ISBN 978-0-265-69969-0
PIBN 11013982

THE CENTURY DICTIONARY AND CYCLOPEDIA

A WORK OF UNIVERSAL REFERENCE
IN ALL DEPARTMENTS OF KNOWLEDGE
WITH A NEW ATLAS OF THE WORLD

IN TEN VOLUMES

VOLUME VI

PUBLISHED BY
The Century Co.
NEW YORK

PUBLISHERS' NOTE ON THE COMPLETED WORK

With the publication of the Atlas which is incorporated in the present edition The Century Dictionary and Cyclopedia has been brought to completion. As the Cyclopedia of Names grew out of the Dictionary and supplemented it on its encyclopedic side, so the Atlas has grown out of the Cyclopedia, and serves as an extension of its geographical material. Each of these works deals with a different part of the great field of words,— common words and names,— while the three, in their unity, constitute a work of reference which practically covers the whole of that field. The total number of words and names defined or otherwise described in the completed work is about 450,000.

The special features of each of these several parts of the book are described in the Prefaces which will be found in the first, ninth, and tenth volumes. It need only be said that the definitions of the common words of the language are for the most part stated encyclopedically, with a vast amount of technical, historical, and practical information in addition to an unrivaled wealth of purely philological material; that the same encyclopedic method is applied to proper names — names of persons, places, characters in fiction, books — in short, of everything to which a name is given; and that in the Atlas geographical names, and much besides, are exhibited with a completeness and serviceableness seldom equaled. Of The Century Dictionary and Cyclopedia as a whole, therefore, it may be said that it is in its own field the most complete presentation of human knowledge — scientific, historical, and practical — that exists.

Moreover, the method of distributing this encyclopedic material under a large number of headings, which has been followed throughout, makes each item of this great store of information far more accessible than in works in which a different system is adopted.

The whole represents fifteen years of labor. The first edition of The Century Dictionary was completed in 1891, and that of the Century Cyclopedia of Names in 1894. During the years that have elapsed since those dates each of these works has been subjected to repeated careful revisions, in order to include the latest information, and the results of this scrutiny are comprised in this edition.

November, 1897.

THE
CENTURY DICTIONARY

AN ENCYCLOPEDIC LEXICON OF THE ENGLISH LANGUAGE

PREPARED UNDER THE SUPERINTENDENCE OF
WILLIAM DWIGHT WHITNEY, PH. D., LL.D.
PROFESSOR OF COMPARATIVE PHILOLOGY AND SANSKRIT
IN YALE UNIVERSITY

PUBLISHED BY
The Century Co.
NEW YORK

By permission of Messrs. Blackie & Son, publishers of The Imperial Dictionary by Dr. Ogilvie and Dr. Annandale, material from that English copyright work has been freely used in the preparation of The Century Dictionary, and certain owners of American copyrights having claimed that undue use of matter so protected has been made in the compilation of The Imperial Dictionary, notice is hereby given that arrangement has also been made with the proprietors of such copyright matter for its use in the preparation of The Century Dictionary.

THE DE VINNE PRESS.

ABBREVIATIONS

USED IN THE ETYMOLOGIES AND DEFINITIONS.

a. adj. .... adjective.
abbr. .... abbreviation.
abl. .... ablative.
acc. .... accusative.
accom. .... accommodated, accommodation.
act. .... active.
adv. .... adverb.
AF. .... Anglo-French.
agri. .... agriculture.
AL. .... Anglo-Latin.
alg. .... algebra.
Amer. .... American.
anat. .... anatomy.
anc. .... ancient.
antiq. .... antiquity.
aor. .... aorist.
appar. .... apparently.
Ar. .... Arabic.
arch. .... architecture.
archæol. .... archæology.
arith. .... arithmetic.
art. .... article.
AS. .... Anglo-Saxon.
astrol. .... astrology.
astron. .... astronomy.
attrib. .... attributive.
aug. .... augmentative.
Bav. .... Bavarian.
Beng. .... Bengali.
biol. .... biology.
Bohem. .... Bohemian.
bot. .... botany.
Braz. .... Brazilian.
Bret. .... Breton.
bryol. .... bryology.
Bulg. .... Bulgarian.
carp. .... carpentry.
Cat. .... Catalan.
Cath. .... Catholic.
caus. .... causative.
ceram. .... ceramics.
cf. .... L. *confer*, compare.
ch. .... church.
Chal. .... Chaldee.
chem. .... chemical, chemistry.
Chin. .... Chinese.
chron. .... chronology.
colloq. .... colloquial, colloquially.
com. .... commerce, commercial.
comp. .... composition, compound.
compar. .... comparative.
conch. .... conchology.
conj. .... conjunction.
contr. .... contracted, contraction.
Corn. .... Cornish.
craniol. .... craniology.
craniom. .... craniometry.
crystal. .... crystallography.
D. .... Dutch.
Dan. .... Danish.
dat. .... dative.
def. .... definite, definition.
deriv. .... derivative, derivation.
dial. .... dialect, dialectal.
diff. .... different.
dim. .... diminutive.
distrib. .... distributive.
dram. .... dramatic.
dynam. .... dynamics.
E. .... East.
E. .... English (*usually meaning* modern English).
eccl., eccles. .... ecclesiastical.
econ. .... economy.
e. g. .... L. *exempli gratia*, for example.
Egypt. .... Egyptian.
E. Ind. .... East Indian.
elect. .... electricity.
embryol. .... embryology.
Eng. .... English.
engin. .... engineering.
entom. .... entomology.
Epis. .... Episcopal.
equiv. .... equivalent.
esp. .... especially.
Eth. .... Ethiopic.
ethnog. .... ethnography.
ethnol. .... ethnology.
etym. .... etymology.
Eur. .... European.
exclam. .... exclamation.
f., fem. .... feminine.
F. .... French (*usually meaning* modern French).
Flem. .... Flemish.
fort. .... fortification.
freq. .... frequentative.
Fries. .... Friesic.
fut. .... future.
G. .... German (*usually meaning* New High German).
Gael. .... Gaelic.
galv. .... galvanism.
gen. .... genitive.
geog. .... geography.
geol. .... geology.
geom. .... geometry.
Goth. .... Gothic (Mœsogothic).
Gr. .... Greek.
gram. .... grammar.
gun. .... gunnery.
Heb. .... Hebrew.
her. .... heraldry.
herpet. .... herpetology.
Hind. .... Hindustani.
hist. .... history.
horol. .... horology.
hort. .... horticulture.
Hung. .... Hungarian.
hydraul. .... hydraulics.
hydros. .... hydrostatics.
Icel. .... Icelandic (*usually meaning* Old Icelandic, *otherwise called* Old Norse).
ichth. .... ichthyology.
i. e. .... L. *id est*, that is.
impers. .... impersonal.
impf. .... imperfect.
impv. .... imperative.
improp. .... improperly.
Ind. .... Indian.
ind. .... indicative.
Indo-Eur. .... Indo-European.
indef. .... indefinite.
inf. .... infinitive.
instr. .... instrumental.
interj. .... interjection.
intr., intrans. .... intransitive.
Ir. .... Irish.
irreg. .... irregular, irregularly.
It. .... Italian.
Jap. .... Japanese.
L. .... Latin (*usually meaning* classical Latin).
Lett. .... Lettish.
LG. .... Low German.
lichenol. .... lichenology.
lit. .... literal, literally.
lit. .... literature.
Lith. .... Lithuanian.
lithog. .... lithography.
lithol. .... lithology.
LL. .... Late Latin.
m., masc. .... masculine.
M. .... Middle.
mach. .... machinery.
mammal. .... mammalogy.
manuf. .... manufacturing.
math. .... mathematics.
MD. .... Middle Dutch.
ME. .... Middle English (*otherwise called* Old English).
mech. .... mechanics, mechanical.
med. .... medicine.
mensur. .... mensuration.
metal. .... metallurgy.
metaph. .... metaphysics.
meteor. .... meteorology.
Mex. .... Mexican.
MGr. .... Middle Greek, medieval Greek.
MHG. .... Middle High German.
milit. .... military.
mineral. .... mineralogy.
ML. .... Middle Latin, medieval Latin.
MLG. .... Middle Low German.
mod. .... modern.
mycol. .... mycology.
myth. .... mythology.
n. .... noun.
n., neut. .... neuter.
N. .... New.
N. .... North.
N. Amer. .... North America.
nat. .... natural.
naut. .... nautical.
nav. .... navigation.
NGr. .... New Greek, modern Greek.
NHG. .... New High German (*usually simply* G., German).
NL. .... New Latin, modern Latin.
nom. .... nominative.
Norm. .... Norman.
north. .... northern.
Norw. .... Norwegian.
numis. .... numismatics.
O. .... Old.
obs. .... obsolete.
obstet. .... obstetrics.
OBulg. .... Old Bulgarian (*otherwise called* Church Slavonic, Old Slavic, Old Slavonic).
OCat. .... Old Catalan.
OD. .... Old Dutch.
ODan. .... Old Danish.
odontog. .... odontography.
odontol. .... odontology.
OF. .... Old French.
OFlem. .... Old Flemish.
OGael. .... Old Gaelic.
OHG. .... Old High German.
OIr. .... Old Irish.
OIt. .... Old Italian.
OL. .... Old Latin.
OLG. .... Old Low German.
ONorth. .... Old Northumbrian.
OPruss. .... Old Prussian.
orig. .... original, originally.
ornith. .... ornithology.
OS. .... Old Saxon.
OSp. .... Old Spanish.
osteol. .... osteology.
OSw. .... Old Swedish.
OTeut. .... Old Teutonic.
p. a. .... participial adjective.
paleon. .... paleontology.
part. .... participle.
pass. .... passive.
pathol. .... pathology.
perf. .... perfect.
Pers. .... Persian.
pers. .... person.
persp. .... perspective.
Peruv. .... Peruvian.
petrog. .... petrography.
Pg. .... Portuguese.
phar. .... pharmacy.
Phen. .... Phenician.
philol. .... philology.
philos. .... philosophy.
phonog. .... phonography.
photog. .... photography.
phren. .... phrenology.
phys. .... physical.
physiol. .... physiology.
pl., plur. .... plural.
poet. .... poetical.
polit. .... political.
Pol. .... Polish.
poss. .... possessive.
pp. .... past participle.
ppr. .... present participle.
Pr. .... Provençal (*usually meaning* Old Provençal).
pref. .... prefix.
prep. .... preposition.
pres. .... present.
pret. .... preterit.
priv. .... privative.
prob. .... probably, probable.
pron. .... pronoun.
pron. .... pronounced, pronunciation.
prop. .... properly.
pros. .... prosody.
Prot. .... Protestant.
prov. .... provincial.
psychol. .... psychology.
q. v. .... L. *quod* (or pl. *quæ*) *vide*, which see.
refl. .... reflexive.
reg. .... regular, regularly.
repr. .... representing.
rhet. .... rhetoric.
Rom. .... Roman.
Rom. .... Romanic, Romance (languages).
Russ. .... Russian.
S. .... South.
S. Amer. .... South American.
sc. .... L. *scilicet*, understand, supply.
Sc. .... Scotch.
Scand. .... Scandinavian.
Scrip. .... Scripture.
sculp. .... sculpture.
Serv. .... Servian.
sing. .... singular.
Skt. .... Sanskrit.
Slav. .... Slavic, Slavonic.
Sp. .... Spanish.
subj. .... subjunctive.
superl. .... superlative.
surg. .... surgery.
surv. .... surveying.
Sw. .... Swedish.
syn. .... synonymy.
Syr. .... Syriac.
technol. .... technology.
teleg. .... telegraphy.
teratol. .... teratology.
term. .... termination.
Teut. .... Teutonic.
theat. .... theatrical.
theol. .... theology.
therap. .... therapeutics.
toxicol. .... toxicology.
tr., trans. .... transitive.
trigon. .... trigonometry.
Turk. .... Turkish.
typog. .... typography.
ult. .... ultimate, ultimately.
v. .... verb.
var. .... variant.
vet. .... veterinary.
v. i. .... intransitive verb.
v. t. .... transitive verb.
W. .... Welsh.
Wall. .... Walloon.
Wallach. .... Wallachian.
W. Ind. .... West Indian.
zoögeog. .... zoögeography.
zoöl. .... zoölogy.
zoöt. .... zoötomy.

KEY TO PRONUNCIATION.

a as in fat, man, pang.
ā as in fate, mane, dale.
ä as in far, father, guard.
â as in fall, talk, naught.
à as in ask, fast, ant.
ã as in fare, hair, bear.

e as in met, pen, bless.
ē as in mete, meet, meat.
ė as in her, fern, heard.

i as in pin, it, biscuit.
ī as in pine, fight, file.

o as in not, on, frog.
ō as in note, poke, floor.
ö as in move, spoon, room.
ô as in nor, song, off.

u as in tub, son, blood.
ū as in mute, acute, few (also new, tube, duty: see Preface, pp. ix, x).
ů as in pull, book, could.
ü German ü, French u.

oi as in oil, joint, boy.
ou as in pound, proud, now.

A single dot under a vowel in an unaccented syllable indicates its abbreviation and lightening, without absolute loss of its distinctive quality. See Preface, p. xi. Thus:

ạ̄ as in prelate, courage, captain.
ẹ̄ as in ablegate, episcopal.
ọ̄ as in abrogate, eulogy, democrat.
ụ̄ as in singular, education.

A double dot under a vowel in an unaccented syllable indicates that, even in the mouths of the best speakers, its sound is variable to, and in ordinary utterance actually becomes, the short *u*-sound (of but, pun, etc.). See Preface, p. xi. Thus:

a̤ as in errant, republican.
e̤ as in prudent, difference.
i̤ as in charity, density.
o̤ as in valor, actor, idiot.

ä̤ as in Persia, peninsula.
ē̤ as in *the* book.
ṳ̄ as in nature, feature.

A mark (◡) under the consonants *t*, *d*, *s*, *z* indicates that they in like manner are variable to *ch*, *j*, *sh*, *zh*. Thus:

t̮ as in nature, adventure.
d̮ as in arduous, education.
s̮ as in pressure.
z̮ as in seizure.

th as in thin.
ᴛʜ as in then.
ch as in German ach, Scotch loch.
ṅ French nasalizing n, as in ton, en.
ly (in French words) French liquid (mouillé) l.
ʹ denotes a primary, ʺ a secondary accent. (A secondary accent is not marked if at its regular interval of two syllables from the primary, or from another secondary.)

SIGNS.

< read *from*; i. e., derived from.
> read *whence*; i. e., from which is derived.
\+ read *and*; i. e., compounded with, or with suffix.
= read *cognate with*; i. e., etymologically parallel with.
√ read *root*.
* read *theoretical* or *alleged*; i. e., theoretically assumed, or asserted but unverified, form.
† read *obsolete*.

SPECIAL EXPLANATIONS.

A superior figure placed after a title-word indicates that the word so marked is distinct etymologically from other words, following or preceding it, spelled in the same manner and marked with different numbers. Thus:

back[1] (bak), *n.* The posterior part, etc.
back[1] (bak), *a.* Lying or being behind, etc.
back[1] (bak), *v.* To furnish with a back, etc.
back[1] (bak), *adv.* Behind, etc.
back[2]† (bak), *n.* The earlier form of *bat*[2].
back[3] (bak), *n.* A large flat-bottomed boat, etc.

Various abbreviations have been used in the credits to the quotations, as "No." for *number*, "st." for *stanza*, "p." for *page*, "l." for *line*, ¶ for *paragraph*, "fol." for *folio*. The method used in indicating the subdivisions of books will be understood by reference to the following plan:

Section only	§ 5.
Chapter only	xiv.
Canto only	xiv.
Book only	iii.
Book and chapter	
Part and chapter	
Book and line	
Book and page	iii. 10.
Act and scene	
Chapter and verse	
No. and page	
Volume and page	II. 34.
Volume and chapter	IV. iv.
Part, book, and chapter	II. iv. 12.
Part, canto, and stanza	II. iv. 12.
Chapter and section or ¶	vii. § or ¶ 3.
Volume, part, and section or ¶	I. i. § or ¶ 6.
Book, chapter, and section or ¶	I. i. § or ¶ 6.

Different grammatical phases of the same word are grouped under one head, and distinguished by the Roman numerals I., II., III., etc. This applies to transitive and intransitive uses of the same verb, to adjectives used also as nouns, to nouns used also as adjectives, to adverbs used also as prepositions or conjunctions, etc.

The capitalizing and italicizing of certain or all of the words in a synonym-list indicates that the words so distinguished are discriminated in the text immediately following, or under the title referred to.

The figures by which the synonym-lists are sometimes divided indicate the senses or definitions with which they are connected.

The title-words begin with a small (lowercase) letter, or with a capital, according to usage. When usage differs, in this matter, with the different senses of a word, the abbreviations [*cap.*] for "capital" and [*l. c.*] for "lower-case" are used to indicate this variation.

The difference observed in regard to the capitalizing of the second element in zoölogical and botanical terms is in accordance with the existing usage in the two sciences. Thus, in zoölogy, in a scientific name consisting of two words the second of which is derived from a proper name, only the first would be capitalized. But a name of similar derivation in botany would have the second element also capitalized.

The names of zoölogical and botanical classes, orders, families, genera, etc., have been uniformly italicized, in accordance with the present usage of scientific writers.

pharmacological (fär″ma-kō-loj′i-kal), *a.* [< *pharmacolog-y* + *-ic-al.*] Of or pertaining to pharmacology: as, *pharmacological* experiments.

Pharmacological considerations certainly render the practical identity of the two solutions very probable.
Lancet, No. 3414, p. 240.

pharmacologist (fär-ma-kol′ō-jist), *n.* [= Sp. *farmacologista* = Pg. *pharmacologista*; as *pharmacolog-y* + *-ist.*] One skilled in pharmacology.

pharmacology (fär-ma-kol′ō-ji), *n.* [= F. *pharmacologie* = Sp. It. *farmacologia* = Pg. *pharmacologia*, < NL. *pharmacologia*, < Gr. φάρμακον, a drug, medicine, + -λογία, < λέγειν, speak: see *-ology.*] 1. The sum of scientific knowledge concerning drugs, including (*a*) pharmacy, or the art of preparing drugs, and (*b*) pharmacodynamics, what is known concerning their action. —2. More specifically, same as *pharmacodynamics*.

pharmacomaniacal (fär″ma-kō-mā-nī′a-kal), *a.* [< Gr. φάρμακον, a drug, medicine, + μανία, madness: see *maniac, maniacal.*] Excessively or irrationally fond of the use or trial of drugs.

pharmacomathy (fär-ma-kom′a-thi), *n.* [< Gr. φάρμακον, a drug, medicine, + -μαθία, < μαθεῖν, μανθάνειν, learn.] Same as *pharmacognostics*.

pharmacon (fär′ma-kon), *n.* [NL. (> It. *farmaco* = Sp. *fármaco*), < Gr. φάρμακον, a drug, whether healing or noxious, a healing drug, a medicine, remedy, a potion, charm, spell, a deadly drug, poison, a dye, color, etc.] A drug; a medicine. Also *pharmacum*.

pharmacopœia (fär″ma-kō-pē′iä), *n.* [= F. *pharmacopée* = Sp. It. *farmacopea* = Pg. *pharmacopea, pharmacopeia*, < NL. *pharmacopœia*, < Gr. φαρμακοποιία, the art of preparing drugs, < φαρμακοποιός, one who prepares drugs, < φάρμακος, a drug, medicine, + ποιεῖν, make.] 1. A book of formulæ or directions for the preparation, etc., of medicines, generally published by authority. The United States Pharmacopœia is revised decennially by delegates in national convention, not more than three each from incorporated medical colleges, incorporated colleges of pharmacy, incorporated pharmaceutical societies, the American Medical Association, and the American Pharmaceutical Association, and not exceeding three each appointed by the surgeon-general of the army, the surgeon-general of the navy, and the surgeon-general of the Marine Hospital. This convention met last in Washington in May, 1890.
2†. A chemical laboratory.

pharmacopœial (fär″ma-kō-pē′ial), *a.* [< *pharmacopœia* + *-al.*] Of or pertaining to a pharmacopœia; made or prepared according to the formula of the pharmacopœia: as, *pharmacopœial* preparations; a *pharmacopœial* solution.

pharmacopolist (fär-ma-kop′ō-list), *n.* [= Pg. *pharmacopolista*; cf. F. *pharmacopole* = Sp. *farmacopola* = Pg. *pharmacopola* = It. *farmacopola*, < L. *pharmacopola*, < Gr. φαρμακοπώλης, one who sells drugs, an apothecary, < φάρμακον, a drug, + πωλεῖν, sell.] A dealer in drugs or medicines; an apothecary.

No *pharmacopolist* could sell one grain of hellebore.
Sterne, Sentimental Journey.

The *pharmacopolist* . . . compounds the drugs after the order of the mediciner. *Scott*, Abbot, xxxii.

pharmacosiderite (fär″ma-kō-sid′ẹ-rīt), *n.* [= F. *pharmacosiderite*, < Gr. φάρμακον, a drug, + σίδηρος, iron: see *siderite.*] A hydrous arseniate of iron: same as *cube-ore*.

pharmacum (fär′ma-kum), *n.* Same as *pharmacon*.

pharmacy (fär′ma-si), *n.*; pl. *pharmacies* (-siz). [< ME. *fermacye*, < OF. *farmacie*, F. *pharmacie* = Sp. It. *farmacia* = Pg. *pharmacia*, < Gr. φαρμακεία, the use of drugs or medicines, pharmacy, < φαρμακεύειν, use drugs, < φάρμακον, a drug, medicine: see *pharmacon.*] 1. The art or practice of preparing, preserving, and compounding medicines, and of dispensing them according to the formulæ or prescriptions of medical practitioners.

Each dose the goddess weighs with watchful eye;
So nice her art in impious *pharmacy!*
Garth, tr. of Ovid's Metamorph., xiv.

Their pain soft arts of *pharmacy* can ease;
Thy breast alone no lenitives appease.
Pope, Iliad, xvi. 38.

2. The occupation of an apothecary or pharmaceutical chemist.—3. A place where medicines are prepared and dispensed; a drug-store; an apothecary's shop. —**Pharmacy Act**, an English statute of 1868 (31 and 32 Vict., c. 121),

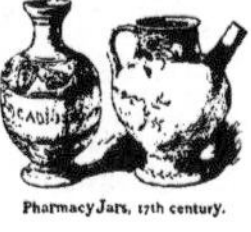
Pharmacy Jars, 17th century.

amended 1869 (32 and 33 Vict., c. 117), regulating the sale of poisons.—**Pharmacy jars**, a name given to vases of majolica and like wares made for use in dispensaries of convents and similar pharmaceutical establishments in Italy, the south of France, and elsewhere, and painted with the name of the drug for which the jar was intended. Vases of the form called *albarello* were used for this purpose, and a pitcher-shaped jar with handle and spout was also common. See cut in preceding column.

Pharnaceum (fär-nā-sē′um), *n.* [NL. (Linnæus, 1753), cf. L. *pharnaceon*, < Gr. φαρνάκειον, a certain plant, a species of panax, so named, according to Pliny, from Pharnaces II. (Gr. Φαρνάκης), son of Mithridates the Great, and King of Pontus or of Bosporus.] An apetalous genus of the order *Ficoideæ* and tribe *Mollugineæ*, characterized by the lacerate or lobed stipules, five sepals, and stamens, styles, and carpels usually three to five. The 16 species are mainly South African. They are low herbs, erect or spreading, with alternate or almost whorled leaves, often bristle-bearing at the apex, and clusters of small white, greenish, or purplish flowers. Some species are cultivated for the flowers, and *P. acidum*, the Longwood samphire of St. Helena, yields an acid salad from its crowded succulent leaves.

pharo[1], *n.* See *faro*.

pharo[2]†, *n.* Same as *pharos*.

pharoh†, *n.* [Cf. Ir. *faram*, noise (?).] A shout or war-cry of Irish soldiers. *Davies*.

That barbarous *Pharoh* and outcry of the Soldiers, which with great straining of their voice they use to set up when they joine battaile. *Holland*, tr. of Camden, ii. 75.

pharology (fā-rol′ō-ji), *n.* [< Gr. φάρος (see *pharos*) + -λογία, < λέγειν, say: see *-ology.*] The art or science of directing the course of ships by means of light-signals from the shore.

Pharomacrus (fā-rom′a-krus), *n.* [NL. (De La Llave, 1832), < Gr. φάρος (?), a lighthouse, + μακρός, long.] A genus of trogons: same as *Calurus*, and of prior date. *P. mocinno* is the paradise-trogon. See cut under *trogon*.

pharos (fā′ros), *n.* [Also *phare*, < F. *phare* = Sp. It. *faro* = Pg. *pharo*; < L. *pharos, pharus*, < Gr. φάρος, a lighthouse, < Φάρος, Pharos, an island in the Bay of Alexandria, famous for its lighthouse.] 1. A lighthouse or tower which anciently stood on the isle of Pharos, at the entrance to the port of Alexandria.

The famous *Pharos*, or light-house, was on a rock at the east end of the island, that was on every side encompass'd with water, and so in a manner a small separate island.
Pococke, Description of the East, I. 2.

Hence—2. Any lighthouse for the direction of seamen; a watch-tower; a beacon.

So high nevertheless it [the Peak of Teneriffe] is as in serene weather it is seen 120 English miles, which some double; serving as an excellent *pharos*.
Sir T. Herbert, Travels in Africa, p. 3.

We pass'd over to the *Pharos*, or Lantern, a towre of very greate height. *Evelyn*, Diary, Oct. 17, 1644.

Here the college, which guided them all till they were ready to launch on the ocean of life, still stands like a *pharos* founded on a sea-girt rock.
Everett, Orations, II. 171.

Pharus (fā′rus), *n.* [NL., < Gr. φᾶρος, a wide cloak or mantle.] 1. In *conch.*, the typical genus of *Pharidæ*. *J. E. Gray*, 1840.—2. In *entom.*, a genus of coleopterous insects of the family *Coccinellidæ*, or ladybirds. Only a few species are known, one Tasmanian and the rest African. *Mulsant*, 1851.—3. A genus of opilionine arachnidans. *Simon*, 1879.—4. An anomalous genus of grasses, classed with the tribe *Oryzeæ*, and characterized by monœcious panicles with spikelets in pairs, one of them pistillate and sessile, the other much smaller, staminate, and pedicelled. The 5 species are found from Florida and the West Indies to Brazil. They are stout grasses, bearing a loose and ample terminal panicle with long slender branches, and are remarkable for their large leaves, which are somewhat feather-veined, unlike those of other grasses, and are often borne reversed on their long-exserted twisted leafstalks. *P. latifolius* is the wild oat of Jamaica; its leaves, which reach 3 inches broad and 8 long, are in use for wrapping small articles, etc. *Linnæus*, 1767.

pharyngalgia (far-ing-gal′ji-ä), *n.* [NL., < Gr. φάρυγξ (φαρυγγ-), throat (see *pharynx*), + ἄλγος, pain.] Pain in the pharynx.

Pharyngea (fā-rin′jẹ-ä), *n. pl.* [NL., < Gr. φάρυγξ (φαρυγγ-), the throat: see *pharynx.*] A group of planarians or *Rhabdocœla* having a pharynx: distinguished from *Apharyngea*.

pharyngeal (fā-rin′jẹ-al), *a.* and *n.* [< NL. *pharynx* (*pharyng-*), pharynx, + *-e-al.*] I. *a.* 1. Of or pertaining to the pharynx; entering into the structure of the pharynx: as, a *pharyngeal* artery, vein, nerve, muscle, gland, etc.—2. Having a pharynx; specifically, of or pertaining to the *Pharyngea*: as, a *pharyngeal* planarian.—3. Having ankylosed pharyngeal bones, as a fish; pharyngognathous.—**Pharyngeal aponeurosis**, the connective-tissue layer of the walls of the pharynx, external to the mucous membrane.—**Pharyngeal arches.** Same as *postoral arches*.—**Pharyngeal artery.** (*a*) *Ascending*, the smallest branch of the external carotid, supplying the prevertebral muscles, the constrictors of the pharynx, the elevator and tensor muscles of the palate, the tonsil, and the Eustachian tube. (*b*) *Superior*. Same as *pterygopalatine artery* (which see, under *pterygopalatine*). —**Pharyngeal bones**, the bones behind the last branchial arch in fishes, generally in a pair below (called *hypopharyngeals*) and in one to four pairs above (called *epipharyngeals*). —**Pharyngeal bursa**, a mucous crypt in the mid-line under the sphenoid bone, just behind the vomer. *Medical News*, Sept., 1889, p. 254.—**Pharyngeal clefts.** Same as *pharyngeal slits*.—**Pharyngeal fascia**, the fascia investing the wall of the pharynx.—**Pharyngeal fishes**, the *Pharyngognathi*.—**Pharyngeal ganglion.** See *ganglion*.—**Pharyngeal glands**, racemose mucous glands, found everywhere in the submucous tissue of the pharynx, but especially numerous at the upper part, around the orifices of the Eustachian tubes.—**Pharyngeal jaws.** (*a*) Jaw-like organs in the pharynx, as in certain nereid worms. (*b*) The pharyngeal bones when they have a jaw-like form or function.—**Pharyngeal nerves**, branches of the vagus, glossopharyngeal, sympathetic, and Meckel's ganglion. The first three unite to form the pharyngeal plexus; the last, after passing through the pterygopalatine canal, is distributed chiefly to the mucous membrane of the pharynx. —**Pharyngeal plexus.** (*a*) A plexus of nerves formed by the branches of the vagus, sympathetic, and glossopharyngeal, and supplying the muscles and mucous membranes of the pharynx. (*b*) A plexus of veins on the outer surface of the pharynx.—**Pharyngeal sac**, a sac or vessel in the head of a butterfly, at the base of the proboscis or spiral tongue, from which it is separated by a valve. By the alternate contraction and expansion of this sac the insect is able to suck up nectar or other liquids.—**Pharyngeal slits**, the postoral visceral clefts or gill-slits which any vertebrate or chordate animal may possess, to the number of not more than eight, temporarily or permanently. The whole tendency is to the reduction in number of these slits in ascending the vertebrate scale, and to their impermanence in the development of the embryos of the higher vertebrates. In adult reptiles, birds, and mammals they have all disappeared, excepting the trace of the first one, which persists as the auditory passage. In batrachians their progressive loss is seen in the transition from gilled tadpoles to the adults with lungs. In fishes and lower vertebrates than fishes more or fewer persist as ordinary gill-slits or branchial apertures. Also called *visceral clefts*, when the structures which separate the slits on each side are known as *visceral arches*.—**Pharyngeal spine.** Same as *pharyngeal tubercle*.—**Pharyngeal teeth**, the teeth on the pharyngeal bones, especially on the lower pharyngeals or hypopharyngeals. They are much used in the taxonomy of the cyprinoid fishes.—**Pharyngeal tubercle**, a small elevation near the middle of the under surface of the basilar process of the occipital bone, for attachment of the fibrous raphe of the pharynx.—**Pharyngeal veins**, tributaries to the internal jugular vein from the pharyngeal plexus.

II. *n.* A structure which enters into the composition of the pharynx: as, the ascending *pharyngeal*, a branch of the external carotid artery, given off at or near the origin of the latter; the ankylosed *pharyngeals* (bones) of some fishes.

pharyngectomy (far-in-jek′tō-mi), *n.* [< Gr. φάρυγξ (φαρυγγ-), throat (see *pharynx*), + ἐκτομή, a cutting out.] The excision of a portion of the pharynx.

pharynges, *n.* New Latin plural of *pharynx*.

pharyngeus (far-in-jē′us), *n.*; pl. *pharyngei* (-ī). [NL., < *pharynx* (*pharyng-*), pharynx.] A pharyngeal muscle. There are several such, distinguished by a qualifying word, generally in composition: as, *stylopharyngeus, palatopharyngeus*. See the compounds.

pharyngismus (far-in-jiz′mus), *n.* [NL., < *pharynx* (*pharyng-*), pharynx.] Spasm of the muscles of the pharynx.

pharyngitic (far-in-jit′ik), *a.* [< *pharyngitis* + *-ic.*] Of, pertaining to, or affected with pharyngitis.

pharyngitis (far-in-jī′tis), *n.* [NL., < *pharynx* (*pharyng-*), pharynx, + *-itis.*] Inflammation of the mucous membrane of the pharynx.—**Granular, follicular, or chronic pharyngitis.** See *granular*.

pharyngobranch (fā-ring′gō-brangk), *a.* and *n.* I. *a.* Of or pertaining to the *Pharyngobranchii*.
II. *n.* A member of the *Pharyngobranchii*.

Pharyngobranchia (fā-ring-gō-brang′ki-ä), *n. pl.* [NL.] Same as *Pharyngobranchii*.

pharyngobranchiate (fā-ring-gō-brang′ki-āt), *a.* [< *Pharyngobranchia* + *-ate*[1].] Same as *pharyngobranch*.

Pharyngobranchii (fā-ring-gō-brang′ki-ī), *n. pl.* [NL., < Gr. φάρυγξ (φαρυγγ-), throat (see *pharynx*), + βράγχια, gills.] An order or class of acranial fish-like vertebrates, so called from the pharynx being perforated at the sides for the branchial apertures. The group was originally constituted as an order of fishes; the name is synonymous with *Cirrostomi, Leptocardii, Entomocrania*, and *Acrania*. It includes only the lancelets. See *Branchiostoma* and *lancelet*, and cut on following page.

pharyngodynia (fā-ring-gō-din′i-ä), *n.* [NL., < Gr. φάρυγξ (φαρυγγ-), throat, + ὀδύνη, pain.] Pain in the pharynx.

pharyngo-esophageal (fā-ring″gō-ē-sō-faj′ẹ-al), *a.* [< *pharyngo-esophagus* + *-e-al.*] Of or pertaining to the pharynx and the esophagus.

pharyngo-esophagus (fā-ring″gō-ẹ-sof′a-gus), *n.* [NL., < Gr. φάρυγξ (φαρυγγ-), throat (see *pharynx*), + οἰσοφάγος, esophagus: see *esopha-*

Anterior End of Body of Lancelet (*Branchiostoma* or *Amphioxus*), representing the *Pharyngobranchii*.

Ch, notochord; *My*, myelon, or spinal cord; *a*, position of olfactory (?) sac; *b*, optic nerve; *c*, fifth (?) pair of nerves; *d*, spinal nerves; *e*, representatives of neural spines or of fin-rays; *f*, *g*, oral skeleton. (The heavy lighter and darker shading represents muscular segments, or myotomes, and their interspaces.)

gus.] A gullet extended to a mouth; a structure representing or consisting of a pharynx and an esophagus combined.

pharyngoglossal (fą-ring-gō-glos'al), *a.* [< Gr. φάρυγξ (φαρυγγ-), throat, + γλῶσσα, tongue: see *glossal.*] Of or pertaining to the pharynx and the tongue; glossopharyngeal: as, a *pharyngoglossal* nerve. *Dunglison.*

pharyngognath (fą-ring'gog-nath), *a.* and *n.* **I.** *a.* Of or pertaining to the *Pharyngognathi.*

II. *n.* A member of the *Pharyngognathi.*

Pharyngognathi (far-ing-gog'ną-thī), *n. pl.* [NL., < Gr. φάρυγξ (φαρυγγ-), throat, + γνάθος, jaw.] In J. Müller's classification, an order of teleost fishes, having the inferior pharyngeals ankylosed and the pneumatic duct closed. It embraced both spine-rayed and soft-rayed fishes. In Günther's system the group was similarly constituted, and contained the families *Labridæ*, *Embiotocidæ*, *Chromides*, and *Pomacentridæ*. In Cope's system the *Pharyngognathi* are an order of physoclistous fishes with the cranium normal, bones of the jaws distinct, third superior pharyngeal bone enlarged and articulating with the cranium, and inferior pharyngeals coalesced. It includes the same fishes as Günther's group.

pharyngognathous (far-ing-gog'ną-thus), *a.* [< *pharyngognath* + *-ous.*] Same as *pharyngognath.*

pharyngographic (fą-ring-gō-graf'ik), *a.* [< *pharyngograph-y* + *-ic.*] Descriptive of the pharynx; of or pertaining to pharyngography.

pharyngography (far-ing-gog'rą-fi), *n.* [= F. *pharyngographie*, < Gr. φάρυγξ (φαρυγγ-), throat, + -γραφία, < γράφειν, write.] An anatomical description of the pharynx.

pharyngolaryngeal (fą-ring"gō-lą-rin'jē-al), *a.* [< Gr. φάρυγξ (φαρυγγ-), throat, + λάρυγξ (λαρυγγ-), larynx: see *laryngeal.*] Of or pertaining to both the pharynx and the larynx: as, a *pharyngolaryngeal* membrane.—**Pharyngolaryngeal cavity.** (*a*) The lower part of the pharynx, into which the larynx opens, separated from the pharyngo-oral cavity by a horizontal plane passing through the tips of the hyoid cornua. (*b*) The part of the pharynx lying below the soft palate in deglutition. See cut under *mouth.*

pharyngological (fą-ring-gō-loj'i-kal), *a.* [< *pharyngolog-y* + *-ic-al.*] Of or pertaining to pharyngology.

pharyngology (far-ing-gol'ō-ji), *n.* [< Gr. φάρυγξ (φαρυγγ-), throat, + -λογία, < λέγειν, speak: see *-ology.*] That part of anatomy which treats of the pharynx.

pharyngomycosis (fą-ring"gō-mī-kō'sis), *n.* [NL., < Gr. φάρυγξ (φαρυγγ-), throat, + NL. *mycosis*, q. v.] The growth of fungi, usually leptothrix, in the pharynx.

pharyngonasal (fą-ring-gō-nā'zal), *a.* [< Gr. φάρυγξ (φαρυγγ-), throat, + L. *nasus*, nose: see *nasal.*] Of or pertaining to both the pharynx and the nose.—**Pharyngonasal cavity**, the uppermost part of the pharynx, separated from that below by a horizontal plane passing through the base of the uvula, or again defined as that part above the soft palate during deglutition; the nasopharynx. See cut under *mouth.*

pharyngo-oral (fą-ring-gō-ō'ral), *a.* [< Gr. φάρυγξ (φαρυγγ-), throat, + L. *os* (*or-*), mouth: see *oral.*] Of or pertaining to both the pharynx and the mouth; oropharyngeal.—**Pharyngo-oral cavity**, the middle part of the pharynx, that into which the mouth opens; the oropharynx.

pharyngopalatinus (fą-ring"gō-pal-ą-tī'nus), *n.*; pl. *pharyngopalatini* (-nī). [NL., < Gr. φάρυγξ (φαρυγγ-), throat, + L. *palatum*, palate: see *palatine*2.] Same as *palatopharyngeus.*

pharyngopathia (fą-ring-gō-path'i-ą), *n.* [NL., < Gr. φάρυγξ (φαρυγγ-), throat, + πάθος, a suffering.] Disease of the pharynx.

pharyngoplegia (fą-ring-gō-plē'ji-ą), *n.* [NL., < Gr. φάρυγξ (φαρυγγ-), throat, + πληγή, a blow, stroke.] Paralysis of the muscles of the pharynx.

pharyngopleural (fą-ring-gō-plö'ral), *a.* [< Gr. φάρυγξ (φαρυγγ-), throat (see *pharynx*), + πλευρά, a rib: see *pleural*1.] Pertaining or common to the pharynx and to the lateral body-walls: as, "the fluted *pharyngo-pleural* membrane" [of a lancelet]. *Encyc. Brit.*, XXIV. 184.

Pharyngopneusta (fą-ring-gop-nūs'tą), *n. pl.* [NL., < Gr. φάρυγξ (φαρυγγ-), throat, + *πνευστός (cf. πνευστικός), verbal adj. of πνεῖν, breathe.] A superordinal division proposed by Huxley to be established for the reception of the tunicates or ascidians and the *Enteropneusta* (*Balanoglossus*).

pharyngopneustal (fą-ring-gop-nūs'tal), *a.* [< *Pharyngopneusta* + *-al.*] Of or pertaining to the *Pharyngopneusta.*—**Pharyngopneustal series**, a name proposed by Huxley in 1877 for the series of animals constituting the *Pharyngopneusta.*

pharyngorhinitis (fą-ring"gō-ri-nī'tis), *n.* [NL., < Gr. φάρυγξ (φαρυγγ-), throat, + ῥίς (ῥιν-), nose, + *-itis.*] Inflammation of the pharynx and the mucous membrane of the nose.

pharyngorhinoscopy (fą-ring"gō-ri-nos'kō-pi), *n.* [< Gr. φάρυγξ (φαρυγγ-), throat, + ῥίς (ῥιν-), nose, + σκοπεῖν, view.] Examination of the posterior nares and adjacent parts of the pharynx with a rhinoscopic mirror.

pharyngoscope (fą-ring'gō-skōp), *n.* [< Gr. φάρυγξ (φαρυγγ-), throat, + σκοπεῖν, view.] An instrument for inspecting the pharynx.

pharyngoscopy (fą-ring'gō-skō-pi), *n.* [< Gr. φάρυγξ (φαρυγγ-), throat, + σκοπεῖν, view.] Inspection of the pharynx.

pharyngospasmus (fą-ring-gō-spaz'mus), *n.* [< Gr. φάρυγξ (φαρυγγ-), throat, + σπασμός, spasm.] Spasm of the pharynx.

pharyngotomy (far-ing-got'ō-mi), *n.* [= F. *pharyngotomie* = Sp. *faringotomia* = Pg. *pharyngotomia* = It. *faringotomia*, < Gr. φάρυγξ (φαρυγγ-), throat (see *pharynx*), + -τομία, < τέμνειν, ταμεῖν, cut.] In *surg.*, incision into the pharynx.

pharynx (far'ingks), *n.*; pl. *pharynges* (fą-rin'jēz), rarely *pharynxes* (far'ingk-sez). [= F. *pharynx* = Sp. It. *faringe* = Pg. *pharynx*, *pharynge*, < NL. *pharynx*, the pharynx, < Gr. φάρυγξ, the throat; technically the joint opening of the gullet and the windpipe, but also applied to the windpipe and the esophagus; cf. φάραγξ, a cleft; < √ φαρ, bore, in φαρᾶν, plow.] **1.** A musculomembranous pouch situated at the back of the nasal cavities, mouth, and larynx, and extending from the base of the skull to the cricoid cartilage. It is continuous below with the esophagus, and communicates above with the nasal passages, Eustachian tubes, mouth, and larynx. It may be conveniently considered to be divided into the pharyngonasal, pharyngo-oral, and pharyngolaryngeal cavities. The pharynx has also been divided into two parts, called *nasopharynx* and *oropharynx*. See cuts under *Branchiostoma*, *mouth*, and *lamprey*.

2. In invertebrates, some tubular or infundibuliform beginning of the alimentary canal or continuation of the oral aperture. A structure to which the name applies is very commonly found in invertebrates, even among those of microscopic size, as rotifers and infusorians. See cut under *Oxyuris*, *Appendicularia*, and *Arctisca*.—**Branchial pharynx.** See *branchial.*—**Constrictor pharyngis superior, medius, inferior.** See *constrictor*, and cut under *muscle.*—**Levator or dilatator pharyngis.** Same as *stylopharyngeus.*—**Nasal pharynx**, the pharyngonasal cavity; the nasopharynx.—**Oral pharynx**, the pharyngo-oral cavity; the oropharynx.

Phascaceæ (fas-kā'sē-ē), *n. pl.* [NL., < *Phascum* + *-aceæ.*] An order of bryaceous mosses, named from the genus *Phascum*. They are very small soft plants, with loosely areolate leaves and globular, immersed, subsessile or short-pedicellate capsules, which rupture irregularly across the middle for the discharge of the spores, there being no deciduous operculum as in most mosses.

Phasceæ (fas'ē-ē), *n. pl.* [NL., < *Phascum* + *-eæ.*] Same as *Phascaceæ.*

Phascogale penicillata.

Phascogale (fas-kog'ą-lē), *n.* [NL. (Temminck, 1827), contr. for **Phascologale*, < Gr. φάσκωλος, a leathern bag, + γαλῆ, a weasel.] A genus of small insectivorous and carnivorous marsupial mammals of the family *Dasyuridæ*, inhabiting the whole of the Australian region. They are of the size of a rat or less, are of arboreal habits, and have a pointed snout, rounded ears, and the fore feet five-toed, the hind feet being variable in this respect. There is usually one more premolar above and below on each side than in the typical dasyures, making a total of 46 instead of 42. There are several species, among them *P. penicillata*, the largest one, with a long bushy tail, somewhat like a squirrel. Some differ in details of form from others, in consequence of which the genera *Chætocercus*, *Antechinomys*, *Antechinus*, and *Podabrus* have been detached from *Phascogale* proper. See cut in preceding column.

Phascogalinæ (fas-kog-ą-lī'nē), *n. pl.* [NL., < *Phascogale* + *-inæ.*] A subfamily of *Dasyuridæ* based on the genus *Phascogale.*

Phascolarctidæ (fas-kō-lärk'ti-dē), *n. pl.* [NL., < *Phascolarctos* + *-idæ.*] The *Phascolarctinæ*, raised to the rank of a family.

Phascolarctinæ (fas"kō-lärk-tī'nē), *n. pl.* [NL., < *Phascolarctos* + *-inæ.*] A subfamily of *Phalangistidæ* based on the genus *Phascolarctos.*

Phascolarctos (fas-kō-lärk'tos), *n.* [NL. (De Blainville, 1816), < Gr. φάσκωλος, a leathern bag, + ἄρκτος, bear.] A genus of *Phalangistidæ*, type of the subfamily *Phascolarctinæ*, having cheek-pouches, 30 teeth, no lower canines, only 11 dorsal vertebræ and as many pairs of ribs, no external tail, the tongue not peculiar, a cardiac gland in the stomach, and a very long cæcum. It contains the koala or native bear of Australia, *P. cinereus*. See cut under *koala.*

Phascolomyidæ (fas-kō-lō-mī'i-dē), *n. pl.* [NL., < *Phascolomys* + *-idæ.*] A family of diprotodont marsupial mammals; the wombats. They have two incisors above and two below, as in rodents, large, scalpriform, enameled in front only; no canines; all the teeth with persistent pulps; the hind feet with four subequal, somewhat syndactylous toes, and hallux rudimentary; the fore feet five-toed; the tail rudimentary; the stomach simple with a cardiac gland; and a short cæcum with a vermiform appendage. There is but one genus, *Phascolomys.*

Phascolomys (fas-kol'ō-mis), *n.* [NL., < Gr. φάσκωλος, a leathern bag, + μῦς, mouse.] The typical genus of the family *Phascolomyidæ*, including the wombats. They are inoffensive terrestrial and fossorial herbivorous animals of the Australian

Wombat (*Phascolomys wombat*).

region. The genus has two sections—one containing the common and broad-nosed wombats, *P. wombat* and *P. platyrhinus*, the other the hairy-nosed wombat, *P. latifrons*. See *wombat.*

Phascolosoma (fas-kō-lō-sō'mą), *n.* [NL., < Gr. φάσκωλος, a leathern bag, + σῶμα, body.] A genus of gephyrean worms of the family *Sipunculidæ*, or spoon-worms. *P. cementarium* is common in deep water on sandy or shelly bottoms along the New England coast, living somewhat like a hermit-crab in the deserted shell of some mollusk, the mouth of which is extended and contracted by sand or mud cemented by the secretion of its own body into a kind of tube.

Phascum (fas'kum), *n.* [NL. (Linnæus), < Gr. φάσκον, same as σφάκος, a kind of tree-moss.] A genus of bryaceous mosses, giving name to the order *Phascaceæ*. They are minute but distinctly caulescent plants, mostly growing on the ground, with costate leaves and monœcious "flowers." The capsule is pedicellate, subglobose or ovate-oblong, dehiscing by irregular ruptures. There are 3 North American species, sometimes called *earth-mosses.*

phase1 (fāz), *n.* [Formerly also, as ML., *phasis* (plural *phases*, whence the E. sing. *phase*); = F. *phase* = Sp. It. *fase* = Pg. *phase*, < ML. *phasis*, < Gr. φάσις, an appearance, < φάειν, shine, = Skt. *bhā*, shine; cf. *phantasm*, etc., and see *face*1, *fable*, etc.] **1.** Aspect, appearance, or guise; the aspect or presentation in which a thing of varying modes or conditions manifests itself to the eye or the mind, or the stage in its history or development which it reaches at a particular time; an era: as, the war entered on a new *phase*; the varying *phases* of life.

Certainly the mansion appeared to enjoy a quieter *phase* of existence than the temple; some of its windows too were aglow. *Charlotte Brontë*, Shirley, ix.

We may congratulate ourselves on having reached a *phase* of civilization in which the rights of life and personal liberty no longer require inculcating.
H. Spencer, Social Statics, p. 131.

That peculiar *phase* in the life of the Greek commonwealths which intervenes between oligarchy and democracy — the age of the tyrannies. *Encyc. Brit.*, XI. 94.

2. In *astron.*, the particular appearance presented by the moon or by a planet at a given time; one of the recurring appearances of the moon or a planet in respect to the apparent form of the illuminated part of its disk.

At such times as these planets show their full *phases* they are found to be sphærical, and only lose this figure by virtue of position to the sun, to whom they owe their light. *Derham*, Astro-Theology, v. 1.

Chief the planter, if he wealth desire,
Should note the *phases* of the fickle moon.
Grainger, The Sugar Cane, i.

3. In *physics*, a particular value, especially at the zero of time, of the uniformly varying angular quantity upon which a simple harmonic motion, or a simple element of a harmonic motion, depends. The position of the moving object may be expressed by means of a sum or sums of terms of the form A sin $(bt + c)$, where t is the time. The value of $bt + c$, at any instant, especially when $t = 0$, is the phase. Two simple harmonic motions A sin $(bt + c)$ and M sin $(bt + n)$ are said to differ in phase, meaning that there is a constant difference in their contemporaneous phases.

The distance whereby one set of waves is in advance of another is called the difference of *phase*.
Spottiswoode, Polarisation, p. 32.

We have within the annular regions two electro-motive forces at right angles, and differing in *phase*.
Science, XIII. 100.

phase[2], *v. t.* A bad spelling of *faze*.

phasel, *n.* See *fasel*[2].

phaseless (fāz'les), *a.* [< *phase*[1] + *-less*.] Unchanging; devoid of change in aspect or state.

A *phaseless* and unceasing gloom.
Poe, Tale of the Ragged Mountains.

Phaseoleæ (fā-sę-ō'lę-ē), *n. pl.* [NL. (Bentham, 1835), < *Phaseolus* + *-eæ*.] A tribe of leguminous plants of the suborder *Papilionaceæ*, distinguished by racemose or fascicled flowers, usually from the axils, stamens diadelphous or nearly so, two-valved pods, pinnate leaves of three entire or lobed leaflets, each with a pair of stipels, and twining or prostrate habit. It includes 6 subtribes and 47 genera, of which the principal are *Phaseolus* (the type), *Apios*, *Butea*, *Cajanus*, *Clitoria*, *Dolichos*, *Erythrina*, *Galactia*, *Kennedya*, *Mucuna*, *Physostigma*, and *Rhynchosia*.

phaseolite (fā-sē'ǫ-līt), *n.* [< *Phaseolus* + *-ite*[2].] A generic name proposed by Unger, under which have been included various remains of fossil plants, principally leaves, which are supposed to belong to the *Leguminosæ*, and some of which appear to be closely allied to the living genus *Phaseolus*.

Phaseolus (fą-sē'ǫ-lus), *n.* [NL. (Rivinus, 1691), < L. *phaseolus*, *fascolus*, also *phasēlus*, *faselus*, < Gr. φάσηλος, also φασήολος, φασίολος, a kind of bean: see *phasel*, *fasel*[2].] A genus of leguminous plants, type of the tribe *Phaseoleæ* and the subtribe *Euphaseoleæ*, distinguished by the spiral keel, orbicular banner, longitudinally bearded style, and flowers clustered above the middle of the peduncle. There are about 60 species, widely dispersed through warmer regions, with about 100 well-marked varieties due to long cultivation. They are twining or prostrate plants, with leaves of three leaflets, persistent striate stipules, white, yellowish, red, violet, or purplish flowers, and long straight or curving pods. To this genus belong most of the beans of culinary use, for which see *bean*[1], *kidney-bean*, *haricot*, and *green gram* (under *gram*[3]). *P. multiflorus*, the scarlet runner, is often cultivated for ornament. *P. perennis*, the wild bean-vine (see cut under *leaf*), and *P. diversifolius*, a trailing plant remarkable for its polymorphous leaves, with two other species, all purplish-flowered, are native to the eastern United States. See *Strophostyles*.

phases, *n.* Plural of *phasis*.

Phasianella (fā"si-ą-nel'ạ̈), *n.* [NL. (Lamarck), fem. dim. of L. *phasianus*, pheasant: see *pheasant*.] The typical genus of *Phasianellidæ*, containing shells brilliantly polished and colored, calling to mind the tints of a pheasant, and hence called *pheasant-shells*.

Pheasant-shell (*Phasianella imperialis*).

Phasianellidæ (fā"si-a-nel'-i-dē), *n. pl.* [NL., < *Phasianella* + *-idæ*.] A family of gastropods; the pheasant-shells. They are generally ranked as a subfamily, called *Phasianellinæ*, of the family *Turbinidæ*. They are distinguished by their nacreous shell. The species abound chiefly in the Australian seas.

Phasianidæ (fā-si-an'i-dē), *n. pl.* [NL., < *Phasianus* + *-idæ*.] A family of rasorial or gallinaceous birds, containing the most magnificent representatives of the order *Gallinæ*, as the peacock, all the various species of pheasants, the domestic hen, the turkey, and the guinea-fowl. The last two, respectively the American and the African representatives, are sometimes excluded as the types of separate families. The *Phasianidæ* are specially characteristic of Asia and the islands zoologically related. There are about 75 species, included in many genera. The leading types are *Pavo* and *Polyplectron*, the peacocks and peacock-pheasants; *Argus* or *Argusianus*, the argus-pheasants; *Phasianus*, the common pheasants, such as have been introduced in Europe; *Chrysolophus* or *Thaumalea*, the golden and Amherstian pheasants; *Pucrasia*, the pucras pheasants; *Crossoptilon*, the eared or snow pheasants; *Euplocamus*, the macartneys, firebacks, kaleeges, and silver pheasants; *Lophophorus*, the monauls or impeyans; *Ceriornis*, the tragopans, satyrs, or horned pheasants; *Gallus*, the domestic cock and hen, descended from the jungle-fowl; *Ithaginis*, the blood-pheasants; *Meleagris*, the turkeys of America; and *Numida*, *Guttera*, *Acryllium*, *Agelastes*, and *Phasidus*, genera of African guinea-fowls. These genera are by Elliot grouped in no fewer than eight subfamilies — *Pavoninæ*, *Lophophorinæ*, *Meleagrinæ*, *Phasianinæ*, *Euplocaminæ*, *Gallinæ*, *Agelastinæ*, and *Numidinæ*. See further under *Phasianus* and *pheasant*.

Phasianinæ (fā"si-a-nī'nē), *n. pl.* [NL., < *Phasianus* + *-inæ*.] The *Phasianidæ*, exclusive of the *Pavoninæ*, *Meleagrinæ*, and *Numidinæ*, or still further restricted to forms resembling the genus *Phasianus*; the pheasants proper. Some authors compose the subfamily of five genera — *Phasianus*, *Thaumalea*, *Euplocamus*, *Lobiophasis*, and *Ithaginis*.

phasianine (fā'si-ą-nin), *a.* Of or pertaining to the *Phasianinæ*.

Phasianomorphæ (fā-si-ā-nǫ-môr'fē), *n. pl.* [NL., < Gr. φασιανός, a pheasant, + μορφή, form.] In Sundevall's system of classification, a cohort of *Gallinæ*, composed of the pheasants proper, or *Phasianidæ*, with the guinea-fowls, partridges, quails, and hemipodes (*Turnicidæ*).

phasianomorphic (fā-si-ā-nǫ-môr'fik), *a.* [< *Phasianomorphæ* + *-ic*.] Of or pertaining to the *Phasianomorphæ*.

Phasianurus (fā"si-ą-nū'rus), *n.* [NL. (Wagler, 1832), < Gr. φασιανός, a pheasant, + οὐρά, tail.] A genus of *Anatidæ*: same as *Dafila*.

Phasianus (fā-si-ā'nus), *n.* [NL., < L. *phasianus*, < Gr. φασιανός, a pheasant: see *pheasant*.] The typical genus of the family *Phasianidæ* and subfamily *Phasianinæ*, formerly nearly conterminous with the family, now restricted to such forms as *Phasianus colchicus*, the common pheasant, and long domesticated in Europe. They have a much-lengthened tail, with long acuminate middle feathers, and the head crestless but provided with lateral tufts. At least 10 species are commonly referred to this genus (in several sections, ranked by some authors as genera). One of the most remarkable is *P.* (*Syrmaticus*) *reevesi*, of northern China, in which the tail reaches the maximum length of 5 or 6 feet. The plumage is beautifully varied with black, white, chestnut, and golden yellow. *P.* (*Catreus*) *wallichi* is the cheer, or Wallich's pheasant, of the Himalayas, with a long, broad tail and much-varied plumage. *P.* (*Graphophasianus*) *soemmeringi* is Sömmering's pheasant, of Japan, with coppery-metallic plumage and very long tail. *P.* (*Calophasis*) *ellioti* is a gorgeously colored pheasant of the mountains near Ningpo, in China. Certain green-breasted pheasants, as *P. versicolor* of Japan and *P. elegans* of China, form a small group. Ring-necked pheasants, as *P. insignis* and *P. mongolicus*, have a white ring around the neck. The above-named approach more and more nearly to the ordinary pheasant as domesticated in Europe, of which the Turkestan *P. shawi* is a near relative. The silver and golden pheasants, though long-tailed, are now placed in other genera (*Euplocamus* and *Thaumalea*). See further under *pheasant*.

Reeves's Pheasant (*Phasianus* or *Syrmaticus reevesi*).

phasic (fā'zik), *a.* [< *phase*[1] + *-ic*.] Pertaining to or of the nature of a phase.

Phasidus (fą-sī'dus), *n.* [NL. (Cassin, 1856), appar. irreg. < Gr. φασ(ιανός), a pheasant, + εἶδος, form.] A notable genus of African guinea-fowls of the family *Numididæ*, having as type *P. niger*, the only species. The head is bare, the tarsi are spurred, and the plumage is black.

phasis (fā'sis), *n.*; pl. *phases* (-sēz). [ML.: see *phase*[1].] In *astron.*, a phase.

phasm (fazm), *n.* [< L. *phasma*, < Gr. φάσμα, an apparition, < φάειν, shine: see *phase*[1]. Cf. *phantasm*.] Appearance; fancied apparition; phantom. [Rare.]

Such *phasms*, such apparitions, are most of those excellencies which men applaud in themselves.
Decay of Christian Piety, p. 83.

phasma (fas'mạ̈), *n.* [NL., < L. *phasma*, < Gr. φάσμα, an apparition: see *phasm*.] 1. Pl. *phasmata* (-mạ-tạ̈). Same as *phasm*.— 2. [*cap.*] A genus of gressorial or ambulatorial orthopterous insects, typical of the family *Phasmidæ*.

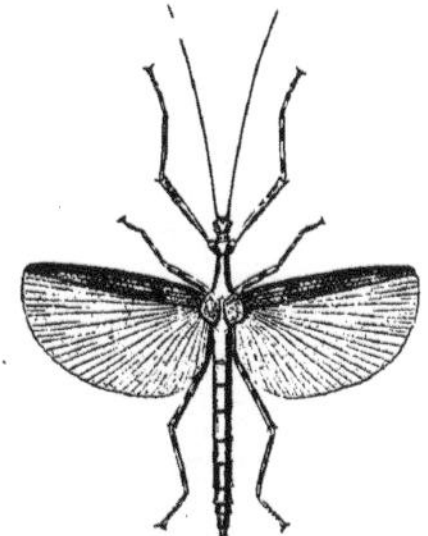

Phasma rubicundum, female. (One half natural size.)

It formerly contained all the curious creatures known as *walking-sticks*, but is now restricted to certain tropical forms. *Lichtenstein*, 1796.

Phasmidæ (fas'mi-dē), *n. pl.* [NL. (Serville, 1831), < *Phasma* + *-idæ*.] A family of *Orthoptera*, typified by the genus *Phasma*, composing with the *Mantidæ* the series *Gressoria* or *Ambulatoria*. They are known as *specters*, *leaf-insects*, *walking-leaves*, *walking-sticks*, etc., from their extraordinary protective mimicry of the twigs and leaves upon which they live. The body is usually long and slender, and the wings, when not abortive, are foliaceous. A member of this family, *Diapheromera femorata*, is the common walking-stick of the northern and eastern United States. See cut under *Phasma*.

Phasmina (fas-mī'nạ̈), *n. pl.* [NL., < *Phasma* + *-ina*[2].] A group of orthopterous insects corresponding to the family *Phasmidæ*.

Phasmomantis (fas-mǫ-man'tis), *n.* [NL., < Gr. φάσμα, an appearance, + μάντις, an insect so called: see *Mantis*.] A genus of *Mantidæ*, containing the common praying-mantis or rear-horse of the United States, *P. carolina*. The female is about three inches long, of a pale pea-green color; the male is smaller, grayish, with dark-barred fore tibiæ. See cut under *Mantis*.

phassachate† (fas'ạ-kāt), *n.* [< Gr. φάσσα, a ring-dove, + ἀχάτης, agate: see *agate*[2].] The lead-colored agate.

phaulographic (fâ-lǫ-graf'ik), *a.* [< Gr. φαῦλος, bad, worthless, + γράφειν, write.] Relating to bad or worthless literature. *Haeckel*. [Rare.]

Ph. B. An abbreviation of the Latin (Middle Latin or New Latin) *Philosophiæ Baccalaureus*, Bachelor of Philosophy.

Ph. D. An abbreviation of the Latin (Middle Latin or New Latin) *Philosophiæ Doctor*, Doctor of Philosophy.

pheasant (fez'ąnt), *n.* [Early mod. E. also *phesant*, *fesunt*; < ME. *fesant*, *fesaunt* (with excrescent *t*), earlier *fesaun*, < AF. *fesant*, *fesaunt*, OF. *faisan*, F. *faisan* = Pr. *faisan*, *fayhan* = Sp. *faisan* = Pg. *feisão* = It. *fagiano*, *fasano* = D. *fazant* = MLG. *fasant*, *phasyan* = MHG. *fasân*, *fasant*, G. *fasan* (also OHG. *fasihuon*, MHG. *pfasehan*, *pfaschuon*, simulating *huon*, hen) (> Bohem. Pol. *bazhant* = Russ. *bazhantŭ*, *fazanŭ* = Hung. *fáczán*) = Dan. Sw. *fasan*, < L. *phasianus* (ML. *fasianus*), m., also *phasiana*, f., < Gr.

φασιανός, a pheasant (abbr. of L. *Phasianus avis*, Gr. Φασιανὸς ὄρνις, the Phasian bird), ‹ φασιανός, Phasian, of Phasis, ‹ Φᾶσις, a river in Colchis, near the mouth of which these birds are said to have been numerous.] A bird of the genus *Phasianus*, family *Phasianidæ*. (See the technical names.) (*a*) *Phasianus colchicus*, the bird originally called *pheasant* from its supposed origin, of which nothing is certainly known, and now for many centuries naturalized in Great Britain and in other parts of Europe. The cock bird in full plumage is nearly three feet long, of which length the tail is more than half. The head and neck are deep steel-blue, glancing greenish in some lights; and there is a bare red skin about the eyes. The general color is golden-brown, varying to chestnut or plain brown, on most parts intimately barred or laced with black. The

Common Pheasant (*Phasianus colchicus*).

hen is more yellowish-brown, and only about two thirds as long. This pheasant runs into some varieties in domestication, and also crosses freely with several related species. The several other forms of the restricted genus are definitely known as to their origin and habitat, all being natives of China and Tibet and more southerly regions of Asia, as well as of Japan and many other islands included in the Oriental fauna. Several of these are often seen in aviaries and in semi-domestication. They are such as Shaw's, *P. shawi*; the Mongolian, *P. mongolicus*; the Yarkand, *P. insignis*; the Formosan, *P. formosanus*; the ring-necked, *P. torquatus*; the Chinese ringless, *P. decollatus*; the Japanese green, *P. versicolor*; the green-backed golden, *P. elegans*; also pheasants known as Reeves's, Wallich's, Sömmering's, Swinhoe's, Elliot's, etc. Pheasants have often been introduced in the United States, where, however, none have been thoroughly naturalized, unless the cases of *P. versicolor* and *P. sœmmeringi* in Oregon should prove successful. (*b*) Hence, any bird of the subfamily *Phasianinæ* or (with a few exceptions) of the family *Phasianidæ*. (*c*) In the United States, the ruffed grouse, *Bonasa umbella*: so called in the Southern and Middle States wherever the bobwhite (*Ortyx virginiana*) is known as the *partridge*, and called *partridge* in the Northern States wherever the bobwhite is known as the *quail*. See cut under *Bonasa*. (*d*) Loosely, one of various birds which resemble or suggest a pheasant, especially in the length of the tail: usually with a qualifying word: (1) The reed-pheasant, or bearded titmouse, *Panurus biarmicus*. [Norfolk, Eng.] (2) The magpie. [Cornwall, Eng.] (3) One of several different American guans (*Cracidæ*). (4) The Australian mallee-bird. See *Leipoa*. (5) A duck, *Dafila acuta*: more fully called *pheasant-duck*, *sea-pheasant*, or *water-pheasant*. [Local, U. S. and Eng.] (6) A merganser; any one of the three species found in the United States: more fully called *pheasant-duck* or *water-pheasant*. [Local, U. S.]—**Amherstian or Lady Amherst's pheasant**, *Chrysolophus* or *Thaumalea amherstiæ*, one of the golden pheasants, with a very long tail, and highly developed ruff around the head, gorgeously arrayed in golden-yellow, green, crimson, white, and other colors. It is sometimes seen in confinement, like *T. picta*.—**Argus-pheasant.** See *Argus*, 3.—**Blood-pheasant**, any member of the genus *Ithaginis*, as *I. cruentatus*. See cut under *Ithaginis*.—**Bohemian pheasant**, a variety of the common pheasant, *Phasianus colchicus*, produced in semi-domestication.—**Copper pheasant**, Sömmering's pheasant, *P. sœmmeringi*, from Japan.—**Cornish pheasant**, the magpie. [Cornwall, Eng.]—**Derbian pheasant.** See *Derbian* and *Oreophasis*.—**Eared pheasant**, a pheasant of the genus *Crossoptilon*, having a tuft of feathers projecting like an ear on each side of the head and neck. They are large birds, not long-tailed, but with a peculiarity of the middle tail-feathers: the males are spurred; the plumage is not so brilliant as that of most pheasants, and the coloration is chiefly massed in large areas of light and dark. There are two Chinese species, *C. mantchuricum* and *C. auritum*; and two Tibetan, *C. thibetanum* and *C. drouyni*. All inhabit high mountain-ranges.—**English pheasant**, the common pheasant, *Phasianus colchicus*, an Asiatic bird naturalized in Great Britain prior to 1050.—**Fire-backed pheasant**, a fireback; a Macartney pheasant; a member of that section of the genus *Euplocamus* in which the plumage is intensely lustrous, part of the back being of a fiery tint. There are several species, as *E. ignitus*, inhabiting the Malay peninsula, Borneo, Sumatra, and Formosa. That of Siam is *E. prælatus*, formerly *Phasianus diardi*, sometimes forming a separate section of the genus, called *Diardigallus*. The Formosan fireback, *E. swinhoei*, has the fiery color of the back replaced by black and blue; it represents a section called *Hierophasis*.—**Golden pheasant**, a magnificent pheasant of the genus *Chrysolophus* or *Thaumalea*, as *C. pictus* or *T. picta*, and *C.* or *T. amherstiæ*. The former has long been known, and is often reared in confinement. It is long-tailed and ruffed; the plumage is scarlet, orange, golden, green, etc. These pheasants are natives of parts of China and Tibet. See cut under *Thaumalea*.—**Green pheasant**, *Phasianus versicolor*, of Japan, much of whose plumage is of an emerald-green.—**Guiana pheasant**, *Ortalida motmot*.—**Horned pheasant**, a pheasant of the genus *Ceriornis*; a satyr or tragopan: so called from the fleshy processes on the head, which resemble horns. See cut under *tragopan*.—**Impey pheasant.** See *Impeyan pheasant*.—**Kaleege or kalij pheasant**, a member of the genus *Euplocamus*, and of that section of the genus called *Gallophasis*. See *kaleege*.—**Macartney pheasant**, a fireback; a pheasant of the fire-backed section of *Euplocamus*, as *E. ignitus*, formerly included in a genus *Macartneya*.—**Native pheasant** of Australia, *Leipoa ocellata*: same as *mallee-bird*.—**Peacock-pheasant**, any pheasant of the genus *Polyplectron*. See cuts under *calcarate* and *Polyplectron*.—**Pucras pheasant.** See *Pucrasia*.—**Ring-necked pheasant**, *Phasianus torquatus*, of China, with a white collar and buff flanks, but in general resembling the common pheasant.—**Silver pheasant**, a pheasant of that section of the genus *Euplocamus* called *Nycthemerus*, in which the upper parts and tail are silvery-white, more or less varied with black, but strongly contrasted with the jet-black of the under parts. The best-known is *E. nycthemerus* of China, whose specific name translates a native designation of the dark and light colors, as if contrasting night and day.—**Snow-pheasant**, an eared pheasant; any species of the genus *Crossoptilon*: so called from their habitat.—**Wallich's pheasant**, *Phasianus* (*Catreus*) *wallichi*, the cheer.—**Water-pheasant**, an aquatic fowl with a long tail, or otherwise suggesting a pheasant, as the pintail duck or a merganser; specifically, *Hydrophasianus chirurgus*. See cut under *Hydrophasianus*.

pheasant-cuckoo (fez'ant-kůk″ö), *n.* Any spur-heeled or lark-heeled cuckoo; a coucal: so called from the length of the tail. See *Centropus*.

pheasant-duck (fez'ant-duk), *n.* Same as *pheasant* (*d*) (5) (6).

pheasant-finch (fez'ant-finch), *n.* An African astrild, *Astrilda undulata*: so called from its general figure and coloration.

pheasantry (fez'ant-ri), *n.*; pl. *pheasantries* (-riz). [‹ *pheasant* + *-ry*, after F. *faisanderie*.] A place where pheasants are bred, reared, and kept.

pheasant's-eye (fez'ants-ī), *n.* 1. See *Adonis*, 2.—2. Same as *pheasant's-eye pink* (which see, under *pink*[2]).

pheasant-shell (fez'ant-shel), *n.* A shell of the genus *Phasianella*. See cut under *Phasianella*.

pheasant-tailed (fez'ant-tāld), *a.* Having a long tail like that of a pheasant: as, the *pheasant-tailed* jacana, *Hydrophasianus chirurgus*, a bird of the family *Parridæ* or *Jacanidæ*, found in eastern and southeastern Asia. See cut under *Hydrophasianus*.

pheasant-wood (fez'ant-wůd), *n.* Same as *partridge-wood*.

phebe, *n.* See *phœbe*[1].

pheer†, pheere†. Bad spellings of *feer*[1] and *feer*[3].

pheese†, pheeze†, *n.* Bad spellings of *feeze*[1].

Phegopteris (fē-gop'te-ris), *n.* [NL. (Presl, 1836), ‹ Gr. φηγός, an oak (= L. *fāgus*, beech, = E. *beech*), + πτερίς, a fern.] A genus of ferns, the beech-ferns. The stipe is continuous with the rootstock, as in the *Aspideæ*, and the sori are naked, small, and borne on the back of the veins, below the apex; the frond is variable. There are about 90 species, of which number 5 are found in North America. By some pteridologists this genus is regarded as a section of the genus *Polypodium*.

Pheidiac, *a.* Same as *Phidian*.

Pheidian, *a.* See *Phidian*.

Phelipæa (fel-i-pē'ä), *n.* [NL. (Tournefort, 1700), named after Louis and Hiér. *Phélipeaux*, French naval officers and patrons of science.] A genus of parasitic plants of the gamopetalous order *Orobanchaceæ*, characterized by the broad and spreading corolla-lobes, equal parallel anther-cells, and five unequal acute calyx-teeth. Two species are Oriental herbs, with a rather smooth, unbranched, leafless stem, bearing a few scales at the base, above becoming a long smooth peduncle bearing a single large scarlet flower. *P. lutea*, of the Old World, has been used for dyeing black. Eight North American species, formerly included in this genus, are now separated, constituting the American genus *Aphyllon*. See *broom-rape*.

phelloderm (fel'ō-dėrm), *n.* [NL., ‹ Gr. φελλός, cork, + δέρμα, skin.] A definite layer of green parenchymatous cells beneath the cork, formed from the inner layers of the phellogen. Phelloderm may be demonstrated in the stems of *Ribes*, *Lonicera*, *Spiræa*, *Deutzia*, etc.

phellogen (fel'ō-jen), *n.* [NL., ‹ Gr. φελλός, cork, + -γενής, producing: see *-gen*.] Cork-meristem, or cork-cambium; the inner layers of cork-tissue, which possess cellular activity and give rise to cork.

phellogenetic (fel″ō-jē-net'ik), *a.* [‹ *phellogen*, after *genetic*.] In *bot.*, pertaining or relating to phellogen: as, *phellogenetic* meristem.

phelloplastics (fel-ō-plas'tiks), *n.* [= F. *phelloplastique*, ‹ Gr. φελλός, cork, + πλαστός, verbal adj. of πλάσσειν, form: see *plastic*.] The art of cutting and manipulating cork, as in making architectural models, etc.

phelonion (fē-lō'ni-on), *n.*; pl. *phelonia* (-ä). [‹ LGr. φελόνιον, φελώνιον, also φελόνης, incorrect forms for φαινόλιον, φαινόλης, ‹ L. *pænula*, *penula*, a cloak, in ML. a chasuble: see *pænula*.] An ecclesiastical vestment corresponding to the Roman Catholic chasuble, worn by patriarchs and priests of the Greek Church.

phenacetin (fē-nas'e-tin), *n.* [‹ *phen*(*ol*) + *acetin*.] An acetyl derivative of amidophenol, occurring in small tasteless colorless crystals but slightly soluble in water, antalgic and antipyretic.

phenacite (fen'a-sīt), *n.* [So called in allusion to its having been mistaken for quartz; ‹ Gr. φέναξ (φενακ-), an impostor, + *-ite*[2].] A rare mineral occurring in transparent rhombohedral crystals, colorless to wine-yellow, and having a vitreous luster. It is a silicate of beryllium (glucinum). It is found in the Urals, also in Switzerland, and on Mount Antoro in Colorado. As a precious stone, the colorless transparent variety is extremely brilliant by artificial light.

phenakism† (fen'a-kizm), *n.* [‹ Gr. φενακισμός, cheating, quackery, ‹ φενακίζειν, cheat, ‹ φέναξ (φενακ-), a cheat, quack, impostor.] The act of conveying false ideas or impressions; deceit. *Bacon.*

phenakistoscope (fen-a-kis'tō-skōp), *n.* [‹ Gr. φενακιστικός, deceitful (‹ φενακίζειν, cheat, deceive, trick, ‹ φέναξ, a cheat: see *phenakism*), + σκοπεῖν, see.] An optical instrument which produces the representation of actual motion, as in leaping, walking, flying, etc. It consists of a disk on which a figure is repeated in successive positions.

Phenakistoscope.

The disk *a* has drawn upon it the figures arranged in successive positions. It is rotated by spinning with the fingers applied to a small boss or nut in the rear (not shown in the cut). *b*, *b* are the slits through which the reflected images are viewed.

When the disk is caused to revolve and is observed through a slit as reflected in a mirror, a single figure appears to the eye, owing to the principle of the persistence of impressions on the retina, to assume in turn the various positions of the separate figures, its motion appearing to be continuous.

phenetol (fen'et-ol), *n.* [‹ *phen*(*ol*) + *-et-* + *-ol*.] Ethyl phenyl ether, $C_2H_5.OC_6H_5$, a volatile aromatic-smelling liquid.—**Phenetol red.** Same as *coccinin*.

phengite (fen'jīt), *n.* [See *fengite*.] A variety of muscovite, or common potash mica. See *muscovite*.

phenic (fē'nik), *a.* [‹ F. *phénique*; as *phen*(*ol*) + *-ic*.] Obtained from coal-tar: as, *phenic* or carbolic acid. See *carbolic*. Also *phenylic*.

Phenician, Phœnician (fē-nish'an), *a.* and *n.* [= F. *Phénicien*, ‹ L. *Phœnicius*, Phenician, ‹ *Phœnice*, ‹ Gr. Φοινίκη, Phenicia, ‹ Φοῖνιξ (› L. *Phœnix*), a Phenician.] **I.** *a.* Of or pertaining to Phenicia.

II. *n.* 1. A native or an inhabitant of Phenicia, an ancient country on the coast of Syria, of which Tyre and Sidon were the chief cities. The Phenicians were probably of Semitic race, and were celebrated for their commerce, colonies, and inventions.—2. The language of the ancient Phenicians. It was a Semitic dialect, akin to Hebrew.

phenicin, phenicine (fen'i-sin), *n.* [Also *phœnicin*; ‹ F. *phénicine*, ‹ Gr. φοῖνιξ, purple-red: see *phenix*.] A brown coloring matter produced by the action of nitrosulphuric acid on carbolic acid (phenol).

phenicious (fē-nish'us), *a.* [Prop. **pheniceous*; < L. *phœniceus*, < Gr. φοινίκεος, purple-red, < φοίνιξ, purple: see *phenix*.] Of or pertaining to phenicin; of the color of phenicin. Also *phœniceous*.

phenicopter†, phœnicopter† (fen-i-kop'tėr), *n.* [< F. *phénicoptère* = Pg. *phenicoptero* = It. *fenicottero, fenicontero*, < L. *phœnicopterus*, < Gr. φοινικόπτερος, a bird, supposed to be the flamingo, lit. red-feathered, < φοίνιξ (φοινικ-), purple-red (see *phenix*), + πτερόν, feather, wing.] A flamingo.

He [Vitellius] blended together the livers of giltheads, the brains of pheasants and peacocks, tongues of *phenicopters*, and the melts of lampreys. *Hakewill*, Apology, p. 381.

Phenicopterus (fē-ni-kop'te-rus), *n.* See *Phœnicopterus*.

phenix, phœnix[1] (fē'niks), *n.* [Formerly *fenix*, but now *phenix* or *phœnix*, after the L. spelling; < ME. *fenix*, < AS. *fenix* = D. *feniks* = MLG. *fēnix* = G. *phönix* = Sw. Dan. *fönix* = F. *phénix* = Sp. *fenix* = Pg. *phenix* = It. *fenice*, < L. *phœnix*, < Gr. φοίνιξ, a fabulous bird, the phenix (see def. 1). The name has no obvious connection with φοῖνιξ, purple-red, purple, red, also the palm, date-palm, date, also a kind of grass, etc., also [*cap.*] a Phenician: see *Phenician*. It is by some identified with Egypt. *bennu*, a bird (supposed to be a small heron) sacred to Osiris, emblem of the soul, and also symbol of a certain cycle of time.] **1.** In *anc. Oriental myth.*, a wonderful bird of great beauty, which, after living 500 or 600 years in the Arabian wilderness, the only one of its kind, built for itself a funeral pile of spices and aromatic gums, lighted the pile with the fanning of its wings, and was burned upon it, but from its ashes revived in the freshness of youth. Hence the phenix often serves as an emblem of immortality. Allusions to this myth are found in the hieroglyphic writings, and the fable survives in popular forms in Arabia, Persia, and India. By heralds the phenix is always represented in the midst of flames.

Than the Brid *Fenix* comethe, and brennethe him self to Askes. *Mandeville*, Travels, p. 48.

For, as there is but one *phœnix* in the world, so there is but one tree in Arabia wherein she buyldeth. *Lyly*, Euphues (ed. Arber), p. 312.

The bird *phœnix* is supposed to have taken that name of this date tree (called in Greek φοίνιξ); for it was assured unto me that the said bird died with the tree, and revived of itself as the tree sprung again. *Holland*, tr. of Pliny, xiii. 4.

Hence—**2.** A person of unique excellence; one of singular distinction or peerless beauty; a paragon.

For God's love let him not be a *phenix*, let him not be alone. *Latimer*, 1st Sermon bef. Edw. VI., 1549.

That incomparable Queene, most deservedly called the *Phœnix* of her sex. *Coryat*, Crudities, I. 43.

The Haji repaid me for my docility by vaunting me everywhere as the very *phœnix* of physicians. *R. F. Burton*, El-Medinah, p. 60.

3. In *entom.*, the geometrid moth *Cidaria ribesiaria*, whose larva feeds on the currant and gooseberry: a collectors' name in England. The small phenix is *C. silaceata*.—**Chinese phenix.** Same as *fung-hwang*.—**Phenix badge**, a medal struck in the reign of Elizabeth about 1574, bearing on the obverse a portrait of Elizabeth, and on the reverse a phenix in flames with cipher and crown above. The inscriptions seem to refer to the plague then raging. It was probably worn by the immediate favorites and courtiers of Elizabeth.—**Phenix fowls.** See *Japanese long-tailed fowls*, under *Japanese*.—**Phenix post.** See *post*[1].

phenix-stone (fē'niks-stōn), *n.* An artificial stone in which furnace-slag is used in place of sand.

phenocryst (fē'nǫ-krist), *n.* [< Gr. φαίνειν, show, + κρύστ(αλλος), crystal: see *crystal*.] One of the prominent crystals in a porphyritic rock.

phenogam, *n.* See *phænogam*.

Phenogamia (fē-nǫ-gā'mi-ạ̈), *n. pl.* See *Phanerogamia*.

phenogamic, phenogamous, *a.* See *phænogamic, phænogamous*.

phenol (fē'nol), *n.* [< F. *phénol*, said to be < Gr. φαίνειν, shine, appear (but prob. < φοίν(ιξ), purple-red), + *-ol*.] **1.** Phenyl alcohol, C_6H_5OH, more commonly called *carbolic acid*.—**2.** The general name of a compound formed from benzene and its homologues by the substitution of hydroxyl for hydrogen in the benzene nucleus. The phenols correspond to tertiary alcohols, as they contain the group COH, and all have weak acid properties.—**Phenol-camphor**, camphorated phenol; camphor combined with carbolic acid.

phenological, phænological (fē-nǫ-loj'i-kal), *a.* [< *phenolog-y* + *-ic-al*.] Pertaining to phenology.

phenologist, phænologist (fę̄-nol'ǫ-jist), *n.* [< *phenolog-y* + *-ist*.] One who is versed in phenology. *Nature*, XXXIX. 12.

phenology, phænology (fę̄-nol'ǫ-ji), *n.* [Short for *phenomenology*, with a restricted application.] That branch of applied meteorology which treats of the influence of climate on the recurrence of the annual phenomena of animal and vegetable life. So far as it concerns plant-growth, phenology is also a branch of botany, and records dates of budding, leafing, blooming, and fruiting, in order to correlate these epochs with the attendant progress of meteorological conditions. Among the phenomena of animal life, the migration of birds has been especially studied as a department of phenology.

phenomena, *n.* Plural of *phenomenon*.

phenomenal (fę̄-nom'e-nạl), *a.* [Also *phænomenal*; = F. *phénoménal* = Sp. *fenomenal*; as *phenomenon* + *-al*.] **1.** Of, pertaining to, or of the nature of phenomena, or the appearances of things, as distinguished from the things in themselves; pertaining to the occurrences or changing phases of matter or mind.

Mill, . . . in holding that all knowledge is only relative and *phenomenal*, and that causation is merely invariable sequence, cuts at the roots of our belief both in matter and force. *Dawson*, Nature and the Bible, p. 188.

The basis of Fichte's system is an absolute Ego, of which the Ego of consciousness is at best *phænomenal*. *Veitch*, Introd. to Descartes's Method, p. lxxix.

The *Phenomenal* is the Real; there is no other real that we can distinguish from it. *H. Sidgwick*, Methods of Ethics, p. 120.

Thought must alter the *phenomenal* sequence, no doubt; but so also does mere emotion, and again sensation. *F. H. Bradley*, Mind, XIII. 26.

2. Of the nature of a phenomenon, or extraordinary fact in nature; so surprising or extraordinary as to arrest the attention or excite wonder; impressively notable or important; beyond what is common or usual; remarkable: as, the *phenomenal* growth of the United States; a brain of *phenomenal* size.—**Phenomenal idealism.** Same as *Berkeleian idealism* (which see, under *idealism*).

II. *n.* That which is in the nature of a phenomenon. [Rare.]

The greatness of the change is sufficiently hinted in the Vision of St. John: "I saw a new heaven and a new earth; for the first heaven and the first earth had passed away, and there was no more sea" (Rev. xxi. 1). In the matter of elementals, the new earth will be identical with the old; in the matter of *phenomenals*, the new earth will be different from the old. *Boardman*, Creative Week, p. 289.

phenomenalism (fę̄-nom'e-nạl-izm), *n.* [= F. *phénoménalisme*; as *phenomenal* + *-ism*.] The philosophical doctrine that the phenomenal and the real are identical—that phenomena are the only realities. Also called *externalism*.

Phenomenalism . . . is that philosophy which holds that all existences, all possible objects of thought, are of two kinds only, external and internal phenomena; or sensuous objects, such as color, shape, hardness, or groups of these, and the unsensuous ideas we have of sensuous objects. *J. C. Shairp*, Culture and Religion, p. 58.

phenomenalist (fę̄-nom'e-nal-ist), *n.* [< *phenomenal-ism* + *-ist*.] An adherent or disciple of phenomenalism.

phenomenality (fę̄-nom-e-nal'ị-ti), *n.* [= F. *phénoménalité*; as *phenomenal* + *-ity*.] The character of being phenomenal, in either sense of that word.

phenomenalize (fę̄-nom'e-nạl-īz), *v. t.*; pret. and pp. *phenomenalized*, ppr. *phenomenalizing*. [< *phenomenal* + *-ize*.] To represent as a phenomenon; cause to figure as a phenomenon.

His [Locke's] integrity is also illustrated in his acknowledgment of the unimaginable, and in this sense incognizable, in our thought of Substance. He tries to *phenomenalize* it; but he finds that it cannot be *phenomenalized*, and yet that we cannot dispense with it. *Encyc. Brit.*, XIV. 760.

phenomenally (fę̄-nom'e-nạl-i), *adv.* **1.** As a phenomenon; as a mere phase or appearance.—**2.** In an extraordinary or surprising manner or degree.

phenomenism (fē-nom'e-nizm), *n.* [< *phenomenon* + *-ism*.] The doctrine or principles of the phenomenists.

phenomenist (fę̄-nom'e-nist), *n.* [< *phenomenon* + *-ist*.] One who believes only in what he observes, or in phenomena, having no regard to their causes or consequences; one who rejects a priori reasoning or necessary primary principles; one who does not believe in an invariable connection between cause and effect, but holds this to be nothing more than a habitually observed sequence.

phenomenize (fę̄-nom'e-nīz), *v. t.*; pret. and pp. *phenomenized*, ppr. *phenomenizing*. [< *phenomen-on* + *-ize*.] To bring into the world of experience.

phenomenological (fę̄-nom'e-nǭ-loj'i-kạl), *a.* [< *phenomenolog-y* + *-ic-al*.] Of or pertaining to phenomenology; related or relating to phenomenology.

My metaphysic is psychological or *phenomenological* metaphysic. *Mind*, IX. 406.

phenomenology (fę̄-nom-e-nol'ǫ-ji), *n.* [= F. *phénoménologie* = Pg. *phenomenologia*, < Gr. φαινόμενα, phenomena, + -λογία, < λέγειν, speak: see *-ology*.] A description or history of phenomena.

phenomenon (fę̄-nom'e-non), *n.*; pl. *phenomena* (-nạ̈). [Formerly also *phænomenon*; = F. *phénomène* = G. *phänomen* = Sw. *fenomen* = Dan. *fænomen* = Sp. *fenómeno* = It. *fenomeno* = Pg. *phenomeno*, < LL. *phænomenon*, < Gr. φαινόμενον, pl. φαινόμενα, that which appears or is seen, neut. of pass. part. of φαίνειν, shine, show, pass. φαίνεσθαι, appear, < √ φαν, extended form of √ φα = Skt. *bhā*, shine: see *phase*[1], *face*[1], etc. Cf. *phantasm*, *phantom*, *phantasy*, *fancy*, etc.] **1.** In *philos.*, an appearance or immediate object of experience, as distinguished from a thing in itself.

How pitifull and ridiculous are the grounds upon which such men pretend to account for the lowest and commonest *phænomena* of nature without recurring to a God and Providence! *South*, Sermons, IV. ix.

The term appearance is used to denote not only that which reveals itself to our observation, as existent, but also to signify that which only seems to be, in contrast to that which truly is. There is thus not merely a certain vagueness in the word, but it even involves a kind of contradiction to the sense in which it is used when employed for *phænomenon*. In consequence of this, the term *phænomenon* has been naturalized in our language as a philosophical substitute for the term appearance. *Sir W. Hamilton*, Metaph., viii.

A *phenomenon*, as commonly understood, is what is manifest, sensible, evident, the implication being that there are eyes to see, ears to hear, and so forth. *J. Ward*, Encyc. Brit., XX. 38.

And do we need any more evidence to convince us that *phenomena*—by which I mean the effects produced upon our consciousness by unknown external agencies—are all that we can compare and classify, and are therefore all that we can know? *J. Fiske*, Cosmic Philos., I. 20.

2. In *science*, a fact directly observed, being either (*a*) an individual circumstance or occurrence, such as the emergence of a temporary star, or more usually (*b*) a regular kind of fact observed on certain kinds of occasion, such as the electrical sparks seen in combing the hair of some persons in cold, dry weather.

In fiction, the principles are given, to find the facts; in history, the facts are given, to find the principles: and the writer who does not explain the *phenomena* as well as state them performs only one half of his office. *Macaulay*, History.

We do not inquire respecting this human nature what are the laws under which its varied *phenomena* may be generalized, and accommodate our acts to them. *H. Spencer*, Social Statics, p. 507.

Last night we watched from our roof that lovely *phenomenon*, the approach of Venus to the moon. *J. F. Clarke*, Self-Culture, p. 119.

3. Any extraordinary occurrence or fact in nature; something strange and uncommon; a prodigy; a very remarkable personage or performer.

"This, sir," said Mr. Vincent Crummles, bringing the Maiden forward, "this is the infant *phenomenon*, Miss Ninetta Crummles." *Dickens*, Nicholas Nickleby, xxiii.

Chess-board phenomenon, the effect produced by crossing the visual axes in front of a chess-board or other similar object, so that there is a partial superposition of the images in the two eyes, and an appearance as if the objects were nearer and smaller.—**Entoptic phenomena.** See *entoptic*.—**Leidenfrost phenomenon.** See *spheroidal condition*, under *spheroidal*.—**Peltier's phenomenon.** See *Peltier effect* (under *effect*), and *thermo-electricity*. = **Syn.** 3. Prodigy, marvel, wonder.

phenozygous (fę̄-noz'i-gus), *a.* [< Gr. φαίνειν, show, + ζυγόν, yoke: see *yoke*.] Having, as a skull, the zygomatic arches visible directly from above; having the bizygomatic diameter greater than the maximum transverse frontal diameter, and the angle of Quatrefages positive.

phenyl, phenyle (fē'nil), *n.* [< F. *phényle*; as *phen(ol)* + *-yl*.] An organic radical (C_6H_5; in the free state, $C_{12}H_{10}$) found in phenol (or carbolic acid), benzol, and aniline. It crystallizes from alcohol in colorless nacreous scales of an agreeable odor, which melt at 70° C. and sublime at a higher temperature.—**Phenyl brown.** See *brown*.

phenylamide (fē-nil-am'id or -īd), *n.* [< *phenyl* + *amide*.] A compound formed by the substitution of one or more amido-groups for the hydrogen of benzene. The phenylamides are very feeble bases. The most important commercially is aniline.

phenylamine (fē-nil-am'in), *n.* [< *phenyl* + *amine*.] Same as *aniline*.

phenyle, *n.* See *phenyl*.

phenylia (fẹ-nil'i-ạ̈), *n.* [NL., < E. *phenyl*, q. v.] Same as *aniline*.

phenylic (fẹ-nil'ik), *a.* [< *phenyl* + *-ic*.] Same as *phenic*.

pheon (fē'on), *n.* [Origin obscure.] **1.** A barbed javelin formerly carried by the royal sergeant-at-arms. *Fairholt.* —**2.** In *her.*, a barbed head, as of an arrow or a fish-spear, differing from the broad-arrow in being engrailed on the inner side of the barbs unless otherwise blazoned. The point is always directed downward unless otherwise stated in the blazon. Also called *ferrum jaculi*. Compare *broad-arrow*.

Pheon, 2.

Pherecratean (fer″ek-rạ-tē'ạn), *n.* [< Gr. Φερεκράτης, Pherecrates (see def.).] In *anc. pros.*, a logaœdic meter (named from Pherecrates, a Greek comic poet), similar to a trochaic tripody, but having a dactyl for the second trochee (also called *Aristophanic*); also, a logaœdic tripody (catalectic or acatalectic) with a dactyl either in the first or second place.

Pherecratic (fer-ek-rat'ik), *n.* Same as *Pherecratean*.

phester†, *n.* A bad spelling of *fester*[1].

phew (fū), *interj.* [A mere exclamation; cf. *phoo*, *pho*, *phy*, etc.] An exclamation of disgust, weariness, or surprise.

phi (fī), *n.* The Greek letter φ, corresponding to the English *ph* (*f*).

phial (fī'ạl), *n.* and *v.* See *vial*.

phiale (fī'ạ-lē), *n.*; pl. *phialæ* (-lē). [< Gr. φιάλη, a patera, saucer: see *vial*.] **1.** A flat saucer-shaped Greek vase used for pouring religious libations: commonly known by its Latin name, *patera*.—**2.** Same as *cantharus*, 2.

Phibalura (fib-ạ-lū'rạ̈), *n.* [A mutilated and corrupt form of *Amphibolura*, q.v.] A genus of birds established by Vieillot in 1816. The type and only species is *P. flavirostris* of Brazil, a bird of the family *Cotingidæ*. The plumage is yellow and black, the beak yellow. The name is derived from the long, deeply forked tail.

Phidian (fid'i-ạn), *a.* [< L. *Phidias*, < Gr. Φειδίας, Phidias (see def.), + *-an*.] Of, pertaining to, or produced by Phidias, the most eminent artist of the most splendid time of ancient Athens, during the fifth century B. C., the artistic director of the monumental works of Pericles, and the sculptor of the decoration of the Parthenon and of the chryselephantine Zeus of Olympia. Hence, in general, noting the Athenian art of the third quarter of the fifth century, including not only the work of Phidias himself, but also that molded by

Phidian School of Sculpture.—The "Gaia and Thalassa" (or Demeter and Kora), from the eastern pediment of the Parthenon.

his example and executed by the galaxy of great artists of whom he was the chief; also, from the artistic standpoint, noting the age when Phidias and his immediate disciples worked. At this time the Greek artists had already won complete command of the material side of their profession, so that they were unhampered by difficulties of execution, and their work was constantly inspired by a high and noble ideal. Also written *Pheidian*.

Phigalian (fi-gā'li-ạn), *a.* [< Gr. Φιγάλεια, Phigalia (see def.), + *-an*.] Pertaining to Phigalia, an ancient town in the Peloponnesus.—**Phigalian marbles**, a series of twenty-three blocks sculptured in alto-rilievo, from the interior frieze of the cella of the temple of Apollo Epikourios at Phigalia or Bassæ, now preserved in the British Museum. They represent the combat of the Centaurs and Lapithæ, and that of the Greeks and Amazons, and are of high artistic excellence, though lacking the dignity and repose of the almost contemporaneous art of the Parthenon.

phil-. See *philo-*.

philabeg† (fil'ạ-beg), *n.* Same as *filibeg*.

Philacte (fi-lak'tē), *n.* [NL. (Bannister, 1870), < Gr. φιλεῖν, love, + ἀκτή, sea-shore.] A genus of arctic maritime *Anatidæ* of the subfamily *Anserinæ*, having a variegated plumage without metallic tints, incised webs, rostral lamellæ exposed posteriorly, and skull with superorbital depression; the painted geese. *P. canagica* is the emperor-goose of Alaska, abounding at the mouth of the Yukon. The color is wavy bluish-gray, with lavender tinting and sharp black crescentic marks, the head, nape, and tail being white, the former often washed with amber, the throat black speckled with white. Its flesh is rank and scarcely fit for food.

philactery†, *n.* See *phylactery*.

Philadelphian[1] (fil-ạ-del'fi-ạn), *a.* and *n.* [< *Philadelphia* (see def.) + *-an*. The name *Philadelphia*, usually explained to mean the 'city of brotherly love' (as if identical with Gr. φιλαδελφία, brotherly love), is taken from the LL. *Philadelphia*, < Gr. Φιλαδέλφεια, the name of a city of Lydia (Rev. i. 11, iii. 7), now Ala-shehr (also the name of a city in Cilicia, and of another in Cœle-Syria), lit. 'city of Philadelphus,' namely, of Attalus II., king of Pergamum, surnamed Philadelphus (Φιλάδελφος) on account of his affection for his brother Eumenes, whom he succeeded; < φιλάδελφος, loving one's brother or sister, < φιλεῖν, love, + ἀδελφός, brother, ἀδελφή, sister.] **I.** *a.* Of or pertaining to Philadelphia, the chief city of Pennsylvania, situated on the Delaware and Schuylkill rivers.

II. *n.* A native or an inhabitant of the city of Philadelphia.

Philadelphian[2] (fil-ạ-del'fi-ạn), *a.* [< L. *Philadelphus* (< Gr. Φιλάδελφος, a man's name: see def.) + *-ian*. Cf. *Philadelphian*[1].] Pertaining to Ptolemy Philadelphus, king of Egypt, 283–247 B. C., a patron of literature, science, and art.

philadelphian[3] (fil-ạ-del'fi-ạn), *n.* [Cf. F. *philadelphe*, member of a society formed in France in the 17th century, < Gr. φιλάδελφος, loving one's brother: see *Philadelphian*[1].] One of a short-lived mystical denomination founded in England in the end of the seventeenth century.

philadelphite (fil-ạ-del'fīt), *n.* [< *Philadelphia* (see def.) + *-ite*[2].] A kind of vermiculite found near Philadelphia in Pennsylvania.

Philadelphus (fil-ạ-del'fus), *n.* [NL. (Linnæus, 1737), < Gr. φιλάδελφον, a sweet-flowering shrub, perhaps jasmine; named after Ptolemy *Philadelphus*, Gr. Φιλάδελφος, king of Egypt: see *Philadelphian*[1].] A genus of shrubs of the order *Saxifrageæ* and the tribe *Hydrangeæ*, characterized by the inferior ovary, numerous stamens, and four or five imbricate petals. The 12 species are natives of central Europe, the southern United States, Japan, and the Himalayas. They bear round opposite branches, opposite leaves, and rather large flowers, corymbed or solitary in the axils, white or straw-colored, and commonly fragrant. They are common in cultivation as ornamental shrubs, under the names *mock-orange* and *syringa*. (For flower-section, see cut under *epigynous*.) *P. grandiflorus* and two other species are wild in the United States from Virginia southward.

Flowering Branch of Syringa or Mock-orange (*Philadelphus coronarius*). *a*, the fruit.

philamot†, *n.* A bad spelling of *filemot*. *Holland*, tr. of Pliny.

Philampelus (fi-lam'pe-lus), *n.* [NL. (Harris, 1839), < Gr. φιλάμπελος, loving the vine, < φιλεῖν, love, + ἄμπελος, a vine.] A genus of sphingid moths of the subfamily *Chærocampinæ*, includ-

Larva of *Philampelus achemon*, slightly reduced.

ing species of large size, with curved antennæ, somewhat pointed fore wings, and produced anal angle of the hind wings. There are four North American species, two of them extending into the West Indies; in the larval state all are vine-feeders, whence the generic name. The larvæ have the head small and globose, the anterior segments slender and retractile into the swollen third segments; and the anal horn is wanting in full-grown individuals, being replaced by a shining lenticular tubercle. *P. achemon* and *P. pandorus* or *satellitia* are abundant, and of economic importance from the damage done in vineyards by their larvæ.

Philampelus achemon, Moth. slightly reduced.

philander (fi-lan'dėr), *n.* [So called in allusion to *Philander*, as the name in old plays and romances of a lover, e. g. "*Philander*, Prince of Cyprus, passionately in love with Erota," one of the dramatis personæ of Beaumont and Fletcher's "Laws of Candy," and *Philander*, the name of a virtuous youth in Ariosto's "Orlando Furioso," between whom and a married woman named Gabrina there were certain tender passages; < Gr. φίλανδρος, loving men, < φιλεῖν, love, + ἀνήρ (ἀνδρ-), man. Cf. *phyllis*, *n.* and *v.*] **1.** A lover.

> This exceeds all precedent; I am brought to fine uses, to become a botcher of second hand marriages between Abigails and Andrews!—I'll couple you!—Yes, I'll baste you together, you and your *Philander!*
> *Congreve*, Way of the World, v. 1.

2. In *zoöl.*, one of several different marsupial mammals. Specifically—(*a*) The Australian bandicoot, *Perameles lagotis*. (*b*) A South American opossum of one of several different species.

philander (fi-lan'dėr), *v. i.* [< *philander*, *n.* Cf. *phyllis*, *v.*] To play the philander; pay court to a woman, especially without serious intention; make love in a foolish way; "spoon."

> Sir Kit was too much taken up *philandering* to consider the law in this case. *Miss Edgeworth*, Castle Rackrent, ii.

> You must make up your mind whether you wish to be accepted: . . . you can't be *philandering* after her again for six weeks. *George Eliot*, Daniel Deronda, xxv.

philanderer (fi-lan'dėr-ėr), *n.* One who philanders; a male flirt.

> At last, without a note of warning, appeared in Beddgelert a phenomenon which rejoiced some hearts, but perturbed also the spirits, not only of the Oxford *philanderers*, but those of Elsley Vavasour.
> *Kingsley*, Two Years Ago, xix.

Philanthidæ (fi-lan'thi-dē), *n. pl.* [NL., < *Philanthus* + *-idæ*.] A family of fossorial hymenopterous insects, founded on the genus *Philanthus*. They have a narrow prothorax, three submarginal cells of the fore wings, the second and third of which receive each a recurrent nervure, and sessile or subsessile abdomen. These wasps are small but beautiful; they prey chiefly on bees and beetles, and their burrows seldom exceed five inches in length. See cut under *Philanthus*.

philanthrope (fil'ạn-thrōp), *n.* [< F. *philanthrope* = Sp. *filántropo* = It. *filantropo* = Pg. *philanthropo*, < Gr. φιλάνθρωπος, humane: see *philanthropy*.] A philanthropist.

> He had a goodness of nature and disposition in so great a degree that he may be deservedly styled a *philanthrope*.
> *Roger North*, Lord Guilford, II. 127. (*Davies.*)

philanthropic (fil-ạn-throp'ik), *a.* [= F. *philanthropique* = Sp. *filantrópico* = Pg. *philantropico* = It. *filantropico*, < ML. **philanthropicus* (in adv. *philanthropice*), < Gr. *φιλανθρωπικός, a false reading for φιλάνθρωπος, humane, a philanthropist: see *philanthropy*.] Of or pertaining to philanthropy; characterized by or springing from love of mankind; actuated by a desire to do good to one's fellows.

> The kindlier feeling of men is seen in all varieties of *philanthropic* effort. *H. Spencer*, Social Statics.

=**Syn.** Benevolent, humane.

philanthropical (fil-ạn-throp'i-kạl), *a.* [< *philanthropic* + *-al*.] Same as *philanthropic*.

philanthropically (fil-ạn-throp'i-kạl-i), *adv.* In a philanthropic manner; benevolently.

philanthropinism (fil-ạn-throp'i-nizm), *n.* [< Gr. *φιλανθρώπινος (a false reading for φιλάνθρωπος, humane: see *philanthropy*) + *-ism*.] A system of education on so-called natural principles, promoted by Basedow and his friends in Germany in the eighteenth century.

philanthropinist (fil-ạn-throp'i-nist), *n.* [< *philanthropin-ism* + *-ist*.] An advocate of philanthropinism.

philanthropism (fi-lan'thrō-pizm), *n.* [= F. *philanthropisme*; as *philanthrop-y* + *-ism*.] Philanthropy.

philanthropist (fi-lan'thrō-pist), *n.* [< *philanthrop-y* + *-ist*.] One who is actuated by a philanthropic spirit; one who loves mankind, or wishes well to his fellow-men and endeavors to benefit them by active works of benevolence or beneficence; one who from philanthropic motives endeavors to do good to his fellows.

> We all know the wag's definition of a *philanthropist*—a man whose charity increases directly as the square of the distance. *George Eliot*, Middlemarch, xxxviii.

philanthropistic (fi-lan-thrọ̄-pis'tik), *a.* [< *philanthropist* + *-ic.*] Relating to or characterizing professional philanthropists. [Rare.]

Over the wild-surging chaos in the leaden air are only sudden glares of revolutionary lightning; then mere darkness with *philanthropistic* phosphorescences, empty meteoric lights. *Carlyle*, Sterling, v. (*Davies.*)

philanthropy (fi-lan'thrọ̄-pi), *n.* [Formerly *philanthropic*; < F. *philanthropie* = Sp. *filantropia* = Pg. *philantropia* = It. *filantropia*, < LL. *philanthropia*, < Gr. φιλανθρωπία, humanity, benevolence, generosity, < φιλάνθρωπος, loving mankind, humane, benevolent, liberal, < φιλεῖν, love, + ἄνθρωπος, man.] Love of mankind, especially as evinced in deeds of practical beneficence and endeavors for the good of one's fellows.

They thought themselves not much concerned to acquire that God-like excellency, a *philanthropy* and love to all mankind. *Jer. Taylor*, Works (ed. 1835), III. i.

=**Syn.** *Philanthropy, Charity.* Originally these words were the same, meaning the love of fellow-man, a sense which *philanthropy* retains, but *charity* (except in Biblical language: see 1 Cor. xiii., authorized version) has lost. Each expresses both spirit and action; but *philanthropy* cannot be applied to a concrete act, while *charity* may; hence we speak of a *charity*, but not of a *philanthropy*; on the other hand, as a spirit, *philanthropy* looks upon human welfare as a thing to be promoted, especially by preventing or mitigating actual suffering, while *charity*, outside of Biblical usage, is simply disposed to take as favorable a view as possible of the character, conduct, motives, or the like, of a fellow-man. As activity, *charity* helps men individually; *philanthropy* helps the individual as a member of the race, or provides for large numbers. *Philanthropy* agitates for prison-reform and the provision of occupation for released convicts; *charity* gives a released convict such personal help as he needs.

Philanthus (fi-lan'thus), *n.* [NL. (Fabricius, 1793), < Gr. φιλανθής, loving flowers (cf. Φίλανθος, a man's name), < φιλεῖν, love, + ἄνθος, flower.] 1. In *entom.*, a notable genus of digger-wasps, typical of the family *Philanthidæ*, having the third submarginal cell narrow and the antennæ inserted in the middle of the face, not far above the clypeus. There are 24 American and 5 European species. The British *P. apivorus* preys especially upon the hive-bee.

Philanthus ventilabris, natural size.

2. In *ornith.*, a genus of meliphagine birds. Also called *Manorrhina*. *Lesson*, 1831.

philantomba (fil-an-tom'bä), *n.* [NL.; supposed to be a native name.] An African antelope of the genus *Cephalophus*, as *C. maxwelli*.

philargurous†, *a.* [< *philargur-y* + *-ous.*] Money-loving; avaricious. *Sir R. L'Estrange.*

philargury† (fi-lär'gụ̄-ri), *n.* [Properly *philargyry*; ML. **philargyria*, *philargiria*, < Gr. φιλαργυρία, love of money, covetousness (the word used in 1 Tim. vi. 10), < φιλάργυρος, loving money, < φιλεῖν, love, + ἄργυρος, silver, money: see *argyrism*, *argent.*] Love of money; avarice.

philatelic (fil-a-tel'ik), *a.* [< *philatel-y* + *-ic.*] Of or relating to philately.

philatelist (fi-lat'e-list), *n.* [< *philatel-y* + *-ist.*] A collector of postage-stamps and revenue-stamps as objects of curiosity or interest.

philately (fi-lat'e-li), *n.* [< F. *philatélie*, intended to mean 'the love of the study of all that concerns prepayment,' i. e. of stamps, absurdly formed (by M. Herpin, a stamp-collector, in "Le Collectionneur," in 1865) < Gr. φίλος, loving (prop. φιλεῖν, love), + ἀτελής, free of tax or charge (taken in the sense of 'prepaid'), < ἀ- priv. + τέλος, tax, duty.] The fancy for collecting and classifying postage-stamps and revenue-stamps as objects of curiosity; also, the occupation of making such collections.

philauty† (fil'â-ti), *n.* [Also *philautie*; < F. *philautie* = Sp. *filaucia* = Pg. *philaucia* = It. *filauzia*, < Gr. φιλαυτία, self-love, < φίλαυτος, loving oneself, < φιλεῖν, love, + αὐτός, self.] Love of self; selfishness.

Then *Philauty* and Pride shall stretch her Soul'
With swelling poison, making her disdain
Heav'ns narrow gate. *J. Beaumont*, Psyche, i. 38.

philazer†, *n.* A bad spelling of *filacer*.

philenor (fi-lē'nor), *n.* [NL., < Gr. φιλήνωρ, φιλάνωρ, loving one's husband, < φιλεῖν, love, + ἀνήρ, man, husband. Cf. *philander.*] A butterfly, *Papilio philenor*, one of the handsomest of the North American swallowtails. The fore wings are black with greenish metallic reflections; the hind are brilliant steel-blue with greenish reflections; the larva is velvety-black, covered with long black fleshy tubercles and shorter orange ones. It feeds upon plants of the genus *Aristolochia*, and is somewhat gregarious in early life. See cuts under *Papilio* and *Papilionidæ*.

Philepitta (fil-e-pit'ä), *n.* [NL. (Isidore Geoffroy St. Hilaire, 1838), < Gr. φιλεῖν, love, + NL. *Pitta.*] The typical genus of *Philepittidæ*, containing two Madagascan species, *P. castanea* and *P. schlegeli*. The systematic position of the genus has been much questioned, it having been classed with the *Pittidæ* or Old World ant-thrushes, the birds of paradise, and the *Nectariniidæ* or honey-suckers. The genus is also called *Brissonia*, *Buddinghia*, and *Paictes*.

Philepittidæ (fil-e-pit'i-dē), *n. pl.* [NL., < *Philepitta* + *-idæ.*] A family of mesomyodian passerine birds peculiar to Madagascar, typified by the genus *Philepitta*. The syrinx is bronchotracheal, with a peculiar modification of the bronchial half-rings and corresponding expansion of the muscular insertions. The tongue is penicillate, the tarsi are taxaspidean, the wing-coverts are long, the tail is short, and the male has a caruncle over the eye.

Philesia (fi-lē'si-ä), *n.* [NL. (Commerson, 1789), < Gr. φίλησις, affection, < φιλεῖν, love.] A genus of liliaceous plants of the tribe *Luzuriageæ*, distinguished by its one-nerved leaves and sepals shorter than the petals. The only species, *P. buxifolia*, is the pepino, a smooth branching shrub from southern Chili and the straits of Magellan, bearing rigid alternate oblong leaves and showy drooping rose-red and waxy flowers, large and bell-shaped. Their contrast with the evergreen leaves makes it one of the handsomest of antarctic plants. It is also remarkable for its structure of bark, wood, and pith, similar to that of exogenous stems.

Philetærus (fil-e-tē'rus), *n.* [NL. (orig. *Philetairus*, Sir Andrew Smith, 1837), < Gr. φιλεῖν, love, + ἑταῖρος, a companion: see *hetæra.*] A genus of sociable weaver-birds of the family *Ploceidæ*, having as type *P. socius* of South Africa, the well-known social weaver, which builds its enormous umbrella-like nest in common with its fellows. See cut under *hive-nest*.

Social Weaver-bird (*Philetærus socius*), with its hive-nest.

philharmonic (fil-här-mon'ik), *a.* [= F. *philharmonique* = Sp. *filarmónico* = Pg. *philarmonico* = It. *filarmonico*, < Gr. as if *φιλαρμονικός, < φιλεῖν, love, + ἁρμονία, harmony: see *harmony.*] Loving harmony; fond of music; music-loving.

Philhellene (fil-hel'ēn), *n.* [< F. *philhellène* = It. *filelleno*, < Gr. φιλέλλην, < φιλεῖν, love, + Ἕλλην, a Greek, pl. Ἕλληνες, Greeks: see *Hellene.*] A friend of Greece; a foreigner who supports the cause and interests of the Hellenes; particularly, one who favored, supported, or actually assisted the modern Greeks in their successful struggle with the Turks for independence.

Philhellenic (fil-he-len'ik), *a.* [As *Philhellene* + *-ic*, after *Hellenic.*] Of or pertaining to Philhellenes; loving the Greeks.

Philhellenism (fil-hel'en-izm), *n.* [As *Philhellene* + *-ism*, after *Hellenism.*] Love of Greece; the principles of the Philhellenes.

Philhellenist (fil-hel'en-ist), *n.* [As *Philhellene* + *-ist*, after *Hellenist.*] Same as *Philhellene*.

Philhydrus (fil-hī'drus), *n.* [NL. (Solier, 1834), < Gr. φίλυδρος, loving water, < φιλεῖν, love, + ὕδωρ (ὑδρ-), water.] In *entom.*, a large genus of water-beetles of the family *Hydrophilidæ*, widely distributed and comprising species which have the last joint of the maxillary palpi shorter than the third. Also *Philydrus* and *Helophilus*.

philiater (fi-lī'a-tėr), *n.* [< Gr. φιλίατρος, a friend of the art of medicine, < φιλεῖν, love, + ἰατρός, a mediciner, physician: see *iatric.*] An amateur student of medicine.

philibeg, philigree†. Bad spellings of *filibeg*, *filigree*.

Philidor's defense. In *chess-playing*. See *opening*, 9.

philip (fil'ip), *n.* [Also contr. *phip*; a particular use of the proper name *Philip* (cf. "*Philip Sparrow*," the name of a poem of Skelton). The name *Philip* is < F. *Philippe* = Sp. *Filipo* = Pg. *Philippo* = It. *Filippo*, < L. *Philippus*, < Gr. Φίλιππος, lit. loving horses, < φιλεῖν, love, + ἵππος, horse.] 1. The common European house-sparrow, *Passer domesticus*.—2. The hedge-sparrow, *Accentor modularis*. [Prov. Eng.]

When *Philip* lyst to go to bed,
It is a heaven to heare my Phippe,
How she can chirpe with chery lip.
Gascoigne, Praise of Philip Sparrow. (*Nares.*)

Philip and Cheiney†. [Also *Philip and Cheyney* (*Cheinie*, *Cheanie*, *Cheny*); from the proper names *Philip* and *Cheiny*, used like *Tom*, *Dick*, *and Harry*. The name *Cheiny*, *Cheyney*, survives in the surnames *Cheney*, *Cheyne.*] 1. "Tom, Dick, and Harry"; any one and every one.

It was not his entent to bryng unto Sylla *philip and cheinie*, mo than a good meiny, but to bryng hable souldiours of manhood approued and well tried to his handes. *Udall*, tr. of Apophthegms of Erasmus, p. 311. (*Davies.*)

Loiterers I kept so meanie,
Both *Philip*, Hob, *and Cheanie*.
Tusser, p. 8. (*Davies.*)

2. Some stuff, apparently coarse or common, the exact character of which is uncertain. [In this use hyphened as one word.]

'Twill put a lady scarce in *Philip-and-cheyney*,
With three small bugle-laces, like a chamber maid.
Beau. and Fl., Wit at Several Weapons, ii. 1.

No cloth of silver, gold, or tissue here;
Philip-and-Cheiny never would appear
Within our bounds.
John Taylor, Praise of Hempseed.

Philipist, *n.* See *Philippist*.

Philippian (fi-lip'i-an), *a.* and *n.* [< L. *Philippianus*, Philippian, < *Philippi*, < Gr. Φίλιπποι, Philippi, < Φίλιππος, Philip: see *philip.*] I. *a.* Of or pertaining to Philippi or its inhabitants.

II. *n.* A native or an inhabitant of Philippi, a city of ancient Macedonia, the seat of an early Christian church, to which Paul addressed his Epistle to the Philippians.—**Epistle to the Philippians**, a letter addressed by the apostle Paul to the church in Philippi, in which he alludes to the close personal relations existing between himself and the members of that church, encourages them to remain in unity, and warns them against various dangers.

Philippic (fi-lip'ik), *n.* [= F. *philippique* = Sp. *filipica* = Pg. *philippica* = It. *filippica*, < L. *philippica*, sc. *oratio*, in plural *philippicæ orationes* (also absolutely *philippica*, neut. pl.), fem. of *Philippicus*, < Gr. Φιλιππικός, pertaining to Philip, < Φίλιππος, Philip: see *philip.*] 1. One of a series of orations delivered, in the fourth century B. C., by the Athenian orator Demosthenes, against Philip, king of Macedon, the father of Alexander the Great, in which the orator proclaims the imminent jeopardy of Athenian liberty, and seeks to arouse his fellow-citizens to a sense of their danger and to stimulate them to timely action against the growing power of Macedon. Hence—2. [*l. c.*] Any discourse or declamation full of acrimonious invective. The orations of Cicero against Mark Antony are called *philippics*.

In a tone which may remind one of the similar *philippic* by his contemporary Dante against his fair countrywomen of Florence. *Prescott*, Ferd. and Isa., i. 8, note 31.

Philippic era. See *era*.

Philippin (fil'ip-in), *n.* [< *Philip* (see def.) + *-in*[1].] A member of a small Russian denomination, chiefly in Lithuania. It was founded by Philip Pustoviat, about 1700; its members have no regular priests, and refuse military service and oaths.

philippine (fil'i-pēn), *n.* Same as *philopena*.

Philippism (fil'ip-izm), *n.* [< *Philip* (see def.) + *-ism.*] The doctrines attributed to Philip Melanchthon by his pupils and followers.

Philippist (fil'ip-ist), *n.* [< *Philip* (see def.) + *-ist.*] A pupil or follower of Philip Melanchthon, a German theologian (1497–1560). Also spelled *Philipist*.

philippize (fil'ip-iz), *v.*; pret. and pp. *philippized*, ppr. *philippizing*. [= F. *philippiser*, < Gr. φιλιππίζειν, be on Philip's side, < Φίλιππος, Philip: see *Philippic*. In defs. I., 2, and II., < *philipp-ic* + *-ize.*] I. *intrans.* 1. To side with Philip of Macedon; support or advocate the cause of Philip.

Its prestige [that of the oracle of Delphi] naturally vanished with the downfall of Greek liberty, after it began, as Demosthenes expressed it, to *philippize*, or to yield its authority to corrupt inducements.
G. P. *Fisher*, Begin. of Christianity, p. 103.

2. To write or utter a philippic or invective; declaim. See *Philippic*.

With the best intentions in the world he naturally *philippizes*, and chaunts his prophetic song in exact unison with their designs. *Burke*, Rev. in France.

II. *trans.* To attack in a philippic; inveigh against.

He argued with us, *philippized* us, denounced us, and, as Nimrod said, "whipped us over the Almighty's back!"
S. Judd, Margaret, iii.

Philister (fi-lis'tėr), *n.* Same as *Philistine*, 3.

Philistian (fi-lis'ti-an), *a.* and *n.* [< *Philistia*, LL. *Philistæa*, *Philisthæa* (see *Philistine*), + *-an.*] **I.** *a.* Of or pertaining to Philistia in Syria, or its inhabitants.

The cis-Jordan country . . . was the scene of a great development of the *Philistian* power.
Encyc. Brit., XVIII. 176.

II. *n.* A Philistine.

But, Colonel, they say you went to Court last night very drunk: nay, I'm told for certain you had been among the *Philistians*.
Swift, Polite Conversation, i. (*Davies.*)

Philistim† (fi-lis'tim), *n.* [< LL. *Philisthiim*, < Heb. *Plishthim*, pl.: see *Philistine*.] A Philistine: properly a plural (Hebrew), but used as a singular.

They serued also the Gods of Aram, Zidon, Moab, Ammon, and the *Philistims*.
Purchas, Pilgrimage, p. 136.

Those *Philistims* put out the fair and farre-sighted eyes of his natural discerning.
Milton, Church-Government, ii., Con.

Philistine (fi-lis'tin), *n.* [= F. *Philistin*, < LL. *Philistini*, also *Philisthiim*, Philistines (cf. Ar. *Filistiy*, Philistines, *Filistin*, Palestine), < Heb. *Plishthi*, pl. *Plishthim*, the original inhabitants of Palestine (Philistia), < *palash*, wander about. In def. 3 *Philistine* is a translation of G. *Philister* (= D. *Philister* = Sw. Dan. *Filister*), a 'Philistine'), applied by German students in the universities, as "the chosen people" or "the children of light," to the townsmen, regarded as their enemies, or "the children of darkness."] **1.** One of a warlike immigrant people, of disputed origin, who inhabited parts of Philistia or Palestine, and contested the possession and sovereignty of it with the Israelites, and continued to harass them with much persistency for several centuries. Hence—**2.** A heathen enemy; an unfeeling foe: used humorously, for example, of a bailiff or sheriff's officer.

She was too ignorant of such matters to know that, if he had fallen into the hands of the *Philistines* (which is the name given by the faithful to bailiffs), he would hardly have been able so soon to recover his liberty.
Fielding, Amelia, v. 6. (*Davies.*)

3. In Germany, one who has not been trained in a university: so called by the students. [Slang.] Hence—**4.** A matter-of-fact, commonplace person; a man upon whom one can look down, as of culture inferior to one's own; one of "parochial" intellect; a satisfied person who is unaware of his own lack of culture.

The people who believe most that our greatness and welfare are proved by our being very rich, and who most give their lives and thoughts to becoming rich, are just the very people whom we call *Philistines*.
M. Arnold, Sweetness and Light, § 13.

Philistinism (fi-lis'tin-izm), *n.* [= F. *philistinisme*; as *Philistine* + *-ism*.] The character or views of Philistines. See *Philistine*, 3, 4.

Out of the steady humdrum habit of the creeping Saxon, as the Celt calls him—out of his way of going near the ground—has come, no doubt, *Philistinism*, that plant of essentially Germanic growth, flourishing with its genuine marks only in the German fatherland, Great Britain and her colonies, and the United States of America. *M. Arnold.*

philizer†, *n.* A bad spelling of *filacer*.

phill-horse†, *n.* A bad spelling of *fill-horse*.

phillibeg, *n.* A bad spelling of *filibeg*.

phillipena, *n.* See *philopena*.

phillipsite (fil'ip-sīt), *n.* [Named after W. *Phillips*, an English mineralogist (died 1828).] In *mineral.*, a hydrous silicate of aluminium, calcium, and potassium, commonly found in cruciform twin crystals. It is a member of the zeolite group, and is closely related to harmotome. It occurs chiefly in basaltic rocks, but was obtained also by deep-sea dredging by the Challenger expedition. Also called *christianite*.

Phillyrea (fi-lir'ē-ä), *n.* [NL. (Tournefort, 1700), fancifully transferred from Gr. φιλλυρέα (Theophrastus), an unidentified shrub, < φιλύρα, the linden-tree.] A plant-genus of the gamopetalous order *Oleaceæ* and the tribe *Oleineæ*, distinguished by broad imbricated corolla-lobes, and a drupe with a thin stone. The 4 species are native of the Mediterranean region and the East. They are smooth shrubs with opposite evergreen leaves, and small greenish-white flowers clustered in the axils, hardy and adapted to seaside planting, forming compact and ornamental roundish masses, called *jasmine box* from the relationship to the jasmine and resemblance to box.

philo-. [F. *philo-* = Sp. It. *filo-* = Pg. *philo-*, < L. *philo-*, < Gr. φιλο-, before a vowel or rough breathing φιλ-, combining form of φιλεῖν (ind. pres. φιλέω), love, regard with affection, be fond of, like or like to do, be wont to do, etc.; < φίλος, loved, beloved, dear, pleasing; as a noun, a friend, neut. φίλον, an object of love; later, in poet. use, in an active sense, loving, friendly, fond; orig. own, one's own (as in Homer); perhaps, with adj. formative -ιλος, and with loss of initial σ, from the root of σφεῖς (dat. σφισι, σφισιν, σφιν, σφι, dial. φιν, ψιν, ψε, etc., acc. σφέας, σφε, etc.), themselves. √ *sva*, = L. *suus*, his, their (own), etc. The element φιλο-, in composition, is usually explained as "φίλος, loving," but the adj. is not so used in composition; the element φιλο- represents φιλεῖν, love, as the element μισο-, of opposite meaning, represents μισεῖν, hate.] An element in many words of Greek origin or formation, representing a verb meaning 'to love.' See etymology, and words following. It is opposed to *miso-*, as in *misogynist*, etc. Before a vowel or *h* it becomes *phil-*, as in *Phil-American*, *Philhellenic*, etc. It occurs terminally (Latin *-philus*, Greek -φιλος, properly passive) in *bibliophile*, *Russophile*, etc.

philobiblical (fil-ǫ-bib'li-kal), *a.* [< Gr. φιλεῖν, love, + LL. *biblia*, the Bible: see *biblical*. Cf. Gr. φιλόβιβλος, loving books.] Devoted to Biblical study.

The Duke of Brunswick, hearing of Hardt's fame, appointed him his librarian shortly after the Orientalist had founded at Leipsic a *philobiblical* society, with the object of determining the sacred text. *Encyc. Brit.*, XI. 475.

philocalist (fil'ǫ-kal-ist), *n.* [< Gr. φιλόκαλος, loving the beautiful (< φιλεῖν, love, + καλός, beautiful), + *-ist*.] A lover of the beautiful. [Rare.]

philodemic (fil-ǫ-dem'ik), *a.* [< Gr. φιλόδημος, a friend of the people, < φιλεῖν, love, + δῆμος, people.] Loving the people.

Philodendreæ (fil-ǫ-den'drẹ-ē), *n. pl.* [NL. (Schott, 1832), < *Philodendron* + *-eæ*.] A tribe of monocotyledonous plants of the order *Araceæ* and the subfamily *Philodendroideæ*, distinguished by their habit as erect sympodial shrubs, often branching or climbing, by their orthotropous or anatropous and often long-stalked ovules, and by the rudimentary stamens sometimes present in the pistillate flowers. It includes 9 genera, all tropical, of which *Philodendron* is the type.

philodendrist (fil-ǫ-den'drist), *n.* [< Gr. φιλόδενδρος, loving trees (< φιλεῖν, love, + δένδρον, a tree), + *-ist*.] A lover of trees. *Lowell*, Study Windows, p. 44.

Philodendroideæ (fil"ǫ-den-droi'dẹ-ē), *n. pl.* [NL. (Engler, 1879), < *Philodendron* + *-oideæ*.] A subfamily of the order *Araceæ*, distinguished by a spadix staminate below, flowers without perianths (usually with distinct stamens), albuminous seeds, an axillary embryo, and abundant tubular unbranched laticiferous ducts. It includes 4 tribes and 12 genera, of which *Philodendron* is the type. See also *Peltandra* and *Richardia*.

Philodendron (fil-ǫ-den'dron), *n.* [NL. (Schott, 1830), < Gr. φιλόδενδρος, loving trees, < Gr. φιλεῖν, love, + δένδρον, a tree.] A genus of araceous plants, type of the tribe *Philodendreæ* and the subfamily *Philodendroideæ*, characterized by a fruit not included in the persistent spathe, stamens united into a prismatic body, and distinct two- to ten-celled ovaries with the orthotropous ovules fixed to the inner angle of the cells. There are about 120 species, natives of tropical America. They are climbing shrubs, with broad coriaceous leaves and short terminal or axillary peduncles, commonly in clusters. They bear fleshy white, red, or yellowish spathes, and a closely flowered spadix, followed by a dense mass of berries. (See *Araceæ*.) Some West Indian species are there known as *wake-robin*.

philofelist† (fi-lof'e-list), *n.* [< Gr. φιλεῖν, love, + L. *felis*, a cat: see *Felis*.] A lover of cats. [Rare.]

Dr. Southey, who is known to be a *philofelist*, and confers honours upon his cats according to their services, has raised one to the highest rank in peerage.
Southey, The Doctor, Fragment of Interchapter. (*Davies.*)

philogalist† (fi-log'ạ-list), *n.* [< Gr. φιλεῖν, love, + γάλα, milk: see *galaxy*.] A lover of milk. [Rare.]

You . . . are a *philogalist*, and therefore understand . . . cat nature. *Southey*, Letters (1821), III. 240. (*Davies.*)

philogarlic (fil-ō-gär'lik), *a.* [< Gr. φιλεῖν, love, + E. *garlic*.] Loving garlic; fond of garlic. *De Quincey*, Spanish Nun. [Rare.]

philogynist (fi-loj'i-nist), *n.* [< *philogyn-y* + *-ist*.] A lover of women: the opposite of *misogynist*.

There are "*philogynists*" as fanatical as any "misogynists," who, reversing our antiquated notions, bid the man look upon the woman as the higher type of humanity; who ask us to regard the female intellect as the clearer and the quicker, if not the stronger.
Huxley, Lay Sermons (1870), p. 21.

philogyny (fi-loj'i-ni), *n.* [= F. *philogynie*, < Gr. φιλογυνία, love of women, < φιλογύνης, φιλόγυνος, loving women, < φιλεῖν, love, + γυνή, woman.] Fondness or admiration for women; love of women: the opposite of *misogyny*.

We will therefore draw a curtain over this scene, from that *philogyny* which is in us.
Fielding, Jonathan Wild, i. 10.

Because the Turks so much admire *philogyny*,
Although their usage of their wives is sad.
Byron, Beppo, st. 70.

Philohela (fi-lō'he-lạ̈), *n.* [NL. (G. R. Gray, 1841), prop. **Philela*, < Gr. φιλεῖν, love, + ἕλος, a marsh.] A genus of *Scolopacidæ*, having short rounded wings, the three outer primaries of which are emarginate and attenuate; the American woodcocks. *P. minor* is the common woodcock of the United States, generically distinct from the European woodcock, *Scolopax rusticula*. See *woodcock*. Also called *Microptera*.

Philohellenian† (fil"ǫ-he-lē'ni-ạn), *n.* [For **Philhellenian*; as *Philhellene* + *-ian*.] Same as *Philhellene*. *Arnold*.

philologer (fi-lol'ǫ-jėr), *n.* [< *philolog-y* + *-er*[1]. Cf. *philologue*.] Same as *philologist*, and formerly in more common use.

philologian (fil-ǫ-lō'ji-ạn), *n.* [< *philology* + *-an*.] Same as *philologist*.

philologic (fil-ǫ-loj'ik), *a.* [= F. *philologique* = Sp. *filológico* = Pg. *philologico* = It. *filologico* (cf. D. *filologisch* = G. *philologisch* = Sw. Dan. *filologisk*), < MGr. φιλολογικός, pertaining to philology or learning, < Gr. φιλολογία, philology, learning: see *philology*.] Of or pertaining to philology, or the study of language: as, *philologic* learning.

philological (fil-ǫ-loj'i-kạl), *a.* [< *philologic* + *-al*.] Relating to or concerned with philology: as, *philological* study; the American *Philological* Association.

philologically (fil-ǫ-loj'i-kạl-i), *adv.* In a philological manner; as regards philology.

philologist (fi-lol'ǫ-jist), *n.* [< *philolog-y* + *-ist*.] One who is versed in philology. Also *philologer*, *philologian*, *philologue*.

Learn'd *philologists*, who chase
A panting syllable through time and space.
Cowper, Retirement, l. 691.

philologize (fi-lol'ǫ-jīz), *v. i.*; pret. and pp. *philologized*, ppr. *philologizing*. [< *philolog-y* + *-ize*.] To discuss questions relating to philology.

Nor is it here that we design to enlarge, as those who have *philologized* on this occasion. *Evelyn.*

philologue (fil'ǫ-log), *n.* [= D. *filoloog* = G. *philolog* = Sw. Dan. *filolog*, < F. *philologue* = Sp. *filólogo* = Pg. *philologo*, *filologo* = It. *filologo* = Russ. *filologŭ*, a philologist; < L. *philologus*, a man of letters, a scholar; as adj., studious of letters, versed in learning, scholarly; < Gr. φιλόλογος, a learned man, student, scholar; prop. adj., fond of learning and literature, etc.: see *philology*.] Same as *philologist*.

This is the fittest and most proper hour wherein to write these high matters and deep sentences, as Homer knew very well, the paragon of all *philologues*.
Urquhart, tr. of Rabelais, i., Author's Prol. (*Davies.*)

The combination . . . was and is a fact in language; and its evolution was the effect of some philological force which it is the business of *philologues* to elucidate.
Latham, Elements of Comparative Philology, ii. 1, 2.

philology (fi-lol'ǫ-ji), *n.* [Formerly *philologie*; = D. *filologie* = G. *philologie* = Sw. Dan. *filologi*; < F. *philologie* = Sp. *filologia* = Pg. *philologia*, *filologia* = It. *filologia* = Russ. *filologiya*, philology (see def.), < L. *philologia*, love of learning and literature (Cicero), explanation and interpretation of writings (Seneca), < Gr. φιλολογία, love of dialectic or argument (Plato), love of learning and literature (Isocrates, Aristotle), the study of language and history (Plutarch, etc.), in later use learning in a wide sense; < φιλόλογος, fond of words, talkative (wine was said to make men so) (Plato), fond of speaking (said of an orator) (Plato), fond of dialectic or argument (Plato), fond of learning and literature, literary, studious, learned (Aristotle, Plutarch, etc.); of books, learned, scientific (Cicero), later also studious of words (Plotinus, Proclus, etc.); as a noun, a learned man, student, scholar (see *philologue*); < φιλεῖν, love, + λόγος, word, speech, discourse, argument: see *Logos*, and cf. *-ology*.] The love or the study of learning and literature; the investigation of a language and its literature, or of languages and literatures, for the light they cast upon men's character, activity, and history. The word is sometimes used more especially of the study of literary and other records, as distinguished from that of language, which is called *linguistics*; often, on the other hand, of the study of language or of languages. See quotation under *comparative philology*, below.

Philology . . . deals with human speech, and with all that speech discloses as to the nature and history of man.
Whitney, Encyc. Brit., XVIII. 765.

Comparative philology, the study of languages as carried on by the comparative method; investigation, by means of a comparison of languages, of their history, relationships, and characteristics, within narrower or wider limits; linguistic science; linguistics; glossology.

Philology, whether classical or oriental, whether treating of ancient or modern, of cultivated or barbarous languages, is an historical science. Language is here treated simply as a means. The classical scholar uses Greek or Latin, the oriental scholar Hebrew or Sanskrit, or any other language, as a key to an understanding of the literary monuments which bygone ages have bequeathed to us, as a spell to raise from the tomb of time the thoughts of great men in different ages and different countries, and as a means ultimately to trace the social, moral, intellectual, and religious progress of the human race. . . . In *comparative philology* the case is totally different. In the science of language, languages are not treated as a means; language itself becomes the sole object of scientific inquiry. Dialects which have never produced any literature at all, the jargons of savage tribes, the clicks of the Hottentots, and the vocal modulations of the Indo-Chinese, are as important, nay, for the solution of some of our problems, more important, than the poetry of Homer or the prose of Cicero. We do not want to know languages, we want to know language; what language is, how it can form a vehicle or an organ of thought; we want to know its origin, its nature, its laws, and it is only in order to arrive at that knowledge that we collect, arrange, and classify all the facts of language that are within our reach.
Max Müller, Science of Language, 1st ser., Lect. 1.

Philomachus (fi-lom'ạ-kus), *n.* [NL. (Moehring, 1752), ‹ Gr. φιλόμαχος, loving fight, ‹ φιλεῖν, love, + μάχη, fight.] A genus of wading birds of the family *Scolopacidæ*; the ruffs and reeves: synonymous with *Machetes* and with *Pavoncella*.

philomath (fil'ọ-math), *n.* [= It. *filomate*, ‹ Gr. φιλομαθής, fond of learning, ‹ φιλεῖν, love, + μάθος, learning, ‹ μανθάνειν, μαθεῖν, learn.] A lover of learning.

A solemn disputation in all the mysteries of the profession, before the face of every *philomath*, student in astrology, and member of the learned societies.
Goldsmith, Citizen of the World, lxviii.

philomathematic† (fil-ọ-math-ẹ-mat'ik), *n.* [‹ Gr. φιλεῖν, love, + μάθημα, learning, › μαθηματικός, mathematic: see *mathematic*.] Same as *philomath*. *Settle.*

philomathic (fil-ọ-math'ik), *a.* [= F. *philomathique* = Sp. *filomático* = Pg. *philomatico*; as *philomath* + *-ic*.] **1.** Of or pertaining to philomathy; also, of or pertaining to philomaths.

The International *Philomathic* Congress, having for its object the discussion of commercial and industrial technical instruction. *Science*, VII. 455.

2. Having a love of letters.

philomathical (fil-ọ-math'i-kạl), *a.* [‹ *philomathic* + *-al*.] Same as *philomathic*.

philomathy (fi-lom'ạ-thi), *n.* [= Pg. *philomacia*; ‹ Gr. φιλομαθία, φιλομάθεια, love of learning, ‹ φιλομαθής, fond of learning: see *philomath*.] Love of learning.

philomel (fil'ọ-mel), *n.* [= F. *philomèle* = Sp. *filomela* = Pg. *philomela* = It. *filomela*, *filomena*, ‹ L. *philomela*, ‹ Gr. φιλομήλα, the nightingale (in tradition, Philomela, daughter of Pandion, king of Athens, who was changed into a nightingale), ‹ φιλεῖν, love, + (prob.) μέλος (lengthened), song: see *melody*.] The nightingale.

By this, lamenting *Philomel* had ended
The well-tuned warble of her nightly sorrow.
Shak., Lucrece, l. 1079.

Philomela (fil-ọ-mē'lạ̈), *n.* [NL. (Rafinesque, 1815), ‹ L. *philomela*: see *philomel*.] A genus of oscine passerine birds, the type of which is the nightingale: now usually called *Luscinia* or *Daulias*.

philomene† (fil'ọ-mēn), *n.* [Appar. a var. of *philomel* (Gr. φιλομήλα), as if ‹ Gr. φιλεῖν, love, + μήνη, the moon.] Same as *philomel*.

To vnderstande the notes of *Phylomene*.
Gascoigne, Complaint of *Philomene*.

philomot, *n.* and *a.* See *filemot*. *Spectator*, No. 265.

philomusical (fil-ọ-mū'zi-kạl), *a.* [‹ Gr. φιλεῖν, love, + μουσική, music: see *music*.] Loving music. *Wright.*

Philonic (fi-lon'ik), *a.* [‹ L. *Philo(n-)*, ‹ Gr. Φίλων, Philo (see def.), + *-ic*.] Of or pertaining to Philo, a Jewish philosopher and writer, who flourished during the first half of the first century of our era.

Philonthidæ (fi-lon'thi-dē), *n. pl.* [NL., ‹ *Philonthus* + *-idæ*.] A family of rove-beetles, named by Kirby in 1837 from the genus *Philonthus*.

Philonthus (fi-lon'thus), *n.* [NL. (Curtis, 1825), ‹ Gr. φιλεῖν, love, + ὄνθος, dung.] A very large and wide-spread genus of rove-beetles, comprising more than 200 species, found in all quarters of the globe. They have the ligula entire, the femora unarmed, and the last joint of the labial palpi slender. They are insects of small size, and of the usual rove-beetle habits, except that some species inhabit ants' nests. Eighty-five species are found in the United States and Canada. See cut under *rove-beetle*.

philopena (fil-ọ-pē'nạ̈), *n.* [A rural or provincial word of undetermined origin and unsettled spelling, being variously written *philopena*, *philipena*, *phillipena*, *filopena*, also *philopene*, *phillipine*, *filipeen*, *fillipeen*, etc., the spelling *philopena* simulating a Greek origin, as if 'a friendly forfeit,' ‹ Gr. φίλος, loving, friendly, + ποινή, a penalty (see *pain*[1], *pine*[2]). The correct form appears to be *philippine* (= F. *philippine*, D. *filippine*, Sw. *filipin*, Dan. *filipine*), ‹ G. *Philippine*, fem. of *Philipp*, Philip, these names being used by the man and woman respectively in greeting the other party to the compact. The use of the name *Philippine* is referred by some to the tradition that St. Philip's two daughters were buried (at Hierapolis) in one sepulcher. The word is commonly said to be a corruption of G. *vielliebchen*, 'sweetheart' (used in address), lit. 'very darling,' ‹ *viel*, much, very, + *liebchen* (= MD. *liefken*), sweetheart, darling: see *feel*[2] and *liefkin*.] **1.** A custom or game of reputed German origin: two persons share a nut containing two kernels, and one of them incurs the obligation of giving something as forfeit to the other, either by being first addressed by the latter with the word *philopena* at their next meeting, or by receiving something from the other's hand, or by answering a question with yes or no, or by some other similar test as agreed upon.—**2.** The salutation in the game or custom thus described.—**3.** The kernel of the nut used in the game.

philopolemic (fil″ọ-pọ-lem'ik), *a.* [‹ Gr. φιλοπόλεμος, φιλοπτόλεμος, loving war, ‹ φιλεῖν, love, + πόλεμος, war: see *polemic*.] Loving war or combat; fond of debate or controversy. [Rare.]

philopolemical (fil″ọ-pọ-lem'i-kạl), *a.* [‹ *philopolemic* + *-al*.] Same as *philopolemic*.

Philoponist (fi-lop'ọ-nist), *n.* [‹ *Philopon-us* (see def.) + *-ist*.] A member of a sect of Tritheists, followers of John Philoponus, an Alexandrian of the sixth century. See *Tritheist*.

philoprogeneity (fil-ọ-prō-jẹ-nē'ị-ti), *n.* [Irreg. ‹ Gr. φιλεῖν, love, + L. *progenies*, offspring, + *-e-ity*.] Love of offspring; philoprogenitiveness. *Science*, XII. 124.

philoprogenitiveness (fil″ọ-prọ-jen'i-tiv-nes), *n.* [Irreg. ‹ Gr. φιλεῖν, love, + L. *progenies* (see *progeny*) + *-itive* + *-ness*.] In *phrenol.*, the love of offspring; the instinctive love of young in general. Phrenologists locate its organ above the middle part of the cerebellum.

One of those travelling chariots or family arks which only English *philoprogenitiveness* could invent.
Thackeray, Pendennis, xxii.

Philopteridæ (fil-op-ter'i-dē), *n. pl.* [NL. (Burmeister, 1838), ‹ *Philopterus* + *-idæ*.] One of the principal families of mallophagous insects, having no tarsal cushions, no maxillary palpi, and filiform antennæ with five or three joints, typified by the genus *Philopterus*. They infest the skins of birds and mammals.

Philopterus (fi-lop'tẹ-rus), *n.* [NL. (Nitzsch, 1818), ‹ Gr. φιλεῖν, love, + πτερόν, a feather.] A genus of bird-lice, or *Mallophaga*, having five-jointed antennæ and two-jointed tarsi, typical of the *Philopteridæ*. They are small insects of much-varied patterns, living in the feathers on the neck and under the wings of birds. *P. hologaster* is a common parasite of the domestic fowl in Europe.

philornithic (fil-ôr-nith'ik), *a.* [Cf. Gr. φιλορνιθία, fondness for birds; ‹ Gr. φιλεῖν, love, + ὄρνις (ὀρνιθ-), a bird.] Bird-loving; fond of birds. [Rare.]

The danger has happily this year been met by the public spirit of a party of *philornithic* gentlemen.
Contemporary Rev., LIV. 184.

philosoph (fil'ọ-sof), *n.* [ME. *filosofe* (AS. *philosoph* = D. *filozoof* = G. *philosoph* = Sw. Dan. *filosof*), ‹ OF. *filosofe*, *philosophe*, F. *philosophe* = Pr. *philosophe* = Sp. *filósofo* = Pg. *philosopho* = It. *filosofo*, ‹ L. *philosophus*, ‹ Gr. φιλόσοφος, a philosopher: see *philosophy*. Cf. *philosopher*.] A philosopher: a word sometimes used with a contemptuous implication as nearly equivalent to *philosophaster*. Also, as French, *philosophe*.

A little light is precious in great darkness; nor, amid myriads of poetasters and *philosophes*, are poets and philosophers so numerous that we should reject such when they speak to us in the hard, but manly, deep, and expressive tones of that old Saxon speech which is also our mother-tongue. *Carlyle*, State of German Literature.

philosophaster (fi-los'ọ-fas-tėr), *n.* [= F. *philosophâtre* = Sp. It. *filosofastro*, ‹ LL. *philosophaster*, ‹ L. *philosophus*, a philosopher, + dim. suffix *-aster*.] A pretender to philosophical knowledge; an incompetent philosopher.

Of necessity there must be such a thing in the world as incorporeal substance, let inconsiderable *philosophasters* hoot and deride as much as their follies please.
Dr. H. More, Immortal. of Soul, i. 14.

philosophate† (fi-los'ọ-fāt), *v. i.* [‹ L. *philosophatus*, pp. of *philosophari* (› It. *filosofare* = Sp. *filosofar* = Pg. *philosophar* = F. *philosopher*, › D. *filozoferen* = G. *philosophiren* = Sw. *filosofera* = Dan. *filosofere*), philosophize, ‹ *philosophus*, a philosopher: see *philosophy*.] To philosophize. *Barrow*, Works, I. xii.

philosophation† (fi-los-ọ-fā'shọn), *n.* [‹ *philosophate* + *-ion*.] The act of philosophizing; philosophical speculation. *Sir W. Pettie*, Advise to Hartlit, p. 18.

philosophdom (fil'ọ-sof-dum), *n.* [‹ *philosoph* + *-dom*.] Philosophs collectively; philosophism. [Rare.]

They entertain their special ambassador in *Philosophedom*. *Carlyle*, Misc., III. 216. (*Davies.*)

philosophe (fil'ọ-sōf), *n.* See *philosoph*.

philosophema (fi-los-ọ-fē'mạ̈), *n.* [NL., ‹ Gr. φιλοσόφημα, a demonstration, ‹ φιλοσοφεῖν, philosophize, ‹ φιλόσοφος, a philosopher: see *philosophy*.] Same as *philosopheme*.

philosopheme (fi-los'ọ-fēm), *n.* [= F. *philosophème*, ‹ NL. *philosophema*: see *philosophema*.] **1.** Properly, a perfect demonstration. Hence —**2.** A theorem; a philosophical truth.

This, the most venerable, and perhaps the most ancient, of the Grecian mythi, is a *philosopheme*. *Coleridge.*

philosopher (fi-los'ọ-fėr), *n.* [‹ ME. *philosophre*, *philosofre*, with term. *-re*, *-er*; earlier *filosofe*, ‹ OF. *filosofe*, *philosophe*, a philosopher: see *philosoph* and *philosophy*.] **1.** One who is devoted to the search for fundamental truth; in a restricted sense, one who is versed in or studies the metaphysical and moral sciences; a metaphysician. The application of the term to one versed in natural science or natural philosophy has become less common since the studies of physicists have been more specialized than formerly.

He said: But who are the true *philosophers*?
Those, I said, who are lovers of the vision of truth.
Plato, Republic (tr. by Jowett), v. § 475.

He who has a taste for every sort of knowledge, and who is curious to learn and is never satisfied, may justly be termed a *philosopher*. Am I not right?
Plato, Republic (tr. by Jowett), v. § 475.

Philosophers, who darken and put out
Eternal truth by everlasting doubt.
Cowper, Progress of Error, l. 472.

2. One who conforms his life to the principles of philosophy, especially to those of the Stoical school; one who lives according to reason or the rules of practical wisdom.

Be mine a *philosopher's* life in the quiet woodland ways,
Where, if I cannot be gay, let a passionless peace be my lot.
Tennyson, Maud, iv. 9.

3†. An alchemist: so called with reference to the search for the philosopher's stone.

But albe that he was a *philosophre*,
Yet hadde he but litel gold in cofre.
Chaucer, Gen. Prol. to C. T., l. 297.

Hence—**4†.** One who deals in any magic art.

"Allas!" quod he, "allas that I bihighte
Of pured gold a thousand pound of wighte
Unto this *philosophre*."
Chaucer, Franklin's Tale, l. 833.

A priori philosopher. See *a priori*.—**Philosopher's egg†**, a medicine compounded of the yolk of an egg, saffron, etc., formerly supposed to be an excellent preservative against all poisons, and against plague and other dangerous diseases. *Nares.*—**Philosopher's game†**, an intricate game, played with pieces or men of three different forms, round, triangular, and square, on a board resembling two chess-boards united. *Halliwell.*—**Philosophers of the garden.** See *garden*.—**Philosopher's oil**, brick-oil (which see, under *oil*).—**Philosopher's stone.** See *elixir*, 1.

philosophess (fi-los'ọ-fes), *n.* [= It. *filosofessa*; as *philosoph* + *-ess*.] A female philosopher. *Carlyle*, Diderot. [Rare.]

philosophic (fil-ọ-sof'ik), *a.* [‹ F. *philosophique* = Sp. *filosófico* = Pg. *philosophico* = It. *filosofico* (cf. D. *filozofisch* = G. *philosophisch* = Sw. Dan. *filosofisk*), ‹ LL. *philosophicus*, ‹ Gr. *φιλοσοφικός (in adv. φιλοσοφικῶς), ‹ φιλοσοφία, philosophy: see *philosophy*.] **1.** Of or pertaining to philosophy, in any sense; based on or in keeping or accordance with philosophy, or the ultimate principles of being, knowledge, or conduct.—**2.** Characteristic of or befitting a philosopher; calm; quiet; cool; temperate: as, *philosophic* indifference; a *philosophic* mind.—**Philosophic cotton.** See *cotton*[1].—**Philosophic wool**, finely divided zinc oxid, resembling tufts of wool or flakes of snow: the *lana philosophica* of the alchemists. Also called *pompholyx*.=**Syn.** 2. Composed, unruffled, serene, tranquil, imperturbable.

philosophical (fil-ǫ-sof′i-kal), *a.* and *n.* [< *philosophic* + *-al.*] I. *a.* 1. Philosophic. (a) Relating or belonging to philosophy or philosophers; proceeding from, based on, in keeping with, or used in philosophy or in philosophic study or research: as, a *philosophical* argument.

> *Philosophical* minds always love knowledge of a sort which shows them the eternal nature not varying from generation and corruption.
> *Plato*, Republic (tr. by Jowett), vi. § 485.

(b) Befitting a philosopher; calm; temperate; wise; controlled by reason; undisturbed by passion; self-controlled.

> Cibber had lived a dissipated life, and his *philosophical* indifference, with his careless gaiety, was the breastplate which even the wit of Pope failed to pierce.
> *I. D'Israeli*, Quar. of Authors, p. 106.

2. Pertaining to or used in the study of natural philosophy: as, *philosophical* apparatus; a *philosophical* instrument.—**Philosophical arrangement**, an Aristotelian category or predicament.—**Philosophical foot.** See *geometrical foot*, under *foot*.—**Philosophical pitch.** See *pitch*1.—**Philosophical presumption**, an inference of the ampliative sort.

II.† *n.* 1. A student of philosophy; a philosopher.—2. *pl.* Philosophical studies; philosophy.

> Hen. Stretsham, a Minorite, who had spent several years here, and at Cambridge, in logicals, *philosophicals*, and theologicals, was one (that supplicated for that degree, B. D.) *Wood*, Fasti Oxon., I. 61.

philosophically (fil-ǫ-sof′i-kal-i), *adv.* In a philosophical manner; according to the rules or principles of philosophy; calmly; wisely; rationally.

philosophicalness (fil-ǫ-sof′i-kal-nes), *n.* The character of being philosophical.

philosophise, philosophiser. See *philosophize, philosophizer*.

philosophism (fi-los′ǫ-fizm), *n.* [< F. *philosophisme* = Sp. It. *filosofismo* = Pg. *philosophismo*; as *philosoph-y* + *-ism.*] Spurious or ill-founded philosophy; the affectation of philosophy.

> Among its more notable anomalies may be reckoned the relations of French *philosophism* to Foreign Crowned Heads. *Carlyle*, Diderot.

philosophist (fi-los′ǫ-fist), *n.* [< F. *philosophiste* = Sp. *filosofista* = Pg. *philosophista*; as *philosoph-y* + *-ist.*] A philosopher; especially, a would-be philosopher.

> This benevolent establishment did not escape the rage of the *philosophists*, and was by them suppressed in the commencement of the republican era.
> *Eustace*, Italy, IV. v.

philosophistic (fi-los-ǫ-fis′tik), *a.* [= Pg. *philosophistico*; as *philosophist* + *-ic*, after *sophistic.*] Pertaining to the love or practice of philosophism, or spurious philosophy. *Wright.*

philosophistical (fi-los-ǫ-fis′ti-kal), *a.* [< *philosophistic* + *-al.*] Same as *philosophistic*.

philosophize (fi-los′ǫ-fiz), *v. i.*; pret. and pp. *philosophized*, ppr. *philosophizing*. [< *philosoph-y* + *-ize.*] To think or reason about the subjects of philosophy; meditate upon or discuss the fundamental principles of being, knowledge, or conduct; reason after the manner of philosophers; form or attempt to form a philosophical system or theory. Also spelled *philosophise*.

> Anaxarchus his pain, though it seems not so sharp, yet his courage appears as great, in that he could *philosophize* so freely while he was by the cruelty of Archelaus braying in a mortar. *Dr. H. More*, Of Enthusiasm, § 59.

> Every one, in some manner or other, either skillfully or unskillfully *philosophizes*.
> *Shaftesbury*, Moralists, iii. § 3, quoted in Fowler, p. 74.

> The most fatal error which a poet can possibly commit in the management of his machinery is that of attempting to *philosophise* too much. *Macaulay*, Milton.

> No *philosophizing* Christian ever organised or perpetuated a sect. *Milman*, Latin Christianity, ix. 8.

philosophizer (fi-los′ǫ-fi-zėr), *n.* [< *philosophize* + *-er*1.] One who philosophizes. Also spelled *philosophiser*.

philosophress† (fi-los′ǫ-fres), *n.* [< *philosopher* + *-ess.*] A female philosopher. [Rare.]

> She is a *philosophress*, augur, and can turn ill to good as well as you. *Chapman*, Cæsar and Pompey, v. 1.

philosophy (fi-los′ǫ-fi), *n.*; pl. *philosophies* (-fiz). [< ME. *philosophie, filosofie*, < OF. *philosophie, filosofie*, F. *philosophie* = Sp. *filosofía* = Pg. *philosophia* = It. *filosofia* = D. *filozofie* = G. *philosophie* = Dan. Sw. *filosofi*, < L. *philosophia*, < Gr. φιλοσοφία, love of knowledge and wisdom, < φιλόσοφος, a philosopher, one who speculates on the nature of things, existence, freedom, and truth; in cool. writers applied to one who leads a life of contemplation and self-denial; lit. 'one who loves wisdom' (a term first used, according to the tradition, by Pythagoras, who preferred to call himself φιλόσοφος, one who loves wisdom, instead of σοφός, a sage); in later use (Hesychius) in the sense 'loving a handicraft or art'; < φιλεῖν, love, + σοφία, wisdom, skill, art, < σοφός, wise, skilful: see *sophist.*] 1. The body of highest truth; the organized sum of science; the science of which all others are branches; the science of the most fundamental matters. This is identified by different schools—(a) with the account of the elementary factors operative in the universe; the science of principles, or the matter, form, causes, and ends of things in general; (b) with the science of the absolute; metaphysics; (c) with the science of science; the theory of cognition; logic. In Greek, *philosophy* originally signified culture; but from Aristotle down it had two meanings—(a) speculative knowledge, and (b) the study of the highest things, metaphysics. Chrysippus defined it as the science of things divine and human. In the middle ages philosophy was understood to embrace all the speculative sciences: hence the faculty and degree of arts in German universities are called the faculty and degree in philosophy.

> In *philosophy*, the contemplations of man do either penetrate unto God or are circumferred to nature, or are reflected or reverted upon himself. Out of which several inquiries there do arise three knowledges, divine *philosophy*, natural *philosophy*, and human *philosophy*, or humanity. *Bacon*, Advancement of Learning, ii.

> *Philosophy* has been defined:—The science of things divine and human, and the causes in which they are contained;—The science of effects by their causes;—The science of sufficient reasons;—The science of things possible, inasmuch as they are possible;—The science of things, evidently deduced from first principles;—The science of truths, sensible and abstract;—The application of reason to its legitimate objects;—The science of the relations of all knowledge to the necessary ends of human reason;—The science of the original form of the ego or mental self;—The science of science;—The science of the absolute;—The science of the absolute indifference of the ideal and real. *Sir W. Hamilton*, Metaphysics, iii.

> All knowledge of reason is . . . either based on concepts or on the construction of concepts; the former being called philosophical, the later mathematical. . . . The system of all philosophical knowledge is called *philosophy*. It must be taken objectively, if we understand by it the type of criticising all philosophical attempts, which is to serve for the criticism of every subjective *philosophy*, however various and changeable the systems may be. In this manner *philosophy* is a mere idea of a possible science which exists nowhere in the concrete, but which we may try to approach on different paths. . . . So far the concept of *philosophy* is only scholastic. . . . But there is also a universal, or, if we may say so, a cosmical concept (conceptus cosmicus) of *philosophy*, which always formed the real foundation of that name. . . . In this sense *philosophy* is the science of the relations of all knowledge to the essential aims of human reason.
> *Kant*, Critique of Pure Reason (tr. by Müller), II. 719.

> *Philosophy* is an all-comprehensive Synthesis of the doctrines and methods of science; a coherent body of theorems concerning the Cosmos, and concerning Man in his relations to the Cosmos of which he is a part.
> *J. Fiske*, Cosmic Philos., I. 9.

> That *philosophy* only means psychology and morals, or in the last resort metaphysics, is an idea slowly developed through the eighteenth century, owing to the victorious advances of science. *Edinburgh Rev.*, CLXV. 95.

2. A special branch of knowledge of high speculative interest. (a) Any such science, as alchemy (in Chaucer).

> Voydeth your man and lat him be theroute,
> And shet the dore, whyls we ben aboute
> Our privetee, that no man us espye
> Whyls that we werke in this *philosophye*.
> *Chaucer*, Canon's Yeoman's Tale, l. 128.

(b†) Theology: this use of the word was common in the middle ages. (c) Psychology and ethics; moral philosophy. (d) Physics; natural philosophy.

3. The fundamental part of any science; propædeutic considerations upon which a special science is founded; general principles connected with a science, but not forming part of it; a theory connected with any branch of human activity: as, the *philosophy* of science; the *philosophy* of history; the *philosophy* of government.—4. A doctrine which aims to be philosophy in any of the above senses.

> But who so coude in other thing him grope,
> Thanne hadde he spent al his *philosophie*.
> *Chaucer*, Gen. Prol. to C. T., l. 645.

> There are more things in heaven and earth, Horatio,
> Than are dreamt of in your *philosophy*.
> *Shak.*, Hamlet, i. 5. 167.

> Of good and evil much they argued then,
> Of happiness and final misery,
> Passion and apathy, and glory and shame;
> Vain wisdom all, and false *philosophy*.
> *Milton*, P. L., ii. 565.

> We may return to the former distribution of the three *philosophies*, divine, natural, and human.
> *Bacon*, Advancement of Learning, ii. 152.

> We shall in vain interpret their words by the notions of our *philosophy* and the doctrines in our schools. *Locke.*

5. A calm temper which is unruffled by small annoyances; a stoical impassiveness under adversity.—**Association philosophy.** See *association*.—**Atomic** or **atomistic philosophy.** See *atomic*.—**Christian philosophy**, the philosophy of St. Augustine and other fathers of the church.—**Constructive philosophy**, the philosophy of Schelling and others, as opposed to the merely destructive philosophy of Kant.—**Corpuscular philosophy**, the doctrine of atoms considered as a philosophy or general explanation of the phenomena of the world, particularly that form of the doctrine advocated by Robert Boyle.—**Critical philosophy.** See *critical*.—**Doctor of philosophy.** See *doctor*.—**Experimental philosophy.** See *experimental*.—**First philosophy**, the science of the principles of being; ontology; metaphysics.—**Inductive, mechanical, moral, natural, Newtonian**, etc., **philosophy.** See the adjectives.—**Italic school of philosophy.** Same as *Pythagorean school of philosophy*.—**Objective philosophy.** Same as *transcendental philosophy*.—**Philosophies of the absolute.** See *absolute*.—**Philosophy of identity**, the philosophy of Schelling and Hegel, as maintaining the absolute identity of identity and non-identity.—**Pneumatic, positive, symbolical**, etc., **philosophy.** See the adjectives.—**Practical philosophy**, philosophy having action as its ultimate end; the laws of the faculties connected with desire and volition.—**Pythagorean school of philosophy.** See *Pythagorean*.—**Theoretical, speculative,** or **contemplative philosophy**, that philosophy which has no other aim than knowledge.—**Transcendental philosophy.** (a) The critical philosophy of Kant. (b) The philosophy of Hegel. Also called *objective philosophy*.

philostorgy† (fil′ǫ-stôr-ji), *n.* [< Gr. φιλοστοργία, tender love, < φιλόστοργος, loving, tenderly affectionate, < φιλεῖν, love, + στοργή, affection, < στέργειν, love.] Natural affection, such as that of a mother for her child.

philotechnic (fil-ǫ-tek′nik), *a.* [= F. *philotechnique*, < Gr. φιλότεχνος, fond of art, < φιλεῖν, love, + τέχνη, art: see *technic*.] Having a fondness for the arts, or a disposition to study or foster them; devoted to study of the arts, or to promoting advancement in them.

philotechnical (fil-ǫ-tek′ni-kal), *a.* [< *philotechnic* + *-al.*] Same as *philotechnic*.

philotheosophical (fil-ǫ-thē-ǫ-sof′i-kal), *a.* [< *philo*(*sophical*) + *theosophical*.] Relating to philosophy and theosophy. [Rare.]

> King of Berytus, to whom Sanchoniathon dedicated his *philo-theosophical* writings. *Cooper*, Arch. Dict., p. 10.

philozoic (fil-ǫ-zō′ik), *a.* [< Gr. φιλεῖν, love, + ζῷον, an animal, + *-ic.*] Having a tenderness for brute creatures; characterized or prompted by fondness for animals. [Rare.]

philter, philtre (fil′tėr), *n.* [Formerly also *filter*; < F. *philtre, filtre* = Sp. *filtro* = Pg. *philtro* = It. *filtro*, < L. *philtrum*, < Gr. φίλτρον, a love-charm; prop. φίλητρον, < φιλεῖν, love: see *philo-*.] A potion supposed to have the power of exciting sexual love; a love-potion.

> They can make friends enemies and enemies friends by *philters*. *Burton*, Anat. of Mel., p. 128.

> The cailliachs (old Highland hags) administered drugs which were designed to have the effect of *philtres*.
> *Scott*, Rob Roy, Int.

philter, philtre (fil′tėr), *v. t.*; pret. and pp. *philtered, philtred*, ppr. *philtering, philtring*. [< *philter, n.*] 1. To impregnate with a love-potion: as, to *philter* a draught.—2. To excite to sexual love or desire by a potion. *Dr. H. More.*

> Soon, like wine,
> Her eyes, in mine poured, frenzy-*philtred* mine.
> *Lowell*, Endymion, ii.

philtrum (fil′trum), *n.* [L.: see *philter*.] A philter.

> Love itself is the most potent *philtrum*.
> *Burton*, Anat. of Mel., p. 434.

Philydor (fil′i-dôr), *n.* [NL. (Spix, 1824), < Gr. φιλεῖν, love, + ὕδωρ, water.] A genus of South

Philydor superciliaris.

American synallaxine birds, of the family *Dendrocolaptidæ*, containing numerous species, such as *P. superciliaris* of Brazil.

Philydraceæ (fil-i-drā′sē-ē), *n. pl.* [NL. (Lindley, 1836), < *Philydrum* + *-aceæ*.] A small order of monocotyledonous plants, of the series *Coronarieæ*, distinguished by the irregular flowers with two petals, one stamen, and two rudiments, three carpels, and numerous ovules. It includes 3 genera, each with one species, mainly Australian. They are small herbs with sword-shaped leaves sheathing at the base, and a few smaller ones along the erect stem, which bears sessile flowers among spathaceous bracts, forming a spike or panicle. In habit they resemble the sedges, and in their flowers the spiderworts.

Philydrum (fil'i-drum), *n.* [NL. (Banks, 1788), so called from its growth in marshes; < Gr. φίλυδρος, loving water, < φιλεῖν, love, + ὕδωρ (ὑδρ-), water.] A genus of plants, type of the order *Philydraceæ*, distinguished by the imperfect partitions of the ovary, and the long undivided spike. The only species, *P. lanuginosum*, ranges from eastern Australia to southern China. It bears a white woolly stem, two-ranked leaves becoming bracts above, and yellow flowers solitary between their broad bracts. It is cultivated for its bright-colored spikes, sometimes under the name of *waterwort*.

phimosed (fī'mōst), *a.* [< *phimosis* + *-ed*[2].] Affected with phimosis.

phimosis (fī-mō'sis), *n.* [NL., < Gr. φίμωσις, a muzzling, < φιμοῦν, muzzle, < φιμός, a muzzle.] Stenosis of the preputial orifice. Compare *paraphimosis*.

phip† (fip), *n.* [A contraction of *philip*.] A sparrow; also, the noise made by a sparrow. See *philip*. *Halliwell.*

And whan I sayd Phyp, Phyp,
Than he wold lepe and skyp,
And take me by the lyp.
Alas! it wyll me slo,
That Phillyp is gone me fro.
Skelton, Phyllyp Sparowe, l. 138.

phisike†, *n.* A Middle English form of *physic*.

phisnomy (fiz'nō-mi), *n.* A corruption of *physiognomy*. *Palsgrave.*

phiton†, *n.* A Middle English form of *python*.

phitonesse†, *n.* A Middle English form of *pythoness*.

phiz (fiz), *n.* [Also *phyz*; an abbr. of *phisnomy*, *physiognomy*.] The face or visage. [Humorous.]

Why, truly a Body would think so by thy slovenly Dress, lean Carcase, and ghastly *Phyz*.
N. Bailey, tr. of Colloquies of Erasmus, I. 51.

Who can see such an horrid ugly *Phiz* as that Fellow's and not be shock'd? *Steele*, Grief A-la-Mode, i. 1.

phlebectasia (flē-bek-tā'si-ạ̈), *n.* [NL., < Gr. φλέψ (φλεβ-), a vein, + ἔκτασις, dilatation: see *ectasis*.] Dilatation of a vein.

phlebectopia (flē-bek-tō'pi-ạ̈), *n.* [NL., < Gr. φλέψ (φλεβ-), a vein, + ἔκτοπος, out of place: see *ectopia*.] Abnormal situation of a vein.

Phlebenterata (flē-ben-te-rā'tạ̈), *n. pl.* [NL. (Quatrefages, 1844), < Gr. φλέψ (φλεβ-), a vein, + ἔντερον, intestine, + *-ata*[2].] In *conch.*, a division of gastropods, characterized by the ramification of the gastric canal (alleged to serve for circulation as well as digestion) termed *gastrovascular*, comprising such genera as *Actæon* or *Elysia*. Quatrefages maintained that these gastric ramifications perform the office of branchial vessels, and that the division he made was of ordinal rank, but by others they are believed to be hepatic. The families *Æolididæ* and *Elysiidæ* exhibit the structure in question. They are now referred to the *Nudibranchiata*. See cuts under *Æolididæ*, *Elysia*, and *Dendronotus*.

phlebenterate (flē-ben'te-rāt), *a.* and *n.* **I.** *a.* Having the characteristics of the *Phlebenterata*, as a nudibranchiate gastropod.

II. *n.* A member of the *Phlebenterata*.

phlebenteric (flē-ben-ter'ik), *a.* [< *phlebenterism* + *-ic*.] Characterized by or exhibiting phlebenterism: as, the *phlebenteric* system.

phlebenterism (flē-ben'te-rizm), *n.* [< Gr. φλέψ (φλεβ-), a vein, + ἔντερον, intestine, + *-ism*.] **1.** Extension of processes of a loose alimentary canal into the legs, as in certain arachnidans (the *Pycnogonida*).—**2.** The doctrine that the gastric ramifications of certain nudibranchiate gastropods (*Phlebenterata*) have a respiratory function.

phlebitic (flē-bit'ik), *a.* [< *phlebitis* + *-ic*.] Pertaining to or affected with phlebitis.

phlebitis (flē-bī'tis), *n.* [NL., < Gr. φλέψ (φλεβ-), a vein, + *-itis*.] Inflammation of a vein.

phlebogram (fleb'ō-gram), *n.* [< Gr. φλέψ (φλεβ-), a vein, + γράμμα, a writing, < γράφειν, write.] A pulse-tracing or sphygmogram from a vein.

phlebographical (fleb-ō-graf'i-kạl), *a.* [< *phlebograph-y* + *-ic-al*.] Descriptive of veins; of or pertaining to phlebography.

phlebography (flē-bog'ra-fi), *n.* [= F. *phlébographie*, < Gr. φλέψ (φλεβ-), a vein, + -γραφία, < γράφειν, write.] A description of the veins.

phleboidal (flē-boi'dạl), *a.* [< Gr. φλέψ (φλεβ-), vein, + εἶδος, form.] Vein-like; in *bot.*, noting moniliform vessels. *Encyc. Brit.*, IV. 87.

phlebolite (fleb'ō-līt), *n.* [= F. *phlébolithe*, < Gr. φλέψ (φλεβ-), a vein, + λίθος, a stone.] In *pathol.*, a calcareous concretion in a vein. Also called *veinstone*.

phlebolith (fleb'ō-lith), *n.* Same as *phlebolite*.

phlebolitic (fleb-ō-lit'ik), *a.* [< *phlebolite* + *-ic*.] Having phlebolites; characterized by phlebolites.

phlebological (fleb-ō-loj'i-kạl), *a.* [< *phlebolog-y* + *-ic-al*.] Of or pertaining to phlebology.

phlebology (flē-bol'ō-ji), *n.* [< Gr. φλέψ (φλεβ-), a vein, + -λογία, < λέγειν, speak: see *-ology*.] That branch of anatomy which treats of the veins; a treatise on the veins. *Dunglison.*

phlebometritis (fleb″ō-mē-trī'tis), *n.* [NL., < Gr. φλέψ (φλεβ-), a vein, + μήτρα, the womb, + *-itis*.] Uterine phlebitis.

phleborrhage (fleb'ō-rāj), *n.* [= F. *phléborrhagie*, < Gr. φλεβορραγία, the bursting of a vein, < φλέψ (φλεβ-), a vein, + -ραγία, < ῥηγνύναι, burst.] Venous hemorrhage.

phleborrhagia (fleb-ō-rā'ji-ạ̈), *n.* [NL.: see *phleborrhage*.] Same as *phleborrhage*.

phleborrhexis (fleb-ō-rek'sis), *n.* [NL., < Gr. φλέψ (φλεβ-), a vein, + ῥῆξις, a rupture, < ῥηγνύναι, break, burst.] The rupture of a vein.

phlebothrombosis (fleb″ō-throm-bō'sis), *n.* [NL., < Gr. φλέψ (φλεβ-), a vein, + θρόμβωσις, a becoming clotted or curdled: see *thrombosis*.] Thrombosis in a vein.

phlebotomic (fleb-ō-tom'ik), *a.* [< *phlebotom-y* + *-ic*.] Of or pertaining to phlebotomy.

phlebotomical (fleb-ō-tom'i-kạl), *a.* [< *phlebotomic* + *-al*.] Pertaining to or of the nature of phlebotomy.

phlebotomise, *v. t.* See *phlebotomize*.

phlebotomist (flē-bot'ō-mist), n. [= F. *phlébotomiste* = Pg. *phlebotomista* (cf. Sp. *flebótomo*, It. *flebotomo*), a phlebotomist; as *phlebotom-y* + *-ist*.] One who practises phlebotomy; a blood-letter.

phlebotomize (flē-bot'ō-mīz), *v. t.*; pret. and pp. *phlebotomized*, ppr. *phlebotomizing*. [= F. *phlébotomiser* = Sp. *flebotomizar* = Pg. *phlebotomisar*; as *phlebotom-y* + *-ize*.] To let blood from; bleed by opening a vein. Also spelled *phlebotomise*.

All body politicks . . . must have an evacuation for their corrupt humours, they must be *phlebotomized*.
Howell, England's Tears (ed. 1645).

Let me beg you not . . . to speak of a "thorough-bred" as a "blooded" horse, unless he has been recently *phlebotomized*. I consent to your saying "blood horse," if you like. *O. W. Holmes*, Autocrat, p. 40.

phlebotomy (flē-bot'ō-mi), *n.* [Formerly spelled *phlebotomie*; < OF. *phlebotomie*, F. *phlébotomie* = Sp. *flebotomia* = Pg. *phlebotomia* = It. *flebotomia*, < LL. *phlebotomia*, < Gr. φλεβοτομία, the opening of a vein, blood-letting, < φλεβοτόμος, opening veins, < φλέψ (φλεβ-), a vein, + τέμνειν, ταμεῖν, cut. Cf. *fleam*[1].] The act or practice of opening a vein for letting blood, as a remedy for disease or with a view to the preservation of health.

Every sin is an incision of the soul, a lancination, a *phlebotomy*, a letting of the soul-blood. *Donne*, Sermons, xi.

Phlegethontius (flej-e-thon'ti-us), *n.* [NL., < Gr. φλεγέθων, ppr. of φλεγέθειν, burn, scorch, burn up.] A genus of sphingid moths, founded by Herrich-Schäffer in 1854, having the thorax tufted, head prominent, palpi well developed, eyes large and scarcely ciliate, and outer border of the wings obliquely rounded. *P. celeus* (formerly called *Macrosila quinquemaculata*) is the common five-spotted sphinx, whose larva is the tomato-worm or potato-worm, abundant in the northern and middle United States upon the tomato, potato, jimson-weed, matrimony-vine, and ground-cherry. *P. carolina* is the tobacco-worm moth, whose caterpillar is found in tobacco-fields and often injures the plant. See cut under *tomato-worm*.

phlegm (flem), *n.* [Also *flegm*, *flegme*, *fleam*, *flem*, etc. (see *fleam*[2]); < ME. *fleme*, *fleume*, < OF. *flegme*, *fleume*, F. *flegme*, *phlegme* = Sp. *flema*, *flegma* = Pg. *flegma*, *fleuma*, *phlegma*, *phleugma* = It. *flemma*, < ML. *phlegma*, *flegma*, phlegm, < Gr. φλέγμα, flame, fire, heat, inflammation; hence, as the result of such heat, phlegm, a humor regarded as the matter and cause of many diseases; < φλέγειν, burn: see *flame*.] **1**†. One of the four humors of which the ancients supposed the blood to be composed.

The II. medicyn is for to hecle the feuere cotidian, the which is causid of putrifaccioun of *fleume* to haboundynge. *Book of Quinte Essence* (ed. Furnivall), p. 21.

The water which is moist and colde
Maketh *fleume*, which is manifolde,
Foryetel [forgetful], slow, and wery sone
Of every thing. *Gower*, Conf. Amant., III. 98.

2. In *old chem.*, the aqueous, insipid, and inodorous products obtained by subjecting moist vegetable matter to the action of heat.—**3.** A thick viscid matter secreted in the digestive and respiratory passages, and discharged by coughing or vomiting; bronchial mucus.

For throughe crudityе and lack of perfect concoction in the stomacke is engendered great abundance of naughty baggage and hurtfull *phlegme*.
Touchstone of Complexions, p. 118.

4. Dullness; sluggishness; indifference; coolness; apathy; calm self-restraint.

They only think you animate your theme
With too much fire, who are themselves all *phlegm*.
Dryden, To Lee, l. 42.

They judge with fury, but they write with *phlegm*.
Pope, Essay on Criticism, l. 662.

But not her warmth, nor all her winning ways,
From his cool *phlegm* could Donald's spirit raise.
Crabbe, Works, I. 76.

His temperament boasted a certain amount of *phlegm*, and he preferred an undemonstrative, not ungentle, but serious aspect to any other. *Charlotte Brontë*, Shirley, xiii.

=**Syn.** 4. *Insensibility*, *Impassibility*, etc. See *apathy*.

phlegma†, n. Same as *phlegm*, 2.

phlegmagogic (fleg-ma-goj'ik), *a.* and n. [< *phlegmagog-ue* + *-ic*.] **I.** *a.* Expelling phlegm; having the character of a phlegmagogue.

II. n. A phlegmagogue.

phlegmagogue (fleg'ma-gog), n. [< F. *phlegmagogue*, *flegmagogue* = Pg. *phlegmagogo* = It. *flemmagogo*, < Gr. φλεγμαγωγός, carrying off phlegm, < φλέγμα, phlegm, + ἀγωγός, carrying off, < ἄγειν, lead, carry off.] A medicine supposed to possess the property of expelling phlegm.

phlegman†, *n.* See *phlegmon*.

phlegmasia (fleg-mā'si-ạ̈), n. [= F. *phlegmasie*, *flegmasie*, < NL. *phlegmasia*, < Gr. φλεγμασία, inflammation, < φλεγμαίνειν, heat, be heated or inflamed, < φλέγμα, flame: see *phlegm*.] In *med.*, inflammation.—**Phlegmasia dolens** (literally, painful inflammation), puerperal tumid leg: an affection presenting thrombosis of the large veins of the part, with swelling, hardness, whiteness of the skin, and much pain, usually affecting the leg, most frequent shortly after childbirth. Also called *phlegmasia alba dolens*, *milk-leg*, and *white-leg*.

phlegmatic (fleg-mat'ik or fleg'ma-tik), *a.* [Also *flegmatic*, and formerly *flegmatick* (ME. *flewmatik*, etc.); < F. *flegmatique*, *phlegmatique* = Sp. *flegmático*, *flemático* = Pg. *phlegmatico*, *flegmatico*, *fleumatico* = It. *flemmatico*, < LL. *phlegmaticus*, < Gr. φλεγματικός, like phlegm, pertaining to phlegm, < φλέγμα, phlegm: see *phlegm*.] **1**†. Of the nature of phlegm; watery; aqueous: as, *phlegmatic* humors.

Spirit of wine . . . grows by every distillation more and more aqueous and *phlegmatic*. *Newton.*

2†. Generating or causing phlegm.

Cold and *phlegmatick* habitations.
Sir T. Browne, Vulg. Err., vi. 10.

3. Abounding in phlegm; lymphatic; hence, cold; dull; sluggish; heavy; not easily excited to action or passion; apathetic; cool and self-restrained: as, a *phlegmatic* temperament. See *temperament*.

ȝitt *flewmatik* men [are occupied] aboute othere [imaginations], but tho men that habounde in blak coler, that is malencoly, ben occupied a thousand part with mo thouȝtis than ben men of ony othere complexioun.
Book of Quinte Essence (ed. Furnivall), p. 17.

The officers' understandings are so *phlegmatic*
They cannot apprehend us.
Fletcher, Mad Lover, ii. 2.

Heavy and *phlegmatick* he trod the stage,
Too proud for tenderness, too dull for rage.
Churchill, The Rosciad.

Many an ancient burgher, whose *phlegmatic* features had never been known to relax, nor his eyes to moisten, was now observed to puff a pensive pipe, and the big drop to steal down his cheek. *Irving*, Knickerbocker, p. 465.

=**Syn.** 3. Frigid, impassive, unsusceptible. See *apathy*.

phlegmatical (fleg-mat'i-kạl), *a.* [< *phlegmatic* + *-al*.] Same as *phlegmatic*.

phlegmatically (fleg-mat'i-kạl-i), *adv.* In a phlegmatic manner; coldly; heavily.

phlegmaticly (fleg-mat'ik-li), *adv.* Same as *phlegmatically*.

phlegmon (fleg'mon), *n.* [Formerly also, erroneously, *phlegman*; < F. *flegmon*, *phlegmon* = Sp. *flegmon*, *flemon* = Pg. *fleimão*, *phlegmão* = It. *flemmone*, < L. *phlegmone*, < Gr. φλεγμονή, inflammation, < φλέγειν, burn: see *phlegm*.] In *pathol.*: (*a*†) Inflammation.

I shall begin with *phlegmon* or inflammation, . . . because it is the first degeneration from good blood, and in its own nature nearest of kin to it.
Wiseman, Surgery, i. 3.

(*b*) Inflammation of the connective tissue, especially the subcutaneous connective tissue, usually suppurative.

phlegmonoid (fleg'mō-noid), *a.* [< Gr. *φλεγμονοειδής, contr. φλεγμονώδης, like an inflamed tumor, < φλεγμονή, an inflamed tumor (see *phlegmon*), + εἶδος, form.] Resembling phlegmon.

phlegmonous (fleg'mǫ-nus), *a.* [< F. *phlegmoneux, flegmoneux* = It. *flemmonoso*; as *phlegmon* + *-ous.*] Of, pertaining to, or of the nature of phlegmon: as, *phlegmonous* inflammation.

phlegmy (flem'i), *a.* Pertaining to, containing, or resembling phlegm.

A *phlegmy* humour in the body. *Chambers's Cyc.*

phlemet, *n.* An obsolete form of *fleam*[1].

Phleum (flē'um), *n.* [NL. (Linnæus, 1737), < Gr. φλέως, also φλέος, φλοῦς, some water-plant, according to Sprengel *Arundo Ampelodesmon.*] A genus of grasses of the tribe *Agrostideæ*, type of the subtribe *Phleoideæ*, and characterized by the dense cylindrical or ovoid spike, with the empty glumes wingless, mucronate, or short-awned, and much longer than the flowering one. There are about 10 species, natives of Europe, central and northern Asia, northern Africa, and northern and antarctic America. They are erect annual or perennial grasses, with flat leaves, and the flowers usually conspicuously hairy, with a purplish cast in blossom from the color of the abundant anthers, which are large and exserted. (See *timothy*, also *cat's-tail grass* (under *cat's-tail*) and *herd's-grass*, names for the most valuable species, in common use in the eastern United States.) P. *alpinum*, the mountain cat's-tail grass, is also an excellent meadow-grass for colder regions.

phlobaphenes (flǫ-baf'e-nēz), *n. pl.* Brown amorphous coloring matters which are present in the walls of the bark-cells of trees and shrubs.

phloëm (flō'em), *n.* [(Nägeli, 1858), irreg. < Gr. φλοιός, bark. Cf. *phlœum.*] In *bot.*, the bast or liber portion of a vascular bundle, or the region of a vascular bundle or axis with secondary thickening which contains sieve-tubes. Compare *xylem.*

phloëm-sheath (flō'em-shēth), *n.* In *bot.*, the sheath of phloëm-tissue sometimes formed about the xylem part in a vascular bundle, as in certain ferns.

Phlœocharina, Phlœocharini (flē"ǫ-ka-rī'nạ̈, -ni), *n. pl.* [NL., < *Phlœocharis* + *-ina*[2], *-ini.*] A group of coleopterous insects named from the genus *Phlœocharis*, and forming a small tribe of the rove-beetle family, *Staphylinidæ*, comprising species of slender, depressed form. Only four genera are known, of which two inhabit the United States.

Phlœocharis (flẹ-ok'ạ-ris), *n.* [NL. (Mannerheim, 1830), < Gr. φλοιός, bark, + χαίρειν, rejoice.] A genus of rove-beetles, typical of the tribe *Phlœocharina*. Few species are known, confined to Europe.

Phlœophora (flẹ-of'ǫ-rạ̈), *n. pl.* [NL., < Gr. φλοιός, bark, + φέρειν = E. *bear*[1].] In Carus's classification, an order of protozoans represented by the sun-animalcules, *Actinophryidæ.*

phlœophorous (flẹ-of'ǫ-rus), *a.* Of or pertaining to the *Phlœophora.*

phlœum (flē'um), *n.* [NL., < Gr. φλοιός, bark.] In *bot.*, the cellular portion of bark lying immediately under the epidermis. It is also termed *epiphlœum* and *bast.* [Not used by later authorities.]

phlogistian (flǫ-jis'ti-ạn), *n.* [< *phlogist-on* + *-ian.*] A believer in the existence of phlogiston.

phlogistic (flǫ-jis'tik), *a.* [< *phlogiston* + *-ic.*] 1. Pertaining or relating to phlogiston.

The mistakes committed in the celebrated *phlogistic* theory. *J. S. Mill*, Logic, v. 4.

2. In *med.*, inflammatory.

phlogisticate† (flǫ-jis'ti-kāt), *v. t.* [< *phlogistic* + *-ate*[2].] To combine phlogiston with.—**Phlogisticated air** or **gas**, the name given by the old chemists to nitrogen.—**Phlogisticated alkali**, prussiate of potash.

phlogistication† (flǫ-jis-ti-kā'shọn), *n.* [= F. *phlogistication*; as *phlogisticate* + *-ion.*] The act or process of combining with phlogiston.

phlogiston (flǫ-jis'ton), *n.* [NL., < Gr. φλογιστός, inflammable, burnt up, verbal adj. of φλογίζειν, burn, < φλόξ, a flame: see *phlox.*] In *old chem.*, the supposed principle of inflammability; the matter of fire in composition with other bodies. Stahl gave this name to a hypothetical element which he supposed to be pure fire fixed in combustible bodies, in order to distinguish it from fire in action or in a state of liberty.

It is only after Stahl's [1660–1734] labors that a scientific chemistry becomes for the first time possible; the essential difference between the teaching of the science then and now being that the phenomena of combustion were then believed to be due to a chemical decomposition, *phlogiston* being supposed to escape, whilst we account for the same phenomena now by a chemical combination, oxygen or some element being taken up.
Roscoe and Schorlemmer, Treatise on Chemistry (1888), I. 14.

phlogogenic (flog-ǫ-jen'ik), *a.* [As *phlogogenous* + *-ic.*] Same as *phlogogenous.*

phlogogenous (flǫ-goj'e-nus), *a.* [< Gr. φλόξ (φλογ-), flame, + -γενής, producing.] Producing inflammation.

phlogopite (flog'ǫ-pit), *n.* [< Gr. φλογωπός (< φλόξ, a flame, + ὤψ, the face), fiery-looking, flaming-red, + *-ite*[2].] A kind of magnesia mica (see *mica*[2], 1) commonly occurring in crystalline limestone and in serpentine. It has often a copper-like color and pearly luster; chemically it is usually characterized by the presence of a small percentage of fluorin.

phlogosis (flǫ-gō'sis), *n.* [NL., < Gr. φλόγωσις, a burning, inflammation, < φλόξ (φλογ-), flame: see *phlox.*] In *med.*, inflammation.

phlogotic (flǫ-got'ik), *a.* [< *phlogosis* (*-ot-*) + *-ic.*] Pertaining to, characterized by, or of the nature of phlogosis; inflammatory.

Phlomis (flō'mis), *n.* [NL. (Tournefort, 1700), < Gr. φλομίς, also φλόμος, also corruptly φλῶμος, φλόνος, mullen, appar. so called in allusion to the use of its thick woolly leaves as wicks (one species being called φλομὶς λυχνῖτις, 'lamp-mullen'); prob. for orig. *φλογμίς, < φλογμός, a flame, < φλέγειν, burn: see *phlegm, phlox, flame.*] A genus of gamopetalous plants of the order *Labiatæ*, the mint family, belonging to the tribe *Stachydeæ* and subtribe *Lamieæ*, and characterized by the villous and concave upper lip, the plicate calyx, and the densely flowered whorls in the axils. There are about 50 species, natives of the Mediterranean region and Asia. They are herbs or shrubs with rugose or puckered leaves, often thick and woolly or hoary, and sessile yellow, purple, or white flowers. They rank among the most showy hardy plants of the mint family. About a dozen species are in common cultivation, especially P. *fruticosa*, the Jerusalem sage (see *sage*), a half-shrubby plant, 3 to 5 feet high, covered with rusty down, and producing many dense whorls of rich-yellow flowers. Several other shrubby species from the Mediterranean are cultivated under the name *Phlomis*. P. *Herba-venti*, the wind-herb, is the best of the herbaceous species. P. *tuberosa* occurs introduced on the south shore of Lake Ontario. See also *lampwick*, 2, and *Jupiter's-distaff.*

phlorizin (flor'i-zin), *n.* [= F. *phloorrhizine*; irreg. < Gr. φλοιόῤῥιζος, having roots covered with coats of rind, < φλοιός, bark, + ῥίζα, root.] A substance ($C_{21}H_{24}O_{10}$) discovered in the fresh bark of the root of the apple, pear, cherry, and plum. It forms fine colorless four-sided silky needles, soluble in water. The solution has a bitter and slightly astringent taste. It has been used with success in intermittents, and while it is administered produces glycosuria.

phloroglucin (flō-rǫ-glō'sin), *n.* [< *phlor(izin)* + *glucin.*] A substance widely distributed in the vegetable kingdom, when pure crystallizing in small yellow crystals with the composition $C_6H_3(OH)_3$; a trivalent phenol. It is used in microscopy as one of the best reagents for testing lignified cell-walls.

Phlox (floks), *n.* [NL. (Linnæus, 1737), < L. *phlox*, < Gr. φλόξ, some flower so named from its color, a particular use of φλόξ, a flame, < φλέγειν, burn: see *flame.*] 1. A genus of ornamental gamopetalous plants of the order *Polemoniaceæ*, characterized by a deeply three-valved loculicidal capsule, included stamens unequally inserted on the tube of a salver-shaped corolla, and entire leaves. The 30 species are natives of North America and Siberia. They are erect or spreading herbs, often tall perennials, bearing chiefly opposite leaves, and showy flowers usually in a flat or pyramidal cyme, red, violet, purplish, white, or blue. Most species are cultivated under the name *phlox*, P. *speciosa* as the pride-of-Columbia, P. *subulata* as the moss-pink. P. *maculata* is the wild sweet-william of the middle and western United States. P. *paniculata*, with large pyramidal clusters of flowers, native of the central and southern States, is the parent of most of the perennial phloxes of the gardens. The annual varieties in gardens are from P. *Drummondii* of Texas, there discovered by Drummond in 1835. P. *divaricata* is the wild phlox of the eastern States, with early bluish-lilac flowers. P. *reptans*, the creeping phlox, is an important spring-flowering species of the south.

2. [*l. c.*] Any plant of this genus.

phloxin (flok'sin), *n.* [< Gr. φλόξ, flame, + *-in*[2].] A coal-tar color used in dyeing, similar to eosin. It is the potassium salt of tetra-brom-dichlor-fluorescein.

phlox-worm (floks'wėrm), *n.* The larva of *Heliothis phlogophagus*, a noctuid moth, closely resembling the well-known boll-worm moth of the cotton. It feeds upon cultivated varieties of phlox, and pupates under ground. See cut in next column.

phlyctena, phlyctæna (flik-tē'nạ̈), *n.*; pl. *phlyctenæ, phlyctænæ* (-nē). [NL. *phlyctæna*, < Gr. φλύκταινα, a blister, pustule, < φλύζειν, φλύειν, boil over.] A small vesicle.

phlyctenar, phlyctænar (flik-tē'nạ̈r), *a.* [< *phlyctena, phlyctæna*, + *-ar*[3].] Affected with phlyctenæ; blistered.

phlyctenoid, phlyctænoid (flik-tē'noid), *a.* [< Gr. φλύκταινα, blister, + εἶδος, form.] Resembling a phlyctena.

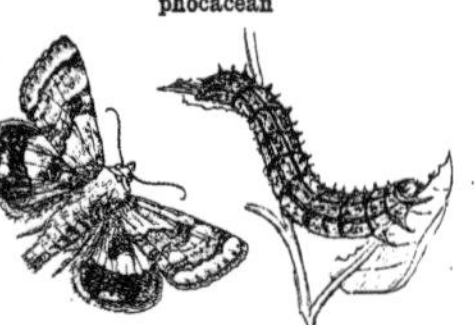

Phlox-worm and Moth (*Heliothis phlogophagus*), natural size.

phlyctenous, phlyctænous (flik-tē'nus), *a.* [< *phlyctena, phlyctæna*, + *-ous.*] Pertaining to, exhibiting, or of the nature of a phlyctena or phlyctenæ.

phlyctenula, phlyctænula (flik-ten'ū-lạ̈), *n.*; pl. *phlyctenulæ, phlyctænulæ* (-lē). [NL., dim. of *phlyctena, phlyctæna.*] In *med.*, a minute phlyctena in the conjunctiva or the cornea.

phlyctenular, phlyctænular (flik-ten'ū-lạ̈r), *a.* [< *phlyctenula, phlyctænula*, + *-ar*[3].] Pertaining to, of the nature of, or accompanied by phlyctenulæ.—**Phlyctenular ophthalmia**, inflammation of the cornea or the conjunctiva with phlyctenulæ on the cornea.

phlyzacium (flī-zā'si-um), *n.*; pl. *phlyzacia* (-ạ̈). [NL., < Gr. φλυζάκιον, a pimple, pustule, < φλύζειν, φλύειν, boil over.] A phlyctena.

pho, *interj.* A bad spelling of *foh.*

phobanthropy (fō-ban'thrǫ-pi), *n.* [< Gr. φοβεῖσθαι, fear (< φόβος, fear), + ἄνθρωπος, man.] A morbid dread of mankind. *Westminster Rev.*

phobophobia (fō-bǫ-fō'bi-ạ̈), *n.* [NL., < Gr. φοβεῖσθαι, fear (< φόβος, fear), + φόβος, fear.] Morbid dread of being alarmed.

Phobos (fō'bos), *n.* [NL., < Gr. Φόβος, Fear, a companion of Ares or Mars (War); a personification of φόβος, fear, terror, dismay, < φέβεσθαι, be scared, fear, flee. Cf. *Deimos.*] The inner of the two satellites of the planet Mars, discovered by Asaph Hall at Washington, in August, 1877. This extraordinary body revolves in the plane of the equator of Mars, at a distance of only about 3,700 miles from the surface of the planet, but as it is probably only about five and a half miles in diameter, it would appear only one sixth of the apparent diameter of our moon at the zenith, and on the horizon, owing to the enormous parallax, only about one fourteenth of the same. At the equinoxes it is in eclipse about one fifth of the time, or double that proportion of the time between sunset and sunrise. At the solstices it does not suffer eclipse. It revolves about its primary in 7 hours, 39 minutes, and 14 seconds, and as Mars revolves on its axis in 24 hours, 37 minutes, and 22.7 seconds, it follows that the satellite appears to an observer on Mars to rise in the west and set in the east, its return to his meridian occurring in 11 hours, 6 minutes, and 23 seconds, but, owing to its close proximity, its velocity will appear to be much greater. At a station on the equator of Mars (where the satellite always passes through the zenith), it will, out of its 11 hours and 6 minutes of period, pass only 3 hours and 20 minutes above the horizon against 7 hours and 46 minutes below.

phoca (fō'kạ̈), *n.* [= F. *phoque* = Sp. It. *foca* = Pg. *phoca*, < L. *phoca*, < Gr. φώκη, a seal.] 1. A seal.—2. [*cap.*] [NL.] A genus of *Phocidæ* or seals, formerly coextensive at least with the

Common Harbor-seal (*Phoca vitulina*).

family, now restricted to the section which is represented by the common harbor-seal, *P. vitulina*, and a few closely related species. See *seal*[1], and cut under *harp-seal.*

phocacean (fǫ-kā'sẹ-ạn), *a.* and *n.* [< *phoca* + *-acean.*] I. *a.* 1. Of or pertaining to the genus *Phoca* in a broad sense; phocine.

II. *n.* A seal of the genus *Phoca* in a broad sense; a phocine.

Phocæna (fō-sē'nä), *n.* [NL., < Gr. φώκαινα, a porpoise; cf. φῶκος, m., a porpoise, φώκη, a seal: see *phoca*.] A genus of delphinoid odontocete cetaceans, containing the true porpoises, such as *P. communis*, as distinguished from the dolphins proper. There are about 64 vertebræ, of which the cervicals are 7, mostly ankylosed, and the dorsals 13; the teeth are from 72 to 100, along nearly the whole length of the jaw, with constricted necks; the symphysis of the mandible is very short, and the rostral is not longer than the cranial section of the skull. The dorsal fin is near the middle of the back (wanting in *P. melas*, which constitutes the subgenus *Neomeris*), triangular, of less height than breadth at the base; the fins have five digits, oval or somewhat falcate. See cut under *porpoise*.

Phocænina (fō-sē-nī'nä), *n. pl.* [NL., < *Phocæna* + *-ina*[2].] A group of cetaceans, typified by the genus *Phocæna*; the porpoises.

phocænine (fō-sē'nin), *a.* [< Gr. φώκαινα, a porpoise, + *-ine*[1].] Resembling a porpoise; of or pertaining to the *Phocænina*.

phocal (fō'kal), *a.* [< *phoca* + *-al*.] Phocacean; phocine. [Rare.]

Phocea (fō-sē'ä), *n.* [NL., prop. *Phocæa*, < L. *Phocæa*, < Gr. Φώκαια, a maritime city of Ionia, a colony of Athens, and the parent city of Massilia, now Marseilles.] The 25th planetoid, discovered by Chacornac at Marseilles in 1853.

Phocian (fō'shian), *a.* and *n.* [< L. *Phocis*, < Gr. Φωκίς, Phocis (see def.), + *-an*.] **I.** *a.* Of or pertaining to Phocis, a state of ancient Greece, or its inhabitants.

II. *n.* A native or an inhabitant of Phocis.

Phocidæ (fō'si-dē), *n. pl.* [NL., < *Phoca* + *-idæ*.] A family of aquatic carnivorous mammals of the order *Feræ* and suborder *Pinnipedia*, having the limbs modified into fins or flippers; the seals. The family was formerly coextensive with the suborder, including the otaries and the walruses as well as the true seals, and divided into three subfamilies: *Arctocephalina*, the otaries; *Trichechina*, the walruses; and *Phocina*, the seals proper. The last alone now constitute the family *Phocidæ*, having the body truly phociform, with the hinder limbs projecting backward, and not capable of being turned forward; the outer ear obsolete; the fore flippers smaller than the hind ones, and having the digits successively shortened and armed with claws, while the hind flippers are emarginated by the shortening of the third and fourth digits, and are usually but not always provided with claws. The incisors are variable in number, and the upper ones are unnotched. The skull has no alisphenoid canals, and the postorbital processes are obsolete. In this restricted sense the *Phocidæ* are represented by about 12 genera, and divided into the subfamilies *Phocinæ*, *Cystophorinæ*, and *Stenorhynchinæ*. See cuts under *harp-seal*, *Pagomys*, *Phoca*, *seal*[1], and *Erignathus*.

phociform (fō'si-fôrm), *a.* [< Gr. φώκη, a seal, + L. *forma*, form.] Resembling a seal in structure; having the form or characters of the *Phocidæ*.

Phocinæ (fō-sī'nē), *n. pl.* [NL., < *Phoca* + *-inæ*.] The leading subfamily of *Phocidæ* proper, typified by the genus *Phoca*, having normally six upper and four lower incisors, and narrow nasal and intermaxillary bones. The genera besides *Phoca* are *Pagomys*, *Pagophilus*, *Erignathus*, *Halichœrus*, and *Monachus*.

phocine (fō'sin), *a.* and *n.* [< Gr. φώκη, a seal, + *-ine*[1].] **I.** *a.* **1.** Seal-like; of or pertaining to the *Phocidæ* at large.—**2.** Belonging to the restricted subfamily *Phocinæ*: distinguished from *otarine*.

II. *n.* Any member of the *Phocinæ*; a phocacean.

Phocodon (fō'kō-don), *n.* [NL. (Agassiz), < Gr. φώκη, a seal, + ὀδούς (ὀδοντ-) = E. *tooth*.] A genus of fossil cetaceans, giving name to the *Phocodontia*. See *Zeuglodon*.

phocodont (fō'kō-dont), *n.* One of the *Phocodontia*.

Phocodontia (fō-kō-don'shi-ä), *n. pl.* [NL., < *Phocodon* (*-odont-*), + *-ia*.] One of the primary groups of the order *Cetacea*, entirely extinct, consisting of the genera *Zeuglodon*, *Squalodon*, and other large cetaceans of the Tertiary epoch, remarkable as furnishing connecting-links between the *Cetacea* and the pinniped aquatic *Carnivora*.

phocodontic (fō-kō-don'tik), *a.* [< *phocodont* + *-ic*.] Pertaining to the *Phocodontia*, or having their characters.

phocoid (fō'koid), *a.* and *n.* [< Gr. φώκη, a seal, + εἶδος, form.] **I.** *a.* Resembling a seal; belonging to the *Phocoidea*.

II. *n.* Any member of the *Phocoidea*.

Phocoidea (fō-koi'dē-ä), *n. pl.* [NL.: see *phocoid*.] A superfamily of pinnipeds, containing the *Otariidæ* and *Phocidæ*, or the eared and earless seals, together contrasted with *Trichechoidea* or *Rosmaroidea*, the walruses. They have no tusks, or highly developed canine teeth, and the incisors are persistent; the lower molars are five on each side, the upper five or six.

phocomelus (fō-kom'e-lus), *n.*; pl. *phocomeli* (-lī). [NL., < Gr. φώκη, a seal, + μέλος, a limb.] In *teratol.*, a monster with very short extremities, the hands and feet being apparently attached directly to the trunk.

Phœbades (fē'bā-dēz), *n. pl.* [L. *Phœbades*, pl. of *Phœbas*, < Gr. Φοιβάς, a priestess of Apollo, < Φοῖβος, Apollo, Phœbus: see *Phœbus*.] Priestesses of the sun.

> Attired like Virginian Priests, by whom the Sun is there adored, and therefore called the *Phœbades*.
> *Chapman*, Masque of the Middle Temple and Lincoln's Inn.

Phœbe[1] (fē'bē), *n.* [Also *Phebe*; < L. *Phœbe*, < Gr. Φοίβη, the moon-goddess, sister of Φοῖβος, Phœbus: see *Phœbus*.] **1.** The moon or moon-goddess.

> To-morrow night, when *Phœbe* doth behold
> Her silver visage in the watery glass.
> *Shak.*, M. N. D., i. 1. 209.

2. [*l. c.*] A Cuban fish, *Haliperca phœbe*. *F. Poey.*

phœbe[2] (fē'bē), *n.* [An imitative name, accom. in spelling to L. *Phœbe*: see *Phœbe*[1]. Cf. *pewit*.] The water-pewee, or pewit flycatcher, *Sayornis fuscus*. See cut under *pewit*.

Phœbean (fē-bē'an), *a.* [< *Phœbus* + *-an*.] Of, pertaining to, or produced by Phœbus Apollo.

> Whose ear
> Is able to distinguish strains that are
> Clear and *Phœbean* from the popular.
> *Shirley*, Love in a Maze, Prol.

phœbe-bird (fē'bē-bėrd), *n.* The phœbe.

phœbium (fē'bi-um), *n.* [NL., < Gr. Φοῖβος, Phœbus, i. e. the sun: see *Phœbus*.] A name suggested by Proctor for the unknown substance which produces the 1474 line of Kirchhoff's scale in the spectrum of the solar corona: commonly called *coronium*.

Phœbus (fē'bus), *n.* [= F. *Phébus* = Sp. It. *Febo* = Pg. *Phebo*, < L. *Phœbus*, < Gr. Φοῖβος, Phœbus (see def.), < φοῖβος, pure, bright, < φάος, φῶς, light, < φάειν, shine: see *phase*[1].] A name of Apollo, often used in the same sense as *Sol* or *Helios*, the sun-god.

> Hark, hark! the lark at heaven's gate sings
> And *Phœbus* 'gins arise. *Shak.*, Cymbeline, ii. 3. 22.

Phœniceæ (fē-nis'ē-ē), *n. pl.* [NL. (Bentham and Hooker, 1883), < *Phœnix* (*Phœnic-*) + *-eæ*.] A tribe of palms, consisting of the genus *Phœnix*, and distinguished by the pinnately divided leaves, with acuminate segments induplicate in the bud, diœcious flowers, and a long, solitary, coriaceous and compressed spathe.

phœniceous (fē-nish'ius), *a.* [< Gr. φοινίκεος, purple-red, < φοῖνιξ (φοινικ-), purple-red.] Same as *phenicious*.

Phœnicercus (fē-ni-sėr'kus), *n.* [NL. (Swainson, 1831, as *Phœnicircus*; emended *Phœnicercus*, Strickland, 1841), prop. *Phœnicocercus* (Cabanis, 1847), and erroneously *Phænicocercus* (Bonaparte, 1850); < Gr. φοῖνιξ (φοινικ-), purple-red, + κέρκος, tail.] A genus of South American non-oscine passerine birds, of the family *Cotingidæ* and subfamily *Rupicolinæ*, closely related to the cock-of-the-rock (see *Rupicola*): so called from the color of the tail. There are two species, *P. carnifex* and *P. nigricollis*, the former of Cayenne and Colombia, the latter found in the vicinity of Pará. Both are chiefly of a scarlet or bloody-red color; in *P. nigricollis* the neck, back, wings, and tip of the tail are black. Also called *Carnifex*.

Phœnician, *a.* and *n.* See *Phenician*.

phœnicin, *n.* See *phenicin*.

Phœnicophilinæ (fē-ni-kof-i-lī'nē), *n. pl.* [NL., < *Phœnicophilus* + *-inæ*.] A subfamily of *Tanagridæ*, represented by the genera *Phœnicophilus* and *Calyptophilus*, peculiar to San Domingo.

Phœnicophilus (fē-ni-kof'i-lus), *n.* [NL. (H. E. Strickland, 1851), < Gr. φοῖνιξ (φοινικ-), the date-palm, + φίλος, loving.] The typical genus of *Phœnicophilinæ*, having a comparatively slender bill, moderate tarsi, and square tail. *P. palmarum* is the leading species.

Phœnicophilus palmarum.

phœnicopter, *n.* See *phenicopter*.

Phœnicopteridæ (fē'ni-kop-ter'i-dē), *n. pl.* [NL., < *Phœnicopterus* + *-idæ*.] A family of birds of the suborder *Odontoglossæ* and order *Lamellirostres*, consisting of the flamingos only. Its systematic position is intermediate between the storks and herons on the one hand and the ducks and geese on the other. The group is called *Odontoglossæ* by Nitzsch, and *Amphimorphæ* by Huxley. See *flamingo*.

phœnicopteroid (fē-ni-kop'te-roid), *a.* Of or resembling the *Phœnicopteroideæ*.

Phœnicopteroideæ (fē-ni-kop-te-roi'dē-ē), *n. pl.* [NL., < *Phœnicopterus* + *-oideæ*.] The flamingos regarded as a superfamily: synonymous with both *Amphimorphæ* and *Odontoglossæ*.

phœnicopterous (fē-ni-kop'te-rus), *a.* [< Gr. φοινικόπτερος, in lit. sense 'red-winged': see *Phœnicopterus*.] Having red wings, as a flamingo; relating to the genus *Phœnicopterus*.

Phœnicopterus (fē-ni-kop'te-rus), *n.* [NL., < L. *phœnicopterus*, the flamingo, < Gr. φοινικόπτερος, a bird, supposed to be the flamingo, lit. 'red-winged,' < φοῖνιξ (φοινικ-), purple-red, red, + πτερόν, feather, wing.] **1.** The typical and leading genus of *Phœnicopteridæ*, usually held to be conterminous with the family, and sometimes divided into four sections—*Phœnicopterus* proper, *Phœniconaias*, *Phœnicorodias*, and *Phœnicoparrus*. *P. antiquorum* is widely distributed in Africa and some parts of Asia and Europe; *P. ignipalliatus* is South American; *P. minor* is African; *P. ruber* inhabits the southern United States, the West Indies, and other parts of tropical America; *P. andinus* is found in the Andes of Peru, Bolivia, and Chili. See cut under *flamingo*. **2.** The constellation Grus.

phœnicurous (fē-ni-kū'rus), *a.* [< L. *phœnicurus*, < Gr. φοινίκουρος, a bird, the redstart, lit. 'having a red tail,' < φοῖνιξ (φοινικ-), purple-red, red, + οὐρά, a tail.] Having a red tail.

phœnix[1], *n.* See *phenix*.

Phœnix[2] (fē'niks), *n.* [NL. (Linnæus, 1737), < Gr. φοῖνιξ, the date-palm; cf. Φοῖνιξ, Phenician: see *Phenician*.] A genus of palms, constituting the tribe *Phœniceæ*, characterized by the three distinct carpels (only one of which matures), containing a single erect cylindrical seed with a deep longitudinal groove, and having the embryo near the base or on the back. The 12 species are the cultivated and the wild date-palms, all natives of the Old World, within or near the tropics of Asia and Africa. The habit of different species varies greatly, the trunks being either short or tall, robust or slender, erect or declined. The trunk is destitute of spines, but is commonly covered with the persistent leaf-bases. The palms grow in close clusters, forming groves. The pinnate leaves are large and terminal, forming a spreading canopy, each consisting of very numerous narrow, rigid, and compressed leaflets, the lower ones shorter and transformed into spines. The abundant yellow and rather small flowers have three sepals and three petals. The staminate trees bear oblong or ovoid flowers on numerous erect and much-branched spadices between the upper leaves. The pistillate trees bear spherical flowers on similar but often nodding spadices, followed by numerous cylindrical orange, brown, or black berries, those of *P. dactylifera* being the dates of commerce. (For this fruit, see *date-palm* and *date*[3]; and for the sugar made from it, see *jaggery* and *goor*.) This species is the chief palm of history and of ceremony, having been used as the emblem of triumph from the Egyptian worship of Isis onward. It is the palm of ancient Palestine, and has been for centuries cultivated for miles along the Italian and French Riviera, to supply palm-branches for festivals. White palm-branches are procured by binding the top of the unfolding leaf-bud, thereby blanching the inner leaves. It does not fruit in Italy nor under glass, and requires for successful growth an average annual temperature of 80° F. In Africa native huts are made from its leaves, its wood is used for building, its fiber for cloth and ropes, its leaf-stalks for brooms, crates, etc., its young leaves are eaten, and an intoxicating drink is made from its sap. It reaches a height of 80 and rarely 120 feet, and bears fruit, though in diminishing abundance, for as long as 200 years. The necessity of artificially fertilizing it first drew attention to the existence of sex in plants. *P. sylvestris*, the wild date-palm of India and Africa, is smaller, reaches a height of 40 feet, bears yellow or reddish berries, and is an important source of sugar and toddy, both prepared from its sap, which it is said can be made to flow from the upper part of its trunk for twenty years. *P. pusilla*, a dwarf from southern China, and *P. reclinata*, a decumbent palm from the Cape of Good Hope, also bear sweet edible berries, and are valued, as is *P. paludosa*, a stout Indian tree, for decorative uses.

pholad (fō'lad), *n.* A member of the family *Pholadidæ*.

Pholadacea (fō-la-dā'sē-ä), *n. pl.* [NL., < *Pholas* (*Pholad-*) + *-acea*.] A family of bivalves: same as *Pholadidæ*. *De Blainville*, 1825.

Pholadidæ (fō-lad'i-dē), *n. pl.* [NL., < *Pholas* (*Pholad-*) + *-idæ*.] A family of lithodomous or lithophagous lamellibranch mollusks, typified by the genus *Pholas*; the piddocks and their allies. The animals have the lobes of the mantle mostly united and everted upon the umbonal region, long siphons with fringed orifices, narrow branchiæ prolonged into the branchial siphon, and a short truncated foot. The shell is gaping and sinupalliate, without hinge or ligament, and besides the pair of large valves there are small accessory valves near the umbones. The family formerly included Teredo, now made the type of *Teredinidæ*. The species are generally classed under at least 8 genera, and occur in various parts of the world, generally boring into stone or wood. See cuts under *accessory* and *piddock*.

Pholadidea (fō-la-did'ē-ä), *n.* [NL., < *Pholas* (*Pholad-*) + *-idea*.] A genus of *Pholadidæ*, characterized by the development of a corneous tubular appendage to the posterior end of the shell, surrounding the siphons at their base, called *siphonoplax*. *P. papyracea*, of the European seas, is the type.

pholadite (fō'la-dīt), *n.* [= F. *pholadite*; < L. *Pholas* (*Pholad-*) + *-ite*[2].] A fossil pholad, or some similar shell.

Pholadomyidæ (fō"la-dō-mī'i-dē), *n. pl.* [NL., < *Pholadomya* (the typical genus) (< Gr. φωλάς (φωλαδ-), lurking in a hole, + μῦς, mussel) + *-idæ*.] A family of bivalves, typified by the genus *Pholadomya*. They are related to the *Anatinidæ*. The mantle-margins are mostly united, and the siphons long and united; the foot is small, with a small process bifurcated behind, and the branchiæ are thick and appendiculate. The shell is equivalve, very thin, nacreous internally and with radiating ribs, without hinge-teeth, and with an external ligament. The living species are few, and are found only in very deep water, but in former ages they were very numerous.

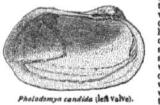

Pholadomya candida (exterior).

Pholadomya candida (left valve).

Pholas (fō'las), *n.* [NL. (Linnæus, 1758), < Gr. φωλάς (φωλαδ-), lurking in a hole, a mollusk that makes holes in stones (*Lithodomus*); cf. φωλεῖν, lurk in a hole, φωλεός, a hole, lurking-place.] 1. The typical genus of the family *Pholadidæ* and the subfamily *Pholadinæ*. It was formerly coextensive with the family, but has been variously subdivided. By recent writers it is restricted to species having the dorsal margin protected by two accessory valves (see *accessory*), anterior and posterior, and with umbonal processes reflected over the beaks. The species are of some economical value, the *Pholas dactylus*, called *piddock*, being marketable and also used as bait in England.

2. [*l. c.*] A species of the genus *Pholas*; a pholad; a piddock. See cut under *piddock*.

Pholcidæ (fol'si-dē), *n. pl.* [NL. (C. Koch, 1850), < *Pholcus* + *-idæ*.] A family of spiders formerly placed in the superfamily *Retitelariæ*, but recently put among the more primitive forms, near the *Dysderidæ*, *Hypochilidæ*, and *Filistatidæ*. They are pale, long-legged spiders, living in dark places and having either six or eight eyes. The male palpi are very peculiar.

Pholcus (fol'kus), *n.* [NL. (Walckenaer, 1805), < Gr. φολκός, squint-eyed.] A genus of spiders, typical of the family *Pholcidæ*, having the eyes in three groups, a cluster of three on each side of the median two. Nine species are known in the United States. They live either in cellars or under rocks in the woods, and construct irregular webs in which they stand upside down. The webs are violently shaken as a defense. The egg-cocoon is carried in the female's mouth. The legs of some species are multiarticulate, indicating a relationship with the *Opiliones*.

pholerite (fol'e-rīt), *n.* [Prop. *pholidite, < Gr. φολίς (φολιδ-), scale, + *-ite*[2].] A clay-like mineral closely related to or identical with kaolinite. It usually occurs in masses consisting of minute scales.

pholidote (fol'i-dōt), *a.* [< Gr. φολιδωτός, armed, clad with scales, < φολίς (φολιδ-), a scale.] Provided with scales; scaly or squamous.

Phoma (fō'mä), *n.* [NL. (Fries, 1828), < Gr. φωίς, a blister.] A genus of parasitic fungi, of the class *Sphærioideæ*, producing little pustules on plants. About 650 species have been referred to this genus, but they probably represent different stages in the development of other forms. *P. uvicola*, of the grape, for instance (see *grape-rot*), is now understood to be only a stage in the life-history of *Physalospora Bidwellii*.

phonal (fō'nal), *a.* [< Gr. φωνή, voice (see *phone*[1]), + *-al*.] Of or pertaining to sound or the voice. [Rare.]

The Thibetan is near in *phonal* structure.
Max Müller, Selected Essays, I. 74.

phonascetics (fō-na-set'iks), *n.* [< Gr. φωνασκεῖν, exercise the voice; cf. φωνασκός, one who exercises the voice: see *phonascus*.] Systematic practice for strengthening the voice; treatment for improving or restoring the voice.

phonascus (fō-nas'kus), *n.*; pl. *phonasci* (-ī). [L., a teacher of singing, LL. a musical director, < Gr. φωνασκός, one who exercises the voice, < φωνή, the voice, + ἀσκεῖν, train, exercise: see *ascetic*.] In *anc. Gr. music*, a trainer of the voice; a teacher of vocal music.

phonate (fō'nāt), *v. i.*; pret. and pp. *phonated*, ppr. *phonating*. [< Gr. φωνή, sound, voice (see *phone*[1]), + *-ate*[2].] To utter vocal sounds; produce a noise with the vocal cords.

In a marked case, on the patient's attempting to *phonate*, the cords remain perfectly movable during the attempt.
Lancet, No. 3417, p. 373.

phonation (fō-nā'shon), *n.* [= F. *phonation*; as *phonate* + *-ion*.] The act of phonating; emission of vocal sounds; production of tone with the vocal cords. *Encyc. Brit.*, XXI. 202.

phonatory (fō'nā-tō-ri), *a.* [< *phonate* + *-ory*.] Of or pertaining to phonation.

phonautogram (fō-nâ'tō-gram), *n.* [< Gr. φωνή, sound, voice, + αὐτός, self, + γράμμα, inscription.] The diagram or record of speech or other sound made by a phonautograph or a gramophone.

phonautograph (fō-nâ'tō-gráf), *n.* [< Gr. φωνή, sound, + αὐτός, self, + γράφειν, write.] 1. An instrument for registering the vibrations of a sounding body. That devised about 1858 by Léon Scott consists of a large barrel-shaped vessel made of plaster of Paris, into the open end of which the sound enters; the

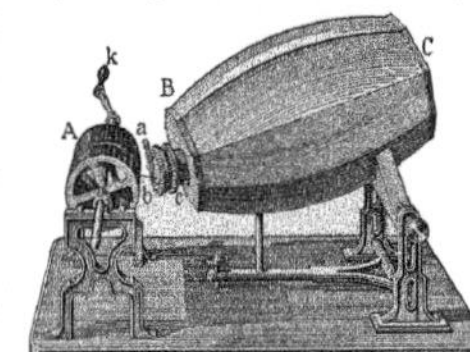

Phonautograph.

BC, barrel with opening at *C*; *c*, brass tube with membrane and style at *b*, and movable piece *a*, by which the position of the nodal points can be regulated; *k*, handle to turn cylinder (*A*) covered with lampblacked paper.

other end, somewhat contracted in shape, is closed by a membrane with a style attached on the outside, whose point rests against a horizontal cylinder covered with lampblacked paper. If the membrane is at rest the trace of the style is a straight line, but when the sound enters the membrane vibrates, and the writing-point registers these vibrations with great perfection.

2. Same as *music-recorder*.

phonautographic (fō-nâ-tō-graf'ik), *a.* [< *phonautograph* + *-ic*.] Of, pertaining to, or made by the phonautograph or gramophone. *Jour. Franklin Inst.*, CXXV. 53.

phonautographically (fō-nâ-tō-graf'i-kal-i), *adv.* By means of the phonautograph. *Jour. Franklin Inst.*, CXXV. 53.

phone[1] (fōn), *n.* [< Gr. φωνή, a sound, tone, sound of the voice (of man or brute), voice, speech, cry, etc., any articulate sound, vowel or consonant (later restricted to vowels as opposed to consonants), also the faculty of speech, language, a language, dialect, also a report, rumor, etc., < √ φα in φήμη, speech, report, etc., = L. *fama*, etc.: see *fame*[1], *fable*.] A sound; a vocal sound; a tone produced by the vibration of the vocal cords; one of the primary elements of utterance. See *phonate*, *phonetic*.

phone[2] (fōn), *n.* [Abbr. of *telephone*, *n.*] A telephone: generally applied to the receiver, but sometimes to the whole apparatus. *Sci. Amer.*, N. S., July 19, 1884, p. 43. [Colloq.]

phone[2] (fōn), *v.*; pret. and pp. *phoned*, ppr. *phoning*. [Abbr. of *telephone*, *v.*] To telephone. [Colloq.]

phoneidoscope (fō-nī'dō-skōp), *n.* [< Gr. φωνή, sound, + εἶδος, form, + σκοπεῖν, view.] An instrument for observing the color-figures of liquid films under the action of sonorous vibrations. *E. H. Knight.*

phoneidoscopic (fō-nī-dō-skop'ik), *a.* [< *phoneidoscope* + *-ic*.] Of or pertaining to the phoneidoscope or the phenomena observed by means of it.

At a meeting of the Physical Society of Paris, Guebhard . . . showed that even the films condensed from the breath may exhibit *phoneidoscopic* properties.
Quoted in *Smithsonian Report*, 1880, p. 274.

phonetic (fō-net'ik), *a.* [= F. *phonétique* = Sp. *fonético* = Pg. *phonetico* = It. *fonetico* (cf. G. *phonetisch*), < NL. *phoneticus*, < Gr. φωνητικός, of or pertaining to sound or voice, phonetic, vocal, < φωνεῖν, produce a sound, speak, < φωνή, a sound, tone, prop. the sound of the voice (of man or brute): see *phone*[1].] 1. Relating or pertaining to the human voice as used in speech; concerning articulate sounds, their mode of production, relations, combinations, and changes: as, *phonetic* science; *phonetic* decay.—2. Representing articulate sounds or utterance: as, a *phonetic* mode of writing (in contradistinction to an ideographic or pictorial mode); a *phonetic* mode of spelling (in contradistinction to a traditional, historical, or so-called etymological mode, such as the current spelling of English, in which letters representing or supposed to represent former and obsolete utterance are retained or inserted according to chances of time, caprice, or imperfect knowledge).—3. In *entom.*, as used by Kirby, noting the collar or prothorax of a hymenopterous insect when it embraces the mesothorax and the posterior angles cover the mesothoracic or so-called vocal spiracles.—**Phonetic shorthand**, a system of shorthand or stenography in which words are represented by their sounds, and not by their spelling as in ordinary longhand writing; phonography. All systems of shorthand in use in writing English are phonetic, the phonetic principle being absolutely necessary to the requisite brevity.—**Phonetic spelling**, spelling according to sound; the spelling of words as they are pronounced.

phonetical (fō-net'i-kal), *a.* [< *phonetic* + *-al*.] Same as *phonetic*.

phonetically (fō-net'i-kal-i), *adv.* In a phonetic manner; as regards the sound and not the spelling of words.

phonetician (fō-ne-tish'an), *n.* [< *phonetic* + *-ian*.] One who is versed in or is a student of phonetics.

We must serve our apprenticeship as *phoneticians*, etymologists, and grammarians before we can venture to go beyond. *Max Müller*, in Fortnightly Rev., N. S., XLI. 700.

phoneticism (fō-net'i-sizm), *n.* [< *phonetic* + *-ism*.] The quality of being phonetic; phonetic character; representation, or faithful representation, of utterance by written signs.

The Egyptian and Chinese alphabets, each of which began as simple picture-writing and developed into almost complete *phoneticism*. *Science*, VIII. 553.

phoneticist (fō-net'i-sist), *n.* [< *phonetic* + *-ist*.] One who adopts or favors phonetic spelling.

phoneticize (fō-net'i-sīz), *v. t.*; pret. and pp. *phoneticized*, ppr. *phoneticizing*. [< *phonetic* + *-ize*.] To make phonetic; render true, or more nearly corresponding, to utterance. *Science*, XV. 7.

phonetics (fō-net'iks), *n.* [Pl. of *phonetic*: see *-ics*.] Phonetic science; that division of language-study which deals with articulate sounds and whatever concerns them; phonology.

phonetism (fō'ne-tizm), *n.* [< *phonet-ic* + *-ism*.] Sound; pronunciation.

phonetist (fō'ne-tist), *n.* [< *phonet-ic* + *-ist*.] A student of or one versed in phonetics.

Different *phonetists* of that time giving different lists.
Trans. Amer. Philol. Ass., XVI. 66.

The author of the Ormulum was a *phonetist*, and employed a special spelling of his own to represent not only the quality but the quantities of vowels and consonants.
Encyc. Brit., VIII. 396.

phonetization (fō"ne-ti-zā'shon), *n.* [< *phonetize* + *-ation*.] The act or art of representing sound by phonetic signs. *Webster's Dict.*; *Imp. Dict.* [Rare.]

phonetize (fō'ne-tīz), *v. t.*; pret. and pp. *phonetized*, ppr. *phonetizing*. [< *phonet-ic* + *-ize*.] To represent phonetically. [Rare.]

I find a goodly number of Yankeeisms in him [Spenser], such as idee (not as a rhyme); but the oddest is his twice spelling dew deow, which is just as one would spell it who wished to *phonetize* its sound in rural New England.
Lowell, Among my Books, II. 195.

phonic (fon'ik), *a.* [= F. *phonique* = Sp. *fónico* = It. *fonico*, < Gr. as if *φωνικός, < φωνή, sound, voice: see *phone*[1]. Cf. *phonetic*.] Of or pertaining to sound; according to sound: as, the *phonic* method. See *phonics*.

phonics (fon'iks), *n.* [Pl. of *phonic*: see *-ics*.] 1. The doctrine or science of sounds, especially those of the human voice; phonetics.—2. The art of combining musical sounds.

phonikon (fō'ni-kon), *n.* [NL., < Gr. as if φωνικόν, neut. of *φωνικός: see *phonic*.] A musical instrument of the metal wind group, with a spherical-shaped bell, invented in 1848 by B. F. Czerveny of Königgrätz, Bohemia.

phonocamptic (fō-nō-kamp'tik), *a.* [= F. *phonocamptique* = Pg. *phonocamptico*, < Gr. φωνή, sound, voice (see *phone*1), + καμπτός, verbal adj. of κάμπτειν, bend.] Reflecting or deflecting sound.

The magnifying the sound by the polyphonisms or repercussions of the rocks and other *phonocamptick* objects. *Derham.*

Phonocamptic center. See *center*1.

phonocamptics (fō-nō-kamp'tiks), *n.* [Pl. of *phonocamptic*: see *-ics*.] That branch of physics which treats of the reflection of sound.

Besides what the masters of . . . *phonocamptics*, otacoustics, etc., have don, something has ben attempted by the Royal Society. *Evelyn*, To Doctor Beale.

phonogram (fō'nō-gram), *n.* [< Gr. φωνή, sound, voice, + γράμμα, a writing, letter: see *gram*2.] 1. A graphic character representing a sound of the human voice.

It is probable that the adoption of the important step by which the advance was made from ideograms to *phonograms* arose out of the necessity of expressing proper names. *Isaac Taylor*, The Alphabet, I. 22.

2. The record of sound produced by a phonograph, or the sheet of tin-foil or cylinder of wax on which it is produced.

There is a brass cylinder, on which the wax *phonogram* is placed. *Nature*, XXXIX. 108.

phonograph (fō'nō-gráf), *n.* [= F. *phonographe*, < Gr. φωνή, sound, voice, + γράφειν, write.] 1. A type or character for expressing a sound; a character used in phonography.— 2. A form of phonautograph, the invention of Thomas A. Edison, by means of which sounds are made to produce on a register permanent tracings, each having an individual character corresponding to the sound producing it. The sounds can be afterward reproduced from the register. In its original form it consists essentially of a curved tube, one end of which is fitted with a mouthpiece, while the other end (about two inches in diameter) is closed with a diaphragm of exceedingly thin metal.

Phonograph (earlier form).

Connected with the center of this diaphragm is a steel point, which, when the sounds are projected on the disk from the mouthpiece, vibrates backward and forward. This part of the apparatus is adjusted to a cylinder which rotates on a horizontal axis. On the surface of the cylinder is cut a spiral groove, and on the axis there is a spiral screw of the same pitch, which works in a nut. When the instrument is to be used, a piece of tin-foil is gummed round the cylinder, and the steel point is adjusted so as just to touch the tin-foil above the line of the spiral groove. If words are now spoken through the mouthpiece, and the cylinder is kept rotating either by the hand or by clockwork, a series of small marks will be made on the foil by the vibratory movement of the steel point, and these markings will each have an individual character corresponding to the various sounds. The sounds thus registered are reproduced by placing the diaphragm with its steel point in the same position with reference to the tin-foil as when the cylinder originally started. When the cylinder is rotated, the indentations previously made cause the steel point to rise or fall, or otherwise vibrate, as they pass under it, and the diaphragm is consequently thrown into a state of vibration exactly corresponding to that which produced the markings, and thus affects the surrounding air so as to produce sounds closely similar to those originally made by the voice. The reproduced sound is, however, more or less metallic and nasal, and some of the consonants, as *s*

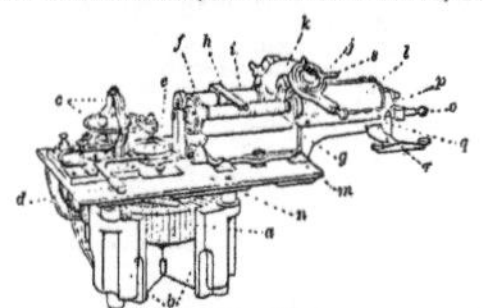

Phonograph (recent form).

a, armature; *b*, field; *c*, governor; *d*, switch; *e*, main pulley on armature-shaft; *f*, pulley on cylinder-shaft; *g*, fixed screw; *h*, spring holding fixed-screw nut; *i*, carriage; *j*, diaphragm; *k*, diaphragm-arm; *l*, cylinder on mandrel; *m*, body; *n*, bed-plate; *o*, lock-bolt; *p*, swinging arm; *q*, stop and start lift; *r*, keys to start lift; *s*, lever for changing diaphragm from recorder to reproducer.

and *z*, are not clearly given. The contents of the strips of foil may be reproduced in sound after any length of time, and repeated until the markings become effaced. The instrument has recently been improved and made in the form shown in the second cut, in which the cylinder is driven by an electric current from a battery, and the tin-foil is replaced by a cylinder of hard wax, which can be turned off to remove marks and thus fitted to register other sounds—a process that may be repeated many times before the cylinder is rendered useless.

phonograph (fō'nō-gráf), *v. t.* [< *phonograph*, *n.*] To register or record by means of the phonograph.

phonographer (fō-nog'ra-fėr), *n.* [< *phonograph*, *phonograph-y*, + *-er*1.] 1. One who is versed in phonography; a writer of phonography, or phonetic shorthand.—2. One who uses or who is skilled in the use of the phonograph.

phonograph-graphophone (fō'nō-gráf-graf'ō-fōn), *n.* See *graphophone*.

phonographic (fō-nō-graf'ik), *a.* [= F. *phonographique*; as *phonograph*, *phonograph-y*, + *-ic*.] 1. Pertaining to or used in the writing or representation of sound.

Although our own writing has reached the alphabetic stage, yet we still continue to employ a considerable number of *phonographic* and ideographic signs. *Isaac Taylor*, The Alphabet, I. 6.

2. Of, pertaining to, or of the nature of phonography, or phonetic shorthand; made in or using phonetic shorthand: as, a *phonographic* note or report; a *phonographic* reporter.—3. Of or pertaining to the phonograph; produced by means of the phonograph.

phonographical (fō-nō-graf'i-kal), *a.* [< *phonographic* + *-al*.] Same as *phonographic*.

phonographically (fō-nō-graf'i-kal-i), *adv.* In a phonographic manner. (*a*) As regards or by means of phonography. (*b*) As regards or by means of the phonograph.

phonographist (fō-nog'ra-fist), *n.* [< *phonograph*, *phonograph-y*, + *-ist*.] A phonographer.

phonography (fō-nog'ra-fi), *n.* [= F. *phonographie*, < Gr. φωνή, sound, voice, + -γραφία, < γράφειν, write.] 1. The science of sound-signs, or the representation of vocal sounds.—2. The representation of words as they are pronounced; specifically, a system of phonetic writing in shorthand introduced by Isaac Pitman of Bath, England, in the year 1837. The consonants are represented by simple lines (called stems), curved or straight, light or heavy, vertical, horizontal, or slanting, with initial and terminal hooks, circles, loops, etc.; the vowels are represented by dots and dashes, light or heavy, by combinations of them, and by small angles and semicircles. In actual use most of the vowel-signs are omitted (though they may in many cases be approximately indicated by the position—above, on, or below the line—of the consonant-stem), and the consonant-stems, by halving, doubling, etc., are made to perform extra duty. To secure further brevity, various arbitrary devices are employed. Mr. Pitman's system has been variously modified and improved by himself and others in England and America. See *shorthand*. 3. The construction and use of phonographs, and the recording of sound by mechanical means, with a view to its reproduction.

phonolite (fō'nō-līt), *n.* [= F. *phonolithe* = Pg. *phonolite*; equiv. to *clinkstone*; < Gr. φωνή, sound, + λίθος, stone.] The name given by Klaproth to certain volcanic rocks of exceedingly variable and complex character, but closely related to the trachytes. The essential constituents of phonolite are sanidine and nephelin, and some authors restrict the name to rocks having this composition. Rocks containing sanidine and leucite are called by Rosenbusch *leucite-phonolites*, varieties of which pass into or are closely allied with leucitophyre and leucite-basalt. Nosean and haüyne are often present in rocks of this class, and give names to varieties known as *nosean-phonolite* and *haüyne-phonolite*. Authors are by no means agreed in opinion with regard to the classification of the many varieties of nephelin and leucite rocks, which frequently pass into each other by insensible gradations. Boricky makes eight divisions of the phonolite family. With the essential constituents of the various phonolites are associated many accessory minerals, especially magnetite, as well as olivin, apatite, zircon, etc. Various zeolitic minerals are of frequent occurrence in the phonolites as alteration products. Phonolite is peculiarly a modern volcanic rock. Auvergne and Bohemia are localities in which it is found in various forms characteristic of volcanic action.

phonolitic (fō-nō-lit'ik), *a.* [< *phonolite* + *-ic*.] Of, pertaining to, or of the nature of phonolite; composed of phonolite.

phonologer (fō-nol'ō-jėr), *n.* [< *phonolog-y* + *-er*1.] Same as *phonologist*.

phonologic, phonological (fō-nō-loj'ik, -i-kal), *a.* [= Sp. *fonológico* = Pg. *phonologico*; as *phonolog-y* + *-ic*, *-ic-al*.] Of or pertaining to phonology.

phonologically (fō-nō-loj'i-kal-i), *adv.* In a phonologic manner; as regards phonology.

phonologist (fō-nol'ō-jist), *n.* [< *phonolog-y* + *-ist*.] One who is versed in phonology.

phonology (fō-nol'ō-ji), *n.* [= F. *phonologie* = Sp. *fonologia* = Pg. *phonologia* = It. *fonologia*, < NL. **phonologia*, < Gr. φωνή, sound, voice, + -λογία, < λέγειν, speak: see *-ology*.] 1. The science or doctrine of the sounds uttered by the human voice, or used in a particular language; phonetics.—2. That part of grammar which treats of pronunciation. Compare *orthoëpy*.—3. The system of sounds and of their combinations in a language.

These common characteristics of the Semitic alphabets consist in the direction of the writing, the absence of true vowels, the unique *phonology*, the number, the names, and the order of the letters. *Isaac Taylor*, The Alphabet, I. 150.

phonomania (fon-ō-mā'ni-ä), *n.* [< Gr. φονή, slaughter, murder, killing, + μανία, madness.] A mania for murder or killing.

phonometer (fō-nom'e-tėr), *n.* [= F. *phonomètre* = Pg. *phonometro*, < Gr. φωνή, sound, voice, + μέτρον, measure.] An instrument for experimentally determining and exhibiting the number of vibrations of a sonorous body (as a string or tuning-fork) in a unit of time. The simplest form comprises apparatus for uniformly moving a paper tape coated with lampblack, in contact with a delicate tracing-point fixed to the vibrating body. By this means an undulating curve is traced having a length corresponding to the time of its motion. The number of undulations in the curve is also the number of vibrations made by the sounding string or fork. By the substitution of sensitized paper for the blackened tape, and a small mirror for the tracing-point, permanent photographic tracings of such curves can be made. See *Savart's wheel* (under *wheel*), and *siren*, and compare *phonautograph*.

phonomotor (fō-nō-mō tor), *n.* [< Gr. φωνή, sound, voice, + L. *motor*, mover: see *motor*.] An instrument by which the energy of sound-waves, as those produced by the human voice, may be made to perform mechanical work. Such an instrument invented by Edison has a mouthpiece like that of a phonograph, and a diaphragm the vibration of which, transmitted by means of a pawl, causes a small wheel to revolve. Compare *phonoscope*.

phonophore (fō'nō-fōr), *n.* [< NL. *phonophorus*, < Gr. φωνή, sound, voice, + φορός, bearing, < φέρειν = E. *bear*1.] 1. An auditory ossicle; one of the phonophori. *Coues*.—2. An apparatus by means of which telephonic communication may be maintained over a telegraph-line without interfering with its use in the ordinary way. The principal feature of the instrument consists in the arrangement of two wires of considerable length, wound in close proximity to but completely insulated from each other, which together act as a condenser. Also called *phonopore*.

phonophori (fō-nof'ō-rī), *n. pl.* [NL., pl. of *phonophorus*: see *phonophore*.] The auditory ossicles, or ossicula auditus, of *Mammalia*, collectively considered as bones subservient to the office of hearing. *Coues*, Amer. Jour. Otology, IV. 19. See cut under *tympanic*.

phonophorous (fō-nof'ō-rus), *a.* [As *phonophore* + *-ous*.] Conveying sound; having the function of the phonophori. *Coues*.

phonoplex (fō'nō-pleks), *n.* [NL., < Gr. φωνή, sound, voice, + πλεκτή, a twisted rope, < πλέκειν, twist.] A system of duplexing on telegraph-lines by the use of condensers and the telephone as a receiver, devised by Edison.

phonopore (fō'nō-pōr), *n.* [< Gr. φωνή, sound, voice, + πόρος, a means of passing: see *pore*1.] Same as *phonophore*, 2.

phonoporic (fō-nō-por'ik), *a.* [< *phonopore* + *-ic*.] Of or pertaining to, or made by, the phonopore. *Electric Rev.* (Amer.), XIV. 6.

phonorganon, phonorganum (fō-nôr'ga-non, -num), *n.* [NL., < Gr. φωνή, sound, voice, + ὄργανον, an instrument: see *organ*1.] An instrument for imitating vocal sounds or speech; a speaking-machine.

phonoscope (fō'nō-skōp), *n.* [< Gr. φωνή, sound, voice, + σκοπεῖν, view.] 1. A machine for recording music as it is played or sung, or for testing the quality of strings for musical instruments.—2. Same as *microphone*.

phonotelemeter (fō-nō-te-lem'e-tėr), *n.* [< Gr. φωνή, sound, voice, + τῆλε, far, + μέτρον, measure.] An instrument for determining distances by means of the velocity with which sound is transmitted.

phonotype (fō'nō-tīp), *n.* [< Gr. φωνή, sound, voice, + τύπος, mark, type: see *type*.] A system of expression which provides a distinct character for every distinct sound of speech; a phonetic alphabet, or writing or printing in phonetic characters.

phonotypic (fō-nō-tip'ik), *a.* [< *phonotype* + *-ic*.] Of or pertaining to phonotypy: as, a *phonotypic* alphabet; *phonotypic* writing or printing.

phonotypical (fō-nō-tip'i-kal), *a.* [< *phonotypic* + *-al*.] Same as *phonotypic*.

phonotypically (fō-nǭ-tip'i-kal-i), *adv.* According to or as regards phonotypy; in phonotypic characters. *Ellis*, Early Eng. Pronunciation, IV. 1182.

phonotypist (fō'nǭ-ti-pist), *n.* [< *phonotyp-y* + *-ist.*] An advocate of phonotypy; one who practises phonotypy.

phonotypy (fō'nǭ-ti-pi), *n.* [< Gr. φωνή, sound, voice, + τύπος, mark, type: see *type.*] A method of representing each of the sounds of speech by a distinct printed character or letter; phonetic printing.

phoo†, *interj.* Same as *pho.*

Phora (fō'rä), *n.* [NL. (Latreille, 1796), < Gr. φορός, bearing, carrying, < φέρειν = E. *bear*[1].] In *entom.*, the typical genus of *Phoridæ*, containing many small active flies whose habits are those of scavengers or, rarely, of parasites. They feed usually on fungi and decaying vegetation. Also called *Noda.*

Phoradendron (fē-ra-den'dron), *n.* [NL. (Nuttall, 1848), so called as being parasitic on trees; < Gr. φώρ (= L. *fur*), a thief, + δένδρον, a tree.] A genus of apetalous plants, the American mistletoes, of the order *Loranthaceæ* and tribe *Visceæ*, characterized by the erect anthers subsessile on the base of the calyx-lobes, vertically two-celled and opening by a longitudinal slit. The 80 species are all American, widely scattered through the warmer regions, extending into the United

American Mistletoe (*Phoradendron flavescens*).
a, branch with the male inflorescence; *b*, branch with the fruit.

States to New Jersey, and especially found in the west, and southward into the Argentine Republic. They are shrubby yellowish-green parasites, generally with abundant short much-jointed branches, flat opposite thickish leaves, and terminal or axillary jointed spikes of small sessile and immersed flowers in several or many rows. *P. flavescens* extends north to New Jersey, on various trees, especially the sour-gum (*Nyssa sylvatica*), and is often destructive to the tree, as in cases of growth on elms, hickories, and wild cherries. (See *mistletoe*, 2.) It is used as a substitute for the European mistletoe.

phoranthium (fǭ-ran'thi-um), *n.*; pl. *phoranthia* (-ä). [NL., < Gr. φορός, bearing (< φέρειν = E. *bear*[1]), + ἄνθος, flower.] In *bot.*, same as *clinanthium.*

phorbeia (fôr-bī'ä), *n.* [NL., < Gr. φορβεία, a mouth-band, a halter by which a horse is tied to the manger, < φορβή, pasture, fodder, < φέρβειν, feed: see *herb.*] Same as *capistrum*, 1.

Phoridæ (for'i-dē), *n. pl.* [NL., < *Phora* + *-idæ.*] A family of cycloraphous *Diptera*, founded on the genus *Phora.* They are small, nearly naked humpback flies with one- or two-jointed antennæ, and large wings with two strong veins and from three to five weak cross-veins. They are everywhere numerous, and feed in the larval state on all sorts of dead animal and vegetable matters, seldom attacking living insects and thus becoming parasites.

phorminx (fôr'mingks), *n.* [NL., < Gr. φόρμιγξ, a kind of lyre, perhaps < φέρειν, carry, = E. *bear*[1], as being a portable lyre.] An ancient Greek stringed musical instrument; a cithara or lyre.

> We beat the *phorminx* till we hurt our thumbs,
> As if still ignorant of counterpoint.
> *Mrs. Browning*, Aurora Leigh, i.

Phormium (fôr'mi-um), *n.* [NL. (J. and G. Forster, 1776), < Gr. φορμίον, a plant, a kind of sage. Cf. Gr. φορμίον, dim. of φορμός, a basket, mat, < φέρειν = E. *bear*[1].] A genus of liliaceous plants of the tribe *Hemerocalleæ*, characterized by the turbinate form of the perianth above its short tube, with three lanceolate erect sepals and three thinner petals slightly spreading at the apex. The 2 species, with several varieties, are natives of New Zealand and Norfolk Island. They are perennials, forming large tufts, with rigid two-ranked sword-shaped radical leaves from a short thickened rootstock. They bear a tall leafless scape branching at the summit, with erect variegated lurid or yellow and red flowers in a terminal panicle. The largest variety produces green and gray leaves from 5 to 6 feet long, and deep orange-red flowers on a stalk 16 feet high. *P. tenax variegata* is the New Zealand flax (which see, under *flax*, 1 (*b*)), also called *flax-bush.* It is a very beautiful variegated-leafed variety, valuable for lawn decoration. The other varieties are cultivated also for their beauty, and especially for their fiber—the strongest vegetable fiber known. The plants are raised from the divided roots or from seeds, and are hardy in England. The fiber is now sold for making cordage, paper, etc., and gardeners use the leaves as cordage when simply torn into shreds.

New Zealand Flax (*Phormium tenax variegata*).

Phoronis (fǭ-rō'nis), *n.* [NL., < Gr. Φορωνίς, of Phoroneus, < Φορωνεύς, Phoroneus, a king of Argos.] A genus of *Gephyrea*, typical of the family *Phoronidæ.* They have a circlet of long tentacular appendages around the mouth, close to which the anus is situated. A pseudohemal system exists, and the fluid is said to contain red corpuscles. The embryo is mesotrochal, but has also two ciliated bands, one around the anus, the other behind the mouth, the latter being produced into a fringe of numerous tentaculiform lobes, in which state it is the so-called *actinotrocha.*

phoronomia† (for-ǭ-nō'mi-ä), *n.* [NL.: see *phoronomy.*] Same as *phoronomics.*

phoronomics (for-ǭ-nom'iks), *n.* [< *phoronom-y* + *-ics.*] That branch of mechanics which treats of bodies in motion; kinematics; the purely geometrical theory of motion.

phoronomy (fǭ-ron'ǭ-mi), *n.* [= F. *phoronomie*, < NL. *phoronomia*, < Gr. φορά, motion (< φέρειν, carry), + -νομία, < νόμος, law: see *nome*[5].] 1. Same as *phoronomics.*

> Matter, quantitatively defined, is "the moveable in space." In this point of view it is the object of a science we may call *Phoronomy.* *E. Caird*, Philos. of Kant, p. 489.

2. The inference of force from motion.

phoroscope (for'ǭ-skōp), *n.* [< Gr. φορά, motion (< φέρειν = E. *bear*[1]), + σκοπεῖν, view.] An instrument for producing at a distance, by means of electricity, a copy of an image as a photograph.

phosgen, phosgene (fos'jen, -jēn), *n.* [= F. *phosgène* = Pg. *phosgeno*; irreg. < Gr. φῶς, contr. of φάος, light, + -γενής, producing: see *-gen.*] Carbonyl chlorid ($COCl_2$), a gas formed by the action of light on a mixture of carbonic oxid and chlorin. Below 8° C. it is a colorless fluid with a suffocating odor.

phosgenite (fos'jen-īt), *n.* [< *phosgen* + *-ite*[2].] A mineral consisting of the chlorid and carbonate of lead. It occurs in white or yellowish tetragonal crystals having an adamantine luster. Also called *corneous lead.*

phosphate (fos'fāt), *n.* [= F. *phosphate* = Sp. *fosfato* = Pg. *phosphato* = It. *fosfato*; as *phosph(orus)* + *-ate*[1].] 1. A salt of phosphoric acid.—2. A name given to various mineral deposits which consist largely of calcium or iron and alumina phosphates, and are used in the manufacture of commercial fertilizers.—**Phosphate of iron**, a native blue ocher, in color similar to the deeper hues of ultramarine ash, but more dull.

phosphated (fos'fā-ted), *a.* [< *phosphate* + *-ed*[2].] Phosphatic: as, *phosphated* deposits. *Nature*, XXXIX. 192.

phosphatic (fos-fat'ik), *a.* [= F. *phosphatique*; < *phosphate* + *-ic.*] Of the nature of or containing a phosphate; characterized by the formation or presence of a phosphate.—**Phosphatic bread**, bread made from bolted meal or white flour to which nutritive salts which have been removed with the bran or gluten coat are restored by the use of an acid phosphate and a carbonated alkali, which, also, by the evolution of carbonic acid, lighten or raise the bread.—**Phosphatic diathesis**, in *med.*, the condition of the system which evinces itself in phosphaturia.—**Phosphatic nodules**, concretions and nodules of phosphate of lime, now largely used for artificial manure.

phosphatization (fos"fā-ti-zā'shǭn), *n.* [< *phosphatize* + *-ation.*] Conversion into a phosphate, or a phosphatic condition. *Amer. Geologist*, I. 256.

phosphatize (fos'fā-tīz), *v. t.*; pret. and pp. *phosphatized*, ppr. *phosphatizing.* [< *phosphate* + *-ize.*] 1. To reduce to the form of a phosphate.

> In most instances these fossils are *phosphatized* more or less completely, in extreme cases to the extent of nearly obliterating the organic structure. *Science*, III. 587.

2. To treat with phosphates, as with phosphatic medicines or fertilizing phosphates.

phosphaturia (fos-fā-tū'ri-ä), *n.* [NL., < *phosphate* + Gr. οὖρον, urine.] The presence of an excessive quantity of phosphates in the urine.

phosphene (fos'fēn), *n.* [= F. *phosphène*; irreg. < Gr. φῶς, light, + φαίνειν, show.] The luminous image produced by pressing the eyeball with the finger or otherwise. It is due to the direct mechanical stimulation of the retina.

> Press the finger into the internal corner of the eye: you perceive a brilliant colored spectrum in the field of view on the opposite or external side. . . . The colored spectra have been called *phosphenes.* *Le Conte*, Sight, p. 67.

phosphide (fos'fid or -fid), *n.* [< *phosph(orus)* + *-ide*[1].] A combination of phosphorus with a single element: as, *phosphide* of iron or copper.

phosphine (fos'fin), *n.* [< *phosph(orus)* + *-ine*[2].] Same as *phosphureted hydrogen* (which see, under *phosphureted*).

phosphite (fos'fit), *n.* [= F. *phosphite* = Sp. *fosfito* = Pg. *phosphito*; as *phosph(orus)* + *-ite*[2].] A salt of phosphorous acid.

phosphochalcite (fos-fē-kal'sit), *n.* [< *phospho(rus)* + *chalcitis.*] Hydrous phosphate of copper. See *pseudomalachite.*

Phosphor (fos'for), *n.* [= F. *Phosphore* = Sp. *Fósforo* = Pg. *Phosphoro* = It. *Fosforo*, Phosphor (in def. 2, F. *phosphore* = Sp. *fósforo* = Pg. *phosphoro* = It. *fosforo* = Dan. Sw. *fosfor*, < NL. *phosphorus*, phosphorus), < L. *Phosphorus*, < Gr. Φωσφόρος, Lucifer, the morning star, < φωσφόρος, bringing light, < φῶς, contr. of φάος, light (< φάειν, shine: see *phase*[1]), + -φορος, < φέρειν, bring, = E. *bear*[1]. Cf. the equiv. *Lucifer.*] 1. The morning star, or Lucifer; the planet Venus, when it precedes the sun and shines in the morning.

> They saw this *Phosphor's* Infant-light, and knew
> It bravely usher'd in a Sun as New.
> *Cowley*, Davideis, ii.

> Bright *Phosphor*, fresher for the night,
> By thee the world's great work is heard
> Beginning. *Tennyson*, in Memoriam, cxxi.

2†. [*l. c.*] Phosphorus.

> Of lambent flame you have whole sheets in a handful of *phosphor.* *Addison.*

phosphorate (fos'fǭ-rāt), *v. t.*; pret. and pp. *phosphorated*, ppr. *phosphorating.* [< *phosphorus* + *-ate*[2].] To combine or impregnate with phosphorus.—**Phosphorated oil.** See *oil.*

phosphor-bronze (fos'for-bronz), *n.* See *bronze.*

phosphor-copper (fos'for-kop"ėr), *n.* A combination of phosphorus with copper, prepared by the reduction of phosphate of copper in a graphite crucible, or in some other similar way, for use in making phosphor-bronze.

phosphoreous† (fos-fō'rē-us), *a.* [< *phosphor* + *-eous.*] Same as *phosphorescent.* *Pennant.*

phosphoresce (fos-fǭ-res'), *v. i.*; pret. and pp. *phosphoresced*, ppr. *phosphorescing.* [< *phosphor* + *-esce.*] To shine, as phosphorus, by exhibiting a faint light without sensible heat; give out a phosphorescent light.

phosphorescence (fos-fǭ-res'ens), *n.* [= F. *phosphorescence* = Sp. *fosforescencia* = Pg. *phosphorescencia* = It. *fosforescenza*; as *phosphorescen(t)* + *-ce.*] The state or character of being phosphorescent; the property which certain bodies possess of becoming luminous without undergoing combustion. Phosphorescence is sometimes a chemical, sometimes a physical action. When chemical, it consists essentially in slow oxidation attended with evolution of light, as in the case of phosphorus. When physical, it consists in the continuation of the molecular vibrations causing the emission of light after the body has ceased to be exposed to the light-radiation (or, more generally, radiant energy) to which this motion is due; this is seen in the case of the diamond, chlorophane, sugar, barium and calcium sulphids, and many other substances. Phosphorescence is also produced in some crystals (diamond, calcite, etc.) by exposure to the electrical discharge in a vacuum-tube. The phosphorescence of the sea is produced by the scintillating or phosphorescent light emitted from the bodies of certain marine animals. The luminosity of plants is a condition under which certain plants (always, so far as now known, *Thallophytes*) evolve light. The so-called luminosity or phosphorescence of decaying wood is due to the presence of the mycelium of *Agaricus melleus.* Other luminous fungi are *Agaricus olearius*, *A. igneus*, *A. noctilus*, and *A. Gardneri.* Various algæ and diatoms also exhibit this phenomenon. See cut under *Noctiluca.*

> What is correctly termed *phosphorescence* has nothing to do with phosphorus, but it is merely a species of fluorescence. *Tait*, Light, § 204.

phosphorescent (fos-fǭ-res'ent), *a.* and *n.* [= F. *phosphorescent* = Sp. *fosforescente* = Pg. *phosphorescente* = It. *fosforescente*; as *phosphor* + *-escent.* Cf. *phosphoresce.*] **I.** *a.* Shining with a faint light or luminosity like that of phosphorus; luminous without sensible heat. Various animals are phosphorescent; as, among infusorians, the noctilucas (see cut under *Noctiluca*); among polyps, certain sea-pens (*Pennatula phosphorea*, for example); among insects, the glow-worm and other beetles of the family *Lampyridæ* (see cuts under *firefly*, *Lampyris*, and *lightning-bug*), and many bugs of the family *Fulgoridæ* (see cut under *lantern-fly*); among ascidians, the pyrosomes or firebodies; and some fishes. A number of mineral substances exhibit a similar property after having been exposed to a bright light, though from a different cause, as calcium chlorid, anhydrous calcium nitrate, the sulphids of barium, strontium, calcium (luminous paint), the diamond, some varieties of fluor-spar, apatite, borax, and many other substances. Some mineral bodies become phosphorescent when strongly heated, as a piece of lime. See *phosphorescence.*—**Phosphorescent dial, paint, photograph,** etc. See the nouns.

II. *n.* A substance having the property of phosphorescence, or luminosity without heat.

The additions used by us as the third constituent are colourless salts, and all of them fusible at the temperature at which the *phosphorescents* are prepared.
Philosophical Mag., 5th ser., XXVIII. 428.

phosphoreted, phosphoretted (fos'fọ-ret-ed), *a.* Same as *phosphureted*.

phosphoric (fos-for'ik), *a.* [= F. *phosphorique* = Sp. *fosfórico* = Pg. *phosphorico* = It. *fosforico*; as *phosphor* + *-ic*.] Pertaining to, obtained from, or resembling phosphorus; phosphorescent.

How the lit lake shines, a *phosphoric* sea,
And the big rain comes dancing to the earth!
Byron, Childe Harold, iii. 93.

The unseen figure . . . had caused to be thrown open the graves of all mankind; and from each issued the faint *phosphoric* radiance of decay. *Poe*, Tales, I. 334.

Glacial phosphoric acid. See *glacial*.—**Phosphoric acid**, H_3PO_4 (sometimes called *orthophosphoric acid* in contradistinction to *metaphosphoric acid*), an acid usually obtained by decomposing bone-ash, which consists chiefly of calcium phosphate, with sulphuric acid, and separating from foreign matters the phosphoric acid thus liberated. It is also produced by the oxidation of phosphorous acid, by oxidizing red phosphorus with nitric acid, by the decomposition of apatite and other native phosphates, and in various other ways. It is a colorless odorless syrup, with an intensely sour taste. It is tribasic, forming three distinct classes of metallic salts. The three atoms of hydrogen may in like manner be replaced by alcohol radicals, forming acid and neutral ethers. Phosphoric acid is used in medicine as a tonic.

phosphorical (fos-for'i-kal), *a.* [< *phosphoric* + *-al*.] Phosphoric.

phosphoridrosis (fos"for-i-drō'sis), *n.* [NL., < *phosphorus* (see *Phosphor*) + Gr. ἱδρωσις, sweat: see *hidrosis*.] Luminous sweat, sometimes seen in the last stages of phthisis. *Lancet.*

Phosphorist (fos'fọ-rist), *n.* [< "*Phosphoros*," a Swedish periodical which was the organ of this movement.] In *Swedish literary hist.*, one of a class of poets and writers of romantic and idealistic tendencies who flourished about the beginning of the nineteenth century.

Among the *Phosphorists*, Atterbom was the man of most genius. *Encyc. Brit.*, XXII. 757.

phosphorite (fos'fọ-rīt), *n.* [= F. *phosphorite* = Sp. *fosforita* = Pg. *phosphorita*; as *phosphor* + *-ite*[2].] A name applied originally to a massive variety of apatite, but now used to embrace the more or less impure earthy to compact calcium phosphate which forms beds of considerable magnitude in some localities (Estremadura in Spain, Bohemia, etc.), and is of much economic importance.

phosphorize (fos'fọ-rīz), *v. t.*; pret. and pp. *phosphorized*, ppr. *phosphorizing*. [= F. *phosphoriser* = Pg. *phosphorisar*; as *phosphor* + *-ize*.] To combine or impregnate with phosphorus.

phosphorogenic (fos"fọ-rọ-jen'ik), *a.* [< NL. *phosphorus*, phosphorus, + Gr. -γενής, producing: see *-gen*.] Producing phosphorescence: specifically noting those rays of the spectrum which possess the property of continuing the phosphorescence of certain substances previously excited by exposure to light.

Glass is only less perfectly permeable than rock-crystal to the *phosphorogenic* rays that accompany the luminous ones. *Miller*, Elem. of Chem., § 112.

phosphorograph (fos-for'ọ-gråf), *n.* [< NL. *phosphorus*, phosphorus, + Gr. γράφειν, write.] A representation, as of the solar spectrum, obtained by phosphorescence, as by projecting it upon a phosphorescent substance like luminous paint: in this way an impression of the invisible infra-red part of the spectrum is obtained.

J. W. Draper has obtained what he calls a *phosphorograph* of the solar spectrum, and has compared it with a photograph of the same spectrum.
Quoted in *Smithsonian Report*, 1881, p. 368.

phosphorographic (fos"fọ-rọ-graf'ik), *a.* [< *phosphorograph* + *-ic*.] Of or pertaining to phosphorography.

Phosphorographic studies for the photographic reproduction of the stars. *Nature*, XXXIII. 431.

phosphorography (fos-fọ-rog'ra-fi), *n.* [< NL. *phosphorus*, phosphorus, + Gr. γράφειν, write.] The art, method, etc., of making phosphorographs.

M. Ch. V. Zenger brought before the Academy of Sciences on August 30th a paper entitled "*Phosphorography* applied to the Photography of the Invisible."
Athenæum, No. 3073, p. 375.

phosphoroscope (fos'fọ-rọ-skōp), *n.* [= F. *phosphoroscope*, < NL. *phosphorus*, phosphorus, + Gr. σκοπεῖν, behold.] 1. An instrument for measuring the duration of evanescent phosphorescence in different substances. It consists of a hollow disk within which is placed the object to be tested. The disk is geared with multiplying-wheels so that it can be rotated at any desired speed, and is so perforated on opposite sides that the substance placed within it is alternately exposed to a light placed behind the disk and to the eye.

M. E. Becquerel has shown experimentally by his beautiful *phosphoroscope* the finiteness of duration of the emission of light in the case of solids in which it was so brief that its emission was described as "fluorescence."
Stokes, Light, p. 150.

2. A philosophical toy consisting of glass tubes containing different phosphorescent substances and arranged in a box. When exposed to sunlight or strong artificial light, and afterward put in a dark place, the tubes glow with lights of different colors.

Alumina, . . . glowing with a rich red colour in the *phosphoroscope*. *Gordon*, Elect. and Mag., II. 116.

phosphorous (fos'fọ-rus), *a.* [= F. *phosphoreux* = Sp. It. *fosforoso* = Pg. *phosphoroso*; as *phosphor* + *-ous*.] Pertaining to, obtained from, or containing phosphorus.—**Phosphorous acid**, H_3PO_3, an acid produced by the action of water on phosphorous anhydrid, by exposing sticks of phosphorus to moist air, and in several other ways. Phosphorous acid exists usually in the form of a thick uncrystallizable syrup, but it may also be obtained crystallized. This acid is dibasic, forming two series of metallic salts, named respectively *neutral* and *acid phosphites*.—**Phosphorous anhydrid**, P_2O_3, a soft, white, readily volatile powder prepared by burning phosphorus in a limited supply of air.

phosphoruria (fos-fọ-rö'ri-ạ̈), *n.* [NL., < *phosphorus*, phosphorus, + Gr. οὖρον, urine.] 1. Phosphaturia.—2. Photuria.

phosphorus (fos'fọ-rus), *n.* [L. (in def. 2 NL.), < Gr. Φωσφόρος, Lucifer: see *Phosphor*.] 1. [*cap.*] The morning star; Phosphor.

John Baptist was that *Phosphorus* or morning star, to signify the sun's approaching.
Rev. T. Adams, Works, III. 224.

2. Chemical symbol, P; atomic weight, 31; specific gravity, 1.826. A solid non-metallic combustible substance, hitherto undecomposed, not found by itself in nature, but occurring chiefly in combination with oxygen, calcium, and magnesium. It is widely distributed, being an essential constituent of all plants and of the bony tissue of animals. It was originally obtained from urine; but it is now manufactured from bones, which consist in large part of calcium phosphate. Common phosphorus, when pure, is semi-transparent and colorless. At common temperatures it is a soft solid, easily cut with a knife, the cut surface having a waxy luster; at 108° F. it fuses, and at 550° is converted into vapor. It is soluble, by the aid of heat, in naphtha, in fixed and volatile oils, and in sulphur chlorid, carbon disulphid, and phosphorus sulphid. It is exceedingly inflammable. Exposed to the air at common temperatures, it undergoes slow combustion, emits a white vapor of a peculiar garlic odor, and appears luminous in the dark. A very slight degree of heat is sufficient to inflame it in the open air. Gentle pressure between the fingers, friction, or a temperature not much above its point of fusion kindles it readily. It burns rapidly even in the air, emitting a splendid white light, and causing intense heat. Its combustion is far more rapid in oxygen gas, and the light far more vivid. The product of the perfect combustion of phosphorus is phosphorous pentoxid (P_2O_5), a white solid which readily takes up water, passing into phosphoric acid (which see, under *phosphoric*). Phosphorus may be made to combine with most of the metals, forming compounds called *phosphides*; when dissolved in fat oils it forms a solution which is luminous in the dark. It is chiefly used in the preparation of lucifer matches, and in the preparation of phosphoric acid. It is used to some extent in medicine in nervous affections, but is virulently poisonous except in very minute doses. Phosphorus presents a good example of allotropy, in that it can be exhibited in at least one other form, known as *red* or *amorphous phosphorus*, presenting completely different properties from common phosphorus. This variety is produced by keeping common phosphorus for a long time slightly below the boiling-point. It is a red, hard, brittle substance, not fusible, not poisonous, and not readily inflammable, so that it may be handled with impunity. When heated to the boiling-point it changes back to common phosphorus.—**Bologna, Bolognian,** or **Bononian phosphorus**, one of the most powerful of the solar phosphoric substances. It is prepared by heating barium sulphate intensely with powdered charcoal, and filling with it while hot glass tubes, which are at once sealed. After exposure to sunlight, the mass phosphoresces in the dark with a bright orange-colored light.—**Phosphorus bottle.** (*a*) A contrivance for obtaining instantaneous light. The light is produced by stirring a piece of phosphorus about in a dry bottle with a hot wire, and introducing a sulphur match. It is now superseded by lucifer matches and similar contrivances. (*b*) A small bottle containing 12 grains of phosphorus melted in half an ounce of olive-oil. On being uncorked in the dark this solution emits light enough to illuminate the dial of a watch, and it will retain this property for several years if not too frequently used.—**Phosphorus paste**, a poisonous compound containing phosphorus, for the destruction of vermin, as rats, mice, cockroaches, etc.

phosphorus-box (fos'fọ-rus-boks), *n.* A box containing oxymuriate matches, which first superseded the tinder-box.

When I was about 16 I joined in partnership with a man who used to make *phosphorus boxes*. I sold them for him. A piece of phosphorus was stuck in a tin tube, the match was dipped into the phosphorus, and it would ignite by friction. *Mayhew*, London Labour and London Poor, I. 373.

phosphuret† (fos'fụ̄-ret), *n.* [= F. *phosphure* = Sp. *fosforeto* = Pg. *phosphureto*; as *phosph*(*orus*) + *-uret*.] Same as *phosphide*.

phosphureted, phosphuretted (fos'fụ̄-ret-ed), *a.* [< *phosphuret* + *-ed*[2].] Combined with phosphorus.—**Phosphureted hydrogen**, PH_3, a gas procured by boiling phosphorus with a caustic alkali. The gas so prepared is spontaneously inflammable, owing to the presence of traces of vapor of a liquid hydrid of phosphorus, and during its combustion there are formed water and phosphoric acid. The pure gas, while very combustible, does not inflame spontaneously; it is colorless, is very poisonous, and has a disgusting smell, resembling that of decaying fish. When mixed with air or oxygen gas it explodes at a temperature of 300° F. It is produced by the decomposition of animal substances. When this gas is cooled below zero (C.) it deposits a liquid, hydrogen phosphide; the gaseous phosphide remaining is no longer spontaneously inflammable. Also called *phosphine*.

photalgia (fọ-tal'ji-ạ̈), *n.* [NL., < Gr. φῶς (φωτ-), light, + ἄλγος, pain.] Pain arising from light.

photantitypimeter (fē-tan-tit-i-pim'e-tėr), *n.* [NL., < Gr. φῶς (φωτ-), light, + ἀντίτυπος, corresponding (see *antitype*), + μέτρον, measure.] A chemical actinometer proposed by Marchand, consisting of a solution of perchlorid of iron and oxalic acid in water. When it is exposed to the sunlight, carbonic-acid gas is set free, the measure of whose volume expresses the chemical intensity of the sun's rays.

photics (fō'tiks), *n.* [< Gr. φῶς (φωτ-), light, + *-ics*.] The science of light.

Photinia (fẹ-tin'i-ạ̈), *n.* [NL. (Lindley, 1821), so called with ref. to the coriaceous and shining evergreen leaves and white flowers; < Gr. φωτεινός, shining, bright, < φῶς (φωτ-), light.] A genus of rosaceous shrubs and trees, of the tribe *Pomeæ*, known by the evergreen leaves and one- to five-celled berry-like pome, with thin partitions. There are about 30 species, natives of Japan, China, and the mountains of India, and one of California. They bear alternate undivided leaves, often with leaf-like stipules, and usually white flowers in terminal corymbs or panicles. The ovoid juicy fruit is crowned by the five ovate calyx-lobes, and is sometimes edible. *P. serrulata* and its varieties (often wrongly called *Cratægus glabra*) are the Chinese hawthorn, and *P. arbutifolia* is the Californian May-bush of ornamental lawn cultivation; both are hardy evergreens, growing to a height of 10 feet. The bark of *P. dubia* is used in Nepal to dye scarlet. *P. Japonica* yields a small scarlet fruit eaten by the Japanese, and is planted for ornament. See *loquat*.

Photinian (fọ-tin'i-ạn), *n.* [< LL. *Photinianus*, an adherent of Photinus, < *Photinus*, < Gr. Φωτεινός, Photinus (see def.), < φωτεινός, shining, bright, < φῶς (φωτ-), light.] One of a sect, disciples of Photinus, a bishop of Sirmium in Pannonia in the fourth century. Photinus denied Christ's essential divinity, and believed that his moral character developed from human to divine.

Photinianism (fọ-tin'i-ạn-izm), *n.* [< *Photinian* + *-ism*.] The system of doctrine held by Photinus.

photo (fō'tō), *n.* A colloquial abbreviation of *photograph*.

photobiotic (fō"tọ-bī-ot'ik), *a.* [< Gr. φῶς (φωτ-), light, + βιωτικός, belonging to life.] Living habitually in the light: said of a class of plant-cells.

photocampsis (fō-tọ-kamp'sis), *n.* [NL., < Gr. φῶς (φωτ-), contr. of φάος, light (< φάειν, shine: see *phase*[1]), + κάμψις, bending, < κάμπτειν, bend.] Refraction of light. *Thomas*, Med. Dict.

photochemical (fō-tọ-kem'i-kạl), *a.* [< Gr. φῶς (φωτ-), light, + E. *chemical*.] Of or pertaining to the chemical action of light.

photochemist (fō-tọ-kem'ist), *n.* [< Gr. φῶς (φωτ-), light, + E. *chemist*.] One who is versed in photochemistry.

photochemistry (fō-tọ-kem'is-tri), *n.* [< Gr. φῶς (φωτ-), light, + E. *chemistry*.] That branch of chemistry which treats of the chemical action of light.

photochromatic (fō"tọ-krọ-mat'ik), *a.* [< *photochrom-y* + *-atic* (after *chromatic*).] Of or pertaining to or produced by photochromy. *Athenæum*, No. 3235, p. 562.

photochromolithograph (fē-tọ-krō-mọ-lith'ọ-gråf), *n.* [< Gr. φῶς (φωτ-), light, + E. *chromolithograph*.] A chromolithograph in the production of which photographic processes have been used.

photochromotype (fō-tọ-krō'mọ-tīp), *n.* [< Gr. φῶς (φωτ-), light, + E. *chromotype*.] A photo-process picture printed in colors in a printing-press by any of the ordinary methods of typography in colors.

photochromy (fō'tō-krō-mi), *n.* [< Gr. φῶς (φωτ-), light, + χρῶμα, color.] The art of reproducing colors by photography, or of producing photographic pictures in which the originals are shown in their natural colors. There is as yet no process by which natural colors can be registered by photography by a single or simple operation, in such form that the resulting picture will be permanent. By the device of taking a separate negative for every color in the subject, using in every case such chemicals or methods as will reproduce only the desired color, and afterward combining prints or matrices from all the negatives, every one in its appropriate color, a remarkably close approximation is made to the natural appearance of the subject. This process is peculiarly adapted to the reproduction of such works of art as jewels, tapestries, potteries, and enamels.

photochronograph (fō-tọ̄-kron'ọ̄-gráf), *n.* [< Gr. φῶς (φωτ-), light, + E. *chronograph.*] **1.** An instrument for taking photochronographic pictures. See *photochronography.*—**2.** A picture taken by this method.

photochronographic (fō-tē-kron-ọ̄-graf'ik), *a.* Of or pertaining to photochronography.

photochronography (fō″tọ̄-krọ̄-nog'ra-fi), *n.* [< Gr. φῶς (φωτ-), light, + χρόνος, time, + γράφειν, write.] The method, practice, etc., of taking instantaneous photographs at regular and generally at short intervals of time, as of a bird, horse, projectile, etc., in motion.

photocrayon (fō-tọ̄-krā'on), *a.* [< Gr. φῶς (φωτ-), light, + E. *crayon.*] Produced by photographic processes giving the effect of work in crayons, or finished in crayons upon a photographic groundwork: said of a picture.

photodermatic (fō″tọ̄-dėr-mat'ik), *a.* [< Gr. φῶς (φωτ-), light, + δέρμα, skin: see *dermatic.*] Having a luminous or phosphorescent skin; phosphorescent, as the mantle of a mollusk. *Nature,* XL. 384.

photodrome (fō'tọ̄-drōm), *n.* [< Gr. φῶς (φωτ-), light, + δρόμος, a running, < δραμεῖν, run.] An instrument for producing optical effects by flashes of light thrown upon revolving disks on which are painted various figures or devices.

photodynamic (fō″tọ̄-di-nam'ik), *a.* [< Gr. φῶς (φωτ-), light, + δύναμις, power: see *dynamic.*] Of or pertaining to the energy or effect of light.

photodysphoria (fō″tọ̄-dis-fō'ri-ạ̈), *n.* [NL., < Gr. φῶς (φωτ-), light, + δυσφορία, pain hard to be borne: see *dysphoria.*] An intolerance of light; photophobia.

photo-electric (fō″tō-ẹ̄-lek'trik), *a.* [< Gr. φῶς (φωτ-), light, + E. *electric.*] Acting by the combined operation of light and electricity; producing light by means of electricity; also noting apparatus for taking photographs by electric light, or by a lamp whose illuminating power is derived from electricity.

photo-electrical (fō″tō-ẹ̄-lek'tri-kạl), *a.* [< Gr. φῶς (φωτ-), light, + E. *electrical.*] Same as *photo-electric.*

photo-electrotype (fō″tō-ẹ̄-lek'trọ̄-tīp), *n.* [< Gr. φῶς (φωτ-), light, + E. *electrotype.*] A photographic picture produced in relief, such as to afford, by the ordinary processes of electrotypy, a matrix for a cast from which impressions in ink may be obtained.

photo-engrave (fō'tō-en-grāv'), *v. t.* [< Gr. φῶς (φωτ-), light, + E. *engrave.*] To produce by or in photo-engraving.

photo-engraving (fō'tō-en-grā'ving), *n.* [< Gr. φῶς (φωτ-), light, + E. *engraving.*] A common name for many processes by which a photograph may be made to afford a plate-matrix from which can be taken prints in ink corresponding to the original of the photographic image. These processes depend upon the property, possessed by potassium bichromate and analogous chemicals, of rendering insoluble, under the action of light, gelatin or some similar body with which they are compounded. By applications of this property, varying according to the process, a picture or design can be produced on a metal surface, and the blank places etched out with acid; or a matrix in relief can be formed, from which an electrotype plate can be made in ordinary ways. In general, the term *photo-engraving* is limited to a relief-block or -plate produced by photographic means for printing in an ordinary printing-press, to the art of making such blocks, and to prints from them; while the term *photogravure* is commonly applied to a photographically engraved plate in intaglio from which prints may be taken in a copperplate-press, to the art of making such an incised plate, and to a print from it. In the Gillet process a zinc plate coated with asphaltum is exposed beneath a negative, and those portions unchanged by light are dissolved. The zinc is then etched. Photographs are reproduced in the form of half-tone plates for use in the printing-press by several methods, all of which depend upon breaking up the surface of the picture by dark lines in regular series. A gelatin film on which such a series of lines has been photographed is placed between the sensitized surface which is to receive the impression and a positive picture. The resulting print will consist of the subject appearing in half-tone on a ground of lines, and from it a typographical matrix is prepared in the usual ways. (For an example of a half-tone plate, see cut under *dekadrachm.*) Also called *photographic engraving, photographic-process printing, photographic process.* See *photo-etching* (Gillet process), and compare *heliotypy* and *photogravure.*

photo-epinastic (fō-tō-ep-i-nas'tik), *a.* [< *photo-epinast-y* + *-ic.*] In *bot.*, of, pertaining to, or of the nature of photo-epinasty.

photo-epinastically (fō-tō-ep-i-nas'ti-kạl-i), *adv.* In *bot.*, in a photo-epinastic manner.

photo-epinasty (fō-tō-ep'i-nas-ti), *n.* [< Gr. φῶς (φωτ-), light, + E. *epinasty.*] In *bot.*, an epinastic movement or state of curvature observed in certain organs when exposed to intense light, due to a more active growth of the dorsal surface. Compare *epinasty.*

photo-etching (fō-tō-ech'ing), *n.* [< Gr. φῶς (φωτ-), light, + E. *etching.*] Any process of photo-engraving or photogravure, or any plate or print produced by such a process, in which a subject in line is transferred by photography to a metal surface in such a manner that either the ground or the lines of the design will resist acid, with which the plate is then etched: most commonly used for relief-plates on zinc, such as those of the Gillet process. See *photo-engraving.*

photogalvanography (fō-tọ̄-gal-va-nog'ra-fi), *n.* [< Gr. φῶς (φωτ-), light, + E. *galvanography.*] A process of obtaining from a photographic positive on glass an intaglio gutta-percha plate for printing like a plate. The gutta-percha plate is a hardened impression from a relief negative in bichromated gelatin, made according to the methods used in photo-process.

photogen (fō'tọ̄-jen), *n.* [F. *photogène*, < Gr. φῶς (φωτ-), light, + -γενής, producing: see *-gen.*] A paraffin-oil: same as *kerosene.*

photogene (fō'tọ̄-jēn), *n.* [< Gr. φῶς (φωτ-), light, + -γενής, producing: see *-gen.*] A more or less continued impression or picture on the retina. *H. Spencer.*

photogenic (fō-tọ̄-jen'ik), *a.* [= F. *photogénique* = It. *fotogenico*; as *photogen-, photogen-ous.*] **1.** Of or pertaining to photogeny.—**2.** In *biol.*, producing light without sensible heat, as an animal or vegetable organism; giving rise to luminosity or phosphorescence; photogenous.

> According to Schulze the males of Lampyris splendidula possess two *photogenic* organs.
> *Huxley*, Anat. Invert., p. 379.

Photogenic drawing. (*a*) A picture produced by the agency of light, according to any of the photographic processes. Specifically—(*b*) A reproduction of the configuration of any flat translucent object, as a leaf, or the wing of an insect, or a drawing upon translucent paper or tracing-cloth, made by confining it under glass in contact with a sensitive film, exposing to the action of light, and fixing or developing the image resulting in the film. A variety of photogenic processes are now in use for copying mechanical drawings. See *blue-printing.*

photogenous (fọ̄-toj'e-nus), *a.* [< Gr. φῶς (φωτ-), light, + -γενής, producing: see *-genous.*] In *biol.*, same as *photogenic.*

> Their further studies . . . enable them to reconcile their theory of *photogenous* fermentation with the hypothesis of the oxidation of a phosphorated substance, as proposed by some biologists.
> *Nature,* XXXVIII. 512.

photogeny (fọ̄-toj'e-ni), *n.* [< Gr. φῶς (φωτ-), light, + -γένεια, < -γενής, producing: see *-geny.*] The art of taking pictures by the action of light on a chemically prepared ground; photography.

photoglyphic (fō-tọ̄-glif'ik), *a.* [< *photoglyph-y* + *-ic.*] Of or relating to photoglyphy.

photoglyphy (fō-tog'li-fi), *n.* [< Gr. φῶς (φωτ-), light, + γλύφειν, engrave.] The art of engraving by means of the action of light and certain chemical processes; particularly, the production by photographic processes of a plate from which copies can be printed in ink. Often restricted to the production of intaglio plates, or photogravure.

photogram (fō'tọ̄-gram), *n.* [< Gr. φῶς (φωτ-), light, + γράμμα, a writing, a drawing, a picture, < γράφειν, write: see *gram*[2].] Same as *photograph.* *Nature,* XXXVI. 317. [Rare.]

photogrammetry (fō-tọ̄-gram'et-ri), *n.* The art of forming an orthogonal projection from two perspectives.

photograph (fō'tọ̄-gráf), *n.* [= F. *photographe* = It. *fotografo*, a photograph (cf. Sp. *fotografia* = Pg. *photographia* = It. *fotografia*, a photograph: see *photography*); Sp. *fotógrafo* = Pg. *photographo* = It. *fotografo* = G. *photograph* = Sw. Dan. *fotograf* = NGr. φωτογράφος, a photographer, < Gr. φῶς (φωτ-), light, + γράφειν, write.] A picture produced by any process of photography.—**Composite photograph.** See *composite.*—**Instantaneous photograph.** See *photography.*—**Phosphorescent photograph**, a photographic picture obtained by coating a plate with a mixture of dextrin, honey, and potassium bichromate, and exposing it under a negative. The parts affected by light through the transparent parts of the negative harden, while those which are protected from the light remain sticky, so that any fine powder dusted over will adhere to them, while having no hold on the hardened parts. If a phosphorescent powder is dusted on this positive, and the plate is then exposed to strong light, there will result a picture appearing luminous in the dark.

photograph (fō'tọ̄-gráf), *v. t.* [< *photograph*, *n.*] To produce a likeness or facsimile of by photographic means

photographer (fọ̄-tog'ra-fėr), *n.* [< *photograph* + *-er*[1].] One who makes pictures by means of photography.

photographic (fō-tọ̄-graf'ik), *a.* [= F. *photographique* = Sp. *fotográfico* = Pg. *photographico* = It. *fotografico*; as *photograph-y* + *-ic.*] Of, pertaining to, using, or produced by photography.—**Photographic engraving.** Same as *photo-engraving.*—**Photographic lens, paper,** etc. See the nouns.—**Photographic process, photographic-process printing.** Same as *photo-engraving.*

photographical (fō-tọ̄-graf'i-kạl), *a.* [< *photographic* + *-al.*] Of or pertaining to photography; more or less directly connected with photographic matters: as, a *photographical* print; a *photographical* society.

photographically (fō-tọ̄-graf'i-kạl-i), *adv.* By means of, or as regards, photography; as in a photograph.

photographometer (fō″tọ̄-gra-fom'e-tėr), *n.* [< *photograph* + Gr. μέτρον, measure.] **1.** In *photog.*, an instrument for determining the sensibility of a film employed in photographic processes, relatively to the amount of radiation, luminous and chemical.—**2.** A rotating photographic apparatus for recording automatically the angular position of objects around a given point.

photography (fọ̄-tog'ra-fi), *n.* [= F. *photographie* = Sp. *fotografia* = Pg. *photographia* = It. *fotografia* = D. *photografie* = G. *photographie* = Sw. Dan. *fotografi*, photography (in Sp. Pg. It. also a photograph), = NGr. φωτογραφία, photography, < Gr. φῶς (φωτ-), light, + -γραφία, < γράφειν, write. Cf. *photograph.*] The art of producing images of objects by an application of the chemical change produced in certain substances, as silver chlorid, bromide, or iodide, by the action of light, or more generally of radiant energy. The rays which are in general most active in this way are those of the upper part of the spectrum, as the blue, violet, and ultra-violet rays. The red and yellow rays produce a much less marked effect on an ordinary sensitive plate; but it has been found possible to prepare a special gelatinobromide plate which is highly sensitive even to the less refrangible rays, as those in the infra-red region of the spectrum. (See *spectrum.*) Photography rests on the fact that silver nitrate and various other chemicals are decomposed by certain solar rays and reduced, becoming dark or black, or in other ways affected, according to the intensity and amount of actinic rays received on them. The process consists (1) in properly exposing a surface made sensitive to actinic rays to a projected image of the object to be reproduced; (2) in rendering visible if merely latent, or in coloring or toning, the reproduction of this image; (3) in removing the sensibility of those parts of the surface which have not been acted on, and in fixing permanently the image produced; and (4), if the image obtained is a negative, as in the majority of processes, in the mechanical production of positive copies from it. The knowledge of the principle on which photography depends reaches back to the time of the alchemists, who discovered that silver chlorid exposed to the sun's rays became black. Wedgwood and Davy in 1802 attempted to apply this fact to artistic purposes by throwing the shadow of an object on a sheet of white paper, or, preferably, of leather, covered with a solution of silver nitrate and exposed to the sun's rays, but they were unable to fix the pictures. About 1814 Niepce, a Frenchman, discovered a method of producing pictures on plates of copper or pewter covered with a sensitive resinous substance called bitumen of Judea, and also of rendering them permanent. This process he called *heliography.* Niepce associated himself with Daguerre, who elaborated, about 1838, from the former process the one which bears his name. (See *daguerreotype.*) This was soon superseded by various processes, especially the *calotype process* (see *calotype*) of Fox-Talbot, first patented in 1841, who revived Wedgwood's process of obtaining pictures on sensitized paper, and the *collodion process* (see *collodion*), first suggested by M. Le Grey, of Paris, and brought into practice by Archer in 1850; and all these later processes have been practically abandoned for the *gelatinobromide dry-plate process*, which is now in almost universal use. Photographs produced by any of these processes may be either *negative* or *positive.* Negative photographs exhibit the lights and shades as opposite to those in nature—that is, the lights appear dark and the shades transparent; positive photographs exhibit the lights and shades in accordance with nature. To produce a positive from a negative, the latter is placed in contact with a surface which has been rendered sensitive to light, and is exposed to the influence of light, which penetrates the negative and affects the parts of the underlying surface opposite the lights of the picture, while the parts opposite the opaque parts of the picture are protected. The operation for obtaining a positive from a negative is called *printing.* Modifications are constantly being introduced in photography. One of the most important has been the *carbon process*, popularized by Swan of Newcastle, according to which a solution of gelatin and potassium bichromate (the latter being the sensitizing agent) is mixed with a pigment, and applied as a coating to a sheet of paper. The positives are printed in the ordinary way on the black cake, or *tissue* as it is called, thus produced, and become visible and permanent by washing, as the pigment-coating is rendered more or less insoluble by the effect of the light passing through the negative. The *autotype process*, invented by Johnson, is a simpler method of carbon-printing than the carbon process proper, but the principles involved are the same. One of the most important developments of the art is the so-called *instantaneous photography*, by means of which, through the use of very sensitive plates and the shortness of the duration of exposure, scenes, motions, etc., are reproduced and registered which are too rapid or evanescent to be distinguishable by the eye. For various mechanical methods of multiplying photographic pictures, see *photo-electrotype, photo-engraving, photogalvanography, photoglyphy, photogravure, photolithography*, and *heliotypy*.

photogravure (fō″tọ̄-grạ̈-vūr′), *n.* [< F. *photogravure*, < Gr. φῶς (φωτ-), light, + F. *gravure*, engraving.] The art of producing on metal, by an application of the action of light on a sensitized surface, often supplemented by etching, an incised engraved plate for printing. There are several processes by which this may be accomplished. According to the Niepce process, which is suitable for the reproduction of line-engravings, a copperplate is coated with bitumen and is then exposed to light beneath a negative. The resulting print is brought out with olive-oil and turpentine, or with oil of spike, which dissolves the parts acted on by light and acts little on the rest, and the lines remain as bare copper. The plate is then etched. In the Fox-Talbot process the gelatin print is transferred to copper which has had a grain given to it by sprinkling the surface with powdered resin and then warming it. (See *aquatint*.) The plate is then etched with ferric acid, which renders the opaque portions of the gelatin film insoluble and impermeable. The acid should be weak and kept in motion during the biting, until the uncovered parts have been sufficiently attacked. To increase the regularity of the erosion, the plate should first be immersed in a weak solution of copper sulphate. In the Woodbury process, which resembles the Goupil process, a gelatin picture in relief is applied under pressure upon a plate of soft metal, and is repeated on the metal in relief and depression. The mold thus formed is filled with pigmented gelatin, over which a sheet of paper which is to receive the picture is placed, and subjected to a level pressure in order to force out the superfluous gelatin. The depressed parts, which represent the dark parts of the picture, retain the most gelatin, and when the paper is lifted it raises the gelatin from the mold in such a manner that it forms a picture in low relief. In order to obtain a grained surface which will hold printing-ink, pounded glass may be mixed with the gelatin.

photogravure (fō″tọ̄-grạ̈-vūr′), *v. t.*; pret. and pp. *photogravured*, ppr. *photogravuring*. [< *photogravure*, *n.*] To produce in photogravure.

photoheliograph (fō-tọ̄-hē′li-ọ̄-gráf), *n.* [< Gr. φῶς (φωτ-), light, + E. *heliograph*.] A photographic telescope designed for making photographs of the sun, particularly at a transit of Venus or at a solar eclipse. There are several forms of the instrument, differing widely in construction.

photoheliographic (fō-tọ̄-hē″li-ọ̄-graf′ik), *a.* [< *photoheliograph* + *-ic*.] Of, pertaining to, or made by means of a photoheliograph: as, *photoheliographic* observations.

photohyponastic (fō-tọ̄-hi-pọ̄-nas′tik), *a.* [< *photohyponast-y* + *-ic*.] In *bot.*, pertaining to or characteristic of photohyponasty.

photohyponasty (fō-tọ̄-hī′pọ̄-nas-ti), *n.* [NL., < Gr. φῶς (φωτ-), light, + E. *hyponasty*.] In *bot.*, a hyponastic movement or curvature brought about by the exposure of organs to intense light after they have had their growth arrested for a period.

photolithograph (fō-tọ̄-lith′ọ̄-gráf), *n.* [< Gr. φῶς (φωτ-), light, + E. *lithograph*.] A print produced by photolithography.

photolithograph (fō-tọ̄-lith′ọ̄-gráf), *v. t.* [< *photolithograph*, *n.*] To produce or reproduce by the aid of photolithography.

photolithographer (fō″tọ̄-li-thog′ra-fėr), *n.* [< *photolithograph-y* + *-er*[1].] One who produces pictures by photolithography.

photolithographic (fō-tọ̄-lith-ọ̄-graf′ik), *a.* [< *photolithograph-y* + *-ic*.] Of, pertaining to, or produced by photolithography.—**Photolithographic process**, any one of the various processes by which photolithography is accomplished. All depend upon the property of a gelatin film, sensitized with potassium bichromate or an analogous chemical, of becoming insoluble when exposed to light, and thus of affording a photographic relief-plate, or a plate which will take lithographic ink in the parts affected by light, and repel it elsewhere, from which the design or picture can be transferred by the ordinary methods of lithography to a stone, or to a plate of zinc, etc.

photolithography (fō″tọ̄-li-thog′ra-fi), *n.* [= F. *photolithographie* = Sp. *fotolitografía*; as Gr. φῶς (φωτ-) + E. *lithography*.] The art of fixing on the surface of a lithographic stone by the agency of the action of light upon bichromated gelatin combined with albumen, and by other manipulations, an image suitable for reproduction in ink by impression in the manner of an ordinary lithograph; also extended to include processes of similar character in which the transfer is not made to stone; specifically, the process of reproducing in ink any design or picture executed on prepared stone by means of photography, either directly or by transfers from photographs. The process is analogous to several photo-engraving processes executed on metal. See *photolithographic process*, under *photolithographic*. Also called *lithophotography*.

photologic (fō-tọ̄-loj′ik), *a.* [= F. *photologique* = Sp. *fotológico* = Pg. *photologico*; as *photolog-y* + *-ic*.] Of or pertaining to photology.

photological (fō-tọ̄-loj′i-kal), *a.* [< *photologic* + *-al*.] Same as *photologic*.

photologist (fọ̄-tol′ọ̄-jist), *n.* [< *photolog-y* + *-ist*.] One who devotes himself to the study or exposition of the science of light.

The painter should never forget that his notion of colour (as compared with that of the *photologist*) is a negative one.
Herschel, Light, § 48.

photology (fọ̄-tol′ọ̄-ji), *n.* [= F. *photologie* = Sp. *fotología* = Pg. *photologia*, < Gr. φῶς (φωτ-), light, + -λογία, < λέγειν, speak: see *-ology*. Cf. MGr. φωτολόγος, announcing light.] The science of light.

photolysis (fọ̄-tol′i-sis), *n.* [NL., < Gr. φῶς (φωτ-), light, + λύσις, a loosing, setting free, < λύειν, loosen, unbind, unfasten.] In *bot.*, the movements of protoplasm under the influence of light: distinguished as *apostrophe* and *epistrophe*. In the first the chlorophyl-grains collect upon the cell-walls which are parallel to the plane of incident light; in the latter, upon those which are at right angles to it. *Moore.*

photomagnetism (fō-tọ̄-mag′net-izm), *n.* [< Gr. φῶς (φωτ-), light, + E. *magnetism*.] The relation of magnetism to light. *Faraday.*

photomechanical (fō″tọ̄-mẹ̄-kan′i-kal), *a.* [< Gr. φῶς (φωτ-), light, + E. *mechanical*.] Pertaining to or consisting in the mechanical production of pictures by the aid of light, as in photo-engraving, photolithography, etc.

Of all the perfected *photomechanical* processes, the collotype is about the most useful for general purposes.
The Engineer, LXVI. 279.

photometallograph (fō″tọ̄-me-tal′ọ̄-gráf), *n.* [< Gr. φῶς (φωτ-), light, + μέταλλον, metal, + γράφειν, write (see *metallography*).] Same as *photozincograph*.

photometer (fọ̄-tom′e-tėr), *n.* [= F. *photomètre* = Sp. *fotómetro* = Pg. *photometro* = It. *fotometro*, < Gr. φῶς (φωτ-), light, + μέτρον, measure.] An instrument used to measure the intensity of light, specifically to compare the relative intensities of the light emitted from different sources. Many forms have been devised, most of which are based upon the determination of the relative distances

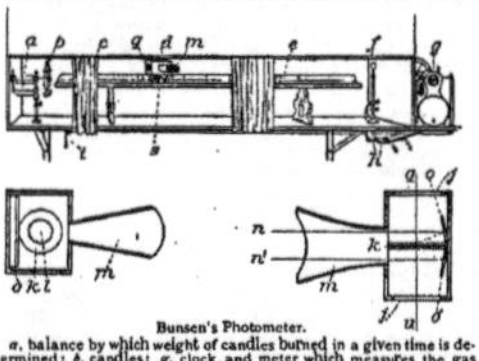

Bunsen's Photometer.

a, balance by which weight of candles burned in a given time is determined; *b*, candles; *g*, clock, and meter which measures the gas consumed in the test; *f*, gas-burner; *h*, flexible pipes for supplying gas to the burner; *d*, sight-box, supported on a carriage *s*; *e*, scale having a guide-way for the carriage of the sight-box, and graduated to show the relative candle-power of gas which gives an illumination having intensity equal to that of the candles. This graduation corresponds with the position of the sight-box when the latter is adjusted so that equal intensity is obtained on both sides of the disk; *c* is a curtain to exclude other light during the adjustment of the sight-box; *i*, cord running over pulleys under the bottom of the instrument, by which an operator can start or stop the clock at the beginning and end of the test; *k*, disk, with the translucent serrated spot *l*; *m*, sight-tube; *o o′*, mirrors. Light enters the sight-box from the candles through the opening *q* in the side of the sight-box, and from the gas-burner on the side of *u*. Images of both sides of the illuminated disk are simultaneously seen at *n n′* by reflection from the mirrors at *o* and *o′*.

at which the light from two sources produces equal intensities of illumination. One of the most common photometers is that of Bunsen, which consists of a screen of white paper with a grease-spot in its center. The lights to be compared are placed on opposite sides of this screen, and their distances are so adjusted that the grease-spot appears neither brighter nor darker than the rest of the paper, from whichever side it is viewed. When the distances have not been correctly adjusted, the grease-spot will appear darker than the rest of the paper when viewed from the side on which the illumination is most intense, and lighter than the rest of the paper when viewed from the other side. The intensities of the two lights are to one another as the squares of the distances from the screen at which they must be placed in order that the grease-spot may appear neither brighter nor darker than the rest of the paper. Another form is Rumford's photometer, which employs a screen in front of which is placed a vertical rod; the positions of the sources of light are so adjusted that the two shadows which they cast are sensibly equal.—**Dispersion photometer**, a form of photometer by means of which the intensity of a brilliant light, as that of an electric arc, may be determined. The dispersive effect of a thin concave lens acts like increase of distance in the common photometer to weaken the bright light to the required degree.—**Polarization photometer**, an instrument in which the measurement depends upon the properties of polarized light.—**Wedge photometer**, an astronomical photometer in which a wedge of neutral-tinted dark glass is used to cause the apparent extinction of a star viewed through it. The thickness of the wedge at the point where the star vanishes determines its brightness.—**Wheel photometer**, an instrument in which the light to be measured is weakened in any required degree by transmission through adjustable apertures in a rapidly revolving wheel.

photometric (fō-tọ̄-met′rik), *a.* [= F. *photométrique* = Pg. *photometrico*; as *photometr-y* + *-ic*.] Pertaining to photometry, or the measurement of the intensity of light, or to the photometer, or instrument by which this is effected; employing or made by a photometer: as, *photometric* researches or observations.—**Lambert's photometric law** [named after Johann Heinrich *Lambert* (1728–77), an eminent mathematician and logician, the discoverer of this law], the fact that a smooth, irregularly reflecting surface appears equally bright under whatever angle it is seen.—**Photometric standard**, a carcel lamp burning 42 grams of refined colza-oil per hour, with a flame 40 millimeters high. It is equal to 9.5 British or 7.6 German standard candles. The *unit of photometry* adopted by the Electrical Congress at Paris (1884) is the amount of light emitted from a surface of one square centimeter of melted platinum at its temperature of solidification; in 1889 one twentieth of this unit was adopted as the practical unit, and called a *candle*. See *candle-power*.

photometrical (fō-tọ̄-met′ri-kal), *a.* [< *photometric* + *-al*.] Same as *photometric*.

photometrically (fō-tọ̄-met′ri-kal-i), *adv.* As regards photometry; by means of a photometer.

photometrician (fō″tọ̄-me-trish′an), *n.* [< *photometric* + *-ian*.] One who is versed in photometry. *R. A. Proctor*, The Sun, p. 302.

photometrist (fọ̄-tom′e-trist), *n.* [< *photometr-y* + *-ist*.] A photometrician.

The best way for a *photometrist* to be certain of his instruments is to test them himself.
W. R. Bowditch, Coal Gas, iii. 67.

photometry (fọ̄-tom′et-ri), *n.* [= F. *photométrie* = Sp. *fotometría* = It. *fotometria*, < Gr. φῶς (φωτ-), light, + -μετρία, < μέτρον, measure.] The measurement of the relative amounts of light emitted by different sources. This is usually accomplished by determining the relative distances at which two sources of light produce equal intensities of illumination. See *photometer*.

photomicrograph (fō-tọ̄-mī′krọ̄-gráf), *n.* [< Gr. φῶς (φωτ-), light, + E. *micrograph*.] An enlarged or macroscopic photograph of a microscopic object; an enlarged photograph. Compare *microphotograph*.

photomicrographer (fō″tọ̄-mī-krog′ra-fėr), *n.* [< *photomicrograph* + *-er*[1].] A maker of photomicrographs; one who enlarges photographs, or makes enlarged pictures of small or microscopic objects.

photomicrographic (fō-tọ̄-mī-krọ̄-graf′ik), *a.* [< *photomicrograph-y* + *-ic*.] Of, pertaining to, or used in photomicrography; obtained or made by photomicrography: as, *photomicrographic* apparatus; a *photomicrographic* representation.

photomicrography (fō″tọ̄-mī-krog′ra-fi), *n.* [= F. *photomicrographie*; < Gr. φῶς (φωτ-), light, + E. *micrography*.] The art or process of enlarging minute objects by means of the microscope, and reproducing the enlarged image by photography. It is to be distinguished from *microphotography*.

photonephograph (fō-tọ̄-nef′ọ̄-gráf), *n.* [< Gr. φῶς (φωτ-), light, + νέφος, a cloud, + γράφειν, write.] A name given by Abney to an apparatus for taking simultaneous photographs of a cloud from two points on the earth. It consists essentially of twin cameras, adjustable at any angle of elevation and azimuth, and, as used at Kew, England, placed 200 yards apart. Two sets of photographs are taken simultaneously at an interval of about a minute, and from these the heights and motions of the clouds are deduced.

photonephoscope (fō-tọ̄-nef′ọ̄-skōp), *n.* [< Gr. φῶς (φωτ-), light, + νέφος, a cloud, + σκοπεῖν, view.] Same as *photonephograph*.

photonosos, photonosus (fọ̄-ton′ọ̄-sos, -sus), *n.* [NL., < Gr. φῶς (φωτ-), light, + νόσος, disease.] Any affection resulting from exposure to a glare of light, as snow-blindness.

photopapyrography (fō-tọ̄-pap-i-rog′ra-fi), *n.* [< Gr. φῶς (φωτ-), light, + E. *papyrography*.] A photo-engraving process in which a relief-print on paper is formed as a matrix from which prints in ink can be struck off.

photophobia (fō-tō-fō′bi-ạ̈), *n.* [= F. *photophobie* = It. *fotofobia*, < NL. *photophobia*, < Gr. φῶς (φωτ-), light, + -φοβία, < φόβος, fear.] An intolerance or dread of light.

photophobic (fō-tọ̄-fō′bik), *a.* [< *photophobia* + *-ic*.] Affected with photophobia; dreading or intolerant of light; unable to bear light.

photophone (fō′tọ̄-fōn), *n.* [< Gr. φῶς (φωτ-), light, + φωνή, sound, voice: see *phone*[1].] An instrument by which a beam of light may be made to transmit spoken words to a distance.

One form consists of a thin mirror of silvered mica which receives the vibrations from the person speaking, and upon which a beam of light falls at the same time. This light is reflected to the receiving-point at a distance. There it falls upon a concave mirror, and is brought to a focus upon a selenium-cell. The variation in the light produces a corresponding variation in the electrical resistance of the selenium, and this reproduces the spoken words in a telephone connected with it.

In the earlier papers describing it [the radiophone] and the experiments which led to its invention it is called *photophone*, because at that time the effects were supposed to be wholly due to light. Afterwards, in order to avoid ambiguity, Bell changed the name to radiophone, and suggested that, to distinguish between instruments depending on the different kinds of radiation, the names *photophone*, thermophone, &c., should be employed.
Encyc. Brit., XXIII. 130.

photophonic (fō-tǫ-fon'ik), *a.* [< *photophone* + *-ic.*] Pertaining to or produced by the photophone.

photophony (fō'tǫ-fō-ni), *n.* [< *photophone* + *-y*³.] The art or practice of using the photophone.

photophosphorescent (fō-tǫ-fos-fǫ-res'ent), *a.* [< Gr. φῶς (φωτ-), light, + E. *phosphorescent.*] Exhibiting phosphorescence under the action of light. See *phosphorescence.*

photophysical (fō-tǫ-fiz'i-kal), *a.* [< Gr. φῶς (φωτ-), light, + E. *physical.*] Pertaining to the physical effect of light: opposed to *photochemical*. *Athenæum*, No. 3235, p. 562.

photopolarimeter (fō-tǫ-pō-lạ-rim'e-tėr), *n.* [< Gr. φῶς (φωτ-), light, + E. *polarimeter.*] A form of polarimeter devised (1885) by Cornu. It has a doubly refracting prism mounted at one end of a tube, which at the other has a diaphragm of such size that the borders of the two images, polarized at right angles, just coincide with each other. A nicol prism suitably mounted is made to revolve until these images have the same intensity, when the angular position of its plane of vibration gives a ready means of determining the degree of polarization in the light under examination.

photo-process (fō'tō-pros''es), *n.* [< Gr. φῶς (φωτ-), light, + E. *process.*] Any process or method by which is produced, by the agency of photography, a matrix in relief or in intaglio from which prints can be made in ink; especially, the photographic production of relief-plates from which impressions are struck off in an ordinary printing-press. It thus includes photogravure, but is especially applicable to such processes of photo-engraving as photolithography and photozincography. The chief kinds of photo-process are differentiated as follows. Heliotype is the production of a matrix in gelatin, from which printing is done directly in a lithographic press. Photogravure is the production of incised or intaglio plates in metal. Photo-engraving is (properly) the production of relief-plates of any kind suited for printing, together with type, in an ordinary printing-press; though the term is often used to include photogravure also. Photo-engraving is particularly applicable to the reproduction of pen-drawings; when used for pictures, such as ordinary photographs, it is necessary, in order to admit of printing, to employ some such device as the formation over the whole surface of the plate of an even series of fine lines, or a finely dotted or stippled ground. Such plates are called *half-tone plates.* (See *half-tone process*, under *photo-engraving.*) Also used attributively to note a relief-plate, or an impression from such a plate, made by photo-process.

photopsia (fǫ-top'si-ạ̈), *n.* [NL., < Gr. φῶς (φωτ-), light, + ὄψις, look, sight, < √ ὀπ, see: see *optic.*] The condition of having the sensation as of light or of flashes of light without external cause.

photopsy (fō'top-si), *n.* [= F. *photopsie* = It. *fotopsia*, < NL. *photopsia*, q. v.] Same as *photopsia.*

photo-relief (fō'tō-rē-lēf'), *a.* [< Gr. φῶς (φωτ-), light, + E. *relief.*] Noting any process for obtaining by photographic means a matrix in relief capable of receiving ink and communicating impressions, or any block, plate, or print produced by such a process. See *photography*, *photo-engraving*.

photoscope (fō'tō-skōp), *n.* [< Gr. φῶς (φωτ-), light, + σκοπεῖν, view.] 1. An instrument or apparatus for exhibiting photographs. *E. H. Knight.*—2. An instrument consisting of a selenium-cell, or an arrangement of some other substance whose electrical resistance varies with the degree of illumination, together with a telephone-receiver placed in the same electrical circuit, by means of which the varying intensities of light may be detected.

photosculpture (fō'tō-skulp''tūr), *n.* [= F. *photosculpture*; < Gr. φῶς (φωτ-), light, + E. *sculpture.*] A process of sculpturing statuettes, medallions, and the like, by the aid of photography. The person whose likeness is to be taken is placed in the focus of a number of photographic cameras, placed at equal distances from one another, and is thus photographed all round. The resulting pictures are projected in succession by means of a magic lantern on a transparent screen. The operator works behind this screen on a piece of modeling-clay, turning it round as he proceeds, and copying the images on the screen by means of a pantograph which has its reducing-point armed with a molding- or cutting-tool, so that, as the longer arm traces every figure on the screen, the shorter one reproduces it in the clay.

photosphere (fō'tǫ-sfēr), *n.* [= F. *photosphère*, < Gr. φῶς (φωτ-), light, + σφαῖρα, sphere: see *sphere.*] An envelop of light; specifically, the luminous envelop, supposed to consist of incandescent matter, surrounding the sun. According to Kirchhoff, the sun's photosphere is either solid or liquid, and is surrounded by an extensive atmosphere, composed of gases and vapors of the substances incandescent in the photosphere. According to the view now more generally accepted, the photosphere is a shell of luminous cloud—that is, the solid or liquid particles which produce the light are minute, and disseminated through the lower strata of the solar atmosphere.

photospheric (fō-tǫ-sfer'ik), *a.* [< *photosphere* + *-ic.*] Of or pertaining to a photosphere, and specifically to the photosphere of the sun.

phototachometer (fō'tǫ-ta-kom'e-tėr), *n.* [< Gr. φῶς (φωτ-), light, + E. *tachometer.*] An instrument for measuring the velocity of light.

phototachometrical (fō-tǫ-tak-ǫ-met'ri-kal), *a.* [< *phototachometr-y* + *-ic-al.*] Pertaining to phototachometry.

phototachometry (fō'tǫ-ta-kom'et-ri), *n.* [< Gr. φῶς (φωτ-), light, + E. *tachometry.*] The measurement of the velocity of light.

phototactic (fō-tǫ-tak'tik), *a.* [< *phototaxis*, after *tactic.*] In *bot.*, pertaining to, characteristic of, or exhibiting phototaxis.

phototaxis (fō-tǫ-tak'sis), *n.* [NL., < Gr. φῶς (φωτ-), light, + τάξις, arrangement: see *taxis.*] In *bot.*, the taking by certain organisms or organs of a definite position with reference to the direction of the incident rays of light, as when the zoöspores of various plants (*Hæmatococcus*, *Ulothrix*, etc.) place their long axes parallel to the direction of the incident rays.

phototelephone (fō-tǫ-tel'e-fōn), *n.* [< Gr. φῶς (φωτ-), light, + E. *telephone.*] Same as *photophone.*

phototheodolite (fō'tǫ-thē-od'ǫ-līt), *n.* [< Gr. φῶς (φωτ-), light, + E. *theodolite.*] An instrument for the performance of triangulation by means of photographs.

phototonic (fō-tǫ-ton'ik), *a.* [< *phototonus* + *-ic.*] In *bot.*, exhibiting phototonus; characterized by phototonus. Compare *paratonic.*

phototonus (fǫ-tot'ǫ-nus), *n.* [NL., < Gr. φῶς (φωτ-), light, + τόνος, tension: see *tone.*] In *bot.*, a term proposed by Sachs for the peculiar condition in which the protoplasm is capable of exhibiting irritability induced in certain plant-organs by exposure to light of a certain intensity. This tonic influence of light is exhibited in the restoration of irritability in organs that have been kept for some days in continuous darkness.

In contrast to the rigidity caused by dark, I have applied the term *Phototonus* to the motile condition resulting from permanent exposure to light.
Sachs, Botany (trans.), p. 790.

phototype (fō'tǫ-tīp), *n.* and *a.* [Cf. F. *phototypie*; < Gr. φῶς (φωτ-), light, + τύπος, type.] I. *n.* 1. A type or plate for printing, of the same nature as an engraved relief-block, produced by an application of the photographic properties of gelatin sensitized with a bichromate (see *photo-engraving*), or by a combination of photographic and etching processes or a combination of photographic and mechanical processes, as when the lines in intaglio are produced by mechanical pressure, these processes when combined being commonly spoken of as a single general process; especially, the process known as photozincography. See *photozincography*, *photolithography*, and *photoglyphy*.—2. A picture printed from a relief-plate prepared by a phototype process.

II. *a.* Pertaining to or produced by means of phototypy: as, a *phototype* process, plate, or print.

phototype (fō'tǫ-tīp), *v. t.*; pret. and pp. *phototyped*, ppr. *phototyping*. [< *phototype*, *n.*] To reproduce in phototype or by phototypy.

phototypic (fō-tǫ-tip'ik), *a.* [< *phototype* + *-ic.*] Of, pertaining to, or produced by means of phototypy.

phototypographic (fō-tǫ-ti-pǫ-graf'ik), *a.* [< Gr. φῶς (φωτ-), light, + τύπος, type, + γράφειν, write.] Of, pertaining to, or using a photographic relief-block adapted for printing in an ordinary press: as, the *phototypographic* process of Poitevin.

phototypy (fō'tǫ-ti-pi), *n.* [< *phototype* + *-y*³.] The art or process of producing phototypes.

A combined albumen and asphalt process of *phototypy*.
Sci. Amer., N. S., LVII. 355.

photovoltaic (fō'tǫ-vol-tā'ik), *a.* [< Gr. φῶς (φωτ-), light, + E. *voltaic.*] Relating to an electric current as produced or varied in intensity by the action of light, as when the electrical resistance of selenium is altered by light.

photoxylography (fō''tǫ-zī-log'rạ-fi), *n.* [< Gr. φῶς (φωτ-), light, + E. *xylography.*] The process of producing an impression of an object on wood by photography and subsequent processes, and then printing from the block.

photozincograph (fō-tǫ-zing'kǫ-gråf), *n.* [< Gr. φῶς (φωτ-), light, + E. *zincograph.*] A plate or picture produced by photozincography. Also *photometallograph.*

photozincographic (fō-tǫ-zing-kǫ-graf'ik), *a.* [< *photozincograph-y* + *-ic.*] Of, pertaining to, or produced by photozincography.

photozincography (fō''tǫ-zing-kog'rạ-fi), *n.* [= F. *photozincographie*; as Gr. φῶς (φωτ-), light, + E. *zincography.*] A process of photo-engraving analogous to photolithography, but having the matrix formed on a plate of zinc instead of a lithographic stone; also, photo-etching executed on zinc. Also *photozincotypy.*

photozincotype (fō-tǫ-zing'kǫ-tīp), *n.* [< Gr. φῶς (φωτ-), light, + E. *zincotype.*] A plate prepared for printing by photozincography.

In place of wood-cuts, *photo-zincotypes* are very often used.
Sci. Amer., N. S., LV. 49.

photozincotypy (fē-tǫ-zing'kǫ-tī-pi), *n.* [< *photozincotype* + *-y*³.] Same as *photozincography.* *Sci. Amer.*, N. S., LV. 94.

photuria (fǫ-tū'ri-ạ̈), *n.* [NL., < Gr. φῶς (φωτ-), light, + οὖρον, urine.] The passage of luminous urine.

Photuris (fǫ-tū'ris), *n.* [NL. (Leconte, 1851), < Gr. φῶς (φωτ-), light, + οὐρά, tail.] A genus of fireflies of the coleopterous family *Lampyridæ*, with nearly 50 species, mainly South American, three only being found in North America. *P. pennsylvanica* is the common firefly or lightning-bug of eastern parts of the United States, about half an inch long and of a yellowish color. Its larva is also luminous. See *firefly*, and cut under *lightning-bug.*

Phoxinus (fok-sī'nus), *n.* [NL. (Agassiz, 1837), < Gr. φοξῖνος, an unknown river-fish.] In *ichth.*, a genus of small cyprinoid fishes; the true minnows, of small size, tapering form, and brilliant colors, the lateral line incomplete if present, the dorsal fin behind the ventrals, and the mouth without barbels. The type is the common European minnow, *P. aphya* or *lævis*; several species of the United States are also described. See cut under *minnow.*

Phractamphibia (frak-tam-fib'i-ạ̈), *n. pl.* [NL., < Gr. φρακτός, fenced, protected (< φράσσειν, fence, protect: see *phragma*), + NL. *Amphibia.*] The mailed or loricate amphibians, as labyrinthodonts: opposed to *Lissamphibia.*

phragma (frag'mạ̈), *n.*; pl. *phragmata* (-mạ-tạ̈). [NL., < Gr. φράγμα, a fence, partition, < φράσσειν, fence in, fence, secure, fortify. Cf. *diaphragm*, etc.] 1. In *bot.*, a spurious dissepiment or partition, as that which occurs at the nodes of certain calamites, and in various fruits.—2. In *zoöl.*, a partition, septum, dissepiment, or diaphragm. Specifically, in *entom.*: (*a*) A transverse partition descending from the dorsal surface into the cavity of the thorax. (*b*) The posterior inflexed border of the prothorax, concealed by the mesothorax and wing-covers: it is found only in those insects in which the prothorax is movable.

phragmacone (frag'mạ-kōn), *n.* [< Gr. φράγμα, a fence, partition (see *phragma*), + κῶνος, cone.] The conical, spiral, or otherwise shaped and chambered or septate internal skeleton of fossil cephalopods, contained in the anterior part of the cavity of a hollow hard structure called the *guard* or *rostrum*. It is homologous with the chambered shell of other cephalopods. See cut under *belemnite.*

phragmaconic (frag-mạ-kon'ik), *a.* [< *phragmacone* + *-ic.*] Having the character of a phragmacone; relating to a phragmacone.

phragmata, *n.* Plural of *phragma.*

Phragmites (frag-mī'tēz), *n.* [L., < Gr. φραγμίτης, growing in hedges, < φράγμα, a fence: see *phragma.*] A genus of grasses of the tribe *Festuceæ* and subtribe *Arundineæ*, distinguished from its relative *Arundo* by spikelets with the lowest flower staminate or sterile. There are 3 species, widely scattered throughout all temperate and subtropical regions. They are the tallest native grasses of the northern United States and of Great Britain, where they are useful in binding together the earth of river-banks by their creeping rootstocks. They are perennials with flat leaves and ample panicles, either dense and erect or loose and nodding, furnished with conspicuous tufts of long silky hairs enveloping the spikelets. *P. communis* is the marsh-reed of England and the Atlantic United States, with the aspect of broom-corn, and bearing ornamental plume-like panicles sought for decoration. Also known in England as *ditch-reed* and *bennets*, and in the western part of the United States as *cane.*

Phragmophora (frag-mof'ō-rä), *n. pl.* [NL., < Gr. φράγμα, a fence, partition (see *phragma*), + φέρειν = E. *bear*[1].] A section of decacerous cephalopods, having a phragmacone or internal shell with a row of air-chambers traversed by a siphon. It includes the extinct families *Belosepiidæ*, *Belopteridæ*, and *Belemnitidæ*.

phragmophorous (frag-mof'ō-rus), *a.* [< *Phragmophora* + *-ous*.] Having the characters of the *Phragmophora*; having a phragmacone.

phraise (frāz), *v. i.*; pret. and pp. *phraised*, ppr. *phraising*. [Appar. merely a particular use of *phrase*.] To use coaxing or wheedling language; cajole; palaver. *Scott*, Rob Roy, xxiii. [Scotch.]

phrampel†, *a.* A bad spelling of *frampel*. *Middleton and Dekker*, Roaring Girl, iii. 1.

phrasal (frā'zal), *a.* [< *phrase* + *-al*.] Of, pertaining to, or consisting of a phrase; consisting of two or more words.

A third series of prepositions are the *phrasal* prepositions consisting of more than one word.
J. Earle, Philology of the Eng. Tongue (4th ed.), p. 501.

phrase (frāz), *n.* [= D. G. *phrase* = Sw. *fras* = Dan. *frase*, < F. *phrase*, OF. *frase* = Sp. *frase*, *frasis* = Pg. *phrase* = It. *frase*, < L. *phrasis*, < Gr. φράσις, speech, manner of speech, phraseology, expression, enunciation, < φράζειν, point out, show, tell, declare, speak.] 1. A brief expression; more specifically, two or more words expressing what is practically a single notion, and thus performing the office of a single part of speech, or entering with a certain degree of unity into the structure of a sentence.

"Convey," the wise it call. "Steal!" foh! a fico for the *phrase!*
Shak., M. W. of W., i. 3. 33.

Now mince the sin,
And mollify damnation with a *phrase*.
Dryden, Spanish Friar, v. 2.

2. A peculiar or characteristic expression; a mode of expression peculiar to a language; an idiom.

The Bible is rather translated into English Words than into English *Phrase*. The Hebraisms are kept, and the *Phrase* of that Language is kept. *Selden*, Table-Talk, p. 20.

And, in his native tongue and *phrase*,
Prayed to each saint to watch his days.
Scott, Rokeby, iv. 9.

Betwixt them blossomed up
From out a common vein of memory
Sweet household talk, and *phrases* of the hearth.
Tennyson, Princess, ii.

3. The manner or style in which a person expresses himself; diction; phraseology; language; also, an expression, or a form of expression.

The chief and principall [subject of poesy] is: the laud, honour, and glory of the immortall gods (I speake now in *phrase* of the Gentiles).
Puttenham, Arte of Eng. Poesie, p. 30.

The Sclauon dooth playnly vnderstande the Moscouite, although the Moscouian toonge be a more rude and harde *phrase* of speach.
R. Eden, tr. of John Faber (First Books on America, ed. [Arber, p. 290).

Thou speak'st
In better *phrase* and matter than thou didst.
Shak., Lear, iv. 6. 8.

A frantic Gipsey now, the House he haunts,
And in wild *Phrases* speaks dissembled Wants.
Prior, Henry and Emma.

4. In *music*, a short and somewhat independent division or part of a piece, less complete than a period, and usually closing with a cadence or a half-cadence. A phrase usually includes four or eight measures. The name is also given less technically to any short passage or figure that is performed without pause or break.

The singer who feels what he sings, and duly marks the *phrases* and accents, is a man of taste. But he who can only give the Values and intervals of the notes without the sense of the *phrases*, however accurate he may be, is a mere machine. *Rousseau*, Dict. Music. (Tr. in *Grove*.)

5. In *fencing*, a period between the beginning and end of a short passage at arms between fencers during which there is no pause, each fencer thrusting and parrying in turn.—**Adverbial, conditional, prepositional**, etc., **phrase**. See the adjectives.—**Extended phrase**, in *music*, a phrase that occupies, by exception, more than the usual number of measures.—**Irregular phrase**, in *music*, a phrase of an unusual number of measures.—**To learn the phrases of a house**, to become familiar with the habits of a family. *Halliwell*. [Cornwall, Eng.]=**Syn.** 1. See *term*.

phrase (frāz), *v.*; pret. and pp. *phrased*, ppr. *phrasing*. [= F. *phraser* = Sp. *frasear* = Pg. *phrasear*; from the noun.] **I.** *intrans.* 1. To employ peculiar phrases or forms of speech; express one's self. [Rare.]

So Saint Cyprian *phraseth*, to expresse effeminate, womanish, wanton, dishonest, mimicall gestures, by the tutorship of an unchast art. *Prynne*, Histrio-Mastix, II., ii. 2.

2. In *music*, to divide a piece in performance into short sections or phrases, so as to bring out the metrical and harmonic form of the whole, and make it musically intelligible; also, to perform any group of tones without pause.

II. *trans.* To express or designate by a particular phrase or term; call; style.

When these suns—
For so they *phrase* 'em—by their heralds challenged
The noble spirits to arms, they did perform
Beyond thought's compass. *Shak.*, Hen. VIII., i. 1. 34.

The Presbyters and Deacons writing to him think they doe him honour enough when they *phrase* him no higher than Brother Cyprian, and deare Cyprian in the 26. Epist.
Milton, Reformation in Eng., i.

phrase-book (frāz'bůk), *n.* A book in which the phrases or idiomatic forms of expression peculiar to a language are collected and explained.

I confess you are pretty well vers'd in *Phrase-Books*, and Lexicons, and Glossaries.
Milton, Answer to Salmasius, i. 32.

phraseless† (frāz'les), *a.* [< *phrase* + *-less*.] Not to be expressed or described.

O, then, advance of yours that *phraseless* hand
Whose white weighs down the airy scale of praise.
Shak., Lover's Complaint, l. 225.

phraseman (frāz'man), *n.*; pl. *phrasemen* (-men). One who habitually uses a set form of words with slight regard to their import; a phrasemonger. [Rare.]

The poor wretch . . .
Becomes a fluent *phraseman*, absolute
And technical in victories and defeats,
And all our dainty terms for fratricide.
Coleridge, Fears in Solitude.

phrase-mark (frāz'märk), *n.* In *musical notation*, a sweeping curve over or under notes that are to be performed connectedly and as forming a single phrase.

phrasemonger (frāz'mung"gėr), *n.* [< *phrase* + *monger*.] One who deals in mere phrases; one who is an adept at stringing words or phrases together.

phraseogram (frā'zē-ō-gram), *n.* [< Gr. φράσις (gen. φράσεος), speech, phrase, + γράμμα, letter: see *gram*[2].] In *phonog.*, a combination of shorthand characters to represent a phrase or sentence.

phraseograph (frā'zē-ō-gråf), *n.* [< Gr. φράσις (gen. φράσεος), speech, phrase, + γράφειν, write.] Same as *phraseogram*.

It contains an exhaustive list of reporting logographs, word signs, *phraseographs*, etc., all of which will, of course, be of great interest to the reporter.
Sci. Amer., N. S., LXI., p. 27 of adv'ts.

phraseography (frā-zē-og'ra-fi), *n.* [< Gr. φράσις (gen. φράσεος), speech, phrase, + -γραφία, < γράφειν, write.] The combining of two or more shortened phonographic or stenographic signs to represent a phrase or sentence; the use of phraseograms.

phraseologic (frā"zē-ō-loj'ik), *a.* [= F. *phraséologique* = Sp. *fraseológico* = Pg. *phraseologico* = It. *fraseologico*; as *phraseolog-y* + *-ic*.] Of or pertaining to phraseology: as, *phraseologic* peculiarities.

phraseological (frā"zē-ō-loj'i-kal), *a.* [< *phraseologic* + *-al*.] Same as *phraseologic*.

It is the vocabulary and the *phraseological* combinations of the man, or class of men, which must serve as the clue to guide us into the secret recesses of their being.
Marsh, Lects. on Eng. Lang., x.

phraseologically (frā"zē-ō-loj'i-kal-i), *adv.* As regards phraseology, or style of expression.

phraseologist (frā-zē-ol'ō-jist), *n.* [= Pg. *fraseologista*; < *phraseolog-y* + *-ist*.] 1. A stickler for phraseology, or a particular form of words; a coiner of phrases.

The author of Poetæ Rusticantis Literatum Otium is but a meer *phraseologist*. *Guardian*, No. 30.

2. A collector of phrases.

phraseology (frā-zē-ol'ō-ji), *n.* [= F. *phraséologie* = Sp. *fraseologia* = Pg. *phraseologia* = It. *fraseologia*, *frasilogia*, < Gr. φράσις (gen. φράσεος), speech, phrase, + -λογία, < λέγειν, speak: see *-ology*.] 1. The form of words used in expressing some idea or thought; mode or style of expression; the particular words or phrases combined to form a sentence, or the method of arranging them; diction; style.

From me they [auctioneers] learned to inlay their *phraseology* with variegated chips of exotic metaphor.
Sheridan, The Critic, i. 2.

Mr. Fox winnowed and sifted his *phraseology* with a care which seems hardly consistent with the simplicity and elevation of his mind.
Macaulay, Mackintosh's Hist. Rev.

2. A collection of phrases and idioms. = **Syn.** 1. *Style*, etc. See *diction*.

phrasical (frā'zi-kal), *a.* [< *phrase* + *-ic-al*.] Having the character of a phrase; idiomatic. [Rare.]

Here it is *phrasical*, and therefore not to be forced.
Rev. T. Adams, Works, I. 395.

phrasing (frā'zing), *n.* [Verbal n. of *phrase*, *v.*] 1. The wording of a speech or passage.—2. In *music*, the act, process, or result of dividing a piece in performance into short sections or phrases, so as to give it form and clearness. Skill in phrasing is one of the chief qualities of a good performer.

phratria (frā'tri-ä), *n.*; pl. *phratriæ* (-ē). [NL.: see *phratry*.] Same as *phratry*.

This tribunal [the Areopagus], however, did not interfere with the ancestral claims of families and *phratriæ*.
Von Ranke, Univ. Hist. (trans.), p. 138.

phratric (frā'trik), *a.* [< *phratr-y* + *-ic*.] Of or pertaining to a phratry.

The *phratric* organization has existed among the Iroquois from time immemorial.
Morgan, Contributions to North Amer. Ethnology, IV. 11.

phratry (frā'tri), *n.*; pl. *phratries* (-triz). [Also *phratria*; = F. *phratrie*, < Gr. φράτρα, φρατρία, a tribe, a political division of people, < φράτηρ, clansman, orig. 'brother,' = L. *frater* = E. *brother*: see *brother*.] A brotherhood or clan; specifically, in the states of ancient Greece, a politico-religious group of citizens, which appears to have been originally based on kinship and to have been a subdivision of the phyle or tribe. By modern ethnologists the term is applied to somewhat analogous brotherhoods existing among the aborigines of Australia and America.

In Australia the *phratries* are still more important than in America. Messrs. Howitt and Fison, who have done so much to advance our knowledge of the social system of the Australian aborigines, have given to these exogamous divisions the name of classes; but the term is objectionable, because it fails to convey (1) that these divisions are kinship divisions, and (2) that they are intermediate divisions; whereas the Greek term *phratry* conveys both these meanings, and is therefore appropriate.
J. G. Frazer, Encyc. Brit., XXIII. 472.

phreatic (frē-at'ik), *a.* [< F. *phréatique*, < Gr. φρέαρ (φρεατ-), an artificial well.] Subterranean, as the sources of wells.

phren (fren), *n.*; pl. *phrenes* (frē'nēz). [NL., < Gr. φρήν, the midriff, diaphragm, also, commonly in pl. φρένες, the parts about the heart, the breast, the heart as the seat of the passions or of the mind.] 1. The thinking principle, or power of thought and perception; mind.—2. The diaphragm. See *phrenic*.

phrenalgia (frē-nal'ji-ä), *n.* [NL., < Gr. φρήν, mind, + ἄλγος, pain.] Psychalgia.

phrenesiac† (frē-nē'si-ak), *a.* [< *phrenesis* + *-iac*.] Same as *phrenetic*.

Like an hypochondriac person, or, as Burton's Anatomia hath it, a *phrenesiac* or lethargic patient.
Scott, Waverley, xlii.

phrenesis (frē-nē'sis), *n.* [< L. *phrenesis*, < Gr. φρένησις, inflammation of the brain, < φρήν, mind: see *frenzy*.] Delirium; frenzy. *Thomas*, Med. Dict.

phrenetic (frē-net'ik), *a.* and *n.* [Also *frenetic*, *frantic* (see *frantic*); < ME. *frenetike*, *frenetik*, *frentik*, < OF. *frenetique*, F. *phrénétique*, *frénétique* = Pr. *frenetic* = Sp. *frenético* = Pg. It. *frenetico*, < L. *phreneticus*, *phreniticus*, < Gr. φρενιτικός, frenzied, distracted, < φρενῖτις, frenzy, phrenitis: see *phrenitis*.] **I.** *a.* See *frenetic*.

II.† *n.* A frantic or frenzied person; one whose mind is disordered.

You did never hear
A *phrenetic* so in love with his own favour!
B. *Jonson*, Devil is an Ass, iv. 3.

phrenetical (frē-net'i-kal), *a.* See *frenetic*.

phrenetically, *adv.* See *frenetically*.

phreniatric (fren-i-at'rik), *a.* [< Gr. φρήν, mind, + ἰατρικός, medicinal: see *iatric*.] Pertaining to the cure of mental diseases; psychiatric.

phrenic (fren'ik), *a.* and *n.* [= F. *phrénique* = Pg. *phrenico* = It. *frenico*, < NL. *phrenicus*, < Gr. as if *φρενικός, of or pertaining to the diaphragm, < φρήν (φρεν-), the diaphragm, the mind: see *phren*.] **I.** *a.* In *anat.*, of or pertaining to the diaphragm; diaphragmatic: as, a *phrenic* artery, vein, or nerve.—**Phrenic arteries**, arteries supplying the diaphragm. (*a*) *Inferior*, two small branches of the abdominal aorta. (*b*) *Superior*, a slender branch from each internal mammary. Also called *comes nervi phrenici*.—**Phrenic ganglion, hernia**, etc. See the nouns.—**Phrenic glands**, a group of small lymphatic glands surrounding the termination of the inferior cava.—**Phrenic nerve**, a deep branch of the fourth cervical nerve, with accessions from the third or fifth, descending through the thorax to be distributed to the diaphragm, giving also filaments to the pericardium and pleura. Also called *internal respiratory nerve of Bell*.—**Phrenic plexus**. See *plexus*.—**Phrenic veins**, tributaries of the inferior vena cava, accompanying the inferior phrenic arteries.

II. *n.* A mental disease; also, a medicine or remedy for such a disease. *Imp. Dict.*

phrenicocolic (fren″i-kō-kol′ik), *a.* Same as *phrenocolic.*

phrenicogastric (fren″i-kō-gas′trik), *a.* Same as *phrenogastric.*

phrenicosplenic (fren″i-kō-splen′ik), *a.* Same as *phrenosplenic.*

phrenics (fren′iks), *n.* [Pl. of *phrenic:* see *-ics.*] Mental philosophy; metaphysics. *R. Parke.* [Rare.]

phrenicus (fren′i-kus), *n.* [NL.: see *phrenic.*] Same as *diaphragm.*

phrenism (fren′izm), *n.* [< *phren* + *-ism.*] The power of one feeling to influence another; thought-force.

phrenitic (frē-nit′ik), *a.* [< *phrenitis* + *-ic.*] Affected with or characterized by phrenitis.

phrenitis (frē-nī′tis), *n.* [NL., < L. *phrenitis*, < Gr. φρενῖτις, inflammation of the brain, < φρήν, the diaphragm, heart, mind: see *phren.*] 1. In *med.*, an inflammation of the brain or its meninges, attended with acute fever and delirium.—2. Delirium; frenzy.

> *Phrenitis* . . . is a disease of the mind, with a continual madness or dotage, which hath an acute feaver annexed, or else an inflammation of the brain. . . . It differs from Melancholy and Madness. . . . Melancholy is most part silent, this clamorous. Burton, Anat. of Mel., i. 1.

phrenocolic (fren-ō-kol′ik), *a.* [< Gr. φρήν (φρεν-), diaphragm, + κόλον, colon: see *colic.*] Pertaining to the diaphragm and the colon.—**Phrenocolic ligament**, a narrow fold of the peritoneum connecting the splenic flexure of the colon with the diaphragm.

phrenogastric (fren-ō-gas′trik), *a.* [< Gr. φρήν (φρεν-), diaphragm, + γαστήρ (γαστρ-), stomach: see *gastric.*] Pertaining to the diaphragm and the stomach.—**Phrenogastric ligament**, a short fold of the peritoneum connecting the diaphragm with the fundus of the stomach.

phrenography (frē-nog′ra-fi), *n.* [< Gr. φρήν (φρεν-), diaphragm, + γράφειν, write.] The observing and descriptive stage of comparative psychology, or phrenology in sense 2. *Smithsonian Report*, 1881, p. 501.

phrenologer (frē-nol′ō-jėr), *n.* [< *phrenology* + *-er*[1].] A phrenologist.

phrenologic (fren-ō-loj′ik), *a.* [= F. *phrénologique* = Sp. *frenológico* = Pg. *phrenologico* = It. *frenologico*; as *phrenolog-y* + *-ic.*] Of or pertaining to phrenology.

phrenological (fren-ō-loj′i-kal), *a.* [< *phrenologic* + *-al.*] Same as *phrenologic.*

> A particularly short, fat, greasy-looking gentleman, with a head as free from *phrenological* development as a billiard-ball. C. Lever, Harry Lorrequer, xxvii.

phrenologically (fren-ō-loj′i-kal-i), *adv.* In a phrenological manner; according to the principles of phrenology; as regards phrenology.

phrenologist (frē-nol′ō-jist), *n.* [= F. *phrénologiste* = Pg. *phrenologista* = It. *frenologista*; as *phrenolog-y* + *-ist.*] One who is versed in phrenology.

phrenology (frē-nol′ō-ji), *n.* [= F. *phrénologie* = Sp. *frenologia* = Pg. *phrenologia* = It. *frenologia*, < Gr. φρήν (φρεν-), heart, mind, + -λογία, < λέγειν, speak: see *-ology.*] 1. The theory that the mental powers of the individual consist of independent faculties, each of which has its seat in a definite brain-region, whose size is commensurate with the power of manifesting this particular faculty. This theory, which originated at the close of the eighteenth century, assumes, moreover, as an essential part, the plasticity of the cranial envelop, by which the skull conforms externally, in the normal subject, to the shape and configuration of the brain within, so that its form and faculties may be determined, with sufficient exactness, from the skull itself, whether in the skeleton or in the living person. The different powers of the mind or faculties are divided into two classes, the feelings and the intellect, or the affective and intellectual faculties, the former of which is again divided into the propensities and sentiments, the latter into the perceptive and reflective faculties. Each of these groups, as well as each of the individual faculties composing them, is located upon the exterior of the skull with more or less exactness, and it is by the prominence or depression of the different regions that the mental powers and faculties are ascertained. The system was founded by Dr. Franz Joseph Gall (1758–1828), a Viennese physician, and was extended and promulgated by his pupil and associate, Dr. Spurzheim, and by George and Andrew Combe and others. The term is sometimes applied, in the phrase *new phrenology*, to the localization of cerebral functions which has been established by experimental and pathological investigations, almost exclusively of the last twenty years, and which has reached such a degree of certainty and definiteness as to furnish a basis for surgical operations on the brain. But there is nothing in common between modern cerebral localization and the views of Gall and Spurzheim. See cut in next column.
2. Comparative psychology; the study of the mind, intellect, or intelligence of man and the lower animals. *Smithsonian Report*, 1881, p. 501.

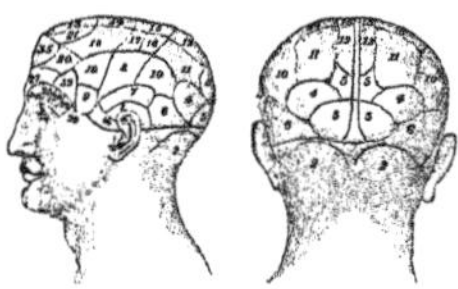

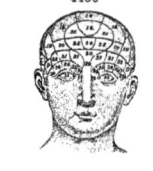

Spurzheim's Phrenological Chart of the Human Head.

AFFECTIVE FACULTIES.—I. *Propensities:* *, alimentiveness; 1, destructiveness; 2, amativeness; 3, philoprogenitiveness; 4, adhesiveness; 5, inhabitiveness; 6, combativeness; 7, secretiveness; 8, acquisitiveness; 9, constructiveness. II. *Sentiments:* 10, cautiousness; 11, approbativeness; 12, self-esteem; 13, benevolence; 14, reverence; 15, firmness; 16, conscientiousness; 17, hope; 18, marvelousness; 19, ideality; 20, mirthfulness; 21, imitation. INTELLECTUAL FACULTIES.—I. *Perceptive:* 22, individuality; 23, configuration; 24, size; 25, weight and resistance; 26, coloring; 27, locality; 28, order; 29, calculation; 30, eventuality; 31, time; 32, tune; 33, language. II. *Reflective:* 34, comparison; 35, causality.

phrenomagnetic (fren″ō-mag-net′ik), *a.* [< Gr. φρήν (φρεν-), mind, + E. *magnetic.*] Pertaining to phrenomagnetism: as, *phrenomagnetic* phenomena. *J. R. Buchanan.*

phrenomagnetism (fren-ō-mag′net-izm), *n.* [< Gr. φρήν (φρεν-), mind, + E. *magnetism.*] Animal magnetism, directed and controlled by will-power; pathetism.

> The simple physiological phænomena known as spirit-rapping, table-turning, *phreno-magnetism.* Huxley, Lay Sermons, p. 90.

phrenomesmerism (fren-ō-mez′mėr-izm), *n.* [< Gr. φρήν (φρεν-), mind, + E. *mesmerism.*] Same as *phrenomagnetism.*

phrenonomy (frē-non′ō-mi), *n.* [< Gr. φρήν (φρεν-), heart, mind, + νόμος, law.] The deductive and predictive stage of phrenology in sense 2. *Smithsonian Report*, 1881, p. 501.

phrenopathia (fren-ō-path′i-ä), *n.* [NL., < Gr. φρήν (φρεν-), mind, + πάθος, disease: see *pathos.*] Mental disease; insanity; psychopathia.

phrenopathic (fren-ō-path′ik), *a.* [< *phrenopathia* + *-ic.*] Of or pertaining to mental disease; psychopathic.

phrenoplegia (fren-ō-plē′ji-ä), *n.* [NL., < Gr. φρήν (φρεν-), mind, + πληγή, a blow, stroke, < πλήσσειν, strike.] Sudden loss of mental power.

phrenosis (frē-nō′sis), *n.* [NL., < Gr. φρήν (φρεν-), heart, mind, + *-osis.*] Psychosis.

phrenosplenic (fren-ō-splen′ik), *a.* Pertaining to the diaphragm and the spleen.—**Phrenosplenic ligament**, a short triangular fold of the peritoneum descending from the diaphragm to the upper end of the spleen.

phrensic† (fren′zik), *a.* [< *phrens-y* + *-ic.* Cf. *phrenetic, frantic.*] Phrenetic; mentally disordered; insane.

> Peace, and be nought! I think the woman be *phrensic.* B. *Jonson*, Tale of a Tub, ii. 1.

phrensy†, **phrenzy**†, *n.* and *v.* Obsolete forms of *frenzy.*

phrentic†, *a.* and *n.* An obsolete form of *frantic.*

phronesis (frō-nē′sis), *n.* [NL., < Gr. φρόνησις, practical wisdom, < φρονεῖν, think, < φρήν, mind: see *phren.*] Practical judgment; the faculty of conducting one's self wisely.

phrontisterion (fron-tis-tē′ri-on), *n.*; pl. *phrontisteria* (-ä). [Also *phrontistery*, < OF. *phrontistere*; < Gr. φροντιστήριον, a place for deep thinking, a "thinking-shop" (as Socrates's school was called by Aristophanes in "The Clouds"), later a school, a monastery, < φροντιστής, a deep thinker, < φροντίζειν, think, consider, meditate, take thought of, be anxious for, < φροντίς, thought, care, < φρονεῖν, think: see *phronesis.*] A school or seminary of learning; a college.

> His lodging! no; 'tis the learn'd *phrontisterion*
> Of most divine Albumazar.
> *T. Tomkis* (?), Albumazar, i. 3.

phrontistery (fron′tis-ter-i), *n.*; pl. *phrontisteries* (-iz). Same as *phrontisterion.*

> As to the scenery [in the old Greek comedies], he holds that the inside of the *phrontistery* is never seen. *Amer. Jour. Philol.*, IX. 344.

Phryganea (fri-gā′nē-ä), *n.* [NL., so called in allusion to the appearance of the cases of caddis-flies; < Gr. φρύγανον, a dry stick, < φρύγειν, roast.] The typical genus of the important neuropterous family *Phryganeidæ.* It formerly included all the caddis-flies then known, and was thus more nearly conterminous with the modern family and equal to the order or suborder *Trichoptera.* It is at present restricted to about 12 species, widely distributed in Europe, Asia, and North America, having rather slender wings with dense pubescence on the anterior pair, and an oblique transverse nervule between the costa and the subcosta.

Phryganeidæ (frig-a-nē′i-dē), *n. pl.* [NL., < *Phryganea* + *-idæ.*] A family of trichopterous neuropterous insects, typified by the genus *Phryganea*, to which different limits have been assigned; the caddis-flies. (*a*) Including all caddis-flies, and synonymous with the order *Trichoptera* or the family *Plicipennes.* (*b*) Restricted to those caddis-flies in which the maxillary palpi of the male are four-jointed, only slightly pubescent, and shaped alike in both sexes. This group contains the giants of the order *Trichoptera*, and occurs only in the northern hemisphere. The larvæ live in still waters and make cylindrical cases of bits of leaves and fibers spirally arranged. See cut under *caddis-worm.*

Phrygian (frij′i-an), *a.* and *n.* [= F. *Phrygien*, < L. *Phrygianus*, < *Phrygius*, < Gr. Φρύγιος, Phrygian, < Φρύξ (Φρυγ-), a Phrygian.] I. *a.* Pertaining to Phrygia, an ancient province or country in the interior of Asia Minor, or to the Phrygians.—**Phrygian cap.** See *cap.*—**Phrygian helmet**, a form of helmet suggesting the classical Phrygian cap. This form, which is very rare in medieval representations, is given to St. George, possibly with intention on the part of the artist to denote the Oriental origin of the saint.—**Phrygian marble.** See *marble*, 1.—**Phrygian mode.** See *mode*[1], 7.—**Phrygian work**, gold embroidery; orphrey-work. See *auriphrygia.*

II. *n.* 1. A native or an inhabitant of Phrygia.—2. In *eccles. hist.*, same as *Montanist.*

Phryma (frī′mä), *n.* [NL. (Linnæus, 1756), of unknown origin.] A genus of plants, of the gamopetalous order *Verbenaceæ*, constituting the tribe *Phrymeæ*, known by the uniformly one-celled ovary in a family characterized by two- or four-celled ovaries. The only species, *P. leptostachya*, is a plant widely diffused but nowhere abundant, native of North America, Japan, and the Himalayan region. It is an erect herb, with a few stiff straggling branches, opposite toothed leaves, and a long slender spike of small scattered purplish flowers, at first erect, then spreading, and in fruit reflexed, whence its popular name, *lopseed.* The fruit is a small, dry, short-stalked utricle, hooked at the apex, and adapted to distribution by catching in the hair of animals.

Phrymeæ (frī′mē-ē), *n. pl.* [NL. (Bentham and Hooker, 1876), < *Phryma* + *-eæ.*] A tribe of plants, of the order *Verbenaceæ*, consisting of the genus *Phryma*, characterized by the one-celled and one-ovuled ovary, erect orthotropous ovule, seed destitute of albumen, and reflexed radicle.

Phrynichus (frin′i-kus), *n.* [NL. (Karsch, 1880).] A genus of arachnids, of the family *Phrynidæ*, in which the tibiæ of the hind legs have no subjoints, the maxillary palpi are much longer than the body, which is slender and tubuliform, and the hand has four finger-like spines. The genus is represented in southern California.

Phrynida (frin′i-dä), *n. pl.* [NL., < *Phrynus* + *-ida.*] An order of pulmonate *Arachnida*: synonymous with *Thelyphonida.* See *Pedipalpi*[2].

Phrynidæ (frin′i-dē), *n. pl.* [NL., < *Phrynus* + *-idæ.*] A family of pulmonate *Arachnida* of the order *Phrynida* or *Thelyphonida*, typified by the genus *Phrynus.* The abdomen is flat, oval, and eleven-jointed; the postabdomen is a mere rudiment, like a button; the cephalothorax is flat, and covered with a horny carapace; the pedipalps are long, strong, six-jointed, and variously armed, but their terminal claw does not form a pincer; the first pair of legs are extremely long, slender, palpiform or even antenniform, and multiarticulate, the fifth and sixth joints being divided into ninety or more subjoints; and the eyes are eight in number, two in the central anterior region, and a cluster of three on each side. The species resemble spiders with (apparently) long feelers and a pair of great claws. They are readily distinguished from the only other family (*Thelyphonidæ*) of this order by not having a long tail like a scorpion. They are nocturnal and sluggish, and live under stones and logs. Compare also cut under *Pedipalpi.*

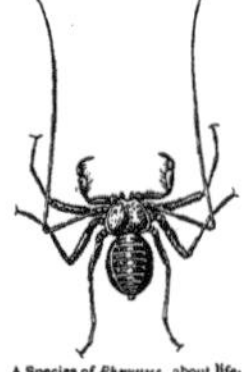

A Species of *Phrynus*, about life-size.

Phrynorhombus (fri-nọ-rom'bus), *n.* [NL. (Günther, 1862), < Gr. φρῦνος, a toad, + ῥόμβος, a turbot.] A genus of flatfishes of the family *Pleuronectidæ*, having no vomerine teeth. *P. unimaculatus* is known as the *topknot*.

Phrynosoma (fri-nọ-sō'mạ̈), *n.* [NL., < Gr. φρῦνος, a toad, + σῶμα, body.] A genus of lizards of the family *Iguanidæ*, including the curious creatures known as *horned toads* or *horned frogs*, as *P. cornutum*, *P. orbiculare*, *P. douglasi*, etc. Some of them are very abundant in most parts of the western and southwestern United States and southward. Some attain a length of six inches, but they are usually small. The body is very flat, and more or less orbicular, with a short tail tapering from a stout base, and shorter legs than

Horned Frog (*Phrynosoma cornutum*).

is usual in related lizards. The head is surmounted with several pairs of stout spines, largest in some of the southerly and Mexican forms, and the whole upper surface of the body is roughly granular or tuberculous; the under side is smooth. The coloration of the upper parts is variegated with black, brown, gray, and reddish, in a blotched pattern, and varies greatly, not only with the different species, but in different individuals of the same kind. The creatures have nothing of the agility of most lizards; they are clumsy in their motions, rather sluggish, and cannot jump. They are perfectly harmless, become tame as soon as handled, and are often kept as pets for their oddity. They feed on flies and other insects, but can fast long, and may be safely sent by mail alive to any part of the United States. They bring forth alive. One species (*P. douglasi*) occurs as far north at least as the British boundary of the United States.

Phrynus (fri'nus), *n.* [NL. (Olivier, 1793), < Gr. φρῦνος, a toad.] The typical genus of the family *Phrynidæ*. See cut under *Phrynidæ*.

Phryxis (frik'sis), *n.* [NL. (Cope, 1872).] A genus of cave-dwelling arachnidans, containing

Phryxis longipes. (Line shows natural size.)

ing such forms as *P. longipes* of the Wyandotte cave in Indiana: now considered synonymous with *Phalangodes*.

Phthartolatræ (thär-tol'ạ-trē), *n. pl.* [NL., < LGr. Φθαρτολάτρης (one of the sect noted in def.), < φθαρτός, corruptible, + λατρεύειν, worship: see *latria*.] A sect of the sixth century: same as *Corrupticolæ*.

phthiriasis (thi-rī'ạ-sis), *n.* [= F. *phthiriase*, *phthiriasis* = Sp. *tiriasis*, < L. *phthiriasis*, < Gr. φθειρίασις, the lousy disease, < φθειριᾶν, have lice or the lousy disease, < φθείρ, a louse.] The presence of lice on the body, with the irritation produced thereby and its effects; the lousy disease, formerly called *morbus pediculosus*.

Phthiriomyiæ (thir"i-ọ-mī'i-ē), *n. pl.* [NL., < Gr. φθείρ, a louse, + μυῖα, a fly.] A division of pupiparous *Diptera*, consisting of the family *Nycteribiidæ*, parasitic upon bats.

Phthirius (thir'i-us), *n.* [NL. (W. E. Leach, 1815), < Gr. φθείρ, a louse.] A genus of *Pediculidæ* or true lice, having the body broad and flat, and the two hinder pairs of legs very much thickened; the crab-lice (so called from their appearance). *P. pubis* or *inguinalis* is found on the hair of the genitals, groin, and perineum, and occasionally on other parts of the body. See cut under *crab-louse*.

phthisic (tiz'ik), *a.* and *n.* [L *a.* (and II. *n.*, 2). Formerly also *phthisick*, *ptisike*; = OF. *tisique*, *tesike*, F. *phthisique*, now *phtisique* = Sp. *tísico* = Pg. *tisico* = It. *tisico*, *ftisico*, < L. *phthisicus*, ML. *ptisicus*, *tisicus*, < Gr. φθισικός, consumptive, < φθίσις, consumption: see *phthisis*. II. *n.* 1. Formerly also *phthisick*, *tisick*, *tissick*, *tizzick*, *tysyke*, *tizic*; < ME. *tisike*, < OF. *tisique*, F. *phtisique* = Sp. *tísica* = Pg. *tisica*, *phthisica* = It. *tisica*, consumption, < L. *phthisica*, fem. of *phthisicus*, < Gr. φθισικός, consumptive: see I.] I. *a.* Same as *phthisical*.

II. *n.* 1. A consumption or wasting away; phthisis.—2. A person affected with phthisis.

> Liberty of speaking, then which nothing is more sweet to man, was girded and straight lac't almost to a broken-winded *tizzick*. *Milton*, On Def. of Humb. Remonst.

phthisical (tiz'i-kạl), *a.* [Formerly *ptisical*, *ptizical*; < *phthisic* + *-al*.] Of or belonging to phthisis; affected by phthisis; wasting the flesh: as, a *phthisical* consumption.

> He . . . sobs me out half a dozen *ptizical* mottos wherever he had them, hopping short in the measure of convulsion-fits. *Milton*, Apology for Smectymnuus, § 3.

phthisicky (tiz'i-ki), *a.* [< *phthisic(k)* + *-y*[1].] Phthisical.

> *Phthisicky* old gentlewomen and frolicsome young ones. *Colman*, The Spleen, i.

phthisiology (tiz-i-ol'ō-ji), *n.* [= F. *phthisiologie*, < Gr. φθίσις, phthisis, + -λογία, < λέγειν, speak: see *-ology*.] The sum of scientific knowledge concerning phthisis.

phthisipneumonia (thiz"ip-nū-mō'ni-ạ̈), *n.* [NL., < Gr. φθίσις, consumption (see *phthisis*), + πνεύμων, lungs: see *pneumonia*.] In *pathol.*, phthisis.

phthisis (thī'sis), *n.* [= F. *phthisie* = Sp. *tisis* = Pg. *phthisis* = It. *tisi*, *ftisi*, *ftisia*, < L. *phthisis*, < Gr. φθίσις, a wasting away, consumption, wane, decline, decay, < φθίειν, waste away, decline, wither, wane, decay.] A disease of the lungs, characterized by progressive consolidation of pulmonary tissue, with breaking down and the formation of cavities. This is so extensively, if not exclusively, pulmonary tuberculosis that the two names are often considered as equivalent. Also called *consumption*.—**Fibroid phthisis**, slow-going phthisis, with considerable production of connective tissue.—**Grinders' phthisis.** Same as *grinders' asthma* (which see, under *grinder*).—**Phthisis florida**, very rapid phthisis; galloping consumption.

phthisozoics (thī-zọ-zō'iks), *n.* [< Gr. φθίειν (φθισ-), consume, destroy, + ζῷον, an animal.] See the quotation.

> [*Phthisozoics.*] From two Greek words: one of which signifies to destroy; the other, an animal . . . :—the art of destroying such of the inferior animals as, in the character of natural enemies, threaten destruction or damage—to himself, or to such animals from which, in the character of natural servants or allies, it is in man's power to extract useful service. *Bentham*, Chrestomathia, note to table I. § 82.

phthongometer (thong-gom'e-tėr), *n.* [NL., < Gr. φθόγγος, the voice, a sound (see *diphthong*), + μέτρον, measure.] An instrument used for measuring vocal sounds. *Whewell.* (*Imp. Dict.*)

phulkari (fụl'kạ-ri), *n.* [Hind. *phūlkari*, a tissued flower on cloth, etc., also an alkaline efflorescence used to adulterate salt, < *phūl*, a flower, + *-kār*, a suffix of agent.] A kind of flower embroidery done by the natives of the Panjāb in India; also, a cloth so embroidered.

phulwara (fụl-wä'rạ̈), *n.* [E. Ind.] Same as *fulwa*.

phy† (fī), *interj.* An obsolete spelling of *fie*[1].

> But, *phy* for shame, when shal we cease this geare?
> I to defie, and you to fly for feare?
> *Sylvester*, tr. of Du Bartas's Weeks, ii., The Trophies.

Phycidæ† (fis'i-dē), *n. pl.* [NL., < *Phycis* + *-idæ*.] A family of pyralid moths, typified by the genus *Phycis*: now called *Phycitidæ*.

Phycinæ (fi-sī'nē), *n. pl.* [NL., < *Phycis* + *-inæ*.] A subfamily of gadoid fishes, named by Swainson in 1839 from the genus *Phycis*; codlings. Two species are known in the United States as *squirrel-hakes*.

Phycis (fī'sis), *n.* [NL. (Artedi, 1738), < Gr. φυκίς, f., φύκης, m., a fish living in seaweed, < φῦκος, seaweed.] 1. In *ichth.*, a genus of gadoid fishes, typical of the subfamily *Phycinæ*, having a ray of the first dorsal more or less elongated and filamentous; squirrel-hakes. *P. chuss* and *P.*

Squirrel-hake (*Phycis chuss*).

tenuis, together with a third species, *P. chesteri*, are found along the Atlantic coast of the United States. They are also known as *codlings*, and *P. tenuis* sometimes as *silver hake*. They are quite different from the fishes more properly called *hake* (which see).

2†. In *entom.*, a genus of pyralid moths, erected by Fabricius in 1798, and giving name to the *Phycidæ* or *Phycitidæ*. The name was changed by Curtis in 1828 to *Phycita*, on account of its preoccupation in ichthyology. See *leaf-crumpler*.

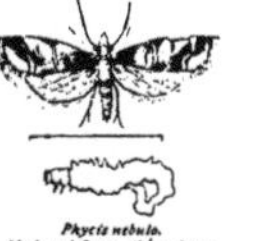

Phycis nebulo. Moth and Case. (Line shows natural size of moth.)

Phycita (fis'i-tạ̈), *n.* [NL. (Curtis, 1828), < Gr. φῦκος, seaweed, fucus: see *fucus*.] The typical genus of *Phycitidæ*, having ciliate antennæ: same as *Phycis*, 2.

Phycitidæ (fi-sit'i-dē), *n. pl.* [NL., < *Phycita* + *-idæ*.] A family of pyralid moths, named from the genus *Phycita*. The maxillary palps are equal in the two sexes; the labial palps are concealed or wanting; the fore wings have eleven, ten, or nine veins, the first one not forked; the hind wings have the middle cell closed and the midrib hairy at the base. It is a large and wide-spread group, whose members differ in habits, some being leaf-crumplers or leaf-folders, others borers, and others carnivorous. Formerly *Phycidæ*.

Phycochromaceæ (fī"kọ-krọ-mā'sẹ-ē), *n. pl.* [NL., < Gr. φῦκος, seaweed, + χρῶμα, color, + *-aceæ*.] Same as *Cryptophyceæ*.

phycochromaceous (fī"kọ-krọ-mā'shius), *a.* Resembling or belonging to the order *Phycochromaceæ*.

phycochrome (fī'kọ-krōm), *n.* [< Gr. φῦκος, seaweed, + χρῶμα, color.] The bluish-green coloring matter of some algæ, a mixture of chlorophyl and phycocyanin.

Phycochromophyceæ (fī"kọ-krō-mọ-fī'sẹ-ē), *n. pl.* [NL., < Gr. φῦκος, seaweed, + χρῶμα, color, + φῦκος, seaweed, + *-eæ*.] An order of *Algæ*: same as *Cryptophyceæ*.

phycocyan (fī-kọ-sī'an), *n.* [< Gr. φῦκος, seaweed, + κυανός, blue.] Same as *phycocyanin*.

phycocyanin, phycocyanine (fī-kọ-sī'ạ-nin), *n.* [< Gr. φῦκος, seaweed, + κυανός, blue, + *-in*[2], *-ine*[2] (cf. *cyanine*).] A blue coloring matter which is present, in addition to chlorophyl, in the cells of certain algæ, and imparts to them a bluish-green color, as in the *Cyanophyceæ* or *Phycochromaceæ*. It is soluble in water, but insoluble in alcohol or ether.

phyco-erythrin (fī"kō-e-rith'rin), *n.* [NL., < Gr. φῦκος, seaweed, + ἐρυθρός, red.] A red coloring matter to which the red seaweeds or *Florideæ* owe their peculiar coloring, which is present, in addition to chlorophyl, in the cells. It is soluble in water.

phycography (fī-kog'rạ-fi), *n.* [< Gr. φῦκος, a seaweed, + -γραφία, < γράφειν, write.] A scientific or systematic description of algæ or seaweeds.

phycologist (fī-kol'ọ-jist), *n.* [< *phycolog-y* + *-ist*.] One who is skilled in phycology; one who studies algæ or seaweeds; an algologist.

phycology (fī-kol'ō-ji), *n.* [= F. *phycologie*, < Gr. φῦκος, seaweed, + -λογία, < λέγειν, speak: see *-ology*.] That department of botanical science which treats of algæ or seaweeds; algology. [Rare.]

phycomater (fī-kọ-mā'tėr), *n.* [NL., < Gr. φῦκος, seaweed, + μήτηρ, Doric μάτηρ = L. *mater*, mother.] The gelatin in which the sporules of algaceous plants first vegetate.

Phycomyces (fī-kom'i-sēz), *n.* [NL. (Kunze), < Gr. φῦκος, seaweed, + μύκης, a fungus.] A genus of phycomycetous fungi of the family *Mucoraceæ*. The spore-bearing hyphæ are erect, not branching, the sporangia spheroid or pyriform, and the spores ovoid or spheroidal and hyaline. Three species are known, of which *P. nitens* is very common, growing on greasy substances, as old bones and oil-casks.

Phycomyceteæ (fī"kọ-mī-sē'tẹ-ē), *n. pl.* [NL. (De Bary), < *Phycomyces* (*-et-*) + *-eæ*.] A division of fungi, named from the genus *Phycomyces* and embracing the families *Mucoreæ*, *Peronosporaceæ*, *Saprolegniaceæ*, *Entomophthoreæ*, *Chytridiaceæ*, and *Protomycetaceæ*. They are mostly parasitic on plants or animals; a few are saprophytic. See the above families or orders for special characterization and illustration.

Phycomycetes (fī-kọ-mī-sē'tēz), *n. pl.* [NL., pl. of *phycomyces*.] Same as *Phycomyceteæ*.

phycomycetous (fī-kọ-mī-sē'tus), *a.* Belonging to the *Phycomyceteæ*: as, *phycomycetous* fungi.

phycophæin (fī-kō-fē'in), *n.* [NL., < Gr. φῦκος, seaweed, + φαιός, dusky, dun.] A reddish-brown coloring matter present in the cells of certain seaweeds. By Schütt it is limited to that part of the compound pigment of the *Fucaceæ* and *Phæosporeæ* which is soluble in water.

phycoxanthin, phycoxanthine (fī-kok-san'thin), *n.* [< Gr. φῦκος, seaweed, + ξανθός, yellow, + *-in*[2], *-ine*[2] (cf. *xanthin*).] A yellow coloring matter: same as *diatomin*.

phygogalactic (fī'gō-ga-lak'tik), *a.* and *n.* [< Gr. φυγεῖν, φεύγειν, shun, avoid, + γάλα (γαλακτ-), milk.] I. *a.* Preventing the formation of milk and promoting the reabsorption of what has been already secreted.

II. *n.* An agent having these qualities.

phyla, *n.* Plural of *phylum*.

phylacter† (fi-lak'tėr), *n.* [< F. *phylactère*: see *phylactery*.] A phylactery. *Sandys.*

phylactered (fi-lak'tėrd), *a.* [< *phylacter-y* + *-ed*².] Wearing a phylactery; hence (because the wearing of phylacteries was assumed to be a sign of bigotry and of a desired separation from the body of worshipers), narrow-minded; bigoted; pharisaical.

> Who for the spirit hug the spleen,
> *Phylacter'd* throughout all their mien;
> Who their ill-tasted home-brewed prayer
> To the State's mellow forms prefer.
> *M. Green*, The Spleen.

phylacteria, *n.* Plural of *phylacterium*.

phylacteric (fil-ak-ter'ik), *a.* [= Sp. *filacterico* = Pg. *phylacterico*; as *phylacter-y* + *-ic*.] Of or pertaining to the phylactery; accompanied by the assumption of the phylactery.

phylacterical (fil-ak-ter'i-kal), *a.* [< *phylacteric* + *-al*.] Same as *phylacteric*. *L. Addison*, Christian Sacrifice, p. 128.

phylacterium (fil-ak-tē'ri-um), *n.*; pl. *phylacteria* (-ä). [NL.: see *phylactery*.] A portable reliquary. See *phylactery*.

Phylacterium found at St. Dunstan's, Fleet Street, London. (From "Archæological Journal.")

phylactery (fi-lak'te-ri), *n.*; pl. *phylacteries* (-riz). [Now written according to the L. spelling; formerly *philactery*, ME. *philaterie*, earlier *filaterie*, < OF. *filaterie*, *philaterie*, also *filatiere*, *philatiere*, later *phylacterie*, *phylactere*, F. *phylactère* = Sp. *filacteria* = Pg. *phylacteria* = It. *filateria*; < LL. *phylacterium*, *fylacterium*, a phylactery, < Gr. φυλακτήριον, a post for watchmen, or a garrison, a fort, castle, outpost, also safeguard, preservative, esp. an amulet (whence the Jewish use), < φυλακτήρ, a guard, < φυλάσσειν, watch, guard.] A charm or amulet.

> And Fathers, Councils, Church, and Church's head
> Were on her reverend *phylacteries* read.
> *Dryden*, Hind and Panther, i. 399.

> Happy are they who verify their amulets, and make their *phylacteries* speak in their lives and actions.
> *Sir T. Browne*, Christ. Mor., iii. 10.

Specifically—(*a*) In *Jewish antiq.*, an amulet consisting of a strip or strips of parchment inscribed with certain texts from the Old Testament, and inclosed within a small leather case, which was fastened with straps on the forehead just above and between the eyes, or on the left arm near the region of the heart. The four passages inscribed upon the phylactery were Ex. xiii. 2–10, 11–17, and Deut. vi. 4–9, 13–22. The custom was founded on a literal interpretation of Ex. xiii. 16, and Deut. vi. 8 and xi. 18.

> He which hath his *Phylacteries* on his head and armes, and his knots on his garment, and his Schedule on his doore, is so fenced that he cannot easily sinne.
> *Purchas*, Pilgrimage, p. 186.

(*b*) Among the primitive Christians, etc., a case in which were inclosed relics of the saints. = **Syn.** (*a*) See defs. of *amulet*, *talisman*, and *mezuzah*.

Phylactolæmata (fi-lak-tō-lē'ma-tä), *n. pl.* [NL., < Gr. φυλακτός, verbal adj. of φυλάσσειν, guard, + λαιμός, throat.] A subclass or order of *Polyzoa*, containing those whose lophophore is bilateral, crescentic, or hippocrepiform, provided with a circlet of tentacles, and defended by an epistoma. These polyzoans are larger, softer, and more homogeneous than the *Gymnolæmata*, and are specially characteristic of fresh water. The families *Plumatellidæ* and *Cristatellidæ* are characteristic components of the group. Also called *Lophopoda* and *Hippocrepia*. See cut under *Polyzoa*.

phylactolæmatous (fi-lak-tō-lē'ma-tus), *a.* Pertaining to the *Phylactolæmata*, or having their characters.

phylæ, *n.* Plural of *phyle*.

phylarch (fī'lärk), *n.* [= F. *phylarque*, < L. *phylarchus*, < Gr. φύλαρχος, chief of a tribe, < φυλή, a tribe (see *phyle*), + ἄρχειν, rule.] In ancient Greece, the chief or head of a tribe; in Athens, the commander of the cavalry of a tribe, the ten phylarchs being under the orders of the two state hipparchs, the commanders-in-chief of the cavalry.

phylarchy (fī'lär-ki), *n.*; pl. *phylarchies* (-kiz). [= F. *phylarchie*, < Gr. φυλαρχία, the office of phylarch, < φύλαρχος, a phylarch: see *phylarch*.] In ancient Greece, the headship of a tribe or clan; the office or authority of a phylarch.

phyle (fī'lē), *n.*; pl. *phylæ* (-lē). [NL., < Gr. φυλή, a body of men joined by ties of birth, a tribe, clan, class, phyle (cf. φῦλον, a tribe: see *phylum*), < φύειν, produce, φύεσθαι, grow: see *be*¹.] In ancient Greece, a tribe or clan; one of the subdivisions normally based on ties of blood, of which the aggregate constituted a community. In Athens the tribes did not rest on family relationship, but were at first geographical divisions, then classes formed according to occupation or wealth. Clisthenes abolished the old tribes, and distributed his fellow-citizens among ten new ones, named after ancient Attic heroes, and arranged upon geographical lines and democratic ideas; and this arrangement persisted through the glorious time of Attic history. Every full citizen of Athens was registered in a phyle, in a deme, and in a phratry. Every phyle was a political unit, to which were allotted the choice of 50 of the 500 senators and that of its due proportion of dicasts and of the higher civil and military officers of the state; and every phyle was required to contribute in a fixed proportion to the military service, to the various liturgies, etc.

phyletic (fi-let'ik), *a.* [< Gr. φυλετικός, < φυλέτης, a tribesman, < φυλή, a tribe: see *phyle*.] 1. Pertaining to a race or tribe. Hence—2. In *biol.*, pertaining to a phylum of the animal kingdom, or to the construction of phyla; phylogenetic.

Phyllactinia (fil-ak-tin'i-ä), *n.* [NL. (Léveillé), < Gr. φύλλον, leaf (see *phyllary*), + ἀκτίς (ἀκτιν-), ray.] A genus of pyrenomycetous fungi of the family *Erysipheæ*. Each perithecium contains several asci, and the appendages are needle-shaped and abruptly swollen at the base. The only well-known species is *P. suffulta*, which grows upon the leaves of a great variety of plants, especially woody plants.

phyllade (fil'äd), *n.* [< Gr. φυλλάς (φυλλαδ-), a bunch of leaves, < φύλλον = L. *folium*, leaf.] In *bot.*, one of the small imperfect leaves in *Isoëtes*, alternating with the fertile leaves. In the submerged species these consist of a small lamina with no sheath, and in the terrestrial species they are reduced to mere scales.

Phyllantheæ (fi-lan'thē-ē), *n. pl.* [NL. (Bartling, 1830), < *Phyllanthus* + *-eæ*.] A tribe of plants of the order *Euphorbiaceæ*, distinguished by carpels with two contiguous ovules in the central angle, and the seed-leaves much broader than the radicle. It includes 54 genera, mainly tropical, of which *Phyllanthus* is the type. For other principal genera, see *Putranjiva* and *Toxicodendron*.

Phyllanthus (fi-lan'thus), *n.* [NL. (Linnæus, 1737), so called from species with flowers seated on leaf-like flattened branches; < Gr. φύλλον, a leaf, + ἄνθος, flower (cf. L. *phyllanthes*, < Gr. φυλλανθές, a plant with prickly leaves, prob. scabious).] A large genus of plants, of the order *Euphorbiaceæ*, type of the tribe *Phyllantheæ*, characterized by the entire alternate leaves and apetalous monœcious flowers, the male in glomerate clusters and with from two to six stamens, and by the pistil consisting of from three to many carpels, their two-cleft styles not dilated below the apex. There are about 450 species, very widely dispersed throughout the warmer parts of the world, rarer in temperate climates. They are either herbs, shrubs, or trees, of great variety in appearance. The leaves are generally two-ranked, and so arranged as to make the branches resemble pinnate leaves. The small greenish flowers are axillary or at the nodes of leafless and often flattened branches, and are often tinged with yellow or purple. Several species are in medicinal repute as diuretics in India, as *P. Niruri* and *P. urinaria*. The bruised leaves of *P. Gonami* are there used to stupefy fish. (Compare *Piscidia*.) Many species are cultivated under the name *leaf-flower*, from the blooming leaf-like branches, or cladodia. (See cut under *cladode*.) The snow-bush, cultivated for its white flowers, is *P. nivalis*, native of the New Hebrides. Many others are cultivated as ornamental evergreen shrubs under the names of *Emblica* and *Xylophylla*, the latter a numerous group of woody-branched shrubs with orange-red flowers, chiefly from the West Indies. For other species, see *Otaheite gooseberry* (under *gooseberry*), *seaside laurel* (under *laurel*, 3), and *emblic myrobalan* (under *myrobalan*). The last produces an edible fruit, used for preserves and in dyeing and tanning, and long famed as an astringent medicine (but not now so used), and a durable wood, used for implements, building, and furniture in India and Burma. The so-called Otaheite gooseberry is also known as star-gooseberry.

phyllary (fil'a-ri), *n.*; pl. *phyllaries* (-riz). [< NL. *phyllarium*, < Gr. φυλλάριον, a leaflet, dim. of φύλλον = L. *folium*, a leaf: see *foil*¹.] In *bot.*, one of the leaflets forming the involucre of composite flowers.

phyllidia, *n.* Plural of *phyllidium*.

Phyllidiobranchiata (fi-lid"i-ō-brang-ki-ā'tä), *n. pl.* [NL., < *phyllidium* + L. *branchiæ*, gills: see *branchiate*.] A suborder of palliate or tectibranchiate opisthobranchiate gastropods, in which the ctenidia are replaced by lateral lamellar functional gills. It contains the limpets only. See *Patellidæ*.

phyllidiobranchiate (fi-lid"i-ō-brang'ki-āt), *a.* Pertaining to the *Phyllidiobranchiata*, or having their characters, as a limpet.

phyllidium (fi-lid'i-um), *n.*; pl. *phyllidia* (-ä). [NL., < Gr. φύλλον, leaf, + dim. suffix -ίδιον.] One of the rudimentary ctenidia of the phyllidiobranchiate gastropods, as limpets, called by Lankester *capitopedal bodies*.

Phyllirhoë (fi-lir'ō-ē), *n.* [NL., prop. *Phyllorrhoë, < Gr. φυλλορρόος, shedding leaves, φυλλοροεῖν, shed leaves, < φύλλον, leaf, + ῥόη, flow, < ῥεῖν, flow.] 1. The typical genus of *Phyllirhoidæ*. *P. bucephalus*, the best-known species, is a highly phosphorescent oceanic organism, bearing little resemblance to a mollusk. It is thin and translucent, without gills, shell, or foot, ending in a rounded tail-like fin with which it swims like a fish, and bearing upon the head a pair of long tentacles. Also *Phyllirhoa* and *Phyllirrhæ*.

Phyllirhoë bucephalus.

2. [*l. c.*] A member of this genus.

phyllirhoid (fil'i-roid), *a.* and *n.* I. *a.* Pertaining to the *Phyllirhoidæ*, or having their characters.

II. *n.* A member of the *Phyllirhoidæ*.

Phyllirhoidæ (fil-i-rō'i-dē), *n. pl.* [NL., < *Phyllirhoë* + *-idæ*.] A family of nudibranchiate gastropods, typified by the genus *Phyllirhoë*. These singularly degenerate and simple mollusks have no ctenidia, cerata, mantle-skirt, or other processes of the body-wall, even the foot being aborted. The intestine ends on the right side, and the head has two long tentacles. They are now sometimes ranked with *Polybranchiata* in a distinct section called *Abranchia*, but were formerly referred to the pteropods, the heteropods, and even the tunicates. Also called *ocean slugs* and *Psilosomata*.

phyllis¹ (fil'is), *n.* [< L. *Phyllis* (Virgil, Horace), < Gr. Φυλλίς, a fem. name: so called in allusion to Phyllis as the name in old plays and romances and pastoral poems of a country girl, or shepherdess, or sweetheart. Cf. *philander*.] A country girl; a shepherdess; a sweetheart: a common name for such in old romances, pastoral poems, etc.

phyllis¹ (fil'is), *v. t.* [< *phyllis*¹, *n.* Cf. *philander*, *v.*] To address or celebrate in amatory verses. [Rare.]

> He passed his easy hours, instead of prayer,
> In madrigals and *phillysing* the fair.
> *Garth*, Dispensary, i.

Phyllis² (fil'is), *n.* [NL. (Linnæus, 1737), so called from the handsome green leaves and their ornamental venation; < L. *phyllis*, an almond-tree, < Gr. φυλλίς, foliage, < φύλλον, a leaf.] A genus of undershrubs of the gamopetalous order *Rubiaceæ* and the tribe *Anthospermeæ*, characterized by stamens inserted on the base of the corolla, and fruit consisting of two pyriform indehiscent carpels. The only species is a native of the Canaries and the island of Madeira. It bears opposite or whorled, broadly lanceolate leaves, stipules united with the petioles into a sheath, and numerous minute whitish flowers in panicles, with thread-like erect stems, nodding in fruit. It is cultivated as a hardy evergreen, sometimes under the name of *bastard hare's-ear* (which see, under *hare's-ear*).

phyllite (fil'īt), *n.* [= F. *phyllithe* (for *phyllite) = Pg. *phyllite* = It. *fillite*, < Gr. φυλλίτης, of or belonging to leaves, < φύλλον, leaf: see *phyllary*.] One of the names given to clay-slate or argillaceous schist. It was introduced by Naumann as a substitute for the *phyllade* of D'Aubuisson. It is little used by authors writing in English. By some later lithologists *phyllite* has been used as the equivalent of *ottrelite-slate*, a schistose rock containing fine lamellæ of the mineral ottrelite.

Phyllites (fi-lī'tēz), *n.* [NL.: see *phyllite*.] A name under which a great variety of fossil leaves have been placed, in regard to whose affinities nothing definite was known.

phyllitic (fi-lit'ik), *a.* [< *phyllite* + *-ic*.] Having the characters of phyllite, or composed of that rock.

> Generally the slates are schistose, *phyllitic*, and chiastolitic.
> *Nature*, XXXIX. 31.

Phyllium (fil'i-um), *n.* [NL., < Gr. φύλλιον, dim. of φύλλον, a leaf: see *phyllary*.] A genus of orthopterous insects belonging to the family *Phasmidæ*, and popularly known by the

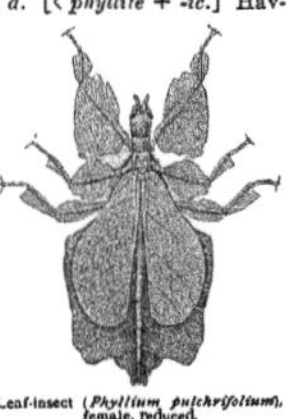

Leaf-insect (*Phyllium pulchrifolium*), female, reduced.

name of *leaf-insects* or *walking-leaves*. Some of them have wing-covers so closely resembling the leaves of plants that they are easily mistaken for the vegetable productions around them. The eggs, too, bear a curious resemblance to the seeds of plants. They are for the most part natives of the East Indies, Australia, and South America. The males have long antennæ and wings, and can fly; the females have short antennæ, and are incapable of flight.

phyllobranchia[1] (fil-ǫ-brang'ki-ạ̈), *n.*; pl. *phyllobranchiæ* (-ē). [< Gr. φύλλον, leaf, + βράγχια (L. *branchiæ*, sing. *branchia*), gills: see *branchiæ*.] One of the lamellar or foliaceous gills of crustaceans.

In the prawns and shrimps, in Gebia and Callianassa, in all the Anomura and Brachyura, the gills are *phyllobranchiæ*. *Huxley*, Proc. Zoöl. Soc., 1878, p. 777.

Phyllobranchia[2] (fil-ǫ-brang'ki-ạ̈), *n. pl.* [NL., < Gr. φύλλον, leaf, + βράγχια, gills: see *branchiæ*.] A division of crustaceans, containing those decapods which are phyllobranchiate.

phyllobranchial (fil-ǫ-brang'ki-ạl), *a.* [< *phyllobranchia*[2] + *-al*.] Lamellar or foliaceous, as gills; of or pertaining to phyllobranchiæ.

phyllobranchiate (fil-ō-brang'ki-āt), *a.* [< *phyllobranchia*[2] + *-ate*[1].] Having phyllobranchiæ, as a crab.

phylloclade (fil'ǫ-klād), *n.* Same as *phyllocladium*.

phyllocladium (fil-ǫ-klā'di-um), *n.*; pl. *phyllocladia* (-ạ̈). [NL., < Gr. φύλλον, leaf, + κλάδος, branch.] In *bot.*, a stem or branch which assumes the functions of foliage. The broad, succulent stems of the *Cactaceæ* are familiar examples.

phyllocyanin (fil-ǫ-si'a-nin), *n.* [< Gr. φύλλον, leaf, + κύανος, blue: see *cyanine*.] See *chlorophyl*.

phyllocyst (fil'ǫ-sist), *n.* [< Gr. φύλλον, leaf, + κύστις, bladder: see *cyst*.] A cyst or cavity in the hydrophyllium of certain oceanic hydrozoans. See cut under *diphyzoöid*.

phyllocystic (fil-ǫ-sis'tik), *a.* [< *phyllocyst* + *-ic*.] Pertaining to or having the character of a phyllocyst.

phyllode (fil'ōd), *n.* [= F. *phyllode*, < NL. *phyllodium*: see *phyllodium*.] Same as *phyllodium*.

phyllodia, *n.* Plural of *phyllodium*.

phyllodineous (fil-ǫ-din'ę-us), *a.* [< *phyllodium* + *-in* + *-eous*.] In *bot.*, resembling or belonging to a phyllodium.

phyllodiniation (fil-ǫ-din-i-ā'shǫn), *n.* [< *phyllodineous* + *-i-ation*.] In *bot.*, the state of being phyllodineous; the formation of twig-like parts instead of true leaves. *R. Brown.*

phyllodium (fi-lō'di-um), *n.*; pl. *phyllodia* (-ạ̈). [NL., < Gr. φυλλώδης, like leaves, rich in leaves, < φύλλον, leaf, + εἶδος, form.] In *bot.*, a petiole which usurps the form and function of a leaf-blade, as in many species of *Acacia*. It has usually been further distinguished from a true blade by the statement that it normally presents the edges instead of the faces to the earth and sky; but recent investigation proves that this does not always hold good, since some undoubted phyllodia are not vertical, but are dorsiventrally placed, like true leaves. The South American *Oxalis bupleurifolia* is an example. Also *phyllode*. See also cut under *petiole*.

Phyllodium (*a*) of *Acacia heterophylla*.

Phyllodoce (fi-lod'ǫ-sē), *n.* [NL. (Brown, 1756), < L. *Phyllodoce*, a sea-nymph, daughter of Nereus and Doris; no corresponding Gr. form appears.] 1. A genus of oceanic hydrozoans of the family *Physophoridæ*. Also *Phyllidoce*. *Lesson*, 1843.—2. The typical genus of *Phyllodocidæ*. *P. viridis* is the palolo, also, however, placed in the genus *Lysidice*, and now in *Palolo*.

Phyllodocidæ (fi-ǫ-dos'i-dē), *n. pl.* [NL., < *Phyllodoce* + *-idæ*.] A family of polychætous annelids, having the parapodia modified as swimming-plates by a widening of the ends of the separated or fused parapodia, or of their cirri: typified by the genus *Phyllodoce*. They are known as *leaf-bearing worms*.

phyllody (fil'ǫ-di), *n.* [< Gr. φυλλώδης, like leaves: see *phyllodium*.] In *bot.*, the condition in which true leaves are substituted for some other organ—that is, in which other organs are metamorphosed into green leaves. This condition may occasionally occur in bracts, the calyx, corolla, ovules, pistils, and stamens. Called *frondescence* by Engelmann, and *phyllomorphy* by Morren.

phyllogen (fil'ǫ-jen), *n.* [< Gr. φύλλον, leaf, + -γενής, producing: see *-gen*.] Same as *phyllophore*.

phyllogenous (fi-loj'e-nus), *a.* [< Gr. φύλλον, leaf, + -γενής, producing: see *-genous*.] Growing upon leaves. *Thomas*, Med. Dict.

Phylloglossum (fil-ǫ-glos'um), *n.* [NL. (Kunze, 1843), < Gr. φύλλον, leaf, + γλῶσσα, tongue.] A peculiar monotypic genus of plants of the natural order *Lycopodiaceæ*. They are acaulescent plants, with a basal rosette of from six to nine linear-subulate leaves, and a peduncled spike crowded with reniform one-celled two-valved sporangia, each subtended by a cuspidate bract. *P. Drummondii*, the only species, is found in Australia, Tasmania, and New Zealand.

phylloid (fil'oid), *a.* [= F. *phylloïde*, < Gr. *φυλλοειδής, contr. φυλλώδης, leaf-like, < φύλλον, leaf, + εἶδος, form.] Leaf-like; foliaceous. Also *phylloideous*.

phylloideous (fi-loi'dę̄-us), *a.* [< *phylloid* + *-eous*.] Same as *phylloid*.

phyllomania (fil-ǫ-mā'ni-ạ̈), *n.* [NL., < Gr. φύλλον, leaf, + μανία, madness (see *mania*). Cf. G . φυλλομανεῖν, run wildly to leaf.] In *bot.*, the production of leaves in unusual numbers or in unusual places.

phyllome (fil'ōm), *n.* [< Gr. φύλλωμα, leafage, foliage, < φυλλοῦν, clothe with leaves, < φύλλον = L. *folium*, leaf: see *foil*[1].] In *bot.*, the leaf in all its modifications; foliage. Also *phylloma*.

We call foliage leaves, tendrils, and anthers in their various adaptations, metamorphosed leaves or *phyllomes*. *De Bary*, Fungi (trans.), p. 256.

Phyllomedusa (fil″ō-mę̄-dū'sạ̈), *n.* [NL. (Wagler), < Gr. φύλλον, leaf, + NL. (L.) *Medusa*.]

Phyllomedusa bicolor.

The typical genus of *Phyllomedusidæ*, having apposable digits, so that the feet can be used for grasping. There are several species, as *P. bicolor* of South America.

Phyllomedusidæ (fil″ǫ-mę̄-dū'si-dē), *n. pl.* [NL. (Günther), < *Phyllomedusa* + *-idæ*.] A family of salient anurous *Batrachia*, typified by the genus *Phyllomedusa*. They have free p a y a y digits, maxillary teeth, ears perfectly developed, parotoids present, and sacral apophyses dilated. The family is now usually merged in *Hylidæ*.

phyllomic (fi-lom'ik), *a.* [< *phyllome* + *-ic*.] In *bot.*, of the nature of a phyllome; resembling a phyllome. *Nature*, XXXIV. 17.

phyllomorphy (fil'ǫ-môr-fi), *n.* [< Gr. φύλλον, leaf, + μορφή, form.] Same as *phyllody*. Also *phyllomorphosis*.

Phyllophaga (fi-lof'ạ-gạ̈), *n. pl.* [NL. (Hartig, 1837), < Gr. φύλλον, leaf, + φαγεῖν, eat.] 1. In *entom.*: (*a*) A series of securiferous hymenopterous insects, including the saw-flies or *Tenthredinidæ*. They have the trochanters two-jointed, anterior tibiæ two-spurred, abdomen connate with the thorax, and the ovipositor formed of two saws which are alternately protruded. (*b*) A section of lamellicorn beetles which are leaf-eaters, as the chafers, conterminous with Macleay's two families *Anoplognathidæ* and *Melolonthidæ*. *Latreille.* Also *Phyllophagi*.—2. In *mammal.*, a group of edentates corresponding to the *Bradypoda*, or sloths. *Owen*, 1842.

phyllophagan (fi-lof'ạ-gạn), *n.* [< *Phyllophaga* + *-an*.] A member of the *Phyllophaga*, in either sense.

phyllophagous (fi-lof'ạ-gus), *a.* [= F. *phyllophage*, < Gr. φύλλον, leaf, + φαγεῖν, eat.] Leaf-eating; feeding on leaves; of or pertaining to the *Phyllophaga* or *Phyllophagi*.

phyllophore (fil'ǫ-fōr), *n.* [< Gr. φυλλοφόρος, bearing leaves: see *phyllophorous*.] In *bot.*, the terminal bud or growing-point in a palm. Also *phyllogen*.

phyllophorous (fi-lof'ǫ-rus), *a.* [< Gr. φυλλοφόρος, bearing leaves, < φύλλον, leaf, + φέρειν = E. *bear*[1].] 1. Leaf-bearing; producing leaves.—2. In *zoöl.*, having foliaceous or leaf-like parts or organs; specifically, provided with a nose-leaf, as a bat.

Phyllopneuste (fil-op-nū'stē), *n.* See *Phyllopseuste*.

phyllopod (fil'ō-pod), *a.* and *n.* [< NL. *phyllopus (-pod-), < Gr. φύλλον, leaf, + πούς (ποδ-) = E. *foot*.] I. *a.* Having foliaceous feet; having the limbs expanded and flattened like leaves; specifically, of or pertaining to the *Phyllopoda*.

II. *n.* A crustacean of the order *Phyllopoda*.

Phyllopoda (fi-lop'ǫ-dạ̈), *n. pl.* [NL.: see *phyllopod*.] 1. An order of entomostracous crustaceans, the leaf-footed crustaceans, sometimes forming (with *Ostracopoda* and *Cladocera*) a suborder of *Branchiopoda*. In Latreille's classification the phyllopods were a section of his branchiopods, corresponding to the modern order of *Phyllopoda*, and divided into (*a*) *Ceratophthalma*, with the genera *Limnadia* and *Estheria* (composing the modern family *Estheriidæ*) and *Artemia* and *Branchipus* (the modern family *Branchipodidæ*), and (*b*) *Aspidophora*, with the genera *Apus* and *Lepidurus* (the modern family *Apodidæ* or *Apusidæ*). The feet in phyllopods are very variable in number, and those of the locomotory series are membranous or foliaceous, as implied in the name. Excepting in *Branchipodidæ*, the body bears a very large carapace, which in the *Limnadiidæ* takes the form of a bivalve shell with a hinge, closed by adductor muscles, into which the legs can be withdrawn. But this carapace is not a cephalothorax as is usual in crustaceans. Two pairs of antennæ are usually present. The mouth-parts are a pair of mandibles, two pairs of maxillæ, and in some forms a pair of maxillipeds. Phyllopods hatch from the egg in the nauplius stage; in some of them parthenogenesis occurs, and the eggs are notable for their ability to withstand desiccation without losing their vitality. Phyllopods inhabit chiefly fresh-water ponds, sometimes swarming in vast numbers. The species of *Artemia*, as *A. salina*, are known as *brine-shrimps*. The phyllopods are an old type, going back to the Devonian, and have some resemblance to trilobites. See cuts under *Apus*, *Estheriidæ*, and *Limnetis*. 2. In *conch.*, in J. E. Gray's classification (1821), one of several orders of *Conchophora*, containing dimyarian bivalve mollusks having the foot lamellar or elongate.

phyllopodal (fi-lop'ǫ-dạl), *a.* [< *phyllopod* + *-al*.] Same as *phyllopod*. *Claus*, quoted in Encyc. Brit., VI. 650, note. [Rare.]

phyllopodan (fi-lop'ǫ-dạn), *a.* and *n.* [< *phyllopod* + *-an*.] Same as *phyllopod*.

phyllopode (fil'ǫ-pōd), *n.* [< Gr. φύλλον, leaf, + πούς (ποδ-) = E. *foot*. Cf. *phyllopod*.] In *bot.*, the dilated sheathing-base of the frond of *Isoëtes*, an organ analogous to the petiole of a leaf. It is hollowed into a pouch which incloses the sporangium. *J. Gay.*

phyllopodiform (fil-ǫ-pod'i-fôrm), *a.* [< NL. *phyllopus (-pod-), a phyllopod. + L. *forma*, form.] Resembling or related to a phyllopod. *Encyc. Brit.*, VI. 650.

phyllopodous (fi-lop'ō-dus), *a.* [< *phyllopod* + *-ous*.] Same as *phyllopod*.

Phyllopseuste (fil-op-sūs'tē), *n.* [NL. (Meyer, 1815), also *Phyllopseustes* (Gloger, 1834), also, appar. by a typographical error long afterward current, *Phyllopneuste* (Boie, 1828), and *Phyllopneustes* (Bonaparte, 1838); appar. so called from some deceptive similarity to leaves; < Gr. φύλλον, leaf, + ψεύστης, a liar, cheat, as adj. false, < ψεύδειν, deceive, cheat, ψεύδεσθαι, lie.] An extensive genus of small warblers of the family *Sylviidæ*, now commonly called *Phylloscopus*. See cut under *Phylloscopus*.

phylloptosis (fil-op-tō'sis), *n.* [NL., < Gr. φύλλον, leaf, + πτῶσις, a falling, < πίπτειν, fall.] In *bot.*, the fall of the leaf.

Phyllorhina (fil-ǫ-rī'nạ̈), *n.* [NL.: see *phyllorhine*.] The typical genus of horseshoe-bats of the family *Rhinolophidæ* and subfamily *Phyllorhininæ*, containing about 20 species which have the leaf not lanceolate behind and not covering the nostrils. They have 1 incisor, 1 canine, 1 or 2 premolars, and 3 molars in each upper half-jaw, and 2 incisors, 1 canine, 2 premolars, and 3 molars in each under half-jaw. See cut on following page.

phyllorhine (fil'ǫ-rin), *a.* and *n.* [< NL. *phyllorhinus, prop. *phyllorrhinus, < Gr. φύλλον, leaf, + ῥίς (ῥιν-), nose.] I. *a.* Having a nose-leaf, as a bat; specifically, of or pertaining to the *Phyllorhininæ*.

II. *n.* A bat of the subfamily *Phyllorhininæ*.

Phyllorhininæ (fil″ō-ri-nī'nē), *n. pl.* [NL., < *Phyllorhina* + *-inæ*.] A subfamily of leaf-nosed bats of the family *Rhinolophidæ*, typified by the genus *Phyllorhina*, having the toes with only two phalanges apiece, and the iliopec-

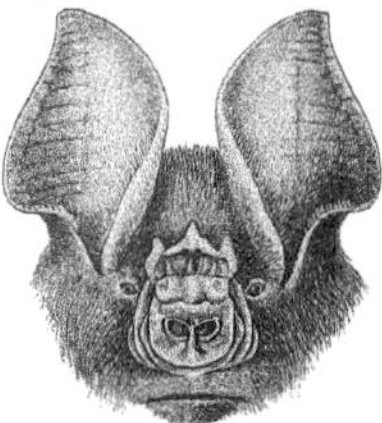

Head of Leaf-nosed Bat (*Phyllorhina tridens*).

tineal spine united with a bony process of the ilium.

Phyllornis (fi-lôr'nis), *n.* [NL. (Temminck, 1829, appar. from a manuscript name of Boie's), < Gr. φύλλον, a leaf, + ὄρνις, bird.] A genus of birds, giving name to the *Phyllornithinæ*; the green bulbuls: synonymous with *Chloropsis*.

phylloscopine (fi-los'kō-pin), *a.* [< *Phylloscopus* + *-ine*¹.] In *ornith.*, resembling a species of *Phylloscopus* in the character of the bill: said of certain warblers. *H. Seebohm.*

Phylloscopus (fi-los'kō-pus), *n.* [NL. (Boie, 1826), < Gr. φύλλον, leaf, + σκοπεῖν, view.] An extensive genus of Old World warblers of the family *Sylviidæ* and subfamily *Sylviinæ*. The type is *Sylvia trochilus*; it has twelve rectrices, yellow axillaries, and the greater wing-coverts with pale tips. The four British species are *P. rufus*, the chiffchaff; *P. trochilus*, the willow-warbler; *P. sibilatrix*, the wood-warbler; and *P. superciliosus*, the yellow-browed warbler. See also cut under *chiffchaff*. Compare *Phyllopseuste*.

Yellow-browed Warbler (*Phylloscopus superciliosus*).

Phyllosoma (fil-ō-sō'mā), *n.* [NL., < Gr. φύλλον, leaf, + σῶμα, body.] A spurious genus of crustaceans, based on certain larval forms called by Leach *Phyllosoma clavicornis*. See *glass-crab*.

Phyllosomata (fil-ō-sō'ma-tā), *n. pl.* [NL., < Gr. φύλλον, leaf, + σῶμα (σωματ-), body.] A spurious group of crustaceans, based on certain larval forms; the glass-crabs. They were by Latreille made the second family of *Stomatopoda*, under the name of *Bipeltata*, composed of forms which are remarkable for their rounded shape and the transparency of their teguments. They are now known to be larval forms of macrurous decapods, as *Palinuridæ* and *Scyllaridæ*. The name is retained for such larvæ. See cut under *glass-crab*.

Phyllostachys (fi-los'tā-kis), *n.* [NL. (Siebold and Zuccarini, 1837), so called with ref. to the leaf-bearing lower branches of the inflorescence; < Gr. φύλλον, leaf, + στάχυς, spike.] A genus of arborescent grasses, of the tribe *Bambuseæ* and subtribe *Arundinarieæ*, characterized by the one- to four-flowered spikelets, in spikes partly included within imbricated spathaceous bracts. They are tall grasses with cylindrical culms and prominent nodes, producing numerous dense or loose panicled spikes, and short-petioled leaves, jointed with the sheath and tessellated with little transverse veinlets. The 4 or 5 species are natives of China and Japan, resemble the bamboo, and furnish material for walking-sticks and bamboo chairs. *P. nigra* is the wanghee-cane of China, with black, nearly solid stems reaching 25 feet. *P. bambusoides* is a dwarf species from which yellowish canes are made.

Phyllosticta (fil-ō-stik'tā), *n.* [NL. (Persoon), < Gr. φύλλον, leaf, + στικτός, spotted, < στίζειν, prick, stab: see *stigma*.] A genus of parasitic fungi of the class *Sphæropsideæ*, order *Sphærioideæ*, probably representing stages in the life-history of other forms. The perithecia, which occupy discolored spots on the leaves, are minute, opening with a terminal pore. About 350 species are recognized, which cause the well-known leaf-spot disease in many plants—*P. Catalpæ* on the catalpa, *P. pirina* on the apple, *P. Rosæ* on roses, *P. Ribis* on cultivated species of *Ribes*, *P. Labruscæ* on the grape (thought to be one form of the black-rot), *P. acericola* on the maple, etc.

Phyllostoma (fi-los'tō-mā), *n.* [NL. (Geoffroy, 1797): see *phyllostomatous*.] A South American genus of phyllostomine bats from which the subfamily and the family each takes its name. *P. hastatum* is one of the largest bats of South America, next in size to *Vampirus spectrum*; *P. elongatum* is smaller, with a larger nose-leaf.

Phyllostomatidæ (fil″ō-stō-mat'i-dē), *n. pl.* [NL., < *Phyllostoma* (*-stomat-*) + *-idæ*.] A family of tropical and subtropical American bats of the emballonurine series. They have a nose-leaf or other cutaneous appendages of the snout (somewhat as in *Rhinolophidæ* or horseshoe-bats, which are, however, of a different alliance (the vespertilionine)), three phalanges of the middle finger, and large middle upper incisors. The eyes are comparatively large, and there is a distinct tragus (wanting in *Rhinolophidæ*). The family includes the vampire-bats, some of which are true blood-suckers, as the genera *Desmodon* and *Diphylla*. The presence of variously formed appendages of the snout has often caused bats of this group to be confused with the horseshoe-bats; but the presence of a tragus alone is sufficient to distinguish the phyllostomes. Leading genera are *Mormops*, *Vampirus*, *Phyllostoma*, *Glossophaga*, *Stenoderma*, and *Desmodon*. The family is divisible into *Phyllostomatinæ* and *Lobostomatinæ*. Also *Phyllostomidæ*.

Phyllostomatinæ (fil-ō-stō-ma-tī'nē), *n. pl.* [NL., < *Phyllostoma* (*-stomat-*) + *-inæ*.] A subfamily of New World bats of the family *Phyllostomatidæ*, having a distinct diversiform nose-leaf and either foliaceous or warty appendages of the chin. See cuts under *Desmodontes*, *Glossophaga*, *Stenoderma*, and *Vampyrus*.

phyllostomatous (fil-ō-stom'a-tus), *a.* [< Gr. φύλλον, leaf, + στόμα, mouth.] Leaf-nosed, as a bat; belonging to the family *Phyllostomatidæ*.

phyllostome (fil'ō-stōm), *n.* [< NL. *phyllostoma*.] A leaf-nosed bat of the genus *Phyllostoma* or family *Phyllostomatidæ*.

Phyllostomidæ (fil-ō-stom'i-dē), *n. pl.* [NL., < *Phyllostoma* + *-idæ*.] Same as *Phyllostomatidæ*.

phyllostomine (fi-los'tō-min), *a.* [< *phyllostome* + *-ine*¹.] Leaf-nosed, as a bat; phyllostomatous or phyllostomous; of or pertaining to the *Phyllostomatinæ*.

phyllostomous (fi-los'tō-mus), *a.* Same as *phyllostomine*.

phyllotactic (fil-ō-tak'tik), *a.* [< *phyllotaxis*, after *tactic*.] Of or pertaining to phyllotaxis.

phyllotaxis (fil-ō-tak'sis), *n.* [NL.: see *phyllotaxy*.] In *bot.*, the distribution or arrangement of leaves on the stem; also, the laws collectively which govern such distribution. Leaves are distributed so as to economize space and give a good exposure to light; and to accomplish this they are arranged in a variety of ways, which all fall under two principal modes. These are the *verticillate* or *cyclical*, in which there are two or more leaves at the same height of the stem, and the *alternate* or *spiral*, in which the leaves stand singly, one after another. In the verticillate arrangement the leaves form a succession of whorls or circles around the stem, with two, three, four, five, or more in each whorl. In the alternate or spiral arrangement the leaves are distributed singly at different heights of the stem and at equal intervals. The simplest is the two-ranked or distichous arrangement, which prevails in all grasses, in the linden, elm, etc., in which the leaves are disposed alternately on exactly opposite sides of the stem. The second leaf is therefore the furthest possible from the first, and the third is the furthest possible from the second, and consequently is exactly over the first, and so on. They thus form two vertical ranks in which the angular divergence is half the circumference, or 180°. In all cases the angular divergence may be represented by a fraction, in which the numerator designates the number of turns of the spiral that are made in passing from one leaf to the next one that is precisely vertical to it, while the denominator expresses the number of vertical rows thus formed, from which the class of phyllotaxis takes its name, as the tristichous or three-ranked ($\frac{1}{3}$), the pentastichous or five-ranked ($\frac{2}{5}$), the octostichous or eight-ranked ($\frac{3}{8}$), and even as high as a thirteen-ranked ($\frac{5}{13}$) phyllotaxis has been made out.

phyllotaxy (fil'ō-tak-si), *n.* [= F. *phyllotaxie*, < NL. *phyllotaxis*, < Gr. φύλλον, leaf, + τάξις, order: see *taxis*.] In *bot.*, same as *phyllotaxis*.

Phyllotreta (fil-ō-trē'tā), *n.* [NL. (Chevrolat, 1834), < Gr. φύλλον, leaf, + τρητός, verbal adj. of τετραίνειν (√ τρα), bore.] A genus of leaf-beetles or *Chrysomelidæ*, of wide distribution in temperate and tropical parts of both the Old and the New World. They are of small size, often of metallic colors, and frequently very destructive to vegetation; the larvæ are white and usually linear. *P. vittata* is the wavy-striped flea-beetle of the United States, abundant in vegetable-gardens, where it attacks cabbages and other cruciferous plants. *P. nemorum* of Europe, known as the *turnip flea-beetle*, has similar habits.

Striped Flea-beetle (*Phyllotreta vittata*), enlarged.

phylloxanthin (fil-ok-san'thin), *n.* [= F. *phylloxanthine*; < Gr. φύλλον, leaf, + ξανθός, yellow, + *-in*².] Same as *xanthophyl*. See *chlorophyl*.

Phylloxera (fil-ok-sē'rā), *n.* [NL. (Fonscolombe, 1834), < Gr. φύλλον, leaf, + ξηρός, dry.] 1. A genus of plant-lice or homopterous insects of the family *Aphididæ* and subfamily *Chermesinæ*, usually of gall-making habits. The front wings have two discoidal veins, and the antennæ are three-jointed, the third joint being much the longest. The young larvæ have one-jointed tarsi, and all forms are destitute of honey-tubes. It is a somewhat large genus, nearly all of whose species are North American, forming galls on the leaves of the hickory in particular, but also on those of the chestnut, butternut, and oak, as *P. rileyi*, the oak-pest. One species, *P. vastatrix*, is a formidable pest of the European grape (*Vitis vinifera*). See def. 2.

2. [*l. c.*] A member of this genus, especially the species just named, known as the *grape-vine phylloxera* and *vine-pest*, the worst enemy of the European or *vinifera* grape. The fact that a vine-disease which had long existed in southern France was due to this insect was discovered in 1865 by Planchon, who described the insect as *P. vastatrix*. The species

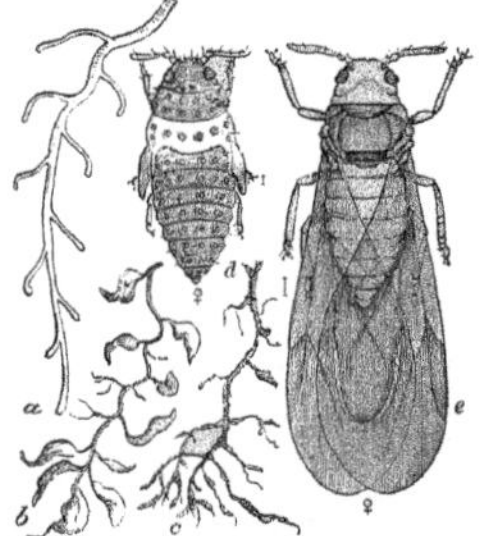

Vine-pest (*Phylloxera vastatrix*).

a, healthy vine rootlet; *b*, rootlet showing nodosities; *c*, rootlet in decay (natural size); *d*, female pupa; *e*, winged female, or migrant. (Hair-lines show natural sizes.) (After Riley.)

had been named before (though Planchon's name holds by common consent); for in 1854 Fitch had described an American gall-louse on grape-leaves as *Pemphigus vitifoliæ*, and this was identified with the European root-louse (*Phylloxera vastatrix*) by Riley in 1870. The same discovery was made by European observers in the same year. It is now established that the native country of this phylloxera is North America east of the Rocky Mountains from Canada to the Gulf of Mexico, whence it spread to Europe, and more recently to California, South Africa, New Zealand, and Australia. The insect exists under two distinct forms: the root-form, called *radicicola*, on the roots of the vine, and the gall-form, called *gallicola*, in galls on the leaves of the grape. The galls are transient, being numerous one year and scarce the next. The root-form is like the gall-form at first, but later acquires certain characteristic tubercles. The phylloxera hibernates as a winter egg above or below ground, or as a young larva on the roots. Late in the summer a generation of winged agamic females is produced; these fly abroad and spread the pest. One of the females lays from three to eight delicate eggs in or on the ground or on the under side of the leaf, and from these eggs issue the true males and females, both of which are wingless. These mate, and the female lays the winter egg. The wingless hypogeal female may occasionally lay eggs which bring forth the sexual brood without the intervention of a winged generation, but this is exceptional. The wingless individuals spread from vine to vine, and the winged ones carry the pest from one vineyard to another. The symptoms of the disease above ground are the yellowing of the leaves the second year and the death of the vine the third year. Below ground, little knots are formed on the small fibrous roots the first year; these roots decay the next year, and the lice settle on the main roots. The third year these rot, and then the vine dies. The vines susceptible to this infestation include all the varieties of the *Vitis vinifera*, the wine-grape of Europe and California and the hothouse-grape—the most valuable of the grape family. The French government early offered a reward of 300,000 francs for a satisfactory remedy, but this prize has never been awarded. The most effectual methods of dealing with the phylloxera thus far ascertained are the underground injection of bisulphid of carbon by means of a specially contrived apparatus, the application of a watery solution of sulphocarbonate of potassium, and the grafting of the European vine upon hardy American varieties, as the Taylor, Clinton, and Jacques. See also cuts under *gall-louse*, *oak-pest*, and *vine-pest*.

3. A genus of lepidopterous insects. *Rambur*, 1869.

phylloxera-mite (fil-ok-sē'rā-mit), *n.* An acarine, *Tyroglyphus phylloxeræ*, one of the natural enemies of the vine-pest, formerly described in its transitional and quiescent stage as *Hoplophora arctata*. *Hoplophora* was supposed to be a genus of *Oribatidæ*, characterized by the hard covering or shield capable of being folded together to inclose the head and limbs, but the members of that ge-

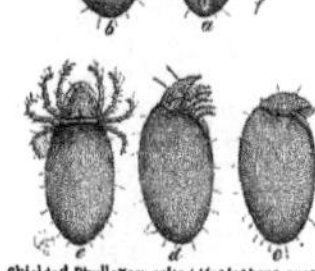

Shielded Phylloxera-mite (*Hoplophora arctata*).
a, b, c, d, e, different attitudes assumed by it; *f*, leg, highly magnified.

nus are now known to belong to *Tyroglyphus*. The figures show the mite in this stage, in several positions.

phylloxerated (fi-lok'sẹ-rā-ted), *a.* [‹ *Phylloxera* + *-ate*[2] + *-ed*[2].] Infested with phylloxeræ. *Edinburgh Rev.*, CLXIV. 378.

phylloxeric (fil-ok-ser'ik), *a.* [‹ *Phylloxera* + *-ic.*] Of or pertaining to the phylloxera or grape-louse.

Phylloxerinæ (fi-lok-sẹ-rī'nē), *n. pl.* [NL., ‹ *Phylloxera* + *-inæ.*] A subfamily of *Aphididæ*, typified by the genus *Phylloxera*; the vine-pests. See *Chermesinæ*.

phylloxerize (fi-lok'sẹ-rīz), *v. t.*; pret. and pp. *phylloxerized*, ppr. *phylloxerizing*. [‹ *Phylloxera* + *-ize.*] To contaminate or infect with phylloxeræ.

phyllula† (fi-lū'lạ̈), *n.* [NL., ‹ Gr. φύλλον, leaf, + οὐλή, scar.] In *bot.*, the scar left on a branch by the fall of a leaf.

phylogenesis (fī-lọ̄-jen'e-sis), *n.* [NL., ‹ Gr. φῦλον, φυλή, a race, tribe (see *phyle*, *phylum*), + γένεσις, origin: see *genesis*.] Same as *phylogeny*.

phylogenetic (fī'lọ̄-jẹ̄-net'ik), *a.* [‹ *phylogenesis*, after *genetic*.] Same as *phylogenic*. *Huxley*, Anat. Invert., p. 43.

phylogenetically (fī'lọ̄-jẹ̄-net'i-kal-i), *adv.* According to the doctrine or principle of phylogenesis; by means of phylogeny.

phylogenic (fī-lọ̄-jen'ik), *a.* [‹ *phylogen-y* + *-ic.*] Of or pertaining to phylogeny, as distinguished from *ontogeny*. Also *phylogenetic*.

phylogeny (fī-loj'e-ni), *n.* [= F. *phylogénie*, ‹ Gr. φῦλον, φυλή, a tribe, + -γένεια, ‹ -γενής, producing: see *-geny*.] That branch of biology which attempts to deduce the ancestral history of an animal or a plant from its ontogeny or individual developmental metamorphoses; tribal history: opposed to *ontogeny*, or the origin and development of individual organisms. Also *phylogenesis*.

Phyloptera (fī-lop'tẹ-rạ̈), *n. pl.* [NL. (Packard), ‹ Gr. φῦλον, φυλή, a tribe, + πτερόν, wing.] A superorder of hexapod insects, including the orders *Neuroptera*, *Pseudoneuroptera*, *Orthoptera*, and *Dermatoptera*.

phylopterous (fī-lop'tẹ-rus), *a.* Pertaining to the *Phyloptera*, or having their characters.

phylum (fī'lum), *n.*; pl. *phyla* (-lạ̈). [NL., ‹ Gr. φῦλον, φυλή, a tribe: see *phyle*.] 1. Any primary division or subkingdom of the animal or vegetable kingdom. Cuvier recognized four animal types which would now be called phyla: the *Radiata*, *Mollusca*, *Articulata*, and *Vertebrata*. Zoölogists now recognize at least seven such phyla: (1) *Protozoa*, (2) *Cœlenterata*, (3) *Echinodermata*, (4) *Vermes*, (5) *Arthropoda*, (6) *Mollusca*, (7) *Vertebrata*. The main branches of a phylum are called *subphyla*.
2. The graphic representation of the evolution of one or several forms of animal life by descent with modification from preëxisting ancestors, on the principle of the construction of a genealogical table or "family tree."

Phymata (fī-mā'tạ̈), *n.* [NL. (Latreille, 1802), ‹ Gr. φῦμα (φυματ-), a tumor (‹ φύειν, produce, φύεσθαι, grow), + *-ata*[1].] The typical genus of *Phymatidæ*, having very broad curved fore femora, of raptorial character. *P. erosa* or *P. wolffi* is a common North American bug of curious form and greenish-yellow color, banded and spotted with black, found on goldenrod and various other plants of meadows and gardens, preying on the insects which come to collect honey or pollen. The species abound in tropical and subtropical America.

Phymata erosa.

Phymatidæ (fī-mat'i-dē), *n. pl.* [NL. (Amyot and Serville, 1843), ‹ *Phymata* + *-idæ.*] A family of raptorial heteropterous insects, typified by the genus *Phymata*, belonging to the coreoid series, and forming a connecting-link with the reduvioids. It contains six genera. Most of the species are tropical or subtropical.

phyogemmaria (fī'ọ̄-je-mā'ri-ạ̈), *n. pl.* [NL., ‹ Gr. φυή, growth (‹ φύεσθαι, grow), + L. *gemma*, bud: see *gemmary*.] The small gonoblastids or reproductive buds of some physophoran hydrozoans, as the *Velellidæ*.

phyogemmarian (fī'ọ̄-je-mā'ri-an), *a.* [‹ *phyogemmaria* + *-an.*] Of or pertaining to phyogemmaria.

Physa (fī'sạ̈), *n.* [NL., ‹ Gr. φῦσα, a pair of bellows, breath, wind.] A large genus of pond-snails or fresh-water gastropods of the family *Limnæidæ*, or made type of the *Physidæ*, having the shell sinistral. There are many species, found on aquatic plants in ponds, as *P. fontinalis* of Europe and *P. heterostropha* of America. The genus was named by Draparnaud in 1801.

Physa fontinalis.

Physalia (fī-sā'li-ạ̈), *n.* [NL. (Lamarck, 1819), ‹ Gr. *φυσαλίς, φυσαλλίς, a bladder: see *Physalis*.] 1. The typical genus of *Physaliidæ*. These oceanic hydrozoans, known as *Portuguese men-of-war*, are remarkable for their size, brilliancy, and power of urticating. There is a large oblong crested float which buoys the animal up, from which hang many processes, some of which attain a length of 12 feet or more in individuals whose float is only a few inches long. *P. atlantica* or *pelagica* is an example.
2. [*l. c.*] A member of this genus.

Portuguese Man-of-war (*Physalia pelagica*).

physalian (fī-sā'li-an), *a.* and *n.* I. *a.* Pertaining to the genus *Physalia*, or having its characters.
II. *n.* A member of the genus *Physalia*.

Physaliidæ (fis-ạ-lī'i-dē), *n. pl.* [NL., ‹ *Physalia* + *-idæ.*] A family of oceanic hydrozoans of the order *Siphonophora* and suborder *Physophora*, represented by the genus *Physalia*. The family is sometimes raised to the rank of a suborder. Also *Physalidæ*, *Physaliadæ*.

Physalis (fis'ạ-lis), *n.* [NL. (Linnæus, 1737), ‹ Gr. *φυσαλίς, prop. φυσαλλίς, some plant with a bladder-like husk or calyx (prob. *Physalis Alkekengi*), ‹ φυσαλλίς, a bladder, ‹ φυσᾶν, blow, blow up, puff, ‹ φῦσα, a pair of bellows: see *Physa*.] A genus of herbaceous plants, of the gamopetalous order *Solanaceæ* and tribe *Solaneæ*, characterized by the five-angled, broadly bell-shaped corolla, and the five- or ten-angled bladdery fruiting calyx remotely inclosing the much smaller globose berry. There are about 30 species, mainly American, especially in Mexico (17 in the United States). They are hairy or clammy annuals or perennials, with sinuate leaves, and rather large flowers, solitary in the axils, violet, yellow, or white, often with a purple eye, and with yellow or violet anthers. Some yellow-flowered species have been cultivated for ornament. The two white-flowered species, once much cultivated in the United States for their edible berries, under the name of *strawberry-tomato* (which see), are *P. Alkekengi*, the winter-cherry of the south of Europe, with red berry and calyx (see *alkekengi* and *bladder-herb*), and *P. Peruviana*, with yellow berries (see *alkekengi*, *winter-cherry* (*a*) (under *cherry*), and *bladder-herb*). Among the native American species, all commonly known as *ground-cherry*, the berries of *P. angulata* are considered edible, and those of *P. viscosa* are strongly diuretic.

physalite (fis'ạ-līt), *n.* [= F. *physalite*, ‹ Gr. *φυσαλίς, prop. φυσαλλίς, a bladder, + *-ite*[2].] A coarse, nearly opaque variety of topaz. Also called *pyrophysalite*.

Physaraceæ (fis-ạ-rā'sẹ̄-ē), *n. pl.* [NL. (Rostafinski, 1875), ‹ *Physarum* + *-aceæ.*] A family of myxomycetous fungi, named from the genus *Physarum*. They have the capillitium (with the tube) delicate, reticulate, hyaline, or pellucid, and the columella is small or wanting.

Physarum (fis'ạ-rum), *n.* [NL. (Persoon), ‹ Gr. φυσάριον, dim. of φῦσα, a pair of bellows: see *Physa*.] A genus of myxomycetous fungi, giving name to the family *Physaraceæ*. The peridium is composed of a simple or double membrane which dehisces irregularly. Sixty species are known. See *fairy ring*, under *fairy*.

Physcia (fis'i-ạ̈), *n.* [NL. (Fries, 1825), ‹ Gr. φύσκη, a sausage, a blister, ‹ φυσᾶν, blow up, ‹ φῦσα, a pair of bellows, breath, wind: see *Physa*.] A large genus of parmeliaceous lichens, with a foliaceous cartilaginous thallus, scutelliform apothecia, and ellipsoid, usually bilocular brown spores. Several of the species are used in the arts for coloring, etc.

physcioid (fis'i-oid), *a.* [‹ *Physcia* + *-oid.*] Belonging to or resembling the genus *Physcia*.

Physcomitrieæ (fis'kọ̄-mi-tri'ẹ̄-ē), *n. pl.* [NL., ‹ *Physcomitrium* + *-eæ.*] A tribe of bryaceous mosses, named from the genus *Physcomitrium*. They are short soft plants with relatively large leaves and a usually corneous or gibbous capsule. The peristome is absent, or has 16 teeth.

Physcomitrium (fis-kọ̄-mit'ri-um), *n.* [NL. (Bridel, 1826), ‹ Gr. φύσκος, something inflated, + μιτρίον, a little cap, dim. of μίτρα, a cap, miter: see *miter*.] A genus of mosses, giving name to the tribe *Physcomitrieæ*. They are simple or sparingly branched plants, with pyriform capsule and no peristome. See cut under *mitriform*.

physema† (fī-sē'mạ̈), *n.* [NL., ‹ Gr. φύσημα, that which is blown, a bubble, ‹ φυσᾶν, blow, blow up, ‹ φῦσα, a pair of bellows, breath, wind: see *Physa*.] 1. A mock pearl; an empty bubble instead of pearl. *E. Phillips*, 1706.—2. The resin of the pine-tree. *E. Phillips*.—3. A swelling or puffing in any part of the body. *E. Phillips*.

Physemaria (fis-ẹ̄-mā'ri-ạ̈), *n. pl.* [NL., ‹ Gr. φύσημα, a bubble: see *physema*.] A group formed by Haeckel for the reception of two genera of low metazoic animals, *Haliphysema* and *Gastrophysema*, which had been confounded partly with the sponges and partly with the protozoans. The validity of the group has been denied.

physemarian (fis-ẹ̄-mā'ri-an), *a.* and *n.* [‹ *Physemaria* + *-an.*] I. *a.* Of or pertaining to the *Physemaria*. *Huxley*.
II. *n.* A member of the *Physemaria*.

physeter (fī-sē'tėr), *n.* [= F. *physétère* = Sp. *fiseter*, *fisetera*, ‹ L. *physeter*, ‹ Gr. φυσητήρ, a blowpipe, a kind of whale, ‹ φυσᾶν, blow, ‹ φῦσα, a pair of bellows, wind: see *Physa*.] 1. A sperm-whale or cachalot.

> When on the surges I perceiue from far
> Th' Ork, Whirl-pool, Whale, or huffing *Physeter*.
> *Sylvester*, tr. of Du Bartas's Weeks, i. 5.

2. [*cap.*] [NL.] The typical genus of *Physeterinæ*, containing the ordinary large spermaceti-whales, or cachalots. The head is very large, truncate in front, and about one third of the total length

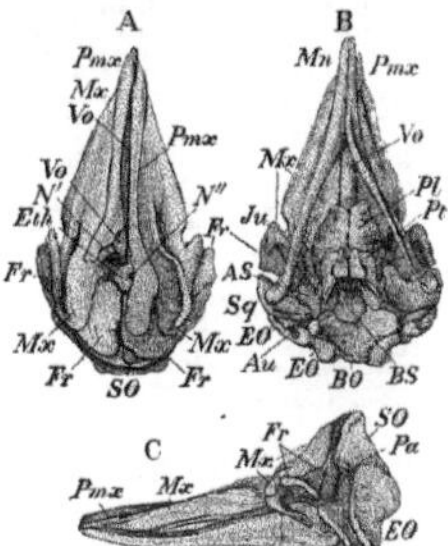

Top (A), Bottom (B), and Side (C) of Skull of Fetal Sperm-whale or Cachalot (*Physeter*). *Au*, auditory; *BO*, basioccipital; *EO*, exoccipital; *Eth*, ethmoid; *Fr*, frontal; *Ju*, jugal (displaced behind in fig. C); *Mn*, mandible; *Mx*, maxilla; *N' N''*, nasal openings, the bones not represented; *Pmx*, *Pmx*, premaxillaries of right and left sides (unsymmetrical); *Pa*, parietal; *Pl*, palatine; *Pt*, pterygoid; *Sq*, squamosal; *SO*, supraoccipital; *Vo*, vomer; *BS*, basisphenoid; *AS*, alisphenoid.

of the body; the blow-hole is near the edge of the snout; and the brain-cavity is declivous. *P. macrocephalus* is the common cachalot, from which spermaceti is obtained. Also called *Catodon*. See also cut under *Catodonta*.

Physeteridæ (fis-ẹ̄-ter'i-dē), *n. pl.* [NL., ‹ *Physeter* + *-idæ.*] 1. A family of existent delphinoid *Cetacea*, of the group *Delphinoidea*, having functional teeth in the lower jaw only, and the skull strongly asymmetrical. To this family belong the sperm-whales proper (*Physeterinæ*), and such forms as the bottle-nosed whale (*Hyperoodon*).
2. In stricter use, a family of sperm-whales, typified by the genus *Physeter*, and containing the subfamilies *Physeterinæ* and *Kogiinæ*, or ordinary and pygmy sperm-whales. They have the head neither rostrate nor marginate: the snout high toward the front and projecting beyond the mouth; the skull high behind or retrorsely convex: the supraoccipital bone projecting forward laterally to or beyond the ver-

tical of the temporal fossæ, and the frontal bones visible above as erect triangular or retrorsely falciform wedges between the maxillaries and the supraoccipital. Sometimes called *Catodontidæ*.

Physeterinæ (fī-sē-te-rī'nē), *n. pl.* [NL., < *Physeter* + *-inæ*.] 1. The typical subfamily of the *Physeteridæ*, containing the genera *Physeter* and *Kogia*.—2. This subfamily restricted, by the exclusion of the genus *Kogia* as the type of a separate subfamily, to the ordinary large sperm-whales of the genus *Physeter*.

physeterine (fī-sē'te-rin), *a.* and *n.* [< *physeter* + *-ine*[1].] I. *a.* Like or related to a sperm-whale; of or pertaining to the *Physeterinæ*.

II. *n.* A member of the *Physeterinæ*.

physeteroid (fī-sē'te-roid), *a.* and *n.* [< *physeter* + *-oid*.] I. *a.* Belonging to the *Physeteroidea*, or having their characters; resembling the genus *Physeter*; xiphioid.

II. *n.* A member of the *Physeteridæ*, in either sense; a xiphioid. *Encyc. Brit.*, XV. 393.

Physeteroidea (fī-sē-te-roi'dē-ä), *n. pl.* [NL., < *Physeter* + *-oidea*.] The *Physeteridæ*, in sense 2, regarded as a superfamily. *Gill.*

physharmonica (fis-här-mon'i-kä), *n.* [NL., < Gr. φῦσα, bellows, + NL. *harmonica*, q. v.] A small reed-organ originally intended to be attached to a pianoforte, so as to sustain melodies. It was invented in 1818, and was the precursor of the harmonium. See *reed-organ*.

physianthropy (fiz-i-an'thrō-pi), *n.* [< Gr. φύσις, nature (see *physic*), + ἄνθρωπος, man.] The science which treats of the constitution and diseases of man, and of medical remedies. [Rare.]

physiatrics† (fiz-i-at'riks), *n.* [< Gr. φύσις, nature, + ἰατρική (sc. τέχνη), medicine, prop. fem. of ἰατρικός, for a physician: see *iatric*.] That department of medical science which treats of the healing powers of nature.

physic (fiz'ik), *n.* [Formerly *physick*, *phisick*, < ME. *phisik*, *fisike*, natural philosophy, the science of medicine, < OF. *fisique*, *fusike*, *phisique*, natural philosophy, the science of medicine, F. *physique*, f., natural philosophy (*physique*, m., natural constitution, physique), = Sp. *fisica* = Pg. *physica* = It. *fisica* = D. *physika* = MHG. *fisike*, G. *physik* = Sw. Dan. *fysik*, natural philosophy, physics; < L. *physica*, *physice*, ML. also *phisica*, *fisica*, natural philosophy, physics, ML. also the science of medicine, < Gr. φυσική, f., φυσικά, neut. pl., natural philosophy, physics; as adj., F. *physique* = Sp. *fisico* = Pg. *physico* = It. *fisico* (G. *physisch* = Sw. Dan. *fysisk*), physical, < L. *physicus*, < Gr. φυσικός, natural; as noun, Sp. *fisico* = Pg. *physico* = It. *fisico*, a natural philosopher, physician, < L. *physicus*, ML. also *phisicus*, *fisicus*, Gr. φυσικός, a natural philosopher, scientist; < φύσις, nature, < φύειν, produce, φύεσθαι, grow: see *be*[1].] 1†. Natural philosophy; physics. See *physics*.

> *Physique* is after the seconde [part of theorike],
> Through which the philosophre hath fonde,
> To techen sondry knoulechinges
> Upon the bodeliche thinges
> Of man, of beste, of herbe, of stone,
> Of fisshe, of foule, of everichone
> That ben of bodely substaunce,
> The nature and the substance.
> *Gower*, Conf. Amant., vii.

Physic should contemplate that which is inherent in matter, and therefore transitory; and metaphysic that which is abstracted and fixed. *Bacon*, Advancement of Learning, ii. 160.

2. The science of medicine; the medical art or profession; the healing art; medicine.

Seynt Luke the Evaungelist was Disciple of seynt Poul, for to lerne *Phisik*; and many othere. *Mandeville*, Travels, p. 124.

Of late yeares I practised bodely *phisick* in Englande, in my lorde of Sumersettes house. *W. Turner*, Spiritual Physic (1555).

3. A medicine; a drug; a remedy for disease; also, drugs collectively.

> The frere with his *phisik* this folke hath enchaunted,
> And plastred hem so esyly thei drede no synne.
> *Piers Plowman* (B), xx. 377.

> Attempre dyete was al hire *phisik*.
> *Chaucer*, Nun's Priest's Tale, l. 18.

> Throw *physic* to the dogs; I'll none of it.
> *Shak.*, Macbeth, v. 3. 47.

> But in this point
> All his tricks founder, and he brings his *physic*
> After his patient's death; the King already
> Hath married the fair lady.
> *Shak.*, Hen. VIII., iii. 2. 40.

4. A medicine that purges; a cathartic; a purge.

The people used *physic* to purge themselves of humours. *Abp. Abbot*, Descrip. of World.

Affliction is my *physic*; that purges, that cleanses me. *Donne*, Sermons, xiv.

5. In *dyeing*, the nitromuriate of tin, or tin-spirits.—**Culver's physic.** See *Culver's-physic*.—**Indian physic.** See *bowman's-root* and *Gillenia*.—**Physic garden**, a botanic garden. = **Syn.** 2. See *surgery*.

physic (fiz'ik), *v. t.*; pret. and pp. *physicked*, ppr. *physicking*. [< *physic*, *n.*] 1†. To treat with physic or medicines; cure; heal; relieve.

> The labour we delight in *physics* pain.
> *Shak.*, Macbeth, ii. 3. 55.

> It *physics* not the sickness of a mind
> Broken with griefs. *Ford*, Broken Heart, ii. 2.

2. To use cathartics or purgatives upon; purge.—3. To mix with some oxidizing body in order to eliminate phosphorus and sulphur, as in the manufacture of iron.

He contended that sulphur could only be eliminated by two processes, "puddling" and "*physicking*." *Ure*, Dict., IV. 474.

physical (fiz'i-kal), *a.* [Formerly also *phisical*; = It. *fisicale*, < ML. *physicalis*, pertaining to physic or medicine, < L. *physica*, natural philosophy, medicine: see *physic*.] 1. Pertaining to physics or natural philosophy: as, *physical* science; *physical* law.—2. Of or pertaining to material nature; in accordance with the laws of nature; relating to what is material and perceived by the senses; specifically, pertaining to the material part or structure of an organized being, as opposed to what is mental or moral; material; bodily: as, *physical* force; *physical* strength.

Labour, then, in the *physical* world is always and solely employed in putting objects in motion; the properties of matter, the laws of nature, do the rest. *J. S. Mill*, Pol. Econ., I. i. § 2.

"Real and *physical* things," Spinoza tells us, "cannot be understood so long as their essence is unknown." *Veitch*, Introd. to Descartes's Method, p. xcvi.

3. External; obvious to the senses; cognizable through a bodily or material organization: as, the *physical* characters of a mineral: opposed to *chemical*. See *mechanical*.—4†. Of or pertaining to physic, or the art of curing disease or preserving health, or one who professes or practises this art; of or pertaining to a physician.

> To take Tobacco thus were *phisicall*,
> And might perhaps doe good.
> *Times' Whistle* (E. E. T. S.), p. 71.

I have therefore sent him just now the following letter in my *physical* capacity. *Tatler*, No. 246.

5†. In need of physic or of a physician; sick; ill. [Rare.]

Thou look'st dull and *physical*, methinks. *Shirley*, Bird in a Cage, iii. 2.

Aimwell. How now? what means this apothecary's shop about thee? art *physical*?
Fowler. Sick, sick. *Shirley*, Witty Fair One, iii. 4.

6†. Of or pertaining to the drugs or medicines used in the healing art; of use in curing disease or in preserving health; medicinal; remedial.

Attalus . . . would plant and set *physicall* herbs, as helleborum. *North*, tr. of Plutarch, p. 739.

> Is Brutus sick? and is it *physical*
> To walk unbraced and suck up the humours
> Of the dark morning? *Shak.*, J. C., ii. 1. 261.

Balmes, Oiles, Medicinals and Perfumes, Sassaparilla, and many other *physicall* drugs. Quoted in *Capt. John Smith's* Works, II. 74.

The tree hath a pretty *physical* smell like an apothecary's shop. *Rob. Knox* (Arber's Eng. Garner, I. 333).

7†. Purgative; cathartic.—**Physical abstraction, equation,** etc. See the nouns.—**Physical astronomy.** See *astronomy*, 1.—**Physical examination**, an examination for the determination of the presence or absence of the various signs of bodily disease.—**Physical-force men.** See *Chartist*.—**Physical fraction.** See *astronomical fraction*, under *fraction*.—**Physical geography**, that branch of science which has for its object the comparison and generalization of geographical facts. It differs chiefly from geology in that it regards the present rather than the past condition of the earth, but many authors include in their text-books of physical geography more or less of that which is generally considered as belonging to geology. Physical geography may be subdivided into various branches, of which the most important are—*orography*, the study of mountain-chains, and in general of the relief of the surface, in which branch geology can only with difficulty be separated from geography; *thalassography*, the study of the ocean, its outline, depths, currents, temperature, salinity, and the nature and distribution of animal and vegetable life on and beneath its surface; *hydrography*, the study of the river-systems, rivers, and lakes; *climatology*, the practical side of meteorology, or the study of the climatic conditions of various parts of the earth's surface; *botanical geography*, the study of the geographical distribution of plants; *zoölogical geography*, the distribution of animal life; and, finally, *ethnology* and *anthropology*, the study of the races of man and their distributions, and their manners and customs. The last two branches, however, are special sciences, and are rarely treated, except in the most succinct manner, in the text-books of physical geography.—**Physical geology**, the study of the geological changes which have taken place on the earth's surface, and of the causes by which these events have been brought about; geology separated, as far as possible, from paleontology, or from any consideration of the order of succession and the nature of organic life upon the globe, and of the classification of the stratified formations in accordance therewith.—**Physical horizon, influx, mineralogy, necessity, optics.** See the nouns.—**Physical influence.** Same as *physical influx*.—**Physical partition**, a partition by which the parts are really separated; real partition: opposed to *ideal partition*.—**Physical perfection, possibility, power.** See the nouns.—**Physical signs**, such features of disease as are directly appreciable by the examiner and are not the expression by the patient of his own feelings, as those elicited by palpation, inspection, auscultation, percussion, etc.—**Physical truth**, the harmony of thought with the phenomena of outward experience.—**Physical whole**, a whole composed of matter and form. = **Syn.** 2. *Corporal*, *Corporeal*, etc. See *bodily*.—3. *Chemical*, etc. See *mechanical*.

physicalist (fiz'i-kal-ist), *n.* [< *physical* + *-ist*.] One who maintains that man's intellectual and moral nature depends on and results from his physical constitution, or that human thought and action are determined by physical organization.

physically (fiz'i-kal-i), *adv.* 1. In a physical manner; according to nature; according to physics or natural philosophy; not intellectually or morally.

I am not now treating *physically* of light or colours. *Locke.*

2†. According to the art or rules of medicine.

And for physic, he [Lord Bacon] did indeed live *physically*, but not miserably. *Rawley*, in Spedding's Bacon, I. 55.

He that lives *physically* must live miserably. *G. Cheyne.*

physicalness (fiz'i-kal-nes), *n.* The state of being physical. *Worcester.*

physician (fi-zish'an), *n.* [Early mod. E. also *physicion*, *phisicion*, *physitian*, *physition*, *phisition*; < ME. *fisicien*, *fizicien*, *fisicion*, *fisician*, *fysycian*, *phisicien*, *phisicyen*, etc., < OF. *fisicien*, *fisician*, *fusicien*, etc., *phisicien*, *physicien*, a natural philosopher, also and usually a medical man, a physician (F. *physicien*, a natural philosopher), = Pr. *phisician* = It. *fisiciano*, a medical man, < ML. as if **physicianus*, < L. *physicus* (> It. *fisico* = Sp. *fisico* = Pg. *physico*), a natural philosopher, a physician, ML. *physica*, physics, medicine, physic: see *physic*.] 1. One who practises the art of healing disease and of preserving health; a prescriber of remedies for sickness and disease; specifically, a person licensed by some competent authority, such as a medical college, to treat diseases and prescribe remedies for them; a doctor; a medical man. The *physician* as a prescriber of remedies is distinguished from the *pharmacist*, whose business is the compounding or preparing of medicines, and from the *surgeon*, who performs remedial operations. The last, however, often follows the practice of medicine, as does the licensed apothecary in England.

Seint Poul him self was there a *Phisicyen*, for to kepen mennes Bodies in hele, before he was converted; and aftre that he was *Phisicien* of Soules. *Mandeville*, Travels, p. 123.

It sometimes falls out that he that visits a sick Man is forced to be a Fighter instead of a *Physician*. *N. Bailey*, tr. of Colloquies of Erasmus, I. 324.

He was less directly embarrassing to the two *physicians* than to the surgeon-apothecaries who attended paupers by contract. *George Eliot*, Middlemarch, xviii.

2†. A student of physics; a naturalist; a physicist; specifically, in medieval universities, a student of the Aristotelian physics.

physiciancy (fi-zish'an-si), *n.*; pl. *physiciancies* (-siz). [< *physician* + *-cy*.] Appointment as physician; the post or office of physician.

He had in the previous year put himself forward as a candidate for a *physiciancy* to St. George's Hospital. *Lancet*, No. 3423, p. 711.

physicianed (fi-zish'and), *a.* [< *physician* + *-ed*[2].] Made a physician; educated or licensed as a physician. [Rare.]

One Dr. Lucas, a *physicianed* apothecary. *H. Walpole.*

physicianly (fi-zish'an-li), *a.* [< *physician* + *-ly*[1].] Pertaining to or characteristic of a physician.

Real knowledge of man and of men, of the causes and courses of human failure, . . . is indescribably rich in *physicianly* force. *Contemporary Rev.*, LIII. 503.

physicianship (fi-zish'an-ship), *n.* [< *physician* + *-ship*.] The post or office of physician. *Lancet*, No. 3543, p. 941.

physicism (fiz'i-sizm), *n.* [< Gr. φυσικός, natural (see *physic*), + *-ism*.] Belief in the material or physical as opposed to the spiritual. [Rare.]

In the progress of the species from savagery to advanced civilization, anthropomorphism grows into theology, while *physicism* (if I may so call it) develops into science. *Huxley*, Lay Sermons, p. 163.

physicist (fiz'i-sist), *n.* [< Gr. φυσικά, physics (see *physics*), + *-ist*.] 1. A student of physics; a natural philosopher.

I do not think there is a doubt in the mind of any competent *physicist* or phys g s that the work done in lifting the weight of the article the mechanical equivalent of a certain proportion of the energy set free by the molecular changes which take place in the muscle.
Huxley, Nineteenth Century, XXI. 495.

2. In *biol.*, one who seeks to explain fundamental vital phenomena upon purely physical or chemical principles; one who holds that life is a form of energy due simply to molecular movements taking place in the ultimate molecules of the protoplasm, and capable of correlation with the ordinary physical and chemical forces: opposed to *vitalist*. *H. A. Nicholson.*

physicky (fiz'i-ki), *a.* [‹ *physic(k)* + *-y*[1].] Like physic or drugs.

Some authors name it cauda pavonis, on account of its inimitable beauty; the flowers have a *physicky* smell.
Grainger, Sugar Cane, i., note 520.

physic-nut (fiz'ik-nut), *n.* See *Jatropha.*

physicochemical (fiz"i-kō-kem'i-kal), *a.* [‹ Gr. φυσικός, physical, + E. *chemical.*] Pertaining or relating to both physics and chemistry; produced by combined physical and chemical action or forces.

physicologic (fiz"i-kō-loj'ik), *n.* [‹ Gr. φυσική, physics, + λογική, logic: see *logic.*] Logic illustrated by physics.

physicological (fiz"i-kō-loj'i-kal), *a.* [‹ *physicologic* + *-al.*] Pertaining to physicologic. *Swift.* [Rare.]

physicomathematics (fiz"i-kō-math-ē-mat'iks), *n.* [= F. *physicomathématique* = It. *fisicomatematico*, ‹ Gr. φυσικά, physics, + μαθηματική, mathematics.] Mixed mathematics. See *mathematics.*

physicomental (fiz"i-kō-men'tal), *a.* [‹ Gr. φυσικός, physical, + E. *mental.*] Pertaining to physical and mental phenomena or their mutual relations.

physicophilosophy (fiz"i-kō-fi-los'ō-fi), *n.* [‹ Gr. φυσικά, physics, + φιλοσοφία, philosophy.] The philosophy of nature.

physicotheological (fiz"i-kō-thē-ō-loj'i-kal), *a.* [‹ *physicotheolog-y* + *-ic-al.*] Of or pertaining to physics and theology, or to physicotheology.

In the first case we have the cosmological and *physicotheological* proofs of the existence of God; in the second, the ontological. *Adamson*, Philos. of Kant.

physicotheology (fiz"i-kō-thē-ol'ō-ji), *n.* [‹ Gr. φυσικά, physics, + θεολογία, theology.] Theology illustrated or enforced by natural philosophy.

physics (fiz'iks), *n.* [Pl. of *physic*, after Gr. φυσικά, neut. pl., physics: see *physic.*] Natural philosophy; experimental philosophy; the science of the principles operative in inorganic nature; the science of forces or forms of energy. Before the rise of modern science, *physics* was usually defined as the science of that which is movable, or the science of natural bodies. It was commonly made to include all natural science. At present, vital phenomena are not considered objects of physics, which is divided into *general* and *applied physics.* General physics investigates the general phenomena of inorganic nature, determines their laws, and measures their constants. It embraces four branches — (1) *mechanics* or *dynamics*, the science of force in general, with extensive mathematical developments; (2) the *science of gravitation*, also mainly mathematical; (3) *molecular physics*, the study of the constitution of matter, and of the forces within and between its molecules, including elasticity and heat (an indivisible subject), cohesion, and chemical forces; and (4) the *physics of the ether*, being the study of light or radiation, electricity, and magnetism. Chemistry is for the time being divorced from physics, being chiefly occupied with the description of the formation of different kinds of substances. Applied physics uses the discoveries of general physics, in connection with special observations, in order to explain the phenomena of the universe. Its chief branches are astronomy, geology, and meteorology; to which may be added terrestrial magnetism, mineralogy, and some other subjects.

Physidæ (fis'i-dē), *n. pl.* [NL., ‹ *Physa* + *-idæ.*] A family of hygrophilous pulmoniferous gastropods, typified by the genus *Physa*, formerly included in *Limnæidæ.* The animal has setiform tentacles; the jaw is single, and has a fibrous prolongation; the radula has central multicuspid teeth; and the lateral as well as the marginal teeth are pectinate or serriform. The shell is sinistral and generally polished. The species abound in fresh water in various parts of the world.

physiform (fis'i-fôrm), *a.* [‹ NL. *Physa*, q. v., + L. *forma*, form.] Having the form of the genus *Physa.*

Physinæ (fi-si'nē), *n. pl.* [NL., ‹ *Physa* + *-inæ.*] The *Physidæ* as a subfamily of *Limnæidæ.*

physiocracy (fiz-i-ok'ra-si), *n.* [‹ Gr. φύσις, nature, + -κρατία, ‹ κρατεῖν, rule.] The economic doctrines and system advocated by the physiocrats; the theory that wealth consists in the products of the soil, that all labor expended in manufactures and in the distribution of wealth, though useful, is sterile, and that the revenue of the state should be raised by a direct tax on land. Also called *physiocratism.*

physiocrat (fiz'i-ō-krat), *n.* [‹ Gr. φύσις, nature, + κρατεῖν, rule: see *physiocracy.*] One who advocates the doctrines of physiocracy; specifically, one of a group of French philosophers and political economists, followers of François Quesnay (1694–1774), which rose to prominence in the latter half of the eighteenth century, and maintained that a natural constitution or order exists in society, the violation of which has been the cause of all the evils suffered by man. A fundamental right derived from this constitution or order was held to be freedom of person, of opinion, of property, and of contract or exchange. The physiocrats regarded land or raw materials as the sole source of wealth, leaving out of account the elements of labor and capital, and denying the dogma of the mercantile system that wealth consists in the precious metals. They maintained that, as wealth consisted entirely in the produce of land, all revenue should be raised by a direct tax on land. They advocated complete freedom of trade and the doctrine of laisser-faire. See *physiocracy.*

There is no other thinker of importance on economic subjects in France till the appearance of the *physiocrats*, which marks an epoch in the history of the science.
Encyc. Brit., XIX. 359.

Commerce, according to the theory of the *physiocrates*, only transfers already existing wealth from one hand to another. *W. Roscher*, Pol. Econ. (trans.), § 49.

physiocratic (fiz"i-ō-krat'ik), *a.* [‹ *physiocrat* + *-ic.*] Of or pertaining to government according to nature; specifically, of or pertaining to the physiocrats or their doctrines: as, *physiocratic* theories; the *physiocratic* school of political economy.

It [the mercantile system] forms the basis of the economic ideas of all writers of the eighteenth century who did not belong to the *physiocratic* school or to that of Adam Smith. *Cyc. Pol. Sci.*, II. 827.

De Gournay, the elder Mirabeau, Morellet, and Dupont de Nemours are well-remembered names of the *physiocratic* school. *Pop. Sci. Mo.*, XXXVI. 481.

physiocratism (fiz-i-ok'ra-tizm), *n.* [‹ *physiocrat* + *-ism.*] Same as *physiocracy.*

physiogenesis (fiz"i-ō-jen'e-sis), *n.* [‹ Gr. φύσις, nature, + γένεσις, generation.] Same as *physiogeny.*

physiogenetic (fiz"i-ō-jē-net'ik), *a.* [‹ *physiogenesis* (after *genetic*).] Same as *physiogenic.*

physiogenic (fiz"i-ō-jen'ik), *a.* [‹ *physiogen-y* + *-ic.*] Of or pertaining to physiogeny or physiogenesis; physiological with special reference to ontogeny and phylogeny; evolutionary or developmental with reference to physiology.

physiogeny (fiz-i-oj'e-ni), *n.* [‹ Gr. φύσις, nature, + -γένεια, ‹ -γενής, producing: see *-geny.*] 1. In *biol.*, the genesis of function; the development or evolution of those functions of living matter which are the province of physiology.— 2. The science or history of the evolution of functions of living matter.

Just as . . . [morphogeny] first opens the way to a true knowledge of organic forms, so will *Physiogeny* afterwards make a true recognition of functions possible, by discovering their historic evolution.
Haeckel, Evol. of Man (trans.), II. 461.

physiognomer (fiz-i-og'nō-mėr), *n.* [‹ *physiognom-y* + *-er*[1].] Same as *physiognomist.*

You erre, fond *physiognomers*, that hold
The inward minde followes the outward molde.
Times' Whistle (E. E. T. S.), p. 23.

physiognomic (fiz"i-og-nom'ik), *a.* [= F. *physionomique* = Sp. *fisionómico* = Pg. *physionomico*, *physiognomico* = It. *fisonomico*, *fisionomico*, ‹ MGr. φυσιογνωμικός, a late and incorrect form for φυσιογνωμονικός: see *physiognomonic.*] Pertaining to physiognomy, the face, or the art of discerning character in the face. Also *physiognomonic.*

From Da Vinci he caught one of the marked *physiognomic* traits of his visages, smiles and dimples.
Encyc. Brit., XIX. 458.

physiognomical (fiz"i-og-nom'i-kal), *a.* [‹ *physiognomic* + *-al.*] Same as *physiognomic.*

In long observation of men he may acquire a *physiognomical* intuitive knowledge; judge the interiours by the outside. *Sir T. Browne.*

physiognomically (fiz"i-og-nom'i-kal-i), *adv.* As regards or by means of physiognomy, or according to its rules or principles; as to the face.

Many a rough and tough old sea-commander, who would have returned a broadside without flinching, has been converted *physiognomically* into an admiral of the blue, white, and red, . . . on having to reply to a volley of thanks. *Hood*, The Elland Meeting.

physiognomics (fiz"i-og-nom'iks), *n.* [Pl. of *physiognomic*: see *-ics.*] Same as *physiognomy*, 1.

physiognomist (fiz-i-og'nō-mist), *n.* [= F. *physionomiste* = Sp. *fisionomista* = Pg. *physionomista* = It. *fisonomista*, *fisionomista*, *fisiognomista*; as *physiognom-y* + *-ist.*] One skilled in physiognomy. (*a*) One who judges of the disposition or qualities of the mind by observation of the countenance. (*b*) One who tells fortunes by scrutiny of the face.

A certain *physiognomist*, or teller of fortune by looking onely upon the face of men and women.
Holland, tr. of Pliny, xxxv. 10.

physiognomize (fiz-i-og'nō-mīz), *v. t.*; pret. and pp. *physiognomized*, ppr. *physiognomizing.* [‹ *physiognom-y* + *-ize.*] To practise physiognomy upon. *Southey.* [Rare.]

physiognomonic (fiz-i-og-nō-mon'ik), *a.* [= F. *physiognomonique*, ‹ Gr. φυσιογνωμονικός, ‹ φυσιογνωμονία, physiognomy: see *physiognomy.*] Same as *physiognomic.*

physiognomy (fiz-i-og'nō-mi), *n.*; pl. *physiognomies* (-miz). [Formerly also *phisiognomie*, also *phisonomie*, *physonomy*, *physnomie*, *phisnomie*, *fisnomy*, etc. (whence colloq. *phiz*, q. v.); ‹ ME. *fysnomye*, *fisnomie*, *visnomie*, *fisnamy*, *fyssnamy*, ‹ OF. *phisonomie*, *physonomie*, *physiognomie*, F. *physionomie* = Pr. *phizonomia* = Sp. *fisonomía* = Pg. *physionomia* = It. *fisiognomia*, *fisionomia*, *fisonomia*, ‹ ML. **physiognomia*, *phisionomia*, *phisonomia*, ‹ MGr. φυσιογνωμία, late and incorrect form of Gr. φυσιογνωμονία, the art of judging a man by his features, ‹ φυσιογνώμων, judging by features, ‹ φύσις, nature, + γνώμων, a judge, interpreter: see *gnomon.*] 1. The art of discovering the characteristic qualities of the mind or temper by observation of the form and movements of the face or body, or both. Also *physiognomics.*

Physiognomy . . . discovereth the disposition of the mind by the lineaments of the body.
Bacon, Advancement of Learning, ii. 184.

2. The face or countenance considered as an index to the mind or disposition; particular configuration, cast, or expression of countenance.

Another [beast] called Aranata, which for the *Physnomie* and subtletie seemes to bee a kinde of Ape.
Purchas, Pilgrimage, p. 825.

Who both in favour and in princely looke,
As well as in the mind's true qualitie,
Doth represent his father's *physnomie.*
Mir. for Mags., p. 756.

Faith, sir, a has an English maine, but his *fisnomy* is more hotter in France then there. *Shak.*, All's Well, iv. 5. 42.

Let the idea of what you are be pourtrayed in your face, that men may read in your *physnomy.*
B. *Jonson*, Every Man in his Humour, i. 2.

The end of portraits consists of expressing the true temper of those persons which it represents, and to make known their *physiognomy.*
Dryden, tr. of Dufresnoy's Art of Painting.

3†. The art of telling fortunes by inspection of the features.

Ger. Let me peruse
Thy face; I'll tell myself how thou hast sped:
Well; is 't not so? . . .
Thor. Your *physiognomy*
Is quite discredited. *Shirley*, Love in a Maze, ii. 3.

4. The general appearance of anything, as the particular configuration of a landscape; the external aspect, without reference to other characteristics.

The changes produced in the *physiognomy* of vegetation on ascending mountains.
Balfour, Botany, § 1158. (*Encyc. Dict.*)

Little details gave each field a particular *physiognomy*, dear to the eyes that have looked on them from childhood.
George Eliot, Middlemarch, xii.

physiogony (fiz-i-og'ō-ni), *n.* [‹ Gr. φύσις, nature, + γονή, generation: see *-gony.*] The production or generation of nature. *Coleridge.*

physiographer (fiz-i-og'ra-fėr), *n.* [‹ *physiograph-y* + *-er*[1].] One versed in, or who practises, physiography. *Amer. Jour. Sci.*, 3d ser., XXX. 261.

physiographic (fiz"i-ō-graf'ik), *a.* [= F. *physiographique* = Sp. *fisiográfico* = Pg. *physiographico* = It. *fisiografico*; as *physiograph-y* + *-ic.*] Belonging or related to physiography: a *physiographic* description of the earth, or a *physiographic* work, is a physico-geographical description or work.—**Physiographic geology**, nearly the same as *orography*, or a discussion of the earth's general features.—**Physiographic mineralogy**, as the phrase is most generally used, nearly or quite the same as *descriptive mineralogy.* The use of this term is rare in English books, except in translations from the German.

physiographical (fiz"i-ō-graf'i-kal), *a.* [‹ *physiographic* + *-al.*] Same as *physiographic.*

Courses of lectures bearing connectively on geographical and *physiographical* subjects. *The American*, VIII. 125.

physiographically (fiz"i-ō-graf'i-kal-i), *adv.* As regards physiography; from a physiographic point of view: as, *physiographically* important.

physiography (fiz-i-og'ra-fi), *n.* [= F. *physiographie* = Sp. *fisiografía* = Pg. *physiographia* = It. *fisiografia*, ‹ Gr. φύσις, nature, + -γραφία, ‹ γράφειν, write.] A word of rather variable meaning, but, as most generally used, nearly or quite the equivalent of *physical geography* (which see, under *physical*). Also called *geophysics*.

This term [*physical geography*] as here used is synonymous with *Physiography*, which has been proposed in its stead. *Geikie*, Elem. Lessons in Phys. Geog., p. 3, note.

[For the use of the word *physiography* by Huxley, as meaning a peculiar kind of physical geography, see the following quotation.

The attempt to convey scientific conceptions without the appeal to observation which can alone give such conceptions firmness and reality appears to me to be in direct antagonism to the fundamental principles of scientific education. *Physiography* has very little to do with this sort of "Physical Geography."
Huxley, Physiography (2d ed.), vii.]

Microscopic physiography. Same as *lithology* or *petrography*: a term thus far used only in the translation from the German of an important work by Rosenbusch, bearing the title "Mikroskopische Physiographie."

physiolatry (fiz-i-ol′a̤-tri), *n.* [< Gr. φύσις, nature, + λατρεία, worship.] The worship of the powers or agencies of nature; nature-worship.

A pantheistic philosophy based on the *physiolatry* of the Vedas. *M. Williams.*

physiologer (fiz-i-ol′ǭ-jėr), *n.* [< *physiolog-y* + *-er*[1].] A physical philosopher, or philosopher of the Ionic school. See *Ionic*.

The generality of the old *phisiologers* before Aristotle and Democritus did pursue the atomical way, which is to resolve the corporeal phenomena, not into forms, qualities, and species, but into figures, motions, and phancies.
Cudworth, Intellectual System, p. 171.

The earliest philosophers or *physiologers* had occupied themselves chiefly with what we may call cosmology.
Encyc. Brit., XVIII. 792.

physiologic (fiz″i-ǭ-loj′ik), *a.* [= F. *physiologique* = Sp. *fisiológico* = Pg. *physiologico* = It. *fisiologico*, < L. *physiologicus*, < Gr. φυσιολογικός, < φυσιολογία, physiology: see *physiology*.] Of or pertaining to physiology.

In early society, incest laws do not recognize *physiologic* conditions, but only social conditions.
J. W. Powell, Science, IV. 472.

No method is more alluring in *physiologic* studies than this of accurate measurement and description.
N. A. Rev., CXXVI. 553.

physiological (fiz″i-ǭ-loj′i-ka̤l), *a.* [< *physiologic* + *-al.*] Of a physiologic character.

The Mosaical philosophy in the *physiological* part thereof is the same with the Cartesian.
Dr. H. More, Def. of Philosophic Cabbala, App. i. § 8.

The most characteristic *physiological* peculiarity of the plant is its power of manufacturing protein from chemical compounds of a less complex nature.
Huxley, Anat. Invert., p. 47.

Physiological antidote, an antidote of opposite pharmacodynamic properties to the poison.—**Physiological botany, chemistry, illusion, optics**, etc. See the nouns.—**Physiological test**, the test for a poison of giving the suspected substance to some living animal.—**Physiological time**, the entire interval of time between an impression on an organ of sense and the muscular reaction; reaction-time.

physiologically (fiz″i-ǭ-loj′i-ka̤l-i), *adv.* According to the principles of physiology; as regards physiology.

physiologist (fiz-i-ol′ǭ-jist), *n.* [= F. *physiologiste* = Sp. *fisiologista* = Pg. *physiologista*; as *physiolog-y* + *-ist.*] One who is versed in physiology.

physiologize (fiz-i-ol′ǭ-jīz), *v. i.*; pret. and pp. *physiologized*, ppr. *physiologizing*. [< *physiolog-y* + *-ize.*] To reason or discourse of the nature of things.

They who first theologized did *physiologize* after this manner. *Cudworth*, Intellectual System, p. 120.

physiology (fiz-i-ol′ǭ-ji), *n.* [Formerly also *phisiologie*; < F. *physiologie* = Sp. *fisiologia* = Pg. *physiologia* = It. *fisiologia*, < L. *physiologia*, < Gr. φυσιολογία, natural philosophy, < φυσιολόγος (> L. *physiologus*), discoursing of nature, as a noun a natural philosopher, < φύσις, nature (see *physic*), + -λογία, < λέγειν, speak: see *-ology*.] 1†. Natural philosophy.

The unparallel'd Des Cartes hath unridled their dark *physiology* and to wonder solv'd their motions.
Glanville, Vanity of Dogmatizing, xviii.

2. The sum of scientific knowledge concerning the functions of living things. The subject comprises two grand divisions, namely *animal* and *vegetable physiology*; when specially applied to the functions in man, the term *human physiology* is used.

Physiology is the science of vital power.
Huxley and Youmans, Physiol., § 370.

physiomedicalism (fiz″i-ǭ-med′i-kal-izm), *n.* [< Gr. φύσις, nature, + E. *medical* + *-ism.*] The doctrines or practices of the physiomedicalists.

physiomedicalist (fiz″i-ǭ-med′i-ka̤l-ist), *n.* [< Gr. φύσις, nature, + E. *medical* + *-ist.*] An adherent or practitioner of that school of medicine which, in its treatment of disease, uses only botanic remedies, discarding those which are poisonous.

physionotrace (fiz-i-on′ǭ-trās), *n.* [F., < *physiono(mie)*, physiognomy, + *trace*, trace.] An instrument for tracing the outlines of a face.

Chrétien, in 1786, had invented an instrument which he denominated the *physionotrace*, by which the profile outline of a face could be taken with mathematical precision, both as to figure and dimensions.
The Century, XXXVIII. 779.

physiophilosophy (fiz″i-ǭ-fi-los′ǭ-fi), *n.* [< Gr. φύσις, nature, + φιλοσοφία, philosophy.] The philosophy of nature.

physiophyly (fiz-i-of′i-li), *n.* [< Gr. φύσις, nature, + φῦλον, a tribe: see *phylum*, *phyle*.] The tribal history of function; that branch of phylogeny which treats of function alone, without reference to form, the tribal history or phylogeny of which latter Haeckel calls *morphophyly*.

Physiophyly, . . . the tribal history of the functions, or the history of the palæontological development of the vital activities, has, in the case of most organisms, not yet been examined. In the case of man, a large part of the history of culture falls under this head.
Haeckel, Evol. of Man (trans.), I. 24.

physiosophic (fiz″i-ǭ-sof′ik), *a.* [< *physiosoph-y* + *-ic.*] Pertaining to physiosophy.

physiosophy (fiz-i-os′ǭ-fi), *n.* [< Gr. φύσις, nature, + σοφία, wisdom.] A doctrine concerning the secrets of nature.

Fanciful ideas of the vaguest kind of *physiosophy*.
Günther, Encyc. Brit., XX. 437.

physiotypy (fiz′i-ǭ-tī-pi), *n.* [< Gr. φύσις, nature, + τύπος, type.] Same as *nature-printing*.

Physiphora (fī-zif′ǭ-rạ̈), *n.* Same as *Physophora*, 2.

physique (fi-zēk′), *n.* [< F. *physique*, m., natural constitution, physique: see *physic*.] Physical structure or organization, especially of a human being.

Out of this strong, ancient, and far-spreading root of domestic piety the powerful *physique* and the healthy mental and moral nature of the Roman grew.
Faiths of the World, p. 191.

physitheism (fiz′i-thē-izm), *n.* [< Gr. φύσις, nature, + θεός, God, + *-ism.*] The attribution of physical or bodily form to the Deity.

physitheistic (fiz″i-thẹ̄-is′tik), *a.* [< Gr. φύσις, nature, + θεός, God, + *-ist-ic.*] Of or pertaining to physitheism. *Pop. Sci. Mo.*, XXXVI. 208.

physiurgic (fiz-i-ėr′jik), *a.* [< Gr. φύσις, nature, + ἔργον, work. Cf. *theurgic.*] See the quotation.

Thus Natural History and Natural Philosophy are respectively represented by *Physiurgic* Somatology and Anthropurgic Somatology: the one signifying the science of bodies, in so far as operated upon in the course of nature, without the intervention of man; the other, the science of bodies so far as man, by his knowledge of the convertible powers of nature, is able to operate upon them.
Bowring, in Int. to Bentham's Works, § 6.

physnomy† (fiz′nǭ-mi), *n.* Same as *physiognomy*.

Physocalymma (fī″sǭ-kạ̄-lim′ạ̈), *n.* [NL. (Pohl, 1827), < Gr. φῦσα, a bladder, + κάλυμμα, a covering (calyx): see *Calymma*.] A genus of polypetalous trees of the order *Lythrarieæ* and tribe *Lythreæ*, characterized by the change of the four-celled ovary in fruit into a small one-celled and many-seeded thin-walled capsule, inclosed within the enlarged bladdery calyx. The only species, *P. floribundum*, is a Brazilian tree with opposite oblong roughish leaves and ample terminal loose-flowered purple panicles. Each flower is composed of two broad concave bracts which at first inclose the roundish flower-bud, an eight-toothed and bell-shaped purple calyx, eight wavy petals, and a row of twenty-four long stamens bearing curved versatile anthers. The beautifully striped rose-colored wood is the *tulip-wood* of English cabinet-makers, also known as *Brazilian pinkwood*. See *tulip-wood*.

physocele (fī′sǭ-sēl), *n.* [< Gr. φῦσα, breath, wind, air-bubble, + κήλη, tumor.] A hernia containing gas.

physoclist (fī′sǭ-klist), *n.* and *a.* **I.** *n.* A member of the *Physoclisti*.

II. *a.* Same as *physoclistous*.

Physoclisti (fī-sǭ-klis′ti), *n. pl.* [NL., pl. of *physoclistus*: see *physoclistous*.] In *ichth.*, a group of teleost fishes having the duct between the air-bladder and the intestine closed: opposed to *Physostomi*. It includes the acanthopterygian fishes, and also the synentognathous fishes, the subbrachial and jugular malacopterygians, the lophobranchiates, and the plectognaths. In Cope's system of classification it is a primary group of actinopterous fishes without a pneumatic duct, with the parietal bones separated by the supraoccipital, and the ventrals thoracic or jugular and without basilar segments.

physoclistic (fī-sǭ-klis′tik), *a.* Same as *physoclistous*. *Encyc. Brit.*, XVI. 671.

physoclistous (fī-sǭ-klis′tus), *a.* [< NL. **physoclistus*, < Gr. φῦσα, bellows, + κλειστός, that may be closed, < κλείειν, close: see *close*[1].] Having no air-bladder, or having the air-bladder closed, as a fish; belonging to the *Physoclisti*, or having their characters.

Physograda (fī-sog′rạ̄-dạ̈), *n. pl.* [NL., neut. pl. of *physogradus*: see *physograde*.] 1. In De Blainville's classification of acalephs, a group of oceanic hydrozoans, provided with hollow vesicular organs which buoy them up and enable them to float.—2. In a restricted sense, an order or suborder of siphonophorous hydrozoans, represented by such forms as the *Physaliidæ*: distinguished from the *Chondrograda*, as *Velellidæ*. See cut under *Physalia*.

physograde (fī′sǭ-grād), *a.* and *n.* [< NL. *physogradus*, < Gr. φῦσα, bellows, + L. *gradi*, step, walk, go.] **I.** *a.* Moving by means of a vesicular float or buoy; of or pertaining to the *Physograda*.

II. *n.* A member of the *Physograda*.

physohematometra, physohæmatometra (fī-sǭ-hem″a̤-tǭ-mē′trạ̈), *n.* [NL., < Gr. φῦσα, a bubble, + αἷμα(τ-), blood, + μήτρα, uterus.] The presence of blood and gas in the uterus.

physohydrometra (fī-sǭ-hī-drǭ-mē′trạ̈), *n.* [NL., < Gr. φῦσα, a bubble, + ὕδωρ (ὑδρ-), water, + μήτρα, uterus: see *hydrometra*[2].] The presence of gas and serum in the uterus.

physoid (fī′soid), *a.* [< NL. *Physa*, q. v., + Gr. εἶδος, form.] Of or relating to the *Physidæ*; like the *Physidæ*, although not of that family; physiform.

Physolobium (fī-sǭ-lō′bi-um), *n.* [NL. (Huegel, 1837), < Gr. φῦσα, bellows, + λοβός, a pod, lobe: see *lobe*.] A section of the plant-genus *Kennedya*. See *bladder-pod*.

physometra (fī-sǭ-mē′trạ̈), *n.* [NL., < Gr. φῦσα, a bubble, + μήτρα, uterus.] The presence of gas in the uterus.

Physomycetes (fī″sǭ-mī-sē′tēz), *n. pl.* [NL., < Gr. φῦσα, bellows, + μύκης, pl. μύκητες, a fungus, mushroom.] A small section of *Fungi*, characterized by the total absence of a hymenium, and by the vesicular fruit inclosing an indefinite number or mass of sporidia. Also called *Vesiculiferi*.

Physonota (fī-sǭ-nō′tạ̈), *n.* [NL. (Boheman, 1854), < Gr. φῦσα, bellows, + νῶτος, back.] An American genus of leaf-beetles or chrysomelids, with about 50 species, characterized by having the third antennal joint longer than the second, and the fourth equal to the third. *P. unipunctata*, var. *quinquepunctata*, is the so-called five-spotted tortoise-beetle, whose larva has 20 smooth spines and feeds on the leaves of sunflowers.

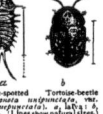

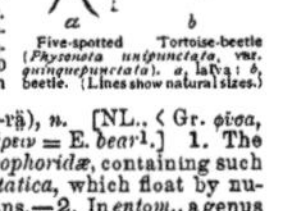

Five-spotted Tortoise-beetle (*Physonota unipunctata*, var. *quinquepunctata*). *a*, larva; *b*, beetle. (Lines show natural sizes.)

Physophora (fī-sof′ǭ-rạ̈), *n.* [NL., < Gr. φῦσα, bellows, + -φόρος, < φέρειν = E. *bear*[1].] 1. The typical genus of *Physophoridæ*, containing such species as *P. hydrostatica*, which float by numerous vesicular organs.—2. In *entom.*, a genus of dipterous insects. Also *Physiphora*. *Fallen*, 1810.—3. [Used as a plural.] Same as *Physophoræ*.

Physophoræ (fī-sof′ǭ-rē), *n. pl.* [NL., pl. of *Physophora*.] An order of siphonophorous oceanic hydrozoans, having the proximal end modified into a float or pneumatophore (as distinguished from a somatocyst). They are mostly monœcious, and are sometimes provided with nectocalyces, and the polypites are united by an unbranched or little-branched cœnosarc, of filiform, globular, or discoidal shape. The group is contrasted with *Calycophoræ*, as one of two orders of *Siphonophora*, and contains a number of families, as *Physophoridæ* and others. Also written *Physophora*, *Physophorida*, *Physophoridæ*. See cuts under *hydranth*, *hydrophyllium*, and *Hydrozoa*.

physophoran (fī-sof′ǭ-ran), *a.* and *n.* [< *Physophora* + *-an.*] **I.** *a.* Of or pertaining to the *Physophoræ*.

II. *n.* A member of the order *Physophoræ*; a physophorous hydrozoan.

physophore (fī′sǭ-fōr), *n.* [< NL. *Physophora*.] Same as *physophoran*.

Physophorida (fī-sǭ-for′i-dạ̈), *n. pl.* [NL., < *Physophora* + *-ida.*] Same as *Physophoræ*.

Physophoridæ (fī-sǭ-for′i-dē), *n. pl.* [NL., < *Physophora* + *-idæ.*] 1. A family of physophorous hydrozoans, represented by the genus *Physophora*; one of several families of the order *Physophoræ*. See cuts under *hydranth*, *hydrophyllium*, and *Hydrozoa*.—2. Same as *Physophoræ*.

physophorous (fī-sof′ǭ-rus), *a.* [< *Physophora* + *-ous.*] Same as *physophoran*.

physopod (fī'sǫ-pod), *a.* and *n.* [< Gr. φῦσα, bellows, + πούς (ποδ-) = E. *foot.*] I. *a.* Having a sort of sucker on the feet; specifically, of or pertaining to the *Physopoda.*

II. *n.* A member of the *Physopoda.*

Physopoda† (fī-sop'ǫ-dạ̈), *n. pl.* [NL., < Gr. φῦσα, bellows, + πούς (ποδ-) = E. *foot.*] Same as *Thysanoptera.*

Physospermum (fī-sǫ-spėr'mum), *n.* [NL. (Cusson, 1782), so called with reference to the looseness of the outer coat of the young fruit; < Gr. φῦσα, bellows, + σπέρμα, seed: see *sperm.*] A genus of umbelliferous plants of the tribe *Ammineæ* and subtribe *Smyrnieæ*, distinguished by the large oil-tubes solitary in their channels, and the very slight ridges on the ovate or compressed fruit. There are about 5 species, natives of Europe and the Caucasus. They are smooth perennials, with ample and minutely dissected leaves, and compound umbels of many white flowers with many linear bracts and bractlets. Several species are cultivated for ornament, under the name *bladder-seed.*

Physostegia (fī-sǫ-stē'ji-ạ̈), *n.* [NL. (Bentham, 1829), so called with reference to the enlarged and somewhat inflated fruiting calyx; < Gr. φῦσα, bellows, + στέγη, a roof or covering.] A genus of erect herbs of the order *Labiatæ*, the mint family, belonging to the tribe *Stachydeæ* and subtribe *Melittеæ*, and characterized by the broad and five-toothed calyx, long-exserted ample corolla-tube, parallel anther-cells, and two-flowered spiked verticillasters. There are 3 species, all North American, called *false dragon's-head* (which see, under *dragon's-head*). They are tall and smooth perennials, with narrow toothed leaves, and showy sessile pink or flesh-colored flowers, forming one or many dense or interrupted terminal spikes. *P. Virginiana*, the variable eastern species, is often cultivated in gardens.

Physostigma (fī-sǫ-stig'mạ̈), *n.* [NL. (Balfour, 1861), so called with reference to the bladder-like apex of the style; < Gr. φῦσα, bellows, + στίγμα, stigma.] A genus of leguminous plants of the tribe *Phaseoleæ* and subtribe *Euphaseoleæ*, characterized by the spiral keel and by the continuation of the bearded style above the stigma into a large and oblique hollow hood. The only species, *P. venenosum*, is a high-twining vine of tropical Africa, with leaves of three large leaflets, and axillary pendulous racemes of purplish flowers, followed by long dark-brown compressed pods, each with two or three thick oblong highly poisonous seeds of valuable medicinal powers. See *Calabar bean* (under *bean*[1]), *chop-nut, eserine,* and *physostigmine.*

physostigmine (fī-sǫ-stig'min), *n.* [< *Physostigma* + *-ine*[2].] An alkaloid constituting the active principle of the Calabar bean. It is highly poisonous, and when separated by the usual process presents the appearance of a brownish-yellow amorphous mass. It is tasteless, being only slightly soluble in water.

physostomatous (fī-sǫ-stom'ạ-tus), *a.* Same as *physostomous.*

physostome (fī'sǫ-stōm), *a.* and *n.* I. *a.* Same as *physostomous.*

II. *n.* A physostomous fish.

Physostomi (fī-sos'tǫ-mī), *n. pl.* [NL., pl. of *physostomus*: see *physostomous.*] An order of teleost fishes established by J. Müller in 1845, containing those whose air-bladder, when present, is connected with the alimentary canal by an air-duct, the bladder thus having an outlet or mouth: contrasted with *Physoclisti.* The order was divided by Müller into 2 suborders and 14 families. It includes most of the abdominal malacopterygian fishes of the older authors. In Cope's system of classification it is ranked as a primary group of actinopterous fishes, with the basilar segments of the ventral fin rudimental and abdominal, the parietal bones usually united, branchiostegal rays developed, and the pneumatic duct open. It includes, in addition to the forms recognized by Müller, certain ganoids, as the *Amiidæ* (order *Halecomorphi*) and *Lepidosteidæ* (order *Ginglymodi*). See cuts under *Percopsis, pike,* and *Esox.*

physostomous (fī-sos'tǫ-mus), *a.* [< NL. *physostomus*, < Gr. φῦσα, bellows, + στόμα, mouth.] Having the mouth and air-bladder connected by an air-duct, as a fish; specifically, of or pertaining to the *Physostomi.* Also *physostomatous, physostome.*

physy† (fiz'i), *n.* [A corrupt form for *fusee*[2] (simulating Gr. φῦσα, a bellows ?).] A fusee.

Some watches . . . are made with four wheels, others with five; . . . some have strings and *physies*, and others none. *Locke*, Human Understanding, III. vi. § 39.

phytalbumose (fī-tal'bū-mōs), *n.* [< Gr. φυτόν, plant, + *album(en)* + *-ose.*] A form of albumen occurring in plants: so named to distinguish it from similar forms occurring in animals.

Phytastra (fī-tas'trạ̈), *n. pl.* [NL., < Gr. φυτόν, plant, + ἀστήρ, star.] In Lankester's classification, one of two orders of *Ophiuroidea*, contrasted with *Ophiastra.*

Phytelephantinæ (fī-tel''ē-fan-tī'nē), *n. pl.* [NL. (Drude, 1887), < *Phytelephas* (*-elephant-*) + *-inæ.*] A tribe of palms, distinguished by the confluence of the ovaries in fruit into a globose syncarp, and including the two genera *Phytelephas* and *Nipa*, both very different from all other palms and from each other, but alike in their growth from partly or wholly prostrate stems, their corneous albumen, and their flowers of one or both sexes crowded upon long drooping spadices resembling catkins.

Phytelephas (fī-tel'ē-fas), *n.* [NL. (Ruiz and Pavon, 1798), so called with reference to the hard albumen, called vegetable ivory; < Gr. φυτόν, plant, + ἐλέφας, ivory: see *elephant.*] An aberrant genus of palms, type of the tribe *Phytelephantinæ*, and from its singularity long separated as an order *Phytelephanteæ* (*Martius*, 1835). It is unlike all other palms in its numerous stamens, filiform stigmas, and unbranched spadices, and in the elongated petals of its female flower. There are 3 species, natives of Peru and the United States of Colombia, known from the nut as *ivory-palm.* They are diœcious trees growing in dense and extensive groves, with a short robust trunk sometimes 6 feet high from a creeping and prostrate base often 20 feet long. They bear a crown of a dozen or more pinnate leaves, reaching 18 or 20 feet in length, resembling those of the cocoanut-palm, and used by the natives in roofing. The male trees are taller, and bear a fleshy and pendulous cylindrical fragrant spadix about 4 feet long, crowded with small flowers between minute bracts, each with about thirty-six stamens, and

Fruiting Female Plant of Vegetable Ivory (*Phytelephas macrocarpa*).

exhaling a penetrating odor of almonds. The female tree produces a shorter and erect spadix, six or eight at once, each with six or seven pure-white flowers, which are far the largest among palms, with from five to ten fleshy petals (each from 2 to 3 inches long), three papery triangular sepals, numerous imperfect stamens, and a roundish ovary with from four to nine furrows, carpels, and stigmas, becoming a drupe in fruit. The mass of six or seven drupes from one spadix consolidates into a heavy pendulous globose syncarp, or multiple fruit (from its size known locally as *negro's-head*), covered with hard woody prominences. Each drupe contains about six large seeds; these, when young, are filled with a clear liquid, which is sought by travelers as a drink, and solidifies first into a pulp eagerly eaten by animals, and later into the hardest albumen known, whence its name *ivory-nut.* This again softens in germinating, turning into a milk and pulp, which feeds the young plant until it has grown for a year or more.

Phyteuma (fī-tū'mạ̈), *n.* [NL. (Linnæus, 1737), < L. *phyteuma*, < Gr. φύτευμα, a kind of plant, perhaps *Reseda phyteuma*; a particular use of φύτευμα, anything planted, < φυτεύειν, plant, < φυτόν, a plant: see *phyton.*] A genus of ornamental plants of the order *Campanulaceæ*, distinguished by a five-parted corolla with narrow spreading or long cohering lobes, and a fruit closed at the apex and dehiscent laterally. There are about 50 species, natives of Europe, the Mediterranean region, and the temperate parts of Asia. They are perennial herbs, with long-stalked radical leaves, and small alternate stem-leaves. The flowers are commonly blue, sessile, and handsome, often in a dense head or spike. Some species are well known in cultivation, especially as hardy ornaments in rockwork, by the name of *horned rampion* (which see, under *rampion*), and often under a former generic name, *Rapunculus.*

phytiform (fī'ti-fôrm), *a.* [< Gr. φυτόν, plant, + L. *forma*, form.] Resembling a plant.

phytiphagan (fī-tif'ạ-gạn), *a.* and *n.* See *phytophagan.*

phytivorous† (fī-tiv'ǫ-rus), *a.* [< Gr. φυτόν, plant, + L. *vorare*, devour.] Feeding on plants or herbage; herbivorous; phytophagous. *Ray*, Works of Creation.

phytobiology (fī-tǫ-bī-ol'ǫ-ji), *n.* [< Gr. φυτόν, plant, + E. *biology.*] That branch of biology which deals with plants; vegetable biology. *Athenæum*, No. 3253, p. 278.

phytobranchiate (fī-tǫ-brang'ki-āt), *a.* [< Gr. φυτόν, plant, + βράγχια, gills.] Having leafy gills; noting a division of isopods, in distinction from *pterygobranchiate.*

phytochemical (fī-tǫ-kem'i-kạl), *a.* [< Gr. φυτόν, plant, + E. *chemical.*] Pertaining or relating to phytochemistry.

phytochemistry (fī-tǫ-kem'is-tri), *n.* [< Gr. φυτόν, plant, + E. *chemistry.*] Vegetable chemistry; the chemistry of plants.

phytochimy (fī'tǫ-kim-i), *n.* [< F. *phytochimie*, < Gr. φυτόν, plant, + F. *chimie*, chemistry: see *alchemy, chemist.*] Same as *phytochemistry.*

phytochlore (fī'tǫ-klōr), *n.* [< Gr. φυτόν, plant, + χλωρός, pale-green: see *chlorin.* Cf. *chlorophyl.*] In *bot.*, same as *chlorophyl.*

Phytocoridæ (fī-tǫ-kor'i-dē), *n. pl.* [NL. (Fieber, 1861), < *Phytocoris* + *-idæ.*] A very large family of heteropterous insects, typified by the genus *Phytocoris*, and collectively called *plant-bugs.* They are mostly of small size, and are extremely variable in form; the base of the wings has usually a looped nervure; and the ocelli are extremely minute or wanting. They are divided into more than a dozen subfamilies, among them being the bugs commonly known as *Capsini* or *Capsinæ.*

Phytocoris (fī-tok'ǫ-ris), *n.* [NL. (Fallen, 1814), < Gr. φυτόν, plant, + κόρις, bug.] A genus of plant-bugs, typical of the family *Phytocoridæ*, having the beak extending to the middle of the abdomen, and the sides of the head angular. There are about 20 species, 7 of which inhabit North America. *P. tripustulatus* is blackish, spotted with orange, and found on nettles.

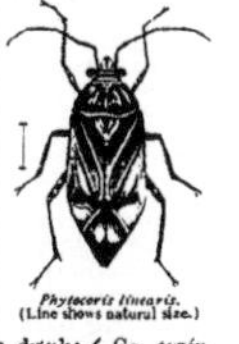

Phytocoris linearis. (Line shows natural size.)

Phytocrene (fī-tǫ-krē'nē), *n.* [NL. (Wallich, 1832), so called with reference to a copious watery sap which flows from the porous wood when pierced, and is used as a drink; < Gr. φυτόν, plant, + κρήνη, fountain.] A genus of polypetalous shrubs of the order *Olacineæ*, type of the tribe *Phytocreneæ*, characterized by capitate flowers with filaments longer than the anthers. The 8 species are natives of tropical Asia and Africa. They are high climbing and twining shrubs, with alternate leaves, and small diœcious hairy flowers, the staminate heads the size of peas and densely crowded in elongated panicles, the pistillate heads solitary and reaching the size of the human head, followed by a globular mass of hairy or spiny drupes with resinous stones. *P. gigantea*, with white flowers, from Martaban in Burma, is cultivated under glass by the names of *water-vine, vegetable fountain*, and *East Indian fountain-tree.*

Phytocreneæ (fī-tǫ-krē'nẹ-ē), *n. pl.* [NL. (Arnott, 1834), < *Phytocrene* + *-eæ.*] A tribe of polypetalous plants of the order *Olacineæ*, characterized by equal and alternate stamens and petals, and broad leaf-like or fleshy cotyledons. It includes 11 genera and about 37 species, all tropical climbers, of which *Phytocrene* is the type.

phytogenesis (fī-tǫ-jen'e-sis), *n.* [NL., < Gr. φυτόν, plant, + γένεσις, origin: see *genesis.*] The doctrine of the generation of plants.

phytogenetic (fī''tǫ-jẹ-net'ik), *a.* [< *phytogenesis*, after *genetic.*] Of or pertaining to phytogeny; of vegetable or plant origin.

phytogenetical (fī-tǫ-jẹ-net'i-kạl), *a.* [< *phytogenetic* + *-al.*] Same as *phytogenetic.*

The morphological and *phytogenetical* study of the higher plants. *Pop. Sci. Mo.*, XXXIII. 479.

phytogeny (fī-toj'e-ni), *n.* [< Gr. φυτόν, plant, + -γένεια, < -γενής, producing: see *-geny.*] Same as *phytogenesis.*

phytogeographer (fī''tǫ-jẹ-og'rạ-fėr), *n.* [< *phytogeograph-y* + *-er*[1].] One who is versed in phytogeography. *Nature*, XL. 98.

phytogeographic (fī-tǫ-jē-ǫ-graf'ik), *a.* [< *phytogeograph-y* + *-ic.*] Of or pertaining to phytogeography.

Islands may be arranged, . . . for *phytogeographic* purposes in three categories, according to their endemic element. *Nature*, XXXIII. 338.

phytogeographical (fī-tǫ-jē-ǫ-graf'i-kạl), *a.* [< *phytogeographic* + *-al.*] Same as *phytogeographic.*

phytogeography (fī''tǫ-jẹ-og'rạ-fi), *n.* [= F. *phytogéographie* = It. *fitogeografia*, < Gr. φυτόν, plant, + γεωγραφία, geography: see *geography.*] The geography or geographical distribution of plants: correlated with *zoögeography.*

phytoglyphic (fī-tǫ-glif'ik), *a.* [< *phytoglyph-y* + *-ic.*] Of or pertaining to phytoglyphy.

phytoglyphy (fī-tog'li-fi), *n.* [< Gr. φυτόν, plant, + γλύφειν, engrave: see *glyph.*] Nature-printing, as applied to the portraying of plants, for which the process was especially devised. Also *phytography*.

phytographer (fī-tog'rạ-fėr), *n.* [< *phytograph-y* + *-er*¹.] One who describes, names, and classifies plants.

phytographic (fī-tǫ-graf'ik), *a.* [< *phytograph-y* + *-ic.*] Of or pertaining to phytography or phytographers; relating or related to the describing, naming, and classifying of plants. *Nature*, XXXVIII. 220.

phytographical (fī-tǫ-graf'i-kạl), *a.* [< *phytographic* + *-al.*] Same as *phytographic*.

phytography (fī-tog'rạ-fi), *n.* [= F. *phytographie* = Sp. *fitografía* = Pg. *phytographia* = It. *fitografia*, < Gr. φυτόν, plant, + -γραφία, < γράφειν, write.] 1. The description of plants; that branch of botany which concerns itself with the rules to be observed in describing, naming, and classifying plants.

> *Phytography* is entirely subordinate to Taxonomy, or Systematic Botany.
> *Henslow*, Descriptive and Physiological Botany, § 3.

2. Same as *phytoglyphy*.

phytoid (fī'toid), *a.* [< Gr. *φυτοειδής (in adv. φυτοειδῶς), contr. φυτώδης, like a plant, < φυτόν, plant, + εἶδος, form.] Plant-like: specifically, in zoölogy, noting animals and organs which resemble plants in appearance.

Phytolacca (fī-tǫ-lak'ạ̈), *n.* [NL. (Tournefort, 1700), so called in allusion to the crimson juice of the berries; < Gr. φυτόν, plant, + NL. *lacca*, lac, F. *lac*, lake: see *lac*², *lake*³.] A genus of plants, type of the order *Phytolaccaceæ* and tribe *Euphytolacceæ*, characterized by the depressed-globose berry of from five to twelve sessile carpels. There are 10 species, mainly tropical and American, a few African and Asiatic. They vary greatly in habit, being shrubs, herbs, or trees, erect or climbing, smooth or hairy, and with round, grooved, or angled branches. They bear alternate undivided leaves, and small flowers in axillary racemes or opposite the leaves, at first apparently terminal. They are usually of marked poisonous and medicinal properties, especially *P. decandra*, one of the most characteristic of American plants (for which see *poke-weed*, also called *coakum*, *scoke*, *redweed*, *red-ink plant*, *ink-berry-weed*, *pigeonberry*, *garget*, and *foxglove*). *P. icosandra*, a small and shrubby plant, is cultivated for its graceful drooping racemes of white flowers, under the name of *hydrangea-leafed poke*. *P. octandra* is the Spanish calalu, or West Indian foxglove. (For *P. dioica*, also called *tree-poke* and *umbra-tree*, see *bellasombra-tree*.) *P. esculenta* has been cultivated, often under the name of *Pircunia*, as a substitute for asparagus and for spinach.

Phytolaccaceæ (fī"tǫ-la-kā'sẹ̄-ē), *n. pl.* [NL. (Lindley, 1835), < *Phytolacca* + *-aceæ.*] An order of apetalous plants of the series *Curvembryeæ*, distinguished by the usually many carpels in a ring, each with an undivided style. It includes about 60 species, of 3 tribes and 10 genera, of which *Phytolacca* (the type), *Rivina*, and *Petiveria* are the best-known. They are trees, shrubs, or herbs with a woody base, bearing alternate entire leaves, generally smooth branches, and racemed flowers, of greenish or whitish tinge, with one bract at the base of the pedicel and two smaller at its middle.

phytolite† (fī'tǫ-līt), *n.* [= F. *phytolithe* = It. *fitolite*, < Gr. φυτόν, plant, + λίθος, stone.] A fossil plant.

phytolithologist (fī"tǫ-li-thol'ǫ-jist), *n.* [< *phytolitholog-y* + *-ist.*] One who is skilled in or who writes upon fossil plants.

phytolithology (fī"tǫ-li-thol'ǫ-ji), *n.* [< Gr. φυτόν, plant, + E. *lithology*.] The science of fossil plants.

phytological (fī-tǫ-loj'i-kạl), *a.* [< *phytolog-y* + *-ic-al.*] Of or pertaining to phytology; botanical.

phytologist (fī-tol'ǫ-jist), *n.* [< *phytolog-y* + *-ist.*] One who is versed in phytology, or the science of plants; a botanist.

> As our learned *phytologist* Mr. Ray has done. *Evelyn.*

phytology (fī-tol'ǫ-ji), *n.* [= F. *phytologie* = Sp. *fitologia* = Pg. *phytologia* = It. *fitologia*, < Gr. φυτόν, plant, + -λογία, < λέγειν, speak: see *-ology*.] The science of plants; botany. [Rare.]

> We pretend not to multiply vegetable divisions by quincuncial and reticulate plants, or erect a new *phytology*.
> *Sir T. Browne*, Garden of Cyrus, Ep. Ded.

phytomer (fī'tǫ-mėr), *n.* [< Gr. φυτόν, plant, + μέρος, part.] In *bot.*, a plant-part, or plant-unit — that is, one of the structures or elements which, produced in a series, make up a plant of the higher grade. The ultimate similar parts into which a plant may be analyzed are the serial leaf-bearing portions, since they are produced from and in time may produce similar parts. Also called *phyton*, *phytomera*.

Phytomyia (fī-tǫ-mī'i-ạ̈), *n.* [NL. (Haliday, 1833), emended from *Phytomyza* (Fallen, 1810), < Gr. φυτόν, plant, + μυῖα, fly.] A genus of dipterous insects formerly of the family *Muscidæ*, now giving name to the *Phytomyidæ*. They are small flies, of a blackish-gray color often spotted with yellow, and characterized by a peculiar venation of the wings. The larvæ are leaf-miners, some transforming to pupæ in the mine, while others pupate in the earth. The genus is large and wide-spread, with over 50 European and 7 North American species.

Phytomyidæ (fī-tǫ-mī'i-dē), *n. pl.* [NL., < *Phytomyia* + *-idæ.*] A family of dipterous insects named from the genus *Phytomyia*, formerly merged in *Muscidæ*. Often called *Phytomyzidæ*, as by Osten Sacken, 1878.

phyton (fī'ton), *n.* [NL., < Gr. φυτόν, plant, < φύειν, produce, pass. φύεσθαι, grow, become: see *be*¹.] 1. In *bot.*, same as *phytomer*.—2. [*cap.*] In *entom.*, a genus of *Cerambycidæ*. *Newman*, 1840.

phytonomy (fī-ton'ǫ-mi), *n.* [= F. *phytonomie* = Sp. *fitonomia* = It. *fitonomia*, *fitonimia*, < Gr. φυτόν, plant, + νόμος, law.] The science of the laws of plant-growth.

phytopaleontologist (fī-tǫ-pā"lẹ̄-on-tol'ǫ-jist), *n.* [< *phytopaleontolog-y* + *-ist.*] Same as *paleobotanist*.

> The nature of some impressions described by *phytopaleontologists* as remains of fossil Algæ. *Science*, I. 252.

phytopaleontology (fī-tǫ-pā"lẹ̄-on-tol'ǫ-ji), *n.* [< Gr. φυτόν, plant, + E. *paleontology*.] Same as *paleobotany*.

> It is to defend his position, and that, indeed, of *phytopaleontology*. *Science*, I. 253.

phytopathological (fī-tǫ-path-ǫ-loj'i-kạl), *a.* [< *phytopatholog-y* + *-ic-al.*] Of or pertaining to phytopathology.

phytopathologist (fī"tǫ-pạ-thol'ǫ-jist), *n.* [< *phytopatholog-y* + *-ist.*] One who is skilled in phytopathology, or in knowledge of the diseases of plants; a mycologist.

phytopathology (fī"tǫ-pạ-thol'ǫ-ji), *n.* [< Gr. φυτόν, plant, + E. *pathology*.] The science of the diseases of plants; an account of the diseases to which plants are liable; mycology.

Phytophaga (fī-tof'ạ-gạ̈), *n. pl.* [NL. (Duméril, 1806): see *phytophagous*.] 1. In *entom.*: (*a*) A very large group of phytophagous tetramerous coleopters, having the head not rostrate, the maxillæ with two lobes, the antennæ linear and of moderate length or short, the body ovate, oblong, or rounded, and the elytra covering the sides of the abdomen. They are found on plants, on which they feed, and number upward of 10,000 described species, representing several different families. The leaf-beetles, *Chrysomelidæ*, are characteristic examples, and the name is sometimes restricted to these, though in a wider sense the *Cerambycidæ*, *Spondylidæ*, and *Bruchidæ* are also included. See also cuts under *Cerambyx*, *Chrysomela*, and *Bruchus*. (*b*) A division of terebrant hymenopterous insects represented by the families *Tenthredinidæ* and *Uroceridæ*, or the saw-flies and horntails; the *Securifera* of Latreille: contrasted with *Entomophaga* and *Gallicolæ*. (*c*) [Used as a singular.] A genus of dipterous insects of the family *Tipulidæ*. *Rondani*, 1840.—2. In *ichth.*, a group of cyprinoid fishes.—3. In *mammal.*: (*a*) One of two primary groups into which the *Edentata* or *Bruta* have been divided, the other being *Entomophaga*. The *Phytophaga* are the vegetable-feeders.

A member of the *Phytophaga* (*Prionus laticollis*), female, natural size.

> The *Phytophaga* are divisible into two groups, one existing, and the other extinct. The former consists of the sloths, or Tardigrada; . . . [the latter are] the Gravigrada.
> *Huxley*, Anat. Vert., p. 333.

(*b*) One of two prime divisions of placental mammals, including the pachyderms, herbivorous cetaceans (*Sirenia*), rodents, and ruminants of Cuvier on the one hand, and the edentates of Cuvier (minus the monotremes) on the other hand, together forming two orders, *Diplodontia* and *Aplodontia*, collectively contrasted with *Zoöphaga*.

phytophagan (fī-tof'ạ-gạn), *a.* and *n.* [< *phytophag-ous* + *-an.*] I. *a.* Same as *phytophagous*.

II. *n.* A phytophagous animal; specifically, a member of the *Phytophaga*, in any sense.

Also *phytiphagan*.

phytophagic (fī-tǫ-faj'ik), *a.* Same as *phytophagous*.

phytophagous (fī-tof'ạ-gus), *a.* [= F. *phytophage* = Pg. *phytiphago* = It. *fitofago*, < Gr. φυτόν, plant, + φαγεῖν, eat.] Plant-eating; feeding on plants; herbivorous; specifically, of or pertaining to the *Phytophaga*, in any sense. Also *phytophagan* and *phytophagic*.

phytophagy (fī-tof'ạ-ji), *n.* [< Gr. φυτόν, a plant, + -φαγία, < φαγεῖν, eat.] The habit of feeding on plants; a phytophagous regimen.

phytophilous (fī-tof'i-lus), *a.* [< NL. *phytophilus*, < Gr. φυτόν, plant, + φιλεῖν, love.] Fond of plants, as an insect.

phytophthire (fī'tof-thīr), *n.* [< Gr. φυτόν, a plant, + φθείρ, louse.] Same as *phytophthirian*.

Phytophthiria (fī-tof-thir'i-ạ̈), *n. pl.* [NL.: see *phytophthire*.] A tribe or suborder of hemipterous insects; plant-lice, etc. They have the thorax normally constructed of three segments; the mouth suctorial without palpi; the wings four, two, or none, and membranous when present; the antennæ of more than five joints; and the tarsi of one or two joints. It contains several families, as the *Coccidæ* or scale-insects, *Aphididæ* or plant-lice proper, *Aleurodidæ*, or moth-blight insects, and *Psyllidæ*, jumping plant-lice, or flea-lice. Also called *Sternorhynchi*. See cuts under *coccus*, *cochineal*, *Aphis*, and *Psylla*.

phytophthirian (fī-tof-thir'i-ạn), *a.* and *n.* [< *phytophthire* + *-an.*] I. *a.* Infesting plants, as a plant-louse, scale-insect, or aphid; specifically, of or pertaining to the *Phytophthiria*.

II. *n.* A member of the *Phytophthiria*; a plant-louse. Also *phytophthire*.

Phytophthora (fī-tof'thǫ-rạ̈), *n.* [NL. (De Bary, 1876), < Gr. φυτόν, a plant, + φθορά, destruction, < φθείρειν, destroy.] A genus of parasitic fungi closely allied to the genus *Peronospora*, from which it differs by the spores being lateral instead of terminal. There are only 2 species, of which *P. infestans*, the downy mildew of the potato or potato-rot, is the most destructive. See *potato-rot*.

phytophysiology (fī-tǫ-fiz-i-ol'ǫ-ji), *n.* [< Gr. φυτόν, a plant, + φυσιολογία, physiology.] Vegetable physiology.

Phytoptidæ (fī-top'ti-dē), *n. pl.* [NL., < *Phytoptus* + *-idæ.*] A family of atracheate *Acarina* with two pairs of hind legs abortive, typified by the genus *Phytoptus*. They are commonly known as *gall-mites* or *rust-mites*.

phytoptosis (fī-top-tō'sis), *n.* [NL., < *Phytoptus* + *-osis.*] A disease of plants caused by the attacks of mites of the genus *Phytoptus*. It is accompanied by an abnormal growth of the plant-tissue. See *erineum*.

Phytoptus (fī-top'tus), *n.* [NL. (Dujardin, 1851), < Gr. φυτόν, plant, + *ὀπτός, verbal adj. of √ὀπ, see: see *optic*.] A genus of gall-mites, giving name to the *Phytoptidæ*, and containing such species as *P. quadripes*, which galls the soft maple in the United States.

phytosis (fī-tō'sis), *n.* [NL., < Gr. φυτόν, plant, + *-osis.*] The presence of vegetable parasites, or the morbid conditions produced by them: especially used in designation of the dermatomycoses.

phytotaxy (fī'tǫ-tak-si), *n.* [< Gr. φύτον, plant, + τάξις, order, arrangement.] The science of the classification of plants; systematic botany. Compare *zoötaxy*. *Lester F. Ward*, Dynamic Sociology, I. 120.

Phytotoma (fī-tot'ǫ-mạ̈), *n.* [NL. (Molina, 1789), < Gr. φυτόν, plant, + -τομος, < τέμνειν, ταμεῖν, cut.] The only genus of *Phytotomidæ*.

Phytotoma rara.

Three species are described, *P. rara*, *P. angustirostris*, and *P. rutila*. These birds are said to do much damage by cutting tender sprouts and buds with their serrated bill. Their voice is harsh and grating.

Phytotomidæ (fī-tộ-tom'i-dē), *n. pl.* [NL., < *Phytotoma* + *-idæ*.] A family of mesomyodian or clamatorial passerine birds, represented by the genus *Phytotoma*, having a conirostral bill with serrate tomia, and certain peculiar cranial characters representing an ancient type of structure. It is peculiar to South America, and contains one genus and a few species of Chili, Bolivia, and the Argentine Republic. Its relationships are with the *Cotingidæ* and *Pipridæ*.

phytotomist (fī-tot'ộ-mist), *n.* [< *phytotom-y* + *-ist*.] One who is versed in phytotomy, or vegetable anatomy.

phytotomous (fī-tot'ộ-mus), *a.* [< Gr. φυτόν, a plant, + -τομος, < τέμνειν, ταμεῖν, cut.] Leaf-cutting or plant-cutting, as a bird or an insect.

phytotomy (fī-tot'ộ-mi), *n.* [= F. *phytotomie* = It. *fitotomia*, < Gr. φυτόν, a plant, + τέμνειν, ταμεῖν, cut.] The dissection of plants; vegetable anatomy.

Phytozoa (fī-tộ-zō'ạ̈), *n. pl.* [NL., pl. of *phytozoön*, < Gr. φυτόν, a plant, + ζῷον, an animal.] 1. Plant-like animals, such as sponges, corals, sea-anemones, and sea-mats.—2. Certain marine animalcules living in the tissues of plants.

phytozoan (fī-tộ-zō'an), *a.* and *n.* **I.** *a.* Phytoid or plant-like, as an animal; zoöphytic; specifically, of or pertaining to the *Phytozoa*.

II. *n.* A plant-like animal; a member of the *Phytozoa*, in either sense; a zoöphyte.

Phytozoaria (fī"tộ-zộ-ā'ri-ạ̈), *n. pl.* [NL., < Gr. φυτόν, a plant, + MGr. ζωάριον, dim. of Gr. ζῷον, an animal.] Same as *Infusoria*, in the widest sense.

Phytozoida (fī-tộ-zō'i-dạ̈), *n. pl.* [NL., as *Phytozoa* + *-ida*.] A prime division of protozoans. It contained the flagellate infusorians. Also called *Filigera*.

phyz, *n.* See *phiz*.

pi¹, **pie**⁴ (pī), *n.* [The more common spelling *pi* is out of analogy, and due to ignorance of the origin of the word, or to the supposition that it is a mere abbr. of *pica*³, with ref. to the common use of that sort of type. The word is otherwise referred to *pie*¹, as a 'mixed mess'; to *pie*², as 'pied' or 'mixed'; and to *pie*³, as an allusion to the (asserted) frequent illegibility of print in the service-book so called.] Printing-types mixed together indiscriminately; type in a confused or jumbled condition or mass.

One night, when, having impos'd my forms, I thought my day's work over, one of them by accident was broken, and two pages reduced to *pi*. I immediately distributed and compos'd it over again before I went to bed.
Franklin, Autobiog., p. 176.

Unordered paradings and clamour, not without strong liquor; objurgation, insubordination; your military ranked arrangement going all (as the typographers say of set types in a similar case) rapidly to *pie*.
Carlyle, French Rev., II. ii. 4.

pi¹, **pie**⁴ (pī), *v. t.* [< *pi*¹, *pie*⁴, *n.*] To reduce (printing-types) to a state of pi.

pi² (pī), *n.* [The name of the Greek letter π, πῖ, the initial letter of περιφέρεια, periphery, circumference.] 1. The name of the Greek letter Π, π, corresponding to the Roman P, p.—2. The name of a symbol (π) used in geometry for the ratio of the circumference of a circle to its diameter, or 3.1415927: first so used by Euler.

pia¹ (pī'ạ̈), *n.* [Abbr. of *pia mater*.] Same as *pia mater*.

pia² (pē'ạ̈), *n.* [Polynesian (Sandwich Islands, Marquesas, etc.).] A perennial herb, *Tacca pinnatifida* (also *T. maculata*), found wild or cultivated throughout Polynesia, and to China and Zanzibar. Its value lies in its large fleshy tubers, from which, after rasping, the starch is washed out and dried to form the South Sea or Tahiti arrowroot. This is widely used as an article of diet in the tropics (in native use not dried, but fermented), and is especially valued in diarrhea and dysentery.

piaba (pi-ä'bä), *n.* [Braz.] A small fresh-water fish of Brazil, of about the size of a minnow, much esteemed for the table. *Imp. Dict.*

piacere (piȧ-chā're), *n.* [It., = E. *pleasure*.] In *music*, in the phrase *a piacere*, at pleasure (same as *ad libitum*).

piacevole (piȧ-chā'vō-le), *a.* [It., pleasant, merry, < *piacere*, please: see *please*.] In *music*, pleasant; playful: noting passages to be so rendered.

piaclet (pī'a-kl), *n.* [< OF. *piacle* = Pg. *piaculo* = It. *piacolo*, *piaculo*, < L. *piaculum*, a sin-offering, expiation, also a sin, < *piare*, appease, < *pius*, devout, dutiful: see *pious*.] A grievous or serious offense; a crime; a sin. Compare *piacular*, 2.

Not to answer me when you mind me is pure Neglect, and no less than a *Piacle*. *Howell*, Letters, I. iv. 16.

281

piacular (pī-ak'ū-lạ̈r), *a.* [= F. *piaculaire*, < L. *piacularis*, expiatory, < *piaculum*, expiation: see *piacle*.] 1. Expiatory; having power to atone: as, *piacular* rites.

In order to our redemption, Christ suffered as a *piacular* victim, which must be understood to mean in our stead. *Waterland*, Works, VII. 76.

The *piacular* sacrifice of his son and heir was the last offering which the king of Moab made to deliver his country. *Encyc. Brit.*, XVI. 696.

2. Requiring expiation; blameworthy; criminal; sinful; wicked.

Our late arch-bishop (if it were not *piacular* for you to read ought of his) could have taught you in his publike writings these five limitations of injoyned ceremonies.
Bp. Hall, Apology against the Brownists.

piacularity (pī-ak-ū-lar'i-ti), *n.* [< *piacular* + *-ity*.] The character of being piacular; criminality; badness. *De Quincey*.

piaculoust (pī-ak'ū-lus), *a.* [< L. *piaculum*, expiation: see *piacle*.] Same as *piacular*.

And so, as Cæsar reports, unto the ancient Britains it was *piaculous* to tast a goose, which dish at present no table is without. *Sir T. Browne*, Vulg. Err., iii. 24.

piaffe (pi-af'), *v. i.*; pret. and pp. *piaffed*, ppr. *piaffing*. [< F. *piaffer*, paw the ground, as a horse, lit. make a show, be ostentatious, strut.] In the *manège*, to advance with the same step as in a trot, flinging the right fore leg and left hind leg diagonally forward, placing them on the ground and balancing on them for a few seconds, while the other two legs are flung forward in the same movement. *Tribune Book of Sports*, p. 41.

Sir Piercie Shafton . . . kept alternately pressing and checking his gay courser, forcing him to *piaffe*, to caracole, to passage, and to do all the other feats of the school.
Scott, Monastery, xv.

piaffer (pi-af'ėr), *n.* [< F. *piaffer*, inf. taken as a noun: see *piaffe*.] The act of piaffing. Sometimes called *Spanish walk*.

The slow *piaffer* is obtained by the slow and alternate pressure of the rider's legs. The quick *piaffer* by quickening the alternate pressure of the leg.
Garrard, Training Cavalry Horses, p. 65.

pial (pī'al), *a.* [< *pia* + *-al*.] Of or pertaining to the pia mater; pia-matral.

In some cases also the appropriate adjectives are employed, e. g. *pial*, dural.
Buck's Handbook of Med. Sciences, VIII. 524.

pia mater (pī'ạ̈ mā'tėr). [= F. *pie-mère* = Sp. *pia-máter* = Pg. *pia-mater* = It. *pia-madre*, < NL. *pia mater*, lit. pious or gentle mother (opposed to *dura mater*), a fanciful name: L. *pia*, fem. of *pius* (see *pious*); *mater*, mother: see *mater*².] The delicate fibrous and very vascular membrane which immediately invests the brain and spinal cord. It is the third or inmost of the three meninges, covered both by the arachnoid and by the dura mater. Also called *pia*.—**Pia mater testis.** Same as *tunica vasculosa*.

pia-matral (pī'ạ̈-mā'tral), *a.* [< *pia mater* + *-al*.] Pertaining to the pia mater; pial.

pian (pi-an'), *n.* [< F. *pian*, yaws.] In *pathol.*, same as *frambœsia*.

pianet, *n.* A Middle English form of *peony*.

pianet¹†, *n.* [Also *pionet*, *piannet*, *pyannet*, *pyannat*, appar. through OF. *pion*, dim. of OF. *pie*, a pie: see *pie*².] The magpie of Europe, *Pica pica*.

pianet²†, *n.* [By confusion with *pianet*¹, a magpie; ult. < L. *picus*, a woodpecker: see *Picus*.] 1. The lesser woodpecker, *Picus minor*.—2. The oyster-catcher, *Hæmatopus ostrilegus*.

pianet³ (pī'a-net), *n.* [Prop. *pionet*, < *pion* + *-et*.] The double peony. [Prov. Eng.]

pianette (pē-a-net'), *n.* [< *piano*² + *-ette*.] In England, a small or miniature upright pianoforte. In France also called a *bibi* (a minced form of *bébé*, baby).

piangendo (piȧn-jen'dộ), *a.* [It., ppr. of *piangere*, *piagnere*, weep: see *plain*².] In *music*, plaintive: noting a passage to be so rendered.

pianino (pē-ȧ-nē'nō), *n.* [It., dim. of *piano*: see *piano*².] An upright pianoforte.

pianism (pi-an'izm), *n.* [< *piano*² + *-ism*.] The act, process, or result of performing music upon the pianoforte; the technique of the pianoforte; the adaptation of a piece of music to effective performance on the pianoforte.

pianissimo (pē-a-nis'i-mō), *a.* [It., superl. of *piano*: see *piano*¹.] In *music*, very soft; with the minimum of force or loudness. Usually abbreviated *pp* or *ppp*.

pianist (pi-an'ist), *n.* [= D. G. Dan. Sw. *pianist* = F. *pianiste* = Sp. *pianista* = Pg. It. *pianista*; as *piano*² + *-ist*.] A performer on the pianoforte.

pianistic (pē-a-nis'tik), *a.* [< *pianist* + *-ic*.] Of or pertaining to a pianist. [Rare.]

piano¹ (piä'nō), *a.* [= F. Sp. Pg. *piano*, < It. *piano*, soft, plane, < L. *planus*, plane: see *plane*, *plain*.] In *music*, soft; with little force or loudness: opposed to *forte*. Usually abbreviated *p.*—**Piano pedal.** See *pedal*.

piano² (pi-an'ō), *n.* [= D. G. Sw. Dan. F. Sp. Pg. *piano*, < It. *piano*, short for *pianoforte*: see *pianoforte*.] A pianoforte.—**Boudoir piano, cabinet piano**, an upright piano.—**Cottage piano.** See *cottage*.—**Dumb piano.** Same as *digitorium*.—**Electric piano**, a pianoforte whose wires are set in vibration by electromagnets, instead of by hammers.—**Grand piano.** See *pianoforte*.—**Pedal piano.** See *pedal*, *a*.—**Piccolo piano.** See *piccolo*.—**Square piano, upright piano.** See *pianoforte*.

piano-case (pi-an'ộ-kās), *n.* The wooden box inclosing the mechanism of a pianoforte.

piano-cover (pi-an'ộ-kuv"ėr), *n.* A cloth or rubber cover for a pianoforte.

pianoforte (pi-an'ō-fōr-te or -fōrt), *n.* [= D. G. Sw. Dan. F. Sp. Pg. *pianoforte*, < It. *pianoforte*, a pianoforte, < *piano*, soft (see *piano*¹), + *forte*, strong, < L. *fortis*, strong: see *fort*, *forte*², *force*¹.] A musical instrument of the percussive group, the tones being produced by blows of hammers upon stretched strings, and the hammers being operated from a keyboard. Essentially, the pianoforte is a large dulcimer with a keyboard; but historically it replaced the clavichord and harpsichord, which

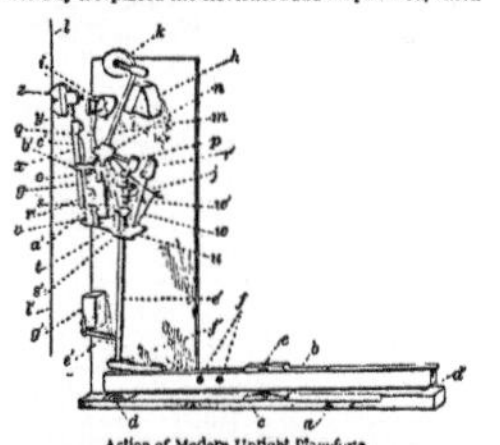

Action of Modern Upright Pianoforte.

a, key-frame; *b*, key; *c*, balance-rail; *d*, *d'*, cushions; *e*, balance key-pin; *f*, balance key-leads, placed where needed to balance the key; *g*, large action-rail; *g'*, small action-rail; *h*, spring-rail or hammer-rest, which is moved by the soft pedal, bringing the hammer nearer to the string and causing it to strike a lighter blow; *i*, spring-rail; *j*, regulating-rail; *k*, hammer; *l l'*, string; *m*, hammer-shank; *n*, hammer-butt; *o*, butt-flange; *p*, counter-check or bumper; *q*, hammer-spring (insuring retreat of hammer from the string promptly after striking); *r*, hammer-check, against which the bumper strikes to steady the hammer after the stroke; *s*, jack, or jack-fly, pivoted to the jack-flange and acting against the hammer-butt to throw the hammer forward when the key is depressed; *s'*, jack-spring (restoring position of jack after the blow); *t*, jack-flange; *u*, whip or jack-whip, which carries the jack-flange, hammer-check, bridle-wire, and damper-lifter, and which is pivoted to the whip-flange *v*, which latter is fastened by a screw to the main action-rail; *w*, bridle-wire, which carries the bridle or flexible tape extending from the bridle-wire to and attached to the hammer-butt, and which pulls the hammer back immediately after its blow upon the string; *w'*, regulating or escapement screw, which releases the jack-fly from the hammer-butt and allows the hammer to be drawn backward by the bridle immediately after striking; *x*, damper-lever; *y*, damper-wire; *z*, damper-head; *a'*, damper-lifter (otherwise called *spoon*, from its shape), which lifts the damper from the spring and holds it away till the key is released from the pressure of the fingers; *b'*, damper-flange, to which the damper-lever is pivoted, and which is rigidly screwed to the main action-rail; *c'*, damper-spring, which presses the damper against the string to stop its vibration when the key is released from pressure; *c''*, action-extension, which may be varied in length, and which simply connects the jack-whip with the rocker *f*, screwed to the key; *r'*, recess in which a horizontal damper-rod (not shown) is placed, which acts by means of forte pedal-action to remove all the dampers simultaneously, thus permitting the strings to vibrate without check.

were keyboard-instruments more akin to the harp than to the dulcimer. The dulcimer has been known in some form from the earliest historic times. Several attempts were made during the sixteenth and seventeenth centuries to combine a keyboard with it, perhaps the most important being the *pantaleone* of Hebenstreit. The chief esthetic motive to these attempts arose from the fact that the keyboard-instruments then known were nearly or entirely incapable of gradation in the loudness of their tone; hence the new instrument, when invented, was called a *piano e forte*, a *fortepiano*, or a *pianoforte*, because its main peculiarity was that its tone might be made either loud or soft at the player's will. The earliest manufacture of pianofortes of which there is certain record was by Bartolomeo Cristofori of Padua, about 1710. Various improvements have been and are still being made in details, but the essential elements of the mechanism have not been radically changed. These elements are as follows. (*a*) The *frame* or *back* is a framework of metal, with various cross-bars and trusses so planned as to offer a stanch resistance to the tension of the strings. This tension in a modern grand pianoforte amounts to several tons. To the frame are attached on one side or end the *string-plate* and on the other the *wrest-plank*, to the former of which one end of the strings is fastened, while in the latter are set the *tuning-pins*, around which their other end is wound, and by turning which their tension may be adjusted. Frames are sometimes made of wood, but usually of iron, preferably cast in a single piece. (*b*) The *strings* are steel wires of graduated thickness and length, the larger being made heavier by being wound with copper wire. For each of the extreme upper and lower tones only one wire is provided, but for most of the others there are two or three wires, which are tuned in unison, and placed so that they shall be struck simultaneously by a single hammer. (c) The *sounding-board* is a thin plate of selected wood so placed under the strings that it is drawn into sympathetic vibration with them. The sonority and quality of the tones depend much upon its material, form, and attachment. At the side or end next the string-plate there is an opening in the sounding-board for the hammers. (d) The *action* comprises the entire system of levers, hammers, etc., by which the player causes the strings to sound. It includes a keyboard (which see) made up of keys or digitals, each of which works on a pivot near its center. When the front end of a key is depressed, the back end is raised, carrying with it a rod called a *jack*, the upper end of which propels a felt-tipped hammer against one or more strings with a blow. At the same instant a *damper* is lifted from the strings so that they can vibrate freely. After the blow is given the hammer falls back against a *check*, while the damper remains lifted until the key is released. Various exceedingly ingenious devices are used to prevent noise, to insure ease, precision, and power, and to provide for extreme rapidity of manipulation. Various mechanical effects are produced by means of pedals, such as the *damper* or *loud pedal*, which lifts the dampers from all the strings at once, so that all the strings sounded shall continue to sound, and other strings shall be drawn into sympathetic vibration until the pedal is released; a *sustaining pedal*, which holds up all the dampers that happen to be raised when it is pressed down, so that selected tones may be prolonged at will; and a *soft pedal*, which either interposes a strip of thin felt between the hammers and the strings, or diminishes the distance from which the hammers strike, or moves them to one side, that they may strike only one instead of two or three strings, so that a soft tone shall be produced. The compass of the keyboard varies from five to seven and a half octaves. Great care is taken that the hammers shall strike the strings at such a point as to bring out their desirable harmonies, and suppress the others. (e) The *case* is a wooden box in which the whole instrument is contained. Its form varies according to the variety of the pianoforte. A *grand piano*, the largest form of which is called a *concert grand*, is harp-shaped, like the harpsichord, and has the strings strung horizontally at right angles to the keyboard. A *square piano*, until lately the commonest form for private use, is rectangular, like the clavichord, and has the strings strung horizontally, parallel with the keyboard. An *upright* or *cabinet piano* is like a square set up on edge, and has the strings strung vertically behind the keyboard. In both these varieties the case is often made of precious woods elaborately carved and inlaid. The importance of the pianoforte rests upon its powerful and finely graduated tone, its convenience for the production of concerted music, and its universal popularity. Its wide-spread use brings into prominence, however, the disadvantages of a percussive tone, which cannot be sustained or varied after the initial stroke, of an ease of manipulation which invites slovenly and vulgar use, and of a temperament which, with the common neglect of frequent tuning, often hopelessly corrupts the player's musical ear. The technique of the pianoforte has developed gradually out of that of the harpsichord and clavichord. Abbreviated *pf.*—**Oblique pianoforte.** See *oblique*.—**Pianoforte-player's cramp**, an occupation-neurosis, allied to writer's cramp, developing in pianoforte-players.—**Sostinente pianoforte**, a name given to various forms of the pianoforte constructed with a view to sustain the full tone like an organ. No such instruments have remained long in use.

pianograph (pi-an'ǫ-gråf), *n.* [< E. *piano* + Gr. -γραφία, < γράφειν, write.] A form of music-recorder. See *music-recorder*.

piano-maker (pi-an'ō-mā"kėr), *n.* A maker of pianofortes.

piano-music (pi-an'ō-mū"zik), *n.* Music written for or performed on a pianoforte.

piano-school (pi-an'ō-sköl), *n.* 1. A school for giving instruction in playing on the pianoforte. —2. A particular method or system of pianoforte instruction; also, a book showing such method.

piano-stool (pi-an'ō-stöl), *n.* A stool, generally adjustable in height, used by a performer on the pianoforte.

piano-violin (pi-an'ō-vī-ǫ-lin"), *n.* Same as *harmonichord*.

piarachnoid (pī-a-rak'noid), *n.* [< *pi*(*a mater*) + *arachnoid*: see *arachnoid*, 2 (*a*).] The pia mater and the arachnoid taken together.

Piarist (pī'ạ-rist), *n.* [< NL. **Piarista*, < L. *pius*, pious: see *pious*.] In the *Rom. Cath. Ch.*, a member of the Pauline Congregation of the Mother of God, a secular order founded at Rome by Joseph Calasanza about 1600 and sanctioned a few years later. In addition to the three usual monastic vows, the Piarists devoted themselves to the free instruction of youth. They are found especially in the Austrian empire.

piarrhæmia (pī-ạ-rē'mi-ạ̈), *n.* [NL., < Gr. πιαρός, fat, + αἷμα, blood.] Same as *lipæmia*.

piassava, piassaba (pi-as'ạ-vạ̈, -bạ̈), *n.* [Pg. *piassava*, *piaçaba*; a Braz. name.] 1. A coarse fiber yielded by two palms, *Attalea funifera* and *Leopoldinia Piassaba*. In South America it is made into coarse but durable ropes; in Europe it is used chiefly for street-brooms. The product of the latter species is less valued, and forms but a small percentage of the commercial article. See *Attalea*, *bast-palm*, *Leopoldinia*, *Para grass*, and cut in next column.

> Since the introduction of *Piassaba* . . . the manufacture of "bass brooms" has become an important branch of the brush-making industry. *Spons' Encyc. Manuf.*, I. 554.

2. Either of the above palms.

Piassava (*Attalea funifera*).
a, the upper part of the stem with the fibers.

piaster, piastre (pi-as'tėr), *n.* [< F. *piastre* = Sp. Pg. *piastra*, piaster, < It. *piastra* (ML. *plastra*, a piaster), a thin plate of any metal, a dollar, < L. *emplastrum*, a plaster: see *plaster*.] 1. The unit of Turkish currency, represented by a silver coin worth about 4.4 United States cents (the Turkish name for it is *ghūrūsh*).—2. The Spanish dollar. See *dollar*, 1, and *peso*.

piation† (pi-ā'shǫn), *n.* [< L. *piatio*(*n*-), an appeasing of the gods by offerings, < *piare*, appease: see *piacle*.] The act of making atonement; expiation. *Imp. Dict.*

piazza (pi-az'ạ̈; It. pron. piät'sä), *n.* [< It. *piazza*, a square, market-place, = Sp. *plaza* = Pg. *praça* = F. *place*, < L. *platea*, place: see *place*[1].] 1. An open square in a town surrounded by buildings or colonnades; a plaza: as, the *piazza* of Covent Garden; the *Piazza* del Popolo in Rome; the *Piazza* dell' Annunziata in Florence.

> Whereupon the next morning, being Sunday, Wolfe came to Chaloner's Chamber, and prayed him familiarly to go walk with him abroad to the *piazza* or marketstead. *Foxe*, Martyrs, an. 1555.

> Din'd at my Lo. Treasurer's, the Earle of Southampton, in Blomesbury, where he was building a noble square or *piazza*, a little towne. *Evelyn*, Diary, Feb. 9, 1665.

> The benediction was much finer than on Thursday, the day magnificent, the whole *piazza* filled with a countless multitude, all in their holiday dresses. *Greville*, Memoirs, April 11, 1830.

2. An arcaded or colonnaded walk upon the exterior of a building; a veranda; a gallery. [A less correct use.]

> The low projecting eaves forming a *piazza* along the front, capable of being closed up in bad weather. *Irving*, Sketch-Book, p. 429.

> He has put a broad verandah (what we so commonly call a *piazza*) all around the house. *Motley*, Correspondence, II. 283.

piazzian (pi-az'i-ạn), *a.* [< *piazza* + *-ian*.] Pertaining to, resembling, or characteristic of a piazza.

> Where in Pluto's gardens palatine
> Mulciber's columns gleam in far *piazzian* line.
> *Keats*, Lamia, i.

pibble†, *n.* An obsolete form of *pebble*.

pibble-pabble (pib'l-pab'l), *n.* [An imitative word, a varied reduplication of **pabble*, equiv. to *babble*.] Tattle; babble. *Worcester*.

pibroch (pē'broċh), *n.* [< Gael. *piobaireachd*, the art of playing on the bagpipe, pipe-music, < *piobair*, a piper, < *piob*, a pipe, bagpipe (see *pipe*[1]), + *fear*, a man.] A wild, irregular kind of music, peculiar to the Scottish Highlands, performed upon the bagpipe. It consists of a ground-theme or air called the *urlar*, followed by several variations, generally three or four, the whole concluding with a quick movement called the *creanluidh*. Pibrochs usually increase in difficulty from the beginning to the end, and are profusely ornamented with grace-notes called *warblers*. They are generally intended to excite a martial spirit. They also often constitute a kind of program-music, intended to represent the various phases of a battle—the march, the attack, the conflict, the flight, the pursuit, and the lament for the fallen. The names they bear are often derived from historical or legendary events, as "The Raid of Kilchrist," attributed to the piper of Macdonald of Glengarry, and supposed to have been composed in 1603. The term is sometimes used figuratively by poets to denote the bagpipe itself.

> *Pibroch* of Donuil Dhu,
> *Pibroch* of Donuil,
> Wake thy wild voice anew,
> Summon Clan Conuil.
> *Scott*, in Albyn's Anthology.

pic[1]†, *n.* A Middle English form of *pike*[1].

pic[2] (pik), *n.* [Turk. *pik*.] A measure of length, varying from 18 to 28 inches, common throughout Moslem nations, and used especially for measuring textile fabrics.

Pica[1] (pī'kạ̈), *n.* [NL. (Brisson, 1760), < L. *pica*, a magpie: see *pie*[2].] 1. A genus of oscine passerine birds of the family *Corvidæ* and subfamily *Garrulinæ*, having an extremely long graduated tail, the nostrils covered with antrorse plumules, and the plumage iridescent black and white; the magpies. The common magpie of Europe is *P. rustica*, *P. caudata*, or *P. pica*. That of America is commonly called *P. hudsonica*, but it is scarcely a distinct species. The yellow-billed magpie of California is *P. nuttalli*. See cut under *magpie*.

2. [*l. c.*] A bird of the genus *Pica*; a pie; a magpie.—**Pica marina**, an old name, not technical, of the oyster-catcher, translating the popular name *sea-pie*.

pica[2] (pī'kạ̈), *n.* [= F. Sp. Pg. It. *pica*, < NL. *pica*, a vitiated appetite, so called in allusion to the omnivorous habits of the magpie; < L. *pica*, a magpie: see *Pica*[1].] In *med.*, a vitiated craving for what is unfit for food, as chalk, ashes, or coal.

pica[3] (pī'kạ̈), *n.* [< ML. *pica*, the ordinal, so called on account of the color and confused appearance of the rules, they being printed in the old black-letter type on white paper, and thus looking pied; < L. *pica*, a magpie: see *Pica*[1] and *pie*[2].] 1. *Eccles.*, same as *ordinal*, 2 (*c*).

> Suppose then one that is sick should have this *Pica*, and long to be annoiled; why might not a lay-friend annoil as well as baptize? *Bp. Hacket*, Abp. Williams, p. 218.

2. An alphabetical catalogue of names and things in rolls and records.

pica[4] (pī'kạ̈), *n.* [So called with ref. to the black-letter type in which the pica or ordinal was printed: see *pica*[3].] A size of printing-type, about 6 lines to the inch, intermediate between the sizes English (larger) and small-pica (smaller). It is equal to 12 points in the new system of sizes. (See *point*[1], 14 (*b*).) The sizes of type respectively called 2-, 3-, 4-, 5-, and 6-line pica have bodies that are equal to 2, 3, 4, 5, and 6 lines of pica. Leads are described by their numerical relation to the pica body, as 6-to-pica or 10-to-pica, according as 6 or 10 set together make a line of pica.

This is Pica Type.

Double pica, in England, a size of type equal to 2 lines of small-pica.—**Double small-pica**, in *printing*, a size of type giving about 3½ lines to the inch. In Great Britain this size is known as *double pica*.—**Two-line pica**, a size of type of about 3 lines to the inch, equal to 2 lines of pica, or to 24 points in the new system of sizes.

picador (pik-a-dōr'), *n.* [Sp., < *pica*, a pike, lance: see *pike*[1].] In *bull-fighting*, one of the horsemen armed with a lance who commence the combat in the arena by pricking the bull to madness with their weapons, but purposely avoid disabling him. The horse of the picador is often disemboweled by the bull; the man has armor for the legs, as much to keep them from being crushed by the weight of the horse falling on them as to protect them against the bull.

> The light darts of the *picador* . . . sting, but do not wound. *G. W. Curtis*, Harper's Mag., LXXVI. 637.

Picæ (pī'sē), *n. pl.* [NL., pl. of *Pica*: see *Pica*[1].] In the Linnean system of classification, the second order of birds, more fully called *Aves picæ*. It consisted of the genera *Psittacus*, *Ramphastos*, *Buceros*, *Buphaga*, *Crotophaga*, *Corvus*, *Coracias*, *Oriolus*, *Gracula*, *Paradisea*, *Trogon*, *Bucco*, *Cuculus*, *Yunx* (*Iynx*), *Picus*, *Sitta*, *Todus*, *Alcedo*, *Merops*, *Upupa*, *Certhia*, and *Trochilus*. Though thus a heterogeneous and artificial group, it corresponds in the main with the modern order *Picariæ*, of which it is the prototype. Elimination of the passerine forms (namely, *Corvus*, *Oriolus*, *Gracula*, *Paradisea*, *Sitta*, and *Certhia*) would leave it very nearly the same as *Picariæ*.

picamar (pik'ạ-mär), *n.* [= F. *picamare*, < L. *pix* (*pic-*), pitch, + *amarus*, bitter.] The bitter principle of tar. It can be separated in the form of a colorless oil.

picaninny, *n.* See *piccaninny*.

Picard[1] (pik'ạ̈rd), *n.* [Perhaps from one *Picard*, the alleged founder.] *Eccles.*, one of a sect in Bohemia about the beginning of the fifteenth century, suppressed by Ziska in 1421. The Picards are accused of an attempt, under the guise of restoring man's primitive state of innocence, to renew the practices of the Adamites, in going absolutely unclothed and in maintaining the community of women, etc. See *Adamite*, 3.

picard[2] (pik'ạ̈rd), *n.* [< F. *Picard*, belonging to Picardy.] A shoe worn by men, introduced into England as the fashion of the French about 1720. It was high-quartered, and not unlike the modern brogan.

Picardist (pik'ạ̈r-dist), *n.* [< *Picard*[1] + *-ist*.] An occasional form of *Picard*[1].

picaresque (pik-ạ-resk'), *a.* [F., < Sp. *picaresco* (= Pg. *picaresco*), < *picaro*, a rogue: see *picaro*.] Pertaining to or dealing with rogues or picaroons: said of literary productions that deal with the fortunes of rogues or adventurers, and especially of works in Spanish literature about the beginning of the seventeenth century, of which "Guzman de Alfarache" was a type.

The rise of the taste for *picaresque* literature in Spain towards the close of the 16th century was fatal to the writers of pastoral. *Encyc. Brit.*, XVIII. 346.

Picariæ (pi-kā'ri-ē), *n. pl.* [NL., fem. pl. of **picarius*, < L. *picus*, a woodpecker: see *Picus*.] In Nitzsch's system of classification, as edited by Burmeister in 1840, an order of birds, instituted for the reception of the *Macrochires*, *Cuculinæ*, *Picinæ*, *Psittacinæ*, and *Amphibolæ* of his earlier arrangement, with the addition of the *Caprimulginæ*, *Todidæ*, and *Lipoglossæ* (the last consisting of the genera *Buceros*, *Upupa*, and *Alcedo*). With various modifications, and especially with the exclusion of the *Psittaci*, the term continues in general use by ornithologists as the name of a group of non-passerine non-raptorial land-birds; but it is so heterogeneous that no diagnostic characters can be assigned, and the tendency now is to drop the term and elevate several of the groups of genera which it formerly covered to ordinal or subordinal rank, under the names *Macrochires*, *Coccyges*, and *Piciformes*, or their equivalents.

picarian (pi-kā'ri-an), *a.* and *n.* [< *Picariæ* + *-an*.] **I.** *a.* Of or pertaining to the *Picariæ*; being or resembling one of the *Picariæ*.

II. *n.* One of the *Picariæ*.

picaro† (pik'a-rō), *n.* [Also *pickaro*; < Sp. *picaro* = Pg. *picaro* = It. *piccaro*, a rogue; cf. F. *picorer*, steal cattle, forage: see *pickeer*, *pickery*.] A rogue; a thief.

The arts . . . used by our Spanish *pickaroes* — I mean filching, foisting, nimming, jilting.
Middleton, Spanish Gypsy, ii. 1.

picaroon[1] (pik-a-rön'), *n.* [Formerly also *pickaroune*, *pickeroon*; < Sp. *picaron*, a rogue, < *picaro*, a rogue: see *pickeer*, *pickery*.] **1.** A rogue or cheat; one who lives by his wits; an adventurer.

I could not recover your Diamond Hatband, which the *Picaroon* snatched from you in the Coach, tho' I used all Means Possible. *Howell*, Letters, I. iii. 30.

I think I see in thy countenance something of the pedlar — something of the *picaroon*. *Scott*, Kenilworth, xx.

2. A plunderer; especially, a plunderer of wrecks; a pirate; a corsair.

This poore vessell . . . the next day was taken by a French *Pickaroune*, so that the Frigot, out of hope of her prize, makes a second time for the West Indies.
Quoted in *Capt. John Smith's* Works, II. 132.

Some frigates should be always in the Downs to chase *picaroons* from infesting the coast. *Lord Clarendon*.

picaroon[2] (pik-a-rön'), *n.* [Origin uncertain.] An instrument like a boat-hook, used in mooring logs or deals. [Canada.]

Picathartes (pik-a-thär'tēz), *n.* [NL. (Lesson, 1828), for **Picacathartes*, < *Pica* + *Cathartes*, in allusion to the long tail, like a magpie's, and the bare head, like that of an American vulture of the genus *Cathartes*.] A remarkable genus of *Corvidæ*. The only species, *P. gymnocephalus*, is found in the forests of Denkera, in the interior of

Vulturine Pie (*Picathartes gymnocephalus*).

the Gold Coast, western Africa. It is 16½ inches long, the tail 7½; the head is bald and of a bright-yellow color, with a round black patch behind; the upper parts are slaty-gray, inclining to blackish on the back, and the under parts are creamy-white. This singular bird was called *tufted grackle* in some of the old books, and Wagler named the genus *Galgulus* in 1827; but the latter name is preoccupied in another connection (*Brisson*, 1760).

picayune (pik-a-yön'), *n.* and *a.* [Prob. for **picayoon* (with term. as *doubloon*, etc.), < F. *picaillon*, a farthing, in slang use cash, "tin"; cf. It. *picciolino*, a farthing; *piccolo*, little.] **I.** *n.* Formerly, in Florida, Louisiana, and adjacent regions, the Spanish half-real, equal to 1/16 of a dollar, or 6¼ cents; now, the five-cent piece or any similar small coin.

Still, the fact remains that the average "Communist" has not one *picayune's* worth of interest in the State as such. *New Princeton Rev.*, I. 38.

II. *a.* Small; petty; of little value or account: as, *picayune* politics. [U. S.]

If only two cents are required, you will have prevented a *picayune* waste. *The Writer*, III. 112.

picayunish (pik-a-yö'nish), *a.* [< *picayune* + *-ish*[1].] Of little value or account; small; petty; paltry; mean. [Colloq., U. S.]

piccadill† (pik'a-dil), *n.* [Also *pickadill*, *pickadil*, *picadill*, *piccadell*, *picadell*, *pickadel*, *pickadell*, *pickardill*; < OF. *piccadille*, *picadille*, a piccadill, with dim. suffix, < Sp. *picado*, pricked, pierced, punctured (cf. *picada*, a puncture, *picadura*, an ornamental gusset), < *picar*, prick, pierce, puncture, < *pica*, a pike: see *pike*[1].] **1.** A large stiff collar in fashion about the beginning of the reign of James I., but the precise character of which is unknown. It appears to have been of French origin.

This [halter] is a coarse wearing;
'Twill sit but scurvily upon this collar;
But patience is as good as a French *pickadel*.
Fletcher, Pilgrim, ii. 2.

Which for a Spanish blocke his lands doth sell,
Or for to buy a standing *pickadell*?
Pasquil's Night-cap (1612). (*Nares*.)

2. An edging of lace or cut-work, forming the ornamental part of the broad collar worn by women early in the seventeenth century.

A short Dutch waist, with a round Catherine-wheel fardingale, a close sleeve with a cartoose collar, and a *pickadil*. *Dekker and Webster*, Northward Ho, iii. 1.

And in her fashion she is likewise thus,
In ev'ry thing she must be monstrous.
Her *picadel* above her crown up-bears,
Her fardingale is set above her ears.
Drayton, Mooncalf.

piccage†, pickage† (pik'āj), *n.* [ME. *picagium*; prob. < OF. *piquer* (?), Norm. *pecker*, break open: see *pick*[1].] Money paid by strolling players and others for the privilege of breaking ground for the erection of their booths at fairs, etc.

Know ye that King Athelstan of famous memory did grant . . . an exemption of all manner of Imposts, Toll, Tallage, Stallage, Tunnage, Lastage, *Pickage*, Wharfage.
Defoe, Tour thro' Great Britain, iii. 188. (*Davies*.)

Courts of pie-powder, stallages, tolls, *piccages*, with the fullest privileges ever enjoyed by the prior in the prepositure of Cartmel.
Quoted in *Baines's* Hist. Lancashire, II. 680.

piccalilli (pik'a-lil-i), *n.* [Origin obscure.] A kind of pickle made up of various vegetables, chopped and seasoned with mustard and pungent spices.

piccaninny, pickaninny (pik'a-nin-i), *n.*; pl. *piccaninnies*, *pickaninnies* (-iz). [Also *picaninny*; Cuban *piquinini*, little, an adj. used by negroes, and applied to persons and things; perhaps an accommodation of Sp. *pequeño niño*, little infant: *pequeño* (= Pg. *pequeno*), little, small (cf. It. *piccolo*, small: see *piccolo*); *niño*, m., a child, boy, *niña*, a girl.] A baby; a child; especially, the child of a member of any negroid race.

You should have seen me coming in state over the paddock with my hair down, and five-and-forty black fellows, lubros, *picaninnies*, and all, at my heels. You would have laughed. *H. Kingsley*, Hillyars and Burtons, xxviii.

You were an exceedingly small *picaninny*
Some nineteen or twenty short summers ago.
F. Locker, The Old Cradle.

A poor puny little *pickaninny*, black as the ace of spades.
Harper's Mag., LXXVI. 800.

picchet†. A Middle English form of *pitch*[1], *pitch*[2], and of *pike*[2].

picchetato (pik-ke-tä'tō), *a.* In music for instruments of the viol family, detached, half-staccato: noting tones produced by short abrupt motions of the bow, without lifting it from the string. Also *piqué*, *spiccato*.

piccolo (pik'ō-lō), *n.* [< It. *piccolo*, small; cf. Sp. *pequeño* = Pg. *pequeño*, small (see *piccaninny*).] **1.** A small flute, sounding an octave higher than the ordinary flute. Also called *flauto piccolo*, *octave-flute*, *ottavino*, and *ottavina*.—**2.** An organ-stop giving tones like those of a piccolo.—**Bombardo piccolo.** Same as *oboe*, 1.—**Piccolo piano**, a small upright pianoforte, introduced by Robert Wornum of London, in 1829.

pice (pis), *n. sing.* and *pl.* [< Marathi *paisa*.] A money of account and a copper coin (one

Obverse. Reverse.
Half-Pice, in the British Museum. (Size of the original.)

fourth of the anna) of India under British rule, equal to about three fourths of a United States cent. Also *paysa*, *pysa*.

Picea (pī'sē-ä), *n.* [NL. (Link, 1827), < L. *picea*, the pitch-pine, or perhaps the spruce or the fir (cf. Gr. πεύκη, the fir), < *pix* (*pic-*), pitch: see *pitch*.] A genus of coniferous trees, of the tribe *Abietineæ*, including the spruce. It is characterized by the evergreen four-sided leaves jointed to the persistent petiole-base, staminate flowers solitary in the axils of the upper leaves, and reflexed cones with persistent scales, hanging near the end of the branches. Great confusion regarding the spruce and fir existed among the Greeks and Romans, and later among moderns; many authors (following Don, 1838) long wrote *Picea* for the fir, *Abies* for the spruce: Asa Gray and others (following Jussieu, 1789) united both under *Abies*; present usage adopts (since Bentham and Hooker, 1880) *Picea* for the spruce, *Abies* for the fir. *Picea* includes about 12 species, natives of n temperate and arctic regions. They bear long and narrow spirally scattered leaves spreading in all directions, and long cones with double thin-margined scales each with two winged seeds. See *spruce* and *king-pine*, and compare *fir* and *pitch*[2].

Picentine (pi'sen-tin), *a.* [< L. *Picentinus*, equiv. to *Picens* (*Picent-*) and *Picenus*, pertaining to Picenum, < *Picenum*, Picenum (see def.).] Of Picenum, a district in the eastern part of Italy noted for its fruits and oil.

Admirable receipt of a salacacaby of Apicius: . . . three crusts of *pycentine* bread, the flesh of a pullet, goat stones, vestine cheese, pine kernels, cucumbers, dried onions minced small; pour a soup over it, garnish it with snow, and send it up in the cacabulum.
W. King, Art of Cookery, letter ix.

piceous (pish'ius), *a.* [= Pg. It. *piceo*, < L. *piceus*, pitchy, pitch-black, < *pix* (*pic-*), pitch: see *pitch*[2].] In *bot.* and *zoöl.*, pitch-black; black with faint dark-red tinge.

piche[1]**†.** A Middle English form of *pitch*[1] and *pitch*[2].

piche[2]**†**, *n.* [Early mod. E., also *pyche*; < ME. *piche*, *pyche*; origin obscure.] A wicker basket; also, a basket or trap for fish. *Cath. Ang.*, p. 277.

picher†, *n.* A Middle English form of *pitcher*[2].

pichiciago (pich"i-si-ä'gō), *n.* [S. Amer.] The

Pichiciago (*Chlamydophorus truncatus*).

little truncate armadillo, *Chlamydophorus truncatus*.

Pichurim bean. A cotyledon of the seed of the South American tree *Nectandra Puchury*. These beans have the medicinal properties of common aromatics, and are said to be used in South America in place of nutmegs. Also *Pitchurim bean*, *Brazilian bean*, and *sassafras-nut*.

Picicorvus (pī-si-kôr'vus), *n.* [NL. (Bonaparte, 1850), lit. 'pie-crow,' < L. *pica*, a magpie, + *corvus*, crow.] A genus of corvine birds of western North America, having the form of the Old World nutcrackers of the genus *Nucifraga*,

Clarke's Crow, or American Nutcracker (*Picicorvus columbianus*).

but the plumage gray, with black and white wings and tail. The only species is *P. columbianus*, commonly called *Clarke's crow* or *American nutcracker*, inhabiting mountainous and especially coniferous regions.

Picidæ (pis'i-dē), *n. pl.* [NL., < *Picus* + *-idæ*.] A large family of scansorial zygodactyl picarian birds, named from the genus *Picus*, characterized by the habit of picking the wood of trees both to procure food and to construct nesting-places; the woodpeckers. (a) In a broad sense, a family including the piculets and wrynecks, which have soft tail-feathers not used in climbing, and divided into *Picinæ*, *Picumninæ*, and *Iynginæ*. See cuts under *Picumnus*, *Picus*, and *wryneck*. (b) By exclusion of the last two as respectively types of different families, the woodpeckers proper, which have stiff acuminate tail-feathers used in climbing, being pressed against the tree, and forming with the feet a tripod of support. The tail consists always of twelve rectrices, but the next to the outer pair are very small and concealed, so that there appear to be only ten. The wing is more or less pointed, with ten primaries, of which the first is short or spurious; the coverts are short, as in passerine birds. The feet are four-toed and zygodactyl (excepting in the genus *Picoides*). The arrangement of the flexor tendons of the toes is antiopelmous, the oil-gland is tufted, the carotid is single, cæca are wanting, and the manubrium of the breast-bone is bifurcate. The principal peculiarities are found in the skull, beak, and tongue. The palatal structure is unique and of the type called by Parker *saurognathous*, and the whole skull is remarkably solid and firm. The beak is eminently fitted, like a gouge or chisel, for boring into wood. In some of the less typical *Picidæ* this instrument is a little curved, acute, and not ridged on the sides; in most woodpeckers, however, it is perfectly straight, very hard, truncated chisel-wise (perpendicularly) at the end, and beveled and strengthened with ridges on the sides. Except in a few genera (as *Sphyropicus*), the tongue is lumbriciform or cylindrical, barbed at the end, and capable of great extension; it is used as a spear to capture insects. The horns of the hyoid bone are very highly developed, as a rule, curling up over the back of the head, even as far as the orbital or nasal cavities, and the salivary glands are very large. The species are numerous (upward of 300), placed in many modern genera, inhabiting nearly all parts of the world. They are chiefly insectivorous, but also frugivorous to some extent, nest in holes which they excavate with the bill, and lay crystal-white eggs. They are not regularly migratory, and not musical. Besides their vocal cries, they make a loud rattling noise by tapping trees. See cuts under *Campophilus*, *Centurus*, *Dryocopus*, *flicker*, *Melanerpes*, *pair-toed*, *Picus*, *pileated*, *pitahaya*, *popinjay*, *sapsucker*, *woodpecker*, and *Xenopicus*.

piciform (pis'i-fôrm), *a.* [< NL. *piciformis*, < L. *picus*, a woodpecker, + *forma*, form.] Having the form or structure of a woodpecker; related to the woodpeckers; picoideous; specifically, of or pertaining to the *Piciformes*.

Piciformes (pis-i-fôr'mēz), *n. pl.* [NL., pl. of *piciformis*: see *piciform*.] 1. In Garrod's classification, a superfamily of anomalogonatous picarian birds, having a tufted oil-gland, one carotid, and no cæca, including the *Picidæ* and some related families: contrasted with *Cypseliformes*.— 2. In Coues's system (1884), the woodpeckers alone as a suborder of *Picariæ*, composed of the three families *Picidæ*, *Picumnidæ*, and *Iyngidæ*.

Picinæ (pi-sī'nē), *n. pl.* [NL., < *Picus* + *-inæ*.] In *ornith.*: (a†) In Nitzsch's classification (1829), a superfamily of birds, equivalent to the *Dendrocolaptæ* of Merrem. (b) A subfamily of *Picidæ* (a), made by elimination of the *Picumninæ* and *Iynginæ*: same as *Picidæ* (b). (c) A subfamily of *Picidæ* (b), containing the most typical woodpeckers, which have the bill perfectly straight, ridged and beveled on the sides, and truncate at the end, and the tongue usually extensile.

picine (pī'sin), *a.* and *n.* [< NL. **picinus*, < L. *picus*, a woodpecker: see *Picus*.] I. *a.* Like a woodpecker; being or resembling one of the *Picidæ*.

II. *n.* One of the *Picidæ*.

pick[1] (pik), *v.* [Early mod. E. also *pike*, *pyke* (partly merged in *pike*[1], *v.*); also *peck*, which is partly differentiated in use (see *peck*[1]); < ME. *picken*, *pikken*, also *pekken*, also *piken*, *pyken* (*pīken*), pick; perhaps < AS. *pycan* (found but once, in the passage 'and lēt him *pycan* ūt his eágan,' 'and caused [one] to pick out his eyes' (AS. Chron., an. 796), where Thorpe prints *pytan*, and Bosworth (ed. Toller) explains the word as *pȳcan* for **pīcan*); the AS. form corresponding to ME. *pikken* would be **piccan*; cf. MD. *picken*, D. *pikken*, pick, = G. *picken*, pick, peck, = Icel. *pikka*, pick, prick; cf. Ir. *piocaim*, I pick, pluck, nibble, = Gael. *pioc*, pick, nip, nibble, = W. *pigo*, pick, peck, prick, choose, = Corn. *pigo*, prick, sting; connected with the noun which appears as E. *pike* and *peak*: see *pike*[1] and *peak*[1]. Cf. also *pitch*[1], an assibilated form of *pick*[1].] I. *trans.* 1. To prick or pierce with some pointed instrument; strike with some pointed instrument; peck or peck at, as a bird with its bill; form with repeated strokes of something pointed; punch: as, to *pick* a millstone; to *pick* a thing full of holes; to *pick* a hole in something.

Beware therefore leaste whyle thou contemne the peaceable princes that god hath sent the, thou bee lyke vnto Isopes frogges, to whom, for theyr vnquietnesse, Iupiter sent a hearon to *picke* them in the hedes.
R. Eden, First Books on America (ed. Arber), p. 53.

Pick an apple with a pin full of holes, not deep, and smear it with spirits, to see if the virtual heat of the strong waters will not mature it. *Bacon.*

The eye that mocketh at his father, and despiseth to obey his mother, the ravens of the valley shall *pick* it out, and the young eagles shall eat it. Prov. xxx. 17.

2. To open with a pointed instrument: said of a lock.

Were beauty under twenty locks kept fast,
Yet love breaks through and *picks* them all at last.
Shak., Venus and Adonis, l. 576.

3. To remove clinging particles from, either by means of a pointed instrument, by plucking with the thumb and finger, or by stripping with the teeth: as, to *pick* one's teeth; to *pick* a thread from one's coat; to *pick* a bone.

Why, he will look upon his boot and sing; mend the ruff and sing; ask questions and sing; *pick* his teeth and sing. *Shak.*, All's Well, iii. 2. 8.

4. To pluck; gather; break off; collect, as fruit or flowers growing: as, to *pick* strawberries.

He . . . hire his trouthe plyghte,
And *piked* of hire al the good he myghte.
Chaucer, Good Women, l. 2467.

'Twas a good lady; we may *pick* a thousand salads ere we light on such another herb. *Shak.*, All's Well, iv. 5. 15.

5. To pluck with the fingers, as the strings of a guitar or banjo; play with the fingers; twitch; twang.

What charming girls, quick of wit, dashing in repartee, who can *pick* the strings, troll a song, and dance a brando! *C. D. Warner*, Their Pilgrimage, p. 11.

Dat nigger, whar nuv'r know how to *pick* a banjer befo', took it up an' play off dat ve'y dance.
Harper's Mag., LXXVIII. 42.

6. To filch or pilfer from; steal or snatch thievishly the contents of: as, to *pick* a pocket or a purse.

The Grekes were full gredy, grippit hom belyue,
Prayen and *pyken* mony priuey chambur.
Destruction of Troy (E. E. T. S.), l. 1371.

Pistol, did you *pick* Master Slender's purse?
Shak., M. W. of W., i. 1. 154.

He found his pocket was *picked!* that being a kind of palmistry at which this race of vermin [gipsies] are very dexterous. *Addison*, Spectator, No. 130.

They *pick'd* my pockets bare.
Battle of Tranent-Muir (Child's Ballads, VII. 173).

Pick my left pocket of its silver dime,
But spare the right—it holds my golden time!
O. W. Holmes, A Rhymed Lesson.

7†. To separate and arrange in order, as a bird its feathers; preen; trim.

He kembeth hym, he proyneth hym and *pyketh*.
Chaucer, Merchant's Tale, l. 767.

8. To separate; pull apart or loosen, as hair, fibers, etc.; pull to pieces; shred: sometimes with *up*: as, to *pick* horsehair; to *pick* oakum; to *pick up* codfish (in cookery).—9. To separate and select out of a number or quantity; choose or cull carefully or nicely: often with *out*: as, to *pick* (or *pick out*) the best.

We vse as much as may be the most flowing words & slippery sillables that we can *picke out*.
Puttenham, Arte of Eng. Poesie, p. 64.

To be honest, as this world goes, is to be one man *picked out* of ten thousand. *Shak.*, Hamlet, ii. 2. 179.

Can nothing then but Episcopacy teach men to speak good English, to *pick* and order a set of words judiciously?
Milton, Apology for Smectymnuus.

Our modern wits are forced to *pick* and cull,
And here and there by chance glean up a fool.
Addison, Prol. to Steele's Tender Husband.

10†. To seek out by ingenuity or device; find out; discover.

He is so wise
That we can *pick* no cause to affront him.
Fletcher (and another), Queen of Corinth, iii. 1.

No key
Could from my bosom *pick* that Mystery.
J. Beaumont, Psyche, ii. 75.

A bone to pick. See *bone*[1].—**To have a crow to pick with one.** See *crow*[2].—**To pick a hole in one's coat,** to find fault with one.—**To pick a quarrel,** to find or make cause or occasion for quarreling.

She 'll *pick a quarrel* with a sleeping child,
Ere she fall out with me.
Beau. and Fl., Coxcomb, iii. 3.

To pick a thank†, to pick thanks†, to procure consideration or favor by servile or underhand means.

He is ashamed to say that which is said already, or else to *pick a thank* with his prince.
Sir T. More, Utopia (tr. by Robinson), i.

As I am not minded to *picke a thanke* with the one, so am I not determined to picke a quarrell with the other.
Lyly, Euphues, Anat. of Wit, p. 107.

By slavish fawning or by *picking thanks*.
Wither, Britain's Remembrancer. (*Nares.*)

To pick fault, to seek out petty occasion for censure; find fault.

They medle with other folkes busines, . . . exhort and glue preceptes, rebuke and correcte, *pyke fautes*.
Hyrde, tr. of Vives's Instruction of a Christian Woman [(ed. 1541), fol. 138 b.

To pick off, to single out, aim at, and kill or wound, as with firearms: as, the riflemen *picked off* the enemy.—**To pick one's way,** to move cautiously or carefully.

He does not fail to observe the entrance of a stalwart old gentleman, who *picks his way* up to the front chairs.
Hallberger's Illus. Mag., I., Ward or Wife?

To pick out. (a) To piece out; form by combining separate or scattered parts or fragments; find or make out. Compare def. 9.

I did prety well *picke out* the sense of the Epitaphe.
Coryat, Crudities, I. 155.

He brings me information, *picked out* of broken words in men's common talk. *Beau. and Fl.*, Woman-Hater, i. 3.

Hopeful . . . called to Christian (for he was learned) to see if he could *pick out* the meaning.
Bunyan, Pilgrim's Progress, p. 170.

(b) To mark as with spots of color or other applications of ornament.

Tall dark houses, with window-frames of stone, or *picked out* of a lighter red. *Thackeray*, Vanity Fair, xlvii.

This flying being [Eros] has his body painted in opaque white; his wings are blue *picked out* with gold.
C. T. Newton, Art and Archæol., p. 388.

To pick pockets, to pick one's pocket. See *pocket*.—**To pick up.** (a) To take up, as with the fingers: as, to *pick up* a stone; to *pick up* a fan; hence, to take up in general; pluck up: as, to *pick up* courage.

I *picked up* courage, and, putting on the best appearance I could, said to them steadily, without trepidation, "What men are these before?"
Bruce, Source of the Nile, I. 195.

The sweet flavor of a frost-bitten apple, such as one *picks up* under the tree in December.
Hawthorne, Seven Gables, x.

(b) To take or get casually; obtain or procure as opportunity offers; acquire by chance or occasional opportunity; gather here and there, little by little, or bit by bit: as, to *pick up* a rare copy of Homer; to *pick up* information; to *pick up* acquaintance; to *pick up* a language or a livelihood.

If in our youths we could *pick up* some pretty estate, 'twere not amiss to keep our door hatched.
Shak., Pericles, iv. 2. 36.

They could find Trade enough nearer home, and by this Trade the Freemen of Malacca *pick up* a good livelihood.
Dampier, Voyages, II. i. 167.

When I was at Grand Cairo I *picked up* several oriental manuscripts, which I have still by me.
Addison, The Vision of Mirza.

If you can *pick* me *up* any fragments of old painted glass, arms, or anything, I shall be excessively obliged to you.
Walpole, Letters, II. 190.

(c) To take (a person found or overtaken) into a vehicle or a vessel, or into one's company: as, to *pick up* a tired traveler; to *pick up* a shipwrecked crew.

On the way Mr. Gowen, who has charge of the first fourteen miles of the aqueduct, was *picked up*.
New York Tribune, Feb. 2, 1890.

(d) See def. 8.—**To pick up one's crumbs, heels,** etc. See the nouns.

II. *intrans.* 1. To strike with a pointed instrument; peck.—2. To take up morsels of food and eat them slowly; nibble.

Why stand'st thou *picking?* Is thy palate sore,
That bete and radishes will make thee roar?
Dryden, tr. of Persius's Satires, iii. 226.

3. To steal; pilfer.—**To pick at,** to annoy by repeated faultfinding; nag: as, she is forever *picking at* the child.—**To pick up,** to improve gradually; acquire vigor or strength, as after illness or failure: as, he is looking better, and beginning to *pick up*. [Colloq.]

This club began to *pick up*, and now it has regained its former prestige. *The Century*, XXXVII. 751.

pick[1] (pik), *n.* [In most uses from the verb; but in senses 1 and 2 prob. a mere var. of *pike*[1], *n.*, which is in part ult. the source of the verb *pick*: see *pick*[1], *v.*, *pike*[1], *n.*] 1. A pointed instrument of various kinds. (a) A tool used for loosening and breaking up closely compacted soil and rock. It is ordinarily a bar of iron tipped with steel at both ends, about eighteen inches long, sometimes straight but more generally slightly curved, and having an eye in

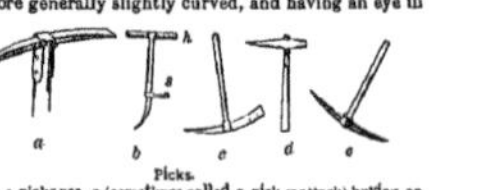

Picks.

a and *c*, pickaxes, *a* (sometimes called a pick-mattock) having an adz-like edge on the end opposite the point, and *c* having its edge in line with the handle, like a common ax; *b*, a push-pick, having a clutch-handle *h*, which is grasped by the hands, and a step *s* for the foot; *d*, a miners' pick; *e*, the common pick used in excavation, etc.

the middle to receive a handle or helve. The tips of the pick are usually sharpened to a point by a square taper; sometimes, however, to a chisel-edge. The tapering extremities of the pick possess the property of the wedge, so that this tool is really hammer and wedge in one. Its form allows it also to be advantageously used as a bent lever. The pick is known in England by the names *pike*, *mandrel*, *slitter*, *mattock*, and *hack*; the last two, however, belong properly to forms of the pick with only one point and that ending in a chisel-edge. The pick is largely employed by miners, especially by coal-miners. (b) An edged or pointed hammer used in dressing stones. (c) A toothpick. [Colloq.] (d†) A fork.

Undone, without redemption, he eats with *picks*.
Fletcher, Monsieur Thomas, i. 2.

(*c*) A four-tined eel-spear with a long handle. [Prov. Eng.]
2†. A pike or spike; the sharp point fixed in the center of a buckler.

Take down my buckler,
And sweep the cobwebs off, and grind the *pick* on 't.
Beau. and Fl., Cupid's Revenge, iv. 3.

3†. The diamond on a playing-card: so called from the point. *Davies.*

Throughout that brave mosaick yard,
Those *picks* or diamonds in the card,
With peeps of harts, of club, and spade,
Are here most neatly interlaid.
Herrick, Oberon's Palace.

4. An instrument for picking a lock; a picklock.—**5.** The bar-tailed godwit, *Limosa lapponica*: from its habit of probing for food. Also *prine*. [Norfolk, Eng.]—**6.** In *weaving*, the blow which drives the shuttle. It is delivered upon the end of the shuttle by the picker-head at the extremity of the picker-staff. The rate of a loom is said to be so many picks per minute.

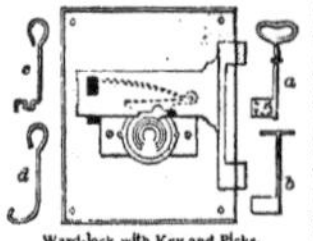

Ward-lock with Key and Picks.
a, key; *b*, instrument for taking impressions of the wards; *c* and *d*, picks or false keys, otherwise called picklocks. These picklocks are made to enter the lock, the maker being guided by the impression of the wards on a coating of wax spread on the flat blade of *b*.

This loom, fitted with Hattersley's patent heald machine, can be worked at a speed of 120 *picks* per minute, the speed of the old loom for the same purpose being about 45 *picks* per minute.
Ure, Dict., IV. 998.

7. In *painting*, that which is picked in, either with a point or with a pointed pencil.—**8.** In the harvesting of hops, cotton, coffee, berries, etc., in which the work is usually done by hand-picking, the quantity of the article which is picked or gathered, or which can be gathered or picked, in a specified time: as, the daily *pick*; the *pick* of last year.—**9.** In *printing*, foul matter which collects on printing-types from the rollers or from the paper impressed; also, a bit of metal improperly attached to the face of stereotype or electrotype plates, which has to be removed by the finisher.—**10.** The right of selection; first choice; hence, the choicest; the most desirable specimens or examples.

France and Russia have the *pick* of our stables.
Bulwer, What will he do with it? vii. 7.

We had had luck with horses this day, however, two or three travellers having been in advance and had the *pick*.
B. Taylor, Northern Travel, p. 44.

Pick and pick, in *weaving*, by or in alternate picks; evenly variegated, as the colors of a fabric.

A fine stripe . . . is got out of twelve bars or threads in the warp and four in the filling; the warp is eight of black and four of white, the filling is *pick and pick*, black and white.
A. Barlow, Weaving, p. 318.

The pick of the basket. See *basket*.

pick[2]† (pik), *v. t.* [An obs. var. of *pitch*[1].] To pitch; throw.

I 'ld make a quarry
With thousands of these quarter'd slaves, as high
As I could *pick* my lance.
Shak., Cor., i. 1. 204.

pick[3] (pik), *n.* A dialectal form of *pitch*[2].

Tho' dark the night as *pick* and tar,
I'll guide ye o'er yon hills fu' hie.
Hobie Noble (Child's Ballads, VI. 100).

pick[4]† (pik), *v. i.* An obsolete form of *peak*[2].

I must hasten it,
Or else *pick* a' famine.
Middleton, Chaste Maid, i. 1.

pick[5] (pik), *n.* [Short for *pickerel*.] A pike or pickerel. [U. S.]

pickaback, pickback (pik'a-bak, pik'bak), *adv.* [Var. of *pickapack*, *pickpack*, simulating *back*[1].] On the back or shoulders like a pack. [Colloq.]

For, as our modern wits behold,
Mounted a *pick-back* on the old,
Much further off, much further he,
Rais'd on his aged beast, could see.
S. Butler, Hudibras, I. ii. 72.

pickable (pik'a-bl), *a.* [< *pick*[1] + *-able*.] Capable of being picked.

pickadil†, **pickadill**†, *n.* See *piccadill*.

pickage†, *n.* See *piccage*.

pickaninny, *n.* See *piccaninny*.

pickapack, pickpack (pik'a-pak, pik'pak), *adv.* [< *pick*[1], *v.*, + obj. *pack*.] Same as *pickaback*.

In a hurry she whips up her darling under her arms, and carries the other a *pickapack* upon her shoulders.
Sir R. L'Estrange.

pickax, pickaxe (pik'aks), *n.* [A corruption, simulating a compound of *pick*[1] + *ax*[1], of ME. *pikeys, pikois, pykeys*, < OF. *picois, pikois, pecois, piquois, picquois*, a pickax, also a goad, a dart, < *piquer*, pick, prick, pierce, < *pic*, a pick, pike: see *pick*[1], *pike*[1].] A pick, especially one with a sharp point on one side of the head and a broad blade on the other. The pointed end is used for loosening hard earth, and the other for cutting the roots of trees. See also cuts under *pick*[1], *n.*, 1.

I'll hide my master from the flies, as deep
As these poor *pickaxes* can dig.
Shak., Cymbeline, iv. 2. 389.

Pickax or Pick-mattock.
a and *b*, steel extremities welded to the iron; *c*, handle.

pickback, *adv.* See *pickaback*.

pickcheese (pik'chēz), *n.* [Prob. imitative.] **1.** The blue titmouse, *Parus cæruleus*. [Norfolk, Eng.]—**2.** The fruit of the common mallow. Compare *cheese-cake*, 3. [Prov. Eng.]

pick-dark†, *a.* Pitch-dark; quite dark. *Halliwell.* [Prov. Eng.]

pick-devant†, *n.* Same as *pike-devant*.

picked[1] (pik'ed), *a.* [< *pick*[1], *n.*, + *-ed*[2]. Cf. equiv. *piked*, of which *picked* is but another form. Cf. also *peaked*[1].] **1.** Having a sharp point; pointed; piked; peaked: as, a *picked* stick. [Obsolete or U. S. (New England).]

Their caps are *picked* like vnto a rike or diamond, broad beneath, and sharpe vpward.
Hakluyt's Voyages, I. 256.

His beard, which he wore a little *picked*, as the mode was, of a brownish colour.
Evelyn, Diary (1623), p. 3.

2. Covered with sharp points; prickly; spinous; echinate: as, the *picked* dogfish.—**Picked dogfish**, *Squalus acanthias* or *Acanthias vulgaris*, a small shark common in British waters: so named from the prickly or spinous skin; also called *bone-dog*, *skittle-dog*, *hoe*, etc. In the United States called simply *dogfish*.

picked[2] (pikt), *p. a.* [Pp. of *pick*[1], *v.*] **1.** Specially selected; hence, choicest or best: as, *picked* men.

A playne tale of faith you laugh at, a *picked* discourse of fancie you meruayle at.
Lyly, Euphues and his England, p. 353.

Ferdinand, on the approach of the enemy, had thrown a thousand *picked* men into the place.
Prescott, Ferd. and Isa., ii. 13.

2†. Choice; affected; refined.

Certain quaint, *pickt*, and neat companions, attired—à la mode de France.
Greene, Def. of C. Catching. (*Nares.*)

He is too *picked*, too spruce, too affected, too odd, as it were, too peregrinate, as I may call it.
Shak., L. L. L., v. 1. 14.

pickedevant†, *n.* See *pike-devant*.

pickedly† (pik'ed-li), *adv.* [< *picked*[2] + *-ly*[2].] Choicely; neatly; finely.

Nor be thei so trymme nor so *pickedly* attired as the other be.
The Table of Cebes, by Poyngs. (*Nares.*)

pickedness[1] (pik'ed-nes), *n.* [< *picked*[1] + *-ness*.] The state of being pointed at the end.

pickedness[2]† (pik'ed-nes), *n.* [< *picked*[2] + *-ness*.] Refinement; affectation.

Too much *pickedness* is not manly.
B. Jonson, Discoveries.

pickeer† (pi-kēr'), *v. i.* [Also *piqueer*; with accom. term *-eer*; earlier *picquour*; < OF. (and F.) *picorer*, forage, maraud: see *pickery*.] To serve in irregular or skirmishing warfare; form part of a body of skirmishers acting in the front or on the wings of an army, or independently, as foragers, etc.; act as a skirmisher.

Ye garrison wth some commons and the scotch horse *picquoring* a while close by the walls on the east.
Tullie's Narrative of the Siege of Carlisle, p. 6. (*Halliwell.*)

So within shot she doth *pickeer*,
Now galls the flank, and now the rear.
Lovelace, Lucasta, ii.

Tiridates on his side *pickeered* about, yet never approached within throw of a dart.
Gordon, tr. of Tacitus's Annals, xiii.

pickeerer† (pi-kēr'ėr), *n.* [Also *pickearer*, *piqueerer*, *picquerer*; < *pickeer* + *-er*[1].] One who pickeers; a skirmisher; hence, by extension, a plunderer.

The club *pickearer*, the robust churchwarden.
Fletcher, Poems, p. 190. (*Halliwell.*)

This I shall do as in other concerns of this history, by following the author's steps, for he is now a *picquerer*, relates nothing but by way of cavil.
Roger North, Examen, p. 406. (*Davies.*)

pickelhaub (pik'el-houb), *n.* [G. *pickelhaube*, earlier *peckelhaube*, *bickelhaube*, *beckelhaube*, MHG. *peckelhûbe*, *beckelhûbe*, *beckenhûbe*, *bechinhûbe* (cf. MLG. *pekelhûve* = Sw. *pickelhufva* = Dan. *pikkelhue*, < G.), < MHG. G. *becken*, a basin, + *haube*, cap: see *basin* and *houve*, and cf. *basinet*.] A kind of helmet formerly worn by arquebusiers, pikemen, etc.: the helmet in use in the present Prussian army is popularly called *pickelhaube*. A similar helmet has been recently adopted by some infantry organizations in the United States and elsewhere. It is round-topped, and has a sharp spear-head projecting at the top.

picker (pik'ėr), *n.* **1.** One who picks, culls, collects, or gathers: as, a rag-*picker*; a hop-*picker*.

O'er twice three *pickers*, and no more, extend
The bin-man's sway.
Smart, The Hop Garden, ii.

2. The workman who removes defects from and finishes electrotype plates.—**3.** A tool or apparatus used in different manufacturing processes involving picking of some sort. (*a*) In *cotton-manuf.*, a machine for opening the tussocks of bale-

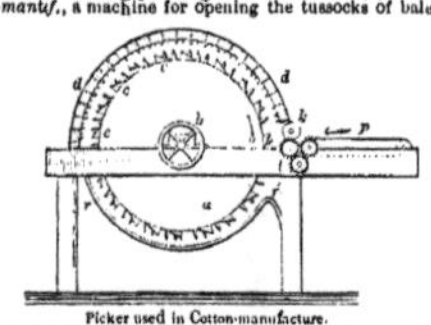

Picker used in Cotton-manufacture.
a, wooden drum having rows of iron spikes alternating on its circumference with upright iron ridges *c*, *c*, *c*, which prevent the cotton from passing through the machine too rapidly; *d*, *d*, wooden lid covering the drum; *r*, wire gauze covering in the lower part of the drum; *r'*, opening through which the clean cotton is removed; *p*, feed-cloth; *k*, *l*, grooved nipping-rollers; *b*, pulley.

cotton, reducing it to a more fleecy condition, and separating it from dirt and refuse. (*b*) A priming-wire for cleaning the vent of a gun: usually applied to that used for muskets. (*c*) In the *manège*, an instrument for dislodging a stone from the crease between the frog and the sole of a horse's foot, or between the heel of the shoe and the frog. (*d*) In *founding*, a light steel rod with a very sharp point, used for picking out small light patterns from the sand. (*e*) In *weaving*, the part of a picker-staff which strikes the shuttle: it is covered with a material not so hard as to injure the shuttle, and yet durable, such as rawhide. (*f*) A utensil for cleaning out small openings: thus, the powder-flasks of the sixteenth century were fitted with pickers to clear the tube, and lamps of both antique and modern make are often fitted with a picker hung by a chain. (*g*) A needle-like instrument used by anglers or fly-tiers in the manufacture of flies. (*h*) A machine for picking fibrous materials to pieces: as, a wool-*picker*. (*i*) In certain machines for disintegrating fire-clay for making fire-bricks, either one of two horizontal shafts armed with spike-like teeth which revolve in opposite directions, acting jointly to tear, break, and disintegrate the lumps of raw clay fed to them through a hopper.

4. One who or that which steals; a pilferer.

If he be a *picker* or a cut-purse, . . . the second time he is taken he hath a piece of his Nose cut off.
Hakluyt's Voyages, I. 241.

Ros. My lord, you once did love me.
Ham. So I do still, by these *pickers* and stealers.
Shak., Hamlet, iii. 2. 348.

5. A young cod, *Gadus morrhua*, too small to swallow bait. [Cape Ann, Massachusetts.]

picker-bar (pik'ėr-bär), *n.* See *mechanical stoker*, under *stoker*.

picker-bend (pik'ėr-bend), *n.* A piece of buffalo-hide, lined but not otherwise dressed, attached to the shuttle by power-loom weavers.

pickerel (pik'e-rel), *n.* [Formerly also *pickrell*; < ME. *pikerel*, *pykerel*; < *pike*[2] + *-er* + *-el*, double dim. as in *cockerel*. Cf. OF. *picarel*, "the small and white cockerel fish" (Cotgrave).] **1**†. A small or young pike, *Esox lucius*.

Old fissh and yonge flessh wolde I han fain,
Bet is, quod he, a pyk than a *pykerel*,
And bet than olde boef is the tendre veel.
Chaucer, Merchant's Tale, l. 175.

When as the hungry *pickerell* doth approach.
Mir. for Mags., 302. (*Nares.*)

2. A kind of pike: so called in the United States. The common pickerel of North America is *Esox reticulatus*. It has scaly cheeks and opercles, and from fourteen to sixteen branchiostegal rays; the color is green-

Common Pond-pickerel (*Esox reticulatus*).

ish, relieved by narrow dark lines in reticulated pattern. It ranges from Maine to the Mississippi, and is the commonest fish of the kind. The vermiculated pickerel, *E. vermiculatus*, has scaly cheeks and opercles, and about twelve branchiostegals, and the color is greenish with

darker streaks combining in a reticulated pattern. It is found chiefly in the Mississippi Valley. The banded pickerel, *E. americanus*, is similar, with about twenty blackish transverse bars. It is the smallest of the genus, and is found chiefly in streams near the coast from Massachusetts to Georgia. The so-called northern pickerel is the true pike, *E. lucius*.

3. A pike-perch or sauger: a commercial name of the dressed fish. See *Stizostedion*.—4. A small wading bird, as a stint, a purre, or a dunlin. [Scotch.]—**Brook-pickerel**, the *Esox americanus*.—**Gray pickerel**, the *Stizostedion vitreum*.—**Little pickerel**, the western trout-pickerel, *Esox vermiculatus*.—**Marsh-pickerel**, *Esox americanus*.—**Pond-pickerel**, *Esox reticulatus*.—**Trout-pickerel**, the banded pickerel, *Esox americanus*.—**Varied pickerel**, *Esox americanus*.—**Yellow pickerel**, the pike-perch.

pickerel-weed (pik'e-rel-wēd), *n.* 1. Any plant of the genus *Pontederia*, but chiefly *P. cordata*, of the eastern half of North America. It is a handsome erect herb common in shallow water, with arrow-head-shaped leaves, all but one from the root, and a dense spike of blue flowers from a spathe-like bract.

2. Any of various species of *Potamogeton*, or pondweed.

Pickerel-weed, of which, I told you, some think pikes are bred. *I. Walton*, Complete Angler, viii.

pickeridge (pik'e-rij), *n.* A tumor on the back of cattle; wornil.

pickering (pik'e-ring), *n.* [A perversion of *pickerel*.] 1. A pickerel. [Local, U. S.]—2. A percoid fish, the sauger, *Stizostedion canadense*.

pickeringite (pik'e-ring-īt), *n.* [Named after one *Pickering*.] A hydrous sulphate of aluminium and magnesium, allied to the alums, occurring in fibrous masses and as an efflorescence.

picker-motion (pik'ėr-mō"shon), *n.* In *weaving*, the system of parts in a loom which have to do with operating the shuttle, including the picker-staff and its connections.

pickeroon† (pik-e-rön'), *n.* See *picaroon*1.

picker-staff (pik'ėr-ståf), *n.* In *weaving*, a bar pivoted at one end and moved automatically by the loom. The disconnected end, called the *picker*, strikes the shuttle with a sharp blow, sending it across the warp first in one direction and then in the other.

pickery† (pik'ėr-i), *n.* [Also *piccory*, *piccorie*; < OF. *picorée* (= Sp. *picorea*), foraging, marauding (*picorer*, forage, maraud), < Sp. *picaro*, a rogue: see *picaro*, *picaroon*1. Cf. *pickeer*.] The stealing of trifles; pilfering.

For *pickerie* ducked at the yards arme, and so discharged. Thomas Nash. *Hakluyt's Voyages*, I. 233.

picket1 (pik'et), *n.* [< OF. *piquet*, *picquet*, a little pickax, a peg, stake, F. *piquet*, a peg, stake, a tent-peg, a military picket, piquet (a game at cards) (= Sp. *piquete* = It. *picchetto*), dim. of *pique*, etc., a pike: see *pike*1.] 1. A pointed post, stake, or bar, usually of wood. Specifically—(*a*) A pointed stake used in military stockading. (*b*) A double-pointed stake used as a defense against cavalry. (*c*) One of a number of vertical pointed bars or narrow boards forming the main part of a fence. (*d*) A pointed stake used in surveying to hold the chain in its place by passing through an end ring. (*e*) A pointed stake used in tethering a horse in open country where there are no trees or other objects to which to attach the line.

2. *Milit.*: (*a*) A guard posted in front of an army to give notice of the approach of the enemy: called an *outlying picket*. (*b*) A detachment of troops in a camp kept fully equipped and ready for immediate service in case of an alarm or the approach of an enemy: called an *inlying picket*. (*c*) A small detachment of men sent out from a camp or garrison to bring in such of the soldiers as have exceeded their leave. See *guard*, *post*, etc.—3. A body of men belonging to a trades-union sent to watch and annoy men working in a shop not belonging to the union, or against which a strike is in progress.—4†. A game at cards. See *piquet*.—5. A punishment which consists in making the offender stand with one foot on a pointed stake.—6. An elongated projectile pointed in front. The point may be conical, but is generally only conoidal, the point being made from the cylindrical body of the projectile by easy curves.

picket1 (pik'et), *v. t.* [< *picket*1, *n.*] 1. To fortify with pickets or pointed stakes; also, to inclose or fence with narrow pointed boards or pales.—2. To fasten to a picket or stake, as a horse.—3. To torture by compelling to stand with one foot on a pointed stake.—4. To place or post as a guard of observation. See *picket*1, *n.*, 2.—5. To make into pickets. [Rare.]

There is a great deal of enchantment in a chestnut rail or *picketed* pine boards. *Emerson*, Farming.

picket2 (pik'et), *n.* [Perhaps < *picket*1, with ref. to the picked tail, which is long and deeply forked, with two slim pointed feathers.] The tern or sea-swallow. Also *pickie*. [Local, Eng.]

picket-clamp (pik'et-klamp), *n.* A device for holding pales while they are being dressed to shape. *E. H. Knight.*

picketee (pik-e-tē'), *n.* Same as *picotee*.

picket-fence (pik'et-fens'), *n.* A fence formed of pickets or narrow vertical boards, often pointed, nailed at close intervals to cross-bars or rails supported by posts, into which they are often mortised.

picket-guard (pik'et-gärd), *n.* *Milit.*, a guard of horse and foot kept in readiness in case of alarm.

picket-line (pik'et-līn), *n.* 1. A position held by an advance-guard of men stationed at considerable intervals.—2. A rope to which cavalry and artillery horses are tied while being groomed.

picket-machine (pik'et-ma-shēn"), *n.* A machine for cutting out and shaping pickets for fences.

picket-pin (pik'et-pin), *n.* A long iron pin with a swivel link at the top, used with a rope or lariat for picketing horses.

picket-pointer (pik'et-poin"tėr), *n.* A machine for dressing the ends of fence-pickets; a picket-machine.

picket-rope (pik'et-rōp), *n.* 1. Same as *picket-line*, 2.—2. The rope with which an animal is tethered to a picket-pin.

pickettail (pik'et-tāl), *n.* The pintail duck, *Dafila acuta*. *G. Trumbull*, 1888. [Connecticut.]

pickfault† (pik'fâlt), *n.* [< *pick*1, *v.*, + obj. *fault*.] A faultfinder.

pick-haired† (pik'hãrd), *a.* Having thin, sparse hair.

Pick-hair'd faces, chins like witches'.
Here and there five hairs whispering in a corner.
Middleton, Changeling, ii. 1.

pickie (pik'i), *n.* Same as *picket*2. [Prov. Eng.]

picking (pik'ing), *n.* [Verbal n. of *pick*1, *v.*] 1. The act of one who picks, in any sense.—2. In *stone-working*, same as *dabbing*, 1.—3. The final dressing or finishing of woven fabrics by going over the surface and removing burs and blemishes by hand, or retouching the color with dye by means of a camel's-hair pencil.—4. *pl.* That which one can pick up or off; anything left to be picked or gleaned.

Compared with the scanty *pickings* I had now and then been able to glean at Lowood, they [books] seemed to offer an abundant harvest of entertainment and information. *Charlotte Brontë*, Jane Eyre, xi.

5. Pilfering; stealing; also, that which is obtained by petty pilfering; perquisites gotten by means not strictly honest.

Heir or no heir, Lawyer Jermyn has had his *picking* out of the estate. *George Eliot*, Felix Holt, Int.

6. Removing picks or defects in electrotype plates with the tools of an electrotype-finisher.—7. *pl.* The pulverized shells of oysters, used in making walks.—8. A hard-burned brick.

picking-peg (pik'ing-peg), *n.* In a hand-loom, the part that directly drives the shuttle. It is usually operated by means of a cord.

picking-stick (pik'ing-stik), *n.* A picker-staff.

pickle1 (pik'l), *v.*; pret. and pp. *pickled*, ppr. *pickling*. [< ME. **pikelen*, in verbal n. **pykeling*, *pykelynge*, cleansing, freq. of *piken*, *pikken*, pick: see *pick*1. Cf. *pickle*2.] I. *trans.* 1. To pick. *Jamieson.*

The wren . . .
Sodainly coms, and, hopping him before,
Into his mouth he skips, his teeth he *pickles*,
Clenseth his palate, and his throat so tickles.
Sylvester, tr. of Du Bartas.

2. To glean.

II. *intrans.* 1. To eat sparingly or squeamishly; pick.—2. To commit small thefts; pilfer. *Jamieson.*

[Obs. or prov. in all uses.]

pickle1 (pik'l), *n.* [< *pickle*1, *v.*] 1. A grain of corn; any minute particle; a small quantity; a few. [Scotch.]

She gi'es the herd a *pickle* nits,
And twa red-checkit apples.
Burns, Halloween.

2. A hay-fork. *Halliwell.* [Prov. Eng.]

pickle2 (pik'l), *n.* [< ME. *pikil*, *pykyl* (ML. reflex *picula*), also *pigell* = D. *pekel* = MLG. *pekel*, *pickel*, LG. *pekel*, *peckel*, *pickel*, *bickel*, > G. *pökel*, *bökel*, pickle, brine; origin uncertain. The Gael. Ir. *picil*, pickle, is from E.] 1. A solution of salt and water in which flesh, fish, or other substance is preserved; brine.

Thou shalt be whipp'd with wire, and stew'd in brine,
Smarting in lingering *pickle*. *Shak.*, A. and C., ii. 5. 66.

2. Vinegar, sometimes impregnated with spices, in which vegetables, fish, oysters, etc., are preserved.—3. A thing preserved in pickle (in either of the above senses); specifically, a pickled cucumber.

A third sort of antiscorbuticks are called astringent, as capers and most of the common *pickles* prepared with vinegar. *Arbuthnot*, Aliments.

4. In *founding*, a bath of dilute sulphuric acid, or, for brass, of dilute nitric acid, to remove the sand and impurities from the surface. *E. H. Knight.*

When removed from the *pickle*, the gilding has the dull ochre appearance, and must be scratch-brushed. *Gilder's Manual*, p. 46.

5. A state or condition of difficulty or disorder; a disagreeable position; a plight. [Colloq.]

How camest thou in this *pickle*?
Shak., Tempest, v. 1. 281.

I am now in a fine *pickle*.
B. *Jonson*, Tale of a Tub, iii. 5.

But they proceed till one drops downe dead drunke, . . .
And all the rest, in a sweet *pickle* brought, . . .
Lie downe beside him. *Times' Whistle* (E. E. T. S.), p. 60.

6. A troublesome child. [Colloq.]

Tummas was a *pickle*—a perfect 'andful, and was took on by the butcher, and got hisself all dirtied over dreadful. *Harper's Mag.*, LXXVI. 140.

To **have a rod in pickle for one**, to have a beating, flogging, or scolding in reserve for one. [Colloq.]

pickle2 (pik'l), *v. t.*; pret. and pp. *pickled*, ppr. *pickling*. [Formerly also *pickel*; = D. *pekelen* = LG. *pekelen*, pickle; from the noun.] 1. To preserve in pickle or brine; treat with pickle; also, to preserve or put up with vinegar, etc.: as, to *pickle* herring; to *pickle* onions.—2. To imbue highly with anything bad: as, a *pickled* rogue. *Johnson.*—3. To prepare, as an imitation, and sell as genuine; give an antique appearance to: said of copies or imitations of paintings by the old masters. *Art Journal.*—4. To subject, as various hardware articles, to the action of certain chemical agents in the process of manufacture. See *pickle*2, *n.*, 4.—5. To treat with brine or pickle, as nets, to keep them from rotting.

pickle3 (pik'l), *n.* [Also *picle*, *pightle*, *pightel*, *pitle*; origin obscure. Cf. *pingle*.] A small piece of land inclosed with a hedge; an inclosure; a close.

pickle-cured (pik'l-kūrd), *a.* Preserved in brine, as fish: distinguished from *dry-salted* or *kench-cured*.

pickled (pik'ld), *p. a.* 1. Preserved in pickle.

I could pick a little bit of *pickled* salmon, with a nice little sprig of fennel and a sprinkling of white pepper. *Dickens*, Martin Chuzzlewit, xxv.

2. Briny. [Rare.]

My *pickled* eyes did vent
Full streams of briny tears, tears never to be spent.
Quarles, Emblems, iv. 12.

3†. Roguish.

His poor boy Jack was the most comical bastard—ha, ha, ha, ha, ha,—a *pickled* dog; I shall never forget him. *Farquhar*, Recruiting Officer, v. 4.

There is a set of merry drolls, whom the common people of all countries admire, those circumforaneous wits whom every nation calls by the name of that dish of meat which it loves best. In Holland they are termed *pickled* herrings; in France Jean Potages; in Italy macaronies; and in Great Britain jack-puddings. *Addison*, Spectator, No. 47.

4. Same as *peckled*.

The head [of the trout-fly] is of black silk or hair; the wings of a feather of a mallard, teal, or *pickled* hen's wing. *W. Lawson* (Arber's Eng. Garner, I. 194).

pickle-herring (pik'l-her"ing), *n.* [= D. *pekelharing*, *pekelhaaring* = MLG. *pekelherink*, *pickelherink*, LG. *pekelhering*, a pickled herring, a merry-andrew, > G. *pökelhering*, a pickled herring (cf. G. *pickelhering*, merry-andrew, from the E. word, which was carried to Germany by English comedians who played in that country in the 17th century); as *pickle*2 + *herring*.] 1. A pickled herring.—2†. A merry-andrew; a zany; a buffoon. Compare second quotation under *pickled*, 3.

pickler (pik'lėr), *n.* One who pickles; specifically, in the *fisheries*, a man detailed to put the fish in pickle.

pickle-worm (pik'l-wėrm), *n.* The larva of a pyralid moth, *Phacellura nitidalis*, of striking aspect, which lays its eggs on young cucumbers and other cucurbitaceous

Moth of Pickle-worm (*Phacellura* (*Eudioptis*) *nitidalis*).

plants. The larva, on hatching, bores into the vegetable, causing it to rot. The moth is found throughout North and South America.

picklock (pik'lok), *n.* [< *pick*[1], *v.*, + obj. *lock*[1].] 1. An instrument for picking or opening a lock without the key; a pick. See cut under *pick*[1], 4.

> Now, sir, in their absence, will we fall to our *picklocks*, enter the chamber, seize the jewels, make an escape from Florence, and we are made for ever. *Fletcher (and another)*, Fair Maid of the Inn, v. 2.

2. A person who picks locks; especially, a thief who tries to enter doors by picking the locks.

> Any state-decypherer, or politic *picklock* of the scene, so solemnly ridiculous as to search out who was meant by the ginger-bread woman. *B. Jonson*, Bartholomew Fair, Ind.

3. A superior selected wool. See the quotation.

> In the woollen trade short-staple wool is separated into qualities, known, in descending series from the finest to the most worthless, as *picklock*, prime, choice, super, head, seconds, abb, and breech. *Encyc. Brit.*, XXIV. 656.

pickman (pik'man), *n.*; pl. *pickmen* (-men). A workman who uses or is provided with a pick. *Ure*, Dict., IV. 631.

pick-mattock (pik'mat″ok), *n.* A mattock having a pointed pick at one end of the head, and at the other a blade set crosswise to the handle. See cut under *pickax*.

pickmaw (pik'mâ), *n.* [Formerly *pykmaw*; appar. < *pick* (uncertain) + *maw*, var. of *mew*[1].] The black-headed or laughing gull of Europe, *Chroicocephalus ridibundus*. Also *pickmire*, *picksea*.

pick-me-up (pik'mē-up), *n.* A stimulating drink. [Slang.]

pickmire (pik'mir), *n.* Same as *pickmaw*. [Roxburgh.]

pick-mirk (pik'mėrk), *a.* Dark as pitch. [Scotch.]

picknick†, *n.* An obsolete form of *picnic*.

pick-over (pik'ō″vėr), *n.* In *weaving*, a thread running loose across the cloth, or detached from the surface of the fabric. *A. Barlow*, Weaving, p. 316.

pickpack, *adv.* See *pickapack*.

pickpenny† (pik'pen″i), *n.* [< *pick*[1], *v.*, + obj. *penny*.] A miser; a skinflint; a sharper. *Dr. H. More.*

pickpocket (pik'pok″et), *n.* [< *pick*[1], *v.*, + obj. *pocket*. Cf. F. *pickpocket*, from the E.] 1. One who picks pockets; one who steals, or makes a practice of stealing, from the pockets of others.—2. A plant, chiefly the shepherd's-purse: so called from its impoverishing the soil. Also *pickpurse*.

pick-pointed (pik'poin″ted), *a.* Having one of its points like that of a pickax: said of a hammer or an ax used as a tool or weapon.

pickpurse (pik'pėrs), *n.* [< ME. *pikepurs*, *pykeporse*; < *pick*[1], *v.*, + obj. *purse*.] 1. One who steals the purse or from the purse of another.

> The *pikepurs* and eek the pale drede. *Chaucer*, Knight's Tale, l. 1140.

> Down with Christ's cross, up with purgatory *pickpurse*. *Latimer*, Sermon of the Plough.

> I think he is not a *pick-purse* nor a horse-stealer. *Shak.*, As you Like it, iii. 4. 24.

2. Same as *pickpocket*, 2.

pickquarrel† (pik'kwor″el), *n.* [< *pick*[1], *v.*, + obj. *quarrel*[1].] A quarrelsome person; one ready to pick quarrels.

> There shall be men that love themselves, covetous, high-minded, proud, railers, disobedient to father and mother, unthankful, ungodly, churlish, promise-breakers, accusers, or *pickquarrels*. *Tyndale*, Ans. to Sir T. More, etc. (Parker Soc., 1850), p. 105.

pick-rake (pik'rāk), *n.* A small rake, with teeth wide apart, used in the oyster-fisheries in gathering oysters from the beds. [Massachusetts.]

pickrell†, *n.* An obsolete form of *pickerel*.

picksea (pik'sē), *n.* [Origin obscure. Cf. *pickmaw*, *pickmire*.] Same as *pickmaw*.

picksome (pik'sum), *a.* [< *pick*[1], *v.*, + *-some*.] Given to picking and choosing; choice; select. [Colloq.]

> We were not quite so *picksome* in the matter of company as we are now. *W. Besant*, Fifty Years Ago, p. 136.

Pick's paint. See *paint*.

picksy†, *n.* An obsolete spelling of *pixy*.

picktarny (pik'tär-ni), *n.* [Also *pictarnie*; cf. *pickie*, *picket*[2], and *tern*.] The tern, *Sterna hirundo*. *Montagu.*

pickthank† (pik'thangk), *n.* [< *pick*[1], *v.*, + obj. *thank*.] One who picks a thank (see under *pick*, *v.*); an officious fellow who does what he is not asked to do, for the sake of gaining favor; a parasite; a flatterer; a toady; also, a talebearer; a busybody. Also used adjectively.

> A pack of *pick-thanks* were the rest,
> Which came false witness for to bear.
> *Gascoigne* (Arber's Eng. Garner, I. 63).

> Which oft the ear of greatness needs must hear,
> By smiling *pick-thanks* and base newsmongers.
> *Shak.*, 1 Hen. IV., iii. 2. 25.

> Whereunto were joined also the hard speeches of her *pickthanke* favourits, who to curry favell spared not, etc. *Knolles*, Hist. Turks, p. 108.

> Be deaf unto the suggestions of tale-bearers, calumniators, *pick-thank* or malevolent delators. *Sir T. Browne*, Christ. Mor., i. 20.

pickthank† (pik'thangk), *v. t.* [< *pickthank*, *n.*] To obtain by the methods of a pickthank.

> It had been a more probable story to have said he did it to *pickthank* an opportunity of getting more money. *Roger North*, Examen, p. 278. (*Davies.*)

picktooth (pik'töth), *n.*; pl. *picktooths*, improperly *pickteeth*. [< *pick*[1], *v.*, + obj. *tooth*.] 1†. An instrument for picking or cleaning the teeth; a toothpick.

> What a neat case of *pick-tooths* he carries about him still! *B. Jonson*, Every Man out of his Humour, iv. 1.

> A curious parke pal'd round with *pick-teeth*. *Randolph's Amyntas*, ii. 6. (*Halliwell.*)

2. An umbelliferous plant, *Ammi Visnaga*, of southern Europe: so called from the use made in Spain of the rays of the main umbel.

pick-up (pik'up), *a.* Composed of such things or fragments as are immediately available, or can be got together; "scratch": as, a *pick-up* dinner. [Slang.]

pickwick (pik'wik), *n.* [< *pick*[1], *v.*, + obj. *wick*[1].] A pointed instrument for picking up the wick of an old-fashioned oil-lamp.

Pickwickian (pik-wik'i-an), *a.* [< *Pickwick* (see def.) + *-ian*.] Relating to or resembling Mr. Pickwick, the hero of Dickens's "Pickwick Papers."—**Pickwickian sense**, a merely technical or constructive sense: a phrase derived from a well-known scene in Dickens's novel (see the first quotation).

> The chairman felt it his imperative duty to demand of the honourable gentleman whether he had used the expression that had just escaped him in a common sense. Mr. Blotton had no hesitation in saying that he had not—he had used the word in its *Pickwickian sense*. (Hear, hear.) *Dickens*, Pickwick Papers, i.

> Unitarianism and Universalism call themselves the church in an altogether *Pickwickian sense* of the word, or with pretensions so affable as to offend nobody. *H. James*, Subs. and Shad., p. 199.

picle, *n.* A variant of *pickle*[3]. *Minsheu.*

picnic (pik'nik), *n.* [Formerly and more prop. *picknick* (> F. *picnic*, *piquenique* (before 1740) = G. *picknick* = Sw. *picknick* (1788) = Dan. *pikkenik*, a picnic); a riming name of popular origin, appar. < *pick*[1], *v.*, + **nick*, for **knick* or *knack* in *knickknack*, *nicknack*, a trifle, but also a picnic. As in many other riming names, the elements are used without precision, but the lit. sense is appar. 'a picking or nibbling of bits,' a snatch, snack (cf. *snatch*, *snack*, in this sense, as related to *snatch*, *v.*).] Formerly, an entertainment in which every partaker contributed his share to the general table; now, an entertainment or pleasure-party the members of which carry provisions with them on an excursion, as from a city to some place in the country: also used adjectively: as, a *picnic* party; *picnic* biscuits (a kind of small sweet biscuits).

picnic (pik'nik), *v. i.*; pret. and pp. *picnicked*, ppr. *picnicking*. [< *picnic*, *n.*] To attend a picnic party; take part in a picnic meal: as, we *picnicked* in the woods.

picnicker (pik'nik-ėr), *n.* One who takes part in a picnic.

picnid (pik'nid), *n.* Same as *pycnidium*.

picnohydrometer (pik″nō-hi-drom'e-tėr), *n.* [< *picno*(*meter*) + *hydrometer*.] A combination of the picnometer and the hydrometer. *E. H. Knight.*

picnometer, *n.* An erroneous spelling of *pycnometer*.

Picnonotus, *n.* See *Pycnonotus*.

Picoideæ (pi-koi'dē-ē), *n. pl.* [NL., < *Picus* + *-oideæ*.] A superfamily of birds, including the families *Picidæ*, *Indicatoridæ*, *Megalæmidæ*, *Rhamphastidæ*, *Galbulidæ*, and *Bucconidæ*, or the woodpeckers, indicators, barbets, toucans, jacamars, and puff-birds.

picoideous (pi-koi'dē-us), *a.* Pertaining to the *Picoideæ*.

Picoides[1] (pi-koi'dēz), *n.* [NL. (Lacépède, 1801), < *Picus* + *-oides*.] A genus of *Picidæ* lacking the first toe, having but one behind and two in front, but in other respects agreeing with *Picus* proper; the three-toed woodpeckers. There are several species, of Europe, Asia, and North America, spotted with black and white, the male with red on the head, as the European *P. tridactylus* and the American *P. americanus* or *hirsutus*. Another common American species is the black-backed three-toed woodpecker, *P. arcticus*. Also called *Tridactyla*, *Apternus*, *Pipodes*, and *Dinopium*.

Picoides[2] (pi-koi'dēz), *n. pl.* [NL., < *Picus* + *-oides* (pl.).] In Blyth's system of classification (1849), a series of his *Zygodactyli*, consisting of the woodpeckers, honey-guides, barbets, and the toucans, touracous, and colies, the first three of these being grouped as *Cuneirostres*, the last three as *Levirostres*.

picot (pē-kō'), *n.* [< F. *picot*, a pearl, purl, OF. *picot*, *piquot*, *picquot*, a point, dim. of *pic*, a point: see *pike*[1].] 1. A small loop forming part of an ornamental edging, but larger than the pearl and thicker, consisting of a thread upon which other thread has been wound, or to which small stitches or knots have been added.—2. The front or outer edge of a flounce or border, as of lace. Compare *footing*, 11.

picotee (pik-ō-tē'), *n.* [Formerly also *picketee*, *piquette*; said to be < F. *picotie*, named after *Picot*, Baron de la Peyrouse (1744–1818), a French botanist.] One of a group of florists' varieties of the carnation, having petals with a white or yellow ground, marked at the outer margin only with red or other color. In older usage the picotee had a white ground, spotted or dusted with the secondary color. Also called *picotee pink*. See *carnation*, and cut under *Dianthus*.

picotite (pik'ō-tit), *n.* [Named after *Picot*, Baron de la Peyrouse (see *picotee*).] A variety of spinel containing 7 or 8 per cent. of chromium sesquioxid. See *spinel*.

picot-ribbon (pē-kō'rib″on), *n.* Ribbon having a pearl-edge or a sort of fringe of loops made by the projecting threads of the weft.

picotté (pi-ko-tā'), *a.* [F. *picoté*, < *picot*: see *picot*.] 1. In *her.*, speckled and spotted.—2. Furnished with picots: as, a *picotté* ground of lace.

picquet, *n.* and *v.* An obsolete spelling of *pique*[1]. *Bp. Parker.*

picquerer†, *n.* See *pickeerer*.

picquet†, *n.* See *piquet*, 2.

picqué-work (pē-kā'wėrk), *n.* Decoration by means of dots or slight depressions. Compare *pounced work*, under *pounced*.

picra (pik'rä), *n.* [LL., a medicine made of aloes, < Gr. πικρός, bitter. Cf. *hiera-picra*.] A powder of aloes with canella, composed of four parts of aloes to one part of canella. It is used as a cathartic.

Picræna (pik-rē'nä), *n.* [NL. (Lindley, 1849), < Gr. πικρος, bitter.] A genus of polypetalous trees of the order *Simarubaceæ* and tribe *Simarubeæ*, characterized by its four or five stamens without hairs, four or five petals not increasing in size, a four- or five-lobed disk, and solitary seeds without albumen. The 3 species are natives of tropical America. They resemble the ailantus-tree in habit, bearing alternate pinnate leaves, and cymose panicles of greenish flowers, followed by small drupes resembling peas. Their wood is whitish or yellow, and extremely bitter. See *bitter-wood*, 2, *bitter ash* (under *ash*[1]), and *quassia*.

Picramnia (pik-ram'ni-ä), *n.* [NL. (Swartz, 1797), < Gr. πικρός, bitter, + θάμνος, shrub.] A genus of shrubs and trees, of the order *Simarubaceæ*, type of the tribe *Picramnieæ*, characterized by carpels with two or more ovules, and diœcious flowers with from three to five stamens opposite as many linear petals. There are about 20 species, natives of tropical America. They bear alternate pinnate leaves, and small green or reddish flowers in clusters forming long slender drooping racemes, followed by two-celled fruits resembling olives. They are known as *bitter-wood*, and *P. Antidesma*, the species most used medicinally, as *cascara amarga bark* (which see, under *bark*[2]), also *macary-bitter*, *majoe-bitter*, *old-woman's-bitter*, and *Tom-Bontryn's-bush*.

Picramnieæ (pik-ram-ni'ē-ē), *n. pl.* [NL. (Bentham and Hooker, 1862), < *Picramnia* + *-eæ*.] A tribe of plants of the order *Simarubaceæ*, distinguished by the entire ovary of from two to five cells. It includes 11 genera of tropical trees or shrubs, of which *Picramnia* (the type) is the chief.

picrate (pik'rāt), *n.* [< *picric* + *-ate*[1].] A salt of picric acid.

picrated (pik'rā-ted), *a.* [< *picrate* + *-ed*[2].] In *pyrotechnics*, mixed with a picrate as in a composition for a whistling rocket.

picric (pik'rik), *a.* [< Gr. πικρός, bitter, + *-ic*.] Same as *carbazotic*.—**Picric acid**, an acid which is used as a dye on silk and wool, but more often in conjunction with other colors as a modifier of shades than as an unmixed dye. Also called *chrysolepic acid*. See *carbazotic*.

Picris (pik'ris), *n.* [NL. (Linnæus, 1737), < L. *picris*, < Gr. πικρίς, a bitter herb, < πικρός, bitter.] A genus of composite plants, of the tribe *Cichoriaceæ* and subtribe *Crepideæ*, distinguished by its plumose pappus. There are about 25 species, in Europe, northern Africa, and temperate regions of Asia;

one, *P. hieracioides*, the German *bitterkraut*, is also widely diffused throughout the northern hemisphere. All are erect, branching, bristly, and rough, with many alternate coarsely cut or entire leaves and bright-yellow flowers. Several species are cultivated for the flowers. *P. echioides* (often called *Helminthia*) is the British wayside weed *ox-tongue*, so called from the shape of its leaves.

picrite (pik'rīt), *n.* [< Gr. πικρός, bitter, + *-ite*[2].] A name proposed for one of the many varieties of olivin-rock, in regard to whose nomenclature lithologists are far from being in accord. Gümbel used the term *palæopicrite* to designate a rock occurring in the Fichtelgebirge, which, as he believed, consisted originally of olivin, with more or less of enstatite, diopside, augite, and magnetite—at present, however, almost entirely altered to serpentine and chlorite. Rosenbusch considers the palæopicrite of Gümbel to be an olivin-diabase destitute of a feldspathic constituent. See *peridotite*.

picrocarmine (pik-rọ̄-kär'min), *n.* [< Gr. πικρός, bitter, + E. *carmine*.] In *histol.*, a stain made from carmine and picric acid.

Picrodendron (pik-rọ̄-den'dron), *n.* [NL. (Planchon, 1846), < πικρός, bitter, + δένδρον, tree.] A genus of polypetalous trees, of the order *Simarubaceæ* and tribe *Picramnieæ*, characterized by the solitary pistillate and amentaceous staminate flowers, the ovary with two pendulous ovules in each of the two cells, and the fruit a one-celled one-seeded drupe. The only species, *P. Juglans*, is a native of the West Indies, a small and exceedingly bitter tree, with alternate leaves of three leaflets, known as *Jamaica walnut* (which see, under *walnut*).

picrolite (pik'rọ̄-līt), *n.* [< Gr. πικρός, bitter, + λίθος, stone.] A fibrous or columnar variety of serpentine.

picromerite (pik-rom'e-rīt), *n.* [< Gr. πικρός, bitter, + μέρος, part, + *-ite*[2].] A hydrous sulphate of magnesium and potassium, obtained in monoclinic crystals and in crystalline crusts at the salt-mines of Stassfurt in Prussia.

picrophyll (pik'rọ̄-fil), *n.* [< MGr. πικρόφυλλος, with bitter leaves, < Gr. πικρός, bitter, + φύλλον, leaf.] A massive, foliated or fibrous, greenish-gray mineral from Sala in Sweden. It is an altered pyroxene.

picrophyllite (pik-rọ̄-fil'īt), *n.* [< *picrophyll* + *-ite*[2].] Same as *picrophyll*.

picrosmine (pik-ros'min), *n.* [< Gr. πικρός, bitter, + ὀσμή, odor, + *-ine*[2].] A mineral occurring in fibrous massive forms, having a bitter argillaceous odor when moistened. It is essentially a hydrous silicate of magnesium, and is found in the iron-mine of Engelsberg, near Pressnitz, in Bohemia.

picrotoxic (pik-rọ̄-tok'sik), *a.* [< *picrotox-in* + *-ic*.] Of or derived from picrotoxin; having picrotoxin as the base: as, *picrotoxic* acid.

picrotoxin, picrotoxine (pik-rọ̄-tok'sin), *n.* [< Gr. πικρός, bitter, + τοξ(ικόν), poison (see *toxic*), + *-in*[2].] A bitter poisonous principle which exists in the seeds of *Anamirta Cocculus* (*A. paniculata*), from which it is extracted by the action of water and alcohol. It crystallizes in small white needles or columns, and dissolves in water and alcohol. It acts as an intoxicating poison.

Pict[1] (pikt), *n.* [= F. *Picte* = It. *Picti*, *Pitti* (pl.), < LL. *Picti* (AS. *Pihtas*, *Peohtas*, pl., > Sc. *Pecht*, *Peaght*, etc.), the Picts (appar. so named from their practice of tattooing themselves), pl. of L. *pictus*, pp. of *pingere*, paint: see *picture*, *paint*; but the name (LL. *Picti*, etc.) may be an accom. of a native name.] One of a race of people, of disputed origin, who formerly inhabited a part of the Highlands of Scotland and other regions. Their language was Celtic. The Picts and Scots were united in one kingdom about the reign of Kenneth Macalpine (in the middle of the ninth century).

> With Arts and Arms shall Britain tamely end,
> Which naked *Picts* so bravely could defend?
> *Steele*, Grief A-la-Mode, Epil.

Picts' houses. See *beehive house*, under *beehive*.

pict[2] (pikt), *v. t.* A dialectal (Scotch) form of *pick*[3] for *pitch*[2].

> Ye'll *pict* her [a ship] well, and spare her not.
> *Sir Patrick Spens* (Child's Ballads, III. 341).

Pictish (pik'tish), *a.* [< *Pict*[1] + *-ish*[1].] Of or pertaining to the Picts.

pictograph (pik'tọ̄-gráf), *n.* [< L. *pictor*, a painter, + Gr. γράφειν, write.] A pictorial symbol or sign, or a record or writing composed of such pictorial signs: as, the *pictographs* of the North American Indians.

> A large, vertical, soft rock on which *pictographs* are still to be observed, although nearly obliterated.
> *Science*, XI. 282.

pictographic (pik-tọ̄-graf'ik), *a.* [< *pictography* + *-ic*.] Of or pertaining to pictography, or the use of pictographs or pictorial signs in recording events or expressing thought; of the nature of or composed of pictographs: as, *pictographic* manuscripts.

pictography (pik-tog'ra-fi), *n.* [< L. *pictor*, a painter, + Gr. γράφειν, write.] Pictorial writing; the use of picture-symbols in recording events or ideas.

Pictor (pik'tor), *n.* [NL., < L. *pictor*, a painter, < *pingere*, pp. *pictus*, paint: see *picture*.] An abbreviated form of *Equuleus pictoris* (which see, under *Equuleus*).

pictorial (pik-tō'ri-al), *a.* [= It. *pittorio*, *pintorio*, < LL. *pictorius*, < L. *pictor*, a painter: see *Pictor*.] 1. Of or pertaining to pictures or the making of them; relating to painting, drawing, etc.: as, the *pictorial* art.—2. Expressed or depicted in pictures; of the nature of a picture or of pictures; consisting of pictures or of pictured symbols: as, *pictorial* illustrations; *pictorial* writing.—3. Illustrated by or containing pictures or drawings: as, *pictorial* publications; a *pictorial* history.

pictorially (pik-tō'ri-al-i), *adv.* In the manner of a picture; as regards pictures; with or by means of pictures or illustrations.

pictoric, pictorical (pik-tor'ik, -i-kal), *a.* [= Sp. *pictórico* = It. *pittorico*; < L. *pictor*, a painter (see *Pictor*), + *-ic*, *-ic-al*.] Same as *pictorial*. [Rare.]

pictura (pik-tū'rä), *n.* [L., painting, picture: see *picture*.] In *zoöl.*, the pattern of coloration; the mode or style of coloring of an animal. *Pictura* differs from *coloration* in noting the disposition and effect of coloring, not the color itself.

picturable (pik'tūr-a-bl), *a.* [< *picture* + *-able*.] Capable of being pictured or painted. *Coleridge*.

pictural (pik'tūr-al), *a.* and *n.* [< *picture* + *-al*.] I. *a.* Relating to or represented by pictures. *Foreign Quarterly Rev.*

II.† *n.* A picture.

> The second rowme, whose wals
> Were painted faire with memorable gestes
> Of famous Wisards, and with *picturals*
> Of Magistrates, of courts, of tribunals.
> *Spenser*, F. Q., II. ix. 53.

picture (pik'tūr), *n.* [< ME. *pycture*, < OF. *picture*, also *peinture*, F. *peinture* (with *n* due to orig. inf.) = Sp. Pg. *pintura* = It. *pittura*, *pintura*, < L. *pictura*, the art of painting, a painting, < *pingere*, fut. part. *picturus*, paint, = Skt. √ *piç*, adorn. From L. *pingere* are also ult. E. *paint*, *depict*, *Pictor*, *pictorial*, etc., *pigment*, *pimento*, *pint*, etc.] 1†. The art or work of a painter; painting.

> *Picture* is the invention of Heaven; the most ancient, and most a-kin to Nature. It is it self a silent Work, And always of one and the same Habit; Yet it doth so enter and penetrate the inmost affection (being done by an excellent Artificer) as sometimes it overcomes the Power of Speech and Oratory. *B. Jonson*, Discoveries.

> Mr. Blemwell was allowed of Lely to have had a very good judgment in the art of *picture*, but his performances were not equal to his skill. *Roger North*.

2. A painting intended to exhibit the image of any person, scene, object, etc., in the natural colors, and with a more or less close approximation to the appearance of reality; especially, such a painting having sufficient merit to rank as a work of art.

> That only should be considered a *picture* in which the spirit, not the materials, observe, but the animating emotion of many such studies, is concentrated, and exhibited by the aid of long studied, painfully chosen forms, idealized in the right sense of the word. *Ruskin*.

3. Hence, any resemblance or representation executed on a surface, as a sketch or drawing, or a photograph.

> The buildings they [the Romans] most used to make were walles for Cities, Calsies [causeways] in high wayes, Bridges ouer Riuers, founteines artificially made, statues, or greate *pictures* ouer gates.
> *Guevara*, Letters (tr. by Hellowes, 1577), p. 14.

4. An image; a representation as in the imagination.

> *Pictures* and shapes are but secondary objects. *Bacon*.

> My eyes make *pictures* when they are shut.
> *Coleridge*, Day Dream.

> But still she heard him, still his *picture* form'd
> And grew between her and the pictured wall.
> *Tennyson*, Lancelot and Elaine.

5. Any actual scene, group, combination, or play of colors, etc., considered as supplying the elements or as a suitable subject of a painting: as, the children at play formed a pretty *picture*. —6. A vivid or graphic representation or description in words.

> A complete *picture* and Genetical History of the Man and his spiritual Endeavour lies before you.
> *Carlyle*, Sartor Resartus, i. 11.

7. In *entom.*, a colored pattern on a white or clear surface: generally used in describing the wings of *Hymenoptera*, *Diptera*, and *Neuroptera*. See *pictura*.—**Dissected picture.** See *dissect*.—**Easel-picture.** See *easel*[1].—**Plane of the picture.** Same as *perspective plane* (which see, under *perspective*).

picture (pik'tūr), *v. t.*; pret. and pp. *pictured*, ppr. *picturing*. [< *picture*, *n.*] 1. To depict or represent pictorially.

> Your death has eyes in 's head then; I have not seen him so *pictured*. *Shak.*, Cymbeline, v. 4. 185.

> An Attic frieze you give, a *pictured* song.
> *Lowell*, To Miss D. T.

2. To form a mental image or picture of; spread out before the mind's eye as in a picture.

> Do *picture* it in my mind. *Spenser*.

> Father Malachi Brennan, P. P. of Carrigaholt, was what I had often *pictured* to myself as the beau ideal of his caste. *Lever*, Harry Lorrequer, vi.

3. To depict or describe in words; give a picture or vivid description of.

> The animated strain of Pindar, where virtue is *pictured* in the successful strife of an athlete at the Isthmian games. *Sumner*, Orations, I. 143.

picture-board (pik'tūr-bōrd), *n.* A deceptive painting of any object or figure on a shaped plank, such as a fierce dog in a garden, a bird on a balcony, or a porcelain bowl on a book-case. This conceit perhaps originated in Holland, but was prevalent in other countries of Europe in the eighteenth century.

picture-book (pik'tūr-bůk), *n.* A book of pictures; also, a book illustrated with pictures.

> To gie good lawful coin for ballants and *picture-books*.
> *Scott*, St. Ronan's Well, vi.

The devil's picture-books. See *book*.

pictured (pik'tūrd), *a.* [< *picture* + *-ed*[2].] In *entom.*, having a definite pictura or colored pattern: said of the wings of insects.

picture-frame (pik'tūr-frām), *n.* The more or less ornamental border put around a picture to protect it and to isolate it, by separating it from other pictures, the decoration of the wall, etc.

picture-gallery (pik'tūr-gal"e-ri), *n.* A gallery, apartment, or building in which pictures are hung up or exhibited.

picture-lens (pik'tūr-lenz), *n.* A large double-convex lens of very long focus, mounted in a frame, and used for examining pictures hung on a wall.

picture-molding (pik'tūr-mōl"ding), *n.* A molded strip of wood, often gilded or colored, secured to an interior wall near the ceiling to allow of the convenient hanging of pictures by means of hooks, which fit over one of the members of the molding. Compare *picture-rod*.

picture-mosaic (pik'tūr-mō-zā"ik), *n.* A name given to Roman mosaic and to mosaic imitated from it, especially that of the imperial factory at St. Petersburg, which derived its processes and methods from the Roman.

picture-nail (pik'tūr-nāl), *n.* A form of nail the shank of which can be driven into a wall without the (more or less ornamental) head, which is afterward screwed on or slid into its place.

picture-plane (pik'tūr-plān), *n.* Same as *perspective plane* (which see, under *perspective*).

picturer† (pik'tūr-ėr), *n.* [< *picture* + *-er*[1].] A painter.

> Zeuxis, the curious *picturer*, painted a boy holding a dish full of grapes in his hand, done so lively that the birds, being deceived, flew to peck the grapes.
> *Fuller*, Holy State, III. xiii. § 10.

picture-rod (pik'tūr-rod), *n.* A rod attached horizontally to a wall near the ceiling as a support for pictures. Brass tubing was much used for this purpose; but the picture-rod has been largely superseded by the picture-molding.

picturesque (pik-tū-resk'), *a.* [= F. *pittoresque*, < It. *pittoresco* (= Sp. *pintoresco* = Pg. *pittoresco*, *pinturesco*), < *pittura*, a picture, painting: see *picture*.] 1. Picture-like; possessing notably original and pleasing qualities such as would be effective in a picture; forming or fitted to form an interesting or striking picture, as a mountain waterfall, or a pine-covered headland, or a gay costume amid appropriate surroundings. The word does not imply the presence of the highest beauty or of sublimity—qualities which belong to a more elevated plane.

> *Picturesque* properly means what is done in the style and with the spirit of a painter; and it was thus, if I am not much mistaken, that the word was commonly employed when it was first adopted in England.
> *D. Stewart*, Philos. Essays, i. 5.

> We all know what we mean by the word *picturesque* as applied to real objects: for example, we all consider that a feudal castle or abbey, when it has become an ivied ruin, is a *picturesque* object. *Encyc. Brit.*, VII. 450.

> Measured by its hostility to our modern notions of convenience, Chester is probably the most *picturesque* city in the world. *Henry James, Jr.*, Trans. Sketches, p. 12.

> If [the traveler] will miss . . . the *picturesque* costumes to which he has become used further south.
> *E. A. Freeman*, Venice, p. 58.

2. Strikingly graphic or vivid; abounding or diversified with striking and vivid imagery: as, *picturesque* language.

The epithet *picturesque* . . . means that graphical power by which Poetry and Eloquence produce effects on the mind analogous to those of a picture.
D. Stewart, Philos. Essays, i. 5.

Where he [Dryden] is imaginative, it is in that lower sense which the poverty of our language, for want of a better word, compels us to call *picturesque*.
Lowell, Among my Books, 1st ser., p. 64.

picturesquely (pik-tū-resk'li), *adv.* In a picturesque manner.

picturesqueness (pik-tū-resk'nes), *n.* The character of being picturesque.

picture-writing (pik'tūr-rī"ting), *n.* 1. The use of pictures or of pictured representations in recording events or expressing ideas; pictography: as, the *picture-writing* of the North American Indians.

There was a period when art and writing were not divorced as they are at present, but so blended into one that we can best express the union by such a compound as *Picture-writing*. *C. T. Newton*, Art and Archæol., p. 9.

2. A writing or inscription consisting of pictures or pictorial signs.

picul, pecul (pik'ul), *n.* [Malay.] A weight in use in China and the East generally, containing 100 kin or catties, and equal to about 133⅓ pounds avoirdupois. By the Chinese it is called *tan*.

picule (pik'ūl), *n.* [< NL. **piculus*, dim. of L. *picus*, a woodpecker: see *Picus*.] A piculet.

piculet (pik'ụ-let), *n.* [< *picule* + *-et*.] Any one of the small soft-tailed woodpeckers of the subfamily *Picumninæ*, family *Picidæ*, of the genera *Picumnus*, *Vivia*, *Sasia*, and *Verreauxia*. See cut under *Picumnus*.

piculule (pik'ụ-lūl), *n.* [< *picule* + *-ule*.] A bird of the family *Dendrocolaptidæ*.

Picumninæ (pik-um-nī'nē), *n. pl.* [NL. (G. R. Gray, 1840), < *Picumnus* + *-inæ*.] A subfamily of *Picidæ*, typified by the genus *Picumnus*, and characterized by the soft non-scansorial tail; the picules, piculets, or pygmy woodpeckers. It is a small group of small woodpeckers of a low or generalized type, inhabiting tropical regions of both hemispheres, as South America, the East Indies, and Africa. The species have generally four toes, yoked in pairs as in the true woodpeckers, but the East Indian genus *Sasia* has only three. Also *Picumnidæ*, as a separate family.

Picumnus (pi-kum'nus), *n.* [NL. (Temminck), < L. *Picumnus*, a deity of the Romans, a personification of the woodpecker, < *picus*, a woodpecker: see *Picus*.] The typical genus of *Picumninæ*, formerly conterminous with the subfamily, now usually restricted to the American species, as *P. lepidotus*, all of which have four toes. Also called *Piculus*, *Asthenurus*, and *Microcolaptes*.

Piculet (*Picumnus lepidotus*).

Picus (pī'kus), *n.* [NL., < L. *picus*, a woodpecker, perhaps < *pingere* (√ *pic*), paint, in allusion to the painted or spotted appearance of the bird. Cf. *Pica*, *pie*[2].] A Linnean genus of woodpeckers, formerly coextensive with the family *Picidæ*, later variously restricted. The name is at present used: (*a*) for the generic group of which the great black woodpecker of Europe, *Picus martius*, is the type, otherwise called *Dryocopus* (see cut under *Dryocopus*); (*b*) for a large series of smaller species, spotted with black and white, such as *P. major* and *P. minor* of Europe, and the hairy and downy woodpeckers of America, *P. villosus* and *P. pubescens*.

Greater Spotted Woodpecker (*Picus major*).

piddle (pid'l), *v. i.*; pret. and pp. *piddled*, ppr. *piddling*. [A var. of *pittle*, the variation being due perhaps to association with *peddle*. Cf. *peddling*, var. of *piddling*.] 1. To deal in trifles; spend time in a trifling way or about trifling or unimportant matters; attend to trivial concerns, or to the small parts rather than to the main; trifle.

She plays and sings too, dances and discourses,
Comes very near essays, a pretty poet,
Begins to *piddle* with philosophy.
Fletcher, Wit without Money, i. 2.

2†. To pick at table; eat squeamishly or without appetite. *Swift.*

Content with little, I can *piddle* here
On brocoli and mutton, round the year.
Pope, Imit. of Horace, II. ii. 137.

3. To make water; urinate: a childish word.

piddler (pid'lėr), *n.* [< *piddle* + *-er*[1].] 1. One who piddles; a mere trifler or good-for-nothing.

Coz. You are good at the sport.
Cal. Who, I? a *piddler*, sir.
Massinger, Great Duke of Florence, iv. 2.

2. A squeamish eater.

piddling (pid'ling), *p. a.* 1. Trifling. Also *peddling*.

Nine geese, and some three larks for *piddling* meat.
Middleton, Mayor of Queenborough, v. 1.

Let children, when they versify, stick here
And there these *piddling* words for want of matter.
Poets write masculine numbers.
Shirley, Love in a Maze, ii. 2.

The ignoble Hucsterage of *pidling* Tithes.
Milton, Reformation in Eng., ii.

2†. Squeamish; difficult to please, especially in eating.

A *piddling* reader . . . might object to almost all the rhymes of the above quotation. *Goldsmith*, Criticisms.

piddock (pid'ọk), *n.* [Origin obscure.] A mollusk of the genus *Pholas* or family *Pholadidæ*; especially, a name of those species which are found in British waters, used rarely for food but much for bait, as *P. dactylus*; a pholad.

Piddocks (*Pholas dactylus*) in their holes.

It has a long ovate shell with a narrowed tongue-like extension in front, and the entire surface marked with longitudinal and concentric grooves and ridges, and radiating rows of sharp spines. The beaks are anterior and covered with callosities. The piddock is capable of perforating the soft rocks, into which it burrows. It is a common inhabitant of European seas, and in winter is frequently killed by the cold when left exposed by low tide. It is edible, and is sought for by digging it out of the clay or shale. After being removed from the water for a day or so, the animal changes color, and is said to shine like a glow-worm. Also called *clam*, *dactyl*, and *long oyster*. See *Pholas*, and cut under *accessory*.

pidet, *a.* An obsolete spelling of *pied*.

pidgeon†, *n.* An obsolete form of *pigeon*.

pidgin (pij'in), *n.* [A Chinese corruption of E. *business*.] Business; affair; thing. [Pidgin-English.]

Pidgin-English (pij'in-ing'glish), *n.* [Also *Pigeon-English*; < *pidgin* + *English*.] An artificial dialect or jargon of corrupted English, with a few Chinese, Portuguese, and Malay words, arranged according to the Chinese idiom, used by Chinese and foreigners for colloquial convenience in their business transactions and other dealings in the treaty ports of China and elsewhere in the China seas; the lingua franca of the ports of China and the Far East.

pie[1] (pī), *n.* [Formerly also *pye*; < ME. *pie*, *pye*, < Ir. *pighe* = Gael. *pigho*, a pie; cf. Ir. *pithan*, Gael. *pigheann*, a pie.] 1. A dish consisting of a thin layer of pastry filled with a preparation of meat, fish, fowl, fruit, or vegetables, seasoned, generally covered with a thicker layer of pastry, and baked: as, beefsteak *pie*; oyster *pie*; chicken *pie*; pumpkin *pie*; custard *pie*. Pies are sometimes made without the under thin layer of pastry. See *pudding*, *tart*, and *turnover*.

Kokes and here knaues crieden "hote *pyes*, hote!
Good goos and grys go we dyne, gowe!"
Piers Plowman (C), i. 226.

Mincing of meat in *pies* saveth the grinding of the teeth.
Bacon.

End now the white loafe and the *pye*,
And let all sports with Christmas dye.
Herrick, Upon Candlemasse Day.

And then there were apple *pies* and peach *pies* and pumpkin *pies*; besides slices of ham and smoked beef.
Irving, Sketch-Book, p. 440.

The *pie* is an English institution, which, planted on American soil, forthwith ran rampant and burst forth into an untold variety of genera and species.
H. B. Stowe, Oldtown, p. 342.

2. A mound or pit for keeping potatoes. *Halliwell*; *Jamieson*. [Prov. Eng. and Scotch.]—3. A compost-heap. [Prov. Eng.]—**A finger in the pie.** See *finger*.—**Minced pie.** See *mince-pie*.—**Périgord pie**, a pie flavored with truffles, which are most abundantly found in Périgord, France.—**To eat humble pie.** See *humble-pie*.

pie[2] (pī), *n.* [Also *pye*; < ME. *pie*, *pye*, < OF. (and F.) *pie* = Sp. Pg. *pega* = It. *pica*, < L. *pica*, a magpie; perhaps, like *picus*, a woodpecker (see *Picus*), so called in allusion to its spotted appearance, < *pingere* (√ *pic*), paint: see *picture*. Otherwise, perhaps both may be derived, with loss of orig. initial *s*, from the root of *specere*, see: see *spy*. To the same source as *picus*, in this view, is referred E. *speight*, a woodpecker. Hence, in comp., *magpie*.] 1. A magpie.

The thef, the chough, and ek the jangelynge *pye*.
Chaucer, Parliament of Fowls, l. 345.

They being all coltish and full of ragery,
And full of gergon as is a flecken *pye*.
W. Cartwright, The Ordinary, ii. 2.

Hence—2. Some similar or related bird; any pied bird: with a qualifying term: as, the smoky *pie*, *Psilorhinus morio*; the wandering *pie* of India, *Temnurus* (or *Dendrocitta*) *vagabundus*; the river-*pie*, or dipper, *Cinclus aquaticus*; the long-tailed *pie*, or titmouse, *Acredula rosea*; the murdering *pie*, or great gray shrike, *Lanius excubitor*; the sea-*pie*, or oyster-catcher; the Scoulton pewit or *pie* (see under *pewit*); etc.—3†. Figuratively, a prating gossip or tattler.

Dredeles it clere was in the wynde
Of every *pie*, and every lette-game.
Chaucer, Troilus, iii. 527.

French pie, the great spotted woodpecker, *Picus major*.

pie[3]† (pī), *n.* [Also *pye*; < ME. **pie* (?), < ML. *pica*: see *pica*[3].] 1. Same as *ordinal*, 2 (c).

The number and hardness of the Rules called the *Pie*.
Book of Common Prayer (Eng.), Concerning the Service of [the Church.

2. An index; a register; a list: as, a *pie* of sheriffs in the reign of Henry VIII.—**By cock and pie†**, a minced and mixed oath, consisting of an adjuration of the Deity (under a corrupted name) and the old Roman Catholic service-book.

By cock and pie, sir, you shall not away to-night.
Shak., 2 Hen. IV., v. 1. 1.

pie[4], *n.* and *v.* See *pi*[1].

pie[5] (pī), *n.* [< Marathi *pā'ī*, a fourth, i. e. a fourth part of an anna.] 1. The smallest Anglo-Indian copper coin, equal to one third of a pice, or one twelfth of an anna—about one fourth of a United States cent.—2. Formerly, a coin equal to one fourth of an anna.

Obverse. Reverse.
Pie of 1809, in the British Museum. (Size of the original.)

piebald (pī'bâld), *a.* [Formerly also *pyebald*, *pieball'd*; < *pie*[2] + *bald*. Cf. F. *pie*, piebald, and see *pied*.] 1. Having spots or patches of white and black or other color; party-colored; pied: as, a *piebald* horse.

The fiery Turnus flew before the rest;
A *pye-ball'd* steed of Thracian strain he press'd.
Dryden, Æneid, ix.

A gold and scarlet chariot drawn by six *piebald* horses.
Mrs. Gaskell, Sylvia's Lovers, xlii.

Hence—2. Mixed; heterogeneous; mongrel.

piece (pēs), *n.* [Early mod. E. also *peece*; < ME. *pece*, *piece*, < OF. *piece*, F. *pièce* = Pr. *pessa*, *pesa*

= Sp. *pieza*, *pedazo* = Pg. *peça*, *pedaço*, *pedasso* = It. *pezza*, *pezzo*, < ML. *petium*, also (after OF.) *pecia*, a piece; origin obscure. Cf. ML. *pedica*, a piece of ground, appar. < L. *pes* (*ped-*) = E. *foot*.] 1. A relatively small portion in bulk or extent forming a part of the whole in which it is or was included; a part; bit; morsel: as, a *piece* of bread or of chalk; a *piece* of ground; a *piece* of history; a *piece* of one's mind.

He alle naked hath a ful scharp Knyf in his hond, and he cuttethe a gret *pece* of his Flessche and castethe it in the face of his Ydole, seyenge his Orysounes, recommendynge him to his God. *Mandeville*, Travels, p. 177.

There is surely a *piece* of divinity in us. *Sir T. Browne*, Religio Medici, ii. 11.

But they relate this *piece* of history of a water about a mile to the south-west of Bethlehem. *Pococke*, Description of the East, II. i. 40.

I'll gie ye a *piece* of advice—bend weel to the Madeira at dinner, for here ye'll get little o't after. *E. B. Ramsay's* Scottish Life and Character, ii.

2. A separate bit; a fragment: as, to fall to *pieces*; to break, tear, cut, or dash to *pieces*.

Many a schene scheld scheuered al to *peces*. *William of Palerne* (E. E. T. S.), l. 3411.

The herte began to swelle with-ynne his cheste,
Soo sore streyned for anguysshe & for peyne
That alle to *pecis* almoste itt to-breste.
Political Poems, etc. (ed. Furnivall), p. 58.

If they fall, they dash themselves to *pieces*. *Shak.*, Rich. III., i. 3. 260.

3. A specimen, instance, example, or sort: as, a *piece* of impudence; a *piece* of carelessness.

Othes, as if they would rend heaven in sunder, . . .
Flie from his mouth, that *piece* of blasphemie.
Times' Whistle (E. E. T. S.), p. 24.

Did you, I say again, in all this progress,
Ever discover such a *piece* of beauty,
Ever so rare a creature? *Fletcher*, Valentinian, I. i.

O, 'twas a *piece*
Of pity and duty unexampled.
Ford, Lover's Melancholy, v. 1.

4. A separate article; a thing: as, a *piece* of plate.

Dumb as a senator, and, as a priest,
A *piece* of mere church-furniture at best.
Cowper, Tirocinium, l. 425.

(*a*) A coin: as, a *piece* of eight (see phrase below); a four-penny *piece*.

Meer. What is 't, a hundred pound?
Eve. No, th' harpy now stands on a hundred *pieces*.
B. *Jonson*, Devil is an Ass, iii. 1.

When a *piece* of silver is named in the Pentateuch, it signifies a sicle; if it be named in the prophets, it signifies a pound; if in the other writings of the Old Testament, it signifies a talent. *Jer. Taylor*, Works (ed. 1835), I. 290.

Harry Fielding . . . was in nowise particular in accepting a few *pieces* from the purses of his rich friends, and bore down upon more than one of them . . . for a dinner or a guinea. *Thackeray*, English Humourists.

(*b*) A cannon or gun; a firearm: as, his *piece* was not loaded; a fowling-*piece*.

He hath great *pieces* of ordnance, and mighty kings and emperors, to shoot against God's people. *Latimer*, Misc. Sel.

Sometimes we put a new signification to an old word, as when we call a *piece* a Gun. *Selden*, Table-Talk, p. 65.

(*c*†) A building; a castle.

Yet still he bet and bounst uppon the dore,
And thundred strokes thereon so hideouslie,
That all the *peece* he shaked from the flore.
Spenser, F. Q., V. ii. 21.

(*d*†) A ship; a vessel.

The wondred Argo, which in venturous *peece*
First through the Euxine seas bore all the flowr of Greece.
Spenser, F. Q., II. xii. 44.

(*e*) A distinct artistic or literary production; a separate article, poem, drama, painting, statue, or other artistic or literary work: as, a *piece* of music; to speak a *piece*; a finely painted *piece*.

I bequeth to Edmund Paston, my sone, a standing *pece* white covered, with a garleek heed upon the knoppe, and a gilt *pece* covered with an unicorne. *Paston Letters*, III. 285.

As I am a gentleman and a reveller, I'll make a *piece* of poetry, and absolve all, within these five days. B. *Jonson*, Poetaster, iii. 1.

I suppose one sha'n't be able to get in, for on the first night of a new *piece* they always fill the house with orders to support it. *Sheridan*, The Critic, i. 1.

This gentleman [Mr. Reynolds] . . . painted a *piece* of me, Lady Lyndon, and our little Bryan, which was greatly admired at the exhibition. *Thackeray*, Barry Lyndon, xvii.

(*f*) A lunch; a snack. [Prov. or colloq.]

5. A distinct job or operation taken separately; the amount of work done or to be done at any one time: as, to work by the *piece*; to do *piece*-work.—6. A definite and continuous quantity; a definite length, as of some textile fabric delivered by a manufacturer to the trade; a whole web of cloth or a whole roll of wall-paper: as, goods sold only by the *piece*; a whole *piece* of lace.

This sorrow works me, like a cunning friendship,
Into the same *piece* with it.
Beau. and Fl., King and No King, iv. 2.

As in little patterns torn from a whole *piece*, this may tell you what all I am. *Donne*, Letters, iii.

7. In *brewing*, a quantity of grain steeped and spread out at one time to make malt. Also called *floor*.

There can be no doubt that it is of importance to the maltster that the law allows him to sprinkle water over the *pieces* on the floor. *Encyc. Brit.*, IV. 268.

8. A plot of ground; a lot; a field; a clearing.

The fire took in the woods down back of our house; it went through Aunt Dolphy's *piece*, and so down to the Horse Sheds. *S. Judd*, Margaret, ii. 10.

9. An individual; a person: now used only contemptuously, and commonly of women: as, she is a bold *piece*.

St. John is called in p. 634 [of the Cursor Mundi] "a wel godd *pece*." *Oliphant*, Old and Middle English, p. 564.

She 's but a sallow, freckled-face *piece* when she is at the best. *Chapman*, Monsieur D'Olive, v. 1.

He is another manner of *piece* than you think for: but nineteen years old, and yet he is taller than either of you by the head. B. *Jonson*, Bartholomew Fair, i. 1.

10. In *chess*, *checkers*, etc., one of the men with which the game is played; specifically, in *chess*, one of the superior men, as distinguished from a pawn.—11†. A cup or drinking-vessel: also used indefinitely for a cask or barrel of wine, as the equivalent of the French *pièce*, which has different values in different parts of France.

Home, Launce, and strike a fresh *piece* of wine. *Fletcher*, Monsieur Thomas, v. 10.

12. In *bookbinding*, a tablet of leather which fills a panel on the back of a book.—13. In *whaling*, specifically, a section or chunk of blubber, more fully called *blanket-piece* (which see, below).—14. In *entom.*, any definitely hardened or chitinized part of the integument, especially of the abdomen, thorax, or head: technically called a *sclerite*. Two pieces may be movable on each other or free, united with a suture between or perfectly connate, so that even the suture is obliterated, and the pieces can be distinguished by their position only.—**A piece of**, a bit of; something of; one who is (a doer of something) to some extent.

If you are *a piece of* a farrier, as every good groom ought to be, get sack, brandy, or strong beer to rub your horses heels every night. *Swift*, Directions to Servants.

At all pieces†, at all points. *Davies.*

The image of a man at Armes on horsebacke, armed *at all peeces*, with a launce in his hand. *Holland*, tr. of Camden, p. 780.

Axis of a piece. See *axis*[1].—**Binding-piece.** See *binding*.—**Blanket-piece,** a strip or section of blubber cut from a whale in a spiral direction, and raised by means of the cutting-tackle. As the blubber is unwound or stripped from the animal it is called a *blanket-piece*, and after being cut in sections and lowered into the blubber-room it still retains the name; but when subdivided for mincing it is known as a *horse-piece*, which in its turn becomes a *book* or *bible*, and when the oil has been extracted the residuum is known as *scrap*.—**Bobstay, characteristic,** etc., **piece.** See the qualifying words.—**Deciduous pieces.** Same as *deciduous cusps* (which see, under *deciduous*).—**Easel-piece.** See *easel*[1].—**Face of a piece.** See *face*[1].—**Nogging-pieces.** See *nogging*.—**Of a piece,** as if of the same piece or whole; of the same nature, constitution, or disposition; of the same sort: generally followed by *with*.

As to the mechanism and scenery, every thing, indeed, was uniform, and *of a piece*. *Steele*, Spectator, No. 14.

The episodes interspersed in this strange story were *of a piece with* the main plot. *Macaulay*, Hist. Eng., vii.

Piece of cambric, linen, or **French lawn,** formerly 13 ells.—**Piece of eight**†, the Spanish *peso duro* (hard dollar) bearing the numeral 8, and of the value of 8 reals. The commercial sign for "dollar" ($) is supposed to have reference to this eight, the vertical strokes representing the Pillars of Hercules, which were formerly stamped on some dollars. According to another account, the sign is derived from the stamp 8 R. (8 reals) accompanied by two vertical strokes.

Tho' the City be then so full, yet during this heat of Business there is no hiring of an ordinary Slave under a *Piece of Eight* a day. *Dampier*, Voyages, I. 179.

A Note of his Hand to pay me 80 *pieces of Eight* for it at Brasil; . . . he offer'd me also 6 *pieces of Eight* more for my Boy Xury. *Defoe*, Robinson Crusoe.

Satisfaction piece, the formal certificate given by one receiving payment of a mortgage or judgment, certifying that it has been paid, and authorizing the public officer in charge of the record to note upon the record that it has been satisfied.—To **cut to pieces.** See *cut*.—To **give one a piece of one's mind,** to pronounce an opinion bluntly to one's face—generally something uncomplimentary, or implying complaint or reproach.

In a majestic tone he told that officer *a piece of his mind*. *Thackeray*, Vanity Fair, xxxviii.

She doubled up an imaginary fist at Miss Asphyxia Smith, and longed to *give her a piece of her mind*. *H. B. Stowe*, Oldtown, p. 199.

To **go to pieces.** See *go*. =**Syn. 1** and **2.** *Section*, *Division*, etc. (see *part*, *n.*), bit, scrap, morsel.

piece (pēs), *v.*; pret. and pp. *pieced*, ppr. *piecing*. [< *piece*, *n.*] **I.** *trans.* **1.** To patch, repair, enlarge, extend, or complete by the addition of a piece or pieces: as, to *piece* a garment or a curtain.

I will *piece*
Her opulent throne with kingdoms.
Shak., A. and C., i. 5. 45.

I went and paid a moccinigo
For *piecing* my silk stockings.
B. Jonson, Volpone, iv. 1.

2. To repair by the use of pieces of the same material, or without the addition of new material, as by bringing the unworn parts to the place where the most wear is; hence, to make good the defects of; strengthen; reinforce.

It is thought the French King will *piece* him up again with new Recruits. *Howell*, Letters, I. iv. 20.

3. To unite or reunite (that which has been broken or separated); make one again; join or rejoin, as one thing to another, or as friends who have fallen out.

Hem. I heard they were out.
Nee. But they are *pieced*, and put together again.
B. *Jonson*, Magnetick Lady, iii. 1.

Gwendolen . . . had conceived a project . . . to place her mother and sisters with herself in Offendene again, and, as she said, *piece* back her life on to that time when they first went there. *George Eliot*, Daniel Deronda, lxv.

To piece out, to form, enlarge, or complete by adding piece to piece.

To those of weaker merits he imparts a larger portion, and *pieces out* the defect of one by the excess of the other. *Sir T. Browne*, Religio Medici, i. 18.

Though his grove was city-planted, and scant of the foliage of the forest, there was Fancy to *piece out* for him . . . far other groves. *Forster*, Goldsmith, iii. 19.

To **piece up,** to patch up; form of pieces or patches; put together bit by bit.

I have known
Twenty such breaches *pieced up* and made whole
Without a bum of noise.
B. *Jonson*, Magnetick Lady, iv. 2.

He tells us that he began this History "about the year 1630, and so *pieced up* at times of leisure afterward." *Bradford*, Plymouth Plantation, p. 444, note.

II. *intrans.* **1.** To unite by coalescence of parts; be gathered as parts into a whole.

The cunning Priest changed his Copy, and chose now Plantagenet to be the Subject his Pupill should personate, because . . . it *pieced* better, and followed more close and handsomely upon the bruit of Plantagenets escape. *Bacon*, Hist. Hen. VII., p. 23.

Those things which have long gone together are, as it were, confederate with themselves; whereas new things *piece* not so well. *Bacon*, Innovations (ed. 1887).

2. To eat a "piece"; eat between meals, as a child. [Colloq., U. S.]

piece-broker (pēs'brō″kėr), *n.* A person who buys shreds and remnants of woolen cloth from tailors, to sell again for use in mending, patching, etc. *Simmonds.*

pieced (pēst), *p. a.* Repaired, strengthened, or completed by the adding or joining of pieces. In bookbinding, those bindings are said to be *pieced* in which the space between the bands upon which the title is to be stamped is covered with colored leather, usually of a different color from the covering of the book.

pièce de résistance (piās dė rā-zēs-toṅs'). [F., lit. 'piece of resistance,' i. e. substantial piece: see *piece*, *de*[2], *resistance*.] The most important piece or feature; the show piece; the main event or incident in any round or series, as the most forcible article in a magazine, the principal exhibition or performance in a show or theatrical entertainment, or the most substantial dish in a dinner.

piece-dyed (pēs'dīd), *a.* Dyed in the piece: said of cloth dyed after weaving, as distinguished from that made of wool dyed before weaving.

piece-goods (pēs'gůdz), *n. pl.* All kinds of cotton, linen, silk, or wool fabrics which are woven in lengths suitable for retail sale by the usual linear measure, as calicoes, shirtings, sheetings, mulls, jaconets, and long cloths.

pieceless (pēs'les), *a.* [< *piece* + *-less*.] Not made of pieces; consisting of something entire or continuous.

In those poor types of God (round circles) so
Religion's types, the *pieceless* centres flow,
And are in all the lines which all ways go.
Donne, To the Countess of Bedford.

piece-liquor (pēs'lik″or), *n.* In *brewing*, a part of a mash which, being of a higher or lower temperature than another part, but having the same density, is added to that other part to change its temperature without altering its strength.

piecely† (pēs'li), *adv.* In pieces; piecemeal. *Huloet.*

piece-master (pēs'màs″tėr), *n.* A middleman coming between an employer and the employed. *Mayhew.* (*Imp. Dict.*) [Eng.]

piecemeal (pēs'mēl), *adv.* [Early mod. E. also *peecemeale*, < ME. *pecemele*; < *piece* + *-meal*, as in *dropmeal*, *flockmeal*, etc.] **1.** By pieces;

bit by bit; little by little; gradually: often pleonastically *by piecemeal*.

Being but yet weak in Body, I am forced to write *by piece-meal*, and break off almost every hour.
Milton, Ans. to Salmasius, Pref., p. 5.

When we may conueniently vtter a matter in one entier speach or proposition, and will rather do it *peecemeale* and by distribution of euery part for amplification sake . . .
Puttenham, Arte of Eng. Poesie, p. 186.

Which little plots I thought they could not otherwise sow but by putting in the corne *by peece-meale* into the earth with their fingers. *Coryat*, Crudities, I. 83.

Piecemeal they win this acre first, then that;
Glean on, and gather up the whole estate.
Pope, Satires of Donne, ii. 91.

All was in ruin. . . . The vaults beneath yawned; the roof above was falling *piecemeal*.
Longfellow, Hyperion, ii. 9.

2†. In pieces; in or into bits or fragments.

Which flitting high) he strook his helm full where his plume did stand,
On which it *piece-meale* brake, and fell from his unhappy hande. *Chapman*, Iliad, iii.

Down goes the top at once; the Greeks beneath
Are *piece-meal* torn, or pounded into death.
Dryden, Æneid, ii.

piecemeal (pēs'mēl), *a.* [< *piecemeal, adv.*] Fragmentary; disconnected.

It appears that this edition [of Shakspere] was printed (at least partly) from no better copies than the prompter's book, or *piece-meal* parts written out for the use of the actors. *Pope*, Pref. to Shakespeare.

piecemealed† (pēs'mēld), *a.* [< *piecemeal* + *-ed*[2].] Divided into small pieces. *Cotgrave*.

piece-mold (pēs'mōld), *n.* In *bronze-casting*, a mold made up of separate pieces which are fitted together one after another upon the model, and beaten with a wooden mallet to make the whole close and solid: between the pieces some powder, such as brick-dust, is introduced to prevent adhesion.

pièce montée (piās môn-tā'). [F., a mounted piece: *pièce*, piece; *montée*, pp. of *monter*, mount: see *mount*[2].] **1.** A fancy dish, such as a salad, prepared for the adornment of the table.—**2.** By extension, a decorative piece for the table, made of paste, sugar, or the like, not necessarily eatable or intended to be eaten; sometimes, a cake or jelly crowned by such a structure; a set piece.

piecen (pē'sn), *v. t.* [< *piece* + *-en*[1].] To extend by adding a part or parts. [Colloq.]

The building [an art-gallery], not designed from the first in its entirety, has been *piecened* and enlarged from time to time. *Nineteenth Century*, XXII. 820.

piecener (pēs'nėr), *n.* [< *piecen* + *-er*[2].] A piecer. See the quotation.

The children whose duty it is to walk backward and forward before the reels on which the cotton, silk, or worsted is wound, for the purpose of joining the threads when they break, are called piecers or *pieceners*.
Mrs. Trollope, Michael Armstrong, viii. (*Davies*.)

piecening (pēs'ning), *n.* [Verbal n. of *piecen*, *v.*] In *textile manuf.*, same as *piecing*.

piece-patched† (pēs'pacht), *a.* Patched up.

There is no manly wisdom, nor no safety,
In leaning to this league, this *piece-patcht* friendship.
Fletcher (and others), Bloody Brother, ii. 1.

piecer (pē'sėr), *n.* [< *piece* + *-er*[1].] One who or that which pieces or patches; a boy or girl employed in a spinning-factory to join broken threads.

piece-work (pēs'wėrk), *n.* Work done and paid for by measure of quantity, or by previous estimate and agreement, in contradistinction to work done and paid for by measure of time.

piece-worker (pēs'wėr"kėr), *n.* One who does piece-work; one who works by the piece or job.

piecing (pē'sing), *n.* [Verbal n. of *piece*, *v.*] **1.** The act of mending by the addition or joining of a piece. Specifically—**2.** In *textile manuf.*, the joining of the ends of laps, slivers, yarns, or threads to make continuous lengths or to repair breaks. Also *piecening*.

pied (pīd), *a.* [Formerly also *pyed*, *pide*, *pyde*; < *pie*[2] + *-ed*[2]. Cf. F. *pie*, piebald.] Party-colored; variegated with spots of different colors; spotted. The word is now used chiefly to note animals which are marked with large spots of different colors. *Speckled* is used when the spots are small. This distinction was not formerly observed, and in some cases *pied* is in good use to express diversity of colors in small pattern.

This *pied* cameleon, this beast multitude.
Lust's Dominion, iii. 4.

Daisies *pied* and violets blue. *Shak.*, L. L. L., v. 2. 904.

I met a fool i' the woods (they said she dwelt here),
In a long *pied* coat. *Fletcher*, Pilgrim, iv. 3.

Guests
Intrusive to thy table and to thy feasts;
Who daub thee with *pyde* flatteries.
Heywood, Dialogues, iv.

There were milk-white peacocks, white and *pyed* pheasants, bantams, and furbelow fowls from the East Indies, and top-knot hens from Hamburg.
J. Ashton, Social Life in Reign of Queen Anne, I. 99.

Pied brant. Same as *harlequin brant* (which see, under *harlequin*).—**Pied dishwasher**, the pied wagtail.—**Pied duck**, the Labrador duck, *Camptolæmus labradorius*, the

Pied or Labrador Duck (*Camptolæmus labradorius*).

male of which is pied with black and white. It has become extremely rare of late years, and is supposed to be approaching extinction. It formerly ranged extensively along the Atlantic coast of the United States.—**Pied finch.** See *finch*[1].—**Pied grallina**, the magpie-lark of Australia, *Grallina picata*.—**Pied hornbill**, *Anthracoceros malabarica*, a bird of the family *Bucerotidæ*.—**Pied kingfisher.** See *kingfisher*.—**Pied seal**, the monk-seal, *Monachus albiventer*.—**Pied wagtail**, *Motacilla lugubris*.—**Pied widgeon.** Same as *garganey*.—**Pied wolf**, a pied variety of *Canis occidentalis*, the common American wolf.

pied-billed (pīd'bild), *a.* Having a pied bill: as, the *pied-billed* dabchick, *Podilymbus podiceps*.

pied-fort (pyā-fôr'), *n.* [F. (a technical term of the French mint), lit. 'strong foot': *pied*, < L. *pes* (*ped-*), foot; *fort*, < L. *fortis*, strong.] In *numis.*, a pattern for a proposed coin, struck on a flan or blank of greater thickness than the ordinary coins. The term is especially applied to French pattern pieces, such as those struck during the seventeenth century.

Piedmontese (pēd-mon-tēs' or -tēz'), *a.* and *n.* [= F. *Piémontais*; as *Piedmont* (It. *Piemonte*), < L. *Pedimontium*, Piedmont.] **I.** *a.* **1.** Of or pertaining to Piedmont, a region in northwestern Italy, bordering on Switzerland and France. In the modern kingdom of Italy, Piedmont is a compartimento, containing the provinces of Turin, Alessandria, Novara, and Cuneo.—**2.** By extension, pertaining to any region situated at or near the foot of mountains: as, the *Piedmontese* districts of Virginia, North Carolina, etc.

II. *n.* A native or an inhabitant of Piedmont.

piedmontite (pēd'mon-tīt), *n.* [< *Piedmont* + *-ite*[2].] A mineral closely related in form and composition to epidote, but containing manganese, hence sometimes called *manganepidote*. It is of a reddish-brown color, and is found at St. Marcel in Piedmont.

piedness (pīd'nes), *n.* The state of being pied; diversity of colors in spots. *Shak.*, W. T., iv. 4. 87.

piedouche (pyā-dösh'), *n.* [< F. *piédouche*, < It. *peduccio*, a corbel; dim. of *piede*, *pie*, foot, < L. *pes* (*ped-*) = E. *foot*: see *foot*.] In *arch.*, a bracket, pedestal, or socle, serving to support a bust, candelabrum, or other ornament.

piedpoudre†, *n.* See *piepowder*.

piedroit (pyā-drwo'), *n.* [< F. *pied-droit*, < L. *pes directus*, 'straight foot': see *pedal* and *direct*.] In *arch.*, an engaged pier, or a square pillar, projecting from the face of a wall. It differs from a pilaster in that it has neither base nor capital.

pied-winged (pīd'wingd), *a.* Having pied wings: specific in the name *pied-winged coot*, the velvet scoter. [New Eng.]

pie-finch (pī'finch), *n.* The chaffinch.

piel (pēl), *n.* [Perhaps a var. spelling and use of *peel*[3].] A wedge for piercing stones. *Simmonds*.

pieled†, *a.* An obsolete spelling of *peeled*.

pie-mag (pī'mag), *n.* Same as *magpie*.

pieman (pī'man), *n.*; pl. *piemen* (-men). A man who sells pies; also, a man who makes pies.

There are fifty street *piemen* plying their trade in London; the year through, their average takings are one guinea a week. *Mayhew*, London Labour and London Poor, I. 224.

pie-nanny (pī'nan"i), *n.* The magpie. Also *nanpie*.

piend (pēnd), *n.* **1.** Same as *peen*.—**2.** In *arch.*, an arris; a salient angle.

piend-check (pēnd'chek), *n.* A rebate on the bottom piend or angle of the riser of a step in a stone stair. It is intended to rest upon the upper angle of the next lower step. [Scotch.]

piend-rafter (pēnd'ráf"tėr), *n.* Same as *angle-rafter*. [Scotch.]

piept, *v. i.* An obsolete spelling of *peep*[1].

pie-plant (pī'plant), *n.* Garden-rhubarb, *Rheum Rhaponticum*: so named from its use for pies.

His *pie-plants* (the best in town), compulsory monastics, blanched under barrels, each in his little hermitage, a vegetable Certosa. *Lowell*, Cambridge Thirty Years Ago.

Wild pie-plant, in Utah and California, *Rumex hymenosepalus*, with acid stem and leaves, used as a pie-plant. See *canaigre*.

piepowder, piepoudre (pī'pou-dėr), *n.* [Also *piedpoudre* (ML. *curia pedis pulverizati*, 'court of dusty foot'); < OF. *piepoudreux* (ML. *pedepulverosus*), a stranger, peddler, or hawker who attends fairs, F. *pied poudreux*, lit. 'dusty foot' (cf. equiv. OF. *pied gris* 'gray foot'): *pied*, < L. *pes* (*ped-*) = E. *foot*; *poudreux*, < *poudre*, powder: see *powder*.] An ancient court of record in England, once incident to every fair and market, of which the steward of the owner or holder of the toll was the judge. It was instituted to administer justice for all commercial injuries done in that fair or market, but not in any preceding one. *Imp. Dict.*

Ffor chyders of Chester were chose many dales
To ben of conceill ffor causis that in the court hangid,
And pledid *pipoudris* alle manere pleyntis.
Richard the Redeless, iii. 319.

Is this well, goody Joan, to interrupt my market in the midst, and call away my customers? can you answer this at the *pie-poudres*? B. *Jonson*, Bartholomew Fair, iii. 1.

The lowest, and at the same time the most expeditious, court of justice known to the law of England is the court of *piepoudre*, curia pedis pulverizati, so called from the dusty feet of the suitors: or, according to Sir Edward Coke, because justice is there done as speedily as the dust can fall from the foot. *Blackstone*, Com., III. iv.

piepowdered (pī'pou-dėrd), *a.* [< *piepowder* (in lit. sense) + *-ed*[2].] Having dusty feet. [Rare.]

One day two peasants arrived in the Eschenheimer Gasse *pie-powdered*, having walked many hundred miles from the Polish backwoods. *Westminster Rev.*, LXXIV. 84.

pier (pēr), *n.* [< ME. *pere*, < OF. *pere*, *piere*, *pierre*, stone, a pier, F. *pierre*, a stone, = Pr. *petra*, *peira*, *peya* = Sp. *piedra* = Pg. *pedra* = It. *pietra*, a stone, rock, < L. *petra*, a mass of rock, crag (ML. also a castle on a rock, a tomb of stone, slate), < Gr. *πέτρα*, Epic and Ionic *πέτρη*, a rock, mass of rock, crag, ridge, ledge, *πέτρος*, a piece of rock, a stone (in prose usually *λίθος*), later also, like *πέτρα*, a mass of rock. From the Gr. *πέτρα*, *πέτρος*, besides *petrary*, *perrier*, etc., are also ult. E. *peter*[1], *petrel*[1], and in comp. *petrific*, *petrify*, *petroleum*, etc., *saltpeter*, *samphire*, etc.] **1.** (*a*) A mole or jetty carried out into the sea, to serve as an embankment to protect vessels from the open sea, to form a harbor, etc. (*b*) A projecting quay, wharf, or other landing-place.

But before he could make his approache, it was of necissitie for him to make a *pere* or a mole, whereby they might passe from the mayne land to the citie.
J. Brende, tr. of Quintus Curtius, fol. 54.

(*c*) One of the supports of the spans of a bridge, or any structure of similar character.—**2.** In *arch.* or *building*: (*a*) The solid support from which an arch springs. See first cut under *arch*[1].

For an interior, an arch resting on a circular column is obviously far more appropriate than one resting on a *pier*.
J. Fergusson, Hist. Arch., I. 305.

(*b*) In medieval architecture, a large pillar or shaft; specifically, a compound or a square pillar.

Pier (*c*) in Cloisters of Ste. Elne, near Perpignan, France; 12th century.

At Siena there is not merely a slight difference in the size of corresponding *piers*, but in many of them the centres, as well as the circumscribing lines of the bases and capitals, are out of line one with another.
C. E. Norton, Church-building in Middle Ages, p. 120.

(*c*) One of the solid parts between openings in a wall, such as doors and windows.

On the façade of the Duomo of Orvieto, upon one of the *piers* at the side of its doors of entrance, were sculptured representations of the Last Judgment and of Hell.
C. E. Norton, Travel and Study in Italy, p. 127.

(*d*) The wall or post, of square or other form, to which a gate or door is hung. (*e*) In a physical laboratory or observatory, a structure, generally of masonry, designed by its stability to prevent vibration in instruments which are supported by it.—**Abutment-pier**, the pier of a bridge next the shore.—**Floating pier**, a decked barge or caisson used as a landing-stage, and connected with the shore by a pivoted bridge that enables it to rise and fall with the tide; a landing-stage.

pierage (pēr'āj), *n.* [< *pier* + *-age.*] Toll paid for using a pier.

pier-arch (pēr'ärch), *n.* An arch resting upon piers.

pierce (pērs, formerly also pērs), *v.*; pret. and pp. *pierced*, ppr. *piercing.* [Early mod. E. also *pierse, pearce, pearse, peerce, perce;* dial. *pearch, peerch;* < ME. *percen, peercyn, persen, parcen, perchen, perishen, perisshen,* < OF. *percer, perser, percier, perchier, parchier,* F. *percer* (Walloon *percher*), pierce, bore; origin uncertain; by some regarded as contracted < OF. *pertuisier,* F. *pertuiser* (= It. *pertugiare*), < *pertuis* = It. *pertugio,* a hole, < ML. **pertusium,* also *pertusus,* a hole, < L. *pertusus,* pp. of *pertundere,* perforate, < *per,* through, + *tundere,* beat: see *pertuse.* Cf. *partizan*[2], from the same source. Cf. also *parch.*] **I.** *trans.* **1.** To thrust through with a sharp or pointed instrument; stab; prick.

> Mordrams to whome almyghty God after that appered & shewed to hym his syde bandes & feet *peryssched* with the spere and nayles.
> *Joseph of Arimathie* (E. E. T. S.), p. 31.

> One of the soldiers with a spear *pierced* his side, and forthwith there came out blood and water. John xix. 34.

> If Percy be alive, I'll *pierce* him.
> *Shak.*, 1 Hen. IV., v. 3. 59.

> If thou wilt strike, here is a faithful heart;
> *Pierce* it, for I will never heave my hand
> To thine. *Beau. and Fl.*, Maid's Tragedy, iii. 2.

2. To cut into or through; make a hole or opening in.

> This must be doon by *persyng* the mountayne,
> The water so to lede into the playne.
> *Palladius*, Husbondrie (E. E. T. S.), p. 176.

> A Cask *pearc't* to be spent,
> Though full, yet runs not till we glue it vent.
> *Sylvester*, tr. of Du Bartas's Weeks, i. 1.

> The mountain of Quarantina, the scene of the forty days temptation of our Saviour, is *pierced* all over with the caves excavated by the ancient anchorites, and which look like pigeons' nests.
> *R. Curzon*, Monast. in the Levant, p. 179.

3. To penetrate; enter into or through; force a way into or through: as, to *pierce* the enemy's center.

> A short orison of the rightuss man or of the iust man thirlith or *perissheth* heuen.
> *Gesta Romanorum* (E. E. T. S.), p. 47.

> Steed threatens steed in high and boastful neighs,
> *Piercing* the night's dull ear.
> *Shak.*, Hen. V., iv., Prol., l. 11.

> The Riuer doth *pierce* many daies iourney the entrailes of that Country. *Capt. John Smith*, Works, II. 194.

> In May, when sea-winds *pierced* our solitudes,
> I found the fresh Rhodora in the woods.
> *Emerson*, The Rhodora.

4. To penetrate with pain, grief, or other emotion; wound or affect keenly; touch or move deeply.

> Did your letters *pierce* the queen to any demonstration of grief? *Shak.*, Lear, iv. 3. 11.

> Tears did gush from every eye, and pithy speeches *pierced* each others heart.
> *N. Morton*, New England's Memorial, p. 24.

=**Syn. 1** and **2.** *Perforate, Transfix,* etc. See *penetrate.*
II. *intrans.* To enter or penetrate; force a way.

> She would not *pierce* further into his meaning than himself should declare. *Sir P. Sidney.*

> These words *pierce* deeper than the wounds I suffer,
> The smarting wounds of loss.
> *Fletcher*, Humorous Lieutenant, ii. 2.

> But see! the mists are stirring, rays of light
> *Pierce* through the haze, as struggling to be free.
> *Jones Very*, Poems, p. 99.

pierceable (pēr'sa-bl), *a.* [< *pierce* + *-able.*] Capable of being pierced. *Spenser,* F. Q., I. i. 7.

pierced (pērst), *p. a.* **1.** Penetrated; entered by force; perforated.—**2.** In *her.*: (*a*) Cut through with an opening not so large as that implied in *cleché,* and not of the shape of the bearing. The shape of the opening should be stated in the blazon, as triangular, lozengy, etc.; when not stated, the opening is supposed to be circular. Compare *quarter-pierced, quarterly pierced,* under *quarterly.* (*b*) Having an arrow, spear, or other weapon thrust into it but not passing through, as an animal used as a bearing. Compare *transfixed.*—**Mullet pierced.** See *mullet*[2].—**Pierced medallion,** a thin plate ornamented by a pattern cut through its whole substance and applied to the surface of a vase or similar object, the body of the piece showing through the openings in the medallion: used in metal-work of some kinds, and in some manufactures of porcelain. Also *perforated medallion.*—**Pierced work,** decoration produced by numerous openings, generally small. The solid pattern is usually heightened by chasing, embossing, or some inlaid ornamentation such as niello.

piercel (pēr'sel), *n.* [< *pierce* + *-el.* Cf. *piercer.*] An instrument for forming vents in casks; a piercer.

piercer (pēr'sėr), *n.* [Early mod. E. also *percer;* < ME. *persour,* < OF. *perceur,* piercer, < *percer,* pierce: see *pierce.*] **1.** One who or that which pierces.

> Such a strong *percer* is money, and such a gredie glotton is auarice. *Hall*, Hen. VI., an. 16.

2. Any sharp instrument used for piercing, boring, perforating, etc., such as an awl, a gimlet, or a stiletto. Specifically—(*a*) A piercel. (*b*) An instrument used in making eyelets. (*c*) A vent-wire used by founders in making holes. (*d*) A bow-drill.
3. In *entom.*, that organ of an insect with which it pierces bodies; the ovipositor. Also called *terebra.*

> The hollow instrument terebra we may English *piercer.*
> *Ray*, Works of Creation.

piercing (pēr'sing), *n.* [Verbal n. of *pierce, v.*] **1.** Penetration. Specifically—**2.** In *metal-working,* the operation of sawing out a pattern or an object from a plate, as distinguished from punching it out. It is done with a jig- or band-saw.

piercing (pēr'sing), *p. a.* **1.** Penetrating; sharp; keen: as, *piercing* eyes; a *piercing* wind.

> The air in this bishopric is pretty cold and *piercing.*
> *Defoe*, Tour thro' Great Britain, III. 220.

2. That touches or moves with pity, alarm, anguish, etc.: as, a *piercing* cry.

> In *piercing* phrases, late,
> The anatomy of all my woes I wrote.
> *Sir P. Sidney* (Arber's Eng. Garner, I. 532).

piercing-drill (pēr'sing-dril), *n.* See *drill*[1].

piercing-file (pēr'sing-fīl), *n.* A sharp narrow file used for enlarging drilled holes. *E. H. Knight.*

piercingly (pēr'sing-li), *adv.* In a piercing manner; with penetrating force or effect; sharply.

piercingness (pēr'sing-nes), *n.* The power of piercing or penetrating; sharpness; keenness.

piercing-saw (pēr'sing-sâ), *n.* A very fine thin saw-blade clamped in a frame, used by goldsmiths and silversmiths for sawing out designs, the blade being introduced into holes previously drilled; a buhl-saw. *E. H. Knight.*

pierelle (pēr-el'), *n.* [< F. *pierre,* stone (see *pier*), + dim. *-elle.*] A filling for a ditch, composed of stones thrown in without regularity, and covered with earth or clay to afford a smooth upper surface.

pier-glass (pēr'glàs), *n.* A mirror used in an apartment to cover the whole or a large part of the wall between two openings; especially, such a mirror set up between two windows, and forming a part of the decoration of a room. Compare *pier-table.*

Pierian (pī-ē'ri-an), *a.* [< L. *Pierius* (> It. Sp. *Pierio*), Pierian, sacred to the Muses, poetic, < *Pieria,* < Gr. Πιερία, a district, Πίερος, a mountain, in the north of Thessaly, haunted by the Muses (hence called *Pierides*).] **1.** Of or belonging to Pieria or the Pierides or Muses.

> A little learning is a dangerous thing;
> Drink deep, or touch not the *Pierian* spring.
> *Pope*, Essay on Criticism, ii. 15.

> And ye, *Pierian* Sisters, sprung from Jove
> And sage Mnemosyne. *Wordsworth*, Ode, 1814.

2. [*l. c.*] In *entom.*, same as *pieridine.*

Pieridæ (pī-er'i-dē), *n. pl.* [NL., < *Pieris* + *-idæ.*] The *Pieridinæ* or *Pierinæ* as a separate family.

Pierides (pī-er'i-dēz), *n. pl.* [L., < Gr. Πιερίδες, < Πίερος, a mountain in northern Thessaly: see *Pierian.*] The nine Muses.

Pieridinæ (pī'e-ri-dī'nē), *n. pl.* [NL., < *Pieris* (*Pierid-*) + *-inæ.*] A very large subfamily of *Papilionidæ,* typified by the genus *Pieris.* They have no concavity of the abdominal edge of the hind wings, the discoidal cellule is closed, the tarsal hook not indented, and the slightly pubescent larva attenuated at the extremity. The subfamily includes about 30 genera and 800 species, and is of world-wide distribution. The larvæ, in many cases, are of great economic importance from their destructive habits. Also *Pierinæ.*

pieridine (pī'e-ri-din), *a.* Of or pertaining to the *Pieridinæ.* Also *pierian.*

Southern Cabbage-butterfly (*Pieris protodice*), female, natural size.

Pieris (pī'ē-ris), *n.* [NL. (Schrank, 1801), < Gr. Πιερίς, sing. of Πιερίδες, the Muses: see *Pierides.*] A genus of butterflies, typical of the *Pieridinæ.* They are rather small whitish or yellowish butterflies, whose fore wings are rounded at the tip and marked with black. The genus as now restricted has over 120 species, of all parts of the world. Most of those of North America are known as *cabbage-butterflies,* with a qualifying word, because their caterpillars feed on the

Southern Cabbage-butterfly (*Pieris protodice*), male, natural size.

cabbage and other cruciferous plants. *P. oleracea* is the pot-herb or northern cabbage-butterfly (see cut under *pot-herb*); *P. protodice,* the southern cabbage-butterfly; *P. monuste,* the larger cabbage-butterfly. The commonest one in the United States now is *P. rapæ,* imported from Europe in 1856 or 1857, and known as the *rape-butterfly* in England. See also cuts under *cabbage-butterfly* and *cabbage-worm.*

pierre perdue (pyãr per-dü'). [F., lit. 'lost stone': *pierre,* stone; *perdue,* fem. of *perdu,* pp. of *perdre,* lose: see *pier* and *perdue.*] In *engin.*, masses of stone thrown down at random on a given site to serve as a subfoundation for regular masonry, as in the construction of a breakwater, etc.

pierriet, *n.* Same as *perry*[3].

pierriert, *n.* See *perrier.*

pierrot (pye-rō'), *n.* [F., dim of *Pierre,* Peter.] **1.** A form of woman's basque cut low in the neck, but having sleeves, worn toward the close of the eighteenth century.—**2.** A buffoon whose costume was white, or white with stripes, large and loose, and with very long sleeves: a popular character in masked balls.

pier-table (pēr'tā'bl), *n.* An ornamental table intended to stand between two windows and to occupy the whole of the lower part of the pier between the windows. It is often combined with a pier-glass, and the glass is sometimes carried down below the top of the table and between its uprights.

piest, *n.* See *pize.*

piet, piot (pī'et, pī'ot), *n.* [Also *pyot, piat, pyat;* < *pie*[2] + *-et.*] **1.** The magpie.—**2.** The water-ouzel or water-piet, *Cinclus aquaticus:* so called from the party-colored plumage. [Scotland.]

pieted, pioted (pī'et-ed, pī'ot-ed), *a.* [< *piet, piot,* + *-ed*[2].] Pied or piebald. [Scotch.]

Pietism (pī'e-tizm), *n.* [= F. *piétisme* = Pg. *pietismo;* as *piet-y* + *-ism.*] **1.** The movement inaugurated by the Pietists, who, from the latter part of the seventeenth century onward, sought to revive the declining piety of the Lutheran churches in Germany; the principles and practices of the Pietists.—**2.** [*l. c.*] Devotion or godliness of life, as distinguished from mere intellectual orthodoxy: sometimes used opprobriously for mere affectation of piety.

Pietist (pī'e-tist), *n.* [= F. *piétiste* = Pg. It. *pietista;* as *piet-y* + *-ist.*] One of a class of religious reformers in Germany in the seventeenth and eighteenth centuries. Their principles as defined by the originator of the movement, Spener (latter part of the seventeenth century), included the more earnest study of the Bible, the participation of the laity in the spiritual work of the church, a more practical type of piety, charity in the treatment of heretics, infidels, and others, a reorganization of the systems of religious and theological instruction in accordance with these principles, and a more enlightened style of preaching. Spener's disciples were led into extravagances of feeling; hence the term is sometimes applied opprobriously to any one who lays stress on mere emotionalism in religion, as distinguished from intelligent belief and practical life.

Pietistic (pī-e-tis'tik), *a.* [= Pg. *pietistico;* as *Pietist* + *-ic.*] **1.** Of or pertaining to the Pietists.—**2.** [*l. c.*] Characterized by strong religious feeling as distinguished from mere intellectual orthodoxy, or doctrinalism.

Pietistical (pī-e-tis'ti-kal), *a.* [< *Pietistic* + *-al.*] Same as *Pietistic,* in either sense.

pietra dura (pyā'trä dö'rä). [It., hard stone: see *pier* and *dure.*] Ornamental work in inlay of hard stones, such as agates and jaspers, especially when on a somewhat large scale.

pietra serena (pyā'trä se-rā'nä). [It., clear stone: see *pier* and *serene.*] A hard gray sandstone quarried in the hills near Fiesole, and much used for building in Florence and other cities of Tuscany.

piety (pī'e-ti), *n.* [Formerly also *pietie* (earlier *pitie*, etc.: see *pity*); < OF. *piete*, F. *piété* = Pr. *pietat*, *pitat*, *pidat* = Sp. *piedad* = Pg. *piedade* = It. *pietà*, < L. *pieta(t-)s*, piety, < *pius*, pious: see *pious*. Cf. *pity*, an earlier form of the same word.] 1. The character of being pious or having filial affection; natural or filial affection; dutiful conduct or behavior toward one's parents, relatives, country, or benefactors.

If any widow have children or nephews, let them learn first to shew *piety* at home, and to requite their parents: for that is good and acceptable before God. 1 Tim. v. 4.

How am I divided
Between the duties I owe as a husband
And *piety* of a parent!
Fletcher, Spanish Curate, iv. 1.

2. Faith in and reverence for the Supreme Being; filial obedience inspired by these sentiments; godliness.

Goodness belongs to the Gods, *Piety* to Men, Revenge and Wickedness to the Devils. *Howell*, Letters, ii. 11.

The Commonwealth which maintains this discipline will certainly flourish in vertu and *piety*.
Milton, Church-Government, ii. 3.

Pelican in her piety. See *pelican*. =**Syn. 2.** *Devotion*, *Sanctity*, etc. See *religion*.

piewipe (pī'wīp), *n.* [Imitative.] Same as *peewit* (*b*).

piezo-electricity (pī″e-zō-ē-lek-tris'i-ti), *n.* [Irreg. < Gr. πιέζειν, press, + E. *electricity*.] Electricity produced by pressure, as that of a sphere of quartz, which becomes electrified by pressure.

piezometer (pī-e-zom'e-tėr), *n.* [= F. *piézomètre* = Pg. *piezometro*; irreg. < Gr. πιέζειν, press, + μέτρον, measure.] 1. Any instrument for ascertaining or testing pressure.—2. An instrument for showing the compressibility of water or other liquid, and the degree of such compressibility under varying pressures. A common form (see figure) consists of a strong glass cylinder, within which is supported a small vessel (C) with a graduated stem containing the liquid under experiment, also a thermometer (T) and manometer (M). The pressure is exerted by the piston moved by a screw at the top, and transmitted by the water with which the cylinder is filled to the liquid in the vessel C. The amount of this pressure is measured by the manometer. The compressibility is shown by the fall of the liquid (and index) in the graduated stem, and its amount can be readily calculated if the capacity of C, in terms of these scale-divisions, is known.

Piezometer.

3. An instrument consisting essentially of a vertical tube inserted into a water-main, to show the pressure of the fluid at that point, by the height to which it ascends in the tube of the piezometer.—4. A sounding-apparatus in which advantage is taken of the compression of air in a tube by the pressure of the water at great depths to indicate the depth of the water.—5. An instrument for testing the pressure of gas in the bore of a gun.

piff (pif), *n.* See *paff*.

piffero (pif'e-rō), *n.* [< It. *piffero*, *piffera*, *pifara*, formerly also *pifera*, *pifaro* = Sp. *pifaro* (also *pifano*) = Pg. *pifaro* (also *pifano*), a fife, < OHG. *pfīfā*, a pipe, fife: see *pipe*[1], *fife*.] 1. A musical instrument, either a small flageolet or a small oboe, used by strolling players in some parts of Italy and Tyrol.—2. The name of an organ-stop: same as *bifara*.

pig[1] (pig), *n.* [Also dial. *peg*; early mod. E. *pigge*; < ME. *pigge*, *pygge* = D. *bigge*, *big* = LG. *bigge*, a pig; origin obscure. An AS. **pecg* is mentioned as occurring "in a charter of Swinford copied into the Liber Albus at Wells" (Skeat, on authority of Earle); but this is doubtful; an AS. **pecg* would hardly produce the E. form *pig*. Whether the word is related to LG. *bigge*, a little child, = Dan. *pige* = Sw. *piga* = Icel. *pika*, a girl, is doubtful.] 1. A hog; a swine; especially, a porker, or young swine of either sex, the old male being called *boar*, the old female *sow*. It is sometimes used in composition to designate some animal likened to a pig: as, a guinea-*pig*. See *hog*, *Suidæ*.

Together with the cottage . . . what was of much more importance, a fine litter of new-farrowed *pigs* no less than nine in number perished. *Lamb*, Roast Pig.

2. The flesh of swine; pork.

Now *pig* it is a meat, and a meat that is nourishing and may be longed for, and so consequently eaten; it may be eaten; very exceedingly well eaten.
B. Jonson, Bartholomew Fair, i. 1.

3. An oblong mass of metal that has been run while still molten into a mold excavated in sand; specifically, iron from the blast-furnace run into molds excavated in sand. The molds are a series of parallel trenches connected by a channel running at right angles to them. The iron thus cools in the form of semi-cylindrical bars, or pigs, united at one end by another bar called the *sow*: so called from a coarse comparison with a litter of pigs suckling.

[We found] many barres of Iron, two *pigs* of Lead, foure Fowlers, Iron shot, and such like heauie things throwne here and there.
Quoted in *Capt. John Smith's* Works, I. 104.

Sometimes a *pig* will solidify partly as white iron partly as grey, the crystallization having commenced in patches, but not having spread throughout the whole mass before it solidified; such iron is known as mottled *pig*.
Encyc. Brit., XIII. 284.

4. A customary unit of weight for lead, 301 pounds.—**All-mine pig**, pig-iron smelted entirely from ore or mine material.—**A pig in a poke.** See *poke*[2].—**Hunt the pig.** See *hunt*.—**Long pig, masked pig**, etc. See the adjectives.—**Pig's whisper.** (*a*) A low or inaudible whisper. (*b*) A very short space of time. [Slang.]

You'll find yourself in bed in something less than a *pig's whisper*. *Dickens*, Pickwick, xxxii.

Please the pigs, if circumstances permit: a trivial rustic substitute for *please God* or *if it please Providence*. *Pigs* is here apparently a mere alliterative caprice; it has been variously regarded as an altered form of *pix*, *pyx*, the box which held the host; or of *pixies*, fairies; or of the "Saxon *piga*, a virgin" (as if meaning the Virgin Mary). These conjectures are all absurd. As to the last, no "Saxon *piga*" exists; the entry "*piga*, puellula," in Somner, Lye, etc., is an error.

I'll have one of the wigs to carry into the country with me, and [if (it)] *please the pigs*. *T. Brown*, Works, ii. 198.

Sussex pig, a vessel in the form of a pig, made at the Bellevue or other Sussex pottery. When empty it stands upon the four feet, but when in use it stands upright, its head is lifted off to allow of its being filled, and it serves as a drinking-cup. The jest of being ordered to drink a "hogshead" of beer in response to a toast, or the like, refers to the emptying of such a cup. See *Sussex rustic ware*, under *ware*.—**To bring one's pigs to a pretty market**, to make a very bad bargain, or to manage anything in a very bad way.

pig[1] (pig), *v. i.*; pret. and pp. *pigged*, ppr. *pigging*. [< *pig*[1], *n.*] 1. To bring forth pigs; bring forth in the manner of pigs; litter.—2. To act as pigs; live like a pig; live or huddle as pigs: sometimes with an indefinite *it*.

But he hardly thinks that the sufferings of a dozen felons *pigging* together on bare bricks in a hole fifteen feet square would form a subject suited to the dignity of history. *Macaulay*, Sir William Temple.

To *pig it* like the prodigal son in the solitudes of ostracism. *Westminster Rev.*, CXXVIII. 873.

The working man here is content to *pig* in, to use an old-country term, in a way that an English workman would not care to do. *The Engineer*, LXV. 480.

pig[2] (pig), *n.* [Abbr. of *piggin*[1].] 1. An earthen vessel; any article of earthenware.

Qubair the *pig* breaks let the shells lie.
Scotch proverb (Ray's Proverbs, 1678, p. 388).

2. A can for a chimney-top.—3. A potsherd. [Scotch in all uses.]

pig-bed (pig'bed), *n.* The bed or series of molds formed of sand into which iron is run from the blast-furnace and cast into pigs.

pig-boiling (pig'boi″ling), *n.* Same as *wet-puddling*. See *puddling*.

pig-cote (pig'kōt), *n.* A pigsty. [Prov. Eng.]

pig-deer (pig'dēr), *n.* The babirussa.

pigeon (pij'on), *n.* [Early mod. E. also *pidgeon*, *pigion*; < ME. *pigeon*, *pijon*, *pygeon*, *pyjon*, < OF. *pigeon*, *pijon*, *pynjon*, *pignon*, also *pipion*, F. *pigeon* = Pr. *pijon* = Sp. *pichon* = It. *piccione*, *pippione*, a pigeon, a young bird, < L. *pipio(n-)*, a young piping or chirping bird, a squab, < *pipire*, chirp: see *pipe*[1], *peep*[1]. For the form, cf. *widgeon*. The native (AS.) word for 'pigeon' is *dove*: see *dove*[1].] 1. Any bird of the family *Columbidæ* (which see for technical characters); a dove. The species are several hundred in number, and are found in nearly all parts of the world. Many kinds are distinguished by qualifying terms, as *fruit-pigeon*, *ground-pigeon*, *passenger-pigeon*, *nutmeg-pigeon*, *rock-pigeon*, and any of them may be called *dove*, as *stock-dove*, *rock-dove*, *ring-dove*, *turtle-dove*, *wood-dove*. (See the compound names, and *dove*1.) Few species are commonly seen in confinement, except in very extensive aviaries, one of the commonest being the ring-dove; but the rock-pigeon or rock-dove, *Columba livia*, is everywhere thoroughly domesticated, and perhaps all the artificial varieties have been produced by careful breeding from this one. Fancy pigeons have naturally received many fanciful names of their breeds, strains, and endless color-variations. Some of these names are—(*a*) from localities, actual or alleged, as Antwerps, barbs (from Barbary), Brunswicks, Burmeses, Damascenes, Florentines, Lahores, Orientals, Swabians; (*b*) from resemblance to other birds, as magpies, owls, starlings, swallows, swifts; (*c*) from characteristic actions, as carriers, croppers, dragoons, homers, pouters, rollers, shakers, trumpeters, tumblers; (*d*) from peculiarities of size, shape, or color, as capuchins, fantails (see cut under *fantail*), fire-pigeons, frills or frill-backs, helmets, hyacinths, ice-pigeons, jacobins (see cut under *jacobin*), nuns, porcelains, priests, runts, shields, turbits. Some names, like *archangel*, *mawmet*, and *victoria*, are unclassifiable, and others are quite peculiar to fanciers' nomenclature, as *blondinette*, *silverette*, and *turbitteen*. Young pigeons are known as *squabs* and *squealers*. The name *pigeon* is also used, with a qualifying word, to designate some bird like or likened to a pigeon, as *prairie-pigeon*, *sea-pigeon*, etc.

Domestic Pigeon, homing variety.

2. A simpleton to be swindled; a gull: opposed to *rook*. See *stool-pigeon*. [Slang.]—**Barbary pigeon.** Same as *barb*[3], 2.—**Blue pigeon**, a deep-sea lead; a sounding-lead.—**Cape pigeon**, a small petrel, spotted black and white, abundant off the Cape of Good Hope; the damier, *Procellaria* or *Daption capensis*, belonging to the family *Procellariidæ*. See cut under *Daption*.—**Clay pigeon.** See *clay*.—**Crown pigeon**, *Goura coronata*. See cut under *Goura*.—**Diving pigeon**, the sea-pigeon, sea-dove, or black guillemot, *Uria grylle*. See cut under *guillemot*.—**Mechanical pigeon.** (*a*) A device to which a flying motion is imparted by means of a spring released by a trigger, or otherwise, to supply the place of living pigeons in shooting-matches, or to afford practice to marksmen in shooting birds on the wing. It may be a strip of sheet-metal with blades bent in a propeller form, and caused to rise by being rotated rapidly, or it may be a ball of glass, terra-cotta, or the like. (*b*) A toy consisting of a light propeller-wheel, which, on being made to revolve rapidly by means of a string wound about a shaft on which it rests, rises in the air in a short flight.—**Nicobar pigeon**, *Calœnas nicobarica*. See cut under *Calœnas*.—**Pigeon's egg**, a bead of Venetian glass, the form and size of which give rise to the name. Such beads were produced as early as the fifteenth century, and very ancient ones are preserved.—**Pigeon's milk**, a non-existent article, in search of which April fools are despatched. *Halliwell*. [Humorous.]—**Tooth-billed pigeon**, *Didunculus strigirostris*. See cut under *Didunculus*.—**To pluck a pigeon**, to swindle; fleece. [Slang.]—**Wild pigeon**, in the United States, specifically, the passenger-pigeon, *Ectopistes migratorius*. See cut under *passenger-pigeon*.

pigeon (pij'on), *v. t.* [< *pigeon*, *n.*] To pluck; fleece; strip of money by the tricks of gambling. [Slang.]

Then hey! at Dissipation's call
To every Club that leads the ton,
Hazard 's the word; he flies at all,
He 's *pigeon'd* and undone.
Observer, No. 27. (*Richardson.*)

pigeonberry (pij'on-ber″i), *n.* The pokeweed. See *garget*, 5, and *Phytolacca*.

pigeon-breast (pij'on-brest), *n.* 1. The breast of a pigeon.—2. A deformity occurring in persons affected with rickets, in which the costal cartilages are bent inward, and the sternum or breast-bone is thrown forward.

pigeon-breasted (pij'on-bres″ted), *a.* Affected with pigeon-breast.

pigeon-cherry (pij'on-cher″i), *n.* Same as *pin-cherry*.

Pigeon-English (pij'on-ing'glish), *n.* See *Pidgin-English*.

pigeon-express (pij'on-eks-pres″), *n.* The conveyance of intelligence by means of a carrier- or homing-pigeon.

pigeon-fancier (pij'on-fan″si-ėr), *n.* One who keeps and breeds pigeons.

pigeonfoot (pij'on-fut), *n.* A plant: same as *dove's-foot*, 1.

pigeon-goose (pij'on-gös), *n.* An Australian goose, *Cereopsis novæ-hollandiæ*.

pigeon-grass (pij'on-gràs), *n.* A grass, *Setaria glauca*, found in stubble-fields, etc., and very widely diffused. It is said to be as nutritious as Hungarian grass, but the yield is small. [U. S.]

pigeon-hawk (pij'on-hâk), *n.* One of the smaller hawks, about as large as a pigeon, or able to prey on birds as large as pigeons. (*a*) A small true falcon of America, *Falco columbarius*, and some closely related species, corresponding to what are termed *merlins* in Europe. (*b*) The sharp-shinned hawk, *Accipiter fuscus* or *A. velox*. See cut at *sharp-shinned*. [U. S.]

pigeon-hearted (pij'on-här″ted), *a.* Timid as a bird; easily frightened.

First Out. The drum, the drum, sir!
Curio. I never saw such *pigeon-hearted* people.
What drum? what danger?—Who 's that that shakes behind there? *Fletcher*, Pilgrim, iii. 4.

pigeonhole (pij'on-hōl), *n.* 1. One of the holes in a dove-cote or pigeon-house through which the birds pass in and out. Hence—2. A little compartment or division in a case for papers, a bureau, a desk, or the like.

Abbé Sieyes has whole nests of *pigeon-holes* full of constitutions already made, ticketed, sorted, and numbered. *Burke.*

3. One of a series of holes in an arch of a furnace through which the gases of combustion pass.—4. One of a series of holes in the block at the bottom of a keir through which its liquid contents can be discharged.—5. *pl.* An old English game, resembling modern bagatelle, in which balls were rolled through little cavities or arches.

Threepence I lost at nynepines; but I got
Six tokens towards that at *pigeon-holes*.
Brome, Antipodes, iv. 5.

In several places there was nine-pins plaid,
And *pidgeon holes* for to beget a trade.
Frost-Fair Ballads (1684). (*Nares.*)

6. In *printing*, an over-wide space between printed words. Also called *rat-hole*.

pigeonhole (pij'on-hōl), *v. t.*; pret. and pp. *pigeonholed*, ppr. *pigeonholing*. [< *pigeonhole*, *n.*] To place or file away in a pigeonhole; hence, to lay aside for future consideration; hence, to lay aside and ignore or forget; "shelve"; treat with intentional neglect: as, to *pigeonhole* an application for an appointment; to *pigeonhole* a scheme.

It is true that in common life ideas are spoken of as being treasured up, forming a store of knowledge: the implied notion being that they are duly arranged and, as it were, *pigeon-holed* for future use.
H. *Spencer*, Prin. of Psychol., § 469.

He had hampered the business of the State Department by *pigeon-holing* treaties for months.
N. A. Rev., CXXVII. 63.

pigeonholed (pij'on-hōld), *a.* Formed with pigeonholes for the escape of gases of combustion, as the arch of a furnace, or for the discharge of liquids, as the bottom of a keir.

pigeon-house (pij'on-hous), *n.* A house for pigeons; a pigeonry; a dove-cote.

pigeon-livered (pij'on-liv"ėrd), *a.* Mild in temper; pigeon-hearted; soft; gentle.

I am *pigeon-liver'd*, and lack gall
To make oppression bitter.
Shak., Hamlet, ii. 2. 605.

pigeon-match (pij'on-mach), *n.* A meeting or contest where pigeons are shot at as they are released from boxes, called traps, placed at a fixed distance from the marksman.

pigeon-pair (pij'on-pãr), *n.* Twins of opposite sex, boy and girl: so called because pigeons lay two eggs which normally hatch a pair of birds, a male and a female.

pigeon-pea (pij'on-pē), *n.* See *Cajanus*.

pigeon-plum (pij'on-plum), *n.* A middle-sized tree, *Coccoloba Floridana*, common in semi-tropical Florida. Its wood is hard and close-grained, of a deep brown tinged with red, and valuable for cabinet-making. Its abundant grape-like fruit is a favorite food of small animals.

pigeonry (pij'on-ri), *n.*; pl. *pigeonries* (-riz). [< *pigeon* + *-ry*.] A place where pigeons are kept; a columbarium; a dove-cote.

pigeon's-blood (pij'onz-blud), *n.* The color of a fine dark ruby, scarcely so dark as the beef's-blood. These two shades are the most admired in that stone.

pigeon's-grass (pij'onz-grȧs), *n.* [Cf. Gr. *περιστερεών*, a kind of verbena, also a dove-cote, < *περιστερά*, a pigeon, dove.] The common vervain, *Verbena officinalis*, said to be frequented by doves, and sometimes fancied to be eaten by them to clear their sight.

pigeontail (pij'on-tāl), *n.* The pintail duck, *Dafila acuta*: so called from the resemblance of the tail to that of the wild pigeon or passenger-pigeon. *W. H. Herbert.* See cut under *Dafila*.

pigeon-toed (pij'on-tōd), *a.* 1. Having that structure of the feet which characterizes pigeons; peristeropod: said of gallinaceous birds. The pigeon-toed fowl are the mound-birds or *Megapodidæ* of the Old World and the curassows or *Cracidæ* of America.—2. Having the toes turned in: said of persons. [Colloq.]

The *pigeon-toed* step and the rollicking motion
Bespoke them two genuine sons of the Ocean.
Barham, Ingoldsby Legends, II. 171.

pigeon-tremex (pij'on-trē"meks), *n.* A hymenopterous insect of the family *Uroceridæ*, or horntails, *Tremex columba*: a hook-name. The adult oviposits in the trunks of maples and other shade-trees, and the larva is a wood-borer.

pigeonwing (pij'on-wing), *n.* 1. A mode of dressing the side hair adopted by men especially in the latter part of the eighteenth century; also, a wig so called.

A young man slightly overdressed. His club and *pigeon-wings* were fastened with three or four pins of gold, and his white-powdered queue was wrapped with a black velvet ribbon shot with silver.
G. W. Cable, Stories of Louisiana, xiii.

2. A brisk fancy step or caper in dancing, skating, etc.: as, to cut a *pigeonwing*.

Shaking off straw and furs, wraps and pattens, the ladies had no sooner swallowed cups of tea than they were whisked into line for the Virginia reel, over against a row of cavaliers arrayed with back-seam coat-buttons coming beneath their shoulder-blades, who cut the *pigeon-wing* in square-toed pumps. Then what life, what joyous frisking! *The Century*, XXXVII. 858.

pigeonwood (pij'on-wůd), *n.* A name of various trees or their wood, from the marking or coloring of the latter. (*a*) *Pisonia obtusata* of the West Indies and Florida: also called *beefwood*, *corkwood*, and *porkwood*. (*b*) *Dipholis salicifolia*, a large fragrant tree; *Diospyros tetrasperma*, a shrub; and several species of *Coccoloba*—all of the West Indies. (*c*) *Guettarda speciosa*, a small evergreen of tropical shores in both hemispheres. (*d*) *Connarus Guianensis* (*Omphalobium Lambertii*) of South America and the West Indies. Also called *zebrawood*.

pigeon-woodpecker (pij'on-wůd"pek-ėr), *n.* Same as *flicker*[2].

pig-eyed (pig'īd), *a.* Having small dull eyes with heavy lids, appearing sunken: said of persons.

pig-faced (pig'fāst), *a.* Having a piggish physiognomy; looking like a pig: as, the *pig-faced* baboon.

pig-fish (pig'fish), *n.* Any one of various fishes which make a grunting noise when taken out of the water. (*a*) A grunt or grunter; a member of the *Hæmulonidæ* or *Pristipomidæ*; specifically, *Orthopristis chrysopterus*. (*b*) A sciænoid fish, the spot or lafayette, *Liostomus obliquus*. (*c*) A cottoid fish, the sculpin, *Cottus octodecimspinosus*. (*d*) A labroid fish of New South Wales, *Cossyphus* or *Bodianus unimaculatus*.

pigfoot (pig'fůt), *n.*; pl. *pigfoots* or *pigfeet* (-fůts, -fēt). A scorpænoid fish, *Scorpæna porcus*, of the Mediterranean and contiguous waters. The cheeks, opercles, and top of the head are naked, and dorsal fins are developed; the form is compressed, and the color is reddish-brown mottled and dotted with black.

pig-footed (pig'fůt"ed), *a.* Having feet like a pig's: as, the *pig-footed* perameles, *Chæropus castanotis*. See cut at *Chæropus*.

piggery[1] (pig'ė-ri), *n.*; pl. *piggeries* (-riz). [< *pig*[1] + *-ery*.] A place where pigs are kept; a pigsty or set of pigsties.

piggery[2] (pig'ė-ri), *n.*; pl. *piggeries* (-riz). [< *pig*[2] + *-ery*.] A place where earthen vessels are made or sold; a pottery. *Jamieson.* [Scotch.]

piggesniet, *n.* See *pigsney*. *Chaucer.*

piggin[1] (pig'in), *n.* [< Gael. *pigean*, a little earthen jar, pitcher, or pot, dim. of *pigeadh* (= It. *pighead*), an earthen jar, pitcher, or pot. Cf. Ir. *pigin*, a small pail, noggin, = W. *picyn*, a piggin, noggin. Hence, by abbr., *pig*[2].] 1. A small wooden vessel with an erect handle formed by continuing one of the staves above the rim.

A *piggin*, to milk in, immulctra. *Holyoke.*

Wooden *piggins*. *Lamb.*

Piggin, "a small wooden vessel with an erect handle, used as a dipper." [Southernisms and Westernisms.]
Trans. Amer. Philol. Ass., XVII. 41.

2. A small earthen vessel; a pitcher; also, a shallow vessel provided with a long handle at one side, used as a dipper.—**Boat-piggin**, a small wooden piggin belonging to a boat's gear, used for bailing.

piggin[2] (pig'in), *n.* [Origin obscure.] The joists to which the flooring is fixed; more properly, the pieces on which the boards of the lower floor are fixed. *Halliwell.* [Prov. Eng.]

piggish (pig'ish), *a.* [< *pig*[1] + *-ish*[1].] Like a pig in disposition, habits, or manners; hoggish; swinish; especially, greedy: said chiefly of persons.

piggishness (pig'ish-nes), *n.* The character of being piggish; especially, greediness.

piggle (pig'l), *v. t.* [A var. of *pickle*[1].] To root up (potatoes) with the hand. *Halliwell.* [Prov. Eng.]

piggle (pig'l), *n.* [< *piggle*, *v.*] A many-pronged hook, with a handle like that of a hoe, used in digging potatoes, and in mixing various materials, as clay, mortar, compost, etc.

pig-headed (pig'hed"ed), *a.* [< *pig*[1] + *head* + *-ed*[2]. Cf. *pig-sconce*.] Stupid and obstinate as a pig; stupidly perverse; unreasonably set in mind.

You should be some dull tradesman by your *pig-headed* sconce now. B. *Jonson*, News from the New World.

If Mr. Tulliver had in the end declined to send Tom to Stelling, Mr. Riley would have thought his friend of the old school a thoroughly *pig-headed* fellow.
George Eliot, Mill on the Floss, i. 3.

pig-headedly (pig'hed"ed-li), *adv.* In a pig-headed, obstinate, or perverse manner.

pig-headedness (pig'hed"ed-nes), *n.* The character of being pig-headed; stupid perversity or obstinacy.

pig-hole (pig'hōl), *n.* In some metallurgic operations, a hole, provided with a cover, in the wall of a furnace, through which a crucible may have an additional supply of pig-metal put in it without the operation of the furnace being interrupted.

pight† (pīt). An obsolete preterit and past participle of *pitch*[1].

pightle (pī'tl), *n.* [See *pickle*[3].] A small meadow; any small inclosed piece of land. [Prov. Eng. and U. S. (eastern end of Long Island).]

pig-iron (pig'ī"ėrn), *n.* 1. Iron in pigs, as it comes from the blast-furnace. See *pig*[1], 3.—2. A flat piece of iron, which is hung so as to be interposed between the fire and meat roasting, when it is desirable to retard the cooking. *Halliwell.*—**Pig-iron breaker**, a power-hammer adapted for breaking pig-iron into pieces suitable for charging a furnace.

pig-lead (pig'led), *n.* Lead in pigs; lead in the form in which it is ordinarily offered for sale after reduction from the ore. See *pig*[1], 3.

pigmean, *a.* See *pygmean*.

pigment (pig'ment), *n.* [< ME. *pigment*, spiced wine (see *piment*), < OF. *pigment* (also *piment*), F. *pigment*, < L. *pigmentum*, a pigment, < *pingere* (√ *pig*), paint: see *picture*.] 1. Any substance that is or can be used by painters to impart color to bodies; technically, a dry substance, usually in the form of a powder or in lumps so lightly held together as to be easily pulverized, which after it has been mixed with a liquid medium can be applied by painters to surfaces to be colored. *Pigment* is properly restricted to the dry coloring matter which when mixed with a vehicle becomes a *paint*; but the two words are commonly used without discrimination. (See *paint*.) In oil-painting, the pigments are ground or triturated to render them smooth, usually in poppy- or nut-oil, since these dry best and do not deaden the colors.

If you will allow me, Pyrophilus, for the avoiding of ambiguity, to employ the word *pigments* to signify such prepared materials (as cochineal, vermilion, orpiment) as painters, dyers, and other artificers make use of to impart or imitate particular colours. *Boyle*, Works, II. 48.

2. In *biol.*, organic coloring matter; any organized substance whose presence in the tissues of animals and plants colors them. *Pigment* is the generic or indifferent term, most kinds of pigment having specific names. Coloring matter of one kind or another is almost universal in animals and plants, comparatively few of which are colorless. Pigments are very generally distributed in the integument and its appendages, as the skin, and especially the fur, feathers, scales, etc., of animals, and the leaves and other soft parts of plants. The dark color of the negro's skin is due to the abundance of pigment in the epidermis. The black appearance of the pupil of the eye is due to the heavy pigmentation of the choroid, and various colors of the iris depend upon specific pigments. Such coloring matters are often collected in special sacs which open and shut, producing the "shot" or play of color of the chameleon, dolphin, cuttlefish, and other animals. In many low animals and plants the color of the pigment is characteristic of genera, families, or even higher groups, as among infusorians, algals, etc. See cut under *cell*.

3†. Highly spiced wine sweetened with honey; piment.

It may be made with puttyng to *pigment*,
Or piper, or sum other condyment.
Palladius, Husbondrie (E. E. T. S.), p. 155.

Pigment color, in *dyeing*, a color prepared in the form of powder, and insoluble in the vehicle by which it is applied to the fabric. *O'Neill*, Dyeing and Calico Printing, p. 375.

pigmental (pig'men-tal), *a.* [< *pigment* + *-al*.] Of or pertaining to pigment; especially, secreting or containing pigment, as a cell or a tissue.

pigmentary (pig'men-tā-ri), *a.* [= F. *pigmentaire*; < *pigment* + *-ary*.] Same as *pigmental*.—**Pigmentary degeneration.** See *degeneration*.—**Pigmentary layer of the iris**, the innermost layer of the iris.—**Pigmentary layer of the retina**, the ectoretina; the outermost layer of the retina, composed of thick hexagonal pigment-cells united by a colorless cement.

pigmentation (pig-men-tā'shon), *n.* [= F. *pigmentation*; as *pigment* + *-ation*.] Discoloration by the deposition of a pigment in the tissues.

pigment-cell (pig'ment-sel), *n.* 1. A cell which secretes or contains pigment. See cut under *cell*.—2. A case or receptacle containing a special pigment; a chromatophore.

pigmented (pig'men-ted), *a.* [< *pigment* + *-ed*[2].] Charged with pigment; colored.

pigment-granule (pig'ment-gran"ūl), *n.* A grain or particle of pigment; one of the minute structureless masses of which pigment usually consists.

pigmentless (pig'ment-les), *a.* [< *pigment* + *-less.*] Free from pigment; destitute of coloring matter.

pigment-molecule (pig'ment-mol"e-kūl), *n.* Same as *pigment-granule.*

pigmentosa (pig-men-tō'sạ̈), *n.* [NL., fem. of **pigmentosus*: see *pigmentose.*] Same as *tapetum.*

pigmentose (pig'men-tōs), *a.* [< NL. **pigmentosus*, < L. *pigmentum*, pigment: see *pigment.*] Full of pigment.

pigmentous (pig'men-tus), *a.* [< *pigment* + *-ous.*] Same as *pigmentose.*

pigment-printing (pig'ment-prin"ting), *n.* A style of calico-printing in which ordinary pigments are mechanically fixed on the fabric by means of albuminous cement. *E. H. Knight.*

pigment-spot (pig'ment-spot), *n.* 1. A definite pigmented spot, or circumscribed pigmentary area; specifically, the so-called eye-spot of certain animalcules, as infusorians and rotifers.—2. In *bot.*, a reddish or brownish spot present in certain spores.

pig-metal (pig'met"al), *n.* Metal in pigs, as it is produced from the ore in the first operation of smelting.—**Pig-metal scales**, a pair of scales arranged for weighing pig-metal. An iron truck of proper dimensions to receive a furnace-charge traverses on rails upon the platform of the scales.

pigmey†, *n.* An obsolete form of *pygmy.*

pigmy, *n.* See *pygmy.*

pignerate, *v. t.* See *pignorate.*

pignon (pin'yon), *n.* [< F. *pignon*, the kernel of a pine-cone, also a gable, gable-end, = Sp. *piñon* = Pg. *pinhão*, the kernel of a pine-cone, < L. *pinea*, a pine-nut, pine-cone, pine: see *pineal.*] 1. An edible seed of the cones of certain pines, as *Pinus Pinea*, the nut- or stone-pine of southern Europe.—2. In *arch.*, a gable: the usual French architectural term, sometimes used in English.

pignorate, pignerate (pig'nō-, -ne-rāt), *v. t.*; pret. and pp. *pignorated, pignerated*, ppr. *pignorating, pignerating.* [< L. *pigneratus* (ML. also *pignoratus*), pp. of *pignerare* (ML. also *pignorare*), pledge, *pignerari*, take as a pledge (> It. *pignorare* = Pg. *penhorar* = OF. *pignorer*, pledge), < *pignus* (*pigner-*, *pignor-*), a pledge: see *pignus.*] 1. To pledge; pawn; mortgage.—2. To take in pawn, as a pawnbroker. *Blount.*

pignorate (pig'nō-rāt), *a.* [< ML. *pignoratus*, pp.: see the verb.] Pignorative.

Pignorate and hypothecary rights were unknown as rights protected by action at the time now being dealt with. *Encyc. Brit.*, XX. 690.

pignoration (pig-nō-rā'shon), *n.* [= OF. *pignoration*, < ML. *pignoratio(n-)*, LL. *pigneratio(n-)*, a pledging, pawning, < L. *pignerare*, pp. *pigneratus*, pledge: see *pignorate.*] 1. The act of pledging or pawning.—2. In *civil law*, the holding of cattle that have done damage as security till satisfaction is made. See *pignus.*

pignorative (pig'nō-rạ̈-tiv), *a.* [= F. *pignoratif* = Sp. *pignorativo* = Pg. *penhorativo* = It. *pignorativo*, < ML. **pignorativus*, < *pignorare*, pp. *pignoratus*, pawn, pledge: see *pignorate.*] Pledging; pawning. *Bouvier.* [Rare.]

pignus (pig'nus), *n.* [< L. *pignus* (*pigner-*, *pignor-*), a pledge, < √ *pac*, in *pangere*, fix, fasten, *pacisci*, agree, contract.] A pledge; the deposit of a thing, or the transfer of possession of it or dominion over it, as security for the performance of an obligation. The essential idea in the Roman and civil law is the putting of property, whether of a chattel, or land, or territorial jurisdiction (or servants or children, when they are regarded as property), under the hand of the creditor or pledgee as security, so that, although the right of the owner was not extinguished, the creditor or pledgee could enforce his claim without legal proceedings or any effort to gain possession; and this is also the essential idea in *pawn* and also in the strict use of *pledge*; while *hypothec* and *mortgage* imply that the owner retains possession, and that the creditor has only a right of action, or a right to demand possession in the contingencies agreed on.

pignut (pig'nut), *n.* 1. Same as *hawknut.*

I with my long nails will dig thee *pig-nuts.*
Shak., Tempest, ii. 2. 172.

First Sold. Fight like hogs for acorns!
Sec. Sold. Venture our lives for *pig-nuts!*
Fletcher, Bonduca, i. 2.

2. The fruit of a North American tree, the brown hickory, *Hicoria glabra* (*Carya porcina*); also, the tree itself. The nut is thin-shelled, oily, at first sweet, then bitterish: it is eaten by swine. The wood is very tough and is used like that of the shellbark, though the tree is not so large.

There are also several sorts of hickories, called *pig nuts*, some of which have as thin a shell as the best French walnuts, and yield their meat very easily; they are all of the walnut kind. *Beverley*, Virginia, ii. ¶ 14.

3. The fruit of *Omphalea triandra* and *O. diandra*, of the West Indies and South America. The kernel with the embryo removed is edible, and yields (one species at least) a fine limpid oil. In Guiana a species of *Omphalea* affords an oil said to be admirably adapted for lubricating, there called *ouabe-oil.* Also called *cobnut* and *breadnut.*

pig-pen (pig'pen), *n.* A pen for pigs; a pigsty.

pig-rat (pig'rat), *n.* The large bandicoot-rat of India, *Nesokia bandicota.* See cut at *Nesokia.*

pigroot (pig'röt), *n.* Any plant of the genus *Sisyrinchium.*

pigsconce (pig'skons), *n.* A pig-headed fellow; a blockhead.

Ding. He is
No *pig-sconce*, mistress.
Secret. He has an excellent headpiece.
Massinger, City Madam, iii. 1.

These representatives of the *pig-sconces* of the population judged by circumstances; airy shows and seems had no effect on them. *G. Meredith*, The Egoist, xxxvii.

pig's-face (pigz'fās), *n.* A plant. See *Mesembryanthemum.*

pigskin (pig'skin), *n.* 1. The skin of a pig, especially when prepared for saddlery, binding, or other purposes.—2. A saddle. [Colloq.]

He was my governor, and no better master ever sat in *pig-skin.* *Dickens.*

pigsney†, **pigsny**† (pigz'ni), *n.* [Also *pigsnye*, *pigsnie*; < ME. *piggesnye*, *piggesneyghe*, lit. 'pig's-eye'; *pigges*, gen. of *pigge*, pig; *neyghe*, a variant, with attracted *n* of indef. art., of *eyghe*, etc., eye: see *eye*[1].] 1. A pig's eye: used, like *eye* and *apple of the eye*, to denote something especially cherished; hence, as a term of endearment used of or to a woman, a darling.

She was a primerole, a *piggesnye.*
Chaucer, Miller's Tale, l. 82.

Miso, mine own *pigsnie*, thou shalt hear news of Dametas. *Sir P. Sidney*, Arcadia, iii.

Thou art,
As I believe, the *pigsney* of his heart.
Massinger, Picture, ii. 1.

2. An eye: applied to a woman's eye. [Humorous.]

Shine upon me but benignly,
With that one, and that other *pigsney.*
S. Butler, Hudibras, II. i. 560.

3. The carnation pink.

pigsticker (pig'stik"ėr), *n.* 1. A pork-butcher; a pig-killer.—2. A boar-hunter. [Anglo-Indian.]

Owing to the courage, horsemanship, and skill with his spear required in the *pigsticker*, . . . it [chasing the wild boar] must be regarded as an admirable training for cavalry officers. *Athenæum*, No. 3226, p. 255.

3. A long-bladed pocket-knife. [Slang.]

pigsty (pig'stī), *n.*; pl. *pigsties* (-stīz). A sty or pen for pigs; a pig-pen.

To go and live in a *pigsty* on purpose to spite Wakem.
George Eliot, Mill on the Floss, ii. 8.

pig's-wash (pigz'wosh), *n.* Swill.

Moral evil is unattainability of *Pig's-wash.*
Carlyle, Latter-Day Pamphlets, Jesuitism.

pig's-wrack (pigz'rak), *n.* The Irish moss, *Chondrus crispus*: so called in England because boiled with meal and potatoes and used as food for pigs.

pigtail (pig'tāl), *n.* 1. The tail of a pig.—2. A cue formed of the hair of the head, as distinguished from that of the periwig. This was retained by certain classes, as the sailors of the British navy, after it had gone out of use in polite society. In this way it survived as late as 1825. See *cue*[1], 1. [Colloq.]

Should we be so apt as we are now to compassionate the misfortunes, and to forgive the insincerity of Charles I., if his pictures had portrayed him in a bob-wig and a *pig-tail!*
Bulwer, Pelham, xliv.

Yonder still more ancient gentleman in powdered hair and *pigtail* . . . walks slowly along.
W. Besant, Fifty Years Ago, p. 40.

3. A person who wears a pigtail or cue. [Colloq.]—4. Tobacco twisted into a rope or cord.

I bequeath to Mr. John Grattan . . . my silver box in which the freedom of the city of Corke was presented to me; in which I desire the said John to keep the tobacco he usually cheweth, called *pigtail.* *Swift*, Will.

pigtailed (pig'tāld), *a.* [< *pigtail* + *-ed*[2].] 1. Having a tail like a pig's.

The additions to the Zoological Society's Gardens during the past week include a *Pigtailed* Monkey.
Nature, XL. 628.

2. Wearing a pigtail or cue; having the hair done up into a cue.

Dapur, i. e. the fortress of Tabor, of the Amorites, defended by *pigtailed* Hittites against Rameses II.
Jour. Anthrop. Inst., XVIII. 229.

Pigtailed baboon, the chacma.—**Pigtailed macaque** or **monkey**, *Macacus nemestrinus* of Java, Sumatra, Borneo, and the Malay peninsula, having a short tail.

pigweed (pig'wēd), *n.* 1. A plant, one of the goosefoots, *Chenopodium album*, also called *lamb's-quarters* and *baconweed.* It is sometimes used as a pot-herb. The name extends more or less to other species of the genus.—2. The green amaranth, *Amarantus retroflexus*, a common weed around sties and barn-yards.—**Winged pigweed**, a coarse branching herb, *Cycloloma platyphyllum*, found from the upper Mississippi westward, resembling goosefoot, but marked by a horizontal wing encircling the calyx in fruit.

pigwiggin†, **pigwidgin**†, *n.* [Also *pigwiggen*, *pigwidgeon*; appar. a fanciful name, prob. based on *Puck* or *pixy.*] A fairy; a dwarf; hence, anything very small: also used adjectively.

Pigwiggen was this fairy knight,
One wond'rous gracious in the sight
Of fair queen Mab. *Drayton*, Nymphidia, st. 12.

By Scotch invasion to be made a prey
To such *pigwidgin* myrmidons as they.
Cleaveland *Revived* (1660). (*Nares.*)

pik (pik), *n.* A Turkish unit of length, a cubit. There are three chief piks—the Stambouli or khalebi, the endazeh, and the beladi or masri. The longest is the Stambouli, which is 26.89 English inches in Constantinople (26.85 in Wallachia, 26.43 in Moldavia, and 26.65 in Egypt). The pik endazeh varies from 25.06 inches in Egypt to 25.70 in Constantinople. The pik beladi is 22.21 inches in Egypt. Formerly the law of Wallachia prescribed that the pik khalebi should be 2 feet 2 inches and 10 lines and the pik endazeh 2 feet 1 inch and 5 lines English measure.

pika (pī'kạ̈), *n.* A small rodent quadruped of the genus *Lagomys*, family *Lagomyidæ*, belonging to the duplicidentate or lagomorphic series of the *Rodentia*, inhabiting alpine regions of the northern hemisphere. It is of about the size of a rat, with soft fur, large rounded ears, and very short tail. There are several species. Also called *calling-hare*, *little chief hare*, *rat-hare*, and *cony.* See cut under *Lagomys.*

pika-squirrel (pī'kạ̈-skwur"el), *n.* A chinchilla; any species of the genus *Chinchilla.*

If the foregoing [species of *Lagidium*] be called rabbit-squirrels, the Chinchilla itself (C. lanigera) may be termed a *pika-squirrel.* *Stand. Nat. Hist.*, V. 80.

pike[1] (pīk), *n.* [Early mod. E. also *pyke*; < ME. *pike*, *pyke*, *pyk*, a sharp point, an iron point or tip of a staff or spear, a piked staff or spear, < AS. *pic*, in earliest form *pilc*, a pike (glossing ML. *acisculum* for **aciculum*, a needle or pin), also in comp. *horn-pic*, a peak, pinnacle (rare in all uses), = MD. *pijcke*, a pike, spear, later *pieke*, D. *piek*, a pike, spear, flourish with the pen, dash, = MLG. *pēk*, LG. *pek*, *pick*, a pike, spear, = G. *pike*, *picke*, a pike, spear, spade at cards, *pick*, a spade at cards, = Sw. *pik*, a pike, spear, = Dan. *pike*, a pike, spear, *pik*, a pike, peak (naut.), = OF. *pique*, *picque*, a pike, spear, pikeman, spade at cards, F. *pique*, pike, spear, spade at cards, = Sp. Pg. *pica*, f., a pike, spear, pikeman, = OIt. *pica*, It. *picca*, a pike, spear, peak (ML. *pica*, a pike, spear, pickax); also Sp. *pico*, m., sharp point, peak, top, point of land, pickax, spout, beak, bill, = Pg. *pico*, m., peak, top, summit, = OIt. *pico*, m., dim. *picchio*, an iron hammer, beetle, pickax, etc. (ML. *picus*, a hook) (the Teut. and Rom. forms and senses show more or less reaction); also in Celtic: Ir. *pice*, a pike, fork, = Gael. *pic*, a pike, spear, pickax, = W. *pig*, a point, pike, bill, beak, = Bret. *pik*, a pike, point, pickax; cf. Ir. *picidh*, a pike, spear, pitchfork; *peac*, a sharp-pointed thing, etc., whence ult. E. *peak* (see *peak*[1]); prob. orig. with initial *s*, < L. *spica*, f., *spicum*, neut., a point, ear of grain, top or tuft of a plant, LL. also a pin, whence ult. E. *spike*: see *spike.* Cf. *pick*[1], the forms *pick*[1] and *pike*[1] in noun and verb uses being more or less confused. Hence *pike*[1], *v.*, *pike*[2], *pike*[3], and, through OF. and F., *pike*[6] and *pique*, as well as *picket*[1], *piquet*, etc.] 1. A sharp point; a spike. Specifically—(*a*) A point of iron or other metal forming the head or tip of a staff or spear. (*b*) A central spike sometimes used in targets and bucklers, to which it was affixed by means of a screw. (*c*) In *turning*, a point or center on which to fasten anything to be turned.

Hard wood, prepared for the lathe with rasping, they pitch between the *pikes.* *J. Moxon.*

(*d*) A thorn; a prickle. (*e*†) The pointed end of a shoe, such as were formerly in fashion, called *piked shoon*, *cracows*, etc. See cut under *cracow.*

It was ordained in the Parliament of Westminster, anno 1463, . . . "that no man weare shoes or boots having *pikes* passing two inches in length."
J. Bryant, On Rowley's Poems. (*Latham.*)

2. A staff or shaft having at the end a sharp point or tip, usually of iron or steel. Specifically—(*a*†) Such a staff used in walking; a pilgrim's staff; a pike-staff.

They were redy for to wende
With *pyke* and with sclavyn
As palmers were in Paynym.
Richard Coer de Lion, l. 611.

That Penitencia his *pyke* he schulde polsche newe.
Piers Plowman (B), v. 482.

(*b*) (1) A sharp-pointed weapon consisting of a long shaft or handle with an iron head. It has been in use from ancient times, but the word dates apparently from the fifteenth century. About that period, and for some time later, it was the arm of a large part of the infantry, and was from 15 to 20 feet long. It continued in use, although reduced in length, throughout the seventeenth century, and was replaced by the bayonet as the latter was improved. It was retained in the British army until a very late date as a mere ensign of rank. (See *half-pike* and *spontoon*.) The pike has always been the arm of hastily levied and unequipped soldiers; thousands were used in the French revolution. Such pikes have usually a round conical head, a mere ferrule of thin iron bent into that form, but long, sharp-pointed, and formidable. The pike of regular warfare had sometimes a round, sometimes a flat or spear-like head.

Pikes. *a*, pike, 2 (*b*) (2); *b*, ordinary infantry pike, 17th century.

In the Court there was a Soldier pourtrayed at length with a blacke *pike* in his hand. Coryat, Crudities, I. 223.

(2) A weapon which replaced for a short time the simple pointed pike: it had an ax-blade on one side and a pointed beak or hook on the other. In this form it was retained in the French army as a badge of rank as late as the first empire. (*c*†) A pitchfork used by farmers.

A rake for to hale up the fitches that lie,
A *pike* for to pike them up, handsome to dry.
Tusser, September's Husbandry.

3. A sharp-pointed hill or mountain summit; a peak. [North. Eng.]

A gathering weight of shadows brown
Falls on the valleys as the sun goes down;
And *Pikes*, of darkness named and fear and storms,
Uplift in quiet their illumined forms.
Wordsworth, Descriptive Sketches.

Masses of broken crag rising at the very head of the valley into a fine *pike*, along whose jagged edges the rain-clouds were trailing.
Mrs. Humphry Ward, Robert Elsmere, I. vii.

4. A point of land; a gore. See *gore*[2], *n.*, 2. [Prov. Eng.]—5. A large cock of hay. [Prov. Eng.]—6†. Same as *pikeman*[1], 1.

Your halbardier should be armed in all points like your *pike*. *Markham*, Soldiers Accidence, p. 4.

7†. A measure of length, originally based on the length of the weapon so called.

He had nineteene and a halfe *pikes* of cloth, which cost in Loudon twenty shillings the *pike*.
Hakluyt's Voyages, II. 249.

pike[1]† (pīk), *v.*; pret. and pp. *piked*, ppr. *piking*. [< ME. *piken*, *pyken*, prob. only or chiefly with a short vowel, *piken*, a var. of *picken*, *pikken*, mod. *pick*[1]: the ref. to *pike*[1], *n.*, being only secondary: see *pike*[1], *pick*[1], *pitch*[1].] I. *trans.* 1. To pick or pluck.—2. To pick or choose; select; cull.

Diligently clodde it, *pyke* oute stones.
Palladius, Husbondrie (E. E. T. S.), p. 62.

Were it soe that the juryes could be *piked* out of such choyse men as you desire, there would nevertheless be as badd corruption in the tryall. *Spenser*, State of Ireland.

3. To bring to a point; taper.

And for this purpose must your bow be well trimmed and *piked* of a cunning man, that it may come round in true compass every where.
Ascham, Toxophilus (ed. 1864), p. 114.

II. *intrans.* To pick or peck, as a hawk smoothing its feathers.

pike[2] (pīk), *n.* [< ME. *pike*, *pyke*, a fish so called from its long slender shape and pointed snout; < *pike*, a sharp point: see *pike*[1]. Cf. the equiv. names, E. *hake*[2], *haked*, etc.; F. *brochet*, a pike, < *broche*, a spit; Bret. *beked*, a pike, < *bek*, beak; D. *snoek*, a pike, < *snoeijen*, cut.] 1. A fish of the genus *Esox*, or of the family *Esocidæ*. The common pike of Europe, Siberia, and northern North America is *E. lucius*. Its cheeks are scaly, the opercles

Pike (*Esox lucius*).

are naked below, the color is grayish with many round whitish spots or pale bars, and the dorsal, anal, and caudal fins are spotted with black. The other pikes of the United States, except the maskalonge, are commonly called *pickerel*. See also cuts under *paraspheno id*, *palatoquadrate*, *Esox*, *optic*, and *teleost*.

2. Some other slender fish with a long snout, or otherwise resembling the pike proper (def. 1). Specifically—(*a*) A cyprinoid fish, *Ptychocheilus lucius*, of slender form with a long snout, inhabiting the Sacramento river and other streams of the Pacific coast. [California.] (*b*) Another cyprinoid fish, *Gila grandis*: a misnomer in the San Francisco market. Also absurdly called *salmon-trout*. (*c*) In Australia, the *Sphyræna novæ-hollandiæ* and S. *obtusata*. (*d*) The sea-pike (a belonid). See also phrases below.—**Bald pike**, a ganoid fish, *Amia calva*. [U. S.]—**Bony pike.** Same as *garpike*, 2.—**Brazilian pike**, a scomberesocid fish, of the genus *Hemirhamphus*. *Pennant*.—**Federation pike**, a pickerel, *Esox americanus*: so called in allusion to the bands with which its body is crossed and rays being often thirteen in number.—**Glass-eyed pike**, the pike-perch, *Stizostedion americanum*, or *S. vitreum*. Also called *goggle-eyed* and *wall-eyed pike*.—**Gray pike.** Same as *blue-pike*.—**Great pike**, the maskalonge, *Esox nobilior*.—**Green pike.** (*a*) The pike-perch, *Stizostedion vitreum*. (*b*) The common pickerel, *Esox reticulatus*.—**Ground-pike**, the sauger, *Stizostedion canadense*.—**Humpbacked pike**, *Esox cypho*. *E. D. Cope*.—**Mud-pike**, the sauger. [Lake Ontario.]—**Sand-pike.** (*a*) The sauger. (*b*) The lizard-fish, *Synodus fœtens*.—**Wall-eyed pike.** Same as *glass-eyed pike*.—**Yellow pike**, the pike-perch, *Stizostedion vitreum*.

pike[3] (pīk), *n.* [Abbr. of *turnpike*, *turnpike road*.] A turnpike; a turnpike road.

pike[3] (pīk), *v. i.* [Appar. < *pike*[3], *n.*] To go rapidly. [Slang.]

pike[4]†, *v. t.* An obsolete form of *pick*[2], *pitch*[1].

pike[5]†, *v. i.* [ME. *piken*: see *peek*[2].] To peep; peek.

Pandarus, that ledde hire by the lappe,
Com ner, and gan in at the curtyn *pike*.
Chaucer, Troilus, iii. 60.

pike[6]†, *n.* An obsolete form of *pique*.

piked† (pī'ked or pīkt), *a.* [< ME. *piked*, *pyked*; < *pike*[1] + *-ed*[2].] Same as *picked*[1].

With scrip and *pyked* staf, y-touked hye.
In every hous he gan to pore and prye
And begged mele or chesse or ellis corn.
Chaucer, Summoner's Tale, l. 29.

His teeth white and even; his hair yellow and not too *piked*. *Sir T. More*, Life of Picus, Int. to Utopia, p. lxxviii.

Their shoes and pattens are snouted and *piked* more than a finger long. *Camden*, Remains.

Pangeas rich in silver, and Massapus for his high steep *piked* rocks to be wondred at. *Sandys*, Travailes, p. 33.

Anne of Bohemia, to whom she had been Maid of Honour, introduced the fashion of *piked* horns, or high heads.
Walpole, Letters, II. 121.

Piked shoon. See *pike*[1], *n.*, 1 (*e*).—**Piked staff.** Same as *pikestaff*.

pike-devant†, *n.* [Also *pickedevant*, *pickadevant*, *pickadevaunt*, *peake-devant*, *pickatevant*, *pickitivant*; < OF. **pique devant* (?), < *pique*, a sharp point, a pike (see *pike*[1]), + *devant*, before (< *de*, from, + *avant*, before: see *avant-*).] A beard cut to a sharp point in the middle, so as to form a peak or pike below the chin. This fashion is illustrated in most of the portraits of the time of Charles I.

And here I vow by my concealed beard, if ever it chance to be discovered to the world, that it may make a *pike-devant*, I will have it so sharp pointed that it shall stab Motto like a poynado. *Lyly*, Midas, v. 2. (*Nares.*)

He must . . . mark . . . how to cut his beard, and wear his lock, to turn up his mushatos, and curl his head, prune his *pickitivant*, or if he wear it abroad, that the east side be correspondent to the west. *Burton*, Anat. of Mel., iii. 2.

pikedevanted†, *a.* [Found as *pittivanted*; < *pike-devant* + *-ed*[2].] Having a pike-devant. [Rare.]

A young, *pittivanted*, trim-bearded fellow.
Burton, Anat. of Mel., p. 480.

pike-fork (pīk'fôrk), *n.* Same as *fork*, 2 (c) (1).

Some made long pikes and lances light,
Some *pike-forks* for to join and thrust.
Old poem on Battle of Flodden.

pike-hammer† (pīk'ham″ėr), *n.* 1. A form of war-hammer with a long and formidable point, like the prolonged blade of a lance, set in the direction of the shaft. One of these weapons now in the museum of artillery at Paris has a pointed blade over 3 feet in length, with a shaft about 6 feet long.
2. The head of the staff of certain military flags, specifically of those carried by the regiments of the first French empire.

pikehead (pīk'hed), *n.* 1. The head of a pike or spear.

His speare . . .
Had riven many a brest with *pikehead* square.
Spenser, F. Q., I. vii. 37.

2. In *ichth.*, a fish of the family *Luciocephalidæ*.

pike-headed (pīk'hed″ed), *a.* 1. Having a sharp-pointed head.—2. Having a head like a pike's, with long snout and jaws.—**Pike-headed alligator**, the common Mississippi alligator: so called as a translation of its specific name, *Alligator lucius*.—**Pike-headed anolis**, *Anolis lucius*.

pike-keeper (pīk'kē″pėr), *n.* The keeper of a turnpike; a tollman.

"What do you mean by a *pike-keeper*?" inquired Mr. Peter Magnus. "The old 'un means a turnpike-keeper, gen'l'm'n," observed Mr. Weller, in explanation.
Dickens, Pickwick, xxii.

pikelet (pīk'let), *n.* [< *pike*[1] (?) + *-let*.] A light cake or muffin; a thin circular tea-cake. *Halliwell*. [Prov. Eng.]

He crumpled up his broad face like a half-toasted *pikelet*. *Anna Seward*, Letters. (*Latham.*)

pikelin (pīk'lin), *n.* [< *pike*[1] (?) + *-lin* for *-ling*[1].] Same as *pikelet*.

pikeman[1] (pīk'man), *n.*; pl. *pikemen* (-men). [< *pike*[1] + *man*.] 1. A soldier armed with a pike; especially, about the sixteenth and seventeenth centuries, a member of a regularly organized body of such soldiers.

The Swiss battalion consisted of *pikemen*, and bore a close resemblance to the Greek phalanx.
Macaulay, Machiavelli.

Pikeman of early 17th century, from print of the time.

2. A miner who works with a pike or crowbar. *Disraeli*, Sybil, ii. 6.

pikeman[2] (pīk'man), *n.* [< *pike*[3] + *man*.] A turnpikeman.

The turnpike has gone, and the *pikeman* with his apron has gone—nearly everybody's apron has gone too—and the gates have been removed.
W. Besant, Fifty Years Ago, p. 42.

pike-perch (pīk'pėrch), *n.* A percoid fish of the genus *Stizostedion* (or *Lucioperca*), of elongate form, with a subconical head, and sharp canines mixed with the villiform teeth of the jaws and palate. The most common pike-perch in Europe is *S. lucioperca*. In the United States two species are common, in the upper Mississippi and Great Lake

Pike-perch (*Stizostedion vitreum*).

regions: *S. vitreum*, attaining a length of 3 feet, and a weight of from 10 to 20 pounds, and *S. canadense*, which is rarely over 15 inches long. (See Lucioperca.) The former is known as *walleye*, *glasseye*, *wall-eyed* or *glass-eyed pike*, *gray pike*, and *jack-salmon*. The other is called *hornfish*, *sauger*, and *sand-pike*.

pike-pole (pīk'pōl), *n.* A pole with a prong and hook at one end, used by lumbermen in driving logs on rivers.

piker (pī'kėr), *n.* [< *pike*[3] + *-er*[1].] A tramp; a vagrant. [Slang.]

The people called in Acts of Parliament sturdy beggars and vagrants, in the old cant language Abraham men, and in the modern *Pikers*.
Borrow, Wordbook of the English Gypsy Language.

pikerel†, *n.* A Middle English form of *pickerel*.

pikestaff (pīk'stâf), *n.*; pl. *pikestaves* (-stävz). [< ME. *pykstaf* (usually *piked staff*); < *pike*[1] + *staff*.] A staff with an iron head more or less pointed and capable of serving as a weapon, formerly used by travelers, pilgrims, and wandering beggars. Also *piked staff*.

He had a *pike-staff* in his hand
That was baith stark and strang.
Robin Hood and the Beggar (Child's Ballads, V. 188).

Plain as a pikestaff. See *plain*[1].

pike-sucker (pīk'suk″ėr), *n.* Any fish of the family *Gobiesocidæ*.

piketail (pīk'tāl), *n.* The pintail duck, *Dafila acuta*. Also *spiketail*. See *pintail*. [Illinois.]

pikeys†, *n.* A Middle English form of *pickax*.

piki, *n.* See *peekee*.

pikke†. A Middle English form of *pick*[1], *pitch*[2].

pila[1] (pī'lạ̈), *n.* [< L. *pila*, a mortar: see *pile*[1], *pile*[2].] In *archæol.* and *art*, a mortar, especially one notable archæologically on account of its antiquity or design. Specimens of ancient mortars have been found in Switzerland, hollowed out of the trunks of large trees and having pestles arranged to be wielded by two men. See *mortar*[1].

pila[2] (pē'lạ̈), *n.* [It.: see *pile*[2].] The holy-water font in an Italian church, usually a stone vase of considerable richness.

Pila[2].—Duomo of Pistoia, Italy.

pila[3], *n.* Plural of *pilum*.

pilage†, *n.* An obsolete form of *pelage*.

pilar (pī'lạ̈r), *a.* Pertaining to or covered

with hair.—**Pilar muscles**, the erector muscles of hairs; arrectores pilorum.

pilary (pil'ạ-ri), *a.* [< L. *pilus*, a hair (see *pile*⁴), + *-ary*.] Of or pertaining to hair or the hair.

> She had never suffered from any *pilary* loss, cutaneous affection, . . . or any other symptom of disorder.
> *Medical News*, LIII. 411.

pilaster (pi-las'tėr), *n.* [Formerly also *pillaster*; = Sp. Pg. *pilastra*, < F. *pilastre*, < It. *pilastro*, < ML. *pilastrum*, a small pillar, dim. of L. *pila*, a pillar: see *pile*² and *-aster*.] A square pillar, with its capital and base, projecting from a pier, or from a wall, to the extent of from one quarter to one third of its breadth; an engaged pillar. In Greek architecture pilasters were not made to correspond in form with the order of columns in connection with which they were used; but in the Roman and later styles they commonly follow closely the design of the accompanying columns. See *anta*¹.

Pilaster. Grand Trianon, Versailles, France (built by Louis XIV.).

pilastered (pi-las'tėrd), *a.* [< *pilaster* + *-ed*².] Furnished with pilasters.

> The polish'd walls of marble be
> *Pilaster'd* round with porphyry.
> *Cotton*, Entertainment to Phillis.

pilau (pi-lâ'), *n.* [Also *pilaw*, *pillau*, *pillaw*, *pilaff*, *pillaffe*; = F. *pilau* = It. *pilao* = G. *pilaw* = Russ. *pilavŭ* = NGr. πιλάφι, < Turk. *pilaw* = Hind. *pulāo*, *palāo*, < Pers. *pilāw*, *pilaw*, a dish of rice boiled with meat, spices, etc.] An Oriental dish consisting of rice boiled with mutton, kid, or fowl, and flavored with spices, raisins, butter, broth, etc. It is a favorite dish among Mohammedans everywhere, and its composition and preparation vary among the different tribes in Turkey, Arabia, Persia, Egypt, etc. It is eaten in Western countries with some Variations, such as the addition of savory herbs and vegetables, and sometimes of beef or pork.

> Their most ordinary food is *pillaw*—that is, Rice which hath been sod with the fat of Mutton.
> *Sandys*, Travailes, p. 51.

> The dinner concluded with a *pillaw* of boiled rice and butter; for the easier discussion of which we were provided with carved wooden spoons.
> *R. F. Burton*, El-Medinah, p. 477.

> Boiled mutton, cold chicken, *pilau* of rice with raisins.
> *G. Kennan*, The Century, XXXVI. 522.

pilch¹ (pilch), *n.* [< ME. *pilch*, *pylch*, *pilche*, *pylche*, *pyls*, < AS. *pylce*, *pylece* (= OF. *pelisse*, > E. *pelisse*), < ML. *pellicea*, erroneously *pelicium*, a furred garment, fem. of L. *pelliceus*, of fur or skin, < *pellis*, skin: see *pell*¹.] 1†. A coat or cloak of skins or fur; later, a buff or leather jerkin: applied also to a coarse garment of other material, worn for warmth.

> And thei clothen hem also with *Pylches*, and the Hyde with outen. *Mandeville*, Travels, p. 247.

> No man caste his *pilche* away. *Chaucer*, Proverbs, l. 4.

> He . . . was blakke and rough, for-rympled and longeberde, and bar-foote, and clothed in a rough *pilche*.
> *Merlin* (E. E. T. S.), iii. 424.

> Thy vesture that thou shalt use ben these, a warme *pylche* for wynter, and oo kirtel, and oo cote for somer.
> *MS. Bodl.* 423, f. 182. (*Halliwell.*)

> He beate fiue pounds out of his leather *pilch*.
> *Dekker*, Satiromastix.

2. A flannel cloth for an infant. *Halliwell.* [Prov. Eng.]

pilch²†, *v. i.* [Perhaps a var. of *pick*¹, accom. to *pilfer* or *filch*.] To pilfer. *Davies.* [Rare.]

> Some steal, some *pilch*,
> Some all away filch.
> *Tusser*, Husbandry, September's Abstract.

pilchard (pil'chạrd), *n.* [With accom. suffix *-ard* for *-er*; earlier *pilcher*, < Ir. *pilseir*, a pilchard; cf. W. *pilcod*, pl., minnows. The F. *pilchard* is from E.] 1. A fish of the family *Clupeidæ*, *Clupea pilchardus*, resembling the herring, but thicker and rounder, with the under

Pilchard (*Clupea pilchardus*).

jaw shorter, the back more elevated, the belly less sharp, and the mouth edentulous. These fishes appear on the Cornish coast in England about the middle of July in immense numbers, and furnish a considerable article of commerce. See *white-bait*.

> Fools are as like husbands as *pilchards* are to herrings.
> *Shak.*, T. N., iii. 1. 39.

2. A fish, *Clupea sagax*, closely related to the pilchard. [California.]—3. A third fish of the family *Clupeidæ*, *Harengula macrophthalma*. [Bermudas.]—4. The young menhaden. [Chesapeake Bay, U. S.]

pilcher¹† (pil'chėr), *n.* [< *pilch* + *-er* (used indefinitely).] 1. One who wears a pilch.

> You mungrels, you curs, you ban-dogs [the serjeants of the Counter]! we are Captain Tucca that talk to you, you inhuman *pilchers*. *B. Jonson*, Poetaster, iii. 1.

2. A pilch.—3. A scabbard. [Cant.]

> Will you pluck your sword out of his *pilcher* by the ears?
> *Shak.*, R. and J., iii. 1. 84.

pilcher²†, *n.* Same as *pilchard*.

> *Doyt.* What meat eats the Spaniard?
> *Pilch.* Dried *pilchers* and poor-john.
> *Middleton*, Blurt, Master-Constable, i. 2.

pilcorn†, *n.* See *pillcorn*.

pilcrow† (pil'krō), *n.* [Formerly also *pillcrow*, *pilkrow*, *pylcrow*, *peelcrow*, corrupted forms, simulating *crow*² (the character ¶, in older form ¶, with its black body, and with its stem variously curled or flourished, suggesting that sable bird), of *pylcrafte*, *parcrafte*, *pargrafte*, corrupted forms of *paragraph*: see *paragraph*.] The character ¶, used to mark the beginning of a new paragraph: same as *paragraph*, 4.

> A lesson how to confer every abstract with his moneth, and how to find out huswifery verses by the *pilcrow*.
> *Tusser*, i.

> *Lapet.* But why a *peel-crow* here?
> *Gal.* I told him so, sir:
> A scare-crow had been better.
> *Fletcher* (*and another?*), Nice Valour, iv. 1.

pile¹ (pīl), *n.* [< ME. *pile*, *pil*, < AS. *pīl*, a sharp stake or stick, as the gnomon of a dial, a stake or pile driven in the bed of a river, a prickle of the holly, a nail, also in comp. an arrow or dart (*hilde-pīl*, 'war-dart,' *orthanc-pīl*, 'subtle dart,' *searo-pīl*, 'subtle dart,' *wælpīl*, 'slaughter-dart'); also *pīle*, a stake, in comp. *tcmes-pīle*; = D. *pijl* = MLG. *pīl* = OHG. *phīl*, *fīl*, MHG. *phīl*, *pfīl*, G. *pfeil*, an arrow, dart, bolt, shaft, = Icel. *pīla* = Sw. Dan. *pil*, an arrow, = OF. *pile*, m., a javelin, = Sp. Pg. *pilo*, a javelin, = It. *pilo*, a javelin, dart, pestle, < L. *pīlum*, a javelin, a heavy javelin used by infantry, lit. a pounder, pestle, contr. of **pislum*, **pisulum* (cf. *pistillum*, a pestle, > E. *pestle* and *pistil*); cf. *pīla*, a mortar (> AS. *pīle*, a mortar, also in comp. *pīl-stæf*, a pestle, *pīlstampe*, a pestle, *pīlstocc*, a pestle, deriv. *pīlstre*, a pestle), contr. of **pisla*, **pisula*; < *pisere*, *pinsere*, pound, beat, bray, crush.] 1. The pointed head of a staff, pike, arrow, or the like, when not barbed, generally of a rounded form and serving as a ferrule; also, an arrow.

Pile of an arrow, 13th or 14th century.

> Cut off the timber of this cursed shaft,
> And let the fork'd *pile* canker to my heart.
> *Chapman*, Gentleman Usher, iv. 1.

> The artist has carefully distinguished the barbed head of the arrow and the *pile* of the crossbow bolt.
> *Hewitt*, Anc. Armour, I., p. xiii.

> With the right hand draw the arrow from the quiver, pass it across the bow until the steel *pile* projects ten inches beyond the handle. *M. and W. Thompson*, Archery, p. 16.

2†. A javelin. [Rare.]

> That was but civil war, an equal set,
> Where *piles* with *piles*, and eagles eagles met.
> *Dryden*, Hind and Panther, ii. 161.

[The above is an imitation of the following passage:

> "Infestisque obvia signis
> Signa, pares aquilas, et *pila* minantia *pilis*."
> *Lucan*, Pharsalia, iii. 7.]

3. A pointed stake; specifically, in *arch.* and *engin.*, a beam, heavy, generally of timber, often the roughly trimmed trunk of a tree, pointed or not at the end and driven into the soil for the support of some superstructure or to form part of a wall, as of a coffer-dam or quay. For permanent works piles are driven in loose or uncertain strata in rows, leaving a space a few feet in width between them, and upon the heads of the piles the foundations of the superstructure are erected. In temporary constructions they are driven close together in single or double rows, so as to inclose a space of water and form a coffer-dam, from which the water is subsequently pumped out, and thus a dry space is obtained for laying the foundation of piers, etc., in bridges and other similar works. Iron piles are used for wharf-walls and other purposes; they are hollow or tubular within, and are cast in various forms. See cuts under *lake-dwelling*, *pile-driver*, and *pilework*.

> They ramme in great *piles* of woodde, which they lay very deepe, upon the which they place their bricke.
> *Coryat*, Crudities, I. 206.

> What rotten *piles* uphold their mason-work.
> *Tennyson*, Sir John Oldcastle, Lord Cobham.

4†. A post such as that used in the exercise of the quintain.

> Of fight, the disciplyne and exercise
> Was this. To have a pale or *pile* upright
> Of mannys hight, thus writeth olde and wise;
> Therwith a bacheler, or a yong knyght,
> Shal first be taught to stonde and lerne to fight.
> And fanne of doubil wight, tak him his shelde
> Of doubil wight, a mace of tre to welde.
> This fanne and mace whiche either doubil wight
> Of shelde, and swayed in conflicte or bataile,
> Shal exercise as well swordmen as knyghtes.
> *MS. Cott. Titus*, A. xxiii. fol. 617.

> And noo man, as they sayn, is seyn prevalle,
> In field or in castell, thoughe he assayle,
> That with the *pile* nathe [*i. e.* ne hath, hath not] firste grete exercise;
> Thus writeth Werrouris olde and wyse.
> *Knyghthode and Batayle* (quoted in Strutt's Sports and Pastimes, p. 185).

False pile, an additional length given to a pile after driving. *E. H. Knight.*—**Gaged piles**, large piles placed at regular distances apart, with horizontal beams called *runners* fitted to each side of them by notching, and secured by bolts. They form a guide for the filling-piles, which are driven between the runners, filling up the spaces between them.—**Hollow pile**, a large wrought- or cast-iron cylinder sunk in sandy strata by digging away or forcing out the sand from the inside. Sections of cylinder are added above, as may be necessary, and secured by flanges and bolts.—**Hydraulic pile**, a pile sunk in sand by means of a water-jet. Two methods are followed. In one, a hollow iron pile is set upright in the sand in the position it is to occupy, while a powerful stream of water is forced into the pile and escapes through a hole at the point of the tube, forcing up the sand, so that the tube rapidly sinks. In the other method, solid wooden piles are sunk in the same manner, the jet being delivered at the foot of the pile by means of an iron pipe let down beside the pile and afterward withdrawn. On stopping the water-jet the sand quickly settles around the pile and holds it firmly in position.—**Pneumatic pile.** See *pneumatic*. (See also *screw-pile*, *sheet-pile*.)

pile¹ (pīl), *v. t.*; pret. and pp. *piled*, ppr. *piling*. [< *pile*¹, *n.*] 1. To furnish with a pile or head.

> At Delops Magus threw
> A speare well *pilde*, that strooke his caske full in the height;
> off flew
> His purple feather, newly made, and in the dust it fell.
> *Chapman*, Iliad, xv.

2. To furnish, strengthen, or support with piles; drive piles into.

pile² (pīl), *n.* [< ME. *pile*, *pyle*, a pile (tower or castle) (the alleged AS. **pīl*, a pillar, is not authorized), < OF. *pile*, f., a pier, mole, pyramid, etc., F. *pile*, a pier, mole, pile or reverse of a coin, = Sp. *pila*, a pillar, font, holy-water font, trough, = OIt. *pila*, a dam, bowl of a font, laver, cistern, It. *pila*, a flat pillar, trough, holy-water font, < L. *pīla*, a pillar, a pier or mole of stone. *Pile* in the senses given below is generally included with *pile*³, 'a heap,' etc.; but see *pile*³. *Pile*² is also more or less confused in various senses with the related *pile*¹. Cf. *peel*⁴.] 1†. A pillar; specifically, a small pillar of iron, engraved on the top with the image to be given to the under side of a coin stamped upon it; hence, the under side or reverse of the coin itself: opposed to the *cross*.—2†. A tower or castle: same as *peel*⁴.

> For to deluen a dyche depe a-boute Vnite,
> That holy-cherche stode in Vnite as it a *pyle* were.
> *Piers Plowman* (B), xix. 360.

> Alle men children in towne & *pile*
> To sleo them, that Ihesus myght with hem die.
> *Hymns to Virgin*, etc. (E. E. T. S.), p. 45.

> The inhabitants at this day call it Milnesse; and as small a village as it is, yet hath it a *pile*.
> *Holland*, tr. of Camden, p. 775. (*Davies.*)

3. A large building or mass of buildings of stone or brick; a massive edifice: as, a noble *pile*; a venerable *pile*.

> Went to see Clarendon House, now almost finish'd, a goodly *pile* to see to. *Evelyn*, Diary, Nov. 28, 1666.

> In the midst of the ruins, there stands up one *pile* higher than the rest, which is the East end of a great Church, probably of the Cathedral of Tyre.
> *Maundrell*, Aleppo to Jerusalem, p. 49.

> High Whitby's cloistered *pile*. *Scott*, Marmion, ii. 1.

4. A pyramid; a pyramidal figure; specifically, in *her.*, a bearing consisting of a pyramidal or wedge-shaped figure (generally assumed to represent an arrow-head), which, unless otherwise blazoned, seems to emerge from the top of the escutcheon with its point downward. It is usually considered one of the subordinaries, but by some authors as an ordinary. See *pile*¹, 1, and phrases below.—**Cross and pile.** See *cross*¹.—**Cross pile**, a pile in which boards, iron bars, or the like are placed in alternate layers at right angles to each other.—**Per pile**, in *her.*, divided by lines in the form of a pile—that is, forming a V-shaped figure in the field. If this V-shaped figure has not its point downward, the blazon must express it as *per pile transposed*, *per pile reversed*, *per pile traverse*, etc.—**Pile solid**, in *her.*, a pile represented as in relief, having three lines, which give it the appearance of a blunt pyramid, projecting upward from the field. One of the three triangles thus formed is of a different tincture from the others, to help the solid appearance.—**Triple pile, triple-pointed pile**, in *her.*, a pile

cut short at the pointed end, and having the end divided into three projecting points.

pile[3] (pil), *n.* [< ME. *pile*, a heap (the AS. **pīl*, a heap, is not authorized, being due to a misinterpretation), < OF. *pile*, f., a heap, pile, stack, F. *pile*, a heap, voltaic pile, etc.; appar. a particular use of *pile*, a pier of stone, etc. (whence any pile of stones or other things, etc.); but according to some < L. *pīla*, a ball (cf. *piles*). Cf. *pile*[2].] 1. A heap consisting of an indefinite number of separate objects, commonly of the same kind, arranged of purpose or by natural causes in a more or less regular (cubical, pyramidal, cylindrical, or conical) form; a large mass, or a large quantity: as, a *pile* of stones; a *pile* of wood; a *pile* of money or of grain.

What *piles* of wealth hath he accumulated
To his own portion! *Shak.*, Hen. VIII., iii. 2. 107.

Yon *pile* of mountains, shining like a white summer cloud in the blue sky. *Irving*, Alhambra, p. 121.

Specifically—2. A funeral pile; a pyre. See *funeral pile*, under *funeral*.

Woe to the bloody city! I will even make the *pile* for fire great. Ezek. xxiv. 9.

The father makes the *pile*: hereon he layes
His bond-led, blind-led Son.
Sylvester, Maiden's Blush (trans.).

3. An oblong rectangular mass of cut lengths of puddled bars of iron, laid together and ready for being rolled after being raised to a welding-temperature in a reheating-furnace. The size of a pile and the quality of the iron of which it is composed vary according to special requirements, the same pile sometimes containing widely different qualities of iron in its different parts.
4. In *elect.*, a series of plates of two dissimilar metals, such as copper and zinc, laid one above the other alternately, with cloth or paper placed between each pair, moistened with an acid solution, for producing a current of electricity. See *electricity*. The term is sometimes used as synonymous with *battery*, for any form of apparatus designed to produce a current of dynamic electricity. It is also applied to an apparatus for detecting slight changes of temperature. See *thermopile*.
5. A large amount of money; a fortune: as, he has made his *pile*. [Slang, U. S.]

Great fortunes grow with the growing prosperity of the country, and the opportunity it offers of amassing enormous *piles* by bold operations.
Bryce, Amer. Commonwealth, II. 704.

Dry pile, an electric pile or battery consisting of a series of disks, generally of paper or leather, coated on one side with silver or tin and on the other with finely powdered binoxid of manganese. These are arranged with the silver of each disk in contact with the manganese of the next, the whole forming a battery the action of which, due to the hygroscopic character of the paper disk, is remarkably permanent.—**Funeral pile.** See *funeral*.

They conveyed them unto the *funerall pile* on beeres.
Sandys, Travailes, p. 65.

Poles of a voltaic pile. See *pole*[2].—**Volta's pile.** See *battery*, 8.

pile[3] (pil), *v. t.*; pret. and pp. *piled*, ppr. *piling*. [< *pile*[3], *n.*] 1. To lay or throw into a heap; heap, or heap up; collect into a pile or mass: as, to *pile* wood or stones.

Or *pile* ten hills on the Tarpeian rock.
Shak., Cor., iii. 2. 3.

The sickening toil
Of *piling* straw on straw to reach the sky.
William Morris, Earthly Paradise, III. 211.

2. To bring into an aggregate; accumulate: as, to *pile* quotations or comments.

Life *piled* on life
Were all too little. *Tennyson*, Ulysses.

3. Same as *fagot*, 2.—**To pile arms**, in *milit. tactics*, to place three muskets or rifles with fixed bayonets in such a relative position that the butts shall remain firm upon the ground, and the muzzles be close together in an oblique direction. Called *to stack arms* in modern tactics.

pile[4] (pil), *n.* [= OF. *peil*, *poil*, F. *poil* = Pr. *pel*, *pelh*, *peil* = Sp. *pelo* = Pg. *pello* = It. *pelo*, < L. *pilus*, a hair, the hair. Hence ult. (from L. *pilus*) E. *depile*, *depilate*, *depilatory*, *pill*[2], *pelluce*, *plush*, *peruke* (with *periwig* and *wig*), and prob. also *pluck*[1].] 1. Hair.

The beard is represented by two tangled tufts upon the chin; where whiskers should be, the place is either bare or thinly covered with straggling *pile*.
R. F. Burton, El-Medinah, p. 320.

2. Specifically, in *hunting*, in the plural, the hair or fur of an animal, as the boar, wolf, fox, etc.; hence, hairs collectively; pelage.—3. The lay or set of the hair.—4. A fiber, as of wool or cotton.—5. In *entom.*, thinly set fine hairs which are ordinarily rather long.—6. Nap of a regular and closely set kind, consisting of threads standing close together and shaved off smooth, so as to form a uniform and even surface. The threads of pile always have a certain inclination in one direction as regards the stuff, and can be smoothed or depressed in that direction, while pressing them the other way roughens the surface. The longest pile of any textile fabric is perhaps that of certain Oriental carpets; this, when of fine goat's hair, has a beautiful gloss. The pile of velvet is sometimes of two different heights or lengths.

Velvet soft, or plush with shaggy *pile*.
Cowper, Task, i. 11.

Cut pile, in a fabric, a pile woven in loops which are afterward cut so as to give a smooth surface composed of the ends of the fibers, as in velvet, plush, etc.—**Double pile.** Same as *pile upon pile*: said of velvet.—**Pile carpet.** See *carpet*.—**Pile upon pile**, an arrangement in which a part of the pile is shorter than another part, as in velvet, in which a pattern is produced in this way, the pile of a flower or leaf being perhaps twice as high as that of the background.

pile[4] (pil), *v. t.*; pret. and pp. *piled*, ppr. *piling*. [< *pile*[4], *n.*] To furnish with pile; make shaggy.

Thou art good velvet; thou 'rt a three-*piled* piece, I warrant thee: I had as lief be a list of an English kersey as be *piled* as thou art *piled* for a French velvet.
Shak., M. for M., i. 2. 33.

His cloak of crimson velvet *piled*,
Trimmed with the fur of marten wild.
Scott, Marmion, v. 8.

pile[5] (pīl), *v. t.*; pret. and pp. *piled*, ppr. *piling*. [< ME. *pilen*, var. of *pillen*, ult. < L. *pīlare*, deprive of hair: see *pill*[2], of which *pile*[5] is thus ult. a variant. Cf. *peel*[1], with which *pile*[5] may have been confused.] To break off the awns of (threshed barley). [Prov. Eng.]

pile[6]†, *v.* A Middle English form of *pill*[1].

Pilea (pī'lẹ̄-ạ̈), *n.* [NL. (Lindley, 1821), so called with ref. to the original species, in which one of the three sepals is enlarged into a hood over the fruit; < L. *pileus*, a felt cap: see *pileus*.] 1. A genus of apetalous herbs of the order *Urticaceæ*, tribe *Urticeæ*, and subtribe *Procrideæ*, distinguished by the equilateral opposite leaves and loosely branched or somewhat condensed greenish cymes. There are about 175 species, for the most part small weedy plants, widely dispersed throughout the tropics except in Australia, with one, *P. pumila*, the clearweed or richweed, with translucent watery stem, common in rich woodlands of the United States. Many species have the peculiarity of developing one leaf of a pair very much larger than that opposite. See *artillery-plant*, *burning-bush*, 2 (*b*), *clearweed*, *coolweed*, and *dwarf elder* (under *elder*), the last peculiar in this genus (mainly of weeds) from having a woody stem.
2. [*l. c.*] Plural of *pileum*.

pileata (pil-ẹ̄-ā'tạ̈), *a.* [L., fem. of *pileatus*, capped: see *pileate*.] Capped—that is, covered or stopped: applied to organ-pipes.—**Pileata diapenta**, a stopped quint.—**Pileata major**, a stopped 16-foot pipe.—**Pileata minor**, a stopped 4-foot pipe.

pileate (pil'ẹ̄-āt), *a.* [< L. *pileatus*, *pilleatus*, capped, bonneted, < *pileus*, *pilleus*, a cap: see *pileus*.] 1. Capped; specifically, in *bot.*, having a pileus or cap, as certain fungi. See *Agaricus*.—2. Having the form of a cap or cover for the head. See cut under *Crypturus*.

A *pileated* echinus taken up with different shells of several kinds. *Woodward*.

pileated (pil'ẹ̄-ā-ted), *a.* [< *pileate* + *-ed*[2].] 1. Same as *pileate*.—2. In *ornith.*, crested; having the feathers of the pileum elongated and conspicuous: as, the *pileated* woodpecker.—**Pileated woodpecker**, *Hylotomus* (or *Ceophlœus*) *pileatus*, the largest woodpecker of North America excepting the ivorybill, locally known as *logcock* or *black logcock*. It is usually 16 to 18 inches long, and about 28 in extent of wings; the color is slaty-black, conspicuously striped with white or pale yellowish on the head and neck, this color also varying the hidden parts of the wings; the male has the whole pileum scarlet; in the female the crest is scarlet on the posterior half only. This fine bird inhabits all the heavily wooded regions of the country, where it represents the great black woodpecker of Europe, *Picus* or *Dryocopus martius*.

Pileated Woodpecker (*Hylotomus pileatus*).

pile-beam (pīl'bēm), *n.* A separate warp-beam, upon which is wound and carried the pile-warp: distinguished from the usual warp-beam of a loom.

pile-bridge (pīl'brij), *n.* A bridge consisting of a platform supported by piles. It is probably the earliest form of bridge, and is still largely used, especially over shallow water and marshy ground.

pile-builder (pīl'bil"dėr), *n.* One who erects a structure on piles; specifically, one of a community which customarily dwells in huts or cabins erected on piles over a body of water, as the ancient lake-dwellers, and some savage peoples of the present day. See *lake-dwelling*, *palafitte*.

As regards India, it seems to me there are good reasons for believing these *pile-builders* are the direct descendants of the pre-Aryan aboriginals. *Nature*, XXX. 169.

pile-cap (pīl'kap), *n.* In *hydraul. engin.*, a beam connecting the heads of piles.

pile-clamp (pīl'klamp), *n.* In *surg.*, an instrument for clamping hemorrhoids previous to excision.

piled (pīld), *a.* [< *pile*[1] + *-ed*[2].] 1. Having a pile, as an arrow.—2. Supported on or by piles.

Among those who build on piles many live and sleep on the ground, using the *piled* part of the house for other purposes. *Nature*, XXX. 169.

pile-dam (pīl'dam), *n.* A dam made by driving piles and filling the interstices with stones. The surfaces are usually protected with planking.

pile-driver (pīl'drī"vėr), *n.* 1. A workman occupied in driving piles.—2. A machine or contrivance, usually worked by steam, for driving piles. A common form, shown in the cut, consists of a

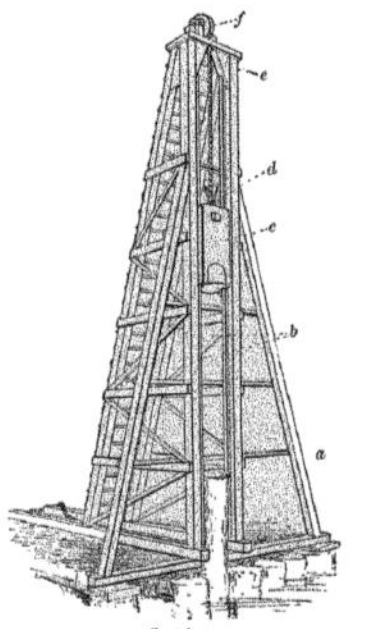

Pile-driver.

a b, framework; *c*, the monkey—a block of cast-iron with guideways which slide on vertical guides on the inner faces of the upright parts *b* of the framework; *d*, nippers; *e*, inclines which engage the arms of the nippers and release the monkey; *f*, hoisting-pulley. The hoisting-rope is attached to the nippers, and the nippers engage a shouldered projection on the top of the monkey.

large ram or block of iron, which slides between two guide-posts. Being drawn up to the top, and then let fall from a considerable height, it comes down on the head of the pile with a violent blow.

pile-dwelling (pīl'dwel"ing), *n.* A dwelling built on piles, especially an ancient lake-dwelling; a palafitte. Compare *pile-builder*.

pile-engine (pīl'en"jin), *n.* An engine for driving piles. See *pile-driver*.

pile-hoop (pīl'hōp), *n.* An iron band put round the head of a timber pile to prevent splitting.

pilei, *n.* Plural of *pileus*.

pileiform (pil'ẹ̄-i-fôrm), *a.* [= F. *piléiforme*, < L. *pileus*, *pilleus*, a cap, + *forma*, shape.] Having the form of a pileus; pileated in shape.

pilement† (pīl'mẹnt), *n.* [< *pile*[3], *v.*, + *-ment*.] An accumulation.

Costly *pilements* of some curious stone.
Bp. Hall, Satires, III. ii. 16.

Pileolares (pil"ẹ̄-ọ̄-lā'rēz), *n.* [NL. (Fries, 1825), < L. *pileolus*, etc., dim. of *pileus*, a cap: see *pileolus*.] A tribe of hymenomycetous fungi of the suborder *Tremellini*, according to Endlicher. The receptacle is membranaceous, and the hymenium inferior, free. Also *Helotici*.

pileolus (pi-lē'ọ̄-lus), *n.*; pl. *pileoli* (-lī). [NL., < L. *pileolus*, *pilleolus*, also *pileolum*, *pilleolum*, dim. of *pileus*, *pilleus*, a cap: see *pileus*.] 1. In *zoöl.* and *bot.*, a little pileus; some small cap-like or lid-like body; specifically, the receptacle of certain fungi.—2. [*cap.*] A genus of gastropods of the family *Neritidæ*, belonging to the Oölite, having no spire, the shell resembling that of a limpet.

Pileopsidæ (pil-ẹ̄-op'si-dē), *n. pl.* [NL., < *Pileopsis* + *-idæ*.] A family of gastropods, named from the genus *Pileopsis*: same as *Calyptræidæ*.

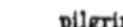

Pileopsis (pil-ǫ-op′sis), *n.* [NL. (Lamarck, 1812), < L. *pileus, pilleus* a cap, + Gr. ὄψις, appearance.] A genus of bonnet-limpets of the family *Calyptræidæ*, having the shell pileate in form, with rounded aperture, posterior spirally recurved apex, and horseshoe-shaped muscular impression. *P. hungarica* is a common European species, known as the *Hungarian bonnet-limpet* or *foolscap-limpet*. *Capulus* is a synonym.

Foolscap-limpet (*Pileopsis hungarica*).

pileorhiza (pil″ē-ǫ-rī′zä), *n.*; pl. *pileorhizæ* (-zē). [NL., < L. *pileus, pilleus*, a cap, + Gr. ῥίζα, a root.] In *bot.*, the root-cap.

pileorhize (pil′ē-ǫ-rīz), *n.* Same as *pileorhiza*.

pileous (pī′lę-us), *a.* [< L. *pilus*, a hair, the hair: see *pile*[4].] Same as *pilous*.

pile-pier (pīl′pēr), *n.* In *hydraul. engin.*, a pier supported on piles.

pile-plank (pīl′plangk), *n.* One of a number of planks, about nine inches broad and from two to four inches thick, sharpened at their lower end, and driven with their edges close together into the ground in hydraulic works, as to make a coffer-dam.

piler[1] (pī′lėr), *n.* [< *pile*[3], *v.*, + *-er*[1].] One who piles or forms into a heap.

piler[2]†, *n.* A Middle English form of *pillar*.

piles (pīlz), *n. pl.* [< NL. *pilæ*, piles, pl. of L. *pila*, a ball: see *pile*[3].] A disease originating in the morbid dilatation of the veins of the lower part of the rectum, and upon the verge of the anus; hemorrhoids. Constipation favors their development.

pile-shoe (pīl′shö), *n.* An iron point fitted on a pile.

pile-start (pīl′stärt), *n.* The pintail duck, *Dafila acuta*. *J. P. Giraud*, 1844. [Long Island.]

pileti, *n.* Plural of *piletus*.

pile-tower† (pīl′tou″ėr), *n.* Same as *pile*[2], 2.

piletus (pi-lē′tus), *n.*; pl. *pileti* (-tī). [ML., < L. *pilum*, a javelin: see *pile*[1].] A form of arrow used in the middle ages, having a knob upon the shaft, near the head, to prevent it from penetrating too deeply.

pileum (pil′ę-um), *n.*; pl. *pilea* (-ä). [NL., < L. *pileum*, a cap: see *pileus*.] In *ornith.*, the cap or whole top of the head, from the base of the bill to the nape, and laterally about to the level of the upper border of the eyes. It is divided into three sections, the forehead or front, the vertex or corona, and the hindhead or occiput. See diagram under *bird*[1].

pileus (pil′ę-us), *n.*; pl. *pilei* (-ī). [L. *pileus*, also *pileum*, also *pilleus, pilleum*, a cap or brimless hat of felt, made to fit close, a felt skull-cap, = Gr. πῖλος, felt, a felt cap or hat, felt cloth, etc.] 1. Among the ancient Romans, a conical cap or hat of felt; a cap or skull-cap.—2. In *bot.*, the expanded cap-like or umbrella-like summit of the stipe, bearing the hymenium, in hymenomycetous fungi: same as *cap*[1], 2 (*a*). See cuts under *Agaricus* and *Fungi*.—3. In *ornith.*, same as *pileum*.—4. [*cap.*] [NL.] A genus of echinoderms.

pile-warp (pīl′wârp), *n.* Same as *nap-warp*.

pile-weaving (pīl′wē″ving), *n.* A process of weaving in which a third thread is introduced, and formed into loops by weaving it over wires laid across the entire breadth of the cloth. The wires are subsequently drawn out, leaving the loops standing, or the loops may be cut so as to form a nap or cut pile.

pile-wire (pīl′wīr), *n.* A wire used in pile-weaving. In the manufacture of cut-pile fabrics grooved pile-wires are used, laid with the grooves facing the outer parts of the loops of the pile. In cutting the pile-threads the knife slides edge upward through the groove or channel in the wire, thus making the cutting uniform, without danger of injuring the warp or weft.

pilework (pīl′wėrk), *n.* Work consisting of piles, as that upon which lacustrine dwellings are supported, or that constructed for many purposes in hydraulic engineering. See cut in next column.

> The wants and habits of the people had changed, and the age of the Swiss *pileworks* was at an end.
> *Sir J. Lubbock*, Pre-historic Times, vi.

pile-worm (pīl′wėrm), *n.* A worm or some similar animal, as a gribble or shipworm, found embedded in the timber of submerged piles. See *Limnoria, Teredo*.

pile-worn (pīl′wōrn), *a.* Worn to such a point that the pile or nap has grown thin, so as to show the threads of the stuff; threadbare.

> Your *pileworn* coat. *Massinger*.

Cast-iron Pilework in Wharves at Deptford and Blackwall, England.
A, elevation; *B*, plan; *C, C′*, sections. *a a*, piles; *b*, a guide-pile; *c*, a stay-pile; *d d*, iron land-ties.

pilewort (pīl′wėrt), *n.* One of the buttercups, *Ranunculus Ficaria*, common in Europe and western Asia. It produces annually grain-like tubers, sometimes gathered for food, and locally fancied to have fallen from above. Also called *celandine* and *figwort*.—**Great pilewort**, an old name of the figwort *Scrophularia nodosa*.

pilfer (pil′fėr), *v.* [< OF. *pelfrer*, rob, plunder, < *pelfre*, plunder, booty, spoil; cf. *pilfeier*, rob: see *pelf*.] **I.** *intrans.* To steal in small quantities; practise petty theft.

> Every string is told,
> For fear some *pilf'ring* hand should make too bold.
> *Dryden*.

> The Malayans, who inhabit on both sides the Streights of Malacca, are in general a bold people: and yet I do not find any of them addicted to Robbery, but only the *pilfering* poorer sort. *Dampier*, Voyages, II. i. 165.

II. *trans.* To steal or gain by petty theft; filch.

> He would not *pilfer* the victory, and the defeat was easy. *Bacon*.

pilferer (pil′fėr-ėr), *n.* One who pilfers or practises petty theft.

> To glory some advance a lying claim,
> Thieves of renown and *pilferers* of fame.
> *Young*, Love of Fame, iii. 88.

=**Syn.** *Thief*, etc. See *robber*.

pilferingly (pil′fėr-ing-li), *adv.* In a pilfering manner; with petty theft; filchingly.

pilfery† (pil′fėr-i), *n.* [< *pilfer* + *-y*[3] (see *-ery*).] The act of pilfering; petty theft; also, the thing stolen.

> They eat bread, and drunk water, as a wholesome penance, enjoined them by their confessors, for base *pilferies*.
> B. *Jonson*, Volpone, ii. 1.

> Proue it when you will, you slow spirited Saturnists, that haue nothing but the *pilfries* of your penne to pollish an exhortation withall, no eloquence but tautologies to tye the cares of your auditory vnto you.
> *Nashe*, Pierce Penilesse, p. 40.

pilgarlick (pil-gär′lik), *n.* [< *pill*[2], *v.*, + obj. *garlic* (formerly *garlick*). See *to pill garlic*, under *pill*[2]. The word came to be applied, with the stress laid on *pill* with ref. to *pilled*, bald, to lepers or to other persons who have become bald by disease, acquiring a particularly opprobrious meaning.] A poor forsaken wretch: a vague term of reproach. [Low.]

> And there got he a knock, and down goes *pilgarlick*.
> *Fletcher*, Humorous Lieutenant, ii. 2.

pilgrim (pil′grim), *n.* and *a.* [Early mod. E. also *pilgrime, pelgrom*; < ME. *pilgrim, pylgrym, pelgrim, pylgreme, pelegrim, pilegrim* = OFries. *pilugrim, pilegrim* = D. *pelgrim* = MLG. *pelegrime, pelgrim, pelgrem* = OHG. *piligrīm, pilikrīm*, MHG. *pilgerīm, pilgrīm, pilgerem, pilgeram, bilgerīn, pilger*, G. *pilger* = Icel. *pílagrímr* = Sw. *pilgrim* = Dan. *pilegrim*, < OF. **pelegrin, pellegrin, pelegri, pelerin, peregrin*, F. *pèlerin* = Pr. *pellegrin* = Sp. Pg. *peregrino* = It. *peregrino, pellegrino*, < ML. *peregrinus, pelegrinus*, a pilgrim, traveler, foreigner, foreign resident, a suburban resident, L. *peregrinus*, a foreigner, stranger, foreign resident, prop. adj., foreign: see *peregrine*.] **I.** *n.* **1.** A traveler; specifically, one who journeys to some place esteemed sacred, either as a penance, or in order to discharge some vow or religious obligation, or to obtain some spiritual or miraculous benefit; hence, a wanderer; a sojourner in a foreign land. The custom of pilgrimages has prevailed especially in India, among Mohammedan peoples, and among Christians in the middle ages. Frequented places of Christian pilgrimage have been (besides Jerusalem and the Holy Land) Rome, Canterbury, Compostela in Spain, Einsiedeln in Switzerland, and in modern times Lourdes in France.

Pilgrim, in the recognized dress worn at Rome in the 18th century.

> And on Mondaye we met with the shyppe with *pylgrymes* that went out of Venyce .iij. wekes before vs, whiche *pylgrymes* had done theyr pylgrymage and retourned homewardes.
> *Sir R. Guylforde*, Pylgrymage, p. 15.

> These all died in faith, not having received the promises, but having seen them afar off, and were persuaded of them, and embraced them, and confessed that they were strangers and *pilgrims* on the earth. Heb. xi. 13.

> With naked foot, and sackcloth vest,
> And arms enfolded on his breast,
> Did every *pilgrim* go.
> *Scott*, L. of L. M., vi. 29.

2. In *Amer. hist.*, specifically, one of the English separatists who sailed from Delfthaven (in the Netherlands) in the "Mayflower," touching at Southampton, England, and founded the colony of Plymouth, Massachusetts, at the end of 1620.—**3.** A new-comer, whether a person or an animal; a "tenderfoot." [Slang, western U. S.]

> *Pilgrim* and "tenderfoot" were formerly applied almost exclusively to newly imported cattle, but by a natural transferrence they are usually used to designate all new-comers, tourists, and business-men.
> L. *Swinburne*, Scribner's Monthly, II. 508.

4. A curtain or screen of silk hanging from the back of a woman's bonnet to protect the neck, worn in the latter part of the eighteenth century.—**Pilgrim-bottle**, a round, flat bottle having on each side of the mouth or neck a ring for the insertion of a cord. The type is a common one in pottery of many nations and times, and is especially frequent in Italian work of the fifteenth and sixteenth centuries, and in imitations of it. The simplest pilgrim-bottles are circular or oval and without a foot; but more elaborate vases, if preserving the flat form and the rings for a cord, are also known by this name. See *costrel*.—**Pilgrim fathers**, in *Amer. hist.*, the founders of Plymouth Colony in 1620. See def. 2, above.—**Pilgrim's pouch**, a badge of lead or other material, having the form of a pouch and hollow like it, but very small: a variety of pilgrim's sign.—**Pilgrim's shell.** (*a*) A scallop- or cockle-shell used as an emblem of pilgrimage, or a sign that one has visited the Holy Land. One of the scallops, *Pecten jacobæus*, is known as *St. James's shell*, from this circumstance. See *Pecten*, 2 (*a*). (*b*) In modern times, a carved pearl shell such as are brought by travelers from the Holy Land. *P. L. Simonds*, Art Jour., N. S., XII. 72.—**Pilgrim's sign**, a small object given to pilgrims at a shrine or sacred place as evidence of their having visited it. It was sometimes a medal, sometimes a small ampulla of lead or pewter, and bore the mark of the monastery, church, etc., which issued it.—**Pilgrim's staff.** (*a*) The long staff which was one of the badges of a pilgrim. (*b*) In *her.*, same as *bourdon*[1].—**Pilgrim's vase**, a decorative vase having a flat and disk-like body, in partial imitation of a pilgrim's bottle.

Pilgrim's Sign.
(From "Journal of the British Archæological Association," 1846.)

II. *a.* Of, pertaining to, used by, or characteristic of a pilgrim, or one who travels to a sacred place in performance of some religious duty; wandering as a pilgrim; consisting of pilgrims.

> A parish priest was of the *pilgrim* train. *Cowley*.

> Till Morning fair
> Came forth, with *pilgrim* steps, in amice gray.
> *Milton*, P. R., iv. 427.

> She remembered the parting words of the *pilgrim* count.
> *Irving*, Moorish Chronicles, p. 31.

pilgrim (pil′grim), *v. i.* [< *pilgrim*, *n.*] To journey or travel as a pilgrim; undertake or accomplish a pilgrimage.

> The ambulo hath no certain home or diet, but *pilgrims* up and down everywhere, feeding upon all sorts of plants.
> *Grew*.

Pilgriming restlessly to so many "Saints' Wells."
Carlyle, Sartor Resartus (ed. 1831), p. 117.

pilgrimage (pil'gri-māj), *n.* [Early mod. E. also *pilgramage*; < ME. *pilgrimage, pylgrymage, pilegrimage*, also *pelrimage, pelrinage*, < AF. *pilrymage*, OF. *pelerinage*, F. *pèlerinage* = It. *pellegrinaggio, peregrinaggio*, < ML. *peregrinaticum*, also, after Rom., *peregrinagium*, a traveling, voyage, pilgrimage, < *peregrinus*, a traveler, pilgrim: see *pilgrim*.] **1.** A journey undertaken by a pilgrim; a traveling on through a strange country or to some place deemed sacred in order to perform some religious vow or duty, or obtain some spiritual or miraculous benefit.

In Southwerk at the Tabard as I lay,
Ready to wenden on my *pilgrimage*.
Chaucer, Gen. Prol. to C. T., l. 21.

We all by one assent auowed a *pylgrymage* to be made in all our behalfes to our blessyd Lady of Loreta.
Sir R. Guylforde, Pylgrymage, p. 68.

Mowbray and myself are like two men
That vow a long and weary *pilgrimage*.
Shak., Rich. II., i. 3. 49.

2. Figuratively, the journey of life; the time spent in passing through the world to the "better land."

And Jacob said unto Pharaoh, The days of the years of my *pilgrimage* are an hundred and thirty years.
Gen. xlvii. 9.

3†. The time occupied by a pilgrimage; hence, a lifetime.

In prison hast thou spent a *pilgrimage*,
And like a hermit overpass'd thy days.
Shak., 1 Hen. VI., ii. 5. 116.

=**Syn. 1.** *Voyage, Tour*, etc. See *journey*.

pilgrimage†, *v. i.* [< *pilgrimage, n.*] To go as a pilgrim. [Rare.]

To Egypt she'll *pilgrimage*, at Meroe fill
Warme drops to sprinkle Isis Temple.
Sir R. Stapleton, tr. of Juvenal's Satires, vi. 555. (*Davies.*)

pilgrimer (pil'gri-mėr), *n.* A pilgrim.

Now, I am Magdalen, a poor *pilgrimer*, for the sake of Holy Kirk.
Scott, Abbot, xv.

pilgrimize (pil'gri-mīz), *v. i.*; pret. and pp. *pilgrimized*, ppr. *pilgrimizing*. [< *pilgrim* + *-ize*.] To wander or journey about as a pilgrim: sometimes with an impersonal *it*.

I'll bear thy charges, an thou wilt but *pilgrimize it* along with me to the land of Utopia.
B. Jonson, Case is Altered, ii. 4.

pili, *n.* Plural of *pilus*.

Pilidium (pī-lid'i-um), *n.* [NL., < Gr. πιλίδιον, a little hat or cap, dim. of πῖλος, a felt hat or cap: see *pileus*.] **1.** A generic name given to the larvæ of rhynchocœle turbellarians, or nemertean worms, under the impression that they are distinct animals. *Pilidium gyrans* is the larva of a species of the genus *Lineus*. The name is retained as a convenient designation of such pileate or helmet-shaped nemertean larvæ: in this use it is written without the capital, and has a plural *pilidia*.

Pilidium gyrans.
A, B, younger and older pilidia: *a*, alimentary canal; *b*, rudiment of the nemertean, more advanced in B than in A; C, newly freed nemertean.

2. In *conch.*, a genus of false limpets of the family *Acmæidæ*. —**3†.** [*l. c.*] In *bot.*, a hemispherical apothecium in certain lichens.

piliferous (pī-lif'e-rus), *a.* [< L. *pilus*, hair (see *pile*⁴), + *ferre* = E. *bear*¹.] **1.** In *bot.*, bearing or tipped with hairs.—**2.** In *zoöl.*, bearing hairs; hairy; piligerous: specifically, in entomology, noting the tubercles of caterpillars whence bundles of hairs arise.—**Piliferous layer**, in *bot.*, the layer of young superficial tissue of active roots that is provided with root-hairs.

piliform (pī'li-fôrm), *a.* [< L. *pilus*, hair, + *forma*, form.] Slender or fine as a hair; filiform; filamentous.

piligerous (pī-lij'e-rus), *a.* [< L. *pilus*, hair, + *gerere*, carry.] Covered with hair or fur; pilous or pilose; piliferous.

piling¹ (pī'ling), *n.* [Verbal n. of *pile*¹, *v.*] **1.** In *engin.*, the operation of placing and driving piles in position.—**2.** Piles collectively; pilework.—**Dovetailed piling**, a combination of piles fixed by mortising them into one another by dovetails or dovetail-tenons.

piling² (pī'ling), *n.* [< *pile*⁴ + *-ing*¹.] In *leather-manuf.*, a slow inward sweating of the leather. C. T. Davis, Leather, p. 297.

piling-iron (pī'ling-ī'ėrn), *n.* An instrument for breaking off the awns of barley.

pilion†, *n.* An obsolete form of *pillion*.

pilkins (pil'kinz), *n.* A corruption of *pillcorn* (?).

The Bantam said he had seen Tom secreting *pilkins* in a sack.
G. Meredith, Ordeal of Richard Feverel, ix.

pill¹† (pil), *v.* [Early mod. E. also *pil, pile, pille*; also *peel* (by confusion with *peel*¹), < ME. *pillen, pyllen, pilen, pylen*, plunder, < OF. *piller*, F. *piller*, plunder, rifle, ransack, loot, = Sp. *pillar*, plunder, pilfer, = Pg. *pilhar* = It. *pigliare* (ML. as if **piliare*), < L. *pilare*, plunder, pillage, rare in the simple form, but common in comp. *compilare*, scrape together and carry off, plunder, pillage (> ult. E. *compile*), and *expilare*, plunder, pillage, and common also in ML., *pilare*, *pillare*; usually explained as a fig. use of *pilare*, deprive of hair (see *pill*²), but no doubt of independent origin.] **I.** *trans.* To rob; plunder; pillage.

Thou sal noght be tyrant til thaim, to *pille* thaime, and spoyle thaim, als the wicked princez duz.
MS. Coll. Eton. 10, f. 5. (*Halliwell.*)

It is more than two yere that thei cessed neuer to robbe and to *pile* oure londes.
Merlin (E. E. T. S.), iii. 556.

The commons hath he *pill'd* with grievous taxes.
Shak., Rich. II., ii. 1. 246.

Having *pilled* a book which no man buys.
B. Jonson, Epigrams, liii.

When he who *pill'd* his province scapes the laws,
And keeps his money, though he lost his cause.
Dryden, tr. of Juvenal's Satires, i. 72.

II. *intrans.* To rob; practise robbery; plunder.

Whan the wolf hath ful his wombe he stynteth to strangle sheepe; but soothly the pilours and destroyours of Goddes hooly chirche ne do nat so, for they ne stynte nevere to *pile*.
Chaucer, Parson's Tale.

The poor man that is wrong'd
Is ready to rebel; he spoils, he *pills*.
Greene, James IV., v.

pill²† (pil), *v.* [Early mod. E. also *pil, pille*; < ME. *pillen, pilen, pilien, pullen, pelen*, < OF. *piller*, *peler, peiller, poiller*, F. *peler*, deprive of hair, hair (hides or skins), scald (pigs), take turf off, = Pr. Sp. *pelar* = Pg. *pellar* = It. *pelare*, deprive of hair, pluck, peel, strip, < L. *pilare*, deprive of hair, depilate, < *pilus*, hair: see *pile*⁴. Cf. *pill*¹, rob, *peel*¹, skin, with which *pill*² has been more or less confused.] **I.** *trans.* **1.** To deprive of hair; make bald. Compare *pilled*. —**2.** To peel; strip; form by stripping off the skin or bark.

Jacob took him rods of green poplar, . . . and *pilled* white strakes in them.
Gen. xxx. 37.

They take limons which they *pil*, anointing themselues thoroughly with the iuice therof.
Hakluyt's Voyages, II. 58.

To pill garlic†, to do some unpleasant office; endure mortification. Compare *pilgarlick*.

And ye shul here how the tapster made the pardonere *pull Garlik* al the long nyghte til it was ner end day;
For the more chere she made of love, the falser was her lay.
The Merry Adventure of the Pardonere and Tapster at the Inn at Canterbury (printed in Urry's ed. of Chaucer, 1721), l. 122.

II. *intrans.* To peel; come off in flakes.

pill²† (pil), *n.* [< *pill*², *v.*; a var. of *peel*¹, *n.*] **1.** Peel; skin; rind; outer covering.

Sweet is the Nut, but bitter is his *pill*.
Spenser, Sonnets, xxvi.

The huske or *pill* of a greene nut which blacketh one's fingers and hands.
Hollyband, Dict., 1593. (*Halliwell.*)

These [hazel-shoots] prune and cleanse of every leaf and spray, . . .
But perish not the rine and utter *pill*.
J. Dennys (Arber's Eng. Garner, I. 149).

2. The refuse of a hawk's prey. *Halliwell.*

pill³ (pil), *n.* [Early mod. E. also *pil, pille* (= MD. *pille, pil* = G. *pille* = Dan. *pille* = Sw. *pil*, *piller*, a pill); an abbr. (as if of *pilule* (= MHG. *pillele*), which actually appears later), perhaps due in part to the written abbr. *pil.*, pl. *pill.*, in physicians' prescriptions, of L. *pilula*, a pill, a little ball, dim. of *pila*, a ball (> OF. *pile*, a ball, a pill): see *pilule*. *Pill* is thus not directly < L. *pila*, which is not used in the sense of 'pill,' but from its dim. *pilula*.] **1.** A globular or ovoid mass of medicinal substance, of a size convenient for swallowing.

Hard is it for the patient which is ill
Fulsome or bitter potions to digest,
Yet must he swallow many a bitter *pill*,
Ere he regaine his former health & rest.
Times' Whistle (E. E. T. S.), p. 127.

Hence—**2.** Something unpleasant that has to be accepted or (metaphorically) swallowed: usually qualified by *bitter*.

Yet cannot thei abyde to swallow down the holsome *pille* of viritie, being bittur in their mouths.
J. Udall, On Luke iv.

He said the renunciation of this interest was a *bitter pill* which they could not swallow.
Jefferson, To Madison (Bancroft's Hist. Const., I. 430).

3. A disagreeable or objectionable person. [Slang.]—**4.** *pl.* A doctor or surgeon. [Milit. and naut. slang.]—**5.** In *varnish-making*, the cooked mass of linseed-oil and gum before turpentine is added to thin it down and complete the varnish.

pill³ (pil), *v. t.* [< *pill*³, *n.*] **1.** To form into pills.—**2.** To dose with pills. [Colloq.]—**3.** To reject by vote; blackball. [Club slang.]

He was coming on for election at Bay's, and was as nearly *pilled* as any man I ever knew in my life.
Thackeray, Newcomes, xxx.

pill⁴ (pil), *n.* [< ME. **pyll*, < AS. *pyll, pull*, a creek, = Icel. *pollr*, a creek, < W. *pwll*, a pool, = Ir. *poll, pull*, a creek. Cf. *pool*¹.] A small creek; one of the channels through which the drainings of a marsh enter a river. *Halliwell.* [Prov. Eng.]

From S. Juste *pille* or creke to S. Manditus creeke is a mile dim. *Leland's Itinerary* (1769), iii. 29. (*Halliwell.*)

The *pills* being the little streams which wear away a sort of miniature tidal estuary in the mud-banks as they empty themselves into the Severn and the Wye.
Seebohm, Eng. Vil. Community, p. 150.

pillaffe, *n.* Same as *pilau*.

pillage (pil'āj), *n.* [< ME. *pillage, pyllage, pilage*, < OF. (and F.) *pillage* = Pr. *pilatge* = Sp. *pillaje* = Pg. *pilhagem*, plunder, pillage, < ML. as if **pilaticum*, after Rom. *pillagium*, plunder, < L. *pilare* (> OF. *piller*, etc.), plunder: see *pill*¹.] **1.** The act of plundering.

Pillage and robbery. *Shak.*, Hen. V., iv. 1. 174.

2. Plunder; spoil; that which is taken from another by open force, particularly and chiefly from enemies in war.

Which *pillage* they with merry march bring home
To the tent-royal of their emperor.
Shak., Hen. V., i. 2. 196.

=**Syn.** *Pillage, Plunder, Booty, Spoil, Prey.* These words denote that which is violently got or carried off; all except *prey* suggest a considerable amount seized. *Pillage* also denotes the act; the others only the thing or things taken. *Pillage* and *spoil* especially suggest the great loss to the owners, completely stripping or despoiling them of their property; *plunder* suggests the quantity and value of that which is taken: as, loaded with *plunder*; *booty* is primarily the spoils of war, but also of a raid or combined action, as of pirates, brigands, or burglars; *spoil* is the only one of these words that is used in the plural, except, rarely, *prey*. *Prey* now seems figurative or archaic when not applied to the objects of pursuit by animals: as, the mouse falls a ready *prey* to both beasts and birds; hence, when applied to that which is pursued or taken by man, it expresses condemnation of the act.

pillage (pil'āj), *v. t.*; pret. and pp. *pillaged*, ppr. *pillaging*. [< *pillage*, *n.*] To strip of money or goods by open violence; plunder; despoil.

Antwerp, the most famous Town of Traffick in all Europe, was miserably *pillaged*. *Baker*, Chronicles, p. 351.

Our modern compilers, like sextons and executioners, think it their undoubted right to *pillage* the dead.
Goldsmith, Essays, Pref.

pillager (pil'ā-jėr), *n.* [< *pillage* + *-er*¹.] One who pillages or plunders by open violence; a plunderer.

pillar (pil'ạr), *n.* [Early mod. E. *piller*; < ME. *piller, pillare, pyllare, pyllour, piler, pyler, pylere, pelere, pyleer, pilour*, < OF. *piler, pilier*, F. *pilier* = Pr. Sp. Pg. *pilar* = It. *piliere* = D. *pilaar* = MLG. *pilere, pilar*, LG. *piler* = OHG. *piliri, pfilari*, MHG. *philære, pfiler*, G. *pfeiler* = Sw. *pelare* = Dan. *piller, pille* = Ir. *pileir*, a pillar, < ML. *pilare*, also *pilarius, pilarium*, and *pillcare*, a pillar, < L. *pila*, a pillar, pier, mole: see *pile*².] **1.** A column; a columnar mass of any form, often composed, or having the appearance of be-

Pillar.—Cathedral of Tours, France, 13th century.

ing composed, of several shafts engaged in a central core, as is frequent in medieval architecture: by architects often distinguished from *column*, inasmuch as it may be of any shape in section, and is not subordinated to the rules of classic architecture. See also cuts under *lat*[6] and *column*.

Eche *piler* is of Penaunce of preyeres to seyntes,
Of Almes-dedes ar the hokes that the gates hangen on.
Piers Plowman (B), v. 602.

The *Piller* is a figure among all the rest of the Geometricall most beawtifull, in respect that he is tall and vpright and of one bignesse from the bottom to the toppe.
Puttenham, Arte of Eng. Poesie, p. 80.

And Jacob set a *pillar* upon her grave. Gen. xxxv. 20.

There are erected two wooden *pillars* in the water.
Coryat, Crudities, I. 3.

2. A support or supporter; one who or that which sustains or upholds.

The *pilere* elm, the cofere unto carayne.
Chaucer, Parliament of Fowls, l. 177.

He is a maine *pillar* of our church, though not yet Deane nor Canon, and his life our Religions best Apologie.
Bp. Earle, Micro-cosmographie, A Graue Diuine.

With grave
Aspect he rose, and in his rising seem'd
A *pillar* of state. *Milton*, P. L., ii. 302.

3. The upright and supporting part of something, as of a table having but one support, or of a candlestick.—**4.** In *anat.* and *zoöl.*, a pillar-like or columnar structure, part, or organ; a column or columella; a crus: as, the *pillar* (columella or modiolus) of a spiral shell; the *pillars* (crura or peduncles) of the brain. See cut under *Discophora*.—**5.** One of the posts which serve to connect the plates of a clock-movement, and also to keep them the necessary distance apart.—**6.** In the *manège*, the raised center of the ring or manège-ground around which a horse turns. There are also pillars at regular intervals around the ground.—**7.** A portable emblem in the form of an ornamented column, formerly carried before an ecclesiastical dignitary as typical of his function as a support to the church.

With worldly p mpe incredible,
Before him rydeth two prestes stronge,
And they bear two crosses right longe,
Gapynge in every man's face.
After them folowe two laye-men secular,
And each of them holdyng a *pillar*
In their handes, steade of a mace.
Skelton, Works. (*Nares.*)

8. Something resembling a pillar in appearance.

And the Lord went before them by day in a *pillar* of cloud, to lead them the way; and by night in a *pillar* of fire, to give them light. Ex. xiii. 21.

9. A solid mass of coal left either temporarily or permanently to support the roof of a mine.—**10.** In *harp-making*, the upright post on the side furthest from the player. It is usually hollow, and contains the rods of the pedal-action.—**11.** A frame for supporting tobacco-pipes in a kiln. *E. H. Knight.*—**12.** The nipple of a firearm. *E. H. Knight.*—**Compound pillar**, in *arch.*, a clustered column.—**From pillar to post**, or **from post to pillar**, from one thing to another without any apparent definite purpose: as, to run or be driven *from pillar to post*. The allusion, according to Brewer, is to the pillar in the center of a manège-ground and the posts placed at regular intervals around its circumference. See def. 6, above.

From thee *poast toe piler* with thoght his rackt wyt he tosseth. *Stanihurst*, Æneid, iv. 296. (*Davies.*)

Our Guards, *from pillar* bang'd *to post*,
He kick'd about till they were lost.
Cotton, Scarronides, p. 62. (*Davies.*)

Knotted pillar. See *knotted*.—**Pillar and breast**, a common method of mining coal, in which the breasts or working-places are rectangular rooms, usually five or ten times as long as they are broad, and opened on the upper side of the gangway, or main haulage-road, or level driven on the strike of the coal. The breasts are made of various widths, usually from five to twelve yards, according to the character of the roof, but not so wide that the roof will not sustain itself. These breasts or rooms are separated by pillars of coal, broken only by cross-headings where these are needed for ventilation. The pillars are sometimes left so narrow that it is not expected they will permanently support the roof of the mine: in such cases the object of the method is to get as much coal as possible in the shortest time and at the least expense. If more economy of coal is considered desirable, the pillars are left wider, and, after the breasts are entirely worked out, are "robbed"—that is, are cut away until all the coal has been obtained from them which can be removed without too great danger to the miners. This method of mining is also called *post and stall*, *pillar and stall*, *pillar and room*, *stoop and room*, *board and pillar*, etc. See *long-wall*.—**Pillar dollar**, a silver coin of Spain (so called from its figure of the Pillars of Hercules), coined especially for use in the former Spanish colonies in America. Also called *peso* and *piece of eight*. See cut in next column.—**Pillar letter-box**, a short pillar placed in a street, containing a receptacle for

Pillar Dollar (reverse), 1661.—British Museum. (Size of the original.)

letters, etc., which are collected at specified hours by post-office letter-carriers. [Eng.]—**Pillars of Corti.** Same as *rods of Corti* (which see, under *rod*).—**Pillars of Hercules**, the two hills on opposite sides of the straits of Gibraltar—Abyla (Jebel-el-Mina), on the African side, and Calpe (Rock of Gibraltar), on the European side—which were said to have been torn asunder by Hercules.—**Pillars of the abdominal ring.** See *columns of the abdominal ring*, under *column*.—**Pillars of the diaphragm.** See *diaphragm*.—**Pillars of the fauces.** See *fauces*.—**Pillars of the fornix**, the more or less compact strands of the fornix passing one pair anteriorly and one pair posteriorly down toward the base of the brain. The anterior pair pass down to the corpora albicantia, and are called *columns of the fornix*, or *radices ascendentes* (by Meynert *descendentes*) *fornicis*. The posterior pillars or crura pass downward to end in the hippocampus major and to form the fimbria.—**Pillars of the palate.** See *palate*, 1.—**Pompey's pillar**, a noted monument of antiquity standing at Alexandria in Egypt. It is a huge Corinthian column of red granite, rising to a height of 98 feet 9 inches, exclusive of the substructure. The shaft is monolithic and unfluted, 73 feet long and 29 feet 8 inches in circumference. The capital is 9 feet high, and the square base measures about 15 feet on the side. Despite the popular name, the monument had nothing to do with Pompey: it was erected in honor of the emperor Diocletian, a statue of whom originally stood upon it.—**Rib and pillar**, in *mining*, a system upon which the so-called "thick coal" was formerly extensively mined. It is a modification of the pillar-and-breast method. [South Staffordshire, Eng.]

pillar-block (pil'ạ̈r-blok), *n.* In *mach.*, a pillow-block or plumber-block.

pillar-box. Same as *pillar letter-box* (which see, under *pillar*).

pillar-brick (pil'ạ̈r-brik), *n.* In the construction of a brick-kiln by building up unburned bricks, one of the bricks which are laid up between the "straight courses," and which form the sides of the arches through which the heated products of combustion flow in the process of burning.

pillar-compasses (pil'ạ̈r-kum"pạs-ez), *n.* A bow-pen; a pair of dividers with an attachment for a pen or pencil.

pillared (pil'ạ̈rd), *a.* [‹ *pillar* + *-ed*[2].] **1.** Having pillars; supported by pillars.

In the ground
The bended twigs take root, and daughters grow
About the mother-tree, a *pillar'd* shade
High over-arch'd, and echoing walks between.
Milton, P. L., ix. 1106.

All that remained [of a vihara] was a series of some twenty cells and four larger halls surrounding a *pillared* court 50 ft. square.
J. Fergusson, Hist. Indian Arch., p. 137.

2. Having the form of a pillar.

Th' infuriate hill that shoots the *pillar'd* flame.
Thomson, Summer.

pillaret (pil'ạ̈r-et), *n.* [‹ OF. *pileret*, dim. of *piler*, a pillar: see *pillar* and *-et*.] A small pillar.

The Pillars and *Pillarets* of Fusill Marble.
Fuller, Worthies (Wiltshire), III. 316.

pillar-file (pil'ạ̈r-fīl), *n.* A narrow, thin, flat hand-file with one safe edge. *E. H. Knight.*

pillaring (pil'ạ̈r-ing), *n.* [‹ *pillar* + *-ing*[1].] A system or series of pillars; a method of applying or employing pillars. *Thearle*, Naval Arch., § 315.

pillarist (pil'ạ̈r-ist), *n.* [‹ *pillar* + *-ist*.] Same as *stylite*.

pillar-lip (pil'ạ̈r-lip), *n.* In *conch.*, the inner or columellar lip of a gastropod.

pillar-plait (pil'ạ̈r-plāt), *n.* In *conch.*, a columellar fold. *P. P. Carpenter.*

pillar-saint (pil'ạ̈r-sānt), *n.* Same as *stylite*.

pillary†, *n.* An obsolete form of *pillory*.

pillas (pil'as), *n.* [Also *pillis*, *pillez*, *pellas*, etc., ‹ Corn. *piles*, *pelez*, bare, bald. Cf. *pill*[2].] The naked oat, *Avena nuda*, by some considered a variety of *A. sativa*. Also called *pillcorn*. *Jago*, Glossary. [Cornwall, Eng.]

pillau, pillaw, *n.* See *pilau*.

pill-beetle (pil'bē"tl), *n.* A coleopterous insect of the family *Byrrhidæ*, especially of the genus *Byrrhus*: so called from its small size and rounded form, which when it draws in or folds away its legs and feigns death make it look like a pill.

Pill-beetle (*Byrrhus pilula*). (Line shows natural size.)

pill-box (pil'boks), *n.* **1.** A box for holding pills.—**2.** Humorously, a kind of carriage.

She drove into town in a one-horse carriage, irreverently called, at that period of English history, a *pill-box*.
Dickens, Little Dorrit, xxxiii.

pill-bug (pil'bug), *n.* An isopod crustacean of the family *Oniscidæ*; a kind of wood-louse, slater, or sow-bug which can roll itself into a ball like a pill. One such species is technically called *Armadillo pilularis*.

pill-coater (pil'kō"tėr), *n.* A machine for coating pills with sugar. The pills are placed in a pan with a compound of sugar, and agitated constantly by a steady rotary motion, exposing their entire surface to the sugar, and yet not allowing them to stick together.

pillcorn (pil'kôrn), *n.* See *pillas*.

pilled† (pild), *p. a.* [Early mod. E. also *pild*; ME. **pilled*, *piled*, *pild*; pp. of *pill*[2], *v.*] **1.** Stripped of hair; bald.

As *piled* as an ape was his skulle.
Chaucer, Miller's Tale, l. 15.

He migte no maistre [ben] kald (for Crist that defended),
Ne puten [no] pylion on his *pild* pate;
But prechen in parfite lijf & no pride vsen.
Piers Plowman's Crede (E. E. T. S.), l. 839.

2. Having scanty hair.

With skalled browes blake and *piled* berd.
Chaucer, Gen. Prol. to C. T., l. 627.

3. Threadbare; hence, forlorn.

I am no such *pilled* Cynick to believe
That beggary is the only happiness.
B. Jonson, Every Man out of his Humour, i. 1.

pilled-garlic† (pild'gär"lik), *n.* Same as *pil-garlick*.

pilledness† (pild'nes), *n.* Baldness; bareness; scantiness; threadbare condition.

Some scorned the *pildnesse* of his garments.
Hakluyt's Voyages, III. 167.

piller[1]† (pil'ėr), *n.* [‹ ME. *pillour*, *pellour*, *pilour*, *pelour*, a robber, ‹ OF. **pillour*, *pilleur*, F. *pilleur*, ‹ LL. **pilator* (in fem. *pilatrix*), ML. *pillator*, a robber, ‹ L. *pilare*, rob: see *pill*[1].] A plunderer; a robber.

To ransake in the tas of bodyes dede,
Hem for to strepe of herneys and of wede,
The *pilours* diden businesse and cure
After the bataille and disconfiture.
Chaucer, Knight's Tale, l. 149.

They haue tooke notable goods of ours,
On this side see, these false *pelours*
Called of Saincte Malo, and ellis where.
Hakluyt's Voyages, I. 190.

piller[2]†, *n.* An obsolete spelling of *pillar*.

pillery[1]† (pil'ėr-i), *n.* [‹ *pill*[1] + *-ery*.] Robbery; plunder; pillage; rapine.

And then concussion, rapine, *pilleries*,
Their catalogue of accusations fill. *Daniel.*

pillery[2]†, *n.* An obsolete spelling of *pillory*.

pillez (pil'ez), *n.* Same as *pillas*.

pilliocausia, pillicoshy (pil"i-ō-kâ'si-ạ, pil'i-kō-shi), *n.* Hiera-picra, or powder of aloes and canella.

pillion (pil'yon), *n.* [Early mod. E. also *pilion*, *pylion*; ‹ ME. *pylion*, *pylliounn*, ‹ Ir. *pillium*, *pillin*, a pack-saddle, = Gael. *pillean*, *pillin*, a pack-saddle, cloth put under a saddle, = W. *pilyn* = Manx *pollan*, a pack-saddle; ‹ Ir. *pill*, a covering, = Gael. *peall*, a skin, coverlet, = L. *pellis*, a skin: see *pell*[1]. In the sense of 'head-dress' perhaps a diff. word, ult. ‹ L. *pileus*, *pilleus*, a felt cap: see *pileus*.] **1**†. A saddle, especially a light and simple saddle without a raised bow and pommel.

His strong brasse bit, his slyding reynes, his shanke *pillion* without stirrups. *Spenser*, State of Ireland.

2. A pad or cushion fitted for adjustment to a saddle behind as a seat for a second person, usually a woman.

Every now and then drop'd a Lady from her *Pillion*, another from her Side Saddle.
Quoted in *Ashton's* Social Life in Reign of Queen Anne, [I. 84.

Why can't you ride your hobby-horse without desiring to place me on a *pillion* behind you?
Sheridan, The Critic, i. 1.

3†. In *mining*, tin recovered from the slags in the smelting of that metal. This is done by repeated stamping, sifting, and washing. [Cornwall, Eng.]—**4**†. A head-dress, as of a priest; a hat.

Ne puten *pylion* [cardinal's hat (Skeat)] on his pild pate;
But prechen in parfite lijf & no pride vsen.
Piers Plowman's Crede (E. E. T. S.), l. 839.

Mercury shall give thee gifts manyfolde;
His *Pillion*, sceptre, his winges, and his harpe.
Barclay, Eclogue, iv.

pillioned (pil'yọnd), *a.* [Early mod. E. *pylyoned*; < *pillion*, *n.*, 4, + *-ed*2.] Having a pillion (the head-dress so called).

The idolatour, the tyrant, and the whoremongar are no mete mynisters for hym, though they be . . . never so fynely forced, *pylyoned*, and scarletted.
Bp. Bale, Vocacion (Harl. Misc., VI. 442).

pill-milleped (pil'mil″e-ped), *n.* A milleped or thousand-legs of the family *Glomeridæ*; a kind of gally-worm that can roll itself into a ball. Also *pill-worm*.

pillorize (pil'ọ-rīz), *v. t.*; pret. and pp. *pillorized*, ppr. *pillorizing*. [< OF. *pilloriser*, *piloriser*, *pyloriser*, *pilloriger* (ML. *pilorisare*), pillorize; as *pillor-y* + *-ize*.] To set in a pillory.

Henry Burton . . . was . . . *pillorized* with Prynne and Bastwicke.
Wood, Fasti Oxon., I. 192.

pillorizing (pil'ọ-rī-zing), *p. a.* Serving to pillorize or set up to ridicule.

Dandin has become a *pillorizing* name adopted (probably from folk-speech) by many French authors—as Rabelais, Racine, La Fontaine, Molière—for types of various forms of folly they have undertaken to scathe.
N. and Q., 7th ser., IX. 150.

pillory (pil'ọ-ri), *n.*; pl. *pillories* (-riz). [Early mod. E. *pillorie*, *pillery*, *pillerie*, *pillary*, *pillarie*, < ME. *pillory*, *pillori*, *pyllery*, *pullery* = MD. *pilorijn*, *pellarin*, < OF. *pilori*, *pilorin*, *pilerin*, *pellorin*, F. *pilori* (= Pg. *pelourinho*), a pillory (cf. OF. *pilori*, *pillory*, *pillori*, a ruff or collar so called, encircling the neck like the boards of a pillory); cf. ML. *pilorium*, *piliorium*, *pellorium*, *pilloricum*, *pellericum*, *pilaricum*, etc. (forms which, like the obs. E. *pillary*, *pillery*, etc., simulate a connection with ML. *pilare*, *pilarium*, *pilorus*, a pillar; cf. OF. *pille*, a pillory, another use of *pile*, *pille*, < L. *pila*, a pillar), also *spiliorium*, a pillory (in ML. also called *collistrigium*), < Pr. *espitlori*, a pillory (supposed, from the fact that the F. form is evidently borrowed, to have been first used, as the name first arose, in Provence or Spain); perhaps lit. 'window,' 'peephole,' or 'lookout' (the prisoner with his head confined in the pillory being humorously regarded as looking out of a window or peephole), < ML. as if **speculatorium*, a lookout, place of observation, neut. of L. *speculatorius*, of or belonging to spies or to observation, < *speculator*, one who looks out, a spy, explorer, examiner, ML. (also *spiculator*) also an under-officer, attendant, jailor, tormentor: see *speculator*. Cf. Cat. *espitllera*, a little window, peephole, loophole, < L. *specularia*, pl. (rarely in sing. *specular*), a window, cf. *specularis*, of or belonging to a looking-glass or mirror (or to looking), < *speculum* (> Cat. *espill*), a looking-glass, mirror: see *speculum*. Forms corresponding to *pillory* do not occur in the other languages, the Sp. being *picota*, It. *berlina*, D. *kaak*, G. *pranger*, Dan. *gabestok*, etc.] A frame of wood erected on a post or pole, with movable boards resembling those in the stocks, and holes through which were put the head and hands of an offender, who was thus exposed to public derision.

Pillory.

In Great Britain it was a common punishment appointed for forestallers, users of deceitful weights, common scolds, political offenders, those guilty of perjury, forgery, libel, seditious writings, etc. It was abolished in 1837.

Cros! thou dost no trouthe
On a *pillori* my fruit to pinne,
He hath no spot of Adam sinne.
Holy Rood (E. E. T. S.), viii. 14.

Er he be put on the *pullery* for [that is, in spite of] eny preier, ich hote!
Piers Plowman (C), iii. 216.

Than they were delyuered to the hangman, and fast bounde layde in a carre and brought with trompettes to the place of execution named ye halles, and there set on the *pillery*, and turned four tymes aboute in the syght of all the people.
Berners, tr. of Froissart's Chron., II. cxlvii.

The jeers of a theatre, the *pillory*, and the whipping-post are very near akin.
Watts, Improvement of Mind, i. 18. § 17.

Public executions gone; *pillory* gone—the last man pilloried was in the year 1830.
W. Besant, Fifty Years Ago, p. 263.

pillory (pil'ọ-ri), *v. t.*; pret. and pp. *pilloried*, ppr. *pillorying*. [< *pillory*, *n.*] **1.** To punish by exposure in the pillory.

He [Lilburne] was condemned to be whipped, *pilloried*, and imprisoned.
Hume, Hist. Eng., lii.

Hungering for Puritans to *pillory*.
Macaulay, Hallam's Const. Hist.

Hence—**2.** Figuratively, to expose to ridicule, contempt, abuse, and the like.

pillour†, *n.* Same as *piller*1.

pillow (pil'ō), *n.* [< ME. *pillowe*, *pylowe*, *pelow*, *pelowe*, *pilwe*, *pulwe*, *pylwe*, *pule* (also *pelwere*, *pulwere*), < AS. **pylwe*, found only in the reduced form *pyle*, = MD. *puluwe*, *pulwe*, D. *peluw*, *peuluw* = MLG. *pole*, *pōl*, LG. *poel* = OHG. *phulwi*, *fulwi*, *phuluwi*, *fuluwi*, *phulawi*, *phuliwi*, *phulwo*, MHG. *phulwe*, *pfulwe*, G. *pfühl*, a pillow; derived at a very early period, with omission of the L. term. *-nus*, < L. *pulvinus*, also *pulvinar*, ML. also dim. *pulvillus*, a pillow, bolster, cushion.] **1.** A head-rest used by a person reclining; specifically, a soft elastic cushion filled with down, feathers, curled hair, or other yielding material, used to support the head during repose. In India, China, Japan, and other warm countries of the East a light bamboo or ratan frame with a slightly concave or crescent-shaped top is used as a pillow.

Weariness
Can snore upon the flint, when resty sloth
Finds the down *pillow* hard.
Shak., Cymbeline, iii. 6. 35.

The second sister, she made his bed,
And laid soft *pillows* under his head.
Lay the Bent to the Bonny Broom (Child's Ballads, VIII. 19).

2. A block or support resembling such a cushion in form or use. (*a*) *Naut.*, the block on which the inner end of a bowsprit is supported. (*b*) In *mach.*, a bearing of brass or bronze for the journal of a shaft, carried by a plumber-block. (*c*) The socket of a pivot; an ink or step. (*d*) In certain industrial arts, a supporter or ground upon which to work, often a stuffed cushion, sometimes hard and resistant; especially, in lace-making, the cushion upon which laces are made. The lace-pillow is in England, and

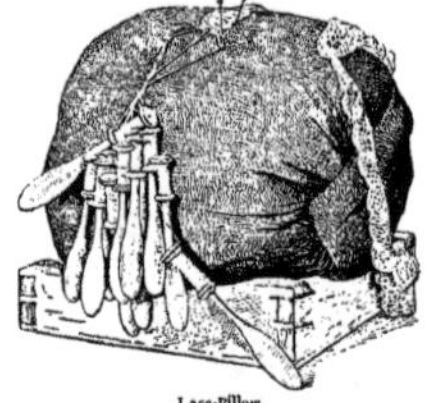
Lace-Pillow.

usually in Belgium, a simple cushion, square or rounded, or rarely oblong, to which the threads are fixed by pins; as the lace is made, the pins have to be taken out and the fabric shifted. In central France the pillow is a box covered with cloth and slightly stuffed on the outside, sloping toward the worker, and having at the side furthest from the worker a cylinder or drum to which the threads are attached by pins, and which can be revolved, carrying the finished lace with it. Another form of pillow is a cylinder set horizontally on a stand high enough to be placed upon the floor in front of the worker.

3. A kind of plain fustian.—**Pillow of a plow**, a cross-piece of wood which serves to raise or lower the beam.

pillow (pil'ō), *v.* [< *pillow*, *n.*] **I.** *trans.* To rest or place on or as on a pillow for support.

So, when the sun in bed,
Curtain'd with cloudy red,
Pillows his chin upon an orient wave.
Milton, Nativity, l. 231.

They lay down to rest,
With corselet laced,
Pillowed on buckler cold and hard.
Scott, L. of L. M., i. 4.

And thou shalt *pillow* on my breast,
While heavenly breathings float around.
J. R. Drake, Culprit Fay, p. 55.

II. *intrans.* To rest the head on or as on a pillow. [Rare.]

pillow-bar (pil'ō-bär), *n.* The ground or filling of pillow-lace, consisting of irregular threads or groups of threads drawn from one part of the pattern to another. These bars may either be plain or have a minute pearl-edge.

pillow-bear, *n.* See *pillow-bier*.

pillow-bier, pillow-beer (pil'ō-bēr), *n.* [Also *pillow-bear*; < ME. *pillowebere*, *pilwebeer*, *pilwebere*, *pelowbere*; < AS. **pylwe*, *pyle*, a pillow, + *bǣr*, a couch, pallet, also a bier: see *pillow* and *bier*.] A pillow-case.

For in his male he hadde a *pilwebeer*,
Which that he seide was oure lady veyl.
Chaucer, Gen. Prol. to C. T., l. 694.

Do not make holes in the *pillow-beers*.
Middleton, Women beware Women, iv. 2.

Your pillow is clean, and your *pillow-beer*,
For I washed 'em in Styx last night, son.
Lamb, Satan in Search of a Wife, i. 9.

pillow-block (pil'ō-blok), *n.* Same as *plumber-block*.—**Ball-and-socket pillow-block.** See *ball*1.

pillow-case (pil'ō-kās), *n.* A movable case or covering which is drawn over a pillow.

When you put a clean *pillowcase* on your lady's pillow, be sure to fasten it well with corking pins.
Swift, Directions to Servants, Chambermaid.

pillow-cup (pil'ē-kup), *n.* A cup or drink taken before going to bed; a "nightcap."

The landlord . . . commanded his waiter Geoffrey to hand round to the company a sleeping-drink, or *pillow-cup*, of distilled water mingled with spices.
Scott, Anne of Geierstein, xix.

pillow-lace (pil'ō-lās), *n.* See *lace*.

pillow-linen (pil'ō-lin″en), *n.* Linen especially made or used for pillow-cases.

pillow-pipe (pil'ō-pīp), *n.* A last pipe smoked before going to bed. [Rare.]

I sat with him whilst he smoked his *pillow-pipe*, as his phrase is.
Fielding, Amelia, iii. 2.

pillow-sham (pil'ō-sham), *n.* An embroidered or otherwise ornamented cover to be laid over a pillow when not in use.

Pillow-shams—one of the hostess's troublesome little household fopperies—neatly folded out of the way.
The Century, XXXVII. 786.

pillow-slip (pil'ō-slip), *n.* An outer covering or case for a pillow; a pillow-case.

pillow-word (pil'ō-wėrd), *n.* A meaningless expression prefixed in Japanese poetry to other words for the sake of euphony. [Rare.]

Almost every word of note has some *pillow-word* on which it may, so to speak, rest its head; and dictionaries of them are often resorted to by the unready Japanese versifier, just as rhyming dictionaries come to the aid of the poetasters of modern Europe.
B. H. Chamberlain, Class. Poetry of the Japanese, [Int., p. 5.

pillowy (pil'ọ̄-i), *a.* [< *pillow* + *-y*1.] Like a pillow; soft; yielding.

Shapes from the invisible world, unearthly singing
From out the middle air, from flowery nests,
And from the *pillowy* silkiness that rests
Full in the speculation of the stars.
Keats, I Stood Tiptoe upon a Little Hill.

pillpate† (pil'pāt), *n.* [< *pill*2, *v.*, + obj. *pate*; or for *pilled pate*.] A shaven head; hence, a friar or monk.

These smeared *pill-pates*, I would say prelates, first of all accused him, and afterward pronounced the sentence of death upon him.
Becon, ii. 315.

pill-tile (pil'tīl), *n.* A metal plate having semicylindrical grooves upon its upper surface, presenting a series of upwardly projecting edges. It is used with a correspondingly grooved roller to cut a small roll of prepared material into equal parts, which are subsequently rounded into pills. See *pill*3.

pill-willet (pil'wil″et), *n.* [Imitative.] The willet, *Symphemia semipalmata*. Also *will-willet*, *pill-will-willet*.

pill-worm (pil'wėrm), *n.* A gally-worm or thousand-legs; a pill-milleped. See *Glomeridæ*.

pillwort (pil'wėrt), *n.* A plant of the genus *Pilularia*; especially, *P. globulifera*, the creeping pillwort of Europe: named from the pellet-like involucres containing the fruit.

pilniewink (pil'ni-wingk), *n.* See *pinnywinkle*.

She shall avouch what it was that she hath given to the wretch Dryfesdale, or the *pilniewinks* and thumbikins shall wrench it out of her finger-joints.
Scott, Abbot, xxxii.

Piloboleæ (pī-lọ̄-bō'lẹ̄-ē), *n. pl.* [NL., < *Pilobolus* + *-eæ*.] A small subfamily of phycomycetous fungi of the family *Mucoraceæ*, having many-spored sporangia.

Pilobolus (pī-lǫ-bō'lus), *n.* [NL., < (?) Gr. πῖλος, felt, + βῶλος, a clod, lump: see *bole*², *bolus*.] A genus of phycomycetous fungi, typical of the subfamily *Piloboleæ*. *P. crystallinus*, the commonest species, occurs on animal dung. Its glutinous spores are forcibly ejected, often to a distance of ten feet.

pilocarpine (pī-lǫ-kär'pin), *n.* [< *pilocarpus* + *-ine*².] An alkaloid ($C_{11}H_{16}N_2O_2$) isolated from pilocarpus, which it resembles in its medicinal properties.

Pilocarpus (pī-lǫ-kär'pus), *n.* [NL. (Vahl, 1796), < Gr. πῖλος, a cap, + καρπός, fruit.] **1.** A genus of polypetalous shrubs of the order *Rutaceæ* and tribe *Zanthoxyleæ*, characterized by the small calyx-teeth, valvate petals, versatile anthers, smooth ovary-lobes, and one-seeded cells, and by the complete numerical symmetry of the flower in circles of fours and fives. The 12 species are natives of the West Indies and tropical America. They bear pellucid-dotted leaves, either thin or coriaceous, pinnate or of one to three leaflets, alternate, opposite, or whorled. The numerous small green or purple flowers form very long terminal or axillary racemes.
2. [*l. c.*] The leaflets of *P. pennatifolius*, a very powerful diaphoretic medicine. Also known as *jaborandi*, though this word has been applied to various pungent sudorific plants.

pilori-rat (pi-lō'ri-rat), *n.* A book-name of the Cuban hutia-conga, *Capromys pilorides*.

Pilori-rat (*Capromys pilorides*).

pilose (pī'lōs), *a.* [Also *pilous*; < L. *pilosus*, hairy, < *pilus*, hair: see *pile*⁴.] Covered with hair; hairy; furry; pilous; especially, covered with fine or soft hair.

pilosity (pi-los'i-ti), *n.* [< *pilose* + *-ity*.] The state of being pilose or pilous; hairiness.

> *Pilosity* is incident to orifices of moisture.
> *Bacon*, Advancement of Learning, ii. 169.

pilot (pī'lot), *n.* [Early mod. E. also *pilotte*, *pylate*; < OF. *pilot*, F. *pilote* = Sp. Pg. *piloto* = It. *piloto*, *pilota* (ML. *pilotus*, *pilota*), a pilot; cf. MD. *pilote*, *piloot*, *pijloot*, *pijlloot* (Kilian), *peilloot* (Sewel), D. *piloot* = MLG. *pilote*, a pilot; origin uncertain; appar., through OF. *piloter*, *pilotier*, "to sound the depth of water with a line and plummet" (Cotgrave), < MD. **peylloot*, **peilloot*, D. *peillood*, a sounding-lead (= G. *peil-loth*, sounding-lead, plummet), < *peylen*, *pijlen* (Kilian), D. *peilen* (= G. *peilen*, take soundings) (contr. of MD. *pegelen*, measure the capacity of anything, < *pegel*, the capacity of a vessel's gage), + *loot*, D. *lood* = G. *loth* = E. *lead*: see *lead*².] **1.** The steersman of a ship; that one of a ship's crew who has charge of the helm and the ship's course; specifically, one who works a ship into and out of harbor, or through a channel or passage. In this specific sense the pilot is a person possessing local knowledge of shallows, rocks, currents, channels, etc., licensed by public authority to steer vessels into and out of particular harbors, or along certain coasts, etc., and rendering such special service for a compensation, fixed usually with reference to the draft of water and the distance.

> And whanne we shuld a take the Porte, Sodenly fell down and Beyde the *Pylate* of our shippe, which we call lodysman. *Torkington*, Diarie of Eng. Travell, p. 60.

> Times answerable, like waters after a tempest, full of working and swelling, though without extremity of storm; but well passed through by the wisdom of the *pilot*.
> *Bacon*, Advancement of Learning, ii. 131.

> Passengers in a ship always submit to their *pilot's* discretion, but especially in a storm. *South*, Sermons, X. v.

> The city remaining . . . without goverument of magistrate, like a ship left without a *pilot*.
> *North*, tr. of Plutarch, p. 601.

> The high-shoed ploughman, should he quit the land
> To take the *pilot's* rudder in his hand, . . .
> The gods would leave him to the waves and wind,
> And think all shame was lost in human kind.
> *Dryden*, tr. of Persius's Satires, v. 148.

2. A guide; a director of the course of others; one who has the conduct of any affair requiring knowledge and judgment.

> All must obey
> The counsell of the *pilot*, & still stand
> Prest at his service, when he doth command.
> *Times' Whistle* (E. E. T. S.), p. 144.

3. Same as *cow-catcher*. See cut under *passenger-engine*. [U. S.]—**4.** A book of sailing-directions.—**5.** Pilot-cloth.

> Linings, rugs, wraps, and heavy friezes, *pilots*, druggets, blankets, etc., in which bulk and warmth more than wear-resisting qualities are required. *Encyc. Brit.*, XXIV. 661.

6. The pilot-fish.—**7.** The black-bellied plover, *Squatarola helvetica*. *G. Trumbull*. [Virginia coast.]—**Coasting-pilot.** Same as *coast-pilot*.—**Pilot's water**, any part of the sea or of a river in which a pilot must be employed. (See also *branch-pilot*.)

pilot (pī'lot), *v. t.* [< F. *piloter*, pilot; from the noun.] To steer; direct the course of, especially through an intricate or perilous passage; guide through dangers or difficulties.

> Where the people are well-educated, the art of *piloting* a state is best learned from the writings of Plato.
> *Bp. Berkeley*, Siris, § 332.

> If all do not join now to save the good old ship of the Union on this voyage, nobody will have a chance to *pilot* her on another voyage. *Lincoln*, in Raymond, p. 89.

pilotage (pī'lot-āj), *n.* [< F. *pilotage*, < *piloter*, pilot: see *pilot*, *v.*] **1.** The act of piloting; direction of a pilot; guidance.

> Under his *pilotage* they anchored on the first of November close to the Isthmus of Darien.
> *Macaulay*, Hist. Eng., xxiv.

2. The employment or services of a pilot: as, incompetent *pilotage*.—**3**†. The knowledge of coasts, rocks, bars, and channels.

> We must for ever abandon the Indies, and lose all our knowledge and *pilotage* of that part of the world. *Raleigh*.

4. The fee or remuneration paid or payable to a pilot for his services.—**Compulsory pilotage**, compulsory employment of pilots in accordance with local law.—**Pilotage authority**, a body of men appointed to test the qualifications of applicants for pilots' licenses, and to grant or suspend such licenses, etc.—**Pilotage district**, the limit of jurisdiction of a pilotage authority.

pilotaxitic (pī"lǫ-tak-sit'ik), *a.* [Irreg. < Gr. πῖλος, felt, + τάξις, arrangement, + *-ite*² + *-ic*.] In *lithol.*, a term introduced by Rosenbusch to designate a holocrystalline structure said by him to be characteristic of certain rocks, and especially of the porphyrites, in which the ground-mass consists of slender lath-shaped microliths of feldspar, with which are frequently connected the phenomena of fluidal structure, amygdules, and the presence of minute vitreous scales.

pilot-balloon (pī'lot-ba-lön"), *n.* A small balloon sent up in advance of a larger one to ascertain the direction and strength of the wind.

pilot-bird (pī'lot-bėrd), *n.* A bird found in the Caribbean Islands: so called because its presence at sea indicates to seamen their approach to these islands.

pilot-boat (pī'lot-bōt), *n.* A boat used by pilots for cruising off shore to meet incoming ships. On the coast of the United States pilot-boats are handy, weatherly schooner-rigged vessels, and frequently

Coast Pilot-boat of the United States.

cruise at a long distance off shore; they are distinguished by a flag and by a number painted conspicuously on the mainsail, and at night by a flare-up light, in addition to a masthead light.

pilot-bread (pī'lot-bred), *n.* Same as *ship-biscuit*.

pilot-cloth (pī'lot-klôth), *n.* A heavy woolen cloth, such as is used by pilots for pea-jackets.

piloteer†, *n.* [< *pilot* + *-eer*.] A pilot.

> Whereby the wand'ring *Piloteer*
> His course in gloomy Nights doth steer.
> *Howell*, Letters, iii. 4.

pilot-engine (pī'lot-en"jin), *n.* A locomotive engine sent on before a railway-train to see the way is clear, especially as a precursor to a train conveying important personages.

pilot-fish (pī'lot-fish), *n.* **1.** A pelagic carangoid fish, *Naucrates ductor*, found in all warm seas, and occasionally on the Atlantic coast of the United States. It somewhat resembles a mackerel, being of fusiform shape, bluish color, with from five to seven dark vertical bars, and the first dorsal fin represented by a few spines. It is a foot or more long. The pilot-fish is supposed by some to have been the pompilus of the ancients, but the traditions respecting it have little foundation in fact. The generic name *Naucrates* was applied by the ancients to species of *Echeneis* and other fishes with a suctorial disk. See cut under *Naucrates*.
2. *pl.* A term extended to all the *Carangidæ*. *D. S. Jordan*.—**3.** A remora or sucking-fish of the family *Echeneididæ*, as *Echeneis naucrates*. [This use of the term is nearer the original meaning of *Naucrates*.]—**4.** A coregonid, *Coregonus quadrilateralis*, the Menomonee white-fish or shad-waiter of New England, some of the Great Lakes, and parts of British America to Alaska.

pilot-flag (pī'lot-flag), *n.* The flag hoisted at the fore by a vessel needing a pilot. In vessels flying the United States flag the pilot-flag is the union-jack. It varies in other nationalities, but is always hoisted at the fore.

pilot-house (pī'lot-hous), *n.* An inclosed place or house on deck which shelters the steering-gear and the pilot or helmsman. In modern sea-going steam-vessels this is usually situated in some commanding position forward, and generally in connection with the officers' bridge. In a very large proportion of vessels, however, there is no pilot-house, the steersmen and steering-gear being left exposed. Also called *wheel-house*.

pilotism (pī'lot-izm), *n.* [< *pilot* + *-ism*.] Pilotage; skill in piloting. *Cotgrave*. [Rare.]

pilot-jack (pī'lot-jak), *n.* A union or other flag hoisted by a vessel as a signal for a pilot.

pilot-jacket (pī'lot-jak"et), *n.* A pea-jacket, such as is worn by seamen. See *pea-jacket*.

pilot-light (pī'lot-līt), *n.* A very small gas-light kept burning beside a large burner, so that when the flow through the main burner is turned on it will be automatically lighted by the pilot-light. It is usually protected by a shield from being accidentally blown out. See *by-pass*.

pilotry (pī'lot-ri), *n.* Same as *pilotism*.

pilot-snake (pī'lot-snāk), *n.* A harmless snake of the United States, *Coluber obsoletus*.

pilotweed (pī'lot-wēd), *n.* Same as *compass-plant*.

pilot-whale (pī'lot-hwāl), *n.* Same as *caaing-whale*.

pilour†, *n.* See *piller*¹.

pilous (pī'lus), *a.* [< L. *pilosus*, hairy: see *pilose*.] **1.** Covered with hair; hairy; pilose.

> That hair is not poison, though taken in a great quantity, is proved by the excrements of voracious dogs, which is seen to be very *pilous*.
> *J. Robinson*, Eudoxa (1658), p. 124.

2. Consisting of hair; hair-like; piliform: as, a *pilous* covering.
Also *pileous*.

pilula (pil'ū-lä), *n.*; pl. *pilulæ* (-lē). [L.: see *pilule*.] In *phar.*, a pill.

pilular (pil'ū-lär), *a.* [< NL. **pilularis*, < L. *pilula*, a pilule: see *pilule*.] Of or pertaining to or characteristic of pills: as, a *pilular* mass; a *pilular* form; a *pilular* consistency.

Pilularia (pil-ū-lā'ri-ä), *n.* [NL. (Vaillant, 1717), so called in allusion to the shape of the reproductive organs; < **pilularis*, like a pill: see *pilular*.] A genus of vascular cryptogamous plants of the order *Marsileaceæ*; the pillworts. They are inconspicuous submerged plants with widely creeping slender rhizomes, with a filiform leaf from the upper side and a tuft of root-fibers from the lower side of each node. Seven species are known, of which only one, *P. Americana*, is found in North America. See *pepper-grass*, 2, and *pillwort*.

pilule (pil'ūl), *n.* [= F. *pilule* = Pg. *pilula*, < L. *pilula*, a pill, dim. of *pila*, a ball. Cf. *pill*³.] A little pill or pellet.

pilulous (pil'ū-lus), *a.* [< *pilule* + *-ous*.] Pertaining to or resembling a pill; pilular; hence, small; inconsiderable; trifling. [Rare.]

> Has any one ever pinched into its *pilulous* smallness the cobweb of pre-matrimonial acquaintanceship?
> *George Eliot*, Middlemarch, ii.

pilum (pī'lum), *n.*; pl. *pila* (-lä). [L.: see *pile*¹.] **1.** A heavy javelin used by the Roman foot-soldiers.—**2.** Any javelin used by barbarous races with whom the Romans had to do, as by the Franks, Burgundians, and others.—**3.** In *phar.*, an instrument used to triturate substances in a mortar; a pestle.

pilus (pī'lus), *n.*; pl. *pili* (-lī). [L., a hair, hair: see *pile*⁴.] **1.** In *bot.*, one of the fine slender bodies, like hair, covering some plants.—**2.** In *zoöl.*, a hair or hair-like body, especially a hair in any way distinguished from those which collectively cover the body.—**Pili gossypii**, cotton.—**Pili tactiles**, tactile hairs. See *hair*[1].

pilwet, *n.* A Middle English form of *pillow*.

pily (pī'li), *a.* [< OF. *pile, < pile, a pile: see *pile*[2].] In *her.*, divided into a number of piles set side by side. Some qualifying term expresses their position if they do not point in a parallel direction and downward. The number of piles must also be mentioned in the blazon.—**Barry pily.** See *barry*[2].—**Pily paly**, in *her.*, pily of the ordinary sort—that is, having the small piles reaching from the top to the bottom of the shield. Also *paly pily*, *palissé*.

pimaric (pī-mar'ik), *a.* [< L. *pi(nus)*, pine, + *mar(itimus)*, maritime, + *-ic.*] Derived from or occurring in the maritime pine: as, *pimaric* acid.

Pimelea (pī-mē'lē-ä), *n.* [NL. (Banks, 1801), so called with ref. to the oily seeds and leaves; < Gr. πιμελή, fat.] A genus of apetalous shrubs of the order *Thymelæaceæ* and tribe *Euthymelæeæ*, known by the two stamens, all others of the family having four, eight, or more. There are 76 species, natives of Australia and New Zealand, slender branching shrubs with tough stringy bark. They bear small opposite or scattered leaves, and white, pink, or yellow flowers in terminal or axillary involucrate clusters, each flower four-lobed, funnel-shaped, and without the appendages usual in the order, followed by a small fruit with thick rind and berry-like pulp. Many species are cultivated as beautiful greenhouse evergreens, of about 3 feet in height, under the name *rice-flower*. Others are known in Australia as *toughbark*, and can be used for textile purposes, especially *P. axiflora*, the curryjong, a tall smooth shrub. Several attain a height of about 10 feet, as *P. drupacea*, the Victorian bird-cherry.

Pimelepteridæ (pim"e-lep-ter'i-dē), *n. pl.* [NL., < *Pimelepterus* + *-idæ.*] A family of percoideous acanthopterygian fishes, typified by the genus *Pimelepterus*. The body is oval, compressed, and developed nearly equally above and below; the scales are small, adherent, and extending over the vertical fins; the lateral line is uninterrupted; and the teeth are generally incisorial or compressed. The species are inhabitants of tropical and temperate seas. Also called *Cyphosidæ*.

Pimelepterinæ (pim-e-lep-te-rī'nē), *n. pl.* [NL., < *Pimelepterus* + *-inæ.*] A subfamily of *Sparidæ*, typified by the genus *Pimelepterus*. They have the front teeth incisiform or lanceolate, and with horizontal backwardly projecting bases, behind which are smaller ones; vomerine teeth are present; and the soft fins are densely scaly. All the species are by some referred to one genus, *Pimelepterus*, while others distinguish two or more additional genera.

Pimelepterus (pim-e-lep'te-rus), *n.* [NL. (Lacépède, 1802), < Gr. πιμελή, fat, + πτερόν, wing, πτέρυξ, wing, fin.] The typical genus of *Pimelepteridæ*, having the skin and scales en-

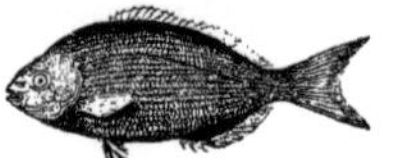
Bermuda Chub (*Pimelepterus* or *Cyphosus bosci*).

croaching on the dorsal and anal fins, which are consequently thickened, whence the name. These fishes are partly herbivorous, and the species are numerous in all warm seas. *P.* (or *Cyphosus*) *bosci* extends from the Isthmus of Panama along the Atlantic coast as far north as Massachusetts.

pimelite (pim'e-līt), *n.* [< Gr. πιμελή, fat, + λίθος, stone.] A mineral of an apple-green color, fat and unctuous to the touch, tender, and not fusible by the blowpipe. It is a hydrous silicate containing some nickel.

pimelitis (pim-e-lī'tis), *n.* [NL., < Gr. πιμελή, fat, + *-itis.*] Inflammation of adipose tissue.

pimelode (pim'e-lōd), *n.* Any catfish of the genus *Pimelodus*.

Pimelodinæ (pim"e-lō-dī'nē), *n. pl.* [NL., < *Pimelodus* + *-inæ.*] A subfamily of catfishes of the family *Siluridæ*, typified by the genus *Pimelodus*, having the anterior and posterior nostrils remote from each other and without barbels. Some have a long spatulate snout, and in others the adipose fin is highly developed. They are characteristic of tropical waters, especially of South America, where they represent the catfishes of North America. A few species are African.

pimelodine (pi-mel'ō-din), *a.* and *n.* **I.** *a.* Belonging to the subfamily *Pimelodinæ*.

II. *n.* A catfish of the subfamily *Pimelodinæ*.

Pimelodus (pim-e-lō'dus), *n.* [NL. (Lacépède), < Gr. πιμελώδης, fatty, < πιμελή, fat, + εἶδος, form.] A genus of silurids, to which very different limits have been assigned. In the old authors it was a very heterogeneous group, embracing a vast number of species and including the common catfishes of the North American lakes and streams, as well as those of the South American, and various others. It was gradually reduced, and is now restricted to South American and Central American forms with two maxillary

Pimelodus maculatus.

and four mental barbels, typical of the subfamily *Pimelodinæ*.

piment†, *n.* [< ME. *piment*, *pyment*, < OF. *piment*, < ML. *pigmentum*, spiced wine, spice: see *pigment*.] Wine with a mixture of spice or honey, once a favorite beverage. Also *pigment*.

He sente hire *pyment*, meeth, and spiced ale.
Chaucer, Miller's Tale, l. 192.

pimenta[1] (pi-men'tä), *n.* Same as *pimento*.

Pimenta[2] (pi-men'tä), *n.* [NL. (Lindley, 1821), < Sp. *pimenta*, allspice (a related tree): see *pimento*.] A genus of fragrant trees of the myrtle family, order *Myrtaceæ* and tribe *Myrteæ*, characterized by the circular or spirally twisted embryo, and from one to six ovules pendulous from the summit of each of the two cells of the ovary. There are 5 species, natives of tropical America. They bear large and coriaceous feather-veined leaves, and many small flowers in axillary cymes. For *P. acris*, called *black cinnamon*, etc., see *bayberry*, 3, *bay-rum*, and *wild clove* (under *clove*[1]). For the important *P. officinalis*, see *pimento*.

pimento (pi-men'tō), *n.* [Also *pimenta*; < Sp. *pimiento*, the pepper-plant, capsicum, *pimienta*, the fruit of this plant, applied also to *Pimenta officinalis*, Jamaica pepper, = Pg. *pimento*, *pimenta* = F. *piment*, pepper (capsicum), < ML. *pigmentum*, spice: see *pigment*.] **1.** Allspice, the berry of *Pimenta officinalis* (*Eugenia Pimenta*), a tree, native of the West Indies, but cul-

Branch of Pimento (*Pimenta officinalis*), with Fruits.
a, flower; *b*, flower in longitudinal section, the stamens removed; *c*, fruit.

tivated almost exclusively in Jamaica, whence called *Jamaica pepper*. The unripe berries, which are of about the size of a pea, are dried in the sun. The shell incloses two seeds, which are roundish and dark-brown, and have a weak aromatic taste and smell, thought to resemble a mixture of those of cinnamon, cloves, and nutmeg, whence the name *allspice*. Pimento is a warm, aromatic stimulant, used chiefly as an adjuvant to tonics and purgatives. Both the fruit and the leaves yield an essential oil closely resembling oil of cloves and often substituted for it. The name *pimento* is sometimes used to include *P. acris*.

2. The tree yielding this spice, a beautiful much-branching evergreen, 30 feet in height.

pimento-walk (pi-men'tō-wâk), *n.* In Jamaica, a plantation of allspice or Jamaica pepper.

pimgenet† (pim'je-net), *n.* [Also *pimgennet*, *pimginit*, *pinjinnet*; origin obscure.] A pimple on the face. [Slang.]

Is it not a manly exercise to stand licking his lips into rubies, painting his cheeks into cherries, parching his *pimginits*, carbuncles, and buboes?
Dunton's Ladies Dictionary, 1694. (*Nares.*)

pimlico (pim'li-kō), *n.* [Imitative. Cf. *pemblico*.] The Australian friar-bird, *Tropidorhynchus corniculatus*: so called from its cry. See *leatherhead*, 2, and cut under *friar-bird*.

pimp[1] (pimp), *n.* [Origin unknown; according to Skeat perhaps orig. 'a fellow,' < F. *pimper*, dress up smartly (= Pr. *pimpar*, *pipar*, render elegant); cf. *pimpant*, ppr., smart, spruce; appar. a nasalized form of *piper*, pipe, beguile, cheat, also excel; cf. Pr. *pimpa*, a pipe, bird-call, snare: see *pipe*[1]. This explanation is, however, inadequate; the word is appar. of low slang origin, without any recorded basis.] One who provides others with the means and opportunity of gratifying their lusts; a pander.

pimp[1] (pimp), *v. i.* [< *pimp*[1], *n.*] To provide for others the means of gratifying lust; pander.

But when to sin our biassed nature leans,
The careful Devil is still at hand with means,
And providently *pimps* for ill desires.
Dryden, Abs. and Achit., i. 81.

pimp[2] (pimp), *n.* [Origin obscure.] A small bavin. See the quotation.

Here they make those . . . small light bavins which are used in taverns in London to light their faggots, and are called in the taverns a Brush, and by the wood-men *Pimps*.
Defoe, Tour thro' Great Britain, I. 138. (*Davies.*)

pimpernel (pim'pėr-nel), *n.* [Early mod. E. *pympernel*; < ME. *pympyrnel*, *pimpernol*, *pympernolle* = D. *pimpernel* = MHG. *pimpenelle*, *bebenelle*, etc., G. *pimpernelle*, < OF. *pimpernelle*, F. *pimpinelle*, *pimprenelle* = Cat. *pampinella* = Sp. *pimpinela* = Pg. *pimpinella* = It. *pimpinella*, Piedmontese *pampinela*, pimpernel, < ML. *pimpinella*, *pimpernella*, *pinpenella*, *penpinela*, also *pampinella* and *pampinaria* (simulating L. *pampinus*, a tendril), with unorig. *m* or *n*; also *pipinella*, *pipenella*, *pippinella*, *pippenella*, *piponella*, *pybenella*, *pipenula*, etc., with initial *p* (due to influence of the following *p*) for orig. initial *b*; also *bipinella*, *bibinella*, *bimpinella*, *bibanella*, prop. **bipennella* or *bipennula*, pimpernel (also burnet), lit. 'the two-winged little plant,' so called by confusion with burnet, which has from two to four scale-like bracts at the base of the calyx; < L. *bipennis*, two-winged: see *bipennate*.] **1**†. The garden-burnet, *Poterium Sanguisorba*.—**2.** The burnet-saxifrage, *Pimpinella Saxifraga*.—**3**†. The selfheal, *Brunella vulgaris*.—**4.** A plant, *Anagallis arvensis*, of the primrose family, sometimes distinguished as *red* or *scarlet pimpernel*, a native of the northern Old World and introduced into the United States and elsewhere. It is a neat procumbent herb with a wheel-shaped corolla, red in color, varying to purple, white, or blue. The flowers close at the approach of bad weather, whence it is named *poor man's* (or *shepherd's*) *weather-glass*; it is also called *red chickweed*, *John-go-to-bed-at-noon*, etc. The name is extended also to the other species of the genus, as *A. tenella*, the bog-pimpernel, and *A. cœrulea* (*A. Monelli*), the Italian or blue pimpernel, a garden species from southern Europe, with large flowers, deep-blue shaded with pink. See cut under *circumscissile*.—**Bastard pimpernel.** Same as *chaffweed*.—**False pimpernel.** See *Ilysanthes*.—**Italian pimpernel.** See def. 4, above.—**Sea- or seaside-pimpernel**, a sandwort, *Arenaria peploides*.—**Water-pimpernel**, the brookweed, *Samolus Valerandi*. See *Samolus*. The name has also been applied to *Veronica Beccabunga* and *V. Anagallis*.—**Yellow pimpernel.** See *Lysimachia*.

Pimpinella (pim-pi-nel'ä), *n.* [NL. (Rivinus, 1699), < ML. *pimpinella*, pimpernel: see *pimpernel*.] A genus of umbelliferous plants of the tribe *Ammineæ* and subtribe *Euammineæ*, characterized by the narrow ribs of the fruit, the two-cleft carpophore, and the usually obsolete bracts and calyx-teeth. There are 75 species, widely distributed throughout the northern hemisphere and South Africa, with a few in South America. They are usually smooth perennial herbs, with pinnate or decompound leaves, and compound umbels of white or yellow flowers. For the three most important species, see *anise*, *sweet cumin* (under *cumin*), *pimpernel*, *breakstone*, and *ninsi*.

pimping (pim'ping), *a.* [Cf. G. *pimpelig*, *pimpelich*, sickly, weak, little, < *pimpeln*, be weak, moan; cf. *pim*, imitative of the sound of a bell. Cf. also *pimp*[2].] Little; petty; sickly. [Colloq.]

He had no paltry arts, no *pimping* ways. *Crabbe.*

"Was I so little?" asked Margaret. "Yes, and *pimpin'* enough."
S. Judd, Margaret, i. 4.

Pimpla (pim'plä), *n.* [NL. (Fabricius, 1804), < Gr. Πίμπλα, usually Πίμπλεια, Pimplea, a city and fountain in Pieria sacred to the Muses.]

Ring-legged Pimpla (*Pimpla annulipes*).
♂, male abdomen; ♀, female. (Lines show natural size.)

1. A genus of pupivorous hymenopterous insects of the family *Ichneumonidæ*, typical of a subfamily *Pimplinæ*. *P. annulipes* preys on the codling-moth (*Carpocapsa pomonella*), the cotton-worm (*Aletia xylina*), and other destructive insects. *P. manifestator* is a large European species parasitic on certain bees. **2.** [*l. c.*] A member of this genus.

pimple (pim′pl), *n.* [Early mod. E. also *pimpel, pumple*; < ME. **pimpel* (?) (not found), perhaps a nasalized form of AS. **pipel*, a pimple, blister, found only in the rare verb *piplian, pypelian*, blister, grow pimply, used only in ppr. *pipligende, pypelgende*, pimply, appar. < L. *papula*, a blister, pimple: see *papula*. For the form, cf. MD. *pimpel, pepel*, a butterfly, < L. *papilio*, a butterfly. The alleged AS. **pinpel*, a pimple (Lye), is an error for *winpel*, a wimple. The W. *pwmp*, a knob, bump (see *bump*²), and F. *pompette*, a pimple, are not connected.] **1.** A small inflammatory dermal tumor or swelling; a papule or pustule, such as are seen in acne.—**2.** A little elevation or protuberance, of any kind, resembling a pimple.

> So do not pluck that flower, lady,
> That has these *pimples* gray.
> *Tom Linn* (Child's Ballads, I. 268).

> On poor pasture land, which has never been rolled, and has not been much trampled on by animals, the whole surface is sometimes dotted with little *pimples*, through and on which grass grows; and these *pimples* consist of old worm-castings. *Darwin*, Vegetable Mould, p. 256.

3†. A jolly boon companion.

> The Sun 's a good *Pimple*, an honest Soaker, he has a Cellar at your Antipodes.
> *Congreve*, Way of the World, iv. 10.

Pimple in a bent†, something very small.

> I could lay down heere sundrye examples, were yt not I should bee thoght ouer curious by prying owt a *pimple in a bent*. *Stanihurst*, Æneid, Ded. (*Davies*.)

pimple (pim′pl), *v. t.*; pret. and pp. *pimpled*, ppr. *pimpling*. [< *pimple*, *n.*] To cover with pimples; cause to abound with pimples; spot or blotch as with pimples.

> Yet you will *pimple* your souls with oaths, till you make them as well-favoured as your faces.
> *Middleton*, Black Book.

pimple-metal (pim′pl-met″al), *n.* See *metal*.

pimple-mite (pim′pl-mit), *n.* A parasitic mite or acarine, *Demodex folliculorum*, occurring in the sebaceous follicles of the face.

pimp-like (pimp′lik), *a.* Like a pimp; vile; infamous; mean.

pimply (pim′pli), *a.* [< *pimple* + *-y*¹.] Covered with pimples; spotted.

pimpship (pimp′ship), *n.* [< *pimp* + *-ship*.] The office, occupation, or person of a pimp. *Imp. Dict.*

pimp-whiskin† (pimp′hwis″kin), *n.* A person of low habits or character. *Ford*, Fancies, i. 3. [Contemptuous.]

pin¹ (pin), *n.* [< ME. *pinne, pynne*, a pin, peg, bolt, bar, peak, < AS. *pinn*, a pin or peg (occurs once, in *hæpsan pinn*, the pin or bolt of a hasp), = MD. *pinne*, D. *pin*, a pin, peg, = MLG. *pinne*, LG. *pinne, pin*, > G. *pinn*, m., *pinne*, f., a pin, peg, = Icel. *pinni* = Sw. *pinne*, a peg, = Dan. *pind*, a pointed stick, = Ir. Gael. *pinne*, a pin, peg, spigot, = W. *pin*, a pin, style, pen, < ML. *pinna*, a pin, nail, peak, pinnacle, probe, appar. later uses of L. *pinna, penna*, feather, wing, fin, pen: see *pen*². The transition from 'feather' to 'pin' (a slender or pointed instrument) appears to have been through 'pen,' a quill, to 'pen,' a style or stylus, hence any slender or pointed instrument: see *pen*².] **1.** A wooden or metal peg or bolt used to fasten or hold a thing in place, fasten things together, or as a point of attachment or support. (*a*) The bolt of a door.

> Then take the sword from my scabbard,
> And slowly lift the *pin*;
> And you may swear, and safe your aith,
> Ye never let Clerk Saunders in.
> *Clerk Saunders* (Child's Ballads, II. 46).

(*b*) A peg or bolt serving to keep a wheel on its axle; a linch-pin. (*c*) A peg on the side of a boat, serving to keep the oar in place; a thole. Also called *thole-pin, boat-pin*. (*d*) A peg of a stringed musical instrument. See *peg*, 1 (*c*).

> Ye'll take a lith o' my little finger bane, . . .
> And ye'll make a *pin* to your fiddle then.
> *The Bonny Bows o' London* (Child's Ballads, II. 362).

(*e*) A peg used to stop a hole.

> Yf thou will haue frute of diuers colours, thou shalt make an hole in a tree ny the roete euyn to the pithe of the tree, and anon doo in yᵉ hole good asure of Almayne so that it be ny full, and stoppe the hole wel and luste wᵗ a short *pynne*. *Arnold's Chron.* (1502), ed. 1811, p. 170.

(*f*) In *mach.*, a short shaft, sometimes forming a bolt, a part of which serves as a journal. (*g*) The axis of a sheave. (*h*) In *joinery*, the projecting part of a dovetail, which fits into the socket or receiving part. (*i*) That part of the stem of a key which enters the lock.

2. A peg, nail, or stud serving to mark a position, step, or degree; hence, a notch; a step; a degree.

> He will
> Imagine only that he shall be cheated,
> And he is cheated; all still comes to passe
> He 's but one *pin* above a natural.
> *W. Cartwright*, The Ordinary, ii. 3.

Specifically—(*a*†) One of a row of pegs let into a drinking-vessel to regulate the quantity which each person was to drink; hence, a drinking-bout; joviality. See *on a merry pin*, below.

> Edgar, away with *pins* i' th' cup
> To spoil our drinking whole ones up.
> *Holborn Drollery* (1673), p. 76. (*Nares*.)

(*b*) A nail or stud (also called a *pike*) marking the center of a target; hence, the center; a central part.

> The very *pin* of his heart cleft with the blind bow-boy's butt-shaft. *Shak.*, R. and J., ii. 4. 15.

> The *pin* he shoots at,
> That was the man deliver'd you.
> *Fletcher*, Island Princess, iv. 1.

> I'll cleave the black *pin* in the midst o' the white.
> *Middleton*, No Wit like a Woman's, ii. 1.

3. One of a number of pieces of wood, of more or less cylindrical form, which are placed upright at one end of a bowling-alley, to be bowled down by the player; a skittle; hence, in the plural form, a game played with such pins. Compare *ninepins, tenpins*.—**4.** A cylindrical roller made of wood; a rolling-pin.—**5.** A leg: as, to knock one off his *pins*. [Slang.]

> Mistake you! no, no, your legs would discover you among a thousand; I never saw a fellow better set upon his *pins*. *Burgoyne*, Lord of the Manor, iii. 3.

6†. A peak; pinnacle.

> Up to this pynnacle now go we;
> I xal the sett on the hyghest *pynne*.
> *Coventry Mysteries*.

7. A small piece of wire, generally brass and tinned, pointed at one end and with a rounded head at the other, used for fastening together pieces of cloth, paper, etc., and for other purposes.

> Yet liberal I was, and gave her *pins*,
> And money for her father's officers.
> *Beau. and Fl.*, Knight of Burning Pestle, v. 3.

Hence—**8.** A thing of very small value; a trifle; a very small amount.

> But when he is to highest power,
> Yet he is not worth a *pin*.
> *Babees Book* (E. E. T. S.), p. 93.

> I do not set my life at a *pin's* fee.
> *Shak.*, Hamlet, i. 4. 65.

> As tho' he cared not a *pin*
> For him and his company.
> *Sir Andrew Barton* (Child's Ballads, VII. 206).

9. A straight, slender, and pointed bar with an ornamental head or attachment, used by women to secure laces, shawls, etc., or the hair, and by men to secure the cravat or scarf, or for mere ornament. Compare *hairpin, safety-pin, scarf-pin, shawl-pin*.—**10†.** A knot in timber.

> The *pinne* or hard corne of a knot in timber, which hurteth sawes. *Nomenclator*. (*Nares*.)

11. A noxious humor in a hawk's foot. *Imp. Dict.*—**Draw-bore pin.** See *draw-bore*.—**Dutch pins**, a game or pastime resembling skittles. *Strutt*.—**Main pin**, in a vehicle, a king-bolt or bolster-pin.—**On or upon a merry pin†, in merry pin**, in a merry humor or mood; disposed to be jolly. See def. 2 (*a*). Compare *to put in the pin*, below.

> Their hartes . . . were set *on so mery a pynne*, for the victory of Montarges. *Hall*, Hen. VI., an. 5.

> Close discourses of the honour of God and our duty to Him are irksome when men are *upon a merry pin*.
> *Charnock*, Works, I. 198.

> The Calend'rer, right glad to find
> His friend *in merry pin*.
> *Cowper*, John Gilpin.

On one's pins, alive and in good condition; on one's legs. [Slang.]

> Glad to hear that he is *on his pins* yet; he might have pegged out in ten years, you know.
> *Harper's Mag.*, LXXX. 269.

Pins and needles, the pricking, tingling sensation attending the recovery of feeling in a limb which has gone to sleep; formication.—**Points and pins.** See *point*¹.—**Steady pin**, in *founding*: (*a*) One of the pins in a flask which fit into openings in the lugs of another flask, so that, after the pattern is drawn, the two parts can be replaced in their original position. (*b*) One of the dowels by which the patterns are held together, when, for convenience in molding, they are made in two or more parts.—**To put in the pin**, to stop; give over; especially, to stop or give over some bad habits or indulgence, such as drunkenness: as, I'll *put in the pin* at the New Year. [Colloq.]

pin¹ (pin), *v. t.*; pret. and pp. *pinned*, ppr. *pinning*. [< ME. *pinnen, pynnen*; < *pin*¹, *n.*] **1.** To fasten or secure with a bolt or peg.

> Conscience held hym
> And made Pees portor to *pynne* the ȝates.
> *Piers Plowman* (C), xxiii. 298.

> I say nothing,
> But smile and *pin* the door.
> *Middleton*, Chaste Maid, i. 2.

2. To fasten with a pin or pins.

> Good Mistriss Orgia, holde your hasty handes!
> Because your insides have not *pind* in your bandes
> According to your minde, must the stick ille
> About their shoulders straight?
> *Times' Whistle* (E. E. T. S.), p. 106.

> Never more
> Will I despise your learning; never more
> *Pin* cards and cony-tails upon your cassock.
> *Beau. and Fl.*, Scornful Lady, iv. 1.

> I tied on my straw bonnet, *pinned* my shawl, took the parcel and my slippers, which I would not put on yet, and stole from my room. *Charlotte Brontë*, Jane Eyre, xxvii.

3. To transfix with or as with a pin; hence, to seize and hold fast in the same spot or position.

> Haven't I come into court twenty afternoons for no other purpose than to see you *pin* the chancellor like a bull-dog? *Dickens*, Bleak House, xxiv.

4. To nab; seize; steal. [Slang.]—**5.** To swage by striking with the peen of a hammer, as in splaying an edge of an iron hoop to give it a flare corresponding to that of the cask. *E. H. Knight*.—**6.** To clog the teeth of: as, to *pin* a file: said of particles which adhere so firmly to the teeth of a file that they have to be picked out with a piece of steel wire.—**To pin one's faith, etc., on or upon**, to rely on; have confidence in.

> The Latins take a great deal of pains to expose this Ceremony as a most shameful imposture. . . . But the Greeks and Armenians *pin their faith upon* it, and make their Pilgrimages chiefly upon this motive.
> *Maundrell*, Aleppo to Jerusalem, p. 97.

To pin the basket†. See *basket*.

pin² (pin), *v. t.*; pret. and pp. *pinned*, ppr. *pinning*. [< ME. *pinnen, pynnen*, var. of *pennen*, E. *pen*¹, with ref. to *pin*¹, *v.*] **1.** To inclose; confine; pen or pound.

> If all this be willingly granted by us which are accused to *pin* the word of God in so narrow room, let the cause of the accused be referred to the accuser's conscience.
> *Hooker*, Eccles. Polity.

2. To aim at or strike with a stone. [Scotch.]

> And who taught me to *pin* a losen [window-pane], to head a bicker, and hold the bannets? *Scott*, Redgauntlet.

pin³† (pin), *n.* [< ME. **pinne*, **penne* (?), < AS. *pinn*, a spot on the eye, prob. = It. *panno*, a spot on the eye, < ML. *pannus*, a spot on the eye, a membrane, a particular use of L. *pannus*, a cloth: see *panel*¹. For the vowel relation, AS. *i* from L. *a*, cf. *pimple*, prob. < L. *papula*.] A spot or web on the eye: usually in the phrase *pin and (or) web*.

> His eyes, good queene, be great, so are they clear and graye,
> He never yet had *pinne or webbe*, his sight for to decay.
> *Gascoigne*, Princely Pl. of Kenelw. (*Nares*.)

> And all eyes
> Blind with the *pin and web* but theirs.
> *Shak.*, W. T., i. 2. 291.

piña¹ (pē′nyä), *n.* [Sp. (Chilian), so called from its shape; a particular use of *piña*, a pine-cone, pineapple, < L. *pinea*, a pine-cone, < *pinus*, pine: see *pine*¹, *pignon*.] The spongy cone of silver left behind, in the treatment of silver amalgam, after all the mercury has been driven off.

piña², *n.* Same as *piña-cloth*.

Pinaceæ (pi-nā′sẹ-ē), *n. pl.* [NL. (Lindley, 1846), < L. *pinus* + *-aceæ*.] The *Coniferæ*.

pinaclet, *n.* A Middle English form of *pinnacle*.

piña-cloth (pē′nyä-klôth), *n.* A thin and translucent fabric made of the fiber of the long leaves of the pineapple-plant, *Ananas sativa*, and other species of the genus. It is highly esteemed by Orientals as a material for fine robes, scarfs, etc. Also *pineapple-cloth, pine-cloth*.

pinacocytal (pin′ạ-kọ̄-si-tạl), *a.* [< *pinacocyte* + *-al*.] Of or pertaining to pinacocytes: as, a *pinacocytal* layer. *Encyc. Brit.*, XXII. 427.

pinacocyte (pin′ạ-kō-sīt), *n.* [< Gr. πίναξ (πινακ-), a tablet, + κύτος, a hollow (cell).] One of the simple pavement-epithelial cells of which the ectoderm of sponges usually consists. Similar or identical pinacocytes form the endodermal epithelium, except in the cases of the ascons and of the flagellated chambers of all sponges, which latter are lined with choanocytes.

pinacoid (pin′ạ-koid), *n.* [< Gr. πίναξ (πινακ-), board, tablet (see *pinax*), + εἶδος, form.] In *crystal.*, a plane parallel to two of the crystallographic axes: as, the basal *pinacoid*, or base parallel to the lateral axes. The *macropinacoid* and *brachypinacoid* are planes in the orthorhombic system parallel to the vertical axis and the longer or shorter lateral axis respectively; similarly the *orthopinacoid* and *clinopinacoid*, in the monoclinic system, are parallel to the vertical axis and the orthodiagonal or clinodiagonal axis respectively.

pinacoidal (pin-ạ-koi′dạl), *a.* [< *pinacoid* + *-al*.] Of the nature of or characteristic of a pinacoid: as, *pinacoidal* cleavage.

pinafore (pin′ạ-fōr), *n.* [< *pin*¹, *v.*, + *afore*.] A sort of apron worn by children to protect the front part of their dress; a child's apron.

pinang (pi-nang′), *n.* [Malay.] The betel-nut palm, or its fruit. See *Areca*, 2, and *areca-nut.*

pinaster (pi-nas′tėr), *n.* [= F. *pinastre* = Sp. It. *pinastro*, < L. *pinaster*, < *pinus*, pine: see *pine*[1].] The cluster-pine. See *pine*[1].

The *pinaster* is nothing else but the wild pine: it groweth wonderfull tall, putting forth armes from the mids of the trunke or bodie upward.
Holland, tr. of Pliny, xvi. 10.

pinax† (pi′naks), *n.* [< L. *pinax*, < Gr. πίναξ, a board, plank, tablet, picture.] A tablet; a list; a register; hence, that on which anything, as a scheme or plan, is inscribed.

Consider whereabout thou art in that old philosophical *pinax* of the life of man. *Sir T. Browne.*

pinball-sight (pin′bâl-sīt), *n.* Same as *bead-sight.*

pinbank† (pin′bangk), *n.* [< *pin*[1] + *bank*[1].] A bank or row of pins or spikes used in torture.

Then was he thrise put to the *pinne banke*, tormented most miserably, to vtter his fetters on, which hee would neuer do. *Foxe*, Martyrs, p. 817 (Hen. VIII., an. 1555).

But alas! when death commeth, than commeth againe his sorow; than wil no soft bed serue, nor no company make him merie. Than he must leaue his outward worship & cumfort of his glory, and lie panting in his bed as it were on a *pin-banke*; than commeth his feare of his euil life, and of his dreadful death.
Sir T. More, Cumfort against Tribulation (1573), fol. 41.

pin-block (pin′blok), *n.* A block of wood split from a larger piece, and of a size adapted to and designed for fashioning into a pin.

pin-borer (pin′bōr″ėr), *n.* The pear-blight beetle, *Xyleborus dispar*, of the family *Scolytidæ*: so called from the small round punctures, like large pinholes, which it makes through the bark. [Canada.]

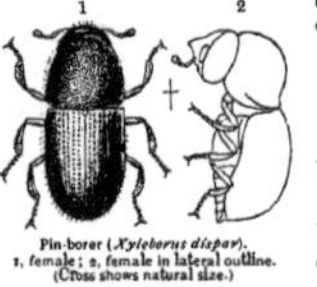

Pin-borer (*Xyleborus dispar*).
1, female; 2, female in lateral outline.
(Cross shows natural size.)

pin-bush (pin′bu̇sh), *n.* A fine reaming- or polishing-tool for delicate metal-work.

pin-buttock† (pin′but″ok), *n.* A sharp angular buttock. *Shak.*, All's Well, ii. 2. 18. [Low.]

pincase (pin′kās), *n.* A case for holding pins.

What do you lack, gentlemen? fine purses, pouches, *pincases*, pipes? *B. Jonson*, Bartholomew Fair, iii. 1.

pince-nez (pans′nā), *n.* [F., < *pincer*, pinch, + obj. *nez*, nose: see *pinch* and *nose*[1].] Eye-glasses kept in place on the nose by a spring.

The lady with whom India had entered put up her *pince-nez*. *Harper's Mag.*, LXXVI. 44.

pincers (pin′sėrz), *n. sing.* and *pl.* [Formerly also *pinsers*; < ME. *pynsour*, < OF. *pinçoir*, *pençoir* (applied to a kind of pincers used as a book-mark, and to a contrivance with iron stakes used in catching fish), < *pincer*, pinch: see *pinch*.] 1. A tool having two hinged jaws which can be firmly closed and held together. See cut under *nippers*.

And with a payre of *pinsers* strong
He pluckt a great tooth out.
Taming of a Shrew (Child's Ballads, VIII. 187).

2. In *zoöl.*, nippers or prehensile claws of certain animals, as insects and crustaceans.

Every ant brings a small particle of that earth in her *pincers*, and lays it by the hole. *Addison*, Guardian.

Specifically — (*a*) A chela, or chelate limb. See *chelal*, and cuts under *lobster* and *Pedipalpi*[2]. (*b*) Anal forceps.

Sometimes called *pinchers*.

Saddlers' pincers, a form of pincers similar to those of shoemakers, but heavier and with straighter grasping-jaws. A lug projects from one of the jaws, and is used as a fulcrum in drawing nails, and in pulling leather forward and holding it firmly while it is tacked or stitched.
E. H. Knight.

pincette (F. pron. pan-set′), *n.* [< F. *pincette*, pincers, tongs, < *pincer*, pinch: see *pinch*. Cf. *pincers*.] Nippers; tweezers.

pinch (pinch), *v.* [< ME. *pinchen*, *pynchen*, pinch, nip, find fault with, < OF. *pincer*, F. *pincer*, pinch, = Sp. *pinchar*, prick; cf. It. *picciare*, *picchiare*, pinch, peck with a beak (*piccio*, *picchio*, a beak), now *pizzare*, pinch, also extended *pizzicare* = Sp. *pizcar*, nip, pinch; cf. also MD. *pitsen*, G. dial. (Bav.) *pfitzen*, *pfetzen*, pinch; It. *pinzo*, a sting, goad. The relations of these forms are undetermined, and the ult. origin unknown.] **I.** *trans.* 1. To compress between the finger and thumb, or between the teeth, or the claws, or with pincers or some similar instrument; squeeze or nip between two hard opposing bodies; nip; squeeze: as, to *pinch* one's self to keep awake.

Yet can you *pinch* out a false pair of sleeves to a friezado doublet. *Middleton*, Anything for a Quiet Life, ii. 2.

The pile was in half a minute pushed over to an old bewigged woman with eye-glasses *pinching* her nose.
George Eliot, Daniel Deronda, i.

Think you Truth a farthing rushlight, to be *pinched* out
when you will
With your deft official fingers, and your politicians' skill?
Lowell, Anti-Apis.

2. To squeeze or press painfully upon: as, his shoes *pinch* his feet.

Stiff in Brocade, and *pinch'd* in Stays,
Her Patches, Paint, and Jewels on; . . .
And Phyllis is but Twenty-one.
Prior, Phyllis's Age.

When you pull on your shoo, you best may tel
In what part it doth chiefely *pinch* you.
Heywood, Dialogues, ii.

3. To seize or grip and bite: said of an animal.

A hound a freckled hind
In full course hunted; on the foreskirts, yet,
He *pinched* and pull'd her down.
Chapman, Odyssey, xix. 318.

4†. To find fault with.

As St. Paul . . . noteth it for a mark of honour above the rest that one is called before another to the Gospel, so is it for the same cause amongst the churches. And in this respect he *pincheth* the Corinths, that, not being the first which received the Gospel, yet they would have their several manners from other churches.
Quoted in *Hooker's* Eccles. Polity, iv. 13.

5†. To plait.

Ful semely hir wympel *pinched* was.
Chaucer, Gen. Prol. to C. T., l. 151.

6. To straiten; distress; afflict: as, to be *pinched* for food; *pinched* with poverty.

There lies the pang that *pinches* me.
Sang of the Outlaw Murray (Child's Ballads, VI. 34).

You . . . that would enjoy,
Where neither want can *pinch*, nor fulness cloy.
Quarles, Emblems, iii., Entertainment.

How hardly will some *pinch* themselves and Families before they will make known their necessities!
Stillingfleet, Sermons, II. vii.

My wife . . . insisted on entertaining them all; for which . . . our family was *pinched* for three weeks after.
Goldsmith, Vicar, vii.

7. To narrow, contract, or nip, as by cold or want or trouble: as, *pinched* features; a mind narrow and *pinched*.

The air hath starved the roses in her cheeks,
And *pinch'd* the lily-tincture of her face.
Shak., T. G. of V., iv. 4. 160.

Pinch'd are her looks, as one who pines for bread.
Crabbe, Works, I. 79.

8. To move with a pinch or crowbar: as, to *pinch* a gun into position.

II. *intrans.* 1. To exert a compressing or nipping pressure or force; bear hard: as, that is where the shoe *pinches*.

I *pinch* not oft, nor doo I often praise;
Yet, must I needs praise the praise-worthy still.
Sylvester, tr. of Du Bartas's Triumph of Faith, Ded.

But thou
Know'st with an equal hand to hold the scale,
Seest where the reasons *pinch*, and where they fail.
Dryden.

2. To lay hold; bite or snap, as a dog.

All held in dismay
Of Diomed, like a sort of dogs, that at a lion bay,
And entertaine no spirit to *pinch*. *Chapman*, Iliad, v.

3. To snarl; carp; find fault.

Every way this office of preaching is *pinched* at.
Latimer, 5th Sermon bef. Edw. VI., 1549.

4. To be sparing, parsimonious, or niggardly.

For to *pinche*, and for to spare,
Of worldes mucke to gette encres.
Gower, Conf. Amant., v.

Surely lyke as the excesse of fare is to be iustely reproued, so in a noble man moche *pinchyng* and nygardshyp of meate and drynke is to be discommended.
Sir T. Elyot, The Governour, iii. 21.

The wretch whom avarice bids to *pinch* and spare,
Starve, steal, and pilfer to enrich an heir. *Franklin.*

Money is exacted (either directly or through raised rent) from the huckster who only by extreme *pinching* can pay her way, from the mason thrown out of work by a strike.
H. *Spencer*, Man vs. State, p. 73.

5†. To encroach.

Yf ich ȝede to the plouh ich *pynchede* on hus half-acre.
Piers Plowman (C), vii. 267.

To know or feel where the shoe pinches, to know by personal experience where the cause of difficulty or trouble in any matter lies.— **To pinch at**†, to find fault with; take exception to.

He speke wol of smale thynges,
As for to *pynchen at* thy rekenynges,
That were nat honeste, if it came to pruf.
Chaucer, Prol. to Manciple's Tale, l. 74.

pinch (pinch), *n.* [< *pinch*, *v.*] 1. The pressure exerted by the finger and thumb when brought together forcibly upon something, or any similar pressure; a nip: as, to give one a *pinch* on the arm.—2. As much of anything as can be lifted between the finger and thumb; hence, a very small quantity: as, a *pinch* of snuff; a *pinch* of salt.

She gave her Charity with a very good Air, but at the same Time asked the Church warden if he would take a *Pinch* (of snuff). *Steele*, Spectator, No. 344.

3. A gripe; a pang.

Rather I abjure all roofs, and choose
To wage against the enmity o' the air;
To be a comrade with the wolf and owl —
Necessity's sharp *pinch!* *Shak.*, Lear, ii. 4. 214.

Now, since some *pinches* have taken them, they begine to reveile yᵉ trueth, & say Mʳ. Robinson was in yᵉ falte.
Cushman, quoted in Bradford's Plymouth Plantation, p. 72.

4. Pressure; oppression; difficulty; need.

The Norman in this narrow *pinch*, not so willingly as wisely, granted the desire.
Selden, Illustrations of Drayton's Polyolbion, xviii. 735.

Where the *pinch* lay, I cannot certainly affirm.
Swift, Tale of a Tub, i.

Steele had the *pinch* of impecuniosity, due rather to excess of expenditure than to smallness of income.
Encyc. Brit., XXII. 528.

5. A pinch-bar.

"*Pinches* or forehammers will never pick upon 't," said Hugh, the blacksmith. *Scott*, Black Dwarf, ix.

In, on, upon, or at a pinch, in an emergency; under the pressure of necessity.

At a pynch a frende is knowen,
I shall put them in adueuture.
Berners, tr. of Froissart's Chron., II. cxviii.

Undone, undone, undone! stay; I can lie yet,
And swear too, *at a pinch*; that 's all my comfort.
Fletcher, Humorous Lieutenant, iv. 4.

Although my proper employment had been to be surgeon or doctor to the ship, yet often *upon a pinch* I was forced to work like a common mariner.
Swift, Gulliver's Travels, ii. 5.

Jack at a pinch. See *Jack*[1].—**Pinch points**, points on a double line at which the two tangent planes coincide.

pinchback (pinch′bak), *n.* [< *pinch*, *v.*, + obj. *back*[1].] A miser who denies himself proper raiment. *Mackay.*

pinch-bar (pinch′bär), *n.* A lever of iron with a projecting snout and a fulcrum-foot, used to move a heavy body by a succession of small lifts. Also called *pinching-bar.*

pinchbeck (pinch′bek), *n.* and *a.* [Short for *Pinchbeck metal*; so called after the inventor, Chr. (Christopher?) *Pinchbeck*, a London watchmaker of the 18th century.] **I.** *n.* An alloy of three or four parts of copper with one of zinc, much used in cheap jewelry.

Illness or sorrow shut us in away from the world's glare, that we may see colors as they are, and know gold from *pinchbeck*. *T. Winthrop*, Cecil Dreeme, xvii.

Many wore ear-hoops of *pinchbeck*, large as a dollar.
S. Judd, Margaret, i. 10.

II. *a.* Sham; spurious; bogus.

Most of these men were of the school of Molyneux, and theirs was *pinchbeck* patriotism.
Westminster Rev., CXXVIII. 795.

The *pinchbeck* heroism that was so ridiculous in that singularly unheroic age . . . had its first exponent in Defoe. *New Princeton Rev.*, VI. 9.

pinch-cock (pinch′kok), *n.* A clamp for compressing a flexible pipe, either to regulate the flow of a liquid through it or to serve as a stopcock by holding the sides of the tube in contact.

An india-rubber tube furnished with a *pinch-cock*.
Ure, Dict., IV. 240.

pinchcommons† (pinch′kom″onz), *n.* [< *pinch*, *v.*, + obj. *commons*, 4.] A parsimonious person; a niggard; a miser.

The crazed projector, and the niggardly *pinch-commons* by which it [a house] is inhabited. *Scott*, Pirate, vi.

pinche, *n.* Same as *pincho.*

pinched (pincht), *p. a.* 1. Compressed; contracted; narrowed; presenting the appearance of being straitened in circumstances or with cold, want, trouble, or the like: as, a *pinched* face; a *pinched* look. Also used occasionally with the meaning of 'narrowing' or 'thinning' in speaking of mineral veins: as, the vein is *pinched*.
2. Narrow; reduced in size; "skimped": said especially of some forms of writing-paper: as, *pinched* post.—3. Petty; contemptible.

He has discover'd my design, and I
Remain a *pinch'd* thing. *Shak.*, W. T., ii. 1. 51.

4. Arrested; apprehended. [Thieves' slang.] —5. Of long, slender growth, as oysters.

pinchem (pin′chem), *n.* [Also *pincher*; imitative of its note.] The note of the titmouse; hence, a titmouse, as *Parus cæruleus.* [Prov. Eng.]

pincher[1] (pin′chėr), *n.* [< ME. **pincher*, *pynchar*; < *pinch* + *-er*[1].] 1. One who or that which pinches.—2. A niggard; a miser. *Prompt. Parv.*, p. 399.—3. Among quarrymen, etc., a person using a pinch, in contradistinction to those moving stones, etc., otherwise.

pincher[2] (pin′chėr), *n.* Same as *pinchem.*

The titmouse foretells cold when crying *Pincher*.
Willsford, Nature's Secrets, p. 132.

pin-cherry (pin'cher"i), *n.* The wild red cherry, *Prunus Pennsylvanica*, found in the northern United States, etc. It is a small tree with clusters of small acid fruits, sometimes used domestically and in cough-mixtures. Also *pigeon-cherry*.

pinchers (pin'chėrz), *n. sing.* and *pl.* [An accom. form of *pincers*, after *pincher*.] 1. Same as *pincers*.—2. A tool for splicing wire rigging.

pinchfist (pinch'fist), *n.* [< *pinch*, *v.*, + obj. *fist*[1].] A niggard; a miser.

pinchgut (pinch'gut), *n.* [< *pinch*, *v.*, + *gut*.] A miserly person.

pinching-bar (pin'ching-bär), *n.* Same as *pinch-bar*.

pinching-bug (pin'ching-bug), *n.* The dobson or hellgrammite. [Western Pennsylvania.]

pinchingly (pin'ching-li), *adv.* Sparingly; parsimoniously.

Giving stingily and *pinchingly*, now and then a little pocket-money or so, to run the hazard of being transgressors of the commandment, and having our portion among the covetous and unmerciful. *Abp. Sharp*, Works, I. vii.

pinching-nut (pin'ching-nut), *n.* A pinch-nut, jam-nut, check-nut, or lock-nut.

pinching-pin (pin'ching-pin), *n.* In a steam-engine, a part of the usual device for keeping a slide-valve packed or tight upon its seat. *E. H. Knight.*

pinching-tongs (pin'ching-tôngz), *n. sing.* and *pl.* In *glass-making*, a kind of tongs used in the manufacture of chandelier-pendants, etc. Each jaw of the tongs is a die, the two jaws when closed forming a mold within which the plastic glass is compressed. The hole for the wire which suspends the drop is formed by a piercer which is inserted into the mold through the ends of the jaws.

Pinching-tongs.
a, jaws; *b*, *b'*, handles pivoted together at *c*.

pincho (pin'chō), *n.* [S. Amer.] A South American marmoset, *Midas œdipus*.

pinchpenny (pinch'pen"i), *n.*; pl. *pinchpennies* (-iz). [< *pinch*, *v.*, + obj. *penny*.] A niggard.

They accompt one . . . a *pynch penny* if he be not prodygall. *Lyly*, Euphues, Anat. of Wit, p. 109.

pinch-plane (pinch'plān), *n.* A singularity of a surface consisting of a generating plane in the developable envelop of the planes having double contact with the surface where the two points of contact coincide.—**Double pinch-plane**, a singularity arising from the coincidence of two pinch-planes.

pinch-point (pinch'point), *n.* A singularity of a surface consisting of a point on a double line or nodal curve where the two tangent-planes coincide.—**Double pinch-point**, a singularity arising from the coincidence of two pinch-points.

pinch-spotted (pinch'spot"ed), *a.* Discolored from having been pinched, as the skin. *Shak.*, Tempest, iv. 1. 261.

pinckanyt, *n.* Same as *pigsney*.

John. Prithee, little *pinckany*, bestow this iewell a me.
Heywood, If you Know not Me (Works, ed. Pearson, I. 308).

Pinckneya (pingk'ni-ä), *n.* [NL. (Richard, 1803), named after Charles Cotesworth *Pinckney*, a South Carolinian statesman.] A genus of small gamopetalous trees of the order *Rubiaceæ* and tribe *Condamineæ*, type of the subtribe *Pinckneyeæ*, characterized by the woolly corolla-lobes and calyx-tube, and by having one sepal dilated into a large rose-colored leaf-like blade. The only species, *P. pubens*, is a native of the southern United States (in the Carolinas and Florida). It bears roundish and closely woolly branchlets, with large thin opposite leaves, and showy pink- and purple-spotted flowers in axillary and terminal corymbs, made more conspicuous by the pinkish bracts, which are ovate and leaf-like and reach 2 inches in length, the flowers 1½ inches. See *fever-tree*, 2, and *Georgia bark* (under *bark*[2]).

pin-clover (pin'klō"vėr), *n.* Same as *alfilerilla*.

pin-connection (pin'ko-nek"shon), *n.* In an iron or steel bridge, a connection of the parts by the use of pins, in contradistinction to connections made with turn-buckles, rivets, etc. This method of connecting parts of bridges is believed to be of American origin.

pin-cop (pin'kop), *n.* A roll of yarn, shaped like a pear, used for the weft in power-looms.

pinc-pinc (pingk'pingk), *n.* [Imitative; cf. *pink*[5].] A name of the reed-warbler, *Drymœca* or *Cisticola schœnicla*, and of other African warblers of the same genus. One of them, *D. textrix*, is remarkable for building a beautiful nest, something like that of the long-tailed titmouse, with a supplementary nest outside for the use of the male. See cut in next column.

pincurtlet, *n.* A pinafore. *Halliwell.* [Prov. Eng.]

Pinc-pinc (*Drymœca textrix*).

pincushion (pin'kush"on), *n.* 1. A cushion into which pins are stuck when not in use. [The first quotation refers to the originally high value of pins.]

Beggar myself with purse and *pincushion*,
When she that is the mistress may be mine?
Shirley, Witty Fair One, iii. 2.

Thou art a Retailer of Phrases, and dost deal in Remnants of Remnants, like a Maker of *Pincushions*.
Congreve, Way of the World, iv. 9.

2. A plant of the genus *Scabiosa*, the scabious: so called with reference to the soft convex flower-head. Also applied locally to various other plants, as the snowball, *Viburnum Opulus*, sometimes called *pincushion-tree*.—**Robin-redbreast's pincushion.** Same as *bedegar*.

pind (pind), *v. t.* [< ME. *pynden*, < AS. **pyndan*, in comp. *for-pyndan*, put in a pound, pound, < *pund*, pound: see *pound*[2]. Cf. *pend*[1], *pen*[1], *pin*[2].] To impound, as cattle, shut up or confine in a pound.

pindal (pin'dal), *n.* [Also *pinda*, *pindar*, *pinder*: said to be of African origin.] The groundnut or peanut, *Arachis hypogæa*. [Southern U. S. and West Indies.]

pindar[1]†, *n.* Same as *pinder*[1].

pindar[2], *n.* Same as *pindal*.

pindara (pin-dä'rä), *n.* [< Hind. *Pindārā*, < Canarese *Pindāra*, *Pendāri*, Marathi *Pindārī*, etc.: see *pindaree*.] Same as *pindaree*.

pindaree (pin-dar'ē), *n.* [Also *pindarry*; < Hind. *Pindārī*, < Marathi *Pindhārī*, prop. *Pendhārī* = Canarese *Pendārī*, a plunderer, freebooter.] A member of a horde of mounted robbers in India, notorious for their atrocity and rapacity. They first appeared about the end of the seventeenth century, and infested the possessions of the East India Company and the surrounding country in the eighteenth century. They were disorderly and mercenary horsemen, organized for indiscriminate raiding and looting. They were dispersed in 1817 by the Marquis of Hastings, then governor-general.

Pindaric (pin-dar'ik), *a.* and *n.* [= F. *pindarique* = Sp. Pg. It. *Pindarico*, < L. *Pindaricus*, < Gr. Πινδαρικός, < Πίνδαρος, Pindar (see def.).] I. *a.* Of or pertaining to Pindar, one of the first of Greek lyric poets (about 522 to 443 B. C.), or resembling or characteristic of his style.

Almighty crowd! thou shortenest all dispute, . . .
Thou leap'st o'er all eternal truths in thy *Pindaric* way!
Dryden, The Medal, l. 94.

You will find, by the account which I have already given you, that my compositions in gardening are altogether after the *Pindaric* manner, and run into the beautiful wildness of nature, without affecting the nicer elegancies of art. *Addison*, Spectator, No. 477.

It was a strange misconception that led people for centuries to use the word *Pindaric* and irregular as synonymous terms; whereas the very essence of the odes of Pindar . . . is their regularity. *Encyc. Brit.*, XIX. 270.

Pindaric hendecasyllabic. See *hendecasyllabic*.

II. *n.* An ode in imitation of the odes of Pindar; an ode in irregular or constantly changing meter. *Addison.*

I sometimes see supreme beauty in Pindar, but English *Pindarics* are to me incomprehensible.
C. A. Ward, N. and Q., 6th ser., IX. 68.

Pindarical (pin-dar'i-kal), *a.* [< *Pindaric* + *-al*.] Same as *Pindaric*.

You may wonder, sir (for this seems a little too extravagant and *pindarical* for prose), what I mean by all this preface. *Cowley*, The Garden.

Pindarism (pin'där-izm), *n.* [= F. *pindarisme*; < *Pindar* + *-ism*.] Imitation of Pindar.

Pindarism prevailed about half a century, but at last died gradually away, and other imitations supply its place.
Johnson, Cowley.

A sort of intoxication of style—a *Pindarism*, to use a word formed from the name of the poet on whom, above all other poets, the power of style seems to have exercised an inspiring and intoxicating effect.
M. Arnold, Study of Celtic Literature, p. 144.

Pindarist (pin'där-ist), *n.* [< *Pindar* + *-ist*.] An imitator of Pindar. *Johnson.*

pindarry (pin-dar'i), *n.* Same as *pindaree*.

pinder[1] (pin'dėr), *n.* [Early mod. E. also *poinder*, also *pinner*, *pynner*; < ME. *pynder*, *pyndare*; < *pind* + *-er*[1]. Cf. *pounder*[2].] The officer of a manor whose duty it was to impound stray cattle.

With that they espy'd the jolly *pinder*,
As he sat under a thorn.
"Now turn again, turn again," said the *pinder*,
For a wrong way you have gone.
Jolly Pinder of Wakefield (Child's Ballads, V. 205).

The *poinder* chafes and swears to see beasts in the corn, yet will pull up a stake, or cut a tether, to find supply for his pin-fold. *Rev. T. Adams*, Works, I. 163.

In the country, at every court leet, ale-tasters were appointed, with the *pinder* or pounder, etc.
S. Dowell, Taxes in England, IV. 56.

pinder[2] (pin'dėr), *n.* Same as *pindal*.

The words by which the peanut is known in parts of the South—goober and *pinder*—are of African origin.
Jour. Amer. Folk-Lore, II. 162.

pindjajap (pin'ja-jap), *n.* A boat of Sumatra and the Malay archipelago, with from one to three masts, generally two, carrying square

Pindjajap of Sumatra.

sails, and having much overhang or projection at both stem and stern. Pindjajaps are employed in bringing spices, etc., to the ports frequented by Europeans, and were also fitted out as pirate vessels.

Pindova palm. See *palm*[2].

pin-drill, *n.* See *drill*[1].

pindrow (pin'drō), *n.* See *king-pine*, under *pine*[1].

pindust (pin'dust), *n.* Small particles of metal produced in the manufacture of pins.

The little particles of *pindust*, when mingled with sand, cannot, by their mingling, make it lighter. *Sir K. Digby.*

pine[1] (pīn), *n.* [< ME. *pine*, *pyne*, *pin*, < AS. **pīn*, in comp. *pīnbeám*, *pīntreów*, pine-tree, = D. *pijn-(boom)* = MHG. *pīne(boum)*, *pīn(boum)* (G. *pinie* = Sw. Dan. *pinie*) = F. Pr. *pin* = Sp. It. *pino* = Pg. *pinho* = Ir. *pīn(chrann)*, < L. *pīnus*, pine; prob. orig. **picnus*, < *pix* (*pic-*), pitch: see *pitch*[2]. Cf. Gr. πίτυς, pine.] 1. Any tree of the genus *Pinus*. The pines are evergreens ranging in size from that of a low bush up to a height of 300 feet. Some of them are of the highest economic importance from the timber obtained from them, which, though not of the finest cabinet quality, is very extensively used in all kinds of construction. In this regard the most important species are—in Europe, the Scotch pine; in North America, the (Canadian) red pine, the common white pine, the long-leafed pine, the yellow pine of the east, and that of the west; in India, the Bhutan, chir, and Khasian pines; and in Japan, the matsu (Japanese pine). (See below.) The resinous products of some are of great value (see *pitch*[2], *tar*, *turpentine*, *resin*, *abietene*, *australene*; also *Aleppo pine*, *cluster-pine*, *Corsican pine*, *long-leafed pine*, *Mugho pine*, and *stone-pine*—all below, and *chir*); and some species are useful for their edible seeds (see *nut-pine*). See also *fir-wood*, and *pine-needle wool* (under *pine-needle*). 2. One of various other coniferous trees, as the Moreton Bay pine and the Oregon pine (see below); also, one of a few small plants suggesting the pine. See *ground-pine*.—3. The wood of any pine-tree.—4. The pineapple.—**Aleppo pine**, a middle-sized tree, *Pinus Halepensis*, of Mediterranean Europe and Asia, occurring along with the Lebanon cedars. It produces a useful wood, and is the source of the Aleppo turpentine.—**Amboyna pine**, *Agathis* (*Dammara*) *orientalis*. Also called *dammar-pine*. See *Dammara*.—**Austrian pine**, a rather tall tree, *Pinus nigricans*, of Austria, etc., having long dark glossy foliage, and resinous wood of moderate worth. Also called *black pine*.—**Bastard pine.** Same as *slash-pine*.—**Bhutan** or **Bhotan pine**, *Pinus excelsa*, of the Himalayas and Afghanistan, a symmetrical tree growing 150 feet high, with a valuable wood, close-grained and easily worked. Also called *lofty pine*. A native name is *kail*.—**Bishop's pine.** Same as *Obispo pine*.—**Black pine.** (*a*) *Pinus Murrayana*, a tree of moderate size and worth, of Pacific North America. Also called *tamarack*, *lodge-pole pine*, *ridge-pole pine*, and *spruce-pine*. (*b*) Same as *Austrian pine*. (*c*) Same as *bull-pine* (*a*). (*d*) Same as *miro*.—**Brazilian pine**, *Araucaria Brasiliensis*, a fine tree growing 100 feet high, which forms large forests in southern Brazil. Its seeds are large and edible, and its wood is fit for boards, masts, etc.—**Broom-pine.** Same as *long-leafed pine.*—**Bull-pine.** (*a*) *Pinus Jeffreyi*, of the Sierra Nevadas, a large tree whose wood affords much coarse lumber. Also called *black pine*, *Truckee pine.* (*b*) Same as *digger-pine.* (*c*) Same as *yellow pine* (*a*). (*d*) Same as *yellow pine* (*c*).—**Bunya-bunya pine.** See *bunya-bunya.*—**Calabrian pine.** See *Corsican pine* and *cluster-pine.*—**Canadian pine.** Same as *red pine* (*a*).—**Canary pine**, *Pinus Canariensis*, forming extensive forests at high elevations on the Canary Islands. Its timber is considered good, and is not subject to insect ravages.—**Candlewood pine**, a resinous Mexican tree, *Pinus Teocote.* Also called *torch-pine.*—**Cedar-pine**, a middle-sized tree, *Pinus glabra*, found locally in the southern United States, and of no great value. Also called *spruce-pine* and *white pine.*—**Celery-pine, celery-leafed pine**, any one of the three species of *Phyllocladus*, beautiful trees, so called from their branchlets resembling a dissected leaf. *P. trichomanoides*, of New Zealand, furnishes a strong durable timber, and is called by the colonists *pitch-pine.* The Tasmanian *P. rhomboidalis* (*P. asplenifolia*) is known as the *celery-top pine*, and yields elastic spars.—**Cembra pine**, the Swiss stone-pine. See *stone-pine*, below.—**Cheel, cheer, or chir pine**, the long-leafed pine of India. See *chir.*—**Chilian pine.** See *Araucaria.*—**Cluster-pine**, the *Pinus Pinaster* of southern Europe. Its stout leaves are set in dense whorls, and its cones are borne in clusters of from four to eight. It furnishes the Bordeaux turpentine (see *barras*[2] and *galipot*), and its timber is of fair worth. It is used on a large scale in southern France to reclaim sandy wastes. It is also called *maritime pine* and *star-pine.* The Calabrian cluster-pine is *P. Brutia.*—**Corsican pine**, *Pinus Laricio*, of Mediterranean Europe, a species reaching a height of 120 feet, notably forming woods on Mount Etna at an altitude of from 4,000 to 6,000 feet. It yields turpentine, and its coarse elastic wood is easily worked and durable. Its variety *Pallasiana*, of the Taurus Mountains, is the *Taurian* or *seaside pine.* Also called *Calabrian pine* and *Corsican larch.*—**Cowdie, cowrie pine.** See *kauri-pine* and *Dammara.*—**Dammar-pine.** Same as *Amboyna pine.*—**Digger-pine**, *Pinus Sabiniana*, a large tree common on the foot-hills of California mountains. It is much used for fuel, and is one of the nut-pines. Also called *bull-pine.*—**Douglas pine.** Same as *Oregon pine.*—**Dwarf pine.** See *Mugho pine.*—**Dye-pine.** Same as *king-pine.*—**Emodi pine.** Same as *cheel pine.*—**Foxtail-pine**, *Pinus Balfouriana*, var. *aristata*, of Nevada, etc., a rather large soft-wooded tree, used in timbering mines. It is now nearly exhausted. Also called *hickory-pine.*—**Frankincense-pine.** Same as *loblolly-pine.*—**Georgia pine.** Same as *long-leafed pine.*—**Giant pine.** Same as *sugar-pine.*—**Ginger-pine**, the Oregon, Port Orford, or white cedar, *Chamæcyparis Lawsoniana*, admired in cultivation, and most valuable for its hard, strong, close-grained, and durable wood, which has many uses. Its odoriferous resin is a powerful diuretic and insecticide.—**Golden pine.** Same as *Chinese* or *golden larch.* See *larch.*—**Gray pine**, *Pinus Banksiana*, a species ranging from the northern borders of the United States northward, of an ashen color, varying in size from 60 feet high down to a straggling bush. Its wood serves for fuel, railway-ties, etc. Also called *Hudson's Bay* or *Labrador pine*, *northern scrub-pine*, and *prince's-pine.*—**Hard pine**, specifically, the long-leafed pine.—**Highland pine**, the horizontal Scotch pine.—**Himalayan pine.** Same as *neoza-pine.*—**Hudson's Bay pine.** See *gray pine.*—**Japanese pine.** See *matsu.* The Japanese red pine is the akamatsu.—**Jersey pine**, *Pinus inops*, a generally small, straggling tree, growing in barren soil on the eastern coast of the United States, in Kentucky, etc., and westward largely used for pump-logs and water-pipes. Also called *scrub-pine.*—**Khasian pine**, *Pinus Khasya*: in the Khasian mountains a small tree; in the Burmese hills sometimes 200 feet high.—**King-pine**, a lofty fir, *Abies Webbiana*, of the Himalayas and Afghanistan, a stout black tree of columnar outline, or flat-headed, sometimes 150 feet high. Its fragrant resinous wood is useful, and its young cones yield a beautiful violet dye, whence it is sometimes called *dye-pine.* The pindrow-fir is a variety of the king-pine.—**Knob-cone pine**, *Pinus tuberculata*, an unimportant species of the western United States.—**Labrador pine.** Same as *gray pine.*—**Lacebark-pine**, *Pinus Bungeana*, of northern China, cultivated by the Chinese in pots. It sheds its outer bark every season.—**Lambert's pine.** Same as *sugar-pine.*—**Lodge-pole pine.** Same as *black pine* (*a*).—**Lofty pine.** Same as *Bhutan pine.*—**Long-leafed pine**, a tree of great economical importance, *Pinus palustris* (*P. australis*), forming extensive forests along the coast of the United States from southern Virginia to Texas, rarely extending inland more than 150 miles. It grows 70 feet high and a yard in diameter, and its needles are nearly a foot long. Its wood is very hard and strong, tough, coarse-grained, and durable, of a reddish color. It is largely manufactured into lumber, and used in ship-building and all kinds of construction. This tree furnishes also nearly all the turpentine, tar, pitch, resin, and spirits of turpentine produced in the United States. Also called *southern* or *Georgia pine*, *yellow pine*, and *hard pine*; sometimes *broom* or *red pine*, and, especially in England, *pitch-pine.*—**Mahogany pine.** Same as *totara.*—**Maritime pine.** Same as *cluster-pine.*—**Meadow-pine.** Same as *slash-pine.*—**Monterey pine**, the Californian *Pinus insignis*, in the wild state rare and local, but now widely cultivated on the Pacific coast for shelter and ornament: a tree of rapid growth, with beautiful fresh green foliage.—**Moreton Bay pine.** Same as *hoop-pine.*—**Mountain-pine.** (*a*) The Mugho pine. (*b*) See *white pine* (*b*).—**Mugho pine**, *Pinus Mughus*, a small tough-wooded tree found on the mountains of southern Europe, and sometimes called *mountain-pine.* A variety, the dwarf pine (*P. Pumilio*) of Austria, etc., yields the Hungarian balsam, sparingly used in medicine. See *knee-pine.*—**Neoza-pine**, *Pinus Gerardiana*, of the northwestern Himalayas, a stout tree growing 60 feet high, with a silvery bark which peels off in long flakes. It yields abundant turpentine, and each cone affords about 100 edible seeds or neoza-nuts, whence it is sometimes called *Nepâl nut-pine.*—**Norfolk Island pine**, *Araucaria excelsa*, a majestic tree, sometimes 200 feet high, abounding on Norfolk Island, and affording a tough and close-grained timber. It is said to produce very large compact knots of a semi-transparent brown, valuable for turnery, etc.—**Norway pine.** See *red pine* (*a*).—**Nut pine.** See *nut-pine* and *piñon*, also *neoza-pine* and *stone-pine.*—**Obispo pine**, a local Californian tree, *Pinus muricata*, of no great value.—**Ocote** or **okote pine.** Same as *candlewood pine.*—**Old-field pine**, the loblolly-pine, which often springs up on abandoned lands, or as second growth after the long-leafed pine.—**Oregon pine**, the Douglas fir or pine, *Pseudotsuga Douglasii.* It ranges from British Columbia to Mexico, but is at its best in Oregon and Washington, where it forms large forests, and sometimes exceeds 300 feet in height. It is the most valuable timber-tree of the Pacific region. Its wood is hard, strong, and durable, difficult to work, largely manufactured into lumber, and used for all kinds of construction, for masts and spars, railway-ties, etc. Lumbermen distinguish varieties of the wood as *red* and *yellow fir*, the red less valuable. The bark is serviceable for tanning.—**Oyster Bay pine**, *Callitris rhomboidea*, a somewhat useful conifer of Tasmania.—**Pinaster-pine**, the cluster-pine.—**Pitch-pine.** (*a*) In America, *Pinus rigida*, a moderate tree of stiff habit, found from New Brunswick to Georgia. Its wood is used for fuel, charcoal, and coarse lumber. Also called *torch-pine.* (*b*) In England, the long-leafed pine, or its imported wood. (*c*) See *celery-pine.*—**Pond-pine**, *Pinus serotina*, a moderate-sized tree of peaty or wet ground from North Carolina to Florida.—**Prince's-pine.** (*a*) The gray pine. (*b*) See *Chimaphila.*—**Red pine.** (*a*) An important tree, *Pinus resinosa*, found throughout Canada, sparingly in northern New England, and at its best in northern Wisconsin and Minnesota. It grows from 70 to 140 feet high. Its wood is of a light-reddish color, resinous, light, hard, tough, and elastic; it is largely manufactured into lumber, and used for spars, piles, and all kinds of construction. Without good reason called *Norway pine.* (*b*) See *Dacrydium.*—**Ridge-pole pine.** Same as *black pine* (*a*).

Ridge-pole pines, which grow close together, and do not branch out until the stems are thirty or forty feet from the ground. *T. Roosevelt*, Hunting Trips, p. 331.

Rosemary-pine. See *loblolly-pine.*—**Running pine.** See *Lycopodium.*—**Sand-pine**, a tree of moderate size, *Pinus clausa*, found in Florida on sandy ridges: of small use. Also called *spruce-pine.*—**Sap-pine.** Same as *pitch-pine* (*a*). [Rare.]—**Scotch pine**, *Pinus sylvestris*, the only indigenous species of *Pinus* in the British Isles, widely spread throughout Europe, especially on mountains, in Scandinavia forming large forests. Its reddish-tinged wood, one of the most generally useful of pine woods, is extensively employed in civil and naval architecture, etc. It is the red or yellow deal of Great Britain. More often called *fir* than *pine*; locally named *redwood*; commercially designated as *Dantzic*, *Riga*, *Swedish*, etc., *fir.* A variety, *horizontalis*, with horizontal branches and red wood, is the *Highland*, *Speyside*, or *horizontal Scotch fir* or *pine.*—**Scrub-pine.** Same as *Jersey pine.* The northern scrub-pine is the same as *gray pine.*—**Seaside pine.** See *Corsican pine.*—**Short-leafed pine.** See *yellow pine* (*a*).—**Siberian pine.** See *stone-pine* (*c*).—**Silver pine.** Same as *yellow pine* (*c*).—**Southern pine**, the long-leafed pine.—**Speyside pine.** See *Scotch pine.*—**Spruce-pine.** Same as *black pine* (*a*), *cedar-pine*, *sand-pine*, and *yellow pine* (*a*).—**Stone-pine.** (*a*) The Italian stone-pine, *Pinus Pinea*, of Mediterranean Europe, a low round-headed tree, in Greece growing 60 feet high. It is much cultivated for ornament and for its large seeds, which are a considerable article of trade as a dessert nut. (*b*) The Swiss stone-pine, or arolla, *Pinus Cembra*, a middle-sized tree with fragrant and resinous, very fine-grained soft wood, much used for carving and cabinet-work. The seeds are edible, and abound in oil. It yields a turpentine called *Carpathian balsam.* (*c*) The Siberian stone-pine, *Pinus Cembra*, var. *Sibirica.*—**Sugar-pine**, *Pinus Lambertiana*, of the Pacific United States, a common tree, sometimes 275 feet high, yielding a light, soft timber, made into lumber, and used for inside finish, etc., but less valuable than the eastern white pine. Burnt or cut trees exude a sweet resinous matter, sometimes used for sugar. The cones are sometimes 1½ feet long. Also called *giant pine*, *Lambert's pine.*—**Swiss pine.** See *stone-pine* (*b*).—**Table-mountain pine**, *Pinus pungens*, of the Alleghanies, in Tennessee forming large forests, in Pennsylvania largely made into charcoal. Also called *hickory-pine.*—**Taurian pine.** See *Corsican pine.*—**Torch-pine.** Same as *candlewood pine*, or *pitch-pine* (*a*).—**Totara pine.** See *totara.*—**Truckee pine.** Same as *bull-pine* (*a*).—**Umbrella pine**, *Sciadopitys verticillata*, of Japan. See *Sciadopitys.*—**Virginian pine**, an old name of the long-leafed pine.—**Water-pine**, the Chinese *Taxodium heterophyllum*, a nearly evergreen tree or bush growing in wet places, and planted along the margins of rice-fields.—**Weymouth pine**, a name, in England, of the common American white pine. It was largely planted by Lord Weymouth soon after its introduction into England.—**White pine.** (*a*) *Pinus Strobus*, found from Newfoundland through Canada and the region of the Great Lakes, and south along the Alleghanies to Georgia. It is at its best in the Upper Lake region, where it forms extensive forests. It rises from 75 to 150 feet, and produces a light, soft, straight-grained timber of a light straw-color, more largely manufactured into lumber than that of any other North American tree, and used in building and for a great variety of purposes. The white pine is also an effective ornamental tree. See *Weymouth pine*, and *yellow pine* (c). (*b*) *Pinus monticola*, a large species of the western United States, not very common, but in Idaho an important timber-tree. (c) The cedar-pine. (d) The Rocky Mountain species *Pinus reflexa*, of Arizona, and *P. flexilis*, which serves for lumber in Nevada, where better is wanting. (*e*) Same as *kahikatea.*—**Yellow pine.** (*a*) *Pinus mitis*, ranging from New Jersey, through the Gulf States, to Texas, and thence to Missouri and Kansas: the most valuable of the yellow pines except the long-leafed, in contrast with which it is called *short-leafed pine.* Its heavy and hard orange-colored wood is largely made into lumber, especially west of the Mississippi, where it is best developed. Also *spruce-pine* and *bull-pine.* (*b*) The long-leafed pine. (c) An important species, *Pinus ponderosa*, found in the Black Hills, and from British Columbia, through the Pacific region, to Texas and Mexico: within its range the most valuable timber-tree after the Oregon pine. It sometimes approaches 300 feet in height, but is commonly much lower, especially in the Rocky Mountains. Its heavy, hard, and strong, but not durable, timber furnishes lumber, railway-ties, etc. Also called *bull-pine*, *silver-pine.* (d) *Pinus Arizonica*, a species of minor importance in the mountains of Arizona. (*e*) A commercial name of the common white pine. (See also *ground-pine*, *heavy-pine*, *hoop-pine*, *huon-pine*, *kauri-pine*, *knee-pine*, *loblolly-pine*, and *slash-pine.*)

1. Cone of Stone-pine (*Pinus Pinea*), on its branch. 2. A fascicle of (two) leaves.

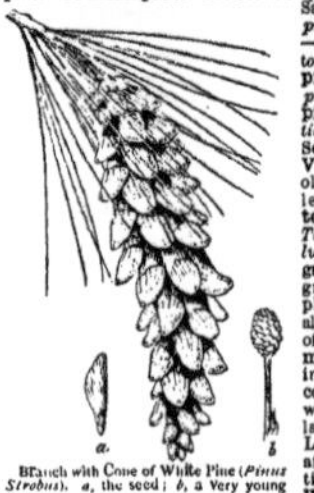

Branch with Cone of White Pine (*Pinus Strobus*). *a*, the seed; *b*, a very young cone.

pine[2]† (pīn), *n.* [< ME. *pine*, *pyne*, < AS. *pīn* = OS. *pīn* = OFries. *pine* = D. *pijn* = MLG. *pine* = OHG. *pīna*, *bīna*, MHG. *pīne*, *pīn*, G. *pein* = Icel. *pīna* = Sw. *pina* = Dan. *pine*, pain, woe, < L. *pœna*, ML. also *pena*, punishment, pain: see *pain*[1]. *Pine*[2] and *pain* are both < L. *pœna*, one coming through the AS., the other through the OF.] Pain; torment; anguish; misery; suffering; wretchedness.

> Doun with Proserpyne,
> Whan I am dede, I wol go wone in *pyne.*
> *Chaucer*, Troilus, iv. 474.

> They shalle be clene of synne & *pyne*
> As Cryste clensed the of thyne.
> *Political Poems*, etc. (ed. Furnivall), p. 125.

> His raw-bone cheekes, through penurie and *pine*,
> Were shronke into his jawes. *Spenser*, F. Q., I. ix. 35.

> O how sall I eat or drink, master,
> Wi' heart sae fu' o' *pine!*
> *Burd Ellen* (Child's Ballads, III. 217).

> The victor hath his foe within his reach,
> Yet pardons her that merits death and *pine.*
> *Fairfax*, tr. of Tasso, xvi. 57.

Done to pine, put to death; starved to death.

> Whether he alive be to be found,
> Or by some deadly chaunce be *done to pine.*
> *Spenser*, F. Q., VI. v. 28.

pine[2] (pīn), *v.*; pret. and pp. *pined*, ppr. *pining.* [< ME. *pinen*, *pynen*, < AS. *pīnian*, torment, torture, = MLG. *pīnen* = OHG. *pīnōn*, MHG. *pīnen* (also extended OFries. *pinigia*, *pingia* = D. *pijnigen* = MHG. *pīnigen*, G. *peinigen*) = Icel. *pīna* = Sw. *pina* = Dan. *pine*, pain, torture; from the noun: see *pine*[2], *n.* Cf. *pain*[1], *v.*, *punish.*] **I.** *trans.* 1. To pain; afflict; torture; starve; wear out or consume, as with sickness, pain, or grief.

> It nedeth nought to *pyne* yow with the corde.
> *Chaucer*, Knight's Tale, l. 888.

> A burning fever him so *pynde* awaye
> That death did finish this his dolefull daye.
> *The Newe Metamorphosis* (1600), MS. (*Nares.*)

> Beare a pleasaunt countenaunce with a *pined* conscience.
> *Lyly*, Euphues, Anat. of Wit, p. 117.

> I left in yonder desert
> A virgin almost *pin'd.*
> *Fletcher*, Sea Voyage, ii. 2.

> This present Spring, Anno Christi 1656, a Quaker, being put into prison at Colechester for his misdemeanours, resolved (as it appeared) to *pine* himself; whereupon he abstained from all manner of food for divers days together.
> *S. Clarke*, Examples, p. 271.

2. To grieve for; bemoan; bewail.

> Abash'd the devil stood, . . . and saw
> Virtue in her shape how lovely; saw, and *pined*
> His loss. *Milton*, P. L., iv. 848.

II. *intrans.* 1. To be consumed with grief or longing; grow thin or waste away with pain, sorrow, or longing; languish: often with *away*: as, she *pined away* and died.

> Ye shall not mourn nor weep; but ye shall *pine away* for your iniquities. Ezek. xxiv. 23.

> There is but One, but One alone,
> Can set the Pilgrim free,
> And make him cease to *pine* and moan.
> *Prior*, Wandering Pilgrim, st. 11.

> Upon the Rebels ill success James Fitz-Eustace, Viscount Baltinglas, fled into Spain, where he *pined away* with Grief. *Baker*, Chronicles, p. 361.

> On the death of the late Duke, it [Parma] was taken possession of by the French, and is now *pining away* under the influence of their iron domination.
> *Eustace*, Italy, I. vi.

2. To long; languish with longing desire: usually with *for* before the object of desire.

Loathing, from racks of husky straw he turns,
And, *pining*, for the verdant pasture mourns.
Rowe, tr. of Lucan, v.

For whom, and not *for* Tybalt, Juliet *pined*.
Shak., R. and J., v. 3. 236.

I *pine* to see
My native hill once more. *Bryant*, Song.

3. To shrink or "render," as fish in the process of curing. = **Syn.** 1. To droop, flag, wither.

pine³ (pīn), *n.* [Origin obscure.] The black-headed gull, *Chroicocephalus ridibundus.* Also *pinemaw.* [Ireland.]

pineal (pin'ē-al), *a.* [= F. *pinéale* = Sp. Pg. *pineal* = It. *pineale*, < L. *pinea*, a pine-cone; prop. fem. of *pineus*, of the pine, < *pinus*, pine: see *pine*¹.] 1. Pertaining to a pine-cone, or resembling it in shape.—2. Pertaining to the pineal body.—**Pineal body**, a small, free, ovoid, conical, reddish organ, attached to the posterior cerebral commissure, and projecting downward and backward between the anterior pair of the corpora quadrigemina. It is believed to be a vestigial sense-organ, probably of sight. Also called *pineal gland*, *conarium*, *pinus*, and *epiphysis cerebri*. See cuts under *corpus*, *encephalon*, and *visceral*.

Courtiers and spaniels exactly resemble one another in the *pineal gland*. *Arbuthnot and Pope.*

Pineal eye, a visual organ on the top of the head of some extinct animals, of which the existing pineal body is supposed to be the persistent vestige. The site of such an organ is indicated by that cavity of the skull of some extinct mammals and reptiles known as the *parietal foramen*, and the eye itself is also called *parietal eye* and *third eye*.—**Pineal peduncles**, the habenæ or habenulæ. See *peduncle*.—**Pineal ventricle**, the cavity sometimes found within the pineal body, as a persistent fetal condition.

pineapple (pin'ap'l), *n.* [Early mod. E. also *pyneapple*, *pyneable*; < ME. *pinappel*, *pynappul*, *pynappylle*, < AS. *pinæppel*, < *pin*, pine, + *æppel*, apple.] 1†. The cone or strobilus of the pine; a pine-cone.

His [the pine's] fruite is great Boulicans or bawles of a brown chestnut colour, and are called *pine-apples*.
Lyte, Dodoens, p. 769.

2. The fruit of *Ananas* (*Ananassa*) *sativa:* so called from its resemblance to a pine-cone. This is a collective fruit, consisting of a matured spike or head of flowers, all parts of which—flowers, bracts, and axis—are consolidated in one succulent mass. In hothouse culture a single fruit has been known to weigh 14 pounds.

Pineapple (*Ananas sativa*).

3. The plant *Ananas sativa*, a native of tropical South America, now widely cultivated and naturalized throughout the tropics. Its short stem rises from a cluster of rigid recurved leaves, like those of the aloe, but thinner. The axis extends beyond the single fruit in a tuft of short leaves called the *crown*. Highly cultivated varieties are seedless, and are propagated by the crown, or (commonly) by suckers, which produce fruit much sooner. The chief seat of pineapple cultivation is the West Indies, whence the fruit is exported in large quantities to the United States and England. The leaves, some 3 feet long, yield a strong fiber, which in the Philippine Islands and elsewhere is woven into a fine fabric. So-called pineapple-cloths are also made from the fiber of other species of *Bromeliaceæ*, as *Bromelia Pinguin*, the wild pineapple.

4. A fish of the family *Diodontidæ*, a kind of porcupine-fish, *Chilomycterus geometricus:* so called from the prickly skin and the shape when inflated.—**Essence of pineapple.** Same as *ethyl butyrate* (which see, under *butyrate*).—**Pineapple cheese.** See *cheese*¹.—**Pineapple rum**, rum flavored with slices of pineapple.

pineapple-cloth (pīn'ap"l-klôth), *n.* Same as *piña-cloth*.

pineapple-flower (pīn'ap-l-flou"ėr), *n.* Any plant of the liliaceous genus *Eucomis*, which consists of four or five bulbous South African plants, moderately ornamental, somewhat cultivated in gardens.

pineapple-tree† (pīn'ap"l-trē), *n.* [< ME. *pyneappyltre*, *pynappul tree*, *pynapple tree*; < *pineapple* + *tree*.] The pine-tree.

Now for *pynappul* tree
The colde or weetisshe land most sowen be.
Palladius, Husbondrie (E. E. T. S.), p. 98.

Heare, amonge certeyne wooddes of date trees and *pyneable trees* of excedyng height, he fownd two natiue sprynges of fresshe water.
R. Eden, tr. of Peter Martyr (First Books on America, ed. Arber, p. 77).

pineaster†, *n.* An improper form of *pinaster*.

pine-barren (pīn'bar"en), *n.* A level sandy tract covered sparsely with pine-trees. [Southern U. S.]

A dreary and extensive forest of pine-trees, or, as it is termed by the Carolinians, a *pine-barren*, where a habitation is seldom seen except at intervals of ten or twelve miles. *Lambert's Travels*, II. 226.

Pine-barren beauty. See *Pyxidanthera*.—**Pine-barren terrapin**, a tortoise of the family *Clemmyidæ*.

pine-beauty (pīn'bū"ti), *n.* A British moth, *Trachea piniperda*, white with a yellow band and red spots, whose larva feeds on coniferous trees.

pine-beetle (pīn'bē"tl), *n.* A xylophagous beetle, as *Hylesinus* or *Hylurgus piniperda*, destructive to pines.

pine-blight (pīn'blīt), *n.* 1. An aphid, *Chermes pinicorticis*, of the subfamily *Chermesinæ*, which blights the bark of the pine.—2. The flocculent substance from this insect.—3. The blighting of the tree caused by this aphid.

pine-bullfinch (pīn'bůl"finch), *n.* Same as *pine-grosbeak*.

pine-carpet (pīn'kär"pet), *n.* A British geometrid moth, *Thera firmata*, whose larva feeds on the Scotch fir.

pine-chafer (pīn'chā"fėr), *n.* A beetle (*Anomala pinicola*) which feeds on the leaves of the pine. [U. S.]

pine-clad (pīn'klad), *a.* Clad or covered with pines.

pine-cloth (pīn'klôth), *n.* Same as *piña-cloth*.

pine-cone (pīn'kōn), *n.* The cone or strobilus of a pine-tree.

pine-drops (pīn'drops), *n. pl.* See *beech-drops* and *Pterospora*.

pine-finch (pīn'finch), *n.* 1. Same as *pine-grosbeak*.—2. A small fringilline bird of North America, *Chrysomitris* or *Spinus pinus*, commonly found in pine-woods. It is about 5 inches long, and entirely covered with pale or flaxen brown and dusky streaks, more or less tinged with yellow, especially on the wings and tail. The bill is very acute, the tail is emarginate, and the wings are pointed. It is an abundant migratory bird in many parts of the United States and British America, and is a near relative of the siskin or linnet of Europe. Also called *pine-linnet* and *pine-siskin*.

pineful† (pīn'fůl), *a.* [< *pine*² + *-ful*.] Full of woe, pain, or misery.

With long constraint of *pineful* penury.
Bp. Hall, Satires, V. ii. 82.

pine-grosbeak (pīn'grōs"bēk), *n.* A large fringilline bird of Europe and North America, *Pinicola enucleator*, found chiefly in coniferous woods in northerly or alpine regions. See *Pinicola*. Also called *pine-bullfinch*, *pine-finch*.

Pine-grosbeak (*Pinicola enucleator*).

pine-grouse (pīn'grous), *n.* Same as *dusky grouse* (which see, under *grouse*). [Western U. S.]

pine-gum (pīn'gum), *n.* A resin, scarcely distinguishable from sandarac, derived from Australian trees of the genus *Callitris* (*Frenela*), as *C. robusta* and *C. rhomboidea*.

pine-house (pīn'hous), *n.* Same as *pinery*, 1.

pine-kernel (pīn'kėr"nel), *n.* The edible seed of some pines. See *pine-nut*.

pine-knot (pīn'not'), *n.* The resinous knot of a pine-tree, used as fuel. [U. S.]

In the remote settlements the *pine-knot* is still the torch of courtship; it endures to sit up by.
C. D. Warner, Backlog Studies, p. 24.

pine-linnet (pīn'lin"et), *n.* Same as *pine-finch*, 2.

pine-lizard (pīn'liz"ärd), *n.* The common brown lizard, or fence-lizard, of the United States, *Sceloporus undulatus*, often found in pine-woods or pine-barrens.

pine-marten (pīn'mär"ten), *n.* A carnivorous quadruped of the family *Mustelidæ*, *Mustela martes* or *Martes abietum*, a native of Europe and Asia: so called in distinction from *beech-marten*. The name is extended to the American representative, which is a different species, *M. americana*. See *marten*¹ and *Mustela*.

pine-mast (pīn'mȧst), *n.* Pine-cones. See *mast*².

pinemaw (pīn'mâ), *n.* Same as *pine*³.

pine-mouse (pīn'mous), *n.* A North American meadow-mouse of the subfamily *Arvicolinæ*, *Arvicola* (*Pitymys*) *pinetorum*, common in many parts of the United States, about 4 inches long, of a rich dark reddish-brown color, with very smooth, glossy fur. This vole lives mostly in dry soils, as of pine-barrens, and represents a section of the large genus *Arvicola* of which the *A.* (or *P.*) *quasiater* is another member found in Mexico, of a blackish color.

Pine-mouse (*Arvicola pinetorum*).

pine-needle (pīn'nē"dl), *n.* The acicular leaf of the pine-tree.

Beneath these trees we walked over a carpet of *pine-needles*, upon which our moccasined feet made no sound.
The Century, XXX. 225.

Pine-needle bath, a bath of water impregnated with an extract of pine-needles.—**Pine-needle wool**, a fibrous substance produced from the leaves of the pine in Norway, Germany, and the southern United States. It is of a light-brown color, and has a pleasant balsamic smell. Garments are made from it when spun and woven on the stocking-loom, and these are supposed to be beneficial to persons threatened with rheumatism or with lung-complaints. In the United States the fibers of pine-needles have been used for coarse bagging. Also *pine-wool* and *fir-wool*.

pine-nut (pīn'nut), *n.* [< ME. *pinnote*, *pynnute*, *pynote*, < AS. *pinhnutu*, < *pīn*, pine, + *hnutu*, nut.] 1. A pine-cone.—2. The edible seed-kernel of several species of pine. See *neozapine* and *stone-pine*, both under *pine*¹. See also *nut-pine* and *piñon*.

In the cottages at the shelter aboue, where we break our cable, we found many *pine-nuts* opened.
Hakluyt's Voyages, III. 422.

Pine-nut tree [< ME. *pinnote tre*], the pine-tree.

Als dede the *pinnote tre*. *Seven Sages*, l. 544.

pine-oil (pīn'oil), *n.* 1. An oil obtained from the resinous exudations of pine- and fir-trees: used in making colors and varnishes. Also called *turpentine-oil*.—2. An essential oil distilled from the leaves and twigs of *Pinus Mughus*, and esteemed in German medicine; also, a similar product of *P. sylvestris*.—3. A fixed oil suitable for lamps, obtained in Sweden and elsewhere from pine- and fir-wood by distillation or chemically.

piner† (pī'nėr), *n.* An obsolete form of *pioneer*.

pinery (pī'nẹ-ri), *n.*; pl. *pineries* (-riz). [< *pine*¹ + *-ry*.] 1. A hothouse in which pineapples are raised. Also called *pine-house* and *pine-stove*.

A little bit of a shrubbery. . . . and a poor little flower-bed or so, and a humble apology for a *pinery*.
Dickens, Dombey and Son, xxxvi.

2. A place where pine-trees grow; especially, a pine-forest in which an extensive lumbering business is carried on, as in the forests of white pine (*P. Strobus*) of Michigan, Wisconsin, and Minnesota.

In *pineries*, on the other hand, valuable timber is obtained, and the population is far superior to the tar heel, the nickname of the dweller in barrens.
Encyc. Americana, I. 190.

pine-sap (pīn'sap), *n.* A tawny or reddish fleshy plant, *Hypopitys multiflora* (*Monotropa Hypopitys*), resembling the Indian-pipe, but having several smaller flowers in a raceme. So named as parasitic on the roots of pine. Also called *false beech-drops*. See *Monotropa*.

1. Flowering Plant of Pine-sap (*Hypopitys multiflora*). 2. Plant with fruits. *a*, a flower; *b*, the fruit.

pine-siskin (pīn'sis"kin), *n.* Same as *pine-finch*, 2.

pine-snake (pīn'snāk), *n.* A snake of the genus *Pituophis*, as *P. bellona*, the bull-snake, of which there are several kinds. They attain a large size, are harmless and inoffensive, and are commonly found in pine-woods. See cut under *Pituophis*.

pine-stove (pīn'stōv), *n.* Same as *pinery*, 1.

pine-thistle (pin'this"l), *n.* A plant, *Carlina* (*Atractylis*) *gummifera*, the root of which abounds with a gummy matter, which exudes when it is wounded. It grows in the south of Europe, where the flower-stalks are dressed with oil and used as food.

pine-tree (pīn'trē), *n.* [< ME. *pinetre*, *pynetre*, < AS. *pīntreów*, < *pīn*, pine, + *treów*, tree.] Same as *pine*[1], 1.—**Pine-tree cod.** See *cod*[2].—**Pine-tree money**, silver coins (the shilling and smaller denominations) of Massachusetts, struck in the latter half of the seventeenth century, and bearing the device of a pine-tree. These pieces were known in their early days as *Boston* or *Bay shillings*, etc. The first application we find of the name of *pine* to them was in May, 1680. *Crosby*, Early Coins of America (1878), p. 62.—**Pine-tree State**, the State of Maine: so called in allusion to its extensive pine-forests.

Obverse.

Reverse.

Pine-tree Shilling, 1652.—British Museum. (Size of the original.)

pinetum (pī-nē'tum), *n.* [L. (> It. *pineto*, *pineta*), a pine-grove, < *pinus*, pine: see *pine*[1], *n.*] 1. A plantation or collection of growing pine-trees of different kinds, especially one designed for ornamental or scientific purposes.—2. A treatise on the pines: as, Gordon's *Pinetum*.

pine-warbler (pin'wâr"blėr), *n.* A small migratory insectivorous bird of North America, *Dendrœca pinus* or *vigorsi*, belonging to the

Pine-warbler (*Dendrœca pinus* or *vigorsi*).

family of wood-warblers (*Mniotiltidæ* or *Sylvicolidæ*). It is about 6 inches long, of an olive-green color above and dull-yellow below, with white blotches on the tail-feathers. It is one of the most abundant of its tribe in some parts of the United States, especially in pine-woods of southern localities.

pineweed (pīn'wēd), *n.* *Hypericum nudicaule*: same as *orange-grass*.

pine-weevil (pīn'wē"vl), *n.* A curculio, *Pissodes strobi*, which lays its eggs on the terminal shoots of the white pine, into which its larvæ bore.

pine-wool (pīn'wůl), *n.* Same as *pine-needle wool* (which see, under *pine-needle*).

pine-worm (pīn'wėrm), *n.* The larva of a sawfly of the genus *Lophyrus*. *L. abbotti* commonly infests the white pine in the United States, and *L. lecontei* the Austrian, Scotch, and pitch pine.

piney, *a.* See *piny*[1].

pin-eyed (pin'īd), *a.* Having the capitate stigma at the throat of the corolla, the stamens standing lower: noting, for instance, the long-styled form of the cowslip, *Primula veris*, and contrasted with *thrum-eyed*, applied to the short-styled form, in which the anthers are above.

> Florists who cultivate the Polyanthus and Auricula have long been aware of the two kinds of flowers, and they call the plants which display the globular stigma at the mouth of the corolla "pin-headed" or "*pin-eyed*."
> *Darwin*, Different Forms of Flowers, p. 14.

pin-feather (pin'feᴛʜ"ėr), *n.* See *feather*.

pin-feathered (pin'feᴛʜ"ėrd), *a.* Covered with pin-feathers; not fully fledged: said of young birds acquiring their first plumage after the downy state, and of old birds renewing their plumage during the molt: sometimes used figuratively.

> Hourly we see some raw *pinfeather'd* thing
> Attempt to mount, and fights and heroes sing,
> Who for false quantities was whipt at school.
> *Dryden*, tr. of Persius's Satires, i.

pin-fire (pin'fīr), *a.* 1. Noting a cartridge for breech-loading guns, invented by Lefaucheux in 1836. Within a recess of the metal base of the cartridge, whose body is of paper, is placed a percussion-cap, the open end of which faces a hole in the side of the base. Into this hole is loosely fitted a brass firing-pin, which penetrates the cap, and, when the cartridge is placed in the gun and the breech closed, projects through a small hole or recess in the barrel. The hammer of the lock strikes the outer end of this pin in firing, driving the pin down upon and igniting the detonating material in the cap. This cartridge is considered the parent of the modern central-fire and rim-fire cartridges.

2. Noting a breech-loading gun in which a pin-fire cartridge is used.—**Pin-fire cartridge**, a cartridge for breech-loading guns. See def. 1. Also called *pin-cartridge*.—**Pin-fire gun**, a breech-loading gun in which a pin-fire cartridge is used.

pinfish (pin'fish), *n.* 1. A sparoid fish, *Lagodon rhomboides*, related to the scup and sheepshead, common along the southern coast of the United States. The body is elliptic-ovate and compressed, the head is pointed, the upper molars are in two rows, the incisors are broad and emarginated at the apex, and there is a precumbent spine in front of the dorsal fin. The color is olive, with silvery sides, six dark vertical bars, a large dark blotch over the pectoral fin, and faint blue and golden stripes on the sides. Also locally called *chopa-spina*, *bream*, *robin*, *sailors' choice*, and *squirrel-fish*. See cut under *Lagodon*.

2. A sparoid fish, *Diplodus holbrooki*, like the *Lagodon rhomboides*, but with entire teeth.—3. A small sunfish of the United States, as the copper-nosed bream, *Lepomis pallidus*.

pin-flat (pin'flat), *n.* 1. A small disk of double cardboard covered with some textile material so arranged that pins can be stuck into the edge.—2. A scow carrying a square sail. *Sportsman's Gazetteer*. [Canada.]

pinfold (pin'fōld), *n.* [Also *penfold*; < ME. *pynfolde*, *punfolde*, *ponfolde*, *pondfolde*, *pyndefolde*; < *pin*, *pound*[2] (cf. derived verb *pind*), + *fold*[2].] 1. A place in which stray cattle are temporarily confined; a pound.

> Heo hath hulpe a thousande oute of the deueles *ponfolde*.
> *Piers Plowman* (B), v. 633.

> His pledge goes to the *pinfold*.
> *Jolly Pinder of Wakefield* (Child's Ballads, v. 205).

2. A fold or inclosure for animals.

> The cattle slept as he went out to the *pinfold* by the light of the stars.
> *The Atlantic*, LXI. 661.

> For the *penfold* [in which was a lion] surrounded a hollow
> Which led where the eye scarce dared follow.
> *Browning*, The Glove.

pinfold† (pin'fōld), *v. t.* [< *pinfold*, *n.*] To confine in a pound or pinfold; impound.

> Had this beene the course in the Primitive time, the Gospel had been *pinfolded* up in a few Cities, and not spread as it is.
> *N. Ward*, Simple Cobler, p. 46.

pin-footed (pin'fůt"ed), *a.* Having pinnate feet; having the toes lobate, as a bird; fin-footed.

ping (ping), *v. i.* [Imitative.] To produce a sound like that of a rifle-bullet whistling through the air.

ping (ping), *n.* [< *ping*, *v.*] The whistling sound made by a bullet, as from a rifle, in passing through the air.

> The *ping* of the rifle bullet or crack of the shot gun have charms that never tire.
> *W. W. Greener*, The Gun, p. 479.

pingle[1]† (ping'gl), *n.* [Perhaps a var. of *pightle*, *pickle*[3].] A small piece of inclosed ground.

> The academy, a little *pingle*, or plot of ground, . . . was the habitation of Plato, Xenocrates, and Polemon.
> *North*, tr. of Plutarch, p. 226. (*Latham.*)

pingle[2] (ping'gl), *v. i.*; pret. and pp. *pingled*, ppr. *pingling*. [Orig. obscure.] To eat with little appetite. [Prov. Eng.]

pingler[1]† (ping'glėr), *n.* [Prob. < *pingle*[1] + *-er*[1].] A cart-horse; a work-horse.

> Perversile doe they alwaies thinke of their lovers, and talke of them scornefullie, judging all to bee clownes which be not courtiers, and all to be *pinglers* that be not coursers.
> *Lyly*, Euphues, Anat. of Wit, p. 109.

pingler[2] (ping'glėr), *n.* [< *pingle*[2] + *-er*[1].] One who eats with little appetite.

> He filleth his mouth well, and is no *pingler* at his meat.
> *Topsell*, Beastes (1607). (*Halliwell.*)

pin-grass (pin'gras), *n.* The stork's-bill. See *alfilerilla*.

Pingster†, *n.* and *a.* See *Pinkster*.

Pinguecula (ping-gwek'ū-lạ̈), *n.* Same as *Pinguicula*, 1.

pinguefy† (ping'gwē-fī), *v. t.* [Also *pinguify*; < L. *pinguefacere*, make fat, < *pinguis*, fat (see *pinguid*), + *facere*, make (see *-fy*).] To fatten.

> The oyl or ointment wherewith women use to anoint the hair of their head hath a certain property in it to *pinguify* withall.
> *Holland*, tr. of Plutarch, p. 944.

> There are they who take pleasure in the incence, fumes, and nidours of sacrifices; wherewith their corporeal and spirituous part is as it were *pinguified*.
> *Cudworth*, Intellectual System, p. 810.

Pinguicula (ping-gwik'ū-lạ̈), *n.* [NL. (in sense 1 so named by Gesner, 1541, with ref. to the popular name *butterwort*), < L. *pinguiculus*, fattish, < *pinguis*, fat: see *pinguid*.] 1. A genus of gamopetalous plants of the order *Lentibularieæ*, characterized by the spreading posterior corolla-lobe, the four- to five-parted calyx, and the terminal one-celled anthers. There are over 30 species, widely dispersed throughout northern temperate regions, and in the Andes to antarctic climates. They are stemless herbs of moist places, with a rosette of radical leaves, and erect leafless scapes bearing a single purple, violet, yellow, or whitish flower. The broad entire leaves have a peculiar surface as of little crystalline drops. The irritation of foreign bodies causes the leaf-margins to roll inward, imprisoning insects caught upon the sticky surface, and assisting in the absorption of their softer parts. Compare *Utricularia*, a related insectivorous plant. Six species occur in North America, mostly either high northern or near the southern coast, of which latter *P. lutea* is the yellow butterwort, a showy plant of the pine-barrens. See *butterwort* (with cut) and *earning-grass*. Also *Pinguecula*. 2. [*l. c.*] A plant of this genus.—3. [*l. c.*] A small painless tumor of the conjunctiva, usually situated close to the edge of the cornea. Also called *interpalpebral blotch*.

pinguid (ping'gwid), *a.* [With unorig. term. *-id* (appar. in imitation of *liquid*, etc.); = Sp. Pg. It. *pingue*, < L. *pinguis*, fat.] Fat; unctuous.

> *Pinguid* juice to nourish and feed the body.
> *Evelyn*, Acetaria.

> A *pinguid* turgid stile, as Tully calls the Asiatic Rhetoric.
> *A. Tucker*, Light of Nature, II. iii. 29.

pinguidinous (ping-gwid'i-nus), *a.* [Also *pinguedinous* = Sp. It. *pinguedinoso*, < L. *pinguedo* (*pinguedin-*), fatness, < *pinguis*, fat: see *pinguid*.] Containing fat; fatty; adipose; greasy; unctuous. *Coles*, 1717.

pinguin[1]†, *n.* An obsolete form of *penguin*[1].

pinguin[2] (ping'gwin), *n.* Same as *penguin*[2].

Pinguipedina (ping"gwi-pẹ̄-dī'nạ̈), *n. pl.* [NL., < *Pinguipes* (*-ped-*) + *-ina*[2].] A group of trachinoid fishes, named from the genus *Pinguipes*; in Günther's system, the third group of *Trachinidæ*, having eyes lateral, the lateral line continuous, and a large tooth on the posterior part of the intermaxillary.

Pinguipedinæ (ping"gwi-pẹ̄-dī'nē), *n. pl.* [NL., < *Pinguipes* (*-ped-*) + *-inæ*.] A subfamily of latiloid fishes, typified by the genus *Pinguipes*.

pinguipedine (ping-gwip'e-din), *a.* and *n.* I. *a.* Of or pertaining to the subfamily *Pinguipedinæ*.

II. *n.* A member of this group.

Pinguipes (ping'gwi-pēz), *n.* [NL. (Cuvier), < L. *pinguis*, fat, + *pes* = E. *foot*.] The typical genus of *Pinguipedinæ*, containing latiloid fishes whose ventral fins are covered with a thick membrane, whence the name.

pinguite (ping'gwīt), *n.* [< L. *pinguis*, fat, + *-ite*[2].] A soft oil-green variety of the hydrous iron silicate chloropal.

pinguitude (ping'gwi-tūd), *n.* [< L. *pinguitudo*, fatness, < *pinguis*, fat: see *pinguid*.] Fatness: a growing fat.

pinhead (pin'hed), *n.* The head of a pin; hence, anything very small.

pin-headed (pin'hed"ed), *a.* Having a head like that of a pin; specifically, in *bot.*, same as *pin-eyed*.

pinhead-sight (pin'hed-sīt), *n.* Same as *bead-sight*.

pinhold (pin'hōld), *n.* A place at which a pin holds or makes fast.

pinhole (pin'hōl), *n.* 1. A small hole made by the puncture or perforation of a pin; hence, any very small aperture.—2. A minute perforation or transparency, as if made with the point of a pin, of which great numbers sometimes appear in the film of a photographic negative from some chemical defect or fault in manipulation.—**False pinhole**, in pillow-lace making, one of those pinholes on the inner side of a rounded strip, as of a collar, which are used to fix the outer curve by carrying the bobbins from the inner to the outer pins, the inner ones acting as centers from which the outer ones are kept equidistant. Also called *false stitch*.

pinic (pī'nik), *a.* [= F. *pinique*; as *pine*[1] + *-ic*.] Pertaining to or derived from the pine-tree; noting one of the acids found in resin: as, *pinic* acid.

Pinicola (pī-nik'ọ̄-lạ̈), *n.* [NL., < L. *pinus*, a pine, pine-tree, + *colere*, inhabit.] 1. A genus of fringilline birds of the family *Fringillidæ*, the type of which is *P. enucleator*; the pine-grosbeaks. The bill is short, obtuse, and turgid, like a bullfinch's; the nostrils are hidden by tufts of nasal plumules; the wings and tail are long—the former pointed, the latter emarginate; and the feet are small. The male is chiefly dull-carmine or lake-red, shaded with black and gray in some places, and varied with white. The female is gray, heightened in some places with saffron-yellow. The genus is restricted to northerly parts of the northern hemisphere, where the birds chiefly inhabit coniferous regions. See cut under *pine-grosbeak*.

2. A genus of hymenopterous insects.

pinicoline (pi-nik'ọ-lin), *a.* [As *pinicol-ous* + *-ine*¹.] Inhabiting or frequenting pines or other coniferous woods: said of various animals. *Coues.*

pinicolous (pi-nik'ọ-lus), *a.* [< L. *pinus*, a pine, pine-tree, + *colere*, inhabit, + *-ous*.] Same as *pinicoline*.

piniform (pī'ni-fôrm), *a.* [< L. *pinus*, a pine, pine-tree, + *forma*, form.] Resembling a pine-cone.—**Piniform decussation**, the decussation of fibers in the oblongata above the decussation of the pyramids: it lies between the pyramids and the central gray matter.

pining (pī'ning), *n.* [< ME. *pining*, *pyning*, < AS. *pīnung*, torment, torture, pain, verbal n. of *pīnian*, torment: see *pine*², *v.*] 1. Punishment; torture.—2. Suffering.

piningly (pī'ning-li), *adv.* In a pining or languishing manner; by wasting away.

pining-stool† (pī'ning-stöl), *n.* [< ME. *pynyng-stole*; < *pining* + *stool*.] A cucking-stool.

To punyshen on pillories and on *pynyng-stoles*.
Piers Plowman (C), iv. 79.

pinion¹ (pin'yọn), *n.* [Formerly also *pinnion*; < ME. *pinion*, *pynyon*, < OF. *pignon*, pennon, *panon*, a pinion, plume, feather of an arrow, same as *pennon*, *penon*, etc., a flag, banner, = Sp. *piñon*, pinion, = It. *pennone*, a bunch of feathers, a pennon, < L. *penna*, *pinna*, wing, feather: see *pin*¹, *pen*², and cf. *pinion*², another use of the same word.] 1. A feather; especially, a remex or flight-feather.

He is pluck'd, when hither
He sends so poor a *pinion* of his wing. *Shak.*, A. and C., iii. 12. 4.

2. The wing of a bird, or the flight-feathers collectively.

Tell me if e'er your tender *Pinions* bore
Such weight of Woe.
Congreve, Tears of Amaryllis.

To Daphne's window speed thy way;
And on quivering *pinions* rise here
And there thy vocal art display.
Shenstone, Sky Lark.

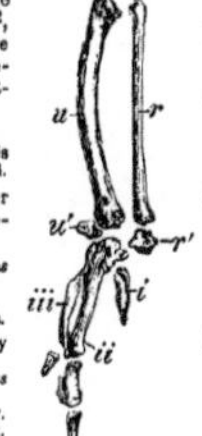
Pinion-bones, or Manus of Adult Fowl, together with *u*, *r*, ulna and radius, bones of the forearm: *u'*, ulnar carpal; *r'*, radial carpal; *i*, phalanx of first digit; *ii*, main metacarpal, bearing two phalanges, with which it is ankylosed; *iii*, another metacarpal, bearing one small phalanx. The first metacarpal is the ankylosed knob on the head of *ii*, bearing *i*.

3. Technically, in *ornith.*, the joint of a bird's wing furthest from the body; the distal segment of the wing; the manus, consisting of the carpus, metacarpus, and phalanges, collectively bearing the primary remiges, or largest flight-feathers, and the alula or bastard-wing. Most adult birds show the seven separate bones of the pinion here figured; but in a few adults, and probably in all embryos, the osseous elements are more numerous.

4. In *entom.*, one of various moths: as, the brown-spot *pinion*, *Anchocelis litura*.—5. [< *pinion*¹, *v.*] A shackle or band for the arm. *Ainsworth.*

pinion¹ (pin'yọn), *v. t.* [Formerly also *pinnion*; < *pinion*¹, *n.*] 1. To bind or confine the wings of (a bird); restrain or confine by binding the wings, or by cutting off the pinions; bind or confine (the wings). A very common but cruel method of pinioning, practised especially upon geese by poulterers, is to twist the pinion over the next joint of the wing, where it is confined by the primaries resting upon the secondaries.

Not like a tame bird, that returns; nor like a hawk, that will shew where she is by her bells; but like an eagle, whose wings thou canst neither clip nor *pinion*.
Rev. T. Adams, Works, I. 432.

2. To bind or confine the arm or arms of (a person) to the body so as to disable or render incapable of resistance; shackle.

Know, sir, that I
Will not wait *pinion'd* at your master's court.
Shak., A. and C., v. 2. 53.

Away with him! I'll follow you. Look you *pinion* him, and take his money from him, lest he swallow a shilling and kill himself. *Beau. and Fl.*, Woman-Hater, v. 1.

All their hands he *pinnioned* behinde
With their owne girdles. *Chapman*, Iliad, xxi.

3. To bind; attach as by bonds or shackles.

Some slave of mine be *pinion'd* to their side.
Pope, Dunciad, iv. 134.

pinion² (pin'yọn), *n.* [Formerly also *pinnion*; < F. *pignon*, a small wheel, pinion, spur-nut, = Sp. *piñon*, the tooth of a wheel, pinion; a particular use of the word represented by *pinion*¹, a wing, etc., < L. *penna*, *pinna*, wing, feather, *pinna*, a float of a water-wheel: see *pen*², *pin*¹, and cf. *pinion*¹.] A small wheel with cogs or teeth which engage the teeth of a larger wheel with cogs or teeth, or sometimes only an arbor or spindle having notches or leaves, which are caught successively by the teeth of the wheel, and the motion thereby communicated. See also cut under *pawl-press*.

Spur-wheel, with Pinion *a*.

—**Flying pinion**, the fly of a clock. See *fly*¹, 3 (*a*).—**Lantern-pinion.** Same as *lantern-wheel*.—**Long pinion**, a pinion whose leaves extend so far along the axis that the wheel into which the pinion works can move along its axis without becoming ungeared.—**Pinion of report**, a smaller pinion moved by the cannon-pinion of a clock.—**Rack and pinion.** See *rack*.

pinion³ (pin'yọn), *n.* Same as *piñon*. [U. S.]

pinion-bone (pin'yọn-bōn), *n.* The bones of the pinion taken together. See *pinion*¹, 3.

pinion-file (pin'yọn-fīl), *n.* A small knife-edged file used by watchmakers.

pinion-gage (pin'yọn-gāj), *n.* Fine calipers used by watchmakers.

pinionist† (pin'yọn-ist), *n.* [< *pinion*¹, *n.*, + *-ist*.] A winged animal; a bird. [Rare.]

All the flitting *pinnionists* of ayre
Attentive sate.
W. Browne, Britannia's Pastorals, i. 4.

pinion-jack (pin'yọn-jak), *n.* In *milling*, a jack for ungearing the pinion which drives the stone.

pinion-wire (pin'yọn-wīr), *n.* Wire formed into the shape and size required for the pinions of clocks and watches. It is drawn, in the same manner as round wire, through plates the holes of which correspond in section to the shape of the wire.

pinite (pin'īt), *n.* [< *Pini*, a mine in Saxony, + *-ite*².] A hydrous silicate of aluminium and potassium, occurring massive of a white to gray or green or brown color and dull waxy luster. It is formed from the alteration of other minerals (as iolite, etc.), and has many varieties; it is probably essentially a compact muscovite.

Pinites (pi-nī'tēz), *n.* [NL., < L. *pinus*, pine: see *pine*¹.] A generic name under which various fragments of plants, chiefly cones, have been described, which were supposed to belong or to be related to the genus *Pinus*, but the affinities of which were uncertain. A specimen described by Steinberg under the name of *Pinites pulvinaris* is referred by Lesquereux to *Knorria*, a lepidodendroid plant occurring in the coal-measures. The great tree-trunk found near Newcastle-on-Tyne, which measured seventy-two feet in length, and was designated as *Pinites Brandlingi* by Lindley and Hutton, has been referred by several recent writers to the *Cycadaceæ*.

pinjinnet†, *n.* Same as *pimgenet*.

pin-joint (pin'joint), *n.* A form of joint in which each part is pierced with an eye and the parts are united by passing a pin through the eye.

The rapidity with which bridges with *pin joints* can be erected is an immense advantage.
Sci. Amer. Supp., p. 8037.

pink¹ (pingk), *v.* [< ME. *pinken*, prick; prob. a nasalized form of *picken*, *pikken*, pick, peck: see *pick*¹, *peck*¹. Cf. F. *piquer*, prick, also pink (pierce with eyelet-holes). *Pink*, ME. *pink*, is a diff. word from ME. *pingen*, < AS. *pyngan*, < L. *pungere*, prick: see *pungent*.] I. *trans.* 1. To pierce; puncture; stab with a rapier or some similar weapon; make a hole or holes in.

We cut not out our clothes, sir,
At half-sword, as your tailors do, and *pink* 'em
With pikes and partizans. *Fletcher*, Mad Lover, i. 1.

I will *pink* your flesh full of holes with my rapier for this. *B. Jonson*, Every Man in his Humour, iv. 1.

"Lovel," said Mr. Coverley, affecting to whisper, "you must certainly *pink* him; you must not put up with such an affront." *Mme. D'Arblay*, Evelina, lxxxiii.

2†. To decorate with punctures or holes; tattoo.

Men and women *pinke* their bodies, putting thereon grease mixed with colour. *Purchas*, Pilgrimage, p. 648.

The sea-hedge-hogge is enclosed in a round shell, . . . handsomely wrought and *pincked*.
R. Carew, Survey of Cornwall, p. 32.

Your Wife,
If once well *pink'd*, is cloth'd for Life.
Prior, Alma, ii.

He found thee savage, and he left thee tame;
Taught thee to clothe thy *pink'd* and painted hide,
And grace thy figure with a soldier's pride.
Cowper, Expostulation, l. 486.

Specifically—3. To decorate, as any garment or article made of textile fabric or leather, by cutting small holes of regular shape in succession, scallops, loops, etc., at the edge, or elsewhere. It is usually done with the pinking-iron, the material being laid upon a block of lead or the like.

Buskins he wore of costliest cordwayne,
Pinckt upon gold, and paled part per part.
Spenser, F. Q., VI. ii. 6.

A doublet of black velvet . . . *pinked* upon scarlet satin.
Scott.

II.† *intrans.* To make a hole.

Hee *pinkes* with heore penne on heore parchemin.
Political Songs (ed. Wright), p. 156.

pink¹ (pingk), *n.* [< *pink*¹, *v.*] 1†. A puncture or small hole made by some sharp slender instrument such as a rapier or dagger; a stab-wound.

A freebooter's *pink*, sir, three or four inches deep.
Middleton, Your Five Gallants, iii. 5.

2. A small hole or eyelet punched in silk or other material with a pinking-iron; a scallop.

You had rather have
An ulcer in your body than a *pink*
More in your clothes.
B. Jonson, Magnetick Lady, iii. 4.

pink² (pingk), *n.* and *a.* [So called as having the edges of the petals delicately pinked or jagged; < *pink*¹, *v.* Cf. F. *pince*, pink, < *pincer*, pinch, nip: see *pinch* (not connected with *pink*²). According to some, so called from the small dots, resembling eyes, on some of the species. Cf. Ir. *pincin*, a gilliflower] I. *n.* 1. A plant of the genus *Dianthus*. The common garden pink is *D. plumarius*, also called *plumed* or *feathered pink*, and in its ring-marked varieties *pheasant's-eye pink*. See *Dianthus*, *carnation*¹, 3, *maiden-pink*, *meadow-pink*, 2, and phrases below.

2. One of various plants of other genera, with some resemblance to the true pinks. See *Lychnis*, 2, *moss-pink*, and phrases below.—3. A red color of low chroma but high luminosity, inclining toward purple.—4. In *painting*, any one of several lakes of a yellow or greenish-yellow color, prepared by precipitating vegetable juices on a white base, such as chalk or alumina.—5. A red coat or badge, or a person wearing one; specifically, a scarlet hunting-coat.

With pea-coats over their *pinks*.
Macmillan's Mag., I. 16.

The *pinks* stand about the inn-door lighting cigars and waiting to see us start, while their hacks are led up and down the market-place on which the inn looks.
T. *Hughes*, Tom Brown at Rugby, i. 4.

6. A small fish, so called from its color. (*a*) A minnow.

And full well may you think,
If you troll with a *pink*,
One [a fishing-rod] too weak will be apt to miscarry.
Cotton, Angler's Ballad.

The Trout is usually caught with a worm, or a minnow, which some call a *penk*, or with a fly.
I. Walton, Complete Angler, p. 90.

(*b*) A young grayling. (*c*) A young salmon before its entry into the sea. See cut under *parr*.

Presently the alevin grows into the fry, or *pink*, which is an absurd little fish about an inch long, goggle-eyed, and with dark bars on its sides. *St. Nicholas*, XIII. 740.

7. A flower; in a figurative use, a beauty; hence, the flower or highest type or example of excellence in some particular; a supremely excellent or choice example or type of excellence: as, the *pink* of perfection.

I am the very *pink* of courtesy.
Shak., R. and J., ii. 4. 61.

He had a pretty *pincke* to his own wedded wife.
Breton, Merry Wonders, p. 7. (*Davies.*)

This is the prettiest pilgrim,
The *pink* of pilgrims! *Fletcher*, Pilgrim, i. 2.

I am happy to have oblig'd the Mirrour of Knighthood and *Pink* of Courtesie in the Age.
Congreve, Old Batchelor, ii. 1.

Brown pink. See *brown*.—**Carolina pink.** See *pink-root*, 1.—**Carthusians' pink**, *Dianthus Carthusianorum*, a somewhat cultivated European species with a dense cluster of small flowers, usually dark-purple or crimson.—**Cheddar pink**, a pretty dwarf species, *Dianthus cæsius*, found at Cheddar in England.—**Cushion-pink.** Same as *moss-pink*.—**Deptford pink**, a European species, *Dianthus Armeria*, with small flowers, pink dotted with white, adventive in the eastern United States.—**Dutch pink.** (*a*) A yellow lake prepared from quercitron bark. It differs from Italian pink in not having as much coloring matter, and in being usually precipitated on a chalk base instead of alumina. It is, in effect, an inferior quality of Italian pink. (*b*) Blood. [Slang.]

That 'll take the bark from your nozzle, and distil the *Dutch pink* for you, won't it?
Cuthbert Bede, Mr. Verdant Green, II. 31.

Fire-pink, *Silene Virginica*, a plant with brilliant scarlet flowers, native in the interior United States, sometimes cultivated.—**Glacier pink**, a species of the Alps and Pyrenees, *Dianthus neglectus*, growing in low tufts whence spring many brilliant flowers.—**Grass-pink**, an orchid, *Calopogon pulchellus*, common in North American bogs. It has a slender stem with a single grass-like leaf at the base, and a short raceme of beautiful pink-purple flowers.—**Indian pink.** (*a*) See *Dianthus*. (*b*) Sometimes same as *pinkroot*, 1 (United States), and *cypress-vine* (West Indies).—**Italian pink**, a yellow lake prepared from quercitron bark.—**Mullen-pink.** See *Lychnis*, 2.—**Old-maid's pink**, the common soapwort or bouncing-bet.—**Pheasant's-eye pink.** See def. 1, above.—**Rose pink**, an inferior kind of red lake, produced by precipitating a decoction of Brazil wood on to a chalk base.—**Sea-pink**, a species of thrift in Europe, *Armeria vulgaris* (*A. maritima*).

II. *a.* Of the color or hue called pink.—**Pink coral.** See coral.—**Pink crystals.** Same as *pink salts*.—**Pink madder.** See *madder lakes*, under *madder*[1].—**Pink salt.** See *salt*.

pink[2] (pingk), *v. t.* [‹ *pink*[2], *a.*] To tinge or dye with a pink color. *Webster.*

pink[3] (pingk), *v. i.* [‹ MD. *pincken*, D. *pinken*, shut the eyes, wink, twinkle; cf. MD. *pinck-oogen*, wink; origin obscure. Cf. *pink-eye*[2].] To wink; peep slyly.

> Though his iye on us therat pleasantlie *pinke*,
> Yet will he thinke that we saie not as we thinke.
> *J. Heywood*, Spider and Fly (1556). (*Nares.*)

> A hungry fox lay winking and *pinking* as if he had sore eyes. *Sir R. L'Estrange.*

> I'll be with ye as soon as daylight begins to *pink* in.
> *Thomas Hardy*, Distracted Preacher, vi.

pink[4]† (pingk), *n.* [‹ MD. *pinck*, D. *pink* = MLG. LG. *pinke* (› G. *pinke*); cf. F. *pinque* = Sp. *pinco*, *pinque* = Pg. *pinque*, from the D. or LG.; appar. the same, with loss of the initial syllable, as MD. *espinck* = Icel. *espingr* = Sw. *esping*, a long boat, ‹ MD. *espe* = Icel. *espi*, asp, aspen-tree: see *asp*[1].] A vessel or boat with a very narrow stern. Now called *pinky*.

> Thus by dividing their squadrons, and spreading the whole sea ouer a mighty way, there could not so much as the least *pinke* passe but she was espied.
> *Hakluyt's Voyages*, I. 610.

> From most parts of Holland or Zealand, *pinks* or shipping may be had at the brewhouses in Saint Katherine's.
> *John Taylor* (Arber's Eng. Garner, I. 245).

> A Dutch *pink* arrived, which had been to the southward a trading. *Winthrop*, Hist. New England, I. 124.

pink[5] (pingk), *n.* [Imitative; cf. *spink* and *finch*, and also *pinc-pinc*. Hence dim. *pinkety*.] A finch; the chaffinch or spink, *Fringilla cœlebs*.

pink[6]†, *n.* [Origin obscure.] A game at cards: the same as *post*[2], 11. Collier's Hist. Dram. Poet., ii. 315. (*Halliwell.*)

pinkcheek (pingk'chēk), *n.* An Australian fish, *Upeneichthys porosus*. [New South Wales.]

pinked (pingkt), *p. a.* Pierced or worked with small holes, sometimes showing a lining of another color; reticulated; scalloped.

> A haberdasher's wife of small wit . . . railed upon me, till her *pinked* porringer fell off her head.
> *Shak.*, Hen. VIII., v. 4. 50.

> The Court is all full of vests, only my Lord St. Albans not *pinked*, but plain black; and they say the King says the pinking upon white makes them look too much like magpies. *Pepys*, Diary, II. 475.

> Letters, long proofs of love, and verses fine
> Round the *pink'd* rims of crisped Valentine.
> *Crabbe*, Works, I. 111.

pinkeen (ping'kēn), *n.* [‹ Ir. *pincin*.] The stickleback. [South of Ireland.]

pinker (ping'kėr), *n.* [‹ *pink*[1] + *-er*[1].] 1. One who scallops silk or other fabric; one who makes eyelets or small ornamental holes or scallops in cloth.—2†. A piercer or stabber; one who stabs another, as in a duel.

pinkety (ping'ket-i), *n.*; pl. *pinketies* (-iz). [Imitative; as *pink*[5] + *-ety*, with dim. force.] The chaffinch, *Fringilla cœlebs*. [Prov. Eng.]

pink-eye[1] (pingk'ī), *n.* [‹ *pink*[2] + *eye*[1].] A contagious influenza of horses. It is a febrile disease, closely allied to scarlet fever in man, named from the pink color of the conjunctiva. There is a similar inflammation of the eye in man.

pink-eye[2] (pingk'ī), *n.* [‹ *pink*[3], *v.*, wink, blink, + *eye*[1], after MD. **pinck-ooghe*, *pimp-ooghe*, one who has small eyes; cf. *pinck-ooghen*, *pimp-ooghen*, make the eyes small, look at with half-shut eyes, contract the eyebrows, wink, blink; ‹ *pincken*, wink, + *ooghe*, eye: see *pink*[3], *v.*, and *eye*[1]. *Pink* in the Shakspere quot. is usually regarded as an adj., with the assumed sense 'winking' or 'blinking'; but if an adj., it must belong to *pink*[2]. Cf. *pinky*[2].] A small eye.

> It was a sport very pleasaunt of theeze beastz, to see the bear with his *pink nyez* leering after his enmiez approach.
> *Laneham*, Letter from Kenilworth. (*Nares.*)

> Plumpy Bacchus with *pink eyne*.
> *Shak.*, A. and C., ii. 7. 121.

pink-eyed[1] (pingk'īd), *a.* [‹ *pink*[2] + *eye*[1] + *-ed*[2].] Having pink eyes, literally, as a white mouse or rabbit. This is the usual color of the eyes in albinism, whether accidentally occurring or artificially produced. It is due to the absence of the natural pigment of the iris and choroid, which are then tinged a light-red color by the blood in the minute vessels.

pink-eyed[2] (pingk'īd), *a.* [‹ *pink-eye*[2] + *-ed*[2].] Having small or blinking eyes.

> Them that were *pink-eyed*, and had veric small cies, they termed ocellæ. *Holland*, tr. of Pliny, xi. 37.

pinkie[1], **pinkie**[2], etc. See *pinky*.

pinkiness (ping'ki-nes), *n.* Pink hue; the pale-red color of the pink.

> Mr. Bult . . . had the general solidity and suffusive *pinkiness* of a healthy Briton on the central table-land of life. *George Eliot*, Daniel Deronda, xxii.

pinking (ping'king), *n.* [Verbal n. of *pink*[1], *v.*] The operation or process of punching a decorative pattern of scallops and small holes or eyes along the margin of silk and other fabrics used for dress or upholstery. Also called *pouncing*.

pinking-iron (ping'king-ī'ėrn), *n.* A tool for cutting out pinked borders. The material is laid upon lead or other suitable substance, and the iron struck upon it with a hammer.

pinkish (pingk'ish), *a.* Somewhat pink.

pink-needle (pingk'nē'dl), *n.* 1. A shepherd's bodkin. *Sherwood.*—2. The stork's-bill, *Erodium cicutarium*, its carpels having long awns like needles for pinking; also, the Venus's-comb, *Scandix Pecten-veneris*. [Prov. Eng.]

pinkroot (pingk'röt), *n.* 1. The root of the Carolina or Indian pink, *Spigelia Marilandica*, a well-known vermifuge officinal in the United States: in large doses narcotic-poisonous.—2. The plant itself, an herb with showy flowers, red outside, yellow inside, common southward in the United States. Also called *Maryland pinkroot* and *worm-grass*. The name extends to the species *S. Anthelmia* of the West Indies and South America, there used as a similar remedy.

pink-saucer (pingk'sâ'sėr), *n.* A small saucer coated with a coloring substance which, when applied to the face, gives a fresh pink color; also, a similar saucer the coating of which was formerly used to give a flesh-tint to silk stockings or ribbons.

Pinkster (pingk'stėr), *n.* and *a.* [Also *Pinxter*, *Pingster*, ‹ D. *Pinkster*, Easter: see *Pentecost*.] Whitsuntide: as, *Pinkster* frolics. [Dutch American.]

> The next day was the first of the three that are devoted to *Pinkster*, the great Saturnalia of the New York blacks. Although this festival is always kept with more vivacity at Albany than in York, it is far from being neglected, even now, in the latter place. *Cooper*, Satanstoe, iv.

pinkster-flower (pingk'stėr-flou'ėr), *n.* The beautiful shrub *Rhododendron* (*Azalea*) *nudiflorum*, common in swamps and on shaded hillsides from Canada to Texas. The flowers have the

Flowering Branch of Purple Azalea, or Pinkster-flower (*Rhododendron nudiflorum*).

style and stamens much exserted, and are quite variable in color—pink, purple, and (in the South) sometimes yellow. Also called *azalea* and *honeysuckle*. [Local, New York and New England.]

pink-stern (pingk'stėrn), *n.* A pinky.

pink-sterned (pingk'stėrnd), *a.* Narrow or sharp in the stern, as a pinky.

pinkweed (pingk'wēd), *n.* The common knotgrass, *Polygonum aviculare*: so called from a pinkish color about the joints.

pinkwood (pingk'wůd), *n.* A Brazilian tree, *Dicypellium* (*Persea*) *caryophyllatum*, scented throughout like the carnation, whence the name; also, an unspecified Australian cabinet-wood.—**Brazilian pinkwood.** See *Physocalymma*.

pinky[1] (ping'ki), *a.* [‹ *pink*[2] + *-y*[1].] Of a pink color; somewhat pink.

pinky[2] (ping'ki), *a.* [Also *pinkie*, *pinkey*; ‹ *pink*[3] + *-y*[1].] Winking; blinking; pink-eyed.

> The bear with his *pinkey* eyes leering after his enemy's approach. *Knight*, Pict. Hist. Eng., II. 875.

pinky[3] (ping'ki), *n.*; pl. *pinkies* (-kiz). [Dim. of *pink*[4].] A narrow-sterned boat; a pink. Also *pinkie*.

pinky-built (ping'ki-bilt), *a.* Built like a pinky—that is, with a sharp stern.

pin-lock (pin'lok), *n.* 1. A form of lock in which the bolt is a projecting cylindrical pin.—2†. A poundmaster's fee.

> The *pinlock*, or pinder's fee, is regulated by an Act of Philip and Mary at fourpence for any number of cattle impounded, which custom has made into one of fourpence for each head. *V. B. Redstone* (N. and Q., 6th ser., X. 197).

pin-machine (pin'ma-shēn'), *n.* 1. A machine for making pins.—2. A machine for cutting and shaping wooden dowels and sash- or blind-pins. It cuts and points pins of all shapes and different sizes.

pin-maker (pin'mā'kėr), *n.* One employed in the making of pins.

pin-mark (pin'märk), *n.* The small circular indentation on one side and near the shoulder of a printing-type. It is made by the pin which dislodges the type from the mold in which it was cast.

pin-mill (pin'mil), *n.* A kind of hide-mill for softening skins after they have been soaked in a weak solution of sulphuric acid, rinsed with clean water, and again steeped in a solution of sal-soda and soap, which neutralizes any traces of acid remaining after the rinsing process. It consists of a large drum, with pins projecting from the interior surface, in which the skins are placed loosely, the drum revolving till they are sufficiently pliable for future operations.

> The Morocco tanners at Lynn, Mass., and other places in New England where it is used, call it a *pin-mill*.
> *C. T. Davis*, Leather, p. 251.

pin-money (pin'mun'i), *n.* 1. An allowance or occasional gift made by a husband to his wife, either voluntarily or as a part of the marriage settlement, for her separate use, to be employed in the purchase of apparel or of ornaments for her person, or for other personal expenditure. Technically, in *law*, it is an annual sum; and arrears can be claimed only for one year, and by the wife, but not by her representatives.

> They have a greater interest in property than either maids or wives, and do not hold their jointures by the precarious tenure of portions or *pin-money*.
> *Addison*, The Ladies' Association.

> The main Article with me is, that Foundation of Wives Rebellion, and Husbands Cuckoldum, that cursed *Pin-Money*—Five-hundred Pound per Annum *Pin-Money*.
> *Steele*, Tender Husband, i. 1.

2. A similar allowance made to any one, as to a daughter.

pinna[1] (pin'ạ̈), *n.*; pl. *pinnæ* (-ē). [NL., ‹ L. *pinna*, *penna*, a feather, wing: see *pen*[2], *pin*[1].] 1. In *anat.* and *zoöl.*: (*a*) A feather. See *penna*. (*b*) A bird's wing. See *pinion*[1]. (*c*) A fish's fin: the usual technical name. (*d*) Some winglike or fin-like part or organ, as the flipper of a seal or cetacean. (*e*) The outer ear, which projects from the head; the auricle, or pavilion of the ear. See cut under *ear*[1]. (*f*) The nostril, or wing of the nose. (*g*) One of the smaller branches of some polyps, as plumularians. (*h*) In entomology, a small oblique ridge forming one of the lines of a pinnate surface. See *pinnate*.—2. In *bot.*, one of the primary divisions of a pinnate leaf: applied most commonly to ferns. In a simply pinnate leaf it is a single leaflet, in a bipinnate leaf it consists of a partial petiole or rachis with the leaflets arranged along the sides. See cut under *Osmunda*.—**Dilatator pinnæ.** Same as *depressor alæ nasi*.—**Pinnæ of the nose**, the alæ nasi; the nostrils.

Pinna[2] (pin'ạ̈), *n.* [NL., ‹ L. *pinna*, *pina*, ‹ Gr. *πίννα*, *πίνα*, a kind of mussel.] 1. A genus of bivalves, typical of the family *Pinnidæ*. They are commonly called *sea-wings*, and are remarkable for the size of the byssus by which they adhere to rocks. It is notably long and delicate, is very strong, has a beautiful silky luster, and is capable of being woven into cloth, upon which a very high value is set. This manufacture was known to the ancients, and is still practised in Italy. Some species of *Pinna* measure about two feet long, with a byssus of the same length. See also cut under *byssus*.

Pinna rotunda. *a*, the byssus.

2. [*l. c.*] A bivalve mollusk of the genus *Pinna*.

pinnace (pin'ās), *n.* [Formerly also *pinace*; ‹ F. *pinasse*, *pinace* = Sp. *pinaza* = Pg. *pinaça*, ‹ It. *pinazza*, *pinassa*, a pinnace, pine, anything made of pine, a ship, ‹ L. *pinus*, pine: see *pine*[1], *n.*] 1. *Naut.*: (*a*†) A small vessel, generally with two masts rigged like those of a schooner, and capable of being propelled by oars; a galley: so called because built of pine wood; poetically, any light sailing-vessel.

> Thou canst safely steer
> My vent'rous *Pinnasse* to her wished Peer.
> *Sylvester*, tr. of Du Bartas's Weeks, ii., Eden.

His fourth Son Edwyn was by his Brother Athelstan, out of Jealousie of State, put into a little *Pinnace*, without either Tackle or Oars. *Baker*, Chronicles, p. 9.

This yeere Master Stickles, the excellent Architect of our time, did, onely to try conclusion, build a *pinnace* in Leaden hall, being of burden about line or sixe tun, which at pleasure might bee taken asunder and ioyned together. *Stow*, Elizabeth, an. 1595.

There came from Virginia into Salem a *pinnace* of eighteen tons, laden with corn and tobacco. *Winthrop*, Hist. New England, I. 67.

> Swift as a swallow sweeps the liquid way,
> The winged *pinnace* shot along the sea. *Pope*.

(*b*) A large double-banked ship's boat.—2†. A procuress; a prostitute. [Old slang.]

> For when all the gallants are gone out o' th' town,
> O then these fine *pinaces* lack their due lading.
> *Songs of the London Prentices*, p. 66. (*Halliwell*.)

She hath been before me—punk, *pinnace*, and bawd—any time these two and twenty years, upon record in the Pie-Poudres. *B. Jonson*, Bartholomew Fair, i. 1.

pinnacle (pin'ạ-kl), *n.* [Early mod. E. also *pinacle*; < ME. *pinnakell*, *pinacle*, *pynacle*, < OF. *pinacle*, *pinnacle*, F. *pinacle* = Sp. *pináculo* = Pg. *pinaculo* = It. *pinacolo*, *pinnacolo*, < LL. *pinnaculum*, a peak, pinnacle; double dim., < L. *pinna*, a pinnacle: see *pin*[1].] 1. A sharp point or peak; the very topmost point, as of a mountain.

He then led me to the highest *pinnacle* of the rock, and placed me on the top of it. *Addison*, Vision of Mirza.

> Far off, three mountain-tops,
> Three silent *pinnacles* of aged snow,
> Stood sunset-flush'd. *Tennyson*, Lotos-Eaters.

2. In *arch.*, any relatively small structure (of whatever form, but commonly terminating in a cone or a pyramid) that rises above the roof or coping of a building, or caps a projecting architectural member, such as a buttress. Its constructive object is to give greater weight to the member which it crowns, in order that this may better resist some lateral pressure. The application of the term is generally limited to an ornamental spire-shaped structure, standing on parapets, angles, and buttresses, and often adorned with rich and varied devices. Pinnacles are very numerous in the fully developed medieval style; their shafts are sometimes formed into niches, and are sometimes paneled or quite plain; in examples of late date, every one of the sides generally terminates in a gablet. The tops are often crocketed, and have finials at the apex. Pinnacles are most often square in plan, but are sometimes octagonal, hexagonal, or pentagonal. See also cut under crocket.

Pinnacle of Buttress, York Minster, England.

> Mony *pynakle* payntet watz poudred ay quere,
> Among the castel carnelez, clambred so thik,
> That pared out of papure purely hit semed.
> *Sir Gawayne and the Green Knight* (E. E. T. S.), l. 801.

> Some renown'd metropolis,
> With glistering spires and *pinnacles* adorn'd.
> *Milton*, P. L., iii. 550.

pinnacle (pin'ạ-kl), *v. t.*; pret. and pp. *pinnacled*, ppr. *pinnacling*. [< ME. *pynaklen*; < *pinnacle*, *n.*] 1. To put a pinnacle or pinnacles on; furnish with a pinnacle or pinnacles.

> A pyȝt coroune ȝet wer that gyrle,
> Of mariorys & non other ston,
> Hiȝe *pynakled* of cler quyt perle,
> Wyth flurted flowreȝ perfet vpon.
> *Alliterative Poems* (ed. Morris), i. 207.

The pediment of the southern transept is *pinnacled*, not inelegantly, with a flourished cross. *T. Warton*, Hist. Kiddington, p. 8.

2. To place on or as on a pinnacle.

> The loftiest star of unascended heaven,
> *Pinnacled* dim in the intense inane.
> *Shelley*, Prometheus Unbound, iii. 4.

pinnacle-work (pin'ạ-kl-wėrk), *n.* In *arch.* and *decoration*, ornamental projections, especially at the top of any object; fleurons, knops, finials, and the like, taken collectively.

pinnadiform (pi-nad'i-fôrm), *a.* [Irreg. < *pinna*[1] + *-ad-* + *form*.] In *ichth.*, having the apparent form modified by an extension or encroachment of the skin and scales on the fins or some of them, as the dorsal and anal, as in the chætodontids. *Gill.*

pinnæ, *n.* Plural of *pinna*[1].

283

pinnage† (pin'āj), *n.* [For **pindage*, < *pind* + *-age*. Cf. equiv. *poundage*[2].] Poundage of cattle. See *pound*[2].

Pinnata (pi-nā'tạ̈), *n. pl.* [NL., < L. *pinnatus*, feathered: see *pinnate*.] In *herpet.*, the marine chelonians; turtles with flippers or fins. See *Euereta*.

pinnate (pin'āt), *a.* [= F. *penné* = Sp. *pinado* = It. *pinnato*, < L. *pinnatus*, feathered, pinnate, < *pinna*, *penna*, feather: see *pen*[2]. Cf. *pennate*.] 1. Shaped like a feather, or resembling a feather in structure. (*a*) In *bot.*, noting leaves of such form. Also *pennate*. (*b*) In *entom.*, noting a surface (especially that of the posterior femora of grasshoppers) having minute parallel oblique lines on each side of a central ridge, so that the whole somewhat resembles a feather. 2. In *zoöl.*: (*a*) Feathered; pinnated. (*b*) Provided with a pinna or pinnæ; having wings, fins, or similar parts.—**Abruptly, alternately, decursively, digitately pinnate.** See the adverbs.—**Articulate-pinnate leaf**, a winged leaf having the common footstalk jointed.—**Equally** or **interruptedly pinnate.** Same as *abruptly pinnate*.—**Oppositely pinnate leaf.** See *oppositely*.—**Pinnate cirrose leaf**, a leaf that is winged and terminates with a tendril.—**Pinnate leaf**, a compound leaf whose leaflets, except the terminal one, are attached to the sides of the main or partial rachis. See cuts under *Jacob's-ladder* and *Phytelephas*.—**Unequally pinnate leaf**, a pinnate leaf with a single terminal leaflet.

pinnated (pin'ā-ted), *a.* Same as *pinnate*.—**Pinnated grouse.** See *grouse*, *prairie-hen*, and cut under *Cupidonia*.

pinnatedly (pin'ā-ted-li), *adv.* Same as *pinnately*.

pinnately (pin'āt-li), *adv.* So as to be pinnate.—**Pinnately cleft.** Same as *pinnatifid*.—**Pinnately lobed.** Same as *pinnatilobed*.—**Pinnately nerved** or **veined.** Same as *penninerved*. See cut under *nervation*.

pinnatifid (pi-nat'i-fid), *a.* [Also *pennatifid*; = F. *pinnatifide*, *pennatifide* = Pg. *pinnatifido*, < L. *pinnatus*, pinnate, + *findere* (√ *fid*), cleave.] In *bot.*, cut or cleft in a pinnate manner, with the divisions half-way down or more, and the sinuses or lobes narrow or acute. Also *pinnisected*.

Pinnatifid Leaf of *Centaurea scabiosa*.

pinnatilobate (pi-nat-i-lō'bāt), *a.* [< L. *pinnatus*, pinnate, + NL. *lobatus*, lobate.] Same as *pinnatilobed*.

pinnatilobed (pi-nat'i-lōbd), *a.* [< *pinnatilobe* + *-ed*[2].] In *bot.*, lobed in a pinnate manner—that is, with the divisions extending more than half-way to the midrib, and with either sinuses or lobes rounded. See cut 7 under *oak*.

pinnation (pi-nā'shọn), *n.* [< *pinnate* + *-ion*.] In *bot.*, the state or condition of being pinnate.

pinnatipartite (pi-nat-i-pär'tīt), *a.* [= F. *pennatipartite*; < L. *pinnatus*, pinnate, + *partitus*, parted: see *partite*.] In *bot.*, parted in a pinnate manner—that is, with the lobes extending almost but not quite to the midrib.

pinnatiped (pi-nat'i-ped), *a.* and *n.* [= Pg. *pinnatipede*; < NL. *pinnatipes* (*-ped-*), < L. *pinnatus*, pinnate, + *pes* (*ped-*) = E. *foot*.] I. *a.* Fin-footed, as a bird; lobiped.

II. *n.* One of the *Pinnatipedes*.

Pinnatipedes (pin-ạ-tip'e-dēz), *n. pl.* [NL., pl. of *pinnatipes*: see *pinnatiped*.] A group of pinnatiped birds. Also *Pinnipedes*. *Schaeffer.*

pinnatisect (pi-nat'i-sekt), *a.* [= F. *pennatiséqué*; < L. *pinnatus*, pinnate, + *sectus*, pp. of *secare*, cut.] In *bot.*, pinnately divided; cut quite down to the midrib, but with the segments not articulated. Also *pinnatisected*.

pinnatulate (pi-naṭ'ụ̄-lāt), *a.* [< LL. **pinnatulus*, *pennatulus*, dim., < L. *pinnatus*, pinnate: see *pinnate*.] In *bot.*, again subdivided: said of the leaflet of a pinnate leaf.

pinna-wool (pin'ạ̈-wůl), *n.* A fabric made from the byssus of a pinna.

pin-necked (pin'nekt), *a.* Pinnated, as a grouse. The pin-necked grouse belong to *Cupidonia*.

pinner[1] (pin'ėr), *n.* [< ME. *pinnere*; < *pin*[1], *v.*, + *-er*[1].] 1. One who pins or fastens with a pin.—2†. A pin-maker. *Destruction of Troy*, Notes, p. 486.—3. An apron with a bib, kept in place by pinning; a pinafore.

She had on a black velvet gown, and a white *pinner* and apron. *Kingsley*, Water-Babies, p. 229.

4†. A woman's head-dress, having long flaps hanging down the sides of the cheeks, worn during the early part of the eighteenth century: generally in the plural.

Pinners.

Four *Pinners* to help narrow Foreheads and long Noses, and Very forward, to make the Eyes look languishing. *Mrs. Centlivre*, Platonick Lady, iii.

It will neither be your crimped *pinners*, Mrs. Lilias (speaking of them with due respect), nor my silver hair, or golden chain, that will fill up the void which Roland Græme must needs leave in our lady's leisure. *Scott*, Abbot, vi.

pinner[2]† (pin'ėr), *n.* [< *pin*[2], *v.*, + *-er*[1]; ult. a var. of *pinder*[1].] A pinder or pound-master.

One George-a-Greene, the *Pinner* of the town. *Greene*, George-a-Greene.

pinnet† (pin'et), *n.* [Dim. of L. *pinna*, a pinnacle: see *pin*[1].] A pinnacle.

> Blazed battlement and *pinnet* high,
> Blazed every rose-carved buttress fair.
> *Scott*, L. of L. M., vi. 23.

Pinnidæ (pin'i-dē), *n. pl.* [NL., < *Pinna*[2] + *-idæ*.] A family of bivalve mollusks, named from the genus *Pinna*; the pinnas. They are closely related to the *Aviculidæ* (with which they are united by some conchologists), but differ in having a triangular or mytiliform shell with two muscular scars, a linear ligament, and a hinge without teeth. The species are mostly inhabitants of warm seas, but one occurs in English waters. Also named *Pinninæ* as a subfamily of *Aviculidæ*. *J. E. Gray*, 1840. See cut under *Pinna*[2].

pinnie, *n.* See *pinny*[2].

pinniewinkle, *n.* See *pinnywinkle*.

pinniform (pin'i-fôrm), *a.* [= F. *pinniforme*, < L. *pinna*, feather, fin, + *forma*, form.] 1. Like a feather; penniform.—2. Like a fin or flipper: as, the *pinniform* wing of the penguin.—3. Pinnate in form, in any sense; slate; lobate; auriculate.—4. Resembling a mollusk of the genus *Pinna*.

Pinnigrada (pi-nig'rạ̈-dạ̈), *n. pl.* [NL., neut. pl. of *pinnigradus*: see *pinnigrade*.] 1. The crinoids as an order of echinoderms. See *Crinoidea*. [Little used.]—2. In *mammal.*, same as *Pinnipedia*. *Owen.*

pinnigrade (pin'i-grād), *a.* and *n.* [< NL. *pinnigradus*, < L. *pinna*, feather, fin, + *gradi*, walk, go.] I. *a.* Moving by means of fins, flippers, or other pinnate parts.

II. *n.* A member of the *Pinnigrada*; a pinniped.

pinninerved (pin'i-nėrvd), *a.* [< L. *pinna*, feather, + *nervum*, nerve, + *-ed*[2].] In *bot.*, same as *penninerved*.

pinning (pin'ing), *n.* [Verbal n. of *pin*[1], *v.*] 1. The act of fastening or securing with a pin.—2. The masonry that supports studwork.—**Pinning in**, the operation of filling in the joints of masonry with spalls or chips of stone.—**Pinning up**, in *building*, the operation of driving in wedges for the purpose of bringing an upper work to bear fully upon an underpinning constructed beneath.

pinniped (pin'i-ped), *a.* and *n.* [< L. *pinna*, feather, fin, + *pes* (*ped-*) = E. *foot*.] I. *a.* Fin-footed, in any sense; having feet like fins or flippers. Specifically—(*a*) Having flippers, as a seal; pinnigrade; belonging to the *Pinnigrada* or *Pinnipedia*, as a mammal. (*b*) Pinnatiped or lobiped, as a bird; belonging to the *Pinnatipedes*. (*c*) Totipalmate or steganopodous, as a bird; belonging to the *Pinnipedes* (see *Pinnipedes*, 1 (*b*)). (*d*) Having alate locomotory appendages, as a pteropod; pteropodous.

II. *n.* A member of the *Pinnipedes* or *Pinnipedia*: opposed to *fissiped*.

Pinnipedes (pi-nip'e-dēz), *n. pl.* [NL., pl. of *pinnipes*: see *pinniped*.] 1. In *ornith.*: (*a*) Same as *Pinnatipedes*. (*b*) Same as *Totipalmatæ* or *Steganopodes*.—2. In *mammal.*, same as *Pinnipedia*.—3. In *Crustacea*, crabs which have some of the limbs like flippers, fitted for swimming; the paddle-crabs, shuttle-crabs, or swimming-crabs. See cut under *paddle-crab*.

Pinnipedia (pin-i-pē'di-ạ̈), *n. pl.* [NL., neut. pl. of *pinnipes*. See *pinniped*.] In *zoöl.*, the pinnigrade, pinniped, or fin-footed aquatic carnivorous quadrupeds, constituting one of the prime divisions of the order *Feræ* or *Carnivora*, the other being the *Fissipedia*. In Illiger's classification (1811) it was the thirteenth order of mammals. The body is prone, not raised from the ground; the limbs are modified into fins or flippers for swimming, and confined within the common integument beyond the elbows and knees; the feet are rotated backward. The first phalanges and digits of the manus and pes are enlarged beyond the others. The deciduous dentition is much reduced or rudimentary. The skull is greatly compressed between the orbits; the lacrymal bone is imperforate, intraorbital, and rarely confluent with the maxillary, which bounds the orbit; the palatines are not produced forward laterally; and there are extensive vacuities between the frontal and maxillary bones and between the tympanics and exoccipitals. There are three families—the *Otariidæ* or eared seals (sea-lions, sea-bears, etc.), the *Phocidæ* or seals proper, and the *Trichechidæ* or walruses. Also called *Pinnipedes* and *Pinnigrada*. See cuts under *otary*, *seal*, and *walrus*.

pinnisected (pin'i-sek-ted), *a.* [< L. *pinna*, feather, + *sectus*, pp. of *secare*, cut, + *-ed*[2].] In *bot.*, same as *pinnatifid*.

pinnitarsal (pin-i-tär'sal), *a.* [‹ L. *pinna*, feather, + NL. *tarsus*, tarsus, + *-al.*] Having pinnate feet, as a swimming-crab.

pinnitentaculate (pin″i-ten-tak'ū-lāt), *a.* [‹ L. *pinna*, a fin, + NL. *tentaculum*, a tentacle, + *-ate*[1].] Having pinnate tentacles, as a polyp; alcyonarian. See *Alcyonaria.*

pinnock[1] (pin'ọk), *n.* [‹ ME. *pinnuc*, hedge-sparrow: said to be so called in imitation of its short piping note (cf. *pink*[5]).] 1. The dunnock or hedge-sparrow, *Accentor modularis.* See cut under *Accentor.* [Prov. Eng.]—2. A titmouse or tomtit.—**Bearded pinnock**, the bearded titmouse, *Panurus biarmicus.*

pinnock[2] (pin'ọk), *n.* [Origin obscure.] A tunnel under a road to carry off water; a culvert. [Local, Eng.]

pinnoite (pin'ọ̄-īt), *n.* [Named after the mineralogist *Pinno.*] A hydrous borate of magnesium, occurring in tetragonal crystals and fibrous massive forms of a yellow color. It is found at Stassfurt in Prussia, where it has probably resulted from the alteration of boracite.

pinnothere (pin'ọ̄-thēr), *n.* [= F. *pinnotère* = Pg. *pinoteres* (pl.), ‹ NL. *Pinotheres, Pinoteres*: see *Pinotheres.*] A crab of the genus *Pinnotheres*; a pea-crab.

Pinnotheres (pin-ọ̄-thē'rēz), *n.* [NL. (Latreille, 1807), prop. *Pinnoteres*, ‹ Gr. πιννοτηρής, a small crab that lives in the pinna's shell, ‹ πίννα, πίννη, the pinna (see *Pinna*[2]), + τηρεῖν, guard.] A genus of small crustaceans, typical of the family *Pinnotheriidæ*, so called because they inhabit the shells of pinnas and other bivalve mollusks, as oysters; the pea-crabs. One of the best-known is *P. ostreum*, the little crab frequently found in the American oyster (*Ostrea virginica*), which when cooked is of a delicate flesh-color with a red band. *P. pisum*, the European pea-crab proper, inhabits mussels. *P. veterum* was known to the ancients as inhabiting the pinnas in the Mediterranean. See cut under *pea-crab.*

pinnotherian (pin-ọ̄-thē'ri-an), *a.* and *n.* [‹ *Pinnotheres* + *-an.*] I. *a.* Relating to pea-crabs; belonging to the genus *Pinnotheres* or the family *Pinnotheriidæ.*

II. *n.* A pea-crab.

Pinnotheriidæ (pin″ọ̄-thẹ-rī'i-dē), *n. pl.* [NL., ‹ *Pinnotheres* + *-idæ.*] A family of brachyurous decapod crustaceans, typified by the genus *Pinnotheres*; the pea-crabs. They are of small size and rounded form, with slender legs and thin, soft integument, owing to their habitual residence inside the shells of the various bivalves of which they are commensals.

pinnula (pin'ū-lạ̈), *n.*; pl. *pinnulæ* (-lē). [NL.: see *pinnule.*] 1. In *zoöl.*: (*a*) A pinnule, or small pinna; some little pinnate part or organ. Specifically—(1) A barb of a feather. See *barb*[1], 3. (2) One of the series of lateral branchlets of the arms of a crinoid. See cut under *Crinoidea.* (3) Same as *pinnulus.* *Sollas.* (*b*) [*cap.*] A genus of bivalve mollusks. *Rafinesque*, 1815.—2. In *bot.*, same as *pinnule*, 3.

pinnulate (pin'ū-lāt), *a.* [‹ NL. *pinnulatus*, ‹ L. *pinnula*, a pinnule: see *pinnule.*] In *zoöl.* and *bot.*, provided with pinnulæ or pinnules.

pinnulated (pin'ū-lā-ted), *a.* [‹ *pinnulate* + *-ed*[2].] Same as *pinnulate.*

pinnule (pin'ūl), *n.* [= F. *pinnule* = It. *pinnola*, ‹ L. *pinnula*, a little plume; dim. ‹ L. *pinna*, a feather: see *pinna*[1], *pen*[2].] 1. A pinnula.—2. In *ichth.*, specifically, a small fin-like appendage. It is developed especially in scombroid fishes, as the mackerel, behind the dorsal and anal fins. Pinnules are really low, short, detached fin-rays, much branched and without membranous connection with one another or with the fin proper. See cut under *mackerel.* 3. In *bot.*, a secondary pinna; one of the pinnately disposed divisions of a pinna: noting especially the ultimate divisions of the frond in ferns. Also *pinnula.* See cuts under *indusium* and *Nothochlæna.*

pinnulus (pin'ū-lus), *n.*; pl. *pinnuli* (-lī). [NL., ‹ L. *pinnula*: see *pinnule.*] A form of sexradiate sponge-spicule resulting from the suppression of the proximal ray and the development of porrect spines on the distal ray. Also *pinnula.* *Sollas.*

pinny[1] (pin'i), *a.* [‹ *pin*[1] + *-y*[1].] Pinned; clogged; choked: as, a *pinny* file.

pinny[2], **pinnie** (pin'i), *n.* [Abbr. dim. of *pinafore.*] A pinafore: a childish or colloquial word.

> When, poor bantling! down she tumbled,
> Daubed her hands, and face, and *pinny.*
> *F. Locker*, Piccadilly.

pinnywinkle, pinniewinkle (pin'i-wing-kl), *n.* [Appar. a particular use and corrupted form of *periwinkle*[2].] An old instrument of torture consisting of a board with holes into which the fingers were thrust and pressed upon with pegs. Also *pinnywinks.* [Scotch.]

> They prick us and they pine us, and they pit us on the *pinny-winkles* for witches.
> *Scott*, Bride of Lammermoor, xxiii.

pinnywinks (pin'i-wingks), *n.* [Also *penny-winks, pilniewinks*, etc.: see *pinnywinkle.*] Same as *pinnywinkle.*

pin-oak (pin'ōk), *n.* A tree, *Quercus palustris*, found in wet places in the eastern half of the United States: so named in allusion to the persistent dead branches, which resemble pins driven into the trunk. It grows from 70 to 90 feet high, and affords a wood of some value. Also called *swamp Spanish oak* and *water-oak.*

pinole (pi-nō'le), *n.* [‹ Sp. *pinole*, ‹ Mex. *pinolli.*] 1. An aromatic powder used in Italy for making chocolate. *Simmonds.*—2. Maize (or, more rarely, wheat) dried, ground, and sometimes mixed with the flour of mesquit-beans, which are quite sweet: used somewhat extensively as an article of food on the borders of Mexico and California.

piñon (pin'yọn), *n.* [Sp.-Amer.: see *pinion*[1].] One of several nut-pines of the Rocky Mountain region, as *Pinus Parryana, P. edulis*, and *P. monophylla*; also, a seed of one of these trees.—**Piñon jay**, the blue-headed or Maximilian's jay: so called from its fondness for piñons and other nut-pines. See *Cyanocephalus*, and cut under *Gymnocitta.*

pinpatch (pin'pach), *n.* The common periwinkle, *Littorina littorea.* [Suffolk, Eng.]

pin-pillow (pin'pil″ō), *n.* A species of prickly-pear, *Opuntia Curassavica.*

pin-point (pin'point), *n.* The point of a pin; hence, a trifle.

pin-poppet (pin'pop″et), *n.* A pincase. [North. Eng.]

pin-rack (pin'rak), *n.* *Naut.*, a rail or frame having holes for holding belaying-pins.

pin-rail (pin'rāl), *n.* 1. A bar or strip, usually of wood, to which are secured pegs or hooks for hanging up various objects.—2. In *organ-building*, a ledge of wood passing under the keys of the manual, in which the key-pins are fixed.—3. *Naut.*, a rail of wood or metal for holding belaying-pins to which ropes are belayed.

pin-rib (pin'rib), *n.* A delicate cord or rib woven in the substance of fine muslin.

pin-rod (pin'rod), *n.* In a locomotive, a tie-rod connecting the brake-shoes on opposite sides.

pinsers†, *n.* An obsolete form of *pincers.*

pinsnet† (pins'net), *n.* [Contr. of **pinsonet*, ‹ *pinson*[2] + *-et.*] Same as *pinson*[2].

> To these their nether-stockes they have corked shooes, *pinsnets*, and fine pantoffles, which bear them up a finger or two from the ground.
> *Stubbes*, Anatomie of Abuses, p. 55.

pinson[1] (pin'sọn), *n.* [Early mod. E. also *pynson*; ‹ ME. *pynsone, pensyn*, pincers, forceps, ‹ OF. **pinçon, pinchon*, dim. of *pince*, pincers, ‹ *pincer*, pinch, nip: see *pinch.*] Pincers; nippers; forceps: usually in the plural. *Halliwell.* [Obsolete or prov. Eng.]

> The *pensynnys*, that drewe the naylys owt
> Of fete and handys, alle a-bowt,
> And losyd thi bodye from the tre,
> Of myn synnys, lord, lose thou me.
> *Holy Rood* (E. E. T. S.), p. 189.

> *Pynsone*, to drawe owt tethe, dentaria.
> *Prompt. Parv.*, p. 400.

> They pull out the haire on their faces with little *pinsons* made for that purpose. *Hakluyt's Voyages*, II. 262.

pinson[2]†, *n.* [Early mod. E. also *pynson*; ‹ ME. *pinson, pynson, pynsone* (see "Prompt. Parv.").] A thin shoe; a kind of pumps.

> Soccatus, that weareth stertups or *pinsons.*
> *Elyot* (1559). (*Halliwell.*)

> Calceamen and calcearium is a shoo, *pinson*, socke.
> *Withals' Dict.* (ed. 1608), p. 286. (*Nares.*)

pin-switch (pin'swich), *n.* A switch in which electric connection is made by means of pins inserted in holes between plates insulated from each other.

pint (pīnt), *n.* [‹ ME. *pinte, pynte, pyynte* (AS. **pynt* is not authorized) = OFries. *pint* = MD. *pinte*, D. *pint* = MLG. *pinte* = MHG. *pinte*, G. *pint*, ‹ OF. (and F.) *pinte* = Sp. Pg. *pinta* (ML. *pinta*), a pint, appar. so called as being a marked part of a larger vessel, ‹ Sp. *pinta*, a mark, ‹ L. *picta*, fem. of *pictus*, painted, marked: see *picture.*] A measure of capacity equal to half a quart. The imperial pint is 34.65925 cubic inches; the United States or old wine-pint, 28$\frac{7}{8}$ cubic inches (see *gallon*); the old customary ale-pint, 35$\frac{1}{4}$ cubic inches; and the old Scotch pint, about 3 old English ale-pints or 105 cubic inches. There was also a local unit of weight of this name for butter, equal to a pound and a quarter.

pinta (pin'tạ̈), *n.* [Sp., a mark: see *pint.*] A skin-affection which prevails in Mexico.

pintado (pin-tä'dō), *a.* and *n.* [Sp., pp. pp. of *pintar*, paint: see *paint.*] I. *a.* Painted—that is, spotted or pied.—**Pintado petrel**, *Daption capensis*, the Cape pigeon. See cut under *Daption.*

II. *n.* 1. The pintado petrel.—2. The common guinea-fowl, *Numida meleagris.* See cut under *Numida.*—3. The West Indian mackerel, *Scomberomorus regalis.*—4. Chintz: the name given to all printed goods in the East Indies, especially those of the finer quality, many of which seem to have been partly painted by hand.

> To Woodcot, when I supped at my lady Mordaunt's at Ashted, where was a room hung with *pintado*, full of figures greate and small, prettily representing sundry trades and occupations of the Indians with their habits.
> *Evelyn*, Diary, Dec. 30, 1665.

> Fresh-colored taffeta lined with their *pintadoes.*
> *Birdwood*, Indian Arts, I. 133.

pintail (pin'tāl), *a.* and *n.* I. *a.* Same as *pin-tailed.*

II. *n.* 1. The pin-tailed duck, *Dafila acuta.* Also called, from the peculiarity of the tail, *pickettail, pigeontail, piketail, sharptail, spiketail, spindletail, splittail, sprigtail, sprittail* or *spreettail*, and *kite-tailed widgeon.* See cut under *Dafila.*—2. The ruddy duck, *Erismatura rubida.* [Delaware, Maryland.]—3. The sharp-tailed or pin-tailed grouse, *Pediœcetes phasianellus*, more fully called *pintail chicken.*

pin-tailed (pin'tāld), *a.* 1. Having the tail narrowly cuneate, with long acute central feathers, as the pintail duck, *Dafila acuta.*—2. Having the individual feathers of the tail stiff, narrow, and pointed, as the pintail ducks of the genus *Erismatura.*

pintle (pin'tl), *n.* [In sense 1 taken to be a dim. of *pin*, but in form and in sense 2 in fact ‹ ME. *pintel, pyntyl*, ‹ AS. *pintel*, dim. of **pint*, = OFries. *pint, penth* = MLG. LG. *pint* = Dan. dial. *pint, pintel*, penis. Cf. It. *pinco, pincio*, the same.] 1. A pin upon which anything revolves, or which holds two things together while one or both are free to move in a certain way. (*a*) In *artillery*, a long iron bolt about which the chassis traverses. (*b*) The pin of a hinge, a dowel, or a plate with pins taking the place of dowels. (*c*) In *carriage-making*, the bolt which allows the forward axle to revolve under the body of the wagon. (*d*) In *ship-building*, that part of the hinge of the rudder which consists of a vertical pin designed to receive the ring of the other part. It is generally set in the stern-post with the pin erect, but in small boats the pintle is often attached to the rudder, in which case the pin projects downward, entering the ring from above.

2. The penis. [Old and prov. Eng.]

pintle-hook (pin'tl-hůk), *n.* In *artillery*, a stout projecting bar of iron, bent upward at a right angle, and bolted to the rear of the limber-axle. It serves to engage the lunette-ring on the end of the trail of the gun-carriage, and attach the latter to the limber for transportation.

pinto (pin'tō), *a.* and *n.* [Sp., painted, ‹ L. *pictus*, painted: see *paint.*] I. *a.* Piebald. [Western U. S.]

> It is often a question whether the pinto, or painted pony of Texas, is the result of a *pinto* ancestry, or of a general coupling of horses of all colors.
> *The Century*, XXXVII. 334.

II. *n.* A piebald animal; specifically, the calico or painted pony of Texas.

pin-tongs (pin'tôngz), *n. sing.* and *pl.* A form of pliers which are closed by a ring sliding on the handles; sliding-tongs.

> For cutting the facets, they are held in small hand-Vises or *pin-tongs.* *Byrne*, Artisan's Handbook, p. 75.

pin-tool (pin'tōl), *n.* In *wood-working*, a tubular cutter or punch for trimming to shape sash-, door-, and other pins of soft wood, for which the stuff is got out in the square. Hard-wood pins are turned. *E. H. Knight.*

pint-pot (pīnt'pot), *n.* 1. A pot made to contain a pint, especially a pewter pot for beer.—2. A person who is addicted to the use of beer, or a seller of beer. [Rare.]

> Peace, good *pint-pot*; peace, good tickle-brain.
> *Shak.*, 1 Hen. IV., ii. 4. 438.

pint-stoup (pīnt'stoup), *n.* A vessel made to hold a pint, properly one made to hold a Scotch pint, which is much larger than the English. See *pint.*

> De'll hae them that hae the least *pint-stoup.*
> *Scotch proverb.*

Pinus (pī'nus), *n.* [NL. (Tournefort, 1700), ‹ L. *pinus*, pine: see *pine*[1].] 1. A genus of coniferous trees of the tribe *Abietineæ*, known by the staminate flowers in numerous short yellowish catkins, and the two forms of leaves, the primary small and scale-like, the secondary long and conspicuous and in clusters of from one to five each, enveloped at the base by a dry sheath.

There are about 70 species, widely distributed throughout north temperate regions, with a very few extending within the tropics in eastern Asia and Central America. They are tall or sometimes low evergreens bearing ovoid or oblong cones of closely imbricated woody scales, with thin or thickened apex. Every scale bears two winged seeds, the embryo with from three to ten seed-leaves set in a circle. (See cut under *cotyledon*.) The scales remain tightly set together over the seeds from fertilization till maturity, and after opening and discharging the seeds are long persistent on the axis. The cones vary in size from 2 inches and less in *P. edulis*, the piñon, to 6 inches in the well-known cones of the white pine, *P. Strobus*, and reach 18 inches or more in *P. Lambertiana*, the sugar-pine. The United States is particularly rich in pines, being the home of half the known species. For species and uses, see *pine1*. See cuts under *cone*, *Abietineæ*, *cotyledon*, and *pollen*.

2. [*l. c.*] Same as *pineal body* (which see, under *pineal*).

pin-vise (pin'vīs), *n.* 1. A hand-vise used by clock-makers for grasping small arbors and pins. *E. H. Knight.*—2. A small vise used by professional and amateur fly-makers to hold a hook while attaching and constructing a fly upon it. *Norris.*

pinwheel (pin'hwēl), *n.* 1. A contrate wheel in which the cogs are pins set into the disk. —2. In *tanning*, a stout circular box containing warm water or water and melted tallow, in which hides are rolled about over strong wooden pins fastened to the inner circumference of the box. *Harper's Mag.*, LXX. 275.—3. A kind of firework, consisting of a long paper case filled with a combustible composition and wound spirally about a disk of pasteboard or wood. When it is supported vertically on a pivot, and ignited, it revolves rapidly, forming a wheel of fire.

pinwheel (pin'hwēl), *v. t.* In *tanning*, to subject to the action of the pinwheel.

pin-wing† (pin'wing), *n.* A penguin. *Encyc. Brit.*, III. 734.

pin-winged (pin'wingd), *a.* Having a short attenuated falcate first primary. The pin-winged doves are pigeons of the genus *Æchmoptila* or *Engyptila*, as *E. albifrons* of Texas and Mexico.

pinwork (pin'wėrk), *n.* In needle-point lace, small and fine raised parts of a design.

pinwork (pin'wėrk), *v. t.*; pret. and pp. *pinworked* or *pinwrought*, ppr. *pinworking*. In *flax-spinning*, to work (flax-yarn) on a pin of wood in a manner to increase its suppleness, when making the yarn up into bundles for packing. Several hanks are operated upon at a time by passing them over a stout arm fixed to a suitable support. A stout pin is then passed through them, and with this the operator jerks and twists the hanks till they are as supple as desired, and will lie as placed while they are being bundled.

pinworm (pin'wėrm), *n.* A small threadworm or nematoid, *Oxyuris vermicularis*, infesting the rectum, especially of children. See *Ascaridæ*, and cut under *Oxyuris*.

pinx. The usual abbreviation of *pinxit*.

pinxit (pingk'sit), *v.* [L., (he) painted (this), 3d pers. perf. ind. of *pingere*, paint: see *paint*.] A word occurring as a part of a marginal note on a picture, noting who painted it: as, Rubens *pinxit*, 'Rubens painted (this).' Abbreviated *pinx.* and *pxt.*

Pinxter, *n.* See *Pinkster*.

pinxter-flower, *n.* See *pinkster-flower*.

piny1 (pī'ni), *a.* [Also *piney*; < *pine1* + *-y1*.] Pertaining to, of the nature of, consisting of, or covered with pines.

> Between the *piney* sides
> Of this long glen. *Tennyson*, Œnone.

We passed the beautiful falls of the Tind Elv, drove for more than twenty miles over wild *piny* hills, and then descended to Kongsberg. *B. Taylor*, Northern Travel, p. 307.

> The thrush that carols at the dawn of day
> From the green steeples of the *piney* wood.
> *Longfellow*, Birds of Killingworth.

Piny resin, the product also called *piny varnish*, *Indian* (sometimes *Manila*) and *liquid copal*, and *white dammar-resin*. See *dammar-resin*.—**Piny tallow**, a concrete fatty substance resembling wax, obtained by boiling with water the fruit of the *Vateria indica*, a tree common upon the Malabar coast. It partakes of the nature of stearine, and forms excellent candles. Also called *Malabar tallow*.

piny2 (pī'ni), *n.*; pl. *pinies* (-niz). A dialectal form of *peony*.

pionet, *n.* A Middle English form of *peony*.

pioned†, *a.* A word variously explained as meaning 'overgrown with marsh-marigolds,' or simply 'dug.' *Aldis Wright.*

> Thy banks with *pioned* and twilled brims.
> *Shak.*, Tempest, iv. 1. 64.

pioneer (pī-o̤-nēr'), *n.* [Formerly also *pioner*, rarely *piner*; < F. *pionnier*, OF. *peonier*, a foot-soldier, sapper, or miner, < *peon*, *pion*, a foot-soldier: see *peon*.] 1. *Milit.*, one of a party or company of foot-soldiers who march before or with an army, and are furnished with digging- and cutting-implements, to clear the way of obstructions, repair the roads, dig intrenchments, etc.

> A thousand horse and foot, a thousand *pioneers*,
> If we get under ground, to fetch us out again,
> And every one an axe to cut the woods down.
> *Fletcher*, Pilgrim, iii. 4.

He [the Russian] useth no Foot but such as are *Pioneers* or Gunners, of both which sort 30000. *Milton*, Hist. Moscovia.

2. One who or that which goes before and opens and leads or prepares the way for others coming after; specifically, a first or early explorer or experimenter in any department of human enterprise.

The colonies and settlements . . . occupied with taming the wild earth, and performing the functions of *pioneers* of civilization. *Sir G. C. Lewis*, Authority in Matters of Opinion, iii. [(*Latham*.)]

Snow-drifts stretch by the roadside, and one by one the *pioneers* of the vast pine-woods of the interior appear. *J. A. Symonds*, Italy and Greece, p. 31.

pioneer (pī-o̤-nēr'), *v.* [< *pioneer*, *n.*] I. *trans.* To go before and open (a way); lead or prepare the way to or for.

I found that miners had *pioneered* the way some distance down the river in search of gold. *The Century*, XXX. 739.

It is true that in the earliest days of the settlement the diggers who found their way to Kimberley were of a more orderly and law-abiding class than those who *pioneered* the gold-mines of California and Australia. *Fortnightly Rev.*, N. S., XLIII. 877.

II. *intrans.* To act as pioneer; clear the way; remove obstructions. *Quarterly Rev.*

pioneering (pī-o̤-nēr'ing), *p. a.* Pertaining to pioneers; serving to pioneer: as, a *pioneering* expedition.

pionert, *n.* An obsolete form of *pioneer*.

Pionias (pī-ō'ni-as), *n.* See *Pionus*.

Pionidæ (pī-on'i-dē), *n. pl.* [NL., < *Pionus* + *-idæ*.] A family of parrots, named from the genus *Pionias* or *Pionus*. It is characterized by a short broad tail half as long as the wings, a short grooved and toothed bill with an extensive naked cere, and coloration chiefly green. There are upward of 80 species, most of which are American, the others being African.

pioning† (pī'o̤-ning), *n.* [< *pion(er)* + *-ing1*.] The working of pioneers; military works raised by pioneers.

> With painefull *pionings*
> From sea to sea he heapt a mighty mound
> *Spenser*, F. Q., II. x. 63.

Pionus (pī'ō-nus), *n.* [NL. (Wagler, 1830), < Gr. πίων, fat.] An extensive genus of parrots of the family *Psittacidæ* (or a family *Pionidæ*), containing such species as *P. menstruus* and *P. senilis* of Brazil. Also, more correctly, *Pionias*.

piony, *n.* An obsolete or dialectal form of *peony*.

Piophila (pī-of'i-lạ̈), *n.* [NL. (Fallen, 1810), < Gr. πίων, fat, + φιλεῖν, love.] A genus of dipterous insects of the family *Muscidæ*, or giving name to a family *Piophilidæ*, species of which inhabit cheese; the cheese-flies. The larva of the cosmopolitan *P. casei*, the common cheese-hopper, lives on cheese, hams, and fat in general, and also, according to Germar, in cooking-salt. One species has been reared on the roots of celery. There are about 30 species, the adults of all of which are small black glistening flies. Three are common to North America and Europe. See cut under *cheese-fly*.

Piophilidæ (pī-ō-fil'i-dē), *n. pl.* [NL. (Macquart, 1835), < *Piophila* + *-idæ*.] A family of acalyptrate dipterous insects, typified by the genus *Piophila*, having the auxiliary vein of the wings coalescent throughout with the first longitudinal vein. Several genera belong to this family, and four of them are represented in North America.

pioscope (pī'ō-skōp), *n.* [< Gr. πίων, fat, + σκοπεῖν, view.] A kind of lactoscope invented by Heeren. It consists of a black vulcanized rubber disk having a central circular recess for holding the milk to be tested. Upon this is fitted a glass cover painted with six sectors of color, ranging from white-gray to deep bluish-gray, around a central unpainted spot. The color of the milk as seen through the unpainted spot in the center of the cover is compared with the colors of the sectors, and the quality of the milk is estimated from the color of the sector which most nearly corresponds to that of the sample.

piot (pī'o̤t), *n.* See *piet*.

pioted, *a.* See *pieted*.

pious (pī'us), *a.* [= F. *pieux*, an extended form of OF. *pie* = Sp. Pg. It. *pio*, < L. *pius*, pious, devout, affectionate, kind. Hence ult. (< L.) *piety*, *pity*, *pittance*, etc.] 1. Having or exhibiting due respect and affection for parents or others to whom respect and affection are due; also, pertaining to or consisting in the duties of respect and affection toward parents or others.

No one Thing preserves and improves Religion more than a Venerable, high, *pious* Esteem of the chiefest Ministers. *Howell*, Letters, ii. 10.

2. Having faith in and reverence for the Supreme Being; actuated by faith in and reverence for God; godly; devout: said of persons.

> Here you stand,
> Adore, and worship, when you know it not;
> *Pious* beyond the intention of your thought;
> Devout above the meaning of your will.
> *Wordsworth*, Excursion, iv.

3. Dictated by reverence for God; proceeding from piety: said of things: as, *pious* awe; *pious* services; *pious* sorrow.

> I have . . . paid
> More *pious* debts to heaven than in all
> The fore-end of my time.
> *Shak.*, Cymbeline, iii. 3. 72.

Sickness itself is appayed with religion and holy thoughts, with *pious* resolutions and penitential prayers. *Jer. Taylor*, Works (ed. 1835), I. 901.

4. Practised under the pretense of religion or for a good end: as, *pious* frauds.

> With devotion's visage
> And *pious* action, we do sugar o'er
> The devil himself. *Shak.*, Hamlet, iii. 1. 48.

Pious uses. See *use*.=**Syn. 2.** Religious, holy, righteous, saintly. See *religion*.

piously (pī'us-li), *adv.* In a pious manner; devoutly; as an act of piety; dutifully.

Encompass'd and in great danger, he was valiantly and *piously* rescu'd by his Son Titus. *Milton*, Hist. Eng., ii.

pious-minded (pī'us-mīn'ded), *a.* Of a pious disposition.

pip1 (pip), *n.* [Early mod. E. also *pipe*, *pype*, < ME. *pippe*, *pyppe* = MD. *pippe*, *pipse*, D. *pip* = MLG. *pip*, LG. *pipp*, *pipps* = OHG. *phiphiz*, *pfipfis*, MHG. *phipfesz*, G. (obs.) *pfips*, *pfipps*, MHG. also *pippusz*, *pippis*, G. *pips*, *pipps* (after LG.) = Sw. *pipp* = Dan. *pip* = F. *pepie* = Pr. *pepida* = Sp. *pepita* = Pg. *pevide*, *pevide* = It. *pipita*, < ML. *pipita*, *picita* (after Rom.), < L. *pituita*, phlegm, rheum, slime, also the pip; prob., with loss of orig. *s-*, < *spuere*, pp. *sputus*, spew: see *spew*.] A disease of fowls, consisting in a secretion of thick mucus in the mouth and throat, often accompanied by the formation of a sheath-like scale on the end of the tongue: not to be confused with *canker* or *roup*.

Choose thou another [friend] of somewhat tougher frame, and that will not die of the *pip* like a young chicken. *Scott*, Monastery, ix.

> A thousand *pips* eat up your sparrow-hawk!
> *Tennyson*, Geraint.

pip2 (pip), *n.* [Short for *pippin1*.] 1. The kernel or seed of fruit, as of an apple or an orange.—2. One of the spots on dice or on playing-cards: thus, the ace has one *pip*; the ten, ten *pips*. —3. One of the rhomboid-shaped spaces into which the surface of a pineapple is divided.—4. A trade-name used by manufacturers and dealers in artificial flowers for an imitation of the central part of a flower which bears the seeds or fruit.

pip2 (pip), *v. t.*; pret. and pp. *pipped*, ppr. *pipping*. [< *pip2*, *n.*] To blackball. [Slang.]

If Buckle were *pipped*, they would do the same to every clergyman. *A. H. Huth*, Buckle, I. 252. (*Encyc. Dict.*)

pip3 (pip), *v.* [A var. of *pipe1*, *peep1*, in like sense.] I. *intrans.* To peep, pipe, or chirp, as a chick or young bird.

It is no unfrequent thing to hear the chick *pip* and cry in the egg before the shell be broken. *Boyle.*

II. *trans.* To crack or chip a hole through (the shell): said of a chick in the egg.

Pipa (pī'pạ̈), *n.* [NL. (Laurenti).] A genus of aglossal tailless amphibians, typical of the family *Pipidæ*. *P. americana* or *surinamensis*, the Surinam toad, is the only species. Its color is brownish-olive above and whitish below. It is some-

Surinam Toad (*Pipa americana*), female.

times 7 inches long, and has a peculiarly hideous aspect. It is particularly interesting on account of its mode of rearing its young. After the female has laid the eggs, the male places them upon her back, fecundates them, and then presses them into cellules, which at that period open for their reception, and afterward close over them. In these cellules on the mother's back the eggs are hatched and the young pass their tadpole state, for they do not leave their domicile till their legs are formed. *Asterodactylus* is a synonym. See *Aglossa*.

Pipæ (pī'pē), *n. pl.* [NL., pl. of *Pipa*.] Same as *Pipidæ*. *Tschudi*, 1838.

pipage (pī'pāj), *n.* [< *pipe*[1] + *-age*.] Conveyance or distribution by pipes, as of water, gas, petroleum, etc.

> The question of *pipage* is one of immense importance.
> *Sci. Amer. Supp.*, p. 8765.

> A public authority which, in dealing with the questions of constant supply, pressure, and *pipage*, should be bound to have regard not only to the convenience of customers, but also to the requirements for the extinction of fire. *Engineer*, LXVII. 343.

pipal (pē'pal), *n.* Same as *pipul-tree*.

> For the discovery of theft they use an ordeal of fire, the person accused carrying a piece of red-hot iron a few paces with nothing between it and the skin but a few *pipal* leaves. *Athenæum*, No. 3202, p. 315.

pipe[1] (pīp), *v.*; pret. and pp. *piped*, ppr. *piping*. [Also, in the orig. sense 'chirp,' *peep* (formerly also spelled *piep*) and *pip*; < ME. *pipen*, *pypen*, = D. *pijpen* = MLG. *pipen*, LG. *piepen*, *pipen* = MHG. *phifen*, *pfifen*, G. *pfeifen*, *piepen*, *pipen* = Sw. *pipa* = Dan. *pibe*, pipe, peep, or chirp, as birds, < OF. *piper*, also *pepier*, F. *piper*, *pipier*, pipe, peep, or chirp, as birds or as frogs, < L. *pipire*, *pipiare*, *piparc* (ML. also *pipulare*) = Gr. πιπίζειν, chirp; imitative of the sound of chirping. In later uses the verb is from the noun. Cf. *peep*[1], *pip*[3].] **I.** *intrans.* **1.** To chirp, whistle, warble, or sing, as a bird.

> It was Autumn, and incessant
> *Piped* the quails from shocks and sheaves.
> *Longfellow*, Pegasus in Pound.

2. To sound shrilly, as wind.

> His big manly voice,
> Turning again toward childish treble, *pipes*
> And whistles in his sound.
> *Shak.*, As you Like it, ii. 7. 162.

> Well *piped* the wind, and, as it swept
> The garden through, no sweet thing slept.
> *William Morris*, Earthly Paradise, II. 124.

3. To cry; weep: sometimes with *up*: as, the children *piped up* at this.—**4.** To play on a pipe, fife, flute, or any similar instrument of music.

> The yonger sorte come *pyping* on apace,
> In whistles made of fine enticing wood.
> *Gascoigne*, Steele Glas (ed. Arber), Epil., p. 82.

> He *pip'd*, I sung; and, when he sung, I *piped*.
> *Spenser*, Colin Clout, l. 76.

> We have *piped* unto you, and ye have not danced.
> Mat. xi. 17.

> From street to street he *piped* advancing,
> And step by step they followed dancing.
> *Browning*, Pied Piper, vii.

5. To make a shrill noise, as bees, in the hive before swarming.—**To pipe in an ivy-leaf.** See *ivy-leaf*.

II. *trans.* **1.** To utter or emit, as notes, in a shrill or piping voice.

> A robin . . . was basking himself in the sunshine, and *piping* a few querulous notes.
> *Irving*, Sketch-Book, p. 256.

> And, while the wood-thrush *pipes* his evening lay,
> Give me one lonely hour to hymn the setting day.
> *Bryant*, A Walk at Sunset.

> When the summer days are bright and long,
> And the little birds *pipe* a merry song.
> *R. H. Stoddard*, Under the Trees.

2. To play; produce on a pipe or similar musical instrument.

> Things without life giving sound, whether pipe or harp, except they give a distinction in the sounds, how shall it be known what is *piped* or harped? 1 Cor. xiv. 7.

> "Piper, *pipe* that song again."
> So I *piped*; he wept to hear.
> *William Blake*, Songs of Innocence, Int.

> *Piping* a ditty sad for Bion's fate.
> *M. Arnold*, Thyrsis.

3. *Naut.*, to call by means of the boatswain's pipe or whistle: as, to *pipe* the crew to grog or to prayers.

> The men are generally in long before they are *piped* down. *Marryat*.

4. To provide or supply with pipes.

> This well was *piped* and used for a while, but, not yielding enough water for cooling purposes, was closed.
> *Sci. Amer.*, N. S., LX. 33.

5. To convey by pipe, as water, gas, oil, etc.

> Wherever the water comes from, it is usually conveyed into a tank or a reservoir, and then *piped* or ditched about over the farm wherever needed.
> *Pop. Sci. Mo.*, XXXVI. 365.

> Natural gas will be *piped* to Chicago.
> *New York Tribune*, July 3, 1887.

6. To furnish with or make into piping, as in dressmaking or upholstery: as, to *pipe* a border.—**7.** In *hydraul. mining*, to direct a stream of water upon, as a bank of gravel, from the hydraulic pipe.—**To pipe one's eye**, to weep; cry. [Nautical slang.]

> Then reading on his 'bacco-box,
> He heav'd a bitter sigh,
> And then began to eye his pipe,
> And then to *pipe his eye*.
> *Hood*, Faithless Sally Brown.

> He was very frail and tearful; for being aware that a shepherd's mission was to pipe to his flocks, and that a boatswain's mission was to pipe all hands, . . . so he had got it into his head that his own peculiar mission was to *pipe his eye*; which he did perpetually.
> *Dickens*, Martin Chuzzlewit, xxxii.

To pipe down (*naut.*), to dismiss from muster, as a ship's company, or to signify by means of a boatswain's whistle that, the duty being finished, the crew have permission to leave their stations.—**To pipe or pipe off**, in *thieves' slang*, to watch (a house or person) closely, in order to obtain information which may be of use in carrying out a criminal plan.

pipe[1] (pīp), *n.* [< ME. *pipe*, *pype*, < AS. *pīpe*, a pipe, = OFries. *pipe* = D. *pijp* = MLG. *pipe*, LG. *pipe* = OHG. *pfīfa*, *fīfa*, MHG. *phīfe*, *pfīfe*, G. *pfeife* = Icel. *pipa* = Sw. *pipa* = Dan. *pibe* = F. *pipe* = Sp. Pg. *pipa* = It. *pipa*, *piva*, a pipe, < ML. *pipa*, a pipe (in various uses); from the verb in the orig. sense 'chirp,' 'peep,' as a bird: see *pipe*[1], *peep*[1], *v.* In later uses the verb is from the noun, while again some later uses of the noun are from modern deflected uses of the verb. Cf. doublet *fife*.] **1.** A simple tubular musical instrument, usually of wood. The typical form is doubtless that of a flageolet or whistle, or perhaps that of an oboe. The term is no longer technically applied to any particular instrument (though it survives in bag*pipe*, Pan's *pipes*, etc.), except in connection with the pipe-organ. See def. 2.

> Tho up they gan their mery *pypes* to trusse,
> And all their goodly heardes did gather rownd.
> *Spenser*, F. Q., III. x. 46.

> They are not a *pipe* for fortune's finger
> To sound what stop she pleases.
> *Shak.*, Hamlet, iii. 2. 75.

> Neyther list I to dance after their *pipe* which ascribe a musicall harmonie to the heauens.
> *Purchas*, Pilgrimage, p. 10.

> These [antic trifles] be the *pipes* that base-born minds dance after. *Quarles*, Emblems, ii. 8.

> A Shepherd now along the Plain he roves,
> And with his jolly *Pipe* delights the Groves.
> *Prior*, Henry and Emma.

2. One of the tubes of metal or of wood from which the tones of an organ are produced; an organ-pipe. Such pipes are either flue- or reed-pipes. The tone is produced in flue-pipes by the fluctuations of a compact focused stream of air impinging upon a sharp edge or lip, and in reed-pipes by the vibration of a metal tongue hung in a stream of air. Metal pipes of either class are usually circular in section, while wooden pipes are usually square or triangular. (*a*) Flue-pipes consist of a *body* and a *foot*, the division between which is marked by an opening on one side of the pipe, called the *mouth*. The upper and lower edges of the mouth are called *lips*, and its sides are often shielded by *ears*. Opposite the lower lip a horizontal shelf, called the *language* or *languid*, is inserted so as nearly to separate the pipe into two distinct cavities. Between this shelf and the lower lip is a narrow slit called the *flue* or *wind-way*, through which the stream of air is directed against the upper lip. The quality of the tone depends upon the general shape of the pipe, and especially upon a delicate adjustment of the language and lips called *voicing*. The pitch of the tone depends upon the length of the vibrating column of air within the body. The upper end of the pipe may be open, or may be closed with a plug: an open pipe gives a tone an octave higher than a stopped pipe of the same length. Tuning is effected by altering the effective length of the air-column in various ways; and the adjustable metal flaps or tongues placed at the top of the pipe for this purpose are called *tuners*. The lower end of the pipe is open for the admission of air from the wind-chest. (*b*) Reed-pipes consist of a *tube* or *body* and a *mouthpiece*, the only communication between which is through a short metallic tube called the *shallot*, or reed proper. The oblong opening into the lower part of the shallot is covered or filled by a thin, elastic piece of brass called the *tongue*, or sometimes the *reed*. When the tongue covers the opening, the reed is *striking*; when it merely fills the opening, the reed is *free*. The quality and power of the tone depend largely upon the material and shape of the body, which serves almost exclusively as a resonance-chamber. The pitch of the tone depends upon the vibrating length of the tongue. Tuning is effected by adjusting a wire spring of peculiar shape so as to lengthen or shorten the part of the tongue left free to vibrate: this spring is called the *tuning-wire*. In the organ, pipes of the same variety are arranged in sets called *stops* or *registers*, containing at least one pipe for each key of the keyboard. (See *stop* and *organ*[1].) The breadth and sonority of a pipe's tone are much influenced by its *scale*—that is, by the general ratio between its width or diameter and its length; broad, bulky pipes giving broad, diapason-like tones, and narrow pipes giving thin, incisive tones. The proportions between the several dimensions of the different kinds of pipes are regulated by somewhat intricate mathematical formulæ. The number of pipes in an organ is approximately equal to the product of the number of keys in the keyboards and the number of stops. The organ at Weingarten is said at one time to have contained 6,666 pipes. The largest pipe in an organ is the deepest one belonging to a 16- or 32-feet open stop of the pedal organ; such a pipe is usually of wood, and is about 16 or 32 feet long. The smallest pipe is the highest one belonging to one of the mixture-stops, and is usually smaller than a common lead-pencil. Pipes are made either of wood or of metal. The metal most in use for this purpose is called *pipe-metal* or *organ-metal*, and is an alloy of tin and lead. Pure tin, zinc, and lead have also been used, and a great variety of their alloys. When a pipe is sounded, it is said to *speak*. When it fails to speak properly, or speaks when not wanted, it is said to *cipher*.

3. Any hollow or tubular thing or part: as, the *pipe* of a key.—**4.** A tube of metal, wood, or earthenware serving for various uses, as in the conveyance of water, gas, steam, or smoke: as, a gas-*pipe*; a stove-*pipe*.—**5.** A large round cell in a bee-hive, used by the queen-bee. *Halliwell*.—**6.** A tube of clay or other material with a bowl at one end, used for smoking tobacco, opium, or other narcotic or medicinal substance. See *chibouk*, *hooka*, *hubble-bubble*, *narghile*.

> The *pipe*, with solemn interposing puff,
> Makes half a sentence at a time enough.
> *Cowper*, Conversation, l. 245.

> The genial stoicism which, when life flouts us, and says, "Put that in your *pipe* and smoke it!" can puff away with as sincere a relish as if it were tobacco of Mount Lebanon in a narghileh of Damascus.
> *Lowell*, Cambridge Thirty Years Ago.

7. A pipeful; a quantity of tobacco sufficient to fill the bowl of a pipe.

> Sir, I am for one *pipe* of tobacco; and I perceive yours is very good by the smell.
> *Cotton*, in Walton's Angler, ii. 235.

> Sir Jeoffrey, to show his good-will towards me, gave me a *pipe* of his own tobacco. *Steele*, Tatler, No. 132.

8. A wine-measure, usually containing about 105 imperial gallons, or 126 wine-gallons. Two pipes, or 210 imperial gallons, make a tun. But in practice the size of the pipe varies according to the kind of wine it contains. Thus, a pipe of port contains nearly 138 wine-gallons; of sherry, 130; of Madeira, 110; and of Lisbon, 140. Sometimes confounded with *butt* (which see).

> The pint you brought me was the best
> That ever came from *pipe*.
> *Tennyson*, Will Waterproof.

9. Same as *pipe-roll*.—**10.** The chief air-passage in breathing and speaking; the windpipe: as, to clear one's *pipe*. [Colloq.]

> Drinke of this licoure wol cure up clene
> The *pipes* and the gomes, as is sure
> This Marcial expert upon this cure.
> *Palladius*, Husbondrie (E. E. T. S.), p. 58.

> I should have quite defeated your oration,
> And slit that fine rhetorical *pipe* of yours.
> *B. Jonson*, Catiline, v. 4.

11. The sound of the voice; the voice; also, a whistle or call of a bird.

> There are who do yet remember him at that period—his *pipe* clear and harmonious. *Lamb*, Old Actors.

> Sad and strange as in dark summer dawns
> The earliest *pipe* of half-awaken'd birds
> To dying ears. *Tennyson*, Princess, iv.

12. *Naut.*, the whistle used by the boatswain and his mates to call or pipe the men to their various duties; also, the sounding of this instrument.—**13.** *pl.* The bagpipe. [Colloq.]—**14†.** A spool, as of thread; a roll or quill on which embroidery-silk was wound.

> I prey yow do byen for me ij. *pypys* of gold [gold thread on pipes or rolls for embroidery]. *Paston Letters*, I. 39.

15. A dingle or small ravine thrown out from a larger one. *Halliwell*. [Local, Eng.]—**16.** In *mining*, an occurrence of ore in an elongated cylindrical or pipe-like mass, such as is characteristic of the so-called pipe-vein. See *pipe-vein*.—**17.** One of the curved flutings of a frill or ruff; also, a pin used for piping or fluting.—**18.** In *hair-dressing*, a cylinder of clay used for curling the peruke.—**19.** In a steam-engine. See *induction-pipe*.—**20.** In *metal.*, a funnel-shaped cavity at the top of an ingot of steel, caused by the escape of occluded gas (largely hydrogen) during the cooling of the metal. This happens chiefly with steel of hard temper. The formation of pipes of this kind is technically known as *piping*.

21. In the manufacture of black-ash or ball-soda (impure sodium carbonate) by the so-called Le Blanc ball-furnace process, one of very numerous hollow characteristic jets of flame which shoot out from the massed mixture of chalk, small coal, and sodium sulphate during the calcining process, and the beginning of the subsidence of which indicates the completion of the calcination. These jets are also called *candles*.—**22.** The puffin or sea-parrot, *Fratercula arctica*. [Cornwall, Eng.]—**Blow-off pipe.** See *blow-off*.—**Celtic pipes.** Same as *fairy pipes*.—**Drip pipe.** See *drip-pipe*.—**Dry pipe**, a pipe for taking steam free from water from a boiler. See *steam-boiler*.—**Dutchman's pipe.** See *Dutchman's-pipe*.—**Elfin pipes.** Same as *fairy pipes*.—**Fairy pipes.** See *fairy*.—**Indian pipe.** See *Indian-pipe*.—**Labial pipe.** See *labial*.—**Laminated pipe.** See *laminate*.—**Oaten pipe.** See *oaten*.—**Open pipe.** See def. 2.—**Pan's pipes,** a primitive musical instrument, consisting of a graduated series of tubes of cane, wood, metal, or stone, closed at the lower end, the tone being produced by blowing with the breath across the upper end. It has been used among barbarous and semi-civilized peoples in various parts of

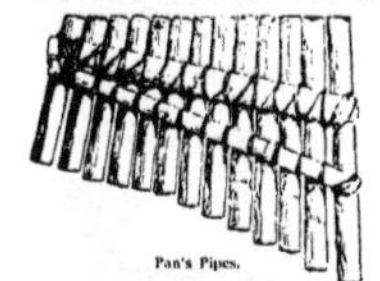

Pan's Pipes.

the world. The tones of the instrument are often sweet and pleasant. Early in the nineteenth century an effort was made in England to form companies of players upon Pan's pipes of various sizes for itinerant performances. Also called *Pandean pipes*, and *syrinx*.—**Pipe gamboge,** gamboge in cylindrical sticks, as shaped by bamboo-joints in which the juice is collected.—**Stopped pipe.** See def. 2.—**To hit the pipe.** See *hit*.

pipe2†, *v.* An obsolete form of *peep*2.

pipe3†, *n.* An obsolete form of *pip*1.

pipe-bender (pīp'ben"dėr), *n.* 1. A machine for bending sheet-iron stove-pipe in the operation of making elbows.—2. A flexible mandrel formed of a strong, closely wound steel helix, which is inserted in a soft metal pipe in order that it may be bent without distortion. *E. H. Knight.*

pipe-box (pīp'boks), *n.* In a vehicle, the box of a hub or nave which receives the arm or spindle of the axle. *E. H. Knight.*

pipe-case (pīp'kās), *n.* (*a*) A case or box lined with soft material to protect a valuable pipe when not in use. (*b*) A similar cover for the bowl of a pipe to protect it from the fingers when in use, as when a meerschaum is being carefully colored, to keep the fingers from touching the bowl.

pipe-clamp (pīp'klamp), *n.* A vise or holder for a pipe; a pipe-vise. *E. H. Knight.*

pipe-clay (pīp'klā), *n.* A white clay suitable for making pipes, and also used for whitening leatherwork, especially by soldiers.

pipe-clay (pīp'klā), *v. t.* 1. To whiten with pipe-clay.

Fellows were singing as they *pipe-clayed* belts or burnished sword-scabbards.
Arch. Forbes, Souvenirs of some Continents, p. 35.

Hence—2. To blot out or wipe off; square or settle: said of accounts. [Slang.]

You . . . would not understand allusions to their [the midshipmen's] *pipe-claying* their weekly accounts.
Dickens, Bleak House, xvii.

pipe-coupling (pīp'kup"ling), *n.* A joint or piece for uniting two pipes so as to form a continuous channel, or for forming a junction between a pipe and another object.—**Flexible pipe-coupling.** See *coupling*.

Pipe-coupling.
a and *b*, pipes to be coupled and male-threaded; *c*, coupling, female-threaded at each end. If one end of the coupling has a left-handed female thread, it is called a right-and-left coupling. If one of the pipes is smaller than the other and the coupling is reduced at one end to fit the smaller pipe, it is called a *reducing-coupling*.

pipe-cutter (pīp'kut"ėr), *n.* 1. A tool for cutting iron pipes. A hook passes under the pipe and serves as a rest, while a cutting-chisel or -disk is forced down upon the pipe, about which the implement is rotated until a complete section is effected.

2. A machine for truing the ends of pipes or cutting them into lengths.

piped (pīpt), *a.* [< *pipe*1 + *-ed*2.] Tubular or fistulous; formed with or into a tube or pipe.—**Piped key,** a key with a hollow barrel which fits upon a pintle contained in the lock. Also *pipe-key*.

pipe-dance (pīp'dȧns), *n.* A dance resembling the sword-dance, in which a number of clay tobacco-pipes are used instead of swords.

Sometimes they do the *pipe-dance*. For this a number of tobacco-pipes, about a dozen, are laid close together on the floor, and the dancer places the toe of his boot between the different pipes, keeping time with the music.
Mayhew, London Labour and London Poor, I. 14.

pipe-die (pīp'dī), *n.* 1. In a press for molding earthenware pipes, the ring-shaped die which shapes the exterior surface of the pipe. A piece called the *core* is supported in such manner that one of its extremities protrudes outwardly into, and is held concentrically within, the pipe-die. This forms an annular opening, through which the plastic clay is forced by heavy pressure, to give it the form of a tube. The inside of the socket on the end of the pipe is shaped by what is called a *lower die*, and the outside of the socket is formed by a device called the *ring*, which is interposed between the outside die and a flange on the lower die. 2. A female screw or nut of hardened and tempered steel used for cutting male threads on the ends of metal pipes. The threads of the die have grooves cut across them parallel with the axis on which the die rotates. In cutting pipe-threads, these grooves afford clearance for escape of the metal cuttings, which would otherwise accumulate in the threads of the die and prevent a clean, uniform cut. 3. Any one of the radially arranged and simultaneously adjustable screw cutting-tools which in some kinds of pipe die-stocks have their inner ends formed like chasers for cutting male screws. (See *chaser*2.) A right-hand die is one that cuts a right-handed screw-thread. One which cuts a left-handed thread is a left-hand die. See *screw-thread*. Also called *outside die*.

pipe-driver (pīp'drī"vėr), *n.* An apparatus for forcing into the ground pipes for driven wells.

pipe-fish (pīp'fish), *n.* One of the several lophobranchiate fishes which have a long tubular snout like a pipe, as any member of the *Syngnathidæ* or *Hippocampidæ*. The members of the latter family are more commonly called *sea-horses*, the pipe-fishes proper having the body as well as the jaws slender. One of the best-known pipe-fishes is *Siphostoma* or *Syngnathus acus*, common in British waters. The best-known American species is *Siphostoma fusca* or *Syngnathus peckianus*.

Great Pipe-fish (*Siphostoma acus*).

Massachusetts Pipe-fish (*Siphostoma fusca*).

pipe-foot (pīp'fůt), *n.* In *organ-building*, the lower part of a flue-pipe. Its lower point is called a *toe*. See *pipe*1, 2.

pipe-grab (pīp'grab), *n.* A clutching tool which is lowered into or upon a well-pipe to lift it to the surface.

pipe-joint (pīp'joint), *n.* A pipe-coupling. *E. H. Knight.*

pipe-key (pīp'kē), *n.* Same as *piped key* (which see, under *piped*).

pipe-layer (pīp'lā"ėr), *n.* 1. A workman who lays gas-, water-, or drainage-pipes.—2. A political intriguer (see the quotation); hence, any schemer. [U. S.]

Among the Glentworth papers was a letter in which he said that the men sent from Philadelphia were to be employed in laying the pipes for the introduction of Croton water. The Whig leaders were immediately stigmatized as *pipe layers*, a term persistently applied to them for several years.
Thurlow Weed, Autobiog., p. 493.

pipe-laying (pīp'lā"ing), *n.* 1. The act of laying down pipes for gas, water, and other purposes.—2. A laying of plans for the promotion or accomplishment of some scheme or purpose, especially a political one; scheming or intriguing. See the quotation under *pipe-layer*, 2.

pipe-lee (pīp'lē), *n.* Tobacco half-smoked to ashes in a pipe. *G. A. Sala.*

pipe-line (pīp'līn), *n.* A conduit of iron pipe, chiefly laid under ground, through which oil is forced by pumping to transport it from an oil-region to storage-tanks at a general market or refinery. The method has been put in operation in the United States on a vast scale, as a substitute for other means of transportation, and carried out with all the refinements of modern pumping-machinery, the result being an enormous reduction in the cost of transportation and in the cost of petroleum products to consumers. The conduits are constructed of lap-welded iron pipes, with pumping-stations at intervals of varying lengths, according as the grade is ascending or descending, the average being about 30 miles. The diameters of the pipes are adapted to the needs of the various lines, 6 inches being the size used on most trunk-lines, and two or more pipes being employed when greater capacity is required. The longest existing trunk-line is that connecting the Pennsylvania oil-region in opposite directions with New York and Chicago. This and other trunk-lines, and lines leading from wells to pumping-stations, etc., make up an aggregate extent of many thousand miles. The pipes are liable to obstruction from deposits of paraffin and foreign matters. Such accumulations are removed by driving a sort of piston (called by the workmen a "go-devil") through the pipes, from station to station, by the pressure of the liquid column behind it.

pipe-loop (pīp'lōp), *n.* In *harness-manuf.*, a long, narrow loop for holding the end of a buckled strap. *E. H. Knight.*

pipe-metal (pīp'met"al), *n.* See *organ-metal*, under *metal*.

pipemouth (pīp'mouth), *n.* A fish of the family *Fistulariidæ*: so called from the pipe-like or tubular snout.

pipe-mouthed (pīp'moutht), *a.* Having a piped, fistulous, or tubular mouth, as a fish: specifically noting fishes of the families *Fistulariidæ* and *Centriscidæ*.

pipe-office (pīp'of"is), *n.* An office, abolished in 1834, in the English court of exchequer, in which the clerk of the pipe made out leases of crown lands, accounts of sheriffs, etc.

pipe-organ (pīp'ôr"gan), *n.* The organ proper, the largest of musical instruments. See *organ*1.

pipe-oven (pīp'uv"n), *n.* A hot-blast oven in which the air passes through pipes exposed to the heat of the furnace. *E. H. Knight.*

pipe-privet† (pīp'priv"et), *n.* A former name of the lilac.

pipe-prover (pīp'prö"vėr), *n.* An apparatus for testing the strength and soundness of steam- and water-pipes by hydraulic pressure.

piper1 (pī'pėr), *n.* [< ME. *piper*, *pyper*, *pipere*, < AS. *pipere* = D. *pijper* = MLG. *piper* = OHG. *phīfāri*, MHG. *phīfære*, *pfīfer*, G. *pfeifer* = Icel. *pīpari* = Sw. *pipare* = Dan. *piber*; as *pipe*1 + *-er*1. Cf. *fifer*.] 1. One who or that which pipes; one who plays on a pipe. In the following quotation from Chaucer the word is used to personify the box-tree, as furnishing the material from which pipes or musical instruments were made.

The box tre *pipere*, holm to whippis lasch.
Chaucer, Parliament of Fowls, l. 178.

The *piper* loud and louder blew;
The dancers quick and quicker flew.
Burns, Tam O'Shanter.

"Please your honours," said he, "I'm able,
By means of a secret charm, to draw
All creatures living beneath the sun . . .
After me so as you never saw, . . .
And people call me the Pied *Piper*."
Browning, Pied Piper, vi.

Specifically—2. In *ornith.*: (*a*) A sandpiper or sandpeep; a bird of the genus *Tringa* or some related genus, as *Ereunetes*. See cuts under *Ereunetes*, *sandpiper*, and *stint*. (*b*) A young squab; a newly hatched pigeon.

Pigeon, . . . literally a nestling bird that pipes or cries out, a "*Piper*"—the very name now in use among Pigeon-fanciers.
A. Newton, Encyc. Brit., XIX. 84.

3. In *ichth.*: (*a*) The most general English name of the lyre-gurnard, *Trigla lyra*. (*b*) An exocœtoid fish, *Hemirhamphus intermedius*, with an elongate body and ensiform lower jaw, common in New Zealand, and esteemed for its flesh as well as for the sport it gives. Also called *garfish*, *ihi*, and *halfbeak*.

I look on the *Piper* as *the* float fish of New Zealand.
The Field (London), Nov. 25, 1871.

4. A kind of caddis-worm. See the quotation.

You are also to know that there be divers kinds of cadis or case-worms, that are to bee found in this nation in several distinct counties, . . . as namely one cadis, called a *Piper*, whose husk or case is a piece of reed about an inch long or longer, and as big about as the compass of a two pence.
I. Walton, Complete Angler, I. 17.

5. The piper-urchin.—6. In *apiculture*, an after-swarm having a virgin queen. *Phin*, Dict. Apiculture, p. 53.—7. See the quotation.

A clever arrangement of screens over which a bushy-tailed dog not unlike a fox—the *piper*, as it is called—is taught to leap at the word of command.
Athenæum, No. 3069, p. 231.

Drunk as a piper, very drunk. [Colloq.]

Jerry thought proper to mount the table, and harangue in praise of temperance: and in short proceeded so long in recommending sobriety, and in tossing off horns of ale, that he became as *drunk as a piper*.
Graves, Spiritual Quixote, x. 29. (*Davies.*)

To **pay the piper.** See *pay*1.

Piper2 (pī'pėr), *n.* [NL. (Linnæus, 1737), < L. *piper*, pepper: see *pepper*.] A genus of plants, the type of the order *Piperaceæ* and tribe *Pipereæ*, characterized by the two to six stamens with distinct anther-cells, and an obtuse or slightly beaked ovary crowned with from two to five stigmas, becoming in fruit a small berry. There are over 650 species, widely dispersed through the tropics. They are most commonly jointed shrubby climbers, rarely trees or tall herbs, bearing alternate entire leaves with several or many conspicuous nerves, and large and often wing-like stipules. The flowers are densely packed together in cylindrical stalked spikes (or in a few species in racemes)—at first terminal, soon becoming opposite the leaves (as in *Phytolacca*), pendulous and slender, with diœcious or perfect flowers without calyx or corolla, each with a shield-shaped protecting bract. The *Piper Æthiopicum* of the shops is now placed in the genus *Xylopia*. See *pepper*, *Chavica*, and *oil of cubebs* (under *oil*); and for important species, see *betel*, *coltsfoot* (and *lizard-tail*), *cubeb*, *kava*, *kawa-kawa*, and *matico*1.

Piperaceæ (pip-e-rā'sē-ē), *n. pl.* [NL. (Richard, 1815), < *Piper* + *-aceæ*.] The pepper family, an order of apetalous plants of the series *Micrembryeæ*, distinguished by the syncarpic ovary with one cell and one ovule, with usually two, three, or four styles or stigmas. They are generally aromatic or pungent herbs or shrubs, bearing alternate entire leaves, commonly with three or more prominent curving nerves, and often pellucid-dotted or fleshy. The minute flowers are usually in unbranched slender stalked spikes. It includes about 1,000 species and 8 genera, of which *Piper* (the type), *Peperomia*, and *Saururus* are the chief. See *pepper*, *cubeb*, and *Peperomia*.

piperaceous (pip-e-rā'shius), *a.* [< *Piperaceæ* + *-ous*.] Of or belonging to the *Piperaceæ* or pepper tribe of plants.

pipe-rack (pīp'rak), *n.* In *organ-building*, a wooden shelf placed above the wind-chests, having perforations in which the pipes are held and supported.

Pipereæ (pi-pē'rē-ē), *n. pl.* [NL. (F. A. W. Miquel, 1843), < *Piper* + *-eæ*.] A tribe of plants of the order *Piperaceæ*, known by the ovary with one cell and one ovule, indehiscent fruit, and by the absence of the perianth. It includes 1,000 species in the two leading genera *Piper* and *Peperomia*, and about four in the three others.

pipe-reducer (pīp'rē-dū"sėr), *n.* A pipe-coupling having one end of less diameter than the other, for connecting pipes of different sizes.

piperic (pi-per'ik), *a.* [< L. *piper*, pepper, + *-ic*.] Produced from plants of the pepper family or from piperine.—**Piperic acid**, $C_{12}H_{10}O_4$, a monobasic acid obtained by boiling piperine with alcoholic potash and acidifying with hydrochloric acid.

piperidge (pip'e-rij), *n.* [Also *pipperage*, *piprage*, and *pepperidge*: said to be a corruption of *berberis*.] 1. The common barberry. Also *piperidge-tree*, *piperidge-bush*. [Eng.]—2. See *pepperidge*.

piperidine (pi-per'i-din), *n.* [< *piperic* + *-id*[2] + *-ine*[2].] A volatile alkaloid ($C_5H_{11}N$) produced by the action of alkalis on piperine.

piperine (pip'e-rin), *n.* [< F. *piperine*, *peperin*, *pépérine*, < It. *peperino*, a cement of volcanic ashes, < L. as if **piperinus*, of pepper, < *piper*, pepper: see *pepper*.] 1. A concretion of volcanic ashes.—2. A crystalline alkaloid ($C_{17}H_{19}NO_3$) extracted from pepper. The crystals of piperine are transparent, colorless, tasteless, inodorous, fusible, not volatile. They are very slightly soluble in water but readily soluble in alcohol, and with oil of vitriol give a red color.

piperitious (pip-e-rish'us), *a.* [< L. *piper*, pepper, + E. *-itious*.] Having a hot, biting, or pungent taste, like that of pepper; peppery.

piperivorous (pip-e-riv'ō-rus), *a.* [< L. *piper*, pepper, + *vorare*, devour.] Eating or feeding upon pepper, as a bird: as, the *piperivorous* toucan, *Pteroglossus piperivorus*.

piperly† (pī'pėr-li), *a.* [< *piper*[1] + *-ly*[1].] Of or resembling a piper.

> Who in London hath not heard of his [Greene's] . . . *piperly* extemporizing and Tarletonizing, his apish counterfeiting of every ridiculous and absurd toy?
> G. Harvey, Four Letters, ii.

pipe-roll (pīp'rōl), *n.* The account kept in the English exchequer containing the summaries and authoritative details of the national treasury: also called the *Great Roll*. It was so named from its shape in the middle ages.

> The *Pipe-Rolls* are complete from the second year of Henry II., and the Chancellor's rolls nearly so.
> *Stubbs*, Const. Hist., § 126.

piper-urchin (pī'pėr-ėr"chin), *n.* A sea-urchin, *Cidaris papillata*, the form of which, with its club-shaped spines, is likened to a bagpipe. [Local, British.]

pipe-staple (pīp'stā"pl), *n.* [OD. *stapel*, a stalk.] 1. The stalk of a tobacco-pipe; also, a stalk of grass; a windle-straw. *Scott*, Black Dwarf, ix. [Scotch.]—2. In *bot.*, the grass *Cynosurus cristatus*, whose stiff stalks are used to clean pipes. [Scotch.]

pipe-stay (pīp'stā), *n.* Any device for holding a pipe in place, or for hanging a pipe. *E. H. Knight.*

pipe-stem (pīp'stem), *n.* The stem of a tobacco-pipe.

pipe-stick (pīp'stik), *n.* A wooden tube used as the stem of a tobacco-pipe. The long German tobacco-pipes have sticks of cherry or birch from which the bark has not been removed.

pipe-stone (pīp'stōn), *n.* Same as *catlinite*.

pipe-stop (pīp'stop), *n.* A spigot in a pipe. *E. H. Knight.*

pipe-tongs (pīp'tôngz), *n. sing.* and *pl.* An implement used by pipe-fitters in screwing together lengths of pipe, or in unscrewing lengths previously screwed together or united by screw-threaded pipe-fittings.

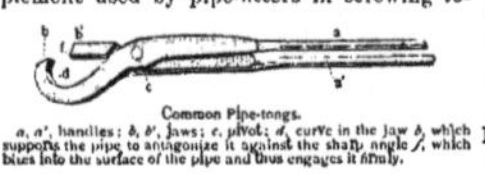

Common Pipe-tongs.
a, *a'*, handles; *b*, *b'*, jaws; *c*, pivot; *d*, curve in the jaw *b*, which supports the pipe to antagonize it against the sharp angle *f*, which bites into the surface of the pipe and thus engages it firmly.

pipe-tree (pīp'trē), *n.* The lilac-tree, *Syringa vulgaris*.—**Pudding pipe-tree**, the purging cassia. See *Cassia*, 1.

pipette (pi-pet'), *n.* [< F. *pipette*, dim. of *pipe*, a pipe: see *pipe*[1].] 1. In porcelain-making, a small can arranged to hold slip, and to allow it to flow through a pipe at one end. Pipettes are sometimes fitted with adjustable pipes of different diameters. See *slip-decoration*.—2. A small tube used to withdraw and transfer fluids or gases from one vessel to another. The shape differs with the special use to which it is adapted. Some are designed to measure fluids accurately as well as to transfer them.—**Absorption pipette**, an apparatus for subjecting gases to the action of a liquid reagent. In the figure, *a* and *b* are absorption bulbs connected by the glass tube *e*. c and *d* are a second pair of bulbs, with

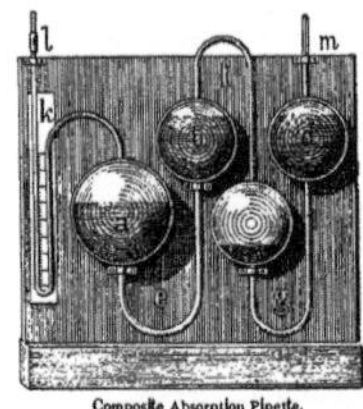

Composite Absorption Pipette.

their connecting tubes *f*, *g*, and *m*, serving as a water-joint to prevent contact with air or escape of fumes. The reagent is introduced through the tube *k*, and connection made by the rubber tube *l*.

pipette (pi-pet'), *v. t.*; pret. and pp. *pipetted*, ppr. *pipetting*. [< *pipette*, *n.*] To take up or transfer by means of a pipette.

> The solution of arsenic acid was *pipetted* into the bottle.
> *Amer. Chem. Jour.*, IX. 177.

pipe-twister (pīp'twis"tėr), *n.* Same as *pipe-wrench*.

pipe-vein (pīp'vān), *n.* A mode of occurrence of metalliferous ores somewhat common in, but not limited to, the lead-mines of Yorkshire and Derbyshire, England. In the so-called "pipes" the ore occupies a more or less nearly cylindrical or pipe-shaped cavity, usually quite irregular in its dimensions, and rarely of any considerable length. Pipe-veins resemble "gash-veins" in some respects; and they also have certain peculiarities in common with the "carbonas" of the Cornish mines. The principal shoot of tin ore in the East Wheal Lovell Mine, Cornwall, was followed from the 40-fathom level down to the 110-fathom as one continuous pipe, in the shape of a long irregular cylindroid with an approximately elliptic section, the dimensions of which were about 14 by 7 feet. *Le Neve Foster.*

pipe-vine (pīp'vīn), *n.* See *Aristolochia*.

pipe-vise (pīp'vīs), *n.* A vise designed for grasping pipes or rods while they are being threaded, etc.; a vise to which is attached a pipe-grip.

pipe-wine (pīp'wīn), *n.* Wine drawn from the cask, as distinguished from bottled wine. When claret was a common drink in English and Scottish taverns, it was customary to keep it on tap.

> I think I shall drink in *pipe-wine* first with him; I'll make him dance.
> *Shak.*, M. W. of W., iii. 2. 90.

pipewood (pīp'wůd), *n.* See *Leucothoë*.

pipework (pīp'wėrk), *n.* 1. See *organ*[1], 6.—2. Same as *piping*, 4.

pipewort (pīp'wėrt), *n.* Any plant of the genus *Eriocaulon*, or indeed of the order *Eriocauleæ* or (as formerly written) *Eriocaulonaceæ*.

pipe-wrench (pīp'rench), *n.* A tool having one jaw movable and the other relatively fixed, the two being so shaped as to bite together when placed on a pipe and rotated in one direction around it. When turned in the opposite direction, the jaws slip over the pipe without turning it, and are thus brought into position for a new effective stroke.

Pipe-wrench.
a, pipe; *b*, hook-shaped jaw, serrated at *g*, and threaded at *c*; *d*, nut which turns in a recess in the block *e*, pivoted at *f* to the shank *h*; the latter is serrated at *g'*, and is supplied with a wooden handle *i*. The jaws *g* and *g'* are adjusted to or from each other by turning the nut *d*, and then a slight rocking motion on the pivot *f* causes them to grip the pipe.

pipi (pē'pē), *n.* [Native name.] The astringent pods of *Cæsalpinia Pipai*, a Brazilian plant, sometimes imported along with divi-divi for tanning, though very inferior.

Pipidæ (pip'i-dē), *n. pl.* [NL., < *Pipa* + *-idæ*.] A family of aglossate amphibians, typified by the genus *Pipa*. They have no teeth, dilated sacral diapophyses, and coracoids and precoracoids which are strongly divergent. It contains the Surinam toad. They are sometimes called *cell-backed toads*. See cut under *Pipa*.

pipient† (pip'i-ent), *a.* [< L. *pipien(t-)s*, ppr. of *pipire*, pipe, chirp: see *pipe*[1], *v.*] Piping; chirping. *Rev. T. Adams*, Works, II. 118.

Pipile (pi-pī'lē), *n.* [NL. (Bonaparte, 1856).] A genus of guans, of the family *Cracidæ* and

Piping-guan (*Pipile jacutinga*).

subfamily *Penelopinæ*, including the piping-guans of South America, as *P. jacutinga* and *P. cujubi*.

Pipilo (pip'i-lō), *n.* [NL. (Vieillot, 1816), also *Pipillo*.] 1. A genus of American fringilline birds, of comparatively large size, with short rounded wings, long rounded tail, and large strong feet; the towhee-buntings. The species are numerous, and found everywhere in the United States

Chewink or Towhee-bunting (*Pipilo erythrophthalmus*).

and adjoining parts of British America, in Mexico, Central America, and parts of South America. They inhabit shrubbery, and keep much on the ground. The common towhee, chewink, or marsh-robin is *P. erythrophthalmus*, about 8 inches long, the male boldly colored with black, white, and chestnut, and with red eyes. The female is plain brown and white. Similar species or varieties inhabit all the western parts of the United States. In the southwest, and thence into Mexico, is another set of species, of plain grayish coloration in both sexes, as the brown towhee, *P. fuscus*, or Abert's towhee, *P. aberti*. Some greenish forms also occur, as Blanding's finch, *P. chlorurus*. 2. [*l. c.*] A species of this genus.

piping (pī'ping), *n.* [Verbal n. of *pipe*[1], *v.*] 1. The act of one who pipes.

> As Poetrie and *Piping* are Cosen germans: so *piping* and playing are of great affinity.
> *Gosson*, Schoole of Abuse.

2. The sound of playing on a pipe or as on a pipe; the music of pipes.—3. Weeping; crying.

> He got the first brash at Whitsunday put ower wi' fair word and *piping*.
> *Scott*, Redgauntlet, letter xi.

4. A system of pipes; pipes, as for gas, water, oil, etc., collectively.—5. Fluting.—6. A kind of covered cord used for trimming dresses, especially along seams.—7. In harness, leather guards or shields encompassing a trace-chain.—8. A cord-like ornament of icing or frosting on the top of a cake.—9. In *jewelry*, a support, usually of a baser metal, attached behind a surface of precious metal which is too thin to preserve its shape unsupported.

> Another smaller diadem found in another tomb may be noted. It is of gold plate, so thick as to require no *piping* at the back to sustain it.
> *Encyc. Brit.*, XIII. 676.

10. In *hort.*, a mode of propagating herbaceous plants having jointed stems, such as pinks, by

taking slips or cuttings consisting of two joints, and planting them in moist sand under glass; also, one of these cuttings.

> No botanist am I, nor wished to learn from you all the Muses that *piping* has a new signification. I had rather that you handled an oaten reed than a carnation one, yet setting layers I own is preferable to reading newspapers, one of the chronical maladies of this age.
> *Walpole*, Letters (1788), iv. 440.

11. A way of dressing the hair by curling it around little pins of wood or baked clay called *bilboquets*.—12. In *metal.* See *pipe*[1], 20.

piping (pī'ping), *p. a.* 1. Playing on a pipe.

> Lowing herds, and *piping* swains. *Swift.*

2. Having a shrill, whistling sound.

> The mother looked wistfully seaward at the changes of the keen *piping* moorland winds.
> *Mrs. Gaskell*, Sylvia's Lovers, i.

3. In *zoöl.*, having or habitually uttering a shrill, whistling cry: said especially of birds.—4. Accompanied by the music of the peaceful pipe, rather than that of the martial trump or fife.

> Why, I, in this weak *piping* time of peace,
> Have no delight to pass away the time.
> *Shak.*, Rich. III., i. 1. 24.

5. Simmering; boiling.—6. The noise made by bees preparatory to swarming.—**Piping hot**, so hot as to hiss or simmer, as a boiling fluid.

> Wafres *pipyng hoot*, out of the gleede.
> *Chaucer*, Miller's Tale, l. 103.

> A nice pretty bit of ox-cheek, *piping-hot* and dressed with a little of my own sauce.
> *Goldsmith*, Citizen of the World, lxv.

piping-crow (pī'ping-krō), *n.* Any bird of the genus *Gymnorhina*, of which there are several Australian species. The best-known is *G. tibicen*, of a black and white color, with great powers of mimicry. It is often domesticated, and can be taught to speak words. See cut under *Gymnorhina*.

piping-guan (pī'ping-gwan), *n.* A bird of the genus *Pipile*.

piping-hare (pī'ping-hãr), *n.* A pika or calling-hare.

piping-iron (pī'ping-ī'ėrn), *n.* A fluting-iron; an Italian iron.

piping-plover (pī'ping-pluv'ėr), *n.* A small ring-necked plover of North America, *Ægialites melodus*, so called from its piping notes. It is of a pale-gray color above and white below, with a narrow

Piping-plover (*Ægialites melodus*).

black frontlet and necklace, and the bill black, orange at the base. It is a near relative of the semipalmated plover, but is rather smaller and lighter-colored, and lacks the semipalmation of the toes.

pipistrel, pipistrelle (pip-is-trel'), *n.* [< F. *pipistrelle*, < It. *pipistrello*, *vispistrello*, *vespistrello*, a var. or dim. of *vespertillo*, *vespertilio*, < L. *vespertilio*, a bat: see *Vespertilio*.] A small European bat, *Vesperugo pipistrellus*, one of the most abundant species, of a reddish-brown color, paler and grayer below.

pipit (pip'it), *n.* [Prob. imitative of its cry.] Any bird of the genus *Anthus* or subfamily *Anthinæ*, of which there are many species, of most parts of the world. The commonest pipit of North America is *A. ludovicianus* or *pennsylvanicus*, usually called *titlark*. Sprague's pipit, also called the *Missouri skylark*, is *A.* (*Neocorys*) *spraguei*. Common British pipits are *A. pratensis*, the meadow-pipit; *A. arboreus* or *trivialis*, the tree-pipit; and *A. obscurus*, the rock-pipit. Others of occasional occurrence in Great Britain are *A. spipoletta*, the European water-pipit; *A. campestris*, the European tawny pipit; and *A. richardi*. The red-throated pipit, *A. cervinus*, of wide distribution in Europe and Asia, has also been found in Alaska and California. See cut under *Anthus*.

pipit-lark (pip'it-lärk), *n.* A pipit.

Pipiza (pi-pī'zạ̈), *n.* [NL. (Fallen, 1816), < Gr. πιπίζειν, pipe, chirp.] A genus of syrphid flies, whose larvæ are useful in destroying plant-lice. Thus, the grub of *P. femoralis* (Loew) or *radicum* (Riley) preys upon the root-louse of the apple (*Schizoneura lanigera*) and upon the vine-pest (*Phylloxera vastatrix*). Of the many species of this wide-spread genus, about 14 are North American. The flies are of small or moderate size, and dark metallic-green or black color. They are thinly

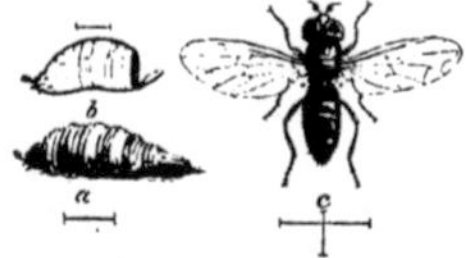

Root-louse Fly (*Pipiza radicum*).
a, larva; *b*, puparium; *c*, fly. (Lines show natural sizes.)

pilose, have the scutellum without points, and have the third longitudinal wing-vein with no projecting stump in the first posterior cell.

pipkin (pip'kin), *n.* [< *pipe*[1] + *-kin*.] 1. A small earthen pot, with or without a cover and with a horizontal handle.—2. A small wooden tub the handle of which is formed by the vertical prolongation of one of the staves.

> The beechen platter sprouted wild,
> The *pipkin* wore its old-time green.
> *Whittier*, Flowers in Winter.

pipkinet (pip'kin-et), *n.* [< *pipkin* + *-et*.] A little pipkin.

> God! to my little meale and oyle
> Add but a bit of flesh to boyle;
> And Thou my *pipkinnet* shalt see
> Give a wave-off'ring unto Thee.
> *Herrick*, To God.

pipowder†, *n.* An obsolete form of *piepowder*.

pipperage, *n.* See *piperidge*.

Pippian (pip'i-an), *n.* [So called because denoted by *P*.] In *math.*, same as *Cayleyan*.

pippin[1]† (pip'in), *n.* [< ME. *pepin*, *popyn*, < OF. *pepin*, F. *pépin*, the seed of a froit, as of the apple, pear, melon, etc.; cf. Sp. *pepita* (with diff. dim. suffix), the seed of a fruit, a grain of gold or other metal; *pipa*, a kernel; orig. applied, it seems, to the conspicuous seeds of the melon and cucumber (cf. Sp. Pg. *pepino*, a cucumber); with dim. suffix (F. *-in*, Sp. *-ino*), < L. *pepo* (*pepon-*), < Gr. πέπων, a melon: see *pepo*, and cf. *pompion*, *pumpion*, now *pumpkin*, from the same source. Hence, by abbr., *pip*[2].] The seed of a fruit, as an apple, pear, melon, etc. Now abbreviated *pip*. *Cotgrave.*

> What thing may be of vyn, of grape dried vnto the *popyn*, thei shulen not eete [later version: "Thei schulen not ete what euer thing may be of the vyner, fro a grape dried til to the draf;" tr. L. *ab uva passa usque ad acinum*].
> *Wyclif*, Num. vi. 4.

> Alle maner *pepins*, cornellis and greynes must be set in ye erth in depnes of iiij. or v. fingers brede, so that eche be from odur half a fote, alwey keping this speciall rule that ye ende or greyne of the *pepin* that stode next the roote be northest in the settinge and that other ende vpward toward heuyn. . . . In vere is most convenable tyme for seedis greynes and *pepins* and in autumpne of springis and plantes. *Arnold's Chron.* (1502), ed. 1811, p. 168.

pippin[2] (pip'in), *n.* [Formerly also *pippine*; < OF. *pepin*, F. dial. (Norm.) *pepin*, a young apple-tree raised from the seed (> *pepinerie*, F. *pépinière*, a seed-plot, a nursery of trees: see *pepinnerie*); < *pepin*, the seed of fruit, as the apple, etc.: see *pippin*[1]. The MD. *pipping*, *pupping* (Kilian), later *pippinck*, *puppinck*, D. *pippeling*, Dan. *pipling*, Sw. *pippin*, pippin, are from E.] One of numerous varieties of the apple, as the golden pippin, the lemon pippin, the Newtown pippin, etc.

> You shall see my orchard, where in an arbour we will eat a last year's *pippin* of my own graffing.
> *Shak.*, 2 Hen. IV., v. 3. 2.

pippin-face (pip'in-fās), *n.* A round smooth face, suggesting a resemblance to a pippin.

> The hard-headed man with the *pippin-face*.
> *Dickens*, Pickwick, vi.

pippin-faced (pip'in-fāst), *a.* Having a round rosy face, suggestive of a pippin.

> A little hard-headed, Ribstone-*pippin-faced* man.
> *Dickens*, Pickwick, vi.

pippin-hearted (pip'in-här"ted), *a.* Chicken-hearted.

> The inhabitants were obliged to turn out twice a year, with such military equipments as it pleased God; and were put under the command of tailors and man-milliners, who, though on ordinary occasions they might have been the meekest, most *pippin-hearted* little men in the world, were very devils at parade. *Irving*, Knickerbocker, p. 301.

pippit, *n.* Same as *pitpit*.

Pipra (pip'rạ̈), *n.* [NL.; of S. Amer. origin (?).] 1. A Linnean genus of birds, formerly including many heterogeneous species, now restricted to certain manikins, and made type of the family *Pipridæ*. They are confined to tropical America. *P. filicauda* has the tail-feathers prolonged in stiff filaments. *P. suavissima* is a beautiful species, velvety-black, varied with bright blue, orange, and white. 2. [*l. c.*] A species of this or some related genus; a manikin. See cut under *Manacus*.

pipraget (pip'rạ̈j), *n.* Same as *piperidge*, *pepperidge*.

Pipridæ (pip'ri-dē), *n. pl.* [NL., < *Pipra* + *-idæ*.] A neotropical family of songless passerine birds, typified by the genus *Pipra*; the pipras or manikins. They are mesomyodian *Passeres*, with bronchotracheal syrinx, heteromerous disposition of the main artery of the leg, exaspidean tarsi, and somewhat syndactylous feet, the outer and middle toes being united to some extent. They are mostly small, of stout thick-set form, with a short stout bill, broad at the base and somewhat hooked at the tip; the coloration is highly varied, often gorgeous or exquisite in the males, the females being usually plain. Black is the prevailing color of the males, relieved by brilliant blues, reds, and yellows, the females being dull-greenish. Their habits are said to resemble those of titmice. The genera and species are numerous, and almost entirely confined to South America.

piprine (pip'rin), *a.* [< *Pipra* + *-ine*[1].] Belonging or related to the genus *Pipra* or family *Pipridæ*.

pipsissewa (pip-sis'e-wạ̈), *n.* [Amer. Ind.] The small evergreen, *Chimaphila umbellata*, the prince's-pine.

Flowering Plant of Pipsissewa (*Chimaphila umbellata*).
1, a branch; 2, the stem with the fruits. *a*, a flower; *b*, a stamen, exterior face; *c*, one of the petals.

Piptadenia (pip-ta-dē'ni-ạ̈), *n.* [NL. (Bentham, 1852), so called in allusion to the deciduous glands crowning the anthers; < Gr. πίπτειν, fall, + ἀδήν, a gland.] A genus of leguminous trees, type of the tribe *Piptadenieæ*, characterized by the globose heads or cylindrical spikes, and flat two-valved pod with the valves entire and continuous within. There are about 30 species, all tropical—2 African, the others American. They are shrubs or trees, with or without thorns, with bipinnate leaves, small and very numerous leaflets, and small white or greenish flowers. The best-known species is the niopo-tree. Another South American species, *P. rigida*, is the source of valuable timber, and of angico-gum, similar to gum arabic.

Piptadenieæ (pip"ta-dē-nī'ē-ē), *n. pl.* [NL. (Durand, 1888), < *Piptadenia* + *-eæ*.] A tribe of leguminous plants, of the suborder *Mimoseæ*, consisting of the genera *Entada*, *Plathymenia*, and *Piptadenia*, trees or shrubs of tropical America and Africa, with sessile flowers in dense spikes or heads, having valvate sepals, ten stamens, and anthers crowned with deciduous glands.

Piptanthus (pip-tan'thus), *n.* [NL. (D. Don, 1823), so called in allusion to the sides of the banner-petal, reflexed as if fallen back on each other; < Gr. πίπτειν, fall, + ἄνθος, flower.] A genus of leguminous shrubs, of the tribe *Podalyrieæ*, characterized by the membranous leaflets, united stipules opposite the leaves, and united keel-petals. The only species, *P. Nepalensis*, a native of the Himalayas, is a shrub with alternate leaves of three radiating leaflets, and large yellow flowers in short racemes terminating the branches. It is cultivated for ornament under the name *Nepal laburnum*. See *laburnum*, 2.

pipul, pipul-tree (pip'ul, -trē), *n.* [Also *pipal*, *pippul-tree*, *peepul-tree*; < Hind. *pipal*, the sacred fig-tree (see *pepper*), + E. *tree*.] The sacred fig-tree, *Ficus religiosa*. See *bo-tree*.

Pipunculidæ (pip-ung-kū'li-dē), *n. pl.* [NL. (Walker, 1834), < *Pipunculus* + *-idæ*.] A small family of dichætous dipterous insects, typified by the genus *Pipunculus*. They are thinly pilose or nearly naked, with large subspherical head composed chiefly of the great eyes, which are contiguous in the male.

Several genera are recognized in Europe, but only *Pipunculus* in America.

Pipunculus (pi-pung'kū-lus), *n.* [NL. (Latreille, 1802).] A genus of flies, typical of the family *Pipunculidæ*, having a seta on the third antennal joint and the head globose. About 40 species are known, 10 of them North American. These flies live on flowers, and the larvæ are parasites of other insects, as the European *P. fuscipes* of tiger-beetles.

pipy (pī'pi), *a.* [< *pipe*[1] + *-y*[1].] Resembling a pipe; formed like a tube; tubular; hollow-stemmed. [Rare.]

> In desolate places, where dank moisture breeds
> The *pipy* hemlock to strange overgrowth.
> *Keats*, Endymion, i.

piquancy (pē'kan-si), *n.* [< *piquan(t)* + *-cy*.] Piquant quality. (*a*) Agreeable pungency or sharpness, as of flavor or taste. (*b*) Pleasing cleverness or raciness, as of manner, style, etc.

> A mind that tasted no *piquancy* in evil-speaking.
> *George Eliot*, Mill on the Floss, vii. 4.

> "How disturbed?" inquired Holgrave. "By things without, or by thoughts within?" "I cannot see his thoughts! How should I?" replied Phœbe, with simple *piquancy*. *Hawthorne*, Seven Gables, xii.

> Our American life is dreadfully barren of those elements of the social picturesque which give *piquancy* to anecdote. *Lowell*, Study Windows, p. 91.

(*c*) Keenness; sharpness; tartness; severity, as of remark or utterance.

> Commonly also satyrical taunts do owe their seeming *piquancy*, not to the speaker or his words, but to the subject and the hearers. *Barrow*, Sermons, I. xiv.

piquant (pē'kant), *a.* [Formerly also *picquant*; < F. *piquant* (= Sp. Pg. *picante* = It. *piccante*), stinging, pungent, piercing, keen, sharp, ppr. of *piquer*, prick, pierce, sting: see *pike*[1], *v.*, and cf. *pique*[2].] **1.** Of an agreeable pungency or sharpness of taste or flavor; sharp; stinging; biting: as, sauce *piquant*.

> He can marinate Fish, make Gellies; he is excellent for a *picquant* sauce. *Howell*, Letters, I. v. 36.

> There are . . . vast mountains of a transparent rock extremely solid, and as *piquant* to the tongue as salt.
> *Addison*, Remarks on Italy.

2. Of a smart, lively, racy, or sparkling nature; keenly interesting, or fitted to produce a sudden or keen interest; "taking": as, a *piquant* anecdote; a *piquant* manner; a *piquant* style of female beauty; a *piquant* hat.

> The most *piquant* passages in the lives of Miss Kennedy, Miss Davis, and Nancy Parsons.
> *Craik*, Hist. Eng. Lit., II. 305.

3. That pierces or wounds, or is fitted to pierce or wound; stinging; sharp or cutting to the feelings; biting; keen; pungent; severe.

> Some . . . think their wits have been asleep, except they dart out somewhat that is *piquant*, and to the quick.
> *Bacon*, Of Discourse.

> Men make their railleries as *piquant* as they can to wound the deeper. *Government of the Tongue.*

> "You can manifestly see their untruths in naming it a *piquant* letter," said Elizabeth, "for it has no sour or sharp word therein." *Motley*, United Netherlands, II. 240.

=Syn. 3. *Poignant*, etc. See *pungent*.

piquantly (pē'kant-li), *adv.* In a piquant manner; with sharpness or pungency; tartly; smartly; lively.

> *Piquantly* though wittily taunted. *Locke.*

pique[1] (pēk), *n.* [< F. *pique*, a point, pike: see *pike*[1].] **1.** A point or peak. [Rare.]

> I turned in my saddle and made its girths tight,
> Then shortened each stirrup, and set the *pique* right.
> *Browning*, From Ghent to Aix.

2†. A point of conduct; punctilio.

> Add long prescriptions of established laws
> And *pique* of honour to maintain a cause.
> *Dryden*, Hind and Panther, iii. 401.

> The ambassador appeared before the Council early in the following month, and demanded, of his own motion, that her [Mary's] officers should be released, and her privilege of worship restored until the Emperor were certified of the position of things. He was told that he spoke without warrant, and could have no answer from the King, and was warned not to move those *piques* without commission.
> *R. W. Dixon*, Hist. Church of Eng., xviii.

3. (*a*) A blind tick, *Argas nigra*, capable of causing painful sores on cattle and men. See *Argas*. (*b*) The jigger, chigoe, or chique. See *Sarcopsylla*.—**4.** In the game of piquet, the winning of thirty points before one's opponent scores at all in the same deal, entitling the winner to add thirty more to his score.

pique[1] (pēk), *v. t.*; pret. and pp. *piqued*, ppr. *piquing*. [Formerly also *picque*; < *pique*[1], *n.*, 4.] To win a pique from. See *pique*[1], *n.*, 4.

> If I go to picquet, though it be but with a novice in 't, he will *picque*, and repicque, and capot me twenty times together. *Dryden*, Sir Martin Mar-All, i.

pique[2] (pēk), *v. t.*; pret. and pp. *piqued*, ppr. *piquing*. [< F. *piquer*, prick, sting, nettle, gall, pique: see *pick*[1], *pike*[1], *v.* Cf. *pique*[1].] **1.** To sting, in a figurative sense; nettle; irritate; offend; fret; excite a degree of anger in.

> I must first have a value for the thing I lose, before it *piques* me. *Cibber*, Careless Husband, iv.

2. To stimulate or excite to action by arousing envy, jealousy, or other passion in a somewhat slight degree.

> *Picqu'd* by Protogenes's fame,
> From Cos to Rhodes Apelles came.
> *Prior*, Protogenes and Apelles.

> I'm afraid to afront People, though I don't like their Faces; or to ruin their Reputations, thou' they *pique* me to it, by taking ever so much pains to preserve 'em.
> *Sir J. Vanbrugh*, Confederacy, i.

> The mystery . . . had not only *piqued* his curiosity, but ruffled his temper. *Barham*, Ingoldsby Legends, I. 45.

> How the imagination is *piqued* by anecdotes of some great man passing incognito! *Emerson*, Conduct of Life.

3. Reflexively, to pride or value (one's self).

> Men *pique themselves* on their skill in them [the learned languages]. *Locke*, Education, § 168.

> We *pique ourselves* upon nothing but simplicity, and have no carvings, gildings, paintings, inlayings, or tawdry businesses. *Walpole*, Letters, II. 340.

=Syn. 1. To displease, vex, provoke. See *pique*[2], *n.*

pique[2] (pēk), *n.* [Formerly also *pike*; < OF. *pique*, F. *pique* (= It. *pica*, *picca*), grudge, pique, < *piquer*, prick, sting, nettle, gall: see *pique*[2], *v.*] **1†.** A quarrel; dispute; strife.

> Consisting of manifold dispositions there was dayly wauering, sometimes *pikes* amongst themselues.
> *Daniel*, Hist. Eng., p. 151.

> It is not only the case of Heresie which renders them obnoxious to the Popes censures, but particular *piques* and quarrels. *Stillingfleet*, Sermons, II. ii.

> This dog and man at first were friends:
> But, when a *pique* began,
> The dog, to gain some private ends,
> Went mad, and bit the man.
> *Goldsmith*, Vicar, xvii.

2. A feeling of anger, irritation, displeasure, or resentment arising from wounded pride, vanity, or self-love; wounded pride; slight umbrage or offense taken.

> Men take up *piques* and displeasures at others.
> *Decay of Christian Piety.*

> Out of personal *pique* to those in service, he stands as a looker on when the government is attacked. *Addison.*

> He had been crossed in love, and had offered his hand from *pique* to a lady who accepted it from interest.
> *Peacock*, Nightmare Abbey, i.

=Syn. 2. *Pique* and *umbrage* differ from the words compared under *animosity* (which see) in that they are not necessarily or generally attended by a desire to injure the person toward whom the feeling is entertained. They are both purely personal. *Pique* is more likely to be a matter of injured self-respect or self-conceit; it is a quick feeling, and is more fugitive in character. *Umbrage* is founded upon the idea of being thrown into the shade or overshadowed; hence, it has the sense of offense at being slighted or not sufficiently recognized; it is indefinite as to the strength or the permanence of the feeling.

piqué (pē-kā'), *a.* [F., prop. pp. of *piquer*, pierce, sting: see *pique*[2], *v.*, and cf. *piquant*.] Slightly soured; beginning to have an acid taste: said of wine which has been exposed to heat, or left insufficiently corked. Also *pricked*.

piqué (pē-kā'), *n.* and *a.* [F., < *piqué*, pp. of *piquer*, prick, pierce: see *pique*[2], *v.*] **I.** *n.* **1.** A cotton material so woven as to have a small pattern in relief, usually rather thick and stiff, used for waistcoats, children's clothing, etc.

> Alpacas, Printed Muslins, or *Piqués* may also be cleaned.
> *Workshop Receipts*, 2d ser., p. 148.

> His silver-buttoned vest of white *piqué* reached low down. *G. W. Cable*, Stories of Louisiana, xii.

2. (*a*) The pattern produced by quilting with the needle, consisting of slightly raised parts between the depressions caused by the rows of stitches. Also called *French quilting*. (*b*) A similar pattern in slight relief obtained in weaving, as in the material called piqué (see def. 1).—**3.** Same as *piqué-work*.

> Bonbonniere of tortoise shell, inlaid with scrolls of gold *piqué*. *Hamilton Sale Cat.*, 1882, No. 1986.

II. *a.* In *music*, same as *picchetato*.

piquedevant†, *n.* Same as *pike-devant*.

piqueer†, piqueerer†. See *pickeer*, *pickeerer*.

piquet (pē-ket'), *n.* [Also *picket*, and formerly *picquet*; < F. *piquet*, a picket, a game at cards: see *picket*[1].] **1.** *Milit.* See *picket*[1].—**2.** A game at cards played between two persons with thirty-two cards, all the deuces, threes, fours, fives, and sixes being set aside: players score for *carte blanche*, or a hand of only plain cards, *point*, or a hand with the strongest suit, *sequence*, *quatorze*, *trio*, and *pique* and *repique*.

> For all Historians say,
> She [Chloe] commonly went up at Ten,
> Unless *Piquet* was in the Way.
> *Prior*, The Dove, st. 11.

piquette (pē-ket'), *n.* [F., < *piquer*, sting: see *pique*[2], *v.*] A drink made by steeping in water the skins, etc., of grapes that have already been pressed for wine-making; hence, thin, small, and sour wine.

piquet-work, *n.* Same as *piqué-work*.

piqué-work (pē-kā'wėrk), *n.* Decoration by means of small points, sometimes pricked or impressed, and then generally forming patterns, sometimes inlaid in other materials flush with the surface or in slight relief.

piquia-oil (pē'ki-ä-oil), *n.* [< S. Amer. *piquia* + E. *oil*.] A sweet concrete food-oil derived from the fruit of *Caryocar Brasiliense*.

piquillin (pi-kwil'in), *n.* [S. Amer.] A bush, *Condalia microphylla*, of the *Rhamneæ*, found in Chili and the Argentine Republic. It bears an edible sweet and succulent drupaceous fruit.

piracy (pī'rä-si), *n.* [< ML. *piratia*, for L. *piratica*, piracy, fem. of *piraticus*, piratic: see *piratic*.] **1.** Robbery upon the sea; robbery by pirates; the practice of robbing on the high seas. Specifically, in the *law of nations*, the crime of depredations or wilful and aggressive destruction of life or property committed on the seas by persons having no commission or authority from any established state. As commonly used it implies something more than a simple theft with violence at sea, and includes something of the idea of general hostility to law. According to the opinion of some, it implies only unlawful interference with a vessel; according to others, it includes also depredations on the coast by a force landing from the sea. The slave-trade was declared piracy by statute in the United States May 15, 1820, by Great Britain in 1824, and since the treaty of 1841 by Austria, Prussia, and Russia.

> The trauel thither [to Japan] both for ciuil discord and great *piracie*, and often shipwracks, is very dangerous.
> *Hakluyt's Voyages*, II. ii. 80.

> *Piracy* is robbery on the sea, or by descent from the sea upon the coast, committed by persons not holding a commission from, or at the time pertaining to, any established state. *Woolsey*, Introd. to Inter. Law, § 137.

2. Literary theft; any unauthorized appropriation of the mental or artistic conceptions or productions of another; specifically, an infringement of the law of copyright.

piragua (pi-rä'gwä), *n.* Same as *periagua*.

pirai (pi-rī'), *n.* Same as *piraya*.

pirameter (pī-ram'e-tėr), *n.* [Irreg. < Gr. πειρᾶν, try, test, + μέτρον, measure.] An instrument or apparatus for testing the relative resistance of roads to the draft of vehicles. The original instrument was a rude form of dynamometer dragged on the ground, and indicating resistance by a finger on a dial. Draft-springs with graduated scales, resembling the ordinary spring-scales for weighing, are now used, the draft-power being applied directly to the springs. Also spelled *peirameter*.

piramidig (pi-ram'i-dig), *n.* [So called, it is said, from its note.] Same as *night-hawk*, 1.

piramis†, *n.* See *pyramis*.

piramuta (pir-ạ-mö'tạ), *n.* [Braz.] A siluroid fish, *Piramutana piramuta*, of the common South American catfish type, but with teeth on the palate and with granulated head. It occurs in the Rio Negro and Rio Madeira.

Piranga (pī-rang'gä), *n.* [NL. (Vieillot, 1807), also *Pyranga* (Vieillot, 1816).] A genus of *Tanagridæ*, having the beak dentate near the middle of the tomia. It is the only genus which is extensively represented in North America. There are several species, extending from Canada to Chili. The common scarlet tanager or black-winged redbird of the United States is *P. rubra*, the male of which is scarlet, with black wings and tail, and the female greenish and yellowish. The summer redbird is *P. æstiva*; the male is entirely rose-red. The Louisiana tanager, *P. ludoviciana*, extensively distributed in the western parts of the United States, is bright-yellow with a black back and wings and scarlet head. The rose-throated tanager, *P. roseigularis*, is a rare and beautiful species found in tropical America. The genus is also called *Phœnicosoma*. See also cut under *tanager*.

Rose-throated Tanager (*Piranga roseigularis*).

pirate (pī'rāt), *n.* [Formerly also *pirat*, *pyrate*, *pyrat*; = D. *piraat* = G. Sw. Dan. *pirat*; < OF. *pirate*, F. *pirate* = Sp. Pg. It. *pirata*, < L. *pirata*, a pirate, < Gr. πειρατής, a pirate, lit. one who attacks or attempts, < πειρᾶν, attempt, try, attack, < πεῖρα, an attempt, trial, attack, assault, akin to περᾶν, pass over or through, pass, < πόρος, passage, etc., and to E. *fare*: see *fare*[1]. Cf. *empiric*, etc.] 1. One who without authority and by violence seizes or interferes with the ship or property of another on the sea; specifically, one who is habitually engaged in such robbery, or sails the seas for the robbery and plunder of merchant vessels; a freebooter or corsair; a sea-robber. See *piracy*.

> There be land-rats and water-rats, water-thieves and land-thieves, I mean *pirates*. *Shak.*, M. of V., i. 3. 25.

> Nor swelling Seas, nor threatening Skies,
> Prevent the *Pirate's* Course.
> *Congreve*, Pindaric Odes, ii.

2. An armed vessel which sails without a legal commission, for the purpose of plundering other vessels indiscriminately on the high seas. —3. A publisher, compiler, or bookseller who appropriates the literary or artistic labors of an author without compensation or permission; specifically, one who infringes on the copyright of another.

> Meres refers to them [Shakspere's "Sonnets"] in 1598 in a manner which implies that though unpublished they were well known among the poet's private friends, . . . and in 1599 two of them were printed by the *pirate* Jaggard. *Shakespeariana*, VI. 106.

4. Any pirate-perch. =**Syn.** 1. *Thief*, *Brigand*, etc. (see *robber*), corsair, bucaneer.

pirate (pī'rāt), *v.*; pret. and pp. *pirated*, ppr. *pirating*. [< *pirate*, *n.*] **I.** *intrans.* **1.** To play the pirate; rob on the high seas.

> They robbed by land, and *pirated* by sea. *Arbuthnot.*

2. To appropriate and reproduce the literary or artistic work of another without right or permission; specifically, to infringe on the copyright of another.

> I am told that, if a book is anything useful, the printers have a way of *pirating* on one another, and printing other persons' copies; which is very barbarous.
> *W. King*, Art of Cookery, letter vii.

> We are doing all the *pirating* in these days; the English used to be in the business, but they dropped out of it long ago. *New Princeton Rev.*, V. 50.

II. *trans.* **1.** To commit piracy upon; play the pirate toward.

> In the yeere 698, a puissant Pirat named Abeuchapeta, passed from Asia into Africa, leading with him 70 Galleyes, and 100 other vessels furnished for his exploite, with which he pilled and *pirated* such as he met with all by Seas. *Guevara*, Letters (tr. by Hellowes, 1577), p. 329.

2. To appropriate and publish without permission or legal right, as books, writings, etc.; use or reproduce illegally.

> They advertised they would *pirate* his edition. *Pope.*

> It [Galignani's edition of Coleridge, Shelley, and Keats] was a *pirated* book, and I trust I may be pardoned for the delight I had in it. *Lowell*, Coleridge.

pirate-fish (pī'rāt-fish), *n.* The glutinous hag, *Myxine glutinosa*. [Local, Eng.]

pirate-perch (pī'rāt-pèrch), *n.* A fish of the family *Aphredoderidæ*, *Aphredoderus sayanus*, of the United States: so named from its voracity.

Pirate-perch (*Aphredoderus sayanus*).

This fish is of a dark-olive color profusely dotted with black, and has two dark bars at the base of the caudal fin. It is notable for the peculiar fins and the position of the anus, which in the adult is under the throat. It occurs in sluggish streams and bayous coastwise from New York to Louisiana and westward to Illinois. It reaches a length of about 5 inches. See *Aphredoderus*.

Pirates (pī-rā'tēz), *n.* [NL. (Burmeister, 1835), < Gr. πειρατής, a pirate: see *pirate*.] A genus of reduvioid bugs, typical of a subfamily *Piratinæ*, having the third joint of the hind tarsi as long as the first and second joints together, and that part of the head which bears the ocelli slightly elevated. They are predaceous, and inhabit both North and South America. *P. biguttatus*, sometimes called the *two-spotted corsair*, occurs from Virginia and Florida to California. It lurks in the branches of trees and bushes for its insect prey, and has been found in houses in beds, where it is supposed to have come in search of bedbugs.

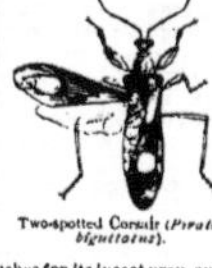

Two-spotted Corsair (*Pirates biguttatus*).

piratic (pī-rat'ik), *a.* [= F. *piratique* = Sp. *piratico* = Pg. It. *piratico*, < L. *piraticus*, < Gr. πειρατικός, of or belonging to a pirate, < πειρατής, a pirate: see *pirate*.] Same as *piratical*.

piratical (pī-rat'i-kal), *a.* [< *piratic* + *-al*.] 1. Of or pertaining to a pirate or piracy; of the nature of piracy: as, *piratical* acts.

> All naval war, not only during the middle ages but down to the seventeenth century, was more or less *piratical*.
> *Stubbs*, Medieval and Modern Hist., p. 190.

2. Engaged in piracy, or robbery on the high seas: as, a *piratical* ship or commander.—3. Pertaining to or practising literary piracy: as, *piratical* publishers.

> The errors of the press were . . . multiplied . . . by the avarice and negligence of *piratical* printers.
> *Pope*, Letters, Pref.

piratically (pī-rat'i-kal-i), *adv.* In a piratical manner; by piracy.

piratously† (pī'rā-tus-li), *adv.* [< **piratous* (< *pirate* + *-ous*) + *-ly*[2].] Piratically.

> Divers merchants . . . have had their goods *piratously* robbed and taken. *State Trials*, Lord Seymour, an. 1549.

piraya (pi-rä'yä), *n.* [S. Amer.] A voracious characinoid fish, *Serrasalmo piraya*, of tropical America. It has a deep compressed body with a keeled serrated belly. The mouth is moderate, but its jaws are armed with lancet-shaped teeth as sharp as those of the shark. Cattle when fording rivers are sometimes badly bitten by it. The natives of Guiana sharpen their tiny arrows for the blow-gun by drawing them between two of the teeth, which shave them to a point with their sharp edges. The fish sometimes becomes 3 or 4 feet in length. Also called *caribe* and *pirai*. See cut under *Serrasalmo*.

pire[1]†, *v. i.* A Middle English form of *peer*[1].

pire[2]†, *n.* A Middle English form of *pear*[1].

pire[3]†, *n.* An obsolete form of *pier*.

pirie†, *n.* A Middle English form of *pear*[1].

piriform (pir'i-fôrm), *a.* [< L. *pirum*, a pear, + *forma*, form.] Having the form of a pear; pear-shaped.

piri-jiri (pē'ri-jē'ri), *n.* [Tasmanian.] A wiry branching herb, *Haloragis micrantha* (*Gonocarpus citriodora*), found from the mountains of India to Japan and southeastward to Australia and Tasmania. Its leaves are said to be scented.

piriwhit†, *n.* Same as *perry*[1].

pirk (pėrk), *v.* Same as *perk*[2].

pirl (pėrl), *v.* and *n.* See *purl*[1].

pirlie-pig (pėr'li-pig), *n.* A tirelire or money-box. [Scotch.]

pirn (pėrn), *n.* [< ME. *pyrne*; origin obscure: cf. *pirl*, *purl*[1]. It is glossed by ML. *panus*.] Anything that revolves or twists. (*a*†) A shuttle.

> *Pyrne* of a webstarys lome, panus.
> *Prompt. Parv.*, p. 462.

(*b*) The reel attached to a fishing-rod for winding up the line. (*c*) A roll of any sort. (*d*†) A stick for twisting on the nose of refractory horses. *Wright.* (*e*) A bobbin; a spool; a reel. [Scotch.] (*f*) The amount of thread or line wound at one time upon a shuttle or reel.

pirnie (pir'ni), *n.* A striped woolen nightcap made in Kilmarnock, Scotland. *Simmonds.* [Scotch.]

Pirogoff's operation. See *operation*.

pirogue (pi-rōg'), *n.* [Also *perogue*; = G. *pirogue* = Dan. *piroge* = Sw. *pirog*, *pirok* = It. Pg. *piroga*; < F. *pirogue*, < Sp. *piragua*, a canoe, dug-out (see *periagua*); orig. W. Ind.] **1.** A canoe made from the trunk of a tree hollowed out. Pirogues are sometimes large, decked, rigged with sails, and furnished with outriggers. In Louisiana the terms *pirogue* and *canoe* are used indifferently. See *periagua*, 2.

> A number of officers, with three hundred and twenty soldiers, twenty women, and seventeen children, left New Orleans on the 27th of February, under the command of an officer named Loftus, in ten boats and two *pirogues*.
> *Gayarré*, Hist. Louisiana, II. 102.

> The earliest improvement upon the canoe was the *Pirogue*, an invention of the whites. Like the canoe, this is hewed out of the solid log; the difference is that the *pirogue* has greater width and capacity, and is composed of several pieces of timber—as if the canoe was sawed in two equal sections and a broad flat piece of timber inserted in the middle, so as to give greater breadth of beam to the Vessel. This was probably the identical process by which Europeans, unable to procure planks to build boats, began in the first instance to enlarge canoes to suit their purposes.
> *James Hall*, Notes on the Western States (1838), p. 218.

> On rounding a point a *pirogue*, skilfully paddled by a youth, shot out.
> *S. L. Clemens*, Life on the Mississippi, App. A, p. 597.

> The white and the red man were on most friendly terms, and the birch canoe and *pirogue* were seen carrying, in mixed company, both races.
> *W. Barrows*, Oregon, p. 39.

2. Same as *periagua*, 3.

> *Pirogue.*—In modern usage in America, a narrow ferry-boat, carrying two masts and a leeboard. *Webster*, 1828.

> She is what they call a *pirogue* here [West Indies], but not at all what is called a pirogue in the United States: she has a long narrow hull, two masts, no deck: she has usually a crew of five, and can carry thirty barrels of tafia.
> *Harper's Mag.*, LXXIX. 851.

pirogue-rig (pi-rōg'rig), *n.* A boat's rig consisting of two leg-of-mutton sails. See *batean*. [Florida.]

pirol (pir'ol), *n.* [= Dan. *pirol*, < G. *pirol*, *pirolt*, < ML. *pirulus*, *pyrrhula*, an oriole, < Gr. πυρρούλας, some red or yellow bird, cf. πύρρα, some red or yellow bird, < πυρρός, flame-colored, red or yellow, < πῦρ, fire: see *fire*.] The European oriole, *Oriolus galbula*. See first cut under *oriole*.

pirouette (pir-ö-et'), *n.* [Formerly also *piroet*; < F. *pirouette*, a whirligig, a whirling about, a pirouette in dancing; OF. also *pirouet*, m.; also *pirevollet*, a whirligig (Cotgrave); dim. of F. dial. *pirone*, a whirligig, a little wheel; cf. *pirr*, *pirry*.] **1.** In *dancing*, a rapid whirling on one leg or on the points of the toes, as performed by ballet-dancers.—**2.** In the *manège*, a quick, short turn or whirl of a horse.

pirouette (pir-ö-et'), *v. i.*; pret. and pp. *pirouetted*, ppr. *pirouetting*. [< F. *pirouetter*, perform a pirouette, < *pirouette*, a pirouette: see *pirouette*, *n.*] To perform a pirouette; turn or whirl on one leg, or on the toes, as in dancing; advance or move along in a series of pirouettes, or short graceful turns, as a horse.

> The mountain stirr'd its bushy crown,
> And, as tradition teaches,
> Young ashes *pirouetted* down,
> Coquetting with young beeches.
> *Tennyson*, Amphion.

pirr (pėr), *n.* [Cf. *birr*[1] and *pirry*.] A gentle wind. [Scotch.]

pirrey†, *n.* An obsolete form of *perry*[1].

pirry† (pir'i), *n.* [Early mod. E. also *pirrie*, *perry*, *perrie*, *pyrry*, *pirie*; < ME. *pirie*, *pyrie*, *perrie*, *pyry*, also *berry*, *berrie*, < Gael. *piorradh* = Ir. *piorra*, a squall, blast. Cf. *pirr* and *birr*[1].] A storm of wind; a squall or gust. *Palsgrave.*

> For sodainly there rose a straunge storme and a quicke *pirie*, so mischevous and so pernicious that nothinge more execrable, or more to be abhorred, could happen in any Christian region. *Hall*, Henry VI., f. 56. (*Halliwell.*)

> A *pirrie* came, and set my ship on sands.
> *Mir. for Mags.*, p. 502. (*Nares.*)

> Nat men and children only, but also . . . horses . . . shulde [by learning to swim] more aptely and boldly passe ouer great riuers, . . . and nat be aferde of *pirries* or great stormes. *Sir T. Elyot*, The Governour, i. 17.

Pisan[1] (pē'zan), *a.* and *n.* [< *Pisa* (see def.) + *-an*.] **I.** *a.* Of or relating to the city of Pisa in northern Italy, or its inhabitants, or its characteristic school of art; of or relating to the province of Pisa.

II. *n.* An inhabitant of Pisa.

pisan[2]†, *n.* [Also *pysane*, *pizain*, *pizaine*, *pusane*; origin obscure.] A part of the armor of the breast and neck; a gorgeret or plastron. Also *pizan-collar*.

pisanite (pi-zä'nīt), *n.* [Named after M. *Pisani*, a French mineralogist.] A hydrous sulphate of iron and copper, allied to the iron sulphate melanterite.

pisasphalt, *n.* See *pissasphalt*.

piscary (pis'ka-ri), *n.* [< L. *piscarius*, belonging to fish, < *piscis*, fish, = E. *fish*: see *fish*[1].] In *law*, the right or privilege of fishing in another man's waters.—**Common of piscary.** See *common*, 4.

piscation† (pis-kā'shon), *n.* [= It. *pescagione*, < LL. *piscatio(n-)*, a fishing, < L. *piscatus*, pp. of *piscari*, fish, < *piscis*, fish: see *fish*[1].] The art or practice of fishing.

> There are extant of his [Oppian's] in Greek . . . five [books] of Halieutics or *piscation*.
> *Sir T. Browne*, Vulg. Err., i. 8.

piscatology (pis-kā-tol'ō-ji), *n.* [Improp. < L. *piscari*, pp. *piscatus*, fish, + Gr. -λογία, < λέγειν, speak.] The scientific study of fishes; ichthyology. *Atwater*, Logic, p. 217.

piscator (pis-kā'tor), *n.* [L., a fisherman, < *piscari*, pp. *piscatus*, fish: see *piscation*.] An angler; a fisherman. *I. Walton.*

Piscatores (pis-kā-tō'rēz), *n. pl.* [NL.: see *piscator*.] In Blyth's system (1849), a group of totipalmate birds corresponding to the *Steganopodes* or *Totipalmatæ* of most authors; the fishers.

piscatorial (pis-kā-tō'ri-al), *a.* [= F. *piscatorial*; as *piscatory* + *-al*.] Same as *piscatory*.

piscatory (pis'kā-tō-ri), *a.* [= Sp. Pg. It. *piscatorio*, < L. *piscatorius*, belonging to fishermen, < *piscator*, a fisherman: see *piscator*.] Pertaining to fishing or to fishermen; connected with angling; given or devoted to fishing.

> On the face of this monument . . . is represented, in bas-relief, Neptune among the Satyrs, to shew that this poet was the inventor of *piscatory* eclogues.
> *Addison*, Remarks on Italy.

piscatrix (pis-kā'triks), *n.* [L., fem. of *piscator*, a fisherman.] 1. The feminine of *piscator*.—2. [*cap.*] [NL.] A genus of gannets of the family *Sulidæ*, the type of which is *Sula piscator*. See *Sula*. *Reichenbach*, 1853.

Pisces (pis'ēz), *n. pl.* [L., the Fishes, a constellation; pl. of *piscis*, a fish: see *fish*1.] 1. A constellation and sign of the zodiac; the Fishes. The figure represents two fishes united by a

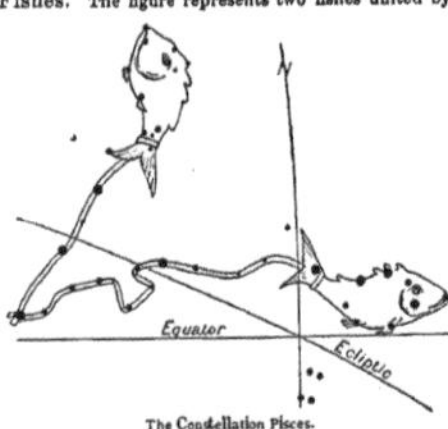

The Constellation Pisces.

ribbon attached to their tails. One of the fishes is east, the other south, of the square of Pegasus.
2. In *zoöl.*, a class of vertebrates, the fishes, to which different limits have been assigned. See *fish*1.

piscicapture (pis'i-kap-tụ̄r), *n.* [< L. *piscis*, fish, + *captura*, taking: see *capture*.] The taking of fish by any means, as angling or netting. [Rare.]

> Snatching is a form of illicit *piscicapture*.
> *Standard*, Oct. 21, 1878. (*Davies*.)

piscicolous (pi-sik'ọ̄-lus), *a.* [< L. *piscis*, fish, + *colere*, inhabit.] Parasitic upon or infesting fishes, as fish-lice.

piscicultural (pis-i-kul'tụ̄-ral), *a.* [< *pisciculture* + *-al*.] Of or pertaining in any way to pisciculture; fish-cultural.

pisciculture (pis'i-kul"tụ̄r), *n.* [= F. *pisciculture* = Pg. *piscicultura*, < L. *piscis*, fish, + *cultura*, cultivation: see *culture*.] The breeding, rearing, preservation, feeding, and fattening of fish by artificial means; fish-culture. Pisciculture has been practised from very early ages. It appears to have been in use in ancient Egypt, and was followed in China in early times on a very large scale. It was introduced in Great Britain by Mr. Shaw of Drumlanrig, in Dumfriesshire, Scotland, in 1837. An important branch of modern pisciculture is the propagation and rearing of young fish in artificial ponds, with the view of introducing fish previously not found in the locality, or of increasing the supply of desirable food-fishes. Salmon- and trout-ova sent from Great Britain have been successfully propagated in Australia and New Zealand. Of late years America has taken the lead in fish-culture, under the administration of the United States Fish Commission, and millions of ova and fry have been planted in various rivers.

pisciculturist (pis'i-kul"tụ̄r-ist), *n.* [< *pisciculture* + *-ist*.] One who practises pisciculture, or is devoted to the breeding and rearing of fishes; a fish-culturist.

Piscidia (pi-sid'i-ạ̈), *n.* [NL. (Linnæus, 1737), < L. *piscis*, fish, + *cædere*, kill.] A genus of plants of the order *Leguminosæ*, tribe *Dalbergieæ*, and subtribe *Lonchocarpeæ*, characterized by wing-petals adherent to the keel, and long thick pods longitudinally four-winged. The only species, *P. Erythrina*, a native of the West Indies, is a tree with alternate pinnate leaves, white and red flowers in short lateral panicles, and many-seeded indehiscent linear pods. It is known as *Jamaica* or *white dogwood*, reaches a height of about 35 feet, extends into Florida and Mexico, and produces a valuable, very hard, close-grained wood, yellowish-brown in color and taking a high polish, used in its native region for boat-building, firewood, and charcoal. (For the use of its powdered leaves and twigs to stupefy fish, see *fish-poison*.) Its gray or brown acrid bark is imported into the United States for its narcotic properties.

piscifactory (pis'i-fak-tọ̄-ri), *n.* [< L. *piscis*, fish, + E. *factory*.] A place where pisciculture is carried on. [Rare.]

> The establishment in 1850 at Huningue (Hüningen) in Alsace by the French Government of the first fish-breeding station, or *piscifactory*, as it was named by Professor Coste, is of great significance. *Encyc. Brit.*, XIX. 128.

piscifauna (pis'i-fâ-nạ̈), *n.* [< L. *piscis*, fish, + NL. *fauna*: see *fauna*.] The fauna of any region or country, in so far as it is composed of fishes: correlated with *avifauna*. See *fauna*.

pisciform (pis'i-fôrm), *a.* [= F. *pisciforme*, < L. *piscis*, fish, + *forma*, form.] Having the form of a fish; like a fish in shape; technically, fish-like in structure or affinities; ichthyopsidan; ichthyomorphic.

piscina (pi-sī'nạ̈), *n.*; pl. *piscinæ* (-nē). [L.: see *piscine*1.] 1. A basin or tank, usually ornamental, as for a fountain or a bath; sometimes, a large shallow vase for ornamental fishes or aquatic plants; also, any tank or cistern of moderate size.

> In the garden of the *piscina* [at Fontainebleau] is an Hercules of white marble. *Evelyn*, Diary, March 7, 1644.

2. *Eccles.*, a stone basin, in old churches generally established within a canopied niche placed close to the altar, used to receive the water in

Piscina in Morning Chapel, Lincoln Cathedral, England.

which the priest washes his hands before the celebration of the eucharist, and washes the chalice after the celebration. Now rarely used in the sanctuary, but often in sacristies.

piscinal (pis'i-nạl), *a.* [< ML. **piscinalis* (LL. *piscinalis*, pertaining to a bath), < L. *piscina*, a fish-pond: see *piscina*.] Of or pertaining to a piscina.

piscine1† (pis'in), *n.* [< ME. *pyscyne*, < OF. (and F.) *piscine* = Sp. Pg. It. *piscina*, < L. *piscina*, a fish-pond, a pool, cistern, basin, < *piscis*, fish: see *fish*1.] A fish-pond.

> And fyll all the *pyscynes*, whiche are in grett nowmber, and myche watir renneth now to waste.
> *Torkington*, Diarie of Eng. Travell, p. 38.

piscine2 (pis'in), *a.* [< NL. *piscinus*, < L. *piscis*, fish: see *fish*1.] Pertaining in any way to fish or fishes; ichthyic: as, *piscine* remains; *piscine* affinities.

Piscis Austrinus (pis'is âs-trī'nus). [NL.: L. *piscis*, fish; *austrinus*, southern: see *austrine*.] An ancient southern constellation, the Southern Fish. It contains the 1.3 magnitude star Fomal-

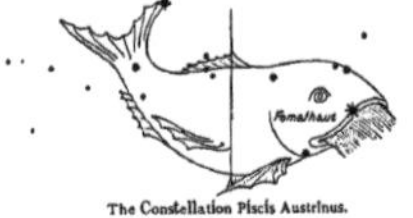

The Constellation Piscis Austrinus.

haut, which is 30 degrees south of the equator, and is in opposition on the 3d of September. The figure represents a fish which swallows the water poured out of the vase by Aquarius.

Piscis Volans (pis'is vō'lanz). [NL.: L. *piscis*, fish; *volans*, flying: see *volant*.] The Flying-Fish, one of the southern constellations introduced by Theodori, or Keyser, at the end of the sixteenth century. It is situated west of the star β Argus, and contains two stars of the fourth magnitude. Also called *Volans*.

piscivorous (pi-siv'ọ̄-rus), *a.* [= F. *piscivore* = Pg. It. *piscivoro*, < L. *piscis*, fish, + *vorare*, devour.] Fish-eating, as a bird; habitually eating or feeding upon fishes; ichthyophagous.

> The meat is swallowed into the crop, or into a kind of antestomach observed in *piscivorous* birds.
> *Ray*, Works of Creation.

pisé (pē-zā'), *n.* [F., < *piser*, build in pisé, < L. *pisere*, *pinsere*, beat, pound, bray, crush.] In *arch.*, stiff earth or clay, as used to form walls or floors, being rammed down until it becomes firm. This method is as old as the days of Pliny, and is still employed in France and in some parts of England.

pisgy (piz'gi), *n.* A dialectal form of *pixy*.

pish (pish), *interj.* [Imitative of a sound made to show contempt.] An exclamation of contempt.

> It is not words that shake me thus. *Pish!* Noses, ears, and lips.—Is 't possible? *Shak.*, Othello, iv. 1. 42.

pish (pish), *v.* I. *intrans.* To express contempt by or as by the exclamation "Pish!"

> Our very smiles are subject to constructions;
> Nay, sir, it 's come to this, we cannot *pish*
> But 'tis a favour for some fool or other.
> *Fletcher*, Wit without Money, iii. 1.

> *Bob.* This is a Toledo! Pish!
> *Step.* Why do you *pish*, captain?
> B. *Jonson*, Every Man in his Humour, iii. 1.

II. *trans.* To say "Pish!" to.

> *Hor.* Pish; ha, ha!
> *Lup.* Dost thou *pish* me? Give me my long sword.
> B. *Jonson*, Poetaster, v. 1.

pishamin (pish'ạ-min), *n.* Same as *persimmon*.—Sweet and sour pishamin, in Sierra Leone, two climbing shrubs, *Carpodinus dulcis* and *C. acida*, of the *Apocynaceæ*, bearing edible fruits resembling the persimmon: so called by colonists from the southern United States.

pishaug (pi-shâg'), *n.* [Amer. Ind.] The female or young of the surf-scoter, a duck, *Œdemia perspicillata*. [Massachusetts.]

pish-pash (pish'pash), *n.* [E. Ind.] A broth of rice mixed with small bits of meat, much used as food for Anglo-Indian children.

> It [a child] surfeits itself to an apoplectic point with *pish-pash*; it burns its mouth with hot curry, and bawls.
> *J. W. Palmer*, The New and the Old, p. 341.

pishymew (pish'i-mū), *n.* A small white gull. [New Eng.]

Pisidiidæ (pis-i-dī'i-dē), *n. pl.* [NL., < *Pisidium* + *-idæ*.] A family of dimyarian bivalves, typified by the genus *Pisidium*. They have the branchial and pedal orifices confluent, the anal siphonate, the foot large, the shell equivalve and oval or cuneiform, with the area in front of the umbones larger than that behind, the hinge with two divergent cardinal teeth in each valve and four lateral teeth in the right and two in the left valve, and an external ligament. These small bivalves inhabit fresh water, and are remarkable for the posterior position of the umbones.

Pisidium amnicum.
b, branchial and pedal orifice; *f*, extended foot; *s*, anal siphon.

Pisidium (pī-sid'i-um), *n.* [NL. (Pfeiffer, 1821), dim. of *Pisum*, q. v.] The typical genus of *Pisidiidæ*, containing such forms as *P. amnicum*.

pisiform (pī'si-fôrm), *a.* and *n.* [< NL. *pisiformis*, < L. *pisum*, a pea (see *pease*1, *Pisum*), + *forma*, form.] I. *a.* Having the form of a pea, as an ossification in tendons at joints; having a structure resembling peas. A variety of iron ore is called *pisiform*, from its being made up of small rounded masses about the size of a pea.

II. *n.* In *anat.*, a sesamoid bone, of about the size and shape of a pea, developed in the tendon of the flexor carpi ulnaris muscle of man and some other animals. It is generally reckoned as one of the carpal bones, making eight in all, in man, but is not morphologically an element of the carpus. It is often of irregular shape, and sometimes one of the largest bones in the carpus, as in the horse. See also cuts under *Artiodactyla*, *Perissodactyla*, *solidungulate*, and *hand*.

Pisiform and other Bones of Right Carpus of Horse, front view, corresponding to back of human wrist. The large bone above is the lower end of the radius. The large bone below is the upper end of the middle metacarpal, or cannon-bone, showing also the ends of the lateral metacarpals, or splint-bones, * *. Between these are the carpal bones—1, cuneiform; 2, lunar; 3, scaphoid; 4, pisiform; 5, unciform; 6, magnum; 7, trapezoid.

pisiforme (pī-si-fôr'mē), *n.*; pl. *pisiformia* (-mi-ạ̈). [NL., neut. of *pisiformis*: see *pisiform*.] The pisiform bone: more fully called *os pisiforme*.

pisk (pisk), *n.* Same as *night-hawk*, 1.

piskashish (pis'kạ-shish), *n.* [Amer. Ind.] Same as *Hutchins's goose* (which see, under *goose*).

pislet, *n.* An obsolete form of *pizzle*. *Purchas*, Pilgrimage, p. 503.

pismire (pis'mīr), *n.* [Early mod. E. also *pismyre*, *pysmyre*; < ME. *pismire*, *pissemyre*, *pys-*

mere, *pismoure*, *pyssmoure* (= MD. *pismierc*), an ant; < *piss* (with ref. to the strong urinous smell of an ant-hill) + *mire*[2], an ant: see *mire*[2]. Cf. MD. *pisimme*, *pisemme*, an ant, < *pissen*, piss, + **emme*, *emte*, ant: see *ant*[1].] An ant or emmet.

He is as angry as a *pissemyre*,
Though that he have al that he kan desire.
Chaucer, Summoner's Tale, l. 117.

Nettled and stung with *pismires*.
Shak., 1 Hen. IV., i. 3. 240.

pismire-hill† (pis'mīr-hil), *n.* [< ME. *pismoure hylle* (also *pysmerys hylle*); < *pismire* + *hill*[1].] An ant-hill. *Cath. Ang.*, p. 281.

pisnet†, *n.* Same as *pinsnet*[2].

pisohamatus (pī"sō-hā-mā'tus), *n.* [NL., < Gr. πίσος, a pea, + L. *hamatus*, furnished with a hook, hooked.] Same as *piso-uncinatus*.

pisolite (pī'sō-līt), *n.* [< Gr. πίσος, a pea, + λίθος, stone.] Limestone having an oölitic structure, in which the individual grains or globules are as large as peas. This mode of occurrence is very characteristic of certain parts of the Oölitic or Jurassic series in England. (See *pea-grit*.) The name "Coral Rag and *Pisolite*" was given by W. Smith, in 1815, to what are now generally called the "Corallian beds," a member of the Middle Oölitic series in England. Also *peastone*.

Pisolitic Structure.

pisolitic (pī-sō-lit'ik), *a.* [< *pisolite* + *-ic*.] Having the structure indicated by the term pisolite: as, *pisolitic* iron ore, etc. See *pisolite*.—**Pisolitic limestone**, a division of the Cretaceous, of some importance in the north of France, where it lies unconformably in patches on the top of the white chalk.

Pisonia (pī-sō'ni-ä), *n.* [NL. (Linnæus, 1737), named after Dr. *Pison*, a traveler in Brazil.] A genus of trees and shrubs, of the order *Nyctagineæ*, type of the tribe *Pisonieæ*, characterized by the terminal stigma and six to ten exserted stamens. There are about 60 species, mainly of tropical America. They bear opposite or scattered oblong-ovate or lanceolate leaves, small diœcious rose, yellow, or greenish funnel-shaped flowers in panicled cymes, and a rigid or stony, rarely fleshy, elongated fruit (an anthocarp), often with rough and glutinous angles. Several species are trees cultivated for ornament. *P. Brunoniana* is the New Zealand para-para tree, a hardy evergreen; others are greenhouse shrubs with green flowers, as the fingrigo or cockspur, a rambling prickly bush of the West Indies with glutinous bur-like fruit, forming thickets. See *beefwood*, 2, *corkwood*, and *loblolly-tree*.

Pisonieæ (pis-ō-nī'ę̄-ē), *n. pl.* [NL. (Bentham and Hooker, 1880), < *Pisonia* + *-eæ*.] A tribe of plants of the apetalous order *Nyctagineæ*, characterized by the straight embryo and the elongated utricle included within the enlarged and closed calyx-tube. It includes about 100 species, of 4 genera, *Pisonia* being the type.

pisophalt† (pis'ǫ-falt), *n.* A corrupt form of *pissasphalt*.

piso-uncinatus (pī-so-un-si-nā'tus), *n.* [NL., < Gr. πίσος, a pea, + L. *uncinatus*, furnished with hooks or tenters, barbed.] A muscle, of rare occurrence, replacing the ligamentum pisohamatum, the short ligament passing from the pisiform to the uncinate bone.

piss (pis), *v.* [< ME. *pissen*, *pyssen*, *pischen* = OFries. *pissia* = D. MLG. LG. *pissen* = G. *pissen* = Icel. Sw. *pissa* = Dan. *pisse*, < F. *pisser* = Pr. *pissar* = It. *pisciare*, piss; supposed to be of imitative origin, perhaps orig. suggested by L. *pitissare*, *pytissare*, < Gr. πυτίζειν, spurt out water, spit frequently, freq. of πτύειν, = L. *spuere*, spew, spit: see *spew*.] **I.** *intrans.* To discharge the fluid secreted by the kidneys and detained in the urinary bladder; urinate.

The moste Synne that ony man may do is to *pissen* in hire Houses that thei dwellen in.
Mandeville, Travels, p. 242.

II. *trans.* To eject as urine. *Shak.*, M. W. of W., v. 5. 16.

piss (pis), *n.* [< ME. *pysse* = D. *pis* = MLG. *pisse* = G. *pisse* = Icel. Sw. *piss* = Dan. *pis*; from the verb.] Urine.

piss-a-bed (pis'a-bed), *n.* [= D. *pissebed*; tr. F. *pissenlit*, dandelion; so called with ref. to the diuretic properties of the expressed juice of the root.] The dandelion. [Vulgar.]

pissasphalt (pis'as-falt), *n.* [= F. *pissasphalte* = Sp. *pisasfalto* = Pg. *pissasphalto* = It. *pissasfalto*, < L. *pissasphaltus*, < Gr. πισσάσφαλτος, a compound of asphalt and pitch, < πίσσα, pitch, + ἄσφαλτος, asphalt.] A variety of bitumen. The word is only used as the equivalent in English of the corresponding Greek and Latin words cited in the etymology. As used by ancient writers, *pissasphalt* seems to have been an occasional designation of the semi-fluid variety of bitumen now called *maltha*. Also *pisasphalt*.

pissasphaltum (pis-as-fal'tum), *n.* [NL., neut. of L. *pissasphaltus*, m.: see *pissasphalt*.] Same as *pissasphalt*.

piss-bowl†, *n.* A chamber-pot. [Low.]

She, beyng moche the more incensed by reason of her housbandes quietnesse and stilnesse, powred doune a *pissebolle* upon hym out of a windore.
Udall, tr. of Apophthegms of Erasmus, p. 25. (*Davies*.)

piss-burnt (pis'bėrnt), *a.* Stained brown, as if scorched with urine: said of clothes. *Johnson*. [Low.]

piss-clam (pis'klam), *n.* The common long clam, *Mya arenaria*: so called from its squirting. [Local, U. S.]

pissing-while† (pis'ing-hwīl), *n.* A very short time. *B. Jonson*, Magnetick Lady, i. 7. [Low.]

Pissodes (pi-sō'dēz), *n.* [NL., < Gr. πισσώδης, like pitch, < πίσσα, pitch, + εἶδος, form.] A genus of weevils of the family *Curculionidæ*. *P. strobi* is a species whose larva injures pines.

White-pine Weevil (*Pissodes strobi*). *a*, larva; *b*, pupa. (Line shows natural size.)

piss-pot (pis'pot), *n.* [= D. *pispot* = MLG. *pissepot* = G. *pisspot* = Sw. *pisspotta* = Dan. *pissepotte*; as *piss* + *pot*.] A chamber-pot. [Low.]

pist[1], **piste** (pist), *n.* [< F. *piste* = Sp. Pg. *pista* = It. *pesta*, a track, < L. *pistus*, pp. of *pinsere*, *pisere*, beat, pound.] The track or footprint of a horseman on the ground he goes over. *Imp. Dict.*

pist[2] (pist), *interj.* [A sibilant syllable like *hist*, *whist*, *'st*.] Same as *hist*.

Pist! where are you?
Middleton, Changeling, v. 1.

pistace†, *n.* A Middle English form of *pistachio*.

pistache (pis-tash'), *n.* [< ME. *pistace*, < OF. and F. *pistache*: see *pistachio*.] Same as *pistachio*.

pistachio (pis-tā'shiō), *n.* [Formerly *pistacho*; < Sp. *pistacho* = F. *pistache* = Pg. *pistacha*, *pistacia* = It. *pistacchio*, *pistacio* = D. *pistasje* = G. *pistazie* = Sw. Dan. *pistacie*, < L. *pistacium*, *pistaceum*, the pistachio-nut, *pistacia*, the pistachio-tree, < Gr. πιστάκιον, in pl. πιστάκια, also βιστάκια, φιττάκια, ψιττάκια, the fruit of the pistachio-tree, itself called πιστάκη, = Ar. *fistaq*, *fustuq* = Hind. *pistah*, < Pers. *pistā*, the pistachio-nut.] Same as *pistachio-nut*.

Pistachoes, so they be good, and not musty, joined with almonds, . . . are an excellent nourisher.
Bacon, Nat. Hist., § 50.

They [the Italians] call it *Pistachi*, a fruit much used in their dainty banquets.
Coryat, Crudities, I. 184.

pistachio-green (pis-tā'shiō-grēn), *n.* A bright green much used in Eastern decoration.

pistachio-nut (pis-tā'shiō-nut), *n.* The nut of the *Pistacia vera*. It contains a greenish-colored kernel of a pleasant almond-like taste, which is extensively used by the Turks, Greeks, etc., as a dessert-nut or in confections, and is also exported. It yields a wholesome food-oil, which, however, soon becomes rancid. Sometimes called *bladdernut*. Also *pistachio*, *pistacia-nut*. See *Pistacia*.

pistachio-tree (pis-tā'shiō-trē), *n.* See *Pistacia*.

Pistacia (pis-tā'shi-ä), *n.* [NL. (Linnæus, 1737), < L. *pistacia*, < Gr. πιστάκη, the pistachio-tree: see *pistachio*.] 1. A genus of trees, of the order *Anacardiaceæ* and tribe *Spondieæ*, distinguished as the one apetalous genus of that polypetalous family. The 8 species are natives of western Asia and the Mediterranean region, the Canary Islands, and Mexico.

Branch of Pistachio-tree (*Pistacia vera*) with fruits.

They are large or small trees, exuding a resin (terebinth or mastic), and bearing alternate evergreen or deciduous leaves, pinnate or of three leaflets, and axillary panicles or racemes of small diœcious flowers. (See *mastic*, *n.*, 1, *mastic-tree*, *lentisk*, *balsam-tree*, *terebinth*, *turpentine-tree*, *Chian turpentine* (under *Chian*), *alk*[2], *alk-gum*, *pistachio-nut*, and *bladder-nut*.) Several species yield useful wood, resins, and galls. The galls of a variety of *P. Khinjuk*, of northwestern India, are sold in the Indian bazaars for tanning, and are there known as *kakra singhi*.

2. [*l. c.*] A tree of this genus.

Pistacia is graffed nowe to growe
In colde lande, and pynapul seede is sowe.
Palladius, Husbondrie (E. E. T. S.), p. 128.

pistacia-nut (pis-tā'shi-ä-nut), *n.* Same as *pistachio-nut*.

pistacio, *n.* Same as *pistachio*.

pistacite (pis'tą-sīt), *n.* [So called from its color; < *Pistacia* + *-ite*[2].] In *mineral.*, same as *epidote*. Also *pistazite*.

pistacite-rock (pis'tą-sīt-rok), *n.* Same as *epidosite*.

pistareen (pis-ta-rēn'), *n.* [Origin uncertain.] In the West Indies, the peseta.

piste, *n.* See *pist*[1].

pistel†, *n.* See *pistle*.

pisteller†, *n.* [ME., by apheresis from *epistler*.] Same as *epistler*.

Pistia (pis'ti-ä), *n.* [NL. (Linnæus, 1737), < Gr. πιστός, liquid, < πίνειν, drink.] A genus of monocotyledonous floating water-plants of the order *Araceæ*, constituting the tribe *Pistioideæ*. It is characterized by the absence of perianth, and the position of the solitary or few staminate flowers on the short tree apex of a spadix which is adnate below to the small white spathe, and bears at the base a single obliquely globose one-celled ovary with thick style and cup-like stigma. The only species, *P. Stratiotes*, is common throughout the tropics excepting Australia and the Pacific islands. It consists of a rosette of pale pea-green rounded and downy leaves. It floats unattached, its tufts of long feathery roots often not reaching the bottom, and increases by runners, often soon covering ponds and tanks, keeping the water fresh and cool. It bears the name of tropical duckweed, and in the West Indies of *water-lettuce*.

pistic† (pis'tik), *a.* [< Gr. πιστικός, in the N. T., qualifying νάρδος, nard; taken to mean 'liquid,' < πιστός, liquid (< πίνειν, drink). By some identified with πιστικός, faithful, genuine, < πιστός, faithful, < πείθειν, πιθεῖν, persuade, πείθεσθαι, πιθέσθαι, believe.] An epithet of nard: as, *pistic* nard.

An alabaster box of nard *pistic* was sent as a present from Cambyses to the king of Ethiopia.
Jer. Taylor, Works (ed. 1835), I. 245.

pistil (pis'til), *n.* [= F. *pistil* = Sp. *pistilo* = Pg. It. *pistillo* = G. Sw. *pistill* = Dan. *pistil*, < NL. *pistillum*, a pistil, so called from the resemblance in shape to the pestle of a mortar; < L. *pistillum*, *pistillus*, a pestle: see *pestle*.] In *bot.*, the female or seed-bearing organ of a flower. A complete pistil consists of three parts, *ovary*, *style*, and *stigma*. The ovary is the hollow part at the base which contains the ovules, or bodies destined to become seeds. The style is simply a prolongation of the ovary, and may sometimes be entirely wanting. The stigma is a part of the surface of the pistil denuded of epidermis, upon which the pollen for fertilizing the ovules is received, and through which it acts upon them. The form of the stigma is very various in different plants, being sometimes a mere knob or point at the apex of the style, a line, or double line, or of various shapes. There are usually several pistils, or at least more than one pistil, in each flower; collectively they are termed the *gynœcium*. See also cuts under *anticous*, *Lemna*, *lily*, *madder*, *Oxalis*, and *pitcher-plant*.—**Compound pistil**. See *compound*[1].

Pistils.
a, *Lilium bulbiferum*; *b*, *Geranium sanguineum*; *c*, *Eleocharis palustris*; *d*, *Oryza sativa*. 1, ovary; 2, style; 3, stigma.

pistillaceous (pis-ti-lā'shius), *a.* [< *pistil* + *-aceous*.] In *bot.*, of or belonging to the pistil.

pistillary (pis'ti-lā-ri), *a.* [= F. *pistillaire* = Pg. *pistillar*, < NL. **pistillaris*, < *pistillum*, pistil: see *pistil*.] In *bot.*, of or belonging to the pistil.—**Pistillary cord**, a channel which passes from the stigma through the style into the ovary.

pistillate (pis'ti-lāt), *a.* [= F. *pistillé*, < NL. *pistillatus*, < *pistillum*, pistil: see *pistil*.] In *bot.*, having a pistil: noting a plant or flower provided with a pistil, and most properly said of one having pistils only. See cuts under *Abietineæ*, *breadfruit*, and *croton*.

pistillation† (pis-ti-lā'shon), *n.* [< L. as if **pistillatio(n-)*, < *pistillum*, *pistillus*, a pestle: see *pestle*.] The act of pounding with a pestle in a mortar.

The best [diamonds] . . . are so far from breaking hammers, that they submit unto *pistillation*, and resist not an ordinary pestle.
Sir T. Browne, Vulg. Err., ii. 5.

pistillidium (pis-ti-lid'i-um), *n.*; pl. *pistillidia* (-ä). [NL., < *pistillum*, a pistil, + Gr. εἶδος, form.] In cryptogams, same as *archegonium*.

pistilliferous (pis-ti-lif'e-rus), *a.* [= F. *pistillifère* = Pg. *pistillifero*, < NL. *pistillum*, a pistil, + L. *ferre* = E. *bear*[1].] In *bot.*, same as *pistillate*.

pistilline (pis'ti-lin), *a.* [< *pistil* + *-ine*[1].] In *bot.*, relating or belonging to the pistil.

The *pistilline* whorl is very liable to changes. *Encyc. Brit.*, IV. 128.

pistillody (pis'ti-lō-di), *n.* [< NL. *pistillum*, pistil, + Gr. εἶδος, form.] In *bot.*, the metamorphosis or transformation of other organs into pistils or carpels. Pistillody may affect the perianth, the sepals, very frequently the stamens, and rarely the ovule. See *metamorphosis*.

Pistioideæ (pis-ti-oi'dē-ē), *n. pl.* [NL. (Durand, 1888), < *Pistia* + *-oideæ*.] A tribe of monocotyledonous plants, of the order *Araceæ*, consisting of the genus *Pistia*, and distinguished by the unappendaged spadix united to the back of the longer spathe, the two connate stamens, the numerous orthotropous ovules, and the single soft berry which constitutes the fruit.

pistlet, pistelt, *n.* [ME. *pistel*, *pystyl*, < AS. *pistol*, with apheresis of initial vowel < L. *epistola*, *epistula*, epistle: see *epistle*. For the apheresis, cf. *postle*, ult. < LL. *apostolus*, and *bishop*, ult. < LL. *episcopus*.] An epistle; a communication.

Tho rowned she a *pistel* in his ere. *Chaucer*, Wife of Bath's Tale, l. 165.

As Paul in a *pistele* of hym bereth witnesse. *Piers Plowman* (C), xvii. 289.

pistle-cloth†, *n.* A covering or wrapper for the books of the epistles.

pistol (pis'tol), *n.* [Formerly also *pistoll*; = D. *pistool* = G. *pistole* = Sw. Dan. *pistol*, < OF. *pistole* = Sp. Pg. *pistola*, < It. *pistola*, "a dag or pistoll" (Florio); cf. *pistolese*, "a great dagger, a wood-knife" (Florio), OF. *pistoyer*, a dagger; said to have been orig. made at Pistoria, < **Pistola*, now *Pistoia*, a town near Florence, < L. *Pistorium*, a city in Etruria, now *Pistoia*. The name appears to have been transferred from a dagger (a small sword) to a pistol (a small gun). Cf. *pistole*, and *pistolet*[1], *pistolet*[2].] A firearm intended to be held in one hand when aimed and fired. It came into use early in the sixteenth century, perhaps as early as 1500, for by 1520 it was common as a weapon of the reiters or German mercenary cavalry,

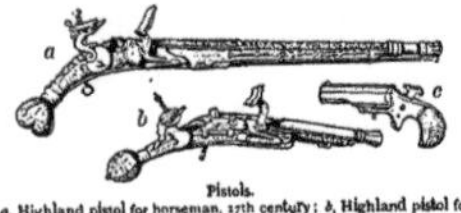

Pistols.
a, Highland pistol for horseman, 17th century; *b*, Highland pistol for the belt, 16th century; *c*, derringer.

who were called *pistoleers* from its use. The early pistol was fitted with the wheel-lock, which was superseded by the flint-lock, and the latter by the percussion-lock. Pistols with more than one barrel have been in use from the introduction of the weapon, those with two having the barrels sometimes side by side, sometimes one over the other. The stock of the pistol has been made of many forms, the old cavalry pistol having it only slightly curved, so that it was held, when pointed at an object, by the right hand, with the lock uppermost, the barrel to the left, the trigger to the right. When accurate aiming was required, as in dueling-pistols, the handle was made much more curved. See *revolver*.—**Volta's pistol**, a metallic vessel, closed by a cork, containing an explosive mixture of gases which may be ignited by an electric spark.

pistol (pis'tol), *v. t.*; pret. and pp. *pistoled* or *pistolled*, ppr. *pistoling* or *pistolling*. [= F. *pistoler*; from the noun.] To shoot with a pistol.

I do not like this humour in thee in *pistoling* men in this sort; it is a most dangerous and stigmatical humour. *Chapman*, Blind Beggar of Alexandria.

This varlet afterwards threatened to *pistol* me. *Evelyn*, Diary, Aug. 1, 1644.

pistoladet (pis-tō-lād'), *n.* [< F. *pistolade*, < *pistoler*, discharge a pistol: see *pistol*, *v.*] The discharge of a pistol; a pistol-shot.

pistol-cane (pis'tol-kān), *n.* A pistol having the form of a cane, the barrel constituting the staff and the lock being concealed; also, a cane which in any form conceals or is combined with a pistol. It is classed in the legal category of concealed weapons (which see, under *weapon*).

pistol-carbine (pis'tol-kär"bin), *n.* A long pistol having its stock so arranged that a shoulder-piece or butt-piece can be adjusted to it, fitting it for firing from the shoulder. See cut in next column.

Pistol-carbine.
a, lock; *b*, detachable butt-piece; *c*, spring-catch; *d*, socket fitting butt of pistol-stock.

pistole (pis-tōl'), *n.* [= G. *pistole* = Pg. *pistola*, < F. *pistole*, a pistole, a coin appar. so called as being smaller than the crown, < OF. *pistole*, a pistol (a small gun): see *pistol*. The name was afterward applied to the gold coins of other countries, especially of Spain.] A gold coin of Spain, worth at the beginning of the nineteenth century nearly $4 United States money. The name was also applied to the French louis d'or of gold

Obverse. Reverse.
Pistole of Charles IV. of Spain, 1790.—British Museum. (Size of the original.)

issued by Louis XIII. in 1640, and to gold coins of various European countries, worth either more or less than the Spanish pistole. About 1835, the Swiss pistole was worth nearly $4.75; the Italian, from $3.45 to $5.55; the German, about $4.—**Double pistole.** See *double*.

pistoleer (pis-tō-lēr'), *n.* [Also *pistolier* = G. *pistolier*; < OF. *pistolier* (= Pg. *pistolero* = It. *pistoliere*), < *pistole*, a pistol: see *pistol*.] One who fires or uses a pistol; a soldier armed with a pistol, especially a German reiter.

Is the Chalk-Farm *pistoleer* inspired with any reasonable belief and determination; or is he hounded on by haggard indefinable fear? *Carlyle*, Misc., iii. 94. (*Davies.*)

pistolet[1]**†** (pis'tō-let), *n.* [Early mod. E. also *pestilett*, *pestelet* (also *pistoletto*, < It.); = D. *pistolet*, < OF. (and F.) *pistolet* = Sp. Pg. *pistolete*, < It. *pistoletto* (ML. *pistolettus*), a little pistol, dim. of *pistola*, a pistol: see *pistol*.] A small pistol.

Pistolets and short swords under their robes. *Marston and Webster*, Malcontent, v. 3.

We had *pestelets* enew [that is, in plenty],
And shot among them as we might.
Raid of the Reidswire (Child's Ballads, VI. 136).

Fetch me my *pestilett*,
And charge me my gonne.
Captain Car (Child's Ballads, VI. 151).

pistolet[2]**†** (pis'tō-let), *n.* [OF. *pistolet*, dim. of *pistole*, a pistole: see *pistole*.] A pistole.

The *pistolet* and roials of plate are most currant there. *Hakluyt's Voyages*, II. 176.

Give a double *pistolet*
To some poor needy friar, to say a Mass.
Beau. and Fl., Spanish Curate, i. 1.

pistolettot (pis-tō-let'ō), *n.* [It.: see *pistolet*[1].] Same as *pistolet*[1].

Give us leave to talk Squibs and *Pistoletto's* charged with nothing but powder of Love and shot of Reason. *N. Ward*, Simple Cobler, p. 88.

pistol-grip (pis'tol-grip), *n.* A handle, shaped like the butt of a pistol, attached to the under side of the small of the stock of fowling-pieces and rifles. It affords a better hold for the hand than the ordinary form of stock. Also *pistol-hand*. See cut under *gun*.

pistolier, *n.* See *pistoleer*.

pistol-pipe (pis'tol-pīp), *n.* In *metal-working*, the twyer of a hot-blast furnace. *E. H. Knight.*

pistol-router (pis'tol-rou"tėr), *n.* A form of carpenters' plane; a router having a handle shaped like a pistol-butt.

pistol-shaped (pis'tol-shāpt), *a.* Having the general form of a pistol—that is, partly straight, with a curved addition or extension like the stock of a pistol.

pistol-shot (pis'tol-shot), *n.* 1. The shot from a pistol, or the report from the firing of a pistol.—2. As an estimate of distance, the range, or the approximate range, of a pistol-ball.—3. One who shoots with a pistol; a marksman with the pistol: as, a good *pistol-shot*.

pistol-splint (pis'tol-splint), *n.* In *surg.*, a splint shaped like a pistol, employed especially in fractures of the lower end of the radius.

pistomesite (pis-tō-mē'sīt), *n.* [< Gr. πιστός, true, + E. *mes(it)ite*.] A carbonate of iron and magnesium like mesitite, intermediate between magnesite and siderite, but more closely related to the latter.

piston (pis'ton), *n.* [< F. *piston*, a piston, formerly also a pestle, = Sp. *piston*, a piston, < It. *pistone*, a piston, var. of *pestone*, a large pestle, < *pestare*, pound, < ML. *pistare*, *pestare*, pound, freq. of L. *pinsere*, *pisere*, pp. *pistus*, beat, pound: see *pestle*, *pistil*.] 1. In *mach.*, a movable piece, generally of a cylindrical form, so fitted as to fill the sectional area of a tube, such as the barrel of a pump or the cylinder of a steam-engine, and capable of being driven alternately in two directions by pressure on one or the other of its sides. One of its sides is fitted to a rod, called the *piston-rod*, to which it imparts reciprocatory motion, as in the steam-engine, where the motion given to the piston-rod is communicated to the machinery, or by which, on the other hand, it is itself made to move, as in the pump. Two sorts of pistons are used in pumps—one hollow with a valve, used in the suction-pump, and the other solid, which is employed in the force-pump. The latter is also called a *plunger*.

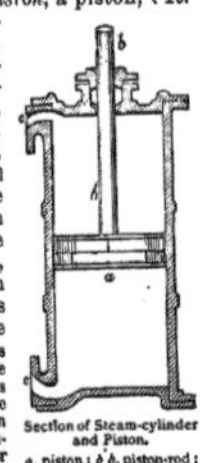

Section of Steam-cylinder and Piston.
a, piston; *b b*, piston-rod; *c c*, steam-ports.

2. In musical wind-instruments of the trumpet family, one of the forms of valve whereby a crook is temporarily added to the tube and the pitch of the tones altered. It is operated by depressing a finger-knob, and thus pushing a plunger into a cylinder. The plunger has channels for changing the direction of the air-column. Pistons have been applied to various instruments, but especially to the cornet, which is therefore called the *cornet-à-pistons*.

3. In *organ-building*, a thumb-knob which may be pushed in like a piston, whereby some change in registration is pneumatically effected; a pneumatic coupler or combination knob.—4. The central retractile part of the acetabulum or sucker of a cephalopod, whose action in producing a vacuum resembles that of the piston of an air-pump.—**Differential piston.** See *differential*.—**Double-piston locomotive.** See *locomotive*.—**Oscillating piston**, an engine-piston which oscillates in a sector-shaped chamber.—**Piston blowing-machine.** See *blowing-machine*.

piston-head (pis'ton-hed), *n.* The disk which is fitted closely to the interior of the cylinder, and is the direct receiver or transmitter of the power developed: distinguished from the *piston-rod*.

piston-knob (pis'ton-nob), *n.* Same as *piston*, 3.

piston-packing (pis'ton-pak"ing), *n.* 1. Any material used to pack or make tight the space between the perimeter of a piston-head and the interior of the cylinder or -barrel in which it moves. Many different materials have been used for piston-packings, among which are hemp (usually in the form of a braided gasket), either by itself or saturated with tallow or mixtures of various oily or fatty materials, india-rubber or compositions of which india-rubber is a principal ingredient, leather, metallic alloys, etc. Piston-packings are usually inserted in a groove or depression in the perimeter of the piston-head, and expanded by mechanical compression to make a steam-tight, air-tight, water-tight, or gas-tight joint.

2. A mechanical device for packing pistons, in which the operation depends more upon the construction than upon the fibrous, plastic, or compressible properties of the packing-material.—**Piston-packing expander**, a steel spring in a piston-head serving to expand the packing against the interior of the cylinder; a piston-spring. *E. H. Knight.*

piston-pump (pis'ton-pump), *n.* A pump consisting of a pump-cylinder or -barrel in which a reciprocating piston works. It is provided with appliances for moving the piston, as a piston-rod or pump-rod, and a hand-lever actuating the pump-rod, or the cross-head of an engine attached to it; an induction-port or -ports covered with valves which permit a fluid to enter the pump-barrel, but prevent its return; and an eduction-port or -ports provided with valves which permit efflux of the fluid from the pump-barrel, but prevent its return. These are the essential features of piston-pumps. They usually also have induction- or suction-pipes, and frequently eduction- or discharge-pipes. See *pump*[1], *lift-pump*, *force-pump*, *plunger-pump*, and *suction-pump*.

piston-rod (pis'ton-rod), *n.* See *piston*, 1.—**Piston-rod packing.** (*a*) A material placed in the stuffing-box of a cylinder to make a steam-tight joint about the piston. (*b*) The stuffing-box of a piston.

piston-sleeve (pis'ton-slēv), *n.* The piston of a trunk-engine, with which the connecting-rod or pitman is directly connected by a pivot. Such a piston has a hollow cylinder (sleeve) cast upon it in order to give it sufficient bearing-length to enable it in itself to perform also the function of a cross-head, the walls of the cylinder then performing the function of the cross-head slides, the pin which directly connects the pitman with the piston taking the place of the ordinary cross-head pin, and no piston-rod being used. This construction enables the engine to be much shortened in the line of its stroke. See *trunk-engine*.

piston-spring (pis'tọn-spring), *n.* A coil around or inside a piston which, by its tension, acts automatically as packing.

piston-valve (pis'tọn-valv), *n.* A reciprocating valve resembling a working piston, moved in a tubular passage to open or close a port or ports for alternately admitting steam to or exhausting it from the cylinder of an engine.

piston-wheel (pis'tọn-hwēl), *n.* **1.** In a rotary engine or pump, a disk or wheel carrying at its outer margin one or more pistons.—**2.** In a chain-pump, a wheel carrying an endless chain to which are attached pistons working in a tube or barrel. See *rotary engine* (under *rotary*), and *chain-pump*.

piston-whistle (pis'tọn-hwis"l), *n.* A whistle in which, by shortening or lengthening the vibrating air-column through the movement of a piston sliding in the tube (or *bell*, as it is called in steam-whistles), a sound of varying pitch is emitted. See *Modoc whistle*, under *whistle*.

Pisum (pī'sum), *n.* [NL., < L.: see *pease*[1], *peal*[1].] **1.** A genus of leguminous plants of the tribe *Vicieæ*, distinguished from the large related genus *Lathyrus* by the dilated summit of the style, which is inflexed and hardened, with reflexed margins above, and bearded on the inner face. There are 2 species, one native of the Taurus in Asia Minor, the other, *P. sativum*, the common garden- and field-pea. *Rivinus*, 1691. See *pea*[1].

2. In *zoöl.*, a genus of bivalves. *Megerle*, 1811.

pit[1] (pit), *n.* [< ME. *pit, put, pyt, pette, putte, pytte*, < AS. *pyt, pytt*, a pit, hole, = OFries. *pet* = D. *put* = OLG. *putte*, MLG. LG. *putte* = OHG. *puzzi, phuzzi, pfuzi*, also *puzza, putza, buzza*, etc., MHG. *butze, bütze, pfütze*, G. *pfütze* = Icel. *pyttr* = Sw. *puss* = Dan. *pyt* = F. *puits* = Wall. *puts* = Pr. *potz, poutz* = Sp. *pozo* = Pg. *poço* = It. *pozzo*, a well, < L. *puteus*, a well, a pit; perhaps orig. a spring of pure water, < √ *pu* in *purus*, pure: see *pure*.] **1.** A hole or cavity in the ground, whether natural or made by digging.

> And faste by it is a lityllo *pytt* in the Erthe, where the foot of the Pilcer is zit entered. *Mandeville*, Travels, p. 94.

> And as the child gan forby for to pace,
> This cursed Jew him hent and held him faste,
> And kitte his throte, and in a *pit* him caste.
> *Chaucer*, Prioress's Tale, l. 119.

Specifically—(*a*) An excavation or hole in the ground, covered or otherwise concealed, for snaring wild beasts; a pitfall. (*b*) A hole dug in the soil of a potato- or turnip-field, for storing potatoes, etc., during the winter. The vegetables stored are usually piled up to some height and covered with earth to keep out the frost. [Great Britain.] (*c*) In *hort.*, an excavation in the soil, generally covered by a glazed frame, for protecting tender plants, or for propagation. (*d*) In *founding*, a cavity scooped in the floor to receive cast-metal. (*e*) The shaft of a coal-mine, or the mine itself. (*f*) A vat, such as is used in tanning, bleaching, dyeing, etc.

2. A cavity or depression in the body: as, the *pit* of the stomach; the arm*pits*.

> For person and complexion, they haue broad and flat visages, . . . thin haired vpon the upper lip and *pit* of the chin, light and nimble-bodied with short legges.
> *Purchas*, Pilgrimage, p. 421.

> I found him lying on his bed with his clothes on, his shoes merely slipped off, and his hat held securely over the *pit* of his stomach. *H. B. Stowe*, Oldtown, p. 415.

3. A very small depression or dent, such as that left on the flesh by a pustule of the smallpox; a dimple.

> Look what a pretty *pit* there's in her chin!
> *Middleton*, Spanish Gypsy, iii. 2.

> The sandstone surface is distinctly marked by raindrop *pits* and by ripple or wave marks. *Science*, IV. 273.

4. In *bot.*, one of the pores or thin places in the more or less lignified cell-walls of many plants. The bordered pits, which are especially characteristic of the wood of the *Coniferæ*, are composed of two concentric circles, which represent thin spots or pores in the walls of the tracheids. They are very regularly arranged.

5. A hollow or cup.

> Flowers on their stalks set
> Like vestal primroses, but dark velvet
> Edges them round, and they have golden *pits*.
> *Keats*, Endymion, i.

6. A deep place; a gulf; an abyss. Specifically—(*a*) The grave.

> Frendes, I am poor and old,
> And almost, God wot, on my *pittes* brynke.
> *Chaucer*, Merchant's Tale, l. 157.

> Thou hast brought up my soul from the grave; thou hast kept me alive, that I should not go down to the *pit*.
> Ps. xxx. 3.

(*b*) The abode of evil spirits; hell.

> We also saw there the Hobgoblins, Satyrs, and Dragons of the *pit*. *Bunyan*, Pilgrim's Progress, p. 131.

> Each one reels
> Under the load towards the *pit* of death.
> *Shelley*, Prometheus Unbound, ii. 4.

7. An inclosed place or area for the exhibition of combats of dogs or cocks, or where dogs are trained or exhibited in killing rats: as, a dog-*pit*; a cock*pit*.

> Sir Thomas Jermin, meaning to make himself merry, and gull all the cockers, sent his man to the *pit* in Shoe-lane with an hundred pounds and a dunghill cock, neatly cut and trimmed for the battle.
> *Harl. MS.*, No. 6395, quoted in Strutt's Sports and [Pastimes, p. 376.

> What though her chamber be the very *pit*
> Where fight the prime cocks of the game for wit.
> *B. Jonson*, An Epigram on the Court Pucell.

8. That part of a theater which is on the floor of the house, somewhat below the level of the stage, and behind the usual station of the musicians. In the United Kingdom the name is now often given to the inferior seats behind the stalls. In the United States it has been superseded by *orchestra* or *parquet*.

> I and my wife sat in the *pitt*, and saw "The Bondman" done to admiration. *Pepys*, Diary, March 26, 1661.

> But we, the Actors, humbly will submit,
> Now, and at any time, to a full *Pit*.
> *Wycherley*, Country Wife, Prol.

> All bad Poets we are sure are Foes,
> And how their Number's swell'd the Town well knows;
> In shoals I've mark'd 'em judging in the *Pit*.
> *Congreve*, Way of the World, Epil.

> The *Pit* is an Amphitheater, fill'd with Bonches without Back boards, and adorn'd and cover'd with green Cloth.
> Quoted in *Ashton's* Social Life in Reign of Queen Anne, [II. 6.

9. Those who occupy the pit in a theater; the people in the pit.

> Now, sir, your soliloquy—but speak more to the *pit*, if you please—the soliloquy always to the *pit*—that's a rule.
> *Sheridan*, The Critic, iii. 1.

> He [King George IV.] was received with immense acclamations, the whole *pit* standing up, hurrahing and waving their hands. *Greville*, Memoirs, Feb. 7, 1821.

10. That part of the floor of an exchange where a special kind of business is carried on: as, a grain-*pit*; a provision-*pit*. [U. S.]—**11.** The cockpit of a ship.—**12.** The framework in a belfry which supports the pivoted yoke of a swinging bell. *Sir E. Beckett*, Clocks and Watches, p. 359. [Now little used.]—**Gjers soaking-pit**, a cavity lined with refractory material, used in metal-working to inclose large ingots, in order to preserve them at a high temperature, and thus avoid the necessity of reheating.—**Olfactory pits**, certain hollows of the embryonic skull which will become nasal passages.—**Pine-pit**, in *hort.*, a pit adapted for raising young plants to replenish pineries.—**Pit and gallows**, in feudal times, the privilege granted by the crown to barons of executing persons convicted of theft by hanging the men on a gallows and drowning the women in a pit. Also *pot and gallows*.—**The bottomless pit**, hell.

> And I saw an angel come down from heaven, having the key of *the bottomless pit* and a great chain in his hand.
> Rev. xx. 1.

> Your deep-conceited cutpurse, who by the dexterity of his knife will draw out the money and make a flame-coloured purse show like *the bottomless pit*, but with never a soul in 't. *Middleton*, The Black Book.

To shoot or fly the pit, to turn tail and try to escape, like a craven cock in a pit.

> The whole nation . . . expressing utmost detestation and abhorrence of the Whig principles, which made the whole party *shoot the pit* and retire.
> *Roger North*, Examen, p. 327. (*Davies.*)

> We were all to blame to make madam here *fly the pit* as she did. *Richardson*, Pamela, ii. 308. (*Davies.*)

pit[1] (pit), *v.*; pret. and pp. *pitted*, ppr. *pitting*. [< *pit*[1], *n.*] **I.** *trans.* **1.** To catch, lay, or bury in a pit.

> They lived like beasts and were *pitted* like beasts.
> *Granger*, On Ecclesiastes (1621), p. 213. (*Latham.*)

2. To form a little pit or hollow in; mark with little dents, as by the pustules of the smallpox.

> An anasarca, a species of dropsy, is characterized by the shining and softness of the skin, which gives way to the least impression, and remains *pitted* for some time.
> *Sharpe.*

> The red acid acts too powerfully and *pits* the copper.
> *Workshop Receipts*, 1st ser., p. 172.

3. To impress with rounded cup-like hollows, as the mold for a metal casting which is to have rounded bosses on it.—**4.** To put or set in the pit or area for fighting; match as contestants or opponents, one against another, as dogs or cocks: used figuratively of any competitors: generally followed by *against*.

> The *pitting* of them [cocks], as they call it, for the diversion and entertainment of man, . . . was, as I take it, a Grecian contrivance. *Archæologia*, III. 133.

> Socrates is *pitted against* the famous atheist from Ionia, and has just brought him to a contradiction in terms.
> *Macaulay*, Athenian Orators.

II. *intrans.* To become marked or spotted with pits or depressions; retain the mark of pressure by or as by the fingers: as, in dropsy the skin *pits* on pressure.

> The Carriage Monthly tells its readers how to remove varnish from a panel after it has *pitted*.
> *Sci. Amer.*, N. S., LVII. 276.

pit[2] (pit), *n.* [A var. of *pip*[2], by confusion with *pit*[1].] The stone of a fruit, as of a cherry or plum. [U. S.]

pit[3] (pit), *v. t.* A Middle English and Scotch form of *put*[1].

pita (pē'tä), *n.* [Sp., < Mex. *pita*.] **1.** The maguey, *Agave Americana*, and other species of the genus.—**2.** The fiber derived from *Agave* leaves. It is of great strength, utilized for cordage, etc., and likely to be of commercial importance. Sometimes called *pita-flax*, *pita-hemp*, or *pita-thread*. The name is applied less properly to the istle-fiber (see *istle*) and to that of *Furcræa* (*Fourcroya*) *gigantea*.

pita-fiber (pē'tä-fī"bėr), *n.* Same as *pita*, 2.

pitahaya (pē-tä-hä'yä), *n.* [Mex. Sp.] Any tall columnar cactus bearing edible fruit, as *Cereus giganteus*, the giant cactus, and *C. Thurberi*. Also *pitajaya*. [Southwestern U. S.]

> Cereus Thurberi is commonly called *pitahaya* by the Mexicans, and this is the name by which it was known to the Aztecs. *Sci. Amer.*, N. S., LXI. 369.

Pitahaya-woodpecker, *Centurus uropygialis*, the Gila woodpecker, which abounds in southern Arizona, and usually nests in the giant cactus. Also called *saguaro woodpecker*.

Pitahaya-woodpecker (*Centurus uropygialis*).

pitaile†, **petaile**†, *n.* [ME., also *pitaill, pitall, pettaill*; < OF. *pitaille, pietaille, pedaile*, foot-soldiers, infantry, the populace, < *piet, pied*, foot, < L. *pes* (*ped-*), foot: see *foot*. Cf. *peon*.] Foot-soldiers; infantry; rabble.

> Than Oriens chese oute of peple as many as hym liked, that were wele xl^m^ with-outen the *petaile* that after hem folowed. *Merlin* (E. E. T. S.), ii. 253.

Pitaka (pit'a-kä), *n.* [Skt., lit. 'basket.'] A collection of Buddhist scriptures, as made in Tibet.

> The great Tibetan teacher . . . had no access to the Pâli *Pitakas*. *Encyc. Brit.*, XIV. 290.

pitance†, *n.* A Middle English form of *pittance*.

pitangua (pi-tang'gwä), *n.* [Braz.] A Brazilian tyrant-flycatcher with an enormous bill, *Megarhynchus pitangua*. See cut under *Megarhynchus*.

Pitangus (pi-tang'gus), *n.* [NL. (Swainson, 1827), < Braz. *pitangua*.] A genus of clamatorial passerine birds of the family *Tyrannidæ*, or tyrant-flycatchers; the Derbian flycatchers, not including the pitangua. They have a long and straight stout bill hooked at the end, rounded wings longer than the nearly square tail, the plumage brown above and yellow below, the head marked with black, white, and orange, the wings and tail extensively rufous. There are several species, inhabiting the warmer parts of America, as *P. sulphuratus*. One is found in Mexico and Texas, *P. derbianus*, about 10½ inches long. Also called *Saurophagus* and *Apolites*.

pitapat (pit'a-pat), *adv.* [Also *pitpat, pitypat, pittypat*; a varied reduplication of *pat*[1].] With a quick succession of beats; in a flutter; with palpitation.

> *V. Arch.* Lord, how my heart leaps!
> *Pet.* 'Twill go *pit-a-pat* shortly.
> *Fletcher*, Loyal Subject, ii. 2.

> His heart kep' goin' *pity-pat*,
> But hern went pity Zekle.
> *Lowell*, The Courtin'.

pitapat (pit'a-pat), *a.* [< *pitapat*, *adv.*] Fluttering.

> She immediately stepped out of her pew and fell into the finest *pitty-pat* air. *Steele*, Spectator, No. 503.

pitapat (pit'a-pat), *n.* [< *pitapat*, *adv.*] A light quick step; a succession of light beats or taps.

> Now again I hear the *pit-a-pat* of a pretty foot through the dark alley. *Dryden*, Don Sebastian, iii. 2.

pitapat (pit'a-pat), *v. i.* [< *pitapat, adv.*] To step or tread quickly.

> Run how'd with burthens to the fragrant Fat,
> Tumble them in, and after *pit-a-pat*
> Vp to the Waste.
> *Sylvester*, tr. of Du Bartas's Weeks, ii., The Magnificence.

pita-wood (pē'tä-wůd), *n.* The pith-like wood of *Furcræa* (*Fourcroya*) *gigantea*, used sometimes in Rio Janeiro as a slow-match, and sometimes to line drawers for holding insects.

Pitaya bark. See *bark*2 and *Cinchona*.

pit-bottom (pit'bot"um), *n.* In *coal-mining*, the entrance to a mine and the underground roads in the immediate vicinity, whether at the bottom of the pit or at any point in it beneath the surface at which the cages are loaded. Also *pit-eye*. [Eng.]

Pitcairnia (pit-kär'ni-ä), *n.* [NL. (L'Héritier, 1786); named after Archibald *Pitcairne* (1652–1713), professor of medicine at Edinburgh.] A genus of monocotyledonous herbs, of the order *Bromeliaceæ*, type of the tribe *Pitcairnieæ*, characterized by the terminal raceme with filiform styles and septicidally three-valved capsules. There are about 70 species, natives of tropical America. They bear close-clustered linear short or elongated rigid leaves, generally with spiny margins, and many showy narrow flowers of scarlet, yellow, or other colors, often with large colored bracts. They are considered handsome greenhouse-plants. See *Bromeliaceæ*.

Pitcairnieæ (pit-kär-ni'ē-ē), *n. pl.* [NL. (Bentham and Hooker, 1883), < *Pitcairnia* + *-eæ*.] A tribe of plants of the order *Bromeliaceæ* and the pineapple family, characterized by the superior ovary, and seeds with linear entire or wing-like appendage. It includes 6 genera, all of tropical America, of which *Pitcairnia* is the type and *Puya* an important genus.

pitch1 (pich), *v.*; pret. and pp. *pitched*, formerly *pight*, ppr. *pitching*. [< ME. *picchen*, *pycchen* (pret. *pighte*, *pigte*, pp. *pight*, *pigt*, *pygt*), pitch, fix, pick, etc.; assibilated form of *picken*, *pikken*, pick: see *pick*1, *v.*] **I.** *trans.* **1**†. To pierce with a sharp point; divide with something sharp and pointed; transfix.

> Christus, thi sone, that in this world alighte
> Upon the cross to suffre his passioun,
> And eek suffred that Longius his herte *pighte*.
> *Chaucer*, A. B. C., l. 163.

2. To thrust into the ground, as a stake or pointed peg; hence, to plant or fix; set up; place: as, to *pitch* a tent or a camp; to *pitch* the wickets in cricket.

> Ther thei *pight* the kynges teynte, by the feirest welle and the moste clere that thei badde seen.
> *Merlin* (E. E. T. S.), ii. 150.

> Sharp stakes . . .
> They *pitched* in the ground.
> *Shak.*, 1 Hen. VI., i. 1. 118.

> Where he spied a parrot or a monkey, there he was *pitched*; . . . no getting him away.
> *B. Jonson*, Bartholomew Fair, i. 1.

> The Southern lords did *pitch* their camp
> Just at the bridge of Dee.
> *Bonny John Seton* (Child's Ballads, VII. 231).

> After their thorrow view of ye place, they began to *pitch* them selves upon their land & near their house.
> *Bradford*, Plymouth Plantation, p. 340.

> Wickets were *pitched* at the orthodox hour of eleven a. m.
> *First Year of a Silken Reign*, p. 84.

3. To fix or set in order; array; arrange; set.

> A hundrith shippes full shene with sharp men of armys, *Pight* full of pepull & mony prise knight.
> *Destruction of Troy* (E. E. T. S.), l. 4056.

> There was no need that the book [the Book of Common Prayer] should mention either the learning of a fit, or the unfitness of an ignorant minister, more than that he which describeth the manner how to *pitch* a field should speak of moderation and sobriety in diet.
> *Hooker*, Eccles. Polity, v. 31.

> Having thus *pitched* the fields, from either part went a Messenger with these conditions.
> Quoted in *Capt. John Smith's* Works, I. 135.

4. To fix, as a rate, value, or price; rate; class;

> Whose vulture thought doth *pitch* the price so high.
> *Shak.*, Venus and Adonis, l. 551.

> They *pitched* their commodities at what rate they pleased.
> Quoted in *Capt. John Smith's* Works, II. 163.

5. To fling or throw; hurl; toss: as, to *pitch* a pike or a dart; to *pitch* a ball or a penny.

> He [his horse] *pighte* him on the pomel of his heed.
> *Chaucer*, Knight's Tale, l. 1831.

> Now, if thou strik'st her but one blow,
> I'll *pitch* thee from the cliff as far
> As ever peasant *pitched* a bar!
> *Scott*, L. of the L., iv. 23.

> As for his cousin Ringwood Twysden, Phil had often entertained a strong desire to wring his neck and *pitch* him down stairs.
> *Thackeray*, Philip, xiii.

6. Specifically, in *base-ball*, to serve (the ball) to the batter. See *base-ball*.—**7.** In *music*, to determine or set the key (tonality) or key-note of; fix the relative shrillness or height of; start or set (a piece) by sounding the key-note or first tone: as, to *pitch* a tune high.—**8.** To pave roughly; face with stones.

> A plaine *pitched* walke subdio, that is vnder the open ayre.
> *Coryat*, Crudities, I. 30.

9. In certain card-games, to lead one of (a certain suit), thereby selecting it as trump.—**Pitched battle.** See *battle*1.—**Pitched work**, in *masonry*, work in rough stones which are neither thrown down indiscriminately nor laid in regular courses, but let fall into place with approximate regularity, so as to bind one another. It is used in hydraulic engineering for the facing of breakwaters, the upper parts of jetties, etc.

II. *intrans.* **1.** To fix a tent or temporary habitation; encamp.

> Laban with his brethren *pitched* in the mount of Gilead.
> Gen. xxxi. 25.

2†. To come to rest; settle down; sit down; alight.

> There *pitching* down, once more adieu, said she,
> Dull home, which no such seat couldst spread for me.
> *J. Beaumont*, Psyche, ii. 19.

> Take a branch of the tree whereon they [the bees] *pitch*, and wipe the hive.
> *Mortimer*, Husbandry.

> A bud which . . . flowers beneath his sight;
> And, in the middle, there is softly *pight*
> A golden butterfly.
> *Keats*, Endymion, ii.

3. To fix or decide: with *on* or *upon*.

> He's the man I've *pitched on*
> My housband for to be.
> *Margaret of Craignargat* (Child's Ballads, VIII. 252).

> *Pitch upon* the best course of life, and custom will render it the most easy.
> *Tillotson*.

> Having *pitched upon* a time for his voyage, when the skies appeared propitious he exhorted all his crews to take a good night's rest.
> *Irving*, Knickerbocker, p. 108.

4. To plunge or fall headlong.

> Thereupon Zed *pitched* headforemost upon him across the streaming pile, and the couple rolled and pounded and kicked and crushed as before.
> *W. M. Baker*, New Timothy, p. 210.

5. *Naut.*, to plunge with alternate fall and rise of bow and stern, as a ship passing over waves. The motion is most marked when running into a head sea.—**6.** To throw, toss, or hurl a missile or other object; throw a ball; specifically, in games of ball, to fill the position of pitcher; serve the ball to the batsman.—**7.** To buck; jump from the ground with the legs bunched together, as a mustang or mule. *Sportsman's Gazetteer.* See cut under *buck*2.—**Pitch and pay**†, pay down at once; pay ready money.

> Let senses rule; the word is "*Pitch and pay*";
> Trust none.
> *Shak.*, Hen. V., ii. 3. 51.

To pitch in, to begin; set to work with promptness or energy. [Colloq.]—**To pitch into**, to attack; assault. [Colloq.]

pitch1 (pich), *n.* [< *pitch*1, *v.* In def. 14 an assibilated form of *pick*1, *n.*, of same ult. origin.] **1.** The highest point or reach; height; acme.

> Boniface the Third, in whom was the *pitch* of pride, and height of aspiring haughtiness.
> *Fuller*.

2. Height (or depth) in general; point or degree of elevation (or of depth); degree; point.

> If a man begin too high a *pitch* in his favours, it doth commonly end in unkindness and unthankfulness.
> *Bacon*, Advancement of Learning, ii. 312.

> To lowest *pitch* of abject fortune thou art fallen.
> *Milton*, S. A., l. 169.

> The chief actor in the poem falls from some eminent *pitch* of honour and prosperity into misery and disgrace.
> *Addison*, Spectator, No. 297.

> To such an absurd *pitch* do the Moos'lims carry their feeling of the sacredness of women that entrance into the tombs of some females is denied to men.
> *E. W. Lane*, Modern Egyptians, I. 224.

3. In *acoustics* and *music*: (*a*) That characteristic of a sound or a tone which depends upon the relative rapidity of the vibrations by which it is produced, a relatively acute or high pitch resulting from rapid vibrations, and a relatively grave or low pitch from slow vibrations. Pitch is therefore coördinate with force, timbre, and duration. It is estimated and stated in terms of the vibration per second of the sounding body. It is experimentally determined either by direct comparison with a standard tuning-fork or by such instruments as the siren. (*b*) A particular tonal standard or example with which given tones may be compared in respect to their relative height: as, concert *pitch*; French *pitch*. Various standards have from time to time been used or promulgated—as, for example, *classical pitch*, during the last half of the eighteenth century, for the A next above middle C about 415 to 430 vibrations per second; *concert pitch* (commonly called *high pitch*), used in concert and operatic music during the middle of the nineteenth century, varying for the same A from about 440 to 455 vibrations; *French pitch* (commonly called *low pitch*), the diapason normal adopted by the French Academy in 1859, for the same A 435 vibrations; *philosophical pitch*, an arbitrary pitch for middle C, obtained by taking the nearest power of 2, that is, 256 vibrations, or for the next A above about 427 vibrations; *Scheibler's pitch*, adopted by the Stuttgart Congress of Physicists in 1834, for the same A 440 vibrations.

Specifically—**4.** The height to which a hawk rises in the air when waiting for game to be flushed, or before stooping on its prey.

> The greatness of thy mind does soar a *pitch*
> Their dim eyes, darken'd by their narrow souls,
> Cannot arrive at.
> *Fletcher* (*and another*), False One, v. 4.

5†. Stature; height.

> So like in person, garb, and *pitch*.
> *S. Butler*, Hudibras, III. iii. 73.

6. Inclination; angle to the horizon.—**7.** In *mech.*: (*a*) The distance between the centers of two adjacent teeth in a cog-wheel, measured on the pitch-line, which is concentric with the axis of revolution, and at such a distance from the base of the teeth as to have an equal rate of motion with a similar line in the cog-wheel with which it engages. (*b*) The distance between the medial lines of any two successive convolutions or threads of a screw, measured in a direction parallel to the axis: the pitch of a propeller-screw is the length measured along the axis of a complete turn. (*c*) The distance between the paddles of a steamship, measured on the circle which passes through their centers. (*d*) The distance between the stays of marine and other steam-boilers. (*e*) The distance from center to center of rivets. (*f*) The rake of saw-teeth (see *rake*).—**8.** A throw; a toss; the act by which something is thrown or hurled from one or at something. Specifically, in *base-ball*: (*a*) A throw or serve of the ball to the batter. (*b*) The right or turn to pitch the ball.

9. A place on which to pitch or set up a booth or stand for the sale or exhibition of something; a stand. [Eng.]

> In consequence of a New Police regulation, "stands" or "*pitches*" have been forbidden, and each coster, on a market night, is now obliged, under pain of the lock-up house, to carry his tray, or keep moving with his barrow.
> *Mayhew*, London Labour and London Poor, I. 12.

10. In *card-playing*, the game all-fours or seven-up played without begging, and with the trump made by leading (pitching) one of a selected suit, instead of being turned up after dealing.—**11.** In *mining*, a certain length on the course of the lode, taken by a tributor, or to work on tribute. Also called *tribute-pitch*. [Cornwall, Eng., chiefly.]—**12.** In *floor-cloth printing*, one of the guide-pins used as registering-marks, corresponding to the register-points in lithographic printing.—**13.** In *naval arch.*, downward angular displacement of the hull of a vessel, measured in a longitudinal vertical plane at right angles with and on either side of a horizontal transverse axis passing through the center of flotation: a correlative of *scend* (which see).—**14.** An iron crowbar with a thick square point, for making holes in the ground. *Halliwell.* [Prov. Eng.]—**Auction-pitch**, a game of pitch in which the player entitled to pitch the trump may sell the privilege to the highest bidder, adding the points bid to his score before play, or may reject all bids and himself lead the play, failure to make as many points as the highest bid reducing the pitcher's score correspondingly.—**Gaining pitch**, in a screw propeller, a pitch which increases from the leading edge of the wings to the following edge. *E. H. Knight.*—**Head of the pitches**, in *angling*. See *head*.—**Natural pitch.** See *natural*.—**Pitch and hustle.** See *hustle*.—**Pitch and toss.** See *pitch-and-toss*.—**Pitch hyperbola.** See *hyperbola*.—**Pitch of an arch**, the rise or height of an arch.—**Pitch of a plane**, the angle at which the iron is set in the stock. *Common pitch*, of 45° from the horizontal line, is used in bench-planes adapted for soft woods; *half pitch*, or 60°, is used in molding-planes for mahogany and other woods difficult to work; *middle pitch*, or 55°, is used in molding-planes for deal and smoothing-planes for mahogany and woods of like character; *York pitch*, or 50° from the horizon, is used in bench-planes for mahogany and other hard or stringy woods, and for wainscoting. The pitch of metal-planes and scraping-planes is 80°.—**Pitch of a roof**, the inclination of a roof. It is expressed in angular measurement, in parts of the span, or in the proportion which the rafters bear to the span. The *common pitch* has a rafter three quarters the length of the span; the *Gothic* has a rafter of the full length of the span; the *Elizabethan*, a rafter longer than the span; the *Greek*, an angle of from 12° to 16°; and the *Roman*, an angle of from 23° to 24°.—**Pitch of a saw**, the inclination of the face of the teeth.

pitch2 (pich), *n.* [< ME. *pich*, *pych*, *pyche*, *pycche*, assibilated forms of *pik*, *pyk*, *pikke*, *pykke* (> Sc. *pick*), < AS. *pic* = OS. OFries. *pik* = MD. *pik*, D. *pek* = MLG. *pik*, *pek* = OHG. *peh*, *pech*, *beh*, MHG. *pech*, *bech*, G. *pech* = Icel. *bik* = Sw. *beck* = Dan. *beg* = Gael. *pic* = W. *pyg* = OF. *peiz*, *pois* (> ME. *peys*, *pays*, *pais*), F. *poix* = Sp. Pg. *pez* = It. *pece*, < L. *pix* (*pic-*), pitch, = Gr. πίσσα, Attic πίττα (for *πίκya), pitch, turpentine, also the fir-tree, = Lith. *pikkis*, pitch; prob. akin to Gr. πίτυς, the pine-tree, L. *pinus* (for **picnus*), the pine-tree: see *pine*1.] **1.** A thick tenacious resinous substance, hard when cold, the residuum of tar after its volatile elements have been expelled: obtained also from the residues of distilled turpentine. It is manufactured mostly in tar-producing countries, especially Russia. It is largely used to cover the seams of vessels after calking, and to protect wood from the effects of moisture; also medicinally in ointments, etc.

> The liquid *pitch* or tarre throughout all Europe is boiled out of the torch tree; and this kind of *pitch* serveth to calke ships withall, and for many other uses.
> *Holland*, tr. of Pliny, xvi. 11.

2. The sap or crude turpentine which exudes from the bark of pines. [An improper use.]—3. Bitumen: a word of indefinite meaning used to designate any kind of bituminous material, but more especially the less fluid varieties (maltha and asphaltum).

> And the streams thereof shall be turned into *pitch*, and the dust thereof into brimstone, and the land thereof shall become burning *pitch*.
> Isa. xxxiv. 9.

Burgundy or **white pitch**, the yellowish, hard and brittle, strongly adhesive aromatic resin derived by incision from the Norway spruce, *Picea excelsa*, and probably other conifers: obtained in various parts of Europe, perhaps formerly in Burgundy. It is used as a mild rubefacient, and for non-medicinal purposes. It is often replaced by inferior artificial substitutes.—**Canada pitch**, a resin exuding from the bark of the hemlock-spruce, *Tsuga (Abies) Canadensis*, in North America. It is used in medicine like Burgundy pitch. Also called *hemlock-pitch* and (improperly) *hemlock-gum*.—**Elastic mineral pitch.** See *elastic*.—**Jew's pitch**, mineral pitch; bitumen.—**Mineral pitch.** See *mineral*.

pitch[2] (pich), *v. t.* [< ME. *pitchen* (= Sw. *becka* = Dan. *bege*); from the noun.] 1. To smear or cover over with pitch: as, to *pitch* the seams of a ship.

> Then into a *pitched* potte he wol hem glene [collect],
> Or salt water oon day and nyght hem lene.
> *Palladius*, Husbondrie (E. E. T. S.), p. 90.

> Great and well *pitched* Cables were twined about the masts of their shippes. *Hakluyt's Voyages*, I. 593.

> *Pitch* it [the ark] within and without with pitch.
> Gen. vi. 14.

2. To make pitch-dark; darken. [Rare.]

> The welkin *pitched* with sudden cloud. *Addison.*

3. In *brewing*, to add to (wort) the yeast for the purpose of setting up fermentation.—**Pitched paper.** See *paper*.

pitch[3] (pich), *v. i.* [An assibilated form of *pick*[4], var. of *peak*[2].] To lose flesh in sickness; fall away; decline. *Halliwell.* [Prov. Eng.]

pitch-and-toss (pich'and-tos'), *n.* A game in which the players pitch coins at a mark, that one whose coin lies nearest to the mark having the privilege of tossing up all the coins together and retaining all the coins that come down "head" up. The next nearest player tosses those that are left, and retains all that come down "head" up, and so on until the coins are all gone.

> Two or three chimney sweeps, two or three clowns
> Playing at *pitch and toss*, sport their "Browns."
> *Barham*, Ingoldsby Legends, II. 109.

pitch-back wheel. See *breast-wheel*.

pitch-black (pich'blak), *a.* Black as pitch.

pitch-blende (pich'blend), *n.* An oxid of uranium, usually occurring in pitchy black masses, rarely in octahedrons. Also *pechblend*, *pechblende*, *pechurane*, *uraninite*.

pitch-block (pich'blok), *n.* In *metal-working*, a bed for supporting the object to be worked in such a manner that it can be turned at any pitch or angle. The bottom of the block is hemispherical, and is supported in a corresponding hollow of a bed or foundation-block. For certain work a pad of leather is interposed between this and the pitch-block. It is used especially to support sheet-metal ware during the operation of chasing.

pitch-board (pich'bōrd), *n.* A guide used by stair-builders in their work, to regulate the angle of inclination. It consists of a piece of thin board cut to the form of a right-angled triangle, of which the base is the exact width of the tread of the steps, and the perpendicular the height of the riser.

pitch-boat (pich'bōt), *n.* A boat in which pitch is melted for paying seams, as a precaution against danger of fire from melting it on board ship.

pitch-chain (pich'chān), *n.* A chain composed of metallic plates bolted or riveted together, to work in the teeth of wheels.

pitch-circle (pich'sėr″kl), *n.* In toothed wheels, the circle which would bisect all the teeth. When two wheels are in gear, they are so arranged that their pitch-circles touch one another. Also called *pitch-line*.

pitch-coal (pich'kōl), *n.* 1. A kind of bituminous coal.—2. Same as *jet*[2]. *Brande and Cox.*

pitch-dark (pich'därk), *a.* Dark as pitch; very dark.

> There was no moon; the night was *pitch dark*.
> *Thackeray*, Bluebeard's Ghost.

pitched (picht), *p. a.* 1. Fully prepared for beforehand, and deliberately entered upon by both sides with formal array: used specifically of a battle.

> In the mean-time, two Armies flye in, represented with foure swords and bucklers, and then what harde heart will not receiue it for a *pitched* fielde?
> *Sir P. Sidney*, Apol. for Poetrie.

> In five *pitched* fields he well maintained
> The honoured place his worth obtained.
> *Scott*, Rokeby, iv. 16.

> The event of a *pitched* battle won gave the rebellion and the Confederate government a standing and a sudden respectability before foreign powers it had hardly dared hope for. *The Century*, XXXVI. 288.

2. Sloped; sloping: as, a high-*pitched* roof.

> Wall fixtures . . . are equally serviceable where roofs are *pitched* as when they are flat.
> *T. D. Lockwood*, Elect., Mag., and Teleg., p. 157.

pitchelongest, *adv.* [ME.; < *pitch*[1] + *-long* + adv. gen. *-es*.] Headlong.

> Hede it that the hedes of hem alle
> Into sum greet diche *pitchelonges* falle.
> *Palladius*, Husbondrie (E. E. T. S.), p. 150.

pitcher[1] (pich'ėr), *n.* [< *pitch*[1] + *-er*[1].] 1. One who pitches. (*a*) In ball-games, the player who serves the ball to the batsman. See *base-ball*. (*b*) The person who pitches reaped grain or hay upon the wagon.

2. In *coal-mining*, one who attends to loading at the shaft or other place of loading. [North. Eng.]—**Pitcher's box**, in *base-ball*, the station of the pitcher.

pitcher[2] (pich'ėr), *n.* [< ME. *picher*, *pycher*, *pychere*, *pychar*, *pycharc*, *pecher*, < OF. *picher*, *pichier*, *pechier*, F. *pichar* (obs.), *pichet*, a small jug, = Sp. *pichel*, mug, = Pg. *picheira*, a pitcher, *pichel*, tankard, = It. *pecchero*, *bicchiere*, a goblet (= OHG. *pechari*, G. *becher*), < ML. *picarium*, *bicarium*, a goblet, < Gr. *βῖκος*, an earthen wine-cup, wine-jar: see *beaker*.] 1. A vessel with an open spout and generally with a handle, used for holding water, milk, or other liquid.

> And . . . behold, Rebekah came forth with her *pitcher* on her shoulder; and she went down unto the well, and drew water. Gen. xxiv. 45.

> I'll take a *pitcher* in ilka hand,
> And do me to the well.
> *Sir William Wallace* (Child's Ballads, VI. 239).

> Dipping deep smooth *pitchers* of pure brass
> Under the bubbled wells.
> *A. C. Swinburne*, At Eleusis.

2. In *bot.*, a specially adapted tubular or cup-shaped modification of the leaf of certain plants, particularly of the genera *Nepenthes* and *Sarracenia*; an ascidium. See *ascidium*, *pitcher-plant*, *Nepenthes*, and *Sarracenia*.—**Pitchers have ears**, there may be listeners overhearing us: a punning proverb. In the form *little pitchers have long ears* it applies to children.

> Not in my house, Lucentio, for, you know,
> *Pitchers have ears*, and I have many servants.
> *Shak.*, T. of the S., iv. 4. 52.

pitcher-man† (pich'ėr-man), *n.* A hard drinker.

> For not one shoemaker in ten
> But are boon blades, true *pitcher-men*.
> *Poor Robin* (1738). (*Nares.*)

pitcher-mold (pich'ėr-mōld), *n.* A terra-cotta mold in which large pieces of stoneware and other pottery were formerly made. See *pitcher-molding*.

pitcher-molding (pich'ėr-mōl″ding), *n.* In *ceram.*, the operation of casting in a pitcher-mold. The mold is filled with the clay in a very diluted form; this being poured out, a little remains adhering to the mold; as soon as this is dry, the operation is repeated, and so on until the requisite thickness is obtained. The Vessel so cast is separated from the mold by drying at a low heat; and the handles, spout, etc., are attached afterward.

pitcher-nose (pich'ėr-nōz), *n.* A form of faucet with a bent-down lip.

pitcher-plant (pich'ėr-plant), *n.* A plant whose leaves are so modified as to form a pitcher or ascidium. See cut under *ascidium*. The pitcher commonly contains a liquid, and is adapted to the capture and assimilation of insects. The common North American pitcher-plant is *Sarracenia purpurea* (see cut in next column), and the parrot-beaked pitcher-plant of Georgia and Florida is *S. psittacina*. (See *Sarracenia*.) The Californian pitcher-plant, sometimes called *calf's-head*, forms the allied genus *Darlingtonia*. *Heliamphora nutans*, of the *Sarraceniaceæ*, is a pitcher-plant of the mountains of Venezuela. A large and quite different group, the East Indian pitcher-plants, is formed by the genus *Nepenthes*. For the Australian pitcher-plant, see *Cephalotus*.

pitcher-shaped (pich'ėr-shāpt), *a.* In *bot.*, having the shape of a pitcher. See *ascidium*, 2.

pitcher-vase (pich'ėr-väs), *n.* A vase having the form of an aiguière with spout and handle on opposite sides: distinguished from a pitcher in that it is merely decorative.

pitch-faced (pich'fāst), *a.* In *masonry*, having the arris cut true, but the face beyond the arris-edge left projecting and comparatively rough, being simply dressed with a pitching-chisel: said of a block or of a whole piece of masonry.

Pitcher-plant (*Sarracenia purpurea*).

a, a flower, showing the calyx, one of the stamens, and the style with its umbrella and hook-like stigmas, the petals removed; *b*, longitudinal section of the whole pistil; *c*, the umbrella of the style, seen from above.

pitch-farthing (pich'fär″ᴛʜing), *n.* [< *pitch*[1], *v.*, + obj. *farthing*.] Same as *chuck-farthing*.

pitch-field† (pich'fēld), *n.* A pitched battle.

> There has been a *pitchfield*, my child, between the naughty Spaniels and the Englishmen.
> *Beau. and Fl.*, Knight of Burning Pestle, ii. 2.

pitchfork (pich'fôrk), *n.* 1. A fork for lifting and pitching hay or the like. (*a*) A fork with a long handle and usually two prongs or tines, used for moving hay, sheaves of grain, straw, etc. (*b*) A fork with a short handle and three or four prongs, used for lifting manure, etc.; a dung-fork.

2. A tuning-fork.

pitchfork (pich'fôrk), *v. t.* [< *pitchfork*, *n.*] 1. To lift or throw with a pitchfork. Hence—2. To put, throw, or thrust suddenly or abruptly into any position.

> Your young city curate *pitchforked* into a rural benefice, when all his sympathies and habits and training are of the streets streety, is the most forlorn, melancholy, and dazed of all human creatures.
> *Nineteenth Century*, XXII. 277.

pitchiness (pich'i-nes), *n.* The state or quality of being pitchy; hence, blackness; darkness.

pitching (pich'ing), *n.* [Verbal n. of *pitch*[1], *v.*] 1. The act of throwing or hurling.—2. A facing of dry stone laid upon a bank as a protection against the wash of waves or current; a lining or sheathing of masonry.

> Timber laden steamers of nearly, if not quite, 1000 tons burthen run up to Wisbech, some twelve miles up the Nene, the banks of which, moreover, are steep, being held up by faggotting and stone *pitching*.
> *The Engineer*, LXVII. 139.

> The channel is to be made of clay with rubble stone *pitching*. *Rankine*, Steam Engine, § 140.

3. In *leather-manuf.*, same as *bloom*[1], 6 (*d*). *Encyc. Brit.*, XIV. 384.—4. In *brewing*, the admixture of yeast with the wort to initiate fermentation. Also called *setting the wort*.

pitching (pich'ing), *p. a.* [< *pitch*[1], *v.*] In *gun.*, noting the fire of cannon at full charge against an object covered in front by a work or a natural obstacle. *Farrow*, Mil. Encyc., II. 531.

pitching-machine (pich'ing-ma-shēn″), *n.* A machine used by brewers for coating the interiors of barrels or casks with pitch.

pitching-pence (pich'ing-pens), *n.* Money paid for the privilege of pitching or setting down merchandise in a fair or market, generally one penny per sack or pack. [Great Britain.]

pitching-piece (pich'ing-pēs), *n.* In *joinery*, same as *apron-piece*.

pitching-stable (pich'ing-stā″bl), *n.* A variety of Cornish granite used for paving.

pitching-temperature (pich'ing-tem″pėr-ā-tūr), *n.* In *brewing*, the temperature of the wort at the time the yeast is added to it. This temperature has an important influence on the activity of the fermentation. The English practice is to cool the wort to from 51 to 64° F. The Bavarian brewers cool the wort to from 45° to 50° F. Between these extremes the temperature is regulated according to the temperature of the tun-room or fermenting-room and the strength of the wort, which is pitched at a lower temperature in summer than in winter, and at a lower temperature with light beers intended for immediate use than for strong stock-ales or porter. Wort for pale ales is also pitched at a low temperature.

pitching-tool (pich'ing-töl), *n.* **1.** A kind of stone-chisel or knapping-tool, made of antler or other hard substance, and anciently used with a hammer for flaking off stone in making arrow-heads, etc.—**2.** In *watch-making*, a tool for placing the wheels of watches in position between the plates.

pitching-yeast (pich'ing-yēst), *n.* In *brewing*: (*a*) Yeast obtained from fermentation of beer, and intended for use in pitching worts. (*b*) Yeast which has been prepared for pitching worts by washing it with pure cold water in the stuff-vat, and allowing it to stand covered in the vat in a cool place for a day or longer.

pitch-kettle (pich'ket"l), *n.* Same as *pitch-pot.*

pitchkettled (pich'ket"ld), *a.* [< *pitch-kettle* + *-ed*[2].] Covered as if with a pitch-kettle, and thus cast into helpless darkness; puzzled. [Rare.]

> Thus, the preliminaries settled,
> I fairly find myself *pitchkettled*,
> And cannot see, though few see better,
> How I shall hammer out a letter.
> *Cowper*, Epistle to Robert Lloyd, l. 32. (*Davies.*)

pitch-ladle (pich'lā"dl), *n.* See *ladle.*

pitch-line (pich'līn), *n.* Same as *pitch-circle.*

pitch-mineral (pich'min"ẹ-ral), *n.* Same as *bitumen* and *asphaltum.*

pitch-opal (pich'ō"pal), *n.* An inferior kind of opal.

pitch-ore (pich'ōr), *n.* Pitch-blende; uraninite.

pitch-pine, *n.* See *pine*[1].

pitch-pipe (pich'pīp), *n.* A small musical pipe of wood or metal to be sounded with the breath, by which the proper pitch of a piece of music may be given, or an instrument tuned. It is either a flue- or a reed-pipe, and may give either a fixed tone, as A or C, or one of several tones. In the latter case the variation is produced either by a movable plug or stopper altering the length of the air-column, or by a spring that alters the free length of the tongue of the reed.

> He had an ingenious servant, by name Licinius, always attending him with a *pitch-pipe*, or instrument to regulate the voice. *Steele*, Spectator, No. 228.

pitch-plaster (pich'plås"tėr), *n.* See *plaster.*

pitch-point (pich'point), *n.* The point of contact on the pitch-line common to two engaged wheels.

> The *pitch-point*, where its teeth are driven by those of the cogged ring, may be in the same vertical plane, parallel to the axis. *Rankine*, Steam Engine, § 153.

pitch-polisher (pich'pol"ish-ėr), *n.* An instrument of metal for polishing curved surfaces of glass, as lenses, specula, etc. It varies in form according to the nature of the work. Its surface is ruled accurately into squares by incised lines, and in use is coated with a prepared pitch. *Byrne*, Artisan's Hand-book.

pitch-pot (pich'pot), *n.* A large iron pot used for the purpose of boiling pitch for paying the seams of wooden ships after calking.

pitchstone (pich'stōn), *n.* An old volcanic rock, resembling hardened pitch in appearance. It is a natural glass resulting from the rapid cooling of those ancient lavas of which common feldspar (orthoclase) forms a considerable part. Some pitchstones have a spherulitic structure. See cut under *fluidal.*

pitch-tankard (pich'tang"kārd), *n.* A tankard covered inside with pitch. The pitch gives a flavor and perhaps a medicinal value to the beverage which the tankard contains. Pitch-tankards are still used in Germany with certain kinds of beer, such as the Lichtenhainer. The modern German pitch-tankards are made of wooden staves held together by wooden hoops, and the ancient English pitch-tankards were made in the same way.

pitch-tree (pich'trē), *n.* The kauri-pine or the Amboyna pine, as the sources of dammar-resins; also, the Norway spruce, as yielding Burgundy pitch.

Pitchurim bean. See *Pichurim bean.*

pitch-wheel (pich'hwēl), *n.* One of two toothed wheels which work together.

pitch-work (pich'wėrk), *n.* Work done in a mine under an arrangement that the workmen shall receive a certain proportion of the output.

pitchy (pich'i), *a.* [< *pitch*[2] + *-y*[1].] **1.** Of, or of the nature of, or resembling pitch; like pitch.

> Native petroleum found floating upon some springs is no other than this very *pitchy* substance, drawn forth of the strata by the water. *Woodward*, On Fossils.

> The *pitchy* taint of general vice is such
> As daubs the fancy, and you dread the touch.
> *Crabbe*, Works, II. 100.

2. Smeared with pitch.

> The sides convulsive shook on groaning beams,
> And, rent with labour, yawn'd their *pitchy* seams.
> *Falconer*, Shipwreck, ii.

3. Black; dark; dismal.

> When saucy trusting of the cozen'd thoughts
> Defiles the *pitchy* night. *Shak.*, All's Well, iv. 4. 24.

> The *pitchy* blazes of impiety. *B. Jonson*, Sejanus, iv. 5.

> *Pitchy* and dark the Night sometimes appears,
> Friend to our Woe, and Parent of our Fears.
> *Prior*, Solomon, i.

4. In *zoöl.*, dark-brown inclining toward black; piceous.

pit-coal (pit'kōl), *n.* Mineral coal, or coal obtained from mines or pits: distinguished from *charcoal.* [Great Britain.]

> Divers . . . of the prime Lords of the Court have got the sole Patent of making all Sorts of Glass with *Pit-coal.* *Howell*, Letters, I. i. 2.

pit-cock (pit'kok), *n.* Same as *pet-cock.* *E. H. Knight.*

pit-crater (pit'krā"tėr), *n.* A volcanic crater at the bottom of a pit or gulf.

> The old cone had, like Mt. Loa or the Maui volcano, a great *pit-crater* at top. *Amer. Jour. Sci.*, 3d ser., XXXII. 251.

pite†, *n.* A Middle English form of *pity.*

piteous (pit'ẹ̄-us), *a.* [< ME. *piteous, pytyous, peteos, pitivous, pytevous, petevous, pitous, pitos,* < OF. *pitos, piteus,* F. *piteux* = Pr. *piatos, pietos, pitos, pidos* = Sp. *piadoso* = Pg. *piadoso, piedoso* = It. *piatoso, pietoso,* < ML. *pietosus,* pitiful, < L. *pieta(t-)s,* piety, ML. pity: see *pity.*] **1.** Full of pity or compassion; compassionate; affected by pity.

> A more suetter, humble, and amyable,
> Gentile, debonair, sage, wise, and connyng,
> Curtois, *piteuous*, and charitable,
> Sche vnto the pore ful gret good doing.
> *Rom. of Partenay* (E. E. T. S.), l. 6247.

> But of his *peteose* tender moder, alasse!
> I am verray sure,
> The wo and payn passis alle othere.
> *MS. Bodl. Mus.*, 160. (*Halliwell.*)

> She gave him (*piteous* of his case,
> Yet smiling at his rueful length of face)
> A shaggy tapestry. *Pope*, Dunciad, ii. 141.

2. Such as to excite pity or move to compassion; affecting; lamentable; sorrowful; mournful; sad: as, a *piteous* look; a *piteous* case.

> And than he seide a *pitouse* worde: "Ha! Cleodalis," quod he, "I crye the mercy of the trespace that I haue don a-gein the, ffor I se well I am come to myn ende." *Merlin* (E. E. T. S.), ii. 354.

> The most *piteous* tale of Lear. *Shak.*, Lear, v. 3. 214.

3†. Pitiful; paltry; poor: as, *piteous* amends. *Milton.*=**Syn. 2.** Doleful, woful, rueful, wretched, distressing.

piteously (pit'ẹ̄-us-li), *adv.* [< ME. *petevously, pitously;* < *piteous* + *-ly*[2].] In a piteous manner; pleadingly; as if for pity or mercy; mournfully; sadly; dreadfully.

> Forsoth to hym spake full *peteuously.* *Rom. of Partenay* (E. E. T. S.), l. 3578.

> Word it, prithee, *piteously.* *Shak.*, A. and C., iv. 13. 9.

piteousness (pit'ẹ̄-us-nes), *n.* The character or condition of being piteous or pitiful.

pit-eye (pit'ī), *n.* Same as *pit-bottom.*—**Pit-eye pillar,** a mass of coal left around the bottom of the shaft to support the ground.

pitfall (pit'fâl), *n.* [< ME. *pitfalle, putfalle, pytfalle;* < *pit*[1] + *fall*[1]. Cf. *pitfold.*] **1.** A pit into which an animal may fall unawares, the opening being so covered as to escape observation. Pitfalls are much used for the capture of large animals in Africa and India and elsewhere, and are sometimes fitted with stout sharp-pointed upright stakes intended to transfix the animal which falls upon them.

> Poor bird! thou'ldst never fear the net nor lime,
> The *pitfall* nor the gin. *Shak.*, Macbeth, iv. 2. 35.

> Now, poor and basely
> Thou sett'st toils to betray me; and, like the peasant
> That dares not meet the lion in the face,
> Digg'st crafty *pit-falls.* *Fletcher*, Pilgrim, ii. 2.

> All around
> Are dim uncertain shapes that cheat the sight,
> And *pitfalls* lurk in shade along the ground.
> *Bryant*, Journey of Life.

Hence—**2.** Figuratively, any concealed danger or source of disaster.

pitfall† (pit'fâl), *v. t.* [< *pitfall, n.*] To lead into a pitfall; insnare. [Rare.]

> Able to shew us the ways of the Lord straight and faithful as they are, not full of cranks and contradictions and *pitfalling* dispenses. *Milton*, Divorce, Pref.

pit-fish (pit'fish), *n.* A small fish of the Indian ocean, about the size of a smelt, colored green and yellow. It has the power of protruding and retracting its eyes at pleasure.

pitfold† (pit'fōld), *n.* [< *pit*[1] + *fold*[2]; appar. an accom. form of *pitfall.*] A pitfall; a trap or snare.

> In her cheek's pit thou didst thy *pitfold* set. *Sir P. Sidney* (Arber's Eng. Garner, I. 508).

pit-frame (pit'frām), *n.* The framework of a coal-pit.

pit-game (pit'gām), *n.* See *game*[1].

pit-guide (pit'gīd), *n.* In a mining-shaft, a bar which serves as a guide for the cage.

pith (pith), *n.* [< ME. *pith, pithe, pythe,* < AS. *pitha,* pith, = MD. *pitte,* D. *pit,* marrow, kernel, = MLG. *pitte, pit,* LG. *pitte, pit,* also *pedik, piek,* pith; root unknown.] **1.** In *bot.*, the medulla, or central cylinder, composed of typical parenchymatous tissue, which occupies the center of the stems of dicotyledonous plants. By Gris the cells of pith have been divided into (*a*) *active cells*, which have the office of storing starch and other assimilated products for a time; (*b*) *crystal-cells*, in which crystals are formed; and (*c*) *inactive cells*, which are empty and have lost the power of receiving starch or other products. See *medulla*, 2, *parenchymatous*, and cuts under *alburnum* and *exogen.* **2.** In *anat.*: (*a*†) The spinal cord or marrow; the medulla spinalis.

> The . . . vertebres . . . [are] all perforated in the middle with a large hole for the spinal marrow or *pith* to pass along. *Ray*, Works of Creation, p. 283.

(*b*) The central or medullary core of a hair.

> In the Peccari the *pith* of the coarse body-hair is crossed by condensed cells, like beams, strengthening the cortex. *Owen*, Anat., III. 621.

3. Strength; vigor; force.

> But age, alas! that al wol envenyme,
> Hath me biraft my beautee and my *pith.*
> *Chaucer*, Prol. to Wife of Bath's Tale, l. 475.

> The paume is the *pith* of the honde, and profreth forth the fyngres,
> To mynystre and to make that myght of hond knoweth.
> *Piers Plowman* (C), xx. 116.

> I shall do what I can for that young man—he 's got some *pith* in him. *George Eliot*, Mill on the Floss, iii. 5.

4. Energy; concentrated force; closeness and vigor of thought and style.

> And hee alone in the *pith* and weight of his Sentences may be compared to Plato or Seneca. *Purchas*, Pilgrimage, p. 439.

> Others, that think whatever I have writ
> Wants *pith* and matter to eternize it.
> *B. Jonson*, Poetaster, v. 1.

5. Condensed substance or matter; quintessence.

> Perhaps you mark'd not what 's the *pith* of all. *Shak.*, T. of the S., i. 1. 171.

> He [Shakspere] could take Ulysses away from Homer, and expand the shrewd and crafty islander into a statesman whose words are the *pith* of history. *Lowell*, Among my Books, 1st ser., p. 226.

6. Weight; moment; importance.

> Enterprises of great *pith* and moment. *Shak.*, Hamlet (ed. Knight), iii. 1. 86.

Discoid pith. See *discoid.*

pith (pith), *v. t.* [< *pith, n.*] To introduce an instrument into the cranial or spinal cavity of (an animal, as a frog), and destroy the cerebrospinal axis or a part of it.

> A spear from above intended to fall upon the head or to *pith* the animal, etc. *Encyc. Brit.*, XIII. 521.

pith-ball (pith'bâl), *n.* A small ball or pellet of pith. Such balls suspended by a silk thread are used in an electroscope. See *electroscope.*

pit-head (pit'hed), *n.* The head or mouth of a mining-shaft or -pit, or the ground surrounding it.—**Pit-head gear,** in *coal-mining*, same as *head-gear*, 3. [Eng.]

pit-headed (pit'hed"ed), *a.* [< *pit*[1] + *head* + *-ed*[2].] Having a pit on the head. It is applied specifically (*a*) to tapeworms, as *Bothriocephalus latus* (*T. S. Cobbald*), and (*b*) to venomous serpents of the family *Crotalidæ*, known as *pit-headed vipers* (see *Bothrophera*, and cut under *pit-viper*).

pithecanthrope (pith-ẹ̄-kan'thrōp), *n.* [< NL. *pithecanthropus*: see *pithecanthropi.*] One of the supposed pithecanthropi.

> Prehistoric man . . . has even been sometimes called man-monkey, or *pithecanthrope.* *N. Joly*, Man before Metals (trans.), p. 17.

pithecanthropi (pith"ẹ̄-kan-thrō'pī), *n. pl.* [NL., pl. of *pithecanthropus*, < Gr. πίθηκος, an ape, monkey, + ἄνθρωπος, man.] Hypothetical ape-men, pithecanthropes, or *Alali.* See *ape-man, Alalus.*

pithecanthropoid (pith-ẹ̄-kan'thrọ̄-poid), *a.* [< *pithecanthrope* + *-oid.*] Relating to the pithecanthropi, or resembling them.

Pithecia (pi-thē'si-ạ̈), *n.* [NL. (Desmarest, 1804), < Gr. πίθηκος, an ape: see *Pithecus.*] The typical genus of the subfamily *Pitheciinæ*, containing such species as *P. satanas*, the black couxio. They are known as *sakis* and *fox-tailed monkeys.* See cut on following page.

Pitheciinæ (pi-thē-si-ī'nē), *n. pl.* [NL., < *Pithecia* + *-inæ.*] A South American subfamily of *Cebidæ*, having the cerebrum overlapping the cerebellum, the hyoid apparatus moderate, the incisors proclivous, and the tail bushy; the sakis and ouakaris. There are 3 genera, *Pithecia* (the type), *Chiropotes*, and *Brachyurus.*

pitheciine (pi-thē'si-in), *a.* Of or pertaining to the *Pitheciinæ.*

pithecoid (pi-thē'koid), *a.* and *n.* [= F. *pithécoïde*; < Gr. πίθηκος, an ape, + εἶδος, form.] **I.** *a.* **1.** Resembling or pertaining to the genus

Black Couxio (*Pithecia satanas*).

Pithecus; belonging to the higher as distinguished from the lower apes; simian; anthropoid, as an ape.—2. Loosely, of or pertaining to an ape: related to an ape.

II. *n*. An anthropoid ape; a simian.

Pithecolobium (pi-thē-kọ-lō'bi-um), *n*. [NL. (K. F. P. von Martius, 1829), so called from the resemblance of the curved pods to a monkey's ear; < Gr. πίθηκος, an ape, + λόβιον, dim. of λοβός, an ear, lobe, or legume.] A genus of leguminous shrubs or trees, of the tribe *Ingeæ*, known by the peculiar rigid pods, which are two-valved and flattened, curved, curled, or twisted, and somewhat fleshy. There are about 110 species, widely dispersed in the tropics, especially of America and Asia. They are either unarmed or thorny with axillary or stipular spines. They bear glandular bipinnate leaves of many small or few larger leaflets, and globose heads of white flowers, with long and very numerous stamens. The most important species, *P. dulce*, a large tree native of Mexico, and there called *guamuchil*, contains in its pods a sweet pulp, for which they are boiled and eaten. Introduced into the Philippine Islands, and thence into India, it is now cultivated there under the name *Manila tamarind*. (Compare *tamarind*.) Several other species produce edible pods, as *P. filifolium*, the wild tamarind-tree of Jamaica, a large tree distinguished by the twice-pinnate leaves from the true tamarind, whose leaves are once-pinnate; and *P. Saman*, the genisaro, also called *saman*, *zamang*, and *rain-tree*. The bark of some species yields a gum, that of others an astringent drug, and that of others, as *P. bigeminum*, the soap-bark tree, and *P. micradenium*, the savonette or shagbark of the West Indies, is a source of soap. Several other species are cultivated as hardy evergreen trees under the name curl *brush-bean*. A smaller species, usually a shrub, is the cat's-claw, also called *nephritic tree* or *black bead-tree*, of Jamaica. See also *algarrobilla*.

Pithecus (pi-thē'kus), *n*. [NL. (Geoffroy, 1812), < L. *pithecus*, < Gr. πίθηκος, an ape.] A genus of anthropoid apes: same as *Simia*.

Pithelemur (pith-ẹ-lē'mėr), *n*. [NL. (Lesson), < *Pithe(cus)* + *Lemur*.] A genus of lemurs: synonymous with *Indris* and *Lichanotus*.

pithful† (pith'fůl), *a*. [< *pith* + *-ful*.] Full of pith; pithy. *W. Browne*, Britannia's Pastorals, ii. 4.

pithily (pith'i-li), *adv*. In a pithy manner; with close application or concentrated force; forcibly; cogently.

pithiness (pith'i-nes), *n*. The character of being pithy; strength; concentrated force: as, the *pithiness* of a reply.

pithless (pith'les), *a*. [< *pith* + *-less*.] 1. Without pith; wanting strength; weak.

> Men who, dry and *pithless*, are debarred
> From man's best joys. *Churchill*, The Times.

2. Lacking cogency or force.

> The *pithless* argumentation which we too often allow to monopolize the character of what is prudent and practical. *Gladstone*, Church and State, ii.

pithole (pit'hōl), *n*. A small hollow or pit; especially, a pit left by a pustule of smallpox.

> I have known a lady sick of the small pocks, only to keep her face from *pitholes*, take cold, strike them in again, kick up the heels, and vanish! *Beau. and Fl.*, Fair Maid of the Inn, ii. 3.

Pithophora (pi-thof'ọ-rạ̈), *n*. [NL. (Wittrock, 1877), < Gr. πίθος, a large storage-vase (see *pithos*), + φέρειν = E. *bear*[1].] A small genus of confervoid algæ first detected in the warm tanks in the Botanic Gardens at Kew, also at Oxford and elsewhere, but since found in tropical America. The thallus is composed of branching filaments of cells resembling *Cladophora*, presenting here and there barrel-shaped cells very rich in chlorophyl. They are further distinguished by the peculiar development of thin rhizoids.

Pithophoraceæ (pith″ọ-fọ-rā'sẹ-ē), *n. pl.* [NL., < *Pithophora* + *-aceæ*.] A doubtfully distinct order of confervoid algæ, containing the single genus *Pithophora*. Reproduction is by means of non-sexual resting spores and prolific cells, no sexual mode of reproduction having as yet been detected.

pithos (pith'os), *n*. [< Gr. πίθος: see def.] In *Gr. antiq.*, a form of earthenware vase, of very large size and spheroid shape, used for the storage of wine, oil, grain, etc., and sometimes for the burial of dead bodies.

Greek Pithos, now in the court-yard of Grace Church, New York.

pith-paper (pith'pā″pėr), *n*. A very thin film cut or prepared from the pith of a plant, and used for paper. See *rice-paper*.

pithsome (pith'sum), *a*. [< *pith* + *-some*.] Strong; robust.

> Beside her *pithsome* health and vigor. *R. D. Blackmore*, Clara Vaughan, lxii. (*Encyc. Dict.*)

pith-tree (pith'trē), *n*. The ambash.

pith-work (pith'wėrk), *n*. Useful or ornamental articles made of the pith of trees, especially those made in India from that of *Æschynomene aspera*. See *Æschynomene*.

pithy (pith'i), *a*. [Early mod. E. also *pitthie*, *pyththy*; < late ME. *pythy*; < *pith* + *-y*[1].] 1. Of the nature of or full of pith; containing or abounding with pith: as, a *pithy* stem; a *pithy* substance.—2. Full of pith or force; forcible; containing much in a concentrated or dense form; of style, sententious: as, a *pithy* saying or expression.

> To teach you gamut in a briefer sort,
> More pleasant, *pithy*, and effectual
> Than hath been taught by any of my trade.
> *Shak.*, T. of the S., iii. 1. 68.

> Your counsel, good Sir Thomas, is so *pithy*
> That I am won to like it.
> *Webster and Dekker*, Sir Thomas Wyat, p. 12.

> Charles Lamb made the most *pithy* criticism of Spenser when he called him the poets' poet. *Lowell*, Among my Books, 2d ser., p. 177.

3. Given to the use of pithy or forcible expressions.

> In his speech he was fine, eloquent, and *pithy*. *Sir T. More*, Utopia (tr. by Robinson), i.

> In all these Goodman Fact was very short but *pithy*; for he was a plain home-spun man. *Addison*.

> A white-haired man,
> *Pithy* of speech, and merry when he would.
> *Bryant*, Old Man's Counsel.

=**Syn.** 2 and 3. Terse, laconic, concise, pointed, sententious.

pitiable (pit'i-ạ-bl), *a*. [< OF. *pitiable*, *piteable*, F. *pitoyable*; as *pity* + *-able*.] Deserving pity; worthy of or exciting compassion: applied to persons or things.

> In the Gospel, he makes abatement of humane infirmities, temptations, moral necessities, mistakes, errors, for every thing that is *pitiable*. *Jer. Taylor*, Sermons, i. vii.

> The *pitiable* persons relieved are constantly under your eye. *Bp. Atterbury*.

> If ye have grieved,
> Ye are too mortal to be *pitiable*,
> The power to die disproves the right to grieve.
> *Mrs. Browning*, Drama of Exile.

pitiableness (pit'i-ạ-bl-nes), *n*. A pitiable state or condition.

pitiably (pit'i-ạ-bli), *adv*. In a pitiable manner.

pitiedly† (pit'id-li), *adv*. In a condition or state to be pitied.

> He is properly and *pittiedly* to be counted alone, that is illiterate. *Feltham*, Resolves, ii. 49.

pitier (pit'i-ėr), *n*. [< *pity* + *-er*[1].] One who pities. *Bp. Gauden*, Hieraspistes, p. 3.

pitiful (pit'i-fůl), *a*. [< *pity* + *-ful*.] 1. Full of pity; tender; compassionate; having a feeling of sorrow and sympathy for the distressed.

> Our hearts you see not; they are *pitiful*;
> And pity to the general wrong of Rome . . .
> Hath done this deed on Cæsar.
> *Shak.*, J. C., iii. 1. 169.

2. Exciting or fitted to excite pity or compassion; miserable; deplorable; sad: as, a *pitiful* condition; a *pitiful* look.

> In faith, 'twas strange, 'twas passing strange,
> 'Twas *pitiful*, 'twas wondrous *pitiful*.
> *Shak.*, Othello, i. 3. 161.

> The Pilgrims . . . stood still, and shook their heads, for they knew that the sleepers were in a *pitiful* case. *Bunyan*, Pilgrim's Progress, p. 336.

3. To be pitied for its littleness or meanness; paltry; insignificant; contemptible; despicable.

> That 's villanous, and shows a most *pitiful* ambition in the fool that uses it. *Shak.*, Hamlet, iii. 2. 49.

> 'Tis *pitiful*
> To court a grin when you should woo a soul.
> *Cowper*, Task, ii. 406.

pitifully (pit'i-fůl-i), *adv*. In a pitiful manner. (*a*) With compassion.

> *Pitifully* behold the sorrows of our hearts. *Book of Common Prayer* (Eng.), Lesser Litany.

(*b*) So as to excite pity; wretchedly.

> Now many Ages since the Greek Tongue is not only impaired, and *pitifully* degenerated in her Purity and Eloquence, but extremely decay'd in her Amplitude and Vulgarness. *Howell*, Letters, ii. 57.

(*c*) Contemptibly.

> Those men who give themselves airs of bravery on reflecting upon the last scenes of others may behave the most *pitifully* in their own. *Richardson*, Clarissa Harlowe.

pitifulness (pit'i-fůl-nes), *n*. The state or quality of being pitiful, in any sense.

pitikins†, *interj*. [< *pity* + *-kin*.] A diminutive of *pity*, used interjectionally, generally in conjunction with *od's* for *God's*. See *ods-pitikins*.

pitiless (pit'i-les), *a*. [< *pity* + *-less*.] 1. Without pity; hard-hearted.

> The pelting of the *pitiless* storm. *Shak.*, Lear, iii. 4. 29.

2. Exciting no pity; unpitied.

> So do I perish *pitiless*, through fear.
> *Sir J. Davies*, Wittes Pilgrimage, sig. G. 1.

=**Syn.** 1. Merciless, cruel, ruthless, inexorable, unmerciful, unpitying.

pitilessly (pit'i-les-li), *adv*. In a pitiless manner.

pitilessness (pit'i-les-nes), *n*. The state of being pitiless.

pit-kiln (pit'kil), *n*. An oven for the manufacture of coke from coal.

pitlet, *n*. Same as *pickle*[3].

pitman (pit'mạn), *n*.; pl. *pitmen* (-men). 1. One who works in a pit, as in coal-mining, in sawing timber, etc. Specifically—2. The man who looks after the pumping machinery within the shaft of a mine.—3. In *mach.*, the rod which connects a rotary with a reciprocating part, either for imparting motion to the latter or

Harvester Pitman.—*a*, knives; *b*, cutter-bar; *c*, pitman connection; *d*, pitman; *e*, crank-wrist.

taking motion from it, as that which couples a crank with a saw-gate, or a steam-piston with its crank-shaft, etc. Also called *connecting-rod*. See also cut under *stone-breaker*.

pitman-box (pit'mạn-boks), *n*. The metal strap and brasses which embrace the crank-wrist of the driving or driven wheel of a pitman. Also called, more commonly, *rod-end*.

pitman-coupling (pit'mạn-kup″ling), *n*. Any means, as a rod-end, for connecting a pitman with the part which drives or is driven by it.

pitman-head (pit'mạn-hed), *n*. The block or enlargement at the end of a pitman where connection is made with the member to which it imparts motion or with the mechanism from which it receives motion.

pitman-press (pit'mạn-pres), *n*. A press which is worked by a pitman connection with a shaft, instead of by an eccentric or other device. Such presses are used for drawing, cutting, shearing, stamping, and for packing materials requiring light pressure.

pit-martin (pit'mär″tin), *n*. The bank-swallow or sand-martin, *Cotile* or *Clivicola riparia*, which nests in gravel-pits and like places. See cut under *bank-swallow*.

pit-mirk (pit'mėrk), *a*. [A corruption of *pick-mirk*, dial. form of **pitch-murk*: see *pitch*[2] and *murk*.] Pitch-dark; dark as pitch. [Scotch.]

> The night is mirk, and it 's very *pit-mirk*.
> *Archie of Ca'field* (Child's Ballads, VI. 90).

> It 's *pit-mirk*—but there 's no ill turn on the road but twa. *Scott*, Guy Mannering, xi.

pitous†, *a*. A Middle English form of *piteous*.

pitously†, *adv*. A Middle English form of *piteously*.

pitpan (pit'pan), *n*. A very long, narrow, flat-bottomed, trough-like canoe, with thin and flat projecting ends, used in navigating rivers and lagoons in Central America. *Imp. Dict.*

pitpat (pit'pat), *adv*. and *n*. Same as *pitapat*.

pitpit (pit'pit), *n*. [Imitative.] An American honey-creeper of the family *Cœrebidæ*; a guit-guit. Also *pippit*.

pit-saw (pit'sâ), *n*. A saw working in a pit, as a large saw used for cutting timber, operated by two men, one of whom (called the *pit-sawyer*) stands in the pit below the log that is being sawed, and the other (called the *top-sawyer*) on the log.

pit-sawyer (pit'sâ"yėr), *n.* See *pit-saw.*

pit-specked (pit'spekt), *a.* Marred by pits or small depressed spots, as fruit.

Pitsaws.

a, a, handles for top-sawyer; *b, b,* handles for pit-sawyer; *c, c,* shanks; *d, d,* blades. In No. 1 *c* is prolonged and curved so that the pit-sawyer may stand out of line with the falling sawdust. No. 2 shows a pit frame-saw, in which the saw, stiffened by a frame *e f,* is longer and thinner than in No. 1.

Pitta (pit'ä), *n.* [NL. (Vieillot, 1816); from the Telugu name.] 1. The typical genus of *Pittidæ*, including most of the Old World ant-thrushes, as *P. coronata.* Also called *Citta.* See *Brachyurus*, and cut under *Pittidæ.*—2. [*l. c.*] Any member of this genus.

pittacal (pit'a-kal), *n.* [Also *pittacall;* = F. *pittacale*, < Gr. πίττα, πίσσα, pitch, + καλός, beautiful.] A blue substance used in dyeing, originally produced from the tar of beech-wood.

pittance (pit'ans), *n.* [< ME. *pitance, pitaunce, pytance, pytaunce*, < OF. *pitance*, an allowance of food in a monastery, F. *pitance* = Sp. *pitanza* = Pg. *pitança* = OIt. *pietanza, piatanza*, It. *pietanza*, dial. *pitanza*, an allowance, daily subsistence (ML. reflex *pitantia, pitancia, pictantia*, allowance of food in a monastery); cf. OF. *robe de pitance*, a uniform; *pitance, pitence*, an anniversary service; lit. 'a pious office or service,' 'a pious dole,' 'an act of piety or pity,' < ML. *pietantia*, < **pietan(t-)s*, ppr. of **pietare*, an assumed verb (> Sp. *pitar*), dole out allowances of food, orig. of any alms, < L. *pieta(t-)s*, piety, pity, mercy: see *piety, pity.* Cf. ML. *misericordia*, a monastic repast, lit. 'pity,' 'mercy': see *misericorde.* According to Du Cange, the word (in the assumed orig. form ML. **pictantia*) meant orig. 'an allowance of the value of a picta,' < *picta*, a small coin issued by the Counts of Poitiers, < LL. *Pictavium*, the capital of the Pictavi, < *Pictavi*, for L. *Pictones*, a people in Gaul. This view is accepted by Skeat as possible, but apart from the consideration of the preceding etymology, which is confirmed by the evidence, ML. *pictantia* is not a likely form to be made from *picta* in such a sense, and there is no evidence that *picta* was in such general circulation as to make it a measure of value.] 1. An allowance or dole of food and drink; hence, any very small portion or allowance assigned or given, whether of food or money; allowance; provision; dole.

> He was an esy man to yeve penaunce
> Ther as he wiste han a good *pitaunce.*
> *Chaucer*, Gen. Prol. to C. T., l. 224.

> Before, Diego,
> And get some pretty *pittance*; my pupil 's hungry.
> *Fletcher*, Spanish Curate, ii. 1.

> I am sensible that the income of your commission, and what I have hitherto allowed you, is but a small *pittance* for a lad of your spirit. *Sheridan*, The Rivals, ii. 1.

2. An allowance of food or money bestowed in charity; a small charitable gift or payment.

> One half of this *pittance* was even given him in money. *Macaulay.*

3. A small portion or quantity; a morsel.

> Our souls shall no longer remain obnoxious to her treacherous flesh and rebellious passions, nor ratiocinate and grow knowing by little parcels and *pittances.*
> *Evelyn*, True Religion, I. 244.

> Far above the mine's most precious ore
> The least small *pittance* of bare mold they prize,
> Scooped from the sacred earth where his dear relics lie.
> *Wordsworth*, Eccles. Sonnets, i. 32.

pittancer (pit'an-sėr), *n.* [< F. *pitancier* (= Sp. *pitancero* = Pg. *pitanceiro*), < *pitance*, pittance: see *pittance.*] The officer in a monastery who distributed the pittance at certain appointed festivals.

pitted (pit'ed), *a.* [< *pit*[1] + *-ed*[2].] Marked thickly with pits or small depressions: as, a face *pitted* by smallpox; specifically, in *bot.*, having pits or punctations, as the walls of many cells; in *zoöl.*, having many punctations, as a surface; foveolate; areolate.—**Pitted teeth**, teeth with pits in the enamel, resulting from defective development.—**Pitted tissue.** See *prosenchyma.*—**Pitted vessel.** See *vessel.*

pitter[1]† (pit'ėr), *v. i.* [A dim. var. of *patter*[2].] To murmur; patter.

> When sommers heat hath dried up the springs,
> And when his *pittering* streames are low and thin.
> *Greene* (Park's Heliconia, III. 67).

pitter[2] (pit'ėr), *n.* [< *pit*[1] + *-er*[1].] 1. One who removes pits or stones from fruit.—2. An implement for removing the stones from such fruit as plums and peaches; a fruit-stoner. [U. S.]

pitteraro†, *n.* Same as *pederero* for *paterero.*

> In an original MS. Accompt of Arms delivered up at Inverary in obedience of the Act of Parliament for securing the peace of the Highlands, 1717, mention is made of Two *pitteraroes*, one broken.
> *N. and Q.*, 7th ser., VIII. 128.

pitticite, *n.* See *pittizite.*

Pittidæ (pit'i-dē), *n. pl.* [NL., < *Pitta* + *-idæ.*] A family of mesomyodian or songless passerine birds, typified by the genus *Pitta;* the Old World ant-thrushes. They are of stout form, with very short tail, and long and strong legs; the plumage is brilliant and varied. The leading genera besides *Pitta* are *Eucichla, Hydrornis*, and *Melanopitta.* These birds are characteristic of the Oriental and Australian regions, though one (*P. angolensis*) is African; they are specially abundant in the islands of the Malay archipelago. About 50 species are known.

Old World Ant-thrush (*Pitta cucullata*).

Pittinæ (pi-tī'nē), *n. pl.* [NL., < *Pitta* + *-inæ.*] The *Pittidæ* regarded as a subfamily of some other family. Before the peculiarities of the Old World ant-thrushes were known, they were wrongly associated with the South American formicarioid birds of somewhat similar superficial aspect, the name *ant-thrush* being given to both. See *ant-thrush*, and compare cuts under *Formicarius* and *Pittidæ.*

pittine (pit'in), *a.* Of or pertaining to the pittas, or ant-thrushes of the Old World.

pitting (pit'ing), *n.* [Verbal n. of *pit*[1], *v.*] 1. The act or operation of digging or sinking a hole or pit.

> The exact situation of the clay is first determined by systematic *pitting*, to a depth of several fathoms, or occasionally by boring. *Spons' Encyc. Manuf.*, I. 636.

2. The act or operation of placing in a pit or in pits: as, the *pitting* of potatoes; the *pitting* of hides.—3. A pit, mark, or hollow depression on the surface, such as that left on the flesh by a pustule of the smallpox.—4. A number of such pits considered collectively; a collection of pitmarks.—5. In *bot.*, the state or condition of being pitted.

> The peculiar *pitting* of the woody fibre of the fir.
> *Encyc. Brit.*, XIV. 411.

6. A corrosion of the inner surface of steam-boilers, whereby the metal becomes gradually covered with small cavities.—7. A corrosion of the bottom of iron ships. Blisters, and afterward pits, are formed, apparently by the action of the carbonic acid and oxygen in sea-water producing ferric oxid under the protecting paint.

pittizite, pitticite (pit'i-zīt, -sīt), *n.* [Irreg. < Gr. *πιττίζειν, πισσίζειν, be like pitch (< πίττα, πίσσα, pitch), + *-ite*[2].] An arsenio-sulphate of iron, occurring in reniform masses; pitchy iron ore.

pittle†, *n.* Same as *pickle*[3], *pightle.* *Minsheu.*

pittle-pattle† (pit'l-pat"l), *v. i.* [A varied reduplication of *patter*[1], *patter*[2]; cf. *pitter*[1], and *prattle, tattle*, etc.] To talk unmeaningly or flippantly.

pittock (pit'ok), *n.* The coalfish. [Prov. Eng.]

Pittosporaceæ (pit"ō-spō-rā'sē-ē), *n. pl.* [NL. (Lindley, 1846), so called from their resinous capsules; < Gr. πίττα, πίσσα, pitch, + σπόρος, seed (see *spore*), + *-aceæ.*] Same as *Pittosporeæ.*

pittosporad (pit'ō-spō-rad), *n.* [< *Pittospor(aceæ)* + *-ad*[1].] A plant of the natural order *Pittosporaceæ.*

Pittosporeæ (pit-ō-spō'rē-ē), *n. pl.* [NL. (R. Brown, 1814), < *Pittosporum* + *-eæ.*] An order of polypetalous plants, of the cohort *Polygalinæ.* It is unlike the two other orders in its numerous ovules, and in its regular flowers with five stamens; it is also characterized by its five imbricated sepals, five petals with their narrow bases or claws commonly forming an incomplete tube, versatile anthers, an ovary usually two-celled, a minute embryo in hard albumen, and loculicidal fleshy or papery fruit. There are about 90 species and 10 genera, of which *Pittosporum* (the type), is the only one widely distributed, the others being all Australian. They are shrubs or shrubby twiners, sometimes procumbent, generally smooth, bearing alternate leaves, and white, blue, yellow, or rarely reddish flowers, solitary, nodding, and terminal, or variously clustered.

Pittosporum (pi-tos'pō-rum), *n.* [NL. (Banks, 1788), so called from the viscous pulp commonly enveloping the seeds; < Gr. πίττα, Attic for πίσσα, pitch, + σπόρος, seed.] A genus of plants, type of the order *Pittosporeæ*, characterized by the thick wingless seeds, and thick loculicidal capsule, which is coriaceous or woody, globose, ovate, or obovate, often compressed and with imperfect partitions. There are about 55 species, natives of Africa, warmer parts of Asia, Pacific islands, Australia, and New Zealand. They are erect shrubs, generally low, sometimes becoming small trees, often with a resinous bark, generally smooth and evergreen. They bear white or yellowish flowers in crowded terminal clusters, or sometimes solitary or few and lateral. Many species have broad shining dark-green leaves, contrasting well with the white fragrant flowers, and are cultivated under the name *hedge-laurel.* Other species are known as *Brisbane laurel, Queensland laurel*, and *hackaro.* From the flowers of *P. undulatum*, the Victorian laurel, a highly fragrant volatile oil is distilled. This species and *P. bicolor*, the Victorian cheesewood or whitewood, yield a wood adapted to turners' use, and sometimes substituted for boxwood. A few sometimes reach the height of 90 feet, as *P. rhombifolium.*

pittypat† (pit'i-pat), *adv.* and *a.* Same as *pitapat.*

pituita (pit-ū-ī'tä), *n.* [L., mucus, phlegm; prob., with loss of initial *s*, < *spuere*, pp. *sputus*, spit out: see *spew.* Cf. *pip*[1].] Phlegm or mucus; especially, the mucous secretion of the pituitary or Schneiderian membrane. Also, rarely, *pituite.*

> As of the *pituita*, or the bile, or the like disorders to which the body is subject.
> *T. Taylor*, tr. of Five Books of Plotinus (1794), p. 102.

pituital (pit-ū-ī'tal), *a.* [< *pituita* + *-al.*] Same as *pituitary.*

pituitary (pit'ū-i-tā-ri), *a.* [= F. *pituitaire* = Pg. It. *pituitario*, < L. *pituitarius*, in fem. *pituitaria* (sc. *herba*), an herb that removes phlegm, < *pituita*, phlegm: see *pituita.*] Mucous; secreting or containing mucus, or supposed to do so; relating to pituita.—**Pituitary body**, a small ovoid pale-reddish body, occupying the sella turcica, and attached to the under surface of the cerebrum by the infundibulum. It consists of two lobes—an anterior, resembling in structure that of a ductless gland, and a posterior, which in the lower vertebrates is composed of nerve-substance, forming an integral part of the brain, and called the infundibular lobe, but in the higher vertebrates showing only slight indications of nervous elements. Also called *pituitary gland, hypophysis cerebri.* See cuts under *brain* (cut 2), *Elasmobranchii*, and *encephalon.*—**Pituitary diverticulum**, a flask-like outgrowth of the middle of the upper posterior part of the buccal cavity in the embryo, which takes part in the formation of the pituitary body.—**Pituitary fossa.** See *fossa*[1], and cuts under *parasphenoid, Struthionidæ, Gallinæ, Crocodilia*, and *skull* (cut 3).—**Pituitary gland.** Same as *pituitary body.*—**Pituitary membrane.** See *membrane.*—**Pituitary space**, in *embryol.*, an open space at the base of the skull, just in advance of the end of the notochord, inclosed by the trabeculæ cranii: it subsequently becomes the seat of the pituitary body, and corresponds to what is known in human anatomy as the sella turcica of the sphenoid bone. See *hypophysis*, and cuts under *chondrocranium* and *periotic* (adult turtle).—**Pituitary stem**, the hollow neck of the pituitary body, by which that body hangs from the brain; the infundibulum of the brain. See cut under *corpus.*

pituite (pit'ū-it), *n.* [< F. *pituite* = Sp. Pg. It. *pituita*, < L. *pituita*, mucus, phlegm: see *pituita.*] Same as *pituita.* [Rare.]

> Phlegm or *pituite* is a sort of semifluid.
> *Arbuthnot*, Aliments, vi., prop. 7, § 7.

pituitous (pit-ū-ī'tus), *a.* [= F. *pituiteux* = Sp. Pg. It. *pituitoso*, < L. *pituitosus*, full of phlegm, < *pituita*, phlegm: see *pituita.*] Same as *pituitary.*

Pituophis (pi-tū'ō-fis), *n.* See *Pityophis.*

pituri (pi-tū'ri), *n.* A plant. See *Duboisia.*

pit-viper (pit'vī"pėr), *n.* A venomous serpent of the family *Crotalidæ*, as a rattlesnake; a pit-headed viper: so called from the characteristic pit between the eyes and the nose. See *Bothrophera.*

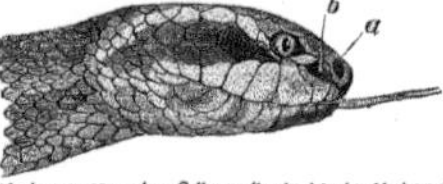

A Pit-viper, the Moccasin or Cottonmouth (*Ancistrodon piscivorus*), three fourths natural size. *a*, nostril; *b*, pit.

pit-wood (pit'wụd), *n.* Timber used for frames, posts, etc., in mines or pits.

> Another consequence of the improvement that has set in with the coal trade is the advance in *pitwood*.
> *The Engineer*, LXVI. 40.

pit-work (pit'wėrk), *n.* The pump and gear connected with it in the engine-shaft of a mine.

pity (pit'i), *n.* [Early mod. E. also *pitty*, *pitie*; < ME. *pitte*, *pite*, *pyte*, *pete*, < OF. *pite*, *pitie*, *pitet*, F. *pitié* = Sp. *piedad* = Pg. *piedade* = It. *pietà*, pity, < L. *pieta(t-)s*, piety, affection, pity: see *piety*. Cf. *pittance*.] **1.** Sympathetic sorrow for and suffering with another; a feeling which inspires one to relieve the suffering of another.

> And sapheris swete that souȝte all wrongis,
> Ypoudride wyth *pete* thor it be ouȝte,
> And traylid with trouthe and treste al aboute.
> *Richard the Redeless*, i. 46.

> For off the peple haue I gret *pitte*.
> *Rom. of Partenay* (E. E. T. S.), l. 3194.

> I am not prone to weeping, as our sex
> Commonly are: the want of which rain dew,
> Perchance, shall dry your *pities*.
> *Shak.*, W. T., ii. 1. 110.

> For *pity* melts the mind to love.
> *Dryden*, Alexander's Feast, l. 96.

> Careless their merits or their faults to scan,
> His *pity* gave ere charity began.
> *Goldsmith*, Des. Vil., l. 162.

> *Pity*, which, being a sympathetic passion, implies a participation in sorrow, is yet confessedly agreeable.
> *Sir W. Hamilton*, Metaph., xliv.

2†. An appeal for pity. [Rare.]

> Let 's have no *pity*.
> For if you do, here 's that shall cut your whistle.
> *Beau. and Fl.*

3. A cause, matter, or source of regret or grief; a thing to be regretted: as, it is a *pity* you lost it; it is a thousand *pities* that it should be so.

> Pendragon was ther deed, and many a-nother gode baron, wher-of was grete *pite* and losse to the cristen partye.
> *Merlin* (E. E. T. S.), i. 66.

> That he is old, the more the *pity*, his white hairs do witness it.
> *Shak.*, 1 Hen. IV., ii. 4. 514.

> They make the King belieue they mend whats amisse, and for money they make the thing worse than it is. Theres another thing in too, the more is the *pity*.
> *Heywood*, 1 Edw. IV. (Works, ed. Pearson, I. 46).

> He 's a brave fellow; 'tis *pity* he should perish thus.
> *Fletcher*, Humorous Lieutenant, iii. 5.

> 'Tis a thousand *pities* (as I told my Lord of Arundel his son) that that jewel should be given away.
> *Evelyn*, Diary, Aug. 23, 1678.

To have pity upon, to take pity upon, generally, to show one's pity toward by some benevolent act.

> He that *hath pity upon* the poor lendeth unto the Lord.
> Prov. xix. 17.

=**Syn. 1.** *Pity, Compassion, Commiseration, Sympathy, Condolence.* *Pity* is the only one of these words that allows even a tinge of contempt; *pity* and *compassion* come from one who is felt to be so far superior. *Sympathy*, on the other hand, puts the sufferer and the one sympathizing with him upon an equality by their fellow-feeling. *Compassion* does not keep so near its derivation; it is deep tenderness of feeling for one who is suffering. *Sympathy* is equal to *compassion* in its expression of tenderness. *Commiseration* is, by derivation, sharing another's misery; *condolence* is sharing another's grief. *Commiseration* may and *condolence* must stand for the communication to another of one's feelings of sorrow for his case. It is some comfort to receive *commiseration* or *condolence*; it gives one strength to receive *sympathy* from a loving heart; it is irksome to need *compassion*; it galls us to be *pitied*. *Sympathy* does not necessarily imply more than kinship of feeling. See also the quotations under *condolence*.

> The Maker saw, took *pity*, and bestowed
> Woman.
> *Pope*, January and May, l. 63.

> In his face
> Divine *compassion* visibly appear'd,
> Love without end.
> *Milton*, P. L., iii. 141.

> Losses . . .
> Enow to press a royal merchant down
> And pluck *commiseration* of his state
> From brassy bosoms, and rough hearts of flint.
> *Shak.*, M. of V., iv. 1. 30.

> With that *sympathy* which links our fate with that of all past and future generations.
> *Story*, Salem, Sept. 18, 1828.

> To Thebes the neighb'ring princes all repair,
> And with *condolence* the misfortune share.
> *Croxall*, tr. of Ovid's Metamorph.

pity (pit'i), *v.*; pret. and pp. *pitied*, ppr. *pitying*. [< *pity*, *n.*] **I.** *trans.* **1†.** To excite pity in; fill with pity or compassion: used impersonally.

> It would *pity* a man's heart to hear that that I hear of the state of Cambridge.
> *Latimer*, 5th Sermon bef. Edw. VI., 1549.

> It *pitied* me to see this gentle fashion
> Of her sincere but unsuccessful Passion.
> *J. Beaumont*, Psyche, ii. 86.

> The poor man would stand shaking and shrinking; I dare say it would have *pitied* one's heart to have seen him; nor would he go back again.
> *Bunyan*, Pilgrim's Progress, p. 295.

2. To feel pity or compassion for; compassionate; commiserate: as, to *pity* the blind or their misfortune; to *pity* the oppressed.

> Like as a father *pitieth* his children, so the Lord *pitieth* them that fear him.
> Ps. ciii. 13.

> He *pities* them whose fortunes are embark'd
> In his unlucky quarrel.
> *Fletcher (and another)*, False One, i. 1.

> A weak man, put to the test by rough and angry times, as Waller was, may be *pitied*, but meanness is nothing but contemptible under any circumstances.
> *Lowell*, Among my Books, 1st ser., p. 19.

=**Syn. 2.** To sympathize with, feel for. See *pity*, *n.*

II. *intrans.* To be compassionate; exercise pity.

> I will not *pity*, nor spare, nor have mercy.
> Jer. xiii. 14.

pityingly (pit'i-ing-li), *adv.* So as to show pity; compassionately.

Pitylinæ (pit-i-lī'nē), *n. pl.* [NL., < *Pitylus* + *-inæ*.] A subfamily of *Tanagridæ*, typified by the genus *Pitylus*; the fringilline tanagers, having for the most part a conical or turgid bill, like a bullfinch's or a grosbeak's. The group is sometimes relegated to the *Fringillidæ*.

pityline (pit'i-lin), *a.* [< *Pitylus* + *-ine*[1].] Sharing the characters of grosbeaks and tanagers; of or pertaining to the *Pitylinæ*.

Pitylus (pit'i-lus), *n.* [NL. (Cuvier, 1817), < Gr. πίτυς, pine.] The typical genus of pityline *Tanagridæ* or grosbeak-tanagers, having a tumid bill, as *P. grossus*.

Pityophis (pi-ti'ō-fis), *n.* [NL. (Hallowell, 1852; orig. *Pituophis*, Holbrook, 1842), < Gr. πίτυς, pine, + ὄφις, serpent.] A genus of North American *Colubridæ*, having carinate scales,

Pine-snake (a species of *Pityophis*).

loral and anteorbital plates present, labials entering into the orbit, posterior gastrostege entire, and all the urosteges bifid. There are several species, growing to a large size, but harmless, as *P. bellona* and *P. melanoleucus*, known as *pine-snakes* and *bull-snakes*.

pityriasis (pit-i-rī'a-sis), *n.* [NL., < LGr. πιτυρίασις, a bran-like eruption, < Gr. πίτυρον, bran; cf. πτίσσειν, winnow.] **1.** In *pathol.*, a condition of the skin or some portion of it in which it sheds more or less fine bran-like scales.—**2.** [*cap.*] In *ornith.*, a genus of piping-crows of the family *Corvidæ*, founded by Lesson in 1837. The only species, *P. gymnocephalus*, inhabits Borneo and Sumatra.—**Pityriasis alba.** Same as *pityriasis simplex*.—**Pityriasis capitis**, alopecia pityrodes capillitii. See *alopecia*.—**Pityriasis maculata et circinata.** Same as *pityriasis rosea*.—**Pityriasis pilaris**, hypertrophy of the epidermis about the orifices of the hair-follicles. Also called *keratosis pilaris* and *lichen pilaris*.—**Pityriasis rosea**, an affection of the skin lasting a few weeks and disappearing spontaneously. It presents round red maculæ, level or slightly raised, and covered with scales; it begins on the thorax usually, and may extend over the entire body. Regarded by some as a form of tinea circinata. Also called *pityriasis circinata*, and *pityriasis rubra maculata* and *circinata*.—**Pityriasis rubra.** (*a*) A rare, usually chronic and fatal, affection in which all or nearly all of the skin is a deep red, and covered with scales; itching and burning are slight or absent. Also called *dermatitis exfoliativa* and *pityriasis rubra essentialis*. (*b*) A scaly eczema. Also called *eczema squamosum* and *psoriasis diffusa*.—**Pityriasis simplex**, a simple scurfy condition of the epidermis, independent of other trouble. Also called *pityriasis alba*.—**Pityriasis tabescentium**, scurfiness of the skin seen in certain debilitated states, due to insufficient secretion of the sebaceous glands and sweat-glands.—**Pityriasis versicolor.** Same as *tinea versicolor* (which see, under *tinea*).

pityroid (pit'i-roid), *a.* [< MGr. πιτυροειδής, Gr. contr. πιτυρώδης, bran-like, < πίτυρον, bran, + εἶδος, form.] Resembling bran; bran-like.

più (pū), *adv.* [It., = F. *plus*, < L. *plus*, more: see *plus*.] More: as, *più allegro*, quicker.

pivot (piv'ot), *n.* [< F. *pivot*, pivot; dim., < It. *piva*, *pipa*, a pipe, a peg, < ML. *pipa*, a pipe: see *pipe*[1].] **1.** A pin on which a wheel or other object turns.—**2.** *Milit.*, the officer or soldier upon whom a line of troops wheels.—**3.** Figuratively, that on which some matter or result hinges or depends; a turning-point.

pivot (piv'ot), *v.* [< *pivot*, *n.*] **I.** *trans.* To place on a pivot; furnish with a pivot.

II. *intrans.* To turn or swing on a pivot, or as on a pivot; hinge.

pivotal (piv'ot-al), *a.* [< F. *pivotal*; as *pivot* + *-al*.] Of the nature of or forming a pivot; belonging to or constituting a pivot, or that upon which something turns or depends: as, a *pivotal* question; a *pivotal* State in an election.

> The slavery question, . . . which both accepted at last as the *pivotal* matter of the whole conflict.
> *The Atlantic*, LVIII. 424.

pivotally (piv'ot-al-i), *adv.* In a pivotal manner; by means of or on a pivot.

pivot-bolt (piv'ot-bōlt), *n.* The vertical bolt which serves as the axis about which a gun swings horizontally.

pivot-bridge (piv'ot-brij), *n.* See *bridge*[1].

pivot-broach (piv'ot-brōch), *n.* In *watch-making*, a fine boring-tool used to open pivot-holes.

pivot-drill (piv'ot-dril), *n.* In *watch-making*, a bow-drill for making pivot-holes.

pivot-file (piv'ot-fīl), *n.* In *watch-making*, a fine file for dressing the pivots on watch-arbors. *E. H. Knight.*

pivot-gearing (piv'ot-gēr″ing), *n.* Any system of gearing so devised as to admit of shifting the axis of the driver, so that the machine can be set in any direction with relation to the power, as in portable drilling-machines, center-grinding attachments, etc.

pivot-gun (piv'ot-gun), *n.* A gun set upon a frame-carriage which can be turned about so as to point the piece in any direction.

pivoting (piv'ot-ing), *n.* [Verbal n. of *pivot*, *v.*] The putting of an artificial crown on the root of a tooth by means of a peg or pivot.

pivot-joint (piv'ot-joint), *n.* A lateral ginglymus joint. See *cyclarthrosis*.

pivot-lathe (piv'ot-lāth), *n.* A small lathe used by watchmakers for turning the pivots on the ends of arbors.

pivot-man (piv'ot-man), *n.* The man at the flank of a line of soldiers, on whom, as a pivot, the rest of the line wheels.

pivot-pin (piv'ot-pin), *n.* A pin serving as a pivot; the pin of a hinge.

pivot-polisher (piv'ot-pol″ish-ėr), *n.* In *watch-making*, an attachment to a bench-lathe for finishing and grinding pivots and other small parts of the mechanism to any desired angle, and for drilling holes at accurately spaced intervals.

pivot-span (piv'ot-span), *n.* The movable span of a pivot-bridge.

pivot-tooth (piv'ot-töth), *n.* In *dentistry*, an artificial crown attached to the root of a natural tooth by means of a dowel-pin. *E. H. Knight.*

piwarrie (pi-wor'i), *n.* [Also *piworrie*; S. Amer.] A fermented liquor made in parts of South America from cassava.

pix†. An obsolete form of *pyx*.

pixie, *n.* See *pixy*.

pix-jury (piks'jö″ri), *n.* In England, a jury of members of the goldsmiths' company, formed to test the purity of the coin.

pixy, pixie (pik'si), *n.*; pl. *pixies* (-siz). [Formerly also *picksy*; dial. *pisky*, *pisgy*: perhaps for **pucksy*, < *puck*, with dim. formative *-sy*.] A fairy: so called in rural parts of England, and associated with the "fairy rings" of old pastures, in which they are supposed to dance by moonlight.

> If thou 'rt of air, let the gray mist fold thee;
> If of earth, let the swart mine hold thee;
> If a *pixie*, seek thy ring.
> *Scott*, Pirate, xxiii.

Pixy ring, a fairy ring or circle. See *fairy ring*, under *fairy*. *Halliwell.*

pixy-led (pik'si-led), *a.* Led by pixies; hence, bewildered.

pixy-puff (pik'si-puf), *n.* A broad species of fungus. *Halliwell.*

pixy-purse (pik'si-pėrs), *n.* The ovicapsule of a shark, skate, or ray; a sea-barrow. See cut under *mermaid's-purse*. [Local, Eng.]

pixy-seat (pik'si-sēt), *n.* A snarl or entangled spot in a horse's mane. [Prov. Eng.]

pixy-stool (pik'si-stöl), *n.* A toadstool or mushroom: sometimes applied specifically to *Cantharellus cibarius*, or edible chanterelle.

pixy-wheel (pik'si-hwēl), *n.* Same as *whorl.* Compare *fairy millstone,* under *fairy.*

pizain, pizaine, *n.* Same as *pisan*[2].

pizan-collar, *n.* Same as *pisan*[2]. *Planché.*

pize[1]†, *n.* An obsolete form of *poise.*

pize[2] (pīz), *n.* [Also *pise, pies;* origin obscure.] A term used in mild execration, like *pox.*

A *pies* upon you; well, my father has made Lucy swear too never to see Truman without his consent. *Cowley,* Cutter of Coleman Street. (*Nares.*)

Pize on 'em, they never think before hand of any thing. *Congreve,* Love for Love, v. 2.

This peevish humour of melancholy sits ill upon you. . . . A *pize* on it, send it off. *Scott,* Kenilworth, i.

pizzicato (pit-si-kä'tō), *a.* [It., twitched, nipped, pp. of *pizzicare,* twitch, nip, pinch: see *pinch.*] In music for stringed instruments of the viol family, noting the manner of playing, or the effect produced, when the strings are plucked or twanged by the finger, as in harp-playing, instead of sounded by means of the bow. The end of a passage to be thus rendered is marked by *col arco,* 'with the bow,' or simply *arco.* Abbreviated *pizz.*

pizzle (piz'l), *n.* [Early mod. E. also *pizzel, pisle;* < LG. *pesel,* a pizzle; dim. of MD. *pese,* D. *pees,* a sinew, string, pizzle, whence also MD. *peserick,* a sinew, string, whip of bull's hide, pizzle, D. *pezerik, peesrik* = MLG. *peserik,* LG. (G. dial.) *peserick,* pizzle. The MHG. *visel,* G. *fisel,* penis, is a diff. word, akin to L. *penis:* see *penis.*] The penis of an animal, as a bull. *Sir T. Browne.*

pk. A common contraction of *park* and *peck.*

pkg. A commercial contraction of *package.*

pl. An abbreviation of *plural.*

placability (plā-ka-bil'i-ti), *n.* [= OF. *placabilite* = Sp. *placabilidad* = Pg. *placabilidade* = It. *placabilità,* < L. *placabilita(t-)s,* < *placabilis,* placable: see *placable.*] The quality of being placable or appeasable; susceptibility of being pacified or placated.

Placability is no lyttell parte of benignitie. *Sir T. Elyot,* The Governour, ii. 6.

placable (plā'ka-bl), *a.* [< OF. (and F.) *placable* = Sp. *placable* = Pg. *placavel* = It. *placabile,* < L. *placabilis,* easily appeased, < *placare,* appease: see *placate.*] Capable of being placated or pacified; easy to be appeased; willing to forgive.

Methought I saw him *placable* and mild. *Milton,* P. L., xi. 151.

So mild and *placable* was Facilidas that he refused to put him [Claudius] to death, but sent him prisoner to the mountain of Wechne. *Bruce,* Source of the Nile, III. 444.

placableness (plā'ka-bl-nes), *n.* Placability.

placably (plā'ka-bli), *adv.* In a placable manner; with readiness to forgive.

placard (plak'ärd or pla-kärd'), *n.* [Formerly also *placart* and *plackard;* = MD. *plackaerd,* < OF. *placard, placart, plaquart,* < F. *placard, plaquard* (= Sp. obs. *placarte*), a placard, a writing pasted on a wall, etc., also rough-cast on walls (OF. also a plate, a part of armor, a piece of money), < *plaquer,* stick or paste on, also rough-cast (< D. *plakken,* glue or fasten up, plaster), < *plaque,* a plate, panel, piece of money, etc.: see *plack, plaque.* Cf. *placcate.*] 1. A written or printed paper displaying some proclamation or announcement, and intended to be posted in a public place to attract public attention; a posting-bill; a poster.—2†. An edict, manifesto, proclamation, or command issued by authority.

And that, vpon the innocencie of my said chancellor declared, it may further please the king's grace to award a *placard* vnto his atturney to confesse the saide enditement to be vntrue. *Foxe,* Martyrs, p. 741.

All Coins bear his Stamp, all *Placarts* or Edicts are published in his Name. *Howell,* Letters, I. ii. 15.

3†. A public permit, or one given by authority; a license.

Euery licence, *placard,* or graunt made to any person or persons, for the hauinge maintenance or keeping of any bowling alleys, dicing houses, or any other vnlawfull game prohibited by the lawes and statutes of this realme, shal be . . . utterly voyde and of none effect. An. 2 & 3 P. and M. cap. 9. *Rastall,* Statutes, fol. 344.

Others are of the contrary opinion, and that Christianity gives us a *placard* to use these sports. *Fuller.*

4†. In *medieval armor,* same as *placcate.*

Some had the helme, the visere, the two bariers and the two *plackardes* of the same curiously graven and conningly costed. *Hall,* Henry IV., f. 12. (*Halliwell.*)

5. A plate or tag on which to place a mark of ownership.

Their Pistolls was the next, which marked Smith upon the *placard.* *Capt. John Smith,* True Travels, I. 17.

6†. Pargeting; parget-work.—7. (*a*) The wood-work or cabinet-work composing the door of a closet, etc., with its framework. Hence—(*b*) A closet formed or built in a wall, so that only the door is visible from the exterior.

placard (pla-kärd' or plak'ärd), *v. t.* [< *placard, n.*] 1. To post placards upon: as, to *placard* the walls of a town.—2. To make known or make public by means of placards: as, to *placard* the failure of a bank.

placate (plā'kāt), *v. t.*; pret. and pp. *placated,* ppr. *placating.* [< L. *placatus,* pp. of *placare* (> It. *placare* = Sp. Pg. *a-placar*), appease; cf. *placere,* please: see *please.*] To appease or pacify; conciliate.

Therefore is he always propitiated and *placated,* both first and last. *Cudworth,* Intellectual System, p. 476.

placation (plā-kā'shon), *n.* [< OF. *placation* = Sp. *a-placacion* = Pg. *a-placação* = It. *placazione;* < L. as if **placatio(n-),* < *placare,* placate: see *placate.*] 1. The act of placating, appeasing, pacifying, or conciliating; propitiation.

They were the first that instituted sacrifices of *placation,* with inuocations and worship. *Puttenham,* Arte of Eng. Poesie, p. 4.

2. A propitiatory act.

The people were taught and perswaded by such *placations* and worships to receaue any helpe, comfort, or benefite to them selues. *Puttenham,* Arte of Eng. Poesie, p. 23.

placatory (plā'ka-tō-ri), *a.* [< *placate* + *-ory.*] Conciliatory; intended to placate or appease or propitiate; betokening pacific intentions.

placcate (plak'āt), *n.* [= MD. *plackaet,* D. *plakkaat,* a placard, an altered form of *plackaerd* (see *placard*); appar. < ML. **placcata,* < *placca, placa,* a plate: see *plack,* and cf. *placard.*] In *medieval armor:* (*a*) A plate of steel used as additional defense, and specifically the doubling of the lower part of the breastplate, often made by bolting on an additional solid thickness of iron: a similar placcate was used for the back. (*b*) A plate of hammered iron reinforcing the gambeson or brigandine in the same parts of the body as (*a*). (*c*) A garment of fence worn in the thirteenth century, consisting of a leather jacket or doublet lined with thin strips or splints of steel; a variety of the brigandine. Also *placket, plaquet.*

place (plās), *n.* [< ME. *place* (= MD. *plaetse,* D. *plaats* = MLG. *plas, plātse, plātze* = MHG. *platz, blatz, blaz,* G. *platz* = Icel. (13th century) *plāz* = Sw. *plats* = Dan. *plads*), < OF. *place,* F. *place,* a place, court, = Sp. *plaza* = Pg. *praça* = It. *piazza,* < L. *platēa,* a street, courtyard, area, < Gr. πλατεῖα, a broad way in a city, a street; prop. fem. (sc. ὁδός, way) of πλατύς, flat, wide, broad: see *plat*[3].] 1. A broad way or open space in a city or town; an area or public courtyard devoted to some particular use or having some specific character; a public square or quadrangle. With a proper or other distinctive name prefixed, *place* is often applied to a street or part of a street, or to a square: as, Waverley *Place,* Waterloo *Place,* Temple *Place.*

The other squirrel was stolen from me by the hangman boys in the market-*place.* *Shak.,* T. G. of V., iv. 4. 60.

In the middle is a little *place,* with two or three cafés decorated by wide awnings. *H. James, Jr.,* Little Tour, p. 176.

2. An area or portion of land marked off or regarded as marked off or separated from the rest, as by occupancy, use, or character; region; locality; site; spot.

The *place* whereon thou standest is holy ground. Ex. iii. 5.

Whilst the mercies of God do promise us heaven, our conceits and opinions exclude us from that *place.* *Sir T. Browne,* Religio Medici, i. 56.

Iron Grates inclose the *Place* called the Choir, so that there 's no Entrance. *N. Bailey,* tr. of Colloquies of Erasmus, II. 26.

There was no convenient *place* in the town for strangers. *Pococke,* Description of the East, II. ii. 44.

3. A particular town or village: as, Hampton is a historic *place;* a thriving *place.*

I am a Devonshire man born, and Tavistock the *place* of my once abiding. *R. Peeke* (Arber's Eng. Garner, I. 632).

This inner part of the bay [of Fana] has a fine beech on the west and south sides for boats to come up to, and seems to be the *place* called Notium by Strabo. *Pococke,* Description of the East, II. ii. 7.

4. A mansion with its adjoining grounds; a residence or dwelling; a manor-house.

The Harringtons had of ancient time a faire manor *place,* within a mile of Horneb Castell. *Leland,* Itinerary, VI. 59.

Yborn he was in fer contree
In Flaundres al biyonde the see,
At Popering in the *place.*
Chaucer, Sir Thopas, l. 9.

5. A building or a part of a building set apart for any purpose; quarters of any kind: as, a *place* of worship; a *place* in the country; a *place* of business.

I do not like the Tower of any place.
Did Julius Cæsar build that *place,* my lord?
Shak., Rich. III., iii. 1. 70.

To see Mr. Spong, and found him out by Southampton Market, and there carried my wife, and up to his chamber, a bye *place,* but with a good prospect of the fields. *Pepys,* Diary, IV. 65.

6. A fortified post; a stronghold.—7. Room to abide in; abode; lodgment; location.

I know that ye are Abraham's seed; but ye seek to kill me, because my word hath no *place* in you. John viii. 37.

Can Discontent find *Place* within that breast? *Congreve,* To Cynthia.

8. Room to stand or sit in; a particular location, as a seat, or a space for sitting or standing, as in a coach, car, or public hall.

Our *places* by the coach are taken. *Dickens,* David Copperfield, xxii.

"No person to be admitted to keep *Places* in the Pit" seems a singular order, were it not explicable by the fact that people used to send their footmen to keep *places* for them until their arrival, and that the manners of these gentry gave great offence to the habitués of the pit. *J. Ashton,* Social Life in Reign of Queen Anne, II. 13.

9. A particular locality; a particular spot or portion of a surface or in a body: as, a sore *place;* a soft *place.*—10. The proper or appropriate location or position: as, a *place* for everything, and everything in its *place.*

This is no *place* for Ladies; we allow
Her absence. *Heywood,* Royal King.

That it may be possible to put a book in its *place* on a shelf there must be (1) the book, and (2), distinct and apart from it, the *place* on the shelf. *J. Ward,* Encyc. Brit., XX. 55.

11. In the abstract, the determinate portion of space occupied by any body.

A mind not to be changed by *place* or time;
The mind is its own *place,* and in itself
Can make a heaven of hell, a hell of heaven.
Milton, P. L., i. 253.

Place . . . stands for that space which any body takes up, and so the universe is in a *place.* *Locke,* Human Understanding, II. xiii. 10.

12. A portion or passage of a book or writing.

The *place* of the Scripture which he read was this. Acts viii. 32.

Hosea, in the person of God, saith of the Jews: They have reigned, but not by me: . . . Which *place* proveth plainly that there are governments which God doth not avow. *Bacon,* Holy War.

This *place* some of the old doctors understood too literally. *Jer. Taylor,* Works (ed. 1835), II. 136.

13. [In this sense a translation of L. *locus,* Gr. τόπος (see *topic*).] In *logic* and *rhet.,* a topic; a class of matters of discourse; an order of considerations comprising all those which have analogous relations to their subjects.

A *place* is the resting corner of an argumente, or els a mark which geveth warning to our memorie what we may speake probably, either in the one parte or the other, upon al causes that fal in question. . . . For these *places* bee nothing elles but covertes or boroughs, wherin, if any one searche diligently, he maye finde game at pleasure. *Wilson,* Rule of Reason (1551).

14. In *falconry,* the greatest elevation which a bird of prey attains in its flight.

A falcon, towering in her pride of *place,*
Was by a mousing owl hawk'd at and kill'd.
Shak., Macbeth, ii. 4. 12.

Eagles can have no speed except when at their *place,* and then to be sure their weight increases their velocity. *Thornton,* Sporting Tour.

15. Room; stead: with the sense of substitution: preceded by *in.*

And Joseph said unto them, Fear not; for am I *in* the *place* of God? Gen. l. 19.

Sir Thomas More is chosen
Lord Chancellor *in* your *place.*
Shak., Hen. VIII., iii. 2. 394.

In place
Of thanks, devise to extirpe the memory
Of such an act. *B. Jonson,* Volpone, iv. 2.

16. A situation; an appointment; an employment; hence, office: as, a politician striving for *place;* a coachman wanting a *place.*

Though he had offered to lay down his *place,* yet, when he saw they went about it, he grew passionate, and expostulated with them. *Winthrop,* Hist. New England, I. 304.

For neither pension, post, nor *place*
Am I your humble debtor.
Burns, The Dream.

17. Official or social status or dignity; vocation, station, or condition in life, etc.: as, to make one know his *place.*

When any of great *place* dyeth, they assemble the Astrologers, and tell the houre of his natiuitie, that they may by their Art finde a Planet fitting to the burning of the corpes. *Purchas,* Pilgrimage, p. 427.

Their summons call'd
From every band and squared regiment
By *place* or choice the worthiest.
Milton, P. L., i. 759.

She teaches him his *place* by an incomparable discipline.
The Century, XXXVII. 231.

18. Precedence; priority in rank, dignity, or importance.

Come, do you think I'd walk in any plot
Where Madam Sempronia should take *place* of me,
And Fulvia come in the rear, or on the by?
B. Jonson, Catiline, iii. 2.

You do not know
What 'tis to be a lady and take *place*.
Shirley, Love in a Maze, i. 2.

19. Point or degree in order of proceeding: as, in the first *place*; in the second *place*; in the last *place*.—**20.** In *geom.* See *locus*, 3.—**21.** Position; specifically, in *astron.*, the bearing of a heavenly body at any instant: as, the moon's *place* (that is, its right ascension and declination, or direction otherwise specified).—**22.** Ground or occasion; room.

There is no *place* of doubting but that it was the very same. *Hammond*, Fundamentals.

23. Position, in general.

By improvement they [of Scio] have all sorts of fruit trees, and the mulberry-tree for their silk has a great *place* among them.
Pococke, Description of the East, II. ii. 9.

Acronychal, aphetical, common, decimal, eccentric place. See the adjectives.—**Apparent place of a star.** See *apparent*.—**Body of a place.** See *body*.—**Heliocentric, high, holy, inward place.** See the adjectives.—**In place.** (*a*) In position or adjustment. (*b*) Into occasion, opportunity, or use.

And gladly ther-of wolde thei ben a-venged, yef thei myght come *in place*. *Merlin* (E. E. T. S.), iii. 444.

(*c*) In *geol.*, in its original position; not moved, especially by currents of water or by other erosive agencies, from its natural bed, or the place which it occupied when the deposit of which it constitutes a part was formed. (*d*) In presence; present.

Thy love is present there with thee *in place*.
Spenser, F. Q., VI. x. 16.

Jumping-off place. See *jump*[1].—**Law of place,** the law in force within a particular jurisdiction: commonly used with reference to the place where a contract is made or to be performed; the lex loci.—**Mean place.** See *mean*[3].—**Most holy place.** See *holy of holies*, under *holy*.—**Out of place.** (*a*) Not properly placed or adjusted in relation to other things; displaced. Hence—(*b*) Ill-assorted; ill-timed; inappropriate; disturbing: as, conduct or remarks *out of place*.—**Place kick.** See *kick*.—**Place of election,** in *surg.* See *election*.—**Place of worship,** a church, chapel, or meeting-house.—**Places of arms,** in *fort.* See *arm*[2].—**Strong place,** a fortress or a fortified town; a stronghold.

At a few miles' distance was the *strong place* of Ripa Candida. *Prescott*, Ferd. and Isa., ii. 2.

To give place, to make room or way; yield.

And when a lady's in the case,
You know all other things *give place*.
Gay, Hare and many Friends.

They heard Jonah and *gave place* to his preaching.
Latimer, Sermon bef. Edw. VI., 1550.

Neither *give place* to the devil. Eph. iv. 27.

To have place. (*a*) To have room, seat, or footing: as, such desires can *have* no *place* in a good heart. (*b*) To have actual existence.—**To make place,** to make room; give way.

Make place! bear back there!
B. Jonson, Cynthia's Revels, v. 2.

To take place. (*a*) To come to pass; happen; occur. (*b*) To take precedence or priority. See def. 18. (*c*) To take effect; avail.

But none of these excuses would *take place*. *Spenser*.

The powder in the touch-hole being wet, and the ship having fresh way with wind and tide, the shot *took place* in the shrouds and killed a passenger.
Winthrop, Hist. New England, I. 271.

place (plās), *v. t.*; pret. and pp. *placed*, ppr. *placing*. [= F. *placer*; from the noun.] **1.** To put or set in a particular place or position.

Place barrels of pitch upon the fatal stake,
That so her torture may be shortened.
Shak., 1 Hen. VI., v. 4. 57.

Hither came Cæsar iorneying night and daye wyth as muche speede as might be, and, taking the towne, *placed* garyson in it. *Golding*, tr. of Cæsar, fol. 30.

The king being dead,
This hand shall *place* the crown on Queen Jane's head.
Webster and Dekker, Sir Thomas Wyat, p. 8.

This seate is admirably *plac'd* for field sports, hawking, hunting, or racing. *Evelyn*, Diary, Sept. 10, 1677.

Over all a Counterpane was *plac'd*.
Congreve, Hymn to Venus.

2. To put or set in position or order; arrange; dispose.

Commend his good choice, and right *placing* of wordes.
Ascham, The Scholemaster, p. 88.

For he obtaineth places of honor which can most fitly *place* his wordes, and most eloquently write of the subiect propounded. *Purchas*, Pilgrimage, p. 438.

3. To put in office or a position of authority; appoint; ordain to a charge.

Thou shalt provide out of all the people able men, such as fear God, men of truth, hating covetousness; and *place* such over them to be rulers of thousands. Ex. xviii. 21.

This gentleman was a Mr. Thompson, the son of a *placed* minister of Melrose.
Mem. of R. H. Barham, in Ingoldsby Legends, I. 89.

4. To find a place, home, situation, etc., for; arrange for the residence, instruction, or employment of.

I am always glad to get a young person well *placed* out. Four nieces of Mrs. Jenkinson are most delightfully situated through my means.
Jane Austen, Pride and Prejudice, xxix.

5. To put out at interest; invest: as, to *place* money in the funds.—**6.** To arrange or make provision for: as, to *place* a loan.—**7.** To set; base; put; repose: as, to *place* confidence in a friend.

Let them shew where the God of our Fathers imposed any of those heavy burdens which the Scribes and Pharisees *place* so much of their Religion in.
Stillingfleet, Sermons, II. i.

The Egyptians *place* great faith in dreams.
E. W. Lane, Modern Egyptians, I. 339.

=**Syn. 1.** *Set*, *Lay*, etc. (see *put*), station, establish, deposit.

placebo (plạ-sē'bō), *n.* [< ME. *placebo*, < OF. *placebo*, < L. *placebo*, I will please; 1st pers. sing. fut. ind. of *placere*, please: see *please*.] **1.** In the *Rom. Cath. Ch.*, the vespers of the office for the dead. It was so called from the initial words of the opening antiphon, *Placebo Domino in regione vivorum* (I shall be acceptable unto the Lord in the land of the living), taken from Psalm cxiv. 9 of the Vulgate (cxvi. 9 of the authorized version).
2. A medicine adapted rather to pacify than to benefit a patient.

Physicians appeal to the imagination in desperate cases with bread pills and *placebos*.
Amer. Jour. Psychol., I. 145.

To sing placebo†, to act with servile complaisance; agree with one in his opinions.

Beth ware, therfore, with lordes how ye pleye,
Syngeth *Placebo*—and I shal if I kan.
Chaucer, Summoner's Tale, l. 367.

Of which comedie . . . when some (to *sing placebo*) aduised that it should be forbidden, because it was somewhat too plaine, . . . yet he would haue it allowed.
Sir J. Harington, Pref. to Ariosto's Orlando Furioso.

place-brick (plās'brik), *n.* In *brickmaking*, an inferior kind of brick, which, having been outermost or furthest from the fire in the clamp or kiln, has not received sufficient heat to burn it thoroughly. Place-bricks are consequently soft, and uneven in texture. They are also termed *peckings*, and sometimes *sandel* or *samel bricks*.

place-broker (plās'brō"kėr), *n.* One who disposes of official place for his own profit; one who traffics in public offices, whether for his personal profit or for that of others.

placeful† (plās'fụl), *a.* [< *place* + *-ful*.] Filling a place.

And in their precinct
(Proper and *placefull*) stood the troughs and pailes
In which he milk'd. *Chapman*, Odyssey, ix.

place-hunter (plās'hun"tėr), *n.* One who seeks persistently for public office.

The multiplication of salaried functionaries creates a population of *place-hunters*.
Sir E. Creasy, Eng. Const., p. 377, note.

placeless (plās'les), *a.* [< *place* + *-less*.] Having no place or office. *Canning*.

placeman (plās'man), *n.*; pl. *placemen* (-men). One who holds or occupies a place; specifically, one who has an office under government.

A cabinet which contains not *placemen* alone, but independent and popular noblemen and gentlemen.
Macaulay, Sir William Temple.

placement (plās'ment), *n.* [< *place* + *-ment*.] A putting, placing, or setting. [Rare.]

They are harmful in proportion as the *placement* of the loan disturbs the market value of the commodities.
Pop. Sci. Mo., XXXI. 415.

placemonger (plās'mung"gėr), *n.* One who traffics in public employments and patronage.

place-name (plās'nām), *n.* The name of a place or locality; such a name as is given to places; a local name: in contradistinction to *personal name*.

placent†, *n.* [< L. *placenta*, a cake, = Gr. πλακοῦς (πλακουντ-), a flat cake, contr. of πλακόεις (πλακοεντ-), flat, < πλάξ (πλακ-), anything flat.] A cake.

Afterwards make a confection of it [flower-de-luce] with clarified hony, which must be so hard that you may make small *placents* or trocisces of it; dry them in the shadow.
T. Adams, Quoted in N. and Q., 7th ser., VII. 29.

placenta (plạ-sen'tạ), *n.*; pl. *placentas* or *placentæ* (-täz, -tē). [= F. Sp. Pg. It. *placenta*, < NL. *placenta*, placenta (something having a flattened circular form), lit. 'cake,' a particular use of L. *placenta*, a cake: see *placent*.] **1.** In *zoöl.*, *anat.*, and *med.*: (*a*) The organ of attachment of a vertebrate embryo or fetus to the wall of the uterus or womb of the female. It is a specially modified part of the surface of the chorion or outside one of the fetal envelops, of a flattened circular form, like a plate or saucer, one side of which is closely applied to the wall of the womb, and from the other side of which proceeds the umbilical cord or navel-string. It is highly vascular, and in intimate vital connection with a similarly vascular area of the uterine walls, serving for the interchange of the constituents of the blood between the female and the fetus, and thus acting during intra-uterine life as the organ of circulation, respiration, and nutrition of the fetus. The human placenta is about as large as a soup-plate, and in connection with the navel-string and membranes is commonly known as the *uterine cake*, *afterbirth*, or *secundines*. The presence of a true placenta is necessarily restricted to viviparous vertebrates, and does not occur in all of these (the two lower subclasses of mammals, the marsupials and monotremes, being implacental). Several forms of placenta have been distinguished among placental mammals, and made a basis of classification. See also cuts under *embryo* and *uterus*. Hence—(*b*) Some analogous part or organ in other animals, having a similar function. (1) In ascidians, the organ by which a fetal sexless ascidiozooid is attached for a time to the wall of the atrial cavity of the parent. See cut under *Salpa*. (2) In infusorians, a name given by Stein to the single mass resulting from the coalescence of the segments of the nuclei of different individuals after the process of conjugation.

Human Placenta (unattached surface), with umbilical cord.

2. In echinoderms, a flat discoidal sea-urchin, as a sand-dollar or cake-urchin: used in a generic sense by Klein, 1734.—**3.** [*cap.*] A genus of bivalve mollusks, now called *Placuna*.—**4.** In *bot.*, that part of the ovary of flowering plants which bears the ovules. It is usually the more or less enlarged or modified margins of the carpellary leaves, and is of a soft cellular texture. When the ovary is composed of a single leaf, both margins give rise to ovules, and they are consequently in two rows. In a compound ovary there are various modifications of the placenta. Thus, when the edges of the carpellary leaves all meet in a common axis, the placentas are said to be *axile*. When, by obliteration of the dissepiments, such an ovary becomes one-celled, the axile placentas remain in a column as a *free central placenta*. Or, when the edges of the carpellary leaves barely meet and slightly incurve, the placentas become *parietal*, being borne on the wall. There are all degrees of incurvation, the placentas being located accordingly. In vascular cryptogams the point giving rise to the sporangia is sometimes called the *placenta*. The placenta is sometimes termed the *trophospermium* and *spermophorum*. See also cut under *ovary*.—**Battledore placenta,** a placenta which has the cord attached to the edge.—**Deciduate placenta,** a placenta which comes away entire at parturition, as in woman and many other mammals.—**Discoidal placenta.** See *discoidal*.—**Non-deciduate placenta,** a placenta which is not deciduate.—**Parietal placenta.** See *parietal*, and def. 4, above.—**Placenta adherent,** a placenta which has, through inflammation during pregnancy, formed adhesions to the uterus.—**Placenta cruoris,** blood-clot.—**Placenta prævia,** that condition of the placenta in which it is attached over the internal os, thus necessitating its rupture or detachment, with consequent hemorrhage, before the contents of the uterus can be expelled.—**Placenta sanguinis,** blood-clot.—**Placenta succenturia,** a supernumerary placental mass, produced by the development of an isolated patch of chorion villi.—**Polycotyledonary placenta,** a placenta whose fetal villi are arranged in distinct tufts or cotyledons, as in the cow.

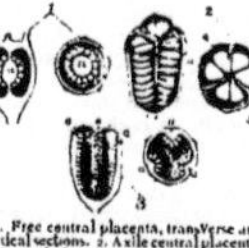

1. Free central placenta, transverse and vertical sections. 2. Axile central placenta. 3. Parietal placenta. *a, a*, Placentas.

placental (plạ-sen'tal), *a.* and *n.* [< NL. *placentalis*, < *placenta*, placenta: see *placenta*.] **I.** *a.* **1.** Of or pertaining to the placenta.—**2.** Forming or constituted by a placenta: as, *placental* gestation; a *placental* part of the chorion.—**3.** Provided with a placenta; placentate or placentary: as, a *placental* mammal.—**Placental dystocia,** difficult birth of the placenta.—**Placental murmur** or **souffle,** a murmur heard on auscultation of the pregnant uterus, and regarded as due to the placental circulation.

II. *n.* A placental mammal; any member of the *Placentalia*.

Placentalia (plas-en-tā'li-ä), *n. pl.* [NL. (Bonaparte, 1837), neut. pl. of *placentalis*: see *placental*.] Placental mammals; those mammals which are placentate or placentiferous: distinguished from *Implacentalia*. The *Placentalia* were formerly one of two prime divisions of mammals, contrasted with marsupials and monotremes together. The division corresponds to *Monodelphia*, and also to *Eutheria*. Also *Placentaria*.

placentalian (plas-en-tā'li-an), *a.* and *n.* **I.** *a.* Of or pertaining to the *Placentalia*; placental.

II. *n.* A member of the *Placentalia*; a placental.

Placentaria (plas-en-tā'ri-ä), *n. pl.* [NL., neut. pl. of *placentarius*: see *placentary*.] Same as *Placentalia*.

placentary (plas'en-tā-ri), *a.* and *n.* [= F. *placentaire*, < NL. **placentarius*, < *placenta*, placenta: see *placenta*.] **I.** *a.* **1.** Of or pertaining to the placenta; placental; pertaining to the *Placentaria*.—**2.** Made or done with reference to the placenta or to placentation: as, a *placentary* classification.

II. *n.*; pl. *placentaries* (-riz). **1.** A member of the *Placentalia*; a placental.—**2.** In *bot.*, a placenta bearing numerous ovules.

Placentata (plas-en-tā'tä), *n. pl.* Same as *Placentalia*.

placentate (plā-sen'tāt), *a.* [< NL. **placentatus*, < *placenta*, placenta: see *placenta*.] Having a placenta; placentiferous; placental.

placentation (plas-en-tā'shon), *n.* [= F. *placentation* = Pg. *placentação*; as *placentate* + *-ion*.] **1.** In *zoöl.*: (*a*) The attachment of the embryo or fetus to the uterus by means of a placenta; uterogestation. (*b*) The mode in which this attachment is effected; the manner of the disposition or construction of the placenta: as, deciduate or discoidal *placentation*.—**2.** In *bot.*, the disposition or arrangement of the placentas.

placentia (plā-sen'shi-ä), *a.* A word found only in the phrase-name *placentia falcon*, apparently noting the large dark area on the belly of that hawk, likened to a placenta. See *falcon*. *T. Pennant.*

placentiferous (plas-en-tif'e-rus), *a.* [< NL. *placenta* + L. *ferre* = E. *bear*[1].] **1.** Provided with a placenta; gestating in the womb, as a mammal.—**2.** In *bot.*, bearing or producing a placenta; having a placenta.

Also *placentigerous*.

placentiform (plā-sen'ti-fôrm), *a.* [= F. *placentiforme*, < NL. *placenta*, placenta, + L. *forma*, form.] **1.** In *zoöl.*, having the form, structure, or character of a placenta.—**2.** In *bot.*, shaped like a placenta; having a thick circular disk, concave in the middle on both upper and lower sides. The root of *Cyclamen* is an example.

placentigerous (plas-en-tij'e-rus), *a.* [< NL. *placenta*, placenta, + L. *gerere*, carry.] Same as *placentiferous*.

placentious† (plā-sen'shus), *a.* [< L. *placen(t-)s*, pleasing (see *pleasant*), + *-ious*.] Pleasant; amiable.

> John Walbye, . . . a *placentious* person, gaining the good-will of all with whom he conversed. — *Fuller*, Worthies, York, III. 467.

placentitis (plas-en-tī'tis), *n.* [NL., < *placenta*, placenta, + *-itis*.] Inflammation of the placenta.

placentoid (plā-sen'toid), *a.* [< NL. *placenta*, placenta, + Gr. *εἶδος*, form.] Like a placenta; placentiform.

place-proud (plās'proud), *a.* Proud of position or rank. *Fletcher*, Wit without Money, iii. 1.

placer[1] (plā'sėr), *n.* [< *place* + *-er*[1].] One who places, locates, or sets.

> Lord of creatures all,
> Thou *placer* of plants both humble and tall.
> — *Spenser*, Shep. Cal., February.

placer[2] (plas'ėr; Amer. Sp. pron. pla-sär'), *n.* [< Sp. *placer*, a place near a river where gold-dust is found (cf. *placel*, a sand-bank), < *plaza*, a place: see *place*.] In *mining*, a place where the superficial detritus is washed for gold or other valuable minerals: a word formerly in common use in California, but now nearly obsolete. Placer-mining has hardly any other meaning in English than that of gold-washing, but it is not used in speaking of washing for gold by the hydraulic method. Washing for tin—a kind of mining not carried on in the United States—is called *streaming*.—**Placer-claim**, a mining claim to a placer deposit; under the United States mining law, a tract of mineral land upon which the owner of the claim is entitled to the ordinary surface rights and all forms of deposit, excepting veins of quartz or other rock in place, under the same circumstances and conditions as in the case of vein- or lode-claims (see *lode*[1], and *mining claim*, under *mining*), except that no location can include more than 20 acres for each individual claimant, and that, where the lands located under such a claim have been previously surveyed by the United States, the exterior limits of the entry must conform to the legal divisions of the public lands and rectangular subdivisions thereof. A patent for a placer-claim includes a vein or lode not at the time known to exist within its limits; but it does not include a known vein or lode, unless so expressed.

placet (plā'set), *n.* [L., it pleases; 3d pers. sing. pres. ind. of *placere*: see *please*.] **1.** An expressed sanction; permission given by one in authority; specifically, sanction granted to the promulgation and execution of an ecclesiastical ordinance, and particularly such sanction granted by a sovereign to papal bulls, briefs, and other edicts.

> Such therefore is that secondary reason which hath place in divinity, which is grounded upon the *placets* of God. — *Bacon*, Advancement of Learning, ii. 364.

2. A vote of assent in a council; a vote of the governing body in a university.

placid (plas'id), *a.* [< F. *placide* = Sp. *plácido* = Pg. It. *placido*, < L. *placidus*, gentle, mild, < *placere*, please: see *please*.] Gentle; quiet; undisturbed; equable; serene; calm; unruffled; peaceful; mild.

> It conduceth unto long life and to the more *placid* motion of the spirits, that men's actions be free. — *Bacon.*

> That *placid* intercourse [with the great minds of former ages] is disturbed by no jealousies or resentments. — *Macaulay*, Bacon.

> That *placid* aspect and meek regard. — *Milton*, P. R., iii. 217.

=**Syn.** *Tranquil, Serene*, etc. See *calm*[1].

placidious† (plā-sid'i-us), *a.* [< *placid* + *-ious*.] Gentle; placid.

> Most easie, peaceable, and *placidious*. — *Topsell*, Four-Footed Beasts, p. 158. (*Halliwell.*)

placidity (plā-sid'i-ti), *n.* [= F. *placidité* = It. *placidità*, < L. *placidita(t-)s*, < *placidus*, placid: see *placid*.] The state or character of being placid; tranquillity; peacefulness; quietness; calmness.

> That habitual *placidity* of temper which results from the extinction of vicious and perturbing impulses. — *Lecky*, European Morals, I. 189.

placidly (plas'id-li), *adv.* In a placid manner; calmly; quietly; without disturbance or passion.

placidness (plas'id-nes), *n.* The state or character of being placid.

placit†, *n.* [= Pg. It. *placito*, < L. *placitum*, that which is pleasing, a maxim, an order, < *placitus*, pp. of *placere*, please: see *please*. Cf. *plea, plead*.] Same as *placet*.

> Sextus Empiricus was but a diligent collector of the *placits* and opinions of other philosophers. — *Evelyn*, To Mr. E. Thurland.

placita, *n.* Plural of *placitum*.

placitory (plas'i-tō-ri), *a.* [< ML. *placitum*, plea (see *placit, plea*), + *-ory*.] Of or relating to pleas or pleading in courts of law.

placitum (plas'i-tum), *n.*; pl. *placita* (-tä). [ML.: see *placit, plea*.] In the middle ages, a public assembly of all degrees of men, where the sovereign presided, usually summoned to consult upon great affairs of state; hence, a resolution taken by such an assembly; also, a penalty or fine, or a plea or suit.

plack (plak), *n.* [< OF. *plaque, placque, plecque, plache*, a coin so called (also *plaquette*), F. *plaque*, a plate, slab, patch, veneer, etc., < MD. *placke, plecke* (= Flem. *placke* = MLG. *placke*, in ML. *placa, placca*), a coin so called, D. *plak*, a thin slice, a ferrule; cf. MD. *placke, plecke*, a spot, a place, village, town, also a patch; mixed, in the form *blecke*, etc., with MD. *bleck, blick*, a plate, as of tin or lead, D. *blik*, white iron, tin, = OHG. *blch, pleh, plech, bleh*, MHG. *blech*, a plate, thin leaf of metal, etc., = Sw. *bleck* = Dan. *blik*, white iron, sheet-metal. Cf. *placard, plaque*.] A Scotch billon coin current in the fifteenth century (from 1468), and also in

Obverse. Reverse.
Plack of Mary, Queen of Scots.—British Museum. (Size of the original.)

the sixteenth century. It was worth 4 pence Scotch (about two thirds of the United States cent), and under James VI. 8 pence Scotch.—**Plack and bawbee**, to the last farthing; fully. [Scotch.]

placket (plak'et), *n.* [< OF. *placquette*, a thin plate (a placket being appar. a patch sewed on), dim. of *plaque*, plate: see *plack*. Cf. *plaquette, placard*.] **1**†. A pocket, especially a pocket in a woman's dress.

> When she comes into a great prease of people, for fear of the cutpurse, on a sudden she'll swap thee into her *plackerd*. — *Greene*, Friar Bacon and Friar Bungay, i. 1.

> Just like a plow-boy tir'd in a browne jacket,
> And breeches round, long leathern point, no *placket*.
> — *Gayton*, Notes on Don Quixote, p. 170. (*Nares.*)

2. The opening or slit in a petticoat or skirt; a fent.

> That a cod-piece were far fitter here than a pinned *placket*. — *Fletcher (and another)*, Love's Cure, i. 2.

3. A petticoat; hence, figuratively, a woman.

> Was that brave heart made to pant for a *placket*? — *Fletcher*, Humorous Lieutenant, iv. 4.

> If the maides a spinning goe,
> Burne the flax, and fire their toe,
> Scorch their *plackets*.
> — *Herrick*, Saint Distaff's Day.

4. Same as *placcate*.

placket-hole (plak'et-hōl), *n.* Same as *placket*, 2.

plackless (plak'les), *a.* [< *plack* + *-less*.] Penniless; without money.

> Poor, *plackless* devils like mysel'! — *Burns*, Scotch Drink.

plack-pie (plak'pī), *n.* A pie formerly sold for a plack. *Scott.* [Scotch.]

Placobranchia (plak-ō-brang'ki-ä), *n. pl.* [NL. (J. E. Gray, 1857), < Gr. *πλάξ* (*πλακ-*), something flat, a tablet, plate, + *βράγχια*, gills.] A suborder of nudibranchiate gastropods, established for the family *Elysiidæ*, characterized by having lamellar or venose gills on the upper surface of the mantle.

placoderm (plak'ō-dėrm), *a.* and *n.* [< Gr. *πλάξ* (*πλακ-*), a tablet, plate, + *δέρμα*, skin, < *δέρειν*, flay.] **I.** *a.* Having the skin covered with broad flat plates, as a fish; belonging to the *Placodermi*.

II. *n.* A ganoid fish of the group *Placodermi*.

placodermal (plak-ō-dėr'mal), *a.* [< *placoderm* + *-al*.] Same as *placoderm*.

Placodermata (plak-ō-dėr'ma-tä), *n. pl.* [NL.: see *placoderm*.] Same as *Placodermi*.

placodermatous (plak-ō-dėr'ma-tus), *a.* Same as *placoderm*.

Placodermi (plak-ō-dėr'mī), *n. pl.* [NL.: see *placoderm*.] An order of fishes, constituted for some remarkable Paleozoic forms of doubtful relationships. It has been variously defined. As usually limited, it includes fishes which had a persistent notochord, neural and hemal spines and interspinals connecting with a dorsal and an anal fin, a jointed pectoral appendage inclosed in a bony covering, the head and front of the body inclosed by bony dorsal and ventral shields, no ventrals, and a distinct lower jaw. Thus limited, it has been made to include the families *Coccosteidæ* and *Dinichthyidæ*. Also *Placodermata, Placoganoidei*.

placodont (plak'ō-dont), *n.* [< *Placodus* (*-odont-*).] A member of the group *Placodontia* or family *Placodontidæ*.

Placodontia (plak-ō-don'shi-ä), *n. pl.* [NL., < Gr. *πλάξ* (*πλακ-*), a tablet, plate, + *ὀδούς* (*ὀδοντ-*) = E. *tooth*.] A group of extinct reptiles, which had double nares (the posterior nares opening directly into the roof of the mouth by horizontal apertures, as in the sauropterygians), no floor to the narial passage, and maxillary as well as palatal teeth. It has been referred to the fishes, and among the reptiles to the *Sauropterygia*; but late systematists regard it as a suborder of the order *Theromora*.

Placodontidæ (plak-ō-don'ti-dē), *n. pl.* [NL., < *Placodus* (*-odont-*) + *-idæ*.] A family of extinct reptiles, represented by the genus *Placodus*. They are the only known members of the group *Placodontia*. The general form is unknown. The skull was broad behind, with an apparently compound temporal arcade and a postorbital bar; the teeth around the palate were like paving-stones. The species lived in the Triassic period.

Placodus (plak'ō-dus), *n.* [NL., < Gr. *πλάξ* (*πλακ-*), a tablet, plate, + *ὀδούς* = E. *tooth*.] A genus of reptiles having pavement-like teeth. *P. gigas* is a species of the Trias.

placoganoid (plak-ō-gan'oid), *a.* and *n.* [< Gr. *πλάξ* (*πλακ-*), a tablet, plate, + E. *ganoid*.] **I.** *a.* Having a placoid exoskeleton, as a ganoid fish; belonging to the *Placoganoidei*.

II. *n.* A member of the *Placoganoidei*.

placoganoidean (plak″ō-ga-noi'dē-an), *a.* and *n.* [< *placoganoid* + *-ean*.] Same as *placoganoid*.

Placoganoidei (plak″ō-ga-noi'dē-ī), *n. pl.* [NL.: see *placoganoid*.] Same as *Placodermi*.

placoid (plak'oid), *a.* and *n.* [< Gr. **πλακοειδής*, contr. *πλακώδης*, flat, < *πλάξ* (*πλακ-*), a tablet, plate, + *εἶδος*, form.] **I.** *a.* **1.** Plate-like: noting the dermal investments of sharks, which take the place of true scales and are the ossified papillæ of the cutis. In combination they form the shagreen of the sharks. The name is also extended to the tubercular or thorn-like armature of the skin in rays.

2. Having placoid scales, as a fish; belonging to the *Placoidei*. See cut under *scale*.—**Placoid exoskeleton**, the shagreen, ichthyodorulites, or other forms of the dermal defenses of the elasmobranchiate fishes.

II. *n.* A member of the *Placoidei*.

Placoidea (plą̄-koi′dē-ą̈), *n. pl.* [NL.] Same as *Placoidei.*

placoidean (plą̄-koi′dē-ąn), *a.* and *n.* [< *placoid* + *-e-an.*] Same as *placoid.*

Placoidei (plą̄-koi′dē-ī), *n. pl.* [NL.: see *placoid.*] In Agassiz's classification, an artificial group of fishes, having placoid scales: correlated with *Ctenoidei, Cycloidei,* and *Ganoidei.* It is mainly equivalent to the class *Elasmobranchii,* but also included the naked marsipobranchs.

placoidian (plą̄-koi′di-ąn), *n.* [< *placoid* + *-ian.*] Same as *placoid.*

Placophora (plą̄-kof′ǭ-rą̈), *n. pl.* [NL., < Gr. πλάξ (πλακ-), a tablet, plate, + φέρειν = E. *bear*[1].] In Gegenbaur's system of classification, one of two primary divisions of the *Mollusca,* consisting of the chitons only. The *Polyplacophora* and *Amphoneura* of Lankester, though of a very different taxonomic grade, are coterminous. See *Polyplacophora,* and cut under *Chitonidæ.*

placophoran (plą̄-kof′ǭ-ran), *a.* and *n.* [< *placophor-ous* + *-an.*] **I.** *a.* Placophorous; belonging to the *Placophora.*

II. *n.* A member of the *Placophora;* a chiton.

placophorous (plą̄-kof′ǭ-rus), *a.* [< Gr. πλάξ (πλακ-), a tablet, plate, + φέρειν = E. *bear*[1].] Same as *placophoran.*

placula (plak′ū-lą̈), *n.*; pl. *placulæ* (-lē). [NL., dim., < Gr. πλάξ (πλακ-), a tablet, plate.] A little plate or plaque: specifically applied to certain discoidal embryos consisting of a mass of cleavage-cells disposed as a plate or layer: see *monoplacula* and *diploplacula. Hyatt,* Proc. Bost. Soc. Nat. Hist., 1884, p. 97.

placular (plak′ū-lär), *a.* [< *placula* + *-ar*[3].] Plate-like; flat and broad; having the character of a placula.

placulate (plak′ū-lāt), *a.* [< *placula* + *-ate*[1].] Having the form of a placula; being a placula or in the placular stage of development, as an embryo.

Placuna (plą̄-kū′nä), *n.* [NL. (Bruguière, 1792), < Gr. πλάξ (πλακ-), a tablet, plate.] The typical genus of *Placunidæ.* They have thin, more

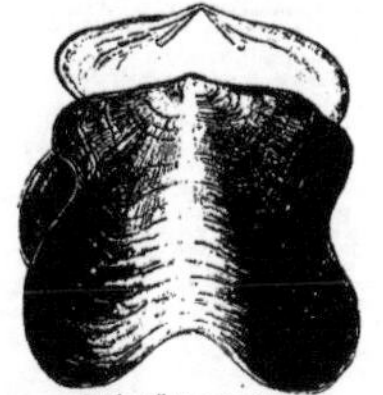

Saddle-shell (*Placuna sella*).

or less translucent shells, which are nearly equivalve, and no byssus. Several species inhabit East Indian seas. *P. placenta* is known as the *window-shell, P. sella* as the *saddle-shell.*

Placunidæ (plą̄-kū′ni-dē), *n. pl.* [NL., < *Placuna* + *-idæ.*] A family of bivalve mollusks, typified by the genus *Placuna,* whose species are generally associated in the same family with the typical *Anomiidæ,* and are known as *window-shells, window-oysters,* and *saddle-shells.*

pladarosis (plad-ą-rō′sis), *n.* [NL., < Gr. πλαδαροῦσθαι, become soft and flabby, < πλαδαρός, wet, damp, flaccid, flabby, < πλαδᾶν, be flaccid.] A soft tumor or wart on the eyelid. Also *pladarotis* and *pladaroma.*

plafond (pla-fond′), *n.* [= Sp. *plafon;* < F. *plafond,* ceiling, < *plat,* flat (see *plate*), + *fond,* bottom: see *fund*[1], *found*[2].] In *arch.,* the ceiling of a room, whether flat or arched; also, the under side of the projection of the larmier of a cornice, and generally any soffit. Also *platfond.*

plaga (plā′gą̈), *n.*; pl. *plagæ* (-jē). [NL., < L. *plaga,* a blow, stroke, wound, stripe: see *plague.*] In *zoöl.,* a stripe or streak of color. —**Plaga scapularis,** in *entom.,* same as *parapsis*[1]. *Haliday.*

plagal (plā′gąl), *a.* [= F. *plagal* = It. *plagale,* < ML. *plagius,* < Gr. πλάγιος, sidewise, slanting, athwart, oblique, < πλάγος, πλᾶγος, side.] 1. In *Gregorian music,* noting a mode or melody in which the final is in the middle of the compass instead of at the bottom: opposed to *authentic.* See *mode*[1], 7.—2. In *modern music,* noting a cadence in which the chord of the tonic is preceded by that of the subdominant. See *cadence.*

plagard†, *n.* Same as *placard,* 4, for *placcate.*

plagate (plā′gāt), *a.* [< *plaga* + *-ate*[1].] Striped or streaked.

plage[1]†, *n.* A Middle English form of *plague.*

plage[2]† (plāj), *n.* [< ME. *plage,* < OF. *plage* (also *plaie*), F. *plage* = Sp. Pg. It. *plaga,* < L. *plaga,* region, quarter, tract. Cf. Gr. πλάγος, the side: see *plagal.*] 1. A region; a district.

> Alle Cristen folk ben fled fro that contree
> Thurgh payens, that conquereden al aboute
> The *plages* of the North by land and see.
> *Chaucer,* Man of Law's Tale, l. 445.

> As far as from the frozen *plage* of heaven
> Unto the watery morning's ruddy bower.
> *Marlowe,* Tamburlaine, I., iv. 4.

2. Quarter of the compass.

> Now hastow her the foure quarters of thin astrelabie, devyded after the foure principals *plages* or quarters of the firmament. *Chaucer,* Astrolabe, i. 5.

Plagianthus (plaj-i-an′thus), *n.* [NL. (J. and G. Forster, 1776), < Gr. πλάγιος, oblique, + ἄνθος, flower.] A genus of polypetalous shrubs of the order *Malvaceæ* and the tribe *Malveæ,* unlike the other genera of its subtribe *Sideæ* in its longitudinally stigmatose style-branches, and characterized by a five-cleft calyx, distant or obsolete bracteoles, many-cleft stamen-column, and one, two, or many carpels, each with one pendulous seed. There are 11 species, all natives of Australia and New Zealand. They bear alternate or clustered, usually entire or angled leaves, and polygamous red, whitish, or yellowish flowers, usually small and densely crowded in the axils or in a terminal spike. Several low shrubby species produce a useful fiber. (See *hemp-bush* and *currajong.*) *P. betulinus,* the ribbon-tree of Otago, New Zealand, also called *cotton-tree, lacebark,* and *ukaroa-tree,* is an evergreen reaching sometimes 70 feet, though usually a tangled bush, and yields a very fine tough fiber resembling flax, derived from the inner bark of the young branches.

plagiarise, *v.* See *plagiarize.*

plagiarism (plā′ji-ą-rizm), *n.* [= Pg. *plagiarismo;* as *plagiar-y* + *-ism.*] 1. The purloining or wrongful appropriation of another's ideas, writings, artistic designs, etc., and giving these forth as one's own; specifically, the offense of taking passages from another's compositions, and publishing them, either word for word or in substance, as one's own; literary theft.

> Sir J. Reynolds has been accused of *plagiarism* for having borrowed attitudes from ancient masters. Not only candour but criticism must deny the force of the charge.
> *Walpole,* Anecdotes of Painting, IV., adv. p. vii., note.

2. A passage or thought thus stolen.

plagiarist (plā′ji-ą-rist), *n.* [< *plagiar-y* + *-ist.*] One who plagiarizes; one who is guilty of plagiarism.

> You glean from the refuse of obscure volumes, where more judicious *plagiarists* have been before you; so that the body of your work is a composition of dregs and sediments—like a bad tavern's worst wine.
> *Sheridan,* The Critic, i. 1.

plagiarize (plā′ji-ą-rīz), *v.*; pret. and pp. *plagiarized,* ppr. *plagiarizing.* [< *plagiar-y* + *-ize.*] **I.** *trans.* To steal or purloin from the writings or ideas of another: as, to *plagiarize* a passage.

II. *intrans.* To commit plagiarism.

Also spelled *plagiarise.*

plagiary (plā′ji-ā-ri), *n.* and *a.* [Formerly *plagiarie;* < F. *plagiaire* = Sp. Pg. It. *plagiario,* a kidnapper, a plagiarist, < L. *plagiarius,* a kidnapper, plagiarist, < (LL.) *plagium,* kidnapping, prob. < *plaga,* a net, snare, trap, prob. orig. **placa,* < *plec-t-ere* = Gr. πλέκειν, weave: see *plait.*] **I.** *n.*; pl. *plagiaries* (-riz). 1†. A manstealer; a kidnapper.

> He was a Cyrenean by birth, and . . . in the time of his minoritie or child-hood he was by some *Plagiary* stolne away from his friends, and sold to the Ismaelite Merchants. *Purchas,* Pilgrimage, p. 243.

2. A plagiarist.

> Why, the ditty 's all borrowed; 'tis Horace's; hang him, *plagiary!* *B. Jonson,* Poetaster, iv. 1.

3. The crime of literary theft; plagiarism.

> *Plagiarie* had not its nativitie with printing, but began in times when thefts were difficult, and the paucity of bookes scarce wanted that invention.
> *Sir T. Browne,* Vulg. Err., i. 6.

II. *a.* 1†. Manstealing; kidnapping.

> *Plagiary* and man-stealing Tartars.
> *Brown,* Travels (1685), p. 49. (*Latham.*)

2. Practising literary theft.

> Or a lios ego from old Petrarch's spright
> Unto a *plagiary* sonnet-wright.
> *Bp. Hall,* Satires, IV. ii. 84.

Plagiaulacidæ (plā′ji-â-las′i-dē), *n. pl.* [NL., < *Plagiaulax* (-*lac*-) + *-idæ.*] A widely distributed family of fossil mammals, typified by the genus *Plagiaulax.* The premolars were obliquely grooved and the last was enlarged, the true molars two on each side and small, and the incisors of the lower jaw inclined forward and two in number. The family was formerly referred to the marsupials, but by recent writers is generally relegated to the *Prototheria,* as a representative of a peculiar order, *Multituberculata.* Remains referred to this family occur in Europe and America, ranging in geologic time from the Triassic to the Eocene.

Plagiaulax (plā-ji-â′laks), *n.* [NL., < Gr. πλάγιος, oblique, + αὖλαξ, furrow.] A genus of fossil primitive mammals from the Purbeck beds of the Upper Oölite, as *P. becclesi, P. minor,* and others. See *diprotodont, polyprotodont.*

plagihedral (plā-ji-hē′drąl), *a.* [= F. *plagiédre,* < Gr. πλάγιος, oblique, + ἕδρα, seat, base.] In *crystal.,* having faces obliquely arranged, as in certain hemihedral forms which are enantiomorphous to their complementary forms—that is, related to them as a right glove is to the left: this is true of the trapezohedral planes on a quartz crystal.

plagiocephalic (plā′ji-ǭ-se-fal′ik or -sef′ą-lik), *a.* [< *plagiocephal-ous* + *-ic.*] 1. Having a broad head with flattened forehead. *Jour. Anthrop. Inst.,* III. 90.—2. Pertaining to or exhibiting plagiocephaly.

plagiocephalous (plā′ji-ǭ-sef′ą-lus), *a.* [< Gr. πλάγιος, oblique, + κεφαλή, head.] Same as *plagiocephalic,* 1.

plagiocephaly (plā′ji-ǭ-sef′ą-li), *n.* [< *plagiocephal-ous* + *-y.*] Oblique deformity of the skull, such that the anterior part of one half is more developed, and similarly the posterior part of the other half.

plagiocitrite (plā′ji-ǭ-sit′rīt), *n.* [< Gr. πλάγιος, oblique, + L. *citrus,* citrus (see *citrus*), + *-ite*[2].] A hydrous sulphate of iron, aluminium, sodium, and potassium, occurring in fibrous crystalline forms of a lemon-yellow color near Bischofsheim vor der Rhön, in Bavaria.

plagioclase (plā′ji-ǭ-klāz), *n.* [< Gr. πλάγιος, oblique, + κλάσις, fracture, < κλᾶν, break.] The name given by Breithaupt to the group of triclinic feldspars the two prominent cleavage-directions in which are oblique to each other. The plagioclase-feldspar group includes albite, anorthite, and the intermediate species, oligoclase, andesin, labradorite; with these the triclinic potash feldspar microcline is sometimes included. See *feldspar.*

plagioclastic (plā′ji-ǭ-klas′tik), *a.* [< Gr. πλάγιος, oblique, + κλαστός, broken; cf. *clastic.*] Breaking obliquely; characterized by two different cleavages in directions oblique to one another, or pertaining to a mineral (as one of the triclinic feldspars) which has this property.

Plagiodon (plā-ji′ǭ-don), *n.* [NL. (orig. *Plagiodontia,* F. Cuvier, 1836), < πλάγιος, oblique, + ὀδούς (ὀδοντ-) = E. *tooth.*] 1. A West Indian genus of small hystricomorphic rodents of the family *Octodontidæ* and subfamily *Echinomyinæ:* so called from the diagonal grooves of the molars. The molars are rootless; the thumb is rudimentary; the tail is short and scaly; the fur is coarse, with silky under-fur; the muzzle is blunt; and the whole form is stout. The genus is closely related to *Capromys.* There is only one species, *P. ædium* of San Domingo.

Plagiodon ædium.

2. A genus of reptiles. *Duméril.*—3. A genus of mollusks. *Isaac Lea.*

plagiodont (plā′ji-ō-dont), *a.* [< Gr. πλάγιος, oblique, + ὀδούς (ὀδοντ-) = E. *tooth.*] Having the teeth oblique: noting the dentition of serpents whose teeth are like one another, those of the palate being set in two converging series.

Plagiodus (plā-ji-ō′dus), *n.* [NL. (orig. *Plagyodus,* Steller, 1811): see *Plagiodon.*] Same as *Alepidosaurus.* See cut under *handsaw-fish.*

plagionite (plā′ji-ǭ-nīt), *n.* [< Gr. πλάγιος, oblique, + *-n-* + *-ite*[2].] A sulphid of antimony and lead, occurring in oblique monoclinic crystals and in massive forms. It has a dark lead-gray color and metallic luster.

Plagiostoma[1] (plā-ji-os′tǭ-mą̈), *n.* [NL. (Sowerby, 1812), fem. sing.: see *plagiostome.*] A genus of bivalve mollusks of the family *Limidæ,* or a subgenus of *Lima,* containing such species as *P. cardiiformis.* See cut under *Lima.*

Plagiostoma[2] (plā-ji-os'tō-mạ̈), *n. pl.* [NL., neut. pl.: see *plagiostome*.] Same as *Plagiostomi*. *Nilsson*, 1832.

Plagiostomata (plā"ji-ō-stō'mạ-tạ̈), *n. pl.* [NL.; cf. *Plagiostoma*[2].] The *Plagiostomi* as an order of *Chondropterygii*. *Günther*.

plagiostomatous (plā"ji-ō-stom'ạ-tus), *a.* [< *Plagiostomata* + *-ous*.] Same as *plagiostomous*.

plagiostome (plā'ji-ō-stōm), *a.* and *n.* [< Gr. πλάγιος, oblique, + στόμα, mouth.] I. *a.* Plagiostomous.

II. *n.* A plagiostomous fish; any member of the *Plagiostomi*, as a selachian.

Plagiostomi (plā-ji-os'tō-mī), *n. pl.* [NL., < Gr. πλάγιος, oblique, + στόμα, mouth.] In the older systems, an order of chondropterygian or elasmobranchiate fishes, including all the sharks and rays. In some recent systems it has been used as a superordinal or subclass name of the same group. Its characteristics are the development of a distinct suspensorium for the mandible (consisting of the undivided palatoquadrate cartilage), five to seven pairs of branchial apertures, and no operculum.

plagiostomous (plā-ji-os'tō-mus), *a.* [As *Plagiostomi* + *-ous*.] Of or pertaining to the *Plagiostomi*. Also *plagiostomatous*.

Plagiotoma (plā-ji-ot'ō-mạ̈), *n.* [NL. (Dujardin), < Gr. πλάγιος, oblique, + -τομος, < τέμνειν, ταμεῖν, cut.] A genus of heterotrichous ciliate infusorians of the family *Bursariidæ*. *P. lumbrici* is known as the *bean-animalcule* of the intestine of the earthworm.

Plagiotremata (plā"ji-ō-trē'mạ-tạ̈), *n. pl.* [NL., < Gr. πλάγιος, oblique, + τρῆμα, hole.] A subclass of *Reptilia*: same as *Lepidosauria*.

plagiotropic (plā"ji-ō-trop'ik), *a.* [< Gr. πλάγιος, oblique, + τρόπος, a turning, direction, < τρέπειν, turn.] In *bot.*, exhibiting or characterized by plagiotropism.

plagiotropically (plā"ji-ō-trop'i-kạl-i), *adv.* With plagiotropism.

plagiotropism (plā-ji-ot'rō-pizm), *n.* [< *plagiotrop-ic* + *-ism*.] In *bot.*, oblique geotropism; a turning by which the organs of certain plants have their long axes more or less divergent from the vertical—that is, across the direction of gravitation or of the ray of light. Compare *orthotropism*.

> The *plagiotropism* of dorsi-ventral organs, such as shoots and leaves, is a more complicated phenomenon. It is the resultant expression of the effect of light and of gravity upon them, promoted, in many cases, by their own weight. In some cases light, and in others gravity, is the determining factor. *Vines*, Physiol. of Plants, p. 502.

plagium (plā'ji-um), *n.* [L., kidnapping: see *plagiary*.] In *civil* and *Scots law*, the crime of stealing men, women, or children, formerly punishable with death.

Plagopterinæ (plā-gop-tẹ-rī'nē), *n. pl.* [NL., < *Plagopterus* + *-inæ*.] A subfamily of cyprinoid fishes: same as *Medinæ*.

Plagopterus (plạ-gop'tẹ-rus), *n.* [NL. (Cope, 1874), so called with ref. to the large dorsal spine, which is capable of inflicting a wound; < L. *plaga*, a wound, + Gr. πτερόν, wing (fin).] A genus of cyprinoid fishes, with a stout spine on the front of the dorsal fin: same as *Meda*.

plague (plāg), *n.* [< ME. *plage*, < OF. *plague*, *plage*, vernacularly *plaie*, F. *plaie* = Sp. *plaga*, plague, *llaga*, wound, sore, ulcer, = Pg. *chaga*, wound, sore, ulcer, = It. *piaga*, wound, sore, calamity, = D. *plaag* = MLG. *plage* = OHG. *plāga*, MHG. *blāge*, *plāge*, *pflāge*, *phlāg*, G. *plage* = Icel. *plāga* = Sw. *plāga* = Dan. *plage*, plague, < LL. *plaga*, a plague, pestilence, affliction, slaughter, destruction; particular uses of L. *plaga*, a blow, shock, cut, thrust, injury, misfortune (= Gr. πληγή, a blow, shock, wound, misfortune), < *plangere* (√ *plag*) = Gr. πλήσσειν, strike.] 1. A blow or calamity; severe trouble or vexation; also, one who or that which troubles or vexes, or ravages or destroys.

> Oh, what a *plague* were it that a strange king, of a strange land and of a strange religion, should reign over us! *Latimer*, 1st Sermon bef. Edw. VI., 1549.

> He had a wife was the *plague* o' his days. *Farmer's Old Wife* (Child's Ballads, VIII. 257).

> But of all *plagues*, good Heaven, thy wrath can send, Save, save, oh, save me from the candid friend! *Canning*, Poetry of the Anti-Jacobin, p. 242.

> In 1280 the Bishop of Hebron, vicegerent of the patriarch, sends the thanks of the Franks, and adds that Armenia and Cyprus have been laid waste by a *plague* of locusts. *Stubbs*, Medieval and Modern Hist., p. 186.

2. Any epidemic disease of high mortality. The disease known specifically as *the plague*, or *bubo plague*, entered Europe from the Levant in the sixth century, and lingered there in scattered localities over a thousand years. It has appeared in various regions (Egypt, Turkey, Persia, etc.) in the nineteenth century; the last occurrence in Europe was in the Volga district, in 1878-9. Typical cases, after a period of incubation of from two to seven days, begin suddenly with prostration, headache, dizziness, and sometimes vomiting and diarrhea; after a few hours or one or two days a chill develops, followed by high fever with noisy delirium, passing into coma; on the second to the fourth day buboes, most frequently inguinal, develop; in non-fatal cases they more frequently suppurate than resolve; there may also be carbuncles, boils, and petechiæ; convalescence begins from the sixth to the tenth day. The mortality is extreme, sometimes running as high as 95 per cent. The black-death of the fourteenth century may have been a modified form of this plague; so, too, the Pali plague. Also called *the pest*, *the pestilence*, *glandular plague* or *pestilence*, *inguinal plague*, Levant or *Levantine plague*, *Justinian plague*.

> Therfore a gret fool were he that wolde presume to cure these *plagis* of pestilence that ben vncurable. *Book of Quinte Essence* (ed. Furnivall), p. 24.

> A *plague* upon the people fell, A famine after laid them low. *Tennyson*, The Victim.

3. As an expletive with the article *the*, used like *the devil*, *the deuce*, etc. Compare *devil*, 7.

> How *the plague* shall I be able to pass for a Jew? *Sheridan*, School for Scandal, iii. 1.

Indian plague, a pestilential disease which prevailed locally in northwestern India during the nineteenth century, similar in some respects to the plague as described under def. 2, and perhaps identical with it. Also called *Pali plague*.—**Plague on** or **upon**, may a plague or curse descend upon (the person or thing mentioned): commonly used lightly, in a diminished sense, and expressing mere annoyance.

> A *plague* o' both your houses! *Shak.*, R. and J., iii. 1. 94.

> *Plague on* your pity, ma'am! I desire none of it. *Sheridan*, School for Scandal, v. 2.

To be at the plague, to take the trouble. [Scotch.]

> But I can seldom *be at the plague*, an' it binna when my bluid 's up. *Scott*, Heart of Mid-Lothian, xxvi.

plague (plāg), *v. t.*; pret. and pp. *plagued*, ppr. *plaguing*. [= MLG. *plagen* = MHG. G. *plagen* = Sw. *plāga* = Dan. *plage* = OF. *plaier*, hurt, = Sp. *llagar*, hurt, *plagar*, plague, = Pg. *chagar*, hurt, = It. *piagare*, wound, hurt, < LL. *plagare*, wound, < L. *plaga*, a blow, wound: see *plague*, *n.*] 1. To vex; harass; trouble; annoy; tease.

> We but teach Bloody instructions, which, being taught, return To *plague* the inventor. *Shak.*, Macbeth, i. 7. 10.

> I think you are very foolish to *plague* yourself so. *Sheridan* (?), The Camp, ii. 1.

2. To infest with disease, calamity, or natural evil of any kind.

> Thus were they *plagued*, And worn with famine. *Milton*, P. L., x. 572.

=**Syn.** 1. *Torment*, *Worry*, etc. (see *tease*), gall, bore.—2. To afflict.

plagueful† (plāg'fụl), *a.* [< *plague* + *-ful*.] Abounding with plagues; infected with plagues. *Mir. for Mags.*

plague-mark (plāg'märk), *n.* Same as *plague-spot*.

plaguer (plā'gėr), *n.* [< *plague* + *-er*[1].] One who plagues or vexes.

plague-sore (plāg'sōr), *n.* A sore resulting from the plague.

> Thou art a boil, A *plague-sore*, an embossed carbuncle, In my corrupted blood. *Shak.*, Lear, ii. 4. 227.

> Come no more near me: Thou art a *plague-sore* to me. *Fletcher*, Humorous Lieutenant, iv. 4.

plague-spot (plāg'spot), *n.* 1. A spot characteristic of the plague or of some foul disease.

> The idea that he had deprived Sybil of her inheritance had . . . been the *plague-spot* of Hatton's life. *Disraeli*, Sybil, vi. 13.

2. A spot or locality where the plague or other foul disease is prevalent.

plaguily (plā'gi-li), *adv.* In a manner to vex, harass, or embarrass; vexatiously; hence also, humorously, greatly. [Colloq.]

> Most wicked woman, that hast so *plaguily* a corrupted mind as thou canst not keep thy sickness to thyself, but must most wickedly infect others. *Sir P. Sidney*, Arcadia, iii.

> I am hurt *plaguily*. *Fletcher*, Humorous Lieutenant, ii. 2.

> He was *plaguily* afraid and humbled. *Swift*, To Stella, xxxi.

plaguy (plā'gi), *a.* [< *plague* + *-y*[1].] 1†. Plague-stricken; infected with the plague; marked by the plague or other foul disease.

> Methinks I see him entering . . . *plaguy* houses, Reaching his dose, walking Moorfields for lepers. *B. Jonson*, Alchemist, i. 1.

> Complaining to me of their bad takings all the last *plaguy* summer. *Middleton*, Black Book.

2. Troublesome; vexatious; annoying. [Humorous.]

> This dragon he had a *plaguy* hide, Which could both sword and spear abide. *Sir Eglamore* (Child's Ballads, VIII. 197).

> Oh, 'twas a *plaguy* thump, charg'd with a vengeance! *Fletcher*, Mad Lover, v. 4.

plaguy (plā'gi), *adv.* [< *plaguy*, *a.*] Vexatiously; deucedly: as, *plaguy* hard; a *plaguy* long time. [Humorous.]

> He looked *plaguy* sour at me. *Steele*, Tatler, No. 25.

> You're so *plaguy* shy that one would think you had changed sexes. *Goldsmith*, Good-natured Man, ii.

plaice (plās), *n.* [Formerly also *plaise*, *place*; < ME. *plaice*, *playce*, *pleise*, < OF. *plais*, *plaïs*, F. *plaise*, also *plateuse*, *plie* = Sp. *platija*, < LL. *platessa*, a flatfish, plaice, < Gr. πλατύς, flat: see *plat*[3]. Cf. *place*, from the same ult. source.] 1. A fish of the family *Pleuronectidæ* and genus *Pleuronectes*, *P. platessa*. It is a well-known British food-fish, not found in American waters, growing to a weight of 8 or 10 pounds. See also cut under *asymmetry*.

Common Plaice (*Pleuronectes platessa*).

2. Hence, by extension, any one of various flatfishes or flounders of the family *Pleuronectidæ*. *Citharichthys sordidus* is a plaice common along the Pacific coast of America. *Rhomboidichthys lunatus* is a Bermuda plaice. The smooth plaice, or smooth-backed flounder, is *Pleuronectes glaber*.

plaice-mouth† (plās'mouth), *n.* A small wry mouth, like that of the plaice.

> Some innocent out of the hospital, that would stand with her hands thus, and a *plaise mouth*, and look upon you? *B. Jonson*, Epicœne, iii. 2.

plaice-mouthed† (plās'moutht), *a.* Having a wry mouth like that of a plaice; wry-mouthed.

> And keep his *plaise-mouth'd* wife in welts and gardes. *Lodge*, in Beloe's Anec. of Scarce Books, II. 113. (*Nares*.)

plaid (plad or plād), *n.* and *a.* [< Gael. *plaide* (= Ir. *plaide*), a blanket, plaid, contr. of *peallaid*, a sheepskin, < *peulle*, a skin, hide: see *pell*[1].] I. *n.* 1. A garment of woolen cloth, often having a tartan pattern. See *tartan*. It is a large rectangular piece of woolen stuff, and is worn in Scotland by both sexes for warmth and for protection against the weather. It is a special dress of the Highlanders, and forms part of the uniform of certain infantry regiments in the British army. A variety of the plaid is called *maud*.

> My *plaid* awa, my *plaid* away, And owre the hills and far awa. *The Elfin Knight* (Child's Ballads, I. 130).

> A himation, worn in the fashion of a shawl, as occasionally on early Greek figures, or as a *plaid*. *Encyc. Brit.*, VI. 465.

Highlander wearing modern Kilt and separate Plaid.

2. In general, any fabric having a pattern consisting of colored bars or stripes crossing each other in imitation of the Scottish tartan.—3. A pattern of bars crossing each other at right angles on anything.—**Belted plaid.** See *belted*.—**Shepherd's plaid.** Same as *shepherd's tartan* (which see, under *tartan*).

II. *a.* 1. Ornamented with a pattern of bars or stripes of color crossing one another at right angles: said especially of textile fabrics: as, a *plaid* silk ribbon; a *plaid* waistcoat.—2. Checkered. [U. S.; an improper use.]

plaided (plad'ed or plā'ded), *a.* [< *plaid* + *-ed*[2].] 1. Made of plaid, or having a similar pattern; tartan.

> A military troop Cheered by the Highland bagpipe, as they marched In *plaided* vest. *Wordsworth*.

2. Wearing a plaid.

> All *plaided* and plumed in their tartan array. *Campbell*, Lochiel's Warning.

plaiden (plad'en or plā'den), *n.* A corruption of *plaiding*.

plaiding (plad'ing or plā'ding), *n.* [< *plaid* + *-ing*[1].] 1. A strong woolen fabric differing from flannel in being twilled. It is used for blankets and plaids, and sometimes for dresses. [Scotch.]—2. Plaid; tartan.—3. A plaided pattern.

I could discern a partiality for white stuffs with apricot-yellow stripes, for *plaidings* of blue and violet, and various patterns of pink and mauve.
Harper's Mag., LXXIX. 844.

plain[1] (plān), *a.* and *n.* [I. *a.* < ME. *plain, playn, pleyn, plaine, playne, pleyne*, < OF. *plain*, F. *plain* = Pr. *plan* = Sp. *plano, llano* = Pg. *plano, lhano* = It. *piano*, < L. *planus*, flat, even, level, plain: see *plane*[1], a later form of the same word. II. *n.* < ME. *plaine, playne, pleyne* = MD. *pleine*, D. *plein* = G. *pläne* = Dan. *plæne* (< F.); cf. MLG. *plān* = MHG. *plān, plāne*, G. *plan* = Sw. *plan* (< L.); < OF. *plain*, m., *plaine, plaigne*, F. *plaine*, f., = Pr. *plana, planha, plaigna* = Sp. *llano*, m., *plana*, f., = Pg. *plano*, m., = It. *piano*, m., a plain; < L. *planum*, level ground, a plain, neut. of *planus*, level, plane: see I.] **I.** *a.* **1.** Flat; level; smooth; even; free from elevations and depressions: as, a *plain* surface or country.

This Contree is gode and *pleyn* and . . . of peple.
Mandeville, Travels, p. 258.

It [Lombardy] is wholly *plaine*, and beautified with . . . abundance of goodly rivers, pleasant meadowes, &c.
Coryat, Crudities, I. 109.

Three Townes situated vpon high white clay clifts; the other side all a low *playne* marish, and the river there but narrow. Quoted in *Capt. John Smith's* Works, I. 185.

Nor does the *plain* country in that land [the East] offer the refuge and rest of our own soft green.
Mrs. Gaskell, Sylvia's Lovers, xxxviii.

2. Open; unobstructed by intervening barriers or defenses.

Ffaire yche furde folowand on other,
And past furth prudly into the *plaine* feld.
Destruction of Troy (E. E. T. S.), l. 7215.

The xj kynges were departed and deseuered, and yeden oute in to the *playn* feldes with-oute the tentes, and made blowe a trompe high and clere.
Merlin (E. E. T. S.), ii. 154.

3. Easy; free from intricacies or difficulties: as, *plain* exercises in shorthand.—**4.** Undisguised; frank; sincere; unreserved.

He cannot flatter, he,
An honest mind and *plain*—he must speak truth!
Shak., Lear, ii. 2. 105.

There is at this time a friend of mine upon the seas—to be *plain* with you, he is a pirate—that hath wrote to me to work his freedom.
Beau. and Fl., Honest Man's Fortune, ii. 2.

If I cannot serve you, I will at once be *plain*, and tell you so.
Steele, Conscious Lovers, i. 2.

5. Clear; evident; manifest; easily perceived or understood: as, to make one's meaning *plain*; it was *plain* he was offended.

It was very *plain* that the Russian commanders were not provided with instructions.
Bruce, Source of the Nile, I. 29.

We have *plain* evidence of crystals being embedded in many lavas whilst the paste or basis has continued fluid.
Darwin, Geol. Observations, i. 6.

6. Unqualified; undisguised; unmistakable; sheer; downright; absolute.

This is *plain* confederacy to disgrace us.
B. Jonson, Cynthia's Revels, v. 2.

Others fell to *plaine* stealing, both night & day, from ye Indeans, of which they greevosly complained.
Bradford, Plymouth Plantation, p. 130.

Through the multitude of them that were to suffer, it could no more be call'd a Persecution, but a *plain* Warr.
Milton, Eikonoklastes, xi.

They suspected some malicious dealing, if not *plain* treachery. *N. Morton*, New England's Memorial, p. 107.

7. Without a figured pattern; unornamented with decorative patterns or designs; also, when applied to fabrics, untwilled or uncolored: as, *plain* black cloth; *plain* muslin.—**8.** Void of ornament or bright color; without embellishment; simple; unadorned.

Hauing obteyned my long expected wish, I doe in all humblenesse prostrate my selfe and this *plaine* discourse of my trauels to your most excellent Maiestie.
Webbe, Travels (ed. Arber), Ded., p. 15.

The women's dress [in Switzerland] is very *plain*, those of the best quality wearing nothing on their heads generally but furs which are to be met with in their own country. *Addison*, Remarks on Italy (ed. Bohn), I. 527.

I took a *plain* but clean and light summer dress from my drawer and put it on; it seemed no attire had ever so well become me. *Charlotte Brontë*, Jane Eyre, xxiv.

9. Without beauty; homely: as, she is *plain*, but clever.

Jer. By this light, she 's as handsome a girl as any in Seville.
Is. Then, by these eyes, I think her as *plain* a woman as ever I beheld. *Sheridan*, The Duenna, ii. 3.

I looked at my face in the glass, and felt it was no longer *plain*; there was hope in its aspect, and life in its colour.
Charlotte Brontë, Jane Eyre, xxiv.

Suppose her fair, her name suppose
Is Car, or Kitty;
She might be Jane—she might be *plain*—
For must the subject of my strain
Be always pretty? *F. Locker*, The Housemaid.

10. Artless; simple; unlearned; without artifice or affectation; unsophisticated.

I am . . . as you know me all, a *plain* blunt man,
That love my friend. *Shak.*, J. C., iii. 2. 222.

Of many *plain* yet pious Christians this cannot be affirmed. *Hammond*, Fundamentals.

You must take what he sayes patiently, because he is a *plaine* man.
Bp. Earle, Micro-cosmographie, A Blunt Man.

Those [Friends] who entered the army illustrated in their *plain* speech and quiet courage the virtues of their lineage. *The Century*, XXXVIII. 563.

11. Not highly seasoned; not rich; not luxuriously dressed: as, a *plain* diet.—**12.** Incomplex; simple.

Plain sounds = simplices sonos.
Hoole, tr. of The Visible World.

13. In *card-playing*, not trumps; lay: as, a *plain* card; a *plain* suit.—**14.** Whole-colored; not variegated: as, *plain* white eggs.—**15.** Smooth; unstriate, as muscular fiber.—**In plain**, plainly; in plain terms.

He tolde him point for point, in short and *playn*.
Chaucer, Clerk's Tale, l. 521.

Plain as a packstaff or **pikestaff**, perfectly plain; quite clear. See quotations under *packstaff*.—**Plain bonito.** See *bonito*.—**Plain cloth**, any untwilled fabric.—**Plain clothes**, the ordinary dress of civil life; non-official dress: opposed to *uniform*: as, a policeman or soldier in *plain clothes*.

They met his Royal Highness in *plain clothes*.
Thackeray, Virginians, lxi.

Plain compass, a simple form of surveyors' instrument, including a compass, a graduated circle, a main plate, sights, and levels. It is supported for use upon the head of the Jacob's-staff.—**Plain couching.** See *couching*[1], 5.—**Plain descant.** See *counterpoint*[2], 3.—**Plain dress**, dress without ornament, as worn by members of the Society of Friends.—**Plain drill.** See *drill*[1].—**Plain embroidery.** (*a*) Embroidery which is without raised work, or padding, or couching of elaborate character—that is, simple needlework on a flat foundation. (*b*) Embroidery in the same color as the ground.—**Plain harmony.** See *harmony*, 2 (*d*).—**Plain muscles** or **muscle-fibers**, unstriated muscles or muscle-fibers.—**Plain paper, sailing, stitch, titmouse**, etc. See the nouns.—**The plain language**, the manner of speech adopted by the Society of Friends. It disallows all merely ceremonious usages, as the plural *you* addressed to an individual, all titles of compliment or rank, etc. =**Syn. 4.** Unaffected, honest, candid, ingenuous, downright.—**5.** *Clear, Evident*, etc. (see *manifest*), distinct, patent, unmistakable, unequivocal, unambiguous, explicit, intelligible.—**8.** Unvarnished, unembellished.

II. *n.* **1.** An extent of level, or nearly level, land; a region not noticeably diversified with mountains, hills, or valleys. *The Plains*, in North America, are the lands lying between the 100th meridian and the eastern base of the Rocky Mountains. This region has a gradual slope from the mountains to the Missouri and Mississippi rivers, but is nowhere broken by any conspicuous ranges of hills. It is a region of small precipitation, wooded only along the banks of the streams, and not always there. The *Plains* and the *prairies* are not properly the same, from either a geographical or a climatological point of view. See *prairie*.

Attre gon men be the hille, besyde the *Pleynes* of Galylee, unto Nazarethe, where was wont to ben a gret Cytee and a fair. *Mandeville*, Travels, p. 112.

Ffrom thens a man may se all Arabye, and the Mownte of Abaryn, and Nebo, and Phasga, the *playnes* of Jordan, and Jherico, and the Dede see vnto the ston of Deserte.
Torkington, Diarie of Eng. Travell, p. 37.

This City of Lyons . . . is situate under very high rocks and hils on one side, and hath a very ample and spacious *plaine* on the other. *Coryat*, Crudities, I. 59.

2. A field; especially, a field of battle.

Pour forth Britannia's legions on the *plain*. *Arbuthnot.*

3. An open space surrounded by houses: as, St. Mary's *Plain*; the Theater *Plain*, in Norwich. *Halliwell*. [Local, Eng.]—**Cock of the plains.** See *cock*[1], and cut under *Centrocercus*.—**Plain of Mars**, in *palmistry*, the space in the middle of the palm of the hand between the line of the heart and the line of life, and surrounded by the mounts.—**The Plain**, in the legislatures of the first French revolution, the floor of the House, occupied by the more moderate party; hence, that party itself, as distinguished from *the Mountain*.

plain[1] (plān), *adv.* [< ME. *playn, pleyn*; < *plain*[1], *a.*] In a plain manner; plainly; clearly; openly; frankly; bluntly.

This is the poynt, to speken short and *pleyn*.
Chaucer, Gen. Prol. to C. T., l. 790.

Sir, to tell you *plain*,
I'll find a fairer face not wash'd to-day.
Shak., L. L. L., iv. 3. 272.

In them is *plainest* taught, and easiest learnt,
What makes a nation happy, and keeps it so.
Milton, P. R., iv. 361.

plain[1]† (plān), *v. t.* [< ME. *playnen*, etc.; < *plain*[1], *a.* Cf. *plane*[1], *v.*] **1.** To make plain, level, or even; smooth; clear.

Discreete demeanour . . . *playneth* the path to felicitie.
Lyly, Euphues, Anat. of Wit, p. 134.

The plot is also *plained* at the cities charges.
Heywood, If you Know not Me (Works, ed. Pearson, I. 280).

The streets of their cities and townes instead of pauing are planked with fir trees, *plained* & layd euen close the one to the other. *Hakluyt's Voyages*, I. 480.

2. To make plain or clear; explain.

His bretheren and his sustern gonne hym freyne
Why he so sorwful was in al his cheere,
And what thyng was the cause of al his peyne?
But al for noght, he nolde his cause *pleyne*.
Chaucer, Troilus, v. 1230.

By Aeromancy to discover doubts,
To *plain* out questions as Apollo did.
Greene, Friar Bacon and Friar Bungay.

What 's dumb in show, I'll *plain* in speech.
Shak., Pericles, iii., Prol.

plain[2] (plān), *v.* [< ME. *plainen, pleinen, pleynen*, < OF. *pleigner*, F. *plaindre* = Pr. *planher, playner, planger, plainer, planer* = Sp. *plañir* = It. *piangere, piagnere*, < L. *plangere*, lament, beat the breast or head as a sign of grief, lit. beat, strike, = Gr. πλήσσειν, strike: see *plague*. Cf. *complain*.] **I.** *intrans.* **1.** To lament; wail; mourn.

But man after his deth moot wepe and *pleyne*,
Though in this world he have care and wo.
Chaucer, Knight's Tale, l. 462.

Tereu, Tereu, and thus she gan to *plaine*
Most piteously, which made my halt to greeue.
Gascoigne, Philomene (ed. Arber), p. 80.

Though he *plain*, he doth not complain; for it is a harm, but no wrong, which he hath received.
Sir P. Sidney, Arcadia, ii.

The air was sad; but sadder still
It fell on Marmion's ear,
It *plain'd* as if disgrace and ill,
And shameful death, were near.
Scott, Marmion, iii. 12.

2†. To whinny: said of a horse.

Right as an hors that can both byte and *pleyne*.
Chaucer, Anelida and Arcite, l. 157.

II. *trans.* To lament; bewail; bemoan; mourn over.

Adam *playning* his case, God sent three Angels after her.
Purchas, Pilgrimage, p. 157.

Who can give tears enough to *plain*
The loss and lack we have?
Sir J. Harington, State of the Church of Eng.

plainant (plā'nant), *n.* [< F. *plaignant*, plaintiff, prop. ppr. of *plaindre*, complain: see *plain*[2], *v.*] In *law*, a plaintiff.

plainbacks (plān'baks), *n.* Bombazet. [Trade-name among weavers.]

plain-chant (plān'chant), *n.* Same as *plain-song*.

plain-clay (plān'klā), *n.* A British noctuid moth, *Noctua depuncta*.

plain-dealer (plān'dē'lėr), *n.* One who expresses his opinions with plainness; one who is frank, honest, and open in speaking and acting.

I the *Plain Dealer* am to act to-day, . . .
An honest man who, like you, never winks
At faults; but, unlike you, speaks what he thinks.
Wycherley, Plain Dealer, Prol.

Every man is more ready to trust the poor *plain-dealer* than the glittering false-tongued gallant.
Rev. T. Adams, Works, I. 29.

plain-dealing (plān'dē'ling), *a.* Dealing with sincerity and frankness; honest; open; speaking and acting without guile.

It must not be denied but I am a *plain-dealing* villain.
Shak., Much Ado, i. 3. 33.

It becomes us well
To get *plain-dealing* men about ourselves,
Such as you all are here.
Beau. and Fl., Maid's Tragedy, iv. 2.

plain-dealing (plān'dē'ling), *n.* Sincere, frank, and honest speech or conduct; conduct or dealing that is without guile, stratagem, or disguise; sincerity and honesty in thought and act.

Too little wit and too much *plain-dealing* for a statesman. *Sir J. Denham*, The Sophy, iii. 1.

plain-edge (plān'ej), *a.* In *lace-making*, not having a pearl-edge, especially in the case of pillow-lace, which is usually so decorated.

plain-hearted (plān'här'ted), *a.* Having a sincere heart; without guile or duplicity; of a frank disposition.

Free-spoken and *plain-hearted* men, that are the eyes of their country. *Milton*, On Def. of Humb. Remonst., § 1.

plain-heartedness (plān'här'ted-nes), *n.* Frankness of disposition; sincerity.

A religion that owns the greatest simplicity and openness and freedom and *plainheartedness*.
Hallywell, Moral Discourses (1692), p. 40. (*Latham.*)

plaining (plā'ning), *n.* [Verbal n. of *plain*[2], *v.*] Mourning; lamenting.

And in your clefts her *plainings* doe not smother,
But let that echo teach it to another!
W. Browne, Britannia's Pastorals, ii. 1.

plainly (plān'li), *adv.* [< ME. *plainly, pleynly, plainliche*, etc.; < *plain*[1] + *-ly*[2].] In a plain manner. (*a*) Smoothly; evenly. (*b*) Clearly; without obstruction or deception; in a way to be easily perceived or understood; unmistakably. (*c*) Without disguise or reserve; sincerely; honestly; bluntly; frankly. (*d*) Without ornament or embellishment; simply; soberly: as, a lady *plainly* dressed.

plainness (plăn'nes), *n.* The state or quality of being plain. (*a*) Evenness of surface; levelness. (*b*) Absence of ornament; lack of artificial show. (*c*) Openness; candor; blunt or unpolished frankness. (*d*) Clearness; distinctness; intelligibility. (*e*) Lack of beauty; homeliness. =Syn. (*d*) *Clearness, Lucidity*, etc. See *perspicuity*.

plain-pug (plăn'pug), *n.* A British geometrid moth, *Eupithecia subnotata*.

plain-singing (plăn'sing"ing), *n.* Same as *plain-song*. *W. Mason*, Eng. Church Music, iii. [Rare.]

plainsman (plānz'mạn), *n.*; pl. *plainsmen* (-men). A dweller on the plains.

> These *plainsmen* are far from being so heterogeneous a people as is commonly supposed.
> *T. Roosevelt*, Hunting Trips, p. 6.

plain-song (plăn'sông), *n.* 1. The unisonous vocal music which has been used in the Christian church from its earliest centuries. Its origin is unknown, but it contains elements taken from the ancient Greek music, and possibly also from the ancient Temple music of the Hebrews. It is often called *Gregorian*, from its most prominent early systematizer, or, in certain details, *Ambrosian*. It rests upon an elaborate system of octave scales or modes. (See *mode*l, 7.) According to the principles and rules of these modes, numerous melodies have been composed or compiled, which have become established by tradition or authority as parts of the liturgies of the Western Church in general and of the modern Roman Catholic Church in particular. This body of melodies includes a great variety of material adapted not only to every part of the liturgy, but to the several seasons of the Christian year. Plain-song melodies are distinguished by adherence to the medieval modes, by independence of rhythmical and metrical structure, and by a limited and austere use of harmony. Their effect is strikingly individual, dignified, and devotional. The style as such is obligatory in the services of the Roman Catholic Church, and has been perpetuated there with remarkable purity, in spite of its contrasts with modern music in general. It has exerted a profound influence upon general musical development, dominating that development until nearly 1600, and furnishing innumerable hints and themes to all subsequent styles. The medieval theory of counterpoint was a direct outgrowth of the melodic principle of plain-song. See *Gregorian, tone, model, antiphon, introit*, and *prick-song*. 2. A cantus firmus or theme chosen for contrapuntal treatment: so called because often an actual fragment of plain-song.—3. The simple notes of an air, without ornament or variation; hence, a plain, unexaggerated statement.

> All the ladies . . . do plainly report
> That without mention of them you can make no sport;
> They are your *playne song*, to singe descant upon.
> *R. Edwards*, Damon and Pythias.

> The humour of it is too hot, that is the very *plain-song* of it.
> *Shak.*, Hen. V., iii. 2. 6.

> *Audi.* Lingua, thou strikest too much upon one string,
> Thy tedious *plain-song* grates my tender ears.
> *Lin.* Tis plain, indeed, for truth no discant needs.
> *Brewer*, Lingua, i. 1.

plain-speaking (plān'spē"king), *n.* Plainness or bluntness of speech; candor; frankness. *Roget.*

plain-spoken (plăn'spō"kn), *a.* Speaking or spoken with plain, unreserved sincerity; frank.

> The reputation of a *plain-spoken*, honest man.
> *Dryden*, All for Love, Pref.

> The convention listened civilly to Mr. Curtis, who presented a very *plain-spoken* address from the New York reformers.
> *G. S. Merriam*, S. Bowles, II. 259.

plainstanes (plăn'stānz), *n. pl.* Flagstones; sidewalks; pavements. [Scotch.]

> I trow no grass grew beneath his feet on the *plainstanes* of London.
> *Galt*, The Steam-Boat, p. 262.

plaint (plānt), *n.* [< ME. *plainte, pleinte, pleynt*, < OF. *pleinte*, F. *plainte* = Pr. *planch* = Sp. *llanto*, OSp. *pranto* = Pg. *pranto* = It. *pianto*, < ML. *plancta*, f., plaint, L. *planctus*, a beating of the breast in lamentation, beating, lamentation, < *plangere*, beat the breast, lament: see *plain*[2].] 1. Lamentation; complaint; audible expression of sorrow; a sad or serious song.

> Greet was the pite for to here hem pleyne,
> Thurgh whiche *pleyntes* gan her wo encresse.
> *Chaucer*, Man of Law's Tale, l. 970.

> Thy accent will excell
> In Tragick *plaints* and passionate mischance.
> *Spenser*, Colin Clout, l. 427.

> Nor Tears can move,
> Nor *Plaints* revoke the Will of Jove.
> *Prior*, Turtle and Sparrow.

2†. Representation made of injury or wrong done; complaint.

> There are . . . three just grounds of war with Spain: one *plaint*, two upon defence.
> *Bacon*, War with Spain.

3. In *law*: (*a*) A statement of grievance made to a court for the purpose of asking redress. (*b*) The first process in an inferior court, in the nature of original process. [Rare.]

plain-table, *n.* See *plane-table*.

plaintful (plānt'fụl), *a.* [< *plaint* + *-ful*.] Complaining; expressing sorrow with an audible voice; also, containing a plaint.

> Hark, *plaintful* ghosts, infernal furies, hark
> Unto my woes the hateful heavens do send.
> *Sir P. Sidney*, Arcadia, iii.

plaintif†, *n.* and *a.* An obsolete form of *plaintiff, plaintive*.

plaintiff (plān'tif), *n.* and *a.* [Formerly also *plaintif, plaintife*; < ME. *plaintif, playntyf*, < OF. *plaintif*, complaining; as a noun, one who complains, a plaintiff: see *plaintive*.] I. *n.* In *law*, the person who begins a suit before a tribunal for the recovery of a claim: opposed to *defendant*.

> And 'tis well that you
> Begin, else I had been the *Plaintiff* now.
> *J. Beaumont*, Psyche, iv. 20.

Calling of the plaintiff. See *calling*.—**Nominal plaintiff**, one who appears by name as plaintiff upon the record, but has no interest in the action. Also *nominal party*.

II.† *a.* Complaining.

> His younger Son on the polluted Ground,
> First Fruit of Death, lies *Plaintiff* of a wound
> Given by a Brother's Hand.
> *Prior*, Solomon, iii.

plaintive (plān'tiv), *a.* [< F. *plaintif*, lamenting; < *plainte*, lament: see *plaint*. Cf. *plaintiff*.] 1†. Lamenting; complaining; giving utterance to sorrow or grief; repining.

> To soothe the sorrows of her *plaintive* son.
> *Dryden*, Iliad, i. 490.

2. Expressive of sorrow or melancholy; mournful; sad: said of things: as, a *plaintive* sound; a *plaintive* air; a *plaintive* song.

> Whose *plaintive* strain each love-sick miss admires,
> And o'er harmonious fustian half expires.
> *Byron*, Eng. Bards and Scotch Reviewers.

=Syn. *Plaintive, Querulous*, woful, rueful. *Plaintive* and *querulous* agree in expressing weakness. He who is *querulous* is ready to find fault over trivial matters, and in a weak, captious, tired way; there is a tone recognized as *querulous*. *Plaintive* is rarely said of persons; a *plaintive* tone or utterance conveys a subdued regret or lamentation: as, the *plaintive* note of the mourning dove. See *petulant*.

> The *plaintive* wave, as it broke on the shore,
> Seemed sighing for rest for evermore.
> *Jones Very*, Poems, p. 120.

> Quickened the fire and laid the board,
> Mid the crone's angry, *querulous* word
> Of surly wonder.
> *William Morris*, Earthly Paradise, III. 69.

plaintively (plān'tiv-li), *adv.* In a plaintive manner; mournfully; sadly.

plaintiveness (plān'tiv-nes), *n.* The quality of being plaintive; mournfulness.

plaintless (plānt'les), *a.* [< *plaint* + *-less*.] Without complaint; unrepining.

> By woe, the soul to daring action swells;
> By woe, in *plaintless* patience it excels.
> *Savage*, The Wanderer, ii.

plain-wanderer (plān'won"dėr-ėr), *n.* A bush-quail of the genus *Pedionomus*: as, the collared *plain-wanderer*, *P. torquatus*. [A book-name.]

plain-wave (plān'wāv), *n.* A British geometrid moth, *Acidalia inornata*.

plain-work (plān'wėrk), *n.* Plain needlework, as distinguished from embroidery.

plaisance†, *n.* [< F. *plaisance*, pleasance: see *pleasance*.] An obsolete form of *pleasance*.

> *Plaisance*, and joy, and a lively spirit, and a pleasant conversation, and the innocent caresses of a charitable humanity, is not forbidden.
> *Jer. Taylor*, Works (ed. 1835), I. 742.

plaise†, *n.* See *plaice*.

plaister, *n.* and *v.* An obsolete or archaic form of *plaster*.

plait (plăt), *n.* [Also *plat, pleat*, and (obs.) *plight*; early mod. E. also *playt, pleyght*, etc.; < ME. *plaite, playte*, < OF. *pleit, plet, ploit*, F. *pli*, a fold, ply, = Pr. *pleg, plec* = Sp. *pliegue* = Pg. *prega* = It. *piega*, a fold, < ML. as if **plictum*, neut., **plicta*, fem., for *plicatum, plicata*, neut. and fem. of L. *plicatus*, pp. of *plicare*, fold: see *ply*.] 1. A flattened gather or fold; an overlapping fold made by doubling cloth or some similar fabric in narrow strips upon itself.

> They vse all one maner of appareyle: as longe coates withowte *pleyghtes* and with narrowe sleaues, after the maner of the Hungaryans.
> *R. Eden*, tr. of Sigismundus Liberus (First Books on America, ed. Arber, p. 320).

> That attire,
> E'en as it sits on thee, not a *plait* alter'd.
> *Middleton*, A Mad World, iv. 4.

> It is very difficult to trace out the figure of a vest through all the *plaits* and folding of the drapery.
> *Addison.*

2. A braid, as of hair, straw, etc.

> But in and cam the Queen hersel,
> Wi' gowd *plait* on her hair.
> *Mary Hamilton* (Child's Ballads, III. 325).

> A high crown of shining brown *plaits*, with curls that floated backward.
> *George Eliot*, Felix Holt, v.

3. Rope-yarn strands braided into sennit.—**Brazilian, Leghorn, etc., plait.** See the qualifying words.

plait (plăt), *v.* [Also *plat, pleat*, and (obs.) *plight*; < ME. *plaiten, playtyn, plaitin, pleten*, < *playte, plaite*, etc.: see *plait, n.*] I. *trans.* 1. To fold; double in narrow strips: as, to *plait* a gown or a sleeve. See *plaiting* and *box-plaiting*.—2. To braid; interweave the locks or strands of: as, to *plait* the hair.

> She has *plaited* her yellow locks
> A little abune her bree.
> *Hynde Etin* (Child's Ballads, I. 294).

> I'll weave her Garlands, and I'll *pleat* her Hair.
> *Prior*, Henry and Emma.

3. To mat; felt. *E. H. Knight.*

II.† *intrans.* To twist; twine.

> The worm lept out, the worm lept down,
> She *plaited* round the stone;
> And ay as the ship came to the land
> She banged it off again.
> *The Laidley Worm of Spindleston-heugh* (Child's Ballads, I. 285).

plaited (plā'ted), *p. a.* 1. Folded; made in or with, or marked by, folds or flattened flutings; pleated: as, a shirt with a *plaited* bosom.

> The Romaines, of any other people most seuere censurers of decencie, thought no vpper garment so comely for a ciuill man as a long *playted* gowne.
> *Puttenham*, Arte of Eng. Poesie, p. 237.

2. In *bot.* and *zoöl.*, folded lengthwise like the plaits of a closed fan; fluted.—3. Wrinkled; contracted; knitted.

> A conflicting of shame and ruth
> Was in his *plaited* brow.
> *Keats*, Endymion, i.

4. Braided; interwoven: as, *plaited* hair.

> Though barks or *plaited* willows make your hive,
> A narrow inlet to their cells contrive.
> *Addison*, tr. of Virgil's Georgics, iv.

5†. Tangled; intricate.

> Time shall unfold what *plaited* cunning hides.
> *Shak.*, Lear, i. 1. 283.

Plaited lace. See *lace*.—**Plaited stitch**, one of the stitches of worsted work or Berlin wool work, in which the threads span a considerable distance at each insertion, the result being a sort of herring-bone pattern.—**Plaited string work**, a kind of fancy work made with small cord, or ordinary string, narrow ribbon, or tape, which is plaited or twisted into simple patterns.—**Plaited worms**, the *Aspidogasteridæ*.

plaiter (plā'tėr), *n.* [< *plait* + *-er*[1].] One who or that which plaits or braids; especially, an implement for producing plaits of regular size, as in cloth.

plaiting (plā'ting), *n.* [Verbal n. of *plait, v.*] 1. The act or process of making plaits or folds, or of interweaving or braiding two or more strands, fibers, etc.

> *Plaiting* appears to have been the process first practised; for short fibers, such as grass, rushes, &c., can be used without the aid of spinning by this means.
> *A. Barlow*, Weaving, p. 404.

2. Plaits, folds, or braids taken collectively.—3. In *hat-making*, the felting or interweaving of the hair to form the body by means of pressure, motion, moisture, and heat. Also called *hardening*.

plaiting-machine (plā'ting-mạ-shēn"), *n.* A machine for forming plaits in cloth; a plaiter. In simple forms it is merely a board with a series of needles hinged to one side, the fabric being folded in plaits under the needles in any manner desired, and held in position by the needles till the form has been impressed by a hot iron. Other machines, whether serving as attachments to sewing-machines or working independently, operate by means of reciprocating blades, which tack or push the fabric into plaits, these plaits being fixed by means of hot irons or heated cylinders.

plait-work (plăt'wėrk), *n.* Decoration by means of interlacing or interwoven bands, seeming as if plaited together. Compare *strap-work*.

plakat (plak'at), *n.* [Siamese name.] The fighting-fish.

plan (plan), *n.* [= D. G. Dan. Sw. *plan*, < F. *plan*, a ground-plot of a building (= Sp. *plan*, *plano* = Pg. *plano* = It. *piano*), < *plan*, flat, a later form than the vernacular *plain*, < L. *planus*, flat, plane: see *plain*[1], *plane*[1].] 1. The representation of anything drawn on a plane, as a map or chart; specifically, the representation of a building or other structure in horizontal section, as it stands or is intended to stand on the ground, showing its extent, and the division and distribution of its area into apartments, rooms, passages, etc., or its method of construction and the relation of its parts. The *raised plan* of a building is the same as an *elevation*. A *geometrical plan* is one drawn to scale, or one in which the solid and vacant parts are represented in their natural proportions. A *perspective plan* is one the lines of which follow the rules of perspective, thus showing more distant parts smaller than they are in fact in relation to the nearer parts. The term *plan* may be applied to the draft or representation of any projected work on paper or on a plane surface: as, the *plan* of a town or city, or of a harbor or fort. See cuts under *camp* and *canal-lock*.

2. Disposition of parts according to a certain design.

> Expatiate free o'er all this scene of man,
> A mighty maze! but not without a *plan*.
> *Pope*, Essay on Man, i. 6.

> Man only mars kind Nature's *plan*,
> And turns the fierce pursuit on man.
> *Scott*, Rokeby, iii. 1.

3. A formulated scheme for the accomplishment of some object or the attainment of an end; the various steps which have been thought out and decided upon for the carrying out of some project or operation.

> Where there seemed nothing but confusion, he can now discern the dim outlines of a gigantic *plan*.
> *H. Spencer*, Social Statics, p. 322.

> The very fact of a *plan* implies a logical procedure.
> *W. L. Davidson*, Mind, XII. 253.

4. A method or process; a way; a custom.

> For why? because the good old rule
> Sufficeth them, the simple *plan*,
> That they should take who have the power,
> And they should keep who can.
> *Wordsworth*, Rob Roy's Grave.

5. A type of structure: as, man is the highest development of the vertebrate *plan*; the *plan* of a mollusk or an insect.—**American plan.** See *American*.—**Common plan**, in *biol.*, an archetype.—**Details of a plan.** See *detail*.—**European plan.** See *European*.—**Half-breadth plan**, in *ship-building*, a plan showing the

Half-breadth Plan.

various lines of one longitudinal half of a ship projected on the horizontal plane.—**Hemal plan**, in mollusks, that modification of the common plan in which, by disproportionate growth of the postabdomen, the intestine acquires a hemal flexure: distinguished from *neural plan*.—**Instalment plan.** See *instalment*.—**Neural plan**, in mollusks, that modification of the common plan in which, by disproportionate growth of the abdomen, the intestine acquires a neural flexure: distinguished from *hemal plan*.—**Plan of campaign.** (*a*) A formulated scheme for carrying on a campaign. (*b*) In Ireland, a system of procedure formed in 1886 and supported by the National League. The officers of the League, acting as trustees, receive the rent of tenants on rack-rented estates; this money, less a certain abatement demanded by the tenants, is offered to the landlord; if the latter refuses it, it is used for support in cases of eviction.—**Working-plan**, a draft, drawn to a large scale, supplied to artisans or workmen to work from.=**Syn. 1.** Draft, delineation, sketch.—**3.** *Plan, Scheme, Project, Design*, plot. *Design* may represent the end which a *plan*, *scheme*, or *project* is intended to promote. They all indicate thought given to the general aim and to the details. *Scheme* is the most likely to represent something speculative or visionary: as, he was full of *schemes*; *project* stands next to it in this respect, but *project* may also be the most definite or concrete: as, a *project* for building a bridge. *Plan* is the least definite; *design* and *plan* may be very indefinite, or have a concrete sense: as, a *design* or plan of going away; a *design* or *plan* of a house. *Scheme* is often used in a bad sense; *design* sometimes.

> Lay square the blocks upon the slip,
> And follow well this *plan* of mine.
> *Longfellow*, Building of the Ship.

> The *scheme* of nature itself is a *scheme* unstrung and mistuned. *Bushnell*, Nature and the Supernat., p. 46.

> And in my ear
> Vented much policy, and *projects* deep
> Of enemies, of aids, battels, and leagues.
> *Milton*, P. R., iii. 391.

> O Painter of the fruits and flowers!
> We thank thee for thy wise *design*,
> Whereby these human hands of ours
> In Nature's garden work with thine.
> *Whittier*, Lines for an Agricultural Exhibition.

plan (plan), *v. t.*; pret. and pp. *planned*, ppr. *planning*. [< *plan*, *n.*] **1.** To lay down on paper the different parts, divisions, dimensions, and methods of construction of (a machine, ship, building, etc.): as, to *plan* an edifice.—**2.** To scheme; lay plans for; devise ways and means for: as, to *plan* the conquest of a country; to *plan* one's escape.

> *Plan* with all thy arts the scene of fate. *Pope*.

=**Syn. 1.** To figure, sketch out, delineate.

planæa (plā̤-nē'ạ̈), *n.* [NL., < L. *planus*, flat: see *plain*[1], *plane*[1].] A theoretical organism, corresponding to the fourth stage in the development of an ovum; a hypothetical multicellular astomatous animal, whose larval form should be that of a ciliated planula. See *planula*. Also called *blastæa*. *Haeckel*.

Planæadæ (plā̤-nē'ạ̈-dē), *n. pl.* [NL., < *planæa* + *-adæ*.] A hypothetical group of animals having the form of a ciliated planula and the morphological valence of a blastula, supposed to have arisen in the primordial geologic period in the direct line of descent of the remote ancestors of the human race. *Haeckel*.

planar (plā'när), *a.* [< L. *planar-ius*, flat: see *planary*.] Lying in a plane; planary; flat.—**Planar dyadic.** See *dyadic*.

Planaria (plā̤-nā'ri-ạ̈), *n.* [NL. (Müller, 1776), < LL. *planarius*, flat.] The typical genus of *Planariidæ*. *P. torva* is an example.

planarian (plā̤-nā'ri-ạn), *a.* and *n.* [< LL. *planarius*, flat (see *planary*), + *-an*.] **I.** *a.* Flat, as a turbellarian; belonging to the *Planarida* or *Dendrocœla*. See cut under *Dendrocœla*.

II. *n.* A member of the suborder *Planarida*.

Planarida (plā̤-nar'i-dạ̈), *n. pl.* [NL., < LL. *planarius*, flat, + *-ida*.] A suborder of *Turbellaria*, containing the rhabdocœlous and dendrocœlous turbellarian worms; the planarians. When the so-called rhynchocœlous turbellarians or nemertean worms are excluded, *Planarida* become the same as *Turbellaria*. They are flatworms, mostly oval or elliptical in form, moving by means of vibratile cilia. They are hermaphrodite. In some the intestine is straight and simple or rhabdocœlous, in others branched and complicated or dendrocœlous. They are mostly aquatic, inhabiting both fresh and salt water; but some, the land-planarians, are found in moist earth. See cut under *Dendrocœla*.

planaridan (plā̤-nar'i-dạn), *a.* and *n.* **I.** *a.* Planarian in a broad sense; turbellarian.

II. *n.* A planarian.

planariform (plā̤-nar'i-fôrm), *a.* [< LL. *planarius*, flat, level, + *forma*, form.] Like a planarian in form; planaridan. Also *planarioid*.

Planariidæ (plan-ạ-ri'i-dē), *n. pl.* [NL., < *Planaria* + *-idæ*.] A family of monogonoporous *Dendrocœla* of an oblong form, without a foot differentiated from the body, typified by the genus *Planaria*.

planarioid (plā̤-nā'ri-oid), *a.* [< LL. *planarius*, flat, + Gr. εἶδος, form.] Same as *planariform*.

planary (plā'nạ-ri), *a.* [< LL. *planarius*, flat, level, < L. *planus*, level, plane: see *plain*[1], *plane*[1].] Lying in one plane; flat.

planate (plā'nāt), *a.* [< NL. **planatus*, < L. *planus*, flat: see *plane*[1].] In *entom.*, flat; forming a plane; flattened.

planceer†, *n.* Same as *plancher*.

planch (planch), *n.* [< F. *planche*, < L. *planca*, a board, plank: see *plank*.] **1**†. A plank. *Fanshaw*.—**2.** In *enameling*, a slab of fire-brick or baked fire-clay used to support the work while it is baked in the oven.—**3.** A flat iron shoe for a mule. *E. H. Knight*.

planch† (planch), *v. t.* [< *planch*, *n.*] To plank; make of or cover with planks or boards. Also *plancher*.

> And to the vineyard is a *planched* gate.
> *Shak.*, M. for M., iv. 1. 30.

> Yet with his hoofes doth beat and rent
> The *planched* floore.
> *Gorges*, tr. of Lucan. (*Nares.*)

plancha (plan'chạ̈), *n.* [Mex.] In the Mexican silver-mines, a charge of ore ready for smelting, and also the disk or plate of argentiferous lead produced by the operation.

plancher† (plan'chėr), *n.* [Also *planceer*; early mod. E. also *plauncher*; < F. *plancher*, a floor or ceiling of boards, < *planche*, a board, plank: see *planch*, *plank*.] **1.** A plank.

> Upon the ground doth lie
> A hollow *plancher*. *Lyly*, Maid's Metamorph.

> Th' anatomized fish, and fowls from *planchers* sprong.
> *Drayton*, Polyolbion, iii. 272

2. A floor of wood.

> The holys that ben made forr hand gunnys, they ben scarse kne hey fro the *plawncher*, and of soche holis ben made fyve. *Paston Letters*, I. 83.

> Oak, cedar, and chestnut are the best builders: some are best for plough timber, as ash: some for *planchers*, as deal. *Bacon*, Nat. Hist., § 658.

3. In *anat.*, the inferior wall or boundary of a cavity.

plancher† (plan'chėr), *v.* [Early mod. E. also *plauncher*; < *plancher*, *n.*] **I.** *intrans.* To make a floor of wood. *Abp. Sancroft*, Letter, 1691, in D'Oyly, II. 16.

II. *trans.* Same as *planch*.

> Towers were *plauncherd*, & battlements and portcolyses of timber set vp. *Golding*, tr. of Cæsar, fol. 133.

planchet (plan'chet), *n.* [< F. *planchette*, a small board, a plane table, a circumferentor, formerly also the bottom of a stump, a bush, etc. (= Sp. *plancheta* = Pg. *prancheta*, a circumferentor), dim. of *planche*, a board: see *planch*, *plank*.] A flat piece of metal intended to receive a die-impression for a coin; a coin-blank.

planchette (plan-chet'; as F., ploṅ-shet'), *n.* [< F. *planchette*, a small board, a circumferentor: see *planchet*.] **1.** A small heart-shaped or triangular board mounted on three supports, of which two, placed at the angles of the base, are easily moving casters, and the third, placed at the apex, is a pencil-point. If the tips of the fingers of one person, or of two, are placed lightly upon it, the board will often, after a time, move without conscious effort on the part of the operator, and the pencil-point will, it is said, trace lines, words, and even sentences. It was invented about 1855, and was for a time an object of not a little superstition.

2. A circumferentor.

plane[1] (plān), *a.* and *n.* [I. *a.* < F. *plan* (fem. *plane*) = Sp. *plano* = Pg. *plano* = It. *piano*, < L. *planus*, flat, level, plane, plain: see *plain*[1], *a.* II. *n.* < F. *plan* = Sp. Pg. *plano* = It. *piano*, < NL. *planum*, a geometrical plane: cf. L. *planum*, level ground, a plain, neut. of L. *planus*, level, flat, plane, plain: see *plain*[1], *n.* Cf. *plan*, *n.* *Plane*[1], *plain*[1], *plan*, *piano*, are from the same L. word.] **I.** *a.* **1.** Having the character of a plane; contained within a plane: as, a *plane* mirror; a *plane* curve. In *n*-dimensional geometry, sometimes applied to a linear manifold of any number of dimensions, for which *flat* is generally used.

2. In *bot.*, having a flat surface or surfaces.—**3.** In *entom.*, flat and not deflexed; flat at the margins: as, *plane* elytra.—**Plane angle.** See *angle*[3], 1.—**Plane ashler.** See *ashler*, 3.—**Plane chart, curve, function, geometry, inflection.** See the nouns.—**Plane cubic parabola.** See *cubic*.—**Plane scale**, in *nav.*, a scale on which are graduated chords, sines, tangents, secants, rhumbs, geographical miles, etc.—**Plane screw**, a disk with a spiral thread upon its side.—**Plane surveying**, the surveying of tracts of moderate extent, without regarding the curvature of the earth.—**Plane trigonometry.** See *trigonometry*.—**Plane wings**, in *entom.*, wings which are extended horizontally in repose.

II. *n.* **1.** A geometrical surface such that if any two points in it are joined by a straight line, the line will lie wholly on the surface; a surface such that two of them which have any three points in common must coincide over their whole extent; hence, a real surface having (approximately) this form. It is thus the simplest of all geometrical surfaces. A plane may also be defined as a surface of the form which is the ideal limit toward which the surfaces of three rigid solids, A, B, C, approximate, if these are ground together in successive pairs, AB, BC, CA, AB, and so on indefinitely. In higher geometry a plane is considered as unlimited; but in elementary geometry a part of such a surface is also called a *plane*.

Specifically—**2.** In *biol.*: (*a*) An ideal surface of extension in any axis of an organism: as, the vertical longitudinal *plane* of the body. (*b*) A surface approximately flat or level: a "horizon": as, the *plane* of the teeth or of the diaphragm.—**3.** In *coal-mining*, any slope or incline on which coal is raised or lowered, but usually applied to self-acting inclines, or those on which the coal is lowered by gravity. [Pennsylvania anthracite region.] In England any main road, whether level or inclined, may be called a *plane*.—**4.** In *crystal.*, one of the natural faces of a crystal.—**5.** Figuratively, a grade of existence or a stage of development: as, to live on a higher *plane*.—**Alveolocondylean plane.** See *craniometry*.—**Aspect of a plane.** See *aspect*.—**Axial, basal, circular plane.** See the adjectives.—**Camper's plane**, the plane passing through the auricular points and the base of the inferior nasal spine. Also called *auriculospinal plane*.—**Cleavage-plane**, in *mineral.*, a surface produced by cleavage.

> The flat surfaces obtained by splitting a crystal are called its *cleavage planes*. *Encyc. Brit.*, XVI. 347.

Composition plane. See *composition*.—**Cyclic planes of a cone of the second order.** See *cyclic*.—**Cyclifying, diagonal, diametral, directing plane.** See the adjectives.—**Double-acting inclined plane**, in *rail.*, etc., an inclined plane worked by the gravity of the load conveyed, the loaded wagons which descend being made to pull up the empty ones by means of a rope passing round a pulley or drum at the top of the plane.—**Double-tangent plane.** See *double*.—**Flecnodal, fleflecnodal, focal, frontal, horizontal plane.** See the adjectives.—**Glabello-lambdoidean plane of Hamy**, the plane of the glabella and lambda, perpendicular to the median plane.—**Glabello-occipital plane**, the plane of the glabello-occipital diameter, perpendicular to the median plane.—**Inclined plane**, in *mech.*, a plane inclined to the horizon, or forming with a horizontal plane any angle whatever excepting a right angle. It is one of the two fundamental simple machines, the other being the lever. In the figure, AC is the inclined plane, CB the height of the plane, BA its base, and BAC the angle of inclination or elevation. The power necessary to sustain any weight on an inclined plane is to

C B A

Inclined Plane.

the weight as the height of the plane to its length, or as CB to CA. This was first proved by Stevinus, as follows. Let the two ends of a chain be joined, and let it be then hung over the inclined plane. Then, the festoon which hangs below AB pulls equally upon the two ends, and consequently the part lying on AC balances the part on BC—that is, weights proportional to the lengths of those two sides of the triangle balance one another. Hence, the less the height of the plane in proportion to its length, or the less the angle of inclination, the greater the mechanical effect, or the less the height in proportion to the length the less in the same proportion will be the weight on the plane which balances a given weight hanging vertically. The name *inclined plane* is sometimes loosely applied to a short railroad of steep grade, where the cars are drawn up the incline by means of a wire rope moved by a stationary engine at the top of the slope, or where special forms of rail and engine are used to overcome the grade. The inclined plane of Mahanoy, Pennsylvania, is an example of the first, the Mount Washington Railroad, New Hampshire, of the second. Inclined planes have been used to lift canal-boats from one level to another, and more recently, as at Cincinnati and at Hoboken, New Jersey, for lifting street-cars and passengers.—**Index of a plane.** See *index*.—**Meckel's plane,** the plane of the auricular and alveolar points.—**Median, mesial plane.** See the adjectives.—**Merkel's plane,** the plane of the auricular points and the lower border of the orbits.—**Metatatic plane,** a plane which contains two metatatic principal axes.—**Naso-iniac plane,** the plane of the nasion and the inion, perpendicular to the median plane.—**Naso-opisthiac plane,** the plane of the nasion and the opisthion, perpendicular to the median plane.—**Nuchal plane,** the surface of the occipital bone between the superior curved line and the foramen magnum.—**Objective, oblique, original plane.** See the adjectives.—**Occipital plane,** the surface of the occipital bone above the superior curved line.—**Orbital plane,** the orbital surface of the superior maxillary bone.—**Osculating plane.** See *osculate*.—**Palatine plane of Barclay,** in *craniom.*, the plane tangent to the arch of the palate along the middle line.—**Pencil of planes.** See *pencil*¹.—**Perspective plane.** See *perspective*.—**Pitch of a plane.** See *pitch*¹.—**Plane at infinity.** See *infinity*, 3.—**Plane of Aeby,** the plane of the nasion and the basion, perpendicular to the median plane.—**Plane of Baer,** in *craniom.*, the plane determined by the superior border of the zygomatic arches.—**Plane of Blumenbach,** in *craniom.*, the horizontal plane upon which the skull, without the mandible, rests.—**Plane of Busk,** the plane of the bregma and the auricular points.—**Plane of comparison,** in *fort.*, a datum-plane; a horizontal plane passing through the highest or lowest part of a fortification or its site.—**Plane of Daubenton,** the plane of the opisthion and the inferior border of the orbits.—**Plane of defilade,** in *fort.*, a plane passing through the interior crest or the highest point of a work, and parallel to the plane of site.—**Plane of flotation.** See *flotation*.—**Plane of mastication,** the plane tangent to the masticating surface of the teeth of the upper jaw.—**Plane of Morton,** the plane passing through the most prominent points of the occipital and parietal protuberances.—**Plane of polarization.** See *polarization*.—**Plane of projection.** Same as *perspective plane*.—**Plane of Rolle,** the plane of the auricular and the alveolar points.—**Plane of the ischium,** in *obstet.*, the lateral wall of the true pelvis, extending from the iliopectineal line to the end of the ischial tuberosity, and including small parts of the ilium and pubis.—**Plane of the picture.** Same as *perspective plane*.—**Polar curve of a plane.** See *polar*.—**Polar plane of a point.** See *polar*.—**Pole of a plane.** See *pole*².—**Popliteal plane,** the popliteal surface of the femur.—**Primitive plane.** See *primitive*.—**Prismatic planes.** See *prismatic*.—**Sagittal plane,** the median longitudinal and vertical plane of bilateral animals: so called because the sagittal suture of the skull lies in this plane.—**Temporal plane,** the temporal surface of the cranium.—**To detail on the plane.** See *detail*.—**Twinning-plane.** See *twin*.=**Syn. 1.** See *plain*¹, n.

plane¹ (plān), *v. t.*; pret. and pp. *planed*, ppr. *planing*. [< *plane*¹, *a.* Cf. *plain*¹ and *plane*², *v.*, ult. the same word.] To make plane or smooth; make clear.

> What student came but that you *planed* her path
> To Lady Psyche? *Tennyson*, Princess, iv.

plane² (plān), *v. t.*; pret. and pp. *planed*, ppr. *planing*. [< ME. *planen*, < OF. (and F.) *planer* = It. *pianare*, < LL. *planare*, plane (with a cutting-tool), make level, < L. *planus*, level: see *plane*¹.] 1. To make smooth, especially by the use of a plane: as, to *plane* wood.—2†. To rub out; erase.

> He *planed* awey the names everichon
> That he biforn had writen in his tables.
> *Chaucer*, Summoner's Tale, l. 50.

plane² (plān), *n.* [< F. *plane*, a carpenters' tool, < ML. *plana*, a carpenters' tool, < LL. *planare*, plane (with a cutting-tool), make level: see *plane*², *v.*] 1. A tool for paring, smoothing, truing, and finishing woodwork. The essential parts of a plane are a stock or frame of wood or metal, having a smooth, concave, or convex base or sole, and a throat in which is placed a steel cutter called the *plane-iron* or *bit*. Various devices are used to keep the bit in position in the stock, the most simple and common being a wedge of wood. Planes are made in a great variety of shapes and sizes, and range from 1 to 72 inches in length. Nearly all are distinguished by names having reference to the particular kind of work for which they are designed, as the *edge-plane*, *molding-plane*, and *smoothing-plane*. Planes are also used for truing soft metal surfaces. Plane-irons are inserted in their stocks at various pitches or angles, according to the duty they are to perform. Common pitch, or 45° from the horizontal line, is used in all bench-planes for soft woods. The pitch is increased with the hardness of the material to be worked. See *pitch*¹ and *plane-stock*, and cut in next column.

2. A metallic gage or test for a true surface; a true plane or plane surface; a surface-plate.—3. An instrument, resembling a plasterers' trowel, used by brickmakers for striking off clay projecting above the top of the mold.—**Box-slipped plane,** a plane provided with slips of boxwood to afford a more durable wearing surface.—**Circular plane,** a plane having a steel sole which is flexible and can be adjusted to the required arc. Also called *round plane* and *rounding-plane*.—**Combination plane.** See *combination*.—**Concave plane.** Same as *compass-plane*.—**Coopers' plane,** a long plane set obliquely, with the sole upward, used for jointing staves. Also called *jointer*.—**Dovetail-plane,** a side rabbet-plane having a very narrow sole, so that it can be used to dress the sides of dovetail-tenons or -mortises.—**Fork-staff plane,** a plane used by joiners for working convex or cylindrical surfaces.—**Hollow plane,** a molding-plane with a convex sole.—**Joiners' plane.** See *joiner*.—**Long plane,** a joiners' plane 27 inches long, used when a piece of stuff is to be planed very true. *E. H. Knight*.—**Mouth of a plane.** See *mouth*.—**Round-nosed plane,** in *joinery*, a bench-plane with a rounded sole, used for coarse work.—**Round plane,** a round-soled plane used for making beads, stair-rails, and other rounded work. Also called *rounding-plane*.—**Scale-board plane,** a plane for splitting off from a block the wide, thin chips or sheets of wood for making a usual form of hat-box, etc. It is either pulled or driven over the stuff, the thickness of each shaving or scale-board depending upon the projection of the iron. Sometimes the iron is fixed and the wood is drawn over it, the scale-board dropping down through an opening in the bench. Also called *scabbard-plane*. (See also *bench-plane*, *block-plane*, *fore-plane*, *jack-plane*, *rabbet-plane*, *trying-plane*.)

Planes.

a, plane-iron; *b*, wooden wedge for front of iron as used in *c* and *d*; *c*, fore-plane; *d*, smoother-plane; *e*, jointer-plane; *f*, iron jack-plane; *g*, iron block-plane; *h*, wooden jack-plane; *i*, wooden block-plane.

plane³ (plān), *n.* [< ME. *plane*, < OF. *plane*, F. *plane*, also *platane* = Sp. *plátano* = Pg. It. *platano*, < L. *platanus*, < Gr. πλάτανος, the plane-tree, < πλατύς, broad: see *plat*³.] The plane-tree.

> In serve and peche, in *plane* and popule.
> *Palladius*, Husbondrie (E. E. T. S.), p. 92.

Mock-plane, the sycamore maple, *Acer Pseudo-platanus*, whose leaves resemble those of the plane-tree. See under *maple*.

plane-bit (plān'bit), *n.* The cutter of a plane; a plane-iron. *E. H. Knight*.—**Plane-bit holder,** a device for holding a plane-bit to the stone while it is ground.

plane-guide (plān'gīd), *n.* In *joinery*, an adjustable guide or attachment to a plane-stock, used in beveling the edges of boards.

plane-iron (plān'ī"ėrn), *n.* The cutting-iron of a plane. Plane-irons are made either double or single, and are armed with a steel cutting edge.

planeness (plān'nes), *n.* The condition of being or having a plane surface.

> On pulling the plates apart the bloom was found to be burnished practically all over both surfaces, showing, of course, that the platinating had not sensibly altered the *planeness* of the surfaces.
> *Philosophical Mag.*, 5th ser., XXVIII. 454.

plane-plane (plān'plān), *a.* Having two plane surfaces perfectly parallel to each other.

plane-polarized (plān'pō"lạr-īzd), *a.* See *polarization*.

planer (plā'nėr), *n.* [< *plane*², *v.*, + *-er*¹.] 1. A tool for planing wood; a plane; also, a planing-machine.—2†. A utensil for smoothing or leveling salt in salt-cellars.

> Than loke your salte be whyte and drye, the *planer* made of Ivory, two inches brode & thre inches longe.
> *Babees Book* (E. E. T. S.), p. 266.

3. In *printing*, a block of wood, about 9 inches long, 3½ wide, and 3 high, on the top of which is a strip of leather, by means of which the projecting types of a form are beaten down to a level by blows of a mallet.—**Compound planer,** a machine-tool which combines two planes in one. *E. H. Knight*.—**Diagonal planer,** a machine for wood-planing in which the planing-cylinder is placed obliquely to the line of motion of the stuff which is to be planed.—**Planer knife-grinder.** See *knife-grinder*.—**Snow-planer,** an implement for removing snow from the surface of ice.

Planera (plan'ẹ-rạ), *n.* [NL. (Gmelin, 1791), named after J. J. *Planer* (1743–89), a German botanist.] A genus of plants of the order *Urticaceæ* and tribe *Ulmeæ*. It is characterized by the fruit, which is wingless, ovoid, nut-like, keeled, and roughened, thick and coriaceous or somewhat fleshy, and containing one cell and one seed. There is but one species, native of North America. See *planer-tree*.

planer-bar (plā'nėr-bär), *n.* An attachment to a planer to enable it to perform within certain limits the work of a slotting- or shaping-machine. *E. H. Knight*.

planer-center (plā'nėr-sen"tėr), *n.* A device, similar to a lathe-center, used to support small work on a planing-machine. *E. H. Knight*.

planer-chuck (plā'nėr-chuk), *n.* A device bolted or keyed to a planer-table, and serving to dog an object under the action of the plane. *E. H. Knight*.

planer-head (plā'nėr-hed), *n.* The slide-rest of a planing-machine.

planerite (plan'ėr-īt), *n.* [After D. J. *Planer*, director of mines in the Ural mountains.] A hydrous phosphate of aluminium, allied to wavellite.

planer-tree (plā'nėr-trē), *n.* A tree of the southern United States, *Planera aquatica*. It is a small tree, with alternate two-ranked toothed leaves, preceded by small axillary clusters of polygamous flowers with bell-shaped calyx and four or five slender projecting stamens. It is most common along the Red River and in southern Arkansas. It resembles the elm, requires wet situations, grows about 30 feet high, and produces a hard compact light-brown wood.

planer-vise (plā'nėr-vīs), *n.* A device to hold work on the bed of a planing-machine by means of a movable jaw.

plane-sailing (plān'sā"ling), *n.* In *nav.*, the art of determining a ship's place on the supposition that she is moving on a plane, or that the surface of the ocean is plane instead of being spherical. This supposition may be adopted for short distances without leading to great errors; and it affords great facilities in calculation, as the place of the ship is found by the solution of a right-angled plane triangle. In plane-sailing the principal terms made use of are the *course*, *distance*, *departure*, and *difference of latitude*, any two of which being given the others can be found. See *sailing*.

plane-stock (plān'stok), *n.* The body of a plane, in which the cutting-iron is fitted. Its under surface, which in use is against the work, is called the *sole* or *face*; the cutting-blade is the *iron*; the device which holds the iron upon the inclined bed is the *wedge*; the opening through which the plane-iron passes is the *mouth*; a projecting portion at the front end is the *horn*; and the pushing-handle which projects above the back end is the toat.

planet (plan'et), *n.* [< ME. *planete* = D. *planeet* = MHG. *plānēte*, G. Sw. Dan. *planet*, < OF. *planete*, F. *planète* = Sp. Pg. *planeta* = It. *pianeta*, < LL. *planeta*, rarely *planetes*, a planet, < Gr. πλανήτης, a wanderer, a wandering star, a planet, lengthened form of πλάνης, pl. πλάνητες, a wanderer, a planet, cf. πλανᾶν, cause to wander, pass. πλανᾶσθαι, wander, < πλάνη, a wandering, perhaps for *πάλνη, akin to L. *palari*, wander.] 1. A star other than a fixed star; a star revolving in an orbit. The sun was formerly considered as a planet, but is now known to be a fixed star. By *planet* is ordinarily meant a *primary planet* of the solar system, or body revolving round the sun in a nearly circular orbit. Of these eight are *major planets*—being, in their order from the sun, Mercury, Venus, the Earth, Mars, Jupiter, Saturn, Uranus, Neptune. There are besides about 300 *minor planets* known. (See *planetoid*.) The periodic comets are not regarded as planets. A *secondary planet* is a satellite, or small body revolving round a primary planet: thus, the moon is a secondary planet. See *solar system* (under *solar*), *gravitation*, *Kepler's laws* (under *law*), and the names of the major planets.

> The *planet* earth, so steadfast though she seem,
> Insensibly three different motions move.
> *Milton*, P. L., viii. 129.

2. Same as *planeta*, 2.—**Interior planets.** See *interior*.—**Limit of a planet.** See *limit*.—**Osculating elements of a planet.** See *osculate*.—**Perturbations of the planets.** See *perturbation*, 4.—**Superior planets.** See *superior*.

planeta (plạ-nē'tạ), *n.*; pl. *planetæ* (-tē). [ML.] 1. Originally, an ample mantle, usually of costly material, similar to the pænula, or chasuble in its earlier or circular form. It was worn by the wealthy, and especially by senators, officials, and nobles, in Rome and other parts of the West during the fifth and sixth centuries.

Hence—2. A chasuble. The name *planeta* (apparently unknown to the Greek Church) seems to have been especially used during the seventh and eighth centuries. After this the vestment was usually called a *casula* or *chasuble*; but *planeta* is still the official term in the Roman Catholic Church. At certain penitential seasons (Advent, Lent, etc.) the deacon and subdeacon in cathedrals and some other churches wear a folded planeta (*planeta plicata*), except in reading the epistle and gospel.

> The *planeta* was worn by bishops as well as by presbyters. *Encyc. Brit.*, VI. 461.

plane-table (plān'tā"bl), *n.* 1. An important instrument of topographical surveying, consisting of a drawing-board mounted upon a tripod, and capable of being leveled and turned in azimuth, sometimes also having two horizontal motions of translation. An indispensable accompaniment of the plane-table is the alidade, which is a straight-edge carrying upon a standard a telescope with cross-wires (generally with a telemeter), which telescope is horizontally fixed relatively to the straight-edge, but has a motion in altitude. The alidade generally carries a delicate magnetic needle. A certain number of points having been geodetically determined and marked by signals, the plane-table is set up at any other point, and the paper upon which the map is to be drawn, having the trigonometric points laid down upon it, is placed upon the table. The latter is then brought into proper orientation, and the position of the station determined graphically by the three-point problem. The plane-table presents some slight difficulties when the scale is to be so large that the board itself appears of considerable size on the map, and especially when irregularly laid out towns are to be surveyed with the last degree of accuracy. On the other hand, the plane-table is of little use in mere reconnaissance. But in most cases it is the chief instrument of the topographer, and is used in all topographical surveys except those of Great Britain.

2. In *mining*, an inclined table or surface of boards on which ore is dressed; a frame, or framing-table.

Also *plain-table*.

plane-table (plān'tā"bl), *v. t.* [< *plane-table, n.*] To survey with a plane-table.

plane-tabler (plān'tā"blėr), *n.* A topographic engineer using a plane-table.

plane-tabling (plān'tā"bling), *n.* The employment of a plane-table; the act or process of making a map by means of a plane-table.

planetarium (plan-e-tā'ri-um), *n.*; pl. *planetariums, planetaria* (-umz, -ạ̈). [= F. *planétaire* = Sp. Pg. It. *planetario*, < NL. *planetarium*, prop. neut. of LL. **planetarius*, planetary: see *planetary*.] An astronomical machine which, by the movement of its parts, represents the motions and orbits of the planets. See *orrery*.

planetary (plan'e-tạ-ri), *a.* [= F. *planétaire* = Sp. Pg. It. *planetario*, < LL. **planetarius*, planetary (only as a noun, *planetarius*, an astrologer), < *planeta*, a planet: see *planet*.] 1. Of or pertaining to a planet or the planets; consisting of planets: as, *planetary* motions; *planetary* inhabitants; the *planetary* system. —2. Having the character attributed to a planet; erratic or wandering.

> I am credibly informed he [Richard Greenham] in some sort repented his removal from his parish, and disliked his own erratical and *planetary* life.
> *Fuller*, Ch. Hist., IX. vii. 68.

3. In *astrol.*, under the dominion or influence of a planet; produced by or under the influence of planets.

> Be as a *planetary* plague, when Jove
> Will o'er some high-viced city hang his poison
> In the sick air. *Shak.*, T. of A., iv. 3. 108.

> Born in the *planetary* hour of Saturn.
> *Addison*, Spectator.

Planetary aberration. See *aberration*.—**Planetary days**, the days of the week as shared among the planets known to the ancients, each having its day.—**Planetary nebula.** See *nebula*.—**Planetary years**, the periods of time in which the several planets make their respective revolutions round the sun.

planeted (plan'et-ed), *a.* [< *planet* + *-ed*[2].] Belonging to planets. [Rare.]

> Tell me, ye stars, ye planets; tell me, all
> Ye starr'd and *planeted* inhabitants—what is it?
> What are these sons of wonder?
> *Young*, Night Thoughts, ix.

planet-gearing (plan'et-gēr"ing), *n.* Any system of gearing in which planet-wheels are introduced; a mechanical device for converting power into speed. It has been employed for driving the cutter-bars of reapers and mowers, and is an element in other machines.

planetic (plạ-net'ik), *a.* [In form < LL. *planeticus*, wandering, < Gr. *πλανητικός*, wandering, irregular, < *πλανητός*, wandering, < *πλανᾶσθαι*, wander: see *planet*. In sense directly dependent on *planet*.] Of or pertaining to a planet; resembling a planet in any way.

planetical (plạ-net'i-kạl), *a.* [< *planetic* + *-al*.] Same as *planetic*.

> According to the *planetical* relations.
> *Sir T. Browne*, Vulg. Err., v. 22.

> Some *planetical* exhalation, or a descending star.
> *J. Spencer*, Prodigies, p. 30.

planeting† (plan'et-ing), *n.* [< *planet* + *-ing*[1].] The music of the planets or spheres.

> Tempering all
> The jarring spheres, and giving to the world
> Again his first and tuneful *planetting*.
> *B. Jonson*, Sad Shepherd, iii. 2.

planetist† (plan'et-ist), *n.* [= F. *planetiste* = Sp. OIt. *planetista*, < LL. **planetista*, < *planeta*, planet: see *planet*.] An observer of the planets. *Minsheu.*

planetoid (plan'et-oid), *n.* [= F. *planétoïde*, < Gr. *πλανήτης*, a planet, + *εἶδος*, form.] One of the group of very small planets revolving round the sun between the orbits of Mars and Jupiter, remarkable for the eccentricity of their orbits and the greatness of their angle of inclination to the ecliptic; a minor planet; an asteroid. The diameter of the largest is supposed not to exceed 450 miles, while most of the others are believed to be very much smaller. Ceres was the first to be detected, being observed for the first time by Piazzi, an Italian astronomer, on January 1st, 1801; since 1847 no year has passed without the discovery of new planetoids. The number now known is over 400.

planetoidal (plan-e-toi'dạl), *a.* [< *planetoid* + *-al*.] Of or pertaining to the planetoids; relating to a planetoid.

plane-tree (plān'trē), *n.* [< *plane*[3] + *tree*.] 1. A tree of the genus *Platanus*, especially *P. orientalis*, the oriental plane-tree, or its variety *acerifolia*, the maple-leafed plane-tree, often regarded as a species. The oriental plane-tree and its variety are found wild from Persia to Italy, and are common in European parks as ornamental trees. The wood is valued for cabinet-work and turnery. (Also called

Branch of the American Plane-tree (*Platanus occidentalis*) with Fruit. *a*, a single nutlet, showing the bristles at its base.

chinar-tree.) The American plane-trees are better known, where native, as *sycamore* or *buttonwood*. The ordinary species is *P. occidentalis*, the largest tree of the Atlantic forests, often from 90 to 120 feet high, found chiefly on bottom-lands. It is not seldom planted for shade and ornament, and its reddish-brown wood is used in various ways. Other names are *buttonball* and *water-beech*. The plane-tree of California is *P. racemosa*, a somewhat smaller tree with very white bark. Plane-trees suffer from a disease caused by the attack of a parasitic fungus, *Glœosporium nerviseqnum*. The entire foliage appears in early summer as if scorched and withered, but later in the season fresh leaves are developed. The trees rarely die from the effects of the fungus. See *Platanus*.

2. The sycamore maple, *Acer Pseudo-platanus*: so called from the similarity of its leaves to those of the plane. Other maples are also sometimes known as *plane-trees*. [Local, Eng. and Scotch.]

planet-stricken (plan'et-strik"n), *a.* Affected by the supposed influence of planets; blasted.

> Like *planet-stricken* men of yore,
> He trembles, smitten to the core
> By strong compunctions and remorse.
> *Wordsworth*, Peter Bell, iii.

planet-struck (plan'et-struk), *a.* Same as *planet-stricken*.

> He battens at the maligned's misery; and if such a man riseth, he falls as if he were *planet-struck*.
> *Rev. T. Adams*, Works, I. 479.

> Since I saw you I have been *planet-struck*. *Suckling.*

planetule (plan'et-ūl), *n.* [< *planet* + *-ule*.] A little planet.

planet-wheel (plan'et-hwēl), *n.* 1. The exterior wheel of the sun-and-planet motion (see *sun*).—2. In the plural, an epicyclic train of mechanism for producing a variable angular motion, such as that of the radius vector of a planet in its orbit. The common contrivance for this purpose consists of two elliptical wheels connected by teeth in gear with each other, and revolving on their foci. While the driving-wheel moves uniformly, the radius vector of the other has the required motion.

Planet-wheels.

The spur-gear to the right, called the planet-gear, is tied to the center of the other, or sun-gear, by an arm which preserves a constant distance between their centers. Each revolution of the planet-gear, which is rigidly attached to the connecting-rod, gives two to the sun-gear, which is keyed to the fly-wheel shaft.

plangency (plan'jen-si), *n.* [< *plangen(t)* + *-cy*.] The state or quality of being plangent; a noisy dashing or beating. [Rare.]

plangent (plan'jent), *a.* [< L. *plangen(t-)s*, ppr. of *plangere*, beat: see *plain*[2].] 1. Beating; dashing, as waves. [Rare.]

> Nor heeds the weltering of the *plangent* wave.
> *Sir H. Taylor*, Ph. van Artevelde (ed. 1852), I., i. 10.

2. Resounding; clashing; noisy.

> The bell on the orthodox church called the members of Mr. Peck's society together for the business meeting with the same *plangent*, lacerant note that summoned them to worship on Sundays. *W. D. Howells*, Annie Kilburn, xxv.

> The shadows and the generations, the shrill doctors and the *plangent* wars, go by into ultimate silence and emptiness. *R. L. Stevenson*, An Apology for Idlers.

plangor† (plang'gọr), *n.* [< L. *plangor*, a striking, beating, a beating the breast in token of grief, < *plangere*, beat: see *plain*[2].] Plaint; lamentation.

> The lamentable *plangors* of Thracian Orpheus for his dearest Eurydice.
> *Meres*, Eng. Literature (Arber's Eng. Garner, II. 99).

Plani (plā'nī), *n. pl.* [NL., pl. of L. *planus*, flat: see *plane*[1].] In Cuvier's classification, the second family of subbrachiate malacopterygian fishes; the flatfishes: same as *Pleuronectidæ* in a wide sense and the suborder *Heterosomata*.

planicaudate (plā-ni-kâ'dāt), *a.* [< L. *planus*, flat, + *cauda*, tail, + *-ate*[1] (see *caudate*).] Having a flattened tail: said of reptiles.

planicipital (plā-ni-sip'i-tạl), *a.* [< L. *planus*, flat, + *caput* (*capit-*, in comp. *-cipit-*), head, + *-al*.] Having a flat head, as an insect.

planidorsate (plā-ni-dôr'sāt), *a.* [< L. *planus*, flat, + *dorsum*, back, + *-ate*[1].] Having a flat back.

planiform (plā'ni-fôrm), *a.* [< L. *planus*, flat, + *forma*, form.] In *anat.*, presenting a plane or flat surface: said of the articular surface of bones whose jointing is arthrodial.

planigraph (plan'i-gráf), *n.* [< NL. *planum*, a plane, + Gr. *γράφειν*, write.] An instrument for reducing or enlarging drawings. It consists of two scales graduated in a definite ratio to each other, attached end to end, and rotating about a pivot at their common origin. Measurements taken on a copy at one side are marked by the operator at the corresponding gradations on the other arm of the instrument. Interchangeable scales are provided for different degrees of enlargement or reduction.

planimeter (plạ-nim'e-tėr), *n.* [= F. *planimètre*; < NL. *planum*, a plane, + Gr. *μέτρον*, measure.] An instrument for measuring a plane area by carrying a tracer round its periphery, and noting the change of reading of a scale. Planimeters are of various constructions; but the most interesting is the polar planimeter (see the first figure). This

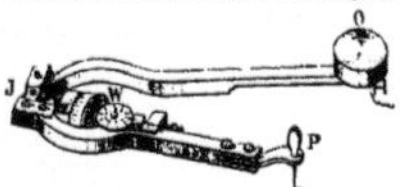

consists of an inner arm OJ, turning about a fixed center O, and an outer arm JP, turning about a joint J, and resting upon a point or tracer P, and upon a wheel W, having its axis coincident with or just below the line JP, and provided with a counting-apparatus, so that the turns and fractions of a turn it makes can be read off. In order to see that the instrument will accurately show the area, consider the second figure, where the tracer is supposed to follow

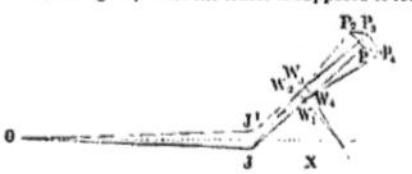

the outline of an infinitesimal parallelogram, $P_1P_2P_3P_4$, so placed that when the tracer moves from P_2 to P_3 and from P_4 to P_1 the wheel moves from W_2 to W_3 and from W_4 to W_1, both these paths of the wheel being in the direction of its axis, so that it only turns in passing from W_1 to W_2 and from W_3 to W_4, during which motions the in-

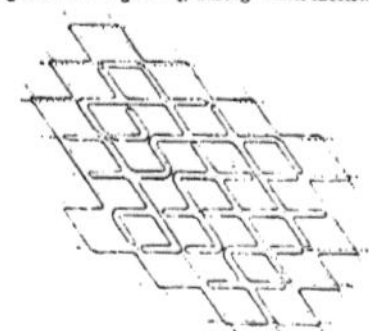

ner arm is stationary. The area of the parallelogram described by the tracer is equal to the base $P_1P_2 = W_1W_2$ $(JP_2 + JW_2)$ multiplied by the altitude, which is evidently equal to W_2W_3, so that the area is $W_1W_2 \times W_2W_3 \times (JP_2 + JW_2)$. The wheel turns one way in passing from W_2 to W_3, and the opposite way in passing from W_4 to W_1. But these two paths are not exactly equal, their difference being plainly $W_1W_2 \times W_2W_3 + JW_2$. The algebraic sum of the rolling multiplied by the constant length JP_2 gives the area. Now, any finite area may be conceived as formed of such infinitesimal parallelograms, and were the peripheries of all these traced out in the direction of the motion of clock-hands, every boundary between two of them would be traced once forward and again backward, so that the final reading of the wheel would be the same as if only the outer boundary of the area were traced. This is illustrated in the third figure. Also called *platometer*.

planimetric (plan-i-met'rik), *a.* [= F. *planimétrique* = Pg. *planimetrico*; as *planimetr-y* + *-ic*.] Pertaining to planimetry or the mensuration of plane surfaces.—**Planimetric function.** See *function*.

planimetrical (plan-i-met'ri-kal), *a.* [< *planimetric* + *-al*.] Same as *planimetric*.

planimetry (plā-nim'et-ri), *n.* [= F. *planimétrie* = Sp. *planometria*, *planimetría* = Pg. It. *planimetria*; < NL. *planum*, a plane, + Gr. *-μετρία*, < *μέτρον*, measure.] The mensuration of plane surfaces, or that part of geometry which regards lines and plane figures.

planing-machine (plā'ning-ma-shēn"), *n.* 1. A machine for planing wood, the usual form of which has cutters on a drum rotating on a

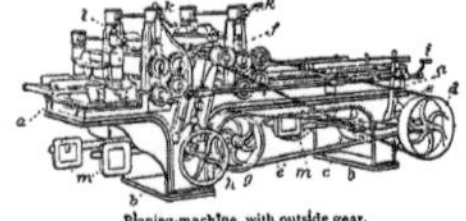

Planing-machine, with outside gear.

a a, bed; *b b*, pedestals; *c*, main driving-pulley, keyed to the same main driving-shaft as the pulley *d*, which transmits motion through the belt *e* to the top cutter-cylinder pulley *f*. The feed-mechanism consists of rollers geared together and driven by the pulley *g*, which derives its motion from the feed-belt *e'*, driven by a small pulley on the main driving-shaft; *h*, a hand-wheel operating screw-mechanism for raising or lowering the top cylinder; *i*, crank operating mechanism for adjusting matching-heads; *k k'*, cranks operating adjusting mechanism for raising or lowering feed-rolls to accommodate different thicknesses of stuff; *l*, crank for regulating the pressure-bar; *m m*, weighted levers for holding the feed-rollers with constant pressure.

horizontal axis over the board, which passes beneath. There may also be cutter-drums underneath and at the edges, so as to plane top, bottom, and edges simultaneously. Also called *wood-planer*. 2. A machine-tool for planing metals, in which the metal object to be planed, fixed to a traversing table, is moved against a relatively fixed cutter. Also called *metal-planer*.

planing-mill (plā'ning-mil), *n.* 1. A shop where planing is done.—2. A planing-machine.

planipennate (plā-ni-pen'āt), *a.* [< L. *planus*, flat, + *penna*, wing, + *-ate*[1] (see *pennate*).] Having flat wings not folded in repose and approximately equal to each other, as a neuropterous insect; specifically, belonging to the *Planipennia*.

Planipennia (plā-ni-pen'i-ä), *n. pl.* [NL., < L. *planus*, flat, + *penna*, wing.] A suborder of neuropterous insects, with nearly equal naked many-veined wings not folded in repose, well-developed jaws, and elongate many-jointed antennæ. The larvæ are mostly terrestrial, and voracious insect-feeders; the pupæ are incomplete and inactive; the perfect insects are generally herbivorous. The suborder includes such forms as the ant-lions (*Myrmeleontidæ*), scorpion-flies (*Panorpidæ*), and sundry other families, which the genera *Ascalaphus*, *Hemerobius*, *Coniopteryx*, *Mantispa*, *Rhaphidia*, and *Sialis* respectively represent. See cuts under *ant-lion* and *Panorpa*.

planipennine (plā-ni-pen'in), *a.* and *n.* [< *Planipennia* + *-ine*[1].] I. *a.* Of or pertaining to the *Planipennia*.

II. *n.* One of the *Planipennia*.

planipetalous (plā-ni-pet'a-lus), *a.* [= Sp. *planipétalo* = Pg. *planipetalo*, < L. *planus*, flat, + NL. *petalum*, petal.] In *bot.*, having flat petals.

planirostral (plā-ni-ros'tral), *a.* [< L. *planus*, flat, + *rostrum*, beak.] Having a broad flat beak, as a bird.

planish (plan'ish), *v. t.* [< OF. *planiss*, stem of certain parts of *planir*, equiv. to *planer*, plane: see *plane*[2], *v.*] 1. To make smooth or plane, as wood.—2. To condense, smooth, and toughen, as a metallic plate, by light blows of a hammer. —3. To polish: as, to *planish* silver goods or tin-plate.

planisher (plan'ish-ėr), *n.* [< *planish* + *-er*[1].] 1. A thin flat-ended tool used by tinners and braziers for smoothing tin-plate and brasswork. —2. A workman who planishes, smooths, or planes.—3. A device for flattening sections cut by a microtome for microscopic examination.

planishing-hammer (plan'ish-ing-ham"ėr), *n.* A hammer used for planishing, having a head with highly polished convex faces, usually rather broader than the face of a common machinists' hammer; also, less correctly, a similar hammer used for flattening, curving, etc.

planishing-roller (plan'ish-ing-rō"lėr), *n.* A highly polished roller used for smoothing surfaces of metal plate, as copper plated with tin or silver. Specifically, one of the second pair of rolls through which coin-metal is passed in preparing it for minting. They are made of case-hardened iron and highly polished. The strips of metal are passed between them cold, and are brought by them to the required thickness.

planishing-stake (plan'ish-ing-stāk), *n.* A small bench-anvil used to support anything being shaped with a planishing-hammer.

planisphere (plan'i-sfēr), *n.* [= F. *planisphère* = Sp. *planisferio* = Pg. *planispherio* = It. *planisferio*, < L. *planus*, flat, + *sphæra*, sphere: see *sphere*.] 1. A projection of the sphere; especially, a polar projection of the celestial sphere. —2. An apparatus consisting of a polar projection of the heavens, with a card over it turning about the pole, and so cut out as to show the part of the heavens visible at a given latitude at a given local sidereal time.

planispheric (plan-i-sfer'ik), *a.* [= F. *planisphérique*; as *planisphere* + *-ic*.] Of or pertaining to a planisphere; resembling a planisphere.

Planispheric representation of the cerebral convolutions. *Nature*, XXX. 161.

planispiral (plā-ni-spī'ral), *a.* [< L. *planus*, flat, + *spira*, a coil, spire: see *spire*.] Coiled in one plane, like a watch-spring or flat spiral, as the antlia of a butterfly; whorled in discoid form, as a shell of the genus *Planorbis*. Also *planospiral*.

plank (plangk), *n.* [< ME. *planke*, < OF. *planke*, assibilated *planche*, F. *planche*, dial. *planke* = Pr. *planca*, *plancha*, *planqua* = Sp. *plancha* = Pg. *prancha* = It. *piana* = OFries. *planke* = D. *plank* = MLG. *planke* = MHG. *planke*, *blanke*, G. *planke* = Sw. *planka* = Dan. *planke*, < L. *planca*, a plank, a nasalized form of **placa*, = Gr. *πλάξ* (*πλακ-*), a flat surface, a plain, tablet, plate. Cf. *plack*. See *planch*, a doublet of *plank*. The Ir. and W. *planc* is appar. < E.] 1. A piece of timber differing from a board in having greater thickness; also, loosely, a board. See *board*.

Ne nevere man dide, sithe the tyme of Noe, saf a Monk that be the grace of God broughte on of the *Plankes* doun; that zit is in the Mynstre, at the foot of the Montayne. *Mandeville*, Travels, p. 148.

Across the fallen oak the *plank* I laid. *Gay*, Shepherd's Week, Monday, l. 107.

2†. A slab (of stone).

Over his [Sir T. Browne's] Grave was soon after erected . . . a Monument of Freestone, with a *Plank* of Marble thereon. *Wood*, Athenæ Oxon., II. 524.

3. In a printing-press, the frame on which the carriage slides.—4. In *ribbon-weaving*, the batten of the Dutch engine-loom or swivel-loom.—5. Figuratively, one of the articles or paragraphs formulating distinct principles which form the program or platform of a political or other party (the word *platform* being taken in a double sense).

In the Chicago platform there is a *plank* on this subject, which should be a general law to the incoming Administration. *Lincoln*, in Raymond, p. 86.

We should get those amendments out of the way before we strike out for the summer campaign. We want two *planks*—non-extension of slavery, and state reform. *S. Bowles*, in Merriam, I. 291.

Walking the plank, a mode of inflicting death formerly practised by pirates by causing their victims to walk along a plank laid across the bulwarks of a ship till they overbalanced it and fell into the sea.

plank (plangk), *v. t.* [= OFries. *plonken* = MD. *planken* = MLG. *planken* = G. *planken* = Sw. *planka* = Dan. *planke*, plank; from the noun. Cf. *planch*, *v.*] 1. To cover or lay with planks: as, to *plank* a floor.

The streets of their cities and townes instead of pauing are *planked* with fir trees, plained & layd euen close the one to the other. *Hakluyt's Voyages*, I. 480.

2. To lay or place as on a plank or table: as, he *planked* down the money. [Colloq.]—3. In *hat-manuf.*, to harden by felting. See *planking*, 4.—4. To unite, as slivers of wool, to form roving.—5. To split, as fish, and cook upon a board. See the quotation. [U. S.]

The principal dish was *planked* shad. By this process four fish are fastened to a board, and held towards a hot fire. Whilst cooking, the fish are constantly basted with a preparation made of butter, salt, and other ingredients. *Science*, V. 426.

plank-hook (plangk'hůk), *n.* A pole armed with an iron hook, used in moving the runs or wheeling-planks in a quarry, a mine, or the like.

planking (plang'king), *n.* [Verbal n. of *plank*, *v.*] 1. The operation of laying down planks or of covering with planks.—2. Planks considered collectively, as in a floor; a piece of work made up of planks; specifically, in *ship-building*, the skin or covering of wooden timbers on the outer and inner surfaces of the ribs, and upon the beams. A *strake* is a line of planking. *Wales* are strakes of thick planking. See cut under *beam*.—3. In *spinning*, the splicing together of slivers of long-stapled wool. See *breaking-frame*.—4. One of the finishing operations in felting hats. The hardened hat-body is passed through a cistern containing a hot acidulated water, and between pressing-rollers, the process compacting the fibers into felt.

5. In a steam-cylinder, the lagging or clothing. —**Anchor-stock planking**, in *ship-building*, planks with one edge straight and the other so cut that the planks taper from the middle in both directions. The middle of one is placed over or under the ends of two others.

planking-clamp (plang'king-klamp), *n.* In *ship-building*, a tool used to bend a strake against the ribs of a vessel, and hold it in position until it can be nailed or bolted. Also called *planking-screw*.

planking-machine (plang'king-ma-shēn"), *n.* A machine for rubbing, pressing, and steaming formed hat-bodies, to give them strength and thickness.

planking-screw (plang'king-skrö), *n.* Same as *planking-clamp*.

plank-sheer (plangk'shēr), *n.* *Naut.*, the gunwale; a timber carried round the ship which covers and secures the timber-heads. Also called *covering-board*.

planky (plang'ki), *a.* [< *plank* + *-y*[1].] Constructed of planks or boards. [Rare.]

He came before the *plankie* gates, that all for strength were wrought. *Chapman*, Iliad, xii.

planless (plan'les), *a.* [< *plan* + *-less*.] Having no plan. *Coleridge*.

planner (plan'ėr), *n.* One who plans or forms a plan; a projector.

planoblast (plā'nō-blåst), *n.* [< Gr. *πλάνος*, wandering, + *βλαστός*, germ.] A wandering bud; the free medusoid of gymnoblastic hydrozoans; the gonophore of such hydroids, detached from the colony, leading an independent locomotory life, and discharging its mature sexual products into the sea: distinguished from the *hedrioblast*, or sedentary bud. With a single known exception (that of *Dicoryne*), planoblasts are craspedote or velum-bearing medusæ, bell-shaped, with the walls of the bell or umbrella mainly of gelatinous consistence; from the bell hangs a tubular body, the manubrium; the opening of the bell-cavity is the codonostoma, partially closed by a membranous velum; and a variable number of filaments, the tentacles, hang from the margin of the umbrella.

To the gonophores belonging to this group [*Gymnoblastea*] the name of *planoblasts* (wandering buds) may be given. *G. J. Allman*, Challenger Reports, Hydroida, XXIII. ii. 26.

planoblastic (plā-nō-blas'tik), *a.* Of the nature of or pertaining to planoblasts; medusoid.

plano-concave (plā"nō-kon'kāv), *a.* [< L. *planus*, plane, + *concavus*, concave: see *concave*.] Plane on one side and concave on the other.

plano-conical (plā"nō-kon'i-kal), *a.* [< L. *planus*, plane, + *conicus*, conic: see *conic*, *conical*.] Plane on one side and conical on the other.

plano-convex (plā"nō-kon'veks), *a.* [< L. *planus*, plane, + *convexus*, convex: see *convex*.] Plane on one side and convex on the other.

planodia (plā-nō'di-ä), *n.* [< Gr. *πλάνος*, wandering, + *ὁδός*, a way, road.] A false passage, such as may be made in using a catheter.

planogamete (plan'ō-ga-mēt), *n.* [< Gr. *πλάνη*, a wandering, + *γαμέτης*, < *γαμεῖν*, marry.] In *bot.*, a motile gamete: same as *zoögamete*. See *gamete*.

planographist (plā-nog'ra-fist), *n.* [< L. *planus*, plane, + Gr. *γράφειν*, write, + *-ist*.] A surveyor; a plan- or map-maker. [Rare.]

All *planographists* of the Holy City. *W. M. Thomson*, Land and Book, p. 421. (*Encyc. Dict.*)

plano-horizontal (plā"nō-hor-i-zon'tal), *a.* [< L. *planus*, plane, + ML. **horizontalis*, horizontal: see *horizontal*.] Having a plano horizontal surface or position.

planometer (plā-nom'e-tėr), *n.* [< L. *planus*, plane, + Gr. *μέτρον*, a measure.] A plane surface used in machine-making as a gage for plane surfaces; a surface-plate.

planometry (plā-nom′et-ri), *n.* [< L. *planus*, plane, + Gr. -μετρία, < μέτρον, measure.] The measurement or gaging of plane surfaces; the art or act of using a planometer.

plano-orbicular (plā″nō-ôr-bik′ū-lär), *a.* [< L. *planus*, plane, + NL. *orbicularis*, orbicular: see *orbicular*.] Flat on one side and spherical on the other.

Planorbinæ (plā-nôr-bī′nē), *n. pl.* [NL., < *Planorbis* + *-inæ*.] A subfamily of pond-snails of the family *Limnæidæ*, typified by the genus *Planorbis*, having a flat discoidal or planispiral shell. The subfamily is one of three, contrasted with *Limnæinæ* and *Ancylinæ*.

planorbine (plā-nôr′bin), *a.* [< L. *planus*, flat, plane, + *orbis*, circle, disk, + *-ine*[1].] Whorled in a round flat spiral; planispiral, as a pond-snail; belonging to the *Planorbinæ*.

Planorbis (plā-nôr′bis), *n.* [NL., < L. *planus*, flat, plane, + *orbis*, circle, disk: see *orb*[1].] The typical genus of *Planorbinæ*.

It is very extensive, including about 150 species, 25 of which are found in the United States. They inhabit ponds and sluggish streams.

Planorbis corneus.

planorbite (plā-nôr′bit), *n.* [< *Planorbis* + *-ite*[2].] A fossil species of *Planorbis*, or some similar planorbine shell.

Planorbulina (plā-nôr-bū-lī′nạ), *n.* [NL., < L. *planus*, plane, + NL. *Orbulina*, q. v.] A genus of foraminifers whose tests are of planorbine figure.

planorbuline (plā-nôr′bū-lin), *a.* [< *Planorbulina*.] Of or pertaining to the genus *Planorbulina*.

Two of the most remarkable modifications of the *planorbuline* type, which strikingly illustrate the extremely wide range of variation among Foraminifera, are Polytrema and Orbitolina. *Encyc. Brit.*, IX. 380.

planospiral (plā-nō-spī′ral), *a.* See *planispiral*.

planosubulate (plā″nō-sub′ū-lāt), *a.* [< L. *planus*, plane, + NL. *subulatus*, awl-shaped: see *subulate*.] Smooth and awl-shaped.

plant[1] (plant), *n.* [< ME. *plante*, *plaunte* (partly < OF.), < AS. *plante* = D. *plant* = MLG. *plante* = OHG. *phlanza*, *flanza*, *planza*, MHG. G. *pflanze* = Icel. *planta* = Sw. *planta* = Dan. *plante* = OF. (and F.) *plante* = Pr. Sp. Pg. *planta* = It. *pianta*, a plant, < L. *planta*, a sprout, shoot, twig, sucker, graft, scion, slip, cutting, a young tree that may be transplanted, a set, hence in general a plant; prob. orig. a spreading sucker (cf. *planta*, the sole of the foot: see *plant*[2]); lit. 'something flat or spreading,' < √ *plat* = Gr. πλατύς, broad: see *plat*[3], *plate*. In the later senses (defs. 5–10) the noun is from the verb. Cf. *clan*.] **1.** A shoot or slip recently sprouted from seed, or rooted as a cutting or layer; especially, such a slip ready for transplanting, as one of the cabbage-*plants*, tomato-*plants*, etc., of the market.

Thoughe that Men bryngen of the *Plauntes*, for to planten in other Contrees, thei growen wel and fayre, but thei bryngen forthe no fructuous thing; and the Leves of Bawme ne fallen noughte. *Mandeville*, Travels, p. 50.

Transplaunte alle hoole the *plaun*e [of cabbage], and it is slaye. *Palladius*, Husbondrie (E. E. T. S.), p. 113.

2. A sapling; hence, a stick or staff; a cudgel.

He caught a *plante* of an appell tre, and caste his shelde to grounde, and toke the barre in bothe handes, and seide he wolde make hem to remeve. *Merlin* (E. E. T. S.), iii. 493.

There is a man haunts the forest, that abuses our young *plants* with carving "Rosalind" on their barks. *Shak.*, As you Like it, iii. 2. 378.

Sir Roger's servants, and among the rest my old friend the butler, had, I found, provided themselves with good oaken *plants*, to attend their master upon this occasion. *Addison*, Sir Roger at the Play.

3. An herb or other small vegetable growth, in contrast with trees.—**4.** An individual living being with a material organism, not animal in its nature; a member of the vegetable kingdom; a vegetable, in the widest sense. While the difference between plants and animals in all their higher forms is clearly marked, science has hitherto been unable to fix upon any one absolutely universal criterion between them. Nothing perhaps is so distinctive of the plant as its power to appropriate and assimilate mineral matter directly, whereas most animals live on the products of previous organization. The plant thus mediates in the scheme of nature between the mineral and the animal world, forming an essential condition of most animal existence. But many plants, including the whole group of *Fungi*, and the saprophytic, parasitic, and carnivorous flowering plants, live wholly or in part on organic matter, while not all animals are confined to organic nutriment. See *animal* and *Protista*. For the fundamental classification of plants, see *Cryptogamia* and *Phanerogamia*.

In some places, those *plants* which are entirely poisonous at home, lose their deleterious quality by being carried abroad. *Goldsmith*, Citizen of the World, xci.

5. The fixtures, machinery, tools, apparatus, appliances, etc., necessary to carry on any trade or mechanical business, or any mechanical operation or process.

What with the *plant*, as Mr. Peck technically phrased a great upas-tree of a total, branching out into types, cases, printing-presses, engines, &c., . . . my father's fortune was reduced to a sum of between seven and eight thousand pounds. *Bulwer*, Caxtons, xi. 6. (*Davies*.)

The entire *plant*, and even the fuel, were transported on heavy waggons across the Karroo, at an enormous cost to the young settlement. *Fortnightly Rev.*, N. S., XLIII. 880.

6. Concealed plunder. [Thieves' slang.]—**7.** A trick; dodge; swindle; artifice. [Slang.]

It wasn't a bad *plant*, that of mine, on Fikey, the man accused of forging the Sou'-Western Railway debentures. *Dickens.*

Such-and-such an author says that so-and-so was "burnt alive," followed by a silly smattering of righteous indignation at what never happened, while the dispassionate scholar finds the whole thing a *plant*. *N. and Q.*, 7th ser., IX. 50.

8. In *fish-culture*, a deposit of fry or eggs.—**9.** *pl.* Oysters which have been bedded: in distinction from *natives*: as, Virginia *plants*. [A market-term, applied chiefly to Virginia oysters bedded in Providence River.]—**10.** *pl.* Young oysters suitable for planting or transplantation. —**Ballast-plants.** See *ballast*.—**Blind, herbaceous, luminous, etc., plants.** See the adjectives.—**Flowering plant.** See *Phanerogamia*.—**Indicative plants**, species which, in their natural habitat, are reputed to indicate the presence of certain minerals. [U. S.]—**Movement of plants.** See *movement*.—**Parasitic plants.** See *parasitic*.—**Pot-plant, potted plant**, a plant grown in a flower-pot, as in conservatories and hothouses. =**Syn.** 4. See *vegetable*, *n.*

plant[1] (plant), *v.* [< ME. *planten*, *plaunten* (partly < OF.), < AS. *plantian* (*ā-plantian*, *geplantian*) = D. *planten* = MLG. *planten* = OHG. *phlanzōn*, *flanzōn*, MHG. G. *pflanzen* = Icel. *planta* = Sw. *planta* = Dan. *plante* = OF. (and F.) *planter* = Pr. Sp. Pg. *plantar* = It. *piantare*, < L. *plantare*, set, plant, transplant, < *planta*, a sprout, shoot, scion, plant: see *plant*[1], *n.*] **I.** *trans.* **1.** To put or set in the ground for growth, as seed, young shoots, cuttings, vegetables with roots, etc.: as, to *plant* potatoes; to *plant* trees.

Nowe onyons sowe, and tasul in his place
Lette *plaunte*; and cunel sowe, eke Armarace [horse-radish]. *Palladius*, Husbondrie (E. E. T. S.), p. 210.

2. To lay out and prepare by putting or setting seed, etc., in the ground; furnish with plants: as, to *plant* a garden or an orchard.

The Lord God *planted* a garden eastward in Eden; and there he put the man whom he had formed. Gen. ii. 8.

3. To implant; sow the seeds or germs of; engender.

It engenders choler, *planteth* anger. *Shak.*, T. of the S., iv. 1. 175.

They *planted* in them a hatred of vices, especially of lying, and in the next place of debt. *Purchas*, Pilgrimage, p. 373.

4. To put; place; set; especially, to post or place firmly in position; fix; set up: as, he *planted* himself in front of me; to *plant* a standard on the enemy's battlements.

Plant yourself there, sir; and observe me. *B. Jonson*, Cynthia's Revels, ii. 1.

The Duke, having *planted* his Ordnance, battered the other side. Quoted in *Capt. John Smith's* True Travels, I. 11.

The Duke of Marlborough *planted* his creatures round his lordship. *Goldsmith*, Bolingbroke.

He *planted* himself with a firm foot in front of the image. *Barham*, Ingoldsby Legends, I. 148.

5. To establish or set up for the first time; introduce and establish: as, to *plant* Christianity among the heathen; to *plant* a colony.

He would entreat your care
To *plant* me in the favour of some man
That 's expert in that knowledge.
Fletcher, Spanish Curate, ii. 1.

When the Romans sent Legions and *planted* Colonies Abroad, it was for divers political Considerations. *Howell*, Letters, ii. 58.

6. To furnish; provide with something that is set in position or in order.

The port of the said Citie is strongly fortified with two strong Castles, and one other Castle within the citie, being all very well *planted* with munition. *Hakluyt's Voyages*, II. 281.

A very goodly strong Castle, well *planted* with Ordinance. *Coryat*, Crudities, I. 93.

Rochdale, by a crosse pale weinigh foure miles long, is also *planted* with houses along the pale. Quoted in *Capt. John Smith's* Works, II. 13.

7. To introduce and establish new settlers in; settle; colonize.

Neither may wee thinke that Moses intended so much a Geographicall history of all the Nations of the world, many of which were not, long after this time, *planted* or peopled. *Purchas*, Pilgrimage, p. 45.

He came hither to return to England for supply, intending to return and *plant* Delaware. *Winthrop*, Hist. New England, II. 396.

This year the towns on the river of Connecticut began to be *planted*. *N. Morton*, New England's Memorial, p. 181.

8. To place or locate as colonists or settlers.

Vpon the twelfth of this Moneth came in a Pinnace of Captaine Bargraues, and on the seuenteenth Captaine Lownes, and one Master Euans, who intended to *plant* themselues at Warraskoyack. Quoted in *Capt. John Smith's* Works, II. 38.

9. To hide; conceal: place in concealment, as plunder or swag. [Thieves' slang.]—**10.** In *fish-culture*, to deposit (eggs or fry) in a river, lake, or pond.—**11.** To bed (oysters); bed down, transplant, or sow (young or small oysters).—**12.** To put, as gold or the like, in the ground, or in a pretended mine, where it can be easily found, for the purpose of affecting the price of the land; also, to treat, as land, in this way; "salt."

A salted claim, a pit sold for a 10£ note, in which a nugget worth a few shillings had before been *planted*. *Percy Clarke*, New Chum in Australia, p. 72.

II. *intrans.* **1.** To sow seed or set shoots, etc., in the soil, that they may grow.

I have *planted*, Apollos watered, but God gave the increase. 1 Cor. iii. 6.

2†. To settle down; locate as settlers or colonists; take up abode as a new inhabitant, or as a settler in a new country or locality; settle.

If we desired to *plant* in Conightecute, they should give up their right to us. *Winthrop*, in Bradford's Plymouth Plantation, p. 349.

Taunton and Bridgewater men are confident that they are *planting* about Assawamsit or Dartmouth, and did yesterday track 200 of them, as they judge, toward Assawamset. *Gov. Winslow*, in App. to New England's Memorial, p. 445.

plant[2]† (plant), *n.* [< F. *plante* = Sp. Pg. *planta* = It. *pianta*, < L. *planta*, the sole of the foot: see *plant*[1].] The sole of the foot, or the foot itself. See *planta*.

Knotty legs, and *plants* of clay,
Seek for ease, or love delay.
B. Jonson, Masque of Oberon.

planta (plan′tạ), *n.*; pl. *plantæ* (-tē). [L., the sole of the foot: see *plant*[2].] **1.** In *vertebrate anat.*, the sole of the foot: corresponding to *palma* of the hand, and opposed to *dorsum* or the *rotular aspect* of the foot. See cuts under *digitigrade* and *plantigrade*.—**2.** In *ornith.*, the back of the shank; the hind part of the tarsometatarsus, corresponding morphologically to the sole of the foot of a mammal. See cut under *booted*.—**3.** In *entom.*, the first joint of the tarsus, when it is large or otherwise distinguished from the rest, which are then collectively called the *digitus*. Also called *metatarsus*, in which case the other joints collectively are the *dactylus*.

plantable (plan′tạ-bl), *a.* [= It. *piantabile*: as *plant*[1] + *-able*.] Capable of being planted, cultivated, settled, placed, etc.

The Land as you go farther from the Sea riseth still somewhat higher, and becomes of a more *plantable* Mould. *Dampier*, Voyages, II. ii. 58.

plant-a-cruive, planta-crew (plant′ạ-krův, plan′tạ-krö), *n.* [Perhaps < OF. *plante*, a plant, *plant*, a plantation, + *acreue*, *acreue*, growth: see *accrue*, *n.*] A small inclosure for the purpose of raising colewort-plants, etc. [Scotch.]

plantage† (plan′tāj), *n.* [< OF. *plantage*, a planting or setting, also plantain, F. *plantage*, plantation, = Sp. *plantaje*, a collection of plants, = Pg. *plantagem*, plants, herbs; cf. ML. *plantagium*, *plantago*, a plantation of trees or Vines; < L. *planta*, a plant: see *plant*[1] and *-age*.] Plants generally.

As true as steel, as *plantage* to the moon,
As sun to day. *Shak.*, T. and C., iii. 2. 184.

[The allusion in this passage is explained by the following:

The poor husbandman perceiveth that the increase of the moon maketh plants fruteful. *Reginald Scott*, Disc. of Witchcraft.]

Plantaginaceæ (plan″tạ-ji-nā′sẹ-ē), *n. pl.* [NL. (Lindley, 1835), < *Plantago* (*Plantagin-*) + *-aceæ*.] Same as *Plantagineæ*.

Plantagineæ (plan-tạ-jin′ẹ̄-ē), *n. pl.* [NL. (Ventenat, 1794), < *Plantago* (*Plantagin-*) + *-eæ*.] The plantain family, an anomalous order of gamopetalous plants, little related to any other, characterized by the scarious corolla with alternate stamens; sepals, petals, and stamens each usually four; and the small entire two-celled pod, usually circumscissile. It includes 3 genera and over 200 species, nearly all of which belong to the typical genus *Plantago*, the other genera, *Bougueria* and *Littorella*, being both monotypic.

Plantago (plan-tā'gō), *n.* [NL. (Tournefort, 1700), < L. *plantago*, plantain: see *plantain*[1].] A genus of plants, type of the order *Plantagineæ*, distinguished by the peltate seeds, two-celled ovary, and circumscissile capsule. It includes over 200 species, known as *plantain* or *ribwort*, and found everywhere, from arctic to tropical regions, in wet or dry ground, but most common in temperate climates. They are annual or perennial herbs, almost stemless, bearing rosettes of spreading leaves, which are characteristically broad, entire, five- to seven-nerved, with dilated-petiole base. The small flowers are usually crowded in a long spike, cross-fertilized by the earlier maturity of the pistils. Many species are dimorphous, or include perfect seed-bearing plants of two kinds, one form having long stamens and short styles, the other the opposite. Most of the American species are introduced weeds (for which see *plantain*[1], *kemp*[4], *hen-plant*, and *way-bread*, and, for *P. lanceolata*, *ribwort*, *rib-grass*, *jackstraw*, and *cocks*). *P. media*, the hoary plantain, lamb's-tongue, or fireweed of English pastures, is a pest on account of its stifling growing crops by its broad flat leaves, close-pressed to the ground; and the common *P. major* is sometimes similarly injurious in America. *P. Coronopus* is a peculiar plant of the British sea-cliffs, called *star-of-the-earth* from its divided radiating leaves, also *herb-ivy*, *buck's-horn*, and *hartshorn-plantain*. For other species, see *fleawort*, 2, and *ispaghul-seed*. See cut under *plantain*[1].

plantain[1] (plan'tān), *n.* [Formerly also *plantan*, *plaintain*; < ME. *planteyne*, *plawnteyne*, < OF. *plantain*, F. *plantain* = Pr. *plantage* = Cat. *plantatge* = Sp. *llanten* (also, after F., *plantaina*) = Pg. *tanchagem* = It. *piantaggine*, < L. *plantago* (*plantagin-*), plantain, so called from its broad spreading leaf; from the same source as *planta*, a spreading sucker, a plant, and *planta*, the sole of the foot: see *plant*[1], *plant*[2].] A plant of the genus *Plantago*, especially *P. major*, the common or greater plantain. This is a familiar dooryard weed, with large spreading leaves close

Flowering Plant of Plantain (*Plantago major*). *a*, the flower; *b*, the fruit (pyxis).

to the ground, and slender spikes; it is a native of Europe and temperate Asia, but is now found nearly everywhere. (See *hen-plant* and *way-bread*.) The English plantain (so called in the United States) is *P. lanceolata*, the ribwort, rib-grass, or ripple-grass, of the same nativity as the former. It has narrow leaves with prominent ribs, and slender stalks a foot or two high, with short thick spikes. (See *cocks* and *jackstraw*.) The sea-plantain or seaside plantain, *P. maritima*, with linear leaves, occurs on muddy shores in both hemispheres. The leaf is bound upon inflamed surfaces with a soothing effect. See also cut under *amphitropous*.

> These poor slight sores
> Need not a *plantain*.
> *Fletcher* (*and another*), Two Noble Kinsmen, i. 2.

> Knot-grass, *plantain* — all the social weeds,
> Man's mute companions, following where he leads.
> *O. W. Holmes*, Poems, The Island Ruin.

Indian plantain, any plant of the genus *Cacalia*. The most common species is *C. atriplicifolia*, a pale-colored plant from 3 to 6 feet high, with palmately veined angulate-lobed and -toothed glaucous leaves.—**Rattlesnake-plantain.** See *Goodyera*. — **Robin's-plantain**, *Erigeron bellidifolius*, a species with few rather broad heads and bluish rays, flowering early, common in the eastern United States.

Plantain (*Musa paradisiaca*).

plantain[2] (plan'tān), *n.* [Formerly also *plantan*; < OF. *plantain*, plane-tree, = Sp. *plátano*, also *plátano*, plantain, plane-tree: see *plane*[3].] A tropical plant, *Musa paradisiaca*, or its fruit. The plantain closely resembles the banana, and is in fact often regarded as a variety of it. It is distinguished to the eye by purple spots on the stem, and by its longer fruit. The plantain-fruit is commonly eaten cooked before fully mature, while the banana is mostly eaten fresh when ripe. The pulp is dried and pulverized to make meal. The fresh fruit is comparable chemically with the potato, the meal with rice. The plantain, together with the banana, supplies the chief food of millions in the tropics. Though less nutritious than wheat or potatoes, it is produced in vastly larger quantities from the same area, and with far less effort. Sometimes called *Adam's apple*, from the fancy that this was the forbidden fruit of the Garden of Eden; the specific name refers to the same fancy. See *Musa* and *banana*.

> They would also bring great store of oranges and *plantans*, which is a fruit that groweth upon a tree, and is very like vnto a cucumber, but very pleasant in eating.
> *Hakluyt's Voyages*, II. ii. 129.

> Berries and chestnuts, *plantains*, on whose cheeks
> The sun sits smiling.
> *Fletcher*, Faithful Shepherdess, i. 1.

Bastard plantain. See *Heliconia*, 2.—**Manila plantain, wild plantain**, *Musa textilis*, the Manila-hemp plant. See *manila* and *Musa*.

plantain-cutter (plan'tān-kut"ėr), *n.* Same as *plantain-eater*. *P. L. Sclater.*

plantain-eater (plan'tān-ē"tėr), *n.* A bird of the family *Musophagidæ*; a plantain-cutter or touracou. See *touracou*.

plantain-lily (plan'tān-lil"i), *n.* See *Funkia*.

plantain-tree (plan'tān-trē), *n.* See *plantain*[2].

plantal† (plan'tal), *a.* [Cf. OF. *plantal*, a plant, set, scion; < ML. **plantalis*, < L. *planta*, a plant: see *plant*[1].] Of or belonging to plants.

> There 's but little similitude betwixt a terreous humidity and *plantal* germinations.
> *Glanville*, Scep. Sci. (*Latham.*)

> The same inequality of temper made him surmise that the most degenerate souls did at last sleep in the bodies of trees, and grew up merely into *plantal* life.
> *Dr. H. More*, Immortal. of Soul, iii. 1.

plantant†, *n.* An obsolete form of *plantain*[1] and *plantain*[2].

plant-animal (plant'an"i-mal), *n.* One of the zoöphytes or *Phytozoa*, as a sea-anemone or coral.

plantar (plan'tär), *a.* [< L. *plantaris*, of or belonging to the sole of the foot, < *planta*, the sole of the foot: see *plant*[2].] Of or pertaining to the planta, or sole of the foot: as, a *plantar* muscle, tendon, or ligament; the *plantar* aspect of the foot or leg: correlated with *palmar*: often in composition: as, *laminiplantar*, *scutelliplantar*.—**Plantar arch**, the arch formed by the external plantar artery.—**Plantar arteries**, the two terminal branches of the posterior tibial artery in the sole of the foot. The external, the larger, passes outward and forward to the base of the fifth metatarsal, where it turns obliquely inward to communicate at the base of the first metatarsal with the dorsal artery, forming the plantar arch. The internal, the smaller, runs along the inner side to the base of the great toe.—**Plantar fascia.** See *fascia*.—**Plantar interossei.** See *interosseus*.—**Plantar ligament**, any ligament of the sole of the foot, especially the long calcaneocuboid ligament.—**Plantar muscle**, the plantaris.—**Plantar nerves**, two branches of the posterior tibial, distributed to many of the small muscles and the integument of the sole of the foot, the external terminating in the skin of the little toe and of the inner side of the fourth, the internal in the contiguous sides of the others.—**Plantar tubercle**, the tubercle on the first metatarsal bone, for attachment of the tendon of the peroneus longus.—**Plantar veins**, the venæ comites of the plantar arteries.

Plantar Arch.

plantaris (plan-tā'ris), *n.*; pl. *plantares* (-rēz). [NL., sc. *musculus*, muscle: see *plantar*.] A small fusiform muscle with a very long tendon ending variably in or near the tendo Achillis. It arises from the femur near the outer head of the gastrocnemius. The muscle is sometimes absent, sometimes double. In man it is very small or vestigial in comparison with its development in some other animals.

plantation (plan-tā'shon), *n.* [< F. *plantation* = Pr. *plantacio* = Sp. *plantacion* = Pg. *plantação* = It. *piantazione*, *piantagione*, < L. *plantatio(n-)*, a planting, < *plantare*, pp. *plantatus*, plant, transplant: see *plant*[1].] 1†. The act of planting seeds or plants.

> In bower and field he sought, where any tuft
> Of grove or garden-plot more pleasant lay,
> Their tendance, or *plantation* for delight.
> *Milton*, P. L., ix. 419.

> In Aprill they begin to plant, but their chiefe *plantation* is in May, and so they continue till the midst of Iune.
> Quoted in *Capt. John Smith's* Works, I. 126.

2. Introduction; establishment.

> Those instruments which it pleased God to use for the *plantation* of the faith.
> *Bacon*, Advancement of Learning, i. 68.

> The first *plantation* of Christianity in this island.
> *Eikon Basilike.*

3. A planting with people or settlers; colonization.

> The first publick attempt against Heaven at Babel after the *plantation* of the world again.
> *Stillingfleet*, Sermons, I. vii.

> Elizabeth thought the time had come for the colonization or *plantation* of Ulster.
> *W. S. Gregg*, Irish Hist. for Eng. Readers, p. 37.

4. A planted place. (*a*) A small wood; a grove; a piece of ground planted with trees or shrubs for the purpose of producing timber or coppice-wood.

> I went to see the New Spring Garden at Lambeth, a pretty contriv'd *plantation*. *Evelyn*, Diary, July 2, 1661.

(*b*) A farm, estate, or tract of land, especially in a tropical or semi-tropical country, such as the southern parts of the United States, South America, the West Indies, Africa, India, Ceylon, etc., in which cotton, sugar-cane, tobacco, coffee, etc., are cultivated, usually by negroes, peons, or coolies: as, a sugar-*plantation*; also used attributively: as, *plantation* life; *plantation* songs.

> From the Euphrates we ascended the hills through *plantations* of pistachio nuts.
> *Pococke*, Description of the East, II. i. 158.

> The house was of the ordinary *plantation* type — large, white, with double piazzas, standing high from the ground; and in the yard was a collection of negro-cabins and stables.
> *The Century*, XXXV. 190.

(c†) An original settlement in a new country; a colony: as, Rhode Island and Providence *plantations*.

> We kept a day of thanksgiving in all the *plantations*.
> *Winthrop*, Hist. New England, I. 35.

5. In Maine and New Hampshire, an unorganized and thinly settled division of a county.—6. An oyster-bed in which the oysters have been artificially planted; a cultivated area of oyster-bottom: a legal term in the State of Delaware.—**Council of Plantations**, in *Eng. hist.*, a committee of the Privy Council, established in the reign of Charles II., for supervision of the colonies (or foreign plantations): it was soon united with the Board of Trade. In the eighteenth century colonial affairs passed to a separate administration.

plantation-mill (plan-tā'shon-mil), *n.* Any one of variously constructed mills adapted for use on a plantation or farm for grinding oats, linseed, etc., moved by hand or other power.

plant-bug (plant'bug), *n.* One of many different heteropterous insects which suck the juices of plants. They belong chiefly to the family *Capsidæ*, as, for example, the tarnished plant-bug, also called *Lygus pratensis*, *Capsus oblineatus*, and *Phytocoris lineolaris*, which does great damage to many different orchard-trees, small fruits, and vegetables in the United States. The dotted plant-bug, a pentatomid, *Euschistus variolarius* or *punctipes*, is also a general plant-feeder, though exceptionally carnivorous. See *Nysius* and *Phytocoris*.

Dotted-legged Plant-bug. (*Euschistus punctipes.*) (Line shows natural size.)

plant-cane (plant'kān), *n.* The original plants of the sugar-cane, produced from germs placed in the ground; or canes of the first growth, in distinction from the *ratoons*, or sprouts from the roots of canes which have been cut. [West Indies.]

plant-cutter (plant'kut"ėr), *n.* 1. A bird of the family *Phytotomidæ*.—2. *pl.* In the early history of Virginia, rioters who went about destroying tobacco-plants.

plant-disease (plant'di-zēz"), *n.* See *disease*.

plant-eating (plant'ē"ting), *a.* Eating or feeding upon plants; phytophagous; specifically, in *entom.*, belonging to the *Phytophaga*.

planted (plan'ted), *p. a.* 1. In *joinery*, wrought on a separate piece of stuff, and afterward fixed in its place: said of a projecting member: as, a *planted* molding.—2. Introduced or naturalized; not indigenous.

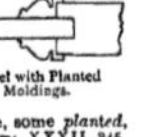

Panel with Planted Moldings.

> There are plenty of foxes, some native, some *planted*, and all wild. *The Century*, XXXII. 345.

planter (plan'tėr), *n.* [= D. *planter* = MHG. *phlanzer*, *phlenzer*, G. *pflanzer* = Sw. *plantorare* = Dan. *planter*; as *plant*[1] + *-er*[1].] 1. One who plants, sets in the ground or in position, introduces, establishes, or sets up: as, a *planter* of maize or of vines; the first *planters* of Christianity; a *planter* of colonies.

> These *Planters* of the ancient Literature in England hoped well of their Mother Tongue.
> *Ascham*, The Scholemaster, p. 4.

> Your lordship hath been a great *planter* of learning.
> *Bacon*, Advancement of Learning, Pref., p. vii.

2. One who owns a plantation, especially in a tropical or semi-tropical country: as, a coffee-*planter*; the *planters* of the West Indies.

The *planters* . . . as well as the negroes were slaves; though they paid no wages, they got very poor work.
Emerson, West Indian Emancipation.

3. A piece of timber, or the naked trunk of a tree, one end of which is firmly planted in the bed of a river while the other rises near the surface of the water: a dangerous obstruction sometimes encountered by vessels navigating the rivers of the western United States. *Bartlett.*—4. A tool or machine for planting seeds: as, a corn-*planter*, a cotton-seed *planter*, etc. Planters are usually simple hand-tools for opening the ground and dropping the seeds in the hill. A planter that distributes seeds in rows is called a *drill*, and one that sows broadcast a *seeder*.

planterdom (plan'tėr-dum), *n.* [‹ *planter* + *-dom.*] Planters collectively.

plantership (plan'tėr-ship), *n.* [‹ *planter* + *-ship.*] The business of a planter, or the management of a plantation.

plant-feeder (plant'fē"dėr), *n.* Any insect which feeds upon plants, as a plant-bug, or plant-feeding beetle. See cuts under *Phytophaga* and *plant-bug*.

plant-feeding (plant'fē"ding), *a.* Feeding upon plants; plant-eating; phytophagous.

plant-food (plant'fōd), *n.* Anything which affords nourishment to vegetation or plants; a fertilizer.

Whilst in the shape of bone-dust it [insoluble phosphate] is sufficiently available as *plant-food* to be of considerable value.
Ure, Dict., IV. 668.

planticle (plan'ti-kl), *n.* [‹ NL. as if **planticula*, dim. of L. *planta*, a plant: see *plant*[1].] A young plant, or a plant in embryo. *Darwin.*

Plantigrada (plan-tig'rā-dā), *n. pl.* [NL., neut. pl. of *plantigradus*, plantigrade: see *plantigrade.*] A subdivision of *Carnivora*, or *Feræ fissipedia*, embracing those carnivorous animals, as the bear and raccoon, which walk with the heel upon the ground. In Illiger's classification (1811), the *Plantigrada* were a family of his *Falculata*, or mammals with claws, and contained carnivorous quadrupeds of several different modern families, as the kinkajou, coati, racoon, badger, wolverine, and bear, yet not all of the members of the families to which the animals named properly belong. [Not now in use, excepting as a convenient collective or descriptive term.]

Plantigrada.—Leg of Polar Bear.
a, femur or thigh; *b*, tibia or leg; *c*, tarsus and metatarsus, or foot; *d*, calx or heel; *e*, planta or sole; *f*, digits or toes.

plantigrade (plan'ti-grād), *a.* and *n.* [‹ NL. *plantigradus*, ‹ L. *planta*, the sole, + *gradi*, go, walk.] I. *a.* Walking on the whole sole of the foot; having the characters of, or pertaining to, the *Plantigrada*: opposed to *digitigrade*. Man is perfectly plantigrade, and the same condition is seen in those quadrupeds, as bears, whose heels touch the ground.

II. *n.* A plantigrade mammal; a member of the *Plantigrada*.

planting (plan'ting), *n.* [‹ ME. *plantynge*; verbal n. of *plant*[1], *v.*] 1. The art of forming plantations of trees; also, the act or art of inserting plants in the soil.—2. A planted place; a grove; a plantation.

That they might be called trees of righteousness, the *planting* of the Lord, that he might be glorified.
Isa. lxi. 3.

3. In *arch.*, the laying of the first courses of stone in a foundation.

planting-ground (plan'ting-ground), *n.* A place where oysters are sown or planted.

plantivorous (plan-tiv'ō-rus), *a.* [‹ L. *planta*, a plant, + *vorare*, devour.] Plant-eating, as most caterpillars. *Westwood.*

plantless (plant'les), *a.* [‹ *plant*[1] + *-less.*] Without plants; destitute of vegetation. *Edinburgh Rev.*

plantlet (plant'let), *n.* [‹ *plant*[1] + *-let.*] A small, undeveloped, or rudimentary plant. Also *plantule*.

plant-louse (plant'lous), *n.* A small homopterous insect which infests plants; specifically, an aphid; any member of the *Aphididæ*. The members of the related family *Psyllidæ* are distinguished as *jumping plant-lice*. The *Coccidæ* are more properly named *bark-lice*. These three families, with the *Aleurodidæ*, are sometimes grouped as *Phytophthiria*. See cuts under *Aphis*, *Phylloxera*, *vine-pest*, *Pemphiginæ*, and *Pemphigus*.

plant-marker (plant'mär"kėr), *n.* A label, plate, or tablet bearing the common and botanical name of a tree or garden-plant, intended to be set in the ground near its roots for its identification. Such markers are often made of terra-cotta, Parian ware, etc.

plant-movement (plant'möv"ment), *n.* See *movement of plants* (under *movement*), *epinasty*, and *hyponasty*.

plantocracy (plan-tok'rā-si), *n.* [‹ L. *planta*, plant, + Gr. *-κρατία*, ‹ *κρατεῖν*, govern.] 1. Government by planters.—2. Planters collectively. *Eclectic Rev.* [Rare.]

plant-of-gluttony (plant'ov-glut'n-i), *n.* The dwarf cornel, *Cornus Canadensis*—its berries being regarded in the Scotch Highlands as stimulating to appetite.

plantosseous (plan-tos'ē-us), *a.* Of or pertaining to the plantossei.

plantosseus (plan-tos'ē-us), *n.*; pl. *plantossei* (-ī). [NL., ‹ L. *planta*, the sole of the foot, + *os* (*oss-*), bone: see *osseous*.] A plantar interosseous muscle; an interosseus of the sole of the foot: correlated with *dorsosseus* and *palmosseus*. *Coues and Shute*, 1887.

plantsman (plants'man), *n.*; pl. *plantsmen* (-men). A florist; a nurseryman. [Colloq.]

plantula (plan'tū-lā), *n.*; pl. *plantulæ* (-lē). [NL., ‹ L. *planta*, the sole of the foot: see *plant*[2].] In *entom.*, a membranous appendage between the claws of certain insects, corresponding to the onychium or spurious claw of other species. It commonly forms a cushion-like organ, by means of which the insect is enabled to walk over smooth surfaces. When this cushion forms a sucking-disk it is called the *pulvillus*.

plantular (plan'tū-lär), *a.* [‹ *plantula* + *-ar*[3].] In *entom.*, of or pertaining to the plantula.

plantule (plan'tūl), *n.* [‹ F. *plantule*, ‹ NL. **plantula*, dim. of L. *planta*, a plant: see *plant*[1].] In *bot.*, same as *plantlet*; also, the embryo of a plant.

planula (plan'ū-lā), *n.*; pl. *planulæ* (-lē). [NL., dim. of L. *planus*, flat: see *plane*[1].] The ordinary locomotory embryo of the cœlenterates, which is of flattened form, mouthless, ciliate, and free-swimming. The term originally applied only to such embryos of certain hydrozoans, but has become more comprehensive. See cut under *blastocœle*.

planulan (plan'ū-lan), *n.* [‹ *planula* + *-an.*] A planula. *Encyc. Brit.*

planular (plan'ū-lär), *a.* [‹ *planula* + *-ar*[3].] Of or pertaining to a planula: as, *planular* cilia; the *planular* stage of an embryo.

planuliform (plan'ū-li-fôrm), *a.* [‹ NL. *planula* + L. *forma*, form.] Resembling a planula in form, or having the morphological valence of a planula. *Huxley*, Anat. Invert., p. 395.

planuloid (plan'ū-loid), *a.* [‹ NL. *planula* + Gr. *εἶδος*, form.] Resembling a planula; planuliform.

planuria, planury (plā-nū'ri-ā, plan'ū-ri), *n.* [NL., ‹ Gr. *πλάνος*, straying, + *οὖρον*, urine.] The discharge of urine through an abnormal passage; uroplania.

planxty† (plank'sti), *n.* [Appar. an adaptation of L. *planctus*, a lament: see *plaint.*] A lament; an Irish or Welsh melody for the harp, often, but not necessarily, of a mournful character.

Dr. Petrie gives a *Planxty* of his in E-major, "Lady Wrixon," from a collection published in Dublin in 1720.
W. K. Sullivan, Introd. to O'Curry's Anc. Irish, p. dcix.

plap (plap), *v. i.*; pret. and pp. *plapped*, ppr. *plapping*. [Imitative; cf. *plash*, *flap*, *slap*, etc.] To plash; fall with a plashing sound.

Bark, there is Barnes Newcome's eloquence still *plapping* on like water from a cistern.
Thackeray, Newcomes, lxvi.

plaquage (plak'āj), *n.* [‹ F. *plaque*, a plate, + *-age.*] A method of producing calico-prints: same as *padding*, 3.

plaque (plak), *n.* [‹ F. *plaque*, a plate (of metal), slab, badge, patch, ticket, etc.: see *plack*.] 1. An ornamental plate; a brooch; the plate of a clasp.

In front of his turban there was a *plaque* of diamonds and emeralds. *W. H. Russell*, Diary in India, II. 239.

2. A square, oblong, or circular tablet of bronze or silver, the largest dimension of which extends to three or four inches, ornamented in relief with some religious, mythological, allegorical, or decorative subject. The Pax, from which the plaque originated, is set in an ornamental framework; the Renaissance plaque was intended to be hung up or inserted in a box or a piece of furniture, or, if circular, to be worn as a hat-medallion. Also called *plaquette*.

3. Any tablet or distinctly flat plate of metal or porcelain, whether plain or ornamented; particularly, an ornamental circular plate intended for a wall-decoration. See cut in next column.

Plaque in Relief of Enameled Pottery, by Bernard Palissy; 16th century.

—4. The especial decoration of a high rank in many honorary orders. See *star*, *insignia*, *order*, 6 (*b*).—5. In *anat.* and *zoöl.*, a small flat object of round figure, as a blood-disk; a little plate. Also *plaquette*.—6. A patch.

Warts, epitheliomn, herpes, and mucous *plaques*.
Lancet, No. 3468, p. 335.

Plaque of blood. Same as *blood-plate*.—**Plaques jaunes**, patches of yellow softening in cerebral cortex.—**Plaques of Peyer.** Same as *Peyerian glands* (which see, under *gland*).

plaquet (plak'et), *n.* [OF.: see *placket.*] In *medieval armor*, same as *placcate*.

plaquette (pla-ket'), *n.* [F., dim. of *plaque*, a plate: see *plaque*. Cf. *placket.*] 1. A small plaque or flat decorative object, as a tile of porcelain or a plate of metal, made for application to a piece of furniture as part of its ornamentation: as, a bureau decorated with bronze *plaquettes*.

On the other hand, the finer of the two medallions . . . bears, in its pseudo-classicality, a considerable resemblance to the work of another North Italian worker in bronze, . . . as will appear from an examination of several *plaquettes* from his hand.
The Academy, Dec. 8, 1888, p. 377.

2. Same as *plaque*, 5.

G. Hayem insists that the elements of the blood, to which he gave the name of hematoblasts, are identical with the *plaquettes*, or corpuscules, described by Bizzozero.
Smithsonian Report, 1883, p. 735.

plash[1] (plash), *v.* [‹ ME. **plashen* (not found except as in the noun), ‹ MD. *plasschen*, *plassen* = MLG. *plasken* = late MHG. *platsen*, *bletschen*, G. *platschen* = Dan. *plaske* = Sw. *plaska*, dabble; with orig. formative *-sk*, from the root seen in AS. *plættan*, *plættian*, strike with the hand, = Sw. *platta*, tap, pat: see *plat*[1], *pat*[1]. The word came to be regarded as imitative, and appears later as *splash.*] I. *intrans.* 1. To dabble in water; also, to fall with a dabbling sound; splash.

Hears, upon turret-roof and wall,
By fits the *plashing* rain-drop fall.
Scott, Rokeby, i. 1.

The bucket *plashing* in the cool, sweet well.
Whittier, Monadnock.

2. To splash water or mud.

His horse is booted
Vp to the flanke in mire; himselfe all spotted
And stain'd with *plashing*.
Heywood, Woman Killed with Kindness (Works, ed. Pearson, 1874, II. 103).

II. *trans.* 1. To make a splashing noise in.—2. To sprinkle with coloring matter so as to produce an imitation of granite: as, to *plash* a wall.

plash[1] (plash), *n.* [Early mod. E. *plasshe*, *plesh*; ‹ ME. *plasche*, *plaische*, ‹ MD. *plasch*, D. *plasch*, *plas*, a pool, puddle; cf. G. *platsch*, *plätsch* = Dan. *plask*, splash, splashing sound; from the verb. Cf. *flash*[2], in like sense.] 1. A small collection of standing water; a puddle; a pool.

Be-twyx a *plasche* and a flode, appone a flate lawnde,
Oure folke fongene theire felde, and fawghte theme agaynes.
Morte Arthure (E. E. T. S.), l. 2799.

Plasche or flasche, where reyne watyr stondythe (or pyt).
Prompt. Parv., p. 403.

Out of the wound the red blood flowed fresh,
That underneath his feet soone made a purple *plesh*.
Spenser, F. Q., II. viii. 36.

The illimitable reed,
And many a glancing *plash* and sallowy isle.
Tennyson, Last Tournament.

2. A sudden downpour of water; a sudden dash or splash: as, a *plash* of rain.—3. A flash; a spot (of light).

The tall grove of hemlocks, with moss on their stems, like *plashes* of sunlight.
Lowell, Fable for Critics (2d ed.), Int.

4. A splash or splashing sound.

Tweed's echoes heard the ceaseless *plash*,
While many a broken band,
Disorder'd, through her currents dash
To gain the Scottish land.
Scott, Marmion, vi. 34.

plash[2] (plash), *v.* [OF. *plassier, plaissier, plessier*, plash (cf. **plesse* (?) (ML. *plessa*), a thicket of woven boughs), a secondary form, < L. *plectere*, weave: see *plait, plat*[4], *pleat*. Cf. *pleach*, a doublet of *plash*[2].] **I.** *trans.* To bend down and interweave the branches or twigs of: as, to *plash* a hedge.

For Nature, loath, so rare a jewels wracke,
Seem'd as she here and there had *plash'd* a tree,
If possible to hinder destiny.
W. Browne, Britannia's Pastorals, ii. 4.

There is a cupola made with pole-work between two elmes at the end of a walk, which, being cover'd by *plashing* the trees to them, is very pretty.
Evelyn, Diary, Oct. 30, 1683.

II. *intrans.* To bend down a branch.

Some of the trees hung over the wall, and my brother did *plash* and did eat. *Bunyan*, Pilgrim's Progress, ii.

plash[2] (plash), *n.* [< *plash*[2], *v.*] A branch of a tree partly cut or lopped, and then bent down and bound to other branches. *Mortimer.*

plashet (plash'et), *n.* [< *plash*[1] + *-et*. Cf. ML. *plassetum*.] A small pond or puddle.

plashing[1] (plash'ing), *n.* [Verbal n. of *plash*[1], *v.*] A dabbling in water; a sound of plunging water.

plashing[2] (plash'ing), *n.* [Verbal n. of *plash*[2], *v.*] A mode of repairing or trimming a hedge, by bending down a part of the shoots, cutting them half through near the ground, to render them more pliable, and twisting them among the upright stems, so as to render the whole effective as a fence, and at the same time preserve all the branches alive.

plashing-tool (plash'ing-töl), *n.* A knife used in plashing hedges; a hedging-knife.

plashoot† (plash'öt), *n.* [Appar. for **plashet*, < *plash*[2] + *-et*, the term. accom. to *shoot* (young twig).] A fence made of branches of trees interwoven.

Woodcocks arrive first on the north coast, where almost every hedge serveth for a road, and every *plashoot* for springles to take them. *R. Carew*, Survey of Cornwall, p. 24.

plash-wheel (plash'hwēl), *n.* Same as *dash-wheel.*

plashy (plash'i), *a.* [< *plash*[1] + *-y*[1].] **1.** Watery; abounding with puddles; full of puddles; wet; moist.

They shed their waters into the valley below, making it *plashy* in sundry places. *Sandys*, Travailes, p. 169.

He also, being past Adrians wall [A. D. 209], cut down Woods, made way through Hills, fast'nd and fill'd up unsound and *plashy* Fens. *Milton*, Hist. Eng., ii.

Along the streaming mountain-side, and through
The dripping woods, and o'er the *plashy* fields.
Bryant, Rain-Dream.

One among many *plashy* meadows, enclosed with stone walls. *E. Dowden*, Shelley, I. 87.

2. Speckled as if plashed or splashed with coloring liquid.

In his grasp
A serpent's *plashy* neck; its barbed tongue
Squeezed from the gorge, and all its uncurl'd length
Dead. *Keats*, Hyperion, ii.

plasm (plazm), *n.* [< LL. *plasma*, < Gr. πλάσμα, a figure formed or molded from clay or wax, an image, counterfeit, an assumed form or manner, < πλάσσειν, form, mold: see *plastic.*] **1.** A mold or matrix in which anything is cast or formed to a particular shape. [Rare.]

The shells served as *plasms* or moulds to this sand.
Woodward.

2. In *biol.*, plasma. See *bioplasm, deutoplasm, protoplasm, plasmogen, sarcode.*

plasma (plas'mạ̈), *n.* [NL.: see *plasm.*] **1.** A variety of translucent quartz, or silica, of a rich grass-green or leek-green color, occurring in large pieces, associated with common chalcedony. Many fine engraved ornaments of this stone have been found among the ruins of Rome.—**2.** The liquid part of unaltered blood, lymph, or milk, as distinguished from the corpuscles of the blood or lymph, or the oil-globules of the milk; also, the juice expressed from fresh muscle; the muscle-plasma.—**3.** The primitive indifferent nitrogenized hydrocarbon which forms the basis of all tissues of plants and animals; the "physical basis of life," in its simplest expression: now generally called *protoplasm*. *Plasma* is now less used in this sense than formerly, as it had originally the more restricted meaning given in def. 2. See *protoplasm* and *starch.*
4. In *phar.*, same as *glycerite of starch.*

plasmasome (plas'mạ-sōm), *n.* [< Gr. πλάσμα, a molded figure (see *plasm*), + σῶμα, body.] A separate particle of plasm; a protoplasmic corpuscle.

The out-wandering *plasmasomes* form the so-called paranuclei. *Micros. Sci.*, XXX. ii. 168.

plasmatic (plas-mat'ik), *a.* [= F. *plasmatique*, < Gr. πλασματικός, imitating, < πλάσμα, a molded figure, an image: see *plasm.*] **1.** In *biol.*, same as *plasmic.*—**2**†. Giving shape; having the power of giving form; plastic. *Imp. Dict.*

plasmatical (plas-mat'i-kạl), *a.* [< *plasmatic* + *-al.*] Same as *plasmatic.*

Working in this, by her [Psyche's] *plasmatical* spirits or archei, all the whole world into order and shape.
Dr. H. More, Philos. Poems (1647), p. 342, notes.

plasmation† (plas-mā'shọn), *n.* [< LL. *plasmatio(n-)*, a forming, creating, < *plasma*, a molded figure, an image: see *plasm.*] Formation.

The *plasmation* or creation of Adam is reckoned among the generations. *Grafton*, Chron. i. 6.

plasmatoparous (plas-mạ-top'ạ-rus), *a.* [< Gr. πλάσμα (πλασματ-), a molded figure, + L. *parere*, bring forth.] In *mycology*, noting germination in which the whole protoplasm of a gonidium issues as a spherical mass which at once becomes invested with a membrane and puts out a germ-tube. *De Bary.*

plasmator†, *n.* [ME., = F. *plasmateur*, < LL. *plasmator*, a former, fashioner, creator, < *plasmare*, form, mold, fashion, < *plasma*, a molded figure: see *plasm.*] One who forms or creates; a creator.

Hayle! fulgent Phebus and fader eternall,
Parfite *plasmator* and god omnipotent.
York Plays, p. 514.

plasmature†, *n.* [< LL. *plasma(t-)*, a molded figure, + *-ure.*] Form; shape.

That so stately frame and *plasmature* wherein the man at first had been created. *Urquhart*, tr. of Rabelais, ii. 8.

plasmic (plaz'mik), *a.* [< *plasm* + *-ic.*] Of the nature of plasma; pertaining to plasma; plastic or formative; blastemic; protoplasmic: as, *plasmic* substances or processes; a *plasmic* origin. Also *plasmatic.*

plasmine (plas'min), *n.* [< Gr. πλάσμα, a molded figure, + *-ine*[2].] A proteid precipitated from blood-plasma on the addition of sodium chlorid and other salts. It coagulates, forming fibrin, when redissolved in water.

plasmochyme (plas'mọ̄-kim), *n.* [< Gr. πλάσμα, a molded figure, + χυμός, juice, chyle: see *chyme*[1].] The thick fluid albuminous substance of a cell. Also *plasmochym. Micros. Sci.*, XXX. ii. 211.

plasmode (plas'mōd), *n.* Same as *plasmodium.*

plasmodia, *n.* Plural of *plasmodium.*

plasmodial (plas-mō'di-ạl), *a.* [< *plasmodi-um* + *-al.*] Having the character or properties of plasmodium. Also *plasmodic.*

Plasmodiata (plas-mō-di-ā'tạ̈), *n. pl.* [NL.: see *plasmodium.*] Plasmodiate organisms: a synonym of *Mycetozoa* when these are regarded as animals. *E. R. Lankester.*

plasmodiate (plas-mō'di-āt), *a.* [< *plasmodium* + *-ate*[1].] Provided with or producing plasmodia; consisting of or contained in plasmodium.

plasmodiation (plas-mō-di-ā'shọn), *n.* [< *plasmodiate* + *-ion.*] In *bot.*, the disposition of plasmodia. *Jour. of Bot. British and Foreign*, 1883, p. 371.

plasmodic (plas-mod'ik), *a.* [< *plasmodi-um* + *-ic.*] Same as *plasmodial.*

plasmodiocarp (plas-mō'di-ọ̄-kärp), *n.* [< NL. *plasmodium* + Gr. καρπός, a fruit.] In *Myxomycetes*, a form of fructification which is more or less irregular in shape. Compare *æthalium*, 2, and *sporangium*. *Cooke*, Myxomycetes of Great Britain, p. 30.

plasmodiocarpous (plas-mō″di-ọ̄-kär'pus), *a.* [< *plasmodiocarp* + *-ous.*] Resembling, characterized by, or producing plasmodiocarps. *Cooke*, Myxomycetes of Great Britain, p. 30.

Plasmodiophora (plas-mō-di-of'ọ̄-rạ̈), *n.* [NL. (Woronin), < *plasmodium* + Gr. φέρειν = E. *bear*[1].] A genus of myxomycetous fungi, giving name to the family *Plasmodiophoreæ*. The spores are free, not quaternate, and are disposed in sori; they emit zoöspores in germination.

Plasmodiophoreæ (plas-mō″di-ọ̄-fō'rẹ̄-ē), *n. pl.* [NL. (Zopf), < *Plasmodiophora* + *-eæ.*] A family of myxomycetous fungi with the fructification disposed in sori.

plasmodium (plas-mō'di-um), *n.*; pl. *plasmodia* (-ạ̈). [NL., < Gr. πλάσμα, a molded figure, + εἶδος, form.] **1.** Protoplasm of protozoans in sheets, masses, or comparatively large quantities, as formed by the plasmodiate members of the *Protozoa*. True plasmodium is formed by the organic fusion of two or several amœbiform bodies, and distinguished from the *aggregate plasmodium* resulting from mere contact. See cut under *Protomyxa.*

2. A definite quantity of plasmodium, or the plasmodium of given individual organisms.

Large masses of gelatinous consistence characteristic of the so-called animal phase of the Myxomycetan, technically known as the *plasmodium*.
W. S. Kent, Infusoria, p. 42.

3. The naked multinucleated mass of protoplasm, exhibiting amœboid movement, which makes up the entire plant-body of the slime-molds (*Myxomycetes*) during the vegetative period of their existence. See *Myxomycetes, slime-mold, Fuligo*, 2, and *Olpidium*.—**Plasmodium malariæ**, a series of forms found in malarial blood, believed to be different stages in the life-history of a single organism which causes paludism. Some of these forms are amœbiform, some crescent-shaped, some rosette-shaped, some ciliate; some contain pigment-granules, and some do not.

plasmogen (plas'mọ̄-jen), *n.* [< Gr. πλάσμα, a molded figure, + -γενής, producing: see *-gen.*] True protoplasm; bioplasm. See the quotation, and *germ-plasma.*

Physiologists have come to use the word "protoplasm" for one of the chemical substances of which Schultze's protoplasm is a structural mixture—namely, that highest point in the chemical elaboration of the molecule which is attached within the protoplasm, and up to which some of the chemical bodies present are tending, whilst others are degradation products resulting from a downward metamorphosis of portions of it. This intangible, unstable, all-pervading element of the protoplasm cannot at present be identified with any visibly separate part of the cell-substance. . . . This "critical" substance, sometimes called "true protoplasm," should assuredly be recognized by a distinct name "*plasmogen.*" *Encyc. Brit.*, XXIV. 817

plasmogony (plas-mog'ọ̄-ni), *n.* [< Gr. πλάσμα, a molded figure, + -γονία, generation: see *-gony.*] The generation or origination of an organism from plasma. *Rossiter.*

plasmology (plas-mol'ọ̄-ji), *n.* [< Gr. πλάσμα, a molded figure, + -λογία, < λέγειν, speak: see *-ology.*] Minute or microscopic anatomy, as a branch of biology; histology; the study of the ultimate corpuscles of living matter, as regards their structure, development, and properties, with the aid of the microscope.

plasmolysis (plas-mol'i-sis), *n.* [NL., < Gr. πλάσμα, a molded figure, + λύσις, a loosing.] In *bot.*, the contraction of the protoplasm in active cells under the action of certain reagents. When the solutions employed are more dense than the fluids within the cell, a certain amount of water will be withdrawn from the contents of the cell by exosmotic action, thereby causing a shrinking which can easily be noted under the microscope, and, when the density of the solution is known, will allow the experimenter to ascertain within very narrow limits the density of the contents of the cell and the relative degree of turgidity.

plasmolytic (plas-mọ̄-lit'ik), *a.* [< *plasmolysis* (*-lyt-*) + *-ic.*] In *bot.*, exhibiting or characterized by plasmolysis; employed in plasmolysis.

plasmolyze (plas'mọ̄-līz), *v. t.*; pret. and pp. *plasmolyzed*, ppr. *plasmolyzing*. [< *plasmolysis.*] To effect plasmolysis in or of; subject to plasmolysis. Also spelled *plasmolyse.*

In order to see the primordial utricle better, *plasmolyse* the cell by running in 10 p. c. salt solution.
Huxley and Martin, Elementary Biology, p. 404.

plaster (plås'tėr), *n.* [Formerly also *plaister, playster*; < ME. *plaster*, also *plastre, playster* (after OF.), < AS. *plaster* = D. *pleister* = MLG. *plāster* = OHG. *phlastar, plastar*, MHG. *phlaster, pflaster, plaster*, G. *pflaster* = Sw. *plåster* = Dan. *plaster* = OF. *plastre, plaistre*, a plaster, plaster, F. *plâtre*, gypsum, = Pr. *plastre*, a plaster, = It. dim. *piastrello*, a plaster (ML. *plastrum*, gypsum); with loss of orig. prefix; ME. *enplastre*, < OF. *emplastre*, F. *emplâtre*, a plaster, < L. *emplastrum*, a plaster for a wound, < Gr. ἔμπλαστρον for ἔμπλαστον, a plaster: see *emplaster.*] **1.** In *phar.*, a solid compound intended for external application, adhesive at the temperature of the human body, and requiring to be softened by heat before being spread.

My myddell woundys they ben derne & depe;
Ther ys no *plaster* that persyth aryght.
Political Poems, etc. (ed. Furnivall), p. 215.

Where any private harm doth grow, we are not to reject instruction as being an unmeet *plaister* to apply unto it.
Hooker, Eccles. Polity, iv. 12.

2. A composition of lime, water, and sand, with or without hair for binding, well mixed so as to form a kind of paste, and used for coating walls and partitions of houses.

A House shou'd be built or with Brick or with Stone;
Why, 'tis *Plaister* and Lath; and I think that's all one.
Prior, Down-Hall, st. 38.

3. Calcined gypsum or calcium sulphate, used, when mixed with water, for finishing walls, for molds, ornaments, casts, luting, cement, etc. Plaster used as a ground for painting in distemper is unburned, and of two kinds, one coarse and one of a finer quality. Both are made from white alabaster, but the latter, which is used also as a ground for gilding, and for working ornaments in relief, is more carefully prepared than the former. The plaster used for taking casts from life or from statues is always burned.

They suppose that this ryuer [Bahuan] hathe made it selfe awaye vnder the grounde by sume passages of *playster* or salte earthe. *Peter Martyr*, tr. in First Books on [America (ed. Arber), p. 172.

Aconite plaster, aconite-root, alcohol, and resin plaster. —**Adhesive plaster.** Same as *resin plaster.*—**Ammoniac plaster**, ammoniac and diluted acetic acid.—**Ammoniac plaster with mercury**, ammoniac, mercury, olive-oil, sublimed sulphur, diluted acetic acid, and lead-plaster.—**Antimonial plaster**, double tartrate of antimony and potassium and Burgundy pitch.—**Arnica plaster**, extract of arnica-root and resin plaster.—**Aromatic plaster.** Same as *spice-plaster.*—**Asafetida plaster**, asafetida, lead-plaster, galbanum, yellow wax, and alcohol.—**Belladonna plaster**, belladonna-root, alcohol, and resin plaster.—**Blistering plaster.** Same as *cantharides plaster.*—**Brown soap plaster.** Same as *soap-cerate plaster.*—**Burgundy-pitch plaster**, Burgundy pitch and yellow wax.—**Calcined plaster.** Same as *plaster of Paris.*—**Canada-pitch plaster**, Canada pitch and yellow wax.—**Cantharides plaster**, cantharides, yellow wax, resin, and lard. Also called *cantharides cerate, blistering plaster, vesicating plaster.*—**Capsicum plaster**, resin plaster and oleoresin of capsicum.—**Carbonate-of-lead plaster**, lead carbonate, olive-oil, yellow wax, lead-plaster, and Florentine orris.—**Chalybeate plaster.** Same as *iron plaster.*—**Court plaster.** See *court-plaster.*—**Diachylon plaster.** Same as *lead-plaster.*—**Fibrous plaster**, plaster of Paris into which fibrous material of some kind is worked to give it coherence: used for patterns in low relief for ceilings, walls, and the like.—**Galbanum plaster**, galbanum, turpentine, Burgundy pitch, and lead-plaster; or galbanum, ammoniac, yellow wax, and lead-plaster.—**Hemlock-pitch plaster.** Same as *Canada-pitch plaster.*—**Iodide-of-lead plaster**, lead iodide, soap plaster, and resin plaster; or lead iodide, lead-plaster, and resin. —**Iron plaster**, oxid of iron, Canada turpentine, Burgundy pitch, and lead-plaster. Also called *chalybeate plaster, strengthening plaster.*—**Isinglass plaster**, isinglass, alcohol, glycerin, and tincture of benzoin. Also called *court-plaster.*—**Lath and plaster.** See *lath*[1].—**Lead plaster.** See *lead-plaster.*—**Litharge plaster.** Same as *lead-plaster.*—**Logan's plaster**, litharge, lead carbonate, Castile soap, butter, olive-oil, and mastic.—**Mahy's plaster.** Same as *carbonate-of-lead plaster.*—**Mercurial plaster**, mercury, olive-oil, resin, and lead-plaster.—**Miraculous plaster**, red oxid of lead, olive-oil, camphor, and alum.—**Opium plaster.** See *opium-plaster.* —**Pitch-plaster**, Burgundy pitch, frankincense, resin, yellow wax, oil of nutmeg, and olive-oil.—**Pitch-plaster with cantharides**, Burgundy pitch and cerate or plaster of cantharides; or cantharides, oil of nutmeg, yellow wax, resin, soap plaster, and resin plaster. Also called *warm plaster.*—**Plaster cast**, a reproduction of an object made by pouring plaster of Paris mixed with water into a mold which has been made from the object to be copied. Many molds are needed for a complicated figure, and the parts separately cast are united, showing raised seams where they are put together.—**Plaster jacket**, a bandage surrounding the trunk, made stiff with gypsum, used in caries of the vertebræ.—**Plaster mull**, a plaster made by coating a thin sheet of gutta-percha, backed with muslin, with the substance that is to be applied to the skin.—**Plaster of Paris.** (*a*) Native gypsum: so called because found in large quantities in the Tertiary of the Paris basin. See *gypsum.* (*b*) Calcined gypsum—that is, gypsum from which the water has been driven off by heat: used in building and in making casts of busts and statues, etc. When diluted with water into a thin paste, plaster of Paris sets rapidly, and at the instant of setting expands or increases in bulk; hence this material becomes valuable for filling cavities, etc., where other earths would shrink.—**Plaster process**, a method of making stereotype plates for printing by the use of plaster. A mold of the type page is made by pouring over it liquid plaster of Paris; this mold, when baked entirely dry, is filled with melted type-metal. *Workshop Receipts*, 4th ser., p. 217.—**Poor man's plaster**, a plaster composed of tar, resin, and yellow wax. *Dunglison.*—**Porous plaster**, a spread plaster having numerous small holes to prevent wrinkling and to render it more pliable.—**Rademacher's plaster**, red lead, olive-oil, amber, camphor, and alum.—**Resin plaster**, resin, lead-plaster, and yellow wax or hard soap. Also called *adhesive plaster, sticking plaster.*—**Soap-cerate plaster**, curd soap, yellow wax, olive-oil, oxid of lead, and vinegar.—**Soap plaster**, soap and lead-plaster, with or without resin.—**Spice plaster**, yellow wax, suet, turpentine, oil of nutmeg, olibanum, benzoin, oil of peppermint, and oil of cloves. Also called *aromatic plaster, stomach-plaster.*—**Sticking plaster.** Same as *resin plaster.*—**Stomach-plaster.** Same as *spice plaster.*—**Stramonium plaster**, extract of stramonium, elemi, and galbanum plaster.—**Strengthening plaster.** Same as *iron plaster.*—**Thapsia plaster**, yellow wax, Burgundy pitch, resin, terebinthina cocta, Venice turpentine, glycerin, and thapsia resin.—**Vesicating plaster.** Same as *cantharides plaster.*—**Vigo plaster**, lead-plaster, yellow wax, resin, olibanum, ammoniac, bdellium, myrrh, saffron, mercury, turpentine, liquid storax, and oil of lavender.—**Warm (or warming) plaster.** Same as *pitch-plaster with cantharides.*—**Zinc plaster**, zinc sulphate and Castile soap.

plaster (plàs'tėr), *v. t.* [Formerly also *plaister, playster*; < ME. *plastren, playsteren, playstren* = D. *pleisteren* = MLG. *plàsteren* = G. *pflastern* = Sw. *plàstra* = Dan. *plastre*; from the noun: see *plaster, n.* Cf. *emplaster, v.*] **1.** To apply a medicative plaster to; cover with a plaster: as, to *plaster* a wound.

And be he bathed in that blode baptised, as it were,
And thanne *plastred* with penaunce and passioun of that babi,
He shulde stonde and steppe. *Piers Plowman* (B), xvii. 95.

2. To cover or overlay with plaster, as the walls of a house, partitions, etc.

The east side [of the aqueduct] is *plaistered* with a very strong cement, probably to prevent any damage from the sands that might be drove against it. *Pococke*, Description of the East, II. i. 59.

The houses [at Rome] are of stone, but *plastered* as at Vienna. *Eustace*, Italy, II. i.

3. To bedaub or besmear: as, to *plaster* the face with powder. [Colloq.]—**4.** To fill or cover over with or as with plaster; hide; gloss: with *up*.

But see here the conueyance of these spirituall gentlemen in *playsteryng vp* their unsauery sorceries. *Bp. Bale*, English Votaries, i.

And suck out clammy dews from herbs and flowers,
To smear the chinks, and *plaster up* the pores.
Addison, tr. of Virgil's Georgics, iv.

5. To treat with plaster; add gypsum to: as, to *plaster* vines by dusting them with gypsum in order to prevent rot or mildew of the berries; to *plaster* wines by adding gypsum in order to neutralize acid or produce other fancied benefits.

plasterbill (plàs'tėr-bil), *n.* The surf-scoter or surf-duck, *Œdemia* (*Pelionetta*) *perspicillata*: so called from a peculiarity of the bill. *G. Trumbull*, 1888. See cut under *surf-duck*. [Massachusetts.]

plaster-clover† (plàs'tėr-klō"vėr), *n.* The sweet clover, *Melilotus officinalis*: so called from its use in ointments.

plasterer (plàs'tėr-ėr), *n.* [= D. *pleisteraar* = G. *pflasterer, pflästerer*; as *plaster, v.*, + *-er*[1].] One who plasters walls; also, one who makes plaster ornaments.

plastering (plàs'tėr-ing), *n.* [< ME. *plasteryng, playsteryng*; verbal n. of *plaster, v.*] **1.** The act or operation of overlaying with plaster.—**2.** The plaster-work of a building; a covering of plaster.—**3.** The treatment of wines by the addition of gypsum or plaster of Paris. See *plaster, v.*, 5.

plastering-machine (plàs'tėr-ing-ma-shēn'), *n.* A machine designed for use in spreading plaster in forming interior walls and ceilings. Attempts to construct a practical machine of this kind, adapted to general use, have not yet succeeded, and the ancient method of plastering with hand-trowels is still universal.

plaster-mill (plàs'tėr-mil), *n.* **1.** A machine consisting of a roller or a set of rollers for grinding lime or gypsum to powder.—**2.** A mortar-mill.

plaster-stone (plàs'tėr-stōn), *n.* Gypsum, or a species of gypsum.

plastery (plàs'tėr-i), *a.* [< *plaster* + *-y*[1].] Resembling plaster; containing plaster.

St. Peter's disappoints me; the stone of which it is made is a poor *plastery* material; and indeed Rome in general might be called a rubbishy place. *A. H. Clough.*

plastic (plas'tik), *a.* [= F. *plastique* = Sp. *plástico* = Pg. It. *plastico* (cf. D. G. *plastisch* = Sw. Dan. *plastisk*), < L. *plasticus*, < Gr. πλαστικός, of or belonging to molding or modeling, < πλαστός, verbal adj. of πλάσσειν, mold or form in clay, wax, etc. Cf. *plaster*.] **1.** Capable of molding or of giving form or fashion to a mass of matter; having power to mold.

Benign Creator, let thy *plastic* Hand
Dispose its own Effect. *Prior*, Solomon, iii.

Plastic Nature working to this end.
Pope, Essay on Man, iii. 9.

The One Spirit's *plastic* stress
Sweeps through the dull dense world.
Shelley, Adonais, xliii.

2. Capable of being modeled or molded into various forms, as plaster, clay, etc.; hence, capable of change or modification; capable of receiving a new bent or direction: as, the mind is *plastic* in youth.

Stuff at hand, *plastic* as they could wish.
Wordsworth, French Revolution.

3. Pertaining to or connected with modeling or molding; produced by or characteristic of modeling or molding: as, the *plastic* art (that is, sculpture in the widest sense, as distinguished from painting and the graphic arts).

Pictorial rather than *plastic* in style, both in action and in the treatment of draperies.
C. C. *Perkins*, Italian Sculpture, p. 152.

4. In *biol.*, specifically, plasmic.—**Plastic bronchitis**, pseudomembranous bronchitis.—**Plastic clay**, clay suitable for making pottery or bricks; specifically, a division of the Eocene in England, especially in the London basin and on the Isle of Wight, where it is characteristically developed. The Plastic clay series was so named by T. Webster, in imitation of the name given by Cuvier and Brongniart (*Argile plastique*) to a division of the series in the Paris basin. The beds thus named by Webster were later designated by Prestwich as the Woolwich and Reading series. Part of the series is very fossiliferous; among the fossils is a bird as large as the dinornis of New Zealand.—**Plastic crystal.** See *crystal.*—**Plastic force**, the sum total of agencies producing growth and organization in living bodies.—**Plastic gum**, gutta-percha.—**Plastic imagination**, the productive or creative imagination.—**Plastic medium**, something intermediate between soul and body, assumed to account for their action one upon the other.—**Plastic nature.** See *nature.*—**Plastic operations, plastic surgery**, operations which have for their object the restoring of lost parts, as when the skin of the cheeks is used to make a new nose (rhinoplasty).—**Plastic solid.** See *solid.*

plastical† (plas'ti-kal), *a.* [< *plastic* + *-al*.] Same as *plastic*. *Dr. H. More*, Philosophical Writings, Pref. Gen., p. xvi.

plastically (plas'ti-kal-i), *adv.* In a plastic manner; by molding or modeling, as a plastic substance.

plasticity (plas-tis'i-ti), *n.* [= F. *plasticité* = Sp. *plasticidad* = Pg. *plasticidade*; as *plastic* + *-ity*.] The property of being plastic. (*a*) The property of giving form or shape to matter.

To show further that this protoplasm possesses the necessary properties of a normal protoplasm, it will be necessary to examine . . . what these properties are. They are two in number, the capacity for life and *plasticity*.
H. *Drummond*, Natural Law in the Spiritual World, p. 290.

(*b*) Capability of being molded, formed, or modeled.

The race must at a certain time have a definite amount of *plasticity*—that is, a definite power of adapting itself to altered circumstances by changing in accordance with them. *W. K. Clifford*, Lectures, I. 102.

Some natures are distinguished by *plasticity* or the power of acquisition, and therefore realise more closely the saying that man is a bundle of habits.
A. Bain, Emotions and Will, p. 473.

plastid (plas'tid), *n.* and *a.* [< NL. *plastidium*, q. v.] **I.** *n.* **1.** A unicellular organism; a simple unit of aggregation of the first order, as an individual protozoan, or a cell considered with reference to its developmental or evolutionary potentiality. The word has no exact zoölogical signification. Haeckel used it for any elementary organism, as a cell or cytode.

If we reduce organized beings to their ultimate organisms—cells or *plastids*.
Dawson, Origin of the World, p. 377.

2. In *bot.*, one of the variously shaped proteid bodies, such as chlorophyl-granules, leucoplastids, chromoplastids, etc., which may be clearly differentiated in the protoplasm of active cells. They have substantially the same chemical and, with the exception of color, the same physical properties as protoplasm. They are regarded as being the centers of chemical activity in cells.

II. *a.* Having the character or quality of a plastid; plastic or plasmic.

plastidium (plas-tid'i-um), *n.*; pl. *plastidia* (-ä). [NL., < Gr. πλαστός, verbal adj. of πλάσσειν, mold, form (see *plastic*), + dim. *-ιδιον*.] Same as *plastid*.

Plastidozoa (plas"ti-dọ-zō'ä), *n. pl.* [NL., < *plastid*(*ium*) + Gr. ζῷον, animal.] Same as *Protozoa*.

plastidular (plas-tid'ụ-lär), *a.* [< *plastidule* + *-ar*[3].] Of or pertaining to plastidules.

plastidule (plas'ti-dūl), *n.* [< *plastid* + *-ule*.] A molecule of protoplasm; chemically, the smallest mass of protoplasm which can exist as such, or the very complex and highly unstable molecule of the chemical substance protein, when invested with vital activities.

plastilina (plas-ti-lī'nä), *n.* [< *plast*(*ic*) + *-il* + *-ina*.] A modeling-clay so compounded as to remain moist for a considerable time, and thus dispense with frequent wetting during the progress of the work.

plastin (plas'tin), *n.* [< Gr. πλαστός, verbal adj. of πλάσσειν, form, mold, + *-in*[2].] In *biol.*, an element in the chemical composition of the cell-nucleus: according to Swartz, who calls it also *cytoplastin*, a viscous extensible mass which resists pepsin- and trypsin-digestion.

Carnoy . . . believes that the single, greatly coiled chromatin thread present in the nucleus in Arthropoda has a "*plastin* envelope," consisting of nuclein substances. . . . Besides the "nuclein" discovered by Miescher, which forms an essential part of the mass of the nucleus, Reinke and Rodewald have found "*plastin*," and Kossel "histon" and "adenin."
Quart. Jour. Micros. Sci., XXX. ii. 166, 169.

plastography (plas-tog'ra-fi), *n.* [< Gr. πλαστός, verbal adj. of πλάσσειν, form, mold, + -γραφία, < γράφειν, write.] Imitation of handwriting; forgery.

plastra, *n.* Plural of *plastrum*.

plastral (plas'tral), *a.* [< *plastr-on* + *-al*.] In *herpet.*, of or pertaining to the plastron; entering into the formation of the under shell: as, *plastral* bones; *plastral* scutes or sutures.

plastron (plas'tron), *n.* [< F. *plastron* (= It. *piastrone*), a breastplate, < OF. *plastre*, a plaster: see *plaster*.] **1.** A breastplate; a garment or part of a garment covering the breast. Specifically—(*a*) The early breastplate worn under the hauberk or broigne: one of the earliest pieces of plate-armor introduced in the European middle ages. *C. Boutell*, Arms and Armour in England. (*b*) A wadded shield of leather which masters hang before the right breast when giving lessons in fencing. (*c*) A detachable part of a woman's dress, made of some soft material, and suspended in loose folds from the throat to the waist and caught in the belt: as, a *plastron* of lace, crape, or silk. (*d*) An ornamental and often jeweled decorative plaque worn on the breast by Hindu women. (*e*) A man's shirt-bosom, especially one of the form fashionable for evening-dress 1875-90, without plaits, presenting a smooth surface of lawn.
2. In *herpet.*: (*a*) The ventral part of the shell of a chelonian or testudinate; the lower shell, or under side of the shell, of a turtle or tortoise: more or less opposed to *carapace*. The plastron is wholly an exoskeletal or integumentary structure, in which no bones belonging to the endoskeleton or skeleton proper are found. It consists of a number, typically nine, of separate dermal bones, developed in membrane, and covered with horny epidermis, or tortoise-shell. The nine typical pieces are one median and four pairs lateral, called *entoplastron*, *epiplastron*, *hyoplastron*, *hypoplastron*, and *xiphiplastron*. Formerly, when these were supposed to contain or represent sternal elements, they were respectively named *entosternum*, *episternum*, *hyosternum*, *hyposternum*, and *xiphisternum*. The plastron is usually immovable, like the carapace, but may be variously hinged, in some cases so as to shut the animal in completely. See also cuts under *carapace*, *Pleurospondylia*, and *Chelonia*. (*b*) One of the similar exoskeletal plates developed upon the under side of the body of certain *Amphibia*, as the *Labyrinthodonta*.—**3.** In *mammal.*, the ventral shield or cuirass of the glyptodons or fossil armadillos.—**4.** In *anat.*, the sternum with the costal cartilages attached, as removed in autopsies.—**5.** In *ornith.*, a colored area on the breast or belly of a bird, like or likened to a shield. *Coues.*

Plastron of Tortoise (*Emys*), ventral surface (outside), showing twelve horny epidermal scales as indicated by the dark lines, one of which traverses each xiphisternal (*xp*) and each hyposternal (*hp*) bony scute; *ic*, interclavicular scute, or entoplastron; *c*, clavicular scute (clavicular; um); *hy*, hyosternal scute.

plastron-de-fer (plas'tron-dė-fer'), *n.* Same as *plastron*, 1 (*a*).

plastrum (plas'trum), *n.*; pl. *plastra* (-trä). [NL., an accom. form of *plastron*; cf. ML. *plastrum*, plaster (gypsum): see *plaster*, *plastron*.] Same as *plastron*.

plat[1] (plat), *v. t.*; pret. and pp. *platted*, ppr. *platting*. [< ME. *platten*, *pletten*, < AS. *plættan*, strike with the hand, slap, = MD. *pletten*, strike, bruise, crush, rub (freq. *pletteren*), = Sw. dial. *plätta*, var. *pjätta*, tap, pat. Cf. *pat*[1], prob. a reduced form of *plat*[1].] To strike with the hand; strike.

His heved of he *plette*. *Havelok*, l. 2626.

Pernel Proud-herte *platte* hire to grounde,
And lay longe ar heo lokede.
Piers Plowman (A), v. 45.

plat[2] (plat), *n.* [Early mod. E. *platte*; a var. of *plot*[1], < ME. *plot*, < AS. *plot*, a plot of ground: see *plot*[1]. The form *plat* may be merely dial., but is prob. due in part to *plat*[3].] **1.** A plot or patch of land laid off for or devoted to some particular purpose: as, a garden-*plat*; a *plat* of ground.

Now therefore take and cast him into the *plat* of ground, according to the word of the Lord. 2 Ki. ix. 26.

2. A flat representation of such plots or patches; a map or plan.

To take by view of eye the *platte* of any thinge.
Booke of Precedence (E. E. T. S., extra ser.), i. 5.

There was no other pastime nor exercise among the youth but to draw *plattes* of Sicile, and describe the situation of Libya and Carthage.
North, tr. of Plutarch, p. 220 B. (*Nares.*)

We followed the shoare or land, which lieth Northnorthwest, . . . as it doth appeare by the *plat*.
Hakluyt's Voyages, I. 275.

3†. A plan or design; scheme; plot.

So shall our *plat* in this one point be larger and much surmount that which Stanihurst first tooke in hand.
Puttenham, Arte of Eng. Poesie, p. 90.

Here might be made a rare scene of folly, if the *plat* could bear it. *Marston*, Antonio and Mellida, I., iii. 2.

To be workmanly wrought, made, and sett up, after the best handlyng and forme of good workmanship, according to a *plat* thereof made and signed with the hands of the lords executors.
Walpole, Anecdotes of Painting, I., App., Indentures, i.

plat[2] (plat), *v. t.*; pret. and pp. *platted*, ppr. *platting*. [< *plat*[2], *n.* Cf. *plot*[1], *v.*] To make a ground-plan of; map or plot; lay down on paper: as, to *plat* a tract of land; to *plat* a town.

The author acknowledges his indebtedness to . . . Wharton's "Hydrographic Surveying," whence he takes the method of *platting* angles by means of chords.
Science, XV. 78.

The work ["Emblematic Mounds"] is illustrated by two hundred and seventy woodcuts, many of them full pages. They represent the effigies both singly and in groups, just as they were when measured and *platted*.
Amer. Antiquarian, XII., adv.

The town was *platted* in 1872, and named in honor of Prince Otto von Bismarck. *Harper's Mag.*, LXXVIII. 360.

plat[3] (plat), *a.* and *n.* [< ME. *plat*, *platt*, *platte* = D. *plat* = MLG. *plat*, LG. *platt* = G. *platt* = Sw. *platt* = Dan. *plat*, flat, level, low; < OF. (and F.) *plat* = Pr. *plat* = Sp. Pg. *plato* = It. *piatto*, flat, level (ML. **platus*, **plattus*, only as a noun, after Rom.: see *plate*), < Gr. πλατύς, flat, wide, broad, = Lith. *platus*, broad, = Skt. *prithu*, wide, broad, < √ *prath*, spread out, broaden; prob. ult. connected with E. *flawn* (OHG. *flado*, etc.), a flat cake (see *flawn*), but not with E. *flat* (see *flat*[1]). From the same ult. source are *plate*, *pate*[1], *place*, *plaza*, *piazza*, *plaice*, *plane*[3], *plateau*, *platina*, *platitude*, *platter*[1], etc.: see esp. *plate*.] **I.** *a.* **1**†. Flat; level; plain.

In another Yle ben folk that han the face all *platt*, alle pleyn, with outen Nese and with outen Mouthe; but thei han 2 smale holes alle rounde, instede of hire Eyen; and hire Mouthe is *platt* also, with outen Lippes.
Mandeville, Travels, p. 204.

He lyeth downe his one eare all *plat*
Unto the grounde, and halt it faste.
Gower, Conf. Amant., I.

2. Specifically, in *lace-making*, flat and of uniform texture: said of the sprigs or flowers; hence, in general, noting the sprigs of bobbin-lace, which are flat, as compared with those of needle-point lace, which may have relief.—**Point plat.** See *point*[1].

II. *n.* **1**†. A beam or plank laid horizontally; a horizontal timber. *Halliwell.*

Thane was the prynce purvayede, and theire places nomene,
Pyghte pavyllyouns of palle, and *plattes* in seegge.
Morte Arthure (E. E. T. S.), l. 2478.

2†. A large flat stone used as the landing-place of a stair.—**3**†. The flat side of a sword.

And what man that is wounded with the strook
Shal never be hool til that yow list, of grace,
To stroke him with the *platte* in thilke place
Ther he is hurt. *Chaucer*, Squire's Tale, l. 154.

4†. The sole of the foot. Compare *plant*[2]. *Withals*, Dict. (1608), p. 284. (*Nares.*)—**5.** In *mining*, an enlargement of a level where it connects with a shaft used for raising ore, its object being to facilitate that operation, especially in mines where the ore is raised in kibbles.

plat[3]† (plat), *adv.* [ME. *plat*, *platte*; < *plat*[3], *a.*] **1.** Flatly; plainly; bluntly.

Thus warned she him ful *plat* and ful pleyn.
Chaucer, Monk's Tale, l. 767.

Whanne we were in the hyghe see, about .xxx. myle in oure waye from Modona, the wynde fell *platte* ayenste vs.
Sir R. Guylforde, Pylgrymage, p. 69.

2. Smoothly; evenly.

plat[3]† (plat), *v. t.* [= D. *pletten* = G. *plätten*, lay flat, flatten; from the adj.: see *plat*[3], *a.*] To lay down flat or evenly; spread.

He *platteth* his butter upon his breed w[t] his thombe as it were a lytell claye. *Palsgrave.* (*Halliwell.*)

plat[4] (plat), *v.*; pret. and pp. *platted*, ppr. *platting*. [< ME. *platten*; a var. of *plait*: see *plait*.] **I.** *trans.* To interweave; make or shape by interweaving; wattle; plait. See *plait*.

When they had *platted* a crown of thorns, they put it upon his head. Mat. xxvii. 29.

Upon her head a *platted* hive of straw,
Which fortified her visage from the sun.
Shak., Lover's Complaint, l. 8.

Some *plat*, like Spiral Shells, their braded Hair.
Congreve, tr. of Ovid's Art of Love, iii.

II. *intrans.* To embrace. [Rare.]

And they twa met, and they twa *plat*,
And fain they wad be near;
And a' the warld might ken right weel,
They were twa lovers dear.
The Douglas Tragedy (Child's Ballads, II. 119).

plat[4] (plat), *n.* [< *plat*[4], *v.*] **1.** A plaited or braided thing; something produced by plaiting or interweaving: as, straw *plat* for hats; a *plat* of hair.—**2.** *Naut.*, a braid of foxes. See *fox*[1], 4. *Dana.*

Platacanthomyinæ (plat-a-kan″thō-mi-ī'nē), *n. pl.* [NL., < *Platacanthomys* + *-inæ*.] A subfamily of *Muridæ*, represented by the genus *Platacanthomys*.

Platacanthomys (plat-a-kan'thō-mis), *n.* [NL. (E. Blyth, 1859), prop. **Platyacanthomys*, < Gr. πλατύς, flat, + ἄκανθα, a spine, + μῦς, mouse.] The only genus of *Platacanthomyinæ*, having transversely laminate molars and the fur mixed with flattened spines. *P. lasiurus* is a small species like a dormouse, with a densely hairy tail, inhabiting mountainous parts of western India.

Platacidæ (plạ-tas'i-dē), *n. pl.* [NL., < *Platax* (*Platac-*) + *-idæ*.] A family of acanthopterygian fishes, typified by the genus *Platax*; the sea-bats. They have a high compressed body, imbricated scales, a long high dorsal with the spines few and crowded in front, a long high anal, well-developed ventrals, setiform teeth in the jaws, and an edentulous palate. About 7 species are known as inhabitants of the Indian and western Pacific oceans.

Platalea (plạ-tā'lē̦-ạ̈), *n.* [NL., < L. *platalea* (also *platea*), the spoonbill, appar. < Gr. πλατύς, flat: see *plat*[3].] The typical genus of *Plataleidæ*, formerly conterminous with the family,

Spoonbill (*Platalea leucorodia*).

now restricted to the Old World spoonbills, such as *P. leucorodia*, in which the intrathoracic parts of the trachea are peculiarly convoluted. Also *Platea*.

Plataleidæ (plat-ạ-lē'i-dē), *n. pl.* [NL., < *Platalea* + *-idæ*.] A family of large grallatorial birds of the order *Herodiones* and suborder *Ibides*, typified by the genus *Platalea*, having the long flat bill dilated at the end like a spoon; the spoonbills, or spoon-billed ibises. There are 5 or 6 species, of various parts of the world, chiefly in tropical latitudes. They were formerly classed with the storks, but are more closely related to the ibises. See cuts under *Aiaia* and *Platalea*.

plataleiform (plạ-tā'lē̦-i-fôrm), *a.* [< L. *platalea*, a spoonbill, + *forma*, form.] Like a spoonbill in form; plataleine in structure and affinity.

plataleine (plạ-tā'lē̦-in), *a.* [< L. *platalea*, a spoonbill, + *-ine*[2].] Pertaining to the spoonbills; belonging to the *Plataleidæ*.

platan, *n.* See *platane*.

Platanaceæ (plat-ạ-nā'sē̦-ē), *n. pl.* [NL. (Lindley, 1836), < *Platanus* + *-aceæ*.] An order of apetalous trees of the series *Unisexuales*, consisting of the genus *Platanus*, and characterized by having monœcious flowers in dense globose heads, without calyx, and with but few or minute bracts, by the ovary with one cell and one ovule, and the fruit a ball of numerous long achenes, each narrowed into a slender base surrounded with long hairs. See cut under *plane-tree*.

platane, platan (plat'ạn, plat'ạn), *n.* [= D. *plataan* = G. *platane* = Sw. Dan. *platan*, < F. *platane* = Sp. *plátano* = Pg. It. *platano*, < L. *platanus*, < Gr. πλάτανος, a plane-tree: see *plane*[3] and *Platanus*, and cf. *plantain*[2].] The plane-tree.

I espied thee, fair indeed and tall,
Under a *platane*. *Milton*, P. L., iv. 478.

Often, where clear-stemm'd *platans* guard
The outlet, did I turn away.
Tennyson, Arabian Nights.

Platanista (plat-ạ-nis'tạ̈), *n.* [NL., < L. *platanista*, < Gr. πλαταvιστής, a fish of the Ganges, appar. this dolphin.] The typical genus of the family *Platanistidæ*, containing the Gan-

Gangetic Dolphin (*Platanista gangetica*).

getic dolphin, *P. gangetica*. This is an entirely fluviatile species, having about 120 teeth, 50 vertebræ, extremely narrow jaws, no pelvic bone, rudimentary eyes, and obsolete dorsal fin. It attains a length of about 8 feet, and feeds on small fishes and crustaceans.

Platanistidæ (plat-ạ-nis'ti-dē), *n. pl.* [NL., < *Platanista* + *-idæ*.] A family of delphinoid odontocete cetaceans, framed to contain the genera *Platanista*, *Inia*, and *Pontoporia*. They are fluviatile or estuarine dolphins of warm waters, having a small or obsolete dorsal fin, broad truncate flippers, distinct flukes, external indication of a neck, free cervical vertebræ, a long mandibular symphysis, no distinct lacrymal bone, distinct tubercular and capitular articulations of the ribs, and long slender jaws with very numerous functional teeth.

Platanus (plat'a-nus), *n.* [NL. (Tournefort, 1700), < L. *platanus*, < Gr. πλάτανος, the plane-tree: see *platane*, *plane*³.] A genus of trees constituting the order *Platanaceæ*, and consisting of 6 species, by some authors reduced to 3, natives of temperate or subtropical parts of the northern hemisphere, 2, or perhaps 3, confined to America, and 2 to the Old World; the plane-trees. They are large trees, with the light-brown bark often scaling off in broad, thin, and roundish flakes, exposing a whitish inner layer, and giving the trunk a naked or spotted appearance wholly unlike that of any other tree. They bear alternate broadly deltoid leaves, palmately nerved and lobed, the dilated leafstalk covering the leaf-bud of the year following. See *buttonball*, *sycamore*, and *chinar-tree*, and cut under *plane-tree*.

Platax (plā'taks), *n.* [NL. (Cuvier, 1829), < Gr. πλάταξ, a fish like a perch, also called κορακῖνος; prob. < πλατύς, flat: see *plat*³.] The typical genus of *Platacidæ*, remarkable for the height or depth of the body.

Sea-bat (*Platax vespertilio*).

platband (plat'band), *n.* [< F. *platebande*, *platband*, lintel, border, OF. *plattebande*, a flat band, < *plate*, fem. of *plat*, flat, + *bande*, band: see *band*¹.] 1. A border of flowers in a garden, or along a wall or the side of a parterre.—2. In *arch.*: (*a*) Any flat rectangular molding the projection of which is much less than its width; a fascia. (*b*) A lintel formed with voussoirs in the manner of an arch, but with the intrados horizontal—a common and vicious modern construction, but employed even in some Roman and medieval work in places where a true arch was not convenient, and when monoliths of sufficient size were not available. See cut of *flat arch*, under *arch*¹. (*c*) The fillets between the flutes of an Ionic or a Corinthian column.

plat-blind† (plat'blīnd), *a.* Entirely blind. *Halliwell.*

plate (plāt), *n.* [< ME. *plate*, a plate, < OF. *plate*, *platte*, *plaite*, *plete*, *plette*, etc., f., a plate of metal, plate-armor, ingot, silver, also *plat*, m., a plate, platter, a flat surface, a low lake, a flatboat, etc., plate, bullion, silver-plate, silver, F. *plat*, m., a dish, plate, scale (of a balance), lid (of a book), sheet (of glass), flat (of the hand), blade (of an oar), etc.; = Sp. *plata*, f., plate, silver, wrought metal, money, *plato*, m., a dish, plate, = Pg. *prata*, f., plate, silver, *prato*, m., a dish, plate, = It. *piatta*, f., a flatboat, *piatto*, m., a dish, plate (ML. *plata*, f., a dish, plate, *platum*, n., a dish, plate, *plattum*, a flat surface, *platus*, m., a dish, plate, also *platta*, f., the clerical tonsure); cf. AS. *platung*, a plate of metal (see *plate*, *v.*); OFries. *platte*, a shaven pate, = D. *plat*, flat side, flat form, = MLG. *plate*, a sheet of metal, = Icel. *plata*, a plate, mounted metal, = Sw. *plåt* = Dan. *plade*, a sheet of metal; MHG. *plate*, G. *platte*, a plate, a shaven or bald pate; from the adj., F. *plat*, etc., flat: see *plat*³. Cf. *pate*¹, the same word, with loss of medial *l*. The uses of *plate* in part overlap those of the related noun *plat*³.] 1. A sheet of metal of uniform thickness and even surface: as, a *plate* of gold; a steel *plate*.

Armor of Plate.
a, plate-armor, as distinguished from *b*, chain-armor.

Over their forehead and eyes they [mules] have three pieces of *plate*, made either of brasse or latten.
Coryat, Crudities, I. 69.

2. A flat piece of metal used to strengthen arms; hence, armor made of sheets of metal, as distinguished from *mail* or *chain-armor*. See cut in preceding column.

> Over that a fyn hauberk
> Was al ywrought of Jewes werk,
> Ful strong it was of *plate*.
> *Chaucer*, Sir Thopas, l. 154.

> Ne *plate*, ne male, could ward so mighty throwes.
> *Spenser*, F. Q., II. v. 9.

> Mangled with ghastly wounds through *plate* and mail.
> *Milton*, P. L., vi. 368.

> Squadrons and squares of men in brazen *plates*.
> *Tennyson*, Fair Women.

3. A shallow dish of pottery, porcelain, or metal, on which food is served at table, or from which it is eaten; also, a plateful; a course or portion at table: as, a soup-*plate*; a fruit-*plate*; a *plate* of soup or of fish.

> Both me and mine he caus'd to dine,
> And serv'd us all with one *plate*.
> *The Kings Disguise* (Child's Ballads, V. 381).

The European pilgrims dine and sup in the refectory with the monks; . . . they are well served with three or four *plates*, and have excellent white-wine of their own making. *Pococke*, Description of the East, II. i. 11.

4. Gold or silver dishes and utensils used at table or in the home, including besides dishes other vessels, as cups, flagons, etc., as well as spoons, knives, forks, etc.: as, a sale of the furniture and *plate*.

> A piece of antique *plate*, bought of St. Mark,
> With which he here presents you.
> *B. Jonson*, Volpone, i. 1.

The *plate* in the hall (all at the Queen's table being gold) was estimated to be worth nearly £400,000.
First Year of a Silken Reign, p. 68.

5. Articles which have been covered with a plating of precious metal not solid gold or silver; plated ware.

Rich *plate*, even to the enamelling on gold, rich stuffs, and curious armour were carried to excess.
Walpole, Anecdotes, I. 2, note.

6. A cup or flagon or other article of gold or silver awarded to the winner in a contest, as to the owner of the winning horse or the crew of the winning boat in a race; a "cup."—7. A beam or piece of timber laid horizontally in a wall to receive the ends of other timbers. The plate for roof-timbers, and also for joists, is called a *wall-plate*. Compare *plat*³, *n.*, 1.—8. A flat piece of metal, as brass, copper, or steel, on which any representation or inscription is engraved: as, a door-*plate*; a coffin-*plate*; especially, such a piece of metal so engraved for impression on paper, etc.: as, a book-*plate*; a card-*plate*; hence, the printed impression from an engraved plate: as, a book illustrated with *plates*.—9. A duplicate, in one piece of metal, of the face of composed types or woodcuts. Such plates are made by electrotype or stereotype process. Plates of book-pages are about one eighth of an inch thick; plates of newspaper-pages are much thicker.

Carpenters' Plates.
a, rafter-plate; *b*, purlin-plate; *c*, crown-plate; *d*, wall-plate.

10. (*a*) In *dentistry*, a piece of metal or composition fitted to the mouth and holding the teeth of a denture. (*b*) In *horology*, one of the two parallel pieces of metal to which the wheels are pivoted in a watch or clock. (*c*) The flat piece of metal forming the side of the lock of a firearm. (*d*) A flat piece of metal usually forming a part of the bed or bosh of a metallurgical furnace. (*e*) A commonly rectangular piece of glass used in photography to receive the picture. (*f*) In *baseball*, the home base.

From the nature of things, a ball so knocked that it cannot be caught or fielded to the *plate* before the man can make the entire circuit of the bases yields an earned, or, as it is in such instance more generally called, a "home run." *The Century*, XXXVIII. 835.

(*g*) *Naut.*, a bar or band of iron, as in *futtock-plates*, *channel-plate*, etc.; specifically, in iron ships, the metal which forms part of the strake on the ship's side.—11. Shale of the coal-measures. It is in these strata that the finest specimens of the coal-plants are most frequently found. Also called *binds*.—12. Plate-glass.

The machine in use for polishing the glass is practically that originally designed for the purpose; it is not only used in plate-glass works, but is the machine used for polishing that description of glass which is known as "patent *plate*." *Glass-making*, p. 168.

13. The finest quality of pewter.—14. In *anat.*, *zoöl.*, and *bot.*, a plate-like part, organ, or structure; a lamina or lamella; a layer: not specific, the thing indicated being designated by a qualifying term. See cuts under *carapace*, *Coluber*, and *whalebone*.—15†. A Spanish money of account. Also called *old plate*. Eight reals of old plate made the *peso de plata*, or piaster—that is, the Spanish dollar.

> Be likche has some new trick for a purse;
> And if he has, he is worth three hundred *plates*.
> *Marlowe*, Jew of Malta, ii.

> Realms and islands were
> As *plates* dropp'd from his pocket.
> *Shak.*, A. and C., v. 2. 92.

Ambulacral plate. See *ambulacral*.—**A pair of plates**†, armor for the breast and back.

> Somme woln have *a peyre plates* large.
> *Chaucer*, Knight's Tale, l. 1262.

Argentine plate, German silver.

The manufacture of German silver, or *Argentine plate*, became an object of commercial importance.
Ure, Dict., III. 414.

Armor of plate. Same as *plate-armor*.—**Auditory plate.** See *auditory crest*, under *auditory*.—**Basilisk plates**, plates of enameled pottery decorated with a basilisk, or similar animal, which are found from time to time in the neighborhood of Quimper, in the department of Finistère in France. They are thought to be specimens of the faience of Quimper, but have often been classed as Rouen ware. See *Quimper pottery*, under *pottery*.—**Bobstay, branchial, buckled plates.** See the qualifying words.—**British plate.** Same as *albata*.—**Bulb plate**, in *iron- and steel-manuf.*, a plate along the margin of which is rolled a rib or bulb thicker than the body of the plate. The plate resembles tee-iron, except that the head of the tee, or what corresponds to it, is more massive. Such plates are used in iron ship-building for keelsons, etc., in bridge-building, and in iron architecture.—**Cardiac, circumesophageal, clinoid plate.** See the adjectives.—**Coat of plates, coif of plate.** See *coat*², *coif*.—**Compound armor-plate.** See under *armor-plate*.—**Correcting-plate.** Same as *compensator* (*a*).—**Costal, cribriform, dry plate.** See the adjectives.—**Dovetail-plates.** See *dovetail*.—**Dumb-plate**, the part at the bottom near the doors of a furnace where there are no air-openings or spaces; the dead-plate.—**Endochrome, gate-end, genital, gular plates.** See the qualifying words.—**Equatorial plate**, in *biol.*, the collection of chromatin-fibers in the equator of the nuclear spindle during karyokinesis.—**Gold plate**, gold vessels for use or ornament; especially, table utensils of gold.—**Half-tone plates.** See *photo-process*.—**Head-block plate.** See *head-block*.—**Horn plate**, in *embryol.*, the remaining ectoderm of a germ, forming the epidermis of the embryo after the formation from ectoderm of the rudiment of the spinal canal.

From this time the remaining portion of the skin-sensory layer is called the *horn-plate* or horn-layer, because the outer skin (epidermis) with its horny appendages—nails, hair, etc.—develops from it.
Haeckel, Evol. of Man (trans.), I. 306.

Induction-plate, a small insulated metal plate placed opposite one of the quadrants of an electrometer, used for reducing the sensitiveness of the instrument. For this purpose the electrified body is connected with the induction-plate instead of with the quadrant directly.

In order that somewhat larger differences may be measured, the *Induction Plate* is introduced to diminish the sensitiveness. *J. E. H. Gordon*, Elect. and Mag., I. 44.

Jugular, madreporic, medullary plate. See the adjectives.—**Locking-plate.** Same as *count-wheel*.—**Main plate**, the principal plate of a lock.—**Muscular plate.** Same as *muscle-plate*.—**Nasal, negative, occipital, ocular, orbital plate.** See the adjectives.—**Patching up plates.** See *patch*.—**Patent plate**, a name given in England to cylinder-glass.—**Perisomatic plates.** See *perisomatic*.—**Plate diamond.** See *diamond*.—**Plate of a furnace.** See *dead-plate*.—**Plate of wind**, in *organ-building*, the flat sheet or jet of air which is projected through the flue of a flue-pipe against the upper lip of the mouth, and by the fluctuations of which the tone is produced.—**Plate-welding hammer**, a steam-hammer of special form. *E. H. Knight*.—**Pterygostomial plates, radial plates.** See the adjectives.—**Ribbed plate**, sheet-metal with its surface alternately ribbed or corrugated.

Ribbed plate is made by using a roller with grooves on its surface. *Workshop Receipts*, 1st ser., p. 55.

Ship-plate, an inferior quality of wrought-iron plate.

Wrought-iron plates . . . are manufactured of . . . coarse, brittle, and uncertain material, sometimes sold as *ship-plate*. *R. Wilson*, Steam Boilers, p. 32.

Terminal plate, in *biol.*, the end-plate of a nerve-fiber.—**Wheel-guard plate** (*milit.*), the rub-iron of a field-artillery carriage. (See also *armor-plate*, *bottom-plate*, *floating-plate*, *horn-plate*, *sieve-plate*, *spreading-plate*, *tie-plate*.)

plate (plāt), *v. t.*; pret. and pp. *plated*, ppr. *plating*. [< ME. **platen*, < AS. **platian* in comp. *āplatian* and verbal n. *platung*, a plate of metal: see *plate*, *n.*] 1. To arm with plate-armor for defense.

> Marshal, ask yonder knight in arms
> Both who he is and why he cometh hither
> Thus *plated* in habiliments of war.
> *Shak.*, Rich. II., i. 3. 28.

2. To overlay or coat with silver, gold, or other metal; specifically, to attach a perma-

nent covering or film of one metal to (the surface of another).—3. To arm or cover (a ship) with armor-plates.—4. To beat into thin flat pieces or laminæ.—5. To implant (micro-organisms) in a thin layer of gelatin spread upon a glass plate. See *plate-culture*.—**Chemical plating or dipping**, a process performed in some cases by the mere immersion of one metal in a hot or cold solution of some salt of another metal, as in plating iron with copper by dipping the former in sulphate-of-copper solution, or the coating of brass with tin by boiling the brass in a solution of cream of tartar to which scraps of tin have been added. Tin-plating of this sort is also variously called *washing, tinning, silvering*, or *whitening*. It is much employed in various arts, particularly in the manufacture of brass pins. The words *plate* and *plating* are often coupled with the prefixed name of the metal which forms the outer surface: as, *silver-plate, silver-plating*, to plate with silver, the process of plating with silver; *nickel-plate, nickel-plating*, to plate with nickel, the process of plating with nickel, etc. See also *electroplate, galvanize*, 3, and *galvanoplastic*.—**Dry plating**, a process of coating the surface of iron by rubbing it over with brass (usually a brass-wire brush) till it is covered with adherent brass. The process is used in mending broken cast-iron articles. Surfaces so coated may first be tinned over, and then soldered with ordinary tin solder.—**Fire-plating** (also called *fire-gilding* when the coating is of gold), plating performed either by a process of soldering the film or coating directly to the surface of the object to be plated, or, when the coating will not directly adhere, by first coating the object with a metal which has an affinity for both the metal of the object to be plated and the metal used for the plating. Thus iron, to which silver cannot be made to adhere directly, may be silver-plated by first coating it with copper, the latter having affinity for both iron and silver. In fire-plating the surface to be covered is laid over with a suitable flux, upon which the silver-foil is smoothly placed, and the whole is then heated till the metals unite.—**Rolled plating**, the soldering together of bars of different metals and of considerable thickness, and then rolling the compound bar out into a thin plate. In this way a thin sheet of some base metal, as copper, may be plated on one side or on both with a much thinner layer of fine metal, as silver. The material called *rolled gold*, much used for cheap watch-cases and jewelry, is thus made.—**To plate a port**, in a steam-engine, to close a port by the land or unperforated part of the plate of a slide-valve. *E. H. Knight.*

Platea (plā'tẹ̄-ä), *n.* [NL.: see *Platalea*.] In *ornith.*, same as *Platalea*. *Brisson*, 1760.

plate-armor (plāt'är"mọr), *n.* Defensive armor consisting of plates of metal.

plateau (pla-tō'), *n.*; pl. *plateaus* (-tōz'), *plateaux* (-tōz'). [< F. *plateau*, dim. of *plat*, a plate: see *plate*.] 1. In *phys. geog.*, an elevated region of considerable extent, often traversed by mountain-ranges. The word is nearly synonymous with *table-land* as that word is used by many geographers. Thus, the Alps are characterized by the absence of plateaus; the Asiatic ranges, from Asia Minor eastward to China, by the presence of table-lands and high, broad, plateau-like valleys.
2. (*a*) A tray for table service. (*b*) A decorative plaque. [French uses.]

plate-basket (plāt'bȧs"ket), *n.* 1. A basket lined with metal, for removing plates and other utensils which have been used at table, preparatory to washing them.—2. A basket, usually divided into compartments, for holding the knives, forks, spoons, etc., in daily use.

plate-bender (plāt'ben"dėr), *n.* A pincers with curved bits used for bending dental plates without leaving marks.

plate-black (plāt'blak), *n.* See *black*.

plate-bone (plāt'bōn), *n.* The blade-bone; the omoplate, shoulder-blade, or scapula.

plate-box (plāt'boks), *n.* 1. A grooved box of appropriate size, for holding photographic plates or finished negatives.—2. A box especially designed to exclude light when closed, for the safe-keeping of photographic dry plates when removed from the manufacturer's package; a safety-box.

plate-brass (plāt'brȧs), *n.* Rolled brass; latten. *E. H. Knight.*

plate-bulb (plāt'bulb), *n.* The swollen part on the edge of beams, having a cross-section of mushroom form.

> The *plate bulb* of beams should be bent before the angle-irons are riveted to their upper edges, after which it is necessary to check and adjust the curvature, which alters slightly in the process of riveting. *Thearle*, Naval Arch., § 310.

platecote†, *n.* A coat of plate-armor.

> An helmette and a Jacke or *platecote* hideth all partes of a manne, sauyng the legges. *Udall*, tr. of Apophthegms of Erasmus, p. 308. (*Davies.*)

plate-culture (plāt'kul"tūr), *n.* The culture of micro-organisms, especially bacteria, in a thin, uniform layer of gelatin spread upon a glass plate.

plated (plā'ted), *p. a.* 1. Strengthened with plates of metal and defensive armor.

> And over all the brasen scales was armd,
> Like *plated* cote of steele, so couched neare
> That nought mote perce. *Spenser*, F. Q., I. xi. 9.

2. Covered or overlaid with a different and especially a richer material: as, *plated* silk hose; *plated* forks and spoons.—3. In *zoöl.*, covered or protected with hard dermal plates or scutes; scutate or loricate; shielded.—**Plated ware**, a name especially given to vessels of base metal, etc., coated or plated with gold or silver, as distinguished from *plate*, *n.*, 4.

plate-fleet† (plāt'flēt), *n.* The vessels engaged in transporting masses of precious metal; especially, the vessels which transported to Spain the products of the mines in Spanish America.

> The [Spanish] admiral's ship was called the Armadillo of Carthagena, one of the greater galleys of the royal *plate-fleet*. *Milton*, Letters of State.
>
> The *Plate-Fleet* also from Lima comes hither with the King's Treasure. *Dampier*, Voyages, I. 179.

plate-frame (plāt'frām), *n.* In *photog.*, a frame of any kind for holding or receiving a plate; a dark-slide; a plate-holder.

plateful (plāt'fůl), *n.* [< *plate* + *-ful*.] As much as a plate will hold.

plate-gage (plāt'gāj), *n.* A plate with notched edges used to measure the thickness of metal plates. The notches are of graduated standard measures of thickness, and are numbered in accordance with the thicknesses they represent. Different standards are in use. The thickness of a plate is definitely specified only when both the number of the notch it fits and the kind of gage used are named: as, No. 16 Birmingham gage; No. 10 Brown and Sharp's gage; etc. See *wire-gage*.

plate-girder (plāt'gėr"dėr), *n.* A girder formed of a single plate of metal, or of a series of plates joined together.

plate-glass (plāt'glȧs), *n.* A superior kind of thick glass used for mirrors, and also for large panes in windows, shop-fronts, etc. (See *plate*, 12.) The materials for this kind of glass are selected and compounded with much greater care than those of ordinary glass. The fused metal is poured upon a true-faced iron table and there rolled out into a plate having parallel faces and a uniform thickness, by means of an iron roller, running on supporting bars at the sides of the table which gage the thickness. By ingenious mechanism the plate while yet hot is transferred to the annealing-oven. It is carried through this oven, retained on flat supports, and is gradually cooled. Both surfaces are then highly polished. Machinery is now universally employed for polishing. See *polishing-machine*, 2.—**German plate-glass.** Same as *broad glass* (which see, under *broad*).—**Rough plate-glass**, unpolished plate-glass. Before grinding and polishing, the surface of plate-glass is not smooth enough to permit distinct vision through it. In this state plate-glass is largely used for sky-lights in sidewalks and roofs, windows opening into halls, etc., where light is desirable, but where distinct vision would be objectionable. Plates of this kind vary in thickness from about $\frac{1}{16}$ inch to 1 inch or more.

plate-hat (plāt'hat), *n.* A hat made with an outer pile or nap of finer material than the body. Such hats are often made water-proof, and stiffened before the nap is added.

plate-holder (plāt'hōl"dėr), *n.* 1. In *photog.*, a movable frame fitted to a camera, used to contain and transport a sensitized plate, which is exposed to the image projected by the lens by withdrawing a slide or shutter after the holder is in position in the camera; a dark-slide; a plate-frame. The plate-holders for dry plates are usually made double, for economy of space, and, after exposure of the plate in one side, are reversed in the camera in order to expose the plate in the other side.
2. A pneumatic device for holding a photographic plate during development or other manipulation.

plate-iron (plāt'ī"ėrn), *n.* Iron pressed into flat plates by being passed between cylindrical rollers; rolled iron.—**Plate-iron girder.** See *girder*[1].

plate-key (plāt'kē), *n.* A flat key notched at the ends or sides, as the key for a Yale lock.

plate-layer (plāt'lā"ėr), *n.* In *rail.*, a workman employed to lay down rails and fix them to the sleepers. [Eng.]

> Sundry new occupations, as those of drivers, stokers, cleaners, *plate-layers*. *H. Spencer*, Universal Progress, p. 54.

plate-leather (plāt'leᴛʜ"ėr), *n.* Chamois leather used for cleaning gold or silver plate, especially when prepared for the purpose, as with rouge-powder, etc., applied to the surface.

platelet (plāt'let), *n.* [< *plate* + *-let*.] In *anat.*, a little plate; a plaque or plaquette.—**Platelet of blood.** Same as *blood-plate*.

platelyt†, *adv.* Same as *platly*.

plate-machine (plāt'ma-shēn"), *n.* A machine for shaping, turning, and finishing plastic materials for making stone or china tableware, plates, dishes, etc.: a variation of the potter's wheel.

plate-mail (plāt'māl), *n.* Same as *scale-armor*.

plate-mark (plāt'märk), *n.* 1. A legal mark or symbol made on certain gold and silver articles for the purpose of indicating their degree of purity, etc. These symbols, according to British regulation, are—(1) The maker's mark or initials. (2) The assay-mark. For gold, the assay-mark is a crown and figures indicating the number of carats fine. For silver, in England, it is a lion passant; in Ireland, a harp crowned; in Glasgow, a lion rampant; and in Edinburgh, a thistle. (3) The hall-mark of the district office. These offices are at London, York, Exeter, Chester, Newcastle,

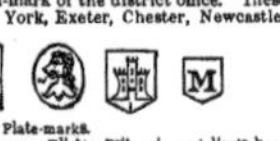
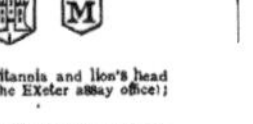

Plate-marks.
El. crowned (maker's name—Eliot); Britannia and lion's head (new standard of silver); castle (mark of the Exeter assay office); M (date-mark—the year 1712).

Birmingham, Sheffield, Edinburgh, Glasgow, and Dublin. The mark is generally the coat of arms of the town. (4) The date-mark, consisting of a letter which is changed every year. (5) The duty-mark, consisting of the head of the sovereign. This indicates that the duty has been paid. (*Imp. Dict.*) All these marks are sometimes called *hall-marks*.
2. In an engraving, the depression in the paper around the edges of an impression taken from an incised plate. It is caused by the force of the press when striking off.

plate-matter (plāt'mat"ėr), *n.* Type cast in a number of stereotype plates for insertion in different newspapers, costing them much less than would have to be paid for setting.

> To-day one of these *plate-matter* manufacturing firms has branch offices and foundries in New York, Boston, Cincinnati, Chicago, Minneapolis, and San Francisco, maintaining a corps of editors and employing a large force of compositors and stereotypers at each point. It furnishes matter for almost every department of a newspaper except editorial articles and local news. *Westminster Rev.*, CXXVIII. 862.

plate-metal (plāt'met"al), *n.* A plate of metal produced in the process of refining pig-iron as preparatory to its being puddled in the reverberatory furnace, according to the method followed in Yorkshire for the production of a high class of iron. Such plates are grooved on the bottom and have been cooled rapidly, so as to be easily broken in pieces. Also called *line-metal, white metal*, or simply *metal*.

plate-mill (plāt'mil), *n.* A mill for rolling metal plates. It usually has long rolls, necessitated by the width of the plates, and the rolls are made very heavy and strong in order to prevent springing and consequent greater thickness of the plates in the middle than at the sides.

platen[1] (plat'en), *n.* [Also *platin, platine*; < F. *platine*, a plate, lock-plate, pillar-plate, scutcheon, plate of a printing-press, covering-plate, etc., < *plat*, flat: see *plat*[3] and *plate*.] In *printing*, the flat part of a press which comes down upon the form, and by which the impression is made.—**Platen press**, any form of printing-press which gives impression from a platen, in distinction from rotary or cylinder presses, which give impression from a cylinder or a curved surface.

platen[2] (plat'en), *n.* [Appar. a reduced form and special use of *platinum*.] An alloy used in making buttons, composed of eight parts of copper and five parts of zinc.

plate-paper (plāt'pā"pėr), *n.* 1. Paper to which a high gloss is imparted on both sides by packing each sheet between smooth plates of copper or zinc, and subjecting a pile of the sheets so packed to heavy pressure in a rolling-press. Supercalendering (which see) has entirely superseded this process.—2. A heavy, spongy paper used for taking impressions from engraved plates.—**Hard plate-paper, soft plate-paper.** See *paper*.

plate-piece (plāt'pēs), *n.* The lower or under half of the fore quarter of beef, used for corning. Also called *rattle-ran*.

plate-powder (plāt'pou"dėr), *n.* A polishing-powder for silverware. One kind, called *jewelers' rouge*, is prepared by mixing solutions of soda and sulphate of iron, and washing, drying, and calcining the precipitated oxid of iron in shallow vessels until it assumes a deep reddish-brown color. Compounds of rouge and prepared chalk, or of oxid of tin and rose-pink, are also termed *plate-powders*.

plate-press (plāt'pres), *n.* A press for printing from engraved plates of steel or copper.

plate-printer (plāt'prin"tėr), *n.* A workman who produces impressions from engraved copper or steel plates, as distinguished from one who prints from types or from stone.

plate-printing (plāt'prin"ting), *n.* The act or process of printing from an engraved plate.

plater (plā'tėr), *n.* 1. One engaged in the manufacture of metallic plates, or in their application in the arts and manufactures.

> When being bent, the plate is lifted by a number of men, under the direction of the *plater* in charge, who hold the plate in the necessary position for obtaining the required curvature and twist. *Thearle*, Naval Arch., § 296.

2. A machine for calendering paper by means of heavy pressure between smooth plates of metal.—3. One who plates or coats articles

with gold or silver: generally in composition: as, silver-*plater*, gold-*plater*, nickel-*plater*.—4. A horse that competes for a plate. *Lever.*

plate-rack (plāt'rak), *n.* 1. An open frame for holding plates and dishes; specifically, a frame in which dishes can be placed in a vertical position to dry after they have been washed.—2. Any arrangement, other than simple shelves, for holding plates in any number, as the inclosed boxes, etc., in the pantries of a ship.—3. A grooved frame for receiving photographic plates while wet, and holding them diagonally on edge to drain; a negative-rack.

plate-rail (plāt'rāl), *n.* In *railway engin.*, a flat rail. *E. H. Knight.*

plate-railway (plāt'rāl"wā), *n.* A tramway in which the wheel-tracks are flat plates. [Eng.]

plateresco (plat-e-res'kō), *a.* [Sp.] Same as *plateresque*.

plateresque (plat-ẹ-resk'), *a.* [< Sp. *plateresco*, < *plata*, silver: see *plate*.] Resembling silverwork: noting a certain class of architectural enrichments. *Ford.*

plate-roller (plāt'rō"lėr), *n.* A smooth roller for making plate- or sheet-iron.

plate-shears (plāt'shērz), *n. sing.* and *pl.* A machine for cutting or shearing plate- or sheet-metal, such as boiler-plate.

Platessa (plạ-tes'ä), *n.* [NL., < L. *platessa*, the plaice: see *plaice*.] A genus of flatfishes of the family *Pleuronectidæ*, having as its type *Pleuronectes platessa*: same as *Pleuronectes* in a strict sense. See cuts under *plaice* and *asymmetry*.

platessiform (plạ-tes'i-fôrm), *a.* [< L. *platessa*, the plaice, + *forma*, form.] In *ichth.*, resembling the plaice in form or structure; related to the plaice or flounder.

plate-tracery (plāt'trā"sėr-i), *n.* In *medieval arch.*, a form of tracery in which the openings are cut or pierced in slabs of stone, as distinguished from ordinary tracery, which is constructed of assembled blocks. This form appeared early in the transition from the round-arched to the point-

Plate-tracery.—Head of a clearstory window, Cathedral of Chartres, France; 13th century.

ed style, and was often employed in subsequent periods in places where stone of the necessary formation and toughness was available. It was particularly esteemed in Italy, where the excellent building-marbles, in addition to their mechanical fitness, supplied a medium adapted for delicacy of outline and profile, and lending itself to high decorative quality in such tracery.

platetrope (plat'e-trōp), *n.* [< Gr. πλατύς, flat, + τρέπειν, turn.] A part symmetrically related to another on the opposite side of the meson; a lateral homologue; a fellow of the opposite side. *Wilder.*

platetropy (plat'e-trō-pi), *n.* [< *platetrope* + *-y*³.] The state or condition of being laterally homologous; bilaterality; bilateral symmetry; reversed repetition of parts or organs on each side of the meson.

plate-vise (plāt'vīs), *n.* In *photog.*, a frame for holding a plate firmly in certain processes, particularly for cleaning or p is ing the glass. It consists essentially of two wooden jaws or sides, grooved to receive the plate, and adjustable by means of a screw.

plate-warmer (plāt'wâr"mėr), *n.* 1. A case with shelves or any other device in which plates are held before a fire, over a hot-air register, etc., to be warmed.—2. A hollow metallic tray, of the size and form of a plate, filled with hot water and placed at table beneath a dinner-plate to keep it warm.

plate-wheel (plāt'hwēl), *n.* A wheel without arms or spokes; a wheel in which the rim and nave are connected by a plate or web.—**Open plate-wheel**, a form of cast-iron wheel having large openings in the web between the arms, hub, and rim. It is used for street-cars, etc.

platey, *a.* See *platy*.

platfond, *n.* Same as *plafond*.

platform (plat'fôrm), *n.* [Formerly also *plotform* (simulating *plat*², *plot*¹); = Sp. Pg. *plataforma* = It. *piattaforma*, < OF. *plateforme*, also *platteforme*, and as two words *plate forme*, *platte fourme*, F. *plateforme*, a platform (terrace), platform (in arch.), prop, mudsill (of a bridge), etc., < *plate*, fem. of *plat*, flat, level, + *forme*, form: see *plat*³ and *form*.] 1†. A ground-plan, drawing, or sketch; a plan; a map.

So I have made a *platform* of a princely garden, partly by precept, partly by drawing—not a model, but some general lines of it. *Bacon*, Gardens (ed. 1887).

The young men meeting in places of exercise, and the old men also in Artificers Shops, and in their compassed Chaires, or halfe circles where they sate talking together, were every one occupied about drawing the *Platforme* of Sicilia, telling the nature of the Sicilian Sea, and reckoning up the Havens and places looking towards Africke. *North*, tr. of Plutarch (ed. 1656), p. 456.

Able so well to limn or paint as to take in paper the situation of a castle or a city, or the *platform* of a fortification. *Leigh* (Arber's Eng. Garner, I. 646).

2†. A plot; a design; a scheme; a plan.

Alexander. Apelles, what peece of worke have you now in hand?
Apelles. None in hand, if it like your majestie: but I am devising a *platforme* in my head.
Lyly, Alexander and Campaspe, v. 4.

And now there rests no other shift but this,
To gather our soldiers, scatter'd and dispersed,
And lay new *platforms* to endamage them.
Shak., 1 Hen. VI., ii. 1. 77.

A sudden *platform* comes into my mind,
And this it is. *Grim*, The Collier of Croydon, ii.

3†. Situation; position.

With your instrument for trying of distances, obserue the *platforme* of the place. *Hakluyt's Voyages*, I. 436.

4. A raised level place; a terrace.

Ham. But where was this?
Mar. My lord, upon the *platform* where we watch'd.
Shak., Hamlet, i. 2. 213.

The buildings we now find on the *platform* at Persepolis may have been dedicated to somewhat different purposes than were those of Nineveh. *J. Fergusson*, Hist. Arch., I. 189.

5. A raised frame or structure with a level surface. Specifically—(*a*) A raised structure in a hall or meeting-place for the use of those who are to speak: a rostrum or stage from which a speaker may conveniently address his audience. (*b*) A raised walk along the track at a railway-station for landing passengers and freight. (*c*) The place where guns are mounted on a fortress or battery.

The Captain commanded them to cast anchor before a certain town called Cris, which had a *platform* or fort with ordnance to defend it. *Eng. Stratagem* (Arber's Eng. Garner, I. 606).

(*d*) *Naut.*, the orlop. (*e*) In a glass-furnace, a bench on which the pots are placed. *E. H. Knight.* (*f*) A projecting floor or landing at the end of a railroad-car or street-car, serving as a means of ingress and egress.

Specifically—6. A systematic scheme or body of principles, especially of religious or political principles, expressly adopted as a policy or basis of action; a syllabus, program, or scheme of principles or doctrines adopted as a basis of action, policy, or belief; specifically, in *U. S. politics*, a statement of political principles and of the course to be adopted with regard to certain important questions of policy, issued by the representatives of a political party assembled in convention to nominate candidates for an election: as, the Genevan *platform*; a political *platform*; the Democratic *platform*.

The wisdom of a lawmaker consisteth not only in a *platform* of justice, but in the application thereof.
Bacon, Advancement of Learning, ii. 355.

Every little society pretending to that venerable name [the church] did the very thing they had complained of: imposed the *platform* of their doctrine, discipline, and worship as divine: and were for rooting out all that opposed or did not comply with it. *Bp. Atterbury*, Sermons, II. xiii.

The Whigs, whether on the Lexington *platform* or some other non-committal *platform*, will be and must be at once known as the party that opposed their country in her just and generous war.
Resolutions of the Democratic National Convention, May 30, [1844, quoted in New York Herald, May 6, 1848.

Conversation in society is found to be on a *platform* so low as to exclude science, the saint, and the poet.
Emerson, Clubs.

7. Figuratively, the function of public speaking, as that of lecturers or political speakers; also, public speeches or public addresses collectively.

It is perfectly true that a great number of foolish and erroneous, sometimes very mischievous, notions are fostered by the periodical press, but the same might be said of the pulpit and the *platform*.
H. N. Oxenham, Short Studies, p. 86.

Cambridge platform, Saybrook platform, declarations of principles respecting church government and doctrine adopted by church synods held respectively at Cambridge, Massachusetts, in 1648, and Saybrook, Connecticut, in 1708. They substantially agree with each other and with the principles still maintained by Congregationalists. See *congregationalism*.—**Feeding-platform**, a platform, generally about two feet by four, placed in the middle of a trout-pond, a few inches above the bottom: used by fish-culturists. If the food is thrown over this platform, all not taken before it reaches the bottom will fall upon it, and, as it can more easily be cleaned than the bottom of the pond, there is less liability of fouling the water. The fish will also take food better from a clean than from a muddy bottom. It serves incidentally, too, as a cover for the young fish.

platform (plat'fôrm), *v. t.* [< *platform*, *n.*] 1†. To sketch or lay down the plan of; set forth in plan; outline.

Some . . . do not think it for the ease of their inconsequent opinions to grant that church-discipline is *platformed* in the Bible, but that it is left to the discretion of men. *Milton*, Church-Government, i. 1.

2. To draw up a platform, or scheme of principles or policy. [Colloq.]—3. To support or rest as on a platform. [Rare.]

Platforming his chin
On the palm left open.
Mrs. Browning, To Flush, my Dog.

platform-bridge (plat'fôrm-brij), *n.* A movable gangway over the space between the platforms of two railroad-cars, designed to protect passengers from falling between the cars. [U. S.]

platform-car (plat'fôrm-kär), *n.* An open

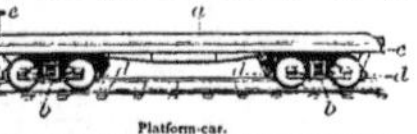

Platform-car.
a, platform; *b*, truck-frames; *c*, buffers; *d*, brake-shoes; *e*, brake-wheel.

railroad-car, having no inclosing sides, or surrounded merely by low ledges.

platform-carriage (plat'fôrm-kar"ạj), *n.* A four-wheeled platform, wagon, or truck used for carrying mortars, guns, or other heavy materials or stores.

platform-crane (plat'fôrm-krān), *n.* 1. A detachable crane on the margin of a railway-car platform or a platform of a truck.—2. A crane permanently mounted on a movable truck, which forms an integral part of the machine.

platformer (plat'fôrm-ėr), *n.* [< *platform* + *-er*¹.] A public speaker; one who draws up or invents a plan of proceedings. [Rare.]

But one divine Aretine in Italy, and two heavenly Tarletons in England, the sole *platformers* of odd elocution, and only singularities of the plain world.
G. Harvey, Four Letters, iii.

platformist (plat'fôrm-ist), *n.* [< *platform* + *-ist*.] A public speaker or lecturer. [Colloq.]

platform-scale (plat'fôrm-skāl), *n.* A weighing-machine or balance with a flat scale or platform for the support of the object to be weighed. The designation is applied especially to a weighing-machine in which the flat scale is placed near to or on a level with a table, counter, floor, or the ground, for the convenient reception of heavy bodies and to save lifting, and is connected with the scale-beam by a system of compound levers and links. Either sliding or detachable counterpoising weights, or both, are used on the beam, which, when sliding weights are used, is graduated to indicate weights and fractions of the unit of weight.

platform-spring (plat'fôrm-spring), *n.* In a vehicle, a compound spring consisting of a rectangular arrangement of four arched springs, each made up of long, thin, curved steel plates of regularly diminishing lengths bolted together. The extremities of the four springs are united at the corners of the rectangle by links or stirrups, two of the springs usually bowing upward and two downward. The name has also been applied to a similar mechanism of three springs arranged as on three sides of a rectangle.

plat-full (plat'fůl'), *a.* [ME. *platful*; < *plat*³ + *full*.] Choke-full.

So that my palays *plat-ful* be pyȝt al aboute.
Alliterative Poems (ed. Morris), ii. 83.

plathelminth, Plathelmintha, etc. See *platyhelminth*, etc.

platiasmus (plat-i-as'mus), *n.* [< Gr. πλατειασμός, a broad manner of speech, a broad Doric accent, < πλατειάζειν, speak or pronounce broadly, < πλατύς, broad: see *plat*³.] Imperfect speech, the result of an abnormal condition of the tongue.

platic† (plā'tik), *a.* [< LL. *platicus*, general, compendious, summary, < Gr. πλατικός, diffuse, detailed, < πλατύς, broad, wide: see *plat*³.] In *astrol.*, pertaining to or in the position of a ray cast from one planet to another, not exactly, but within the orbit of its own light: opposed to *partile*.—**Platic conjunction.** See *conjunction*.

platilla (plạ-til'ä), *n.* A white linen fabric made in Silesia.

platin (plat'in), *n.* See *platen.*

platina (pla-tē'nạ̈), *n.* [= D. G. Sw. Dan. *platina* = F. *platine*, < Sp. *platina* = Pg. *platina* (NL. *platina*), platina, so called from its resemblance to silver, < *plata*, plate, silver: see *plate.*] 1. Same as *platinum*: the older name. —2. Twisted silver wire.—3. An iron plate for glazing stuff.

platinate (plat'i-nāt), *v. t.* Same as *platinize. Philos. Mag.*, 5th ser., XXVIII. 454.

plating (plā'ting), *n.* [Verbal n. of *plate*, *v.*] 1. The art or operation of covering articles with a thin coating or film of metal, especially of overlaying articles made of the baser metals with a thin coating of gold, silver, or nickel. It is effected in various ways; sometimes the plating-metal is attached to and rolled out with the other metal by pressure; sometimes the one metal is precipitated from its solution upon the other, electrochemical decomposition being now much employed for this purpose. See *electrotype.*

2. A thin coating of one metal laid upon another.

plating-hammer (plā'ting-ham"ėr), *n.* A steam-hammer of from 500 to 700 pounds weight, used for bending plates and for other operations in armor-plating vessels.

platinic (plạ-tin'ik), *a.* [< *platinum* + *-ic.*] In *chem.*, of or pertaining to platinum.

platiniferous (plat-i-nif'e-rus), *a.* [< NL. *platinum* + L. *ferre* = E. *bear*[1].] Producing platinum: as, *platiniferous* sand.

platiniridium (plat"in-i-rid'i-um), *n.* [NL., < *platin(um)* + *iridium.*] An alloy of platinum and iridium, occurring in isometric crystals and crystalline grains together with native platinum.

platinization (plat"i-ni-zā'shon), *n.* The process of platinizing, or the condition of being platinized.

platinize (plat'i-nīz), *v. t.*; pret. and pp. *platinized*, ppr. *platinizing.* [< *platin(um)* + *-ize.*] To coat with platinum in a fine state of division: as, to *platinize* the negative plate (silver) of a Smee's battery. Silver is platinized by dipping it or washing it in a solution of platinum chlorid, and then heating it in a closed vessel till the salt decomposes. The negative plates of Urquhart's potassium-bichromate cell—which consist each of a copper plate having one face and its edges covered with platinum-foil soldered to the copper, and its other face covered with lead—have their platinum sides platinized by a deposit of metallic platinum, obtained by decomposition of platinum chlorid with the aid of a galvanic current, the lead being temporarily covered with an acid-proof varnish or cement. Also spelled *platinise.*—**Platinized glass.** See *glass.*

platinochlorid (plat"i-nọ-klō'rid), *n.* [< *platinum* + *chlorid.*] A double chlorid containing platinum: as, potassium *platinochlorid.*—**Ethylene platinochlorid.** See *ethylene.*

platinode (plat'i-nōd), *n.* [< NL. *platinum*, platinum, + Gr. ὁδός, way (see *cathode*).] The negative or non-oxidizable plate of a voltaic cell, which often consists of a sheet of platinum, as in the Grove cell.

platinoid (plat'i-noid), *n.* [< NL. *platinum* + Gr. εἶδος, form.] One of the metals with which platinum is invariably found associated. The platinoids are palladium, rhodium, iridium, osmium, and ruthenium.

platinotype (plat'i-nọ-tīp), *n.* [< *platinum* + *type.*] 1. A process of photographic printing in which the paper is coated with a solution of platinum chlorid and ferric oxalate. When exposed to the light under a negative and subsequently immersed in a hot solution of potassic oxalate, the metal is reduced in proportion to the action of the light. The picture is then finished by simply washing in slightly acidulated water. Some patented platinum processes, as that of Pizzighelli, simplify greatly the operations of development.

2. A print made by any platinotype process.

> Excellent specimens of *platinotypes* were shown.
> *Sci. Amer.*, N. S., LIV. 66.

platinous (plat'i-nus), *a.* [< NL. *platinum* + *-ous.*] Containing or consisting of platinum.

platinum (plat'i-num), *n.* [= F. *platine* = Sp. Pg. It. *platino*, < NL. *platinum* (with term. *-um* added, in analogy with other names of metals), < *platina*, < Sp. *platina*, platina (the orig. name): see *platina.*] Chemical symbol, Pt; atomic weight, 194.9. An important metal, introduced into Europe about the middle of the eighteenth century from South America. It does not occur as an ore, but alloyed with other metals, especially with rhodium, osmium, iridium, and palladium, all of which, together with iron, copper, and gold, are almost always present in it in small quantity in what is called its native state. Platinum is surpassed in ductility only by gold and silver, and in malleability only by those metals and copper. It is easily rolled into sheets or drawn into wire. Its specific gravity is 21.5, which is higher than that of any other known substance except osmium and iridium. It is not oxidized in the air at any temperature, and is not attacked by any of the simple acids. It is infusible in the strongest heat of a blast-furnace, but can be melted in the flame of the oxyhydrogen blowpipe or by means of the electric current. It is a rare metal, and the regions which supply it are few. Most of the platinum of commerce comes from the Urals, South America, and Borneo. It is used chiefly in chemical manufacture and analysis, where its resistance to heat and acids is of special value, and in electrical work. It was used for coinage in Russia from 1828 to 1845.—**Platinum chlorid.** Same as *chloroplatinic acid* (which see, under *chloroplatinic*).—**Platinum luster.** See *luster*[2].

platinum-black (plat'i-num-blak'), *n.* A black dull powder consisting of very finely divided metallic platinum. It was first obtained by E. Davy, and considered to be a nitrite of platinum; later it was recognized by Liebig as metallic, and prepared by him by warming a solution of platinum chlorid in potash with alcohol. According to Liebig, platinum-black absorbs more than 800 times its volume of oxygen. It can be prepared in a variety of ways, and is used in organic chemistry as an oxidizing agent.

platinum-lamp (plat'i-num-lamp), *n.* In *elect.*, an electric lamp in which the incandescent filament is of platinum.

platitude (plat'i-tūd), *n.* [< F. *platitude*, flatness (of taste), vapidness, a flat remark, < *plat*, flat: see *plat*[3].] 1. Flatness; dullness; insipidity of thought; triteness.—2. A trite, dull, or stupid remark; especially, such a remark uttered as if it were a novelty; a truism.

> It does not seem so easy for a preacher to trade upon his capacity of reserve, yet even in the clerical profession many have gained the reputation of profound divines and able judges in the spiritual life by a judicious management of solemn *platitudes.*
> *H. N. Oxenham*, Short Studies, p. 76.

platitudinarian (plat-i-tū-di-nā'ri-an), *a.* and *n.* [< *platitude* (*-din-*) + *-arian.*] **I.** *a.* Of the nature of or characterized by platitude; given to the utterance of platitudes.

II. *n.* One who is addicted to or indulges in platitudes.

> You have a respect for a political *platitudinarian* as insensible as an ox to everything he can't turn into political capital. *George Eliot*, Daniel Deronda, xxii.

platitudinize (plat-i-tū'di-nīz), *v. i.*; pret. and pp. *platitudinized*, ppr. *platitudinizing.* [< *platitude* (*-din-*) + *-ize*, as in *attitudinize.*] To utter platitudes; make dull, stale, or insipid remarks.

platitudinous (plat-i-tū'di-nus), *a.* [< *platitude* (*-din-*) + *-ous.*] Relating to or characterized by platitude or platitudes; stale; trite; flat; dull; insipid.

platitudinousness (plat-i-tū'di-nus-nes), *n.* The state or quality of being platitudinous; dullness; flatness; staleness; insipidity; triteness.

platly† (plat'li), *adv.* [< ME. *platly*; < *plat*[3] + *-ly*[2].] Flatly; plainly; certainly; surely.

> This synne is *platly* agayns the Hooly Goost.
> *Chaucer*, Parson's Tale.
>
> If ȝou barnes bowe the brede of an hare,
> *Platly* ȝe be putte to perpetuell pyne.
> *York Plays*, p. 328.

platness†, *n.* [< *plat*[3] + *-ness.*] Flatness. *Palsgrave.*

platode (plat'ōd), *a.* Same as *platoid*: correlated with *cestode*, *trematode*, and *nematode.*

platoid (plat'oid), *a.* [Irreg. < Gr. πλατύς, broad, flat, + εἶδος, form.] Broad or flat, as a worm.

platometer (plạ-tom'e-tėr), *n.* [Irreg. < Gr. πλατύς, flat, + μέτρον, measure.] Same as *planimeter.*

platometry (plạ-tom'et-ri), *n.* [< Gr. πλάτος, breadth, + -μετρία, < μέτρον, measure.] The art of measuring the breadth of rivers. *Dee*, 1570.

Platonia (plā-tō'ni-ä), *n.* [NL. (Martius, 1829), < *Plato*, < Gr. Πλάτων, the Greek philosopher: see *Platonic*[1].] A small genus of tropical American trees, belonging to the natural order *Guttiferæ* and the tribe *Moronobeæ.* It is chiefly distinguished from the other genera of the tribe by the anthers being borne above the middle of the numerous filaments into which the phalanges of stamens are divided. The genus embraces only two (perhaps only one) species, large trees with coriaceous, delicately penninerved leaves, solitary and showy pink flowers, and five-celled fleshy edible berries. The fruit of *P. insignis*, called *pacoury-uva* in Brazil, is said to be highly delicious, its seeds almond-flavored.

Platonic[1] (plā-ton'ik), *a.* and *n.* [Formerly also *Platonick*, *Platonike*; = F. *Platonique* = Sp. *Platónico* = Pg. It. *Platonico*, < L. *Platonicus*, < Gr. Πλατωνικός, of or pertaining to Plato, < Πλάτων, L. *Plato*, a Greek philosopher, son of Ariston, orig. named Aristocles, and surnamed Πλάτων with ref. to his broad shoulders, < πλατύς, broad: see *plat*[3].] **I.** *a.* Pertaining to Plato (about 427–347 B. C.), or to his doctrines. Reference to the school of Plato and to his followers is more usually expressed by the adjective *Platonistic.* Plato wrote in dialogues, which are equally admirable from a literary and from a philosophical point of view. He held that the object of philosophy is beauty; that without a deep sense of ignorance no man can philosophize; that judgments of common sense are open to doubt; that the senses may err, and at best can afford only likelihood (εἰκασία); that experience (δόξα), built out of perceptions, though safer, does not know the reasons of phenomena; and that man is the measure of things, not in his experience of particular facts, as Protagoras would have it, but in his knowledge of reasons, which alone is ennobling. Philosophy according to Plato has three branches—dialectic, physics, and ethics. Dialectic, the art of discussion, proceeds by definition and division. Division should be by dichotomy. He holds strongly to the truth of cognition; the process of mind and the process of nature are one. Neither the Eleatic doctrine that all is One, and the Many mere illusion, nor the Heraclitan doctrine that there is only a fluid manifold without unity, is the truth; there is a mixed being (μικτὴ οὐσία): being has an eternal and an evanescent element, and only a compound of these can be an object of science. The One in the Many is the Idea, the active force prescribing regularity (as we should say, the law of nature), which in supercelestial place subsists while individual cases arise and perish. The ideas make up an organism, or living system (ζῷον). They are themselves regulated by an idea of a teleological character, the Good, or ultimate purpose of all things, identical with Reason, the true Being (ὄντως ὄν), the One, King of heaven and earth, which, immutable, draws all things toward itself. This Reason is God, who is related to the ideas as a poet to the ideals he has created and intends to embody. That other element which in the actual condition of things in this world has not yet been eliminated so as to leave pure Reason is extended quantity (μικρὸν καὶ μέγα) or body (σῶμα), nearly Aristotle's matter (ὕλη). This is the secondary principle (συναίτιον) of the universe. God, the father, implants the seed of the Good in space, the mother, and without his further intervention the Cosmos, the only begotten son of God, made in his likeness, grows up. This is a second blessed god, instinct with Reason. Plato was a political philosopher. He abhorred alike the sway of oligarchy and of democracy, and still more the outcome of the latter, the one-man power—tyranny. He believed in aristocracy supported by an iron socialism. The relations of the sexes should be so regulated as to stop all increase in the population, which should be limited to 5,040 households. Private property and family relations should be abolished. Three classes should be recognized—workmen, soldiers, and lawyers. The education of a lawyer should begin with music, gymnastic, and mathematics. In his thirtieth year (up to which age he should be seen and not heard) he is to begin the study of dialectic. His education should be completed at the age of fifty, when he is to take his share in the government. The above is an outline of the general views of Plato; many of his special opinions are celebrated. He strongly maintains the immortality and previous existence of the soul. The tie which holds body and soul together is music. Virtue is not natural, nor can it be commanded by the will, but it is the result of discipline. The cardinal virtues are wisdom (σοφία), courage (ἀνδρία), prudence (σωφροσύνη), and justice (δικαιοσύνη). The unjust alone prosper; the perfect man would suffer on the cross. Reason resides in the head, desire in the abdomen, prophesy in the liver. Time is an image of eternity; it is produced by circular motions. Nature abhors a vacuum. Like attracts like. The constellations and the earth are living divinities. Plato was a mathematician, and is said to have invented the ancient method of analysis. His thoughts constantly show the influence of mathematical studies, and the desire to import mathematically distinct conceptions into philosophy. Aristotle, who was Plato's scholar, declared that the Platonic ideas were numbers. Plato no doubt attributed active virtues to the ideas of One, Two, Three, and Four.

> Now the first Christians many of them were *Platonick* Philosophers. *Selden*, Table-Talk, p. 53.
>
> We are apt to ridicule the sublime *Platonic* notions they had, or personated, in love and friendship.
> *Swift*, Conversation.

Platonic bodies, the five regular geometrical solids which inwrap the center only once—namely, the tetrahedron, the hexahedron or cube, the octahedron, the dodecahedron, and the icosahedron.—**Platonic idea.** See *idea.*—**Platonic love**, a pure spiritual affection subsisting between the sexes, unmixed with sensual desire, and regarding the mind only and its excellences.

> The Court affords little News at present, but that there is a Love called *Platonic Love.* *Howell*, Letters, I. vi. 15.

Platonic year. See *year.*

II. *n.* 1. A follower of Plato; a Platonist.

> Other things which he with great paines hath gathered out of the *Platonikes*, stamped with Zoroasters name, are many of them diuine. *Purchas*, Pilgrimage, p. 367.

2. One who loves with a Platonic affection.

> A talking dull *Platonic* I shall turn;
> Learn to be civil when I cease to burn.
> *Prior*, Ode, st. 5.

Platonic[2] (plạ-ton'ik), *a.* [< Gr. Πλάτων, Plato (see def.).] Pertaining to the Greek comic poet Plato (about 427–388 B. C.).—**Platonic meter**, in *anc. pros.*, a meter or period consisting of an iambic penthemimeres between two dactylic penthemimeres.

Platonical (plạ-ton'i-kal), *a.* [< *Platonic*[1] + *-al.*] Same as *Platonic*[1]. *Bp. Atterbury*, Sermons, I. xi., Pref.

Platonically (plā-ton'i-kal-i), *adv.* In a Platonic manner. *Sir H. Wotton.*

Platonise, Platoniser, *n.* See *Platonize*, *Platonizer.*

Platonism (plā'tọ-nizm), *n.* [< Gr. Πλάτων, Plato, + *-ism.*] 1. The doctrines, opinions, or philosophy of Plato, or of the Academic school. —2. A Platonic saying or proposition.

> The striking *Platonisms* of Coleridge.
> *R. Choate*, Addresses, p. 165.

Platonist (plā'tọ̄-nist), *n.* [< Gr. Πλάτων, Plato, + *-ist*.] One who adheres to the philosophy of Plato; a follower of Plato.

Or, self-conceited, play the humorous Platonist,
Which boldly dares affirm that Spirits themselves supply
With bodies, to commix with frail mortality.
Drayton, Polyolbion, v. 180.

Platonistic (plā-tọ̄-nis'tik), *a.* [< *Platonist* + *-ic*.] Of or pertaining to Plato or his followers, or the Platonic doctrines; characteristic of the Platonists.

Platonize (plā'tọ̄-nīz), *v.*; pret. and pp. *Platonized*, ppr. *Platonizing*. [< Gr. Πλάτων, Plato, + *-ize*.] **I.** *intrans.* To follow the opinions or philosophy of Plato; reason like Plato; emulate Plato.

Hitherto Philo; wherein, after his usual wont, he *platonizes*: the same being in effect to be found in Plato's Timæus. *Hakewill*, Apology, II. vi. § 2.

The imagination instinctively *Platonizes*, and it is the essence of poetry that it should be unconventional, that the soul of it should subordinate the outward parts. *Lowell*, Study Windows, p. 402.

II. *trans.* To explain on the principles of the Platonic school, or to accommodate to those principles.

Also spelled *Platonise*.

Platonizer (plā'tọ̄-nī-zėr), *n.* One who Platonizes; a Platonist. Also spelled *Platoniser*.

Philo the Jew, who was a great *platonizer*, calls the stars divine images, and incorruptible and immortal souls. *Dr. A. Young*, Idolatrous Corruptions in Religion, I. 109.

platoon (pla-tön'), *n.* [< F. *peloton* (pron. plọ̄-tôn'), a platoon, lit. a 'ball,' i. e. cluster, a particular use of *peloton*, a ball, tennis-ball, dim. of *pelote*, a ball, pellet: see *pellet*.] **1†.** A small body of soldiers or musketeers, drawn out of a battalion of foot to form a hollow square to strengthen the angles of some military formation or position; or, a small body acting together, but separate from the main body.—**2.** A number of soldiers, as large as is convenient for drill, etc., drawn up in two ranks, usually from 15 to 25 in each rank; hence (since a company of infantry is habitually divided into two platoons), half of a company considered as a separate body.—**Platoon firing**, firing by platoons, or subdivisions of companies.

platopic (pla-top'ik), *a.* Same as *platyopic*. *Jour. of Anthrop. Inst.*, p. 156.

platte[1]†, *v. t.* A Middle English form of *plat*[1].

platte[2]†, *a.* A Middle English form of *plat*[3].

platte[3] (plat), *n.* [OF.: see *plate*.] Same as *placcate* (c).

platté (pla-tā'), *a.* [OF., < *platte*, a plate: see *plate*.] In *her.*, semé with plates—that is, with roundels argent.

platted (plat'ed), *a.* Same as *plaited*.

platten (plat'en), *v. t.* [< *plat*[3] + *-en*[1].] In *glass-manuf.*, to open out and flatten into a plate or sheet: said of a blown cylinder of glass. The hot cylinder is first cracked on one side in a straight line longitudinally by the application of a cold iron rod; then it is laid in the flattening-oven (which has a smooth stone bottom), and kept there in a soft state till it opens out; and lastly it is smoothed out with an implement called a *flattener*. Sometimes the cylinders are cut longitudinally with a diamond, and then placed in the furnace or flattening-arch for opening and smoothing. The flattening of crown-glass is called *flashing*.

plattening (plat'en-ing), *n.* [Verbal n. of *platten*, *v.*] In *glass-manuf.*, the process of forming glass into plates or sheets. See *platten*.

platter[1] (plat'ėr), *n.* [< ME. *plater*, *platere*, appar. orig. **platel*, < OF. *platel*, dim. of *plat*, a plate: see *plate*, and cf. *plateau*.] A plate; a large shallow dish for holding eatables; especially, a flat dish in which a fowl, a joint, or the like is placed to be carved.

In the Lond of Prestre John ben many dyverse thinges, and many precious Stones so grete and so large that men maken of hem Vesselle; as *Plateres*, Dissches, and Cuppes. *Mandeville*, Travels, p. 272.

Earthen *Platters* held their homely Food. *Congreve*, tr. of Juvenal's Satires, xi.

The attendants bustled to and fro, and speedily brought in several large smoking *platters*, filled with huge pieces of beef, boiled and roasted. *Scott*, Monastery, xxiv.

platter[2] (plat'ėr), *n.* [< *plat*[4] + *-er*[1].] One who plats, braids, or interweaves.

platting (plat'ing), *n.* [Verbal n. of *plat*[4], *v.*] **1.** The process of making interwoven or platted work.—**2.** A fabric made of fibers, bundles of fibers, or thin slips of any pliable material, such as cane or straw.

Bermuda hats are worn by our ladies; they are made of a sort of mat or (as they call it) *platting* made of the palmetto leaf. *Bp. Berkeley*, Proposals for Better Supplying of Churches.

plattnerite (plat'nėr-īt), *n.* [Named after K. F. *Plattner* (1800–58), a German chemist and mineralogist.] Native lead dioxid (PbO_2), a rare mineral occurring in iron-black massive forms, of high specific gravity. It was originally described as found at Leadhills, Scotland, but was regarded as a doubtful species until recently identified from the lead-mines of northern Idaho.

Plattner's process. See *process*.

platty (plat'i), *a.* [< *plat*[2] + *-y*[1].] Having plats or bare spots, as grain-fields sometimes have. *Halliwell*. [Prov. Eng.]

plature (plā'tûr), *n.* [< NL. *Platurus*, q. v.] A broad-tailed humming-bird of the genus *Platurus*.

platurous (plạ̄-tū'rus), *a.* [Prop. **platyurous*, < Gr. πλατύουρος, broad-tailed, < πλατύς, broad, flat, + οὐρά, tail.] Having a broad tail.

Platurus (plạ̄-tū'rus), *n.* [NL. (Latreille), prop. **Platyurus*, < Gr. πλατύουρος, broad-tailed: see *platurous*.] **1.** A genus of venomous marine serpents of the family *Hydrophidæ*, having wide and flat gastrosteges and two pairs of frontal shields.—**2.** A genus of broad-tailed *Trochilidæ*, named by Lesson in 1829; the platures.

Platurus fasciatus.

platy (plā'ti), *a.* [Also *platey*; < *plate* + *-y*[1].] Like a plate; consisting of plates.

platybasic (plat-i-bā'sik), *a.* [< Gr. πλατύς, broad, flat, + βάσις, foot, base: see *basic*.] Having the occipital bone about the foramen magnum pressed upward; having the negative angle of Daubenton more than 80°. See *craniometry*.

platybrachycephalic (plat-i-brak-i-se-fal'ik or -sef'ạ-lik), *a.* [< *platy(cephalic)* + *brachycephalic*.] Flat and broad; both platycephalic and brachycephalic: said of a skull.

platybregmete (plat-i-breg'mēt), *n.* [< Gr. πλατύς, broad, + βρέγμα, the front part of the head: see *bregma*.] A wide bregma, as seen in Mongolian skulls.

platycarpous (plat-i-kär'pus), *a.* [< Gr. πλατύς, broad, + καρπός, fruit.] In *bot.*, having broad fruit.

platycephalic (plat″i-se-fal'ik or -sef'ạ-lik), *a.* [< *platycephal-ous* + *-ic*.] Same as *platycephalous*.

Platycephalidæ (plat″i-se-fal'i-dē), *n. pl.* [NL., < *Platycephalus* + *-idæ*.] A family of acanthopterygian fishes, typified by the genus *Platycephalus*; the flatheads. They have an elongated body depressed in front, a wide depressed head, imbricated scales, two dorsals (the anterior shorter than the posterior), a long anal, and perfect ventrals behind the pectorals. Nearly 50 species are known as inhabitants of the tropical Pacific and Indian oceans.

Platycephalinæ (plat-i-sef-a-lī'nē), *n. pl.* [NL., < *Platycephalus* + *-inæ*.] The *Platycephalidæ* as a subfamily of scorpænoid fishes.

platycephalous (plat-i-sef'ạ-lus), *a.* [< Gr. πλατυκέφαλος, broad-headed, < πλατύς, broad, flat (see *plat*[3]), + κεφαλή, head.] Having the vault of the skull flattened; having a vertical index of less than 70.

Platycephalus (plat-i-sef'ạ-lus), *n.* [NL.: see *platycephalous*.] **1.** The typical genus of *Platycephalidæ*: so called from the broad depressed head. *Bloch and Schneider*, 1801.—**2.** [*l. c.*] A broad flat skull, deformed from synosteosis of frontal and parietal bones.

Flathead (*Platycephalus tentaculatus*).

platycephaly (plat-i-sef'ạ-li), *n.* [< *platycephal-ous* + *-y*.] The condition of having a platycephalic skull.

Platycercidæ (plat-i-sėr'si-dē), *n. pl.* [NL., < *Platycercus* + *-idæ*.] The broad-tailed parrakeets as a separate family of parrots.

Platycercinæ (plat″i-sėr-sī'nē), *n. pl.* [NL., < *Platycercus* + *-inæ*.] A subfamily of *Psittacidæ*, typified by the genus *Platycercus*, to which varying limits have been ascribed; the broad-tailed parrakeets. It is properly restricted to those parrots which have no ambiens and no furculum. In a common acceptation, it contains parrakeets with a short beak of greater height than length, a small cere (frequently feathered), and a long tail, usually exceeding the wings in length, and in some cases with broad feathers. All the *Platycercinæ* belong to the Old World, and they are most numerous in species and individuals in the Australian region. About 70 species are described, among them the grass-, ground-, and zebra-parrakeets. See *grass-parrakeet*, *Euphema*, *Melopsittacus*, and *Platycercus*.

platycercine (plat-i-sėr'sin), *a.* Broad-tailed; belonging to the *Platycercinæ*.

Platycercus (plat-i-sėr'kus), *n.* [NL. (Vigors and Horsfield, 1825), < Gr. πλατύκερκος, broad-tailed, < πλατύς, broad, + κέρκος, tail.] The leading genus of *Platycercinæ*, containing more than half the species of this subfamily, having the tail long and ample, with its feathers broad to their ends, and the four middle ones longer than the rest. They are beautifully and variously colored, and range from the Malay archipelago to the islands of the Pacific ocean. Several are favorite cage-birds, as the rosella or rose-parrakeet, *P. eximius*, and the king-parrakeet, *P. scapulatus*. See cut under *rosella*.

Platycerium (plat-i-sē'ri-um), *n.* [NL., < Gr. πλατύς, broad, + κηρίον, a honeycomb, < κηρός, wax: see *cere*.] A very distinct and remarkable genus of ferns, commonly associated with the *Acrosticheæ*. It has been proposed to place it in a separate section, from its producing its sori in large amorphous patches, not, as in the true *Acrosticheæ*, universal over the fertile portions. The species are few in number, chiefly Eastern or Australian, and for the most part tropical.

Platycerus (plạ̄-tis'ẹ-rus), *n.* [NL. (Geoffroy, 1762) (cf. L. *platyceros*, < Gr. πλατύκερως, having broad horns), < Gr. πλατύς, broad, + κέρας, horn.] A genus of stag-beetles of rather small size, chiefly characterized by the distinctness of the sixth ventral abdominal segment. The few species known are found in Asia, Europe, and North America. Four inhabit the United States, as *P. quercus*, found in oak-stumps throughout North America, ½ inch long and brownish-black.

Platycerus quercus. (Line shows natural size.)

platycnemia (plat-ik-nē'mi-ạ̈), *n.* [NL.: see *platycnemic*.] The condition of being platycnemic; platycnemism.

platycnemic (plat-ik-nē'mik), *a.* [< Gr. πλατύς, broad, + κνήμη, the lower leg: see *Cnemis*.] Broad and flat, as a tibia; having such tibiæ, as a person.

platycnemism (plat-ik-nē'mizm), *n.* [< *platycnem-ic* + *-ism*.] The state of being platycnemic; breadth and flatness of the tibia.

Platycœlia (plat-i-sē'li-ạ̈), *n.* [NL. (Dejean, 1833), < Gr. πλατύς, flat, + κοῖλος, hollow.] A genus of lamellicorn beetles of the family *Rutelidæ*, or typical of a family *Platycœlidæ*. They are large and handsome South American insects, with a very convex head of a beautiful green color. Also *Platycœlus*.

platycœlian (plat-i-sē'li-ạn), *a.* [< *platycœl-ous* + *-ian*.] Same as *platycœlous*.

Platycœlidæ (plat-i-sē'li-dē), *n. pl.* [NL., < *Platycœlia* + *-idæ*.] A family of coleopterous insects, named from the genus *Platycœlia*. *Burmeister*, 1844.

platycœlous (plat-i-sē'lus), *a.* [< Gr. πλατύς, flat, + κοῖλος, hollow.] Plano-concave, as a vertebra; plane or flat in front and cupped behind, as the bodies of the vertebræ of the cetiosaurians: now usually called *opisthocœlian*.

platycoria (plat-i-kō'ri-ạ̈), *n.* [NL., < Gr. πλατύς, broad, + κόρη, the pupil of the eye.] In *med.*, an undue dilatation of the pupil; mydriasis.

Platycrinidæ (plat-i-krin'i-dē), *n. pl.* [NL., < *Platycrinus* + *-idæ*.] A family of Paleozoic crinoids or encrinites, typified by the genus *Platycrinus*.

platycrinite (plat'i-kri-nīt), *n.* An encrinite of the genus *Platycrinus* or *Platycrinites*.

platycrinoid (plat'i-kri-noid), *n.* [< NL. *Platycrinus*, q. v., + Gr. εἶδος, form.] A platycrinite.

Platycrinoidea (plat″i-kri-noi'dẹ̄-ạ̈), *n. pl.* [NL., < *Platycrinus* + *-oidea*.] Same as *Platycrinidæ*.

Platycrinus (plā-tik'ri-nus), *n.* [NL., < Gr. πλατύς, broad, flat, + κρίνον, lily (see *crinoid*).] The typical genus of *Platycrinidæ*, from the limestone of the coal-measures: so named from the flatness and breadth of the radial plates on the receptacle. Originally *Platycrinites*.

platydactyl, platydactyle (plat-i-dak'til), *a.* and *n.* [< NL. *platydactylus*, < Gr. πλατύς, broad, + δάκτυλος, finger.] **I.** *a.* Having broad or thick digits; specifically, in *herpet.*, having toes dilated at the ends; discodactyl; belonging to the *Discodactyla*: distinguished from *oxydactyl*.

II. *n.* A platydactyl batrachian.

Platydactyla (plat-i-dak'ti-lạ̈), *n. pl.* [NL., neut. pl. of *platydactylus*: see *platydactyl*.] In Günther's classification, a group of opisthoglossate batrachians, having the toes dilated: distinguished from *Oxydactyla*. Also called *Discodactyla*.

Platydactylus (plat-i-dak'ti-lus), *n.* [NL. (Cuvier, 1817): see *platydactylous*.] **1.** A genus of gecko lizards. *P. fascicularis* or *muralis* is the wall-gecko. *P. mauritanicus*, of the countries bordering the Mediterranean, is known as the *tarente*. **2.** In *entom.*, a genus of orthopterous insects. *Brullé*, 1835.

Platydactylus mauritanicus.

platydolichocephalic (plat-i-dol″i-kọ̄-se-fal'ik or -sef'ạ-lik), *a.* [< *platy*(*cephalic*) + *dolichocephalic*.] Flat and narrow; both platycephalic and dolichocephalic: said of a skull.

Platyelmia (plat-i-el'mi-ạ̈), *n. pl.* [NL., < Gr. πλατύς, flat, + ἕλμινς (ἑλμινθ-), worm.] Same as *Platyhelmintha*.

Platygaster (plat-i-gas'tėr), *n.* [NL. (Latreille, 1809) (cf. Gr. πλατυγάστωρ, flat-bellied), < Gr. πλατύς, broad, flat, + γαστήρ, stomach: see *gaster*[2].] **1.** A genus of parasitic hymenopterous

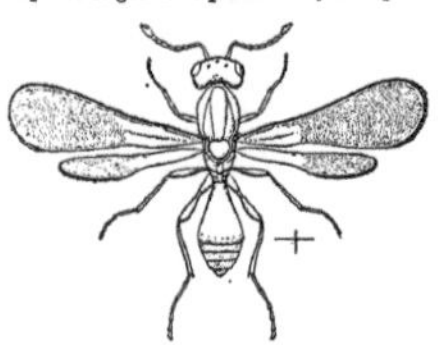

Platygaster herricki. (Cross shows natural size.)

insects of the family *Proctotrypidæ*, typical of the subfamily *Platygasterinæ*. It is separated from other genera by negative characters, and contains a large number of species, more than 100 being known in Europe alone. *P. herricki* is a common parasite of the Hessian fly in North America. **2.** A genus of true bugs of the family *Lygæidæ*, erected by Schilling in 1829.—**3.** A genus of fishes erected by Swainson in 1839.—**4.** A genus of flies of the family *Acroceridæ*, erected by Zetterstedt in 1840: same as *Sphærogaster*.

Platygasterinæ (plat-i-gas-tẹ-rī'nē), *n. pl.* [< *Platygaster* + *-inæ*.] An important subfamily of the parasitic hymenopterous family *Proctotrypidæ*, consisting of minute black insects having the fore tibiæ one-spurred, the mandibles toothed, and the anterior wings without marginal and stigmal veins. Over 20 genera have been founded, though the group has been little studied. The species seem to be mainly parasitic on dipterous larvæ.

platygastric (plat-i-gas'trik), *a.* [< Gr. πλατύς, broad, + γαστήρ, stomach: see *gastric*.] Having broad or wide gastric cavities: belonging to the *Platygasterinæ*.

platyglossal (plat-i-glos'ạl), *a.* [< Gr. πλατύγλωσσος, broad-tongued, < πλατύς, broad, + γλῶσσα, tongue.] Having a broad or wide tongue.

Platyglossus (plat-i-glos'us), *n.* [NL. (Bleeker, 1861, after Klein), < Gr. πλατύγλωσσος, broad-tongued: see *platyglossal*.] A genus of labroid fishes of the wrasse family. They have the teeth of the jaws distinct, the pharyngeal teeth not confluent, the posterior canines well developed, 3 anal spines, 9 dorsal spines, and the cheeks and opercles naked or nearly so. They are known as *doncellas*. *P. radiatus*, 16 inches long, inhabits West Indian and Floridan waters. *P. semicinctus* is a kelp-fish of the Pacific coast of North America.

platygonidium (plat″i-gọ̄-nid'i-um), *n.*; pl. *platygonidia* (-ạ̈). [NL., < Gr. πλατύς, broad, flat, + NL. *gonidium*.] See *gonidium*, 3.

Platygonus (plạ̄-tig'ọ̄-nus), *n.* [NL., < Gr. πλατύς, broad, flat, + γόνυ, knee.] A genus of fossil peccaries of the family *Dicotylidæ*, founded by Le Conte in 1848 upon remains of the late Tertiary of America. Also called *Hyops*, *Protochœrus*, and *Euchœrus*.

platyhelminth (plat-i-hel'minth), *n.* [< NL. *Platyhelmintha*.] A member of the *Platyhelmintha*, in any sense; a flatworm, as a cestoid, trematoid, turbellarian, or nemertean.

Platyhelmintha, Platyhelminthes (plat″i-hel-min'thạ̈, -thēz), *n. pl.* [NL., < Gr. πλατύς, broad, flat, + ἕλμινς (ἑλμινθ-), a worm: see *helminth*.] A superordinal or other high group of worms, variously named and rated, including forms more or less flattened, usually ovate, and indistinctly segmented; the flatworms, or cestoids, trematoids, and turbellarians, together contrasted with the roundworms or nemathelminths. In some of the older arrangements, under the name *Platyelmia*, they were divided into the non-parasitic order *Turbellaria* and the two parasitic orders *Tæniada* and *Trematoda*. In another classification the platyhelminths are a prime division of *Vermes*, divided into *Turbellaria* (rhabdocœlous and dendrocœlous turbellarians), *Nemertina* (rhynchocœlous turbellarians), *Trematoda*, and *Cestoda*. In Lankester's latest arrangement they are called *Platyhelmia*, and are divided into two branches, *Ciliata* and *Cotylophora*. The former is the order *Turbellaria* in a broad sense, here divided into three classes, *Rhabdocœla*, *Dendrocœla*, and *Nemertina* (or *Rhynchocœla*). The *Cotylophora* are divided into three classes, *Trematoidea*, *Cestoidea*, and *Hirudinea*, the two former of these, each with numerous orders, corresponding in a general way with the families of other authors. The *Mesozoa* of Van Beneden (see *Dicyemida*) are regarded as probably classable with the *Ciliata*. This arrangement is peculiar in bringing the leeches and *Dicyemida* under this head. Otherwise it resembles its predecessors. The many arrangements of the flatworms differ more in nomenclature and taxonomic rating than in actual significance. Also *Plathelmintha*, *Plathelminthes*.

Platylobium (plat-i-lō'bi-um), *n.* [NL. (Smith, 1794), < Gr. πλατύς, broad, + λόβιον, dim. of λοβός, pod.] A genus of leguminous shrubs of the tribe *Genisteæ* and subtribe *Bossiææ*, characterized by the two-lipped calyx, orbicular banner-petal, monadelphous stamens, uniform versatile anthers, and broad flat two-valved pod, opening elastically along the lower suture, broadly winged upon the other. The 3 species are Australian shrubs, with slender branches, opposite undivided leaves, and handsome orange-yellow flowers solitary in the axils, occasionally red, resembling the sweet-pea. They are pendent-branching evergreens, cultivated under the name *flat pea*.

Platylophus (plạ̄-til'ọ̄-fus), *n.* [NL., < Gr. πλατύς, flat, broad, + λόφος, a crest.] **1.** A genus of birds of the family *Corvidæ* and subfamily *Garrulinæ*, containing several species of crested jays from Java, Sumatra, Borneo, etc., such as *P. galericulatus*, *P. coronatus*, and others. *Swainson*, 1831.—**2.** A genus of arachnidans. *Koch*, 1839.—**3.** A genus of polypetalous plants of the order *Saxifrageæ* and the tribe *Cunonieæ*, characterized by the two-celled, two-seeded, and two-valved capsules, the two awl-shaped recurved styles, four or five calyx-lobes, as many smaller petals, and eight or ten stamens, of the length of the petals, and inserted with them on the base of an urn-shaped disk. *D. Don*, 1830. The only species, *P. trifoliatus*, the white alder or white ash of Cape Colony, is a very smooth and handsome tree, casting abundant shade, and bearing multitudes of small white flowers in long-stalked axillary panicles, followed by small white capsules. The coriaceous opposite and stalked leaves are each composed of three toothed and veiny lanceolate leaflets. See *alder*[1], 2.

platymesaticephalic (plat-i-mes″ạ-ti-se-fal'ik or -sef'ạ-lik), *a.* [< *platy*(*cephalic*) + *mesaticephalic*.] Both platycephalic and mesaticephalic: said of a skull. Also *platymesocephalic*.

platymeter (plạ̄-tim'e-tėr), *n.* [< Gr. πλατύς, flat, + μέτρον, measure.] An apparatus for measuring the inductive capacity of dielectrics. It consists essentially of two cylindrically shaped condensers of equal size, having their inner coatings connected.

Platymiscium (plat-i-mis'i-um), *n.* [NL. (Vogel, 1837), so called with ref. to the compressed stalk of the pod; < Gr. πλατύς, flat, + *μίσκος for μίσχος, a stalk, also, in form μίσκος, husk or shell.] A genus of leguminous trees and shrubs, of the tribe *Dalbergieæ* and the subtribe *Lonchocarpeæ*, characterized by the free wing-petals, the opposite leaves and leaflets, and the indehiscent one-seeded long-stalked pod, which is thin, flat, and oblong. In its opposite or whorled leaves it is almost alone in this large order. The 13 species are natives of tropical America. They bear yellow flowers in racemes on the branches. *P. platystachyum* is called *roble* in the West Indies.

Platynota (plat-i-nō'tạ̈), *n. pl.* [NL.: see *platynote*.] A group of existing *Lacertilia*, with a columella and an orbital septum, procœlous vertebræ, not more than nine cervical vertebræ, and the nasal bone single. It embraces the monitors or varanoids of the Old World, with the American genus *Heloderma*. See *monitor*, *Heloderma*.

platynotal (plat-i-nō'tạl), *a.* [< *platynote* + *-al*.] Broad-backed, as a lizard; specifically, of or pertaining to the *Platynota*.

platynote (plat'i-nōt), *a.* and *n.* [< Gr. πλατύνωτος, broad-backed, < πλατύς, broad, flat, + νῶτος, back.] **I.** *a.* Broad-backed, as a lizard: applied to the varans or monitors.

II. *n.* A monitor or varanoid lizard.

Platynotus (plat-i-nō'tus), *n.* [NL.: see *platynote*.] In *zoöl.*, a generic name variously used. (*a*) By Fabricius, 1801, for a genus of coleopterous insects. (*b*) By Schilling, 1829, for a genus of hemipterous insects. (*c*) By Wagler, 1830, for a genus of reptiles, whence the name *Platynota*. (*d*) By Haan, 1835, for a genus of crustaceans.

Platynus (plat'i-nus), *n.* [NL., irreg. < Gr. πλατύνειν, widen, make wide, < πλατύς, wide, broad: see *plat*[3].] A genus of caraboid beetles. *P. maculicollis* is at times so abundant in California as to be a nuisance. It is popularly called the *overflow-bug*.

Platynus maculicollis, enlarged.

platyodont (plat'i-ọ̄-dont), *a.* and *n.* [< Gr. πλατύς, broad, + ὀδούς (ὀδοντ-) = E. *tooth*.] **I.** *a.* Having broad teeth.

II. *n.* A broad-toothed animal.

Platyonychus (plat-i-on'i-kus), *n.* [NL., < Gr. πλατυώνυχος, with broad nails or hoofs, < πλατύς, broad, flat, + ὄνυξ (ὀνυχ-), claw.] A genus of

Lady-crab (*Platyonychus ocellatus*).

crabs of the family *Portunidæ*. *P. ocellatus* is a beautiful species known as the *lady-crab*. Incorrectly written *Platyonichus*.

platyope (plat'i-ōp), *n.* [< Gr. πλατύς, broad, + ὤψ (ὀπ-), face.] A broad-faced animal, person, or skull.

platyopic (plat-i-op'ik), *a.* [< *platyope* + *-ic*.] Broad-faced; wide across the eyes: applied to skulls or persons whose nasomalar index is below 107.5, as in the Mongolian races generally. Also *platopic*.

platypetalous (plat-i-pet'ạ-lus), *a.* [< Gr. πλατύς, broad, + πέταλον, a leaf (in mod. bot. a petal).] In *bot.*, having very broad petals. [Rare.]

Platypeza (plat-i-pē'zạ̈), *n.* [NL. (Meigen, 1804), < Gr. πλατύς, broad, flat, + πέζα, foot.] The typical genus of *Platypezidæ*, having the four basal joints of the posterior tarsi broad and flattened, whence the name. They are small velvety-black or gray flies, whose larvæ live in fungi. Fifteen European and five North American species are known. *P. cingulatus* of the District of Columbia is an example.

Platypezidæ (plat-i-pez'i-dē), *n. pl.* [NL. (Fallen, 1817), < *Platypeza* + *-idæ*.] A family of dichætous brachycerous dipterous insects, typified by the genus *Platypeza*. They are of minute size, and resemble the *Dolichopodidæ*, but the body is depressed and the head hemispherical, almost entirely occupied by the eyes; the legs are short and spineless, and the hind tarsi are often dilated. The antennæ are porrect and three-jointed; the bare eyes are contiguous in the male; the abdomen is short, and pulvilli are present. The genera are four in number.

platyphylline (plat-i-fil'in), *a.* [< *platyphyllous* + *-ine*[1].] In *bot.*, broad-leaved; flat.

Thallus sub-membranaceous, stellate, appressed. *platyphylline*. *E. Tuckerman*, N. A. Lichens, I. 74.

platyphyllous (plat-i-fil'us), *a.* [< Gr. πλατύφυλλος, broad-leafed, < πλατύς, flat, + φύλλον, leaf.] In *bot.*, having broad leaves.

platypod (plat'i-pod), *a.* and *n.* [< NL. *platypus* (*-pod-*), < Gr. πλατύπους, broad-footed, < πλατύς, broad, + πούς (ποδ-) = E. *foot.*] **I.** *a.* **1.** Having broad feet, in any sense; belonging to the *Platypoda.*—**2.** In *ornith.*, having the toes extensively coherent, forming a broad sole; syndactyl.

II. *n.* A broad-footed animal.

Platypoda (plạ-tip'ọ-dạ̈), *n. pl.* [NL.: see *platypod.*] **1.** In *mammal.*, a group of monotremes, named from the genus *Platypus*. See *Ornithorhynchidæ*, and cut under *duckbill.*—**2.** In *conch.*, a group of rostriferous gastropods with broad flat foot fitted for crawling. It includes most of the rostriferous gastropods, among the best-known of them being the *Cypræidæ*, *Littorinidæ*, *Melaniidæ*, *Cerithiidæ*, and *Viviparidæ*. *J. E. Gray.* See cuts under *Cerithium*, *Cypræa*, *Littorinidæ*, and *Viviparidæ*.

platypode (plat'i-pōd), *a.* and *n.* Same as *platypod.*

Platypsyllidæ (plat-ip-sil'i-dē), *n. pl.* [NL. (Le Conte, 1872), < *Platypsyllus* + *-idæ.*] A family of clavicorn *Coleoptera*, typified by the genus *Platypsyllus*. They have the dorsal segments of the abdomen partly membranous, ventral segments free; the tarsi five-jointed (at least one pair of tarsi); the mentum large, and prolonged in three obtuse lobes behind; and the palpi distant at base. The family is certainly coleopterous, and its true position seems to be between the *Hydrophilidæ* and the *Silphidæ*; but the form is degraded by parasitism to the semblance of a mallophagous insect.

Platypsyllus (plat-ip-sil'us), *n.* [NL. (Ritsema, 1869), < Gr. πλατύς, broad, flat, + ψύλλα, a flea.] A remarkable genus of insects, type of the family *Platypsyllidæ*, referred by some to the order *Aphaniptera*, by others to the *Diptera*, by Westwood made type of an order *Achreioptera*, by Le Conte placed in the order *Coleoptera* among the clavicorns. *P. castoris*, a parasite of the beaver, is a small eyeless and wingless beetle with short elytra leaving five abdominal segments exposed. Also called *Platypsylla*.

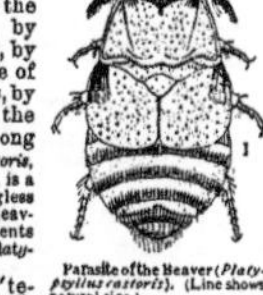

Parasite of the Beaver (*Platypsyllus castoris*). (Line shows natural size.)

Platyptera (plạ-tip'tẹ-rạ̈), *n.* [NL., < Gr. πλατύς, broad, + πτερόν, wing, = E. *feather.*] A genus of fishes, typical of the family *Platypteridæ*. The only known species, *P. aspro*, is an inhabitant of fresh water in islands of the Sunda-Moluccan archipelago.

Platypteridæ (plat-ip-ter'i-dē), *n. pl.* [NL., < *Platyptera* + *-idæ.*] A family of acanthopterygian fishes, represented by the genus *Platyptera*. They are related to the *Gobridæ*, and by many referred to that family, but differ from it by having the ventrals widely separate from each other, and from the *Callionymidæ* by the scaly body, unarmed preoperculum, and moderately wide gill-openings.

Platypterna (plat-ip-tėr'nạ̈), *n.* [NL. (Hitchcock, 1848), < Gr. πλατύς, broad, flat, + πτέρνα, the heel.] A genus of gigantic animals, formerly supposed to be birds, now believed to be dinosaurian reptiles, known by their footprints in the Triassic formation of the Connecticut valley.

Platypterygidæ (plạ-tip-tẹ-rij'i-dē), *n. pl.* [NL., < *Platypteryx* (*-pteryg-*) + *-idæ.*] A family of bombycid moths, typified by the genus *Platypteryx*. The antennæ of the male are pectinate, those of the female generally filiform; the abdomen is slender, and the wings are small but comparatively broad, and sometimes hooked at the tip; the larvæ have 14 legs.

Platypteryx (plạ-tip'tẹ-riks), *n.* [NL., < Gr. πλατύς, broad, flat, + πτέρυξ, wing.] In *entom.*, the typical genus of *Platypterygidæ*. The species are known as *hook-tip moths*.

Platypus (plat'i-pus), *n.* [NL., < Gr. πλατύπους, broad-footed, < πλατύς, broad, + πούς (ποδ-), = E. *foot.*] **1.** In *entom.*, a genus of xylophagous beetles of the family *Scolytidæ*: synonymous in part with *Bostrychus*. *Herbst*, 1793.—**2.** In *mammal.*: (*a*) A genus of monotremes, now called *Ornithorhynchus*. *Shaw*, 1799. (*b*) [*l. c.*] The species of this genus; the duck-billed platypus. See cut under *duckbill.*—**3.** In *ornith.*, a genus of sea-ducks of the family *Anatidæ* and the subfamily *Fuligulinæ*: synonymous with *Fulix*. *Brehm*, 1831.

platypygous (plat-i-pī'gus), *a.* [< Gr. πλατύπυγος, broad-bottomed, < πλατύς, broad, + πυγή, rump, buttocks.] Having broad buttocks.

platyrhine, Platyrhini, etc. See *platyrrhine*, etc.

Platyrhynchi (plat-i-ring'kī), *n. pl.* [NL., pl. of *Platyrhynchus*, q. v.] In Merrem's classification of birds (1813), a group equivalent to the *Steganopodes* or *Totipalmati* of authors, containing such genera as *Pelecanus*, *Phaëton*, and *Plotus*, or the pelicans, gannets, cormorants, anhingas, tropic-birds, etc.

platyrhynchine (plat-i-ring'kin), *a.* [< *Platyrhynchus* + *-ine*1.] Broad-billed, as a bird.

Platyrhynchus (plat-i-ring'kus), *n.* [NL. (Desmarest, 1805), prop. **Platyrrhynchus*, < Gr. πλατύρρυγχος, broad-snouted, broad-beaked, < πλατύς, broad, + ῥύγχος, snout, beak.] **1.** In *ornith.*: (*a*) A genus of American tyrant-flycatchers, belonging to the family *Tyrannidæ*, and typical of the subfamily *Platyrhynchinæ*, having a very broad flat bill with long vibrissæ, whence the name. There are several species, of South and Central America, as *P. mystaceus*. *Megarhynchus* is a synonym. (*b*) Same as *Eurylæmus*. *Vieillot*, 1825.—**2.** In *entom.*, a genus of coleopterous insects. *Thunberg*, 1815.—**3.** In *herpet.*, a genus of batrachians. Also *Platyrhincus*. *Duméril*, 1854.

Head of *Platyrhynchus mystaceus*, top and side views, natural size.

platyrrhine, platyrhine (plat'i-rin), *a.* and *n.* [< Gr. πλατύρρις (-ριν-), broad-nosed, < πλατύς, broad, + ῥίς (ῥιν-), nose.] **I.** *a.* **1.** Broad-nosed, as any American monkey; belonging to the *Platyrrhini.*—**2.** In *craniom.*, having a flat nose; having a nasal index of from 51.1 (Frankfort agreement) or 53 (Broca) to 58.

II. *n.* A platyrrhine monkey.

Platyrrhini, Platyrhini (plat-i-rī'nī), *n. pl.* [NL.: see *platyrrhine.*] A division of *Quadrumana*, contrasted with *Catarrhini* and *Strepsirrhini*, including all the American or New World members of the order *Primates* and families *Cebidæ* and *Hapalidæ* or *Mididæ*; the platyrrhine monkeys. There is no bony external auditory meatus, the tympanic bone being annular; the premolars are three above and below on each side; the nasal septum is usually broad and flat, and the nostrils are proportionately far apart, presenting forward or laterally and not downward; the thumb, when present, is scarcely or not apposable; there are no cheek-pouches nor ischial callosities; and the tail is generally long and prehensile or bushy. Also written *Platyrrhina*, *Platyrrhinæ*, and in all forms with single or double r. See cuts under *Cebinæ* and *Hapalidæ*.

platyrrhinian (plat-i-rin'i-ạn), *a.* and *n.* [< *platyrrhine* + *-ian.*] **I.** *a.* **1.** In *zoöl.*, platyrrhine, as a monkey.—**2.** In *anthropol.*, having broad flat nasal bones, as a person, a people, or a skull.

II. *n.* A platyrrhinian animal, person, or skull.

platyrrhiny, platyrhiny (plat'i-rī-ni), *n.* [< Gr. πλατύρρις (-ριν-), broad-nosed: see *platyrrhine.*] The condition of having a platyrrhine skull.

Platyschistæ (plat-i-skis'tē), *n. pl.* [NL., < Gr. πλατίσχιστος, with broad clefts, < πλατύς, broad, + σχιστός, cloven, parted, divided, < σχίζειν, split, part.] In Günther's classification, the first subfamily of *Murænidæ*, with the branchial openings in the pharynx in the form of wide slits, including all the true apodal fishes excepting the typical *Murænidæ*.

platyscopic (plat-i-skop'ik), *a.* [< Gr. πλατύς, broad, flat, + σκοπεῖν, view.] In *optics*, having a wide and flat field of view: used as a trade-name for certain achromatic combinations of lenses, as for photographic use, or for hand-magnifiers.

platysma (plạ-tis'mạ̈), *n.*; pl. *platysmata* (-mạ-tạ̈). [NL., < Gr. πλάτυσμα, a flat piece or plate, < πλατύνειν, broaden, extend, < πλατύς, broad, flat: see *plat*[3].] A thin broad muscle situated immediately beneath the skin at the side of the neck, and extending from the chest and shoulder to the face. It represents the panniculus carnosus of many mammals, which produces the movements of the skin, as in the horse.—**Platysma myoides.** Same as *platysma*. See *panniculus*, and cut 3, λ, under *muscle*.

Platysomata (plat-i-sō'mạ-tạ̈), *n. pl.* [NL., < Gr. πλατύς, broad, + σῶμα (σωματ-), body.] In Latreille's system of classification, the third family of tetramerous *Coleoptera*, corresponding to the genus *Cucujus* of Fabricius, and to the modern family *Cucujidæ*, which, however, is now differently located, among the clavicorn pentamerous coleopters.

platysome (plat'i-sōm), *n.* An insect of the group *Platysomata*.

Platysomidæ (plat-i-som'i-dē), *n. pl.* [NL., < *Platysomus* + *-idæ.*] A family of fossil lepidosteoid ganoid fishes, represented by the genus *Platysomus*. The body is generally high, covered with rhomboganoid scales arranged in dorsiventral rows; the notochord is persistent, but vertebral arches are developed; the vertebral column is heterocercal; the fins have fulcra; the dorsal fin is long, occupying the posterior half of the back; the branchiostegals are numerous; and the teeth are tubercular or obtuse. All these fishes are extinct.

Platysomus (plat-i-sō'mus), *n.* [NL., < LGr. πλατύσωμος, with a broad body, < Gr. πλατύς, broad, + σῶμα, body.] A genus of fossil ganoid fishes, typical of the family *Platysomidæ*. *Agassiz*, 1833.

Platystemon (plat-i-stē'mon), *n.* [NL. (Bentham, 1831), so called in allusion to the dilated filaments; < Gr. πλατύς, broad, + στήμων, warp (stamen).] A genus of polypetalous plants of the order *Papaveraceæ* and tribe *Romneyeæ*, characterized by its three sepals, six petals, many broad flat stamens, numerous coalescent carpels distinct at maturity, and separate linear stigmas. The only species, *P. Californicus*, common on the lower hills of California and Arizona, is a hairy spreading annual, with yellow long-stalked flowers, and narrow entire leaves, alternate or whorled in threes, blooming profusely in dense dwarf tufts in early spring, and known as *cream-cups*.

Platysternæ (plat-i-stėr'nē), *n. pl.* [NL., < Gr. πλατύστερνος, broad-breasted: see *platysternal.*] An order of birds in Nitzsch's classification of 1840. It is the subclass *Ratitæ* of Merrem reduced to ordinal rank and placed between *Gallinæ* and *Grallæ*, and consists of the struthious or ratite birds—ostriches, cassowaries, the apteryx, and other ecarinate birds. See *Ratitæ*. [Little used.]

platysternal (plat-i-stėr'nạl), *a.* [< Gr. πλατύστερνος, broad-breasted, < πλατύς, broad, + στέρνον, breast, chest.] Having a broad flat breastbone, as a bird; ratite; non-carinate; specifically, of or pertaining to the *Platysternæ*.

Platystoma (plạ-tis'tọ-mạ̈), *n.* [NL., < Gr. πλατύστομος, broad-mouthed: see *platystomous.*] **1.** A genus of dipterous insects. *Meigen*, 1803.—**2.** A genus of South American catfishes of the family *Siluridæ*, having a long flattened spatulate snout, a large mouth, six barbels, and scaleless skin. There are several species: some of them attain a large size, and *P. tigrinum* of South American rivers, called by the natives *corutto*, *colite*, and *cronni*, is one of the most beautiful and delicious of fresh-water fishes. The Indians take it both by hook and line and by shooting it with arrows.
3. In *conch.*, a genus of gastropods. *Conrad*, 1842.

platystomous (plạ-tis'tọ-mus), *a.* [< Gr. πλατύστομος, broad-mouthed, < πλατύς, broad, + στόμα, mouth.] Having a broad mouth.

Platystomus (plạ-tis'tọ-mus), *n.* [NL.: see *platystomous.*] **1.** A genus of sirenians: same as *Dugungus.*—**2.** A genus of flycatchers: same as *Peltops*.

plaud (plâd), *v. t.* [< L. *plaudere*, applaud, clap the hands in applause, clap, strike, beat. From the same source are *applaud*, *displode*, *explode*, *applause*, *explosion*, *implosion*, etc., *plausible*, etc.] To applaud. [Rare.]

> At our banquet all the gods may 'tend.
> *Plauding* our victory and this happy end.
> *Chapman*, Blind Beggar of Alexandria.

plaud (plâd), *n.* [< *plaud*, *v.*; or short for *plaudit.*] Claim to applause; plaudit; applause. [Obsolescent.]

> To patient judgments we appeal our *plaud*.
> *Marlowe*, Faustus (cho.).

> Shekels of gold may shrink to grains
> Into this treasury as they fall,
> While a poor widow's hard-earned gains
> May win the *plaud* "More than they all."
> *Pulpit Treasury*, July, 1886, p. 201.

plaudit (plâ'dit), *n.* [Formerly *plaudite* (in 3 syllables), sometimes spelled *plaudity*; < L. *plaudite*, 2d pers. pl. pres. impv. of *plaudere*, clap the hands, applaud, as an audience at the theater (*plaudite* or *vos plaudite*, 'clap!' 'applaud!' a formula craving the approbation of the audience, used by actors at the end of a performance): see *plaud.*] An expression or round of applause; praise bestowed with audible demonstrations: in the plural, equivalent to *applause.*

Augustus Cæsar . . . desired his friends about him to give him a *Plaudite*, as if he were conscious to himself that he had played his part well upon the stage.
Bacon, Advancement of Learning, ii. 322.

Chuse whether you will let my notes have you by the ears or no; hiss or give *plaudites.*
Dekker, Gull's Hornbook.

Our poet, could he find forgiveness here,
Would wish it rather than a *plaudit* there.
Dryden, Prol. to Univ. of Oxford (1673), l. 39.

Now I have him that neer of ought did speak
But when of plays or players he did treat—
Hath made a common-place book out of plays,
And speaks in print: at least what e'er he says
Is warranted by Curtain *plaudities.*
Marston, Scourge of Villanie, xi. 45.

When the committee read the report, the house passed his accounts with a *plaudite*, without further examination.
Steele, Spectator, No. 248.

plaudite†, *n.* An obsolete form of *plaudit.*

plauditory (plâ'di-tọ̄-ri), *a.* [< *plaudit* + *-ory.*] Applauding; commending.

plaudity† (plâ'di-ti), *n.* An obsolete form of *plaudit.*

plausibility (plâ-zi-bil'i̧-ti), *n.* [= F. *plausibilité* = Sp. *plausibilidad* = Pg. *plausibilidade* = It. *plausibilità*; < L. as if **plausibilita(t-)s*, < *plausibilis*, plausible: see *plausible.*] 1. The quality of being plausible or worthy of praise or acceptance; especially, a specious or superficial appearance of being right or worthy of acceptance, approval, or applause.

He insists upon the old Plea of his Conscience, honour, and Reason; using the *plausibility* of large and indefinite words to defend himself. Milton, Eikonoklastes, xi.

Covetousness is apt to insinuate also by the *plausibility* of its pleas. South, Sermons, IV. x.

To give any *plausibility* to a scheme of perpetual peace, war must already have become rare, and must have been banished to a prodigious distance.
De Quincey, Philos. of Rom. Hist.

The Austrian diplomatists propounded a new scheme of politics, which, it must be owned, was not altogether without *plausibility*. Macaulay, Frederic the Great.

2†. A praiseworthy act or quality; whatever deserves or commands applause.

Being placed in the upper part of the world, [he] carried on his dignity with that justice, modesty, integrity, fidelity, and other gracious *plausibilities*, that in a place of trust he contented those who could not satisfy, and in a place of envy procured the love of those who emulated his greatness. Vaughan, Life, etc., of Dr. Jackson. (Trench.)

3†. Applause.

With great admiration and *plausibility* of the people running plentifully on all sides.
Hakluyt's Voyages, I. 287.

plausible (plâ'zi-bl), *a.* [< F. *plausible* = Sp. *plausible* = Pg. *plausivel* = It. *plausibile*, < L. *plausibilis*, praiseworthy, pleasing, acceptable, < *plaudere*, pp. *plausus*, applaud: see *plaud.*] 1†. Deserving applause or approval; meritorious; praiseworthy; commendable.

The dactil is commendable inough in our vulgar meetres, but most *plausible* of all when he is sounded vpon the stage. Puttenham, Arte of Eng. Poesie, p. 105.

The *plausible* examples of Tully, Cato, Marius, Scipio, divers such virtuous Romans, and sundry excellent Greeks, are famously known. G. Harvey, Four Letters, iii.

This objection seems very *plausible* and cordiall to covetous earthworms.
Prynne, Treachery and Disloyalty, iv. 14.

Beauty, composed of blood and flesh, moves more,
And is more *plausible* to blood and flesh,
Than spiritual beauty can be to the spirit.
B. Jonson, Poetaster, iv. 6.

These Comedies, bearing the title of The fair Maid of the West: if they proved but as gratious in thy private reading as they were *plausible* in the publick acting, I shall not much doubt of their successe.
Heywood, Fair Maid of the West (Works, ed. Pearson, [II. 259).

2. Seemingly worthy of acceptance or approval; apparently right, meritorious, or worthy of confidence; having a specious or superficial appearance of truth or trustworthiness: as, a *plausible* excuse; a *plausible* theory or doctrine.

Go you to Angelo; answer his requiring with a *plausible* obedience; agree with his demands to the point.
Shak., M. for M., iii. 1. 253.

Well dissembling his untimely joys,
And veiling truth in *plausible* disguise.
Pope, Odyssey, xiii. 304.

The undermining smile becomes at length habitual; and the drift of his *plausible* conversation is only to flatter one that he may betray another.
Dryden, tr. of Virgil's Georgics, Ded.

I am not at all clear that I could not write a fairly *plausible* answer to myself; only I am much surer that I could write a rejoinder to that answer which should be something more than *plausible.*
E. A. Freeman, Amer. Lects., p. 38.

3. Fair-spoken and apparently worthy of confidence; using or presenting discourse or arguments that seem right and worthy of acceptance: as, a *plausible* person.

My boy—that delightful contradiction, who was always *plausible*, yet never right.
C. W. Stoddard, South-sea Idyls, p. 259.

4†. Applauding; applausive.

That when the epilogue is done we may with franke intent,
After the plaudite stryke vp our *plausible* assente.
Drant, tr. of Horace's Art of Poetry.

Euarchus, though neither regarding a prisoner's passionate prayer nor bearing over-*plausible* ears to a many-headed motion, yet [was] well enough content to win their liking with things in themselves indifferent.
Sir P. Sidney, Arcadia, v.

I will haste to declare of what virtue and strength the true and Christian prayer is, that men, knowing the efficacy and dignity, yea, and the necessity thereof, may with the pure *plausible* and joyful minds delight in it.
Becon, Works, I. 141. (Davies.)

=**Syn.** 2. *Colorable, Specious*, etc. See *ostensible.*

plausibleize (plâ'zi-bl-īz), *v. t.* [< *plausible* + *-ize.*] To render plausible; recommend. [Rare.]

He [Richard III.] endeavoured to work himself into their good will by erecting and endowing of religious houses, so to *plausibleize* himself, especially among the clergy. Fuller, Church Hist., IV. iv. 7.

plausibleness (plâ'zi-bl-nes), *n.* Same as *plausibility.*

It is no trusting either to outward favour or to *plausibleness* of disposition; but the true fear of God is that the comfort whereof will stick by us always.
Bp. Hall, Hard Texts, Prov. xxxi. 30.

plausibly (plâ'zi-bli), *adv.* In a plausible manner. (*a*†) With expressions of applause or approval; with acclamation.

The Romans *plausibly* did give consent
To Tarquin's everlasting banishment.
Shak., Lucrece, l. 1854.

(*b*) With fair show; speciously; so as to command attention or win approbation.

They could talk *plausibly* about what they did not understand. Collier.

If they be well considered they will convince any reasonable man that, how *plausibly* soever this objection looks at the first sight, yet there is nothing in the world in it, but it is all mere cavill. Abp. Sharp, Works, II. viii.

Great crimes alarm the conscience, but it sleeps,
While thoughtful man is *plausibly* amus'd.
Cowper, Task, iii. 186.

plausive (plâ'siv), *a.* [< L. *plaudere*, pp. *plausus*, applaud, + *-ive.*] 1. Applauding; manifesting praise or approval.

Those *plausiue* shouts which giue you entertain
Eccho as much to the Almighties cares.
Heywood, If you Know not Me, i.

No mightier work had gained the *plausive* smile
Of all-beholding Phœbus!
Wordsworth, Sonnets, ii. 34.

The young graduate, when the Commencement anniversary returned, though he were in a swamp, would see a festive light, and find the air faintly echoing with *plausive* academic thunders. Emerson, Works and Days.

2†. Plausible.

His *plausive* words
He scatter'd not in ears, but grafted them,
To grow there and to bear.
Shak., All's Well, i. 2. 53.

plaustral (plâs'trạl), *a.* [< L. *plaustrum*, also *plostrum*, *plaustra*, a wagon, cart, + *-al.*] Of or relating to a wagon or cart. [Rare.]

Whether this contention between three carts of different parishes was promoted by a subscription among the nobility, or whether the grand jury . . . had . . . combined to encourage *plaustral* merit, I cannot take upon me to determine. Goldsmith, Citizen of the World, lxxxvi.

Plautidæ (plâ'ti-dē), *n. pl.* [NL., < *Plautus* + *-idæ.*] The auk family, named from the genus *Plautus*; the *Alcidæ*. *Henry Bryant.*

Plautine (plâ'tin), *a.* [< *Plautus* (see def.) + *-ine*[1].] Of, pertaining to, or characteristic of Plautus, a Roman comic poet (died 184 B. C.): as, *Plautine* diction.

It is needless to dwell further upon the details of *Plautine* scansion. Encyc. Brit., XIV. 330.

Plautus (plâ'tus), *n.* [NL. (Klein, 1759), < L. *plautus*, also (Umbrian) *plotus*, flat, flat-footed.] 1. An old book-name of the great auk, *Alca impennis*, lately used in a generic sense.— 2. A genus of gulls: synonymous with *Larus*. *Reichenbach*, 1853.

plaw[1]†, *v.* A Middle English form of *play*[1].

plaw[2] (plâ), *v.* [Also *play*; ME. *plawen*, *playen*, boil.] I.† *intrans.* To boil.

Take a pot full of wyne, and steke yt wele aboue that no thynges go ynne nor owte, and put it ynne a cowdrun ful of water, and layt yt *play* longe therin, and yt schal be gode ayselle sone.
Sloane MS. 3548, f. 16, quoted in Prompt. Parv., p. 403.

Item, a grete lede to brew v comb malte with one *plawyng.* Paston Letters, III. 435.

II. *trans.* To boil; especially, to boil slightly. [Prov. Eng.]

play[1] (plā), *v.* [< ME. *playen*, *pleyen*, *pleien*, *plegen*, also *plawen*, *plahen*, *plagen*, < AS. *plegan* (pret. *plægde*), *plegian*, *plegean*, *plægian* (pret. *plegode*, *plegede*, *pleogede*), *plagian* (pret. *plagade*), move briskly, play, amuse oneself, exercise, strive, play on an instrument, clap the hands, etc., = OS. *plegan* = OFries. *plegia*, *pligia*, be wont or accustomed, use, = D. *plegen*, be wont or accustomed, use, commit, = MLG. LG. *plegen* = OHG. *phlegan*, *pflegan*, *plegen*, MHG. *phlegen*, *pflegen*, G. *pflegen*, be wont or accustomed, care for, cherish, administer, indulge, apply, etc., = Icel. *plaga* = Sw. *pläga*, be wont or accustomed, use, entertain, treat, = Dan. *pleje*, be accustomed; the AS. senses refer only to physical activity, the orig. sense of all the forms being appar. 'be in action,' whence 'be busy,' 'be concerned' (with a thing), 'be wont or accustomed' (to do something), senses leading to those of the derivative *plight*. Hence *play*[1], *n.*, and *plight*[1].] I. *intrans.* 1. To move lightly and quickly; move with a brisk, lively, and more or less irregular and capricious motion, as water in waves or in a fountain, light and shadow on agitated water, leaves in the wind, tremulous flames, etc.; flutter; flicker; dart; dance; in *mech.*, to move freely.

And Cytherea all in sedges hid,
Which seem to move and wanton with her breath,
Even as the waving sedges *play* with wind.
Shak., T. of the S., Ind., ii. 55.

But soon their pleasures pass'd; at noon of day
The sun with sultry beams began to *play.*
Dryden, Flower and Leaf, l. 373.

This [garden] of the Tuilleries is vastly great, has shaded Tarrasses on two sides, one along the River Seine, planted with Trees, very diverting, with great Parters in the middle, and large Fountains of Water, which constantly *Play.*
Lister, Journey to Paris, p. 181.

The self-same shadows now as then
Play through this grassy upland glen.
M. Arnold, Resignation.

And hark the clock within, the silver knell
Of twelve sweet hours that past in bridal white,
And died to live, long as my pulses *play.*
Tennyson, Maud, xviii. 8.

The window was open, and barbs of fire, like serpents' tongues, *played* over it. R. D. Blackmore, Erema, I. 211.

The motion [of an anchor] may be limited by a second pin through the shoulder, *playing* in a long hole in the flukes. Luce, Seamanship, p. 233.

2. To engage in active exercise; exercise or contend in any way, but especially with weapons; technically, to contend with swords or sticks; fence: said of persons.

Us he dude lede
Into a galeie
With the se to *pleie.*
King Horn (E. E. T. S.), l. 186.

Betere him were in Scotlond,
With is ax in ys hond,
To *pleyen* o the grene.
Execution of Sir Simon Fraser (Child's Ballads, VI. 282).

When you *play* at weapons, I would have you get thick caps and bracers [gloves].
Sir P. Sidney (Arber's Eng. Garner, I. 309).

And Abner said to Joab, Let the young men now arise, and *play* before us. 2 Sam. ii. 14.

He sends to know if your pleasure hold to *play* with Laertes. Shak., Hamlet, v. 2. 206.

3. To contend in a game of skill or chance: as, to *play* at chess or cards; specifically, to gamble.

He wule come the nier
And bidde the *pleie* at the escheker.
Whane thescheker is forth ibrogt
Bithute panes ne *plei* thu nogt.
Floriz and Blauncheflur (E. E. T. S.), l. 344.

He made him to ben clept Melechmanser: the whiche on a Day *pleyed* at the Chesse, and his Swerd lay besyde him. Mandeville, Travels, p. 37.

I'll follow
The ladies, *play* at cards, make sport, and whistle.
Ford, Lady's Trial, v. 2.

After they [the Chinese] have lost their Money, Goods, and Cloaths, they will stake down their Wives and Children: and lastly, as the dearest thing they have, will *play* upon tick, and mortgage their Hair upon honour.
Dampier, Voyages, II. i. 42.

4. To engage in exercise or occupation of any kind for diversion, amusement, or recreation; amuse one's self, as with games or diversion, or with any occupation which is not a task or for profit; sport; frolic; gambol.

Han pardoun thorw purgatorie to passen ful sone,
With patriarkes in paradys to *pleyen* ther-aftur.
Piers Plowman (A), viii. 12.

He . . . preyed hath Daun John
That he sholde come to Seint Denys, to *pleye*
With hym and with his wyf a day or tweye.
Chaucer, Shipman's Tale, l. 59.

The people sat down to eat and to drink, and rose up to *play.* Ex. xxxii. 6.

O come ye here to fight, young lord,
Or come ye here to *play?*
Katharine Janfarie (Child's Ballads, IV. 31).

It seems so little while ago since I used to see you *playing* about the door of the old house, quite a small child!
Hawthorne, Seven Gables, iv.

5. To take part in a game or games; join in sport or frolic: as, to *play* with the children.—6. To act thoughtlessly or wantonly; trifle; toy; dally.

Do not *play* with mine anger, do not, wretch!
Beau. and Fl., Maid's Tragedy, iv. 1.

O golden hair, with which I used to *play*
Not knowing! O imperial-moulded form,
And beauty such as never woman wore.
Tennyson, Guinevere.

7. To act; behave; deal: as, to *play* fair or false.

If she have *played* loose with me, I'll cut her throat.
B. *Jonson*, Cynthia's Revels, iv. 1.

You *play* false with us, madam—I saw you give the baronet a letter. *Sheridan*, The Rivals, ii. 2.

8. To act on the stage; personate a character.

There is a lord will hear you *play* to-night.
Shak., T. of the S., Ind., i. 93.

Courts are theatres where some men *play*. *Donne.*

9. To perform on an instrument of music: as, to *play* on a flute or a violin.

With musicke sweete that did excell
Hee *plaies* under her window then.
The Merchant's Daughter (Child's Ballads, IV. 329).

We sat round a pan of coals, and three Mahometans sung Arab songs, beating time with their hands, and *playing* on a tambour. *Pococke*, Description of the East, I. 82.

10. To operate or act with continuous blows or strokes, or with repeated action: as, the cannon *played* on the enemy's works; the firemen *played* upon the burning building.

Upon the seauenteenth day of Aprill [the Archduke] planted his Cannon against the towne, and *played* upon it.
Coryat, Crudities, I. 8.

Here, as before, the firemen were not permitted to *play* on the flames. *The Century*, XXXVII. 929.

To play against the bank. See *bank*2.—**To play at duck and drake.** See *duck*2.—**To play false.** See *false*, *adv.*—**To play fast and loose.** See *fast*1, *a.*—**To play for love.** See *love*1.—**To play in**, to begin at once. *Halliwell.* [Prov. Eng.]—**To play in and out**†. Same as *to play fast and loose*.—**To play into the hands of some one**, to act in such a way as to give the advantage to one's opponent or a third party.

Why *play* . . . *into the devil's hands*
By dealing so ambiguously?
Browning, Ring and Book, vi. 1883.

To play loose, in *fencing*, to practise attack and defense. *Encyc. Brit.*, IX. 71.—**To play off**, to simulate; feign; make pretense: as, the man is not ill, he is *playing off*.—**To play on** or **upon**. (*a*) To make sport of; trifle with; mock; delude; befool, especially for advantage or through malice: as, to *play upon* one's feelings.

Art thou alive?
Or is it fantasy that *plays upon* our eyesight?
Shak., 1 Hen. IV., v. 4. 138.

Is 't not enough
That you have *played upon* me all this while,
But still to mock me, still to jest at me?
B. *Jonson*, Case is Altered, iv. 5.

You rely upon the mildness of my temper—you do, you dog! you *play upon* the meekness of my disposition!
Sheridan, The Rivals, ii. 1.

(*b*) To give a humorous or fanciful turn to: as, to *play upon* words.

He jested with all ease, and told
Free tales, and took the word and *play'd upon* it,
And made it of two colours. *Tennyson*, Geraint.

To play up. (*a*) To work forward. (*b*) To play (music) more vigorously.—**To play upon advantage**†, to cheat.—**To play with edged tools.** See *tool*, and compare *edge-tool*.—**To play with fire.** See *fire*.—**To play with one's beard**†, to deceive one. *Nares.*

Yet have I *play'd with his beard*, in knitting this knot
I promist friendship, but . . . I meant it not.
R. Edwards, Damon and Pythias.

=**Syn.** 4. To gambol, romp, caper, frisk.

II. *trans.* 1. To divert or amuse with or as with sports or pastimes: used reflexively. [Obsolete or prov. Eng.]

They goon and *pleye hem* al the longe day.
Chaucer, Shipman's Tale, l. 177.

Lete vs go for to *pley vs* and disporte in this foreste, to assay yef we tynde eny aventure.
Merlin (E. E. T. S.), iii. 562.

Bot fyn I am put to a poynt that pouerte hatte,
I schal me poruay pacyence, & *play me* with bothe.
Alliterative Poems (ed. Morris), iii. 36.

2. To take part as a contestant in (a game or pastime engaged in at a particular time and place); also, to be in the habit of engaging in (a particular kind of game), be able to join in (it), or be skilled in (it): as, to *play* a rubber of whist; to *play* a round of golf; he does not *play* chess, but he can *play* billiards.—3. To engage in a game, contest, or competition with.

I will *play* you for a hundred pounds.
Warren, Diary of a Late Physician, II. xxv.

4. To put forward, move, throw, or lay on the table, etc., in carrying on a game or contest: as, *play* a swift ball; to *play* the knave of clubs.—5. To use as a plaything; trifle or fool with.

Some wise Men, and some Fools we call:
Figures, alas, of Speech, for Destiny *plays* us all.
Cowley, Pindaric Odes, vi. 2.

6. To manœuver; handle or play with, as a hooked fish in angling.

The river is large and free from obstacles, and when you are landed *to play* him, you have little to do except to exercise the ordinary give and take which is within the competence of any angler for pike or carp.
Quarterly Rev., CXXVI. 340.

7. To produce music from; perform upon: as, to *play* the flute or the organ.

The dancing-master, having to *play* the kit besides, was thoroughly blown. *Dickens*, Battle of Life.

8. To perform on a musical instrument; execute: as, to *play* a tune.—9. To operate or cause to operate with continuous or repeated action; put into and keep in action: as, to *play* the hose on a burning building.

The water is brought from a river which is lower than the basin; it commonly rises eighty feet, and, by *playing* another pipe, it throws the water a hundred and twenty feet high. *Pococke*, Description of the East, II. ii. 226.

10. To give out or discharge freely: as, to *play* a steady stream.

In 1711 there were shown Sea Gods and Goddesses, Nymphs, Mermaids, and Satirs, all of them *playing* of water as suitable, and some Fire mingling with the water, and Sea Triumphs round the Barrel that *plays* so many Liquors; all which is taken away after it had perform'd its part, and the Barrel is broken in Pieces before the Spectators. Quoted in *Ashton's* Social Life in Reign of Queen [Anne, I. 293.

11. To perform or act on the stage; represent in character with appropriate action and accessories: as, to *play* a comedy.

Two persons *plaied* a dialogue, the effect whereof was whether riches were better than love.
Hall, Hen. VIII., an. 1528.

The old comedies were *plaid* in the broad streets vpon wagons or carts vncouered.
Puttenham, Arte of Eng. Poesie, p. 29.

Luscus, what 's *play'd* to-day? Faith now I know
I set thy lips abroach, from whence doth flow
Naught but pure Juliet and Romeo.
Marston, Scourge of Villanie, xi. 37.

12. To take or assume the rôle of; act the part or perform the duties of; act or behave like: as, to *play* Hamlet; to *play* the tyrant; to *play* the hostess.

I have a will, I am sure, howe'er my heart
May *play* the coward.
Beau. and Fl., Laws of Candy, iii. 3.

To *play* the fool by authority is wisdom.
B. *Jonson*, Poetaster, iv. 3.

Remember how thou *playedst* the man at Vanity-fair, and wast neither afraid of the chain nor cage, nor yet of bloody death. *Bunyan*, Pilgrim's Progress, p. 177.

Why, every Man *plays* the Fool once in his Life;
But to marry is *playing* the Fool all ones Life long.
Congreve, Old Batchelor, iii. 10.

Neither the Pope nor the most Christian King will *play* the devil. *Walpole*, Letters, II. 435.

13. To do; operate; enact; perform: as, to *play* tricks; to *play* a part.

But man, proud man, . . .
Plays such fantastic tricks before high heaven
As make the angels weep. *Shak.*, M. for M., ii. 2. 121.

No law nor justice frights 'em; all the town over
They *play* new pranks and gambols.
Fletcher, Loyal Subject, iv. 3.

Who can call him a wise man who *playeth* the part of a Foole or a Vice? *Stubbes*, Anat. of Abuses.

I have indeed observed in several inscriptions of this country that your men of learning are extremely delighted in *playing* little tricks with words and figures.
Addison, Remarks on Italy (ed. Bohn), p. 522.

This man had *played* an important part in all the revolutions which, since the time of Surajah Dowlah, had taken place in Bengal. *Macaulay*, Warren Hastings.

14†. To use; apply; ply.

Yif thow wolt *pleie* this craft with the arisyng of the mone, loke thow rekne wel her cours howre by howre.
Chaucer, Astrolabe, ii. 40.

15. To make a pretense of; make believe: as, children *play* being devoured by lions.

We [merchants] may wel make chiere and good visage,
And dryve forth the world as it may be,
And kepen our estant in pryvetee
Til we be ded: or elles that we *pleye*
A pilgrymage, or goon out of the weye.
Chaucer, Shipman's Tale, l. 233.

Played out. (*a*) Played to an end; finished; used up; done for. [Colloq.]

Brown thinks to himself that after all there is some refreshing sense of the primeval about this *played-out* country. *Fortnightly Rev.*, N. S., XLIII. 88.

(*b*) Exhausted and brought to land or killed, as a fish that has been played.—**To play bob tool**†, **booty**, **ducks and drakes**, **first** (or **second**) **fiddle**, **gooseberry**, **hob**, **hooky**, etc. See *fool*1, *booty*, *duck*2, *fiddle*, etc.—**To play off**, to display; show: as, to *play off* tricks.—**To play off a person**, to exhibit or expose a person for the entertainment or merriment of others.—**To play one false.** See *false*.—**To play possum.** See *possum*.—**To play the deuce** or **dickens.** See *deuce*1, *dickens*.—**To play the devil, the fool, the hangment, the mischief**, etc., **with.** See the nouns.—**To play up**, to start or begin playing; strike up.

Play uppe The Brides of Enderby.
Jean Ingelow, High Tide on the Coast of Lincolnshire.

play1 (plā), *n.* [< ME. *play*, *pley*, *pleye*, *pleie*, *pleze*, also *plawe*, *plahe*, *plage*, < AS. *plega*, brisk motion, play, sport, game, also fight, battle (cf. OFries. *plega*, *pliga*, custom, habit, practice, MLG. *plege*, care, custom, also *plage*, LG. *plege*, OHG. *phlega*, MHG. *phlege*, *pflege*, G. *pflege*, care, nursing, custom, etc., Icel. *play*, manner, Dan. *pleje*, nursing, tendance, care, maintenance, cultivation, encouragement, administration, etc.); from the verb: see *play*1, *v.*] 1. Brisk or free motion; movement, whether regular or irregular: as, the *play* of water in a fountain; the *play* of a wheel or piston; hence, freedom or room for motion.

The *play* and slight agitation of the water, in its upward gush, wrought magically with these variegated pebbles.
Hawthorne, Seven Gables, vi.

The saw, with restless *play*,
Was cleaving through a fir-tree
Its long and steady way. *Bryant*, Saw-Mill.

Any *play* or lost motion between the threads of the cross-feed screw and its nut.
Joshua Rose, Practical Machinist, p. 34.

2. Liberty and room for action or display; scope; swing; ease or freedom in performance.

Give him [the chub] *play* enough before you offer to take him out of the water.
I. Walton, Complete Angler, p. 68.

He dares not give his Imagination its full *play*.
Addison, Spectator, No. 315.

The Mercian scribes appear to have been very excellent penmen, writing a very graceful hand with much delicate *play* in the strokes. *Encyc. Brit.*, XVIII. 159.

3. Action; use; employment.

The senseless plea of right by Providence
Was by a flattering priest invented since,
And lasts no longer than the recent sway,
But justifies the next who comes in *play*.
Dryden, Character of a Good Parson, l. 120.

Every kind of vehicle is brought into *play* on this day to carry people down who prefer to drive over the magnificent country roads between London and Epsom.
T. C. Crawford, English Life, p. 15.

4. Active exercise; especially, exercise in trial of skill: as, sword-*play*.—5. Any exercise intended for recreation, amusement, or pleasure; a game or sport, such as cricket, foot-ball, curling, skittles, quoits, graces, etc.

And suche *pleyes* of desport thei make, til the takynge up of the Boordes. *Mandeville*, Travels, p. 238.

They say that this Philosopher [Lycurgus] did inuent the Olympiades, which were certeine *playes* vsed euery fourth yeere in the mounteine Olympus.
Guevara, Letters (tr. by Hellowes, 1577), p. 21.

See that *plaies* be published,
Mai-games and maskes, with mirthe and minstrelsie,
Pageants and school-feastes, beares and puppet-*plaies*.
Three Lords of London, in Strutt's Sports and Pastimes, [p. 32.

The *plays* of children are nonsense, but very educative nonsense. *Emerson*, Experience.

6. Amusement, diversion, recreation, or pastime; sport; frolic; fun; merry-making: as, "all work and no *play* makes Jack a dull boy."

Al the loze of oure herte nou is went a-wey,
For into serwe & into wo tornid is al oure *pley*.
Political Poems, etc. (ed. Furnivall), p. 232.

Come forth than, my maidens, an show them some *play*.
Baron of Braikley (Child's Ballads, VI. 194).

A tiger . . . by chance hath spied
In some purlieu two gentle fawns at *play*.
Milton, P. L., iv. 404.

But the instinct of *play* and the desire for amusement is not exhausted in childhood.
J. F. Clarke, Self-Culture, p. 386.

7. Fun; jest; sport: opposed to *earnest*: as, it was done in *play*.—8. Gaming; the practice of contending for amusement, or for wager, as at dice, cards, billiards, etc.: as, to lose money at *play*.

They [the gamesters] will change the cards so often that the old ones will be a considerable advantage by selling them to coffee-houses, or families who love *play*.
Swift, Directions to Servants (Butler).

What are they to do who love *play* better than wine?
Sheridan, School for Scandal, iii. 3.

A sportsman keen, he shoots through half the day,
And, skill'd at whist, devotes the night to *play*.
Crabbe, Works, I. 15.

He left his wine and horses and *play*.
Tennyson, Maud, xix. 7.

9. A dramatic composition; a literary composition in which characters are represented by dialogue and action; a written tragedy, comedy, or other such production intended for representation on the stage.

And when his *plays* come forth, think they can flout them,
With saying he was a year about them.
B. *Jonson*, Volpone, Prol.

The first *play* of this kind [miracle-play] specified by name, I believe, is called "St. Catherine," and, according to Matthew Paris, was written by Geofrey, a Norman, afterwards abbot of Saint Albans. *Strutt*, Sports and Pastimes, p. 227.

10. Representation or exhibition of a comedy, tragedy, or other form of drama; dramatic performance.

The *play* 's the thing
Wherein I'll catch the conscience of the king.
Shak., Hamlet, ii. 2. 633.

For a *play* is still an imitation of nature; we know we are to be deceived, and we desire to be so. *Dryden*, Essay on Dram. Poesy.

The King went to the *play* last night (Drury Lane) for the first time, the Dukes of York and Clarence and a great suite with him. *Greville*, Memoirs, Feb. 7, 1821.

I am just come from the *play* at Richmond. *Walpole*, Letters, II. 126.

11. Style or manner of playing; style of performing or executing a play or game; execution; performance; skill: as, he made clever *play* with the foils.

There were Billiard Rooms, where a young man from the country who prided himself upon his *play* could get very prettily handled. *W. Besant*, Fifty Years Ago, p. 135.

12. Manner of acting or dealing, or of treating another: as, fair *play*; foul *play*.

Good my friends, consider
You are my guests; do me no foul *play*, friends.
Shak., Lear, iii. 7. 31.

13. A country wake. *Halliwell*. [Prov. Eng.] —**A play upon words**, punning; a pun.—**Benefit play.** See *benefit*.—**Child's play.** See *child*.—**Fair play.** See *fair*¹.—**In play**, in *foot-ball* and some other games, alive; that can be legitimately played; not dead: said of the ball: the opposite of *out of play*.—**Out of play**, in *foot-ball* and some other games, dead: the opposite of *in play*.—**Play of colors**, an appearance of several prismatic colors in quick succession on the surface of an object, as on a diamond.—**To hold in play**, to keep occupied or engaged; hold the attention of.

I, with two more to help me,
Will *hold* the foe *in play*.
Macaulay, Horatius.

To make good play, to proceed or take action with spirit or advantage.=**Syn.** 4. Activity, exercise.—6. Pastime.

play²† (plā), *v.* A variant of *plaw*².

playa (plä'yä), *n.* [Sp., 'shore,' 'strand.'] In *geol.*, a general name for various desiccated lake-basins in the Western States. [U. S.]

playable (plā'a-bl), *a.* [< *play*¹ + *-able*.] Capable of being played: as, a ball touching the balk-line is not *playable*.

play-acting (plā'ak″ting), *n.* Theatrical performance; stage-playing.

play-actor (plā'ak″tor), *n.* A stage-player; an actor.

If any *play-actors* or spectators think themselves injured by any censure I have past upon them. *Prynne*.

play-actorism (plā'ak″tor-izm), *n.* [< *play-actor* + *-ism*.] The profession, habits, manner, style, etc., of a play-actor; a stilted, theatrical, affected style or manner; histrionism.

Sterling's view of the Pope, as seen in these his gala days, doing his big *playactorism* under God's earnest sky, was much more substantial to me than his studies in the picture galleries. *Carlyle*, Sterling, ii. 7. (*Davies*.)

playbill (plā'bil), *n.* A bill or placard displayed as an advertisement of a play, with or without the parts assigned to the actors; a bill of the play; a program.

Nicholas found himself poring with the utmost interest over a large *playbill* hanging outside a minor theatre. *Dickens*, Nicholas Nickleby, xlviii.

play-book (plā'bůk), *n.* 1. A book containing material for amusement or pastime; a picture-book or book of games for children.

There was compiled and printed "A *Play Book* for Children, to allure them to read as soon as they can speak plain." *Ashton*, Social Life in Reign of Queen Anne, I. 12.

2. A book of plays or dramatic compositions.

I would have them [women] well read, but in scripture and goode bookes, not in *playbookes* and love-bookes.
Quoted in *The Atlantic*, LXIV. 522.

That ridiculous passion, which has no being but in *play-books* and romances. *Swift*.

play-club (plā'klub), *n.* In *golf*, a wooden-headed club with a full-length handle, used in driving a ball to a great distance.

play-day (plā'dā), *n.* A day given to pastime or diversion; a day exempt from work; a holiday.

Livius Drusus said of himself, he never had any *play-days* or days of quiet when he was a boy. *Jer. Taylor*, Holy Dying, i. 4.

player (plā'ėr), *n.* [< ME. *playere*, < AS. *plegere*, a player (of a wrestler), < *plegian*, play: see *play*¹.] One who plays. (*a*) One who takes part in sports, pastimes, or amusements of any kind. (*b*) An idler; a trifler.

Saints in your injuries, devils being offended,
Players in your housewifery.
Shak., Othello, ii. 1. 113.

(*c*) A contestant in a game or match of any kind; also, one who is in the habit of playing, or who is skilled in, a particular game: as, a chess-*player*; a billiard-*player*.

If two play, then each one covers two divisions, the one nearest to the wall being the inband, the other one the cuthand *player*. *Tribune Book of Sports*, p. 128.

(*d*) A dramatic performer; an actor; one who enacts characters on the stage.

The propertie and condition of *Players* is sometymes to haue greate abundance, and at other times to suffer greate lacke.
Guevara, Letters (tr. by Hellowes, 1577), p. 318.

All the world 's a stage,
And all the men and women merely *players*.
Shak., As you Like it, ii. 7. 140.

To give a poor soul a farthing at that door where you give a *player* a shilling is not equal dealing, for this is to give God the refuse of the wheat. *Donne*, Sermons, viii.

The *player* feigns for no other end but to divert or instruct you. *Steele*, Spectator, No. 370.

(*e*) One who performs on an instrument of music.

Seek out a man who is a cunning *player* on an harp.
1 Sam. xvi. 16.

Then *playeris* played, and songsters song,
To gled the mirrie host.
Battle of Balrinnes (Child's Ballads, VII. 220).

playerly (plā'ėr-li), *a.* [< *player* + *-ly*¹.] Player-like.

All which, together with the satyricall invectiues of Juuenall and others against this infamous *playerlie* emperor, are a sufficient euidence.
Prynne, Histrio-Mastix, II. ii. 1.

playfeer†, *n.* [Also improp. *playpheer*; < ME. *playfere*; < *play*¹ + *feer*¹.] A playfellow.

Pouerte & pacyence are nedes *play-feres*.
Alliterative Poems (ed. Morris), iii. 45.

Learn what maids have been her companions and *play-pheers*. *Fletcher* (*and another*), Two Noble Kinsmen, iv. 3.

She was wont to call him her dear son,
Her little *play-feer*, and her pretty bun.
Drayton, Moon-Calf.

The minion of delight, faire from thy birth,
Adonis *play-pheere*, and the pride of earth.
Heywood, Fair Maid of the Exchange (Works, ed. Pearson, [II. 13).

playfellow (plā'fel″ō), *n.* A companion in amusements or sports.

Heart's discontent and sour affliction
Be *playfellows* to keep you company!
Shak., 2 Hen. VI., iii. 2. 301.

Danger 's my *playfellow*;
Since I was a man, 't has been my best companion.
Fletcher, Wife for a Month, v. 3.

playful (plā'fůl), *a.* [< ME. *pleiful*; < *play*¹ + *-ful*.] 1. Full of play; sportive; frolicsome; frisky: as, a *playful* child.

The *playful* children just let loose from school.
Goldsmith, Deserted Village, l. 120.

2. Showing a sportive fancy or sprightly humor; pleasantly jocular: as, a *playful* remark; a *playful* style; *playful* attentions.

playfully (plā'fůl-i), *adv.* In a playful manner; sportively.

playfulness (plā'fůl-nes), *n.* The quality or state of being playful; sportiveness.

I think the word that Cowper was at a loss for was *playfulness*, the most delightful ingredient in letters, for Gray can hardly be said to have had humor in the deeper sense of the word. *Lowell*, New Princeton Rev., I. 167.

playgame (plā'gām), *n.* Sport; child's play; a play of children.

Liberty alone gives the true relish to their ordinary *playgames*. *Locke*.

playgoer (plā'gō″ėr), *n.* One who habitually attends theatrical performances.

I now became a confirmed *playgoer*.
T. Hook, Gilbert Gurney. (*Latham*.)

playground (plā'ground), *n.* A piece of ground set apart for open-air recreation; especially, such a piece of ground connected with a school, etc.

playhouse (plā'hous), *n.* [< ME. **playhous*, < AS. *pleghūs*, a theater, < *plega*, play, + *hūs*, house.] A house appropriated to dramatic performances; a theater.

These are the youths that thunder at a *playhouse*.
Shak., Hen. VIII., v. 4. 64.

Is your *playhouse* an inn, a gentleman can not see you without crumpling his taffeta cloak?
Middleton, Spanish Gypsy, ii. 1.

His lordship's avocations as a statesman prevented him from attending the *playhouse* very often.
Thackeray, Pendennis, xiv.

playing-card (plā'ing-kärd), *n.* One of a pack of cards used for playing games; especially, one of a set composed of fifty-two cards, of four suits—diamonds, hearts, spades, and clubs.

playing-passage (plā'ing-pas″āj), *n.* The galley of the bower-bird. See cut under *bower-bird*.

The Bower-birds, by tastefully ornamenting their *playing-passages* with gayly-colored objects, . . . offer additional evidence that they possess a sense of beauty.
Darwin, Descent of Man, I. 61.

playless (plā'les), *a.* [< *play*¹ + *-less*.] Without play; not playing. *Coleridge*. [Rare.]

play-lome†, *n.* [ME., < *play*, exercise, as sword-play, + *lome*, implement: see *loom*¹.] A weapon.

Go reche me my *playlome*,
And I salle go to hym sone;
Hym were better hafe bene at Rome,
So ever mote I thryfe!
Perceval, 2013. (*Halliwell*.)

play-maker (plā'mā″kėr), *n.* A writer of plays.

play-mare†, *n.* Same as *hobby-horse*, 1.

This exhibition, the *play-mare* of Scotland, stood high among holyday gambols. It must be carefully separated from the wooden chargers of our nurseries. It gives rise to Hamlet's ejaculation—
"But oh, but oh, the hobby-horse is forgot!"
Scott, Abbot, xiv., note.

playmate (plā'māt), *n.* A playfellow; a companion in play or amusement.

Patience, discreetnesse, and benignitie, . . .
These be the lovely *playmates* of pure veritie.
Dr. H. More, Psychathanasia, III. iii. 58.

Nature does not like to be observed, and likes that we should be her fools and *playmates*. *Emerson*, Experience.

playne†. A Middle English form of *plain*¹ and *plain*².

playnte†, *n.* A Middle English form of *plaint*.

playock (plā'ok), *n.* [< *play*¹ + *-ock*.] A plaything; a toy. [Scotch.]

play-pleasure† (plā'plezh″ūr), *n.* Idle amusement; mock pleasure; pretended pleasure. [Rare.]

He taketh a kind of *play-pleasure* in looking upon the fortunes of others. *Bacon*, Envy (ed. 1887).

play-right (plā'rīt), *n.* The proprietary right of the author of a dramatic or musical composition to its exclusive production or performance, as distinguished from the right to multiply copies by printing. See *stage-right*.

playse†, *n.* An obsolete form of *plaice*.

playsome (plā'sum), *a.* [< *play*¹ + *-some*.] Playful; wanton.

All pleasant folk, well-minded, malicious, and *playsome*.
Shelton, tr. of Don Quixote, iii. 3. (*Latham*.)

playsomeness (plā'sum-nes), *n.* The quality of being playsome; playfulness; wantonness; sportiveness.

playstow† (plā'stō), *n.* [Also *pleystow*, corruptly *plestor*; < ME. **pleystow*, < AS. *plegstōw*, a place for play, a wrestling-place, gymnasium, palestra, < *plega*, play, + *stōw*, place.] A wrestling-place. [Prov. Eng.]

playte†, *n.* An obsolete form of *plait*.

playten†, *v. t.* To plait; fold.

plaything (plā'thing), *n.* A toy; anything that serves to amuse.

A child knows his nurse, and by degrees the *playthings* of a little more advanced age. *Locke*.

playtime (plā'tīm), *n.* Time for playing; time devoted to or set aside for amusement.

Upon festivals and *playtimes* they should exercise themselves in the fields by riding, leaping, fencing, mustering, and training. *Cowley*, The School.

playwright (plā'rīt), *n.* A writer or adapter of plays for the stage.

Nor is it without reluctance that we name him [Grillparzer] under this head of *playwrights*, and not under that of dramatists, which he aspires to.
Carlyle, German Playwrights.

play-writer (plā'rī″tėr), *n.* One who writes plays; a dramatist.

plaza (plä'zä), *n.* [Sp., = It. *piazza* = F. *place*, > E. *place*: see *place*.] A public square or open space surrounded by houses in a Spanish or Spanish-American town or city; a market-place in such a town: as, the *Plaza* of San Francisco.

Overlooking the *Plaza*, . . . you had before you, across the midst of the open space, the Parker House, famous as the first of Californian hotels.
J. W. Palmer, The New and the Old, p. 70.

ple†, *n.* A Middle English form of *plea*.

plea (plē), *n.* [< ME. *plee*, *ple*, *play*, *plait*, < OF. *plait*, *plaid*, *plat*, *play*, *plet*, *plez*, F. *plaid* = Pr. *plait*, *plag* = Sp. *pleito* = Pg. *pleito*, *preito* = It. *piato*, < ML. *placitum* (also contr. *plactum*, *placdum*, and, after Rom., *plaitum*), a decree, sentence, suit, plea, etc., L. an opinion, determination, prescription, order, lit. 'that which is pleasing,' 'pleasure,' neut. of *placitus*, pp. of *placere*, please: see *please*, and cf. *placit*.

Hence *plead*, *v.*] **1.** In *law:* (*a*) A suit or action; the presentation of a cause of action to the court. Pleas were formerly distinguished as *pleas of the crown*, or public prosecutions, usually in criminal cases, and *common pleas*, or suits between subjects or commoners in civil controversies, whence this name was given to a court for such actions, the original of which was held in an outer court of the Tower of London, while the King's Bench was held in an inner court. *Davis*, Law in Shak. (*b*) In a general sense, that which is urged by or on behalf of a litigant, in support of his claim or defense; the contention of either party. (*c*) Specifically, in modern practice: (1) At common law, a document (or in some inferior courts an oral statement) on the defendant's part, denying the allegations of the plaintiff's declaration, or alleging new matter (that is, matter not shown by the plaintiff's pleading) as cause why the action should not be maintained. (2) In equity, a document alleging new matter as a cause why the defendant should not be required to answer the complainant's bill. (*d*) In Scots law, a short and concise note of the grounds on which the action or defense is to be maintained, without argument.—**2.** That which is alleged in support, justification, or defense; an urgent argument; a reason; a pleading; an excuse; an apology: as, a *plea* for the reduction of taxation; a *plea* for rationalism.

And thus I leave it as a declared truth that neither the feare of sects, no, nor rebellion, can be a fit *plea* to stay reformation. *Milton*, Church-Government, i. 7.

Hast thou no other *plea* for thy self but that thy sins were fatal? *Stillingfleet*, Sermons, I. ii.

Nor is it possible to urge in defense of this act of James those *pleas* by which many arbitrary acts of the Stuarts have been vindicated or excused. *Macaulay*, Hist. Eng., vii.

3. Pretext; pretense.

The Spaniards subdued the Indians under *plea* of converting them to Christianity. *H. Spencer*, Social Statics, p. 178.

The invasion of private property under the doctrinaire's *plea* of the general good. *N. A. Rev.*, CXLIII. 295.

4†. Proposition; proposal.

And yet shall I make to yow a feire *plee:* com with me to Bredigan, where the kynge Arthur me abideth, and do hym homage, as the barouns seyen that ye owe for to do, and I shall yelde yow the castell all quyte. *Merlin* (E. E. T. S.), ii. 365.

5†. A dispute or controversy; a quarrel.

Make a *plee* betwyx glotony and thy pursse. Nevyrthelesse be ware to which of thise two thow be advocate, or what sentens thou geue betwyx them, for glotony hath effectualle wytnes. *Political Poems*, etc. (ed. Furnivall), p. 30.

And wow but they were lovers dear,
And loved fu' constantlie;
But aye the mair when they fell out,
The sairer was their *plea*.
Young Benjie (Child's Ballads, II. 300).

Court of Common Pleas. See *court*.—**Declinatory, dilatory, equitable plea.** See the adjectives.—**Double plea,** in *law*, a plea in which the defendant alleges two different matters in bar of the action.—**Foreign plea.** (*a*) In *old Eng. law*, a plea in either a civil or a criminal case that the matter arose or the prisoner was taken in another county than that where it is sought to try him, and therefore that the court or judge of the latter place has no jurisdiction of the case. It was one kind of plea to the jurisdiction, but distinguished from other kinds by the fact that it resulted in removing the cause. (*b*) Another litigation elsewhere, on the same subject, and between the same parties, or between the creditor and a third party sought to be held for the same debt. When used in this sense it is commonly in reference to the question whether arrest in one action is a satisfaction or bar to the other.—**Issuable, non-issuable,** etc., **plea.** See the adjectives.—**Plea in abatement, plea in avoidance, plea in bar,** etc. See *abatement*, etc.—**Plea of auterfois acquit, of auterfois attaint, of auterfois convict,** pleas in criminal cases, that the accused has been already acquitted, attainted, or convicted, as the case may be, on a former trial for the same offense, the object of which is to invoke the protection of the rule in law that a man cannot be twice put in jeopardy for the same cause.—**Plea of non-claim.** See *non-claim*.—**Plea of panel,** in Scotland, the plea of guilty or of not guilty.—**Plea of parole demurrer.** Same as *age-prayer*.—**Plea of pregnancy.** See *pregnancy*.—**Pleas of the crown,** public prosecution in criminal cases; hence, the body of English criminal law.—**Plea to the jurisdiction.** See *jurisdiction*.—**Special plea,** a plea which admits the truth of the declaration, but alleges special or new matter in avoidance.=**Syn. 1.** *Argument, Plea.* See *argument*.—**2.** *Excuse*, etc. See *apology*.

pleach (plēch), *v. t.* [< ME. *plechen*, < OF. *plescier*, *plessier*, *plesser*, also *plaissier*, *plassier*, plash, plait: see *plash*[2], of which *pleach* is a doublet.] **1.** To unite (the branches of shrubs, vines, etc.) by plaiting, weaving, or braiding together; plash; mingle.

Bende as a bowe, or vynes that men *pleche*,
And cleme it, mose it, bynde it softe aboute.
Palladius, Husbondrie (E. E. T. S.), p. 76.

Round thee blow, self-*pleached* deep,
Bramble roses, faint and pale,
And long purples of the dale.
Tennyson, A Dirge.

Seeing I have sworn by the pale temples' band
And poppied hair of gold Persephone,
Sad-tressed and *pleached* low down about her brows.
A. C. Swinburne, At Eleusis.

2. To form by intermingling or interweaving.

The prince and Count Claudio, walking in a thick-*pleached* alley in mine orchard, were thus much overheard. *Shak.*, Much Ado, i. 2. 10.

Plundered vines, teeming exhaustless, *pleach'd*
New growth. *Keats*, Endymion, iii.

3. To fold, as the arms.

Wouldst thou be window'd in great Rome and see
Thy master thus with *pleach'd* arms, bending down
His corrigible neck, his face subdued
To penetrative shame? *Shak.*, A. and C., iv. 14. 73.

[Obsolete or archaic in all uses.]

pleacher (plē'chėr), *n.* One who pleaches.

The topiarius, or *pleacher*, was kept actively at work trimming the hedges and trellis walks. *Portfolio*, No. 240, p. 231.

plead (plēd), *v.*; pret. and pp. *pleaded*, rarely *pled*, *plead* (pled), ppr. *pleading*. [< ME. *pleden*, *pleten*, *plaidien* (?), < OF. *plaider*, *pleidier*, F. *plaider* (> G. *plädiren*) = Pr. *plaidejar*, *plaideiar*, *playejar*, *plaegar* = Sp. *pleitear* = Pg. *pleitear* = It. *piateggiare*, *piatire*, plead, offer a plea, < *plait*, a plea: see *plea*.] **I.** *intrans.* **1.** In *law*, to present an answer to the declaration or complaint of a plaintiff, or the charge of a prosecutor; deny the plaintiff's declaration or complaint, or allege facts relied on as showing that he ought not to recover in the suit. The plaintiff is said to *declare*, *complain*, or *allege;* the defendant *pleads* to his complaint or declaration. The crown or the state prosecutes an offender, and the offender *pleads* guilty or not guilty, confessing or denying the charge.

Be ye noght ware how false Polyphete
Is now aboute eftsones for to *plete*
And brynge on yow advocacies newe?
Chaucer, Troilus, ii. 1468.

2. To urge a plea, an argument, or an excuse for or against a claim, or in support, justification, extenuation, etc.; endeavor to persuade by argument or supplication; urge reasons or use argument: as, to *plead* with a judge for a criminal or in his favor; to *plead* with a wrong-doer, urging him to reform.

A! lorde, a-yeenst the wee wole nat *plette*,
For as thou wouledyst, hit is, and was.
Political Poems, etc. (ed. Furnivall), p. 168.

I will *plead* against it with my life. *Shak.*, M. for M., iv. 2. 192.

The drooping child who prays in vain to live,
And *pleads* for help its parent cannot give.
O. W. Holmes, Ded. of Pittsfield Cemetery.

3†. To sue; make application; enter a plea or an argument.

If a Woman can prove her Husband to have been thrice drunk, by the ancient Laws of Spain she may *plead* for a Divorce from him. *Howell*, Letters, ii. 54.

4. To argue or prosecute causes; contend.

Whan shal your cursed *pletynge* have an ende?
Chaucer, Parliament of Fowls, l. 495.

There do the Advocats and Civilians *pleade*, and discusse matters of controvercie. *Coryat*, Crudities, I. 31.

II. *trans.* **1.** To discuss, defend, and attempt to maintain by arguments or reasons offered to the person or tribunal that has the power of determining; argue: as, to *plead* a cause before a court or jury.—**2.** To urge or allege in extenuation, justification, or defense; adduce in proof, support, or vindication: as, to *plead* poverty as an excuse for stealing.

What *plead* you to your father's accusation?
Beau. and Fl., Laws of Candy, v. 1.

But who are we to make complaint,
Or dare to *plead*, in times like these,
The weakness of our love of ease?
Whittier, Thy Will be Done.

3. To set forth in a plea or defense: interpose a plea of: as, to *plead* a statute of limitations.

I . . . humbly crave pardon at adventure, having nothing that I can think of to *plead*. *N. Ward*, Simple Cobler, p. 91.

The punishment for this, by *pleading* benefit of clergy, which of course was always done, was reduced to a very minimum—something amounting to the supposed burning of the hand with a barely warm or cold iron.
Ashton, Social Life in Reign of Queen Anne, II. 105.

pleadable (plē'da-bl), *a.* [< *plead* + *-able*.] Capable of being pleaded; capable of being alleged in proof, defense, or vindication: as, a right or privilege *pleadable* at law.

Nor bargaine or sale that he [an excommunicate] maketh is auaileable in law, neither anie of his acts whatsoever *pleadable*, whereby he liueth as an outlaw.
Holinshed, Descrip. of England, ii. 15.

Pleadable briefs†, in *Scots law*, precepts directed to the sheriffs, who thereupon cite parties, and hear and determine.

pleader (plē'dėr), *n.* [< ME. *pledere*, *pletere*, *pletour*, *plaidur*, < OF. *plaideur*, a pleader, < *plaidier*, plead: see *plead*.] **1.** One who pleads; one who presents pleas for or against a claim, allegation, etc.; technically, a lawyer who pleads a cause or argues in a court of justice (the original meaning of the term), or who drafts, prepares, or devises pleadings.

The thridde buffet signifieth these false *pletours*, men of lawe, that sellen and a-peire theirs neyghbours be-hinde here bakke for couetise and envye. *Merlin* (E. E. T. S.), iii. 434.

So fair a *pleader* any cause may gain. *Dryden*, Aurengzebe, iii. 1.

2. The party whose pleading is under consideration.—**Special pleader,** one of a class of the English bar, whose business consists in giving opinions, and especially in drawing special and difficult pleadings and other documents. In the days of technical common-law procedure, when the statement of the cause of action was presented in different counts varying as to details so as to cover every anticipated variation of circumstances, the function of the special pleader was important to the English practitioner, whether in preparing documents or in detecting defects in those of the adversary.

pleading (plē'ding), *n.* [< ME. *pledyng*, *pletyng;* verbal n. of *plead*, *v.*] **1.** The act of advocating any cause; specifically, the act or practice of advocating clients' causes in courts of law.

The lawyer is judged by the virtue of his *pleading*, and not by issue of the cause.d *Bacon*, Advancement of Learning, ii. 159.

I fling my heart into your lap
Without a word of *pleading*.
Whittier, Among the Hills.

2. In *law:* (*a*) The document (or in some inferior courts an oral statement) formally setting forth the cause of action or the defense of a party. The objects of pleading are to inform the adverse party what questions he must be prepared to meet at the trial; to inform the court what questions are to be determined; and to preserve a record which, with the verdict or judgment, shall show what matters are not afterward to be drawn in question. The term *pleadings* is applied to the documents on either side, whether a declaration, complaint, or bill with demurrer, or a declaration with plea, etc., or a bill or complaint with plea or answer, etc., which form the issue on which it is proposed to try the cause. See *issue*, 10. (*b*) The formal allegation on the record of that which is to be relied on as the support of the party's case in evidence. (*c*) The rules and usages of framing such documents, and of the sufficiency of their contents; the art of drawing pleadings. (*d*) *pl.* (1) The written allegations made in alternate series by the plaintiff and the defendant of their respective grounds of action and defense, terminating in propositions distinctly affirmed on one side and denied on the other, called the *issue*. *Heard.* (2) In a more limited sense, only those allegations or altercations which are subsequent to the count or declaration. *Gould.*—**Code pleading, Color in pleading†, oral pleading.** See *code*, *color*, *oral*.—**Pleading over,** going on to respond by pleading, after a previous pleading has been adjudged insufficient, or has been withdrawn.—**Special pleading.** (*a*) The allegation of special or new matter, as distinguished from a direct denial of matter previously alleged on the other side. (*b*) The science of pleading, which, until the English Common-law Procedure Act, in 1852, constituted a distinct branch of the law, having the merit of developing the points in controversy with great precision. Its strictness and subtlety were frequently a subject of complaint, and one of the objects of the act was to relax and simplify its rules. (*c*) In popular use, the specious but unsound or unfair argumentation of one whose aim is victory rather than truth.

Not one of these [medieval wars] was simply a war of aggression, . . . except perhaps the Norman Conquest; and we all know what an amount of *special pleading* was thought necessary to justify that.
Stubbs, Medieval and Modern Hist., p. 217.

pleadingly (plē'ding-li), *adv.* In a pleading manner; by supplication.

pleading-place (plē'ding-plās), *n.* A court of justice. *Cowley*, Pindaric Odes, xiii. 5. [Rare.]

pleasable† (plē'za-bl), *a.* [< *please* + *-able*.] Capable of being pleased.

I love not to have to do with men which be neither grateful nor *pleasable*.
Northumberland, quoted in R. W. Dixon's Hist. Church of Eng., xx., note.

pleasance (plez'ans), *n.* [Early mod. E. also *pleasaunce;* < ME. *plesance*, *plesaunce*, *pleasaunce*, < OF. *plaisance*, F. *plaisance* = Pr. *plazensa* = It. *piacenza*, pleasure, < LL. *placentia*, suavity, courteousness, lit. 'pleasingness,' < L. *placen(t-)s*, pleasing, dear: see *pleasant*.] **1.** Pleasant manners; agreeable behavior; complaisance.

Wrapped under humble chere, . . .
Under *plesaunce*, and under bisy peyne.
Chaucer, Squire's Tale, l. 501.

2. Pleasure; satisfaction; enjoyment; delight.

He beholdethe in alle whiche of hem is most to his *plesance*, and to hire anon he sendethe or castethe a Ryng fro his Fyngre. *Mandeville*, Travels, p. 39.

Of love I seke nothir *plesance*, ne ease,
Nor grete desire, nor righte grete affiance.
Political Poems, etc. (ed. Furnivall), p. 62.

The nymphs
With *pleasance* laugh to see the satyrs play.
Greene, Orlando Furioso.

When my passion seeks
Pleasance in love-sighs.
Tennyson, Lilian.

It was a pageant befitting a young and magnificent chief, in the freshness and *pleasance* of his years.
Irving, Moorish Chronicles, p. 18.

3. Pleasure; will.

Doth your *plesaunce*; I wol your lust obeye.
Chaucer, Clerk's Tale, l. 602.

Ser, if it be your will and your *pleasaunce*,
Her am I come to offer my seruice
To your lordshippe, right as ye list to devise.
Generydes (E. E. T. S.), l. 654.

4. A garden, especially a pleasure-garden, or part of a garden attached to a mansion but secluded or screened by trees, shrubs, and close hedges.

The window . . . commanded a delightful view of what was called the *Pleasance*—a space of ground enclosed and decorated with arches, trophies, statues, fountains, and other architectural monuments, which formed one access from the castle itself into the garden.
Scott, Kenilworth, xxvi.

Meanwhile the party had broken up, and wandered away by twos and threes, among trim gardens, and *pleasaunces*, and clipped yew-walks. *Kingsley*, Westward Ho.

5. A kind of lawn or gauze in use in the fifteenth and sixteenth centuries. In one instance at least it is mentioned as used for a napkin. It was sometimes black.

Moreover there is j. kome in to Englond a knyght out of Spayne, with a kercheff of *plesaunce* i wrapped aboute hys arme; the wych knyght wyl renne a cours wyth a sharpe spere for his sovereyn lady sake.
Paston Letters, I. 41.

Over their garmentes were vochettes of *pleasauntes*, rouled with crymosyne velvet, and set with letters of gold like carrettes, their heades rouled in *pleasaunces* and typpers lyke the Egipcians.
Hall, Henry VIII., f. 7. (*Halliwell*.)

[Archaic in all senses.]

Kerchief of pleasance†. See *kerchief*.

pleasancy† (plez'an-si), *n.* [As *pleasance* (see *-cy*).] Pleasantness.

pleasant (plez'ant), *a.* and *n.* [Early mod. E. also *pleasaunt*; < ME. **plesant*, *pleasaund*, < OF. *pleisant*, *plesant*, *plaisant*, F. *plaisant* = It. *piacente*, *piagente*, < L. *placen(t-)s*, pleasing, charming, dear, ppr. of *placere*, please: see *please*.] **I.** *a.* **1.** Pleasing; delightful; agreeable; grateful to the mind or to the senses.

The bocher sweet, the *pleasant* flounder thin.
J. Dennys (Arber's Eng. Garner, I. 175).

How good and how *pleasant* it is for brethren to dwell together in unity! Ps. cxxxiii. 1.

This summer morning makes vs couetous
To take the profit of the *pleasant* aire.
Heywood, If you Know not Me, ii.

This latter [Lord Weston] goes to France, Savoy, Venice, and so returns by Florence—a *pleasant* Journey, for he carrieth Presents with him from King and Queen.
Howell, Letters, I. v. 38.

The *pleasant* savoury smell
So quicken'd appetite that I, methought,
Could not but taste. *Milton*, P. L., v. 84.

A *pleasant* spot in spring, where first the wren
Was heard to chatter.
Bryant, Little People of the Snow.

2. Merry; lively; cheerful; gay.

'Tis merry,
And meant to make ye *pleasant*, and not weary.
Fletcher, Spanish Curate, Prol.

Nay, then, I'm heartily *pleasant*, and as merry
As one that owes no malice.
Middleton, More Dissemblers besides Women, iii. 2.

Happy who in his verse can gently steer
From grave to light, from *pleasant* to severe.
Dryden and Soames, tr. of Boileau's Art of Poetry, i. 76.

3. Jocular; witty; facetious.

They all agreed; so, turning all to game
And *pleasaunt* bord, they past forth on their way.
Spenser, F. Q., IV. iv. 13.

It does become you well to make us merry:
I have heard often of your *pleasant* vein.
Beau. and Fl., Captain, iii. 3.

Can a ghost laugh . . . when you are *pleasant* with him?
Lamb, New-Year's Eve.

=**Syn. 1.** *Pleasant, Pleasing, Agreeable, Congenial*, gratifying, acceptable, welcome. *Pleasing* is the strongest, and *agreeable* the weakest of the first four words. *Pleasant* may be, and generally is, applied to things in the concrete: as, *pleasant* weather. *Pleasing* applies generally to things not physical: as, a *pleasant* face; a *pleasing* aspect, variety. *Pleasant* suggests the effect produced, *pleasing* the power of producing it; hence we may say a *pleasant* or a *pleasing* variety. *Pleasing* must be objective, *pleasant* may be subjective: as, he was in a *pleasant* mood. *Agreeable* and *congenial* are used of social qualities and relations, but the latter goes deeper, expressing a natural suitableness, on the part of a person or thing, to the tastes, habits, temperament, or passing mood of the person concerned.

It was worth while to hear the croaking and hollow tones of the old lady, and the *pleasant* voice of Phœbe, mingling in one twisted thread of talk.
Hawthorne, Seven Gables, v.

Sallies of wit and quick replies are very *pleasing* in conversation. *Johnson.*

Politeness and good breeding are equally necessary to make you welcome and *agreeable* in conversation and common life. *Chesterfield*, Letters.

The natural and *congenial* conversations of men of letters and of artists must be those which are associated with their pursuits.
I. D'Israeli, Lit. Char. of Men of Genius, p. 147.

II.† *n.* A humorist; a droll; a jester; a buffoon.

They bestow their silver on courtesans, *pleasants*, and flatterers. *Holland*, tr. of Plutarch, p. 169. (*Encyc. Dict.*)

pleasantly (plez'ant-li), *adv.* **1.** In a pleasant manner. (*a*) So as to please or gratify the senses or the mind.

It standeth very *pleasantly* in a clift betweene two hilles.
Hakluyt's Voyages, II. 104.

All these things were carried so *pleasantly* as within a weeke they became Masters, making it their delight to heare the trees thunder as they fell.
Quoted in *Capt. John Smith's* Works, I. 197.

(*b*) Merrily; cheerfully; happily.

It is impossible to live *pleasantly* without living wisely, and well, and justly; and it is impossible to live wisely, and well, and justly without living *pleasantly*.
Quoted in *W. Wallace's* Epicureanism, p. 155.

2†. Jestingly; jocularly.

This embellishment carries an odd appearance, and has occasioned strangers sometimes to ask us *pleasantly*, "Whether we fastened our walls with tenpenny nails?"
Gilbert White, Nat. Hist. of Selborne, letter iv.

pleasantness (plez'ant-nes), *n.* **1.** Pleasing or agreeable character or quality; the quality of being pleasing or of affording pleasure.

Her ways are ways of *pleasantness*, and all her paths are peace. Prov. iii. 17.

All the way from the white Promontory to this Plain is exceeding Rocky; but here the *pleasantness* of the Road makes you amends for the former labour.
Maundrell, Aleppo to Jerusalem, p. 53.

Bewitched with the *pleasantnesse* of the fruit to the taste and sight. *Purchas*, Pilgrimage, p. 25.

In all satisfaction of desire there is pleasure, and thus *pleasantness* in an object is a necessary incident of its being good. *T. H. Green*, Prolegomena to Ethics, § 171.

2. Vivacity; gaiety.

It was refreshing, but composed, like the *pleasantness* of youth tempered with the gravity of age. *South.*

3†. Jocularity; pleasantry.

pleasantry (plez'an-tri), *n.*; pl. *pleasantries* (-triz). [< F. *plaisanterie* = It. *piacenteria*, *piagenteria*, pleasantry; as *pleasant* + *-ry*.] **1.** Good humor; cheerfulness; sprightliness.

The harshness of reasoning is not a little softened and smoothed by the infusions of mirth and *pleasantry*.
Addison.

But let us leave the serious reflections, and converse with our usual *pleasantry*.
B. Franklin, Autobiography, p. 295.

2. Humorousness; jocularity; witticism; raillery; wit.

He saw my distress, and, with a kind of benevolent *pleasantry*, asked me if I would let him guess any more.
Miss Burney, Evelina, lxii.

The harmless play of *pleasantry* and mirth.
Cowper, Epistle to J. Hill.

The keen observation and ironical *pleasantry* of a finished man of the world. *Macaulay.*

3. A sprightly or humorous saying; a jest.

The grave abound in *pleasantries*, the dull in repartees and points of wit. *Addison.*

4. A laughable trick; a prank; a caper: as, the *pleasantries* of monkeys. *Addison.* (*Worcester.*) =**Syn. 2.** Sport, fun, facetiousness, jocoseness, drollery.

pleasant-spirited (plez'ant-spir"i-ted), *a.* Having a pleasant spirit; cheerful; merry.

D. Pedro. A *pleasant-spirited* lady.
Leon. There's little of the melancholy element in her.
Shak., Much Ado, ii. 1. 355.

pleasant-tongued (plez'ant-tungd), *a.* Having pleasing speech.

pleasaunce†, *n.* An obsolete form of *pleasance*.

please (plēz), *v.*; pret. and pp. *pleased*, ppr. *pleasing*. [< ME. *plesen*, < OF. *plesir*, *plaisir*, also *plere*, *pleire*, F. *plaire* = Pr. *placer* = Sp. *placer* = Pg. *prazer* = It. *piacere*, *piagere*, < L. *placere*, please, be agreeable, welcome, or acceptable, satisfy, impers. *placet* (with dat. *mihi*, etc.), it pleases, suits (me, etc.), it is (my) opinion or resolve, etc. From the L. *placere* are also ult. E. *pleasant*, *pleasance*, *pleasure*, *plea*, *plead*, *complacent*, *complaisant*, *placid*, *placate*, etc. In constructions and development *please* is similar to *like*[3], *v.*] **I.** *trans.* **1.** To be agreeable to; suit; satisfy; seem good to: used impersonally, and followed by an object, originally dative, of the person: same as *like*[3], I., 1. This impersonal construction with the indirect object of the person has given way in more familiar use to a personal construction, the original dative *you*, in *if you please*, for example, being now taken as the subject. (See II., 1.) The word in this sense was formerly common in polite request, *may it please you*, or *if it please you*, or, elliptically, *please you*: a mode of speech still common in addressing a judge or persons of rank or position: as, may it *please* the court; if it *please* your honor; *please* your worship; etc. Compare II., 1.

It *pleased* the Father that in him should all fulness dwell.
Col. i. 19.

Please you, lords,
In sight of both our battles we may meet.
Shak., 2 Hen. IV., iv. 1. 178.

The toils and troubles,
All that is burthenous in authority,
Please you lay it on me.
Middleton (and another), Mayor of Queenborough, i. 1.

It is very likely, an 't *please* your Worship, that I should bullock him; I have marks enow about my body to show of his cruelty to me. *Fielding*, Tom Jones, ii. 6.

2. To excite agreeable sensations or emotions in; impart satisfaction, gratification, pleasure, or delight to; gratify; content.

The elther suster vndirstode hym wele, and gretly was *plesed* with his doctryne. *Merlin* (E. E. T. S.), i. 5.

I know a Trout taken with a fly of your own making will *please* you better than twenty with one of mine.
Cotton, in Walton's Angler, ii. 247.

What next I bring shall *please* . . .
Thy wish exactly to thy heart's desire.
Milton, P. L., viii. 449.

Pleas'd in Mind, he calls a Chair,
Adjusts, and combs, and courts the Fair.
Congreve, An Impossible Thing.

'Tis certainly very commendable in the King, who *pleases* himself in Planting and Pruning the Trees with his own Hand, to make use of no other Trees but what the Neighbouring Woods afford. *Lister*, Journey to Paris, p. 209.

If it were not to *please* you, I see no necessity of our parting. *Dryden*, Mock Astrologer, iv.

Pleased with his daily task, or, if not *pleased*,
Contented. *Wordsworth*, Prelude, vi.

Please the pigs. See *pig*[1].—**To be pleased** (followed by an infinitive with *to*). (*a*) To be willing or well inclined.

Here also they *are pleased to* shew a stone, which, they say, spoke on that question.
Pococke, Description of the East, II. i. 9.

Many of our most skillful painters . . . *were pleased to* recommend this author to me.
Dryden, Parallel of Poetry and Painting.

(*b*) To think fit or have the complaisance or kindness; condescend; be good enough; be so kind as: an expression of courtesy, often used ironically.

They *are pleas'd*, I hear,
To censure me extremely for my pleasures.
Fletcher, Valentinian, i. 3.

To be pleased in, to take pleasure in.

And lo a voice from heaven, saying, This is my beloved Son, *in* whom I *am* well *pleased*. Mat. iii. 17.

=**Syn. 2.** To rejoice, gladden, make glad.

II. *intrans.* **1.** To like; choose; think fit: as, do as you *please*.

Their troops we can expel with ease,
Who vanquish only when we *please*.
Dryden, Fair Stranger, l. 12.

The Aga sent for my servant, and told him I might stay as long as I *pleased*, but that I should see nothing more.
Pococke, Description of the East, I. 119.

Since I last attended your Lordship here, I summoned my Thoughts to Counsel, and canvassed to and fro within myself the Business you *pleased* to impart to me, for going upon the King's Service into Italy.
Howell, Letters, I. iv. 25.

Spirits, freed from mortal laws, with ease
Assume what sexes and what shapes they *please*.
Pope, R. of the L., i. 69.

[In this use common in polite request: as, *please* let me pass; especially in the phrase *if you please* (see I., 1), by ellipsis, in familiar use, *please*: as, let me pass, *please*.]

2. To give pleasure; win approval.

For we that live to *please* must *please* to live.
Johnson, Prol. on Opening of Drury Lane Theatre.

Let her be comprehended in the frame
Of these illusions, or they *please* no more.
Wordsworth, Sonnets, iii. 3.

pleasedly (plē'zed-li), *adv.* In a pleased manner; with pleasure or satisfaction.

Surely, he that would be *pleasedly* innocent must refrain from the tast of offence. *Feltham*, Resolves, ii. 40.

He . . . that can look upon another man's lands evenly and *pleasedly*, as if they were his own.
Jer. Taylor, Holy Dying, i. 3.

pleaseman†, *n.* [< *please*, *v.*, and obj. *man*.] An officious or servile person who courts favor; a pickthank.

Some carry-tale, some *please-man*, some slight zany, . . .
Told our intents before. *Shak.*, L. L. L., v. 2. 463.

pleaser (plē'zėr), *n.* One who pleases or gratifies.

No man was more a *pleaser* of all men, to whom he [St. Paul] became all honest things, that he might gain some.
Jer. Taylor (?), Artif. Handsomeness, p. 190.

pleasing (plē'zing), *n.* [< ME. *plesynge*; verbal n. of *please*, *v.*] 1. Pleasure given or afforded; pleasurable or pleasure-giving quality; gratification; charm.

He capers nimbly in a lady's chamber
To the lascivious *pleasing* of a lute.
Shak., Rich. III., i. 1. 13.

2. Satisfaction; approbation.

That ye might walk worthy of the Lord unto all *pleasing*, being fruitful in every good work, and increasing in the knowledge of God. Col. i. 10.

3†. A matter of pleasure.

Swiche manere necessaries as bee *plesynges*
To folk that han ywedded hem with rynges.
Chaucer, Man of Law's Tale, l. 613.

pleasing (plē'zing), *p. a.* [< ME. *plesynge*; ppr. of *please*, *v.*] Giving pleasure or satisfaction; agreeable to the senses or to the mind; gratifying: as, a *pleasing* prospect; a *pleasing* reflection; *pleasing* manners.

It were *plesynge* to god that he hadde my doughter spoused. *Merlin* (E. E. T. S.), ii. 226.

I do
Protest my ears were never better fed
With such delightful *pleasing* harmony.
Shak., Pericles, ii. 5. 28.

I know there is no music in your ears
So *pleasing* as the groans of men in prison.
Massinger and Field, Fatal Dowry, i. 2.

To be exempt from the passions with which others are tormented is the only *pleasing* solitude.
Steele, Spectator, No. 4.

She formed a picture, not bright enough to dazzle, but fair enough to interest; not brilliantly striking, but very delicately *pleasing*. *Charlotte Brontë*, Shirley, xvi.

=**Syn.** *Agreeable*, *Congenial*, etc. See *pleasant*.

pleasingly (plē'zing-li), *adv.* In a pleasing manner; so as to give pleasure.

While all his soul,
With trembling tenderness of hope and fear,
Pleasingly pain'd, was all employ'd for her.
Mallet, Amyntor and Theodora, iii.

pleasingness (plē'zing-nes), *n.* The quality of being pleasing or of giving pleasure.

Stafford's speech was esteemed full of weight, reason, and *pleasingness*; and so affectionate it was that it obtained pity and remorse in the generality.
Wood, Athenæ Oxon., II. 36.

pleasurable (plezh'ūr-a̤-bl), *a.* [< *pleasure* + *-able*.] 1. Pleasing; giving or capable of giving pleasure; gratifying; pleasant.

On the restoration of his Majesty of *pleasurable* memory, he hastened to court, where he rolled away and shone as in his native sphere.
Brooke, Fool of Quality, I. 2. (*Davies*.)

By feeling is meant any state of consciousness which is *pleasurable* or painful.
J. Sully, Outlines of Psychol., p. 449.

2. Pleasure-seeking; capable of receiving pleasure. [Rare.]

A person of his *pleasurable* turn and active spirit could never have submitted to take long or great pains in attaining the qualifications he is master of.
Richardson, Clarissa Harlowe, I. xii. (*Davies*.)

I think we are a reasonable, but by no means a *pleasurable* people; and to mend us we must have a dash of the French and Italian; yet I don't know how.
Gray, Letters, I. 126.

pleasurableness (plezh'ūr-a̤-bl-nes), *n.* The quality of being pleasurable or of giving pleasure: as, the *pleasurableness* of the benevolent emotions.

Able to discern the fraud and fained *pleasurableness* of the bad. *Feltham*, Resolves, ii. 61.

The Sensations that have been considered have no inherent quality of *pleasurableness* or painfulness.
Mind, IX. 339.

pleasurably (plezh'ūr-a̤-bli), *adv.* In a pleasurable manner; with pleasure; with gratification of the senses or the mind.

Woe to those that live securely and *pleasurably* in Zion, and that trust to the impregnable situation of the City of Samaria. *Bp. Hall*, Hard Texts, Amos vi. 1.

pleasurance†, *n.* Pleasure. *Destruction of Troy* (E. E. T. S.), l. 3471.

pleasure (plezh'ūr), *n.* [Early mod. E. also *pleasur*, *plesur*; with termination accommodated to the noun suffix *-ure* (as also in *leisure*), < OF. *plesir*, *plaisir*, F. *plaisir* = Pr. *plazer* = Sp. *placer* = Pg. *prazer* = It. *piacere*, *piagere*, please, inf. used as noun: see *please*.] 1. That character of a feeling by virtue of which it gratifies the sentient being that experiences it, so that there is an impulse to its continuance or renewal. As being a character of a mere feeling, *pleasure* is distinguished from *happiness*, which is a general state of consciousness arising from such an adaptation of circumstances to desires as to produce a prevalent sense of satisfaction. According to hedonistic writers, happiness consists in an excess of pleasure over pain. Pleasure is measured by its intensity, its duration, the freedom from consequent pain, the number of persons whom it affects, etc.

And Salomon saithe, "The harte full of enuie
Of him selfe hath no *pleasure* nor commoditie."
Babees Book (E. E. T. S.), p. 349.

There is a *pleasure*, sure,
In being mad which none but madmen know.
Dryden, Spanish Friar, ii.

About three quarters of the way up the hill we came to a level spot where there is a fountain, and every thing made very convenient for those who come here for their *pleasure*. *Pococke*, Description of the East, II. i. 146.

How shall we define *pleasure*? It seems obvious to define it as the kind of feeling which pleases us, which we like or prefer. *H. Sidgwick*, Methods of Ethics, p. 114.

2. Sensual gratification; indulgence of the appetites.—3. That which pleases or gratifies the senses or the mind; that which is delightful or beautiful.

Wiche Galyes went to the Turke Ambasset, and they Caryed with them Riches and *pleasurs*, as clothe of gold and Crymsyn velvett, and other thyngs mor than I knewe.
Torkington, Diarie of Eng. Travell, p. 18.

O bonny, bonny was my love,
A *pleasure* to behold.
James Herries (Child's Ballads, I. 209).

4. A favor; gratification.

Felix, willing to shew the Jews a *pleasure*, left Paul bound. Acts xxiv. 27.

He [Domitian] would have done us some *pleasure* in driving away those flies. *Coryat*, Crudities, I. 151.

5. Will; desire; preference, or whatever one chooses, desires, or wills: as, it is my *pleasure* to remain.

My counsel shall stand, and I will do all my *pleasure*.
Isa. xlvi. 10.

It is his worship's *pleasure*, sir, to bail you.
Middleton (*and others*), The Widow, ii. 2.

Cannot a man of fashion, for his *pleasure*, put on, now and then, his working-day robes of humility, but he must presently be subject to a beadle's rod of correction?
Dekker and Ford, Sun's Darling, i. 1.

There is a prerogative of God and an arbitrary *pleasure* above the letter of his own law.
Sir T. Browne, Religio Medici, i. 57.

At pleasure, as or whenever one pleases: as, an officer removable *at pleasure*.

Here are many Tortoises, and abundance of all sorts of foules, whose young ones we tooke and eate *at our pleasure*. Quoted in *Capt. John Smith's* Works, I. 107.

But if love be so dear to thee, thou hast a chamber-sted
Which Vulcan purposely contriu'd with all fit secrecie;
There sleepe *at pleasure*. *Chapman*, Iliad, xiv. 288.

Positive pleasure. See *positive*.—**To take pleasure in**, to have satisfaction or enjoyment in; regard with approbation or favor.

The Lord *taketh pleasure in* them that fear him.
Ps. cxlvii. 11.

=**Syn.** 1. *Joy*, *Delight*, etc. (see *gladness*), satisfaction, comfort, solace.—2. Self-indulgence; luxury, sensuality, voluptuousness.—4. Kindness.

pleasure (plezh'ūr), *v. t.*; pret. and pp. *pleasured*, ppr. *pleasuring*. [< *pleasure*, *n.*] To give pleasure to; please; gratify.

I count it one of my greatest afflictions, say, that I cannot *pleasure* such an honourable gentleman.
Shak., T. of A., iii. 2. 63.

Silvius doth shew the citty dames brave sights,
And they for that doe *pleasure* him a nightes.
Times' Whistle (E. E. T. S.), p. 90.

You're in the happiest way t' enrich yourself
And *pleasure* me. *Middleton*, Chaste Maid, iii. 3.

Aristides . . . would do no man wrong with *pleasuring* his friends; nor yet would anger them by denying their requests. *North*, tr. of Plutarch, p. 273.

The Birds rural Musick too
Is as melodious and free
As if they sung to *pleasure* you.
Cowley, The Mistress, Spring.

Tost his ball and flown his kite and roll'd
His hoop, to *pleasure* Edith.
Tennyson, Aylmer's Field.

pleasureful (plezh'ūr-fůl), *a.* [< *pleasure* + *-ful*.] Pleasant; agreeable. [Rare.]

This country, for the fruitfulness of the land and the conveniency of the sea, hath been reputed a very commodious and *pleasureful* country.
Abp. Abbot, Descrip. of the World.

pleasure-ground (plezh'ūr-ground), *n.* Ground ornamented and appropriated to pleasure or amusement.

On his Tuscan villa he [Pliny] is more diffuse; the garden makes a considerable part of the description; and what was the principal beauty of that *pleasure-ground*?
Walpole, Modern Gardening.

pleasure-house (plezh'ūr-hous), *n.* A house to which one retires for recreation or pleasure.

I built my soul a lordly *pleasure-house*,
Wherein at ease for aye to dwell.
Tennyson, Palace of Art.

pleasureless (plezh'ūr-les), *a.* [< *pleasure* + *-less*.] Devoid of pleasure; without enjoyment or satisfaction.

He himself was sliding into that *pleasureless* yielding to the small solicitations of circumstance which is a commoner history of perdition than any single momentous bargain. *George Eliot*, Middlemarch, lxxix.

pleasurer (plezh'ūr-ėr), *n.* A pleasure-seeker.

Let us turn now to another portion of the London population; . . . we mean the Sunday *pleasurers*.
Dickens, Sketches, Scenes, ix.

pleasure-train (plezh'ūr-trān), *n.* A railway excursion-train. [Colloq.]

pleasure-trip (plezh'ūr-trip), *n.* A trip or excursion for pleasure.

pleasurist† (plezh'ūr-ist), *n.* [< *pleasure* + *-ist*.] A person devoted to worldly pleasure; a pleasure-seeker.

Let intellectual contests exceed the delights wherein mere *pleasurists* place their paradise.
Sir T. Browne, Christ. Mor., iii. § 23.

pleat, *n.* and *v.* See *plait*.

pleb (pleb), *n.* [< L. *plebs*: see *plebe*.] One of the common people; a plebeian; a low-born person.

The muggur [broad-snouted crocodile] is a gross *pleb*, and his features stamp him lowborn.
P. *Robinson*, Under the Sun, p. 78.

plebe (plēb), *n.* [< OF. *plebe* = Sp. Pg. It. *plebe*, < L. *plebs*, the common people: see *plebs*.] 1†. The common people; the populace; plebs; plebeians.

Which . . . wrought such impression in the hearts of the *plebe* that in short space they excelled in civility and government.
Heywood, Apology for Actors (1612). (*Halliwell*.)

2. A member of the lowest class in the United States naval and military academies; a freshman. [Slang.]

The *plebes* of the last fall had passed through squad and company drill, and the battalion was now proficient in the most intricate manœuvre. *The Century*, XXXVII. 464.

plebeian (plẹ̄-bē'a̤n), *a.* and *n.* [< OF. *plebeien*, F. *plébéien*, extended with suffix *-en*, E. *-an* (cf. Sp. *plebeyo* = Pg. *plebeo* = It. *plebeo*, *plebejo*, plebeian), < L. *plebeius*, of or belonging to the common people, < *plebs*, *plebes*, the common people: see *plebs*.] I. *a.* 1. Of or pertaining to or characteristic of the plebs or common people; vulgar.

Distinguishing the senator's garded robe
From a *plebeian* habit.
Massinger, Believe as you List, i. 2.

Wordsworth . . . confounded *plebeian* modes of thought with rustic forms of phrase, and then atoned for his blunder by absconding into a diction more Latinized than that of any poet of his century.
Lowell, Among my Books, 1st ser., p. 156.

2. Belonging to the lower ranks.

He through the midst unmark'd,
In show *plebeian* angel militant
Of lowest order, pass'd. *Milton*, P. L., x. 442.

II. *n.* One of the common people or lower ranks: first applied to the common people of ancient Rome, comprising those free citizens who were not descended from the original or patrician families. See *plebs*.

They haue no gentlemen, but euery man is a *Plebeian* vntill his merits raise him. *Purchas*, Pilgrimage, p. 438.

The word *plebeian*, in its strict sense, is no more contemptuous than the word commoner in England.
Encyc. Brit., XVII. 526.

plebeianism (plẹ̄-bē'a̤n-izm), *n.* [< *plebeian* + *-ism*.] The state or character of being plebeian; the conduct or manners of plebeians; vulgarity.

Thor himself engages in all manner of rough manual work, scorns no business for its *plebeianism*. *Carlyle*.

plebeianize (plẹ̄-bē'a̤n-īz), *v. t.*; pret. and pp. *plebeianized*, ppr. *plebeianizing*. [< *plebeian* + *-ize*.] To render plebeian or common. *Imp. Dict.*

plebicolist (plẹ̄-bik'ọ̄-list), *n.* [< L. *plebicola*, one who courts the common people (< *plebs*, the common people, + *colere*, cultivate), + *-ist*.] One who courts the favor of the common people; a friend of the people; a demagogue. [Rare.]

plebification (pleb'i-fi-kā'shọn), *n.* [< L. *plebs*, the common people, + *-ficatio(n-)*, < *-ficare*, make: see *-fy*.] The act of making plebeian or common; the act of deteriorating by vulgarizing.

You begin with the attempt to popularize learning and philosophy; but you will end in the *plebification* of knowledge. *Coleridge*.

What is practically meant by the *plebification* of opinion, as a danger to be dreaded, is, when put in its extremest form, the tyranny of unintelligent or half intelligent mobs.
H. N. Oxenham, Short Studies, p. 127.

plebify (pleb'i-fī), *v. t.*; pret. and pp. *plebified*, ppr. *plebifying*. [< L. *plebs*, the common people, + *-ficare*, make: see *-fy*.] To make plebeian; bring into accord with plebeian ideals or methods. *Coleridge*.

plebiscita, *n.* Plural of *plebiscitum*.

plebiscitary (pleb'i-si-tā-ri), *a.* [< *plebiscite* + *-ary.*] Pertaining to or of the nature of a plebiscite.

The *plebiscitary* confirmation makes the reform illusory.
The Nation, May 12, 1870, p. 297.

plebiscite (pleb'i-sit or -sēt), *n.* [< F. *plébiscite* = Sp. Pg. It. *plebiscito*, < L. *plebiscitum*, a decree or ordinance of the people, < *plebs*, the people, + *scitum*, a decree, neut. of *scitus*, pp. of *scire*, know: see *science*.] **1.** Same as *plebiscitum*.—**2.** An expression of the will or pleasure of the whole people in regard to some measure already decided upon; a vote of the whole people for the ratification or disapproval of some matter: chiefly a French usage.

If people by a *plebiscite* elect a man despot over them, do they remain free because the despotism was of their own making?
H. *Spencer*, Man vs. State, p. 14.

Plebiscite we have lately taken, in popular use, from the French. The word previously belonged, however, to the language of the civil law.
F. Hall, Mod. Eng., p. 310.

plebiscitum (pleb-i-sī'tum), *n.*; pl. *plebiscita* (-tä). [L.: see *plebiscite*.] A law enacted in ancient Rome by the lower rank of citizens meeting in the assembly called the *comitia tributa*, under the presidency of a tribune or some other plebeian magistrate; a decree of the plebs. At first these decrees bound only the plebs, but by a law generally assigned to 449 B. C., and confirmed by later legislation (339 and 286 B. C.), their effect was extended to the patricians.

plebity† (pleb'i-ti), *n.* [< L. *plebita(t-)s*, the rank of a common citizen, < *plebs*, the common people: see *plebs*.] The common people; the plebs. *Wharton.*

plebs (plebz), *n.* [L., also less commonly *plebes*, in OL. *pleps*, also *plebis*, the common people; akin to *plenus*, full, *plerique*, many, etc.: see *plenty*.] The lower order of citizens in ancient Rome; the plebeians; hence, in general, the populace. The members of this order were originally of pure Latin blood, but were not among the founders of Rome; they were recruited from the ranks of the clients and of the Latin peoples who had been annexed by Rome; while citizens, they did not figure in the three tribes or in the curiæ and gentes of the patricians, and were thus excluded from the comitia, the senate, and all public, civil, and religious offices. They had all the duties and burdens of citizens with greatly restricted privileges. After the establishment of the republic there took place a long struggle between the two orders. The plebeians secured the institution of the tribunate, various reforms, and an increased share in the government; their efforts culminated when, by the Licinian laws (about 367 B. C.), they secured one of the two consulships. The offices of dictator, censor, and pretor were soon opened to them, and finally, by the Ogulnian law (300 B. C.), the sacred colleges. The strife practically ended by the final confirmation of the extended plebiscitum, about 286 B. C. (See *plebiscitum*.) Under the kings and the republic a plebeian could be raised to patrician rank only by a lex curiata; Julius Cæsar and the emperors conferred the distinction by personal decree. Patrician families or individuals sometimes went over to the plebeian order, for various reasons.

Cæsar, as I stated in another Lecture, divides all the Continental Celtic tribes into the Equites and the *Plebs*.
Maine, Early Hist. of Institutions, p. 132.

Bethink you that you have to deal with *plebs*,
The commonalty. *Browning*, Ring and Book, I. 153.

pleck (plek), *n.* [< ME. *pleck*, *plek*; a var. of *plack*.] A plot of ground. [Prov. Eng.]

For the bourȝ watz so brod & so bigge alce,
Stalled in the fayrest stud the sterrez an-vnder,
Prudly on a plat playn, *plek* alther-fayrest.
Alliterative Poems (ed. Morris), ii. 1379.

plecolepidous (plek-ǭ-lep'i-dus), *a.* [< Gr. πλέκειν, twine, twist, + λεπίς (λεπιδ-), a scale: see *lepis*.] In *bot.*, having the bracts coherent that form the involucre in the order *Compositæ*.

plecopter (plę̄-kop'tėr), *n.* [< Gr. πλέκειν, twine, twist, + πτερόν, wing, = E. *feather*.] A pseudoneuropterous insect whose wings fold. Also *plecopteran*.

Plecoptera (plę̄-kop'tę-rä), *n. pl.* [NL.: see *plecopter*.] In *entom.*, a division of pseudoneuropterous insects, having the reticulated wings folded in repose, whence the name. The antennæ are long, setaceous, and many-jointed, and the jaws rudimentary. The family *Perlidæ* represents this division. In Brauer's classification (1885), it is one of 16 orders of insects. See cut under *Perla*.

plecopteran (plę̄-kop'tę-ran), *n.* [< *plecopter* + *-an*.] Same as *plecopter*.

plecopterous (plę̄-kop'tę-rus), *a.* [< *plecopter* + *-ous*.] Having reticulated wings which are folded in repose, as a perlid; specifically, of or pe a n ng to the *Plecoptera*.

Plecostomus (plę̄-kos'tō-mus), *n.* [NL. (Gronovius, 1754), < Gr. πλέκειν, twine, twist, + στόμα, mouth.] A South American genus of catfishes of the family *Siluridæ*.

Plecotinæ (plek-ǭ-tī'nē), *n. pl.* [NL., < *Plecotus* + *-inæ*.] A subfamily of *Vespertilionidæ*, exemplified by the genus *Plecotus*, having rudimentary nasal appendages or grooves and very large ears; the eared bats. The genera *Plecotus*, *Synotus*, *Otonycteris*, *Nyctophilus*, and *Antrozous* are contained in this group. Also called *Plecoti*.

plecotine (plek'ǭ-tin), *a.* Belonging to the *Plecoti*.

Plecotus (plę̄-kō'tus), *n.* [NL. (Geoffroy), < Gr. πλέκειν, twine, twist, + οὖς (ὠτ-), ear.] A genus of eared bats of the family *Vespertilionidæ* and subfamily *Plecotinæ*, having the incisors and premolars each two above and three below on each side, as the long-eared bat of Europe, *P. auritus*, and the North American *P. macrotis*.

Plectellaria (plek-te-lā'ri-ä), *n. pl.* [NL., < L. *plectere*, plait, twine, twist, + *-ell-* + *-aria*.] A suborder of nassellarians, whose skeleton consists of a simple silicious ring or of a triradiate framework of spicules, usually furnished with processes forming simple or branched spicules. The branches of the latter may be united into a loose plexus, without, however, forming a chambered fenestrated shell. The skeleton is entirely wanting only in the simplest form.

plectellarian (plek-te-lā'ri-an), *a.* and *n.* [< *Plectellaria* + *-an*.] **I.** *a.* Of or pertaining to the *Plectellaria*.

II. *n.* A member of the *Plectellaria*.

plectile (plek'til), *a.* [< L. *plectilis*, plaited, < *plectere*, plait: see *plait*.] Woven; plaited.

The crowns and garlands of the Ancients . . . were made up after all the ways of art, compactile, sutile, *plectile*.
Sir T. Browne, Misc. Tracts, ii.

Plectocomia (plek-tǭ-kō'mi-ä), *n.* [NL. (Martius and Blume, 1830), so called in allusion to the slender filaments; < Gr. πλεκτός, plaited, twisted (verbal adj. of πλέκειν, plait, twist), + κόμη, hair.] A genus of ratan-palms of the tribe *Lepidocaryeæ* and subtribe *Calameæ*. It is characterized by an axillary diœcious inflorescence, with numerous persistent spathes, and the spadix divided into many very long tail-like branches, every branch sheathed with numerous two-ranked closely imbricated shell-shaped secondary spathes, each inclosing a short spike 3 inches or less long, bearing coriaceous perianths. The 6 species are natives of mountains in eastern India and the Malayan archipelago. They are climbing palms, with slender or robust, very much prolonged stems. The one-seeded fleshy fruits are densely covered with overlapping rough-fringed, almost prickly scales. The large leaves are pinnate, with narrowly elliptical segments, and the midrib extended into long whip-like tails, covered beneath with exceedingly strong compound claw-like spines, which take firm hold of branches of trees, and support the climbing stem, which in *P. elongata*, the rotang-dahown of Indian jungles, is said to extend to a length of 500 feet.

plectognath (plek'tog-nath), *a.* and *n.* **I.** *a.* Pertaining to the *Plectognathi*, or having their characters. Also *plectognathic*, *plectognathous*.

II. *n.* A member of the *Plectognathi*.

Plectognathi (plek-tog'nā-thī), *n. pl.* [NL., < Gr. πλεκτός, plaited, twisted, + γνάθος, jaw.] An order of physoclistous fishes, with the cranium normal, the premaxillaries usually coössified behind with the maxillaries, the dentary coössified with the articular and angular bones, and the lower pharyngeals distinct: so called from the extensive ankyloses of the jaws. The order includes the porcupine-fishes, swell-fishes, box-fishes, globe-fishes, egg-fishes, file-fishes, and related forms, as of the families *Triacanthidæ*, *Balistidæ*, *Triodontidæ*, *Ostraciontidæ*, *Tetrodontidæ*, *Diodontidæ*, and *Molidæ*.

plectognathic (plek-tog-nath'ik), *a.* [< *plectognath* + *-ic*.] Same as *plectognath*.

plectognathous (plek-tog'nā-thus), *a.* [< *plectognath* + *-ous*.] Same as *plectognath*.

Plectoptera (plek-top'tę-rä), *n. pl.* [NL., < Gr. πλεκτός, plaited, twisted, + πτερόν, wing, = E. *feather*.] In Packard's classification (1888), one of 15 orders of insects, corresponding to the pseudoneuropterous family *Ephemeridæ* alone. These had before (in 1885) been raised to ordinal rank by Brauer, but without a new name.

plectospondyl (plek-tǭ-spon'dil), *a.* and *n.* [< Gr. πλεκτός, plaited, twisted, + σπόνδυλος, σφόνδυλος, the backbone: see *spondyl*.] **I.** *a.* Having some joints of the back-bone coössified or ankylosed together, as a fish; having the characters of the *Plectospondyli*. Also *plectospondylous*.

II. *n.* Any fish of the order *Plectospondyli*.

Plectospondyli (plek-tǭ-spon'di-lī), *n. pl.* [NL.: see *plectospondyl*.] An order of fishes having a precoracoid arch, a symplectic but no coronoid bones, and the anterior vertebræ coössified and connected with the auditory apparatus by a chain of little bones. It contains the cyprinids, characinids, and gymnonotous fishes—all of fresh water.

plectospondylous (plek-tǭ-spon'di-lus), *a.* [< *plectospondyl* + *-ous*.] Same as *plectospondyl*.

plectra, *n.* Plural of *plectrum*.

Plectranthus (plek-tran'thus), *n.* [NL. (L'Héritier, 1784), so called in allusion to the spurred corolla of many species; < Gr. πλῆκτρον, spur (see *plectrum*), + ἄνθος, flower.] A genus of gamopetalous plants of the order *Labiatæ*, tribe *Ocimoideæ*, and subtribe *Euocimeæ*, characterized by the longer and concave anterior corolla-lobe, four perfect stamens, calyx with five equal or unequal teeth, the posterior tooth sometimes larger, and this or the corolla often prolonged below into a spur or sac. There are about 80 species, natives of the tropics, especially in Africa, Asia, and the Pacific, and also in Japan and at the Cape of Good Hope. They are usually herbs, rarely tall shrubs, bearing two-lipped flowers with a long tube, in large or small cymes, which are variously racemed or panicled, and are commonly blue or purple. The name *cockspur-flower* is sometimes used for the cultivated species, which are either tender annuals or herbs and shrubs grown under glass. *P. nudiflorus* is the Chinese basil, and *P. ternatus* the omime-root of Madagascar.

plectre (plek'tėr), *n.* [< F. *plectre*, < L. *plectrum*, plectrum: see *plectrum*.] A plectrum. [Rare.]

He'd strike that lyre adroitly—speech,
Would but a twenty-cubit *plectre* reach.
Browning, Sordello.

plectron (plek'tron), *n.* Same as *plectrum*.

Plectrophanes (plek-trof'ạ-nēz), *n.* [NL. (Temminck, 1820), < Gr. πλῆκτρον, a cock's spur (see *plectrum*), + φαίνειν, show.] A genus of *Fringillidæ*, so named from the long straightened hind claw or plectrum characteristic of some of its members; the snow-buntings or longspurs. The bill is small and conic, with a nasal ruff or tuft of plumules; the wings are long and pointed; and the tail is short, and square or emarginate. The common snow-bunting is usually called *P. nivalis*, but has been placed in a different genus (*Plectrophenax*). The Lapland longspur is *P. lapponicus*. The collared and the painted longspurs are *P. ornatus* and *P. pictus*. Excluding the snow-bunting, the members of this genus are now usually called *Centrophanes* or *Calcarius*. See cut under *Centrophanes*.

Plectrophenax (plek-trof'e-naks), *n.* [NL., < Gr. πλῆκτρον, a cock's spur (see *plectrum*), + φέναξ, a cheat.] A genus of *Fringillidæ* dismembered from *Plectrophanes*, having *P. nivalis* as its type; the snow-buntings.

Plectropteridæ (plek-trop-ter'i-dē), *n. pl.* [NL., < *Plectropterus* + *-idæ*.] The spur-winged geese regarded as a family apart from *Anatidæ*. See cut under *Plectropterus*.

Plectropterinæ (plek-trop-tę-rī'nē), *n. pl.* [NL., < *Plectropterus* + *-inæ*.] A subfamily of *Anatidæ*, represented by the genus *Plectropterus*; the spur-winged geese.

plectropterine (plek-trop'tę-rin), *a.* Belonging to the *Plectropterinæ*.

Plectropterus (plek-trop'tę-rus), *n.* [NL. (W. E. Leach, 1824), < Gr. πλῆκτρον, a cock's spur (see *plectrum*), + πτερόν, wing, = E. *feather*.]

Spur-winged Goose (*Plectropterus gambensis*).

An African genus of geese having a spur on the wing, as *P. gambensis*.

plectrum (plek'trum), *n.*; pl. *plectra* (-trä). [NL., < L. *plectrum*, < Gr. πλῆκτρον, a thing to strike with, as an instrument for striking the lyre, a spear-point, a cock's spur, a punting-pole, < πλήσσειν (πληκ-), strike: see *plague*.] **1.** A small instrument of ivory, horn, or metal used for plucking or twanging the strings of a lyre, cithara, or other similar instrument.

I heard the forlorn but melodious note of a hooting owl indefinitely far: such a sound as the frozen earth would yield if struck with a suitable *plectrum*.
Thoreau, Walden, p. 292.

2. Something like or likened to a plectrum. (*a*†) In *anat.*: (1) The stylohyal bone, or styloid process of the temporal bone. (2) The uvula. (3) The tongue. *Encyc. Dict.* (*b*) In *ornith.*, a spur or claw on the wing or foot. (*c*) In *entom.*, a small bristle or point on the costal margin of the wing, and standing out from it.

pled (pled). An occasional (less correct) preterit and past participle of *plead*.

pledge (plej), *n.* [< ME. *plegge*, < OF. *plege*, *pleige*, *plaige*, *ploige*, *ploge*, *plage*, m., = Pr. *plieu*, *pleya* = OIt. *pieggio*, a pledge, surety, bail (person or thing), prob. < LL. **præbium*, found only in ML. forms reflecting the Rom., *plivium*, *pluvium*, *plegium*, neut., a pledge, surety, *plirius*, *plegius*, m., one who gives a pledge, surety (cf. L. *præbrum*, in pl. *præbra*, an amulet), < L. *præbere*, proffer, offer, give, grant, afford (*præbere fidem*, give promise or security): see *prebend*, and cf. *plevin*, from the same source. Hence *pledge*, *v.*] 1. In *law*: (*a*†) A person who goes surety or gives bail for another; especially, a surety whom early English law required of a plaintiff on bringing an action. After a time "John Doe" and "Richard Roe" did duty as such pledges. (*b*) A bailment of personal property as a security for some debt or engagement. *Story, J.* It differs from a *chattel mortgage* in three essential characteristics: (1) it may be constituted without any contract in writing, merely by delivery of the thing pledged; (2) it requires a delivery of the thing pledged, and is continued only so long as the possession remains with the creditor; (3) it does not generally pass the title to the thing pledged, but gives only a lien to the creditor, and the debtor retains the general property. But, as regards choses in action, the distinction that a *mortgage* is a transfer of the title, while a *pledge* is a mere lien without a transfer of title, does not always hold good; for in most cases a pledge of choses in action can be made effectual only by a transfer of the legal title. (See *mortgage*.) A pledge of a chose in action is now more commonly termed *collateral security*, or *collateral*. (*c*) The thing pawned or delivered as security; a pawn. —2. Anything given or considered as security for the performance of an act; a guaranty. Thus, a man gives his word or makes a promise to another, which is received as a *pledge* for fulfilment; a candidate for parliamentary honors gives promises or *pledges* to support certain measures; the mutual affection of husband and wife is a *pledge* for the faithful performance of the marriage covenant; mutual interest is the best *pledge* for the performance of treaties.

> Him litle answerd th' angry Elfin knight, . . .
> But threw his gauntlet, as a sacred *pledge*,
> His cause in combat the next day to try.
> *Spenser*, F. Q., I. iv. 43.

> I had been insulted by the boy that belonged to the gate, who demanded money of me, and snatched my handkerchief from me as a *pledge*.
> *Pococke*, Description of the East, II. i. 7.

(*a*) Figuratively, a child; offspring.

> 'Tis the curse
> Of great estates to want those *pledges* which
> The poor are happy in: they, in a cottage,
> With joy behold the models of their youth.
> *Fletcher*, Spanish Curate, i. 3.

(*b*) A surety; a hostage.

> Command my eldest son, nay, all my sons,
> As *pledges* of my fealty and love.
> *Shak.*, 2 Hen. VI., v. 1. 50.

> Samuel, their other consort, Powhatan kept for their *pledge*. Quoted in *Capt. John Smith's* Works, I. 213.

(*c*) A formal obligation whereby one voluntarily binds himself to abstain from the use of intoxicating drink.

3. A token or sign of favor, agreement, etc.

> Let it therefore suffice us to receive Sacraments as sure *pledges* of God's favour, signs infallible that the hand of his saving mercy doth thereby reach forth itself towards us. *Hooker*, Eccles. Polity, v., App. 1.

> Here, boldly take
> My hand in *pledge*, this hand, that never yet
> Was given away to any.
> *Fletcher*, Faithful Shepherdess, i. 3.

4. An expression of good will, or a promise of friendship and support, conveyed by drinking together; hence, in a more general sense, the act of drinking together; the drinking of a health.

> Suppose that you winked at our friends drinking those *pledges*. *Scott*.

To hold in pledge, to keep as security.—**To put in pledge**, to pawn.—**To take the pledge**, to bind one's self to observe principles of temperance or of total abstinence from intoxicating drink.=**Syn. 2.** *Covenant*, etc. See *promise*, *n.*, and *earnest*.

pledge (plej), *v. t.*; pret. and pp. *pledged*, ppr. *pledging*. [< ME. *pleggen*, < OF. *pleiger*, ML. reflex *plegiare*, *plegire* (beside *plevire*, *plivire*, etc., after the OF. *plevir*, pledge: see *plevin*); from the noun: see *pledge*, *n.*] 1. To give as a pledge or pawn; deposit in pawn; deposit or leave in possession of a person as security. See *pledge*, *n.*—2. To give or formally and solemnly offer as a guaranty or security.

> Aud so her father *pledg'd* his word,
> And so his promise plight.
> *The Gay Goss-Hawk* (Child's Ballads, III. 281).

> *Abs.* But my vows are *pledged* to her.
> *Sir A.* Let her foreclose, Jack; let her foreclose; they are not worth redeeming. *Sheridan*, The Rivals, ii. 1.

> We mutually *pledge* to each other our lives, our fortunes, and our sacred honour. *Declaration of Independence*.

3. To bind to something by a pledge, promise, or engagement; engage solemnly: as, to *pledge* one's self.

> Here [shall] Patriot Truth her glorious precepts draw,
> *Pledged* to Religion, Liberty, and Law.
> *Story*, Life and Letters, I. 127.

4†. To guarantee the performance of by or as by a pledge.

> Yes, I accept her, for she well deserves it;
> And here, to *pledge* my vow, I give my hand.
> *Shak.*, 3 Hen. VI., iii. 3. 250.

5. To give assurance of friendship to, or promise friendship to, by or in the act of drinking; hence, to drink a health to or with. [The use of the word in this sense is said to have arisen from the fact that, in the rude and lawless society of former times, the person who called upon another to drink virtually pledged himself that the other would not be attacked while drinking or poisoned by the liquor.]

> *Pledge* me, my Friend, and drink till thou be'st Wise.
> *Cowley*, Ode.

> I'll *pledge* you, Sir: so, there 's for your ale, and farewell.
> *Cotton*, in Walton's Angler, ii. 228.

> Sipping beverage divine,
> And *pledging* with contented smack
> The Mermaid in the Zodiac.
> *Keats*, Lines on the Mermaid Tavern.

> Reach me my golden cup that stands by thee,
> And *pledge* me in it first for courtesy.
> *M. Arnold*, Tristram and Iseult.

6. To assure solemnly or in a binding manner; guarantee.

> Ye have *plegged* me vpon youre lyves that I shall have no drede of deth. *Merlin* (E. E. T. S.), i. 35.

=**Syn. 1-3.** To pawn, hypothecate. See *plight*¹, *v.*

pledge-cup (plej'kup), *n.* A cup for drinking healths or pledges; especially, a large cup designed to pass from hand to hand.

pledgee (ple-jē'), *n.* [< *pledge* + *-ee*¹.] The person to whom anything is pledged.

pledgeless (plej'les), *a.* [< *pledge* + *-less*.] Having no pledges.

pledgeor (plej'or), *n.* [< *pledge* + *-or*¹.] In *law*, one who gives a pledge; a pledger.

pledger (plej'ėr), *n.* 1. One who pledges or offers a pledge.

> If a pawnbroker receives plate or jewels as a pledge or security for the repayment of money lent thereon at a day certain, he has them upon an express contract or condition to restore them if the *pledger* performs his part by redeeming them in due time. *Blackstone*, Com., II. xxx.

2. One who accepts an invitation to drink after another, or who pledges himself, his honor, word, etc., to another by drinking with him.

> If the *pledger* be inwardlye sicke, or have some infirmitie, whereby too much drinke doe empayre his health.
> *Gascoigne*, Delicate Diet for Droonkardes.

pledge-ring (plej'ring), *n.* A ring capable of being divided into three parts, each of which could be worn separately, one part for each of the parties to an agreement and one for the witness.

pledgery† (plej'ėr-i), *n.* [< OF. *plegerie*, *pleigerie*, etc., < *pleger*, pledge: see *pledge*, *v.*] Suretyship. *Bailey*, 1731.

pledget (plej'et), *n.* [Perhaps for **pludget*, assibilated dim. of *plug*: see *plug*.] A small plug; in *surg.*, a small flat mass of lint, absorbent cotton, etc., used, for example, to lay over a wound to absorb the matter discharged.

> Get my rollers, bolsters, and *pledgets* armed.
> *Middleton*, Anything for a Quiet Life, ii. 4.

pleet†, *n.* An early modern English and Middle English spelling of *plea*.

Plegadis (pleg'a-dis), *n.* [NL. (Kaup, 1829).] A genus of *Ibididæ*, having the plumage more or less metallic and iridescent; the glossy ibises. The type is the common bay ibis, *P. falcinellus*. *P. guarauna* is the white-faced ibis of America.

Glossy Ibis (*Plegadis falcinellus*).

plegaphonia (pleg-a-fō'ni-ä), *n.* [NL., < Gr. πληγή, a blow, stroke, + -φωνία, < φωνεῖν, produce a sound or tone.] The sound yielded in auscultation of the chest when the larynx is percussed.

pleghan (pleg'an), *n.* [Cf. Gael. *ploicean*, a plump-cheeked boy.] A stripling; a lad; a baflin. [Scotch.]

> The ordinary farmer's household consisted of a big man, a little man, and a *pleghan*, i. e. a lad of fifteen to drive the plough. *Quarterly Rev.*, CXLVI. 39.

plegometer (ple-gom'e-tėr), *n.* [< Gr. πληγή, a stroke, + μέτρον, measure.] Same as *pleximeter*.

Pleiad (plī'ad), *n.*; pl. *Pleiads*, *Pleiades* (-adz, -a-dēz). [< L. *Pleias*, *Pleias* (-*ad*-), < Gr. Πληϊάς, Πλειάς (-αδ-), pl. Πλειάδες, one of the Pleiads or Seven Stars, traditionally so called as indicating by their rising the time of safe navigation; < πλεῖν, sail.] One of a close group of small stars in the constellation Taurus, very conspicuous on winter evenings, about twenty-four degrees north of the equator, and coming to the meridian at midnight in the middle of November. For some unknown reason, there were anciently said to be seven Pleiads, although only six were conspicuous then as now; hence the suggestion of a lost Pleiad. In mythology the Pleiads were said to be the daughters of Atlas and Pleione, and were named Alcyone, Merope, Celæno, Electra, Sterope or Asterope, Taygeta, and Maia. These names, with those of the parents, have been applied by modern astronomers since Ricciolo (A. D. 1665) to the principal stars of the group. Four of the brightest stars are at the corners of a trapezoid, with one in the base near the star at the northern angle, and one outside the trapezoid, like a handle to a dipper. Alcyone, the brightest of the group, is a greenish star, of magnitude 3.0, at the east end of the base of the trapezoid; it is η Tauri. Electra is a very white star, of magnitude 3.8, at the westernmost corner of the trapezoid, on the short side opposite the base. Taygeta is a yellowish star, of magnitude 4.4, at the northern corner on the base. Merope is a yellowish star, of magnitude 4.2, at the southernmost corner, not on the base. It is surrounded by a faint nebula, discovered by Tempel many years ago, and visible with a telescope of moderate dimensions. But photographs show that the cluster is also full of invisible wisps and filaments of nebulosity, which are for the most part attached to the larger stars. Maia is a yellowish star, of magnitude 4.0, on the base of the trapezoid, close to the northern angle, but not in it. Asterope is a double star, of magnitude 5.7, not very conspicuous, forming an equilateral triangle with Taygeta and Maia, and lying outside of the trapezoid. Celæno is a star of magnitude 5.2, half-way between Electra and Taygeta, just a little outside the western slanting side of the trapezoid. Atlas is a yellowish star, of magnitude 3.8, the second or third brightest in the group, which lies out of the trapezoid, considerably to the east, as in the handle of the dipper. Pleione is a star of magnitude 5.1, a little north of Atlas.

> Canst thou bind the sweet influences of *Pleiades*, or loose the bands of Orion? Job xxxviii. 31.

> Many a night I saw the *Pleiads*, rising thro' the mellow shade,
> Glitter like a swarm of fire-flies tangled in a silver braid.
> *Tennyson*, Locksley Hall.

plein†, *a.* [ME., < OF. *plein*, F. *plein* = Sp. Pg. *pleno* = It. *pieno*, < L. *plenus*, full: see *plenty*.] Full; perfect. *Chaucer*.

pleinly†, *adv.* [ME. *pleynly*; < *plein* + *-ly*².] Fully. *Chaucer*.

pleio-. For words so beginning and not found below, see forms beginning with *plio-*.

pleiochasium (plī-ǫ-kā'si-um), *n.* [NL., < Gr. πλείων, more, + χάσις, separation, < χαίνειν, gape, yawn: see *chasm*.] In *bot.*, a cyme with three or more lateral axes. Also called *multiparous cyme*.

pleiomorphic (plī-ǫ-môr'fik), *a.* [< *pleiomorphism* + *-ic*.] In *bot.*, exhibiting or characterized by pleiomorphism.

pleiomorphism (plī-ǫ-môr'fizm), *n.* [< *pleiomorphy* + *-ism*.] In *bot.*, the occurrence of more than one independent stage or form in the life-cycle of a species, as in certain uredineous fungi, such as *Puccinia graminis*, which passes through three stages. See *heterœcism*, *Puccinia*, *Uredineæ*, etc. Also spelled *pleomorphism*.

pleiomorphy (plī'ǫ-môr-fi), *n.* [< Gr. πλείων, more, + μορφή, form.] 1. In *bot.*, same as *pleiomorphism*.—2. In *vegetable teratol.*, the state of a normally irregular flower when it becomes regular by the increase in the number of its irregular elements. It is due to an excessive development. Compare *peloria*. Also spelled *pleomorphy*.

pleiophyllous (plī-ǫ-fil'us), *a.* [< Gr. πλείων, more, + φύλλον, leaf.] In *bot.*, exhibiting or characterized by pleiophylly; also, having several or many leaves.

pleiophylly (plī'ǫ-fil-i), *n.* [< *pleiophyll-ous* + *-y*³.] In *vegetable teratol.*, a condition in which there is an abnormal increase in the number of leaves starting from a particular point; also, that condition in which the number of leaflets in a compound leaf is abnormally increased. *Masters.*

pleiosporous (plī'ọ̄-spō-rus), *a.* [< Gr. πλείων, more, + σπόρος, seed: see *spore.*] In *bot.*, having or containing several or many spores.

pleiotaxy (plī'ọ̄-tak-si), *n.* [< Gr. πλείων, more, + τάξις, arrangement, order.] In *bot.*, a multiplication of the number of whorls—that is, the production of additional distinct whorls, as in many so-called double flowers. Pleiotaxy may affect the bracts, calyx, corolla, andrœcium, gynœcium, or perianth as a whole.

pleiothalamous (plī-ọ̄-thal'a̤-mus), *a.* [< Gr. πλείων, more, + θάλαμος, a bedchamber.] In *bot.*, several- or many-chambered or -celled.

pleiotrachea (plī''ọ̄-trā-kē'ạ̈), *n.* [NL., < Gr. πλείων, more, + τραχεῖα, the windpipe.] In *bot.*, a membranous tube or trachea containing a compound spiral fiber. *Cooke.*

Pleistocene (plīs'tọ̄-sēn), *n.* [< Gr. πλεῖστος, most (superl. of πολύς, much), + καινός, recent.] The name given by geologists, with more or less vagueness, to the lower division of the Quaternary or Post-tertiary deposits, or to that division which cannot properly be included under the designation *recent.* See *Post-tertiary*, *Tertiary*, and *Quaternary*.

plek†, *n.* A Middle English form of *pleck*.

plenal† (plē'na̤l), *a.* [< ML. **plenalis* (in adv. *plenaliter*), < L. *plenus*, full (see *plein* and *plenty*), + *-al.*] Full; complete.

> This free and *plenall* act I make.
> *J. Beaumont*, Psyche, ix. 231.

plenally† (plē'na̤l-i), *adv.* Fully; entirely.

> Yours *plenally* devoted, Thomas Heyvvood.
> *Heywood*, Ep. Ded. to Fair Maid of the West.

plenar†, *a.* See *plener*.

plenargyrite (plẹ̄-när'ji-rīt), *n.* [< L. *plenus*, full, + Gr. ἄργυρος, silver, + *-ite*[2].] A sulphid of bismuth and silver found near Schapbach in Baden: it is supposed to be similar in form to miargyrite.

plenarily (plē'nạ̄-ri-li), *adv.* In a plenary manner; fully; completely.

plenariness (plē'nạ̄-ri-nes), *n.* The state of being plenary; fullness; completeness.

plenarly†, *adv.* See *plenerly*.

plenarty (plē'nạ̈r-ti), *n.* [< OF. *plenerete*, *plenierte*, fullness, < *plenier*, < ML. *plenarius*, full, entire: see *plenary*. Cf. *plener.*] The state of an ecclesiastical benefice when occupied; occupancy by an incumbent: opposed to *vacancy* or *avoidance:* as, the plea of *plenarty* (that is, the plea that the benefice was already filled by valid appointment) was urged.

> When the clerk was once instituted . . . the church became absolutely full; so the usurper by such *plenarty*, arising from his own presentation, became in fact seised of the advowson. *Blackstone*, Com., III. xvi.

plenary (plē'nạ̄-ri), *a.* and *n.* [< ML. *plenarius*, entire, < L. *plenus*, full: see *plenty*. Cf. *plener.*] **I.** *a.* **1.** Full; entire; complete: as, a *plenary* license; *plenary* consent; *plenary* indulgence.

> In a vawght vnderneth ys the very self Place wher our blyssyd lady was born. And ther ys *Plenarie* Remission.
> *Torkington*, Diarie of Eng. Travell, p. 31.

> The King, to shew his *plenary* Authority of being at full Age, removed the Archbishop of York from being Lord Chancellor, and put in his Place William Wickham, Bishop of Winchester. *Baker*, Chronicles, p. 146.

> Do not confound yourself with Multiplicity of Authors; two is enough upon any Science, provided they be *plenary* and orthodox. *Howell*, Letters, I. v. 9.

2. In *law*, noting an ordinary suit which passes through all its gradations and formal steps: opposed to *summary*. Plenary causes in the ecclesiastical courts are now three—(*a*) suits for ecclesiastical dilapidations; (*b*) suits relating to seats or sitting-places in churches; and (*c*) suits for tithes.

> The cause is made a *plenary* cause.
> *Aylife*, Parergon. (*Latham.*)

3. Having full power; plenipotentiary.

> The chambers called into existence by the League of the Three Kings met at Erfurt in March, 1850. Austria, as an answer to the challenge, summoned a *plenary* assembly of the German Diet to meet at Frankfort in September.
> *Quarterly Rev.*, CXLV. 334.

Plenary indulgence, the remission of all the temporal punishment due to sin. See *indulgence*, 4.—**Plenary inspiration**, complete inspiration of Scripture in all its utterances. See *inspiration*, 3.

> What is meant by "*plenary inspiration*"? A divine influence full and sufficient to secure its end. The end in this case secured is the perfect infallibility of the Scriptures in every part, as a record of fact and doctrine, both in thought and verbal expression.
> *A. A. Hodge*, Outlines of Theology, iv. 7.

Plenary missal. See *missal*.

II.† *n.* In *law*, decisive procedure. *Ayliffe.*

plener†, *a.* [ME., also *plenar;* < OF. *plenier*, F. *plénier* = Pr. *plener*, *plenier* = Sp. *llenero* = Pg. It. *plenario*, < ML. *plenarius*, full, entire: see *plenary.*] Full; abundant; plenary.

> Anon conueid to sitte att the table,
> Thys fest *plener* and ryght delectable.
> *Rom. of Partenay* (E. E. T. S.), l. 2751.

> Oute of this woo he will you wynne,
> To plese hym in more *plener* place.
> *York Plays*, p. 80.

plenere†, *adv.* [ME., < *plener*, *a.*] Fully; completely.

> Whan the peple was *plenere* comen, the porter vnpynned the ʒate. *Piers Plowman* (B), xi. 108.

> Now was Jason a seemely man withalle, . . .
> And goodly of his speche and famulere,
> And koude of love al craft and arte *plenere*
> Withoute boke. *Chaucer*, Good Women, l. 1607.

plenerly†, *adv.* [ME., also *plenarly*, *plenerliche;* < *plener* + *-ly*[2].] Fully; completely.

> Not only upon ten ne twelve,
> But *plenerliche* upon us alle.
> *Gower*, MS. Soc. Antiq. 134, f. 34. (*Halliwell.*)

> Wherfore I say yow *plenerly* in a clause.
> *Chaucer*, Merchant's Tale, l. 187. (*Harl. MS.*)

plenicorn (plen'i-kôrn), *a.* [< L. *plenus*, full, + *cornu*, horn.] Solid-horned, as a ruminant: opposed to *cavicorn*.

plenilunar† (plen-i-lū'nạ̈r), *a.* [< *plenilune* + *-ar*[3].] Pertaining to the full moon.

plenilunary† (plen-i-lū'na̤-ri), *a.* Same as *plenilunar*. See the quotation under *interlunary*.

plenilune† (plen'i-lūn), *n.* [< L. *plenilunium*, the time of full moon, < *plenus*, full, + *luna*, moon: see *luna.*] The full moon.

> Whose glory (like a lasting *plenilune*)
> Seems ignorant of what it is to wane.
> *B. Jonson*, Cynthia's Revels, v. 3.

plenipo† (plen'i-pō), *n.* A colloquial abbreviation of *plenipotentiary*.

> I'll give all my silver amongst the drawers, make a bonfire before the door, say the *plenipos* have signed the peace, and the Bank of England 's grown honest.
> *Vanbrugh*, Provoked Wife, iii. 1.

plenipotence (plẹ̄-nip'ọ̄-tẹns), *n.* [= Sp. Pg. *plenipotencia* = It. *plenipotenza;* as *plenipoten(t)* + *-ce.*] Fullness or completeness of power.

> A whole parliament . . . endewed with the *plenipotence* of a free nation. *Milton*, Eikonoklastes, § 6.

plenipotency (plē-nip'ọ̄-tẹn-si), *n.* Same as *plenipotence*.

plenipotent (plẹ̄-nip'ọ̄-tẹnt), *a.* [< ML. **plenipoten(t-)s*, having full power, < L. *plenus*, full, + *poten(t-)s*, having power: see *potent.*] Possessing full power.

> My substitutes I send ye, and create
> *Plenipotent* on earth, of matchless might
> Issuing from me. *Milton*, P. L., x. 404.

plenipotentiary (plen''i-pọ̄-ten'shi-ạ̄-ri), *a.* and *n.* [= F. *plénipotentiaire* = Sp. Pg. *plenipotenciario* = It. *plenipotenziario*, < ML. *plenipotentiarius*, < **plenipoten(t-)s*, having full power: see *plenipotent.*] **I.** *a.* Invested with, having, or bestowing full power: as, *plenipotentiary* authority; ministers *plenipotentiary*.

> I hear the Peace betwixt Spain and Holland is absolutely concluded by the *Plenipotentiary* Ministers at Munster.
> *Howell*, Letters, ii. 43.

II. *n.*; pl. *plenipotentiaries* (-riz). A person invested with full power to transact any business; specifically, an ambassador or envoy to a foreign court, furnished with full powers to negotiate a treaty or to transact other business. A plenipotentiary is not necessarily accredited to any specified foreign court. Frequently meetings of plenipotentiaries for concluding peace, negotiating treaties, etc., are held in some neutral place, so that they may conduct their negotiations and despatch their business uninfluenced by any special power.

> The treaty of Blois had not received the ratification of the Navarrese sovereigns; but it was executed by their *plenipotentiaries*, duly authorized.
> *Prescott*, Ferd. and Isa., ii. 23.

> The terms or propositions of peace should have been fully, frankly, and unreservedly laid before the *plenipotentiaries* assembled at Utrecht.
> *Lecky*, Eng. in 18th Cent., i.

=**Syn.** See *ambassador*, 1.

plenish (plen'ish), *v. t.* [< OF. *pleniss-*, stem of certain parts of *plenir*, < ML. **plenire*, fill up, < L. *plenus*, full: see *plenty*. Cf. *replenish.*] **1.** To fill.

> How art thou then for spread tables and *plenished* flaggon's? *Reeve*, God's Plea for Nineveh (1657). (*Latham.*)

> He must be a Jew, intellectually cultured, morally fervid—in all this a nature ready to be *plenished* from Mordecai's. *George Eliot*, Daniel Deronda, xxxviii.

2. To furnish; provide (a dwelling) with furniture, etc.; stock (a farm) with cattle, horses, farm implements, etc.

[Old Eng. and Scotch in both senses.]

plenishing (plen'ish-ing), *n.* [Verbal n. of *plenish*, *v.*] Household furniture or furnishing. [Scotch.]

> We hae gude *plenishing* o' our ain, if we had the cast o' a cart to bring it down. *Scott*, Old Mortality, viii.

Outsight plenishing. See *outsight*.

plenishing-nail (plen'ish-ing-nāl), *n.* In *carp.*, a large flooring-nail.

plenist (plē'nist), *n.* [< *plenum* + *-ist.*] One who maintains that all space is full of matter; one who denies the possibility of a vacuum or the reality of empty space.

> The generality of the *plenists* . . . did not take a vacuum in so strict a sense. *Boyle*, Works, I. 75.

plenitude (plen'i-tūd), *n.* [< F. *plénitude* = Sp. *plenitud* = Pg. *plenitude* = It *plenitudine*, < L. *plenitudo*, fullness, < *plenus*, full: see *plenty.*] **1.** Fullness; abundance; completeness.

> In him a *plenitude* of subtle matter,
> Applied to cautels, all strange forms receives.
> *Shak.*, Lover's Complaint, l. 302.

> You know the *plenitude* of the power and right of a king, as well as the circle of his office and duty.
> *Bacon*, Advancement of Learning, ii. 280.

> A clime
> Where life and rapture flow in *plenitude* sublime.
> *Wordsworth*, Desultory Stanzas.

2†. Repletion; animal fullness; plethora. *Arbuthnot.*—**The moon in her plenitude**, in *her.*, the full moon.

plenitudinarian† (plen-i-tū-di-nā'ri-a̤n), *n.* [< L. *plenitudo* (*-din-*), plenitude, + *-arian.*] A plenist. *Shaftesbury.*

plenitudinary (plen-i-tū'di-nā-ri), *a.* [< L. *plenitudo* (*-din-*), plenitude, + *-ary.*] Characterized by plenitude, fullness, or completeness.

plente†, *n.* A Middle English form of *plenty*.

plenteous (plen'tẹ̄-us), *a.* [< ME. *plenteus*, *plentevous*, *plentivous*, *plentefous*, *plentuos*, < OF. *plentious*, *plentivos*, *plentivous*, *plentevous*, *plentuous*, etc., < *plentif*, plenty, < *plente*, plenty: see *plenty.*] **1.** Abundant; copious; full; plentiful; wholly sufficient for every purpose or need: as, a *plenteous* supply of provisions.

> I shall think it a most *plenteous* crop
> To glean the broken ears after the man
> That the main harvest reaps.
> *Shak.*, As you Like it, iii. 5. 101.

2. Yielding abundance; fruitful; productive.

> Toward that land he toke the waye full right,
> Whiche was callid a *plentevous* contre.
> *Generydes* (E. E. T. S.), l. 1031.

> The seven *plenteous* years. Gen. xli. 34.

3. Bountifully or abundantly supplied; well provided for; rich; characterized by plenty: formerly sometimes followed by *of* before the thing that abounds or is plentiful: as, *plenteous* in grace; *plenteous of* good fish.

> It is a fair Cytee, and *plentevous of* alle Godes.
> *Mandeville*, Travels, p. 211.

> Thys Ile ys a grett Ile and a *Plenteous of* all maner of thynges. *Torkington*, Diarie of Eng. Travell, p. 20.

> The Lord shall make thee *plenteous* in goods.
> Deut. xxviii. 11.

> The *plenteous* horn
> Of autumn, filled and running o'er
> With fruit, and flower, and golden corn!
> *Whittier*, Autumn Festival.

4†. Bounteous or bountiful in giving; generous; open-handed.

> Ne beth *plentyuous* to the pore as pure charite wolde.
> *Piers Plowman* (B), x. 80.

> Be a man neuer so valiaunt, so wise, so liberall or *plentuous*, . . . if he be sene to exercise iniustyce, . . . it is often remembred. *Sir T. Elyot*, The Governour, iii. 4.

=**Syn. 1.** *Copious*, etc. See *ample*.

plenteously (plen'tẹ̄-us-li), *adv.* In a plenteous manner; copiously; plentifully; bountifully; generously.

> Al myhten tho same thinges betere and more *plentevously* ben couth in the mowth of the poeple.
> *Chaucer*, Boëthius, i. prose 5.

plenteousness (plen'tẹ̄-us-nes), *n.* The state of being plenteous; abundance; copious supply; plenty.

plentiful (plen'ti-fụl), *a.* [< *plenty* + *-ful.*] **1.** Existing in great plenty; copious; abundant; ample.

> The satirical rogue says here that old men have grey beards, . . . and that they have a *plentiful* lack of wit.
> *Shak.*, Hamlet, ii. 2. 202.

> Alcibiades . . . a young man of noble birth, excellent education, and a *plentiful* fortune.
> *Swift*, Contests and Dissensions, ii.

> Can anybody remember when sensible men, and the right sort of men, and the right sort of women were *plentiful?* *Emerson*, Works and Days.

2. Yielding abundance; affording ample supply; fruitful.

If it be a long winter, it is commonly a more *plentiful* year. *Bacon*, Nat. Hist.

For as *plentiful* springs are fittest, and best become large aquaducts, so doth much virtue such a steward and officer as a Christian. *Donne*, Letters, lxxxix.

3†. Lavish.

He that is *plentiful* in expenses of all kinds will hardly be preserved from decay. *Bacon*, Expense (ed. 1887).

=**Syn.** 1 and 2. Profuse, luxuriant. *Plentiful* is essentially the same as *plenteous*. See comparison under *ample*.

plentifully (plen'ti-fụl-i), *adv.* In a plentiful manner; copiously; abundantly; with ample supply.

Berne is *plentifully* furnished with water, there being a great multitude of handsome fountains planted at set distances. *Addison*, Remarks on Italy.

Sometimes the Cashit sent for me to dine with him, when the drams went round very *plentifully* whilst we were eating. *Pococke*, Description of the East, I. 59.

plentifulness (plen'ti-fụl-nes), *n.* The state of being plentiful; abundance.

plentify† (plen'ti-fī), *v. t.* [< *plenty* + *-fy*.] To make plenteous; enrich.

For alms (like levain) make our goods to rise,
And God His owne with blessings *plentifies*.
Sylvester, tr. of Du Bartas's Weeks, ii., The Vocation.

plentivous†, *adv.* A Middle English form of *plenteous*.

plenty (plen'ti), *n.* and *a.* [< ME. *plentee*, *plente*, < OF. *plente*, *plentet*, < L. *plenita(t-)s*, fullness, repletion, abundance, < *plenus*, full; cf. Gr. πλέως, full; akin to E. *full*: see *full*[1].] **I.** *n.* **1.** Fullness; abundance; copiousness; a full or adequate supply; sufficiency.

There ben Hilles where men geten gret *plentee* of Manna, in gretter habundance than in ony other Contree. *Mandeville*, Travels, p. 152.

The fyer towards the element flew,
Out of his mouth, where was great *plentie*.
Ballad of King Arthur (Child's Ballads, I. 239).

God give thee . . . *plenty* of corn and wine. Gen. xxvii. 28.

They have great *plenty* of very large carp in this river. *Pococke*, Description of the East, II. ii. 86.

2. Abundance of things necessary for man; the state in which enough is had and enjoyed.

It ne may han togidere al the *plente* of the lyf. *Chaucer*, Boëthius, v. prose 6.

Ye shall eat in *plenty* and be satisfied, and praise the name of the Lord. Joel ii. 26.

Thy lopp'd branches point
Thy two sons forth; . . . whose issue
Promises Britain peace and *plenty*.
Shak., Cymbeline, v. 5. 458.

3. A time of abundance; an era of plenty.

Peace,
Dear nurse of arts, *plenties*, and joyful births.
Shak., Hen. V., v. 2. 35.

If a man will goe at Christmas to gather Cherries in Kent, though there be plenty in Summer, he may be deceiued; so here these *plenties* haue each their seasons. *Capt. John Smith's* Works, II. 196.

Horn of plenty. See *horn*.=**Syn.** *Plenty*, *Abundance*, *Exuberance*, *Profusion*. These words are in the order of strength. *Plenty* is a full supply, all that can possibly be needed. *Abundance* is a great plenty, as much as can be wanted or more. *Exuberance* is an overflowing plenty, an abundance that bursts out with fullness: as, the *exuberance* of the harvest. *Profusion* is a plenty that is poured or scattered abroad; *profusion* naturally applies to a large number of units: as, a *plenty* of food; a *profusion* of things to eat. *Exuberance* and *profusion* may mean an amount that needs to be restrained or reduced. See *ample*.

Enough is a *plenty*. *Old proverb.*

All they did cast in of their *abundance*; but she of her want. Mark xii. 44.

With an *exuberance* of thought and a splendour of diction which more than satisfied the highly raised expectation of the audience, he [Burke] described the character and institutions of the natives of India. *Macaulay*, Warren Hastings.

One boundless blush, one white-empurpled shower
Of mingled blossoms, where the raptur'd eye
Hurries from joy to joy, and, hid beneath
The fair *profusion*, yellow Autumn spies.
Thomson, Spring, l. 112.

II. *a.* Being in abundance; plentiful: an elliptical use of the noun, now chiefly colloquial.

Thei ordeyned hir a litier vpon two palfrayes, and leide ther-ynne fresch gras and erbes *plente* and clothes, and than leide her ther-ynne softely. *Merlin* (E. E. T. S.), ii. 301.

For he maye not lese at the moost but a lyne or an hoke: of whyche he maye haue store *plentee* of his owne makynge, as this symple treatyse shall teche hym. *Juliana Berners*, Treatyse of Fysshynge, fol. 2.

They seem formed for those countries where shrubs are *plenty* and water scarce. *Goldsmith.*

When labourers are *plenty*, their wages will be low. *Franklin.*

plenum (plē'num), *n.* [< L. *plenum*, neut. of *plenus*, full: see *plenty*.] **1.** The fullness of matter in space: the opposite of *vacuum*: also used to denote fullness in general.—**2.** A quantity of a gaseous body in an inclosed space greater than would remain there under normal atmospheric pressure.—**Plenum method** (or **system**) **of ventilation**, a system in which the air is forced by artificial means into the space to be ventilated, while vitiated or heated air is forced out by displacement.

plenytide†, *n.* [Irreg. (appar. after *plenitude*) < L. *plenus*, full, + E. *tide*.] A full tide; flood-tide.

Let rowling teares in *pleny-tides* oreflow,
For losse of England's second Cicero.
Greene, Groats-worth of Wit.

pleochroic (plē-ọ-krō'ik), *a.* [< Gr. πλέων, πλείων, more, + χρόα, color, + *-ic*.] Exhibiting pleochroism. The epithet includes *dichroic* and *trichroic*. Also *pleochromatic*, *pleochroous*, *polychroic*.—**Pleochroic halo** or **aureole**, a spot within a mineral (for example, biotite) characterized by strong pleochroism. Such spots are frequently observed in sections when examined under the microscope, and are usually immediately associated with microscopic inclusions.

pleochroism (plē-ok'rọ-izm), *n.* [< *pleochro-ic* + *-ism*.] In *crystal.*, the variation in color observed in some crystals when viewed in different directions, due to the fact that the rays having vibrations in different planes suffer absorption in different degrees. In general, a uniaxial crystal may be *dichroic*, or have two axial colors, corresponding respectively to the ordinary ray, whose vibrations are transverse to the axis, and the extraordinary ray, with vibrations parallel to this axis; biaxial crystals may be *trichroic*, and the axial colors are generally taken as those determined by the absorption of the rays which are propagated by vibrations parallel to the three axes of elasticity. Tourmalin is a striking example of a dichroic species, epidote and hornblende of trichroic species. A more general epithet for both is *pleochroic*.

pleochromatic (plē"ọ-krọ-mat'ik), *a.* [< Gr. πλέων, πλείων, more, + χρῶμα(τ-), color, + *-ic*.] Same as *pleochroic*.

pleochromatism (plē-ọ-krō'ma-tizm), *n.* [< *pleochromatic* + *-ism*.] Same as *pleochroism*.

pleochroous (plē-ok'rọ-us), *a.* [< *pleochro-ic* + *-ous*.] Same as *pleochroic*.

plěodont (plē'ọ-dont), *a.* [< Gr. πλέως, full, + ὀδούς (ὀδοντ-) = E. *tooth*.] Solid-toothed: opposed to *cœlodont*.

pleomastia (plē-ọ-mas'ti-ä), *n.* [NL., < Gr. πλέων, more, + μαστός, one of the breasts.] The presence of more than one nipple to one mammary gland.

pleomazia (plē-ọ-mā'zi-ä), *n.* [NL., < Gr. πλέων, πλείων, more, + μαζός, Ionic and epic for μαστός, one of the breasts.] The presence of a greater number of mammary glands than is normal.

pleomorphic (plē-ọ-môr'fik), *a.* [< *pleomorph-y* + *-ic*.] Same as *pleomorphous*. *E. R. Lankester*, Nature, XXXIII. 413.

pleomorphism (plē-ọ-môr'fizm), *n.* [< *pleomorph-y* + *-ism*.] **1.** Same as *polymorphism*. *Nature*, XXX. 433.—**2.** Same as *pleiomorphism*.

pleomorphous (plē-ọ-môr'fus), *a.* [< *pleomorph-y* + *-ous*.] Having the property of pleomorphism; polymorphic.

pleomorphy (plē'ọ-môr-fi), *n.* [< Gr. πλέων, πλείων, more, + μορφή, form.] **1.** Same as *polymorphism*.—**2.** Same as *pleiomorphy*.

pleon[1] (plē'on), *n.* [NL., < Gr. πλέων, πλείων, more: see *plus*.] In *bot.*, a term proposed by Nägeli for those aggregates of molecules which cannot be increased or diminished in size without changing their chemical nature, as distinguished from *micellæ*, or aggregates that can be so increased or diminished. See *micella*.

pleon[2] (plē'on), *n.* [NL., < Gr. πλέων, ppr. of πλέειν, πλεῖν, sail, swim.] **1.** In *Crustacea*, the abdomen: distinguished from *cephalon* (head) and *pereion* (thorax). *C. Spence Bate*, Encyc. Brit., VI. 634.—**2.** The tail-spine or telson of some crustaceans, as the king-crab: so named by Owen, on the supposition that it represents the abdomen: correlated with *thoracetron* and *cephaletron*.

pleonal (plē'ọ-nal), *a.* [< *pleon*[2] + *-al*.] Of or pertaining to the pleon or abdomen of a crustacean. [Rare.]

pleonasm (plē'ọ-nazm), *n.* [= F. *pléonasme* = Sp. Pg. It. *pleonasmo*, < L. *pleonasmus*, < Gr. πλεονασμός, abundance, exaggeration, in gram. pleonasm, < πλεονάζειν, be or have too much, abound, < πλέων, πλείων, more, compar. of πολύς, much: see *plus*.] **1.** Redundancy of language; the use of more words than are necessary to express an idea. Pleonasm may be justifiable when the intention is to present thoughts with particular perspicuity or force.

The first surplusage the Greekes call *Pleonasmus* (I call him too full speech), and is no great fault: as if one should say, I heard it with mine eares, and saw it with mine eyes, as if a man could heare with his heeles, or see with his nose. *Puttenham*, Arte of Eng. Poesie, p. 264.

2. A redundant phrase or expression; an instance of redundancy of language.

Harsh compositions, *pleonasms* of words, tautological repetitions. *Burton*, Anat. of Mel., p. 25.

3. In *med.*, excess in number or size.=**Syn.** 1. *Pleonasm*, *Verbosity*, *Tautology*, *Circumlocution*, *Periphrasis*, *Verbiage*, *Redundancy*. "By *pleonasm* is meant the employment of more words than usual, or of redundant words. When properly employed, it is productive of a high degree of emphasis. . . . By *Verbosity* is meant an excessive use of words; it arises from a natural gift of fluent expression, which has not been sufficiently chastened and corrected. . . . *Tautology* arises from verbosity, and may be defined as the repetition of the same idea in different words. . . . *Circumlocution* is another characteristic of verbosity; it means a roundabout mode of speech, where, instead of a direct statement of meaning, the words are multiplied to an unnecessary extent. When properly employed, this is a recognized figure of speech, *periphrasis*. . . . *Periphrasis* is also known as *circumlocution*, but the term *periphrasis* generally refers to those cases where the figure is used with effect, while *circumlocution* refers to its faulty use. *Periphrasis* may be defined as naming a thing indirectly by means of some well-known attribute, or characteristic, or attendant circumstance." *J. De Mille*, Rhetoric, §§ 27, 28, 29, 132, 218. *Verbiage* and *verbosity* are contemptuous words, *verbiage* being more often applied to the things said or written that are verbose: as, his speech was mere *verbiage*. *Pleonasm* and *periphrasis* are terms of rhetoric, with some general use; the others are in common use. *Redundancy* expresses without contempt the fact that more words are used than are necessary.

A work on style might fitly take, from these documents which our Government annually lays before all the world, warning instances of confusions, and illogicalities, and *pleonasms*. *H. Spencer*, Study of Sociol., p. 268.

A relentless clock that has curbed the exuberant *verbosity* of many a lecturer before me. *Nature*, XXX. 135.

"In fine," added he, with his usual *tautology*, "it is right that a man should do his duty." *Motley*, Dutch Republic, I. 279.

The *circumlocutions* which are substituted for technical phrases are clear, neat, and exact. *Macaulay*, Dryden.

As the master [Pope] had made it an axiom to avoid what was mean and low, so the disciples endeavored to escape from what was common. This they contrived by the ready expedient of the *periphrasis*. They called everything something else. *Lowell*, Study Windows, p. 392.

Verbiage may indicate observation, but not thinking. *Irving.*

He [Wordsworth] . . . lacked the critical sagacity or the hardy courage to condemn and strip away his own *redundancies*. *D. G. Mitchell*, Bound Together, p. 104.

pleonast (plē'ọ-nast), *n.* [< LGr. πλεόναστος, abundant, < Gr. πλεονάζειν, abound: see *pleonasm*.] One who uses more words than are needed; one given to redundancy in speech or writing.

Ere the mellifluous *pleonast* had done oiling his paradox with fresh polysyllables . . . he met with a curious interruption. *C. Reade*, Hard Cash, xxv. (*Davies.*)

pleonaste (plē'ọ-nast), *n.* [So called in allusion to the four facets sometimes found on each solid angle of the octahedron; < LGr. πλεόναστος, abundant, rich, < Gr. πλεονάζειν, abound: see *pleonasm*.] In *mineral.*, same as *ceylonite*. See *spinel*.

pleonastic (plē-ọ-nas'tik), *a.* [= Sp. *pleonástico* = Pg. *pleonastico*, < Gr. *πλεοναστικός, redundant, < πλεόναστος, verbal adj. of πλεονάζειν, abound: see *pleonasm*.] Characterized by pleonasm or redundancy; of the nature of pleonasm; redundant.

pleonastical (plē-ọ-nas'ti-kal), *a.* [< *pleonastic* + *-al*.] Same as *pleonastic*.

pleonastically (plē-ọ-nas'ti-kal-i), *adv.* In a pleonastic manner; with redundancy.

pleonexia (plē-ọ-nek'si-ä), *n.* [NL., < Gr. πλεονεξία, greediness, < πλεονέκτης, greedy, grasping, having or claiming more than one's due, < πλέων, πλείων, more, + ἔχειν, hold, have.] Morbid greediness or selfishness.

pleopod (plē'ọ-pod), *n.* [< Gr. πλέειν, swim, + πούς (ποδ-) = E. *foot*.] One of the abdominal limbs of a crustacean; a swimmeret. The pleopods are the typical natatory limbs, or swimming-feet, succeeding the pereiopods or walking-feet.

pleopodite (plẹ-op'ọ-dīt), *n.* [< *pleopod* + *-ite*[2].] A pleopod.

pleroma (plẹ-rō'mä), *n.* [NL., < Gr. πλήρωμα, a filling up, < πληροῦν, fill up, < πλήρης, full: see *plenty*.] **1.** Fullness; abundance; plenitude: in *gnosticism*, the spiritual world, or world of light, including the body of eons.

In his system he [Heracleon] appears to have regarded the divine nature as a vast abyss in whose *pleroma* were æons of different orders and degrees—emanations from the source of being. *Encyc. Brit.*, XI. 861.

2. In *bot.*, same as *plerome*.

pleromatic (plē-rọ-mat'ik), *a.* [< *pleroma(t-)* + *-ic*.] Pertaining to the pleroma or fullness of divine being.

plerome (plē'rōm), *n.* [NL. (Hanstein, 1868), < Gr. πλήρωμα, a filling up: see *pleroma*.] **1.** In *gnosticism*, same as *pleroma*.—**2.** In *bot.*, the cylinder or shaft of nascent fibrovascular elements at the growing-points of the axis of plants.

Enclosed by this [the periblem] is a central cellular mass, out of which the fibro-vascular bundles and the structures of the central part of the shoot or root are formed; this has been termed *plerome*. *Encyc. Brit.*, IV. 92.

plerome-sheath (plē'rōm-shēth), *n.* In *bot.*, a limiting layer of surrounding cellular tissue which incloses ordinarily a group of fibrovascular bundles: with some authors the same as *bundle-sheath*.

pleromorph (plē'rō-môrf), *n.* [‹ Gr. πλήρωμα, a filling up, + μορφή, form.] A kind of pseudomorph formed by the filling of a cavity left by the removal of a crystal of some species with another mineral or mineral substance.

plerophoria (plē-rō-fō'ri-ä), *n.* [NL.] Same as *plerophory*.

plerophory (plē-rof'ō-ri), *n.* [‹ NL. *plerophoria*, ‹ Gr. πληροφορία, full conviction, certainty, ‹ πληροφορεῖν, give full satisfaction or certainty, in pass. be fully convinced, ‹ πλήρης, full, + φέρειν = E. *bear*[1].] Full persuasion or confidence; perfect conviction or certitude. [Rare.]

Young men apprehend not the necessities of knowledge, old men presume of a *plerophory* and abundance.
Rev. T. Adams, Works, I. 317.

Abraham had a *plerophory* that what was promised God was able to perform. *Barrow*, Sermons, II. iv. (*Latham.*)

The *plerophory* or full assurance of faith.
Schaff, Christ and Christianity, p. 8.

plesance†, plesaunce†, *n.* Obsolete forms of *pleasance*.

plesant†, plesaunt†, *a.* Obsolete forms of *pleasant*.

plesh†, *n.* An obsolete variant of *plash*[1].

Plesiarctomys (plē-si-ärk'tō-mis), *n.* [NL., ‹ Gr. πλησίος, near, + NL. *Arctomys*, q. v.] A Miocene genus of sciuromorphic rodents, somewhat resembling marmots.

Plesiochelyidæ (plē''si-ō-ke-lī'i-dē), *n. pl.* [NL., ‹ *Plesiochelys* + *-idæ*.] A family of pleurodirous turtles, typified by the genus *Plesiochelys*. They were distinguished by the total absence of the mesoplastral element in the plastron and the union of the pubis above with the epiplastral. They were of Mesozoic age.

Plesiochelys (plē-si-ok'e-lis), *n.* [NL., ‹ Gr. πλησίος, near, + χέλυς, a tortoise.] An extinct genus of turtles, typical of the family *Plesiochelyidæ*.

plesiomorphic (plē''si-ō-môr'fik), *a.* [‹ *plesiomorph-ous* + *-ic*.] Same as *plesiomorphous*.

plesiomorphism (plē''si-ō-môr'fizm), *n.* [‹ *plesiomorph-ous* + *-ism*.] In *crystal.*, the relation of crystallized substances the forms of which closely resemble each other, but are not absolutely identical.

plesiomorphous (plē''si-ō-môr'fus), *a.* [‹ Gr. πλησίος, near, + μορφή, form, + *-ous*.] Nearly alike in form; exhibiting plesiomorphism.

Plesiopidæ (plē-si-op'i-dē), *n. pl.* [NL., ‹ *Plesiops* + *-idæ*.] A family of acanthopterygian fishes, typified by the genus *Plesiops*, generally embraced in the family *Pseudochromididæ*.

Plesiops (plē'si-ops), *n.* [NL., ‹ Gr. πλησίος, near, + ὤψ, eye, face.] A genus of pseudo-

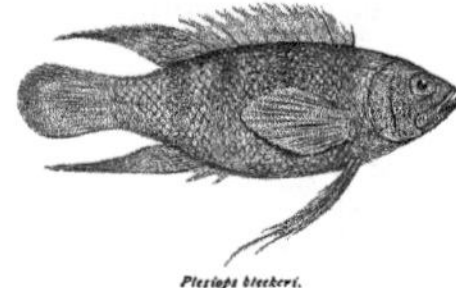

Plesiops bleekeri.

chromidoid fishes, regarded by some as the type of a family *Plesiopidæ*. It contains fishes of the Indian and Pacific oceans, as *P. bleekeri*.

plesiosaur (plē'si-ō-sâr), *n.* An animal of the order *Plesiosauria*.

Plesiosauri (plē''si-ō-sâ'rī), *n. pl.* [NL., pl. of *Plesiosaurus*.] Same as *Plesiosauria*.

Plesiosauria (plē''si-ō-sâ'ri-ä), *n. pl.* [NL.: see *Plesiosaurus*.] An order of extinct marine *Reptilia*, having the limbs fitted for swimming, the body fish-like, the neck long, and the head quite small. The fore and hind limbs both constitute flippers or paddles like those of cetacean mammals, having numerous phalanges inclosed in a common integument like a fin. The pectoral arch is complete, with triradiate scapular and large coracoid and clavicular elements, and the pelvis is large, with separate ilium, ischium, and pubis. There is no sternum, nor are there any sternal ribs, but floating abdominal ribs are present. The skull has a fixed quadrate bone, one postorbital bar, and no free paroccipital; the vertebræ are amphicœlous, with neurocentral sutures, and only two of them compose a sacrum. The ribs are one-headed. The eyeball has no sclerotic ring of bones, and the teeth are socketed in a single row in both jaws. The order contains many genera of gigantic fish-like saurians from the Trias, Lias, and Chalk, whose affinities are with the chelonians, notwithstanding the wide difference in form. The order is also called *Sauropterygia*, but *Plesiosauria* is its prior and proper name. See cut under *Plesiosaurus*.

plesiosaurian (plē''si-ō-sâ'ri-an), *a.* and *n.* [‹ *Plesiosauria* + *-an*.] **I.** *a.* Of or pertaining to the *Plesiosauria*; plesiosauroid; sauropterygian.

II. *n.* A member of the *Plesiosauria*; a plesiosaur.

Plesiosauridæ (plē''si-ō-sâ'ri-dē), *n. pl.* [NL., ‹ *Plesiosaurus* + *-idæ*.] A family of gigantic animals represented by the genus *Plesiosaurus* and related forms, having both fore and hind limbs perfectly natatory. The pterygoids diverge backward, and do not overlie the basisphenoid, and there are small infra-orbital vacuities in the palate. They lived from the uppermost Triassic to the Cretaceous epoch. Some of the species were of huge dimensions.

plesiosauroid (plē'si-ō-sâ'roid), *a.* [‹ *plesiosaur* + *-oid*.] Resembling a plesiosaur; plesiosaurian. *Owen.*

Plesiosaurus (plē''si-ō-sâ'rus), *n.* [NL. (Conybeare), ‹ Gr. πλησίος, near, + σαῦρος, lizard.] A

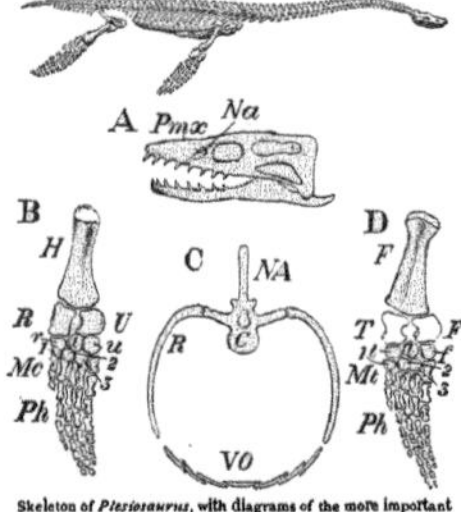

Skeleton of *Plesiosaurus*, with diagrams of the more important parts.

A, skull: *Na*, nasal aperture; *Pmx*, premaxilla. B, left fore limb: *H*, humerus; *R*, *U*, radius and ulna; *r*, *i*, *u*, radiale, intermedium, and ulnare of carpus; 1, 2, 3, distal carpalia; *Mc*, metacarpus; *Ph*, phalanges. C, dorsal vertebra, with *R*, ribs, and *VO*, ventral ossifications; *C*, centrum; *NA*, neural arch. D, left hind limb: *F*, femur; *T*, tibia; *F'*, fibula; *t*, *i*, *f*, tibiale, intermedium, and fibulare of tarsus; 1, 2, 3, distal tarsalia; *Mt*, metatarsus; *Ph*, phalanges.

genus of *Reptilia*, typical of the order *Plesiosauria*, and formerly conterminous with it, now restricted to forms from the Upper Triassic (Rhætic) and the Liassic, as *P. dolichodirus*, with extremely long neck.

plesire†, *n.* A Middle English variant of *pleasure*.

plessimeter (ple-sim'e-tėr), *n.* Same as *pleximeter*.

plet (plet), *n.* [Also *plete*, *plitt*; ‹ Russ. *pletŭ*, a whip.] A whip, especially one of the form used by the Russian penal administration for the chastisement of refractory prisoners.

There is another flagellator, however, called the *plete*, a whip of twisted hide, which is still retained at a few of the most distant Siberian prisons, and only for the most incorrigible, on whom irons, the birch, and other punishments have had no effect. *Encyc. Brit.*, XIX. 762.

plete[1]**†**, *v.* A Middle English form of *plead*.

plete[2], *n.* See *plet*.

pletere†, *n.* A Middle English form of *pleader*.

plethora (pleth'ō-rä), *n.* [Formerly also *plethory*; = F. *pléthore* = Sp. *plétora* = Pg. *plethora* = It. *pletora*, ‹ NL. *plethora*, ‹ Gr. πληθώρη, fullness, in med. plethora, ‹ πλῆθος, fullness, ‹ πλήθειν, be or become full, ‹ √ πλη in πιμπλάναι, fill, πλήρης, L. *plenus*, full: see *full*[1], *plenty*.] 1. In *pathol.*, overfullness of blood; a redundant fullness of the blood-vessels.

At the same time he is full and empty, bursting with a *plethory*, and consumed with hunger.
Jer. Taylor, Works (ed. 1835), I. 910.

Your character at present is like a person in a *plethora*, absolutely dying from too much health.
Sheridan, School for Scandal, iv. 3.

2. Overfullness in any respect; superabundance.

A *plethora* of dull fact is . . . especially the characteristic of . . . [this] volume on ancient history.
Athenæum, Jan. 7, 1888, p. 11.

plethoretic (pleth-ō-ret'ik), *a.* [‹ *plethora* + *-etic*, as in *diuretic*, etc.] Same as *plethoric*.

plethoretical (pleth-ō-ret'i-kal), *a.* [‹ *plethoretic* + *-al*.] Same as *plethoric*.

plethoric (plē-thor'ik or pleth'ō-rik), *a.* [‹ Gr. πληθωρικός, ‹ πληθώρη, plethora: see *plethora*.] Having a full habit of body, or the vessels overcharged with fluids; characterized by plethora, in any sense.

And late the nation found, with fruitless skill,
Its former strength was but *plethoric* ill.
Goldsmith, Traveller, l. 144.

At length he broke out into a *plethoric* fit of laughter that had well nigh choked him, by reason of his excessive corpulency. *Irving*, Sketch-Book, p. 169.

The pockets, *plethoric* with marbles round,
That still a space for ball and pegtop found.
Lowell, Biglow Papers, 1st ser., Int.

plethorical (plē-thor'i-kal), *a.* [‹ *plethoric* + *-al*.] Same as *plethoric*.

plethorically (plē-thor'i-kal-i), *adv.* In a plethoric manner; with plethora.

plethory† (pleth'ō-ri), *n.* An obsolete form of *plethora*.

Plethospongiæ (plē-thō-spon'ji-ē), *n. pl.* [NL., ‹ Gr. πλῆθος, fullness, + σπόγγος, sponge.] In Sollas's classification of sponges, same as *Micromastictora*.

plethron, plethrum (pleth'ron, -rum), *n.*; pl. *plethra* (-rä). [‹ Gr. πλέθρον (see def.).] In ancient Greece, a fundamental land-measure, being the square of 100 feet, or 10,000 square feet. As a measure of length, the plethron was the side of this square, the sixth part of a stadium, or about 101 English feet.

plethysmograph (plē-this'mō-gràf), *n.* [‹ Gr. πληθυσμός, increasing, enlargement (‹ πληθύειν, be or become full, πληθύνειν, make full, ‹ πλῆθος, πληθύς, fullness), + γράφειν, write.] An instrument for obtaining tracings indicating the changes in the volume of a part of the body, especially as dependent on the circulation of blood in it. The part, as the arm, is inclosed in a tight vessel and surrounded by water, which is forced up or allowed to recede in a tube as the volume increases or diminishes.

plethysmographic (plē-this-mō-graf'ik), *a.* [‹ *plethysmograph* + *-ic*.] Of or pertaining to the plethysmograph, or its use. *Medical News*, XLIX. 276.

pleting†, *n.* A Middle English form of *pleading*.

pletour†, *n.* A pleader; a lawyer.

pleugh, pleuch (plüch), *n.* and *v.* Scotch forms of *plow*.

pleugh-paidle (plüch'pā''dl), *n.* A plow-staff. *Scott*, Old Mortality, xxxv. [Scotch.]

pleura[1] (plö'rä), *n.*; pl. *pleuræ* (-rē). [NL., ‹ Gr. πλευρά, a rib, in pl. (also in sing.) the side, side of a triangle, a page of a book; cf. neut. πλευρόν, a rib, pl. πλευρά, the ribs, the side.] 1. The principal serous membrane of the thorax; the shut sac, having a serous surface, which lines the walls of the chest, and is reflected over the surface of each lung. There are two pleuræ, right and left, completely shut off from each other. Each is divided into a parietal or costal layer and a visceral or pulmonary layer. (See the phrases below.) Like the other serous membranes, the pleuræ are moistened with a serous secretion, which serves to facilitate the movements of the lungs in the chest. See cuts under *peritoneum* and *thorax*.

2. In *conch.*, one of the lateral tracts on each side of the rachis of the lingual ribbon of the odontophore: generally used in the plural.

The teeth of the *pleuræ* are termed uncini; they are extremely numerous in the plant-eating gastropods.
Woodward.

3. In *compar. anat.*, the lateral portion of one of the rings composing the integument of an arthropod or articulate animal, lying between the tergum and sternum, and in insects and crustaceans consisting of two pieces, the epimeron and episternum. In descriptive entomology the term is generally restricted to the side of the thorax, as in *Diptera*.—**Cavity of the pleura**, the space between the parietal and pulmonary layers of the pleura. In the normal state these layers are in contact. See cut under *thorax*.—**Parietal pleura.** (*a*) Same as *pleura costalis*. (*b*) All the parts of the pleura except the pulmonary portion.—**Pericardial pleura.** See *pericardial*.—**Pleura costalis**, the costal part of the pleura, lining the walls of the thorax.—**Pleura mediastinalis**, that part of the pleura which enters into the formation of the mediastinum.—**Pleura pericardiaca.** Same as *pericardial pleura*.—**Pleura phrenica**, that part of the pleura which invests the upper surface of the diaphragm; the diaphragmatic pleura.—**Pleura pulmonalis**, the pulmonary or visceral part of the pleura, investing the lungs.—**Visceral pleura**, the pleura pulmonalis.

pleura[2], *n.* Plural of *pleuron*.

pleuracanth (plö'ra-kanth), *a.* and *n.* [‹ NL. *Pleuracanthus*.] Same as *pleuracanthoid*.

Pleuracanthidæ (plö-ra-kan'thi-dē), *n. pl.* [NL., < *Pleuracanthus* + *-idæ*.] A family of fishes of the order *Xenacanthini*, typified by the genus *Pleuracanthus*. The body was moderately long; the head roundish; the mouth terminal and well slit; the dorsal double, the first short, armed with an anterior spine, and mostly above the head, the second extending from the first to the caudal fin; the anals were double, and the caudal was long and diphycercal; the pectorals had a biserial arrangement of cartilaginous rays, and the ventrals were shark-like; the teeth had two divergent cones and an intermediate denticle. The species lived during the Carboniferous and Permian periods.

Pleuracanthini (plö'ra-kan-thī'nī), *n. pl.* [NL., < *Pleuracanthus* + *-ini*.] An order of fishes otherwise called *Xenacanthini* and *Ichthyotomi*. See *Xenacanthini*.

pleuracanthoid (plö-ra-kan'thoid), *a.* and *n.* I. *a.* Of or resembling the *Pleuracanthidæ*.

II. *n.* A member of the family *Pleuracanthidæ*.

Also *pleuracanth*.

Pleuracanthus (plö-ra-kan'thus), *n.* [NL. (Agassiz, 1837), < Gr. πλευρόν, a rib, + ἄκανθα, spine.] A remarkable extinct genus of fishes, typical of the family *Pleuracanthidæ*.

pleural[1] (plö'ral), *a.* [< *pleura*[1] + *-al*.] Of or pertaining to a pleura or the pleuræ: as, the *pleural* investment of the lungs; the *pleural* cavity; *pleural* effusion or adhesions. Also *pleuric*.

pleural[2] (plö'ral), *a.* [< *pleuron* + *-al*.] 1. Pertaining to a rib or a pleuron, or to the ribs or the pleura collectively; costal; situated on the side of the thorax or chest.—2. Lateral, in general; situated on the side of the body: correlated with *dorsal*, *ventral*, etc.—3. In arthropods, pertaining to an arthropleura or pleurite: applied to the lateral limb-bearing section of an arthromere, between the sternite and the tergite. See cuts under *Brachyura* and *Trilobita*.—4. Especially, in *entom.*, lateral and thoracic: as, a *pleural* sclerite; a *pleural* segment of a thoracic somite.—**Pleural facet** of the movable pleura of a crustacean, the anterior part of a pleuron which is overlapped by the preceding pleuron in flexion of the body.—**Pleural spine**, a spine connected with a pleuroid. *G. Baur.*

pleuralgia (plö-ral'ji-ä), *n.* [NL., < Gr. πλευρά, the side, + ἄλγος, pain.] Pain in the pleura or side; pleurodynia.

pleuralgic (plö-ral'jik), *a.* [< *pleuralgia* + *-ic*.] Pertaining to or affected with pleuralgia.

pleuralia (plö-rā'li-ä), *n. pl.* [NL., neut. pl. of **pleuralis*, < Gr. πλευρά, the side: see *pleural*[1], *pleura*[1].] In sponges, spicules forming a fur. *F. E. Shulze.*

pleurapophysial (plö-rap-ō-fiz'i-al), *a.* [< *pleurapophysis* + *-al*.] Having the morphological character of a pleurapophysis; of the nature of a rib; costal; costiferous.

pleurapophysis (plö-ra-pof'i-sis), *n.*; pl. *pleurapophyses* (-sēz). [NL., < Gr. πλευρόν, a rib, + ἀπόφυσις, a process: see *apophysis*.] A lateral process of a vertebra, having the morphological character of a rib, or forming a true rib. Such processes in the thoracic region of the spine are commonly highly developed, and movably articulated both with the centra and with the diapophyses of the thoracic vertebræ, and they are then ribs in an ordinary sense. They are mostly rudimentary in other parts of the spinal column, but sometimes are very evident, as in the cervical ribs of various vertebrates, including man. In man, in the neck, they bound the vertebrarterial foramen in front, and produce the tubercles known as *anterior* on the transverse process. Pleurapophyses are also by some considered to be represented in the lateral mass of the human sacrum. Developed and movably articulated pleurapophyses, forming true ribs, often extend into the sacral as well as cervical region, as in various birds; and in all of this class more or fewer of them bear accessory processes called *uncinate*. (See cut under *epipleura*.) In serpents they run in unbroken series from head to tail, and assist in locomotion. (See *gastrostege*.) In some reptiles they support a patagium (see cut under *dragon*); in the cobra they spread the hood. In Owen's nomenclature the term *pleurapophysis* is restricted to the true bony part of a rib, the gristly part or costal cartilage being called *hemapophysis*. See cuts under *vertebra* and *endoskeleton*.

pleurarthron (plö-rär'thron), *n.*; pl. *pleurarthra* (-thrä). [NL., < Gr. πλευρά, a rib, + ἄρθρον, a joint.] The articulation of a rib. *Thomas*, Med. Dict.

pleurecbolic (plö-rek-bol'ik), *a.* [< Gr. πλευρά, the side, + ἐκβολή, a throwing out: see *ecbolic*.] Eversible or capable of protrusion by a forward movement of the sides of the containing tube, as an invert: correlated with *acrembolic*, and distinguished from *pleurembolic*. [Rare.]

It is clear that, if we start from the condition of full eversion of the tube and watch the process of introversion, we shall find that the *pleurecbolic* variety is introverted by the apex of the tube sinking inwards.
Lankester, Encyc. Brit., XVI. 652.

pleurembolic (plö-rem-bol'ik), *a.* [< Gr. πλευρά, the side, + ἐμβολή, a putting into: see *embolic*.] Introversible or capable of being withdrawn by a backward movement of the parts into which it sinks, as an evert: correlated with *acrecbolic*, and distinguished from *pleurecbolic*. [Rare.]

It [the pleurecbolic variety of eversion] may be called acrembolic, whilst conversely the acrecbolic tubes are *pleurembolic*. *Lankester*, Encyc. Brit., XVI. 652.

pleurenchyma (plö-reng'ki-mä), *n.* [NL., < Gr. πλευρά, the side, + ἔγχυμα, what is poured in: see *enchymatous*, *parenchyma*.] In *bot.*, the woody tissue of plants. See *wood-cell*.

pleurenchymatous (plö-reng-kim'a-tus), *a.* [< *pleurenchyma*(*t-*) + *-ous*.] Of, pertaining to, or of the nature of pleurenchyma.

pleuric (plö'rik), *a.* [< *pleura*[1] + *-ic*.] Same as *pleural*[1].

pleurisy (plö'ri-si), *n.* [Formerly also *plurisy*, partly associated (as in the equiv. ML. *plurior*, *pluritas*, plethora) with L. *plus* (gen. *pluris*), more, as if implying a plethora of blood; < F. *pleurésie* = Pr. *pleurezia* = Sp. *pleuresia* = Pg. *pleuriz* = It. *pleurisia*, < LL. *pleurisis*, a later form of the reg. L. *pleuritis*: see *pleuritis*.] Inflammation of the pleura. It may be acute or chronic, and may or may not be accompanied by effusion. The effusion may be serous, seropurulent, purulent, or hemorrhagic. Also called *pleuritis*.

The *Pleurisie* stabs him with desperate foyl
Beneath the ribs, where scalding blood doth boyl.
Sylvester, tr. of Du Bartas's Weeks, ii., The Furies.

Virtue in a chafe should change her linen quick,
Lest *pleurisy* get start of providence.
Browning, Ring and Book, I. 194.

Dry pleurisy, pleurisy without effusion.

pleurisy-root (plö'ri-si-röt), *n.* A plant of the milkweed family, *Asclepias tuberosa*: so named

1. Part of the Inflorescence of Pleurisy-root (*Asclepias tuberosa*). 2. The root and the lower part of the stem. *a*, a flower; *b*, the anthers and the stigma; *c*, the fruit; *d*, a seed.

from its medicinal use. Also called *butterfly-weed*.

pleurite (plö'rīt), *n.* [< Gr. πλευρά, the side, + *-ite*[2].] 1. In arthropods, a pleural sclerite; a lateral piece or segment of a somitic ring or somite, between the tergite and the sternite.—2. In a restricted sense, the lateral or pleural part of an abdominal segment of an insect.

pleuritic[1] (plö-rit'ik), *a.* [< L. *pleuriticus*, < Gr. πλευριτικός, suffering from pleurisy, < πλευρῖτις, pleurisy: see *pleuritis*.] 1. Pertaining to or suffering from pleurisy: as, *pleuritic* symptoms or affections; a *pleuritic* patient.—2. Causing or bringing pleurisy.

For while the effluence of the skin maintains
Its native measure, the *pleuritic* Spring
Glides harmless by.
Armstrong, Art of Preserving Health, iii.

pleuritic[2] (plö-rit'ik), *a.* [< *pleurite* + *-ic*.] 1. In arthropods, of or pertaining to a pleurite; pleural, as a segment of a somite.—2. In *entom.*, specifically, lateral or pleural and abdominal; of or pertaining to a pleurite.

pleuritical (plö-rit'i-kal), *a.* [< *pleuritic*[1] + *-al*.] Same as *pleuritic*[1].

pleuritis (plö-rī'tis), *n.* [NL., < L. *pleuritis*, < Gr. πλευρῖτις, pleuritis (cf. πλευρίτης, on or at the side), < πλευρα, the side: see *pleura*[1].] Same as *pleurisy*.

pleuroblastic (plö-rō-blas'tik), *a.* [< Gr. πλευρά, the side, + βλαστός, a germ.] In *bot.*, in the *Peronosporeæ*, producing vesicular lateral outgrowths which serve as haustoria. *De Bary.*

Pleurobrachia (plö-rō-brā'ki-ä), *n.* [NL., < Gr. πλευρά, the side, + βραχίων, the arm.] A genus of ctenophorans: same as *Cydippe*, 1.

pleurobranchia[1] (plö-rē-brang'ki-ä), *n.*; pl. *pleurobranchiæ* (-ē). [NL., < Gr. πλευρά, the side, + βράγχια (NL. *branchiæ*, sing. *branchia*), gills.] A pleural gill; a branchial organ borne upon an epimeron of any thoracic segment of a crustacean. Some of the thoracic segments, as in the crawfish, may bear on each side four branchiæ, a coxopoditic podobranchia, anterior and posterior arthrobranchiæ, and epimeral pleurobranchiæ.

Pleurobranchia[2] (plö-rō-brang'ki-ä), *n. pl.* [NL., < Gr. πλευρά, the side, + βράγχια, gills.] Same as *Pleurobranchiata*. *J. E. Gray*, 1821.

pleurobranchial (plö-rō-brang'ki-al), *a.* [< *pleurobranchia*1 + *-al*.] Of or pertaining to a pleurobranchia: as, a *pleurobranchial* process.

Pleurobranchiata (plö-rō-brang-ki-ā'tä), *n. pl.* [NL., neut. pl. of *pleurobranchiatus*: see *pleurobranchiate*.] An order of opisthobranchiate gastropods, whose gills are tufts on the sides under a fold of the mantle, and which have generally a spiral shell in the adult as well as the young. Also *Pleurobranchia*, *Tectibranchiata*.

pleurobranchiate (plö-rē-brang'ki-āt), *a.* [< NL. *pleurobranchiatus*, < Gr. πλευρά, the side, + βράγχια, gills.] 1. Having pleurobranchiæ, as a crustacean.—2. Having gills along the sides; specifically, pertaining to the *Pleurobranchiata*, or having their characters.

Pleurobranchidæ (plö-rō-brang'ki-dē), *n. pl.* [NL., < *Pleurobranchus* + *-idæ*.] A family of notaspidean nudibranchiate gastropods, typified by the genus *Pleurobranchus*. They have distinct buccal tentacles forming a veil, branchiæ on the right side of the body under the border of the mantle, a proboscidiform mouth, and numerous falciform marginal teeth on the radula.

Pleurobranchus (plö-rō-brang'kus), *n.* [NL., < Gr. πλευρά, the side, + βράγχια, gills.] A genus of nudibranchiates, typical of the family *Pleurobranchidæ*.

Pleurobranchus membranaceus.

Pleurocarpi (plö-rō-kär'pī), *n. pl.* [NL., < Gr. πλευρά, the side, + καρπός, fruit.] A division of bryaceous mosses in which the fructification is lateral on the stems, having proceeded from the axils of the leaves. Sometimes called *Pleurocarpæ*.

pleurocarpous (plö-rō-kär'pus), *a.* [< Gr. πλευρά, the side, + καρπός, fruit.] In *bot.*, having the fructification proceeding laterally from the axils of the leaves, as in some mosses. *Sachs.*

pleurocele (plö'rō-sēl), *n.* [< Gr. πλευρά, the side, + κήλη, tumor.] Same as *pneumocele*.

pleurocentral (plö-rō-sen'tral), *a.* [< *pleurocentrum* + *-al*.] Of or pertaining to a pleurocentrum; hemicentral.

pleurocentrum (plö-rō-sen'trum), *n.*; pl. *pleurocentra* (-trä). [NL., < Gr. πλευρά, the side, + κέντρον, the center.] One of the lateral elements of the centrum of a vertebra; a hemicentrum.

Pleurocera (plö-ros'e-rä), *n.* [NL., < Gr. πλευρά, the side, + κέρας, horn.] A genus of American fresh-water univalves, typical of the family *Pleuroceridæ*. Also called *Trypanostoma*.

pleurocerebral (plö-rō-ser'ē-bral), *a.* [< Gr. πλευρά, the side, + L. *cerebrum*, the brain: see *cerebral*.] Connecting the side of the body with the head: specifically, in mollusks and some other invertebrates, noting a nervous cord connecting a cerebral with a pleural ganglion.

Pleuroceridæ (plö-rō-ser'i-dē), *n. pl.* [NL., < *Pleurocera* + *-idæ*.] A family of tænioglossate gastropods, typified by the genus *Pleurocera*. It comprises a great number of species, mostly occurring in the fresh waters of the United States, referred by the old writers to the melanians. They are distinguished, however, by their unfringed mantle, want of a distinct male organ, and oviparity. Also called *Ceriphasiidæ* and *Strepomatidæ*.

pleurocœle (plö'rō-sēl), *n.* [< Gr. πλευρά, the side, + κοῖλον, a hollow, neut. of κοῖλος, hollow.] One of two lateral spaces of the posterior part of the splanchnocœle of a brachiopod.

I propose to give the name *pleurocœles* to these spaces, simply from their position as side chambers.
Davidson, Trans. Linn. Soc., XIV. iii. 210.

pleurocolic (plö-rō-kol'ik), *a.* [< Gr. πλευρόν, a rib, + L. *colon*, colon: see *colon*[2].] Same as *costocolic*.—**Pleurocolic ligament.** Same as *costocolic ligament* (which see, under *costocolic*).

pleurocollesis (plö'rō-ko-lē'sis), *n.* [NL., < Gr. πλευρά, the side, + κόλλησις, a gluing, < κολλᾶν, glue, < κόλλα, glue.] Adhesion of the pleura.

Pleuroconchæ (plö-rō-kong'kē), *n. pl.* [NL., < Gr. πλευρά, the side, + κόγχη, a mussel, shell.] A suborder of inequivalve *Conchifera*, comprising the families *Aviculidæ*, *Pectinidæ*, *Spondylidæ*, *Ostreidæ*, and *Chamidæ*.

Pleurodeles (plö-rod'e-lēz), *n.* [NL.] A genus of tailed amphibians, typical of the family *Pleurodelidæ*.

Pleurodelidæ (plö-rọ-del'i-dē), *n. pl.* [NL., < *Pleurodeles* + *-idæ*.] A family of gradient or tailed amphibians, typified by the genus *Pleurodeles*. They have palatine teeth in two longitudinal series diverging behind, inserted on the inner margin of two palatine processes, which are much prolonged posteriorly; the parasphenoid toothless; and a postfrontal arch, sometimes ligamentous.

Pleurodira (plö-rọ-dī'rạ̈), *n. pl.* [NL.: see *Pleurodires*.] A superfamily of tortoises with the neck bending in a horizontal plane, and pelvis ankylosed to carapace and plastron. It includes the recent families *Sternothæridæ*, *Podocnemididæ*, *Chelydidæ*, and several extinct ones. *Chelodines* is a synonym.

pleurodiran (plö-rọ-dī'ran), *a.* Same as *pleurodirous*. *Amer. Nat.*, XXII. 36.

Pleurodires (plö-rọ-dī'rēz), *n. pl.* [NL., < Gr. πλευρά, the side, + δειρή, the neck.] In Gray's classification, a suborder of tortoises whose necks bend sidewise; the pleurodirous tortoises: same as *Pleurodira*. See cut under *Chelydidæ*.

pleurodirous (plö-rọ-dī'rus), *a.* [< Gr. πλευρά, the side, + δειρή, the neck.] In *Chelonia*, bending the neck sidewise: noting those tortoises, as the matamata, which thus fold the head and neck in the shell: opposed to *cryptodirous*. See cut under *Chelydidæ*.

pleurodiscous (plö-rọ-dis'kus), *a.* [< Gr. πλευρά, the side, + δίσκος, a disk.] In *bot.*, attached to the sides of a disk.

pleurodont (plö'rọ-dont), *a.* and *n.* [< NL. **pleurodus* (*pleurodont-*), < Gr. πλευρά, the side, + ὀδούς (ὀδοντ-) = E. *tooth*.] I. *a.* 1. Ankylosed to the side of the socket, as teeth; laterally fixed

Anterior Part of Right Ramus of Lower Jaw of an Iguana, showing Pleurodont Dentition.

in the jaw: distinguished from *acrodont*.—2. Having or characterized by pleurodont teeth or dentition, as a lizard; belonging to the *Pleurodontes*; not acrodont: as, a *pleurodont* reptile.

II. *n.* A pleurodont lizard; a member of the *Pleurodontes*.

Pleurodontes (plö-rọ-don'tēz), *n. pl.* [NL., pl. of **pleurodus* (*pleurodont-*): see *pleurodont*.] A group of pleurodont lizards, comprising such as the American iguanoids. *J. Wagler*, 1830.

pleurodynia (plö-rọ-din'i-ạ̈), *n.* [NL., < Gr. πλευρά, the side, + ὀδύνη, pain.] In *pathol.*, pain in the muscles of the chest.

pleuro-esophageus (plö-rọ-ē-sọ-fā'jẹ-us), *n.* [NL., < Gr. πλευρά, the side, + οἰσόφαγος, esophagus.] A band of smooth muscle-fibers connecting the left pleura behind with the esophagus.

pleurogenic (plö-rọ-jen'ik), *a.* [< Gr. πλευρά, the side, + -γενής, produced: see *-genous*.] Originating from the pleura: as, *pleurogenic* phthisis.

pleurogynous (plọ-roj'i-nus), *a.* [< Gr. πλευρά, the side, + γυνή, female (in mod. bot. pistil).] In *bot.*, having a glandular or tubercular elevation rising close to and parallel with the ovary.

pleurogyrate (plö-rọ-jī'rāt), *a.* [< Gr. πλευρά, the side, + L. *gyratus*, pp. of *gyrare*, turn: see *gyrate*.] In *bot.*, having the ring on the theca (of ferns) placed laterally.

pleurogyratous (plö-rọ-jī'rạ̄-tus), *a.* [< *pleurogyrate* + *-ous*.] Same as *pleurogyrate*.

pleurohepatitis (plö-rọ-hep-ạ-tī'tis), *n.* [NL., < Gr. πλευρά, the side, + ἧπαρ (ἡπατ-), liver, + *-itis*. Cf. *hepatitis*.] Inflammation of the liver and adjacent pleura.

pleuroid (plö'roid), *n.* [< Gr. πλευρόν, a rib, + εἶδος, form. Cf. Gr. πλευροειδῶς, adv., after the manner of ribs.] One of the pair of distinct pleural elements which compose the pleural arch of a vertebra; a pleurapophysis: correlated with *neuroid*. *G. Baur*, Amer. Nat., XXI. 945.

pleurolepidal (plö-rọ-lep'i-dal), *a.* [< NL. *Pleurolepis* (*-lepid-*) + *-al*.] Of or pertaining to the *Pleurolepididæ*; having oblique rows of ribbed rhomboid scales interlocking. Each scale has upon its inner anterior margin a thick, solid, bony rib extending upward, and sliced off obliquely below, thus forming splices with the inverse parts of the upper and lower scales.

Pleurolepididæ (plö″rọ-le-pid'i-dē), *n. pl.* [NL., < *Pleurolepis* (*-lepid-*) + *-idæ*.] A family of fossil pycnodont fishes, typified by the genus *Pleurolepis*. By some they are united with the *Dapediidæ*. The vertebral column was homocercal, the fins had fulcra, and the body was not very high. They flourished in the Liassic. Also *Pleurolepidæ*.

Pleurolepis (plọ-rol'e-pis), *n.* [NL., < Gr. πλευρά, the side, + λεπίς, a scale.] The typical genus of the *Pleurolepididæ*, having riblike rows of scales, whence the name. *Agassiz*.

Pleuroleura (plö-rọ-lū'rạ̈), *n.* [NL., < Gr. πλευρά, the side, + λευρός, smooth, level.] A genus of nudibranchiates, typical of the family *Pleuroleuridæ*. Also called *Dermatobranchus*.

Pleuroleuridæ (plö-rọ-lū'ri-dē), *n. pl.* [NL., < *Pleuroleura* + *-idæ*.] A family of inferobranchiate nudibranchiate gastropods, typified by the genus *Pleuroleura* (or *Dermatobranchus*). They are destitute of specialized branchiæ, and respiration is effected by the skin. Also called *Dermatobranchidæ*.

pleuromelus (plọ-rom'e-lus), *n.*; pl. *pleuromeli* (-lī). [NL., < Gr. πλευρά, the side, + μέλος, a limb.] In *teratol.*, a monster with supernumerary limbs attached to the lateral regions of the trunk.

Pleuromonadidæ (plö″rọ-mọ-nad'i-dē), *n. pl.* [NL., < *Pleuromonas* (*-monad-*) + *-idæ*.] A family of pantostomatous flagellate *Infusoria*, typified by the genus *Pleuromonas*. These animalcules are free-swimming, and naked or illoricate, and have a single lateral or dextral flagellum and no distinct oral aperture.

Pleuromonas (plọ-rom'ọ-nas), *n.* [NL., < Gr. πλευρά, the side, + NL. *Monas*, < Gr. μονάς (μοναδ-), a unit: see *monad*.] The typical genus of *Pleuromonadidæ*. *P. jaculans* is an example.

pleuron (plö'ron), *n.*; pl. *pleura* (-rạ̈). [NL., < Gr. πλευρόν, a rib: see *pleura*[1].] A lateral piece, part, or aspect of the body; especially, the side of the thorax: chiefly used of invertebrates. Specifically—(*a*) In *Crustacea*, a lateral piece or part of any somite below the tergum and above the insertion of the legs; an epimeron. (*b*) In *Trilobita*, one of the flattened lateral sections of a thoracic or pygidial somite, lying on each side of the axis or tergum. See cut under *Trilobita*. (*c*) In *entom.*, the lateral section of the thorax; the pleural part of any one of the three thoracic somites. There are consequently three pleura on each side, called from their position the *propleuron*, *mesopleuron*, and *metapleuron*, according to their respective seats on the prothorax, mesothorax, and metathorax.

Pleuronectæ (plö-rọ-nek'tē), *n. pl.* [NL., pl. of *Pleuronectes*.] The flatfishes. See *Pleuronectidæ*.

Pleuronectes (plö-rọ-nek'tēz), *n.* [NL. (Artedi, Linnæus), < Gr. πλευρά, the side, + νήκτης, a swimmer.] A genus of flatfishes, giving name to the family *Pleuronectidæ*, formerly conterminous with the family, later variously restricted. By most recent writers the name has been limited to the group typified by the common plaice, *P. platessa*, sometimes to the few species much like this type, sometimes extended to a larger assemblage. By others it has been used for the turbots, otherwise called *Bothus* and *Psetta*. By others still it has been employed for the genus otherwise called *Arnoglossus*. In a common European acceptation it includes flounders of northern seas, having the eyes and the color on the right side, the colored side of each jaw usually toothless, the blind side with close-set teeth in one (rarely two) series, the body ovate or elliptical, the small scales ctenoid or cycloid, the lateral line nearly straight or more or less arched anteriorly, and the small gill-rakers widely set. About 12 species of *Pleuronectes* in this sense are found in North America, a majority of them on the Pacific coast, as *P.* (*Platichthys*) *stellatus*, the California flounder, one of the largest and most important. *P.* (*Limanda*) *ferrugineus* is the sand-dab of the Atlantic coast. *P.* (*Pseudopleuronectes*) *americanus* is the mud-dab or winter flounder, common on this coast from New York northward.

pleuronectid (plö-rọ-nek'tid), *n.* and *a.* I. *n.* A flatfish; any member of the *Pleuronectidæ*; a pleuronectoid.

II. *a.* Of or pertaining to the *Pleuronectidæ*.

Pleuronectidæ (plö-rẹ-nek'ti-dē), *n. pl.* [NL., < *Pleuronectes* + *-idæ*.] A family of teleocephalous fishes, of the suborder *Heterosomata*, or flatfishes, or the *Anacanthini pleuronectoidei* of Günther, comprising the flatfishes or flounders.

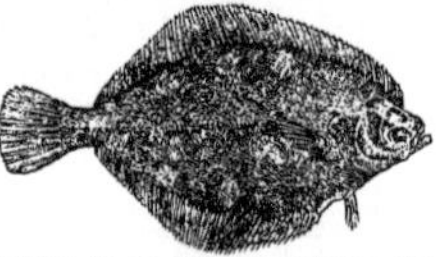

Lepidopsetta bilineata, of California, one of the *Pleuronectidæ*.

In the widest sense, it includes all the representatives of the suborder. The head is unsymmetrical, with both eyes on one side; one surface is colored, the other colorless; and the dorsal and anal fins are long and soft. The genera are about 40 in number, with 400 species, mostly carnivorous, inhabiting sandy bottoms of all seas, sometimes ascending rivers, and including such important food-fishes as the halibut, turbot, plaice, and sole. With more restricted limits, it embraces those which have the general physiognomy of the plaice or halibut, distinctly outlined preopercle and other bones, little twisted mouth, generally subacute snout, and nostrils little dissimilar on two sides. It thus excludes the true soles and like fishes (see *Soleidæ*). See also cuts under *halibut*, *plaice*, *flounder*, *Paralichthys*, *sole*, and *turbot*. Also *Pleuronectoidei*.

pleuronectoid (plö-rọ-nek'toid), *a.* and *n.* [< *Pleuronectes* + *-oid*.] I. *a.* Resembling a fish of the genus *Pleuronectes*; belonging to the *Pleuronectidæ* or *Pleuronectoidei*.

II. *n.* A member of the *Pleuronectoidei*; a pleuronectid.

Pleuronectoidei (plö″rọ-nek-toi'dẹ-ī), *n. pl.* [NL.: see *pleuronectoid*.] Same as *Pleuronectidæ*.

pleuropathia (plö-rọ-path'i-ạ̈), *n.* [NL., < Gr. πλευρά, the side, + πάθος, suffering.] Disease of the pleura.

pleuropedal (plö-rọ-ped'ạl), *a.* [< Gr. πλευρά, the side, + L. *pes* (*ped-*) = E. *foot*.] Connecting the side of the body with the foot: specifically said of a nervous cord which connects a pleural with a pedal ganglion, as in mollusks. Also *pedopleural*.

pleuropericarditis (plö-rọ-per″i-kär-dī'tis), *n.* [NL., < Gr. πλευρά, the side, + NL. *pericardium*, q. v., + *-itis*.] Inflammation of the pleura and the pericardium.

pleuroperipneumony (plö-rọ-per-ip-nū'mọ-ni), *n.* Same as *pleuropneumonia*.

pleuroperitoneal, pleuroperitonæal (plö-rọ-per″i-tọ-nē'ạl), *a.* [< *pleuroperitoneum* + *-al*.] In *zoöl.* and *anat.*, of or relating to the pleura and the peritoneum, or the general body-cavity or perivisceral cavity of a vertebrate animal when it is not divided by a partition (diaphragm) into a pleural or thoracic and a peritoneal or abdominal cavity. It is formed in the early embryo by the splitting of the laminæ ventrales into inner or splanchnopleural and outer or somatopleural layers, and the union of the latter layers of right and left sides in the ventral midline of the body.

pleuroperitoneum, pleuroperitonæum (plö-rō-per″i-tọ-nē'um), *n.* [NL., < Gr. πλευρά, the side, + περιτόναιον, peritoneum: see *peritoneum*.] A serous membrane, representing both pleura and peritoneum, which lines a pleuroperitoneal cavity, as in vertebrates below mammals.

Pleurophthalma (plö-rof-thal'mạ̈), *n. pl.* [NL., < Gr. πλευρά, the side, + ὀφθαλμός, the eye.] A group of toxoglossate gastropods with the eyes at the external borders of the tentacles, comprising the families *Conidæ*, *Pleurotomidæ*, and *Cancellariidæ*.

pleuroplegia (plö-rọ-plē'ji-ạ̈), *n.* [NL., < Gr. πλευρά, the side, + πληγή, a stroke. Cf. *hemiplegia*.] Absence of the power of conjugate movement of the eyes to the right or left, though convergence may be preserved.

pleuropneumonia (plö″rọ-nū-mō'ni-ạ̈), *n.* [NL., < Gr. πλεύρα, the side, + πνεύμων, lung: see *pleura*[1] and *pneumonia*.] A specific contagious disease, peculiar to cattle, affecting the lungs and the pleura, supposed to be caused by some form of micro-organism. It was recognized as far back as the eighteenth century, and now occurs in all the countries of western Europe, in the United States, in southern Africa, and in Australia. The losses which it causes are frequently enormous. The disease first appears in the interlobular tissue of the lungs, whence it invades the pleura and the lung-tissue proper. The latter becomes solidified, and dark-red in color, which varies in later stages. The interlobular tissue becomes thickened into broad yellowish or grayish bands, which give the cut surface of the lungs a peculiar marbled appearance. The disease may be limited to a single lobe or involve one entire lung. A lung becomes very heavy, weighing in some cases over fifty pounds. The disease appears after a period of incubation of from three to six weeks with a feeble cough, which grows more troublesome from week to week. There is slight fever, associated with partial cessation of rumination and milk-secretion. The back is arched and the head is stretched out horizontally during fits of coughing. After a period of from two to six weeks the animal may recover, or the disease may enter a second or acute stage, in which all the symptoms mentioned become greatly aggravated. This stage may last two or three weeks, ending fatally in from 30 to 50 per cent. of all the cases.

pleuropous (plö'rọ-pus), *a.* [< Gr. πλευρά, the side, + πούς = E. *foot*.] In *bot.*, having side supports: noting in the genus *Polyporus* those species which have several supports or stipes instead of one as is usually the case. [Rare.]

Pleuroptera (plọ-rop'tẹ-rạ̈), *n. pl.* [NL., < Gr. πλευρά, the side, + πτερόν, wing.] A group of mammals, containing such as the *Galeopithecidæ*, or so-called flying-lemurs (of the order *Insectivora*): so named from the lateral extension of the skin, which forms a kind of parachute. See cut under *Galeopithecus*.

Pleuropygia (plö-rọ̄-pij′i-ạ̈), *n. pl.* [NL., ‹ Gr. πλευρά, the side, + πυγή, the rump, buttocks.] A division of *Brachiopoda*, containing the inarticulate or lyopomatous members of that class: contrasted with *Apygia*: same as *Lyopomata*.

pleuropygial (plö-rọ̄-pij′i-al), *a.* [‹ *Pleuropygia* + *-al*.] Of or pertaining to the *Pleuropygia*.

pleurorhizal (plö-rọ̄-rī′zal), *a.* [‹ Gr. πλευρά, the side, + ῥίζα, root, + *-al*.] In *bot.*, having the embryo with the radicle against one edge of the cotyledons—that is, with the cotyledons accumbent. *Gray*.

pleurorrhea, pleurorrhœa (plö-rọ̄-rē′ạ̈), *n.* [NL., ‹ Gr. πλευρά, the pleura, + ῥοία, a flow, flux.] Effusion into the pleural cavity.

Pleurosauridæ (plö-rọ̄-sâ′ri-dē), *n. pl.* [NL., ‹ *Pleurosaurus* + *-idæ*.] A family of extinct reptiles referred by some to the order *Rhynchocephalia*, and represented by the genus *Pleurosaurus*. They had an extremely elongated body with many presacral vertebræ, and a long narrow skull with slit-like nares. Their remains have been found in the Kimmeridgian rocks of Bavaria.

Pleurosaurus (plö-rọ̄-sâ′rus), *n.* [NL., ‹ Gr. πλευρόν, a rib, + σαῦρος, lizard.] An extinct genus of lizard-like reptiles, typical of the family *Pleurosauridæ*.

Pleurosigma (plö-rọ̄-sig′mạ̈), *n.* [NL., ‹ Gr. πλευρά, the side, + σίγμα, the letter Σ, σ.] A genus of *Diatomaceæ*, containing species in which the valves show, with a good microscope, a series of lines, capable, under high powers and a favorable light, of resolution into dots, and therefore furnishing excellent tests for the power of a microscope.

Pleurospondylia (plö″rọ̄-spon-dil′i-ạ̈), *n. pl.* [NL., ‹ Gr. πλευρόν, a rib, + σπόνδυλος, a vertebra.] One of the primary groups into which *Reptilia* are divisible. It is characterized by the immobility of the dorsal vertebræ upon one another, and of the ribs upon these vertebræ (and by the absence of transverse processes from all the vertebræ), this fixity being secured by the union of superficial bony plates into which the ribs and vertebræ pass, forming a carapace, and further carried out by the development, in the ventral walls of the thorax and abdomen, of dermal bones, usually nine in number, of which one is median and asymmetrical, the others lateral and paired, the whole forming a plastron. The group contains the single order *Chelonia* or *Testudinata*, and is alone contrasted with *Herpetospondylia*, *Perospondylia*, and *Suchospondylia* collectively, which together include all other *Reptilia*. See these words; also cuts under *Chelonia*, *Chelonidæ*, *carapace*, and *plastron*.

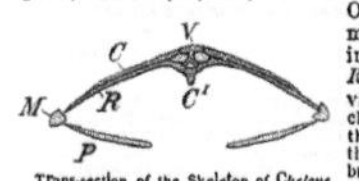

Trans-section of the Skeleton of *Chelone midas* in the dorsal region, showing the disposition of Vertebra and ribs, forming the carapace, and characteristic of *Pleurospondylia*. C′, centrum of a vertebra; V, expanded neural plate; R, a rib; C, expanded costal plate; M, marginal plate; P, a lateral element of the plastron.

pleurospondylian (plö″rọ̄-spon-dil′i-ạn), *a.* and *n.* [‹ *Pleurospondylia* + *-an*.] **I.** *a.* Having the ribs fixed immovably upon the vertebræ; belonging to the *Pleurospondylia*, as a turtle or tortoise; chelonian; testudinate.

II. *n.* A member of the *Pleurospondylia*, as a turtle or tortoise.

pleurosteal (plọ̈-ros′tẹ̄-ạl), *a.* [‹ *pleurosteon* + *-al*.] Lateral and costiferous, as a part of a bird's sternum; pertaining to the pleurosteon.

pleurosteon (plọ̈-ros′tẹ̄-on), *n.*; pl. *pleurostea* (-ạ̈). [NL., ‹ Gr. πλευρά, the side, + ὀστέον, a bone.] In *ornith.*, the anterior lateral piece of the breast-bone; that element of the sternum which forms the costal process and with which ribs articulate: distinguished from *lophosteon*, *coracosteon*, and *metosteon*. See cuts under *carinate* and *epipleura*.

Pleurosternidæ (plö-rọ̄-stėr′ni-dē), *n. pl.* [NL., ‹ *Pleurosternum* + *-idæ*.] A family of pleurodirous turtles, represented by the genus *Pleurosternum*. The plastron had a mesoplastral bone and an intergular shield, and the entoplastron was rhomboidal. The species lived during the Oölitic and Cretaceous periods.

Pleurosternum (plö-rọ̄-stėr′num), *n.* [NL., ‹ Gr. πλευρόν, rib, + στέρνον, the chest.] A genus of extinct turtles, typical of the family *Pleurosternidæ*.

pleurosthotonos (plö-ros-thot′ọ̄-nos), *n.* Same as *pleurothotonos*.

pleurostict (plö′rọ̄-stikt), *a.* [‹ NL. *pleurostictus*, ‹ Gr. πλευρά, the side, + στικτός, verbal adj. of στίζειν, prick, stab: see *stigma*.] In *entom.*, having the abdominal spiracles pleural, or situated on the dorsal part of the ventral segments; specifically, of or pertaining to the *Pleurosticta*: opposed to *laparostict*.

Dr. Horn exhibited seven species of Pleocoma from California, of which three were new, and supported the views of the late Dr. Le Conte of the position of this genus, which he insisted was a Laparostict, and not a Pleurostict Lamellicorn. *Amer. Naturalist*, XXII. 951.

Pleurosticta (plö-rọ̄-stik′tạ̈), *n. pl.* [NL., pl. of *pleurostictus*: see *pleurostict*.] In *entom.*, one of the two main divisions of the family *Scarabæidæ*, including those forms which have the abdominal spiracles (except the anterior ones) situated in the dorsal part of the abdominal segments, forming rows which diverge strongly, and with the last spiracle usually visible behind the elytra. The ligula is always connate with the mentum, and the larvæ have the lobes of the maxillæ connate. The other main division is *Laparosticta*. Also *Pleurostictica*.

pleurothotonic (plö″rọ̄-thọ̄-ton′ik), *a.* [‹ *pleurothotonos* + *-ic*.] Pertaining to, of the nature of, or affected with pleurothotonos.

pleurothotonos (plö″rọ̄-thot′ọ̄-nos), *n.* [NL., ‹ Gr. πλευρόθεν, from the side (‹ πλευρά, the side, + -θεν, from, an adverbial suffix), + τόνος, tension: see *tone*.] Tonic spasm in which the body is bent sidewise: correlated with *emprosthotonos* and *opisthotonos*.

Pleurotoma babylonica.

Pleurotoma (plö-rot′ọ̄-mạ̈), *n.* [NL. (Lamarck, 1801), ‹ Gr. πλευρά, the side, + -τομος, ‹ τέμνειν, ταμεῖν, cut.] In *conch.*, the typical genus of *Pleurotomidæ*: so called from the notch or slit in the outer lip of the aperture. Formerly the name was used for all the members of the family, but it is now restricted to forms more or less like *P. babylonica*.

Pleurotomaria (plö-rọ̄-tọ̄-mā′ri-ạ̈), *n.* [NL. (Defrance, 1826), ‹ Gr. πλευρά, the side, + τομάριον, prop. dim. of τόμος, a cut, slice, ‹ τέμνειν, ταμεῖν, cut.] The typical genus of *Pleurotomariidæ*.

Pleurotomaria anglica, from the Lias.

Pleurotomariidæ (plö-rọ̄-tom-ạ-rī′i-dē), *n. pl.* [NL., ‹ *Pleurotomaria* + *-idæ*.] A family of scutibranchiate gastropods, typified by the genus *Pleurotomaria*. The animal has the muzzle simple; there is no frontal veil, the tentacles are simple, and the eyes on pedicels exterior to their bases; two nearly symmetrical gills are developed, and lateral fringes, but no cirri, project from the sides; the shell is trochiform, and has a deep slit in the outer lip, leaving a fasciole on the completed whorls; the operculum is horny and multispiral or subspiral. Four living species, inhabiting deep tropical seas, are known, and many extinct species, ranging from the Silurian epoch upward, as the Liassic *Pleurotomaria anglica*. An ancient genus, ranging from the Devonian to the Trias, is *Porcellia*, of which a typical species is *P. puzosi*.

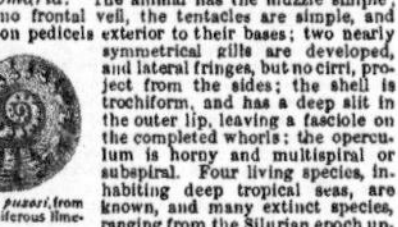

Porcellia puzosi, from the Carboniferous limestone.

pleurotomarioid (plö″rọ̄-tọ̄-mā′ri-oid), *a.* and *n.* **I.** *a.* Of or relating to the *Pleurotomariidæ*.

II. *n.* A species of the family *Pleurotomariidæ*.

Pleurotomidæ (plö-rọ̄-tom′i-dē), *n. pl.* [NL., ‹ *Pleurotoma* + *-idæ*.] A family of toxoglossate gastropods, typified by the genus *Pleurotoma*. Most of them have the shell spindle-shaped, with a prolonged canaliculate aperture notched near the suture. It contains about 500 species, sometimes known as *fissure-shells*. See cuts under *Lachesis* and *Pleurotoma*.

pleurotomine (plọ̈-rot′ọ̄-min), *a.* [‹ *Pleurotoma* + *-ine*[1].] Of or related to shells of the genus *Pleurotoma*.

pleurotomoid (plọ̈-rot′ọ̄-moid), *a.* and *n.* [‹ *Pleurotoma* + *-oid*.] **I.** *a.* Of or relating to the *Pleurotomidæ*.

II. *n.* A shell of the family *Pleurotomidæ*.

pleurotransversalis (plö-rọ̄-trans-vėr-sā′lis), *n.*; pl. *pleurotransversales* (-lēz). [NL., ‹ Gr. πλευρά, the pleura, + NL. *transversalis*, q. v.] An anomalous muscular slip arising from the transverse process of the seventh cervical vertebra, and inserted into the top of the pleural sac.

pleurotribe (plö′rọ̄-trīb), *a.* [‹ Gr. πλευρά, the side, + τρίβειν, rub.] In *bot.*, touching the side: said of certain zygomorphic flowers, especially adapted for cross-fertilization by external aid, in which the stamens and styles are so arranged or turned as to strike the visiting insect on the side. Such flowers are especially adapted to bees. *Phaseolus*, *Lathyrus sylvestris*, and *Polygala myrtifolia* are examples. Compare *nototribe* and *sternotribe*.

pleurotropous (plọ̈-rot′rọ̄-pus), *a.* [‹ Gr. πλευρά, the side, + τρέπειν, turn.] In *bot.*, having the faces flat: noting the stems of certain species of *Selaginella*. Compare *goniotropous*.

pleurovisceral (plö-rọ̄-vis′ẹ-ral), *a.* [‹ Gr. πλευρά, the side, + L. *viscera*, the internal organs: see *visceral*.] Pertaining to the side of the body and to viscera: specifically said of the connecting cord or loop between a pleural and a visceral nervous ganglion of an invertebrate, as a mollusk. Also *visceropleural*.

plevin† (plev′in), *n.* [Also *plevine*, ‹ ME. **plevine*, ‹ OF. *plevine*, *plevigne*, *pleurine*, *plevene* (ML. *plevina*, *pleuvina*, *pluvina*), a pledge, warrant, assurance, ‹ *plevir*, *pleivir*, *pleuvir*, *pluvir*, also *plever*, *pluver* = Pr. *plevir* (ML. reflex *plevire*, *plivire*), promise, engage, pledge, give in pledge, warrant, ‹ L. *præbere*, p[ræbere fid]e[m], offer, give (*præbere fidem*, give a pledge): see *prebend*. Cf. *pledge* and *replevin*, *replevy*.] In *law*, a warrant or an assurance.

plex (pleks), *v. i.* [‹ *plexus*.] To form a plexus.

plexal (plek′sạl), *a.* [‹ *plex-us* + *-al*.] Of or pertaining to a plexus.

plexed (plekst), *a.* [‹ L. *plexus*, plaited (see *plexus*), + *-ed*[2].] Plaited, netted, or made plexiform; plexiform.

plexiform (plek′si-fôrm), *a.* [‹ L. *plexus*, a twining, plaiting (see *plexus*), + *forma*, form.] 1. In the form of network; complicated. *Quincy*.—2. In *anat.*, specifically, formed into a plexus, as nerves; plaited; plexed.

pleximeter, plexometer (plek-sim′e-tėr, plek-som′e-tėr), *n.* [‹ Gr. πλῆξις, percussion (‹ πλήσσειν, strike: see *plague*), + μέτρον, measure.] In *med.*, an elongated plate, composed of ivory, india-rubber, or some similar substance, from 1½ to 2 inches in length, placed in contact with the body, commonly on the chest or abdomen, and struck with the percussion-hammer, in diagnosis of disease by mediate percussion. Also *plessimeter*, *plegometer*.

pleximetric (plek-si-met′rik), *a.* [‹ *pleximeter* + *-ic*.] Of or pertaining to the pleximeter or its use.

plexometer, *n.* See *pleximeter*.

plexor (plek′sor), *n.* [NL., irreg. ‹ Gr. πλῆξις, percussion, ‹ πλήσσειν, strike: see *plague*.] That which strikes in percussion; a percussion-hammer.

plexure (plek′şūr), *n.* [‹ L. as if **plexura* (ML. ?), ‹ *plectere*, pp. *plexus*, interweave: see *plexus*.] An interweaving; a texture; that which is woven together.

plexus (plek′sus), *n.* [‹ L. *plexus*, an interweaving, twining, plaiting, ‹ *plectere*, pp. *plexus*, interweave, twine, plait: see *plait*.] 1. A network; any collection of intimately coherent parts, as of an argument.

Antecedent and consequent relations are therefore not merely linear, but constitute a *plexus*; and this *plexus* pervades nature. *Amer. Jour. Sci.*, 3d ser., XXXI. 286.

A perfect *plexus* of ideas that mutually support and interpret one another. *Encyc. Brit.*, II. 55.

2. In *anat.*, an interlacing of nerves, vessels, or fibers; a net-like arrangement of parts, or the parts so disposed: especially said of certain delicate vascular membranes chiefly composed

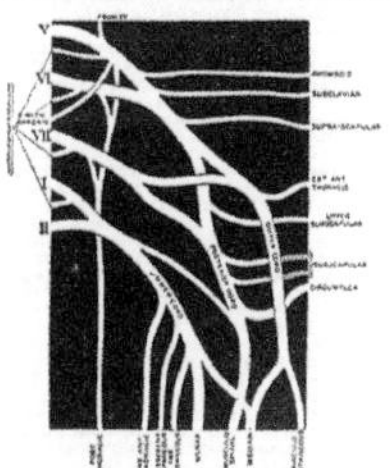

Brachial Plexus of Nerves in Man.
V, VI, VII, I, II, the five main roots (anterior divisions of cervical and dorsal spinal nerves) of the plexus; other cords and continuations of the plexus are named in the figure.

of minute anastomosing blood-vessels, as the choroid plexus, and of similar arrangements of nerves of the spinal and sympathetic systems. —3. In *math.*, a system of one-fold relations. —**Aortic plexus**, the network of sympathetic nerves on the side and front of the abdominal aorta, between the origins of the superior and inferior mesenteric arteries. Also called *intermesenteric plexus*.—**Auerbach's plexus**, an extensive gangliated plexus of nerves lying between the longitudinal and the circular layer of the small intestine. Also called *myenteric plexus*.—**Axillary plexus.** Same as *brachial plexus*.—**Basilar plexus.** Same as *transverse sinus* (which see, under *sinus*).—**Brachial plexus.** See *brachial*.—**Cardiac plexus**, one of the three great prevertebral plexuses of the sympathetic, situated in the upper thoracic region in front, and between the aorta and the pulmonary artery, where these vessels are in contact. It receives the cardiac branches from the cervical ganglia and those of the vagus nerves, and gives off the nerves which supply the heart, together with some smaller branches which contribute to the nervous supply of the lungs. That division (the smaller) which lies in the concavity of the arch of the aorta is called the *superficial cardiac plexus*, while the *deep cardiac plexus* is placed behind the arch of the aorta, between it and the end of the trachea.—**Carotid plexus.** See *carotid*.—**Caudal plexus.** Same as *coccygeal plexus*.—**Cavernous plexus.** (*a*) The continuation of the carotid plexus in the cavernous sinus. (*b*) The continuation of the prostatic plexus, supplying the erectile tissue of the penis. Also called *cavernous nerves*.—**Cervical plexus**, the network of nerves formed by the anterior divisions of the four upper cervical nerves, giving off numerous nerves to the head, neck, and chest, and the phrenic nerve to the diaphragm. A similar plexing of posterior divisions of the three upper cervical nerves is known as the *posterior cervical plexus*.—**Choroid plexuses.** See *choroid*.—**Ciliary plexus**, a fine gangliated network formed from the ciliary nerves, spread over the choroid, and within the ciliary muscle, from which the nerves of the cornea, of the ciliary muscle, and of the iris are derived.—**Coccygeal plexus**, the connection formed between the anterior divisions of the fourth and fifth sacral and first coccygeal nerves.—**Cœliac plexus**, the sympathetic plexus of the cœliac artery, continued from the solar plexus, and dividing into the gastric, hepatic, and splenic plexuses.—**Colic plexuses**, divisions of the superior and inferior mesenteric plexuses accompanying the colic arteries.—**Coronary plexus.** (*a*) One of two plexuses, right and left, derived from the cardiac plexus, and accompanying the respective coronary arteries. (*b*) Same as *gastric plexus* (*b*).—**Cystic plexus**, a secondary plexus of the hepatic, to the gall-bladder.—**Deep jugular plexus**, a plexus of lymphatic vessels extending along the internal jugular vein to the base of the cranium.—**Deferential plexus**, the continuation of the vesical plexus upon the vasa deferentia and the seminal vesicles.—**Diaphragmatic plexus**, the phrenic plexus.—**Dorsispinal plexus**, a network of veins investing the arches of the vertebræ, and receiving branches from the contiguous muscles and skin of the back.—**Epigastric plexus**, the solar plexus, or solariplex.—**Esophageal plexus**, plexiform branches of the pneumogastric nerve on the esophagus. Also called *plexus gulæ*.—**Gastric plexus.** (*a*) One of two plexuses, anterior and posterior, formed by the left and right vagus nerves respectively. (*b*) A secondary plexus of the cœliac, accompanying the gastric artery. Also called *coronary plexus*.—**Gastro-epiploic plexuses**, secondary plexuses of the hepatic and splenic, accompanying the gastro-epiploic arteries.—**Hemorrhoidal plexus.** (*a*) A plexus of fine nerves derived from the pelvic, vesical, and inferior hemorrhoidal plexuses, penetrating the coats of the rectum. (*b*) A large and copiously anastomosing network of veins in the lower wall of the rectum, beneath the mucous coat, from which the hemorrhoidal veins proceed.—**Hepatic plexus**, the largest division of the cœliac plexus, accompanying the hepatic artery in the substance of the liver.—**Hypogastric plexus**, an intricate sympathetic plexus, formed by the prolongation of the aortic plexus on each side, lying in the interval of the common iliac arteries, invested by a sheath of areolar tissue. It divides into two parts below, one on each side of the pelvic viscera, forming the pelvic plexuses. Also called *superior hypogastric plexus*.—**Ileocolic plexus**, the division of the superior mesenteric plexus accompanying the ileocolic artery.—**Inferior dental plexus**, a plexus formed by the communications of the branches of the inferior dental nerve within the lower jaw.—**Inferior hypogastric plexus.** Same as *pelvic plexus*.—**Inferior mesenteric plexus**, a sympathetic plexus derived from the left lateral part of the aortic plexus, and surrounding the artery of the same name.—**Infra-orbital plexus**, a plexus formed by the union of the labial branches of the superior maxillary nerve with branches of the facial nerve.—**Interepithelial plexus**, the fine network of nerves among the cells of the epithelium of the cornea.—**Intermesenteric plexus.** Same as *aortic plexus*.—**Intermuscular plexuses**, gangliated nerve-plexuses in the substance of organs having unstriated muscle-fibers.—**Intraspinal plexus**, an irregular network of veins investing the spinal canal, emptying into the intercostal, lumbar, vertebral, and lateral sacral veins.—**Ischiatic plexus**, the upper part of the sacral plexus.—**Lumbar plexus.** See *lumbar*[1].—**Meissner's plexus**, the gangliated plexus of the submucous layer of the small intestine, formed by branches derived from Auerbach's plexus.—**Meningeal plexus**, the continuation of the carotid plexus upon the middle meningeal artery.—**Mesenteric plexus**, the sympathetic plexus accompanying a mesenteric artery. The superior is derived from the great solar plexus; the inferior chiefly from the aortic plexus.—**Myenteric plexus.** Same as *Auerbach's plexus*.—**Obturator plexus**, the plexus of veins surrounding the obturator foramen.—**Ophthalmic plexus**, the continuation of the cavernous plexus on the ophthalmic artery.—**Ovarian plexus.** See *pampiniform plexus*.—**Pampiniform, pancreatic, patellar, pelvic plexus.** See the adjectives.—**Pancreaticoduodenal plexus**, a secondary plexus of the hepatic, accompanying the superior pancreaticoduodenal artery.—**Parotid plexus**, the anastomoses formed by loops of the seventh nerve on the side of the face. Also called *plexus* or *pes anserinus*.—**Pharyngeal plexus.** See *pharyngeal*.—**Phrenic plexus**, the sympathetic plexus which accompanies the phrenic artery to the diaphragm, arising from the semilunar ganglion.—**Plexus anserinus.** Same as *parotid plexus*.—**Plexus anserinus nervi mediani**, the bundles from the eighth cervical nerve that go to form the median nerve.—**Plexus brachialis**, the brachial plexus.—**Plexus cervicalis**, the cervical plexus.—**Plexus choroideus**, the choroid plexus of a lateral ventricle.—**Plexus choroideus inferior**, the choroid plexus of the fourth ventricle.—**Plexus choroideus medius**, the choroid plexus of the third ventricle.—**Plexus choroideus ventriculi lateralis**, the choroid plexus of a lateral ventricle.—**Plexus choroideus ventriculi quarti**, the choroid plexus of the fourth ventricle.—**Plexus choroideus ventriculi tertii**, the choroid plexus of the third ventricle.—**Plexus gangliiformis**, the lower ganglion, or ganglion of the trunk, of the vagus nerve.—**Plexus gulæ.** Same as *esophageal plexus*.—**Plexus lumbalis**, the lumbar plexus.—**Plexus nodosus**, the ganglion of the trunk of the vagus.—**Plexus patellæ**, the plexiform network of the kneepan, formed by cutaneous nerves, especially the long saphenous.—**Plexus sacralis**, the sacral plexus.—**Plexus submucosus.** Same as *Meissner's plexus*.—**Posterior cervical plexus**, a plexus often formed by the internal branches of the posterior divisions of the first three cervical nerves.—**Prevertebral plexuses**, the three large median plexuses formed by the two sympathetic nerves, situated in front of the spine, in the cavity of the thorax, abdomen, and pelvis, and respectively known as the *cardiac*, *solar*, and *hypogastric plexuses*.—**Prostatic plexus.** (*a*) The continuation of the vesical plexus supplying the prostate body. (*b*) A plexus of veins surrounding the base of the prostate, formed mainly from the dorsal veins of the penis.—**Pterygoid plexus**, a close network of veins covering both surfaces of the external pterygoid muscle, receiving tributaries mostly corresponding to the branches of the internal maxillary artery, and emptying into the internal maxillary vein.—**Pudendal plexus.** (*a*) A close net of large veins occupying the upper part of the pubic arch, between the layers of the triangular ligament, and mainly derived from the dorsal veins of the penis or clitoris. (*b*) The lower section of the sacral plexus (*a*).—**Pulmonary plexuses**, the two plexuses, the anterior and posterior, formed by branches of the vagus and sympathetic on the front and back side respectively of each lung at its root.—**Pyloric plexus**, a secondary plexus of the hepatic, accompanying the pyloric artery.—**Renal plexus**, a plexus formed of nerves from the semilunar ganglion, the solar and aortic plexuses, and the smallest splanchnic nerve, accompanying the renal artery and terminating in the substance of the kidney.—**Sacral plexus.** (*a*) A plexus formed by the union of the lumbosacral cord and anterior divisions of the three upper sacral nerves, together with a portion of that of the fourth. Its branches of distribution are the superior and inferior gluteal, great and small sciatic, pudic, and muscular. (*b*) A plexus of veins in the back of the pelvis, tributary to the middle sacral vein.—**Sacrococcygeal plexus**, the series of loops formed by the anastomoses of the external branches of the posterior divisions of the first three sacral nerves, the fourth and fifth posterior sacrals, and the posterior coccygeal.—**Santorinian plexus**, the pudendal plexus of veins.—**Solar plexus**, the largest of the three great sympathetic plexuses, situated at the upper part of the abdomen, behind the stomach, and in front of the aorta. It consists of an intricate network of nerves, associated with ganglia, receiving the upper splanchnic nerves and some branches of the vagus, and giving off numerous branches which accompany the arteries to the principal viscera of the abdomen, constituting secondary plexuses. Its two principal masses, right and left, are known, from their form, as the *semilunar ganglia*. Also called *epigastric plexus*, *solar ganglion*.—**Spermatic plexus.** (*a*) A small plexus, derived from the renal and aortic plexuses, accompanying the artery to the testis in the male, to the ovary and uterus in the female. (*b*) Same as *pampiniform plexus*.—**Spiral plexus**, the plexiform arrangement assumed in the spiral lamina by the nerve-filaments given off from the spiral ganglion of the cochlea.—**Splenic plexus**, one of the divisions of the cœliac plexus, accompanying the splenic artery into the substance of the spleen.—**Subepithelial plexus**, the delicate network, formed by the terminal filaments of the ciliary nerves, ramifying on the basement membrane of the ectocornea, or surface of the cornea proper, beneath the epithelium.—**Superficial jugular plexus**, lymphatic tributaries to the jugular trunk from the occipital, ear, and temporal regions.—**Superior dental plexus**, the series of loops formed by branches of the dental nerves of the upper jaw, from which the filaments given to the teeth are derived.—**Suprarenal plexus**, a secondary plexus derived from the solar plexus, terminating in the suprarenal body, and receiving branches from one of the splanchnic nerves.—**Tonsilar plexus**, a plexus formed around the tonsil by the tonsilar branches of the glossopharyngeal nerve.—**Triangular plexus**, the plexiform arrangement assumed by the bundles of fibers of the sensory root of the fifth nerve before ending in the Gasserian ganglion.—**Tympanic plexus**, a plexus formed by the branches of the tympanic nerve, in union with others from the facial and sympathetic, in the mucous lining of the middle ear.—**Uterine plexus.** (*a*) A plexus derived from the pelvic plexus, passing through the broad ligament with the uterine artery to be distributed to the uterus. (*b*) Venous channels at the sides of the uterus, and in the broad ligaments, emptying into the ovarian veins.—**Vaginal plexus**, a network of veins surrounding the vagina, especially in its lower part.—**Venous plexus**, an anastomosing set of veins, forming a network. There are several such, as the ovarian, pampiniform, pharyngeal, prostatic, pterygoid, spermatic, uterine, and vaginal.—**Vertebral plexus**, the sympathetic plexus on the vertebral artery, joined by filaments from the lower cervical nerves.—**Vesical plexus.** (*a*) A plexus of veins surrounding the muscular coat of the bladder. (*b*) A plexus derived from the pelvic plexus, distributed to the lower part and side of the bladder, the prostate, and the seminal vesicle.—**Vesicovaginal plexus**, a plexus derived from the pelvic plexus, distributed to the vagina and bladder.—**Vidian plexus**, the plexus formed by the Vidian nerve about the Vidian artery.

pleyt, *v.* and *n.* A Middle English form of *play*[1].

pleyn†, pleyne†. Obsolete forms of *plain*[1], *plain*[2], *plain*[3].

pliability (pli-a-bil'i-ti), *n.* [< *pliable* + *-ity* (see *-bility*).] The quality of being pliable; flexibility; pliableness.

Sweet *pliability* of man's spirit, that can at once surrender itself to illusions which cheat expectation and sorrow of their weary moments! — *Sterne*, Sentimental Journey, p. 84.

Pliability in politics, if accompanied by honesty, is a virtue. — *H. Adams*, Gallatin, p. 577.

pliable (pli'a-bl), *a.* [< F. *pliable* = Pr. *plicable*, flexible, pliant, pliable, < L. as if **plicabilis*, that can be bent, < *plicare*, fold, bend: see *ply*.] 1. Easy to be bent; readily yielding to force or pressure without rupture; flexible: as, willow is a *pliable* plant.

The younger they are when they begin with that art [music], the more *pliable* and nimble their fingers are touching the instrument. — *Sharp*, Works, VI. viii.

2. Flexible in disposition; easy to be bent, inclined, or persuaded; readily yielding to influence, arguments, persuasion, or discipline.

At the last, having found the citys *plyable* to theyr desyer, they bounde the one to another by othe, and wrought sure wyth hostages and money. — *Golding*, tr. of Cæsar, fol. 148.

So is the heart of some men; when smitten by God it seems soft and *pliable*. — *Jer. Taylor*, Works, II. xii.

Since I was of understanding to know we knew nothing, my reason hath been more *pliable* to the will of faith. — *Sir T. Browne*, Religio Medici, i. 10.

=**Syn.** 1. Pliant, supple.—2. Compliant, yielding, tractable.

pliableness (pli'a-bl-nes), *n.* The quality of being pliable; flexibility; the quality of yielding readily to force or to moral influence; pliability: as, the *pliableness* of a plant; *pliableness* of disposition.

The chosen vessel hath by his example taught me this charitable and holy *pliablenesse*. — *Bp. Hall*, Satan's Fiery Darts, iii. 5.

Compare . . . the ingenuous *pliableness* to virtuous counsels in youth, as it comes fresh and untainted out of the hands of nature, with the confirmed obstinacy in most sorts of sin that is to be found in an aged sinner. — *South*, Sermons.

pliably (pli'a-bli), *adv.* In a pliable manner; yieldingly; compliantly.

This worthy Doctor [George Morley] . . . was . . . not of the number of those lukewarm irreligious Temporizers who had learn'd *pliably* to tack about, as still to be ready to receive whatever revolution and turn of affairs should happen. — *Wood*, Athenæ Oxon., II. 771.

pliancy (pli'an-si), *n.* [< *plian(t)* + *-cy*.] The quality of being pliant, or easily bent or inclined in any desired direction; readiness to be persuaded or influenced: as, the *pliancy* of a rod; *pliancy* of disposition.

To be overlooked for want of political *pliancy* is a circumstance I need not blush to own. — *Anecdotes of Bp. Watson*, I. 305.

Avaunt all specious *pliancy* of mind
In men of low degree, all smooth pretence!
I better like a blunt indifference.
— *Wordsworth*, A High-Minded Spaniard.

Jane, you please me, and you master me—you seem to submit, and I like the sense of *pliancy* you impart. — *Charlotte Brontë*, Jane Eyre, xxiv.

Insolence had taken the place of *pliancy*, and the former slave now applied the chain and whip to his master. — *Motley*, Dutch Republic, III. 158.

There was in Bacon an invariable *pliancy* in the presence of great persons which disqualified him for the task of giving wise and effectual counsel. — *E. A. Abbott*, Bacon, p. 21.

pliant (pli'ant), *a.* [< ME. *plyaunt*, < OF. *pliant*, *pleiant*, *ploiant*, F. *pliant*, flexible, supple, pliant, folding, < L. *plican(t-)s*, ppr. of *plicare* (> F. *plier*), fold: see *ply*.] 1. Capable of being easily bent; flexible; supple; limber; lithe: as, a *pliant* twig.

So *pliant* were
His goodly timber'd Limbs, and yet so stout,
That wax and steel seem'd kindly marry'd there.
— *J. Beaumont*, Psyche, i. 61.

Me of a *pliant* metall you shall finde;
See then you cast and shape me to your minde.
— *Heywood*, Dialogues.

Who foremost now delight to cleave
With *pliant* arm thy glassy wave?
— *Gray*, Prospect of Eton College.

A well organized and very *pliant* hand may determine to occupations requiring manual dexterity. — *Beddoes*, Mathematical Evidence, note.

Pliant as a wand of willow. — *Longfellow*, Hiawatha, vi.

Paint that figure's *pliant* grace. — *M. Arnold*, Switzerland, i.

2. Easily bent or inclined to any particular course; readily influenced for good or evil; easy to be persuaded; yielding.

I . . .
Took once a *pliant* hour, and found good means
To draw from her a prayer of earnest heart.
— *Shak.*, Othello, i. 3. 151.

No man has his servant more obsequious and *pliant*. — *B. Jonson*, Every Man out of his Humour, i. 1.

Whatsoever creates fear . . . is apt to entender the spirit, and make it devout and *pliant* to any part of duty.
Jer. Taylor, Holy Living, iv. 7.

His *pliant* soul gave way to all things base,
He knew no shame, he dreaded no disgrace.
Crabbe, Works, I. 63.

pliantly (plī'ant-li), *adv.* In a pliant manner; flexibly; yieldingly.

pliantness (plī'ant-nes), *n.* The quality of being pliant; flexibility.

plica (plī'kạ), *n.*; pl. *plicæ* (-sē). [NL., < L. *plicare*, fold: see *ply*.] 1. In *pathol.*, a matted, filthy condition of the hair, from disease. Also called *plica polonica*, *helosis*, and *trichosis*.—2. In *bot.*, a diseased state in plants in which the buds, instead of developing true branches, become short twigs, and these in their turn produce others of the same sort, the whole forming an entangled mass.—3. In *zoöl.* and *anat.*, a fold or folding of a part.—4. In *entom.*, a prominent ridge or carina, often turned over or inclined to one side, so that it appears like a fold; specifically, a longitudinal ridge on the internal surface of each elytron, near the outer edge; an elytral ridge, found in certain *Coleoptera*.—5. In *herpet.*: (*a*) [*cap.*] A genus of American iguanoid lizards: named from the folds of skin on the sides. *J. E. Gray.* (*b*) A lizard of this genus: as, the dotted *plica*, *P. punctata*.—6. In *mensural music*: (*a*) A kind of grace-note. (*b*) A kind of ligature. (*c*) The stem or tail of a note.—**Elytral plica.** See def. 4, and *elytral*.—**Plica alaris**, in *ornith.*: (*a*) The feathered fold of skin on the fore border of the wing which occupies the reëntrant angle made by the bones of the upper arm and forearm, stretching from the shoulder to the wrist. (*b*) The bend or flexure of the wing at the carpal joint. [Rare.]—**Plicæ adiposæ.** Same as *alar ligaments* (which see, under *alar*).—**Plicæ rectovesicales.** Same as *plicæ semilunares Douglasii*.—**Plicæ semilunares Douglasii**, two folds of the peritoneum between the rectum and the bladder. See cut under *peritoneum*.—**Plica gubernatrix**, that peritoneal fold which is in relation with the gubernaculum testis.—**Plica interdigitalis**, in *ornith.*, the webbing or palmation of the toes; the palama.—**Plica primitiva**, in *embryol.*, the primitive fold; either lip of the primitive furrow of the early embryo of a vertebrate.—**Plica semilunaris**, in *human anat.*, a fold of conjunctival mucous membrane at the inner corner of the eye: the rudiment of a nictitating membrane or third eyelid. See cut under *eye*[1].

Plicacea (plī-kā'sẹ̄-ạ̈), *n. pl.* [NL., < *plica*, a fold, + *-acea*.] In *conch.*, a family of trachelipod gastropods, having the columella plaited, and containing the genera *Tornatella* and *Pyramidella*. *Latreille*, 1825.

plical (plī'kạl), *a.* [< *plica* + *-al*.] In *bot.*, of or pertaining to plica.

Plicaria (plī-kā'ri-ạ̈), *n.* [NL., < *plica*, a fold, + *-aria*.] In *conch.*, same as *Cancellaria*. *Fabricius*, 1823.

plicata (plī-kā'tạ̈), *n.*; pl. *plicatæ* (-tē). [ML., fem. of L. *plicatus*, pp. of *plicare*, fold: see *plicate*.] In the *Rom. Cath. Ch.*, the folded chasuble worn at certain penitential seasons by the deacon and subdeacon, or by a priest when officiating as deacon. *McClintock and Strong.*

plicate (plī'kāt), *a.* [< L. *plicatus*, pp. of *plicare*, fold, bend, lay or wind together, double up: see *ply*.] 1. In *bot.*, folded like a fan; plaited: as, a *plicate* leaf.—2. In *zoöl.* and *anat.*, plaited, plexed, or folded; formed into a plication.—3. In *entom.*, having parallel raised lines which are sharply cut on one side, but on the other descend gradually to the next line, as a surface; plaited or folded. Also *plicative*, *plicated*.—**Plicate elytra**, elytra having two or three conspicuous longitudinal folds or furrows, as in the coleopterous family *Pselaphidæ*.—**Plicate wings**, in *entom.*, same as *folded wings* (which see, under *folded*).

Plicate Leaf of *Alchemilla vulgaris*.

plicated (plī'kā-ted), *a.* [< *plicate* + *-ed*[2].] Same as *plicate*.

plicately (plī'kāt-li), *adv.* In a plicate or folded manner; so as to be or make a plication.

plicatile (plik'ạ-til), *a.* [< L. *plicatilis*, that may be folded together, < *plicare*, fold: see *plicate*.] 1†. Capable of being folded or interwoven; pliable.

Motion of the *plicatile* fibers or subtil threds of which the brain consists.
Dr. H. More, Antidote against Atheism, App., x.

2. In *entom.*, folding lengthwise in repose, as the wings of a wasp.

plication (plī-kā'shon), *n.* [< ML. **plicatio(n-)*, a folding, < L. *plicare*, fold: see *ply*.] 1. The act or process of folding, or the state of being put in folds; a folding or putting in folds, as duplication or triplication. Also *plicature*.

The peculiar surface-marking . . . consists in a strongly marked ridge-and-furrow *plication* of the shelly wall.
W. B. Carpenter, Micros., § 487.

2. That which is plicated; a plica or fold. Also *plicature*.

Why the deuce should you not be sitting precisely opposite to me at this moment, . . . thy juridical brow expanding its *plications*, as a pun rose in your fancy?
Scott, Redgauntlet, letter i.

3. In *geol.*, a bending of the strata; a fold or folding.

In Western Europe the prevalent lines along which terrestrial *plications* took place during Palæozoic time were certainly from S.W. or S.S.W. to N.E. or N.N.E.
Geikie, Text-Book of Geol. (2d ed.), p. 270.

plicative (plik'ạ-tiv), *a.* [< *plicate* + *-ive*.] Same as *plicate*.

plicatopapillose (plī-kā-tō-pap'i-lōs), *a.* [< L. *plicatus*, plicate, + NL. *papillosus*, papillose.] In *entom.*, plicate and papillose; forming a series of elevations and depressions resembling folds, as the papillose surfaces of certain larvæ.

plicator (plī-kā'tọr), *n.* [< L. as if **plicator* (cf. L. fem. *plicatrix*), a folder (ML. *plicator*, a collector of taxes), < L. *plicare*, fold: see *ply*.] A device for forming a fold or plait: an attachment to some forms of sewing-machine, etc.

Plicatula (plī-kaṭ'ụ̄-lạ̈), *n.* [NL. (Lamarck, 1801), < L. *plicatus*, pp. of *plicare*, fold: see *plicate*, *ply*.] In *conch.*, a genus of bivalve mollusks of the family *Spondylidæ*, having the shell irregular, attached by the umbo of the right valve, which is plicate, the cartilage internal, and the hinge-teeth two in each valve.

Plicatula cristata.

plicatulate (plī-kaṭ'ụ̄-lāt), *a.* [< NL. **plicatulus*, dim. of L. *plicatus*, folded: see *plicate*.] In *bot.*, minutely plicate.

plicature (plik'ạ-ṭụ̄r), *n.* [< L. *plicatura*, a folding, < *plicare*, pp. *plicatus*, fold: see *plicate*.] Same as *plication*, 1, 2.

The many *plicatures* so closely prest.
Dr. H. More, Psychozoia, I. 18.

plicidentine (plis-i-den'tin), *n.* [< NL. *plica*, a fold, + E. *dentine*.] Plicated or folded dentine; a kind of dentine which is folded on a series of vertical plates, causing the surface of the tooth to be fluted. *Brande and Cox.*

pliciferous (pli-sif'ẹ-rus), *a.* [< NL. *plica*, a fold, + L. *ferre* = E. *bear*[1].] Provided with folds or plicæ: specifically, in entomology, said of those elytra which have an internal plica or ridge.—**Pliciferous Coleoptera**, those *Coleoptera* which have pliciferous elytra.

pliciform (plis'i-fôrm), *a.* [< NL. *plica*, a fold, + L. *forma*, form.] In *bot.* and *zoöl.*, plait-like; having the form of a plait or fold.

Plicipennes (plis-i-pen'ēz), *n. pl.* [NL., < *plica*, a fold, + L. *penna*, a feather.] In Latreille's classification, the third family of neuropterous insects; the caddis-flies. It corresponds to the *Phryganeidæ* in a broad sense, or the *Trichoptera* of Leach. Also *Plicipennia*.

plicipennine (plis-i-pen'in), *a.* Belonging to the *Plicipennes*.

Plictolophinæ (plik-tol-ō-fī'nē), *n. pl.* [NL., < *Plictolophus* + *-inæ*.] Cockatoos as a subfamily of *Psittacidæ*: same as *Cacatuinæ*.

Plictolophus (plik-tol'ọ̄-fus), *n.* [NL., orig. *Plyctolophus* (Vieillot, 1816), later *Plectolophus* (Bourjot St. Hilaire, 1837–8), *Pluctolophus* (Nitzsch, 1840), *Plissolophus* (C. W. L. Gloger, 1842), and *Plictolophus* (Otto Finsch, 1867), < Gr. *πλικτός, assumed verbal adj. of πλίσσειν, cross one's leg in walking, stride, + λόφος, a crest.] A genus of cockatoos: same as *Cacatua*.

plie†, *v.* An obsolete spelling of *ply*.

plié (plē-ā'), *a.* [F. *plié*, bent, pp. of *plier*, bend: see *ply*, *plicate*.] In *her.*, same as *close*[2]: said of a bird.

plier (plī'ėr), *n.* [Also, less prop., *plyer* (cf. *crier*, *flier*, *trier*); < *ply* + *-er*[1].] 1. One who or that which plies.—2. *pl.* In *fort.*, a kind of balance used in raising and letting down a drawbridge, consisting of timbers joined in the form of a St. Andrew's cross.—3. *pl.* Small pincers with long jaws, adapted for handling small articles, and also for bending and shaping wire. See cut under *nipper*.—**Saw-set pliers**, a form of adjustable pliers sometimes used in place of the saw-set for bending the teeth of saws.

plif (plif), *n.* A dialectal form of *plow*. *Halliwell.* [Yorkshire, Eng.]

pliform† (plī'fôrm), *a.* [Prop. **plyform*; < *ply* + *form*.] In the form of a fold or doubling. *Pennant.*

plight[1] (plīt), *n.* [< ME. *plight*, *plyght*, *pligt*, *pliht*, danger, pledge, < AS. *pliht*, danger, damage, = OFries. *plicht*, danger; cf. OFries. *plicht*, care, concern, = MD. *plicht*, *plecht*, duty, debt, D. *pligt*, duty, = MLG. LG. *plicht* = OHG. *phliht*, *fliht*, MHG. *pfliht*, *phliht*, friendly care, concern, service, duty, G. *pflicht*, duty, = Sw. Dan. *pligt* (< LG. ?), duty; with abstract formative *-t*, from the verb found in the rare AS. **pléon*, *plión* (a strong verb, pret. *pleah*, *plēh*), expose to danger, risk (whence also *pleoh*, *plioh*, contr. *pleó*, *plió* = OFries. *plē*, *plī*, danger), or in the related weak verb, OS. *plegan*, promise, pledge, = OFries. *plegia*, *pligia*, be wont, = MD. *pleghen*, be wont, practise, take care of, D. *plegen*, pledge, be wont, = MLG. *plegen* = OHG. *pflegan*, *phlegan*, *phlekan*, *plegan*, MHG. *phlegen*, *pflegen*, G. *pflegen*, promise or engage to do, take care of, keep, be accustomed (etc.), = Sw. *pläga* = Dan. *pleje*, be wont, = AS. *plegan*, *plegian*, play, orig. be in active motion: see *play*[1]. The OF. *plevir*, pledge, cannot be from the Teut. (OS. *plegan*, etc.), but is to be referred, with the OF. *pleige*, ML. *plegium*, etc. (whence E. *pledge*), to the L. *præbere*, proffer, give: see *plevin*, *pledge*. The word *plight*[1] has been confused with *plight*[2], state, condition: see *plight*[2].] 1†. Peril; danger; harm; damage.

He (hath) mi lond with mikel onrith,
With michel wrong, with mikel *plith*,
For I ne misdede him nevere nouth,
And havede me to sorwe brouth.
Havelok (1370). (*Halliwell.*)

2. A solemn promise or engagement concerning a matter of serious personal moment; solemn assurance or pledge.

That lord whose hand must take my *plight* shall carry
Half my love with him. *Shak.*, Lear, i. 1. 103.

So these young hearts, not knowing that they loved,
Not she at least, nor conscious of a bar
Between them, nor by *plight* or broken ring
Bound . . . *Tennyson*, Aylmer's Field.

In plight†, under promise or pledge.

Thus they justtyd tylle hyt was nyght,
Then they departyd *in plyght*,
They had nede to reste.
MS. Cantab. Ff. ii. 38, f. 76. (*Halliwell.*)

plight[1] (plīt), *v. t.* [< ME. *plighten*, *plyghten*, *pligten*, *plygten*, *plihten*, pledge, < AS. *plihtan*, imperil, bring danger upon; = D. *ver-pligten*, *ver-plichten* = MLG. *plichten* = MHG. *pflihten*, *phlihten*, G. *bei-pflichten*, *ver-pflichten* = Sw. *be-pligta*, *för-pligta* = Dan. *for-pligte*, *til-pligte*, pledge, engage, bind; from the noun.] To engage by solemn promise; pledge; engage or bind one's self by pledging: as, to *plight* one's hand, word, honor, faith, truth, vows, etc.

Ye woot right wel what ye bihighten me,
And in myn hand your trouthe *plighten* ye
To love me best. *Chaucer*, Franklin's Tale, l. 600.

Pylgrimis and palmers *plyghten* hem to-gederes,
To seche seint Iame and seyntys of rome.
Piers Plowman (C), i. 47.

And for to put hir out of fere,
He swore, and hath his trouth *plight*
To be for ever his owne knight.
Gower, Conf. Amant., iv.

Dearer is love then life, and fame then gold:
But dearer then them both your faith once *plighted* hold.
Spenser, F. Q., V. xi. 63.

By this fair fount hath many a shepherd sworn,
And given away his freedom, many a troth
Been *plight*. *Fletcher*, Faithful Shepherdess, i. 2.

Have we not *plighted* each our holy oath,
That one should be the common good of both?
Dryden, Pal. and Arc., i. 291.

=**Syn.** *Pledge*, *Plight*. *Pledge* is applied to property as well as to word, faith, truth, honor, etc. *Plight* is now chiefly poetic or rhetorical; to *plight* honor is, as it were, to deposit it in *pledge* for the performance of an act—not often for the truth of a statement—to be forfeited if the act is not performed.

plight[2] (plīt), *n.* [An erroneous spelling, due to confusion with *plight*[1], of *plite*[1], < ME. *plite*, *plyte*, *plit*, state, condition, < OF. *plite*, *pliste*, condition, < ML. **plicita*, prop. fem. of L. *plicitus*, pp. of *plicare*, fold: see *ply*. Cf. *plight*[3].] Condition; position; state; situation; predicament.

Certes I not how,
Ne when, allas, I shal the tyme se,
That in this *plit* I may ben eft with yow.
Chaucer, Troilus, iii. 1480.

When Paris persayuit the *plit* of his brother,
How he was dolfully ded, and drawen in the ost.
Destruction of Troy (E. E. T. S.), l. 10363.

Never knight I saw in such misseeming *plight*.
Spenser, F. Q., I. ix. 23.

For-thy appease your griefe and heavy *plight*.
Spenser, F. Q., II. i. 14.

Some stone horses came over in good *plight*.
Winthrop, Hist. New England, I. 34.

I think myself in better *plight* for a lender than you are.
Shak., M. W. of W., ii. 2. 172.

I am lately arrived in Holland in a good *Plight* of Health.
Howell, Letters, I. i. 7.

We continued here three weeks in this dismal *plight*.
Addison, Frozen Words.

In piteous *plight* he knock'd at George's gate,
And begg'd for aid, as he described his state.
Crabbe, Works, I. 126.

In particular—(*a*) A bad condition or state; a distressed or distressing condition or predicament; misfortune.

And ther was no man that hadde seyn hym in that *plite* but he wolde haue hadde pite. *Merlin* (E. E. T. S.), ii. 354.

Have comfort, for I know your *plight* is pitied
Of him that caused it. *Shak.*, A. and C., v. 2. 33.

(*b*†) A good condition or state.

He that with labour can use them aright,
Hath gain to his comfort, and cattel in *plight*.
Tusser, February's Husbandry, x.

All wayes shee sought him to restore to *plight*.
Spenser, F. Q., III. vii. 21.

plight^{3}†, *v. t.* [An erroneous spelling of *plite*^{2}, < ME. *pliten*, *plyten*, var. of *plaiten*, plait: see *plait*, and cf. *pleat*, *plat*^{4}, *v.*] **1.** To weave; plait; fold. See *plait*.

Now, gode nece, be it never so lite
Yif me the labour it [a letter] to sow and *plyte*.
Chaucer, Troilus, ii. 1204.

Her locks are *plighted* like the fleece of wool
That Jason with his Grecian mates atchiev'd.
Greene, Menaphon's Eclogue.

On his head a roll of linnen *plight*,
Like to the Mores of Malaber, he wore.
Spenser, F. Q., VI. vii. 43.

A long love-lock on his left shoulder *plight*.
P. Fletcher, Purple Island, vii. 23.

2. To combine or put together in one's mind.

So she gan in hire thought argue
In this matere, of which I have yow told,
And what to done best were, and what teschue,
That *plytede* she ful ofte in many folde.
Chaucer, Troilus, ii. 697.

plight^{3}† (plīt), *n.* [Also *pleight*; an erroneous spelling of *plite*^{2}, < ME. *plite*, *plyte*, a var. of *plaite*, a fold, plait: see *plait*, and cf. *pleat*, *plat*^{4}, *n.*] A fold; a plait.

He perced through the *plites* of his haubreke vndir the side, that the spere hede shewed on the tother side.
Merlin (E. E. T. S.), ii. 265.

Straunge was her tyre, and all her garment blew,
Close rownd about her tuckt with many a *plight*.
Spenser, F. Q., II. ix. 40.

If a Tailour make your gowne too little, you couer his fault with a broad stomacher; if too great, with a number of *plights*. *Lyly*, Euphues and his England, p. 222.

Our Gentlewomens dutch Fans, that are made either of paper, or parchment, or silke, or other stuffe, which will with certaine *pleights* easily runne and fold themselues together. *Hakluyt's Voyages*, I. 610.

plight^{4}†. An obsolete preterit and past participle of *pluck*^{1}.

plighter (plī'tėr), *n.* One who or that which plights, engages, or pledges.

This kingly seal
And *plighter* of high hearts!
Shak., A. and C., iii. 13. 126.

plightful† (plīt'fůl), *a.* [ME. *plihtful*; < *plight*^{1} + *-ful*.] Dangerous.

plightly†, *adv.* [ME. *plihtlic*, < AS. *plihtlic*, dangerous, < *pliht*, danger: see *plight*^{1}.] Dangerously; with peril.

pliht†, *n.* and *v.* A Middle English form of *plight*^{1}.

plim (plim), *v. i.* [Appar. related to *plump*; see *plump*^{1}.] To swell. *Grose.* [Prov. Eng.]

Plimsoll's mark. See *mark*^{1}.

Plinian (plin'i-an), *a.* and *n.* [< *Pliny* + *-an*.] **I.** *a.* Of or pertaining to Pliny; specifically, in *nat. hist.*, pertaining to C. Plinius Secundus (Pliny), a celebrated Roman author and naturalist (A. D. 23–79): as, *Plinian* names.

II. *n.* [*l. c.*] A variety of cobaltiferous arsenopyrite, erroneously supposed by Breithaupt to be distinct in crystallization.

plinth (plinth), *n.* [= F. *plinthe* = Sp. *plinto* = Pg. *plintho* = It. *plinto*, < L. *plinthus*, < Gr. πλίνθος, a brick, tile, plinth: see *flint*.] In *arch.*, the flat square table or slab under the molding of the base of a Roman or Renaissance column, of which it constitutes the foundation, and the bottom of the order; also, an abacus; also, a square molding or table at the base of any architectural part or member, or of a pedestal, etc. See phrases below, and cuts under *base*, *column*, and *capital*.

The lower *plinth* is made a seat for people to sit on; and so 'tis no more to be seen in its antient state.
Pococke, Description of the East, I. 8.

One grey *plinth*,
Round whose worn base the wild waves hiss and leap.
Shelley, Revolt of Islam, ii. 18.

Course of a plinth. See *course*^{1}.—**Plinth of a statue**, a flat base, whether round or square.—**Plinth of a wall**, a plain projecting band at the base of a wall, upon which the wall rests. In classical and medieval buildings the plinth is sometimes divided into two or more gradations.

plinthoid (plin'thoid), *n.* [< Gr. πλινθοειδής, like a brick, < πλίνθος, a brick, + εἶδος, form.] A mathematical surface having the general shape of a water-worn brick.

Pliocene (plī'ǭ-sēn), *n.* [= F. *pliocène*; for **Plionocene*, < Gr. πλείων, more, + καινός, recent.] In *geol.*, the most recent of the divisions of the Tertiary proper. See *Tertiary*. Also spelled *Pleiocene*.

Pliohippus (plī-ǭ-hip'us), *n.* [NL. (Marsh, 1874), < *Plio(cene)* + Gr. ἵππος, horse.] **1.** A genus of fossil horses or *Equidæ* from the Pliocene of North America.—**2.** [*l. c.*] A horse of this genus.

Pliolophidæ (plī-ǭ-lof'i-dē), *n. pl.* [NL., < *Pliolophus* + *-idæ*.] A family of fossil perissodactyl hoofed quadrupeds, typified by the genus *Pliolophus*, related to the *Lophiodontidæ*. The nasal region was compressed and extended forward, the supramaxillaries being excluded from the nasal aperture; the long nasal bones extended far forward, and articulated with the premaxillaries; and the upper molars had two transverse rows of tubercles separated by an intervening valley, with a cingulum anteriorly and internally. The external lobes of the upper molars were well separated and little flattened, and the lobes of the lower molars scarcely united. It also includes the genera *Hyracotherium* and *Systemodon*, of Eocene age. Also called *Hyracotheriidæ* and *Hyracotheriinæ*.

pliolophoid (plī-ol'ǭ-foid), *a.* and *n.* **I.** *a.* Pertaining to the *Pliolophoidea*, or having their characters.

II. *n.* A member of the *Pliolophoidea*.

Pliolophoidea (plī-ol-ǭ-foi'dẹ̄-ä̤), *n. pl.* [NL., < *Pliolophus* + *-oidea*.] A superfamily of *Perissodactyla*, framed by Gill in 1872 for the reception of the family *Pliolophidæ*.

Pliolophus (plī-ol'ǭ-fus), *n.* [NL. (Owen, 1858), < Gr. πλείων, more, + λόφος, a crest.] The typical genus of *Pliolophidæ*. *P. vulpiceps* is a species from the London clay.

Plioplatycarpidæ (plī-ǭ-plat-i-kär'pi-dē), *n. pl.* [NL., < *Plioplatycarpus* + *-idæ*.] A family of pythonomorph or mosasaurian reptiles, represented by the genus *Plioplatycarpus*. They are distinguished by the presence of interclavicles and a sacrum. They lived in the Upper Cretaceous period.

Plioplatycarpus (plī-ǭ-plat-i-kär'pus), *n.* [NL., < *Plio(cene)* + Gr. πλατύς, broad, flat, + καρπός, the wrist.] An extinct genus of mosasaurian reptiles, representing the family *Plioplatycarpidæ*.

pliosaurian (plī-ǭ-sâ'ri-an), *a.* Of or pertaining to the genus *Pliosaurus*.

Further indications of *Pliosaurian* affinities are, moreover, shown by the teeth themselves.
Quart. Jour. Geol. Soc., XLV. 50.

Pliosaurus (plī-ǭ-sâ'rus), *n.* [NL. (Owen, 1866), < *Plio(cene)* + Gr. σαῦρος, lizard.] A genus of plesiosaurs from the Middle and Upper Oölite, having the head large and the neck comparatively short. Also *Pleiosaurus*.

pliskie (plis'ki), *n.* [Origin obscure.] **1.** A mischievous trick.—**2.** Plight; condition.

[Scotch in both uses.]

plit†, **plite**^{1}†, *n.* Obsolete forms of *plight*^{2}.

plite^{2}†, *v. t.* An obsolete form of *plait*.

plitt (plit), *n.* Same as *plet*. *North British Rev.*

ploc (plok), *n.* [< F. *ploc*, sheathing-hair, cow's hair, waste wool.] A mixture of hair and tar for covering a ship's bottom. *Simmonds.*

Plocamobranchia (plok″a-mǭ-brang'ki-ä̤), *n. pl.* [NL., < Gr. πλόκαμος, fringe (< πλέκειν, weave, plait), + βράγχια, gills.] A group of tænioglossate gastropods, with rigid filamentary branchial processes, proposed for the families *Capulidæ* or *Calyptræidæ* and *Hipponycidæ*.

Plocaria (plǭ-kā'ri-ä̤), *n.* [NL., < Gr. πλόκος, something woven or plaited, < πλέκειν, weave, plait: see *plait*.] A genus of algæ, of the order or suborder *Ceramiaceæ*. *P. helminthochorton* is the Corsican moss of the shops, once of some reputation as a vermifuge. *P. candida*, or Ceylon moss, is used to a considerable extent as an article of food in the East.

ploce (plō'sē), *n.* [< Gr. πλοκή, a plaiting, < πλέκειν, plait, twist.] In *rhet.*, repetition of a word one or more times in close succession; especially, such repetition with a change of meaning or application: as, a man should be a *man*.

Ploceidæ (plǭ-sē'i-dē), *n. pl.* [NL., < *Ploceus* + *-idæ*.] A family of Old World oscine passerine birds having ten primaries and a conirostral bill; the weavers, weaver-birds, or weaver-finches. They are a large and diversified family, many of them resembling finches or buntings, but always distinguished from *Fringillidæ* by the presence of ten instead of nine primaries. They are specially characteristic of the Ethiopian region, where more than three fourths of the species occur, but also extend into the Oriental and Australian regions. The weavers are named and noted for the construction of their nests, in some cases of immense size, in others highly artificial. (See cuts under *hive-nest* and *Ploceus*.) About 250 species are recognized, referred to some 60 genera, divided into 3 subfamilies, *Ploceinæ*, *Viduinæ*, and *Spermestinæ*. Many of the last-named are common cage-birds, as amadavats, strawberry-finches, and the like.

ploceiform (plō'sẹ̄-i-fôrm), *a.* [< NL. *Ploceus* + L. *forma*, form.] Resembling or related or belonging to the genus *Ploceus* or family *Ploceidæ*.

Ploceinæ (plō-sẹ̄-ī'nē), *n. pl.* [NL., < *Ploceus* + *-inæ*.] **1.** The *Ploceidæ* as a subfamily of *Fringillidæ*.—**2.** The characteristic subfamily of *Ploceidæ*, represented by such genera as *Ploceus*, *Textor*, *Hyphantornis*, *Malimbus*, *Philetærus*, *Nigrita*, and *Plocepasser*. See cuts under *hive-nest*, *Philetærus*, and *Ploceus*.

Ploceus (plō'sẹ̄-us), *n.* [NL. (Cuvier, 1817), < Gr. πλοκεύς, a plaiter, braider, < πλέκειν, plait, braid, weave: see *plait*.] The typical genus of *Ploceidæ*, formerly of great extent, now restricted to the Indian and Oriental baya-birds, as *P. philippinus*, *P. bengalensis*, and others.

Baya-bird (*Ploceus philippinus*).

plod^{1}† (plod), *n.* [< ME. *plod*, a puddle; cf. Dan. *pladder*, mire; prob. < Ir. Gael. *plod*, a pool (also a clod), *plodan*, a small pool (also a small clod), *plodach*, a puddle.] A puddle.

plod^{2} (plod), *v.*; pret. and pp. *plodded*, ppr. *plodding*. [< ME. **plodden* (found only in deriv. *plodder*); prob. orig. splash through water and mud; < *plod*^{1}, *n.* Cf. *plodge*, and *plout*^{1}, *plouter*, *plotter*^{2}, *plowder*, of like sense.] **I.** *intrans.* **1.** To trudge; travel or work slowly and perseveringly; go on in any pursuit with steady, laborious diligence.

Why, universal *plodding* poisons up
The nimble spirits in the arteries.
Shak., L. L. L., iv. 3. 305.

I'le take my blew blade all in my hand,
And *plod* to the green-wood with thee.
Jolly Pinder of Wakefield (Child's Ballads, V. 206).

She reason'd without *plodding* long,
Nor ever gave her judgement wrong.
Swift, Cadenus and Vanessa.

I, with my fate contented, will *plod* on,
And hope for higher raptures when life's day is done.
Wordsworth, Skylark.

2. To lag behind or puzzle upon the scent: said of hounds.=**Syn. 1.** To trudge, jog.

II. *trans.* To go or walk over in a heavy, laboring manner; accomplish by heavy, toilsome walking or exertion.

If one of mean affairs
May *plod* it in a week, why may not I
Glide thither in a day?
Shak., Cymbeline, iii. 2. 53.

The plowman homeward *plods* his weary way.
Gray, Elegy.

ploddant†, *n.* [Prob. < Gael. *plaide*, a blanket, plaid: see *plaid*.] The checkered plaid of the Scotch. See *plaid*.

Coarse cloth of 2 or 3 colours in checker-work, vulgarly called *ploddan*.
English Traveller in Scotland, 1598 (Planché's History of Costume).

plodder (plod'ėr), *n.* [< ME. *plodder*; < *plod*^{2} + *-er*^{1}.] **1**†. One who trudges or wanders about; a "moss-trooper."

There come out of castels & of cloise townes
Ffro the bowerdurs aboute, that hom bale wroght,
Pilours [robbers] and *plodders*, piked [stole] there goodes.
Destruction of Troy (E. E. T. S.), l. 12862.

2. One who plods; a drudge; a dull, laborious person.

Small have continual *plodders* ever won
Save base authority from others' books.
Shak., L. L. L., i. 1. 86.

plodding (plod'ing), *p. a.* Moving or working with slow and patient diligence; patiently laborious: as, a man of *plodding* habits.

Some stupid, *plodding*, money-loving wight.
Young, Love of Fame, ii. 161.

Fortune . . . fixes on the *plodding* mechanic, who stays at home and minds his business.
Goldsmith, Citizen of the World, lxx.

ploddingly (plod'ing-li), *adv.* In a plodding manner; drudgingly.

plodge (ploj), *v. i.*; pret. and pp. *plodged*, ppr. *plodging*. [Appar. an extended form of *plod*[2], *v.*] To walk in mud or water; plunge. *Halliwell.* [Prov. Eng.]

Ploima (plō'i-mä), *n. pl.* [NL. (C. T. Hudson, 1884), < Gr. πλώϊμος, fit for sailing, < πλώειν, var. of πλέειν, sail, float.] One of three orders of lipopod *Rotifera*, contrasted with *Bdelloygrada* and *Rhizota*, containing those wheel-animalcules which move only by swimming. Most rotifers, whether loricate or illoricate, are ploïmate.

ploïmate (plō'i-māt), *a.* [< *Ploima* + *-ate*[1].] Of or pertaining to the order *Ploima*.

plokke†, *v. t.* A Middle English form of *pluck*[1].

plom†, *n.* A Middle English form of *plumb*[2].

plomb†, *n.* and *v.* An obsolete form of *plumb*[2].

plombée, plommée (plom-bā', -mā'), *n.* [OF., < *plomb*, lead: see *plumb*[2].] 1. A variety of the mace or martel-de-fer to which weight was given by lead combined with the head: a common form bore a mass of lead at the end of the handle, and projecting from it in opposite directions two points of steel.—2. A variety of the war-flail. Compare *morning-star* (*b*).

Plombée (def. 1), middle of 15th century.

plombgomme, *n.* Same as *plumbogummite*.

plombierite (plom'bėr-it), *n.* [< *Plombières* (see def.) + *-ite*[2].] A hydrated calcium silicate occurring in gelatinous forms (hardening on exposure) at Plombières, Vosges, France, where, with several zeolites, it is the result of the action of thermal waters upon the brick and mortar of a Roman aqueduct.

plome†, *n.* A Middle English form of *plum*[1].

plomet†, *n.* A Middle English form of *plummet*.

plommé, plommée, *n.* See *plombée*.

plonge[1]†, *v.* A Middle English form of *plunge*.

plonge[2] (plonj), *v. t.*; pret. and pp. *plonged*, ppr. *plonging*. [< F. *plonger*, plunge: see *plunge*, *v.*] To cleanse, as open sewers, by stirring up the mud with a pole as the tide in a tidal river is on the ebb. Plonging is distinguished from *flushing*, the method used for covered sewers. *Mayhew.*

plonge[2] (plonj), *n.* [F.: see *plunge*, *n.*] 1. *Milit.*, the superior slope of a parapet.—2. The course of a bomb from its greatest altitude to the point of fall; the descending branch of its trajectory.

plongée (plôṅ-zhā'), *n.* [F.: see *plonge*[2], *n.*] Same as *plonge*[2].

plook, plooky, *n.* See *plowk*, *plowky*.

plop (plop), *v. i.*; pret. and pp. *plopped*, ppr. *plopping*. [Imitative. Cf. *plap*.] To fall or plump into water. *Mrs. Gaskell*, Mary Barton. [Prov. Eng.]

plot[1] (plot), *n.* [Also *plat* (see *plat*[2]); < ME. *plot*, *plotte*, < AS. *plot* (rare), a plot of ground; cf. Goth. *plats*, a patch: see *patch*. The sense 'scheme' (whence later 'stratagem, conspiracy') appar. arose from that of 'plan' or 'plat' of a piece of ground, as *plan*, 'scheme,' from *plan*, 'plat,' 'draft.' The sense has prob. been affected by association with *complot*, but *plot*, 'scheme,' can hardly be an abbr. of *complot*. Instances of the loss of the prefix *com-*, *con-* are scarcely to be found except recently in humorous or childish use (as in *'fess* for *confess*).] 1. A piece of ground; specifically, a small piece of ground of well-defined shape; a patch or spot of ground.

Loke ye, take gode hede of this *plotte* of grounde that ye now sitte on, whan that ye be agein repeired.
Merlin (E. E. T. S.), ii. 150.

They [the cities] be all set and situate alike, and in all points fashioned alike, as far forth as the place or *plot* suffereth. *Sir T. More*, Utopia (tr. by Robinson), ii. 1.

This blessed *plot*, this earth, this realm, this England.
Shak., Rich. II., ii. 1. 50.

I saw an Innumerable company of little *plots* of corne, not much bigger then little beds (as we call them) in our English Gardens. *Coryat*, Crudities, I. 83.

Love paced the thymy *plots* of Paradise.
Tennyson, Love and Death.

2†. A patch, spot, or splotch of any kind, as in a garment.

He had a cote of Crystendome as holykirke bileueth,
Ac it was moled in many places with manye sondrio *plottes*.
Of Pruyde here a *plotte*, and there a *plotte* of unbuxome speche. *Piers Plowman* (B), xiii. 275.

3. In *surv.*, a plan or draft of a field, farm, estate, etc., surveyed and delineated on paper; a map or plan.

I am a young beginner, and am building
Of a new shop, an't like your worship, just
At corner of a street:—Here is the *plot* on 't.
B. Jonson, Alchemist, i. 1.

In another roome are represented at large mapps and *plotts* of most countries in the world.
Evelyn, Diary, Jan. 18, 1645.

4. A fully formulated scheme or plan; a systematized purpose; design; aim.

Thus was not the law of England ever properly applyed unto the Irish nation as by a purposed *plott* of government, but as they could insinuat and steale themselves under the same by theyr humble carriadge and submission. *Spenser*, State of Ireland.

Then doth the crafty fox begin to fill
His braines with cunning; if his *plotes* doe hit
To his desire, his landlordes want of wit
Shall make him rich for ever.
Times' Whistle (E. E. T. S.), p. 65.

All things cannot
But suit aright when Heav'n do's lay the *plot*.
J. Beaumont, Psyche, ii. 93.

5. A stratagem or secret plan; a secret project; an intrigue; a conspiracy.

I thank you, fine fool, for your most fine *plot*;
This was a subtle one, a stiff device
To have caught dotterels with.
Beau. and Fl., Scornful Lady, iv. 1.

But the Gunpowder *Plot*—there was a get-penny!
B. Jonson, Bartholomew Fair, v. 1.

Oh think what anxious moments pass between
The birth of *plots* and their last fatal periods.
Addison, Cato, i. 3.

The *plot* was the most wicked and desperate ever known.
Macaulay, History.

6. The story of a play, poem, novel, or romance, comprising a complication of incidents which are at last unfolded by unexpected means; the intrigue.

If the *plot* or intrigue must be natural, and such as springs from the very subject, as has been already urged, then the winding-up of the *plot*, by a more sure claim, must have this qualification, and be a probable consequence of all that went before.
Le Bossu, tr. in Pref. to Pope's Odyssey.

O lud, sir, if people who want to listen or overhear were not always connived at in a tragedy, there would be no carrying on any *plot* in the world. *Sheridan*, The Critic, ii. 2.

7. Contrivance; deep reach of thought; ability to plan.

Who says he was not
A man of much *plot*
May repent that false accusation.
Sir J. Denham, Return of Mr. Killegrew.

Gunpowder plot. See *gunpowder*.—**Popish plot**, in *Eng. hist.*, an alleged conspiracy of Roman Catholics in 1678, by which, according to the testimony of Titus Oates and other informers, the king, Charles II., was to be killed, and the government and the Protestant religion were to be overthrown. Several Roman Catholics were executed for supposed complicity in these measures.—**Rye House plot**, in *Eng. hist.*, a conspiracy of some radical Whigs for the assassination of Charles II. at Rye House, Hertfordshire, in 1683. Algernon Sidney and Lord Russell were executed for alleged implication in this plot. =**Syn.** 5. Combination, machination, cabal.

plot[1] (plot), *v.*; pret. and pp. *plotted*, ppr. *plotting*. [< *plot*[1], *n.*] **I.** *trans.* 1. To make a map or plan of; lay down on paper according to scale: as, to *plot* a farm or an estate; to *plot* a ship's course on a chart.—2. To determine or fix by measurements on a map or chart.

The position of 97 [water-]spouts, occurring on 60 different dates, . . . has been *plotted* with respect to the centre of low pressure areas. *Amer. Meteor. Jour.*, III. 121.

3. To plan; form plans for; devise; contrive; conspire to effect or bring about: now rarely used in a good sense.

Let your reason
Plot your revenge, and not your passion.
Beau. and Fl., Maid's Tragedy, iv. 2.

Conning Submission's language as he went,
And *plotting* how his Brethren to content.
J. Beaumont, Psyche, i. 125.

Plotting an unprofitable crime.
Dryden, Cock and Fox, l. 775.

The good man and woman are long since in their graves who used to sit and *plot* the welfare of us their children.
Steele, Spectator, No. 263.

=**Syn.** 3. To concoct, brew, hatch, plan.

II. *intrans.* To form a plan or plot; scheme; especially, to conspire.

The wicked *plotteth* against the just. Ps. xxxvii. 12.

plot[2] (plot), *v. t.*; pret. and pp. *plotted*, ppr. *plotting*. [Also *plout*; cf. Gael. *plodach*, lukewarm, parboiling.] 1. To scald; steep in very hot water.—2. To make (any liquid) scalding hot. [Scotch in both senses.]

plotch† (ploch), *n.* [A var. of *plot*, perhaps due to association with *splotch*.] A patch; splotch; blotch; scab.

An idle vagrant person . . . who stood at the Temple gate demanding of almes, with certaine counterfait *plotches* of a leper.
Benvenuto, Passengers' Dialogues (1612). (*Nares.*)

Ploteres (plō-tē'rēz), *n. pl.* [NL. (F. *plotères*—Latreille), < Gr. πλωτήρ, a sailor, < πλώειν, sail.] A group of hemipterous insects of the tribe *Geocores*, or land-bugs, containing such as have very long legs and run on the surface of the water.

plotform†, *n.* An obsolete form of *platform*.

plotful (plot'fůl), *a.* [< *plot*[1] + *-ful*.] Abounding with plots. *Wright.*

Plotidæ (plot'i-dē), *n. pl.* [NL., < *Plotus* + *-idæ*.] A family of totipalmate birds of the order *Steganopodes*; the darters, anhingas, or snake-birds. They have a very long, slim, sinuous neck; long, slender, straight, and acute bill; broad fan-shaped tail, with stiff rectrices, of which the middle pair are crinkled or fluted; naked lores; and rudimentary gular sac. There is only one genus, *Plotus* or *Anhinga*, with several species, inhabiting swamps and marshes of warm countries in both hemispheres. See *anhinga*, *darter*, *Plotus*.

Plotinian (plǫ-tin'i-an), *a.* [< *Plotinus* (see *Plotinism*) + *-ian*.] Of or pertaining to Plotinus or the Plotinists, or their doctrines.

Plotinism (plǫ-tī'nizm), *n.* [< LL. *Plotinus*, < Gr. Πλωτῖνος, Plotinus, a Greek philosopher of the 3d century, + *-ism*.] The doctrine of Plotinus or of the Plotinists.

Plotinist (plǫ-tī'nist), *n.* [< *Plotin-us* + *-ist*.] A disciple of Plotinus. See *Neoplatonism*.

plot-proof (plot'pröf), *a.* Proof against plots; not to be hurt by a plot or plots. [Rare.]

The harlot-king
Is quite beyond mine arm, out of the blank
And level of my brain, *plot-proof*.
Shak., W. T., ii. 3. 6.

plotter[1] (plot'ėr), *n.* [< *plot*[1], *v.*, + *-er*[1].] One who plots, in any sense; especially, one who contrives; a contriver; a conspirator.

plotter[2] (plot'ėr), *v. i.* Same as *plouter*.

Miss's pony has trodden dahn two rigs o' corn, and *plottered* through, raight o'er into t' meadow.
E. Brontë, Wuthering Heights, ix.

plottie (plot'i), *n.* [< *plot*[2].] A sort of mulled wine. [Scotch.]

Get us a jug of mulled wine—*plottie*, as you call it.
Scott, St. Ronan's Well, xxviii.

plotting[1] (plot'ing), *n.* [Verbal n. of *plot*[1], *v.*] The act of making a plot. Specifically—(*a*) The act of making a plan or map. (*b*) The act of forming or attempting a stratagem or conspiracy.

plotting[2] (plot'ing), *n.* [Verbal n. of **plot*, *v.*, < F. *peloter* (pron. plo-tā'), form into a ball, < *pelote*, a ball: see *pellet*. Cf. *platoon*.] In *soap-making*, the operation of forming the paste into cakes by means of heavy pressure.

The soap is ready for the final operation, known as *plotting* (from the French pelotage), in which the paste is subjected to enormous pressure, sometimes 3000–4000 lb. a sq. in., to form it into cakes, or into continuous bars from which cakes may be cut.
W. L. Carpenter, Soap and Candles, p. 200.

plottingly (plot'ing-li), *adv.* In a plotting manner; as a plotter.

The walls were covered with curious old Dutch prints. . . . There was Frederick the Great, with head drooped *plottingly*, and keen sidelong glance from under the three-cornered hat. *Lowell*, Cambridge Thirty Years Ago.

plotting-machine (plot'ing-ma-shēn"), *n.* A form of press for shaping soap-paste into bars or cakes. See *plotting*[2].

plotting-scale (plot'ing-skāl), *n.* A scale used for setting off the lengths of lines in surveying. It consists of two graduated scales, made of ivory, silver, brass, or boxwood. One of these scales is pierced along nearly its whole length by a dovetail-shaped groove, for the reception of a sliding-piece. The second scale is attached to this sliding-piece, and moves along with it, the edge of the second scale being always at right angles to the edge of the first. By this means the rectangular coordinates of a point are measured at once on the scales, or the position of the point is laid down on the plan.

Plotus (plō'tus), *n.* [NL. (Linnæus, 1766), < Gr. πλωτός, sailing, floating, < πλώειν, var. of πλέειν, sail: see *flow*[1].] The only genus of the family *Plotidæ*. *P. anhinga* is the common darter, anhinga, snake-bird, or water-turkey of America; *P. levaillanti* is African; *P. melanogaster*, Indian; *P. novæ-hollandiæ*, Australian. Also called *Plynx* and *Plottus*. See cut under *anhinga*.

plough, ploughable, etc. See *plow*, etc.

plounce† (plouns), *v. i.*; pret. and pp. *plounced*, ppr. *plouncing*. [Appar. a var. of *plunge* (ME.

plongen, ploungen, etc.), accom. to *flounce*[1].] To plunge.

Our observation must not now launch into the whirlpool, or rather *plounce* into the mudd and quagmire, of the people's power and right pretended, That the sovereignty is theirs, and originally in them.
Bp. Hacket, Abp. Williams, II. 200. (*Davies.*)

plounge†, *v.* A Middle English form of *plunge*.

plousiocracy, *n.* See *plusiocracy*.

plout[1] (plout), *v. i.* [Cf. *plod*[2]. Hence freq. *plouter, plotter*[2], etc.] To wade or flounder through water or mire. [North. Eng. and Scotch.]

plout[2] (plout), *v. t.* Same as *plot*[2]. [Scotch.]

plouter (plou'tėr), *v. i.* [Also *plotter, plowder*; freq. of *plout*[1].] To dabble or paddle in water or mire. [North. Eng. and Scotch.]

plouter (plou'tėr), *n.* [< *plouter, v.*] A dabbling or playing in water; a splashing bath. [Scotch.]

Shepherd. Faith, I think I shall tak a *plouter*. (Shepherd retires into the marble bath. . . . The hot water is let on with a mighty noise.)
Wilson, Noctes Ambrosianæ, III. 226.

plout-net (plout'net), *n.* [Appar. var. of *poutnet* (perhaps affected by *plait*).] A small stocking-shaped river-net attached to two poles. [Eng.]

ploutocracy, ploutocrat, etc. See *plutocracy*, etc.

plover (pluv'ėr), *n.* [< ME. *plover, plovere*, < OF. *plovier*, F. *pluvier*, a plover, < ML. **pluviarius, pluvarius*, a plover, so called because it appears during the rainy season; prop. adj., equiv. to L. *pluvialis*, of the rain (cf. NL. *Pluviales*, pl., the plovers), < *pluvia*, rain: see *pluvious*.] **1.** A bird of the family *Charadriidæ* and genus *Charadrius*, C. *pluvialis*. This bird, more fully called the *golden, yellow*, or *green plover*, is very widely distributed in the Old World, breeding in high latitudes, and performing extensive migrations during the spring and fall. It is about 10½ inches long and 22½ in extent of wings, the wing 7 inches, the bill ⅞ inch, the tarsus 1⅜ inches. The upper parts are black, and profusely spotted with yellow and white; the under parts are black in the breeding-dress, whitish in winter, variously mottled or speckled during the changes of plumage. The bill and feet are black; the feet are three-toed. The plover lays four eggs, 1⅞ inches long by 1¼ broad, of a piriform shape, drab color, with heavy brownish or blackish blotches.

Golden Plover (*Charadrius pluvialis*), in autumn plumage.

Crook-billed Plover (*Anarhynchus frontalis*).

Hence—**2.** Some or any bird of the family *Charadriidæ*; a charadriomorphic grallatorial bird. The American golden plover, or field-plover, is *Charadrius dominicus*, very closely resembling C. *pluvialis*, but having ashy-gray instead of white axillars. The Swiss bullhead, or black-bellied plover, is *Squatarola helvetica*, inhabiting most parts of the world, and having four toes. (See cut under *Squatarola*.) Many small plovers with white under parts, and rings or bands of black on the head, neck, or breast, are known as *ring-plovers* or *ring-necks*, and mostly belong to the genus *Ægialites*. (See also *killdee*.) The most singular of these is the crook-billed plover, *Anarhynchus frontalis*, having the bill bent sidewise. It inhabits New Zealand. The mountain-plover of the western United States is *Podasocys montanus*. Some plovers are known as *dotterels*. (See *dotterel* and *Eudromias*.) The thickknees, stone-plovers, or stone-curlews are birds of the family *Œdicnemidæ*. (See cut under *Œdicnemus*.) Stilt-plovers are the stilts, *Himantopinæ*. (See cut under *stilt*.) The crab-plover is *Dromas ardeola*. "Plovers' eggs," so called in England, are laid by the lapwing, *Vanellus cristatus*.

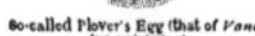
So-called Plover's Egg (that of *Vanellus cristatus*).

3. In various parts of the United States, the Bartramian sandpiper, *Bartramia longicauda*, more fully called *upland, highland, pasture, field, corn-field, prairie, grass*, and *plain plover*. See cut under *Bartramia*.—**4.** The greater or lesser yellowshanks, *Totanus melanoleucus* or *T. flavipes*, commonly called *yellow-legged plovers*. [Local, U. S.]—**5†.** A loose woman: otherwise called a *quail*.

Here will be Zekiel Edgworth, and three or four gallants with him at night, and I have neither *plover* nor quail for them; persuade this . . . to become a bird o' the game.
B. *Jonson*, Bartholomew Fair, iv. 3.

Bastard plover. See *bastard*.—**Bishop plover**, the turnstone, *Strepsilas interpres*. [Massachusetts.]—**Black-bellied plover.** See def. 2.—**Black-breasted plover.** (*a*) The golden plover in full plumage. [Ireland.] (*b*) The black-heart plover. [Local, U. S.]—**Black-heart plover**, the black-bellied or black-breasted sandpiper; the American dunlin. [Local, Canada.]—**Bullhead-plover.** See *bullhead*, 4.—**Golden plover.** See def. 1.—**Gray plover.** (*a*) A misnomer of the knot, *Tringa canutus*, a sandpiper in winter plumage. [Scotland.] (*b*) The golden plover when young. [Ireland.]—**Great plover**, the stone-plover.—**Green plover**, the lapwing, *Vanellus cristatus*. [Ireland.]—**Helvetian plover**, the Swiss plover, *Squatarola helvetica*.—**Highland plover**, the Bartramian sandpiper. Also called *Bartram's highland snipe*.—**Hill-plover**, the golden plover. [Forfar.]—**Kentish plover**, *Ægialites cantianus*, a small ring-plover of wide distribution in the eastern hemisphere: so called because the specimens from which it was first described (by Dr. John Latham) were received from Mr. Boys of Sandwich in Kent, England.—**Long-legged plover**, a longshanks or stilt; a bird of the genus *Himantopus*.—**Mud-plover**, *Squatarola helvetica*. [Local, British.]—**Norfolk plover**, the stone-plover, *Œdicnemus crepitans*.—**Oyster-plover**, the oyster-catcher.—**Plover's page.** See *page*[2].—**Red-legged plover**, the turnstone, *Strepsilas interpres*; the red-legs. [Massachusetts.]—**Ringed plover.** See *Ægialites* and *killdee*.—**Rock-plover**, *Squatarola helvetica*. [Wexford, Ireland.]—**Ruddy plover**, the sanderling or three-toed sandpiper, *Calidris arenaria*, when in full plumage: chiefly a book-name.—**Sea-plover**, *Squatarola helvetica*. [Local, British.]—**Silver plover.** Same as *gray plover* (*a*).—**Spanish plover**, the willet, or semipalmated tattler, *Symphemia semipalmata*. *March.* [Jamaica.]—**Speckled-back** or **streaked-back plover**, the turnstone, *Strepsilas interpres*. [Massachusetts.]—**Spur-winged plover.** See *Chettusia*.—**Strand plover**, *Squatarola helvetica*. [Cork, Ireland.]—**Whistling plover.** (*a*) The golden plover. (*b*) *Squatarola helvetica*. (*c*) The Norfolk plover. [Various localities.]—**Wry-billed plover**, the crook-billed plover. See second cut above.—**Yellow plover**, the golden plover. [East Lothian.] (See also *lark-plover, marsh-plover, piping-plover, stone-plover*.)

plover-quail (pluv'ėr-kwāl), *n.* Any bird of the genus *Pedionomus*.

plover-snipe (pluv'ėr-snīp), *n.* Any bird of the group *Pressirostres*.

plow, plough (plou), *n.* [Also dial. (Sc.) *pleugh, pleuch*; < ME. *plow, plowe, plough, ploughe, plowghe, plouz, plouh, ploghe, plughe, ploh*, a plow, a plowland, < AS. *plōh* (rare), a plowland (not found in AS. in the sense of 'plow,' for which the reg. word was *sulh*, > E. dial. *sull, sullow*), = OFries. *plōch* = D. *ploeg* = MLG. *plōch, plūch* = OHG. *pfluog, pfluoh, phluog, fluog, fluoc, plōh, pluag*, MHG. *phluoc, pfluoc*, G. *pflug* = Icel. *plōgr* = Sw. *plog* = Dan. *plov*, a plow; perhaps from the root of *play*[1] (AS. *plegan*) and *plight*[1] (AS. *pliht*), with ref. to the activity or labor involved: cf. MHG. *phluoc, pfluoc*, business, occupation, maintenance. Like *play* and *plight*, the word *plow* belongs only to Teut. (the Slav., etc., forms, OBulg. *plugŭ* = Russ. *plugŭ*, etc., = Lith. *plugas*, are from OHG.). It is not found in Goth., where *hōha*, plow. Cf. Icel. *ardhr*, Norw. *ar, al*, plow, related to L. *aratrum*, a plow (see *aratrum terræ*), MHG. *arl*, a plowshare, from the same ult. root (see *ear*[3]). The explanations which connect *plow* with the Gr. πλοῖον = Skt. *plava*, a ship, or with the Gael. *ploc*, a block of wood, stump of a tree (and hence, as Skeat supposes, a primitive plow), are untenable.] **1.** An agricultural implement, drawn by animals or moved by steam-power, used to cut the ground and turn it up so as to prepare it for the reception of seeds. The soil is cut to a depth of several inches, raised up, and turned over by the progress of the plow, the object being to expose a new surface to the air and, by pulverizing and loosening the soil, to fit it for the reception of seed and the vigorous growth of crops. The plow, in various forms, is also much used for other purposes. In its modern form, the common agricultural plow essentially consists of a *plow-beam* provided with a *clevis* for attachment of draft-animals; *handles*, connected with each other and cross-braced by the *rounds*; a *mold-board*, usually of cast-iron; a *plowshare*, usually of steel, or steel-pointed, and bolted to the mold-board; a *land-side*, usually of cast-iron, attached to the mold-board near the front edge of the latter and in line with the beam; a *colter*, of wrought-iron with a tempered-steel edge, attached to the beam in line with the front edge of the mold-board; and a *standard* or *sheth*, projecting upward from and usually integral with the mold-board, and connecting the latter with the beam. The rear end of the beam is attached to the land-side handle, one handle being attached to the rear part of the land-side and the other to the rear part of the mold-board. Often a wheel is adjustably attached to the beam near the clevis, for gaging the depth of the furrow.

American Plow.
a, handles; *b*, beam; *c*, mold-board; *d*, share; *e*, slip-point (can be replaced when broken or worn); *f*, colter; *g*, colter-brace; *h*, wheel (gages depth of furrow); *i*, arc by which the wheel is set to regulate depth of furrow; *j*, clevis; *k*, land-side.

2. Figuratively, tillage; culture of the earth; agriculture. *Johnson.*—**3.** A tool that furrows, grooves, planes, cuts, or otherwise acts by pushing or shoving, like a plow. (*a*) In *woodworking*, a kind of plane used for grooving door-stiles and similar work. It has an adjustable fence, and is usually adapted to carry eight different widths of plane-irons, for different widths of grooves. (*b*) In *cloth-manuf.*, an instrument for cutting the flushing parts of the pile or nap of fustian. (c) The cutting-knife of a plow-press. (d) In *bookbinding*, a hand-implement for cutting or trimming the edges of books. Machines for the same purpose have rendered the bookbinders' plow almost obsolete. (*e*) A narrow shovel used in malting to bring the grains underneath to the surface. (*f*) A rimmer or fatting-knife: as, a mackerel-*plow*. See *rimmer*. (*g*) A hanging connection extending from a car propelled by electricity through the slot of the underground conduit, by means of which the current is conveyed to the motor on the car.

4†. A plowland.

And I'll gie him to his dowry
Full fifty *ploughs* of land.
Childe Vyet (Child's Ballads, II. 76).

Black-land plow, a plow specially adapted to plowing rich soil free from stones, as the black lands of prairies.—**Double mold-board plow**, a plow which, instead of a land-side, has a second mold-board with curvature the reverse of the ordinary mold-board, so that it turns a double furrow, throwing the earth in opposite directions. It is used for making surface-drains, ridging up, etc.—**Double plow.** (*a*) A plow by which two furrows can be turned at the same time; a gang-plow consisting of two single plows. (*b*) A plow which can be adjusted to turn a furrow either to the right or to the left. Also called *drill-plow, reversible plow*, and *turning mold-board plow*.—**Gang-plow**, two or more plows attached to a single stock or frame, generally having wheels as a sulky-plow has, with adjustable devices for regulating the depth of furrows, and also a seat for the plowman, except when moved by steam. Compare *steam-plow*.—**Hand-plow**, a light small plow sometimes used in gardening, drawn or pushed by hand.—**Hoe-plow.** Same as *horse-hoe*.—**Mole-plow**, a plow with a long standard or sheth, to the lower part of which is attached an iron shoe or burrowing-tool which makes a burrow under the surface without turning a furrow. It is used for under-draining. The shoe is sometimes so attached to the lower part of the sheth as to permit its free motion around stones, etc.—**Paring-plow.** Same as *sod-plow* (which see).—**Pillow of a plow.** See *pillow*.—**Reversible plow.** Same as *double plow* (*b*).—**Seeding-plow**, a plow with a box for holding and scattering seed in the path of the furrow.—**Shim-colter plow**, a plow having in advance of the mold-board of the principal plow a small inclined share or scraper, which cuts off weeds and scrapes them, and sometimes spread manure, into the furrow previously plowed, where the main plow covers them.—**Shim-plow**, a plow cutting off a shallow slice from the surface of land, for killing out weeds. Also called *shim*.—**Side-hill plow**, a plow with a reversible mold-board, which can be turned to throw the furrow downhill in plowing in opposite directions along the side or slope of a hill. Also called *hillside-plow* and *turn-wrest plow*.—**Shovel-plow**, a plow with a triangular share, but having no mold-board. It is used for cultivating growing crops. The double shovel-plow has a very broad triangular share attached to two standards.—**Skeleton-plow**, a plow in which the parts bearing against the soil are made in skeleton form, to lessen friction. *E. H. Knight.*—**Steam-plow**, a heavy plow or gang of plows driven

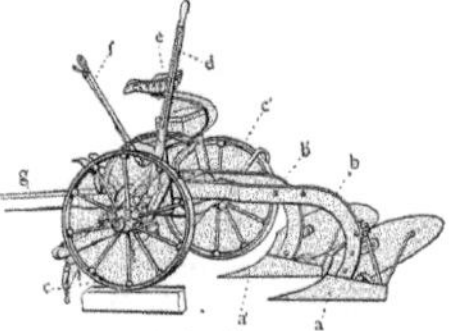

Gang-plow.
a, rear plow; *a'*, front plow; *b*, long beam; *b'*, short beam; *c*, wheel running on land; *c'*, wheel running in furrow; *d*, lever; *e*, seat; *f*, ratchet-adjusting lever; *g*, pole.

by steam-power. Steam-plows, operating on various principles, are in use in farming on a large scale. Some are driven by a single stationary engine, which winds an endless rope (generally of wire) passing over pulleys attached to an apparatus called the *anchor*, fixed at the opposite headland, and round a drum connected with the engine itself. Others are driven by two engines, one at each headland, thus superseding the anchor. As steam-plowing apparatus are usually beyond both the means and the requirements of any but the largest farmers, companies have been formed at various places for hiring them out. Locomotive engines drawing gangs of plows have been tried, but compact the soil so injuriously that their use has been practically abandoned.—**Straddle-plow**, a plow with two triangular parallel shares set a little apart, used for running on each side of a row of dropped corn for covering the seed. *E. H. Knight.*—**Subsoil-plow**, a plow with a long standard and a share, but having no mold-board. Following the ordinary plow, it loosens the earth in the bottom of the ordinary furrow, while itself turning no furrow.—**Sulky-plow**, a plow attached to an axle with two wheels, the axle carrying a seat for the plowman and mechanism for adjusting and guiding the plow. *E. H. Knight.*—**The Plow**, the prominent seven stars in the constellation of the Great Bear; Charles's Wain.—**To hold the plow.** See *hold*[1].—To **put one's hand to the plow**, figuratively, to begin a task; commence an undertaking.—**Turn-wrest plow.** Same as *side-hill plow*.—**Wheel-plow.** (*a*) A plow in which the depths of furrows are gaged by a wheel or wheels attached to the plow and running upon the surface of the land. (*b*) A plow having a wheel in the space between the land-side and the mold-board, reducing the friction of the plow by bearing the weight. *E. H. Knight.* (See also *balance-plow*, *ice-plow*, *prairie-plow*, *snow-plow*, *sod-plow*.)

plow, plough (plou), *v.* [< ME. *plowen* (?), *plowghen* = D. *ploegen* = MLG. *plogen* = MHG. *phluogen*, *pfluogen*, G. *pflügen* = Icel. *plægja* = Sw. *plöja* = Dan. *pløje*, plow; from the noun. The older verb for 'plow' is *ear*: see *ear*[3].] **I.** *trans.* **1.** To turn up with a plow; till.

I should be vnwilling to go thither, . . . much lesse to carry an Oxe or an Horse with me to *plough* the ground.
Coryat, Crudities, I. 88.

It 's I hae fifty acres of land;
It 's a *plow'd* and sawn already.
Glasgow Peggy (Child's Ballads, IV. 78).

2. To make furrows, grooves, or ridges in, as with a plow; furrow; figuratively, to move through like a plow; make one's way through.

Let
Patient Octavia *plough* thy visage up
With her prepared nails.
Shak., A. and C., iv. 12. 38.

Here 's a health to the mariners
That *plough* the raging main.
Mary Hamilton (Child's Ballads, III. 125).

3. To effect as with a plow; traverse like a plow.

A Fleet for Gaul addrest
Ploughs her bold course across the wondering seas.
Wordsworth, Eccles. Sonnets, ii. 15.

4. To trim or square, as the edges of paper, with a plow. See *plow*, *n.*, 3 (*d*).

Cutting or *ploughing* the edges [of a book] with a knife-edged instrument called the plough. *Encyc. Brit.*, IV. 43.

5. To cut or gash (a fish) with the plow or rimmer. [American fisheries.]—**6.** To reject, as a candidate in an examination; pluck. [British university slang.]

"I have been cramming for smalls; and now I am in two races at Henley, and that rather puts the snaffle on reading and gooseberry pie, . . . and adds to my chance of being *ploughed* for smalls." "What does it all mean?" inquired mamma. "'gooseberry pie' and 'the snaffle' and '*ploughed*!'" "Well, the gooseberry pie is really too deep for me; but '*ploughed*' is the new Oxfordish for 'plucked.'"
C. Reade, Hard Cash, Prol.

To plow in, to cover by plowing: as, to *plow in* wheat.—**To plow up** or **out**, to turn out of the ground by plowing.

All Egypt shall be *plough'd up* with dishonour.
Fletcher (and another), False One, iv. 1.

The Arctic glaciers reach the sea, enter it, often *ploughing up* its bottom into submarine moraines.
Tyndall, Forms of Water, p. 134.

II. *intrans.* To turn up the soil with a plow; till the soil with a plow.

He that *plougheth* shall *plough* in hope. 1 Cor. ix. 10.

plowable, ploughable (plou'ạ-bl), *a.* [< *plow*, *plough*, + *-able*.] Capable of being plowed; arable.

plow-alms† (plou'ämz), *n.* A small coin paid to the church in England, in the early Anglo-Saxon period, for every plowland, or for every use of a plow between certain fixed dates.

plow-beam (plou'bēm), *n.* [< ME. *plow-beem*, *ploghe-beme*; < *plow* + *beam*.] The solid horizontally projecting part of the frame of a plow, by which it is drawn. See cuts under *plow*.

He was a little annoyed when Magill, getting down from the *plow-beam*, stopped him.
E. Eggleston, The Graysons, xvi.

plow-bolt (plou'bōlt), *n.* A bolt for securing the share, land-side, or mold-board of a plow to the stock. The head is chamfered or countersunk, and in the former case generally has a square or fin, to prevent it from turning when the nut is screwed on. *E. H. Knight.*

plow-bote (plou'bōt), *n.* In *old Eng. law*: (*a*) Wood or timber allowed to a tenant for the repair of instruments of husbandry. (*b*) A strip of land set apart in the open-field system of cultivation in the ancient village community for the carpenter on a manor for the repair of the plows and other farm implements.

plowboy, ploughboy (plou'boi), *n.* A boy who drives or guides a team in plowing; hence, a rustic boy; an ignorant country fellow.

plow-clevis (plou'klev'is), *n.* A clevis of special form used on a plow at the end of the plow-beam. It is a stirrup-shaped piece with three loops, one over another, in any one of which the open ring of the doubletree may be placed, according to the depth of furrow desired. *E. H. Knight.*

plower, plougher (plou'ėr), *n.* [< ME. *plougher* = D. *ploeger* = G. *pflüger* = Icel. *plōgari*; as *plow* + *-er*[1].] One who plows land; a cultivator.

The countrey people themselves are great *plowers* and small spenders of corne. *Spenser*, State of Ireland.

plow-foot†, *n.* [ME. *plouhfot*; < *plow* + *foot*.] A plow-tail; a plow-handle.

My *plouh-fot* shal be my pyk-staf and picche a-two the rotes,
And help my culter to kerue and clanse the forwes.
Piers Plowman (C), ix. 64.

plow-gang (plou'gang), *n.* Same as *plowland*, 2. In Scotland a plow-gang of land was formerly the property qualification to hunt under the game-laws.

plow-gate (plou'gāt), *n.* Same as *plow-gang*.

plow-handle (plou'han'dl), *n.* [< ME. *ploghe handylle*.] Same as *plow-tail*.

plow-head (plou'hed), *n.* [< ME. *ploghe-hede*.] A plowshare: same as *bridle*, 5.

plowing-machine (plou'ing-mạ-shēn'), *n.* A steam-plow.

plow-iron (plou'ī'ėrn), *n.* The colter of a plow. *Shak.*, 2 Hen. IV., v. 1. 20.

plowk, *n.* [Also (dial.) *plook*, *pluke*; < late ME. *plowke*, a pimple; cf. *plowked*, pimply.] A pimple. *Cath. Ang.*, p. 284. [Obsolete or Scotch.]

plowked†, *a.* [ME. *plowked*, *pluccid*; < *plowk* + *-ed*[2].] Covered with pimples; pimply.

Polidarius was *pluccid* as a pork fat.
Destruction of Troy (E. E. T. S.), l. 3837.

plow-knife (plou'nīf), *n.* In *bookbinding*, a flat knife (about 6 inches long, 1½ inches wide, and ¼ inch thick) with a rounded and pointed cutting-face, sharpened on one side only, which follows the groove of the bookbinders' plow in cutting books or paper.

plowky, *a.* [Also *plooky*; < ME. *plowkky*; < *plowk* + *-y*[1].] Pimply. [Obsolete or Scotch.]

For hyme that is smetyne of his awenne biode, and spredis alle over his lymmes, and waxes *plowkky* and brekes owte. Quoted in *Cath. Ang.*, p. 284.

Plooky, *plooky* are your cheeks,
And *plooky* is your chin.
Sir Hugh le Blond (Child's Ballads, III. 256).

His face was as *plooky* as a curran' bun, and his nose as red as a partan's tae. *Galt*, Provost, xxxii. (*Davies.*)

plowland, ploughland (plou'land), *n.* [< ME. *plowlond*, *plowe-lond*, *plouȝ-lond* (= D. *ploegland* = MLG. *plochlant* = G. *pflugland* = Icel. *plōgsland* = Sw. *plogland* = Dan. *pløjeland*); < *plow* + *land*[1].] **1.** Land that is plowed or that is suitable for tillage.—**2.** In early English tenures, as much land as could be tilled with the use of one plow; a hide of land; a carucate. It was a descriptive term by which land might be granted with the buildings thereon. The difference in early authorities as to the area is probably to be explained by differences in local customs of husbandry and in the arableness of the soil, and especially by the fact that in some districts, and perhaps most generally, the plow was drawn by eight oxen, while in others it may have been drawn by four. It seems generally to have contained about 100 acres more or less. Compare *oxland*.

The pris of a *plouȝ-lond* of penyes so rounde
To aparaile that pyler were pure lytel.
Piers Plowman's Crede (E. E. T. S.), l. 160.

Jugum terræ, or half a *plow land*, is as much as two oxen can till. *Sheppard*, Touchstone.

Others say that one oxgange of land containeth 15 acres, and 8 oxganges make a *plow land*. *Coke upon Littleton.*

plowman, ploughman (plou'man), *n.*; pl. *plowmen*, *ploughmen* (-men). [< ME. *plowman*, *plougman* (= G. *pflugmann*); < *plow* + *man*.] One who plows or guides a plow; a farm laborer who is or may be engaged in plowing.

Wille . . . wrougte that here is wryten, and other werkes bothe
Of Peres the *Plowman*, and mechel puple al-so.
Piers Plowman (A), xii. 102.

The merchant gains by peace, and the soldiers by war, the shepherd by wet seasons, and the *ploughmen* by dry.
Sir W. Temple.

Like any *Ploughman* toil'd the little God,
His Tune he whistled, and his Wheat he sow'd.
Prior, Cupid turned Ploughman (trans.).

Plowman's fee. See *fee*[2].—**Plowman's spikenard.** See *spikenard*.

plowmbet, plowmet, *n.* Obsolete (Middle English) forms of *plum*[1].

plowmeat† (plou'mēt), *n.* Cereal food, as distinguished from flesh-meat.

Some countryes lack *plough-meat*,
And some do lack cow-meat.
Tusser, Husbandry, April's Abstract.

Plow Monday (plou mun'dā). The Monday after Twelfth-day, or the termination of the Christmas holidays, when the labors of the plow usually began, observed in England as a rustic festival. On that day it is the custom of plowmen to draw a plow from door to door, soliciting drink-money. Also called *Rock Monday*.

Plough Monday next, after that Twelfth tide is past,
Bids out with the plough, the worst husband is last.
Tusser, Husbandry, Ploughman's Feasting Days.

plowngy†, *a.* An obsolete form of *plungy*.

plow-point (plou'point), *n.* A detachable share at the front end of a plow-body, forming an apex to the junction of mold-board, sole, and land-side. *E. H. Knight.*

plow-press (plou'pres), *n.* In *bookbinding*, same as *cutting-press*, 2.

plow-service (plou'sėr'vis), *n.* In early English tenancies, the service rendered by villeins or other tenants in plowing the lands of the lord's manor, or furnishing oxen to the team therefor.

plowshare, ploughshare (plou'shãr), *n.* [< ME. *plouhschare* (= MLG. *plōchschare* = MHG. *pfluocschar*, G. *pflugschar*); < *plow* + *share*[2].] **1.** The share of a plow, or that part which cuts the ground at the bottom of the furrow, and raises the slice to the mold-board, which turns it over; the sock of a plow. See first cut under *plow*.

Countries by future *Plow-shares* to be torn,
And Cities rais'd by Nations yet unborn.
Prior, Solomon, i.

2. In *anat.*, the vomer.

plowshare-bone (plou'shãr-bōn), *n.* **1.** In *anat.*, the vomer.—**2.** In *ornith.*, the pygostyle.

plow-shoe (plou'shö), *n.* A block of wood fitted under the point of a plowshare when not in use, to prevent it from penetrating the soil.

plow-silver (plou'sil'vėr), *n.* In *old Eng. law*, money paid by tenants and retainers in commutation of service due in plowing the lands of the lord of the manor.

plow-sock (plou'sok), *n.* Same as *plowshare*, 1. *Scott.* [Scotch.]

plow-staff (plou'ståf), *n.* [< ME. *ploghe-staffe*.] A kind of paddle to clear the colter and share of a plow when choked with earth or weeds: called in Scotland a *pattle* or *pettle*.

plow-star (plou'stär), *n.* See *the Plow*, under *plow*.

Thee lights starrye noting in globe celestial hanging:
Thee seun stars stormy, twise told thee *plowstar*, eke Arcture. *Stanihurst*, Æneid, iii. 528. (*Davies.*)

plow-stert†, *n.* [ME. (= D. *ploegstaart* = MLG. *plochstert* = G. *pflugsterz*, *pflugsterze* = Sw. *plogstjert* = Dan. *plovstjert*), < *plow* + *stert*, tail.] Same as *plow-tail*.

plow-stilt (plou'stilt), *n.* A handle of a plow.

plow-swain (plou'swān), *n.* A plowman.

Beasts leave their stals, *plough-swains* their fires forego,
Nor are the meadows white with drifts of snow.
Sir T. Hawkins, tr. of Odes of Horace, i. 4. (*Davies.*)

plow-tail (plou'tāl), *n.* That part of a plow which the plowman holds; the handle of a plow.

plow-team (plou'tēm), *n.* In early English times, usually a team of eight oxen, commonly yoked four abreast. The estimated work of such a team served as a measure of land. See *plowland*, 2.

plow-tree (plou'trē), *n.* A plow-handle.

I whistled the same tunes to my horses, and held my *plow-tree* just the same, as if no King nor Queen had ever come to spoil my tune or hand.
Blackmore, Lorna Doone, lxxiv.

plow-truck (plou'truk), *n.* An attachment to a plow, in the form of a riding-seat supported on two wheels, to enable the plowman to ride at his work. See *sulky-plow*, under *plow*.

plow-wise (plou'wīz), *a.* Going alternately forward and backward in parallel lines, as in plowing.

This was succeeded by Boustrophedon, or *plough-wise* writing. *Isaac Taylor*, The Alphabet, II. 33.

plow-witcher (plou'wich'ėr), *n.* One of a company of plowmen and other field-laborers who drag a plow from house to house, soliciting drink-money, with mumming, dancing, and other sports, preparatory to the first plowing after the Christmas holidays. See *Plow Monday*. [Local, Eng.]

Seven companies of *plough-witchers* waited upon me in my South Lincolnshire home; and some of the performers—Bessy, the Doctor, the Valiant Soldier, &c.—went through the recital of their little play.
N. and Q., 7th ser., I. 86.

plowwright, ploughwright (plou'rīt), *n.* One who makes and repairs plows.

Ploughwrite, cartwright, knacker, and smith.
Tusser, Husbandry, Corn Harvest.

ploy[1] (ploi), *n.* [Abbr. of *employ*.] **1.** Employment.—**2.** A harmless frolic; a merrymaking. [Scotch.]

ploy[2] (ploi), *v. i.* [Cf. *deploy*.] *Milit.*, to move from line into column: the opposite of *deploy*.

ployment (ploi'ment), *n.* [< *ploy*[2] + *-ment*.] *Milit.*, the formation of column from line.

Pluchea (plō'kē-ạ̈), *n.* [NL. (Cassini, 1817), named after N. A. *Pluche*, a French abbé who wrote upon natural history in 1732.] A genus of composite plants of the tribe *Inuloideæ*, type of the subtribe *Plucheineæ*, characterized by the corymbose heads of flowers with dry broad bracts, each head containing numerous truncate thread-shaped pistillate flowers in many outer rows, and a few perfect but sterile five-cleft flowers in the center. There are about 35 species, natives of warmer parts of America, Africa, Asia, and Australia, a few herbaceous and extending into the central or northern United States on the coast, the others shrubs or undershrubs. They are woolly or glutinous, with a strong or camphoric odor, bearing alternate toothed leaves, and white, yellow, or purplish flowers. *P. camphorata* is the salt-marsh fleabane of the Atlantic coast, sometimes called *camphor-plant*. *P. odorata* is the riverside tobacco of the West Indies.

pluck[1] (pluk), *v. t.* [< ME. *plukken*, *plokken*, *plockien* (pret. *pluckede*, *plukkede*, pp. *plukked*, irreg. pret. *plyghte*, pp. *plyght*), < AS. *pluccian*, *pluccigean*, *ploccan* (pret. *pluccede*, pp. *plucced*) = D. *plukken* = MLG. *plucken*, LG. *plukken* = OHG. **pfluccheu* (not found), MHG. *phlücken*, *pflücken*, G. *pflücken* = Icel. *plukka*, *plokka* = Sw. *plocka* = Dan. *plukke*, pick, pluck; hardly a Teut. word, the Scand. forms being appar. borrowed from AS. or LG., and these prob. derived, through OHG. or Goth. (where, however, the word is not recorded), from an early Rom. (LL.) verb **pilicare*, **pilucare*, found in OIt. *pelucare*, *peluccare*, *piluccare*, It. *piluccare*, pluck (grapes), pick off (grapes) one by one, = Pr. *pelucar*, pick out, = OF. *plocquer*, in secondary form **pluquier*, *plusquier*, *pelukier*, *peluchier*, F. dial. (Picard) *pluquer*, *pluskier*, *ploki*, *plucher*, F. in comp. *éplucher*, pick, gather (the F. forms prob. in part reflections of the LG.); the ref. to plucking grapes (which suggests the means of its early introduction into Teut. use) being a particular application or transfer of the orig. sense (OIt. *pelucare*, etc.) 'pick out hairs one by one,' as explained under the derivative *peruke*, the verb (LL. **pilicare*, **pilucare*) being derived, with freq. formative (L. *-ic-are*, LL. **-uc-are*, It. *-uc-are*, *-ucc-are*, etc., the same occurring in *plunge*, ult. < ML. **plumbicare*), from L. *pilus*, hair, a hair: see *pile*[4], *peruke* (and *periwig* and *wig*), and also *plush*, from the same source. No evidence of the existence of the Rom. (LL.) verb at a period early enough to produce the earliest Teut. forms is found; analogous verbs in *-icare* are, however, found, and the explanation here given meets all the other conditions. It will be observed that *pluck* still refers in most instances to pulling hair or feathers or berries or flowers, and that L. *pilus*, hair, has had in other respects a remarkable development.] **1.** To pull off, as feathers from a fowl, or fruit or flowers from a plant; pick off; gather; pick or cull, as berries or flowers.

Hise disciplis *pluckiden* eeris of corn, and thei frotynge with her hondis eeten.
Wyclif, Luke vi. 1.

Al sodeynly thre leves have I *plyght*
Out of his book right as he radde.
Chaucer, Prol. to Wife of Bath's Tale, l. 790.

I'll show thee the best springs;
I'll *pluck* thee berries;
I'll fish for thee.
Shak., Tempest, ii. 2. 164.

As thro' the land at eve we went,
And *pluck'd* the ripen'd ears.
Tennyson, Princess, i. (song).

2. To pull; draw; drag: used either literally or figuratively.

Pluck him headlong from the usurped throne.
Shak., Rich. II., v. 1. 65.

What poor fate follow'd thee, and *pluck'd* thee on,
To trust thy sacred life to an Egyptian?
Fletcher (and another), False One, ii. 1.

The best part of himselfe he had lost before in Apostasie, which *plucked* this destruction upon him.
Purchas, Pilgrimage, p. 357.

It is their Custom to make Men sit on the Floor, as they do, cross-legg'd like Taylors; But I had not strength then to *pluck* up my Heels in that manner.
Dampier, Voyages, I. 502.

Especially—**3.** To pull sharply; pull with sudden force or jerk; give a tug or twitch to; twitch; snatch; twang, as the strings of a harp or guitar.

Sodeynly he *plyghte* his hors aboute.
Chaucer, Prol. to Man of Law's Tale, l. 15.

Merlin caught the flayle of the yate and *plukked* it to hym, and yede oute as lightly as it hadde not haue ben lokked, and than departed oute mag[r]e how it grucchid.
Merlin (E. E. T. S.), ii. 206.

You are the hare of whom the proverb goes,
Whose valour *plucks* dead lions by the beard.
Shak., K. John, ii. 1. 138.

I have been *pluck'd* and tugg'd by th' hair o' th' head
About a gallery half an acre long.
Fletcher (and another), Nice Valour, iii. 2.

E'en children followed, with endearing wile,
And *pluck'd* his gown, to share the good man's smile.
Goldsmith, Des. Vil., l. 184.

4. To strip, as a fowl, by pulling off its feathers; strip the feathers from: as, to *pluck* a fowl.

Since I *plucked* geese, played truant, and whipped top, I knew not what 'twas to be beaten till lately.
Shak., M. W. of W., v. 1. 26.

The King of Great Britain used to send for his Ambassadors from Abroad to *pluck* Capons at Home.
Howell, Letters, I. v. 31.

5. To reject, after a university or other examination, as not coming up to the required standard. [College slang, Eng.]

He went to college, and he got *plucked*, I think they call it.
Charlotte Brontë, Jane Eyre, x.

If a man is *plucked*—that is, does not get marks enough to pass—his chance of a Fellowship is done for.
C. A. Bristed, English University, p. 258.

I trust that I have never *plucked* a candidate in the Schools without giving him every opportunity of setting himself right.
Stubbs, Medieval and Modern Hist., p. 336.

Plucked instrument, in *music*. See *instrument*, 3 (*c*).—**To pluck a crow with one**, to pick a quarrel with one.

O, these courtiers, neighbours, are pestilent knaves; but, ere I'll suffer it, I'll *pluck a crow with some* of 'em.
Dekker and Ford, Sun's Darling, iv. 1.

To pluck a pigeon. See *pigeon*.—**To pluck down a side.** See the quotation.

Other that never learned to shoot, nor yet knoweth good shaft nor bow, will be as busy as the best, but such one commonly *plucketh down a side* [to *pluck down a side*, I believe, is to shoot on one side into the ground], and crafty archers which be against him will be both glad of him, and also ever ready to lay and bet with him: it were better for such one to sit down than shoot.
Ascham, Toxophilus (ed. 1864), p. 8.

To pluck off†, to descend in regard to rank or title; descend lower.

Pluck off a little;
I would not be a young count in your way.
Shak., Hen. VIII., ii. 3. 40.

To pluck up. (*a*) To pull or haul up suddenly; remove entirely or by the roots; eradicate; hence, to exterminate; destroy: as, to *pluck up* weeds.

They *pluckt up* anchor, and away did sayle.
The Noble Fisherman (Child's Ballads, V. 331).

But if they will not obey, I will utterly *pluck up* and destroy that nation, saith the Lord.
Jer. xii. 17.

I observed that the corn here was *plucked up* by the roots, according to the antient usage, which is retained also in the upper Ægypt.
Pococke, Description of the East, II. i. 131.

(*b*) To summon or muster up: as, to *pluck up* courage, spirit, etc.

Pluk vp thi hert, my dere mayster.
Robin Hood and the Monk (Child's Ballads, V. 2).

Pluck up thy spirits; look cheerfully upon me.
Shak., T. of the S., iv. 3. 38.

Why did not Little-faith *pluck up* a greater heart?
Bunyan, Pilgrim's Progress, p. 188.

Pluck up a little resolution, and we shall soon be out of the reach of her malignity.
Goldsmith, She Stoops to Conquer, v.

(c) *Intrans.*, to collect one's self; gather spirit or courage.

Bene. You break jests as braggarts do their blades. . . .
D. Pedro. But, soft you, let me be. *Pluck up*, my heart, and be sad [serious].
Shak., Much Ado, v. 1. 207.

pluck[1] (pluk), *n.* [= D. *pluk*, plucking, gathering, crop, = Sw. *plock* = Dan. *pluk*, gathering; from the verb: see *pluck*, *v.* In def. 4 the same word, the heart, liver, and lights being 'plucked out' in preparing the carcass for market. In def. 5 a colloq. fig. use of sense 4, like *heart* and *liver* in similar expressions.] **1.** A pull; a tug; a twitch; a snatch: as, he gave the sword a *pluck*.

Were they [the bones] dry, they could not . . . without great difficulty yield to and obey the *plucks* and attractions of the motory muscles.
Ray, Works of Creation, ii.

2†. A blow; a stroke.—**3†.** A bout; a round.

Why, wylt thou fyght a *plucke*?
Playe of Robyn Hode (Child's Ballads, V. 423).

4. The heart, liver, and lungs or lights of a sheep, ox, or other animal used as butchers' meat: also used figuratively or humorously of the like parts of a human being.

It vexes me to the *pluck* that I should lose walking this delicious day.
Swift, Journal to Stella, xviii.

There were lower depths yet: there were the purl houses, where "Tradesmen flock in their Morning gowns, by Seven, to cool their *Plucks*."
J. Ashton, Social Life in Reign of Queen Anne, I. 234.

Hence—**5.** Heart; courage; spirit; determined energy; resolution in the face of difficulties.

Decay of English spirit, decay of manly *pluck*.
Thackeray.

Be firm! one constant element in luck
Is genuine, solid, old Teutonic *pluck*.
O. W. Holmes, A Rhymed Lesson.

Attracted by the fame of Botta's discoveries, he [Layard] set to work digging at Nineveh with that *pluck*, that energy, and at the same time that discriminating judgment, which he has since shown on other occasions.
Max Muller, Biograph. Essays, p. 289.

pluck[2] (pluk), *n.* [Origin obscure; cf. Ir. Gael. *pluc*, a lump, knot, bunch, *ploc*, a club, plug, block: see *plug* and *block*[1].] The pogge, *Agonus cataphractus*. [Scotch.]

plucked[1] (plukt), *p. a.* Having the long stiff hairs removed: said of the pelt of a fur-seal.

plucked[2] (plukt), *a.* [< *pluck*[1], *n.*, 5, spirit, courage, + *-ed*[2].] Endowed with pluck or courage: with a qualifying adjective. [Colloq.]

"What, going?" said he, "and going for good? I wish I was such a good-*plucked* one as you, Miss Anville."
Thackeray, Roundabout Papers, On a Peal of Bells, note.

A very sensible man, and has seen a deal of life, and kept his eyes open, but a terrible hard-*plucked* one. Talked like a book to me all the way, but be hanged if I don't think he has a thirty-two-pound shot under his ribs instead of a heart.
Kingsley, Two Years Ago, iv. (*Davies*.)

plucker (pluk'ėr), *n.* **1.** One who or that which plucks.

Thou setter up and *plucker* down of kings.
Shak., 3 Hen. VI., ii. 3. 37.

2. A machine for straightening and cleaning long wool to render it fit for combing. It has a traveling apron which feeds the ends of the tufts to a pair of spiked rollers, by which tufts and locks are opened, and whence they proceed to a fanning apparatus for cleaning. It is usually managed by a boy.

Plückerian (plü-kē'ri-an), *a.* [< *Plücker* (see def.) + *-ian*.] Pertaining to the geometrician Julius Plücker (1801–68).—**Plückerian characteristic**, one of the quantities entering into the Plückerian equations.—**Plückerian equations**, equations published in 1834, substantially as follows: Let m be the order of a plane curve, n its class, δ its nodes, κ its cusps, τ its bitangents, and ι its inflections. Then

$$3m - \kappa = 3n - \iota;$$
$$2\delta = m^2 - m - n - 3\kappa;$$
$$2\tau = n^2 - n - m - 3\iota.$$

Plücker's formulæ. See *formula*.

pluckily (pluk'i-li), *adv.* In a plucky manner; with courage or spirit. [Colloq.]

"No," said Frank, *pluckily*, as he put his horse into a faster trot.
Trollope, Dr. Thorne, xxix.

pluckiness (pluk'i-nes), *n.* The character of being plucky; pluck; courage.

Her quaint, queer expression, in which curiosity, *pluckiness*, and a foretaste of amusement mingled.
Mrs. Whitney, Leslie Goldthwaite, vi.

pluckless (pluk'les), *a.* [< *pluck*[1], *n.*, 5, + *-less*.] Without pluck; faint-hearted. [Colloq.]

plucky (pluk'i), *a.* [< *pluck*[1], *n.*, 5, + *-y*[1].] Possessing pluck, or spirit and courage; spirited; courageous. [Colloq.]

If you're *plucky*, and not over-subject to fright,
And go and look over that chalk-pit white,
You may see, if you will,
The Ghost of old Gill.
Barham, Ingoldsby Legends, II. 146.

pluff (pluf), *v. t.* [Imitative of a sudden puff; cf. *puff* and *fluff*[2].] To throw out smoke or fine dust in quick whiffs, as by igniting gunpowder or throwing out hair-powder from a puffball. [Scotch.]

pluff (pluf), *n.* [< *pluff*, *v.*] **1.** A puff of smoke or dust, as from gunpowder or hair-powder. [Scotch.]

The gout took his head, and he went out of the world like a *pluff* of powther.
Galt, Steam-Boat, p. 78. (*Jamieson*.)

2†. An instrument used in powdering the hair, made like a sort of bellows, by which the powder was blown in a cloud. Also *powder-puff*.—**3.** In *bot.*, a Scotch name for a species of puffball, *Bovista lycoperdon*.

pluffy (pluf'i), *a.* [< *pluff* + *-y*[1].] Fluffy; puffy; blown up.

Light *pluffy* hair.
Albert Smith, Pottleton Legacy, xxvii.

A good-looking fellow—a thought too *pluffy*, perhaps, and more than a thought too swaggering.
Lever, One of Them.

plug (plug), *n.* [< MD. *plugge*, D. *plug*, a bung, peg, plug, = MLG. *plugge*, LG. *plugge*, *plügge*, a plug, = MHG. *pfloc* (*pflock-*), *pflocke*, G. *pflock*, a peg, plug, = Sw. *plugg*, *pligg* = Norw. *plug* = Dan. *plög*, *plök* (prob. < LG.), plug, peg; cf. W.

ploc, a plug, block, = Ir. *ploc*, a plug, block, club: see *block*[1].] 1. A piece of wood or other substance, usually in the form of a peg or cork, used to stop a hole in a vessel; a stopple; a bung or stopper of any kind.—2. A peg, wedge, or other appliance driven in, or used to stop a hole or fill a gap. (*a*) A piece of wood driven horizontally into a wall, its end being then sawed away flush with the wall, to afford a hold for nails. (*b*) In *civil engin.*, a heavy peg or stake driven in flush with the surface of the ground as a permanent reference-point, as distinguished from a *stake*, one projecting above the ground. (*c*) A piece of boxwood cut to cylindrical form, used by wood-engravers. If any part of an engraved block has been injured, a circular hole is drilled through the block, large enough to remove the damaged part. A plug is then driven into the hole, and a new surface thus obtained which can be reëngraved.

This mode of repairing a block was practised by the German wood engravers of the time of Albert Durer. The *plug* which they inserted was usually square, and not circular as at present. *Chatto*, Wood Engraving, p. 369.

(*d*) A wedge-pin forced between a rail and its chair on a railway. (*e*) A spigot driven into place, as in a barrel, in contradistinction to one screwed in. (*f*) A wooden stopper fitted in the opening of the pump on a ship's deck during a storm, to protect the water-tanks against lightning; a pump-stopper.

3. A small piece of some substance, as metallic foil, used by a dentist to fill the cavity of a decayed tooth.—4. A branch pipe from a water-main, leading to a point where a hose can be conveniently attached, and closed by a cap or plug: a fire-plug.—5. In *die-sinking*, a cylindrical piece of soft steel the end of which is fitted to a matrix. When matrix and plug are forced together under heavy pressure, the intaglio design of the matrix is impressed in relief upon the plug. The plug is then hardened, and becomes a punch, which can be used to make impressions on die-faces, as for coining, etc.

6. A flat oblong cake of pressed tobacco.

Tom brought out a corncob pipe for the preacher, and shaved him tobacco from a *plug*. *The Century*, XXXVIII. 89.

7. A man's silk or dress hat; a plug-hat. [Slang.] —8. A worn, damaged, unfashionable, or otherwise injured article, which, by reason of its defects, has become undesirable, unsalable, or in a condition rendering it difficult to sell without a large reduction of its price, as a shelf-worn book, or an old horse worn down by hard work. Also *old plug*. [Colloq.]—9. A short, thick-set person. [Slang.]—10. A workman who has served no regular apprenticeship. [Slang.]—11. A sort of fishing-boat. [Cape Ann.]—12. Same as *plug-rod*, 1.—**Cutting plug**, in a chronographic apparatus for registering velocities of projectiles from one position in the bore of a gun to another, one of a series of plugs inserted into holes drilled radially in the gun-barrel from its exterior into the bore. The plug is connected with a looped electric conducting-wire of a primary circuit, and at its inner end is a small knife pivoted to the body of the plug in such manner that it slightly projects into the bore of the gun, and so arranged that, when forced radially outward by the passage of the projectile over it, it cuts the loop of the wire, and breaks the primary circuit. This induces a brief current in the secondary coil, which has one of its terminals arranged at the edge of one of a series of rapidly, uniformly, and synchronously rotating thin disks of equal diameter attached to a common shaft. The edges of the disks are coated with lampblack. The induced current of the secondary coil produces a spark at the terminal, which burns off a small dot in the peripheral coating. A number of the cutting plugs are inserted at uniform intervals in the gun. Each is serially related to one of the disks, in the order of succession from breech to muzzle of the gun; and when the gun is fired it records the instant the shot passes it on the edge of its related disk. From the angular distance between these records, the known diameter and rotating speed of the disks, the time occupied by the shot in moving from plug to plug is readily calculated; and it is asserted that intervals of time as small as one millionth of a second can be measured. The data thus obtained are of great value in the investigation of the action of explosives.—**Fusible plug**. See *fusible*.—**Plug-and-collar gage**. See *gage*[2].—**Plug and feathers**, a flat iron wedge (the *plug*) used in connection with two semi-cylindrical pieces of iron (the *feathers*), placed in a hole bored in a rock, with their flat surfaces toward each other, between which the wedge is driven with a sledge-hammer, the object being to split the rock. See *feather*, 2 (*d*).—**Plug center-bit**. See *center-bit*.

plug (plug), *v. t.*; pret. and pp. *plugged*, ppr. *plugging*. [= MLG. *pluggen* = Sw. *pligga* = Dan. *plökke*, plug; from the noun.] 1. To stop with a plug; make tight by stopping a hole: as, to *plug* a decayed tooth; to *plug* a wound with lint.—2. To hit with a ball or bullet: as, to *plug* a buck with a rifle. [Slang, western U.S.]—3. To cut out a plug from: said of watermelons when a tapering plug is cut out to see if the fruit is ripe, and then replaced. [Eastern U. S.]

plug-arbor (plug'är"bor), *n.* A lathe attachment for mounting drill-chucks. *E. H. Knight.*

plug-basin (plug'bā"sn), *n.* A standing wash-basin with a plug-hole at the bottom for emptying. *E. H. Knight.*

plug-bayonet (plug'bā"o-net), *n.* A bayonet of the early type, which the soldier fixed into the muzzle of his piece. The haft or plug was often of horn, more commonly of wood, and the steel was secured to this by brass or iron mounting.

plugboard (plug'bōrd), *n.* A switchboard in which the connections are made by means of brass or other conducting plugs.

plug-cock (plug'kok), *n.* A cock in which a plug with a transverse hole in it is fitted into a transverse hole in a hollow barrel or cylinder, the diameter of the plug being greater than the interior diameter of the cylinder, and therefore permitting liquid to flow through the latter only when the transverse hole in the plug is so turned as to form a continuous passage with the hollow in the cylinder. The plugs are sometimes covered or packed with a yielding material, and are usually tapored, so that pressing them into their seats keeps them tight.

Plug-cock.
a, body or barrel; *b*, tapered plug; *c*, tightening-screw fitted to the bottom of *b*, and bearing upon a washer, *c'*; *d*, thumb-piece, in large cocks replaced by a hand-lever or wrench.

plug-finisher (plug'fin"ish-ėr), *n.* In *dentistry*, a fine file, of a great variety of shapes, used for finishing the surfaces of plugs or fillings.

plugger (plug'ėr), *n.* One who or that which plugs; specifically, a dentists' instrument, of various forms, for driving and packing a filling material into a hole in a carious tooth. See *dental hammer*, under *hammer*[1]. *E. H. Knight.*

plugging-forceps (plug'ing-fôr"seps), *n.* A dentists' instrument or plugger used to compress a filling in a carious tooth. *E. H. Knight.*

plug-hat (plug'hat), *n.* Same as *chimney-pot hat* (which see, under *hat*[1]). [Slang.]

plughet, *n.* An obsolete dialectal form of *plow*.

plug-hole (plug'hōl), *n.* A hole for a plug; a hole left by the removal of a plug.

A surbase had been taken down, leaving large *plug-holes* to be filled up. *Paper-hanger*, p. 21.

plug-joggle (plug'jog"l), *n.* The name given by Smeaton to a stone such as the center-stones of the Eddystone-lighthouse foundation, which were joggled into the surrounding stones, and also secured to the corresponding stones above and below by a central plug of stone.

plug-machine (plug'ma-shēn"), *n.* A machine combining a cutter and shaper for making wooden plugs for the draught-holes of beer- and liquor-casks.

plug-rod (plug'rod), *n.* 1. In a condensing engine, a rod connected with the working-beam and serving to drive the working-gear of the valves. Also called *plug*, *plug-tree*.—2. The air-pump rod of a steam-engine. *E. H. Knight.*

plug-switch (plug'swich), *n.* An arrangement in which electrical connection between two conductors is established by the insertion of a metallic plug.

plug-tap (plug'tap), *n.* 1. A cylindrical tap for cutting the dies of a screw-stock; a master-tap.—2. A tap slightly tapered at the end to facilitate its entrance in tapping a hole. *E. H. Knight.*

A *plug-tap* has the full depth of screw-thread all along its length. *Campin*, Hand-turning, p. 111.

plug-tree (plug'trē), *n.* Same as *plug-rod*, 1.

plug-ugly (plug'ug'li), *n.* A city ruffian; one of a band of rowdies who indulged in wanton assaults upon persons and property in streets and public places: first used in Baltimore. [Slang.]

plug-valve (plug'valv), *n.* A valve closed by a tapering plug at right angles to the flow of the liquid.

plum[1] (plum), *n.* [Formerly also, erroneously, *plumb* (as in *limb* for *lim*, *numb* for *num*, etc.); < ME. *plumme*, with vowel shortened, earlier *ploume*, < AS. *plūme*, *plȳme* = D. *pruim* = MLG. *plūme*, LG. *plumme* = OHG. *pfrūma*, *pflūmo*, MHG. *pflūme*, *phlūme*, *phrūme*, *prūme*, *prūne*, G. *pflaume* = Icel. *plōma* = Sw. *plommon* = Dan. *blomme*, plum, = F. *prune* (> E. *prune*) = Pr. *pruna* = Sp. dial. *pruna* = It. *pruna*, *prugna*, f., a plum, < ML. *prūna*, f., a plum, L. *prūnum* (pl. *prūna*), neut., a plum, *prūnus*, f., a plum-tree, < Gr. προῦνον, neut., προῦνος, f., earlier προύμνον, neut., a plum, προύμνη, f., a plum-tree. Cf. Ir. *pluma* = Corn. *pluman* = Gael. *plumbas*, *plumbais*, plum (< E.). For the change of L. *r* to *l* and of *n* to *m*, cf. *pilgrim*, ult. < L. *peregrinus*. For the introduction of a Latin and Greek fruit-name into Teut., cf. *peach*[1] and *pear*[1], also *quine*, *quince*.] 1. A fruit of any of the trees called *plums* (see defs. 2 and 3); specifically, the fruit of a tree of the genus *Prunus*, distinguished from the peach and apricot by its smooth surface, smaller size, and unwrinkled stone, and from the cherry by the bloom on its surface and commonly larger size. Plums are of use chiefly as a dessert fruit (the green gage being esteemed the best of all varieties), and as a dried fruit in the form of prunes. (See *prune*[1].) Locally a liquor is manufactured from them, and sometimes an oil is expressed from the kernels.

2. One of several small trees of the genus *Prunus*, forming the section *Prunus* proper. The numerous varieties of the common garden-plum are often classed as *P. domestica*; but all these, together with the bullace-plum, known as *P. insititia* (see *bullace*), are believed to be derived ultimately from *P. spinosa* (*P. communis*), the blackthorn or sloe of Europe and temperate Asia, in its truly wild state a much-branched shrub, the branches often ending in a stout thorn. Plum-wood is useful in cabinet-work and turnery. The plum is chiefly cultivated in France (in the valley of the Loire), in Germany, and in Bosnia, Servia, and Croatia. In America the plum suffers greatly from the ravages of the curculio. (See *plum-curculio*.) The Japanese plum, *P. Japonica*, though not insect-proof, is a valued acquisition in California and the southern United States. For native species, see *beach-plum*, *cherry-plum*, and *wild plum*, below.

In Aimauot, in himself, in malo, in pecho,
Ys graffed *plumme*.
Palladius, Husbondrie (E. E. T. S.), p. 216.

The harvest white *plum* is a base *plum*.
Bacon, Nat. Hist., § 509.

It is as if the rose should pluck herself,
Or the ripe *plum* finger its misty bloom.
Keats, Posthumous Sonnets, xiv.

3. One of numerous trees of other genera bearing plum-like fruit. See phrases below.—4. A grape dried in the sun; a raisin.

So when you've swallow'd the Potion, you sweeten your Mouth with a *Plumb*. *Congreve*, Double-Dealer, iii. 4.

The dried grapes which the French term raisins secs, or raisins passés, we term simply raisins when used for eating uncooked, and *plums* when they form an ingredient in the famous English plum pudding.
S. Dowell, Taxes in England, IV. 37.

5. A good thing; the best or choicest part; a sugar-plum: in allusion to the use of plums or raisins in cakes, plum-pudding, etc.

The reviewer who picks all the *plums* out of a book is a person who is regarded with reasonable terror and resentment by both authors and publishers.
The Academy, Nov. 2, 1889, p. 280.

Often, indeed, the foot-note contains the very *plum* of the page. *The Writer*, III. 120.

6. The sum of £100,000 sterling; hence, any handsome sum or fortune generally; sometimes, also, a person possessing such a sum. [Colloq., Eng.]

The Miser must make up his *Plumb*,
And dares not touch the hoarded Sum.
Prior, The Ladle, Moral.

Several who were *plums*, or very near it, became men of moderate fortunes. *Addison*, Vision of Justice.

An honest gentleman who sat next to me, and was worth half a *plumb*, stared at him. *Steele*, Tatler, No. 244.

My brother Heidelberg was a warm man, a very warm man, and died worth a *plumb* at least: a *plumb!* ay, I warrant you, he died worth a *plumb* and a half.
Colman, Clandestine Marriage, iii.

Assyrian plum. See *sebesten*.—**Australian plum**, a date-plum or persimmon, *Diospyros* (*Cargillia*) *australis*, the black plum of Illawarra. For other Australian plums, see *Queensland plum* and *wild plum* (*e*).—**Beach-plum**, *Prunus maritima*, a straggling bush on the coast from Maine to Mexico, with a rather pleasant red or purple fruit, often preserved.—**Black plum**. See *Australian plum*.—**Blood-plum**. (*a*) See *Hæmatostaphis*. (*b*) A recently introduced Japanese plum with red flesh. [U. S.] —**Canada plum**. See *wild plum* (*b*), below.—**Cherry-plum**, a cherry-like form of the common plum, the variety *myrobalana*. Also called *myrobalan plum*.—**Chickasaw plum**, *Prunus angustifolia* (*P. Chicasa*), a species probably native in the southern Rocky Mountains, now naturalized widely eastward and northward. It bears a globose red or yellow fruit, thin-skinned and of pleasant flavor. It is often cultivated, receiving special attention as less subject than the common plum to the attacks of the curculio.—**Cocoa-plum**, *Chrysobalanus Icaco*. See *Chrysobalanus*.—**Damask plum**. Same as *damson plum*. —**Damson plum**. See *damson*.—**Darling plum**, the red ironwood, *Reynosia latifolia*, a small tree of the West Indies and southern Florida. It bears an agreeable fruit, and its dark-brown wood is very hard and strong.—**Date plum**. See *date-plum*, *Diospyros*, and *persimmon*.—**Downward plum**, a small tree of the West Indies and Florida: same as *ant's-wood*. Also called *saffron plum*.—**East Indian plum**, *Flacourtia Cataphracta* and *F. Ramontchi* (including *F. sapida*). The latter is common, wild or cultivated, throughout India, and found also in the Malay archipelago and in Madagascar, thence called *Madagascar plum*. —**French plum**, a very superior plum grown in the valley of the Loire, entering the market in the form of prunes.—**Gopher plum**. Same as *Ogeechee lime* (which see, under *lime*[3]).—**Gray plum**, in Sierra Leone, *Parinarium excelsum*, a large tree with a fruit having a large stone and a thin, rather dry, and insipid pulp. Also called *rough-skinned plum* and *Guinea plum*.—**Green-gage plum**. See def. 1, and *gage*[3].—**Guiana plum**, a small euphorbiaceous tree, *Drypetes crocea*, of the West Indies and southern Florida. Also called *whitewood*.—**Guinea plum**. See *gray plum*.—**Imperatrice plum**, a variety of the common plum.—**Jamaica plum**, *Spondias lutea*, one of the hog-plums.—**Japan plum**, **Japanese plum**. (*a*) An improper name for the loquat. [Southern U. S.] (*b*) *Prunus Japonica* and other true plums of Japan. See def. 2, and *blood-plum* (b).—**Java plum**, the Jambolana.—**Madagascar plum.** See *East Indian plum*.—**Malabar plum**, the jamrosade or rose-apple.—**Mola plum**, in the region of the Zambesi, *Parinarium Mobola*, which yields very oily two-celled stones called *mabo-seeds*.—**Myrobalan plum.** See *cherry-plum*.—**Natal plum**, an evergreen shrub, *Carissa grandiflora* of the *Apocynaceæ*.—**Pigeon plum.** (a) See *pigeon-plum*. (b) In Sierra Leone, either of two species of *Chrysobalanus*, *C. ellipticus* and *C. luteus*.—**Port Arthur plum**, a small handsome Tasmanian tree, *Cenarrhenes nitida*, the foliage smooth and bright-green, the drupe inedible.—**Queensland plum.** See *Owenia*, 1.—**Rough-skinned plum.** See *gray plum*.—**Saffron plum.** Same as *downward plum*.—**Sapodilla plum.** See *Achras* and *sapodilla*.—**Seaside plum.** Same as *mountain-plum*. [West Indies.]—**Sebesten plum.** See *Cordia* and *sebesten*.—**Sour plum, sweet plum.** See *Owenia*, 1.—**Spanish plum**, one of the hog-plums (*Spondias purpurea*), also *Mammea humilis*, both West Indian and South American.—**St. Julien plum**, a variety of the common plum known as *Juliana*, yielding part of the French plums.—**Tamarind plum**, a leguminous tree, *Dialium indum*, whose fruit has a delicious pulp resembling that of the tamarind.—**Tasmanian plum.** Same as *Port Arthur plum*.—**Wild-goose plum**, an improved variety of the Chickasaw, said to have been raised from a stone found in the crop of a wild goose.—**Wild plum**, any undomesticated plum. Specifically—(a) The *Prunus spinosa*. See def. 2. (b) In eastern North America, the wild yellow or red plum, or Canada plum, *P. Americana*. It has a well-colored fruit with pleasant pulp, but tough acerb skin. It is common along streams, etc., and sometimes planted. (c) In western North America, *P. subcordata*, whose red fruit, which is large and edible, is often gathered. (d) In South Africa, *Pappea Capensis*. (e) In New South Wales, a tree, *Sideroxylon australis*, with drupaceous fruit, sometimes very tall, having a hard, prettily marked wood, available for cabinet purposes. See also *Podocarpus*. (See also *gingerbread-plum, hog-plum, horse-plum, maiden-plum, mountain-plum, olive-plum*.)

plum²† (plum), *adv.* and *a.* An obsolete spelling of *plumb²*.

pluma (plö'mạ̈), *n.*; pl. *plumæ* (-mē). [L.: see *plume*.] In *ornith.*, a plume or feather of pennaceous structure; a contour-feather, as distinguished from a down-feather; a quill-feather or penna: opposed to *plumule*.

plumaceous (plọ̈-mā'shius), *a.* [‹ NL. **plumaceus*, ‹ L. *pluma*, plume: see *plume*.] Having the character of a pluma; pennaceous, as a feather: distinguished from *plumulaceous*.

plumage (plö'māj), *n.* [‹ F. *plumage* (= Sp. *plumaje* = Pg. *plumagem* = It. *piumaggio*), feathers, ‹ *plume*, feather: see *plume*.] The feathery covering of birds; feathers collectively; ptilosis. See *feather* and *pterylosis*.

> Will the falcon, stooping from above,
> Smit with her varying *plumage*, spare the dove?
> *Pope*, Essay on Man, iii. 54.

Autumnal plumage. See *autumnal*.—**Laced plumage.** See *lacing*, 3.—**Nuptial plumage.** See *nuptial*.

plumaged (plö'mạ̈jd), *a.* [‹ *plumage* + *-ed²*.] Covered with plumage; feathered: usually in composition with a qualifying term: as, full-*plumaged*.

plumaile†, *n.* [ME. *plomayle*; ‹ OF. *plumail*, a plume, plumage, ‹ *plume*, plume: see *plume*.] Plumage.

> They plucked the *plomayle* ffrom the pore skynnes,
> And schewed her signes ffor men shulde drede
> To axe ony mendis ffor her mys-dedis.
> *Richard the Redeless*, ii. 32.

plumassary† (plọ̈-mas'ạ-ri), *n.* [Prop. **plumassery*, ‹ F. *plumasserie*, the feather-trade (also feathers collectively), ‹ *plumassier*, a dealer in or dresser of feathers: see *plumassier*.] A plume or collection of ornamental feathers.

plumassier (plö-ma-sēr'), *n.* [Formerly also *plumasier*; ‹ F. *plumassier*, a dealer in or dresser of feathers, ‹ *plume*, feather, plume: see *plume*.] One who prepares or deals in plumes or feathers for ornamental purposes. See *plumist*.

> The couerings of his tent . . . are all of gold, adorned with stones of great price, and with the curious workemanship of *plumasiers*.
> *Hakluyt's Voyages*, I. 250.

plumate (plö'māt), *a.* [‹ L. *plumatus*, pp. of *plumare*, feather, ‹ *pluma*, feather: see *plume*.] In *entom.*, resembling a plume: said of a hair or bristle when it bears smaller hairs.—**Plumate antenna**, an aristate antenna with the arista covered with fine hairs, as in many flies.

Plumatella repens; a single polypid in its cell or case, magnified. *a*, ectocyst; *b*, endocyst; *m*, calyx at base of tentacles, *q*, on the lophophore, or oral disk; *k*, mouth; *f*, esophagus; *g*, *g*, stomach; *h*, intestine; *i*, anus; *n*, muscle; *w*, nervous ganglion; *z*, *z*, statoblasts; *θ*, funiculus, or gastroparietal band.

Plumatella (plö-mạ-tel'ạ̈), *n.* [NL. (Lamarck), dim., ‹ L. *plumatus*, plumate: see *plumate*.] The typical genus of *Plumatellidæ*, having a tubular cœnœcium and pergamentaceous ectocyst, as *P. repens*. See also cut under *Polyzoa*.

Plumatellidæ (plö-mạ-tel'i-dē), *n. pl.* [NL., ‹ *Plumatella* + *-idæ*.] A family of phylactolæmatous polyzoans, typified by the genus *Plumatella*. They are fresh-water polyzoans of various forms, branching or massive, but always fixed. There are several genera. See cuts under *Plumatella* and *polyzoarium*.

plumb¹†, *n.* An obsolete spelling of *plum¹*.

plumb² (plum), *n.* [Early mod. Eng. also *plomb*; ‹ ME. *plom*, ‹ OF. *plom*, *plomb*, F. *plomb*, lead, a plummet, = Pr. *plom* = Sp. *plomo* = Pg. *chumbo* = It. *piombo*, ‹ L. *plumbum*, lead (*plumbum album* or *candidum*, 'white lead,' tin, *plumbum nigrum*, 'black lead'), a leaden ball, a leaden pipe, a scourge with a leaden ball on the end of it; cf. Gr. *μόλυβος*, *μόλιβος*, *μόλυβδος*, lead (see *molybdena*). Hence ult. (‹ L. *plumbum*) E. *plummet*, *plumber*, *plump²*, *plunge*, *plumbago*, etc.] 1. A mass of lead attached to a line, used to test the perpendicularity of walls, etc.; a plummet.—2. The position of a plumb or plummet when freely suspended; the vertical or perpendicular.—**Out of plumb**, not vertical.

plumb² (plum), *a.* [An ellipsis of *in plumb*. Cf. *plumb²*, *adv.*] 1. True according to a plumb-line; vertical.

> I . . . cannot take a *plumb*-lift out of it, for my soul.
> *Sterne*, Tristram Shandy, ix. 13.

2. Of persons, upright in character or conduct; thoroughgoing.

> Neither can an opposition, neither can a ministry be always wrong. To be a *plumb* man therefore with either is an infallible mark that the man must mean more and worse than he will own he does mean.
> *Richardson*, Clarissa Harlowe, IV. 262. (*Davies.*)

plumb² (plum), *adv.* [Formerly also *plum*; an adverbial use of *plumb²*, *n.*; in part an ellipsis of *in plumb*. Cf. *plump²*, *adv.*] 1. In a vertical direction; in a line perpendicular to the plane of the horizon; straight down.

> Instantly the stony storm of Hail
> Which flew direct a-front, direct now falls
> *Plumb* on their heads, and cleaues their sculs and cauls.
> *Sylvester*, tr. of Du Bartas's Weeks, ii., The Captaines.

> You might mistake it for a ship,
> Only it stands too *plumb* upright.
> *Lowell*, Appledore.

2. Exactly; to a nicety; completely: as, he hit the target *plumb* in the bull's-eye. [Colloq., U. S.]—3. Downright; entirely; altogether. [Colloq., U. S.]

> O Sal, Sal, my heart ar' *plum* broke!
> *The Century*, XXXVI. 900.

plumb² (plum), *v. t.* [Formerly also *plum*; ‹ *plumb²*, *n.*] 1. To adjust by a plumb-line; set in a vertical position: as, to *plumb* a wall or a building.

> The Genius trims our lamps while we sleep. It *plumbs* us by day and levels us by night. *Alcott*, Tablets, p. 201.

2. To sound with or as with a plummet, as the depth of water.

> Where, red and hot with his long journey, He
> *Plummed* the cool bath of th' Atlantic Sea.
> *J. Beaumont*, Psyche, iv. 58.

> I consulted the most experienced seamen upon the depth of the channel, which they had often *plumbed*.
> *Swift*, Gulliver's Travels, i. 5.

3. To ascertain the measure, dimensions, capacity, or the like, of; test.

> He did not attempt to *plumb* his intellect. *Bulwer.*

> I should have *plumbed* the utmost depths of terrified boredom. *Forster*, Dickens, xlix.

4. To supply, as a building, with lead pipes for water, sewage, etc.

Plumbaginaceæ (plum-baj-i-nā'sẹ̄-ē), *n. pl.* [NL. (Lindley, 1835), ‹ *Plumbago* (*-gin-*) + *-aceæ*.] Same as *Plumbagineæ*.

Plumbagineæ (plum-bạ-jin'ẹ̄-ē), *n. pl.* [NL. (Ventenat, 1794), ‹ *Plumbago* (*Plumbagin-*) + *-eæ*.] An order of dicotyledonous gamopetalous plants, the leadwort family, of the cohort *Primulales*, characterized by a tubular or funnel-shaped calyx with five, ten, or fifteen ribs, five stamens opposite the five equal corolla-lobes, five styles, and a free one-celled ovary with one ovule pendulous from a long central stalk (funiculus) which rises from the bottom of the cell. Both in its ovary and its farinaceous albumen it is unlike all other gamopetalous orders. It includes 8 genera, of which *Plumbago* is the type, and from 200 to 270 species, all but 20 of which are contained in the large genera *Statice*, *Acantholimon*, and *Armeria*. They are maritime herbs, natives especially of the Mediterranean region, with a few widely diffused. They are commonly smooth stemless plants, with densely tufted or rosulate leaves, and a branching inflorescence bearing dry rigid bracts and flowers usually having a rose, violet, blue, or yellow corolla, with a calyx of a different color.

plumbaginous (plum-baj'i-nus), *a.* [‹ L. *plumbago* (*-gin-*), plumbago, + *-ous*.] Resembling plumbago; consisting of or containing plumbago, or partaking of its properties.

plumbago (plum-bā'gō), *n.* [‹ L. *plumbago*, black-lead, molybdena, also a plant, leadwort, ‹ *plumbum*, lead: see *plumb²*.] 1. Black-lead; graphite. See *graphite¹*.—2. [*cap.*] [NL. (Tournefort, 1700).] A genus of plants, the leadworts, of the order *Plumbagineæ* and tribe *Plumbageæ*, characterized by a glandular calyx with five short erect teeth, a salver-shaped corolla with slender tube, free stamens, and five styles united into one nearly to the top. The 10 species are natives of warm climates, extending to southern Europe and central Asia. They are usually perennial herbs, with long branches, or partly climbing, bearing alternate clasping leaves, and spikes of blue flowers (or of other colors) at the end of the branches. Several species, bearing the name *leadwort*, are in common cultivation; another, *P. scandens*, a trailing white-flowered species, is native to the south of Florida, extending thence to Brazil, and known, like *P. Europæa*, as *toothwort*, from the use to which its caustic leaves and roots are put. *P. rosea* is used in India to produce blisters.

Plumb-bobs.

a, plumb-bob in common use, made of brass, with cap to attach cord, and steel point at bottom; *b*, plumb-bob with reel inclosed; *c*, common cast-iron plumb-bob; *d*, common lead plumb-bob with wire core.

plumb-bob (plum'bob), *n.* A conoid-shaped metal bob or weight attached to the end of a plumb-line. See also cut under *plumb-rule*.

plumbean (plum'bẹ̄-ạn), *a.* [‹ *plumbeous* + *-an*.] Of, pertaining to, or resembling lead; leaden; hence, dull; heavy.

> There will be a *plumbean* flexible rule.
> *Ellis*, Knowledge of Divine Things, p. 411.

plumbeous (plum'bẹ̄-us), *a.* [‹ L. *plumbeus*, of or belonging to lead, ‹ *plumbum*, lead: see *plumb²*.] 1. Leaden; heavy.

> Attend and throw your ears to mee . . . till I have endoctrinated your *plumbeous* cerebrosities.
> *Sir P. Sidney*, Wanstead Play, p. 622. (*Davies.*)

2. Lead-colored; metallic gray.—**Plumbeous falcon.** See *falcon*.

plumber (plum'ėr), *n.* [Formerly also *plummer*; ‹ ME. *plummer*, *plomere*, ‹ OF. *plombier*, F. *plombier* = Sp. *plomero* = Pg. *chumbeiro* = It. *piombajo*, OIt. *piombaro*, ‹ LL. *plumbarius*, a worker in lead, a plumber, prop. adj. (sc. *artifex*), L. *plumbarius*, pertaining to lead, ‹ *plumbum*, lead: see *plumb²*. Cf. OF. *plombeur* = OIt. *piombatore*, ‹ ML. *plumbator*, a plumber, ‹ L. *plumbare*, solder with lead, ‹ *plumbum*, lead: see *plumb²*.] One who works in lead; especially, one who fits lead pipes and other apparatus for the conveyance of gas and water, covers the roofs of buildings with sheets of lead, etc.

> Take thenne a *plummers* wire that is euyn and streyte & sharpe at the one ende.
> *Juliana Berners*, Treatyse of Fysshynge, fol. 3.

> Early in the morning will I send
> To all the *plumbers* and the pewterers,
> And buy their tin and lead up.
> *B. Jonson*, Alchemist, ii. 1.

plumber-block (plum'ėr-blok), *n.* A metal box or case for supporting the end of a revolving shaft or journal. It is adapted for being bolted to the frame or foundation of a machine, and is usually furnished with brass bearings for diminishing the friction of the shaft, and a movable cover secured by bolts for tightening the bearings as they wear. Also *plummer-block*, *plummer-box*, *pillow-block*.

Plumber-block.

a, brasses; *b*, cap; *c*, *c*, bolts; *e*, oil-hole.

plumbery (plum'ėr-i), *n.* [Also *plummery*; ‹ F. *plomberie*, f., lead-making, lead-works, ‹ L. *plumbaria*, sc. *officina*, lead-works, also (LL.) *plumbarium*, neut., a place to keep leaden vessels in; ‹ *plumbarius*, pertaining to lead: see *plumber*.] 1. Works in lead collectively; manufactures of lead.

> Whose shrill saint's-bell hangs on his lovery,
> While the rest are damned to the *plumbery*!
> *Bp. Hall*, Satires, V. i. 120.

2. A place where plumbing is carried on.—3. The business of a plumber.

plumbic (plum'bik), *a.* [‹ L. *plumbum*, lead, + *-ic*.] Of or pertaining to lead; derived from lead: as, *plumbic* acid.

plumbiferous (plum-bif'e-rus), *a.* [‹ L. *plumbum*, lead, + *ferre* = E. *bear¹*.] Producing lead.

plumbing (plum'ing), *n.* [Verbal n. of *plumb*², *v.*] 1. The art of casting and working in lead (also, by extension, in other metals put to similar uses), and applying it to various purposes connected with buildings, as in roofs, windows, pipes, etc.—2. The act or process of ascertaining the depth of anything.—3. Lead pipes and other apparatus used for conveying water or other liquids through a building.

plum-bird (plum'bėrd), *n.* The bullfinch, *Pyrrhula vulgaris.* Also called *plum-budder.* [Local, Eng.]

plumbism (plum'bizm), *n.* [< L. *plumbum*, lead (see *plumb*²), + *-ism.*] Lead-poisoning.

plumb-joint (plum'joint), *n.* A lap-joint in sheet-metal the edges of which are not bent or seamed, but merely laid over one another and soldered; a soldered lap-joint.

plumbless (plum'les), *a.* [< *plumb*² + *-less.*] Incapable of being measured or sounded with a plummet or lead-line; unfathomable.

The moment shot away into the *plumbless* depths of the past, to mingle with all the lost opportunities that are drowned there. *Dickens*, Hard Times, xv.

plumb-level (plum'lev'el), *n.* A plumb or plummet considered with reference to its use in testing the level of a plane. Also called *pendulum-level.*

plumb-line (plum'lin), *n.* A cord or line to one end of which is attached a metal bob or weight, used to determine vertical direction, depth of water, etc.; a plummet.

plumb-line (plum'lin), *v. t.* [< *plumb-line, n.*] To measure, sound, or test by means of a plumb-line. *G. H. Lewes*, Probs. of Life and Mind, II. ii. § 77.

plumbocalcite (plum-bọ-kal'sit), *n.* [< L. *plumbum*, lead, + E. *calcite.*] A variety of calcite containing a small percentage of lead carbonate.

plumbogummite (plum-bọ-gum'it), *n.* [< L. *plumbum*, lead, + *gummi*, gum, + *-ite*².] A hydrous phosphate of lead and alumina occurring in globular or reniform crusts of a yellow to brown color, looking like gum (whence the name).

plumbostib (plum'bọ-stib), *n.* [< L. *plumbum*, lead, + *stibium*, antimony.] A variety of boulangerite from Siberia.

plum-broth (plum'brôth), *n.* Broth containing plums or raisins.

Good bits hee holds breedes good positions, and the pope hee best concludes against in *plum-broth.* *Sir T. Overbury*, Characters, A Puritane.

plumb-rule (plum'röl), *n.* [< ME. *plom-rewle*; < *plumb*² + *rule.*] A narrow board with parallel edges having a straight line drawn through the middle, and a string carrying a metal weight attached at the upper end of the line. It is used by masons, bricklayers, carpenters, etc., for determining a vertical.

Set thy pyn by a *plom-rewle* evene upryht. *Chaucer*, Astrolabe, ii. 38.

Bevel plumb-rule, a surveyors' instrument for adjusting the slope of embankments. *E. H. Knight.*

Masons' Plumb-rule. *a*, center of suspension; *b*, plumb-line; *c*, straight edge; *d*, plumb-bob.

plum-budder (plum'bud-ėr), *n.* Same as *plum-bird.*

plumbum (plum'bum), *n.* [L.: see *plumb*².] Lead.

plum-cake (plum'kāk'), *n.* A cake containing raisins, currants, and often other fruit.

plum-color (plum'kul'or), *n.* One of various shades of purple and violet used in textile fabrics and as a ground color in Oriental porcelain, in the latter use sometimes flat, sometimes mottled, and sometimes in streaks, as if allowed to run freely down the side of the vase or vessel.

plum-colored (plum'kul'ọrd), *a.* Of the color of a plum; dark-purple.

plum-curculio (plum'kėr-kū'li-ō), *n.* A weevil, *Conotrachelus nenuphar*, which damages the plum, peach, and cherry. It is one of the most noxious of the *Curculionidæ*, and is commonly called the *little Turk*, from the characteristic crescent-shaped mark made by the female in the fruit in oviposition. See cut under *Conotrachelus.*

plum-duff (plum'duf'), *n.* A stiff kind of flour-pudding containing raisins and boiled in a bag: a favorite sea-dish.

plume (plöm), *n.* [< ME. *plume*, *plome*, < OF. *plume*, F. *plume* = Sp. Pg. *pluma* = It. *piuma*, a feather, plume, = MD. *pluym*, D. *pluim*, plume, feather, = MLG. *plume* = G. *pflaum*, *flaum*, down; < L. *plūma*, a small soft feather, in pl. *plūmæ*, soft feathers, down; hence the down of the first beard, the scales on a coat of mail; cf. W. *pluf* = Bret. *plu*, plumage; < √ *plu*, float, Skt. √ *plu*, swim, float, fly: see *fleet*¹, *float*, *fly*¹. Cf. *feather*, ult. from another root meaning 'fly.'] 1. A feather. (*a*) Technically, a pluma or penna: distinguished from *plumule.* See cut under *Oreortyx.* (*b*) A long, large, ornamental, specially modified, or in any way conspicuous feather: as, an ostrich-*plume*; the *plumes* of paradise-birds. 2. A tuft of feathers; a set or bunch of plumes worn as an ornament; an egret; plumery.

Plume as worn at tourneys and ceremonials, 16th century. (From a print of the time.)

His high *plume* that nodded o'er his head. *Dryden*, Iliad, vi. 148.

3. Plumage. [Rare.]

The bird of Jove, stoop'd from his aëry tour,
Two birds of gayest *plume* before him drove.
Milton, P. L., xi. 186.

4†. A token of honor; a prize won by contest.

But well thou comest
Before thy fellows, ambitious to win
From me some *plume.* *Milton*, P. L., vi. 161.

5. In *bot.*, same as *plumule*, 3.—6. In *entom.*: (*a*) A hair with many fine branches, resembling a little soft feather; a plumate hair. (*b*) A plume-moth.—7. A plumose part or formation, as of the gill of a crustacean or a mollusk.

At the upper end this stem on the gills divided into two parts, that in front, the *plume*, resembling the free end of one of the gills. *Huxley*, Crayfish, p. 78.

Apical plume. See *podobranchia.*

plume (plöm), *v. t.*; pret. and pp. *plumed*, ppr. *pluming.* [< *plume, n.*] 1. To dress the plumage of, as a bird; preen.

Swans must be kept in some incloséd pond, where they may have room to come on shore and *plume* themselves. *Mortimer*, Husbandry.

2. To strip off the plumage of, as a bird; pluck.

Madam, you take your hen,
Plume it, and skin it, cleanse it o' the inwards.
B. Jonson, Devil is an Ass, iv. 1.

And, after they have *plum'd* ye, return home,
Like a couple of naked fowls, without a feather.
Fletcher (and another), Elder Brother, v. 2.

3. To adorn with feathers or plumes; feather; set as a plume; hence, to decorate or adorn (the person) in any way.

The mother of the Sirens was not thus *plumed* on the head. *Bacon*, Moral Fables, vi., Expl.

His stature reach'd the sky, and on his crest
Sat horrour *plumed.* *Milton*, P. L., iv. 989.

This gentlewoman being a very rich merchantman's daughter, upon a time was invited to a bridal or wedding which was solemnized in that towne; against that day she made great preparation for the *pluming* of herself in gorgeous array. *J. Cooke*, Green's Tu Quoque, note 3.

The lists were ready. Empanoplied and *plumed*
We enter'd in, and waited. *Tennyson*, Princess, v.

4. To pride; boast: used reflexively: as, to *plume one's self* on one's skill.

Can anything in nature induce a man to pride and *plume himself* in his deformities? *South.*

What business have I, forsooth, to *plume myself* because the Duke of Wellington beat the French in Spain? *Thackeray*, Men and Pictures.

Plumed adder, a kind of horned viper of the genus *Cerastes*, as *C. cornutus*, having a plume-like formation of the scales over each eye.—**Plumed bird.** Same as *plume-bird.*—**Plumed pink.** See *pink*², I.

plume-alum (plöm'al'um), *n.* A kind of alum occurring in feathery, plumose forms.

plume-bird (plöm'bėrd), *n.* A member of the subfamily *Epimachinæ*, and especially of the genus *Epimachus.*

plume-holder (plöm'hōl'dėr), *n.* Anything made to secure a plume, as to the head or dress; especially, an extra piece screwed on a helmet and having a slender pipe or tube, used for this purpose.

plumeless (plöm'les), *a.* [< *plume* + *-less.*] Featherless, as an animal; having no plumage.

Borne on unknown, transparent, *plumeless* wings [a bat]. *Eusden*, tr. of Ovid's Metamorph., iv.

plumelet (plöm'let), *n.* [< *plume* + *-let.*] 1. In *ornith.*, a plumule or plumula; a down-feather. —2. Anything resembling a small plume, as a tuft of leaves or leaflets, or needles of a coniferous tree.

When rosy *plumelets* tuft the larch.
Tennyson, In Memoriam, xci.

3†. In *bot.*, a little plumule.

plume-maker (plöm'mā'kėr), *n.* A feather-dresser; a maker of plumes. See *plumist.*

plume-moth (plöm'môth), *n.* One of the small delicate moths which compose the family *Pterophoridæ* (or *Alucitidæ*): so called from the division of the wings into plume-like parts or feathery lobes. Their larvæ usually feed upon the leaves of plants, and transform to naked pupæ. The grape-vine plume-moth is *Pterophorus periscelidactylus*, whose larva loosely webs with silk the leaves on which it feeds. This caterpillar is yellowish-green with dull-yellow tubercles, and is usually found singly, though sometimes several feed together. The pupa is reddish-brown with darker spots, and the moth itself is yellowish-brown with a metallic luster, marked with several dull-white streaks and spots. See *Pterophoridæ.*

Grape-vine Plume-moth (*Pterophorus periscelidactylus*).
a, caterpillars in their retreat; *b*, chrysalis; *c*, one of the dorsal processes of chrysalis, enlarged; *d*, moth; *e*, one joint of larva, enlarged, side view.

plume-nutmeg (plöm'nut'meg), *n.* A large tree of Australia and Tasmania, *Atherosperma moschata* of the *Monimiaceæ.* It is aromatic in all its parts, and the fruit-carpels bear each a persistent plumose style.

plume-plucked (plöm'plukt), *a.* Stripped of a plume or plumes; hence, figuratively, humbled; brought down. [Rare.]

Great Duke of Lancaster, I come to thee
From *plume-pluck'd* Richard.
Shak., Rich. II., iv. 1. 108.

Plumeria (plọ̈-mē'ri-ạ̈), *n.* [NL. (Tournefort, 1700), named after Charles *Plumier* (1646–1706), author of many works on American plants.] A genus of trees of the gamopetalous order *Apocynaceæ*, type of the tribe *Plumerieæ*, and of the subtribe *Euplumerieæ.* It is characterized by the numerous ovules in many rows in two carpels which ripen into two rigid diverging follicles, a calyx glandular within, stamens near the base of the tube of a salver-shaped corolla, winged seeds, and unappendaged anthers. There are about 45 species, natives of tropical America, some of them naturalized in the Old World. They are trees with thick branches, alternate long-stalked and prominently feather-veined leaves, and large white, yellow, or purplish flowers in terminal cymes. See *jasmine-tree*, *kambodja*, *nosegay-tree*, and *pagoda-tree.*

Plumerieæ (plö-mẹ-ri'ẹ̄-ē), *n. pl.* [NL. (Endlicher, 1836), < *Plumeria* + *-eæ.*] A tribe of plants of the order *Apocynaceæ*, the dogbane family, characterized by the distinct carpels of the ovary, peltate seeds, and unappendaged base of the anther-cells, which are filled with pollen throughout. It includes 41 genera, mainly tropical trees or shrubs—two, *Vallesia* and *Amsonia*, occurring in the United States, and another, the herbaceous genus *Vinca*, extending into Europe, and widely naturalized in the Atlantic States. The four subtribes are typified by the genera *Rauwolfia*, *Cerbera*, *Plumeria*, and *Tabernæmontana.*

plumery (plö'mẹ-ri), *n.* [< *plume* + *-ery.*] Plumes collectively; a number of plumes taken together; a display of plumes.

Helms or shields
Glittering with gold and scarlet *plumery.* *Southey.*

plumetty, plumetté (plö'met-i, plö-me-tā'), *a.* [Heraldic F. *plumetté*, < OF. *plumette*, a little feather, dim. of *plume*, feather: see *plume.*] In *her.*, covered with feathers, or feather-like decorations: said especially of the field when divided into fusils each of which is filled with a feather. The decorations are then of different tinctures, usually a metal and a color alternately.

plum-fir (plum'fėr), *n.* See *Podocarpus.*

plum-gouger (plum'gou'jėr), *n.* A kind of cur-

Plum-gouger (*Coccotorus prunicida*). (Line shows natural size.)

culio or weevil, *Coccotorus prunicida.* It is common in the Mississippi valley, where it damages plums, nectarines, and allied fruits. Both sexes in the adult state gouge the fruit when feeding, and the larva feeds upon the contents of the pit or stone. It is single-brooded, and passes the winter in the beetle state.

plumicome (plö'mi-kōm), *n.* [< L. *pluma*, a feather, + *coma* (< Gr. *κόμη*), the hair of the head: see *coma*[2].] In sponges, a hexaster whose rays end in a number of plumose branches. Compare *floricome.*

plumicomous (plọ̈-mik'ọ̈-mus), *a.* [< *plumicome* + *-ous.*] Having the character of a plumicome.

plumicorn (plö'mi-kôrn), *n.* [< L. *pluma*, a feather, + *cornu*, a horn.] One of the pair of tufts of feathers, or egrets, also called *ears* and *horns*, on the head in sundry owls, as species of *Bubo, Scops, Otus*, or *Asio*; a feather-horn. Also (rarely) called *corniplume.* See cuts under *Buboninæ* and *Otus.*

plumigerous (plọ̈-mij'ẹ-rus), *a.* [< L. *plumiger*, feather-bearing, < *pluma*, feather, + *gerere*, bear.] Plumaged; feathered; having plumes. *Bailey.*

plumiped, plumipede (plö'mi-ped, -pēd), *a.* and *n.* [< L. *plumipes* (*-ped-*), feather-footed, < *pluma*, feather, + *pes* (*ped-*) = E. *foot.*] **I.** *a.* Having feathered feet.

II. *n.* A plumiped bird.

plumist (plö'mist), *n.* [< F. *plumiste*, a worker in feathers, < *plume*, feather: see *plume.*] A feather-dresser; a maker of ornamental plumes.

> Fine and feathery artisan,
> Best of *plumists* (if you can
> With your art so far presume),
> Make for me a prince's plume.
> *Moore*, Anacreontic to a Plumassier.

plum-juniper (plum'jö″ni-pėr), *n.* A handsome Oriental juniper, *Juniperus drupacea*, whose fleshy drupe-like cones are highly esteemed as a fruit.

plum-loaf (plum'lōf), *n.* A loaf with raisins or currants in it.

plummer† (plum'ėr), *n.* An obsolete form of *plumber.*

plummer-block (plum'ėr-blok), *n.* Same as *plumber-block.*

plummer-box (plum'ėr-boks), *n.* Same as *plumber-block.*

plummery, *n.* Same as *plumbery.*

plummet (plum'et), *n.* [< ME. *plomet*, < OF. *plomet, plommet, plombet, plummet*, a piece of lead, a ball of lead, a plummet, dim. of *plom*, lead, a lead, plummet: see *plumb*[2].] **1.** A piece of lead or other metal attached to a line, used in sounding the depth of water, determining the vertical, etc.

> I'll seek him deeper than e'er *plummet* sounded.
> *Shak.*, Tempest, iii. 3. 101.

> My conscience is the *plummet* that does press
> The deeps, but seldom cries O fathomless.
> *Quarles*, Emblems, iii. 11.

They would plunge, and tumble, and thinke to ly hid in the foul weeds, and muddy waters, where no *plummet* can reach the bottome. *Milton*, Reformation in Eng., i.

It is an oblong square well, which I found by a *plummet* to be a hundred and twenty two feet deep.
Pococke, Description of the East, II. i. 25.

2. An instrument used by carpenters, masons, and others in adjusting erections to a vertical line; a plumb-rule.—**3**†. The pommel or knob on the hilt of a sword.

> Dickie coud na win to him wi' the blade o' the sword,
> But feld 'im wi' the *plumet* under the eie.
> *Dick o' the Cow* (Child's Ballads, VI. 75).

4†. A weight.

> For when sad thoughts perplex the mind of man,
> There is a *plummet* in the heart that weighs,
> And pulls us, living, to the dust we came from.
> *Beau. and Fl.*, Laws of Candy, iv. 1.

> What hath hung *plummets* on thy nimble soul?
> What sleepy rod hath charm'd thy mounting spirit?
> *Shirley*, Love in a Maze, iv. 2.

5†. A piece of lead formerly used by schoolboys to rule paper for writing.

plummet (plum'et), *v. t.*; pret. and pp. *plummeted* or *plummetted*, ppr. *plummeting* or *plummetting.* [< *plummet, n.*] To weight with plummets, or as with plummets.

A rich *plummetted* worsted fringe valance may be preferred to drapery. *Paper-hanger*, p. 91.

plummet-level (plum'et-lev″el), *n.* A plummet used as a level. Any plummet may be used as a level provided its base is approximately perpendicular to the mean position of the plumb-line. If this hangs the same way when the whole is rotated 180°, the support is level. Also called *masons' level.*

plum-moth (plum'môth), *n.* A tortricid moth whose larva infests plums. See *Grapholitha.*

plummy (plum'i), *a.* [< *plum*[1] + *-y*[1].] Full of plums or excellences; hence, good; desirable. [Colloq.]

The poets have made tragedies enough about signing one's self over to wickedness for the sake of getting something *plummy.* *George Eliot*, Daniel Deronda, xvi.

plumose (plö'mōs), *a.* [= F. *plumeux* = Sp. Pg. *plumoso* = It. *piumoso*, < L. *plumosus*, full of feathers or down, < *pluma*, feather, down: see *plume.*] **1.** Feathery; plumous; resembling a feather, as something light, airy, and spray-like.—**2.** Feathered; plumed or plumaged; provided with plumes or feathers.—**3.** In *bot.*, feathery or feathered: specifically noting bristles, etc., which have fine hairs on opposite sides like the vane of a feather. A *plumose pappus* is one composed of feathery hairs. See fig. *b* under *pappus.*—**Plumose anemone.** See *anemone.*

plumosity (plọ̈-mos'ị-ti), *n.* [= It. *piumosità*; as *plumose* + *-ity.*] The state of being plumose.

plumous (plö'mus), *a.* Same as *plumose.*

plump[1] (plump), *a.* [< ME. *plomp*, rude, clownish (not found in lit. sense), = D. *plomp* = MLG. LG. *plump, plomp*, bulky, unwieldy, dull, clownish, = G. *plump* = Sw. Dan. *plump*, bulky, massive, clumsy, coarse (the G., and prob. Scand., from the D.); prob. orig. 'swollen,' from the pp. of the dial. (orig. strong) verb *plim*, swell; but more or less associated with *plump*[2], *plumb*[2].] **1.** Full and well-rounded; hence, of a person, fleshy; fat; chubby: as, a *plump* figure; a *plump* habit of body; of things, filled out and distended; rounded: as, a *plump* seed.

> Banish *plump* Jack, and banish all the world.
> *Shak.*, 1 Hen. IV., ii. 4. 527.

> The ploughman now . . .
> Sows his *plump* seed.
> *Fanshawe*, tr. of Guarini's Pastor Fido, iv. 6.

> Like a childe, she 's pleasant, quick, and *plump.*
> *Sylvester*, tr. of Du Bartas's Weeks, ii., The Magnificence.

Of medium height, *plump*, but not stout, with a rather slender waist and expansive hips, and a foot which stepped firmly and nimbly at the same time, she was as cheerful a body as one could wish to see.
B. *Taylor*, Northern Travel, p. 72.

2. Figuratively, round; fat; large; full.

> Will no *plump* fee
> Bribe thy false fists to make a glad decree?
> *Quarles*, Emblems, ii. 3.

3. Dry; hard. *Halliwell.* [Prov. Eng.]

plump[1]† (plump), *n.* [< ME. *plump, plomp*, a cluster, clump; < *plump*[1], *a.* Cf. *clump*[1].] A knot; a cluster; a group; a clump; a number of persons, animals, or things closely united or standing together; a covey.

Whan thei wil fighte, thei wille schokken hem to gidre in a *plomp.* *Mandeville*, Travels, p. 252.

By means wherof such as were chief officers in his campe reuolted by *plumpes* vnto Seleucus.
Golding, tr. of Justine, fol. 83.

> Here 's a whole *plump* of rogues.
> *Fletcher*, Double Marriage, iii. 2.

> So spread upon a lake, with upward eye,
> A *plump* of fowl behold their foe on high.
> *Dryden*, Theodore and Honoria, l. 316.

plump[1] (plump), *v.* [< *plump*[1], *a.*] **I.** *intrans.* To grow plump; enlarge to fullness; swell. *Johnson; Imp. Dict.*

II. *trans.* To make plump, full, or distended; extend to fullness; dilate; fatten.

The golden films, whilst they were in a liquor that *plumped* them up, seemed to be solid wires of gold.
Boyle, Subtilty of Effluviums, ii.

I can with another experiment *plump* him and heighten him at my pleasure. *Shirley*, Maid's Revenge, iii. 2.

The action of the saltpetre on the hides or skins, it is claimed, is to *plump* or "raise" them, as it is called.
C. T. Davis, Leather, p. 249.

plump[2] (plump), *v.* [< ME. *plumpen* = D. *plompen* = G. *plumpen, plumpsen*, fall like a stone in the water, = Sw. *plumpa* = Dan. *plumpe*, plump, plunge; connected with *plump*[2], *adv.*: words felt to be imitative, and so subject to variation (G. *plumpsen*, etc.), but prob. ult. due to L. *plumbum*, lead, whence also ult. E. *plunge*, plump: see *plumb*[2], *plunge.*] **I.** *intrans.* **1.** To plunge or fall like a heavy mass or lump of dead matter; fall suddenly.

It will give you a notion how Dulcissa *plumps* into a chair. *Steele*, Spectator, No. 402.

> He *plump'd* head and heels into fifteen feet water!
> *Barham*, Ingoldsby Legends, II. 335.

2. To vote for a single candidate, when one has the right to vote for two or more. In British parliamentary and other elections, when there are more persons than one to be elected, a voter, while having the right to vote for as many candidates as there are vacancies, may cast a single vote for one only. He is then said to *plump* for that candidate. In British school-board elections the voting is cumulative; a voter may *plump*, by giving as many votes as there are vacancies to any one candidate, or he may distribute that number among the candidates in any way he chooses.

They refused to exercise their right of electing local members, and *plumped* for Earl Grey himself in 1848.
Westminster Rev., CXXV. 62.

II. *trans.* To cause to fall suddenly and heavily: as, to *plump* a stone into water.—**To plump** (a thing) **out**, to come out plump or rudely with (something).

"But if it ain't a liberty to *plump* it *out*," said Mr. Boffin, "what do you do for your living?"
Dickens, Our Mutual Friend, viii.

plump[2] (plump), *adv.* [An elliptical use of *plump*[2], *v.* Cf. *plumb*[2], *adv.*] At once, as with a sudden heavy fall; suddenly; heavily; without warning or preparation; very unexpectedly; downright; right.

> The art of swimming he that will attain to't,
> Must fall *plump* and duck himself at first.
> *Beau. and Fl.*, Wit at Several Weapons, i. 1.

Just as we were a-going up Snow-hill, *plump* we comes against a cart, with such a jog it almost pulled the coach-wheel off. *Miss Burney*, Evelina, lv.

How refreshing to find such a place and such a person *plump* in the middle of New York.
T. Winthrop, Cecil Dreeme, vi.

plump[2] (plump), *a.* [< *plump*[2], *v.* Cf. *plumb*[2], *a.*] Blunt; downright; unreserved; unqualified: as, a *plump* lie. *Wright.*

plump[2] (plump), *n.* [< *plump*[2], *v.*] A sudden heavy downfall of rain. [Scotch.]

The thunder-*plump* that drookit me to the skin. *Galt.*

The whole day was showery, with occasional drenching *plumps.* *R. L. Stevenson*, Inland Voyage, p. 89.

plumper (plum'pėr), *n.* **1.** One of a pair of balls or rounded masses of some light material kept in the mouth to give the cheeks a rounded appearance.

> And that the cheeks may both agree,
> Their *plumpers* fill the cavity.
> *The London Ladies Dressing Room.* (*Nares.*)

> Now dext'rously her *plumpers* draws,
> That serve to fill her hollow jaws.
> *Swift*, A Beautiful Young Nymph.

2. One who votes for a single candidate in an election, when he has a right to vote for more than one; also, the vote (sometimes the total number of votes collectively) which one thus gives to a single candidate. See *plump*[2], *v. i.*, 2. [Great Britain.]

Mr. Brooke's success must depend either on *plumpers*, which would leave Bagster in the rear, or on the new minting of Tory votes into reforming votes.
George Eliot, Middlemarch, li.

3. An unqualified lie; a downright falsehood; a "corker." [Colloq.]

plump-faced (plump'fāst), *a.* Having a plump or full, round face.

plum-pig (plum'pig'), *n.* A dish consisting of figures of pigs molded in pie-crust or cake, with raisins or currants for eyes.

plumply (plump'li), *adv.* Fully; roundly; without reserve: as, to assert a thing *plumply.* [Colloq.]

plumpness (plump'nes), *n.* The state or quality of being plump; fullness of skin; distention to roundness: as, the *plumpness* of a boy; *plumpness* of the cheek.

plum-porridge (plum'por'ij), *n.* Porridge made with plums, raisins, or currants.

All those new statutes [promulgated by the Senate of Venice on Aug. 25th, 1626] principally reguard the English, whom they thincke so inamored with *plumporredge*, cakes, and pies, as they will with currents swallow any thing.
Sir Thomas Roe, quoted in N. and Q., 7th ser., IV. 504.

Nearly two centuries had elapsed since the fiery persecution of poor mince-pies throughout the land; when *plum porridge* was denounced as mere popery, and roast-beef as anti-Christian.
Irving, Sketch-Book, Christmas Day, p. 266.

plum-pudding (plum'pụd'ing), *n.* A pudding composed of flour and finely chopped beef suet, with raisins, currants, various spices, and wine, brandy, or rum. It is tied in a pudding-cloth and boiled for some hours. It should be served with a blazing sauce of brandy or rum. In the United States a plainer pudding, resembling the above but without the brandy, is sometimes called by this name.

plum-puddinger (plum'pụd'ing-ėr), *n.* A small whaling-vessel which makes only short voyages: so called because the crew has fresh provisions and an abundant supply of plum-pudding or plum-duff. [U. S.]

Provincetown has ever been foremost with her numerous fleet of *plum-puddingers*, or, in whaling phrase, "plum-pudnrs," which are small vessels employed on short voyages in the Atlantic Ocean.
C. M. Scammon, Marine Mammals, p. 241.

plumpy (plum'pi), *a.* [< *plump*[1] + *-y*[1].] Plump; fat.

> Come, thou monarch of the vine,
> *Plumpy* Bacchus with pink eyne!
> *Shak.*, A. and C., ii. 7. 121.

Plumstead Peculiars. Same as *Peculiar People* (which see, under *peculiar*).

plum-tree (plum'trē), *n.* [< ME. *plumtre*, < AS. *plūmtreów* (= Sw. *plommonträd* = Dan. *blommetræ*), < *plūme*, plum, + *treów*, tree.] A tree that produces plums. See *plum*[1].

plumula (plö'mū-lä), *n.*; pl. *plumulæ* (-lē). [NL., < L. *plumula*, a little feather: see *plumule*.] Same as *plumule*.

plumulaceous (plö-mū-lā'shius), *a.* [< NL. *plumulaceus*, < L. *plumula*, a plumule: see *plumule*.] Downy; of or pertaining to a plumule; in *ornith.*, not pennaceous. See *plumule*.

plumular (plö'mū-lär), *a.* [< *plumula* + *-ar*[3].] In *ornith.*, of or pertaining to a plumula or plumule; plumulaceous.

Plumularia (plö-mū-lā'ri-ä), *n.* [NL. (Lamarck), < L. *plumula*, a little feather: see *plumule*.] The typical genus of *Plumulariidæ*. *P. filicula* is an example.

Plumularia filicula, natural size.

plumularian (plö-mū-lā'ri-an), *a.* and *n.* [< *Plumularia* + *-an*.] **I.** *a.* Pertaining to the genus *Plumularia* or the family *Plumulariidæ*, or having their characters: correlated with *sertularian* and *campanularian*.

II. *n.* A member of the *Plumulariidæ*.

Plumulariidæ (plö"mū-lā-rī'i-dē), *n. pl.* [NL., < *Plumularia* + *-idæ*.] A family of hydroid polyps or calyptoblastic *Hydromedusæ*, typified by the genus *Plumularia*, having sessile polypites in hydrothecæ on only one side of the branched polyp-stock. They are colonial, and include gastrozoöids, generative zoöids, and machopolyps, the first-named with one verticel of filiform tentacles.

plumulate (plö'mū-lāt), *a.* [< *plumula* + *-ate*[1].] In *bot.*, minutely plumose.

plumule (plö'mūl), *n.* [< L. *plumula*, a little feather, dim. of *pluma*, a feather: see *plume*.] **1.** In *ornith.*, a down-feather; a feather of plumulaceous structure throughout.—**2.** In *entom.*: (*a*) A little plume-like organ or ornament. (*b*) One of the peculiar obcordate scales found on the wings of certain lepidopterous insects, as *Pieridæ*.—**3.** The bud of the ascending axis of a plant while still in the embryo, situated at the apex of the caulicle (or radicle), above the base of the cotyledon or cotyledons, and inclosed by them when there are two or more. In such seeds as the bean and beechnut it consists of a rudimentary pair of leaves of a feather-like appearance, while in the pea and acorn it is a rudimentary stem which will develop leaves only when germination is considerably advanced. In these examples the plumule is manifest, but often it is scarcely visible to the naked eye until the seed begins to germinate. See also cuts under *exogen* and *monocotyledonous*.

1, the seed of *Vicia Faba*, one cotyledon detached; 2, germinating plantlet of *Cyperus vegetus*; 3, germinating plantlet of *Ipomœa paniculata*; 4, germinating plantlet of *Rheum Moorcroftianum*, showing the plumule breaking through the tubular base of the petioles of the cotyledons. *Cot*, cotyledon; *P*, plumule; *R*, root.

plumuliform (plö'mū-li-fôrm), *a.* [< L. *plumula*, a plumule, + *forma*, form.] Having the appearance of a small feather. *Thomas*, Med. Dict.

plumulose (plö'mū-lōs), *a.* [< *plumule* + *-ose*.] In *entom.*, branching laterally, as the hairs of an insect, and thus resembling downy feathers or plumules.

plum-weevil (plum'wē'vl), *n.* A weevil which infests the plum; the plum-curculio. See cuts under *Conotrachelus* and *plum-gouger*.

plumy (plö'mi), *a.* [< *plume* + *-y*[1].] **1.** Resembling a feather; feathery.

> As thicke as when a drift wind shakes
> Black clouds in pieces, and plucks now in great and *plumie* flakes
> From their soft bosomes, till the ground be wholly cloth'd in white.
> *Chapman*, Iliad, xii.

2. Plumed; adorned with plumes.

> Appeared his *plumy* crest, besmeared with blood.
> *Addison.*

> And Murray's *plumy* helmet rings—
> Rings on the ground, to rise no more.
> *Scott*, Cadyow Castle.

3. Plumaged; feathered.

> Angels on full sail of wings flew nigh,
> Who on their *plumy* vans received him soft.
> *Milton*, P. R., iv. 583.

> A well
> Shrouded with willow-flowers and *plumy* fern.
> *Wordsworth*, Excursion, i.

plunder (plun'dėr), *n.* [< MD. *plunder*, *plonder*, household effects, furniture, < G. *plunder*, household effects, furniture, baggage, lumber, trumpery, rags, late MHG. *plunder*, *blunder*, household effects, clothing, washing (also bedclothing?); cf. MLG. *plunder*, *plunde* (in comp.), clothing, *plunder*, *plonder*, spoil, booty, LG. *plunne*, *plunn*, in pl. *plunnen*, *plunden*, household trumpery, rags, = D. *plunje*, sailor's luggage, etc.; ulterior origin obscure. In defs. 2 and 3 from the verb: see *plunder*, *v.*] **1.** Household or personal effects; baggage; luggage. [Local, U. S.]

> An American, by his boasting of the superiority of the Americans generally, but more especially in their language, once provoked me to tell him that "on that head the least said the better, as the Americans presented the extraordinary anomaly of a people without a language. That they had mistaken the English language for baggage (which is called *plunder* in America), and had stolen it."
> *Coleridge*, Letters, Conversations and Recollections, p. 214.

> "Help yourself, stranger," added the landlord, "while I tote your *plunder* into the other room."
> *Hoffman*, Winter in the West, letter xxxiii. (*Bartlett.*)

2. The act of plundering; robbery.

> *Plunder*, both name and thing, was unknown in England till the beginning of the war; and the war began not till September, anno 1642.
> *Heylin*, Examen Historicum (1659), i. 248, quoted in F. [Hall's Mod. Eng., p. 113.

> For my part I abhor all violence, *plunder*, rapine, and disorders in souldiers.
> *Prynne*, Treachery and Disloyalty, iv. 29.

> The Biscains were almost quite disheartned by reason of the frequent inrodes and *plunders* of the Saracens.
> *North*, tr. of Plutarch (ed. 1676), ii. 35.

3. That which is taken from an enemy by force; pillage; prey; spoil; booty.

> The prospect of *plunder* reconciled all disputes. Dutch and English, admirals and generals, were equally eager for action. *Macaulay*, War of the Succession in Spain.

4. Hence, that which is taken by theft, robbery, or fraud: as, the cashier escaped with his *plunder*.=**Syn. 3.** *Booty*, *Spoil*, etc. See *pillage*.

plunder (plun'dėr), *v. t.* [< MD. and D. *plunderen*, *plonderen* = MLG. *plunderen* = Sw. *plundra* = Dan. *plyndre*, plunder, < G. *plündern*, steal household effects, pillage, plunder, prop. remove household effects, < *plunder*, household effects, trumpery, baggage: see *plunder*, *n.* The word appears to have been carried from Germany to the other countries during the Thirty Years' War, in which many foreign mercenaries were engaged, and much plundering was done. For the development of sense from 'household effects,' 'clothing,' etc., to 'pillage,' 'rob,' cf. *rob*, *reave*, as similarly developed from *robe* (AS. *reáf*), clothing.] **1.** To take goods or valuables forcibly from; pillage; spoil; strip; rob.

> He [Raleigh] hath fired and *plundered* Santo Thoma, a Colony the Spaniards had planted with so much blood.
> *Howell*, Letters, I. i. 4.

> It is not demonstrated that kings and aristocracies will *plunder* the people, unless it be true that all men will *plunder* their neighbours if they can.
> *Macaulay*, West. Reviewer's Def. of Mill.

2. To take by pillage or open force: as, the enemy *plundered* all the goods they found.

> A treasure richer far
> Than what is *plundered* in the rage of war. *Dryden.*

=**Syn. 1.** To despoil, sack, rifle, ravage. See *pillage*, *n.*

plunderage (plun'dėr-āj), *n.* [< *plunder* + *-age*.] In *maritime law*, the embezzlement of goods on board a ship.

plunderer (plun'dėr-ėr), *n.* One who plunders.

> It was a famous saying of William Rufus, . . . "Whosoever spares perjured men, robbers, *plunderers*, and traitors, deprives all good men of their peace and quietness."
> *Addison*, Freeholder, No. 31.

plunderous (plun'dėr-us), *a.* [< *plunder* + *-ous*.] Plundering; pillaging.

plunge (plunj), *v.*; pret. and pp. *plunged*, ppr. *plunging*. [< ME. *plungen*, *plonngen*, *plongen*, < OF. *plonger*, *plonchier*, F. *plonger* = Picard *plonker*, < LL. **plumbicare*, freq., plunge; cf. Pr. *plombar*, plunge, = It. *piombare*, fall heavily like lead, plunge, throw, hurl (see also *plump*[2], *v.*); < L. *plumbum*, lead: see *plumb*[2]. The L. *plumbare* means only 'solder with lead,' 'make of lead.' For the LL. freq. **plumbicare*, cf. *pluck*[1], prob. < LL. **pilicare*, **piluccare*.] **I.** *trans.* **1.** To cast or thrust suddenly into water or some other fluid, or into some penetrable substance; immerse; thrust: as, to *plunge* one's hand into the water; to *plunge* a dagger into one's breast.

> What if the breath that kindled those grim fires,
> Awaked, should blow them into sevenfold rage,
> And *plunge* us in the flames? *Milton*, P. L., ii. 172.

2. Figuratively, to cast or throw into some thing, state, condition, or action: as, *plunged* in grief; to *plunge* a nation into war.

> Agrausyn, that was *plonged* in to the presse, smote on bothe sides hym a-boute, and began yeve so grete strokes that sore thei hym douted. *Merlin* (E. E. T. S.), ii. 194.

> Without a prudent determination in matters before us, we shall be *plunged* into perpetual errors. *Watts.*

> Yet he listen'd, *plunged* in thought.
> *M. Arnold*, Sohrab and Rustum.

3†. To entangle or embarrass: used chiefly in the past participle.

> For thou well know'st I have been so *plung'd*, so torn
> With her resolv'd rejection and neglect.
> *Beau. and Fl.*, Knight of Malta, i. 1.

> *Plunged* and gravelled with three lines of Seneca.
> *Sir T. Browne*, Religio Medici, § 21.

II. *intrans.* **1.** To dive, leap, or rush (into water or some fluid).

> Bid me go find some desp'rate rock from whence
> Down I may *plunge* into the deepest Main.
> *J. Beaumont*, Psyche, ii. 158.

> Through the forest, like a wild beast, roared and *plunged* the Saco's falls. *Whittier*, Mary Garvin.

2. To fall or rush headlong into some thing, action, state, or condition: as, to *plunge* into debt or into a controversy.

> Bid me for honour *plunge* into a war
> Of thickest foes, and rush on certain death.
> *Addison*, Cato, i. 1.

3. To throw the body forward and the hind legs up, as an unruly horse.

> But th' angry Steed . . .
> Calls for the Combat, *plunges*, leaps, and praunces.
> *Sylvester*, tr. of Du Bartas's Weeks, ii., The Handy-Crafts.

4. To descend precipitously or vertically, as a cliff.

> While she sat on an ivied stone, on the edge of the *plunging* wall, I stood there and made a speech.
> *H. James, Jr.*, Pass. Pilgrim, p. 236.

5. To bet recklessly; gamble for large stakes; speculate. [Sporting slang.]

> *Plunging* was the order of the day, and lansquenet was the game at which most of this *plunging* was done.
> *Fortnightly Rev.*, N. S., XXXIX. 319.

plunge (plunj), *n.* [< *plunge*, *v.*] **1.** A sudden dive, leap, or dip into something: as, a *plunge* in the sea.—**2.** An immersion in difficulty, embarrassment, or distress; the condition of being surrounded or overwhelmed; a strait; difficulty. [Obsolete or obsolescent.]

> Do you observe the *plunges* that this poor gallant is put to, signior, to purchase the fashion?
> *B. Jonson*, Every Man out of his Humour, iv. 5.

> Then be thou in these *plunges*
> A patron to thy mother in her pains.
> *Greene and Lodge*, Looking Glass for Lond. and Eng.

3. A sudden and violent pitching forward of the body, and pitching up of the hind legs, as by an unruly horse.—**At a plunge**, at a pinch; in a strait.

> He [Collins] had a pressing and immediate objection to remove. And as he had no great stock of argument, and but small forecast, any thing *at a plunge* would be received which came to his relief.
> *Warburton*, Divine Legation, vi. § 6.

Flow-and-plunge structure, in *geol.* See *flow*[1].

plunge-bath (plunj'bath), *n.* A bath sufficiently large to admit of the complete immersion of the bather.

plunge-battery (plunj'bat"ėr-i), *n.* See *battery*.

plungeon (plun'jon), *n.* [< F. *plongeon*, a plungeon, the diver, also diving, < *plonger*, dive, plunge: see *plunge*.] A diving bird. *Ainsworth.*

plunge-pole (plunj'pōl), *n.* The hollow pump-rod of a pumping-engine. [Eng.]

plunger (plun'jėr), *n.* **1.** One who or that which plunges.—**2.** A cavalryman; in the plural, cavalry. [Milit. slang.]

It's an insult to the whole Guards, my dear fellow, after refusing two of us, to marry an attorney, and after all to bolt with a *plunger*. *Kingsley*, Two Years Ago, xvi.

3. A reckless better; a dashing or venturesome gambler or speculator. [Sporting slang.] —4. A part of a machine or piece of mechanism that plunges. (*a*) The piston of a Cornish pump. It is a cylindrical mass of iron which plays through a stuffing-box up and down in the plunger-case, and forces the water into the lift or tube, in which it rises to the surface, adit-level, or other desired point. (*b*) Any solid piston. See *plunger-piston*. (*c*) The dasher of a churn. (*d*) The firing-pin or striker used in some breech-loading firearms. (*e*) A metallic cylinder, hollow or solid, sometimes surrounding and sometimes within the coil of wire of a small inductorium, by the movement of which the intensity of the induced current may be regulated. (*f*) Any compression-machine in which the force is applied by means of a plunger. See cuts under *hydraulic*, *percussion-fuse*, and *pump*. (*g*) A cylindrical graduated rod used in blasting to ascertain whether the cartridge has reached the bottom of the drilled hole, when charging the hole for a blast.

5. In *pottery*, a vessel in which clay is beaten by a wheel to the required consistency. *E. H. Knight.*

plunger-bucket (plun'jėr-buk"et), *n.* 1. In a pump, a bucket having no valve.—2. Same as *plunger-piston*, 2.

plunger-case (plun'jėr-kās), *n.* The cylinder in which a plunger works.

plunger-lift (plun'jėr-lift), *n.* 1. In a pump, a bucket having no valve. See cut under *pump*. —2. Same as *plunger-piston*, 2.

plunger-piston (plun'jėr-pis"ton), *n.* 1. In a pump, a solid cylindrical piston, either operated by a special piston-rod with a crosshead, or protruding from the pump-barrel sufficiently for the direct attachment of a pitman to it outside of the pump-cylinder.—2. The solid piston of a pressure-gage, steam-indicator, or some similar instrument. Also called *plunger-lift* and *plunger-bucket*.

plunger-pump (plun'jėr-pump), *n.* A pump in which the liquid confined in the pump-barrel by a foot-valve or check-valve is forced by displacement, during the inward stroke of a plunger, through another check-valve into the discharge-pipe or -passage, or the air-chamber, of the pump.

plunging (plun'jing), *p. a.* Directed from above downward; poured down from a higher plane: as, to subject the enemy to a *plunging* fire. See *fire*, *n.*, 13.

plunging-siphon (plun'jing-sī"fon), *n.* A small tube with open ends which is thrust into liquor in bulk in order to withdraw a sample by closing the upper end with the finger.

plungy (plun'ji), *a.* [< ME. *plowngy*; < *plunge* + *-y*[1].] Rainy. [Prov. Eng.]

The wynd Nothus leteth his *plowngy* blastes. *Chaucer*, Boëthius, iii. meter 1.

plunket† (plung'ket), *n.* Same as *blunket*.

Out came six ladies all in crimosin satin and *plunket*, embroudered with golde and perle, with Frenche hoodes on their beddes. *Hall*, quoted in Strutt's Sports and Pastimes, p. 240.

plup. An abbreviation of *pluperfect*.

pluperfect (plö'pėr"fekt), *a.* and *n.* [Abbr. of L. (NL.) *plusquam-perfectum* (sc. *tempus*), the pluperfect tense, lit. 'more than perfect': L. *plus*, more (see *plus*); *quam*, than; *perfectum*, neut. of *perfectus*, perfect: see *perfect*.] **I.** *a.* Noting the time, or the expression of time, of an action occurring prior to another specified time: as, the *pluperfect* tense.

II. *n.* In *gram.*, the pluperfect tense of a verb, or an equivalent verb-phrase: for example, Latin *amaveram*, English 'I had loved.'

plural (plö'ral), *a.* and *n.* [< ME. *plurelle*, < OF. *plurel*, F. *pluriel* = Sp. Pg. *plural* = It. *plurale* = G. *plural*, < L. *pluralis*, of or belonging to more than one, or to many; in gram. *pluralis*, sc. *numerus*, the plural number; < *plus* (*plur-*), more: see *plus*.] **I.** *a.* 1. Containing more than one; consisting of two or more, or designating two or more.

Better have none
Than *plural* faith, which is too much by one.
Shak., T. G. of V., v. 4. 52.

Specifically—2. In *gram.*, noting the form of a word (primarily of a noun or pronoun, then of an adjective qualifying it, and finally of a verb of which it is subject) which marks it as signifying or relating to more than one, as distinguished from *singular*, signifying only one; in some languages, which have a dual form for two, signifying more than two: thus, *boys* is the plural number of *boy*, *men* of *man*, *we* of *I*, *these* of *this*, *are* of *is*, and *were* of *was*.—**Plural marriage.** See *marriage*.

II. *n.* 1. The state of being manifold or more than one.

If respect be had to the severall arts there professed, Sigebert founded schools in the *plurall*. But if regard be taken of the cyclopædy of the learning resulting from those several sciences, he erected but one grand school. *Fuller*, Ch. Hist., II. ii. 56.

2. That form of a word which expresses plurality, or the plural number. Abbreviated *pl.*

pluralisation, pluralise, etc. See *pluralization*, etc.

pluralism (plö'ral-izm), *n.* [< *plural* + *-ism.*] 1. The character of being plural.—2. The holding by one person of two or more offices at the same time; specifically, the holding of two or more livings or benefices at the same time, or the ecclesiastical system under which this is possible.

pluralist (plö'ral-ist), *n.* [< *plural* + *-ist.*] A clergyman who holds at the same time two or more ecclesiastical benefices.

Who, being a *pluralist*, may under one Surplice, which is also linnen, hide foure benefices besides the metropolitan toe. *Milton*, Apology for Smectymnuus.

Many ecclesiastics, some even of those who affected to be evangelical, were *pluralists*, and left their numerous parishes to the care of those who would serve at the lowest price. *Bancroft*, Hist. U. S., I. 215.

pluralistic (plö-ra-lis'tik), *a.* [< *pluralist* + *-ic.*] Holding to the existence of many reals.

plurality (plö-ral'i-ti), *n.*; pl. *pluralities* (-tiz). [< ME. *pluralite*, < OF. *pluralite*, F. *pluralité* = Sp. *pluralidad* = Pg. *pluralidade* = It. *pluralità*, < LL. *pluralita(t-)s*, the plural number, < L. *pluralis*, plural: see *plural*.] 1. The character of being plural; the fact of expressing or of consisting of more than one; also, a number greater than unity: as, a *plurality* of gods; a *plurality* of worlds.

And bigge ȝow benefices *pluralite* to haue. *Piers Plowman* (C), iv. 33.

The wantonnesse
Of their insatiat appetite, that feeds
On such *plurality* of viands, breeds
Offensive humors.
Times' Whistle (E. E. T. S.), p. 57.

We are now led to recognise the doctrine of the "*plurality* of causes" in our explanations of things; and the instances of this *plurality* are both numerous and familiar. *A. Bain*, Emotions and Will, p. 213.

2. The greater number; the majority.

Take the *plurality* of the world, and they are neither wise nor good. *Sir R. L'Estrange.*

The two avoyers are elected by the *plurality* of suffrages of all the citizens. *J. Adams*, Works, IV. 332.

3. In *U. S. politics*, the number by which the votes cast for the candidate who receives the greatest number exceed the votes cast for the candidate who receives the next greatest number, when there are more than two candidates and no one candidate receives a majority of the votes. If A receives 5,000 votes, B 4,000, and C 3,000, no one has a majority, but A has a plurality of 1,000 over B. In most of the States a plurality elects a candidate; in others, as Connecticut and Rhode Island, if no candidate (as for governor) receives a popular majority, the election goes to the legislature. Compare *majority*.

4. *Eccles.*: (*a*) The holding of two or more benefices by the same person at the same time; pluralism.

The most part of them were such as had preach'd and cri'd down, with great show of zeale, the avarice and *pluralities* of Bishops and Prelats. *Milton*, Hist. Eng., iii.

(*b*) One of two or more livings held by the same incumbent. See *living*, 4 (*a*).

Who engross many *pluralities* under a non-resident and slubbring dispatch of souls. *Milton*, Apology for Smectymnuus.

pluralization (plö"ral-i-zā'shon), *n.* [< *pluralize* + *-ation.*] The act of pluralizing; the attribution of plurality to a person or thing. Also spelled *pluralisation*.

"Inferiors invariably use the third person plural in addressing their superiors:" a form which, while dignifying the superior by *pluralization*, increases the distance of the inferior by its relative indirectness. *H. Spencer*, Pop. Sci. Mo., XIII. 300.

pluralize (plö'ral-īz), *v.*; pret. and pp. *pluralized*, ppr. *pluralizing*. [< *plural* + *-ize.*] **I.** *trans.* To make plural by using the termination of the plural number; attribute plurality to; express in the plural form.

II. *intrans. Eccles.*, to hold two or more benefices at the same time.

Also spelled *pluralise*.

pluralizer (plö'ral-ī-zėr), *n.* *Eccles.*, a pluralist. Also spelled *pluraliser*.

plurally (plö'ral-i), *adv.* As a plural; in a sense implying more than one.

Plato . . . often spoke of Gods *plurally*. *Cudworth*, Intellectual System, p. 402.

pluricapsular (plö-ri-kap'sū-lär), *a.* [< L. *plus* (*plur-*), more, + NL. *capsula*, capsule: see *capsular*.] Having several capsules; specifically, polycyttarian, as a radiolarian.

pluricellular (plö-ri-sel'ū-lär), *a.* [< L. *plus* (*plur-*), more, + *cellula*, cell: see *cellular*.] Consisting of many cells; composed of two or more cells: as, *pluricellular* tissues. See cut under *hair*, 4.

pluricuspid (plö-ri-kus'pid), *a.* [< L. *plus* (*plur-*), more, + *cuspis* (*cuspid-*), a point; see *cusp*, 5.] Having several cusps, as teeth. Also *pluricuspidate*.

pluridentate (plö-ri-den'tāt), *a.* [< L. *plus* (*plur-*), more, + *den(t-)s* = E. *tooth*: see *dentate*.] In *zoöl.*, having numerous tooth-like processes: opposed to *parcidentate* or *paucidentate*.

pluries (plö'ri-ēz), *n.* [So called from the LL. word *pluries*, often, which occurs in the first clause; < L. *plus* (*plur-*), more: see *plus*.] In *law*, a writ that issues in the third instance, after the first and the alias have been ineffectual.

plurifarious (plö-ri-fā'ri-us), *a.* [< L. **plurifarius*, manifold, in adv. *plurifariam*, in many parts, in many ways, < *plus* (*plur-*), more, + *-farius*, as in *bifarius*: see *bifarious*.] Manifold; multifarious. [Rare.]

pluriflagellate (plö-ri-flaj'e-lāt), *a.* [< L. *plus* (*plur-*), more, + NL. *flagellum*, flagellum: see *flagellum*.] Having several flagella, as an infusorian; polymastigate.

plurifiorous (plö-ri-flō'rus), *a.* [< L. *plus* (*plur-*), more, + *flos* (*flor-*), a flower.] Having several or many flowers.

plurifoliate (plö-ri-fō'li-āt), *a.* [< L. *plus* (*plur-*), more, + *folium*, leaf: see *foliate*.] In *bot.*, having several leaves.

plurifoliolate (plö-ri-fō'li-ō-lāt), *a.* [< L. *plus* (*plur-*), more, + NL. *foliolum*, dim. of *folium*, leaf, + *-ate*[1].] In *bot.*, having several leaflets: said of a compound leaf.

pluriguttulate (plö-ri-gut'ū-lāt), *a.* [< L. *plus* (*plur-*), more, + *guttula*, dim. of *gutta*, drop: see *guttulate*.] In *bot.*, containing many fine drops or drop-like particles, as the sporules of certain fungi.

pluriliteral (plö-ri-lit'e-ral), *a.* and *n.* [< L. *plus* (*plur-*), more, + *littera*, *litera*, a letter: see *literal*.] **I.** *a.* Containing several letters.

II. *n.* A word consisting of several letters.

plurilocular (plö-ri-lok'ū-lär), *a.* [< L. *plus* (*plur-*), more, + *loculus*, a cell: see *loculus*.] In *bot.* and *zoöl.*, many-celled; having several or many cells or loculaments; multilocular. See cut under *hair*, 4.

plurinominal (plö-ri-nom'i-nal), *a.* [< L. *plus* (*plur-*), more, + *nomen* (*nomin-*), name: see *nominal*.] In *zoöl.* and *bot.*, same as *polynomial*.

plurinucleate (plö-ri-nū'klē-āt), *a.* [< L. *plus* (*plur-*), more, + *nucleus*, a kernel: see *nucleate*.] In *bot.* and *zoöl.*, having several nuclei; multinucleate.

plurinucleated (plö-ri-nū'klē-ā-ted), *a.* [< *plurinucleate* + *-ed*[2].] Same as *plurinucleate*.

pluripara (plö-rip'a-rä), *n.*; pl. *pluriparæ* (-rē). [NL.: see *pluriparous*.] A female parturient for the second or some subsequent time, or one who has borne two or more children.

pluriparity (plö-ri-par'i-ti), *n.* [< *pluripara* + *-ity.*] The state of being a pluripara.

pluriparous (plö-rip'a-rus), *a.* [< NL. *pluripara*, < L. *plus* (*plur-*), more, + *parere*, bear.] 1. Having several young at a birth; multiparous. *H. Spencer.*—2. Of or pertaining to a pluripara.

pluripartite (plö-ri-pär'tīt), *a.* [< L. *plus* (*plur-*), more, + *partitus*, pp. of *partire*, divide, < *pars* (*part-*), a part: see *part*, *v.*] In *bot.* and *zoöl.*, having several septa or partitions.

pluripresence (plö-ri-prez'ens), *n.* [< L. *plus* (*plur-*), more, + *præsentia*, presence: see *presence*.] Presence in more places than one. [Rare.]

Toplady. Does not their invocation of saints suppose omnipresence in the saints?
Johnson. No, Sir; it supposes only *pluri-presence*.
Boswell, Johnson, an. 1773.

pluriseptate (plö-ri-sep'tāt), *a.* [< L. *plus* (*plur-*), more, + NL. *septum*, a partition: see *septate*.] In *bot.*, having several septa, partitions, or dissepiments; pluripartite.

pluriserial (plö-ri-sē'ri-al), *a.* [< L. *plus* (*plur-*), more, + *series*, a row: see *serial*.] Consisting of several series. *Encyc. Brit.*, XXII. 190.

pluriseriate (plö-ri-sē'ri-āt), *a.* [< L. *plus* (*plur-*), more, + *series*, a row: see *seriate*.] In *bot.*, disposed in many rows.

plurisetose (plö-ri-sē'tōs), *a.* [< L. *plus* (*plur-*), more, + *seta*, a bristle: see *setose*.] Having several or many setæ.

plurispiral (plö-ri-spī'ral), *a.* [< L. *plus* (*plur-*), more, + *spira*, a coil, fold: see *spiral*.] Having several or many spiral turns; multispiral: specifically said of the opercula of some shells.

plurisporous (plö-ri-spō'rus), *a.* [< L. *plus* (*plur-*), more, + Gr. σπορά, seed: see *spore*.] In *bot.*, having two or more spores.

plurisubinvariant (plö-ri-sub-in-vā'ri-ant), *n.* A function, ϕ, of a, b, c, etc., of a', b', c', etc., of a'', b'', c'', etc., such that $(aD_b + 2bD_c + 3cD_d + \text{etc.} + a'D_{b'} + \text{etc.} + a''D_{b''} + \text{etc.})\,\phi = 0$.

plurisy† (plö'ri-si), *n.* [An altered spelling of *pleurisy*, simulating L. *plus* (gen. *pluris*), more, and taking sense accordingly.] **1.** Superabundance.

> Oh, great corrector of enormous times,
> . . . that heal'st with blood
> The earth when it is sick, and cur'st the world
> O' the *plurisy* of people.
> *Fletcher (and another)*, Two Noble Kinsmen, v. 1.

> Thy *plurisy* of goodness is thy ill.
> *Massinger*, Unnatural Combat, iv. 1.

2. Superabundance of blood; a plethora.

> You are too insolent;
> And those too many excellencies, that feed
> Your pride, turn to a *plurisy*, and kill
> That which should nourish virtue.
> *Beau. and Fl.*, Custom of the Country, ii. 1.

plurivalve (plö'ri-valv), *a.* [< L. *plus* (*plur-*), more, + *valva*, a folding door: see *valve*.] **1.** In *entom.*, having several valves or sheathing-plates.—**2.** In *bot.*, having many valves: said especially of capsules.—**3.** In *conch.*, same as *multivalve*.

Plurivalvia (plö-ri-val'vi-ä), *n. pl.* [NL.: see *plurivalve*.] In *conch.*, same as *Multivalvia*.

plus (plus), *a.* [< L. *plus* (*plur-*), more, pl. *plures*, OL. *pleores*, more, several, the majority (compar. of *multus*, much), = Gr. πλείων, πλέων, pl. πλείονες, more, compar. of πολύς, many (= E. *feel*[2]); cf. πλέως, full, L. *plenus*, full: see *plenty*.] **1.** More (by a certain amount); increased (by a specified addition): followed by a noun as an apparent object (a preposition, *by*, to be supplied): as, the interest *plus* the disbursements amounts to so much; 6 *plus* 9 is 15: in this and the next two uses correlative to *minus*. In algebra and arithmetic this sense is indicated by the sign +, called the plus sign or sign of addition: as, $a + b = x$, which is read "*a* plus *b* equals *x*." [A sign like this was formerly sometimes used as a contraction of Latin *et*, and.]

> His prose, then, is that of a wise man *plus* a poet.
> *E. C. Stedman*, Poets of America, p. 134.

2. More than nothing; belonging to the positive side, as of an account; above zero, or above the lowest point of positive reckoning: as, a *plus* quantity in an equation (that is, one having the plus sign, or when initial having no sign, before it).—**3.** Marking more than zero; positive: as, the *plus* sign.

> Success goes invariably with a certain *plus* or positive power. *Emerson*, Complete Prose Works, II. 352.

4. In *etym.*, in composition with; with the addition of (the word or element following): expressed, as in mathematics, by the sign + (see the etymologies in this work). The same sign is occasionally used to indicate cognate or related forms.—**Logarithmic plus and minus.** See *logarithmic*.

plush (plush), *n.* [Formerly also *pelluce*; = D. *pluis*, a tuft or lock of wool or hair, plush, = G. *plusch* = Sw. *plys*, *plysch* = Dan. *plyds*, < F. *pluche*, *peluche*, shag, plush, = Sp. *peluzza*, *pelussa*, *pelusa* = Pg. *pellucia*, plush, nap, = It. *peluzzo*, *pelucio*, dial. *plusia*, plush, nap, down; < ML. as if **pilucius*, hairy, shaggy, < L. *pilus*, hair: see *pile*[4], and cf. *peruke* and *pluck*[1].] A cloth of silk or cotton, and sometimes of wool (especially of camel's and goat's hair), having a softer and longer nap than that of velvet. Plush is used especially for upholstery, women's cloaks, expensive liveries, and men's silk hats, and since 1870 as a ground for embroidery in house-decoration, for curtains, and the like.

> The rich Tartars sometimes fur their gowns with *pelluce* or silke shag, which is exceeding soft, light, and warme.
> *Hakluyt's Voyages*, I. 98.

> My tailor brings me home my fine, new, coloured-cloth suit, my cloak lined with *plush*—as good a suit as ever I wore in my life. *Pepys*, Diary, Oct. 28, 1664.

Banbury plush, woolen plush used for upholstery and the like, first made in the town of Banbury, England. (See also *furniture-plush*.)

plush-copper (plush'kop'ėr), *n.* A capillary variety of cuprite, or red oxid of copper: same as *chalcotrichite*.

plusher† (plush'ėr), *n.* [Origin obscure.] A kind of dogfish.

> The Pilcherd are pursued and devoured by a bigger kinde of fish, called a *Plusher*, being somewhat like the Dog-fish.
> *R. Carew*, Survey of Cornwall, p. 34.

plush-stitch (plush'stich), *n.* In worsted- or wool-work, a stitch that forms freely hanging loops which can be cut, thus producing a long soft nap similar to that of plush, or can be left uncut, as a kind of fringe.

plush-velvet (plush'vel'vet), *n.* Plush having a shorter nap than is common, and thus resembling velvet.

plush-velveteen (plush'vel-ve-tēn'), *n.* Cotton plush closely imitating plush made of silk.

plushy (plush'i), *a.* [< *plush* + *-y*[1].] Consisting of or resembling plush; shaggy and soft.

> Then followed a long gaze out of the window, across the damp gravel and *plushy* lawn.
> *H. Kingsley*, Geoffry Hamlyn, iv.

Plusia (plö'si-ä), *n.* [NL. (Ochsenheimer, 1816), with ref. to the silver or gold markings; < Gr. πλούσιος, rich, < πλοῦτος, riches: see *Plutus*.] **1.** A notable genus of noctuid moths, having the body stout, the proboscis rather long, the abdomen crested, and the fore wings as a rule partly gilded or silvery. More than 100 species are known, and the genus is represented in all parts of the

Cabbage-plusia (*Plusia brassicæ*).
a, caterpillar; *b*, chrysalis in cocoon; *c*, moth, male.
(All natural size.)

world. Many of the species are wide-spread, several being common to Europe and North America, and one to Europe and South Africa. The larvæ of many are injurious to growing crops, and *P. brassicæ* of the United States is one of the worst enemies of the cabbage and other cruciferous plants. In Europe the gamma-moth or silver-Y, *P. gamma*, is equally destructive to the same vegetables. *P. chrysitis* is the burnished-brass moth.

2. [*l. c.*] A member of this genus; especially, in the United States, *P. brassicæ*, known as the *cabbage-plusia*.

Plusidæ (plö'si-dē), *n. pl.* [NL.] Same as *Plusiidæ*.

Plusiidæ (plö-sī'i-dē), *n. pl.* [NL. (Guenée, 1852), < *Plusia* + *-idæ*.] A family of noctuid moths, typified by the genus *Plusia*, having the palpi slender and ascending, and the wings often golden or silvered. It contains 8 genera.

plusiocracy, plousiocracy (plö-si-ok'rā-si), *n.* [< Gr. πλούσιος, rich, wealthy, + -κρατία, < κρατεῖν, rule.] Same as *plutocracy*. [Rare.]

> To say a word against . . . the cruel punishments of the Game-laws, or against any abuse which a rich man inflicted and a poor man suffered, was treason against the *plousiocracy*. *Sydney Smith*, in Lady Holland, ii.

Plusiotis (plö-sī'ō-tis), *n.* [NL. (Burmeister), < Gr. πλούσιος, rich; cf. πλουσιότης, wealth.] A genus of lamellicorn beetles of the family *Scarabæidæ*, containing American species of large size and burnished silvery or golden color. Three species are known in the United States; the others are Mexican.

plutarchy (plö'tär-ki), *n.* [< Gr. πλοῦτος, wealth, + -αρχία, < ἄρχειν, rule.] Same as *plutocracy*. *Southey*, The Doctor, cii.

plutei, *n.* Plural of *pluteus*.

pluteiform (plö'tē-i-fôrm), *a.* [< NL. *pluteus* (see *pluteus*, 3) + L. *forma*, form.] **1.** Having the morphological value of a pluteus: as, the *pluteiform* larva of an echinoderm. See cut under *echinopædium*.—**2.** Less exactly, like or likened to a pluteus in any way; echinopædic.

Plutella (plö-tel'ä), *n.* [NL. (Schrank, 1802), < Gr. πλοῦτος, wealth, + dim. *-ella*.] **1.** A genus of tineid moths, typical of the family *Plutellidæ*.

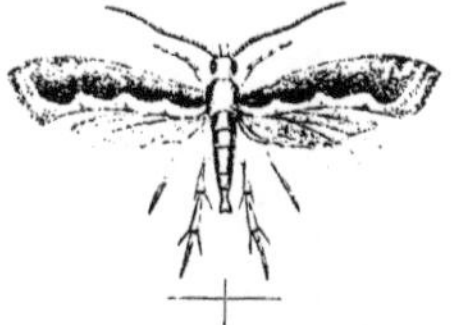

Plutella cruciferarum. (Cross shows natural size.)

They are small, with antennæ not thickened at the base, erect palpi, and the sixth and seventh veins of the hind wings separate. The larva skeletonizes leaves, and pupates in a gauzy cocoon. *P. cruciferarum* (*xylostella*) is a turnip- and cabbage-pest of cosmopolitan distribution.

2. [*l. c.*] A member of this genus; especially, in the United States, *P. cruciferarum*, known as the *cabbage-plutella*. In England and the British colonies it is known as the *diamond-back*.

Plutellidæ (plö-tel'i-dē), *n. pl.* [NL., < *Plutella* + *-idæ*.] A family of tineid moths, typified by the genus *Plutella*. The head is woolly, and the palpi are provided with a strong bunch of scales on the middle joint below; they have the peculiar habit of holding the antennæ straight forward when at rest (most other tineids holding the antennæ back on the wings). The family contains about 6 genera, of which *Cerostoma* is the most extensive.

pluteus (plö'tē-us), *n.*; pl. *plutei* (-ī). [L., also *pluteum*, a shed or mantlet to protect besiegers, a breastwork, parapet, a headboard of a couch or bed, a partition, etc.] **1.** In *anc. Rom. arch.*, a barrier, as any construction of boards, osiers, grating, or other light work, placed between the columns of a portico; a light wall occupying the lower part of an intercolumniation; a balustrade or parapet crowning a building or a part of a building; also, a shelf fixed to the wall; the headboard of a bed.—**2.** In *anc. Rom. milit. engin.*: (*a*) Boards or planks placed on the fortifications of a camp, or on movable towers or other military engines, to form a kind of roof or shed for the protection of the soldiers. (*b*) A movable gallery on wheels, shaped like an arch-covered wagon, in which a besieging party made their approaches.—**3.** In *zoöl.*, a larval stage of the echinopædia of certain echinoderms, as a holothurian, ophiurian, or echinid. It is known as the

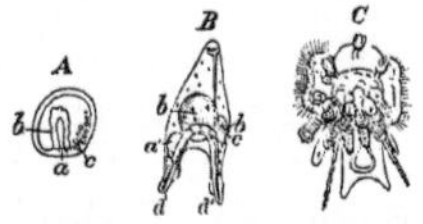

A. Echinopædium of *Echinus pulchellus*, gastrula stage: *a*, mouth; *b*, intestine; *c*, anus. *B*. Fully developed echinopædium or pluteus of the same: *a'*, mouth; *b*, stomach and intestine; *c*, anus; *d*, *d*, processes of body containing prolongations of internal skeleton. *C*. Echinopædium of an echinid advanced so far that spines, pedicels, and pedicellariæ are visible.

painter's-easel larva, from its shape, and was originally described as a distinct genus by Müller in 1846. Compare cuts under *Bipinnaria* and *echinopædium*.

Pluto (plö'tō), *n.* [L., < Gr. Πλούτων, poet. also Πλουτεύς, Pluto, orig. epithet of Hades, the underworld (as a source of grain, etc.), < πλοῦτος, wealth: see *Plutus*.] In *Rom. myth.*, the lord of the infernal regions, son of Saturn and brother of Jupiter and Neptune. He is represented as an elderly man with a dignified but severe aspect, often holding in his hand a two-pronged fork. He was generally called by the Greeks *Hades*, and by the Romans *Orcus*, *Tartarus*, and *Dis*. His wife was Proserpine, daughter of Jupiter and Ceres, whom he seized in the island of Sicily while she was plucking flowers, and carried to the lower world. See cut on following page.—**Pluto monkey**, *Cercopithecus pluto*, of western Africa.

plutocracy (plö-tok'rā-si), *n.* [< Gr. πλουτοκρατία, an oligarchy of wealth, < πλοῦτος, wealth, + -κρατία, < κρατεῖν, rule.] Government by the wealthy class; the rule of wealth; also, a class ruling by virtue of its wealth. Also *plutarchy*.

plutocrat (plö'tō-krat), *n.* [< Gr. πλουτοκρατ-, base of πλουτοκρατία, an oligarchy of wealth: see *plutocracy*.] One who rules or sways a

Pluto, enthroned, with Proserpine. (From a vase-painting.)

community or society by virtue of his wealth; a person possessing power or influence solely or mainly on account of his riches; a member of a plutocracy.

We have had *plutocrats* who were patterns of every virtue. *Gladstone*, Nineteenth Century, XXI. 17.

The *plutocrats* and bureaucrats, the money-changers and devourers of labour. *Kingsley*, Alton Locke, xli. (*Davies.*)

plutocratic (plö-tō̦-krat'ik), *a.* [< *plutocrat* + *-ic.*] Pertaining to or characteristic of a plutocracy or a plutocrat: as, a *plutocratic* government; *plutocratic* ideas.

plutologist (plö-tol'ō̦-jist), *n.* [< *plutolog-y* + *-ist.*] One skilled in plutology, or the science of wealth and its distribution.

As the *plutologists* have explained, the means of happiness are immensely increased by that complex system of mutual co-operation which has been gradually organized among civilised men. *H. Sidgwick*, Methods of Ethics, p. 406.

plutology (plö-tol'ō̦-ji), *n.* [< Gr. πλοῦτος, wealth, + -λογία, < λέγειν, speak: see *-ology.*] The science of wealth; the body of natural laws governing the production and distribution of wealth; political economy.

Several authors have tried to introduce totally new names [for political economy], such as *plutology*, chrematistics, catallactics. *Jevons*, Pol. Econ. (2d ed.), Pref.

Plutonian (plö̦-tō'ni-a̦n), *a.* and *n.* [< L. *Plutonius*, < Gr. Πλουτώνιος, of Pluto or the nether world, < Πλούτων, Pluto: see *Pluto.*] **I.** *a.* Of or pertaining to Pluto; Plutonic.

The night's *Plutonian* shore. *Poe*, The Raven.

II. *n.* A Plutonist.

Plutonic (plö̦-ton'ik), *a.* [< L. *Pluto(n-)*, < Gr. Πλούτων, Pluto, + *-ic.*] **1.** Of or relating to Pluto or the regions of fire; subterranean; dark.—**2.** Pertaining to or designating the system of the Plutonists: as, the *Plutonic* theory.—**3.** In *geol.*, formed deep below the surface. Plutonic rocks are such igneous rocks as have been formed under conditions of depth and pressure, and have cooled slowly, so as to have acquired in general a distinctly crystalline structure: the term *Plutonic* is opposed to *volcanic*, the former designating rocks formed at some depth beneath the surface, the latter rocks of igneous origin but of superficial formation. As used by Lyell, the word is nearly the equivalent of *metamorphic*.

Granite is thus a decidedly *plutonic* rock — that is, it has consolidated at some depth beneath the surface, and in this respect differs from the superficial volcanic rocks, such as lava, which have flowed out above ground from volcanic orifices. *A. Geikie*, Text-Book of Geology, II. ii. § 7.

Plutonic theory, the geological theory that the present aspect and condition of the earth's crust are mainly due to igneous action.

Several modern writers, without denying the truth of the *Plutonic* or metamorphic *theory*, still contend that the crystalline and non-fossiliferous formations, whether stratified or unstratified, such as gneiss and granite, are essentially ancient as a class of rocks. *Lyell*, Prin. of Geol. (11th ed.), I. 129.

Plutonism (plö'tō̦-nizm), *n.* [< *Pluton-ist* + *-ism.*] The doctrines of the Plutonists.

Plutonist (plö'tō̦-nist), *n.* [< *Pluton-ic* + *-ist.*] One who adopts the Plutonic theory.

Plutus (plö'tus), *n.* [L., < Gr. Πλοῦτος, the god of riches, a personification of πλοῦτος, riches, wealth; prob. from the root of πλέως, full, L. *plus*, more, etc.: see *plus.*] In *classical myth.*, a personification of wealth, described as a son of Iasion and Demeter, and intimately associated with Eirene or Peace, who is often represented in art grouped with the infant Plutus. Zeus is said to have blinded him, in order that he might not bestow his favors exclusively on good men, but should distribute his gifts without regard to merit.

pluvial (plö'vi-a̦l), *a.* and *n.* [I. *a.* = F. *pluvial* = Pr. Sp. Pg. *pluvial* = It. *piuviale*, < L. *pluvialis*, of or pertaining to rain, < *pluvia*, rain, < *pluvius*, rainy: see *pluvious.* II. *n.* < F. *pluvial* (Sp. *capa pluvial*), < ML. *pluvialis*, etc., a rain-cloak: see I.] **I.** *a.* **1.** Rainy; humid; relating to rain; also, very rainy; characterized by great or extensive rainfall.—**2.** In *geol.*, depending on or arising from the action of rain.

The particular kind of denudation effected by means of rain is called *pluvial* denudation. *Huxley*, Physiography, p. 131.

II. *n. Eccles.*, a cope: so called from its use in outdoor processions, etc., as a protection from the weather.

Pluviales (plö-vi-ā'lēz), *n. pl.* [NL., pl. of L. *pluvialis*, pertaining to rain: see *pluvial.*] The plovers and plover-like birds: synonymous with *Charadriomorphæ*.

pluvialiform (plö-vi-al'i-fôrm), *a.* [< NL. *pluvialiformis*, < *Pluviales*, q. v., + L. *forma*, form.] Plover-like; pluvialine; charadriomorphic.

Pluvialiformes (plö-vi-al-i-fôr'mēz), *n. pl.* [NL., pl. of *pluvialiformis*: see *pluvialiform.*] The schizognathous water-birds, an extensive series of wading and swimming birds more or less related to the plovers, corresponding to the *Charadriomorphæ* and *Cecomorphæ* of Huxley, or the orders *Limicolæ*, *Longipennes*, and *Pygopodes*.

pluvialine (plö'vi-a̦-lin), *a.* [< *Pluvial-es* + *-ine*[1].] In *ornith.*, of or pertaining to a plover; resembling or related to the plovers; charadriomorphic: as, *pluvialine* characters; a *pluvialine* genus of birds.

pluviameter (plö-vi-am'e-tėr), *n.* Same as *pluviometer.*

pluviametrical (plö"vi-a̦-met'ri-ka̦l), *a.* Same as *pluviometric.*

Pluvianellus (plö"vi-a̦-nel'us), *n.* [NL. (Hombron and Jacquinot), dim. of *Pluvianus*: see *Pluvianus.*] A genus of small wading birds related to the turnstones and surf-birds, with a hind toe and very short tarsus, containing one species, *P. sociabilis*, from the southern regions of South America.

Pluvianellus sociabilis.

Pluvianus (plö-vi-ā'nus), *n.* [NL. (Vieillot, 1816), < L. *pluvia*, rain: see *pluvial.*] A genus of plovers, belonging to the subfamily *Cursorinæ*; the crocodile-birds. *P. ægyptius*, the only species, inhabits northern Africa, and is among the birds supposed to be the trochilus of Herodotus (the *Hoplopterus spinosus* being another). See *trochilus*, and cut under *spur-winged*. Also called *Cursorius*, *Hyas*, *Ammoptila*, and *Chilodromus*.

Crocodile-bird (*Pluvianus ægyptius*).

pluviograph (plö'vi-ō̦-grȧf), *n.* [< L. *pluvia*, rain, + Gr. γράφειν, write.] A self-recording rain-gage.

In Beckley's *pluviograph* a pencil, attached to a vessel which sinks as it receives the rain, describes a curve on a sheet of paper fixed round a rotating cylinder. *Encyc. Brit.*, XX. 257.

pluviometer (plö-vi-om'e-tėr), *n.* [Also *pluviameter*; < L. *pluvia*, rain, + Gr. μέτρον, measure.] An instrument for collecting and measuring the quantity of water that falls in rain, snow, etc., at a particular place; a rain-gage. See cut in next column.

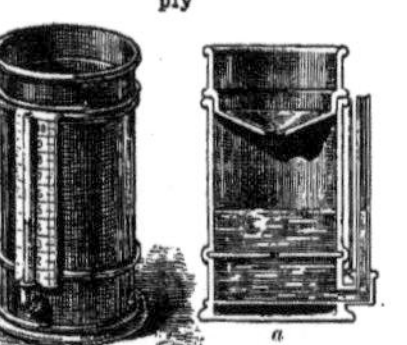

Pluviometer. *a*, vertical section.

pluviometric (plö"vi-ō̦-met'rik), *a.* [< *pluviometer* + *-ic.*] Made by means of a pluviometer: as, *pluviometric* observations.

pluviometrical (plö"vi-ō̦-met'ri-ka̦l), *a.* [< *pluviometric* + *-al.*] Same as *pluviometric.*

pluviometrically (plö"vi-ō̦-met'ri-ka̦l-i), *adv.* In a pluviometric manner; by means of pluviometry; by the use of the pluviometer.

pluviometry (plö-vi-om'et-ri), *n.* [< L. *pluvia*, rain, + Gr. *-μετρία*, < *μέτρον*, measure.] The measurement of the amount of precipitation of rain or snow; the use of the pluviometer.

pluvioscope (plö'vi-ō̦-skōp), *n.* [< L. *pluvia*, rain, + Gr. *σκοπεῖν*, view.] A rain-gage; a pluviometer.

The results are here tabulated of the pluviometric observations taken at Paris during the years 1860–70 with the *pluvioscope* invented by the author [M. Hervé Mangon]. *Nature*, XXXV. 479.

Pluviose (plö'vi-ōs), *n.* [F., < L. *pluviosus*, full of rain, < *pluvia*, rain.] The fifth month of the French revolutionary calendar, from January 20th to February 18th inclusive in the year 1794.

pluvious (plö'vi-us), *a.* [< ME. *pluvyous* = F. *pluvieux* = Pr. *ploios* = Sp. *pluvioso* = Pg. *pluvioso*, *chuvoso* = It. *piovoso*, < L. *pluvius*, rainy, causing or bringing rain, < *pluere*, rain, impers. *pluit*, it rains.] Rainy; pluvial.

In places over oolde
And *pluvyous*, clyves is to doon.
Palladius, Husbondrie (E. E. T. S.), p. 161.

The fungus parcels about the wicks of candles . . . only signifieth a moist and *pluvious* air about them, hindering the avolation of the light and favillous particles. *Sir T. Browne*, Vulg. Err., v. 24.

ply (plī), *v.*; pret. and pp. *plied*, ppr. *plying*. [< ME. *plyen*, *plien*, bend, mold (as wax), < OF. *plier*, *pleier*, *ploier*, fold, bend, plait, ply, F. *plier*, also *ployer*, fold, bend, etc., = Pr. *pleiar*, *plegar* = Sp. *plegar* = Pg. *pregar* = It. *piegare*, fold, bend, < L. *plicare* (pp. *plicātus* and *plĭcitus*), fold, lay or wind together, double up, = Gr. πλέκειν, twine, twist, weave, tie, infold, etc.; akin to L. *plectere*, weave, whence ult. *plait*, etc.: see *plait*. From L. *plicare* are ult. E. *ply*, *apply*, *comply*, *imply*, *reply*, etc., also *ploy*, *deploy*, *employ*, etc., *display*, *splay*, etc., *plicate*, *complicate*, *explicate*, *implicate*, *supplicate*, etc., *explicit*, *implicit*, etc., *complex*, *complice*, *accomplice*, etc., *simple*, *duplex*, *double*, *triple*, *quadruple*, etc., *multiple*, etc., *supple*, etc., *pliable*, *pliant*, etc.; from the related L. *plectere*, weave, are ult. E. *plait*, *pleat*, *plat*[4], *plight*[3], *pleach*, *plash*[2], *plexus*, *complexion*, *perplex*, etc.] **I.** *trans.* **1**†. To bend; mold; shape.

Womman of manye scoles half a clerk is:
But certeynly a yonge thyng may men gye,
Right as men may warm wex with handes *plye*.
Chaucer, Merchant's Tale, l. 186.

2†. To draw; work.

Then all his letters will be such ecstasies, such vows and promises, which you must answer short and simply, yet still *ply* out of them your advantages. *Dryden*, Sir Martin Mar-all, i. 2.

3. To use or employ diligently; keep on using with diligence and persistence; apply one's self steadily to; keep busy with; toil at.

Who shall bear your part,
And be in Padua here Vincentio's son,
Keep house and *ply* his book, welcome his friends,
Visit his countrymen and banquet them?
Shak., T. of the S., i. 1. 201.

Lord George Gordon the left wing guided,
Who well the sword could *ply*.
Battle of Alford (Child's Ballads, VII. 239).

The bold swain, who *plies* his oar,
May lightly row his bark to shore.
Scott, Rokeby, ii. 31.

So lustily did Van Poffenburgh *ply* the bottle that in less than four short hours he made himself and his whole garrison, who all sedulously emulated the deeds of their chieftain, dead drunk. *Irving*, Knickerbocker, p. 331.

4. To practise or perform with diligence and persistence; pursue steadily: as, to *ply* one's trade.

Then, laying aside those their holy garments, they *plie* their worke till the euening. *Purchas*, Pilgrimage, p. 145.

The needle *plies* its busy task. *Cowper*, Task, iv. 150.

"When first"—(he so began)—"my trade I *plied*,
Good master Addle was the parish-guide."
Crabbe, Works, I. 120.

Gambling is not permitted on the grounds at Epsom, but there were many gamblers on the grounds, and they sought every occasion to *ply* their vocation. *T. C. Crawford*, English Life, p. 19.

5. To attack or assail briskly, repeatedly, or persistently.

They so warmly *plied* our divided fleets that whilst in conflict the merchants sail'd away, and got safe into Holland. *Evelyn*, Diary, March 12, 1672.

The hero stands above, and from afar
Plies him with darts and stones, and distant war.
Dryden, Æneid, viii.

Again he [Apollo] took
The harnessed steeds, that still with horror shook,
And *plies* 'em with a lash, and whips 'em on,
And, as he whips, upbraids them with his son.
Addison, tr. of Ovid's Metamorph., ii.

6. To address with importunity or persistent solicitation; urge, or keep on urging or soliciting, as for a favor.

He *plies* the duke at morning and at night.
Shak., M. of V., iii. 2. 279.

A courtier would not *ply* it so for a place.
B. Jonson, Volpone, iii. 4.

I have been always *plying* you to walk and read.
Swift, Journal to Stella, xxxiv.

Sunderland was *plied* at once with promises and menaces. *Macaulay*, Hist. Eng., vi.

7. To offer with persistency or frequency; press upon for acceptance; continue to present or supply: as, to *ply* one with drink, or with flattery.

If you perceive that the untravelled company about you take this down well, *ply* them with more such stuff. *Dekker*, Gull's Hornbook, p. 113.

With cup full ever *plied*,
And hearts full never dried.
Chapman, The Blind Beggar of Alexandria (song).

They adore him, they *ply* him with flowers, and hymns, and incense, and flattery. *Thackeray*.

8†. To apply; devote with persistency or perseverance.

Ne ever cast his mind to covet prayse,
Or *ply* himselfe to any honest trade.
Spenser, F. Q., III. vii. 12.

9†. To exert; acquit.

But it is worthy of memorie to see how the women of ye towne did *plie* themselues with their weapons, making a great massacre vpon our men. *Webbe*, Travels (ed. Arber), p. 23.

II. *intrans.* 1†. To bend; yield; incline.

The gold of hem hath now so badde alayes
With bras that, though the coyne be fair at ye,
It wolde rather breste atwo than *plye*.
Chaucer, Clerk's Tale, l. 1113.

To *plie* this waie or that waie to good or to bad, ye shall haue as ye vse a child in his youth. *Ascham*, The Scholemaster, p. 46.

As like a lion he could pace with pride,
Ply like a plant, and like a river slide.
Sir J. Davies, Dancing.

2. To keep at work or in action; busy one's self; work steadily; be employed.

All D'Aulnay's company *plied* for their fortifying with palisadoes, and the friars as busy as any. *Winthrop*, Hist. New England, II. 162.

Ere half these authors be read (which will soon be with *plying* hard and daily), they cannot choose but be masters of any ordinary prose. *Milton.*

In vain their airy Pinions *ply*.
Congreve, Pindaric Odes, ii.

And around the bows and along the side
The heavy hammers and mallets *plied*.
Longfellow, Building of the Ship.

3. To proceed in haste; sally forth.

Thither he *plies*,
Undaunted to meet there whatever power
Or spirit of the nethermost abyss
Might in that noise reside. *Milton*, P. L., ii. 954.

Adriaen Block . . . *plied* forth to explore the vicinity. *Bancroft*, Hist. U. S., II. 33.

4. To go back and forth or backward and forward over the same course; especially, to run or sail regularly along the same course, or between two fixed places or ports; make more or less regular trips: as, the boats that *ply* on the Hudson; the steamers that *ply* between New York and Fall River; the stage *plied* between Concord and Boston: said both of the vessels or vehicles that make the trips and of those who sail or run them.

And then they *ply* from th' caues vnto the ground,
With mud-mixt Reed to wall their mansion round.
Sylvester, tr. of Du Bartas's Weeks, ii., The Handy-Crafts.

Cæsar, causing all his Boats and Shallops to be fill'd with Souldiers, commanded to *ply* up and down continually with relief where they saw need. *Milton*, Hist. Eng., ii.

Busy housewives *plied* backwards and forwards along the lines, helping everything forward by the nimbleness of their tongues. *Irving*, Knickerbocker, p. 129.

5. *Naut.*, to beat; tack; work to windward: as, to *ply* northward.

That day we *plyed* downe as farre as our Ladie of Holland, and there came to an anker. *Hakluyt's Voyages*, I. 310.

The Currents at Cape La Vela do seldom shift, therefore Ships that *ply* to Wind-ward to get about it do not *ply* near the shore, but stand off to Sea. *Dampier*, Voyages, II. iii. 101.

She was flying dead into the east, and every minute her keel passed over as many fathoms of sea as would take her hours of *plying* to recover. *W. C. Russell*, Death Ship, xli.

6. To offer one's services for trips or jobs, as boatmen, hackmen, carriers, etc.

He was forced to *ply* in the streets, as a porter, for his livelihood. *Spectator.*

There is at Edinburgh a society or corporation of errand-boys called Cawdies, who *ply* in the streets at night with paper lanterns, and are very serviceable in carrying messages. *Smollett*, Humphrey Clinker (J. Melford to Sir Watkin [Phillips).

[It] will be readily pointed out by any one of the fifty intelligent fly-drivers who *ply* upon the pier. *Barham*, Ingoldsby Legends, II. 139.

ply (plī), *n.* [< *ply*, *v.*] 1. A fold; a thickness: often used in composition to designate the number of thicknesses or twists of which anything is made: as, three-*ply* thread; three-*ply* carpets.

I found myself at last on the diver's platform, twenty pounds of lead upon each foot, and my whole person swollen with *ply* and *ply* of woollen underclothing. *R. L. Stevenson*, Education of an Engineer.

2. Bent; turn; direction; bias.

Custom is most perfect when it beginneth in young years; . . . late learners cannot so well take up the *ply*. *Bacon*, Custom and Education (ed. 1887).

He bent all the subordinate branches of their government to the *ply* of his own favourite passion. *Goldsmith*, Seven Years' War, v.

Under Elizabeth the growing taste for theatrical representations had begun gradually to displace it [the baiting of animals, and especially of bulls and bears], and to give a new *ply* and tone to the manners of the rich. *Lecky*, Eng. in 18th Cent., iv.

He [Hamilton] accepted the constitution as it was, and did his best to give it the *ply* which he desired by practical interpretation. *Nineteenth Century*, XXIII. 105.

Plyctolophinæ, Plyctolophus. See *Plictolophus*, etc.

plyer, *n.* See *plier*.

plyght[1]†, *n.* and *v.* A Middle English form of *plight*[1], *plight*[2], etc.

plyght[2]†, **plyghte**†. Middle English forms of the preterit and past participle of *pluck*[1].

Plymouth Brethren. See *brother*.

Plymouth cloak†. A staff; a cudgel. [Slang.]
[That is, a cane, a staff; whereof this is the occasion. Many a man of good extraction, coming home from far voyages, may chance to land here, and, being out of sorts, is unable for the present time and place to recruit himself with clothes. Here (if not friendly provided) they make the next wood their draper's shop, where a staff cut out serves them for a covering. For we use, when we walk *in cuerpo*, to carry a staff in our hands, but none when in a cloak. *Ray*, Proverbs (1742), p. 238.]

Reserving still the embleme of a souldier (his sword) and a *Plimouth cloake*, otherwise called a battoone. *Lenten's Characterismi*, Char. 30. (*Nares.*)

Shall I walk in a *Plymouth cloak* (that 's to say) like a rogue, in my hose and doublet, and a crab-tree cudgel in my hand? *Dekker*, Honest Whore, ii.

Plymouthism (plim'uth-izm), *n.* [< *Plymouth* + *-ism.*] The doctrines of the Plymouth Brethren. See *Plymouth Brethren*, under *brother*.

Plymouthist (plim'uth-ist), *n.* [< *Plymouth* + *-ist.*] An adherent of Plymouthism; one of the Plymouth Brethren; a Plymouthite.

There are therefore at least five official divisions or sects of *Plymouthists*. *Encyc. Brit.*, XIX. 239.

Plymouthite (plim'uth-īt), *n.* [< *Plymouth* + *-ite*[2].] One of the Plymouth Brethren.

Plymouth Rock. A large and serviceable variety of the domestic hen, of American origin. Both cock and hen have the plumage finely and evenly barred transversely throughout with blue-black on a ground of pearl-gray. The legs and beak are clear-yellow, and the tail is very small. The normal variety has an upright comb; but there are also pea-combed Plymouth Rocks. White Plymouth Rocks have been introduced recently.

plyt†, **plyte**†, *n.* Middle English forms of *plight*[2].

P. M. An abbreviation: (*a*) of *post meridiem*, 'after noon or midday' (also P. M., p. m.): frequently used as synonymous with *afternoon* or *evening*; (*b*) of *postmaster*; (*c*) of *peculiar meter*.

pm. In dental formulæ, an abbreviation of *premolar*.

pneodynamics (nē"ō-dī-nam'iks), *n.* [Irreg. < Gr. πνεῖν, breathe, + δύναμις, power: see *dynamics*.] The science of the mechanics of respiration.

pneogaster (nē-ō-gas'tėr), *n.* [Irreg. < Gr. πνεῖν, breathe, + γαστήρ, the stomach.] The respiratory tract; the respiratory or branchial intestine considered as a part of the general intestinal system, being developed from the embryo in connection therewith. It consists of air-passages in the widest sense, as lungs, windpipes, etc., or their equivalents.

pneogastric (nē-ō-gas'trik), *a.* [< *pneogaster* + *-ic.*] Of or pertaining to the pneogaster.

pneograph (nē'ō-grāf), *n.* [Irreg. < Gr. πνεῖν, breathe, + γράφειν, write.] An instrument invented by Dr. Mortimer Granville for testing and indicating the duration, force, and continuity of expiration in diverse conditions of the lungs. It consists of a delicately suspended and counterpoised semi-disk of talc, which is moved by the breath when held in front of the mouth. The disk carries a needle, which makes a tracing on smoked paper caused to move uniformly in relation with the needle. The tracings indicate by their undulations the character of the expiratory movement, from which the condition of the lungs may be inferred.

pneometer (nē-om'e-tėr), *n.* [Irreg. < Gr. πνεῖν, breathe, + μέτρον, measure.] A spirometer.

pneometry (nē-om'et-ri), *n.* [Irreg. < Gr. πνεῖν, breathe, + μετρία, < μέτρον, measure.] Measurement of inspired or expired air.

pneoscope (nē'ō-skōp), *n.* [Irreg. < Gr. πνεῖν, breathe, + σκοπεῖν, view.] An instrument for measuring the extent of movement of the thorax.

pneuma (nū'mạ̈), *n.* [NL., < Gr. πνεῦμα, breath, < πνεῖν, blow, breathe. Cf. *neume*, *neuma*.] 1. Breath; spirit; soul.—2. A breathing. In *early church music*: (*a*) A form of ligature at the end of certain plain-chant melodies, resembling the periclesis, but differing from it in being sung to an unmeaning syllable having no connection with the text. Its use can be traced with certainty to the fourth century, and it is still employed in the services of the Roman Catholic Church, especially at high mass. (*b*) Same as *neume*, 2.

pneumarthrosis (nū-mär-thrō'sis), *n.* [NL., < Gr. πνεῦμα, air, + ἄρθρωσις, a jointing: see *arthrosis*.] The presence of air in the cavity of a joint.

pneumathorax (nū-mạ-thō'raks), *n.* An erroneous form of *pneumothorax*.

pneumatic (nū-mat'ik), *a.* and *n.* [= F. *pneumatique* = Sp. *pneumático* = Pg. It. *pneumatico*, < L. *pneumaticus*, < Gr. πνευματικός, relating to wind or air, < πνεῦμα, wind, air, breath, spirit, < πνεῖν, blow, breathe.] I. *a.* 1. Of or pertaining to air, or gases in general, or their properties; also, employing (compressed) air or other gas as a motive power: as, *pneumatic* experiments; a *pneumatic* engine. *Pneumatic* notes numerous instruments, machines, apparatus, etc., for experimenting on elastic fluids, or for working by means of the compression or exhaustion of air.

2. Consisting of or resembling air; having the properties of an elastic fluid; gaseous.

The *pneumatic* substance being in some bodies the native spirit of the body. *Bacon.*

3. Moved or played by means of air: as, a *pneumatic* instrument of music.—4. In *zoöl.*: (*a*) Filled with air; fitted to receive or contain air; pneumatized, as the air-cells or the bones of birds. (*b*) Of or pertaining to the respiratory system of any animal.—**Pneumatic action**, in *organ-building*, an action in which the keys, stop-knobs, or pedals merely make connections whereby the desired motions may be pneumatically effected. The pneumatic principle involved is either that of a small bellows which is inflated or emptied by the key or coupler, or that of a tube with pistons or valves at the ends which work sympathetically.—**Pneumatic bellows, coupler**, etc. See *pneumatic action*, above.—**Pneumatic cabinet**, in *med.*, an air-tight cabinet in which a patient is placed, so that the atmospheric pressure on the surface of the body may be increased or diminished.—**Pneumatic caisson.** See *caisson*, 3 (*c*).—**Pneumatic car, clock, conductor, drill.** See the nouns.—**Pneumatic despatch**, the transmission of articles from one point to another by air-pressure through a tube specially prepared for the purpose. Practically this is limited to the sending of small articles, as letters, telegraphic despatches, etc., for short distances, as between different stations in a large city. They are inclosed in a suitable box, which is propelled by compressed air through a tube from 2 to 3 inches in diameter; the return takes place by the atmospheric pressure, the air in the tube being exhausted at the first station.—**Pneumatic-despatch tube**, a tube traversed by a car or carrier which receives and delivers letters or parcels at stations along a route. Motion is caused by pressure of air, which is either forced into the tube from behind the car or exhausted in front of it, or both simultaneously. Special devices have been contrived for perfecting the construction of the cars and for arresting them at the points desired. The Brisbane carrier is a hollow ball which rolls along the interior of the pneumatic tube.—**Pneumatic differ-**

entiation, in *med.*, the causing a patient to breathe air of a different tension from that which surrounds his body.—**Pneumatic duct**, in *comp. anat.* See *ductus pneumaticus*, under *ductus*.—**Pneumatic elevator, excavator, gun**, etc. See the nouns.—**Pneumatic jig**, in *mining*, an air-jig; a jig in which the separation is effected by blasts of air instead of an intermittent current of water.—**Pneumatic organ.** See *organ*1.—**Pneumatic paradox**, that peculiar exhibition of atmospheric pressure which retains a valve on its seat under a pressure of gas, allowing only a film of gas to escape.—**Pneumatic pen.** See *pen*2.—**Pneumatic philosophy**†, the science of metaphysics or psychology; pneumatology.—**Pneumatic physicians**, a school of physicians, at the head of which was Athenæus, who made health and disease to consist in the different proportions of a fancied spiritual principle, called *pneuma*, from those of the other elementary principles.—**Pneumatic pile.** (*a*) A tube open at the lower or penetrating end, and closed from the air at the top, but communicating with a receiver from which air is exhausted. The pressure of the air acts to force the pile downward, and at the same time the silt within it is pressed upward and discharged into the receiver. (*b*) A caisson within which compressed air excludes the water, permitting necessary operations to be carried on inside it.—**Pneumatic spring, tube**, etc. See the nouns.—**Pneumatic trough**, a form of trough used by the physicist or chemist in experiments with gases. By its use the gas can be collected in a bell-jar or other receptacle over a surface of water or mercury.

II. *n.* 1. In *organ-building*, one of the members of a pneumatic action, whether a bellows or a tube. See *pneumatic action*, above.—2. Same as *pneumatology*, 2, where see quotation.

pneumatical (nū-mat'i-kal), *a.* and *n.* [< *pneumatic* + *-al.*] I. *a.* Same as *pneumatic*.

> This body then accompanying the soul he calls *pneumatical*, that is (not spiritual in the Scripture sense, but) spirituous, vaporous, or airy.
> *Cudworth*, Intellectual System, p. 785.

II.† *n.* A vaporous substance; a gas. *Bacon.*

pneumatically (nū-mat'i-kal-i), *adv.* By means of pneumatic force or of some pneumatic contrivance: as, *pneumatically* sunk caissons.

pneumaticity (nū-ma-tis'i-ti), *n.* [< *pneumatic* + *-ity.*] The state of being pneumatic, or hollow and filled with air; capacity of being inflated with air; inflation by air: applied to air-passages of animals, the hollow bones of birds, etc.

pneumatics (nū-mat'iks), *n.* [Pl. of *pneumatic*: see *-ics.*] 1. That branch of physics which treats of the mechanical properties of gases, and particularly of atmospheric air. Pneumatics treats of the weight, pressure, equilibrium, elasticity, density, condensation, rarefaction, resistance, motion, etc., of gases; it treats of them also considered as media of sound (acoustics), and as vehicles of heat, moisture, etc. It also comprises the description of those machines which depend for their action chiefly on the pressure and elasticity of air, as the various kinds of pumps, artificial fountains, etc.

2†. The doctrine of spiritual substances; pneumatology.

pneumatize (nū'ma-tiz), *v. t.*; pret. and pp. *pneumatized*, ppr. *pneumatizing*. [< *pneumat(ic)* + *-ize.*] To fill with air; render pneumatic, as bones. *Coues*, Key to N. A. Birds, p. 135.

pneumatocyst (nū'ma-tō-sist), *n.* [< Gr. πνεῦμα(τ-), air, + κύστις, bladder: see *cyst.*] 1. The air-sac, float, or pneumatophore of an oceanic hydrozoan or siphonophorous hydromedusan; one of the several appendages of the stem of these organisms, serving to buoy them in the water. See cuts under *Athorybia* and *Hydrozoa*. When pneumatocysts are wanting, they may be replaced by a general inflation of the stem, called then a *somatocyst*.

2. In *ornith.*, an air-sac or air-space; one of the cavities in a bird's body filled with air. *Coues.*

pneumatocystic (nū'ma-tō-sis'tik), *a.* [< *pneumatocyst* + *-ic.*] Of or having the character of a pneumatocyst, in any sense.

pneumatogram (nū'ma-tō-gram), *n.* [< Gr. πνεῦμα(τ-), breath, + γράμμα, a writing: see *gram*2.] A tracing of respiratory movements.

pneumatographic (nū'ma-tō-graf'ik), *a.* [< *pneumatograph-y* + *-ic.*] Of or pertaining to pneumatography: as, a *pneumatographic* communication; a *pneumatographic* medium.

pneumatography (nū-ma-tog'ra-fi), *n.* [< Gr. πνεῦμα(τ-), wind (in def. 1, a spirit), + -γραφία, < γράφειν, write.] 1. So-called spirit-writing, independent of the hand of a medium or other material instrument. Also called *independent writing* and *direct writing*.—2. The observing and descriptive stage of pneumatology (sense 3). *O. T. Mason*, Smithsonian Report, 1881, p. 500.

pneumatological (nū'ma-tō-loj'i-kal), *a.* [< *pneumatolog-y* + *-ic-al.*] Pertaining to pneumatology.

pneumatologist (nū-ma-tol'ō-jist), *n.* [< *pneumatolog-y* + *-ist.*] One versed in pneumatology.

pneumatology (nū-ma-tol'ō-ji), *n.* [< Gr. πνεῦμα(τ-), air, + -λογία, < λέγειν, speak: see *-ology.*] 1†. The doctrine of or a treatise on the properties of elastic fluids; pneumatics.—2. The branch of philosophy which treats of the nature and operations of mind or spirit, or a treatise on it.

> The terms Psychology and *Pneumatology*, or Pneumatic, are not equivalent. The latter word was used for the doctrine of spirit in general, which was subdivided into three branches, as it treated of the three orders of spiritual substances—God, Angels and Devils, and Man.
> *Sir W. Hamilton*, Metaphysics, vi., foot-note.

3. The study of the beliefs, practices, and organizations of men with reference to a supposed world of spirits; spiritual philosophy.

> Various terms have been suggested, as comparative mythology, spiritology, *pneumatology*, daimonology, &c.
> *O. T. Mason*, Smithsonian Report, 1881, p. 500.

4. In *theol.*, the doctrine of the Holy Spirit.

> The *pneumatology* of Ephesians resembles that of John, as the christology of Colossians resembles the christology of John.
> *Schaff*, Hist. Christ. Church, I. § 95.

Pneumatomachian (nū'ma-tō-mā'ki-an), *n.* and *a.* [< Gr. πνευματομάχος, hostile to the Holy Spirit, < πνεῦμα(τ-), spirit, + μάχεσθαι, quarrel.] I. *n.* An adversary of the Holy Ghost; one who denies the existence, personality, or godhead of the Holy Spirit; specifically, one of a sect or party, or group or succession of parties and sects, in the fourth century holding such doctrines. The Pneumatomachians in general taught that the Holy Ghost is a creature, a ministering spirit. Some combined this view with the Arian view that God the Son is a creature, and a few taught the extreme doctrine that the Spirit is the creature of a creature (the Son). Most of them, however, accepted the Homoiousian doctrine of the person of the Son, and these were known as *Macedonians* or *Marathonians*, and also as *Semi-Arians*—the Semi-Arians having as a whole adopted these views. The views of the Pneumatomachians were developed out of Arianism, after the Nicene Council (A. D. 325), and first showed themselves distinctly about 358. The heresy declined rapidly after the Constantinopolitan Council of 381.

II. *a.* Pertaining to the Pneumatomachians.

pneumatometer (nū-ma-tom'e-tėr), *n.* [< Gr. πνεῦμα(τ-), air, breath, + μέτρον, measure.] An instrument for measuring the quantity of air inhaled into the lungs at a single inspiration and given out at a single expiration; a pulmometer; a spirometer. Also called *pneumometer*, *pneumonometer*.

pneumatometry (nū-ma-tom'et-ri), *n.* [As *pneumatometer* + *-y*3.] The measurement of the air inspired or expired, as with a pneumatometer.

pneumatophonic (nū'ma-tō-fon'ik), *a.* [< *pneumatophon-y* + *-ic.*] Of or pertaining to pneumatophony. [Rare.]

pneumatophony (nū'ma-tō-fō-ni), *n.* [< Gr. πνεῦμα(τ-), spirit, + φωνή, voice.] So-called spirit-speaking; the supposed production of articulate sounds, resembling the human voice or speech, and conveying intelligence, by disembodied spirits. [Rare.]

pneumatophore (nū'ma-tō-fōr), *n.* [< Gr. πνεῦμα(τ-), air, + -φόρος, < φέρειν = E. *bear*1. Cf. LGr. πνευματόφορος, borne by the wind, also inspired.] A pneumatocyst, or a structure which supports such a float; especially, the proximal dilatation of the cœnosarc or hydrosome of the *Physophoridæ*. See cuts under *Athorybia* and *Hydrozoa*.

pneumatophorous (nū-ma-tof'ō-rus), *a.* [< *pneumatophore* + *-ous.*] In *zoöl.*, bearing a pneumatocyst; pertaining to a pneumatophore, or having its character.

pneumatosic (nū-ma-tō'sik), *a.* [< *pneumatosis* + *-ic.*] Affected with pneumatosis.

pneumatosis (nū-ma-tō'sis), *n.* [NL., < Gr. πνευμάτωσις, a blowing up, inflation, < πνευματοῦν, blow up, fill with wind, < πνεῦμα(τ-), wind: see *pneumatic*.] A morbid accumulation of gas in any part of the body. See *emphysema*.

pneumatothorax (nū'ma-tō-thō'raks), *n.* Same as *pneumothorax*.

pneumectomy (nū-mek'tō-mi), *n.* [For *pneumonectomy*, < Gr. πνεύμων, lung, + ἐκτομή, excision.] Excision of a portion of a lung.

pneumo-. In the following compounds of Greek πνεύμων, lung, *pneumo-* is short for the proper form *pneumono-*.

pneumoactinomycosis (nū-mō-ak"ti-nō-mi-kō'sis), *n.* [NL., < Gr. πνεύμων, lung, + NL. *actinomycosis*.] Actinomycosis of the lung.

Pneumobranchia (nū-mō-brang'ki-ä), *n. pl.* [NL., < Gr. πνεύμων, lung, + βράγχια, gills.] In Gray's classification (1840), same as *Pneumobranchiata*, 3.

Pneumobranchiata (nū-mō-brang-ki-ā'tä), *n. pl.* [NL., < Gr. πνεύμων, lung, + NL. *Branchiata*.] 1. An order of gastropods, including those which breathe air in a closed chamber lined with pulmonic vessels: applied by J. E. Gray to the typical pulmonates or pulmonifers, and including most of the inoperculate land-shells as well as the fresh-water forms related to them.—2. In Lamarck's classification (1819), a section of gastropods, containing his family *Limacea*.—3. In Gray's classification (1821), a subclass of *Gasteropodophora*, comprising all terrestrial gastropods, and divided into *Inoperculata* and *Operculata*.

pneumocace (nū-mok'a-sē), *n.* [< Gr. πνεύμων, lung, + κακή, badness, < κακός, bad.] Gangrene of the lungs.

pneumocarcinoma (nū-mō-kär-si-nō'mä), *n.* [NL., < Gr. πνεύμων, lung, + L. *carcinoma*.] Carcinoma of the lungs.

pneumocele (nū'mō-sēl), *n.* Same as *pneumonocele*.

pneumoconiosis (nū-mō-kō-ni-ō'sis), *n.* Same as *pneumonoconiosis*. Also *pneumokoniosis*.

pneumoderm (nū'mō-dėrm), *n.* [< Gr. πνεύμων, lung, + δέρμα, skin.] A gymnosomatous pteropod of the family *Pneumodermidæ*.

pneumoderma1 (nū-mō-dėr'mä), *n.* [NL., < Gr. πνεῦμα, air, + δέρμα, skin.] Subcutaneous emphysema.

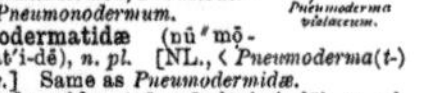
Pneumoderma violaceum.

Pneumoderma2 (nū-mō-dėr'mä), *n.* [NL. (Péron and Lesueur, 1810), < Gr. πνεύμων, lung, + δέρμα, skin.] A genus of gymnosomatous pteropods, typical of the *Pneumodermonidæ*, in which processes of the integument perform the function of gills. Also called *Pneumodermis*, *Pneumodermon*, *Pneumodermum*, *Pneumonodermum*.

Pneumodermatidæ (nū"mō-dėr-mat'i-dē), *n. pl.* [NL., < *Pneumoderma(t-)* + *-idæ.*] Same as *Pneumodermidæ*.

Pneumodermidæ (nū-mō-dėr'mi-dē), *n. pl.* [NL., < *Pneumoderma*2 + *-idæ.*] A family of gymnosomatous pteropods, typified by the genus *Pneumoderma*, having the head and mouth tentaculate. They have a specialized branchial apparatus consisting of at least a lateral gill on one (right) side and generally a posterior gill, suckers on the ventral side of the protrusible anterior part of the buccal cavity, and a jaw. Twelve or more species, of three genera, are known. Also called *Pneumodermatidæ*, *Pneumodermonidæ*, *Pneumonodermatidæ*.

Pneumodermis (nū-mō-dėr'mis), *n.* [NL.] Same as *Pneumoderma*2. *Oken.*

Pneumodermon (nū-mō-dėr'mon), *n.* [NL. (Lamarck, 1819): see *Pneumoderma*2.] Same as *Pneumoderma*2.

Pneumodermonidæ (nū"mō-dėr-mon'i-dē), *n. pl.* [NL., < *Pneumodermon* + *-idæ.*] Same as *Pneumodermidæ*.

pneumoenteritis (nū-mō-en-te-rī'tis), *n.* [NL., < Gr. πνεύμων, lung, + ἔντερον, intestine, + *-itis.*] Hog-cholera; swine-plague. See *cholera*.

pneumogastric (nū-mō-gas'trik), *a.* and *n.* [< Gr. πνεύμων, lung, + γαστήρ, stomach.] I. *a.* Pertaining to the lungs and the stomach, or to the functions of respiration and digestion: specifically, in anatomy, noting several nervous structures.—**Pneumogastric ganglion.** See *ganglion*.—**Pneumogastric lobule.** Same as *flocculus*, 2.—**Pneumogastric plexus.** See *gastric plexus* (under *plexus*), and *vagus*.

II. *n.* The pneumogastric nerve. See *vagus*.

pneumogram (nū'mō-gram), *n.* [< Gr. πνεύμων, lung, + γράμμα, a writing: see *gram*2.] The tracing yielded by the pneumograph.

pneumograph (nū'mō-graf), *n.* [< Gr. πνεύμων, lung, + γράφειν, write.] In *pathol.*, same as *stethograph*.

pneumographic (nū-mō-graf'ik), *a.* [< *pneumograph-y* + *-ic.*] Descriptive of the lungs and air-passages, or the organs of respiration.

pneumography (nū-mog'ra-fi), *n.* [< Gr. πνεύμων, lung, + -γραφία, < γράφειν, write.] 1. Descriptive pneumology; a treatise on or description of the lungs and air-passages, or organs of respiration.—2. The recording of the movements of respiration.

pneumohemothorax (nū-mō-hem-ō-thō'raks), *n.* [NL., < Gr. πνεῦμα, air, + αἷμα, blood, + θώραξ, chest.] The presence of gas and blood or bloody serum in the pleural cavity.

pneumohydrothorax (nū-mō-hi-drō-thō'raks), *n.* [NL., < Gr. πνεῦμα, air, + ὕδωρ (ὑδρ-), water, + θώραξ, chest.] The presence of gas and serous liquid in the pleural cavity.

pneumological (nū-mō-loj'i-kal), *a.* [< *pneumolog-y* + *-ic-al.*] Of or pertaining to pneumology.

pneumology (nū-mol'ọ-ji), *n.* [< Gr. πνεύμων, lung, + -λογία, < λέγειν, speak: see *-ology.*] The sum of scientific knowledge concerning the lungs and air-passages, or the organs and processes of respiration.

pneumometer (nū-mom'o-tėr), *n.* Same as *pneumatometer.*

pneumometry (nū-mom'et-ri), *n.* Same as *pneumatometry.*

pneumomycosis (nū'mọ-mi-kō'sis), *n.* [NL., < Gr. πνεύμων, lung, + μύκης, fungus, + *-osis.*] The presence of fungi in the lungs. Also *pneumonomycosis.*

pneumonalgia (nū-mọ-nal'ji-ạ), *n.* [NL., < Gr. πνεύμων, lung, + ἄλγος, pain.] Pain in the lungs.

pneumonatelectasis (nū-mọ-nat-e-lek'tā-sis), *n.* [NL., < Gr. πνεύμων, lung, + NL. *atelectasis.*] Atelectasis of the lungs.

pneumonedema (nū'mọ-nē-dē'mạ), *n.* [< Gr. πνεύμων, lung, + οἴδημα, swelling.] Edema of the lungs; pulmonary edema.

pneumonia (nū-mō'ni-ạ), *n.* [= F. *pneumonie* = Sp. Pg. *pneumonia*, < NL. *pneumonia*, < Gr. πνευμονία, Attic also πλευμονία, a disease of the lungs, < πνεύμων, Attic also πλεύμων, = L. *pulmo(n-)*, a lung, < πνεῖν, breathe: see *pneumatic.* Cf. *pulmonary.*] Inflammation of the tissues of the lung, as distinct from inflammation of the bronchial tubes (bronchitis) and from inflammation of the serous covering of the lungs (pleuritis). Also called *pneumonitis.*—**Bilious pneumonia,** croupous pneumonia with icterus.—**Catarrhal pneumonia,** pneumonia in which the exudate contains mucin and pus, but does not coagulate. Also called *bronchopneumonia* and *lobular pneumonia.*—**Central pneumonia,** pneumonia of the central part of a lung.—**Cheesy pneumonia,** bronchopneumonia with consolidation of more or less extensive areas of lung-tissue, with degeneration resulting in the formation of cheese-like masses of debris. Such cases are usually if not always tuberculous, and are usually designated as *phthisis.*—**Chronic interstitial lobular pneumonia,** a chronic pneumonia with excessive increase of the interstitial connective tissue. Such cases are often tuberculous in origin, and are sometimes called *fibroid phthisis.*—**Croupous pneumonia,** pneumonia in which the exudate coagulates from the contained fibrin. Also called *fibrinous pneumonia*, or, from its distribution to one or more lobes in their entirety, *lobar pneumonia.*—**Desquamative pneumonia,** catarrhal pneumonia in which the alveolar epithelium is shed in considerable quantity.—**Intermittent pneumonia,** croupous pneumonia with frequent marked remissions of pyrexia, not pertaining to malarial poisoning.—**Lobular pneumonia,** a pneumonia which in its distribution affects the areas belonging to small bronchi scattered here and there, as distinct from lobar pneumonia, in which entire lobes are affected. Also called *catarrhal pneumonia* from the character of the exudate, and *bronchopneumonia* because it invades the lung-tissue from the bronchi, which are primarily affected.—**Pneumonia migrans,** a croupous pneumonia which invades progressively from day to day adjacent parts of the lungs.—**Typhoid pneumonia,** croupous pneumonia with exceptionally severe general effects, exhibited in great prostration, delirium, dry tongue, enlarged spleen, often slight icterus, and albuminuria.

pneumonic (nū-mon'ik), *a.* and *n.* [< Gr. πνευμονικός, pertaining to the lungs, < πνεύμων, lung: see *pneumonia.* Cf. *pulmonic.*] **I.** *a.* **1.** Pertaining to the lungs; pulmonary.—**2.** Pertaining to pneumonia; affected with pneumonia; pulmonitic: as, *pneumonic* patients.

II. *n.* A remedy used in diseases of the lungs.

pneumonitic (nū-mọ-nit'ik), *a.* [< *pneumonitis* + *-ic.*] Pertaining to or of the nature of pneumonitis.

pneumonitis (nū-mọ-nī'tis), *n.* [NL., < Gr. πνεύμων, lung, + *-itis.*] Inflammation of the lungs; pneumonia.

pneumonocarcinoma (nū'mọ-nọ-kär-si-nō'mạ), *n.* [NL., < Gr. πνεύμων, lung, + NL. *carcinoma*, carcinoma.] Carcinoma of the lungs.

pneumonocele (nū'mọ-nọ-sēl), *n.* [< Gr. πνεύμων, lung, + κήλη, tumor.] Hernia of the lung, as through an opening in the diaphragm.

Pneumonochlamyda (nū'mọ-nọ-klam'i-dạ), *n. pl.* [NL., < Gr. πνεύμων, lung, + χλαμύς (χλαμυδ-), a cloak, mantle.] A suborder of *Gasteropoda*, having the pallial chamber converted into a lung-sac, but no gills, as in the families *Cyclostomidæ, Helicinidæ, Aciculidæ*, etc.

pneumonochlamydate (nū'mọ-nọ-klam'i-dāt), *a.* [< *Pneumonochlamyda* + *-ate*[1].] Belonging to the *Pneumonochlamyda.*

pneumonocirrhosis (nū'mọ-nọ-si-rō'sis), *n.* [NL., < Gr. πνεύμων, lung, + NL. *cirrhosis.*] Cirrhosis of the lungs.

pneumonoconiosis (nū'mọ-nọ-kō-ni-ō'sis), *n.* [NL., < Gr. πνεύμων, lung, + κόνις, dust, + *-osis.*] Inflammatory disease of the lungs due to inhalation of irritating particles.

Pneumonoderma (nū'mọ-nọ-dėr'mạ), *n.* [NL.] Same as *Pneumoderma*[2].

pneumonodynia (nū'mọ-nọ-din'i-ạ), *n.* [NL., < Gr. πνεύμων, lung, + ὀδύνη, pain.] Pain in the lungs.

pneumonomelanosis (nū'mọ-nō-mel-ạ-nō'sis), *n.* [NL., < Gr. πνεύμων, lung, + NL. *melanosis.*] Pulmonary melanosis, or anthracosis.

pneumonometer (nū-mọ-nom'e-tėr), *n.* [< Gr. πνεύμων, lung, + μέτρον, measure.] Same as *pneumatometer.*

pneumonophthisis (nū'mō-nof-thī'sis), *n.* [NL., < Gr. πνεύμων, lung, + φθίσις, consumption.] Pulmonary phthisis.

pneumonorrhagia (nū'mọ-nọ-rā'ji-ạ), *n.* [NL., < Gr. πνεύμων, lung, + -ραγία, < ῥηγνύναι, break, burst.] Same as *pneumorrhagia.*

pneumony (nū'mọ-ni), *n.* Same as *pneumonia.*

Pneumoötoka (nū-mọ-ot'ọ-kạ), *n. pl.* Same as *Pneumotoca.*

pneumoötokous (nū-mọ-ot'ọ-kus), *a.* Same as *pneumotocous.*

pneumopericarditis (nū-mọ-per″i-kär-dī'tis), *n.* [NL., < *pneumo(pericardium)* + *pericarditis.*] Pneumopericardium with pericarditis.

pneumopericardium (nū-mọ-per-i-kär'di-um), *n.* [NL., < Gr. πνεῦμα, air, + περικάρδιον, pericardium: see *pericardium.*] The presence of gas in the pericardial cavity.

pneumophthisis (nū-mof-thī'sis), *n.* [NL., < Gr. πνεύμων, lung, + φθίσις, consumption: see *phthisis.*] Pulmonary phthisis.

pneumopleuritis (nū″mọ-plọ-rī'tis), *n.* [NL., < Gr. πνεύμων, lung, + πλευρῖτις, pleuritis: see *pleuritis.*] Inflammation of the lungs and the pleura; pleuropneumonia.

pneumopyothorax (nū-mọ-pī-ọ-thō'raks), *n.* [NL., < Gr. πνεῦμα, air, + πύον, pus, + θώραξ, the chest: see *thorax.*] The presence of gas and pus in the pleural cavity. Also called *pyopneumothorax.*

pneumorrhagia (nū-mọ-rā'ji-ạ), *n.* [NL., < Gr. πνεύμων, lung, + -ραγία, < ῥηγνύναι, break.] Pulmonary hemorrhage.—**Diffuse pneumorrhagia,** an escape of blood into the substance of the lung, with laceration. Also called *pulmonary apoplexy.*

pneumoskeletal (nū-mọ-skel'e-tal), *a.* [< *pneumoskeleton* + *-al.*] Of or pertaining to the pneumoskeleton.

pneumoskeleton (nū-mō-skel'e-tọn), *n.* [< Gr. πνεύμων, lung, + σκελετόν, a dry body: see *skeleton.*] An exoskeleton or hard tegumentary structure developed in connection with a respiratory or pulmonary organ. Thus, the shell of a mollusk, being developed from the pallium or mantle, which has a respiratory function, constitutes a *pneumoskeleton.* *H. A. Nicholson.*

pneumothorax (nū-mọ-thō'raks), *n.* [NL., < Gr. πνεῦμα, air, + θώραξ, the chest: see *thorax.*] The presence of air in the pleural cavity. Also *pneumatothorax.*

Pneumotoca (nụ-mot'ọ-kạ), *n. pl.* [NL.: see *pneumotocous.*] A division of *Vertebrata*, including air-breathing oviparous vertebrates, as birds and reptiles. *Owen.*

pneumotocous (nụ-mot'ọ-kus), *a.* [< Gr. πνεύμων, lung, + ᾠοτόκος, egg-laying: see *oötocous.*] Breathing air and laying eggs, as a vertebrate; belonging to the *Pneumotoca.*

pneumotomy (nụ-mot'ọ-mi), *n.* [< Gr. πνεύμων, lung, + τομή, a cut, < τέμνειν, ταμεῖν, cut.] In *surg.*, incision into the lung, as for the evacuation of an abscess.

pneupome (nū'pōm), *n.* [For **pneumonopome*, < Gr. πνεύμων, lung, + πῶμα, lid.] An operculate pulmonate gastropod.

pnigalion (nī-gā'li-ọn), *n.* [< Gr. πνιγαλίων, the nightmare, cf. πνίξ, suffocation, < πνίγειν, choke.] In *med.*, an incubus; a nightmare.

Pnoëpyga (nō-e-pī'gạ), *n.* [NL. (Hodgson, 1844), < Gr. πνοή, breath, + πυγή, the rump.] A genus of birds of wren-like character, having booted tarsi, and very short tail-feathers hidden by their coverts, commonly referred to the family *Troglodytidæ.* There are several species, all Asiatic, as *P. squamata* (or *albiventer*), *P. pusilla*, and *P. caudata.* The genus had before been called *Tesia* by Hodgson, from the Nepålese name of some bird of this kind. The latest authority refers the genus to the *Timeliidæ.* *R. B. Sharpe*, Cat. Birds Brit. Mus., VI. 301.

Pnoëpyga albiventer.

Pnyx (niks), *n.* [Gr. πνύξ (gen. πυκνός), a place of assembly (see def.), < πυκνός, crowded, close.] A public place of assembly in ancient Athens, where the people met for the discussion of political affairs of the state; also, a popular assembly convened in this place.

po†, *n.* A Middle English form of *pea*[2].

P. O. An abbreviation: (*a*) of *post-office;* (*b*) (*naut.*) of *petty officer.*

Poa (pō'ạ), *n.* [NL. (Linnæus, 1737), < Gr. πόα, dial. ποία, ποίη, grass, esp. as fodder, an herb or plant.] A genus of grasses of the tribe *Festuceæ* and subtribe *Eufestuceæ*, characterized by the commonly two- to six-flowered spikelets in a lax panicle, the smooth grain free from the palets, and the keeled and obtuse awnless flowering glume with five nerves converging at the apex. There are 100, or according to some over 200, species, widely dispersed, few in the tropics, most abundant in north temperate regions. They are known in general as *meadow-grass* or *spear-grass.* Some are low annuals, as *P. annua*, the low spear-grass, abundant by American roadsides and paths in parks, and blooming in the south from midwinter onward. The other American species are perennials, with tufted stems, often tall, and soft leaves, flat or less often convolute. The genus contains several valuable hay- and pasture-grasses, of which the most important is *P. pratensis*, the Kentucky blue-grass, June-grass, etc. (See *blue-grass* and *meadow-grass.*) *P. amabilis* is cultivated under the name *love-grass*, *P. trivialis* as *bird-grass*, etc., and *P. cæspitosa* as *Australian grass.* For other species, see *bunch-grass, daggers* (under *dagger*[1], 6), *fowl-grass* (under *fowl*[1]), *June-grass, silver-grass, teff,* and *wire-grass.*

Flowering Plant of Kentucky blue-grass (*Poa pratensis*). *a*, a spikelet; *b*, the empty glumes; *c*, flowering glume, palet, and perfect flower.

Poaceæ (pọ-ā'sẹ-ē), *n. pl.* [NL. (R. Brown, 1814), < *Poa* + *-aceæ.*] A series or division of the order *Gramineæ*, the grasses, distinguished from the other similar division, *Paniceæ*, by the absence of a joint to the pedicel beneath the glumes, and by the presence of a stalk or empty glumes or imperfect flowers above the fertile flowers. It includes the larger part of the grasses, or about 200 genera (*Poa* being the type), in 7 tribes and 21 subtribes.

poach[1] (pōch), *v.* [Early mod. E. also *poatch, potch, poche, poch;* according to Cotgrave, who gives only the pp. *poché*, < OF. *pocher, poucher*, thrust, poke (given by Cotgrave 'thrust or dig out with the fingers'), F. *pocher*, hit (the eye, so as to give one a black eye), also OF. *pocher*, blur (with ink), < LG. *poken*, poke, thrust, = MD. *pochen*, thrust: see *poke*[1], of which *poach*[1] is thus ult. an assibilated form. Some refer this OF. *pocher, poucher*, to *pouce, poulce*, the thumb, < L. *pollex* (*pollic-*), the thumb: see *pollex.*] **I.** *trans.* **1†.** To poke; thrust; push; put.

> Pull out my heart: O! *poach* not out mine eyes.
> *Sylvester*, tr. of Du Bartas's Weeks, ii., The Decay.

> His [Charlemagne's] horse, *poching* one of his legs into some hollow ground, made way for the smoking water to break out, and gave occasion for the Emperor's building that city [Aix]. *Sir W. Temple*, On the United Provinces, i.

2. To stab; pierce; spear: as, to *poach* fish.

> They vse also to *poche* them [fish] with an instrument somewhat like the sammon-speare.
> *R. Carew*, Survey of Cornwall, p. 31.

3. To tread; break up or render slushy by frequent treading; mark with footprints.

> The cattle of the villagers . . . had *poached* into black mud the verdant tuft. *Scott.*

> The *poach'd* filth that floods the middle street.
> *Tennyson*, Merlin and Vivien.

II. *intrans.* **1.** To make a thrust in or as in sword-play.

> For where
> I thought to crush him in an equal force,
> True sword to sword, I'll *potch* [*potche*, folio 1623] at him
> some way,
> Or wrath or craft may get him. *Shak.*, Cor., i. 10. 15.

> To speak truly of latter times, they [the Spaniards] have rather *poached* and offered at a number of enterprises than maintained any constantly. *Bacon*, War with Spain.

2. To be penetrable, as soft muddy or marshy ground; be damp and swampy.

> Chalky and clay lands burn in hot weather, chap in summer, and *poach* in winter. *Mortimer*, Husbandry.

poach[2] (pōch), *v.* [Formerly also *poch* (and *poche*?); appar. < OF. *pocher*, found in the phrase "*pocher le labeur d'autruy*, to poch into, or incroach upon, another man's imployment, practice in trade" (Cotgrave), where the exact sense is undetermined; it might be translated 'to pocket another man's labor' (*pocher*, pocket, < *poche*, a pocket, pouch: see *pouch*, *poke*[2]); or *pocher* may be identical with *pocher*, thrust: see *poach*[1]. Cf. OF. *pocher*, imitate, counterfeit.] **I.** *intrans.* To intrude or encroach upon another's preserves for the purpose of stealing game; kill and carry off game in violation of law.

His greatest fault is he hunts too much in the purlieus; would he would leave off *poaching!*
Beau. and Fl., Philaster, iv. 1.

II. *trans.* To trespass upon, especially for the purpose of killing and stealing game.

So shameless, so abandoned are their ways,
They *poach* Parnassus, and lay claim for praise.
Garth, Claremont.

But he, triumphant spirit! all things dared,
He *poach'd* the wood, and on the warren snared.
Crabbe, Works, I. 67.

poach[3] (pōch), *v. t.* [Early mod. E. also *poatch*, *potch*, *poche*, *poch*; < F. *pocher*, poach (eggs), first appar. in the pp., *œuf poché*, a poached egg, perhaps orig. an egg 'scooped out' (or simply 'broken'), the verb being then a particular use of OF. *pocher*, thrust, poke, dig out with the fingers: see *poach*[1]. Cf. *poach*[2], perhaps of the same ult. origin.] To cook by breaking the shell and dropping the contents whole into boiling water: said of eggs.

Tho. Has drest his excellence such a dish of eggs ——
P. jun. What, *potched?*
B. Jonson, Staple of News, iii. 1.

Is a man therefore bound in the morning to *potcht* eggs and vinnegar? *Milton*, On Def. of Humb. Remonst.

poachard†, *n.* An obsolete form of *pochard*.

poacher[1] (pō'chėr), *n.* [< *poach*[2] + *-er*[1].] **1.** One who poaches; one who intrudes on the preserves of another for the purpose of stealing game; one who kills game unlawfully.—**2.** The sea-poacher, a fish.—**3.** The widgeon, *Mareca americana*: so called from its habit of seizing the food for which other ducks have dived. *G. Trumbull.* [Michigan.]

poacher[2] (pō'chėr), *n.* [< *poach*[3] + *-er*[1].] A contrivance for poaching eggs.

poachiness (pō'chi-nes), *n.* The state of being poachy.

The vallies, because of the *poachiness*, they keep for grass. *Mortimer*, Husbandry.

poachy (pō'chi), *a.* [< *poach*[1] + *-y*[1].] Wet and soft; easily penetrated, as by the feet of cattle: said of land.

But marsh lands lay not up till April, except your marshes be very *poachy*. *Mortimer*, Husbandry.

Poacites (pō-a-sī'tēz), *n.* [NL., < Gr. πόα, grass, + *-c-* (insignificant) + *-ite*[2].] A generic name, originated by Brongniart, under which have been described a large number of leaves of fossil plants supposed to belong to the *Gramineæ*.

poad-milk (pōd'milk), *n.* The first milk given by cows after calving; beestings. *Halliwell.* [Prov. Eng.]

poak[1]†, *v.* An obsolete spelling of *poke*[1].

poak[2] (pōk), *n.* [Also *poake*; origin obscure.] Waste arising from the preparation of skins, composed of hair, lime, oil, etc. It is used as manure.

pocan (pō'kan), *n.* [See *poke*[4].] The poke or pokeweed, *Phytolacca decandra*.

pocard†, *n.* An obsolete form of *pochard*.

Bosca [It.], a bird called a *pocard*. *Florio*, 1598.

poccoon, *n.* Same as *puccoon*.

pochard (pō'chärd), *n.* [Also *poker*, and formerly *poachard*, *pocard*; said to be a var. of *poacher*. Cf. *poacher*, 3.] A duck, *Fuligula* or *Æthyia ferina*, belonging to the family *Anatidæ* and subfamily *Fuligulinæ*, more fully called the *red-headed* or *red-eyed pochard*, also *dunbird*. This duck is very common in Europe and many other parts of the Old World, and a variety or very closely related species, *F.* or *Æ. americana*, is equally so in North America, and known as the *redhead*. In the male the head is puffy, and with the neck is rich chestnut-red with coppery or bronzy reflections. The lower neck, foreparts of the body above and below, and rump and tail-coverts are black. The back is white, finely vermiculated with wavy or zigzag black lines. The bill is dull-blue with a black belt at the end, and the feet are grayish-blue with dusky webs. The eyes are orange. The female has the head dull-brown. The length is from 20 to 23 inches, the extent of wings about 33 inches. The pochard is a near relative of the canvasback. The name is extended to some or all of the species of *Fuligula* in a broad sense: as, the white-eyed *pochard*. See cuts under *Nyroca*, *redhead*, and *scaup*.

poche[1]† (pōch), *v.* An obsolete form of *poach*[1].

poche[2]†, *n.* A Middle English form of *poke*[2], *pouch*.

pochette (pō-shet'), *n.* [F.] A small violin: see *kit*[5].

pock[1] (pok), *n.* [< ME. *pokke*, pl. *pokkes*, < AS. *poc* (*pocc-*), a pustule, = MD. *pocke*, D. *pok* = MLG. *pocke*, *poche*, LG. *pokken*, pl., = G. dial. *pfocke* (G. *pocke*, < LG.), a pustule, G. *pocken*, pl., smallpox; cf. Gael. *pucaid*, a pimple, Ir. *pucoid* (?), a pustule, *pucadh*, a swelling up; akin to *poke*[2], a bag. Hence pl. *pocks*, taken, esp. in *small pocks*, as a singular, and spelled disguisedly *pox*.] **1.** A pustule raised on the surface of the body in an eruptive disease, as the smallpox.

Of *pokkes* and of scabbe, and every sore,
Shal every sheep be hool that of this welle
Drinketh a draughte.
Chaucer, Prol. to Pardoner's Tale, l. 72.

2. A pox; an eruptive disease, as smallpox. [Obsolete or vulgar.]

If God punish the world with an evil *pock*, they immediately paint a block and call it Job, to heal the disease.
Tyndale, Ans. to Sir T. More, etc. (Parker Soc., 1850), p. 105.

Glad you got through the *pock* so well — it takes a second time, some say. *S. Judd*, Margaret, ii. 5.

As soon as ever the *pock* began to decay it took away my eyes altogether.
Mayhew, London Labour and London Poor, I. 451.

pock[2], *n.* A Scotch form of *poke*[2].

pockarred† (pok'ärd), *a.* [< *pock*[1] + *arr*[1] + *-ed*[2].] Pitted with the smallpox; pock-pitted.

pock-broken (pok'brō″kn), *a.* Broken out or marked with smallpox.

pocked (pokt), *a.* [< *pock*[1] + *-ed*[2].] Pitted; marked with pustules, or pits left by them, or with other small lesions, suggesting the appearance of the skin during or after smallpox.

The posterior parts of both lungs were *pocked* with tubercle in the softening stage. *Lancet*, No. 3435, p. 1314.

And of this tufty, flaggy ground, *pocked* with bogs and boglets, one special nature is that it will not hold impressions. *R. D. Blackmore*, Lorna Doone, lix.

pocket (pok'et), *n.* [< ME. *pocket*, *poket*, < AF. **poquet* (Norm. *pouquet*), OF. assibilated *pochet*, *pouchet*, m., also *pochette* (F. *pochette*), f., a pocket, dim. of *poque*, OF. assibilated *poche*, a poke, pocket: see *poke*[2], *pouch*.] **1.** A small pouch or bag; specifically, a small pouch inserted in a garment for carrying money or other small articles.

Cered *pokets*, sal peter, vitriole.
Chaucer, Prol. to Canon's Yeoman's Tale, l. 255.

He took a little horn out of his *pocket*,
And he blew 't baith loud and schill.
Lady Marjorie (Child's Ballads, II. 340).

A fellow that has but a groat in his *pocket* may have a stomach capable of a ten-shilling ordinary. *Congreve.*

About 25 lbs. or 35 lbs. of ungummed silk are enclosed in bags of coarse canvas, called *pockets*. *Ure*, Dict., I. 392.

2. That which is carried in the pocket; money; means; financial resources.

For tho there were Fowls to be bought at every house where I lay, yet my *pocket* would not reach them.
Dampier, Voyages, II. i. 93.

They [shippers] have been more cautious since, but have more than once again glutted our markets, and been punished in *pocket*. *Quarterly Rev.*, CXLV. 315.

3. One of the small bags or nets at the corners and sides of some billiard-tables.

At the commencement of the last century the billiard-table was square, having only three *pockets* for the balls to run in, situated on one of the sides.
Strutt, Sports and Pastimes, p. 396.

4. Any cavity or opening forming a receptacle: as, a brace-*pocket*, a post-*pocket*, etc.—**5.** In a window fitted with sashes, the hole for a pulley.—**6.** In *mining*, an irregular cavity filled with veinstone and ore; a swelling of the lode in an irregular manner, in which a more or less isolated mass of ore occurs. A pockety lode is one in which the ore is thus distributed, instead of being disseminated somewhat uniformly through the body of the lode.

7. A glen or hollow among mountains. [U. S.]

In many of the *pockets* or glens in the sides of the hill the trees grow to some little height.
T. Roosevelt, Hunting Trips, p. 136.

8. A certain quantity of hops, wool, etc., equal to about 168 pounds.—**9.** In *racing slang*, a position in a race where one contestant is surrounded by three or more others, so that, owing to the impeding of his advance, he has no chance to win.—**10.** In *zoöl.* and *anat.*: (*a*) A blind sac; a sac-shaped cavity. (*b*) The external cheek-pouch of a rodent, as of the *Geomyidæ* and *Saccomyidæ*. See cuts under *Geomyidæ* and *Perognathus*. (*c*) The abdominal pouch of a marsupial. (*d*) The abdominal cavity of a halibut or other fish.—**11.** The trap of a weir, in which the fish are retained or caught. The fish pass from the little pound into the pocket, which is a frame about 16 feet long and 10 feet wide, with sides of netting and a board floor. The fish are left in the pocket by the receding tide, and are taken out at low water. In a deep-water weir the fish are not left by the tide, but must be lifted out with a seine or purse-net. See *weir*.—**Patch-pocket**, a pocket made by sewing a piece of stuff upon the outside of a garment, forming one side of the pocket, the other side being formed by the material of the garment itself. The piece so sewed on is usually of the same material as the garment.—**Pocket borough.** See *borough*[1].—**Pocket veto**, a mode of veto of a bill by a president, governor, or other executive officer, employed at the end of a legislative session. If the President does not interpose the ordinary veto, a bill becomes law at the expiration of ten days; but if the bill was passed within ten days of the adjournment of Congress, the President may retain ("pocket") the bill, which is thus killed at the end of the session without the interposition of a direct veto, and without risking the chances of its passage over the veto. [U. S.]—**To be in pocket**, to have gain or profit.—**To be out of pocket**, to expend or lose money: as, to *be out of pocket* by a transaction.—**To have** or **carry in one's pocket**, to have complete control of.

Dr. Proudie had interest with the government, and the man *carried*, as it were, Dr. Proudie *in his pocket*.
Trollope, Barchester Towers.

To pick one's pocket, to pick pockets, to steal from one's pocket; be in the habit of stealing from the pockets of others.

pocket (pok'et), *v. t.* [< *pocket*, *n.* Cf. F. *pocheter*, carry in the pocket.] **1.** To put in a pocket or in one's pocket: as, to *pocket* a ball in billiards; to *pocket* a penknife.

On one occasion he *pocketed* very complacently a gratuity of fifty pistoles. *Macaulay*, Hist. Eng., vii.

He locked the desk, *pocketed* all the property, and went.
Charlotte Brontë, Shirley, xxix.

2. To appropriate to one's self or for one's own use; take possession of.

They [kings] seized the goods of traders, sold them, and *pocketed* a large part of the proceeds.
H. Spencer, Social Statics, p. 463.

3. In *racing slang*, to surround in such a way as to leave no room for getting out or in front: as, he was *pocketed* at the beginning of the race.—**4.** To carry in or as in the pocket; specifically, of a president, governor, or other executive officer, to prevent (a bill) from becoming law by retaining it unsigned. See *pocket veto*, under *pocket*, *n.* [Colloq., U. S.]—**5.** To accept meekly or without protest or resentment; submit to tamely or without demand for redress, apology, etc.: as, to *pocket* an insult.

If I calmly *pocket* the abuse, I am laughed at.
Goldsmith, Citizen of the World, xix.

6. To conceal; give no indication of; suppress: as, to *pocket* one's pride.—**7.** To control or have the control of, as if carried in one's pocket: as, to *pocket* a borough.

They [the English] say they will *pocket* our carrying trade as well as their own. *Jefferson*, Correspondence, II. 11.

He [the poor white of Virginia] was fond of his State and its great men, and loyal to some one of the blood families who contended for the honor of *pocketing* the borough in which he voted. *Schouler*, Hist. U. S., I. 10.

8. In *mech.*, placed in a case or pocket: as, a *pocketed* valve. See *valve*.—**To pocket up.** (*a*) To put up in or as in a pocket; bag.

I'll step but up and fetch two handkerchiefs
To *pocket up* some sweetmeats.
Middleton, Women Beware Women, iii. 1.

Letting Time *pocket up* the larger life.
Lowell, Voyage to Vinland.

(*b*†) To submit tamely to; accept without protest or murmur.

Patience hath trained me to *pocket-up* more heinous indignities, and even to digest an age of iron.
G. Harvey, Four Letters, ii.

pocket-book (pok'et-bụk), *n.* **1.** A book to be carried in the pocket; a note-book.

Nor let your *Pocket-Book* two Hands contain.
Congreve, tr. of Ovid's Art of Love, iii.

2. A book worthy to be constantly used, small enough to be carried in the pocket.

La Rochefoucauld ranks among the scanty number of *pocket-books* to be read and re-read with ever new admiration, instruction, and delight. *Encyc. Brit.*, XIV. 318.

3. A small book or pouch, usually of flexible leather, divided into compartments, made for carrying money or memoranda in the pocket.—**4.** Pecuniary resources, especially of one person. [In the last two senses usually without a hyphen.]

pocket-cloth† (pok'et-klôth), *n.* A pocket-handkerchief.

Cannot I wipe mine eyes with the fair *pocket-cloth*, as if I wept for all your abominations?
Tom Brown, Works, I. 3. (*Davies.*)

pocket-dial (pok'et-dī″al), *n.* A portable sundial of small size. See *ring-dial*.

pocket-drop (pok'et-drop), *n.* *Theat.*, a drop-scene made to be doubled up so as to be taken out of sight, where the roof above the stage is low.

pocket-edition (pok'et-ē-dish'on), *n.* A book issued in a small size, as for convenience in carrying in the pocket.

pocket-flap (pok'et-flap), *n.* A narrow piece of cloth sewed above the opening of a pocket in a garment, and hanging over it like a small flounce.

pocketful (pok'et-fůl), *n.* [< *pocket* + *-ful.*] Enough to fill a pocket; as much as a pocket will hold.

pocket-gopher (pok'et-gō'fėr), *n.* An American rodent quadruped of the family *Geomyidæ*: so called from the large pockets or external cheek-pouches. Also *pocket-rat*. See cut under *Geomyidæ*.

pocket-hammer (pok'et-ham'ėr), *n.* A hammer adapted for carrying in the pocket; a geologists' hammer.

pocket-handkerchief (pok'et-hang'kėr-chif), *n.* A handkerchief intended to be carried in the pocket.

pocketing-sleeve† (pok'et-ing-slēv), *n.* A large and loose sleeve worn in the fourteenth and fifteenth centuries.

Of the long *pocketting-sleeves* in the time of King Henry the fourth, Hocclive, a master of that age, sung.
Camden, Remains, Apparell.

pocket-judgment (pok'et-juj'ment), *n.* Formerly, in England, a recognizance given to secure a private debt, as distinguished from a recognizance taken as a public obligation. The Statute of Merchants, 13 Edward I., stat. 3, authorized recognizances to be taken for the securing of debts in certain cases, and allowed enforcement against property without the formality of a suit. A recognizance so taken was technically termed a *statute merchant*, and this, too, has been called a *pocket-judgment*.

pocket-knife (pok'et-nīf), *n.* A knife with one or more blades which fold into the handle, suitable for carrying in the pocket; loosely, a penknife.

pocket-lid (pok'et-lid), *n.* A pocket-flap.

pocket-money (pok'et-mun'i), *n.* Money for the pocket or for occasional or trivial expenses.

pocket-mouse (pok'et-mous), *n.* An American rodent quadruped of the family *Saccomyidæ*: so called from its pockets or external cheek-pouches. Various species are found in the United States, belonging to the genera *Dipodomys* and *Perognathus*. The larger kinds, which leap well, are also known as *kangaroo-mice* and *kangaroo-rats*. See cuts under *Dipodomys* and *Perognathus*.

pocket-net (pok'et-net), *n.* A fishing-net in which the fish are caught in certain special compartments or pockets.

pocket-piece (pok'et-pēs), *n.* A coin kept in the pocket and not spent, generally a coin that is not current.

pocket-pistol (pok'et-pis'tol), *n.* 1. A pistol designed to be carried in the pocket.—2. A small liquor-flask, arranged with a screw-stopper, or in other ways safely closed, and often fitted with a cup; a small traveling-flask. [Slang.]

He . . . swigged his *pocket-pistol*.
Naylor, Reynard the Fox, p. 42. (*Davies.*)

pocket-rat (pok'et-rat), *n.* Same as *pocket-gopher*.

pocket-relay (pok'et-rē-lā'), *n.* An instrument which can be carried in the pocket to make telegraphic connection at any point on a line. It is employed in case of accidents, etc., and hence is often called a *wrecking-instrument*.

pocket-sheriff (pok'et-sher'if), *n.* A sheriff appointed by the sole authority of the sovereign, and not one of the three nominated by the exchequer. [Eng.]

pockety (pok'et-i), *a.* [< *pocket* + *-y*[1].] In *mining*, noting a lode in which the ore occurs in pockets, or small irregular bunches, instead of being somewhat uniformly distributed through the mass of the veinstone.

pock-fretten† (pok'fret'n), *a.* Pock-marked; marked with smallpox; pitted with smallpox. *Richardson*, Clarissa Harlowe, VI. 137.

pock-house (pok'hous), *n.* A smallpox hospital. [Prov. U. S.]

A *Pock House* was established, . . . and a general beating up for patients was had throughout the region.
S. Judd, Margaret, ii. 6.

pockiness (pok'i-nes), *n.* The state of being pocky.

pockmanky, pockmanty (pok-mang'ki, -man'ti), *n.* Scotch corruptions of *portmanteau*.

pock-mark (pok'märk), *n.* A mark or scar made by the smallpox; a pock.

pock-marked (pok'märkt), *a.* Pitted or marked with smallpox, or with pits resembling those of smallpox; pock-pitted.

pock-pitted (pok'pit'ed), *a.* Pitted or marked with smallpox.

pock-pitten (pok'pit'n), *a.* Same as *pock-pitted*. *Tennyson*, Aylmer's Field. [Rare.]

pock-pudding (pok'pud'ing), *n.* A bag-pudding: sometimes applied to persons as a term of opprobrium. [Scotch.]

pockwood (pok'wůd), *n.* The lignum-vitæ, *Guaiacum officinale*.

pocky (pok'i), *a.* [< *pock*[1] + *-y*[1].] 1. Having pocks or pustules; infected with an eruptive distemper, but particularly with syphilis.

He might, forewarnd, have left his *pockie* drabbes.
Times' Whistle (E. E. T. S.), p. 80.

2. Vile; rascally; mischievous; contemptible. [Vulgar.]

That *Pocky*, Rotten, Lying, Cowardly, and most perfidious knave, Sir Hugh Caulverly, Knight.
Quoted in *Ashton's* Social Life in Reign of Queen Anne [II. 268, Appendix.

Pocky cloud. Same as *mammato-cumulus*.

poco (pō'kō), *adv.* [It., little, = Sp. *poco* = Pg. *pouco* = F. *peu*, < L. *paucus*, few: see *paucity*.] In *music*, a little; somewhat; rather: as, *poco adagio*, somewhat slow.

pococurante (pō'kǫ-kǫ-rän'te), *n.* [< It. *poco*, little, + *curante*, ppr. of *curare*, care: see *cure*, *v.*] A person characterized by want of care, interest, attention, or the like; an apathetic, careless, easy, inaccurate person.

Leave we my mother (truest of all the *Pococurantes* of her sex!) careless about it, as about everything else in the world which concerned her.
Sterne, Tristram Shandy, vi. 20.

pococurantism (pō'kǫ-kǫ-rän'tizm), *n.* [< *pococurante* + *-ism*.] The character, disposition, or habits of a pococurante; extreme indifference, apathy, or carelessness; inaccuracy.

The doom of Fate was, Be thou a Dandy! Have thy eye-glasses, opera-glasses, thy Long-Acre cabs with white-breeched tiger, thy yawning impassivities, *pococurantisms*.
Carlyle, Past and Present, ii. 17.

pococurantist (pō'kǫ-kǫ-rän'tist), *a.* [< *pococurante* + *-ist*.] Careless; inaccurate.

pocok†, *n.* A Middle English variant of *peacock*.

pocosin, *n.* See the quotation.

These swamps [of Virginia and North Carolina] are locally known through the region where they occur as "dismals" or "*pocosins*."
J. D. Whitney, Encyc. Brit., XXIII. 509.

poculary† (pok'ų-lā-ri), *n.*; pl. *poculuries* (-riz). [< L. *poculum*, a goblet: see *poculent*.] A drinking-cup.

Some brought forth . . . *pocularies* for drinkers, some manuaries for handlers of relicks, some pedaries for pilgrims. *Latimer*, Sermons and Remains, I. 49. (*Davies.*)

poculent† (pok'ų-lent), *a.* [< L. *poculentus*, drinkable, < *poculum*, a goblet, cup, < √ *po* in *potare*, drink: see *potation*.] Fit for drink.

Some of those herbs which are not esculent are, notwithstanding, *poculent*. *Bacon*, Nat. Hist., § 630.

poculiform (pok'ų-li-fôrm), *a.* [= F. *poculiforme*; < L. *poculum*, cup, + *forma*, form.] Cup-shaped; of the shape of a drinking-cup or goblet.

pod (pod), *n.* [Prob. a var. of *pad*[3].] 1. In *bot.*, a more or less elongated cylindrical or flattish seed-vessel, as of the pea, bean, catalpa, etc.; technically, a legume or silicle, but applied commonly to any dry dehiscent (mostly) several-seeded pericarp, whether of one carpel (follicle, legume) or of several (capsule). See cuts under *Arachis*, *balloon-vine*, *circumscissile*, *Cruciferæ*, *divi-divi*, and *Eriodendron*.—2. The straight channel or groove in the body of certain forms of augers and boring-bits.—3. The pike when nearly full-grown. *Halliwell*. [Prov. Eng.]—4. A school or shoal, as of fishes or whales; a group or number, as of seals or walruses.

Different kinds of Pod.
1, legume of common vetch (*Vicia sativa*); 2, follicle of peony (*Pæonia officinalis*); 3, siliqua of bitter cress (*Cardamine hirsuta*); 4, silicle of field penny-cress (*Thlaspi arvense*).

A *pod* of whales was seen in the offing.
C. M. Scammon, Marine Mammals, p. 36.

These groups of walrus on the ice are by the whalers called *pods*. *Fisheries of U. S.*, V. ii. 313.

To set around a pod, to inclose a school of fish in a net. [New Eng.]

pod (pod), *v. i.*; pret. and pp. *podded*, ppr. *podding*. [< *pod*, *n.*] 1. To swell and assume the appearance of a pod.—2. To produce pods.—3. To drive seals or walruses into a pod or bunch for the purpose of clubbing them.

A singular lurid green light suddenly suffuses the eye of the fur-seal at intervals when it is very much excited, as the *podding* for the clubbers is in progress.
Fisheries of U. S., V. ii. 360.

Podager (pod'ā-jėr), *n.* [NL. (Wagler, 1832), < L. *podager*, < Gr. ποδαγρός, gouty: see *podagra*.] An American genus of *Caprimulgidæ*, typical of the subfamily *Podagerinæ*, having long, strong, entirely naked tarsi. *P. nacunda*, the only species, inhabits South America. It is 11 inches long, fuscous, vermiculated and maculated with black; the throat, belly, and tip of the tail (in the male) are white; the primaries are black with a broad white bar.

Podagerinæ (pod'ā-je-rī'nē), *n. pl.* [NL., < *Podager* + *-inæ*.] A subfamily of *Caprimulgidæ*, typified by the genus *Podager*, having the wings long and the bill glabrirostral, corresponding to the *Caprimulginæ glabrirostres* of Sclater, and composed of the genera *Podager*, *Lurocalis*, and *Chordeiles*. The best-known example is the common night-hawk, bull-bat, pisk, or piramidig of the United States. See cut under *night-hawk*.

podagerine (pǫ-daj'ẹ-rin), *a.* Belonging to the *Podagerinæ*.

podagra (pǫ-dag'rạ̈), *n.* [In ME. *podagre*, < OF. (and F.) *podagre* = Sp. Pg. It. *podagra* = D. G. Dan. *podagra* = Sw. *podager*; < L. *podagra*, < Gr. ποδάγρα, gout in the feet, < πούς (ποδ-), foot, + ἄγρα, a catching (cf. *chiragra*).] Gout in the foot. See *gout*[1], 3.

I cured him of the gout in his feet, and now he talks of the chargeableness of medicine. . . . His *podagra* hath become a chiragra; . . . the gout has got into his fingers, and he cannot draw his purse. *Scott*, Abbot, xxvi.

podagral (pod'ạ-grạl), *a.* [< *podagra* + *-al*.] Same as *podagric*.

podagric (pǫ-dag'rik), *a.* [= It. *podagrico*; < L. *podagricus*, gouty, < Gr. ποδαγρικός, gouty, < ποδάγρα, gout in the feet: see *podagra*.] 1. Pertaining to the gout; gouty.—2. Afflicted with the gout.

podagrical (pǫ-dag'ri-kạl), *a.* [< *podagric* + *-al*.] Same as *podagric*.

I shall return to kiss your Hands, and your Feet also, could I ease you of that *podagrical* Pain which afflicts you.
Howell, Letters, iv. 42.

A loadstone held in the hand of one that is *podagrical* doth either cure or give great ease in the gout.
Sir T. Browne, Vulg. Err., ii. 3.

Podagrion (pǫ-dag'ri-on), *n.* [NL. (Spinola, 1811), < Gr. ποδαγρός, gouty, < ποδάγρα, gout: see *podagra*.] A notable genus of chalcid hymenopterous insects, having a very long ovipositor and enlarged and dentate hind thighs. It is of cosmopolitan distribution, but mainly tropical, and its species are invariably parasitic in the egg-cases of orthopterous insects of the family *Mantidæ*.

podagrous (pod'ạ-grus), *a.* [= It. *podagroso*, < L. *podagrosus*, gouty, < *podagra*, gout: see *podagra*.] Same as *podagric*.

podalgia (pǫ-dal'ji-ạ̈), *n.* [NL., < Gr. ποδαλγία, pain in the feet, < πούς (ποδ-), foot, + ἄλγος, pain.] Pain in the foot; especially, neuralgia in the foot.

podalic (pǫ-dal'ik), *a.* [Irreg. < Gr. πούς (ποδ-), = E. *foot*, + *-al* + *-ic*. Cf. *pedal*.] Pertaining to the feet.—**Podalic version**, in *obstet.*, the operation of turning the fetus within the uterus so as to bring down the feet or some part of the lower extremities: distinguished from *cephalic version*.

Podalyria (pod-ạ-lir'i-ạ̈), *n.* [NL. (Lamarck, 1793), < L. *Podalirius*, < Gr. Ποδαλείριος, in myth. son of Æsculapius.] A genus of leguminous shrubs, type of the tribe *Podalyrieæ*, characterized by the broad obtuse keel-petals united on the back, the turgid, ovoid, coriaceous pod, simple short-petioled rigid leaves, and a calyx remarkably indented at its broadly bell-shaped base. The 17 species are natives of South Africa, and are silvery-pubescent or villous shrubs, with alternate leaves, awl-shaped stipules, and pink, purple, or blue axillary flowers, usually only one or two together. *P. sericea*, the African satin-bush, and several other species are cultivated for their flowers and silky leaves.

Podalyrieæ (pod'ạ-li-rī'ẹ̄-ē), *n. pl.* [NL. (Bentham, 1840), < *Podalyria* + *-eæ*.] A tribe of leguminous plants, characterized by its united sepals, papilionaceous petals, ten separate stamens, and simple or radiately compound leaves. The *Sophoreæ*, the only other papilionaceous tribe with ten free stamens, is different in its pinnate leaves. The *Podalyrieæ* include 26 genera, mainly Australian shrubs, with unjointed pods, and usually simple leaves not jointed to their short petiole. For the best-known genera. see *Podalyria* (the type), *Baptisia* (the only genus in the eastern United States), *Piptanthus*, *Pultenæa*, *Jacksonia*, and *Gompholobium*.

podanencephalia (pod-an-en-se-fā'li-ạ̈), *n.* [NL., < Gr. πούς (ποδ-), = E. *foot*, + NL. *anencephalia*, q. v.] In *teratol.*, anencephalia with a pedunculated head.

Podargidæ (pọ̄-där'ji-dē), *n. pl.* [NL., < *Podargus* + *-idæ*.] A family of fissirostral picarian birds, typified by the genus *Podargus*, related to the *Caprimulgidæ*, and usually included in that family. They have very broad palatine bones with posterolateral processes, rudimentary basipterygoid processes, no elæodochon or oil-gland, and a pair of powder-down tracts, one on each side of the rump. These birds are confined to the Oriental and Australian regions; some of them are known as *frogmouths*, from the great breadth and deep fissure of the beak. They are nocturnal and insectivorous, and resemble goatsuckers and owls. The genera are *Podargus*, *Batrachostomus*, and *Ægotheles*. Also *Podarginæ* as a subfamily of *Caprimulgidæ*.

podargine (pọ̄-där'jin), *a.* Of or pertaining to the *Podargidæ* or *Podarginæ*.

podargue (pọ̄-därg'), *n.* A bird of the genus *Podargus*.

Podargus (pọ̄-där'gus), *n.* [NL. (Cuvier, 1829), < Gr. πόδαργος, swift-footed, < πούς (ποδ-), foot, + ἀργός, swift, bright.] 1. The typical genus of the family *Podargidæ*. There are several species, confined to the Australian and Papuan regions, as *P. strigoides*, or *P. cuvieri*, known to the colonists as *more-pork*, from its cry. — 2. [*l. c.*] A species of this genus; a podargue.

More-pork (*Podargus cuvieri*).

podarthral (pọ̄-där'thral), *a.* [< *podarthr-um* + *-al*.] In *ornith.*, joining the toes to the shank; pertaining to the podarthrum: as, the *podarthral* joint or articulation.

podarthritis (pod-är-thrī'tis), *n.* [NL., < Gr. πούς (ποδ-), foot, + ἀρθρῖτις, joint-disease: see *arthritis*.] Inflammation of the joints of the foot.

podarthrum (pọ̄-där'thrum), *n.*; pl. *podarthra* (-thrạ̈). [NL., < Gr. πούς (ποδ-), foot, + ἄρθρον, a joint.] In *ornith.*, the foot-joint; the metatarsophalangeal articulation; the juncture of the toes collectively with the metatarsus.

pod-auger (pod'â"gėr), *n.* See *auger*, 1.

Podaxineæ (pod-ak-sin'ẹ̄-ē), *n. pl.* [NL. (Saccardo), < Gr. πούς (ποδ-), foot, + L. *axis*, axle: see *ax*[2].] A subfamily of gasteromycetous fungi of the family *Lycoperdaceæ*.

Podaxonia (pod-ak-sō'ni-ạ̈), *n. pl.* [NL., < Gr. πούς (ποδ-), foot, + ἄξων, axis: see *ax*[2].] A phylum of molluscoids, composed of three classes, *Sipunculoidea*, *Brachiopoda*, and *Polyzoa*, having a secondary long axis of the body at right angles with an original oro-anal long axis. It corresponds nearly to *Molluscoidea*, except in including the gephyreans.

podaxonial (pod-ak-sō'ni-al), *a.* [< *Podaxonia* + *-al*.] Of or pertaining to the *Podaxonia*.

pod-bit (pod'bit), *n.* A boring-tool used in a brace. It is semi-cylindrical in shape, with a hollow barrel, and a cutting lip projecting from the extremity of the barrel.

podder (pod'ėr), *n.* [< *pod* + *-er*[1].] 1. A gatherer of pods. — 2. *pl.* Beans, peas, tares, vetches, and other podded or leguminous plants in general. [Prov. Eng. in both uses.]

poddy (pod'i), *a.* [< *pod* + *-y*[1].] Round and stout in the belly; paunchy. *Halliwell.* [Prov. Eng.]

podelcoma (pod-el-kō'mạ̈), *n.* [NL., < Gr. πούς (ποδ-), foot, + ἕλκωμα, a sore.] A perforating ulcer of the foot.

podencephalus (pod-en-sef'ạ-lus), *n.*; pl. *podencephali* (-lī). [NL., < Gr. πούς (ποδ-), foot, + ἐγκέφαλος, brain.] In *teratol.*, an exencephalus in which the brain is contained in a pedicellate sac.

poder (pọ̄-der'), *n.* [< Sp. *poder*, power: see *power*.] In *Spanish-Amer. law*, a power of attorney formally made before a notary public; a procuration.

podestà (pō-des-tä'), *n.* [It. (> F. *podestat* = Pg. *podestade*), < L. *potestas* (*potestat-*), power, a magistrate: see *potestate*.] One of certain magistrates in Italy. (*a*) A foreign magistrate, placed by the emperor Frederick Barbarossa over various Italian cities. (*b*) A chief magistrate in Italian towns and in medieval republics, often clothed with nearly despotic power. His functions were largely judicial.

The Venetians haue alwayes their *Podesta*, or Gouernour, with his two Counsellours resident therein.
Hakluyt's Voyages, II. 104.

(*c*) In many Italian cities, a subordinate municipal judge.

podestate†, *n.* [< F. *podestat*, < It. *podestate*, *podestà*: see *podestà*, *potestate*.] A magistrate: same as *potestate*.

I haue sene of the greatest *podestates* and grauest judges and Presidentes of Parliament in Fraunce.
Puttenham, Arte of Eng. Poesie, p. 308.

podesterate (pọ̄-des'tẹ-rāt), *n.* [As It. *podesteria*, *podestaria*, magistracy (< *podestà*, a magistrate: see *podestà*), + *-ate*[3].] The office, dignity, or jurisdiction of a podestà; the term of office of a podestà.

In the next year, 1280, in the *podesterate* of Alberigo Signoregi of Bologna, the palaces of the Incontri were burnt and demolished by the fury of the people.
J. Adams, Works, V. 230.

podetia, *n.* Plural of *podetium*.

podetiiform (pọ̄-dē'shi-i-fôrm), *a.* [< NL. *podetium* + L. *forma*, form.] Of the shape of a podetium; resembling a podetium. *E. Tuckerman*, Genera Lichenum, p. 232.

podetium (pọ̄-dē'shi-um), *n.*; pl. *podetia* (-ạ̈). [NL., < Gr. πούς (ποδ-), foot.] In *bot.*, in certain lichens, the shrubby or stalk-like outgrowth of the thallus, bearing exposed hymenia; also, any stalk-like elevation. See cuts under *Cladonia*.

podex (pō'deks), *n.*; pl. *podices* (pod'i-sēz). [L.] In *zoöl.*: (*a*) The rump; the uropygium; the anus or anal region. (*b*) In *entom.*, the pygidium.

pod-fern (pod'fėrn), *n.* A singular aquatic fern, *Ceratopteris thalictroides*, very variable in form, found in the tropics of both hemispheres: so called from the pod-like segments of the fertile frond, which are everywhere covered with sori. The stipes are inflated with large air-cells.

pod-gaper (pod'gä"pėr), *n.* A bivalve mollusk of the family *Solenomyidæ*.

podge[1] (poj), *n.* [Perhaps for *plodge*; cf. *plod*[1].] A puddle; a plash.

podge[2] (poj), *v. i.*; pret. and pp. *podged*, ppr. *podging*. [Perhaps for *plodge*; cf. *plod*[2].] To plod.

My dames will say I am a *podging* asse.
Historie of Albino and Bellama (1638). (*Nares.*)

podgy (poj'i), *a.* Same as *pudgy*.

podia, *n.* Plural of *podium*.

podial (pō'di-ạl), *a.* [< *podium* + *-al*.] Of or pertaining to the podium.

Podica (pod'i-kạ̈), *n.* [NL. (Lesson, 1831), < LL. *podicus*, belonging to a foot, < Gr. πούς (ποδ-), foot.] The African genus of *Heliornithidæ*, the sunbirds or finfoots, containing several species, as *P. senegalensis* and *P. petersi*. Also called *Podoa* and *Rhigelura*.

African Finfoot (*Podica senegalensis*).

podical (pod'i-kạl), *a.* [< L. *podex* (*podic-*), rump, + *-al*.] Of or pertaining to the podex; uropygial; anal or pygidial, as with reference to the terminal somite of the abdomen of an insect.—**Podical plates**, in *entom.*, two or more small pieces surrounding the opening of the intestinal canal: when present, they are generally concealed by the last external abdominal segments. Anatomists have regarded these plates as the rudiments of the eleventh abdominal segment.

Podiceps (pod'i-seps), *n.* The original and usual form of *Podicipes*.

podices, *n.* Plural of *podex*.

Podicipedidæ (pod"i-si-ped'i-dē), *n. pl.* [NL., < *Podicipes* (*-ped-*) + *-idæ*.] A family of birds of the order *Pygopodes*, typified by the genus *Podicipes*; the grebes. The family has many peculiarities, causing it to rank as a suborder called *Podicipedes*, whose characters are the same as those of the family. They have no ambiens, femorocaudal, or accessory tendinosus muscle, only one carotid, short xiphisternum, long narrow pelvis, from fifteen to nineteen cervical vertebræ, a long cnemial process of the tibia and a very large patella, no superorbital depression for a nasal gland, and a special pyloric sac. Cæca are present, and the oil-gland is tufted. The feet are four-toed and lobate, not webbed; the nails are flat and blunt; the tail is rudimentary; the primaries are eleven in number; the lores are naked; the head is usually crested; and the bill is of variable shape. The leading genera are *Æchmophorus*, *Podicipes*, *Tachybaptes*, and *Podilymbus*. *Colymbidæ* is a synonym in one of its senses. Also *Podicipidæ*, *Podicepidæ*, *Podicipitidæ*. See cuts under *Æchmophorus* and *grebe*.

Podicipes (pọ̄-dis'i-pēz), *n.* [NL., orig. *Podiceps* as a specific name (Linnæus, 1766), later as a generic name (Latham, 1790), tr. E. *arse-foot*; < L. *podex* (*podic-*), rump, + *pes* = E. *foot*.] The typical genus of the family *Podicipedidæ*. It formerly contained all the grebes, but is now usually restricted to those which have the bill moderately stout, not longer than the head, and not hooked at the end, the tarsus not longer than the middle toe and claw, the dimensions over ten inches, and the head usually crested and ruffed. There are numerous species, such as the crested grebe, *P. cristatus*; the red-necked grebe, *P. grisëigena*; the horned grebe, *P. cornutus*; and the eared grebe, *P. auritus*. Also called *Colymbus*. Usually *Podiceps*. See cut under *grebe*.

Podilymbus (pod-i-lim'bus), *n.* [NL. (Lesson, 1831), < *Podi*(*ceps*) + (*Co*)*lymbus*.] A genus of *Podicipedidæ*, containing American grebes with a thick stout epignathous bill, and no crests or ruffs, the frontal feathers being mucronate. *P. podiceps* is the commonest grebe of the United States, commonly called the *pied-billed dabchick*. The genus is also called *Hydroka* and *Nexiteles*.

podismus (pọ̄-dis'mus), *n.* [NL., < Gr. ποδισμός, a measuring by feet (taken in sense of 'a binding of the feet'), < ποδίζειν, measure by feet, also bind the feet, < πούς (ποδ-), foot.] Spasm of the muscles of the foot.

Podisus (pod'i-sus), *n.* [NL. (Herrich-Schäffer, 1853), < Gr. πούς (ποδ-), foot, + ἴσος, equal.] A genus of pentatomid bugs, with over 30 species, all American. They are of medium size and usually light colors, predaceous in habit, and provided with a strong beak wherewith to impale their prey. *P. placidus* is a North American species, notable as an enemy of the imported currant-worm, *Nematus ventricosus*. *P. spinosus* is common and wide-spread; it attacks many injurious larvæ. See also cut under *soldier-bug*.

Podisus placidus.
a, enlarged; *b*, natural size.

podite (pod'īt), *n.* [< Gr. πούς (ποδ-), foot, + *-ite*.] A limb or leg of a crustacean, especially when developed as an ambulatory appendage, or leg fitted for walking. See *endopodite*, *exopodite*, *epipodite*; also *basipodite*, *coxopodite*, *dactylopodite*, *ischiopodite*, *meropodite*, *propodite*, and cuts under *Podophthalmia*.

These *podites* are usually seven-jointed.
Encyc. Brit., VI. 685.

poditic (pọ̄-dit'ik), *a.* [< *podite* + *-ic*.] Of or pertaining to a podite.

poditti (pọ̄-dit'i), *n.* [Australian.] The Australian saw-beaked kingfisher, *Syma flavirostris*. See cut under *Syma*.

podium (pō'di-um), *n.*; pl. *podia* (-ạ̈). [L. (> It. *podio* = F. *podium*), < *podium* (see def.), < Gr. πόδιον, a little foot, dim. of πούς (ποδ-), foot: see *pew*[1].] 1. In *arch.*, a continuous pedestal; a stylobate; also, a raised platform which surrounded the arena of the ancient amphitheater, upon which sat persons of distinction, or a bench surrounding a room. — 2. In *zoöl.* and *anat.*, the foot; the pes: usually applied in ornithology to the toes collectively, without the shank of the foot. — 3. In *conch.*, the foot of a mollusk. Its parts are distinguished as *propodium*, *mesopodium*, *metapodium*, and *epipodium*, or *fore*, *middle*, *hind*, and *side parts*. See cuts under *Gasteropoda*, *Leptonidæ*, *Myidæ*, and *Pisidiidæ*. 4. In *bot.*: (*a*) A footstalk, stipe, or the like. [Rarely used except in compounds.] (*b*) A joint, internode, or independent unit in the growth of the axis of a plant.

podje (poj'e), *n.* [Native name.] The spectral tarsier, *Tarsius spectrum*, of Borneo and Celebes. See cut under *Tarsius*.

pod-lover (pod'luv'ėr), *n.* The noctuid moth *Dianthœcia capsophila*: an English collectors' name, translating the specific term.

podobranchia (pod-ǫ-brang'ki-ặ), *n.*; pl. *podobranchiæ* (-ē). [NL., ‹ Gr. πούς (ποδ-), foot, + βράγχια, gills.] A foot-gill; one of the respiratory organs of crustaceans which are attached to the legs. Parts of a podobranchia are distinguished as the *base*, *stem*, *expanded lamina*, and *apical plume*, besides the proper *branchial filaments*. Podobranchiæ are coxopoditic, or borne upon the coxopodites of the limbs to which they are respectively attached, and of which they are the modified epipodites. See cuts under *Podophthalmia*, especially *M* and *N*.

podobranchial (pod-ǫ-brang'ki-ạl), *a.* [‹ *podobranchia* + *-al.*] Of or pertaining to a podobranchia.

podobranchiate (pod-ǫ-brang'ki-āt), *a.* [‹ *podobranchia* + *-ate*[1].] Having podobranchiæ.

Podocarpeæ (pod-ǫ-kär'pę-ē), *n. pl.* [NL. (Endlicher, 1847), ‹ *Podocarpus* + *-eæ.*] Same as *Taxoideæ*.

Podocarpus (pod-ǫ-kär'pus), *n.* [NL. (L'Héritier, 1817), so called in allusion to the thick fleshy stalk which supports the fruit (not so in other conifers); ‹ Gr. πούς (ποδ-), foot, + καρπός, fruit.] A genus of coniferous trees of the tribe *Taxoideæ*, characterized by solitary or twin pistillate flowers surrounded by a few scales, bearing a somewhat stalked and projecting blade, which envelops the single adnate and inverted ovule. In fruit this blade usually becomes fleshy, forming a pulpy covering to the hard shell-like seed, which contains a thin embryo with two seed-leaves only, in fleshy albumen. The staminate flowers are solitary or in clusters of from two to five, or in long catkins, the stamens forming a long dense column covered with sessile two-celled anthers in spiral rows. There are from 40 to 60 species, forming much the largest coniferous genus except *Pinus*. They are chiefly natives of the southern hemisphere beyond the tropics, and also frequent in montane and eastern tropical Asia. They are evergreen trees, with much diversity in foliage: the leaves are either scattered, opposite, two-ranked, or crowded; scale-like, linear, or broad; and veinless or with many fine parallel veins. The fruit is a globular or ovoid drupe or nut, 1½ inches or less in diameter, in some species edible, as *P. andina*, the plum-fir of Chili, with clusters of cherry-like fruits, and *P. spinulosa*, the native plum or damson of New South Wales, also called *Illawarra pine* and *white pine*. Several other species are known as *fir* or *pine* among the colonists of New Zealand, Australia, and Cape Colony. Compare *fir* and *pine* 1, and for individual species see *kahikatea*, *matai*, and *miro*. Many species are among the most important timber-trees of the southern hemisphere, as (besides the preceding) *P. Totara*, the mahogany-pine; *P. cupressina*, the kaw-tabua, one of the chief timber-trees of Java; and the various yellow-woods of Cape Colony. (See *yellow-wood*.) Others are a source of valuable gums, as *P. polystachya*, the wax-dammar of Singapore. Some are but bushes, others reach a great height, as *P. amara* of Java (200 feet), and the yacca-tree of the West Indies (100 feet). Some botanists use the name of the section *Nageia* for the whole genus.

podocephalous (pod-ǫ-sef'ạ-lus), *a.* [‹ Gr. πούς (ποδ-), foot, + κεφαλή, head.] In *bot.*, having a head of flowers elevated on a long peduncle: said of a plant.

Podoces (pǫ-dō'sēz), *n.* [NL. (Fischer, 1823), ‹ Gr. ποδώκης, swift-footed, ‹ πούς (ποδ-), foot, + ὠκύς, swift.] A genus of oscine passerine birds of the family *Corvidæ* and subfamily *Fregilinæ*, with short wings, characteristic of the desert regions of central Asia; the desert-choughs. Four species are described—*P. panderi*, *P. hendersoni*, *P. biddulphi*, and *P. humilis*.

Desert-chough (*Podoces panderi*).

Podocoryne (pod''ǫ-kǫ-rī'nē), *n.* [NL. (Sars, 1842), ‹ Gr. πούς (ποδ-), foot, + κορύνη, a club.] The typical genus of *Podocorynidæ*. *P. carnea* is an example. Also *Podocoryna*.

Podocorynidæ (pod''ǫ-kǫ-rin'i-dē), *n. pl.* [NL., ‹ *Podocoryne* + *-idæ.*] A family of gymnoblastic hydromedusans, typified by the genus *Podocoryne*.

pododynia (pod-ǫ-din'i-ặ), *n.* [NL., ‹ Gr. πούς (ποδ-), foot, + ὀδύνη, pain.] Pain in the foot; podalgia.

podogyn (pod'ǫ-jin), *n.* [‹ F. *podogyne*, ‹ NL. *podogynium*, q. v.] Same as *podogynium*.

podogynium (pod-ǫ-jin'i-um), *n.*; pl. *podogynia* (-ặ). [NL., ‹ Gr. πούς (ποδ-), foot, + γυνή, female (in mod. bot. pistil).] In *bot.*, same as *basigynium*.

Podolian (pǫ-dō'li-ạn), *a.* [‹ It. *Podolia* (see def.) + *-an.*] Of or pertaining to Podolia, a district of western Russia.—**Podolian cattle**, a breed of cattle widely distributed throughout Italy, usually with white or gray coat and enormous horns.—**Podolian marmot**, the *Spalax typhlus*. *Pennant.*

podology (pǫ-dol'ǫ-ji), *n.* [= F. *podologie*, ‹ Gr. πούς (ποδ-), foot, + -λογία, ‹ λέγειν, speak: see *-ology*.] A treatise on or a description of the foot. *Dunglison.*

podometer (pǫ-dom'e-tėr), *n.* [‹ Gr. πούς (ποδ-), foot, + μέτρον, measure.] Same as *pedometer*.

Podophthalma (pod-of-thal'mặ), *n. pl.* [NL.: see *Podophthalmia*.] 1. In *Crustacea*, same as *Podophthalmia*. *Leach*, 1815.—2. In *conch.*, a division of rostriferous gastropods, having eyes at the ends of cylindrical peduncles which are separated from and at the outer edges of the long subulate tentacles. It includes the family *Ampullariidæ*. *J. E. Gray*, 1840.—3. [Used as a sing.] A genus of spiders, type of the *Podophthalmidæ*.

Podophthalmata (pod-of-thal'mạ-tặ), *n. pl.* [NL., pl. of *Podophthalma*.] Same as *Podophthalmia*.

podophthalmate (pod-of-thal'māt), *a.* [‹ Gr. πούς (ποδ-), foot, + ὀφθαλμός, eye, + *-ate*[1].] Same as *podophthalmic*.

podophthalmatous (pod-of-thal'mạ-tus), *a.* [‹ *podophthalmate* + *-ous.*] Same as *podophthalmic*.

Podophthalmia (pod-of-thal'mi-ặ), *n. pl.* [NL., ‹ Gr. πούς (ποδ-), foot, + ὀφθαλμός, eye: see *ophthalmia*.] A division of malacostracous *Crustacea*, having the eyes borne upon movable eye-stalks or ophthalmites, and the cephalothorax forming a carapace; the stalk-eyed crustaceans: distinguished from *Edriophthalmia*. The group is divisible into two orders, *Stomatopoda* and *Decapoda*, the latter containing the most familiar crustaceans, as prawns, shrimps, crawfish, lobsters, and crabs. See also cuts under *Astacidæ*, *Astacus*, *Copepoda*, *copepod-stage*, *endopodite*, *lobster*, *prawn*, and *stalk-eyed*.

Parts of the Crawfish (*Astacus fluviatilis*), with the nomenclature of the appendages of the stalk-eyed crustaceans (*Podophthalmia*) and the higher crustaceans (*Malacostraca*) in general.

A, mandible: *e*, its terminal joints, being the palpus of the mandible; *B*, first maxilla; *C*, second maxilla: *cd*, scaphognathite; *D*, first maxilliped; *E*, second maxilliped; *F*, third maxilliped. (*B* right; the others left.) In *A* to *F*, *ab*, endopodite; *c*, exopodite; *d*, epipodite; *e*, setaceous filaments of coxopodite. *M*, cross-section of half a thoracic somite: *a*, the somite; *b*, the coxopodite; *c*, basipodite; *d*, ischiopodite; *h*, branchiferous epipodite; *f*, *g*, branchiæ; *e*, filiform appendage. *N*, a branchiferous epipodite, enlarged: *a*, its point of attachment; *b*, basal enlargement; *c*, *c*, branchial filaments; *d*, terminal lobes.

podophthalmian (pod-of-thal'mi-ạn), *a.* and *n.* I. *a.* Same as *podophthalmic*.

II. *n.* A member of the *Podophthalmia*.

podophthalmic (pod-of-thal'mik), *a.* [‹ Gr. πούς (ποδ-), foot, + ὀφθαλμός, eye (see *ophthalmia*), + *-ic.*] Stalk-eyed, as a crustacean; belonging to the *Podophthalmia*.

Podophthalmidæ (pod-of-thal'mi-dē), *n. pl.* [NL. (Cambridge, 1877), ‹ *Podophthalma* + *-idæ.*] A family of spiders, allied to the *Lycosidæ* and *Agalenidæ*, and having the eyes placed in four rows, the legs long and slender, and the abdomen long and cylindrical: typified by the genus *Podophthalma*. It is represented in the southern United States by the genus *Tetragonophthalma*.

podophthalmite (pod-of-thal'mīt), *n.* [‹ Gr. πούς (ποδ-), foot, + E. *ophthalmite*.] The distal or terminal joint of the movable two-jointed ophthalmite or peduncle of the eye of a stalk-eyed crustacean, the other being the *basiophthalmite*. See cut under *stalk-eyed*.

podophthalmitic (pod''of-thal-mit'ik), *a.* [‹ *podophthalmite* + *-ic.*] Of or pertaining to a podophthalmite.

podophthalmous (pod-of-thal'mus), *a.* [‹ *podophthalm-ic* + *-ous.*] Same as *podophthalmic*.

podophyllic (pod-ǫ-fil'ik), *a.* [‹ *podophyll-in* + *-ic.*] Pertaining to or derived from podophyllin.

podophyllin (pod-ǫ-fil'in), *n.* [= F. *podophylline*; ‹ *Podophyllum* + *-in*[2].] A resin obtained from the rootstalk of *Podophyllum peltatum*. It is used in medicine as a purgative, and seems to have the power of stimulating the secretion of bile.

podophyllous (pod-ǫ-fil'us), *a.* [= F. *podophylleux*, ‹ Gr. πούς (ποδ-), foot, + φύλλον, a leaf.] In *entom.*, having the feet or locomotive organs compressed into the form of leaves.

Podophyllum (pod-ǫ-fil'um), *n.* [NL. (Linnæus, 1737), so called in allusion to the 5- to 7-parted leaf, thought to resemble the foot of some animal; ‹ Gr. πούς (ποδ-), foot, + φύλλον, leaf.] A genus of polypetalous plants of the order *Berberideæ* and tribe *Berbereæ*, characterized by having the ovules in many rows, the flower with six sepals, from six to nine petals, as many or twice as many stamens, and a large peltate stigma crowning the ovary, which becomes in fruit a berry. There are 2 species, one being *P. peltatum*, the May-apple or wild mandrake of North America, the other a Himalayan species. They are singular herbs, with thick and prolonged poisonous creeping rootstocks, from which rise long-stalked orbicular peltate and deeply lobed leaves, known among children as *umbrellas*, from their resemblance both when folded and when expanded; also called *duck's-foot*. The flowering stem, unlike the other, bears two leaves, peltate near the edge, and between them a single large flat white flower. The leaves are poisonous, but the sweetish yellow egg-shaped fruit is sometimes eaten. See *May-apple*, 1, *mandrake*, 2, *hog-apple*, and *podophyllin*.

podopter (pǫ-dop'tėr), *n.* [‹ Gr. πούς (ποδ-), foot, + πτερόν, wing, = E. *feather*.] A member of the *Podoptera*.

podoscaph (pod'ǫ-skaf), *n.* [‹ Gr. πούς (ποδ-), foot, + σκάφος, a ship: see *scaphus*.] A hollow apparatus, like a small boat, attached one to each foot, and serving to support the body erect on the water.

Podosomata (pod-ǫ-sō'mạ-tặ), *n. pl.* [NL., neut. pl. of *podosomatus*: see *podosomatous*.] In Leach's system, an order of aporobranchiate *Arachnida*, constituted by the single family *Pycnogonidæ*.

podosomatous (pod-ǫ-som'a-tus), *a.* [‹ NL. *podosomatus*, ‹ Gr. πούς (ποδ-), foot, + σῶμα(τ-), body.] Having the legs of conspicuous size in comparison with the body; specifically, of or pertaining to the *Podosomata*.

podosperm (pod'ǫ-spėrm), *n.* [= F. *podosperme*, ‹ Gr. πούς (ποδ-), foot, + σπέρμα, seed: see *sperm*.] In *bot.*, same as *funicle*, 4.

podospermium (pod-ǫ-spėr'mi-um), *n.* [NL.: see *podosperm*.] In *bot.*, same as *funicle*, 4.

Podosphæra (pod-ǫ-sfē'rặ), *n.* [NL. (Kunze), ‹ Gr. πούς (ποδ-), foot, + σφαῖρα, a ball.] A genus of pyrenomycetous fungi of the family *Erysipheæ*. The appendages are free from the mycelium, and dichotomously branched at the end. The perithecium contains but a single ascus. *P. Oxyacanthæ* is the cherry-blight.

Podostemaceæ (pod''ǫ-stę-mā'sę-ē), *n. pl.* [NL. (Lindley, 1835), ‹ *Podostemon* + *-aceæ.*] A peculiar order of apetalous plants of little-known affinity, characterized by the ovary of two or three cells, with numerous ovules in each cell, and by the aquatic habit, with creeping or expanded disks in place of roots, united to stones under water, from which arise stems with small leaves like mosses, or fronds resembling algæ. The flowers are minute, with one, two, few, or many stamens, one ovary and two or three styles, a three- or five-cleft perianth, or in its place a row of little scales, and the fruit a small capsule. There are about 116 species, belonging to 4 tribes and 23 genera, of which *Podostemon* is the type. They are small plants of rapid rivers and brooks, growing firmly attached to stones under water, natives of the tropics, mainly in America, Africa, and Asia.

Podostemon (pod-ǫ-stē'mon), *n.* [NL. (Michaux, 1803), so called in allusion to the elevation of the two stamens on a stalk supporting the ovary; ‹ Gr. πούς (ποδ-), foot, + στήμων, warp (stamen).] A genus of aquatic plants, type of the order *Podostemaceæ* and tribe *Eupodostemeæ*, characterized by the two stamens with filaments united more than half their length, the two awl-shaped and entire stigmas, and an equally two-valved, oval, obtuse pod with two cells and eight ribs. There are about 20 species, natives of North America, Brazil, Madagascar, and the East Indies, with one, the type species, *P. ceratophyllus*, the threadfoot or river-weed, extending into the northern United States. They have erect or branching stems, growing fast to stones, or in some the plant forms a lichen-like crust, sending up short branches only. Their usual aspect is much that of a filamentous or membranous seaweed.

Podostomata (pod-ọ-stō'ma-tạ̈), *n. pl.* [NL., neut. pl. of **podostomatus*: see *podostomatous*.] A class of *Arthropoda*, composed of the orders *Trilobita* and *Merostomata* (the latter containing the *Xyphosura*, *Synziphosura*, and *Eurypterida*): so called from the foot-like or ambulatory character of the mouth-parts. They are an ancient generalized type, represented at the present day by the king-crabs only.

podostomatous (pod-ọ-stom'ạ-tus), *a.* [< NL. **podostomatus*, < Gr. πούς (ποδ-), foot, + στόμα, mouth.] Having foot-like mouth-parts; belonging to the *Podostomata*.

podotheca (pod-ọ-thē'kạ̈), *n.*; pl. *podothecæ* (-sē). [NL., < Gr. πούς (ποδ-), foot, + θήκη, sheath.] 1. In *ornith.*, the covering of the foot, in so far as it is bare of feathers; the tarsal envelop and the sheaths of the toes.—2. In *entom.*, a leg-case, or that part of the integument of a pupa covering a leg.

podothecal (pod-ọ-thē'kạl), *a.* [< *podotheca* + *-al.*] Sheathing or investing the foot; of or pertaining to a podotheca.

podotrochilitis (pod-ọ-trō-ki-lī'tis), *n.* [NL., < Gr. πούς (ποδ-), foot, + τροχιλία, pulley, + *-itis.*] An inflammatory disease of the fore foot in the horse, involving the synovial sheath between the sesamoid or navicular bone of the third phalanx (or hoof) and the flexor perforans playing over it: commonly called *navicular disease*. It is a frequent cause of lameness.

Podoura, podouran, etc. See *Podura*, etc.

pod-pepper (pod'pep"ėr), *n.* See *Capsicum*.

pod-shell (pod'shel), *n.* A bivalve mollusk of the family *Pharidæ*.

pod-shrimp (pod'shrimp), *n.* An entomostracous crustacean whose carapace is hinged or valvular, and thus capable of inclosing the legs as in a pod. The existing pod-shrimps are all small, but the type is an old one, formerly represented by large entomostracans. It is illustrated in the cuts under *Estheriidæ* and *Limnetis*.

> The once giant *pod-shrimps* of Silurian times.
> *Encyc. Brit.*, VI. 663.

pod-thistle (pod'this"l), *n.* The stemless thistle, *Cnicus* (*Carduus*) *acaulis*.

> The people at Brackley . . . always spoke of the stemless thistle as the *pod-thistle*.
> *Academy*, Jan. 11, 1890, p. 30.

Podura, Podoura (pọ-dū'rạ̈, pọ-dö'rạ̈), *n.* [NL. (Linnæus, 1748), < Gr. πούς (ποδ-), foot, + οὐρά, tail.] 1. A Linnean genus of apterous insects, corresponding to the modern order *Thysanura*, used by later naturalists with various restrictions, and now typical of the family *Poduridæ*. They have but one tarsal claw. Some forms are found on standing water, others on the snow. They are known as *springtails* and *snow-fleas*. See cut under *springtail*.
2. [*l. c.*] A species of this genus; a poduran.

poduran, podouran (pọ-dū'ran, pọ-dö'ran), *a.* and *n.* [< *Podura* + *-an.*] I. *a.* Same as *podurous*.
II. *n.* A member of the genus *Podura* or the family *Poduridæ*.

Podurellæ, Podourellæ (pod-ū-rel'ē, pod-ọ-rel'ē), *n. pl.* [NL., dim. of *Podura*.] In early systems of classification, as Leach's and Latreille's, a group of thysanurous insects, typified by the genus *Podura*, inexactly corresponding to the modern order or suborder *Collembola*.

Poduridæ, Podouridæ (pọ-dū'ri-dē, pọ-dö'ri-dē), *n. pl.* [NL. (Burmeister, 1838), < *Podura* + *-idæ*.] A family of thysanurous insects of the order *Collembola*, typified by the genus *Podura*, to which various limits have been assigned. It was formerly nearly equivalent to *Collembola*, but is now restricted to forms with the body cylindrical and the appendage of the fourth abdominal segment developed into a saltatory apparatus. The mouth-parts are very rudimentary. The respiration is tracheal, though the podurans are supposed also to breathe directly through the integument. They are found almost everywhere in damp places. There are several genera besides *Podura*, as *Anura*, *Achoreutes*, *Tomocerus*, *Orchesella*, and *Lepidocyrtus*. See *snow-flea*, and cut under *springtail*.

podurous (pọ-dū'rus), *a.* [< Gr. πούς (ποδ-), foot, + οὐρά, tail.] Belonging or pertaining to the genus *Podura* in any sense.

pod-ware (pod'wãr), *n.* Pulse growing in pods or cods. See *podder*, 2. *Halliwell*. [Prov. Eng.]

podyperidrosis (pod-i-per-i-drō'sis), *n.* [NL., < Gr. πούς (ποδ-), foot, + ὑπέρ, over, beyond, + ἱδρωσις, perspiration: see *hidrosis*.] Excessive sweating of the feet.

poe[1], *n.* See *poi*.

poe[2] (pō'e), *n.* [Also *pue*; a New Zealand name.] The poe-bird, originally called the *poe bee-eater*. *Latham*, 1782.

poe-bird (pō'e-bėrd), *n.* [< *poe*[2] + *bird*[1].] The poe, tui, or parson-bird, *Prosthemadera cincinnata* or *novæ-zealandiæ*, a meliphagine bird of New Zealand and Auckland. It is about as large as a blackbird, iridescent-black in color, with a patch of long curly white plumes on each side of the neck, and a white band on the wings. It is valued both by the natives for its plumage, which contributes to the ornamentation of the feather mantles worn by them, and also as a cage-bird, from the fineness of its song and its powers of mimicry. See cut under *parson-bird*.

pœcile (pē'si-lē), *n.* [< Gr. ποικίλη, sc. στόα, a porch adorned with fresco-paintings, fem. of ποικίλος, many-colored, mottled, pied, variegated, various, manifold; akin to L. *pingere* (√ *pic*), paint: see *picture*, *paint*.] A stoa or porch on the agora of ancient Athens: so called from the paintings of historical and religious subjects with which its walls were adorned. See *stoa*.

pœcilite (pē'si-līt), *n.* Same as *bornite*. Also *poikilite*.

pœcilitic (pē-si-lit'ik), *a.* and *n.* [Also *poikilitic*, and incorrectly *pæcilitic*; < Gr. ποικίλος, many-colored, mottled, + *-it-ic*.] A name suggested by Conybeare as an equivalent for *New Red Sandstone*, in allusion to its variegated color, the rocks of which this group is made up consisting chiefly of red, yellow, and variegated sandstones, conglomerates, and marls, with occasional beds of limestone. See *sandstone*, *Permian*, and *New Red Sandstone* (under *sandstone*).

pœcilocyte (pē'sil-ọ-sīt), *n.* [< Gr. ποικίλος, many-colored, + κύτος, a hollow.] A red blood-corpuscle of abnormal shape.

pœcilocytosis (pē"si-lọ-sī-tō'sis), *n.* [NL., as *pœcilocyte* + *-osis*.] The presence of pœcilocytes in the blood.

pœcilonym (pē'si-lọ-nim), *n.* [< Gr. ποικίλος, various, manifold, + ὄνυμο, ὄνομα, a name: see *onym*.] One of two or more names for the same thing; a synonym. *Wilder*; *Leidy*.

pœcilonymic (pē-si-lọ-nim'ik), *a.* [< *pœcilonym-y* + *-ic*.] Characterized by or pertaining to pœcilonymy.

> An unusually complete combination of *pœcilonymic* ambiguities. *Buck's Handbook Med. Sci.*, p. 528.

pœcilonymy (pē-si-lon'i-mi), *n.* [< *pœcilonym* + *-y*[3].] The use of several different names for the same thing; application of different terms indifferently to a thing; varied or varying nomenclature. *The Nation*, July 18, 1889.

Pœcilopoda (pē-si-lop'ọ-dạ̈), *n. pl.* [NL., < Gr. ποικίλος, many-colored, manifold, + πούς (ποδ-) = E. *foot*.] In Latreille's system of classification, the second order of his *Entomostraca*, divided into two families, *Xiphosura* and *Siphonostoma*. It was a highly artificial group, including *Limulus* with numerous parasitic crustaceans, fish-lice, etc., as *Argulus*, *Caligus*, etc. Divested of these and restricted to the *Xiphosura*, the term is synonymous with *Merostomata* in one sense. See *Merostomata*.

pœcilopodous (pē-si-lop'ọ-dus), *a.* Of or pertaining to the *Pœcilopoda*.

pœcilothermic (pē"si-lọ-ther'mik), *a.* [< Gr. ποικίλος, various, + θέρμη, heat.] Varying in bodily temperature with that of the surrounding medium, as is particularly the case with cold-blooded animals. Also *poikilothermic*. [Rare.]

> Most of the lower animals are *poikilothermic*, or, as they have less appropriately been called, cold-blooded.
> *Claus*, Zoöl. (trans.), I. 74.

poem (pō'em), *n.* [< OF. *poëme*, F. *poème* = Sp. Pg. It. *poema*, < L. *poēma*, < Gr. ποίημα, anything made or done, a poem, < ποιεῖν, make. Cf. *poet*.] 1. A written composition in metrical form; a composition characterized by its arrangement in verses or measures, whether in blank verse or in rime: as, a lyric *poem*; a pastoral *poem*.

> The first and most necessarie poynt that euer I founde meete to be considered in making of a delectable *poeme* is this, to grounde it upon some fine inuention.
> *Gascoigne*, Notes on Eng. Verse, § 1 (Steele Glas, etc., ed. Arber).

> A *poem* is not alone any work or composition of the poets in many or few verses; but even one alone verse sometimes makes a perfect *poem*. *B. Jonson*, Discoveries.

> A *poem*, round and perfect as a star.
> *Alex. Smith*, A Life Drama, ii.

> There is no heroic *poem* in the world but is at bottom a biography, the life of a man. *Carlyle*, Sir Walter Scott.

> It is not metres, but a metre-making argument, that makes a *poem*. *Emerson*, The Poet.

2. A written composition which, though not in verse, is characterized by imaginative and poetic beauty in either the thought or the language: as, a prose *poem*.

poematic (pō-e-mat'ik), *a.* [< Gr. ποιηματικός, poetical, < ποίημα, a poem: see *poem*.] Relating to a poem; poetical. *Coleridge*.

pœnology, *n.* See *penology*.

Poephaga (pọ-ef'ạ-gạ̈), *n. pl.* [NL. (Owen, 1839), neut. pl. of *poephagus*: see *poephagous*.] A division of *Marsupialia*, including the kangaroos and others which feed on grass and herbage; the herbivorous marsupials.

poephagous (pọ-ef'ạ-gus), *a.* [< NL. *poephagus*, < Gr. ποηφάγος, grass-eating, < πόα, grass, + φαγεῖν, eat.] Eating grass; feeding on herbage; phytophagous or herbivorous; specifically, belonging to the *Poephaga*.

Poephagus (pọ-ef'ạ-gus), *n.* [NL. (J. E. Gray, 1846), < Gr. ποηφάγος, grass-eating: see *poephagous*.] A genus of *Bovidæ*, of the subfamily *Bovinæ*; the yaks. The common yak is *P. grunniens*. See cut under *yak*.

Poephila (pọ-ef'i-lạ̈), *n.* [NL. (J. Gould, 1842), < Gr. πόα, grass, + φιλεῖν, love.] An Australian genus of *Ploceidæ*, of the subfamily *Spermestinæ*. There are several species, as *P. acuticauda*, *P. personata*, *P. cincta*, *P. leucotis*, and *P. gonediæ*.

poeple†, *n.* A Middle English spelling of *people*.

poesy (pō'e-si), *n.* [Formerly also *posy* (q. v.); < ME. *poesie*, *poyse* = D. *poëzy*, *poëzie* = G. *poesie* (formerly also *poesei*, *poesey*) = Sw. Dan. *poesi*, < F. *poésie* = OSp. *poesi*, Sp. *poesía* = Pg. It. *poesia*, < L. *poesis*, poesy, poetry, < Gr. ποίησις, a making, creation, poesy, poetry, < ποιεῖν, make. Cf. *poem*, *poet*.] 1. The art of poetic composition; skill in making poems.

> *Poesie* therefore is an arte of imitation, for so Aristotle termeth it in his word Mimesis—that is to say, a representing, counterfetting, or figuring foorth.
> *Sir P. Sidney*, Apol. for Poetrie.

> *Poesy* is a part of learning in measure of words for the most part restrained, but in all other points extremely licensed. *Bacon*, Advancement of Learning, ii. 141.

> A poem . . . is the work of the poet, the end and fruit of his labour and study. *Poesy* is his skill or craft of making, the very fiction itself, the reason or form of the work.
> *B. Jonson*, Discoveries.

2. Poetry; metrical composition.

> By the many formes of *Poesie* the many moodes and pangs of louers throughly to be discouered.
> *Puttenham*, Arte of Eng. Poesie, p. 36.

> Simonides said that picture was a dumb *poesie*, and *poesie* a speaking picture. *Holland*, tr. of Plutarch, p. 805.

> Music and *poesy* used to quicken you.
> *Shak.*, T. of the S., i. 1. 36.

> I am satisfied if it cause delight; for delight is the chief, if not the only, end of *poesy*; instruction can be admitted but in the second place; for *poesy* only instructs as it delights. *Dryden*, Def. of Essay on Dram. Poesy.

> The lofty energies of thought,
> The fire of *poesy*.
> *Whittier*, The Female Martyr.

3†. A poem.

> Some few ages after came the poet Geffery Chaucer, who, writing his *poesies* in English, is of some called the first illuminator of the English tongue.
> *Verstegan*, Rest. of Decayed Intelligence, vii.

4†. A motto or sentimental conceit engraved on a ring or other trinket. See *posy*.

> A hoope of Gold, a paltry Ring
> That she did giue me, whose *Poesie* was
> For all the world like Cutlers Poetry
> Vpon a knife; Loue mee, and leaue mee not.
> *Shak.*, M. of V. (folio 1623), v.

> Nay, and I have *poesies* for rings too, and riddles that they dream not of. *B. Jonson*, Cynthia's Revels, ii. 1.

poet (pō'et), *n.* [< ME. *poete*, < OF. *poëte*, F. *poète* = Sp. Pg. It. *poeta* = D. *poëet* = G. Sw. Dan. *poet*, < L. *poeta*, < Gr. ποιητής, a maker, poet, < ποιεῖν, make. Cf. *poem*, *poesy*.] 1. One who composes or indites a poem; an author of metrical compositions.

> A *poet* is a maker, as the word signifies; and he who cannot make, that is invent, hath his name for nothing.
> *Dryden*.

> Search'd every tree, and pry'd on every flower,
> If anywhere by chance I might espy
> The rural *poet* of the melody.
> *Dryden*, Flower and Leaf, l. 125.

2. One skilled in the art of making poetry, or of metrical composition; one distinguished by the possession of poetic faculties or susceptibilities; one endowed with the gift and power of imaginative invention and creation attended by corresponding eloquence of expression, commonly but not necessarily in a metrical form.

> Semblably they that make verses, expressynge therby none other lernynge, but the crafte of versifienge, be not of auncient writers named *poetes*, but only called versifyers. *Sir T. Elyot*, The Governour, i. 13.

> I begin now, elevated by my Subject, to write with the Emotion and Fury of a *Poet*, yet the Integrity of an Historian. *Wycherley*, Love in a Wood, Ded.

The *poet* represents the things as they are impressed on his mind by the hand of the Creator.
Landor, Chesterfield and Chatham.

The *poet* is the man whose emotions, intenser than those of other men, naturally find a vent for themselves in some form of harmonious words, whether this be the form of metre or of balanced and musical prose.
J. C. Shairp, Poetic Interpretation of Nature, i.

Poet laureate. See *laureate*.—**Poet's cassia.** See *Osyris*.

poetaster (pō′et-as-tėr), *n.* [= OF. *poëtastre* = Sp. It. *poetastro*, < NL. **poetaster*, < L. *poeta*, a poet (see *poet*), + dim. *-aster*.] A petty poet; a feeble rimester, or a writer of indifferent verses.

He [Voltaire] was well acquainted with all the petty vanities and affectations of the *poetaster*.
Macaulay, Frederic the Great.

He makes no demand on our charity in favor of some *poetaster* for whom he may have imbibed a strange affection.
Whipple, Ess. and Rev., I. 32.

poetastry (pō′et-as-tri), *n.* [< *poetaster* + *-y*[3].] The rimed effusions of a poetaster; paltry verses.

poetess (pō′et-es), *n.* [= F. *poëtesse* = Sp. *poetisa* = Pg. *poetiza* = It. *poetessa*, < ML. *poetissa*, fem. of L. *poeta*, a poet: see *poet* and *-ess*.] A woman who is a poet.

poethood (pō′et-hu̇d), *n.* [< *poet* + *-hood*.] The state or quality of being a poet; the inherent qualifications or the conditions that constitute a poet. *S. Lanier*, The English Novel, p. 47.

poetic (pọ̄-et′ik), *a.* [= F. *poëtique* = Sp. *poético* = Pg. It. *poetico* (cf. D. G. *poetisch* = Sw. Dan. *poetisk*), < L. *poeticus*, < Gr. ποιητικός, creative, poetic, < ποιεῖν, make (> ποιητής, poet): see *poet*.] 1. Of or pertaining to poetry; of the nature of or expressed in poetry; possessing the qualities or the charm of poetry: as, a *poetic* composition; *poetic* style.

In our own day such *poetic* descriptions of Nature have burst the bonds of metre altogether, and filled many a splendid page of *poetic* or imaginative prose.
J. C. Shairp, Poetic Interpretation of Nature, viii.

2. Of or pertaining to a poet or poets; characteristic of or befitting a poet: as, *poetic* genius; *poetic* feeling; *poetic* license.

Then farewell hopes o' laurel boughs,
To garland my *poetic* brows!
Burns, To James Smith.

He [Faraday] was always in the temper of the poet, and, like the poet, he continually reached that point of emotion which produces *poetic* creation. *Stopford Brooke*, Faraday.

3. Endowed with the feeling or faculty of a poet; having the susceptibility, sensibility, or expression of a poet; like a poet: as, a *poetic* youth; a *poetic* face.

What warm, *poetic* heart but inly bleeds,
And execrates man's savage, ruthless deeds!
Burns, Brigs of Ayr.

4. Celebrated, or worthy to be celebrated, in poetry: as, a *poetic* scene.

When you are on the east coast of Sicily you are in the most *poetic* locality of the classic world.
C. D. Warner, Roundabout Journey, p. 104.

Mere trade became *poetic* while dealing with the spices of Arabia, the silks of Damascus, the woven stuffs of Persia, the pearls of Ceylon.
C. E. Norton, Church-building in Middle Ages, p. 41.

5. Of or pertaining to making or shaping, especially to artistic invention and arrangement. [Recent.]

Poetic philosophy is a form of knowledge having reference to the shaping of material, or to the technically correct and artistic creation of works of art.
Ueberweg, Hist. Philos. (trans.), I.

Poetic justice, an ideal distribution of rewards and punishments such as is common in poetry and works of fiction, but seldom exists in real life.

And so it came to pass that quite unintentionally, and yet by a sort of *poetic justice*, Rodrigue's letter to Rose, as hers to him, was written by a third person.
The Century, XXXVII. 584.

Poetic license, a privilege or liberty taken by a poet in using words, p ra es, or matters of fact in order to produce a desired eff ect.

poetical (pọ̄-et′i-kạl), *a.* [< *poetic* + *-al*.] Same as *poetic*.

Poetical expression includes sound as well as meaning. "Music," says Dryden, "is inarticulate poetry."
Johnson, Pope.

poetically (pọ̄-et′i-kạl-i), *adv.* In a poetical sense or manner; according to the laws of poetry.

The critics have concluded that it is not necessary the manners of the hero should be virtuous. They are *poetically* good if they are of a piece. *Dryden*, Æneid, Ded.

poetics (pọ̄-et′iks), *n.* [Pl. of *poetic*: see *-ics*. Cf. F. *poëtique* = Sp. Pg. It. *poetica*, f., poetics.] That branch of criticism which treats of the nature and laws of poetry.

poeticule (pọ̄-et′i-kūl), *n.* [< L. *poeta*, a poet, + dim. term. *-culus*.] A petty poet; a poetaster.

A study which sets before us in fascinating relief the professional *poeticule* of a period in which as yet clubs, coteries, and newspapers were not.
A. C. Swinburne, Nineteenth Century, XXI. 97.

poetization (pō″et-i-zā′shọn), *n.* [< *poetize* + *-ation*.] Composition in verse; the act of rendering in the form of poetry. Also spelled *poetisation*.

The great movement for the *poetization* of Latin prose which was begun by Sallust ran its course till it culminated in the monstrous style of Fronto. *Encyc. Brit.*, XX. 187.

poetize (pō′et-īz), *v.*; pret. and pp. *poetized*, ppr. *poetizing*. [< F. *poétiser* = Sp. Pg. *poetizar* = It. *poetizzare*, *poeteezzare*, < ML. *poetizare*, *poetisare*, compose poetry, < L. *poeta*, a poet: see *poet* and *-ize*.] I. *intrans.* To compose poetry; write as a poet.

I versify the truth, not *poetize*. *Donne.*

II. *trans.* To make poetic; cause to conform to poetic standards; express in a poetic form.

What Ovid did but *poetize*, experience doth moralise, our manners actually perform. *Rev. T. Adams*, Works, I. 212.

Virgil has, upon many occasions, *poetized* . . . a whole sentence by means of the same word.
Goldsmith, Poetry Distinguished from other Writing.

Instead of the sublime and beautiful, the near, the low, the common, was explored and *poetized*.
Emerson, Misc., p. 93.

Also spelled *poetise*.

poet-musician (pō″et-mū-zish′ạn), *n.* One in whom the gifts and skill of the poet and the musician are united; a bard.

poetress† (pō′et-res), *n.* [< OF. *poeteresse*, as if < ML. **poetrissa* for L. *poetris*, *poetria*, a poet, < Gr. ποιήτρια, fem. of ποιητής, a poet: see *poet*. Cf. *poetess*.] Same as *poetess*.

Most peerless *poetress*,
The true Pandora of all heavenly graces. *Spenser.*

poetry (pō′et-ri), *n.* [< ME. *poetrye*, *poetrie*, < OF. *poetrie*, *poeterie*, *poterie*, *poetrerie* = OIt. *poetria*, < ML. *poetria*, poetry (cf. L. *poetria*, < Gr. ποιήτρια, a poetess), < L. *poeta*, a poet: see *poet* and *-ry*.] 1. That one of the fine arts which addresses itself to the feelings and the imagination by the instrumentality of musical and moving words; the art which has for its object the exciting of intellectual pleasure by means of vivid, imaginative, passionate, and inspiriting language, usually though not necessarily arranged in the form of measured verse or numbers.

By *poetry* we mean the art of employing words in such a manner as to produce an illusion on the imagination, the art of doing by means of words what the painter does by means of colours. *Macaulay*, Milton.

Poetry is itself a thing of God;
He made his prophets poets; and the more
We feel of poesie do we become
Like God in love and power — under-makers.
Bailey, Festus, Proem.

The grand power of *Poetry* is its interpretative power, by which I mean . . . the power of so dealing with things as to awaken in us a wonderfully full, new, and intimate sense of them, and of our relations with them.
M. Arnold, Maurice de Guérin.

We shall hardly make our definition of *poetry*, considered as an imitative art, too extended if we say that it is a speaking art of which the business is to represent by means of verbal signs arranged with musical regularity everything for which verbal signs have been invented.
Encyc. Brit., IX. 207.

2. An imaginative, artistic, and metrical collocation of words so marshaled and attuned as to excite or control the imagination and the emotions; the language of the imagination or emotions metrically expressed. In a wide sense poetry comprises whatever embodies the products of the imagination and fancy, and appeals to these powers in others, as well as to the finer emotions, the sense of ideal beauty, and the like. In this sense we speak of the *poetry* of motion.

The essence of *poetry* is invention: such invention as, by producing something unexpected, surprises and delights. *Johnson*, Waller.

Poetry is not the proper antithesis to prose, but to science. *Poetry* is opposed to science, and prose to metre. . . . The proper and immediate object of science is the acquirement or communication of truth; the proper immediate object of *poetry* is the communication of immediate pleasure. *Coleridge.*

No literary expression can, properly speaking, be called *poetry* that is not in a certain deep sense emotional whatever may be its subject matter, concrete in its method and its diction, rhythmical in movement, and artistic in form.
Encyc. Brit., XIX. 257.

3. Composition in verse; a metrical composition; verse; poems: as, heroic *poetry*; lyric or dramatic *poetry*; a collection of *poetry*.

Oon seyde that Omere made lyes
Feyninge in his *poetries*.
Chaucer, House of Fame, l. 1477.

And this young birkie here, . . . will his . . . *poetries* help him here? *Scott*, Rob Roy, xxiii.

Arcadic, lyric, etc., poetry. See the adjectives.

poetship (pō′et-ship), *n.* [< *poet* + *-ship*.] The state of being a poet; poethood.

poet-sucker (pō′et-suk″ėr), *n.* A suckling poet; an immature or precocious poet. [Low.]

What says my *poet-sucker*?
He 's chewing his muse's cud, I do see by him.
B. Jonson, Staple of News, iv. 1.

pogamoggan (pog-ạ-mog′ạn), *n.* [Amer. Ind.] A weapon used by some tribes of North American Indians, consisting of a rounded stone inclosed in a net of woven fibers ending in a strong braid, by which it can be whirled. Compare *slung-shot*.

pogge (pog), *n.* A cottoid fish, the armed bullhead, *Agonus cataphractus*.

Pogge (*Agonus cataphractus*).

poggy[1] (pog′i), *n.*; pl. *poggies* (-iz). [Also *poggie*.] A small arctic whale, yielding only about 20 or 25 barrels of oil, supposed to be the young of the bow-head whale, *Balæna mysticetus*. *C. M. Scammon*, Marine Mammals, p. 60. See cut under *whale*.

poggy[2] (pog′i), *n.* Same as *porgy*.

poghaden (pog-hā′dn), *n.* [Amer. Ind.] The menhaden. Also *pauhagen*.

pogie, *n.* Same as *pogy*.

Pogonia[1] (pọ̄-gō′ni-ạ̈), *n.* [NL. (Jussieu, 1789), so called in allusion to the frequently fringed lip; < Gr. πωγωνίας, bearded, < πώγων, beard.] A genus of terrestrial orchids of the tribe *Neottieæ* and subtribe *Arethuseæ*, characterized by the distinct and usually erect sepals, the long wingless column, and the undivided or three-lobed lip. There are over 30 species, widely dispersed over the world, of which 5 occur in the United States. The typical species (including the most common American, *P. ophioglossoides*, sometimes called *snake's-mouth orchis*) grow in bogs, especially in the neighborhood of peat, and produce a tuberous root, and a slender stem bearing a single handsome and fragrant pale-rose nodding flower, a single leaf, and a single bract; others have two or three leaves, and few or many flowers; a few bear a single flower surmounting a whorl of leaves; and many of the Old World species produce first a one-sided raceme of nodding flowers and later a single broad or roundish leaf. *P. pendula* is the three-birds orchis of the United States, named from the form of the fruit.

Flowering Plant and Leaf of Snake's-mouth Orchis (*Pogonia ophioglossoides*).

pogonia[2], *n.* Plural of *pogonium*.

Pogonias (pō-gō′ni-as), *n.* [NL. (Lacépède, 1802), < Gr. πωγωνίας, bearded, < πώγων, beard.] 1. In *ichth.*, a genus of sciænoids, having numerous barbels on the lower jaw (whence the name); the drums or drumfish, as *P. chromis*. See cut under *drum*[1], 11 (*a*).—2. In *ornith.*, same as *Pogonorhynchus*. *Illiger*, 1811.

pogoniasis (pō-gọ̄-nī′ạ-sis), *n.* [NL., < Gr. πώγων, beard (cf. πωγωνίας, bearded), + *-iasis*.] Excessive growth of beard, especially in a woman.

pogoniate (pọ̄-gō′ni-āt), *a.* [< Gr. πωγωνιάτης, bearded, < πώγων, beard.] 1. In *zoöl.*, bearded or barbate.—2. In *ornith.*, webbed, as a feather; having webs or pogonia; vexillate.

pogonium (pọ̄-gō′ni-um), *n.*; pl. *pogonia* (-ạ̈). [NL., < Gr. πωγώνιον, dim. of πώγων, a beard.] In *ornith.*, the web, vane, or vexillum of a feather.

Pogonorhynchinæ (pọ̄-gō″nọ̄-ring-kī′nē), *n. pl.* [NL., < *Pogonorhynchus* + *-inæ*.] A subfamily of *Megalæmidæ* (or *Capitonidæ*), typified by the genus *Pogonorhynchus*, and containing the African barbets.

Pogonorhynchus (pọ̄-gō-nọ̄-ring′kus), *n.* [NL. (Van der Hoeven, 1835), < Gr. πώγων, beard, + ῥύγχος, snout.] A genus of African barbets, typical of the subfamily *Pogonorhynchinæ*, having a large sulcate and dentate beak which is strongly pogoniate. *P. dubius* is glossy-black, blood-red, and white. *P. hirsutus* (or *flavipunctata*) is a barbet of the Gaboon, forming the type of the subgenus *Tricholæma*. See cut on following page.

Pogostemon (pō-gō-stē'mon), *n.* [NL. (Desfontaines, 1815), so called in allusion to the long hairs often clothing the filaments; < Gr. *πώγων*, beard, + *στήμων*, warp (stamen).] A genus of gamopetalous plants of the mint family, order *Labiatæ*, and tribe *Satureineæ*, type of the subtribe *Pogostemoneæ*, and characterized by the four perfect stamens, which are protruding, distant, straight, and little unequal, and by the terminal roundish one-celled anthers, five-toothed calyx, four-cleft corolla with one lobe spreading, and the flowers close-crowded in large verticillasters, in an interrupted spike or panicle. There are about 32 species, natives of the East Indies, the Malay archipelago, and Japan. They are herbs or shrubby plants, with opposite leaves, and the numerous small flowers are whitish and purple, or of other colors. See *patchouli* for the principal species.

Pogonorhynchus hirsutus.

pogue (pōg), *n.* [< Ir. Gael. *pog* = W. *poc*, a kiss.] A kiss. [Irish.]

> I axed her for a *pogue*,
> The black-eyed saucy rogue,
> For a single little *pogue*,
> An' she scornful turned away!
> *The Century*, XXXVIII. 892.

pogy (pō'gi), *n.*; pl. *pogies* (-giz). [Also *poggy*, *poggie*, *pogie*, *porgy*, etc.] 1. The menhaden, *Brevoortia tyrannus*. [New England.]—2. A kind of small fishing-boat used in the Bay of Fundy and along the New England coast. *Perley.*

pogy-catcher (pō'gi-kach″ėr), *n.* A sailing vessel or steamer employed in the capture of menhaden.

pogy-gull (pō'gi-gul), *n.* A sea-gull found at Cape Cod, Massachusetts (where so called), perhaps *Larus argentatus.*

poh (pō), *interj.* Same as *pooh.*

pohutukawa (pọ̄-hō-tọ̄-kä'wạ̈), *n.* [Maori: see the quotation.] A conspicuous tree, *Metrosideros tomentosa*, growing on rocky coasts in New Zealand. It has leathery shining leaves, and is very handsome in blossom. Its bark yields a brown dye, and its hard strong reddish wood is suitable for the frames of ships, agricultural implements, etc.

> Here every headland is crowned with magnificent *pohutukawa*-trees, literally rendered the 'brine-sprinkled,' . . . known to the settlers as the Christmas tree, when boughs of its glossy green and scarlet are used in church decoration as a substitute for the holly-berries of Old England.
> *Constance F. Gordon Cumming*, The Century, XXVII. 920.

poi (pō'i), *n.* [Hawaiian.] An article of food of the Sandwich Islanders, prepared from the root of the taro, *Colocasia antiquorum*. After being mixed with water, the taro-root is beaten with a pestle till it becomes an adhesive mass like dough; it is then fermented, and in three or four days is fit for use. Also *poe*. C. W. Stoddard, South Sea Idyls, p. 135.

> *Poi* is generally eaten from a bowl placed between two people, by dipping three fingers into it, giving them a twirl round, and then sucking them.
> *Lady Brassey*, Voyage of Sunbeam, II. xvi.

poignancy (poi'nạn-si), *n.* [< *poignan(t)* + *-cy*.] 1. The power of stimulating the organs of taste; piquancy.—2. Point; sharpness; keenness; power of irritation; asperity: as, the *poignancy* of wit or sarcasm.—3. Painfulness; keenness; bitterness: as, the *poignancy* of grief.

poignant (poi'nạnt), *a.* [Early mod. E. *poynant*, < ME. *poynant*, < OF. (and F.) *poignant* (= Sp. Pg. *pungente* = It. *pungente*, *pugnente*, < L. *pungen(t-)s*, ppr. of *pungere*, prick: see *pungent*, and cf. *point*.] 1†. Sharp to the taste; biting; piquant; pungent.

> Wo was his cook, but if his sauce were
> *Poynaunt* and sharp, and redy al his gere.
> *Chaucer*, Gen. Prol. to C. T., l. 352.

> No *poignant* sauce she knew, nor costly treat;
> Her hunger gave a relish to her meat.
> *Dryden*, Cock and Fox, l. 21.

2†. Pointed; keen; sharp.

> His *poynant* speare, that many made to bleed.
> *Spenser*, F. Q., I. vii. 19.

3. Keen; bitter; satirical; hence, telling; striking.

> Always replying to the sarcastic remarks of his wife with complacency and *poignant* good humour.
> *Sir T. More*, Family of Sir T. More, Int. to Utopia, p. xiv.

> Example, whether for emulation or avoidance, is never so *poignant* as when presented to us in a striking personality. *Lowell*, Books and Libraries.

4. Severe; piercing; very painful or acute: as, *poignant* pain or grief.

> Our recent calamity . . . had humbled my wife's pride, and blunted it by more *poignant* afflictions.
> *Goldsmith*, Vicar, xxii.

=**Syn.** 3 and 4. *Piquant*, etc. (see *pungent*), sharp, penetrating, intense, biting, acrid, caustic.

poignantly (poi'nạnt-li), *adv.* In a poignant, stimulating, piercing, or irritating manner; with keenness or point.

poignard, *n.* [F.] Same as *poniard.*

poignet (poin), *n.* [< F. *poing*, fist: see *poing*.] Fist; hand.

> The witnesses which the faction kept in *poigne* (like false dice, high and low Fullhams), to be played forth upon plots and to make discoveries as there was occasion, were now chapfallen.
> *Roger North*, Examen, p. 108. (*Davies.*)

poimenics (poi-men'iks), *n.* [< Gr. *ποιμήν*, a shepherd, LGr. a pastor: see *-ics*.] Pastoral theology. See *pastoral.*

poinado†, *n.* Same as *poniard.*

> My Peece I must alter to a *Poynado*, and my Pike to a Pickadevant.
> *Heywood*, Royal King (Works, ed. Pearson, 1874, VI. 70).

poinard†, *n.* An obsolete form of *poniard.*

Poinciana (poin-si-ā'nạ̈), *n.* [NL. (Tournefort, 1700), named after *Poinci*, a governor-general of the West Indies in the middle of the 17th century, who wrote on the natural history of the Antilles.] A genus of leguminous plants of the suborder *Cæsalpinieæ* and tribe *Eucæsalpinieæ*, characterized by the five valvate calyx-lobes, five nearly equal orbicular petals, ten distinct declined stamens, and hard flat two-valved many-seeded pods. The 3 species are natives of warm regions in eastern Africa, the Mascarene Islands, and western India, but have long been introduced into the West Indies and other tropical countries. They are handsome trees with bipinnate leaves and showy orange or scarlet flowers. *P. regia*, with crimson flowers, is known as royal peacock-flower, flame-acacia, and gold mohur-tree. *P. pulcherrima*, with red and yellow flowers, is the Barbados-pride, flower-pride, or flower-fence. *P. Gilliesii* is the crimson thread-flower. They are also sometimes called *flamboyants*. See *flamboyant.*

poind (poind), *v. t.* 1. A dialectal (Scotch) form of *pind* or *pound*[2].—2. To seize; distrain; seize and sell under warrant, as a debtor's goods. [Scotch.]

> He slew my knight, and *poin'd* his gear.
> *Lament of the Border Widow* (Child's Ballads, III. 87).

poinder (poin'dėr), *n.* A dialectal form of *pinder.*

poinding (poin'ding), *n.* [Verbal n. of *poind*, *v.*] In *Scotch law*, a process by which a creditor may enforce his demand by seizure of movable property. It is carried into effect either by sale and payment of the proceeds to the creditor, or by appraisal of the goods and their delivery to the creditor on account. *Personal poinding* cannot be prosecuted, except against a tenant for rent, until the debtor has been charged to pay or perform and the days allowed therefor have expired. The right of a private creditor to reach things in action and some other movables, such as money and ornaments on the person, has been questioned. *Real poinding*, or *poinding of the ground*, is the remedy of one who is enforcing a lien or burden on land, as distinguished from a personal obligation to seize movables found on the land, other than those of strangers, and other than those of a tenant in excess of rent actually due from him.

poinette, *n.* See *poynet.*

poing (pwań), *n.* [F., the fist, = Sp. *puño* = Pg. *punho* = It. *pugno*, < L. *pugnus*, fist.] In *her.*, a fist or closed hand used as a bearing.

Poinsettia (poin-set'i-ạ̈), *n.* [NL. (Graham, 1836), named after Joel R. *Poinsett*, American minister to Mexico, who discovered the plant there in 1828.] 1. A former genus of American apetalous plants of the order *Euphorbiaceæ* and tribe *Euphorbieæ*, now included as a section of the vast genus *Euphorbia*.—2. [*l. c.*] The *Euphorbia* (*Poinsettia*) *pulcherrima*, a plant much cultivated in conservatories. It is conspicuous for the large scarlet floral leaves surrounding its crowded yellowish cymes of small flowers, and is much used for decoration, especially in churches. Also called *Christmas-flower* or *Easter-flower*, in England *lobster-flower* and *Mexican flame-leaf*, and in Mexico *flora de pasqua.*

point[1] (point), *n.* and *a.* [< ME. *point*, *poynt*, *pointe*, *poynte*; < (*a*) OF. *point*, *poinct*, *puint*, F. *point*, m., a point, dot, full stop, period, speck, hole, stitch, point of time, moment, difficulty, etc., = Sp. *punto* = Pg. *ponto* = It. *punto*, m., = OFries. *punt*, *pont* = D. *punt* = MLG. *punte*, LG. *punt*, *pünt* = MHG. *punct*, *punt*, *puncte*, *punte*, G. *punkt* = Icel. *punktr* = Sw. Dan. *punkt*, a point, < L. *punctum*, a point, puncture, spot on dice, small part or weight, moment, point in space, etc., prop. a hole punched in, neut. of *punctus*, pp. of *pungere*, prick, pierce, punch: see *punch*[1], *pungent* (cf. L. *punctus* (*punctu-*), a pricking, stinging, also a point, < *pungere*, prick, punch); (*b*) < OF. *pointe*, *poincte*, *puinte*, F. *pointe*, f., a point, bodkin, small sword, place, etc.; also sharpness, pungency, etc., = Sp. *punta* = Pg. *ponta* = It. *punta*, f., < ML. *puncta*, f., a point, etc., fem. of L. *punctus*, pp. of *pungere*, prick, pierce, punch: see above.] **I.** *n.* **1.** The sharp end of something, as of a thorn, pin, needle, knife, sword, etc.

> With the egge of the knyfe youre trenchere vp be ye reysande
> As nyghe the *poynt* as ye may.
> *Babees Book* (E. E. T. S.), p. 138.

> Eight forky arrows from this hand have fled,
> And eight bold heroes by their *points* lie dead.
> *Pope*, Iliad, viii. 362.

> This barbed the *point* of P.'s hatred.
> *Dickens*, Great Expectations, II. 217.

2. That which tapers to or has a sharp end; a tapering thing with a sharp apex. (*a*†) A sword.

> Why, I will learn you, by the true judgment of the eye, hand, and foot, to control any enemy's *point* in the world.
> B. *Jonson*, Every Man in his Humour, i. 4.

(*b*) In *etching*, an engraving-tool consisting of a metallic point, a sewing-needle or a medium embroidery-needle, or a rat-tail file ground to an evenly rounded tapering point, not too sharp if intended for use on an etching-ground, but much more trenchant if it is to be employed in dry-point on the bare copper.

> There were also many fragments of boxwood, on which were designs of exquisite beauty, drawn with the *point*.
> *C. T. Newton*, Art and Archæol., p. 379.

(*c*) In *printing*, a projecting pin on a press for marking the register by perforating the paper. (*d*) A small diamond or fragment of a diamond used for cutting glass. (*e*) A punch used by stone-masons to form narrow ridges in the face of a stone which is to be afterward dressed down. (*f*) A wedge-shaped chisel for nigging ashler. (*g*) A triangular piece of zinc for holding glass in the sash before the putty is put in. (*h*) *pl.* In *rail.*, the switches or movable guiding-rails at junctions or stations. [Eng.]

> For horse traction fixed *points* of chilled cast-iron or steel are sufficient, as the driver can turn his horses and direct the car on to either line of rails.
> *Encyc. Brit.*, XXIII. 507.

(*i*) A branch of a deer's antler. See *antler.*

> He was a fine buck of eight *points.*
> *T. Roosevelt*, Hunting Trips.

(*j*) In *backgammon*, one of the narrow tapering spaces on which the men are placed. (*k*) *pl.* Spurs or stout needles suitably fastened in a flat board, on which printed sheets are placed by passing the needles through the point-holes; this is done to insure the exact cutting of printed sheets that have uneven margins. *Knight*, Bookbinding.

3. A salient or projecting part; a part of an object projecting abruptly from it, as a peak or promontory from the land or coast.

> And the sayde yle Cirigo is directely ayeust the *poynt* of Capo Maleo in Morrea.
> *Sir R. Guylforde*, Pylgrymage, p. 13.

> The splintered *points* of the crag are seen,
> With water howling and vexed between.
> *Whittier*, Mogg Megone.

4. A salient feature or physical peculiarity; especially, a feature which determines the excellence of an animal; characteristic; trait.

> So remarkable was their resemblance [two horses] in *points*, action, and color that . . . even the grooms came out to see. *J. W. Palmer*, After his Kind, p. 226.

5. The salient feature of a story, discourse, epigram, or remark; that part or feature of a saying, etc., which gives it application; the directly effective part; hence, the possession of such a feature; force or expression generally: as, he failed to see the *point* of the joke; his action gave *point* to his words.

> Every author has a way of his own in bringing his *points* to bear. *Sterne*, Tristram Shandy, i. 9.

> Both her [Madame de Lieven's] letters and her conversation are full of *point*. *Greville*, Memoirs, Feb. 3, 1819.

> An epigram now is a short satire closing with a *point* of wit. *I. D'Israeli*, Amen. of Lit., II. 352.

6. The precise question or matter in dispute or under consideration; the principal thing to be attended to; the main difficulty to be met or obviated: as, these are side issues—let us come to the *point.*

> He maintained, which was in fact the *point* at issue, that the opinions held at that day by the Quakers were the same that the Ranters had held long ago.
> *Southey*, Bunyan, p. 42.

> "You haven't told me about the Greek yet," says Charles Wall, clinging to the *point.*
> *W. M. Baker*, New Timothy, p. 115.

7. An indivisible part of an argument, narrative, or account; a particular; a detail; an item. See *at all points* and *in point of*, below.

> Where she no *point* had of diffame no dais.
> *Rom. of Partenay*, l. 3392.

But for y am a lewed man, paraunter y migte
Passen par aventure & in som poynt erren.
Piers Plowman's Crede (E. E. T. S.), l. 846.

Told him every poynt how he was slayn.
Chaucer, Nun's Priest's Tale, l. 202.

But in what particular *points* the oracle was, in faith I know not. *Sir P. Sidney*, Arcadia, i.

You are now beyond all our fears, and have nothing to take heed on your self but fair ladies. A pretty *point* of security, and such a one as all Germany cannot afford. *Sir John Suckling*, Letters (1648), p. 86.

8. Particular end, aim, purpose, or concern; object desired: as, to gain one's *point*.

The constant design of both these orators, in all their speeches, was, to drive some one particular *point*. *Swift*, To a Young Clergyman.

Our Swain,
A very hero till his *point* was gained,
Proved all unable to support the weight
Of prosperous fortune.
Wordsworth, Excursion, vi.

I suppose the *point* of the exhibition lay in hearing the notes of love and jealousy warbled with the lisp of childhood; and in very bad taste that *point* was. *Charlotte Brontë*, Jane Eyre, xi.

The rain always made a *point* of setting in just as he had some out-door work to do. *Irving*, Rip Van Winkle.

9†. Case; condition; situation; state; plight.

He departed that Ryvere in 360 smale Ryveres, because that he had sworn that he scholde putte the Ryvers in suche *poynt* that a Woman myghte wel passe there withouten castynge of hire Clothes. *Mandeville*, Travels, p. 41.

He was a lord ful fat and in good *poynt*.
Chaucer, Gen. Prol. to C. T., l. 136.

And over yere thai wol been in goode *pointe*,
Withouten scorf or scalle in cors or jointe.
Palladius, Husbondrie (E. E. T. S.), p. 154.

Amaunt be-thought hym that he myght come neuer in better *poynt* to conquere his Castell that he so longe hadde loste, and sente after peple. *Merlin* (E. E. T. S.), ii. 350.

10†. A deed or feat; an exploit.

Yf thow durst, par ma fay,
A *poynt* of armys undyrtake,
Thow broke her wille fore ay.
Torrent of Portugal, p. 36. (*Halliwell*.)

11. A mark made by the end of a sharp instrument, such as a pin, needle, pen, etc.; a dot or other sign to mark separation, to measure from, etc. Specifically—(*a*) A mark of punctuation; a character used to mark the divisions of composition, or the pauses to be observed in reading or speaking, as the comma (,), the semicolon (;), the colon (:), and especially the period or full stop (.).

There abruptly it did end,
Without full *point*, or other Cesure right.
Spenser, F. Q., II. x. 68.

Who shall teach the propriety and nature of *points* and accents of letters? *Purchas*, Pilgrimage, p. 168.

But thy Name all the Letters make;
Whate'er 'tis writ, I find That there,
Like *Points* and Comma's ev'ry where.
Cowley, The Mistress, The Thief.

Hence—(*b*) A stop; a conclusion; a period.

And ther a *pount*; for ended is my tale.
Chaucer, Canon's Yeoman's Tale, l. 469.

(*c*) A diacritical mark, indicating a vowel, or other modification of sound: especially in Hebrew, Arabic, etc. (*d*) A dot used in writing numbers—(1) inserted after the units' place to show where the decimals begin (specifically called a *decimal point*); or (2) placed over a repeating decimal, or over the first and last figures of a circulating decimal: thus, $\frac{8}{9} = .\dot{8}\dot{8}$; $\frac{??}{?} = 1.\dot{2}56\dot{7}$; or (3) used to separate a series of figures representing a number into periods of a certain number of figures each. (*e*) In *musical notation*, a dot affixed to a note, either after it, to increase its time-value (see *dot*), or above or below it, as a sign of a staccato effect (see *staccato*). (*f*) A speck or spot; a jot; a trace; hence, figuratively, a very small quantity.

Thei cowde not in hym espi no *poynte* of covetise.
Merlin (E. E. T. S.), i. 106.

12. An object having position but not extension. (*a*) A place having spatial position but no size; the uninterrupted common limit of four three-dimensional spaces.

We sometimes speak of space, or do suppose a *point* in it, at such a distance from any part of the universe. *Locke*.

All rays proceeding from a *point* pass through a single *point* after reflexion, because they undergo a change in their direction greater in proportion as the *point* of the mirror struck is distant from the principal axis.
Lommel, Light (trans.), p. 42.

(*b*) In *astron.*, a certain place marked in the heavens, or distinguished for its importance in astronomical calculations: as, vertical *points* (the zenith and the nadir); equinoctial *points*; solstitial *points*. (*c*) In *persp.*, any definitive position with reference to the perspective plane: as, *point* of sight; vanishing-*point*. (*d*) That which has position in time, but no definite continuance; an instant of time.

And a-noon as he was comen his felowes recouered that were in *pointe* to leve place. *Merlin* (E. E. T. S.), iii. 459.

The period of his [Henry V.'s] accession is described as a *point* of time at which his character underwent some sort of change. *Stubbs*, Const. Hist., § 645.

13. Precise limit or degree; especially, the precise degree of temperature: as, the boiling-*point* of water.

Oh, furious desire, how like a whirlwind
Thou hurriest me beyond mine honour's *point*!
Beau. and Fl., Knight of Malta, i. 1.

They [the Jesuits] appear to have discovered the precise *point* to which intellectual culture can be carried without risk of intellectual emancipation.
Macaulay, Hist. Eng., vi.

14. A small unit of measurement. (*a*) A linear unit, the tenth part of a geometrical line, the twelfth part of a French line. (*b*) In *typog.*, a type-founding unit of measure; in the United States about one seventy-second of an inch. It regulates the bodies and defines numerically different sizes of types. The body of pica, for instance, is 12 points in size, and the new designation for pica is 12 *point*. The French (Didot) point is larger. Twelve points French are nearly equal to thirteen points American. The point system was introduced in 1737 by Fournier the younger, a type-founder of Paris. As made by him, this point was not a regular fraction of any legally prescribed measure. François-Ambroise Didot readjusted this point as a fraction of the standard royal foot, in which form it was gradually accepted by the printing-trades of France and Germany. The American point was adopted by the United States Type-Founders' Association in 1883, and made of smaller size, to prevent a too marked disturbance of the sizes then in regular use. The old names of types and their relation to each other are shown by the number of points assigned to each size in the following table:

4 Point.
5 Point.
6 Point.
7 Point.
8 Point.
9 Point.
10 Point.
11 Point.
12 Point.

Points.	Name of Type.	Points.	Name of Type.
3	Excelsior	14	English
3½	Brilliant	16	Two-line brevier
4	Semi-brevier	18	Great primer
4½	Diamond	20	Paragon
5	Pearl	22	Two-line small pica
5½	Agate	24	Two-line pica
6	Nonpareil	28	Two-line English
7	Minion	32	Four-line brevier
8	Brevier	36	Three-line pica
9	Bourgeois	40	Double paragon
10	Long primer	44	Four-line small pica
11	Small pica	48	Four-line pica.
12	Pica		

(*c*) *Naut.*, an angular unit, one eighth of a right angle, or 11¼°, being the angle between adjacent points of the compass (see *compass*, *n.*, 7): as, to bring the ship up half a *point*.

I find the compass of their doctrine took in two and thirty *points*. *Swift*, Tale of a Tub, viii.

15. A unit of fluctuation of price per share or other standard of reference on the exchanges, etc. In stock transactions in the United States a point is $1 (or in Great Britain £1); in coffee and cotton it is the hundredth part of a cent, and in oil, grain, pork, etc., one cent: as, Erie preferred has declined five *points*; coffee has gone up 200 *points*.

In the afternoon there had been one of the usual flurries in the "street." Zenith and Nadir preferred had gone off three *points*. *The Century*, XXXVIII. 209.

16. A unit of count in a game (compare def. 19); hence, an advantage in any struggle: as, I have gained a *point*.

Charles's impudence and bad character are great *points* in my favour. *Sheridan*, School for Scandal, iv. 2.

17. In *piquet*, the number of cards in the longest suit of a hand: as, what is your *point*? Six.—18. In *lace-making*, needle-point lace: as, Alençon *point*; Dresden *point*; a collar of *point*. See cut under *lace*. Used in the plural, the term denotes lace, especially fine lace in general: as, a christening-robe trimmed with French *points*; especially so used in the eighteenth century, in such phrases as "he is well in *points*"—that is, well supplied with lace. *Point* is also used freely in English in connection with the decorative arts (as a tapestry of Beauvais *point*), referring to some peculiar kind of work, and is even applied to bobbin-lace and the like. It also denotes vaguely a pattern or a feature of a pattern in works of embroidery and the like, usually in connection with the stitch or the peculiar method of work which produces it. Thus, *dentelle, point d'Angleterre*, means literally lace, English style of work, but the phrase *English point* is more often used for it, causing great confusion with the proper sense of needle-point lace. See *lace*.

We shall all ha' bride-laces
Or *points*. *B. Jonson*, Tale of a Tub, i. 2.

19. A lace with tags at the end. Such laces, about eight inches long, consisting often of three differently colored strands of yarn twisted together and having their ends wrapped with iron, were used in the middle ages to fasten the clothes together, but gave place to buttons in the seventeenth century. They were also made of silk or leather. They or their tags were much used as small stakes in gaming, as forfeits, counters, and gratuities—uses explaining many allusions in old writers, especially the figurative use of the word for a small value, or a thing of small value.

Points in Costume.

Al in a kirtel of a lyght waget,
Ful faire and thikke been the *poyntes* set.
Chaucer, Miller's Tale, l. 136.

I pray yow bryng hom *poynts* and lasys of silk for you and me. *Paston Letters*, II. 358.

He made his pen of the aglet of a *point* that he plucked from his hose. *Latimer*, 4th Sermon bef. Edw. VI., 1549.

In matters not worth a blewe *poinct* . . . we will spare for no cost. *Udall*, tr. of Apophthegms of Erasmus, p. 8.

Full large of limbe and every joint
He was, and cared not for God or man a *point*.
Spenser, F. Q., I. ii. 12.

20. A fastening resembling a tagged lacing. (*a*) A short narrow strip of leather sewed to any part of harness to form a buckling-strap. (*b*) *Naut.*, a short piece of rope or sennit used in reefing sails. See *reefing-point*.

21. In *fencing*, a stab or puncture with the point of a sword; a blow with the button of the foil when properly directed: as, he can give me three *points* in ten (i. e., he can make ten hits or points on me while I make seven on him).—22. In *her.*: (*a*) One of the nine recognized positions on the shield which denote the local-

The Nine Points of the Shield.
A, dexter chief point; B, chief point; C, sinister chief point; D, honor point; E, fesse-point; F, nombril; G, base or flank point; H, dexter base point; I, sinister base point.

ity of figures or charges. (*b*) The middle part of either the chief or the base as distinguished from the dexter and sinister cantons. (*c*) A bearing which occupies the base of the escutcheon. It is usually considered as a pile reversed—that is, rising from the base and reaching to the upper edge of the escutcheon; but it is very often of less height, reaching only to the fesse-point or to the nombril, and sometimes is merely the base itself bounded by a horizontal line separating it from the rest of the field. Plain point is especially treated in the way last mentioned. The bearing is very rare in English armory, and hence some writers treat it as synonymous with *base*, and others as synonymous with *pile reversed*. It is also customary to represent the sides of the sharply angled point as concavely curved, while those of the pile are straight. (*d*) A division of the field barwise: thus, three *points* gules, argent, and azure, means that the field is divided into three horizontal stripes, of which the uppermost is red, the middle one silver, etc.—23†. Ordinance; law; act.

The comyns of this present yeld affermen and enacte alle the *poyntes* of this yeld, for the grete ease, pease, profitz, and tranquilite of the Cyte.
English Gilds (E. E. T. S.), p. 404.

24†. A slur; an indignity.

But the triet men of Troy traitur hym cald,
And mony *pointtes* on hym put for his pure shame,
That disseruet full duly the dethe for to haue.
Destruction of Troy (E. E. T. S.), l. 7900.

25. The action or attitude of a dog in pointing game: as, he comes to a *point* well.

In the pointer and setter, the fit almost always occurs just after a *point*, the excitement of which appears to act upon the brain. *Dogs of Great Brit. and America*, p. 349.

26. In games: (*a*) In *cricket*, a fielder who stands at a short distance to the right of the batsman, and slightly in front of him. See diagram under *cricket*[2]. (*b*) In *lacrosse*, a player who stands a short distance in front of the goal, and whose duty is to prevent the ball from passing through the goal. (*c*) *pl.* In *base-ball*, the position occupied by the pitcher.—27. A thing to be pointed at, or the mere act of pointing; especially, a flitch of bacon or the like, which is not eaten, but only pointed at as a pretense for seasoning: as, to dine on potatoes and *point* (that is, on nothing but potatoes): a jocular expression in vogue in Ireland.

Their universal sustenance is the root named potato, . . . generally without condiment or relish of any kind, save an unknown condiment named *point*.
Carlyle, Sartor Resartus.

28†. A particular signal given, as by the blast of a trumpet or the beat of a drum; hence, a note; a call.

On a sudden we were alarmed with the noise of a drum, and immediately entered my little godson to give me a *point* of war. *Steele*, Tatler, No. 95.

The trumpets and kettledrums of the cavalry were next heard to perform the beautiful and wild *point* of war, appropriated as a signal for that piece of nocturnal duty.
Scott, Waverley, xlvi.

29. In *music*, the entrance of a voice or an instrument with an important theme or motive.—Accidental point. See *accidental*.—Acting point, in *physics*, the exact point at which any impulse is given.—

Alençon point. See *Alençon lace*, under *lace*.—**Alveolar point.** See *alveolar*, and cut under *craniometry*.—**Apparent double point.** See *apparent*.—**Archimedean point**, the initial recognition of one's own existence as given in consciousness: so called because this was supposed to supply the necessary point or fulcrum of indubitable fact on which to raise the structure of philosophy.—**Armed at all points.** See *armed*.—**At all points** (formerly **of all points**), in every particular; completely.

The thirde was Monevall, that was a noble knyght and richely armed *of alle pointes*. *Merlin* (E. E. T. S.), iii. 562.

Young Eustace is a gentleman *at all points*,
And his behaviour affable and courtly.
Fletcher (and another), Elder Brother, iii. 1.

At or in (the) point, on the point; ready; about (to): sometimes used with *on* or *upon*.

My son *in point* is for to lete
The holy lawes of oure Alkaron.
Chaucer, Man of Law's Tale, l. 233.

And Esau said, Behold, I am *at the point* to die; and what profit shall this birthright do to me? Gen. xxv. 32.

I knock'd and, bidden, enter'd; found her there
At point to move. *Tennyson*, Princess, iii.

At (or on) the point of, in the act of; very near to: as, *on the point of* leaving; *at the point of* death.

Shah Alum had invested Patna, and was *on the point of* proceeding to storm. *Macaulay*, Lord Clive.

Auricular point. See *auricular*, and cut under *craniometry*.—**Base point**, in *her.* See def. 22 (*a*).—**Bone-point**, a name given to some rich varieties of rose point-lace—it is said because of its appearance as if richly sculptured in ivory or bone. See *bone-lace*.—**Breaking-point**, in *engineering*, *mechanics*, etc., the degree of strain under which a structure or part will give way.—**Cardinal point.** (*a*) One of the four points of the horizon, due north, south, east, and west. (*b*) In *astrol.* See *cardinal*. (*c*) In *optics*, six points on the axis of a lens or system of lenses, including (1) two *focal points*, which are the foci for parallel rays; (2) two *nodal points*, so situated that an incident ray through one emerges in a parallel direction through the other; (3) two *principal points*—those points on the axis through which the so-called *principal planes* pass: these planes are parallel to the axis, and so situated that the line joining the points in which an incident ray meets the first and the corresponding emergent ray meets the second is parallel to the axis; under certain conditions the principal points may coincide with the nodal points.—**Conical, conjugate, consecutive, corresponding, etc., points.** See the adjectives.—**Critical point.** See *critical*.—**Cut over point**, in *fencing*. See *cut*, *n.*—**Cut point**, cut work or cut-and-drawn work, a phrase adapted from the French *point coupé*.—**Dead-point**, in *mech.* See *dead-center*.—**Decimal, diacritical, diagonal, double point.** See the adjectives.—**English point.** See *English point-lace* (*a*), under *lace*.—**Equinoctial points.** See *equinoctial*.—**Fixed point**, in *mech.*, a center around which any part moves.—**From point to point**, from one particular to another.

He can al devyse
Fro point to point, nat o word wol he faille.
Chaucer, Monk's Tale, l. 472.

Frontal points. Same as *antiæ*.—**Genoa point**, a kind of bobbin-made guipure, especially that which has a réseau instead of detached and irregular brides for its ground.—**Heads and points.** See *head*.—**Imaginary point.** See *imaginary*.—**Indented in point.** See *indented*.—**Index of a point.** See *index*.—**In good point**† [OF. *en bon point*: see *embonpoint*], in good case or condition. See def. 9.—**In point.** (*a*†) See *at point*. (*b*) Applicable; apposite; appropriate; exactly fitting the case.

When history, and particularly the history of our own country, furnishes anything like a case *in point*, . . . he will take advantage of it. *Sheridan*, The Critic, ii. 1.

In point of, as regards; with respect or regard to.

If I transgress *in point of* manners, afford me
Your best construction.
B. Jonson, Devil is an Ass, iii. 1.

Providence had created the inhabitants of the peninsula of India under many disadvantages *in point of* climate.
Bruce, Source of the Nile, I. 371.

In point of fact, as a matter of fact; in fact.

In point of fact, he expired about half-past four that same afternoon. *R. H. D. Barham*, Memoir of R. H. Barham [(Ingoldsby Legends, I. 116).

Irish point. See *Irish*[1].—**Jugal point.** See *craniometry*.—**Limiting points.** See *limit*.—**Lubber's point.** Same as *lubber-line*.—**Lunistitial points.** See *lunistitial*.—**Malar point.** See *craniometry*.—**Mental, metoptic, multiple, nasal, navel point.** See the qualifying words.—**Needle-point**, needle-made lace: a phrase especially applied to Alençon and Argentan laces, as being formerly the only important French laces and the only fashionable ones not made with the bobbins. See under *lace*.—**Neutralization point.** See *neutralization*, 1.—**Neutral points**, points on the commutator of a dynamo upon which the collecting brushes rest: generally the extremities of a diameter at right angles to the resultant lines of force.—**Nodal points.** See *nodal*.—**Objective, occipital, original, parabolic point.** See the adjectives.—**Painful points**, points painful on pressure, occurring in many cases of neuralgia in the course of any affected nerve: described by Valléix in 1841.—**Petit point.** Same as *tent-stitch*.—**Pinch points.** See *pinch*.—**Point à brides.** (*a*) The ground of lace when made of brides or bars. (*b*) Lace having a bride ground, as opposed to that having a réseau ground.—**Point appliqué.** See *appliqué*.—**Point à réseau**, lace which has a net ground worked together with the pattern, as is the case with Mechlin.—**Point at infinity.** See *infinity*, 3.—**Point d'Alençon.** Same as *Alençon lace* (which see, under *lace*).—**Point d'Angleterre.** See *English point-lace* (*a*), under *lace*.—**Point d'appui.** See *appui*.—**Point d'Argentan.** Same as *Argentan lace* (which see, under *lace*).—**Point de gaze**, a very fine needle-made ground for lace, generally identified with the finest Brussels lace when wholly made with the needle.—**Point de raccroc**, a method of fastening together the different pieces of lace as in Brussels and Bayeux laces: it is not sewing, but a fresh row of meshes imitating in part the ground of the lace.—**Point d'esprit**, in *lace-making*: (*a*) Originally, a small oval figure occurring in various kinds of guipure, and usually consisting of three short lengths of cord or parchment laid side by side and covered with the thread: such ovals were arranged in various patterns, but especially in rosettes. (*b*) A much smaller solid or mat surface, square or oblong, used to diversify the net ground of certain laces.—**Point de Valenciennes.** Same as *Valenciennes lace* (which see, under *lace*).—**Point de velin.** Same as *velum point*.—**Point diamond.** See *diamond*.—**Point duchesse.** Same as *duchesse lace* (which see, under *lace*).—**Point for point**, in detail; precisely; exactly.

This sergeaunt cam unto his lord ageyn,
And of Grisildes wordes and hir chere
He tolde him *point for point*.
Chaucer, Clerk's Tale, l. 521.

Point impaled, in *her.*, a point divided vertically or palewise, the two parts of different tinctures.—**Point of alteration or duplication**, in *medieval musical notation*, a dot placed after and properly above the first of two short notes in perfect rhythm as a sign that the second note after it is long.—**Point of attack**, that part of a defended position which is chosen for the main assault or onset; in siege operations, that part of the defenses which must be reduced in order to force the garrison to surrender.

Up to that time I had felt by no means certain that Crump's landing might not be the *point of attack*.
U. S. Grant, Personal Memoirs, I. 336.

Point of coincidence. See *coincidence*.—**Point of contrary flexure**, a point on a plane curve at which a tangent moving along the curve ceases to turn in one direction and begins to turn in the opposite way.—**Point of day**, dawn; daybreak. [Obsolete or poetical.]

So shall I sey to alle the princes that thei be redy at the *poynte of day* for to ride. *Merlin* (E. E. T. S.), iii. 585.

Point of dispersion, in *optics*, that point from which the rays begin to diverge, commonly called the *virtual focus*.—**Point of distance.** See *distance*.—**Point of division or imperfection**, in *medieval musical notation*, a dot placed between two short notes to indicate a rhythmic division like that marked by the modern bar.—**Point of election.** See *election*.—**Point of fall**, in *gun.*, the point first struck by the projectile. *Tidball*, Manual of Artillery.—**Point of fusion of metals.** See *fusion*.—**Point of honor.** (*a*) See *honor*. (*b*) In *her.*, a point in the escutcheon immediately above the center: also called the *heart*.—**Point of horse**, in *mining*, the spot where a vein, as of ore, is divided by a mass of rock into one or more branches.—**Point of incidence**, in *optics*, that point on a surface upon which a ray of light falls.—**Point of law**, a specific legal principle or rule. The term is generally used to indicate a discriminating application, or the precise effect on a given state of facts, of the appropriate legal principle or provision.—**Point of magnetic indifference.** See *magnetic*.—**Point of order**, in deliberative bodies, a question raised as to whether proceedings are in conformity with parliamentary law and with the special rules of the particular body itself.—**Point of osculation.** See *osculation*.—**Point of perfection**, in *medieval musical notation*, a dot placed after a long note in triple or perfect rhythm to prevent its being made duple or imperfect by position.—**Point of reflection**, in *optics*, the point from which a ray is reflected.—**Point of refraction**, in *optics*, that point in the refracting surface where the refraction takes place.—**Point of regard**, the point at which the eye is directly looking. Its image falls in the middle of the macula lutea of the retina.—**Point of sight.** Same as *point of vision*.

Therefore, as in perspective, so in tragedy, there must be a *point of sight* in which all the lines terminate, otherwise the eye wanders, and the work is false.
Dryden, Grounds of Criticism in Tragedy.

Point of view, a position from which one looks, or from which a picture is supposed to be taken; hence, the state of mind, or predisposition, which consciously or unconsciously modifies the consideration of any subject.—**Point of vision**, the position from which anything is observed, or is represented as being observed; the position of the eye of the observer. Also called *point of sight*, *point of view*, *center of projection*, *center of vision*, etc.—**Point plat**, in *lace-making*: (*a*) Flowers or sprigs of bobbin-work, as opposed to needle-point work. See *plat*[3], *a.*, 2. (*b*) Application-lace in which such pillow-made flowers are applied to a net ground. See *application-lace* and *Brussels lace* (both under *lace*).—**Points and pins**, an old game similar to skittles.—**Points of support**, in *arch.*, those points or surfaces on the plan of the piers, walls, columns, etc., upon which an edifice rests, or in which the various pressures are collected and met.—**Points of the compass.** See *compass*, *n.*, 7.—**Point-to-point**, in a straight line; across country.

To test a good hunter there is nothing like a four-mile *point-to-point* steeplechase. *Edinburgh Rev.*, CLXVI. 409.

Poristic points. See *poristic*.—**Power of points**, in *elect.*, the effect of fine points in promoting electrical discharge. The density (electrical) at any point of a charged body is inversely as the radius of curvature, and is, therefore, relatively great at the extremity of a fine point. When it reaches a certain limit, the electricity escapes easily, and charged bodies may thus be silently discharged.—**Principal points**, in *optics*, of a lens or a combination of lenses, the two points on the optical axis which possess the property (among others) that the line drawn from the first principal point to any point in the object is parallel to the line drawn from the second principal point to the corresponding point in the image. The angle subtended by the object at the first principal point, therefore, equals that subtended by the image at the second. Gauss first discovered these points, and introduced the term *Hauptpunkt*, of which *principal point* is the translation.—**Rose-point**, in *lace-making*, the peculiar style identified with Venetian needle-point lace of the early part of the seventeenth century. The pattern is rather large, with beautifully designed conventional flowers, and is especially distinguished by the decided relief which is given to it, so that it is often said to resemble carved ivory. The pattern is so distributed that there is but little space for the ground to occupy, and this ground is composed of large brides or bars decorated with picots.—**Spanish point**, galloons and passements of silk, silk and gold, silver, and the like, which were in demand during the latter part of the seventeenth and in the eighteenth century. Much of it was made in the Spanish Netherlands, and much also in Genoa.—**Spinal point.** See *craniometry*.—**Subnasal, supra-auricular, supraclavicular, etc., point.** See the adjectives, and cut under *craniometry*.—**Supranasal point.** Same as *ophryon*.—**Supraorbital point.** Same as *ophryon*.—**The Five Articles and the Five Points.** See *article*.—**To back a point**, in *sporting*, to come to a point on observing that action in another dog: said of pointers and setters.—**To be at a point**†, to be determined or resolved.

Be at a point with yourselves, as the disciples of Christ which had forsaken themselves, to follow not your will but God's will.
J. Bradford, Letters (Parker Soc., 1853), II. 120.

To blow heads and points. See *head*.—**To cast a point of traverse.** See *cast*[1].—**To come to points**†, to fight with swords.

They would have *come to points* immediately, had not the gentlemen interposed.
Smollett, Sir L. Greaves, iii. (*Davies.*)

To control the point. See *control*.—**To give points to.** (*a*) To give odds to; have the advantage of.

Any average Eton boy could *give points to* his Holiness in the matter of Latin verses. *The American*, 1883, VI. 333.

(*b*) To give a valuable or advantageous hint, indication, or piece of information to: as, he can *give* us *points* on that subject. [Slang.]—**To make a point.** (*a*) To rise in the air with a peculiar motion over the spot where quarry is concealed: said of a hawk. (*b*) To make a particular desired impression; "score."—**To make a point of**, to be resolved to (do something) and do it accordingly; insist upon: as, to *make a point of* rising early.—**To point**†, in every detail; completely.

A faithlesse Sarazin, all armde *to point*.
Spenser, F. Q., I. ii. 12.

Hast thou, spirit,
Perform'd *to point* the tempest that I bade thee?
Shak., Tempest, i. 2. 194.

To stand upon points, to be punctilious; be overnice or over-scrupulous.

This fellow doth not *stand upon points*.
Shak., M. N. D., v. 1. 118.

To strain a point, to exceed the reasonable limit; make an exception or concession, as of a rule in business, or a position in an argument.—**Tressed point**, a lace made of human hair.—**Tritactic, quadritactic, quinquetactic, sextactic, etc., point**, a point where two plane curves have three, four, five, six, etc., consecutive points in common.—**Vellum point**, lace worked on a pattern drawn on parchment, to correspond with which the main lines of the threads are laid; hence, needle-point lace of almost any sort.—**Venice point.** Same as *rose-point*: indicating both the lace itself and the method of working it.—**Vowel points**, in the Hebrew and other Eastern alphabets, certain marks placed above or below the consonants, or attached to them, as in the Ethiopic, representing the vocal sounds or vowels which precede or follow the consonant sounds.

II. *a.* Made with the needle: said of lace. Compare *needle-point*.

The principal *point* (i. e., strictly, needle-made) laces are the ancient laces of Italy, Spain, and Portugal, and the more modern lace of France, called point d'Alençon.
Industrial Arts (S. K. Handbook), p. 261.

point[1] (point), *v.* [< ME. *pointen*, *poynten*, < OF. (and F.) *pointer*, *poynter*, also *pointier* = Pr. *ponchar* = Sp. *puntar*, also *puntuar* = Pg. *pontuar* = It. *puntare*, point, = D. *punten*, point, sharpen, *punteren*, stipple, point, dot, = MLG. *punten*, appoint, settle, fix, = G. *punkten*, *pünkten* (also *punktieren*, *punctieren* = Sw. *punktera* = Dan. *punktere*, < F.), point, punctuate, stipple, dot, < ML. *punctare*, also *punctuare*, prick, punch, point, mark, < L. *punctum*, neut., *punctus*, m., a point: see *point*[1], *n.*] **I.** *trans.* **1**†. To prick with a pointed instrument; pierce.

Aftirward they prile and *poynten*
The folk right to the bare boon.
Rom. of the Rose, l. 1058.

2. To supply or adorn with points. See *point*, *n.*, 19.

And *pointed* on the shoulders for the nonce,
As new come from the Belgian garrisons.
Bp. Hall, Satires.

3. To mark with characters for the purpose of separating the members of a sentence and indicating the pauses; punctuate: as, to *point* a written composition.—**4.** To direct toward an object; aim: as, to *point* a gun; to *point* the finger of scorn at one.

The girl recognized her own portrait without the slightest embarrassment, and merely *pointed* her pencil at her master. *H. W. Preston*, Year in Eden, viii.

5. To direct the observation or attention of.

Whosoever should be guided through his battles by Minerva, and *pointed* to every scene of them, would see nothing but subjects of surprise. *Pope.*

6. To indicate; show; make manifest: often with *out*.

But O vaine judgement, and conditions vaine,
The which the prisoner *points* unto the free!
Spenser, F. Q., IV. xii. 11.

Are. What will you do, Philaster, with yourself?
Phil. Why, that which all the gods have *pointed out* for me. *Beau. and Fl.*, Philaster, i. 2.

And will ye be sae kind, fair may,
As come out and *point* my way?
The Broom of Cowdenknowes (Child's Ballads, IV. 46).

What a generous ambition has this man *pointed* to us! *Steele*, Tatler, No. 251.

7. To indicate the purpose or point of.

If he means this ironically, it may be truer than he thinks. He *points* it, however, by no deviation from his straightforward manner of speech. *Dickens.*

8. To give in detail; recount the particulars of.

Of what wight that stant in swich disjoynte,
His wordes alle or every look to *poynte*.
Chaucer, Troilus, iii. 497.

9. In *masonry*, to fill the joints of (brickwork or stonework) with mortar, and smooth them with the point of a trowel: as, to *point* a wall: often with *up*.

Point all their chinky lodgings round with mud.
Addison, tr. of Virgil's Georgics, iv.

10. To give a point to; sharpen; forge, grind, file, or cut to a point: as, to *point* a dart or a pin; also, to taper, as a rope (see below). Hence— 11. Figuratively, to give point, piquancy, or vivacity to; add to the force or expression of.

There is a kind of drama in the forming of a story, and the manner of conducting and *pointing* it is the same as in an epigram. *Steele*, Guardian, No. 42.

Beauty with early bloom supplies
Her daughter's cheek, and *points* her eyes. *Gay.*

He left the name at which the world grew pale
To *point* a moral or adorn a tale.
Johnson, Vanity of Human Wishes, l. 222.

With joys she'd griefs, had troubles in her course,
But not one grief was *pointed* by remorse.
Crabbe, Works, I. 93.

To point a rope, to taper a rope at the end, as by taking out a few of its yarns, and with these working a mat over it, for neatness, and for convenience in reeving through a block.—**To point a sail**, to rig points through the eyelet-holes of the reefs in the sail. [Rare.]—**To point the leaders**, in *four-in-hand driving*, to give the leaders an intimation with the reins that they are to turn a corner.—**To point the yards of a vessel**, to brace the yards up sharp: often done when steaming, to expose less surface to the wind.

II. *intrans.* 1. To indicate direction or direct attention with or as with the finger.

They are portentous things
Unto the climate that they *point* upon.
Shak., J. C., i. 3. 32.

This fable seems to *point* at the secrets of nature.
Bacon, Physical Fables, vii., Expl.

Their neighbors scorn them, Strangers *poynt* at them.
Dekker, Seven Deadly Sins, p. 15.

Thus having sumarily *pointed* at things wch Mr. Brewster (I thinke) hath more largly write of to Mr. Robinson, I leave you to the Lords protection.
Cushman, quoted in Bradford's Plymouth Plantation, p. 38.

2. To lead or direct the eye or the mind in some specified direction: with *to:* as, everything *points to* his guilt; to *point* with pride *to* one's record.

None of these names can be recognised, but they *point to* an age when foreign kings, possibly of the Punjab, ruled this country by satraps.
J. Fergusson, Hist. Indian Arch., p. 151.

How Latin, together with Greek, the Celtic, the Teutonic, and Slavonic languages, together likewise with the ancient dialects of India and Persia, *points* back *to* an earlier language, the Mother, if we so may call it, of the whole Indo-European or Aryan family of speech.
Macmillan's Mag., I. 35.

Everything *pointed* to a struggle that night or early next morning. *Cornhill Mag.*, Oct., 1888.

3. To indicate the presence of game by standing in a stiff position, with the muzzle directed toward the game. See *pointer*, 1 (*c*).—4. To show positively by any means.

To *point* at what time the balance of power was most equally held between the lords and commons at Rome would perhaps admit a controversy.
Swift, Contests and Dissensions in Athens and Rome, iii.

5. In *surg.*, to come to a point or head: said of an abscess when it approaches the surface and is about to burst.—6. In *printing*, to make point-holes in the operation of printing, or to attach printed sheets on previously made point-holes; in *bookbinding*, to put printed sheets on pointing-needles.—7. *Naut.*, to sail close to windward: said of a yacht.

point[2]† (point), *v. t.* [By apheresis from *appoint.*] To appoint.

First to his Gate he *pointed* a strong gard.
Spenser, Mother Hub. Tale, l. 1115.

Go! bid the banns and *point* the bridal day.
Bp. Hall, Satires, IV. i. 124.

Has the duke *pointed* him to be his orator?
Shirley, Love's Cruelty, ii. 2.

pointable (poin'ta-bl), *a.* [< *point* + *-able.*] Capable of being pointed, or pointed out.

You know, quoth I, that in Elias' time, both in Israel and elsewhere, God's church was not *pointable;* and therefore cried he out that he was left alone.
J. Bradford, Works (Parker Soc.), I. 552. (*Davies.*)

pointal (poin'tal), *n.* [< F. *pointal*, strut, girder, prop, OF. *pointal, pointel*, a point, = Sp. *puntal*, a prop, stanchion, < ML. as if **punctale* (f), < L. *punctum*, point: see *point*. Cf. *pointel.*] 1. A king-post. *Imp. Dict.*—2. Same as *pointel*, 2.—3. Same as *pointel*, 3.

point-blank (point'blangk'), *n.* [< F. *point blanc*, white spot: *point*, point; *blanc*, white: see *point*[1] and *blank.*] 1. A direct shot; a shot with direct aim; a point-blank shot.

Against a gun more than as long and as heavy again, and charged with as much powder again, she carried the same bullet as strong to the mark, and nearer and above the mark at a *point blank* than their's.
Pepys, Diary, IV. 156.

2. The second point (that is, that furthest from the piece) at which the line of sight intersects the trajectory of a projectile.

When the natural line of sight is horizontal, the point where the projectile first strikes the horizontal plane on which the gun stands is the *point-blank*, and the distance to the *point-blank* is the point-blank range.
U. S. Army Tactics.

point-blank (point'blangk'), *adv.* [An ellipsis of *at point-blank.*] Directly; straight; without deviation or circumlocution.

This boy will carry a letter twenty mile as easy as a cannon will shoot *point-blank* twelve score.
Shak., M. W. of W., iii. 2. 34.

There is no defending of the Fact; for the Law is *point-blank* against it.
N. Bailey, tr. of Colloquies of Erasmus, I. 408.

Pointblank, directly, as, an arrow is shot to the point-blank or white mark. *Johnson.*

Point-blank, positivement, directement [F.], Recta ad scopum, directis verbis [L.]. *Bailey.*

Philip has contradicted him *point-blank*, until Mr. Hobday turned quite red. *Thackeray*, Philip, xxii.

point-blank (point'blangk'), *a.* [< *point-blank*, *n.* and *adv.*] 1. In *gun.*, having a horizontal direction: as, a *point-blank* shot. In point-blank shooting the ball is supposed to move directly toward the object without describing an appreciable curve.
2. Direct; plain; explicit; express: as, a *point-blank* denial.—**Point-blank range**, the distance to which a shot is reckoned to range straight, without appreciably drooping from the force of gravity.

The difference between the proper method of shooting at short, that is *point blanc*, *range*, and that of shooting at the great distances used in the York Round, is radical.
M. and W. Thompson, Archery, p. 1.

point-circle (point'sėr″kl), *n.* A point considered as an infinitesimal circle.

point-coördinate (point'kọ̄-ôr″di-nạ̄t), *n.* One of a system of coördinates of points.

point-device†, **point-devise**† (point'dẹ̄-vīs'), *n.* [< ME. *point devys:* see *point* and *device*. No OF. form of the term appears.] Used only in the following phrase.—**At point-device**, exactly; particularly; carefully; nicely.

Whan that the firste cok hath crowe anon,
Up rist this joly lovere Absolon,
And him arraieth gay, *at poynt devys.*
Chaucer, Miller's Tale, l. 503.

Hym self armyd *atte poynte-devise.*
Generydes (E. E. T. S.), l. 3307.

So noble he was of stature,
So faire, so joly, and so fetys,
With lymes wrought *at poynt devys*,
Delyver, smert, and of grete myght,
Ne sawe thou nevere man so lyght.
Rom. of the Rose, l. 830.

point-device† (point'dẹ̄-vīs'), *adv.* [By ellipsis from *at point device.*] Same as *at point-device* (which see, under *point-device*, *n.*).

The wenche she was full proper nyce,
Amonge all other she bare great price,
For sche coude fricke it *point device*,
But fewe like her in that countree.
The Miller of Abington. (*Halliwell.*)

point-device (point'dẹ̄-vīs'), *a.* [< *point-device*, *adv.*] Precise; nice; finical; scrupulously neat. [Obsolete or archaic.]

Then your hose should be ungartered, your bonnet unbanded, your sleeve unbuttoned, your shoe untied, and every thing about you demonstrating a careless desolation. But you are no such man; you are rather *point-device* in your accoutrements, as loving yourself, than seeming the lover of any other. *Shak.*, As you Like it, iii. 2. 401.

Men's behaviour should be like their apparel, not too strait or *point device*, but free for exercise or motion.
Bacon, Ceremonies and Respects (ed. 1887).

Otto looked so gay, and walked so airily, he was so well-dressed and brushed and frizzled, so *point-de-vice*, and of such a sovereign elegance.
R. L. Stevenson, Prince Otto, ii. 1.

pointe (F. pron. pwaṅt), *n.* [F.: see *point*[1].] A triangular scarf; a half-shawl folded in a point: usually of lace or other fine and delicate fabric.

pointé (pwaṅ-tā'), *a.* [F., pp. of *pointer*, p in, prick: see *point*[1].] In *her.*, leafed: said of a flower or plant.

pointed (poin'ted), *a.* [< *point*[1] + *-ed*[2].] 1. Sharp; having a sharp point: as, a *pointed* rock.

The various-colour'd scarf, the shield he rears,
The shining helmet, and the *pointed* spears.
Pope, Iliad, x. 86.

2. Aimed at or expressly intended for some particular person; directly applicable or applied; emphasized: as, a *pointed* remark.

Only ten days ago had he elated her by his *pointed* regard. *Jane Austen*, Northanger Abbey, xxix.

This is a comprehensive, brief, *pointed*, and easily understood exposition of the whole subject.
Science, XII. 229.

3. Epigrammatical; abounding in conceits or lively turns; piquant; sharp.

His moral pleases, not his *pointed* wit.
Pope, Imit. of Horace, II. i. 76.

They cast about them their *pointed* antitheses, and often subsided into a clink of similar syllables, and the clinch of an ambiguous word. *I. D'Israeli*, Amen. of Lit., II. 352.

Pointed arch, an arch bounded by two arcs each less than 90°. The arch of this form is characteristic of European medieval architecture from the middle of the twelfth century, though examples of its use occur earlier. Its logical and consistent use was devised and perfected in France. The pointed arch of much Oriental architecture is an independent development, which never led to the logical conclusions and constructive methods of the French pointed architecture. See *Pointed style*, below.

Gothic architecture differs from Romanesque far more fundamentally than by the use of *pointed arches* in place of round arches, or by the substitution of one decorative system for another.
C. H. Moore, Gothic Architecture, p. 7.

Pointed ashler. See *ashler*, 3.—**Pointed box**, in *mining*, a box in the form of an inverted pyramid, forming one of a series of three or four, and used for dressing ore according to the method devised by Von Rittinger. Also called a *V-vat*, and frequently by the German name *Spitzkasten* (that is, 'point-box').—**Pointed cross**, in *her.*, a cross having every one of its four arms pointed abruptly, or with a blunt point, differing from the cross fitché of all four, which is like a four-pointed star.—**Pointed style**, in *arch.*, a general phrase under which are included all the different varieties of advanced medieval architecture, generally called *Gothic*, from the common application of the pointed arch and vault in the twelfth century until the general diffusion of Renaissance architecture toward the beginning of the sixteenth century. This style, as fully developed by the middle of the thirteenth century, exhib-

Pointed Style.—Typical scheme of a fully developed French cathedral of the 13th century. (From Viollet-le-Duc's "Dict. de l'Architecture.")

its great flexibility and adaptability to all purposes, and is thoroughly in accord with the conditions imposed upon the architect by northern climates, which demand, among other things, spacious and well-lighted interiors for public meetings, and high-pitched roofs which can shed rain rapidly and upon which heavy masses of snow cannot lodge. While the pointed arch and vault are the most obvious characteristics of this style, they are in fact merely necessary details of it. It is fundamentally a system of construction in stone in which a skeleton framework of ribs and props forms the essential organic part of the building. All the weights and strains are collected in a relatively small number of points, where the loads are supported by vertical props or piers, while the lateral pressures are counterbalanced by buttresses and flying-buttresses. Upon the ribs rest shells of masonry constituting the vaults or ceiling, and between those of the props which fall in the exterior boundary of the building thin inclosing walls are carried up, which walls may be, and in the most perfect examples often are, almost entirely done away with, giving place to light-transmitting screens of colored glass supported by a slender secondary framework of stone and metal. The use of the pointed arch and vault has the advantage over that of the earlier semicircular forms that the pressures outward are less strong and more easily counteracted; and good examples of the style are as carefully studied, and founded upon principles as scientific and proportions as subtle, as the best Greek work. See *medieval architecture*, under *medieval*, for an outline of the history of the style, and *Decorated*, *Flamboyant*, *Perpendicular*, and *Tudor* for the characteristics of some of its varieties. See also *early English architecture*, under *early*.

pointedly (poin'ted-li), *adv.* In a pointed manner. (*a*) With point or force; with lively turns of thought or expression.

He often wrote too *pointedly* for his subject. *Dryden.*

(*b*) With direct assertion; with explicitness; with direct reference to a subject.

pointedness (poin'ted-nes), *n.* 1. The state or quality of being pointed; sharpness.

High, full of rock, mountain, and *pointedness*. B. *Jonson*, Discoveries.

2. Epigrammatical smartness or keenness.

In this [you] excel him [Horace], that you add *pointedness* of thought. *Dryden*, Ded. of tr. of Juvenal.

pointel (poin'tel), *n.* [< ME. *poyntel*, < OF. *pointel*, F. *pointeau*, a point, prick, = Sp. *puntel*, a glass-blowers' pipe, < ML. **punctellum*, LL. *punctillum*, a little point, dim. of L. *punctum*, a point: see *point*1. Cf. *pontil*, *ponty*, etc., and *pointal*.] 1. A point or sharp instrument; especially, such an instrument used in writing; in the middle ages, a style used with ivory tablets or for writing on a soft surface, as of wax.

His felawe hadde a stafe tipped with horn,
A peyre of tables al of yvory,
And a *poyntel* polysshed fetisly,
And wroot the names alwey as he stood
Of alle folk that gaf hym any good.
Chaucer, Summoner's Tale, l. 34.

Take a scharp *poyntel*, or a pricke of yren, and peerse into the wex that hongith in the mouth of the glas azens the erthe. *Book of Quinte Essence* (ed. Furnivall), p. 5.

2. Any sharp-pointed thing resembling a pencil, as the pistil of a plant. Also *pointal*.

It [the basilisk] is not halfe a foot long, and hath three *pointels* (Galen saith) on the head, or, after Solinus, strakes like a Mitre. *Purchas*, Pilgrimage, p. 560.

A breathless ring was formed about
That sudden flower: get round at any risk
The gold-rough *pointel*, silver-blazing disk
O' the lily! *Browning*, Sordello.

3. A pavement formed of materials of a lozenge shape, or of squares set diagonally. *Imp. Dict.* Also *pointal*.

pointeling†, *adv.* See *pointling*.

point-equation (point'ē-kwā"shọn), *n.* An equation in point-coördinates.

pointer (poin'tėr), *n.* [< *point*1 + -*er*1. Cf. F. *pointeur*, < ML. *punctator*, < *punctare*, point; cf. Sp. *puntero* = Pg. *ponteiro*, < ML. as if **punctarius*, < L. *punctum*, point: see *point*1.] 1. One who or that which points. Specifically—(*a*) One of the hands of a clock or watch; the index-hand of a circular barometer, anemometer, or the like. (*b*) A long tapering stick used by teachers or lecturers in pointing out places on a map, or words, figures, diagrams, etc., on a blackboard. (*c*) One of a breed of sporting-dogs. A pointer is a modified hound, of medium size, differing from the setter in being close-haired. When game is scented the pointer stands stiffly, with the muzzle raised and stretched toward the game, the tail straight out behind, and usually one fore foot raised. Most setters are now trained to this same action, instead of to drop before game as formerly. Pointers are usually liver-colored, or liver and white, but many retain the tan marks of the foxhound, and some are black. They are used chiefly for hunting birds, and make excellent retrievers.

The *pointer* is known to have come originally from Spain. *The Century*, XXXI. 122.

(*d*) *pl.* With the definite article, the two stars of the constellation Ursa Major which guide the eye of the observer to the pole-star.

2. A light pole with a black ball on the end of it, used at the masthead of a whaler when the boats are down. *Macy*.—3. *Naut.*, one of the pieces of timber fixed fore-and-aft, and diagonally inside of a vessel's run or quarter, to connect the stern-frame with the after-body. See *counter*3, 4. Also called *snake-piece*.—4. A pointed tool; especially, one used for cutting, graving, boring, and the like: a term common to many trades: as, a stone-cutters' *pointer*; a silversmiths' *pointer*.—5. A tool used by bricklayers for clearing out the old mortar in pointing brickwork.—6. The lever of a railroad-switch.—7. In *printing*, the workman who adjusts sheets by means of the point-holes on a press.—8. A hint; an indication; a point; an item of information which may be used with advantage: as, *pointers* in a race or a game. [Slang.]

pointer-dog (poin'tėr-dog), *n.* Same as *pointer*, 1 (*c*).

point-finder (point'fin"dėr), *n.* In *persp.*, an instrument employed for determining the vanishing-point in making projections.

point-hole (point'hōl), *n.* In *printing*, one of the needle-holes made in the margins of paper when printed on the first side or in the first color. If the sheet is fitted by means of these point-holes when printing on the second side or in the second color, the second impression will be in the same position, or in exact register.

-pointic. An adjectival suffix used in mathematical language. An *m-pointic* contact is a contact consisting in two curves having *m* consecutive points in common.

pointillé (F. pron. pwañ-tē-lyā'), *a.* [F., pp. of *pointiller*, dot, stipple, < *pointe*, point, dot: see *point*1.] See *pounced work*, under *pounced*1.

pointing (poin'ting), *n.* [Verbal n. of *point*1, *v.*] 1. The art of indicating the divisions of a writing; punctuation.—2. The marks or points made, or the system of marks employed, in punctuation.—3. The act of removing mortar from between the joints of a stone or brick wall, and replacing it with new mortar; also, the material with which the joints are refilled.—4. In *sculp.*, the operation of marking off into regular spaces by points the surface of a plaster or clay model, preliminary to reproducing it in marble, as well as the reproduction of these points on the marble block. The distances between the points being easily measurable, accuracy is insured. Both the Greeks and the Romans pointed the marble blocks out of which their sculptures were to be cut. Pointing-marks are visible on a head of Alcibiades in the Louvre, and at Rome on the colossal statues in the Quirinal and the Discobolus in the Vatican.

5. In *milling*, the first treatment of grain in the high-milling process. It consists in rubbing off the points of the grain, clipping the brush, and removing the germ-end, and is performed either by a machine similar to a smut-mill or by millstones set at an appropriate distance apart.

6. In *chanting*, the act, process, or result of indicating exactly how the words shall be adapted to the music, or of making such an adaptation. Since the same melody may be used with many different texts, and the same melody and text may be variously adapted to each other, pointing becomes an intricate art, if both rhetorical and musical propriety is to be maintained. No method of pointing is yet recognized as standard, and the differences between different editors are considerable.

7. The conical softish projection, of a light-yellow color, observable in an abscess when nearly ripe. *Thomas*, Med. Dict.—8. *Naut.*, the operation of tapering the end of a rope and covering the tapered portion with the yarns that have not been removed for tapering.—**Cross pointing**, a peculiar kind of braiding made by using the outer yarns of a rope after it has been tapered. The yarns are twisted up into nettles; every alternate one is turned up and the intermediate one down; an upper nettle is brought down to the right of its corresponding lower one and the lower one is laid up, all round the rope; then what are now the upper nettles are brought down to the left of the lower ones, and so on.—**Flat-joint pointing**, the operation of filling the joints of masonry evenly with mortar, and of marking them with a trowel.—**Tuck-joint pointing**, the operation of finishing the joints of masonry with fine mortar, left projecting slightly, and formed to parallel edges; tuck-pointing.

pointingly† (poin'ting-li), *adv.* Pointedly; perspicuously. *B. Jonson*, Volpone, Ded.

pointing-machine (poin'ting-ma-shēn"), *n.* 1. A machine for cutting something (as a picket, a peg, a match, etc.) to a point.—2. A machine for finishing the ends of pins, nails, etc. —3. A machine or, more properly, an apparatus used by sculptors in the production of stone or marble copies of clay models, to locate accurately any point in the copy of the modeled figure. It consists of a round standard *a*, and three round cross-bars *b*, *c*, *d*, made adjustable by means of the sliding-crosses and set-screws *k*, *l*, *m*. On *b* are two adjustable stocks *i*, *j*, with steel points, and at *h* is a third point rigidly attached to d. In the clay model, or, more usually, in a plaster cast of it, are fixed small metal socket-plates *s*, *t*, *r*, each with a small countersink or socket. To these three points the standard is adjusted, the axis of the standard being, when applied to *s*, *t*, *r*, always coincident with the intersection of two fixed planes. To the stone to be cut three socket-plates *s′*, *t′*, *r′* are fixed in such positions that the points will exactly fit their countersinks. The cross-bar c being adjustable vertically on the standard, its axis may be made to coincide with any third plane of projection cutting at right angles the two fixed vertical planes intersecting in the axis of the standard. On *c* is another cross-bar *e*, with an adjustable universal-motion sliding-cross *n*, and to *e* is also attached at *p* a socket holding a bar *f* that also carries at *q* a friction-spring holder for the pointer *g*, the sliding motion of which in the holder is limited by the stop *o*. Suppose the instrument to be set on the socket-plates, and the pointer *g* arranged to just touch the tip of the cat's

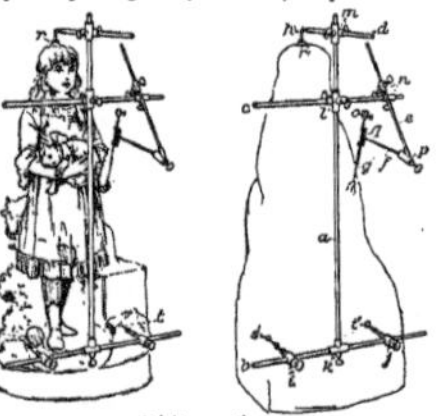

Pointing-machine.

tail in the model. It is then applied to the stone, and if it does not simultaneously touch the bottoms of all the sockets when the point of *g* touches the stone, the latter is cut carefully away till *s*, *t*, and *r* all bed home in their sockets and the point of *g* just touches the bottom of the cut. Other points in the surface are located similarly as guides for the cutting, and intermediate points are located as the cutting proceeds. The instrument is also used to test the accuracy of the work as it progresses, and remarkable fidelity in the copy is attainable by its use.

4. A machine for preparing printed sheets for cutting.

pointing-stock (poin'ting-stok), *n.* An object of scandal or scorn. Compare *laughing-stock*.

I, his forlorn duchess,
Was made a wonder and a *pointing-stock*
To every idle rascal follower.
Shak., 2 Hen. VI., ii. 4. 46.

point-lace (point'lās), *n.* See *lace*.

pointless (point'les), *a.* [< *point* + -*less*.] 1. Having no point; terminating squarely or in a rounded end.

After the procession folowed therle of Northumberlande with a *poinctless* sword naked. *Hall*, Rich. III., an. 2.

An arrow with a *pointless* head will fly further than a pointed one. *M. and W. Thompson*, Archery, p. 34.

2. Without point or force: as, a *pointless* joke.

O'er the protracted feast the suitors sit,
And aim to wound the prince with *pointless* wit.
Fenton, in Pope's Odyssey, xx.

3. In *bot.*, same as *muticous*.

pointleted (point'let-ed), *a.* [< *point* + -*let* + -*ed*2.] In *bot.*, having a small distinct point; apiculate.

pointling†, *adv.* [Also *pointeling*; ME. *poyntelynge*; < *point* + -*ling*2.] With the point directed forward.

He myght wel see a spere grete and longe that came streyghte upon hym *poyntelynge*.
Morte d'Arthur, ii. 165. (*Nares*.)

pointment†, *n.* [By apheresis for *appointment*.] Appointment; arrangement.

Two kynges mo were in his *poyntement*,
With the nowmber of knyghtes accordeng.
Generydes (E. E. T. S.), l. 2178.

To this *poyntment* euery man was agreed, and on the Monday in the mornyng Sir Johan Bouchyer and his company came to the house.
Berners, tr. of Froissart's Chron., II. xix.

He made *poyntment* to come to my house this daye.
Udall, Flowers, fol. 45.

point-pair (point'pãr), *n.* A degenerate conic consisting of two coincident straight lines connected by two points. It may also be considered as two points, the line between them being a bitangent. The two conceptions are equally legitimate.

point-paper (point'pā"pėr), *n.* Pricked paper used for copying or transferring designs. *E. H. Knight.*

pointrel (poin'trel), *n.* [Cf. *pointel*.] A graving-tool. *E. H. Knight.*

pointsman (points'man), *n.*; pl. *pointsmen* (-men). A man who has charge of the points or switches on a railway; a switchman. [Eng.]

Hast thou ne'er seen rough *pointsmen* spy
Some simple English phrase—"With care"
Or "This side uppermost"—and cry
Like children? No? No more have I.
C. S. Calverley, Thoughts at a Railway Station.

point-sphere (point'sfēr), *n.* A point considered as an infinitesimal sphere.

point-tool (point'tōl), *n.* In *turning*, a flat tool having a V-shaped point.

pointy (poin'ti), *a.* [< *point* + -*y*1.] Well-put; pithy; full of point. [Slang.]

poise (poiz), *v.*; pret. and pp. *poised*, ppr. *poising*. [Formerly also *poize*, *peise*, *peize*, *peiz*, *pease*, *peaze*, *paise*, *paize*, *payse*; < ME. *poisen*, *peisen*, *peysen*, *paysen*, < OF. *poiser*, *peiser*, F.

peser = Sp. Pg. *pesar*, *pensar* = It. *pesare*, *pensare*, weigh, poise (cf. OF. and F. *penser* = Sp. Pg. *pensar* = It. *pensare*, think, consider), < L. *pensare*, weigh, counterbalance, compensate, etc., also weigh, ponder, consider, freq. of *pendere*, pp. *pensus*, weigh: see *pendent*. Cf. *poise*, *n.*] **I.** *trans.* **1.** To weigh; ascertain by weighing or balancing; figuratively, to weigh; ponder; consider.

Ac the pounde that she payed by *poised* a quarteroun more
Than myne owne auncere who-so weyzed treuthe.
Piers Plowman (B), v. 218.

Payse euery thyng in gowre lust aduertence.
Political Poems, etc. (ed. Furnivall), p. 46.

And *poise* the cause in justice' equal scales,
Whose beam stands sure, whose rightful cause prevails.
Shak., 2 Hen. VI., ii. 1. 204.

Much more lett 's *peiz* and ponder
Th' Almighties Works, and at his Wisedom wonder.
Sylvester, tr. of Du Bartas's Weeks, i. 2.

2. To counterbalance; be of equal weight with.

Your good opinion shall in weight *poise* me
Against a thousand ill.
Fletcher (and another), Love's Cure, ii. 2.

Thou continent of wealth, whose want of store,
For that it could not *peise* th' unequal scale
Of avarice, giv'st matter to my moan!
Middleton, Family of Love, ii. 4.

Be it the weightiest and most rich affair
That ever was included in your breast,
My faith shall *poise* it.
B. Jonson, Case is Altered, i. 2.

3. To balance; make of equal weight; hold or place in equilibrium: as, to *poise* the scales of a balance.

Moderatly exercise your body with some labour, or playeng at the tennys, or castyng a bowle, or *paysyng* weyghtes or plommettes of leede in your handes, or some other thyng, to open your poores, & to augment naturall heate.
Babees Book (E. E. T. S.), p. 247.

The just skale of even, *paized* thoughts.
Marston, What you Will, Prol.

The world, who of itself is *peised* well,
Made to run even upon even ground.
Shak., K. John, ii. 1. 575.

Chaos wild
Reign'd where these heavens now roll, where earth now rests
Upon her centre *poised*. *Milton*, P. L., v. 579.

The falcon, *poised* on soaring wing,
Watches the wild-duck by the spring.
Scott, Rokeby, iii. 1.

He became conscious of a soul beautifully *poised* upon itself, nothing doubting, nothing desiring, clothed in peace. *R. L. Stevenson*, Will o' the Mill.

4†. To hold suspended or in suspense; delay.

I speak too long; but 'tis to *peize* the time,
To eke it and to draw it out in length.
Shak., M. of V., iii. 2. 22.

5. To weigh or press down; force.

Chawmbyrs with chymnes, and many cheefe inns;
Paysede and pelid downe playsterede walles.
Morte Arthure (E. E. T. S.), l. 3043.

II. *intrans.* To be balanced or suspended; hence, figuratively, to hang in suspense.

Breathless racers whose hopes *poise* upon the last few steps. *Keats.*

And everywhere
The slender, graceful spars
Poise aloft in the air.
Longfellow, Building of the Ship.

poise (poiz), *n.* [Formerly also *poize*, *peise*, *peize*, *paise*; < ME. *poyse*, *peis*, (*a*) < OF. *pois*, *peis*, m., F. *poids* (the *d* introduced during the sixteenth century on account of a supposed derivation from L. *pondus*, weight) = Pr. *pens*, *pes* = Sp. Pg. It. *peso*, m., a weight; (*b*) < OF. *poise*, *peise*, f., weight, balance; < L. *pensum*, anything weighed, prop. neut. of *pensus*, pp. of *pendere*, weigh: see *poise*, *v.*] **1.** Weight; ponderosity; gravity.

Full heauie is the *paise* of Princes ire.
Puttenham, Arte of Eng. Poesie, p. 110.

Some others were in such sort bound vnto pillers with their faces turned to the wall, hauing no staie vnder their feet, and were violentlie weighed downe with the *peise* of their bodies. *Foxe*, Martyrs, The Ten First Persecutions.

When I have suit, . . .
It shall be full of *poise* and difficult weight,
And fearful to be granted. *Shak.*, Othello, iii. 3. 82.

A stone of such a *paise*
That one of this time's strongest men, with both hands, could not raise. *Chapman*, Iliad, xii.

2. A weight; especially, the weight or mass of metal used in weighing with steelyards to balance the substance weighed.

They make many smaule diamundes, whiche . . . are soulde by a *poyse* or weight which they caule Mangiar.
R. Eden, tr. of Antonio Pigafetta (First Books on America, [ed. Arber, p. 265).

Laborynge with *poyses* made of leadde or other metall.
Sir T. Elyot, The Governour, i. 16.

3. A thing suspended or attached as a counterweight; hence, that which counterbalances; a counterpoise.

Men of an unbounded imagination often want the *poise* of judgment. *Dryden.*

4. A state of balance; equipoise; equilibrium; hence, equanimity.

The particles that formed the earth must convene from all quarters toward the middle, which would make the whole compound to rest in a *poise*. *Bentley*, Sermons.

It is indeed hard for the weak and unsteady hearts of men to carry themselves in such a *poize* between both as not to make the shunning of one inconvenience the falling into another. *South*, Sermons, XI. vii.

But what was most remarkable, and, perhaps, showed a more than common *poise* in the young man, was the fact that, amid all these personal vicissitudes, he had never lost his identity. *Hawthorne*, Seven Gables, xii.

5. The condition of balancing or hovering; suspended motion.

Like water-reeds the *poise*
Of her soft body, dainty thin.
D. G. Rossetti, Staff and Scrip.

The tender *poise* of pausing feet.
A. C. Swinburne, Life of Blake.

poiseless (poiz'les), *a.* [Formerly also *peizless*; < *poise* + *-less*.] Without weight; light.

poiser (poi'zėr), *n.* [Formerly also *peizer*, *payser*; < *poise* + *-er*¹.] **1.** One who poises or weighs; a weigher.

The officers deputed to manage the coynage are porters to beare the tynne, *peizers* to weigh it, a steward, comptroller, and receiver to keepe the account.
Carew, Survey of Cornwall, fol. 14.

2. That which poises or balances; specifically, in *entom.*, the halter or balancer of a dipterous insect or a male coccid. See cut under *halter*.

poison (poi'zn), *n.* [< ME. *poisoun*, *poyson*, *poysone*, *puyson*, *puisun*, a potion, poison, < OF. *poison*, *puison*, potion, poison, F. *poison*, poison, = Pr. *poizo* = Sp. *pocion*, potion (*ponzoña*, poison, = Pg. *peçonha*, poison), = It. *pozione*, potion, < L. *potio(n-)*, drink, a draught, a poisonous draught, a potion, < *potare*, drink: see *potion*, of which *poison* is but an older form.] **1†.** A drink; a draught; a potion.

And nailede hym [Christ] with thre nayles naked on the rode,
And with a pole *poyson* putten to hus lippes,
And beden hym drynke, hus deth to lette, and hus dayes lengthen. *Piers Plowman* (C), xxi. 52.

2. Any substance which, introduced into the living organism directly, tends to destroy the life or impair the health of that organism.

Hereby was signified that, as glasse by nature holdeth no *poyson*, so a faythful counsellor holdeth no treason.
Norton and Sackville, Ferrex and Porrex, ii.

Tobacco, coffee, alcohol, hashish, prussic acid, strychnine, are weak dilutions; the surest *poison* is time.
Emerson, Old Age.

3. Hence, that which taints or destroys moral purity or health or comfort: as, the *poison* of evil example.

Plato also, that diuine Philosopher, hath many Godly medicines agaynst the *poyson* of vayne pleasure.
Ascham, The Scholemaster, p. 77.

Why linger We? see, see your Lover's gone;
Perhaps to fetch more *poison* for your heart.
J. Beaumont, Psyche, ii. 115.

Aërial poison. Same as *miasma*.—**Arrow-poison**, the juice of various plants used by savages in Africa, South America, Java, etc., for anointing arrows to render them deadly. The plants so used include several euphorbias, two species of *Strychnos*, the manchineel, and the poison-bulb. See especially *curari*.—**Poison of Pahonias** or **Phonias**, an exceedingly violent poison obtained from the seeds of *Strophanthus hispidus*, an apocynaceous plant of the Gaboon, where it is used as an arrow-poison, under the name of *inée*, *onaye*, or *onage*.

poison (poi'zn), *v. t.* [< ME. *poisonen*, *poysnyn*, < OF. *poisonner* = Sp. *ponzoñar* (cf. Pg. *peçonhentar*), poison; from the noun.] **1.** To infect with poison; put poison into or upon; add poison to: as, to *poison* an arrow.

This even-handed justice
Commends the ingredients of our *poison'd* chalice
To our own lips. *Shak.*, Macbeth, i. 7. 11.

The *poysoned* weed is much in shape like our English Iuy.
Capt. John Smith, Works, II. 113.

None knew, till guilt created fear,
What darts or *poison'd* arrows were.
Roscommon, tr. of Horace's Odes, i. 22.

2. To administer poison to; attack, injure, or kill by poison.

He was so discouraged that he *poisoned* himself and died.
2 Mac. x. 13.

How easy 'twere for any man we trust
To *poison* one of us in such a bowl.
Beau. and Fl., Maid's Tragedy, iv. 2.

3. To taint; mar; impair; vitiate; corrupt.

My rest
Was *poison'd* with th' extremes of grief and fear.
Quarles, Emblems, iv. 11.

Constantine with his mischevous donations *poyson'd* Silvester and the whole Church. *Milton*, Eikonoklastes, xvii.

poisonable (poi'zn-a-bl), *a.* [< *poison* + *-able*.] **1†.** Capable of poisoning; venomous.

Tainted with Arianism and Pelagianism, as of old, or Anabaptism and Libertinism, or such like *poisonable* heresies, as of late.
Tooker, Fabrick of the Church (1604), p. 54. (*Latham.*)

2. Capable of being poisoned.

poison-ash (poi'zn-ash), *n.* Same as *poison-sumac*.

poison-bag (poi'zn-bag), *n.* Same as *poison-sac*.

poison-bay (poi'zn-bā), *n.* An evergreen shrub, *Illicium Floridanum*, whose leaves are reputed poisonous.

poison-berry (poi'zn-ber"i), *n.* Any one of the various species of *Cestrum*; also, the boraginaceous shrub *Bourreria succulenta*. [West Indies.]

poison-bulb (poi'zn-bulb), *n.* The South African herb *Buphane* (*Hæmanthus*) *toxicaria* of the *Amaryllideæ*, whose coated bulb is said to furnish the Kafirs an arrow-poison.

poison-cup (poi'zn-kup), *n.* A name given to certain old glass beakers, tankards, etc., from the belief that poison poured into them would break them and thus be detected.

poison-dogwood (poi'zn-dog"wůd), *n.* Same as *poison-sumac*.

poison-elder (poi'zn-el"dėr), *n.* Same as *poison-sumac*.

poisoner (poi'zn-ėr), *n.* One who poisons or corrupts, or that which poisons or corrupts.

poison-fang (poi'zn-fang), *n.* One of the superior maxillary teeth of certain serpents, as the viper and rattlesnake, having a channel in it through which the poisonous fluid is conveyed into the wound when they bite; a venom-fang. The fang ordinarily lies recumbent, but when the serpent bites it is erected and the poison-gland is at the same time compressed and emptied of its secretion, which is injected through the hollow fang into the wound. See cut under *Crotalus*.

poisonful† (poi'zn-fůl), *a.* [< *poison* + *-ful*.] Poisonous; full of poison.

The spider, a *poisonfull* vermine, yet climes to the roof of the king's palace. *White*, Sermons (1665), p. 53.

poison-gland (poi'zn-gland), *n.* A gland which secretes poison, as in a venomous serpent. See cuts under *chelicera* and *Hymenoptera*.

poison-hemlock (poi'zn-hem"lok), *n.* Same as *hemlock*, 1.

poisonie†, *a.* Same as *poisony*.

poison-ivy (poi'zn-ī"vi), *n.* A shrub-vine of North America, *Rhus Toxicodendron*, sometimes low and erect, but commonly a climber on trees, rocks, fences, etc. It poisons many persons either by contact or by its effluvium, causing a severe cutaneous eruption with intense smarting and itching. It is popularly distinguished as *three-leafed ivy* from the innocuous Virginia creeper, *Ampelopsis quinquefolia*, the five-leafed ivy, their leaves having respectively three and five leaflets. It is often confounded with the common clematis (*Clematis Virginiana*), but the trifoliate leaves of that plant are opposite, not alternate as in the poison-ivy. See *poison-oak*.

poison-nut (poi'zn-nut), *n.* **1.** The nux vomica. —**2.** The fruit of *Cerbera Tanghin*, and doubtless of *C. Odollam*.

poison-oak (poi'zn-ōk), *n.* The poison-ivy, or properly its low form; also, the kindred plant of Pacific North America, *Rhus diversiloba*, which is similarly poisonous and not high-climbing. The latter is also called *yeara*.

poison-organ (poi'zn-ôr"gan), *n.* Any part or organ capable of inflicting a poisoned wound; an organic apparatus for poisoning.

poisonous (poi'zn-us), *a.* [Formerly also *poisnous*, *poysnous* (= Sp. *ponzoñoso*); as *poison* + *-ous*.] Having the properties of a poison; containing poison; venomous; hence, corrupting, vitiating, or impairing.

O sovereign mistress of true melancholy,
The *poisonous* damp of night disponge upon me.
Shak., A. and C., iv. 9. 13.

Serpents & *poysnous* toads, as in their bowers,
Doe closely lurke vnder the sweetest flowers.
Times' Whistle (E. E. T. S.), p. 23.

poisonously (poi'zn-us-li), *adv.* In a poisonous manner; with fatal or injurious effects.

poisonousness (poi'zn-us-nes), *n.* The character of being poisonous.

poison-pea (poi'zn-pē), *n.* See *Swainsona*.

poison-plant (poi'zn-plant), *n.* (*a*) One of various species of *Gastrolobium*. (*b*) The Swainson pea. See *Swainsona*. (*c*) A bird's-foot trefoil, *Lotus australis*. [All Australian.]

poison-sac (poi'zn-sak), *n.* A sac or pouch containing or secreting poison; a poison-gland.

poisonsome† (poi'zn-sum), *a.* [< *poison* + *-some*.] Poisonous. *Holland.*

poison-sumac (poi'zn-shö"mak), *n.* A small handsome tree, *Rhus venenata*, of swamp-borders in eastern North America. It is even more poisonous by contact or vicinity than the poison-ivy. Its leaves have from seven to thirteen leaflets, and, like those of the other sumacs, become brilliantly red in the autumn. In this condition it is often unwittingly gathered for ornament. It is distinguishable from the others by its smooth leaves, entire leaflets, axis not winged between the leaflets, and white fruit. Also called *poison-* or *swamp-dogwood*, *poison-elder*, *poison-ash*.

poison-tooth (poi'zn-töth), *n.* Same as *poison-fang* or *venom-fang*.

poison-tower (poi'zn-tou"ėr), *n.* In the production of arsenic, as practised in Saxony and Silesia, one of the chambers in which the fumes of arsenic and sulphur are condensed.

poison-tree (poi'zn-trē), *n.* Any tree of poisonous character, especially species of *Rhus*; also *Croton Verreauxii*, a small Australian tree.

poison-vine (poi'zn-vīn), *n.* 1. The poison-ivy.—2. The milk-vine, *Periploca Græca*.

poisonwood (poi'zn-wůd), *n.* 1. A small poisonous tree, *Rhus Metopium*, of the West Indies and southern Florida, whose bark yields upon incision a gum with emetic, purgative, and diuretic properties. Also called *burnwood*, *coral-sumac*, *mountain manchineel*, *hog-plum*, etc. —2. A small euphorbiaceous tree, *Sebastiania lucida*, of the same habitat. Its wood, which is hard and close-grained, dark-brown streaked with yellow, is manufactured into canes, and is also valued for fuel.

poisony†, *a.* [< *poison* + *-y*1.] Poisonous.

> Eunomus, who at the first had sowne
> His *poisony* seeds.
> *Sylvester*, tr. of Du Bartas's Triumph of Faith, ii. 43.

poisure† (poi'zūr), *n.* [< *poise* + *-ure*.] Weight; poise.

> Nor is this forc'd,
> But the mere quality and *poisure* of goodness.
> *Fletcher*, Wit without Money, i. 1.

poitrel (poi'trel), *n.* [Formerly also *peitrel*, *peytrel*, *petrel*, etc., < ME. *peytrel*, *peitrel*, *paytrelle*, *payetrelle*, < OF. *poitral*, *poictral*, *poictrail*, F. *poitrail* = Sp. *petral*, *pretal* = Pg. *peitoral* = It. *pettorale*, < L. *pectorale*, a breastplate, neut. of *pectoralis*, of the breast: see *pectoral*.] A piece of armor that protected the breast of a horse. The use of the poitrel lingered long after the other parts of the bards had been abandoned.

Poitrel, 15th century.

> Curious harneys, as in sadeles, in crouperes, *peytrels* and bridles covered with precious clothing, and riche barres and plates of gold and of silver.
> *Chaucer*, Parson's Tale.

> His *petrell* and reins were embroidered with feathers.
> *Sir P. Sidney*, Arcadia, iii.

poitrine (poi'trin), *n.* [< OF. *poictrine*, a breastplate, the breast, also *peitrine*, *petrine*, F. *poitrine*, the breast, = Sp. *petrina*, *pretina*, a girdle, = Pg. *petrina* = It. *pettorina*, *petturina*, a breast-girdle, < L. as if **pectorina*, < *pectus* (*pector-*), breast: see *pectoral*.] 1. The breastplate of a knight.—2. Same as *poitrel*.

poivrette (pwo-vret'), *n.* [F., < *poivre*, pepper: see *pepper*.] Same as *pepperette*.

poize†, *v.* and *n.* An obsolete form of *poise*.

pokal (pō-käl'), *n.* [= Sw. Dan. *pokal*, < G. *pokal*, < F. *bocal*, a drinking-vessel: see *bocal*.] A drinking-vessel of ornamental character, large and showy; a vessel shaped like a drinking-vessel: a term recently borrowed from the German, and applied especially to vessels of silver and of enameled glass of German make.

Pokal of Rock-crystal.

poke1 (pōk), *v.*; pret. and pp. *poked*, ppr. *poking*. [< ME. *poken*, *pouken*, *pukken* = D. *poken* = MLG. LG. *poken*, poke, = Walloon *poquer*, knock: cf. D. *pook*, MLG. *pōk*, LG. *poke*, a dagger; Sw. *påk*, a stick; prob. of Celtic origin: Gael. *puc*, push, Ir. *poc*, a blow, kick, = Corn. *poc*, a shove. Hence the assibilated form *poach*1.] I. *trans.* 1. To thrust or push against; prod, especially with something long or pointed; prod and stir up: as, to *poke* a person in the ribs.

> He helde the swerde in his honde all naked, and griped his shelde, and come to hym that yet lay on the grene, and putte the poynte of his swerde on his shelde and be-gan to *pouke* hym.
> *Merlin* (E. E. T. S.), ii. 367.

> The impressions . . . which a man receives from *poking* objects with the end of his walking-stick.
> *H. Spencer*, Prin. of Psychol. (2d ed.), § 79.

> The crowning human virtue in a man is to let his wife *poke* the fire.
> *C. D. Warner*, Backlog Studies, p. 4.

2. To push gently; jog.

> And Pandare wep as he to water wolde,
> And *poked* ever his nece newe and newe.
> *Chaucer*, Troilus, iii. 116.

3. To thrust or push.

> The end of the jib-boom seemed about to *poke* itself into the second story window of a red-brick building.
> *Scribner's Mag.*, IV. 611.

4. To force as if by thrusting; urge; incite.

> "3us," quod Pieres the plowman, and *pukked* hem alle to gode.
> *Piers Plowman* (B), v. 643.

> You must still be *poking* me, against my will, to things?
> *B. Jonson*, Poetaster, ii. 1.

5. To put a poke on: as, to *poke* an ox or a pig. See *poke*1, *n.*, 3. [U. S.]—6†. To set the plaits of (a ruff).

> My poor innocent Openwork came in as I was *poking* my ruff.
> *Middleton and Dekker*, Roaring Girl, iv. 2.

To poke fun, to joke; make fun. [Colloq.]—**To poke fun at**, to ridicule; make a butt of. [Colloq.]

II. *intrans.* 1. To stoop or bend forward in walking.—2. To grope; search; feel or push one's way in or as in the dark; also, to move to and fro; dawdle.

> Hang Homer and Virgil; their Meaning to seek
> A man must have *pok'd* into Latin and Greek.
> *Prior*, Down-Hall, st. 3.

> Full licence to *poke* about among what there is to *poke* about in the shattered castle.
> *E. A. Freeman*, Venice, p. 342.

poke1 (pōk), *n.* [< *poke*1, *v.*] 1. A gentle thrust or push, especially with something long or pointed; a prod; a dig.

> "But," concluded Uncle Jack, with a sly look, and giving me a *poke* in the ribs, "I've had to do with mines before now, and know what they are."
> *Bulwer*, Caxtons, xvii. 1.

2. A poke-bonnet.

> Governesses don't wear ornaments. You had better get me a grey frieze livery and a straw *poke*, such as my aunt's charity children wear. *George Eliot*, Daniel Deronda, xxiv.

3. A sort of collar or ox-bow from the lower part of which a short pole projects, placed about the neck of a cow or steer in order to prevent it from jumping fences. [U. S.]—4. A lazy person; a dawdler. [U. S.]

> They're only worn by some old-fashioned *pokes*.
> *Lowell*, Fitz Adam's Story.

poke2 (pōk), *n.* [< ME. *poke*, also irreg. *palke* = MD. *poke* (> OF. *poque*, *pouque*, assibilated *poche*, *pouche*, > ME. *pouche*, E. *pouch*), a bag, = Icel. *poki*, a bag; prob. of Celtic origin, < Ir. *poc*, Gael. *poca*, a bag. Cf. AS. *poha*, *pohha*, a purse, etc. Hence ult. *pocket*, *pucker*. Cf. the doublet *pouch*. No connection with AS. *pung*, a bag, = Icel. *pungr*, a pouch, purse, = Goth. *puggs*, a bag.] 1. A pocket; a pouch; a bag; a sack.

> "Trewely, frere," quath y tho, "to tellen the the sothe,
> Ther is no peny in my *palke* to payen for my mete."
> *Piers Plowman's Crede* (E. E. T. S.), l. 399.

> And in the floor, with nose and mouth to-broke,
> They walwe as doon two pigges in a *poke*.
> *Chaucer*, Reeve's Tale, l. 358.

> And then he drew a dial from his *poke*.
> *Shak.*, As you Like it, ii. 7. 20.

2†. A large, wide, bag-like sleeve formerly in vogue. Same as *poke-sleeve*.

> An hool cloith of scarlet may not make a gowne,
> The *pokes* of purchace hangen to the erthe.
> *MS. Digby* 41, f. 7. (*Halliwell.*)

3. A bag or bladder filled with air and used by fishermen as a buoy.

> When the *pokes* are used, the officer gives the order to "Blow up! Blow up!" and a man with sound lungs grasps one of these membranous pouches and inflates it. . . . It is then attached to the whale, and, being of a white color, may be readily seen at quite a distance from the ship.
> *Fisheries of U. S.*, V. ii. 270.

4. The stomach or swimming-bladder of a fish. —5. A cock, as of hay. [Prov. Eng.]

> I pray thee mow, and do not go
> Until the hay 's in *pokes*.
> Ballad *of the Mower*, quoted in N. and Q., 7th ser., VI. [287.

6. A customary unit of weight for wool, 20 hundredweight.—**A pig in a poke**, a pig in a bag.

poke3 (pōk), *n.* [Also *pocan*; appar. Amer. Ind.] Same as *pokeweed* or *garget*.—**Hydrangea-leafed poke.** See *Phytolacca*.—**Indian poke**, the American, false, or white hellebore, *Veratrum viride*.

poke4 (pōk), *n.* The small green heron more fully called *shitepoke*. [U. S.]

poke5†, *n.* Scrofula.

> Aubanus Bohemus referres that struma or *poke* of the Bavarians and Styrians to the nature of their waters.
> *Burton*, Anat. of Mel., p. 71. (*Davies.*)

poke-bag (pōk'bag), *n.* [So called in allusion to the shape of the nest; < *poke*2 + *bag*.] The bottletit: same as *feather-poke*. [Local, Eng.]

pokeberry (pōk'ber"i), *n.*; pl. *pokeberries* (-iz). The fruit of the pokeweed.

poke-bonnet (pōk'bon"et), *n.* A bonnet having a projecting front of a nearly conical form, worn about the beginning of the nineteenth century and later.

> His mamma . . . came fawning in with her old *poke-bonnet*. *Thackeray*, Lovel the Widower, vi.

poke-dial† (pōk'dī"al), *n.* A pocket-dial; specifically, a ring-dial.

poke-milkweed (pōk'milk"wēd), *n.* An American plant, *Asclepias phytolaccoides*, with some resemblance to pokeweed.

poke-net (pōk'net), *n.* A pole-net.

poker1 (pō'kėr), *n.* [< *poke*1 + *-er*1.] 1. One who or that which pokes. (*a*) An iron or steel bar or rod used in poking or stirring a fire.

> If the *poker* be out of the way, or broken, stir the fire with the tongs.
> *Swift*, Advice to Servants, General Directions.

(*b*†) A small stick or iron used for setting the plaits of ruffs; a poking-stick.

> Now your Puritans *poker* is not so huge, but somewhat longer; a long slender poking-sticke is the all in all with your Suffolke Puritane.
> *Heywood*, If you Know not Me (Works, ed. Pearson, I. 258).

(*c*) An iron instrument used for driving hoops on masts. It has a flat foot at one end and a round knob at the other.—**Red-hot-poker.** Same as *flame-flower*.

poker2 (pō'kėr), *n.* [Cf. Sw. *pocker*, Dan. *pokker*, the devil, deuce, and see *puck*. Cf. *hodge-poker*.] Any frightful object; a bugbear. [Colloq.]—**Old Poker**, the devil. [Slang.]

> The very leaves on the horse-chesnuts are little snotty-nosed things that cry and are afraid of the north wind, and cling to the bough as if *Old Poker* was coming to take them away. *Walpole*, Letters, iv. 359.

poker3 (pō'kėr), *n.* [Origin obscure; perhaps a particular use, as orig. applied, of *poker*1 or *poker*2, but, as with some other names of card-games (e. g. *euchre*), the origin is without literary record.] A game of cards played by two or more persons with a full pack of fifty-two cards, which rank as in whist. After each player has deposited an *ante* or preliminary bet in the pool, hands of five cards are dealt. Any player not satisfied can demand in place of from one to five cards in his hand as many new ones from the undealt part of the pack; the eldest hand must then deposit an additional bet in the pool or withdraw from the game, the second hand having then the privilege of betting higher, or *calling* (that is, merely equaling the bet and demanding a show of hands), or retiring, and so on all around. If all the players but one retire, that one takes the pool; if a player calls the bet, those who follow him may bet the same amount, and the highest hand wins the pool. The hands rank as follows, beginning with the lowest: (1) the highest card in any hand; (2) one pair; (3) two pairs; (4) three of the same denomination; (5) a "straight"—a sequence of five cards not of the same suit (sometimes omitted); (6) a flush—five cards of the same suit not in sequence; (7) a full—three cards of the same denomination and a pair; (8) four cards of the same denomination; and (9) a straight flush—a sequence of five cards of the same suit. There are varieties of the game known as *whisky-poker*, *straight poker*, etc. [U. S.]

poker4 (pō'kėr), *n.* [Cf. *pochard*.] One of various kinds of wild ducks, especially the pochard. [Local, Eng.]

pokerish1 (pō'kėr-ish), *a.* [< *poker*1 + *-ish*1.] Like a poker; stiff. [Colloq.]

> Maud Elliott, the most reserved and diffident girl of her acquaintance—"stiff and *pokerish*," Elia called her.
> *The Century*, XXXVI. 35.

pokerish2 (pō'kėr-ish), *a.* [< *poker*2 + *-ish*1.] Frightful; causing fear, especially to children; uncanny: as, a *pokerish* place. [Colloq.]

> There is something *pokerish* about a deserted dwelling, even in broad daylight. *Lowell*, Fireside Travels, p. 144.

pokerishly (pō'kėr-ish-li), *adv.* Like a poker; stiffly. [Colloq.]

> "I'm afraid I'm interrupting a pleasant tete-a-tete?" says the old lady, *pokerishly*.
> *R. Broughton*, Cometh up as a Flower, xxxvi.

poke-root (pōk'röt), *n.* The Indian poke (see under *poke*3), or its root; also, the root of the pokeweed.

poker-painting (pō'kėr-pān"ting), *n.* The process or act of producing poker-pictures.

poker-picture (pō'kėr-pik"tūr), *n.* An imitation of a sepia drawing, executed by singeing the surface of wood with a heated poker.

poke-sleeve† (pōk'slēv), *n.* A loose sleeve having a part hanging below the arm like a bag.

poke-stick (pōk'stik), *n.* A stick rounded at the end, used by some tribes of American Indians to aid them in gorging food at a feast.

pokeweed (pōk'wēd), *n.* A plant of the genus *Phytolacca*, especially *P. decandra* of eastern North America. This is a strong-growing branching herb, bearing racemes of white flowers and deep-purple juicy berries, their coloring principle too evanescent for use. The young shoots are boiled like asparagus, and the berries and root, especially the latter, are emetic, purgative, and somewhat narcotic, officinal in the United States. Also called *poke, scoke, garget, inkberry-weed*, and *pigeon-berry*. Obscure names are *coakum* and *pocan*.

poking (pō'king), *p. a.* [Ppr. of *poke*[1], *v.*] Drudging; servile. [Colloq.]

Some *poking* profession or employment in some office of drudgery. *Gray*, Works, II. xxxvi.

poking-stick† (pō'king-stik), *n.* An instrument formerly used to adjust the plaits of ruffs.

Pins and *poking-sticks* of steel. *Shak.*, W. T., iv. 4. 228.

The horning-busk and silken bridelaces are in good request with the parson's wife; your huge *poking-sticke*, and French periwig, with chambermaids and waiting gentlewomen. *Heywood*, If you Know not Me (Works, ed. Pearson, I. 258).

poky (pō'ki), *a.* [< *poke*[1] + *-y*[1].] **1.** Slow; dull; stupid: said of persons.—**2.** Confined; cramped; musty; stuffy: said of places.—**3.** Poor; shabby. [Colloq. in all uses.]

The ladies were in their *pokiest* old head-gear and most dingy gowns when they perceived the carriage approaching. *Thackeray*, Newcomes, lvii.

Polabian (pō̤-lā'bi-a̤n), *a.* and *n.* [< *Polab*, one of a tribe dwelling 'on the Elbe' (< Bohem. *po*, near, on, + *Labe*, L. *Albis*, G. *Elbe*, the Elbe), + *-ian*.] **I.** *a.* Of or pertaining to the Polabs or to their language.

II. *n.* A Slavic language, allied to Polish or to Czech, formerly spoken in northern Germany.

Polabish (pō̤-lā'bish), *a.* and *n.* [= G. *Polabisch*; as *Polab(ian)* + *-ish*[1].] Same as *Polabian*.

polacca[1] (pō̤-lak'ạ̈), *n.* [Also *polacre, polaque* (< F.), and *polacre*; < It. *polacca*, a vessel so called.] A vessel with two or three masts, used on the Mediterranean. The masts are usually of one piece.

polacca[2] (pō̤-lak'ạ̈), *n.* [It. *polacca*, fem. of *Polacco*, Polish: see *Polack*.] In *music*, same as *polonaise*.—**Alla polacca**, in the style of a polonaise.

Polack (pō'lak), *n.* [< D. *Polak* = G. Sw. *Polack* = Dan. *Polak* = Sp. Pg. *Polaco* = It. *Polacco*, Polish, a Pole, < Pol. *Polak* = Russ. *Polyakŭ*, a Pole: see *Pole*[3].] A Pole; a Polander.

His nephew's levies . . . appear'd
To be a preparation 'gainst the *Polack*.
Shak., Hamlet, ii. 2. 63.

These vsed to make sudden inrodes vpon the *Polachs*. *Purchas*, Pilgrimage, p. 421.

polacre (pō̤-lā'kėr), *n.* **1.** Same as *polacca*[1].—**2.** A mast of one piece, without tops.

polant, *n.* Same as *poulaine*.

Poland bill. See *bill*[3].

Polander (pō'la̤n-dėr), *n.* [< *Poland* (see def.) + *-er*[1]. The name *Poland* is an accom. (simulating *land*) of **Polen*, < D. G. Sw. Dan. *Polen* = F. *Pologne* = Sp. Pg. It. *Polonia*, ML. *Polonia*, Poland: see *Pole*[3].] A Pole, or native of Poland.

The Grand Council of the *Polanders*. *Milton*, Letters of State, Feb. 6, 1650.

Poland manna. Same as *manna-seeds*.

Polanisia (pol-a-nis'i-ä), *n.* [NL. (Rafinesque, 1824), so called in allusion to the many differences between the stamens and those of the related genus *Cleome*; irreg. < Gr. πολύς, many, + ἄνισος, unequal, dissimilar, < ἀν- priv. + ἴσος, equal.] A genus of polypetalous plants of the order *Capparideæ* and tribe *Cleomeæ*, distinguished by its short receptacle, four entire petals, eight or more free stamens, and numerous reniform seeds in a long two-valved pod. There are 15 species, all tropical or subtropical, with one, *P. graveolens*, extending north to Vermont. They are annual herbs, commonly glandular and of a strong peculiar odor, bearing palmate or undivided leaves, and small flowers in terminal clusters, which are purplish, greenish, etc. Several species with white, pink, or yellow flowers are occasionally cultivated.

Flowering Branch of *Polanisia viscosa*. *a*, a flower; *b*, a pod; *c*, a seed; *d*, the rhizome and roots.

polaque (pō̤-lak'), *n.* Same as *polacca*[1].

polar (pō'lär), *a.* and *n.* [= F. *polaire* = Sp. Pg. *polar* = It. *polare*, < NL. *polaris*, < L. *polus*, pole: see *pole*[2], *n.*] **I.** *a.* **1.** Of or pertaining to a pole or the poles of a sphere. (*a*) Of or pertaining to either extremity of the axis round which the earth, or any other sphere, revolves. (*b*) Pertaining to the points in which the axis of the earth meets the sphere of the heavens.

2. Proceeding, issuing from, or found in the regions near the poles of the earth or of the heavens: as, the *polar* ocean; a *polar* bear.

Two *polar* winds, blowing adverse
Upon the Cronian sea. *Milton*, P. L., x. 289.

3. Pertaining to a magnetic pole or poles; pertaining to the points of a body at which its attractive or repulsive energy is concentrated. —**4.** In *anat.*, having poles in any way distinguished, as a cell: said especially of ovum-cells and nerve-cells. There may be one, two, or several poles, when the cell is distinguished as *unipolar*, *bipolar*, or *multipolar*.

5. In *higher geom.*, reciprocal to a pole; of the nature of a polar. See II.—**Polar angle**, the angle at a pole formed by two meridians.—**Polar axis**, that axis of an astronomical instrument, as an equatorial, which is parallel to the earth's axis.—**Polar bands.** Same as *Noah's ark*, 3.—**Polar bear.** See *bear*[2], 1, and cut under *Plantigrada*.—**Polar cells**, in *Dicyemida*, cells of the cortical layer which invest the head-end of the body: distinguished from *parapolar cells*, further back.—**Polar circles**, two small circles of the earth parallel to the equator, the one north and the other south, distant 23° 28' from the pole. The north polar circle is called the *arctic circle*, and the south polar circle the *antarctic circle*. The distance of each from its own pole is equal to the obliquity of the ecliptic, and the spaces within the two circles are called the *frigid zones*.—**Polar clock**, an optical apparatus whereby the hour of the day is found by means of the polarization of light.—**Polar coördinates.** See *coördinate*.—**Polar curve** with respect to a line, the locus in tangential coördinates corresponding to the polar curve with respect to a point.—**Polar developable.** See *developable*.—**Polar dial.** See *dial*.—**Polar distance**, the distance of a point on a sphere from one of the poles of the sphere.—**Polar equation**, an equation in polar coördinates.—**Polar forces**, in *physics*, forces that are developed and act in pairs, with opposite tendencies, as in magnetism, electricity, etc.—**Polar formation.** See *formation*.—**Polar globule**, in the maturation of the ovum, a small globule, composed of a part of the germinal vesicle together with a small amount of the vitellus, which is extruded into the perivitelline space. Also called *polar vesicle*, *extrusion-globule*.—**Polar hare.** See *hare*[1], 1.—**Polar lights**, the aurora borealis or australis.—**Polar line**, the last of the polar curves with respect to a point.—**Polar line of a skew curve.** See *line*[2].—**Polar map-projection.** See *projection*.—**Polar multiplication.** See *multiplication*.—**Polar nucleus**, in *bot.*, the fourth nucleus in each group at the two extremities of the embryo-sac, which move toward the middle of the embryo-sac and there coalesce to form the secondary nucleus of the embryo-sac. *Goebel*.—**Polar opposite of a point** with respect to two conics in a plane, the point of intersection of the polars of the first point with respect to the two conics.—**Polar pantograph.** See *pantograph*. —**Polar plane of a point** with respect to a conicoid or quadric surface, the plane of tangency with the conicoid of a cone having its vertex at the point.—**Polar projection**, a map-projection in which the earth's pole is taken as the center of projection: generally, either the gnomical or the equal-distance projection is chosen.—**Polar reciprocal.** See *reciprocal*.—**Polar star**, the pole-star. *Tennyson*.—**Polar surface**, in *solid geometry*, a locus in all respects analogous to the polar curve of plane geometry.—**Polar triangle**, in *spherical trigonometry*, a spherical triangle formed from any triangle by the intersections of the great circles having the vertices of the first triangle for their poles.—**Polar vesicle.** Same as *polar globule*. —**Polar whale.** See *whale*.=**Syn. 2.** *Polar, Arctic.* That which is *polar* belongs to or is connected with the north or south pole; that which is *arctic* belongs to a limited region about the north pole. See definitions of *arctic* and *antarctic*.

II. *n.* A plane curve whose point-equation is derived from that of another plane curve (with respect to which it is said to be a polar) by operating one or more times (according as it is *first*, *second*, etc., *polar*) with the symbol $x'.d/dx+y'.d/dy+z'.d/dz$, where x', y', z' are the trilinear coördinates of a fixed point (of which the curve is said to be a polar). The first polar of a point with respect to a curve is a curve of the next lower order, cutting the primitive curve at all the points of tangency of tangents to the primitive from the fixed point, as well as at all the nodes of the primitive, and tangent to the primitive at every cusp of the latter. Thus the polar of a point with respect to a conic is simply the straight line joining

Nodal cubic with its conic polar.

the points of tangency of tangents from that point to the conic. The harmonic mean of the distances from the fixed point, measured along any given radius of the intersections of any polar of that point, is the same as that of the distances of the intersections of the primitive curve; and the same is equally true of products of pairs or triplets or any number of intersections. In a generalized sense, mathematicians speak of a polar of a curve with respect to another curve: if the tangential equation of the first curve is $(a, b, c, \ldots \between u, v, w)^n$, and the point-equation of the second curve is $(A, B, C, \ldots \between x, y, z)^m$, where $m > n$, then the polar of the first with respect to the second is

$$(a, b, c, \ldots \between d/dx, d/dy, d/dz)^n (A, B, C, \ldots \between x, y, z)^m.$$

But if $n > m$, the polar of the second curve with respect to the first is

$$(A, B, C \ldots \between d/du, d/dv, d/dw)^m (a, b, c \ldots \between u, v, w)^n.$$

polar-bilocular (pō'lär-bī-lok'ụ̄-lär), *a.* In *bot.*, having two cells or loculi, as certain spores.

polaric (pō̤-lar'ik), *a.* [< *polar* + *-ic*.] Polar. [Rare.]

polarily† (pō'lär-i-li), *adv.* In a polary manner; with respect to polarity.

If an iron be touched before, it varieth not in this manner; for then it admits not this magnetical impression, as being already informed by the loadstone, and *polarily* determined by its preaction. *Sir T. Browne*, Vulg. Err., ii. 2.

polarimeter (pō-la̤-rim'e-tėr), *n.* [= F. *polarimètre*; < NL. *polaris*, polar, + Gr. μέτρον, measure.] A polariscope; more specifically, an instrument for measuring the amount of polarized light in the light received from a given source, or for measuring the angular rotation of the plane of polarization. See *photo-polarimeter*, *polaristrobometer*, and *saccharimeter*.

polarimetry (pō-la̤-rim'et-ri), *n.* [< NL. *polaris*, polar, + Gr. -μετρία, < μετρεῖν, measure.] The art or process of measuring or analyzing the polarization of light.

Polaris (pō̤-lā'ris), *n.* [NL., < L. *polus*, pole: see *polar*, *pole*[2].] The pole-star.

polarisable, polarisation. See *polarizable*, *polarization*.

polariscope (pō̤-lar'i-skōp), *n.* [= F. *polariscope*; irreg. < NL. *polaris*, polar, + Gr. σκοπεῖν, view.] An optical instrument, various forms of which have been contrived, for exhibiting the polarization of light, or for examining substances in polarized light. The essential parts of the instrument are the polarizing and analyzing plates or prisms, and these are formed either from natural crystals or of a series of reflecting surfaces, as of glass, artificially joined together. (See *polarization*.) A polariscope employing parallel light, and designed to find the extinction-directions — that is, planes of light-vibration — in a crystal section, is called a *stauroscope*. One using converging light, and employed in examining the interference figures, as of uniaxial and biaxial crystals, is sometimes called a *conoscope*. The *tourmalin tongs*, consisting of two transparent plates of tourmalin, cut parallel to the axis, and mounted in circular pieces of cork held in a kind of wire pincers, form the simplest kind of polariscope for viewing axial interference figures. The more complex and convenient forms have polarizing prisms of Iceland spar mounted in a vertical stand resembling that of a microscope, with a movable stage, coarse adjustment, and other arrangements. When the polariscope is essentially a microscope with Nicol prisms and attachments for viewing crystal-sections in polarized light, it is usually called a *polarization-microscope* or *polarizing microscope*. The *saccharimeter* and the *polaristrobometer* are special forms of polariscope designed to measure the angular rotation of the plane of polarization of an optically active substance, as a sugar solution, quartz, etc. See *rotation*, and *rotatory power* (under *rotatory*).

Polariscope (Tourmalin Tongs).

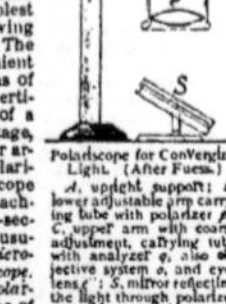

Polariscope for Converging Light. (After Fuess.)
A, upright support; *B*, lower adjustable arm carrying tube with polarizer *p*; *C*, upper arm with coarse adjustment, carrying tube with analyzer *q*, also objective system *o*, and eye-lens *e'*; *S*, mirror reflecting the light through polarizer *p* and lenses *e*, *e'* in parallel rays upon the converging system *n*; *h*, support for object under examination, revolving with the collar *l*, having a graduated circle at *l*, also index and vernier at *h*; *s*, quartz wedge for determination of character of double refraction; *r*, glass micrometer adjusted by screw at *a*.

polariscopic (pō-lar-i-skop'ik), *a.* [< *polariscope* + *-ic*.] Pertaining to a polariscope; ascertained by the polariscope.

polariscopist (pō-lar'i-skō-pist), *n.* [< *polariscope* + *-ist*.] One who is expert in the use of the polariscope.

polariscopy (pō-lar′i-skō-pi), *n.* [NL. *polaris*, polar, + Gr. σκοπεῖν, view.] That branch of optics which deals with polarized light and the use of the polariscope.

polarise, polariser. See *polarize, polarizer.*

polaristic (pō-la-ris′tik), *a.* [< *polar* + *-ist-ic.*] Pertaining to or exhibiting poles; having a polar arrangement or disposition. [Rare.]

polaristrobometer (pō″lar-i-strō-bom′e-tėr), *n.* [< NL. *polaris*, polar, + Gr. στρόβος, a whirling around, + μέτρον, measure.] A form of polarimeter or saccharimeter devised by Wild. Its special feature is the use of a double calcite interference-plate, which produces, in monochromatic light, a set of parallel black lines or fringes, which disappear in a certain relative position of the polarizer and analyzer; this gives a delicate means of fixing the plane of polarization as rotated by the sugar solution under examination. See *saccharimeter.*

polarity (pō-lar′i-ti), *n.* [= F. *polarité* = Sp. *polaridad* = Pg. *polaridade* = It. *polarità*, < NL. *polarita(t-)s*, < *polaris*, polar: see *polar.*] 1. The having two opposite poles; variation in certain physical properties, so that in one direction they are the opposite of what they are in the opposite direction: thus, a magnet has *polarity.* Usually, as in electrified or magnetized bodies, these are properties of attraction or repulsion, or the power of taking a certain direction: as, the *polarity* of the magnet or magnetic needle. (See *magnet.*) A substance is said to possess *magnetic polarity* when it possesses poles, as shown by the fact that it attracts one pole of a magnetic needle and repels the other.

> A magnetical property which some call *polarity.*
> *Boyle*, Works, III. 309.

2. The being attracted to one pole and repelled from the other; attraction of opposites: literal or figurative: as, electricity has *polarity.*

> It seemed Clifford's nature to be a Sybarite. It was perceptible even there, in the dark old parlor, in the inevitable *polarity* with which his eyes were attracted towards the quivering play of sunbeams through the shadowy foliage.
> *Hawthorne*, Seven Gables, vii.

3. The having of an axis with reference to which certain physical properties are determined.—4. The having, as a ray, variation of properties in reference to different inclinations to a plane through the ray; polarization. [This use of the word is objectionable.]

polarizable (pō′lār-ī-za-bl), *a.* [< *polarize* + *-able.*] Capable of being polarized. Also spelled *polarisable.*

polarization (pō″lār-i-zā′shon), *n.* [= F. *polarisation* = It. *polarizzazione*; as *polarize* + *-ation.*] 1. The state, or the act producing the state, of having, as a ray, different properties on its different sides, so that opposite sides are alike, but the maximum difference is between two sides at right angles to each other. This is the case with polarized light.—2. Less properly, the acquisition of polarity, in any sense.

Also spelled *polarisation.*

Angle of polarization, circular polarization. See *polarization of light.*—**Electrolytic polarization,** in *elect.*: (*a*) The process of depositing a film of gas upon the plate in a voltaic cell, or upon the electrodes in electrolysis. (*b*) The condition thus produced. Thus, in the electrolysis of water polarization of the electrodes takes place, the one becoming coated with a film of oxygen, the other with a film of hydrogen gas. The phrase is most frequently used to describe the process by which the negative plate in a voltaic cell becomes coated with hydrogen, with the result of giving rise to a reverse electromotive force, and thus of weakening the current. On the methods of preventing this, see *cell*, 8.—**Elliptic polarization.** See *polarization of light.*—**Plane of polarization,** the plane which includes the incident ray and the ray which is reflected (or refracted) and polarized.—**Polarization of a dielectric,** or **dielectric polarization,** a phrase introduced by Faraday to describe the condition of a non-conductor or dielectric, as he conceived it, when in a state of strain under the action of two adjacent charges of positive and negative electricity, as, for example, in the condenser.—**Polarization of light,** a change produced in light by reflection from or transmission through certain media by which the transverse vibrations of the ether (see *light*[1]) are limited to a single plane, while in a ray of ordinary light these vibrations take place indifferently in any plane about the line of propagation. Polarization may be effected (1) by reflection from a surface of glass, water, or similar substance, and it is most complete if the angle of incidence has a certain value, depending upon the substance, called the *angle of polarization* (for glass 54½°), the tangent of this angle being equal to the refractive index of the given substance (Brewster's law); (2) by transmission through a series of transparent plates of glass placed in parallel position at the proper angle to the incident ray; and (3) by double retraction in any transparent anisotropic crystal (see *refraction*). In the last case the two rays into which the incident ray is separated upon refraction are polarized in planes at right angles to each other, as, for example, in transparent calcite (Iceland spar), in which this double retraction is most marked. A prism of Iceland spar may be prepared in such a way that one of the two refracted rays suffers total reflection and is extinguished; the other ray, which passes through, is polarized, its vibrations taking place in the direction of the shorter diagonal of the cross-section. Such a prism is called a *Nicol prism*, or simply a *nicol.* If two such prisms are placed in the path of a beam of ordinary light, it will pass through them if their positions are parallel; if, however, the nicols are crossed—that is, have their shorter diagonals, or, in other words, their vibration-planes, at right angles to each other—the light which passes through the first prism (called the *polarizer*) will be extinguished by the second (called the *analyzer*). Two sections of a crystal of tourmalin, another doubly refracting substance, cut parallel to the vertical axis, will act in the same way as the nicols, transmitting the light if placed parallel, arresting it if placed with axes at right angles to each other. In the tourmalin one of the rays is almost entirely absorbed by the crystal, and that which passes through is polarized with its vibrations parallel to the axis. In addition to the above *linear plane polarization* of a light-ray, there is also what is called *circular* and *elliptical polarization*, in which the vibrations of the ether-particles take place in circles and ellipses. This property, belonging to certain substances, as quartz, cinnabar, and solution of sugar, has the effect of rotating the plane of polarization of the light transmitted through them to the right (right-handed) or to the left (left-handed). A light-ray passing through a transparent medium in a strong magnetic field, or reflected from the pole of a powerful electromagnet, also suffers a rotation of the plane of polarization. See *rotation*, and *rotatory power*, under *rotatory.*

polarization-microscope (pō″lār-i-zā′shon-mī′krō-skōp), *n.* An instrument consisting essentially of a microscope and a polariscope combined. See *microscope.*

polarize (pō′lār-īz), *v. t.*; pret. and pp. *polarized*, ppr. *polarizing.* [= F. *polariser* = Sp. *polarizar* = It. *polarizzare*; as *polar* + *-ize.*] 1. To develop polarization in, as in a ray of light which is acted upon by certain media and surfaces; give polarity to. See *polarization.*

> If sound's sweet influence *polarize* thy brain,
> And thoughts turn crystals in the fluid strain.
> *O. W. Holmes*, A Rhymed Lesson.

2. In *elect.*, to coat with a film of gas, as the negative plate in a voltaic cell.

Also spelled *polarise.*

Polarizing angle. Same as *angle of polarization*, for which see *polarization of light*, under *polarization.*—**Polarizing microscope.** See *polariscope.*

polarized (pō′lār-īzd), *p. a.* 1. Having polarization; affected by polarization: as, *polarized* light; *polarized* radiant heat.—2. In *elect.*, having the surface covered with a film of gas, as the negative plate of a simple voltaic cell (with hydrogen) after a brief use.

Also spelled *polarised.*

Polarized rings. See *interference figures*, under *interference*, 5.

polarizer (pō′lār-ī-zėr), *n.* In *optics*, that part of a polariscope by which light is polarized: distinguished from *analyzer.* Also spelled *polariser.*

polar-plant (pō′lār-plant), *n.* Same as *compass-plant.* [Rare.]

polary† (pō′la-ri), *a.* [< NL. *polaris*: see *polar.*] Tending to a pole; turning toward a pole.

> All which acquire a magnetical *polary* condition, and, being suspended, convert their lower extream unto the North; with the same attracting the Southern point of the needle.
> *Sir T. Browne*, Vulg. Err., ii. 2.

polatouche (pol-ä-tösh′), *n.* [F.] The small flying-squirrel of Europe and Asia, a species of the genus *Sciuropterus.* Also *palatouche.*

polayne†, *n.* Same as *poulaine.*

poldavis†, *n.* Same as *poledavy.*

polder (pōl′dėr), *n.* [D.] A boggy or marshy soil; a morass; specifically, a tract of marshy land in the Netherlands, Flanders, and northern Germany, which has been reclaimed and brought under cultivation.

polder-land (pōl′dėr-land), *n.* In the Netherlands and adjoining regions, marshy land which has been reclaimed and brought under cultivation.

> Thus the privileges of the Abbey of St. Pierre of Ghent of about the year 830 mention the existence of a partnership of fifty members for the working of some *polder-land.*
> *W. K. Sullivan*, Introd. to O'Curry's Anc. Irish, p. ccxii.

poldern†, **poldron**†, *n.* Obsolete forms of *pauldron.*

poldway†, *n.* Same as *poledavy.* *Weale.*

pole[1] (pōl), *n.* [< ME. *pole*, < AS. *pāl*, a pole, = OFries. *pāl*, *pēl* = D. *paal* = MLG. *pāl* = OHG. *phāl*, MHG. *phāl*, *pfāl*, G. *pfahl* = Icel. *páll* = Sw. *påle* = Dan. *pæl*, a pale, post, stake, = OF. *pal* (> ME. *pal*, *pale*, E. *pale*[1]), F. *pal* = Sp. *palo* = Pg. *pao*, *pau* = It. *palo*, a stake, stick, < L. *pālus*, a stake, pale, prop, stay: see *pale*[1], from the same L. source, derived through OF.] 1. A long, slender, tapering piece of wood, such as the trunk of a tree of any size, from which the branches have been cut; a piece of wood (or metal) of much greater length than thickness, especially when more or less rounded and tapering.

> In the euenyng they entred with a thousand Spaniards & other, & slewe one citizen & set his bed on a *polle*, & caused it to be borne afore them.
> *Hall*, Hen. VIII., an. 19.

> Vines that grow not so low as in France, but vpon high *poles* or railes.
> *Coryat*, Crudities, I. 95.

Specifically—(*a*) A rod used in measuring. (*b*) In a two-horse vehicle, a long tapering piece of wood, forming the shaft or tongue, carrying the neck-yoke or the pole-straps, and sometimes the whiffletrees, by means of which the carriage is drawn. (*c*) A fishing-rod. (*d*) A bean-pole or hop-pole. (*e*) A ship's mast.

2. A perch or rod, a measure of length containing 16½ feet or 5½ yards; also, a measure of surface, a square pole denoting 5½ × 5½ yards, or 30¼ square yards.

> In dyuers odur placis in this lande they mete grounde by *pollis*, gaddis, and roddis; som be of xviij foote, som of xx. fote, and som xxi. fote in lengith.
> *Arnold's Chron.*, p. 173.

3. A flatfish, *Pleuronectes* or *Glyptocephalus cynoglossus*, also called *pole-dab.* [Local, Eng.]—4. That part of the sperm-whale's lower jaw which holds the teeth. See *pan*[1], 12.—**Barber's pole.** See *barber.*—**Setting pole,** a pole with which a boat is pushed through the water.—**To set a pole.** See *set.*—**Under bare poles.** See *bare*[1].

pole[1] (pōl), *v.*; pret. and pp. *poled*, ppr. *poling.* [< *pole*[1], *n.*] **I.** *trans.* 1. To furnish with poles for support: as, to *pole* beans.—2. To bear or convey on poles.—3. To impel by means of a pole, as a boat; push forward by the use of poles.—4. In *copper-refining*, to stir with a pole.

II. *intrans.* To use a pole; push or impel a boat with a pole.

> From the beach we *poled* to the little pier, where sat the Bey in person to perform a final examination of our passports.
> *R. F. Burton*, El-Medinah, p. 120.

pole[2] (pōl), *n.* [< ME. *pol* = D. *pool* = G. Sw. Dan. *pol*, < OF. *pol*, F. *pôle* = Sp. Pg. It. *polo*, < L. *polus*, < Gr. πόλος, a pivot, hinge, axis, pole, < πέλειν, πέλεσθαι, be in motion; prob. of like root with κέλεσθαι, urge on, κέλλειν, drive on, L. *-cellere* in *percellere*, urge on, impel, strike, beat down, etc.] 1. One of the two points in which the axis of the earth produced cuts the celestial sphere; the fixed point about which (on account of the revolution of the earth) the stars appear to revolve. These points are called the *poles of the world*, or the *celestial poles.*

> She shook her throne that shook the starry *pole.*
> *Pope*, Iliad, viii. 241.

2. Either of the two points on the earth's surface in which it is cut by the axis of rotation. That one which is on the left when one faces in the direction of the earth's motion is the *north pole*, the other the *south pole.*

3. In general, a point on a sphere equally distant from every part of the circumference of a great circle of the sphere. Every great circle has two such poles, which lie in a line passing through the center of the sphere and perpendicular to the plane of the great circle—that is, in an axis of the sphere. Thus, the zenith and nadir (on the celestial sphere) are the poles of the horizon. So the poles of the ecliptic are two points on the surface of the celestial sphere equally distant (90°) from every part of the ecliptic.

Hence—4. In any more or less spherical body, one of two opposite points of the surface in any way distinguished; or, when there is a marked equator, one of the two points most remote from it: as, in botany, the *poles* of certain spores or sporidia.—5. The star which is nearest the pole of the earth; the pole-star.—6. The firmament; the sky.

> The God that made both sky, air, earth, and heaven,
> Which they beheld, the moon's resplendent globe,
> And starry *pole.*
> *Milton*, P. L., iv. 724.

7. One of the points of a body at which its attractive or repulsive energy is concentrated, as the free ends of a magnet, one called the *north*, the other the *south pole*, which attract more strongly than any other part. See *magnet.*—8. In *math.*: (*a*) A point from which a pencil of lines radiates: as, the *pole*—that is, the origin—of polar coördinates. (*b*) A point to which a given line is polar. (*c*) A curve related to a line as a polar is to a point, except that tangential are substituted for point coördinates; the result of operating upon the equation of a curve with the symbol $(u'.d/du + v'.d/dv + w'.d/dw)$, where u', v', w' are the coördinates of the line of which the resulting curve is pole relative to the primitive curve. See *polar*, *n.*—**Altitude** or **elevation of the pole.** See *altitude.*—**Analogous pole,** that end of a pyro-electric crystal, as tourmalin, at which positive electricity is developed with a rise, and negative electricity with a fall, in temperature. See *pyro-electricity.*—**Antilogous pole,** that end of a pyro-electric crystal, as tourmalin, at which negative electricity is developed with a rise, and positive with a fall, in temperature. See *pyro-electricity.*—**Austral, blue, boreal, chlorous pole.** See the adjectives.—**Consecutive poles, consequent poles.** See *mag-*

net.—**Galactic poles.** See *galactic.*—**Magnetic pole.** (*a*) One of the points on the earth's surface where the dipping-needle stands vertical. The term has also sometimes been improperly applied to the points of maximum magnetic intensity, of which there are two in each hemisphere, neither of them near the pole of dip. (*b*) In a magnetic body, either of the two points about which two opposite magnetic forces are generally most intense. A line joining these points is called the *magnetic axis*, and generally a magnet may be considered as if the magnetic forces were concentrated at the extremity of this line. When a magnetic body is freely suspended, the magnetic axis assumes a direction parallel with the lines of force of the magnetic field in which it is. On the surface of the earth this direction is in a vertical plane approximately north and south, and that end of the magnet which points to the north is generally called the *north pole* or the *north-seeking pole*. The fact that the real magnetism of this pole is opposite in character to that of the north pole of the earth gives rise to some confusion in the nomenclature of the poles. Some physicists have used the epithets *marked* and *unmarked* to designate the north-seeking and south-seeking poles respectively. The words *austral* and *boreal* are also used. A magnet may have more than two poles, or points of maximum magnetic intensity, and in fact it may be assumed that all parts of a magnet are in a state of polarity, the actual poles of the magnet being the result of all polarization.—**Multiple pole.** Same as *multipolar.*—**Pole of a glass**, in *optics*, the thickest part of a convex lens, or the thinnest part of a concave lens; the center of its surface. *Hutton.*—**Pole of a line** with reference to a conic, the point of intersection of the tangents to the conic having their points of contact at the intersections of the conic with the line.—**Pole of a plane** with reference to a conicoid, the vertex of the cone tangent to the conicoid on the plane.—**Pole of revolution.** When a globe or sphere revolves about one of its diameters as an axis, each extremity of such diameter is called a *pole of revolution.*—**Pole of verticity**, the earth's magnetic pole, at which a freely suspended magnetic needle assumes a vertical position.—**Poles of a voltaic pile or battery**, the plates at the extremities of a voltaic battery, or the wires which join them, the end which is chemically passive being called the *positive pole*, and that which is chemically active the *negative pole*. See *battery, cell, electrode.*—**Poles of maximum cold.** See *temperature.*—**Red pole**, the boreal pole.—**Strength of pole**, the force exerted between a magnetic pole and a unit pole at a unit distance.—**The marked pole of a magnet.** See *marked.*—**To depress the pole.** See *depress.*—**Unit pole**, a magnetic pole between which and another of equal strength, separated from it by a unit's distance, a unit's force is exerted.

Pole[3] (pōl), *n.* [= G. *Pole* = D. *Pool*, a Pole (*Polen*, Poland); < Pol. *Polak*, a Pole (see *Polack*); cf. *Polsko*, Poland, *Polski*, Polish.] A native or an inhabitant of Poland, a former kingdom of Europe, divided, since the latter part of the eighteenth century, between Russia, Prussia, and Austria.

pole[4]†, *n.* An obsolete spelling of *pool*[1].

pole[5]†, *n.* and *v.* An obsolete spelling of *poll*[1].

poleax, pollax (pōl'aks), *n.* [Also *polleaxe*; commonly *polcax*, as if < *pole*[1] + *ax*[1], but prop. *pollax*, < ME. *pollax*, < MLG. *polexe*, a poleax, < *pol*, poll, head, + *exe* = E. *ax*[1]: see *poll*[1] and *ax*[1].] 1. Formerly, a weapon or tool consisting of an ax-head on a long handle, and often combined with a hook at the end, or a blade like a pick on the side opposite the blade of the ax; later, more loosely, a battle-ax.

> The Pentioners with their *poleaxes* on each side of her Maiestie. *Books of Precedence* (E. E. T. S., extra ser.), i. 22.

2. (*a*) A weapon used in the navy by boarders and also to cut away rigging, etc. It is a hatchet with a short handle at the end of which is a strong hook. (*b*) An ax for slaughtering cattle.

pole-bean (pōl'bēn), *n.* Any one of the twining varieties of the common garden bean, requiring the support of a pole. See *bean*[1], 2.

pole-burn (pōl'bėrn), *v. i.* To discolor and lose flavor by overheating, as tobacco when hung too closely on poles in the first stage of the curing process.

pole-brackets (pōl'brak"ets), *n. pl.* Brackets placed upon poles for supporting telegraph-wires.

polecat (pōl'kat), *n.* [Early mod. E. also *polecatte, polcat*; < ME. *polcat, polkat, pulkat*, prob. orig. **polecat* or **poulecat*, < **pole*, **poule*, a hen, chicken (< OF. **pole, poule*, F. *poule*, a hen, a chicken), + *cat*. The polecat is well known as a chicken-thief. The word **polc*, **poule*, a hen, chicken, is not elsewhere found in ME. (except as in the derivatives *poult, poultry, pullet, pullen*, etc.), and the first element of *polecat* has been variously identified with (*a*) *Pole*[3] or *Polish*; (*b*) OF. *pulent*, stinking; or (*c*) ME. *pol*, E. *pool*, in the assumed sense of 'hole' or 'burrow.'] 1. The fitchew or foulmart, *Putorius fœtidus* of Europe, of a dark-brown color, with a copious fine pelage much used in furriery and for making artists' brushes. See *fitch*[2].—2. One of several other quadrupeds, mostly of the family *Mustelidæ*, which have a strong offensive smell. Specifically—(*a*) Any American skunk, especially the common one, *Mephitis mephitica.* See *skunk.* (*b*) The African zoril, *Zorilla striata* or *Z. capensis.* (*c*) A kind of paradoxure.

Fitch or Polecat (*Putorius fœtidus*).

polecat-weed (pōl'kat-wēd), *n.* The skunk-cabbage, *Symplocarpus fœtidus.*

pole-chain (pōl'chān), *n.* A chain on the front end of a carriage-pole. It is connected with the collar or the breast-chains of the harness. *E. H. Knight.*

pole-changer (pōl'chān"jėr), *n.* A device by means of which the direction of the current in an electric circuit may conveniently be reversed. Also called *pole-changing key* or *switch.*

pole-clipt† (pōl'klipt), *a.* Entwined or embraced by means of supporting poles: said of a vineyard. See *clip*[1].

> Thy *pole-clipt* vineyard. *Shak.*, Tempest, iv. 1. 68.

pole-crab (pōl'krab), *n.* A double loop attached to the metallic cap or pole-tip on the end of the pole of a vehicle. The loops receive the breast-straps of the harness. When pole-chains are used, they are attached to rings added to the pole-crab.

pole-dab (pōl'dab), *n.* Same as *pole*[1], 3. [Local, Eng.]

poledavy† (pōl'dā-vi), *n.* [Also *poledavie, polldavy, pouldavies, poldway*, etc.; origin obscure. Cf. *oulderness.*] A coarse linen; hence, any coarse ware. *Nares; Halliwell.*

> Your deligence, knaves, or I shall canvase your *poledavyes*; deafen not a gallant with your anon, anon, sir, to make him stop his eares at an over-reckoning. *The Bride*, sig. C. iii. (*Halliwell.*)

> You must be content with homely *Polldavie* Ware from me, for you must not expect from us Country-folks such Urbanities and quaint Invention that you, who are daily conversant with the Wits of the Court, and of the Inns of Court, abound withal. *Howell*, Letters, I. ii. 10.

pole-evil†, *n.* An obsolete form of *poll-evil.*

pole-hammer (pōl'ham"ėr), *n.* A martel-de-fer with a long handle. See *Lucerne hammer*, under *hammer*[1].

> In the fourteenth century the war hammer was in general use, and was often of considerable weight. The foot soldiers had it fixed on a long pole, whence the name *Pole-hammer*, given to it in England. *W. K. Sullivan*, Introd. to O'Curry's Anc. Irish, p. ccccclix.

pole-head (pōl'hed), *n.* [For **pollhead* (?); < *poll*[1] + *head.* Cf. *tadpole.*] A tadpole. *Halliwell.* [Prov. Eng.]

pole-hook (pōl'hůk), *n.* 1. A hook on the end of a carriage-tongue.—2. Same as *boat-hook. E. H. Knight.*

pole-horse (pōl'hôrs), *n.* A shaft-horse as distinguished from a leader; a wheeler.

pole-lathe (pōl'lāᴛʜ), *n.* Same as *center-lathe*, 2.

poleless (pōl'les), *a.* [< *pole*[1] + *-less.*] Without a pole.

> Horses that draw a *pole-lesse* chariot. *Sir R. Stapleton*, tr. of Juvenal, x. 155.

polemarch (pol'e-märk), *n.* [= F. *polémarque* = Pg. *polemarco*, < Gr. πολέμαρχος, one who leads a war, polemarch, < πόλεμος, war, + ἄρχειν, be first.] A title of several officials in ancient Greek states. At Athens the polemarch was the third archon, who was as late as Marathon the titular military commander-in-chief, and was later a civil magistrate having under his especial care all strangers and temporary sojourners in the city, and all children of parents who had lost their lives in the service of their country.

pole-mast (pōl'mȧst), *n.* *Naut.*, a mast composed of a single piece or tree, in contradistinction to one built up of several pieces.

polemic (pọ̄-lem'ik), *a.* and *n.* [= F. *polémique* = Sp. *polémico* = Pg. It. *polemico*, polemic (F. *polémiques* = Sp. *polémica* = Pg. It. *polemica*, n., polemics), < Gr. πολεμικός, warlike, < πόλεμος, war.] I. *a.* Of or pertaining to controversy; controversial; disputative: as, a *polemic* essay or treatise; *polemic* divinity or theology; *polemic* writers.

> The nullity of this distinction has been solidly shewn by most of our *polemick* writers of the Protestant church. *South*, Sermons.

II. *n.* 1. A disputant; one who carries on a controversy; a controversialist; one who writes in support of an opinion or a system in opposition to another.

> Each staunch *polemic*, stubborn as a rock. *Pope*, Dunciad, iv. 196.

2. A controversy; a controversial argument.

> It is well that, in our *polemic* against metaphysics, there should be no room left for ambiguity or misconception. *J. Fiske*, Cosmic Philos., I. 125.

> Prof. Huxley, in his *polemic* against Herbert Spencer, states quite rightly that the most perfect zoological beings present that subordination pushed to the extreme degree. *Contemporary Rev.*, L. 433.

polemical (pọ̄-lem'i-kạl), *a.* [< *polemic* + *-al.*] Of or pertaining to polemics or controversy; controversial; polemic: as, *polemical* logic.

> The former [error in doctrine] I must leave to the conviction of those *polemicall* discourses which have been so learnedly written of the several points at difference. *Bp. Hall*, Christ. Moderation, ii. § 1.

polemically (pọ̄-lem'i-kạl-i), *adv.* In a polemical manner; controversially; disputatively; in polemic discourse or argument; in the manner of polemics.

polemicist (pọ̄-lem'i-sist), *n.* [< *polemic* + *-ist.*] One given to controversy; a polemic. [Rare.]

polemics (pọ̄-lem'iks), *n.* [Pl. of *polemic*: see *-ics.*] The art or practice of disputation; controversy; specifically, that branch of theology which is concerned with the history or conduct of ecclesiastical controversy: the word more particularly denotes offensive as distinguished from defensive controversy: opposed to *irenics.*

polemist (pol'e-mist), *n.* [= F. *polémiste*; < Gr. πολεμιστής, a combatant, < πολεμίζειν, fight, < πόλεμος, war.] A controversialist; a polemic. [Rare.]

> Other political *polemists* of his kind. *The Century*, XXXV. 201.

Polemoniaceæ (pol-e-mō-ni-ā'sẹ̄-ē), *n. pl.* [NL. (Ventenat, 1794), < *Polemonium* + *-aceæ.*] The phlox family, an order of gamopetalous plants, the type of the cohort *Polemoniales.* It is characterized by the five stamens inserted on the corolla-tube alternate to its five equal and convolute lobes, the three-cleft thread-like style, the superior three-celled ovary, with two or more ovules in each cell, and a capsular fruit. There are about 150 species, belonging to 8 genera, of which *Polemonium, Phlox, Gilia, Cobæa*, and *Cantua* yield many handsome species in cultivation. They are chiefly natives of western North America, with others in the Andes, and a few in Europe and temperate parts of Asia, mostly herbs, of mild and innocent properties, with ornamental and bright-colored flowers. See cuts under *Cobæa* and *Jacob's-ladder.*

polemoniaceous (pol-e-mō-ni-ā'shius), *a.* Of or pertaining to the *Polemoniaceæ.*

Polemoniales (pol-e-mō-ni-ā'lēz), *n. pl.* [NL. (Bentham and Hooker, 1876), < *Polemonium*, q. v.] A cohort of gamopetalous plants, characterized by a regular corolla with five lobes and five alternate stamens, as in the related cohort *Gentianales*, from which it is distinguished by its alternate leaves. It includes 5 orders, the *Solanaceæ, Convolvulaceæ, Boragineæ, Hydrophyllaceæ*, and *Polemoniaceæ*, in part distinguished respectively by rank odor, twining habit, fruit of four nutlets, pods with two cells, and pods with three cells.

Polemonium (pol-e-mō'ni-um), *n.* [NL. (Tournefort, 1700) (cf. L. *polemonia*, valerian), < Gr. πολεμώνιον, valerian (?), said by Pliny to be from πόλεμος, war, because the cause of war between two kings; by others, to be so named from the philosopher *Polemon* of Athens, or from King *Polemon* of Pontus.] A genus of plants, the type of the order *Polemoniaceæ*, characterized by its declined stamens, pilose filament-bases, bractless calyx, deeply three-valved capsule, and from two to twelve ovules in each cell. There are 8 or 9 species, natives of Europe, Asia, North America, Mexico, and Chili. They are delicate plants with pinnate leaves and terminal cymes of ornamental blue, violet, or white flowers, commonly broadly bell-shaped. *P. cæruleum* is known as *Jacob's-ladder*, also *Greek valerian*, and sometimes in England as *makebate* or *charity.* *P. reptans* is locally known as *abscess-root*, and improperly as *forget-me-not.*

polemoscope (pol'e-mọ̄-skōp), *n.* [= F. *polémoscope* = Sp. Pg. *polemoscopio*, < Gr. πόλεμος, war, + σκοπεῖν, view.] A perspective glass fitted with a mirror set at an angle, designed for viewing objects that do not lie directly before the eye: so named from its possible use in warfare to observe the motions of the enemy from behind defenses. Opera-glasses also are sometimes constructed in this way, to admit of seeing persons obliquely without apparently directing the glass at them.

polemy† (pol'e-mi), *n.* [< Gr. πόλεμος, war.] War; warfare; hence, contention; resistance. *Sir E. Dering.*

pole-net (pōl'net), *n.* A net attached to a pole for fishing; a shrimping-net; a poke-net.

polenta (pọ̄-len'tạ̈), *n.* [= F. *polente, polenta* = Sp. Pg. It. *polenta*, "a meate vsed in Italie, made of barlie or chesnut flowre soked in water, and then fride in oyle or butter" (Florio, 1598), "barley-grotes, a meate much used in Italie" (Florio, 1611), now generally applied to porridge of maize, < L. *polenta, polentum*, peeled barley; cf. Gr. πάλη, the finest meal.] 1. In Italy: (*a*) A porridge made of Indian meal (maize-meal), the principal food of the poorer people throughout large sections of the country. The meal is yellow and not very fine, with a sharp granulated character. The porridge is made very stiff, and usually poured out while hot into a flat pan about half an inch deep. It is cut with a string when partly cool.

A kind of meal called *polenta* made of Indian corn, which is very nourishing and agreeable. *Smollett*, Travels, xx.

(*b*) A porridge made of chestnut-meal, much used in autumn.—2. In France, a porridge made of barley-meal, not common except in the south.

pole-pad (pōl'pad), *n.* In *artillery*, a stuffed leather pad fixed on the end of the pole of a field-carriage to preserve the horses from injury.

pole-piece (pōl'pēs), *n.* A mass of iron forming the end of an electromagnet, by means of which the lines of magnetic force are concentrated and directed. In dynamos the pole-pieces are shaped so as to inclose the surface in which the armature revolves.

pole-plate (pōl'plāt), *n.* In *building*, a small wall-plate resting on the ends of the tie-beams of a roof, and supporting the lower ends of the common rafters.

pole-prop (pōl'prop), *n.* In *artillery*, a short rod or bar fastened under the pole of a gun-carriage, to support it when the horses are unhitched.

pole-rack (pōl'rak), *n.* In *tanning, dyeing*, and other industries, a rack which supports the poles on which articles are suspended or laid for drying, draining, etc.

pole-rush (pōl'rush), *n.* The bulrush, *Scirpus lacustris*. Also *pool-rush*. [Prov. Eng.]

pole-sling (pōl'sling), *n.* A pole, about twenty-five feet long, from which are suspended a leather seat and a board for the feet, carried by two or more bearers: used for traveling in Dahomey. *N. A. Rev.*, CXLV. 361.

pole-staff (pōl'stȧf), *n.* The pole of a net.

pole-star (pōl'stär), *n.* 1. The star Polaris, of the second magnitude, situated near the north pole of the heavens. It served in former times, and still serves among primitive peoples, as a guide in navigation. It is now about 1¼° from the pole, very nearly in a line with the two stars in the Dipper (α and β) which form the further edge of the bowl. About 5,000 years ago the pole-star was α Draconis, and in about 12,000 it will be α Lyræ.

It is wel knowen (moste noble prince) that the starre which we caule the *pole starre*, or northe starre (cauled of the Italians Tramontana), is not the very poynte of the pole Artyke vppon the whiche the axes or extremities of heauens are turned abowte.
R. Eden, tr. of Peter Martyr (First Books on America, ed. [Arber, p. 90).

2. Hence, that which serves as a guide or director; a lodestar.—3. In *biol.*, a polar star; one of the two stellate figures which may be borne upon the poles of the fusiform nucleus-spindle in the process of karyokinesis.

pole-strap (pōl'strap), *n.* A heavy strap for connecting a carriage-pole with the collar of a horse; a pole-piece. See cut under *harness*.

polete†, *n.* A Middle English form of *pullet*.

pole-tip (pōl'tip), *n.* A cylindrical cap fixed on the front end of the pole of a vehicle.

pole-torpedo (pōl'tôr-pē″dō), *n.* A torpedo projected on the end of a pole, and operated from a boat or vessel: usually called *spar-torpedo*.

pole-vault (pōl'vâlt), *n.* A vault, generally over a horizontal bar, performed with the aid of a pole.

pole-vaulting (pōl'vâlt″ing), *n.* The act or practice of vaulting with the aid of a pole.

pol-evil†, *n.* An obsolete spelling of *poll-evil*.

poleward, polewards (pōl'wärd, -wärdz), *adv.* [< *pole*[2] + *-ward, -wards*.] Toward the pole (either north or south).

The waters at the equator, and near the equator, would produce steam of greater elasticity, rarity, and temperature than that which occupies the regions further *polewards*. *Whewell.*

polewig (pōl'wig), *n.* A fish, the spotted goby, *Gobius minutus*, which inhabits British and neighboring shores. It is of a transparent golden-gray color, with a multitude of tiny black dots upon the back, and generally marked with dark blotches upon the sides and a black spot on the dorsal fin. Also called *polly-bait*. [Prov. Eng.]

poley[1]**†**, *n.* An obsolete form of *poly*.

poley[2] (pō'li), *a.* [For **polly*, < *poll*[1] + *-y*[1].] Without horns; polled. [Eng.]

If it had been any other beast which knocked me down but that *poley* heifer, I should have been hurt.
H. Kingsley, Geoffry Hamlyn, xxix. (*Davies.*)

poleyn†, *n.* See *poulaine*.

polhode (pol'hōd), *n.* [Irreg. formed (by Poinsot, in 1852) < Gr. πόλος, axis, pole, + ὁδός, way, path.] A non-plane curve, the locus of the point of contact with an ellipsoid of a plane tangent at once to that surface and to a concentric sphere.—**Associate of the polhode**, the locus of the point of contact of a plane with an ellipsoid rolling upon it and having a fixed center; herpolhode.

Polian (pō'li-an), *a.* [< *Poli* (see def.) + *-an*.] Described by or named from the Neapolitan naturalist Poli (1746–1825).—**Polian vesicles**, cæcal diverticula of the circular vessel of the ambulacral system of *Echinodermata*. They are of the nature of arrested or abortive madreporic canals which have blind ends, and therefore do not place the cavity of the ambulacral system in communication with the perivisceral cavity of the animal. See cuts under *Holothurioidea, Echinoidea*, and *Synapta*.

polianite (pol'i-an-īt), *n.* [Named in allusion to its gray color, < Gr. πολιός, gray, + *-an-* + *-ite*[2].] Anhydrous manganese dioxid (MnO_2), a mineral of a light steel-gray color and hardness nearly equal to that of quartz. It crystallizes in tetragonal forms, and is isomorphous with rutile (TiO_2), cassiterite (SnO_2), and zircon (ZrO_2SiO_2). It has often been confounded with the commoner mineral pyrolusite.

polianthea (pol-i-an'thē-ä), *n.* [NL., < Gr. πολύς, many, + ἄνθος, flower.] A commonplace-book containing many flowers of eloquence, etc.

Your reverence, to eke out your sermonings, shall need repair to postils or *poliantheas*.
Milton, On Def. of Humb. Remonst., Postscript.

Polianthes (pol-i-an'thēz), *n.* [Also *Polyanthes*; NL. (Linnæus, 1737), from the pure-white flowers; = Sp. *poliantes*, < Gr. πολιός, white, + ἄνθος, flower.] A genus of ornamental plants of the order *Amaryllideæ* and tribe *Agaveæ*, characterized by the long undivided raceme bearing twin flowers with a prominent and incurved tube dilated upward into thick, spreading lobes, by the conical ovary within the base of the perianth, and by the short, erect, tuberous rootstock. There are 3 species, natives of Mexico and Central America. They produce a tall unbranched wand-like stem, with a tuft of linear leaves at its base, and many showy fragrant white flowers clothing the upper portion. *P. tuberosa* is the tuberose.

police (pō-lēs'), *n.* [< F. *police* = Sp. *policía* = Pg. *policia* = It. *polizia, pulizia* = D. *policie, politie* = MLG. *policie, polici, pollicie* = G. *polizei, policei* = Sw. Dan. *politi*, civil government, police; < L. *politia*, the state, < Gr. πολιτεία, citizenship, government, the state, < πολίτης, a citizen, < πόλις, a city. Cf. *policy*[1], *polity*.] 1. Public order; the regulation of a country or district with reference to the maintenance of order; more specifically, the power of each state, when exercised (either directly by its legislature or through its municipalities) for the suppression or regulation of whatever is injurious to the peace, health, morality, general intelligence, and thrift of the community, and its internal safety. In its most common acceptation, *the police* signifies the administration of the municipal laws and regulations of a city or incorporated town or borough by a corps of administrative or executive officers, with the necessary magistrates for the immediate use of force in compelling obedience and punishing violation of the laws, as distinguished from judicial remedies by action, etc. The primary object of the police system is the prevention of crime and the pursuit of offenders; but it is also subservient to other purposes, such as the suppression of mendicancy, the preservation of order, the removal of obstructions and nuisances, and the enforcing of those local and general laws which relate to the public health, order, safety, and comfort.

But here are no idle young Fellows and Wenches begging about the Streets, as with you in London, to the Disgrace of all Order, and, as the French call it, *Police*.
Burt, Letters from the North of Scotland (1720), quoted in [N. and Q., 7th ser., IV. 346.

Rome was the centre of a high *police*, which radiated to Parthia eastwards, to Britain westwards, but not of a high civilization. *De Quincey*, Philos. of Roman Hist.

Where Church and State are habitually associated, it is natural that minds even of a high order should unconsciously come to regard religion as only a subtler mode of *police*. *Lowell*, Among my Books, 1st ser., p. 77.

2. An organized civil force for maintaining order, preventing and detecting crime, and enforcing the laws; the body of men by whom the municipal laws and regulations of a city, incorporated town or borough, or rural district are enforced. A police force may be either open or secret. An open police is a body of officers dressed in uniform, and known to everybody; a secret police consists of officers whom it may be difficult or impossible to distinguish from ordinary citizens, the dress and manners of whom they may think it expedient to assume, in order that they may the more easily detect crimes, or prevent the commission of such as require any previous combination or arrangement. See *detective, constable*.

Time out of mind the military department has had a name; so has that of justice; the power which occupies itself in preventing mischief, not till lately, and that but a loose one, the *police*.
Bentham, Introd. to Morals and Legislation, xvi. 17, note 2.

3. In the United States army, the act or process of policing (see *police*, *v.*, 2): a kind of fatigue duty: as, to go on *police*; to do *police*.—**Commissioners of police.** See *commissioner*.—**Military police.** (*a*) An organized body employed within an army to maintain civil order, as distinct from military discipline. (*b*) A civil police having a military organization. Such are the French gendarmerie, the sbirri of Italy, and the Irish constabulary.—**Mounted police**, a body of police who serve on horseback.—**Police board**, in several of the United States, a board constituted by the justices of the county for the control of county police, public buildings, roads, bridges, ferries, county funds, lunatics, paupers, vagrants, etc. *Murfree*, Justices' Practice.—**Police burgh.** See *burgh*.—**Police captain**, in some of the larger cities of the United States, as in New York, a subordinate officer in the police force having general charge of the members of the force serving in his precinct, and special powers of search and entry for purposes of search.—**Police commissioner.** (*a*) See *commissioner*. (*b*) In Scotland, one of a body elected by the ratepayers to manage police affairs in burghs.—**Police constable**, a member of a police force; a policeman. Abbreviated *P. C.*—**Police court**, a court for the trial of offenders brought up on charges preferred by the police.—**Police inspector**, a superintendent or superior officer of police, or of a subordinate department therein.—**Police jury**, the designation in Louisiana of the local authority in each parish (corresponding nearly to the board of supervisors of each county in many other States), invested with the exercise of ordinary police powers within the limits of the parish, such as prescribing regulations for ways, fences, cattle, taverns, drains, quarantine, support of the poor, etc.—**Police magistrate**, a judge who presides at a police court.—**Police office.** Same as *police station*.—**Police officer**, a policeman; a police constable.—**Police power**, in *constitutional law*, in a comprehensive sense, the whole system of internal regulation of a state, by which the state seeks not only to preserve the public order and to prevent offenses against the state, but also to establish for the intercourse of citizens with citizens those rules of good manners and good neighborhood which are calculated to prevent a conflict of rights and to insure to each the uninterrupted enjoyment of his own so far as is reasonably consistent with a like enjoyment of rights by others. (*Cooley.*) Definitions of the *police power* must be taken subject to the condition that the State cannot, in its exercise, for any purpose whatever, encroach upon the powers of the general government, or rights granted or secured by the supreme law of the land. (*Supreme Court of U. S.*) The question as to what are the proper limits of the police power in the United States is a judicial one, depending in each case upon the relation of the act in question to the situation of the people and the condition of the federal legislation. In a long and fluctuating line of decisions it has been held to include quarantine laws, fire and building laws, laws for draining marshes, licensing slaughter-houses, excluding paupers and immigrants, caring for the poor, regulating highways, bridges, carriers, peddlers, etc., within the limits of the State (so far as not interfering with interstate commerce or an equality of freedom), laws prohibiting and abating nuisances, prohibiting lotteries, the sale of adulterated and simulated food-products, and the manufacture and sale of intoxicating liquors, but not, however, the sale in the original package of articles of interstate commerce, nor discriminating against sales by persons from without the State as compared with those within it.—**Police rate**, a tax levied for the purposes of the police. [Brit.]—**Police sergeant**, a petty officer of police.—**Police station**, the station or headquarters of the police force in a municipality or district thereof, usually, if not always, containing a lock-up for the temporary detention of accused or suspected persons, and accommodations for officers and magistrate. Also *police office*.—**Prefect of police.** See *prefect*.

police (pō-lēs'), *v. t.*; pret. and pp. *policed*, ppr. *policing*. [< *police*, *n.*] 1. To watch, guard, or maintain order in; protect or control by means of a body of policemen: as, to *police* a district; to *police* the inland waters of a country.

Princes . . . are as it were inforced to . . . entend to the right *pollicing* of their states, and haue not one houre to bestow vpon any other ciuill or delectable Art.
Puttenham, Arte of Eng. Poesie, p. 36.

From the wilds she came
To *policed* cities and protected plains.
Thomson, Liberty, iv.

2. To clean up; clear out; put in order: as, to *police* the parade-ground. [U. S.]

policeman (pō-lēs'man), *n.*; pl. *policemen* (-men). 1. One of the ordinary police, whose duty it usually is to patrol a certain beat for a fixed period, for the protection of property and for the arrest of offenders, and to see that the peace is kept.—2. In *entom.*, a soldier-ant. *Pascoe.*—3. In *coal-mining*, a wood or iron guard around or covering the mouth of a pit, or placed at mid-workings.—4. A kind of swab, used for cleaning vials, etc., made by slipping a piece of rubber tubing over the end of a glass rod.

police-nippers (pō-lēs'nip″ėrz), *n. pl.* Handcuffs or foot-shackles. Compare *nipper*[1], 5 (*j*). [Slang.]

policial (pō-lish'al), *a.* [= Pg. *policial*; < *police* + *-al*.] Of or pertaining to the police. [Rare.]

It thus happened that he found himself the cynosure of the *policial* eyes. *Poe*, Tales, I. 215.

policiant, *n.* [Early mod. E., written *politien*; < OF. *policien*, a public man, a statesman, < *policie*, *police*, government, policy: see *police*, *policy*[1].] An officer of state. *Puttenham*, Arte of Eng. Poesie, p. 122.

policlinic (pol-i-klin'ik), *n.* [= G. *poliklinik*; as Gr. πόλις, city, + E. *clinic*. Sometimes written *polyclinic* (= F. *polyclinique*), as if 'a clinic for many'; as Gr. πολύς, many, + E. *clinic*.] A general city hospital or dispensary.

policy[1] (pol'i-si), *n.* [Early mod. E. also *policie*, *pollicie*; < ME. *policie*, < OF. *policie*, < L. *politia*, < Gr. πολιτεία, polity: see *police*, *polity*.] 1†. Polity; administration; public business.

In alle governaunce and *policye*. *Chaucer*, Pardoner's Tale, l. 138.

2. Object or course of conduct, or the principle or body of principles to be observed in conduct; specifically, the system of measures or the line of conduct which a ruler, minister, government, or party adopts and pursues as best for the interests of the country, as regards its foreign or its domestic affairs: as, a spirited foreign *policy*; the commercial *policy* of the United States; a *policy* of peace; public *policy*.

As he is a Spirit, vnseen he sees
The plots of Princes, and their *Policies*.
Sylvester, tr. of Du Bartas's Weeks, i. 1.

This was the Serpents *policie* at first, Balsams *policie* after, Babels *policy* now. *Purchas*, Pilgrimage, p. 38.

The legislation and *policy* of Mary were directed to uproot everything that Edward VI. had originated. *Stubbs*, Medieval and Modern Hist., p. 322.

3. Prudence or wisdom in action, whether public or private; especially, worldly wisdom: as, honesty is the best *policy*.

That maner of iniurie whiche is done with fraude and deceyte is at this present tyme so communely practised that, if it be but a little, it is called *policie*. *Sir T. Elyot*, The Governour, iii. 4.

In these days 'tis counted *pollicie*
To vse dissimulation.
Times' Whistle (E. E. T. S.), p. 94.

It is my *Policy* at this time to thank you most heartily for your late copious Letter, to draw on a second. *Howell*, Letters, I. ii. 9.

The politic nature of vice must be opposed by *policy*. *Sir T. Browne*, Christ. Mor., i. 18.

4. In Scotland, the pleasure-grounds around a nobleman's or gentleman's country house. [In this use its primary sense is 'the place or tract within which one has authority to administer affairs.']

My father is just as fond of his *policy* and his gardens; but it's too little for a *policy*, and it's more than a garden. *Mrs. Oliphant*, Joyce, xvii.

Policy of pourboire. See *pourboire*.—**Policy of the law.** See *law*[1].=**Syn.** 2 and 3. *Policy*, *Polity*, address, shrewdness. *Polity* is now confined to the constitution or structure of a government. It may be used of civil government, but is more often used of ecclesiastical government: as, Hooker's "Laws of Ecclesiastical *Polity*"; Congregational or Presbyterian *polity*. *Policy* has the sense of the management of public affairs: as, a certain bequest is pronounced invalid by the courts as being contrary to public *policy*. *Polity* has neither a narrower nor a lower sense; *policy* has both. The narrower sense of *policy* is system of management, especially wise management; the lower sense is cunning or worldly wisdom.

The Pope's *policy* was to have two Italian interests which could be set against one another, at the pleasure of the Roman See, which thus secured its own safety and influence. *Woolsey*, Introd. to Inter. Law, § 44.

Protestantism may be described as that kind of religious *polity* which is based upon the conception of individual responsibility for opinion. *J. Fiske*, Evolutionist, p. 266.

Public policy. See *public*.

policy[1]† (pol'i-si), *v. t.* [= Pg. *policiar*; < *policy*[1], *n.*] To reduce to order; regulate by laws; police.

It is a just cause of war for another nation, that is civil or *policied* to subdue them. *Bacon*, Holy War.

Towards the *policying* and perpetuating of this your new Republic, there must be some special Rules for regulating of Marriage. *Howell*, Letters, iv. 7.

policy[2] (pol'i-si), *n.*; pl. *policies* (-siz). [< F. *police*, a bill, policy, = Sp. *póliza*, a written order, policy, = Pg. *apolice*, policy, = It. *polizza*, a note, bill, ticket, lottery-ticket, policy, = Sw. *pollict*, a ticket, < ML. *politicum*, *poletum*, *poleticum*, *polecticum*, *polegium*, prop. *polyptychum* (LL. *polyptycha*, pl.), a register, < Gr. πολύπτυχον, neut. of πολύπτυχος, with many folds or leaves, < πολύς, many, + πτύξ (πτυχ-), fold, leaf, < πτύσσειν, fold. Cf. *diptych*, etc.] 1. A written contract by which a person, company, or party engages to pay a certain sum on certain contingencies, as in the case of fire or shipwreck, in the event of death, etc., on the condition of receiving a fixed sum or percentage on the amount of the risk, or certain periodical payments. See *insurance*.

A *policy* of insurance is a contract between A. and B. that, upon A.'s paying a premium equivalent to the hazard run, B. will indemnify or insure him against a particular event. *Blackstone*, Com., II. xxx.

2. A ticket or warrant for money in the public funds. [Eng.]—3. A form of gambling in which bets are made on numbers to be drawn by lottery. [U. S.]—**Endowment policy.** See *endowment*.—**Open policy,** a policy of insurance in which the value of the ship or goods insured is not fixed, but left to be ascertained in case of loss; or in which the subject of insurance is not limited, so that other things may be added from time to time.—**Time policy,** a policy of insurance in which the limits of the risk as regards time are clearly specified.—**Valued policy.** See the quotation.

A *valued policy* is one in which a value has been set upon the property or interest insured, and inserted in the policy, the value thus agreed upon being in the nature of liquidated damages, and so saves any further proof of damages. *Angell*, on Ins., § 5.

Wagering policy, or **wager policy,** a pretended insurance founded on an ideal risk, where the insured has no interest in the thing insured, and can therefore sustain no loss by the happening of any of the misfortunes insured against. Such insurances were often expressed by the words "interest or no interest." Notwithstanding the general principle that insurance is a contract of indemnity, such policies came in England to be held as legal contracts at common law; and the gambling thus legalized became so prevalent and injurious that wager policies, as above defined, were prohibited by statute 19 Geo. III., c. 37, and are generally invalid in the United States.

Wager Policies are such as are "founded upon a mere hope and expectation, and without some interest," and "are objectionable as a species of gaming." *Angell*, on Ins., § 55, p. 96.

policy-book (pol'i-si-bůk), *n.* In an insurance-office, a book in which the policies issued are entered or recorded.

policy-holder (pol'i-si-hōl'dėr), *n.* One who holds a policy or contract of insurance.

policy-shop (pol'i-si-shop), *n.* A place for gambling by betting on the drawing of certain numbers in a lottery. [U. S.]

policy-slip (pol'i-si-slip), *n.* The ticket given on a stake of money at a policy-shop. [U. S.]

poliencephalitis (pol″i-en-sef-ạ-lī'tis), *n.* [NL., < Gr. πολιός, gray, + ἐγκέφαλος, the brain, + *-itis*.] Inflammation of the gray matter of the brain: applied to inflammation of the nuclei of origin of cranial nerves, and also to inflammation of the cortex. Also *polioëncephalitis*.—**Poliencephalitis inferior.** Same as *progressive bulbar paralysis*. See *paralysis*.—**Poliencephalitis superior.** Same as *ophthalmoplegia progressiva*. See *ophthalmoplegia*.

poligar (pol'i-gär), *n.* [Also *polligar*, *polygar*, etc.; < Canarese *pālegāra*, Telugu *palegādu*, Marathi *pālegār*, Tamil *pālaiyakāran*, a petty chieftain.] Originally, a subordinate feudal chief, generally of predatory habits, occupying tracts more or less wild in the presidency of Madras, India, or a follower of such a chieftain; now, nearly the same as *zemindar*. *Yule and Burnell.*

poling (pō'ling), *n.* [Verbal n. of *pole*[1], *v.*] 1. The act of using a pole for any purpose.—2. A process used in toughening copper. It consists in plunging a long pole of green wood (birch is preferred) into the fused metal on the floor of the refining furnace. This process reduces the oxid which the refined metal still holds, and brings the copper to what is called "tough pitch," or to the highest attainable degree of malleability. A somewhat similar process, known by the same name, is employed in the refining of tin.

3. In *hort.*, the operation of scattering worm-casts on garden-walks with poles.—4. The boards (collectively) used to line the inside of a tunnel during its construction, to prevent the falling of the earth or other loose material.—5. Cramming for examination; hard study. [College slang, U. S.]

polioëncephalitis (pol″i-ọ-en-sef-ạ-lī'tis), *n.* Same as *poliencephalitis*.

poliomyelepathy (pol″i-ọ-mī-e-lep'ạ-thi), *n.* [NL., < Gr. πολιός, gray, + μυελός, marrow, + -πάθεια, < παθεῖν, 2d aor. of πάσχειν, suffer: see *pathos*.] Disease of the gray matter of the spinal cord.

poliomyelitis (pol″i-ọ-mī-e-lī'tis), *n.* [NL., < Gr. πολιός, gray, + μυελός, marrow, + *-itis*.] Inflammation of the gray matter of the spinal cord.—**Anterior poliomyelitis,** inflammation of the anterior horns of the gray matter of the spinal cord. In children called *infantile paralysis*.

Polioptila (pol-i-op'ti-lạ̈), *n.* [NL. (Sclater, 1854), < Gr. πολιός, gray, + πτίλον, wing, = E. *feather*.] An isolated genus of oscine passerine birds, typical of the subfamily *Polioptilinæ*; the American gnatcatchers: so called from the hoary edgings of the wings. *P. cærulea* is the blue-gray gnatcatcher, a very common small migratory insectivorous bird of eastern parts of the United States and Canada. *P. plumbea* inhabits the southwestern United States. *P. melanura* and about ten others are found in warmer parts of America. Also called *Culicivora*. See cut under *gnatcatcher*.

Polioptilinæ (pol-i-op-ti-lī'nē), *n. pl.* [NL. (Sclater, 1862), < *Polioptila* + *-inæ*.] A subfamily of birds, represented by the genus *Polioptila*, formerly referred to the *Paridæ*, now associated with the sylviine *Passeres*. The bill is muscicapine, with well-developed rictal bristles and exposed nostrils; the tarsi are scutellate; the toes are short; the primaries are ten, the first of which is spurious; the wings are rounded; and the tail is graduated. The size is very small, and the coloration is bluish-gray above, white below, the tail black, with white lateral feathers.

poliorcetics (pol″i-ôr-sē'tiks), *n.* [= F. *poliorcétique*, < Gr. πολιορκητικός, concerning besieging, < πολιορκητής, taker of cities, < πολιορκεῖν, besiege, < πόλις, city, + ἕρκος, fence, inclosure.] The art or science of besieging towns. *De Quincey.* [Rare.]

poliosis (pol-i-ō'sis), *n.* [NL., < Gr. πολίωσις, a making or becoming gray, < πολιοῦν, make gray, πολιός, gray.] In *pathol.*, same as *canities*.

polipragmatick†, *a.* An obsolete form of *polypragmatic*.

polish[1] (pol'ish), *v.* [< ME. *polischen*, *pollischen*, *polyshen*, *polschen*, *pullischen*, *pulischen*, *pulschen* = D. *polijsten*, < OF. (and F.) *poliss-*, stem of certain parts of *polir* (> MLG. *pollēren* = MHG. *polieren*, *pollieren*, *bollieren*, *pulieren*, *palieren*, *pallieren*, *ballieren*, G. *polieren* = Sw. *polera* = Dan. *polere*) = Sp. *pulir*, OSp. *polir* = Pg. *polir* = It. *polire*, *pulire*, < L. *polire*, polish, make smooth. Cf. *polite*.] **I.** *trans.* 1. To make smooth and glossy, as a surface of marble, wood, etc., whether by rubbing or by coating with varnish, etc., or in both ways. Polishing is often done with the object of bringing out the color and markings of the material, as of colored marble, agate, jasper, etc., and richly veined wood.

Bryght *y-pullished* youre table knyve, semely in sygt to sene;
And thy spones fayre y-wasche; ye wote welle what y meene.
Babees Book (E. E. T. S.), p. 120.

The whiteness and smoothness of the excellent pargeting was a thing I much observed, being almost as even and *polished* as if it had been of marble. *Evelyn*, Diary, Rome, Nov. 10, 1644.

2. Figuratively, to render smooth, regular, uniform, etc.; remove roughness, inelegance, etc., from; especially, to make elegant and polite.

Rules will help, if they be laboured and *polished* by practice. *Bacon*, Advancement of Learning, ii. 247.

Such elegant entertainments as these would *polish* the town into judgment in their gratifications. *Steele*, Spectator, No. 370.

3. To beat; chastise; punish. [Slang.]—**To polish off,** to finish off quickly, as a dinner, a contest, or an adversary, etc. [Slang.]

I fell them [the Sepoys] in against the wall, and told some Sikhs who were handy to *polish* them *off*. This they did immediately, shooting and bayoneting them. *W. H. Russell*, Diary in India, II. 296.

=**Syn.** 1. To burnish, furbish, brighten, rub up.—2. To civilize.

II. *intrans.* 1. To become smooth; receive a gloss; take a smooth and glossy surface.

A kind of steel . . . which would *polish* almost as white and bright as silver. *Bacon*, Nat. Hist., § 849.

2. Figuratively, to become smooth, regular, uniform, elegant, or polite.

polish[1] (pol'ish), *n.* [< *polish*[1], *v.*] 1. Smoothness of surface, produced either by friction or by the application of some varnish, or by both means combined. *Polish* denotes a higher degree of smoothness than *gloss*, and often a smoothness produced by the application of some liquid, as distinguished from that produced by friction alone.

Another prism of clearer glass and better *polish* seemed free from veins. *Newton*, Opticks.

It never seems to have occurred to Waller that it is the substance of what you polish, and not the *polish* itself, that insures duration. *Lowell*, Study Windows, p. 396.

2. A substance used to give smoothness or to help in giving smoothness to any surface. See *French polish*, *varnish-polish*, etc., below.—3. Smoothness; regularity; elegance; refinement; especially, elegance of style or manners.

What are these wondrous civilizing arts,
This Roman *polish*, and this smooth behaviour?
Addison, Cato, i. 4.

As for external *polish*, or mere courtesy of manner, he never possessed more than a tolerably educated bear. *Hawthorne*, Blithedale Romance, iv.

Black polish, the highest polish of iron or steel or other non-precious metal.—**French polish.** (*a*) A glossy surface p u e by shellac dissolved in alcohol or similar liquid, applied with abundant friction. (*b*) A liquid application prepared by dissolving gum-shellac in alcohol, or an imitation of this. It is applied with a sponge or rag, and the surface is then rubbed very thoroughly, the operation being usually repeated two or three times.—**Shoe-polish,** a liquid or pasty compound which, when applied to the surface of leather and rubbed with a brush, imparts to the leather a black and polished surface.—**Stove-polish,** plumbago, or a composition of which plumbago is a considerable ingredient, which, when applied with benzin or a similar liquid, or with water, and brushed with a broom or a stove-brush, imparts a black and polished surface to iron plates.—**Varnish-polish**, polish produced by a coat of varnish which covers the solid substance with a transparent coat, as distinguished from *French polish*, which is supposed to fill the pores only and to bring the surface to uniform smoothness.—**Wax-polish.** (*a*) A glossy surface produced by the application of a paste composed of wax and some liquid in which it is dissolved or partly dissolved. It requires hard and constant rubbing, and frequent renewal. (*b*) The paste by which such a polish is produced.

Polish[2] (pō'lish), *a.* and *n.* [‹ *Pole*[3] + *-ish*[1]. Cf. D. *Poolsch*, G. *Polnisch*, Sw. Dan. *Polsk*, Pol. *Polski*, Polish.] **I.** *a.* Pertaining to Poland, a country of Europe, or to its inhabitants.—**Polish berry**, *Porphyrophora polonica*, a bark-louse or scale-insect very similar to the kermes-berry, furnishing a kind of cochineal used as a red dyestuff in parts of Russia, Turkey, and Armenia.—**Polish checkers** or **draughts.** See *checker*[1], 2.—**Polish manna.** Same as *manna-seeds.*

II. *n.* **1.** The language of the Poles. It is a Slavic language belonging to the western division, nearly allied to Bohemian (Czech), and is spoken by about 10,000,000 persons in western Russia, eastern Prussia, and eastern Austria.

2. Same as *Polish checkers.*

> Can you play at draughts, *polish*, or chess?
> *Brooke*, Fool of Quality.

3. A highly ornamental breed of the domestic hen, characterized especially by the large globular crest, and in most varieties having also a full muff or beard. Among the principal varieties are the white, the silver-, gold-, and buff-laced, and the white-crested black Polish, the last presenting an especially striking appearance from the contrast of their large white crests and glossy-black body-plumage.

polishable (pol'ish-a-bl), *a.* [‹ *polish*[1] + *-able.*] Capable of taking a polish: thus, marble is *polishable*, and may be defined as a *polishable* crystalline limestone.

polished (pol'isht), *p. a.* **1.** Made smooth by polishing. (*a*) Smooth; perfectly even: as, *polished* plate-glass. (*b*) Made smooth and lustrous by friction or by covering with polish or varnish. See cut under *conglomerate.*

> Fro that Temple, towardes the Southe, right nyghe, is the Temple of Salomon, that is righte fair and wel *polisscht.*
> *Mandeville*, Travels, p. 88.

> Gentleman in white pantaloons, *polished* boots, and Berlins.
> *Forster*, Dickens, II. 259.

2. Having naturally a smooth, lustrous surface, like that produced by polishing; specifically, in *entom.*, smooth and shining, but without metallic luster.

> Bright *polish'd* amber precious from its size,
> Or forms the fairest fancy could devise.
> *Crabbe*, Works, I. 110.

3. Brought by training or elaboration to a condition void of roughness, irregularity, imperfections, or inelegances; carefully elaborated; especially, elegant; refined; polite.

> The Babylonians were a people the most *polished* after the Egyptians.
> *Bruce*, Source of the Nile, I. 428.

> The frivolous work of *polished* idleness.
> *Sir J. Mackintosh*, Works, I. 235.

> Those large and catholic types of human nature which are familiarly recognizable in every *polished* community.
> *Bulwer*, Misc. Prose Works, I. 121.

> His [Shaftesbury's] cold and monotonous though exquisitely *polished* dissertations have fallen into general neglect, and find few readers and exercise no influence.
> *Lecky*, Rationalism, I. 190.

4†. Purified; absolved.

> I halde the *polysed* of that plyȝt, & pured as clene
> As thou hadeȝ neuer forfeted, sythen thou watȝ fyrst borne.
> *Sir Gawayne and the Green Knight* (E. E. T. S.), l. 2393.

polisher (pol'ish-ėr), *n.* One who or that which polishes. Specifically—(*a*) A workman whose occupation is the polishing of wood, marble, or other substances.

> The skill of the *polisher* fetches out the colours.
> *Addison*, Spectator, No. 215.

(*b*) In *bookbinding*, a steel tool of rounded form, used for rubbing and polishing leather on book-covers.

polishing-bed (pol'ish-ing-bed), *n.* A machine for smoothing and polishing the surface of stone by the attrition of rubbers. These, for plane surfaces, are wooden blocks covered with felt, and are charged with emery in the first stages of the operation and with putty-powder for finishing. Rubbers for moldings are formed of old bagging cut into strips, folded, and nailed to blocks in such a way as to present edges or folds of the cloth to enter into the hollows of the moldings.

polishing-cask (pol'ish-ing-kȧsk), *n.* A tumbling- or rolling-barrel in which light articles of metal are placed with some polishing-powder, and cleaned and burnished by attrition against one another. A similar apparatus is used for polishing grained gunpowder.

polishing-disk (pol'ish-ing-disk), *n.* In *dentistry*, one of a number of small instruments of different shapes and sizes for polishing the surfaces of teeth, dentures, or fillings; a small polishing-wheel. They are rotated by means of a drill-stock, and used with a fine polishing-powder. Disks of sandpaper or emery-paper are also used.

polishing-hammer (pol'ish-ing-ham'ėr), *n.* A hammer with a polished face, for the fine dressing of metal plates. Compare *planishing-hammer.*

polishing-iron (pol'ish-ing-ī'ėrn), *n.* **1.** A burnishing-tool for polishing the covers of books.—**2.** A laundry-iron for polishing shirt-fronts, collars, cuffs, and other starched pieces. It sometimes has a convex face.

Laundry Polishing-iron. *a*, polishing-iron; *b*, polishing-surface.

polishing-jack (pol'ish-ing-jak), *n.* A polishing-machine armed with a lignum-vitæ slicker, for polishing leather when considerable pressure is required. *E. H. Knight.*

polishing-machine (pol'ish-ing-ma-shēn'), *n.* A machine which operates a rubbing-surface for bringing to a polish the surfaces of materials or articles to which a polish is desired to be given, as in polishing metals, stone, glass, wood, horn, or articles made from these or other materials. The rubbing may be reciprocatory or rotary; or it may be irregular, as where small articles are polished by the tumbling process, in a rotating cylinder containing abrasive or smoothing substances. Specifically—(*a*) A machine for grinding and polishing plate-glass. In one form of glass-polishing machine, the plate is supported on a bed which has a slow reciprocating motion, and the polishing is effected by rubbers carried in a frame moved by a reciprocating arm. The rubbing-surfaces are of felt. Moist sand and afterward different grades of emery are used for grinding. The polishing-powder is Venetian pink, and is used with water. The final polish is given by hand with tripoli, crocus, or dry putty-powder. (*b*) In *stone-working*, a polishing-bed. (*c*) In *agri.* and *milling*, a machine for removing by trituration the inner cuticle of rice or barley; a whitening-machine. (*d*) In *cotton-manuf.*, a machine for smoothing or burnishing cotton threads by brushing after the sizing. (*e*) In *wood-working*, a machine for smoothing wood surfaces, employing an emery-wheel, or a wheel armed with sand-paper or emery-paper.

polishing-mill (pol'ish-ing-mil), *n.* A lap of metal (lead, iron, or copper), leather, list, or wood used by lapidaries in polishing gems.

> Thus we have the slitting-mill, the roughing-mill, the smoothing-mill, and the *polishing-mill*, all generally of metal.
> *Byrne*, Artisan's Handbook, p. 197.

polishing-paste (pol'ish-ing-pāst), *n.* Polish of any kind made in the form of a paste.

polishing-powder (pol'ish-ing-pou'dėr), *n.* **1.** Any pulverized material used to impart a smooth surface by abrasive or wearing action, as corundum, emery, Venetian pink, crocus, tripoli, putty-powder, or oxid of tin for glass-polishing; whiting for cleaning and polishing mirrors and window-glass; corundum, emery, and the dust of diamonds, sapphires, and rubies for lapidaries' work; corundum, emery, pumice-stone, rottenstone, chalk, rouge, and whiting for metals; and pumice-stone for wood. Powders which, like plumbago and its various compounds, adhere to other surfaces to form a superimposed polished surface are generally called *polishes*, as stove-polish. Specifically—**2.** Same as *plate-powder.*

polishings (pol'ish-ingz), *n. pl.* The fine particles removed from a surface by polishing; particularly, the dust produced in polishing articles made from precious metals, which is saved, and reduced again to concrete form; also, particularly, the dust produced in cutting hard precious stones, which is saved, and used for arming tools in lapidary work.

polishing-slate (pol'ish-ing-slāt), *n.* **1.** A slate, usually gray or yellow, composed of microscopic infusoria, found in the coal-measures of Bohemia and in Auvergne in France, and used for polishing glass, marble, and metals.—**2.** A kind of whetstone used for sharpening or polishing the edges of tools after grinding on a revolving grindstone.

polishing-snake (pol'ish-ing-snāk), *n.* A kind of serpentine quarried near the river Ayr in Scotland, and formerly used for polishing the surfaces of lithographic stones.

polishing-stone (pol'ish-ing-stōn), *n.* Same as *polishing-slate.*—**Blue polishing-stone**, a dark slate of uniform density, used by jewelers, clock-makers, silversmiths, etc.—**Gray polishing-stone**, a slate similar in character to the blue, but paler and of coarser texture. See *honestone* and *hone*[1].

polishing-tin (pol'ish-ing-tin), *n.* A thin plate of tinned iron, usually the full size of the leaf, placed between the cover and first leaf and between the cover and last leaf of a book, to prevent the progress of dampness in a newly pasted-up book, and to keep the linings smooth.

polishing-wheel (pol'ish-ing-hwēl), *n.* **1.** A wheel armed with some kind of abrasive material, as sandpaper, emery, corundum, etc., and used for smoothing rough surfaces.—**2.** A wheel having its perimeter covered with leather, felt, cotton, or other soft smoothing material, for bringing partly polished surfaces to a fine degree of polish. See *emery-wheel*, *buff-wheel*, etc.

polishment (pol'ish-ment), *n.* [‹ OF. *polissement*; as *polish* + *-ment.* Cf. F. *poliment* = Sp. *pulimento* = Pg. *polimento* = It. *pulimento.*] **1.** The act of polishing.—**2.** The condition of being polished.

> In the mind nothing of true celestial and virtuous tendency could be, or abide, without the *polishment* of art and the labour of searching after it.
> *Waterhouse*, Apology for Learning (1653), p. 5. (*Latham.*)

[Rare in both senses.]

polish-powder (pol'ish-pou'dėr), *n.* Same as *polishing-powder.*

polissoir (F. pron. po-lē-swor'), *n.* [F., ‹ *polir*, polish: see *polish*[1].] In *glass-manuf.*, an implement, consisting of a smooth block of wood with a rod of iron for a handle, used for flattening sheet-glass while hot on the polishing-stone. Also called *flattener.*

> The flattener now applies another instrument, a *polissoir*, or rod of iron furnished at the end with a block of wood.
> *Glass-making*, p. 129.

Polistes (pǭ-lis'tēz), *n.* [NL. (Latreille, 1804), ‹ Gr. πολιστής, founder of a city, ‹ πολίζειν, build a city, ‹ πόλις, a city: see *police.*] A genus of social wasps of the family *Vespidæ*, containing long-bodied black species with subpedunculate abdomen and wings folding in repose. They have the abdomen subsessile or subpetiolate, long, and fusiform,

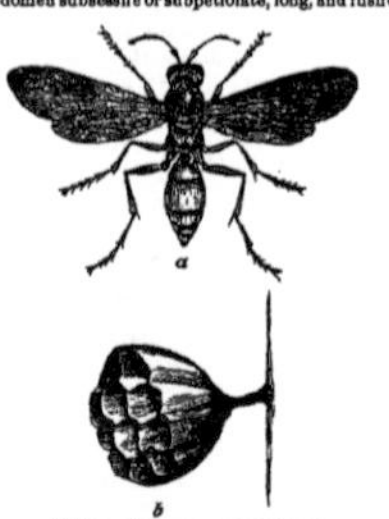

Polistes rubiginosus. *a*, wasp; *b*, nest.

and the metathorax as long as broad, and oblique above; the basal nervure joins the subcostal at the base of the stigma. It is a large genus of variable species, which build combs or a series of paper cells in sheltered places, chiefly on rafters, without a complete covering. *P. gallicus* is a common European species. *P. rubiginosus* is common in North America.

polite (pǭ-līt'), *a.* [= F. *poli* = Sp. *pulido* = Pg. *polido* = It. *pulito*, *polito*, ‹ L. *politus*, polished, polite, pp. of *polire*, polish: see *polish*[1].] **1**†. Polished; smooth; lustrous; bright.

> Where there is a perfeyte mayster prepared in tyme, . . . the brightnes of . . . science appereth *polite* and clere.
> *Sir T. Elyot*, The Governour, iii. 23.

> *Polite* bodies, as looking-glasses.
> *Cudworth*, Intellectual System, p. 731.

2. Polished, refined, or elegant in speech, manner, or behavior; well-bred; courteous; complaisant; obliging: said of persons or their speech or behavior, etc.: as, *polite* society; he was very *polite.*

> The court of Turin is reckoned the most splendid and *polite* of any in Italy; but by reason of its being in mourning, I could not see it in its magnificence.
> *Addison*, Remarks on Italy (ed. Bohn), I. 507.

> He is just *polite* enough to be able to be very unmannerly with a great deal of good breeding.
> *Colman*, Jealous Wife, ii.

3. Polished or refined in style, or employing such a style: now rarely applied to persons: as, *polite* learning; *polite* literature (that is, belles-lettres).

> Some of the finest treatises of the most *polite* Latin and Greek writers are in dialogue, as many very valuable pieces of French, Italian, and English appear in the same dress.
> *Addison*, Ancient Medals, ii.

> He [Cicero] had . . . gone through the studies of humanity and the *politer* letters with the poet Archias.
> *Middleton*, Cicero (ed. 1755), I. 36.

> The study of *polite* literature is generally supposed to include all the liberal arts. *Goldsmith*, Origin of Poetry.

=**Syn. 2.** *Civil, Polite, Courteous, Urbane, Complaisant*, gracious, affable, courtly, gentlemanly, ladylike. *Civil*, literally, applies to one who fulfils the duty of a citi-

son; it may mean simply not rude, or observant of the external courtesies of intercourse, or quick to do and say gratifying and complimentary things. *Polite* applies to one who shows a polished civility, who has a higher training in ease and gracefulness of manners; politeness is a deeper, more comprehensive, more delicate, and perhaps more genuine thing than civility. *Polite*, though much abused, is becoming the standard word for the bearing of a refined and kind person toward others. *Courteous*, literally, expresses that style of politeness which belongs to courts: a *courteous* man is one who is gracefully respectful in his address and manner—one who exhibits a union of dignified complaisance and kindness. The word applies to all sincere kindness and attention. *Urbane*, literally city-like, expresses a sort of politeness which is not only sincere and kind, but peculiarly suave and agreeable. *Complaisant* applies to one who pleases by being pleased, or obliges and is polite by yielding personal preferences; it may represent mere fawning, but generally does not. See *genteel*.

A man of sober life,
Fond of his friend, and *civil* to his wife.
Pope, Imit. of Horace, II. ii. 189.

A *polite* country esquire shall make you as many bows in half an hour as would serve a courtier for a week.
Addison, Spectator, No. 119.

Like a very queen herself she bore
Among the guests, and *courteous* was to all.
William Morris, Earthly Paradise, II. 303.

So I the world abused—in fact, to me
Urbane and *civil* as a world could be.
Crabbe, Works, VIII. 169.

He was a man of extremely *complaisant* p esen e, and suffered no lady to go by without a complimentto her complexion, her blonde hair, or her beautiful eyes, whichever it might be. *Howells*, Venetian Life, xx.

polite† (pǭ-līt'), *v. t.* [< L. *politus*, pp. of *polire*, polish: see *polish*[1], *v.*] To polish; refine.

Those exercises . . . which *polite* men's spirits, and which abate the uneasiness of life.
Ray, Works of Creation, i.

politely (pǭ-līt'li), *adv.* 1†. Smoothly; with a polished surface.

The goodly Walks *politely* paved were
With Alabaster. *J. Beaumont*, Psyche, ii. 195.

2. In a polite manner; with elegance of manners; courteously.

politeness (pǭ-līt'nes), *n.* 1. The character of being polite; smoothness; polish; finish; elegance.

Here was the famous Dan. Heinsius, whom I so long'd to see, as well as the Elzivirian printing house and shop, renown'd for the *politeness* of the character and editions of what he has publish'd through Europe.
Evelyn, Diary, Aug. 28, 1641.

Nay, persons of quality of the softer sex, and such of them as have spent their time in well-bred company, shew us that this plain, natural way, without any study or knowledge of grammar, can carry them to a great degree of elegance and *politeness* in the language.
Locke, Education, § 168.

2. Good breeding; polish or elegance of mind or manners; refinement; culture; ease and grace of behavior or address; courteousness; complaisance; obliging attentions.

All the men of wit and *politeness* were immediately up in arms through indignation. *Swift*, Tale of a Tub, Apol.

A foreigner is very apt to conceive an idea of the ignorance or *politeness* of a nation from the turn of their public monuments and inscriptions.
Addison, Thoughts in Westminster Abbey.

Forgetting *politeness* in his sullen rage, Malone pushed into the parlour before Miss Keeldar.
Charlotte Brontë, Shirley, xv.

Politeness has been well defined as benevolence in small things. *Macaulay*, Samuel Johnson.

=**Syn.** 2. Courtesy, civility, urbanity, suavity, courtliness. See *polite*.

politesse (pol-i-tes'), *n.* [< F. *politesse* = Pg. *polidez*, < It. *pulitezza*, politeness, < *pulito*, polite: see *polite*.] Politeness.

I insisted upon presenting him with a single sous, merely for his *politesse*. *Sterne*, Sentimental Journey, p. 37.

politic (pol'i-tik), *a.* and *n.* [I. *a.* Formerly also *politick*, *politique*; < F. *politique* = Sp. *político* = Pg. It. *politico* (cf. D. G. *politisch* = Sw. Dan. *politisk*), < L. *politicus*, < Gr. πολιτικός, of or pertaining to citizens or the state, civic, civil, < πολίτης, a citizen, < πόλις, a city: see *police*, *policy*[1], *polity*. II. *n.* < F. *politique* = Sp. *político* = Pg. It. *politico*, < ML. *politicus*, m., < Gr. πολιτικός, a politician, statesman; from the adj. As an abstract noun (in E. in pl. *politics*), F. *politique* = Sp. *política* = Pg. It. *politica* = D. *politiek* = G. Sw. Dan. *politik*, < L. *politica*, < Gr. πολιτική, the science of politics, neut. pl. πολιτικά, political affairs, politics; fem. or neut. pl. of πολιτικός, adj., pertaining to the state: see above.] I. *a.* 1†. Of or pertaining to politics, or the science of government; having to do with politics.

I will be proud, I will read *politic* authors.
Shak., T. N., ii. 5. 174.

2†. Of or pertaining to civil as distinguished from religious or military affairs; civil; political.

When the Orater shall practize his schollers in the excrcixe thereof, he shall chiefly do yt in Orations made in English, both *politique* and militare.
Sir H. Gilbert, Queene Elyzabethes Achademy (E. E. T. S., extra ser., III. i. 2).

He made Religion conform to his *politick* interests.
Milton, Reformation in Eng., ii.

Hence—3†. Of or pertaining to officers of state; official; state.

I hope
We shall be call'd to be examiners,
Wear *politic* gowns garded with copper lace,
Making great faces full of fear and office.
Beau. and Fl., Woman-Hater, iii. 2.

4. That constitutes the state; consisting of citizens: as, the body *politic* (that is, the whole body of the people as constituting a state).

We, . . . the loyal subjects of . . . King James, . . . do by these presents solemnly and mutually, in the presence of God and one another, covenant and combine ourselves together into a civil body *politick*.
Covenant of Plymouth Colony, in New England's Memorial, p. 37.

5. Existing by and for the state; popular; constitutional.

The *politic* royalty of England, distinguished from the government of absolute kingdoms by the fact that it is rooted in the desire and institution of the nation, has its work set in the task of defence against foreign foes in the maintenance of internal peace. *Stubbs*, Const. Hist., § 365.

6. In keeping with policy; wise; prudent; fit; proper; expedient: applied to actions, measures, etc.

This land was famously enrich'd
With *politic* grave counsel.
Shak., Rich. III., ii. 3. 20.

It would be *politic* to use them with ceremony.
Goldsmith, The Bee, No. 5.

Pillage and devastation are seldom *politic*, even when they are supposed to be just.
Woolsey, Introd. to Inter. Law, § 130.

7. Characterized by worldly wisdom or craftiness; subtle; crafty; scheming; cunning; artful: applied to persons or their devices: as, a *politic* prince.

I have flattered a lady; I have been *politic* with my friend, smooth with mine enemy.
Shak., As you Like it, v. 4. 46.

Carthaginian Hanniball, that stout
And *politicke* captaine.
Times' Whistle (E. E. T. S.), p. 100.

It is not quite clear that Xenophon was honest in his credulity; his fanaticism was in some degree *politic*.
Macaulay, History.

Body politic. See def. 4 and *body*. =**Syn.** 6 and 7. Discreet, wary, judicious, shrewd, wily. *Political* goes with *politics* and the older meaning of *polity*; *politic* chiefly with the lower meaning of *policy*. See *policy*[1].

II.† *n.* A politician.

Every sect of them hath a diverse posture, or cringe, by themselves, which cannot but move derision in worldlings and depraved *politics*, who are apt to contemn holy things.
Bacon, Unity in Religion (ed. 1887).

political (pǭ-lit'i-kal), *a.* and *n.* [= Pg. *political*; as *politic* + *-al*.] I. *a.* 1. Relating or pertaining to politics, or the science of government; treating of polity or government: as, *political* authors.

The malice of *political* writers, who will not suffer the best and brightest of characters . . . to take a single right step for the honour or interest of the nation.
Junius, Letters, iii.

2. Possessing a definite polity or system of government; administering a definite polity.

The next assertion is that, in every independent *political* community, that is, in every independent community neither in a state of nature on the one hand nor a state of anarchy on the other, the power of using or directing the irresistible force stored up in the society resides in some person or combination of persons who belong to the society themselves.
Maine, Early Hist. of Institutions, p. 358.

3. Relating to or concerned in public policy and the management of the affairs of the state or nation; of or pertaining to civil government, or the enactment of laws and the administration of civil affairs: as, *political* action; *political* rights; a *political* system; *political* parties; a *political* officer.

The distinct nationalities that composed the empire [Rome], gratified by perfect municipal and by perfect intellectual freedom, had lost all care for *political* freedom.
Lecky, Europ. Morals, I. 310.

Within any territory which appears on the map as a Roman province there was a wide difference of *political* conditions; all that appears geographically as the province was not in the provincial condition.
E. A. Freeman, Amer. Lects., p. 321.

4†. Politic; sagacious; prudent; artful; skilful.

I cannot beget a project with all my *political* brain yet.
B. Jonson, Bartholomew Fair, iii. 1.

Orthodox school in political economy, that school of economists which follows the doctrines laid down by Adam Smith, Ricardo, J. S. Mill, and their disciples.—**Political arithmetic.** See *arithmetic*.—**Political assessments.** See *assessment*.—**Political economist**, one who is versed in political economy; a teacher or writer on economic subjects; an economist.—**Political economy**, the science of the laws and conditions which regulate the production, distribution, and consumption of all products, necessary, useful, or agreeable to man, that have an exchangeable value; the science of the material welfare of human beings, particularly in modern society, considered with reference to labor, and the production, distribution, and accumulation of wealth. It includes a knowledge of the conditions which affect the existence and prosperity of useful industry, and the laws or generalizations which are deduced from an observation of the relations between the industrial and commercial methods of a people and their prosperity and physical well-being. The principal topics discussed in political economy are—(1) labor (including the distinction between productive and unproductive labor), wages, increase of population (or the Malthusian doctrine), production on a large or on a small scale, strikes, etc.; (2) capital, including interest, risk, wages of superintendence, credit, etc.; (3) rent; (4) money, or the circulating medium of exchange; (5) competition and governmental interference with the natural course of trade; (6) value, including price, cost of production, and the relative demand and supply; (7) international trade, including the questions of free trade and protection; (8) the influence of government upon economic relations; and (9) the progress of civilization.—**Political geography.** See *geography*.—**Political law**, that part of jurisprudence which relates to the organization and polity of states, and their relations to each other and to their citizens and subjects.—**Political liberty, power**, etc. See the nouns.—**Political science**, the science of politics, including the consideration of the form of government, of the principles that should underlie it, of the extent to which it should intervene in public and private affairs, of the laws it establishes considered in relation to their effects on the community and the individual, of the intercourse of citizen with citizen as members of a state or political community, etc.—**Political verse**, in *medieval* and *modern Greek poetry*, a verse composed without regard to quantity and always having an accent on the next to the last syllable. The name is especially given to a verse of fifteen syllables, an accentual iambic tetrameter catalectic. Lord Byron has compared with this measure the English line,

"A captain bold of Halifax, who lived in country quarters."

This is the favorite meter in modern Greek poetry. *Political* in this connection means 'common,' 'usual,' 'ordinary.' =**Syn.** See *politic*.

II. *n.* 1. A political officer or agent, as distinguished from military, commercial, and diplomatic officers or agents; specifically, in India, an officer of the British government who deals with native states or tribes and directs their political affairs.—2. A political offender or prisoner.

As the *politicals* in this part of the fortress are all persons who have not yet been tried, the [Russian] Government regards it as extremely important that they shall not have an opportunity to secretly consult one another.
G. Kennan, The Century, XXXV. 528.

politicalism (pǭ-lit'i-kal-izm), *n.* [< *political* + *-ism*.] Political zeal or partisanship.

politically (pǭ-lit'i-kal-i), *adv.* 1. In a political manner; with relation to the government of a nation or state; as regards politics.—2†. In a politic manner; artfully; with address; politicly.

The Turks *politically* mingled certain Janizaries, harquebusiers, with their horsemen. *Knolles*, Hist. Turks.

politicaster (pǭ-lit'i-kas-tėr), *n.* [= Sp. It. *politicastro*; as *politic*, *n.*, + *-aster*.] A petty politician; a pretender to political knowledge or influence.

We may infallibly assure our selvs that it will as wel agree with Monarchy, though all the Tribe of Aphorismers and *Politicasters* would perswade us there be secret and misterious reasons against it.
Milton, Reformation in Eng., ii.

politician (pol-i-tish'an), *n.* and *a.* [Formerly also *polititian*, *polititien*; < F. *politicien*, a politician; as *politic* + *-ian*.] I. *n.* 1. One who is versed in the science of government and the art of governing; one who is skilled in politics.

The first *polititiens*, deuising all expedient meanes for th' establishment of Common wealth, to hold and containe the people in order and duety.
Puttenham, Arte of Eng. Poesie, p. 5.

He is the greater and deeper *politician* that can make other men the instruments of his will and ends.
Bacon, Advancement of Learning, ii. 169.

2. One who occupies himself with politics; one who devotes himself to public affairs or to the promotion of the interests of a p i a party; one who is practically interested in politics; in a bad sense, one who concerns himself with public affairs not from patriotism or public spirit, but for his own profit or that of his friends, or of a clique or party.

This is the masterpiece of a modern *politician*, how to qualify and mould the sufferance and subjection of the people to the length of that foot that is to tread on their necks; how rapine may serve itself with the fair and honourable pretences of public good; how the puny law may be brought under the wardship and control of lust and will: in which attempt if they fall short, then must a superficial colour of reputation by all means, direct or indirect, be gotten to wash over the unsightly bruise of honour. *Milton*, Reformation in Eng., ii.

A *politician*, where factions run high, is interested not for the whole people, but for his own section of it. *Macaulay*, Hallam's Const. Hist.

A sincere Utilitarian, therefore, is likely to be an eager *politician*. *H. Sidgwick*, Methods of Ethics, p. 459.

3†. A politic or crafty person; a petty and generally an unscrupulous schemer; a trickster.

The Diuell . . . was noted . . . to be a greedie pursuer of newes, and so famous a *politician* in purchasing that Hel, which at the beginning was but an obscure village, is now become a huge citie, whervnto all countreys are tributarie. *Nashe*, Pierce Penilesse, p. 9.

The *politician*, whose very essence lies in this, that he is a person ready to do any thing that he apprehends for his advantage, must first of all be sure to put himself into a state of liberty as free and large as his principles, and so to provide elbow-room enough for his conscience to lay about it, and have its free play in. *South*, Sermons (1737), I. 324.

Pot-house politician, a politician of low aims and motives; a professional politician, ignorant, irresponsible, and often venal: so called from the favorite resorts of such men. =**Syn. 1** and **2**. This word has degenerated so as generally to imply that the person busies himself with partizanship, low arts, and petty management, leaving the enlightened and high-minded service of the state to the *statesman*. A man, however, would not properly be called a *statesman* unless he were also of eminent ability in public affairs.

The Eastern *politicians* never do anything without the opinion of the astrologers on the fortunate moment. . . . *Statesmen* of a more judicious prescience look for the fortunate moment too; but they seek it, not in the conjunctions and oppositions of planets, but in the conjunctions and oppositions of men and things. Burke, To a Member of the Nat. Assembly, 1791.

II. *a.* 1†. Politic; using artifice.

Your ill-meaning *politician* lords. *Milton*, S. A., l. 1195.

2. Of or pertaining to politicians or their methods. [Rare.]

A turbulent, discoloured, and often unsavory sea of political or rather *politician* quasi-social life. *Arch. Forbes*, Souvenirs of some Continents, p. 155.

politicise, *v. i.* See *politicize*.

politicist (pọ̄-lit'i-sist), *n.* [‹ *politic* + *-ist*.] A student or observer of politics; one who writes upon subjects relating to politics. [Rare.]

politicize (pọ̄-lit'i-sīz), *v. i.*; pret. and pp. *politicized*, ppr. *politicizing*. [‹ *politic* + *-ize*.] To occupy one's self with politics; discuss political questions. Also spelled *politicise*.

But while I am *politicizing*, I forget to tell you half the purport of my letter. *Walpole*, To Mann (1758). (*Davies*.)

Politicizing sophists threaten to be a perfect curse to India. *Contemporary Rev.*, LII. 711.

politicly (pol'i-tik-li), *adv.* In a politic manner; artfully; cunningly.

politico†, *n.* [‹ Sp. *politico* = It. *politico*, a politician: see *politic*, *n.*] A politician; hence, one whose conduct is guided by considerations of policy rather than principle.

He is counted cunning, a meere *politico*, a time-server, an hypocrite. *Bp. Gauden*, Tears of the Church, p. 256. (*Davies*.)

politics (pol'i-tiks), *n.* [Early mod. E. *politicks*, *polytykes*; pl. of *politic* (see *-ics*).] 1. The science or practice of government; the regulation and government of a nation or state for the preservation of its safety, peace, and prosperity. *Politics*, in its widest extent, is both the science and the art of government, or the science whose subject is the regulation of man in all his relations as the member of a state, and the application of this science. In other words, it is the theory and practice of obtaining the ends of civil society as perfectly as possible. The subjects which political science comprises have been arranged under the following heads: (1) natural law; (2) abstract politics — that is, the object or end of a state, and the relations between it and individual citizens; (3) political economy; (4) the science of police, or municipal regulation; (5) practical politics, or the conduct of the immediate public affairs of a state; (6) history of politics; (7) history of the political systems of foreign states; (8) statistics; (9) positive law relating to state affairs, commonly called constitutional law; (10) practical law of nations; (11) diplomacy; (12) the technical science of politics, or an acquaintance with the forms and style of public business in different countries.

Hence the stress which Utilitarians are apt to lay on social and political activity of all kinds, and the tendency which Utilitarian ethics have always shewn to pass over into *politics*. *H. Sidgwick*, Methods of Ethics, p. 459.

Machiavelli . . . founded the science of *politics* for the modern world by concentrating thought upon its fundamental principles. *Encyc. Brit.*, XV. 150.

2. In a narrower and more usual sense, the art or vocation of guiding or influencing the policy of a government through the organization of a party among its citizens — including, therefore, not only the ethics of government, but more especially, and often to the exclusion of ethical principles, the art of influencing public opinion, attracting and marshaling voters, and obtaining and distributing public patronage, so far as the possession of offices may depend upon the political opinions or political services of individuals; hence, in an evil sense, the schemes and intrigues of political parties, or of cliques or individual politicians: as, the newspapers were full of *politics*.

When we say that two men are talking *politics*, we often mean that they are wrangling about some mere party question. *F. W. Robertson*.

I always hated *politics* in the ordinary sense of the word, and I am not likely to grow fonder of them. *Lowell*, Biglow Papers, 2d ser., Int.

3. Political opinions; party connection or preference.

Politics, like religion, are matters of faith on which reason says as little as possible. *Froude*, Sketches, p. 85.

politient†, *n.* See *polician*.

Politique (pol-i-tēk'), *n.* [‹ F. *politique*: see *politic*.] In *French hist.*, a member of a party, formed soon after the massacre of St. Bartholomew (1572), which aimed at the reconciliation of the Huguenots and the Catholics.

At Court three great parties were contending for power in the King's name — the Guises, the Reformers, and the *Politiques*. *Quarterly Rev.*, CXLVI. 21.

The middle party, the *Politiques* of Europe — the English, that is, and the Germans — sent help to Henry, by means of which he was able to hold his own in the north-west and south-west throughout 1591. *Encyc. Brit.*, IX. 564.

polititious†, *a.* [For **politicious*, ‹ *politic* + *-ious*.] Politic; crafty.

The *polititious* Walker
By an intreague did quail them again.
Undaunted Londonderry (Child's Ballads, VII. 249).

politize† (pol'i-tiz), *v.* [‹ *polit-y* + *-ize*.] I. *intrans.* 1. To play the politician; act in a politic manner.

Let us not, for feare of a scarecrow, or else through hatred to be reform'd, stand hankering and *politizing* when God with spread hands testifies to us. *Milton*, Reformation in Eng., ii.

II. *trans.* To educate in politics or in polity; make a politician or politicians of. [Rare.]

Its inhabitants [the state's] must be *politized*, for they [according to Feuerbach], all of them, constitute the polis. *Rae*, Contemporary Socialism, p. 116.

politure† (pol'i-ṭūr), *n.* [= D. *politoer*, *polituur* = G. Dan. *politur* = Sw. *politur*, *polityr*, ‹ OF. *politure* = Pg. *polidura* = It. *politura*, *pulitura*, ‹ L. *politura*, a polishing, ‹ *polire*, polish: see *polish*1.] Polish; the gloss given by polishing.

The walls are brick, plaster'd over wth such a composition as for strength and *politure* resembles white marble. *Evelyn*, Diary, Feb. 7, 1645.

polity (pol'i-ti), *n.* [‹ F. *politie*, *policie*, etc., ‹ L. *politia*, ‹ Gr. πολιτεία, polity, policy, the state: see *policy*1, the same word in another form.] 1. Government; form, system, or method of government: as, civil *polity*; ecclesiastical *polity*.

To our purpose therefore the name of Church-*Polity* will better serve, because it containeth both government and also whatsoever besides belongeth to the ordering of the Church in public. *Hooker*, Eccles. Polity, iii. 1.

They alledge 1. That the Church government must be conformable to the civill *politie*. *Milton*, Reformation in Eng., ii.

2. Any body of persons forming a community governed according to a recognized system of government.—3†. Policy; art; management; scheme.

It was no *polity* of court,
Albe the place were charmed,
To let in earnest, or in sport,
So many Loves in, armed.
B. *Jonson*, Masque of Beauty.

=**Syn. 1.** See *policy*1.

politzerize (pol'it-sėr-īz), *v. t.*; pret. and pp. *politzerized*, ppr. *politzerizing*. [Named after Adam *Politzer*, of Vienna.] To inflate the Eustachian tube and tympanum of, by blowing into the anterior nares while the way down the pharynx is closed by the patient's swallowing at the instant of inflation. Also spelled *politzerise*.

polive†, *n.* A Middle English form of *pulley*.

polk1†, *v.* A Middle English form of *poke*1.

polk2, *n.* [Cf. *pool*1.] A pool. [Old and prov. Eng.]

polk3 (pōlk), *v. i.* [‹ F. *polker*, dance the polka, ‹ *polka*, polka: see *polka*.] To dance a polka. [Colloq.]

Gwendolen says she will not waltz or *polk*. *George Eliot*, Daniel Deronda, xi.

polka (pōl'kạ̈), *n.* [‹ F. *polka* = G. *polka*, a polka, so called with ref. to the half-step provalent in it, ‹ Bohem. *pulka*, half; cf. Pol. *pol*, half, Russ. *polovina*, a half.] 1. A lively round dance which originated in Bohemia about 1830, and was soon after introduced into Austria, France, and England, where it immediately attained a remarkable popularity.—2. Music for such a dance or in its rhythm, which is duple, and marked by a capricious accent on the second beat, frequently followed by a rest.—**Polka mazurka**, a modification of the mazurka to the movement of a polka.

polka-dot (pōl'kạ̈-dot), *n.* In textile fabrics, a pattern of round dots or spots, especially in printed stuffs for women's wear.

polka-gauze (pōl'kạ̈-gâz), *n.* Gauze into which are woven spots or dots of more solid texture.

polka-jacket (pōl'kạ̈-jak"et), *n.* A knitted jacket worn by women.

poll1 (pōl), *n.* [Formerly also *pole*, *pol*; Sc. *pow*; ‹ ME. *poll*, *pol*, head, list (AF. *poll*, list), ‹ MD. *polle*, *pol*, also *bol*, the head, = LG. *polle*, the head, top of a tree, bulb, = Sw. dial. *pull*, the head, = Dan. *puld*, crown (of a hat); according to some, a variant or connection of *bowl*1, etc.; according to Skeat, the same, by the occasional interchange of initial *p* and *k*, as Icel. *kollr*, top, shaven crown, = OSw. *kull*, *kulle*, crown of the head, Sw. *kulle*, crown, top, peak; cf. Ir. *coll*, head, neck, = W. *col*, peak, top, summit: cf. *kill*1. Hence *poll*1, *v.*, *pollard*, etc.; in comp. *catchpoll*, etc.] 1. The head, or the rounded back part of the head, of a person; also, by extension, the head of an animal.

And preyen for the *pol* bi *pol*.
Piers Plowman (B), xi. 57.

His beard was as white as snow,
All flaxen was his *poll*.
Shak., Hamlet, iv. 5. 196.

Have you a catalogue
Of all the voices that we have procured
Set down by the *poll*? *Shak.*, Cor., iii. 3. 9.

You shall sometimes see a man begin the offer of a salutation, and observe a forbidding air, or escaping eye, in the person he is going to salute, and stop short in the *poll* of his neck. *Steele* Spectator, No. 259.

Hence — 2. A person, an individual enumerated in a list.—3. An enumeration or register of heads or persons, as for the imposition of a poll-tax, or the list or roll of those who have voted at an election.—4. The voting or registering of votes at an election, or the place where the votes are taken: in the United States used chiefly in the plural: as, to go to the *poll*; the *polls* will close at four.—5. A poll-tax.

According to the different numbers which from time to time shall be found in each jurisdiction upon a true and just account, the service of men and all charges of the war be borne by the *poll* [that is, by a tax of so much per head]. *Winthrop*, Hist. New England, II. 123.

When, therefore, in 1379, an immediate sum of money was required for "instant operations" on the continent, recourse was again had to a *poll*. *S. Dowell*, Taxes in England, III. 6.

6. The broad end or butt of a hammer.

Jake began pounding on it [the door] with the *poll* of an ax. *E. Eggleston*, The Graysons, xxv.

7. The chub or cheven, *Leuciscus cephalus*. Also called *pollard*.—**At the head of the poll**, in Great Britain, having the highest number of votes in an election: as, the Gladstonian candidate was *at the head of the poll*.—**Challenge to the polls**. See *challenge*, 9.—**Hours of Poll Act**. See *Elections Act*, under *election*.

poll1 (pōl), *v.* [‹ *poll*1, *n.* Cf. *kill*1, *v.*, etym.] I. *trans.* 1. To remove the top or head of; hence, to cut off the tops of; lop; clip; also, to cut off the hair of; also, to cut, as hair; shear; cut closely; mow; also, to remove the horns of, as cattle: as, to *poll* tares, hair, wool, or grass.

So was it here in England till her Maiesties most noble father, for diuers good respects, caused his owne head and all his Courtiers to be *polled*, and his beard to be cut short. *Puttenham*, Arte of Eng. Poesie, p. 239.

Neither shall they shave their heads, nor suffer their locks to grow long; they shall only *poll* their heads. Ezek. xliv. 20.

Ev'ry man that wore long hair
Should *poll* him out of hand.
Queen Eleanor's Fall (Child's Ballads, VII. 294).

So may thy woods, oft *poll'd*, yet ever wear
A green and (when she list) a golden hair.
Donne, Letters, To Mr. J. P.

Since this *polling* and shaving world crept up, locks were locked up, and hair fell to decay. *Dekker*, Gull's Hornbook, p. 88.

2. In *law*, to cut even without indenting, as a deed executed by one party. See *deed poll*, under *deed*.

A deed made by one party only is not indented, but *polled* or shaved quite even, and therefore called a deed-poll, or a single deed. *Blackstone*, Com., II. xx.

3. To rob; plunder; despoil, as by excessive taxation. [In this sense associated with, and perhaps suggested by, the synonymous *pill*1.]

Neither can justice yield her fruit with sweetness among the briars and brambles of catching and *polling* clerks and ministers. *Bacon*, Judicature (ed. 1887).

Great man in office may securely rob whole provinces, undo thousands, pill and *poll*. *Burton*, Anat. of Mel., To the Reader, p. 41.

4. To enumerate one by one; enroll in a list or register, as for the purpose of levying a poll-tax.—**5.** To pay, as a personal tax.

The man that *polled* but twelve pence for his head. *Dryden*, tr. of Juvenal's Satires, iii. 268.

6. To canvass or ascertain the opinion of.

I believe you might have *polled* the North, and had a response, three to one: "Let the Union go to pieces, rather than yield one inch." *W. Phillips*, Speeches, etc., p. 379.

7. To receive at the polls: as, A *polled* only 50 votes; also, to cast at the polls: as, a large vote was *polled*.—**8.** To vote at the polls; bring to the polls.

And *poll* for points of faith his trusty vote. *Tickell*, From a Lady to a Gentleman at Avignon.

The Greenbackers in 1880 *polled* 307,740 votes in the whole country. *The Nation*, July 31, 1884, p. 81.

II. *intrans.* To vote at a poll; record a vote, as an elector.

I should think it no honour to be returned to Parliament by persons who, thinking me destitute of the requisite qualifications, had yet been wrought upon by cajolery and importunity to *poll* for me in despite of their better judgment. *Macaulay*, in Trevelyan, I. 251.

poll[2] (pol), *n.* [Abbr. of *Polly* (for *Molly*), a familiar form of *Mary* and a common name of parrots.] A parrot: also called *poll-parrot* and *polly*.

poll[3] (pol), *n.* [So called as being one of 'the many,' Gr. *οἱ πολλοί*, the many, pl. of *πολύς*, much, many: see *feel*[2].] A student at Cambridge University in England who merely takes a degree, but receives no honors; one who is not a candidate for honors.—**The poll**, such students collectively.—**Captain of the poll.** See *captain*.

Pollachius (po-lā'ki-us), *n.* [NL. (Nilsson; Bonaparte, 1846), < E. *pollack*.] In *ichth.*, a genus of gadoid fishes closely resembling *Gadus* proper, but having the lower jaw protrusive, with a rudimentary or obsolete barbel, and the teeth of the upper jaw subequal. It contains the true pollack and the green pollack, or coalfish, of the North Atlantic, both sometimes called *green-cod*, and *P. chalcogrammus* of the North Pacific. See cut under *coalfish*.

pollack, pollock (pol'ak, -ok), *n.* [Cf. D. G. *pollack* (< E.); < Gael. *pollag*, a whiting, = Ir. *pullog*, a pollack.] A fish of the genus *Pollachius*. The true pollack, of European waters only, is *P. pollachius* or *P. typus*, also called *green-cod*, *greenfish*, *greenling*, *laithe*, *laits*, *leeat*, *lect*, *leets*, *lythe*, *lob*, *skeet*, and *whiting-pollack*. The green pollack of Atlantic waters, both European and American, is a closely related species, *P. virens* or *P. carbonarius*, called *coalfish* (and by many other names) in England. Both these fishes are greenish-brown above, with the sides and the belly silvery, the lateral line pale, and the fins mostly pale; but the true pollack has a much more projecting under jaw, the snout twice as long as the eye, the vent more in advance (being below the anterior half of the first dorsal fin), and the first anal fin much longer. The pollack of Pacific waters, *P. chalcogrammus*, is more decidedly different. Like the cod, hake, and haddock, the pollacks are among the important food-fishes of the family *Gadidæ*.

poll-adz (pōl'adz), *n.* An adz with a striking-face on the head or poll, opposite the bit. *E. H. Knight.*

pollage† (pō'lāj), *n.* [< *poll*[1] + *-age*.] A poll-tax; hence, extortion.

It is unknowne to any man what minde Paul, the Bishop of Rome, beareth to us for deliuering of our realme from his greuous bondage and *pollage*. *Foxe*, Martyrs, p. 990.

pollam (pol'am), *n.* [Hind. (?).] A fief; a district held by a poligar. [Hindustan.]

pollan (pol'an), *n.* [= Sc. *powan*; cf. *pollack*.] The so-called fresh-water herring of Ireland, a variety of whitefish technically known as *Coregonus pollan*, found in the various loughs. The corresponding variety of the Scotch lochs is called *powan* and *vendace*. See *Coregonus* and *whitefish*.

pollarchy (pol'är-ki), *n.* [< Gr. *πολύς*, many (pl. *οἱ πολλοί*, the many), + *ἀρχή*, rule.] The rule of the many; government by the mob or masses. [Rare.]

A contest . . . between those representing oligarchical principles and the *pollarchy*. *W. H. Russell*, My Diary, North and South, II. 340. (*Davies*.)

pollard (pol'ärd), *n.* [< *poll*[1] + *-ard*. In def. 2, < ME. *pollard*, AF. *pollard*.] **1.** A tree cut back nearly to the trunk, and thus caused to form a dense head of spreading branches, which are in turn cut for basket-making and fagot-wood. Willows and poplars especially are so treated.—**2.** A clipped coin. The term was applied especially to the counterfeits of the English silver penny imported into England by foreign merchants in the reign of Edward I.

He then retourned into England, and so vnto London, where, by the aduyce of some of his counsayle, he sodeynly dampned certayne coynes of money, called *pollardes*, crocardes, and rosaries, and caused theym to be broughte vnto newe coynage to his great aduantage. *Fabyan*, Chron., II., an. 1350.

3. A polled animal, as a stag or an ox without horns.—**4.** Same as *poll*[1], 7.—**5.** A coarse product of wheat.

The coarsest of bran, vsuallie called gurgeons, or *pollard*. *Harrison*, Descrip. of Eng., ii. 6.

pollard (pol'ärd), *v. t.* [< *pollard*, *n.*] To make a pollard of; convert (a tree) into a pollard by cutting off the head.

Elm and oak, frequently *pollarded* and cut, . . . increases the bulk and circumference. *Evelyn*, Sylva, III. ii.

pollax, pollaxe†, *n.* See *poleax*.

poll-book (pōl'bůk), *n.* A register of persons entitled to vote at an election.

poll-clerk (pōl'klėrk), *n.* A clerk appointed to assist the presiding officer at an election. In British elections that officer may do by poll-clerks any act which he may do at a polling-station, except to arrest, eject, or exclude a person. In South Australia and Queensland the duties of a poll-clerk are to have charge of the ballots and furnish them to voters, as required of the ballot-clerk in New York and Massachusetts.

polled (pōld), *p. a.* [Pp. of *poll*[1], *v.*] **1.** Deprived of the poll; lopped, as a tree having the top cut off.—**2.** Cropped; clipped; also, bald; shaven.

These *polled* locks of mine, . . . while they were long, were the ornament of my sex. *Sir P. Sidney*, Arcadia, ii.

The *polled* bachelor. *Beau. and Fl.*

3. Having no horns or antlers: noting a stag or other deer that has cast its antlers, or a hornless breed of cattle, or an animal that has lost its horns or whose horns have been removed: as, a *polled* cow. Also called, in Scotland, *dodded*.

The Drumlanrig and Ardrossan herds are extinct. These herds were horned, the latter having latterly become *polled* on the introduction of *polled* bulls from Hamilton. *Amer. Naturalist*, XXII. 789.

pollen (pol'en), *n.* [= F. *pollen* = Sp. *pólen* = Pg. *pollen* = It. *polline*, < NL. *pollen* (*pollin-*), pollen, < L. *pollen* (*pollin-*), also *pollis* (*pollin-*), fine flour, mill-dust, also fine dust of other things; cf. Gr. *πάλη*, the finest meal.] A fine yellowish dust or powder produced in the anther of a flower (whence it is discharged when mature), which when magnified is found to consist of separate grains of definite size and shape; the male or fecundating element in flowering plants: the homologue of the microspore in cryptogams. The individual grains are usually single-celled and of a globular or oval form, but they may occasionally be composed of two or several cells, curiously irregular in shape. They are often beautifully ornamented with spines, angles, lines, etc., and while they are very uniform in the same species they often differ widely in different species or families. Pollen-grains are usually formed in fours by the division of the contents of mother-cells into two parts and these again into two parts. Each grain has two coats, the inner of which is called the *intine* and the outer the *extine*. See *pollen-tube*.

Grains of Pollen of (*a*) *Œnothera biennis*, (*b*) *Cichorium Intybus*, (*c*) *Hibiscus Moschentos*, (*d*) *Passiflora cærulea*, and (*e*) *Pinus sylvestris*.

pollen (pol'en), *v. t.* [< *pollen*, *n.*] To cover or dust with pollen; supply with pollen. *Tennyson*, Voyage of Maeldune.

pollenarious (pol-e-nā'ri-us), *a.* [Prop. **pollinarious*; < *pollen* (NL. *pollen*, *pollin-*) + *-arious*.] Consisting of pollen or meal.

pollenarium (pol-e-nā'ri-um), *n.* An erroneous form for *pollinarium*. *Hoffman.*

pollenation (pol-e-nā'shon), *n.* Same as *pollenization*.

Experiments to show, by cross-*pollenations*, the relation between gonotropic irritability and appropriate nutrition upon the growth and direction of pollen-tubes. *Amer. Naturalist*, XXIV. 369.

pollen-brush (pol'en-brush), *n.* The corbiculum of a bee. See cut under *corbiculum*.

pollen-catarrh (pol'en-ka-tär"), *n.* Same as *hay-fever*.

pollen-cell (pol'en-sel), *n.* In *bot.*, a cell or chamber of an anther in which pollen is developed.

pollen-chamber (pol'en-chām"bėr), *n.* In gymnosperms, the cavity at the apex of the ovule in which the pollen-grains lie after pollenization. It is beneath the integuments. Also called *pollinic chamber*.

pollen-fever (pol'en-fē"vėr), *n.* Same as *hay-fever*.

pollenger† (pol'en-jėr), *n.* [< **pollager*, < *poll*[1] + *-age* (cf. *pollage*) + *-er*[1]. Cf. *pollard*; and for the form, cf. *porringer*, etc.] **1.** A pollard tree. See quotation under *husband*, *n.*, 5.—**2.** Brushwood. *Tusser*, Husbandry, January.

pollen-grain (pol'en-grān), *n.* See *pollen*.

polleniferous (pol-e-nif'e-rus), *a.* [< NL. *pollen* (*pollin-*), pollen, + L. *ferre* = E. *bear*[1].] An erroneous form of *polliniferous*.

pollenization (pol"en-i-zā'shon), *n.* [< *pollenize* + *-ation*.] The act or process of supplying or impregnating with pollen.

pollenize (pol'en-iz), *v. t.*; pret. and pp. *pollenized*, ppr. *pollenizing*. [< *pollen* + *-ize*.] To supply with pollen; impregnate with pollen.

pollen-mass (pol'en-mås), *n.* In *bot.*, same as *pollinium*.

The sterility of the flowers, when protected from the access of insects, depends solely on the *pollen-masses* not coming into contact with the stigma. *Darwin*, Fertil. of Orchids by Insects, p. 29.

pollen-paste (pol'en-pāst), *n.* Pollen mixed with a little honey, as it is stored by bees for the sustenance of their young. Kneaded with more honey and with a secretion from the mouth of the insects, it becomes bee-bread.

pollen-plate (pol'en-plāt), *n.* In *entom.*, a flat or hollowed surface fringed with stiff hairs, used as a receptacle for pollen. These plates are found on the inner sides of the tibiæ and tarsi, or on the sides of the metathorax, of various species of bees. Those on the legs are called *corbiculæ*. See cut under *corbiculum*.

pollen-sac (pol'en-sak), *n.* The sac in which the pollen is produced; the anther-cell: the homologue of the microsporangium in cryptogams.

pollen-spore (pol'en-spōr), *n.* Same as *pollen-grain*. See *pollen*.

pollent (pol'ent), *a.* [< L. *pollen(t-)s*, ppr. of *pollere*, be strong.] Powerful; prevailing.

We had no arms or merely lawful ones,
An unimportant sword and blunderbuss,
Against a foe *pollent* in potency.
Browning, Ring and Book, II. 100.

pollen-tube (pol'en-tūb), *n.* In *bot.*, the tube through which the fecundating element is conveyed to the ovule. When a pollen-grain is deposited upon a fitting stigma, at a time when the stigmatic secretion is sufficiently abundant, it increases somewhat in size, and soon a tube (sometimes more than one) is thrust forth and passes immediately into the loose tissue of the stigmatic surface. The tube consists of a protrusion of the intine. During its descent the pollen-tube is slender, of about the same caliber throughout, and has extremely thin walls. It extends through the conducting tissue of the style, being nourished by the nutrient matter secreted from the cells of that tissue, until it at last reaches the cavity of the ovary and penetrates the micropyle of the ovule.

poller (pō'lėr), *n.* [Formerly also *powler*; < *poll*[1] + *-er*[1].] One who polls. (*a*) One who shaves persons or cuts their hair; a barber; a hair-dresser. [Rare.]

R. I know him not; is he a deaft barber?
G. O yea; why, he is mistress Lamia's *powler*.
Promos and Cassandra, v. 4. (*Nares.*)

(*b*) One who lops or polls trees. (*c*) A pillager; a plunderer; one who fleeces by exaction.

The *poller* and exacter of fees. *Bacon*, Judicature (ed. 1887).

(*d*) One who registers voters; also, one who casts a vote at the polls.

pollet† (pol'et), *n.* [For **paulet*, for *epaulet*, q. v.] Same as *pollette*.

pollette† (pol'et), *n.* [For **paulette*, for *epaulette*, < F. *épaulette*, an epaulet, dim. of *épaule*, the shoulder: see *epaulet*.] The pauldron or epaulet worn with the suits of armor of the sixteenth century.

poll-evil (pōl'ē"vl), *n.* A swelling or aposteme on a horse's head, or on the nape of the neck between the ears. Formerly also *pole-evil*.

pollex (pol'eks), *n.*; pl. *pollices* (-i-sēz). [L., the thumb, the great toe, perhaps < *pollere*, be strong: see *pollent*.] **1.** In *anat.*, the innermost digit of the hand or foot, when there are five; the thumb or the great toe, especially the thumb, the great toe being usually distinguished as *pollex pedis*, or *hallux*.—**2.** In *zoöl.*: (*a*) The innermost digit of the fore limb only, when there are five; the digit that corresponds to the human thumb. (*b*) The thumb of a bird; the short digit bearing the alula or bastard wing, regarded as homologous with either the human thumb or the forefinger.—**Abductor longus pollicis.** Same as *extensor ossis metacarpi pollicis*.—**Adductor pollicis pedis.** See *adductor*.—**Extensor brevis or minor pollicis.** Same as *extensor primi internodii pollicis*.—**Extensor ossis metacarpi pollicis.** See *extensor*.—**Extensor pollicis longus or major.** Same as *extensor secundi internodii pollicis*.—**Extensor primi internodii pollicis.** See *extensor*.—**Extensor pro-**

prius pollicis. See *extensor*.—**Extensor secundi internodii pollicis.** See *extensor*.—**Flexor longus pollicis.** See *flexor*.—**Pollex pedis,** the hallux.

pollical (pol'i-kal), *a.* [< L. *pollex* (*pollic-*), thumb, + *-al.*] Of or pertaining to the pollex: as, the *pollical* muscles.—**First pollical extensor.** Same as *extensor ossis metacarpi pollicis.* See *extensor.*—**Second pollical extensor.** Same as *extensor primi internodii pollicis.* See *extensor.*—**Third pollical extensor.** Same as *extensor secundi internodii pollicis.* See *extensor.*

Pollicata (pol-i-kā'tä), *n. pl.* [NL., neut. pl. of *pollicatus*: see *pollicate.*] In Illiger's classification (1811), the second order of mammals, containing those with apposable thumbs, consisting chiefly of the quadrumanous quadrupeds, but including also most of the marsupials.

pollicate (pol'i-kāt), *a.* [< NL. *pollicatus*, < L. *pollex* (*pollic-*), the thumb: see *pollex.*] Having thumbs; specifically, of or pertaining to the *Pollicata*.

pollices, *n.* Plural of *pollex*.

pollicie†, *n.* An obsolete form of *policy*[1].

pollicitation (po-lis-i-tā'shon), *n.* [= F. *pollicitation* = Sp. *policitacion* = Pg. *pollicitação* = It. *pollicitazione*; < L. *pollicitatio(n-)*, a promising, < *pollicitari*, promise, < *polliceri*, hold forth, promise, < *por-*, forth, + *liceri*, bid for, offer.] 1. A promise; a voluntary engagement; also, a paper containing such an engagement.

> It seems he granted this following *pollicitation* or promise. *Herbert*, Hist. Reign Hen. VIII., p. 220. (*Latham.*)

2. In *civil law*, a promise without mutuality; a promise not yet accepted by the person to whom it is made. As a general rule, such a promise could be revoked at any time before it was accepted, but a vow made in favor of a public or religious object was irrevocable from the moment it was made. This principle has been reaffirmed by the canon law. In some cases the promiser could be released from the effect of his vow by paying a fifth part of his property.

polligar, *n.* See *poligar*.

pollinar (pol'i-när), *a.* [< LL. *pollinaris* (L. *pollinarius*), belonging to fine flour, < L. *pollen* (*pollin-*), fine flour (NL. pollen): see *pollen.*] In *bot.*, covered with a very fine dust resembling pollen.

pollinarium (pol-i-nā'ri-um), *n.* [NL., < *pollen* (*pollin-*), pollen (see *pollen*), + *-arium.*] In *bot.*: (*a*) In phanerogams, same as *pollinium*. (*b*) In cryptogams, same as *cystidium*.

pollinate (pol'i-nāt), *v. t.*; pret. and pp. *pollinated*, ppr. *pollinating*. [< L. *pollen* (*pollin-*), fine flour (NL. pollen), + *-ate*[2].] In *bot.*, to convey pollen to the stigma of; pollenize. See *pollination*.

pollinated (pol'i-nā-ted), *a.* [< *pollinate* + *-ed*[2].] In *bot.*, supplied with pollen: said of anthers.

pollination (pol-i-nā'shon), *n.* [= F. *pollination*; as *pollinate* + *-ion.*] 1. In *bot.*, the supplying of pollen to the part of the female organ prepared to receive it, preliminary to fertilization. See *pollen-tube*.

> By *pollination* is meant the conveyance of the pollen from the anthers to the stigma of Angiosperms or to the nucleus of Gymnosperms. *Sachs*, Botany (trans.), p. 429.

2. The fertilization of plants by the agency of insects that carry pollen from one flower to another.

pollinctor (po-lingk'tor), *n.* [L., < *pollingere*, pp. *pollinctus*, wash and prepare a corpse for the funeral pile.] One who prepares materials for embalming the dead.

> The Egyptians had these several persons belonging to and employed in embalming, each performing a distinct and separate office: viz., a designer or painter, a dissector or anatomist, a *pollinctor* or apothecary, an embalmer or surgeon, and a physician or priest. *Greenhill*, Art of Embalming, p. 177. (*Latham.*)

polling-booth (pō'ling-böth), *n.* See *booth*.

polling-pence†, *n.* Same as *poll-tax*.

polling-place (pō'ling-plās), *n.* A place in which votes are taken and recorded at an election.

polling-sheriff (pō'ling-sher"if), *n.* In Scotland, the presiding officer at a polling-place.

polling-station (pō'ling-stā"shon), *n.* Same as *polling-place*.

pollinia, *n.* Plural of *pollinium*.

pollinic (po-lin'ik), *a.* [< *pollen* (*pollin-*) + *-ic.*] Of or pertaining to pollen, or concerned with its conveyance from anther to stigma. *R. Bentley*, Botany, p. 765.—**Pollinic chamber.** Same as *pollen-chamber*.

polliniferous (pol-i-nif'e-rus), *a.* [= F. *pollinifère* = Pg. *pollinifero*, < NL. *pollen* (*pollin-*), pollen, + L. *ferre* = E. *bear*[1].] 1. Producing or containing pollen.—2. Bearing pollen: applied in zoölogy to the brushes, plates, etc., by which insects gather or transport pollen.

pollinigerous (pol-i-nij'e-rus), *a.* [< NL. *pollen*, pollen, + L. *gerere*, carry.] 1. Fitted for collecting and carrying pollen; polliniferous.—2. Collecting and carrying pollen: a term applied to bees which collect pollen for the sustenance of their young.

pollinium (po-lin'i-um), *n.*; pl. *pollinia* (-ä). [NL., < *pollen* (*pollin-*), pollen: see *pollen*.] In *bot.*, an agglutinated mass or body of pollen-grains, composed of all the grains of an anther-cell. A pollinium is especially characteristic of the families *Asclepiadaceæ* and *Orchideæ*, and is an adaptation for cross-fertilization by insect aid. Also called *pollen-mass*, *pollinarium*.

pollinivorous (pol-i-niv'ọ-rus), *a.* [< NL. *pollen* (*pollin-*), pollen, + L. *vorare*, devour, eat.] Feeding upon pollen, as an insect.

pollinodial (pol-i-nō'di-al), *a.* [< *pollinodi-um* + *-al.*] In *bot.*, characteristic of, produced by, or resembling a pollinodium. *Encyc. Brit.*, XX. 426.

pollinodium (pol-i-nō'di-um), *n.*; pl. *pollinodia* (-ä). [NL., < *pollen* (*pollin-*), pollen, + Gr. εἶδος, form.] In *bot.*, the male sexual organ in *Ascomycetes*, which, either directly or by means of an outgrowth, conjugates with the oögonium, or female sexual organ.

> A second branch (termed the *pollinodium*) is formed in the immediate neighbourhood of the first. *Huxley and Martin*, Elementary Biology, p. 420.

pollinoid (pol'i-noid), *n.* [< NL. *pollen* (*pollin-*), pollen, + Gr. εἶδος, form.] In *bot.*, the non-motile male organ in the *Florideæ* and *Ascomycetes*: the same, or nearly the same, as *pollinodium*.

pollinose (pol'i-nōs), *a.* [< NL. *pollen* (*pollin-*), pollen, + *-ose*.] In *entom.*, covered (as if with pollen) with a loose or light powdery substance, often of a yellow color.

polliwog, polliwig (pol'i-wog, -wig), *n.* [Also *pollywog*, *pollywig*; early mod. E. *polewigge*; < ME. *polwygle*, later *porwigle*; appar. < *poll*[1] + *wig(gle)*.] A tadpole.

> Tadpoles, *polewigges*, yonge frogs. *Florio*, p. 212.

> Dame, what ails your ducks to die?
> Eating o' *pollywigs*, eating o' *pollywigs*.
> *Whiter's Specimen* (1794), p. 19. (*Halliwell.*)

poll-mad (pōl'mad), *a.* [< *poll*[1] + *mad*[1].] Wrong in the head; crazy; mad or eager to the point of mental derangement. [Prov. Eng.]

pollman (pol'man), *n.*; pl. *pollmen* (-men). [< *poll*[3] + *man*.] A student at Cambridge University, England, who is a candidate for the ordinary degree and not for honors.

> It is related of some Cambridge *pollman* that he was once so ill-advised as to desert a private tutor . . . in order to become the pupil of the eminent "Shilleto." *Academy*, March 2, 1889.

poll-money† (pōl'mun"i), *n.* Same as *poll-tax*.

pollock, *n.* See *pollack*.

poll-pick (pōl'pik), *n.* A form of pick in common use by miners in various parts of Great Britain. The form used in Cornwall has a stem or arm about 12 inches long from the end of the eye, and a stump which forms the poll or head. The face of the poll is steeled like a sledge to form a peen, so that it can be used for striking a blow.

poll-silver† (pōl'sil"vėr), *n.* Same as *poll-tax*.

poll-suffrage (pōl'suf"rāj), *n.* Universal manhood suffrage.

poll-tax (pōl'taks), *n.* A tax levied at so much per head of the adult male population; a capitation-tax: formerly common in England, and still levied in some of the United States, as well as in a few of the countries of continental Europe. Formerly also called *poll-money*, *polling-pence*, and *poll-silver*.

pollucite (pol'ū-sīt), *n.* [< L. *Pollux* (*Polluc-*), Pollux, + *-ite*[2].] Same as *pollux*, 3.

pollute (po-lūt'), *v. t.*; pret. and pp. *polluted*, ppr. *polluting*. [< L. *pollutus*, pp. of *polluere* (> Pg. *polluir* = F. *polluer*), soil, defile, as with blood, slime, etc., hence defile morally, pollute, prob. orig. wash or smear over; cf. *proluvies*, an overflow, inundation, < *pol-*, *por-*, forth, + *luere*, wash.] 1. To make foul or unclean; render impure; defile; soil; taint.

> In those wide wounds thro' which his spirit fled,
> Shall flies and worms obscene *pollute* the dead?
> *Pope*, Iliad, xix. 30.

2. To corrupt or defile in a moral sense; destroy the perfection or purity of; impair; profane.

> That I hadde *polut* and defowled my conscience with sacrilege. *Chaucer*, Boëthius, i. prose 4.

> Power, like a desolating pestilence,
> *Pollutes* whate'er it touches.
> *Shelley*, Queen Mab, iii.

3. Specifically, to render legally or ceremonially unclean, so as to be unfit for sacred services or uses.

> Neither shall ye *pollute* the holy things of the children of Israel, lest ye die. Num. xviii. 32.

4. To violate sexually; debauch or dishonor. =**Syn.** 1 and 2. *Defile*, *Corrupt*, etc. (see *taint*), deprave, degrade, debase.—4. To ravish.

pollute (po-lūt'), *a.* [Formerly also *polute*; = F. *pollu* = Sp. *poluto* = Pg. It. *polluto*, < L. *pollutus*, pp. of *polluere*, defile: see *pollute*, *v.*] Polluted; defiled. [Rare.]

> And on her naked shame,
> *Pollute* with sinful blame,
> The saintly veil of maiden white to throw.
> *Milton*, Nativity, l. 41.

pollutedly (po-lū'ted-li), *adv.* With pollution.

pollutedness (po-lū'ted-nes), *n.* The state of being polluted; defilement.

polluter (po-lū'tėr), *n.* [< *pollute* + *-er*[1].] One who pollutes or profanes; a defiler. *Dryden*, Æneid, xi.

pollutingly (po-lū'ting-li), *adv.* In a polluting manner; with pollution or defilement.

pollution (po-lū'shon), *n.* [= F. *pollution* = Pr. *pollucio* = Sp. *polucion* = Pg. *pollução* = It. *polluzione*, < LL. *pollutio(n-)*, defilement, < L. *polluere*, pp. *pollutus*, defile: see *pollute*, *v.*] 1. The act of polluting; also, the state of being polluted; defilement; uncleanness; impurity.

> Their strife *pollution* brings
> Upon the temple. *Milton*, P. L., xii. 355.

2. Specifically, legal or ceremonial uncleanness, disqualifying a person for sacred services or for intercourse with others, or rendering anything unfit for sacred use.—3. The emission of semen at any other time than during coition: more frequently called *self-pollution*.—**Nocturnal pollution,** the emission of semen during sleep, usually accompanied by erotic dreams. =**Syn.** 1. Vitiation, corruption, foulness (see *taint*, *v.*), violation, debauching.

Pollux (pol'uks), *n.* [NL., < L. *Pollux* (*Polluc-*), also *Polluces*, Pollux, one of the Gemini or Twins, < Gr. Πολυδεύκης, Pollux.] 1. An orange star of magnitude 1.2 (β Geminorum) in the head of the following twin.—2. In *meteor.* See *Castor and Pollux*, 2.—3. [*l. c.*] A rare mineral found with castor (petalite) in the island of Elba, Italy. It occurs in isometric crystals and massive; it is colorless and has a vitreous luster, and is essentially a silicate of aluminium and cæsium.

polly (pol'i), *n.* Same as *poll*[2].

pollybait (pol'i-bāt), *n.* Same as *polewig*.

pollywog, pollywig, *n.* See *polliwog*.

polment†, *n.* [ME., < OF. *polment*, *pulment*, < L. *pulmentum*, anything eaten with bread, a sauce, condiment, relish.] A kind of pottage.

> Messeȝ of mylke he merkkeȝ bytwene,
> Sythen potage & *polment* in plater honest;
> As sewer in a god assyse he serued hem fayre,
> Wyth sadde semblaunt & swete of such as he hade.
> *Alliterative Poems* (ed. Morris), ii. 638.

polo[1] (pō'lō), *n.* [E. Ind.] A game of ball resembling hockey, played on horseback. It is of Eastern origin, and is played in India, whence it has been introduced into Europe and America.

polo[2] (pō'lō), *n.* A Spanish gipsy dance which originated in Andalusia, and closely resembles certain Eastern dances in its wild contortions of the body. The song to which it is danced is low and melancholy, with startling pauses, and is sung in unison with a rhythmic clapping of hands. The words, called *coplas*, are generally of a jocose character without refrains. Also called *ole*.

polonaise (pō-lo-nāz'), *n.* [< F. *Polonais*, m., the Polish language, *polonaise*, f., a polonaise (dress), polonaise (music), prop. adj., Polish, < *Pologne* (ML. *Polonia*), Poland: see *Pole*[3].] 1. A light open gown looped up at the sides, showing the front of an elaborate petticoat, and longer behind, worn toward the close of the eighteenth century; also, a similar but plainer gown, not so much drawn back, and draped more simply, worn at the present time.—2. A kind of overcoat, short and usually faced and bordered with fur, worn by men who affected a semi-military dress during the first quarter of the nineteenth century.—3. A Polish dance, consisting mainly of a march or promenade of the dancers in procession.—4. Music for such a promenade, or in its peculiar rhythm, which is triple and stately, with a characteristic division of the first beat of the measures, and a capricious ending of the phrases on the last beat. The origin of the form is uncertain. It was first described by Mattheson in 1739, and it has since been frequently used by various instrumental composers. It received the most elaborate and original treatment from Chopin, many of whose finest works are in this form. The rhythm of the bolero is very similar to that of the polonaise. Also called *polacca*.

Polonese (pō-lọ-nēs′ or -nēz′), *n.* [< F. *Polonais*, the Polish language: see *polonaise*.] 1. The Polish language.—2. [*l. c.*] Same as *polonaise*, 1.

Polonian (pọ-lō′ni-ạn), *a.* and *n.* [< ML. *Polonia* (OF. *Polonie*), Poland, + *-ian*.] **I.** *a.* Of or pertaining to Poland or the Poles; Polish.

The hardness and fortitude of the *Polonian* Army.
Milton, Letters of State, May 22, 1674.

II. *n.* A Pole. *Milton*, Declaration for Election of John III.

Polonize (pō′lọ-nīz), *v. t.*; pret. and pp. *Polonized*, ppr. *Polonizing*. [< ML. *Polonia*, Poland, + *-ize*.] To render Polish in character or sympathies. *Contemporary Rev.*, XLIX. 286.

polony (pọ-lō′ni), *n.*; pl. *polonies* (-niz). [Prob. corrupted from *Bologna* (sausage).] A kind of high-dried sausage made of partly cooked pork.

They were addicted to *polonies*; they did not disguise their love for Banbury cakes; they made bets in ginger-beer.
Thackeray, Newcomes, xviii.

polos (pō′los), *n.* [< Gr. πόλος, a pivot, the vault of heaven, etc.] In *Gr. archæol.*, a tall cylindrical cap or head-dress, usually worn with a veil depending at the back and side. It is a usual attribute of the more powerful Oriental female deities, and is frequently worn by some Greek goddesses, as Persephone, particularly by such as have Oriental affiliations. It is often very similar to the modius. See cut under *modius*.

Europa sometimes holds a sceptre surmounted by a bird, and wears upon her head a *polos*, showing that she was regarded at Gortyna in the light of a powerful goddess.
B. V. *Head*, Historia Numorum, p. 394.

polront, polrondt, *n.* Obsolete variants of *pauldron*.

polrose, polroze (pol′rōz), *n.* [Cornish.] In mines, the pit underneath a water-wheel. Also written *polroz*. [Cornwall, Eng.]

polska (pōl′skạ), *n.* [Sw., < *Polsk*, Polish: see *Polish*[2].] 1. A Swedish dance resembling somewhat a Scotch reel.—2. Music for such a dance, or in its rhythm, which is triple, and moderate in movement. It is usually in the minor mode.

polt[1] (pōlt), *n.* [Prob. a var. of *palt*, *pelt*[1]. Cf. L. *pultare*, beat, Sw. *bulta*, beat.] A thump or blow.

If he know'd I'd got you the knife, he'd go nigh to give me a good *polt* of the head.
Miss Burney, Cecilia, ii. 9. (*Davies*.)

polt[2]†, *n.* An obsolete spelling of *poult*.

polt-foot, *n.* and *a.* See *poult-foot*.

poltront, poltronryt, *n.* Obsolete forms of *poltroon*, *poltroonery*.

poltroon (pol-trön′), *n.* and *a.* [Formerly *poltron*; < F. *poltron*, a coward, dastard, knave, rascal, also a sluggard, = Sp. *poltron* = Pg. *poltrão*, a coward, < It. *poltrone* (ML. *pultro(n-)*, a coward), < *poltro*, lazy, cowardly, as a noun a sluggard, coward, cf. *poltrare*, *poltrire*, lie in bed, be idle, < *poltro*, bed, couch, < OHG. *polstar*, *bolstar*, MHG. G. *bolster*, a pillow, cushion, bolster, quilt, = E. *bolster*: see *bolster*.] **I.** *n.* A lazy, idle fellow; a sluggard; a fellow without spirit or courage; a dastard; a coward.

K. *Hen.* Be patient, gentle Earl of Westmoreland.
Clif. Patience is for *poltroons*. *Shak.*, 3 Hen. VI., i. 1. 62.

Out, you *poltroon!*—you ha'n't the valour of a grasshopper. *Sheridan*, The Rivals, iv. 1.

=**Syn.** *Craven*, *Dastard*, etc. See *coward*.

II.† *a.* Base; cowardly; contemptible.

He is like to be mistaken who makes choice of a covetous man for a friend, or relieth upon the reed of narrow and *poltroon* friendship.
Sir T. Browne, Christ. Mor., i. § 36.

poltroonery (pol-trön′ẹ-ri), *n.* [Formerly *poltronry*; < F. *poltronnerie* (= Sp. *poltroneria* = Pg. It. *poltroneria*), cowardice, < *poltron*, a coward: see *poltroon*.] The character or nature of a poltroon; cowardice; baseness of mind; want of spirit.

You believed rather the tales you heard of our *poltroonery*, and impotence of body and mind.
B. Franklin, Autobiography, p. 294.

poltroonish (pol-trön′ish), *a.* [< *poltroon* + *-ish*[1].] Resembling a poltroon; cowardly.

polverin, polverine (pol′vẹ-rin), *n.* [< It. *polverino* (= Sp. *polvorin* = Pg. *polverino*), < *polvere*, dust, < L. *pulvis* (*pulver-*), dust, powder: see *powder*[1].] The calcined ashes of a plant, probably *Salsola Kali*, of the nature of pot- and pearl-ashes, brought from the Levant and Syria, and used in the manufacture of glass.

poly (pō′li), *n.* [Formerly also *poley*; = Sp. Pg. It. *polio*, < L. *polium*, *polion*, < Gr. πόλιον, an aromatic plant having glaucous leaves, perhaps *Teucrium Polium*, < πολιός, gray, white, akin to πελός or πελλός, dusky, L. *pullus*, dusky, and E. *fallow*[1], etc.: see *fallow*[1].] A species of germander, *Teucrium Polium*, an aromatic herb of southern Europe. The name is also used for some other plants of the genus *Teucrium*.—**Poly-mountain.** Same as *poly*; also, a British plant, *Calamintha Acinos*.

poly-. [L., etc., *poly-*, < Gr. πολυ-, combining form of πολύς, dial. πουλύς, πολλός, many, much, neut. πολύ, as adv. much, very, many times, often, long, etc.; = Goth. *filu* = AS. *fela*, E. obs. *feel*, much: see *feel*[2].] An element in many compounds of Greek origin or formation, meaning 'many' or 'much.' It is equivalent to *multi-* of Latin origin. It is sometimes, but rarely, used in composition with a word of non-Greek origin, as in *polygrooved*, *polypage*.

polyacanthid (pol″i-a-kan′thid), *a.* [< *polyacanth-ous* + *-id*[2].] Having pluriserial adambulacral spines, as a starfish: correlated with *monacanthid* and *diplacanthid*.

polyacanthous (pol″i-a-kan′thus), *a.* [< Gr. πολυάκανθος, having many thorns, used only as the name of a kind of thorn, < πολύς, many, + ἄκανθα, thorn, spine.] In *bot.*, having many thorns or spines. *Thomas*, Med. Dict.

polyacoustic (pol″i-ạ-kös′tik), *a.* and *n.* [= Sp. *policústico*, < Gr. πολύς, many, + ἀκουστικός, of or pertaining to hearing: see *acoustic*.] **I.** *a.* Multiplying or magnifying sound.

II. *n.* An instrument for multiplying or magnifying sounds.

polyacoustics (pol″i-a-kös′tiks), *n.* [Pl. of *polyacoustic* (see *-ics*).] The art or science of multiplying sounds.

polyact (pol′i-akt), *a.* [< Gr. πολύς, many, + ἀκτίς (ἀκτιν-), ray.] Having numerous rays: specifically said of sponge-spicules of the stellate kind.

polyactinal (pol-i-ak′ti-nạl), *a.* [< Gr. πολύς, many, + ἀκτίς (ἀκτιν-), a ray, + *-al*.] Many-rayed; multiradiate; in sponges, polyact.

polyad (pol′i-ad), *n.* [< Gr. πολύς, many, + term. -ας (-αδ-) as in τριάς (τριαδ-), triad: see *-ad*[1].] In *chem.*, an element whose valence or quantivalence is greater than two, as a triad, tetrad, hexad, etc.

polyadelph (pol′i-a-delf), *n.* [< Gr. πολυάδελφος, having many brothers, < πολύς, many, + ἀδελφός, brother.] In *bot.*, a plant having its stamens united in three or more bodies or bundles by the filaments.

Polyadelph.

Polyadelphia (pol″i-ạ-del′fi-ạ), *n. pl.* [NL.: see *polyadelph*.] In *bot.*, the eighteenth class of the Linnean system, in which the stamens are united by their filaments into three or more sets or brotherhoods.

polyadelphian (pol″i-ạ-del′fi-ạn), *a.* [< *Polyadelphia* + *-an*.] Same as *polyadelphous*.

polyadelphite (pol″i-ạ-del′fit), *n.* [< Gr. πολυάδελφος, having many brothers (see *polyadelph*), + *-ite*[2].] A massive brownish-yellow variety of iron garnet occurring in the zinc-mines in Sussex county, New Jersey.

polyadelphous (pol″i-ạ-del′fus), *a.* [= F. *polyadelphe* = Pg. *polyadelpho* = It. *poliadelfo*, < Gr. πολυάδελφος, having many brothers: see *polyadelph*.] In *bot.*, having the stamens united in three or more bundles or parcels, as in some species of *Hypericum*. Also *polyadelphian*.

polyadenia (pol″i-a-dē′ni-ạ), *n.* [NL., < Gr. πολύς, many, + ἀδήν, gland: see *adenia*.] Pseudoleucemia.

polyadenitis (pol-i-ad-e-nī′tis), *n.* [NL., < Gr. πολύς, many, + ἀδήν, gland, + *-itis*. Cf. *adenitis*.] Inflammation of numerous glands.

polyadenopathy (pol-i-ad-e-nop′ạ-thi), *n.* [< Gr. πολύς, many, + ἀδήν, gland, + πάθος, disease. Cf. *adenopathy*.] Disease of numerous glands.

polyadenous (pol-i-ad′e-nus), *a.* [< Gr. πολύς, many, + ἀδήν, gland.] In *bot.*, bearing many glands. *Thomas*, Med. Dict.

polyæmia, *n.* See *polyhemia*.

polyæsthesia, polyesthesia (pol″i-es-thē′si-ạ), *n.* [NL., < Gr. πολύς, many, + αἴσθησις, sensation.] The production, by the stimulation of a single point on the skin, of a sensation as if two or more points were stimulated: observed in tabes dorsualis. Also *polyæsthesis*, *polyesthesis*.

polyæsthetic, *a.* See *polyesthetic*.

Polyalthia (pol-i-al′thi-ạ), *n.* [NL. (Blume, 1828), so called with ref. to its supposed healing properties; < Gr. πολυαλθής, healing many diseases, < πολύς, many, + ἀλθαίνειν, heal (> ἀλθήεις, wholesome).] A genus of polypetalous shrubs or trees of the order *Anonaceæ* and tribe *Unoneæ*, characterized by six thick, flat, ovate or narrow petals, and numerous carpels each with only one or two ovules. The 40 species are natives of tropical Asia, tropical and southern Africa, and Australasia. They bear obliquely feather-veined alternate leaves, and solitary or clustered flowers, followed by globose or oblong one-seeded stalked berries. See *mast-tree*, 2.

polyandria (pol-i-an′dri-ạ), *n.* [NL.: see *polyandry*.] 1. Same as *polyandry*.—2. [*cap.*] [Used as a plural.] In *bot.*, according to the Linnean system, a class of hermaphrodite flowering plants having more than twenty hypogynous stamens of equal length, free from each other and from the pistils.

polyandrian (pol-i-an′dri-ạn), *a.* [< *polyandry* + *-an*.] Same as *polyandrous*.

polyandric (pol-i-an′drik), *a.* [= F. *polyandrique* = Pg. *polyandrico*; as *polyandr-y* + *-ic*.] Relating to or characterized by polyandry. Also *polyandrous*. *Westminster Rev.*, April, 1868, p. 410.

polyandrion (pol-i-an′dri-on), *n.*; pl. *polyandria* (-ạ). [< Gr. πολυάνδριον, a place where many assemble, neut. of πολυάνδριος, with many men, < πολύς, many, + ἀνήρ (ἀνδρ-), man.] In *Gr. antiq.* and *archæol.*, a monument or a burial inclosure provided by the state for a number of men, usually for those of its citizens who had fallen in a battle. The famous "Lion of Chæronea" which stood within the burial inclosure of the Thebans who died in the battle with Philip of Macedon, 338 B. C., was a monument of this class; and this was itself a close copy throughout of that recently excavated at Thespiæ, which is believed to have commemorated the Thespians who fell at Platæa, 479 B. C.

polyandrious (pol-i-an′dri-us), *a.* In *bot.*, same as *polyandrous*.

polyandrist (pol-i-an′drist), *n.* [< *polyandr-y* + *-ist*.] One who practises polyandry.

polyandrous (pol-i-an′drus), *a.* [< Gr. πολύανδρος, with many men, LGr. with many husbands, < πολύς, many, + ἀνήρ (ἀνδρ-), man, male (in mod. bot. stamen).] 1. In *bot.*: (*a*) Belonging to the Linnean class *Polyandria*. (*b*) Having the stamens indefinitely numerous, at least more than ten.—2. In *zoöl.*, having several male mates; polygamous, as a female animal.—3. In *sociology*, same as *polyandric*.

polyandry (pol-i-an′dri), *n.* [= F. *polyandrie* = Sp. *poliandria* = Pg. *polyandria* = It. *poliandria*, < LG. πολυανδρία, taken in sense of 'a condition of having many husbands' (in bot. stamens), found in sense of 'a condition of having many men, populousness,' < πολύανδρος, having many men: see *polyandrous*.] The state of having more husbands than one at the same time; plurality of husbands. Polyandry is believed to have had its origin in unfertile regions, in an endeavor to check the undue pressure of population on the means of subsistence. It formerly prevailed to some extent in Europe, and is now observed in Tibet, Ceylon, parts of India, among certain tribes in America and the islands of the Pacific, etc. It is sometimes limited to the marriage of the woman to two or more brothers.

In the one type, called by M'Lennan Nair *polyandry*, the woman remains with her own kin, but entertains at will such suitors as she pleases.
W. R. Smith, Kinship and Marriage, p. 122.

polyangular (pol-i-ang′gụ̈-lạ̈r), *a.* [< Gr. πολύς, many, + L. *angulus*, an angle: see *angular*.] Having many angles.

polyantheat, *n.* Same as *polianthea*.

Polyanthes (pol-i-an′thēz), *n.* See *Polianthes*.

polyanthous (pol-i-an′thus), *a.* [< NL. *polyanthus*, < Gr. πολύανθος, also πολυανθής, much-blossoming, having many flowers, < πολύς, many, + ἄνθος, a flower.] Bearing many flowers. *Thomas*, Med. Dict.

polyanthus, polyanthos (pol-i-an′thus, -thos), *n.* [NL., < Gr. πολύανθος, having many flowers: see *polyanthous*.] A garden variety of *Primula veris*, most nearly allied to the variety *elatior*, the oxlip, whose flowers are umbeled on a common peduncle several inches high. It is an old garden favorite, which has passed through countless subvarieties. Florists require that a good polyanthus should possess a strong scape, a well-filled truss, a corolla with a short tube, a bright-yellow eye, and a deep, rich brown-crimson limb, bordered with a well-defined yellow edging. See *primrose*.—**Polyanthus Narcissus.** See *Narcissus*.

polyarchist (pol′i-är-kist), *n.* [< *polyarch-y* + *-ist*.] One who favors polyarchy.

Plato . . . was no *polyarchist*, but a monarchist, an assertor of one supreme God.
Cudworth, Intellectual System, p. 403.

polyarchy (pol′i-är-ki), *n.* [= F. *polyarchie* = Sp. *poliarquia* = Pg. *polyarchia* = It. *poliarchia*, < Gr. πολυαρχία, the government of many, < πολύς, many, + ἄρχειν, rule.] A government by many, whether by a privileged class (aristocracy) or by the people at large (democracy); any government by several rulers.

Yet he [Aristotle] absolutely denied πολυκοιρανίην, and πολυαρχίαν, a *polyarchy* or mundane aristocracy: that is, a multiplicity of first principles and independent deities. *Cudworth*, Intellectual System, II. 83.

polyarsenite (pol-i-är'se-nīt), *n.* [< Gr. πολύς, many, + E. *arsen(ic)* + *-ite*².] In *mineral.*, same as *sarkinite*.

polyarthritis (pol″i-är-thrī'tis), *n.* [NL., < Gr. πολύς, many, + NL. *arthritis*, q. v.] Arthritis involving a number of joints.

polyarthrous (pol-i-är'thrus), *a.* [< Gr. πολύς, many, + ἄρθρον, a joint.] Having many joints or jointed parts; multiarticulate.

polyarticular (pol″i-är-tik'ū-lär), *a.* [< Gr. πολύς, many, + L. *articulus*, a joint: see *articular*.] Pertaining to a number of joints: as, *polyarticular* rheumatism.

polyatomic (pol″i-a-tom'ik), *a.* [= F. *polyatomique*; < Gr. πολύς, many, + ἄτομον, atom: see *atom*, *atomic*.] In *chem.*, noting elements or radicals which have an equivalency greater than two; also, noting compounds having three or more hydroxyl groups, in which hydrogen is easily replaceable by other elements or radicals without otherwise changing the structure of the original compound: thus, glycerol is a *polyatomic* alcohol.

polyautography (pol″i-â-tog'ra-fi), *n.* [< Gr. πολύς, many, + αὐτός, self, + -γραφία, < γράφειν, write. Cf. *autography*.] The act of multiplying copies of one's own handwriting or of manuscripts, as by printing from stone: a form of lithography.

polyaxial (pol-i-ak'si-al), *a.* [< Gr. πολύς, many, + L. *axis*, axis, + *-ial*.] Having several axes.

polyaxon (pol-i-ak'son), *a.* and *n.* [NL., < Gr. πολύς, many, + ἄξων, axis.] I. *a.* Having several or many (more than six) axes of growth, as a sponge-spicule; polyaxial, as the form of spicule known as a *sterraster*.

II. *n.* A polyaxial sponge-spicule.

polybasic (pol-i-bā'sik), *a.* [= F. *polybasique*; < Gr. πολύς, many, + βάσις, base: see *base*², *basic*.] In *chem.*, capable of combining with more than two univalent bases: as, *polybasic* acids or radicals.

polybasicity (pol″i-bā-sis'i-ti), *n.* [< *polybasic* + *-ity*.] The character or property of being polybasic.

polybasite (pō-lib'a-sīt), *n.* [= F. *polybasite*; < Gr. πολύς, many, + βάσις, base, + *-ite*².] An iron-black ore of silver, consisting of silver, sulphur, and antimony, with some copper and arsenic.

Polybia (pō-lib'i-ä), *n.* [NL. (St. Fargean, 1836), < Gr. πολύβιος, with much life, < πολύς, much, + βίος, life.] A genus of hymenopterous insects of the family *Vespidæ*, or wasps, resembling *Polistes* closely, but differing in the shape of the abdomen. The species are all Central or South American except *P. flavitarsis*, which is found in California. *P. palmarum* is the palm-wasp, so called because it makes its nests on palms.

Polyborinæ (pol″i-bō-rī'nē), *n. pl.* [NL., < *Polyborus* + *-inæ*.] A subfamily of *Falconidæ*, typified by the genus *Polyborus*, and including the genera *Phalcobænus*, *Senex*, *Milvago*, *Ibycter*, and *Daptrius*; the caracaras, or American vulture-hawks. There is a coracoclavicular articulation, a centric nasal tubercle, an anterior palatal keel, and a superorbital shield, in which respects the *Polyborinæ* resemble falcons; but the external aspect is rather that of vultures. The bill is toothless, and the sternum is single-notched. See cuts under *caracara* and *Ibycter*.

polyborine (pol'i-bō-rin), *a.* Of or pertaining to the *Polyborinæ*.

Polyborus (pō-lib'ō-rus), *n.* [NL. (Vieillot, 1816), < Gr. πολυβόρος, much-devouring, < πολύς, much, + βορός, gluttonous.] The typical genus of the subfamily *Polyborinæ*; the caracaras proper. There are several species, of temperate and tropical America, as *P. cheriway*, *P. auduboni*, and *P. lutosus*. See cut under *caracara*.

polybrachia (pol-i-brā'ki-ä), *n.* [NL., < Gr. πολύς, many, + L. *brachium*, properly *bracchium*, the arm: see *brachium*.] In *teratol.*, the presence of supernumerary arms.

polybrachus (pō-lib'ra-kus), *n.*; pl. *polybrachi* (-kī). [NL.: see *polybrachia*.] In *teratol.*, a monster with supernumerary arms.

polybranch (pol'i-brangk), *a.* and *n.* [< Gr. πολύς, many, + βράγχια, gills.] I. *a.* Having many gills or numerous branchiæ, as a mollusk or crustacean; of or pertaining to the *Polybranchia* or *Polybranchiata*. Also *polybranchiate*.

II. *n.* A polybranch mollusk or crustacean.

Polybranchia (pol-i-brang'ki-ä), *n. pl.* [NL.: see *polybranch*.] 1. In J. E. Gray's classification (1821), one of two orders (the other being *Pygobranchia*) of nudibranchiate gastropods, having lamellar or plumose gills on the upper surface of the mantle, and containing the families *Tritoniadæ*, *Scyllæidæ*, and *Tethyadæ*.—2. In later systems, a suborder or superfamily comprising the same forms, but subdivided among numerous families: same as *Polybranchiata*, 1.

polybranchian (pol-i-brang'ki-an), *a.* and *n.* Same as *polybranch*.

Polybranchiata (pol-i-brang-ki-ā'tạ), *n. pl.* [NL.: see *polybranchiate*.] 1. A suborder or superfamily of nudibranchiate gastropods, characterized by the development of dorsal gill-like appendages variously distributed, but never disposed in a rosette round the anus. It comprised numerous species, classified by modern malacologists among 12 to 15 families. Also called *Polybranchia*. 2. In De Blainville's classification (1825), one of five orders of his second section of *Paracephalophora monoica symmetrica*, composed of the two families *Tetracerata* and *Dicerata*.

polybranchiate (pol-i-brang'ki-āt), *a.* [< NL. *polybranchiatus*, < Gr. πολύς, many, + βράγχια, gills.] Same as *polybranch*.

polycarpellary (pol-i-kär'pe-lā-ri), *a.* [< Gr. πολύς, many, + NL. *carpellum*, carpel: see *carpel*, *carpellary*.] In *bot.*, composed of two or many carpels. Compare *monocarpellary*.

polycarpic (pol-i-kär'pik), *a.* [< *polycarp-ous* + *-ic*.] In *bot.*, producing fruit many times or indefinitely: applied by De Candolle to perennial herbs. Compare *monocarpous* (*a*).

Polycarpon (pol-i-kär'pon), *n.* [NL. (Linnæus, 1737), so called in allusion to the many little fruits (cf. L. *polycarpon*; < Gr. πολύκαρπον, a plant, a kind of cratægus), < πολύκαρπος, with much fruit, fruitful: see *polycarpous*.] A genus of diffuse polypetalous herbs of the order *Caryophylleæ*, type of the tribe *Polycarpeæ*, and characterized by the five keeled and entire sepals, the five small entire hyaline petals, the three to five stamens, and the one-celled ovary with many ovules, crowned with a short three-cleft style, and becoming a small three-valved capsule. There are 6 species, generally diffused throughout temperate and warmer regions. They are slender annuals, bearing opposite ovate or oblong flat leaves, dry and thin bracts and stipules, and very numerous densely compacted little whitish flowers in much-branched cymes. From the great quantity of its seed, the European species, *P. tetraphyllum*, is called *allseed*.

polycarpous (pol-i-kär'pus), *a.* [< Gr. πολύκαρπος, with much fruit, fruitful, < πολύς, many, + καρπός, fruit.] In *bot.*, having a gynœcium composed of two or more distinct ovaries or carpels. Compare *monocarpous*, and cuts under *carpel* and *gynobase*.

polycellular (pol-i-sel'ū-lär), *a.* [< Gr. πολύς, many, + NL. *cellula*, a cell: see *cellular*.] In *bot.*, containing or composed of many cells.

polycentric (pol-i-sen'trik), *a.* [< Gr. πολύς, many, + κέντρον, point: see *center*¹.] Having several centers or nucleal points.

But a complexity is introduced as soon as the sap-vacuoles appear, in many cases making the cell not monocentric but *polycentric*. *H. Marshall Ward*, Nature, XXXV. 301.

Polycentridæ (pol-i-sen'tri-dē), *n. pl.* [NL., < *Polycentrus* + *-idæ*.] A family of acanthopterygian fishes, typified by the genus *Polycentrus*. They have a symmetrical compressed body without lateral line, compressed head with very projectile jaws, a long dorsal and anal fin with many spines, and perfect ventrals. The family contains a few South American fresh-water fishes, somewhat related to the centrarchoids of North America. In Günther's classification it was referred to the *Acanthopterygii perciformes*.

Polycentrus (pol-i-sen'trus), *n.* [NL. (Müller and Troschel, 1848), < Gr. πολύς, many, + κέντρον, point: see *center*¹.] The typical genus of *Polycentridæ*: so called from the many spines, especially of the anal fin.

polycephalist† (pol-i-sef'a-list), *n.* [< Gr. πολυκέφαλος, having many heads (see *polycephalous*), + *-ist*.] One who has or acknowledges many heads or superiors. *Bp. Gauden*, Tears of the Church, p. 541. (*Davies.*)

polycephalous (pol-i-sef'a-lus), *a.* [< Gr. πολυκέφαλος, having many heads, many-headed, < πολύς, many, + κεφαλή, head.] In *bot.*, bearing or consisting of many heads.

Polycera (pō-lis'e-rä), *n.* [NL., < Gr. πολύκερως, many-horned, < πολύς, many, + κέρας, horn.]

Polycera quadrilineata. (Line shows natural size.)

The typical genus of *Polyceridæ*. A true representative species is *P. quadrilineata* of Europe. *P. lessoni* is a beautiful sea-slug of a pale flesh-color marked with green and yellow, found in the North Atlantic ocean, referred by some to a distinct genus *Palio*.

Polyceridæ (pol-i-ser'i-dē), *n. pl.* [NL., < *Polycera* + *-idæ*.] A family of phanerobranchiate doridoid gastropods having a simple pharyngeal bulb, typified by the genus *Polycera*. The branchiæ are not retractile, the labial armature is variable, and the radula is narrow. The species are numerous, and have been grouped by some under three or more subfamilies, elevated by others to family rank.

Polychæta (pol-i-kē'tä), *n. pl.* [NL., neut. pl. of *polychætus*: see *polychætous*.] An order or other group of chætopodous annelids, having the body segmented, the false feet or parapodia with many chætæ, setæ, or bristles (whence the name), and the head tentaculate; the polychætous worms. It is a very large group, of numerous families, including a majority of the annelids, as all the sedentary or tubicolous and the errant marine worms. It is contrasted with the order *Oligochæta*. See cuts under *elytrum*, *Polynoë*, *Protula*, *cerebral*, *esophageal*, *præstomium*, and *pygidium*.

polychæte (pol'i-kēt), *a.* Same as *polychætous*.

polychætous (pol-i-kē'tus), *a.* [< NL. *polychætus*, < Gr. πολυχαίτης, with much hair, < πολύς, many, + χαίτη, long hair, mane: see *chæta*.] Having numerous chætæ, setæ, or bristles of the parapodia, as an annelid; belonging to the *Polychæta*. See cut under *elytrum*.

Forms of *Polychætous* Annelidan larvæ which are called Telotrocha. *Huxley*, Anat. Invert., p. 164.

polychœrany†, *n.* An erroneous form of *polycœrany*.

polycholia (pol-i-kō'li-ä), *n.* Excessive secretion of bile.

polychord (pol'i-kôrd), *a.* and *n.* [= Pg. *polychordo*; < Gr. πολύχορδος, many-stringed, < πολύς, many, + χορδή, string, chord.] I. *a.* Having many chords or strings.

II. *n.* A musical instrument invented by F. Hillmer in 1799, but never generally used. It was shaped like a bass viol with a movable fingerboard, and had ten gut strings. It was played either with a bow, or by the fingers, like a lute.

polychorion (pol-i-kō'ri-on), *n.* [< Gr. πολύς, many, + χόριον, membrane.] In *bot.*, a polycarpous fruit, like that of *Ranunculus*. *Treasury of Botany*.

polychorionic (pol-i-kō-ri-on'ik), *a.* [< *polychorion* + *-ic*.] Having the character of a polychorion.

polychotomous (pol-i-kot'ō-mus), *a.* [< *polychotom-y* + *-ous*.] Divided into more than two groups or series; made or done on the principle of polychotomy, as a classification.

polychotomy (pol-i-kot'ō-mi), *n.* [< Gr. πολύχοος, πολυχόος, manifold, + -τομία, < τέμνειν, ταμεῖν, cut.] In *zoöl.*, division of a given group of animals into more than two other groups or series: correlated with *dichotomy*. *Amer. Nat.*, XXI. 915.

polychrest† (pol'i-krest), *n.* [= F. *polychreste*, = Pg. *polycresto*, < Gr. πολύχρηστος, very useful, < πολύς, much, + χρηστός, useful, < χρῆσθαι, use: see *chrestomathy*.] A medicine that serves for many uses, or that cures many diseases.—**Polychrest salt**, in *old chem.*, potassic sulphate; also, sodiopotassic tartrate.

polychrestic (pol-i-kres'tik), *a.* [< *polychrest-y* + *-ic*.] Admitting of use in various ways, as a drug, or in various connections (as in naming different things), as a word.

polychresty (pol'i-kres-ti), *n.* [< Gr. πολυχρηστία, great usefulness, < πολυχρηστός, very useful: see *polychrest*.] The character of being polychrestic; the use of polychrestic words. *Buck's Handbook of Med. Sciences*, VIII. 518.

polychroic (pol-i-krō'ik), *a.* Same as *pleochroic*.

Optical properties of the *polychroic* aureolas present in certain minerals, by M. A. Michel Lévy. *Nature*, XLI. 215.

polychroism (pol'i-krō-izm), *n.* [= F. *polychroïsme*; < Gr. πολύχροος, many-colored, < πολύς, many, + χροιά, color.] Same as *pleochroism*.

polychroite (pol-i-krō'īt), *n.* [= F. *polychroïte*, < Gr. πολύχροος, many-colored (see *polychroism*), + *-ite*².] The coloring matter of saffron: so named in consequence of the variety of colors which it exhibits when acted upon by various reagents.

polychromatic (pol″i-krō-mat'ik), *a.* [< Gr. πολυχρώματος, many-colored (see *polychrome*), + *-ic*. Cf. *chromatic*.] 1. Many-colored: as, *polychromatic* light.—2. In *mineral.*, exhibiting a play of colors.—**Polychromatic acid.** See *polychromic acid*, under *polychromic*.—**Polychromatic process**, a carbon photographic process invented by Vidal, analogous to chromolithography in method and object. The first step is to make from the subject as many negatives as there are colors to be represented, each of these being appropriated for a particular tint, while all parts otherwise tinted in the original are masked on the negative with an opaque pigment. Gelatin pictures of the required tints are then prepared from the negatives, and superimposed in turn by a system of registration over a print of the whole subject previously made with a neutral ground, thus completing the polychromatic picture. This process gives strikingly naturalistic results in the reproduction of goldsmiths' work, enamels, mosaics, etc.

polychrome (pol'i-krōm), *a.* and *n.* [= F. *polychrome;* < Gr. πολύχρωμος, also πολυχρώματος, many-colored, < πολύς, many, + χρῶμα (χρωματ-), color: see *chrome.*] **I.** *a.* Having or tinted with several or many colors; executed in the manner of polychromy: as, *polychrome* sculpture; *polychrome* architecture.

A large panorama of Pergamon, . . . exhibited in conjunction with a full-size plastic restoration and *polychrome* reconstruction of the eastern front of the Olympian temple. *Tenth Report of the Archæol. Institute of America,* [1888–9, p. 55.

Polychrome printing, the art or process of printing in several colors at the same time.

II. *n.* A fluorescent substance ($C_{21}H_{24}O_{13}$), forming prismatic crystals, odorless, with a bitter taste and slight acid reaction. It is obtained from the bark of the horse-chestnut and from quassia-wood, etc. A solution of polychrome appears colorless by transmitted light, but blue by reflected light. Acids destroy the fluorescence of the liquid; alkalis increase it.

polychromic (pol-i-krō'mik), *a.* [< *polychrome* + *-ic.*] Same as *polychromatic.*—**Polychromic acid** (also called *aloetic acid*), an acid produced by the action of nitric acid upon aloes.

polychromy (pol'i-krō-mi), *n.* [= F. *polychromie,* < Gr. as if *πολυχρωμία, < πολύχρωμος, many-colored: see *polychrome.*] Decoration or execution in many colors; specifically, the practice of coloring more or less completely statues and the exteriors and interiors of buildings. This practice dates from the highest antiquity, and reached its greatest artistic perfection in Greece, where it was consistently applied to all sculpture and architecture. In archaic examples the coloring was the most complete and strong, and in the case of sculpture was to a great extent conventional—men's flesh, for instance, being colored deep-brown or red, and women's white or yellowish. In the architecture of the best time, while surfaces of considerable extent were still brilliantly colored, as in red or blue, the chief part of many features, as of columns, was left in the natural color of the marble, or perhaps merely slightly tinted, and discreetly set off with meanders or other ornaments in gilding or strong color. Throughout Europe, during the twelfth and thirteenth centuries, architectural polychromy was employed with admirable effect.

Polychrus (pol'i-krus), *n.* [NL. (Cuvier, 1817), < Gr. πολύς, many, + χρώς, color of the skin, complexion.] **1.** A leading genus of lizards of the family *Iguanidæ*, having smooth scales, a small dewlap, no dorsal crest, and the squarish head covered with numerous plates: so called from its versicoloration. *P. marmoratus* inhabits Central America and portions of South America.—**2.** [*l. c.*] A member of this genus: as, the marbled *polychrus.*

polycladous (pol-i-klā'dus), *a.* [< Gr. πολύκλαδος, with many boughs and branches, < πολύς, many, + κλάδος, a young slip or shoot.] In *bot.*, much-branched.

polyclady (pol'i-klā-di), *n.* [< Gr. πολύκλαδος, with many boughs and branches: see *polycladous.*] In *bot.*, the production of a number of branches where there is normally but one. See *plica*, 2.

Polycletan (pol-i-klē'tan), *a.* [< L. *Polycletus, Polyclitus,* < Gr. Πολύκλειτος, Polycletus (see def.), + *-an.*] Pertaining to the great Greek sculptor Polycletus of Argos and Sicyon, a contemporary and emulator of Phidias, to the school of art inspired by him, or to the sculptural canon of perfect human proportions which he established (see *doryphorus*).

Polycletan School of Sculpture.—Amazon, in the Museum of Berlin.

polyclinic, *n.* See *policlinic.*

polycoccous (pol-i-kok'us), *a.* [NL., < Gr. πολύς, many, + κόκκος, berry: see *coccus.*] In *bot.*, having several cocci: said of a dry pericarp whose lobes separate at maturity.

Polycœlia[1] (pol-i-sē'li-ä), *n.* [NL., fem. sing., < Gr. πολύς, many, + κοιλία, cavity: see *cœlia.*] A genus of fossil rugose corals of the family *Stauridæ*, from the Permian formation.

Polycœlia[2] (pol-i-sē'li-ä), *n. pl.* [NL., < Gr. πολύς, many, + κοιλία, cavity.] Animals whose encephalocœle is segmented into several cœliæ, as all skulled vertebrates. They have the neuron partly preaxial, the axon vertebrated, and the heart with more than a single cavity. *Wilder,* Amer. Nat., XXI. 914.

polycœlian (pol-i-sē'li-an), *a.* [< *Polycœlia*[2] + *-an.*] Having several cœliæ; of or pertaining to the *Polycœlia.*

polycœrany† (pol-i-sē'ra-ni), *n.* [Also *polycœranie;* < Gr. (Ionic) πολυκοιρανίη, rule of many, < πολύς, many, + κοίρανος, a ruler.] A government by many rulers, lords, or princes. [Rare.]

The world would be a *polycœrany* or aristocracy of Gods. *Cudworth,* Intellectual System, p. 411.

polyconic (pol-i-kon'ik), *a.* [= F. *polyconique,* < Gr. πολύς, many, + κῶνος, a cone: see *cone, conic.*] Pertaining to or based upon many cones.—**Polyconic map-projection.** See *projection.*

polycoria (pol-i-kō'ri-ä), *n.* [NL., < Gr. πολύς, many, + κόρη, the pupil of the eye.] The presence of more than one pupil in an eye.

Polycotylea (pol-i-kot-i-lē'ä), *n. pl.* [NL., < Gr. πολύς, many, + κοτύλη, a vessel, cup: see *cotyle*, 2.] A section of octopod cephalopods characterized by two or three rows of suckers on each arm, comprising the *Octopodidæ, Tremoctopodidæ,* and *Argonautidæ:* contrasted with *Monocotylea.*

polycotyledon (pol-i-kot-i-lē'don), *n.* [NL., < Gr. πολύς, many, + κοτυληδών, cavity: see *cotyledon.*] A plant whose embryo has a whorl of more than two cotyledons or seed-leaves. This is normally the case with the pines and most *Coniferæ.* It is true in appearance in a few aberrant dicotyledons, as the genus *Amsinckia* of the *Boragineæ,* whose cotyledons are two-parted, and one species of *Lepidium,* whose cotyledons are three-parted. See cut under *cotyledon.*

polycotyledonary (pol-i-kot-i-lē'don-ā-ri), *a.* [< *polycotyledon* + *-ary*[1].] In *zoöl.*, having many cotyledons, or tufts of fetal villi, as the chorion or placenta of a mammal.

polycotyledonous (pol-i-kot-i-lē'don-us), *a.* [< *polycotyledon* + *-ous.*] Possessing more than two cotyledons, as an embryo; producing an embryo with more than two cotyledons, as a plant.

polycotyledony (pol-i-kot-i-lē'don-i), *n.* [< *polycotyledon* + *-y*[3].] In *bot.*, an aberrant increase in the number of cotyledons, as in *Cola acuminata*, where they vary from two to five.

polycracy (pō-lik'rā-si), *n.* [< Gr. πολύς, many, + -κρατία, < κρατεῖν, rule.] Government by many rulers; polyarchy.

polycrase (pol'i-krāz), *n.* [< Gr. πολύς, many, + κρᾶσις, a mixing: see *crasis.*] A rare titanoniobate of uranium, the metals of the yttrium group, and other bases: it is found in Norway, and also in North Carolina.

polycrotic (pol-i-krot'ik), *a.* [< Gr. πολύς, many, + κρότος, a rattling noise, beat, clash: see *dicrotic.*] Having several beats; having several secondary waves: said of some pulses.

Polyctenes (pō-lik'te-nēz), *n.* [NL. (Westwood; Giglioli, 1864), < Gr. πολύς, many, + κτείς (κτεν-), a comb.] A genus of true lice, typical of the family *Polyctenidæ.* The head is armed beneath with rows of long flat spines, whence the name. The species are parasites of bats in Jamaica and China, and doubtless elsewhere. This remarkable form has been of disputed location, being by some referred to the pupiparous dipterous insects.

Polyctenidæ (pol-ik-ten'i-dē), *n. pl.* [NL., < *Polyctenes* + *-idæ.*] A family of true lice, or *Hemiptera parasitica*, represented by the genus *Polyctenes.* *Westwood*, 1874.

polycyclic (pol-i-sik'lik), *a.* [< Gr. πολύκυκλος, with many circles, < πολύς, many, + κύκλος, a ring, circle.] Having many rounds, turns, or whorls, as a shell.

polycystic (pol-i-sis'tik), *a.* [< Gr. πολύς, many, + κύστις, a bag: see *cyst.*] Having many cysts or sacs, as a tumor.

Polycystida (pol-i-sis'ti-dä), *n. pl.* [NL., < Gr. πολύς, many, + κύστις, bag (see *cyst*), + *-ida.*] A family of *Nassellaria.* The skeleton is an irregular fenestrated shell, composed of several unequal chambers, piled usually irregularly (rarely in definite order varying from that of the *Cyrtidea*) round a primary capitulum (derivable from the twin shell of the *Sphyroida*), with or without spicules.

polycystidan (pol-i-sis'ti-dan), *a.* and *n.* **I.** *a.* Of or pertaining to the *Polycystida.*

II. *n.* A member of the *Polycystida.*

Polycystina (pol″i-sis-ti'nä), *n. pl.* [NL., < Gr. πολύς, many, + κύστις, bag (see *cyst*), + *-ina*[2].] Ehrenberg's name (given by him in the form *Polycistina*) of all those radiolarians which were known to him: loosely synonymous with *Radiolaria.*

polycystine (pol-i-sis'tin), *a.* and *n.* **I.** *a.* Of or pertaining to the *Polycystina:* now noting one of the divisions of *Radiolaria.*

II. *n.* A member of the *Polycystina.*

polycythemia (pol″i-si-thē'mi-ä), *n.* [NL. *polycythæmia*, < Gr. πολύς, many, + κύτος, a hollow (cell), + αἷμα, blood.] Excess of red corpuscles in the blood.

Polycyttaria (pol″i-si-tā'ri-ä), *n. pl.* [NL., < Gr. πολύς, many, + κύτταρος, a cell, < κύτος, a hollow.] A family or other group of *Radiolaria*, containing compound or colonial forms having many central capsules connected by extracapsular protoplasm; the polycyttarian radiolarians. The capsules are multinuclear, multiplying by fission, and the skeleton is spherical and fenestrated or composed of loose spicules, or absent. Leading forms are *Collosphæra, Sphærozoum,* and *Collozoum.* Also called *Collozoa.*

polycyttarian (pol″i-si-tā'ri-an), *a.* and *n.* [< Gr. πολύς, many, + κύτταρος, a cell, + *-ian.*] **I.** *a.* Having several central capsules; pluricapsular, as a radiolarian; of or pertaining to the *Polycyttaria.*

II. *n.* A member of the *Polycyttaria.*

polydactyl, polydactyle (pol-i-dak'til), *a.* and *n.* [< Gr. πολυδάκτυλος, many-toed, < πολύς, many, + δάκτυλος, a finger, a toe: see *dactyl.*] **I.** *a.* Having many digits, whether fingers or toes; exhibiting or characterized by polydactylism.

II. *n.* A polydactyl animal.

polydactylism (pol-i-dak'ti-lizm), *n.* [= F. *polydactylisme;* as *polydactyl* + *-ism.*] The condition of having many digits—that is, more than the normal number of fingers or toes; the state of being polydactyl.

Polydactylism of Hand.

polydactylous (pol-i-dak'ti-lus), *a.* Same as *polydactyl.*

polydactyly (pol-i-dak'ti-li), *n.* [< *polydactyl* + *-y*[3].] Same as *polydactylism.*

polydelphous (pol-i-del'fus), *a.* An improper form of *polyadelphous.*

polydimensional (pol″i-di-men'shon-al), *a.* [< Gr. πολύς, many, + E. *dimension* + *-al.*] Of more than three dimensions. *Nature*, XXX. 24.

polydipsia (pol-i-dip'si-ä), *n.* [NL., < Gr. as if *πολυδιψία, great thirst, < πολυδίψιος, very thirsty, πολύδιψος, making very thirsty, < πολύς, much, + δίψα, thirst.] In *pathol.*, excessive thirst. It is usually accompanied by hydruria.

polydromic (pol-i-drom'ik), *a.* Same as *polytropic.*

polydymite (pō-lid'i-mīt), *n.* A sulphid of nickel, occurring in isometric octahedrons and in massive forms, of a light-gray color and brilliant metallic luster. A ferriferous variety from Ontario carries a small amount of platinum.

polyedral, polyedron, etc. Same as *polyhedral*, etc.

polyembryonate (pol-i-em'bri-ō-nāt), *a.* [As *polyembryon-y* + *-ate*[1].] In *bot.*, pertaining to polyembryony; consisting of or having several embryos.

polyembryonic (pol-i-em-bri-on'ik), *a.* [As *polyembryon-y* + *-ic.*] Same as *polyembryonate.*

polyembryony (pol-i-em'bri-ō-ni), *n.* [< Gr. πολύς, many, + ἔμβρυον, an embryo: see *embryo.*] In *bot.*, the production or existence of two or more embryos in one seed—a phenomenon occurring, sometimes regularly and sometimes abnormally, in the development of the ovules of flowering plants. In angiospermous plants several germinal masses usually occur in the unfertilized embryo-sac, but in most cases only one of these is impregnated, and, although occasionally more than one commence the course of development, as in the *Orchideæ*, generally all but one become subsequently obliterated. In the orange, however, this is not the case, and its ripe seeds are met with containing more than one embryo.

polyemia, *n.* See *polyhemia.*

polyergic (pol-i-ėr'jik), *a.* [< Gr. πολύεργος, much-working, < πολύς, much, + ἔργον, work.] Acting, or endowed with the power of acting, in many ways.

Polyergus (pol-i-ėr′gus), *n.* [NL. (Latreille, 1802), < Gr. πολύεργος, much-working, < πολύς, much, + ἔργον, work.] A genus of *Formicidæ*, having the mandibles almost cylindrical, curved, very narrow, and acute at the tip, ocelli present, and the wings of the female with only one discoidal cell; the Amazon-ants. Two species are found in the United States, but most are tropical or subtropical. *P. rufescens* is a slave-making ant which has lost the building instinct and shows no care for its young, and in which the mandibles have lost their teeth — all as a result of their entire dependence upon slaves.

polyesthesia, *n.* See *polyæsthesia*.

polyesthesis (pol″i-es-thē′sis), *n.* Same as *polyæsthesia*.

polyesthetic, polyæsthetic (pol″i-es-thet′ik), *a.* [< *polyæsthesia* (-*thet*-) + -*ic* (cf. *esthetic*).] Of or pertaining to polyæsthesia.

polyethnic (pol-i-eth′nik), *a.* [< Gr. πολύς, many, + ἔθνος, a nation, people.] Inhabited by or containing many races or nationalities.

polyfoil (pol′i-foil), *n.* and *a.* [< Gr. πολύς, many, + E. *foil*[1]. Cf. *multifoil* and *polyphyllous*.] **I.** *n.* In *arch.*, an opening or ornament consisting of several combined foliations; specifically, a combination of more than five foils; a multifoil.

II. *a.* Consisting or composed of, or decorated with, more than five foils or foliations: as, a *polyfoil* arch.—**Polyfoil arch**, an arch the head of which is divided into a number of foils or foliations.

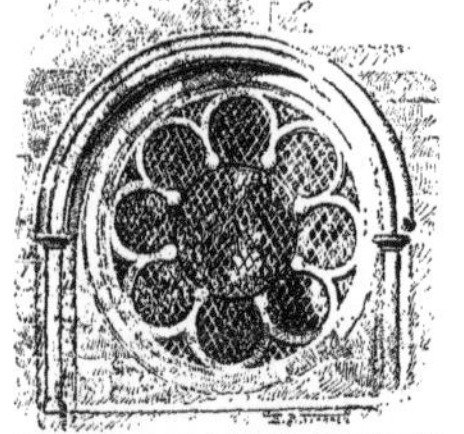

Polyfoil Window.—Hereford Cathedral, England; 13th century.

Polyfoil Arch.—Main Portal of Lichfield Cathedral, England.

Such arches occur especially in medieval architecture later than the time of highest perfection.

Polygala (pǭ-lig′a-lä̤), *n.* [NL. (Malpighi, 1675), < L. *polygala*, < Gr. πολύγαλον, milkwort, < πολύς, much, + γάλα, milk.] **1.** A genus of herbaceous plants, the milkworts, type of the order *Polygaleæ*, characterized by the great enlargement of the two petaloid inner sepals of its irregular calyx, and by its eight anthers, its two-celled compressed roundish capsule, and its three small petals united into a tube, and often augmented by a lobed crest at the top. There are about 260 species, natives of temperate and warm regions, widely prevalent except in Australia. They are small herbs or sometimes shrubby plants, usually with alternate leaves, and terminal spikes of small or showy flowers of red, yellow, green, white, and other colors. Several cultivated purple-flowered species from the Cape of Good Hope are evergreen shrubs reaching 9 feet in height. *P. lutea* of the southern United States is known locally as *bachelor's-buttons*. *P. paucifolia*, another handsome species, is the fringed polygala or flowering wintergreen of the United States; this and *P. polygama* of the Atlantic States are remarkable for their two kinds of flowers, having crimson or purple open flowers above ground, and also abundant white or green unexpanding but fertile subterranean flowers on slender white branches. The root of *P. Senega* is a stimulating expectorant and diuretic, and in large doses cathartic and emetic. It is called *senega* in medicine. (See *senega-root*.) *P. thesioides* is the chinchin of Chili, a powerful diuretic, and *P. venenosa*, the katu-tutum of Java, is poisonous to the touch. Many species are claimed as remedies against snake-bites, as *P. sanguinea* and *P. purpurea*, common reddish-flowered plants of the United States, and others in the West Indies, Cape Colony, and the Himalayas. For *P. vulgaris*, also sometimes called *procession-flower* or *passion-flower*, see *milkwort*, *cross-flower*, *gang-flower*, and *rogation-flower*.

2. [*l. c.*] A plant of this genus.

Polygalaceæ (pol″i-gā̤-lā′sē̤-ē), *n. pl.* [NL. (Lindley, 1835), < *Polygala* + -*aceæ*.] Same as *Polygaleæ*.

polygalaceous (pol″i-gā̤-lā′shius), *a.* [< *Polygalaceæ* + -*ous*.] Of or pertaining to the *Polygaleæ*.

Polygaleæ (pol-i-gā′lē̤-ē), *n. pl.* [NL. (Jussieu, 1809), < *Polygala* + -*eæ*.] An order of polypetalous plants, unlike the others in the cohort *Polygalinæ* in its irregular flowers, and characterized by its three or five petals, usually eight monadelphous stamens, straight embryo in fleshy albumen, and five sepals, of which the two inner are larger, wing-like, and petaloid. The fruit is either a capsule or a dry or fleshy indehiscent fruit. The order is without close affinity, but often shows in its keeled flowers a superficial resemblance to the *Leguminosæ* or bean family. It includes about 470 species, widely dispersed throughout temperate and warm climates, belonging to 15 genera, of which *Polygala* is the type. They are herbs or undershrubs, rarely becoming small trees, erect or sometimes twining or climbing, with usually entire alternate leaves, and solitary, spiked, or racemed flowers.

Polygalinæ (pol″i-gā̤-lī′nē), *n. pl.* [NL. (Bentham and Hooker, 1862), < *Polygala* + -*inæ*.] A cohort of polypetalous plants of the series *Thalamifloræ*, characterized by an ovary of two cells or carpels, many horizontal ovules or a single pendulous one, fleshy albumen, and absence of stipules. It includes 3 orders, of which the *Pittosporum* and *Tremandra* families are small groups of Australian shrubs, while the *Polygala* family (the type) is of nearly universal distribution.

polygaline (pǭ-lig′a̤-lin), *n.* [= F. *polygaline*; as *Polygala* + -*ine*[2].] A substance obtained from *Polygala Senega*, apparently identical with *saponin*. Also called *polygalic acid* and *senegin*.

polygam (pol′i-gam), *n.* [< *Polygam-ia*.] A plant of the Linnean class *Polygamia*.

Polygamia (pol-i-gā′mi-ä̤), *n. pl.* [NL., < Gr. πολύγαμος, polygamous: see *polygamous*.] In the Linnean system of classification, a class of plants bearing both hermaphrodite flowers and those with the sexes separated, the different flowers being scattered either on the same plant or on two or three distinct individuals.

polygamian (pol-i-gā′mi-a̤n), *a.* [< *Polygamia* + -*an*.] Belonging or relating to the *Polygamia*; producing hermaphrodite flowers, and also male or female flowers, or both.

polygamist (pǭ-lig′a̤-mist), *n.* [= Pg. *polygamista*; as *polygam-y* + -*ist*.] A person who practises polygamy, or who maintains its propriety.

polygamize (pǭ-lig′a̤-mīz), *v. i.*; pret. and pp. *polygamized*, ppr. *polygamizing*. [< *polygam-y* + -*ize*.] To practise polygamy. *Sylvester*, tr. of Du Bartas's Weeks, ii., The Handy-Crafts.

polygamodiœcious (pǭ-lig″a̤-mō-dī-ē′shus), *a.* [< LGr. πολύγαμος, polygamous, + NL. *diœcius*, diœcious.] Same as *diœciously polygamous*. See *polygamous*, 3.

polygamous (pǭ-lig′a̤-mus), *a.* [= F. *polygame* = Sp. *polígamo* = Pg. *polygamo* = It. *poligamo*, polygamous, a polygamist; < LGr. πολύγαμος, often-married, polygamous, < Gr. πολύς, many, + γάμος, marriage.] **1.** Relating to or characterized by polygamy: as, *polygamous* marriage (a union including more than one spouse of either sex, sanctioned in respect to plurality of wives by the law of some countries, but not recognized as marriage by the law of Christian states).—**2.** In *zoöl.*, mating with more than one individual of the opposite sex; polyandrous or polygynous, especially the latter, which is more frequent among animals than the former.—**3.** In *bot.*, bearing both unisexual and bisexual or hermaphroditic flowers in the same species. According to the tendency to become either monœcious or diœcious, they are called *monœciously* or *diœciously polygamous* respectively. In the case of mosses having both barren and fertile inflorescences (flowers) variously disposed on the same plant, *polygamous* is also used for *polygamian*.

polygamy (pǭ-lig′a̤-mi), *n.* [Formerly *polygamie*, *poligamy* < F. *poligamie*, now *polygamie*, = Sp. *poligamia* = Pg. *polygamia* = It. *poligamia*, < LGr. πολυγαμία, polygamy, < πολύγαμος, polygamous: see *polygamous*.] **1.** Marriage with more than one spouse; the having of a plurality of wives or husbands at the same time. In Christian countries, when a man has more wives than one, or a woman more husbands than one, at the same time, he or she is punishable for polygamy; but if there was a separate marriage with each the first marriage would be valid notwithstanding the subsequent ones, and the later ones would be void. The offense of contracting the subsequent marriage is now termed *bigamy*. But polygamy in the form of polygyny is allowed in some countries, especially among Mohammedans, and was held a matter of faith and duty by the Mormons. Compare *polyandry*.

2. In *zoöl.*, the practice or habit of having more than one mate of the opposite sex; polyandry or polygyny. In mammals, polygamy is the rule with pinniped and various other carnivorous quadrupeds, with the hoofed quadrupeds in general, and in many other groups, especially in its polygynous form. In the class of birds, where monogamy is the rule, polygamy is conspicuous in the rasorial or gallinaceous order, and is exceptionally witnessed in some members of the monogamous orders, as in the cowbirds and cuckoos among passerine and picarian birds.

polygar (pol′i-gär), *n.* See *poligar*.

polygarchy (pol′i-gär-ki), *n.* [= F. *poligarchie* (Cotgrave) = Sp. *poligarquia* = Pg. *polygarchia*; an erroneous form (appar. simulating *oligarchy*, etc.) for *polyarchy*: see *polyarchy*.] An erroneous form of *polyarchy*.

polygastrian (pol-i-gas′tri-a̤n), *a.* and *n.* [< *polygastria* + -*an*.] Same as *polygastric*.

polygastric (pol-i-gas′trik), *a.* and *n.* [< Gr. πολύς, many, + γαστήρ (γαστρ-), stomach.] **I.** *a.* Having or appearing to have many stomachs, as an animalcule; specifically, of or pertaining to the *Polygastrica*.

II. *n.* A polygastric animalcule.

Polygastrica (pol-i-gas′tri-kä̤), *n. pl.* [NL.: see *polygastric*.] Ehrenberg's name (1830) of those animalcules the appearance of whose movable food-vacuoles led him to suppose they had many proper digestive cavities or stomachs. The term had special application to ciliate infusorians, of which it is now a disused synonym, and less exactly of *Infusoria* at large.

polygastrulation (pol-i-gas-trǫ-lā′shǫn), *n.* [< Gr. πολύς, many, + E. *gastrulation*.] Multiple gastrulation.

polygenesis (pol-i-jen′e-sis), *n.* [< Gr. πολύς, many, + γένεσις, origin: see *genesis*.] In *biol.*, generation or origination from several separate and independent germs; the doctrine that organisms took rise from cells or embryos of different kinds. It is akin, as a biological theory, to the notion of special creations, and in its application to man is commonly called *polygeny*.

polygenetic (pol″i-jē̤-net′ik), *a.* [< *polygenesis*, after *genetic*.] **1.** Formed by several different causes, in several different ways, or of several different parts.

> A composite or *polygenetic* range or chain, made up of two or more monogenetic ranges combined.
> *Amer. Jour. Sci.*, 3d ser., V. 429.

2. Pertaining to or characterized by polygenesis.

polygenic (pol-i-jen′ik), *a.* [< *polygen-ous* + -*ic*.] Same as *polygenous*, 1. *Fallows.*

polygenism (pǭ-lij′e-nizm), *n.* [< *polygen-ous* + -*ism*.] Same as *polygeny*.

polygenist (pǭ-lij′e-nist), *n.* and *a.* [< *polygen-ous* + -*ist*.] **I.** *n.* An adherent of or believer in polygeny; a special-creationist; particularly, one who advocates the view that the human race consists of several distinct zoölogical races or species.

> The granting of the *Polygenist* premises does not, in the slightest degree, necessitate the *Polygenist* conclusion.
> *Huxley*, Critiques and Addresses, p. 163.

II. *a.* Same as *polygenous*.

polygenistic (pol″i-jē̤-nis′tik), *a.* [< *polygenist* + -*ic*.] Having independent origins, as the races of man or the domestic animals; of or pertaining to polygeny.

polygenous (pǭ-lij′e-nus), *a.* [< LGr. πολυγενής, of many kinds or families, < Gr. πολύς, many, + γένος, kind: see *genus*, -*genous*.] **1.** Containing or consisting of many different sorts or kinds of things; heterogeneous; composite: as, a *polygenous* mountain (one made up of different strata of rocks).—**2.** Of or pertaining to polygeny.

polygeny (pǭ-lij'e-ni), *n.* [< LGr. πολυγενής, of many kinds or families: see *polygenous* and *-geny*.] In *anthropol.*, the multiple genesis of man; the supposed independent origin of the human races, as opposed to *monogenism*, or the theory of unity of genesis.

polyglossary (pol-i-glos'a̤-ri), *n.*; pl. *polyglossaries* (-riz). [< Gr. πολύς, many, + ML. *glossarium*, glossary: see *glossary*.] A glossary or dictionary in several languages. *Gent. Mag.*

polyglot, polyglott (pol'i-glot), *a.* and *n.* [= F. *polyglotte* = Sp. *poligloto* = Pg. *polyglotto* = It. *poliglotto*, < ML. *polyglottus*, < Gr. πολύγλωττος, πολύγλωσσος, many-tongued, speaking many languages, < πολύς, many, + γλῶττα, γλῶσσα, tongue, language.] **I.** *a.* Using or containing many languages; many-languaged: as, a *polyglot* lexicon or Bible.

II. *n.* **1.** A book containing in parallel columns versions of the same text in several different languages. The most important polyglots are editions of the Bible in which the original Hebrew and Greek texts are given along with the chief versions in other languages. The chief polyglots are — the London polyglot (published in 1657), giving versions in whole or in part in Hebrew, Greek, Chaldee, Syriac, Arabic, Ethiopic, Latin, etc.; the Complutensian polyglot (see *Complutensian*); and the Antwerp and Paris polyglots. A recent collection is Bagster's polyglot.

2. One who understands or uses many languages.

> A *Polyglot*, or good Linguist, may be also termed a useful learned Man, especially if versed in School-Languages.
> Howell, Letters, iii. 8.

polyglottic (pol-i-glot'ik), *a.* [< *polyglot* + *-ic*.] Same as *polyglottous*.

polyglottous (pol-i-glot'us), *a.* [< Gr. πολύγλωττος, speaking many languages: see *polyglot*, *a.*] Speaking many languages.

> While working as a Missionary among the *Polyglottous* tribes of America. *Max Müller*, Sci. of Lang., p. 139.

polygon (pol'i-gon), *n.* [Formerly *polygone*; = F. *polygone* = Sp. *poligono* = Pg. *polygono* = It. *poligono*, a polygon, polygonal, < LL. *polygonum*, < Gr. πολύγωνον, a polygon, neut. of πολύγωνος, having many angles, < πολύς, many, + γωνία, corner, angle.] In *geom.*, a closed figure formed by the intersections of a number of straight lines, each with two others; especially, a plane figure of this sort; a figure with numerous angles.—**Acceleration-polygon.** Same as *acceleration-diagram* (*a*) (which see, under *diagram*).—**Closed polygon,** a plane polygon inclosing an area: opposed to *open polygon*, which is only a part of a plane polygon.—**Complete polygon,** a plane figure connecting every one of a number of angular vertices with every one of the others.—**Concave polygon.** Same as *reëntering polygon*.—**Conjugate polygon of *n* sides,** two sets of *n* lines, each cutting all the lines of the other set upon one curve of the *n*th order.—**Convex polygon,** a plane rectilinear figure without reëntrant angles: opposed to *concave polygon*.—**Displacement-polygon.** Same as *displacement-diagram* (*a*) (which see, under *diagram*).—**Funicular polygon,** originally an open polygon representing a series of connected ties, but extended to a closed polygon representing a series of virtual ties and struts.—**Gauche polygon.** See *gauche*.—**Inscriptible polygon,** a polygon with all its vertices lying on one circle.—**Polygon of forces,** a diagram used in graphical statics, depending on a theorem of the same name due to Leibnitz; a polygon each side of which represents in magnitude and direction one of the component forces acting on a material point: if then the polygon is closed, it represents forces in equilibrium. See diagram under *force*[1], 8.—**Reëntering polygon,** a polygon containing one or more reëntrant angles.—**Regular polygon,** a polygon all whose sides and angles are equal: it is further generally understood that the perimeter wraps around the interior only once.—**Similar polygon.** See *similar*.—**Skew polygon,** a non-plane polygon.—**Spherical polygon,** a polygon whose vertices lie on a sphere; also, a similar figure formed by arcs of great circles on a sphere.—**Steinerian polygon,** a polygon in the Steinerian sense — that is, a figure composed of a number of vertices with connecting lines.—**Stellated polygon,** a polygon which wraps its interior more than once.

Polygonaceæ (pol'i-gǭ-nā'sẹ-ē), *n. pl.* [NL. (Lindley, 1836), < *Polygonum* + *-aceæ*.] A very distinct order of apetalous plants of the series *Curvembryeæ*. It is characterized by a colored or greenish calyx with four, five, or six imbricated segments, an ovary with one cell and one orthotropous ovule, two or three styles or style-branches, from six to nine perigynous stamens, and stipules with each pair united into a cylindrical sheath (ocrea), or at least leaving, on falling away, a scar forming a completering around the stem. It includes about 750 species, belonging to 6 tribes and 30 genera, varying in habit according to distribution, the numerous herbaceous species being mainly in temperate or montane regions, represented by shrubs in western Asia and the Mediterranean, and by trees in tropical America. They bear alternate and usually entire leaves, generally with dilated and clasping petiole-base. The fruit is a small seed-like nut, three-angled or compressed, and inclosed by the withering, persistent flower. Many of the species are weedy plants, especially in the large genera *Rumex* (dock), *Eriogonum*, and *Polygonum* (the type). The most useful genera are *Fagopyrum* (buckwheat) and *Rheum* (rhubarb). See also *Oxyria*, *Coccoloba*, *Kœnigia*.

polygonaceous (pol'i-gǭ-nā'shius), *a.* In *bot.*, like or belonging to the *Polygonaceæ*.

polygonal (pǭ-lig'ǭ-nal), *a.* [= F. Pg. *polygonal*; as *polygon* + *-al*.] Having the form of a polygon; having many angles.—**Polygonal numbers,** in *arith.*, the successive sums from unity up of a series of numbers in arithmetical progression beginning with 1. When the common difference of the series is 1, the sums of the terms give the *triangular* numbers; when the common difference is 2, the sums give the *square* numbers; when it is 3, the sums give the *pentagonal* numbers, and so on. (See *figurate numbers*, under *figurate*.) These numbers are understood to be called *polygonal numbers* from possessing the property that the same number of points may be arranged according to a certain rule in the form of that polygonal figure to which it belongs. In the cut, 5, 12, and 22 points are shown arranged in pentagonal forms, 5, 12, and 22 being pentagonal numbers.

polygonate (pǭ-lig'ǭ-nāt), *a.* [< Gr. πολύς, many, + γόνυ (γονατ-), knee, joint: see *knee*.] Many-jointed: said of some plants and animals. *Thomas*, Med. Dict.

Polygonateæ (pol'i-gǭ-nā'tẹ-ē), *n. pl.* [NL. (Bentham and Hooker, 1883), < *Polygonatum* + *-eæ*.] A tribe of liliaceous plants, typified by the genus *Polygonatum*, the Solomon's-seal. It is characterized by a herbaceous leafy stem, nearly or quite unbranched, an inflorescence of axillary flowers or a raceme, rarely a panicle, anthers introrsely dehiscent, the fruit a berry, and anatropous ovules. It includes 7 genera and about 42 species. See *Polygonatum*, *Smilacina*, *Maianthemum*, *Streptopus*.

Polygonatum (pol-i-gon'a̤-tum), *n.* [NL. (Tournefort, 1700), < L. *polygonatum*, < Gr. πολυγόνατον, Solomon's-seal (so called from the many-jointed rootstocks), < πολύς, many, + γόνυ (γονατ-), knee.] A genus of liliaceous plants, the Solomon's-seal, type of the tribe *Polygonateæ*. It is characterized by the nodding cylindrical flowers, having six short little-spreading lobes, and placed one or two or rarely more together at an axil, and by the undivided style and small stigma. There are 23 species, widely scattered through all north temperate regions. They bear a single erect leafy stem from a horizontal thickened deep-buried or creeping rootstock, which is terminated by the upturned bud for the stem of the following year, and is marked by the circular scars of previous similar stems. These seal-like impressions gave the rootstock great fame for magic powers in the middle ages, as able to seal up and heal all wounds, having been stamped with the seal of Solomon, or of the Virgin Mary, whence the popular names *Solomon's-seal* and *Our-Lady's-seal*, the former of which is still in use. (See *Solomon's-seal* and *lady's-seal*.) From its bell-like flowers, resembling a string of tintinnabula, by the monks ascribed to King David, the common English species, *P. multiflorum*, has derived the name *David's-harp*; also, from its upward series of leaves, *ladder-to-heaven*, and, from resemblances to other plants, *lily-of-the-mountain* and *fraxinell*.

polygoneutic (pol'i-gǭ-nū'tik), *a.* [< Gr. πολυγονεῖσθαι, multiply, < πολύς, many, + γόνος, offspring.] In *entom.*, many-brooded; having several broods during a single year.

polygoneutism (pol'i-gǭ-nū'tizm), *n.* [< *polygoneut-ic* + *-ism*.] The state or character of being polygoneutic.

polygonometric (pol-i-gon-ǭ-met'rik), *a.* [< *polygonometr-y* + *-ic*.] Pertaining to polygonometry.

polygonometry (pol'i-gǭ-nom'et-ri), *n.* [= F. *polygonométrie*, < Gr. πολύγωνος, many-angled (see *polygon*), + -μετρία, < μετρεῖν, measure.] An extension of trigonometry to polygons; the doctrine of polygons, as trigonometry is the doctrine of triangles.

Polygonopoda (pol'i-gǭ-nop'ǭ-dä), *n. pl.* [NL., < Gr. πολύγωνος, many-angled, + πούς (ποδ-) = E. *foot*.] The sea-spiders: a synonym of *Podosomata* and *Pycnogonida*.

polygonoscope (pol'i-gon-ǭ-skōp), *n.* [< Gr. πολύγωνος, many-angled, + σκοπεῖν, view.] An instrument of the nature of the kaleidoscope, used to produce a great variety of geometrical patterns by the reflections from two mirrors supported in a case and connected by an adjustable hinge; specifically, a compact form of carpet-exhibitor for the multiple reproduction of a pattern.

polygonous (pǭ-lig'ǭ-nus), *a.* [< Gr. πολύγωνος, having many angles: see *polygon*.] Polygonal.

Polygonum (pǭ-lig'ǭ-num), *n.* [NL. (Tournefort, 1700), < L. *polygonum*, < Gr. πολύγονον, knot-grass, polygony: see *polygon*.] A large genus of plants, type of the order *Polygonaceæ* and tribe *Eupolygoneæ*. It is characterized by a stem with swollen joints and conspicuous stipular sheaths, flowers with eight or six stamens, two or three styles, and a five-parted and commonly colored perianth, remaining with little change around the black and shining or opaque hard three-angled or compressed nutlet, which is of nearly the same length as the sepals. The species are variously estimated at 150 to 300, widely distributed, and some of them nearly or quite cosmopolitan. They are most abundant in the northern hemisphere, but also extend into arctic, alpine, and tropical regions. Although of polymorphous habit, they are easily distinguished by the swollen joints sheathed with the united stipules. (See cut under *node*.) Nearly all are herbs, a few shrubby at the base. Some are tall and erect, as *P. orientale*, the prince's-feather (also called *ragged-sailor*); a very few are floating, some erect and aquatic, and others climbing or trailing, as *P. scandens*, now esteemed for baskets in greenhouses, and *P. vaccinifolium*, the rock-knotweed, from the Himalayas, used for ornamental rockeries. The majority are, however, spreading weedy plants, especially in the section *Avicularia*, a group of about 50 species with wiry and short or prostrate stems, typified by *P. aviculare* (see *knot-grass*, *doorweed*, and *bird's-tares*), also known by many other names, as *allseed*, *armstrong*, *beggar-weed*, *cow-grass*, *crab-weed*, *goose-grass*, *iron-grass*, *knotwort*, *ninety-knot*, *pink-weed*, *sparrow-tongue*, *swine's-grass*, etc. Another section, also of about 50 species, *Persicaria*, with erect but weak and juicy stems, is typified by the abundant weed *P. Persicaria*, the lady's-thumb, also called, from the peach-leaf shape of the leaves, *persicary* and *peachwort*, from their dark central spot, *heart's-ease* and *spotted knotweed*, and, from the jointed stem, *crab's-claw* and *redshanks*. Several related species are known as *smartweed*, especially *P. Hydropiper*, also called in England *redknees*, *ciderage*, *lake-weed*, etc., and for which see also *water-pepper*, *culrage*, and *arse-smart*. A related and handsome-flowered species of American river-margins, introduced into cultivation as a source of tannin, is *P. amphibium*, the willow-grass or water-persicaria. The general name *knotweed* is a book-name for many of the species. Many are mild astringents, others strongly diuretic and acid; the most important in medicine is *P. Bistorta* (see *bistort*, *snakeweed*, *adder's-wort*, *astrology*, and *dragonwort*), also known in England as *redlegs*, *twice-writhen*, *Easter-ledges*, etc. *P. Fagopyrum* of many authors, the cultivated buckwheat, is now separated (see *Fagopyrum*). *P. tinctorium* is the Chinese indigo-plant, cultivated in France and Belgium, as also in Japan, as a source of a blue dye, a substitute for indigo. The leaves of *P. hispidum* are used in South America as a substitute for tobacco. For the climbing weed *P. Convolvulus*, also called *cornbind*, *bearbine*, *climbing buckwheat*, and *black bindweed*, see *ivy-bindweed*. For other species, see *serpent-grass*, *jointweed*, *false buckwheat* (under *buckwheat*), *tear-thumb* (and cut of leaf under *hastate*), and *scratch-grass*. See also cut under *ocrea*.

polygony (pǭ-lig'ǭ-ni), *n.* [= OF. *polygone* (F. *polygonum*) = Sp. *poligono* = Pg. *polygono* = It. *poligono*; < L. *polygonos*, *polygonon*, *polygonium*, < Gr. πολύγονον, knot-grass, < πολύς, many, + γόνυ, knee, joint, = E. *knee*.] A plant of the genus *Polygonum*; specifically, the *Polygonum aviculare*, or knot-grass.

Polygordiidæ (pol'i-gôr-dī'i-dē), *n. pl.* [NL., < *Polygordius* + *-idæ*.] A family of worms, typified by the genus *Polygordius*, of a low and generalized type of structure.

Polygordius (pol-i-gôr'di-us), *n.* [NL. (Schneider, 1866), < Gr. πολύς, many, + Γόρδιος, Gordius (with ref. to the Gordian knot): see *Gordian*, *Gordius*.] The typical genus of the family *Polygordiidæ*, referred to the annelids as type of a group, *Archiannelida*. *P. purpureus* and *P. luteus* are two species, the former hermaphroditic, the latter diœcious.

polygram (pol'i-gram), *n.* [= Pg. *polygramo* = It. *poligramma*, < Gr. πολύγραμμος, marked with many stripes, < πολύς, many, + γραμμή, a stroke, line, γράμμα, a mark, line, etc., < γράφειν, write.] A figure consisting of many lines.

polygrammatic (pol'i-gra-mat'ik), *a.* [As *polygram* + *-atic*[2] (cf. *grammatic*).] Pertaining or relating to polygrams.—**Polygrammatic telegraph,** a form of semaphore invented by Captain Pasley in 1804.

polygraph (pol'i-gråf), *n.* [= F. *polygraphe* = Pg. *polygrapho* = It. *poligrafo*, < Gr. πολυγράφος, writing much, < πολύς, much, + γράφειν, write.] **1.** An instrument for multiplying copies of a writing; a gelatin copying-pad.—**2.** An author of many works.—**3.** A collection of different works written either by one or by different authors; a book containing articles or treatises on different subjects.

polygraphic (pol-i-graf'ik), *a.* [= F. *polygraphique* = Pg. *polygraphico*; as *polygraph* + *-ic*.] **1.** Pertaining to multiplication of copies of a writing: as, a *polygraphic* instrument.—**2.** Done with a polygraph: as, a *polygraphic* copy or writing.—**Polygraphic paper.** See *paper*.

polygraphical (pol-i-graf'i-kạl), *a.* [< *polygraphic* + *-al*.] Same as *polygraphic*.

polygraphy (pǭ-lig'ra̤-fi), *n.* [= F. *polygraphie* = Sp. *poligrafía* = Pg. *polygraphia* = It. *poligrafia*, < LGr. πολυγραφία, a writing much, < Gr. πολύς, much, + γράφειν, write.] **1.** Voluminous writing.

> No less admirable his [Dr. Willet's] industry, appearing in his Synopses, Comments, and Commentaries, insomuch that one, considering his *polygraphy*, said merrily that he must write while he slept.
> *Fuller*, Worthies, Cambridgeshire.

2. The art of writing in various ciphers, and also of deciphering such writings.

polygroove (pol'i-gröv), *v. t.*; pret. and pp. *polygrooved*, ppr. *polygrooving*. [< Gr. πολύς, many, + E. *groove*.] To make many grooves in.

> [The guns] are similar in construction, and will both be *polygrooved* in the rifling. *Times* (London).

polygyn (pol'i-jin), *n.* [< *Polygyn-ia.*] In *bot.*, a plant of the order *Polygynia.*

polygynia[1] (pol-i-jin'i-ä), *n.* [NL.] Same as *polygyny.*

In certain cantons of Media, according to Strabo, *polygynia* was authorised by express law, which ordained every inhabitant to maintain at least seven wives.
M'Lennan, Primitive Marriage (ed. 1865), viii.

Polygynia[2] (pol-i-jin'i-ä), *n. pl.* [NL., < Gr. πολύς, many, + γυνή, female (in mod. bot. pistil).] One of the orders in the fifth, sixth, twelfth, and thirteenth classes of the Linnean system, comprehending those plants which have flowers with more than twelve styles or stigmas.

polygynian (pol-i-jin'i-an), *a.* [< *polygynia*[1] + *-an.*] Same as *polygynous.*

polygynic (pol-i-jin'ik), *a.* [< *polygyn-ous* + *-ic.*] Same as *polygynous.*

polygynious (pol-i-jin'i-us), *a.* Same as *polygynous.*

polygynist (pō-lij'i-nist), *n.* [< *polygyn-y* + *-ist.*] One who or that which practises polygyny; an advocate of polygyny.

polygynœcial (pol"i-ji-nē'shal), *a.* [< Gr. πολύς, many, + NL. *gynœcium* + *-al.*] In *bot.*, formed by the united pistils of many flowers: said of multiple fruits.

polygynous (pō-lij'i-nus), *a.* [= F. *polygyne*; as *polygyn* + *-ous.*] 1. In *bot.*, having many styles; belonging to the order *Polygynia.*— 2. Polygamous, as a male; having more than one female as wife or mate.

Few, perhaps, would stigmatize a legal *polygynous* connexion as impure, however they might disapprove of the law and of the state of society in which such a law was established.
H. *Sidgwick*, Methods of Ethics, p. 337.

polygyny (pō-lij'i-ni), *n.* [< NL. *polygynia*, < Gr. *πολυγυνία, the condition of having many wives, < πολυγύνης, πολυγύναιος, having many wives, < πολύς, many, + γυνή, woman, wife.] Marriage or cohabitation of one man with more than one woman at the same time; polygamy as practised by the male. Polygyny is more frequent than polyandry, being the usual case of polygamy as practised by man and the lower animals.

polygyral (pol-i-jī'ral), *a.* [< Gr. πολύγυρος, with many windings, < πολύς, many, + γῦρος, a circle, ring: see *gyre.*] Having many whorls or gyres, as a univalve shell. *W. G. Binney.*

polyhæmia, *n.* See *polyhemia.*

polyhalite (pol-i-hal'īt), *n.* [< Gr. πολύς, many, + ἅλς (ἁλ-), salt, + *-ite*[2].] A mineral or salt occurring in masses of a fibrous structure, of a brick-red color, being tinged with iron. It is a hydrous sulphate of calcium, magnesium, and potassium. It is found at Ischl in Austria, and also at Berchteagaden in Bavaria.

polyhedra, *n.* Plural of *polyhedron.*

polyhedral (pol-i-hē'dral), *a.* [< *polyhedron* + *-al.*] Having many faces, as a solid body; of or pertaining to a polyhedron. Also *polyhedric, polyhedrous, polyedral, polyedrous.*— **Polyhedral function**, an algebraic function which remains unchanged when the variable undergoes any of those transformations which would carry a polyhedron, stereographically projected upon the plane of an imaginary quantity, into a congruent position.

polyhedric (pol-i-hē'drik), *a.* [= F. *polyédrique*; as *polyhedr-on* + *-ic.*] Same as *polyhedral.*

polyhedrical (pol-i-hē'dri-kal), *a.* [< *polyhedric* + *-al.*] Same as *polyhedric.* [Rare.]

polyhedrometric (pol-i-hē-drō-met'rik), *a.* [< *polyhedrometr-y* + *-ic.*] Pertaining to polyhedrometry.

polyhedrometry (pol"i-hē-drom'et-ri), *n.* [< *polyhedron* + Gr. μετρία, < μετρεῖν, measure.] The system of theorems concerning the numbers of faces, edges, and summits of polyhedra, the numbers of edges belonging to the different faces and summits, and other allied matters. The name is ill formed to express this idea.

polyhedron (pol-i-hē'dron), *n.*; pl. *polyhedra*, *polyhedrons* (-drä, -dronz). [Also *polyedron*; = F. *polyèdre* = Sp. *poliedro* = Pg. *polyedro* = It. *poliedro*, < Gr. πολύεδρον, neut. of πολύεδρος, with many bases, < πολύς, many, + ἕδρα, seat, base.] 1. In *geom.*, a solid bounded by plane faces.— 2. In *optics*, a multiplying glass or lens consisting of several plane surfaces disposed in a convex form, through each of which an object is seen; a polyscope.— 3. In *bot.*, in *Hydrodictyon* or water-net, one of the special angular cells with horn-like processes formed by the swarm-cells produced in the zygospore, within each of which a new cœnobium is developed. *Goebel.*— **Conjugate polyhedra**, two polyhedra each having a summit for every face of the other.— **Doubly reversible polyhedron**, a polyhedron which exhibits, in the faces touching the base, a series repeated twice. So in a *trebly reversible polyhedron*, etc., the series is repeated thrice, etc.— **Generator of a polyhedron.** See *generator.*— **Regular polyhedron**, a polyhedron that has all its summits alike in all respects and composed of plane angles of the same magnitude: sometimes understood as excluding the stellated polyhedra. See cut under *octahedron.*— **Semi-regular polyhedron**, a polyhedron all the summits of which are alike, while the plane angles which compose the summits are not all alike.— **Stellated polyhedron**, a polyhedron that inwraps its center more than once.

polyhedrous (pol-i-hē'drus), *a.* [= F. *polyèdre* = Sp. *poliedro* = Pg. *polyedro* = It. *poliedro*, < Gr. πολύεδρος, with many bases: see *polyhedron.*] Same as *polyhedral.*

polyhemia, polyhæmia (pol-i-hē'mi-ä), *n.* [NL., < Gr. πολυαιμία, fullness of blood, < πολύς, much, + αἷμα, blood.] Excess of blood; plethora. Also *polyemia, polyæmia.*

polyhistor (pol-i-his'tor), *n.* [< L. *polyhistor* (as a title of the grammarian Cornelius Alexander), < Gr. πολυΐστωρ, very learned, < πολύς, much, + ἵστωρ, ἵστωρ, knowing: see *history.*] A person of great learning; one who is versed in various departments of study.

I haue much read of admirable things of them [storks] in Ælianus the *polyhistor.* *Coryat*, Crudities, I. 38, sig. E.

Polyhymnia (pol-i-him'ni-ä), *n.* [L., also *Polymnia* (> F. *Polymnie*), < Gr. Πολύμνια, one of the Muses, < πολύς, many, + ὕμνος, a hymn.] In *Gr. antiq.*, the Muse of the sublime hymn, and of the faculty of learning and remembering: according to some poets, inventor of the lyre, and considered during the final centuries of the Roman empire as the patroness of mimes and pantomimes. In art she is usually represented as in a meditative attitude, voluminously draped, and without any attribute.

polylemma (pol-i-lem'ä), *n.* [< Gr. πολύς, many, + λῆμμα, a proposition, assumption: see *dilemma.*] A dilemma with several alternatives: opposed to *dilemma* in the narrow sense.

polylepidous (pol-i-lep'i-dus), *a.* [< Gr. πολύς, many, + λεπίς (λεπιδ-), a scale.] In *bot.*, having many scales.

polylithic (pol-i-lith'ik), *a.* [< Gr. πολύλιθος, of many stones, < πολύς, many, + λίθος, stone.] Consisting of many stones; built up of several blocks, as a shaft or column: opposed to *monolithic.*

polylogy† (pō-lil'ō-ji), *n.* [= It. *polilogia*, < Gr. πολυλογία, loquacity, talkativeness, < πολύλογος, much-talking, talkative, < πολύς, much, + λέγειν, speak: see *-ology.*] Talkativeness; garrulity.

Many words (battology or *polylogy*) are signs of a fool.
Granger, On Ecclesiastes (1621), p. 115. (*Latham.*)

polyloquent† (pō-lil'ō-kwent), *a.* [< Gr. πολύς, much, + L. *loquen(t-)s*, ppr. of *loqui*, speak.] Talking much; talkative.

polymagnet (pol'i-mag-net), *n.* [< Gr. πολύς, many, + E. *magnet.*] An instrument consisting of two or more electromagnets so arranged that the resultant field of force may be varied in many ways. Such an apparatus devised by Tyndall, to be used in exhibiting diamagnetic and other similar phenomena, consists of two electromagnets standing vertically, with adjustable pole-pieces of soft iron, and between them a helix of copper wire. The diamagnetic substance—for example, a bar of bismuth—is supported horizontally in the direction passing through the axis of the helix.

polymastia (pol-i-mas'ti-ä), *n.* [NL., < Gr. πολύς, many, + μαστός, breast.] The presence of supernumerary breasts or nipples.

Polymastiga (pol-i-mas'ti-gä), *n. pl.* [NL., < Gr. πολύς, many, + μάστιξ (μαστιγ-), a whip.] Infusorians with six, ten, or many flagella, of whatever other character. The genera included by Diesing (1865) under this head were *Chloraster*, *Spondylomorum*, *Phacelomonas*, and *Lophomonas.*

polymastigate (pol-i-mas'ti-gāt), *a.* [< Gr. πολύς, many, + μάστιξ (μαστιγ-), a whip, + *-ate*[1].] Having more than four flagella, as an infusorian; pluriflagellate.

polymastigous (pol-i-mas'ti-gus), *a.* [< Gr. πολύς, many, + μάστιξ (μαστιγ-), a whip, + *-ous.*] Same as *polymastigate.*

Polymastodon (pol-i-mas'tō-don), *n.* [NL., < Gr. πολύς, many, + μαστός, teat, + ὀδούς (ὀδοντ-) = E. *tooth*: see *Mastodon.*] 1. A genus of American Mesozoic mammals from the Puerco beds, having numerous tubercles on the molars, typical of the family *Polymastodontidæ.*— 2. [*l. c.*] A member of this genus.

polymastodont (pol-i-mas'tō-dont), *a.* and *n.* [< Gr. πολύς, many, + μαστός, breast, + ὀδούς (ὀδοντ-) = E. *tooth.*] I. *a.* Having many molar tubercles; of or pertaining to the *Polymastodontidæ.*

II. *n.* A polymastodon.

Polymastodontidæ (pol-i-mas-tō-don'ti-dē), *n. pl.* [NL., < *Polymastodon(t-)* + *-idæ.*] A family of extinct North American Eocene marsupial mammals, represented by the genus *Polymastodon.* They had molars with numerous tubercles arranged in three imperfect or two longitudinal rows. They were of small size.

polymath (pol'i-math), *n.* [= F. *polymathe* = Sp. *polimato*, < Gr. πολυμαθής, having learned much, knowing much, < πολύς, much, + μανθάνειν, μαθεῖν, learn.] A person of various learning. Also *polymathist.*

polymathic (pol-i-math'ik), *a.* [= F. *polymathique* = Pg. *polymathico*; as *polymath-y* + *-ic.*] Pertaining to or characterized by polymathy.

polymathist (pō-lim'a-thist), *n.* [< *polymath-y* + *-ist.*] Same as *polymath.*

Those *Polymathists* that stand poring all Day in a Corner upon a Moth-eaten Author. *Howell*, Letters, iii. 8.

polymathy (pō-lim'a-thi), *n.* [= F. *polymathie* = Sp. *polimatía* = Pg. *polymathia*, < Gr. πολυμαθία, much learning, < πολυμαθής, having learned much: see *polymath.*] The knowledge of many arts and sciences; acquaintance with many branches of learning, or with various subjects.

That high and excellent learning which men, for the large extent of it, call *polymathy.*
Hartlib, tr. of Comenius's Reformation of Schools (1642), [p. 53. (*Latham.*)

polymatype (pol'i-ma-tīp), *n.* [Irreg. < Gr. πολύς, many, + τύπος, type.] A now disused system of type-making by which 150 or 200 types were cast at one operation twice a minute.

polymazia (pol-i-mā'zi-ä), *n.* [NL., < Gr. πολύς, many, + μαζός, breast.] Polymastia.

polymechany† (pol-i-mek'a-ni), *n.* [< Gr. πολυμηχανία, the having many resources, inventiveness, < πολυμήχανος, having many resources, inventive, < πολύς, many, + μηχανή, contrivance, means: see *machine, mechanic.*] Practical invention.

In actual experiments and *polymechany*, nothing too profound; a superficial slightness may seem fine for sheets, but prooveth good for nothing.
G. Harvey, Four Letters, iv.

polymelia (pol-i-mē'li-ä), *n.* [NL.] Same as *polymely.*

polymelian (pol-i-mē'li-an), *a.* [< *polymel-y* + *-ian.*] In *teratol.*, having supernumerary members.

polymelius (pol-i-mē'li-us), *n.*; pl. *polymelii* (-ī). [NL., < Gr. πολυμελής, with many limbs: see *polymely.*] In *teratol.*, a monster with supernumerary members.

polymely (pol'i-mē-li), *n.* [< NL. *polymelia*, < Gr. πολυμελής, with many limbs or members, < πολύς, many, + μέλος, a limb.] In *teratol.*, monstrosity by redundancy of parts, or the appearance of supernumerary members, as extra digits and the like.

polymer (pol'i-mėr), *n.* [< *polymer-ous.*] In *chem.*, a compound which is polymeric with some other compound; a polymeride.

We speak of "polymeric" bodies when the several formulæ are intermultiples of the same primitive group (e. g., ethylene, 2 × CH_2, and butylene, 4 × CH_2, are *polymers* to one another). *Encyc. Brit.*, XVIII. 237.

polymeria (pol-i-mē'ri-ä), *n.* [NL., < Gr. πολύς, many, + μέρος, a part.] In *teratol.*, the possession of many parts.

polymeric (pol-i-mer'ik), *a.* [< *polymer-ous* + *-ic.*] In *chem.*, pertaining to or characterized by polymerism: as, butyric acid ($C_4H_8O_2$) and aldehyde (C_2H_4O) are *polymeric.*

polymeride (pō-lim'e-rid or -rīd), *n.* [< *polymer-ous* + *-ide*[1].] In *chem.*, a compound that exhibits the properties of polymerism with reference to some other compound.

polymerism (pō-lim'e-rizm), *n.* [= F. *polymérisme*; as *polymer-ous* + *-ism.*] 1. In *chem.*, that property of certain compounds by virtue of which they differ in their molecular weights and in their chemical properties, though formed from the same elements, combined in the same proportion. Thus, the molecular weights of butyric acid ($C_4H_8O_2$) and aldehyde (C_2H_4O) are 88 and 44 respectively and their chemical properties are wholly unlike, but both contain the same elements—carbon, hydrogen, and oxygen—combined in the same proportion. See *isomerism, metamerism.*— 2. Multiplicity of parts; presence of many parts in one whole.

polymerization (pol-i-mer-i-zā'shon), *n.* [< *polymerize* + *-ation.*] The apparent fusion or union of two or more molecules of a compound, forming a more complex molecule with a higher atomic weight and somewhat different physical and chemical properties. Also spelled *polymerisation.*

In the quenched globule we may possibly encounter a *polymerization* of the molecular structure of the annealed globule. *Amer. Jour. Sci.*, 3d ser., XXXII. 182.

polymerize (pō-lim'e-rīz), *v. t.* and *i.*; pret. and pp. *polymerized*, ppr. *polymerizing*. [< *polymer-ous* + *-ize*.] To combine or cause to combine so as to form polymerides. Also spelled *polymerise*.

Prof. Armstrong found hydrocarbons . . . which are readily *polymerised* by sulphuric acid. *Jour. Franklin Inst.*, CXXI. 172.

Polymerosomata (pol-i-mer-ō-sō'ma-tä), *n. pl.* [NL., neut. pl. of *polymerosomatus*: see *polymerosomatous*.] In Leach's system of classification, an order of pulmonate *Arachnida*, synonymous with Latreille's *Pedipalpi*, containing the scorpions and their allies, as the *Thelyphonidæ* and *Phrynidæ*: so called from the numerous flexible segments of the body, and contrasted with *Dimerosomata*, *Monomerosomata*, and *Podosomata*.

polymerosomatous (pol-i-mer-ō-som'a-tus), *a.* [< NL. *polymerosomatus*, < Gr. πολύς, many, + μέρος, part, + σῶμα, body.] Having the body segmented into many joints, as a scorpion; of or pertaining to the *Polymerosomata*.

polymerous (pō-lim'e-rus), *a.* [= F. *polymère*; < Gr. πολυμερής, consisting of many parts, < πολύς, many, + μέρος, part.] 1. Composed of many parts; specifically, in *bot.*, having numerous members in each series or circle. *Gray*.— 2. Of or pertaining to polymerism.

polymetameric (pol-i-met-a-mer'ik), *a.* [< Gr. πολύς, many, + E. *metamere*: see *metameric*.] Of or pertaining to several metameres; lying upon or extending over more than two metameres, as a muscle innervated by different spinal nerves. *Nature*, XXXIX. 151.

polymeter (pō-lim'e-tėr), *n.* [< Gr. πολύς, many, + μέτρον, measure.] 1. An instrument for measuring angles.—2. An apparatus for testing the distance between the rails of a railway line, and detecting inequalities of elevation. *E. H. Knight*.

polymetochia (pol″i-me-tō'ki-ä), *n.* [NL., < Gr. πολύς, many, + μετοχή, a participle.] Use of many participles or participial clauses in composition: opposed to *oligometochia*.

polymicroscope (pol-i-mī'krō-skōp), *n.* [< Gr. πολύς, many, + E. *microscope*.] A microscope arranged on the principle of the revolving stereoscope. The objects to be examined are mounted on plates fastened to a band, and may be presented in succession to the focus of the instrument.

polymignite (pol-i-mig'nīt), *n.* [Irreg. < Gr. πολύς, much, + μιγνύναι, mix, + *-ite*[2].] A rare mineral which occurs in small prismatic crystals of a black color and submetallic luster. It is found at Frederiksvaern in Norway, and has received its name from the variety of its constituents—consisting of titanic and niobic acids, zirconia, thoria, lime, yttria, and oxids of iron, cerium, and manganese.

polymite†, *a.* [ME. *polimite*, < OF. *polimite*, ML. *polymitus*, *polimitus*, < Gr. πολύμιτος, consisting of many threads, woven of many (different) threads, < πολύς, many, + μίτος, thread.] Many-colored.

> Of ȝonge Josephe the cote *polimite*,
> Wrouȝte by the power of alle the Trinite.
> *Lydgate*, MS. Soc. Antiq. 134, f. 13. (*Halliwell*.)

Polymixia (pol-i-mik'si-ä), *n.* [NL. (Lowe, 1836), < Gr. πολυμιξία, promiscuous mingling, < πολύς, many, + μῖξις, mixing, mingling.] The typical genus of the family *Polymixiidæ*: so called as formerly supposed to indicate a mixture or combination of several diverse forms. There are three species, *P. nobilis* of Madeira, *P. lowei* of Cuba, and *P. japonica*. Also *Polymyxia*.

Polymixiidæ (pol″i-mik-si'i-dē), *n. pl.* [NL., < *Polymixia* + *-idæ*.] A family of acanthopterygian fishes, typified by the genus *Polymixia*, having an oblong compressed body, blunt head with a pair of barbels on the chin, long dorsal fin with three or four spines, and ventrals with a spine and six or seven rays. It contains three species, inhabiting rather deep water of both the Atlantic and the Pacific.

Polymnia[1] (pō-lim'ni-ä), *n.* See *Polyhymnia*.

Polymnia[2] (pō-lim'ni-ä), *n.* [NL. (Linnæus, 1753), < Gr. Πολύμνια, Polyhymnia, one of the Muses: see *Polyhymnia*.] A genus of composite plants of the tribe *Helianthoideæ* and subtribe *Melampodieæ*. It is characterized by ample leaves, either opposite or alternate above, and corymbose flower-heads with broad involucres, the outer row of bracts often large, leaf-like, and spreading, the ray-flowers in a single row or lacking altogether, and smooth, thick, and nearly cylindrical obovoid achenes, without awns. The 12 species are natives of America, and are found from Canada to Buenos Ayres. They are perennial herbs, shrubs, or trees, often viscid, with yellow flowers, and large angled, lobed, or entire leaves, generally appendaged at the petiole-base with a cup-like membrane, whence their name *leafcup*.

polymnite (pol'im-nīt), *n.* [For **polymniite*, < Gr. πολύμνιος, full of moss (< πολύς, much, + μνίον, moss), + *-ite*[2].] A stone marked with dendrites and black lines, and so disposed as to represent rivers, marshes, and ponds.

polymorph (pol'i-môrf), *n.* [< Gr. πολύς, many, + μορφή, form.] 1. In *chem.*, a substance which crystallizes in two or more forms distinct from each other. See *dimorphism* and *trimorphism*.— 2. In *biol.*, an organism exhibiting or characterized by polymorphism; an individual member of a species or other group which differs from other members of the same group to an unusual degree.

Polymorphi (pol-i-môr'fī), *n. pl.* [NL., pl. of *polymorphus*: see *polymorphous*.] One of the six main divisions of *Braconidæ*, a family of hymenopterous parasites, including those subfamilies in which the clypeus fits closely to the mandibles and the second submarginal cell of the fore wings is large, quadrangular, or wanting. It includes 12 subfamilies and many genera.

polymorphic (pol-i-môr'fik), *a.* [< *polymorph-ous* + *-ic*.] Same as *polymorphous*.

Polymorphina (pol″i-môr-fī'nä), *n.* [NL. (D'Orbigny), < Gr. πολύς, many, + μορφή, form, + *-ina*.] The typical genus of *Polymorphininæ*.

Polymorphininæ (pol-i-môr-fi-nī'nē), *n. pl.* [NL., < *Polymorphina* + *-inæ*.] A subfamily of *Lagenidæ*, typified by the genus *Polymorphina*, having the cells of the test arranged spirally or irregularly around the long axis, or (rarely) biserial and alternate.

polymorphism (pol-i-môr'fizm), *n.* [= F. *polymorphisme*; as *polymorph-ous* + *-ism*.] 1. The property of being polymorphous, or capable of existing in different forms; specifically, in *crystal.*, the property of crystallizing in two or more fundamental forms: thus, carbon crystallizes in isometric forms in the diamond, and in hexagonal forms in graphite. When the substance assumes two forms it is said to be *dimorphic*, or to present the phenomenon of *dimorphism*; when three, it is said to be *trimorphic*.

2. In *zoöl.*, difference of form, structure, or type; existence in, or exhibition by, a group of animals, as a species, genus, family, or order, of different types of structure; heterogeneousness.

A considerable number of what have been classed as varieties are really cases of *polymorphism*. *A. R. Wallace*, Nat. Select., p. 145.

New complications of structure among the Hydromedusæ are summed up under the head of *polymorphism*. The differentiation of hydriform and medusiform persons is a case of dimorphism; a further distribution of functions, with corresponding modification of form, gives us *polymorphism*. *Encyc. Brit.*, XII. 554.

3. In *bot.*, the comprisal of numerous definite or indefinite subtypes under a given type.

polymorphous (pol-i-môr'fus), *a.* [= F. *polymorphe* = Pg. *polymorpho* = It. *polimorfo*, < NL. *polymorphus*, < Gr. πολύμορφος, multiform, manifold, < πολύς, many, + μορφή, form.] 1. Having or exhibiting many forms; characterized by polymorphism; not isomorphous or monomorphous.

I . . . find it difficult to form any judgment of any author so "many-sided" (to borrow a German expression)—*polymorphous* as Herder. *De Quincey*, Herder.

2. Specifically, in *zoöl.*: (*a*) Undergoing a series of marked changes during development, as most insects. (*b*) Varying much in appearance, form, or structure in the same species or group.—3. In *bot.*, same as 2 (*b*).—4. In *music*, noting a contrapuntal composition, as a canon or a fugue, in which the themes are or may be treated in various ways, as by augmentation, diminution, inversion, etc.

Also *polymorphic*.

polymorphy (pol'i-môr-fi), *n.* [= F. *polymorphie*; < LGr. πολυμορφία, manifoldness, < Gr. πολύμορφος, manifold: see *polymorphous*.] Same as *polymorphism*.

poly-mountain (pō-li-moun'tān), *n.* See *poly*.

Polymyaria (pol″i-mī-ā'ri-ä), *n. pl.* [NL., < Gr. πολύς, many, + μῦς, muscle, + *-aria*.] One of three principal divisions of the *Nematoidea*, containing those threadworms in which the muscles of the body-wall are divided into many series, each made up of many muscle-cells. See *Meromyaria*, *Holomyaria*.

polymyarian (pol″i-mī-ā'ri-an), *a.* and *n.* I. *a.* Of or pertaining to the *Polymyaria*.

II. *n.* A polymyarian worm.

Polymyodi† (pol″i-mī-ō'dī), *n. pl.* [NL., < Gr. πολύς, many, + μῦς, muscle, + ᾠδή, song.] In Johannes Müller's system of classification (1847), a tribe of birds of an order *Insessores*, including singing birds whose lower larynx is provided with the full number (five pairs) of song-muscles: thus distinguished from the tribes *Tracheophonæ* and *Picarii* of the same author. The term is nearly equivalent to *Oscines* or *Acromyodi* of later authors.

polymyodian (pol″i-mī-ō'di-an), *a.* Same as *polymyoid*.

polymyoid (pol'i-mī-oid), *a.* [< Gr. πολύς, many, + μῦς, muscle, + ᾠδή, song. Cf. *Polymyodi*.] In *ornith.*, having several distinct intrinsic muscles of the syrinx: opposed to *oligomyoid*. The word is nearly synonymous with *acromyodian*, but is of less exact signification. The group of birds it denotes is that of the *Oscines* or singing birds.

polymyositis (pol-i-mī-ō-sī'tis), *n.* [NL., < Gr. πολύς, many, + μῦς (μυός), muscle, + *-itis*: see *myositis*.] Inflammation of a number of muscles.

Polymyxia, *n.* See *Polymixia*.

polyneme (pol'i-nēm), *n.* [< NL. *polynemus*, q. v.] A fish of the genus *Polynemus*.

Polynemidæ (pol-i-nem'i-dē), *n. pl.* [NL., < *Polynemus* + *-idæ*.] A family of acanthopterygian fishes, typified by the genus *Polynemus*. They have a subfusiform shape, with a blunt snout, subabdominal ventrals with a spine and five rays, two dorsals separated by a considerable interval, anal with one or two spines, forked caudal, and pectorals with an entire upper part and several free elongated filiform rays below. Numerous species occur in tropical seas, some of much importance, as the mango-fish of India, *P. paradiseus*.

polynemiform (pol-i-nem'i-fôrm), *a.* [< NL. *Polynemus* + L. *forma*, form.] Having the form of a polyneme; belonging to the *Polynemidæ*.

polynemoid (pol-i-nē'moid), *a.* and *n.* I. *a.* Belonging or relating to the *Polynemidæ*; polynemiform.

II. *n.* A polynemiform fish; a polyneme.

Polynemus (pol-i-nē'mus), *n.* [NL. (Gronovius, 1754), < Gr. πολύς, many, + νῆμα, thread: see *nematoid*.] The typical genus of the family *Polynemidæ*, with the lower pectoral rays separated as numerous long slender filaments (whence the name). *P. plebeius* is a very common Indian species.

Polynemus plebeius.

Polynesian (pol-i-nē'sian), *a.* and *n.* [= F. *polynésien* = Pg. *polynesiano*; < NL. *Polynesia* (see def.), < Gr. πολύς, many, + νῆσος, island.] I. *a.* 1. [*l. c.*] Full of islands, as an archipelago.—2. Specifically, of or pertaining to Polynesia.—**Polynesian region**, Polynesia, or the Pacific islands, zoögeographically considered. It is sometimes regarded as a division of a very comprehensive Australian region, and is then known more precisely as the *Polynesian subregion*. It consists of all the Pacific islands excepting those that pertain zoölogically to the Papuan or Austromalayan group and to New Zealand. Wallace, who defined this region, divides it into Polynesia proper and the Hawaiian Islands, the former being then considered under the four subdivisions of the Ladrone and Caroline Islands, New Caledonia and the New Hebrides, the Fiji, Tonga, and Samoa Islands, and the Society and Marquesas Islands.

II. *n.* A native or an inhabitant of Polynesia, a division of Oceania east of Australia and Malaysia, or, in the more modern and restricted sense, a division of Oceania east of Micronesia and Melanesia.

polyneuritis (pol″i-nū-rī'tis), *n.* [NL., < Gr. πολύς, many, + νεῦρον, nerve, + *-itis*. Cf. *neuritis*.] Neuritis affecting a number of nerves; multiple neuritis.

polynia (pō-lin'i-ä), *n.* [Russ. *poluinya*, an open place in the midst of ice.] An open or unfrozen place in the midst of the ice of a river or lake or in the ocean: a word used in English only by navigators in arctic seas. By some writers it was formerly used with the meaning of an open or unfrozen (theoretical) sea at the north pole, apparently from the (erroneous) idea that *polynia* is connected with *pole*[2].

> In such places as Robeson and Kennedy Channels and Bellot's Straits . . . *polynias* or water-pools are met with on rare occasions throughout the winter.
> *Nares*, Voyage to the Polar Sea, I. 234.

Polynoë (pǭ-lin'ǭ-ē), *n.* [NL. (Savigny), ‹ Gr. πολύς, much, many, + νέειν, swim.] A genus of marine errant annelids of the family *Aphroditidæ*: a name used in different senses. (*a*) Applied by Savigny and most authors to such species as the British *P. squamata*, an inch or two long, with large ovate and reniform ciliated scales imbricated in a double row of 12 along the whole length of the worm, and the body of equal width at both ends. This worm is *Aphrodite squamata* of Linnæus, also known as *Lepidonotus squamatus*. (*b*) After Oersted, 1842, applied to worms resembling (*a*), but with not less than 70 segments covered forward with small scales in pairs, naked behind, as *P. scolopendrina* of the British Islands.

a b b' c e g c' e g f

Polynoë squamata, from above, enlarged.
a, prestomial tentacle; *b*, *b'*, superior and inferior prestomial cirrus; *c*, *c'*, notopodial and neuropodial cirrus; *e*, *e*, elytra; *f*, space between the posterior elytra; *g*, *g*, setæ and fimbriæ of the elytra.

polynome (pol'i-nōm), *n.* [= F. *polynôme* = Pg. *polynomo*, n., *polynomio*, adj., = It. *polinomio*; ‹ Gr. πολύς, many, + L. *nomen*, name.] A polynomial.

polynomial (pol-i-nō'mi-al), *a.* and *n.* [‹ *polynome* + *-ial*. Cf. *binomial*.] **I.** *a.* **1.** Containing many names or terms.—**2.** In *zoöl.* and *bot.*, specifically, noting a method of nomenclature in which the technical names of species are not confined to two terms, the generic and the specific, as they are in the binomial system of nomenclature: as, a *polynomial* name; a *polynomial* system of nomenclature: contrasted with *binomial* and *mononomial*.

Also *multinomial*, *plurinominal*.

Polynomial theorem, the theorem for raising a polynomial to any power.

II. *n.* **1.** A technical name consisting of more than two terms; a polyonym.—**2.** An algebraical expression consisting of two or more terms united by addition: as,

$$ax + by + cz - exy - fxz + gyz.$$

Also *multinomial*.

Appell's polynomial, a form

$$A_n x = a_0 x^n + \binom{n}{1} a_1 x^{n-1} + \binom{n}{2} a_2 x^{n-2} + \ldots + a_n.$$

Homogeneous polynomial, a polynomial in which all the terms are of the same degree in the variables.

polynomialism (pol-i-nō'mi-al-izm), *n.* [‹ *polynomial* + *-ism*.] Polynomial nomenclature; the method or practice of using polynomials.

polynomialist (pol-i-nō'mi-al-ist), *n.* [‹ *polynomial* + *-ist*.] In *zoöl.* and *bot.*, one who uses polynomials, or a polynomial system of nomenclature, as the pre-Linnean writers usually did.

polynuclear (pol-i-nū'klē-ạr), *a.* [‹ Gr. πολύς, many, + NL. *nucleus*: see *nuclear*.] Having several nuclei, as a cell.

Polyodon (pǭ-lī'ǭ-don), *n.* [NL., ‹ Gr. πολύς, many, + ὀδούς (ὀδοντ-) = E. *tooth*.] **1.** In *ichth.*, a genus of selachostomous fishes, named by Lacépède in 1798, the type of the family *Polyodontidæ*, having many teeth crowded in band-like masses during the youth of its members, these teeth being lost at maturity. *P. spatula* is an example. Also called *Spatularia*. See cuts under *paddle-fish*.—**2.** In *conch.*, a genus of pulmonate gastropods. *Desmarest*.

polyodont (pol'i-ǭ-dont), *a.* and *n.* [‹ Gr. πολύς, many, + ὀδούς (ὀδοντ-) = E. *tooth*.] **I.** *a.* Having many teeth; multidentate; specifically, of or pertaining to the *Polyodontidæ*.

II. *n.* In *ichth.*, a member of the *Polyodontidæ*.

Polyodontidæ (pol″i-ǭ-don'ti-dē), *n. pl.* [NL., ‹ *Polyodon(t-)* + *-idæ*.] A family of selachostomous ganoid fishes, typified by the genus *Polyodon*, including the paddle-fishes of the Mississippi basin and related forms of China and Japan. The body is naked, or rough with minute stellate ossifications; the snout is much produced; the very wide mouth contains many minute teeth, in youth at least; the nostrils are double; and the dorsal and anal fins are near the heterocercal fin. Also called *Spatulariidæ*.

polyommatous (pol-i-om'ạ-tus), *a.* [‹ Gr. πολυόμματος, many-eyed, ‹ πολύς, many, + ὄμμα (ὀμματ-), eye, ‹ √ ὀπ, see: see *optic*.] Many-eyed; having many eyes or eye-like organs.

Polyommatus (pol-i-om'ạ-tus), *n.* [NL. (Latreille), ‹ Gr. πολυόμματος, many-eyed: see *polyommatous*.] **1.** In *entom.*, a genus of butterflies of the family *Lycænidæ*, having many ocelli on the wings (whence the name). There are many species, known as *blues*, as *P. alexis*, the common blue, and *P. argiolus*, the azure blue.—**2.** A genus of worms. *Quatrefages*, 1850.

polyonomous (pol-i-on'ǭ-mus), *a.* Same as *polyonymous*.

polyonomy (pol-i-on'ǭ-mi), *n.* Same as *polyonymy*.

polyonym (pol'i-ǭ-nim), *n.* [‹ *polyonym-ous*.] A name consisting of several (specifically, more than three) terms; a polynomial name in zoölogy: correlated with *mononym*, *dionym*, and *trionym*.

polyonymal (pol-i-on'i-mal), *a.* [‹ *polyonym* + *-al*.] Of or pertaining to a polyonym; polynomial.

polyonymic (pol″i-ǭ-nim'ik), *a.* [‹ *polyonym-y* + *-ic*.] Consisting of more than two terms, as a name in anatomy or zoölogy; polyonymal; polynomial. *Buck's Handbook of Med. Sciences*, VIII. 516.

polyonymist (pol-i-on'i-mist), *n.* [‹ *polyonym* + *-ist*.] Same as *polynomialist*.

polyonymous (pol-i-on'i-mus), *a.* [‹ Gr. πολυώνυμος, having many names, ‹ πολύς, many, + ὄνυμα, name.] Having many names or titles; many-titled.

polyonymy (pol-i-on'i-mi), *n.* [Also *polyonomy*; = F. *polyonymie*, ‹ Gr. πολυωνυμία, a multitude of names, ‹ πολυώνυμος, having many names: see *polyonymous*.] **1.** Variety or multiplicity of names for the same object. Specifically—**2.** In *zoöl.*, same as *polynomialism*.

Polyophthalmus (pol″i-of-thal'mus), *n.* [NL., ‹ Gr. πολύς, many, + ὀφθαλμός, eye.] A genus of remarkable polychætous annelids, having a pair of visual organs on every somite of the body, besides the usual cephalic eyes.

polyopia, polyopy (pol-i-ō'pi-ạ̈, pol'i-ǭ-pi), *n.* [NL., ‹ Gr. πολύς, many, + ὤψ, face.] The appearance as of two or more objects when there is but one; multiple vision.

polyoptrum, polyoptron (pol-i-op'trum, -tron), *n.*; pl. *polyoptra* (-trạ̈). [= F. *polyoptre* = It. *poliottro*; ‹ NL. *polyoptrum*, *polyoptron*, ‹ Gr. πολύς, many, + √ ὀπ, see: see *optic*.] A glass through which objects appear multiplied but diminished. It consists of a lens one side of which is plane, while in the other are ground several spherical concavities, every one of which becomes a piano-concave lens, through which an object appears diminished.

polyopy, *n.* See *polyopia*.

polyorama (pol″i-ǭ-rä'mạ̈), *n.* [= F. *polyorama*, ‹ NL. *polyorama*, ‹ Gr. πολύς, many, + ὅραμα, view, sight, ‹ ὁρᾶν, see.] **1.** A view of many objects.—**2.** An optical apparatus presenting many views. See *panorama*.

polyorganic (pol″i-ôr-gan'ik), *a.* [‹ Gr. πολύς, many, + ὄργανον, organ: see *organic*.] Having several diversified or differentiated organs.

> In the natural world some beings are monorganic, others are *polyorganic*.
> *Science*, IX. 534.

polyp, polype (pol'ip), *n.* [= F. *polype* (also *poulpe*: see *poulp*) = Sp. *pólipo* = Pg. *polypo* = It. *polipo* = D. *polyp*, *poliep* = G. Sw. Dan. *polyp*, ‹ L. *polypus*, a polyp, a polypus in the nose, ‹ Gr. πολύπους, a polyp, a polypus in the nose, prop. adj., many-footed, ‹ πολύς, many, + πούς = E. *foot*.] In *zoöl.*, an animal with many feet or foot-like processes. Specifically—(*a*†) An octopus, or eight-rayed cephalopod: an old usage, often in the form *polypus*, still found in *poulp* or *poulpe*. (*b*) Some isopod crustacean, as a wood-louse, slater, sow-bug, or pill-bug. See *Oniscidæ*. (*c*) Since the middle of the eighteenth century: (1) A hydroid or hydrozoan; an actinoid or actinozoan; some cœlenterate or hollow animal, soft or hard, fixed or free, of variable or no determinate form: as, an actinarian, alcyonarian, tubularian, sertularian, campanularian, or pennatularian *polyp*; a coralligenous *polyp*; a medusiform *polyp*; a ctenophoran *polyp*. In this sense the word is coextensive with *Cœlentera*, though not applicable to all the members thereof. See cuts under *Plumularia*, *Corynida*, and *Obelia*. (2) A polyzoan or bryozoan; especially, an aggregate or colonial one, as a sea-mat, like or likened to a polyp in the preceding sense. (3) Some echinoderm, as a sea-lily, stone-lily, crinoid, or encrinite. (4) Some other animal, as a rotifer, an infusorian, or a sponge: a loose or mistaken usage. (*d*) One of the individuals, persons, or zooids of a compound, colonial, or aggregate polyp, the whole of which is a polypidom or polypary, or a polyzoary; a polypide or polypite, as of a hydrozoan, actinozoan, or polyzoan: a common present usage, especially with reference to hydriforms. See cut under *Coralligena*.—**Ascidian polyps**†, the polyzoans or bryozoans; the moss-animalcules.—**Funnel-like polyps.** See *funnel-like*.

polypage (pol'i-pāj), *a.* [‹ Gr. πολύς, many, + E. *page*[1].] Containing several pages.—**Polypage plate**, a stereotype-plate including the matter of several pages.

polypantograph (pol-i-pan'tǭ-gråf), *n.* [‹ Gr. πολύς, many, + E. *pantograph*.] A form of pantograph by which a number of identical designs may be produced simultaneously from a single pattern.

polyparia (pol-i-pā'ri-ạ̈), *n.*; pl. *polypariæ* (-ē). [NL.: see *polypary*.] The stock of the *Anthozoa* and related polyps; a polypary.

polyparian (pol-i-pā'ri-ạn), *a.* [‹ *polypar-y* + *-ian*.] Of or pertaining to a polypary.

polyparium (pol-i-pā'ri-um), *n.*; pl. *polyparia* (-ạ̈). [NL.: see *polypary*.] Same as *polypary*.

polyparous (pǭ-lip'ạ-rus), *a.* [‹ Gr. πολύς, many, + L. *parere*, produce. Cf. *multiparous*.] Same as *polytocous*, 1.

polypary (pol'i-pạ̄-ri), *n.*; pl. *polyparies* (-riz). [‹ NL. *polyparium* = F. *polypier*; ‹ L. *polypus*, a polyp: see *polyp* and *-ary*.] The stock of the *Anthozoa* and related polyps; a polyp-stock, polypidom, or polyparia; the horny or chitinous outer covering or envelop with which many of the *Hydrozoa* are furnished. The term is also not uncommonly applied to the very similar structures produced by the *Polyzoa*; but for these *polyzoary* is used by those who desire to keep *polypary* for the *Actinozoa* and *Hydrozoa*. The polypary-producing polypides are propagated by budding, and live together in groups or colonies so associated that each group forms a compound animal, whose united coverings form a compound polypary or polypidom, which is their common home, and is at the same time the central stem or stock sustaining the whole. Every individual polyp thus lives in its own proper cavity in the common polypary, from which it protrudes its body and into which it retracts it at pleasure. Also *polypiarium*.

polyp-colony (pol'ip-kol″ǭ-ni), *n.* A colony of polyps; a compound or aggregate polyp.

polype, *n.* See *polyp*.

polypean (pǭ-lip'ẹ̄-ạn), *a.* and *n.* [‹ *polyp* + *-e-an*.] **I.** *a.* Of or pertaining to a polyp or polypus in any sense.

II. *n.* A polyp; any polyp-like organism.

Polypedetes (pol″i-pẹ̄-dē'tēz), *n.* [NL., ‹ Gr. πολύς, many, + πεδήτης, one fettered, a prisoner.] The typical genus of the family *Polypedetidæ*, containing numerous species, chiefly Oriental. *P. maculatus* is a common Indian tree-toad. *P. eques* is called the *spurred tree-toad*. Also, erroneously, *Polypedates*, *Polypedotes*.

Polypedetidæ (pol″i-pẹ̄-det'i-dē), *n. pl.* [NL., ‹ *Polypedetes* + *-idæ*.] A family of anurous salient batrachians, typified by the genus *Polypedetes*, containing the so-called glandless tree-toads. It is an ill-characterized group; the species which have been referred to it belong mostly to the *Ranidæ*. Also *Polypedatidæ*.

Polypetalæ (pol-i-pet'ạ-lē), *n. pl.* [NL. (Tournefort, 1694), fem. pl. of **polypetalus*: see *polypetalous*.] A division or group of dicotyledonous plants, characterized by distinct or separate petals, forming a circle inside the calyx, as in the single rose, or several circles, as in the water-lily, magnolia, and cactus. It includes 82 orders, classed in 15 cohorts, and grouped in the 3 series *Thalamifloræ*, *Discifloræ*, and *Calycifloræ*, with the stamens inserted respectively on the receptacle, disk, or calyx, and having the buttercup, maple, and rose as examples. See *dicotyledon*. Also called *Dialypetalæ*.

polypetalous (pol-i-pet'ạ-lus), *a.* [= F. *polypétale* = Sp. *polipétalo* = Pg. *polypetalo* = It. *polipetalo*; ‹ NL. **polypetalus*, ‹ Gr. πολύς, many, + πέταλον, leaf (NL. petal).] In *bot.*, having two or more separate petals: as, a *polypetalous* corolla. Also *apopetalous*, *dialypetalous*, *choripetalous*. See cut under *corolla*.

polyphagia (pol-i-fā'ji-ạ̈), *n.* [NL.: see *polyphagy*.] **1.** In *med.*, excessive desire of eating; voracity. *Dunglison*.—**2.** In *zoöl.*, same as *polyphagy*.

polyphagic (pol-i-faj'ik), *a.* [‹ *polyphag-y* + *-ic*.] Exhibiting or characterized by polyphagy; polyphagous.

polyphagous (pǭ-lif'ạ-gus), *a.* [= F. *polyphage* = It. *polifago* (‹ L. *polyphagus*, a glutton), ‹ Gr. πολυφάγος, eating too much, ‹ πολύς, much, + φαγεῖν, eat.] Eating many different kinds of food; almost pamphagous or omnivorous; not monophagous.

> Its [a scale-insect's] *polyphagous* habit, or the ease with which it accommodates itself to so great a variety of plants.
> *C. V. Riley*, U. S. Entom. Bull., No. 15, 1887, p. 12.

polyphagy (pǭ-lif'ạ-ji), *n.* [= F. *polyphagie*; ‹ NL. *polyphagia*, ‹ Gr. πολυφαγία, excess in eating, ‹ πολυφάγος, eating too much: see *polyphagous*.] The habit or practice of subsisting on many different kinds of food; polyphagous regimen. Also *polyphagia*.

polypharmacy (pol-i-fär'mạ-si), *n.* [= F. *polypharmacie*, ‹ Gr. πολυφάρμακος, having to do with many drugs, ‹ πολύς, many, + φάρμακον, a drug: see *pharmacon*, *pharmacy*.] The prescribing of too many medicines, especially in one prescription. *Dr. J. Brown*, Spare Hours.

polyphase (pol'i-fāz), *a.* [< Gr. πολύς, many, + E. *phase*[1], *n.*] In *elect.*, having components of various phase.

polypheme† (pol'i-fēm), *n.* [< *polyphemus.*] One of a group of snail-shells, such as *Halia priamus.*

Polyphemidæ (pol-i-fem'i-dē), *n. pl.* [NL., < *Polyphemus* + *-idæ.*] A family of cladocerous or daphniaceous crustaceans, typified by the genus *Polyphemus.*

polyphemous (pol-i-fē'mus), *a.* [< L. *Polyphemus*, < Gr. Πολύφημος, a one-eyed Cyclops: see *polyphemus.*] One-eyed; monoculous; cyclopean.

polyphemus (pol-i-fē'mus), *n.* [NL., < L. *Polyphemus*, < Gr. Πολύφημος, a Cyclops so named, < πολυφήμος, many-voiced, also famous, < πολύς, many, + φήμη, voice, fame: see *fame*[1].] 1. An animal which has only one eye, whether naturally or abnormally; a cyclops.—2. The specific name of the king-crab, *Limulus polyphemus.*—3. [*cap.*] In *Crustacea*, the typical genus of the family *Polyphemidæ:* so called from the large solitary and apparently single eye formed by the coalescence of a pair of eyes. *P. stagnorum* is an example.—4. Any member of the family *Polyphemidæ.*—5. In *Lepidoptera*, the technical specific and (absolutely) the vernacular name of one of the largest American silkworms or silkworm-moths, *Telea polyphemus.* The caterpillar feeds on many different native trees, as oak, walnut, hickory, willow, elm, maple, poplar, etc., and is of a clear apple-green color with

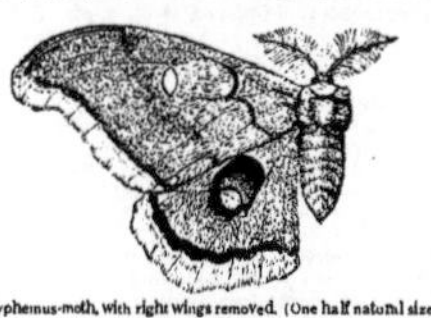

Polyphemus-moth, with right wings removed. (One half natural size.)

yellow lateral lines. The cocoon is oval and usually wrapped in a leaf, sometimes falling to the ground, but often hanging on the tree all winter. The moth is normally single-brooded in the northern United States, but double-brooded in the southern. The silk can be reeled, but with considerable difficulty, and is lustrous and strong. The moth has a wing-spread of five or six inches, and is of a buff color, with a large eye-spot on each hind wing.

polyphlœsbœan (pol'i-fles-bē'an), *a.* [< Gr. πολυφλοισβος (gen. πολυφλοίσβοιο), loud-roaring, frequent in Homer as an epithet of θάλασσα, the sea; < πολύς, much, + φλοῖσβος, roar, noise.] Loud-roaring.

> Two men are walking by the *polyphlœsbœan* ocean.
> *O. W. Holmes*, Autocrat, iv.

polyphobia (pol-i-fō'bi-ä), *n.* [NL., < Gr. πολύς, many, + -φοβία, < φέβεσθαι, fear.] Morbid fear of many things: nearly equivalent to *pantophobia.*

polyphone (pol'i-fōn), *n.* [< Gr. πολύς, many, + φωνή, voice, sound: see *phone*[1].] A written sign capable of being read in more than one way, or standing for two or more phonetic signs.

> The different phonetic values of the *polyphones.*
> *Encyc. Brit.*, XI. 801.

polyphonia (pol-i-fō'ni-ä), *n.* [NL.: see *polyphony.*] Same as *polyphony.*

polyphonian (pol-i-fō'ni-an), *a.* [< *polyphon-ous* + *-ian.*] Many-voiced; polyphonic.

> I love the air; her dainty sweets refresh
> My drooping soul, and to new sweets invite me;
> Her shrill mouth'd choir sustain me with their flesh,
> And with their *Polyphonian* notes delight me.
> *Quarles*, Emblems, v. 6.

polyphonic (pol-i-fon'ik), *a.* [= F. *polyphonique* = Pg. *polyphonico;* as *polyphon-ous* + *-ic.*] 1. Capable of being read or pronounced in more than one way: said of a written character.

> The particular value to be assigned to each of the *polyphonic* characters. *Isaac Taylor*, The Alphabet, I. 46.

2. Consisting of or having many voices or sounds.

> The barking crow possesses the most remarkable *polyphonic* powers. It can shriek, laugh, yell, shout, whistle, scream, and bark. *Saturday Rev.*, XXV. 469.

3. In *music:* (*a*) Noting a method of composition or a work in which two or more voice-parts are simultaneously combined without losing their independent character, but with harmonious effect; contrapuntal: opposed on one side to *monodic, monophonic*, and *homophonic*, and on another to *harmonic:* as, a fugue is a *polyphonic* form of composition. (*b*) Noting an instrument which is capable of producing more than one tone at a time, as an organ or a harp.

Also *polyphonous.*

polyphonism (pol'i-fō-nizm), *n.* [= Pg. *polyphonismo;* as *polyphon-ous* + *-ism.*] 1. Multiplicity of sounds, as in the reverberations of an echo.

> I have chosen to single out the passages which relate to the *polyphonisms*, or repercussions of the rocks and caverns, and other phonocamptic . . . objects below in the mount. *Derham*, Physico-Theology, i. 3.

2. In *music*, the use of polyphony, or the state of being polyphonic in structure.

polyphonist (pol'i-fō-nist), *n.* [< *polyphon-y* + *-ist.*] 1. One who professes the art of multiplying sounds, or who makes a variety of sounds; an imitator of a variety of sounds; a ventriloquist.—2. One who understands or uses polyphony; a contrapuntist.

polyphonium (pol-i-fō'ni-um), *n.* [NL., < Gr. πολυφωνία, variety of tones: see *polyphony.*] In *music*, a polyphonic composition.

polyphonous (pol'i-fō-nus), *a.* [= F. *polyphone*, < Gr. πολύφωνος, having many tones, < πολύς, many, + φωνή, sound, voice, tone: see *phone*[1].] Same as *polyphonic.*

polyphony (pol'i-fō-ni, oftener pō-lif'ō-ni), *n.* [= F. *polyphonie* = Pg. *polyphonia*, < NL. *polyphonia*, < Gr. πολυφωνία, variety of tones, < πολύφωνος, having many tones: see *polyphonous.*] 1. The capability of being pronounced in various ways characterizing some written characters.

> It will be seen how great an element of ambiguity was introduced by the *polyphony* which arose from the adaptation of a Turanian syllabary to a Semitic language.
> *Isaac Taylor*, The Alphabet, I. 45.

2. In *music*, the act, process, art, or result of simultaneously combining two or more voice-parts so that they shall maintain their individuality and independent interest, and yet shall harmonize with each other; counterpoint. It is opposed to *monody, monophony*, and *homophony*, in which a single voice-part is raised into decided prominence, and to *harmony* (in one of its senses), in which the attention is centered upon the successive chords as such rather than upon the voice-parts that constitute them. See *counterpoint*[2], 3.

polyphore (pol'i-fōr), *n.* [= F *polyphore*, < Gr. πολυφόρος, bearing much, < πολύς, much, + φέρειν = E. *bear*[1].] In *bot.*, a fleshy receptacle with numerous ovaries, as that of a strawberry.

polyphotal (pol'i-fō-tal), *a.* [< *polyphote* + *-al.*] Same as *polyphote.*

polyphote (pol'i-fōt), *a.* [< Gr. πολύς, many, + φῶς (φωτ-), light.] An epithet applied to electric arc-lamps which are so constructed that more than one may be used on the same electric circuit. Monophote lamps require a separate circuit for each lamp.

polyphyletic (pol"i-fī-let'ik), *a.* [< Gr. πολύς, many, + φυλή, tribe: see *phyle, phyletic.*] 1. Pertaining to or derived from several phyla; having several different lines of descent: as, a *polyphyletic* origin.—2. Of or pertaining to the doctrine or theory that animals are not monophyletic, but are severally and specially created, or at least derived from many different sources.

polyphylline (pol-i-fil'in), *a.* [< *polyphyll-ous* + *-ine*[1].] In *bot.*, same as *polyphyllous.*

polyphyllous (pol-i-fil'us), *a.* [= F. *polyphylle* = Pg. *polyphillo* = It. *polifillo*, < NL. *polyphyllus*, < Gr. πολύφυλλος, with many leaves, < πολύς, many, + φύλλον, leaf.] In *bot.*, many-leafed: as, a *polyphyllous* calyx or perianth.

polyphylly (pol'i-fil-i), *n.* [< NL. **polyphyllia*, < *polyphyllus*, many-leafed: see *polyphyllous.*] In *bot.*, an increase in the number of members or organs in a whorl, as when a normally pentamerous calyx has six or more sepals, as is occasionally the case in the plum. Foliage, leaves, and all the parts of the flowers may be so affected.

polyphyodont (pol-i-fī'ō-dont), *a.* and *n.* [< Gr. πολυφυής, manifold (< πολύς, many, + φύειν, produce), + ὀδούς (ὀδοντ-) = E. *tooth.*] I. *a.* Having several sets of teeth, as a fish: opposed to *monophyodont* and *diphyodont.*

II. *n.* A polyphyodont animal.

Polypi (pol'i-pī), *n. pl.* [NL., pl. of L. *polypus*, a polyp: see *polyp.*] 1. The polyps as a class or other high group of low invertebrate animals, of which the nearest modern synonym is *Cœlentera* or *Cœlenterata.* Specifically—(*a*) In Cuvier's system of classification, *Polypi* were the fourth class of his *Radiata*, divided into three orders—*Carnosi*, including *Actinia* and *Lucernaria; Gelatinosi*, including Hydra and the *Polyzoa;* and *Coralliferi*, or the corals at large, with *Pennatula, Alcyonium*, and also the sponges. (*b*) In Leuckart's system (1848), they were one of two classes of *Cœlentera*, distinguished from *Acalephæ*, and divided into two orders, *Anthozoa* and *Cylicozoa.* (*c*) In Milne-Edwards's system (1855), an alternative name of his *Corallaria*, or the third class of his *Radiaria*, distinguished from echinoderms and acalephs. Also *Polypiaria, Polypifera, Polypiphera.*

2. [*l. c.*] Plural of *polypus.*

Polypiaria (pol"i-pi-ā'ri-ä), *n. pl.* [NL., < L. *polypus*, a polyp: see *polyp.*] Same as *Polypi.*

polypiarian (pol"i-pi-ā'ri-an), *a.* and *n.* [< *Polypiaria* + *-an.*] I. *a.* Of or pertaining to the *Polypiaria;* polypiferous; cœlenterate.

II. *n.* A member of the *Polypiaria.*

polypiarium (pol"i-pi-ā'ri-um), *n.;* pl. *polypiaria* (-ä). [NL.: see *polypary.*] Same as *polypary.*

polypide (pol'i-pid), *n.* [< *polyp* + *-ide*[2].] An individual zoöid of a polyzoarium, or compound polyzoan; the individual organism contained in one of the cells or cups of the ectocyst of a polyzoarium, just as an individual of a compound coralligenous actinozoan is contained in a cup of the polypidom. The polypide of a polyzoan thus corresponds to the polypite of a cœlenterate. See *polypary*, and cuts under *Plumatella* and *Polyzoa.*

polypidom (pol'i-pi-dum), *n.* [< Gr. πολύπους, a polyp, + δόμος, house.] An aggregate of polypites or polypides; a compound polypary, or the dermal system of a colony of individual actinozoans, hydrozoans, or polyzoans; a polyp-stock, or the stem of a colony of zoöphytes, containing the cells of the individual polypites or polypides which fabricate it. Thus, a piece of coral is the *polypidom* of an actinozoan or hydrozoan; a sea-mat is the *polypidom* (more exactly, the *polyzoary*) of a polyzoan. See cuts under *Coralligena* and *Polyzoa.*

polypier (pol'i-pėr), *n.* and *a.* [< F. *polypier*, < NL. *polypiarium:* see *polypary.*] I. *n.* 1. A polyp in sense (*d*); a polypite or polypide; one individual, or a single cell, of a compound polyp.—2. A polypidom, polypary, or polyp-stock; a compound or aggregate polyp; a polyzoarium.

> Sometimes each polyp has a distinct *polypier*, but in general it is the common portion of a mass of aggregated polypi which presents the characters peculiar to these bodies, and thus these form aggregated *polypiers*, the volume of which may become very considerable, although each of its constituent parts has dimensions which are very small. *Milne-Edwards*, Manual of Zoology, § 610.

II. *a.* Composed of the stony material of some polypidoms; coral-like: as, *polypier* beads. *Catalogue Boban Collection*, 1887.

polypiety (pol-i-pī'e-ti), *n.* [< Gr. πολύς, many, + E. *piety.*] Belief in or reverence for anything and everything; tolerance of all kinds of piety or belief. [Rare.]

> *Polypiety* is the greatest impiety in the world. To say that men ought to have liberty of conscience is impious ignorance. N. Ward, Simple Cobler, p. 5.

polypifer (pol'i-pi-fėr), *n.* [< L. *polypus*, polyp, + *ferre* = Gr. φέρειν = E. *bear*[1].] A polyp or polyp-stock; a member of the *Polypifera.*

Polypifera (pol-i-pif'e-rä), *n. pl.* [NL.: see *polypifer.*] Same as *Polypi.*

polypiferous (pol-i-pif'e-rus), *a.* [< L. *polypus*, polyp, + *ferre* = E. *bear*[1].] Bearing polyps; producing polypites: as, the *polypiferous* surface of a coral. Also *polypiparous, polypigerous.*

polypiform (pol'i-pi-fôrm), *a.* [< L. *polypus*, polyp, + *forma*, form.] 1. Having the form, structure, or character of a polyp; polypomorphic.—2. Having the form or appearance of a polypus.

polypigerous (pol-i-pij'e-rus), *a.* [< L. *polypus*, polyp, + *gerere*, carry.] Same as *polypiferous.*

polypiparous (pol-i-pip'a-rus), *a.* [< L. *polypus*, polyp, + *parere*, produce.] Same as *polypiferous.*

polypite (pol'i-pīt), *n.* [= F. *polypite;* as *polyp* + *-ite*[2].] 1. The fundamental element in the structure of a polyp, as a hydrozoan or an actinozoan; an individual zoöid of a compound polyp; one of the individuals or persons which together fabricate and constitute a polyp-stock or polypary; a hydranth. The term is sometimes extended to the corresponding elements of a polyzoarium, or compound polyzoan, but these are more strictly called *polypides.* See cut under *Athorybia.*

2. A fossil polyp.

polyplacid (pol'i-plas-id), *a.* [< Gr. πολύς, many, + πλακοῦς, a flat cake: see *placent.*] Having more than one madreporic plate, as a starfish; not monoplacid. Abbreviated *p.*

Polyplacophora (pol″i-plā̤-kof′ō-rä̤), *n. pl.* [NL. (J. E. Gray, 1821), neut. pl. of *polyplacophorus*: see *polyplacophorous*.] An order of isopleurous gastropods, exhibiting bilateral symmetry and metameric segmentation. The dorsal shell is in eight successive pieces, sometimes embedded in shell-sacs; there are numerous gill-combs and olfactory tracts, or ctenidia and osphradia; paired genital

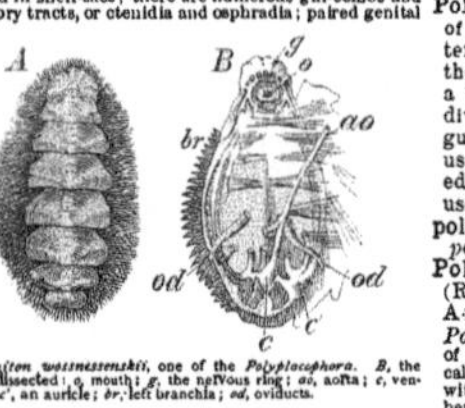

A, Chiton wossnessenskii, one of the *Polyplacophora*. *B*, the same, dissected: *o*, mouth; *g*, the nervous ring; *ao*, aorta; *c*, ventricle; *c′*, an auricle; *br*, left branchia; *od*, oviducts.

ducts distinct from the paired nephridia; and there is a well-developed odontophore with numerous lingual teeth on the radula. The order is conterminous with the family *Chitonidæ* in a broad sense. In J. E. Gray's classification (1821) it was one of 9 orders of cryptobranchiate gastropods. The original form was *Polyplaxiphora*. In Gray's system of the mollusks it was considered as a suborder of heteroglossate scutibranchiate gastropods, and defined as having the gills in two lamellar series on each side of the binder part of the under side of the mantle-edge, and the shell formed of eight imbricate valves.

polyplacophoran (pol″i-plā̤-kof′ō-ran), *a.* and *n.* Same as *polyplacophore*.

polyplacophore (pol-i-plak′ō-fōr), *a.* and *n.* [< NL. *polyplacophorus*: see *polyplacophorous*.] I. *a.* Bearing many plates, as a chiton; of or pertaining to the *Polyplacophora*.

II. *n.* A member of the *Polyplacophora*; a chiton, or coat-of-mail shell.

polyplacophorous (pol″i-plā̤-kof′ō-rus), *a.* [< NL. *polyplacophorus*, < Gr. πολύς, many, + πλάξ (πλακ-), a tablet, plate, + φέρειν = E. *bear*[1].] Same as *polyplacophore*.

polyplastic (pol-i-plas′tik), *a.* [< Gr. πολύς, many, + πλαστικός, plastic: see *plastic*.] Having or assuming many forms.

Polyplaxiphora (pol″i-plak-sif′ō-rä̤), *n. pl.* Same as *Polyplacophora*. *De Blainville*, 1825, etc.

polyplectron, polyplectrum (pol-i-plek′tron, -trum), *n.* [= F. *polyplectron*; < Gr. πολύς, many, + πλῆκτρον, plectrum: see *plectrum*.] **1.** Pl. *polyplectra* (-trä̤). An obsolete variety of harpsichord or spinet.—**2.** [*cap.*] [NL. (Temminck, 1815).] A magnificent genus of *Phasianidæ*, of the subfamily *Pavoninæ*, having the tarsi with

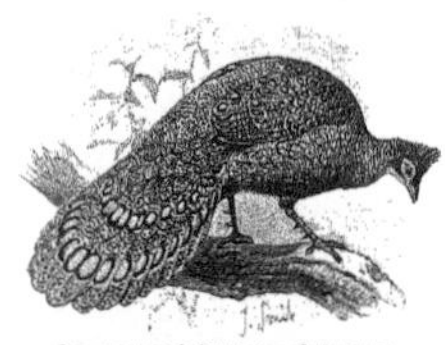

Peacock-pheasant (*Polyplectron bicalcaratum*).

two or more spurs, and the plumage more or less ocellated, as in the peacock; the peacock-pheasants. The best-known species is *P. bicalcaratum* or *chinquis*; others are *P. germaini*, *helenæ*, *schleirmachi*, and *thibetanum*. More different than these are the Napoleon pheasant of the Moluccas, *P. emphanum* (or *napoleonis*), and the Sumatran *P. chalcurum*. Also called *Diplectropus*, *Diplectron*, *Diplectrum*.

Polyplectroninæ (pol-i-plek-trō-nī′nē), *n. pl.* [NL., < *Polyplectron*, 2, + *-inæ*.] Same as *Pavoninæ*.

polyplectrum, *n.* See *polyplectron*.

polypnœa (pol-ip-nē′ä̤), *n.* [NL., < Gr. πολύς, many, + πνοιά, πνοή, breathing, < πνεῖν, breathe.] Increased frequency of respiration.

polypod (pol′i-pod), *a.* and *n.* [< Gr. πολύπους, many-footed, < πολύς, many, + πούς (ποδ-) = E. *foot*. Cf. *polyp*.] I. *a.* Having many legs, feet, arms, or rays. (*a*) In *Crustacea*, more than decapod; having more than ten and fewer than fifty legs. Compare *amphipod*, *isopod*. (*b*) In *Mollusca*, more than octopod; decapod or decacerous; of or pertaining to the *Polypoda*. (*c*) In *Annelida*, having indefinitely many foot-stumps or parapodia; of or pertaining to the *Polypoda*. (*d*) In entom.: (1) myriapod; of or pertaining to the *Polypoda*. (2) Many-footed, as the larvæ of certain hexapods.

II. *n.* **1.** A member of the *Polypoda*, in any sense.—**2.** Same as *polypody*.

Also *polypode*.

Polypoda (pō-lip′ō-dä̤), *n. pl.* [NL., neut. pl. of *polypus*: see *polypod*.] **1.** In Kirby's system (1826), a class of insects corresponding to the modern class *Myriapoda*.—**2.** In *Annelida*, a large division of worms which are polypod, divided into *Nereidina* and *Serpulina*: distinguished from *Apoda*. *Macleay*, 1840. [Little used.]—**3.** An order of cephalopods represented by the nautiloids. See *Nautilidæ*. [Little used.]

polypode (pol′i-pōd), *n.* [= F. *polypode*: see *polypod*.] Same as *polypod*.

Polypodiaceæ (pol-i-pō-di-ā′sē̤-ē), *n. pl.* [NL. (Robert Brown, 1810), < *Polypodium* + *-aceæ*.] A natural order of ferns, named from the genus *Polypodium*. This order includes the largest number of genera and species, and may be regarded as the typical order of ferns. They are usually herbaceous plants, with a permanent stem, which remains buried or rooted beneath the soil, or creeps over the stems of trees, or forms a scarcely moving point of growth around which new fronds are annually produced in a circle, or it rises into the air in the form of a simple stem bearing a tuft of fronds at its apex, and sometimes attaining the height of 40 feet or more, as in the tree-ferns. The sporangia are collected in dots, lines, or variously shaped clusters on the back or margins of the frond or its divisions, and are provided with an incomplete vertical annulus so that they dehisce transversely. It embraces the tribes *Polypodieæ*, *Grammatideæ*, *Pterideæ*, *Blechneæ*, *Asplenieæ*, *Aspidieæ*, *Woodsieæ*, *Dicksonieæ*, etc. See cuts under *Nothochlæna* and *Onoclea*.

polypodiaceous (pol-i-pō-di-ā′shius), *a.* [< *Polypodiaceæ* + *-ous*.] Of or pertaining to the *Polypodiaceæ*.

Polypodieæ (pol″i-pō-dī′ē̤-ē), *n. pl.* [NL., < *Polypodium* + *-eæ*.] A tribe of ferns of the order *Polypodiaceæ*, embracing the genus *Polypodium*. The sori are on the back of the frond, on the veins, or at the ends of the veins, in roundish clusters, and without indusium of any kind.

Polypodium (pol-i-pō′di-um), *n.* [NL., < L. *polypodium*, a kind of fern: see *polypody*.] The largest and most widely distributed genus of ferns, typical of the suborder *Polypodiaceæ* and tribe *Polypodieæ*. The fronds are very various in outline, with the sori round, naked, dorsal, in one or more rows on each side of the midrib, or irregularly scattered. About 400 species are known, of which only 9 are found in North America, *P. vulgare*, which occurs also in the Old World, being the most common. See *polypody*.

The complete plant of Polypody (*Polypodium vulgare*). *a*, pinnule with sori; *b*, a sporangium.

polypody (pol′i-pō-di), *n.* [< ME. *polypodye* = F. *polypode* = Sp. *polipodio* = Pg. *polypodio* = It. *polipodio*, < L. *polypodium*, < Gr. πολυπόδιον, a kind of fern, so called with ref. to the branching rootstock, < πολύπους, many-footed: see *polypode*[1], *polyp*.] A fern of the genus *Polypodium*, chiefly *P. vulgare*, the common polypody, growing commonly on rocks: in England locally called *adder's-fern*, *wall-* or *wood-fern*, *polypody of the oak* or *of the wall*, etc. The hoary polypody is *P. incanum*, a smaller species abounding in tropical America and reaching north to Ohio, having the fronds grayish-scurfy beneath, growing on trees and roofs, also on rocks. Also *polypod*, *polypode*.

> Take the stinking oil drawn out of *polypody of the oak* by a retort, mixed with turpentine and hive-honey, and anoint your bait therewith.
> *I. Walton*, Complete Angler, p. 128.

Polypogon (pol-i-pō′gon), *n.* [NL. (Desfontaines, 1798), so called in allusion to the many long awns; < Gr. πολύς, much, + πώγων, beard.] A genus of grasses of the tribe *Agrostideæ* and subtribe *Euagrosteæ*. It is characterized by the usually dense and spike-like inflorescence, the one-flowered spikelets with the pedicel not prolonged beyond the flower, and the three-awned glumes, the flowering glume much the smaller, and bearing its awn below the apex. There are about 10 species, widely distributed over temperate and subtropical regions, mainly annuals with decumbent stems and flat leaves. They bear cylindrical spikes almost concealed by their abundant awns, or spicate panicles, which are larger and irregular. See *beard-grass*.

polypoid (pol′i-poid), *a.* [< Gr. πολύπους, polyp, + εἶδος, form.] Resembling a polyp or polypus; polypiform or polypomorphic.

polypoidal (pol-i-poi′da̤l), *a.* [< *polypoid* + *-al*.] Resembling a polypus.

Polypomedusæ (pol″i-pǫ-mę̄-dū′sē), *n. pl.* [NL., < L. *polypus*, polyp, + NL. *Medusa*: see *Medusa*, 2.] A group of epithelarian *Cœlentera*, consisting of the hydrozoans and actinozoans, thus together distinguished from the ctenophorans by the possession of cnidoblasts. According to the presence or absence of phacellæ, the *Polypomedusæ* are divided into *Phacellotæ* and *Aphacellæ*, the former consisting of the *Scyphomedusæ* and *Actiniaria*, the latter of the *Hydromedusæ* alone. The polypomedusans are simply the cœlenterates divested of the ctenophorans.

polypomedusan (pol″i-pō-mę̄-dū′sa̤n), *a.* and *n.* I. *a.* Pertaining to the *Polypomedusæ*, or having their characters.

II. *n.* A member of the *Polypomedusæ*.

Polypomorpha (pol″i-pǫ-môr′fä̤), *n. pl.* [NL., < Gr. πολύπους, polyp, + μορφή, form.] Polyps or polypiform cœlenterates, a prime group or grade of *Hydrozoa*: used when the ctenophores are included in that class, the two divisions then being *Polypomorpha* and *Ctenophora*.

polypomorphic (pol″i-pǫ-môr′fik), *a.* [< Gr. πολύπους, polyp, + μορφή, form, + *-ic*.] Having the form or character of a polyp; polypoid; polypiform; of or pertaining to the *Polypomorpha*.

Polypora (pǫ-lip′ǫ-rä̤), *n.* [NL. (McCoy, 1844), < Gr. πολύπορος, with many passages or pores: see *polyporous*.] A genus of coralligenous hydrozoans or *Hydrocorallinæ*, belonging to the family *Stylasteridæ*.

Polyporiaceæ (pol i-pō-ri-ā′sę̄-ē), *n. pl.* [NL., < *Polyporus* + *-aceæ*.] An order of hymenomycetous fungi, typified by the genus *Polyporus*.

polyporite (pǫ-lip′ǫ-rīt), *n.* [< *polyporus* + *-ite*[2].] In *geol.*, a fungus-like organism resembling *Polyporus versicolor*.

polyporoid (pǫ-lip′ǫ-roid), *a.* [< *Polyporus* + *-oid*.] In *bot.*, similar to, characteristic of, or belonging to the genus *Polyporus*.

polyporous (pǫ-lip′ǫ-rus), *a.* [< Gr. πολύπορος, with many pores, < πολύς, many, + πόρος, a passage, pore: see *pore*[2].] Having many pores; cribrate; ethmoid; foraminulate.

Polyporus (pǫ-lip′ǫ-rus), *n.* [NL. (Fries, 1836–1838), < Gr. πολύς, many, + πόρος, a passage, pore.] A very large, widely distributed genus of hymenomycetous fungi, typical of the order *Polyporiaceæ*, having the hymenium lining long, narrow, round, or angular tubes. They are very familiar objects, forming little shelves or brackets attached to dead or decaying wood, some being very small, others several or many inches in circumference. *P. officinalis* is the white or purging agaric, or larch-agaric, used internally to check sweats, sometimes as a purgative and emetic, and externally as a styptic. See *agaric* and *amadou*.

Polyporus igneus. *a*, longitudinal section, showing the tubular pores; *b*, transverse section through a part of one of the pores, showing the basidia and the hyphæ.

polypose (pol′i-pōs), *a.* [< L. *polyposus*: see *polypous*.] Same as *polypous*. *Arbuthnot*, Aliments, vi.

polypostem (pol′i-pǫ-stem), *n.* Same as *polypstem*.

polypostylar (pol″i-pō-stī′lä̤r), *a.* [< *polypostyle* + *-ar*[3].] Pertaining to a polypostyle, or having its character.

polypostyle (pol′i-pō-stīl), *n.* [< Gr. πολύπους, many-footed (see *polyp*), + στῦλος, a pillar: see *style*[2].] A reduced or imperfect nutritive zoöid of a hydroid hydrozoan, without mouth or tentacles; a dactylozoöid.

polypotome (pol′i-pǫ-tōm), *n.* [< Gr. πολύπους, polypus, + -τομος, < τέμνειν, ταμεῖν, cut.] An instrument for excising a polypus.

polypous (pol′i-pus), *a.* [= F. *polypeux* = Sp. *poliposo* = Pg. *polyposo* = It. *poliposo*, < L. *polyposus*, having polypus in the nose, < *polypus*, polypus: see *polypus*.] Of the nature of a polypus; having many feet or roots, like a polypus.

polypragmatic (pol″i-prag-mat′ik), *a.* and *n.* [Formerly *polipragmatick*; < Gr. πολυπράγματος, having many things to do, meddlesome, inquisitive, < πολύς, many, + πρᾶγμα, a thing to do, affair, pl. πράγματα, business: see *pragmatic*.] I. *a.* Overbusy or meddlesome; forward; officious. [Rare.]

II. *n.* A meddlesome or officious person.

Jesuited *polipragmaticks.* *Burton.* (*Davies.*)

polypragmatical (pol″i-prag-mat′i-kal), *a.* [< *polypragmatic* + *-al.*] Same as *polypragmatic.*

His [the busybody's] actions are *polypragmatical*, his feet peripatetical. Erasmus pictures him to the life: "He knows what every merchant got in his Voyage, what plots are at Rome, what stratagems with the Turk, &c."
Rev. T. Adams, Works, I. 502.

polypragmaty (pol-i-prag′ma-ti), *n.* [As *polypragmat-ic* + *-y*[3].] The state of being over-engaged in business or affairs. [Rare.]

polypragmon (pol-i-prag′mon), *n.* [Formerly *polipragmon, polipragman*; < OF. *polipragmon*, < Gr. πολυπράγμων, a busybody, < πολύς, much, many, + πρᾶγμα, affair, πράσσειν, act.] A busybody; an officious person.

polypragmonist† (pol-i-prag′mǫ-nist), *n.* [< *polypragmon* + *-ist.*] Same as *polypragmon.*

Dry tobacco with my [hornbook's] leaves, you good dry-brained *polypragmonists.* *Dekker*, Gull's Hornbook.

Polyprion (pol-i-pri′on), *n.* [NL. (Cuvier, 1817), < Gr. πολύς, many, + πρίων, a saw.] A genus of serranoid fishes; the stone-basses. The anal spines are strong, the dorsal spines serrated, the branchiostegals seven, and the teeth all villiform; the tail is not forked, and there is a rough ridge on the operculum. *P. cernium* is a large fish, 6 feet long, of the coasts of southern Europe and Africa, sometimes known as the *stone-bass, wreck-fish*, and *cernier*, and *P. oxygeneios* is an inhabitant of the temperate Pacific.

polyprism (pol′i-prizm), *n.* [< Gr. πολύς, many, + πρίσμα, a prism: see *prism.*] A compound prism formed of several prisms of different materials, but of the same angle, connected at their ends, and used to show the unequal refracting power of different media.

polyprismatic (pol″i-priz-mat′ik), *a.* [= It. *poliprismatico*, < Gr. πολύς, many, + πρίσμα, a prism: see *prism, prismatic.*] In *mineral.*, having crystals presenting numerous prisms in a single form.

polyprotodont (pol-i-prō′tǭ-dont), *a.* and *n.* [< Gr. πολύς, many, + πρῶτος, first, + ὀδούς (ὀδοντ-) = E. *tooth.*] I. *a.* Having several front teeth: noting the insectivorous or carnivorous dentition of marsupials, in which the incisors are small, several, and much alike, and the canines large and specialized: contrasted with *diprotodont.*

II. *n.* A polyprotodont marsupial.

Polyprotodontia (pol-i-prō-tǭ-don′shi-ạ̈), *n. pl.* [NL., neut. pl.: see *polyprotodont.*] The carnivorous or polyprotodont marsupials, a prime division of *Marsupialia*, having more than two incisors (at least in the lower jaw) and specialized canines.

polyp-stem (pol′ip-stem), *n.* A polyp-stock; the stem of a polypidom, common to several polypites. Also *polypostem.*

polyp-stock (pol′ip-stok), *n.* The stock of a polyp; a polypary or polypidom.

Polypteridæ (pol-ip-ter′i-dē), *n. pl.* [NL., < *Polypterus* + *-idæ.*] A family of crossopterygian ganoid fishes, typified by the genus *Polypterus*; the bichirs. They have lozenge-shaped ganoid scales, fins without fulcra, a series of dorsal spines, to which an articulated finlet is attached, anal situated close to the caudal fin, the vent near the end of the tail, the abdominal part of the vertebral column much longer than the caudal portion, and no pseudobranchiæ.

polypteroid (pǭ-lip′tẹ-roid), *a.* and *n.* I. *a.* Resembling or related to the fin-fishes; belonging to the *Polypteroidei.*

II. *n.* A member of the *Polypteroidei.*

Polypteroidei (pǭ-lip-tẹ-roi′dē-ī), *n. pl.* [< NL. *Polypterus*, q. v., + Gr. εἶδος, form.] A suborder of ganoid fishes, represented by the *Polypteridæ* and some related families.

Polypterus (pǭ-lip′tẹ-rus), *n.* [NL. (Geoffroy, 1802), < Gr. πολύπτερος, many-winged, < πολύς, many, + πτερόν, feather, wing.] The typical genus of *Polypteridæ*, remarkable for the number of the dorsal spines bearing rays behind. It contains the bichir.

polyptoton (pol-ip-tō′ton), *n.* [L. (> F. *polyptote*), < Gr. πολύπτωτον, neut. of πολύπτωτος, with many cases, < πολύς, many, + πτωτός, verbal adj. of πίπτειν, fall (> πτῶσις, a case).] In *rhet.*, a figure consisting in the use of different cases or inflections of the same word, or of words of the same immediate derivation, in the same context. One of the most celebrated examples is the distich,

Mors mortis morti mortem nisi morte tulisset,
Æternæ vitæ janua clausa foret.

(Unless the *death of Death* had brought *death to death by* [his] *death*, the door of eternal life would have been closed.)

polyptych (pol′ip-tik), *n.* [= F. *polyptique*, < ML. *polyptychum*, a register, roll, < Gr. πολύπτυχον, a writing folded into many leaves, a register, roll, neut. of πολύπτυχος, with many leaves or folds, < πολύς, many, + πτύξ (πτυχ-) or πτυχή, fold. Cf. *policy*[2], from the same source.] A combination of panels or frames, more than three in number, for receiving paintings on one or both sides of every leaf. Compare *diptych* and *triptych.* *Maskell*, Russian Art, S. K. M. Handbook.

Polyptychodon (pol-ip-tik′ǭ-don), *n.* [NL. (Owen), < Gr. πολύπτυχος, with many folds (see *polyptych*), + ὀδούς (ὀδοντ-) = E. *tooth.*] A genus of cretaceous plesiosaurians: same as *Basilosaurus.*

polypus (pol′i-pus), *n.*; pl. *polypi* (-pī). [NL., < L. *polypus* (pl. *polypi*), < Gr. πολύπους (pl. πολύποδες, poet. or dial. πολύποι), a polypus: see *polyp.*] 1. In *zoöl.*: (*a*) A poulp or cuttle. (*b*) A polyp, in any sense. (*c*) [*cap.*] (1) A genus of cuttles. (2) A genus of polyps.—2. In *pathol.*, any kind of tumor growing from a mucous membrane, of rounded form, and more or less distinctly pedunculated. The term is most frequently applied to benign growths.—**Polypus-forceps**, a forceps for grasping and tearing off polypi.

polyrhizal (pol-i-rī′zal), *a.* [< Gr. πολύρριζος, with many roots: see *polyrhizous.*] Same as *polyrhizous.*

polyrhizous (pol-i-rī′zus), *a.* [Prop. **polyrrhizous*; = F. *polyrrhize*; < L. *polyrrhizos*, < Gr. πολύρριζος, with many roots, < πολύς, many, + ῥίζα, root.] In *bot.*, possessing numerous rootlets independently of those by which the attachment is effected.

polysarcia (pol-i-sär′si-ạ̈), *n.* [NL., < Gr. πολυσαρκία, fleshiness, < πολύσαρκος, fleshy: see *polysarcous.*] 1. Excess of flesh.—2. In *bot.*, an excess of sap, giving rise to unnatural or abnormal growth. *Thomas*, Med. Dict.—**Polysarcia adiposa**, obesity.—**Polysarcia cordis**, obese heart.

polysarcous (pol-i-sär′kus), *a.* [< Gr. πολύσαρκος, having much flesh, fleshy, < πολύς, much, + σάρξ (σαρκ-), flesh.] Affected with polysarcia; obese.

polyscelia (pol-i-sē′li-ạ̈), *n.* [NL., < Gr. πολύς, many, + σκέλος, the leg.] In *teratol.*, a monster having many legs.

polyschematic (pol″i-skẹ-mat′ik), *a.* Same as *polyschematist.*

polyschematist (pol-i-skē′mạ-tist), *a.* [< LGr. πολυσχημάτιστος, multiform, < Gr. πολύς, many, + σχηματίζειν, assume form, < σχῆμα(τ-), form: see *scheme.*] Characterized by or existing in many forms or fashions; specifically, in *anc. pros.*, admitting as substitutes feet not metrically equivalent, or containing such feet.

polyscope (pol′i-skōp), *n.* [= F. *polyscope* = Sp. *poliscópio* = Pg. *polyscopo, polyscopio*, < Gr. πολύς, many, + σκοπεῖν, view. Cf. Gr. πολύσκοπος, far-seeing.] 1. In *optics*, a lens plane on one side and convex on the other, but having the convex side formed of several plane surfaces or facets, so that an object seen through it appears multiplied.—2. In *surg.*, an instrument for illuminating the cavities of the body by means of an electric light.

polysepalous (pol-i-sep′ạ-lus), *a.* [< Gr. πολύς, many, + NL. *sepalum*, sepal.] In *bot.*, having the sepals separate from each other: said of a calyx.

Polysiphonia (pol″i-sī-fō′ni-ạ̈), *n.* [NL. (Greville): see *polysiphonous.*] A very large, widely distributed, and extremely variable genus of red algæ. The fronds are filamentous or subcompressed, distichously or irregularly branching, formed of a monosiphonous axis and several siphons, and either naked or with a cortical layer of irregular cells, furnished with numerous tufts of hyaline, monosiphonous, dichotomous filaments. The tetraspores are in one, rarely two, rows, in slightly altered upper branches; cystocarps ovate-globose or urceolate; spores piriform, on short pedicles. See *dough-balls, niggerhair, lobster-claws.*

polysiphonous (pol-i-sī′fǭ-nus), *a.* [< Gr. πολύς, many, + σίφων, a tube: see *siphon.*] In *bot.*: (*a*) Having several or many siphons: said of certain algæ. Compare *monosiphonous*, and see *siphon.* (*b*) Resembling, belonging to, or characteristic of the genus *Polysiphonia.*

polysomatic (pol″i-sǭ-mat′ik), *a.* [< Gr. πολυσώματος, with many bodies, < πολύς, many, + σῶμα, body.] Consisting of an aggregation of smaller grains: used by some lithologists to note a grain or chondrus of this character.

polysomitic (pol″i-sǭ-mit′ik), *a.* [< Gr. πολύς, many, + E. *somite* + *-ic.*] Consisting of a number of primitively distinct somites which have united or become grouped into a segment or region of the body in any way distinguished from another part of the body: thus, the head, or thorax, or abdomen of an arthropod, such as an insect or a crustacean, is *polysomitic.* *Huxley*, Anat. Invert., p. 220.

polyspast† (pol′i-spast), *n.* [= Sp. *polispástos* = It. *polispasto*, < L. *polyspaston*, < Gr. πολύσπαστον, a hoisting-tackle with many pulleys, neut. of πολύσπαστος, drawn by many cords, < πολύς, many, + σπᾶν, draw: see *spasm.*] 1. A machine consisting of a combination of pulleys, used for raising heavy weights: a term formerly used by writers on mechanics.—2. An apparatus of the same character formerly used in surgery to reduce dislocations.

polysperm (pol′i-spėrm), *n.* [< Gr. πολύσπερμος, with many seeds: see *polyspermous.*] A tree whose fruit contains many seeds.

All of them easily raised of the kernels and roots, which may be got out of their *polysperms.*
Evelyn, Sylva, II. iii. § 1. (*Latham.*)

polyspermal (pol-i-spėr′mal), *a.* [< *polysperm-ous* + *-al.*] Same as *polyspermous.*

polyspermous (pol-i-spėr′mus), *a.* [= Sp. *polispermo* = Pg. *polyspermo* = It. *polispermo*, < Gr. πολύσπερμος, with many seeds, < πολύς, many, + σπέρμα, seed: see *sperm.*] Containing many seeds: as, a *polyspermous* capsule or berry.

polyspermy (pol′i-spėr-mi), *n.* [< Gr. πολύς, many, + σπέρμα, seed.] Impregnation of an ovum by more than one spermatozoön.

polyspire (pol′i-spīr), *n.* [< Gr. πολύς, many, + σπεῖρα, coil.] In *zoöl.*, a structure resulting from continued spiral growth through several revolutions. *Encyc. Brit.*, XXII. 417.

polysporangium (pol″i-spǭ-ran′ji-um), *n.*; pl. *polysporangia* (-ạ̈). [NL., < Gr. πολύς, many, + NL. *sporangium.*] In *bot.*, a sporangium containing many spores.

polyspore (pol′i-spōr), *n.* [< Gr. πολύς, many, + σπόρος, seed: see *spore.*] In *bot.*, a compound spore; in certain algæ, a compound spore composed of several or many spores or cells.

Polysporea (pol-i-spō′rẹ-ạ̈), *n. pl.* [NL., < Gr. πολύς, many, + σπόρος, seed, + *-ea.*] An ordinal name of those coccidiid sporozoans whose cyst-contents are converted into a great many spores, as in the genus *Klossia.* *Aimé Schneider.*

polysporean (pol-i-spō′rẹ-ạn), *a.* and *n.* I. *a.* Polysporous; of or pertaining to the *Polysporea.*

II. *n.* A member of the order *Polysporea.*

polyspored (pol′i-spōrd), *a.* [< *polyspore* + *-ed*[2].] In *bot.*, containing or producing many spores, as the asci of certain lichens, which contain from twenty to one hundred instead of eight, the usual number.

polysporic (pol-i-spor′ik), *a.* [< *polyspor-ous* + *-ic.*] In *bot.*, same as *polysporous.*

polysporous (pol-i-spō′rus), *a.* [= F. *polyspore*, < Gr. πολύσπορος, with many seeds or crops, < πολύς, many, + σπόρος, seed: see *spore.*] Producing many spores. Specifically—(*a*) In *bot.*, same as *polyspored.* (*b*) In *zoöl.*, polysporean.

polystachous (pǭ-lis′tạ-kus), *a.* [< Gr. πολύς, many, + στάχυς, an ear of corn, a spike.] In *bot.*, having many spikes.

polystaurium (pol-i-stâ′ri-um), *n.* [NL.: see *polystauron.*] Same as *stauracin.*

polystauron (pol-i-stâ′ron), *n.* [< Gr. πολύς, many, + σταῦρον, a stake, pale, cross.] Same as *stauracin.*

polystemonous (pol-i-stem′ǭ-nus), *a.* [< Gr. πολύς, many, + στήμων, warp (stamen).] Having many stamens; having stamens more than double the number of sepals and petals: said of flowers. *Encyc. Brit.*, IV. 135.

polystichous (pǭ-lis′ti-kus), *a.* [< Gr. πολύς, many, + στίχος, row, line.] In *nat. hist.*, arranged in numerous rows or ranks; multifarious. Compare *monostichous* and *distichous.*

Polysticta (pol-i-stik′tạ̈), *n.* [NL. (T. C. Eyton, 1836), < Gr. πολύστικτος, much-spotted, < πολύς, many, + στικτός, verbal adj. of στίζειν, prick, spot.] 1. A genus of ducks related to the eiders, but having the bill not gibbous, without frontal processes, and not feathered to the nostrils, and its tomial edge dilated and leathery. There is only one species, *P. stelleri* or *dispar*, known as *Steller's eider*, a beautiful duck of circumpolar distribution. The male is chiefly white, black, and chestnut-brown, tinged with sea-green on the head. Also called *Macropus, Stelleria*, and *Eniconetta* or *Heniconetta.* 2. In *entom.*, a genus of coleopterous insects. *Hope*, 1840.

polystigm (pol′i-stim), *n.* [< Gr. πολύς, many, + στίγμα, point, mark.] A figure composed of a number of points.

polystigmous (pol-i-stig′mus), *a.* [< Gr. πολύς, many, + στίγμα, mark: see *stigma.*] In *bot.*, having many carpels, every one bearing a stigma: said of a flower.

Polystoma (pō-lis'tǫ-mạ̈), *n.* [NL., < Gr. *πολύστομος*, having many mouths, < *πολύς*, many, + *στόμα*, mouth.] Same as *Polystomum*.

Polystomata (pol-i-stō'ma-tạ̈), *n. pl.* [NL., neut. pl. of *polystomatus*: see *polystomatous*.] 1. The sponges or *Porifera*, as metazoic organisms contrasted with all other *Metazoa*, or *Monostomata*: so called from their many mouths or oscula.—2. In Saville Kent's system of classification, one of four sections of *Protozoa*, consisting of the suctorial or tentaculiferous animalcules, or the acinetiform infusorians, having many tentacular organs, each of which serves as a tubular sucking-mouth: contrasted with *Eustomata*, *Discostomata*, and *Pantostomata*. The group is oftener called *Tentaculifera*.

polystomatous (pol-i-stom'ạ-tus), *a.* [< NL. *polystomatus* (cf. Gr. *πολύστομος*), < Gr. *πολύς*, many, + *στόμα*, mouth.] Having many mouths or apertures for the ingestion of food; specifically, of or pertaining to the *Polystomata*.

polystome (pol'i-stōm), *n.* [= F. *polystome*, < Gr. *πολύστομος*, having many mouths, < *πολύς*, many, + *στόμα*, mouth.] An animal with many mouths. (*a*) A member of the *Polystomata*, in either sense, as a sponge or an acinetiform infusorian. (*b*) A trematoid of the suborder *Polystomea*; a polystome-fluke.

Polystomea (pol-i-stō'mẹ-ạ̈), *n. pl.* [NL., < Gr. *πολύστομος*, having many mouths: see *polystome*.] A suborder of *Trematoidea*, containing trematoid worms with two small lateral suckers on the head and several posterior suckers, with which a pair of large chitinous hooks are often found. Some species are elongated, and present a kind of segmentation. They are for the most part ectoparasitic. The term is contrasted with *Distomea*.

Polystomeæ (pol-i-stō'mẹ-ē), *n. pl.* Same as *Polystomea*.

polystome-fluke (pol'i-stōm-flök), *n.* A fluke or trematoid of the family *Polystomidæ*.

polystomia, *n.* Plural of *polystomium*.

Polystomidæ (pol-i-stom'i-dē), *n. pl.* [NL., < *Polystomum* + *-idæ*.] A family of polystomatous *Trematoidea*, typified by the genus *Polystomum*, having several posterior suckers, usually paired and disposed in two lateral rows, and reinforced by an armature of chitinous hooks.

polystomium (pol-i-stō'mi-um), *n.*; pl. *polystomia* (-ạ̈). [NL.: see *polystome*.] One of the numerous fine pores at the ends of the ramifications of the oral arms in some acalephs, replacing the original mouth, which has become closed by the gradual union of the arms.

Polystomum (pō-lis'tǫ-mum), *n.* [NL.: see *polystome*.] The typical genus of *Polystomidæ*, having an oral but no lateral sucker on the anterior end, four eyes, and at the posterior end six suckers, two median hooks, and sixteen small hooks. The species are parasitic, as *P. integerrimum* in the bladder of frogs, and *P. ocellatum* in the pharynx of turtles. A fluke formerly called *P. sanguinicola*, now *Hexathyridium venarum*, is found in venous blood. Also *Polystoma*.

polystyle (pol'i-stīl), *a.* [= F. *polystyle* = It. *polistilo*, < Gr. *πολύστυλος*, with many columns, < *πολύς*, many, + *στῦλος*, a column: see *style*².] In *arch.*, having, characterized by, or supported by many columns; surrounded by several rows of columns, as some Moorish or Arabic courts.

polystylous (pol-i-stī'lus), *a.* [< Gr. *πολύστυλος*, with many columns, < *πολύς*, many, + *στῦλος*, column (style). Cf. *polystyle*.] In *bot.*, bearing many styles. *Gray.*

polysyllabic (pol″i-si-lab'ik), *a.* [= F. *polysyllabique*; as *polysyllab-le* + *-ic*.] Of or pertaining to a polysyllable; consisting of many syllables, specifically of more than three.

polysyllabical (pol″i-si-lab'i-kạl), *a.* [< *polysyllabic* + *-al*.] Same as *polysyllabic*.

polysyllabicism (pol″i-si-lab'i-sizm), *n.* [< *polysyllabic* + *-ism*.] Polysyllabic character; the quality of having or of being composed of many (specifically more than three) syllables.

polysyllabism (pol-i-sil'ạ-bizm), *n.* [< *polysyllab-le* + *-ism*.] Same as *polysyllabicism*.

polysyllable (pol-i-sil'ạ-bl), *n.* [= F. *polysyllabe* = Sp. *polisílabo* = Pg. *polysyllabo* = It. *polisillabo*, a polysyllable, < Gr. *πολυσύλλαβος*, polysyllabic, < Gr. *πολύς*, many, + *συλλαβή*, syllable: see *syllable*.] A word of several syllables; usually, a word of four or more syllables, words of one syllable being called *monosyllables*, those of two *dissyllables*, and those of three *trisyllables*.

polysyllogism (pol-i-sil'ǫ-jizm), *n.* [< Gr. *πολύς*, many, + *συλλογισμός*, syllogism: see *syllogism*.] A combination of syllogisms; a chain of reasoning.—**Manifest polysyllogism.** See *manifest*.

polysyllogistic (pol-i-sil-ǫ-jis'tik), *a.* [< *polysyllog-ism* + *-istic* (cf. *syllogistic*).] Consisting of a chain of syllogisms.

polysymmetrical (pol″i-si-met'ri-kạl), *a.* [As *polysymmetry* + *-ic-al*.] Divisible into exactly similar halves by more than one plane, as is the case with all regular flowers. *Actinomorphous* is a synonym.

polysymmetrically (pol″i-si-met'ri-kạl-i), *adv.* In a polysymmetrical manner; in accordance with polysymmetry.

polysymmetry (pol-i-sim'et-ri), *n.* [< Gr. *πολύς*, many, + *συμμετρία*, symmetry: see *symmetry*.] Susceptibility of division into like halves by more than one plane; the state of being polysymmetrical.

polysyndeton (pol-i-sin'de-ton), *n.* [NL., = F. *polysyndète* = Sp. *polisíndeton* = Pg. *polysyndeton*, < NL. *polysyndeton*, < Gr. **πολυσύνδετον*, prop. neut. of **πολυσύνδετος*, joined in various ways, < *πολύς*, many, + *σύνδετος*, bound together: see *asyndeton*.] In *rhet.*, a figure consisting in the use of a number of conjunctions in close succession; introduction of all the members of a series of coördinate words or clauses with conjunctions: opposed to *asyndeton*. Asyndeton produces an accelerated, polysyndeton a retarded movement in the sentence. Asyndeton gives an effect of accumulation and energy, polysyndeton demands special and deliberate attention to each separate word and clause introduced. Rom. viii. 35, 38, 39 is an example.

polysynthesis (pol-i-sin'the-sis), *n.* [NL., < Gr. *πολύς*, many, + *σύνθεσις*, composition: see *synthesis*.] Composition of many elements; specifically, in *philol.*, composition from an abnormal number and variety of elements.

polysynthetic (pol″i-sin-thet'ik), *a.* [= F. *polysynthétique*, < Gr. *πολυσύνθετος*, much-compounded, < *πολύς*, much, + *σύνθετος*, compounded: see *synthetic*.] 1. In *philol.*, compounded of a number and variety of elements beyond the usual norm; exhibiting excessive intricacy of synthetic structure, as by the incorporation of objective and adverbial elements in the verb forms; incapsulated: as, a *polysynthetic* word; characterized by such compounds: as, a *polysynthetic* language: first applied by Du Ponceau to the class of languages spoken by the Indian tribes of America. Also *incorporative* and (rarely) *megasynthetic*.—2. In *mineral.*, compounded of a number of thin lamellæ in twinning position to each other, or characterized by this kind of structure: as, a *polysynthetic* twin. See *twin*.

> Felspar, very fresh and clear, sometimes with distinct *polysynthetic* twin lines. *Nature*, XXX. 12.

polysynthetical (pol″i-sin-thet'i-kạl), *a.* [< *polysynthetic* + *-al*.] Same as *polysynthetic*.

polysynthetically (pol″i-sin-thet'i-kạl-i), *adv.* In a polysynthetic manner; by polysynthesis.

polysyntheticism (pol″i-sin-thet'i-sizm), *n.* [< *polysynthetic* + *-ism*.] The character of being polysynthetic.

polysynthetism (pol-i-sin'the-tizm), *n.* [< *polysynthet-ic* + *-ism*.] Polysynthetic structure; polysyntheticism.

> If we cannot prove the American languages related except by the characteristic of *polysynthetism*. *Whitney*, Life and Growth of Lang., p. 268.

polytechnic (pol-i-tek'nik), *a.* and *n.* [= F. *polytechnique* = Sp. *politécnico* = Pg. *polytechnico* = It. *politechnico*, < Gr. *πολύτεχνος*, skilled in many arts, < *πολύς*, many, + *τέχνη*, art: see *technic*.] I. *a.* Concerning or comprehending many arts: noting specifically educational institutions in which instruction is given in many arts, more particularly with reference to their practical application.

II. *n.* 1. An exhibition of objects belonging to the industrial arts and manufactures.—2. An educational institution, especially for instruction in technical subjects. A number of such institutions are in successful operation in London.

polytechnical (pol-i-tek'ni-kạl), *a.* [< *polytechnic* + *-al*.] 1. Same as *polytechnic*.—2. Practising many arts.

> The trade guilds of the great *polytechnical* cities of India are not, however, always exactly coincident with the sectarian or ethnical caste of a particular class of artisans. *Sir George C. M. Birdwood*, Indian Arts, I. 138.

polytechnics (pol-i-tek'niks), *n.* [Pl. of *polytechnic* (see *-ics*).] The science of the mechanical arts.

polyterpene (pol-i-tėr'pēn), *n.* [< *poly(meric)* + *terpene*.] In *chem.*, any one of a class of substances polymeric with the terpenes. The class includes, among other substances, caoutchouc, gutta-percha, balata, dammar-resin, and the fossil resins fichtelite, hartite, etc. See *polymeric* and *terpene*.

Polythalamacea (pol-i-thal-ạ-mā'sẹ-ạ̈), *n. pl.* [NL., < Gr. *πολύς*, many, + *θάλαμος*, chamber, + *-acea*.] An order of cephalopods whose shell is polythalamous, as the ammonites, belemnites, nautili, and related forms.

polythalamaceous (pol-i-thal-ạ-mā'shius), *a.* Same as *polythalamous*, 2: said of the *Polythalamacea*.

Polythalamia (pol″i-thạ̈-lā'mi-ạ̈), *n. pl.* [NL., < Gr. *πολύς*, many, + *θάλαμος*, chamber.] A division of reticulate amœbiform protozoans, whose test is many-chambered or polythalamian: opposed to *Monothalamia*. The name is less exactly used as a synonym of *Foraminifera*.

polythalamian (pol″i-thạ̈-lā'mi-ạn), *a.* [< *Polythalamia* + *-an*.] Many-chambered; multilocular; having many compartments: especially, noting *Foraminifera* of such character, in distinction from *monothalamian*. See cut under *Foraminifera*.

polythalamic (pol-i-thal'ạ-mik), *a.* [< *Polythalamia* + *-ic*.] Having many chamberlets, as a foraminifer; thalamophorous; of or pertaining to the *Polythalamia*.

polythalamous (pol-i-thal'ạ-mus), *a.* [= F. *polythalame*, < Gr. *πολύς*, many, + *θάλαμος*, chamber.] 1. In *entom.*, having several or many chambers: applied to the nests of insects, and to galls, when they contain many cells or compartments, each destined for or inhabited by a single larva.—2. In *conch.*, having many compartments; multilocular.

polythecial (pol-i-thē'si-ạl), *a.* [< *polythecium* + *-al*.] Forming a polythecium; pertaining to a compound zoöthecium; compositely zoöthecial.

polythecium (pol-i-thē'si-um), *n.*; pl. *polythecia* (-ạ̈). [NL., < Gr. *πολύς*, many, + *θήκη*, a box.] A compound or aggregate zoöthecium, consisting of several conjoined loricæ, found in various infusorians. *W. S. Kent*, Infusoria, p. 329.

polytheism (pol'i-thē-izm), *n.* [= F. *polythéisme* = Sp. *politeismo* = Pg. *politheismo* = It. *politeismo*, < NL. **polytheismus*, < Gr. *πολύθεος*, of or belonging to many gods (*δόξα πολύθεος*, polytheism): see *polytheous*, and cf. *theism*.] Belief in more gods than one; the doctrine of a plurality of divine beings superior to man, and having part in the government of the world.

> The first author of *polytheism*, Orpheus, did plainly assert one supreme God. *Stillingfleet.*

polytheist (pol'i-thē-ist), *n.* [= F. *polythéiste* = Sp. *politeista* = Pg. *politheista* = It. *politeista*, < NL. **polytheista*, < Gr. *πολύθεος*, of or belonging to many gods: see *polytheism* and *theist*.] One who believes in or maintains polytheism, or the doctrine of a plurality of gods.

> The emperor [Hadrian] indeed himself, though a *polytheist*, was very little of an idolater till the conquest by the Arabs. *S. Sharpe*, Hist. Egypt, xv. § 21.

polytheistic (pol″i-thẹ̄-is'tik), *a.* [= It. *politeistico*; as *polytheist* + *-ic*.] 1. Pertaining to, of the nature of, or characterized by polytheism: as, *polytheistic* belief or worship.

> In all *polytheistic* religions among savages, as well as in the early ages of heathen antiquity, it is the irregular events of nature only that are ascribed to the agency and power of the gods. *Adam Smith*, Hist. Astron., iii.

2. Believing in a plurality of gods: as, a *polytheistic* writer.

polytheistical (pol″i-thẹ̄-is'ti-kạl), *a.* [< *polytheistic* + *-al*.] Of a polytheistic character.

polytheistically (pol″i-thẹ̄-is'ti-kạl-i), *adv.* In the manner of a polytheist or of polytheism; as regards polytheism.

polytheize (pol'i-thē-īz), *v. i.*; pret. and pp. *polytheized*, ppr. *polytheizing*. [= F. *polythéiser*; as *polythe-ism* + *-ize*.] To adhere to, advocate, or inculcate the doctrine of polytheism; believe in a plurality of gods. *Milman.*

polytheous†, *a.* [< Gr. *πολύθεος*, of or belonging to many gods, < *πολύς*, many, + *θεός*, god: see *theism*. Cf. *atheous*.] Characterized by polytheism; polytheistical.

> Heav'n most abhor'd *Polytheous* piety. *J. Beaumont*, Psyche, xxi. 58.

polythore†, *n.* [Origin obscure.] See the quotation.

> I went to that famous physitian Sir Fr. Prujean, who shew'd me his laboratorie. . . . He plaied to me likewise on the *polythore*, an instrument having something of the harp, lute, theorbo, &c. It was a sweete instrument, by none known in England, or describ'd by any author, nor us'd but by this skilfull and learned doctor. *Evelyn*, Diary, Aug. 9, 1661.

polytocous (pǭ-lit'ǫ-kus), *a.* [< Gr. *πολυτόκος*, bringing forth many young ones, < *πολύς*, many, + *-τοκος*, < *τίκτειν*, *τεκεῖν*, bring forth.] 1. Producing many or several at a birth; multiparous. Also *polytokous*, *polyparous*.—2. In *bot.*, fruiting year after year, as perennials: a term proposed by Gray in place of De Candolle's *polycarpous*.

polytomous (pọ̄-lit'ọ̄-mus), *a.* [< Gr. πολύς, many, + τέμνειν, ταμεῖν, cut.] 1. In *bot.*, subdivided into many distinct subordinate parts, which, however, not being jointed to the petiole, are not true leaflets: said of leaves.—2. Dividing once or repeatedly into sets of three or more branches: opposed to *dichotomous*.

polytomy (pọ̄-lit'ọ̄-mi), *n.* [< *polytom-ous* + *-y*[3].] Division into more than two parts: distinguished from *dichotomy*.

polytope (pol'i-tōp), *n.* [< Gr. πολύς, many, + τόπος, a place.] A form in *n*-dimensional geometry corresponding to a polygon or polyhedron.

Polytrichaceæ (pol″i-tri-kā'sẹ̄-ē), *n. pl.* [NL., < *Polytrichum* + *-aceæ*.] Same as *Polytricheæ*.

Polytricheæ (pol-i-trik'ẹ̄-ē), *n. pl.* [NL., < *Polytrichum* + *-eæ*.] A tribe of acrocarpous bryaceous mosses, typified by the genus *Polytrichum*. It embraces plants that are very variable in size and appearance, of woody or strong texture. The capsule is long-pedicellate, erect or cernuous, and cylindrical or angular, provided with a cucullate calyptra, which may be naked, spinulose, or hairy, and with a peristome of 32, 64, or rarely 16 teeth.

polytrichous (pọ̄-lit'ri-kus), *a.* [< Gr. πολύτριχος, having much hair, < πολύς, many, + θρίξ (τριχ-), a hair.] Very hairy; densely or uniformly ciliate, as an embryo or an animalcule.

Polytrichum (pọ̄-lit'ri-kum), *n.* [NL. (Dillenius, 1719), < Gr. πολύτριχος, having much hair: see *polytrichous*.] A genus of tall showy mosses, type of the tribe *Polytricheæ*. They grow in wide, large tufts from creeping shoots. The stems are erect, woody, and triangular; the leaves are rigid and coriaceous, linear-lanceolate, sheathing below, and spreading above. The capsule is from four- to six-sided, oblong or ovate, and long-pediceled with a cuculliform calyptra, which is covered with long hairs forming a dense mat, whence the name of *haircap-moss*. The peristome is single, of 64 teeth. The genus is widely distributed in north temperate and arctic countries, there being 6 species and several varieties in North America. See *bear's-bed*, *silver heather* (under *heather*), *goldilocks*, 5, *haircap-moss*, *golden maidenhair* (under *maidenhair*), and cut under *paraphysis*.

polytroch (pol'i-trok), *n.* [< *Polytrocha*.] A polytrochal or polytrochous organism.

Polytrocha (pọ̄-lit'rọ̄-kạ̈), *n. pl.* [NL. (Ehrenberg), < Gr. πολύς, many, + τροχός, a wheel.] A division of natant *Rotifera* or wheel-animalcules, in which the wheel or swimming-organ has several lobes surrounding the anterior end of the body.

polytrochal (pọ̄-lit'rọ̄-kạl), *a.* [< *Polytrocha* + *-al*.] 1. Having several ciliate zones, or girdles of cilia, as an embryo worm: correlated with *mesotrochal*, *telotrochal*.—2. In *Rotifera*, of or pertaining to the *Polytrocha*.

polytrochous (pọ̄-lit'rọ̄-kus), *a.* [< Gr. πολύς, many, + τροχός, a wheel.] Same as *polytrochal*.

polytropic (pol-i-trop'ik), *a.* [< Gr. πολύς, many, + τρέπειν, turn.] Turning several times round a pole.—**Polytropic function.** See *function*.

polytypage (pol'i-ti-pāj), *n.* [= F. *polytypage*; as *polytype* + *-age*.] A peculiar mode of stereotyping, by which facsimiles of wood-engravings, etc., are produced in metal, from which impressions are taken as from types. See *polytype*.

polytype (pol'i-tīp), *n.* and *a.* [= F. *polytype*; < Gr. πολύς, many, + τύπος, type: see *type*.] I. *n.* A cast or facsimile of an engraving, matter in type, etc., produced by pressing a woodcut or other plate into semi-fluid metal. An intaglio matrix is the result; and from this matrix, in a similar way, a polytype in relief is obtained.

II. *a.* Pertaining to polytypage; produced by polytypage.

polytype (pol'i-tīp), *v. t.*; pret. and pp. *polytyped*, ppr. *polytyping*. [< *polytype*, *n.*] To reproduce by polytypage: as, to *polytype* an engraving.

polytypic (pol-i-tip'ik), *a.* [< Gr. πολύς, many, + τύπος, type: see *typic*. Cf. *polytype*.] Same as *polytypical*.

A new species may be one that has been formed by monotypic transformation, the old form disappearing with the production of the new, or it may be one that has arisen through *polytypic* transformation.
Amer. Jour. Sci., 3d ser., XXXIX. 22.

polytypical (pol-i-tip'i-kạl), *a.* Having several or many types; represented by numerous forms: opposed to *monotypical*: as, a *polytypical* family of animals.

polyuresis (pol″i-ụ̄-rē'sis), *n.* [NL., < Gr. πολύς, many, + οὔρησις, urination, < οὐρεῖν, urinate, < οὖρον, urine: see *urine*.] Same as *polyuria*.

polyuria (pol-i-ū'ri-ạ̈), *n.* [NL., < Gr. πολύς, much, + οὖρον, urine.] The passing of an excessive quantity of urine, especially of normal urine.

polyuric (pol-i-ū'rik), *a.* and *n.* [< *polyuria* + *-ic*.] I. *a.* Of, pertaining to, or affected with polyuria.

II. *n.* One affected with polyuria.

polyvoltine (pol-i-vol'tin), *n.* [< Gr. πολύς, many, + It. *volta*, turn, time, + *-ine*[1].] A silkworm which yields more than one crop of cocoons a year: usually applied only to those races which have more than four yearly generations.

For the protection of the mulberry-trees, the raising of *polyvoltines*, or worms that hatch several broods a year, is forbidden in many countries. *Pop. Sci. Mo.*, XXXVI. 500.

polyzoa[1]† (pol-i-zō'ạ̈), *n.*; pl. *polyzoæ* (-ē). [NL.: see *polyzoön*.] The original name of one of the animals afterward grouped as *Polyzoa* and *Bryozoa*; a kind of polyzoan or bryozoan.

On *Polyzoa*, a new animal, an inhabitant of some zoophytes. *J. Vaughan Thompson*, Zoöl. Researches (1830).

Polyzoa[2] (pol-i-zō'ạ̈), *n. pl.* [NL., pl. of *polyzoön*, q. v.] 1. A class of molluscoid invertebrated animals; the moss-animalcules, sea-mosses, or sea-mats. They are invariably compound, forming aggregated or colonial organisms originating by germination from a single parent polyzoon, and inhabit a polyzoary or polyzoarium comparable to the polypary or polypidom of a compound hydrozoan. (See *polypary*.) The individual or person of such a stock is called a *polypide*, and differs from the polypite of a cœlenterate in having a complete and distinct alimentary canal suspended freely in a body-cavity or cœloma, and in many other respects. There are definite oral and anal apertures, not communicating directly with the perivisceral cavity. The mouth is within an oral disk or lophophore supporting a circlet of ciliated tentacles, the lophophore being comparable to the wheel-organ of rotifers. The intestine is bent on itself toward the oral end of the body, bringing the anus near the mouth, either within or without the circlet of lophophoral tentacles, whence the terms *entoproctous* and *ectoproctous*. There is a well-defined nervous system, the nerve-ganglion being situated in the reëntering angle of the alimentary canal, between the mouth and the anus. The respiratory system is represented by the ciliated tentacles exsertile from the body-sac. There is no heart. The *Polyzoa* are hermaphrodite, and the sexual organs are contained within the body-walls. Besides the true sexual reproduction, and propagation by budding or gemmation, they exhibit in many cases a process of discontinuous gemmation. These creatures are chiefly marine, and are found incrusting submerged stones, shells, wood, seaweed, and other objects; but some inhabit fresh water. There is great diversity in size, form, and outward aspect. Some resemble corals, or polyps of various kinds, and all were confounded with various cœlenterates under the name of *corallines*. Though quite definite as a class, the systematic position of the *Polyzoa* has been much disputed. Besides having been classed as radiates, zoöphytes, and polyps, they have been regarded (*a*) as worms, and approximated to the *Rotifera*, being sometimes associated with the rotifers as a class of *Vermes*; (*b*) as worms, and approximated to the *Gephyrea*; (*c*) as molluscoids, and associated with the brachiopods as a division apart called *Malacoscolices*; (*d*) as molluscoids, and associated with brachiopods and tunicates in a division *Molluscoidea*; (*e*) or as mollusks, classed with brachiopods and lamellibranchs in a group called *Lipocephala*. Their proper position is near or with the brachiopods. The division of the *Polyzoa* into orders, etc., is not less disputed. Regarded as related to the siphunculoid gephyrean worms, the *Polyzoa* have been considered to form a third section, called *Eupolyzoa*, or *Polyzoa* proper, of such organisms (the other two being *Pterobranchia* and *Vermiformia*), and then divided into two subclasses—*Ectoprocta*, with anus external to the circlet of tentacles, and *Endoprocta*, with anus internal to the tentacles—the former consisting of two orders, *Phylactolæmata* and *Gymnolæmata*. Again, the *Polyzoa* proper have been directly divided into (*a*) *Gymnolæmata*, consisting of the *Chilostomata*, *Cyclostomata*, and *Ctenostomata*, without an epistome, and (*b*) *Phylactolæmata*, with an epistome, these latter being commonly called the *fresh-water polyzoans*. The families and genera are numerous, and date back to the Silurian. A member of the class was named a *polyzoa* by J. Vaughan Thompson in 1830; in 1831 Ehrenberg named the class *Bryozoa*, and the two names have since continued in alternative usage.

A Portion of the Polyzoarium of *Plumatella repens*, one of the *Polyzoa*, with several polypides protruding from the cells of the ectocyst.

2. In *Protozoa*, the polyzoan radiolarians: another name of the *Polycyttaria* or *Collozoa*.

polyzoal (pol-i-zō'ạl), *a.* [< *polyzoa* + *-al*.] Same as *polyzoan*.

polyzoan (pol-i-zō'ạn), *a.* and *n.* [< *polyzoa* + *-an*.] I. *a.* Consisting of many zoöids, polypides, or persons in one compound or colonial aggregate; specifically, pertaining to the *Polyzoa*, or having their characters; bryozoan.

II. *n.* 1. A member of the *Polyzoa*; a polyzoön.—2. An individual element of a compound polyzoön; a polypide.

polyzoarial (pol″i-zọ̄-ā'ri-ạl), *a.* [< *polyzoarium* + *-al*.] 1. Of or pertaining to a polyzoary.—2. Relating to polyzoans or the *Polyzoa*. *Encyc. Brit.*, XIX. 431.

polyzoarium (pol″i-zọ̄-ā'ri-um), *n.*; pl. *polyzoaria* (-ạ̈). [NL.: see *polyzoary*.] A compound polyzoan; the common stock of a set of polyzoan polypides, the result of repeated gemmation from a single embryo. Every individual zoöid of the aggregation is a polypide; the common stock consists of an ectocyst and an endocyst, the former furnishing the special cells or cups in which each polypide is contained. See cuts under *Polyzoa*, *Plumatella*, and *vibraculum*.

polyzoary (pol-i-zō'ạ-ri), *n.*; pl. *polyzoaries* (-riz). [< NL. *polyzoarium*, < *polyzoön* + *-arium*.] The polypary or polypidom of a polyzoan; a colony of polypides; a compound or aggregate polyzoan; a polyzoal cœnœcium.

polyzoic (pol-i-zō'ik), *a.* [< Gr. πολύζωος, named from many animals, < πολύς, many, + ζῷον, an animal. Cf. *polyzoön*.] Filled with imaginary animals and other beings, as primitive religious conceptions; zoölatrous. *Encyc. Brit.*, XX. 367. [Rare.]

polyzonal (pol-i-zō'nạl), *a.* [< Gr. πολύς, many, + ζώνη, belt: see *zone*.] Composed of many zones or belts: used by Sir D. Brewster to note burning-lenses composed of pieces united in rings. Lenses of a large size are constructed on this principle for lighthouses, as they can be obtained freer from defects, and have but slight spherical aberration.

Polyzoniidæ (pol″i-zọ̄-nī'i-dē), *n. pl.* [NL., < *Polyzonium* + *-idæ*.] A family of chilognath or diplopod *Myriapoda*, typified by the genus *Polyzonium*: called *Siphonophoridæ* by Newport and *Siphonizantia* or *Sugentia* by Brandt. Also *Polyzonidæ*.

Polyzonium (pol-i-zō'ni-um), *n.* [NL. (Brandt, 1834), < Gr. πολύς, many, + ζώνη, belt.] The typical genus of *Polyzoniidæ*.

polyzoöid (pol-i-zō'oid), *a.* [< Gr. πολύς, many, + E. *zoöid*.] Consisting of many zoöids.

The *polyzoöid* nature of these [sponge-stocks] is made apparent by the presence of many oscula.
Claus, Zoölogy (trans.), p. 210.

polyzoön (pol-i-zō'on), *n.*; pl. *polyzoa* (-ạ̈). [NL., also *polyzoum*; < Gr. πολύς, many, + ζῷον, animal. Cf. Gr. πολύζωος, named from many animals.] A member of the class *Polyzoa*; a polyzoan.

polyzoum (pol-i-zō'um), *n.*; pl. *polyzoa* (-ạ̈). [NL.] Same as *polyzoön*.

poma (pō'mạ̈), *n.*; pl. *pomata* (pō'mạ-tạ̈). [NL., < Gr. πῶμα, lid, cover.] The so-called occipital operculum of a monkey's brain, which overlaps parts in front of itself and thus forms a supergyre over the pomatic or external occipital fissure. *Buck's Handbook of Med. Sciences*, VIII. 161.

Pomacanthus (pō-ma-kan'thus), *n.* [NL. (Lacépède, 1802), < Gr. πῶμα, a lid, cover, + ἄκανθα, a thorn.] A genus of chætodont fishes in which the preoperculum has a strong spine at its angle. They are numerous in tropical seas, and many of them are brilliantly colored. *P. ciliaris* is a West Indian fish, occasional on the south Atlantic coast of the United States, called *angel-fish* and *isabelite*. See *angel-fish*, 2.

pomace (pum'ạ̄s), *n.* [Formerly also *pummace*, *pomice*; < OF. as if **pomace*, < ML. *pomacium*, cider, < L. *pomum*, an apple, etc.: see *pome*. Cf. *pomage* and *pomade*[1].] 1. The substance of apples or of similar fruit crushed by grinding.—2. Fish-scrap or refuse of fishes from which the oil has been extracted. It is dried by exposure to the sun and ground up into fish-guano. Pomace is very extensively manufactured from the menhaden. Crude pomace is called *chum*.
3. The cake left after expressing castor-oil from the beans.

Pomaceæ (pọ̄-mā'sẹ̄-ē), *n. pl.* [NL. (Jussieu, 1789), fem. pl. of *pomaceus*: see *pomaceous*.] Same as *Pomeæ*.

Pomacentridæ (pō-mạ-sen'tri-dē), *n. pl.* [NL., < *Pomacentrus* + *-idæ*.] A family of pharyngognathous fishes, typified by the genus *Poma-*

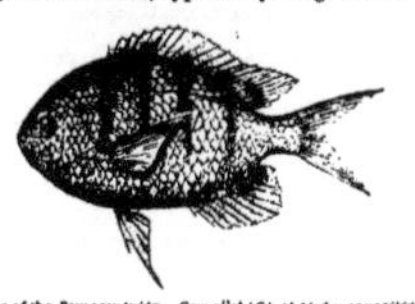

One of the *Pomacentridæ*. Cow-pilot (*Glyphidodon saxatilis*).

centrus, with pseudobranchiæ, ctenoid scales, 3½ gills, and from 5 to 7 branchiostegals; the coral-fishes. They are fishes of tropical seas, like the chætodonts, feeding on animals and vegetable organisms on coral reefs. There are about 15 genera and 160 species. The principal genera are *Pomacentrus* and *Glyphidodon*; seven species of the former and two of the latter, among them *G. saxatilis*, reach the coast of the United States or its vicinity. Also called *Ctenolabridæ* and *Glyphidodontidæ*.

pomacentroid (pō-ma-sen'troid), *a.* and *n.* I. *a.* Resembling, related to, or belonging to the family *Pomacentridæ*.

II. *n.* A fish of the family *Pomacentridæ*.

Pomacentrus (pō-ma-sen'trus), *n.* [NL. (Lacépède, 1802), prop. *Pomatocentrus*, < Gr. πῶμα, lid, + κέντρον, center.] The typical genus of *Pomacentridæ*, having incisiform teeth fixed in one series. Numerous species inhabit tropical seas, a few reaching southern waters of the United States. These

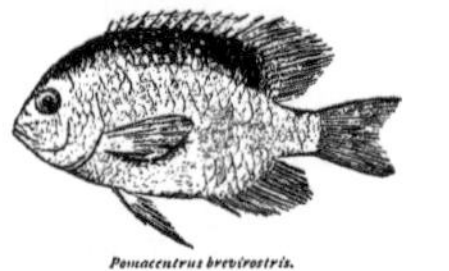

Pomacentrus brevirostris.

fishes are collectively known by the book-name of *demoiselles*. *P. leucostictus* is West Indian and Floridian. *P. brevirostris* is a Cuban species. *P. rubicundus* is the well-known garibaldi of the California coast, sometimes placed in another genus, *Hypsypops*, having the opercle and teeth entire. Also *Pomatocentrus*.

pomaceous[1] (pō-mā'shius), *a.* [< NL. *pomaceus*, of or pertaining to apples, etc., < L. *pomum*, a fruit (as an apple, peach, plum, etc.): see *pome*.] 1. Of, pertaining to, or consisting of apples.

> Autumn paints
> Ausonian hills with grapes: whilst English plains
> Blush with *pomaceous* harvests, breathing sweets.
> *J. Philips*, Cider, ii.

2. Having the character of a pome; belonging to the *Pomeæ*.

pomaceous[2] (pō-mā'shius), *a.* [< *pomace* + *-ous*.] Consisting of or resembling pomace.

Pomadasys (pō-mad'a-sis), *n.* [NL. (Lacépède, 1802), < Gr. πῶμα, lid, cover, + δασύς, hairy.] A genus of hæmulonid fishes, better known under the later name of *Pristipoma*. *P. davidsoni* is the sargo of California, a typical member of the genus, having the second anal spine longer than the third. *P. fulvomaculatus* (usually called *Orthopristis chrysopterus*) is the hog-fish or sailor's-choice, a food-fish of some importance from New York southward. Several other fishes of the United States have been ascribed to this genus.

pomade[1]†, *n.* [ME., < OF. **pomade*, vernacularly *pomee*, *pommee*, *pomeye*, f., also *pomat*, vernacularly *pomé*, *pommé*, *pomey*, m., < ML. *pomata*, f., a drink made from apples, cider, < L. *pomum*, apple: see *pome*. Cf. *pomace*.] Cider.

> May no pyement ne *pomade* ne presiouse drynkes
> Moyste me to the fulle ne my thurst slake,
> Til the vendage valle in the vale of Iosaphat.
> *Piers Plowman* (C), xxi. 412.

pomade[2] (pō-mād'), *n.* [Formerly also *pomado* (after It.) (also *pomatum*, q. v.), = D. G. *pomade*, *pommade* = Sw. *pomada* = Dan. *pomade*; < F. *pommade* (= Sp. Pg. *pomada*), < It. *pomata*, *pomada*, an ointment, < ML. **pomata*, *pomatum*, an ointment (said to be so called because orig. made with apples), < L. *pomum*, apple: see *pome*.] 1. A fat saturated with the odorous principles of flowers by enfleurage.—2. An ointment, especially a perfumed ointment used for the scalp and in dressing the hair. Also *pomatum*.

pomade[2] (pō-mād'), *v. t.*; pret. and pp. *pomaded*, ppr. *pomading*. [< *pomade*[2], *n.*] To anoint with pomade.

> A powdered and *pomaded* woman like Mrs. Sam. Crockford. *Mrs. Oliphant*, Poor Gentleman, xliv.

Pomaderris (pō-ma-der'is), *n.* [NL. (La Billardière, 1804), in allusion to the loose covering of the fruit formed by the calyx-tube; < Gr. πῶμα, a lid or cover, + δέρρις, a skin.] A genus of polypetalous shrubs of the order *Rhamneæ* and tribe of the same name, characterized by a capsule free at the apex, deciduous bracts, and petals, if present, five, shorter than the filaments, and surpassed by the oblong anthers. The ovary is coherent with the calyx-tube, and encircled at the base of the calyx-lobes by a slight disk. There are 22 species, natives of Australia and New Zealand. They are erect branching shrubs, hoary with star-shaped hairs on the young branches, and on the under surface of the alternate revolute leaves, which are either narrow or broad and flat. The abundant flowers are arranged in oblong panicles or corymbs, and are whitish- or yellowish-brown. *P. apetala* and *P. lanigera* are small evergreen trees of Australia, there known as *hazel*, the former sharing with *Alphitonia excelsa* the name of *cooper's-wood*. *P. elliptica* is the kumerahou of New Zealand, with crisped and fragrant yellow flowers, and *P. ericifolia* is the tauhinu, both shrubs with white branches. Several other species are cultivated for their flowers in Australia.

pomado[1]†, *n.* Same as *pomade*[2].

pomado[2], *n.* See *pommado*.

pomage†, *n.* [OF. *pomage*, F. *pommage* (ML. *pomagium*), cider, < *pome*, *pomme*, apple: see *pome*.] Same as *pomace*.

> Where of late daies they used much *pomage*, or cider, for want of barley, now that lacke is more commonly supplied with oates. *Lambard's Perambulation* (1596), p. 10. (*Halliwell.*)

pomalology (pō-ma-lol'ō-ji), *n.* Same as *pomology*, 1.

pomander (pō-man'dėr), *n.* [Corrupted from earlier *pomeambre*, < OF. *pomme d'ambre*, a ball of amber: see *pome*, *de*[2], *amber*[2].] 1. A perfume-ball, or a mixture of perfumes, formerly carried in the pocket or suspended from the neck or the girdle, especially as an amulet, or to prevent infection in time of plague.

> Your only way to make a good *pomander* is this. Take an ounce of the purest garden mould, cleans'd and steeped seven days in change of motherless rose-water; then take the best labdanum, benjoin, both storaxes, ambergris, civit, and musk. Incorporate them together and work them into what form you please. This, if your breath be not too valiant, will make you smell as sweet as my lady's dog. *A. Brewer* (?), Lingua, iv. 3.

> He . . . walks all day hanged in *pomander* chains for penance. *B. Jonson*, Every Man out of his Humour, ii. 1.

2. A hollow ball or round box used for carrying about the person the ball above described, and sometimes pierced with small openings to allow the perfume to escape.

> I have sold all my trumpery; not a counterfeit stone, not a ribbon, glass, *pomander*, brooch, table-book, ballad, knife, tape, glove, shoe-tie, bracelet, horn-ring, to keep my pack from fasting. *Shak.*, W. T., iv. 4. 609.

> He himself carried a *pomander* of silver in the shape of an apple, stuffed with spices, which sent out a curious faint perfume through small holes.
> *J. H. Shorthouse*, John Inglesant, xxxiii.

pomander-ball (pō-man'dėr-bâl), *n.* Same as *pomander*.

Pomard (pō-mär'), *n.* [F.: see def.] A good red Burgundy wine produced near the village of Pomard, in the department of Côte-d'Or, France. The wine from the whole district that comes up to a certain degree of excellence is included under this name.

pomarine (pom'a-rin), *a.* [< NL. *pomarinus*, irreg. for *pomatorhinus*: see *pomatorhine*.] In *ornith.*, pomatorhine: only applied to the *pomarine* jäger or skua-gull, *Stercorarius pomarinus* or *pomatorhinus*.

pomata, *n.* Plural of *poma*.

Pomatiacea (pō-mā-ti-ā'sē-ā), *n. pl.* Same as *Pomatiidæ*.

Pomatias (pō-mā'ti-as), *n.* [NL., < Gr. πωματίας, an operculated shell, < πῶμα, a lid, cover.] A genus of operculated land-shells, typical of the family *Pomatiidæ*.

Pomatias obscurus. (Line shows natural size.)

pomatic (pō-mat'ik), *a.* [< *poma*(*t*-) + *-ic*.] Pertaining to the poma; caused by the overlapping of the poma, as an apparent fissure of the monkey's brain; opercular. *Buck's Handbook of Med. Sciences*, VIII. 161.

Pomatiidæ (pō-ma-ti'i-dē), *n. pl.* [NL., < *Pomatias* + *-idæ*.] A family of terrestrial tænioglossate gastropods, typified by the genus *Pomatias*. The animal has a characteristic lingual dentition, the central tooth being narrow, the lateral and internal marginal unicuspid, and the external marginal very small; the shell is turreted, and the operculum multispiral. The species are inhabitants of the European zoölogical region.

Pomatobranchiata (pō'ma-tō-brang-ki-ā'tä), *n. pl.* [NL., < Gr. πῶμα (πωματ-), lid, cover, + βράγχια, gills.] A division of opisthobranchiate gastropods, corresponding to *Monopleurobranchiata*.

pomatobranchiate (pō'ma-tō-brang'ki-āt), *a.* Of or pertaining to the *Pomatobranchiata*.

Pomatocentrus (pō'ma-tō-sen'trus), *n.* [NL.] Same as *Pomacentrus*.

Pomatomidæ (pō-ma-tom'i-dē), *n. pl.* [NL., < *Pomatomus* + *-idæ*.] A family of fishes closely related to the *Carangidæ*, represented by the genus *Pomatomus*. The form is compressed and fusiform, the scales are moderate, the lateral line is gradually curved and not plated behind, and the jaws are armed with small compressed incisorial teeth.

Pomatomus (pō-mat'ō-mus), *n.* [NL. (Lacépède, 1812), prop. **Pomatotomus*, so called from the emarginate opercle; < Gr. πῶμα (πωματ-), lid, cover, + τέμνειν, ταμεῖν, cut.] 1. A genus of carangoid fishes, the type of the family *Pomatomidæ*, containing only the well-known bluefish, greenfish, or skipjack, *P. saltatrix*. This fish was called by Linnæus *Gasterosteus saltatrix*, and by Cuvier *Temnodon saltator*. It is common in nearly all warm and some temperate seas, attains a length of from 2 to 3 feet, and is highly valued as a food-fish, besides being prized for sporting. It is extremely voracious and destructive to other fishes. See cut under *bluefish*. 2. Among European ichthyologists, a genus of perciform fishes, distinguished by its very large eyes, and represented by a single species, now known as *Telescops telescopium*, inhabiting the deep water of the Mediterranean and neighboring Atlantic.

pomatorhine (pō-mat'ō-rin), *a.* [< NL. *pomatorhinus*, prop. **pomatorrhinus*, < Gr. πῶμα (πωματ-), lid, cover, + ῥίς (ῥιν-), nose.] In *ornith.*, having the nostrils overlaid with a lid-like operculum or false cere.

pomatum (pō-mā'tum), *n.* [NL.: see *pomade*[2].] Same as *pomade*[2], 2.

> A collection of receipts to make pastes for the hands, *pomatums*, lip-salves, white pots, etc. *Tatler*, No. 245.

pomatum (pō-mā'tum), *v. t.* [< *pomatum*, *n.*] To apply pomatum to, as the hair.

> Their hair, untortured by the abominations of art, was scrupulously *pomatumed* back from their foreheads with a candle. *Irving*, Knickerbocker, p. 172.

pombe (pom'be), *n.* [African.] A kind of beer made throughout central and eastern Africa.

pome (pōm), *n.* [< ME. *pome*, < OF. *pome*, *pomme*, an apple, ball, etc., F. *pomme*, an apple, = Sp. *pomo*, fruit, apple, scent-bottle, nosegay, *poma*, apple, perfume-box, = Pg. *pomo*, fruit, apple, = It. *pomo*, apple, ball, pommel, etc., < L. *pomum*, fruit, as an apple, pear, peach, cherry, fig, date, nut, grape, truffle, etc., in ML. esp. an apple; also a fruit-tree (*pomus*, a fruit-tree).] 1. An apple; a fruit of the apple kind; specifically, in *bot.*, a fleshy fruit composed of the thickened walls of the adnate calyx embracing one or more carpels, as the apple, pear, etc.

> Oxe dounge about her rootes yf that me trete,
> The *pomes* sadde and brawny wol it gete.
> *Palladius*, Husbondrie (E. E. T. S.), p. 87.

2†. A ball or globe; the kingly globe, mound, or ball of dominion.

> Dressid one me a diademe, that dighte was fulle faire,
> And syne profres me a *pome* pighte fulle of faire stonys, . . .
> In sygne that I sothely was soverayne in erthe.
> *Morte Arthure* (E. E. T. S.), l. 3355.

3. In the *Western Church*, in medieval times, a small globe of silver or other metal filled with hot water and placed on the altar during mass in cold weather, so that the priest might keep his fingers from becoming numb, and thus avoid danger of accident to the elements.

pome† (pōm), *v. i.* [< F. *pommer*, grow round, < *pomme*, apple: see *pome*.] To grow to a head, or form a head in growing.

> Cauly-flowers over-spreading to *pome* and head (before they have quite perfected their heads) should be quite eradicated. *Evelyn*, Kalendarium, Aug.

Pomeæ (pō'mę-ē), *n. pl.* [NL. (Lindley, 1835), < L. *pomum*, fruit, + *-eæ*.] A tribe or suborder of rosaceous plants, the apple family, characterized by the one to five carpels, each with two ovules, the fruit a pome, and crowned with the calyx-lobes, or in some becoming a drupe by the hardening of the inner layer. It includes over 200 species of 14 genera, natives of the northern hemisphere, chiefly in temperate regions. They are small trees, mainly with hard, compact, and durable wood, but of very irregular and twisted grain. They are among the most valuable fruit-bearing trees, and are most ornamental in flower, as the apple, pear, quince, medlar, service-berry, hawthorn, thorn-apple, shad-bush, and loquat. See *Pyrus*, *Cratægus*, and *Photinia* for the principal genera; also *Cotoneaster*.

pomeambre†, *n.* Same as *pomander*.

pomecitron (pōm'sit-ron), *n.* [< OF. *pome*, apple (see *pome*), + *citron*, a citron, pomecitron: see *pome* and *citron*.] 1. A citron.—2. A variety of apple.

> There's a fine little barrel of *pome-citrons*
> Would have serv'd me this seven year.
> *Middleton* (*and others*), The Widow, v. 1.

pomegarnet†, *n.* A Middle English form of *pomegranate*.

pomegranate (pom'- or pum'gran-āt), *n.* [Formerly also *pomegranet*; < ME. *pomegarnet*, *pomgarnet*, *pomgarnat*, *pomegarnade*, *pomgarnad*, < OF. *pome grenate*, *pome de grenate*, *pun de grenat*, *pomme de grenade* = It. *pomogranato*, < ML. *pomum granatum*, in L. *malum granatum*, pomegranate, lit. apple with many seeds (also called in L. *malum Punicum*, Punic apple): L. *pomum*, fruit, apple (see *pome*); *granatum*, neut. of *granatus*, with many seeds (*granatum*, > F. *grenade* = Sp. *granada*, pomegranate), < *granum*, seed, grain: see *grain*[1], *grenade*, *garnet*[1].] 1. The fruit of the tree *Punica Granatum*. It is of the size of an orange, has six rounded angles, and bears at the summit the remains of the calyx-lobes. It has a hard rind filled

Branch of Pomegranate (*Punica Granatum*) with Flowers. *a*, the fruit; *b*, the fruit, transverse section; *c*, flower, longitudinal section, the petals removed.

with numerous seeds, each inclosed in a layer of pulp of reddish color and pleasant subacid taste (the edible part of the fruit). It affords a cooling drink, and in Persia a wine is derived from it, as in Mexico an ardent spirit. The rind contains a large amount of tannin, and has been employed in tanning and as an astringent medicine. The pomegranate is outwardly of a beautiful orange color shaded with red.

> There were, and that wot I ful wel,
> Of *pome-garnettys* a ful gret del.
> *Rom. of the Rose*, l. 1356.

> They brought of the *pomegranates* and of the figs.
> Num. xiii. 23.

2. The tree, *Punica Granatum*, which produces the fruit pomegranate. A native of western Asia to northwestern India. It is now widely cultivated and naturalized in subtropical regions. It is a deciduous tree, 15 or 20 feet high, with numerous slender branches, some of them armed with thorns, the leaves lance-shaped or oblong. It is a fine ornamental plant, the flowers scarlet, large, and sometimes doubled. The latter are used in medicine like the fruit-rind, under the name of *balaustines*, and they also afford a red dye. The bark supplies the color of yellow morocco leather, and that of the root is an efficient tænicide, this property residing in an alkaloid, pelletierine, contained in it. It also yields punicotannic acid and mannit. The pomegranate has been known as a fruit-tree from the earliest times; it was common in Italy in the third century B. C., was familiar to the Hebrews, and its fruit was copied on Egyptian and Assyrian monuments, and later on the pillars of Solomon's temple. It thrives in the southern United States, and can be grown with moderate protection even in the climate of New York.

> An orchard of *pomegranates*, with pleasant fruits.
> Cant. iv. 13.

3. In Queensland, a small tree, *Capparis nobilis*, with some resemblance to the pomegranate. —**Pomegranate pattern**, a pattern much used in rich stuffs of European make in the fourteenth and fifteenth centuries, the chief motive in the design of which is a fruit-like figure supposed to imitate a pomegranate.

pomegranate-tree (pom'gran-āt-trē), *n.* [< ME. *pomgarnat-tree*.] Same as *pomegranate*, 2.

> In Aprille and in Marche in tempur lande
> *Pomgarnattree* is sette, in boote and drie.
> *Palladius*, Husbondrie (E. E. T. S.), p. 115.

pomeis, *n.* [OF., < *pome*, F. *pomme*, an apple.] In *her.*, a roundel vert: so called because considered the representation of an apple.

pomel†, *n.* An obsolete form of *pommel*.

pomelee†, *a.* See *pomely*.

pomelo, pummelo (pom'-, pum'e-lō), *n.* [Also *pumelo*: see *pompelmous*.] A variety of the shaddock, smaller than the shaddock proper, but much larger than an orange; the grape-fruit. Also called *forbidden-fruit*. Compare *pompelmous*.

pomely†, *a.* [ME., also *pomelee*, < OF. *pomele*, F. *pommelé* (= It. *pomellato*), dappled, < *pomme*, apple: see *pome*.] Spotted like an apple; dapple.

> This reeve sat upon a ful good stot,
> That was al *pomely* gray and highte Scot.
> *Chaucer*, Gen. Prol. to C. T., l. 616.

Pomeranian (pom-e-rā'ni-an), *a.* and *n.* [< *Pomerania* (see def.) + *-an*.] **I.** *a.* Pertaining to Pomerania, a former duchy, and now a province of northern Prussia.—**Pomeranian bream**, a fish, *Abramis buggenhagi*, supposed to be a hybrid between the common bream, *A. brama*, and the roach, *Leuciscus rutilus*. —**Pomeranian dog**, a variety of dog, about 14 inches high, having a sharp nose, pricked ears, bushy tail curled over the back, and a long thick silky coat of a white, creamy, or black color; a Spitz dog.

II. *n.* A native or an inhabitant of Pomerania.

pomeria, *n.* Plural of *pomerium*.

pomeridian (pō-me-rid'i-an), *a.* [= Pg. *pomeridiano*, < L. *pomeridianus*, postmeridian: see *postmeridian*.] 1. Postmeridian.

> I thank God . . . that I can pray to him every Day of the Week in a several Language, and upon Sunday in seven, which in Orisons of my own I punctually perform in my private *pomeridian* devotions.
> *Howell*, Letters, I. vi. 32.

2. In *entom.*, flying in the afternoon, as a lepidopterous insect.—3. In *bot.*, blossoming, etc., in the afternoon.

Pomeridianа† (pō-me-rid-i-ā'nä), *n. pl.* [NL. (Stephen, 1829), neut. pl. of L. *pomeridianus*, postmeridian: see *pomeridian*, *postmeridian*.] In *entom.*, a group of lepidopterous insects which are pomeridian, corresponding to the families *Hepialidæ*, *Bombycidæ*, *Notodontidæ*, and *Arctiidæ* combined.

pomerium (pō-mē'ri-um), *n.*; pl. *pomeria* (-ä). [L., < *post*, behind, + *murus*, wall.] In *Rom. antiq.*, an open space prescribed to be left free from buildings within and without the walls of a town, marked off by stone pillars, and consecrated by a religious ceremony.

pomeroy (pom'roi), *n.* [< OF. *pome roy*, king-apple (cf. *pomeroye*, apple marmalade): *pome*, < L. *pomum*, apple (see *pome*); *roy*, < L. *rex*, king (see *roy*).] The king-apple.

> Hauing gathered a handfull of roses, and plucking off an apple called a *Pome-roie*, hee returned.
> *Breton*, Strange Fortunes of Two Princes, p. 19. (*Davies*.)

pomeroyal† (pom-roi'al), *n.* [< OF. *pome royal*, royal apple: *pome*, < L. *pomum*, fruit; *royal*, < L. *regalis*, royal: see *royal*.] Same as *pomeroy*.

pometiet, pomettie†, *a.* Obsolete forms of *pommetty*.

pomewater† (pōm'wâ"tėr), *n.* [Also *pomwater*; < ME. *pomewater*; < *pome* + *water*.] A kind of apple.

> Ripe as the *pomewater*, who now hangeth like a jewel in the ear of caelo, the sky, the welkin, the heaven.
> *Shak.*, L. L. L., iv. 2. 4.

> The captain loving you so dearly, ay, like the *pomewater* of his eye, and you to be so uncomfortable: fie, fie!
> *Middleton* (?), The Puritan, i. 4.

pomey (pō'mi), *n.* [< F. *pommé*, pp. of *pommer*, grow round: see *pome*, *v.*] In *her.*, the figure of an apple or a roundel, always of a green color.

pomfret (pom'fret), *n.* [Appar. corrupted from the equiv. Pg. *pombo* or *pampo*.] 1. In the East Indies, a fish of the genus *Stromateoides*, distinguished from the other stromateoids by the restricted lateral branchial apertures. The white pomfret is *S. sinensis*, having no distinct free spines be-

White Pomfret (*Stromateoides sinensis*).

fore the dorsal and anal fins, and the caudal lobes subequal. It is highly esteemed for its flesh. The gray pomfret is *S. cinereus*, which has free truncated spines before the dorsal and anal fins, and the lower caudal lobe much longer than the upper; young specimens are called *silver pomfrets*.

2. Loosely, any fish of the family *Stromateidæ*. —3. A bramoid fish, *Brama rayi*, Ray's sea-bream or hen-fish.

pomgarnat†, pomgarnate†, *n.* Middle English forms of *pomegranate*.

pomicet, *n.* Same as *pomace*.

pomiferous (pō-mif'e-rus), *a.* [= F. *pomifère* = Sp. *pomifero* = Pg. It. *pomifero*; < L. *pomifer*, fruit-bearing, < *pomum*, fruit, + *ferre* = E. *bear*[1].] Pome-bearing: noting all plants which produce pomes or any of the larger fruits, as cucumbers, pumpkins, etc., in distinction from the bacciferous plants, which yield berries and other small fruits.

pomiform (pō'mi-fôrm), *a.* [< L. *pomum*, apple, + *forma*, form.] Having the form of a pome or apple.

Pomino (pō-mē'nō), *n.* [It., < *pomo*, apple: see *pome*.] A red wine of Tuscany, dry and of good flavor. It is one of several wines that are sold in some countries under the general name of *Chianti*.

pommado (pō-mā'dō), *n.* [Also *pomado*, *pommada*; < F. *pommade*, a trick in vaulting, < *pomme* in the sense of *pommeau*, pommel: see *pommel*.] An exercise of vaulting on a horse by laying one hand over the pommel of the saddle, and without the aid of stirrups.

> How many great horse he hath rid that morning, or how oft he hath done the whole or half the *pommado* in a seven-night before.
> *B. Jonson*, Cynthia's Revels, ii. 1.

Pommado reversa, the act or method of vaulting off a horse by resting the hand on the pommel.

pommage†, *n.* Same as *pomage* for *pomace*.

pomme-blanche (pom-blońsh'), *n.* [F., white apple: see *pome* and *blank*.] See *Psoralea*.

pomme-de-prairie (pom-dė-prā-rē'), *n.* [F., meadow apple: see *pome*, *de*[2], and *prairie*.] See *Psoralea*.

pommée (po-mā'), *a.* [< F. *pommé*, *pommée*, pp. of *pommer*, grow round: see *pomey*.] Same as *pommetty*.

pommel (pum'el), *n.* [Also *pummel*; early mod. E. also *pomel*; < ME. *pomel*, < OF. *pomel*, *pommel*, a ball, knob, pommel, F. *pommeau*, pommel, dim. of *pome*, *pomme*, apple, ball: see *pome*.] 1. A knob or ball, or anything of similar shape. Especially—(*a*) The rounded termination of the handle or grip of a sword, dagger, martel-de-fer, or the like, serving to keep the hand from slipping, and for striking a heavy blow at an adversary who is too close for the sweep of the weapon. The pommel in medieval weapons was often highly ornamented, and was a favorite place for the armorial bearings of the owner. These bearings, when engraved at the point opposite the junction with the blade, were sometimes used in affixing the owner's seal. See cut under *hilt*.

> Gawein lepte to hym, and smote hym so with the *pomell* of his swerde on the temple that he fill to the erthe vpright.
> *Merlin* (E. E. T. S.), iii. 457.

> Too other to offer his swerd, the *pomell* and the Crosse foreward. *Booke of Precedence* (E. E. T. S., extra ser.), i. 35.

(*b*) The protuberant part of a saddle-bow.

> He came within the target of the gentleman who rode against him, and, taking him with incredible force before him on the *pummel* of his saddle, he in that manner rid the tournament over. *Steele*, Spectator, No. 109.

(*c*) The top (of the head).

> His hors for feere gan to turne, . . .
> And . . . pighte him on the *pomel* of his heed.
> *Chaucer*, Knight's Tale, l. 1831.

(*d*) A round knob on the frame of a chair. (*e*) A ball-shaped ornament used as a finial to the conical or dome-shaped roof of a turret, pavilion, etc.

> And aboven the chief Tour of the Palays ben 2 rounde *Pomeles* of Gold; and in everyche of hem ben 2 Carboncles grete and large, that schynen fulle brighte upon the nyght.
> *Mandeville*, Travels, p. 275.

> Two wreaths to cover the two *pommels* of the chapiters which were on the top of the pillars. 2 Chron. iv. 12.

(*f*) In a ceremonial mace, the lower or butt end; in the case of a crowned mace, the end opposite the crown.

2. A piece of hard wood, grooved like a crimping-board, and attached to the hand by means of a strap, used in giving a granular appearance to leather and in making it supple.—3. The bat used in the game of nur-and-spell.

pommel (pum'el), *v. t.*; pret. and pp. *pommeled* or *pommelled*, ppr. *pommeling* or *pommelling*. [Also *pummel*; early mod. E. also *pomel*; < *pommel*, *n.*] To beat as with a pommel or with something thick or bulky; beat, as with the fists; bruise.

> Ye duke by pure strength tooke hym about the necke, and *pomeled* so aboute the hed that the bloud yssued out of his nose. *Hall*, Hen. VIII., an. 6.

> I was *pummeled* to a mummy by the boys, showed up by the ushers, etc. *Observer*, No. 96.

pommelé (pom-e-lā'), *a.* [F.: see *pomely*.] In *her.*, same as *pommetty* (*a*).

pommeled, pommelled (pum'eld), *a.* [< *pommel* + *-ed*[2].] In *her.*, having a rounded knob which terminates in a second smaller one: differing from *bottony* in that the lobes are of different sizes, the final one being much the smaller.

pommeler (pum'el-ėr), *n.* One who or that which pommels.

pommelion†, *n.* The cascabel or knob at the rear end of a cannon: the common term in early artillery, as of the sixteenth century.

pommetty (pom'e-ti), *a.* [Also *pommetté*, *pommettee*, *pomettie*, *pometie*; < F. *pommetté*, *pommetée*, ornamented with knobs (= It. *pometto*), < *pommette*, a knob, dim. of *pomme*, apple, ball: see *pome*.] In *her.*: (*a*) Terminating in a small roundel or knob: said especially of a cross. Also *pommelé*. (*b*) Double pommeled

Cross pommetty (*b*).

—that is, ending in two knobs or lobes side by side.—**Fesse pommetty.** Same as *fesse bottony* (which see, under *fesse*).

pommeture (pom'e-tūr), *n.* [< F. *pommeture*, < *pommetté*, pommetty: see *pommetty*.] In *her.*, the fact of being pommetty.

pommy (pom'i), *a.* In *her.*, same as *pommetty*.

Pomolobus (pō-mol'ō-bus), *n.* [NL. (Rafinesque, 1820), < Gr. πῶμα, lid, cover, + λοβός, lobe.] A genus of clupeoid fishes, or a subgenus of *Clupea*, differing from the typical herrings in having no vomerine teeth. The type is *P. chrysochloris*, the Ohio shad; besides this species the genus contains most of the American herrings which have usually been placed in *Clupea*. *P. mediocris* is the tailor-herring, or fall herring; *P. vernalis* is the alewife, or branch herring; *P. æstivalis* is the glut-herring or blue-back.

pomological (pō-mō-loj'i-kal), *a.* [Cf. F. *pomologique*; as *pomolog-y* + *-ic-al*.] Of or pertaining to pomology.

pomologist (pō-mol'ō-jist), *n.* [< *pomolog-y* + *-ist*.] One who is versed in pomology; a cultivator of fruit-trees.

pomology (pō-mol'ō-ji), *n.* [= F. *pomologie* = It. *pomologia*; < L. *pomum*, fruit, + Gr. -λογία, < λέγειν, speak: see *-ology*.] 1. That department of knowledge which deals with fruits; that branch of gardening which embraces the cultivation of fruit-trees or fruit-bearing shrubs. Also *pomonology*.—2. A treatise on fruits considered as esculents. *Gray.*

Pomona (pō-mō'nạ̈), *n.* [L., < *pomum*, fruit: see *pome*.] In *Rom. myth.*, the goddess who fostered fruit-trees and promoted their culture.—**Pomona green.** Same as *apple-green*.

pomonal (pō-mō'nal), *n.* [< *Pomona* + *-al*.] A place sacred to Pomona. *Encyc. Brit.*, XIX. 443.

Pomotis (pō-mō'tis), *n.* [NL. (Rafinesque, 1819), < Gr. πῶμα, a lid, cover, + οὖς (ὠτ-), ear.] An extensive genus of small American centrarchoid fishes, having the operculum prolonged backward into an ear-like flap; the sunfishes: synonymous with *Lepomis*. Various fishes which have been included in *Pomotis* are also referred to *Eupomotis*, *Apomotis*, *Bryttus*, etc. The genus has also comprised some forms not now included in *Lepomis*. They are popularly known as *sunfishes*, *pond-perches*, *tobacco-boxes*, *pumpkin-seeds*, *breams*, and by various more special names. Also *Pomatotis*.

Pomoxys (pō-mok'sis), *n.* [NL. (Rafinesque, 1818, in the form *Pomoxis*), < Gr. πῶμα, lid, cover, + ὀξύς, sharp.] In *ichth.*, a genus of American centrarchoid fishes, having long slender gill-rakers, the dorsal scarcely longer than the anal fin and obliquely opposite it, the spinous dorsal with five to eight spines and shorter than its soft part, and the anal spines six or seven. It contains two familiar fishes, *P. annularis*, the crappie, newlight, or campbellite, and *P. sparoides*, the bar-fish, or calico-, grass-, or strawberry-bass, both of fresh waters of the United States, and valuable as food-fishes. See cut under *crappie*.

pomp (pomp), *n.* [< ME. *pompe*, < OF. (and F.) *pompe* = Sp. Pg. It. *pompa* = D. *pomp* = LG. *pump* = G. *pomp*, obs. *pump* = Sw. Dan. *pomp*, < L. *pompa*, a procession, pomp, < Gr. πομπή, a sending, a solemn procession, pomp, < πέμπειν, send. Cf. *pump*[2].] 1. A procession distinguished by splendor or magnificence; a pageant; an ostentatious show or display.

> In olden dayes, good kings and worthy dukes . . .
> Contented were with *pompes* of little pryce,
> And set their thoughtes on regal gouernement.
> *Gascoigne*, Steele Glas (ed. Arber), p. 58.

> The king hereof vseth great pride and solemnitie; his *pompes* and triumphes are in maner incredible.
> *R. Eden*, tr. of Sebastian Munster (First Books on [America, ed. Arber, p. 14).

> With goddess-like demeanour forth she went,
> Not unattended; for on her, as queen,
> A *pomp* of winning Graces waited still.
> *Milton*, P. L., viii. 61.

2. Display; ostentation; parade; splendor; magnificence.

> Pomp and circumstance of glorious war.
> *Shak.*, Othello, iii. 3. 356.

> They did promise . . . that I should renounce . . . the *pomps* and vanity of this wicked world.
> *Book of Common Prayer*, Catechism.

> Yet, because he [the Son of God] came not with the *pomp* and splendour which they expected, they despise his Person, revile his Doctrine, persecute his Followers, and contrive his ruin. *Stillingfleet*, Sermons, I. vi.

> Where the Verse is not built upon Rhymes, there *Pomp* of Sound, and Energy of Expression, are indispensably necessary to support the Stile.
> *Addison*, Spectator, No. 285.

> Give me health and a day, and I will make the *pomp* of emperors ridiculous. *Emerson*, Misc., p. 22.

=**Syn. 2.** State, ostentation, grandeur, pride, display, show, flourish. See *pompous*.

pomp† (pomp), *v. i.* [= Pg. *pompear* = It. *pompare*; < LL. *pompare*, make or do with pomp, < L. *pompa*, pomp: see *pomp*, *n.*] To exhibit pomp or magnificence; make a pompous display: with indefinite *it*.

> What is the cause you *pomp it* so, I ask?
> And all men echo, you have made a masque.
> *B. Jonson*, Expost. with Inigo Jones.

pompadour (pom'pa-dōr), *n.* [Named after Marquise de *Pompadour*, influential at the French court in the middle of the 18th century.] A head-dress worn by women about the middle of the eighteenth century; also, a mode of dressing the hair by rolling it off the forehead over a cushion, later in use.—**Pompadour parasol**, a form of parasol used by women about 1860, having a folding handle, and generally covered with moire antique, or other heavy silk.—**Pompadour pattern**, a pattern for silk in which some small design of leaves and flowers, with the colors pink and blue intermingled, and frequently heightened with gold, is used. There are many modifications of this style.

pompal (pom'pal), *a.* [< LL. *pompalis*, pompous, showy, < L. *pompa*, pomp: see *pomp*.] Proud; pompous.

> Dionysian *pompal* processions.
> *C. O. Müller*, Manual of Archæol. (trans.), § 336.

pompano (pom-pä'nō), *n.* [Sp. *pampano*, applied to the fish *Stromateus fiatola*.] 1. A carangoid fish of the West Indies and South Atlantic and Gulf States, *Trachynotus carolinus*, attaining a length of about 18 inches, and highly esteemed for food. It is of an oblong rhomboid figure, with blunt snout, the spinous dorsal fin atrophied and rep-

Common Pompano (*Trachynotus carolinus*).

resented by free spines, and the soft dorsal and anal fins falciform. The color is uniformly bluish above, without dark bands or black on the vertical fins, and silvery or golden on the sides. The name extends to other members of the same genus, as the ovate, round, or short pompano, *T. ovatus*, of tropical seas (and north as far as Virginia), having the vertical fins largely black; and the glaucous or long-finned pompano, *T. glaucus*, of tropical seas (and north as far as Virginia and Lower California), having dark vertical bands on the body. 2. In California, a fish, *Stromateus simillimus*, abundant in summer along the coast, and highly esteemed for food. It is quite different from the foregoing, and is closely related to the harvest-fish, and to the butter-fish or dollar-fish. It has an ovate body rounded in front, the dorsal and anal fins not falciform, and no series of pores along the sides of the back. It is about a foot long, bluish above and bright-silvery below, with punctulate fins, and the dorsal and anal fins edged with dusk. 3. Along the western coast of Florida, a gerroid fish, *Gerres olisthostoma*. It has an oblong form with a high rounded back, rather large and very

Irish Pompano (*Gerres olisthostoma*).

smooth scales, and a nearly double dorsal, the anterior part of which has nine spines. It is specifically known as the *Irish pompano*.

pompano-shell (pom-pä'nō-shel), *n.* A wedge-shell of the genus *Donax*: so called because it is eaten by the pompano. See cut under *Donax*. [Florida.]

pompatic† (pom-pat'ik), *a.* [< LL. *pompaticus*, pompous, < *pompatus*, pp. of *pompare*, do anything with pomp: see *pomp*, *v.*] Pompous; splendid; ostentatious.

> *Pompatic*, foolish, proud, perverse, wicked, profane words. *Barrow*, Pope's Supremacy.

Pompeian (pom-pē'an), *a.* [< L. *Pompeianus*, belonging to Pompeii, < *Pompeii* (see def.).] Of or pertaining to Pompeii, a city of Italy, which with Herculaneum and other towns was overwhelmed by an eruption of Mount Vesuvius in the year 79, and of which the ruins have been in part laid bare by excavations begun in 1755. Hence, in *art* and *decoration*, noting the style of wall-painting in both fresco and plain colors which was usual among the Romans at the beginning of the Christian era, and was first made familiar by the excavations at Pompeii.—**Pompeian red**, a red color similar to that found on the walls of many houses in Pompeii. It is an oxid-of-iron color such as would be produced by a light Indian red without too much purple tone, or by a dark Venetian red.

pompelmous, pompelmoose (pom'pel-mus, -mōs), *n.* [Also *pampelmoes*, *pampelmoose*, *pompelmoes*, *pompoleon*; also *pompelo*, *pomelo*, *pummelo*, *pumelo*; prob. of E. Ind. origin.] The shaddock, especially in its larger forms. Compare *pomelo*.

pompelo (pom'pe-lō), *n.* Same as *pompelmous*.

pompeon†, *n.* Same as *pumpion*.

pomperkin†, *n.* [Appar. a drink made from apples (cf. *pomace*, *pomade*[1]), ult. < OF. *pome*, apple: see *pome*.] See the quotation.

> The sixt sort of Brittish drinkes is *Pomperkin*, a drinke whose originall was from Pomeranea (a Province in Germany), as some writers relate. Some derive it from the Pomponii (a Noble Roman family). However Authors differ about it, it is not much materiall; most certaine it is that it is made of Apples, as the name of it imports; being nothing but the Apples bruised and beaten to mash, with water put to them, which is a drinke of so weake a condition that it is no where acceptable but among the Rusticks and Plebeyans. *John Taylor*, Drinke and Welcome, [all Drinkes, and all Waters.

pompet†, **pumpet**† (pum'pet), *n.* [< OF. *pompette*, *pompete*, a tuft, topknot, pompon; "*pompette d'imprimeur*, a printer's pumpet-ball" (Cotgrave); dim. of *pompe*, pomp: see *pomp*.] In *printing*, an elastic ball formerly used to ink the types.

Pompey's pillar. See *pillar*.

pompholyx (pom'fō-liks), *n.* [L. (> F. *pompholix*, *pompholyx*), < Gr. πομφόλυξ, a bubble, slag, < πομφός, a blister.] 1. The white oxid which sublimes during the combustion of zinc: formerly called *flowers of zinc*. It rises and adheres to the dome of the furnace and the covers of the crucibles.—2. In *med.*, an eruption of deep-seated vesicles suggesting sago-grains, occurring principally on the palms of the hands and the soles of the feet. Also called *chiropompholyx* and *dysidrosis*.—3. [*cap.*] [NL.] In *zoöl.*, a generic name variously used. (*a*) A genus of rotifers of the family *Brachionidæ*. (*b*) A genus of mollusks of the family *Limnæidæ*. (*c*) A genus of hymenopterous insects of the family *Tenthredinidæ*, having wingless males. *Freymuth*, 1870. (*d*) A genus of orthopterous insects of the family *Acrididæ*. *Stål*, 1873.

Pompilidæ (pom-pil'i-dē), *n. pl.* [NL. (Leach, 1819), < *Pompilus* + *-idæ*.] A family of aculeate hymenopterous insects, typified by the genus *Pompilus*. It is a large and important group, whose members are commonly called *sand-wasps*. They are slender, usually black, with oval abdomen on a short petiole. Most of them burrow in sandy places and provision their nests with insects of various kinds which they have stung to death. Ten genera are represented in North America. The members of one genus, *Ceropales*, appear to be inquilinous.

pompillion†, *n.* Same as *popilion*.

Pompilus (pom'pi-lus), *n.* [NL., < L. *pompilus*, < Gr. πομπίλος, a fish which follows ships, < πομπή, conduct, escort, procession: see *pomp*.] 1. In *ichth.*, a genus of stromateoid fishes: same as *Centrolophus*.—2. In *conch.*, a genus of octopod cephalopods. *Schneider*, 1784.—3. In *entom.*, the typical genus of *Pompilidæ*, founded by Fabricius in 1798. These sand-wasps have strongly spinose legs, and the submedian cell of the fore wings as long as the median cell on the externomedian nervure. Over 200 species are known: one of the most notable is *P. formosus*, the so-called *tarantula-killer* of the southwestern parts of the United States.

pompion, *n.* Same as *pumpion*.

pompire† (pom'pīr), *n.* [Irreg. < L. *pomum*, fruit, apple, + *pirum*, pear.] A kind of apple; a sort of pearmain. *Ainsworth.*

pompoleon (pom-pō'lẹ̄-ọn), *n.* Same as *pompelmous*.

pompon[1]†, *n.* See *pumpion*.

pompon[2] (pom'pon; F. pron. pôṅ-pôṅ'), *n.* [Also *pompoon*; < F. *pompon*, an ornament, < *pompe*, splendor: see *pomp*.] An ornamental tuft of feathers, silk, etc., for a bonnet or hat; a topknot; specifically (*milit.*), a ball of colored wool worn on the front of a shako.

> Marian drew forth one of those extended pieces of black pointed wire with which, in the days of toupees and *pompoons*, our foremothers were wont to secure their fly-caps and head-gear. *Barham*, Ingoldsby Legends, I. 129.

pomposity (pom-pos'ị-ti), *n.* [= It. *pompositá*; < ML. *pomposita(t-)s*, < LL. *pomposus*, pompous: see *pompous*.] Pompous conduct or character; pompousness; ostentation.

> Too impatient of dullness or *pomposity*, she is more sarcastic now than she became when after-years of suffering had softened her nature. *Thackeray*, Newcomes, xxiv.

=**Syn.** *Pompousness* may be used in a good sense; *pomposity* always expresses something objectionable. See *pomp* and *pompous*.

pomposo (pom-pō'sō), *a.* [It.: see *pompous.*] In *music*, dignified; grand: noting a passage or movement to be rendered in a grand and dignified style.

pompous (pom'pus), *a.* [= D. *pompeus* = G. *pompös*, *pompos* = Sw. Dan. *pompös*, < F. *pompeux* = Sp. Pg. It. *pomposo*, < LL. *pomposus*, stately, pompous, < L. *pompa*, pomp: see *pomp.*] 1. Full of or characterized by pomp or showy display; ostentatiously grand, dignified, or magnificent; splendid; stately: as, a *pompous* triumph; a *pompous* procession.

I will make relation of those *pompous* ceremonies that were publiquely solemnized.
Coryat, Crudities, I. 36, sig. D.

But nothing is here so *pompous* as double red and stript stocks; which they multiply with care; and their Pains are justly Rewarded. *Lister*, Journey to Paris, p. 194.

2. Exhibiting self-importance or an exaggerated sense of dignity; ostentatiously dignified or self-important; lofty: as, a *pompous* style; *pompous* in manners.

We reprove a sinning brother, but do it with a *pompous* spirit; we separate from scandal, and do it with glory and a gaudy heart. *Jer. Taylor*, Works (ed. 1835), I. 679.

The *pompous* vanity of the old school-mistress . . . annoyed her. *Thackeray*, Vanity Fair, ii.

=**Syn.** 1. Superb, grand, august, lofty, dignified.—2. Magisterial, swelling, inflated, bombastic, grandiloquent, pretentious. That which gives *pompous* its distinctive character among these words and the words used in defining it is the idea of the display of magnificence for the sake of enhancing, properly or improperly, the dignity, etc., of the person or thing most concerned. A *pompous* procession gives dignity to a person thus welcomed to a city; a *pompous* deportment or manner of speech arises from the feeling of one's own importance and the effort to seem what one thinks himself to be. *Pompous* is used in a good sense now only when applied to public ceremonies or celebrations or the ways of courts.

pompously (pom'pus-li), *adv.* In a pompous manner; with great parade or display; magnificently; splendidly; ostentatiously; loftily.

pompousness (pom'pus-nes), *n.* The character of being pompous; also, pompous conduct; magnificence; splendor; great display or show; ostentatiousness.

In verse he [Dryden] had a pomp which, excellent in itself, became *pompousness* in his imitators.
Lowell, Among my Books, 1st ser., p. 76.

=**Syn.** See *pomposity*.

pomster, *v. i.* [Origin obscure.] To doctor or play the quack with salves and slops; apply a medicament to a wound or contusion, or administer medicine internally. *Halliwell.* [Prov. Eng.]

pomum (pō'mum), *n.* [L., an apple: see *pome.*] 1. An apple.—2. In *anat.*, the apple of the throat; Adam's apple, more fully called *pomum Adami*. See *Adam*.—3. Same as *calefactory*.

pomwater†, *n.* Same as *pomewater*.

ponceau[1] (pon-sō'), *n.* [< F. *ponceau*, < L. as if **punicellus*, dim. of *puniceus*, red, < *punicus*, red, prop. Punic, i. e. Phenician: see *Punic.*] 1. In *bot.*, a corn-poppy.—2. Corn-poppy color; a flame-color.—3. In *dyeing*, the name for various coal-tar colors of different red shades.

ponceau[2] (pon-sō'), *n.* [F., a culvert, dim. of *pont*, < L. *pon(t-)s*, a bridge: see *pons.*] In *engin.*, a small bridge or culvert.

poncelet (pons'let), *n.* [Named after J. V. *Poncelet*, a French mathematician (1788–1867).] A unit of rate of expenditure of energy, equivalent to 100 kilogrammeters per second.

poncer†, *n.* See *pouncer*[1].

poncho (pon'chō), *n.* [< Sp. (S. Amer.) *poncho*, a poncho; cf. Sp. *poncho*, lazy, indolent.] 1. A sort of cloak or loose garment worn by the South American Indians, and also by many of the Spanish inhabitants of South America and Mexico. It resembles a narrow blanket with a slit in the middle for the head to pass through, so that it hangs down before and behind, leaving the arms free. Garments similar to the above in general shape are made and used elsewhere, especially by sportsmen as rain-cloaks.

2. A trade-name for camlet or strong worsted.

pond[1] (pond), *n.* [< ME. *pond*, *ponde*, *poonde*, a pond: another use and form of *pound*, an inclosure: see *pound*[2].] A body of water, natural or artificial, of less extent than a lake: as, a mill-*pond*.

Make choice of such a place for your *pond* that it may be refreshed with a little rill, or with rain water, running or falling into it. *I. Walton*, Complete Angler, p. 199.

Big pond. See *pasture*, 4.—**Great pond,** in the fishery laws of Massachusetts, a pond exceeding 20 acres in area, as distinguished from a *small pond*, or one of not more than 20 acres.—**Sale-pond,** a fish-pond used only for fish ready to be sold.

pond[1] (pond), *v.* [< *pond*[1], *n.*] **I.** *trans.* To dam or pen up; make into a pond by damming; collect in a pond by stopping the current of a river.

Another flood-gate . . . *ponds* the whole river, so as to throw the waste water over a strong stone weir into its natural channel.
Defoe, Tour thro' Great Britain, I. 379. (*Davies.*)

II. *intrans.* To form pools or ponds; collect in the manner of water in a pond.

The use of turning the paper upside down is to neutralise the increase of darkness towards the bottom of the squares, which would otherwise take place from the *ponding* of the colour. *Ruskin*, Elements of Drawing.

pond[2]†, *n.* A Middle English form of *pound*[1].

pond[3]† (pond), *v. t.* [Abbr. of *ponder.*] To ponder.

O my liege Lord, the God of my Life,
Pleaseth you *pond* [in later editions, *ponder*] your Suppliants Plaint.
Spenser, Shep. Cal., February (ed. 1750), l. 151.

pondage[1] (pon'dāj), *n.* [< *pond*[1] + *-age.*] In the construction of dams for mills, reservoirs, etc., the amount of water (usually estimated in feet for mill purposes, and in gallons for waterworks) that can be restrained from overflow by the dam. It is the content of the irregular concavity below a horizontal plane on a level with the upper edge of the dam.

The stream was surveyed, . . . and . . . demonstrated the practicability of *pondage* far beyond the necessities of city supply. *Sanitary Engineer*, XIII. 80.

Basins having limited *pondage* or available storage of rainfall. *J. T. Fanning*, Water-Supply Engineering, § 47.

pondage[2]†, *n.* Same as *poundage*[1].

pond-apple (pond'ap"l), *n.* A small tree, *Anona laurifolia*, of the West Indies and southern Florida; also, its scarcely edible fruit, which is from half a foot to a foot long.

pond-carp (pond'kärp), *n.* The common carp, *Cyprinus carpio*, as bred in ponds: distinguished from *river-carp*. It is fleshier than the latter, but not so well-flavored. See cut under *carp*.

pond-dogwood (pond'dog"wůd), *n.* The button-bush, a North American shrub of wet places. See *button-bush*.

ponder (pon'dėr), *v.* [= F. *pondérer* = Sp. Pg. *ponderar* = It. *ponderare*, < L. *ponderare*, weigh, ponder, ML. also load, < *pondus* (*ponder-*), weight, < *pendere*, weigh: see *pendent* and *pound*[1].] **I.** *trans.* 1†. To weigh.

An innocent with a nocent, a man ungylty with a gylty, was *pondered* in an eqall balaunce.
Hall, Hen. IV., fol. 14 (*a*).

2. To weigh carefully in the mind; consider carefully; think about; reflect upon.

Let vs heare, and as well as wee can *ponder*, what obiections may bee made against this Arte.
Sir P. Sidney, Apol. for Poetrie.

Mary kept all these things, and *pondered* them in her heart. Luke ii. 19.

Tell me, that I may *ponder* it when gone.
M. Arnold, Balder Dead.

=**Syn.** 2. To consider, reflect upon, etc. See list under *contemplate*.

II. *intrans.* To think; muse; reflect; deliberate: with *on* or *over*: as, to *ponder over* what one has heard.

This tempest will not give me leave to *ponder*
On things would hurt me more.
Shak., Lear, iii. 4. 24.

The forest sages *pondered*, and at length
Concluded in a body to escort her
Up to her father's home of pride and strength.
Whittier, Bridal of Pennacook, v.

ponder† (pon'dėr), *n.* [< *ponder*, *v.*] Something to ponder on. [Rare.]

He laughed a little, and soon after took his leave, not without one little flight to give me for a *ponder*.
Mme. D'Arblay, Diary, IV. 27. (*Davies.*)

ponderability (pon"dėr-a-bil'i-ti), *n.* [= F. *pondérabilité* = It. *ponderabilità*; as *ponderable* + *-ity* (see *-bility*).] The property of being ponderable; the property of having weight.

ponderable (pon'dėr-a-bl), *a.* and *n.* [= F. *pondérable* = Sp. *ponderable* = Pg. *ponderavel* = It. *ponderabile*, < LL. *ponderabilis*, that can be weighed, < L. *ponderare*, weigh: see *ponder.*] **I.** *a.* Capable of being weighed; having weight.

If the bite of an asp will kill within an hour, yet the impression scarce visible, and the poison communicated not *ponderable*; we cannot as impossible reject this way of destruction. *Sir T. Browne*, Vulg. Err., iii. 27.

Immense as is the difference in density between ether and *ponderable* matter, the waves of the one can set the atoms of the other in motion.
H. Spencer, Prin. of Biol., I. 30.

II. *n.* A substance that has weight.

ponderableness (pon'dėr-a-bl-nes), *n.* Ponderability.

ponderal (pon'dėr-al), *a.* [= F. *pondéral* = Sp. *ponderal*, < LL. **ponderalis* (in neut. *ponderale*, the public scales), < L. *pondus* (*ponder-*), weight: see *ponder* and *pound*[1].] Estimated or ascertained by weight, as distinguished from *numeral* or *monetary*. [Rare.]

Thus did the money drachma in process of time decrease; but all the while we may suppose the *ponderal* drachma to have remained the same.
Arbuthnot, Anc. Coins.

ponderance (pon'dėr-ans), *n.* [< L. *ponderan(t-)s*, ppr. of *ponderare*, weigh: see *ponder.*] Weight; gravity. [Rare.]

ponderate (pon'dėr-āt), *v.*; pret. and pp. *ponderated*, ppr. *ponderating*. [< L. *ponderatus*, pp. of *ponderare*, weigh, ponder: see *ponder.*] **I.**† *trans.* To ponder; consider. *Wright.*

II. *intrans.* To weigh; have weight or ponderosity.—**Ponderating sinker,** an anglers' sinker made in two sections of lead like truncated cones, fitting closely together and held fast by means of a brass screw.

ponderation (pon-de-rā'shon), *n.* [< OF. *ponderation*, F. *pondération* = Sp. *ponderacion* = Pg. *ponderação* = It. *ponderazione*, < L. *ponderatio(n-)*, a weighing, < *ponderare*, pp. *ponderatus*, weigh: see *ponder.*] 1†. The act of weighing.

While we perspire we absorb the outward air, and the quantity of perspired matter, found by *ponderation*, is only the difference between that and the air imbibed.
Arbuthnot.

2. Weight. [Rare.]

It is not the *ponderation* of personal evidence for or against a word that should accredit or discredit it.
F. Hall, Mod. Eng., p. 35.

3†. Something that has weight; a consideration.

Now, because his heart told him how light those proofs were, he lays in the scales with them certaine grave *ponderations*, which, all put together, will prove almost as weighty as the feather he wrote withall.
Bp. Hall, Honour of Married Clergy, iii. 13.

ponderer (pon'dėr-ėr), *n.* [< *ponder* + *-er*[1].] One who ponders or reflects; one who weighs in his mind.

ponderingly (pon'dėr-ing-li), *adv.* In a pondering manner; with consideration or deliberation. *Hammond*, Works, IV. 497.

ponderling (pon'dėr-ling), *n.* [< *ponder* + *-ling*[1].] A thing of little weight. [Rare.]

She hushed her *ponderling* against her bosom, and stood aloof watching, whilst another woman brought her child to scale. *C. Reade*, Cloister and Hearth, xxxvi.

ponderment (pon'dėr-ment), *n.* [< *ponder* + *-ment.*] The act of pondering. [Rare.]

In deep and serious *ponderment*
I watch'd the motions of his next intent.
Byron, Robbery of the Cambridge Coach.

ponderomotive (pon"dėr-ō-mō'tiv), *a.* [Irreg. < L. *pondus* (*ponder-*), weight, + ML. *motivus*, motive: see *motive.*] Tending to produce motion in a body; specifically, in *elect.*, noting the electrodynamic force excited between two adjacent conductors carrying currents, in distinction from electromotive force.

ponderose† (pon'dėr-ōs), *a.* [< L. *ponderosus*, of great weight: see *ponderous.*] Same as *ponderous*.

A grand alliance with the Emperor and Spain brought down a *ponderose* army out of Germany.
Roger North, Examen, p. 470. (*Davies.*)

ponderosity (pon-de-ros'i-ti), *n.* [< F. *pondérosité* = Sp. *ponderosidad* = It. *ponderosità*, < ML. *ponderosita(t-)s*, weightiness, ponderousness, < L. *ponderosus*, weighty, ponderous: see *ponderous.*] 1. Weightiness; heaviness; ponderous character or quality; gravity: literally and figuratively.

And th' Earle of Surrey with Syr Thomas Wyat, the most excellent makers of their time, more peraduenture respecting the fitnesse and *ponderositie* of their wordes then the true cadence or simphonie, were very licencious in this point. *Puttenham*, Arte of Eng. Poesie, p. 145.

All the mynes which yow shall fynde, . . . after that at the fyrste syght they haue shewed them selues to bee mynes of metals, yow owght to consyder of what *ponderositie* of weyght they are.
R. Eden, tr. of Vannuccio Biringuccio (First Books on America, ed. Arber, p. 358).

Gold is remarkable for its admirable ductility and *ponderosity*. *Ray*, Works of Creation, p. 98.

2. A weight; something heavy, literally or figuratively; heavy matter.

Learned Ducange denies this fact, which the Vermandois genealogists maintain; these contests sport amidst the *ponderosities* of archæology.
Sir F. Palgrave, Hist. Eng. and Normandy, II. 197.

ponderous (pon'dėr-us), *a.* [< F. *pondéreux* = Sp. Pg. It. *ponderoso*, < L. *ponderosus*, of great weight, weighty, heavy, < *pondus* (*ponder-*), weight: see *ponder*, *pound*[1].] 1. Having weight; weighty; heavy; especially, very heavy; hence, clumsy or unwieldy by reason of weight: used both literally and figuratively.

The sepulchre . . .
Hath oped his *ponderous* and marble jaws.
Shak., Hamlet, i. 4. 50.

> Pressed with the *ponderous* blow,
> Down sinks the ship within the abyss below.
> *Dryden*, tr. of Ovid's Metamorph., x.

> In cases doubtfull it is dangerous
> T' admitte light Councells; for, for want of weight,
> 'Twil make the case to be more *ponderous*
> The whilst such Councells prove Aëreous.
> *Davies*, Microcosmos, p. 50.

> O, the temptation! To make of his *ponderous* sorrow a security! To sink, with its leaden weight upon him, and never rise again! *Hawthorne*, Seven Gables, xvi.

2†. Weighty; important; momentous.

> Your more *ponderous* and settled project
> May suffer alteration. *Shak.*, W. T., iv. 4. 535.

3†. Disposed to ponder; thinking; thoughtful. [Rare.]

> The next perplexed Question, with pious and *ponderous* men, will be—What should bee done for the healing of these comfortlesse exulcerations? *N. Ward*, Simple Cobler, p. 3.

Ponderous spar, heavy-spar, or barytes. See *barite*. = **Syn.** 1. *Massive*, *Burly*, etc. See *bulky*.

ponderously (pon'dėr-us-li), *adv.* In a ponderous manner; with great weight.

ponderousness (pon'dėr-us-nes), *n.* Ponderous character or quality; ponderosity; weight.

> Such downy feathers as these will never make up the *ponderousness* of a mill-stone.
> *Jer. Taylor* (?), Artif. Handsomeness, p. 126. (*Latham.*)

pond-fish (pond'fish), *n.* One of various fishes found in ponds. (*a*) The pond-carp. (*b*) A pond-perch; a sunfish of the genus *Pomotis* or *Lepomis*, many species of which abound in the United States.

pondfold† (pond'fōld), *n.* An obsolete variant of *pinfold*.

pond-hen (pond'hen), *n.* The American coot. See *Fulica*. [Massachusetts.]

pond-lily (pond'lil"i), *n.* 1. A plant of the aquatic genus *Nymphæa* (*Nuphar*); a coarse plant with yellow globular flowers, and large shining leaves floating or erect (more fully, *yellow pond-lily*; also *yellow water-lily*); spatter-dock. *N. lutea* is the common European plant; *N. advena*, the common species of eastern North America. The yellow pond-lily of Oregon, etc., is *N. polysepala*, the largest species of the genus, with flowers sometimes 5 inches across, and having large nutritious seeds largely gathered by the Indians. See *Nymphæa*1, 1.
2. A plant of the American species of *Castalia* (*Nymphæa*), the white pond-lily, more properly called *water-lily*. See *Nymphæa*1, 2.

pond-mullet (pond'mul"et), *n.* A cyprinodont fish, *Fundulus bermudæ*. [Bermudas.]

pond-mussel (pond'mus"l), *n.* A fresh-water mussel, as a unio or an anodon. A very common species is the swan-mussel, *Anodonta cygneus*. See cut under *Anodonta*.

pond-perch (pond'pėrch), *n.* A sunfish; any fish of the genus *Pomotis* or *Lepomis*.

pond-pickerel (pond'pik"e-rel), *n.* See *pickerel*.

pond-pine (pond'pin), *n.* See *pine*1.

pond-scum (pond'skum), *n.* Any free-floating fresh-water alga that forms a scum on water; specifically, one of the order *Zygnemaceæ*.

pond-shrimp (pond'shrimp), *n.* A phyllopod crustacean of the family *Branchipodidæ*. See cut under *fairy-shrimp*.

pond-snail (pond'snāl), *n.* A gastropod of the family *Limnæidæ*, and especially of the genus *Limnæa*, as *L. stagnalis*. These have spiral turreted shells. Members of *Ancylus* and related genera are similar pond-snails. Those whose shells are a flat or discoid spiral belong to *Planorbis* and related genera. The left-handed or sinistral pond-snails are of a different family, *Physidæ*. Members of a third family, *Paludinidæ*, are also called *pond-snails*. See the technical names, and cuts under *Limnæa*, *Limnæidæ*, *Paludina*, *Physa*, and *Planorbis*. Also called *mud-snail*.

pond-spice (pond'spis), *n.* A shrub, *Litsea* (*Tetranthera*) *geniculata*, of pine-barren ponds from Virginia to Florida. It has small yellow flowers in clustered umbels appearing before the coriaceous leaves, globose red drupes, and remarkably zigzag branches.

pond-turtle (pond'tėr"tl), *n.* A common name in the United States of the *Emydidæ*, most of which are also called *terrapins*, and some of them *mud-turtles*.

pondweed (pond'wēd), *n.* An aquatic herb of the genus *Potamogeton*, found in numerous species in both hemispheres. *P. natans* is a species found floating or wholly immersed in ponds and ditches in most parts of the world.—**Cape pondweed**, a desirable aquarium plant from the Cape of Good Hope, *Aponogeton distachyon* of the *Naiadaceæ*. It puts forth fragrant flowers with pure-white bracts in the midst of bright-green floating leaves. Compare *Ouvirandra*.—**Choke-pondweed**, a fresh-water plant, *Elodea* (*Anacharis*) *Canadensis* (*A. Alsinastrum*), introduced into Europe from North America, and in both continents so thriving as often to obstruct canal navigation. [Eng.]—**Horned pondweed**, a slender submerged plant, *Zannichellia palustris*, widely distributed over the world: so called from the beaked nutlets of the fruit.—**Tassel pondweed.** Same as *ditch-grass*.

Fruit-bearing Plant of Pondweed (*Potamogeton natans*). *a*, a flower.

pone1 (pōn), *n.* [Formerly also *paune*; ‹ Amer. Ind. *oppone* (see first quot.).] 1. Cornbread; in the southwestern United States, any bread made of Indian corn, especially coarse kinds used by the negroes and poorer whites, commonly called *corn-pone*; also, finer bread, made with milk and eggs, in flat cakes about an inch thick, very light and delicate. See *johnny-cake*, *hoe-cake*.

> The bread in gentlemen's houses is generally made of wheat, but some rather choose the *pone*, which is the bread made of Indian meal, . . . not so called from the Latin panis, but from the Indian name oppone.
> *Beverley*, Virginia, iv. ¶ 72.

2. A loaf or cake of such bread.

> Holding a *pone* of corn bread in one hand, the half of a roasted chicken in the other.
> *W. Baker*, New Timothy, p. 74.

[Southern United States in both uses.]

pone2 (pō'nē), *n.* [‹ L. *pone*, impv. of *ponere*, place: see *ponent*.] In *old Eng. law*: (*a*) A writ whereby an action depending in an inferior court might be removed into the Court of Common Pleas. (*b*) A writ whereby the sheriff was commanded to take security of a person for his appearance upon an assigned day.

pone3 (pō'nē), *n.* [‹ L. *pone*, impv. of *ponere*, place: see *ponent*. Cf. *pone*2.] In the game of vingt-et-un, the player to the left of the dealer; the eldest hand.

ponent (pō'nent), *a.* [‹ OF. *ponent* = Sp. *poniente* = Pg. It. *ponente*, ‹ ML. *ponen(t-)s*, the west, the place of the setting sun, ‹ L. *ponen(t-)s*, ppr. of *ponere*, set, put, lay down, intrans. poet. fall, abate (of winds); prob. contr. of **posnere*, **posinere*, let down, ‹ *po-*, forward, down, + *sinere*, let: see *site*.] 1. Western. [Rare.]

> Forth rush the Levant and the *Ponent* winds,
> Eurus and Zephyr. *Milton*, P. L., x. 704.

2. [*cap.*] A division of the Paleozoic strata in Pennsylvania, according to the nomenclature suggested by H. D. Rogers: it corresponds to the Catskill group of the New York survey, forming one of the divisions of the Upper Devonian.

ponente (pọ-nen'te), *n.* [It.: see *ponent*.] In Italy, the west; the region in the west: as, the Riviera di *Ponente*; hence, the west wind.

Ponera (pọ-nē'rạ̈), *n.* [NL. (Latreille, 1804), ‹ Gr. πονηρός, bad, useless, ‹ πονεῖν, be in distress.] An important genus of ants, typical of the family *Poneridæ*, distributed throughout the tropics. *P. ferruginea* is a Mexican species. The females and workers are armed with spines; the abdomen is elongated, with its first segment comparatively large and often cubical.

Poneridæ (pọ-ner'i-dē), *n. pl.* [NL., ‹ *Ponera* + *-idæ*.] One of the five families into which the true ants or *Heterogyna* are now divided. They have the abdominal petiole single-jointed, the abdomen proper constricted between the first and second segments, and the mandibles inserted close together. Four genera are represented in the United States.

ponerology (pon-ẹ-rol'ọ-ji), *n.* [‹ Gr. πονηρός, bad, + -λογία, ‹ λέγειν, speak: see *-ology*.] In *theol.*, the doctrine of wickedness.

Pongamia (pon-gā'mi-ạ̈), *n.* [NL. (Ventenat, 1803), ‹ E. Ind. *pongam*.] A genus of leguminous trees of the tribe *Dalbergieæ* and subtribe *Lonchocarpeæ*, characterized by its short, thick, smooth, compressed, and wingless pod, by the union of the ten stamens above into a tube, and by the partial adherence of the wing-petals to the keel. The only species, *P. glabra*, is a native of the tropics from India and China to Australia and the Fiji Islands. It bears smooth pinnate leaves, and white or yellow flowers in racemes, ornamental in cultivation under glass. The seeds yield kurung- or poonga-oil.

pongee (pon-jē'), *n.* [Said to be a corruption of Chinese *pŭn-ki*, 'own loom,' or of *pŭn-chih*, 'own weaving' (as if 'home-made'); but all silks woven in China are stamped with one or other of these phrases, along with the name of the house selling them. According to another suggestion, a corruption of Chinese *pun-shih*, 'native (or wild) silk.'] A soft, unbleached washing silk resembling the tasar silk of India, woven in China, chiefly in the province of Shantung, from cocoons of a wild silkworm (*Attacus pernyi*) which feeds on a scrub-oak. The finer kinds, bleached, dyed, or figured after importation, are known in the trade as *China silks*.

pongo (pong'gō), *n.* [= F. *pongo* (NL. *Pongo*); from a native name in Borneo.] 1. A large anthropoid ape of Borneo, *Simia* (or *Pithecus*) *wurmbi*, not known to be distinct from the ordinary orang-utan, *Simia satyrus*.—2. [*cap.*] [NL.] A genus of apes, including the gorilla (*P. gorilla*) and the chimpanzee (*P. troglodytes*). *Lacépède.* [Little used.]

poniard (pon'yạ̈rd), *n.* [An altered form of earlier *poiniard*, *poinard* (also corruptly *poinado*, *poinadoe*) = MD. *poniaerd*, D. *ponjaard*, ‹ F. *poignard*, a poniard, ‹ *poing*, fist, ‹ L. *pugnus*, fist: see *pugnacious*. Cf. Sp. *puñal* = Pg. *punhal* = It. *pugnale*, a poniard, of the same ult. origin.]

Poniard, entirely of steel, 17th century.

A stabbing-weapon; a dagger: applied to any such weapon, without reference to shape or make.

> Those bloody brothers, Hastings and the rest,
> Sheath'd their sharp *poniards* in his manly breast.
> *Drayton*, Miseries of Queen Margaret.

poniard (pon'yạ̈rd), *v. t.* [= F. *poignarder*; from the noun.] To stab with or as with a poniard.

> But may be it is your ladyship's pleasure that this young esquire shall *poniard* the servants, as well as switch and baton them. *Scott*, Abbot, iv.

ponibility† (pō-ni-bil'i-ti), *n.* [‹ L. *ponere*, place (see *ponent*), + *-ibility*.] The capability of being placed. *Barrow.* [Rare.]

pons (ponz), *n.*; pl. *pontes* (pon'tēz). [L. (› It. *ponte* = Sp. *puente* = Pg. *ponte* = F. *pont* = W. *pont*), a bridge: see *path*.] In *anat.*, a part which connects two parts, as if bridging the interval between them. Except in phrases, it designates the ventral part of the epencephalon, of which the cerebellum constitutes the remaining dorsal part. The ventral part of the pons is formed by the heavy masses of transverse fibers coming from the middle peduncles of the cerebellum. Also called *pons Varolii* and *pons cerebelli*.—**Brachium pontis.** See *brachium*.—**Pons asinorum.** [L., 'bridge of asses,' F. *pont aux ânes*, 'bridge for asses.' The Latin expression was applied early in the sixteenth century to a diagram showing how to find middle terms to arguments, and "commonly called the *pons asinorum* on account of its apparent difficulty"; OF. *pont aux asnes de logicque* (Rabelais), "the conversion of propositions" (Cotgrave); hence, "*c'est le pont aux asnes* (applicable when such as are ignorant of the true reason or cause of things impute them to witchcraft, fortune, etc.), a shift, evasion, help at a pinch, for a dunce" (Cotgrave), in mod. use equiv. to "everybody knows that," "it is a trite thing." The original allusion seems to have been to the difficulty of getting asses to cross a bridge; hence, to the difficulty of getting students to apprehend what is in fact simple enough if attempted.] A name given to the fifth proposition of the first book of Euclid, which sets forth that, if a triangle has two of its sides equal, the angles opposite to these sides are also equal. This proposition affords a difficulty to the learner, because it is the first one involving any mathematical puzzle. The name is also carelessly given to the Pythagorean proposition (Euc. I. 47).—**Pons hepatis**, a prolongation, often present, of the substance of the left lobe of the liver, uniting it with the square lobe across the umbilical fissure.—**Pons Tarini**, the posterior perforated space at the base of the brain; a depressed gray tract between the diverging crura cerebri and behind the corpora albicantia.—**Pons Varolii**, or **pons cerebelli**. See def.

Pontacq (pon'tak), *n.* [From *Pontacq*, in the Basses-Pyrénées, France, where it is made.] A white wine from southern France, similar to Barsac in flavor.

pontage (pon'tạ̄j), *n.* [‹ OF. *pontage* = Sp. *pontaje*, *pontazgo* = It. *pontaggio*, ‹ ML. *pontaticum* (also, after OF., *pontagium*), bridge-toll, ‹ L. *pon(t-)s*, bridge: see *pons*.] A toll or tax for the privilege of using a bridge, or a tax for the maintenance and repair of bridges.

> The citizens of Hereford fined, in the second year of Henry III., in a hundred marks and two palfreys, . . . that they might be quit throughout England of toll and lastage, of passage, *pontage*, and stallage, and of leve, and danegeld, and gaywite, and all other customs and exactions. *S. Dowell*, Taxes in England, I. 26.

pontal (pon'tạl), *a.* [‹ L. *pon(t-)s*, a bridge, + *-al*.] Same as *pontile*.

Pontederia (pon-tẹ-dē'ri-ạ̈), *n.* [NL. (Linnæus, 1737), named after Giulio *Pontedera*, 1688–1757, professor of botany at Padua, author of a compend of botany, etc.] A genus of monocotyledonous aquatic plants, type of the order *Pontederiaceæ*, characterized by the funnel-shaped and two-lipped corolla, six stamens, versatile anthers, and compound ovary with one cell and one ovule. There are but 7 or 8 species, all American, growing in shallow water, with rootstocks creeping in the mud or floating, and covered by long sheaths. The long stout leafstalks rise erect often 2 feet above the water, each bearing a single arrow-shaped, lanceolate, or roundish leaf, with many fine parallel curving veins. The flowers rise a little higher, forming a dense cylindrical spike, blue or purple, or rarely white, and remarkable for their trimorphous stamens, having three lengths of filaments, and three reciprocally different lengths of styles, present in different flowers, facilitating cross-fertilization. *P. cordata*, which is found throughout nearly the whole length of America, is known in the northern United States as *pickerel-weed*, and in the southern as *wampee*. Several former species are now separated as the genus *Eichhornia*, as *E. azurea*, the water-plantain of Jamaica, and *E. crassipes*, the bladder-stalked pickerel-weed or gamalote of Guiana, cultivated (under the name *Pontederia*) in tanks under glass as a singular bladder-bearing and floating plant.

Pontederiaceæ (pon-tē-dē-ri-ā'sē-ē), *n. pl.* [NL. (Achille Richard, 1828), < *Pontederia* + *-aceæ*.] An order of monocotyledonous plants of the series *Coronarieæ*. It is characterized by a perianth of three petals and three similar sepals, all united below into a tube and forming unequal lobes above, by a superior ovary of three complete or imperfect carpels, forming a dry fruit, and by a straight cylindrical embryo extending through the center of copious farinaceous albumen. It includes 35 species, in 5 genera, of which *Pontederia* and *Heteranthera* are the chief, natives of warm northern and extratropical southern regions, extending to Canada, China, and Japan, but lacking in Europe. They are aquatics, erect or floating in fresh water from rootstocks which lie horizontally in the mud, or which extend as runners floating on the water.

pontee (pon-tē'), *n.* Same as *pontil*.

pontes, *n.* Plural of *pons*.

Pontic[1] (pon'tik), *a.* [= F. *pontique* = Pg. It. *pontico*, < L. *Ponticus*, < Gr. Ποντικός, Pontic, < Πόντος, the Black Sea, a particular use (also applied to the Ægean and to the whole Mediterranean) of πόντος, the sea, esp. the open sea.] Of or pertaining to the Pontus, Euxine, or Black Sea, or the regions near it.

> Like to the *Pontic* sea,
> Whose icy current and compulsive course
> Ne'er feels retiring ebb. *Shak.*, Othello, iii. 3. 452.

pontic[2] (pon'tik), *a.* [< L. *pon(t-)s* + *-ic*.] Of or pertaining to the pons of the brain.

> Thirteen of the cases occurred between the ages of ten and twenty-nine, the only case over forty being one of *pontic* abscess. *Lancet*, No. 3475, p. 739.

pontifex (pon'ti-feks), *n.*; pl. *pontifices* (pon-tif'i-sēz). [L.: see *pontiff*.] 1. In *Rom. antiq.*, a member of the principal college of priests who was not assigned to the service of any particular god, but performed general functions of the state religion. The chief of the pontifices was styled *pontifex maximus*, and was ex officio the highest religious authority in the state.— 2. *Eccles.*, a bishop; specifically, the Pope.

> Well has the name of *pontifex* been given
> Unto the Church's head, as the chief builder
> And architect of the invisible bridge
> That leads from Earth to Heaven.
> *Longfellow*, Golden Legend, v.

pontiff (pon'tif), *n.* [< F. *pontife*, OF. *pontif* = Sp. *pontifice* = Pg. It. *pontifice*, a pontiff, < L. *pontifex*, *pontufex* (*-fic-*), a high priest, pontifex (see *pontifex*), LL. eccl. a bishop, ML. NL. the Pope, lit. (and so used in ML.) 'bridge-maker, bridge-builder' (prob. orig. so called as having charge of the making or maintenance of a bridge — it is said, of the Sublician bridge built over the Tiber by Ancus Marcius), < *pon(t-)s*, bridge, + *facere*, make: see *fact*.] 1. In *Rom. antiq.*, a chief priest: same as *pontifex*, 1.

> The reverence which the people showed for the emperors was due to the fact that they all, from Augustus to Theodosius, were sovereign *Pontiffs*. *Faiths of the World*, p. 205.

> The supreme *pontiff* was in the religion of the state what the father was in the religion of the family. His dwelling was in the regia close to the altar of Vesta, the sacred hearth of the state. *Encyc. Brit.*, XIX. 455.

2. A Jewish high priest.—3. *Eccles.*, a bishop; especially, the Bishop of Rome, as the head of the church; the Pope. Also called the *supreme pontiff*.

> To secure the papal recognition he empowered the bishops of Durham and St. David's to perform that "filial and catholic obedience which was of old due and accustomed to be paid by the kings of England to the Roman *pontiffs*." *Stubbs*, Const. Hist., § 361.

pontific (pon-tif'ik), *a.* [Irreg. accom. to adjectives in *-fic*; = Sp. Pg. It. *pontificio*, < L. *pontificius*, of or belonging to a pontiff, pontifical, < *pontifex* (*-fic-*), pontiff: see *pontifex*.] 1. Of or pertaining to the pontifices of ancient Rome.

> The *Pontifick* College with their Augurs and Flamins taught them [the Romans] in Religion and Law. *Milton*, Areopagitica, p. 8.

2. Of or pertaining to a pope; papal.

> Nor yet surceas'd with John's disastrous fate
> *Pontific* fury! *Shenstone*, Ruined Abbey.

pontifical[1] (pon-tif'i-kal), *a.* and *n.* [< F. *pontifical* = Sp. Pg. *pontifical* = It. *pontificale*, < L. *pontificalis*, of or belonging to a pontiff, ML. of or belonging to a bishop or the Pope (as a noun *pontificale*, neut., a book of offices, *pontificalia*, neut. pl., pontifical vestments), < *pontifex* (*-fic-*), pontiff: see *pontiff*.] I. *a.* 1. Of, belonging to, or befitting a pontiff or high priest.

> Thus did I keep my person fresh and new;
> My presence, like a robe *pontifical*,
> Ne'er seen but wonder'd at.
> *Shak.*, 1 Hen. IV., iii. 2. 56.

2. Of or pertaining to a bishop.—3. Of or pertaining to the Pope of Rome; papal; popish.

> Than she came to the Pope's palays in Auignon, and there alighted and went to see the Pope, who sat in consystory in a chayre *pontyficall*. *Berners*, tr. of Froissart's Chron., II. clv.

> Guibert the Antipope, who, by the aid of the Imperial arms, . . . had filled Rome with every kind of violence, crime, and bloodshed, invaded the *pontifical* throne, and driven forth the rightful Pope. *Milman*, Latin Christianity, III. 208.

Pontifical choir, the choir of the Sistine Chapel in Rome.—**Pontifical indiction.** See *indiction*, 3.—**Pontifical mass**, a mass celebrated by a bishop wearing his insignia.

II. *n.* 1. In *liturgics*, an office-book of the Western Church, containing the forms for the sacraments and other rites and ceremonies which can be performed only by a bishop (especially those for ordination, confirmation, and consecration of churches), the changes in the rubrics necessary when a bishop officiates, benedictions, and other forms, some of which can be used by priests who have received special commission from the bishop. Pontificals were probably first introduced in the eighth century. In the Anglican Church since the Reformation the office of confirmation is contained in the Book of Common Prayer, to which the ordinal also is united. In the Greek Church the offices for confirmation and ordination are included in the Euchologion.

2. *pl.* The insignia of a pontiff; the dress, ornaments, etc., of a bishop or pope, or, more loosely, those of a priest. See *pontificalia*.

> Robed in their *pontificals*,
> England's ancient prelates stood.
> *Whittier*, Curse of the Charter-Breakers.

3†. A kind of ouch in use in the sixteenth century. *Fairholt*.

pontifical[2]† (pon-tif'i-kal), *a.* [< L. *pontifex* (*-fic-*), lit. sense, as in ML., 'bridge-builder': see *pontiff*. Cf. *pontifical*[1].] Of or pertaining to bridge-building. [Rare.]

> Now had they brought the work by wondrous art
> *Pontifical*, a ridge of pendent rock,
> Over the vex'd abyss. *Milton*, P. L., x. 313.

pontificalia (pon-tif-i-kā'li-ä), *n. pl.* [ML.: see *pontifical*[1].] The insignia of a bishop. In the Western Church these are the pastoral staff, miter, ring, pectoral cross, cathedra or diocesan throne, episcopal vestments, gloves, and sandals. In the Greek Church they are the pateressa, encolpion, throne, and special vestments with omophorion, polystaurion or saccos, and epigonation.

pontificality† (pon-tif-i-kal'i-ti), *n.* [< OF. *pontificalité*; as *pontifical*[1] + *-ity*.] 1. The state, dignity, and government of the Pope; the papacy.

> Charles the fifth, emperor, who was accounted one of the Pope's best sons, yet proceeded in matters temporal towards Pope Clement with strange rigour, never regarding the *pontificality*, but kept him prisoner thirteen months in a pestilent prison. *Bacon*, Charge against William Talbot.

> When the *pontificality* was first set up in Rome, all nations from East to West did worship the Pope no otherwise than of old the Cæsars. *Usher*, Judgment on the See of Rome, p. 20.

2. *pl.* Same as *pontifical*[1], 2.

> He himself [the Bishop of Paris] was that day in his sumptuous *Pontificalities*, wearing religious ornaments of great price. *Coryat*, Crudities, I. 37, sig. D.

pontifically (pon-tif'i-kal-i), *adv.* In a pontifical manner; specifically, after the manner of a bishop; officially as bishop.—**To assist pontifically**, to be present officially as bishop without being celebrant or officiant. In the Anglican Church the bishop when present at the eucharist pronounces the absolution and gives the benediction.

> After sermon yᵉ Bishop (Dr. Wren) gave us the blessing very *pontifically*. *Evelyn*, Diary, Feb. 10, 1661.

pontificate (pon-tif'i-kāt), *n.* [< F. *pontificat* = Sp. Pg. *pontificado* = It. *pontificato*, < L. *pontificatus*, the office of a pontiff, < *pontifex* (*-fic-*), pontiff: see *pontiff*.] 1. The office or dignity of a pontiff, high priest, or pope.

> He turned hermit in the view of being advanced to the *pontificate*. *Addison*.

2. The time during which a pontifical office is held by any given incumbent.

> After the *pontificate* of Clement V. the hold of the papacy on the nation was relaxing. *Stubbs*, Medieval and Modern Hist., p. 308.

pontificate (pon-tif'i-kāt), *v. i.*; pret. and pp. *pontificated*, ppr. *pontificating*. [< ML. *pontificatus*, pp. of *pontificare*, perform a pontiff's duties, < L. *pontifex* (*-fic-*), pontiff: see *pontiff*.] To act officially as pontiff or bishop; especially, to say pontifical mass.

> The golden reed is used to this day by the Pope whenever he solemnly *pontificates*. *Rock*, Church of our Fathers, I. 167.

pontifice (pon'ti-fis), *n.* [< L. *pon(t-)s*, a bridge, + *-ficium*, < *facere*, make. Cf. ML. *pontifex* (*-fic-*), a bridge-builder: see *pontiff*.] Bridge-work; the structure or edifice of a bridge; a bridge. [Rare.]

> At the brink of Chaos, near the foot
> Of this new, wondrous *pontifice*.
> *Milton*, P. L., x. 348.

pontifices, *n.* Plural of *pontifex*.

pontificial† (pon-ti-fish'al), *a.* [< L. *pontificius* (see *pontific*) + *-al*.] Of or pertaining to a pontiff; pontifical; hence, papal; popish.

> I have my puritan news, my protestant news, and my *pontificial* news. *B. Jonson*, World in the Moon.

pontifician† (pon-ti-fish'an), *a.* and *n.* [< L. *pontificius*, of or belonging to a pontiff (see *pontific*), + *-an*.] I. *a.* Of or pertaining to the Pope; pontificial.

> The *pontifician* laws. *Bp. Hall*, Peace-maker, ii. § 2.

II. *n.* An adherent of the Pope or of the papacy.

> In some of our hands they [the keys of heaven] are suffered to rust for want of use, in others (as the *Pontificians*) the wards are altered, so as they can neither open nor shut. *Bp. Hall*, Righteous Mammon.

> That in the Public Office or Liturgy of the Church of England is nothing but what is consonant to the faith, the *pontificians* grant. *Evelyn*, True Religion, II. 353.

pontil (pon'til), *n.* [Also *puntel* (and *pontee*, *puntee*, *ponty*, *punty*); < F. *pontil*, dim. of *point*, a point: see *point*. Cf. *pointel*.] An iron rod used in glass-making for handling, and especially for revolving rapidly, the soft glass in the process of formation, especially in the making of crown-glass.

pontile (pon'til), *a.* [< LL. *pontilis*, belonging to a bridge, < L. *pon(t-)s*, a bridge.] Of or pertaining to the pons of the brain. Also *pontal*, *pontine*.

pontinal (pon'ti-nal), *a.* and *n.* [< L. *pon(t-)s*, a bridge.] I. *a.* Bridging; forming a bridge over a gap, as among cranial bones.

II. *n.* A bone of the skull of some fishes; a modified bone of the infra-orbital chain of bones bridging the interval between the second suborbital and the preoperculum, as in the *Dactylopteroidea*. *Gill*, Amer. Nat. (1888), p. 358.

Pontine[1] (pon'tin), *a.* [Also *Pomptine*; = F. *pontins* (pl.) = It. *pontine* (pl.), < L. *Pontinus*, *Pomptinus*, an appellation given to a district in Latium near Pometia, and particularly used of extensive marshes there; appar. a var. of *Pometinus*, of or belonging to Pometia, < *Pometia*, an old town of the Volscians.] Of or relating to an extensive marshy district southeast of Rome, called the *Pontine Marshes*.

pontine[2] (pon'tin), *a.* [< L. *pon(t-)s*, bridge, + *-ine*[1].] Same as *pontile*.

> Pontile (sometimes, incorrectly, *pontine* or pontal). *Buck's Handbook of Med. Sciences*, VIII. 524.

Pont l'Evêque cheese. See *cheese*[1].

pontlevis (pont-lev'is), *n.* [< F. *pontlevis*, a drawbridge, the rearing of a horse, < *pont* (< L. *pon(t-)s*), bridge, + *levis*, OF. *leveïs*, *levadis* = Pr. *levadis* = Sp. *levadizo* = Pg. *levadiço*, that may be raised or drawn up, < L. as if **levaticius*, < *levare*, raise: see *levy*[1]. Cf. It. *levatojo*, a drawbridge.] 1. A drawbridge.

> Yonder 's a plum-tree, with a crevice
> An owl would build in, were he but sage,
> For a lap of moss, like a fine *pontlevis*
> In a castle of the middle age,
> Joins to a lip of gum pure amber.
> *Browning*, Sibrandus Schafnaburgensis.

2. In the *manège*, the resistance of a horse by rearing repeatedly so as to be in danger of falling over.

Pontocaspian (pon-tō-kas'pi-an), *a.* [< *Pontic* + *Caspian*.] Relating to the regions which drain into the Caspian and Black seas.

> The water-shed of the *Pontocaspian* area. *Huxley*, Crayfish, vi.

ponton†, *n.* An obsolete form of *pontoon*.

pontonier (pon-tō-nēr'), *n.* [Also *pontonnier*; = It. *pontoniere*, < F. *pontonnier*, < *ponton*, a pontoon: see *pontoon*.] A soldier who has charge of pontoons; also, one who constructs pontoon-bridges.

pontoon (pon-tön'), *n.* [Formerly *ponton*; < F. *ponton* = Sp. *ponton* = Pg. *pontão* = It. *pontone*, < LL. *ponto(n-)*, a pontoon, L. *ponto(n-)*, a kind of Gallic transport, a punt, < *pon(t-)s*, a bridge: see *pons*, *path*. Cf. *punt*[1].] 1. In *milit. engin.*, a flat-bottomed boat, or any light framework or floating structure, used in the construction of a temporary bridge over a river. One form of pontoon is a hollow cylinder of tin-plate, with hemispherical ends, divided by several longitudinal and transverse partitions to act as braces and to prevent sinking if pierced by a shot or accidentally. Another is in the form of a decked canoe, consisting of a timber frame covered with sheet-copper, and formed in two distinct parts, which are locked together for use and dislocated for transportation, and also divided into air-tight chambers.

Pontoons in place for Pontoon-bridge.
a, balks for supporting the roadway; *b*, roadway complete.

2. *Naut.*, a lighter; a low flat vessel resembling a barge, furnished with cranes, capstans, and other machinery, used in careening ships, chiefly in the Mediterranean. *Admiral Smyth.* —3. In *hydraul. engin.*: (*a*) A water-tight structure or frame placed beneath a submerged vessel and then filled with air to assist in refloating the vessel. (*b*) A water-tight structure which is sunk by filling with water and raised by pumping it out, used to close a sluiceway or entrance to a dock. Also spelled *ponton*.—4. In *anat.*, a loop or knuckle of the small intestine: so called from the way it appears to float in the abdominal cavity. See the quotation under *mesentery*. —5. In *brewing*, one of the cleansing-rounds or cleansing-squares used for clarifying ale.

pontoon-bridge (pon-tön'brij), *n.* A platform or roadway supported upon pontoons.

Pontoon-bridge at Coblentz on the Rhine.

pontoon-train (pon-tön'trān), *n.* *Milit.*, the carriages or wagons and materials carried with an army to construct bridges.

pontophidian (pon-tọ-fid'i-an), *n.* [< Gr. πόντος, the sea, + ὀφίδιον, dim. of ὄφις, a snake.] A sea-serpent.

Pontoporia (pon-tọ-pō'ri-ạ̈), *n.* [NL., < Gr. πόντος, the sea, + πόρος, passage, pore: see *pore*[2].] A genus of delphinoid odontocete cetaceans. It contains a small estuarine American dolphin, *P. blainvillei*, about 5 feet long, with a developed

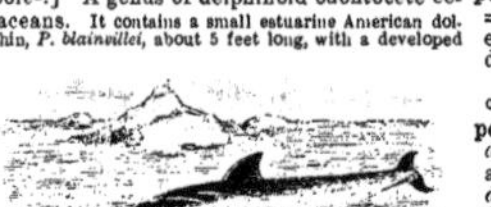

Pontoporia blainvillei.

dorsal fin, long slender jaws with from 200 to 240 teeth, about 40 vertebræ, the sternum of two pieces, the ribs 10 in number, of which 4 join the sternum, and the blow-hole transverse and crescentic. This genus connects the *Platanistidæ* or fluviatile dolphins with the *Delphinidæ* or true marine dolphins, porpoises, grampuses, etc. Also called *Stenodelphis*. Also *Pontoporus*.

Pontoporiinæ (pon-tọ-pō-ri-ī'nē), *n. pl.* [NL., < *Pontoporia* + *-inæ*.] A subfamily of *Delphinidæ*, represented by the genus *Pontoporia*. There is an evident external neck; the frontal area is expanded and little depressed; the postorbital process of the frontal bone and the zygomatic process of the squamosal project outward; and the maxillary is crested, with a free margin over the orbital region.

pont-volant (pont-vọ-lant'), *n.* [< F. *pont volant*: *pont*, bridge (see *pons*); *volant*, flying: see *volant*.] *Milit.*, a flying-bridge; a kind of bridge used in sieges for surprising a fort or outwork that has but a narrow moat. It is composed of two small bridges laid one above the other, and so contrived that, by the aid of cords and pulleys, the upper one may be pushed forward till it reaches the destined point.

ponty (pon'ti), *n.*; pl. *ponties* (-tiz). Same as *pontil*.

ponty-sticker (pon'ti-stik"ėr), *n.* In *glass-making*, a workman who affixes a quantity of blown glass to the ponty or pontil.

pony (pō'ni), *n.*; pl. *ponies* (-niz). [Formerly also *poney*, *powney*; prob. < OF. *poulenet*, a colt; cf. *poulenet*, *poulinel*, a colt, dim. of *poulain*, a colt: see *pullen*. The word is thus ult. connected with Gr. πῶλος, a foal: see *foal*. The Gael. *ponaidh*, as well as Ir. *poni*, a pony, F. *poney*, a pony, are from E.] 1. A very small horse; specifically, a horse less than 13 hands in height. The Shetland breed of ponies are stoutly built, active and hardy, with very full mane and tail, and of gentle, docile disposition. In western parts of the United States all the small hardy horses (mustangs or broncos) used by the Indians are called *ponies*.

I have bought two more *ponies*, so we are strong in pigmy quadrupeds.
Sydney Smith, To Mrs. Holland, June 3, 1835.

A *pony* must be less than 52 inches (13 hands) from the ground to the top of the withers. . . . *Ponies*, as a rule, will do far more work than a full-sized horse.
Encyc. Brit., XII. 191.

2. The sum of £25. [English sporting slang.]

He is equally well amused whether the play is high or low, but the stake he prefers is fives and *ponies*.
Greville, Memoirs, Aug. 15, 1818.

3. A translation of a Greek or Latin author used unfairly in the preparation of lessons; hence, any book so used: same as *horse*[1], 9. [School and college slang.]—4. A very small drinking-glass. (*a*) A glass holding about a mouthful of spirits, as brandy. (*b*) A glass holding about a gill of beer.

5. The quantity (of liquor) contained in such a glass.—6. A small raft of logs. [Delaware.] —7. In the West Indies, a small tree, *Tecoma serratifolia*. [Pony is used in composition to denote something small of its kind, as *pony-saw*, *pony-engine*, etc.]—**Jerusalem pony**, an ass. [Slang.]=**Syn.** 1. *Pony*, *Colt*, *Filly*. A *pony* is a small horse, especially of a small breed, as a Shetland pony; a *colt* is a young horse, and distinctively a male; a *filly* is a young mare.

pony (pō'ni), *v. t.*; pret. and pp. *ponied*, ppr. *ponying*. [< *pony*, *n.*] To use a pony in translating: as, to *pony* a piece of Latin. [School and college slang.]

pony-engine (pō'ni-en"jin), *n.* On a railroad, a small drill-engine, or a yard-engine used at stations for moving cars and making up trains.

pony-saw (pō'ni-sâ), *n.* A small gang-saw used for sawing timber into boards.

pony-truck (pō'ni-truk), *n.* A two-wheeled leading truck used in some forms of locomotives.

P. O. O. An abbreviation of *post-office order*, a money-order issued by the post-office.

pooa, puya[2] (pö'ạ̈, pö'yạ̈), *n.* [E. Ind.] An urticaceous plant, *Maoutia* (*Bœhmeria*) *Puya*, of northern India. Its stem is 6 or 8 feet high, and yields a fiber similar to ramie (that of *Bœhmeria nivea*). Also *pooah*.

pood (pöd), *n.* [Formerly also *pode* (= F. *poude* = G. *pud*); < Russ. *pudŭ*.] A Russian weight, equal to 40 Russian pounds, or 36 pounds avoirdupois.

I haue bought . . . for 77. robles foure hundred *podes* of tried tallowe.
Hakluyt's Voyages, I. 302.

poodle (pö'dl), *n.* [= Sw. Dan. *pudel* = D. *poedel(-hond)*, < LG. *pudel*, G. *pudel*, *pudel-hund*, a poodle, poodle-dog; prob. < LG. *pudeln*, *puddeln*, waddle; cf. G. *pudeln*, splash. Cf. *puddle*[2].] One of a breed of usually undersized fancy or toy dogs, with long curly hair. They are intelligent and affectionate, and are much used as pets. There are many varieties, one of which is the French barbet. Poodles are said, perhaps without sufficient reason, to be especially liable to rabies.

Poœcetes (pō-ẹ̄-sē'tēz), *n.* [NL. (Baird, 1858, in the form *Poocætes*), < Gr. πόα, grass, + οἰκητής, an inhabitant.] A genus of North American fringilline birds, having the inner secondaries lengthened, the tail long and emarginate, with white lateral feathers, the wing pointed, with bay on the bend, and the whole plumage streaked. The only species, *P. gramineus*, is the well-known grassfinch, bay-winged bunting, or vesper-bird, one of the commonest sparrows of the United States, migratory, granivorous, a sweet songster, and nesting on the ground. See cut under *grassfinch*.

pooh (pö or pû), *interj.* [Also *poh*, and formerly *puh*, *pough*, *pow*; cf. Icel. *pū*, pooh; cf. *pugh*, *pho*, *phoo*, *phy*, *fie*[1], etc.] An exclamation of dislike, scorn, or contempt.

Pough! pr'ythee never trouble thy Head with such Fancies.
Prior, The Thief and the Cordelier.

pooh-pooh (pö'pö), *interj.* [Reduplication of *pooh*.] An exclamation indicating contempt. —The pooh-pooh theory of language. See *language*[1].

pooh-pooh (pö'pö), *v. t.* [< *pooh*, *pooh*, a repeated form of *pooh*, *interj.*] To turn aside from with a "Pooh"; express dislike, scorn, or contempt for; sneer at.

George *pooh-poohed* the wine and bullied the waiters royally.
Thackeray, Vanity Fair, xxvi.

Surely if we could recall that early bitterness . . . we should not *pooh-pooh* the griefs of our children.
George Eliot, Mill on the Floss, i. 7.

pookoo (pö'kö), *n.* [African.] A kind of kob or water-antelope of Africa, *Kobus vardoni*. See *kob*.

pool[1] (pöl), *n.* [< ME. *pool*, *pole*, *pol*, < AS. *pōl* = OFries. *pol* = D. *poel* = MLG. *pōl*, LG. *pōl*, *pohl*, *pul* = MHG. *phuol*, *pfuol*, G. *pfuhl* = Icel. *pollr* = Sw. Dan. *pöl*, pool; prob. of Celtic origin: < Ir. *poll*, *pull*, a hole, pit, also mire, dirt, = Gael. *poll*, a hole, pit, bog, pond, pool, also mire, mud, = W. *pwll* = Corn. *pol* = Manx *poyll*, a pool, puddle, = Bret. *poull*, a pool; cf. L. *pālus* (*pālūd-*), a marsh, = Gr. πηλός, mud: see *palus*. Cf. *pill*[4], from the same source.] 1. A small body of standing water; a small pond.

At last I left them
I' the filthy mantled *pool* beyond your cell.
Shak., Tempest, iv. 1. 182.

2. A part of a small stream where the bed suddenly deepens and broadens, forming a relatively still, deep, and wide stretch of water.

Such *pools* as be large and have most gravel, and shallows where fish may sport themselves, do afford fish of the purest taste.
I. Walton, Complete Angler, p. 199.

The sleepy *pool* above the dam,
The *pool* beneath it never still.
Tennyson, Miller's Daughter.

3. (*a*) In Pennsylvania, on some of the rivers of the mining regions, a stretch of water lying between two river-dams. Hence—(*b*) The country adjacent to such pools.

During a strike last fall on one of the *pools* of the Monongahela river, a body of miners from one of the other *pools* came up in a steamboat with a brass band and paraded around the mines, while a committee urged the men who had remained at work despite the strike to come out and join them.
N. A. Rev., CXLIII. 275.

4. A measure of work in slating, or covering houses with slate, equal to 168 square feet in all, or to 84 square feet on each side of the roof. *Halliwell*. [Prov. Eng.]—5. In *decorative art*, a rounded depression, small and short in comparison with its width. Compare *fluting*. —**Pool fishway.** See *fishway*.—**Salmon-pools**, eddies where the salmon collect. Formerly, in some parts of New England, these pools or eddies were numbered, and the fishermen living near the streams had certain rights in them. *Mass. Rep.*, 1866, p. 32.

pool[2] (pöl), *n.* [Formerly *poule*; < F. *poule*, pool, stakes (= Sp. *polla*, pool, stakes, = Pg. *polha*, a mark or counter in certain games), lit. 'the hen' (the stakes being regarded as eggs to be gained from the hen), a particular use of F. *poule* (= Sp. *polla* = Pg. *polha*, a hen), < ML. *pulla*, f., hen, < L. *pullus*, m., a chicken, a young animal: see *pullet*. The same element occurs prob. in *polecat*.] 1. The stakes in certain games of cards, billiards, etc.—2. A game played on a billiard-table with six pockets by two or more persons. (*a*) In the United States, a game played with fifteen balls, each ball numbered and counting from one to fifteen. The object of each player is to pocket the balls, the number on each ball being placed to his credit. Also called *pyramid pool*. (*b*) In Great Britain, a game in which each player is provided with a differently colored or numbered ball, with which, playing on the others in a fixed order, he endeavors to pocket as many of them as possible.

3. In *horse-racing*, *ball-games*, etc., the combination of a number of persons, each staking a sum of money on the success of a horse in a race, a contestant in a game, etc., the money to be divided among the successful betters according to the amount put in by each; also, the money so staked.—4. In *rifle-shooting*, firing for prizes on the principle that every competitor pays a certain sum for every shot, and the proceeds after a certain deduction are divided among the successful competitors.—5. A set of players, as at the game of quadrille or comet; also, one of the counters used in such games.

What say you to a *poule* at comet at my house?
Southerne. (*Latham.*)

She had also asked him twice to dine at Rosings, and had sent for him only the Saturday before, to make up her *pool* of quadrille in the evening.
Jane Austen, Pride and Prejudice, xiv.

Quadrille *pools* are the fishes or other counters used in playing the old-fashioned game of quadrille.
N. and Q., 7th ser., I. 477.

6. A combination intended by concert of action to make or control changes in market rates. More specifically — (*a*) A joint adventure by several owners of a specified stock or other security temporarily subjecting all their holdings to the same control for the purposes of a speculative operation, in which any sacrifice of the shares contributed by one, and any profit on the shares contributed by another, shall be shared by all alike. (*b*) A combination of the interests of several otherwise competing parties, such as rival transportation lines, in which all take common ground as regards the public, and distribute the profits of the business among themselves equally or according to special agreement. In this sense pooling is a system of reconciling conflicting interests, and of obviating ruinous competition, by which the several competing parties or companies throw their revenue into one common fund, which is then divided or redistributed among the members of the pool on a basis of percentages or proportions previously agreed upon or determined by arbitration.—**Blind pool**, a pool or combination the purpose of which is known only to the organizers, to whom the other members of the pool leave the entire management of the transaction. See def. 6 (*a*).—**Pin-pool**, a game played on a billiard-table with three balls, and five small pins, numbered from one to five. The object of each player is, with the pins he upsets and a number assigned specially to himself, to score 31 points.

pool[2] (pöl), *v.* [< *pool*[2], *n.*] **I.** *trans.* To put into one common fund or stock for the purpose of dividing or redistributing in certain proportions; make into a common fund: as, to *pool* interests.

The common method of accomplishing this [dividing the traffic between competing lines] is to *pool* the receipts and to redistribute them on percentages based upon experience and decided by an arbitrator. *Pop. Sci. Mo.*, XXVIII. 587.

To pool issues. See *issue*.

II. *intrans.* To form a pool; make common cause in some matter.

Most of the class who may be called railroad professors favor "*pooling* under regulation."
The Nation, XLVII. 444.

pool[3]†, *n.* A Middle English form of *pole*[1].

pool-ball (pöl'bâl), *n.* One of the ivory balls used in the game of pool.

pooler (pö'lėr), *n.* An instrument for stirring a tan-vat.

pool-room (pöl'röm), *n.* A room in which pools on races, etc., are sold.

pool-rush, *n.* See *pole-rush*.

pool-seller (pöl'sel"ėr), *n.* One who sells pools on any event, as a horse-race, boat-race, election, etc.

pool-snipe (pöl'snīp), *n.* The redshank, *Totanus calidris*: so called from its haunts. [Eng.]

pool-ticket (pöl'tik"et), *n.* A ticket entitling the holder to a share in the proceeds of a pool. See *pool*[2], *n.*

poon (pön), *n.* See *poon-wood*.

poonahlite (pö'nạ-līt), *n.* [< *Poonah* (see def.) + Gr. λίθος, stone.] A variety of scolecite from Poonah in India.

poona-wood (pö'nạ-wůd), *n.* Same as *poon-wood*.

poonay-oil, poon-oil (pö'nā-oil, pön'oil), *n.* A thick dark-green oil of strong scent and bitter taste, derived from the seeds of *Calophyllum Inophyllum* in India, used in lamps and medicinally. Also called *poonseed-oil* and *keena-oil*.

poondet, *n.* A Middle English form of *pond*[1].

poondy-oil (pön'di-oil), *n.* A yellowish concrete oil derived from the seeds of *Myristica Malabarica* in India, used as an application to ulcers and otherwise.

poonga-oil (pöng'gạ-oil), *n.* A fixed oil derived from the seeds of *Pongamia glabra* in India, there used as an inferior lamp-oil alone or in mixture, and as a medicinal stimulant.

poongi, *n.* Same as *pungi*.

poongy, poonghee (pöng'gi, -gē), *n.* [< Burm. *p'hun-gyi*, 'great glory.'] In Burma, a Buddhist priest or monk.

The yellow-draped and meditative *poonghee*, barefooted and with shaven crown, attended by a boy.
J. W. Palmer, Up and Down the Irrawaddi, p. 190.

poon-oil, *n.* See *poonay-oil*.

poonseed-oil (pön'sēd-oil), *n.* Same as *poonay-oil*.

poon-spar (pön'spär), *n.* A spar made of poon-wood.

poon-wood (pön'wůd), *n.* [< E. Ind. (Malay) *poon* + E. *wood*.] The commercial name for several East Indian woods suitable for various uses, but particularly for making spars, for which they are specially fitted by a straight growth, light weight, and good degree of stiffness. They appear to be derived mainly from species of *Calophyllum*—*C. Burmanni*, *C. tomentosum*, *C. Inophyllum*, and for the region of Penang the doubtful *C. angustifolium* being assigned as sources. Also *poona-wood*.

poop[1] (pöp), *n.* [Formerly also *poup*, *poupe*, *puppe*, < OF. *poupe*, *pouppe*, F. *poupe* = Pr. Sp. Pg. *popa* = It. *poppa*, < L. *puppis*, the stern of a ship.] **1.** The stern or aftermost part of a ship.

The waues did ryse so high and thicke, breaking sometime vpon the *puppes* of the shippes, and sometimes vp on the side, that the shypmen began to vale the sailes.
J. Brende, tr. of Quintus Curtius, fol. 203.

The barge she sat in like a burnish'd throne
Burn'd on the water; the *poop* was beaten gold.
Shak., A. and C., ii. 2. 197.

2. A deck above the ordinary deck in the aftermost part of a ship.—**Break of the poop.** See *break*.—**In poop** [OF. *en pouppe*], astern.

Ship of War with High Poop, 17th century.

The windes blow firmely for certaine times, with the which they goe to Pegu with the winde *in poope*.
Hakluyt's Voyages, II. 237.

poop[1] (pöp), *v. t.* [Formerly also *poupe*; < *poop*[1], *n.*] **1.** *Naut.*, to break heavily over the stern or quarter of (a ship); drive in the stern of.

He was *pooped* with a sea that almost sent him to the bottom. *Smollett*, Sir L. Greaves, xvii.

2. To trick; cheat; cozen. [Prov. Eng.]

But there ich was *powpte* indeed.
Bp. Still, Gammer Gurton's Needle, ii. 1.

poop[2] (pöp), *n.* [< F. *poupée*, in arch., poppy, poppy-head: see *poppy*[2].] In *arch.*, a poppy-head.

poop[3] (pöp), *v. i.* [< D. *poepen*, break wind; imitative; cf. *pop*[1], and ME. *poupen*, blow a horn.] To break wind. [Vulgar.]

poop[3] (pöp), *n.* [< D. *poep*, a breaking of wind, from the verb.] An act of breaking wind. [Vulgar.]

poop-cabin (pöp'kab"in), *n.* A cabin under the poop-deck. See *deck*, 2.

Every part of the ship was already occupied. Another order soon came for the construction of a *poop-cabin*.
W. Colton, Deck and Port, p. 14.

poop-lantern (pöp'lan"tėrn), *n.* A lantern carried at night on the taffrail to denote a flagship, or to serve as a signal.

poor (pör), *a.* [< ME. *pour*, *poure*, *pore*, *pover*, *povere*, *povre*, < OF. *povre*, *poure*, *povere*, F. *pauvre* = Sp. Pg. *pobre* = It. *povero*, < L. *pauper*, poor: see *pauper*.] **1.** Possessing little; destitute of wealth: opposed to *rich*: as, a *poor* man; a *poor* community.

Ther made the loud full *povere*, the folk ded thei slo.
Rob. of Brunne, p. 7.

Pore of possessioùn in purse and in coffre.
Piers Plowman (B), xiii. 301.

He, being rich, shall be born of a *poor* Maid.
Howell, Letters, iv. 43.

You may think I do not deserve to be rich; but I hope you will likewise observe I can ill afford to be *poor*.
Steele, Tatler, No. 124.

2. Lacking means to procure the comforts of life; indigent; needy; necessitous; specifically, in *law*, so destitute or impoverished as to be dependent upon charity, or upon the poor-rates; pauper.

In good feith yet had I lever
Than to coveite in such a weye
To ben for ever till I deie
As *povere* as Job and loveless.
Gower, Conf. Amant., II. 211.

In prison thou shalt find me *poor* and broken.
Fletcher, Beggars' Bush, iii. 2.

What *poor* attend my charity to-day, wench?
Fletcher, Pilgrim, i. 1.

He [Linnæus] was so *poor* as to be obliged to mend his shoes with folded paper, and often to beg his meals of his friends. *J. F. Clarke*, Self-Culture, p. 41.

I have observed, the more public provisions are made for the *poor*, the less they provide for themselves.
Franklin.

3. Deficient in or destitute of desirable or essential qualities; lacking those qualities which render a thing valuable, desirable, suitable, or sufficient for its purpose; inferior; bad: as, *poor* bread; *poor* health; cattle in *poor* condition.

The Erian flora is comparatively *poor*, and its types are in the main similar to those of the Carboniferous.
Dawson, Geol. Hist. of Plants, p. 204.

In particular — (*a*) Of little consequence; trifling; insignificant; paltry: as, a *poor* excuse.

That I have wronged no man will be a *poor* plea or apology at the last day. *Calamy*, Sermons.

Poor is the contentment that can be found in virtue and religion, if it stretch no farther than to the end of this life. *Bp. Atterbury*, Sermons, I. xi., Pref.

(*b*) Mean; shabby: as, a *poor* outfit; *poor* surroundings.

On the North side, a large square Piazza, encompass'd with Pillars, and on the East some *poor* remains of a great Church. *Maundrell*, Aleppo to Jerusalem, p. 59.

As shines the moon through clouded skies
She in her *poor* attire was seen.
Tennyson, The Beggar Maid.

(*c*) Lean; meager; emaciated: as, *poor* cattle.

Thin and *poor* as a late chicken. *S. Judd*, Margaret, i. 4.

(*d*) Lacking in fertility; barren; exhausted: as, *poor* land.

Part of the distance lay over *poor* country, covered with ti-tree, box, and ironbark saplings.
A. C. Grant, Bush Life in Queensland, I. 46.

(*e*) Lacking in spirit or vigor; feeble; impotent.

I have very *poor* and unhappy brains for drinking.
Shak., Othello, ii. 3. 35.

His spirit is but *poor* that can be kept
From death for want of weapons.
Beau. and Fl., Maid's Tragedy, v. 4.

Art thou so *poor* to blench at what thou hast done?
Is conscience a comrade for an old soldier?
Fletcher (*and another*), False One, iv. 3.

(*f*) Destitute of merit or worth; barren; jejune: as, a *poor* discourse; a *poor* essay.

4. Unfortunate; to be pitied or regretted: much used colloquially as a vague epithet indicative of sympathy or pity for one who is sick, feeble, or unhappy, or of regret for one who is dead.

And in gret reverence and charitee
Hire olde *poure* fader fostred she.
Chaucer, Clerk's Tale, l. 876.

Poor Jack, farewell!
I could have better spared a better man.
Shak., 1 Hen. IV., v. 4. 103.

Poor little pretty, fluttering Thing,
Must we no longer live together?
Prior, Imit. of Hadrian's Address to his Soul.

Poor things! as the case stands with them even now, you might take the heart out of their bodies, and they never find it out, they are sae begrutten. *Scott*, Monastery, viii.

Get out, and don't come slandering, and backbiting, and bullying that *poor* devil of a boy any more.
Thackeray, Philip, xxi.

My *poor* dear! What has made thy heart so sore as to come and cry a-this-ons? *Dickens*, Lizzie Leigh, iii.

5. Miserable; wretched: used in contempt.

The sufferings of those *poor* bigotted creatures, the martyrs, made mighty impressions upon men.
Bp. Atterbury, Sermons, I. iii.

As a murderer, he was a *poor* creature; as an artist in gold, he was inimitable. *De Quincey*, Secret Societies, i.

6. Humble; slight; insignificant: used modestly in speaking of things pertaining to one's self.

And for mine own *poor* part,
Look you, I'll go pray. *Shak.*, Hamlet, i. 5. 131.

The estate which I should leave behind me of any estimation is my *poor* fame in the memory of my friends.
Donne, Letters, xiv.

I had carried my *poor* pitcher to that well often enough, I thought, and was resolved never again to risk its fracture.
Lowell, Address in behalf of International Copyright,
[Nov. 28, 1887.

Guardians of the poor. See *guardian*.—**Overseers of the poor.** See *overseer*.—**Poor Clares.** See *Clarisse*.—**Poor debtor.** See *debtor*.—**Poor in spirit**, spiritually humble. Mat. v. 3.—**Poor Knight of Windsor.** Same as *Windsor Knight* (which see, under *knight*).—**Poor law.** See *law*[1].—**Poor man's herb**, in England, the hedge-hyssop, *Gratiola officinalis*.—**Poor man's parmacety**, in England, the shepherd's-purse, *Capsella Bursa-pastoris*.—**Poor man's pepper.** See *pepper*.—**Poor man's plaster.** See *plaster*.—**Poor man's treacle**, in England, the onion, *Allium Cepa*.—**Poor man's weather-glass.** Same as *pimpernel*, 4.—**Poor Priests.** See *priest*.—**Poor Robin**, an almanac: said to be so called from a series of almanacs brought out by Robert Herrick in the seventeenth century.

• I was informed she discern'd by the beat of the pulse a Feast from a Feria, without the help of *poor Robin*.
Gentleman Instructed, p. 120. (*Davies.*)

Poor's box, a box for receiving contributions for the poor; a poor-box.

She draws her mouth till it positively resembles the aperture of a *poor's box*, and all her words appear to slide out edgewise. *Sheridan*, School for Scandal, ii. 2.

The policeman took me off to Clerkenwell, but the magistrates, instead of sending me to prison, gave me 2s. out of the *poor's-box*.
Mayhew, London Labour and London Poor, II. 88.

poorblind†, *a.* An obsolete form of *purblind*.

poor-box (pör'boks), *n.* A box for receiving contributions of money for the poor, usually set at the entrance of a church.

pooren (pör'n), *v. t.* [< *poor* + *-en*[1].] To make poor; impoverish. [Rare or provincial.]

A foolish wife and a back door *pooren* a man.
Booke of Precedence (E. E. T. S., extra ser.), i. 69, marginal
[note.

poor-farm (pör'färm), *n.* A farm maintained at public expense for the housing and support of paupers.

poorfu' (pör'fü), *a.* A Scotch form of *powerful*.

poorful† (pör'fůl), *a.* [< ME. **poreful*, *porful*; < *poor* + *-ful*.] Poor; mean; shabby.

Iesu, swete sone dere!
On *porful* bed list thou here;
And that me greveth sore;
For thi cradel is ase a bere.
Political Poems, etc. (ed. Furnivall), p. 226.

poorhead†, *n.* [ME. *pouerehede;* < poor + *-head.*] Poverty.

The ȝothe milde loueth pouerté . . . vor the guodes thet byeth in guode *pouerehede.*
Ayenbite of Inwit (E. E. T. S.), p. 138.

poorhouse (pör'hous), *n.* An establishment in which persons receiving public charity are lodged and cared for; an almshouse.

poor-John† (pör'jon), *n.* The hake when salted and dried.

'Tis well thou art not fish; if thou hadst, thou hadst been *poor John.* *Shak.*, R. and J., i. 1. 37.

And then, if you scape with life, and take a faggot-boat and a bottle of usquebaugh, come home, poor man, like a type of Thames-street, stinking of pitch and *poor-John.*
Beau. and Fl., Scornful Lady, ii. 3.

Poor John was haik when salted and dried. It was always beaten before it was cooked.
Shirley, Maid's Revenge, iii. 2, note.

poor-lights (pör'līts), *n. pl.* *Eccles.*, lights or candles provided for the burial ceremonies of the poor. *Rock*, Church of our Fathers, ii. 472, note.

poorliness (pör'li-nes), *n.* The state of being poorly; ill health. *Mrs. Gore.*

poorly (pör'li), *a.* [< *poor* + *-ly*[1].] Somewhat ill; indisposed; not in health; unwell. [Colloq.]

Sympathetic inquiries about the state of her health, which was always "only tol'able," or "rather *poorly.*"
The Atlantic, XVIII. 84.

poorly (pör'li), *adv.* [< ME. *poureliche;* < *poor* + *-ly*[2].] In a poor manner or condition. (*a*) In indigence or want of the conveniences and comforts of life: as, to live *poorly.*

For *poureliche* yfostred up was she.
Chaucer, Clerk's Tale, l. 157.

(*b*) With little or no success; insufficiently; defectively: as, *poorly* constructed; *poorly* adapted to the purpose.

You meaner beauties of the night,
That *poorly* satisfie our eies.
Sir H. Wotton, On his Mistress, the Queen of Bohemia.

(*c*) Humbly; without spirit; ignobly.

The duke of Juliers, his cosyn, of his owne free wyll was come to see hym, and to put himselfe *poorely* without any reseruacyon vnto his obeysaunce and commaundement.
Berners, tr. of Froissart's Chron., II. xciii.

Dare you do ill, and *poorly* then shrink under it?
Were I the Duke Medina, I would fight now.
Fletcher, Rule a Wife, v. 5.

poor-man-of-mutton (pör'man-ov-mut'n), *n.* Cold mutton broiled; especially, the remains of a shoulder of mutton broiled. [Scotch.]

poormaster (pör'mås"tėr), *n.* A parish or county officer who superintends the relief and maintenance of paupers, or such other persons as are dependent on public aid or support.

The Agent of the United States to the Sioux Indians was to act as a sort of national *poor-master*, and deal out rations. *Amer. Miss.*, XXXIX. 8.

poorness (pör'nes), *n.* The state, condition, or quality of being poor, in any of the senses of the word; poverty; meanness.

When I mock *poorness*, then heaven make me poor.
B. Jonson, Case is Altered, iii. 1.

Landaff, . . . for the *poorness* thereof, lay Bishopless for three years after the death of Bishop Kitchin.
Fuller, Worthies, Wales, III. 495.

There is over and above a peculiar *poorness* and vileness in this action. *South*, Sermons, IX. v.

Ovid and Lucan have many *Poornesses* of Expression upon this account. *Addison*, Spectator, No. 285.

poor-rate (pör'rāt), *n.* An assessment or tax imposed by law for the relief or support of the poor.

poor-spirited (pör'spir"i-ted), *a.* Of a poor or tame spirit; cowardly.

Mr. Tulliver would never have asked anything from so *poor-spirited* a fellow for himself.
George Eliot, Mill on the Floss, iii. 1.

poor-spiritedness (pör'spir"i-ted-nes), *n.* Tameness or baseness of spirit; cowardice.

That meanness and *poor-spiritedness* that accompanies guilt. *South*, Sermons.

poortith (pör'tith), *n.* [A var. of *poverty.*] Poverty. [Scotch.]

poor-will (pör'wil), *n.* [Imitative; cf. *whip-poorwill.*] A bird of the genus *Phalænoptilus*, as *P. nuttalli:* so called from its characteristic dissyllabic note. Nuttall's poor-will is a common bird in most parts of the western United States, where it mainly replaces the whippoorwill. See *Phalænoptilus.*

At nightfall the *poor-wills* begin to utter their boding call from the wooded ravines back in the hills; not "whip-poorwill," as in the East, but with two syllables only.
T. Roosevelt, The Century, XXXV. 664.

Poöspiza (pō-ō-spī'zä), *n.* [NL. (Cabanis, 1847), < Gr. πόα, grass, + σπίζα, a finch.] A genus of South American fringilline birds. The United States black-chinned and Bell's buntings, long called respectively *P. bilineata* and *P. belli*, are now placed in the genus *Amphispiza.* See cut under *sage-sparrow.*

poostet, *n.* A variant of *poust.*

pop[1] (pop), *v.*; pret. and pp. *popped*, ppr. *popping.* [Imitative; cf. Gr. ποππύζειν, pop, smack, whistle or chirp with the lips compressed; cf. also *pop*[2].] **I.** *intrans.* **1.** To make a quick sudden explosive report.

Neesing and *popping* or smacking with the mouthe.
Touchstone of Complexions, p. 124. (*Encyc. Dict.*)

They convinced him that any of his men could . . . *pop* away at him with a gun. *The Century*, XL. 219.

2. To appear or issue forth with a quick sudden motion; come suddenly into view; also, to disappear suddenly.

He that hath . . .
Popp'd in between the election and my hopes.
Shak., Hamlet, v. 2. 65.

I startled at his *popping* upon me unexpectedly.
Addison.

So, diving in a bottomless sea, they [the Roman Church] *pop* sometimes above water to take breath.
Donne, Sermons, iv.

Others have a trick of *popping* up and down every moment from their paper to the audience, like an idle schoolboy. *Swift.*

When company comes, you are not to *pop* out and stare, and then run in again, like frightened rabbits in a warren.
Goldsmith, She Stoops to Conquer, ii.

3. To propose marriage.—**Popping widgeon**, one of various ducks which dive with celerity; a diving duck, or ducker; a merganser. [Local, Eng.]—**To pop off**, to disappear or depart suddenly; die.

The Gineral he was thick-set and short-necked, and drank pretty free, and was one o' the sort that might *pop off* any time. *H. B. Stowe*, Oldtown, p. 37.

II. *trans.* **1.** To cause to make a sudden explosive report.

And all round the glad church lie old bottles
With gunpowder stopped,
Which will be, when the Image re-enters,
Religiously *popped.*
Browning, Englishman in Italy.

2. To thrust forward, or offer suddenly or abruptly; put or thrust suddenly: with *in*, *into*, *out*, or *upon.*

My daughter Nell shall *pop* a posset *upon* thee, when thou goest to bed.
Heywood, 1 Edw. IV. (Works, ed. Pearson, 1874, I. 47).

These our Prelates, who are the true Successors of those that *popt* them *into* the other world.
Milton, On Def. of Humb. Remonst.

Eat your porridge now, little ones. Charlotte, *pop* a bit of butter *in* Carrick's porridge. *Thackeray*, Philip, xvi.

While some of the small fry *popped out* their heads to have a look. *W. Black*, House-boat, viii.

3. To thrust aside or put off abruptly or unexpectedly.

That is my brother's plea and none of mine;
The which if he can prove, a' *pops* me out
At least from fair five hundred pound a year.
Shak., K. John, i. 1. 68.

And do you *pop* me off with this slight answer?
Fletcher (*and another*), Noble Gentleman, i. 1.

4. To put suddenly: as, to *pop* the question. See phrase below.

Plagued with his doubts and your own diffidences; afraid he would now, and now, and now, *pop* out the question which he had not the courage to put.
Richardson, Grandison, vi. 103.

5. To pawn, or pledge with a pawnbroker. [Slang.]—**To pop corn**, to parch or roast a particular variety of maize until it pops or bursts open. [U. S.]—**To pop the question**, to propose unexpectedly the important question (or its equivalent) "will you marry me?" hence, without implication of unexpectedness, to make an offer of marriage. [Colloq.]

Growing faint at this sudden proposal to wed,
As though his abruptness, in *popping the question*
So soon after dinner, disturb'd her digestion.
Barham, Ingoldsby Legends, II. 39.

pop[1] (pop), *n.* [< *pop*[1], *v.*] **1.** A smart explosive sound or small report like that made in drawing a cork from a bottle.

I cannot bear people to keep their minds bottled up for the sake of letting them off with a *pop.*
George Eliot, Daniel Deronda, xxxix.

2. An effervescent beverage: so called from the sound made by the expulsion of the cork: as, ginger-*pop.*

With lobsters and whitebait, and other swatemeats,
And wine, and nagus, and imperial *pop.*
Barham, Ingoldsby Legends, I. 277.

Home-made *pop* that will not foam,
And home-made dishes that drive one from home.
Hood, Miss Kilmansegg, Her Misery.

3. A pistol. [Slang or thieves' cant.]

A pair of *pops*, silver-mounted. . . . I took them loaded from the captain. *Smollett*, Roderick Random, viii.

pop[1] (pop), *adv.* [An elliptical use of *pop*[1], *v.* and *n.*] Suddenly; abruptly; with unexpected entrance or exit.

Into that bush
Pop goes his pate, and all his face is comb'd over.
Fletcher, Pilgrim, iii. 2.

There were three or four bidders, I cannot tell whether,
But they never could come two upon me together;
For as soon as one spoke, then immediately *pop*
I advanc'd something more, fear the hammer should drop.
Byrom, To Henry Wright, Esq.

pop[2]† (pop), *v. t.* [< ME. *poppen*, strike; origin obscure.] **1.** To strike. *Cath. Ang.*, p. 286. —**2.** To smear (the face) with white lead or other cosmetics; powder (the face).

Fetys she was and smale to se,
No wyntred browes hedde she,
Ne *popped* hir, for it nedede noughte
To wyndre hir, or to peynte hir ought.
Rom. of the Rose, l. 1019.

The aungelle ansuered, for whanne she was on luye she plucked, *popped* and peinted her visage forto plese the sighte of the worlde. . . . Alas whi take women none hede of the gret loue that God bathe yeue hem to make hem after hys figure? and whi *popithe* they, and *paintithe* and plucke the her visage otherwise than God hathe ordeined?
Book of the Knight of La Tour Landry, p. 68.

pop[2]† (pop), *n.* [ME. *poppe;* < *pop*[2], *v.*] A stroke. *Cath. Ang.*, p. 286.

pop[3] (pop), *n.* [Origin obscure.] The red-winged thrush, *Turdus iliacus.* *C. Swainson.* [Local, Eng.]

pop[4] (pop), *n.* A contraction of *popular:* as, the Monday *pops* (popular concerts). [Low.]

pop-corn (pop'kôrn'), *n.* **1.** One of several varieties of Indian corn suitable for "popping." They have small ears and kernels, the latter white, yellow, or red, sharp-pointed or not. Pop-corn abounds in oil, the expansion of which under heat causes an explosion, in which the contents of the kernel become puffed out, nearly hiding the seed-coat, and assuming a pure-white color.

2. Corn thus prepared; popped corn.

pop-dock (pop'dok), *n.* The foxglove, *Digitalis purpurea:* so called from its large coarse leaves, and the use made of the corolla by children after inflating it. Also *pop-glove*, *pops*, *poppy.* [Prov. Eng.]

pope[1] (pōp), *n.* [< ME. *pope*, *pape*, < AS. *pāpa*, pope, = D. *paap*, priest, pope, *pope*, pope (of the Greek Church), = Icel. *papi*, a pope, priest, = Sw. *påfve* = Dan. *pave*, pope, also with terminal *-s* (perhaps due to the OF. nom. *papes*), OFries. *pâves*, *pâvis*, *pâus* = D. *paus* = OLG. *pâvos*, MLG. *paves*, *pawes*, later *pawest*, *pauwst*, pope, = OHG. *bâbes*, MHG. *bâbes*, *bâbest*, *bâbst*, G. *papst*, priest, pope, = OF. *pape*, also in nom. *papes*, F. *pape* = Sp. Pg. It. *papa*, pope, < LL. *papa*, a bishop, ML. pope: see *papa*[2].] **1.** The Bishop of Rome as head of the Roman Catholic Church and hierarchy. The title *pope* (Latin *papa* or *papas*, Greek πάπας, πάππας), literally 'papa' or 'father,' was given in the early church, both in the East and West, to bishops in general, and has from the middle of the third century to the present day been an especial title of the patriarch of Alexandria. In the Western Church it began to be restricted to the Bishop of Rome in the sixth century, and in 1073 the assumption of the title by any other bishop was formally forbidden. In the Eastern Church the same word (with a different accentuation, παπᾶς) became a familiar title of ordinary priests, and is commonly so used at the present day. According to Roman Catholic teaching, the Pope is not only bishop, metropolitan, and patriarch, but, as incumbent of the Roman see, is successor of St. Peter, and as such vicar of Christ and visible head of the whole church, and supreme pastor and teacher of all Christians. From his decision there is no appeal; and when he speaks ex cathedra — that is, in discharge of his office and by virtue of his supreme apostolic authority — his teaching regarding faith and morals is to be accepted as infallible. (See *infallibility*, 1.) Even in very early times the Bishop of Rome addressed other churches in a tone of authority. The first great asserter of the privileges of the Roman see was Leo I. (440–461); and the medieval papacy reached its climax of spiritual and temporal power under Gregory VII. (1073–85).

2. The patriarch of Alexandria.—**3.** A priest in the Greek or Russian Church.—**4.** The head of any church or ecclesiastical system.

And in that Yle dwellethe the *Pope* of hire Lawe, that they clepen Lobassy. *Mandeville*, Travels, p. 308.

Adoration of the Pope. See *adoration.*—**Pope's crown**, in *her.*, same as *tiara.*—**Pope's size**, a size so named as a trade-term. See the quotation.

A year or two ago I bought a merino vest. On the bill I noticed P. S. after it, and by enquiry I elicited that P. S. stood for *pope's size*, and that *pope's size* meant short and stout. *N. and Q.*, 7th ser., VII. 225.

pope[2] (pōp), *n.* [Of various uncertain origin; cf. *pape*[2], E. dial. *mwope* for *mawp*, etc.] **1.** The blacktail, a fish: same as *ruff*[3]. [Local, Eng.] —**2.** The bullfinch, *Pyrrhula vulgaris.* [Dorsetshire, Eng.]—**3.** The red-backed shrike, *Lanius collurio.* [Hants, Eng.]—**4.** The puffin, *Fratercula arctica.* *Montagu.* [Local, Eng.]—**5.** The painted finch, or nonpareil. See cut under *Passerina.* [Louisiana.]

popedom (pōp'dum), *n.* [< ME. *popedom*, < AS. *pāpdōm* (= D. *pausdom* = MLG. *pavesdôm* = MHG. *bâbestuom*, G. *papstthum* = Sw. *påfvedöme* = Dan. *pavedömme*), < *pāpa*, pope, + *dōm*, jurisdiction: see *-dom.*] The office or dignity of pope; also, the temporal or spiritual jurisdiction of a pope.

> All that world of wealth I have drawn together
> For mine own ends; indeed, to gain the *popedom*,
> And fee my friends in Rome.
> *Shak.*, Hen. VIII., iii. 2. 212.

> The next default was in the Bishops, who, though they had renounc't the Pope, they still hugg'd the *Popedome*.
> *Milton*, Reformation in Eng., i.

> The Crusades, too, had now made the Western world tributary to the *Popedom*. *Milman*, Latin Christianity, i. 9.

pope-holy†, *a.* [ME. *popeholy, poope-holy*; appar. an accom., as if ‹ *pope*[1] + *holy*, of OF. *papelard*, hypocritical.] Hypocritical. [In the first quotation it is used as a noun, as a quasi-proper name.]

> Another thing was don there write
> That semede lyk an ipocrite,
> And it was clepid *Poope-holy* [OF. *papelardie*].
> *Rom. of the Rose*, l. 415.

> Was none suche as hym-self ne none so *pope-holy*.
> *Piers Plowman* (B), xiii. 284.

> There be *pope-holy*, which, following a righteousness of their own feigning, resist the righteousness of God in Christ.
> *Tyndale*, Ans. to Sir T. More, etc. (Parker Soc., 1850), p. 36.

popehood (pōp'hụd), *n.* [‹ *pope*[1] + *-hood*.] The condition of being pope; papal character or dignity.

> To all Popes and Pope's Advocates . . . the answer of the world is: Once for all your *Popehood* has become untrue. *Carlyle*.

pope-Joan (pōp'jōn'), *n.* [From *Pope Joan*, a female pope who, according to tradition, reigned in the middle of the 9th century, now generally regarded as a fictitious personage.] A game of cards played by any number of persons with a pack from which the eight of diamonds has been removed, on a board divided into eight compartments for holding the bets, which are won by the player who turns up or plays certain cards.

popekin (pōp'kin), *n.* [‹ *pope*[1] + *-kin*.] A little pope; a term of contempt.

popeleret, *n.* See *popler*[2].

popeling (pōp'ling), *n.* [‹ *pope*[1] + *-ling*[1].] A little or insignificant pope; one who apes the Pope.

> After these losses came other troubles vpon him, with other as great or more great enemies (that is, with the Pope and his *popelings*). *Foxe*, Martyrs, I. 282.

popelott, *n.* [ME.; perhaps ‹ OF. *papillot*, a butterfly; dim. of *popet*: see *puppet*.] A butterfly (?).

> In al this world, to seken up and doun,
> Ther nas no man so wys that koude thenche
> So gay a *popelote*, or swich a wenche.
> *Chaucer*, Miller's Tale, l. 68.

popery (pō'pẹ-ri), *n.* [‹ *pope*[1] + *-ery*.] The doctrines, customs, ceremonies, and polity associated with the office and person of the Pope, or with the Roman Catholic Church, of which he is the supreme head; papacy: used in opprobrium.

> The name of *popery* is more odious than very paganism amongst divers of the more simple sort.
> *Hooker*, Eccles. Polity, iv. 4.

> That prime and leading article of all *popery*, the Pope's supremacy. *South*, Sermons, VI. i.

pope's-eye (pōps'ī), *n.* A large lymphatic gland, or cluster of such glands, in the leg of an ox or a sheep, surrounded with fat. It is regarded as a delicacy.

> You should have the hot new milk, and the *pope's-eye* from the mutton. *R. D. Blackmore*, Lorna Doone, l.

pope's-head (pōps'hed), *n.* **1.** A large round brush with a long handle, for dusting ceilings, cornices, etc. [Local.]

> *Bloom.* You're no witch indeed if you don't see a cobweb as long as my arm. Run, run, child, for the *pope's head*.
> *House.* *Pope's head*, ma'am?
> *Bloom.* Ay, the *pope's head*, which you'll find under the stairs. *Miss Edgeworth*, Love and Law, i. 5. (*Davies.*)

2. See *Melocactus*.

popeship (pōp'ship), *n.* [= D. *pausschap*; as *pope*[1] + *-ship*.] The office or dignity of pope; popehood.

> *Popeship*, spiritual Fatherhood of God's Church, is that a vain semblance, of cloth and parchment? It is an awful fact. *Carlyle*.

pope's-nose (pōps'nōz), *n.* The fleshy part of the tail of a bird; the part on which the tail-feathers are borne; the coccyx and its coverings. Also called *parson's-nose*. See cut under *elæodochon*. [Colloq.]

popett, *n.* A Middle English form of *puppet*. *Chaucer*.

popetryt, *n.* See *puppetry*.

pop-eyed (pop'īd), *a.* Having pop-eyes. [U. S.]

pop-eyes (pop'īz), *n. pl.* Full, bulging, or prominent eyes. [U. S.]

> His hair stood up in front, he had wide *pop-eyes*, and long ears, and a rabbit-like aspect.
> *M. N. Murfree*, Great Smoky Mountains.

pop-gun (pop'gun), *n.* A small gun or tube with a piston or rammer for shooting pellets, which makes a pop by the expansion of compressed air when the pellet is expelled.

> You liked *pop-guns* when you were schoolboys, and rifles and Armstrongs are only the same things better made.
> *Ruskin*, Crown of Wild Olive, p. 71.

popify† (pō'pi-fī), *v. t.* [‹ *pope*[1] + *-i-fy*.] To make a papist of.

> As if all were well so they be not *Popified*, though they have departed from the Church in which they were baptized. *Bp. Hacket*, Abp. Williams, i. 121. (*Davies.*)

popilion† (pō-pil'yọn), *n.* [Also *pompillion*; ME. *popilion*, ‹ OF. *populeon*, ‹ *populier*, *poplier*, F. *peuplier*, poplar: see *poplar*.] A pomatum or ointment prepared from black-poplar buds.

> To cure the frenesye and woodnes, or ellis at the leeste to swage it, take a greet quantite of *popilion*, and the beste vynegre that ȝe may haue.
> *Book of Quinte Essence* (ed. Furnivall), p. 22.

popin†, *n.* A Middle English form of *poppin*.

popingay†, *n.* An obsolete form of *popinjay*.

popinjay (pop'in-jā), *n.* [Formerly also *popingay*; ‹ ME. *popinjay*, *popynjay*, *popingay*, *popyngay*, *papinjay*, *papingay*, *papyngay*, *popejay*, *papejay* = D. *papegaai* = MLG. *papagoie*, *papegoie*, LG. *papegoje* = MHG. *papegān*, G. *papagei* = Sw. *papegoja* = Dan. *papegöje*, ‹ OF. *papejaye*, *papegai* (F. *papegai*, *papegaut*), also *papegau*, *papegaut* = Pr. *papagai* = Sp. *papagayo* = Pg. *papaguio* = It. *papagallo*, ‹ ML. *papagallus*, ‹ NGr. παπαγάλλος, a parrot; altered by popular etym. (simulating OF. *gai*, *geai*, E. *jay*, a bright garrulous bird, comparable in these respects to the parrot, or L. *gallus*, a cock: the first part being perhaps taken as also imitative: cf. Bav. *pappel*, a parrot, ‹ *pappeln*, chatter) ‹ MGr. παπαγάς, a parrot; perhaps of Eastern origin; but the Ar. *babaghā*, Pers. *bapga*, a parrot, are appar. borrowed from the Sp. word. Cf. Malay *bayan*, a parrot.] **1.** A parrot.

> Bryddeȝ on semeȝ,
> As *papiayeȝ* paynted pernyng bitwene.
> *Sir Gawayne and the Green Knight* (E. E. T. S.), l. 611.

> Certeyn men . . . that kepen Bryddes, as Ostrycches, Gerfacouns, Sparehaukes, . . . *Papyngayes* wel spekynge, and Briddes syngynge. *Mandeville*, Travels, p. 238.

> The *popynjay* ful of delicasye.
> *Chaucer*, Parliament of Fowls, l. 359.

> Young *popinjays* learn quickly to speak. *Ascham*.

> Likewise there be *popiniayes* very great and gentle, and some of them haue their foreheads yellow, and this sort do quickly learne to speak, and speak much.
> *Hakluyt's Voyages*, III. 700.

2. A woodpecker; especially, the green woodpecker of Europe, *Gecinus viridis*.

> The daughters of Pierius, who were turned into *popinjays* or woodpeckers.
> *Peacham*, On Drawing. (*Latham.*)

Popinjay, or Green Woodpecker (*Gecinus viridis*).

3. The figure of a parrot or other bird used as a mark for archery or firearms. For this purpose, it was usually hung to the top of a pole so as to swing in the wind.

> When the musters had been made and duly reported, the young men, as was usual, were to mix in various sports, of which the chief was to shoot at the *popinjay*, an ancient game formerly practised with archery, but at this period with firearms. This was the figure of a bird, decked with party-colored feathers, so as to resemble a popinjay or parrot. It was suspended to a pole, and served for a mark at which the competitors discharged their fusees and carabines in rotation, at the distance of sixty or seventy paces. He whose ball brought down the mark held the proud title of Captain of the *Popinjay* for the remainder of the day.
> *Scott*, Old Mortality, i.

4. In *her.*, a parrot used as a bearing: always, unless otherwise mentioned in the blazon, represented green, with red legs and beak.—**5.** A coxcomb; a fop.

> To be so pester'd with a *popinjay*.
> *Shak.*, 1 Hen. IV., i. 3. 50.

> A number of these *popinjays* there are.
> *B. Jonson*, Every Man out of his Humour, ii. 2.

popish (pō'pish), *a.* [‹ *pope*[1] + *-ish*[1].] Of or pertaining to the Pope or the Roman Catholic Church: used in opprobrium: as, *popish* doctrines or practices; *popish* forms and ceremonies.

> Yet, for I know thou art religious,
> And hast a thing within thee called conscience,
> With twenty *popish* tricks and ceremonies,
> Which I have seen thee careful to observe,
> Therefore I urge thy oath. *Shak.*, Tit. And., v. 1. 76.

Popish Methodists. Same as *Dialectic Methodists* (which see, under *Methodist*).—**Popish plot.** See *plot*[1].=**Syn.** See *papal*.

popishly (pō'pish-li), *adv.* To or toward popery; as regards popery: used in opprobrium: as, to be *popishly* inclined.

> Owen's unkle, who was a papist, or at least *popishly* affected (from whom he expected legacies), dash'd his name out from his last will and testament.
> *Wood*, Athenæ Oxon., I.

popit, *n.* In *mach.*, same as *poppet*.

popjoying (pop'joi-ing), *n.* [Verbal n. of **popjoy*, appar. an accom. dial. form of **popinjay*, *v.*, ‹ *popinjay*, *n.*, 3.] Idle pastime; sport.

> Benjy had carried off our hero to the canal in defiance of Charity, and between them, after a whole afternoon's *popjoying*, they had caught three or four small coarse fish and a perch.
> *Hughes*, Tom Brown's School Days, I. ii. (*Davies.*)

poplar (pop'lạ̈r), *n.* [Early mod. E. *popler*; ‹ ME. *popler*, *poplere*, *populere* = D. *populier*, *popelier*, ‹ OF. *poplier*, *peuplier*, F. *peuplier*, a poplar-tree, poplar, ‹ *peuple*, poplar, ‹ L. *populus*, poplar: see *popple*[2], *Populus*.] **1.** A tree of the genus *Populus*; also, the wood of the tree. The poplars are trees of rapid growth, mostly of moderate size, producing varieties of light soft wood, useful for many purposes requiring lightness and moderate strength; in America the wood is largely converted into pulp for paper-making. Various species are planted for shade and ornament. The aspens and cottonwoods are true poplars, though less called by that name. See *asp*[1], *aspen*, and *cottonwood*.

2. A tree of some other genus in some way resembling a poplar.—**Balsam-poplar**, *Populus balsamifera*, the tacamahack. Also called (especially the variety *candicans*) *balm of Gilead*.—**Black Italian poplar**, a name in England of the balm-of-Gilead tree, which abounds in Italy, but its origin is not well known.—**Black poplar**, *Populus nigra*, a native of central and southern Europe and temperate Asia, planted as a forest-tree elsewhere in Europe. Its wood is used for flooring, joiners' and coopers' work, and in the making of gunpowder, charcoal, etc., and its buds in the preparation of an ointment. See *ointment of poplar-buds*, under *ointment*.—**Carolina poplar.** Same as *necklace-poplar*.—**Downy poplar**, *Populus heterophylla*, the river- or swamp-cottonwood, a moderate-sized tree of no great value, found in bottom-land swamps from Connecticut to Louisiana and Arkansas.—**Gray poplar**, a variety or hybrid of the white poplar, its wood esteemed best of European poplars.—**Lombardy poplar**, a species, *Populus pyramidalis* (*P. dilatata*, Ait.), or probably a remarkable variety of the black poplar, of Oriental origin. Its fastigiate habit gives it a striking columnar or spire-shaped outline, on account of which it is planted to some extent. It is said that in America only male-flowered individuals are known.—**Necklace-poplar**, the common cottonwood, *Populus monilifera*, translating the specific name: so called on account of its raceme of pods, which resembles a string of beads. It is a large tree, sometimes 150 feet high, found from Vermont to Texas and the base of the Rocky Mountains, bordering all streams of the great plains. Its light soft wood is used for packing-cases, fence-boards, and fuel, and largely for paper-pulp. Also *Carolina poplar*.—**Ointment of poplar-buds.** See *ointment*.—**Ontario poplar.** Same as *balsam-poplar*.—**Poplars of Yarrum**†, buttermilk. [Cant.] (*Davies.*)

> Here's pannum and lap, and good *poplars of Yarrum*.
> *Brome*, Jovial Crew, ii.

Queensland poplar, *Homalanthus populifolius*, one of the *Euphorbiaceæ*, a large shrub with poplar-like leaves, found in Australia and the Pacific islands.—**Silver** or **silver-leaf poplar.** Same as *white poplar*.—**Trembling poplar**, the European aspen. See *asp*[1] and *populin*.—**Tulip-poplar.** Same as *yellow poplar*.—**Weeping poplar**, the variety *pendula* of *Populus grandidentata*, the large-toothed aspen. Both species and variety are used ornamentally.—**White poplar**, *Populus alba*, native in Europe and middle Asia, notable for the silvery-white under surface of its wavy-toothed leaves, and often planted, but highly objectionable on lawns, on account of suckers from the roots. Also called *silver poplar*, *silver-leaf poplar*, *white asp*, and *abele*.—**Yellow poplar**, the tulip-tree or white-wood. See *Liriodendron*.

poplar-birch (pop'lạ̈r-bėrch), *n.* A European tree, *Betula alba*. See *birch*, 1.

poplar-borer (pop'lạ̈r-bōr″ėr), *n.* A longicorn beetle, *Saperda calcarata*, the larva of which bores the trunks of various poplars.

poplar-dagger (pop'lạ̈r-dag″ėr), *n.* A bombycid moth, *Acronycta populi*, whose larva feeds on poplar-leaves. See cut under *dagger*[1], 4.

poplared (pop'lạ̈rd), *a.* [‹ *poplar* + *-ed*[1].] Covered with or containing poplars.

poplar-girdler (pop'lạ̈r-gėr″dlėr), *n.* A longicorn beetle, *Saperda concolor*, whose larva girdles the trunks of poplar-saplings.

poplar-gray (pop'lạ̈r-grā), *n.* A British moth, *Acronycta megacephala*.

poplar-kitten (pop'lạ̈r-kit″n), *n.* A British puss-moth, *Cerura bifida*.

poplar-lutestring (pop'lặr-lût″string), *n.* A British moth, *Cymatophora or.*

poplar-spinner (pop'lặr-spin″ėr), *n.* A geometrid moth, *Biston ursaria*, whose larva defoliates poplars in the United States.

poplar-tree (pop'lặr-trē), *n.* Same as *poplar.*

poplet†, *n.* Squirrel-fur. *Fairholt.*

popler[1]†, *n.* An obsolete form of *poplar.*

popler[2]†, *n.* [ME., also *popelere*, a bird; glossed by ML. *populus.*] A sea-gull. *Halliwell.* [In the quotation, the name in parentheses is that of the shoveler duck.]

> *Popelere*, byrd (or schovelerd, infra), *Populus.*
> *Prompt. Parv.*, p. 408.

poples (pop'lēz), *n.*; pl. *poplites* (-li-tēz). [L.] The ham, or back of the knee; the popliteal space.

poplexy†, *n.* An aphetic form of *apoplexy.*

> *Poplexie* shente not hire heed.
> *Chaucer*, Nun's Priest's Tale, l. 21.

poplin (pop'lin), *n.* [= Sp. *populina, popelens*, < F. *popeline*, formerly *papeline*, poplin; origin obscure.] A fabric having a silk warp and a weft of wool heavier than the silk, which gives it a corded surface somewhat resembling that of rep. It may be watered, brocaded, or plain.—**Double poplin**, poplin in which both the silk warp and wool weft are very heavy, the heavy wool weft making the corded appearance very prominent and the woven stuff much stiffer and heavier than single poplin.—**Irish poplin**, a light variety of poplin, sometimes also called *single poplin*, made in Dublin, and celebrated for its uniformly fine quality.—**Terry poplin**, a very durable fabric in which, by throwing up to the surface alternate threads of the silk warp, an appearance somewhat resembling Terry velvet is obtained.

poplitæus, popliteus (pop-li-tē'us), *n.*; pl. *poplitæi, poplitei* (-ī). [NL., < L. *poples* (*poplit-*), the ham of the knee, the hock.] A flat triangular muscle at the back of the knee-joint, covered by the gastrocnemius. It arises from the outer side of the external femoral condyle, and is inserted into the upper back part of the tibia.

popliteal (pop-li-tē'ạl), *a.* [< *poplitæus* + *-al.*] Of or pertaining to the ham, or back of the knee.—**External popliteal nerve.** Same as *peroneal nerve* (which see, under *peroneal*).—**Popliteal aneurism**, aneurism of the popliteal artery.—**Popliteal artery**, the continuation of the femoral artery in the popliteal space, after passing through the foramen in the adductor magnus. It divides, below the popliteal muscle, into the anterior and posterior tibial arteries.—**Popliteal aspect**, the posterior aspect of the leg.—**Popliteal bursæ**, bursæ beneath the heads of the gastrocnemius muscles, and sometimes others, in the popliteal space, often communicating with the knee-joint.—**Popliteal glands**, four or five lymphatic glands surrounding the popliteal artery.—**Popliteal ligament**, the posterior ligament of the knee-joint.—**Popliteal line.** See *line*[2].—**Popliteal nerve**, the larger division of the great sciatic, passing down the middle of the popliteal space to the lower border of the popliteus muscle, where it becomes the posterior tibial. It gives off muscular and articular branches and the external saphenous nerve. Also called *internal popliteal nerve.*—**Popliteal notch, plane**, etc. See the nouns.—**Popliteal region.** Same as *popliteal space.*—**Popliteal space** a lozenge-shaped space at the back of the knee, bounded above by the hamstring-muscles, below by the inner and outer heads of the gastrocnemius; the ham. Also called *popliteal interval.*—**Popliteal surface**, the surface of the femur between the supracondylar lines.—**Popliteal tendons**, the tendons of the muscles forming the boundaries of the popliteal space; the hamstrings.—**Popliteal vein**, the vein accompanying the popliteal artery, formed from the venæ comites of the tibial arteries, and continued as the femoral vein.

poplites, *n.* Plural of *poples.*

popliteus, *n.* See *poplitæus.*

poplitic (pop-lit'ik), *a.* [= OF. *poplitique*, n., < L. *poples* (*poplit-*), the ham of the knee.] Of or pertaining to the poples; popliteal.

popper[1] (pop'ėr), *n.* [< *pop*[1] + *-er*[1].] 1. A utensil for popping corn; a corn-popper. It is made of wire gauze with a cover and a long wooden handle. [U. S.]—2. Anything that pops or makes a popping sound, as a firecracker or pistol.

> And all round the glad church lie old bottles
> With gunpowder stopped,
> Which will be, when the Image re-enters,
> Religiously popped.
> And at night from the crest of Calvano
> Great bonfires will hang,
> On the plain will the trumpets join chorus,
> And more *poppers* bang.
> *Browning*, Englishman in Italy.

popper[2]† (pop'ėr), *n.* [ME., < (?) *pop*[2], strike, + *-er*[1].] A dagger.

> A joly *poppere* baar he in his pouche.
> *Chaucer*, Reeve's Tale, l. 11.

poppet (pop'et), *n.* [A var. of *puppet.*] 1†. A puppet. *London Gazette*, Feb. 15, 1705.—2. A term of endearment. See *puppet.*—3. A shore or piece of timber placed between a vessel's bottom and the bilgeways, at the foremost and aftermost parts, to support her in launching. See cut under *launching-ways.*—4. One of the heads of a lathe. Also *popit.* See cut under *lathe-head.*—5. A puppet-valve.—6. Small bits of wood upon a boat's gunwale, to support the rowlocks and washstrake.

poppet-head (pop'et-hed), *n.* 1. The adjustable head of a lathe which supports the back or dead-center.—2. In *mining*, the pulley-frame or head-gear over a shaft, supporting the pulleys over which the ropes used in winding or hoisting pass. Also called *pulley-frame, shaft-tackle, head-gear, head-stocks*, and *pit-head frame.*

poppet-valve (pop'et-valv), *n.* Same as *puppet-valve.*

poppied (pop'id), *a.* [< *poppy* + *-ed*[2].] 1. Producing or covered or grown over with poppies; mingled with poppies: as, *poppied* fields; "*poppied* corn," *Keats*, Endymion, i.—2. Resulting from or produced by the use of poppy-juice or opium; listless.

> The end of all—the *poppied* sleep. *Swinburne*, Ilicet.

popping†, *n.* [ME. *poppinge, poppynge*; verbal n. of *pop*[2], *v.*: see *pop*[2].] The act of smearing the face with white lead (ceruse).

> The aungelle saide it was but litelle merualle though this lady, for her *poppinge* and peintynge, suffre this payne.
> *Knight of La Tour Landry* (E. E. T. S.), p. 68.

popping-crease (pop'ing-krēs), *n.* In *cricket.* See *crease*[1], 2.

popple[1] (pop'l), *v. i.*; pret. and pp. *poppled*, ppr. *poppling.* [Dim. and freq. of *pop*[1].] 1†. To flow; rush; foam; bubble.

> And on the stany's owt thar barnys [he] dang,
> Quhil brayn and eyn and blude al *poplit* owt.
> *Gavin Douglas*, tr. of Virgil, l. 167.
> His brains came *poppling* out like water.
> *Cotton*, Burlesque upon Burlesque, p. 226. (*Davies.*)

2. To bob or move up and down: said of a floating object.

popple[1] (pop'l), *n.* [< *popple*[1], *v.*] A ripple.

popple[2] (pop'l), *n.* [< ME. *popul-(tre)* = MLG. *poppele, poppeleone, popplione*, LG. *poppele, poppelo* = MHG. *popel, papel*, G. *poppel, pappel* = Sw. Dan. *poppel* = OF. **pople, peuple, pouple, pouble, pible* = Sp. *pobo, chopo* = Pg. *choupo, chopo* = It. *pioppo, pioppa*, < L. *populus*, a poplar; perhaps for **palpulus*, < √ *palp* in *palpitare*, tremble.] Same as *poplar.* [Prov. Eng. and U. S.]

popple[3] (pop'l), *n.* The corn-cockle, *Lychnis Githago.* [Prov. Eng.]

poppy (pop'i), *n.*; pl. *poppies* (-iz). [< ME. *popy*, < AS. *popig, papig* = F. *pavot*, Norm. *papi* = Pr. *paver, papaver* = Sp. *ababol*, corn-poppy, *amapola*, poppy, corn-poppy, = Pg. *papoula* = It. *papavero*, < L. *papaver*, poppy. The Gr. word was *μήκων*; cf. *meconium.* The L. *papaver* suffered considerable change in passing into vernacular use in later languages. With *poppy* in the architectural sense, cf. F. *poupée* in same sense (whence E. *poop*[2]), appar. an extended use of *poupée*, the bunch of flax on a distaff, hence a distaff, also a crown-graft, particular uses of *poupée*, a doll, rag-baby: see *puppet.*] 1. A plant of the genus *Papaver.* The poppies are showy herbs, in the New World cultivated chiefly in gardens, and wild or cultivated in the Old. The opium-poppy, *P. somniferum*, is of importance as the source of opium and as yielding, in its seeds, a valuable oil. (See *poppy-oil* and *maw-seed.*) Its capsules afford also a syrup or extract used as a sedative, and in hot decoction serve as an anodyne application. The opium-poppy is a glaucous plant, with wavy clasping leaves. The petals and seeds vary in color. The variety chiefly cultivated in India and Persia has white petals and white seeds, that in Asia Minor purple petals and dark seeds; they are called respectively *white* and *black poppy.* The common red poppy, corn-poppy, or corn-rose is *P. Rhœas*, abounding in central and southern Europe and western Asia. The petals are deep-red or scarlet with a dark eye, or when doubled varying in color. The long-headed poppy, *P. dubium*, has smaller flowers of a lighter red, the capsule elongated. The Oriental poppy, *P. orientale*, has a very large deep-red flower on a tall peduncle, and is the most showy species.

Poppy (*Papaver somniferum*).
a, the upper part of the stem with the flower; *b*, the lower part of the plant; *c*, the fruit.

> Nowe *popy* seede in grounde is goode to throwe.
> *Palladius*, Husbondrie (E. E. T. S.), p. 81.

2. One of several plants belonging to other genera of the *Papaveraceæ.*—3. The foxglove.—4. In *arch.*, same as *poppy-head.*—**Black poppy.** See def. 1.—**California poppy.** See *Eschscholtzia.*—**Corn-poppy.** See def. 1.—**Field-poppy.** Same as *corn-poppy.*—**Garden poppy**, specifically, the opium-poppy.—**Horn-poppy**, or **horned poppy**, a small seaside plant of the poppy family, *Glaucium luteum*, with clasping leaves and solitary yellow flowers: so named from the long curved horn-like seed-pods. Also *sea-poppy.*—**Long-headed poppy.** See def. 1.—**Mexican poppy.** See *prickly poppy.*—**Oriental poppy.** See def. 1.—**Poppy trash.** See *trash.*—**Prickly poppy**, *Argemone Mexicana*, the Mexican poppy, now widely diffused, often a weed. The pods and leaves are prickly, the latter blotched with white; the flowers are yellow, a variety being white. Its seeds are regarded as cathartic and yield a useful oil. See *poppy-oil.*—**Red poppy.** See def. 1.—**Sea-poppy, or seaside poppy.** Same as *horn-poppy.*—**Spatling** or **frothy poppy**, an old name of *Silene inflata*: so called on account of the spittle-like froth produced upon it by the puncture of an insect.—**Tree-poppy**, *Dendromecon rigidum*, of California, remarkable as a shrub in the almost wholly herbaceous order *Papaveraceæ*, 6 or 8 feet high, with bright-yellow flowers from 1 to 3 inches broad.—**Welsh poppy.** See *Meconopsis.*—**White poppy.** See def. 1.

poppy-bee (pop'i-bē), *n.* An upholsterer-bee, *Anthocopa papaveris*, which furnishes its nest with the petals of poppies. See cut under *upholsterer-bee.*

poppycock (pop'i-kok), *n.* [Appar. < *pop*[1] in dim. form, + *cock*[1], in vague addition of contempt.] Trivial talk; nonsense; stuff and rubbish. [U. S. vulgarism.]

poppy-head (pop'i-hed), *n.* A carved finial in decorative woodwork and other ornamental work, on a smaller scale than architectural ornament in stone; especially, such a finial at the top of the end of a bench or a pew.

Poppy-head.—Choir-stalls of Lincoln Cathedral, England.

poppy-mallow (pop'i-mal″ō), *n.* Any plant of the genus *Callirrhoë*, of the mallow family: so named from the poppy-like flowers. Various species are beautiful in cultivation, among them *C. involucrata*, the purple poppy-mallow, with stems spreading on the ground.

poppy-oil (pop'i-oil), *n.* 1. A fixed oil expressed from the seeds of the opium-poppy. The pure oil is of a golden-yellow color and an agreeable flavor. It serves as a food and an illuminating oil, and is used in soap-making. The finer qualities of that produced in France are used to adulterate olive-oil, very extensively in grinding artists' colors, and as a medium in painting. 2. A limpid light-yellow oil obtained, chiefly in India, from the seeds of the Mexican or prickly poppy. It saponifies readily, burns well, is recommended for lubricating, and credited with medicinal properties.—3. An oil, little utilized, obtained from the seeds of the horned poppy.

poppy-seed (pop'i-sēd), *n.* The seed of the poppy, chiefly of the opium-poppy.—**Poppy-seed oil.** Same as *poppy-oil.*

pops (pops), *n.* Same as *pop-dock.* [Prov. Eng.]

pop-shop (pop'shop), *n.* A pawnbroker's shop. [Slang.]

populace (pop'ụ̄-lạ̄s), *n.* [< F. *populace*, OF. *populas* = Sp. *populacho, populazo* = Pg. *populaça, populacho*, < It. *popolaccio, popolazzo*, the common people, the populace, with a depreciative suffix *-accio* (see *-ace*), < *popolo*, people, < L. *populus*, people: see *people.*] The common people; the vulgar; the multitude, comprehending all persons not distinguished by rank, education, office, or profession.

The *populace* hooted and shouted all day before the gates of the royal residence.
Macaulay, Nugent's Hampden.

=**Syn.** *Populace, Mob, Rabble*, crowd, masses. *Populace* is used to represent the lower classes, the body of those without wealth, education, or recognized position; it is, however, much less opprobrious than *mob* or *rabble*. *Mob* is a very strong word for a tumultuous or even riotous assembly, moved to or toward lawlessness by discontent or some similar exciting cause. *Rabble* is a contemptuous word for the very lowest classes, considered as confused or without sufficient strength or unity of feeling to make them especially dangerous.

That vast portion, lastly, of the working class which, raw and half-developed, has long lain half-hidden amidst its poverty and squalor, and is now issuing from its hiding-place to assert an Englishman's heaven-born privilege of doing as he likes, and is beginning to perplex us by marching when it likes, meeting where it likes, bawling what it likes, breaking what it likes — to this vast residuum we may with great propriety give the name of *Populace*.
M. Arnold, Culture and Anarchy, iii.

A *mob* is at first an irregular, then a regular army; but in every stage of its progress the mere blind instrument of its leaders.
Ames, Works, II. 228.

Follow'd with a *rabble* that rejoice
To see my tears and hear my deep-fet groans.
Shak., 2 Hen. VI., ii. 4. 32.

populacy† (pop'ū-lā-si), *n.* [< *populace*, irreg. conformed to nouns in *-acy*.] The populace or common people; the rabble. *Decay of Christian Piety.*

popular (pop'ū-lạ̈r), *a.* [= D. *populair* = G. *populär*, *populär* = Sw. *populär* = Dan. *populær*, < F. *populaire* = Sp. Pg. *popular* = It. *populare*, *popolare*, < L. *popularis*, of the people, belonging to the people, of the same people or country (as a noun, a fellow-countryman), agreeable to the people, popular, attached or devoted to the people, democratic, etc., < *populus*, the people: see *people*.] 1. Of or pertaining to the people; constituted by or depending on the people, especially the common people: as, the *popular* voice; *popular* elections; *popular* government.

Autinous, by my shame observe
What a close witchcraft *popular* applause is.
Beau. and Fl., Laws of Candy, v. 1.

2. Suitable to or intended for common people; easy to be comprehended; not technical or abstruse; plain; familiar: as, a *popular* treatise on astronomy.

Homilies are plain and *popular* instructions.
Hooker, Eccles. Polity.

"Piers Ploughman" is the best example I know of what is called *popular* poetry — of compositions, that is, which contain all the simpler elements of poetry, but still in solution, not crystallized around any thread of artistic purpose.
Lowell, Study Windows, p. 263.

3. Enjoying the favor of the people; pleasing to people in general: as, a *popular* preacher; a *popular* war or peace.

In their sermons they were apt to enlarge on the state of the present time, and to preach against the sins of princes and courts, a topic that naturally makes men *popular*.
Bp. Burnet.

An author may make himself very *popular*, however, and even justly so, by appealing to the passion of the moment, without having anything in him that shall outlast the public whim which he satisfies.
Lowell, Study Windows, p. 117.

4†. Desirous of obtaining the favor of the people; courting the vulgar; of demagogic proclivities.

Divers were of opinion that he [Caius Gracchus] was more *popular* and desirous of the common people's good will and favour then his brother had been before him. But indeed he was clean contrary.
North, tr. of Plutarch, p. 690. (*Trench.*)

5. Prevailing among the people; epidemic. *Johnson.* [Rare.]

The world 's a *popular* disease, that reigns
Within the froward heart and frantic brains
Of poor distemper'd mortals.
Quarles, Emblems, i. 8.

6†. Plebeian; vulgar.

Discuss unto me; art thou officer?
Or art thou base, common, and *popular*?
Shak., Hen. V., iv. 1. 38.

7. Conceited. [Vulgar, U. S.]

Popular: conceited. . . . "*Pop'lar* as a hen with one chicken."
Lowell, Biglow Papers, 2d ser., Int.

Popular action, in *law*, an action for a penalty given by statute to the person who sues for the same.—**Popular sovereignty**, in *U. S. hist.*, the theory that the right to decide whether slavery should exist in a territory rested with the people of that territory, and not with Congress. It was advocated especially by Democrats during the period 1847-61, and its leading champion was Douglas. It was often termed "squatter sovereignty," with which it was nearly identical. =**Syn.** 3. Favorite, current, prevailing.

popularisation, popularise, etc. See *popularization*, etc.

popularity (pop-ū-lar'i̦-ti), *n.* [= F. *popularité* = Sp. *popularidad* = Pg. *popularidade* = It. *popolarità* = D. *populariteit* = Sw. Dan. *popularitet*, < L. *popularita(t-)s*, a being of the same country, also a courting of popular favor, popular bearing, < *popularis*, of the people: see *popular*.] 1. Popular character or quality; favor in the eyes of the people; acceptance or acceptability among the people; the fact of being favored by or of having the approbation of the people: as, the *popularity* of a measure; the *popularity* of a public officer; the *popularity* of a book or of a preacher.

The best temper of minds desireth good name and true honour; the lighter, *popularity* and applause; the more depraved, subjection and tyranny.
Bacon.

2†. That which catches public favor; anything suited to the vulgar fancy; a piece of claptrap.

Popularities . . . which sway the ordinary judgement.
Bacon.

3†. A desire to obtain favor with the people; a currying of favor with the people.

Harold, lifted up in mind, and forgetting now his former shows of *popularity*, defrauded his soldiers their due and well-deserved share of the spoils.
Milton, Hist. Eng., vi.

4†. Vulgarity; commonness.

This gallant, labouring to avoid *popularity*, falls into a habit of affectation ten thousand times hatefuler than the former.
B. Jonson.

popularization (pop'ū-lạ̈r-i-zā'shọn), *n.* [= F. *popularisation*; < *popularize* + *-ation*.] The act of making popular; adaptation to popular needs or capacities: as, the *popularization* of science. Also spelled *popularisation*.

popularize (pop'ū-lạ̈r-īz), *v. t.*; pret. and pp. *popularized*, ppr. *popularizing*. [= F. *populariser* = Sp. *popularizar* = Pg. *popularisar*; as *popular* + *-ize*.] To make popular; treat in a popular manner, or so as to be generally intelligible to common people; spread among the people. Also spelled *popularise*.

The *popularizing* of religious teaching.
Milman.

popularizer (pop'ū-lạ̈r-ī-zėr), *n.* One who popularizes, or treats scientific or abstruse subjects in a popular manner. Also spelled *populariser*. *Athenæum.*

popularly (pop'ū-lạ̈r-li), *adv.* 1. In a popular manner; so as to please the populace.

Why then should I, encouraging the bad,
Turn rebel and run *popularly* mad?
Dryden, Abs. and Achit., i. 336.

2. Among the people at large; currently; commonly; prevalently.

popularness (pop'ū-lạ̈r-nes), *n.* The state of being popular; popularity.

Meretricious *popularness* in literature.
Coleridge.

populate (pop'ū-lāt), *v.*; pret. and pp. *populated*, ppr. *populating*. [< ML. *populatus*, pp. of *populare* (> It. *popolare*), people, populate, < L. *populus*, people: see *people*, *n.*, and cf. *people*, *v.* Cf. L. *populari*, *populare*, devastate, lay waste: see *depopulate*.] I. *trans.* To furnish with inhabitants, either by natural increase or by immigration or colonization; people.

II. *intrans.* To breed; propagate; increase in number.

Great shoals of people which go on to *populate*.
Bacon, Vicissitudes of Things.

populate (pop'ū-lāt), *a.* [= It. *popolato*, *populato*; < ML. *populatus*, pp. of *populare*, populate: see *populate*, *v.*] Populated; populous.

The countrie of Caldea, the situation whereof is vnder the fourth Climate, the Region after the floud first inhabited and *populate*.
Guevara, Letters (tr. by Hellowes, 1577), p. 376.

A prince . . . in the prime of his years, owner of the entire isle of Britain, enjoying Ireland *populate* and quiet.
Bacon, Notes of a Speech on Spain.

population (pop-ū-lā'shọn), *n.* [= F. *population* = Sp. *populacion*, *poblacion* = Pg. *populaçåo* = It. *popolazione*, < ML. *populatio(n-)*, population (LL. a people, multitude), < *populare*, pp. *populatus*, people: see *populate*.] 1. The act or process of populating or peopling: as, the rapid *population* of the country still continues.

The first radical impact of the principle of *population*, working in harmony with the repellent forces of savagery, tends to the speediest possible diffusion of population throughout the most accessible parts of the habitable world.
Amer. Anthropologist, I. 17.

2. The whole number of people or inhabitants in a country, county, city, or other locality: as, the *population* has increased 20,000 in four years; also, a part of the inhabitants in any way distinguished from the rest: as, the German *population* of New York.

A country may have a great *population* and yet not be populous.
Tooke.

In countries of the highest civilization which has yet been reached, armed with the resources of the best government, purest justice, truest morality, soundest economy, and most fruitful science attained by men, we find the greatest density of *population*, because the limits of *population* revolve more and more within the sphere of man's material, mental, and moral freedom.
Amer. Anthropologist, I. 11.

3. The state of a locality with regard to the number of its inhabitants; populousness.

Neither is the *population* to be reckoned only by number, for a smaller number, that spend more and earn less, do wear out an estate sooner than a greater number that live low and gather more.
Bacon, Seditions and Troubles.

populator (pop'ū-lā-tọr), *n.* [= It. *popolatore*, < ML. *populator*, one who peoples, < *populare*, pp. *populatus*: see *people* and *populate*.] One who or that which populates or peoples.

populicide (pop'ū-li-sīd), *n.* [= F. *populicide*; < L. *populus*, people, + *cædere*, kill.] Slaughter of the people. *Eclectic Rev.* [Rare.]

populin (pop'ū-lin), *n.* [= F. *populine*; < L. *populus*, poplar, + *-in*[2].] A crystallizable substance ($C_{20}H_{22}O_8$) found in the bark, root, and leaves of the aspen, *Populus Tremula*, along with salicin. It forms delicate white needles, which have a sweet taste like that of licorice.

populinate (pop'ū-lin-āt), *v. t.* [< *populin* + *-ate*[2].] To impregnate with populin, as lard, to prevent a tendency to rancidity. *U. S. Dispensatory*, p. 1489.

Populist (pop'ū-list), *a.* and *n.* I. *a.* Of or pertaining to the People's party, a political organization established in the United States in 1891, having for its chief objects expansion of the currency, state control of railways, and the placing of restrictions upon the ownership of land.

II. *n.* A member of the People's party.

populosity† (pop-ū-los'i̦-ti), *n.* [= F. *populosité*, < LL. *populosita(t-)s*, < L. *populosus*, populous: see *populous*.] Populousness.

The length of men's lives conduced unto the *populosity* of their kind.
Sir T. Browne, Vulg. Err., vi. 6.

populous (pop'ū-lus), *a.* [< F. *populeux* = Sp. Pg. *populoso* = It. *populoso*, *popoloso*, < L. *populosus*, full of people, populous, < *populus*, people: see *people*.] 1. Full of people; containing many inhabitants in proportion to the extent of the country.

You will finde it a *populous* towne, and well inhabited.
Coryat, Crudities, I. 9.

They passed not farre frome an other Ilande which the captyues sayde to bee verye *peopulous*, and replenyshed with all thynges necessarie for the life of man.
Peter Martyr (tr. in Eden's First Books on America, ed. [Arber, p. 69).

2†. Numerous; multitudinous.

Yt was shewed hym that Kynge Rycharde was at hande wyth a stronge powre and a *populous* armye.
Hall, Rich. III., fol. 29, a., quoted in Wright's Bible [Wordbook.

The dust
Should have ascended to the roof of heaven,
Raised by your *populous* troops.
Shak., A. and C., iii. 6. 50.

3†. Pleasing or acceptable to the people; popular.

He I plead for
Has power to make your beauty *populous*.
Webster, Appius and Virginia, ii. 1.

4†. Suited to the populace; coarse; vulgar.

It should have been some fine confection,
That might have given the broth some dainty taste;
This powder was too gross and *populous*.
Arden of Feversham, i. 3.

populously (pop'ū-lus-li), *adv.* In a populous manner; with many inhabitants in proportion to the extent of the country.

populousness (pop'ū-lus-nes), *n.* The state of being populous, or of having many inhabitants in proportion to extent of territory.

Populus (pop'ū-lus), *n.* [NL. (Tournefort, 1700), < L. *populus*, poplar: see *popple*[2], *poplar*.] A genus of dicotyledonous trees of the order *Salicineæ*, including the poplar and aspen, having diœcious flowers in catkins without floral envelops, and distinguished from *Salix*, the willow, by the numerous ovules, obliquely lengthened and cup-shaped disks, broad and toothed bracts, loosely flowered and generally pendulous catkins, and broad leaves. The 18 species are all natives of the northern hemisphere. They are trees with angled or sometimes cylindrical branches, scaly resinous buds coated externally with varnish before opening, and catkins appearing before the leaves, which are alternate and slender-petioled, feather-veined and three-nerved, sometimes entire and triangular, often toothed or lobed. Most species present a very characteristic appearance when in flower, from the long drooping catkins and their red anthers and white-fringed scales. The fertile catkins discharge innumerable seeds, each enveloped in white cottony down, which fill the air about the trees in May, and collect in small drifts like snow; hence the name *cottonwood*, which is in use for several American species. *P. Tremula* of Europe and *P. tremuloides* of America, the aspens, are remarkable for the tremulous motion of their leaves, due to the vertical flattening of their leafstalks (see cut under *petiole*). See *quaking asp* (under *asp*1), *aspen*, *auld wives' tongues* (under *auld*), and *corticine*. For other species, see *poplar*, the general name of the genus.

popweed (pop'wēd), *n.* The common bladderwort. See *Utricularia*.

I stuck awhile with my toe-balls on the slippery links of the *pop-weed*, and the world was green and gliddery, and I durst not look behind me.
R. D. Blackmore, Lorna Doone, vii.

poquauhock, *n.* [Said to be Algonkin, a fuller form of *quahaug*.] The round hard clam, or quahaug, *Venus mercenaria*. Also *poquanhock*. See *sequannock*.

por-. [L. *por-*: see *pro-*.] A prefix of Latin origin, ultimately a form of *pro-*. It occurs in *portend*, *portent*, etc.

poraillet, *n.* [ME., < OF. *povraille*, poor people, < *povre*, poor: see *poor*.] The poor; poor people.

For the parisch prest and the pardonere parten the siluer,
That the *poraille* of the parisch shold haue ʒif thei nere:
Piers Plowman (B), Prol., l. 82.

It is not honest, it may not avaunce,
For to delen with no swich *poraille*.
Chaucer, Gen. Prol. to C. T., l. 247.

Al be it the *porayll* and needy people drewe vnto hym, & were parteners of yᵗ ille. *Fabyan*, Chron., I., an. 1550.

poral (pō'ral), *a.* [< *pore*2 + *-al*.] Of or pertaining to the pores of the body.

Giving only of our waste; . . . by form of perspiration, radiation, if you like; unconscious *poral* bountifulness.
G. Meredith, The Egoist, xiv.

porbeagle (pôr'bē"gl), *n.* [Said to be for *porc-beagle, < F. *porc*, hog, + E. *beagle* (applied to several sharks). Cf. *porpoise*.] Any shark of the family *Lamnidæ*, and especially of the genus *Lamna*; a kind of tope or mackerel-shark. The name originally applied to *L. cornubica*, a British species occurring also in the North Atlantic at large, and also known as the *Beaumaris shark*. It is a large fierce shark, of a gray color. Species of *Isurus* are mackerel-sharks to which the name also applies, as *I. glaucus* or *I. oxyrhynchus* of the Atlantic. See cut under *mackerel-shark*.

porcate (pôr'kāt), *a.* [< L. as if *porcatus, < *porca*, a ridge between two furrows: see *furrow*.] Ridged; formed in ridges; specifically, in *entom.*, marked by longitudinal deep furrows separated from one another by narrow ridges.

porcated (pôr'kā-ted), *a.* [< *porcate* + *-ed*1.] Same as *porcate*.

porcelain1 (pôrs'lān or pōrs'lān), *n.* and *a.* [Formerly also *porcellan*, *porcelane*, also irreg. *purslaine*, *purslane*, *purslen* (by confusion with *purslane*1, which was also written *porcelain*); = D. *porselein* = G. *porzellan*, *porcellan* = Dan. *porcellæn* = Sw. *porslin*, < OF. *porcellaine*, *pourcelaine*, *porchelaine*, *porcelaine*, porcelain, china, chinaware, also the purple-fish, the Venus-shell, F. *porcelaine*, porcelain, china, cowry, sea-snail, = Sp. *porcelana* = Pg. *porcellana*, *porcelana*, porcelain, < It. *porcellana*, porcelain (so called because its finely polished surface was compared with that of the Venus-shell), also the purple-fish, the Venus-shell, so called because the curved shape of the upper surface resembles the curve of a pig's back, < *porcella*, a little pig, a pig, dim. of *porco*, m., *porca*, f., a hog, pig: see *pork*.] **I.** *n.* A ceramic ware having a translucent body, and when glazed (see *biscuit*, 3) a translucent glaze also. It is of various kinds: (*a*) Hard-paste (or natural) porcelain, of which the principal material is a peculiar clay commonly known as *kaolin*, with which is combined some silicious material (in China, petuntse; at Sèvres and elsewhere in Europe, white sand, and sometimes chalk, or roasted and ground flints). The glaze is of similar composition, the silicious ingredient being sometimes rock-crystal ground to powder. (*b*) Soft-paste (or artificial) porcelain, of which the composition varies; it was originally an attempted imitation of the hard porcelain brought from China and Japan. Sand, niter, soda (or other alkaline substance), gypsum, salt, and other ingredients enter into it, and, in order to make it plastic, glue or some similar material is added. The glaze is hard, and the ware is not exposed to the great heat of the hard-porcelain furnace. (*c*) Hybrid or mixed porcelain, which is also a compound produced in attempted imitation of Oriental porcelain, but contains a certain amount of a kaolinic clay. Of these three varieties, Chinese and Japanese porcelain, the porcelain of Dresden, Vienna, and Sèvres (since about 1770), and in England that of Bristol, Plymouth, and Lowestoft are of the first; St. Cloud, Sèvres (before 1770), and most English wares are of the second; and the medieval Italian wares, with some English ones and perhaps some modern ones of the European continent, belong to the third; but the distinction between the second and third is often hard to fix or ascertain.—**Alcora porcelain**, a rich porcelain having a metallic luster not unlike that of majolica, made at Alcora in Spain, toward the end of the eighteenth century. The mark is an A in gold-colored luster.—**Amstel porcelain**, porcelain made near Amsterdam in the Netherlands, first at a factory called Old Amstel from 1782 to 1807, and then at the factory of New Amstel for two or three years only. The ware of both is marked Amstel in full, or with an A, and is of great excellence of manufacture, rarely in decorative pieces, but in table-services of great variety, and decorated in a simple way, especially with small paintings of birds.—**Arita porcelain**, the more exact name of the fine Japanese porcelain commonly known as Old Japan, Hizen porcelain, and Imari porcelain, the greater part of which was made at the town of Arita. See *Hizen porcelain*.—**Berlin porcelain**, porcelain made at Berlin, Prussia, especially a hard-paste porcelain made at the royal factory (founded by a private person in 1750, and bought by Frederick the Great thirteen years later). This ware has been made down to the present day. The mark has usually been a scepter in blue under the glaze, to which has been added K. P. M., for Königl. Porzellan Manufaktur; but the recent productions are marked with a circular seal having the above German words in full around the rim and the royal eagle in the middle. The uses to which this ware is put are extremely varied, and decoration of every sort has been tried in it, and generally with success. Lithophane belongs to it, as well as a curious manufacture called *porcelain-lace*, which is added to decorative figures, and is produced by soaking lace or a similar fabric in the porcelain-slip, and then firing, by which the threads are destroyed and the pattern left in thin filaments of porcelain.—**Bone porcelain**. See *bone*1.—**Bow porcelain**, a soft-paste porcelain made at Stratford-le-Bow, near London, generally decorated by figures in relief and in painting of the simplest character. It is the earliest English porcelain. A frequent decoration is what is called the hawthorn pattern (thorny branches covered with blossoms, frequently in slight relief). A frequent mark of Bow china is a bent bow with an arrow on the string.—**Brandenburg porcelain**, porcelain made at a factory near Brandenburg between 1713 and 1719. The founder of the factory appears to have been a workman from Meissen.—**Bristol porcelain**, porcelain made at Bristol in England, especially a ware made in the eighteenth century from the Cornwall china-stone, and directed by a potter named Champion, who bought out Cookworthy's interest. See *Cookworthy porcelain*.—**Budweis porcelain**, a hard-paste porcelain made at Budweis in Bohemia in modern times.—**Burslem porcelain**, a name given to some of the finer wares made at the first Wedgwood factory in Burslem. They are not strictly porcelain in any sense, but are described by Wedgwood, in catalogues, etc., as "fine porcelain bisque" and the like, whence probably the term came to be used.—**Caen porcelain**, porcelain made at Caen in Normandy, especially a hard-paste ware made during the early years of the French revolution, and commonly marked with the word Caen in full. It is extremely rare, the manufacture having lasted but a few years.—**Capodimonte porcelain**, porcelain made at Capodimonte, a suburb of Naples, especially that of the royal factory, which was continued through the greater part of the eighteenth century. The most celebrated variety is that which is decorated with figures in high relief, not very finely modeled, but decorative in their disposition, and then touched with red applied in the pointillé manner to the less prominent parts of the relief, as if with the intention of giving a flesh-like warmth to the shadows.—**Cast porcelain**, a semi-transparent or milky-white glass made of silica and cryolite with oxid of zinc. Also called *milk-glass*, *fusible porcelain*, *cryolite glass*, and *hot-cast porcelain*.—**Chantilly porcelain**, porcelain made at Chantilly, near Paris. Especially—(*a*) A soft-paste porcelain made under the patronage of the Prince de Condé from 1725, the mark of which was a hunting-horn in blue under the glaze. The glaze of this porcelain was made opaque by tin, so as to be practically a thin coat of enamel. A design consisting of small detached flowers painted in blue became very popular, and was known as the *Chantilly sprig pattern*. (*b*) A hard-paste porcelain made in the early part of the nineteenth century. (c) See *Petit porcelain*.—**Chelsea porcelain**, a porcelain made at Chelsea in England, especially a soft-paste porcelain made from 1735, the most admired of the old English porcelains.—**Chemical porcelain** a fine porcelain nearly completely vitrified, so as to be almost an opaque glass, made at the works of Granger & Co. at Worcester, England, about 1860.—**Cookworthy porcelain**, porcelain made at Plymouth, England, from about 1755, by W. Cookworthy, who discovered the Cornish clay (see *china-stone* (*b*)) independently of Chaffers. This was the most important of the Plymouth porcelain manufactures.—**Copenhagen porcelain**, porcelain made at Copenhagen. Especially—(*a*) A hard-paste porcelain made from 1760 for a few years, and from 1772, soon after which time it was taken up by the government. The well-known mark is three waving or rippling lines supposed to represent the waves of the sea. (*b*) A modern porcelain, of which the variety best known is unglazed works of art, such as statuettes and groups. Thorwaldsen's works, especially, have been copied in this ware.—**Crown Derby porcelain**, a variety of Derby porcelain, bearing a royal crown as a distinguishing mark. In some cases a D only is crowned, sometimes the monogram D. K., or D with a St. Andrew's cross, this mark being sometimes in red, sometimes in violet, and sometimes impressed.—**Derby crown porcelain**, a modern porcelain made at Derby in imitation of the old Crown Derby ware and also from new designs. The mark adopted by the company is a cipher of D. D. surmounted by a crown.—**Derby porcelain**, porcelain made at Derby in England, especially a soft-paste porcelain made from 1751. The ware is very translucent, and some of the colors are of unusual brilliancy, especially the blue. One of the specialties of the Derby fabric is the unglazed biscuit-ware, of which figures and groups were made for the decoration of the table; this is unmatched by any recent wares, the Parian being generally inferior to it. An old mark of Derby ware is a D and the name of the potter Bloor, with the word Derby, and a crown has been used since 1830.—**Dresden porcelain**, a hard-paste porcelain made at the royal factory of Meissen, near Dresden in Saxony, beginning with the year 1707. This was the first hard-paste porcelain made in Europe, and the manufacture has continued to the present day, including pieces for decoration, for uses of every kind and decoration of every variety, both in relief and in color and gold. The small figures and groups, brilliantly painted, and especially those in which shepherds and shepherdesses are represented, have been especially popular for many years. A common name for the old Dresden porcelain is *vieux Saxe*. The best-known mark of this factory is two swords crossed, but a number of Oriental marks are roughly imitated on certain pieces. Pieces that are sent out from the royal factory white can be known by a cut or scratch through the two swords which form the mark; such pieces, if decorated, have been decorated outside. Compare *Sèvres porcelain*.—**Egg-shell porcelain**. See *egg-shell*.—**Egyptian porcelain**. See *Egyptian*.—**Embossed porcelain**, porcelain the decoration of which is in slight relief. Especially—(*a*) When the relief is obtained by the decoration itself, as in *pâte sur pâte*. (*b*) Less properly, when the decoration is produced by casting or pressing the whole surface before the color is applied.—**False porcelain**, a name given by the first makers of hard-paste porcelain in England to the artificial or soft-paste porcelain.—**Frit porcelain**. See *frit*.—**Fusible porcelain**. Same as *cast porcelain*.—**Hizen porcelain**, porcelain made in Japan, in the province of Hizen, and often known as *Imari porcelain*, from the name of the seaport whence it is exported. The ware specially known as *Hizen* or *Imari* is decorated with blue under the glaze, and with red and sometimes green and gold upon the glaze, the green forming translucent enamels in slight relief. This ware was brought to Europe by the Dutch during the seventeenth and eighteenth centuries, and was known as Old Japan, until the recent investigation into the history of Japanese ceramics. Compare *Arita porcelain*.—**Hot-cast porcelain**. See *cast porcelain*.—**Hybrid porcelain**. See *hybrid*.—**Imari porcelain**, Japanese porcelain exported from the seaport of Imari, in the province of Hizen. See *Hizen porcelain*.—**Imperial yellow porcelain**. See *imperial*.—**Iran porcelain**, a name given to a hard white ware, with blue decoration in the Chinese style, which has many of the characteristics of porcelain. See *Kashee ware*, under *ware*2.—**Kiyomidzu porcelain**, a variety of Japanese porcelain the body of which is said to be artificial, composed of clay mixed with powdered silicious stone and having peculiarities also in the composition of the glaze.—**Kouan-Ki porcelain**, a name given to certain vases of Chinese porcelain of blue decoration, and marked with one or other of certain well-known emblems of the Chinese magistracy, such as the pearl (considered the emblem of talent or ability), the sacred ax, the sonorous stone, and a group of writing-materials.—**Limoges porcelain**, porcelain made at Limoges, in the department of Haute-Vienne, France. Especially—(*a*) A soft-paste porcelain made from 1773. (*b*) A hard-paste porcelain made from 1779 to the present day. The kaolin was obtained from St. Yrieix in the neighborhood, and the ware was especially brilliant and translucent as long as this alone was used. The modern porcelain includes much of the most important ceramic production of modern France.—**Lowestoft porcelain**, a porcelain made at Lowestoft in Suffolk, from 1757 to 1804, especially a hard-paste porcelain made after 1775: one of the most admired wares of English manufacture. The pieces were usually for table-services, and are remarkable for rich borders in which festoons are a common detail.—**Lunéville porcelain**, a soft-paste porcelain made at Lunéville in France, especially famous for the statuettes and groups in biscuit, of which the chief maker was Paul Louis Cyfflé. The paste of these seems to have been gradually improved by Cyfflé or others from the original *terre-de-Lorraine*, and the improved paste was called *pâte-de-marbre*. The name Cyfflé is commonly marked on these pieces.—**Mandarin porcelain**. See *mandarin*.—**May-flower porcelain**. See *May-flower*.—**Medici porcelain**, a translucent ceramic ware produced in or near Florence, under the Medicean grand dukes, in the sixteenth century. Pieces of this ware are of great rarity. The mark is sometimes the balls (palloni) of the Medici, and sometimes a rude picture of the dome of the Cathedral of Florence.—**Meissen-Saxony porcelain**, the name more properly given to the Dresden porcelain.—**Nankin porcelain**. Same as *blue china* (which see, under *china*).—**Natural soft-paste porcelain**, a name given by M. Brogniard, chief of the Sèvres works for many years, to those soft-paste porcelains which have clay for their basis, and therefore are properly ceramic wares.—**Parian porcelain**. See *Parian*.—**Petit porcelain**, porcelain made from 1834 at Paris by a potter named Jacob Petit, and of late years at Chantilly. This ware is of remarkable excellence, and the pieces of original design are important in the development of ceramic decoration; but the greater number of the present products are imitations of Dresden and other celebrated wares.—**Porcelain jasper**. See *jasper*, 2.—**Réaumur's porcelain**, an artificial or hybrid production of the eminent scientist Réaumur, differing from all porcelains properly so called, and not strictly a soft-paste porcelain, but rather a glass that has been exposed to a long-continued heat, which makes it opaque and of a milky white. This substance is called by the Germans *milch-glass*. The discovery had no important results.—**Rose porcelain**, Chinese porcelain in the decoration of which large surfaces of brilliant red enamel are used. Plates and dishes of which the outside is covered with this enamel are called *rose-back plates*, etc. The rose porcelain is to be distinguished from the porcelain of the so-called rose family, or *famille rose*.—**Royal Worcester porcelain**. See *Worcester porcelain*.—**Sèvres porcelain**, porcelain made at Sèvres, near Paris. Especially—(*a*) A soft-paste porcelain made from 1740, in which year the manufacture was removed from Vincennes. The celebrated colors *bleu du roi*, *bleu turquoise*, *rose Pompadour* (more commonly called *rose du Barry*), and others, were introduced for the soft-paste ware; and the decoration in gold raised in slight relief above the glaze, the addition of jewels, and the style of the paintings in medallions, all have their origin in this soft-paste ware, which was the only ware made at Sèvres before 1769, although the true hard porcelain had already been made at Meissen sixty years before. (See *Dresden porcelain*.) The soft-paste porcelain, now greatly in demand as a rarity, has one advantage over the hard-paste—in the slight absorption of the color by the paste, giving a pleasant softness of effect. (*b*) A hard-paste porcelain made from 1769, in consequence of the discovery of deposits of kaolin in France. This manufacture has reached greater merit of late years than before the revolution; in size and perfection the pieces surpass anything produced elsewhere, and the painting shows unparalleled skill and mastery of the material, whatever may be thought of its appropriateness and good taste as decoration. The mark under the kings of the old régime was always the royal cipher L L, front to front, crossing above and below, and within the space so inclosed a letter denoting the year of manufacture, a double alphabet beginning in 1778, AA, etc. Under the republic, the word Sèvres, and R. F. for République Française, were used; under the empire, M. Imple. de Sèvres, sometimes with the imperial eagle, was used. The restored kings used a cipher of LL and one of CC; Louis Philippe, a cipher L. P., and often the name of the palace for which the ware was made. The 1848 republic restored the R. F.; and the second empire, a crowned N, with S for Sèvres, and the date, as 56, 57. But since about 1830 all pieces are marked before decorating with the letter S, and a date in green included in a cartouche, and, when the piece is sold undecorated, this mark is cut through by a touch to a grinding-wheel.—**Solon porcelain**, porcelain made either at Paris or at the national factory at Sèvres, and decorated by a potter named Solon; especially, those pieces decorated in low relief by layers or coats of kaolinic slip applied one upon another, producing a bas-relief more or less translucent, according as the application is less or more thick.—**Swansea porcelain**, porcelain made at Swansea from about 1814 till 1820, when the factory was removed to Coalport. But little porcelain was made, as the factory was devoted chiefly to delf and what was called *opaque china*; but the quality of it was excellent, and it is ranked by some as the most perfect porcelain ever produced in England. The word Swansea, sometimes combined with a trident or with two tridents crossed, and sometimes with the name of the director for the time being, is used as a mark.—**Tender porcelain**, a ceramic ware in which the composition of hard-paste or natural porcelain is imitated. The clay of which it is made is an imperfect kaolin—that is to say, it contains too much of other substances in combination with the feldspar to furnish a natural porcelain.—**Worcester porcelain**, a soft-paste porcelain made at Worcester in England, from 1751, by an association called the Worcester Porcelain Company. Transfer printing was used in this ware at a very early time, and the association also produced a blue and white ware imitated from the Chinese, and made up in decorative pieces. A peculiar mottled quality of the blue, produced by the running of the color in firing, was especially admired. The manufacture is still continued by a joint-stock company. The epithet "Royal," often prefixed to the name "Worcester Porcelain," dates from 1788, when George III., on the occasion of a visit to the factory, conferred this appellation upon it. The paste was a very artificial composition, having little or no clay in it. The old Worcester porcelain seems to have had no mark peculiarly its own, but used a crescent, or some one of several "seal-marks" copied from Chinese porcelain, or a group of characters imitating Chinese but without signification. But from about 1828 the mark of Chamberlain & Co., and later a combination of W. W. W. with a date in the middle, have been used by the chief factory.

II. *a.* Of the nature of or consisting of porcelain: as, *porcelain* adornments.—**Porcelain mosaic**, a name given to tile-work in which the separate tiles are of uniform or nearly uniform color and composed of porcelain or fine pottery such as white stoneware.

porcelain²†, *n.* An obsolete form of *purslane.*

porcelain-cement (pôrs'lạn-sẹ-ment"), *n.* A cement, variously constituted, for mending chinaware or glassware.

porcelain-clay (pôrs'lạn-klā), *n.* Kaolin.

porcelain-color (pôrs'lạn-kul"ọr), *n.* A pigment used for painting on porcelain. Such pigments are either colored glasses reduced to powder, which, when fired or subjected to the action of heat, fuse upon the surface of the biscuit, or fluxes combined with metallic colors, usually oxids.

porcelain-crab (pôrs'lạn-krab), n. A crab of the genus *Porcellana:* so called from its shell, which is smooth and polished, as if made of porcelain. Several species are found on British coasts, the most interesting being the broad-clawed porcelain-crab, P. *platycheles*, taking its name from its singular flat broad claws, each of which is almost as large as the whole body. See *Porcellana*, 1.

porcelain-gilding (pôrs'lạn-gil"ding), *n.* A gold pigment used in decorating porcelain. It is a magma of gold, quicksilver, and flux, thinned with oil and turpentine. When fired, the volatile ingredients are sublimed, and the black magma assumes a dead-gold surface, which must be burnished to acquire the bright metallic appearance. Other compounds give a bright metallic surface from simple firing, but this is less durable than the burnished gold.

porcelainised, *a.* See *porcelainized.*

porcelainist (pôrs'lạn-ist), *n.* [< *porcelain*¹ + *-ist.*] 1. A student or collector of porcelain; also, an authority on porcelains.—2. A decorator of porcelain.

porcelainite (pôrs'lạn-īt), *n.* [< *porcelain*¹ + *-ite*².] A trade-name of certain kinds of fine white stoneware, jasper-ware, etc.

porcelainized (pôrs'lạn-īzd), *a.* [< *porcelain*¹ + *-ize* + *-ed*².] Baked like potters' clay; specifically, in *geol.*, hardened and altered, by contact or other metamorphism, so as to resemble in texture porcelain or earthenware: said of clays, shales, and other stratified rock. Also spelled *porcelainised.*

porcelain-jasper (pôrs'lạn-jas"pėr), *n.* See *jasper*, 2.

porcelain-lace (pôrs'lạn-lās), *n.* See *Berlin porcelain*, under *porcelain*¹.

porcelain-oven (pôrs'lạn-uv"n), n. The firing-kiln used in baking porcelain. Each oven is heated by a number of fireplaces arranged radially around its base, with flues converging to a central opening in the floor, through which the heated gases enter the oven. Other flues pass from the fireplaces (or *mouths*, as they are technically called) up in the sides of the ovens, and open into the interior about four feet above the floor. The oven is conoidal in form, and has an opening at its apex for the escape of gases and vapor. A number of these ovens or kilns are clustered about a central furnace called a *hovel.*

porcelain-paper (pôrs'lạn-pā"pėr), n. A glazed French paper, plain, gilt, painted, or figured.

porcelanaceous (pôr"se-lạ-nā'shius), *a.* [< *porcelain*¹ (*porcellan*) + *-aceous.*] Same as *porcelanous.*

porcelane (pôr'se-lān), n. [< Sp. *porcelana* = Pg. *porcellana*, *porcelana*, < It. *porcellana*, Venus-shell, porcelain: see *porcelain*¹.] The money-cowry, *Cypræa moneta.*

The cowry shells, which, under one name or another—changos, zimbis, bouges, *porcelanes*, etc.—have long been used in the East Indies as small money.
Jevons, Money and the Mechanism of Exchange, p. 24.

porcelane, porcellane (pôr'se-lān), *a.* [< *porcelain*¹ (*porcellan*).] Same as *porcelanous.*

porcelaneous (pôr-se-lā'nẹ-us), *a.* [< *porcelain*¹ (*porcellan*) + *-ous.*] Same as *porcelanous.*

porcelanian, porcellanian (pôr-se-lā'ni-ạn), *a.* [< *porcelain*¹ (*porcellan*) + *-ian.*] Porcelanous; specifically, noting the porcelain-crabs.

porcelanite, porcellanite (pôr'se-lạ-nīt), *n.* [= F. *porcellanite* = Pg. *porcelanite* = It. *porcellanite;* as *porcelain*¹ (*porcellan*) + *-ite*².] Clay metamorphosed into a rock resembling porcelain or earthenware in texture and appearance.

porcelanous, porcellanous (pôr'se-lạ-nus), *a.* [< *porcelain*¹ (*porcellan*) + *-ous.*] 1. Pertaining to or of the nature of porcelain.—2. Resembling porcelain in structure or appearance; hard, smooth, and opaque-white, as the shell of a mollusk or the carapace of a crustacean. Among foraminifers, a type of test is distinguished as *porcelanous* from *hyaline* or *vitreous;* and the three-layered type of mollusk-shell, each layer composed of plates set on edge, is called *porcelanous.*

porcellant†, *n.* and *a.* An obsolete form of *porcelain*¹.

Porcellana (pôr-se-lā'nạ̈), *n.* [NL., < It. *porcellana*, porcelain: see *porcelain*¹.] 1. The typical genus of *Porcellanidæ*, founded by Lamarck in 1801. *P. platycheles* and *P. longicornis* are two European species of porcelain-crabs.—2. A genus of porcelanous foraminifers.

porcellanaceous (pôr"se-lạ-nā'shius), *a.* [< *porcelain*¹ (*porcellan*) + *-aceous.*] Same as *porcelanous.*

porcellane, *a.* See *porcelane.*

porcellaneous (pôr-se-lā'nẹ-us), *a.* [< *porcelain*¹ (*porcellan*) + *-ous.*] Same as *porcelanous.*

porcellanian, *a.* See *porcelanian.*

Porcellanidæ (pôr-se-lan'i-dē), *n. pl.* [NL., < *Porcellana* + *-idæ.*] 1. A family of short-tailed ten-footed crustaceans, typified by the genus *Porcellana*, so called from the smoothness and hardness of the shell; the porcelain-crabs. The antennæ are very long, and the chelæ of great size.—2. In *conch.*, a family of gastropods: commonly called *Marginellidæ.*

porcellanite, *n.* See *porcelanite.*

porcellanous, *a.* See *porcelanous.*

porch (pōrch), *n.* [< ME. *porche*, < OF. *porche*, F. *porche* (also *portique*) = Pr. *porge*, *porgue* = Sp. *pórtico*, also (after F.) *porche*, a covered walk, = Pg. It. *portico*, porch, < L. *porticus*, porch, colonnade, gallery, < *porta*, door, gate: see *port*².] 1. In *arch.*, an exterior appendage to a building, forming a covered approach or vestibule to a doorway; a covered way or entrance, whether inclosed or uninclosed. Many church and cathedral porches are magnificent in proportions and decoration. See also cut under *caryatid.*

Porch.— South door of Gloucester Cathedral, England.

Into a church-*porch* then they went,
To stand out of the raine and wet.
Dutchess of Suffolk's Calamity (Child's Ballads, VII. 303).

To the *porch*, belike with jasmine bound
Or woodbine wreaths.
Wordsworth, Descriptive Sketches.

2. A covered walk, or portico; a stoa.

And in a *porche*, bilt of square stones
Full mightily enarched enuiron,
Where the domes and ples [pleas] of the town
Were executed, and lawes of the king.
Lydgate, Story of Thebes, ii.

Repair to Pompey's *porch*, where you shall find us.
Shak., *J. C.*, i. 3. 147.

3. A veranda. [Local, U. S.]—4. Figuratively, the beginning or entrance.

Cet. No age was spared, no sex.
Cat. Nay, no degree.
Cet. Not infants in the *porch* of life were free.
B. *Jonson*, Catiline, i. 1.

Solomon's Porch, a porch connected with and forming a part of Herod's Temple at Jerusalem, minutely described by Josephus.—**The Porch**, the Stoa Pœcile, one of the public porticos on the agora of ancient Athens, whither the Stoic philosopher Zeno resorted with his disciples. It was called the *Painted Porch*, from the pictures of Polygnotus and other eminent painters with which it was adorned. Hence, *the Porch* is equivalent to the *school of the Stoics.*

porcine (pôr'sin), *a.* [= F. *porcine* = Sp. Pg. It. *porcino*, < L. *porcinus*, of a hog, < *porcus*, hog: see *pork.*] 1. In *zoöl.*, resembling or related to swine; suilline: as, *porcine* characters or affinities.—2. Swinish; hoggish; piggish: applied to persons in derision or contempt.

His large *porcine* cheeks, round, twinkling eyes, and thumbs habitually twirling, expressed a concentrated effort not to get into trouble. *George Eliot*, Felix Holt, xx.

porcupig† (pôr'kụ-pig), *n.* Same as *porcupine.*

You would have thought him for to be
Some Egyptian *porcupig.*
Dragon of Wantley, l. 84. (*Percy's Reliques.*)

porcupike†, *n.* Same as *porcupine.* *Holyoke.*

porcupine (pôr'kụ-pīn), *n.* [< ME. *porkepyn*, also, then or later, reduced to *porkpen*, *porpyn*, *porpin*, *porpint*, *porkpoint*, *porpoint*, *perpoint*, *porpoynte* (simulating *point*), whence *porpentine*, *purpentine;* < OF. *porc espin*, *porch espin*, also *porc d'espine*, F. *porte-espine* (simulating *porter*, carry, as if 'carry-spine') (OF. also *porc-espic*, *porc-espi*, F. *porc-épic* (whence obs. E. *porkespick*, also *porcupike*, simulating *pike*¹, and *porcupig*, simulating *pig*¹) = Pr. *porc-espi:* simulating OF. *espic*, spike) = Sp. *puerco espin* = Pg. *porco espinho* = It. *porco spino* (also *porco spinoso*, < ML. *porcus spinosus*), a porcupine, lit. 'spine-hog,' < L. *porcus*, a hog, + *spina*, ML. also *spinus*, a spine, thorn: see *pork* and *spine.* Cf. equiv. D. *stekel-varken*, *stekelzwijn*, G. *stachelschwein*, 'thorn-hog'; Sw. *piusvin* = Dan. *pindsvin*, 'pin-hog.'] 1. A hystricomorphic rodent quadruped of the family *Hystricidæ*, of which there are several genera and many species, representing two subfamilies, the *Hystricinæ* or Old World porcupines, which are all terrestrial and fossorial animals, and the *Sphingurinæ* or New World porcupines, more or less arboreal, and in some cases having a prehensile tail. The spines or quills with which these animals are beset reach their highest development in species of *Hystrix* proper, as *H. cristata*,

European Porcupine (*Hystrix cristata*).

the common porcupine of southern Europe and northern Africa. Such quills may be a foot long; they are prettily variegated in color, and much used for penholders. Brush-tailed porcupines constitute the genus *Atherura*, and inhabit the Malay region and Africa. The only North American porcupines belong to the genus *Erethizon*, of which there are 2 species, the common eastern *E. dorsatus*, and the western yellow-haired *E. epixanthus;* in both the spines are only an inch or two long, and mostly hidden in long hair. They are of large size, reaching 2½ feet in length, and of ungainly form and ugly visage, with an extremely stout and clumsy body and broad, flat, blunt tail. One or the other species is found from the northern limit of trees through the greater part of the United States.

The spines grow mostly on the rump and back of the broad flat tail; they are quite loosely attached, and when the animal slaps with its tail (its usual mode of defense) some quills may be flirted to a distance. Something like this, no doubt, gives rise to the popular notion that the porcu-

Urson, or Canada Porcupine (*Erethizon dorsatus*).

pine "shoots" its quills at an enemy. These small quills are strikingly like the spines of the prickly-pear (*Opuntia*) in size and shape, and like them are minutely barbed at the end, so that they stick in the flesh of one who receives a blow from the tail. They are much used by the Indians for trimming buckskin garments and ornamenting moccasins. Other American tree-porcupines constitute the genera *Sphingurus* and *Chætomys*; they are of smaller size and arboreal habits, and range from southern Mexico through a great part of South America. See *Hystricidæ*, *Hystrix*; also cut under *prehensile-tailed*.
2. (*a*) An apparatus for heckling flax. (*b*) A cylindrical heckle for worsted yarn. *E. H. Knight.* —**Porcupine ant-eater**, a monotreme of the family *Echidnidæ* or *Tachyglossidæ*, having spines or quills in the pelage resembling those of the porcupine. *Echidna* or *Tachyglossus hystrix* is the best-known species, inhabiting Australia. There are several others. See cut under *Echidnidæ*.

porcupine† (pôr'kū̦-pīn), *v. t.* [< *porcupine*, *n.*] To cause to stand up like a porcupine's quills. [Rare.]

Thus did the cooks on Billy Ramus stare,
Whose frightful presence *porcupined* each hair.
Wolcot (Peter Pindar), The Lousiad, iv.

porcupine-crab (pôr'kū̦-pīn-krab), *n.* A kind of crab, *Lithodes hystrix*, inhabiting Japan, having the carapace and limbs spiny.

porcupine-disease (pôr'kū̦-pīn-di-zēz"), *n.* Same as *hystricismus*.

porcupine-fish (pôr'kū̦-pīn-fish), *n.* A diodontoid fish, as *Diodon hystrix*, whose skin is studded with prickles; a sea-porcupine. The various species inhabit tropical seas. See *Diodontidæ*, and cuts under *Diodon* and *swell-fish*.

porcupine-grass (pôr'kū̦-pīn-gràs), *n.* A grass, *Stipa spartea*, found from Illinois and Michigan northwestward: so named from the long, strong awns of its flowering glume.

porcupine-wood (pôr'kū̦-pīn-wu̇d), *n.* The outer wood of the cocoanut-palm, which is very hard and durable, and when cut horizontally displays beautiful markings resembling those of porcupine-spines.

pore[1] (pōr), *v. i.*; pret. and pp. *pored*, ppr. *poring*. [Early mod. E. also *poar*; < ME. *poren*, *pouren*, prob. < Sw. dial. *pora*, *pura*, *påra*, work slowly and gradually, do anything slowly, Sw. *purra*, turn out; cf. D. *porren*, p ke, stir, move, endeavor, attempt, = MLG. LG. *purren* = Dan. *purre*, poke, stir; perhaps of Celtic origin: cf. Gael. Ir. *purr*, push, thrust, drive, urge. Prob. in part confused with *peer*, ME. *piren*, *puren*, look: see *peer*[1].] To gaze earnestly or steadily; look with close and steady attention or application; read or examine anything with steady perseverance: generally followed by *on*, *upon*, or *over*.

What [why] sholde he studie and make hymselven wood
Upon a book in cloystre alwey to *poure*?
Chaucer, Gen. Prol. to C. T., l. 185.

Painfully to *pore upon* a book
To seek the light of truth. *Shak.*, L. L. L., i. 1. 74.

Many of the Pilgrims, by *poaring on* hot bricks, do voluntarily perish their sights. *Sandys*, Travailes, p. 97.

pore[2] (pōr), *n.* [< F. *pore* = Pr. *pors* = Sp. Pg. It. *poro* = D. *porie* = G. *pore* = Sw. *por* = Dan. *pore*, < L. *porus*, a pore, < Gr. πόρος, a pore, ford, passage, way, means, pore, fiber of the nerves, etc., < √ περ in περᾶν, pass: see *fare*[1], *ford*.] 1. A small opening or orifice; a hole, aperture, or perforation; a foramen; an opening in general: as, the *pores* of a sponge. The term is especially used for a minute perforation, invisible to the naked eye, in a membrane, through which fluids may pass. Such are the pores of the skin, formed by the ducts of the sweat-glands.

The sweats came gushing out of euery *pore*.
Chapman, Odyssey, xi.

And gathering virtue in at every *pore*.
Lowell, Under the Willows.

2. One of the small interstices between the particles or molecules of the matter of which a body is composed. The compressibility of matter, its expansion and contraction with changes of temperature, and other considerations lead to the conclusion that even the densest bodies are porous—that is, that the molecules forming them are not in actual contact, but separated by spaces which, though extremely minute, may have a magnitude considerable as compared with their own size.

Which Atoms are still hovering up and down, and never rest till they meet with some *Pores* proportionable and cognate to their Figures, where they acquiesce.
Howell, Letters, iv. 50.

3. In *bot.*, a small aperture or hole, as that at the apex of the anthers in certain *Ericaceæ*; in *Pyrenomycetes*, same as *ostiole*; in *Hymenomycetes*, same as *tubulus*. See cut under *anther*. —**Abdominal, branchial, calycine pore.** See the adjectives.—**Cortical pore**, in *bot.*, same as *lenticel*.—**Crural** or **femoral pores.** See *crural*.—**Metasternal pores.** See *metasternal*.

pore[3]†, *v.* An obsolete form of *pour*[1].

pore[4], *a.* An obsolete or dialectal form of *poor*.

poreblind†, *a.* An obsolete form of *purblind*.

porencephalia (pō-ren-se-fā'li-ạ), *n.* [NL., < Gr. πόρος, pore, + ἐγκέφαλος, brain.] The presence of a defect in the cerebral hemisphere such that a depression or hollow, which may lead into the ventricle, is formed. It is congenital, or from early life, and may be caused by inflammation, embolus, or hemorrhage.

porencephalic (pō-ren-se-fal'ik or po-ren-sef'a-lik), *a.* [< *porencephal-y* + *-ic.*] Of or pertaining to or of the nature of porencephaly; porencephalous.

porencephalous (pō-ren-sef'a-lus), *a.* [< *porencephal-y* + *-ous.*] Pertaining to, of the nature of, or characterized by porencephalia.

porencephaly (pō-ren-sef'a-li), *n.* [< NL. *porencephalia.*] Same as *porencephalia*.

poret†, *n.* See *porret*.

porfilt, *v.* and *n.* See *purfle*.

porgy (pôr'gi), *n.*; pl. *porgies* (-giz). [Also *porgie*, *poggy*, *poggie*, *paughie*; said to be corrupted from NL. *pagrus*: see *Pagrus*.] One of several different fishes. (*a*) A fish of the genus *Sparus* in a restricted sense, or of the genus *Pagrus*; specifically, *Sparus pagrus* or *Pagrus vulgaris*, supposed to be

Porgy (*Sparus pagrus*).

the *pagrus* of the ancients, inhabiting the Mediterranean and Atlantic waters, of a silvery color, with the back rosy. (*b*) A fish of the related genus *Stenotomus*. *S. argyrops* is the well-known porgy, scup, or scuppaug, found from Cape Cod to Florida. See *scup*. (*c*) An ephippioid fish, *Chætodipterus faber*, the angel-fish. See cut under *Chætodipterus*. (*d*) One of several viviparous perches, or embiotocoids, as *Ditrema jacksoni* or *Damalichthys argyrosomus* (or *vacca*). [California.] (*e*) A clupeoid fish, the menhaden, *Brevoortia tyrannus*: by confusion with a different word, *pogy*. [Local, U. S.] (*f*) The toadfish, *Chilomycterus geometricus*. [Florida.] (*g*) With a qualifying word, one of several other fishes. See phrases below.—**Flannel-mouthed porgy**, *Orthopristis chrysopterus*.—**Goat-head porgy**, *Calamus megacephalus*. [Bermudas.]—**Rhomboidal porgy**, *Lagodon rhomboides*.—**Sheep's-head porgy**, *Calamus orbitarius*. [Bermudas.]—**Spanish porgy.** (*a*) The rhomboidal porgy. [Bermudas.] (*b*) A scaroid fish, *Scarus radians*.—**Three-tailed porgy**, the moonfish, *Chætodipterus* or *Parephippus faber*.

pori, *n.* Plural of *porus*.

porifer (pō'ri-fėr), *n.* [< NL. *porifer*, having pores: see *poriferous*.] That which has pores, as a sponge; a member of the *Porifera*.

Porifera (pō-rif'e-rạ), *n. pl.* [NL., neut. pl. of *porifer*, q. v.] 1. The sponges as a prime division of cœlenterates, or superclass of *Cœlentera*, having a system of pores or incurrent and excurrent openings, but no stinging-or-

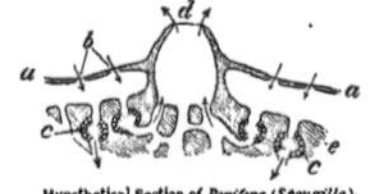

Hypothetical Section of *Porifera* (*Spongilla*).

a, superficial layer; *b*, inhalent apertures; *c*, ciliated or flagellated chambers, lined with a layer of sponge-cells which are the individual animalcules (closely resembling choanoflagellate infusorians), all the rest of the structure being the fibrous skeleton which they produce in common; *d*, an osculum, or exhalent aperture; *e*, deeper substance of the sponge.

gans: contrasted with *Nematophora*, and more fully called *Cœlentera porifera*. It is a name of sponges when these are regarded as cœlenterates, to distinguish them from the true cœlenterates, then called *Nematophora*. A usual division of *Porifera* is into *Calcispongiæ* or *Megamastictora*, the chalk-sponges; and *Silicospongiæ* or *Micromastictora*, all other sponges; but nearly every writer on sponges has his own classification. See *Spongiæ*, and cuts under *sponge* and *Spongilla*. Also called *Poriferata*.
2. Same as *Foraminifera*.

poriferal (pō̦-rif'e̦-ral), *a.* [< *porifer-ous* + *-al.*] Poriferous, as a sponge; of or pertaining to the *Porifera* or *Spongiæ*.

poriferan (pō̦-rif'e̦-ran), *n.* and *a.* [< *porifer-ous* + *-an.*] I. *n.* A porifer; a sponge.
II. *a.* Same as *poriferous*.—**Poriferan theory**, that theory which considers the tracheæ or tubes of some animals as having a common origin with the incurrent tubes of the *Porifera* or sponges.

poriferous (pō̦-rif'e̦-rus), *a.* [< NL. *porifer*, having pores, < L. *porus*, pore, + *ferre* = E. *bear*[1].] Provided with pores; specifically, of or pertaining to the *Porifera*; poriferal: distinguished from *osculiferous*.

poriform (pō'ri-fôrm), *a.* [< L. *porus*, a pore, + *forma*, form.] Having the character or form of a pore.

porime (pō'rim), *n.* Same as *porism*.

porism (pō'rizm), *n.* [ME. *porysme*, < OF. (and F.) *porisme* = Sp. *porisma* = It. *porisma*, *porismate*, *porismato*; < Gr. πόρισμα(τ-), a corollary, < πορίζειν, bring about, procure, deduce, < πόρος, a way, passage: see *pore*[2], *n.*] A form of mathematical proposition among the Greeks, concerning the nature of which there continues to be much dispute. The corollaries to Euclid's elements—that is, extra propositions, inserted by commentators and readily deducible from his theorems—are called by this name. But the word had a more general meaning, which Chasles defines as follows: A porism is an incomplete theorem expressing a relation between things variable according to a common law, the statement being left incomplete in regard to some magnitude which would be stated in the theorem properly so called. For example, to say that there is within every triangle a point every line through which has for the sum of its distances from the two vertices which lie on one side of it its distance from the third vertex, is a porism in substance. But the porism was further distinguished by a peculiar mode of enunciation, namely, that which in modern language is made to be constant, is called in the porism "given." The definition of Playfair, which has had great currency, is as follows: A porism is a proposition affirming the possibility of finding such conditions as will render a certain problem indeterminate, or capable of innumerable solutions. This is the sense in which the word would ordinarily be understood to-day. Other widely different definitions have been given.

Ryht as thyse geometryens, whan they have shewyd hyr proposiciouns, ben wont to bryngen in thinges that they clepen *porysmes*, or declaraciouns of forseyde thinges.
Chaucer, Boëthius, iii. prose 10.

=**Syn.** See *inference*.

porismatic (pō-ris-mat'ik), *a.* [< Gr. πόρισμα(τ-), a porism, + *-ic.*] Of or pertaining to a porism. [As used by modern mathematicians, it usually refers to Playfair's sense of *porism*. See *porism*.]

porismatical (pō-ris-mat'i-kal), *a.* [< *porismatic* + *-al.*] Same as *porismatic*.

poristic (pō̦-ris'tik), *a.* [= F. *poristique* = Pg. *poristica* = It. *poristico*; < Gr. ποριστικός, able to bring about or procure, < πορίζειν, bring about, procure: see *porism*.] Reducing a determinate problem to an indeterminate one.—**Poristic points**, a set of points of the number which usually suffice to determine a curve of a given order, but so situated that an indefinite number of such curves can be drawn through them.

poristical (pō̦-ris'ti-kal), *a.* [< *poristic* + *-al.*] Same as *poristic*.

porite (pō'rit), *n.* [< NL. *Porites*.] A coral of the family *Poritidæ*.

Porites (pō̦-rī'tēz), *n.* [NL., < L. *porus*, a pore: see *pore*[2].] 1. The typical genus of the family *Poritidæ*, established by Lamarck.—2. A genus of millepores. Also *Heliolites*. *Lonsdale*, 1849.

Porites clavaria.

Poritidæ (pō̦-rit'i-dē), *n. pl.* [NL., < *Porites* + *-idæ*.] A family of perforate sclerodermatous corals, typified by the genus *Porites*. The corallum is composed of reticulated sclerenchyme, with well-developed septa in the form of stylate processes which unite in a kind of latticework. The walls are reticulate, not distinct from the sclerenchyme, and there are few dissepiments and no tabulæ.

pork (pōrk), *n.* [< ME. *pork*, *poork*, *porc*, < OF. (and F.) *porc* = Sp. *puerco* = Pg. It. *porco*, a hog, pork, < L. *porcus* (= Gr. (Italic ?) πόρκος), a swine, hog, pig (*porca*, f., or *porcus femina*, a sow), = Lith. *parszas* = W. *porch* = Ir. *orc* (with reg. loss of initial *p*) = AS. *fearh*, E. *farrow*, a pig: see *farrow*[1].] 1. A swine; hog; pig; porker.

> Poveralle and pastorelles passede one aftyre,
> With *porkes* to pasture at the price gates.
> *Morte Arthure* (E. E. T. S.), l. 3122.

2. The flesh of swine, used as meat.

> Then for ten days did I diet him
> Only with burnt *pork*, sir, and gammons of bacon.
> *Fletcher (and another)*, Love's Cure, iii. 2.

3†. A stupid, obstinate, or ignorant person; a pig-headed fellow.

> I mean not to dispute philosophy with this *pork*, who never read any. *Milton*, Colasterion.

Mess pork, the best quality or grade of pork: so called originally because in the navy the best pork was supplied to the officers' mess.

pork-butcher (pōrk'bůch″ėr), *n.* One who kills pigs.

pork-chop (pōrk'chop'), *n.* A slice from the ribs of a pig.

pork-eater (pōrk'ē″tėr), *n.* One who feeds on swine's flesh.

> If we grow all to be *pork-eaters*, we shall not shortly have a rasher on the coals for money.
> *Shak.*, M. of V., iii. 5. 27.

porker (pōr'kėr), *n.* [< *pork* + *-er*[1]; perhaps orig. for *porket*.] A hog; a pig; especially, one fatted for killing.

> Straight to the lodgments of his herd he run,
> Where the fat *porkers* slept beneath the sun.
> *Pope*, Odyssey, xiv. 86.

porkespick†, *n.* Same as *porcupine*.

> He gaue for his deuice the *porkespick* with this posie, pres et loign, both farre and neare.
> *Puttenham*, Arte of Eng. Poesie, p. 118.

porket (pōr'ket), *n.* [< OF. *porquet*, *porchet*, *pourchet* (= It. *porchetto*), dim. of *porc*, a hog: see *pork*.] A young hog.

> We now are Gergesites, that would rather lose Christ than our *porkets*.
> *J. Bradford*, Letters (Parker Soc., 1853), II. 64.

porkling (pōrk'ling), *n.* [< *pork* + *-ling*[1].] A young pig.

> Through plenty of acorns the *porklings* to fat.
> *Tusser*, October's Husbandry, st. 34.

porknell†, *n.* [ME., < *pork* + double dim. *-n-el*.] A little pig; also, a gross, fat person.

> Polidárius, the *porknell*, and his pere Machaon,
> Suet with the xvij, sad men & noble.
> *Destruction of Troy* (E. E. T. S.), l. 6368.

pork-pie (pōrk'pī'), *n.* A pie made of pastry and minced pork.—**Pork-pie hat**, the popular name of a hat resembling a deep meat-pie, worn by both men and women about 1860, distinguished by a brim which turned up around the crown, leaving but a narrow space between the crown and itself, the crown being low and the brim sloping slightly outward.

pork-pit (pōrk'pit), *n.* That part of the floor of a produce-exchange in which dealers in pork congregate and transact their business.

pork-pork† (pōrk'pōrk), *v. i.* [Imitative. Cf. *more-pork*.] To utter the cry of the raven; sound like the cry of a raven.

> From the mountains nigh,
> The rav'ns begin with their *pork-porking* cry.
> *Sylvester*, tr. of Du Bartas's Weeks, ii., The Schisme.

pork-sausage (pōrk'sâ″sāj), *n.* A sausage made of minced pork with various seasoning or flavoring ingredients.

porkwood (pōrk'wůd), *n.* The pigeonwood, beefwood, or corkwood, *Pisonia obtusata*.

porky (pōr'ki), *a.* [< *pork* + *-y*[1].] 1. Pork-like: as, a *porky* odor permeated the whole place.—2. Fat; plump.

pornial (pôr'ni-al), *a.* [< Gr. πορνεία, prostitution, a prostitute, + *-al*.] Lawlessly passionate; meretricious.

> To the "*pornial* fire" of the Elizabethan period had succeeded an age of patient research and cool criticism.
> *The American*, VI. 41.

pornocracy (pôr-nok'rā-si), *n.* [< Gr. πόρνη, a prostitute (prob. orig. 'a bought female captive,' < περνάναι (πέρνημι), send or export for sale, sell, esp. of captives who were transported and sold: akin to L. *pretium*, price: see *price*), + -κρατία, < κρατεῖν, rule.] The rule of prostitutes; dominating influence of courtezans.—**The Pornocracy**, a party which controlled the government of Rome and the elections to the papacy throughout the first half of the tenth century; the rule or government of this party: so called from the paramount influence of three women of noble family but profligate lives, Theodora and her daughters Theodora and Marozia (Mary).

pornograph (pôr'nǫ-grȧf), *n.* [< LGr. πορνογράφος, writing of prostitutes: see *pornography*.] An obscene picture or writing.

pornographer (pôr-nog'rạ-fėr), *n.* [< *pornograph-y* + *-er*.] One who writes of prostitutes or obscene subjects.

> The literary offences of French *pornographers* and coprologists. *Fortnightly Rev.*, N. S., XLIII. 745.

pornographic (pôr-nǫ-graf'ik), *a.* [< *pornograph-y* + *-ic*.] Of, pertaining to, or of the nature of pornography; describing or descriptive of prostitutes; having to do with pornographs.

pornography (pôr-nog'rạ-fi), *n.* [= F. *pornographie*; LGr. as if *πορνογραφία, < πορνογράφος, writing of prostitutes, painting prostitutes, < Gr. πόρνη, a prostitute, + γράφειν, write.] A description of or treatise on prostitutes or prostitution; hence, obscene writing.

porodinic (pō-rǫ-din'ik), *a.* [< Gr. πόρος, a pore, + ὠδίς, the pangs of labor.] Reproducing or bringing forth by means of a special pore or opening of the body, through which the genital products are extruded: distinguished from *schizodinic*. Two porodinic methods are distinguished as *nephrodinic* and *idiodinic*. *Encyc. Brit.*, XVI. 682.

porophyllous (pō-rō-fil'us), *a.* [< Gr. πόρος, pore, + φύλλον, leaf.] Having leaves sprinkled with transparent points. *Thomas*, Med. Dict.

Porosa (pǫ-rō'sạ̈), *n. pl.* [NL., neut. pl. of *porosus*: see *porose*.] Perforate or porose corals: distinguished from *Aporosa* or *Eporosa*. *Perforata* is a synonym.

porose (pō'rōs), *a.* [< NL. *porosus*, full of pores: see *porous*.] 1. Containing pores; porous; perforate. Specifically—(*a*) Of corals, perforate: distinguished from *aporose* or *eporose*. (*b*) Of the sculpture of insects, dotted or pitted as if full of little holes. The elytra of species of *Apion*, for example, are porose.

2. In *bot.*, pierced with small holes or pores.

porosis (pǫ-rō'sis), *n.* [NL., < Gr. πώρωσις, the process by which the extremities of fractured bones are reunited, < πωροῦν, cause a callus to form, unite (fractured bones) by a callus, < πῶρος, a node on the bones.] Formation of callus, as in the knitting together of broken bones.

porosity (pō-ros'i-ti), *n.* [= F. *porosité* = Sp. *porosidad* = Pg. *porosidade* = It. *porosità*, < NL. *porosita(t-)s*, < *porosus*, porous: see *porous*.] 1. The state or quality of being porose, porous, or pervious; perforation.

> The fifteenth [cause] is the *porosity* or imporosity betwixt the tangible parts, and the greatness or smallness of the pores. *Bacon*, Nat. Hist., § 846.

> All matter is porous or possesses *porosity*. Hydrogen gas leaks through white-hot iron under pressure; cold water can be pressed through iron . . . or through lead.
> *Daniell*, Prin. of Physics, p. 194.

2. A pore or perforation.

> The nerves with their invisible *porosities*.
> *Dr. H. More*, Immortal. of Soul, ii. 8.

porotype (pō'rǫ-tīp), *n.* [< Gr. πόρος, a pore, + τύπος, impression.] A print produced by exposing another print or a writing, placed on the surface of chemically prepared paper, to a gas which permeates those parts of the thing to be copied which are not rendered impervious by the ink, and thus acts upon the chemical surface in the same way that light acts upon the sensitized film of paper exposed under a photographic negative.

porous (pō'rus), *a.* [= D. *poreus* = G. Sw. Dan. *porös* = OF. *poreux*, F. *poreux* = Pr. *poros* = Sp. Pg. It. *poroso*, < NL. *porosus*, porous, < L. *porus*, pore: see *pore*[2].] Having pores; porose; pervious by means of minute interstices.

> Through veins
> Of *porous* earth, with kindly thirst up drawn,
> Rose a fresh fountain. *Milton*, P. L., iv. 228.

> According to what is here presented, what is most dense and least *porous* will be most coherent and least discernible. *Glanville*, Vanity of Dogmatizing, v.

> A sponge is *porous*, having small spaces between the solid parts.
> *Theodore Parker*, Ten Sermons, Justice and her Conscience.

Porous cup, a vessel of unglazed earthenware used in a voltaic cell to separate the two liquids employed. See *cell*, 8.—**Porous plaster.** See *plaster*.

porously (pō'rus-li), *adv.* By means of pores; in a porous manner; perviously; interstitially.

porousness (pō'rus-nes), *n.* 1. Porosity.

> Some fish have no mouths, but are nourished and take breath by the *porousness* of their gills.
> *I. Walton*, Complete Angler, p. 73.

2. The pores or porous parts of anything. [Rare.]

> They will forcibly get into the *porousness* of it, and pass between part and part. *Sir K. Digby*, Nature of Bodies.

porpaise†, *n.* An obsolete form of *porpoise*.

porpentine†, *n.* Same as *porcupine*.

porpesse†, *n.* An obsolete form of *porpoise*.

porpezite (pôr'pez-īt), *n.* [< *Porpez* (see def.) + *-ite*[2].] A variety of native gold containing a small percentage of palladium. That first described was from Porpez in Brazil.

porphire†, *n.* An obsolete variant of *porphyry*.

porphurie†, *n.* An obsolete variant of *porphyry*.

Porphyra (pôr'fi-rạ̈), *n.* [NL. (Agardh), < Gr. πορφύρα, purple: see *porphyry*.] A small genus of floridcous algæ, giving name to the suborder *Porphyreæ*. The fronds are gelatinous, membranaceous, and composed of a single layer of brownish-red cells bearing the spores on the margin of the frond, eight in number, arising from a single mother-cell. *P. laciniata*, the laver, is the best-known and most widely distributed species. It has fronds from 3 to 18 inches in length, of a livid-purple color. See *laver*[2], 1, and *marine sauce* (under *marine*).

porphyraceous (pôr-fi-rā'shius), *a.* [< *porphyr-y* + *-aceous*.] Same as *porphyritic*.

porphyre† (pôr'fīr), *n.* An obsolete form of *porphyry*.

> Consider the red and white colours in *porphyre*; hinder light but from striking on it, its colours vanish, and produce no such ideas in us; but upon the return of light it produces these appearances again. *Locke*.

Porphyreæ (pôr-fir'ę̄-ē), *n. pl.* [NL., < *Porphyra* + *-eæ*.] A small suborder of floridcous algæ, typified by the genus *Porphyra*, and characterized by having brownish-purple fronds, which are composed of cells embedded in a gelatinous network, and arranged in filaments or in membranes formed of a single layer of cells. The spores, of which there are eight, formed by a division of each mother-cell, are arranged by fours in two layers; the antherozoids are spherical, colorless, and formed by the division of a mother-cell into 32 or 64 parts.

Porphyrio (pôr-fir'i-ō), *n.* [NL. (Brisson, 1760), < L. *porphyrio(n-)* (> It. *porfirione* = Sp. *porfirion* = Pg. *porfirião* = F. *porphyrion*), < Gr. πορφυρίων, the purple gallinule (*Porphyrio veterum*), < πορφύρα, purple: see *porphyry*.] 1. A genus of *Rallidæ*, representing a subfamily *Porphyrioninæ*; the porphyrios, sultans, hyacinths, or hyacinthine gallinules. These birds are closely related to the common gallinules or water-hens, but are generally of larger size, with stouter bill and longer legs, and more stately carriage; the plumage is very rich and elegant, with intense blue, purple, and other striking tints. There are about 12 species, inhabiting warm temperate and tropical countries of both hemispheres. They live in marshes, like other ralliform or paludicole birds of the same family, and their habits are similar. *P. veterum* is the form of

Black-backed Sultan (*Porphyrio melanotus*).

southern Europe and northern Africa; *P. smaragnotus* is African, *P. melanotus* Australian. The purple gallinule of America is *P. martinicus*, often placed in a separate genus *Ionornis*. See *gallinule*.

2. [*l. c.*] A bird of this genus; a sultan; a purple gallinule.

Porphyrioninæ (pôr-fir″i-ǫ-nī'nē), *n. pl.* [NL., < *Porphyrio(n-)* + *-inæ*.] A subfamily of paludicole or ralliform wading birds of the family *Rallidæ*, represented by the genus *Porphyrio*, having the bill stout, with the base of the culmen mounting on the forehead as a frontal shield, the legs long and strong, and the toes margined; the purple gallinules, usually retained in *Gallinulinæ*.

porphyrionine (pôr-fir'i-ǭ-nin), *a.* [< NL. *Porphyrioninæ*, q. v.] Belonging to the *Porphyrioninæ*.

porphyrisation, porphyrise. See *porphyrization*, *porphyrize*.

porphyrite (pôr'fi-rīt), *n.* [< L. *porphyrites*: see *porphyry*.] The name given to those porphyries in which the ground-mass consists chiefly of a triclinic feldspar, together with either augite or hornblende, or, in some cases, of biotite: in this ground-mass larger crystals of the same species are porphyritically developed. The porphyrites are classed by some authors as diorite- or diabase-porphyrites: in the former the ground-mass contains hornblende; in the latter, augite in connection with the plagioclase. With these occur certain accessory minerals, such as magnetite, titaniferous iron, etc. Various names are given to these rocks, in accordance with the nature of the minerals porphyritically developed in the ground-mass, as hornblende *porphyrite*, mica *porphyrite*, augite *porphyrite*, etc.

porphyritic (pôr-fi-rit'ik), *a.* [= F. *porphyritique* = It. *porfiritico*, < L. *porphyrites*: see *por-*

phyry.] Containing or resembling porphyry; composed of a compact homogeneous rock in which distinct crystals or grains of feldspar or some other minerals are embedded: as, *porphyritic* granite. Also *porphyraceous*, and sometimes, incorrectly, *porphyroid*.

porphyritical (pôr-fi-rit'i-kal), *a.* [< *porphyritic* + *-al.*] Same as *porphyritic*.

Porphyritic Structure.

porphyritically (pôr-fi-rit'i-kal-i), *adv.* In a porphyritic manner; as in porphyry.

They [crystals of black hornblende] are *porphyritically* scattered through the gray ground-mass. *Amer. Jour. Sci.*, 3d ser., XXXI. 40.

porphyrization (pôr″fi-ri-zā'shọn), *n.* [= F. *porphyrisation* = Pg. *porphyrisação*; as *porphyrize* + *-ation.*] 1. The act of porphyrizing, or the state of being porphyrized.—2. The process of grinding a substance with a muller on a slab of porphyry or other hard stone. It is much used in the preparation of colors, and takes its name from the especial suitability of porphyry, from its hardness, as a bed for grinding upon.

Also spelled *porphyrisation*.

porphyrize (pôr'fi-rīz), *v. t.*; pret. and pp. *porphyrized*, ppr. *porphyrizing*. [= F. *porphyriser* = Pg. *porphyrisar*; < *porphyr-y* + *-ize*. Cf. Gr. πορφυρίζειν, be purplish.] 1. To cause to resemble porphyry.—2. To grind with a muller upon a slab of porphyry, as painters' colors.

Also spelled *porphyrise*.

porphyrogeniti, *n.* Plural of *porphyrogenitus*.

porphyrogenetic (pôr″fi-rọ̄-jẹ-net'ik), *a.* [< *porphyr-y* + Gr. γεννητικός, productive: see *genetic*.] Producing or generating porphyry.

porphyrogenitism (pôr″fi-rọ̄-jen'i-tizm), *n.* [< *porphyrogenitus* + *-ism.*] That principle of succession in royal families, especially in the families of the Byzantine emperors, in accordance with which a younger son, if born in the purple—that is, after the succession of his parents to the throne—was preferred to an older son who was not.

Henry the porphyrogenitus, though a younger son relatively to Otho, who was the eldest son of royal blood, first-born after the accession of Duke Henry to the throne of Charlemagne, the first-born of Henry, King of Germany. . . . The doctrine of *porphyrogenitism*, congenial to popular sentiment, and not without some foundation in principle, prevailed influentially and widely in many countries and through many ages. *Sir F. Palgrave*, Hist. Eng. and Normandy, II. 210.

porphyrogenitus (pôr″fi-rọ̄-jen'i-tus), *n.*; pl. *porphyrogeniti* (-tī). [ML. (> It. *porfirogenito* = Pg. *porphyrogenito* = F. *porphyrogénète*, a.); adapted (with L. *genitus*) < LGr. πορφυρογέννητος, born in the purple, < Gr. πορφύρα, purple (see *purple*), + γεννητός, begotten, < γενναῖν, beget: see *genetic*.] A title given, especially in the Byzantine empire, to those sons of a sovereign who are born after his accession to the throne. See *porphyrogenitism*.

porphyroid (pôr'fi-roid), *n.* [< Gr. πορφύρα, purple, + εἶδος, form.] A sedimentary rock, originally (in some cases at least) a clay slate, or quartzite, which has been altered by dynamic metamorphism or by some other metamorphic agency so as to take on a slaty and more or less perfectly developed porphyritic structure. The occurrence of this slaty structure is accompanied by the development of some micaceous mineral, usually sericite or paragonite. Rocks to which the name *porphyroid* has been applied, and in regard to the exact nature and origin of which lithologists are not entirely in agreement, have been described from Saxony, the Ardennes, Westphalia, Nevada, etc.

Porphyrophora (pôr-fi-rof'ọ̄-rä), *n.* [NL., < Gr. πορφύρα, purple, + φέρειν = E. *bear*[1].] A genus of *Coccidæ* or scale-insects. *P. polonica*, formerly *Coccus polonicus*, the Polish berry, is a scale long known as yielding a kind of red dye. Compare *Margarodes*.

porphyry (pôr'fi-ri), *n.* [Formerly also *porphiric* (and *porphire, porphyre*); < ME. *porphuric, porfuric* = D. *porfier, porphier* = G. *porphyr* = Sw. Dan. *porfyr*, < OF. *porphyre*, F. *porphyre* = Pr. *porfire* = Sp. *pórfiro, pórfido* = Pg. *porphyro, porfido* = It. *porfiro, porfido*, porphyry; in form as if < Gr. πόρφυρος, purple, but in sense depending on L. *porphyrites*, < Gr. πορφυρίτης (sc. λίθος), porphyry, prop. adj., like purple, < πορφύρα, purple: see *purple*.] 1. The English form of the Latin word *porphyrites*, used by the Romans to designate a certain rock having a dark-crimson ground through which are scattered small crystals of feldspar. In Pliny's time this rock, which was quarried in Egypt, was used extensively for architectural and ornamental purposes, and especially for the base or lower part of busts of which the upper part was made of bronze or marble. Later on, a similar stone appears to have been procured from nearer localities, as from the island of Sardinia. To the Italians it became known as *porfido rosso antico*. Other rocks having a similar structure, commonly called *porphyritic*, were used in Italy, and designated, in accordance with the predominating color, as *porfido nero, porfido verde*, etc. In modern times the term *porphyry* has come to be used as the name of any rock consisting of a very fine-grained or microcrystalline ground-mass through which are disseminated distinctly recognizable crystals of some mineral; but the popular use of the word is frequently extended so as to include rocks which are dark-colored, fine-grained, and very hard, and which do not appear to belong either to the marbles or granites, and this is done even when the porphyritic structure is not at all or only very indistinctly marked. The varieties of porphyry are numerous, and their nomenclature by no means definitely established. The most generally accepted are the following: *quartz-porphyry*, of which the ground-mass consists of an intimate or cryptocrystalline admixture of orthoclase and quartz, in which distinct crystals or large grains of quartz are developed; *feldspar, felsitic* or *felstone porphyry*, having a similar base with porphyritically inclosed crystals of feldspar, which is commonly orthoclase; but similar crystals of this mineral are not infrequently found occurring with the quartz in quartz porphyry, so that no very distinct line can be drawn separating the two varieties mentioned. These porphyries are of most frequent occurrence in the Paleozoic rocks, but they are also found in abundance in other Pre-tertiary formations, presenting the characters of a truly eruptive material. See *porphyrite*, and cut under *porphyritic*.

Now, far from noise, he creepeth covertly
Into a Caue of kindly *Porphyry*.
Sylvester, tr. of Du Bartas's Weeks, ii., Eden.

Within the which [labyrinth] a number of columns and statues there be, all of *porphyrit* or red marble. *Holland*, tr. of Pliny, xxxvi. 13.

And pedestals with antique imagery
Emboss'd, and pillars huge of *porphyry*.
West, Abuse of Travelling.

2†. A slab of porphyry, used in alchemy.

Our grounden litarge eek on the *porphurie*.
Chaucer, Prol. to Canon's Yeoman's Tale, l. 222.

3. In *zoöl.*, a porphyry-moth.—**Augitic porphyry.** See *augitic*.—**Red porphyry.** See *pebbleware*.

porphyry-moth (pôr'fi-ri-môth), *n.* A pyralid moth, *Botys porphyralis*, found throughout Europe: an English collectors' name.

porphyry-shell (pôr'fi-ri-shel), *n.* A shell of the genus *Murex*. From members of this genus was formerly obtained a liquor that produced the Tyrian purple.

porpice†, *n.* An obsolete form of *porpoise*.

porpin (pôr'pin), *n.* [See *porcupine*.] 1†. An obsolete form of *porcupine*.—2. A hedgehog. *Halliwell*. [Prov. Eng.]

porpint†, **porpoint**†, *n.* Obsolete forms of *porcupine*.

porpoise (pôr'pus), *n.* [Formerly also *porpess, porpus, porposs, porpass, porpas, porpesse, porpese, porpaise, porpice, purpose, purpesse, porcpisce*; < ME. *porpeys, purpeys*, < AF. *porpeis, purpeis*, OF. *porpeis, porpeys, porpais, porpaiz, porpaix, porpois, pourpais, pourpois*, F. dial. *pourpeis* (ML. *porpecia*) (= Pg. *peixe porco* = OIt. *pesce porco*, in transposed order), lit. 'hog-fish,' < L. *porcus*, a hog, + *piscis* = E. *fish*: see *pork* and *fish*[1]. Cf. It. Sp. *puerco marino* = It. *porco marino*, porpoise, lit. 'sea-hog': see *pork* and *marine*.] A small toothed cetacean of the family *Delphinidæ* and subfamily *Delphininæ*, and especially of the genus *Phocæna*, of which there are several species, the best-known being *P. communis*, which attains a length of about 5 feet and has a blunt head not produced into a long beak, and a thick body tapering toward the tail. It is common in the North Atlantic, and usually goes in herds or shoals. It feeds almost entirely on fish. A fine oil is prepared from its blubber, and the skin is made into leather; the flesh is eatable. Several genera and numerous species of small cetaceans share the name *porpoise*, among them the dolphin. See *Delphinus, Lagenorhynchus*, and *Tursiops*.

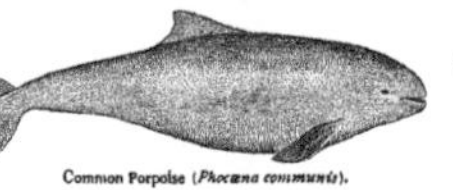

Common Porpoise (*Phocæna communis*).

Wallowing *porpice* sport and lord it in the flood.
Drayton.

Then I drag a bloated corpus,
Swell'd with a dropsy like a *porpus*.
Swift, From a Physician to his Mistress.

With such accoutrements, with such a form,
Much like a *porpoise* just before a storm.
Churchill, Independence.

Porpoise sperm-whale. See *sperm-whale*.—**Right-whale porpoise,** *Leucorhamphus borealis* of the Pacific coast of North America. A similar species, not determined, occurs on the New England coast.—**Skunk-porpoise,** a porpoise streaked with white, as *Lagenorhynchus obliquidens* of the Pacific coast of North America, *L. leucopleurus* (or *acutus*), or *L. perspicillatus* of the eastern coast. See cut under *Lagenorhynchus*.—**Sperm-whale porpoise,** a species of *Hyperoödon*. [Cape Cod.]

porpoise-oil (pôr'pus-oil), *n.* A fine oil obtained from the porpoise and other small cetaceans, especially from the head, used as a lubricant for watches, sewing-machines, etc. Also called *clock-oil*.

porporino (pôr-pọ̄-rē'nō), *n.* [It., purple color, < *porpora*, purple: see *purple*.] An alloy of quicksilver, tin, and sulphur, constituting a yellow powder, used by artists in the middle ages in place of gold.

porpus (pôr'pus), *n.* An obsolete or dialectal spelling of *porpoise*.

porraceous (po-rā'shius), *a.* [= F. *porracé, poracé* = Sp. Pg. *poraceo* = It. *porracceo*, < L. *porraceus*, like leeks, leek-green, < *porrum*, a leek: see *porret*.] Resembling the leek in color; greenish.

If the lesser intestines be wounded, he will be troubled with *poracious* vomitings. *Wiseman*, Surgery, vi. 7.

porrage†, *n.* An obsolete form of *porridge*.

porray†, *n.* See *porrey*.

porrect (po-rekt'), *v. t.* [< L. *porrectus*, pp. of *porrigere*, stretch out before oneself, reach out, extend, < *por-*, forth, + *regere*, stretch, direct: see *regent, rector*.] To thrust out horizontally.

An elongated proboscis capable of being *porrected* in front of the head. *Westwood*.

porrect (po-rekt'), *a.* [< L. *porrectus*, pp.: see the verb.] Extended forward; stretched forth horizontally; antrorse; prorsal.

porrectate (po-rek'tāt), *a.* Same as *porrect*.

porrection (pọ-rek'shọn), *n.* [= F. *porrection*; < L. *porrectio(n-)*, a stretching, < *porrigere*, pp. *porrectus*, stretch out: see *porrect*.] The act of holding in outstretched hands to deliver; delivery.

Varied groups of bowing and saluting figures, appearing and retiring, falling and rising, before the altars, . . . carried gradually forward the expression of forms and the *porrection* of symbols, in devices so intricate as to require the frequent consultation of the directing Volumes of the Pontificals, lest anything should be omitted or performed amiss. *R. W. Dixon*, Hist. Church of Eng., xvii.

porret† (por'et), *n.* [< ME. *poret, porette*, < OF. *poret, porret, purret*, m., F. dial. *pourret*, m., a leek, OF. also *porette, porete*, F. *porrette, pourete, purete*, f. (= Sp. *porreta* = It. *porretta*), a leek; cf. OF. *porreau*, F. *porreau, poireau*, a leek; dim. of OF. **porre* (f) = Sp. *puerro* = Pg. It. *porro*, a leek, < L. *porrum*, also *porrus*, a leek, orig. **porsum* = Gr. πράσον, a leek. From the same source are *porridge, porringer, puree*, etc.] A leek or small onion; a scallion.

Ac I haue percil and *porettes* and many koleplantes,
And eke a cow and a kalf. *Piers Plowman* (B), vi. 288.

porrey†, *n.* [ME., also *porray, porree, porre, purre, poree*, also *perrey, perraye*, < OF. *poré, porray, porrey*, m., leek, a pottage of leeks, also OF. *poree, porree, puree*, leek, also pot-herbs, pulse, etc., pottage, pottage made of beets or of other herbs, F. *purée*, soup of peas, beans, etc., = It. *porrata*, leek-pottage (Florio), < ML. *porrata*, also corruptly *porreta, porrecta*, broth made with leeks, < L. *porrum, porrus*, a leak: see *porret*. Hence *porridge, porringer*.] Porridge; pottage.

porridge (por'ij), *n.* [Formerly also *porredge, porrage*; Sc. *parritch*, etc.; with accom. suffix *-idge, -age* (due to confusion with *pottage*), < ME. *porrey, porray*, etc., porridge, pottage: see *porrey*.] 1. A food made by boiling vegetables in water, with or without meat; broth; soup; pottage.

King. You shall fast a week with bran and water.
Cost. I had rather pray a month with mutton and *porridge*. *Shak.*, L. L. L., i. 1. 305.

A very extraordinary miscellaneous sermon, in which there are some good moral and religious sentiments, and not ill mixed up with a sort of *porridge* of various political opinions and reflections. *Burke*, Rev. in France.

2. A food made by slowly stirring a meal or flour of oats, dried pease, or wheat-flour, or other grain, into water or milk while boiling till a thickened mass is formed. The singular form *porridge* (like *broth, kale, soup*, etc.) is often used, especially in Scotland, as a plural.

The halesome *parritch*, chief o' Scotia's food.
Burns, Cottar's Saturday Night.

"They're gude *parritch* enough," said Mrs. Wilson, "if ye wad but tak time to sup them. I made them mysell."
Scott, Old Mortality, vi.

Nettle porridge. See *nettle*[1].

porridge (por'ij), *v.*; pret. and pp. *porridged*, ppr. *porridging*. [< *porridge*, *n.*] **I.** *intrans.* To take the form of porridge.

Let my son Henry provide such peas as will *porridge* well, or else none. *Winthrop*, Hist. New England, I. 435.

II. *trans.* To provide with porridge.

porriginous (po-rij'i-nus), *a.* Of, pertaining to, or of the nature of porrigo; affected with porrigo.

porrigo (po-rī'gō), *n.* [L. (> It. *porrigine* = F. *porrigo*), scurf, dandruff.] A vague name for a number of diseases of the scalp, especially tinea favosa, tinea tonsurans, and eczema.

porringer (por'in-jėr), *n.* [Formerly *porrenger*, with inserted *n* (as in *messenger*, *passenger*, etc.), < *porridge* + *-er*[1]. Partly confused with or suggested by *pottenger*, < *pottage*. Cf. *porridge* as confused with *pottage*.] **1.** Originally, a porridge-dish; hence, a small vessel deeper than a plate or saucer, usually having upright sides, a nearly flat bottom, and one or two ears.

The Charity Meat, which charitable disposed Persons send in every Thursday, whereon Earthen Dishes, *Porringers*, Pans, Wooden Spoons, and Cabbage Nets are Stirring about against Dinner Time.
Quoted in *Ashton's* Social Life in Reign of Queen Anne, [II. 244.

And often after sunset, sir,
When it is light and fair,
I take my little *porringer*,
And eat my supper there.
Wordsworth, We are Seven.

2†. A head-dress shaped like a porringer: so called in jest.

A haberdasher's wife of small wit . . . rail'd upon me, till her pink'd *porringer* fell off her head.
Shak., Hen. VIII., v. 4. 50.

Porro's operation. See *operation*.

porrum (por'um), *n.* [NL., < L. *porrum*, a leek, scallion: see *porret*.] The bulb of *Allium Porrum*, the leek, sometimes used in medicine.

porry (por'i), *n.* [Origin obscure.] In *weaving*, the length of the warp-threads stretched out between the heddles or harness and the warp-beam.

porset†, *n.* and *v.* A Middle English form of *purse*.

porselyn†, *n.* An obsolete form of *porcelain*[1].

port[1] (pōrt), *n.* [< ME. *port*, *poort*, < AS. *port*, a port, harbor, also a town, city, = MHG. G. *port* = OF. and F. *port* = Pr. *port* = Sp. *puerto* = Pg. It. *porto*, a port, harbor, = W. *porth* = Gael. Ir. *port*, a port, ferry, < L. *portus* (*portu-*), a harbor, haven, fig. a place of refuge, LL. also a warehouse, OL. also a house; orig. 'entrance'; akin to *porta*, a city gate, a gate, door (see *port*[2]); with formative *-tu*, < √ *por*, go (cf. Gr. πόρος, a way), = E. *fare*: see *fare*[1]. Cf. *port*[3]. Hence ult. *port*[5].] **1.** A bay, cove, inlet, or recess of the sea, or of a lake or the mouth of a river, where vessels can be protected from storms; a harbor or haven, whether natural or artificial.

And for the more surer defence y[t] they shuld not efte lande in Kent, prouysyon was made to defende the hauens and *portys* vpon the sees syde. *Fabyan*, Chron., an. 1460.

And beyonde Grece, ouer a branche of the see, is Asya, wherin almoste at thentre standynge Troia, with the chyef *porte* the yle of Tenedos.
Sir R. Guylforde, Pylgrymage, p. 13.

From isles of Greece
The princes orgulous, their high blood chafed,
Have to the *port* of Athens sent their ships.
Shak., T. and C., Prol.

Farcing his letter with like fustian, calling his own court our most happy and shining *port*, a *port* of refuge for the world. *Sandys*, Travailes, p. 37.

2. A place where there is a constant resort of vessels for the purpose of loading and unloading; specifically, in *law*, a place where persons and merchandise are allowed to pass into and out of the realm and at which customs officers are stationed for the purpose of inspecting or appraising imported goods. In this sense a port may exist on the frontier, where the foreign communication is by land.

The King has the prerogative of appointing *ports* and havens, or such places only for persons and merchandize to pass into and out of the realm as he in his wisdom sees proper. Blackstone, Com., I. vii.

Under the fierce competition of rival companies, the vast shipping business of the *Port* of London stimulated the accumulation along the river side of a mass of labour underpaid, irregularly employed, [and] immensely overstocked. *Nineteenth Century*, XXVI. 729.

Barons of the Cinque Ports. See *baron*.—**Boston Port Bill.** See *bill*3.—**Cinque Ports.** See *cinque*.—**Close port.** See *close*2.—**Establishment of the port.** See *establishment*.—**Free port,** a port where importations are not subject to any tariff or customs duty on landing. Hence the term has been sometimes used of the like privilege enjoyed by a class of merchants, or in respect to particular classes of goods. *Free port* is specifically applied to a port (such as the Hanse towns, Lübeck, Hamburg, and Bremen, until 1888), or part of a harbor (such as the island made for the purpose on the Elbe when those cities surrendered their privileges as free ports), where goods are allowed to be landed free of all duty, on condition that they be not carried thence into the country without payment of duty, the object being to facilitate traffic by reshipment to other countries.—**Port admiral,** the admiral commanding at a naval port.—**Port charges,** in *com.*, charges to which a ship or its cargo is liable in a harbor, as wharfage, etc. Also called *port dues*.—**Port of call,** a port at which vessels are in the habit of touching for repairs, stores, coal, etc.—**Port of entry,** a port where a custom-house is maintained for the entry of goods.—**Port of recruit** (*naut.*), a recruiting-station.—**Port warden.** See *warden*.

port[1]† (pōrt), *v. t.* [< *port*[1], *n.*] To carry or bring into port.

So hoist we
The sails, that must these vessels *port* even where
The heavenly limiter pleases.
Fletcher (and another), Two Noble Kinsmen, v. 1.

port[2] (pōrt), *n.* [< ME. *port*, *porte*, < AS. *port* = OS. *porta* = OFries. *porte* = D. *poort* = MLG. *porte* = OHG. *porta*, *phorta*, MHG. *porte*, *borte*, *phorte*, G. *pforte* = Icel. Sw. Dan. *port* = OF. *porte*, F. *porte* = Sp. *puerta*, OSp. *porta* = Pg. It. *porta*, a gate, entrance, = W. *porth*, a gate, gateway, = Ir. *port*, a door, < L. *porta*, a city gate, a gate, door, entrance; akin to *portus*, a harbor, orig. 'entrance'; with formative *-ta*, < √ *por*, go, = E. *fare*[1]: see *port*[1]. Cf. *port*[3]. Hence ult. *porter*[1], and in comp. *portcullis*, etc.] **1.** A gate; an entrance; a portal; specifically, the gate of a town or fortress.

So, let the *ports* be guarded; keep your duties,
As I have set them down. *Shak.*, Cor., i. 7. 1.

The mind of man hath two *ports*, the one always frequented by the entrance of manifold vanities, the other desolate and overgrown with grass, by which enter our charitable thoughts and divine contemplations.
Raleigh (Arber's Eng. Garner, I. 199).

Each order, age, and sex amazed at other,
And at the *ports* all thronging out.
B. Jonson, Catiline, iii. 4.

Towards the streete, at a back gate, the *port* is so handsomely cloath'd with ivy as much pleas'd me.
Evelyn, Diary, Nov. 28, 1644.

2. An opening in the side of a ship; specifically, an embrasure in the side of a ship of war, through which cannon are pointed; a port-hole; also, the covering or shutter of such an opening. Ports in merchant ships are square openings in the sides, bow, or stern of the vessel for loading and discharging cargo or ballast. See cut under *lumber-port*.
3. In *her.*, the door or gate of a castle, used as a bearing.—**4.** An aperture for the passage of steam, air, water, etc. In steam-engines the ports are two passages leading from the steam-chest to the inside of the cylinder, by means of which the steam enters and returns above and below the piston: the former is called the *steam-* or *induction-port*, the latter the *exhaust-* or *eduction-port*. See cut under *piston*.
5. In harness, a curved piece of metal used as a mouthpiece in some forms of bit. Such a bit is called a *port-bit*.—**6.** In *armor*, the socket or bucket in which the butt of the lance was set when held upright: it was secured to the saddle or stirrup.—**Half-port.** Same as *port-lid* (which see, under *lid*).—**Port-pendant,** a rope spliced through a ringbolt on the outside of the lid of a lower-deck port, and used to trice up the lid by means of the tackle inboard.—**Port-sash,** a half-port fitted with glass for lighting a cabin.—**Port-sill,** in a ship, a timber forming the frame for a port, and called, according to its position, *upper*, *side*, or *lower port-sill*.—**Port-tackleman,** one of the members of a gun's crew whose duty it is to trice up or swing aside the covering of the port to admit of the free training of the gun.—**Rudder-port,** the aperture in a ship's counter through which the rudder-head passes.—**To plate a port.** See *plate*.

port[2] (pōrt), *v. t.* [< *port*[2], *n.*] To furnish with doors or gates.

We took the seven-fold *ported* Thebes when yet we had not there
So great helps as our fathers had. *Chapman*, Iliad, iv.

port[3] (pōrt), *v. t.* [< F. *porter* = Sp. *portar* = It. *portare*, < L. *portare*, carry, bear, bring, convey, fig. convey, import, betoken; akin to *porta*, gate, *portus*, harbor, < √ *por*, go, = E. *fare*[1]: see *port*[1], *port*[2], *fare*[1]. Hence ult. (< L. *portare*) in comp. *comport*, *deport*, *disport* (and *sport*), *export*, *import*, *purport*, *report*, *support*, *transport*, etc., *important*, etc., *portass*, *porter*[2], etc.] **1†.** To bear; carry; convey.

Lady L. Her love and zeal transport her.
Com. I am glad
That anything could *port* her hence.
B. *Jonson*, Magnetick Lady, i. 1.

They [fresh-water coalfish] are easily *ported* by boat into other shires. *Fuller*, Worthies, Shropshire, III. 53.

2. To carry in military fashion; carry (a weapon, as a rifle) with both hands in a slanting direction upward and toward the left, crossing the body in front, in execution of the military command "*Port* arms," or, as now given, "Arms *port*."

The angelic squadron bright
Turn'd fiery red, sharpening in mooned horns
Their phalanx, and began to hem him round
With *ported* spears. *Milton*, P. L., iv. 980.

port[3] (pōrt), *n.* [< ME. *port*, *poort*, < OF. *port*, F. *port* = Sp. Pg. *porte* = It. *porto*, carriage, demeanor; from the verb: see *port*[3], *v.*] **1.** Bearing; carriage; demeanor; air; mien: as, the *port* of a gentleman.

Of his *port* as meke as is a mayde.
Chaucer, Gen. Prol. to C. T., l. 69.

Then should the warlike Harry, like himself,
Assume the *port* of Mars. *Shak.*, Hen. V., i. (cho.).

Mark well his *port*! his figure and his face
Nor speak him vulgar, nor of vulgar race.
Pope, Iliad, xiv. 553.

The consciousness of a train of great days and victories behind. . . . That is it which throws thunder into Chatham's voice, and dignity into Washington's *port*.
Emerson, Essays, 1st ser., p. 52.

King Arthur, like a modern gentleman
Of stateliest *port*. *Tennyson*, Morte d'Arthur.

2†. State; style; establishment; retinue.

What time as, most Gracious Prince, your Highness, this last year past, took that your most honourable and victorious journey into France, accompanied with such a *port* of the Nobility and Yeomanly of England as neither hath been like known by experience, nor yet read of in history. *Ascham*, Toxophilus (ed. 1864), p. 1.

Sir, when we lie in garrison, 'tis necessary
We keep a handsome *port*, for the king's honour.
Fletcher, Rule a Wife, iv. 3.

Many millions of reuenue doe besides accrew vnto his [the king's] coffers; yet his *Port* and Magnificence is not so great as of many other Princes.
Purchas, Pilgrimage, p. 477.

=**Syn.** 1. Deportment, address.

port[4] (pōrt), *v.* [Origin uncertain.] **I.** *trans.* *Naut.*, to turn or shift to the left or larboard side of a ship: as, to *port* the helm (that is, to shift the tiller over to the port or left side).

The William had her sterne post broken, that the rudder did hang clean besides the sterne, so that she could in no wise *port* her helm. *Hakluyt's Voyages*, I. 448.

II. *intrans.* *Naut.*, to turn or shift to the left or larboard, as a ship.

port[4] (pōrt), *n.* [See *port*[4], *v.*] *Naut.*, the larboard or left side of a ship (when one is looking forward): as, "the ship heels to *port*"; "hard a *port*." The left side of the ship is now called *port* in preference to the old *larboard*, to prevent confusion with *starboard* in orders, from resemblance of sound.

U. S. Navy Department, Washington, Feb. 18, 1846.
It having been repeatedly represented to the Department that confusion arises from the use of the words "larboard" and "starboard" in consequence of their similarity of sound, the word "*port*" is hereafter to be substituted for "larboard." *George Bancroft*, Sec. of the Navy.

The whalemen are the only class of seamen who have not adopted the term *port* instead of larboard, except in working ship. The larboard boat was this boat to their great-grandfathers, and it is so with the present generation. More especially is this the case in the Atlantic and South Pacific fleets; but recently the term *port-boat* has come into use in the Arctic fleet. *Fisheries of U. S.*, V. ii. 243.

port[5] (pōrt), *n.* [= F. *porto*; abbr. of *port wine*, prop. *Port wine*, *Port* being an English form of Pg. *Oporto* or *Porto* (orig. *o porto*, 'the port' or 'harbor'), a city in Portugal, whence the wine was orig. shipped: *o*, the, < L. *ille*, that; *porto*, < L. *portus*, harbor: see *port*[1].] A wine of Portugal, named from Oporto (see above). The name is usually given to a very dark-red or purplish wine, but it is sometimes pale. The wine usually sold under the name of *port* is partly artificial, prepared or "doctored" by blending, etc. Wine of absolutely pure growth is seldom to be got under the name. This wine is a favorite for imitation by blending and sweetening, etc., in American wines, both east and west, which are sold as American port.

In England *port* is adulterated with the red Spanish wine of Tarragona, which is a true wine, but procurable at half the cost of the cheapest port.
Encyc. Brit., XVII. 795.

In fact, when people spoke of wine in these days, they generally meant *port*. They bought *port* by the hogshead, had it bottled, and laid down. They talked about their cellars solemnly; they brought forth bottles which had been laid down in the days when George the Third was king; they were great on body, bouquet, and beeswing; they told stories about wonderful *port* which they had been privileged to drink; they looked forward to a dinner chiefly on account of the *port* which followed it; real enjoyment only began when the cloth was removed, the ladies were gone, and the solemn passage of the decanter had commenced. *W. Besant*, Fifty Years Ago, p. 166.

port[6] (pōrt), *n.* [< Gael. Ir. *port*, a tune.] Martial music adapted to the bagpipes.

The pipe's shrill *port* aroused each clan.
Scott, L. of L. M., v. 14.

Port. An abbreviation of *Portugal* and *Portuguese*.

porta (pōr'tạ̈), *n.*; pl. *portæ* (-tē). [NL., < L. *porta*, a gate, door: see *port*[2].] In *anat.*: (*a*) The entrance or great transverse fissure of the liver: especially in the term *vena portæ*, the portal vein (which see, under *portal*[1]). See cut under *liver*. (*b*) The foramen of Monro; especially, the lateral orifice of the Y-shaped foramen which opens communication between each of the lateral ventricles of the brain and the third ventricle.—**Porta hepatis**, the transverse fissure of the liver.—**Porta lienis**, the hilum of the spleen.—**Porta pulmonis**, the hilum of the lung, an elongate elliptical recess where the bronchus, vessels, etc., enter or emerge from the lung.—**Porta renis**, the notch or hilum of the kidney.

portability (pōr-tạ-bil'i-ti), *n.* [= F. *portabilité*; < *portable* + *-ity* (see *-bility*).] The state of being portable; fitness to be carried; portableness.

By unscrewing the pillar, the whole is made to pack into a small flat case, the extreme *portability* of which is a great recommendation. *W. B. Carpenter*, Micros., § 43.

portable (pōr'tạ-bl), *a.* [= F. *portable* = It. *portabile*, < LL. *portabilis*, that may be carried, < L. *portare*, carry: see *port*[3].] 1. Capable of being carried in the hand or about the person; capable of being carried or transported from place to place; easily carried or conveyed.

In Wales where there are *portable* boats . . . made of leather. *Sir T. Browne*, Vulg. Err., ii. 3.

They [poems] are caskets which inclose within a small compass the wealth of the language—its family jewels, which are thus transmitted in a *portable* form to posterity. *Irving*, Sketch-Book, p. 170.

2†. Supportable; tolerable.

How light and *portable* my pain seems now!
Shak., Lear, iii. 6. 115.

3†. Capable of carrying or transporting.

If you find great plentie of tymber on the shore side, or vpon any *portable* riuer, you were best to cut downe of the same the first winter to be seasoned for ships, barkes, boates, and houses. *Hakluyt's Voyages*, III. 46.

4†. Accessible (?).

Had his designes beene to have perswaded men to a mine of gold; . . . or some new Invention to passe to the South Sea; or some strange plot to invade some strange Monastery or some *portable* Countrie, . . . what multitudes of both people and mony would contend to be first imploied! Quoted in *Capt. John Smith's* Works, II. 264.

Casella's portable anemometer. See *anemometer*.—**Portable boiler and furnace**, a furnace mounted on wheels, used to heat tar or other material, as for paving or roofing.—**Portable dial.** See *dial*.—**Portable gas**, gas furnished to consumers in portable reservoirs which serve to supply small holders or tanks at the place of consumption.

portableness (pōr'tạ-bl-nes), *n.* The character of being portable; portability.

portace†, *n.* Same as *portass*.

portæ, *n.* Plural of *porta*.

portage[1] (pōr'tāj), *n.* [< F. *portage* = Sp. *portaje*, *portazgo* = Pg. *portagem* = It. *portaggio*, < ML. *portaticum*, also, after Rom., *portagium*, carriage, portage, < L. *portare*, carry: see *port*[3].] 1. The act of carrying; carriage; transportation.

Fiue hundred pounds here haue they sent by me,
For the easier *portage*, all in angel gold.
Heywood, 1 Edw. IV. (Works, ed. Pearson, 1874, I. 89).

If the hundred-weight were of gold or jewels, a weaker person would think it no trouble to bear that burden, if it were the reward of his *portage*. *Jer. Taylor*, Works (ed. 1835), I. 248.

2. That which is carried or transported; cargo; freight; baggage.

The Muses bacely hegge or hibbe,
Or both, and must, for why?
They finde as bad bestoe as is
Their *portage* beggerly.
Warner, Albion's England, v. 27.

These two gallions are laden for the king, neither doe they carie any particular mans goods, sauing the *portage* of the Mariners and souldiers. *Hakluyt's Voyages*, II. 228.

3†. Tonnage; burden of a vessel.

Their shippe, ships, barke, pinnesses, and all other vessels, of whatsoeuer *portage*, bulke, quantitie, or qualitie they may be. *Hakluyt's Voyages*, I. 271.

4. The price paid for carriage; freight-charges. —5. A break in a chain of water-communication over which goods, boats, etc., have to be carried, as from one lake, river, or canal to another, or along the banks of rivers round waterfalls, rapids, or the like; a carry.

A rumor was spread through the intrenched camp . . . that a chosen detachment of fifteen hundred men was to depart, with the dawn, for William Henry, the post at the northern extremity of the *portage*.
J. F. Cooper, Last of Mohicans, i.

Expeditions of the gravest magnitude have not infrequently depended for their success upon the passage of brief *portages* from stream to stream, or from sea to sea.
Harper's Mag., LXXVI. 374.

portage[2]† (pōr'tāj), *n.* [< *port*[2], *n.*, + *-age*. Cf. OF. *portage*, a fee for admission paid at a gate.] An opening; a port or port-hole.

Let it pry through the *portage* of the head
Like the brass cannon. *Shak.*, Hen. V., iii. 1. 10.

Portage group. See *group*[1].

portal[1] (pōr'tạl), *n.* [< OF. *portal*, F. *portail* = Sp. Pg. *portal* = D. *portaal* = G. Sw. Dan. *portal*, < ML. *portale*, entrance, vestibule, portal, neut. of *portalis*, pertaining to a gate (see *portal*[2]), < L. *porta*, a gate, door: see *port*[2].] 1. A door or gate; an entrance or opening for passage;

Portal.—West front of Peterborough Cathedral, England.

specifically, the entire architectural treatment of the entrance and its surroundings of a great or splendid building, as a cathedral.

The *portall* postes and threshold vp are throwen and doores of halles. *Phaer*, Æneid, ii.

King Richard doth himself appear,
As doth the blushing discontented sun
From out the fiery *portal* of the east.
Shak., Rich. II., iii. 3. 64.

The lips that open to this fruit 's a *portal*
To let in death, and make immortal mortal.
Quarles, Emblems, i. 1.

She . . . gazed through the dusty side-lights of the *portal* at the young, blooming, and very cheerful face which presented itself for admittance into the gloomy old mansion. *Hawthorne*, Seven Gables, iv.

On the ground-story of the central compartment [of a transept] there is a great *portal*, while the aisle ends usually have windows instead of doors.
C. H. Moore, Gothic Architecture, p. 102.

2†. A square corner of a room separated from the rest by a wainscot, and forming a short passage or vestibule.

portal[1] (pōr'tạl), *a.* [< ML. *portalis*, pertaining to a gate (as a noun, a porter), < L. *porta*, a gate. Cf. *portal*[1], *n.*] In *anat.*: (*a*) Pertaining to the hepatic porta, or great transverse fissure of the liver. (*b*) Pertaining to the vena portæ, or portal vein.—**Accessory portal veins**, a number of small veins which collect blood from the areolar tissue and peritoneal folds around the liver, and discharge into branches of the portal vein.—**Portal canals**, tubular passages in the substance of the liver, invested by the capsule of Glisson, and containing each a branch of the portal vein, hepatic artery, and hepatic duct.—**Portal circulation**, the passage of venous blood from the capillaries of one organ to those of another before reaching the heart. There are two such circulations, through the liver and through the kidneys, distinguished as *hepatoportal* and *reniportal*. Only the former occurs in man, whence the specific use of the phrase in reference to this only. In this form of portal circulation, the venous blood from the capillaries of the stomach, spleen, and intestine or chylopoietic viscera collectively is gathered by the gastric, splenic, and mesenteric veins into a common venous channel, the vena portæ or portal vein, which conducts it into the liver. See *reniportal*, and cuts under *embryo* and *liver*.—**Portal fissure.** See *fissure*.—**Portal system**, the portal vein with its tributaries and its distributing branches.

With a dose of cleansing calomel
Unload the *portal system* (that sounds well!).
O. W. Holmes, Rip Van Winkle, M. D.

Portal vein, a large, short trunk receiving the blood from the chylopoietic viscera, formed from the union of the splenic and superior mesenteric veins. It enters the transverse fissure of the liver, where it divides into a right and a left branch, which again subdivide to be distributed to the substance of the liver. Also called *vena portæ* or *portarum*.

portal[2]†, *n.* Same as *portass*.

portamento (pōr-tä-men'tō), *n.* [It. (> Pg. *portamento*), carriage, < ML. *portamentum*, carrying, carriage, action, < L. *portare*, carry: see *port*[3].] In music for the voice or an instrument of the viol family, a gradual change or gliding from one pitch or tone to another without break or perceptible step. It is similar to a legato in the first particular, but different from it in the second. As an effect, it is valuable when judiciously introduced, but readily passes into a vulgar mannerism. The term is sometimes loosely applied to legato effects on keyed instruments.

Trills, graces, and a good *portamento* or direction of voice.
Della Valle, tr. in Burney's Hist. Music, IV. 40.

portance† (pōr'tạns), *n.* [< *port*[3] + *-ance*.] Carriage; port; demeanor; air; mien.

A woman of great worth,
And by her stately *portance* borne of heavenly birth.
Spenser, F. Q., II. iii. 21.

Through what a grace
And goodly countenance the rascal speaks!
What a grave *portance*! *Tomkis* (?), Albumazar, iv. 2.

portant (pōr'tạnt), *a.* [< F. *portant*, ppr. of *porter*, carry: see *port*[3].] In *her.*, same as *portate*.—**Cross double portant.** Same as *cross double* (which see, under *cross*[1]).

Port Arthur plum. See *plum*[1].

portass† (pōr'tas), *n.* [Early mod. E. also *portasse*, *portase*, *portace*, *portus*, *portesse*, *portise*, *portat*, *portuas*, *portuous*, *portuis*, *pertuse*, *porteus*, *portos*, *porthose*, < ME. *portas*, *portos*, *porthos*, *portus*, *portous*, *poortos*, *porthous*, prop. *porthors*, < OF. *porte-hors* (ML. *portiforium*), a breviary, < *porter*, carry (see *port*[3]), + *hors*, *fors*, outside, out, < L. *foris*, out of doors, abroad, < *fores*, doors: see *door*.] A breviary; a prayer-book. Also called *portuary*.

On my *porthors* I make an oath.
Chaucer, Shipman's Tale, l. 130.

An old priest always read in his *portass* mumpsimus domine for sumpsimus. *Camden*.

Almost nothing remaineth in them simple and vncorrupt, as in the usuall *portus* woont to be read for dailie seruice is manifest and euident to be seene.
Foxe, Martyrs, p. 85.

The friar ready with his *portace* there,
To wed them both. *Greene*, Friar Bacon.

Not only clerks, but some lay folks, and those of high degree, used to carry about with them a *portous*, out of which their daily wont was to read matins and even-song.
Rock, Church of our Fathers, III. ii. 143.

portate (pōr'tāt), *a.* [< L. *portatus*, pp. of *portare*, carry: see *port*[3].] In *her.*, in a position as if being carried. See *cross portate*, under *cross*[1]. Also *portant*.

Cross Portate.

portatile (pōr'tạ-til), *a.* [= Sp. *portátil* = Pg. *portatil*, < ML. *portatilis*, portable, movable (said of bishops without a charge), < L. *portare*, carry: see *port*[3].] Portable.—**Portatile altar**, a portable altar.

portative (pōr'tạ-tiv), *a.* [< ME. *portatif*, < OF. (and F.) *portatif* = It. *portativo*, < L. **portativus*, < *portare*, pp. *portatus*, carry: see *port*[3].] 1. Portable; easily carried.

As whanne hit hadde of the folde flesch and blod ytake,
Tho was it *portatyf* and pershaunt as the poynt of a neldo.
Piers Plowman (C), ii. 154.

As fer forth . . . as may be shewyd in so smal an instrument *portatif* aboute. *Chaucer*, Astrolabe, Prol.

Its weight and size seem to have originated a distinction between portable and stationary organs, which began early, and was perpetuated in the terms frequently used of "*Portative*" and "Positive." *Grove's Dict. Music*, II. 575.

2. Of or pertaining to carrying or the power of carrying: as, a "*portative* memory," *Encyc. Brit.*, VIII. 780.—**Portative force of a magnet.** See *magnet*.—**Portative organ.** See *organ*[1], and compare *regal*.

Portax (pōr'taks), *n.* [NL. (Hamilton Smith, 1827), < Gr. πόρταξ, equiv. to πόρτις, a calf.] A genus of *Bovidæ*, containing only the nilgau, *Portax pictus*. This is an Indian antelope, another of whose names is *Boselaphus tragocamelus*, and which is also known as *blue cow* (a translation of its native name) and *blue antelope* (a name properly belonging to the African blauwbok). See cut under *nilgau*.

port-bar (pōrt'bär), *n.* *Naut.*: (*a*) A strong bar of oak used to secure the ports in a gale, by bracing the closed port on the inside. (*b*) A boom formed of spars or trees lashed together, and moored across the entrance of a port to prevent entrance or egress. (*c*) Same as *bar*[1], 4 (*a*).

port-bit (pōrt'bit), *n.* In harness, any bit having a port, or curved mouthpiece. *E. H. Knight*.

port-cannons† (pōrt'kan'ọnz), *n. pl.* In *costume*, ornamental appendages worn at the knees. See *cannon*, 7.

He walks in his *port-cannons* like one that stalks in long grass. *S. Butler*, Genuine Remains, II. 83. (*Nares*.)

port-caustic (pōrt'kâs'tik), *n.* A small case, usually cylindrical, used for carrying a caustic substance in the pocket, or for applying the caustic.

portcluse†, *n.* An obsolete form of *portcullis*.

port-crayon, porte-crayon (pōrt'krā'ọn), *n.* [< F. *porte-crayon*, < *porter*, carry, + *crayon*, pencil: see *port*[3] and *crayon*.] A holder for chalk, charcoal, crayon, or the like, used in drawing. It is usually a kind of tube of metal, split at

Port-crayon.

one or both ends, and tending to spring open there, but held fast by rings which slide upon it, so that the drawing-material is nipped and held firmly.

portcullis (pōrt-kul'is), *n.* [Early mod. E. also *portcullize, porcullis, purculleise, percullis, percollis, percollice, percollois*, etc.; < ME. *portcullise, portcolise, poort colyce, porte colyse*, < OF. *porte coleïce, porte coulisse, porte colice*, a sliding gate, portcullis, < *porte* (< L. *porta*, door) + *coleïce, coulisse*, adj. (also as a noun, *coulisse*, a sliding gate, portcullis, F. *coulisse*, a groove), fem. of *coleis, coulis*, F. *coulis*, sliding, < ML. **colaticius*, < *colatus*, pp. of *colare*, flow, < L. *colare*, strain: see *colander, cullis*[1], *cullis*[2], etc.] 1. In *fort.*, a strong grating of timber or iron, somewhat resembling a harrow, made to

Portcullis.

slide in vertical grooves in the jambs of the entrance-gate of a fortified place, to protect the gate in case of assault. The vertical bars were made either of iron or of wood pointed with iron at the bottom, in order to demolish whatever the portcullis might fall upon. There was usually a series of portcullises in the same gateway. They were probably of Italian origin, and not older than the twelfth century.

In to the town were but two entrees, and at eche entre two *portecolyses* and stronge yates covered with Iren nailed, that shet with two leves well and strongly barred.
Merlin (E. E. T. S.), ii. 254.

Everich hadde, withoute fable,
A *porte-colys* defensable. *Rom. of the Rose*, l. 4168.

Pull up *portcullize!* down draw-brigg!
My nephews are at hand.
Auld Maitland (Child's Ballads, VI. 226).

Where be those rosy cheeks that lately scorn'd
The malice of injurious fates?
Ah! where's that pearl *portcullis* that adorn'd
Those dainty two-leav'd gates?
Quarles, Emblems, ii. 9.

Battering all the wall over the *percullis*.
J. Randolph, Honour Advanced, p. 3. (*Davies.*)

If I had you out once,
I would be at charge of a *percullis* for you.
Fletcher, Wit without Money, iv. 5.

2. In *her.*: (*a*) Same as *lattice*, 3. (*b*) The representation of a portcullis: a rare bearing, but familiar in English art of the fifteenth century from its adoption as a badge by the Tudors and in the city arms of Westminster.—3. One of the pursuivants of the English College of Heralds: so called from his distinctive badge.—4†. A coin struck in the reign of Queen Elizabeth, with a portcullis stamped on the reverse. Portcullis money consisted of crowns, half-crowns, shillings, and sixpences (regulated according to the weight of the Spanish piaster or dollar and its divisions), and was struck for the use of the East India Company (whence it was also called *India money*).

Obverse.

Reverse.

Portcullis Shilling.—British Museum. (Size of the original.)

I had not so much as the least *portcullis* of coin before.
B. Jonson, Every Man out of his Humour, iii. 1.

portcullis (pōrt-kul'is), *v. t.* [< *portcullis, n.*] To arm or furnish with a portcullis; hence, to bar; obstruct.

Within my mouth you have engaol'd my tongue,
Doubly *portcullis'd* with my teeth and lips.
Shak., Rich. II., i. 3. 167.

And all those towns great Longshanks left his son,
Now lost, which once he fortunately won,
Within their strong *port-cullis'd* ports shall lie,
And from their walls his sieges shall defy.
Drayton, Mortimer to Queen Isabel.

port de voix (pōr dė vwo). [F., compass of the voice: *port*, bearing, carriage; *de*, of; *voix*, voice: see *port*[3], *n.*, *de*[2], *voice*.] In *harpsichord music*, an embellishment consisting of an appoggiatura and a single or double pincé.

Porte (pōrt), *n.* [< F. *Porte* (= Sp. Pg. It. *Porta*), short for *Sublime Porte* (> E. *Sublime Porte*), lit. lofty gate (see *sublime* and *port*[2]), tr. Turk. *bâbi 'aliy* (*Babi Ali*), the chief office of the Ottoman government, so called from the gate of the palace at which justice was administered, lit. 'high gate': *bâb*, gate; *'aliy*, high.] The Ottoman court; the government of the Turkish empire.

porte-acid (pōrt'as'id), *n.* An instrument for holding a drop or more of acid for local application.

porteaiguille (pōrt'ā-gwēl'), *n.* [F., < *porter*, carry, + *aiguille*, needle: see *aiguille*.] In *surg.*, same as *needle-holder*.

porte-bonheur (pōrt'bo-nėr'), *n.* [F., < *porter*, carry, + *bonheur*, good luck.] A charm, an amulet, or a trinket carried after the fashion of an amulet, suspended to a bracelet or other article of personal adornment.

porte-cochère (pōrt'kō-shãr'), *n.* [< F. *porte cochère*: *porte*, gate; *cochère*, < *coche*, coach: see *coach*.] A carriage-entrance in a building; a gate and passage for carriages leading through a building, as a town-house or hotel, from the street to an interior court.

Philip was at the Hôtel des Bains at a very early hour next morning, and there he saw the general, with a woe-worn face, leaning on his stick, and looking at his luggage, as it lay piled in the *porte-cochère* of the hotel.
Thackeray, Philip, xvi.

The great, wide *porte-cochère* in front, and the little back gate on the street in the rear.
New Princeton Rev., IV. 363.

porte-crayon, *n.* See *port-crayon*.

ported† (pōr'ted), *a.* [< *port*[2] + *-ed*[2].] Having gates.

These bright keys
Designing power to ope the *ported* skies.
B. Jonson, Masque of Hymen.

porte-drapeau (pōrt'dra-pō'), *n.* [F., < *porter*, carry, + *drapeau*, standard, banner, flag.] An appliance for raising and displaying a flag.

Port Egmont hen. See *hen*[1].

porteguet, *n.* See *portague*.

port-electric (pōrt'ę-lek'trik), *a.* [< F. *porter*, carry, + E. *electric*.] Carrying by electricity: noting a proposed system for the rapid transmission of mail-packages, etc., the principal feature of which consists in drawing a car through a series of coils that are momentarily energized as the car approaches.

porte-lumière (pōrt'lü-miãr'), *n.* [F., < *porter*, carry, + *lumière*, a light.] An apparatus consisting of a plane mirror so mounted and fitted with adjusting screws that the user can easily control the direction of the reflected rays. It is much employed in physical experimentation as a substitute for the more elaborate and expensive heliostat.

porte-monnaie (pōrt'mo̤-nā'), *n.* [F., < *porter*, carry, + *monnaie*, money: see *money*.] A pocket-book; especially, a small book or leather pouch with clasps, for holding money.

portenaunce†, *n.* Same as *purtenance*.

portend (pōr-tend'), *v. t.* [= It. *portendere*; < L. *portendere*, point out, indicate, foretell, an archaic collateral form, belonging to religious language, of *protendere*, stretch forth, < *pro*, forth, + *tendere*, stretch.] 1†. To stretch forth; protend.

Thy fate was next, O Phæstus! doom'd to feel
The great Idomeneus' *portended* steel.
Pope, Iliad, v. 58. (*Richardson.*)

2. To betoken; presage; signify in advance; foreshow.

Their [the Longobardes'] comming into Italy . . . was *portended* by divers fearfull prodigies.
Coryat, Crudities, I. 109.

Their mouths
With hideous orifice gaped on us wide,
Portending hollow truce. *Milton*, P. L., vi. 578.

=**Syn.** 2. To forebode, augur, presage, threaten, foreshadow. See *omen*.

portent (pōr-tent' or pōr'tent), *n.* [< OF. *portente* = Sp. Pg. It. *portento*, < L. *portentum*, a sign, token, omen, portent, prop. neut. of *portentus*, pp. of *portendere*, portend: see *portend*.] That which portends or foretokens; a sign or token; an omen, generally of ill, or of something to be feared.

My loss by dire *portents* the god foretold. *Dryden.*

=**Syn.** *Sign, Presage*, etc. See *omen*, and *foretell, v. t.*

portention† (pōr-ten'sho̤n), *n.* [< L. *portendere*, pp. *portentus*, point out, portend: see *portend*.] The act of portending or foreshowing; a portent.

Why, although the red comets do carry the *portentions* of Mars, the brightly white should not be of the influence of Jupiter or Venus, . . . is not absurd to doubt.
Sir T. Browne, Vulg. Err., vi. 14.

portentive† (pōr-ten'tiv), *a.* [< *portent* + *-ive*.] Portentous. *Brome.*

portentous (pōr-ten'tus), *a.* [< OF. *portenteux* = Sp. Pg. It. *portentoso*, < L. *portentosus*, monstrous, portentous, < *portentum*, a portent: see *portent*.] 1. Of the nature of a portent; ominous; foreshowing ill.

This *portentous* figure
Comes armed through our watch, so like the king
That was. *Shak.*, Hamlet, i. 1. 100.

All is deep silence, like the fearful calm
That slumbers in the storm's *portentous* pause.
Shelley, Queen Mab, iv.

2. Monstrous; prodigious; wonderful.

On the banke of this ryuer there is a towne of such *portentous* byggenes as I dare not speake.
R. Eden, tr. of Peter Martyr (First Books on America, ed. [Arber, p. 194).

Let us see whether we can discover in any part of their schemes the *portentous* ability which may justify these bold undertakers in the superiority which they assume over mankind. *Burke*, Rev. in France.

The neck was thrice encircled by a white muslin cravat tied in a *portentous* bow with drooping ends.
Fortnightly Rev., N. S., XLII. 200.

portentously (pōr-ten'tus-li), *adv.* In a portentous manner; ominously; monstrously; wonderfully.

porter[1] (pōr'tėr), *n.* [< ME. *porter, portere, portour*, < OF. (and F.) *portier* = Sp. *portero* = Pg. *porteiro* = It. *portiere*, < LL. *portarius*, a doorkeeper, < L. *porta*, a door, gate: see *port*[2].] One who has the charge of a door or gate; a doorkeeper or gate-keeper.

Com forth, I wol unto the gate go,
Thise *portours* ben unkonnynge evermo.
Chaucer, Troilus, v. 1139.

Bar but your Gate, and let your *Porter* cry
Here's no Admittance.
Congreve, tr. of Ovid's Art of Love.

Porter's lodge, a room or cottage near an entrance door or gate for the use of the keeper.

porter[2] (pōr'tėr), *n.* [< ME. *portour, portowre*, < OF. (and F.) *porteur* = Sp. Pg. *portador* = It. *portatore*, < ML. *portator* (cf. LL. fem. *portatrix*), a carrier, < L. *portare*, pp. *portatus*, carry: see *port*[3].] 1. One who bears or carries; a bearer; a carrier; specifically, a person who carries burdens, etc., or runs errands for hire: as, a railway or dock *porter*.

Simon of Cyrene is forced to be the *porter* of Thy cross.
Bp. Hall, Contemplations, V. 343.

On the Fourth of July, at five o'clock in the morning, the *porters* called the sleepers out of their berths at Wickford Junction. *C. D. Warner*, Their Pilgrimage, p. 84.

2. A law officer who carries a white or silver rod before the justices in eyre. [Eng.]—3. *Eccles.*, same as *ostiary*.—4. That which is used in bearing, supporting, or carrying. (*a*†) A lever. *Withals.* (*b*) A bar of iron attached to a heavy forging, by which it is guided beneath the hammer or into the furnace, being suspended by chains from a crane above; also, a bar from whose end an article is forged. *E. H. Knight.* (*c*) In *agri.*, a light two- or three-wheeled carriage used in steam-plowing to hold up from the ground the wire rope by which the plows are drawn. (*d*) In *weaving*, a term used in Scotland to denote twenty splits or dents in the reed, in plain work. In England called a *beer*.—**Porter's knot.** See *knot*[1].

porter[3] (pōr'tėr), *n.* [Short for *porter-beer* (> F. *porter-bière*) or **porters' beer*: said to have been a favorite beverage of the London porters (see *porter*[2]), but perhaps so called in allusion to its strength and substance. There is no evidence that London porters, as distinguished from London cabmen or London artisans, favored this sort of beer.] A dark-brown malt liquor, of English origin. It is made either wholly or partially of high-dried malt, which gives color and imparts a special flavor to the liquor. Top-fermentation in large tuns, lasting from 48 to 60 hours, is followed by after-fermentation in smaller casks or transport-barrels, lasting several days. The after-fermentation clarifies the liquor, from which the air is then excluded by bunging the casks.—**Fettled porter.** See *fettle*.

porterage[1] (pōr'tėr-āj), *n.* [< *porter*[1] + *-age*.] The business or duties of a porter or doorkeeper.

porterage[2] (pōr'tėr-āj), *n.* [< *porter*[2], q. v., + *-age.*] 1. Carrying; carriage; transportation; porters' work.

My mother used to take me with her to help with the *porterage* of her purchases. *Academy*, No. 878, p. 142.

A great deal of the *porterage* of Lisbon is done by women and girls, who also do most of the unloading of the lighters on the quays. *Harper's Mag.*, LXXVII. 868.

2. The cost of carrying; money charged for porters' services.

Perpetually grumbling at the expense of postage and *porterage*. *Fortnightly Rev.*, N. S., XLIII. 355.

porteress, portress (pōr'tėr-es, -tres), *n.* [Formerly also *porteresse*; < *porter*[1] + *-ess.*] A female porter or keeper of a gate.

porter-house (pōr'tėr-hous), *n.* A house at which porter, ale, and other malt liquors are retailed; an ale-house; also, such a house at which steaks, chops, etc., are served up; a chop-house. —**Porter-house steak**, a beefsteak consisting of a choice cut of the beef between the sirloin and the tenderloin, the latter being the under cut: it is supposed to derive its name from a well-known porter-house in New York, where this particular cut of the meat was first introduced. [U. S.]

porterly (pōr'tėr-li), *a.* [< *porter*[2] + *-ly*[1].] Like a porter; hence, coarse; vulgar. [Rare.]

The *porterly* language of swearing and obscenity. *Dr. Bray*, Essay on Knowledge (1697), Pref. (*Latham.*)

portesse†, *n.* Same as *portass.*

port-face (pōrt'fās), *n.* The flat surface in the steam-chest of a steam-engine which includes the openings into the ports of the engine-cylinder, and upon which a slide-valve works. See *valve-seat* and *slide-valve.*

port-fire (pōrt'fīr), *n.* [< *port*[3], *v.*, + obj. *fire*; tr. F. *porte-feu.*] A kind of slow-match or match-cord formerly used to discharge artillery.—**Port-fire clipper**, nippers for cutting off the ends of port-fires. *E. H. Knight.*

port-flange (pōrt'flanj), *n.* A wooden or metallic batten fitted on a ship's side over a port to keep out water.

portfolio (pōrt-fō'liō), *n.* [< Sp. *portafolio* = It. *portafoglio* = F. *portefeuille*, a case for carrying papers, etc.; < L. *portare*, carry, + *folium*, a leaf: see *port*[3] and *folio.*] 1. A movable receptacle for detached papers or prints, usually in the form of a complete book-cover with a flexible back, and fastened with strings or clasps. *E. H. Knight.*

I sat down, and turned over two large *portfolios* of political caricatures. *Macaulay*, in Trevelyan, I. 209.

2. Figuratively, the office of a minister of state: as, he holds the *portfolio* of education (that is, he has charge of the documents, etc., connected with that department); he has received the *portfolio* of the home department.

portglave†, **portglaive**† (pōrt'glāv), *n.* [< F. *porte-glaive*, < *porter*, carry, + *glaive*, sword: see *port*[3] and *glave.*] 1. An attendant or retainer armed with a glave. Hence—2. A subordinate officer of the law, whose badge of office was the glave. Compare *halberdier*, 2.

portgrave† (pōrt'grāv), *n.* [Also *portgreve*; < ME. **portgreve* (not found); cf. AS. *portgerēfa* (> E. *portreeve*) = Icel. *portgreifi*, a portreeve: see *portreeve* and *grave*[5].] Same as *portreeve.*

His Ordinances were chiefly for the Meridian of London; for where before his Time the City was governed by *Portgraves*, this King [Richard I.] granted them to be governed by two Sheriffs and a Mayor. *Baker*, Chronicles, p. 66.

port-hole (pōrt'hōl), *n.* 1. An aperture in a ship's side, especially one of the apertures through which the guns are protruded and fired. —2. The opening to the steam-passages into or from a cylinder, or to the exhaust-passage. See *port*[2], 4.

port-hook (pōrt'hůk), *n.* One of the hooks in the side of a ship to which the hinges of a port-lid are hooked.

porthors†, *n.* Same as *portass.*

portico (pōr'ti-kō), *n.*; pl. *porticos* or *porticoes* (-kōz). [< It. *portico* = Sp. *pórtico* = Pg. *portico* = F. *portique*, < L. *porticus*, a porch, portico: see *porch.*] In *arch.*, a structure consisting essentially of a roof supported on at least one side by columns, sometimes detached, as a shady walk, or place of assemblage, but generally, in modern usage, a porch or an open vestibule at the entrance of a building; a colonnade. Porticos are called tetrastyle, hexastyle, octastyle, decastyle, etc., according as they have four, six, eight, ten, or more columns in front; in classical examples they are also distinguished as prostyle or in antis, according as they project before the building or are inclosed between its side walls prolonged.—**Philosophers of the Portico**, the Stoics. See *The Porch* (under *porch*), and cuts under *octastyle* and *pantheon.*

porticoed (pōr'ti-kōd), *a.* [< *portico* + *-ed*[2].] Having a portico or porticos.

porticus† (pōr'ti-kus), *n.* [L.: see *portico, porch.*] A portico. [Rare.]

Till the whole tree become a *porticus*,
Or arched arbor. *B. Jonson*, Neptune's Triumph.

portière (pōr-tiār'), *n.* [F., a door-curtain, < *porte*, door: see *port*[2], *n.*] A curtain hung at a doorway, or entrance to a room, either with the door or to replace it, to intercept the view or currents of air, etc., when the door is opened, or for mere decoration.

portiforium (pōr-ti-fō'ri-um), *n.*; pl. *portiforia* (-ä). [ML.: see *portass.*] In the medieval church in England, an office-book containing the offices for the canonical hours. It was also known as the *breviary*, and answered to the Roman Catholic breviary. The name assumed many forms in popular use, such as *portfory, portuary, porthors, portous, portuis*, etc. See *portass.*

portify (pōr'ti-fī), *v. t.*; pret. and pp. *portified*, ppr. *portifying*. [< *port*[5] + *-i-fy*; in allusion to the saying, "Claret would be port if it could."] To give (one's self) more value or importance than belongs to one. [Humorous and rare.]

I grant you that in this scheme of life there does enter ever so little hypocrisy; that this claret is loaded, as it were; but your desire to *portify* yourself is amiable, is pardonable, is perhaps honourable. *Thackeray*, Roundabout Papers, Small-Beer Chron.

portigue†, *n.* Same as *portugue.*

Portingal†, **Portingall**† (pōr'ting-gal), *a.* and *n.* Obsolete forms of *Portugal.*

portio (pōr'shi-ō), *n.*; pl. *portiones* (pōr-shi-ō'-nēz). [L.: see *portion.*] In *anat.*, a part, portion, or branch.—**Portio aryvocalis**, short muscular fibers attached in front to the vocal cord, and behind to the vocal process of the arytenoid.—**Portio axillaris**, the second part of the axillary artery; the part behind the pectoralis minor.—**Portio brachialis**, the third part of the axillary artery; the part below the pectoralis minor. —**Portio cervicalis**, the third division of the subclavian artery.—**Portio dura of the seventh nerve of Willis**, the facial nerve.—**Portio inter duram et mollem of Wrisberg**, the pars intermedia Wrisbergii.—**Portio intermedia.** (*a*) Same as *pars intermedia* (which see, under *pars*). (*b*) The middle part of the cervix uteri, which is vaginal behind and supravaginal in front.—**Portio major trigemini**, the sensitive root of the trifacial.—**Portio minor trigemini**, the motor root of the trifacial.—**Portio mollis of the seventh nerve of Willis**, the auditory nerve.—**Portio muscularis**, the second division of the subclavian artery.—**Portio pectoralis**, the first division of the subclavian artery.—**Portio supravaginalis**, the supravaginal division of the cervix uteri.—**Portio thoracica**, the first part of the axillary artery; the part above the pectoralis minor.—**Portio vaginalis**, that part of the cervix uteri which is free within the vagina.

portion (pōr'shon), *n.* [< ME. *porcioun, porcion, porcyone* = D. *portie* = G. Sw. Dan. *portion*, < OF. *portion, porcion*, F. *portion* = Sp. *porcion* = Pg. *porção* = It. *porzione*, < L. *portio(n-)*, a share, part, portion, relation, proportion, akin to *par(t-)s*, part: see *part*. Cf. *proportion.*] 1. A part of a whole, whether separated from it, or considered by itself though not actually separated.

These are parts of his ways: but how little a *portion* is heard of him? Job xxvi. 14.

Some other *portions* of Scripture were read, upon emergent occasions. *Jer. Taylor*, Works (ed. 1835), II. 256.

2. A part assigned or contributed; a share; an allowance or allotment; hence, a helping at table.

And gif . . . he ne hath nougt of his owene to helpe hymself withe, that the bretheren helpe hym, eche man to a *porcioun*, what his wille be, in wey of charite, sauynge his estaat. *English Gilds* (E. E. T. S.), p. 9.

The priests had a *portion* assigned them of Pharaoh, and did eat their *portion* which Pharaoh gave them. Gen. xlvii. 22.

They . . . carry certaine dayes provision of victuals about with them. Nor is it a cumber; it being no more than a small *portion* of rice and a little sugar and hony. *Sandys*, Travailes, p. 38.

3. Lot; fate; destiny.

The lord of that servant . . . shall cut him asunder, and appoint him his *portion* with the hypocrites. Mat. xxiv. 51.

If length of days be thy *portion*, make it not thy expectation. *Sir T. Browne*, Christ. Mor., iii. 30.

This tradition tells us further that he had afterwards a sight of those dismal habitations which are the *portion* of ill men after death. *Addison*, Tale of Marraton.

4. The part of an estate given to a child or heir, or descending to him by law, or to be distributed to him in the settlement of the estate.—5. A wife's fortune; a dowry.

I give my daughter to him, and will make
Her *portion* equal his. *Shak.*, W. T., iv. 4. 397.

Thy beauty is *portion*, my joy and my dear.
Catskin's Garland (Child's Ballads, VIII. 178).

O, come to me—rich only thus—in loveliness.—Bring no *portion* to me but thy love. *Sheridan*, The Rivals, iii. 3.

Falcidian portion. See *Falcidian.*—**Marriage portion**, a share of the patrimonial estate or other substantial gift of property made by a parent, or one acting in the place of a parent, to a bride upon her marriage, usually intended as a permanent provision.=**Syn. 2.** *Share, Division*, etc. See *part.*

portion (pōr'shon), *v. t.* [= F. *portionner*, portion; from the noun. Cf. *apportion, proportion*, *v.*] 1. To divide or distribute into portions or shares; parcel; allot in shares.

Where my Ulysses and his race might reign,
And *portion* to his tribes the wide domain.
Fenton, in Pope's Odyssey, iv. 238.

2. To endow with a portion or an inheritance.

Him *portion'd* maids, apprenticed orphans bless'd,
The young who labour, and the old who rest.
Pope, Moral Essays, iii. 267.

portionable (pōr'shon-a-bl), *a.* [ME. *porcionable*; as *portion* + *-able*. Cf. *proportionable.*] Proportional. *Chaucer*, Boëthius, iii. meter 9.

portioner (pōr'shon-ėr), *n.* [< ME. **portionere*, < OF. *portionnier* = Pg. *porcionario*, < ML. *portionarius*, a portioner, < L. *portio(n-)*, a portion: see *portion.*] 1. One who divides or assigns in shares.—2. In *Scots law:* (*a*) The proprietor of a small feu or portion of land. (*b*) The subtenant of a feu; an under-feuar.—3. *Eccles.*, a person in part possession of a benefice which is occupied by more than one incumbent at a time. —**Heirs portioners**, two or more females who succeed jointly to a heritable estate in default of heirs male.

portiones, *n.* Plural of *portio.*

portionist (pōr'shon-ist), *n.* [= OF. *portioniste* = Sp. Pg. *porcionista*; as *portion* + *-ist.*] 1. *Eccles.*, same as *portioner*, 3.—2. In Merton College, Oxford, same as *postmaster*, 3.

portionless (pōr'shon-les), *a.* [< *portion* + *-less.*] Having no portion or share; specifically, having no dowry: as, a *portionless* maid.

Port Jackson fig. See *fig*[2], 1.

Portland arrowroot. See *arrowroot* and *Arum.*

Portland beds. See *Portland stone*, under *stone.*

Portland cement. See *cement.*

Portlandian (pōrt-lan'di-an), *n.* [< *Portland* (Isle of Portland), a peninsula of Dorset, England, + *-ian.*] Same as *Portland beds.* See *Portland stone*, under *stone.*

Portland moth. A British noctuid moth, *Agrotis præcox.*

Portland powder, sago, screw, stone, tern, vase. See *powder, sago*, etc.

port-lanyard (pōrt'lan"yärd), *n.* See *lanyard*, 1.

portlast (pōrt'läst), *n.* [< *port*[3], *v.*, + *last*[3].] The gunwale of a ship. Also called *portoise.*

port-lid (pōrt'lid), *n.* See *lid.*

port-lifter (pōrt'lif"tėr), *n.* A contrivance for raising and lowering heavy ports in ships.

portliness (pōrt'li-nes), *n.* The character or state of being portly in manner, appearance, or person; dignified bearing or stately proportions.

Such pride is praise; such *portlinesse* is honor.
Spenser, Sonnets, v.

portly (pōrt'li), *a.* [< *port*[3] + *-ly*[1].] 1. Stately or dignified in mien; of noble appearance and carriage.

Portly his person was, and much increast
Through his Heroicke grace and honorable gest.
Spenser, F. Q., III. ii. 24.

Rudely thou wrongest my deare harts desire,
In finding fault with her too *portly* pride.
Spenser, Sonnets, v.

My sister is a goodly, *portly* lady,
A woman of a presence.
Fletcher, Wit without Money, i. 2.

What though she want
A portion to maintain a *portly* greatness?
Ford, Lover's Melancholy, i. 3.

2. Stout; somewhat large and unwieldy in person.

It was the *portly* and, had it possessed the advantage of a little more height, would have been the stately figure of a man considerably in the decline of life. *Hawthorne*, Seven Gables, viii.

3†. Swelling.

Where your argosies with *portly* sail . . .
Do overpeer the petty traffickers.
Shak., M. of V., i. 1. 9.

portman (pōrt'man), *n.*; pl. *portmen* (-men). [AS. *portman*, a townsman, citizen, < *port*, a port, town, city, + *man*, man.] An inhabitant or burgess of a port-town, or of one of the Cinque Ports. *Imp. Dict.*

portman-mote (pōrt'man-mōt), *n.* See *portmote.*

portmanteau (pōrt-man'tō), *n.* [Formerly also *portmanteaw, portmantue, portmantua* (also *portmantle*, accom. to *mantle*); = Sp. Pg. *portamanteo*, < F. *portemanteau* (= It. *portamantello*), < *porter*, carry, + *manteau*, cloak, mantle: see *port*[3] and *mantle, manteau.*] 1. A case used in journeying for containing clothing: originally adapted to the saddle of a horseman, and therefore nearly cylindrical and of flexible make.

There are old leather *portmanteaus*, like stranded porpoises, their mouths gaping in gaunt hunger for the food with which they used to be gorged to repletion.
O. W. Holmes, Poet at the Breakfast Table, I.

2. A trunk, especially a leather trunk of small size.—**3.** A hook or bracket on which to hang a garment, especially one which holds a coat or cloak securely for brushing.

port-mantick†, *n.* A corrupt form of *portmanteau*.

He would linger no longer, and play at cards in King Philip's palace, till the messenger with the *port-mantick* came from Rome.
Bp. Hacket, Abp. Williams, i. 160. (*Davies.*)

portmantle† (pōrt-man'tl), *n.* [An accom. form of F. *portemanteau*: see *portmanteau*.] A portmanteau.

And out of the sheriffs *portmantle*
He told three hundred pound.
Robin Hood and the Butcher (Child's Ballads, V. 38).

portmantua†, *n.* Same as *portmanteau*.

Fol. Where be the masking-suits?
Maw. In your lordship's *portmantua*.
Middleton, Mad World, ii. 2.

Your cunningest thieves . . . use to cut off the *portmantua* from behind, without staying to dive into the pockets of the owner.
Swift, To a Young Poet.

port-mote (pōrt'mōt), *n.* [AS. **port-gemōt* (not found), < *port*, a town, + *gemōt*, meeting: see *port*[1] and *mote*[3], *moot*[1].] In *early Eng. hist.*, a court or moot composed of the portmen or burghers of a port-town, corresponding to the leet of other places. Also called *portman-mote*.

These legal ports were undoubtedly at first assigned by the crown; since to each of them a court of *portmote* is incident, the jurisdiction of which must flow from the royal authority.
Blackstone, Com., I. vii.

portoir†, *n.* [< OF. *portoir*, m., a bearing branch (sc. *de vigne*, of a vine), < *porter*, bear: see *port*[3].] One who or that which bears; hence, one who or that which produces.

Branches which were *portoirs* and bear grapes the year before.
Holland. (*Encyc. Dict.*)

portoise† (pōr'tiz), *n.* [Appar. for **portoire*, < OF. *portoire*, f., a bearer, support, as a barrow, basket, etc., the span of the door of a coach, etc., < *porter*, bear, carry: see *port*[3]. Cf. *portlast*.] The gunwale of a ship: in the phrase *à portoise*, said of yard-arms resting on the gunwale.

Port Orford cedar. See *Chamæcyparis*, and *ginger-pine* (under *pine*[1]).

portos†, portoos†, portous†, *n.* Middle English forms of *portass*.

portour†, *n.* A Middle English form of *porter*[2].

port-pane† (pōrt'pān), *n.* [< OF. *porte-pain*, < *porter*, carry, + *pain*, bread: see *port*[3] and *pain*[2].] A cloth in which bread was carried in order that it might not be touched by the hands.

port-piece† (pōrt'pēs), *n.* [< OF. *porte-piece*, a part of armor, also (as in F. *porte-pièce*) a shoemaker's awl; < *porter*, carry, + *piece*, piece: see *port*[3] and *piece*.] A kind of cannon used in the sixteenth century, mentioned as employed on board ship.

portrait (pōr'trạ̄t), *n.* [Formerly also *pourtrait*, *pourtraict*, *portract* (= D. *portret* = G. *porträt* = Sw. *porträt* = Dan. *portræt*); < OF. *portrait*, *pourtrait*, *portraict*, *pourtraict*, F. *portrait*, < ML. *protractus*, a portrait, prop. an image, portrait, plan, pp. of *protrahere* (> OF. *portraire*, etc.), depict, portray: see *portray*.] **1.** A drawing, representation, delineation, or picture of a person or a thing; specifically, a picture of a person, drawn from life; especially, a picture or representation of the face; a likeness, whether executed in oil or water-color, in crayon, on steel, by photography, in marble, etc., but particularly in oil: as, a painter of *portraits*.

The sayde Besson left, in witnesse of his excellencie in that Art, a booke in prynt, conteyning the fourmes or *portractes* of syxtie engins of marueylous strange and profytable deuice, for diuers commodious and necessary vses.
R. Eden, First Books on America (ed. Arber, p. xlvii.).

Even in *portraits* the grace, and we may add the likeness, consists more in taking the general air than in observing the exact similitude of every feature.
Sir J. Reynolds, Discourses, iv.

2. A vivid description or delineation in words.

But, if Jonson has been accused of having servilely given *portraits*—and we have just seen in what an extraordinary way they are *portraits*—his learning has also been alleged as something more objectionable in the dramatic art; and we have often heard something of the pedantry of Jonson.
I. D'Israeli, Amen. of Lit., II. 245.

Berlin portraits, in *photog.* See *gray*, *v.*, 3.—**Composite portrait.** See *composite photograph*, under *composite*.

portrait† (pōr'trạ̄t), *v. t.* [Also *pourtraict*; < *portrait*, *n.*] To portray; draw.

I labour to *pourtraict* in Arthure, before he was king, the image of a brave knight.
Spenser, F. Q., To the Reader.

A Painter should more benefite her to *portraite* a most sweet face, wryting Canidia vpon it, then to paint Canidia as she was.
Sir P. Sidney, Apol. for Poetrie.

portraitist (pōr'trā-tist), *n.* [= F. *portraitiste*; as *portrait* + *-ist*.] A maker of portraits; a portrait-painter; one who devotes his attention particularly to portraits, as a photographer.

A young French artist, who is among the "really good" as a *portraitist*.
Contemporary Rev., LIV. 86.

portrait-lens (pōr'trạ̄t-lenz), *n.* One of a class of double or triple photographic lenses especially adapted for taking portraits.

Petzval designed the *portrait-lens* [in photography], in which two achromatic lenses, placed at a certain distance apart, combine to form the image.
Lord Rayleigh, Encyc. Brit., XVII. 805.

portrait-painter (pōr'trạ̄t-pān'tėr), *n.* One whose occupation is the painting of portraits.

portrait-stone (pōr'trạ̄t-stōn), *n.* In *gem-cutting*, a lask, or flat diamond, occasionally with several rows of small facets around the edge, used to cover miniatures or small portraits.

portraiture (pōr'trā-tūr), *n.* [Formerly also *portrature*, *pourtraiture*; < ME. *portreiture*, *portreture*, *portratowre*, < OF. *pourtraicture*, F. *portraiture*, < OF. *pourtraire*, F. *portraire*, portray: see *portrait*.] **1.** A representation or picture; a painted resemblance; a likeness or portrait.

We will imitate the olde paynters in Greece, who, drawing in theyr Tables the *portraiture* of Jupiter, were euery houre mending it, but durst neuer finish it.
Lyly, Euphues and his England, p. 257.

There is an exquisite *pourtraiture* of a great horse made of white stone.
Coryat, Crudities, I. 35, sig. D.

2. Likenesses or portraits collectively.

The *portreiture* that was upon the wal
Withinne the temple of mighty Mars the reede.
Chaucer, Knight's Tale, l. 1110.

Unclasp me, Stranger, and unfold
With trembling care my leaves of gold,
Rich in Gothic *portraiture*.
Rogers, Voyage of Columbus (inscribed on the original MS.).

3. The art of making portraits; the art or practice of portraying or depicting, whether in pictures or in words; the art of the portraitist.

Portraiture, which, taken in its widest sense, includes all representation not only of human beings, but also of visible objects in nature.
C. T. Newton, Art and Archæol., p. 26.

portraiture† (pōr'trā-tūr), *v. t.* [< *portraiture*, *n.*] To paint; portray. *Shaftesbury.*

portray (pōr-trā'), *v.* [Formerly also *pourtray*; < ME. *portrayen*, *portreyen*, *pourtraien*, *purtrayen*, *purtreyen*, < OF. *portraire*, *pourtraire* (ppr. *portrayant*), F. *portraire* = It. *protraere*, *protrarre*, < ML. *protrahere*, paint, depict, a later use of L. *protrahere*, draw forth, reveal, extend, protract, < *pro*, forth, + *trahere*, draw: see *tract*[1], *trait*. Cf. *protract*.] **I.** *trans.* **1.** To depict; reproduce the lineaments of; draw or paint to the life.

I haue him *portreide* an paynted in mi hert withinne,
That he sittus in mi sigt me thinkes euermore.
William of Palerne (E. E. T. S.), l. 445.

Take thee a tile, and lay it before thee, and *pourtray* upon it the city, even Jerusalem.
Ezek. iv. 1.

2. To depict or describe vividly in words; describe graphically or vividly.

Ther was nothinge that she loved so moche, ffor he was so like the kynge Ban as he hadde be *portreyed*.
Merlin (E. E. T. S.), iii. 675.

Scott *portrayed* with equal strength and success every figure in his crowded company.
Emerson, Walter Scott.

3†. To adorn with pictures or portraits.

Portreid it was with briddes freshly,
Thys fair pauilon rich was in seing.
Rom. of Partenay (E. E. T. S.), l. 1003.

Rigid spears and helmets throng'd, and shields
Various, with boastful argument *portray'd*.
Milton, P. L., vi. 84.

=**Syn. 1** and **2.** To delineate, sketch, represent.

II.† *intrans.* To paint.

He coude songes make and wel endite,
Juste and eek daunce and wel *purtreye* and write.
Chaucer, Gen. Prol. to C. T., l. 96.

portrayal (pōr-trā'al), *n.* [< *portray* + *-al*.] The act of portraying; delineation; representation.

portrayer (pōr-trā'ėr), *n.* [< ME. *portrayer*, *portreyour*, < OF. *portraior*, *pourtrayeur*, a painter, < *portraire*, portray: see *portray*.] One who portrays; a painter; one who paints, draws, or describes to the life.

Ne *portreyour* ne kervere of ymages.
Chaucer, Knight's Tale, l. 1041.

Remembre my brotheris ston. . . . It is told me that the man at Sent Bridis is no kienly *portrayer*; therfor I wold fayn it myth be portrayed be sum odir man and he to grave it up.
Paston Letters, III. 268.

A poet . . . is the faithful *portrayer* of Nature, whose features are always the same, and always interesting.
Irving, Sketch-Book, p. 169.

portreeve (pōrt'rēv), *n.* [< ME. *portreve* (ML. *portireve*, *portyrevius*), < AS. *portgerēfa*, a portreeve, < *port*, a port, town, + *gerēfa*, reeve: see *port*[1] and *reeve*.] The chief magistrate of a port or maritime town; in *early Eng. hist.*, the representative or appointee of the crown having authority over a mercantile town. The appointment was made with especial reference to the good order of a crowded commercial population, and the collection of royal revenues there, the functions of this officer having a general correspondence to those of a shirgerefa (sheriff) in a county. Formerly also *portgrave*.

The chief magistrate of London in these times is always called the *Port-Reeve*.
E. A. Freeman, Norman Conquest, III. 491.

portreise†, *n.* Same as *portass*. *Ascham*, The Scholemaster, p. 7.

portress, *n.* See *porteress*.

portrey†, *v.* An obsolete form of *portray*.

port-rope (pōrt'rōp), *n.* A rope or tackle for hauling up and suspending the ports or covers of port-holes. Also *port-tackle* and *port-lanyard*.

port-rule (pōrt'röl), *n.* An instrument, or a system of mechanism, which carries, moves, or regulates the motion of a rule in a machine.

port-sale (pōrt'sāl), *n.* [< *port*[1] + *sale*.] A public sale of goods to the highest bidder; an auction.

I have repaired and rigged the ship of knowledge, . . . that she may safely pass about and through all parts of this noble realm, and there make *port sail* of her wished wares.
Harman, Caveat for Cursetors, p. iv.

When Sylla had taken the citie of Rome, he made *port-sale* of the goods of them whom he had put to death.
North, tr. of Plutarch, p. 466.

port-sill (pōrt'sil), *n.* In *ship-building*, a piece of timber let in horizontally between two frames, to form the upper or lower side of a port.

port-stopper (pōrt'stop'ėr), *n.* A heavy piece of iron, rotating on a vertical axis, serving to close a port in a turret-ship.

port-tackle (pōrt'tak'l), *n.* Same as *port-rope*.

port-town (pōrt'toun), *n.* A town having a port, or situated near a port.

portuary† (pōr'tū-ā-ri), *n.* Same as *portass*.

Portugal (pōr'tū-gal), *a.* and *n.* [Formerly also *Portingal*, *Portingall* (cf. OF. *Portingalois*, Sp. *Portugalese*, ML. *Portugalensis*, Portuguese); < Pg. Sp. *Portugal* (ML. *Portugalia*), Portugal, orig. (ML.) *Portus Cale*, 'the port Cal,' the fuller name of the city now called *Oporto* ('the port'), transferred to the kingdom itself: L. *portus*, port; *Cale*, the city so called, now Oporto.] **I.** *a.* Pertaining to Portugal; Portuguese.—**Portugal crakeberry, laurel**, etc. See the nouns.

II.† *n.* A native or an inhabitant of Portugal; a Portuguese.

The Spaniards and *Portugales* in Barbarie, in the Indies, and elsewhere haue ordinarie confederacie and traffike with the Moores.
Hakluyt's Voyages, III., Ded.

portugue†, porteguet†, *n.* [Also *portague*, *portigue*; < OF. *portugaise* (also *portugalle*, *portugaloise*), a Portuguese coin so called (see def.); fem. of *portugais*, Portuguese: see *Portuguese*.] A gold coin of Portugal, current in the sixteenth century, and weighing about 540 grains, worth about $22.50 United States money.

An egge is eaten at one sup, and a *portague* lost at one cast.
Lyly, Midas, ii. 2.

For the compounding of my wordes, therein I imitate rich men, who, hav-

Obverse.

Reverse.

Portugue of John III., 1521-57.—British Museum. (Size of the original.)

ing store of white single money together, convert a number of those small little sentes into great peeces of gold, such as double pistoles and *portugues*.
Nashe, quoted in Int. to Pierce Penilesse, p. xxx.

Face. No gold about thee?
Drug. Yes, I have a *portague* I have kept this half-year.
B. *Jonson*, Alchemist, i. 1.

And forthwith he drew out of his pocket a *portegué*, the which you shall receive enclosed herein.
Sir T. More, To His Daughter (Utopia, Int., p. xxiv.).

Portuguese (pōr-tū̦-gēs′ or -gēz′), *a.* and *n.* [= D. *Portugees* = G. *Portugiese* = Sw. *Portugis* = Dan. *Portugiser*, n. (cf. D. *portugeesch* = G. *portugiesisch* = Sw. Dan. *portugisisk*, a.) (< E. or F.); < F. *Portugais* = Sp. *Portugués* = Pg. *Portuguez* = It. *Portoghese*, Portuguese; with omission of the final element *-al* (retained in OF. *Portugalois*, *Portingalois* = Sp. *Portugalese*, ML. *Portugalensis*), < *Portugal* (ML. *Portugalia*), Portugal: see *Portugal*.] **I.** *a.* Of or pertaining to Portugal, a kingdom of Europe, situated west of Spain. Abbreviated *Pg.*, *Port.*—**Portuguese cut.** See *brilliant*.—**Portuguese man-of-war.** See *man-of-war*, and cut under *Physalia*.

II. *n.* **1.** An inhabitant of Portugal; as a collective plural, the people of Portugal.—**2.** The language of Portugal. It is one of the Romance group of languages, and is nearly allied to Spanish.

portuist, portuise†, *n.* Same as *portass*.

Portulaca (pōr-tū̦-lā′kạ̈, often -lak′ạ̈), *n.* [NL. (Tournefort, 1700), < L. *portulaca*, also *porcilaca*, purslane: see *purslane*[1].] **1.** A genus of polypetalous plants, type of the order *Portulaceæ*. It is characterized by a one-celled ovary, with many ovules, half-coherent with the calyx, and surrounded at its middle by the two calyx-lobes, four to six petals, and eight or many stamens—all others in the order having the ovary free. There are about 20 species, natives of the tropics, especially in America, and one, *P. oleracea*, the purslane, a weed widely scattered throughout temperate regions. All are fleshy herbs, prostrate or ascending, with thick juicy and often cylindrical leaves, mainly alternate, and bearing terminal flowers, yellow, red, or purple, often very bright and showy. Many species are in cultivation, under the name *portulaca*, *P. grandiflora* bearing also the name of *sun-plant*, the flowers expanding in bright sunshine.
2. [*l. c.*] A plant of this genus.

Portulacaceæ (pōr′tū-lạ̈-kā′sē-ē), *n. pl.* [NL. (Lindley, 1835), < *Portulaca* + *-aceæ*.] Same as *Portulaceæ*.

Portulacaria (pōr″tū̦-lạ̈-kā′ri-ạ̈), *n.* [NL. (N. J. von Jacquin, 1786), < *Portulaca* + *-aria*.] A genus of plants of the order *Portulaceæ*, having two short sepals, four or five longer petals, and from four to seven stamens, unlike any other member of its family in its single ovule, and also in its winged fruit. The only species, *P. Afra*, is a smooth South African shrub, with fleshy and obovate opposite leaves, and small rose-colored flowers clustered in the upper axils, or forming a leafy panicle, followed by three-winged capsules which do not split open when ripe. It is the spek-boom of the Cape colonists, and affords in many places the principal food of the elephant, besides giving by its pale-green foliage a characteristic aspect to the country. Also called *purslane-tree*.

Portulaceæ (pōr-tū̦-lā′sē̦-ē), *n. pl.* [NL. (A. L. de Jussieu, 1789), < *Portulaca* + *-eæ*.] A small order of polypetalous plants of the cohort *Caryophyllinæ* and series *Thalamifloræ*, characterized by a one-celled ovary with a free central placenta, and by the usual presence of scarious stipules, two sepals, five petals, and either numerous or less than five stamens. It includes 18 genera and about 145 species, natives mainly of America, with a few in all continents. Nearly half of the species are contained in the tropical genus *Calandrinia*, being fleshy-leafed herbs of America or Australia: of the others, *Portulaca* (the type) and *Claytonia* (containing the well-known spring-beauty of the United States) are the chief. They are usually smooth succulent herbs, with entire and often fleshy or even pulpy leaves, either alternate or opposite, and commonly with very bright ephemeral flowers.

portunian (pōr-tū′ni-ạn), *a.* and *n.* [< *Portunus* + *-ian*.] **I.** *a.* Of or pertaining to the genus *Portunus* or the family *Portunidæ*.

II. *n.* A crab of the family *Portunidæ*, as the common blue edible crab of the United States, *Callinectes hastatus*. See cut under *paddle-crab*.

Portunidæ (pōr-tū′ni-dē), *n. pl.* [NL., < *Portunus* + *-idæ*.] A family of short-tailed ten-footed crustaceans, typified by the genus *Portunus*, containing many crabs, some of whose legs are fitted for swimming, known as *paddle-crabs*, *shuttle-crabs*, and *swimming-crabs*. See cuts under *paddle-crab* and *Platyonychus*.

Portunus (pōr-tū′nus), *n.* [NL. (Fabricius, 1798), < L. *Portunus*, the protecting god of harbors, < *portus*, a harbor: see *port*[1].] The typical genus of the family *Portunidæ*.

portoust†, *n.* Same as *portass*.

porturature†, **porture**[2]†, *n.* Corrupt forms of *portraiture*. *Udall*, tr. of Apophthegms of Erasmus, pp. 208 and 99.

porture[1]† (pōr′tū̦r), *n.* [< *port*[3] + *-ure*.] Carriage; behavior. *Halliwell.*

porture[2]†, *n.* See *porturature*.

port-way[1]† (pōrt′wā), *n.* [< *port*[1] + *way*.] A paved highway.

The *Port-way*, or High paved street named Bath-gate.
Holland, tr. of Camden, p. 557. (*Davies.*)

port-way[2] (pōrt′wā), *n.* [< *port*[2] + *way*.] One of the steam-passages connecting the steam-chest of a steam-engine with the interior of the steam-cylinder. Also called *port*.

port-wine (pōrt′wīn′), *n.* Same as *port*[5].

porus (pō′rus), *n.*; pl. *pori* (-rī). In *anat.* and *zoöl.*, a pore: used in a few phrases: as, *porus excretorius*, an excretory pore; *porus ejaculatorius*, an ejaculatory pore.—**Porus opticus.** Same as *optic disk*. See *optic*.

porwiggle† (pôr′wig-l), *n.* [A var. of *polliwig*.] A tadpole.

That which the ancients called gyrinus, we a *porwigle* or tadpole. *Sir T. Browne*, Vulg. Err., iii. 13.

pory† (pōr′i), *a.* [< *pore*[2] + *-y*[1].] Porous or porose.

The stones hereof are so light and *pory* that they will not sink when thrown into the water.
Sandys, Travailes, p. 217.

porzana (pōr-zā′nạ̈), *n.* [NL.] **1.** An old name of the small water-rail or crake of Europe, and now a specific name of the same. See *Ortygometra*, 2, and *Crex*.—**2.** [*cap.*] An extensive genus of rails of the family *Rallidæ*, founded by Vieillot in 1816, having a short stout bill; the crakes. The species are numerous and of almost world-wide distribution. The common crake or short-billed

Sora Rail (*Porzana carolina*).

water-rail of Europe is *Porzana porzana* or *P. maruetta*. In the United States the best-known species is *P. carolina*, the Carolina crake or rail, also called *sora*, *soree*, and *ortolan*. The small yellow crake or rail of North America is *P. noveboracensis*. The little black crake or rail of America is *P. jamaicensis*.

pos (poz), *a.* An abbreviation of *positive*. Also *poz*. [Slang.]

She shall dress me and flatter me, for I will be flattered, that 's *pos*. *Addison*, The Drummer, iii.

posada (pō-sä′dạ̈), *n.* [Sp., < *posar*, lodge, rest, < ML. *pausare*, put, lodge: see *pose*[2], *n.*] An inn. *Southey.*

posaune (pọ̄-zou′ne), *n.* [G., also *bosūne*, *basūne*, *busūne*, *busine* (= D. *bazuin* = Sw. Dan. *basun*), < OF. *buisine* = It. *buccina*, < L. *buccina*, prop. *bucina*, a trumpet: see *buccina*.] The German name of the trombone.

pose[1]† (pōz), *n.* [< ME. *pose*, < AS. *geposu*, pose, catarrh, < W. *pas*, a cough. Cf. *wheeze*.] A cold in the head; catarrh.

He yexeth, and he speketh thurgh the nose,
As he were on the quakke or on the *pose*.
Chaucer, Reeve's Tale, l. 232.

Distillations called rewmes or *poses*.
Sir T. Elyot, The Governour, iii. 22.

Now haue we manie chimnies, and yet our tenderlings complaine of rheumes, catarhs, and *poses*.
Quoted in Forewords to *Manners and Meals* (E. E. T. S.), [XXXII. lxiv.

pose[2] (pōz), *v.*; pret. and pp. *posed*, ppr. *posing*. [< ME. *poser*, < OF. *poser*, F. *poser*, put, place, lay, settle, lodge, etc., refl. *se poser*, put oneself in a particular attitude, = Sp. *posar*, *pausar* = Pg. *pausar*, *poisar*, *pousar* = It. *posare*, *pausare*, put, place, < ML. *pausare*, cease, cause to rest, place, < L. *pausare*, cease, < *pausa*, pause, < Gr. παῦσις, pause: see *pause*, *n.* This verb, OF. *poser*, etc., acquired the sense of L. *ponere*, pp. *positus*, put, place, etc., and came to be practically identified with it in use, taking all its compounds, whence E. *appose*, *compose*, *depose*, *dispose*, *propose* (and *purpose*), *repose*, *suppose*, etc., which verbs coexist in E., in some cases, with forms from the L. *ponere*, as *compound*[1], *depone*, *expone* (and *expound*), *impone*, *propone* (and *propound*), etc., with derived forms like *opponent*, *component*, *deponent*, etc., *apposition*, *composition*, *deposition*, etc.] **I.** *trans.* **1**†. To put; place; set.

But XXX[ti] footes *pose*
Iche order of from other; croppe and tail
To save in setting hem is thyne advail.
Palladius, Husbondrie (E. E. T. S.), p. 78.

2†. To put by way of supposition or hypothesis; suppose.

I *pose* I hadde synned so and shulde now deye,
And now am sory, that so the seint spirit aguite,
Confesse me, and crye his grace god that al made.
Piers Plowman (B), xvii. 293.

I *pose* that thow lovedest hire biforn.
Chaucer, Knight's Tale, l. 304.

Yet *pose* I that it myght amended be.
Palladius, Husbondrie (E. E. T. S.), p. 11.

3. To lay down as a proposition; state; posit. [Recent.]

It is difficult to leave Correggio without at least *posing* the question of the difference between moralised and merely sensual art.
J. A. Symonds, Italy and Greece, p. 280.

M. Janet, with perhaps pardonable patriotism, *poses* the new psychology as of French origin, but it is really connected with the past by many roots. *Science*, XI. 256.

4. To place in suitable or becoming position or posture; cause to assume a suitable or effective attitude: as, to *pose* a person for a portrait.

It was no unusual thing to see the living models *posed* in his [Gainsborough's] painting-room.
Geo. M. Brock-Arnold, Gainsborough, p. 55.

5. To bear; conduct. [Rare.]

Mr. Avery was a cheerful, busy, manly man, who *posed* himself among men as a companion and fellow-citizen, whose word on any subject was to go only so far as its own weight and momentum should carry it.
H. B. Stowe, Oldtown, p. 441.

Interchangeably posed, in *her*. See *interchangeably*.

II. *intrans.* **1**†. To make a supposition; put the case.—**2.** To assume a particular attitude or rôle; endeavor to appear or be regarded (as something else); attitudinize, literally or figuratively: as, to *pose* as a model; to *pose* as a martyr.

He . . . *posed* before her as a hero of the most sublime kind. *Thackeray*, Shabby Genteel Story, vi.

These solemn attendants simply *posed*, and never moved.
T. C. Crawford, English Life, p. 35.

pose[2] (pōz), *n.* [< F. *pose*, standing, attitude, posture, pose, < *poser*, put, refl. put oneself in an attitude: see *pose*[2], *v.*] **1.** Attitude or position, whether taken naturally or assumed for effect: as, the *pose* of an actor; especially, the attitude in which any character is represented artistically; the position, whether of the whole person or of an individual member of the body: as, the *pose* of a statue; the *pose* of the head. In physiology the pose of a muscle is the latent period between the stimulation of a muscle-fiber and its contraction.
2. A deposit; a secret hoard. [Scotch.]

Laying by a little *pose*, even out of such earnings, to help them in their old age.
Noctes Ambrosianæ, April, 1832.

=**Syn. 1.** *Position*, *Attitude*, etc. See *posture*.

pose[3] (pōz), *v. t.*; pret. and pp. *posed*, ppr. *posing*. [Formerly also *poze*; < ME. *posen*, by apheresis from *apposen*, *aposen*, a corruption of *oposyn*, *opposen*: see *oppose*. The method of examination in the schools being by argument, to examine was to oppose. Hence *puzzle*.] **1**†. To put questions to; interrogate closely; question; examine.

If any man rebuke them with that, they persecute him immediately, and *pose* him in their false doctrine, and make him an heretic.
Tyndale, Ans. to Sir T. More, etc. (Parker Soc., 1850), p. 104.

She . . . *posed* him, and sifted him, to try whether he were the very Duke of York or no.
Bacon, Hist. Henry VII., p. 119.

2. To puzzle, nonplus, or embarrass by a difficult question.

I still am *pos'd* about the case,
But wiser you shall judge.
J. Beaumont, Psyche, i. 110.

A thing which would have *pos'd* Adam to name.
Donne, Satires (ed. 1819).

A sucking babe might have *posed* him.
Lamb, South-Sea House.

posé (pō-zā′), *a.* [F., pp. of *poser*, place: see *pose*[2].] In *her.*, standing still, with all the feet on the ground; statant: said of a lion, horse, or other animal used as a bearing.

posed† (pōzd), *p. a.* [< *pose*[2] + *-ed*[2].] Balanced; sedate: opposed to *flighty*.

An old settled person of a most *posed*, staid, and grave behaviour. *Urquhart*, tr. of Rabelais, iii. 19. (*Davies.*)

Poseideon (pō-sī'dē-on), *n.* [Gr. Ποσειδεών: see def.] The sixth month of the ancient Athenian year, corresponding to the latter half of our December and the first half of January.

Poseidon (pō-sī'don), *n.* [< Gr. Ποσειδῶν: see def.] 1. In *Gr. myth.*, one of the chief Olympians, brother of Zeus, and supreme lord of the sea, sometimes looked upon as a benignant promoter of calm and prosperous navigation, but more often as a terrible god of storm. His consort was the Nereid Amphitrite, and his attendant train

Poseidon overwhelming the giant Polybotes, for whom Ge or Gaia (on the left) makes intercession. (From a Greek red-figured vase of the 4th century B. C.)

was composed of Nereids, Tritons, and sea-monsters of every form. In art he is a majestic figure, closely approaching Zeus in type. His most constant attributes are the trident and the dolphin, with the horse, which he was reputed to have created during his contest with Athena for supremacy in Attica. The original Roman or Italic Neptune became assimilated to him.
2. In *zoöl.*: (*a*) A genus of worms. (*b*) A genus of hemipterous insects of the family *Scutelleridæ*. *Snellen*, 1863. (*c*) A genus of crustaceans.

Poseidonian (pō-sī-dō'ni-an), *a.* [< Gr. Ποσειδώνιος, of Poseidon (< Ποσειδῶν, Poseidon), + *-an*.] Of or pertaining to Poseidon.

Poseidon, the great and swarthy race-god of the South, is readily enough conceived of as coming into conflict with Zeus, when immigrants arriving in the country bring with them a *Poseidonian* worship.
Gladstone, Contemporary Rev., LI. 766.

poser (pō'zėr), *n.* [< *pose*3 + *-er*1.] 1. One who poses or puts questions; one who questions or interrogates closely; an examiner.

Let his questions not be troublesome, for that is fit for a *poser*. Bacon, Discourse (ed. 1887).

The university [of Cambridge] . . . appointed Doctor Cranmer (afterwards Archbishop of Canterbury) to be the *poser*-general of all candidates in Divinity.
Fuller, Worthies, Norfolk, II. 462.

2. A question that poses or puzzles; a puzzling or difficult question or matter.

"What do you think women are good for?" "That's a *poser*." *C. D. Warner*, Backlog Studies, p. 161.

posied (pō'zid), *a.* [< *posy* + *-ed*2.] Inscribed with a posy or motto.

Some by a strip of woven hair
In *posied* lockets bribe the fair.
Gay, To a Young Lady, with some Lampreys.

posit (poz'it), *v. t.* [< L. *positus*, pp. of *ponere*, place: see *position*.] 1. To dispose, range, or place in relation to other objects.

That the principle that sets on work these organs and worketh by them is nothing else but the modification of matter, or the natural motion thereof, thus or thus *posited* or disposed, is most apparently false.
Sir M. Hale, Orig. of Mankind, p. 49.

2. To lay down as a position or principle; assume as real or conceded; present as a fact; affirm.

In *positing* pure or absolute existence as a mental datum, immediate, intuitive, and above proof, he mistakes the fact. *Sir W. Hamilton.*

When it is said that the ego *posits* itself, the meaning is that the ego becomes a fact of consciousness, which it can only become through the antithesis of the non-ego.
Chambers's Encyc.

position (pō-zish'on), *n.* [< F. *position* = Sp. *posicion* = Pg. *posição* = It. *posizione*, < L. *positio(n-)*, a putting, position, < *ponere*, pp. *positus*, put, place: see *ponent*. Cf. *apposition*, *composition*, *deposition*, and the similar verbs *appose*, *compose*, *depose*, etc.: see *pose*2.] 1. The aggregate of spatial relations of a body or figure, considered as rigid, to other such bodies or figures; the definition of the place of a thing; situation.

We have different prospects of the same thing according to our different *positions* to it. *Locke.*

The absolute *position* of the parties has been altered; the relative *position* remains unchanged.
Macaulay, War of the Succession in Spain.

Position, Wren said, is essential to the perfecting of beauty; — a fine building is lost in a dark lane; a statue should stand in the air. *Emerson*, Woman.

The exceptional miracles were those of exorcism, which occupied a very singular *position* in the early Church.
Lecky, Europ. Morals, I. 404.

Hence — 2. Status or standing; social rank or condition: as, social *position*; a man of *position*.

Such changes as gave women not merely an advisory but an authoritative *position* on this and similar boards.
N. A. Rev., CXXXIX. 400.

3. The act of positing or asserting; also, the assertion itself; affirmation; principle laid down.

From Gods word I'me sure you never tooke
Such damnable *positions*.
Times' Whistle (E. E. T. S.), p. 12.

In order to be a truly eloquent or persuasive speaker, nothing is more necessary than to be a virtuous man. This was a favourite *position* among the ancient rhetoricians.
H. *Blair*, Rhetoric, xxxiv.

4. A place occupied or to be occupied. (*a*) *Milit.*, the ground occupied by a body of troops preparatory to making or receiving an attack. (*b*) An office; a post; a situation: as, a *position* in a bank. (c) In *music*: (1) The disposition of the tones of a triad or other chord with reference to the lowest voice-part — the *first*, original, or fundamental position having the root of the chord in that part, the *second* position having the next or second tone of the chord there, etc., and all positions except the first being also called *inverted positions* or *inversions*. (2) The disposition of the tones of a triad or other chord with reference to their nearness to each other, *close* position having the tones so near together that an outer voice-part cannot be transposed so as to fall between two middle parts, and *open* or dispersed position being the reverse of this. See *open* and *close harmony*, under *harmony*, 2 (d). (3) In viol-playing, same as *shift*.

5. Posture or manner of standing, sitting, or lying; attitude: as, an uneasy *position*.

Miss Eyre, draw your chair still a little farther forward; you are yet too far back; I can not see you without disturbing my *position* in this comfortable chair, which I have no mind to do. *Charlotte Brontë*, Jane Eyre, xiv.

6. Place; proper or appropriate place: as, his lance was in *position*; specifically (*milit.*), the proper place to make or receive an attack.

As I expected, the enemy was found in *position* on the Big Black. *U. S. Grant*, Personal Memoirs, I. 523.

7. In *arith.*, the act of assuming an approximate value for an unknown quantity, and thence determining that quantity by means of the data of a given question. A value of the unknown quantity is posited or assumed, and then, by means of the given connection between the unknown and a known quantity, from the assumed value of the unknown a value of the known is calculated. A new value of the unknown is then assumed, so as to make the error less. In the rule of *simple position*, only one assumption is made at the outset, and this is corrected by the rule of three. In the far superior rule of *double position*, two values are assumed, and the corrected value of the unknown is ascertained by the solution of a linear equation. Also called the *rule of supposition*, *rule of false*, and *rule of trial and error*.

8. In *logic*, the laying down of a proposition, generally an arbitrary supposition; also, the proposition itself. Thus, in the school disputations, the opponent would say: "*Pono* that a man says that he is lying." Then this act, as well as the proposition so advanced, is a *position*.

9. In *anc. pros.*, the situation of a vowel before two or more consonants or a double consonant, tending to retard utterance and consequently to lengthen the syllable; such combination of consonants, or the prosodic effect produced by it. A short vowel so situated is said to be *in position*, the syllable to be *long by position*, and the consonants to *make position*. A mute with succeeding liquid does not always make position, and the situation of a short vowel before such a combination, or the combination itself, is known as *weak position*.

10. In *obstet.*, the relation between the body of the fetus and the pelvis of the mother in any given presentation. There are in vertex presentations four positions, named according to the direction of the occiput, which the fetal head may occupy: (1) *first* or *left occipitocotyloid position*, in which the occiput points to the left foramen ovale — the most frequent position; (2) *second* or *right occipitocotyloid position*, in which the occiput points to the right foramen ovale; (3) *third* or *right sacro-iliac position*, in which the occiput points to the right sacro-iliac synchondrosis; (4) *fourth* or *left occipito-sacro-iliac position*, in which the occiput points to the left sacro-iliac synchondrosis. See *presentation*1, 6. — **Absolute position, apparent position.** See the adjectives. — **Angle of position**, in *astron.*, the angle which the line joining two neighboring celestial objects makes with the hour-circle passing through that one of the two which is regarded as the principal one, and is taken as the point of reference. The angle is reckoned from the north point through the east, counter-clockwise, completely around the circumference. — **Center of position**, the same as the center of gravity and center of inertia: but when a body is viewed as composed of physical points, and the center of gravity is considered in relation to their positions, geometers designate that point the *center of position*. — **Contrariety of position.** See *contrariety*. — **Eastward position.** See *eastward*. — **Energy of position.** See *energy*, 7. — **Geographical position.** See *geographical*. — **Geometry of position.** See *geometry*. — **Guns of position.** See *gun*1. — **Inverted position.** See def. 4 (c) (1). — **Long by position.** See *long*1. — **Mean position.** See *mean*3. — **Original position**, in *music*, that disposition of the tones of a triad or chord in which the root is at the bottom: opposed to *inversion* or *inverted position*. — **Position angle.** See *angle*3. = **Syn.** 1. Station, spot, locality, post. — 3. Thesis, assertion, doctrine. — 5. *Attitude*, *Pose*, etc. See *posture*.

position (pō-zish'on), *v. t.* [< *position*, *n.*] To place with relation to other objects; set in a definite place.

They are always *positioned* so that they stand upon a solid angle with the "basal plane." *Encyc. Brit.*, XVI. 348.

positional (pō-zish'on-al), *a.* [< *position* + *-al*.] Of or pertaining to position; relating to or depending on position.

A strange conceit, ascribing unto plants *positional* operations, and after the manner of the loadstone.
Sir T. Browne, Vulg. Err., ii. 7.

position-finder (pō-zish'on-fīn"dėr), *n.* An arrangement of apparatus whereby a gunner may point a cannon to the exact position of an object not visible to him. In the form now used in the United States army, the region within range is accurately mapped and laid out in squares, and the elevation corresponding to each square is tabulated. Two telescopes at distant stations are electrically connected with movable bars which are so arranged over the map that the direction of each corresponds to that of its controlling telescope. When both telescopes are directed to the object the two bars cross each other over the square in which the object is, and thus the gunner, knowing the horizontal position and the range, can accurately direct his fire. Compare *range-finder*.

position-micrometer (pō-zish'on-mī-krom'e-tėr), *n.* A micrometer for measuring angles of position (see *angle of position*, under *position*), which are read upon a graduated circle. It has a single thread, or a pair of parallel threads, which can be revolved around the common focus of the object-glass and eye-glass in a plane perpendicular to the axis of the telescope.

positive (poz'i-tiv), *a.* and *n.* [< ME. *positif* (= D. *positief* = G. Sw. Dan. *positiv*), < OF. (and F.) *positif* = Sp. Pg. It. *positivo*, < L. *positivus*, settled by arbitrary appointment or agreement, positive, < *positus*, pp. of *ponere*, put: see *position*.] I. *a.* 1. Laid down as a proposition; affirmed; stated; express: as, a *positive* declaration. — 2. Of an affirmative nature; possessing definite characters of its own; of a kind to excite sensation or be otherwise directly experienced; not negative. Thus, light is *positive*, darkness negative; man is *positive*, non-man negative.

To him, as to his uncle, the exercise of the mind in discussion was a *positive* pleasure. *Macaulay.*

The force of what seems a *positive* desire for an object is in many cases derived from a negative desire or aversion to some correlative pain.
J. Sully, Outlines of Psychol., p. 581.

3. Arbitrarily laid down; determined by declaration, enactment, or convention, and not by nature: opposed to *natural*. Thus, the phenomenon of onomatopœia shows that words are in some degree natural, and not altogether *positive*; so, *positive* law, *positive* theology. [This sense, the original one in Latin, is a translation of Greek θέσει.]

4. Imperative; laid down as a command to be followed without question or discretion: as, *positive* orders.

In laws, that which is natural bindeth universally; that which is *positive*, not so. . . . Although no laws but *positive* are mutable, yet all are not mutable which be *positive*.
Hooker.

5. Unquestionable; indubitable; certain; hence, experiential.

'Tis *positive* against all exceptions, lords,
That our superfluous lackeys . . . were enow
To purge this field of such a hilding foe.
Shak., Hen. V., iv. 2. 25.

The unity and identity of structure in an organism in which a law of action may be inferred form the condition of *positive* science.
E. Mulford, The Nation, The Foundation of Civil Order, i.

6. Confident; fully assured.

I am sometimes doubting when I might be *positive*.
Rymer.

7. Over-confident in opinion and assertion; dogmatic.

Some *positive* persisting fops we know,
That, if once wrong, will needs be always so.
Pope, Essay on Criticism, l. 568.

Where men of judgment creep and feel their way,
The *positive* pronounce without dismay.
Cowper, Conversation.

8†. Actually or really officiating or discharging the duties of an office.

I was, according to the Grand Signior his commandement, very courteously interteined by Peter, his *positiue* prince. *Hakluyt's Voyages*, II. 289.

9. Not reversed. (*a*) Greater than zero; not measured in a reversed direction: signifying the absence of such reversal. (*b*) In *photog.*, representing lights by lights and shades by shades, and not the reverse. (c) Being that one of two opposite kinds which is arbitrarily considered as first: as, *positive* electricity. In all these senses opposed to *negative*.

10. Not comparative. Especially, in *gram.*, signifying a quality without an inflection to indicate comparison as to the intensity of that quality.—**Positive allegation**, in *law*, an allegation made without reserve, as distinguished from an allegation made on information and belief or argumentatively.—**Positive attribute**, an attribute whose real nature is analogous to the form of a positive term.—**Positive colors.** See *color*.—**Positive crystal.** See *refraction* and *hemihedrism*.—**Positive degree**, in *gram.*, the simple value of an adjective or adverb, without comparison or relation to increase or diminution: used by antithesis to *comparative* and *superlative degree*: see *comparison*, 5.—**Positive discrepancy**, the relation between the testimony of two witnesses one of whom explicitly affirms what the other explicitly denies.—**Positive distinction**, a distinction which distinguishes two real existences: opposed to *negative distinction*, which distinguishes an existence from a non-existence.—**Positive electricity, ens, entity, evidence, eyepiece.** See the nouns.—**Positive judgment**, in *logic*, an affirmative proposition.—**Positive law**, in the philosophy of jurisprudence and legislation, the body of laws prescribed or controlling human conduct, as distinguished from laws so called which are merely generalizations of what has been observed to take place; law set as a rule to which itself requires conformity. Some have included divine law, others only human law; judicial as well as statutory law is included.—**Positive misprision, motion, organ.** See the nouns.—**Positive philosophy**, a philosophical system founded by Auguste Comte (1798–1857). Its main doctrines are as follows. All speculative thought passes through three stages—the theological, the metaphysical, the positive. The theological stage is that in which living beings with free will are supposed to account for phenomena; the metaphysical is that in which unverifiable abstractions are resorted to; the positive is that which contents itself with general descriptions of phenomena. The sciences are either abstract or concrete. The abstract discover regularities, the concrete show in what manner these regularities are applicable to special cases. The abstract sciences are (1) mathematics, (2) astronomy, (3) physics, (4) chemistry, (5) biology, (6) sociology. They must be studied in this order, since each after the first rests on the preceding. Especially, sociology must be founded on biology. The development of civilization has taken place according to certain laws or regularities. The civilized community is a true organism—a Great Being—to which individuals are related somewhat as cells to an animal organism. This Great Being should be an object of worship; and this worship should be systematized after the model of the medieval church.—**Positive pleasure** or **pain**, a state of pleasure or pain exceeding the neutral point; a pleasure or pain which is such irrespective of comparison with other states.—**Positive pole of a voltaic pile** or **battery.** See *pole*[2] and *electricity*.—**Positive precision.** See *precision*.—**Positive prescription.** See *prescription*, 3 (*a*).—**Positive proof**, direct proof deducing the conclusion as a particular case of some general rule, without the use of the reductio ad absurdum, etc.—**Positive quantity**, in *alg.*, an affirmative or additive quantity, which character is indicated by the sign + (plus) prefixed to the quantity, called in consequence the *positive sign*. *Positive* is here used in contradistinction to *negative*.—**Positive term**, a term not in form affected with the negative sign.—**Positive whole**, a whole which has parts: opposed to a *negative whole*, or something called a whole as being indivisible.

II. *n.* 1. That which settles by absolute appointment.

Positives . . . while under precept cannot be slighted without slighting morals also.
Waterland, Scripture Vindicated, iii. 37.

2. That which is capable of being affirmed; reality.

Rating *positives* by their privatives.
South, Sermons, I. ii.

3. In *gram.*, the positive degree.—4. In *photog.*, a picture in which the lights and shades are rendered as they are in nature: opposed to *negative*. Positives are usually obtained by printing from negatives. See *negative* and *photography*.—5. Same as *positive organ*.—**Alabastrine positive.** See *alabastrine*.

positively (poz'i-tiv-li), *adv.* In a positive manner. (*a*) Absolutely; by itself; independently of anything else; not comparatively.

The good or evil which is removed may be esteemed good or evil comparatively, and not *positively* or simply.
Bacon.

(*b*) Not negatively; really; in its own nature; directly; inherently: thus, a thing is *positively* good when it produces happiness by its own qualities or operation: it is *negatively* good when it prevents an evil or does not produce it. (*c*) Certainly; indubitably; decidedly.

Give me some breath, some little pause, my lord,
Before I *positively* speak herein.
Shak., Rich. III., iv. 2. 25.

So, Maria, you see your lover pursues you; *positively* you sha'n't escape.
Sheridan, School for Scandal, i. 1.

(*d*) Directly; explicitly: as, the witness testified *positively* to the fact. (*e*) Peremptorily; in positive terms; expressly.

I would ask . . . whether the whole tenor of the divine law does not *positively* require humility and meekness?
Bp. Sprat.

The Queen found it expedient to issue an order *positively* forbidding the torturing of state-prisoners on any pretence whatever.
Macaulay, Lord Bacon.

(*f*) With full confidence or assurance: as, I cannot speak *positively* in regard to the fact. (*g*) By positive electricity: as, *positively* electrified. See *electricity*.

positiveness (poz'i-tiv-nes), *n.* The state of being positive; actualness; reality of existence; not mere negation; undoubting assurance; full confidence; peremptoriness.

positivism (poz'i-tiv-izm), *n.* [= F. *positivisme*; as *positive* + *-ism*.] 1. Actual or absolute knowledge.

The metaphysicians can never rest till they have taken their watch to pieces and have arrived at a happy *positivism* as to its structure.
Lowell, Among my Books, 1st ser., p. 150.

2. [*cap.*] The Positive philosophy (which see, under *positive*).

Positivist (poz'i-tiv-ist), *n.* [= F. *positiviste*; as *positive* + *-ist*.] One who maintains the doctrines of the Positive philosophy.

positivistic (poz"i-ti-vis'tik), *a.* [< *Positivist* + *-ic*.] Of or pertaining to the Positivists or Positivism.

positivity (poz-i-tiv'i-ti), *n.* [= F. *positivité*; as *positive* + *-ity*.] Positiveness in any sense.

There is a time, as Solomon . . . teaches us, when a fool should be answered according to his folly, lest he be wise in his own conceit, and lest others too easily yield up their faith and reason to his imperious dictates. Courage and *positivity* are never more necessary than on such an occasion.
Watts, Improvement of Mind, i. 9.

The property which renders a structure capable of undergoing excitatory change is expressed by relative *positivity*, the condition of discharge by relative negativity.
Nature, XXXVIII. 141.

positor† (poz'i-tor), *n.* [< L. *positor*, one who lays, a builder, founder, < *ponere*, pp. *positus*, put, lay: see *posit*.] A depositor. *Hakluyt's Voyages*, II. 249.

positure† (poz'i-tūr), *n.* [< OF. *positure* = Sp. Pg. It. *positura*, < L. *positura*, position, posture, < *ponere*, pp. *positus*, put, place: see *posit*, and cf. *posture*.] Posture.

First he prayed, and then sung certain Psalmes, . . . resembling the Turks in the *positure* of their bodies and often prostrations.
Sandys, Travailes, p. 96.

posnet (pos'net), *n.* [Early mod. E. also *postnet*, *posenet*; < ME. *posnett*, *posnette*, *postnet*, < OF. *pocenet*, a little basin. The W. *posned*, a porringer, a round body, is appar. from E.] A small basin or porringer; also, a small vessel of fanciful form.

The cunning man biddeth set on a *posnet*, or some pan with nayles, and seeth them, and the witch shal come in while they be in seething, and within a fewe daies after her face will be all bescratched with the nayles.
Gifford, Dialogue on Witches (1603). (*Halliwell.*)

Then skellets, pans, and *posnets* put on,
To make them porridge without mutton.
Cotton's Works (1734), p. 17. (*Halliwell.*)

A silver *posnet* to butter eggs. *Steele*, Tatler, No. 245.

posologic (pos-ǫ-loj'ik), *a.* [= F. *posologique*; < *posolog-y* + *-ic*.] Of or pertaining to posology.

posological (pos-ǫ-loj'i-kal), *a.* [< *posologic* + *-al*.] Same as *posologic*.

posology (pǫ-sol'ǫ-ji), *n.* [= F. *posologie*; < Gr. πόσος, how much, + -λογία, < λέγειν, speak: see *-ology*.] The doctrine of quantity. (*a*) A name suggested by Bentham for the science of quantity. (*b*) That part of medical science which is concerned with the doses or quantities in which medicines ought to be administered.

poss, *v.* An obsolete or dialectal form of *push*.

posse (pos'ē), *n.* [< ML. *posse*, power, a noun use of the L. inf. *posse*, be able: see *potent* and *power*.] 1. Possibility. A thing is said to be *in posse* when it may possibly be (in familiar language, often a softened denial of existence; in philosophical language, ready to be, in germ); *in esse*, when it actually is.

Those are but glorious dreams, and only yield him
A happiness *in posse*, not in esse.
Fletcher (*and another*), Elder Brother, i. 1.

2. A sheriff's posse comitatus (see below); in general, a body or squad of men.

It was high noon, and the *posse* had been in saddle since dawn.
M. N. Murfree, Prophet of Great Smoky Mountains, p. 20.

Posse comitatus, the power of the county; in *law*, the body of men which the sheriff is empowered to call into service to aid and support him in the execution of the law, as in case of rescue, riot, forcible entry and occupation, etc. It includes all male persons above the age of fifteen. In Great Britain peers and clergymen are excluded by statute. The word *comitatus* is often omitted, and *posse* alone is used in the same sense (see def. 2).

possede†, *v. t.* [< OF. *posseder*, possess: see *possess*.] To possess.

None other persone may . . . *possede* it or clayme it.
Sir T. Elyot, The Governour, iii. 3.

possess (pǫ-zes'), *v. t.* [< ME. *possessen*, < OF. *possesser*, possess, < L. *possessus*, pp. of *possidere* (> It. *possedere*, *possidere* = Sp. *poseer* = Pg. *possuir* = Pr. *possedir*, *possider* = F. *posséder*), have and hold, be master of, possess, perhaps orig. 'remain near,' < *po-*, **post-*, akin to *pro-*, before, + *sedere*, sit, dwell: see *sit*. Cf. *obsess*, *assessor*, *siege*, etc.] 1. To own; have as a belonging, property, characteristic, or attribute.

So shall you share all that he doth *possess*,
By having him. *Shak.*, R. and J., i. 3. 93.

These *possess* wealth as sick men *possess* fevers,
Which truller may be said to *possess* them.
B. Jonson, Volpone, v. 8.

St. Peter's can not have the magical power over us that the red and gold covers of our first picture-book *possessed*.
Emerson, Domestic Life.

2. To seize; take possession of; make one's self master of.

Let us go up at once and *possess* it; for we are well able to overcome it. Num. xiii. 30.

Remember
First to *possess* his books.
Shak., Tempest, iii. 2. 100.

The English marched toward the river Eske, intending to *possess* a hill called Under-Eske. *Sir J. Hayward.*

3. To put in possession; make master or owner, whether by force or legally: with *of* before the thing, and now generally used in the passive or reflexively: as, to *possess one's self of* another's secret; to be or stand *possessed of* a certain manor.

Sithe god bathe chose the to be his knyȝt,
And *possesside the* in thi right,
Thoue him honour with al thi myght.
Political Poems, etc. (ed. Furnivall), p. 4.

The plate, coin, revenues, and moveables,
Where*of* our uncle Gaunt did stand *possess'd*.
Shak., Rich. II., ii. 1. 162.

We here *possess*
Thy son *of* all thy state.
B. Jonson, Volpone, v. 8.

Five hundred pound a yeare 's bequeath'd to you,
Of which I here *possesse* you: all is yours.
Heywood, Fair Maid of the West (Works,
[ed. Pearson, 1874, II. 305).

Our debates *possessed* me so fully *of* the subject that I wrote and printed an anonymous pamphlet on it.
Franklin, Autobiography, p. 113.

4. To have and hold; occupy in person; hence, to inhabit.

Houses and fields and vineyards shall be *possessed* again in this land. Jer. xxxii. 15.

They report a faire Riuer and at least 30. habitations doth *possesse* this Country.
Capt. John Smith, Works, II. 194.

5. To occupy; keep; maintain; entertain: mostly with a reflexive reference.

In your patience *possess* ye [ye shall win, revised version] your souls. Luke xxi. 19.

Then we [anglers] sit on cowslip-banks, hear the birds sing, and *possess* ourselves in as much quietness as these silent silver streams, which we now see glide so quietly by us. *I. Walton*, Complete Angler, p. 109.

It is necessary to an easy and happy life to *possess* our minds in such a manner as to be always well satisfied with our own reflections. *Steele*, Tatler, No. 251.

6. To imbue; impress: with *with* before the thing.

It is of unspeakable advantage to *possess* our minds *with* an habitual good intention. *Addison.*

Hence . . . it is laid down by Holt that to *possess* the people *with* an ill opinion of the government—that is, of the ministry—is a libel. *Hallam.*

7. To take possession of; fascinate; enthrall; affect or influence so intensely or thoroughly as to dominate or overpower: with *with* before the thing that fills or dominates.

A poets brayne, *possest with* layes of loue.
Gascoigne, Steele Glas (ed. Arber), p. 56.

Sin of self-love *possesseth* all mine eye
And all my soul and all my every part.
Shak., Sonnets, lxii.

I have been touched, yea, and *possessed with* an extreme wonder at those your virtues.
Bacon, Advancement of Learning, i. 2.

This [fancy] so *possessed* him and so shook his mind that he dared not stand at the door longer, but fled for fear the tower should come down upon him.
Southey, Bunyan, p. 16.

8. To have complete power or mastery over; dominate; control, as an evil spirit, influence, or passion: generally in the passive, with *by*, *of*, or *with*.

They also which saw it told them by what means he that was *possessed of* the devils was healed. Luke viii. 36.

Unless you be *possess'd with* devilish spirits,
You cannot but forbear to murder me.
Shak., 2 Hen. VI., iv. 7. 80.

One of those fanatic infidels *possessed by* the devil who are sometimes permitted to predict the truth to their followers. *Irving*, Granada, p. 23.

9†. To put in possession of information; inform; tell; acquaint; persuade; convince.

Possess us, *possess* us; tell us something of him.
Shak., T. N., ii. 3. 149.

The merchants are *possess'd*
You've been a pirate.
Middleton, Anything for a Quiet Life, i. 1.

I see it don with some artifice and labour, to *possess* the people that they might amend thir present condition by his or by his Sons restorement.
Milton, Eikonoklastes, xxvii.

Whether they were English or no, it may be doubted; yet they believe they were, for the French have so *possessed* them. N. *Morton*, New England's Memorial, p. 57.

10†. To attain; achieve; accomplish.

Where they in secret counsell close conspird,
How to effect so hard an enterprize,
And to *possesse* the purpose they desird.
Spenser, F. Q., III. iii. 51.

=**Syn.** *Have, Possess, Hold, Own, Occupy.* *Have* is the most general of these words; it may apply to a temporary or to a permanent *possession* of a thing, to the *having* of that which is one's own or another's: as, to *have* good judgment; to *have* another's letter by mistake. *Possess* generally applies to that which is external to the possessor, or, if not external, is viewed as something to be used: as, to *possess* a library; if we say a man *possesses* hands, we mean that he *has* them to work with; to *possess* reason is to *have* it with the thought of what can be done with it. To *hold* is to *have* in one's hands to control, not necessarily as one's own: as, to *hold* a fan or a dog for a lady; to *hold* a title-deed; to *hold* the stakes for a contest. To *own* is to have a good and legal title to; one may *own* that which he does not *hold* or *occupy* and cannot get into his *possession*, as a missing umbrella or a stolen horse. *Occupy* is chiefly physical: as, to *occupy* a house; one may *occupy* that which he does not *own*, as a chair, room, office, position.

Let me *have* the land
Which stretches away upon either hand.
Whittier, Mogg Megone, i.

Frederic was succeeded by his son, Frederic William, a prince who must be allowed to have *possessed* some talents for administration. *Macaulay*, Frederic the Great.

Holding Corioli in the name of Rome. *Shak.*, Cor., i. 6. 37.

Habitually savages individually *own* their weapons and implements, their decorations, their dresses.
H. Spencer, Prin. of Sociol., § 202.

Palaces which ought to be *occupied* by better men.
Macaulay, Hist. Eng., xvi.

possessed (pǫ-zest′), *p. a.* Controlled by some evil spirit or influence; demented; mad.

He 's coming, madam; but in very strange manner. He is, sure, *possessed*, madam. *Shak.*, T. N., iii. 4. 9.

Corv. The man is mad!
Corb. What 's that?
Corv. He is *possesst.* B. *Jonson*, Volpone, v. 6.

possession (pǫ-zesh′ǫn), *n.* [< ME. *possession, possessyone, possessioun*, < OF. (and F.) *possession* = Sp. *posesion* = Pg. *possessão* = It. *possessione, possessio*, < L. *possessio(n-)*, a seizing, possession, < *possessus*, pp. of *possidere*, possess: see *possess.*] **1.** The act of possessing, or the state of being possessed; the having, holding, or detaining of property in one's power or control; the state of owning or controlling; actual seizing or occupancy, either rightful or wrongful. One man may have the *possession* of a thing, and another may have the right of property in it.

Ministering light prepared, they set and rise;
Lest total darkness should by night regain
Her old *possession*, and extinguish life
In nature and all things. *Milton*, P. L., iv. 666.

It is ill going to law for an estate with him who is in *possession* of it, and enjoys the present profits, to feed his cause. *Dryden*, Ded. of Third Misc.

You see in their countenances they are at home, and in quiet *possession* of their present instant as it passes.
Steele, Spectator, No. 49.

If the *possession* be severed from the property, if A. has the jus proprietatis, and B. by some unlawful means has gained *possession* of the lands, this is an injury to A. Thus . . . B. . . . hath only . . . a bare or naked *possession*. *Blackstone*, Com., III. x.

If . . . mere *possession* could confer sovereignty, they had that *possession*, and were entitled to that sovereignty.
Story, Discourse, Sept. 18, 1828.

2. In *law*, the physical control which belongs of right to unqualified ownership; the having a thing in such manner as to exclude the control of other persons; that detention of or dominion over a thing by one person which precludes others from the adverse physical occupancy of or dominion over it. In modern law the legal conception of possession is intermediate between the conception of right and that of physical occupancy, and shares something of the qualities of both; but there is great difference of view as to the precise signification and the resulting proprieties of use. In general, all are agreed that a master has possession of a thing which belongs to him but is in the hand of his servant, however far away; but a lender has not possession of a chattel in the hand of the borrower. In respect to real estate, the landlord was formerly said to have possession, and the tenant was not said to *possess* or *have possession*, but only to *be in possession*. The distinction is now more commonly expressed by saying that the tenant has actual possession (*pedis possessio*), although the legal possession may be in the landlord. The servant's or tenant's possession is legal in the sense of being lawful, but is not the legal possession in the sense in which that term is used in contrast to mere physical occupancy without any right of ownership. *Possession* is sometimes said to involve the intent to exclude others, but a man may have possession without such intent, as where he has given a thing away, and it has not been removed; or even without the consciousness of possessing, as where a thing is forgotten or supposed to be lost. In Roman law, *possession* required not only physical control, but also the animus domini. When these two elements concurred, there existed a right which was protected against everybody, including the rightful owner. If he disturbed the possession, he could not in defense to the action (interdict) brought by the possessor plead title, but he had to resort to a separate action in order to assert his right. It was not necessary in order to make this protection that the possession should be in good faith, but good faith was necessary in order to make possession ripen into title by prescription. In some modern systems of law, for example the French code, possession acquired in good faith gives an ownership of chattels.

3. The thing possessed; in the plural, goods, land, or rights owned; belongings: as, your friendship is one of my richest *possessions*; the French *possessions*.

The house of Jacob shall possess their *possessions*.
Obadiah 17.

When the young man heard that saying, he went away sorrowful; for he had great *possessions*. Mat. xix. 22.

Neither your letters nor silence needs excuse: your friendship is to me an abundant *possession*, though you remember me but twice in a year. *Donne*, Letters, xli.

Hence—**4.** Property; wealth.

Fy on *possessioun*
But if a man be Vertuous withal.
Chaucer, Prol. to Franklin's Tale, l. 14.

5. In *international law*, a country or territory held by right of conquest. *Bouvier.*—**6.** Persuasion; conviction.

I have a strong *possession* that with this five hundred I shall win five thousand. *Cibber*, Provoked Husband, i.

Whoever labours under any of these *possessions* is as unfit for conversation as a madman in Bedlam.
Swift, Conversation.

7. The state of being under the control of evil spirits or of madness; madness; lunacy: as, demoniacal *possession*.

I knew he was not in his perfect wits. . . .
How long hath this *possession* held the man?
Shak., C. of E., v. 1. 44.

There are some sins so rooted, so rivetted in men, so incorporated, so consubstantiated in the soul, by habitual custom, as that those sins have contracted the nature of ancient *possessions*. *Donne*, Sermons, xiv.

Forms of madness which were for ages supposed to result from *possession* are treated successfully in our hospitals. *Lecky*, Europ. Morals, I. 375.

Actual possession, sometimes called *natural possession*, occupancy to the actual exclusion of possession by any others, except such as hold as the servants of the possessor or as representing him, and so hold without any right to detain as against him. Thus, a man is in *actual possession* of his house when he leaves it in charge of his wife or servant, but not when he leaves it in charge of a tenant having a right to retain it.—**Adverse possession.** See *adverse*.—**Chose in possession.** See *chose*[2].—**Constructive possession**, possession in law, sometimes called *civil* or *juridical possession*, a possession through the occupancy of others, or that possession which is imputed by the law to one who has title to a thing of which no one is in *actual possession*, as for instance wild and unoccupied land. See *seizin*.—**Delivery of juridical possession.** See *delivery*.—**Demoniacal possession.** See *demoniacal*.—**Envoi in possession**, the authority granted by a court to the presumptive heirs of an absentee, who has not been heard of for a certain period of years, to take possession of his property.—**Estate in possession**, technically, an estate so created as to vest in the owner thereof a present right of present enjoyment: referring not to the fact of the thing owned being in the owner's possession, which may or may not be the case, but to the fact that the right of present possession is an estate or title in the owner, as distinguished from an *expectant estate*.—**In possession**, said of a person in actual possession of a thing, or a thing in the actual possession of a person, as distinguished from mere ownership. Thus, when a testator gives all his possessions or everything which he may possess at death, he gives not only the things of which he may be in possession, but also his property of which others may be in possession. When used of an estate, it designates such an estate or interest as gives a right of possession, as distinguished from an expectant estate. Thus, a gift to one person to take effect after the death of another is said to vest *in possession* when the death occurs irrespective of actual taking possession.—**Juridical possession.** See *constructive possession*, above, and *delivery*.—**Naked possession**, mere possession without color of right.—**Natural possession.** Same as *actual possession*.—**To give possession**, to put into another's control or occupancy.—**To take possession**, to enter upon or to take under control or occupancy.

The Lord of Love went by
To *take possession* of his flowery throne.
William Morris, Earthly Paradise, I. 221.

Unity of possession. See *estate in joint tenancy*, under *estate*.—**Vacant possession**, a phrase used occasionally of lands not in the possession of any person.—**Writ of possession**, in *law*, a process directing a sheriff to put a person in peaceable possession of property recovered in ejectment. =**Syn. 1.** Ownership, occupation, tenure, control. See *possess*.

possession† (pǫ-zesh′ǫn), *v. t.* [< *possession*, *n.*] To invest with property.

Sundry more gentlemen this little hundred possesseth and *possessioneth*. *Carew.*

possessional (pǫ-zesh′ǫn-al), *a.* [= F. *possessionnel* = Sp. *posesional*; as *possession* + *-al*.] Same as *possessive*. *Imp. Dict.*

possessionary (pǫ-zesh′ǫn-ā-ri), *a.* [< ML. **possessionarius*, < L. *possessio(n-)*, possession: see *possession*.] Relating to or implying possession. *Imp. Dict.*

possessioner† (pǫ-zesh′ǫn-ėr), *n.* [< ME. *possessioner*, < OF. *possessionaire* = Sp. *posesionero*, < ML. **possessionarius*: see *possessionary*.] **1.** One who owns or has actual possession of a thing, or power over it; a possessor.

They were a kind of people who, having been of old freemen and *possessioners*, the Lacedæmonians had conquered them. *Sir P. Sidney*, Arcadia, i.

This term, "the *Possessioners*," was a popular circulating coinage struck in the mint of our reformer [Robert Crowley], and probably included much more than meets our ear. Every land-owner, every proprietor, was a *Possessioner*. *I. D'Israeli*, Amen. of Lit., I. 378.

2. A member of a religious order endowed with lands, etc., as distinguished from those orders whose members lived entirely by alms; a member of one of the orders possessing lands and revenues; a beneficed clergyman.

Ne ther it nedeth nat for to be geve,
As to *possessioners*, that mowen lyve,
Thanked be God, in wele and habundaunce.
Chaucer, Summoner's Tale, l. 14.

Thise *possessioneres* preche. *Piers Plowman* (B), v. 144.

possessive (pǫ-zes′iv), *a.* and *n.* [< F. *possessif* = Sp. *posesivo* = Pg. It. *possessivo*, < L. *possessivus*, possessive (in gram.), < *possessus*, pp. of *possidere*, possess: see *possess*.] **I.** *a.* Pertaining to or denoting possession; expressing possession: as in a *lady's* dress, *their* house, a mere notion of *John's*.

What mean these liv'ries and *possessive* keys?
What mean these bargains, and these needless sales?
Quarles, Emblems, v. 9.

Possessive case, in *gram.*, the genitive case, or the case of nouns, pronouns, etc., which expresses possession and other kindred and derived relations.

The supposition that the apostrophe 's as a mark of the *possessive case* is a segment of his, a question which has been lately revived, is here denied.
A. Hume, Orthographie (E. E. T. S.), p. 37.

Possessive pronoun, a derivative adjective formed from a personal pronoun, and denoting possession or property, as in *my* book, *your* hand.

II. *n.* **1.** A pronoun or other word denoting possession.—**2.** The possessive case.

Their and theirs are the *possessives* likewise of they, when they is the plural of it, and are therefore applied to things. *Johnson*, English Grammar.

possessively (pǫ-zes′iv-li), *adv.* In a manner denoting possession.

possessor (pǫ-zes′ǫr), *n.* [Formerly *possessour*; < F. *possesseur* = Sp. *poseedor* = Pg. *possessor* = It. *possessore*, < L. *possessor*, possessor, < *possidere*, pp. *possessus*, possess: see *possess*.] One who possesses; one who has or enjoys anything; one who owns; one who holds, occupies, or controls any species of property, real or personal.

Whereby great riches, gathered manie a day,
She in short space did often bring to nought,
And their *possessours* often did dismay.
Spenser, F. Q., IV. i. 29.

And yet he lived as chearfully and contentedly, by the faith he had in God's goodness, as if he had been *possessor* of the whole world. *Sharp*, Works, V. iv.

Riches are the instruments of serving the purposes of heaven or hell, according to the disposition of the *possessor*. *Steele*, Spectator, No. 466.

Bona-fide possessor. See *bona fide*. =**Syn.** Owner, proprietor, holder, master, lord.

possessory (pǫ-zes′ō-ri), *a.* [< F. *possessoire* = Sp. *posesorio* = Pg. It. *possessorio*, < LL. *possessorius*, possessory, < L. *possessor*, a possessor: see *possessor*.] **1.** Pertaining to possession.

A *possessory* feeling in the heart. *Chalmers.*

But it will be based upon fear, and, among lower animals, inherited habit, rather than upon any sense of *possessory* right. *Westminster Rev.*, CXXVI. 134.

2. Having possession: as, a *possessory* lord.

Absolute equality among nations is established, and their commercial rights are to be held the same as those of the *possessory* government. *N. A. Rev.*, CXLII. 125.

3. In *law*, arising from possession: as, a *possessory* interest.

The motive of the guardian must not be tainted by a selfish greed to get the land which the ward held by *possessory* right. *N. A. Rev.*, CXLIII. 438.

Possessory action, an action to determine the right of possession, as distinguished from one to determine the title to the thing. See *petitory*.

If a *possessory action* be brought within six months after the avoidance, the patron shall (notwithstanding such usurpation and institution) recover that very presentation which gives back to him the seisin of the advowson. *Blackstone*, Com., III. xvi.

Possessory judgment, in *Scots law*, a judgment which entitles a person who has been in uninterrupted possession for seven years to continue his possession until the question of right shall be decided at law.

Either touching *possessory judgments* of ecclesiastical livings, or concerning nominations thereunto.
Hooker, Eccles. Polity, viii. 6.

posset (pos′et), *n.* [< ME. *posset*, *possett*, *possyt* (cf. F. *possel*, *possette*, < E. †); perhaps < Ir. *pusoid*, a posset; cf. W. *posel*, curdled milk, a posset, < *posiaw*, gather, heap. The L. *posca*, a drink of mingled vinegar and water, is prob. not concerned.] A drink composed of hot milk curdled by some infusion, as wine or other liquor, formerly much in favor both as a luxury and as medicine.

> I have drugg'd their *possets*,
> That death and nature do contend about them,
> Whether they live or die. *Shak.*, Macbeth, ii. 2. 6.

After supper to dancing and singing till about twelve at night; and then we had a good sack *possett* for them, and an excellent cake. *Pepys*, Diary, Jan. 6, 1667.

Having had several violent fits of an ague, recourse was had to . . . drinking carduus *posset*, then going to bed and sweating. *Evelyn*, Diary, Feb. 7, 1682.

Posset is an excellent mixture of hot ale, milk, sugar, spices, and sippets or dice of bread or oat cake, almost if not quite universal for supper on Christmas eve.
L. *Jewitt*, Ceramic Art of Gr. Britain (first ed.), I. 108.

posset† (pos'et), *v. t.* [< *posset*, *n.*] To curdle; coagulate. [Rare.]

> And with a sudden vigour it doth *posset*
> And curd, like eager droppings into milk,
> The thin and wholesome blood.
> *Shak.*, Hamlet, i. 5. 68.

posset-ale (pos'et-āl), *n.* Posset made with ale, used in medicine in the seventeenth century.

posset-cup (pos'et-kup), *n.* A large bowl or

Posset-cup.

porringer, often having a cover, used for containing posset.

posset-pot (pos'et-pot), *n.* Same as *posset-cup*.

possett†, *n.* A Middle English form of *posset*.

posshe†, *v.* A Middle English form of *push*.

Possibilist (pos'i-bil-ist), *n.* [< F. *possibiliste* = Sp. *Posibilista*; as L. *possibilis*, possible, + *-ist*.] 1. A member of a Spanish political party which aims at the establishment of a republic by constitutional means.

Thus Castelar and his followers constitute what is called the *Possibilist* party, which, although numbering few partisans among the people, yet comprises several distinguished and upright individuals.
Fortnightly Rev., XXXIX. 115.

2. A member of a modern socialistic faction in France.

possibility (pos-i-bil'i-ti), *n.*; pl. *possibilities* (-tiz). [< ME. *possibilitee*, *possybilite*, < OF. *possibilite*, F. *possibilité* = Sp. *posibilidad* = Pg. *possibilidade* = It. *possibilità*, < LL. *possibilita(t-)s*, possibility, < L. *possibilis*, possible: see *possible*.] 1. The mode of that which is possible; the fact of being possible.

There is no let but that, as often as those books are read, and need so requireth, the stile of their differences may expressly be mentioned to bar even all *possibility* of error. *Hooker*.

It is pleasant to see great works in their seminal state, pregnant with latent *possibilities* of excellence. *Johnson*.

He looked so virtuous that he might commit any crime and no one would believe in the *possibility* of his guilt.
Lady Holland, Sydney Smith, vi.

2. A thing possible; that which may take place or come into being.

Consider him antecedently to his creation, while yet he lay in the barren womb of nothing, and only in the number of *possibilities*, and consequently could have nothing to recommend him to Christ's affection. *South*.

Never country had such a fortune, as men call fortune, as this, in its geography, its history, and in its majestic *possibilities*. *Emerson*, Fortune of the Republic.

3. Specifically, in *law*, a chance or expectation; an uncertain thing which may or may not happen. It is *near* or *ordinary*, as where an estate is limited to one after the death of another; or *remote* or *extraordinary*, as where it is limited to a man provided he shall be married to a certain woman, and then that she shall die, and he be married to another. *Wharton*.—**Logical possibility.** See *logical*.—**Permanent possibility.** See *permanent*.—**Physical possibility**, compatibility with the laws of nature.—**Possibility of issue extinct**, a term, formerly of some importance in the law of real property, used to designate the effect of the age of a woman under a gift conditioned on having issue. The highest authorities in medical jurisprudence sustain the proposition that a woman beyond the age of fifty-five has, in the legal sense, no possibility of issue. Extinction of possibility may be inferred at an earlier age, varying with the evidence as to the length of married life and the condition of health.—**Practical possibility**, capability of being realized by means within the power of the persons considered.—**Real possibility**, indeterminateness in things as to the future happening or non-happening of something which lies within the power of a free agent.

possible (pos'i-bl), *a.* [< ME. *possible*, *possybylle*, < OF. (and F.) *possible* = Sp. *posible* = Pg. *possivel* = It. *possibile*, *possevole*, < L. *possibilis*, possible, < *posse*, be able: see *power*.] That may be; not known not to be true; not known not to be true in some hypothetical state of information. The only kind of object which in strict propriety of language can be called *possible* is the truth of a proposition; and when a kind of *thing* is said to be *possible*, this is to be regarded as an elliptical expression, meaning that it is of such a general description that we do not know it does not exist. So an event or act is said to be *possible*, meaning that one would not know that it would not come to pass. But it is incorrect to use *possible* meaning *practicable*; *possible* is what may be, not what can be. A proposition is *logically possible*, if it would not be known not to be true by a person who should know nothing but the principles of logic and the meanings of words; *physically possible*, if it would not be known not to be true by one who should know all the laws of nature, but none of the particular facts; *practically possible*, if it were not known not to be about to be accomplished to one who should know what was in the power of the persons concerned, but not their dispositions, etc.

> Desire things *possible*,
> Thou foolish young man; nourish not a hope
> Will hale thy heart out. *Fletcher*, Mad Lover, ii. 2.

I take it those things are to be held *possible* which may be done by some person, though not by every one.
Bacon, Advancement of Learning, ii. 118.

In such an age, it is *possible* some great genius may arise, to equal any of the ancients; abating only for the language. *Dryden*, Orig. and Prog. of Satire.

Is it *possible* that, when the necessities of life are supplied, a man would flatter to be rich!
Steele, Tatler, No. 251.

The marvellous is so fascinating that nine persons in ten, if once persuaded that a thing is *possible*, are eager to believe it probable, and at last cunning in convincing themselves that it is proven.
Lowell, Among my Books, 2d ser., p. 144.

Possible intellect. See *intellect*, 1. =**Syn.** *Possible*, *Practicable*. See *practicable*.

possibly (pos'i-bli), *adv.* 1. In a possible manner; by any power, moral or physical, really existing; by possibility.—2. Perhaps; perchance.

possum (pos'um), *n.* [Formerly also *possoune*, *possowne*, etc.; by apheresis from *opossum*.] Same as *opossum*. [Colloq.]

Amongst the Beasts in Virginia there are two kinds most strange. One of them is the Female *Possowne*, which hath a bag under her belly, out of which she will let forth her young ones, and take them in again at her pleasure.
S. Clarke, Four Plantations in America (1670), p. 14.

To play possum, to act possum, to feign; dissemble: in allusion to the habit of the opossum, which feigns death on the approach or attack of an enemy, and may allow itself to be tormented to death without showing a sign of life.

possum (pos'um), *v. i.* [< *possum*, *n.*] To play possum; feign death. [Colloq.]

When disturbed they [certain beetles] drop to the ground . . . after *possuming* awhile.
Insect Life, Jan., 1889, p. 220.

possum-oak (pos'um-ōk), *n.* Same as *water-oak*.

post[1] (pōst), *n.* [< ME. *post*, < AS. *post*, a post, stake, = OFries. *post* = D. MLG. *post*, post (of a door), = OHG. *pfosto*, MHG. *pfoste*, G. *pfoste* = Sw. Dan. *post*, a post, = OF. *poste*, *poust* (dim. *posteau*, F. *poteau*) = Sp. Pg. *poste*, < L. *postis*, a post, door-post (ML. a post, beam, rod, pole), also a door; prob. < *postus*, contr. of *positus*, pp. of *ponere*, put, set: see *posit*, *position*. Cf. *post*[2].] 1. A piece of timber, metal (solid or built up), or other solid substance, of considerable size, set upright, and intended as a support to a weight or structure resting upon it, or as a firm point of attachment for something: as, the *posts* of a door or of a gate; a king-*post*, queen-*post*, truss-*post*, bed-*post*; iron *posts* supporting the floor of a building; a hitching-*post*, etc.

And Samson . . . took the doors of the gate of the city, and the two *posts*, and went away with them, bar and all.
Judges xvi. 3.

> Through the glass the clothes-line *posts*
> Looked in like tall and sheeted ghosts.
> *Whittier*, Snow-Bound.

Specifically—(*a*†) A piece of timber set in any position; a beam.

Vse all possible diligence in well vpholdynge and fortyfyinge the caue with arches of waules trauersed with stronge *postes* of tymber after the maner of framed beames, susteyned with grose and stronge pyles made of good and stronge tymber of oke or other great trees.
R. Eden, tr. of Biringuccio's Pyrotechnia (First Books on America, ed. Arber, p. 359).

(*b*†) An upright piece of timber upon which proclamations were fixed; also, an upright piece of timber used for keeping a score when marked with chalk or notches.

> I from my mistress come to you in post;
> If I return, I shall be *post* indeed,
> For she will score your fault upon my pate.
> *Shak.*, C. of E., i. 2. 64.

(*c*†) A staff.

A *post* in hand he bare of mighty pyne, and therewithall
He felt his way, and led his sheepe. *Phaer*, Æneid, iii.

(*d*) In *violin-making*. See *sound-post*.

2. In *coal-mining*: (*a*) A pillar or wall of coal left to support the roof of the mine. (*b*) Fine-grained sandstone, such as often occurs forming a part of the coal-measures.—3. The stern-post of a vessel.

The queene's majestic commanded her bargemen to row round her, and viewed her from *post* to stemme.
Observations of Sir R. Hawkins, p. 11. (*Latham*.)

4†. Figuratively, a prop; a support.

> I thenke, . . . sith Love of his godenesse
> Hath the converted oute of wikkydnesse,
> That thou shalt ben the beste *post*, I leeve,
> Of alle his lay, and moost his foes to greve.
> *Chaucer*, Troilus, i. 1000.

5. In *paper-manuf.*, a pile of 144 sheets of hand-made paper fresh from the mold, arranged alternately with pieces of felt, ready to be placed in the screw-press; a felt-post. When the felts are removed, the pile of paper sheets is termed a *white post*.—6. [< *post*[1], *v.*, 4.] The state of being posted as rejected in a college examination in the University of Cambridge, England.—**Arm-post**, in *furniture-making*, a small upright member supporting the arm of a sofa, or of an arm-chair, at the end furthest from the back.—**Deaf as a post.** See *deaf*.—**False post**, a piece of timber fixed on the after part of the stern-post of a vessel, to make good a deficiency in it.—**From pillar to post.** See *pillar*.—**Knight of the post**†. See *knight*.—**Middle post**, in *carp.*, a king-post.—**Pendent post.** See *pendent*.—**Phenix post**, a trade-name for a wrought-iron column or post formed of rolled plates riveted together at the edges: largely used in the elevated railways of New York.—**Post and paling**, a close wooden fence, constructed of posts fixed in the ground and having pales nailed between them.—**Post and pane, post and petrail**, phrases noting a system of construction consisting of timber framings filled in with panels of brick or lath and plaster.—**Post and railing**, a kind of open wooden fence for the protection of young quickset hedges, consisting mainly of posts and rails.—**Post and stall.** Same as *pillar and breast* (which see, under *pillar*).—**Principal post.** See *principal*.—**Side post**, in *arch.*, one of a pair of truss-posts set each at the same distance from the middle of the truss, as a support to the principal rafters and to suspend the tie-beam below. Two or three pairs of side posts are sometimes used in roofs of extended span: such posts are called *primary* and *secondary side posts*.—**To kiss the post**†. See *kiss*.

post[1] (pōst), *v. t.* [< *post*[1], *n.*] 1. To fix to a post; nail or otherwise fasten up in a public place, as a notice or an advertisement: as, to *post* a bill; to *post* a notice.

The attempts of which sort of man I can liken to nothing so properly as to those pretences to infallible cures which we daily see *posted* in every corner of the streets.
South, Sermons, III. vi.

2. To bring before the public notice by means of a placard fastened up in some public place; placard: as, to *post* one for nomination; hence, to expose to reproach by overt declaration: brand; stigmatize: as, to *post* a man as a coward.

> On pain of being *posted* to your sorrow,
> Fail not at four to meet me. *Granville*.

3. To raise to the rank of post-captain; make a post-captain of. [Great Britain.]

Whispers were afloat which came to the ears of the Admiralty, and prevented him from being *posted*.
Marryat, Peter Simple, lv. (*Davies*.)

4. Specifically, in the University of Cambridge, England, to placard as rejected in a college examination.

Should a man be *posted* twice in succession, he is generally recommended to try the air of some small college, or devote his energies to some other walk of life.
C. A. Bristed, English University, p. 100.

5. To placard with handbills; fix notices upon.

He had the whole printed in great black letters on a staring broadsheet, and he caused the walls to be *posted* with it. *Dickens*, Hard Times, iii. 4.

=**Syn.** To placard, advertise, announce, blaze abroad.

post[2] (pōst), *n.* [(*a*) < F. *poste*, m., a post, station, guard-house, employment, situation, military post, naval station, = Pg. *posto* = It. *posto*, station, post (> D. *post* = G. *posten* = Sw. Dan. *post*); < ML. **postus*, m., a station. (*b*) < F. *poste*, f., a post (establishment for post-horses), post (manner of traveling), stage, post-house, post-office, post-boy, mail-carrier, mail, also a military post, = Sp. Pg. It. *posta* (> D. G. Sw. Dan. *post*), post, post-office, mail, etc., < ML. *posta*, f., a station, a fixed place on a road, < L. *postus*, contr. of *positus*, pp. of *ponere*, put, place, set, fix: see *posit*, *position*, and cf. *post*[1].] 1. A fixed point or place; the place where some person or thing is stationed or fixed; a station or position occupied: as, a *post* of observation;

a sentry at his *post;* specifically, the place where a body of troops is stationed; a military station.

The waters rise everywhere upon the surface of the earth; which new *post* when they had once seized on they would never quit. *T. Burnet*, Theory of the Earth.

The squadrons among which Regulus rode showed the greatest activity in retreating before the French, and were dislodged from one *post* and another which they occupied with perfect alacrity on their part. *Thackeray*, Vanity Fair, xxxii.

Uncle Venner, who had studied the world at street-corners, and at other *posts* equally well adapted for just observation, was as ready to give out his wisdom as a town-pump to give water. *Hawthorne*, Seven Gables, x.

2. The occupants, collectively, of a military station; a garrison.—3. Hence, a subdivision of the organization of veteran soldiers and sailors called the *Grand Army of the Republic* (which see, under *republic*).—4. An office or employment; a position of service, trust, or emolument; an appointment; a position.

When vice prevails, and impious men bear sway,
The *post* of honour is a private station.
Addison, Cato, iv. 4.

Unpaid, untrammelled, with a sweet disdain
Refusing *posts* men grovel to attain.
Lowell, To G. W. Curtis.

5. One of a series of fixed stations, as on a given route or line of travel.

Thence with all convenient speed to Rome, . . .
With memorandum book for ev'ry town
And ev'ry *post*. *Cowper*, Progress of Error, l. 374.

And there thro' twenty *posts* of telegraph
They flash'd a saucy message to and fro
Between the mimic stations.
Tennyson, Princess, Prol.

6. One who travels through fixed stations on a given route, to carry messages, letters, papers, etc.; a postman; hence, in general, a messenger.

What good news hast thou brought me, gentle *post?*
Beau. and Fl., Coxcomb, iv. 6.

He was also dispatching a *Post* lately for Spain; and the *Post* having received his Packet, and kissed his Hands, he called him back. *Howell*, Letters, I. iii. 3.

7†. A post-horse.

I have speeded hither with the very extremest inch of possibility; I have foundered nine score and odd *posts*.
Shak., 2 Hen. IV., iv. 3. 40.

8. An established system for the conveyance of letters, especially a governmental system; the mail; the transmission of all the letters conveyed for the public at one time from one place to another; also, a post-office.

He chides the tardiness of ev'ry *post*,
Pants to be told of battles won or lost.
Cowper, Retirement, l. 475.

9†. Haste; speed. Compare *post-haste*.

As Ferardo went in *post*, so hee retourned in hast.
Lyly, Euphues, Anat. of Wit, p. 82.

The mayor towards Guildhall hies him in all *post*.
Shak., Rich. III., iii. 5. 73.

10. A size of writing-paper varying in dimensions from $22\frac{1}{2} \times 17\frac{1}{2}$ inches to $19 \times 15\frac{1}{4}$ inches, and in weight from 25 to 7 pounds per ream: so called because its original water-mark was a postman's horn. *E. H. Knight.*—11†. An old game of cards, in which the hands consisted of three cards, that one being the best which contained the highest pair royal, or, if none contained a pair royal, the highest pair. *Nares.* Also called *post and pair*, and *pink*.
—**Advance posts**, positions in front of an army, occupied by detachments of troops for the purpose of keeping a watch upon the enemy's movements, to learn his position and strength, and, in case of an advance, to hold him in check until the main body is prepared for his attack.—**Parcels post**. See *parcel*.—**Penny post**, a post or postal establishment which conveys letters, etc., for a penny. The original penny post was set up in London about 1680 by William Dockwra and Robert Murray, for the conveyance to all parts of the city of London and suburbs of letters, and packets weighing less than a pound, for the sum of one penny each. In course of time, this and all other posts throughout the country having been assumed by the government, a uniform rate of one penny per half-ounce for all places within the United Kingdom of Great Britain and Ireland was ordained by Parliament, August 17th, 1839, to take effect January 10th, 1840. This rate continued till 1871, when the minimum weight was increased to one ounce, which is now carried for one penny—there being reduced rates for larger weights.—**Post adjutant**. See *adjutant*.—**Post and pair†**. See def. 11.

If you cannot agree upon the game, to *post and paire*.
Heywood, Woman Killed with Kindness.

At *Post and Paire*, or Slam, Tom Tuck would play
This Christmas, but his want wherwith says nay.
Herrick, Upon Tuck.

Post folio. See *folio*, 4.—**Post fund**. See *fund*[1].—**Post surgeon**. See *surgeon*.

post[2] (pōst), *v.* [= D. *posteren* = G. *postieren* = Sw. *postera* = Dan. *postere*, < F. *poster* = Sp. *a-postar*, wager, = Pg. *postar* = It. *postare*, station, post; from the noun: see *post*[2], *n.*] **I.** *trans.* 1. To station; place.

I had *posted* myself at his door the whole morning.
Goldsmith, Citizen of the World, xxx.

To discharge cannon against an army in which a king is known to be *posted* is to approach pretty near to regicide.
Macaulay.

2. To place in the post-office; transmit by post.

Mrs. Fairfax had just written a letter which was waiting to be *posted;* so I put on my bonnet and cloak and volunteered to carry it to Hay.
Charlotte Brontë, Jane Eyre, xii.

3. To send or convey by or as by means of post-horses.

The swiftest harts have *posted* you by land;
And winds of all the corners kiss'd your sails,
To make your vessel nimble.
Shak., Cymbeline, ii. 4. 27.

4. In *bookkeeping*, to carry (accounts or items) from the journal to the ledger; make the requisite entries in, as a ledger, for showing a true state of affairs: often followed by *up*.—5. To supply with information up to date; put in possession of needed intelligence; inform; communicate facts to: as, to be *posted* in history. [Colloq.]—**To post off†**, to put off carelessly; thrust aside.

Thinking that of intention to delude him, they *posted* the matter *off* so often. *Hakluyt's Voyages*, I. 247.

I have not stopp'd mine ears to their demands,
Nor *posted off* their suits with slow delays.
Shak., 3 Hen. VI., iv. 8. 40.

=**Syn.** 1. To set, put, establish.

II. *intrans.* 1. To travel with post-horses; hence, to travel rapidly; travel with speed; hasten away.

Thou must *post* to Nottingham,
As fast as thou can dree.
Robin Hood and Queen Katherine (Child's Ballads, V. 313).

Riding as fast as our horses could trot (for we had fresh horses almost thrise or foure times a day), we *posted* from morning till night. *Hakluyt's Voyages*, I. 65.

Thousands at his bidding speed,
And *post* o'er land and ocean without rest.
Milton, Sonnets, xiv.

2. In the *manège*, to rise and sink on the saddle in accordance with the motion of the horse, especially when trotting. *Imp. Dict.*

post[2] (pōst), *adv.* [An elliptical use of *post*[2], *n.*] With post-horses; as a post; by post; hence, with speed; hastily: as, to ride *post;* to journey *post*.

I am a knight that took my journey *post*
Northward from London.
Beau. and Fl., Knight of Burning Pestle, iii. 4.

Send him *post* on errands
A thousand miles. *B. Jonson*, Devil is an Ass, i. 2.

A journey of seventy miles to be taken *post* by you, at your age, alone, unattended!
Jane Austen, Northanger Abbey, xxviii.

Post alone†, quite alone. *Davies.*

Her self loft also she deemed
Post aloan, and soaly from woonted coompanye singled.
Stanihurst, Æneid, iv. 492.

To talk post†, to speak hastily.

'Twere no good manners to speak hastily to a gentlewoman, to *talk post* (as they say) to his mistress.
Shirley, Love in a Maze, i. 1.

post[2] (pōst), *a.* [< *post*[2], *adv.*] Hasty; hurried.

What should this fellow be, i' the name of Heaven,
That comes with such *post* business?
Beau. and Fl., Coxcomb, iv. 6.

post[3]† (pōst), *p. a.* [For *posted*, pp. of *post*[2], *v.* Cf. F. *aposter*, place for a bad purpose (= Sp. Pg. *apostar*, post, = It. *apostare*, lie in ambush), < *à* (< L. *ad*, to) + *poster*, station: see *post*[2], *v.*] Suborned; hired to do what is wrong.

These men, in blacking the lives and actions of the reformers, . . . partly suborned other *post* men to write their legends.
Sir E. Sandys, State of Religion, sig. I. 2 b. (*Latham.*)

post[4]†, *n.* See *poust*.

post[5] (pōst), *adv.* and *prep.* [L., *post*, adv., behind, back, backward, after, afterward; prep., behind, after.] A Latin adverb and preposition, meaning 'behind,' 'after,' 'afterward,' 'since,' etc. It occurs in many Latin phrases sometimes used in English, and is also very common as a prefix. See *post-*.—**Post hoc, ergo propter hoc**, after this, therefore on account of this; B follows A, therefore it is the effect of A: the formula of a fallacy noticed especially by the Arabian physicians, into which there was in medicine a particular tendency to fall, on account of the old objections to making experiments.

post-. [L. *post-*, prefix, *post*, adv. and prep., after, etc.: see *post*[5].] A prefix of Latin origin, meaning 'behind' or 'after.' It occurs in some compounds of Latin formation, and is freely used as an English prefix: opposed to *ante-* and to *pre-*. See *ante-* and *pre-*.

postabdomen (pōst-ab-dō'men), *n.* [NL., < L. *post*, behind, + *abdomen*, abdomen.] A posterior abdominal part of the body in any way distinguished, as in an insect or a crustacean; in mollusks, the postanal part or region of the body; in ascidians, the prolongation of the abdomen beyond the alimentary canal. The tail of a scorpion, or the telson of a king-crab, is a *postabdomen*. See cut under *Pedipalpi*.

postabdominal (pōst-ab-dom'i-nal), *a.* [< *postabdomen* (*-min-*) + *-al* (cf. *abdominal*).] Forming or formed by a postabdomen; situated behind the abdomen proper; pertaining to the postabdomen.

postable† (pōs'ta-bl), *a.* [< *post*[2], *v.*, + *-able*.] Capable of being posted or carried. [Rare.]

postacetabular (pōst-as-e-tab'ū-lär), *a.* [< L. *post*, behind, + *acetabulum*, the socket of the hip-bone: see *acetabular*, *acetabulum*, 2.] Situated behind the acetabulum or cotyloid cavity of the hip-bone.

post-act (pōst'akt), *n.* An after-act; an act done after a particular time.

post-adjutant (pōst-aj'ö-tant), *n.* See *adjutant*.

postage (pōs'tāj), *n.* [< *post*[2], *n.*, + *-age*.] 1†. The act of posting or going by post; hence, passage; journey.

The transient and skin-deep pleasures that we fondly smack after in this *postage* of life in this world.
Feltham, Resolves, p. 277.

2. The rate or charge levied on letters or other articles conveyed by post.

"Never mind the *postage*, but write every day, you dear darling!" said the impetuous and woolly-headed, but generous and affectionate Miss Swartz.
Thackeray, Vanity Fair, i.

Postage currency. See *currency*.

postage-stamp (pōs'tāj-stamp), *n.* An official mark or stamp, either affixed to or embossed on letters, etc., sent through the mails, as evidence of the prepayment of postage. Also called *post-stamp*. See *stamp*.

postal (pōs'tal), *a.* and *n.* [< F. *postal* = Pg. *postal* = It. *postale;* as *post*[2], *n.*, + *-al*.] **I.** *a.* Relating to the post or mails; belonging or pertaining to a mail service: as, *postal* arrangements; *postal* regulations; *postal* service.—**Postal car**, a railroad-car especially designed for carrying mail.—**Postal card**, a stamped official blank provided by postal authorities for the writing and mailing of short messages at a less rate of postage than that required for ordinary letters. Called *post-cards* in the United Kingdom.—**Postal note**, in the postal system of the United States, a note which, on the payment of a small fee, is issued by a postmaster at one office, requiring the postmaster of any other money-order office to pay to the bearer a designated sum, less than five dollars, which the purchaser or remitter has deposited at the issuing office. Also called *post-note*.—**Postal order**, in the United Kingdom, a note or order, similar to the postal note of the United States, but differing from this in being issued only for a fixed amount, which is printed on the order.—**Postal tube**, a tubular case, made of strawboard or millboard, used for the transmission through the mails of any article requiring to be rolled up.—**Universal Postal Union**, the single territory and administration for purposes of international postal communication formed by the countries and colonies which have become parties to the postal convention of Bern in 1874, extended by later conventions, and including most civilized countries.

II. *n.* A postal card or postal order. [Colloq.]

postament (pōs'ta-ment), *n.* [= G. Sw. Dan. *postament*, < NL. *postamentum*, postament, < L. *postis*, post: see *post*[1].] A foot or pedestal, as for an ornamental vase; also, a mounting for a bas-relief, large cameo, or the like, showing moldings in a sort of frame around the principal piece. [Rare.]

postanal (pōst-ā'nal), *a.* [< L. *post*, behind, + *anus*, anus: see *anal*.] Situated behind the anus.

post-angel (pōst'ān"jel), *n.* An angelic messenger. [Rare.]

Let a *post-angel* start with thee,
And thou the goal of earth shalt reach as soon as he.
Cowley, Hymn to Light.

post-apostolic (pōst-ap-os-tol'ik), *a.* [< L. *post*, after, + LL. *apostolus*, apostle: see *apostolic*.] Subsequent to the era of the apostles.

postarytenoid (pōst-ar-i-tē'noid), *a.* and *n.* [< L. *post*, behind, + E. *arytenoid*.] **I.** *a.* Situated behind the arytenoid; of or pertaining to the postarytenoideus.

II. *n.* The postarytenoideus.

postarytenoideus (pōst-ar"i-tē-noi'dē-us), *n.*; pl. *postarytenoidei* (-ī). [NL.: see *postarytenoid*.] The posterior crico-arytenoid muscle.

postauditory (pōst-â'di-tō-ri), *a.* [< L. *post*, behind, + E. *auditory*.] In *anat.*, situated behind the auditory nerve or chamber: opposed to *preauditory*.—**Postauditory processes**, in *ichth.*, processes situated behind the auditory chamber. See cut under *Squatina*.

postaxial (pōst-ak'si-al), *a.* [< L. *post*, behind, + *axis*, axis: see *axial*.] Of or pertaining to, or situated upon, that side of the axis of either fore or hind limb of a vertebrate which is posterior when the limb is extended at a right angle to the long axis of the body: opposed to *preaxial*.

post-bag (pōst'bag), *n.* A bag for carrying mail-matter; a mail-bag.

post-bill (pōst'bil), *n.* 1. Same as *bank post-bill* (which see, under *bill*[3]).—2. A way-bill of the letters despatched from a post-office. [Great Britain.]

post-bird (pōst'bėrd), *n.* The spotted flycatcher, *Muscicapa grisola*: so called from its habit of perching on posts.

post-book (pōst'bůk), *n.* A book containing the regulations of a post-service.

> I pulled out the *postbook*, and began to read with great vociferation the article which orders that the traveller who comes first shall be first served.
> *Smollett*, Travels (ed. 1766), I. 137.

post-box[1] (pōst'boks), *n.* In *mach.*, a shafting-box attached to a post instead of to a hanging or standing pedestal.

post-box[2] (pōst'boks), *n.* A mail-box.

postboy (pōst'boi), *n.* A boy who rides post; a boy or man who carries mail; the driver of a post-chaise; a postilion.

postbrachial (pōst-brā'ki-al), *a.* [< L. *post*, after, + *brachium*, upper arm: see *brachial*.] In *human anat.*, situated upon the back of the brachium, or upper arm: specifically applied to a group of muscles represented by the divisions of the triceps. *Coues*, 1887.

postbranchial (pōst-brang'ki-al), *a.* [< L. *post*, behind, + *branchiæ*, gills: see *branchial*.] Placed behind the gills; posterior to any one gill: opposed to *prebranchial*. *Micros. Sci.*, XXIX. 179.

post-butt (pōst'but), *n.* A block of stone or wood sunk in the ground as a support for a fence-post.

post-calcaneal (pōst-kal-kā'nē-al), *a.* [< L. *post*, behind, + NL. *calcaneum* + *-al*.] Situated behind the calcaneum: noting a lobe of the interfemoral membrane of the *Chiroptera*.

post-canonical (pōst-ka-non'i-kal), *a.* Of later date than the canon; written after the close of the canon of Scripture.

post-captain (pōst'kap'tān), *n.* See *captain*, 1 (*b*).

post-card (pōst'kärd), *n.* Same as *postal card* (which see, under *postal*). [Great Britain.]

post-carochet, *n.* A post-chaise.

> And, being to travel, he sticks not to lay
> His *post-caroches* still upon his way.
> *Drayton*, Moon-Calf.

postcava (pōst-kā'vä), *n.*; pl. *postcavæ* (-vē). The inferior vena cava; the caval vein which is below in man, and behind or posterior in other animals: opposed to *præcava*.

postcaval (pōst-kā'val), *a.* and *n.* I. *a.* Of or pertaining to or constituting the postcava.

II. *n.* The postcava, or postcaval vein.

post-cedar (pōst'sē"där), *n.* See *incense-cedar*.

postcephalic (pōst-se-fal'ik or pōst-sef'a-lik), *a.* [< L. *post*, behind, + Gr. κεφαλή, head: see *cephalic*.] Situated behind the head; more specifically, in myriapods, situated behind the cephalic segment: as, a *postcephalic* segment of the body.

postcerviciplex (pōst-sėr'vi-si-pleks), *n.* [< L. *post*, behind, + *cervix* (*cervic-*), neck, + NL. *plexus*, q. v.: see *cerviciplex*.] The posterior cervical plexus (which see, under *plexus*). *Coues*.

post-chaise (pōst'shāz), *n.* A chaise or carriage let for hire for conveying travelers from one station to another.

> A heroine in a hack *post-chaise* is such a blow upon sentiment as no attempt at grandeur or pathos can withstand.
> *Jane Austen*, Northanger Abbey, xxix.

post-chaise (pōst'shāz), *v. i.* [< *post-chaise*, *n.*] To travel by post-chaise. *Thackeray*, Newcomes, xv.

post-chariot (pōst'char"i-ot), *n.* A post-chaise. *Thackeray*, English Humorists, Steele.

postclassic (pōst-klas'ik), *a.* [< L. *post*, after, + *classicus*, classic: see *classic*.] Same as *postclassical*.

postclassical (pōst-klas'i-kal), *a.* [As *postclassic* + *-al*.] Occurring or existing after the times of those Greek and Latin writers who take rank as classical, and previous to the literature classified as medieval: as, the *postclassical* poets.

postclavicle (pōst-klav'i-kl), *n.* [< L. *post*, behind, + NL. *clavicula*, clavicle: see *clavicle*.] In *ichth.*, a posterior element of the scapular arch of some fishes, which, like the supraclavicle and interclavicle, is variously homologized by different writers.

postclavicular (pōst-kla-vik'ū-lär), *a.* [< *postclavicle*, after *clavicular*.] Of or pertaining to the postclavicle.

postclitellian (pōst-kli-tel'i-an), *a.* [< L. *post*, behind, + NL. *clitellum*, q. v., + *-ian*.] Having the ducts of the testes opening behind, and not before or in, the clitellum, as certain earthworms.

post-coach (pōst'kōch), *n.* Same as *post-chaise*.

postcommunicant (pōst-ko-mū'ni-kant), *a.* [< L. *post*, behind, + *communican(t-)s*, ppr. of *communicare*, communicate: see *communicant*.] Communicating behind: said of the posterior communicating artery of the circle of Willis, at the base of the brain.

post-communion (pōst-ko-mū'nyon), *n.* and *a.* I. *n.* 1. The part of the liturgy or eucharistic office which succeeds the act of communion.—2. A collect or prayer, or one of several prayers, said after communion.

II. *a.* In *liturgics*, succeeding or following the act of communion; also, used after communion: as, a *post-communion* collect; the *post-communion* veil.

postcostal (pōst-kos'tal), *a.* [< L. *post*, behind, + *costalis*, costal: see *costal*.] Placed next behind the costal nervure or vein of the wing, as a nervure of some insects' wings.—**Postcostal cellules** or **areolets**, a name given by some of the older authors to one or more cells in the costal area exterior to the stigma: they are now generally known as the *marginal* or *radial cells*.—**Postcostal vein** or **nervure**, the second main longitudinal vein immediately behind the costal vein: it is generally called the *subcostal vein* or *cubitus*.

postcoxal (pōst-kok'sal), *a.* [< L. *post*, behind, + NL. *coxa*, q. v., + *-al*.] In *entom.*, situated behind the coxæ, or coxal cavities.

postcruciate (pōst-krö'shi-āt), *a.* [< L. *post*, behind, + NL. *cruciatus*, cross-shaped, also tormented: see *cruciate*[1], 2.] Posterior to the cruciate fissure of the cerebrum. *Alien. and Neurol.* (trans.), VI. 9.

postcubital (pōst-kū'bi-tal), *a.* [< L. *post*, behind, + *cubitus*, forearm: see *cubital*.] Situated upon the back of the forearm: specifically noting a group or set of cubital muscles. *Coues*.

postdate (pōst'dāt), *n.* [= F. *postdate* = Pg. *posdata*; as *post-* + *date*[1].] A date put on a document later than the actual date on which it was written.

postdate (pōst-dāt'), *v. t.*; pret. and pp. *postdated*, ppr. *postdating*. [= F. *postdater* = Pg. *posdatar*; from the noun: see *postdate*, *n.*] 1. To affix a later date to than the real one: as, to *postdate* a contract (that is, to date it as if, for instance, it were made six months later than the actual date).—2. To date afterward; give a previous date to. *South*. [Rare.]

post-day (pōst'dā), *n.* A day on which the post or mail arrives or departs.

postdiastolic (pōst-dī-a-stol'ik), *a.* [< L. *post*, behind, + Gr. διαστολή, dilatation: see *diastolic*.] After the diastole: said infelicitously of a cardiac murmur occurring at the beginning of the diastole.

postdicrotic (pōst-dī-krot'ik), *a.* [< L. *post*, behind, + E. *dicrotic*, q. v.] Coming after the dicrotic wave: said of a secondary wave indicated in the sphygmograms of some pulses.

postdiluvial (pōst-di-lū'vi-al), *a.* [< L. *post*, after, + *diluvium*, deluge: see *diluvial*.] Existing or occurring after the deluge.

postdiluvian (pōst-di-lū'vi-an), *a.* and *n.* [= F. *postdiluvien* = Sp. *postdiluviano* = Pg. *posdiluviano* = It. *postdiluviano*, *posdiluviano*, < L. *post*, after, + *diluvium*, deluge: see *diluvian*.] I. *a.* Same as *postdiluvial*.

> But this was very obscurely discovered as yet, as sometimes by dreams and visions, till the *postdiluvian* and more prophetic days. *Evelyn*, True Religion, II. 15.

II. *n.* One who has lived since the deluge.

> Methusalem might be half an hour in telling what o'clock it was; but as for us *post-diluvians*, we ought to do everything in haste. *Steele*, Tatler, No. 264.

post-disseizin (pōst-dis-sē'zin), *n.* In *law*, a subsequent disseizin; also, a writ that lay for him who, having recovered lands or tenements by force of novel disseizin, was again disseized by the former disseizor. *Wharton*.

post-disseizor (pōst-dis-sē'zor), *n.* A person who disseizes another of lands which he had before recovered of the same person.

postdorsulum (pōst-dôr'sū-lum), *n.*; pl. *postdorsula* (-lä). [NL., < L. *post*, behind, + NL. *dorsulum*, q. v.] In *entom.*, the metascutum, or scutum of the metathorax. *Kirby*.

post-drill (pōst'dril), *n.* A drill supported on a standard; a lever-drill or pillar-drill. *E. H. Knight*.

post-driver (pōst'drī"vėr), *n.* A bird, the stake-driver.

postet, *n.* See *poust*.

postea (pōs'tē-ä), *n.* [So called from the first word in the orig. (Latin) form of the return: namely, L. *postea*, after this, < *post*, after, + *eā*, abl. fem. of *is*, fem. *ea*, this.] In *law*, entry upon the record of a court, stating the proceedings at the trial. The name was derived from the usual beginning of the entry, which signified that, issue having been joined, afterward (*postea*) the cause came on for trial, etc.

postelt, *n.* See *postle*[1].

postembryonic (pōst-em-bri-on'ik), *a.* [< L. *post*, after, + NL. *embryon*, embryo: see *embryonic*.] Subsequent to the embryonic stage or state of any animal; postnatal.

> The *post-embryonic* development, when the larva is free-swimming and can procure its own food.
> *C. Claus*, Zoölogy, p. 116.

post-entry (pōst-en'tri), *n.* 1. In *com.*, an addition to the manifest of a vessel of an item or items of merchandise found on the vessel, and not enumerated on the manifest at the time of the entry of the vessel at the custom-house.—2. In *bookkeeping*, a subsequent or additional entry.

poster[1] (pōs'tėr), *n.* [< *post*[1], *v.*, + *-er*[1].] 1. One who posts bills; a bill-poster.—2. A broadside or placard intended for pasting or nailing upon a post or wall in some public place; an advertisement.

> Before the Great Fire the space for foot-passengers in London was defended by rails and posts; the latter served for theatrical placards and general announcements, which were therefore called *posters* or posting-bills.
> *Brewer*, Dict. Phrase and Fable.

> The official *poster* at the door [of Notre Dame] asserts that the great bell in the tower is the largest in the world.
> *Harper's Mag.*, LXXIX. 94.

poster[2] (pōs'tėr), *n.* [< *post*[2], *v.*, + *-er*[1].] 1. One who posts, or travels as post; one who travels expeditiously.

> The weird sisters, hand in hand,
> *Posters* of the sea and land,
> Thus do go about, about.
> *Shak.*, Macbeth, i. 3. 33.

2. A post-horse.

> Two travellers . . . were slowly dragged by a pair of jaded *posters* along the commons.
> *Bulwer*, Night and Morning, ii. 10.

poste restante (pōst res-tänt'). [F., < *poste*, post-office, + *restante*, remaining, left, fem. of *restant*, ppr. of *rester*, remain: see *post*[2] and *restant*.] In France and other countries of Europe and America, a department in a post-office where letters specially addressed are kept till the owners call for them. It is intended particularly for the convenience of persons passing through a country or town where they have no fixed residence.

posterial (pos-tē'ri-al), *a.* [For **posterioral*, < *posterior* + *-al*.] Of or relating to the posterior or posteriors; posterior.

> No license of fashion can allow a man of delicate taste to adopt the *posterial* luxuriance of a Hottentot.
> *Carlyle*, Sartor Resartus (ed. 1831), p. 193.

posterior (pos-tē'ri-or), *a.* and *n.* [Formerly also *posteriour*; < OF. *posterieur*, F. *postérieur* = Sp. Pg. *posterior* = It. *posteriore*, < L. *posterior*, compar. of *posterus*, coming after, following, next, next in order, time, or place, later, latter, hinder, < *post*, after: see *post*[5].] I. *a.* 1. Later in position in a series or course of action; coming after.

> So it is manifest that, where the anteriour body giveth way as fast as the *posteriour* cometh on, it maketh no noise, be the motion never so great or swift.
> *Bacon*, Nat. Hist., § 115.

2. Especially, later or subsequent in time: opposed to *prior*.

> Hesiod was *posterior* to Homer. *W. Broome*.

> No care was taken to have this matter remedied by the explanatory articles *posterior* to the report. *Addison*.

> What is *posterior* in the order of things does not act from itself, but from something prior to it.
> *Swedenborg*, Christian Psychol. (tr. by Gorman), p. 64.

3. Situated behind; hinder: opposed to *anterior*. In most cases, in anatomy and zoölogy, *posterior* is said of parts lying behind the head, or fore end of the body; in man, also of parts lying behind the front of the body: in the former case synonymous with *caudal*, in the latter with *dorsal*. See cuts under *bivalve* and *Dromæus*.

4. In *bot.*, situated on the side nearest the axis; superior: said of the parts of an axillary flower. Compare *anterior*.—**Posterior area of the medulla**, a somewhat oval area seen in transverse sections of the lower part of the oblongata on each side, at the posterior part, bounded in front by bundles of nerve-

root fibers of the spinal accessory.—**Posterior communicating artery of the brain**, a branch connecting the internal carotid with the posterior cerebral artery, and forming part of the circle of Willis; the postcommunicant artery.—**Posterior ethmoidal canal.** See *ethmoidal*.—**Posterior extremity**, the leg of man, or the hind leg of any animal.—**Posterior line**, or **posterior basal line**, a more or less angulated and curved line crossing the anterior wing about midway between the base and the center, found in many moths.—**Posterior margin**, in *conch.*, that side of the bosses of acephalous bivalves which contains the ligament.—**Posterior margin of the wing**, in *entom.*, generally the edge of the wing opposed to the costa or front border; but in those *Lepidoptera* and *Hymenoptera* which have the borders of the wings naturally divided into three parts *posterior margin* is often understood to mean the outer one, or that between the apex and the inner angle, the latter being also called the *posterior angle*.—**Posterior mediastinum, nares**, etc. See *mediastinum*, *naris*, etc.—**Posterior palpi**, in *entom.*, those palpi that are on the labium; the labial palpi.—**Posterior sulcus of Reil**, a deep groove between the island of Reil and the upper surface of the temporosphenoidal lobe.

II. *n.* 1. The hinder part; in the plural, the hinder parts of the body of man or any animal.

When [matters] . . . are resolved upon, I believe then nothing is so advantageous as Speed, . . . for Expedition is the Life of Action, otherwise Time may shew his bald occiput, and shake his *Posteriors* at them in Derision.
Howell, Letters, ii. 17.

2†. *pl.* The latter part. [A whimsical use.]

Sir, it is the king's most sweet pleasure and affection to congratulate the princess at her pavilion in the *posteriors* of this day, which the rude multitude call the afternoon.
Shak., L. L. L., v. 1. 94.

posterioristic (pos-tē"ri-o-ris'tik), *a.* [< *posterior* + *-istic.*] Pertaining to the two books of the Posterior Analytics of Aristotle. There are some discrepancies between the doctrine of the Prior and that of the Posterior Analytics, and these are distinguished as the *prioristic* and the *posterioristic doctrines*.—**Posterioristic universal**, a proposition de omni according to the definition given in Anal. Post. I. cap. 4, where the term is limited to true propositions: opposed to *prioristic universal*, a proposition de omni according to the definition given in Anal. Prior. I. cap. 1, according to which a false proposition may be said de omni.

posteriority (pos-tē-ri-or'i-ti), *n.* [= F. *postériorité* = Sp. *posterioridad* = Pg. *posterioridade*, < NL. *posteriorita(t-)s*, < L. *posterior*, posterior: see *posterior*.] The state of being later or subsequent: opposed to *priority*.

A priority and *posteriority* of dignity as well as order.
Cudworth, Intellectual System, p. 598.

posteriorly (pos-tē'ri-or-li), *adv.* In a posterior manner; subsequently; behind; specifically, in *zoöl.*, toward or near the posterior or caudal end of an animal; caudad; in *human anat.*, toward the back; dorsad: as, a line directed *posteriorly*; organs situated *posteriorly*.

posterity (pos-ter'i-ti), *n.* [Formerly also *posteritie*; < F. *postérité* = Sp. *posteridad* = Pg. *posteridade* = It. *posterità*, < L. *posterita(t-)s*, posterity, < *posterus*, coming after, in pl. as noun, *posteri*, coming generations, posterity: see *posterior*.] 1. Descendants collectively; the race that proceeds from a progenitor.

Yet it was said
It [the crown] should not stand in thy *posterity*.
Shak., Macbeth, iii. 1. 4.

From whom a Race of Monarchs shall descend,
And whose *Posterity* shall know no End.
Congreve, Hymn to Venus.

2. Succeeding generations collectively.

Methinks the truth should live from age to age,
As 'twere retail'd to all *posterity*.
Shak., Rich. III., iii. 1. 77.

My lords, how much your country owes you both,
The due reward of your desertful glories,
Must to *posterity* remain.
Beau. and Fl., Laws of Candy, i. 2.

What has *posterity* done for us,
That we, lest they their rights should lose,
Should trust our necks to gripe of noose?
J. Trumbull, McFingal, ii. 124. (*Bartlett.*)

3. Posteriority. [Rare.]

There is no difference of time with him [God]; it is dangerous to dispute of priority or *posterity* in nature.
Baxter, Saints' Rest, i. 8.

=**Syn.** 1. *Issue, Progeny*, etc. See *offspring*.

postern (pōs'tėrn), *n.* [< ME. *posterne*, *postyrn*, *postorne*, *postrene*, < OF. *posterne*, *posterle*, F. *poterne* = Pr. *posterlla* = Sp. Pg. *poterna* = It. *postierla*, < LL. *posterula* (also, after OF., *posterna*), a small back door, a back way, dim. (sc. *janua*, door, or *via*, way), < L. *posterus*, hinder: see *posterior*.] 1. A back door or gate; a private entrance; hence, any small door or gate. See cuts under *castle* and *barbican*.

Thanne Anasor remembered that ther was
A *postrene* yssuyng owt of the Citee,
And thederward they drowe to haue entree.
Generydes (E. E. T. S.), l. 2559.

Go on, good Eglamour,
Out at the *postern* by the abbey-wall.
Shak., T. G. of V., v. 1. 9.

I love to enter pleasure by a *postern*,
Not the broad popular gate that gulps the mob.
Lowell, Under the Willows.

2. In *fort.*, a covered passage closed by a gate, usually in the angle of the flank of a bastion, or in that of the curtain, or near the orillion, descending into the ditch.

postern-door (pōs'tėrn-dōr), *n.* A postern.

The conscious priest, who was suborn'd before,
Stood ready posted at the *postern door*.
Dryden, Sig. and Guis., l. 152.

postern-gate (pōs'tėrn-gāt), *n.* [< ME. *posterne gate*; < *postern* + *gate*[1].] A postern.

Weren passed priuell the paleys bi a *posterne gate*.
William of Palerne (E. E. T. S.), l. 2870.

posterolateral (pos"te-rō-lat'e-ral), *a.* [< L. *posterus*, hinder, + *lateralis*, lateral: see *lateral*.] Posterior and lateral; placed at the posterior end of a lateral margin or surface: as, *posterolateral* angles.—**Posterolateral groove**, the groove along the spinal cord where the posterior roots issue. Also called *sulcus lateralis dorsalis*.

posteroparietal (pos"te-rō-pā-rī'e-tal), *a.* [< L. *posterus*, hinder, + NL. *parietalis*, parietal.] Situated in a posterior part of the parietal lobe of the brain.—**Posteroparietal lobule.** Same as *superior parietal lobule*. See *parietal lobule*.

posterosuperior (pos"te-rō-sū-pē'ri-or), *a.* [< L. *posterus*, hinder, + *superior*, superior.] Posterior and superior; placed backwardly on top of something.—**Posterosuperior lobe of the cerebellum.** See *lobe*.

posterotemporal (pos"te-rō-tem'pō-ral), *a.* [< L. *posterus*, hinder, + NL. *temporalis*, temporal.] Posterior and temporal: noting a bone of the scapular arch of most fishes, behind the post-temporal, between this and the proscapula. *Gill.* Also called *scapula* and *supraclavicle*.

posteroterminal (pos"te-rō-tėr'mi-nal), *a.* [< L. *posterus*, hinder, + NL. *terminalis*, terminal.] Situated at the hind end; ending something behind.

posteroventral (pos"te-rō-ven'tral), *a.* [< L. *posterus*, hinder, + *venter*, stomach: see *ventral*.] Posterior and ventral; placed backwardly on the ventral aspect of something.

postesophageal, postœsophageal (pōst-ē-sō-faj'ē-al), *a.* [< L. *post*, behind, + NL. *œsophagus*, the gullet: see *esophageal*.] 1. Situated behind (dorsad of) the gullet.—2. Situated behind (caudad of) the esophageal ring or ganglion of the nervous system of an invertebrate. See cuts under *leech*[2] and *stomatogastric*.

post-exilian (pōst-eg-zil'i-an), *a.* [< L. *post*, after, + *exilium*, exile: see *exile*[1].] Subsequent to the Babylonian captivity of the Jews; belonging to or characteristic of times subsequent to the exile of the Jews (about 586 to 537 B. C.).

post-exilic (pōst-eg-zil'ik), *a.* Same as *post-exilian*.

post-exist (pōst-eg-zist'), *v. i.* [< L. *post*, after, + *existere*, exist: see *exist*.] To exist afterward; live subsequently. [Rare.]

Anaxagoras could not but acknowledge that all souls and lives did pre- and *post-exist* by themselves, as well as those corporeal forms and qualities, in his similar atoms.
Cudworth, Intellectual System, p. 37.

post-existence (pōst-eg-zis'tens), *n.* Subsequent or future existence.

As he [Simonides] has exposed the vicious part of women from the doctrine of pre-existence, some of the ancient philosophers have . . . satirized the vicious part of the human species in general from a notion of the soul's *post-existence*. *Addison*, Spectator, No. 211.

post-existent (pōst-eg-zis'tent), *a.* Existent or living after or subsequently.

As for the conceit of Anaxagoras, of præ and *post-existent* atoms endued with all those several forms and qualities of bodies ingenerably and incorruptibly, it was nothing but an adulteration of the genuine atomical philosophy.
Cudworth, Intellectual System, p. 35.

postfact (pōst-fakt'), *a.* and *n.* [L. *post factus*, done after (ML. *post factum*, after the deed, after): *post*, after; *factus*, done: see *fact*.] I. *a.* Relating to a fact that occurs after another.

II. *n.* A fact that occurs after another.

postfactor (pōst-fak'tor), *n.* [< L. *post*, after, + *factor*, doer: see *factor*.] The latter factor of two combined by non-commutative multiplication.

postfebrile (pōst-fē'bril), *a.* [< L. *post*, after, + *febris*, fever: see *febrile*.] Occurring after a fever: as, *postfebrile* insanity.

postfemoral (pōst-fem'ō-ral), *a.* [< L. *post*, behind, + *femur*, thigh: see *femoral*.] Situated on the back of the thigh: specifically noting a group of muscles.

postferment† (pōst-fėr'ment), *n.* [< L. *post*, behind, + *ferre*, bear, + *-ment* (in imitation of *preferment*).] Removal to an inferior office: the opposite of *preferment*. [Rare.]

That his translation was a *Post-ferment*, seeing the Archbishoprick of Saint Andrews was subjected in that age unto York. *Fuller*, Worthies, Durham, I. 329. (*Davies.*)

postfine (pōst'fīn), *n.* In *Eng. law*, a fine due to the king by prerogative. Also called the *king's silver* (which see, under *silver*). See *alienation-office*.

postfix (pōst-fiks'), *v. t.* [< *post-* + *fix*, *v.*] To add or annex (a letter, syllable, or word) to the end of a word.

postfix (pōst'fiks), *n.* [< *postfix*, *v.*] In *gram.*, a letter, syllable, or word added to the end of a word; a suffix.

postfixal (pōst'fik-sal), *a.* [< *postfix* + *-al.*] Having the character of a postfix, or characterized by postfixes; suffixal.

The *postfixal* languages of Central Asia.
Jour. Anthrop. Inst., XVII. 170.

post-free (pōst'frē), *a.* Deliverable by the post-office without charge.

postfrenum (pōst-frē'num), *n.* [NL., < L. *post*, behind, + *frenum*, a bridle, curb, bit: see *frenum*.] In *entom.*, a part of the upper surface of the metathorax in a beetle, lying next to the abdomen, and often connected at the sides with the bases of the lower or membranous wings, preventing them from being pushed too far forward. *Kirby.*

postfrontal (pōst-fron'tal), *a.* and *n.* [< L. *post*, behind, + *fron(t-)s*, forehead: see *frontal*.] I. *a.* 1. Situated behind the forehead: as, a *postfrontal* bone.—2. Posterior with respect to certain gyres of the frontal lobe of the cerebrum.—**Postfrontal process**, in many quadrupeds and birds, a process of bone upon the upper and posterior part of the brim of the orbital cavity; a postorbital process, sometimes a distinct bone. See further under *postorbital*, 1.

II. *n.* A bone of the skull of sundry vertebrates, situated at the back part of the brim of the orbit of the eye. It is not recognized as a distinct bone in animals above birds. See cut under *Ichthyosauria*.

postfurca (pōst-fėr'kä), *n.*; pl. *postfurcæ* (-sē). [NL., < L. *post*, behind, + *furca*, a fork: see *furca*.] In *entom.*, the posterior forked or double apodeme which projects from the sternal wall into the cavity of a thoracic somite.

postfurcal (pōst-fėr'kal), *a.* [< *postfurca* + *-al.*] In *entom.*, of or pertaining to or constituting a postfurca: as, a *postfurcal* apodeme.

postgeniculatum (pōst-jē-nik-ū-lā'tum), *n.*; pl. *postgeniculata* (-tä). [NL. (Wilder), < L. *post*, after, + NL. *geniculatum*.] The internal geniculate body of the brain, an elevation at the side of the diencephalon, between the optic tract and the cimbia. *Wilder and Gage.*

postgenital (pōst-jen'i-tal), *a.* [< L. *post*, behind, + *genitalis*, genital: see *genital*.] In *entom.*, situated behind the genital orifice.—**Postgenital segments**, segments of the abdomen following the eighth: in the perfect insect they are concealed under the other rings.

post-geniture (pōst-jen'i-tūr), *n.* [< L. *post*, after, + *genitura*, begetting: see *geniture*.] The state or position of a child born after another in the same family: used specifically of the second born of twins.

Naturally a king, though fatally prevented by the harmless chance of *post-geniture*. *Sir T. Browne.*

post-glacial (pōst-glā'shial), *a.* [< L. *post*, after, + E. *glacial*.] In *geol.* See *Post-tertiary*.

postglenoid (pōst-glē'noid), *a.* and *n.* [< L. *post*, behind, + Gr. γληνοειδής, like a ball-and-socket joint: see *glenoid*.] I. *a.* Situated behind the glenoid fossa for the articulation of the lower jaw. Compare *preglenoid*.

II. *n.* The postglenoid process of the squamosal bone.

postglenoidal (pōst-glē-noi'dal), *a.* [< *postglenoid* + *-al.*] Same as *postglenoid*.

The squamosal [of the rhinoceros] sends down an immense *post-glenoidal* process. *Huxley*, Anat. Vert., p. 308.

postgraduate (pōst-grad'ū-āt), *a.* and *n.* [< L. *post*, after, + ML. *graduatus*, pp. of *graduare*, confer a degree upon: see *graduate*.] I. *a.* Belonging or relating to or prosecuting a course of study pursued after graduation: as, *postgraduate* lectures; a *postgraduate* course of study; a *postgraduate* student. [U. S.]

The "graduate" (sometimes even called *postgraduate*) work of our candidates for the Ph. D. degree is carried on either in Europe or in the United States.
Classical Rev., IV. 53.

II. *n.* A graduate; one studying after graduation. [U. S.]

[An objectionable form in both uses.]

post-hackney (pōst'hak″ni), *n.* A post-horse.

Teach *post-hackneys* to leap hedges. *Sir H. Wotton*, Remains.

post-haste (pōst-hāst'), *n.* Haste or speed like that of a post or courier in traveling.

Norfolk and myself,
In haste, *post-haste*, are come to join with you.
Shak., 3 Hen. VI., ii. 1. 139.

I have continually been the man and the mean that have most plainly dehorted her from such *post-haste*. *Lord Sackville*, quoted in Motley's Hist. Netherlands, II. 250.

post-haste (pōst-hāst'), *adv.* With the haste of a post; with speed or urgent expedition: as, he traveled *post-haste*.

Old John of Gaunt is grievous sick, my lord,
Suddenly taken; and hath sent *post haste*
To entreat your majesty to visit him.
Shak., Rich. II., i. 4. 55.

To see him die, across the waste
His son and heir doth ride *post-haste*,
But he'll be dead before.
Tennyson, Death of the Old Year.

Travelling *post-haste*, Bismarck arrived in Berlin on the 19th September. *Lowe*, Bismarck, I. 283.

post-haste (pōst-hāst'), *a.* Expeditious; speedy; immediate.

The duke does greet you, general,
And he requires your haste-*post-haste* appearance,
Even on the instant. *Shak.*, Othello, i. 2. 37.

[The edition of 1623 reads "haste, *post-haste*."]

Write from us to him; post-*post-haste* dispatch.
Shak., Othello, i. 3. 46.

[The edition of 1623 reads "post, *post-haste*."]

posthetomist (pos-thet'ō-mist), *n.* [= F. *posthétomiste*; < *posthetom-y* + *-ist*.] One who performs the operation of posthetomy or circumcision.

posthetomy (pos-thet'ō-mi), *n.* [< Gr. *πόσθη*, penis, prepuce, + *-τομία*, < *τέμνειν*, *ταμεῖν*, cut.] Circumcision.

posthioplastic (pos″thi-ō-plas'tik), *a.* [< Gr. *πόσθη*, penis, prepuce, + *πλαστός*, verbal. adj. of *πλάσσειν*, mold: see *plastic*.] Pertaining to the plastic surgery of the prepuce.

post-hippocampal (pōst-hip-ō-kam'pal), *a.* [< L. *post*, behind, + NL. *hippocampus*.] Situated behind the hippocampus: specifically in Owen's name, *post-hippocampal* fissure, of the calcarine fissure or sulcus.

posthitis (pos-thī'tis), *n.* [NL., < Gr. *πόσθη*, penis, prepuce, + *-itis*.] Inflammation of the prepuce.

post-holder (pōst'hōl″dėr), *n.* One who holds a post or place under government; a civil official at a foreign or colonial station.

Serah and Larat, both islets of the Timorlaut group, where the Government had just then placed *Postholders* (civil officials of subordinate rank) charged with initiatory work of these new colonies. *H. O. Forbes*, Eastern Archipelago, p. 289.

post-hole (pōst'hōl), *n.* A hole cut in the ground to receive the end of a fence-post.—**Post-hole auger.** See *auger*, 2.—**Post-hole borer**, a post-hole auger.—**Post-hole digger**, a pair of pointed segmental spades so jointed together as to cut in the ground, by rotation, a cylindrical hole for a fence-post.

post-horn (pōst'hôrn), *n.* A postman's horn; a horn blown by the driver or guard of a mail-coach, and at present used on four-in-hands for pleasure driving. It is a straight tube of brass or copper, from two to four feet long, the bore gradually enlarging downward, with a small, shallow, cupped mouthpiece. Its pitch varies with its length. It is occasionally used as a musical instrument by exceptional players.

But let eternal infamy pursue
The wretch, to nought but his ambition true,
Who, for the sake of filling with one blast
The *posthorns* of all Europe, lays her waste.
Cowper, Table Talk, l. 32.

post-horse (pōst'hôrs), *n.* A horse kept or hired for forwarding post-riders or travelers with speed from one station to another.

I, from the orient to the drooping west,
Making the wind my *post-horse*, still unfold
The acts commenced on this ball of earth.
Shak., 2 Hen. IV., Ind., l. 4.

post-house (pōst'hous), *n.* 1. A house where relays of post-horses are kept for the convenience of travelers.

We repos'd this night at Piperno, in the *post-house* without the towne. *Evelyn*, Diary, Jan. 25, 1645.

Posthouses were at convenient stages all over the kingdom, and the postmaster was bound to provide horses for all comers, either to ride or drive. *J. Ashton*, Social Life in Reign of Queen Anne, II. 109.

2†. A post-office.

I found yours of the first of February in the *Post-house*, as I casually had other Business there, else it had miscarried. *Howell*, Letters, iv. 35.

I will now put an end to my letter, and give it into the *posthouse* myself. *Swift*, Journal to Stella, xxxvi.

posthume†, **postume†**, *a.* [< F. *posthume*, posthumous: see *posthumous*.] Posthumous.

Oh! if my soul could see their *posthume* spite,
Should it not joy and triumph in the sight?
Bp. Hall, Satires, iv., Int.

Pliny observeth that *posthume* children, born after the death of their father, . . . prove very happy in success. *Fuller*, Worthies, Cumberland, I. 346.

posthumeral (pōst-hū'me-ral), *a.* [< L. *post*, behind, + *humerus*, shoulder: see *humeral*.] In *entom.*, lying behind the humeri or anterolateral angles of the thorax or elytra: as, a *posthumeral* sinus.

posthumous (pos'tū-mus), *a.* and *n.* [Prop. *postumous*; = F. *posthume* = Sp. *póstumo* = Pg. *posthumo* = It. *postumo*, < L. *postumus*, last, applied esp. to the youngest children or to one born after the father's death ("qui post patris mortem natus est"); also written, erroneously, *posthumus*, simulating a derivation from *post humum*, lit. 'after the ground,' but forced into the sense of 'after the father has been put into the ground,' i. e. inhumed, buried; prop. superl. of *posterus*, coming after: see *posterior*.] **I.** *a.* **1.** Born after the death of the father: as, a *posthumous* son.

I was a *posthumous* child. My father's eyes had closed upon the light of this world six months when mine opened on it. *Dickens*, David Copperfield, i.

2. Appearing or existing after the death or cessation of that to which its origin is due; especially, of books, published after the death of the author: as, *posthumous* works.

The sufficiency of Christian immortality frustrates all earthly glory, and the quality of either state after death makes a folly of *posthumous* memory. *Sir T. Browne*, Urn-burial, v.

The desire of *posthumous* fame and the dread of *posthumous* reproach and execration are feelings from the influence of which scarcely any man is perfectly free. *Macaulay*, Mill on Government.

II. *n.* A posthumous child. [Rare.]

My brother Thomas was a *posthumous*, as being born some weeks after his father's death. *Lord Herbert of Cherbury*, Life (ed. Howells), p. 32.

posthumously (pos'tū-mus-li), *adv.* After one's death; especially, after an author's death.

The third [edition], however, appeared *posthumously*. *Science*, III. 390.

postic† (pos'tik), *a.* [< L. *posticus*, hinder, back, posterior, < *post*, after: see *post*5.] Posterior or hinder.

The *postick* and backward position of the feminine parts in quadrupedes. *Sir T. Browne*, Vulg. Err., iii. 17.

postiche (pos-tēsh'), *a.* [< F. *postiche* = Sp. *postizo* = Pg. *postiço*, < It. *posticcio*, superadded, for *apposticcio*, *appositiccio*, < L. *appositus*, pp. of *apponere*, superadd, put beside, < *ad*, to, + *ponere*, place: see *position*. Cf. *apposite*.] Superadded; done after the work is finished: noting a superadded ornament of sculpture or architecture, especially when inappropriate or in false taste. Also *postique*.

posticous (pos-tī'kus), *a.* [< L. *posticus*, hinder, back: see *postic*.] In *bot.*, hinder; back. (*a*) In an inflorescence, posterior; toward the axis. (*b*) Extrorse: said of an adnate anther, the stamen being regarded as facing the axis.

posticum (pos-tī'kum), *n.* [L. (> It. *postico* = Sp. Pg. *postigo*), a back door; prop. neut. of *posticus*, hinder, back, posterior: see *postic*.] **1.** A back door; a postern.—**2.** The term used by Vitruvius, and adopted from him in English, for the open vestibule of an ancient temple in the rear of the cella, corresponding to the *pronaos* at the front of the temple. In Greek architecture the proper name for this feature is *opisthodomos*. It has also been called *epinaos*. See cut under *opisthodomos*, and compare *anticum*.
3. *Eccles.*, a reredos.

postil (pos'til), *n.* [Also *postle*, and formerly *postill*; < ME. *postille*, < OF. (and F.) *postille* = Sp. *postila* = Pr. Pg. It. *postilla* = D. *postil* = G. *postille* = Sw. *postilla* = Dan. *postille*, < ML. *postilla*, a marginal note in a Bible, a gloss in addition, < L. *post illa*: *post*, after; *illa*, neut. pl. of *ille*, that.] **1.** A note or comment on some passage of Scripture, written in the margin of a Bible, and so called because it followed the text; any explanatory remark or comment on the text of the Bible; hence, any marginal note.

The said Langton also made *postils* vpon the whole bible. *Foxe*, Martyrs, p. 248.

This was the main Substance of his Majesty's late Letter; yet there was a *Postil* added, that, in case a Rupture happen 'twixt the two Crowns, the Earl should not come instantly and abruptly away. *Howell*, Letters, I. iii. 12.

That which is the main point in their Sermons affecting the comments and *postils* of Friers and Jesuits, but scorning and slighting the reformed writers. *Milton*, Apology for Smectymnuus.

2. A series of comments, specifically on Scripture; a commentary, or written exposition.—3. A sermon or homily; specifically, a homily following and treating of the liturgical gospel; also, a collection of such homilies.

But in the homes the old prayer-books and the old Lutheran *postils* were still gladly and frequently used. *Bibliotheca Sacra*, XLV. 136.

postil† (pos'til), *v.* [Also *postel*; < OF. *postiller* = Sp. *postilar* = Pg. *postillar* = It. *postillare*, < ML. *postillare*, write a postil: see *postil*, *n.*] **I.** *intrans.* To write or deliver a postil.

To *postell* vpon a kyry. *Skelton*, Colyn Cloute, l. 755.

II. *trans.* To explain or illustrate by a postil.

I doe remember to haue seene long since a book of accompt of Empson's that . . . was in some places *postilled* in the margent with the King's hand. *Bacon*, Hist. Hen. VII., p. 211.

postiler, **postiller** (pos'til-ėr), *n.* [< *postil* + *-er*1.] One who writes or delivers a postil.

Shew yourselves skilful workmen, such as have been brought up not only in morals of the heathen, subtilties of schoolmen, sentences and conceits of *postillers*, . . . but in the wholesome word of faith. *S. Ward*, Sermons, p. 38.

It hath been observed by many holy writers, commonly delivered by *postillers* and commentators. *Sir T. Browne.*

postilion (pōs-til'yon), *n.* [Formerly also *postillion*, *postillon*, < F. *postillon* (= Sp. *postillon* = Pg. *postilhão* = It. *postiglione*), a postilion, < *poste*, post: see *post*2, *n.*] **1†.** A post-boy; one who rides a post-horse; a guide or forerunner.

Albeit you be upon an Island, and I now upon the Continent (tho' the lowest part of Europe), yet those swift *Postilions*, my Thoughts, find you out daily and bring you unto me. *Howell*, Letters, I. i. 8.

2. One who rides the near horse of the leaders when four or more horses are used in a carriage or post-chaise, or who rides the near horse when one pair only is used and there is no driver on the box.

The coachman, however, did not drive all six, one of the leaders being always ridden by a *postilion*. *J. Ashton*, Social Life in Reign of Queen Anne, II. 173.

3. Same as *postilion-basque*.

postilion-basque (pōs-til'yon-bȧsk), *n.* A woman's basque having its skirt cut at the back into short square tabs or coat-tails, after the fashion of a postilion's coat.

postilion-belt (pōs-til'yon-belt), *n.* A leather belt with a large buckle, worn by ladies about 1860.

postilioness (pōs-til'yon-es), *n.* [< *postilion* + *-ess*.] A female postilion. [Rare.]

At Vik, where we found the same simple and honest race of people, we parted with the *postillioness* and with our host of Kettbo. *B. Taylor*, Northern Travels, p. 423.

postilize† (pos'til-īz), *v. t.* [< *postil* + *-ize*.] Same as *postil*.

Postilizing the whole doctrine of Duns Scotus. *Wood*, Athenæ Oxon., I. 9.

postillate (pos'til-āt), *v.*; pret. and pp. *postillated*, ppr. *postillating*. [< ML. *postillatus*, pp. of *postillare*, postil, write postils: see *postil*, *v.*] **I.** *intrans.* To write or deliver a postil.

II. *trans.* To explain or illustrate by a postil.

postillation (pos-ti-lā'shon), *n.* [= Sp. *postilacion*, < ML. *postillatio(n-)*, postillation, < *postillare*, pp. *postillatus*, postillate: see *postillate*.] The act of writing or delivering a postil, or of explaining or illustrating by a postil.

postillator (pos'ti-lā-tor), *n.* [= Sp. *postilador* = Pg. *postillador* = It. *postillatore*, < ML. *postillator*, < *postillare*, pp. *postillatus*, postillate: see *postillate*.] One who writes or delivers a postil, or explains or illustrates by a postil.

postiller, *n.* See *postiler*.

postillion, *n.* See *postilion*.

postime†, *n.* An obsolete form of *apostem*.

posting-house (pōs'ting-hous), *n.* A house or hotel where post-horses are kept.

posting-inn (pōs'ting-in), *n.* Same as *posting-house*. *Harper's Mag.*, LXXIX. 628.

postique (pos-tēk'), *a.* Same as *postiche*.

postischial (pōst-is'ki-al), *a.* [< L. *post*, behind, + NL. *ischium*: see *ischial*.] Situated behind the ischium.

post-jack (pōst'jak), *n.* An implement for lifting posts out of the ground. It is a form of crowbar pivoted in a base-piece, and having a claw which seizes the post. *E. H. Knight.*

postle1†, *n.* [ME., also *postel*; by apheresis from *apostle*.] An apostle; a preacher.

Suffreth my *postles* in pays and in pees gange.
Piers Plowman (B), xvi. 159.

postle², *n.* See *postil.*

postle-spoon†, *n.* Same as *apostle-spoon.*

postliminary, postliminiary (pōst-lim'i-nā-ri, pōst-li-min'i-ā-ri), *a.* [< *postliminy* + *-ary.*] Pertaining to or involving the right of postliminy.

We follow Heffter . . . principally in our brief representation of the rights and obligation of a state restored in this *postliminary* way.
Woolsey, Introd. to Inter. Law, § 247.

postliminiar† (pōst-li-min'i-ạr), *a.* Same as *postliminary.*

It may be said that it is possible the soul may be rap't from this terrestrial body, and carried to remote and distant places, from whence she may make a *postliminiar* return.
Hallywell, Melampronœa (1681), p. 70.

postliminiary, *a.* See *postliminary.*

postliminious (pōst-li-min'i-us), *a.* [< *postliminy* + *-ous.*] Same as *postliminary.*

postliminium (pōst-li-min'i-um), *n.* [L.: see *postliminy.*] Same as *postliminy.*

postliminy (pōst-lim'i-ni), *n.* [= Sp. Pg. It. *postliminio*, < L. *postliminium*, < *post*, after, + *limen* (*limin-*), threshold: see *limit.*] 1. In *Rom. antiq.*, the return of a person who had been banished, or taken prisoner by an enemy, to his old condition and former privileges.—2. In *international law*, that right by virtue of which persons and things taken by an enemy in war are restored to their former status when coming again under the power of the nation to which they belonged.

Prisoners of war in a neutral port, escaping on shore from the vessel where they are confined, . . . cannot be recaptured, since they enjoy the benefit of the right of *postliminy*.
Woolsey, Introd. to Inter. Law, § 145.

post-line (pōst'līn), *n.* A railway constructed upon posts, usually of wrought iron, which support stringers and cross-ties upon which the rails are laid and fastened; an elevated railway.

postlude (pōst'lūd), *n.* [< L. *post*, after, + *ludus*, play, < *ludere*, play.] In *music*, an organ-piece at the end of a church service; a concluding voluntary: correlated with *prelude* and *interlude.*

postman¹ (pōst'man), *n.* [< *post*¹ + *man.*] A barrister in the Court of Exchequer in England, now merged in High Court of Justice, who had precedence in motions: so called from the place where he sat. The postman was one of the two most experienced barristers in the court, the other being called the *tubman.*

In the courts of exchequer, two of the most experienced barristers, called the *post-man* and the tub-man (from the places in which they sit), have also a precedence in motions.
Blackstone, Com., III. iii., note.

postman² (pōst'man), *n.*; pl. *postmen* (-men). [< *post*² + *man.*] 1†. A post; a messenger; a courier; one who rides post.

The *Post-Man* was in the Fault that you have had no Letters from me.
N. Bailey, tr. of Colloquies of Erasmus, I. 117.

2. A mail-carrier.

The *postman* coming along, and knowing her well enough, stopped and gave her the letter he had for her.
W. Black, In Far Lochaber, xix.

General postman. See *general.*

postmark (pōst'märk), *n.* The mark or stamp of a post-office placed on a letter, paper, card, or package sent through the mail; an official stamp on a letter, etc., giving the place and date of sending or the place and date of receipt.

postmark (pōst'märk), *v. t.* [< *postmark*, *n.*] To affix the stamp or mark of the post-office to, as letters, etc.

postmaster (pōst'mȧs"tėr), *n.* [= D. *postmeester* = G. *postmeister* = Sw. *postmästare* = Dan. *postmester*; as *post*² + *master*¹.] 1. The official who has charge of a post-station and provides post-horses, etc.

After the first stage, she had been indebted to the *postmasters* for the names of the places which were then to conduct her to it, so great had been her ignorance of her route.
Jane Austen, Northanger Abbey, xiv.

2. The official who has the superintendence and general direction of a post-office, of the receipt and despatch of mails, etc. In the United States postmasters are classed with reference to their salaries: all those receiving $1,000 or over annually are appointed by the President; all who receive under that sum are appointed by the Postmaster-General. Abbreviated *P. M.*

All those that will send letters to the most parts of the habitable world, or to any part of our King of Great Britain's Dominions — let them repair to the General *Post Master* Thomas Withering, at his house in Sherburne Lane.
John Taylor (Arber's Eng. Garner, I. 240).

3. In Merton College, Oxford, a scholar who is supported on the foundation. Also called *portionist.*

postmaster-general (pōst'mȧs"tėr-jen'e-ral), *n.* The chief executive head of the postal and telegraphic systems of Great Britain, or of the postal system of the United States. In Great Britain the postmaster-general is often a member of the cabinet; he exercises authority over all the departments of the postal system, including money-orders, savings-bank, insurances, and annuities. The postmaster-general of the United States has been a member of the cabinet since the administration of Andrew Jackson.

postmaster-generalship (pōst'mȧs"tėr-jen'e-ral-ship), *n.* [< *postmaster* + *general* + *-ship.*] The office of a postmaster-general.

postmastership (pōst'mȧs"tėr-ship), *n.* [< *postmaster* + *-ship.*] The office of a postmaster; also, the time during which a postmaster holds office.

postmedian (pōst-mē'di-an), *a.* [< L. *post*, behind, + *medianus*, middle: see *median*¹.] Situated behind the middle transverse plane of the body.

postmediastinal (pōst-mē-di-as'ti-nal), *a.* [< *postmediastin-um* + *-al.*] Situated in or pertaining to the postmediastinum: as, *postmediastinal* arteries; the *postmediastinal* space.

postmediastinum (pōst-mē-di-as-tī'num), *n.* [< L. *post*, behind, + NL. *mediastinum*, q. v.] The posterior mediastinum or mediastinal space.

postmeridian (pōst-me-rid'i-an), *a.* and *n.* [Also *pomeridian*, q. v.; = F. *postméridien* = Sp. Pg. *postmeridiano*, Pg. also *pomeridiano* = It. *pomeridiano*, < L. *postmeridianus*, *pomeridianus*, belonging to the afternoon, < *post*, after, + *meridies*, noon: see *meridian.*] I. *a.* Occurring after the sun has passed the meridian; of or pertaining to the afternoon.

Over-hasty digestion . . . is the inconvenience of *postmeridian* sleep.
Bacon, Nat. Hist., § 57.

II. *n.* 1. The afternoon.

'Twas *post-meridian* half-past four
By signal I from Nancy parted. *C. Dibdin.*

2. In the nomenclature suggested by H. D. Rogers for the Paleozoic rocks of Pennsylvania, the equivalent of the Corniferous and Cauda-galli divisions of the New York survey, or that part of the Devonian series which lies between the Oriskany sandstone and the Hamilton group.

post meridiem (pōst me-rid'i-em). [L.: see *postmeridian.*] After midday: applied to the time between noon and midnight. Regularly abbreviated P. M., P. M., or p. m.

postmeridional (pōst-me-rid'i-on-al), *a.* [< *postmeridian*, after *meridional.*] Same as *postmeridian.*

"After our *postmeridional* refection," rejoined Hypertatus, "we will regale with a supernumerary compotation of convivial ale."
Campbell, Lexiphanes, p. 9.

post-mill (pōst'mil), *n.* A form of windmill so constructed that the whole fabric rests on a vertical axis, and can be turned by means of a lever according as the direction of the wind varies. It thus differs from the smock-mill, of which the cap (including the gudgeon and pivot-bearings resting upon it) turns.

postmillenarian (pōst-mil-e-nā'ri-an), *n.* [< L. *post*, after, + NL. *millennium*, millennium: see *millenarian.*] A believer in the doctrine of postmillennialism.

postmillenarianism (pōst-mil-e-nā'ri-an-izm), *n.* [< *postmillenarian* + *-ism.*] Same as *postmillennialism.*

postmillennial (pōst-mi-len'i-al), *a.* [< L. *post*, after, + NL. *millennium*, millennium: see *millennial.*] Relating to what may occur in the period following the millennium. *Princeton Rev.*, March, 1879, p. 425.

postmillennialism (pōst-mi-len'i-al-izm), *n.* [< *postmillennial* + *-ism.*] The doctrine that the second coming of Christ will follow the millennium.

postmillennialist (pōst-mi-len'i-al-ist), *n.* [< *postmillennial* + *-ist.*] Same as *postmillenarian.* *Princeton Rev.*, March 1879, p. 419.

postminimus (pōst-min'i-mus), *n.*; pl. *postminimi* (-mī). [NL., < L. *post*, after, + *minimus* (sc. *digitus*), the little finger: see *minimum.*] An additional little finger or little toe of some mammals, on the ulnar or fibular side of the hand or foot, opposite to the prepollex or prehallux. *Proc. Zoöl. Soc. Lond.*, 1889, p. 260.

postmistress (pōst'mis"tres), *n.* [< *post*² + *mistress.*] A woman who has charge of mails or of a post-office.

post-money (pōst'mun'i), *n.* The charge made for the use of post-horses; cost of posting or traveling post.

We were charged additional *post-money* for the circuits we were obliged to make to keep our runners on the snow.
B. *Taylor*, Northern Travel, p. 192.

post-morning (pōst'môr"ning), *n.* The morning of a post-day. *Sterne*, Tristram Shandy, vi. 22.

post-mortem (pōst-môr'tem), *a.* and *n.* [< L. *post mortem*, after death: *post*, after; *mortem*, acc. of *mors*, death: see *mort*¹.] I. *a.* Subsequent to death: as, a *post-mortem* examination of the body; *post-mortem* changes.

It [Gawain Douglas's poetry] is a mere bill of parcels, a *post-mortem* inventory of nature, where imagination is not merely not called for, but would be out of place.
Lowell, Among my Books, 2d ser., 131.

II. *n.* A post-mortem examination; an examination of the body after death; an autopsy. Also *post-obit.*

post-mortuary (pōst-môr'tū-ā-ri), *a.* [< L. *post*, after, + *mortuarius*, of the dead: see *mortuary.*] Occurring after death; post-mortem; posthumous.

postmultiply (pōst-mul'ti-plī), *v. t.*; pret. and pp. *postmultiplied*, ppr. *postmultiplying.* To multiply into a postfactor, by which the direct object is said to be *postmultiplied.*

postnarial (pōst-nā'ri-al), *a.* [< *postnares* + *-ial.*] Of or pertaining to the postnares.

postnaris (pōst-nā'ris), *n.*; pl. *postnares* (-rēz). [NL. (Wilder), < L. *post*, behind, + *naris*, a nostril.] One of the posterior nares or choanæ; either one of the paired openings of the nasal chamber into the pharynx. *Wilder and Gage*, Anat. Tech., p. 513.

postnasal (pōst-nā'zal), *a.* [< *postnasus* + *-al.*] Posterior, with reference to the nose, nostrils, or nasal passages: as, the *postnasal* spine of the palate-bone.

postnasus (pōst-nā'sus), *n.* [NL., < L. *post*, behind, + *nasus* = E. *nose*¹.] A division of the clypeus of many insects, including the upper part with extensions down the sides: now commonly called *supraclypeus.* *Kirby and Spence.*

postnatal (pōst-nā'tal), *a.* [< L. *post*, after, + *natus*, born: see *natal*¹.] Subsequent to birth: as, a *postnatal* disease.

postnate† (pōst'nāt), *a.* [< ML. *postnatus*, born after, younger (> OF. *puisne*, > E. *puny*¹), < L. *post*, after, + *natus*, born: see *natal.* Cf. *puisne*, *puny*¹.] Subsequent to birth or occurrence; appearing or occurring later.

Of these [pretended prophecies] some were *postnate*, cunningly made after the thing came to pass.
Fuller, Ch. Hist., VI. iv. 2.

The graces and gifts of the Spirit are *postnate*, and are additions to art and nature.
Jer. Taylor, Works (ed. 1835), II. 269.

postnatus (pōst-nā'tus), *n.*; pl. *postnati* (-tī). [ML.: see *postnate.*] In *law*: (*a*) The second son. (*b*) One born after a particular event: as, one born in the United States after the Declaration of Independence (1776) is a *postnatus*; a *postnatus* in Scotland is one born in that country after the accession (1603) of James VI. to the English throne as James I. Compare *antenati.*—**Case of the postnati.** See *Calvin's case*, under *case*¹.

post-Nicene (pōst-nī'sēn), *a.* [< L. *post*, after, + *Nicænus*, Nicene: see *Nicene.*] After the first general council held at Nice, A. D. 325: as, *post-Nicene* Christianity. See *Nicene.*—**Post-Nicene fathers.** See *fathers of the church*, under *father.*

post-night (pōst'nīt), *n.* The evening of a post-day.

It being *post-night*, I wrote to my Lord to gi e him notice that all things are well.
Pepys, Diary, I. 103.

post-note¹ (pōst'nōt), *n.* [< *post*² + *note*¹.] Same as *postal note.* See *postal.*

post-note² (pōst'nōt), *n.* [< L. *post*, after (see *post*⁵), + E. *note*¹.] A note issued by a bank, payable at some future time, and not on demand.

post-nuptial (pōst-nup'shal), *a.* [< L. *post*, after, + *nuptiæ*, nuptials: see *nuptial.*] Being or happening after marriage: as, a *post-nuptial* settlement on a wife.

post-oak (pōst'ōk), *n.* An oak-tree, *Quercus obtusiloba.* It grows in sandy or barren soils throughout a great part of the eastern half of the United States and especially in Texas. It grows to a height of 70 feet; the wood is hard, close-grained, and very durable in contact with the soil, and is largely used, especially in the southwest, for fencing, railroad-ties, fuel, etc. Also called *iron-oak* and *rough* or *bax white oak.*

All the way from Hoppleton merely *post-oak* and sands.
W. M. Baker, New Timothy, p. 51.

Swamp post-oak, a tree, *Quercus lyrata*, of deep river-swamps in the southern United States, especially in the valley of the Red River and adjacent regions, but extending northward into Maryland. It has a height of from 70 to 90 feet, and its hard, strong, and tough wood has the same uses as white oak. See *oak*, 1. Also called *overcup-oak* and *water white oak*.

post-obit (pōst-ō'bit), *n.* [< L. *post*, after, + *obitus*, death: see *obit*.] 1. A bond given for the purpose of securing to a lender a sum of money on the death of some specified individual from whom the borrower has expectations: sometimes used attributively: as, a *post-obit* bond. Such loans are not only made at usurious rates of interest, but usually the borrower has to pay a much larger sum than he has received, in consideration of the risk that he may die before the person from whom he has expectations. If, however, there is in the proportions a gross inadequacy amounting to fraud, a court of equity will interfere.

Now I propose, Mr. Premium, if it 's agreeable to you, a *post-obit* on Sir Oliver's life.
Sheridan, School for Scandal, iii. 3.

2. Same as *post-mortem*.

postoblongata (pōst-ob-long-gā'tä), *n.* [NL., < L. *post*, behind, + NL. *oblongata*, q. v.] The oblongata proper, lying behind the pons.

postocular (pōst-ok'ū-lär), *a.* [< L. *post*, behind, + *oculus*, the eye: see *ocular*.] 1. Lying behind the eye (on the surface of the body of any animal); running back from the eye, as a streak of color; postorbital.

Parallel curved white superciliary and *postocular* stripes.
Sportsman's Gazetteer, p. 209.

2. In *entom.*, situated behind or beneath the compound eyes.—**Postocular lobes**, anterior projections of the lower sides of the prothorax, impinging on the eyes when the head is retracted.

postœsophageal, *a.* See *postesophageal*.

post-office (pōst'of"is), *n.* 1. An office or place where letters are received for transmission to various destinations, and from which letters are delivered that have been received from places at home and abroad. Abbreviated *P. O.*

If you are sent to the *post-office* with a letter in a cold rainy night, step to the ale-house and take a pot.
Swift, Directions to Servants (Footman).

2. A department of the government charged with the conveyance of letters, etc., by post.—**General post-office**, the principal post-office in a large city or town.—**Post-office annuity** and **insurance**, in Great Britain, a system whereby the postmaster-general is empowered to insure lives between the ages of fourteen and sixty-five for not less than £5 nor more than £100, and also to grant annuities of not more than £100.—**Post-office box**, one of a series of pigeonholes into which the mail for a person or firm, or for a particular destination, is distributed in a post-office or postal car. Such boxes in a post-office are generally numbered, and either have glass backs, to display their contents from the outside, or are provided with locking doors at the back, to which the lessee of the box holds the key, and are then called *lock-boxes*. [U. S.]—**Post-office car.** See *mail-car*.—**Post-office Department**, that branch of a government which supervises the business of the post: in Great Britain the telegraph-lines are also under its management. See *department*.—**Post-office order.** See *money-order*.—**Post-office savings-bank**, in the British postal system, a bank connected with a local post-office where deposits not exceeding £30 in any year are received to an amount not exceeding £150, on government security, at a rate of interest of 2½ per cent. per annum.—**Railway post-office**, a railroad-car, or part of a railroad-car, in which the distribution of mail-matter is made: in England styled a *traveling post-office*.

postolivary (pōst-ol'i-vā-ri), *a.* [< NL. *postolivaris*, < L. *post*, behind, + NL. *olivaris*, L. *olivarius*, olivary: see *olivary*.] Posterior to the oliva, or olivary body.—**Postolivary sulcus.** Same as *sulcus postolivaris* (which see, under *sulcus*).

postomosternal (pōst-ō-mō-stėr'nal), *a.* [< *postomostern-um* + *-al*.] Pertaining to the postomosternum.

postomosternum (pōst-ō-mō-stėr'num), *n.*; pl. *postomosterna* (-nä). [NL., < L. *post*, behind, + NL. *omosternum*, q. v.] A posterior omosternum.

post-operative (post-op'e-rā-tiv), *a.* [< L. *post*, after, + E. *operat(ion)* + *-ive*.] Occurring after an operation, as an examination made after a surgical operation.

postoral (pōst-ō'ral), *a.* [< L. *post*, behind, + *os* (*or-*), the mouth: see *oral*.] Situated behind the mouth: specifically applied to certain of the visceral arches and clefts of the vertebrate embryo.—**Postoral arches**, visceral arches posterior to the mouth. Also called *pharyngeal arches*.—**Postoral segments**, in arthropods, those primary or theoretical segments which are situated behind the mouth, as distinguished from the *preoral segments*, which are morphologically anterior to the mouth, but are turned back to form the front or top of the head. The postoral cephalic segments of insects are the mandibular, first maxillary, and second maxillary or labial, each corresponding to the appendages from which they are named, and which answer to the ambulatory limbs of the thoracic segments; in spiders the labial segment is transferred to the thorax, the anterior pair of legs in that group being the homologues of the labium of insects. The postoral segments are closely united with one another and with the preoral segments, so that it is very difficult to trace them; probably the genæ, occiput, gula, and cervical sclerites represent them in the head of the perfect insect.

postorbital (pōst-ôr'bi-tal), *a.* and *n.* [< L. *post*, behind, + *orbita*, orbit: see *orbital*.] I. *a.* 1. In *anat.* and *zoöl.*: (*a*) Situated on the hinder part of the bony brim of the orbit of the eye. Since the frontal bone usually circumscribes more than half of this orbit, a postorbital process is usually also a postfrontal process. This process, when formed of the frontal bone, varies much in size and shape, and may be present or absent in the skulls of animals closely related, therefore furnishing a useful zoölogical character. Compare, for example, the large hooked postorbital process of the skull of the hare, figured under *Leporidæ*, with the absence of such a formation in the skull of another rodent, the beaver, figured under *Castor*. In man the corresponding formation is known as the *external angular process* of the frontal bone. (*b*) Bounding the orbit behind, as a separate bone of sundry reptiles. See the noun. (*c*) Lying backward (caudad) of the orbit of the eye, on the surface of the body; postocular: as, the *postorbital* part of the head. *Encyc. Brit.*, XII. 636.—2. In *entom.*, lying behind the compound eyes of an insect.

II. *n.* In *herpet.*, a separate bone which in some reptiles forms a posterior part of the orbit of the eye. Such a bone may come in behind another regarded as a postfrontal (see cut under *Ichthyosauria*), and is then unequivocal; but when only one bone, apart from the frontal, bounds the orbit in any part of its posterior half, it may be regarded as either a postfrontal or a postorbital.

post-paid (pōst'pād), *a.* Having the postage prepaid: as, a *post-paid* letter.

postpalatal (pōst-pal'ā-tal), *a.* and *n.* [< L. *post*, behind, + *palatum*, palate: see *palatal*.] I. *a.* Situated behind the palate or palate-bones.

II. *n.* A postpalatal bone; a postpalatine.

postpalatine (pōst-pal'ā-tin), *n.* [< L. *post*, behind, + *palatum*, palate: see *palatine*[2].] One of the so-called pterygoid bones of certain reptiles, as the crocodile.

postparietal (pōst-pą-rī'e-tal), *a.* and *n.* [< L. *post*, behind, + *paries* (*pariet-*), wall: see *parietal*.] I. *a.* In *herpet.*, situated behind the parietal plates of a serpent's head.

II. *n.* A postparietal plate.

post-partum (pōst-pär'tum), *a.* [< L. *post partum*, after birth: *post*, after; *partum*, acc. of *partus*, birth, < *parere*, bear, bring forth.] Taking place after the birth of a child: as, *post-partum* hemorrhage.

postpectoral (pōst-pek'tō-ral), *a.* [< *postpectus* (*-pector-*) + *-al*.] Of or pertaining to the postpectus.—**Postpectoral legs**, in *entom.*, the third pair, or hind legs.

postpectus (pōst-pek'tus), *n.* [NL., < L. *post*, behind, + *pectus*, breast: see *pectus*.] 1. In *zoöl.*, the hind-breast, or hinder part of the breast.—2. In *entom.*, a region corresponding to the metathorax.

postpeduncular (pōst-pē-dung'kū-lär), *a.* [< *postpedunculus* + *-ar*[3].] Of or pertaining to the postpedunculus.

postpedunculus (pōst-pē-dung'kū-lus), *n.*; pl. *postpedunculi* (-lī). [NL. (Wilder), < L. *post*, behind, + LL. *pedunculus*, a peduncle or pedicel: see *peduncle*.] The inferior peduncle of the cerebellum.

postpetiole (pōst-pet'i-ōl), *n.* [< L. *post*, behind, + *petiolus*, a petiole: see *petiole*.] In *entom.*, that part of a petiolate abdomen immediately behind the petiole or narrow basal section: generally the second segment is understood, especially if it is somewhat narrower than the succeeding segments.

postpharyngeal (pōst-fā-rin'jē-al), *a.* [< L. *post*, behind, + NL. *pharynx*, pharynx: see *pharyngeal*.] Behind the pharynx; retropharyngeal; situated in the posterior pharyngeal wall: as, a *postpharyngeal* abscess.

postpituitary (pōst-pit'ū-i-tā-ri), *a.* [< L. *post*, behind, + E. *pituitary*.] Situated behind the pituitary fossa.

Post-pliocene (pōst-plī'ō-sēn), *a.* and *n.* [= F. *post-pliocène*; as L. *post*, after, + E. *pliocene*.] In *geol.*, same as *Post-tertiary*.

post-pocket (pōst'pok"et), *n.* In a railway stock-car, etc., an iron casting attached to the outside of the sill to receive and hold a post.

postponable (pōst-pō'nạ-bl), *a.* [< *postpone* + *-able*.] Admitting of postponement or delay.

postpone (pōst-pōn'), *v. t.*; pret. and pp. *postponed*, ppr. *postponing*. [= Sp. *posponer* = Pg. *pospor* = It. *posporre*, < L. *postponere*, put after, < *post*, after, + *ponere*, put: see *position*. Cf. *postpose*.] 1. To put off; defer to a future or later time; delay.

I will *postpone* common and every-day topics.
Peter Martyr, quoted in Bradford's Works (Parker Soc., 1853), II. 403.

His pray'r preferr'd to saints that cannot aid;
His praise *postpon'd*, and never to be paid.
Cowper, Truth, l. 86.

2. To set below (something else) in value or importance; rate as less important or inferior.

All other considerations should give way and be *postponed* to this. *Locke*, Education.

So shall each youth, assisted by our eyes, . . .
To headless Phœbe his fair bride *postpone*,
Honour a Syrian prince above his own.
Pope, Dunciad, iv. 367.

But the philosopher, not less than the poet, *postpones* the apparent order and relations of things to the empire of thought. *Emerson*, Nature.

=**Syn.** 1. To adjourn, procrastinate, stave off.

postponement (pōst-pōn'ment), *n.* [= It. *posponimento*; as *postpone* + *-ment*.] 1. The act of postponing, or deferring to a future time; temporary delay.

Persons and events may stand for a time between you and justice, but it is only a *postponement*. You must pay at last your own debt. *Emerson*, Compensation.

2. The act of placing after or below in importance or esteem; a subordinating.

The opportunities for that *postponement* of self to others which constitutes altruism as ordinarily conceived must, in several ways, be more and more limited as the highest state is approached. H. *Spencer*, Data of Ethics, § 96.

postponence† (pōst-pō'nens), *n.* [< L. *postponen(t-)s*, ppr. of *postponere*: see *postpone*.] Same as *postponement*, 2.

Noting preference, or *postponence*.
Johnson, in def. of Of.

postponer (pōst-pō'nėr), *n.* [< *postpone* + *-er*[1].] One who postpones; one who delays or puts off.

postpontile (pōst-pon'til), *a.* [< L. *post*, behind, + *pon(t-)s*, bridge: see *pontile*.] Situated behind the pons Varolii: opposed to *prepontile*: as, the *postpontile* recess, more commonly called *foramen cæcum*.

postpose† (pōst-pōz'), *v. t.* [< F. *postposer*, < L. *post*, after, + F. *poser*, put: see *pose*[2].] 1. To place after (something else).

We utter our wil be verbes signifying the form of our wil, or *postposing* the supposit [subject].
A. Hume, Orthographie (E. E. T. S.), p. 31.

2. To postpone; put off. *Fuller*. (*Imp. Dict.*)

postposit† (pōst-poz'it), *v. t.* [< L. *postpositus*, pp. of *postponere*: see *postpone*.] To postpone; treat or regard as of inferior value.

Often, in our love to her, our love to God is swallowed and *postposited*. *Feltham*, On St. Luke, 328. (*Latham*.)

postposition (pōst-pọ-zish'ọn), *n.* [< F. *postposition* = Pg. *posposição* = It. *posposizione*; < L. *postpositus*, pp. of *postponere*, put after: see *postpone*.] 1. The act of postposing or placing after; the state of being put behind.

Nor is the *post-position* of the nominative case to the verb against the use of the tongue.
J. Mede, Daniel's Weeks, p. 36.

For purely intellectual writing, then, it seems that the French usage of *postposition* [of the adjective] is the best.
Amer. Jour. Philol., VI. 347.

2. In *gram.*, a word or particle placed after or at the end of a word: opposed to *preposition*. [Rare.]

In almost all the native languages of Asia, what we call prepositions follow their noun; often, like the article and reflective pronoun, coalescing with it, so as to form, or simulate, an inflection. The inconvenience of such a term as preposition is now manifest; nor is it much remedied when we allow ourselves to use the contradictory phrase postpositive preposition. What is really wanted is a general name for that part of speech under which preposition and *postposition* may stand as co-ordinate terms.
Latham, Dict., II. 568.

postpositional (pōst-pọ-zish'ọn-al), *a.* [< *postposition* + *-al*.] Pertaining to a postposition.

postpositive (pōst-poz'i-tiv), *a.* [< F. *postpositif* = It. *pospositivo*, < L. *postpositus*, pp. of *postponere*, place after: see *postpone* and *positive*.] Placed after something else; suffixed; appended: as, a *postpositive* word.

We find here the *postpositive* article which constitutes so notable a feature of the Scandinavian languages.
The Nation, XLVIII. 391.

postprandial (pōst-pran'di-al), *a.* [< L. *post*, after, + *prandium*, dinner: see *prandial*.] Happening, uttered, done, etc., after dinner: as, a *postprandial* speech.

I was much cheered by the announcement of this Carlton Club; the very name seemed to have been chosen with an eye to the drooping condition of *post-prandial* business.
Noctes Ambrosianæ, Sept., 1832.

postpredicament (pōst-prē-dik'ą-ment), *n.* [< ML. *postprædicamentum* (Abelard), < L. *post*, after, + ML. *prædicamentum*, predicament: see *predicament*.] One of the five subjects treated by Aristotle at the end of his book on the categories or predicaments, namely the explanations concerning the conceptions of 'opposite,' 'before,' 'at once,' 'motion,' and 'to have.'

post-pridie (pōst-prid'i-ē), *n.* [L., < *post*, after, + *pridie*, day before.] In the *Mozarabic liturgy*, a variable prayer said immediately after the words of institution. It seems originally to have regularly contained the great oblation and epiclesis, as is apparent in a number of extant examples. In the Gallican office it is called the collect (*collectio*) *post Mysterium* or *post Secreta*. The present Mozarabic title, literally 'after the Pridie' (day before), seems to refer to the institution in its Roman and Gallican form, beginning "Who (or, "For he) on the day before he suffered," rather than the Mozarabic "Our Lord . . . in the night in which he was betrayed."

postpubic (pōst-pū'bik), *a.* [< *postpubis*, after *pubic*.] Of or pertaining to the postpubis.

postpubis (pōst-pū'bis), *n.*; pl. *postpubes* (-bēz). [NL., < L. *post*, behind, + NL. *pubis*, q. v.] The postacetabular part of the pubic bone: said especially of the so-called pubis of birds and some other *Sauropsida*, as dinosaurs. It is very well developed in birds, in which class the prepubis or pubis proper is small, and forms only a part of the pectineal process, or is quite rudimentary. See cuts under *epipleura* and *sacrarium*.

post-pyramidal (pōst-pi-ram'i-dal), *a.* [< L. *post*, after, + *pyramis* (*-mid-*), pyramid: see *pyramidal*.] **1.** Occurring or existing since the Egyptian pyramids were built. *R. A. Proctor.* —**2.** In *anat.*, pertaining to the funiculus gracilis, formerly sometimes called *posterior pyramid*.—**Postpyramidal nucleus**, the nucleus funiculi gracilis. See *funiculus*.

post-redemption (pōst-rē-demp'shon), *a.* [< L. *post*, after, + *redemptio(n-)*, redemption.] Subsequent to redemption: used of reissues of United States government notes after their return to the Treasury in payment of dues to the government, or redemption in coin. The act of Congress of May 31st, 1878, forbade the Treasury to cancel unmutilated notes which had been received back, and required them to be reissued and kept in circulation, and such reissues were called *post-redemption issues*.

post-remote (pōst-rē-mōt'), *a.* More remote in subsequent time or order. *Darwin.* (*Imp. Dict.*)

postrhinal (pōst-rī'nal), *a.* [< L. *post*, behind, + Gr. ῥίς (ῥιν-), nose: see *rhinal*.] Posterior and rhinal: applied by Wilder to a fissure of the brain called by Owen *basirhinal*.

post-rider (pōst'rī'dėr), *n.* One who rides post; a mounted mail-carrier.

post-road (pōst'rōd), *n.* **1.** A road on which are stations where relays of post-horses can be obtained.—**2.** In the United States, any road, way, or street, including water-routes, over which the United States mail is carried.

postrolandic (pōst-rē-lan'dik), *a.* [< L. *post*, after, + E. *Rolandic*.] Situated behind the Rolandic or central fissure of the cerebrum.

postrorse (pos-trôrs'), *a.* [< NL. **postrorsus*, irreg. < L. *post*, back, + *versus*, turned (in imitation of *introrse*, *retrorse*, *antrorse*).] Turned back; directed backward; retrorse: the opposite of *antrorse*.

postsacral (pōst-sā'kral), *a.* [< L. *post*, behind, + NL. *sacrum*: see *sacral*.] Situated behind the sacrum; succeeding the sacral vertebræ, as the caudal or coccygeal vertebræ; urosacral.

postscalene (pōst-skā'lēn), *a.* [< NL. *postscalenus*.] Pertaining to the scalenus posticus, or postscalenus. *Coues.*

postscalenus (pōst-skā-lē'nus), *n.*; pl. *postscaleni* (-nī). [NL., < L. *post*, behind, + NL. *scalenus*, q. v.] The posterior scalene muscle of the neck; the scalenus posticus. *Coues.* See cut under *muscle*.

postscapular (pōst-skap'ū-lär), *a.* [< L. *post*, behind, + NL. *scapula*, the shoulder-blade: see *scapular*.] Situated behind or below the spine of the scapula or shoulder-blade; infraspinous, with reference to the scapula: the opposite of *prescapular*: as, the *postscapular* fossa (the infraspinous fossa).

postscapularis (pōst-skap-ū-lā'ris), *n.*; pl. *postscapulares* (-rēz). [NL.: see *postscapular*.] A muscle of the postscapular or infraspinous aspect of the scapula; the infraspinatus. *Coues.*

postscenium (pōst-sē'ni-um), *n.* [L., also *postscænium*, *poscænium*, *postcenium*, *poscenium* (> It. *postscenio* = F. *postscénium*), < *post*, after, behind, + *scena*, *scæna*, stage: see *scene*.] In *arch.*, the back part of the stage of a theater, behind the scenes.

postschwartzian (pōst-schwärt'si-an), *n.* [< L. *post*, after, + E. *Schwartzian*.] In *math.*, a form obtained by operating on the Schwartzian with the generator for mixed reciprocants.

postscribe (pōst-skrīb'), *v. t.*; pret. and pp. *postscribed*, ppr. *postscribing*. [< L. *postscribere*, write after, < *post*, after, + *scribere*, write: see *scribe*.] To write after; append to.

And the second is but a consequent of the first, *post-scribed* with that word of inference "Now then," &c., Rom. vii. 25. *Rev. T. Adams*, Works, I. 325.

postscript (pōst'skript), *n.* [= F. *postscript*, *postscriptum* = Pg. *postscripto* = It. *poscritto*, *poscritta*, < ML. *postscriptum*, a postscript, neut. of L. *postscriptus*, pp. of *postscribere*, write after, < *post*, after, + *scribere*, write.] An addition made to a written or printed composition as an afterthought, or to state something that has been omitted. (*a*) A supplement or appendix, as to a book or newspaper.

In the early days of the reign both these papers had manuscript *postscripts*, or supplements, when any fresh news arrived that was not in their last edition.
J. Ashton, Social Life in Reign of Queen Anne, II. 68.

(*b*) More commonly, a paragraph added to a letter which has already been concluded and signed by the writer.

Laer. Know you the hand?
King. 'Tis Hamlet's character. "Naked!"
And, in a *postscript* here, he says "alone."
Shak., Hamlet, iv. 7. 54.

Then came a *postscript* dash'd across the rest.
Tennyson, Princess, v.

Abbreviated *P. S.*

postscriptal (pōst'skrip-tal), *a.* [< *postscript* + *-al*.] Of or relating to a postscript; of the nature of a postscript.

The *postscriptal* speech which he had to deliver six years after, in 1794, in answer to the pleas of Hastings's counsel.
Mrs. Oliphant, Sheridan, p. 142.

postscripted (pōst'skrip-ted), *a.* [< *postscript* + *-ed*[2].] Having a postscript; written afterward. *J. Quincy Adams.* (*Imp. Dict.*) [Rare.]

postscutel (pōst-skū'tel), *n.* In *entom.*, same as *postscutellum*.

postscutellar (pōst-skū'te-lär), *a.* [< *postscutell-um* + *-ar*[3].] In *entom.*, situated behind the scutellum; of or pertaining to the postscutellum.

postscutellum (pōst-skū-tel'um), *n.*; pl. *postscutella* (-ä). [NL., < L. *post*, behind, + NL. *scutellum*, q. v.] In *entom.*, the fourth and last of the sclerites into which the pronotum, mesonotum, and metanotum of insects are severally typically divisible, situated behind the scutellum.

postsphenoid (pōst-sfē'noid), *n.* [< L. *post*, behind, + E. *sphenoid*.] The posterior part of the compound sphenoid bone, including the basisphenoid, alisphenoids, and pterygoids, separable in infancy.

postsphenoidal (pōst-sfē-noi'dal), *a.* [< *postsphenoid* + *-al*.] Pertaining to the postsphenoid: as, the *postsphenoidal* parts or elements of the sphenoid bone.

post-stamp (pōst'stamp), *n.* Same as *postage-stamp.* [Great Britain.]

postsylvian (pōst-sil'vi-an), *a.* [< L. *post*, behind, + E. *Sylvian*.] Situated behind the Sylvian fissure of the brain.

post-systolic (pōst-sis-tol'ik), *a.* [< L. *post*, after, + NL. *systole*.] In *physiol.*, following the systole.

post-temporal (pōst-tem'pō-ral), *a.* and *n.* [< L. *post*, after, + *tempus* (*tempor-*), temple: see *temporal*[2].] **I.** *a.* Situated behind the temporal region of the skull.

II. *n.* In *ichth.*, a bone of the scapular arch of some fishes by means of which that arch is attached to the back part of the skull. It may form an integral part of the skull. Also called *suprascapula* and *supraclavicle*. See first cut under *teleost*.

post terminum (pōst tėr'mi-num). [L.: *post*, after; *terminum*, acc. of *terminus*, a term, limit: see *term*.] In *law*, after the term.

Post-tertiary (pōst-tėr'shi-ā-ri), *a.* and *n.* The most recent division of the geological series, including all that is later than that which can properly be denominated Tertiary: frequently called *Quaternary*. The line of division between the Tertiary and the Quaternary is, in many regions, one which cannot be sharply drawn, and geologists differ essentially in regard to the nomenclature of the groups more or less vaguely designated by the terms *Post-tertiary*, *Pleistocene*, *Quaternary*, *recent*, and *diluvial*, as well as to the meaning and limitation of the term *glacial*, all these being subdivisions in use as designating more or less of the deposits later than the Tertiary. In general it is stated in the text-books that none of the Post-tertiary species are extinct; but this applies only to the mollusks: deposits containing extinct forms of the higher animals, and probably also of plants, are by many geologists unhesitatingly called Post-tertiary. In the region where geology has been longest cultivated (northwestern Europe) ice has played an important part in Post-tertiary times; hence, a classification of deposits of this age is largely influenced by this circumstance, and a parallelism of the more recent deposits of glaciated and non-glaciated regions — the latter comprising much the larger part of the earth's surface — is greatly increased in difficulty. See *Quaternary* and *Pleistocene*.

post-tibial (pōst-tib'i-al), *a.* [< L. *post*, after, + *tibia*, tibia.] Situated upon the back of the lower leg; sural: as, a *post-tibial* muscle; the *post-tibial* nerve.

post-time (pōst'tīm), *n.* The time for the arrival of a postman, or for the despatch of letters by mail.

I was detained till after *post-time*.
Macaulay, in Trevelyan, II. 147.

post-tonic (pōst-ton'ik), *a.* [< L. *post*, after, + Gr. τόνος, tone: see *tonic*.] Following the accent or accented syllable.

In French the first of the two *post-tonic* vowels of a Latin proparoxytone always disappears. *Encyc. Brit.*, XIX. 860.

post-town (pōst'toun), *n.* **1.** A town on a post-route, where relays of post-horses can be obtained.—**2.** A town in which a post-office is established.

post-trader (pōst'trā'dėr), *n.* A trader at a military post: the official designation of a sutler. [U. S.]

post-tympanic (pōst-tim-pan'ik), *a.* and *n.* [< L. *post*, after, + E. *tympanic*.] **I.** *a.* Situated behind the tympanic bone, or external auditory meatus.—**Post-tympanic bone**, a small ossicle which lies over the squamosal and opisthotic bones of the bear and probably some other carnivores. *H. Allen*, 1880.—**Post-tympanic process**, a formation of the united squamosal and opisthotic bones in some carnivores.

II. *n.* The post-tympanic bone. *Huxley*, Anat. Vert., p. 308.

postulant (pos'tū-lant), *n.* [< F. *postulant* = Pg. It. *postulante*, an applicant, candidate, prop. adj., < L. *postulan(t-)s*, ppr. of *postulare*, demand: see *postulate*, *n.*] One who or that which postulates, demands, or asks; specifically, a candidate for membership in a religious order during the period preparatory to his admission into the novitiate; in the American Episcopal Church, an applicant for admission to candidateship for the ministry, not yet received as candidate.

As some words, instinctively avoided, are constantly falling into desuetude, so others, often answering to calls too subtile for analysis, are constantly presenting themselves as *postulants* for recognition.
F. Hall, Mod. Eng., p. 98.

postulata, *n.* Plural of *postulatum*.

postulate (pos'tū-lāt), *v.*; pret. and pp. *postulated*, ppr. *postulating*. [< L. *postulatus*, pp. of *postulare* (> OIt. *postulare* = Sp. Pg. Pr. *postular* = F. *postuler*), ask, demand, require, summon, prosecute, impeach, etc., also require or need; perhaps, as a freq. form, < *poscere* (pp. **posctus*, **postus*), ask, demand, perhaps orig. **porscere*, akin to *procare*, ask, demand, *procus*, a wooer, and *precari*, pray: see *procacious* and *pray*[1].] **I.** *trans.* **1.** To invite; solicit; require by entreaty. See def. 3.

A great alliance was projected among many Protestant Princes to disturb Cardinal Furstemberg in the possession of Cologne, to which he was *postulated* by the majority of the chapter. *Bp. Burnet*, Hist. Own Time, an. 1688.

2. To assume without proof; lay down as something which has to be assumed, although it cannot be proved; take for granted.

We conclude, therefore, that Being, intelligent, conscious Being, is implied and *postulated* in thinking.
J. D. Morell.

Symmetry and simplicity, before they were discovered by the observer, were *postulated* by the philosopher.
Max Müller, Sci. of Lang., 1st ser., p. 20.

3. In *eccles. law*, to ask legitimate ecclesiastical authority to admit (a nominee) by dispensation, when a canonical impediment is supposed to exist. *Lee*, Glossary.

II. *intrans.* To make postulates or demands; urge a suit.

The excellent Doctor had not even yet discovered that the King's commissioners were delighted with his postulates; and that to have kept them *postulating* thus five months in succession . . . was one of the most decisive triumphs ever achieved by Spanish diplomacy.
Motley, Hist. Netherlands, II. 397.

postulate (pos'tū-lāt), *n.* [= F. *postulat* = Sp. Pg. *postulado* = It. *postulato*, < L. *postulatum*, a demand, prop. neut. of *postulatus*, pp. of *postulare*, demand: see *postulate*, *v.*] **1.** A petition; a suit; solicitation.

With the honest pride of a protocol-maker, he added, "our *postulates* do trouble the King's commissioners very much, and do bring them to despair."
Motley, Hist. Netherlands, II. 397.

2. A proposition proposed for acceptance without proof; something taken for granted; an assumption. Thus, the postulates of Euclid were as follows: (1) that a straight line may be drawn between any two points; (2) that any terminated straight line may be produced indefinitely; (3) that about any point as a center a circle with any radius may be described; (4) that all right angles are equal; (5) that if two straight lines lying in a plane are met by another line, making the sum of the internal angles on one side less than two right angles, then those straight lines will meet, if sufficiently produced, on the side on which the sum of the angles is less than two right angles. See *axiom*.

'Tis a *postulate* to me that Methusalem was the longest lived of all the children of Adam.
Sir T. Browne, Religio Medici, i. 22.

When you assume a premise without demonstrating it, though it be really demonstrable, this, if the learner is favorable and willing to grant it, is an assumption or hypothesis valid relatively to him alone, but not valid absolutely; if he is reluctant or adverse, it is a *postulate*, which you claim whether he is satisfied or not. *Grote*, Aristotle, vii.

3. A self-evident practical proposition, to the effect that something is possible: opposed to an *axiom*, as a self-evident proposition that something is impossible. The fourth and fifth of Euclid's postulates (see def. 2) being converted into axioms in the modern editions, and his proved propositions being distinguished into theorems and problems, this new conception of a postulate naturally arose.

Before the injunction — Do this, there necessarily comes the *postulate* — It can be done. *H. Spencer*, Social Statics.

4. A condition for the accomplishment of anything.

The earnestness with which peace is insisted on as a *postulate* of civic well-being shows what the experience had been out of which Dante had constructed his theory.
Lowell, Among my Books, 2d ser., p. 29.

postulate† (pos'tū-lāt), *a.* [< L. *postulatus*, pp.: see *postulate, v.*] Postulated; assumed.

And if she [Nature] ever gave that boon
To man, I'll prove that I have one:
I mean, by *postulate* illation [that is, begging the question].
S. Butler, Hudibras, II. i. 763.

postulation (pos-tū-lā'shon), *n.* [< F. *postulation* = Sp. *postulacion* = Pg. *postulação* = It. *postulazione*, < L. *postulatio(n-)*, a demanding, < *postulare*, demand: see *postulate, v.*] 1. Supplication; prayer. [Rare.]

Presenting his *postulations* at the throne of God.
Bp. Pearson, Expos. of Creed. (*Latham.*)

2. The act of postulating, or assuming without proof; supposition; assumption.

I must have a second *postulation*, that must have an ingredient to elicit my assent, namely, the veracity of him that reports and relates it.
Sir M. Hale, Orig. of Mankind, p. 129.

3. In *eccles. law*, the presentation or election to any office of one who is in some way disqualified for the appointment.

By this means the cardinal's *postulation* was defective, since he had not two-thirds [of the voices].
Bp. Burnet, Hist. Own Time, an. 1688.

Nicolas IV. ordered that all *postulations*, that is, elections of persons disqualified, including translations, should be personally sued out at Rome.
Stubbs, Const. Hist., § 383, note.

postulatory (pos'tū-lā-tō-ri), *a.* [= Pg. It. *postulatorio*, < L. *postulatorius*, < *postulator*, one who demands or claims, < *postulare*, demand: see *postulate, v.*] 1. Supplicatory. [Rare.]

He easily recovers the courage to turn that deprecatory prayer into a *postulatory* one.
Clarendon, Tracts, 392. (*Latham.*)

2. Postulating; assuming without proof. *Johnson.*—3. Assumed without proof. *Sir T. Browne*, Vulg. Err., ii. 6.

postulatum (pos-tū-lā'tum), *n.*; pl. *postulata* (-tä). [L.: see *postulate, n.*] A postulate.

postumbonal (pōst-um'bō-nal), *a.* [< L. *post*, behind, + NL. *umbo(n-)*, umbo: see *umbo.*] In *conch.*, situated behind the umbo. See *Pholas*.

postume[1]†, *n.* [ME.: see *apostem.*] Same as *impostume*. *Chaucer*, Boëthius, iii. prose 4.

postume[2]†, *a.* See *posthume*.

postural (pos'tū-ral), *a.* [< *posture* + *-al.*] Pertaining or relating to posture: as, the *postural* treatment of a fractured limb. *Dunglison.*

posture (pos'tūr), *n.* [Formerly also *positure* (< L.); < F. *posture* = Sp. *postura*, *positura* = Pg. *postura* = It. *postura*, *positura*, < L. *positura*, position, posture: see *positure.*] 1. Position; situation; condition; state: as, the *posture* of public affairs.

This growing *posture* of affairs is fed by the natural depravity. *Bacon*, Political Fables, viii., Expl.

Concerning the *Posture* of Things here, we are still involved in a Cloud of Confusion, 'specially touching Church Matters. *Howell*, Letters, iv. 44.

They do speak very sorrowfully of the *posture* of the times. *Pepys*, Diary, III. 156.

Everybody clamored around the governor, imploring him to put the city in a complete *posture* of defence.
Irving, Knickerbocker, p. 223.

2. The disposition of the several parts of anything with respect to one another, or with respect to a particular purpose; especially, position of the body as a whole, or of its members; attitude; pose.

Some strange commotion
Is in his brain: he bites his lip and starts;
Stops on a sudden; . . . in most strange *postures*
We have seen him set himself.
Shak., Hen. VIII., iii. 2. 118.

The statues of the Sibyls are very finely wrought, each of them in a different air and *posture*, as are likewise those of the prophets underneath them.
Addison, Remarks on Italy (ed. Bohn), I. 409.

3†. Disposition; attitude of mind.

A good Christian . . . must always be in a travelling *posture*, and so taste sensual pleasures as one that is about to leave them. *Bp. Atterbury*, Sermons, I. xi.

=Syn. 2. *Position, Posture, Attitude, Pose.* These words agree in expressing the manner of standing, sitting, lying, etc. The first three may be used in a figurative sense: as, my *position* on that question is this; his *attitude* was one of hostility to the measure. *Position* is the most general word, and is applicable to persons or things. *Posture* is generally natural, and may be awkward. *Attitude* is generally studied for the sake of looking graceful; hence it is sometimes affected, the practice of it being then called *attitudinizing*. An *attitude* is often taken intentionally for the purpose of imitation or exemplification; generally *attitude* is more artistic than *posture*. *Posture* is generally used of the whole body; *attitude* has more liberty in referring to the parts of the body, especially the head; but *position* is more common in such cases. *Pose* is now confined to artistic positions, taken generally for effect, of part or the whole of a body or representation of a body, as a statue or a picture.

The absolute *position* of the parties has been altered; the relative *position* remains unchanged.
Macaulay, War of the Succession in Spain.

I have seen the goats on Mount Pentelicus scatter at the approach of a stranger, climb to the sharp points of projecting rocks, and attitudinize in the most self-conscious manner, striking at once those picturesque *postures* against the sky with which Oriental pictures have made us . . . familiar. *C. D. Warner*, In the Wilderness, iv.

It is the business of a painter in his choice of *attitudes* to foresee the effect and harmony of the lights and shadows with the colours which are to enter into the whole.
Dryden, tr. of Dufresnoy's Art of Painting, § 4.

Placed, . . . with the instinct of a finished artist, in the best light and most effective *pose*.
Lathrop, Spanish Vistas, p. 108.

posture (pos'tūr), *v.*; pret. and pp. *postured*, ppr. *posturing*. [< *posture, n.*] **I.** *trans.* 1. To place; set.

As pointed Diamonds, being set,
Cast greater Lustre out of Jet,
Those Pieces we esteem'd most rare
Which in Night-shadows *postur'd* are.
Howell, Letters, I. v. 22.

2. To place in a particular attitude; dispose for a particular purpose.

He was raw with *posturing* himself according to the direction of the chirurgeons. *Brook.*

II. *intrans.* 1. To dispose the body in a particular posture or attitude; put one's self in an artificial posture; specifically, to contort one's self.

What is meant by *posturing* is the distortion of the limbs, such as doing the splits, and putting your leg over your head, and pulling it down your back, . . . and such like business.
Mayhew, London Labour and London Poor, III. 98.

2. To assume an artificial position of the mind or character; change the natural mental attitude; hence, to be affected; display affectation.

Not proud humilities of sense
And *posturing* of penitence,
But love's unforced obedience.
Whittier, The Meeting.

She had forced her intelligence to *posture* before her will, as the exigencies of her place required.
O. W. Holmes, Elsie Venner, viii.

They are so affected! . . . You would say that they *posture* before the whole universe.
E. Schuyler, tr. of Turgénieff's Fathers and Sons, x.

posture-maker (pos'tūr-mā"kėr), *n.* A contortionist; an acrobat.

I would fain ask any of the present mismanagers — why should not rope-dancers, vaulters, tumblers, ladderwalkers, and *posturemakers* appear again on our stage?
Steele, Spectator, No. 258.

posture-making (pos'tūr-mā"king), *n.* The art or practice of posturing, or making contortions of the body.

Your comedy and mine will have been played then, and we shall be removed, O how far, from the trumpets, and the shouting, and the *posture-making!*
Thackeray, Vanity Fair, lxi.

posture-master† (pos'tūr-màs"tėr), *n.* Same as *posture-maker*.

Posture masters, as the acrobats were then called, abounded, and one of the chief among them was Higgins, . . . who could dislocate and deform himself at pleasure.
J. Ashton, Social Life in Reign of Queen Anne, I. 280.

posturer (pos'tūr-ėr), *n.* [< *posture* + *-er*[1].] A posture-maker; an acrobat.

posturist (pos'tūr-ist), *n.* [< *posture* + *-ist.*] Same as *posturer*.

post-uterine (pōst-ū'te-rin), *a.* [< L. *post*, behind, + *uterus*, uterus: see *uterine.*] Situated behind the uterus: retro-uterine.

postvene† (pōst-vēn'), *v. t.* [< L. *post*, after, + *venire*, come.] To come after.

postventional† (pōst-ven'shon-al), *a.* [< L. *post*, after, + *ventio(n-)*, a coming, < *venire*, come: see *postvene.*] Coming after.

A *postventional* change of the moon, i. e. a change that happens after some great movable feast, planetary aspect, appearance of a comet, etc. *E. Phillips.*

postvermis (pōst-vėr'mis), *n.*; pl. *postvermes* (-mēz). [NL., < L. *post*, behind, + NL. *vermis*, q. v.] The vermis inferior of the cerebellum.

postvide† (pōst-vīd'), *v. i.* [< L. *post*, after, + *videre*, see.] To take measures too late: opposed to *provide*.

"When the daughter is stolen, shut Peppergate;" . . . when men instead of preventing *postvide* against dangers.
Fuller, Worthies Chester, I. 200. (*Davies.*)

post-wagon (pōst'wag"on), *n.* A wagon for posting; a stage-wagon; a diligence.

We took our leave of those friends that had accompanied us thither, and began our journey in the common *post-wagon* to Osnabrug, where we came the fourth day following in the evening.
Penn, Travels in Holland, etc. (Works, III. 394).

postward (pōst'wärd), *adv.* [< *post*[2] + *-ward.*] Toward the post.

post-warrant† (pōst'wor"ant), *n.* An official warrant for accommodation for one traveling by post; a passport.

For better Assurance of Lodging where I pass, in regard of the Plague, I have a *Post-Warrant* as far as Saint David's: which is far enough, you will say, for the King hath no Ground further on this Island. *Howell*, Letters, I. iv. 28.

post-windlass (pōst'wind"las), *n.* A winding-machine worked by brakes or handspikes which have a reciprocating movement. *E. H. Knight.*

postzygapophysial (pōst-zī"gap-ō-fiz'i-al), *a.* [< *postzygapophysis* + *-al.*] Posterior or inferior and zygapophysial or serving for articulation, as a process of a vertebra; pertaining to a postzygapophysis, or having its character.

postzygapophysis (pōst-zī-ga-pof'i-sis), *n.*; pl. *postzygapophyses* (-sēz). [NL., < L. *post*, after, + NL. *zygapophysis.*] In *anat.* and *zoöl.*, an inferior or posterior zygapophysis; in man, an inferior oblique or articular process of a vertebra: opposed to *prezygapophysis*. See cuts under *lumbar*, *vertebra*, *dorsal*, and *endoskeleton*.

posy (pō'zi), *n.*; pl. *posies* (-ziz). [Contr. of *poesy*, q. v.] 1. A verse of poetry attached to or inscribed on a ring, knife, or other object; hence, in general, a motto; an epigram; a legend; a short inscription.

And the tente was replenyshed and decked with this *posie*: After busy labor commeth victorious rest.
Hall, Hen. V., an. 7.

We call them [short epigrams] *Posies*, and do paint them now a dayes vpon the backe sides of our fruite trenchers of wood, or vse them as deuises in rings and armes and about such courtly purposes.
Puttenham, Arte of Eng. Poesie, p. 47.

A hoop of gold, a paltry ring
That she did give me, whose *posy* was
For all the world like cutler's poetry,
Upon a knife, "Love me, and leave me not."
Shak., M. of V., v. 1. 148.

2. A bunch of flowers, or a single flower; a nosegay; a bouquet. [Perhaps so called from the custom of sending verses with flowers as gifts.]

And I will make thee beds of roses,
And a thousand fragrant *posies*.
Marlowe, Passionate Shepherd to his Love.

Nature pick'd several flowers from her choice banks,
And bound 'em up in thee, sending thee forth
A *posy* for the bosom of a queen.
Fletcher (and another), Queen of Corinth, iii. 1.

Y' are the maiden *posies*,
And so grac't
To be plac't
'Fore damask roses. *Herrick*, To Violets.

A girl came with violet *posies*, and two
Gentle eyes, like her violets, freshened with dew.
F. Locker, Mr. Placid's Flirtation.

posy-ring (pō'zi-ring), *n.* A ring inscribed with a posy or short poetical motto. In some cases the posy consists of a single word formed by the initial letters of stones set around the ring. Also called *chanson*.

pot[1] (pot), *n.* [< ME. *pot*, *potte*, < AS. *pott* = OFries. *pot* = D. *pot* = MLG. *pot*, *put*, LG. *pot* (> G. *pott*) = Icel. *pottr* = Sw. *potta* = Dan. *potte* (cf. F. *pot* = Pr. *pot* = Sp. Pg. *pote*, a pot, < Teut.), a pot; of Celtic origin: < Ir. *pota*, *puite* = Gael. *poit* = W. *pot* = Bret. *pôd*, a pot; prob. orig. a drinking-vessel; cf. Ir. *potaim*, I drink, L. *potare*, drink: see *potation.*] 1. A vessel of earth, iron, brass, or other metal, usually of circular section and in shape rather deep than broad, employed for domestic and other purposes. (*a*) A vessel used in cooking, generally made of metal.

As the crackling of thorns under a *pot*, so is the laughter of the fool. Eccl. vii. 6.

A little *pot*, and soon hot. *Shak.*, T. of the S., iv. 1. 6.

(*b*) An earthen vessel, often for holding something distinctively specified; a jar or jug: as, a flower-*pot*; a cream-*pot*.

For he caused of all kindes of serpentes to be put into earthen *pots*, the whiche in the middes of the battell were cast into the enemyes shippes.
Golding, tr. of Justine, fol. 131.

In the Monastery of blake monkys callyd Seynt Nicholas De Elio ther lyes the body of Seynt Nicholas, as they sey, also oon of the *Pottis* that ower lord turnyd watir in to wyne.
Torkington, Diarie of Eng. Travell, p. 10.

Doe we not commonly see that in painted *pottes* is hidden the deadlyest poyson?
Lyly, Euphues, p. 53.

At an open window of a room in the second story, hanging over some *pots* of beautiful and delicate flowers, . . . was the figure of a young lady.
Hawthorne, Seven Gables, xiii.

In order to lighten the weight of the solid plaster, earthen *pots* have been placed between the joists and the spaces filled up with the mortar [practice in Paris in respect of floors with iron joists].
Encyc. Brit., IV. 455.

2. A drinking-vessel; a vessel containing a specified quantity of liquor, usually a quart or a pint; a mug.

Fill me a thousand *pots*, and froth 'em, froth 'em!
Fletcher, Pilgrim, iii. 7.

No carved cross-bones, the types of Death,
Shall show thee past to Heaven:
But carved cross-pipes, and, underneath,
A pint-*pot*, neatly graven.
Tennyson, Will Waterproof.

3. The contents of a pot; that which is cooked in a pot; specifically, the quantity contained in a drinking-pot, generally a quart (in Guernsey and Jersey, about 2 quarts). A *pot* of butter was by statutes of Charles II. made 14 pounds.

He maketh the deep to boil like a *pot*. Job xli. 31.

Let's each man drink a *pot* for his morning's draught, and lay down his two shillings.
I. Walton, Complete Angler, p. 181.

They will wait until you slip into a neighbouring alehouse to take a *pot* with a friend.
Swift, Directions to Servants, iv.

4. Stoneware: a trade-term.

A street seller who accompanied me called them merely *pots* (the trade term), but they were all *pot* ornaments. Among them were great store of shepherdesses, of greyhounds, . . . and some *pots* which seem to be either shepherds or musicians.
Mayhew, London Labour and London Poor, I. 333.

5. In *sugar-manuf.*, an earthen mold used in refining; also, a perforated cask in which sugar is placed for drainage of the molasses.—6. In *founding*, a crucible.—7. In *glass-manuf.*, the crucible in which the frit is melted. Those used for glass of fine quality, such as flint-glass, are closed to guard against impurities. —8. The metal or earthenware top of a chimney; a chimney-pot.—9. A size of writing-paper whose original water-mark is said to have been a pot. The smallest sheets measure 15½ × 12½ inches. Also spelled *pott*.—10. In *fishing*: (*a*) The circular inclosed part of a pound-net, otherwise called the *bowl*, *pound*, or *crib*. (*b*) A hollow vessel for trapping fish; a lobster-pot.—11. In *card-playing*: (*a*) The aggregate stakes, generally placed together in the center of the table; the pool. (*b*) In faro, the name given to the six-, seven-, and eight-spots in the lay-out.—12. A large sum of money. [Betting slang.]

The horse you have backed with a heavy *pot*.
Lever, Davenport Dunn (ed. Tauchnitz), I. 191. (*Hoppe.*)

13†. A simple form of steel cap, sometimes plain, like the skull-cap, sometimes having a brim.—14. In *pyrotechny*, the head of a rocket, containing the decorations.—**Double pot.** See *double*.—**Glass-melting pot.** See *glass*.—**Little pot†.** See *little*.—**Pot of money.** See *money*.—**To boil the pot.** Same as *to keep the pot boiling* (*a*).

No tav'ring patrons have I got,
But just enough to *boil the pot*.
W. Combe, Dr. Syntax, i. 23. (*Davies.*)

To go to (the) pot, to be destroyed, ruined, or wasted; come to destruction: possibly in allusion to the sending of old metal to the melting-pot.

Then *goeth* a part of little flock *to pot*, and the rest scatter.
Tyndale, Ans. to Sir T. More, etc. (Parker Soc., 1850), p. 110.

Your mandate I got,
You may all *go to pot*.
Goldsmith, Reply to Invitation to Dinner at Dr. Baker's.

The number of common soldiers slain not amounting to fewer than seven hundred. . . . But where so many officers *went to the pot*, how could fewer soldiers suffer?
Court and Times of Charles I., I. 285.

To keep the pot boiling. (*a*) To provide the necessaries of life.

Whatsoever Kitching found it, it was made poor enough before he left it; so poor that it is hardly able to *keep the pot boiling* for a parson's dinner.
Heylin, Hist. Reformation, p. 212. (*Davies.*)

(*b*) To "keep things going"; keep up a brisk and continued round of activity.

"*Keep the pot a bilin'*, sir," said Sam; and down went Wardle again, and then Mr. Pickwick, and then Sam, and then Mr. Winkle, and then Mr. Bob Sawyer, and then the fat boy, and then Mr. Snodgrass, following closely upon each other's heels.
Dickens, Pickwick, xxx.

To make the pot with two ears†, to set the arms akimbo. *Davies.*

Thou sett'st thy tippet wondrous high,
And rant'st, there is no coming nigh;
See what a goodly port she bears,
Making the pot with the two ears.
Cotton, Burlesque upon Burlesque, p. 236.

pot[1] (pot), *v.*; pret. and pp. *potted*, ppr. *potting*. [< *pot*[1], *n.*] **I.** *trans.* 1. To put into pots.—2. To preserve in pots, usually in the form of paste and often with high seasoning: as, *potted* meats or lobster.

I was invited to excellent English *potted* venison at Mr. Hobbson's, a worthy merchant.
Evelyn, Diary, March 22, 1646.

Meat will also keep fresh for a considerable period when surrounded with oil, or fat of any kind, so purified as not to turn rancid of itself, especially if the meat be previously boiled. This process is called *potting*.
Ure, Dict., III. 673.

3. To stew; cook in a pot as a stew: as, to *pot* pigeons.—4. To plant or set in pots: as, to *pot* plants.

Pot them [Indian tuberoses] in natural (not forc'd) earth.
Evelyn, Calendarium Hortense, April.

5. To put in casks for draining: as, to *pot* sugar by taking it from the cooler and placing it in hogsheads with perforated heads, from which the molasses percolates.—6. To shoot; bring down by shooting; bag: as, to *pot* a rabbit, a turkey, or an enemy; hence, to catch; secure: as, to *pot* an heiress. [Slang.]

The arrow flew, the string twanged, but Martin had been in a hurry to *pot* her, and lost her by an inch.
C. Reade, Cloister and Hearth, viii.

It being the desire of puntsmen to *pot* as many birds as possible by one shot, . . . punt-guns are not required to shoot close, the main object being a large killing circle.
W. W. Greener, The Gun, p. 531.

7†. To cap. See *to cap verses*, under *cap*[1], *v.*

The boies of divers schooles did cap or *potte* verses, and contend of the principles of grammar.
Stowe, Survey (1599), p. 53. (*Latham.*)

8. To manufacture, as pottery or porcelain; especially, to shape and fire, as a preliminary to the decoration.—**Potted meats**, viands parboiled and seasoned and put up in the form of paste covered with oil or fat in small porcelain pots, or in hermetically sealed tin cans or glass jars.

II. *intrans.* 1. To drink; tipple.

Cas. 'Fore God, an excellent song [a drinking-song].
Iago. I learned it in England: where, indeed, they are most potent in *potting*.
Shak., Othello, ii. 3. 79.

The increase in drinking—that unfailing criterion, alas! of increase in means in the lower classes in England—carried your English in potency of *potting* above even "your Dane, your German, and your swag-bellied Hollander."
S. Dowell, Taxes in England, I. 200.

2. To shoot at an enemy or at game; especially, to shoot to kill.

The jovial knot of fellows near the stove had been *potting* all night from the rifle-pit.
Lever, Davenport Dunn (ed. Tauchnitz), III. 292. (*Hoppe.*)

pot[2] (pot), *n.* [A var. of *put*[2] for *pit*[1]; but prob. in part associated with *pot*[1].] A pit; a hole; especially, a deep hole scooped out by the eddies of a river.

The deepest *pot* in a' the linn
They fand Erl Richard in.
Earl Richard (Child's Ballads, III. 7).

Pot and gallows. See *pit and gallows*, under *pit*[1].

pot[3] (pot), *v. t.*; pret. and pp. *potted*, ppr. *potting*. [Origin uncertain; perhaps a slang use of *pot*[1].] To deceive. *Halliwell.*

potable (pō'tạ-bl), *a.* and *n.* [< F. *potable* = Sp. *potable* = Pg. *potavel* = It. *potabile*, < L. *potabilis*, drinkable, < *potare*, drink: see *potation*.] **I.** *a.* 1. Drinkable; suitable for drinking.

Dig a pit upon the sea shore, somewhat above the high-water mark, and sink it as deep as the low water mark; and as the tide cometh in it will fill with water fresh and *potable*.
Bacon, Nat. Hist.

They [the Chinese] bore the Trunk with an Awger, and there issueth out sweet *potable* Liquor.
Howell, Letters, ii. 54.

The product of these vineyards [of England] may have proved *potable*, in peculiarly favourable seasons, if mixed with honey.
S. Dowell, Taxes in England, IV. 75.

Hence—2. Liquid; flowing.

Therefore, thou best of gold art worst of gold;
Other, less fine in carat, is more precious,
Preserving life in medicine *potable*.
Shak., 2 Hen. IV., iv. 5. 163.

What wonder then if fields and regions here
Breathe forth elixir pure, and rivers run
Potable gold.
Milton, P. L., iii. 608.

II. *n.* Anything that is drinkable; a drink.

The damask'd meads,
Unforc'd, display ten thousand painted flowers
Useful in *potables*.
J. Philips, Cider, i.

potableness (pō'tạ-bl-nes), *n.* The quality of being potable or drinkable.

potage†, *n.* An obsolete form of *pottage*.

potager†, *n.* An obsolete form of *pottinger*.

Potameæ (pọ-tā'mẹ-ē), *n. pl.* [NL. (Jussieu, 1828), < Gr. ποταμός, river, + *-eæ*.] A tribe of monocotyledonous water-plants of the order *Naiadaceæ*, by some botanists erected into a separate order, characterized by an ovary with four carpels having one half-coiled ovule in each containing a curved embryo. It includes 2 genera, *Potamogeton* (the type) and *Ruppia*, the latter an inhabitant of salt and the other of fresh waters throughout the world. See cut under *pondweed*.

potamic (pọ-tam'ik), *a.* [< Gr. ποταμός, a river (see *potation*), + *-ic*.] Pertaining to, connected with, or dependent on rivers. [Rare.]

The commercial situation of the trading towns of North Germany, admirable so long as the trade of the world was chiefly *potamic* or thalassic in character, lost nearly all its value when at the opening of the sixteenth century commerce became oceanic.
The Academy, Oct. 26, 1889, p. 265.

Potamobiidæ (pot″ạ-mō-bī'i-dē), *n. pl.* [NL., < Gr. ποταμός, river, + βίος, life, + *-idæ*.] Huxley's name (1878) of a family of fluviatile crawfishes, confined to the northern hemisphere and represented only by the genera *Astacus* and *Cambarus*, the other genera of *Astacidæ* in a usual sense forming a contrasted family *Parastacidæ*.

Potamochœrus (pot″ạ-mọ-kē'rus), *n.* [NL., < Gr. ποταμός, river, + χοῖρος, hog.] An African genus of *Suidæ* or swine, containing such

Red River-hog (*Potamochœrus penicillatus*).

species as *P. penicillatus*, of a reddish color with tufted ears; the river-hogs. Also called *Chœropotamus*.

Potamogale (pot-ạ-mog'ạ-lē), *n.* [NL. (Du Chaillu, 1860), < Gr. ποταμός, river, + γαλῆ, contr. of γαλέη, a weasel.] The typical genus of the family *Potamogalidæ*; the otter-shrews. The tibia and fibula are ankylosed, the muzzle is broad and flat with valvular nostrils, the limbs are short, the feet are not webbed, and the long cylindroid body is continued into the thick vertically flattened tail, which constitutes a powerful swimming-organ. The dental formula is 3 incisors, 1 canine, 3 premolars, and 3 molars in each half-jaw. *P. velox*, the only species known, is a large animal (for this order), being about 2 feet long, of which the tail is about half, dark-brown above and whitish below, of aquatic habits, and in general resembling a small otter, whence the name *otter-shrew*.

Potamogalidæ (pot″ạ-mọ-gal'i-dē), *n. pl.* [NL., < *Potamogale* + *-idæ*.] A family of aquatic mammals of the order *Insectivora*, of equatorial Africa, containing the genus *Potamogale*; the otter-shrews.

Potamogeton (pot″ạ-mọ-jē'ton), *n.* [NL. (Tournefort, 1700), < L. *potamogeton*, < Gr. ποταμογείτων, pondweed, < ποταμός, river, + γείτων, neighbor, inhabitant.] A genus of fresh-water plants known as pondweeds, the type of the tribe *Potameæ* in the order *Naiadaceæ*. It is distinguished from the allied genus *Ruppia* by the sessile nutlets and also by the presence of a calyx; and is further characterized by its numerical plan in fours, each flower having four roundish sepals, four stamens, four styles, and four distinct ovaries producing four small rounded drupes or nutlets, each with a thick, rigid, or spongy pericarp, and a single seed containing an annular or spirally coiled embryo. There are over 50 species, scattered throughout the world, growing in still rivers, ponds, and lakes, with one or two in brackish waters. (See *pondweed*.) A few species have acquired other names in local use, as, in England, *P. densus*, the frog's lettuce or water-caltrops, and *P. natans*, the tench-weed or devil's-spoons, and in America *P. amplifolius*, the cornstalk-weed. (See *heterophyllous*, 1.) A large number of aquatic plants, supposed to belong to the genus *Potamogeton*, have been described under that name by paleobotanists: they come from various regions, and from several divisions of the Tertiary.

potamography (pot-ạ-mog'rạ-fi), *n.* [= F. *potamographie* = It. *potamografia*; < Gr. ποταμός, river, + -γραφία, < γράφειν, write.] A description of rivers.

potamological (pot″ạ-mọ-loj'i-kạl), *a.* [< *potamology* + *-ic-al*.] Of or pertaining to potamology: as, a *potamological* table.

potamology (pot-a-mol'ǫ-ji), *n.* [< Gr. ποταμός, river, + -λογία, < λέγειν, say: see *-ology.*] The science or scientific study of rivers; also, a treatise on rivers.

potance (pō'tans), *n.* See *potence.*

potargo† (pǫ-tär'gō), *n.* Same as *botargo.*

> There 's a fishmonger's boy with caviare, sir,
> Anchovies, and *potargo*, to make you drink.
> *Fletcher (and another)*, Elder Brother, iii. 3.

potash (pot'ash), *n.* [= D. *potasch* = G. *pottasche* = Sw. *pottaska* = Dan. *potaske*; as *pot*[1] + *ash*[1]. The F. *potasse* = Sp. *potasa* = Pg. It. *potassa*, with NL. *potassa*, are from G. or E.] A substance obtained by leaching wood-ashes, evaporating the solution obtained, and calcining the residuum; one of the fixed alkalis; the so-called vegetable alkali; more or less impure or crude potassium carbonate, or carbonate of potash as formerly generally (and still very frequently) designated; any combination of which potassium forms the base, whether containing oxygen or not. Potash-salts play a most important part in vegetable life, existing in all plants in various proportions, and in various combinations with both inorganic and organic acids. When plants are burned, the inorganic constituents remain behind in the ashes, and it is by the lixiviation or leaching of these ashes that potash was first obtained, a process with which the Greeks and Romans were acquainted, although they were unable clearly to distinguish potash from soda, calling them both by the same name (νίτρον, nitrum). The name *potash* is of comparatively modern origin, and is derived from the fact that the potassiferous solution from wood-ashes was boiled down or concentrated in pots. It was not until about the middle of the eighteenth century that the two alkalis, soda and potash, were clearly distinguished from each other; but they were considered to be simple substances until after the beginning of the nineteenth century, when their metallic bases were separated from them by Davy (1807–8). Up to comparatively recent times the potash compounds used in the arts—and they are numerous and of great importance—were chiefly obtained in the form of crude potash after the method indicated as having given origin to the name of this alkali, and this method is still in use, although much less important than it formerly was. Saltpeter, or the nitrate of potash, had been long known, and obtained in a very different way. (See *saltpeter.*) Since the beginning of the present century potash has been obtained in considerable quantity from the refuse of beet-root used in the manufacture of sugar, and from sheep's wool. It has also been got (in the form of the chlorid) from sea-water; but the most important source of supply is the region near Stassfurt in Prussia, where two minerals containing potassic compounds (carnallite, a double chlorid of potassium and magnesium, and cænite, containing sulphates of potash and magnesia with chlorid of magnesium) are found in abundance, and mined on a large scale. From these naturally occurring potassiferous compounds all the various salts of potash used in the arts are manufactured, and it is by using the potash-salts obtained at Stassfurt that the Chili saltpeter (nitrate of soda) is converted into common saltpeter or niter (nitrate of potash), a substance important as the principal ingredient in the manufacture of gunpowder.—**Caustic potash.** See *caustic.*—**Fish and potash-salts.** See *fish*[1].—**Lump-potash,** the trade-name for a crude potash containing about 6 per cent. of water.—**Potash alum.** See *alum.*—**Potash feldspar.** See *orthoclase, microcline, feldspar.*—**Potash kettle country.** See *kettle-moraine.*—**Potash lye,** the strong aqueous solution of caustic potash or of potassium carbonate.—**Potash mica.** See *muscovite*, 2, *mica*[2].—**Potash-water,** an aërated beverage consisting of carbonic-acid water to which is added potassium bicarbonate.

potass (pǫ-tas'), *n.* [< F. *potasse*, < NL. *potassa*: see *potassa.*] Same as *potash.*

potassa (pǫ-tas'ä), *n.* [NL.: see *potash.*] Potash.

potassamide, potassiamide (pot-as-am'id, pǫ-tas-i-am'id), *n.* [< NL. *potassium* + E. *amide.*] An olive-green compound (KNH_2) formed by heating potassium in ammonia gas.

potassic[1] (pǫ-tas'ik), *a.* [= F. *potassique*; as *potassium* + *-ic.*] Relating to potassium; containing potassium as an ingredient.

potassic[2] (pǫ-tas'ik), *a.* [< *potassa* + *-ic.*] Consisting of or related to potash.

potassiferous (pot-a-sif'e-rus), *a.* [< NL. *potassa*, potash, + L. *ferre* = E. *bear*[1].] Containing or yielding potash or potassic salts.

potassium (pǫ-tas'i-um), *n.* [= F. *potassium* = Sp. *potasio* = Pg. *potassio, potassium* = It. *potassio*; < NL. *potassium*, < *potassa*, potash: see *potassa.*] Chemical symbol, K (for *kalium*); atomic weight, 39.1. The metallic base of the alkali potash, a substance not occurring uncombined in nature, but in various combinations widely diffused and of the highest importance. See *potash.* Potassium is silvery-white, and has a decided metallic luster. Its specific gravity is 0.875, and it is the lightest of all the metals with the exception of lithium. At the freezing-point of water it is brittle and has a crystalline fracture; at the ordinary temperature it is soft and may easily be cut with the knife. It was first obtained by Davy, in 1807, by the electrolysis of potash; but its preparation in the large way is effected by the ignition of a mixture of charcoal and potassium carbonate in a mercury bottle or iron tube coated with clay. In perfectly pure and dry air it undergoes no change; but in ordinary air it soon becomes coated with a film of potassium hydrate and carbonate. Its affinity for water is so great that when brought into contact with it immediate decomposition is effected, and sufficient heat evolved to set on fire the liberated hydrogen, which burns with the characteristic violet flame of potassium. Next to cæsium and rubidium it is the most electropositive element. It is a most powerful reducing agent, and hence has been largely employed for separating other metals from their various combinations; but at the present time sodium, being cheaper, is more generally employed for that purpose. Among the most important salts of potassium are the *chlorid* or *muriate*, KCl, mined at Stassfurt, Germany, and used as a fertilizer as well as the starting-point for the manufacture of other potash-salts; *potassium chlorate*, $KClO_3$, which is used in the arts as an oxidizing agent and in the manufacture of explosives; *potassium nitrate*, KNO_3, niter or saltpeter, made at present by the double decomposition of sodium nitrate and potassium chlorid, which is used in medicine and pyrotechny, but chiefly in the manufacture of gunpowder; *potassium carbonate*, K_2CO_3, which, under the commercial names of *potash* and *pearlash*, is largely used in the manufacture of soap and glass, and as a basis for making other potash-salts; *potassium cyanide*, KCN, a violent poison, used in photography and as a reducing agent; and *potassium bichromate*, $K_2Cr_2O_7$, red chromate of potash, much used in dyeing and calico-printing.—**Carbovinate of potassium,** more properly *ethyl-potassium carbonate*, $C_2H_5K.CO_3$, a white crystalline ether obtained by the action of carbon dioxid upon perfectly dry potassium hydrate in absolute alcohol.—**Cobalticyanide of potassium.** See *cobalticyanide.*—**Potassium bitartrate.** Same as *cream of tartar* (which see, under *cream*[1]).—**Potassium-chlorate battery,** an electric battery in which depolarization is produced by means of potassium chlorate with sulphuric acid.—**Potassium cyanide, ferrocyanide, myronate, etc.** See *cyanide*, etc.

potate†, *a.* [< L. *potatus*, pp. of *potare*, drink: see *potation.*] In *alchemy*, liquefied, as a metal; potable.

> Eight, nine, ten days hence
> He [Mercury] will be silver *potate*, then three days
> Before he citronize. *B. Jonson*, Alchemist, iii. 2.

potation (pǫ-tā'shǫn), *n.* [< OF. *potation, potacion* = OSp. *potacion* = It. *potagione, potazione*, < L. *potatio(n-)*, a drinking, < *potare*, pp. *potatus*, drink (= Ir. *potaim*, I drink); cf. *potus*, drunken (= Gr. ποτός, drunk: see below), *potus* (*potu-*), a drinking, *potio(n-)*, a drinking, drink; < √ *po* = Gr. √ πο in ποτός, drunk, for drinking (neut. ποτόν, what is drunk, drink), πότος, a drinking, prob. ποταμός, river, stream, √ πι in πίνειν, drink, = Skt. √ *pā*, drink. From the same (L.) source are ult. *potable, potion, poison, compotation*, and (from Gr.) *symposium*, etc.] 1. The act of drinking; drinking.

> Upon the account of these words so expounded by some of the fathers concerning oral manducation and *potation*, they believe themselves bound by the same necessity to give the eucharist to infants as to give them baptism.
> *Jer. Taylor*, On the Real Presence, iii. 3.

2. A drinking-bout; a drinking-party; a compotation; especially, an annual entertainment formerly given by schoolmasters to their pupils. See *potation-penny.*

> The Count and other nobles from the same country [Holland] were too apt to indulge in those mighty *potations* which were rather characteristic of their nation and the age. *Motley*, Hist. Netherlands, II. 138.

> Statutes of Hartlebury, Worcestershire, "the seventh year of our Sovereign Lady Queen Elizabeth": "The said Schoolmaster shall and may have, use, and take the profits of all such cock-fights and *potations* as are commonly used in Schools, and such other gifts as shall be freely given them, . . . over and besides their wages, until their salary and stipend shall be augmented" (vol. ii. p. 759).
> *N. and Q.*, 7th ser., IX. 90.

3. A drink; a draught.

> Roderigo,
> Whom love hath turn'd almost the wrong side out,
> To Desdemona hath to-night caroused
> *Potations* pottle-deep. *Shak.*, Othello, ii. 3. 56.

4. A liquor drunk; a drink; a beverage.

> If I had a thousand sons, the first humane principle I would teach them should be, to forswear thin *potations* and to addict themselves to sack.
> *Shak.*, 2 Hen. IV., iv. 3. 135.

potation-penny (pǫ-tā'shǫn-pen″i), *n.* Money paid by the scholars or their friends to the master of a school to enable him to give an entertainment (usually in Lent) to the scholars on quitting school. In some counties of England this is still continued, and is called "the drinking." *Wharton*, Hist. Manchester Grammar School, p. 25.

> Under the head of Manchester School, Carlisle gives a copy of an indenture of feoffment by Hugh Bexwyke and Johnne Bexwyke, on April 1, 1524, containing ordinances, one of which is: "Item, that every schoolmaster . . . shall teach freely . . . without any money or other rewards taken therefore, as Cock-penny, Victor-penny, *Potation penny*, or any other whatsoever it be" (vol. i. p. 677).
> *N. and Q.*, 7th ser., IX. 90.

potato (pǫ-tā'tō), *n.*; pl. *potatoes* (-tōz). [Early mod. E. also *potatoe, pottatoe, potatus, potades* (quasi NL.); also *botatas* = G. *potate*, sweet potato, = Dan. *potet, poteles* = Sw. *potät, potates, potatis*, white potato (< E.); = F. *patate*, sweet potato (cf. *pomme de terre*, 'earth-apple,' white potato), < Sp. *patata*, white potato, *batata*, sweet potato, = Pg. *batata*, sweet potato (NL. *batatas*), < Haytian *batata*, sweet potato.] 1†. The sweet potato. See below. [This was the original application of the name, and it is in this sense that the word is generally to be understood when used by English writers down to the middle of the seventeenth century.]

> This Plant (which is called of some Sisarum Peruvianum, or Skyrrets of Peru) is generally of us called *Potatus* or *Potato's.* It hath long rough flexible branches trailing upon the ground, like unto those of Pompions, whereupon are set greene three cornered leaves very like those of the wilde Cucumber. . . . Clusius calleth it Batata, Camotes, Amotes, and Ignames: in English, *Potatoes, Potatus*, and *Potades.* *Gerarde*, Herball (1636), Of *Potato's.*

> Candied *potatoes* are Athenians' meat.
> *Marston*, Scourge of Villanie, iii.

2. One of the esculent tubers of the common plant *Solanum tuberosum*, or the plant itself. The potato is a native of the Andes, particularly in Chili and Peru, but in the variant *boreale* it reaches north to New Mexico. It was probably first introduced into Europe from the region of Quito by the Spaniards, in the earlier part of the fifteenth century. In 1586 it was brought to England from Virginia, where, however, it was probably derived from a Spanish source. Its progress in Europe was slow, its culture, even in Ireland, not becoming general till the middle of the eighteenth century; but it is now a staple food in most temperate climates. The fruit of the potato-plant is a worthless green berry; its useful product is the underground tubers, which in the wild plant are small, but are much enlarged under cultivation. These tubers, which are of a roundish or oblong shape, sometimes flattish, are set with "eyes," really the axils of rudimentary leaves, containing ordinarily several buds, and it is by means of these that the plant is usually propagated. The food-value of the potato lies mostly in starch, of which it contains from 15 to 20 or 25 per cent. It is deficient in albuminoids and phosphates. Besides their ordinary food-use, potatoes are a source of manufactured starch; and spirits are now distilled from them to a considerable extent, chiefly in Germany. The tops (in America called *vines*, in England *halms*, in Scotland *shaws*) contain, together with the fruit, a poisonous alkaloid, solanin, absent in the tubers except when exposed to the sun. The varieties of the potato are numerous. The crop is often seriously injured by the potato-beetle and the potato-rot. To distinguish it from the yellow sweet potato, this plant is sometimes called *white potato* or (from its being one of the chief food-staples in Ireland) *Irish potato.*

> Virginian *Potato* hath many hollow flexible branches trailing upon the ground, three square, uneven, knotted or kneed in sundry places at certaine distances: from the which knots cometh forth one great leaf made of divers leaves. . . . Because it hath not only the shape and proportion of Potato's, but also the pleasant taste and vertues of the same, we may call it in English *Potatoes* of America or Virginia.
> *Gerarde*, Herball (1636), Of *Potatoes* of Virginia.

> They dygge also owte of the ground certeyne rootes growynge of theim selues, whiche they caule *Botatas.* . . . The skyn is sumwhat towgher than eyther of nauies or mussheroms, and of earthy coloure: But the inner meate thereof is verye whyte.
> *Peter Martyr* (tr. in Eden's First Books on America, ed. [Arber, p. 131).

Canada potato, the Jerusalem artichoke.—**Chat potatoes.** See *chat*[4].—**Cree potato,** *Psoralea esculenta*: so called as used by the Cree Indians.—**Hog's potato,** in California, the death-camass, *Zygadenus venenosus*, whose tubers are said to be eaten eagerly by hogs.—**Indian potato.** (*a*) The groundnut or wild bean, *Apios tuberosa*: so called on account of its small edible tubers. (*b*) The liliaceous genus *Calochortus*: so called from its bulb or corm.—**Irish potato.** See def. 2.—**Native potato,** of New South Wales, *Marsdenia viridiflora*; of Tasmania, *Gastrodia sesamoides*, an orchid with a rootstalk thickened into a tuber.—**Oil of potatoes,** an amylic alcohol obtained from spirits made from potatoes. It is somewhat oily in appearance, has a strong smell, at first pleasant but afterward nauseous, and a very acrid taste.—**Potato starch,** a fecula obtained from the potato, and also called *English arrowroot.*—**Seaside potato,** *Ipomæa biloba* (*I. Pes-capræ*), a twining and creeping plant of tropical shores in both hemispheres, said to reach a length sometimes of 100 feet.—**Small potatoes,** something petty or insignificant or contemptible. [Slang, U. S.]

> All our American poets are but *small potatoes* compared with Bryant. Quoted in *De Vere's* Americanisms.

> I took to attendin' Baptist meetin', because the Presbyterian minister here is such *small potatoes* that 't wan't edifying to sit under his preachin'.
> *Mrs. Whitcher*, Widow Bedott Papers, p. 188.

Spanish potato, the sweet potato.—**Sweet potato.** (*a*) A plant of the convolvulus family, *Ipomæa Batatas*, or one of its spindle-shaped fleshy esculent roots. The plant is a creeping, rarely twining, vine, with variously heart-shaped, halberd-shaped, or triangular (sometimes cut-lobed) leaves, and a blossom like that of the common morning-glory, but less open, and rose-purple with a white border. Its value lies in the roots, which are richer in starch, and still more in sugar, than the common potato. Their use is very much that of the latter, but in Mexico they are said to be regarded as a sweetmeat, and in Spain they are made into a preserve. They are red, yellow, or white in different varieties, and range in weight from that of the common potato up to many pounds. A variety in the southern United States is called *yam.* The sweet potato appears to have originated in tropical America, but is referred by some to the East Indies, or to both hemispheres. It is widely cultivated in warm climates, and is successfully grown in the United States as far north as New Jersey and Illinois, and even Michigan. (*b*) In Bengal, the yam.—**Telinga potato,** *Amorphophallus campanulatus*, an araceous plant much cultivated in India for its esculent tubers.—**White potato.** See def. 2.—

Wild potato, in Jamaica, *Ipomœa fastigiata*, a tuber-bearing plant, unlike the sweet potato in its climbing habit.

potato-beetle (pǫ-tā'tō-bē″tl), *n.* A chrysomelid beetle, the notorious *Doryphora decemlineata*, which up to 1855 or 1856 lived in the Rocky Mountain region, feeding upon the wild *Solanum rostratum*, but which, as the cultivated potato reached its habitat, increased enormously and began to spread to the east. In 1874 it reached the Atlantic coast at several points, and it has since been a pest in almost the entire country. It has several times made its way to Europe, but has been stamped out. Both larva and beetle feed upon the leaves of the potato, and the pupa is formed in the earth at the foot of the plant. There are three generations annually, and the perfect beetles hibernate. The most common and effective remedy is Paris green. See cut under *beetle*[2].

potato-bing (pǫ-tā'tō-bing), *n.* A heap of potatoes. [Scotch.]

> Potato-bings are snugged up frae skaith
> Of coming Winter's biting frosty breath.
> *Burns*, Brigs of Ayr.

potato-blight (pǫ-tā'tō-blīt), *n.* See *potato-rot.*

potato-bogle (pǫ-tā'tō-bō″gl), *n.* A scarecrow. [Prov. Eng. and Scotch.]

potato-bread (pǫ-tā'tō-bred), *n.* A bread made of potatoes which have been boiled, pressed till they are dry, beaten up, kneaded with wheat-flour, aniseed, and yeast, and then baked.

potato-bug (pǫ-tā'tō-bug), *n.* Same as *potato-beetle.*

potato-digger (pǫ-tā'tō-dig″ėr), *n.* An implement, resembling a plow, used to remove potatoes from the ground. Some of these implements simply leave the potatoes on the surface, others screen the earth from the tubers, and other more complicated machines remove the potatoes from the soil, divest them of adherent earth, and deposit them in a receptacle.

potato-disease (pǫ-tā'tō-di-zēz″), *n.* See *potato-rot.*

potato-eel (pǫ-tā'tō-ēl), *n.* A small threadworm or nematoid, of the family *Anguillulidæ*, infesting the potato.

potato-fern (pǫ-tā'tō-fėrn), *n.* A New Zealand fern, *Marattia fraxinea.* Its rootstock is a rounded, hard, fleshy mass, as large as the head, roasted and eaten by the natives, who call it *para.*

potato-finger† (pǫ-tā'tō-fing″gėr), *n.* A long thick finger, like a sweet potato: used in a loose, contemptuous sense. It is otherwise explained as 'a provocative.' [Rare.]

> How the devil Luxury, with his fat rump and *potato-finger*, tickles these together! *Shak.*, T. and C., v. 2. 56.

potato-fungus (pǫ-tā'tō-fung″gus), *n.* See *potato-rot.*

potato-grant (pǫ-tā'tō-grȧnt), *n.* A patch of land for growing vegetables, formerly granted by the owner to each of his slaves. *Bartlett.* [West Indies.]

potato-hook (pǫ-tā'tō-hůk), *n.* A hand-tool with bent fork-like tines, used for digging potatoes from the ground.

potato-mold (pǫ-tā'tō-mōld), *n.* Same as *potato-rot.*

potato-murrain (pǫ-tā'tō-mur″ạn), *n.* The potato-rot.

potato-oat (pǫ-tā'tō-ōt), *n.* A variety of the common oat. See *oat*, 1 (*a*).

potato-oil (pǫ-tā'tō-oil), *n.* Same as *oil of potatoes* (which see, under *potato*).

potato-onion (pō-tā'tō-un″yǫn), *n.* See *Egyptian onion*, under *onion.*

potato-pen (pǫ-tā'tō-pen), *n. Naut.*, a wooden compartment or pen on deck, built with a view to thorough ventilation, for keeping potatoes and other vegetables during a voyage.

potato-planter (pǫ-tā'tō-plan″tėr), *n.* An implement for planting seed-potatoes and covering them with soil. A planting-share plows a furrow, into which the potatoes are dropped by an automatic device, and a following covering-share turns the soil over them.

potator (pǫ-tā'tǫr), *n.* [= OF. *potateur* = It. *potatore*, < L. *potator*, a drinker, < *potare*, pp. *potatus*, drink: see *potation.*] A drinker.

> Barnabee, the illustrious *potator*, saw there the most unbecoming sight that he met with in all his travels.
> *Southey*, The Doctor, xliv. (*Davies.*)

potato-rot (pǫ-tā'tō-rot), *n.* A very destructive disease of the potato, caused by a parasitic fungus, *Phytophthora infestans.* It seems to have been introduced from South America, about the year 1840, and since that time has been the cause of very serious losses, sometimes involving almost the entire crop. The fungus attacks the stem and leaves as well as the tubers, and when confined to the leaves and stem is usually called *potato-blight.* On the leaves it first appears as pale-yellowish spots, which soon turn brown and finally black, indicating the total destruction of the tissues. On the tubers the parasite attains a considerable growth within the tissues before there is any external manifestation of its presence. After a time depressed spots appear, and the skin covering these dies and becomes discolored. Underlying these spots the tissue will be found to be dark-colored to a considerable depth. The flesh in the center of the tuber may remain for some time healthy and normal, but in the end it also decays, with either dry or wet rot. See *Phytophthora* and *mildew.*

Potato-rot (*Phytophthora infestans*).

Transverse Section of Leaf of Potato (*Solanum tuberosum*), showing the hyphæ ramifying among the cells, and a branch or conidiophore bearing a single conidium, which has issued from a stoma (highly magnified); *h*, a hair of the leaf. *a*, a leaflet, half natural size, showing the dark spots caused by the fungus; *b*, a conidium.

potatory (pō'tā-tǫ-ri), *a.* [< LL. *potatorius*, belonging to drinking, < L. *potator*, a drinker, < *potare*, pp. *potatus*, drink: see *potation.*] Potable; drinkable. [Rare.]

> I attempted the soup, and . . . helped myself to the *potatory* food with a slow dignity that must have perfectly won the heart of the solemn waiter.
> *Bulwer*, Pelham, xxxix.

potato-scoop (pǫ-tā'tō-sköp), *n.* A hand-screen in the form of a grated shovel for taking up potatoes which have been dug by a potato-digger. The soil sifts through the grating-bars, which detain the tubers.

potato-spirit (pǫ-tā'tō-spir″it), *n.* An alcohol distilled from potatoes: it is made chiefly in Germany.—**Potato-spirit oil.** See *oil.*

potato-sugar (pǫ-tā'tō-shůg″ạr), *n.* A sugar obtained from potatoes.

potato-vine (pǫ-tā'tō-vīn), *n.* The potato-plant, especially the part above ground. [U. S.]—**Wild potato-vine.** See *Ipomœa* and *man-of-the-earth.*

pot-barley (pot'bär″li), *n.* See *barley*[1].

pot-bellied (pot'bel″id), *a.* Having a prominent belly; abdominous.

> He appears to be near forty; a little *pot-bellied* and thick-shouldered, otherwise no bad figure.
> *Gray*, To Mason. (*Latham.*)

pot-belly (pot'bel″i), *n.* **1.** A protuberant belly.—**2.** A person having a protuberant belly.

> He will find himself a forked straddling animal, and a *pot-belly*. *Arbuthnot and Pope.*

3. The lake-trout, *Salvelinus* (*Cristivomer*) *namaycush.* [Lake Huron.]

pot-boiler (pot'boi″lėr), *n.* **1.** A work of art or literature produced merely "to keep the pot boiling"—that is, for the sake of providing the necessaries of life.

> His [Raff's] very fertility is a misfortune; . . . writing *pot-boilers* has injured the development of a delicate feeling for what is lofty and refined.
> *Grove's Dict. Music*, III. 65.

> Murillo executed a few portraits about the time he was painting *pot-boilers* for sale at fairs and to sea-captains.
> *The American*, XIV. 301.

2. A housekeeper. Compare *pot-waller*, *pot-walloper.* *Halliwell.* [Prov. Eng.]

pot-boiling (pot'boi″ling), *n.* The practice of producing pot-boilers; working for a living rather than for love of art.

> Most earnestly is it to be hoped that a writer who has the faculty displayed in this book will not, like so many of his contemporaries, dissipate it in *pot-boiling* on a colossal scale. *The Academy*, July 20, 1889, p. 34.

pot-boy (pot'boi), *n.* A boy or young man who has the charge of beer-pots. (*a*) An attendant on a bar; a young man who assists the barmaid in serving customers with porter, ale, or beer. (*b*) One who carries beer or ale in pots to customers, or for sale to passers-by. [Eng.]

> I could get a *pot-boy's* place again, but I'm not so strong as I were, and it 's slavish work in the place I could get.
> *Mayhew*, London Labour and London Poor, II. 17.

pot-cake (pot'kāk), *n.* A light Norfolk dumpling. *Halliwell.*

pot-celt (pot'selt), *n.* A celt having the hollow or opening comparatively large. This form of celt was long thought to be an ax-head, but is now regarded as a ferrule. See *amgarn.*

potch[1] (poch), *v. i.* A variant of *pouch*[1].

potch[2]† (poch), *v. t.* An obsolete form of *poach*[3].

potch[3] (poch), *v. t.* In *paper-manuf.*, to perform gas-bleaching upon (paper-stock) in a potching-engine. The bleaching reagent is chlorin dissolved in water, or chlorin generated in the mass by the action of dilute sulphuric acid upon a solution of common salt, or a solution of salt and chlorid of manganese, called *bleaching-liquid.* The stock is placed in a machine constructed much like a breaking- or washing-engine, and called a *potching-engine.* The acid is very slowly dropped into the bleaching-liquid when the chlorin is to be generated in the mass, and, after the liberated chlorin has performed its work, the stuff is discharged into stone or earthenware chests having zinc strainers at the bottom, where the bleaching-liquid is drained off. When a solution of chlorin in water is used, it is added in proper quantity to the stock after washing, and the latter, after sufficient treatment, is drained as above described. See *bleaching* and *gas-bleaching.*

pot-cheese (pot'chēz), *n.* See *cheese*[1].

potcher (poch'ėr), *n.* Same as *potching-engine.*

> From this main tank the solution is pumped to the bleaching mill, . . . and is there discharged into *potchers* which contain the paper bulk to be bleached.
> *Elect. Rev.* (Amer.), XIII. xxiv. 2.

potcher-engine (poch'ėr-en″jin), *n.* In *paper-manuf.*, a machine for saturating washed rags thoroughly with a bleaching-solution of chlorid of lime. Also called *potching-machine.*

potching (poch'ing), *n.* [Verbal n. of *potch*[3], *v.*] In *paper-manuf.*, gas-bleaching. See *potch*[3].

potching-engine (poch'ing-en″jin), *n.* In *paper-manuf.*, a machine in which both washing and gas-bleaching are performed. It resembles in general construction a breaking- or washing-engine. In it the rags are first washed. The washer is then lifted out, and the bleaching-liquid introduced. The process thereafter proceeds as described under *potch*[3]. Also called *potcher.*

potching-machine (poch'ing-mạ-shēn″), *n.* Same as *potcher-engine.*

pot-claw (pot'klâ), *n.* A hook hung in an open chimney to support a pot or kettle. See *trammel.*

pot-clep (pot'klep), *n.* Same as *pot-claw.*

pot-companion (pot'kǫm-pan″yǫn), *n.* A comrade in drinking; a boon companion: applied generally to habitual topers.

> One *pot companion* and his fashion
> I will describe, and make relation
> Of what my selfe have scene.
> *Times' Whistle* (E. E. T. S.), p. 59.

> For fuddling they shall make the best *pot-companion* in Switzerland knock under the table.
> *Sir R. L'Estrange*, tr. of Quevedo. (*Latham.*)

pote (pōt), *v.*; pret. and pp. *poted*, ppr. *poting.* [< ME. *poten*, < AS. *potian*, push, thrust, as an ox with its horns; cf. Sw. *påta*, poke; D. freq. *poteren*, *peuteren*, dig, poke, pry into, search; of Celtic origin; cf. W. *pwtio* = Corn. *poot* = Gael. *put*, poke, put: see *put*[1], a var. of *pote*, and *potter*[2], a freq. form.] **I.** *trans.* . To push; kick. *Halliwell.* [North. Eng.]—**2**†. To plait. See *poke*[1], 6.

> He keepes a startcht gate, weares a formall ruffe,
> A nosegay, set face, and a *poted* cuffe.
> *Heywood*, Troia Britannica (1609), p. 89. (*Halliwell.*)

II. *intrans.* To creep about listlessly or moodily; poke.

potecary† (pot'ẹ-kā-ri), *n.* An obsolete aphetic form of *apothecary.*

poteen (po-tēn'), *n.* [Also *potteen*, *potheen*; < Ir. *poitin*, a small pot, dim. of *poite*, a pot, *pota*, a pot, a vessel: see *pot*, *potation.*] Whisky made in Ireland, especially that which is illicitly distilled, sometimes very strong.

poteline (pot'e-lin), *n.* [< *Potel*, the name of its inventor, + *-ine*[2].] A mixture of gelatin, glycerin, and tannin in variable proportions, according to its intended application, in which also may be incorporated zinc sulphate or barium sulphate. It may or may not be tinted by vegetable coloring matters. It is plastic or liquid when heated, according to the degree of heat, and hard enough at ordinary temperatures to be bored, turned, filed, or polished. It has various adaptations. In a liquid state it is used for sealing bottles, and meats can be preserved by coating them with it.

potellt, *n.* An obsolete form of *pottle.*

potelot (pot'e-lot), *n.* [< F. *potelot*, < D. *potlood* (> also G. *pottloth*), black-lead, < *pot*, pot, + *lood*, lead.] Sulphid of molybdenum.

potence (pō'tẹns), *n.* [Also, in some uses, *potance*; < OF. *potence*, power, a crutch, F. *potence*, a crutch, gibbet, etc., = Sp. Pg. *potencia* = It. *potenza*, power, < L. *potentia*, power, ML. also a crutch, < *poten(t-)s*, powerful: see *potent.*] **1.** Power; potency.

> I've seen the oppressor's cruel smile
> Amid his hapless victim's spoil,
> And for thy *potence* vainly wish'd,
> To crush the villain in the dust.
> *Burns*, Lines Written on a Bank Note.

2. In *her.*: (*a*) A bearing of the shape of a capital T—that is, a cross tau. (*b*) The termination of an ordinary or other bearing when of that form.—**3.** In *watch-making*, the counter-bridge to the main cock or bridge on the top plate of a watch, holding the jeweling for the balance-staff, cylinder, or verge.

potencée (pō-ten-sā'), *a.* [< OF. *potence*, < *potence*, a cross: see *potence.*] In *her.*, terminating in a potence—that is, in the figure of a cross tau. Also, rarely, *enhendé.*

potence-file (pō'tens-fīl), *n.* A small hand-file with flat and parallel sides. *E. H. Knight.*

potency (pō'ten-si), *n.*; pl. *potencies* (-siz). [As *potence* (see *-cy*).] **1.** The quality of being potent; power; inherent strength. (*a*) Physical, mental, or moral power or influence.

> Heavenly [Father], that admonisheth us of his *potency* and ability, that is ruler over all things.
> *Latimer*, First Sermon on the Lord's Prayer.

> When we will tempt the frailty of our powers,
> Presuming on their changeful *potency*.
> *Shak.*, T. and C., iv. 4. 99.

> 'Tis always Springtime here; such is the grace
> And *potency* of her who has the bliss
> To make it still Elysium where she is.
> *J. Cook*, Green's Tu Quoque.

> Her spirit resembled, in its *potency*, a minute quantity of ottar of rose in one of Hepzibah's huge, iron-bound trunks, diffusing its fragrance through . . . whatever else was treasured there. *Hawthorne*, Seven Gables, ix.

(*b*) Potentiality; capability of development.

> Books are not absolutely dead things, but doe contain a *potencie* of life in them to be as active as that soule was whose progeny they are. *Milton*, Areopagitica.

> By an intellectual necessity I cross the boundary of the experimental evidence, and discern in that Matter which we, in our ignorance of its latent powers, and notwithstanding our professed reverence for its Creator, have hitherto covered with opprobrium, the promise and *potency* of all terrestrial Life. *Tyndall*, Belfast Address, 1874, p. 75.

(*c*) Efficacy; capability of producing given results: as, the *potency* of a medicine.

> Use almost can change the stamp of nature,
> And either master the devil, or throw him out
> With wondrous *potency*.
> *Shak.*, Hamlet, iii. 4. 170. (*Furness.*)

(*d*) Specifically, in *homeopathy*, the power of a drug as induced by attenuation. Two scales of dilution or attenuation are employed, known as the *centesimal* and the *decimal*, the former being the one advocated by Hahnemann, and the latter of more recent introduction. In the decimal scale, one drop of the mother tincture is added to nine of the diluent, which is usually alcohol, with certain manipulations, and from this first decimal solution or potency one drop is taken, to form, with nine others of the diluent, the second decimal solution. This process is repeated till the required solution or potency is reached. Drugs of high potency are those of which the dilution has been frequently repeated, and the medicinal substance correspondingly attenuated; drugs of low potency, on the other hand, are those in a less diluted, more concentrated condition. The thirtieth (centesimal) potency was the highest recommended by Hahnemann.

2. Power dependent on external circumstances; material strength or force; authority.

> Read
> The cardinal's malice and his *potency*
> Together. *Shak.*, Hen. VIII., i. 1. 105.

> Afterwards, there coming a company of Indians into these parts, that were driven out of their country by the *potency* of the Pequots, they solicited them to go thither.
> *N. Morton*, New England's Memorial, p. 171.

3. Influence; power; sovereignty.

> Strange thunders from the *potency* of song.
> *Keats*, Sleep and Poetry.

> Whose mighty *potencies* of verse
> Move through the plastic universe.
> *The Academy*, June 15, 1889, p. 407.

4†. Same as *potence*, 2.—**Objective potency.** See *objective*.—**Potency of two circles**, in *math.*, the square of the distance between their centers less the sum of the squares of their radii.

potent (pō'tent), *a.* and *n.* [I. *a.* < OF. **potent* = Sp. Pg. It. *potente*, < L. *poten(t-)s*, powerful, strong, potent, ppr. of *posse* (ind. *possum*), be able, < *potis*, able, powerful, orig. a lord, master, = Gr. *πόσις, later πόσις, husband, orig. master, lord, = Skt. *pati*, master, lord, = Lith. *patis*, lord. The same element occurs also in *despot*, *host*², q. v. II. *n.* < ME. *potent*, *potente*, a crutch, equiv. to *potence*, a crutch: see *potence*.] **I.** *a.* **1.** Powerful; possessed of inherent strength. (*a*) Powerful in a physical sense; effective; efficacious.

> Moses once more his *potent* rod extends.
> *Milton*, P. L., xii. 211.

> A beautiful crimson flower, the most gorgeous and beautiful, surely, that ever grew; so rich it looked, so full of *potent* juice. *Hawthorne*, Septimius Felton, p. 119.

(*b*) Powerful in a moral sense; having great influence; cogent; prevailing; convincing: as, *potent* arguments; *potent* interest.

> I do believe,
> Induced by *potent* circumstances, that
> You are mine enemy. *Shak.*, Hen. VIII., ii. 4. 76.

> Rise, madam; those sweet tears are *potent* speakers.
> *Fletcher*, Wife for a Month, v. 3.

> We may well think there was no small Conflict in King Edward's Mind between the two great commanders, Love and Honour, which of them should be most *potent*.
> *Baker*, Chronicles, p. 205.

> Such a majesty
> As drew of old the people after him . . .
> Is *potent* still on me in his decline.
> *M. Arnold*, Empedocles on Etna.

2. Having great authority, control, or dominion.

> The Jews imagining that their Messiah should be a *potent* monarch upon earth. *Hooker*, Eccles. Polity, vii. 15.

> Most *potent*, grave, and reverend signiors.
> *Shak.*, Othello, i. 3. 76.

3. In *her.*, divided or included by a line or lines forming a series of potents: as, a fesse *potent*. [In this sense originally *potenté*.]—**Cross potent.** See *cross*¹.=**Syn. 1** and **2**. Puissant, cogent, influential.

II. *n.* **1†.** A prince; a potentate.

> Cry "havock" ! kings; back to the stained field,
> You equal *potents*, fiery kindled spirits!
> *Shak.*, K. John, ii. 1. 358.

2†. A crutch; a walking-staff.

> Fro the bench he droof awey the cat,
> And leyde adoun his *potente* and his hat.
> *Chaucer*, Summoner's Tale, l. 68.

> A pyk is in that *potent* to punge a-doun the wikkede,
> That wayten eny wikkednesse.
> *Piers Plowman* (A), ix. 88.

3. In *her.*: (*a*) A figure resembling the head of a crutch, and consisting of a parallelogram laid horizontally on the top of a small square. (*b*) A fur made up of patches or figures. There are four varieties. Of these, the first is the most common, and is generally called *potent*; the second is generally called *counter-potent*; and the others are varieties which different authors describe by the above names, or by the term *potent counter-potent*, which is applied to one or the other indifferently.

Potent Counter-potent.

4. In *watch-making*, a journal plate or bearing. *E. H. Knight.*

potentacy† (pō'ten-tā-si), *n.* [< *potenta(te)* + *-cy*.] Sovereignty.

> That observation of Socrates, that long before his time the Roman episcopacy had advanced itself beyond the priesthood into a *potentacy*. *Barrow*, Works, VII. 371.

potentate (pō'ten-tāt), *n.* [< F. *potentat* = Sp. Pg. *potentado* = It. *potentato*, a potentate, < LL. *potentatus*, might, power, political power, ML. a potentate, prince, < L. *poten(t-)s*, powerful: see *potent*.] **1.** A person who possesses power or sway; a prince; sovereign; monarch; ruler.

> The blessed and only *Potentate*, the King of kings, and Lord of lords. 1 Tim. vi. 15.

> Kings and mightiest *potentates* must die.
> *Shak.*, 1 Hen. VI., iii. 2. 136.

2†. A power; state; sovereignty.

> Carthage grew so great a *Potentate*, that at first was but incircled in the thongs of a Bulls skinne, as to fight with Rome for the Empire of the world.
> Quoted in *Capt. John Smith's* Works, [I. 242.

potenté (pō-ten-tā'), *a.* [< *potent*, *n.*, 3.] Same as *potented*.

potented (pō'ten-ted), *a.* [< *potent*, *n.*, 3, + *-ed*².] In *her.*, having the outer edge stepped or battlemented in the form of potents.

Argent, a Fesse Potented Purpure.

potential (pō-ten'shal), *a.* and *n.* [< ME. *potencial*, < OF. *potential*, *potentiel*, F. *potentiel* = Pr. Sp. Pg. *potencial* = It. *potenziale*, < LL. **potentialis*, of power (in adv. *potentialiter*), < L. *potentia*, power: see *potence*.] **I.** *a.* **1†.** Potent; powerful; mighty.

> O most *potential* love! vow, bond, nor space,
> In thee hath neither sting, knot, nor confine,
> For thou art all, and all things else are thine.
> *Shak.*, Lover's Complaint, l. 264.

2. Possible, as opposed to actual; capable of being or becoming; capable of coming into full being or manifestation.

> *Potential* merit stands for actual,
> Where only opportunity doth want,
> Not will, nor power.
> *B. Jonson*, Cynthia's Revels, v. 3.

> Nor doth it [ice] only submit unto an actual heat, but not endure the *potential* calidity of many waters.
> *Sir T. Browne*, Vulg. Err., ii. 1.

> Alfenus was a cobbler, even when not at work: that is, he was a cobbler *potential*; whereas, when busy in his booth, he was a cobbler actual.
> *Sir W. Hamilton*, Metaphysics, vii.

> We cannot form any idea of a *potential* existence of the universe as distinguished from its actual existence.
> *H. Spencer*, First Principles, p. 32.

3. In *physics*, existing in a positional form, not as motion: especially in the phrase *potential energy*.—**4.** In *gram.*, expressing power or possibility: as, the *potential* mode; *potential* forms.—**Potential being.** See *being*.—**Potential cautery.** See *cautery*, 1.—**Potential composition**, in *metaph.*, the union of two things related as power and act.—**Potential difference.** Same as *difference of potentials* (which see, under *difference*).—**Potential energy.** See *energy*, 7.—**Potential essence**, in *metaph.*, the essence of something that does not actually exist.—**Potential existence**, existence in an undeveloped state; preparedness such that on an appropriate occasion the subject will come into existence.—**Potential function.** See *function*.—**Potential group.** See *group*¹.—**Potential mode**, in *gram.*, a name sometimes given to verb-forms or verb-phrases that express power, possibility, or liberty of action or of being: as, I *may go*; he *can write*.—**Potential part.** (*a*) A species as contained under a genus. (*b*) See phrase under *part*.—**Potential whole**, a genus as containing species under it.

> Because universal contains not subjected species's and individuals in act, that is actually, but power, it is come to pass that this *whole* is called *potential*.
> *Burgersdicius*, tr. by a Gentleman, I. xiv. 9.

II. *n.* **1.** Anything that may be possible; a possibility.—**2.** In *dynamics*: (*a*) The sum of the products of all the pairs of masses of a system, each product divided by the distance between the pair. The conception is due to Lagrange, the name to Green (1828) and independently to Gauss (1840). The *potential* is so called because its product by one constant differs only by another constant from the total *vis viva* of the system. In case there is but one attracting point, the potential is the sum of the masses, each divided by its distance from the point. (*b*) More generally, the line-integral of the attractions of a conservative system from a fixed configuration to its actual configuration; the work that would be done by a system of attracting and repelling masses (obeying the law of energy) in moving from situations infinitely remote from one another (or from any other fixed situations) to their actual situation. In this sense, the *potential* is the negative of the potential energy, to a constant *près*. But some writers limit the use of the word to the case in which the bodies in $(s+1)$-dimensional space attract one another inversely as the sth power of the distance. (*c*) In *electrostatics*, at any point near or within an electrified body, the quantity of work necessary to bring a unit of positive electricity from an infinite distance to that point, the given distribution of electricity remaining unaltered. See *equipotential*. (*d*) A scalar quantity distributed through space in such a way that its slope represents a given vector quantity distributed through space.—**Difference of potentials.** See *difference*.—**Logarithmic potential**, the potential for a force varying inversely as the distance. It is proportional to the logarithm of the distance, and is important in reference to the theory of functions.—**Magnetic potential**, at any point in a magnetic field, the quantity of work expended in bringing a positive unit magnetic pole from a given distance to that point.—**Newtonian potential.** See *Newtonian*.—**Potential difference.** Same as *difference of potentials* (which see, under *difference*).—**Potential of dilatation**, the function whose partial differential coefficients are the components of a dilatation.—**Velocity potential**, a scalar quantity such that the velocity of a mass of fluid in irrotational motion is everywhere equal to the slope of this quantity—that is to say, coincides in direction and in amount with the most rapid change of the value of the potential with the space. See *slope*.—**Zero potential**, in *elect.*, strictly, the potential of a point infinitely distant from all electrified bodies; practically, the potential of the earth, this being taken as an arbitrary zero, analogous to the sea-level in measuring altitudes. A body which is positively electrified is said to be at a higher potential, one negatively electrified at a lower, than the assumed zero of the earth. *Potential* in electricity is analogous to *temperature*; and, as heat tends to pass from a point at a higher to one at a lower temperature, so electricity tends to move from a higher to a lower potential. Two bodies, then, one or both of which are electrified, if brought into metallic connection with each other, will assume the same potential, which will be determined by their original potential and their capacity. (See *capacity*.) The time necessary for this equalization of potential will depend on the resistance of the connecting conductor. Thus, an electrified body connected with the earth loses its electricity—that is, takes the zero potential of the latter—the capacity of the earth being indefinitely great. If the difference of potentials between two connected bodies is kept up in any way—by the expenditure of mechanical work as in turning a Holtz machine, or of chemical energy as in a voltaic battery—there results an electric current. Hence, in *electrokinetics*, the difference of potential determines the electromotive force of the electric current, being analogous to the difference of level between two reservoirs of water, which determines the pressure causing the flow.

potentiality (pō-ten-shi-al'i-ti), *n.*; pl. *potentialities* (-tiz). [< F. *potentialité* = Sp. *potencialidad* = It. *potenzialità*, < LL. **potentialita(t-)s*, < **potentialis*, potential: see *potential*.] **1.** The state of being potential; mere being without actualization; the state of being capable of development into actuality: as, to exist in *potentiality*: opposed to *entelechy*.—**2.** A potential state, quality, or relation; the inherent capability of developing some actual state or quality; possibility of development in some particular direction; capability; possibility.

> For space and time, if we abstract from their special determination by objects, are mere *potentialities* or possibilities of relations. *E. Caird*, Philos. of Kant, p. 246.

> Rudimentary organs sometimes retain their *potentiality*; this occasionally occurs with the mammæ of male mammals, for they have been known to become well developed, and to secrete milk. *Darwin*, Origin of Species, p. 405.

> An old-fashioned American rustic home; not a peasant-home—far above that in refinement and *potentialities*—but equally simple, frugal, and devout.
> *E. C. Stedman*, Poets of America, p. 117.

> In using the notion of self-development we must carefully exclude the apparent implication that we are beings

with perfectly definite *potentialities*, which we have only the alternatives of developing or not developing.
H. Sidgwick, Methods of Ethics, p. 170.

3. A potential being; a being, or capacity for existence, not yet actualized, but which may be developed into actuality.

The self-creation of such a potential universe would involve over again the difficulties here stated — would imply behind this potential universe a more remote *potentiality*.
H. Spencer, First Principles, p. 33.

The seed is the *potentiality* of the plant.
Encyc. Brit., II. 522.

potentialize (pọ̄-ten'shạl-iz), *v. t.* and *i.*; pret. and pp. *potentialized*, ppr. *potentializing*. [< *potential* + *-ize*.] To convert into or assume a potential or positional form: said of energy.

The problem proposed is to find an expression for the distribution of *potentialized* energy throughout the passive mass.
Amer. Jour. Sci., 3d ser., XXXI. 119.

With a given metal, there is large *potentializing* in the first stages of strain, and large dissipation in the final stages.
Nature, XL. 562.

potentially (pọ̄-ten'shạl-i), *adv.* 1†. Powerfully; potently; efficaciously.

Indeed the wordes of holy scripture doe worke their effectes *potentiallie* and thorowly by the mightie operation of the spirit of God.
Foxe, Martyrs, p. 1256, an. 1549.

2. In a potential manner or state; in an undeveloped or unrealized manner or state; possibly; latently.

Anaximander's infinite was nothing else but an infinite chaos of matter, in which were either actually or *potentially* contained all manner of qualities.
Cudworth, Intellectual System, p. 128.

Blackness is produced upon the blade of a knife that has cut sour apples, if the juice, though both actually and *potentially* cold, be not quickly wiped off.
Boyle, On Colours.

The apple already lies *potentially* in the blossom, as that may be traced also in the ripened fruit.
Lowell, Study Windows, p. 121.

potentiary (pọ̄-ten'shi-ạ̄-ri), *n.*; pl. *potentiaries* (-riz). [< ML. **potentiarius*, < L. *potentia*, power: see *potence*. Cf. *plenipotentiary*.] A person invested with or assuming power; one having authority or influence.

The last great *potentiary* had arrived who was to take part in the family congress.
Thackeray, Newcomes, xxx.

potentiate (pọ̄-ten'shi-āt), *v. t.*; pret. and pp. *potentiated*, ppr. *potentiating*. [< L. as if **potentiatus*, < *potentia*, power: see *potence*.] To give power to.

Substantiated and successively *potentiated* by an especial divine grace.
Coleridge.

The power of the steam-engine derives its force and effect, its working capacity, from the appliances by which it is *potentiated* — i. e., from road-beds, rolling-stock, etc., in railroads, and from fly-wheels, cog-wheels, spindles, etc., in manufactories.
Amer. Anthropologist, I. 20.

potentiation (pọ̄-ten-shi-ā'shọn), *n.* [< *potentiate* + *-ion*.] The state or quality of being made potent; capacitation for certain ends.

Estimating the increased *potentiation* [of steam-engines] at the average of forty-seven times, we shall have, from railroads alone, a working capacity equal to that of 5,293,250,000 living horses or of 31,407,750,000 laboring men.
Amer. Anthropologist, I. 20.

Potentilla (pō-ten-til'ạ̈), *n.* [NL. (Linnæus, 1737), so called in allusion to the repute of some species in medieval medicine; < L. *poten(t-)s*, potent: see *potent*.] 1. A large genus of rosaceous plants, type of the tribe *Potentilleæ*, characterized by the numerous pistils on the dry receptacle, styles not lengthened after flowering, four or five bracts below the calyx, and many stamens in a single row. The number of species has been estimated at from 160 to 200, most common in temperate and cold northern regions, only two being as yet known south of the equator. They are herbs or undershrubs, with mainly alternate pinnate or palmate leaves, adnate stipules, and usually white or yellow, often clustered, flowers. Several species are frequently called *wild strawberry*, as *P. Canadensis* in the Atlantic States and *P. Fragariastrum* in England, but, while they are often very much like the true strawberry, *Fragaria*, in habit, the latter is always different in its fleshy receptacle. (See *cinquefoil* and *fivefinger*.) Many brilliant-flowered species are occasional in cultivation, under the name *potentilla*. *P. anserina* is called in England *goose-tansy*, *wild tansy*, *goose-grass*, and *silverweed*. For *P. Tormentilla*, the most in repute in medicine, also known as *septfoil*, see *tormentil* and *bloodroot*, 1. 2. [*l. c.*] A plant of this genus.

Flowering Plant of Cinquefoil (*Potentilla Canadensis*).

Potentilleæ (pō-ten-til'ē-ē), *n. pl.* [NL. (Bentham and Hooker, 1865), < *Potentilla* + *-eæ*.] A tribe of dicotyledonous plants of the order *Rosaceæ*, characterized by a superior ovary, four or sometimes numerous carpels, each with a single ovule, and the four or five calyx-lobes provided with alternate bracts. It includes 14 genera of herbs and shrubs, mainly of the north temperate zone, of which *Potentilla* is the type, and the strawberry, *Fragaria*, the best-known. See also *Geum* and *Dryas*.

potentiometer (pọ̄-ten-shi-om'e-tėr), *n.* [< L. *potentia*, power, + Gr. μέτρον, measure.] An instrument used for measuring the difference of electrical potential between two points. There are many forms of the instrument, as the conditions under which it is used differ widely.

The *potentiometer* employed its own working battery, mirror galvanometer, and Clark standard cell.
Electric Rev. (Eng.), XXV. 642.

potentize (pō'tẹn-tīz), *v. t.*; pret. and pp. *potentized*, ppr. *potentizing*. [< *potent* + *-ize*.] In *homeopathy*, to induce power in, as drugs, by attenuation. See *potency*, 1 (*d*).

In the most characteristic feature of Hahnemann's practice — "the *potentizing*," "dynamizing," of medicinal substances — he appears to have been original.
Encyc. Brit., XII. 127.

potently (pō'tẹnt-li), *adv.* 1. In a potent manner; with potency; powerfully; with great energy or force.

You are *potently* opposed, and with a malice
Of as great size.
Shak., Hen. VIII., v. 1. 134.

What is there in thee, Moon! that thou shouldst move
My heart so *potently*!
Keats, Endymion, iii.

2. Hence, extremely; emphatically.

From my own experience I begin to doubt most *potently* of the authenticity of many of Homer's stories.
Irving, Knickerbocker, p. 388.

potentness (pō'tẹnt-nes), *n.* The state or property of being potent; powerfulness; strength; potency.

Poterieæ (pot-ḗ-rī'ẹ̄-ē), *n. pl.* [NL. (Bentham and Hooker, 1865), < *Poterium* + *-eæ*.] A tribe of rosaceous plants, characterized by an inferior ovary with one ovule, and fruit of one, two, or three dry achenes inclosed within the calyx-tube. It contains 11 genera, mainly of temperate regions, both herbs and shrubs, generally without petals, producing a dry fruit resembling a rose-hip in structure, and having the five-lobed calyx provided with alternate bractlets. See *Poterium* (the type) and *agrimony*.

Poterium (pọ̄-tē'ri-um), *n.* [NL. (Linnæus, 1737), so called in allusion to the former use of the leaves of *P. Sanguisorba*, which have a cucumber-like flavor, in preparing a medicinal drink called *cool-tankard*, q. v.; < L. *poterium*, < Gr. ποτήριον, a drinking-cup, < ποτήρ, a drinking-cup, < √ πο- (in ποτός, verbal adj.), drink: see *potation*.] A genus of rosaceous plants, type of the tribe *Poterieæ*, characterized by pinnate leaves, absence of bractlets and petals, imbricated calyx, and herbaceous habit; the burnets. There are about 20 species, natives of north temperate and warm regions. They are leafy perennial herbs, erect from a decumbent base, rarely becoming spiny shrubs. The pinnate leaves are alternate, with long sheathing petioles and toothed and stalked leaflets. The small perfect or polygamodiœcious flowers are borne in dense heads or spikes on long peduncles, and are green, purplish, pink, or white, conspicuous chiefly for the several or numerous slender stamens. The former genus *Sanguisorba* is here included. *P. Sanguisorba* is the common burnet. A tall American species, *P. Canadense*, with white flowers in cylindrical spikes, appearing late in summer, is the wild or Canadian burnet. See *burnet*[2], 2.

Flowering Plant of Canadian Burnet (*Poterium Canadense*).
a, male flower, seen from the side; *b*, female flower, seen from above.

poterner†, *n.* Same as *pautener*[2].

He plucked out of his *poterner*,
And longer wold not dwell;
He pulled forth a pretty mantle,
Betweene two nut-shells.
The Boy and the Mantle (Child's Ballads, I. 8).

potestas (pọ̄-tes'tas), *n.* [L., power: see *potestate*.] In *Rom. antiq.*, personal sovereignty or dominion of a man over persons dependent on him; the authority which the head of a household possessed over wife, descendants, and slaves, as distinguished from official authority, called *imperium*; more specifically, such personal authority over children and descendants as members of the household (*patria potestas*, which see) and over slaves (*dominica potestas*, also called *dominium*), as distinguished from authority over a wife, called *manus*. The conception of *potestas* is substantially that of the patriarchal authority — consisting of the aggregate of the powers of punishment even to death, of control, and of disposal — which in early times the chief of the household has generally been allowed to exercise, the ground of this authority being connected with the fact that retributive justice dealt rather with the family than with individuals, and held the chief responsible for offenses committed by members of the household, and did not interfere with him in his discipline. Hence, *potestas* was often used as the equivalent of *jus* or right, those who were subject to it being said to be *alieni juris*, or under the right of another, and those who were not subject to it *sui juris*, or living in their own right.

potestate† (pō'tes-tāt), *n.* [< ME. *potestat*, < OF. *potestat* = Sp. *potestad* = Pg. *potestade* = It. *potestà*, *potestate*, *potestade*, dominion, *podestà*, a magistrate, < L. *potesta(t-)s*, power, a supreme monarch, < *potis*, powerful: see *potent*. Cf. the doublets *podestà* and *poust*.] A potentate; a ruler.

Whilom ther was an irous *potestat*.
Chaucer, Summoner's Tale, l. 300.

Still hee stood a *potestate* at sea.
Marston, What you Will, i. 1.

potestative (pō'tes-tạ̄-tiv), *a.* [= F. *potestatif* = Sp. Pg. *potestativo*; < LL. *potestativus*, denoting power, < L. *potesta(t-)s*, power: see *potestate*.] Authoritative; befitting a ruler or potentate. [Rare.]

So I might contemplate him [Christ] in a judiciary posture, in a *potestative*, a sovereign posture, sitting, and consider him as able, as willing to relieve me.
Donne, Sermons, xi.

Potestative condition. See *conditional obligation*, under *conditional*.

pot-eye (pot'ī), *n.* 1. In a spinning-frame, the glass or metal guide-eye through which the yarn passes from the rollers to the flyer.—2. In *bleaching*, a glass or earthenware ring through which the moist cloth is passed, in order to guide it and prevent its coming in contact with other objects.

pot-fish (pot'fish), *n.* [= D. *potrissh* = G. *pottfisch* = Sw. *pottfisk*; as *pot*[1] + *fish*[1].] The sperm-whale, *Physeter macrocephalus*.

pot-fisher (pot'fish"ėr), *n.* 1. Same as *pot-fisherman*.—2. Same as *pot-hunter*.

pot-fisherman (pot'fish"ėr-mạn), *n.* One who fishes while floating on the surface of the water, supported by an earthen pot. The vessel not only buoys up the fisherman, but serves as a receptacle for the fish caught. This method is much practised in some Asiatic rivers.

potful (pot'fủl), *n.* [< ME. *potful*; < *pot*[1] + *-ful*.] The contents of a pot; as much as a pot can hold.

Honger was nat hardy on hem for to loke,
For a *potful* of potage that Peersses wyf made.
Piers Plowman (C), ix. 182.

potgun† (pot'gun), *n.* 1. A popgun.

Bryng with thee my *potgunne*, hangyng by the wall.
Udall, Roister Doister, iv. 7.

They are but as the *potguns* of boys.
Bp. Hall, Honour of Married Clergy, p. 148.

2. A short wide cannon for firing salutes; a mortar: so called from its resemblance to a pot in shape.

They haue . . . a great many of morter pieces or *pot-guns*, out of which pieces they shoote wild fire. *Hakluyt's Voyages*, I. 316.

pot-gutted (pot'gut"ed), *a.* Pot-bellied. *Graves*, Spiritual Quixote, iv. 8.

pot-hanger (pot'hang"ėr), *n.* Same as *pothook*.

pot-hanglet (pot'hang"gl), *n.* Same as *pothook*.

Item, a fryeng panne and a peyre of *pot-hangles* sold to the seyd Scudamour. *Inventory of Goods*, 30 Hen. VIII. (*Nares.*)

pot-hat (pot'hat), *n.* Same as *chimney-pot hat* (which see, under *hat*[1]).

pothead (pot'hed), *n.* A stupid fellow.

She was too good for a poor *pot-head* like me. *Kingsley*, Westward Ho, xv. (*Davies.*)

pothecary†, *n.* An obsolete aphetic form of *apothecary*.

potheen (po-thēn'), *n.* Same as *poteen*.

pot-hellion (pot'hel"ion), *n.* A large pie made of beef, pork, potatoes, and onions baked in a pan. [Gloucester, Massachusetts.]

pot-helmet (pot'hel"met), *n.* In a general sense, any defensive head-covering which has little opening, and covers the head completely, like the great heaume of the twelfth and thirteenth centuries. Compare *pot*[1], 13.

pother (poᴛʜ'ėr), *n.* [Also *pudder*; origin uncertain. The sense 'a suffocating cloud' seems to rest on the assumption that *pother* stands for *powder* (dial. *pouther*, etc.). Cf. *pothery*.] A tumult; disturbance; confusion; bustle; flutter.

Let the great gods,
That keep this dreadful *pother* o'er our heads,
Find out their enemies now. *Shak.*, Lear, iii. 2. 50.

And suddenly unties the poke,
Which out of it sent such a smoke
As ready was them all to choke,
So grievous was the *pother*.
Drayton, Nymphidia, st. 82.

Lucretius keeps a mighty *Pother*
With Cupid, and his fancy'd Mother.
Prior, Alma, i.

The *Pother* that is made about Precedence. *Steele*, Grief A-la-Mode, i. 1.

pother (poᴛʜ'ėr), *v.* [See *pother*, *n.*] I. *intrans.* To make a pother or bustle; make a stir.
II. *trans.* To harass and perplex; bother; puzzle; tease. *Locke.* (*Imp. Dict.*)

pot-herb (pot'ėrb), *n.* Any herb prepared for use by boiling in a pot; particularly, one of which the tops or the whole plant is boiled.

A gentleman,
Well read, deeply learned, and thoroughly
Grounded in the hidden knowledge of all sallads
And *pot-herbs* whatsoever.
Beau. and Fl., Woman-Hater, i. 3.

Black pot-herb, in old use, the *Smyrnium Olusatrum* (see *alexanders*), in distinction from the corn-salad, *Valerianella olitoria*, the white pot-herb.—**Pot-herb butterfly**, *Pieris oleracea*, an American congener of the imported

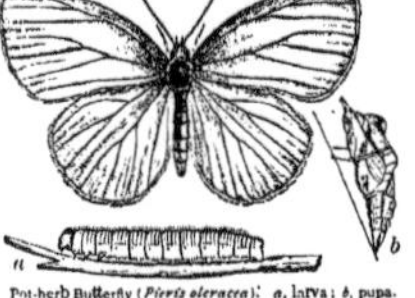

Pot-herb Butterfly (*Pieris oleracea*): *a*, larva; *b*, pupa.

cabbage-butterfly, *P. rapæ*. The wings are white, the body is black, and the larva is pale-green.

pothery (poᴛʜ'ėr-i), *a.* [< *pother* + *-y*[1].] Hot; close; muggy. *Halliwell.* [Prov. Eng.]

pothicar (poth'i-kär), *n.* An aphetic form of *apothecary*. *Scott*, Abbot. [Scotch.]

Pothoideæ (poth-ọ-id'ẹ̄-ē), *n. pl.* [NL. (A. Engler, 1879), < *Pothos* + *-ideæ*.] A subfamily of monocotyledonous plants, of the order *Araceæ*, characterized by the netted-veined or lateral-veined two-ranked or spiral leaves, by the flowers usually having both stamens and pistils and anatropous ovules, and by the absence of laticiferous vessels and intercellular hairs. It includes in 6 tribes about 15 genera, of which *Pothos* (the type), *Anthurium*, and *Culcasia* are in cultivation for their handsome leaves. See *Calla*, 1, *Acorus*, *Orontium*, and *Symplocarpus* for important genera native in the United States.

pot-hole (pot'hōl), *n.* A cavity more or less nearly cylindrical in form, and from a few inches to several feet in depth and diameter, made by an eddying current of water, which causes a stone or a collection of detrital material to revolve and thus wear away the rock with which it is in contact. Such pot-holes are common, especially in and near the beds of streams running over bare rocks, and under glaciers, in regions of present or past glaciation, or in any locality where there is, or was formerly, a rapid current of water. A group of pot-holes, some of which are of great size, is one of the curiosities of Lucerne in Switzerland (the "Glacier Garden"), where they appear to have been made at the time of the former greater extension of the glaciers in the Alpine range: also called *giants' kettles*. The large conical or more rarely pot-shaped cavities formed by water in the chalk and other limestone rocks of England and the United States are called, besides *pot-holes*, by various names, as *swallow-holes*, *sink-holes*, *butter-tubs*, *water-sinks*, and *pots*. See *swallow-hole*.

pothook (pot'hůk), *n.* **1.** A hook, secured in a chimney in any manner (as upon a crane), for supporting a pot over a fire.

The great black crane . . . swung over it, with its multiplicity of *pot-hooks* and trammels. *H. B. Stowe*, Oldtown, p. 62.

2. A short bar or rod of iron, usually curved, and with a hook at the end, used to lift hot pots, irons, or stove-lids from a stove.—**3.** A letter, character, or curve shaped like a pothook (def. 1); an elementary character consisting of a stroke terminating in a curve, practised upon by children in learning to write; hence, any irregular, straggling written character.
Also *pot-hanger*.

Pothooks and hangers. See *hanger*.

Pothos (pō'thos), *n.* [NL. (Linnæus, 1737), < *potha*, a native name in Ceylon.] A genus of plants, of the order *Araceæ*, type of the tribe *Pothoideæ*, characterized by an ovary with three cells, each with one ovule, a large embryo without albumen, and a spathe enlarging after flowering. It includes about 29 species, natives of Asia, the Pacific islands, Australia, and Madagascar. They are shrubby climbers, fastening themselves by rooting branches below and more spreading above. When grown under glass, they often adhere, perfectly flat, to damp vertical wooden surfaces, forming a sinuous upward line with the leaves facing the horizon. The leaves are two-ranked, oblique, and usually ovate or narrower, sometimes replaced by a broad leaf-like petiole (phyllodium). The small green reflexed spathe is ovate or shell-shaped, and contains a short or roundish spadix, sometimes twisted or bent, bearing small close or scattered flowers above, each with a six-parted perianth.

pot-house (pot'hous), *n.* An ale-house; a liquor-saloon.—**Pot-house politician.** See *politician*.

pot-hunter (pot'hun"tėr), *n.* One who hunts or fishes for profit, regardless of close seasons, the waste of game, or the pleasure to be derived from the pursuit. *Sportsman's Gazetteer.*

Poachers and *pot-hunters* are encouraged [in Rumania], that they may keep the tables of their friends in office well supplied with game. *W. W. Greener*, The Gun, p. 570.

pot-hunting (pot'hun"ting), *n.* The act or practice of hunting for the sake of profit, regardless of the regulations or conventionalities of the sport.

The Chinese have an original and effective manner of *pot-hunting* after Wild-fowl. *W. W. Greener*, The Gun, p. 575.

poticary†, *n.* An aphetic form of *apothecary*.

potiche (F. pron. pọ-tēsh'), *n.* [F., < *pot*, pot: see *pot*[1].] A vase or jar of rounded form and short neck, with or without a cover. The shape usually denoted by this term approaches more or less that of an inverted truncated cone below, finished above in a hemispheroidal form, and with a cylindrical neck.

Potiche.

potichomania (pot"i-kọ-mā'ni-ä), *n.* [Also *potichomanie*, < F. *potichomanie*; < F. *potiche*, a kind of pot (see *potiche*), + L. *mania*, madness.] Cheap decoration, consisting in coating a glass vessel with paintings on paper or linen, the interstices being filled with opaque paint, or varnish.

potin (F. pron. pọ-tań'), *n.* [F., < OF. *potin*, *potain*, *potein*, *pottin*, a mixed metal (see def.), < *pot*, pot: see *pot*[1], *n.* Cf. *putty*.] A mixed metal, consisting of copper, zinc, lead, and tin, of which certain coins of ancient Gaul were composed. The term is sometimes, though incorrectly, applied by numismatists to some ancient coins (for example, those of Alexandria) of mixed metal into the composition of which some silver enters: such coins should be called *billon*.

potinger, *n.* See *pottinger*.

poting-stick†, *n.* [< *poting*, ppr. of *pote*, *v.*, + *stick*.] Same as *poking-stick*.

Pins, points, and laces,
Poting-sticks for young wiues, for young wenches glasses,
Ware of all sorts, which I bore at my back.
Heywood, If you Know not Me (Works, ed. Pearson, 1874, [I. 285).

potion (pō'shon), *n.* [< ME. *pocion*, < OF. *pocion*, *potion* (also *poison*, > E. *poison*), F. *potion* = Sp. *pocion* = Pg. *poção* = It. *pozione*, < L. *potio(n-)*, a drink; cf. *potus*, drunken, *potare*, drink: see *potation*. Cf. *poison*, a doublet of *potable*.] A drink; a draught; especially, a liquid medicine.

Would you haue one *potion* ministered to the burning Feuer and to the cold Palsey? *Lyly*, Euphues, p. 43.

Here, thou incestuous, murderous, damned Dane,
Drink off this *potion*. *Shak.*, Hamlet, v. 2. 337.

potion† (pō'shon), *v. t.* [< *potion*, *v.* Cf. *poison*, *v.*] To drug.

Lord Roger Mortimer, . . . hauing corrupted his keepers, or (as some others write) hauing *potioned* them with a sleepy drinke, escaped out of the Tower of London. *Speed*, Hist. Great Britain, ix. 11. (*Davies.*)

pot-knight (pot'nīt), *n.* A drunken fellow. *Halliwell.*

pot-lace (pot'lās), *n.* See *lace*.

potlatch (pot'lach), *n.* [Also *potlache*; < Amer. Ind. (Nootka) *potlatsh*, *pahtlatsh*, a gift; as a verb, give.] **1.** Among some American Indians, a gift.

They [Klickatat Indians] . . . expressed the friendliest sentiments, perhaps with a view to a liberal *potlatch* of trinkets. *Theodore Winthrop*, Canoe and Saddle, iv.

2. An Indian feast, often lasting several days, given to the tribe by a member who aspires to the position of chief, and whose reputation is estimated by the number and value of the gifts distributed at the feast.

It may also, very probably, happen that delay arises because the man about to give the *potlatch* has not obtained the requisite number of blankets. *Pop. Sci. Mo.*, XXX. 350.

On his return he again called the people together and held a big *potlatch*, giving the Indians what appeared to them at that time great curiosities. *Amer. Antiquarian*, XII. 75.

pot-lead (pot'led), *n.* Black-lead or graphite: as, a *pot-lead* crucible. [The word is now used chiefly of graphite in stove-polish applied to the hulls of racing-yachts below the water-line to diminish the friction of the water by giving a smooth surface.]

pot-lead (pot'led), *v. t.* [< *pot-lead*, *n.*] To coat with pot-lead: as, to *pot-lead* a yacht.

pot-leech† (pot'lēch), *n.* One who sucks at the pot; hence, one who drinks to excess; a drunkard.

This valiant *pot-leach*, that upon his knees
Has drunke a thousand pottles up-se-freese.
John Taylor, Works (1630). (*Nares.*)

pot-lid (pot'lid), *n.* **1.** The lid or cover of a pot.—**2.** A concretion occurring in various sandstones and shales, especially those of different parts of the Jurassic series. [In this sense properly *potlid*.]—**Pot-lid valve.** See *valve*.

pot-liquor (pot'lik"ėr), *n.* The liquor in which meat has been boiled; thin broth.

Mr. Geoffry ordered her to come daily to his mother's kitchen, where, together with her broth or *pot-liquor*, he contrived to slip something more substantial into Dorothy's pipkin. *Graves*, Spiritual Quixote, i. 9. (*Davies.*)

pot-luck (pot'luk'), *n.* What may chance to be in the pot, in provision for a meal; hence, a meal at which no special preparation has been made for guests.

He never contradicted Mrs. Hackit—a woman whose *pot-luck* was always to be relied on. *George Eliot*, Amos Barton, i. (*Davies.*)

To take pot-luck, to accept an impromptu invitation to a meal; partake of a meal in which no special preparation has been made for guests.

Do, pray, stop and dine—
You will *take* our *pot-luck*—and we've decentish wine.
Barham, Ingoldsby Legends, I. 294.

pot-man (pot'man), *n.* **1.** A pot-companion.

Eddisbury carried it by the juniors and *pot-men*, he being one himself. *Life of A. Wood*, p. 286. (*Latham.*)

2. Same as *pot-boy*.

The *potman* thrust the last brawling drunkards into the street. *Dickens*, Uncommercial Traveller, xiii. (*Davies.*)

pot-marigold (pot'mar"i-gōld), *n.* See *Calendula*[1].

pot-metal (pot'met"al), *n.* **1.** An alloy of copper and lead, formerly used for making faucets and various large vessels employed in the arts.—**2.** Same as *pot-metal glass* (which see, under *glass*).—**3.** A kind of cast-iron suitable for making hollow ware.

pot-miser (pot'mī"zėr), *n.* See *miser*[2].

poto, *n.* See *potto*.

potomania (pō-tọ-mā'ni-ä), *n.* [NL., < L. *potus*, drinking (see *potation*), + *mania*, < Gr. *μανία*, madness: see *mania*.] Dipsomania.

potometer (pọ̄-tom'e-tėr), *n.* [< Gr. ποτόν, drink, + μέτρον, measure.] An instrument for measuring the amount of water absorbed by a transpiring plant in a given time. *F. Darwin.*

potoo (pọ̄-tö'), *n.* [Jamaican; imitative.] A caprimulgine bird, *Nyctibius jamaicensis.*

pot-paper (pot'pā"pėr), *n.* An old brand of paper bearing the figure of a pot as a water-mark. See *pot*[1], *n.*, 9.

pot-pie (pot'pī), *n.* **1.** A pie made by lining the inner surface of a pot or pan with pastry and filling it with meat, as beef, mutton, fowl, etc., seasoning it, and then baking.—**2.** A dish of stewed meat with pieces of steamed pastry or dumplings served in it; a fricassee of meat with dumplings. [U. S.]

pot-piece† (pot'pēs), *n.* Same as *potgun*, 2.

pot-plant (pot'plant), *n.* **1.** Any plant grown in a pot.—**2.** The pot-tree, or monkey-pot tree. See *Lecythis* and *pot-tree.*

pot-plate (pot'plāt), *n.* A plate of Chinese porcelain, or of some fine European faïence, in

Pot-plate of Chinese blue and white porcelain.

the decoration of which appears a vase, basket, or the like, of broad rounded form, usually very conventional.

potpourri (pō-pö-rē'), *n.* [Formerly also *pot porrid* (Cotgrave); < F. *pot-pourri*, < *pot*, pot, + *pourri*, pp. of *pourrir*, < L. *putrere*, rot: see *putrefy.* Cf. equiv. *olla podrida.*] **1.** A dish of different kinds of meat and vegetables cooked together; a stew. Hence — **2.** A miscellaneous collection; a medley. Specifically—(*a*) A mixture of the dried petals of rose-leaves or other flowers with spices and perfumes. It is usually kept in jars for its fragrance. (*b*) An incense for burning, made of a mixture of gums, seeds, and the like, recipes for which were highly valued, especially in the eighteenth century. (*c*) Same as *potpourri-jar.* (*d*) Same as *medley.* (*e*) A literary composition consisting of parts put together without unity or bond of connection.—**Potpourri-jar**, a covered jar or vase for holding potpourri. (See def. 2 (*a*).) Rich jars of the enameled pottery of the eighteenth century having covers are often called by this name.

Potpourri-jar.

potrack (pot-rak'), *v. i.* [Imitative.] To cry as a guinea-fowl. [Rare.]

That the dusting of chickens, cackling of geese, and the *potracking* of Guinea-hens have not given rise to an elaborate series of weather proverbs is, I think, surprising.
Pop. Sci. Mo., XXVIII. 640.

pot-roast (pot'rōst), *n.* Meat (generally beef) cooked in a pot with a little water, and allowed to become brown as if roasted. [Local, U. S.]

pot-setting (pot'set"ing), *n.* In *glass-manuf.*, the operation of placing in their proper position in the furnace pots which have previously been annealed at a red heat.

potshard, *n.* Same as *potsherd.*

potshare†, *n.* Same as *potsherd.*

potsheen†, *n.* Same as *poteen. Miss Edgeworth*, Absentee, x.

potshell (pot'shel), *n.* A potsherd. *Harper's Mag.*, LXXIX. 248.

potsherd (pot'shėrd), *n.* [Also *potshard*; < *pot*[1] + *sherd.*] A piece or fragment of an earthenware pot; any broken fragment or piece of earthenware.

And he took him a *potsherd* to scrape himself withal.
Job ii. 8.

In upper Egypt, it is true, the *potsherd*, the ostrakon, takes the place of the papyrus.
Amer. Jour. Philol., VIII. 508.

pot-shop (pot'shop), *n.* A small public house. [Slang.]

Mr. Ben Allen and Mr. Bob Sawyer betook themselves to a sequestered *pot-shop* on the remotest confines of the Borough.
Dickens, Pickwick, lii.

pot-shot[1] (pot'shot), *n.* **1.** A shot taken for the purpose of filling the pot, little heed being paid to skill in shooting or to the preservation of the appearance of the animal.

Shooting flying was not an ordinary accomplishment: it was just coming in, and most people took *pot shots*, and would not risk shooting at a bird on the wing.
J. Ashton, Social Life in Reign of Queen Anne, I. 313.

2. Hence, a shot carefully aimed.

In consequence of the sepoys stealing through the thick brushwood and dense woods, and taking *pot shots* at their sentries and pickets.
W. H. Russell, Diary in India, II. 327.

pot-shot[2]† (pot'shot), *a.* Drunk; fuddled with drink.

And being mad perhaps, and hot *pot-shot*,
A crazed crowne or broken pate hath got.
John Taylor, Works (1630). (*Nares.*)

pot-sick† (pot'sik), *a.* Intoxicated; tipsy. *Florio*, p. 68.

pot-stick (pot'stik), *n.* [Early mod. E. *potstycke*, < ME. *potstyk*; < *pot*[1] + *stick.*] A stick for stirring porridge, etc.

The next had in her hand a sword, another a club, another a *pot-sticke.*
Quoted in Capt. *John Smith's* Works, I. 196.

pot-still (pot'stil), *n.* A still to which heat is applied directly as to a pot, in contradistinction to one heated by a steam-jacket. See *still.*

potstone (pot'stōn), *n.* **1.** A concretion or mass of flint, of a pear-shaped form, and having a central cavity passing through the longer axis. These concretions occur in the chalk, singly or in vertical rows like columns, at irregular distances from each other, but usually from 20 to 30 feet apart. They were formerly particularly conspicuous near Horstead, about six miles from Norwich, England, in a quarry, now closed, where they were mostly pear-shaped, and about 3 feet in height and 1 foot in diameter. Their origin is not easily explained.

2. Same as *soapstone* or *steatite.*

pot-sure† (pot'shör), *a.* Full of confidence through drink; cock-sure.

When these rough gods beheld him thus secure,
And arm'd against them like a man *pot-sure*,
They stint vain storms; and so Monstrifera
(So hight the ship) touch'd about Florida.
Legend of Captain Jones (1659). (*Halliwell.*)

pott†, *n.* An obsolete spelling of *pot*[1].

pottage (pot'āj), *n.* [< ME. *potage*, < OF. *potage*, pottage, F. *potage* (= Sp. *potaje* = Pg. *potagem* = It. *potaggio*, *pottaggio*), porridge, soup, < *pot*, pot: see *pot*[1].] **1.** A dish consisting of meat boiled to softness in water, usually with vegetables; meat-broth; soup.

Though a man be falle in jalous rage,
Let maken with this water his *potage*,
And never shal he more his wyf mistriste.
Chaucer, Prol. to Pardoner's Tale, l. 82.

Blow not thy *Pottage* nor Drinke,
For it is not commendable.
Babees Book (E. E. T. S.), p. 79.

Jacob sod *pottage*: and Esau came from the field, and he was faint.
Gen. xxv. 29.

2. Oatmeal or other porridge.

Thei have not, in many places, nouther Pesen ne Benes, ne non other *Potages*, but the Brothe of the Flessche.
Mandeville, Travels, p. 250.

pottage-ware†, *n.* [ME. *potageware*; < *pottage* + *ware*[2].] Pottage-herbs; pulse.

Nowe *potageware* in askes mynge & kepe
In oilbarelles or salt tubbes doone.
Palladius, Husbondrie (E. E. T. S.), p. 100.

pottain† (pot'ān), *n.* [< OF. *potain*, pot-metal: see *potin.*] Same as *pot-metal*, 1.

potteen, *n.* See *poteen.*

pottenger, *n.* See *pottinger.*

potter[1] (pot'ėr), *n.* [= D. *potter*, a hoarder, = MLG. *potter*, LG. *pottjer* = G. *pötter*, potter; < OF. *potier*, F. *potier*, a potter, < *pot*, pot: see *pot*[1].] **1.** One whose occupation is the making of pots or earthenware vessels of any kind.

We are the clay, and thou our *potter*; and we all are the work of thy hand.
Isa. lxiv. 8.

2. One who peddles earthenware or crockery. [Prov. Eng.]

Rough *potters* seemed they, trading soberly,
With paniered asses driven from door to door.
Wordsworth, Guilt and Sorrow, xlvi.

3. One who pots meats, vegetables, etc.—**4.** A fresh-water clemmyoid turtle, *Deirochelys serrata*, of the United States.—**5.** The slider, or red-bellied terrapin, *Pseudemys rugosa.* See *slider.* [Local, U. S.]—**Potters' clay.** (*a*) A clay used for ordinary earthenware, and of some shade of brown, red, or yellow after burning. (*b*) In a larger sense, any earth used in the ceramic art, including kaolin, a so-called blue clay which is of a grayish color and when fired is white, and a black clay so called, which also results in a white biscuit. —**Potter's field**, a piece of ground reserved as a burial-place for strangers and the friendless poor. The name is derived from its use in the following passage:

And they took counsel, and bought with them [thirty pieces of silver] the *potter's field*, to bury strangers in.
Mat. xxvii. 7.

Potters' lathe. Same as *potters' wheel.*—**Potters' ore**, one of the many miners' terms for galena: lead ore in lumps and sufficiently free from gangue to be used by potters for glazing their ware.—**Potters' wheel**, an implement used in shaping earthenware vessels of rounded form, serving to give the mass of clay a rotary motion while the potter manipulates it. The primitive form is a small round table set on a pivot, and free to revolve; it is turned by the hand at intervals. An improved form has a lower shelf or foot-piece connected with the table, so that

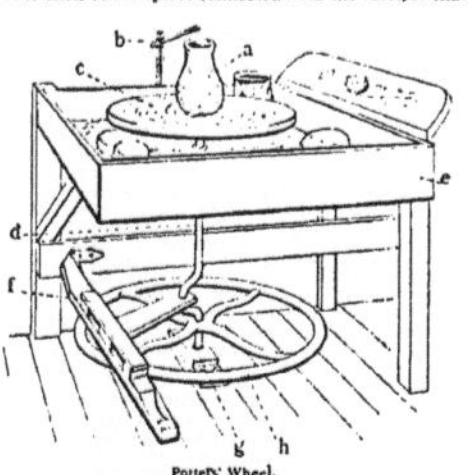

Potters' Wheel.

a, partly molded clay; *b*, guiding measure; *c*, revolving wheel, screwed on shaft *d*, which is propelled by horizontally moving treadle-apparatus *f*, and steadied by fly-wheel *h*, pivoted on block *g*; *e*, box for containing balls of clay, water-vessel, sponge, tools, etc.

the potter can give it continuous motion by the action of his foot. The wheel is also used in applying rings of color, by revolving the vessel while the brush is firmly held stationary and in contact with it.

potter[2] (pot'ėr), *v.* [Also *putter*, dial. (Sc.) *pouter*, *pudder*; cf. D. *poteren*, *peuteren*, poke, pry, search; freq. of *pote*, and secondarily of *put*[1], push: see *pote*, *put*[1].] **I.** *intrans.* **1.** To be busy in doing little, or what is of little or no practical value; busy one's self over trifles; trifle; work with little energy or purpose. [Colloq.]

His servants stayed with him till they were so old and *pottering* he had to hire other folks to do their work.
George Eliot, Adam Bede, xvii.

Lord John Russell's Government *pottered* with the difficulty rather than encountered it.
J. McCarthy, Hist. Own Times, xvii.

2. To hobble; walk slowly and with difficulty; move slowly; loiter.

Past the old church and down the footpath *pottered* the old man and the child, hand-in-hand.
T. Hughes, Tom Brown at Rugby, i. 2.

I . . . *pottered* about Beaune rather vaguely for the rest of my hour.
H. James, Jr., Little Tour, p. 252.

3. To walk upon or leap from piece to piece of floating ice. *Bartlett.* [Local, U. S.]—**To potter about**, to wander idly to and fro; move about in a purposeless and ineffectual manner.

II. *trans.* To poke; push; disturb. [Colloq.]

potterer (pot'ėr-ėr), *n.* One who or that which potters; one who moves slowly or loiters.

Potterton hen. See *hen*1.

potter-wasp (pot'ėr-wosp), *n.* A wasp of one of the genera *Odynerus*, *Eumenes*, etc., which builds mud cells in any convenient cylindrical

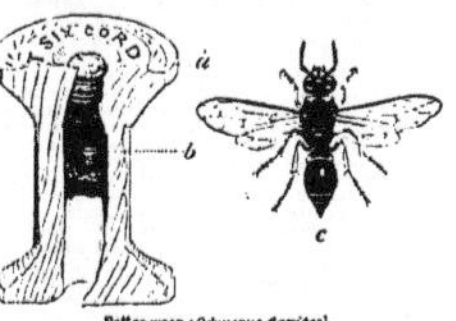

Potter-wasp (*Odynerus flavipes*).

a, mass of tempered clay used by wasp to close the nest in a wooden spool; *b*, one cell of the nest; *c*, the wasp.

cavity, such as a hollow reed, an accidentally folded paper, or the hole in a spool. *O. flavipes* and *E. fraterna* are good examples.

pottery (pot'ėr-i), *n.*; pl. *potteries* (-iz). [< F *poterie* (= Pr. *potaria*), pottery, < *pot*, a pot: see *pot*[1].] 1. The ware or vessels made by potters; baked earthenware, glazed or unglazed. —2. A place where earthen vessels are made. —3. The business of a potter; the manufacture of earthenware.—**Abruzzi pottery**, a name given to the decorative potteries made in the provinces of Abruzzi in Italy. The traditions of the majolica decoration lingered long in this region, although gradually modified. The most important of these wares are known by the name of *Castelli pottery*.—**Amstel pottery**, a common name for the decorative enameled pottery of Amsterdam, perhaps from the river Amstel, on which many of the furnaces were situated, but also by confusion with *Amstel porcelain*.—**Anatolian pottery**. See *Anatolian*.—**Apulian pottery**. See *Apulian*.—**Assyrian pottery**, the pottery found in the ruins of Assyrian antiquity. Its most important forms are—(*a*) architectural tiles and bricks, which are frequently decorated with enamel of the most brilliant colors, and arranged to form simple or elaborate designs, and sometimes painted with engobes, the bricks of each of these two kinds being frequently molded in relief; (*b*) cylinders, prisms, and so-called barrels, all intended to receive inscriptions which are impressed upon them; (*c*) flat tablets or tiles inscribed in the same way, and stored together in immense collections, forming libraries or collections of records, according to their subjects; (*d*) vessels for various uses—not generally rich in decoration, and for the most part of plain unglazed clay.—**Awata pottery**. Same as *Awata ware*. See *ware*.—**Bendigo pottery**, pottery made by the Bendigo Pottery Company at Epsom, near Sandhurst, in Victoria, Australia. It has a coarse body; but the surface is modeled in relief with flowers, etc., in a partial imitation of majolica.—**Bizen pottery**, pottery made in the Japanese province of Bizen; especially, a fine and hard pottery, unglazed or having a slight vitrification of the surface the nature of which is uncertain. It is of several colors, most commonly a grayish-white. Figures and grotesques are made of this ware, generally well modeled and spirited.—**Broussa pottery**, pottery with a coarse and soft brown paste and white enamel, made at Broussa or Brusa in Asia Minor. It is generally decorated in a style similar to the Persian or Rhodian ware, and is used especially for wall-tiles.—**Burslem pottery**, pottery made at Burslem in Staffordshire, of which there are many varieties, made by many different potters from the seventeenth century to the present day. The name is sometimes used for the early work of the Wedgwoods, especially that made by Thomas and John Wedgwood from about 1740 to 1770, and also the earliest work of Josiah Wedgwood, before his removal to the Etruria works.—**Cambrian pottery**. See *Cambrian*.—**Castelli pottery**. See *Abruzzi pottery*.—**Celtic pottery**, pottery found in northern Europe in burial-places and occasionally among ruins, evidently pre-Roman in character, and supposed to belong to times before the Roman domination in Gaul, Britain, and elsewhere. Among the most common forms are large jars used as cinerary urns; but utensils of many kinds are also found. This pottery is usually soft, fragile, and gray or black in color.—**Chartreuse pottery**. See *Chartreuse*.—**Cognac pottery**, a decorative enameled pottery made at Cognac in France at the beginning of the nineteenth century. It seems to have been generally similar to the pottery of Nevers.—**Corean, Corinthian, Cypriote**, etc., **pottery**. See the adjectives.—**Damascus pottery**, enameled pottery decorated with conventional flowers, scrolls, etc., made in various parts of the Levant, and known otherwise as Rhodian, Anatolian, Lindus, and Persian. An attempt has been made to discriminate between these, and to class as Damascus only the finer pieces having a very even surface and more subdued coloring.—**Dresden pottery**, a name given to the fine pottery made by Böttger before his discovery of porcelain. See *Böttger ware*, under *ware*[2].—**Etruscan, Etrusco-Campanian, German pottery**. See the adjectives.—**Faenza pottery**, a variety of the Italian enameled and decorated pottery known as *majolica*, made at the town of Faenza in the province of Ravenna in Italy. In this place decorated pottery was made at a very early epoch; in the fifteenth and sixteenth centuries several important establishments existed there, and the amount of work done was very great. A distinguishing mark of the arabesque decoration of Faenza is the dark-blue ground, upon which the scrolls are often in yellow or orange. Faenza ware is generally decorated at the back, especially with an imbricated pattern, or still more simply with concentric circles.—**Hard pottery**, a name given to all manufactures of baked clay which are not translucent and are hard enough not to be scratched by an iron point. [This definition includes stoneware, which, however, is by some writers separated from pottery to constitute a third class, between pottery and porcelain. See *stoneware*.]—**Inlaid pottery**, a name given to the few varieties of decorated pottery in which the design is produced by cut-out patterns either incised in the surface of the paste or cut through the enamel to the paste beneath, which patterns are then filled up with clay of a different color. The earthenware tiles of the European middle ages, inlaid in red, yellow, and black, are an instance of this. The most remarkable is the Oiron ware. See cut under *biberon*.—**Mexican, Moorish, nonesuch pottery**. See the qualifying words.—**Nuremberg pottery**, pottery made at Nuremberg in Bavaria, a town which has always been a center of the potters' art. The most celebrated maker was Veit Hirschvogel, who was working in 1470, and after him his son Augustin, until 1560. The most important works of these and other potters of their time are tiles or panels with figures in relief, hand-modeled in fine clay, hard and thickly enameled, and colored dark-green, yellow, or brown.—**Palissy pottery**. (*a*) Decorative pottery made by Bernard Palissy in the sixteenth century, and from his molds or his designs after his death. Palissy's works were first at Saintes, near La Rochelle, and afterward at Paris, where the greater part of his finest productions were completed. The pottery by which he is best known has a hard paste and a rich glaze, decorated in many colors of great richness and depth. Some of his dishes, cups, and other pieces are pierced through, leaving an openwork pattern; some are decorated with marbled and jaspered surfaces, with moldings or marks in slight relief; and others are covered with lizards, serpents, fish, etc., modeled directly from life, and painted in close imitation of nature. (*b*) Imitations of the true Palissy ware, made by modern manufacturers, and often extremely successful, so as to be deceptive.—**Peasant pottery**. See *peasant*.—**Persian pottery**, pottery made in Persia, of several kinds, including an extremely hard and semi-translucent sort, which is probably an artificial porcelain. The ware commonly known as Persian is (*a*) a coarse brown paste with a white enamel, upon which flowers, scrolls, etc., are painted in vivid colors, and covered with a silicious glaze, and (*b*) a ware of similar composition with figures in relief and similarly decorated. Each of these two sorts has sometimes a copper luster, and it is not uncommon for pieces otherwise alike to differ in having more or less luster, so that it seems that the luster is not in all cases an important object with the decorator. Rhodian, Damascus, and Anatolian wares are often classed as Persian.—**Quimper pottery**, pottery made at Quimper, in the department of Finistère, France, especially enameled faïence made from 1650 and throughout the eighteenth century. The style of decoration is usually very similar to that of either Nevers or Rouen, according to the time.—**Rhodian pottery**, pottery made in the Isle of Rhodes. This pottery is similar in decoration to Persian and Damascus ware, but is distinguished from it by a somewhat bolder decoration and more brilliant colors, and by the more frequent use of enamel color put on so thickly as to remain in slight relief. In material and character, this ware is similar to the Persian. Also called *Lindus pottery*, from the town of Lindus, now called Lindo, a seaport of the isle.—**Roman pottery**, pottery made in the city of Rome since the tenth century; especially—(*a*) a variety of Italian majolica marked as being made in Rome, of which but few pieces are known to exist; and (*b*) a white-glazed earthenware, of which the factory was established by Volpato the engraver, about 1790, and was continued by his sons and others. Figures and groups were made of this ware. The color of the pieces varies from pure white through different shades of buff to a sort of stone-color.—**Rouen pottery**, pottery made at Rouen in Normandy, especially that made during the seventeenth century and later: an enameled faïence of excellent make and fine finish, and decorated generally in excellent taste, according to the style of the day. The chief varieties, considered with regard to the decoration, are—(*a*) that ornamented with scrolls and arabesques of grayish blue on a bluish-white ground, the ground thickly covered with the ornament, which is generally disposed with great skill, so as to be effective both near at hand and at a distance; (*b*) that painted in full color with bouquets and single flowers, and more rarely with figure-subjects in medallions, the ground of this variety being generally of a purer white; and (*c*) that in which the two preceding styles are mingled, the dark-blue scrolls alternating with bouquets and festoons in color, and the ground of the enamel bluish. There are also exceptional varieties, as that closely imitating Chinese painting on porcelain, and that in which carefully made white enameled pieces are decorated only by a coat of arms, or a device or emblem in imitation of an effective Italian style.—**Rough-cast pottery**, a pottery whose surface is roughened by being dusted, before being fired, with pottery either in small fragments or pounded fine, or with small bits of dry clay. In most cases the vessel is dipped in thin slip before being fired.—**Semi-porcelain pottery**, a name given to pottery of a fine body made at the Royal China Works at Worcester about 1850: an excellent ware for table-services and the like, hard, very perfectly vitrified, and white throughout the paste.—**Sèvres pottery**, pottery made at Sèvres near Paris—either (*a*) at the National Porcelain Factory, which at different epochs has produced a limited number of pieces of enameled faïence, or (*b*) at private factories, of which there have been a number at different times since about 1775. Compare *Sèvres porcelain*, under *porcelain*[1].—**Sicilian pottery**, a name given to certain varieties of lustered ware akin to the Hispano-Moresque, and with decoration frequently resembling Damascus pottery. The names *Siculo-Arabian* and *Siculo-Moresque* have been given to the above, and some attempt has been made to distinguish between these two alleged varieties. The pieces offered for sale in the towns of Sicily are roughly decorated in a style similar to that of the Italian peninsula.—**Soft pottery**, common pottery which is not hard-baked. The test is that it can be easily scratched with an iron point. All common flower-pots are of soft pottery; but there are many kinds of pottery much softer, some of which can be cut with a knife.—**Unglazed pottery**, earthenware made by modeling the vessel in clay, and firing it without the addition of a glaze. Ordinary flower-pots, terra-cotta, and common bricks are instances of unglazed pottery.—**Upchurch pottery**, a name given to the ancient pottery found in the Upchurch marshes in Kent, and also to that found elsewhere which appears to have come from that region. In a district five or six miles long many ancient kilns and immense quantities of this pottery have been found. The ware is gray or black, more rarely brownish-red, generally thin, and well made. It is undoubtedly of the Roman period.—**Varages pottery**, pottery made at Varages, in the department of Var, France, beginning about 1730. It is an enameled faïence whose decoration imitates that of other factories, especially that of Moustiers. There were many potters engaged in this manufacture, whose work it is not possible to distinguish. (See *thrown-ware*.)

pottery-bark tree. See *Licania*.

pottery-tissue (pot'ėr-i-tish″ö), *n*. In *ceram*., a thin paper used in transfer-printings for taking the impression of the engraved plate and transferring it to the biscuit. See *transfer-printing*.

pottery-tree (pot'ėr-i-trē), *n*. 1. See *caraipi*. —2. Same as *pottery-bark tree*.

pottery-ware (pot'ėr-i-wãr), *n*. Same as *pottery*, 1.

Pottia (pot'i-ä), *n*. [NL. (Ehrhart), after J. F. *Pott*, a German botanist.] A genus of bryaceous mosses, the type of the tribe *Pottieæ*. They are small annual or biennial plants, growing on newly exposed soil, with entire obovate-oblong or obovate-lanceolate leaves, an erect obovate- or oval-oblong capsule with cuculliform calyptra, and peristome either absent or composed of sixteen flat teeth. There are 9 North American species.

Pottieæ (po-tī'ę-ē), *n. pl.* [NL., < *Pottia* + *-eæ*.] A small tribe of bryaceous mosses, taking its name from the genus *Pottia*.

potting (pot'ing), *n*. [Verbal n. of *pot*[1], *v*.] 1. In *hort*., the transfer of plants from beds or benches to flower-pots, or from one pot to another.—2. The operation of putting up cooked and seasoned meats in pots, where they are preserved by the action of the salt, spices, etc., with which they are prepared, and by the exclusion of air.—3. In *sugar-manuf*., the act or operation of transferring raw sugar from the crystallizing-pans to perforated casks. *Ure*, Dict., III. 942.—4. In *sulphuric-acid manuf*., the placing of pots containing either potassium nitrate or sodium nitrate and sulphuric acid in the kilns used for the manufacture of sulphuric acid from sulphurous acid obtained from the combustion of sulphur in air. The decomposition of the nitrate by the sulphuric acid supplies nitric acid, by which the sulphurous acid is oxidized into sulphuric acid, nitrogen being set free in the process. See *sulphuric acid*, under *sulphuric*.

potting-cask (pot'ing-kȧsk), *n*. In *sugar-manuf*., a cask vat used for draining molasses from imperfectly crystallized sugar. It has holes in the bottom, into each of which is inserted an end of a crushed stalk of sugar-cane, which is long enough to reach to the top of the sugar. The molasses drains off through the porous channels which these stalks afford, leaving the product much drier and more perfectly crystallized.

pottinger, pottenger (pot'in-jėr, -en-jėr), *n*. [Also (in def. 2) *potinger*, *potenger*; with inserted *n* as in *passenger*, *messenger*, etc., for **pottager*, < ME. *potager*, a pottage-maker, < *potage*, pottage: see *pottage*. Cf. *porringer*.] 1. A pottage-maker; a cook. [Obsolete or archaic.]

> I haue be cook in here kychene and the couent serued
> Meny monthes with hem and with monkes bothe.
> Ich was the prioresse *potager*.
> *Piers Plowman* (C), vii. 232.

> Before that time . . . the wafers, flamms, and pastry-meat will scarce have had the just degree of fire which learned *pottingers* prescribe as fittest for the body.
> *Scott*, Monastery, xvi.

2†. A porringer.

> Her treasure was . . . only thynges necessary to bee vsed, as cheyars, stooles, settels, dyskes, *potingers*, pottes, pannes, basons, treyes, and suche other howsholde stuffe and instrumentes.
> *Peter Martyr* (tr. in Eden's First Books on America, [ed. Arber, p. 85).

> A *potenger*, or a little dish with cares.
> *Baret*, 1580. (*Halliwell*.)

potting-house (pot'ing-hous), *n*. A house in which plants are potted.

potting-stick (pot'ing-stik), *n*. A flat stick with a blunt end, used by gardeners, in potting plants, for compacting the earth in the space between the roots or ball of the plant and the sides of the pot.

pottle (pot'l), *n*. [< ME. *potel*, < OF. *potel*, a little pot, dim. of *pot*, pot: see *pot*[1].] 1. A liquid measure of two quarts; the contents of such a measure; hence, a measure of wine or other beverage; any large tankard; a pot.

> Go brew me a *pottle* of sack finely.
> *Shak*., M. W. of W., iii. 5. 30.

> He calls for a *pottle* of Rhenish wine,
> And dranke a health to his queene.
> *Robin Hood and Queen Katherine* (Child's Ballads, V. 313).

> Certain Canes as bigge as a mans legge, which between the knots contained a *pottle* of water, extracted from the dewes. *Purchas*, Pilgrimage, p. 877.

> Put them [ant-flies] into a glass that will hold a quart or a *pottle*. *I. Walton*, Complete Angler, p. 184.

2. A dish made by Connecticut fishermen by frying pork in the bottom of a kettle, then adding water, and stewing in the water pieces of fresh fish. *Muddle*, made by Cape Ann fishermen, is the same dish with the addition of crackers.—3. A small wicker basket or vessel for holding fruit.

> Strawberry *pottles* are often half cabbage leaves, a few tempting strawberries being displayed on the top of the *pottle*. *Mayhew*, London Labour and London Poor, I. 63.

4. A children's game. [Prov. Eng.]

> I have as little inclination to write verses as to play at *pottle* or whip a top.
> *Southey*, To Rev. H. Hill, Oct. 14, 1822.

pottle-bellied (pot'l-bel″id), *a*. Same as *pot-bellied*.

pottle-bodied (pot'l-bod″id), *a*. Same as *pot-bellied*.

> A something-*pottle-bodied* boy,
> That knuckled at the taw.
> *Tennyson*, Will Waterproof.

pottle-bottle†, *n.* A bottle holding two quarts, or a pottle.

Item, j payre of *potell botellys* of one sorte.
Item, j. nother *potell bottell.* *Paston Letters*, I. 488.

pottle-deep (pot'l-dēp), *a.* As deep as the pottle; to the bottom of the pottle.

Now, my sick fool Roderigo,
Whom love hath turn'd almost the wrong side out,
To Desdemona hath to-night caroused
Potations *pottle-deep.* *Shak.*, Othello, ii. 3. 56.

pottle-draught (pot'l-dräft), *n.* The drinking of a pottle of liquor at one draught; hence, a deep draught. [Prov. Eng.]

pottle-pot† (pot'l-pot), *n.* A vessel holding two quarts; also, the contents of such a vessel.

Great rattels swellyng bygger than the belly of a *pottale pot.* *W. Patten*, quoted in N. and Q., 7th ser., VI. 217.

Shal. By the mass, you'll crack a quart together, ha! will you not, Master Bardolph?
Bard. Yea, sir, in a *pottle-pot.*
Shak., 2 Hen. IV., v. 3. 68.

potto (pot'ō), *n.* [Also *poto;* African (?).] 1. A small West African lemuroid quadruped, *Perodicticus potto.* See *Perodicticus.*—2. The kinkajou, *Cercoleptes caudivolvulus.* See cut under *kinkajou.* [A misnomer.]

pot-tree (pot'trē), *n.* The monkey-pot tree: both names are from the large woody seed-vessels furnished with lids. See *Lecythis.*

Pott's curvature, disease, fracture. See *curvature*, etc.

Pottsville conglomerate. See *millstone-grit.*

pottu (pot'ö), *n.* The circular caste-mark worn on the forehead of a Brahman.

The right line alone, or *pottu*, the mystic circle, describes the sublime simplicity of his soul's aspiration.
J. W. Palmer, The New and the Old, p. 263.

potulent† (pot'ū-lent), *a.* [= It. *potulento*, < L. *potulentus*, drinkable, drunken, < *potus*, drunken: see *potation.*] 1. Nearly drunk; rather tipsy. *Bailey.*—2. Fit to drink; drinkable. *Johnson.*

pot-valiant (pot'val″yant), *a.* Courageous through drink; fighting-drunk.

"Perhaps we had better retire," whispered Mr. Pickwick. "Never, sir," rejoined Pott, *pot-valiant* in a double sense, "never." *Dickens*, Pickwick, li.

pot-valiantry (pot'val″yant-ri), *n.* The courage excited by drink; Dutch courage.

The old man is still mercurial; but his *pot-valiantry* is gone; cold water is his only fog-breaker.
S. Judd, Margaret, iii.

pot-verdugo† (pot'vėr″dū-gō), *n.* [*Verdugo* for *vertigo.*] Giddiness produced by hard drinking.

Have you got the *pot-verdugo?*
Beau. and Fl., Scornful Lady, ii. 1.

pot-wabbler (pot'wob″lėr), *n.* Same as *pot-walloper. Halliwell.*

pot-waller (pot'wol″ėr), *n.* Same as *pot-walloper.*

pot-walliner†, pot-walloner†, *n.* Same as *pot-walloper.*

The election of members here [Taunton] is by those whom they call *pot-walloners*—that is to say, every inhabitant, whether housekeeper or lodger, who dresses his own victuals: to make out which, several inmates or lodgers will, some little time before the election, bring out their pots, and make fires in the street, and boil victuals in the sight of their neighbours, that their votes may not be called in question.
De Foe, Tour thro' Great Britain, II. 18. (*Davies.*)

pot-walloper (pot'wol″op-ėr), *n.* [< *pot* + *walloper.* Cf. *pot-waller, pot-walliner*, and *pot-boiler*, 2.] One who boils a pot. Specifically—(*a*) One who prepares his own food; a housekeeper or a lodger who prepares his own food; in particular, a parliamentary voter in some English boroughs before the passing of the Reform Bill of 1832. Every male inhabitant, whether housekeeper or lodger, who had resided six months in the borough, and had not been chargeable to any township as a pauper for twelve months, was entitled to vote.

All manner of Utilitarians, Radicals, refractory *Potwallopers*, and so forth. *Carlyle*, Sartor Resartus, p. 198.

(*b*) A cook aboard ship; a pot-wrestler. [Slang.] (*c*) A scullion. *Bartlett.* [U. S.]

pot-walloping (pot'wol″op-ing), *n.* The sound made by a pot in boiling.

The trumpet that once announced from afar the laurelled mail . . . has now given way for ever to the *pot-wallopings* of the boiler. *De Quincey*, Eng. Mail Coach.

pot-walloping (pot'wol″op-ing), *a.* Boiling a pot: applied to boroughs in which, before the Reform Act of 1832, pot-wallopers were entitled to vote. *Encyc. Dict.*

A *pot-walloping* borough like Taunton.
Southey, Letters, IV. 39.

pot-wheel (pot'hwēl), *n.* A bucket-wheel for raising water; a noria.

potwork (pot'wėrk), *n.* A small establishment for the making of pottery, or one for the production of the commoner wares only. *Jewitt*, II. i.

pot-works (pot'wėrks), *n. pl.* and *sing.* A manufactory of fish-oil; an oil-factory.

pot-wrestler (pot'rest″lėr), *n.* 1. The cook on a whale-ship. [Slang.]—2. A kitchen-maid. [Slang, U. S.]

pouce¹, *n.* An obsolete or dialectal form of *pulse¹*.

pouce² (pous), *n.* [Appar. a reduced form of *pounce²* (cf. *powsoned* for *pounsoned*). Hence *poucy.*] 1. Dust. See the quotation.

The name under which the flax dust is known among the workers is "*pouce*," and those suffering from its effects are said to be "*poucey*," a word coming directly from the French. *Lancet*, No. 3423, p. 668.

2. Nastiness. *Halliwell.* [Prov. Eng.]

pouch (pouch), *n.* [< ME. *pouche*, var. of *poche*, < OF. *poche*, a pouch, pocket: see *poke²*.] 1. A bag or sack of any sort; especially, a poke or pocket, or something answering the same purpose, as the bag carried at the girdle in the fifteenth and sixteenth centuries, and serving as a purse to carry small articles.

A joly poppere baar he in his *pouche.*
Chaucer, Reeve's Tale, l. 11.

Tester I'll have in *pouch*, when thou shalt lack.
Shak., M. W. of W., i. 3. 96.

A dirk fell out of William's *pouch*,
And gave John a deadly wound.
The Twa Brothers (Child's Ballads, II. 353).

Mony a time he wad slip in to see me wi' a brace o' wild deukes in his *pouch.* *Scott*, Antiquary, xv.

2. A mail-pouch. See *mail-bag.*

At 3 o'clock A. M. the European mails closed, and the *pouches* put on board the Aller carried the usual copies for the foreign circulation. *The Century*, XXXVIII. 806.

3. In *zoöl.*, a dilated or sac-like part, capable of containing something. (*a*) A sac-like dilatation of the cheeks, commonly called *cheek-pouch.* See *cheek-pouch*, and cuts under *Geomys* and *Perognathus.* (*b*) The gular sac of totipalmate or steganopodous birds, as pelicans. See cut under *pelican.* (*c*) The marsupium of marsupial mammals. See *marsupium.* (*d*) The gill-sac or marsupium of a marsipobranchiate, as a lamprey or hag. See cut under *basket*, 10. (*e*) A brood-pouch, of whatever character. See *brood-pouch*, and cuts under *Nototrema* and *Pipa.* (*f*) The scent-bag of various animals, as the musk, the civet, and the beaver.

4. In *bot.*, a silicle; also, some other purse-like vessel, as the sac at the base of some petals.—5. In *anat.*, a cæcum, especially when dilated or saccular, or some similar sac or recess. See cut under *lamprey.*—6. A bag for shot or bullets; hence, after the introduction of cartridges, a cartridge-box.—7. A small bulkhead or partition in a ship's hold to prevent grain or other loose cargo from shifting.—**Anal, branchial, copulatory, gular pouch.** See the adjectives.—**Fabrician pouch.** See *bursa Fabricii*, under *bursa.*—**Laryngeal pouch**, a membranous sac, conical in form, placed between the superior vocal cord and the inner surface of the thyroid cartilage. Also called *saccule of the larynx.*—**Leaden pouch**, an ampulla of the kind used for pilgrims' signs.—**Needham's pouch** or **sac**, an enlargement or cæcal diverticulum of the seminal duct of a cephalopod, forming a hollow muscular organ serving as a receptacle for the seminal ropes or spermatophores which are formed in the glandular parts of the same duct.—**Pilgrim's pouch.** See *pilgrim.*—**Pouch gestation.** See *gestation.*—**Recto-uterine pouch.** Same as *rectovaginal pouch.*—**Rectovaginal pouch**, the pouch formed by the peritoneum between the rectum behind and the vagina and uterus in front. Also called *pouch of Douglas.*—**Rectovesical pouch**, the peritoneal pouch between the rectum and the bladder, bounded laterally by the semilunar folds.—**Vesico-uterine pouch**, the peritoneal pouch between the bladder and the uterus.

pouch (pouch), *v.* [< *pouch, n.*] **I.** *trans.* 1. To pocket; put into a pouch or pocket; inclose as in a pouch or sack.

Come, bring your saint *pouch'd* in his leathern shrine.
Quarles, Emblems, i. 9.

They [letters] have next to be *pouched.* For this purpose a large semicircular table is provided with a range of large sized pigeon holes whose floors are inclined downward in the rear. These are marked with the names of railroads, cities, etc. The packages of letters are thrown dexterously into the proper compartments.
Sci. Amer., N. S., LXII. 56.

2. To swallow, as a bird or fish. *Norris.*

The common heron hath . . . a long neck . . . to reach prey, a wide extensive throat to *pouch* it.
Derham, Physico-Theology, I. 364.

3. To pocket; submit quietly to.

I will *pouch* up no such affront. *Scott.*

4. To fill the pockets of; provide with money.

He had been loaded with kindness, . . . and, finally, had been *pouched* in a manner worthy of a Marquess and of a grandfather. *Disraeli*, Coningsby, i. 11.

5. To purse up.

He *pouched* his mouth, and reared himself up, and swelled.
Richardson, Sir Charles Grandison, V. 58. (*Davies.*)

II. *intrans.* To form a pouch; bag.

Pouchings and irregularities of the bladder.
Lancet, No. 3470, p. 813.

pouch-bone (pouch'bōn), *n.* A marsupial bone; one of the ossa marsupialia of marsupials and monotremes.

pouched (poucht), *a.* [< *pouch* + *-ed²*.] Having a pouch.—**Pouched animals**, the marsupials.—**Pouched ant-eaters**, the marsupials of the family *Myrmecobiidæ.*—**Pouched badgers**, the marsupials of the family *Peramelidæ.*—**Pouched dog.** See *dog.*—**Pouched frog.** Same as *pouch-toad.* See cut under *Nototrema.*—**Pouched lion**, a large extinct carnivorous marsupial of Australia. See *Thylacoleo.*—**Pouched marmot**, a spermophile; a ground-squirrel of the subfamily *Spermophilinæ*, having cheek-pouches. See cut under *Spermophilus.*—**Pouched mouse**, a rodent of the family *Saccomyidæ*; a pocket-mouse, having external cheek-pouches. See cut under *Perognathus.*—**Pouched rat**, some rat-like animal with cheek-pouches. Specifically—(*a*) An animal of the family *Geomyidæ*, including the two genera *Geomys* and *Thomomys*, to which belong the gophers proper, camass-rats, or sand-rats of North America; one of the pocket-gophers, having external cheek-pouches. See cuts under *Geomyidæ* and *camass-rat.* (*b*) One of the African hamsters of the genus *Cricetomys.*—**Pouched stork.** Same as *adjutant-bird.*—**Pouched weasel**, a marsupial of the genus *Phascogale.*

pouchet-box (pou'chet-boks), *n.* Same as *pounce-box.*

pouch-gill (pouch'gil), *n.* 1. One of the *Marsipobranchii*; a lamprey or hag, having the gills in a pouch.—2. The so-called basket of the marsipobranchiates. *Haeckel.* See cut under *basket*, 10.

pouch-gilled (pouch'gild), *a.* Having the gills in a pouch; marsipobranchiate, as a lamprey or hag.

pouch-hook (pouch'hůk), *n.* A hook used for suspending mail-bags while assorting the mails. *Car-Builder's Dict.*

pouchless (pouch'les), *a.* [< *pouch* + *-less.*] Having no pouch.

The opossum was absolutely forced to acquire a certain amount of Yankee smartness, or else to be improved off the face of the earth by the keen competition of the *pouchless* mammals. *Pop. Sci. Mo.*, XXXIII. 687.

pouch-maker (pouch'mā″kėr), *n.* One whose business is the making of pouches or bags. *York Plays*, Index, p. lxxvii.

pouch-mouse (pouch'mous), *n.* One of the smaller pocket-gophers, *Thomomys talpoides.* [Manitoba.]

pouch-mouth† (pouch'mouth), *n.* and *a.* **I.** *n.* A mouth with pursed or protruded lips. *Ash.*

II. *a.* Same as *pouch-mouthed.*

(Players, I mean), theaterians, *pouch-mouth* stage-walkers. *Dekker*, Satiromastix.

pouch-mouthed† (pouch'moutht), *a.* Blubber-lipped. *Ainsworth.*

pouch-toad (pouch'tōd), *n.* A toad of the genus *Nototrema*, as *N. marsupiatum*, which hatches its eggs and carries its tadpoles in a hole in its back. Also called *pouched frog.* See cut under *Nototrema.*

poucy (pou'si), *a.* [< *pouce²* + *-y¹*.] 1. Dirty; untidy. [Prov. Eng.]—2. See quotation under *pouce²*, 1.

poudre†, *n.* A Middle English form of *powder.*

poudré (pö-drā'), *a.* [F., pp. of *poudrer*, powder: see *powder, v.*] In *her.*, same as *semé.*

poudre-marchant†, *n.* [ME., also *pouder marchant, poudre marchaunt;* < OF. *poudre* (see *powder*) + *marchant, marchand*, "well traded, much used, very common" (Cotgrave): see *merchant.*] A kind of flavoring powder used in the middle ages.

A cook they hadde with hem for the nones,
To boylle chyknes with the mary bones,
And *poudre-marchaunt* tart and galingale.
Chaucer, Gen. Prol. to C. T., l. 381.

poudrette (pö-dret'), *n.* [F., dim. of *poudre*, powder: see *powder.*] A manure prepared from night-soil dried and mixed with charcoal, gypsum, etc.

Speculators have not traced a sufficient distinction between the liquid manure of the sewers and the *poudrette* or dry manure.
Mayhew, London Labour and London Poor, II. 464.

pouer¹†, *a.* An obsolete form of *poor.*

pouer²†, *n.* An obsolete form of *power¹*.

pouert†, *n.* An obsolete form of *poverty.*

pouf (pöf), *n.* [F.: see *puff.*] A plaited piece of gauze worn in the hair, forming part of a head-dress of the second half of the eighteenth century; hence, a head-dress in which such pieces of gauze, and the like, were used, and to which were sometimes added very elaborate ornaments, as figures of men and animals, or even a ship or a windmill.

pouffe (pöf), *n.* [F.: see *puff.*] Anything rounded and soft. Especially—(*a*) In *dressmaking*, material gathered up so as to produce a sort of knot or bunch for decorative effect. (*b*) In *upholstery*, a cushion, or ottoman, made very soft with springs and stuffing.—Double-pouffe ottoman. See *ottoman*[2].

pougonie, pougonné (pö-go-nē′, -nā′), *n.* The Indian palm-cat or palm-marten, a kind of paradoxure, *Paradoxurus typus*.

pouke[1]†, *n.* An obsolete form of *puck*.

pouke[2]†, *n.* See *powk*.

poukenel†, *n.* [Also *powkenel*, *powke-needle*; said to be so called in allusion to the long beaks of the seed-vessels; ‹ *pouke*, older form of *puck*, + *needle*.] The plant Venus's-comb, *Scandix Pecten-Veneris*.

poulaine (pö-lān′), *n.* [Also *poulain*; ME. *polayne*, *polayn*, *polan*, *poleyn*, ‹ OF. *poulaine*, *poullaine*, "*souliers à poulaine*, old fashioned shoes, held on the feet by latchets running overthwart the instup, which otherwise were all open; also, those that had a fashion of long hooks sticking out at the end of their toes" (Cotgrave). Cf. Sp. Pg. *polaina*, usually in pl. *polainas*, gaiters, spatterdashes, from the F.] A long, pointed

Poulaines, close of 14th century.
A, slipper; *B*, jambe and solleret with poulaine; *C*, riding-boot; *D*, sole of clog for wearing with either *A* or *C*.

shoe worn in the fourteenth century. See *cracow*.

The half-boots or shoes distinguished as *poulaines* continued to be long and very sharply pointed.
Encyc. Brit., VI. 469.

Poulaine de varlet, a poulaine with shorter projecting toe, such being the only ones allowed to working people and domestics, not merely for convenience or utility, but by express ordinances.

poulce†, *n.* A Middle English form of *pulse*[1].

pouldavis†, *n.* Same as *poledavy*.

poulder†, *v.* An obsolete form of *powder*.

pouldred†, *a.* An obsolete form of *powdered*.

pouldron, *n.* A variant of *pauldron*.

poule (pöl), *n.* [F.: see *pool*[2], *n.*] 1. In *card-playing*. See *pool*[2].—2. One of the movements of a quadrille.

pouleine†, *n.* A Middle English form of *pullen*.

poulet (pö-lā′), *n.* [F., a note: see *pullet*.] A note; a familiar note.

Miss Tristram's *poulet* ended thus: "Nota bene,
We meet for croquet in the Aldobrandini."
Locker, Mr. Placid's Flirtation.

poulp, poulpe (pölp), *n.* [‹ F. *poulpe*, ‹ L. *polypus*: see *polypus*.] A cuttlefish or octopus. See *polyp* (*a*).

The description of the *poulpe* or devil-fish, by Victor Hugo, in "The Toilers of the Sea," with which so many readers have recently become familiar, is quite as fabulous and unreal as any of the earlier accounts, and even more bizarre. His description represents no real animal whatever. He has attributed to the creature habits and anatomical structures that belong in part to the polyps and in part to the *poulpe* (Octopus), and which appear to have been derived largely from the several descriptions of these totally distinct groups of animals contained in some cyclopedia. *Verrill.*

poult (pōlt), *n.* [Early mod. E. also *powlt* (and *polt*: see *poult-foot*); also dial. *pout*, *powt*; ‹ ME. *pulte*, a contr. of *polete*, a pullet, fowl: see *pullet*. Cf. *poulter*, *poultry*.] The young or chick of the domestic fowl, turkey, pheasant, guinea-fowl, and similar birds.

I' th' camp
You do not feed on pheasant *poults*.
Chapman, Revenge for Honour, i. 1.

The third [dish] contained a turkey-*pout* on a marmalade of berengena. *Smollett*, tr. of Gil Blas, ix. 4.

A turkey *poult* larded with bacon and spice.
Barham, Ingoldsby Legends, I. 109.

poult (pōlt), *v. t.* [‹ *poult*, *n.*] To kill poultry. *Halliwell.*

poult-de-soie (pö-dė-swo′), *n.* A heavy corded silk material used for dresses.

poulter† (pōl′tėr), *n.* [Early mod. E. also *powlter*, *pulter*; ‹ ME. *pulter*, ‹ OF. *pouletier*, *poletier*, *pulletter*, a dealer in fowls, ‹ *poulet*, a pullet, fowl: see *poult*, *pullet*.] Same as *poulterer* (and the earlier form).

His eyes are set,
Like a dead hare's hung in a *poulter's* shop!
B. Jonson, Volpone, v. 8.

The costermongers fruite vs,
The *poulters* send vs in fowl,
And butchers meate without controul.
Heywood, 1 Edw. IV. (Works, ed. Pearson, 1874, I. 11).

Poulters' measure†, a kind of verse combining lines of twelve and fourteen syllables. See the quotations.

The commonest sort of verse which we vse now adayes (viz. the long verse of twelue and fourtene sillables) I know not certainly howe to name it, vnlesse I should say that it doth consist of *Poulter's measure*, which giueth xii. for one dozen and xiiij. for another.
Gascoigne, Steele Glas, etc. (ed. Arber), p. 39.

The first or the first couple hauing twelue sillables, the other fourteene, which versifyers call *poulters measure*, because so they tallie their wares by dozens.
W. Webbe, Discourse of Eng. Poetrie, p. 62. (*Davies.*)

poulterer (pōl′tėr-ėr), *n.* [‹ *poulter* + *-er*[1]; the suffix being needlessly added as in *fruiterer*, *upholsterer*, etc.] 1. One whose business is the sale of poultry, and often also of hares, game, etc., for the table.

Yesterday the lords past the bill for the preservation of the game, in which is a clause that if any *poulterer*, after the 1st of May next, sells hare, pheasant, partridge &c., [he] shall forfeit 5*l.* for every offence, unless he has a certificate from the lord of the mannor that they were not taken by poachers. *Luttrell*, Diary, March 15, 1707.

2†. Formerly, in England, an officer of the king's household who had supervision of the poultry.

poult-foot (pōlt′fůt), *n.* and *a.* [Formerly also *powlt-foot*, commonly *polt-foot*; lit. 'chicken-foot'; ‹ *poult*, *polt*[2], + *foot*.] I. *n.* A club-foot.

Venus was content to take the blake Smith with his *powlt foote*. *Lyly*, Euphues, Anat. of Wit, p. 97.

She hath a crooked backe, he a *polte-foote*.
Times' Whistle (E. E. T. S.), p. 98.

II. *a.* Club-footed.

What 's become of . . . Venus, and the *polt-foot* stinkard her husband? *B. Jonson*, Poetaster, iv. 7.

The rough construction and the *poltfoot* metre, lame sense and limping verse. *Swinburne*, Shakespeare, p. 185.

[Obsolete or archaic in both uses.]

poult-footed† (pōlt′fůt″ed), *a.* [‹ *poult-foot* + *-ed*[2].] Club-footed.

I will stand close up anywhere to escape this *polt-footed* philosopher, old Smug here of Lemnos, and his smoky family. *B. Jonson*, Mercury Vindicated.

poultice (pōl′tis), *n.* [Early mod. E. also *pultis*, *pultesse*; ‹ OF. as if **pultice*, ‹ ML. **pulticium*, poultice (cf. OF. *pulte* = It. *polta*, poultice, It. also *poltiglia*, formerly also *pultiglia*, pap, porridge, formerly also poultice), ‹ L. *pul(t-)s*, thick pap, porridge: see *pulse*[2].] A soft and usually warm mass of meal, bread, herbs, or the like, used as an emollient application to sores, inflamed parts of the body, etc.; a cataplasm.

Is this the *poultice* for my aching bones?
Shak., R. and J., ii. 5. 65.

Pultisse made of green herbs.
Burton, Anat. of Mel., p. 380.

Treating it [a stiff joint] . . . with *poultices* of marshmallows, . . . bonus Henricus, white lilies, and fenugreek.
Sterne, Tristram Shandy, vii. 21.

And silence like a *poultice* comes
To heal the blows of sound.
O. W. Holmes, Organ-grinder.

poultice (pōl′tis), *v. t.*; pret. and pp. *poulticed*, ppr. *poulticing*. [‹ *poultice*, *n.*] To cover with a poultice; apply poultices to.

Back into the friendly shadows of the mountain the young man carried his *poulticed* ear and picturesque scars.
The Century, XXXVI. 904.

poultice-boot (pōl′tis-böt), *n.* A large boot with soft leather sides and a heavy sole-leather bottom, used for applying a poultice to a horse's leg. *E. H. Knight.*

poultice-shoe (pōl′tis-shö), *n.* Same as *poultice-boot*. *Encyc. Brit.*, XXIV. 202.

poultry (pōl′tri), *n.* [Early mod. E. also *pultrie*; ‹ ME. *pultrie*, *pultrye*, ‹ OF. *pouleterie*, *poulleterie*, *pouletrie*, *polletrie*, fowls collectively, poultry, ‹ *poulet*, a pullet, fowl: see *poult*, *pullet*.] 1. Domestic fowls collectively; those birds which are ordinarily kept in a state of domestication for their flesh, eggs, or feathers, as the domestic hen, turkeys, guinea-fowl, geese, and ducks. Pigeons are not ordinarily included in the term, nor are pheasants or other birds which are kept in preserves for sporting purposes.

His lordes scheep, his neet, . . . and his *pultrie*.
Chaucer, Gen. Prol. to C. T., l. 598.

It is ryght lykely that within a shorte space of yeares our familiar *pultrie* shal be as scarce as be now partriche and fesaunt. *Sir T. Elyot*, The Governour, i. 18.

2. A number of specimens of the common hen, as distinguished from ducks, geese, etc.; particularly, chickens dressed for market.

The fat cook—or probably it might be the housekeeper—stood at the side-door, bargaining for some turkeys and *poultry*, which a country-man had brought for sale.
Hawthorne, Seven Gables, xiii.

poultry-farm (pōl′tri-färm), *n.* A place where poultry are reared and kept; an extensive establishment for the breeding and fattening of poultry and the commercial production of eggs.

poultry-feeder (pōl′tri-fē″dėr), *n.* 1. A hopper for grain the contracted open bottom of which extends below the rim of a feeding-trough for fowls, and allows fresh grain to descend into the trough as fast as it is emptied by the fowls.—2. An épinette, or gavage apparatus.

poultry-house (pōl′tri-hous), *n.* A building in which poultry are sheltered or reared; a hen-house or chicken-house.

poultry-yard (pōl′tri-yärd), *n.* A yard or inclosure for poultry, including usually the buildings and appliances commonly connected with such a yard.

poun[1]†, *n.* An obsolete form of *pound*[2].

poun[2]†, *n.* An obsolete variant of *pawn*[2]. *Chaucer.*

pounage†, *n.* An obsolete form of *pannage*.

pounce[1] (pouns), *v.*; pret. and pp. *pounced*, ppr. *pouncing*. [‹ ME. *pounsen*, a var. of *punchen*, punch, pierce (see *punch*); in part prob. an abbr. of *pounsonen*, punch: see *pounson*[1], *v.*] I. *trans.* 1. To punch; prick; perforate; make holes in; specifically, to ornament by perforating or cutting; ornament with holes, especially eyelet-holes.

A shorte coate garded and *pounced* after the galliarde fashion. *Sir T. Elyot*, The Governour, ii. 3.

They make holes in their faces, and, foorthwith sprinkelynge a pouder theron, they moiste the *pounced* place with a certeyne blacke or redde iuise.
Peter Martyr (tr. in Eden's First Books on America, ed. Arber, p. 182).

The women with an Iron *pounce* and race their bodies, legs, thighes, and armes, in curious knots and portraitures of fowles, fishes, beasts, and rub a painting into the same, which will neuer out. *Purchas*, Pilgrimage, p. 768.

2†. To cut, as glass or metal; ornament by cutting.

Item, ij. ewers, gilt, *pounsed* with floures and braunches, weiyng xxxix. unces. *Paston Letters*, I. 468.

Punzonare, . . . to *pounce*, or work pouncing work.
Florio.

A *pounced* decanter would be what we now term a cut decanter. *Halliwell.*

3. To seize with the pounces; strike suddenly with the claws or talons.

As if an eagle flew aloft, and then—
Stoop'd from its highest pitch to *pounce* a wren.
Cowper, Table Talk, l. 553.

4. In *hat-making*, to raise a nap on (a felt hat). See *pouncing-machine*.

II. *intrans.* To fall on and seize with the pounces or talons; dart or dash upon, like a bird of prey upon its victim; seize suddenly: used with *on* or *upon*.

The eagle *pounces on* the lamb. *Scott*, Rokeby, iii. 1.

Eagles such as Brandon do not sail down from the clouds in order to *pounce upon* small flies, and soar airwards again, contented with such an ignoble booty.
Thackeray, Shabby Genteel Story, iv.

Crime being meant, not done, you punish still
The means to crime you haply *pounce upon*,
Though circumstance have balked you of their end.
Browning, Ring and Book, II. 98.

pounce[1] (pouns), *n.* [‹ *pounce*[1], *v.*; in part prob. an abbr. of *pounson*[1]: see *pounson*[1]. Cf. *punch*[1], *n.*] 1†. A punch or puncheon; a stamp.

A *pounce* to print the money with.
Withals, Dict., p. 147. (*Nares.*)

2†. A sharp-pointed graver.—3†. Cloth pounced, or worked with eyelet-holes.

One spendeth his patrimony upon *pounces* and cuts.
Book of Homilies, Against Excess of Apparel, ii.

4. A claw or talon of a bird of prey; the claw or paw of any animal.

He did fly her home
To mine own window; but I think I soused him,
And ravished her away out of his *pounces*.
B. Jonson, Devil is an Ass, iv. 3.

We saw an eagle in close pursuit of a hawk that had a great fish in his *pounces*. *Beverley*, Virginia, ii. ¶ 24.

A lion may be judg'd by these two claws of his *pounce*.
Bp. Hacket, Abp. Williams, i. 71. (*Davies.*)

pounce[2] (pouns), *n.* [‹ F. *ponce* = Sp. *pómez* = Pg. *pomes* = It. *pomice*, ‹ L. *pumex* (*pumic-*), pumice: see *pumice*.] 1. A substance, such as powdered sepia-bone or powdered sandarach, used to prevent blotting in rewriting over erasures, and in medicine as an antacid; also, a similar powder used in the preparation of parchment or writing-paper.

It [sandarach] is used as a varnish, dissolved in spirits of wine, and the powder is used, under the name of *pounce*, to give writing-paper a surface after erasure. *McCulloch*, Dict. Commerce, p. 1210.

2. A powder (especially, the gum of the juniper-tree reduced to a finely pulverized state, or finely powdered pipe-clay darkened by charcoal) inclosed in a bag of some open stuff, and passed over holes pricked in a design to transfer the lines to a paper underneath. This kind of pounce is used by embroiderers to transfer their patterns to their stuffs; also by fresco-painters, and sometimes by engravers.

3†. A powder used as a medicine or cosmetic.

Of the flesh thereof is made *pounces* for sicke men, to refresh and restore them. *Benvenuto*, Passengers' Dialogues. (*Nares.*)

pounce[2] (pouns), *v. t.*; pret. and pp. *pounced*, ppr. *pouncing*. [< *pounce*[2], *n.*] **1.** To sprinkle or rub with pounce; powder.—**2.** To trace by rubbing pounce through holes pricked in the outline of a pattern: as, to *pounce* a design. See *pouncing*[2].—**3.** To imprint or copy a design upon by means of pounce. See *pouncing*[2].—**4.** In *hat-making*, to grind or finish (felt hats) by dressing them with sandpaper.

Pouncing is a term for rubbing down the outside of a hat with a piece of pumice stone, sand paper, or emery paper. *J. Thomson*, Hat-making, p. 48.

pounce-bag (pouns'bag), *n.* A bag of unsized muslin filled with pulverized charcoal, black or red chalk, black-lead, or pounce of any other kind, used to transfer a design from one surface to another by dusting through holes pierced along the lines of the design to be reproduced.

pounce-box (pouns'boks), *n.* A small box with a perforated lid, used for sprinkling pounce on paper, or for holding perfume for smelling. The term was retained in use for the powder-box used on the writing-table, whether holding pounce or black sand, until the general disappearance in England and America of the object itself when supplanted by blotting-paper, about the middle of the nineteenth century. Also *pouncet-box*.

pounced[1] (pounst), *a.* [< ME. *pounsed*; pp. of *pounce*[1], *v.*] **1.** Ornamented with holes or indentations upon the surface, or with cut-work; perforated.

Pounsed (var. *pounsoned*) and dagged clothyng. *Chaucer*, Parson's Tale.

Gilt bowls *pounced* and pierced. *Holinshed.*

2. Powdered; mealy.

Where rich carnations, pinks with purple eyes, . . .
Tulips tall-stemm'd, and *pounced* auriculas rise.
Crabbe, Works, I. 41.

Pounced work, ornament made by means of a small pointed punch and a hammer. The punch was sometimes shaped at the end into a circle, triangle, or other form, which every blow marked upon the metal. This was a common style of decoration in the fourteenth century, sometimes alone, and sometimes used for the borders of enameled or embossed articles, as is seen in the sepulchral statues of Richard II. and his queen at Westminster.

pounced[2] (pounst), *a.* [< *pounce*[1], *n.*, 3, + *-ed*[2].] Furnished with pounces or talons.

Some haggard Hawk, who had her eyry nigh,
Well *pounc'd* to fasten, and well wing'd to fly.
Dryden, Hind and Panther, iii. 1117.

High from the summit of a craggy cliff
The royal eagle draws his vigorous young
Strong *pounced*. *Thomson*, Spring.

pounce-paper (pouns'pā'pėr), *n.* A kind of tracing-paper used in pouncing.

pouncer[1] (poun'sėr), *n.* In the *medieval church* in England, a gold or silver thumb-stall placed upon the thumb of a bishop's right hand after it had been dipped in chrism or holy oil, used out of reverence for the hallowed oils and in order to avoid soiling his vestments until he had washed his hands. Also *poncer*, *ponser*, *ponsir*, *thumb-stall*.

pouncer[2]†, *n.* Same as *pounce*[1], 2.

Bulino, a kind of *pouncer* that gravers vse. *Florio*, 1611.

pouncet-box (poun'set-boks), *n.* Same as *pounce-box*.

He was perfumed like a milliner,
And 'twixt his finger and his thumb he held
A *pouncet-box*, which ever and anon
He gave his nose. *Shak.*, 1 Hen. IV., i. 3. 38.

pounce-tree (pouns'trē), *n.* The arar-tree, *Callitris quadrivalvis*.

pouncing[1] (poun'sing), *n.* [Verbal n. of *pounce*[1], *v.*] **1.** The act of punching holes in or perforating anything for ornament: same as *pinking*.—**2.** Any design or ornamental effect produced by holes.

pouncing[2] (poun'sing), *n.* [< ME. *pounsyng*; verbal n. of *pounce*[2], *v.*] **1.** The operation of transferring the outline of a design from one surface to another, as from a cartoon to a wall or from a sheet of paper to a canvas or a piece of muslin, by perforating the surface on which the drawing has been made with small holes along the outlines, then laying it on the surface intended to receive the transfer and dusting over it with a pounce-bag, thus leaving a dotted repetition of the design. This may be fixed with a soft lead-pencil or a reed pen.—**2.** A pattern so produced.—**3†.** Same as *pounce*[2], 3.

What can you do now,
With all your paintings and your *pouncings*, lady?
Beau. and Fl., Knight of Malta, ii. 1.

pouncing-machine (poun'sing-ma-shēn'), *n.* In *hat-making*, a machine for raising a nap upon felt hats by a grinding action. The hat-body is rotated against a revolving cylinder of sandpaper, which shaves off loose fibers and gives the proper surface.

pound[1] (pound), *n.* [< ME. *pound*, *pownd*, *pund*, < AS. *pund*, a pound (weight), a pound (money), a pint, = OS. *punt* = OFries. *pund*, *pond* = D. *pond* = MLG. *punt* = OHG. *phunt*, MHG. *phunt*, *pfunt*, G. *pfund* = Icel. Sw. Dan. *pund* = Goth. *pund*, a pound, < L. *pondo*, a pound, short for *pondo libra*, a pound by weight: *libra*, pound (see *libra*); *pondo*, by weight, heteroclitical abl. of *pondus* (*ponder-*), a weight, the weight of a pound, weight, heaviness, < *pendere*, weigh, *pendēre*, hang: see *pendent*. Cf. *ponder*, *ponderous*, etc. *Pound*, as used in comp. in designating the sizes of nails, has suffered alteration to *penny*: see *penny*.] **1.** A fundamental unit of weight or mass. In the English system, both in the more antiquated form retained in the United States and under the improvements established by the British government, two pounds are used—the pound avoirdupois (divided into 16 ounces) for all ordinary commodities, and the troy pound (divided into 12 ounces) for bullion, and in the United States for a few other purposes. But, while troy ounces and their subdivisions are often used, the pound itself is hardly employed. In Great Britain and its colonies the legal original standard weight since 1856 has been the imperial pound avoirdupois, which is a cylindrical mass of platinum, having a groove round it near the top, and marked P. S. 1844 1lb. The letters P. S. stand for "Parliamentary Standard." The so-called "commercial pound" is only an ideal brass pound to be weighed in air. The troy pound in Great Britain is defined as 5,760 grains of which the avoirdupois pound contains 7,000. From 1824 to 1856 the only legal original standard weight in Great Britain was a troy pound constructed in 1758 and denominated the imperial standard troy pound; and the avoirdupois pound was defined as 7,000 grains of which the troy pound contained 5,760. The present imperial pound avoirdupois probably does not differ by $\frac{1}{100}$ grain from the p e us avoirdupois pound. Before 1824 the legal standards had been certain weights, both troy and avoirdupois, constructed under Queen Elizabeth in 1588. These standards had not been very accurately constructed, and became worn by continual use; but it is probable that the avoirdupois pound had been equal to 7,002 of our present grains, of which the troy pound may have contained 5,750. The two pounds were not supposed to be commensurable. The Elizabethan avoirdupois pound remains, in theory, the legal avoirdupois pound in the United States; but of late years the practice has been to copy the British imperial pound avoirdupois. Congress has made a certain pound-weight kept in Philadelphia the troy pound of the United States; but this is a hollow weight (and therefore of an inferior character, and such as no European nation would be content to take for a prototype), and consequently its buoyancy is uncertain, and its mass cannot be ascertained with great accuracy. Practically, the British troy pound is copied. The pound avoirdupois was made a standard by Edward III., according to official evidence. From his 56-pound weight Elizabeth's standards were copied, although standards had been made in 1497, direct copies from which still exist. The troy pound was the pound of the city of Troyes, where a great annual fair was held. In 1497 it was made the legal weight in England for gold and silver, and it was generally used for other costly things, such as silk. The old books say it was used for bread; but Kelly, writing before the abolition of the assize of bread, says the pound used for that purpose was one of 7,600 grains, which he calls "the old commercial weight of England." The monetary pound which the troy pound displaced had been used from Saxon times. It was equal to 5,400 or 5,420 of our present grains, and was divided into 12 ounces or 20 shillings. Contemporaneously with it there existed a merchants' pound containing 15 of the same ounces, making 6,775 grains. The avoirdupois and troy pounds are respectively about 453.6 and 373.26 grams. Other pounds have been in use in England. An act of 12 Charles II. legalizes the Venetian pound for weighing Venetian gold. This pound was a variation of the ancient Roman pound. The pound of Jersey and Guernsey was the French *poids de marc*. The Scottish Troyes or tron pound varied at different times, but latterly it was about 492 grams, being identical with the Dutch pound. Local pounds of 17, 18, 21, 22, and 24 ounces were in use until recently. Before the metric system, many hundreds of different pounds were in use in Europe, mostly divided into 16 ounces, but many into 12 ounces. The principal types were as follows. (1) Polish pounds, of values clustering about 405 grams, containing 16 ounces of about 25 grams each, from the old Warsaw pound of 378.8 grams to the old Cracow pound of 405.9 grams. The latest Polish pound was 405.504 grams. (2) The pounds of High Languedoc and the "table-weight" pounds of Provence, of values clustering about 410 grams, from the pound of Salon of 376.6 to that of Embrun of 425.0 grams. Some of the table pounds, as that of Ain (438.3 grams), were divided into 14 ounces; so the chocolate pound of Vienna had 28 loth, weighing 490 grams. Also, certain silk-pounds were divided into 15 ounces; but these were of greater weight. This was the case with the ordinary pound of Geneva of 458.9 grams, which was equal to the silk-pound of Lyons. The silk-pound of Patras in the Morea had also 15 ounces, but its value amounted to 480 grams. The 15-ounce merchants' pound of England of 437 grams had ounces of the same value as the old 12-ounce moneyers' pound of the Saxons. (3) Baltic pounds, of values clustering about 422 grams (making the ounce about 26¼ grams), from the Russian pound of 409.5174 grams to the Dantzic pound of 435.5 grams. The Swedish pound was 425.04 grams. (4) The Italian pounds, of values clustering about 326 grams (having 12 ounces of about 27 grams each), the great majority between 300 and 350 grams. The following are examples:

	Grams.
Venice, light pound	301.29
Sicily	319.06
Naples, silk-pound	320.70
Milan, light pound	327.02
Rome	339.16
Tuscany	339.58
Piedmont	368.88
Ragusa, in Dalmatia	374.07
Venice, heavy pound	477.12

Those pounds would seem to be mostly modifications of the ancient Roman pound, the value of which was, according to the extant standards, 325.8 grams, but according to the coins 327.4 grams. There were, however, anciently other widely different pounds in Italy, from which some of the modern Italian pounds may have been derived. Many of the Italian cities had light and heavy pounds, the latter belonging to the class of pounds about 490 grams, or being still larger and containing more than 16 ounces. (5) Light-weight pounds, having ounces of about 29 grams. These include Spanish and Portuguese pounds, mostly ranging from 458.5 to 460.5 grams, Netherlands pounds, ranging mostly from 463 to 470 grams, and German light-weight pounds, ranging mostly from 467 to 468.5 grams. The Saxon moneyers' pound comes into this category, being 350 grams, or 467 grams for 16 ounces. The avoirdupois pound of 453.6 grams is either a very light Spanish pound or a very heavy Provençal pound. The German pounds are divided not into 16 ounces but into 32 loth. Some of the Spanish pounds contain only 12 ounces, the ounce retaining the same value. The following are examples:

	Grams.
Portugal	459.00
Spain	460.14
Liège	467.09
Antwerp	470.17
Saxony	467.15
Prussia	467.7110
Würtemberg	467.75
Frankfort	467.88

(6) The German 12-ounce medicinal pounds, of values clustering about 358 grams (the ounce about 30), and mostly between 357 and 360. The Nuremberg pound, 357.854 grams, had much currency in different parts of Germany. (7) The heavy-weight pounds of France and Germany, of values clustering about 490 grams (making the ounce about 30⅝ grams), being mostly included between 488¼ and 498¼ grams. But there were a few half-heavy pounds between the heavy and the light, having ounces of 29¾ grams. There were also a few extra-heavy, having ounces of 31¾ grams. The following are German examples:

	Grams.
Nuremberg, goldsmiths' (half-heavy)	477.138
Hamburg	484.12
Cassel	484.24
Lübeck	484.72
Hanover	489.57
Dutch troy	492.16772
Bremen	498.50
Denmark	499.26
Nuremberg, commer. (extra-heavy)	510.22

But the most important pound of this class was the French mark-weight pound, of 489.50585 grams. This unit was so called because it had double the mass of a certain nest of weights, called a *mark*, which had been preserved in the Paris mint with scrupulous care from time immemorial. There is evidence that Charlemagne, under whom Western medieval coinage commenced, used a 12-ounce pound, the *livre esterlin*, whose ounces agreed with those of the Paris mark. It is said that Haroun al Raschid sent a standard pound to Charlemagne, and it has commonly been inferred that the *livre esterlin* was conformed to that, especially as Queipo found an authentic rotl of the same weight. Rotls, however, are of almost all weights, and there is no sufficient evidence of what one Haroun would have sent; besides, the fact that he sent a weight to Charlemagne affords no reason for thinking that Charlemagne would adopt it. We know that Dagobert, 150 years before, had kept a standard of weight in his palace, and it is quite likely that Charlemagne continued the use of that. Indeed, he had neither motive nor power to change the customary weight, such changes being effected only by changes in the course of commerce or by the hands of strong governments. (8) The South German pounds, of values clustering about 560 grams (making the ounce about 35¼ grams), from that of Fiume, in Croatia, of 558.7 to that of Münster of 576.4 grams. The Bavarian and Vienna commercial pounds were, by law, 560 grams. Besides the pounds above mentioned, there were some containing more than 16 ounces. The heavy pounds of Valencia (524.4 grams), Zürich (528.6), and Geneva (550.6) had 18 ounces. There is said to have been a heavy pound (575 grams) in the Swiss canton of Schaffhausen, having 20 ounces. The commercial pound of the Asturias, equal to 690.1 grams, seems to have been divided into 24 ounces. The heavy pound of Milan of 763.13 grams had 28 ounces, that of Bergamo (815.2 grams) 30 ounces, and the meat-pound of Valencia (1069 grams) 36 ounces. See *mark*[2], *mina*1, *rotl*.

2. A money of account, consisting of 20 shillings, or 240 pence, originally equivalent to a pound weight of silver (or of the alloy used). It is usually discriminated from the pound weight by the epithet *sterling*. The pound Scots was equal to a twelfth only of the pound sterling; it also was divided into 20 shillings, the shilling being worth only an English penny. In the currency of the American colonies the pound had different values: in New England and Virginia it was equal at the time of the Revolution to 15*s.* sterling, or $3.33⅓; in New York and North Carolina, to 11*s.* 3*d.* sterling, or $2.50; in New Jersey, Pennsylvania, Delaware, and Maryland, to 12*s.*, or $2.66⅔; in Georgia, to 18*s.*, or $4.00. These units of value did not at once disappear from local use on the adoption of the decimal system of coinage by the United States.

3†. A balance.

> Mongst them al no change hath yet beene found;
> But, if thou now shouldst weigh them new in *pound*,
> We are not sure they would so long remaine.
> *Spenser*, F. Q., V. ii. 36.

Five-pound Act, Ten-pound Act, statutes of the colony of New York (1759, 1769) giving to justices of the peace and other local magistrates jurisdiction of civil cases involving not more than the sums named.—**Pound for pound**, in equal measure or proportions: applied in cookery, especially in preserving, to ingredients which are taken in equal weights.—**Ten-pound Act.** See *Five-pound Act*, above.—**Turkish pound.** See *lira*[1], 2.

pound[1] (pound), *v. t.* [< *pound*[1], *n.* Cf. *pond*[2].] 1†. To weigh. *Levins.*—2. To wager a pound on. [Slang.]

> "Don't be out of temper, my dear," urged the Jew, submissively. "I have never forgot you, Bill, never once." "No! I'll *pound* it that you han't," replied Sikes, with a bitter grin. *Dickens*, Oliver Twist, xxxix.

pound[2] (pound), *n.* [< ME. *pound, *pond*, < AS. *pund, an inclosure, only in the derived *pyndan, shut up, dam, in verbal noun *pynding*, a dam, and comp. *forpyndan*, turn away (shut out), *gepyndan*, shut up, impound: see *pind*, *pinder*[1], and cf. *pond*[1], a doublet of *pound*[2].] 1. An inclosure, maintained by authority, for confining cattle or other beasts when taken trespassing, or going at large in violation of law; a pinfold. Pounds were also used for the deposit of goods seized by distress.

> *Pro.* You are astray, 'twere best pound you.
> *Speed.* Nay, sir, less than a pound shall serve me for carrying your letter.
> *Pro.* You mistake: I mean the *pound*—a pinfold.
> *Shak.*, T. G. of V., i. 1. 113.

> Some captured creature in a *pound*,
> Whose artless wonder quite precludes distress.
> *Browning*, Sordello.

> There is no more ancient institution in the country than the Village *Pound*. It is far older than the King's Bench, and probably older than the kingdom.
> *Maine*, Early Hist. of Institutions, p. 263.

2†. A pond.—3. In a canal, the level portion between two locks.—4. A pound-net; also, either one, inner or outer, of the compartments of such a net, or the inclosure of a gang of nets in which the fish are finally entrapped. See cut under *pound-net*.

> We concluded the day by accompanying the fisherman and a neighbor as they went to "lift" their *pounds*.
> *New York Evening Post*, Aug. 28, 1885.

Big pound, one of the compartments of a weir where the fish, directed by the leader, first enter the weir; the largest part of the weir, inclosed by a row of stakes.—**Hob's pound.** See *hob*[2].—**Inner pound**, the first inclosure of a pound-net, at the extremity of the run, shaped like an obtuse arrow-head, the entrance being between the two barbs or hooks.—**Little pound**, a compartment of a weir into which the fish pass from the big pound.—**Outer pound**, the inclosure of a pound-net connecting with the inner pound.—**Pound overt**, an open pound—that is, one not roofed, or perhaps one accessible to the owner of goods or cattle—as distinguished from a *pound covert* or *close*.

> A pound (parcus, which signifies any enclosure) is either *pound-overt*, that is, open overhead; or *pound-covert*, that is, close. *Blackstone*, Com., III. i.

Round pound, one of the divisions of the deep-water weir, through which the fish pass, between the pasture and the fish-pound.—**To go to pound**, to go to prison; be imprisoned. [Slang.]

pound[2] (pound), *v. t.* [< *pound*[2], *v.* Cf. *impound*. The older verb is *pind*, q. v.] 1. To shut up in a pound; impound; confine as in a pound; hence, to imprison; confine.

> We'll break our walls,
> Rather than they shall *pound* us up.
> *Shak.*, Cor., i. 4. 17.

> In a lone rustic hall for ever *pounded*,
> With dogs, cats, rats, and squalling brats surrounded.
> *Colman*, Epil. to Sheridan's School for Scandal.

2. Figuratively, to keep within narrow limits; cramp; restrain.

> This was the civil and natural habit of that prince; and more might be said if I were not *pounded* within an epistle. *Sir H. Wotton*, Reliquiæ, p. 246.

> He is balked or *pounded* at every step, always trying back, but never by any chance hitting off the right road to his object. *Lever*, Davenport Dunn, III. 164. (*Hoppe.*)

3. To form into pounds, bins, or compartments.

> In the hair-seal fishery, on the coast of Newfoundland, the vessel's hold is *pounded off* into bins only a little larger than the skins. *Fisheries of U. S.*, V. ii. 426.

pound[3] (pound), *v.* [Early mod. E. *poun*, *pown*; < ME. *pounen*, < AS. *punian* (once), *gepunian* (rare), pound. Cf. *pun*[1].] I. *trans.* 1. To beat; strike as with a heavy instrument and with repeated blows; pommel.

> On the left the Mediterranean was *pounding* the sand and the clam-shells, for the wind had been blowing some days from the south, and a good surf was on.
> *C. D. Warner*, Roundabout Journey, p. 60.

2†. To inflict; strike: as, to *pound* blows.

> An hundred knights had him enclosed round, . . .
> All which at once huge strokes on him did *pound*,
> In hope to take him prisoner.
> *Spenser*, F. Q., IV. iv. 31.

3. To pulverize; break into fine pieces by striking with a heavy instrument; crush; reduce to powder.

> Which (after) th' Indians parch, and *pun*, and knead,
> And thereof make them a most holesom bread.
> *Sylvester*, tr. of Du Bartas's Weeks, i. 3.

> Oh, brauely said, Ned Spicing! the honestest lad that euer *pound* spice in a mortar.
> *Heywood*, 1 Edw. IV. (Works, ed. Pearson, 1874, I. 10).

> I care not, though, like Anacharsis, I were *pounded* to death in a mortar. *Webster*, White Devil, v. 1.

II. *intrans.* 1. To strike repeated blows; hammer continuously.

> I found all our guns *pounding* at the Martinière.
> *W. H. Russell*, Diary in India, xviii.

2. To walk with heavy steps; plod laboriously or heavily.

> What you don't know about cross-country riding in these parts that horse does, . . . for he 's *pounded* up and down across this Territory for the last five years.
> *The Century*, XXXVII. 900.

pound[3] (pound), *n.* [< *pound*[3], *v.*] A blow; a forcible thrust given to an object, thus generally occasioning a noise or report; also, the sound thus produced.

poundage[1] (poun'dāj), *n.* [Also *pondage*; < ME. *poundage (= ML. *pondagium*); < *pound*[1], *n.*, + *-age*.] 1. A certain sum or rate per pound sterling; a tax, duty, or deduction of so much per pound; specifically, in *Eng. hist.*, a duty of 12*d.* in the pound on exported or imported merchandise. See *tonnage and poundage* (under *tonnage*), and *subsidy*.

> *Poundage*, . . . an allowance or abatement of twelve Pence in the Pound, upon the receipt of a Summ of Money; Also a Duty granted to the Queen of 12 Pence for every 20 Shillings Value of all Goods exported or imported, except such as pay Tunnage, Bullion, and a few others. *E. Phillips*, 1706.

> There were considerable additions made to it last year: the ruins of a priory, which, however, make a tenant's house, that pays me tolerable *poundage*.
> *Shenstone*, Letters, lxxi.

> *Poundage* was a duty imposed *ad valorem*, at the rate of 12*d.* in the pound, on all other merchandise whatsoever.
> *Blackstone*, Com., I. viii.

2. In *law*, an allowance to a sheriff or similar officer, computed by a percentage on the value of property seized by him or the amount of the judgment or process satisfied, as a compensation for his service.

> *Poundage* also signifies a fee paid to an officer of a court for his services, e. g. to a sheriff's officer, who is entitled by 28 Eliz. c. 4 to a *poundage* of a shilling in the pound on an execution up to £100, and sixpence in the pound above that sum. *Encyc. Brit.*, XXIII. 443.

3. In *salt-manuf.*, the number of pounds of salt contained in one cubic foot of brine.

poundage[1] (poun'dāj), *v. t.*; pret. and pp. *poundaged*, ppr. *poundaging*. [< *poundage*[1], *n.*] To assess or rate by poundage; collect as poundage.

> The custom-house of certain Publicans that have the tunaging and the *poundaging* of all free spok'n truth.
> *Milton*, Areopagitica.

poundage[2] (poun'dāj), *n.* [< *pound*[2] + *-age*.] 1. The confinement of cattle in a pound.—2. A charge levied upon the owners of impounded cattle, both as a fine for trespass and to defray the cost of caring for the animals.

> *Poundage*, . . . the fee paid to the pounder of cattle.
> *E. Phillips*, 1706.

> Molly I've known ever since she was dropt; she has brought in the strays, and many is the *poundage* she has saved Uncle Ket. *S. Judd*, Margaret, ii. 5.

poundal (poun'dal), *n.* [< *pound*[1] + *-al*.] A name proposed by Prof. James Thomson for the British kinetic unit of force—the force which, acting for one second upon a mass of one pound, gives it a velocity of one foot per second: g poundals (g being the acceleration of gravity at a given place) are equal to the action of gravity upon (that is, to the weight of) one pound; one poundal = 13,825 dynes.

pound-boat (pound'bōt), *n.* A fishing-boat used on Lake Erie. It is a flat-bottomed, wide-beamed type, very simply constructed from rough boards, usually 40 feet in length, with a large center-board, carrying two very tall spars, and a wide spread of canvas. It is fast before the wind, and very roomy, and is used in transporting fish from the nets to the warehouses and freezing-houses.

pound-breach (pound'brēch), *n.* [ME. *pund-breche*; < *pound*[1] + *breach*.] The forcible recovery, by the owner, of impounded chattels.

> The taking them [chattels] back by force is looked upon as an atrocious injury, and denominated a rescous, for which the distrainor has a remedy in damages, either by writ of rescous, in case they were going to the pound, or by writ [of] . . . *pound-breach*, in case they were actually impounded. *Blackstone*, Com., III. ix.

pound-cake (pound'kāk), *n.* A rich sweet cake, so named because its principal ingredients are measured by the pound.

pounder[1] (poun'dėr), *n.* 1. A thing or person weighing a specified number of pounds: only in composition, with a numeral; specifically, of artillery, a gun that discharges a missile of the specified weight: thus, a 64-*pounder* is a cannon firing balls weighing each 64 pounds.

> There was the story of Doffue Martling, a large blue-bearded Dutchman, who had nearly taken a British frigate with an old iron nine-*pounder* from a mud breastwork, only that his gun burst at the sixth discharge.
> *Irving*, Sketch-Book, p. 442.

2. A person who promises or pays a specified number of pounds sterling. Before the passing of the Reform Act of 1867 the term *ten-pounders* was applied in Great Britain to those paying the lowest amount of yearly rent (£10) entitling them to vote in parliamentary elections in cities and boroughs.

3†. A kind of pear, supposed to weigh a pound.

> Alcinoüs' orchard various apples bears;
> Unlike are bergamots and *pounder* pears.
> *Dryden*, tr. of Virgil's Georgics, ii.

pounder[2] (poun'dėr), *n.* [< *pound*[2] + *-er*[1]. Cf. *pinder*.] A pound-keeper.

pounder[3] (poun'dėr), *n.* [< *pound*[3] + *-er*[1].] 1. One who pounds.—2. An instrument for pounding. (*a*) A pestle. (*b*) The beater of a fulling-mill.

poundfold† (pound'fōld), *n.* An obsolete form of *pinfold*.

> Fro the poukes *poundfalde* no maynprise may ous fecche.
> *Piers Plowman* (C), xix. 282.

pound-foolish (pound'fōl'ish), *a.* Neglecting the care of large sums or concerns in attending to little ones: used only in the phrase *penny-wise and pound-foolish*. See *penny-wise*.

pounding (poun'ding), *n.* In *coining*, the process of testing repeatedly the weight of a given number of blanks punched from a sheet of gold or silver.

pounding-barrel (poun'ding-bar"el), *n.* A barrel to hold clothes which are pounded in hot water with a heavy pestle or pounder to clean them. *H. B. Stowe*, Oldtown, p. 340.

pounding-machine (poun'ding-ma-shēn"), *n.* A stamping-mill; specifically, a powder-mill. *E. H. Knight.*

pound-keeper (pound'kē"pėr), *n.* One who has the care of a pound.

poundman (pound'man), *n.*; pl. *poundmen* (-men). A fisherman employed in weir- or pound-fishing; a pound-fisherman.

poundmaster (pound'màs"tėr), *n.* A pound-keeper.

poundmeal†, *adv.* [ME. *poundmele*; < *pound*[1] + *-meal* as in *dropmeal*, *piecemeal*, etc.] By the pound.

> Pardoners . . . ȝaf pardun for pons *poundmele* a-boute.
> *Piers Plowman* (A), ii. 198.

pound-net (pound'net), *n.* In *fishing*, a kind of weir; a wall-net with wings (*c*, *c* in the cut), a leader (*a*), and a pocket, bowl, or pound (*b*). The leader is an upright net which is extended in a straight line to the shore to guide the fish into the mouth of an outer netted inclosure called the *heart*. A contracted opening at the extremity of the heart admits the fish into another inclosure called the *bowl* or *pound*, with a bottom of netting, where they remain until removed for market. The fish, in coasting along the shore, keep near the land, and, meeting the wing of the pound, follow the obstruction to its outer extremity, in order to get around it, and thus enter the trap, from which there is no escape. The wings are in many cases a thousand yards in length.

b
a
c
c
CHANNEL
MARSH

Pound-net.

pound-rate (pound'rāt), *n.* A rate or payment at a certain proportion per pound.

> Houses in London pay an annual *pound-rate* in the name of tithes by virtue of an arbitration or decree confirmed by act of parliament.
> *Toller* (ed. 1808), Law of Tithes, I. 151.

poundrel[1]† (poun'drel), *n.* [ME., appar. < *pound*[1].] A weight, of unknown amount.

All that falsen or vse false measures . . . or false wightes, poundes or *poundrelles*, or false ellen yerdes, wetyngly other than the lawe of the lond woll.
J. Myrc, Instructions for Parish Priests (E. E. T. S.), p. 22.

poundrel[2]† (poun'drel), *n.* [Appar. a particular use of *poundrel*[1] (?).] The head.

So nimbly flew away these scoundrels,
Glad they had 'scap'd, and sav'd their *poundrels*.
Cotton, Works (ed. 1734), p. 14. (*Halliwell.*)

pound-scoop (pound'sköp), *n.* A scoop-net used in taking fish out of a pound.

pound-weight (pound'wāt), *n.* A piece of metal used in weighing to determine how much makes a pound.

No man can by words only give another an adequate idea of a foot-rule, or a *pound-weight*.
Blackstone, Com., I. vii.

poundwort (pound'wėrt), *n.* Same as *Hercules' allheal* (which see, under *Hercules*).

pounsed†, *a.* See *pounced*[1].

pounson[1]†, *n.* A Middle English form of *puncheon*.

pounson[1]†, *v.* [ME. *pounsonen* (in verbal n. and pp.); < *pounson*[1], *n.* Cf. *pounce*[1], *v.*] Same as *pounce*[1], 1.

pounson[2] (poun'son), *n.* In coal-mines, a dense, soft clay underlying the coal-seam. Also called *under-clay, seat, pavement, floor*, or *thill* in different mining districts in England.

pounsoned†, *a.* [ME.: see *pounson*[1], *v.*] Same as *pounced*[1], 1.

Pounsoned [var. *pownsonyd, pownsoned*, also *pounsed*] and dagged clothyng.
Chaucer, Parson's Tale.

pounsoning†, *n.* [ME., verbal n. of *pounson*[1], *v.*] Punching.

So muche *pounsonynge* [var. *pownsenynge, pownsonynge*, also *pounsyng*] of chisel to maken holes.
Chaucer, Parson's Tale.

Poupart's ligament. See *ligament*.

poupe[1]†, *v. i.* [ME.; cf. *pop*[1], *poop*[3].] To make a sudden sound or blast with a horn; blow.

Of bras they broughten beemes, and of box,
Of horn, of boon, in which they blew and *powped*.
Chaucer, Nun's Priest's Tale, l. 579.

poupe[2]†, *n.* [< OF. **poupe*, < L. *pupa*, a doll, puppet: see *pupa*.] A puppet. *Palsgrave.*

poupeton† (pö'pe-ton), *n.* [< OF. **poupeton*, dim. of *poupette*, a puppet: see *puppet*.] 1. A little baby; a puppet; a doll. *Palsgrave.*—2. A stew consisting of either meat or fish, or of both; a ragout.

Poupeton, . . . a Mess made in a Stew-pan, as it were a Pie, with thin slices of Bacon laid underneath.
E. Phillips, 1706.

pour[1] (pōr), *v.* [Early mod. E. also *poure, powre, power*; < ME. *pouren, powren, poweren, poren*, pour; perhaps < W. *bwrw*, cast, throw, rain (*bwrw gwlaw*, 'cast rain,' rain, *bwrw dagrau*, shed tears, *bwrw eira*, 'cast snow,' snow); cf. Gael. *purr*, push, thrust, drive, urge. Cf. D. *porren* = LG. *purren*, stir: see *pore*[1].] **I.** *trans.* 1. To cause to flow or stream, as a liquid or granular substance, either out of a vessel or into one; discharge in a stream: as, to *pour* out wine; to *pour* in salt or sand.

Peny-ale and podyng-ale hue *pourede* to-gedere.
Piers Plowman (C), vii. 226.

It is a figure in rhetoric that drink, being *poured* out of a cup into a glass, by filling the one doth empty the other.
Shak., As you Like it, v. 1. 46.

Orontes is a Riuer which ariseth in Cœlesyria, and . . . in fine *powreth* himselfe into the lappe of Neptune.
Purchas, Pilgrimage, p. 83.

Mean while, Syneidesis *pour'd* this loud Cry
In Psyche's ear. *J. Beaumont*, Psyche, ii. 113.

The soft-eyed well-girt maidens *poured*
The joy of life from out the jars long stored
Deep in the earth.
William Morris, Earthly Paradise, I. 293.

2. To cause to flow or fall in a succession of streams or drops; rain.

There was *powred* downe a great deale of water.
Coryat, Crudities, I. 3.

This day will *pour* down,
If I conjecture aught, no drizzling shower,
But rattling storm of arrows barb'd with fire.
Milton, P. L., vi. 544.

3. To send forth as in a stream; discharge; emit; send forth in profusion or as in a flood, as words.

And Daniel likewyse, cap. 9., *powereth* forth his herte before God. *Joye*, Expos. of Daniel iv.

They *poured* out a prayer when thy chastening was upon them. Isa. xxvi. 16.

Now will I shortly *pour* out my fury upon thee.
Ezek. vii. 8.

How London doth *pour* out her citizens!
Shak., Hen. V., v., Prol., l. 24.

A multitude, like which the populous north
Pour'd never from her frozen loins, to pass
Rhene or the Danaw. *Milton*, P. L., i. 352.

Here nature all her sweets profusely *pours*,
And paints th' enamell'd ground with various flowers.
Gay, The Fan, I.

Tun'd at length to some immortal song,
It sounds Jehovah's name, and *pours* his praise along.
Cowper, Conversation, l. 908.

Over the waving grass-fields of June, the bobolink, tipsy with joy, *pours* his bubbling laughter.
G. S. Merriam, S. Bowles, I. 14.

Hence—4. To shed; expend: as, to *pour* out one's blood.

Four sprightly coursers with a deadly groan
Pour forth their lives, and on the pyre are thrown.
Pope, Iliad, xxiii. 209.

The Babylonian, Assyrian, Medean, Persian monarchies must have *poured* out seas of blood in their destruction.
Burke, Vind. of Nat. Society.

To pour oil on the fire. See *fire*.—**To pour water on the hands.** See *hand*.

II. *intrans.* 1. To flow; issue forth in a stream: as, the water *poured* over the rocks.

Through the fair scene roll slow the ling'ring streams,
Then foaming *pour* along, and rush into the Thames.
Pope, Windsor Forest, l. 218.

The torrent brooks of hallow'd Israel
From craggy hollows *pouring*, late and soon,
Sound all night long, in falling thro' the dell.
Tennyson, Fair Women.

2. To fall, as a torrent of rain; rain hard.

In such a night
To shut me out! *Pour* on; I will endure.
Shak., Lear, iii. 4. 18.

May he who gives the rain to *pour* . . .
Protect thee frae the driving shower!
Burns, On the Birth of a Posthumous Child.

3. To rush on as in a stream; come forth in great numbers.

A nation of barbarians *pours* down on a rich and unwarlike empire. *Macaulay*, Gladstone on Church and State.

Roll of cannon and clash of arms,
And England *pouring* on her foes.
Tennyson, Death of Wellington.

The slaves *poured* into the Roman provinces of the East in nearly the same character in which the Teutons *poured* into the Roman provinces of the West.
E. A. Freeman, Amer. Lects., p. 431.

4. To spread; become diffused.

The universal calm of southern seas *poured* from the bosom of the ship over the quiet, decaying old northern port. *G. W. Curtis*, Prue and I, p. 67.

pour[1] (pōr), *n.* [< *pour*[1], *v.*] 1. Continuous motion as of a stream; flow.

The author's striking experiment of comparing solar radiation directly with the *pour* of molten steel from a Bessemer converter. *Science*, XI. 143.

2. A heavy fall of rain; a downpour.

He mounted his horse, and rode home ten miles in a *pour* of rain. *Miss Ferrier*, Destiny, xx. (*Davies.*)

pour[2]†, *v. i.* A Middle English form of *pore*[1].

pour[3]†, *n.* A Middle English form of *power*[1].

pour[4]†, *a.* A Middle English form of *poor*.

pourboire (pör-bwor'), *n.* [F., < *pour*, for, + *boire*, drink, < L. *bibere*, drink: see *bib*[1].] Drink-money; a douceur; a "tip."—**Policy of pourboire**, in international political transactions, the practice of giving equivalents or returns for particular courses of governmental action.

In 1866—for the *policy of pourboire* was known then, although the name had not, I think, been invented—Italy asked at Paris whether she was to join Austria or Prussia in the war, as both of them had made to her the same promise, that Venice was to be the price of her alliance.
Fortnightly Rev., N. S., XLI. 2.

pourchace†, *v. t.* A Middle English form of *purchase*.

pourchas†, *n.* A Middle English form of *purchase*.

poure†. A Middle English form of *pour*[1], *poor*, *pore*[1].

pourer (pōr'ėr), *n.* One who or that which pours.

pourfill†, *v. t.* An obsolete form of *purfle*.

pourge†, *v.* An obsolete form of *purge*.

pourie (pö'ri), *n.* [< *pour*[1] + dim. *-ie*.] 1. A small quantity of any liquid.—2. A vessel for holding beer or other liquids, with a spout for pouring; a pitcher, as distinguished from a mug; a decanter; a cream-jug. *Jamieson.* [Scotch.]

pouring-gate (pōr'ing-gāt), *n.* In *founding*. See *gate*[1], 5 (*a*).

pouriwinkle†, *n.* An obsolete form of *periwinkle*. *Palsgrave.*

pourlich†, *adv.* An obsolete form of *poorly*.

pourlieu†, *n.* An obsolete form of *purlieu*.

pourparler (pör-pär'lā), *n.* [F., a conference, parley, < OF. *pourparler, porparler, purparler*, confer, parley, < *pour-* (< L. *pro-*), before, + *parler*, speak: see *parle*, *v.*] A preliminary conference of a more or less informal nature; a consultation preliminary to subsequent negotiation.

A young man and maid, who were blushing over tentative *pourparlers* on a life-companionship, sat beneath the corner cupboard. *T. Hardy*, The Three Strangers.

pourparty†, *n.* See *purparty*.

pourpoint (pör'point), *n.* [< F. *pourpoint* (OF. *pourpoint, purpoint*, > ME. *purpeynte*) = Pr. *perpong, perpoing, perponh* = Sp. *perpunte* = Pg. *perpoente*, < ML. *perpunctum*, a quilted garment, prop. neut. pp. of LL. *perpungere*, pierce through, < L. *per*, through, + *pungere*, pierce: see *pungent, point*[1].] 1. A stuffed and quilted garment, as a military coat of fence, stuffed like the gambeson.

The knight wears a studded *pourpoint*.
J. Hewitt, Ancient Armour, II. 23.

2. A close-fitting garment worn by men in the fourteenth century and later, as distinguished from the doublet, which superseded it. Representations of it show a smoothly drawn garment, without wrinkles or folds.

Item, j. coveryng of whyte lynen clothe. Item, j. *purpoynt*.
Paston Letters, I. 482.

The slashed velvets, the ruffs, the jeweled *purpoints* of the courtiers around.
Green, Short History of the English People, p. 389.

Pourpoint, 2.—From a contemporary engraving of Henry II. of France.

pourpoint (pör'point), *v. t.* [< *pourpoint*, *n.*] To stuff and quilt, as a coat of fence.

The Jack of Defence . . . appears to have been of four kinds: it was a quilted coat; or it was *pourpointed* of leather and canvas in many folds; or it was formed of mail; or of small plates like the brigandine armour.
J. Hewitt, Ancient Armour, II. 131.

pourpointerie (F. pron. pör-pwan-te-rē'), *n.* [F.] Quilted work.

The hood is sometimes shewn as made of a cloth-like material (cloth, leather, or *pourpointerie*).
J. Hewitt, Ancient Armour, I. 237.

pourpointing (pör'poin-ting), *n.* [Verbal n. of *pourpoint*, *v.*] Stuffing and quilting, especially of garments of fence, as the gambeson; quilted work. Compare *gamboised*.

pourpointwise†, *adv.* [< *pourpoint* + *-wise*.] By quilting; as if quilted.

Item, j cover of white clothe, tyne and well-wrought, *purpeynte wyse*. *Paston Letters*, I. 478.

pourpre†, *n.* A Middle English form of *purple*.

pourpresture, *n.* See *purpresture*.

pourridié (pö-rē-di-ā'), *n.* [F., < *pourrir*, rot, < *putrere*, rot: see *putrid*.] A comprehensive term for certain diseases of the roots of the cultivated vine, caused by several fungi, such as *Agaricus melleus, Dematophora necatrix, D. glomerata, Vibrissea hypogæa*, etc., and frequently very destructive to the vineyards of southern Europe. The only really efficacious remedy is to remove and burn all roots showing traces of the disease.

poursuivant†, *n.* An obsolete form of *pursuivant*.

pourtraict†, *v. t.* Same as *portrait*.

pourtraie†, *v.* A Middle English form of *portray*.

pourtraiour†, *n.* A Middle English form of *portrayer*.

pourtraiture†, *n.* An obsolete form of *portraiture*.

pourtray†, *v.* An obsolete form of *portray*.

pourvey, *v.* See *purvey*.

pourveyance, *n.* See *purveyance*.

pous†, *n.* A Middle English form of *pulse*[1]. *Chaucer.*

pouse, pouss (pous), *v.* and *n.* A dialectal (Scotch) form of *push*.

What tho' at times, when I grow crouse,
I gi'e their wames a random *pouse*.
Burns, To a Tailor.

poush†, *n.* An obsolete form of *push*.

pousse†, *n.* An obsolete form of *pulse*[2].

pousse-café (pös'ka-fā'), *n.* [F., < *pousser*, push, + *café*, coffee.] A drink served after coffee at dinner, composed of several cordials (generally two parts of maraschino and one each of chartreuse, absinthe, vermouth, and benedictine, with a film of brandy), forming successive layers in the glass. The name is often given to any cordial taken after coffee.

poussette (pö-set′), *v. i.*; pret. and pp. *poussetted*, ppr. *poussetting*. [< F. *poussette*, push-pin, < *pousser*, push: see *push*.] To swing round in couples, as in a country-dance.

> Came wet-shot alder from the wave;
> Came yews, a dismal coterie;
> Each pluck'd his one foot from the grave,
> *Poussetting* with a sloe-tree.
> *Tennyson*, Amphion.

poussie (pö′si), *n.* A Scotch form of *pussy*.

poust†, poustie†, *n.* [< ME. *pouste, powste, post, poste*, also *poustee*, < OF. *poeste, poest, poestre, podeste, poesté, pousté, poestet, podestet*, etc., < L. *potesta(t-)s*, power: see *potestate*.] 1. Power; might.

> And so I wille my *post* proue,
> By creaturis of kyndis clene.
> *York Plays*, p. 9.

> Richesse hath *pouste*. *Rom. of the Rose*, l. 6484.

> The est he put in my *powste*,
> And the north at my will to be.
> *Holy Rood* (ed. Morris), p. 63.

> With al thi myght and thi *pooste*
> Thou schalt him serue, and othir noone.
> *Hymns to Virgin*, etc. (E. E. T. S.), p. 43.

2. Violence; violent attack.

> Thow hast ben warned ofte
> With *poustees* of pestilences, with pouerte and with angres.
> *Piers Plowman* (B), xii. 11.

In poust†, in one's power; hence, possible.

> Yef it were *in poste*, he wolde it not haue do for all the reme of grete Breteigne, for sore he dredde oure lorde.
> *Merlin* (E. E. T. S.), iii. 610.

pou sto (pö stō). [Gr. ποῦ στῶ: ποῦ, where; στῶ, 1st pers. sing. second aor. subj. of ἱστάναι, set, place, stand: see *stand*.] A place to stand; a basis of operations, either physical or metaphysical. According to Diogenes Laertius, Archimedes said, "Give me where I may stand (ποῦ στῶ), and with a lever I could move the world."

> She perhaps might reap the applause of Great,
> Who learns the one *pou sto* whence after-hands
> May move the world. *Tennyson*, Princess, iii.

pout¹ (pout), *n.* [< ME. **poute*, < AS. **pûte*, in comp. *ǣle-pûte*, eel-pout (see *eel-pout*); cf. MD. *puyt*, D. *puit*, a frog; MD. *pudde*, an eel-pout; ulterior origin unknown.] One of several fishes which have swollen or inflated parts. (*a*) An eel-pout. (*b*) The bib or blens, *Gadus luscus*; the whiting-cod: more fully called *whiting-pout*. (*c*) In the United States,

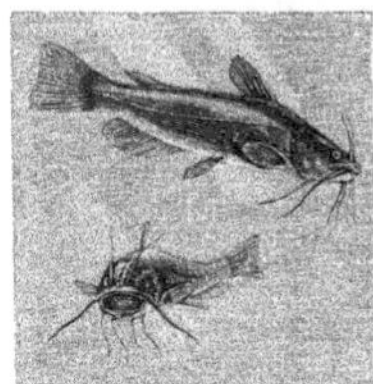

Horn-pout (*Amiurus catus*).

a kind of catfish, *Amiurus catus*, and others of this genus; a horn-pout.

pout¹ (pout), *v. i.* [< *pout¹*, *n.*] To fish or spear for pouts.

pout² (pout), *v.* [< ME. *pouten*; perhaps < W. *pwdu*, be sullen, pout. Cf. F. *bouder*, pout (see *boudoir*). Cf. also F. dial. *pot, pout, potte*, lip (*faire la potte*, 'make a lip,' pout), = Pr. *pot*, lip, mod. Pr. kiss. The relations of these forms are undetermined.] I. *intrans.* 1. To thrust out the lips, as in displeasure or sullenness; hence, to look sullen.

> Be not gapynge nor ganynge, ne with thy mouth to *powt*.
> *Babees Book* (E. E. T. S.), p. 135.

> Thou *pout'st* upon thy fortune and thy love.
> *Shak.*, R. and J., iii. 3. 144.

> *Pouting* is generally accompanied by frowning, and sometimes by the utterance of a booing and whooing noise.
> *Darwin*, Express. of Emotions, p. 232.

2. To swell out; be plump and prominent: as, *pouting* lips; *pouting* clusters of grapes.

> Her mouth! 'twas Egypt's mouth of old,
> Push'd out and *pouting* full and bold.
> *Joaquin Miller*, Ship in the Desert.

3. To puff out or swell up the breast, as a pigeon. See *pouter¹*, 2.

II. *trans.* To thrust out; protrude.

> Her lips are sever'd as to speak:
> His own are *pouted* to a kiss.
> *Tennyson*, Day-Dream, Sleeping Palace.

pout² (pout), *n.* [< *pout²*, *v.*] 1. A protrusion of the lips as in pouting; hence, a fit of sullenness or displeasure: as, she has the *pouts*.

> Sideway his face reposed
> On one white arm, and tenderly unclosed,
> By tenderest pressure, a faint damask mouth
> To slumbery *pout*. *Keats*, Endymion, ii.

2. A pouter pigeon. See *pouter¹*, 2.

pout³ (pout), *n.* [A reduction of *poult*. The LG. and G. *pute* are prob. < E.] 1. A young fowl or bird: same as *poult*. [Prov. Eng. and Scotch.]

> *Fasanello* [It.], a phesant *pout*.
> *Florio*, p. 181. (*Halliwell*.)

> As soon 's the cloakin' [brooding] time is by,
> An' the wee *pouts* begin to cry.
> *Burns*, Epistle to John Rankine.

2. Figuratively, a young girl; a sweetheart. [Scotch.]

> The Squire, returning, mist his *poute*,
> And was in unco rage, ye needna doubt.
> *Ross's Helenore*, p. 93. (*Jamieson*.)

pout³ (pout or pöt), *v. i.* [< *pout³*, *n.*] To go gunning for young grouse or partridges. *Imp. Dict.*

pout⁴ (pout), *n.* [Prob. < **pout* for *pote*, *v.*] In *coal-mining*, a tool used for knocking out timbers in the workings. [North. Eng.]

poutassou (pö-tas′ö), *n.* A name of the *Micromesistius* (or *Gadus*) *poutassou*, a fish of the family *Gadidæ*.

pouter¹ (pou′tėr), *n.* [< *pout²* + *-er¹*.] 1. One who or that which pouts. Specifically— 2. A long-legged breed of domestic pigeons, named from their characteristic habit of pout-

English Pouter.

ing, or puffing up the breast, sometimes to surprising size and almost globular shape. They occur in many different color-varieties. Pygmy pouters have the same form and habit, but are of very small size, like the bantams among chickens.

3. Same as *pout¹* (*b*).

> Small haddocks and rock *pouters*—cheap, common fish—are often . . . sold at a high price for whiting.
> *Lancet*, No. 3455, p. 1024.

pouter² (pou′tėr or pö′tėr), *n.* [< *pout³* + *-er¹*.] A sportsman whose game is poults or young grouse. *Imp. Dict.*

pouting¹ (pou′ting), *n.* [Verbal n. of *pout¹*, *v.*] The act or art of taking pouts (the fish).

pouting² (pou′ting), *n.* [Verbal n. of *pout²*, *v.*] The act of protruding the lips petulantly; a pout.

> Never look coy, lady;
> These are no gifts to be put off with *poutings*.
> *Fletcher*, Humorous Lieutenant, iii. 2.

pouting³ (pou′ting or pö′ting), *n.* [Verbal n. of *pout³*, *v.*] The act or art of taking pouts (the bird).

poutingly (pou′ting-li), *adv.* In a pouting or sullen manner.

> "I suppose I hesitate without grounds." Gwendolen spoke rather *poutingly*, and her uncle grew suspicious.
> *George Eliot*, Daniel Deronda, xiii.

pout-net (pout′net), *n.* Same as *plout-net*.

povert, *a.* An obsolete variant of *poor*.

poverish†, *v. t.* [By apheresis for *impoverish*.] To impoverish; make poor.

> No violent showr
> *Poverish* the Land, which frankly did produce
> All fruitfull vapours for delight and vse.
> *Sylvester*, tr. of Du Bartas's Weeks, ii., Eden.

povertet, *n.* A Middle English form of *poverty*.

poverty (pov′ėr-ti), *n.* [< ME. *povertee, poverte*, < OF. *poverte, povrete, povreteit, pourete, pauvrete*, F. *pauvreté* = Pr. *paupretat, paubretat, pauretat* = OCat. *pobretat* = OSp. *pobredad* (cf. Sp. Pg. *pobreza*) = It. *povertà*; < L. *paupertа(t-)s*, poverty, < *pauper*, poor: see *poor* and *pauper*.] 1. The state or condition of being poor; need or scarcity of means of subsistence; needy circumstances; indigence; penury.

> For pacyence is payn for *pouerte* hym-seiue,
> And sobrete swete drynke and good leche in sykenesse.
> *Piers Plowman* (B), xiv. 313.

> Glad *poverte* is an honest thyng, certeyn.
> *Chaucer*, Wife of Bath's Tale, l. 327.

> The destruction of the poor is their *poverty*. Prov. x. 15.

> It is still her [Fortune's] use
> To let the wretched man outlive his wealth,
> To view with hollow eye and wrinkled brow
> An age of *poverty*. *Shak.*, M. of V., iv. 1. 271.

> A carpenter thy father known, thyself
> Bred up in *poverty* and straits at home.
> *Milton*, P. R., ii. 415.

2. The quality of being poor; a lack of necessary or desirable elements, constituents, or qualities. (*a*) Lack of fertility or productiveness: as, the *poverty* of the soil. (*b*) Lack of ideas or of skill; lack of intellectual or artistic merit: as, the *poverty* of a sermon or a picture. (*c*) Lack of adequate means or instrumentality: as, *poverty* of language.

> When Lucretius complains of our *poverty* in language, he means only in terms of art and science.
> *Landor*, Imaginary Conversations (Tibullus and Messala).

(*d*) Lack of richness of tone; thinness (of sound).

> The peculiar quality of tone commonly termed *poverty*, as opposed to richness, arises from the upper partials being comparatively too strong for the prime tone.
> *Helmholtz*, Sensations of Tone (trans.), i. 5.

3. Dearth; scantiness; small allowance.

> In places glade and warme if vyne abounde
> In leef, and have of fruite but *povertee*,
> Now kitte hem short and thai wol be feconde.
> *Palladius*, Husbondrie (E. E. T. S.), p. 219.

4†. Poor things; objects or productions of little value.

> Alack, what *poverty* my Muse brings forth!
> *Shak.*, Sonnets, ciii.

5†. The poor; poor people collectively. Compare *the quality*, used for persons of quality.

> I have diuers tymes taken a waye from them their lycences, of both sortes, wyth such money as they haue gathered, and haue confiscated the same to the *pouerty* nigh adioyninge to me.
> *Harman*, Caveat for Cursetors (1567).

> There is no people in the world, as I suppose, that liue so miserably as do the *pouerty* in those parts.
> *Hakluyt's Voyages*, I. 323.

=**Syn.** 1. *Poverty, Want, Indigence, Penury, Destitution, Pauperism, Need*, neediness, necessitousness, privation, beggary. *Poverty* is a strong word, stronger than *being poor*; *want* is still stronger, indicating that one has not even the necessaries of life; *indigence* is often stronger than *want*, implying especially, also, the lack of those things to which one has been used and that befit one's station; *penury* is poverty that is severe to abjectness; *destitution* is the state of having absolutely nothing; *pauperism* is a poverty by which one is thrown upon public charity for support; *need* is a general word, definite only in suggesting the necessity for immediate relief. None of these words is limited to the lack of property, although that is naturally a prominent fact under each.

> Yet a little sleep, a little slumber, a little folding of the hands to sleep: so shall thy *poverty* come as one that travelleth, and thy *want* as an armed man. Prov. vi. 10, 11.

> *Want* can quench the eye's bright grace.
> *Scott*, Marmion, i. 28.

> The luxury of one class is counterbalanced by the *indigence* of another. *Thoreau*, Walden, p. 38.

> Chill *penury* repressed their noble rage,
> And froze the genial current of the soul.
> *Gray*, Elegy, st. 13.

> Pity and *need*
> Make all flesh kin. . . .
> My strength is waned now that my *need* is most.
> *Edwin Arnold*, Light of Asia, vi. 73, 113.

2 and 3. Meagerness, jejuneness.

poverty-grass (pov′ėr-ti-grȧs), *n.* A low branching grass, *Aristida dichotoma*, common eastward and southward in the United States: so named as inhabiting poor soils. The name is sometimes extended to the genus.

poverty-plant (pov′ėr-ti-plant), *n.* A cistaceous plant, *Hudsonia tomentosa*, a little heath-like shrub of sandy shores. [New Jersey.]

poverty-stricken, poverty-struck (pov′ėr-ti-strik″n, -struk), *a.* Reduced to a state of poverty; suffering from the effects of poverty; needy; indigent.

> *Poverty-stricken*, hunger-pinched, and tempest-tortured, it [the pine] maintains its proud dignity, grows strong by endurance, and symmetrical by patient struggle.
> *H. Macmillan*, quoted in Word-hunter's Note-book, iv.

poverty-weed (pov′ėr-ti-wēd), *n.* The purple cow-wheat, *Melampyrum arvense*, a deleterious grain-field weed with showy red and yellow flowers. [Isle of Wight.]

povey (puv'i), *n.* The white owl, or barn-owl. C. *Swainson.* [Gloucestershire, Eng.]

pow[1] (pou), *n.* A Scotch form of *poll*[1].

> But now your brow is beld, John,
> Your locks are like the snaw;
> But blessings on your frosty *pow*,
> John Anderson, my jo.
> *Burns*, John Anderson.

pow[2]† (pou), *interj.* A variant of *pooh*.

> *Vir.* The gods grant them true!
> *Vol.* True! *pow, wow.* *Shak.*, Cor., ii. 1. 157.

powan, *n.* Same as *pollan*. [Scotch.]

powder (pou'dėr), *n.* [Early mod. E. also *pouder, poulder;* < ME. *powder, powdyr, powdur, pouder, poudre,* dust, powder (= D. *poeder*, hair-powder, = MLG. *puder, pudel*, powder, = G. *puder* = Sw. *puder* = Dan. *pudder*, hair-powder), < OF. *poudre, poldre, puldre, pouldre*, F. *poudre* = Sp. *polvo, pólvora* = Pg. *po, polvora* = It. *polve, polvere* = D. *pulver* = MLG. *pulver* = MHG. *pulver, bulver*, G. *pulver* = Sw. Dan. *pulver*, powder, < L. *pulvis* (*pulver-*), ML. also *pulver*, dust, powder; cf. *pollen*, fine flour (see *pollen*). From L. *pulvis* are also ult. E. *pulverize, pulverulent*, etc.] 1. Fine, minute, loose, uncompacted particles, such as result from pounding or grinding a solid substance; dust.

> On his face than fell he downe,
> And kest *pouder* opon his croune.
> *Holy Rood* (ed. Morris), p. 66.

> The *poudre* in which myn herte ybrend shal turne,
> That preye I the thow tak, and it conserve
> In a vesselle that men clepeth an urne.
> *Chaucer*, Troilus, v. 309.

Therfore, whan thei wil schryven hem, thei taken Fyre, and sette it besyde hem, and casten therin *Poudre* of Frank encens. *Mandeville*, Travels, p. 120.

They [the Indians] haue amongst them Physicians or Priests, whose dead bodies they burne with great solemnitie, and make *poulder* of the bones, which the kinsmen a yeare after drink. *Purchas*, Pilgrimage, p. 774.

2. A preparation or composition, in the form of dust or minute loose particles, applied in various ways, as in the toilet, etc.: as, hair-*powder*; face-*powder*.

> The fische in a dische oleniy that ye lay
> With vineger and *powdur* ther vppon, thus is vsed ay.
> *Babees Book* (E. E. T. S.), p. 159.

3. A composition of saltpeter, sulphur, and charcoal, mixed and granulated: more particularly designated *gunpowder* (which see).

> These violent delights have violent ends,
> And in their triumph die, like fire and *powder*.
> *Shak.*, R. and J., ii. 6. 10.

> Like their great Marquis, they could not
> The smell of *powder* bide.
> *Marquis of Huntley's Retreat* (Child's Ballads, VII. 272).

4. Seasoning, either of salt or of spices.—5. A medical remedy, or a dose of some medical remedy, in the form of powder, or minute loose or uncompacted particles: as, he has to take three *powders* every hour.—**Antacid powder**, compound powder of rhubarb.—**Antimonial powder**, oxid of antimony and precipitated calcium phosphate. Also called *James's powder*.—**Aromatic powder**, cinnamon, ginger, and cardamom, with or without nutmeg.—**Brass-powder.** See *brass*[1].—**Compound chalk powder**, prepared chalk, acacia, and sugar.—**Compound effervescing powder**, a compound of two ingredients (35 grains of tartaric acid and a mixture of 40 grains of sodium bicarbonate with 120 grains of potassium and sodium tartrate) dissolved separately and the solutions mixed immediately before use. Also called *Seidlitz powder*.—**Compound licorice powder**, senna, glycyrrhiza, and sugar, with or without fennel and washed sulphur.—**Compound powder of catechu**, catechu, kino, rhatany-bark, cinnamon-bark, and nutmeg.—**Compound powder of morphine**, morphine, camphor, glycyrrhiza, and precipitated calcium carbonate. Also called *Tully's powder*.—**Compound powder of opium**, opium, black pepper, ginger, caraway-fruit, and tragacanth.—**Compound powder of rhubarb**, rhubarb, magnesia, and ginger.—**Compound powder of tragacanth**, tragacanth, gum acacia, starch, and sugar.—**Cubical powder.** Same as *cube-powder*.—**Cyanide powder.** See *cyanide*.—**Detonating powders.** See *detonating*.—**Dover's powder**, the more common name for powder of ipecac and opium. As originally prepared by the English physician Thomas Dover (died 1742), it was composed of potassium nitrate and sulphate, each 4 parts, opium, ipecac, and licorice-root, each 1 part.—**Effervescing powder.** Same as *soda powder*.—**Flour of powder.** See *flour*.—**Fulminating powders.** Same as *detonating powders*.—**Goa powder.** [So called from the Portuguese colony of *Goa* in India, where the substance, imported from Bahia in Brazil, appears to have been introduced about the year 1852.] A powder found in the longitudinal canals and interspaces of the wood of *Andira araroba*, a tree growing in Brazil and the East Indies. Its color varies from ocher to chocolate-brown. It has a bitter taste, and is used sometimes in medicine in the treatment of skin-diseases. It consists chiefly of chrysarobin, and is used for the preparation of chrysophanic acid. Also called *chrysarobin*.—**James's powder**, a celebrated nostrum of Dr. James, an English physician (died 1776), composed of calcium phosphate and antimony oxid. The phrase is often used for *antimonial powder*.—**Jesuits' powder.** See *Jesuit*.—**Knox's powder**, chlorinated lime.—**Mealed powder**, powder pulverized by treatment with alcohol. Also called *meal-powder*. *E. H. Knight*.—**Mica-powder.** See *mica*[2].—**Molded powder**, a gunpowder whose grains are formed in a mold.—**Oilstone-powder.** See *oilstone*.—**Portland powder**, gentian-root, aristolochia-root, germander, ground-pine, and lesser centaury.—**Powder of Algaroth**, the powder precipitated from the aqueous solution of the terchlorid of antimony by an excess of water. It is chiefly composed of the oxychlorid.—**Powder of aloes and canella**, socotrine aloes and canella. Also called *hiera-picra*.—**Powder of ipecac and opium**, ipecac 1 part, opium 1 part, and sugar of milk (or potassium sulphate) 8 parts: a powder widely used as an anodyne diaphoretic under the more common name of *Dover's powder*.—**Powder of iron**, reduced iron.—**Powder of projection.** See *projection*.—**Powder of sympathy.** Same as *sympathetic powder*.—**Prismatic powder**, a gunpowder adapted for heavy cannon. The grains are hexagonal prisms, with six cylindrical holes pierced parallel to the axis and symmetrically disposed around it. In putting up the cartridges, the prisms are arranged so that the orifices are continuous throughout the length.—**Seidlitz powder.** Same as *compound effervescing powder*.—**Soda powder**, sodium bicarbonate 30 grains, tartaric acid 25 grains.—**Styptic powder**, alum, gum acacia, and colophony, or argil, tragacanth, and colophony.—**Sympathetic powder**, a powder "said to have the faculty, if applied to the blood-stained garments of a wounded person, to cure his injuries, even though he were at a great distance at the time. A friar, returning from the East, brought the recipe to Europe somewhat before the middle of the seventeenth century" (*O. W. Holmes*, Med. Essays, p. 8).—**Talcum powder**, powdered soapstone: used as a local application for inflamed and chafed surfaces.—**Tennant's powder**, chlorinated lime.—**To fluff powder†.** See *fluff*[2].—**Tully's powder.** Same as *compound powder of morphine*: so named from Dr. William Tully, an American physician, who originated it.—**Vienna powder**, potassa and lime.—**Vigo's powder**, red oxid of mercury.—**Violet powder**, a toilet-powder made of pulverized starch scented with so-called violet extract.

powder (pou'dėr), *v.* [Early mod. E. also *pouder, poulder, pouldre;* < ME. *powderen, poudren* (= D. *poederen*, powder, = MLG. *puderen*, season, spice, = G. *pudern* = Sw. *pudra* = Dan. *pudre*, powder), < OF. *poudrer, pouldrer, poldrer*, F. *poudrer* = Sp. *polvorear*, < ML. *pulverare*, powder, < L. *pulvis* (*pulver-*), powder: see *powder*, *n.*] I. *trans.* 1†. To reduce to powder; pulverize; triturate; pound, grind, or rub to fine particles.

> And, were not hevenly grace that did him blesse,
> He had beene *pouldred* all as thin as flowre.
> *Spenser*, F. Q., I. vii. 12.

2. To sprinkle with powder, dust, ashes, etc.; specifically, to put powder upon: as, to *powder* the hair or the face.

> Thou sal make sorow in goddes sight;
> Fall to erth and *powder* the.
> *Holy Rood* (ed. Morris), p. 65.

If the said Ambassador were here among us, he would think our modern Gallants were also mad, . . . because they ash and *powder* their Pericraniums all the Year long. Howell, Letters, iv. 5.

> He came back late, laid by cloak, staff, and hat,
> *Powdered* so thick with snow it made us laugh.
> *Browning*, Ring and Book, II. 15.

3. To sprinkle with salt, spices, or other seasoning; hence, to corn; pickle.

> Seththe sche brouȝt hom in haste
> Ploverys *poudryd* in paste.
> *Sir Degrevant*, l. 1402.

If thou embowel me to-day, I'll give you leave to *powder* me and eat me too to-morrow. *Shak.*, 1 Hen. IV., v. 4. 112.

One amongst the rest did kill his wife, *powdered* her, and had eaten part of her before it was knowne. Quoted in *Capt. John Smith's* Works, II. 12.

4. To sprinkle as with powder; stud; ornament with a small pattern, continually repeated.

> No patchwork quilt, all seams and scars,
> But velvet, *powder'd* with golden stars.
> Hood, Miss Kilmansegg, Her Dream.

5. To whiten by some application of white material in the form of a powder: thus, lace which has grown yellow is *powdered* by being placed in a packet of white lead and beaten.—6. To scatter; place here and there as if sprinkled like powder: as, to *powder* violets on a silk ground.

> Gilofre, gyngure, & gromylyoun,
> & pyonys *powdered* ay betwene.
> *Alliterative Poems* (ed. Morris), i. 44.

II. *intrans.* 1. To fall to dust; be reduced to powder.—2. To apply powder to the hair or face; use powder in the toilet.

The Deacon . . . went to the barber's, where the bi-weekly operation of shaving and *powdering* was performed. *S. Judd*, Margaret, ii. 8.

3. To attack violently; make a great stir.

Whilst two companions were disputing it at sword's point, down comes a kite *powdering* vpon them, and gobbets up both. *Sir R. L'Estrange.*

He had done wonders before, but now he began to *powder* away like a raving giant. *Dickens.*

powder-blower (pou'dėr-blō"ėr), *n.* 1. A surgical instrument for throwing powder upon a diseased part.—2. A small bellows, or compressible bulb, with a long and slender nozle, used for blowing insect-powder into crevices, or among aphides, etc., which infest green-house-plants; an insect-gun.

powder-box (pou'dėr-boks), *n.* A box in which powder is kept. Especially—(*a*) A box for toilet-powder, large enough to contain a puff.

Betty, bring the *powderbox* to your lady; it gives one a clean look (tho' your complexion does not want it) to enliven it. *Steele*, Lying Lover, iii. 1.

(*b*) A box for powder or sand used on the writing-table, generally rather small and with a cover pierced with holes. Compare *pounce-box*.

powder-cart (pou'dėr-kärt), *n.* A two-wheeled covered cart that carries powder and shot for artillery.

powder-chamber (pou'dėr-chām"bėr), *n.* See *chamber*, 5 (*b*) (2).

powder-chest (pou'dėr-chest), *n.* A small box or case charged with powder, old nails, etc., formerly secured over the side of a ship and discharged at an enemy attempting to board.

powder-division (pou'dėr-di-vizh"on), *n.* On a man-of-war, a division of the crew detailed to supply ammunition during action.

powder-down (pou'dėr-doun), *n.* In *ornith.*, certain down-feathers or plumulæ, technically called *pulviplumes*, which grow indefinitely, and continually break down at their ends into a kind of powdery or scurfy exfoliation. Such plumules are not found on most birds; they occur in various representatives of the raptorial, psittacine, and gallinaceous tribes, and especially in the heron tribe and some other wading birds, where they form matted masses of peculiar texture and appearance, called *powder-down tracts* or *patches*. These tracts are definite in number and situation in the several kinds of birds on which they occur. Thus, in the true herons, there are three pairs, one on the lower back over each hip, one on each side of the lower belly under each hip, and one on each side of the breast along the track of the furcula. Bitterns have two pairs (none under the hips); boatbills have one extra pair over the shoulder-blades.

powdered (pou'dėrd), *a.* 1. Having the appearance of powder, or of a surface covered with fine powder: as, a *powdered* glaze in porcelain; in *zoöl.*, marked as if powdered or dusted over: as, the *powdered* quaker, *Tæniocampa gracilis*, a moth; the *powdered* wainscot, *Simyra venosa*, a moth.—2. Ornamented with a small pattern, as a flower or the like, continually repeated. This sort of design differs from diaper in not covering the surface so completely, and in showing the pattern isolated with background between.

3. In *her.*, same as *semé*.—4. Burnt in smoking, as a herring.—**Powdered gold**, aventurin.

powder-flag (pou'dėr-flag), *n.* A plain red flag hoisted at the fore, to denote that the vessel is taking in or discharging powder. *Preble*, Hist. Flag, p. 676.

powder-flask (pou'dėr-flȧsk), *n.* A flask in which gunpowder is carried. The powder-flask was developed from the earlier powder-horn. It was made of metal, of a size convenient for handling and carrying about the person, in shape usually something like a flattened Florence flask, and fitted with a special device for measuring and cutting off a charge of powder to be dropped into the fowling-arm. The powder-flask has nearly disappeared with the disuse of the old-fashioned muzzle-loading shotgun and the invention of special contrivances for loading shells or cartridges.

Powder-horns.
1, of stag's horn, 17th or 18th century; 2, of cow's horn.

powder-gun (pou'dėr-gun), *n.* An instrument for diffusing insect-powder.

powder-horn (pou'dėr-hôrn), *n.* A powder-flask made of horn, usually the horn of an ox or cow, the larger end fitted with a wooden or metal bottom, and the small end with a movable stopper or some special device for measuring out a charge of powder. Whenever gunpowder has been used for loading apart from cartridges and the like, powder-horns have been common. See cut on preceding page.

> The father bought a *powder-horn*, and an almanac, and a comb-case; the mother a great fruztower, and a fat amber necklace. *Congreve*, Old Batchelor, iv. 8.

powder-hose (pou'dėr-hōz), *n.* A tube of strong linen filled with a combustible compound, used for firing mines; a fuse.

powderiness (pou'dėr-i-nes), *n.* The state or property of being powdery, or of being divided into minute particles; resemblance to powder; pulverulence.

powdering (pou'dėr-ing), *n.* [Verbal n. of *powder, v.*] 1. *pl.* Small pieces of fur powdered or sprinkled on other furs, in resemblance to the spots on ermine; also, bands of ermine. Powderings have been worn on the capes of the robes of English peers as part of the insignia of rank; and the design has been often reproduced in heraldic bearings.

> A dukes daughter is borne a Marchionesse, and shall weare as many *Poudringes* as a Marchionesse. *Booke of Precedence* (E. E. T. S., extra ser.), i. 14.

2. Decoration by means of numerous small figures, usually the same figure often repeated. See *powdered*, 2.

powdering-gown (pou'dėr-ing-goun), *n.* A loose gown formerly worn by men and women to protect their clothes when having the hair powdered; a dressing-gown.

> I will sit in my library, in my night-cap and *powdering-gown*, and give as much trouble as I can. *Jane Austen*, Pride and Prejudice, xv.

powdering-mill (pou'dėr-ing-mil), *n.* A grinding- or pulverizing-mill, as for ore, snuff, etc.

powdering-tub (pou'dėr-ing-tub), *n.* 1. A tub or vessel in which meat is corned or salted.—2. A heated tub in which an infected lecher was cured by sweating.

> From the *powdering-tub* of infamy
> Fetch forth the lazar kite of Cressid's kind,
> Doll Tearsheet. *Shak.*, Hen. V., ii. 1. 79.

powder-magazine (pou'dėr-mag-a-zēn'), *n.* 1. A place where powder is stored, as a bomb-proof building in fortified places, etc.—2. A specially constructed place on board a man-of-war for the storage and issue of explosives. See *magazine*, 1.

powder-man (pou'dėr-man), *n.* 1. On a man-of-war, a member of a gun's crew detailed to fetch powder for the gun.—2. A man in charge of explosives in an operation of any nature requiring their use.

> In driving the heading, each of the three shifts is made up of a boss, 4 drill men, 4 helpers on drills, 1 *powder man*, 1 car man, and 2 laborers. *Sci. Amer.*, N. S., LIV. 85.

powder-mill (pou'dėr-mil), *n.* A mill in which gunpowder is made.

powder-mine (pou'dėr-mīn), *n.* An excavation filled with gunpowder for the purpose of blasting rocks, or for blowing up an enemy's works in war.

powder-monkey (pou'dėr-mung"ki), *n.* A boy employed on ships to carry powder from the magazine to the guns. [Obsolete or colloquial.]

> One poet feigns that the town is a sea, the playhouse a ship, the manager the captain, the players sailors, and the orange-girls *powder-monkies*. *Sir J. Hawkins*, Johnson (ed. 1787), p. 195.

powder-paper (pou'dėr-pā"pėr), *n.* A substitute for gunpowder, consisting of paper impregnated with a mixture of potassium chlorate, nitrate, prussiate, and chromate, powdered wood-charcoal, and a little starch. It is stronger than gunpowder, produces less smoke and less recoil, and is not so much affected by humidity.

powder-plot† (pou'dėr-plot), *n.* See *gunpowder plot*, under *gunpowder*.

powder-post (pou'dėr-pōst), *n.* Wood decayed to powder, or eaten by a worm which leaves its holes full of powder. [Local, U. S.]

> The grubs of the law have gnawed into us, and we are all *powder-post*. *S. Judd*, Margaret, ii. 7.

powder-prover (pou'dėr-prö"vėr), *n.* A device or apparatus for testing the efficiency of gunpowder; a ballistic pendulum; an eprouvette.

powder-puff (pou'dėr-puf), *n.* 1. A soft feathery ball, as of swansdown, by which powder is applied to the skin.—2. Same as *pluff*, 2.

powder-room (pou'dėr-röm), *n.* The room in a ship in which gunpowder is kept. See *magazine*, 1.

powder-scuttle (pou'dėr-skut"l), *n.* A small opening in a ship's deck for passing powder from the magazine for the service of the guns.

powder-shoot (pou'dėr-shöt), *n.* A canvas tube for conveying empty powder-boxes from the gun-deck of a ship to a lower deck.

powder-traitor† (pou'dėr-trā"tor), *n.* A conspirator in a gunpowder plot.

> When he has brought his design to perfection, and disposed of all his materials, he lays his train, like a *powder-traitor*, and gets out of the way, while he blows up all those that trusted him. *Butler*, Remains, II. 453.

powder-treason† (pou'dėr-trē"zn), *n.* Conspiracy involving the use of gunpowder; a gunpowder plot.

> *Powdertreason* surpasses all the barbarities of the Heathens. *Bacon*, Works (ed. 1765), III., Index.

> How near were we going in '88- and in the *powder-treason?* *Rev. S. Ward*, Sermons and Treatises, p. 90.

powdery (pou'dėr-i), *a.* [< *powder* + *-y*[1].] 1. In the form of powder; resembling powder in the fineness of its particles; pulverulent.

> Her feet disperse the *powdery* snow
> That rises up like smoke. *Wordsworth*, Lucy Grey, ii. 85.

> The niched snow-bed sprays down
> Its *powdery* fall. *M. Arnold*, Switzerland, ii.

> The bee,
> All dusty as a miller, takes his toll
> Of *powdery* gold, and grumbles. *Lowell*, Under the Willows.

2. Sprinkled or covered with powder; specifically, in *bot.* and *zoöl.*, covered with a fine bloom or meal resembling powder; powdered; farinose.

> News is often dispersed as thoughtlessly and effectively as that pollen which the bees carry off (having no idea how *powdery* they are). *George Eliot*, Middlemarch, II. 191.

> Delicate golden auriculas with *powdery* leaves and stems. *J. A. Symonds*, Italy and Greece, p. 291.

3. Friable; easily reduced to powder.

> A brown *powdry* spar which holds iron is found amongst the iron ore. *Woodward*, On Fossils.

Powdery grape-mildew. See *grape-mildew*.

powdike (pou'dīk), *n.* A dike made in a marsh or fen for carrying off its waters. *Halliwell*. [Prov. Eng.]

> By statute of 22 Hen. VIII. c. 11, perversely and maliciously to cut down or destroy the *powdike* in the fens of Norfolk and Ely is felony. *Blackstone*, Com., IV. xvii.

powe†, *n.* and *v.* An obsolete form of *paw*[1].

power[1] (pou'ėr), *n.* [< ME. *poer, pouer, power*, < OF. *poer, poeir, poueir, pooir, povoir*, F. *pouvoir* = Pr. Sp. Pg. *poder* = It. *potere*, power, prop. inf., be able, < ML. **potere*, for L. *posse*, be able: see *potent*.] 1. In general, such an absence of external restriction and limitation that it depends only upon the inward determination of the subject whether or not it will act.

> Knowledge itself is a *power* whereby he [God] knoweth. *Bacon*, Of Heresies.

2. An endowment of a voluntary being whereby it becomes possible for that being to do or effect something. The power is said to belong to the being exercising it, and to be a power to act or of acting in a specified way. The person or thing affected by the action is said to be under the power of the subject, which is said to have power over or upon that object.

> Hath not the potter *power* over the clay, of the same lump to make one vessel unto honour and another unto dishonour? Rom. ix. 21.

> And brought thee out of the land of Egypt with his mighty *power*. Deut. iv. 36.

> The devil hath *power*
> To assume a pleasing shape. *Shak.*, Hamlet, ii. 2.

> I know my soul hath *power* to know all things,
> Yet is she blind and ignorant in all. *Sir J. Davies*, Immortal. of Soul, Int.

> Not heaven upon the past has *power*. *Dryden*, Imit. of Horace, III. xxix.

3. A property of an inanimate thing or agency, especially a property of modifying other things.

> Not that nepenthe which the wife of Thone
> In Egypt gave to Jove-born Helena
> Is of such *power* to stir up joy as this. *Milton*, Comus, l. 675.

> The spot he loved has lost the *power* to please. *Cowper*, Retirement.

> Or alum styptics with contracting *power*. *Pope*, R. of the L., ii. 131.

4. Used absolutely, with specification of the effect: (*a*) The property whereby anything fulfils its proper functions well or strongly: as, a medicine of great *power*. (*b*) A gift or talent for influencing others.

> Her beauty, grace, and *power*
> Wrought as a charm upon them. *Tennyson*, Guinevere.

5. The ability or right to command or control; dominion; authority; the right of governing.

> All *power* is given unto me in heaven and in earth. Mat. xxviii. 18.

> There are some things which are issues of an absolute *power*, some are expresses of supreme dominion some are actions of a judge. *Jer. Taylor*, Works (ed. 1835), I. 24.

> All empire is no more than *power* in trust. *Dryden*, Abs. and Achit., i. 411.

> Who never sold the truth to serve the hour,
> Nor palter'd with Eternal God for *power*. *Tennyson*, Death of Wellington.

> *Power* means nothing more than the extent to which a man can make his individual will prevail against the wills of other men, so as to control them. *J. Bryce*, American Commonwealth, I. 213.

6†. The domain within which authority or government is exercised; jurisdiction.

> No brewestere out of fraunchyse, ne may browe wᵗ-ynne the *power* of the Citee. *English Gilds* (E. E. T. S.), p. 355.

7. In *law*: (*a*) Legal capacity: as, the *power* to contract; the *power* of testation, or making a will. (*b*) Legal authority conferred, and enabling one to do what otherwise he could not do; the dominion which one person may exercise over the property of another: as, the *power* of an agent, which is his delegated authority to act in the name or on behalf of his principal. In Roman law, *power* (*potestas*), in its largest sense, was held to comprise the control of the head of the household over slaves, children, descendants, and wife. In its more limited sense, it was used for the control over children and descendants, the power over the wife being distinguished by the name *manus*.

> He had assumed no *powers* to which he was not entitled by his services and peculiar situation. *Prescott*, Ferd. and Isa., ii. 19.

> Henry was a prince who had only to learn the extent of his *powers* in order to attempt to exercise them. *Stubbs*, Medieval and Modern Hist., p. 253.

(*c*) In the law of conveyancing, an authority to do some act in relation to the title to lands or the creation of estates therein or to charges thereon, either conferred by the owner on another or reserved to himself when granting the lands or some interest therein; usually a *power of appointment*, which is the conferring on a person of the power of disposing of an interest in lands, quite irrespective of the fact whether or not he has any interest in the land itself. *Digby*. If the donee of the power has no interest in the land, the power is said to be *collateral*, as distinguished from a *power appendant* or *appurtenant*, as it is called when the interest he may dispose of must be carved out of or reduce his own interest; and from a *power in gross*, as it is called when the interest he may appoint will not take effect until his own interest has terminated: as, a *power* to a tenant for life to appoint the estate after his death among his children. A *general power* is one that may be exercised in favor of any one whatever, even the donee himself; a *special* or *particular power* can be exercised only in favor of a person or some of a class of persons specified in the document creating the power, or for specified purposes: as, a *power* to sell, to exchange, to lease, and the like.

8. A written statement of legal authority; a document guaranteeing legal authority.

> When I said I was empowered, etc., he desired to see my *powers*. *Swift*, Letter, Oct. 10, 1710.

9†. Pecuniary ability; wealth.

> Eche brother other suster thᵗ ben of the fraternite, ȝif he be of *power*, he schal ȝeue somewhat in maintenance of the bretherhede, what hym lyketh. *English Gilds* (E. E. T. S.), p. 4.

10. A large quantity; a great number. [Colloq.]

> I am providing a *power* of pretty things for her against I see her next. *Richardson*, Pamela, II. 389. (*Davies.*)

> They ate a *power*, and they drank bottle after bottle. *Harper's Mag.*, LXXIX. 49.

11. (*a*) [Tr. of ML. *potestas*.] An active faculty of the mind whose exercise is dependent on the will.

> When *power* is applied to the soul, it is used in a larger signification than faculty; for by it we designate the capacities that are acquired, as well as those that are original. *Porter*, Human Intellect, § 36.

(*b*) [Tr. of L. *potentia*.] A capacity for acting or suffering in any determinate way.

> There are nations in the East so enslaved by custom that they seem to have lost all *power* of change except the capability of being destroyed. *W. K. Clifford*, Lectures, I. 105.

12. In *Aristotelian metaph.*, the state of being of that which does not yet exist, but is in germ, ready to exist, the general conditions of its existence being fulfilled; the general principle of existence.

> We say in *power*, as in the wood a statue, and in the whole a part, because it may be brought out; and a theo-

rem not yet discovered, but capable of discovery, which is the actuality. . . . For as a person building is to a builder, and the thing waking to the thing sleeping, and the seeing to him who has his eyes shut though he has sight, and that which is severed from matter to matter, and work done to material unworked, so is act to *power*.
Aristotle, Metaphysics, viii. 6.

13. In *mech.*, that with which work can be done. (*a*) Energy, whether kinetic or potential (as of a head of water or a steam-engine), considered as a commodity to be bought and sold in definite quantities. Hence (since this is usually provided in the kinetic form)—(*b*) Kinetic energy.

If the *power* with which a system is moving at any instant be denoted by T, its expression becomes $T = \frac{1}{2} mv^2$.
B. *Peirce*, Anal. Mechanics, p. 307.

(*c*) The mechanical advantage of a machine. (*d*) A simple machine. (*e*) Mechanical energy as distinguished from hand-labor.

14. In *arith.* and *real alg.*, the result of multiplying a quantity into itself a specified number of times. The first power of a quantity is the quantity itself; the nth power, where n is any positive integer, is the continued product of the quantity taken n times—that is, the quantity composed of n factors each equal to the quantity. A negative power, where n is a negative integer, is the reciprocal of the corresponding positive power: thus,

$$x^{-n} = \frac{1}{x^n}.$$

A fractional power is that root of the power of the quantity denoted by the numerator of the fraction which is denoted by the denominator: thus, $x^{\frac{m}{n}}$ is the nth root of x^m. (See *exponent*.) In imaginary algebra the definition of a power is extended.

15. In *geom.*, the square of the distance of a point from the point of tangency to a given circle of a line through that point. This quantity is said to be the power of the point with respect to the circle.—16. A spiritual being in general. Specifically [*pl.*], in the celestial hierarchy, the sixth order of angels, ranking last in the second triad. The word translates the 'Εξουσίαι (*Potestates*) of Eph. i. 21 and Col. i. 16. See *hierarchy*.

Thrones, dominations, princedoms, virtues, *powers*.
Milton.

The lord of spirits and the prince of *powers*.
2 Mac. iii. 24.

17. A person in authority or exercising great influence in his community.

You have, by fortune and his highness' favours,
Gone slightly o'er low steps and now are mounted
Where *powers* are your retainers.
Shak., Hen. VIII., ii. 4. 113.

Are all teachers? Are all *powers*? 1 Cor. xii. 29.

A *power* is passing from the earth. *Wordsworth*.

18. A government; a governing body.

There is no power but of God; the *powers* that be are ordained of God. Rom. xiii. 1.

19. That which has power; specifically, an army or navy; a military or naval force; a host.

Than com Merlin to Arthur, and bad hym sende for all his *power* in all haste with-oute taryinge.
Merlin (E. E. T. S.), iii. 566.

K. *Rich.* What says Lord Stanley, will he bring his *power*?
Mess. My lord, he doth deny to come.
K. Rich. Off with his son George's head!
Shak., Rich. III., v. 3. 344.

20. A token of subjection to power; in the New Testament, a covering for the head; a veil.

For this cause ought the woman to have *power* [a "sign of authority," revised version] on her head because of the angels. 1 Cor. xi. 10.

21. In *optics*, the degree to which an optical instrument, as a telescope or microscope, magnifies the apparent linear or superficial dimensions of an object. See *magnify*.—22. The eyepiece of a telescope or the objective of a microscope.—**Absolute power**, unlimited power; power uncontrolled by law.—**Abutting power.** See *abut*.—**Accumulation of power.** See *accumulation*.—**Active power.** See *active*.—**Agonistic power**, power in strife.—**Animal power.** See *animal*.—**Animate power**, a faculty of the soul or mind.—**Appetitive power**, a faculty of desiring.—**Apprehensive power**, faculty of cognition.—**Artificial power**, an art considered as a power.—**Augmentative power**, the power of growth.—**Balance of power.** See *balance*.—**Civil power.** Same as *political power*.—**Cognoscitive power.** Same as *apprehensive power*.—**Commanding, directing,** and **executive powers**, three faculties of the mind, in the psychology of Aquinas, of which the first determines what shall be done, the last does it, and the second secures the correspondence of the action with the intention.—**Commensurable in power**, in *math.* See *commensurable*.—**Connate power**, a faculty possessed from birth, not developed by education.—**Corporeal power**, the virtue of an inanimate substance or thing.—**Creative power**, the power of creating.—**Doctrine of enumerated powers, of implied powers.** See *enumerate*, *imply*.—**Emissive, entitative, existent power.** See the adjectives.—**Essential power**, power in an essence to receive actual existence.—**Existential power**, power in a thing that actually exists to do or become something.—**Free power**, a faculty which the mind is free to exercise or not.—**Generative power**, the faculty of propagating the kind.—**Habitual power**, power resulting from custom.—**High power.** See *objective*, n., 3.—**Impassive power**, the power of resisting a force tending to produce a change.—**Inanimate power**, a power not belonging to the soul.—**Incommensurable in power.** See *incommensurable*.—**In power**, in control of the administrative and executive functions of a government: a phrase noting the position of ministers or political parties when a majority vote or some other influence has given them the ascendancy.

In power a servant, out of power a friend.
Lord Melcombe, quoted in Pope's Epil. to Satires, ii. 161.

He [Pitt] had often declared that, while he was *in power*, England should never make a peace of Utrecht.
Macaulay, Frederic the Great.

Irrational power, as defined by the advocates of the freedom of the will, a power which is determined to one or another of two opposites, so that it either can act but cannot refrain, or can refrain but cannot act.—**Judicial, justiciary, legislative, locomotive power.** See the adjectives.—**Logical power**, logical possibility; the not involving any contradiction.—**Low power.** See *objective*, n., 3.—**Magnetic rotatory power.** See *magnetic*.—**Medicinal power**, the power of healing.—**Ministerial powers.** See *ministerial*.—**Mixed power**, a power of changing the subject of the power itself; a power at once active and passive: *mixed act* is used in an analogous sense.—**Motive power.** See *motive*.—**Natural power.** (*a*) Power to produce a natural motion. (*b*) Power within nature, not supernatural. Also called *physical power*.—**Nutritive power**, power of assimilating nutriment.—**Obediential power**, the power of a person, an animal, or a thing to do that which is beyond his or its natural powers, in consequence of miraculous interposition.—**Objective power.** See *objective*.—**Occult power**, an occult virtue or property of a natural thing. See *occult*.—**Passive power.** See *passive*.—**Perspective power**, the faculty of supersensuous cognition.—**Physical power.** Same as *natural power*.—**Police power.** See *police*.—**Political power**, power of governing; influence in the government.—**Power of attorney.** See *attorney*².—**Power of contradiction**, the power in an individual of being determined to one or the other of two contradictory predicates. The corresponding power in a genus to be determined to one or the other of two species is not called by this name.—**Power of life and death**, authority to inflict or to remit capital punishment.—**Power of points.** See *point*¹.—**Power of sale**, a clause inserted in securities for debt, conferring on the creditor a power to sell the subject of the security if the debt is not paid as specified; also, in wills, conferring on the executor authority to convert property into money.—**Power of the keys.** See *key*¹.—**Power to license.** See *license*.—**Practical power**, the power of doing something; the power conferred by a practical science.—**Pure power**, force which wants all form; the state of first matter.—**Rational power**, a faculty connected with the reason, as that part of the soul which distinguishes man from the beasts.—**Real power**, a power of doing, or suffering, or becoming: opposed to *logical power*.—**Receptive power.** Same as *subjective power*.—**Resolving power.** See *objective*, n., 3.—**Rhetorical power**, the power of eloquence.—**Rotatory power.** See *rotatory*.—**Sensitive power**, the capacity of sensation.—**Signatory power.** See *signatory*.—**Sovereign power**, the supreme power in a state.—**Subjective power**, the capability of a subject of receiving contradictory predicates, or of being determined in different ways: usually confounded with *passive power*.—**The powers, the great powers of Europe**, in *modern diplomacy*, phrases designating the principal nations of Europe. The great powers long recognized were Great Britain, France, Austria, Prussia, and Russia. Later Prussia was replaced by the new German Empire, Italy was recognized, and in 1887 Spain was admitted to the European concert.—**Transmutative power**, the power of producing a change in an object.—**Treaty-making power.** See *treaty*.—**Violent power**, the power of producing violent motion.—**Vital power**, the power of living. = **Syn.** *Power, Strength, Force*. *Power* and *strength* may be active or inactive; *force* is active. *Strength* is rather an inward capability; *force* an outward; *power* may be either: we speak of *strength* of character, *power* of habit, *force* of will; *strength* of timber, *power* of a steam-engine, *force* of a projectile.

power²†, *a.* An obsolete form of *poor*.

power³†, *v.* An obsolete form of *pour*¹.

powerable† (pou'ėr-a-bl), *a.* [< *power*¹ + *-able*.] Endowed with power; powerful.

That you may see how *powerable* time is in altering tongs as all things else. *Camden*, Remains, Languages.

poweration (pou-e-rā'shon), *n.* [< *power*¹ + *-ation*.] A great quantity. *Halliwell*. [Prov. Eng.]

power-capstan (pou'ėr-kap"stan), *n.* See *capstan*.

powered (pou'ėrd), *a.* [< *power* + *-ed*².] Having power (of a specified kind or degree): used especially in composition: as, high-*powered* or low-*powered* rifles or guns. The measure of a gun's power is its muzzle-velocity, or the velocity with which the projectile leaves the muzzle. This in modern guns is about 2,000 feet per second, but there is no exact dividing-line between guns of high power and those of low power.

powerful (pou'ėr-fůl), *a.* [< *power* + *-ful*.] 1. Exerting great force or power; able to produce great physical effects; strong; efficient: as, a *powerful* engine; a *powerful* blow; a *powerful* medicine.

The cedar . . .
Whose top-branch overpeer'd Jove's spreading tree,
And kept low shrubs from winter's *powerful* wind.
Shak., 3 Hen. VI., v. 2. 15.

When first that sun too *powerful* beams displays,
It draws up vapours which obscure its rays.
Pope, Essay on Criticism, l. 470.

2. Having great authority; puissant; potent; mighty: as, a *powerful* nation.

The Lords of Ross, Beaumond, and Willoughby,
With all their *powerful* friends, are fled to him.
Shak., Rich. II., ii. 2. 55.

He that had seen Pericles lead the Athenians which way he listed haply would have said he had been their prince; and yet he was but a *powerfull* and eloquent man in a Democracy. *Milton*, Prelatical Episcopacy.

3. Characterized by great intellectual power.

In his turn, he knew to prize
Lord Marmion's *powerful* mind, and wise.
Scott, Marmion, iv. 13.

4. Having great influence or moral power; cogent; efficacious.

God makes sometimes a plain and simple man's good life as *powerful* as the most eloquent sermon.
Donne, Sermons, v.

What had I
To oppose against such *powerful* arguments?
Milton, S. A., l. 862.

5. Great; numerous; numerically large. Compare *power*¹, 10. [Colloq.]

This piano was sort o' fiddle like—only bigger—and with a *powerful* heap of wire strings.
Carlton, New Purchase, II. 8. (*Bartlett.*)

= **Syn.** Puissant, forcible, cogent, influential; vigorous, robust, sturdy.

powerful (pou'ėr-fůl), *adv.* [< *powerful*, *a.*] Very: as, *powerful* good; *powerful* weak. [Local, U. S.]

powerfully (pou'ėr-fůl-i), *adv.* In a powerful manner; with great force or energy; potently; strongly.

All which, sir, though I most *powerfully* and potently believe, yet I hold it not honesty to have it thus set down.
Shak., Hamlet, ii. 2. 203.

powerfulness (pou'ėr-fůl-nes), *n.* The character of being powerful; force; power; might; potency; efficacy.

The *powerfulness* of Christ's birth consists in this, that he is made of God. *Donne*, Sermons, iii.

power-hammer (pou'ėr-ham"ėr), *n.* A hammer actuated by machinery.

power-house (pou'ėr-hous), *n.* In water-works, and other works in which machinery is driven by power from steam, electric, or other prime motors, a building especially provided to contain the prime motor or motors from which power is conveyed to the driven machinery by a main shaft and gearing, or by a belt or cable.

power-lathe (pou'ėr-lāтн), *n.* A lathe in which the live head-stock mandrel is driven by steam, water, or other power, independently of the operator. The transmission of power from line-shafting and counter-shafts to lathes is usually performed by pulley-and-belt mechanism, variable speed being secured by cone-pulleys.

powerless (pou'ėr-les), *a.* [< *power* + *-less*.] Lacking power; weak; impotent; unable to produce any effect.

I give you welcome with a *powerless* hand,
But with a heart full of unstained love.
Shak., K. John, ii. 1. 15.

With no will,
Powerless and blind, must he some fate fulfil,
Nor knowing what he is doing any more.
William Morris, Earthly Paradise, I. 403.

powerlessly (pou'ėr-les-li), *adv.* In a powerless manner; without power; weakly.

powerlessness (pou'ėr-les-nes), *n.* The state or character of being powerless; absence or lack of power.

power-loom (pou'ėr-löm), *n.* A loom worked by water, steam, or some other mechanical power.

power-machine (pou'ėr-ma-shēn"), *n.* A machine actuated by a mechanical force, as distinguished from one worked by hand.

power-press (pou'ėr-pres), *n.* A printing-press worked by steam, gas, or other mechanical agency, as distinguished from a hand-press.

powitch (pou'ich), *n.* [Chinook Indian.] The Oregon crab-apple, *Pyrus rivularis*, a small tree often forming dense thickets, the wood very hard, and the fruit eaten by the Indians.

powke-needle† (pouk'nē"dl), *n.* Same as *poukenel*.

powldron†, *n.* An obsolete form of *pauldron*.

powler†, *n.* An obsolete form of *poller*.

pownage†, *n.* An obsolete form of *pannage*.

powney (pou'ni), *n.* A Scotch form of *pony*.

powst, powse¹†. Obsolete forms of *pulse*¹.

powse²†, *n.* An obsolete form of *pulse*².

powsoned†, *a.* See *pounson*.

powsoning†, *n.* See *pounsoning*.

powsowdy (pou-sou'di), *n.* [Also *powsowdie*; appar. < *pow*¹, = *poll*¹, + *sodden*.] Any mixture of incongruous sorts of food. Specifically—(*a*) Sheep's-head broth. (*b*) Porridge. (*c*) A Yorkshire pudding. (*d*) A mixed drink. See the quotation. [Prov. Eng. or Scotch in all uses.]

The principal charm of the "gathering" [in Westmoreland] was not assuredly diminished to the men by the anticipation of excellent ale, . . . and possibly of still more excellent *pow-sowdy* (a combination of ale, spirits, and spices). *De Quincey*, Autobiog. Sketches, II. 109. (*Davies.*)

powstet, *n.* See *poust.*

powting-clotht, *n.* A kerchief for the head or neck.

A crosse-cloath, as they tearme it, a *powting-cloth*, plagula. *Withals*, Dict. (ed. 1608), p. 275. (*Nares.*)

powwow (pou'wou), *n.* [Formerly also *pawwow, pawwaw;* Amer. Ind.] 1. As applied to the North American aborigines: (*a*) A priest; a conjurer.

When all other means fail to recover their sick, they send for their *Pawaw* or Priest, who, sitting down by them, expects a Fee, and works accordingly, calling sometimes on one God, sometimes on another, beating his naked breast till he sweat and be almost out of breath.
Hist., Geog., etc., *Dict.*, ed. Collier, 2d ed. (1701), s. v. [New York.

Let them come if they like, be it sagamore, sachem, or *pow-wow.* *Longfellow*, Miles Standish, i.

Many a church member saw I, walking behind the music, that has danced in the same measure with me when Somebody was fiddler, and, it might be, an Indian *powwow* or a Lapland wizard changing hands with us!
Hawthorne, Scarlet Letter, xxii.

(*b*) A conjuration performed for the cure of diseases. (*c*) A dance, feast, or other public celebration preliminary to a grand hunt, a council, a war expedition, or some similar undertaking. Hence—2. Any uproarious meeting or conference; a meeting where there is more noise than deliberation. [Colloq., U. S.]

powwow (pou'wou), *v. i.* [< *powwow*, *n.*] 1. As applied to the North American aborigines, to perform a ceremony with conjurations for the cure of diseases and for other purposes.

And if any shall hereafter *Powwow*, both he that shall *Powwow*, & he that shall procure him to *Powwow*, shall pay 20s. apeece.
T. Shepard, Clear Sunshine of the Gospel, p. 5.

The Angekok of the tribe [of Esquimaux] . . . prescribes or *pow-wows* in sickness and over wounds.
Kane, Arctic Explorations, xliii.

Hence—2. To hold a consultation; deliberate over events. [Colloq., U. S.]

We would go to the cave and *pow-wow* over what we had done. *S. L. Clemens*, Huckleberry Finn, iii.

The young bucks, having had insufficient rations, are now out hunting for game. When they can, they will come in and *pow-wow* with Generals Sheridan and Miles.
New York Herald.

3. To hold any noisy meeting. [Colloq., U. S.]

pox (poks), *n.* [An irreg. spelling and adaptation of *pocks*, pl. of *pock:* see *pock*[1].] A disease characterized by eruptive pocks or pustules upon the body. As used by the writers of the sixteenth and seventeenth centuries, the word generally means *smallpox*, but also, and especially in later use, the *French pox*, or syphilis. See *chicken-pox, smallpox, syphilis.*

In al the Ilandes of this Archipelagus rayneth the disease of saynt Iob (whiche wee caule the frenche *poxe*) more then in any other place in the worlde.
R. Eden, tr. of Antonio Pigafetta (First Books on America, [ed. Arber, p. 260).

A number here [in Egypt] be afflicted with sore eyes, either by the reflecting heat, the salt dust of the soyle, or excessive venery: for the *pocks* is uncredible frequent among them. *Sandys*, Travailes, p. 85.

A pox on, a pox of, a plague on: a mild imprecation much used by the old dramatists.

Ros. O that your face were not so full of O's!
Kath. A pox of that jest! *Shak.*, L. L. L., v. 2. 46.

I must needs fight yet; for I find it concerns me.
A pox on 't! I must fight.
Fletcher, Wildgoose Chase, ii. 3.

poxt (poks), *v. t.* [< *pox*, *n.*] To communicate the pox or venereal disease to. *Pope*, Imit. of Horace, II. i. 84.

pox-stone (poks'stōn), *n.* A very hard stone of a gray color found in some of the Staffordshire mines. *Halliwell.*

poy (poi), *n.* [Also *puy;* by apheresis from OF. *apoi, appoi*, F. *appui*, support, prop: see *appui* and *pew*[2].] 1. A prop or support.—2. A rope-dancers' pole. *Johnson.*—3. A pole to impel or steer a boat. *Halliwell.* [Prov. Eng.]

poy-bird (poi'bėrd), *n.* Same as *poe-bird. Worcester.*

poynadot, *n.* See *poinado.*

poynauntt, *a.* An obsolete form of *poignant.*

poyndt, *v. t.* An obsolete form of *poind.*

poynet (poi'net), *n.* 1. A bodkin or punch.—2. An aglet or tag.
Also *poinette.*

poyntt, poyntet, *n.* and *v.* Obsolete forms of *point*[1].

poyntellt, *n.* An obsolete form of *pointel.*

poyntementt, *n.* A variant of *pointment.*

poyou (po.'ö), *n.* [Native name.] The six-banded armadillo, *Dasypus sexcinctus*, or *D. encoubert.* See *armadillo*, 1.

poyset, *n.* An obsolete form of *poise.*

poz (poz), *a.* Same as *pos.*

I will have a regiment to myself, that 's *poz.*
Thackeray, Catharine.

pozet, *v.* An obsolete form of *pose*[3].

pozzo (pot'sō), *n.*; pl. *pozzi* (-sē). [It., a well, < L. *puteus*, a well: see *pit*[1].] In Venice, one

Pozzo.

of the curbs or heads of the cisterns which are filled with water from the neighboring mainland; a well-curb: a common abbreviation of *vera di pozzo.*

pozzuolana (pot"sö-ọ-lä'nä), *n.* [It., also *pozzolana*, < *Pozzuoli:* see def.] A material of volcanic origin, first found at Pozzuoli, near Naples, and afterward in many other localities, and of great importance in the manufacture of hydraulic cement. It is a volcanic ash, generally somewhat pulverulent, of various colors, and of different qualities in different localities. It closely resembles in origin and quality the so-called trass of Germany and the Netherlands. These substances consist chiefly of silicate of alumina with a small percentage of the alkalis, oxids of iron, etc. For making cement the pozzuolana is pulverized and mixed with lime and sand. The use of this material was well known to the Romans, and the preparation of hydraulic cement is described in detail by Vitruvius. Also *pozzolana, puzzolana, puzzuolana, puzzolite, puzzolano.*

pozzuolanic (pot"sö-ọ-lan'ik), *a.* Consisting of or resembling pozzuolana.

pp. An abbreviation (*a*) of *pages* (as *p.* for *page*); (*b*) of *past participle* or *perfect participle;* (*c*) of *pianissimo.*

P. P. C. An abbreviation of the French phrase *pour prendre congé*, 'to take leave': written upon a visiting-card to indicate that the bearer or sender is making a farewell call or otherwise bidding farewell to the recipient of the card. Sometimes English *T. T. L.*, to take leave, is used instead.

ppr. An abbreviation of *present participle.*

pr. An abbreviation of *pronoun.*

Pr. An abbreviation of *Provençal.*

praam (präm), *n.* See *pram*[1].

practict (prak'tik), *a.* and *n.* [I. *a.* Also *practick;* < OF. *practic, practiq*, usually *pratiq, pratique*, F. *pratique* = Pr. *practic* = Sp. *práctico* = Pg. It. *pratico* (cf. D. *praktisch* = G. *practisch, praktisch* = Sw. Dan. *praktisk*), < LL. *practicus*, active, < Gr. πρακτικός, of or pertaining to action, concerned with action or business, active, practical, < πράσσειν (√ πραγ-), do. Cf. *pragmatic, praxis*, etc., from the same source, and see *prat, praty, pretty.* II. *n.* 1. Also *practick, practique, pratic, prattic, pratique*, < ME. *practike, practique, praktike*, < OF. *practique, pratique, prattique*, F. *pratique* = Pr. *practica* = Sp. *práctica* = Pg. It. *pratica* = D. *praktijk* = G. *practik, praktik* = Sw. *praktik*, < ML. *practica*, practical or familiar knowledge, execution, accomplishment, intrigue, practice, < Gr. πρακτική, practical knowledge, fem. of πρακτικός, practical: see I. Cf. *practice* and *pratique.*] I. *a.* 1. Concerned with action; practical, as distinguished from theoretical.

The art and *practic* part of life
Must be the mistress to this theoric.
Shak., Hen. V., i. 1. 51.

Discipline is the *practick* work of preaching directed and apply'd as is most requisite to particular duty.
Milton, Church-Government, i. 1.

2. Skilled; skilful; practised.

Right *practicke* was Sir Priamond in fight,
And throughly skild in use of shield and speare.
Spenser, F. Q., IV. iii. 7.

See if I hit not all their *practic* observance, with which they lime twigs to catch their fantastic lady-birds.
B. Jonson, Cynthia's Revels, v. 2.

II. *n.* 1. Practice, as opposed to theory; practical experience.

Spareth for no man,
And teche us yonge men of youre *praktike.*
Chaucer, Wife of Bath's Tale, l. 187.

Poison thyself, thou foul empoisoner!
Of thine own *practique* drink the theory!
Middleton and Rowley, Fair Quarrel, iii. 2.

2. One concerned with action or practice, as opposed to one concerned with theory. See the quotation.

These Essenes were again divided into *Practicks* and Theoricks. The first spent their time in Handy-Crafts, the latter only in Meditation. The *Practicks* had Dinner and Supper; the Theoricks, only Supper.
Hist., Geog., etc., *Dict.*, ed. Collier, 2d ed. (1701), s. v. [Essenes.

practicability (prak"ti-ka-bil'i-ti), *n.* [< *practicable* + *-ity* (see *-bility*).] The state or character of being practicable; feasibility; capacity for being practised.

They all attend the worship of the kirk, as often as a visit from their minister or the *practicability* of travelling gives them opportunity. *Johnson*, Jour. to Western Isles.

This third method brings the attempt within the degree of *practicability* by a single person.
Mason, Supplement to Johnson's Dict., p. vi.

practicable (prak'ti-ka-bl), *a.* [< F. *praticable* = Sp. *practicable* = Pg. *praticavel* = It. *praticabile* = G. Sw. Dan. *praktikabel*, < ML. **practicabilis*, < *practicare*, execute, practise: see *practise.*] 1. Capable of being performed or effected; performable; possible in point of execution.

It is sufficient to denominate the way *practicable;* for we esteem that to be such which in the trial oftener succeeds than misses. *Dryden*, Essay on Dram. Poesy.

In seeking the causes of change which worked through Solon, and also made *practicable* the reorganization he initiated, we shall find them to lie in the direct and indirect influences of trade. *H. Spencer*, Prin. of Sociol., § 488.

The rule for us, in whatever case, is one: to make the best *practicable* use of the best available means for thinking truly and acting rightly.
Gladstone, Might of Right, p. 185.

2. Capable of being practised.

An heroick poem should be more like a glass of nature, figuring a more *practicable* virtue to us than was done by the ancients. *Dryden.*

3. Capable of being used: as, a *practicable* road; a *practicable* breach.

We descended the hill to the north, by a very easy way, *practicable* by camels.
Pococke, Description of the East, I. 36.

Nemours, finding it impossible to force the works in this quarter, rode along their front in search of some *practicable* passage. *Prescott*, Ferd. and Isa., ii. 12.

4. In *theat.*, capable of real use, in distinction from something merely simulated: as, a *practicable* door, bridge, or window.—5. Suitable for practice, fulfilment, or execution; hence, desirable; advantageous.

Naturally, people did not tell each other all they felt and thought about young Grandcourt's advent; on no subject is this openness found prudentially *practicable.*
George Eliot, Daniel Deronda, ix.

= **Syn.** 1. *Practical, Practicable* (see *impracticable*). *Possible, Practicable. Possible* notes that which may or might be performed if the necessary powers or means can or could be obtained; *practicable* is limited to things which may be performed by the means that one possesses or can obtain.

practicableness (prak'ti-ka-bl-nes), *n.* The character of being practicable; practicability.

practicably (prak'ti-ka-bli), *adv.* In a practicable manner; with action or performance.

practical (prak'ti-kal), *a.* [< *practic* + *-al.*] 1. Relating or pertaining to action, practice, or use: opposed to *theoretical, speculative*, or *ideal.* (*a*) Engaged in practice or action; concerned with material rather than ideal considerations.

Nothing can be conceived more whimsical than the conferences which took place between the first literary man and the first *practical* man of the age. . . . The great poet would talk of nothing but treaties and guarantees, and the great king of nothing but metaphors and rhymes.
Macaulay, Frederic the Great.

(*b*) Educated by practice or experience: as, a *practical* gardener. (*c*) Derived from experience: as, *practical* skill: *practical* knowledge. (*d*) Used, or such as may advantageously be used, in practice; capable of being used or turned to account; contributing to one's material advantage; possessing utility.

Time and experience may forme him to a more *practical* way than that he is in of University lectures and erudition. *Evelyn*, Diary, March 5, 1673.

Little Phœbe was one of those persons who possess, as their exclusive patrimony, the gift of *practical* arrangement. *Hawthorne*, Seven Gables, v.

(*e*) Exemplified in practice.

The moral code, while it expanded in theoretical catholicity, had contracted in *practical* application.
Lecky, Europ. Morals, I. 309.

(*f*) Spent in practice; devoted to action or material pursuits.

The idea of a future life is one which we ourselves read into the Bible; the idea which we find there, pervading it from first to last, is one which belongs altogether to *practical* life. *J. R. Seeley*, Nat. Religion, p. 165.

2. In effect and result; to all intents and purposes; equivalent to (something) in force or influence; virtual: as, a victory may be a *practical* defeat.

That imagined "otherwise" which is our *practical* heaven. *George Eliot*, Middlemarch, II. 49.

We are not to be guilty of that *practical* atheism which, seeing no guidance for human affairs but its own limited foresight, endeavours itself to play the god, and decide what will be good for mankind, and what bad. *H. Spencer*, Social Statics, p. 518.

The great advantage of our *practical* republic over your avowed republic . . . is the power of changing the actual ruler at any moment, while you must keep the chief magistrate once chosen till the end of a fixed term. *E. A. Freeman*, Amer. Lects., p. 390.

Practical agriculture, arithmetic, chemistry, cognition, geometry, etc. See the nouns.—**Practical conviction**, a conviction relating to morals or practice.—**Practical joke**, a jest carried into action; a trick played upon a person, to annoy him and amuse the performers and others.—**Practical judgment**, the judgment that something can or ought to be done.—**Practical knowledge**, knowledge the end of which is action.—**Practical location**, in the *law of real property*, the actual location or establishment (of a boundary-line) with the continued acquiescence of the adjoining owners.—**Practical logic**, logic as an art teaching how to reason well.—**Practical metaphysics**, the theory of the nature of duty and the end of living.—**Practical meteorology, philosophy, possibility, power,** etc. See the nouns.—**Practical Proposition**, the statement of the solution of a problem.—**Practical reason**, the thinking will: the will determining itself according to general laws; that which gives imperative laws of freedom.—**Practical sentiments**, sentiments accompanying the conative powers. =**Syn.** 1. *Practical, Practicable.* See *impracticable*.

practicalist (prak'ti-kal-ist), *n.* [< *practical* + *-ist.*] One who derives his knowledge from or relies upon experience or practice; an empiric. [Rare.]

practicality (prak-ti-kal'i-ti), *n.* [< *practical* + *-ity.*] The character of being practical, or concerned with material considerations; practicalness.

The fair Susan, stirring up her indolent enthusiasm into *practicality*, was very successful in finding Spanish lessons, and the like, for these distressed men. *Carlyle*, Sterling, x. (*Davies.*)

practicalize (prak'ti-kal-īz), *v. t.*; pret. and pp. *practicalized*, ppr. *practicalizing*. [< *practical* + *-ize.*] To make practical; convert into actual work or use. [Rare.]

While he [my father] saved me from the demoralizing effects of school life, he made no effort to provide me with any sufficient substitute for its *practicalizing* influences. *J. S. Mill*, Autobiography, p. 37.

practically (prak'ti-kal-i), *adv.* 1. In a practical manner; from a practical point of view; by actual experience; not merely theoretically: as, to be *practically* acquainted with a business.

Not childhood alone, but the young man till thirty, never feels *practically* that he is mortal. *Lamb*, New Year's Eve.

Differences of definition are logically unimportant; but *practically* they sometimes produce the most momentous effects. *Macaulay*, Mitford's Hist. Greece.

2. In effect; actually, so far as results and relations are concerned; as a matter of fact.

Eventually, the head executive agent [in Florence], nominally re-elected from time to time, but *practically* permanent, became, in the person of Cosmo de' Medici, the founder of an inherited leadership. *H. Spencer*, Prin. of Sociol., § 488.

Formally, the Imperial power was bestowed by a special grant of the Senate: *practically*, it was the prize of any Roman that could grasp it. *E. A. Freeman*, Amer. Lects., p. 337.

practicalness (prak'ti-kal-nes), *n.* Practicality.

practice, *v.* See *practise*.

practice (prak'tis), *n.* [Formerly also *practise*; < ME. **practise*, *prattise*; < *practice, practise, v.*; a later noun taking the place of the earlier noun *practic*. The spelling *practice* (with *c* instead of *s*) is appar. in conformity with *practic, practical*, etc.] 1. Action; exercise; performance; the process of accomplishing or carrying out; performance or execution as opposed to speculation or theory.

It was with difficulty that he [Archimedes] was induced to stoop from speculation to *practice*. *Macaulay*, Lord Bacon.

We study Ethics, as Aristotle says, for the sake of *Practice*; and in *practice* we are concerned with particulars. H. *Sidgwick*, Methods of Ethics, p. 191.

The world of *practice* depends on man in quite a different sense from that in which nature, or the world of experience, does so. *T. H. Green*, Prolegomena to Ethics, § 87.

2. An action; act; proceeding; doing: in the plural, generally in a bad sense.

Heauens make our presence and our *practises*
Pleasant and helpfull to him.
Shak., Hamlet (folio 1623), ii. 2.

Our *practises* haue hitherto beene but assayes, and are still to be amended. *Capt. John Smith*, Works, I. 59.

Loose principles, and bad *practices*, and extravagant desires naturally dispose men to endeavour changes and alterations, in hopes of bettering themselves by them. *Stillingfleet*, Sermons, II. iv.

3. Frequent or customary performance; habit; usage; custom.

When I was a Student as you are, my *Practice* was to borrow rather than buy some sort of Books. *Howell*, Letters, ii. 21.

He [a Maronite priest] prepared a supper for us, and we lay on the top of the house, which is a very common *practice* in this country during the summer season. *Pococke*, Description of the East, II. i. 99.

4. The regular pursuit of some employment or business; the exercise of a profession; hence, the business of a practitioner: as, to dispose of one's *practice*; a physician in lucrative *practice*.

Some lawyers are already said to be called upon either to bring certificates of their communicating, or to pay their fines and give over their *practice*. *Court and Times of Charles I.*, I. 65.

His predecessor in this career had "bettered" himself . . . by seeking the *practice* of some large town. *Trollope*, Doctor Thorne.

5. Exercise for instruction or discipline; training; drill: as, *practice* makes perfect.

Proceed in *practice* with my younger daughter;
She 's apt to learn and thankful for good turns.
Shak., T. of the S., ii. 1. 165.

Practice is the exercise of an art, or the application of a science, in life, which application is itself an art, for it is not every one who is able to apply all he knows. *Sir W. Hamilton*, Metaph., x.

6. The state of being used; customary use; actual application.

Reduc'd to *practice*, his beloved rule
Would only prove him a consummate fool.
Cowper, Conversation, l. 139.

7. Skill acquired through use; experience; dexterity.

This disease is beyond my *practice*. *Shak.*, Macbeth, v. 1. 65.

What *practice*, howsoe'er expert, . . .
Hath power to give thee as thou wert?
Tennyson, In Memoriam, lxxv.

8. Artifice; treachery; a plot; a stratagem.

And in this first yere also this realme was troubled with ciuile sedition, and the craftie *practises* of the Frenchmen. *Grafton*, Hen. IV., an. 1.

His vows were but mere courtship; all his service
But *practice* how to entrap a credulous lady.
Fletcher (and another), Queen of Corinth, i. 2.

About this time were *Practices* plotted against Queen Elizabeth in behalf of the Queen of Scots, chiefly by Francis Throgmorton, eldest Son of John Throgmorton, Justice of Chester. *Baker*, Chronicles, p. 362.

But Vivien . . . clung to him and hugg'd him close
And call'd him dear protector in her fright,
Nor yet forgot her *practice* in her fright,
But wrought upon his mood and hugg'd him close.
Tennyson, Merlin and Vivien.

9. In *arith.*, a rule for expeditiously solving questions in proportion, or rather for abridging the operation of multiplying quantities expressed in different denominations, as when it is required to find the value of a number of articles at so many pounds, shillings, and pence each.—10. The form and manner of conducting legal proceedings, whether at law, or in equity, or in criminal procedure, according to the principles of law and the rules of the court; those legal rules which direct the course of proceeding to bring parties into court, and the course of the court after they are brought in. *Bishop*. *Pleading* is generally considered as another branch of the law, because it involves questions of substantive right.—**Corrupt and Illegal Practices Prevention Act**. See *corrupt*.—**In practice** (or **out of practice**). (*a*) In (or not in) the actual performance or exercise (of some function or occupation): as, a physician who is *in practice*. (*b*) Hence, in possession of (or lacking) that skill or facility which comes from the continuous exercise of bodily or mental power.—**Practice Act**, a name under which are known statutes of several of the United States, regulating procedure of the courts in civil cases.—**Practice cases, practice reports**, cases or reports of cases decided on questions of practice, as distinguished from those decided on the merits of controversies.—**Privateer practice**. Same as *privateerism*.—**To break of a habit or practice**. See *break*.—**To put in practice**, to apply practically; execute; carry out.

Their conceits are [not] the fittest things to bee *put in practice*, or their own countenances [to] maintaine Plantations. *Capt. John Smith*, Works, II. 242.

=**Syn.** 3. *Habit, Usage*, etc. See *custom*.—5. *Practice, Experience*. *Practice* is sometimes erroneously used for *experience*, which is a much broader word. *Practice* is the repetition of an act: as, to become a skilled marksman by *practice*. *Experience* is, by derivation, a going clear through, and may mean action, but much oftener views the person as acted upon, taught, disciplined, by what befalls him.

practiced, practicer. See *practised, practiser*.

practice-ship (prak'tis-ship), *n.* A ship used for the training of boys and young seamen.

Sailing cutters cluster about a long wharf that reaches deep water, and holds in safe moorings the *practice-ship* Constellation and the school-ship Santee. *Harper's Mag.*, LXXVII. 168.

practician (prak-tish'an), *n.* [< OF. *practicien, praticien*, F. *praticien*, a practiser, practitioner, as adj. practising, practical; as *practic* + *-ian*.] 1†. A practitioner.

He was ane right Courticiane,
And in the Law ane *practiciane*.
Sir D. Lyndsay, Squyer Meldrum (E. E. T. S.), l. 1636.

2. One who practises or performs, in distinction from one who theorizes or speculates.

They . . . must shun, on one hand, the blind pride of the fanatic theorist, and, on the other, the no less blind pride of the libertine *practician*. *Guizot*, Hist. Civilization (trans., ed. Appleton, 1872), I. 84.

practick†, *a.* and *n.* See *practic*.

practics† (prak'tiks), *n.* [Pl. of *practic*.] The name formerly given to the reported decisions of the Court of Session in Scotland with reference to their authority in fixing and proving the practice and consuetudinary rules of law. They are now termed *decisions*. Also *practiques*.

The latter spoke disparagingly of Sir James Balfour's "*practiques*." *Quarterly Rev.*, CXLVI. 60.

practisant† (prak'ti-zant), *n.* [< OF. *practisant*, ppr. of *practiser*, practise: see *practise, v.*] One who practises or acts; an agent; especially, an agent in treachery; a confederate.

Here enter'd Pucelle and her *practisants*. *Shak.*, 1 Hen. VI., iii. 2. 20.

practise, practice (prak'tis), *v.*; pret. and pp. *practised, practiced*, ppr. *practising, practicing*. [< ME. *practisen, prattisen* (= D. *praktiseren* = Sw. *praktisera* = Dan. *praktisere*), < OF. *practiser, pratiser* (ML. *practizare*), for the usual *practiquer, pratiquer*, F. *pratiquer* = Pr. *proticar* = Sp. *practicar* = Pg. *praticar* = It. *praticare*, < ML. *practicare, praticare*, do, perform, execute, propose, practise, exercise, be conversant with, contrive, conspire, etc., < *practica*, practical affairs, business, etc.: see *practic*.] I. *trans.* 1. To put into action or practice; execute; perform; enact.

I laugh to see your ladyship so fond
To think that you have aught but Talbot's shadow
Whereon to *practise* your severity.
Shak., 1 Hen. VI., ii. 3. 47.

And (strange to tell!) he *practis'd* what he preach'd. *Armstrong*, Art of Preserving Health, iv.

He *practised* every pass and ward,
To thrust, to strike, to feint, to guard.
Scott, L. of the L., v. 15.

Things learned on earth we shall *practise* in heaven. *Browning*, Old Pictures in Florence.

2. To do or perform frequently or habitually; make a practice of; observe or follow usually: as, to *practise* the Christian virtues; to *practise* deception.

The lawe of god is litel studied, . . . lesse kept & taught; but the olde testament for wynnyng of tythes & offryngis is sumwhat *practised*. *Wyclif*, Office of Curates (E. E. T. S.), xxv.

I have pardon'd,
And pardon'd, and by that have made her fit
To *practise* new sins, not repent the old.
Beau. and Fl., King and no King, i. 1.

Why the Essenes, as an orthodox Jewish sect, should have *practised* any secrecy, Josephus would have found it hard to say. *De Quincey*, Essenes, i.

3†. To make use of; frequent.

The court he *practised*, not the courtier's art. *Dryden*, Abs. and Achit., i. 825.

After having *practised* the Paris Coaches for four mouths, I once rid in the easiest Chariot of my Lord's, which came from England. *Lister*, Journey to Paris, p. 12.

4. To exercise or pursue as a profession, art, or occupation: as, to *practise* law.

2 *Fish*. Canst thou catch any fishes, then?
Per. I never *practised* it. *Shak.*, Pericles, ii. 1. 71.

The art of architecture continues to be *practised* with considerable success in parts of India remote from European influence. *J. Fergusson*, Hist. Indian Arch., p. 35.

5. To exercise one's self in, with the object of acquiring skill or experience; study or learn by repeated performance: as, to *practise* a piece of music.

Perhaps the ladies will condescend to hear a march and chorus, which some recruits are *practising* against his majesty comes to the camp. *Sheridan* (?), The Camp, ii. 3.

I wish I had ever *practised* a love scene—I doubt I shall make a poor figure. *Sheridan*, The Duenna, ii. 2.

6. To cause to practise; teach by practice or exercise; train; drill.

But *practise* him a little in men, and brush him ore with good companie, and hee shall out ballance those glisterers as much as a solid substance do's a feather, or Gold Goldlace. *Bp. Earle*, Micro-cosmographie, A Downe-right Scholler.

Whoso is to rule over his passions in maturity must be *practised* in ruling over his passions during youth.
H. Spencer, Social Statics, p. 206.

So soon as knowledge of this kind has been attained, the captain *practises* his company in all the phases of war.
Fortnightly Rev., N. S., XLIII. 24.

7. To scheme; plot; contrive craftily or treacherously.

My uncle *practises* more harm to me.
Shak., K. John, iv. 1. 20.

What do you read? Is it yet worth your care,
If not your fear, what you find *practised* there?
B. *Jonson*, Catiline, v. 4.

8†. To influence; entice; tamper with; bribe.

The Switzers, being *practised* under hand by a great summe of money, . . . did mutinously demand their pay.
Coryat, Crudities, I. 110.

To *practise* the city into an address to the queen. *Swift.*

9†. To make; construct; build.

A door or window so called [Venetian] from being much *practised* at Venice, by Palladio and others.
Pope, Moral Essays, iv. 36, note.

I copied an inscription set up at the end of a great road, which was *practised* through an immense solid rock by bursting it asunder with gunpowder.
Walpole, To Richard West, Nov. 11, 1739.

II. *intrans.* 1. To perform certain acts repeatedly or usually; exercise, train, or drill one's self: as, to *practise* upon the piano; to *practise* with the rifle.—2. To form a habit of action; act or do habitually; hence, to behave; conduct one's self.

I send you here a bullock which I did find amongst my bulls, that you may see how closely in time past the foreign prelates did *practise* about their prey.
Bp. Latimer, Sermons and Remains (Parker Soc.), II. 378.

Verily, a man knows no more rightly than he *practises*.
Rev. S. Ward, Sermons and Treatises, p. 170.

3. To exercise a profession; follow a vocation.

E'en Radcliffe's doctors travel first to France,
Nor dare to *practise* till they've learned to dance.
Pope, Imit. of Horace, ii. 1. 184.

4. To experiment.

I am little inclined to *practise* on others, and as little that others should *practise* on me. *Sir W. Temple*, Misc.

5. To negotiate secretly; have a secret understanding.

Opechankanough the last yeare had *practised* with a King on the Basterne shore to furnish him with a kind of poison which onely growes in his Country, to poison vs.
Quoted in *Capt. John Smith's* Works, II. 71.

One Mr. William Vassall had *practised* with such as were not members of our churches to take some course, . . . that the distinctions which were maintained here, both in civil and church estate, might be taken away.
Winthrop, Hist. New England, II. 319.

Syph. But what's this messenger?
Sem. I've *practised* with him,
And found a means to let the victor know
That Syphax and Sempronius are his friends.
Addison, Cato, ii. 6.

6. To use schemes or stratagems; conspire; plot.

I was hated by some lewde Gunners, who, envying that I should haue the Title to be Master Gunner in Fraunce, *practised* against me, and gaue me poyson in drinke that night.
E. Webbe, Travels (ed. Arber), p. 35.

If he do not mightily grace himself on thee, he will *practise* against thee by poison.
Shak., As you Like it, i. 1. 156.

To whom he shows his uncle's discontent,
And of his secret dangerous *practising*.
Daniel, Civil Wars, i.

You have *practised* on her,
Perplext her, made her half forget herself,
Swerve from her duty to herself and us.
Tennyson, Aylmer's Field.

practised, practiced (prak'tist), *p. a.* Skilled through practice; expert; proficient; experienced.

The transportation of the company was committed to Captaine Christopher Newport, a Marriner well *practised* for the Westerne parts of America.
Quoted in *Capt. John Smith's* Works, I. 150.

A scholar and a *practiced* controversialist.
Macaulay, Hist. Eng., vi.

We know that it requires a *practised* and well-educated eye to distinguish between the capitals of the Pantheon of Agrippa and those last executed at Baalbec or Palmyra.
J. Fergusson, Hist. Indian Arch., p. 177.

= **Syn.** Experienced, versed, accomplished, proficient.

practiser, practicer (prak'ti-sėr), *n.* [Early mod. E. also *practyser*, *pratiser*; < ME. *practisour*, *praktisour*, < OF. **practisour*, < *practiser*, *pratiser*, practise: see *practise*.] 1. One who practises or performs, or carries out in action or conduct.

A champion roughe, and *practyser*
Of vertue straite and sounde.
Drant, tr. of Horace's Epistles to Mæcenas.

If we pass to the professors and *practicers* of an higher philosophy, the Apostles and primitive Christians, who ever so overflowed with spiritual joy as they did?
South, Sermons, IV. xi.

I therefore apprehend and do attach thee
For an abuser of the world, a *practiser*
Of arts inhibited and out of warrant.
Shak., Othello, i. 2. 78.

2. One who exercises a profession; a practitioner.

And did him assaye his surgerye on hem that syke were,
Til he was parfit *practisoure* if any peril felle.
Piers Plowman (B), xvi. 107.

He was a verray parfit *praktisour*.
Chaucer, Gen. Prol. to C. T., l. 422.

3. One who uses schemes or stratagem; one who plots; a conspirator.

It is true that Buckingham and Suffolk were the *practisers* and contrivers of the duke's death.
Raleigh, Hist. World, Pref., p. xi.

Virgil, Horace, and the rest
Of those great master-spirits did not want
Detractors then, or *practicers* against them.
B. *Jonson*, Apol. to Poetaster.

practisour†, *n.* A Middle English form of *practiser*.

practitioner (prak-tish'ǫn-ėr), *n.* [Formerly *practicioner* for **practicianer*, < *practician* + *-er*[1] (the suffix unnecessarily added, as in *musicianer*, etc.).] 1. A practiser; one who acquires knowledge from actual practice; one who has practical experience.

He that would be a *practitioner* in those affaires I hope will allow them not only needfull but expedient.
Capt. John Smith, Works, II. 252.

Believe an old *practitioner*, whoever out of malice to a fellow servant carries a tale to his master shall be ruined by a general confederacy against him.
Swift, Directions to Servants in General.

2. One who is engaged in the actual practice or exercise of any art or profession, as law or medicine.

There are several Fictions still exercising powerful influence on English jurisprudence which could not be discarded without a severe shock to the ideas, and considerable change in the language, of English *practitioners*.
Maine, Ancient Law, p. 27.

The surgeon who has not sufficient courage to propose a useful operation, and sufficient skill to perform it, is as open to censure as the reckless *practitioner* who is swayed by the unworthy lure of notoriety.
J. M. Carnochan, Operative Surgery, Pref., p. iii.

3†. One who uses schemes or artifices; a plotter; a conspirator.

There are some papistical *practitioners* among you.
Abp. Whitgift.

General practitioner, one who practises both medicine and surgery. Formerly in England the general practitioner, also called *surgeon apothecary* or *apothecary*, was the ordinary family medical attendant, supplying drugs as well as advice to his patients. He was licensed to practise by the Apothecaries' Company (incorporated 1617), and was in rank below the physician or surgeon. This distinction is now passing away, and the word *general practitioner* may be applied, as in the United States, to a physician who practises also surgery and obstetrics. See *apothecary*.

It was clear that Lydgate, by not dispensing drugs, intended to cast imputations on his equals, and also to obscure the limit between his own rank as a *general practitioner* and that of the physicians who, in the interests of the profession, felt bound to maintain its various grades.
George Eliot, Middlemarch, ii. 18.

practive†, *a.* [A variant, with accom. suffix *-ive* (as in *active*), of *practic*: see *practic*.] Active; actual.

practively†, *adv.* Actively; actually.

Then true religion might be sayd
With vs in primitiue;
The preachers and the people both
Then *practively* did thriue.
Warner, Albion's England, viii. 39.

prad (prad), *n.* [< D. *paard*, a horse: see *palfrey*.] A horse. *Tufts*, Glossary of Thieves' Jargon, 1798. [Thieves' cant.]

It would never do to go to the wars on a rickety *prad*.
Barham, Ingoldsby Legends, I. 93.

prad-holder (prad'hōl″dėr), *n.* A bridle. *Tufts*, Glossary of Thieves' Jargon, 1798. [Thieves' cant.]

præ-. See *pre-*.

præanal, præauditory, etc. See *preanal*, etc.

præcava, precava (prē-kā'vạ̈), *n.* [NL., < L. *præ*, before, + (*vena*) *cava*.] The vena cava superior of man and the corresponding vein of other animals; the anterior caval vein.

præcaval, *a.* and *n.* See *precaval*.

præcinctio (prē-singk'ti-ō), *n.*; pl. *præcinctiones* (prē-singk-ti-ō'nēz). [L.: see *precinction*.] In the ancient Roman theater, a passage running parallel to the seats: equivalent to *diazoma* in the Greek theater. See cut under *diazoma*.

præcipe, *n.* See *precipe*.

Præcoces† (prē'kǭ-sēz), *n. pl.* [NL., pl. of L. *præcox*, *præcoquis*, *præcoquus*, premature, precocious: see *precoce*.] Precocial birds; in some systems, as Bonaparte's, a prime division of the class *Aves*, including those birds whose young are able to run about and feed themselves as soon as they are hatched: opposed to *Altrices*, and synonymous with *Grallatores* in one sense. Gallinaceous birds, all the wading birds except the herons and their allies, and the duck tribe are *Præcoces*. Also called *Dasypædes* and *Ptilopædes*. Also *Precoces*.

præcocial, *a.* See *precocial*.

præcognitum (prē-kog'ni-tum), *n.*; pl. *præcognita* (-tạ̈). [NL., < L. *præcognitus*, pp. of *præcognoscere*, foreknow, foresee: see *precognition*.] Something a knowledge of which precedes or must precede the understanding of something else.

præconize, præcoracoid, etc. See *preconize*, etc.

præcordia, precordia (prē-kôr'di-ạ̈), *n.* [= It. *precordio*, < L. *præcordia*, neut. pl., the midriff, the stomach, also the breast or heart, < *præ*, before, + *cor*(*d-*), the heart.] Same as *precordial region* (which see, under *precordial*).

præcornu (prē-kôr'nū), *n.*; pl. *præcornua* (-nū-ạ̈). [NL. (Wilder), < L. *præ*, before, + *cornu* = E. *horn*.] The anterior horn of the lateral ventricle of the brain; the forward part of the cerebral procœlia.

præcuneal, *a.* See *precuneal*.

præcuneus, precuneus (prē-kū'nē-us), *n.*; pl. *præcunei*, *precunei* (-ī). [< L. *præ*, before, + *cuneus*, wedge: see *cuneus*.] The quadrate lobule, on the median surface of the cerebral hemisphere, just in front of the cuneus. Its anterior boundary is marked by the upturned end of the callosomarginal sulcus. See cuts under *cerebral* and *corpus*.

prædelineation, *n.* See *predelineation*.

prædial, *a.* See *predial*.

Prædones (prē-dō'nēz), *n. pl.* [NL. (Latreille, 1807), < L. *prædo*, one that makes booty, < *præda*, booty, prey: see *prey*[2].] A subsection of aculeate hymenopterous insects, proposed by Latreille and adopted by Westwood, including the families *Crabronidæ*, *Larridæ*, *Bembecidæ*, *Sphegidæ*, *Scoliidæ*, *Mutillidæ*, *Formicidæ* (in the broad sense), and *Vespidæ*. In Hartig's arrangement, now in vogue, the *Prædones* would correspond to the three series *Heterogyna*, *Fossores*, and *Diploptergya*.

præesophageal, *a.* See *preësophageal*.

præfatio (prē-fā'shi-ō), *n.* [ML., < L. *præfatio*, preface: see *preface*.] In the celebration of high mass in the Roman Catholic Church, a prayer which immediately precedes the Sanctus. On ferial days it is recited; on Sundays and festival days it is sung.

præfect, præfloration, etc. See *prefect*, etc.

prælabrum (prē-lā'brum), *n.*; pl. *prælabra* (-brạ̈). [NL., < L. *præ*, before, + *labrum*, lip.] In *entom.*, the clypeus or epistoma.

prælect, prælection, etc. See *prelect*, etc.

præmaxilla (prē-mak-sil'ạ̈), *n.*; pl. *præmaxillæ* (-ē). Same as *premaxilla*.

præmaxillary, *a.* and *n.* See *premaxillary*.

præmetial (prē-mē'shi-al), *a.* [< L. *præmetium*, the offering of the first fruits measured out beforehand for Ceres, < *præ*, before, + *metiri*, measure: see *mete*[1].] Of or pertaining to the first fruits.

If we should not, therefore, freely offer to your Majesty some *præmetial* handfuls of that crop whereof you may challenge the whole harvest, how could we be but shamelessly unthankful? *Bp. Hall*, Ded. to K. James. (*Davies.*)

præmolar, *a.* and *n.* See *premolar*.

præmonish†, *v.* An obsolete form of *premonish*.

Præmonstratensian, *a.* and *n.* See *Premonstratensian*.

Præmunientes (prē-mū-ni-en'tēz), *n.* [< ML. *præmunientes*, pl. of *præmunien*(*t-*)*s*, ppr. of *præmunire*, for L. *præmonere*, forewarn, admonish: see *præmunire*.] In *Eng. law*, the summons addressed to the bishops or archbishops admonishing them to cause the ecclesiastics to convene whose attendance was required in Parliament: so called from the characteristic word used in the introduction of the writ.—**Præmunientes writ.** Same as *Præmunientes*.

As the part of the writ described as the *Præmunientes Writ* was not disused, and the Clergy are still summoned to attend Convocation by what may be termed the Parliamentary form, it is contended that Convocation must owe its origin to the time when that form was first adopted.
Quarterly Rev., CXLVI. 140.

præmunire, premunire (prē-mū-nī'rē), *n.* [So called from the first word of the writ, which began "*Præmuniri facias* . . . ," etc., 'cause A. B. to be forewarned that he appear before us,' etc.; *præmuniri* being pass. of ML. *præmunire*, a corruption (by confusion with L. *præmunire*, fortify, protect: see *premunition*) of L. *præmonere*, forewarn, admonish: see *premonish*.] 1. In *Eng. law*, a species of writ, or the offense for which it is granted, or the penalty incurred. Originally the offense contemplated was the introduction of a foreign power into the kingdom. Whenever it is said that a person by any act incurs a *præmunire*, it is meant to express that he thereby incurs the penalty of being out of the crown's protection, of having his lands and tenements, goods and chattels, forfeited to the crown, and his body remain in prison during the sovereign's pleasure. This penalty attached in former times to the offenses of asserting the jurisdiction of the Pope, especially by impleading other subjects in foreign ecclesiastical courts, and denying the sovereign's supremacy. By later statutes, acts of a very miscellaneous nature have been rendered liable to the penalties of præmunire, as refusing to take the oaths of allegiance and supremacy.

He [Henry VIII.] saw that the *Præmunire* made him absolutely master of the clergy, and, as absolute master, the primary owner of all Church property.
Stubbs, Medieval and Modern Hist., p. 254.

2†. A serious or awkward position; a predicament.

If the law finds you with two wives at once,
There 's a shrewd *premunire*.
Middleton, Massinger, and Rowley, Old Law, v.

Præmunire case, or the case of præmunire, the name by which reference is frequently made to the conviction and attainder of Robert Lalor, priest, indicted in 1606 (Sir John Davis, Ireland, Rep., 83 b: 2 How. St. Tr., 534) for having exercised the office of vicar-general of Dublin, etc., by appointment of the Pope, in violation of the Statute of Præmunire (16 Rich. II., c. 5).—**Statute of Præmunire.** (*a*) An English statute or ordinance of 1353, imposing outlawry, forfeiture, and imprisonment on those who should sue in foreign courts for matters cognizable in England, and thereafter not appear, when summoned, to answer for their contempt. (*b*) Another English statute, of 1392, designed to check the power of the Pope in England, by punishing those who procured from the papal authority any process against the king, or his crown or realm.

præmunire, premunire (prē-mū-nī'rē), *v. t.* [< *præmunire*, *n.*] To bring within the penalties of a præmunire.

For you must know that Horn desir'd
To have good Bonner *præmunired*.
T. Ward, England's Reformation, p. 160.

præmunitory, *a.* See *premunitory*.

prænarial (prē-nā'ri-al), *a.* [< *prænaris* + *-al.*] Pertaining to the prenares.

prænaris (prē-nā'ris), *n.*; pl. *prænares* (-rēz). [NL. (Wilder), < L. *præ*, before, + *naris*, a nostril: see *naris*.] The anterior nostril; the anterior opening of the nasal chamber; the nostril of ordinary language: distinguished from *postnaris*.

prænomen, prenomen (prē-nō'men), *n.*; pl. *prænomina*, *prenomina* (prē-nom'i-nạ). [< L. *prænomen*, a first or personal name, < *præ*, before, + *nomen*, name: see *nomen*.] 1. Among the ancient Romans, a name prefixed to the family name, answering to the modern Christian or personal name, as *Gaius*, *Lucius*, *Marcus*, etc.

The Roman child received its *prænomen* with a lustration at about the same age [one week].
E. B. Tylor, Prim. Culture, II. 397.

2. In *zoöl.*, the generic name, or name of the genus to which a species belongs, which invariably precedes the specific or trivial name in the binomial system of nomenclature. Thus, *Felis* is the prænomen in the term *Felis leo*, which is the technical name of the lion.

prænominal, *a.* See *prenominal*.

præœsophageal, præopercular, etc. See *preœsophageal*, etc.

præoperculum, preoperculum (prē-ọ-pėr'kū-lum), *n.*; pl. *præopercula*, *preopercula* (-lạ). [NL., < L. *præ*, before, + *operculum*, q. v.] 1. In *bot.*, the fore lid or operculum in mosses.—2. In *ichth.*, one of the four principal opercular bones. See *operculum* (*b*) (5), and cut under *teleost*.

præpelvisternum, prepelvisternum (prē-pel-vi-stėr'num), *n.*; pl. *præpelvisterna*, *prepelvisterna* (-nạ). [NL., < L. *præ*, before, + *pelvisternum*.] An anterior pelvisternum.

præperforatus (prē-pėr-fọ-rā'tus), *n.*; pl. *præperforati* (-tī). [NL., < L. *præ*, before, + *perforatus*, perforate: see *perforate*, *a.*] The anterior perforated space at the base of the brain; the precribrum.

præscutellum (prē-skū-tel'um), *n.* [NL., < L. *præ*, before, + NL. *scutellum*, q. v.] In *entom.*, a rarely differentiated sclerite between the mesoscutum and the mesoscutellum.

præscutum (prẹ-skū'tum), *n.*; pl. *præscuta* (-tạ). [NL., < L. *præ*, before, + *scutum*, a shield: see *scutum*.] The first or anterior one of the four sclerites or pieces of hard integument into which the pronotum, mesonotum, and metanotum of insects are severally divisible; the foremost piece of the tergum of each one of the three thoracic segments, situated in advance of the piece called the *scutum*.

præseminal, *a.* See *preseminal*.

Præsepe (prẹ-sē'pē), *n.* [L., also *præsepes*, *præsepis*, *præsepium*, an inclosure, fold, pen, stall, manger, crib, < *præsepire*, fence in front, < *præ*, before, + *sepire*, fence: see *septum*.] A loose cluster of stars, appearing as a nebula to the naked eye, in the breast of the Crab; r Cancri.

præsepium (prẹ-sē'pi-um), *n.*; pl. *præsepia* (-ạ). [NL., < L. *præsepium*, *præsæpium*, manger, crib: see *Præsepe*.] A representation of the nativity of Christ when treated decoratively, as in wood-carving or the like. It commonly contains at least two separate views or subjects—the babe lying in the manger and adored by the mother, and the adoration by the shepherds.

præsternum, presternum (prẹ-stėr'num), *n.* [NL., < L. *præ*, before, + NL. *sternum*, q. v.] 1. The fore part of the sternum; the part of any sternum which corresponds to the manubrium of the human breast-bone; the part immediately preceding the mesosternum or gladiolus. See cut under *mesosternum*.—2. In *entom.*, same as *prosternum*.

præstomial, *a.* See *prestomial*.

præstomium (prẹ-stō'mi-um), *n.*; pl. *præstomia* (-ạ). [NL., < L. *præ*, before, + Gr. στόμα, mouth.] In *Annelida*, a distinct cephalic segment of the higher polychætous worms, bearing the eyes and tentacles. Also *prestomium*. See also cut under *Polynoë*.

Anterior Extremity of *Polynoë*, a polychætous annelid (*B*, from above; *C*, from below): *a*, præstomial tentacle; *b*, *b'*, superior and inferior præstomial cirri; *c*, *c'*, notopodial and neuropodial cirri; *e*, peduncle of first elytron; *l*, præstomium; *m*, parapodium of peristomium.

præter†, *a.* and *n.* See *preter*.

præter-. See *preter-*.

præterhuman, *a.* See *preterhuman*.

præterit†, *a.* and *n.* An obsolete spelling of *preterit*.

præterition, *n.* See *preterition*.

prætexta (prẹ-teks'tạ), *n.*; pl. *prætextæ* (-tē). [L., fem. of *prætextus*, pp. of *prætexere*, weave in front, edge, border: see *pretex*, *pretext*.] In ancient Rome: (*a*) A white toga or wrap with a broad purple border, worn by children of both sexes. It was laid aside by young men upon becoming entitled to assume the toga virilis, not before completion of their fourteenth year. Girls wore it till their marriage. (*b*) A white toga with a broad border of purple, worn as their official dress by higher magistrates and priests, and upon certain ceremonial occasions, as the discharge of vows or the celebration of religious rites, by those citizens who were chiefly concerned. Compare *clavus*.

The *prætexta*, on the other hand, with its purple border, could only be worn along with a white tunic under it with a purple stripe (clavus).
Encyc. Brit., VI. 456.

prætor, prætympanic, etc. See *pretor*, etc.

pragmatic (prag-mat'ik), *a.* and *n.* [< F. *pragmatique* = Sp. *pragmático* = Pg. *pragmatico* = It. *prammatico*, *pragmatico* (cf. D. G. *pragmatisch* = Sw. Dan. *pragmatisk*), adj., pragmatic (as a noun, masc., in def. 1; fem. F. *pragmatique* = Sp. *pragmática*, n., = Pg. *pragmatica*, n., = It. *prammatica*, *pragmatica*, in def. 3); < LL. *pragmaticus*, relating to civil affairs (*pragmatica sanctio* or *jussio* or *annotatio* or *constitutio*, a pragmatic sanction, i. e. an imperial decree relating to the affairs of a community, ML. simply *pragmatica*, a decree); in L., as a noun, a person versed in the law who furnished arguments and points to advocates and orators, a kind of attorney; < Gr. πραγματικός, active, versed in affairs, etc., < πρᾶγμα (> LL. *pragma*), a thing done, a fact, pl. πράγματα, affairs, state affairs, public business, etc., < πράσσειν (√ πραγ), do: see *practic*, *practice*, etc.] **I.** *a.* 1. Relating to civil affairs; relating or pertaining to the affairs of a community. See *pragmatic sanction*, below.—2. Same as *pragmatical*, in any sense.

Nor can your Palace be a dwelling-place
For Safety, whilst *pragmatic* Logos or
Sly Charis revel in your princely Grace.
J. Beaumont, Psyche, v. 153.

I love to hit
These *pragmatic* young men at their own weapons.
B. Jonson, Devil is an Ass, i. 3.

3. In the *Kantian philos.*, practical in a particular way—namely, having reference to happiness.—**Pragmatic method, pragmatic treatment**, the treatment of historical phenomena with special reference to their causes, antecedent conditions, and results. Also *pragmatism*.—**Pragmatic sanction**, a term first applied to certain decrees of the Byzantine emperors, regulating the interests of their subject provinces and towns; then to a system of limitations set to the spiritual power of the Pope in European countries: as, for instance, the French *pragmatic sanction* of 1268, and that of 1438. Lastly, it became the name for an arrangement or family compact, made by different potentates, regarding succession to sovereignty—the most noted being the instrument by which the emperor Charles VI., being without male issue, endeavored to secure the succession to his female descendants, settling his dominions on his daughter Maria Theresa.

II. *n.* 1†. A man of business; one who is versed or active in affairs.

He 's my attorney and solicitor too; a fine *pragmatic*.
B. Jonson.

2†. A busybody; a meddlesome person.

Such *pragmaticks* . . . labour impertinently.
Bp. Gauden, Tears of the Church, p. 502. (*Davies.*)

Keep to your problems of ten groats; these matters are not for *pragmaticks* and folkmooters to babble in.
Milton, Prose Works, I. 330.

3. A decree or ordinance issued by the head of a state.

A *pragmatic* was issued, September 18th, 1495, prescribing the weapons and the seasons for a regular training of the militia.
Prescott, Ferd. and Isa., ii. 26, note.

pragmatica (prag-mat'i-kạ), *n.* [ML.: see *pragmatic*.] Same as *pragmatic*, *n.*, 3.

Royal *pragmaticas* began to take the place of constitutional laws.
Encyc. Brit., IX. 811.

pragmatical (prag-mat'i-kạl), *a.* and *n.* [< *pragmatic* + *-al.*] **I.** *a.* 1†. Versed in affairs; skilled in business; engaged in business pursuits.

Pragmatical men may not go away with an opinion that learning is like a lark, that can mount, and sing, and please herself, and nothing else.
Bacon, Advancement of Learning, ii. 323.

2. Active; diligent; busy.

I received instructions how to behave in town, with directions to masters and books to take in search of the antiquities, churches, collections, etc. Accordingly, the next day, Nov. 6th, I began to be very *pragmatical*.
Evelyn, Diary, Nov. 4, 1644.

3. Pertaining to business or to material interests; hence, material; commonplace.

Low *pragmatical* earthly views of the gospel. *Hare.*

"In One Town," though a little *pragmatical* and matter of fact, is not uninteresting. *Athenæum*, No. 3068, p. 203.

4†. Practical; authoritative.

Can a man thus imployd find himselfe discontented or dishonour'd for want of admittance to have a *pragmaticall* voyce at Sessions and Jayle deliveries?
Milton, On Def. of Humb. Remonst.

5. Unduly busy over the affairs of others; meddlesome; interfering; officious.

The fellow grew so *pragmatical* that he took on him the management of my whole family. *Arbuthnot.*

6. Characterized by officiousness; performed or delivered by an officious person; intrusive.

It is like you to give a *pragmatical* opinion without being acquainted with any of the circumstances of the case.
Charlotte Brontë, The Professor.

Suddenly an unknown individual, in plain clothes and with a *pragmatical* demeanor, interrupted the discourse by giving a flat contradiction to some of the doctrines advanced.
Motley, Dutch Republic, I. 544.

7. Busy over trifles; self-important; busy.

You cannot imagine what airs all the little *pragmatical* fellows about us have given themselves since the reading of those papers.
Addison, The Tall Club.

II.† *n.* A professional opinion or decision.

The eloquent persuasions and *pragmaticals* of Mr. Secretary Windwood.
Bacon, To the King, 1617, July 25, Works, XIII. 232.

pragmatically (prag-mat'i-kạl-i), *adv.* In a pragmatic manner.

Over busy, or *pragmatically* curious.
Barrow, Sermons, I. 597.

pragmaticalness (prag-mat'i-kạl-nes), *n.* The character of being pragmatical, in any sense; especially, meddlesomeness; officiousness; excessive zeal.

pragmatism (prag'mạ-tizm), *n.* [< *pragmat(ic)* + *-ism.*] 1. Pragmatical character or conduct; officiousness; busy impertinence.

Mrs. Dollop, the spirited landlady of the Tankard in Slaughter Lane, . . . had often to resist the shallow *pragmatism* of customers disposed to think that their reports from the outer world were of equal force with what had "come up" in her mind. *George Eliot*, Middlemarch, lxxi.

2. In *hist.*, same as *pragmatic method*. See *pragmatic*, *a.*

pragmatist (prag'mạ-tist), *n.* [< *pragmat(ic)* + *-ist.*] One who is impertinently busy or meddling.

We may say of *pragmatists* that their eyes look all ways but inward. *Bp. Reynolds*, The Passions, xvi.

pragmatize (prag'mạ-tīz), *v. t.*; pret. and pp. *pragmatized*, ppr. *pragmatizing*. [< *pragmat(ic)*

+ *-ize*.] To make real or material; attribute a practical objective existence to (some product of imagination or fancy).

The merest shadowy fancy or broken-down metaphor, when once it gains a sense of reality, may begin to be spoken of as an actual event. . . . One of the miraculous passages in the life of Mohammed himself is traced plausibly by Sprenger to such a *pragmatized* metaphor. *E. B. Tylor*, Prim. Culture, I. 407.

pragmatizer (prag'ma-ti-zėr), *n.* [< *pragmatize* + *-er*1.] One who pragmatizes, or attributes objective existence to what is subjective, imaginary, or fanciful.

The *pragmatizer* is a stupid creature; nothing is too beautiful or too sacred to be made dull and vulgar by his touch. *E. B. Tylor*, Prim. Culture, I. 368.

prahme, *n.* See *pram*1.

prahu (prä'hö), *n.* Same as *proa*.

We . . . decided to alter our course for Malacca, where we arrived at half-past nine; the Doctor at once went on shore in a native *prahu*. *Lady Brassey*, Voyage of Sunbeam, II. xxiv.

praiert, *n.* An early modern English spelling of *prayer*1.

Prairial (prā'ri-al), *n.* [F., < *prairie*, a meadow: see *prairie*.] The ninth month in the French revolutionary calendar. In the year 1794 it began May 20th and ended June 18th.

prairie (prā'ri), *n.* [< F. *prairie* = Pr. *pradaria* = Sp. *pradera*, *praderia* = Pg. *praderia* = It. *prateria*, a meadow, < ML. *prataria*, meadow-land, prop. fem. of *pratarius*, adj., < L. *pratum*, a meadow. Cf. *prayere*, *prayell*.] A meadow; level grassy land: a word frequently used by Hennepin and other French writers in describing the country adjacent to the Mississippi river, and now in common use, designating the level or slightly undulating treeless areas which cover a large part of Illinois, Wisconsin, Iowa, Minnesota, and other States further south. The prairies are never by the inhabitants of the prairie regions called *plains*, as are the treeless regions further west. They are characterized by a highly fertile soil, often of great thickness, and they often occur where the rainfall is even considerably larger than on parts of the adjacent forest-covered regions. The cause of the absence of trees upon them cannot, therefore, be deficiency of moisture; in all probability it is the physical character of the soil, and especially its extreme fineness, which renders it more suitable for the growth of the grasses than for that of arboreal vegetation. In the extreme northwestern region of the United States, especially in Montana, certain level treeless areas surrounded by the mountains are now by some called *prairies*: some of these had been previously denominated *holes*. Further south in the Rocky Mountains they are known as *parks*, or sometimes as *basins*. See *hole*1, 6, and *plain*1.

The *prairie* alluded to was one of those small natural meadows, or pastures, that are to be found in Michigan, and may have contained four or five thousand acres of open land. *Cooper*, Oak Openings, i.

These are the gardens of the Desert, these
The unshorn fields, boundless and beautiful,
For which the speech of England has no name,
The *Prairies*. *Bryant*, The Prairies.

In general, however, the term *prairie* is used to designate tracts of land nearly or quite destitute of forests, or over which the trees are, as a general rule, limited to the "bluffs"—the more or less precipitous slopes which separate the upland, or prairie proper, from the river bottom. *J. D. Whitney*, Encyc. Brit., XXIII. 811.

Prairie State, the State of Illinois.—**Trembling** or **shaking prairie**. See under *tremble*.

prairie-alligator (prā'ri-al″i-gā-tor), *n.* An insect of the family *Phasmidæ*; one of the walking-sticks, usually the thick-thighed walking-stick, *Diapheromera femorata*. [Local, U. S.]

prairie-apple (prā'ri-ap″l), *n.* Same as *prairie-turnip*.

prairie-bean (prā'ri-bēn), *n.* See *bean*1, 2.

prairie-bird (prā'ri-bėrd), *n.* Same as *prairie-hen*.

prairie-bitters (prā'ri-bit″ėrz), *n. pl.* See *bitters*.

prairie-brant (prā'ri-brant), *n.* Same as *harlequin brant* (which see, under *harlequin*).

prairie-burdock (prā'ri-bėr″dok), *n.* See *burdock*.

prairie-chicken (prā'ri-chik″en), *n.* Same as *prairie-hen*.—**Prairie-chicken of the Northwest**, the sharp-tailed grouse, pintail, or sprigtail, *Pediœcetes phasianellus columbianus*. See cut under *Pediœcetes*.

prairie-clover (prā'ri-klō″vėr), *n.* See *Petalostemon*.

prairie-cocktail (prā'ri-kok″tāl), *n.* A raw egg, peppered and salted, and drunk in vinegar or spirits. Also called *prairie-oyster*. [Western U. S.]

prairied (prā'rid), *a.* [< *prairie* + *-ed*2.] Abounding in prairies; skirted by prairies.

And he whose grave is holy by our calm
And *prairied* Sangamon,
From his gaunt hand shall drop the martyr's palm,
To greet thee with "Well done!"
Whittier, Freedom in Brazil.

prairie-dock (prā'ri-dok), *n.* Same as *prairie burdock* (which see, under *burdock*).

prairie-dog (prā'ri-dog), *n.* A sciuromorphic rodent quadruped of the family *Sciuridæ*, subfamily *Spermophilinæ*, and genus *Cynomys*, of which there are two species, *C. ludovicianus* and *C. columbianus*, the former living east and the latter west of the Rocky Mountains: so called from their habitat and from their cry, which is like the barking of a dog. These animals are generally but irregularly distributed in the prairie

Prairie-dogs (*Cynomys ludovicianus*).

regions of the Western States and Territories, from the British nearly to the Mexican boundary of the United States; they are gregarious, and many thousands together populate some places called *prairie-dog towns* or *villages*, where they dig deep burrows, the entrance of each of which is surmounted by a mound of earth thrown up in making the excavation. (See second cut under *owl*.) Some of the larger towns include many hundred acres. Prairie-dogs are about a foot long, of very stout, squat, paunchy form, with low ears, a very short tail, and long strong fore claws; they are of a uniform reddish-gray or fawn color, paler underneath. They subsist entirely on vegetable food. Also called *prairie-marmot* and *wistonwish*.

prairie-falcon (prā'ri-fâ″kn), *n.* See *falcon*.

prairie-fly (prā'ri-flī), *n.* One of various species of flies of the family *Tabanidæ* which attack cattle. [Western U. S.]

prairie-fox (prā'ri-foks), *n.* The kit, or swift fox, *Vulpes velox*, inhabiting the prairies of North America. See cut under *kit*.

prairie-goose (prā'ri-gös), *n.* Same as *Hutchins's goose* (which see, under *goose*). [Texas.]

prairie-grass (prā'ri-gràs), *n.* 1. Any grass growing on prairies.—2. Specifically, in Australia, the grass *Bromus* (*Ceratochloa*) *unioloides*, once called there *Californian prairie-grass*, though not found in California. See *rescue-grass*.

prairie-hawk (prā'ri-hâk), *n.* The American sparrow-hawk, *Falco sparverius*, which abounds on the prairies as elsewhere in North America, and has the habit of hovering on wing like the European kestrel or windhover.

The *prairie-hawk* that, poised on high,
Flaps his broad wings, yet moves not.
Bryant, The Prairies.

prairie-hen (prā'ri-hen), *n.* (*a*) The pinnated grouse, *Cupidonia* or *Tympanuchus cupido*, a gallinaceous bird of North America belonging to the family *Tetraonidæ*; or (*b*) the sharp-tailed grouse, *Pediœcetes phasianellus columbianus*. See cuts under *Cupidonia* and *Pediœcetes*. The range of these two different birds, though somewhat overlapping, especially of late years, is complementary. The true prairie-hen or pinnated grouse belongs properly to the fertile prairies of the United States, especially Illinois, Iowa, Missouri, the eastern half of Minnesota, South Dakota (especially eastward), middle and eastern Kansas and Nebraska, Arkansas, and eastern Texas—a variety (*pallidicincta*) occurring in western Texas. It also still lingers in some localities in the Middle States and New England; but with the settlement of the country it has followed the railroads, as these have been pushed westward and northwestward, to the Rocky Mountains and far up the Missouri river. The sharp-tailed grouse, the prairie-hen or -chicken of the Northwest, locally called *whitebelly*, is a bird of more arid regions, resembling the sage-grouse in this respect, and its eastward range has contracted with the extension of the pinnated grouse westward. It is found in suitable country of the central plateau to the Sierra Nevadas of California and the Cascade ranges of Oregon and Washington, and northward in much of British America, where it occurs in its typical form, *Pediœcetes phasianellus*, as distinguished from the United States variety called *columbianus*.

prairie-marmot (prā'ri-mär″mot), *n.* The prairie-dog.

prairie-mole (prā'ri-mōl), *n.* The silvery shrew-mole, *Scalops aquaticus argentatus*, a variety of the common mole of the United States occurring on the prairies.

prairie-oyster (prā'ri-ois″tėr), *n.* Same as *prairie-cocktail*.

prairie-pigeon (prā'ri-pij″on), *n.* 1. The American golden plover, *Charadrius dominicus*. Also called *prairie-plover* and *prairie-snipe*.—2. Bartram's sandpiper, *Bartramia longicauda*. This bird abounds on the fertile alluvial prairies from Indiana and Illinois to the Dakotas, but not on the arid plains further west.

prairie-plover (prā'ri-pluv″ėr), *n.* Same as *prairie-pigeon*, 1.

prairie-plow (prā'ri-plou), *n.* A large plow with wheels in front, a broad sharp share, and a long mold-board, used for paring the sod and for turning a broad, shallow furrow.

prairie-rattler (prā'ri-rat″lėr), *n.* A prairie-rattlesnake.

prairie-rattlesnake (prā'ri-rat″l-snāk), *n.* One of several different rattlesnakes inhabiting the prairies, as the massasauga, *Sistrurus catenatus*, and especially *Crotalus confluentus*, the most common and widely distributed rattler in the West.

prairie-rose (prā'ri-rōz), *n.* A wild rose, *Rosa setigera*, of the interior United States, the only American climbing rose. The flowers are large, in flat corymbs, and of a deep rose-color when first expanded. This is the original of the queen-of-the-prairie, Baltimore-belle, and other double roses. Also called *Michigan rose*. See cut under *rose*.

prairie-schooner (prā'ri-skö″nėr), *n.* The white-tilted wagon used by emigrants in freighting on the prairies and great plains before the construction of transcontinental railroads. [Slang, U. S.]

prairie-snipe (prā'ri-snīp), *n.* Same as *prairie-pigeon*, 1.

prairie-squirrel (prā'ri-skwur″el), *n.* A spermophile or ground-squirrel of North America; a sciuromorphic rodent quadruped of the subfamily *Spermophilinæ* and genus *Spermophilus*, numerous species of which inhabit the prairies of western North America. These animals are commonly known as *gophers*, from their burrowing in the ground, but they have little resemblance to the myomorphic rodents of the family *Geomyidæ* to which the name *gopher* properly applies. They vary much in size, color, and general appearance, some having the stout form, short tail, and low ears of the prairie-dog, as *S. richardsoni*; others have longer tail and ears, a slenderer form, and are very prettily spotted or striped, or both, as *S. tridecemlineatus*; in some the tail is so long and bushy that they resemble true arboreal squirrels, as *S. franklini*. Some are numerous enough in cultivated regions to threaten agriculture seriously. They form a characteristic feature of the mammalian fauna in the whole prairie region. See cut under *Spermophilus*.

prairie-turnip (prā'ri-tėr″nip), *n.* The tuber-bearing plant *Psoralea esculenta*.

prairie-warbler (prā'ri-wâr″blėr), *n.* A small insectivorous migratory bird of the eastern parts of the United States, *Dendrœca discolor*,

Prairie-warbler (*Dendrœca discolor*).

belonging to the family *Sylvicolidæ* or *Mniotiltidæ*. It is 4½ inches long, olive-yellow above and bright-yellow below varied with black spots, with a patch of brick-red spots on the middle of the back and white blotches on the lateral tail-feathers. It does not occur in the prairie regions proper of the West.

prairie-wolf (prā'ri-wůlf), *n.* A small wolf, *Canis latrans*, characteristic of the prairie regions of western North America. See cut under *coyote*.

praisable† (prā'za-bl), *a.* [< ME. *praysable*, *preisable*; < *praise* + *-able*.] Praiseworthy.

Which bene so chiualrous in your doing,
And which for to do is *preisable* thyng.
Rom. of Partenay (E. E. T. S.), l. 1911.

praisably† (prā'za-bli), *adv.* In a praisable manner; praiseworthily; admirably.

Then doth our tung naturallie and *praisablie* vtter her meaning, when she boroweth no conterfeitness of other tunges. *Ascham*, The Scholemaster, p. 5.

praise (prāz), *v. t.*; pret. and pp. *praised*, ppr. *praising*. [< ME. *praisen*, *praysen*, *preisen*, *preysen*, < OF. *praisier*, *proisier*, *prisier*, F. *priser* = Pg. *prezar* = It. *pregiare*, *prezzare*, value, prize, < LL. *pretiare*, value, prize: see *prize*2, of which *praise* is a doublet.] 1. To express approbation or admiration of; laud; applaud; eulogize; commend.

When the Citezins herde Gawein thus speke, thei hym comended and *preysed* moche, and seide he myght not faile to be a worthy man; and thei hym loved hertely a-bove alle thynge, and *preised* the grete gentilenesse that thei hym founden. *Merlin* (E. E. T. S.), ii. 202.

Fondly we think we honour merit then
When we but *praise* ourselves in other men.
Pope, Essay on Criticism, l. 455.

2. To extol in gratitude and devotion for blessings received; especially, to offer grateful homage to; worship; glorify.

And to worschipe and *preyse* suche an holy Lond, that broughte forthe suche Fruyt, thorghe the whiche every Man is saved, but it be his owne defaute.
Mandeville, Travels, p. 3.

Oh that men would *praise* the Lord for his goodness, and for his wonderful works to the children of men!
Ps. cvii. 8.

Praise God for the merry year.
Shak., 2 Hen. IV., v. 3. 19.

3†. To appraise; set a price upon; value.

Many folk worschipen tho Bestes, whan thei meeten hem first at Morwe, for here gret vertue and for the gode smelle that thei han; and thei Skynnes thei *preysen* more than thoughe thei were Plate of fyn Gold.
Mandeville, Travels, p. 217.

That no seriaunt take . . . for ther fees, when the goodes be *preised*, but iiij. d. *English Gilds* (E. E. T. S.), p. 391.

And let them that shall *praise* the moveable goods to be delivered unto the creditor take good heed that they do set a reasonable price upon them.
Statute of Merchants, 11 Edw. I., st. I. (1283), tr. in [Statutes of the Realm, I. 53 (1810).

=**Syn. 1** and **2.** *Praise, Applaud, Extol*, laud, eulogize, celebrate, exalt, bless. *Praise* is the general word; it is positive, but of varying degrees of strength. We *praise, applaud*, and *extol* by words written or spoken; we may *applaud* also by clapping the hands or by other physical demonstrations of approbation. To *extol* is to praise very highly, generally at some length. See *eulogy*.

He *praised* her taste, and she commended his understanding: an age could not have made them better acquainted. *Goldsmith*, Vicar, v.

Rome approves my act;
Applauds the blow which costs me life, but keeps
My honour spotless. *Browning*, Ring and Book, II. 287.

The young minister had in private *extolled* Hastings as a great, a wonderful man, who had the highest claims on the government. *Macaulay*, Warren Hastings.

praise (prāz), *n.* [< ME. *prayse, preis, preys*, praise; from the verb.] 1. The expression of approbation or esteem because of some virtue, meritorious performance, or pleasing quality; bestowal of commendation or admiration for something excellent or beautiful; laudation; applause.

O, flatter me; for love delights in *praises*.
Shak., T. G. of V., ii. 4. 148.

Their *praise*
Was to the poet money, wine, and bays.
B. Jonson, Epicœne, Prol.

If their words have any meaning at all, by *praise* they must mean the exercise or testimony of some sorts of esteem, respect, and honourable regard.
Edwards, On the Will, iii. 1.

Compliment is a name for the more familiar forms of *praise*. *A. Bain*, Emotions and Will, p. 109.

2†. The expression of any opinion, whether in commendation or otherwise; hence, fame; reputation.

Laus, Anglice, good *preys*; vel vituperum, Anglice, bad *preys*. *MS. Bib. Reg.* (*Halliwell*.)

Your *praise* is come too swiftly home before you.
Know you not, master, to some kind of men
Their graces serve them but as enemies?
Shak., As you Like it, ii. 3. 9.

3. The expression of love and gratitude for benefits received; devotion with thanksgiving; especially, a tribute of grateful homage to God.

My lips shall utter *praise*, when thou hast taught me thy statutes. Ps. cxix. 171.

In devotion spend my latter days,
To sin's rebuke and my Creator's *praise*.
Shak., 3 Hen. VI., iv. 6. 44.

Prayer causeth the first Shower of Rain, but *Praise* brings down the second. *Howell*, Letters, ii. 67.

4. A ground or reason for praise.

You have the honey still, but these the gall;
So to be valiant is no *praise* at all.
Shak., T. and C., ii. 3. 145.

A restless crowd, . . .
Whose highest *praise* is that they live in vain.
Cowper, Retirement, l. 23.

5. A subject for praise; a person or thing worthy to be praised.

He is thy *praise*, and he is thy God. Deut. x. 21.

Praise at parting, praise in departing, proverbial phrases current among the old writers to express good wishes at parting.

Now *praise at thy parting*.
Tom Tyler, etc. (1598). (*Nares*.)

Pros. [Aside.] *Praise in departing.*
Fran. They vanish'd strangely.
Shak., Tempest, iii. 3. 39.

Prick and praise†. See *prick*.=**Syn.** 1. Encomium, honor, panegyric, plaudit, acclaim. See *praise*, *v.*, and *eulogy*.

praiseful (prāz'ful), *a.* [< *praise* + *-ful*.] Abounding in praise; worthy of praise; laudable.

Of whose high praise, and *praiseful* bliss,
Goodness the pen, heaven paper is:
The ink immortal fame doth lend.
Sir P. Sidney, Arcadia, ii.

praiseless (prāz'les), *a.* [< *praise* + *-less*.] Without praise; undeserving of praise; without merit.

If . . . speech, next to reason, bee the greatest gyft bestowed vpon mortalitie, that cannot be *praiselesse* which dooth most pollish that blessing of speech.
Sir P. Sidney, Apol. for Poetrie (Arber rep., II. 50).

praise-meeting (prāz'mē″ting), *n.* In the United States, a religious service of congregational worship in which singing is a conspicuous feature.

praisement† (prāz'ment), *n.* [< ME. *prayesment*; < *praise* + *-ment*. Cf. *appraisement*.] Appraisement; valuation.

Also I will that my chalice, wt my ij. crewetts and pax of siluer, before the *praysement* or division made of my foresaid moveables, . . . remayn styll to her.
Fabyan, Chron., I., Pref., vii.

praiser (prā'zėr), *n.* [< ME. *preiser*; < *praise* + *-er*[1].] 1. One who praises, commends, or extols; a eulogist.

Thou shalt rather drede and flee fro the swete wordes of flateringe *preiseres* than fro the egre wordes of thy freend that seith thee sothes. *Chaucer*, Tale of Melibeus.

We men and *praisers* of men should remember that, if we have such excellencies, it is reason to think them excellent creatures of whom we are. *Sir P. Sidney*.

2†. An appraiser.

He . . . talked himself with the *praisers*, and made them set high prises upon every thing that was to be sold.
North, tr. of Plutarch, p. 649. (*Davies*.)

praiseworth†, *a.* Praiseworthy.

Whose *praise-worth* vertures, if in verse I now should take in hand
For to comprize. *Holland*, tr. of Camden, p. 290. (*Davies*.)

praiseworthily (prāz'wėr″ᴛʜi-li), *adv.* In a manner deserving of praise.

Her name was Envie, knowen well thereby,
Whose nature is to grieve and grudge at all
That ever she sees doen *prays-worthily*.
Spenser, F. Q., V. xii. 31.

praiseworthiness (prāz'wėr″ᴛʜi-nes), *n.* The character of being praiseworthy.

praiseworthy (prāz'wėr″ᴛʜi), *a.* [< *praise* + *worthy*.] Deserving of praise; laudable; commendable.

Thou hast taught us to admire onely that which is good, and to count that onely *praiseworthy* which is grounded upon thy divine Precepts.
Milton, On Def. of Humb. Remonst.

In surrendering her western territory, North Carolina showed *praiseworthy* generosity.
J. Fiske, Critical Period of Amer. Hist., v.

praithee†. An obsolete variant of *prithee*.

Prakrit (prä'krit), *n.* [Skt. *prākrita*, that which is natural, not accomplished, vulgar, < *prakriti*, nature.] The collective name of those dialects which succeed the Sanskrit in the historical development of the language of India. They assumed a literary position first in the Sanskrit dramas, where female characters and the lower male characters are introduced as speaking Prakrit instead of the Sanskrit used by kings, noblemen, and priests.

The inscriptions of Asoka are written in three local Pali or *Prakrit* dialects, evidently derived by long continued detrition from the Sanskrit of the Vedas.
Isaac Taylor, The Alphabet, II. 296.

Prakritic (prä-krit'ik), *a.* [< *Prakrit* + *-ic*.] Belonging or pertaining to Prakrit, or to one of the dialects constituting Prakrit.

The next stage of Indian language, to which the inscriptions just referred to belong, is called the *Prakritic*.
W. D. Whitney, Life and Growth of Lang., p. 187.

praline (prä'lēn), *n.* [F.] A confection made by stirring almonds (or other kernels of nuts) in boiling sugar and water till they are brown and will crackle between the teeth; also, in Louisiana, a flat cake made by stirring the kernels of nuts (generally pecan-nuts) in sugar. Also, corruptly, *prawling*.

pram[1] (präm), *n.* [Also *praam, prame, prahme*; < F. *prame* = MD. *prame*, D. *praam* = MLG. *prām*, LG. *praam* = G. *prahm, prahme* = Icel. *prāmr* = Sw. *prâm* = Dan. *pram*; of Slavic origin: OBulg. *pramŭ*.] 1. A flat-bottomed boat or lighter, used in the Netherlands and the Baltic ports for loading and unloading merchant vessels.

Around us lay the foreign steamers, mostly English, each with its crowd of boats and *prams*. These *prams* are huge barges roofed over, and resemble for all the world gamepies or old-fashioned monitors.
Rae, Land of the North Wind (1875), p. 158. (*Davies*.)

He steers the leading *prame* into the bay.
R. D. Blackmore, Springhaven, xxxviii.

2. *Milit.*, a similar barge or lighter mounted with guns, and used as a floating battery.

One of the *praams* mounted ten guns and the other eight. *Marryat*, Peter Simple, III. xvi.

pram[2] (pram), *n.* [Contr. of **peram*, abbr. of *perambulator*.] A perambulator. [Vulgar.]

I am told that it is now common amongst the lower classes to call perambulators *p'rams*.
N. and Q., 6th ser., IX. 420.

prance (prȧns), *v. i.*; pret. and pp. *pranced*, ppr. *prancing*. [< ME. *prancen, prauncen*, prance, lit. show off; an assibilated form of *prank*. Cf. G. dial. (Bav.) *prangezen, prangsen*, assume airs, Swiss *spranzen*, strut.] 1. To make a show in walking; move proudly, lifting the feet with a rearing or capering motion: used of horses in high mettle.

Upon the first setting out, my Steed falls a *prancing*; you would have said he was a Horse of Mettle; he was plump, and in good Case.
N. Bailey, tr. of Colloquies of Erasmus, I. 413.

As the proud horse, with costly trappings gay,
Exulting *prances* to the bloody fray.
Falconer, Shipwreck, ii.

2. To ride with a rearing or capering motion; ride gaily, proudly, or insolently.

I see
The insulting tyrant *prancing* o'er the field.
Addison, Cato, i. 1.

Anon to meet us lightly *pranced*
Three captains out. *Tennyson*, Princess, v.

3. To walk, strut, or caper in an elated, proud, or conceited manner.

Trimm'd like a younker *prancing* to his love.
Shak., 3 Hen. VI., ii. 1. 24.

'Tis so, those two that there deride him,
And with such graces *prance* beside him
In pomp, infallibly declare
Themselves the sheriffs; he the Mayor.
D'Urfey, Colin's Walk, ii.

Rawdon . . . *pranced* off to engage the lodgings with all the impetuosity of love. *Thackeray*, Vanity Fair, xvi.

prancer (prȧn'sėr), *n.* [< *prance* + *-er*[1].] A prancing horse.

Then came the captaine or governor of the castle of St. Angelo upon a brave *prancer*.
Evelyn, Diary, Nov. 22, 1644.

And fleeter now she skimm'd the plains
Than she whose elfin *prancer* springs
By night to eery warblings.
Tennyson, Lancelot and Guinevere.

prancing (prȧn'sing), *n.* [Verbal n. of *prance*, *v.*] The rearing or capering action of a horse.

Thrace feels thro' all her realms their furious course,
Shook by the *prancings* of the thund'ring horse.
Pitt, Æneid, xii.

prancing (prȧn'sing), *p. a.* [Ppr. of *prance*, *v.*] Rearing; bounding; capering; riding with gallant show.

Now rule thy *prancing* steeds, lac'd charioteer.
Gay, Trivia, ii. 528.

prancingly (prȧn'sing-li), *adv.* In a prancing manner.

prancome†, *n.* [For **prankum* (cf. *prinkum-prankum*), a Latinized form of *prank*.] Something odd or strange.

Gog's hart, I durst have laid my cap to a crown,
Ch' would learn of some *prancome* as soon as ich cham to town. *Bp. Still*, Gammer Gurton's Needle.

prandial (pran'di-al), *a.* [< L. *prandium*, a breakfast or an early dinner or luncheon, usually taken at noon.] Relating or pertaining to a dinner or other meal: as, *prandial* preparations.

pranet, *n.* An obsolete form of *prawn*. *Palsgrave*.

Prangos (prang'gos), *n.* [NL. (Lindley, 1824), from an E. Ind. name.] 1. A genus of umbelliferous plants of the tribe *Seselineæ* and subtribe *Cachrydeæ*. It is characterized by a very broadly excavated seed, the p ma y ridges of the fruit some or all of them expanded into wings, and a tall smooth stem, sometimes woolly at the base. There are about 40 species, natives of the Mediterranean region and of Asia. They are perennial herbs, with pinnate or pinnately decompound leaves, compound many-rayed umbels of yellow flowers, numerous bracts and bractlets, and smooth oblong fruit containing many oil-tubes. *P. pabularia*, the prangos of Cashmere, is called *hay-plant*.
2. [*l. c.*] A plant of this genus.

Praniza (prạ-nī'zạ), *n.* [NL. (Leach), irreg. < Gr. πρηνίζειν, throw headlong, < πρανής, Dor. for πρηνής, with the face downward.] A supposed genus of isopods, founded on the female form of the genus *Anceus*.

prank (prangk), *v.* [< ME. *pranken*, prank, arrange one's dress, = MD. *proncken, pronken*, D. *pronken*, make a show, arrange one's dress (*pronckeprinken*, glitter in a fine dress): in relation with *prink*, and with MLG. *prunken* = MHG. *brunken*, G. *prunken* = Sw. *prunka* = Dan. *prunke*, make a show, prank, and with MLG. *prangen* = MHG. *prangen, brangen*, G. *prangen* = Icel. *pranga* = Sw. *prånga, pranga* = Dan.

prange, make a show, G. dial. *prangezen*, *prangsen*, assume airs, and further connected with *brank*, etc., and W. *prangcio*, prank, and with D. and MLG. *pracht*, OHG. MHG. *praht*, *braht*, G. *pracht*, Icel. *prakt*, Sw. *prakt*, Dan. *pragt*, pomp, splendor. Cf. *prance*.] **I.** *trans.* **1.** To decorate; adorn; deck; especially, to deck out in a showy manner.

To *prancke* your selues in a lookinge Glasse.
Lyly, Euphues and his England, p. 433.

Circled with children, *pranking* up a girl,
And putting jewels in her little ears.
Middleton, Chaste Maid, iii. 3.

False rules *prank'd* in reason's garb.
Milton, Comus, l. 759.

Some *prank* up their bodies, and have their minds full of execrable vices. *Burton*, Anat. of Mel., p. 35.

When violets *pranked* the turf with blue.
Holmes, Poems, Old-Year Song.

2†. To adjust; set in order.

Some frounce their curled heare in courtly guise;
Some *prancke* their ruffes. *Spenser*, F. Q., I. iv. 14.

II. *intrans.* **1.** To present a showy or gaudy appearance; make a brilliant show.

It was on a Wednesday that the *pranking* army of high-mettled warriors issued forth from the ancient gates of Antiquera. *Irving*, Granada, p. 87.

White houses *prank* where once were huts.
M. Arnold, Obermann Once More.

2†. To be crafty or subtle. *Palsgrave.*

prank (prangk), *n.* and *a.* [< *prank*, *v.*] **I.** *n.* A playful or mischievous act; a trick played sometimes in malice, but more commonly in sport; an escapade; a gambol.

His *pranks* have been too broad to bear with.
Shak., Hamlet, iii. 4. 2.

Both old and young commended the maid
That such a witty *prank* had play'd.
Friar in the Well (Child's Ballads, VIII. 125).

His dog, . . . with many a frisk
Wide-scamp'ring, snatches up the drifted snow. . . .
Heedless of all his *pranks*, the sturdy churl
Moves right toward the mark. *Cowper*, Task, v. 52.

=**Syn.** *Whim*, etc. (see *freak*[2]), antic, vagary.

II.† *a.* Frolicsome; mischievous.

If I do not seem *pranker* now than I did in those days, I'll be hang'd. *A. Brewer* (?), Lingua, iv. 7.

pranker (prang'kėr), *n.* [< *prank* + *-er*[1].] One who pranks, or dresses ostentatiously; a person fond of show or ostentation.

If she be a noted reveller, a gadder, a singer, a *pranker* or dancer, then take heed of her.
Burton, Anat. of Mel., p. 539.

prankingly (prang'king-li), *adv.* In a pranking manner; showily; ostentatiously.

prankish (prang'kish), *a.* [< *prank* + *-ish*[1].] Mischievous; frolicsome; full of pranks.

prankle[1] (prang'kl), *v. i.*; pret. and pp. *prankled*, ppr. *prankling*. [Freq. of *prank*, *v.*] To prance. *Halliwell.* [Prov. Eng.]

prankle[2] (prang'kl), *n.* [Prob. a reduction of *periwinkle*[2], accom. to *prawn* (formerly *prane*).] A prawn. *Halliwell.* [Prov. Eng.]

pranksome (prangk'sum), *a.* [< *prank* + *-some*.] Prankish; mischievous; frolicsome.

Ah, but he drove a *pranksome* quill!
With quips he wove a spell.
Harper's Mag., LXXIX. 972.

prase (prāz), *n.* [< F. *prase*, leek-green, < Gr. πράσον, a leek: see *prason*.] A cryptocrystalline variety of quartz, of a leek-green color. See *quartz*.

prasine (pras'in), *a.* [< OF. *prasin*, fem. *prasine*, < L. *prasinus*, < Gr. πράσινος, leek-green, < πράσον, leek: see *prason*.] **1.** Of a light-green color, inclining to yellow.—**2.** In *her.*, same as *vert*. Also *prasin*.

prasinous (pras'i-nus), *a.* [< *prasine* + *-ous*.] Same as *prasine*.

prasoid (prā'soid), *a.* [< Gr. πρασοειδής, like a leek, < πράσον, leek, + εἶδος, form.] Resembling prase.

prason† (prā'son), *n.* [< Gr. πράσον, leek, = L. *porrum*, leek: see *porret*.] A leek; also, a seaweed of leek-green color.

prat[1]**†** (prat), *n.* [< ME. *prat*, < AS. *præt*, *prætt*, a trick, craft: see *pretty*.] A trick.

prat[2] (prat), *n.* [Origin obscure.] The buttock. [Slang.]

Fiddle, Patrico, and let me sing.
First set me down here on both my *prats*.
Brome, Jovial Crew, ii.

pratal (prā'tal), *a.* [< L. *pratum*, a meadow.] In *bot.*, growing in meadows. Compare *pascual*.

prate (prāt), *v.*; pret. and pp. *prated*, ppr. *prating*. [< ME. *praten*, < MD. D. *praten* = MLG. LG. *praten* = Icel. Sw. *prata* = Dan. *prate*, talk, prate. Hence freq. *prattle*.] **I.** *intrans.* To talk idly or boastfully; be loquacious; chatter; babble.

To speke or *prate*, or vse much talke, ingenders many lyes. *Babees Book* (E. E. T. S.), p. 94.

Quoth bold Robin Hood, "Thou dost *prate* like an ass."
Robin Hood and Little John (Child's Ballads, V. 218).

Hear not my steps, which way they walk, for fear
Thy very stones *prate* of my whereabouts.
Shak., Macbeth, ii. 1. 58.

II. *trans.* To utter foolishly; chatter.

He that *prates* his secrets,
His heart stands a' th' side.
Tourneur, Revenger's Tragedy, iii. 5.

He *prates* Latin
An it were a parrot, or a play-boy.
B. Jonson, New Inn, i. 1.

prate (prāt), *n.* [= D. *praat* = Sw. Dan. *prat*, talk; from the verb.] Idle or childish talk; prattle; unmeaning loquacity; twaddle.

If I talk to him, with his innocent *prate*
He will awake my mercy which lies dead.
Shak., K. John, iv. 1. 25.

Will the child kill me with her foolish *prate*?
Tennyson, Guinevere.

=**Syn.** See *prattle*.

prate-apace† (prāt'a-pās"), *n.* A prater; a talkative person; a chatterbox. [Rare.]

Prince of passions, *prate-apaces*, and pickl'd lovers.
Heywood, Love's Mistress, ii. 1.

prateful† (prāt'fụl), *a.* Inclined to prate; loquacious; idly talkative.

The French character seems to me much altered; . . . the people are more circumspect, less *prateful*.
Taylor of Norwich, 1802 (Memoir, I. 208). (*Davies.*)

prater (prā'tėr), *n.* [< *prate* + *-er*[1].] One who prates; an idle talker; a loquacious person; one who speaks much to little purpose; a babbler.

What! a speaker is but a *prater*.
Shak., Hen. V., v. 2. 166.

A Yorkshire girl herself, she hated to hear Yorkshire abused by such a pitiful *prater*.
Charlotte Brontë, Shirley, vi.

pratic†, *n.* See *pratique*.

praticien (F. pron. pra-tē-si-aṅ'), *n.* [F.: see *practician*.] In *French law*, a person appointed by the court to examine into a question of account and to report; an expert referee.

Praticola (prā-tik'ō-lạ̈), *n.* [NL., < L. *pratum*, a meadow, + *colere*, inhabit.] **1.** In *ornith.*, same as *Pratincola*. *Kaup*, 1819.—**2.** In *conch.*, a genus of land-snails or *Helicidæ*. *Strebel*, 1879.

pratily†, *adv.* An obsolete form of *prettily*.

Pratincola (prā-ting'kō-lạ̈), *n.* [NL.: see *pratincole*.] **1.** In *ornith.*, a genus of chats or saxicoline birds; the whinchats, such as *P. rubicola* and *P. rubetra* of Europe. Also called *Praticola*, *Fruticicola*, and *Rubetra*.—**2.** [*l. c.*] Same as *pratincole*.

pratincole (prat'ing-kōl), *n.* [< NL. *pratincola*, < L. *pratum*, a meadow, + *incola*, an inhabitant: see *incolant*.] A glareole, as *Glareola pratincola*; any bird of the family *Glareolidæ*. See cut under *Glareola*.

prating (prā'ting), *p. a.* Chattering; talking idly; loquacious.

prating (prā'ting), *n.* [Verbal n. of *prate*, *v.*] Idle or boastful talk. =**Syn.** *Chatter*, etc. See *prattle*.

pratingly (prā'ting-li), *adv.* In a prating manner; with much idle talk; with loquacity.

pratique, pratic (prat'ēk, -ik), *n.* [Formerly also *prattic*, *prattick*, etc.; in later use conformed to the F., *pratique*, *prattique*, < F. *pratique*, practice: see *practic*.] **1.** In *com.*, intercourse; the communication between a ship and the port in which she arrives; hence, a license or permission to hold intercourse and trade with the inhabitants of a place, especially after quarantine, or certificate of non-infectiveness.

We remain yet aboard, and must be content to be so, to make up the month before we have *pratic*—that is, before any be permitted to go ashore and negotiate, in regard we touched at some infected Places.
Howell, Letters, I. i. 26.

At first, indeed, *Prattick* was allow'd, though only to two or three of our Seamen out of every Ship, who had the Favour to go ashoar. *Milton*, Letters of State, May, 1658.

Almost as soon as we had anchored, the quarantine officer came on board and gave us *pratique*.
E. Sartorius, In the Soudan, p. 93.

2†. Experience; practice.

One (either of Venice or Padoa) hath written unto a certain Florentine, of great *prattick* with strangers, to enquire after me amongst the Dutch nation.
Sir H. Wotton, Reliquiæ, p. 663.

How could any one of English education and *prattique* swallow such a low rabble suggestion? Much more monstrous is it to imagine readers so imposable upon to credit it upon any one's bare relation.
Roger North, Examen, p. 306. (*Davies.*)

prattic†, *n.* An obsolete variant of *pratique*.

prattle (prat'l), *v.*; pret. and pp. *prattled*, ppr. *prattling*. [Freq. and dim. of *prate*.] **I.** *intrans.* To talk artlessly and childishly; talk freely and idly, like a child; chatter; be loquacious; prate.

The office of the woman is to spin and *prattle*, and the office of the man is to holde his peace and fight.
Guevara, Letters (tr. by Hellowes, 1577), p. 161.

Now we *prattle*
Of handsome gentlemen, in my opinion
Malfato is a very pretty fellow.
Ford, Lady's Trial, i. 2.

II. *trans.* **1.** To force or effect by talking; bring or lead by prattling.

Tongue, I must put you into a butter-woman's mouth, and buy myself another of Bajazet's mule, if you *prattle* me into these perils. *Shak.*, All's Well, iv. 1. 46.

2. To utter in a babbling or childish manner.

Frequent in park with lady at his side,
Ambling and *prattling* scandal as he goes.
Cowper, Task, ii. 382.

prattle (prat'l), *n.* [< *prattle*, *v.*] Artless or childish talk; hence, puerile loquacity; twaddle.

Mere *prattle*, without practice,
Is all his soldiership. *Shak.*, Othello, i. 1. 26.

=**Syn.** *Prattle*, *Prating*, *Chat*, *Chatter*, *Babble*, *Tattle*, *Gossip*, *Gabble*, *Palaver*, *Twaddle*, *Gibberish*, *Jargon*, *Balderdash*, *Rigmarole*. *Prattle* is generally harmless, if not pleasant, as the *prattle* of a child, or of a simple-minded person; *prating* now generally suggests the idea of boasting or talking above one's knowledge; *chat* is easy conversation upon light and agreeable subjects, as social *chat* beside an open fire; *chatter* is incessant or abundant talk, seeming rather foolish and sounding pretty much alike; *babble* or *babbling* is talk that is foolish to inaneness, as that of the drunkard (Prov. xxiii. 29); *tattle* is talk upon subjects that are petty, and especially such as breed scandal; *gossip* is the small talk of the neighborhood, especially upon personal matters, perhaps dealing with scandal; *gabble* is a contemptuous word, putting the talk upon the level of the sounds made by geese; *palaver* implies that the talk is either longer than is necessary, or wordy, or meant to deceive by flattery and plausibility; *twaddle* is mere silliness in talk; *gibberish* is mere sounds strung together without sense; *jargon* is talk that is unintelligible by the mingling of sounds or by the lack of meaning; *balderdash* is noisy nonsense; *rigmarole* is talk that has the form of sense, but is really incoherent, confused, or nonsensical.

prattle-basket† (prat'l-bås"ket), *n.* A prattle-box.

But if she be ilfauor'd, blind and old,
A *prattle-basket*, or an idle slut.
Breton, Mother's Blessing, st. 74. (*Davies.*)

prattlebox (prat'l-boks), *n.* A chatterbox; a prattler.

The old *prattlebox* . . . made a short pause to recover breath. *Peter Wilkins*, I. ii.

prattlement (prat'l-mẹnt), *n.* [< *prattle* + *-ment*.] Prattle.

The childish *prattlement* of pastoral composition.
Cowper, Letter to Unwin, Oct. 31, 1779.

prattler (prat'lėr), *n.* [< *prattle* + *-er*[1].] One who prattles; a puerile or trifling talker.

Poor *prattler*, how thou talk'st!
Shak., Macbeth, iv. 2. 64.

praty[1]**†**, *a.* An obsolete form of *pretty*.

praty[2] (prā'ti), *n.* A dialectal (Irish) corruption of *potato*.

prau, *n.* Same as *proa*. *H. O. Forbes*, Eastern Archipelago, p. 126.

praunce†, *v. i.* An obsolete form of *prance*.

pravilege†, *n.* [< L. *pravus*, bad, + *lex* (*leg-*), law; formed in contrast with *privilege*.] A bad law. [Rare.]

And whatsoeuer colour of right, in Exemptions, Customes, Priuiledges, and *prauileges* . . .
Purchas, Pilgrimage, p. 133.

pravity (prav'i-ti), *n.*; pl. *pravities* (-tiz). [= OF. *pravité* = Sp. *pravedad* = Pg. *pravidade* = It. *pravità*, < L. *pravitas*, crookedness, badness, deformity, < *pravus*, crooked, bad. Cf. *deprave*, *depravity*.] Evil or corrupt state; moral perverseness; depravity; wickedness; depraved action.

As these *pravities* have corrupted him [the devil], we must hate him. *Rev. T. Adams*, Works, II. 41.

Give me leave first to make an inquisition after this antichristian *pravity*. *Jer. Taylor*, Works (ed. 1835), II. 94.

prawling (prâ'ling), *n.* An accommodated form of *praline*. *Workshop Receipts*, 2d ser., p. 159.

prawn (prân), *n.* [Early mod. E. also *praun*, *prane*; < ME. *prane*, a prawn; perhaps transposed from an unrecorded OF. **purne*, **perne*, a prawn (?), = Sp. *perna*, a flat shell-fish, = OIt. *perna*, "a nakre or narre-fish" (Florio), cf. dim. *parnocchie*, pl., "shrimps or prawne fishes" (Florio), < L. *perna*, a sea-mussel, so called from its shape, < *perna* (> OF. *perne*), ham.] A long-tailed ten-footed crustacean, *Palæmon serratus*, abundant on the shores of Great Britain, resembling the shrimp, but having a long serrate rostrum; hence, any species of the family *Palæmonidæ*. The common prawn is 3 or 4 inches long, and is marketed in vast numbers. Among the species known as prawns in the United States, and available for food, are

Prawn (*Palæmon serratus*).

Palæmonetes vulgaris, *Palinurus interruptus* (the California sea-crawfish), and the shrimp (*Peneus brasiliensis*) of the southern United States. Æsop's prawn is a member of the genus *Hippolyte*.

Praxean (prak'sē-an), *n.* [< *Praxeas* (see def.) + *-an.*] A follower of Praxeas, a Patripassian leader belonging to the close of the second and the beginning of the third century. See *Monarchian* and *Patripassian*.

Praxeanist (prak'sē-an-ist), *n.* [< *Praxean* + *-ist.*] Same as *Praxean*.

praxinoscope (prak'si-nọ̄-skōp), *n.* [Irreg. < Gr. *πρᾶξις*, a doing, + *σκοπεῖν*, view.] An instrument allied to the phenakistoscope and zoetrope, and giving like effects. Pictures representing a cycle of positions of a moving object, as a running horse or a dancer, are arranged in due order on the inside surfaces of a polygonal box in the center of which is also placed a polygonal prism having one side facing each picture in the cycle. On each face of the prism is affixed a flat mirror. The box with its contained pictures and mirrors is rotated horizontally. The eye, fixed upon the central arrangement of mirrors, then sees the object apparently performing its natural movements.

praxis (prak'sis), *n.* [< NL. *praxis*, < Gr. *πρᾶξις*, a doing, action, practice, condition, < *πράσσειν*, make, do: see *practic*.] 1. Use; practice; especially, practice or discipline for a specific purpose, as the acquisition of a specific art.

An impious treatise of the elements and *praxis* of necromancy. *Coventry*, Philemon to Hydaspes, iii.

There are few sciences more intrinsically valuable than mathematics. . . . They are the noblest *praxis* of logick, or universal reasoning. *J. Harris*, Hermes, Pref.

2. An example or a collection of examples for practice; a representative specimen; a model.

A *praxis* or example of grammatical resolution. *Bp. Lowth*, Introd. to Eng. Gram. (ed. 1763), p. 185.

The pleadings of the Ancients were *praxises* of the art of oratorical persuasion. *Gillies*, tr. of Aristotle, II. 348.

3. [*cap.*] [NL.] In *zoöl.*: (*a*) A genus of lepidopterous insects of the family *Noctuidæ*, erected for two handsome Australian species. *Guenée*, 1852. (*b*) A genus of mollusks. *Adams*, 1858.

Praxitelean (praks-it-e-lē'an), *a.* [< L. *Praxiteles*, < Gr. *Πραξιτέλης*, Praxiteles (see def.), + *-ean.*] Of or pertaining to Praxiteles, of the fourth century B. C., one of the greatest of ancient Greek sculptors; executed by or characteristic of Praxiteles or his school. The art of Praxiteles was more luxurious than that of his predecessors; his types were sympathetic, abounding in pathos, and his expression of sentiment and character very subtly rendered. An original work by him has been recovered in the Hermes and Infant Dionysus at Olympia (see cut under *Greek*). See also cut under *Aphrodite*.

pray[1] (prā), *v.* [< ME. *prayen*, *preyen*, *preien*, < OF. *preier*, *praier*, *proier*, *preer*, *prier*, F. *prier* = Pr. *preyar*, *pregar* = It. *pregare*, pray, < L. *precari*, ML. also *precare*, ask, beg, entreat, beseech, pray, supplicate; cf. *prex* (*prec-*), usually in pl. *preces*, a prayer, *procare*, ask, demand, *procus*, a wooer; cf. Skt. √ *prachh*, ask: see *frain*[1], and cf. *postulate*. Hence ult. (from L. *precari*) E. *prayer*[1], *precarious*, *precative*, *deprecate*, *imprecate*, etc.] I. *intrans.* 1. To ask earnestly; beg; entreat; supplicate, as for a personal grace or favor.

The guilty rebel for remission *prays*. *Shak.*, Lucrece, l. 714.

Had you cried, or knelt, or *pray'd* to me,
I should not less have kill'd him. *Tennyson*, Geraint.

2. In religious usage, to make devout petition to God, or (in some forms of religion) to any object of worship, as a saint or an angel; more generally, to enter into spiritual communion with God, usually through the medium of speech. See *prayer*[1].

It was moche more comforte and gladnesse to vs to have suche wether as we hadde longe desyred and *prayde* for. *Sir R. Guylforde*, Pylgrymage, p. 74.

When thou *prayest*, enter into thy closet, and, when thou hast shut thy door, *pray* to thy Father which is in secret, and thy Father which seeth in secret shall reward thee openly. Mat. vi. 6.

We do *pray* for mercy;
And that same prayer doth teach us all to render
The deeds of mercy. *Shak.*, M. of V., iv. 1. 200.

Pray for my soul. More things are wrought by prayer
Than this world dreams of. *Tennyson*, Morte d'Arthur.

I pray, usually, by ellipsis, **pray**, a common formula introducing a question, invitation, suggestion, or request. Compare *prithee*.

My father
Is hard at study; *pray* now, rest yourself. *Shak.*, Tempest, iii. 1. 20.

Pray, leave these frumps, sir, and receive this letter. *Beau. and Fl.*, Scornful Lady, v. 1.

II. *trans.* 1. To ask earnestly; beg; entreat; supplicate; urge.

Pacience apposed hym fyrste and *preyed* hym he sholde hem telle
To Conscience, what crafte he couthe an to what countree he wolde. *Piers Plowman* (B), xiii. 222.

Call to remembrance (I *prai* thee) the vaine youthfull fantasie and ouertimelie death of fathers and thy brethren. *Holinshed*, Hist. Eng., an. 640.

We *pray* you in Christ's stead, be ye reconciled to God. 2 Cor. v. 20.

You are passing welcome,
And so I *pray* you all to think yourselves. *Shak.*, T. of the S., ii. 1. 114.

She *pray'd* me not to judge their cause from her
That wrong'd it. *Tennyson*, Princess, vii.

2. In religious usage, to address a desire or petition to (specifically to God) devoutly and with reverence.

And I will *pray* the Father, and he shall give you another Comforter. John xiv. 16.

Cham. There is hope
All will be well.
Anne. Now, I *pray* God, amen! *Shak.*, Hen. VIII., ii. 3. 56.

She was ever *praying* the sweet heavens
To save her dear lord whole from any wound. *Tennyson*, Geraint.

3. To offer up, as a prayer; utter in devotion.

I haue had no time to *pray* my houres, much lesse to aunswere your leters missiue. *Guevara*, Letters (tr. by Hellowes, 1577), p. 126.

I'll *pray* a thousand prayers for thy death,
No word to save thee. *Shak.*, M. for M., iii. 1. 146.

4. To make entreaty or petition for; crave; implore: as, the plaintiff *prays* judgment of the court.

I know not how to *pray* your patience. *Shak.*, Much Ado, v. 1. 280.

He that will have the benefit of this act must *pray* a prohibition before a sentence in the ecclesiastical court. *Ayliffe*, Parergon.

An address was presented to the king, *praying* that Impey might be summoned home to answer for his misdeeds. *Macaulay*, Warren Hastings.

5. To effect, move, or bring by prayer or entreaty: followed by an adverb or a preposition particularizing the meaning.

I *pray* you *home* to dinner with me. *Shak.*, M. for M., ii. 1. 292.

Occiduus is a pastor of renown:
When he has *pray'd* and preach'd the Sabbath *down*,
With wire and catgut he concludes the day. *Cowper*, Progress of Error, l. 125.

Praying souls *out* of purgatory, by masses said on their behalf, became an ordinary office. *Milman*, Latin Christianity, xiv. 2.

To pray in aid, in *law*, to call in, as aid, one who has an interest in the cause (see *aid-prayer*); hence, to become an advocate for.

You shall find
A conqueror that will *pray in aid* for kindness,
Where he for grace is kneel'd to. *Shak.*, A. and C., v. 2. 27.

Without *praying in aid* of alchymists, there is a manifest image of this in the ordinary course of nature. *Bacon*, Friendship (ed. 1887).

=**Syn.** 1. To crave, implore, beseech, petition, importune. See *prayer*[1].

pray[2]†, *n.* and *v.* An obsolete spelling of *prey*[2].

pray[3] (prā), *v. i.* A dialectal form of *pry*.

praya[1] (prī'ä), *n.* [< Pg. *praia*, shore, beach, bank.] In some cities of India, an embanked road; a public walk or drive on a river-bank or water-front; a bund.

A more practical scheme is the proposed building of the whole river front of the city, the reclamation of a considerable amount of frontage, and the construction of a broad *praya* suitable for wheeled conveyances, and lighted by electricity. *The Engineer*, LXIX. 65.

Praya[2] (prā'ä), *n.* [NL.] The typical genus of *Prayidæ*.

prayant† (prā'ant), *a.* [< OF. *preiant*, ppr. of *preier*, pray: see *pray*[1].] Being in the mood or attitude of prayer.

Fanatick Errour and Levity would seem an Euchite as well as an Eristick, *Prayant* as well as predicant. *Bp. Gauden*, Tears of the Church, p. 93.

prayell†, *n.* [< OF. *prayel*, *prael*, *pratel*, < ML. *pratellum*, < L. *pratulum*, dim. of *pratum*, a meadow. Cf. *prayere*, *prairie*.] A little meadow. *Halliwell*.

prayer[1] (prãr), *n.* [< ME. *prayer*, *prayere*, *proer*, *preyer*, *preyre*, *preyere*, *preiere*, < OF. *preiere*, *preere*, *proiere*, *priere*, F. *prière* = It. *pregaria*, < ML. *precaria*, a supplication, prayer, prop. fem. of L. *precarius*, obtained by entreaty or favor, hence depending on favor, doubtful, transient, < *precari*, entreat, supplicate: see *pray*[1], and cf. *precarious*.] 1. The act of beseeching, entreating, or supplicating; supplication; entreaty; petition; suit.

That ys to seye sothliche ȝe sholde rather deye
Than eny dedliche synne do for drede other for *preyere*. *Piers Plowman* (C), viii. 210.

He sought to have that by practice which he could not by *prayer*. *Sir P. Sidney*, Arcadia, ii.

Thy threats have no more strength than her weak *prayers*. *Shak.*, M. N. D., iii. 2. 250.

2. In religious usage, a devout petition to an object of worship, as God, or a saint or an angel; an orison: confined in Protestant usage to such petitions addressed to God; more generally, any spiritual communion with God, including confession, petition, adoration, praise, and thanksgiving. See *dulia*.

When thou comes to tho chirche dore,
Take the haly water stondand on flore;
Rede or synge or byd *prayeris*
To crist, for alle thy crysten ferys. *Babees Book* (E. E. T. S.), p. 304.

What is *prayer* but an ascent of the mind towards God? *Bp. Atterbury*, Sermons, II. xx.

Prayer is the soul's sincere desire,
Uttered or unexpressed. *J. Montgomery*, Hymn.

Thrice blest whose lives are faithful *prayers*. *Tennyson*, In Memoriam, xxxii.

3. The practice of praying, or of communing with God.

He is famed for mildness, peace, and *prayer*. *Shak.*, 3 Hen. VI., ii. 1. 156.

It hath been well said of *prayer*, that *prayer* will either make a man leave off sinning, or sin will make him leave off *prayer*. *Paley*, Sermons, i.

So keep I fair thro' faith and *prayer*
A virgin heart in work and will. *Tennyson*, Sir Galahad.

4. The form of words used in praying; a formula of worship: as, the Lord's *Prayer*.

He . . . made those two excellent *prayers*, which were published after his death. *Bp. Fell*, Hammond, p. 212.

Not a bell was rung, not a *prayer* was read. *Tennyson*, Maud, xxvii.

5. A form of religious service; a religious observance, either public or private, consisting mainly of prayer to God; a liturgy: often in the plural: as, the service of morning *prayer*; family *prayers*.

She went from opera, park, assembly, play,
To morning walks, and *prayers* three hours a-day. *Pope*, To Miss Blount, ii.

Prayers and calling-over seemed twice as short as usual. T. *Hughes*, Tom Brown at Rugby, i. 8.

6. That part of a memorial or petition to a public body, or of a bill of complaint in equity, which specifies the thing desired to be done or granted, as distinct from the recital of facts or reasons for the grant.—**Apostleship of prayer.** See *apostleship*.—**Book of Common Prayer**, the book containing the appointed forms for public worship and for the words and acts used in the rites and ceremonies of the Church of England, or a similar book authorized by one of the other branches of the Anglican Church: briefly and popularly known as the *Prayer-book*. After the publication in English of the Litany in 1544, and of the parts of the communion office relating to the communion of the people in 1548, the First Book of Common Prayer was issued in 1549, the second year of Edward VI. Almost the whole book is taken from the medieval liturgical books, especially the missal, portiforium (breviary), and manual according to the Use of Sarum (see *use*), but with omissions, condensations, and the addition of a number of addresses to the people. English was substituted for Latin, all the offices were united in one book, and a uniform use was established for the whole Church of England. Successive revisions were made in 1552, 1559, and 1662. The greatest changes were those introduced in the Second Prayer-book of Edward VI. (1552), especially in the communion office (see *communion*) and at confirmation and burial. This book never came into actual use, but was in the main followed in the revision under Elizabeth in 1559 and in the present English book as issued in 1662, after the restoration of Charles II., but with material modifications, especially in 1662, returning toward the standard of 1549. The Prayer-book authorized in 1637 for use in Scotland, and differing from the English book mainly in the communion office, met with serious opposition at the time, but came into use afterward in the Scotch Episcopal Church. The American Prayer-book, authorized in 1789, differs from the English mainly in the omission of the Athanasian Creed and of the form of private absolution in the visitation of the sick, the restoration of the great oblation and invocation to their primitive places in the prayer of consecration (see *consecration*), and the later addition of the offices of consecration of churches and institution of ministers. In 1886 a new revision took place, resulting chiefly in a return to the English book in several points: this revision was completed in 1892. The Psalter, Ordinal, and Thirty-nine Articles are always bound with the Book of Common Prayer, and usually considered parts of it,

though technically speaking they are distinct from it. —Commendatory, common, Lord's, passive, etc., **prayer**. See the qualifying words.—**Hours of prayer.** Same as *canonical hours* (which see, under *canonical*).—**House of prayer.** See *house of God*, under *house*[1].—**Prayer of humble access.** See *access*.—**The long prayer**, in non-liturgical churches, the chief prayer of the service. It is usually offered just before the sermon, or before the hymn preparatory to the sermon. Also called *pastoral prayer*.—**To lead in prayer.** See *lead*[1]. =**Syn.** *Prayer, Petition, Request, Entreaty, Supplication, Suit, Appeal*, invocation, orison. *Prayer* is always addressed to God, but *a prayer* may be addressed to a sovereign, legislative body, court, or the like, always to a person or body recognized as having authority in some way, and asking for something especially important. A *petition* may be a single point in a *prayer*: thus, the Lord's *Prayer* contains one address, three loyal desires, four *petitions*, and a closing ascription. A *petition* may also be a formal and public *request* or *prayer*, but still generally covering only a single thing desired. *Request* is the most general and least forcible of these words, indicating nothing as to the degree of formality of the act or as to the rank of the persons concerned. An *entreaty* is an urgent, perhaps tender, request, generally from and to a person. A *supplication* is still more urgent, the request being made with passion, and humbly, as to a superior. The word *entreaty* is not often followed by the mention of that which is desired, but may be: as, *entreaty* for aid. A *suit* is a petition or an entreaty prolonged for any reason: hence we speak of a lover's *suit* or a *suit* at law. An *appeal* is an urgent request, of the nature of a call or demand. See *ask*[1].

> Whence can comfort spring,
> When *prayer* is of no avail?
> *Wordsworth*, Force of Prayer.

> This one *prayer* yet remains, might I be heard,
> No long *petition*, speedy death,
> The close of all my miseries, and the balm.
> *Milton*, S. A., l. 650.

> I will marry her, sir, at your *request*.
> *Shak.*, M. W. of W., i. 1. 253.

> Yet not with brawling opposition she,
> But manifold *entreaties*, many a tear, . . .
> Besought him. *Tennyson*, Enoch Arden.

> I have attempted one by one the lords, . . .
> With *supplication* prone and father's tears,
> To accept of ransom for my son their prisoner.
> *Milton*, S. A., l. 1459.

> They make great *sute* to serue her.
> *Ascham*, The Scholemaster, p. 77.

> Meanwhile must be an earnest motion
> Made to the queen, to call back her *appeal*
> She intends unto his holiness.
> *Shak.*, Hen. VIII., ii. 4. 234.

prayer[2] (prā'ėr), *n.* [< ME. *prayere*, < OF. *preieur*, F. *prieur*, < L. *precator*, one who prays, < *precari*, pray: see *pray*[1], *v.*] One who prays; a suppliant; a petitioner.

prayer-bead (prãr'bēd), *n.* A seed of the plant Indian licorice, *Abrus precatorius*.

prayer-book (prãr'bůk), *n.* 1. A book of forms for public or private devotion, consisting chiefly or solely of forms for prayers. See *Book of Common Prayer*, under *prayer*[1].—2. *Naut.*, a small stone used in scrubbing the deck and other woodwork of a vessel: so called from its shape and size. Compare *holystone*.

> Smaller hand-stones, which the sailors call *prayer-books*, are used to scrub in among the crevices and narrow places, where the large holystone will not go.
> *R. H. Dana, Jr.*, Before the Mast, p. 208.

prayer-carpet (prãr'kär"pet), *n.* A prayer-rug.

> The rich use a *prayer-carpet* (called segga'deh) about the size of our hearth-rugs.
> *E. W. Lane*, Modern Egyptians, I. 81.

prayer-cure (prãr'kūr), *n.* The cure of disease by means of prayer.

prayere†, *n.* [ME., < OF. *praiere*, *praere*, *proiere*, a meadow, < ML. *prataria*, a meadow: see *prairie*, and cf. *prayell*.] A meadow.

> A castel the comlockest that euer knygt agte,
> Pyched on a *prayere*, a park al aboute.
> *Sir Gawayne and the Green Knight* (E. E. T. S.), l. 768.

prayerful (prãr'fůl), *a.* [< *prayer*[1] + *-ful*.] 1. Praying much; devout.

> They melt, retract, reform, and are watchful and *prayerful* to prevent similar miscarriages in future.
> *Jay*, Sermons, p. 70. (*Latham.*)

2. Devotional; given to prayer; occupied with prayer: as, a *prayerful* spirit.

> He had sunk back in his chair, . . . and was pursuing a sort of *prayerful* meditation.
> *George Eliot*, Felix Holt, xxxviii.

prayerfully (prãr'fůl-i), *adv.* In a prayerful manner; with prayer.

prayerfulness (prãr'fůl-nes), *n.* The state of being prayerful.

prayerless (prãr'les), *a.* [< *prayer*[1] + *-less*.] Without prayer; not having the habit of prayer: as, a *prayerless* family; also, not having the blessing or protection of prayer.

> Let a servant or child go *prayerless* to their work, and few regard it; but they will not go without meat, or drink, or clothes. *Baxter*, Self-denial, iv.

> Never on *prayerless* bed
> To lay thine unblest head.
> *Margaret Mercer*, Exhortation to Prayer.

prayerlessly (prãr'les-li), *adv.* In a prayerless manner; without prayer.

prayerlessness (prãr'les-nes), *n.* The state of being prayerless; total or habitual neglect of prayer.

prayer-meeting (prãr'mē"ting), *n.* A meeting for prayer; especially, a service devoted to prayer, sacred song, and other religious exercises, in which laymen take part.

> Hence the importance he justly attaches to his accurate family worship, morning and night; to his exact attendance on the Wednesday night *prayer-meeting*, which he prizes as a sort of Sabbath hour in the centre of the week.
> *W. M. Baker*, New Timothy, p. 160.

prayer-mill (prãr'mil), *n.* Same as *praying-wheel*.

prayer-monger (prãr'mung"gėr), *n.* One who offers prayers. [Contemptuous.]

> I have led
> Some camel-kneed *prayer-monger* through the cave.
> *Southey*, Thalaba, v. 34.

prayer-rug (prãr'rug), *n.* A rug or small carpet intended to be spread on the floor of a mosque, the roof of a house, or the ground by a Moslem when engaged in his devotions. He stands on it, with his face turned toward Mecca, and prostrates himself, touching the carpet with his forehead from time to time. In many of the prayer-rugs of Persia and Arabia the place to receive the forehead in prostration is indicated in the pattern at one end of the carpet. Compare *doorshek*.

prayer-stick (prãr'stik), *n.* A decorated stick used by the Zuñi Indians in their religious ceremonies.

> It was nearly hidden by symbolic slats and *prayer-sticks* most elaborately plumed. *The Century*, XXVI. 29.

prayer-thong (prãr'thông), *n.* Same as *phylactery* (*a*). [Rare.]

> Phylactery (φυλακτήριον) is the name given in the New Testament to the . . . (tefillin) or *prayer-thongs* of the Jews. *Encyc. Brit.*, XIX. 1.

prayer-wheel (prãr'hwēl), *n.* Same as *praying-wheel*.

Prayidæ (prā'i-dē), *n. pl.* [NL., < *Praya* + *-idæ*.] A family of oceanic hydrozoans of the order *Calycophora*, typified by the genus *Praya*. It is related to *Diphyidæ*, and often merged in that family.

praying (prā'ing), *n.* [Verbal n. of *pray*[1], *v.*] A service of prayer.

> That purgatory, saintes worshippinge, masses, and *prayinges* for the dead, with such like, were mooste deuelyshe inuencions. *Bp. Bale*, English Votaries, ii.

praying-desk (prā'ing-desk), *n.* A piece of furniture affording a desk to support books for prayer and worship and a platform on which to kneel; especially, such an article forming a piece of furniture in a private house, as in a bedroom or an oratory. Also called *prie-dieu*.

> A man and his wife are kneeling at an old-fashioned *praying-desk*, and the woman clasps a little sickly-looking child in her arms, and all three are praying as earnestly as their simple hearts will let them.
> *Thackeray*, Men and Pictures.

praying-insect (prā'ing-in"sekt), *n.* A gressorial and raptorial orthopterous insect of the family *Mantidæ*: so called from the peculiar attitude and position of the fore legs, which are raised and held as in the act of prayer. See cut under *Mantis*.

prayingly (prā'ing-li), *adv.* In a praying manner; with devout supplication.

> It is indeed the same ability to speak affirmatively, or doctrinally, and only by changing the mood to speak *prayingly*. *Milton*, Apology for Smectymnuus.

praying-machine (prā'ing-ma-shēn"), *n.* See *praying-wheel*.

praying-mantis (prā'ing-man"tis), *n.* A praying-insect. See cut under *Mantis*.

praying-wheel (prā'ing-hwēl), *n.* A revolving apparatus used for prayer. (*a*) Among the Buddhists of Tibet and other parts of the East, a wheel or cylinder, varying in size, used as a mechanical aid to prayer. One variety contains the Buddhist canon; to another written prayers are attached, and upon being set in motion each revolution of the wheel or cylinder counts as an uttered prayer. Sometimes the wheel is fixed in the bed of a stream, and kept in motion by the current, thus praying night and day for the person who has placed it there. See cut in next column. (*b*) In western Europe, a wheel set with bells and fastened to the ceiling of certain medieval chapels. This contrivance was used as a means of divination, being set in motion during high mass or on feast-days, when its position on coming to rest was supposed to denote a favorable or an unfavorable response to the prayer of the applicant. Also called *wheel of fortune*.

> The *praying-wheel* exists in old chapels in Brittany as a religious toy, formerly used with rites half magical under the sanction of the local clergy.
> *The Century*, XXXVII. 371.

prayset, *v. t.* An obsolete form of *praise*.

pre-. [In L. form also *præ-*; = F. *pré-* = Sp. Pg. It. *pre-*, < L. *præ-* (ML. usually *pre-*), prefix,

Praying-wheel in the Buddhist Temple at Asakusa, Tokio, Japan.

præ, adv., before, in front, prep., before, in front of, in advance of: in comparison, with, on account of, etc.; OL. **prai*, akin to Skt. *pra-*, before, etc.: see *pro-* and *fore-*[1]. This prefix occurs disguised or absorbed in *preach*, *premium*, *prey*[2], *prison*, *prize*[1], etc., and as *pro-* in *provand*, *provender*, *provost*, etc.] A prefix in words of Latin origin, meaning 'before,' in place, time, or rank. By reason of its great frequency in compounds of Latin origin or formation, it has been used and felt as an English formative, whether with words of Latin or Greek origin, as in *preact*, *prehistoric*, etc., or with other words, as in *preraphaelite*, *preadamite*, etc., though rarely with native English verbs, as in *pre-look*. In zoölogy *pre-* (or *præ-*) is a frequent prefix, used almost at will, indicating precedence, whether in time or place; it is quite synonymous with *ante-*, and to some extent with *pro-* or *proto-*, and is opposed to *post-* or *meta-* in any sense. In recent technical terms it is often in the Latin form *præ-*, such words, whether Latin or English in termination, having *pre-* or *præ-* almost indifferently. Strictly, in all such words having a Latin termination the prefix should be *præ-*; in words fully Englished, the form *pre-* is to be used. It is sometimes interchanged with *pro-*.

preaccusation (prē-ak-ū-zā'shon), *n.* [< *pre-* + *accusation*.] Previous accusation.

preacet, *n.* An obsolete form of *press*[1].

preacetabular (prē-as-e-tab'ū-lär), *a.* [< L. *præ*, before, + L. *acetabulum*, the socket of the hip-bone: see *acetabular*.] Situated in front of the acetabulum or cotyloid cavity of the hip-bone: as, the *preacetabular* area of the ilium.

preach (prēch), *v.* [< ME. *prechen*, < OF. *precher*, *prechier*, *precher*, *preecher*, *preescher*, *preeschier*, F. *prêcher* = Pr. *predicar*, *prezicar* = Sp. *predicar* = Pg. *pregar* = It. *predicare* = AS. *predician* = OS. *predicōn* = D. *prediken* = MLG. *prediken*, *predigen* = OHG. *predigōn*, *bredigōn*, MHG. *bredigen*, G. *predigen* = Icel. *prēdika* = Sw. *predika* = Dan. *prædike*, *præke*, preach, < L. *prædicare*, declare in public, publish, proclaim, LL. and ML. preach, < *præ*, before, + *dicare*, declare, proclaim, < *dicere*, say, tell: see *diction*, and cf. *predicate*.] I. *intrans.* 1. To make a public announcement; especially, to pronounce a public discourse upon a religious subject, or from a text of Scripture; deliver a sermon.

> But *precheth* nat, as freres doon in lente,
> To make us for our olde synnes wepe.
> *Chaucer*, Prol. to Clerk's Tale, l. 12.

> Now, good Conscience, and thou wolt *preche*,
> Goo stele an abite, & bicome a frere.
> *Hymns to Virgin*, etc. (E. E. T. S.), p. 67.

> How oft, when Paul has serv'd us with a text,
> Has Epictetus, Plato, Tully, *preach'd!*
> *Cowper*, Task, ii. 540.

2. To give earnest advice, especially on religious or moral subjects; also, to give advice obtrusively on religious or moral matters.

> His form and cause conjoin'd, *preaching* to stones,
> Would make them capable. *Shak.*, Hamlet, iii. 4. 126.

> Old Father Time deputes me here before ye,
> Not for to *preach*, but tell his simple story.
> *Burns*, Prol. Spoken at the Theatre, Dumfries.

> If it had been an unnamed species, surely it ought to have been called Diabolicus, for it is a fit toad to *preach* in the ear of Eve. *Darwin*, Voyage of Beagle, I. 124.

Preaching friars, a name sometimes given to the Dominicans, on account of the stress which they laid upon preaching.

II. *trans.* 1. To proclaim as a herald; declare; make known; publish.

> The Lord hath anointed me to *preach* good tidings unto the meek. Isa. lxi. 1.

> A world that seems
> To toll the death-bell of its own decease,
> And by the voice of all its elements
> To *preach* the gen'ral doom. *Cowper*, Task, ii. 53.

A heated pulpiteer,
Not *preaching* simple Christ to simple men,
Announced the coming doom.
Tennyson, Sea Dreams.

2. To inculcate (especially religious or moral truth or right conduct) in public or private discourse.

I have *preached* righteousness in the great congregation. Ps. xl. 9.

Ungracious wretch,
Fit for the mountains and the barbarous caves,
Where manners ne'er were *preach'd!*
Shak., T. N., iv. 1. 53.

Now as for spelling, I have always *preached* the extremest doctrine of liberty of spelling. At the utmost, I have only asked to be allowed to indulge my own fancies and to allow other people to indulge theirs. *E. A. Freeman*, Amer. Lects., p. 41.

3. To deliver, as a public religious discourse; pronounce, as a sermon.

A lytylle thens, 28 Pas, is a Chapelle, and there in is the Ston on the whiche oure Lord sat whan he *prechede* the 8 Blessynges. *Mandeville*, Travels, p. 96.

4. To affect by preaching, in a manner indicated by the context: as, to *preach* one into a penitent or a rebellious mood.—**To preach a funeral**, to pronounce a public funeral discourse. [Colloq.]

We are almost at the end of books: these paper-works are now *preaching* their own *funerals*. *Goad*, Preface to Dell's Works. (*Davies.*)

To preach down. (*a*) To decry; oppose in public discourse.

Last week came one to the county town,
To *preach* our poor little army *down*,
And play the game of the despot kings.
Tennyson, Maud, x.

(*b*) To silence or suppress by preaching: as, to *preach down* unbelief.—**To preach the cross**, to proclaim the death of Christ as the ground of salvation.—**To preach up**, to discourse in favor of.

Can they *preach up* equality of birth? *Dryden.*

preach (prēch), *n.* [< OF. *preche*, F. *prêche*, a preaching; from the verb.] A sermon; a religious discourse. [Colloq.]

According to this forme of theirs, it must stand for a rule: No sermon, no seruice. Which ouersight occasioned the French spitefully to terme religion in that sort exercised a mere *preach*. *Hooker*, Eccles. Polity, v. 28.

A word of his is as much as a whole *preach* of anybody's else. He says a word now and then, and it hits. *Mrs. Whitney*, Leslie Goldthwaite, v.

preacher (prē'chėr), *n.* [< ME. *precher*, *prechour*, < OF. *precheor*, *precheur*, F. *prêcheur* = Pr. *predicaire*, *prezicaire* = Sp. *predicador* = Pg. *pregador* = It. *predicatore* (cf. AS. *predicere*, D. *prediker* = MLG. *prediker*, *predeger* = OHG. *predigāri*, *bredigāri*, MHG. *bredigære*, G. *prediger* = Icel. *prēdikari*, with diff. suffix), a preacher, < L. *prædicator*, one who declares in public, a proclaimer, LL. and ML. a preacher, < *prædicare*, declare, preach: see *preach*.] 1. One who preaches; one who discourses publicly, especially on religious subjects; specifically, a clergyman.

There, where a few torn shrubs the place disclose,
The village *preacher's* modest mansion rose.
Goldsmith, Des. Vil., l. 140.

2. One who inculcates or asseverates anything with earnestness.

They are our outward consciences,
And *preachers* to us all. *Shak.*, Hen. V., iv. 1. 9.

We have him still a perpetual *Preacher* of his own vertues. *Milton*, Eikonoklastes, xii.

Friars preachers. See *Dominican*.—**Lay preacher**, a layman, or one not ordained to the ministry, who preaches.—**Local preacher.** See *local*.—**The Preacher.** See *Ecclesiastes*.

preacher-in-the-pulpit (prē'chėr-in-thē-pul'pit), *n.* The showy orchis, *Orchis spectabilis*. [Pennsylvania.]

preachership (prē'chėr-ship), *n.* [< *preacher* + *-ship*.] The office of a preacher.

preachify (prē'chi-fī), *v. i.*; pret. and pp. *preachified*, ppr. *preachifying*. [< *preach* + *-i-fy*.] To preach in a tedious or obtrusive way; give prolonged, tiresome moral advice. [Colloq.]

"Shut up your sarmons, Pitt, when Miss Crawley comes down," said his father; "she has written to say that she won't stand the *preachifying*." *Thackeray*, Vanity Fair, x.

preaching (prē'ching), *n.* [< ME. *prechynge*; verbal n. of *preach*, *v.*] 1. The act or practice of delivering public discourses, particularly upon moral or religious subjects; the art of delivering sermons.

If *preaching* decay, ignorance and brutishness will enter again. *Latimer*, 2d Sermon bef. Edw. VI., 1550.

2. That which is preached; a sermon; doctrine; theory.

His *preaching* was a striking contrast to the elegant Addisonian essays of Parson Lothrop. It was a vehement address to our intelligent and reasoning powers—an address made telling by a back force of burning enthusiasm. *H. B. Stowe*, Oldtown, p. 441.

Missionaries . . . rarely make rapid way unless their *preachings* fall in with the prepossessions of the multitude of shallow thinkers. *Huxley*, Pop. Sci. Mo., XXXVI. 761.

preaching-cross (prē'ching-krôs), *n.* A cross, sometimes simple, sometimes architecturally elaborate, connected with a small chapel,

Preaching-cross at Inveraray, Argyllshire, Scotland.

erected on a highway or in an open place, to mark a point where monks and others could assemble the people for religious services. See *cross*[1].

preachman† (prēch'man), *n.*; pl. *preachmen* (-men). [< *preach* + *man*.] A preacher. *Howell*, Letters, ii. 33. [Contemptuous.]

preachment (prēch'ment), *n.* [< OF. *prechement*, *preschement*, *preechement*, preaching, discourse, < ML. *prædicamentum*, preaching, discourse, declaration, < L. *prædicare*, declare, LL. and ML. preach: see *preach*, and cf. *predicament*.] A sermon; a lecture upon moral or religious subjects; hence, in contempt, any discourse affectedly solemn, or full of obtrusive or tedious advice.

No doubt, such lessons they will teach the rest
As by their *preachments* they will profit much.
Marlowe, Edward II.

Was 't you that revell'd in our parliament,
And made a *preachment* of your high descent?
Shak., 3 Hen. VI., i. 4. 72.

The sum of her iniquities is recounted by Knox in his *preachment* to the citizens of Edinburgh. *Stedman*, Vict. Poets, p. 407.

preachy (prē'chi), *a.* [< *preach* + *-y*[1].] Inclined to preach or give long-winded moral advice; of a tedious moralizing tendency. [Colloq.]

She has the art of making her typical good women real and attractive, while she never makes them prudish or *preachy*. *The Academy*, Oct. 19, 1889, p. 260.

preacquaint (prē-a-kwānt'), *v. t.* [< *pre-* + *acquaint*.] To acquaint beforehand; inform previously.

You have been *pre-acquainted* with her birth, education, and qualities. *B. Jonson*, Epicœne, ii. 3.

I'll *pre-acquaint* her, that she mayn't be frightened. *Steele*, Grief A-la-Mode, iv. 1.

preacquaintance (prē-a-kwān'tans), *n.* [< *pre-* + *acquaintance*.] Previous acquaintance or knowledge.

preact (prē-akt'), *v. t.* [< *pre-* + *act*.] To act beforehand; perform previously; rehearse.

Those which, though acted after evening service, must needs be *preacted* by the fancy . . . all the day before. *Fuller.* (*Webster.*)

preaction (prē-ak'shon), *n.* [< *pre-* + *action*.] Previous or antecedent action. *Sir T. Browne*, Vulg. Err., ii. 2.

pread†, *v.* See *prede*.

preadamic (prē-a-dam'ik), *a.* [< *pre-* + *Adamic*.] Existing prior to Adam; preadamite.

preadamite (prē-ad'a-mit), *n.* and *a.* [< NL. *præadamita*, < L. *præ*, before, + LL. *Adam*, Adam: see *Adamite*.] I. *n.* 1. One who lived before Adam; an inhabitant of the earth before the date assigned to Adam.

He is of great antiquity, perhaps before the creation, at least a *præadamite*; for Lucifer was the first of his family. *Butler*, Remains (ed. 1759), II. 408.

In the *preadamite* she [Nature] bred valor only, by-and-by she gets on to man, and adds tenderness, and thus raises virtue piecemeal. *Emerson*, N. A. Rev., CXXVI. 406.

The black races, then, are *preadamites*; and there is no objection to allowing all the time requisite for their divergence from some common stock. *Pop. Sci. Mo.*, XIII. 499.

2. One who holds that there were men in existence upon the earth before Adam.

II. *a.* 1. Existing or being prior to Adam.

Some feign that he is Enoch; others dream
He was *pre-Adamite*, and has survived
Cycles of generation and of ruin. *Shelley*, Hellas.

The Ginn are said to be of *preadamite* origin, an intermediate class of beings between angels and men. *E. W. Lane*, Modern Egyptians, I. 283.

2. Pertaining to the preadamites; relating to the period of the world's history prior to the time of Adam: as, the *preadamite* theory.

preadamitic (prē-ad-a-mit'ik), *a.* [< *preadamite* + *-ic*.] Same as *preadamite*.

preadamitical (prē-ad-a-mit'i-kal), *a.* Same as *preadamitic*.

Upon what memorials do you ground the story of your *pre-adamitical* transactions? *Gentleman Instructed*, p. 414. (*Davies.*)

preadaptation (prē-ad-ap-tā'shon), *n.* [< *pre-* + *adaptation*.] Previous adaptation; previous adjustment or conformation to some particular end.

The movements ["instinctive" appetites] are only more definite than those simply expressive of pain because of inherited *pre-adaptation*, on which account, of course, they are called "instinctive." *J. Ward*, Encyc. Brit., XX. 73.

preadjustment (prē-a-just'ment), *n.* [< *pre-* + *adjustment*.] Previous adjustment or arrangement. *J. Sully*, Outlines of Psychol., p. 90.

preadministration (prē-ad-min-is-trā'shon), *n.* [< *pre-* + *administration*.] Previous administration. *Bp. Pearson*, Expos. of Creed, x.

preadmission (prē-ad-mish'on), *n.* [< *pre-* + *admission*.] Previous admission.

An effect of lead is to cause *preadmission*—that is to say, admission before the end of the back stroke—which, together with the compression of steam left in the cylinder when the exhaust port closes, produces the mechanical effect of "cushioning." *Encyc. Brit.*, XXII. 501.

preadmonish (prē-ad-mon'ish), *v. t.* [< *pre-* + *admonish*.] To admonish previously.

These things thus *preadmonished*, let us enquire what the undoubted meaning is of our Saviour's words. *Milton*, Judgement of M. Bucer on Divorce, xxx.

preadmonition (prē-ad-mō-nish'on), *n.* [< *pre-* + *admonition*.] Previous warning or admonition.

The fatal *preadmonition* of oaks bearing strange leaves. *Evelyn.*

preadvertise (prē-ad'vėr-tīz), *v. t.*; pret. and pp. *preadvertised*, ppr. *preadvertising*. [< *pre-* + *advertise*.] To advertise or inform beforehand; preacquaint.

Adam, being *pre-advertised* by the vision, was presently able to pronounce, This is now bone of my bone, and flesh of my flesh. *Dr. H. More*, Def. of Lit. Cabbala, ii.

præstival, *a.* See *prēestival*.

pre-albuminuric (prē-al-bū-mi-nū'rik), *a.* Preceding the occurrence of albuminuria: as, the *prealbuminuric* stage of Bright's disease.

preallably†, *adv.* [Tr. OF. *prealablement*, previously; < **preallable* (< OF. *prealable*, former, forerunning, first, < *pre-*, before, + *aller*, go) + *-ly*[2].] Previously. [Rare.]

No swan dieth until *preallably* he have sung. *Urquhart*, tr. of Rabelais, iii. 21. (*Davies.*)

preamble (prē'am-bl), *v.*; pret. and pp. *preambled*, ppr. *preambling*. [= Pg. *preambular* = It. *preambolare*, < LL. *præambulare*, walk before, < L. *præ*, before, + *ambulare*, walk, proceed: see *pre-* and *amble*.] I. *intrans.* 1. To go before; precede; serve as a preamble.

Ere a foot furder we must bee content to heare a *preambling* boast of your valour. *Milton*, On Def. of Humb. Remonst.

2. To make a preamble; preface one's remarks or actions; prelude.

So we seemed to take leave one of another; my Lord of me, desiring me that I would write to him, . . . which, put together with what he *preambled* with yesterday, makes me think that my Lord do truly esteem me still. *Pepys*, Diary, II. 148.

II. *trans.* 1†. To walk over previously; tread beforehand.

Fifthly [I will] take a through view of those who have *preambled* this by path. *N. Ward*, Simple Cobler, p. 17.

2. To preface; introduce with preliminary remarks.

Some will *preamble* a tale impertinently. *Feltham*, Resolves, i. 93.

preamble (prē'am-bl), *n.* [< ME. *preamble*, < OF. **preamble*, *preambule*, F. *préambule* = Sp. *preámbulo* = Pg. *preambulo* = It. *preambulo*, *preambolo*, < ML. *præambula*, *præambulum*, a preamble, preface, fem. or neut. of LL. *præambulus*, walking before, going before, < *præambulare*, walk before: see *preamble*, *v.*] 1. A preliminary statement; an introductory paragraph or division of a discourse or writing; a preface; prologue; prelude.

This is a long *preamble* of a tale.
Chaucer, Prol. to Wife of Bath's Tale, l. 831.

After this fabulous *preamble*, they proceeded to handle the matter of fact with logical precision.
Motley, Hist. Netherlands, II. 228.

Specifically—2. The introductory part of a statute or resolution, which states or indicates the reasons and intent of what follows. = **Syn.** *Preface, Prologue*, etc. See *introduction*.

preambular (prē-am'bū-lär), *a.* [< L. *præambulus*, going before, + *-ar*2.] Same as *preambulary*.

preambulary (prē-am'bū-lā-ri), *a.* [< LL. *præambulus*, walking before (see *preamble*), + *-ary*.] Having the character of a preamble; serving as a prelude; introductory.

I must begin with the fulfilling of your Desire in a *preambulary* Way, for the Subject admits it.
Howell, Letters, ii. 8.

These three evangelical resuscitations are so many *preambulary* proofs of the last and general resurrection.
Bp. Pearson, Expos. of Creed, xi.

This famous revenue stands, at this hour, on all the debate, as a description of revenue not as yet known in all the comprehensive (but too comprehensive!) vocabulary of finance—a *preambulary* tax.
Burke, American Taxation.

preambulate† (prē-am'bū-lāt), *v. i.* [< LL. *præambulatus*, pp. of *præambulare*, walk or go before: see *preamble*, *v.*] To walk or go before.

Mistress, will it please you to *preambulate?*
Chapman, Humorous Day's Mirth.

When fierce destruction follows to hell gate,
Pride doth most commonly *preambulate*.
Jordan, Poems, §§ 3 b. (*Latham.*)

preambulation† (prē-am-bū-lā'shon), *n.* [< ME. *preambulacioun*, < LL. **præambulatio(n-)*, < *præambulare*, walk before: see *preamble*, *preambulate*.] 1. The act of walking or going before.—2. A preamble: a sense given to the word in the following quotation in consequence of the previous use of *preamble*.

What spekestow of *preambulacioun?*
What? amble, or trotte, or pees, or go sit doun!
Thou lettest our disport in this manere.
Chaucer, Prol. to Wife of Bath's Tale, l. 837.

preambulatory† (prē-am'bū-lā-tō-ri), *a.* [< *preambulate* + *-ory*. Cf. *ambulatory*.] Going before; preceding; previous.

Simon Magus had *preambulatory* impieties; he was covetous and ambitious long before he offered to buy the Holy Ghost. *Jer. Taylor*, Works (ed. 1835), I. 855.

preambulous† (prē-am'bū-lus), *a.* [< LL. *præambulus*, going before: see *preamble*.] Preambulary; introductory.

He . . . undermineth the base of religion, and destroyeth the principle *preambulous* unto all belief.
Sir T. Browne, Vulg. Err., i. 10.

preambulum (prē-am'bū-lum), *n.* In *music*, same as *prelude*, 2.

preanal, præanal (prē-ā'nal), *a.* [< L. *præ*, before, + *anus*, anus: see *anal*.] Placed in front of the anus: as, the *preanal* pores of a lizard.—**Preanal gastrostege.** See *gastrostege*.—**Preanal segment**, the antepenultimate segment of the abdomen, or the section immediately anterior to the anal segment. It is often hidden in the perfect insect, or appears only as a small piece on the end of the dorsal surface, called the *preanal* or *supra-anal plate* or *lamina*.

preantepenultimate (prē-an"tē-pē-nul'ti-māt), *a.* [< *pre-* + *antepenultimate*.] Preceding the antepenultimate; being the fourth from the last: as, a *preantepenultimate* syllable.

pre-aortic (prē-ā-ôr'tik), *a.* [< L. *præ*, before, + NL. *aorta*: see *aortic*.] Situated in front of or before the aorta.

preappoint (prē-a-point'), *v. t.* [< *pre-* + *appoint*.] To appoint previously. *Sir E. Creasy*, Eng. Const., p. 195.

preappointment (prē-a-point'ment), *n.* [< *pre-* + *appointment*.] Previous appointment.

preapprehension (prē-ap-rē-hen'shon), *n.* [< *pre-* + *apprehension*.] An apprehension or opinion formed before examination.

A conceit not to be made out by ordinary inspection, or any other eyes then such as, regarding the clouds, behold them in shapes conformable to *pre-apprehensions*.
Sir T. Browne, Vulg. Err., ii. 6.

prearm† (prē-ärm'), *v. t.* [< *pre-* + *arm*2.] To forearm. *Rev. T. Adams*, Works, II. 478.

prearrange (prē-a-rānj'), *v. t.*; pret. and pp. *prearranged*, ppr. *prearranging*. [< *pre-* + *arrange*.] To arrange previously.

prearrangement (prē-a-rānj'ment), *n.* [< *pre-* + *arrange* + *-ment*.] Previous arrangement.

prease†, *v.* An obsolete form of *press*1.

preaspection† (prē-as-pek'shon), *n.* [< *pre-* + *aspection*.] A seeing beforehand; previous view.

To believe . . . (pygmies) should be in the stature of a foot or span requires the *preaspection* of such a one as Philetas the poet, in Athenæus, who was fain to fasten lead unto his feet, lest the wind should blow him away.
Sir T. Browne, Vulg. Err., iv. 11.

preaudience (prē-â'di-ens), *n.* [< ML. *præaudientia*, < L. *præaudire*, hear beforehand, < *præ*, before, + *audire*, hear: see *audient*, *audience*.] Right of previous audience; precedence or rank at the English bar among serjeants and barristers; the right to be heard before another. The preaudience of the English bar is as follows: (1) The queen's attorney-general; (2) the queen's solicitor-general; (3) the queen's advocate-general; (4) the queen's premier serjeant; (5) the queen's ancient serjeant, or the eldest among the queen's serjeants; (6) the queen's serjeants; (7) the queen's counsel; (8) serjeants-at-law; (9) the recorder of London; (10) advocates of the civil law; (11) barristers. *Imp. Dict.*

A custom has of late years prevailed of granting letters-patent of precedence to such barristers as the crown thinks proper to honour with that mark of distinction, whereby they are entitled to such rank and *preaudience* as are assigned in their respective patents.
Blackstone, Com., III. iii.

preauditory, præauditory (prē-â'di-tō-ri), *a.* [< *pre-* + *auditory*.] In *anat.*, situated in front of the auditory nerve: opposed to *postauditory*.

preaxal (prē-ak'sal), *a.* [< L. *præ*, before, + *axis*, axis, + *-al*.] Placed in advance of the axon; prechordal.

preaxial (prē-ak'si-al), *a.* [< L. *præ*, before, + *axis*, axis, + *-al*. Cf. *axial*.] Of, pertaining to, or situated upon that side of the axis of either fore or hind limb of a vertebrate which is anterior when the limb is extended at a right angle with the long axis of the body: the opposite of *postaxial*.

prebacillary (prē-bas'i-lā-ri), *a.* [< *pre-* + *bacillary*.] Prior to invasion by bacilli: as, a *prebacillary* stage.

prebalancer (prē-bal'an-sėr), *n.* [= F. *prébalancier*; < *pre-* + *balancer*: see *balancer*, 4.] One of the prehalteres of an insect. See *prehalter*.

prebasal (prē-bā'sal), *a.* [< *pre-* + *base*2: see *basal*.] Placed in front of a base or basal part: as, the *prebasal* plate of a myriapod.

prebasilar (prē-bas'i-lär), *a.* [< *pre-* + *basilar*.] Placed in front of a basilar part.

prebend (preb'end), *n.* [< ME. *prebende* = F. *prébende* = Pr. *prebenda*, *prevenda* = Sp. Pg. It. *prebenda*, < ML. *præbenda*, f., a portion of food and drink supplied (a pittance), also an ecclesiastical living, a prebend; cf. L. *præbenda*, neut. pl., things to be offered or supplied; fem. sing. or neut. pl. gerundive of L. *præbere*, hold forth, proffer, offer, furnish, grant, contr. of *præhibere*, hold forth, proffer, etc., < *præ*, before, + *habere*, have, hold: see *habit*. Cf. *provand*, *provend*, *provender*, doublets of *prebend*. From the same L. verb are prob. also ult. *pledge*, *plevin*.] 1. In *canon law*, a stated income derived from some fixed source; hence, especially, a stipend allotted from the revenues of a cathedral or collegiate church for the performance of certain duties by a person hence called a *prebendary*. Originally a prebend was the portion of food, clothing, or money allowed to a monk or cleric, independent of a benefice. When in the eleventh century canons ceased to live in common, each canon received a share of the cathedral revenues, called a *prebend*, and some of their number a prebendal residence. A prebend may be held by a layman.

Many noblemen and gentlemen's sons had *prebends* given them on this pretence, that they intended to fit themselves by study for entering into orders; but they kept them, and never advanced in their studies.
Lords' Journals, quoted in R. W. Dixon's Hist. Church of [Eng., xxi., note.

To each [canon] was assigned . . . a decent provision, called a *prebend*, for the support of himself and his household. *Rock*, Church of our Fathers, ii. 83.

2†. A prebendary.

To make Amends for the suppressing of so many Monasteries, the King instituted certain new Bishopricks, . . . and assigned certain Canons and *Prebends* to each of them.
Baker, Chronicles, p. 286.

3. A prebendaryship.

Another writes to desire that I would prevail on the Archbishop of Dublin to give him the best *prebend* of St. Patrick's. *Swift*, Letter, Sept. 30, 1735.

Deaneries and *prebends* may become void, like a bishopric, by death, by deprivation, or by resignation to either the king or the bishop. *Blackstone*, Com., I. xi.

prebendal (preb'en-dal), *a.* [< OF. *prebendal*, < ML. *præbendalis*, < *præbenda*, a prebend: see *prebend*.] Of or pertaining to a prebend or a prebendary.—**Prebendal stall**, the seat of the prebendary in a church.

prebendary (preb'en-dā-ri), *n.*; pl. *prebendaries* (-riz). [< ME. *prebendary* = F. *prébendier* = Pg. *prebendeiro* = It. *prebendario*, < ML. *præbendarius*, a prebendary, < *præbenda*, a prebend: see *prebend*.] 1. One who holds a prebend. A clerical prebendary is necessarily a canon. At present in the Church of England all resident prebendaries are by law styled *canons*, but the holders of disendowed prebendal stalls are still known as *prebendaries*.

One Dr. Lark, a *Prebendary* of St. Stephen's.
Baker, Chronicles, p. 273.

That ease be mine, which, after all his cares,
The pious, peaceful *prebendary* shares.
Crabbe, Works, II. 21.

2. A prebendaryship.

First, whereas the hope of honour maketh a souldier in England, byshopricks, deanries, *prebendaries*, and other priuate dignities animate our diuines to such excellence.
Nashe, Pierce Penilesse, p. 26.

prebendaryship (preb'en-dā-ri-ship), *n.* [< *prebendary* + *-ship*.] The office of a prebendary. See *prebend*.

prebendate (preb'en-dāt), *v. t.*; pret. and pp. *prebendated*, ppr. *prebendating*. [< ML. *præbendatus*, pp. of *præbendari*, receive a prebend, < *præbenda*, a prebend: see *prebend*.] To make a prebendary of; raise to the rank of prebendary.

He falleth into commendation of Stephen Langton his cardinall, declaryng howe learned he was in the liberall artes, and in diuinitie, insomuch as he was *prebendated* at Paris. *Grafton*, K. John, an. 11.

prebendry†, *n.* [< *prebend* + *-ry*.] A prebend. *Cotgrave.*

prebendship (preb'end-ship), *n.* [< *prebend* + *-ship*.] A prebendaryship. *Foxe*, Martyrs, p. 216, an. 1190.

prebrachial (prē-brā'ki-al), *a.* and *n.* [< L. *præ*, before, + *brachium*, upper arm: see *brachial*.] **I.** *a.* In *human anat.*, situated upon the front of the brachium, or upper arm: specifically noting a group of muscles composed of the biceps, coracobrachialis, and anticobrachialis. *Coues and Shute*, 1887.

II. *n.* A vein of the wing of some insects, between the cubitus and the postbrachial.

prebranchial, præbranchial (prē-brang'ki-al), *a.* Placed in advance of the gills.

The *prebranchial* zone, which separates the branchial sac behind from the branchial siphon in front.
Encyc. Brit., XXIII. 611.

prebuccal (prē-buk'al), *a.* [< L. *præ*, before, + *bucca*, cheek: see *buccal*.] Placed in front of the m u or buccal cavity; preoral; prostomial. o th

precant (prē'kant), *n.* [< L. *precan(t-)s*, ppr. of *precari*, pray: see *pray*1. Cf. *prayant*.] One who prays. *Coleridge.* (*Imp. Dict.*)

precardiac (prē-kär'di-ak), *a.* [< L. *præ*, before, + Gr. καρδία, heart: see *cardiac*.] Situated in front of the heart—that is, cephalad of the heart. Compare *precordial*.

precaria, *n.* Plural of *precarium*.

precarious (prē-kā'ri-us), *a.* [= F. *précaire* = Sp. Pg. It. *precario*, < L. *precarius*, pertaining to entreaty or petition, obtained by entreaty or by mere favor, depending on favor, < *precari*, pray: see *pray*1.] 1. Dependent on the will or pleasure of another; liable to be lost or withdrawn at the will of another; hence, uncertain; insecure.

This little happiness is so very *precarious* that it wholly depends on the will of others. *Addison.*

Men of real sense and understanding prefer a prudent mediocrity to a *precarious* popularity.
Goldsmith, English Clergy.

To be young is surely the best, if the most *precarious*, gift of life. *Lowell*, Study Windows, p. 379.

2. Specifically, in *law*, of uncertain tenure; revocable at the will of the owner or creator: as, a *precarious* right or loan.

His holding was, in the language of the Roman lawyers, *precarious*—that is, upon his request to the owner, and with that owner's leave.
W. E. Hearn, Aryan Household, p. 425.

3†. Dependent only upon the will of the owner or originator; hence, arbitrary; unfounded.

That the fabrick of the body is out of the concurse of atomes is a mere *precarious* opinion.
Dr. H. More, Immortal. of Soul, ii. 10.

4. Dependent upon chance; of doubtful issue; uncertain as to result.

Both succeeded in establishing themselves on the throne after the most *precarious* vicissitudes.
Prescott, Ferd. and Isa., ii. 16.

Hence—5. Dangerous; hazardous; exposed to positive peril, risk of misunderstanding, or other hazard. [Recent and objectionable.]

It would be *precarious* to say that every course of thought has an ideally best order.
J. F. Genung, Rhetoric, p. 262.

precariously (prē-kā'ri-us-li), *adv.* In a precarious manner; dependently; hence, with risk of detriment, alteration, failure, total loss, or removal.

precariousness (prẹ̄-kā'ri-us-nes), *n.* The state or character of being precarious; uncertainty; dependence on the will or pleasure of others, or on unknown events: as, the *precariousness* of life or health.

precarium (prẹ̄-kā'ri-um), *n.*; pl. *precaria* (-ạ̈). [L., neut. of *precarius*, obtained by entreaty: see *precarious*.] In *Rom.* and *Scots law*, a loan or grant revocable at the discretion of the lender or grantor.

Very early in Roman legal history we come upon tenancy-at-will, under the name of *precarium*, which of itself showed that there must have been large estates capable of subdivision. *Encyc. Brit.*, XIV. 260.

precartilaginous (prē-kär-ti-laj'i-nus), *a.* [< *pre-* + *cartilage*: see *cartilaginous*.] Prior to the formation of cartilage, as a stage or state of an embryo.

precary† (prek'ạ-ri), *n.* [< ML. *precaria*, also *precarium*, a precary (see def.), fem. (sc. *charta*) or neut. of *precarius*, depending on favor: see *precarious*. Cf. *precarium*.] A charter or grant, also known as *precarious* or *precatorious letters*, by which a person obtained from a church or monastery the use for an annual rent of an estate previously donated by him to the church or monastery. *Hist., Geog.*, etc., *Dict.*, 2d ed., ed. Collier (1701), s. v. *precary*.

precation† (prẹ̄-kā'shọn), *n.* [Early mod. E. *precacion*, < OF. *precation*, *precacion*, F. *précation* = Pg. *precação* = It. *precazione*, < L. *precatio(n-)*, a praying, a form of prayer, < *precari*, pp. *precatus*, pray: see *pray*[1].] The act of praying; supplication; entreaty; hence, a prayer; an invocation.

Beside our daily praiers and continual *precacions* to God and his saintes for prosperus successe to ensue in your merciall exployte and royall passage. *Hall*, Hen. V., f. 5. (*Halliwell.*)

precative (prek'ạ-tiv), *a.* [< L. *precativus*, prayed for, obtained by entreaty, < *precari*, pp. *precatus*, pray: see *pray*[1].] Suppliant; beseeching; expressing an entreaty or a desire: as, the *precative* mode.

This is not to be called an imperative sentence, . . . but rather, if I may use the word, 'tis a sentence *precative* or optative. *Harris*, Hermes, i. 2.

precatorious†, *a.* [< L. *precatorius*, pertaining to entreaty or petition: see *precatory*.] Same as *precatory*. See *precary*.

precatory (prek'ạ-tọ̄-ri), *a.* [< L. *precatorius*, pertaining to entreaty or petition, < *precari*, pp. *precatus*, pray: see *pray*[1].] Relating to prayer; being in the form of a prayer or supplication.

Perfect models of *precatory* eloquence. *Sir J. Hawkins*, Johnson, p. 270.

Precatory words, in *law*, expressions in a will praying or recommending that a thing be done. Such words do not raise a trust nor bind the person to whom they are addressed, unless properly capable of an imperative construction, when they are sometimes deemed to establish what is called a *precatory trust*.

precaudal (prē-kâ'dạl), *a.* [< *pre-* + *caudal*.] Situated in advance of the caudal or coccygeal series of vertebræ: as, a *precaudal* vertebra.

precausation (prē-kâ-zā'shọn), *n.* [< *pre-* + *causation*.] Foreordination.

As if God were not able to make a faculty which can determine its own comparative act to this rather than to that, by his sustentation, and universal *precausation* and concourse, without the said predetermining premotion. *Baxter*, Life of Faith, ii. 9.

precaution (prẹ̄-kâ'shọn), *n.* [< OF. *precaution*, F. *précaution* = Sp. *precaucion* = Pg. *precaução* = It. *precauzione*, < LL. *præcautio(n-)*, precaution, < L. *præcavere*, pp. *præcautus*, guard against beforehand, < *præ*, before, + *cavere*, be on one's guard: see *caution*.] 1. Previous caution; prudent foresight; care previously employed to prevent mischief or secure good results.

She like a new disease, unknown to men,
Creeps, no *precaution* used, among the crowd.
Tennyson, Guinevere.

2. A measure taken beforehand; an act of foresight, designed to ward off possible evil or to secure good results.

The same notion of predestination makes them [the Turks] use no *precautions* against the plague; but they even go and help to bury the bodies of those that die of it. *Pococke*, Description of the East, I. 181.

precaution (prẹ̄-kâ'shọn), *v. t.* [< *precaution*, *n.*] To caution beforehand; warn.

To *precaution* posterity against the like errours. *Dryden*, Vind. of Duke of Guise.

precautional (prẹ̄-kâ'shọn-ạl), *a.* [< *precaution* + *-al*.] Of the nature of precaution; preventive of mischief; precautionary. [Rare.]

Wherefore this first filiall fear is but virtuous and *precautionall*. *W. Montague*, Devoute Essays, I. vi. 3.

precautionary (prẹ̄-kâ'shọn-ạ̄-ri), *a.* and *n.* [< *precaution* + *-ary*.] **I.** *a.* 1. Advising precaution; containing or expressing precaution.

Recollecting the *precautionary* letter she had written me on the subject, I felt that I wished Miss Marshall at Jericho. *T. Hook*, Gilbert Gurney, I. iv. (*Latham.*)

2. Taking precautions; characterized by previous caution: as, *precautionary* measures.

II.† *n.* A precaution; a preliminary measure taken for prudential reasons.

Thou seest, Belford, by the above *precautionaries*, that I forget nothing. *Richardson*, Clarissa Harlowe, IV. 49. (*Davies.*)

precautious (prẹ̄-kâ'shus), *a.* [< *precauti(on)* + *-ous*. Cf. *cautious*.] Using precaution; displaying previous care or caution; provident.

It was not the mode of the Court in those days to be very penetrant, *precautious*, or watchful. *Roger North*, Examen, p. 93. (*Davies.*)

precautiously (prẹ̄-kâ'shus-li), *adv.* With precaution.

precava, *n.* See *præcava*.

precaval, præcaval (prē-kā'vạl), *a.* and *n.* [< *præcava* + *-al*.] **I.** *a.* Anterior or (in man) superior, as a caval vein: distinguished from *postcaval*.

II. *n.* The precaval vein, or præcava.

prece†, *v.* An obsolete variant of *press*[1].

precedaneous† (prē-sẹ̄-dā'nẹ̄-us), *a.* [< *precede* + *-aneous*.] Going before in time; preceding; antecedent; anterior.

Faith is in Holy Scripture represented in nature *precedaneous* to God's benevolence. *Barrow*, Sermons, II. iv. (*Latham.*)

precede (prẹ̄-sēd'), *v.*; pret. and pp. *preceded*, ppr. *preceding*. [< OF. *preceder*, F. *précéder* = Pr. Sp. Pg. *preceder* = It. *precedere*, < L. *præcedere*, go before, precede, surpass, excel, < *præ*, before, + *cedere*, go, move, walk: see *cede*.] **I.** *trans.* 1. To go before in place; walk in front of; advance before; hence, specifically, to go before in rank or importance; take precedence of.

Such a reason of precedence St. Cyprian giveth in another case, because (saith he) Rome for its magnitude ought to *precede* Carthage. *Barrow*, The Pope's Supremacy.

Room for my lord! three jockeys in his train;
Six huntsmen with a shout *precede* his chair.
Pope, Dunciad, ii. 193.

2. To go before in the order of time; occur or take place before; exist before.

Imagination ever *precedeth* voluntary motion. *Bacon*, Advancement of Learning, ii. 206.

Both families lived together in all that harmony which generally *precedes* an expected alliance. *Goldsmith*, Vicar, ii.

3. To put something before; preface; introduce as by a preface or prelude.

It has been usual to *precede* hostilities by a public declaration communicated to the enemy. *Chancellor Kent*, Com. (7th ed.), I. 61.

II. *intrans.* 1. To go before in place; walk in front; specifically, to take precedence; have superior authority; hence, to prevail.

Then heaven and earth renew'd shall be made pure
To sanctity that shall receive no stain:
Till then, the curse pronounced on both *precedes*.
Milton, P. L., x. 640.

2. To come first in the order of time; occur or exist previously.

Of six *preceding* ancestors, that gem,
Conferr'd by testament to the sequent issue,
Hath it been owed and worn.
Shak., All's Well, v. 3. 196.

An antecedent proposition may be separated from its consequent by other propositions; but a *preceding* proposition is closely followed by another. *Crabb*, Eng. Synonymes, p. 85.

precedence (prẹ̄-sē'dẹns), *n.* [< OF. *precedence*, F. *précédence* = Sp. Pg. *precedencia* = It. *precedenza*, < ML. *præcedentia*, precedence, < L. *præceden(t-)s*, ppr. of *præcedere*, go before: see *precedent*.] 1. The act of going before; specifically, the right of preceding others in public or private ceremonies; the right to a more honorable place in public processions or assemblies, or in the formalities of social life; social superiority; advantage in rank. In many countries precedence is a matter of strict regulation. See *order of precedence*, below.

For me now,
That hitherto have kept the first, to know
A second place, or yield the least *precedence*
To any other, 's death.
Beau. and Fl., Thierry and Theodoret, ii. 1.

2. Prior place; superior position; position indicative of superior rank.

Precedence
None sure will claim in hell.
Milton, P. L., ii. 33.

That form, the labour of almighty skill,
Fram'd for the service of a free-born will,
Asserts *precedence*, and bespeaks control.
Cowper, Tirocinium, l. 9.

3. Previous occurrence, or existence before; priority in time.—4†. That which goes before; a preceding act or speech.

Mess. But yet, madam ——
Cleo. I do not like "but yet"; it does allay
The good *precedence*. *Shak.*, A. and C., ii. 5. 51.

Order of precedence, the whole body of rules which fix gradation of rank, especially with regard to the right of certain officials and persons of rank to a prescribed place in any ceremony. In Great Britain precedence is formed by statute, patent, or usage, but the chief regulations regarding the order of precedence were settled by Parliament in the reign of Henry VIII. Some of the leading rules are thus summarized from Burke: precedence is conferred by men's rank; men of official rank who have higher personal precedence are placed according to that precedence; peers and peeresses rank in the order of England, Scotland, Great Britain, Ireland, United Kingdom and Ireland, according to the dates of patents; younger sons of persons of higher rank come after eldest sons of persons of next lower rank; daughters of peers, baronets, etc., rank after the wives of their eldest brothers; wives and children of great officers of state have no consequent precedence; a lady having precedence by birth retains her precedence although married to a commoner; baronets rank according to dates of their patents; ambassadors rank after members of royal families, ministers and envoys after dukes.—**Patent of precedence**, a grant from the crown to such barristers as it thinks proper to honor with that mark of distinction, whereby they are entitled to such rank and preaudience as are assigned in their respective patents.—**Personal precedence**, precedence in right of birth or family, as distinguished from that which is conferred by official position.—**To take precedence of**, to come before, as superior in rank or importance; have a prior claim to attention or respect. =**Syn.** 1. *Preëminence*, etc. See *priority*.

precedency (prẹ̄-sē'dẹn-si), *n.* [As *precedence* (see *-cy*).] Same as *precedence*.

Me thinkes the *Precedencie* which God gave this Iland, to be the first Restorer of buried Truth, should have beene followed with more happy successe, and sooner attain'd Perfection. *Milton*, Reformation in Eng., i.

precedent (prẹ̄-sē'dẹnt as an adj., pres'ẹ̄-dẹnt as a noun), *a.* and *n.* [< OF. *precedent*, F. *précédent* = Sp. Pg. It. *precedente*, < L. *præceden(t-)s*, ppr. of *præcedere*, go before: see *precede*.] **I.** *a.* (prẹ̄-sē'dẹnt). Preceding; going before in the order of time; antecedent; anterior; previous; former.

A slave that is not twentieth part the tithe
Of your *precedent* lord. *Shak.*, Hamlet, iii. 4. 98.

Cordus, a writing fellow, they have got
To gather notes of the *precedent* times,
And make them into Annals.
B. *Jonson*, Sejanus, ii. 2.

Precedent condition, or condition precedent. See *condition*, 8 (*a*). =**Syn.** See *previous*.

II. *n.* (pres'ẹ̄-dẹnt). 1. A preceding action or circumstance which may serve as a pattern or example in subsequent cases; an antecedent instance which creates a rule for following cases; a model instance.

Set it down to thyself as well to create good *precedents* as to follow them. *Bacon*, Great Place.

The *Precedent* may dangerous prove, and wrack
Thy throne and kingdom, if thy People read
Highest Rebellion's Lesson in their Head.
J. Beaumont, Psyche, iii. 157.

2. Specifically, in *law*: (*a*) A judicial decision, interlocutory or final, which serves as a rule for future determinations in similar or analogous cases. (*b*) A form of proceeding or of an instrument followed or deemed worthy to be followed as a pattern in similar or analogous cases.

He hath lately found out, among the old Records of the Tower, some *Precedents* for raising a Tax called Ship-Money. *Howell*, Letters, I. vi. 11.

3. A custom, habit, or rule established; previous example or usage.

The unconquered powers
Of *precedent* and custom interpose
Between a king and virtue.
Shelley, Queen Mab, iii.

Precedent is only another name for embodied experience, and . . . counts for even more in the guidance of communities of men than in that of the individual life. *Lowell*, Study Windows, p. 164.

4†. A presage; sign; indication.

With this she seizeth on his sweating palm,
The *precedent* of pith and livelihood.
Shak., Venus and Adonis, l. 26.

5†. An original, as the original draft of a writing.

My Lord Melun, let this be copied out,
And keep it safe for our remembrance:
Return the *precedent* to these lords again.
Shak., K. John, v. 2. 3.

=**Syn.** 1. *Pattern*, *Model*, etc. See *example*.

precedented (pres'ẹ̄-den-ted), *a.* [< *precedent* + *-ed*[2].] Authorized by precedent; in accordance with precedent or established custom.

He opposed a bill which . . . was right and wise in principle, and was *precedented* in the best times.
Burke, Works, VII. 240.

precedential (pres-ẹ̄-den'shạl), *a.* [< *precedent* + *-i-al.*] Of the nature of a precedent; suitable for imitation; followed as a precedent.

I have read that, by act of parliament, it [the church] was settled on the city to maintain and repair, and hope their practice hath proved *precedential* to other places in the same nature.
Fuller, Worthies, Gloucestershire, I. 549.

precedently (prẹ̄-sē'dẹnt-li), *adv.* Beforehand; antecedently.

precel† (prẹ̄-sel'), *v.* [< OF. *preceller*, < L. *præcellere*, surpass, excel, < *præ*, before, + *-cellere*, as in *excellere*, surpass: see *excel.*] **I.** *trans.* To excel; surpass.

A princely graffe which as far *precels* her which he hath lighted upon as a damask rose doth the cowslip.
Howell, Vocall Forrest, p. 132.

Thou shalt be Janus; hard 'tis to *precel*
Thy father; if thou equal'st him, 'tis well.
Owen's Epigrams. (*Nares.*)

II. *intrans.* To excel others; display unusual superiority.

For it is conueniente that he whiche *precelleth* in honor should also *precelle* in vertues. *J. Udall*, On Timothy, iii.

precellence† (prẹ̄-sel'ẹns), *n.* [< *precellen(t)* + *-ce.*] Same as *precellency*.

precellency† (prẹ̄-sel'ẹn-si), *n.* [As *precellence* (see *-cy*).] Excellence; superiority.

As you have the *precellency* of the women of the world for beauty and feature, so assume the honour to give, and not take Law from any, in matter of attire.
N. Ward, Simple Cobler, p. 29.

Nor thought I it fit to rhetoricate in proposing the great variety of things, and *precellency* of one above another.
Dr. H. More, Antidote against Atheism, Pref.

precellent† (prẹ̄-sel'ẹnt), *a.* [< OF. *precellent* = Sp. *precelente*, < L. *præcellen(t-)s*, ppr. of *præcellere*, excel: see *precel.*] Excellent; surpassing; conspicuously superior.

Even so the rectitude of reason in the *precellent* knowledge of the truth is one puissance.
Holland, tr. of Plutarch, p. 653.

precentor (prẹ̄-sen'tọr), *n.* [< LL. *præcentor*, a leader in music, < *præcinere*, sing or play before, < *præ*, before, + *canere*, sing: see *cant*[2], *chant.*] A leader or director of a church choir or congregation in singing. Specifically, the leader or manager of the choir or musical services in a cathedral, or in a monastic or collegiate church; in the Church of England, an official, often ranking next to the dean, who has charge of the choir, of the musical service, and often of other matters; a musical director. The precentor's place in the choir-stalls is on the left of the altar; hence that side is called *cantoris*, 'the precentor's.'

The Spirit of Christ is the *precentor*, or rector chori, the master of the choir. *Jer. Taylor*, Works (ed. 1835), I. 637.

In 1204, when the see of Winchester was vacant, the chapter was divided between the dean of Salisbury and the *precentor* of Lincoln. *Stubbs*, Const. Hist., § 382.

precentorship (prẹ̄-sen'tọr-ship), *n.* [< *precentor* + *-ship.*] The office or duties of a precentor; the condition of being a precentor.

precentral (prē-sen'trạl), *a.* [< NL. *præcentralis*, < L. *præ*, before, + *centrum*, center: see *central.*] In *anat.*: (*a*) Situated in front of the central sulcus or Rolandic fissure of the brain. (*b*) Placed in front of a vertebral centrum.—**Precentral convolution**, the anterior central or ascending frontal convolution.—**Precentral sulcus**, a sulcus of the frontal lobe, parallel with the fissure of Rolando, and limiting the anterior central convolution in front. Also called *vertical sulcus*.

precept (prē'sept), *n.* [< OF *precept*, *precipt*, F. *précepte* = Sp. *precepto* = Pg. *preceito* = It. *precetto*, < L. *præceptum*, a rule, injunction, doctrine, maxim, precept, neut. of *præceptus*, pp. of *præcipere*, take or seize beforehand, admonish, advise, give rules to, instruct, teach, < *præ*, before, + *capere*, take: see *capable*. Cf. *precipe.*] **1.** A commandment or direction given as a rule of action; teaching; instruction; especially, an injunction as to moral conduct; a rule of conduct; a maxim.

For *precept* must be upon *precept*, *precept* upon *precept*; line upon line, line upon line; here a little, and there a little. Isa. xxviii. 10.

Thy learned *precepts*
Shall call me back and set my footings straight.
Ford, Broken Heart, i. 3.

2. In *law*: (*a*) A command or mandate in writing issued by a court or judge, as for bringing a person, record, or other matter before him, or for the collection of costs, etc., or for summoning jurors, etc. (*b*) In English law, a command or mandate in writing issued pursuant to law by an administrative officer: as, a sheriff's *precept* for a municipal election.

Sord. Who brought this same, sirrah?
Hind. Marry, sir, one of the justice's men; he says 'tis a *precept*, and all their hands be at it.
B. *Jonson*, Every Man out of his Humour, i. 1.

Precept of clare constat, in *Scots law*. See *clare constat*.—**Precept of sasine**, the order of a superior to his bailie to give infeftment of certain lands to his vassal. See *sasine*.=**Syn. 1.** *Dogma*, *Tenet*, etc. (see *doctrine*); *Rule*, etc. (see *principle*); *Axiom*, *Maxim*, etc. (see *aphorism*), instruction, law.

precept†, *v. t.* [< *precept*, *n.*] **1.** To teach; lead by precept.

I do not find but it may well become a man to *precept* himself into the practice of virtue. *Feltham*, Resolves.

2. To order by rule; ordain.

The two commended rules by him [Aristotle] set down, whereby the axioms of sciences are *precepted* to be made convertible, . . . are the same thing, in speculation and affirmation, which we now observe.
Bacon, Works (ed. Montagu), I. 284.

preceptial† (prẹ̄-sep'shạl), *a.* [Irreg. < *precept* + *-i-al.*] Consisting of precepts; instructive. [Rare.]

Men
Can counsel, and speak comfort to that grief
Which they themselves not feel; but, tasting it,
Their counsel turns to passion, which before
Would give *preceptial* medicine to rage.
Shak., Much Ado, v. 1. 24.

preception† (prẹ̄-sep'shọn), *n.* [< OF. *preception*, < L. *præceptio(n-)*, a taking or receiving beforehand, an injunction, < *præcipere*, pp. *præceptus*, take or receive beforehand, admonish, teach: see *precept.*] A precept; an injunction.

Their Leo calls these words [let him be the husband of one wife] a *preception*; I did not.
Bp. Hall, Honour of Married Clergy, § xviii.

preceptive (prẹ̄-sep'tiv), *a.* [< OF. *preceptif* = Sp. Pg. *preceptivo* = It. *precettivo*, < L. *præceptivus*, didactic, pertaining to a precept, < *præcipere*, pp. *præceptus*, take or receive beforehand, admonish, teach: see *precept.*] Giving or containing precepts or rules of conduct; instructive; admonitory.

Not expounding, but obeying the *preceptive* words of their Lord. *Jer. Taylor*, Works (ed. 1835), I. 116.

For it is the same thing which is denominated the law (of Moses, or of Christ) from the *preceptive* part, and a covenant from the terms, or sanction, especially the promissory part. *Baxter*, Divine Appointment of the Lord's [Day, v., Postscript.

preceptor (prẹ̄-sep'tọr), *n.* [= F. *précepteur* = Sp. Pg. *preceptor* = It. *precettore*, < L. *præceptor*, an anticipator, a teacher, < *præcipere*, pp. *præceptus*, take or receive beforehand, teach: see *precept.*] **1.** A teacher; an instructor; a tutor.

Folly is soon learn'd;
And under such *preceptors* who can fail!
Cowper, Task, ii. 284.

2. The head of a preceptory of the Knights Templars.

This establishment of the Templars was seated amidst fair meadows and pastures, which the devotion of the former *preceptor* had bestowed upon their order.
Scott, Ivanhoe, xxxv.

preceptorial (prē-sep-tō'ri-ạl), *a.* [< *preceptor* + *-ial.*] Pertaining or belonging to a preceptor: as, *preceptorial* functions.

preceptory (prẹ̄-sep'tọ̄-ri), *a.* and *n.* [< ML. *præceptorius*, preceptory (fem. *præceptoria*, a preceptory), < L. *præceptor*, a preceptor: see *preceptor.*] **I.**† *a.* Giving precepts; preceptive. *Rev. T. Adams*, Works, III., Memoir, p. 1.

II. *n.*; pl. *preceptories* (-riz). A subordinate religious house where instruction was given. Preceptories were establishments of the Knights Templars, the superiors of which were called preceptors, or knights preceptors. All the preceptories of a province were subject to a provincial superior, three of whom held rank above all the rest, viz., those of Jerusalem, Tripolis, and Antioch.

The establishments of the order [Templars], which bore the name of *preceptories*, to the number of twenty-three, were at first seized by the King and other lords, but afterwards, by a bull from the Pope and an Act of Parliament, transferred to the rival order of the Hospitallers.
R. W. Dixon, Hist. Church of Eng., v.

preceptress (prẹ̄-sep'tres), *n.* [< *preceptor* + *-ess*. Cf. OF. *preceptrice.*] A female preceptor or teacher. *Cowper*, Task, iii. 505.

precerebellar (prē-ser-ẹ̄-bel'ạ̈r), *a.* [< L. *præ*, before, + *cerebellum*, cerebellum: see *cerebellar.*] Anterior or superior with respect to the cerebellum: noting the superior cerebellar artery.

precerebral (prē-ser'ẹ̄-brạl), *a.* [< L. *præ*, before, + *cerebrum*, brain: see *cerebral.*] Anterior with respect to the cerebrum: noting the anterior cerebral artery.

preces (prē'sēz), *n. pl.* [ML., pl. of L. *prex* (*prec-*), a prayer: see *pray*[1].] The alternate petitions, such as the versicles and suffrages, which pass conjointly between the clergyman and the congregation in liturgical churches; specifically, in the English choral service, those versicles (with the *Gloria Patri*) which immediately precede the Psalms, beginning "O Lord, open thou our lips."

The occasional presence of *preces*, a series of short intercessions resembling the Greek Ektene, or deacon's litany. *Encyc. Brit.*, XIV. 707.

precession (prẹ̄-sesh'ọn), *n.* [< ME. *precession*, < OF. *precession*, F. *précession* = Sp. *precesion* = Pg. *precessão* = It. *precessione*, < ML. *præcessio(n-)*, a going before, advance, < L. *præcedere*, pp. *præcessus*, go before: see *precede.*] **1.** The act of going before or of moving forward; advance.

Iij women I met with *precession*,
I askyd hem whedir that thei were bone.
Political Poems, etc. (ed. Furnivall), p. 208.

2†. Precedence.

The legates of Pope Leo did take in dudgeon this preferment of Dioscorus, and would not sit down in the synod, because the *precession* was not given to their Holy See.
Barrow, The Pope's Supremacy, p. 197.

3. In *philol.*, a weakening of a vowel due to a change of accent; a change from a full strong vowel to a thinner one: opposed to *progression*. *March*, Anglo-Saxon Gram., p. 26.—**Lunisolar precession.** See *lunisolar*.—**Precession of the equinoxes**, in *astron.*, a slow retrograde motion of the equinoctial points, viz. from east to west, or contrary to the order of the signs. The equinoctial points do not retain the same position in the heavens, but have a slow retrograde motion, at the rate of about 50."24 in a year, or about a degree in 71.66 years, the equator moving on the ecliptic while the ecliptic retains its position nearly unchanged among the stars. This phenomenon is caused by the combined action of the sun and moon on the mass of matter accumulated about the earth's equator, and is called the precession of the equinoxes because it makes the equinoxes succeed each other in less time than they would otherwise do. In consequence of the precession of the equinoxes, the longitudes of the heavenly bodies are continually increasing, the latitudes remaining unchanged. The right ascensions and declinations are, of course, both changing. The precession of the equinoxes was discovered by Hipparchus more than a century before the Christian era. The equinoctial points will make an entire revolution in about 25,800 years.

precessional (prẹ̄-sesh'ọn-ạl), *a.* [< *precession* + *-al.*] Pertaining to or resulting from the precession of the equinoxes: as, *precessional* force.

precessor† (prẹ̄-ses'ọr), *n.* [= It. *precessore*, < L. *præcessor*, a predecessor, a superior, < *præcedere*, pp. *præcessus*, go before: see *precede.*] A predecessor.

Fordham was herein more court-like and civil to this Eudo than Thomas Arundel, his *Precessour*, Bishop of Ely.
Fuller, Hist. Camb., iii. 62. (*Davies.*)

prechet, *v.* A Middle English form of *preach*.

prechordal (prē-kôr'dạl), *a.* [< L. *præ*, before, + *chorda*, < Gr. χορδή, chord: see *chordal.*] **1.** Situated in front of the notochord: applied to those parts of the brain which are anterior to the end of the chorda dorsalis: correlated with *epichordal* and *parachordal*.—**2.** Prior in time to the existence of the *Chordata* or chordate animals; before the evolution of a notochord in animals. [Rare.]

In what we may call *præ-chordal* times.
Encyc. Brit., XXIV. 187.

prechoroid (prē-kō'roid), *a.* [< *pre-* + *choroid.*] Situated before the choroid.—**Prechoroid artery**, the anterior choroid artery.

prechristian (prē-kris'tiạn), *a.* [< *pre-* + *Christian.*] Relating to or existent or occurring in times prior to the Christian era: as, the *prechristian* system; *prechristian* speculations. *Princeton Rev.*, July, 1879, pp. 148, 149.

prechristianic (prē-kris-ti-an'ik), *a.* [< *pre-* + *Christian* + *-ic.*] Same as *prechristian*. *Encyc. Brit.*, XV. 89.

precinct (prē'singt), *n.* [= Pg. It. *precinto*, < ML. *præcinctum*, circuit, boundary line, < L. *præcinctus*, a girding, < *præcingere*, pp. *præcinctus*, gird, gird about, < *præ*, before, + *cingere*, surround, gird: see *cincture.*] **1.** The exterior line or boundary encompassing a place; bound; limit; boundary line.

I think never man could boast it without the *precincts* of paradise but he that came to gain us a better Eden then we lost. *Glanville*, Vanity of Dogmatizing, xii.

2. An inclosed or bounded space; an inclosure or a space definitely marked off by boundaries; a peribolus.

God made a winde to passe in Commission, and, as a common vmpire, to end their vnnaturall strife, forcing the Waters into their ancient *precincts* aboue and beneath the Firmament. *Purchas*, Pilgrimage, p. 41.

She made the House of the Seven Gables like a home to him, and the garden a familiar *precinct*.
Hawthorne, Seven Gables, xii.

I like the silent church, before the service begins, better than any preaching. How far off, how cool, how chaste the persons look, begirt each one with a *precinct* or sanctuary! *Emerson*, Self-reliance.

You retain a single broad image of the vast gray edifice [a cathedral], with its towers, its tone of color, and its still, green *precinct*. *H. James, Jr.*, Trans. Sketches, p. 35.

3. A district within certain boundaries and under certain jurisdiction; a minor territorial or jurisdictional division: as, a police *precinct*; in several of the United States, the principal subdivision of the county, corresponding generally to the township in other States. These subdivisions in Nebraska and Oregon are called *precincts*. In California, Colorado, Florida, Illinois, Mississippi, and Nevada they are called *election precincts*. The counties of Texas are each divided into four *commissioners' precincts*, also into from four to eight *justices' precincts*, and into from four to eleven *election precincts*. Some of the counties of Kentucky are divided into *voting precincts*. In colonial Massachusetts a *precinct* was a part set off from a town and made independent of it in respect to some matters of local administration, but not in respect to choosing a representative to the General Court.

As easily may you get the soldan's crown
As any prizes out of my *precinct*.
Marlowe, Tamburlaine the Great, I., i. 2.

I am the king's vicegerent by my place:
His right lieutenant in mine own *precinct*.
Beau. and Fl., Love's Cure, iii. 1.

The extent of the old Hans was from Nerve in Livonia to the Rhine, and contained 62 great mercantile Towns, which were divided into four *Precincts*. *Howell*, Letters, I. vi. 3.

4. A region; a tract. [A loose use.]

The vessel, . . . now slowly pushed by the wind against the turbid current, now warping along the fragrant *precincts* of orange or magnolia groves or fields of sugar-cane . . . *G. W. Cable*, The Grandissimes, p. 13.

precinction (prē-singk'shon), *n.* [< L. *præcinctio(n-)*, < *præcingere*, gird about: see *precinct*.] Same as *præcinctio*.

preciosity (presh-i-os'i-ti), *n.* [< ME. *precyosite*, < OF. *preciosite*, F. *préciosité* = Sp. *preciosidad* = Pg. *preciosidade* = It. *preziosità*, < L. *pretiosita(t-)s*, costliness, ML. also a costly thing, < *pretiosus*, valuable, precious: see *precious*.] 1†. Costliness; value; great worth; preciousness.

Among ye which ye blacke crosse of Scotlande is specyally namyd, a relyke accomptyd of great *precyosyte*. *Fabyan*, Chron., II., an. 1327.

2†. Anything of great price or value.

The index or forefinger was too naked whereto to commit their *pretiosities*. *Sir T. Browne*, Vulg. Err., iv. 4.

Barbarians seem to exceed them in the curiosity of their application of these *preciosities*. *Dr. H. More*, Divine Dialogues.

3. The quality of being overnice; fastidiousness; excessive refinement. *Saturday Rev.*, No. 1474.

precious (presh'us), *a.* [Early mod. E. also *pretious*; < ME. *precious*, *precyous*, *precius*, < OF. *precios*, *precieus*, *precieux*, valuable, costly, precious, beloved, also affected, finical, F. *précieux* = Sp. Pg. *precioso* = It. *prezioso*, < L. *pretiosus*, of great value, costly, dear, precious, < *pretium*, value, price: see *price*.] 1. Of great price; costly; having a high money-value.

Sweet are the uses of adversity,
Which, like the toad, ugly and venomous,
Wears yet a *precious* jewel in his head.
Shak., As you Like it, ii. 1. 14.

To leave a little snuffe
Is petty treason, and such *pretious* stuffe
Must not be throwne away.
Times' Whistle (E. E. T. S.), p. 60.

A gold-adorned pillared temple round,
Whose walls were hung with rich and *precious* things,
Worthy to be the ransom of great kings.
William Morris, Earthly Paradise, I. 258.

2. Of great worth; held in high esteem; intrinsically valuable.

But she stode som what bynethe, byfore her dere sone, face to face, at the tyme of his *precyous* dethe. *Sir R. Guylforde*, Pylgrymage, p. 27.

Health is *precious* because sickness doth breed that pain which disableth action. *Hooker*, Eccles. Polity, v. 76.

By thy *precious* Death and Burial; . . .
Good Lord, deliver us.
Book of Common Prayer, Litany.

O, what a *precious* book the one would be
That taught observers what they're not to see!
O. W. Holmes, A Rhymed Lesson.

3. Worthless; good-for-nothing. [Ironical.]

Your worship is a *precious* ass! *B. Jonson*, Volpone, i. 1.

Oh, you're a *precious* man! two days in town,
And never see your old friend!
Fletcher, Mad Lover, iii. 3.

Sir Oliver S. Well, Sir Peter, I have seen both my nephews in the manner we proposed.
Sir Peter T. A *precious* couple they are!
Sheridan, School for Scandal, v. 2.

4. Considerable; great. [Colloq.]

It 's hard enough to see one's way, a *precious* sight harder than I thought last night. *T. Hughes*, Tom Brown at Rugby, ii. 7.

5. Particular; scrupulous; fastidious; overnice.

In swich estaat as God hath cleped us,
I wol persever, I nam nat *precius*.
Chaucer, Prol. to Wife of Bath's Tale, l. 148.

Precious blood, the blood shed by Christ on the cross: it gives name to various orders, confraternities, and relics in the Roman Catholic Church, and to the Feast of the Most Precious Blood on the first Sunday in July.—**Precious metals**, gold and silver: so called on account of their value. Platinum is also sometimes included with the precious metals: it is more valuable than silver, and has been used in coinage. Mercury also has been by some called one of the precious metals. In general, *precious* means valuable enough to be used as a standard of value and abundant enough for coinage. Only gold and silver have these requisites.—**Precious stone**, a stone distinguished for its beauty and rarity, and prized for use in ornamentation, especially in jewelry; a gem; a jewel.

Beauty of color, hardness, and rarity are the essential qualities which entitle a mineral to be called precious. Strictly speaking, the only *precious stones* are the diamond, ruby, sapphire, and emerald, though the term is often extended to the opal, notwithstanding its lack of hardness, and to the pearl, which is not a mineral, but strictly an animal product. *Geo. F. Kunz*, Gems and *Precious Stones* of North America, [p. 3].

To be precious of, to prize; value highly. Compare *choice of*, under *choice*, 3. [Local, New Eng.]

We set everything by that little bird, Bartholomew! . . . He understands now that we're *precious of* it. *Mrs. A. D. T. Whitney*, The Other Girls, vii.

=**Syn.** 1 and 2. *Costly*, etc. See *valuable*.

precious (presh'us), *adv.* [< *precious*, *a.*] Very; exceedingly; extremely. [Colloq.]

For I had brought Lizzie something dear, and a *precious* heavy book it was. *R. D. Blackmore*, Lorna Doone, xxvii.

Precious glad he is to be rid of us girls, I know. *Harper's Mag.*, LXXVI. 294.

preciously (presh'us-li), *adv.* [< ME. *preciousely*; < *precious* + *-ly*2.] 1. In a costly manner; at a great price or expense.

It nys but wast to burye hem *preciously*. *Chaucer*, Prol. to Wife of Bath's Tale, l. 500.

Some *preciously* by shattered porcelain fall,
And some by aromatic splinters die.
Dryden, Annus Mirabilis, st. 29.

2. Valuably; in a manner productive of worth; to good purpose.

The time 'twixt six and now
Must by us both be spent most *preciously*.
Shak., Tempest, i. 2. 241.

3. Very much; exceedingly; extremely. [Colloq.]—4. Fastidiously; scrupulously; with extreme care in matters of detail.

If, on the other hand, you fall short of this point [the limit to imitation of details], your art of painting from nature is not yet quite perfectly and *preciously* imitative. *P. G. Hamerton*, Thoughts about Art, ii.

preciousness (presh'us-nes), *n.* 1. The character of being precious; valuableness; worth; costliness.—2. Anything of great price or value; a valuable article, object, or part of a thing.

The enemies of the Lord shall be as the fat of lambs [marginal note: the *preciousness* of lambs]. Ps. xxxvii. 20.

3. Fastidiousness; excessive refinement; scrupulous attention to detail, particularly in art.

As on the one hand their works have none of the majesty of imagination, so on the other they lack the *preciousness* of genuine imitation. *P. G. Hamerton*, Thoughts about Art, ii.

precipe, præcipe (pres'i-pē), *n.* [< ME. *precipe*, *presipe*, *presepe*, *pricipe*; < L. *præcipe*, imperative of *præcipere*, take or seize beforehand, admonish: see *precept*.] 1. In *law*: (*a*) A writ commanding something to be done, or requiring a reason for neglecting it.

For a wrytte called *Pricipe*. A wrytte which is called *p'cipe* from hensforth shall not be made to any man of ani freeholde wherthurgh a free man lese his courte. *Arnold's Chron.* (1502), ed. 1811, p. 210.

(*b*) A note of instructions delivered by a plaintiff or his solicitor to the officer of the court to procure a writ of summons.—2†. A precept; an order.

Clense wele our eghne, and standis on bakke,
For here es comene a *presepe*, swylke menne to take.
MS. Lincoln A. i. 17, f. 148. (*Halliwell.*)

precipice (pres'i-pis), *n.* [< OF. *precipice*, F. *précipice* = Sp. Pg. *precipicio* = It. *precipizio*, a precipice, < L. *præcipitium*, a falling down headlong, an abrupt descent, a steep place, < *præceps* (*præcipit-*), head foremost, headlong, < *præ*, before, + *caput*, head: see *capital*1. Cf. *precipitate*.] 1†. A headlong fall; an abrupt descent.

Stay me in my *precipice* to ruin. *Massinger*, The Picture, iv. 4.

His (Job's) fall is with a *precipice*, from a sublime pinnacle of honour to a deep puddle of penury. *Rev. T. Adams*, Works, III. 293.

2. A bank or cliff extremely steep, or even perpendicular or overhanging; a headlong declivity.

The sulphurous hail
Shot after us in storm, o'erblown, hath laid
The fiery surge, that from the *precipice*
Of heaven received us falling. *Milton*, P. L., i. 173.

3. The brink of a steep declivity; hence, a dangerous place; a critical position; a perilous location.

My fortunes standing in this *precipice*,
'Tis counsel that I want, and honest aids.
B. Jonson, Devil is an Ass, iv. 3.

But surely it cannot be safe for any man still to walk upon a *precipice*, to stand upon an indivisible point, and to be always upon the very border of destruction. *South*, Sermons, VI. xi.

They are at present in a frenzy, and will not be recovered from it till they shall have leaped the *precipice* they are now so boldly advancing to. *Jefferson*, Correspondence, II. 2.

precipient (prē-sip'i-ent), *a.* [< L. *præcipien(t-)s*, ppr. of *præcipere*, admonish, instruct: see *precept*.] Commanding; directing.

precipitability (prē-sip"i-ta-bil'i-ti), *n.* [< *precipitable* + *-ity* (see *-bility*).] The quality or state of being precipitable.

precipitable (prē-sip'i-ta-bl), *a.* [< *precipit-ate* + *-able*.] Capable of being precipitated or thrown down, as a substance in solution.

precipitance (prē-sip'i-tans), *n.* [= It. *precipitanza*, < L. *præcipitantia*, a falling headlong, < *præcipitan(t-)s*, falling headlong: see *precipitant*.] The quality of being precipitant; rash haste; headlong hurry.

Thither they
Basted with glad *precipitance*.
Milton, P. L., vii. 291.

Rashness and *precipitance* of judgment. *Watts*, Logic, ii. 4, § 5.

precipitancy (prē-sip'i-tan-si), *n.* [As *precipitance* (see *-cy*).] Precipitance; impatience to reach a conclusion or result; overhaste in inference or action.

When the *precipitancy* of a man's wishes hurries on his ideas ninety times faster than the vehicle he rides in — wo be to truth! *Sterne*, Tristram Shandy, vii. 8.

As a revising tribunal the Upper House has continually counteracted the evils of *precipitancy*, impatience, and ill-digested legislation, to which a numerous assembly, representing or delegated by larger constituent bodies, is necessarily and continually prone. *Quarterly Rev.*, CLXII. 255.

=**Syn.** Rashness, temerity, hastiness.

precipitant (prē-sip'i-tant), *a.* and *n.* [< OF. *precipitant*, F. *précipitant* = Sp. Pg. It. *precipitante*, < L. *præcipitan(t-)s*, ppr. of *præcipitare*, cast down headlong: see *precipitate*.] **I.** *a.* 1. Falling headlong; headlong.

From pole to pole
He views in breadth; and, without longer pause,
Downright into the world's first region throws
His flight *precipitant*. *Milton*, P. L., iii. 563.

Take care
Thy muddy beverage to serene, and drive
Precipitant the baser, ropy lees.
J. Philips, Cider, ii.

2. Rushing hastily onward.

But soon recovering speed he ran, he flew
Precipitant. *Addison*, Æneid, iii.

3. Rashly hasty; precipitate; characterized by rapid movement or progress; impatient to reach a conclusion.

There may be some such decays as are *precipitant* as to years.
Jer. Taylor (?), Artif. Handsomeness, p. 73. (*Latham.*)

The stormy bluster of men more audacious and *precipitant* then of solid and deep reach. *Milton*, Reformation in Eng., ii.

These fits being not so ordinary as our naturall sleep, these dreams the *precipitant* and unskilfull are forward to conceit to be representations extraordinary and supernatural. *Dr. H. More*, Enthusiasm, § 27.

II. *n.* In *chem.*, an agent which, when added to a solution, separates something dissolved and causes it to precipitate, or fall to the bottom in a concrete state.

precipitantly (prē-sip'i-tant-li), *adv.* In a precipitant manner; precipitately; rashly; with ill-advised haste.

Men *precipitantly* quit their new undertakings. *Bacon*, Physical Fables, ii., Expl.

How much less will he hear when we cry hereafter, who, once deliver'd by him, . . . are returning *precipitantly*, if he withhold us not, back to the captivity from whence he freed us! *Milton*, Free Commonwealth.

precipitantness (prē-sip'i-tant-nes), *n.* The quality of being precipitant.

precipitate (prē-sip'i-tāt), *v.*; pret. and pp. *precipitated*, ppr. *precipitating*. [< L. *præcipitatus*, pp. of *præcipitare* (> It. *precipitare* = Sp. Pg. *precipitar* = F. *précipiter*), cast down headlong, < *præceps* (*præcipit-*), head foremost, headlong, < *præ*, before, + *caput*, head: see *capital*. Cf. *precipice*.] **I.** *trans.* **1.** To cast down headlong; fling from a precipice or height; hurl downward.

Few men have frowned first upon Fortune, and *precipitated* themselves from the top of her wheel, before they felt at least the declination of it. *Dryden*, Amboyna, Ded.

He trembles to think that a single touch might bury him under a crag *precipitated* from above. *Eustace*, Italy, I. i.

2. To cause to fall as a sediment to the bottom of a vessel; reduce from a state of solution to a solid form, as by means of a reagent or chemical force.—**3.** To drive forcibly; cause to hasten onward.

Hence, then, and evil go with thee along, . . .
Ere . . . some more sudden vengeance, wing'd from God, *Precipitate* thee with augmented pain.
Milton, P. L., vi. 280.

4. To hasten; bring hastily to pass; hurry up: as, to *precipitate* a flight.

But they allow him [the Son of God] not the liberty of a fair tryal; they hasten and *precipitate* the sentence, that they might do so the execution. *Stillingfleet*, Sermons, I. vi.

Hostilities had been *precipitated* by the impolitic conduct of Navarre. *Prescott*, Ferd. and Isa., ii. 23.

5. To hasten intemperately or rashly; hence, to spoil; ruin.

That they like vertuous fathers have regard thereunto, and not to suffer the pope's holiness, if he would thus wilfully, without reason or discretion, to *precipitate* himself and the said see. *Bp. Burnet*, Records, I. ii. 22.

We sat whole nights drinking strong liquors without eating a bit; which disposed us to sloth, enflamed our bodies, and *precipitated* or prevented digestion.
Swift, Gulliver's Travels, iv. 6.

Precipitated calomel, calomel obtained by precipitation from a solution of corrosive sublimate by a stream of sulphurous acid.—**Precipitated carbonate of calcium or lime**, a white, minutely crystalline powder prepared by precipitation from a solution of calcium chlorid by sodium carbonate: used in medicine as an astringent and antacid.—**Precipitated carbonate of iron**, a reddish-brown powder prepared by precipitation from an iron sulphate solution by sodium carbonate. In composition it is a hydrated ferric oxid containing a little ferrous carbonate. Also called *sesquioxid of iron*, *red oxid of iron*, *aperitive saffron of Mars*.—**Precipitated carbonate of zinc**, a white, impalpable, odorless, and tasteless powder obtained from a solution of zinc sulphate by precipitating with sodium carbonate.—**Precipitated extract of bark.** Same as *chinoidine*.—**Precipitated oxid of mercury**, yellow oxid of mercury.—**Precipitated phosphate of calcium or lime**, normal calcium orthophosphate, a fine white amorphous powder prepared by precipitation from a hydrochloric acid solution of bone-ash by ammonia. Also called *bone-phosphate*.—**Precipitated sulphate of iron**, a pale bluish-green crystalline powder precipitated by alcohol from an aqueous solution of ferrous sulphate.—**Precipitated sulphid of antimony**, sulphurate of antimony.—**Precipitated sulphur**, a fine yellowish-white odorless amorphous powder prepared by heating a mixture of sublimed sulphur, lime, and water, and treating the resulting solution with hydrochloric acid.

II. *intrans.* **1.** To fall headlong.

Hadst thou been aught but gossamer, feathers, air,
So many fathom down *precipitating*,
Thou'dst shiver'd like an egg. *Shak.*, Lear, iv. 6. 50.

2. To make haste; hurry; proceed without deliberation.

Neither did the rebels spoil the country, neither on the other side did their forces increase, which might hasten him to *precipitate* and assail them. *Bacon.*

3. In *chem.*, to separate from a solution as a precipitate.

precipitate (prẹ̄-sip'i-tạ̄t), *a.* and *n.* [< L. *præcipitatus*, pp.: see the verb.] **I.** *a.* **1.** Hurled headlong; plunging or rushing down, as by a steep descent; headlong.

Precipitate the furious Torrent flows. *Prior*, Solomon, ii.

Disparting towers,
Tumbling all *precipitate* down dash'd,
Rattling around, loud thundering to the moon.
J. Dyer, Ruins of Rome.

2. Steep; precipitous.

No cliff or rock is so *precipitate*
But down it eyes can lead the blind a way.
Lord Brooke, Tragedy of Alaham. (*Latham.*)

3. Hasty; acting without due deliberation; rash.

Rules to be observed in choosing of a wife, . . . not to be too rash and *precipitate* in his election.
Burton, Anat. of Mel., p. 587.

I fear I have already been too *precipitate*. I tremble for the consequences. *Colman*, Jealous Wife, ii.

4. Hastily brought to pass; speedy; hurried; sudden.

His downfall too will not be more *precipitate* than awkward. *Poe*, Prose Tales, I. 280.

The danger of a *precipitate* abandonment of Virginia continued to be imminent. *Bancroft*, Hist. U. S., I. 100.

=**Syn.** **3** and **4.** *Precipitous* now always expresses the physical attribute of a headlong steepness; *precipitate* the moral quality of being very hasty or overhasty. Other uses are obsolete or figurative.

II. *n.* In *chem.*, any substance which, having been dissolved in a fluid, falls to the bottom of the vessel on the addition of some other substance capable of producing decomposition of the compound. The term is generally applied when the separation takes place in a flocculent or pulverulent form, in opposition to *crystallization*, which implies a like separation in an angular form. But chemists call a mass of crystals a *precipitate* when they subside so suddenly that their proper crystalline shape cannot be distinguished by the naked eye. Substances which fall or settle down, as earthy matter in water, are called *sediments*, the operating cause being mechanical and not chemical.—**Flocculent precipitate.** See *flocculent*.—**Precipitate per se**, red precipitate.—**Red precipitate**, red oxid of mercury.—**Sweet precipitate**, mercurous chlorid or calomel.—**White precipitate**, mercurammonium chlorid, NH_2HgCl. Also called *hydrargyrum ammoniatum*, or *ammoniated mercury*.

precipitately (prẹ̄-sip'i-tạ̄t-li), *adv.* In a precipitate manner; with sudden descent; headlong; hastily; without due deliberation; with a sudden subsiding motion.

Ill-counsell'd force by its own native weight *precipitately* falls. *Francis*, tr. of Horace's Odes, iii. 4.

Driven to that state of mind in which we are more ready to act *precipitately* than to reason right.
Goldsmith, Vicar, xviii.

Not so brave Arnall: with a weight of skull,
Furious he dives, *precipitately* dull.
Pope, Dunciad, ii. 316.

precipitateness (prẹ̄-sip'i-tạ̄t-nes), *n.* The state or character of being precipitate; precipitation; hastiness.

precipitation (prẹ̄-sip-i-tā'shọn), *n.* [= OF. *precipitation*, F. *précipitation* = Sp. *precipitacion* = Pg. *precipitação* = It. *precipitazione*, < L. *præcipitatio(n-)*, a falling headlong, headlong haste, < *præcipitare*, pp. *præcipitatus*, cast down headlong: see *precipitate*.] **1.** The act of casting down from a height, or the state of being flung or hurled downward.

We . . . banish him our city,
In peril of *precipitation*
From off the rock Tarpeian, never more
To enter our Rome gates. *Shak.*, Cor., iii. 3. 102.

2. Rapid motion; a hurrying or rushing onward.

That could never happen from any other cause than the hurry, *precipitation*, and rapid motion of the water, returning, at the end of the deluge, towards the sea.
Woodward, Nat. Hist.

Pacing along Cheapside with my accustomed *precipitation* when I walk westward. *Lamb*, Chimney-Sweepers.

3. Haste; hurry; unwise or rash rapidity.

Precipitation in our works makes us unlike to God. Heady fool, art thou wiser than thy Maker?
Rev. T. Adams, Works, III. 119.

We were forced to eat with great *precipitation*, having received advice of General Carpenter's march as we were at dinner. *Addison*, Freeholder, No. 3.

Precipitation, . . . incited by the pride of intellectual superiority, is very fatal to great designs.
Johnson, Rambler, No. 43.

4. In *chem.*, the process by which any substance is made to separate from another or others in solution, and fall to the bottom.—**5.** Moisture from the atmosphere deposited on the earth's surface, including dew, mist, rain, frost, snow, sleet, hail, etc.

It [visibility] is no doubt, to some extent, the effect of previous rains, the *precipitation* having washed the atmosphere of its dust.
Rev. W. C. Ley, in Modern Meteorology, p. 128.

Precipitation process, in the smelting of lead. See *process*.=**Syn. 1.** See list under *precipitancy*. *Precipitancy* is always a quality; *precipitation* is primarily an act, but may be a quality.

precipitative (prẹ̄-sip'i-tạ̄-tiv), *a.* [< *precipitate* + *-ive*.] Pertaining to precipitation; tending to precipitate.

The *precipitative* tendencies of tidal action may exceed those resulting from resistances encountered in planetary space. *Winchell*, World-Life, p. 491.

precipitator (prẹ̄-sip'i-tā-tọr), *n.* [= It. *precipitatore*, < L. *præcipitator*, one who overthrows, < *præcipitatus*, pp. of *præcipitare*, cast down headlong: see *precipitate*.] **1.** One who precipitates; especially, one who urges on with undue haste; one who rashly brings to pass.

Zelots, . . . as it prov'd, [were] the hast'ners and *precipitators* of the destruction of that kingdom.
Hammond, Works, IV. 590.

2. That which brings about the precipitation or downfall of atmospheric moisture.

For the slopes of elevations towards the sea are great *precipitators* of rain. *The American*, XI. 166.

3. That which causes or favors chemical precipitation; an apparatus for inducing precipitation. Specifically, a tank in which carbonates held in solution by free carbonic acid in water are precipitated by caustic lime, which neutralizes the free carbonic acid and permits the carbonates to fall to the bottom. This method of purifying water is used by dyers, and also in fitting hard water for use in steam-boilers.

The mother-liquor is conducted through the pipe for mother-water to the *precipitators*, which are constructed of 2 in. tongued and grooved timber, lined with sheet-lead.
Workshop Receipts, 2d ser., p. 350.

precipitious† (pres-i-pish'us), *a.* [< L. *precipitium*, a precipice (see *precipice*), + *-ous*. Cf. *precipitous*.] Precipitous.

I perswaded him fairly . . . to keep them from any such *precipitious* and impertinent rupture as might preclude all meditation of accord. *Sir H. Wotton*, Reliquiæ, p. 288.

The descent was *precipitious*: so that, save by ragged steps, and those not a little dangerous, [there] was no riding down. *Sir T. Herbert*, Travels, p. 152. (*Latham.*)

precipitiously† (pres-i-pish'us-li), *adv.* Precipitously.

Headlong riot *precipiciously* will on, wherever strong desire shall drive, or flattering lust allure.
Decay of Christian Piety, p. 174.

precipitous (prẹ̄-sip'i-tus), *a.* [< OF. *precipiteux*, F. *précipiteux* = Sp. Pg. It. *precipitoso*; as L. *præceps* (*-cipit-*), head foremost, headlong (see *precipice*), + *-ous*. Cf. *precipitious*.] **1.** Headlong; descending rapidly, or rushing onward.

The sweep
Of some *precipitous* rivulet to the wave.
Tennyson, Enoch Arden.

2. Steep; like a precipice; consisting of precipices: as, *precipitous* cliffs.

Tangled swamps and deep *precipitous* dells.
Shelley, Alastor.

3†. Hasty; rash; precipitate.

She [Nature] useth to act by due and orderly gradations, and takes no *precipitous* leaps from one extream to another.
Glanville, Pre-existence of Souls, xiii.

Thus framed for ill, he loosed our triple hold
(Advice unsafe, *precipitous*, and bold).
Dryden, The Medal, l. 65.

4†. Hastily appearing or passing; sudden.

How precious the time is, how *precipitous* the occasion, how many things to be done in their just season.
Evelyn, Calendarium Hortense, Int.

=**Syn. 1** and **2**. See *precipitate*, *a*.

precipitously (prẹ̄-sip'i-tus-li), *adv.* **1.** In a precipitous manner; with sudden descent; in violent haste.

Till the victim hear within and yearn to hurry *precipitously*
Like the leaf in a roaring whirlwind, like the smoke in a hurricane whirl'd. *Tennyson*, Boädicea.

2†. Hastily; with precipitation; precipitately.

Some . . . *precipitously* conclude they [chameleons] eat not any at all. *Sir T. Browne*, Vulg. Err., iii. 21.

precipitousness (prẹ̄-sip'i-tus-nes), *n.* **1.** The state or quality of being precipitous or steep; steepness.—**2.** Hastiness; precipitation; rash haste.

As simplicity ordinarily signifies sencelessness, *precipitousness*, as Trismegistus defines it, μάνιας εἶδος, a species of madness in one place, and τις μέθη, a kind of drunkenness in another, a wild irrational acting.
Hammond, Works, IV. iii.

précis (prā-sē'), *n.* [F., an abstract, < L. *præcisum*, a piece cut off (ML. also an abstract?), neut. of *præcisus*, cut off: see *precise*.] **1.** A concise statement; a summary; an abstract.

Any gentlemen who are willing to co-operate are requested to send in their names, and in return they will be supplied with a *précis* of the case.
Fortnightly Rev., N. S., XL. 45.

Contrast the newspaper *précis* of some important negotiation and the Blue Book—there is the difference at a glance. *Contemporary Rev.*, XLIX. 669.

2. The act or process of drawing up a précis or abstract.

precise (prẹ̄-sīs'), *a.* [< ME. **precis* (in adv. **precisly*, *percysly*), < OF. *precis*, m., *precise*, f., F. *précis* = Sp. Pg. It. *preciso*, cut off, definite, precise, strict, < L. *præcisus*, cut short, shortened, brief, pp. of *præcidere*, cut off in front, cut short, abridge, < *præ*, before, + *cædere*, cut. Cf. *concise*.] **1.** Definite; exact; neither more nor less than; just, with no error.

I know not well what they are: but *precise* villains they are, that I am sure of. *Shak.*, M. for M., ii. 1. 54.

What special hinderers the Apostle means, we shall have *precise* occasion in some future passages to demonstrate. *Rev. T. Adams*, Works, II. 336.

End all dispute, and fix the year *precise*
When British bards begin to immortalise.
Pope, Imit. of Horace, II. i. 53.

2. Exactly stated, defined, marked off, or measured, etc.; strictly expressed, stated, etc.

John Villani has given us an ample and *precise* account of the state of Florence in the early part of the fourteenth century. *Macaulay*, Machiavelli.

Not a Christian thought exists which must go outside of the English tongue for a clear, *precise*, forcible utterance. *A. Phelps*, English Style, p. 55.

The distinct is that which is so *precise* and different from all other objects as to comprehend in itself only what is clear. *Veitch*, Introd. to Descartes's Method, p. lv.

3. Being just what it purports or is alleged to be, and not something else; particular.

Abs. Well, sir, and what did you say?
Fag. O, I lied, sir—I forget the *precise* lie; but you may depend on 't he got no truth from me. *Sheridan*, The Rivals, ii. 1.

4. Containing or committing no error: as, a *precise* measurement; measuring or reckoning with extreme exactness, so as to reduce the errors in an unusual degree: as, a *precise* instrument or operator.—5. Exact in conduct or requirements; strict; punctilious; express; formal; over-exact or over-scrupulous; prim; precisian; also, conformed to over-scrupulous requirements.

He was ever *precise* in promise-keeping. *Shak.*, M. for M., i. 2. 76.

The Venetians are extraordinarily *precise* herein, insomuch that a man cannot be receiued into Venice without a bill of health. *Coryat*, Crudities, i. 74.

I think the purest and *precisest* reformers . . . of religion can hardly order this matter better than God hath done. *Rev. T. Adams*, Works, II. 361.

They would tell me I was too *precise*, and that I denied myself of things, for their sakes, in which they saw no evil. *Bunyan*, Pilgrim's Progress, p. 122.

Grave without dullness, learned without pride;
Exact, yet not *precise*; though meek, keen-ey'd.
Cowper, Conversation, l. 610.

The extravagance of the Independent preachers in the camp, the *precise* garb, the severe countenance, the petty scruples, the affected accent, . . . which marked the Puritans. *Macaulay*, Hist. Eng.

6†. Specifically, Puritan; puritanical.

A sort of sober, scurvy, *precise* neighbours,
That scarce have smiled twice since the king came in.
B. Jonson, Alchemist, i. 1.

My fine *precise* artisan, that shuns a tavern as the devil doth a cross, is as often drunk as the rankest. His language doth not savour of the pot; he swears not, but "indeed!" But trust him, and he will cozen you to your face. *Rev. T. Adams*, Works, II. 445.

7. In *logic*, containing nothing superfluous.

The definition should be *precise*: that is, contain nothing unessential, nothing superfluous. *Sir W. Hamilton*, Logic, xxiv.

=**Syn.** 1. *Accurate*, Correct, *Exact*, etc. (see *accurate*), distinct, express.—5. Stiff, ceremonious.

precise† (prē-sīs'), *adv.* [< *precise*, *a.*] Precisely; exactly.

Sum follow so *precyse*
A learned man that oftentymes
They imitate his vyce.
Drant, tr. of Horace's Epistles to Mæcenas.

precisely (prē-sīs'li), *adv.* [< ME. **precisly*, *percysly*; < *precise* + *-ly*².] 1. In a precise or exact manner; accurately; definitely; exactly; just.

We declare, that is to weten, that all and euery Alderman of yᵉ forsayd cite euery yere for euermore in yᵉ feste of Saynt Gregory yᵉ Pope, from yᵉ office of aldyrmanry vtterly aud *percysly* to cessen and therof holych to be remeuyd. *Charter of London*, in Arnold's Chron., p. 37.

Many cases happen, in which a man cannot *precisely* determine where it is that his lawful liberty ends, and where it is that it begins to be extravagant and excessive. *Sharp*, Works, I. vii.

It is *precisely* these impulses and emotions which are so hard to control that give dignity and worth to life. *J. R. Seeley*, Nat. Religion, p. 141.

2. With strict conformity to rule; punctiliously; nicely; with over-scrupulous exactness in ceremony or behavior.

Some craven scruple
Of thinking too *precisely* on the event.
Shak., Hamlet, iv. 4. 41.

preciseness (prē-sīs'nes), *n.* The character of being precise; exactness; precision; particularity; punctiliousness; scrupulousness; primness; squeamishness.

But they thinke this *precisenes* in reformation of apparell not to be so materiall, or greatly pertinent. *Spenser*, State of Ireland.

Is all your strict *preciseness* come to this? *Shak.*, 1 Hen. VI., v. 4. 67.

Among their *preciseness* was a qualm at baptism; the water was to be taken from a basin, and not from a fount. *Disraeli*, Quarrels of Authors, p. 362, note.

precisian (prē-sizh'an), *a.* and *n.* [= F. *précisien*; as *precise* + *-ian*.] I. *a.* 1. Precise; punctiliously or ostentatiously observant of rules or doctrines.—2. Characteristic of precisians; puritanical.

If a man be a Herod within and a John without, a wicked politician in a ruff of *precisian* set, God can distinguish him. *Rev. T. Adams*, Works, II. 465.

II. *n.* One who adheres punctiliously to certain rules or observances; especially, one who is precise in matters of religion: often used depreciatingly with reference to the English Puritans of the seventeenth century.

Hypocriticall *precisians*,
By vulgar phrase entitled Puritanes.
Times' Whistle (E. E. T. S.), p. 10.

These men (for all the world) like our *Precisions* be,
Who for some Cross or Saint they in the window see
Will pluck down all the Church.
Drayton, Polyolbion, vi. 301.

Married he was, and to as bitter a *precisian* as ever eat flesh in Lent. *Scott*, Kenilworth, ii.

He is no *precisian* in attire. *R. L. Stevenson*, Inland Voyage, Epil.

precisianism (prē-sizh'an-izm), *n.* [< *precision* + *-ism*.] The quality or state of being a precisian; the doctrine or conduct of precisians.

It is *precisianism* to alter that
With austere judgment that is given by nature.
B. Jonson, Case is Altered, ii. 3.

precisianist (prē-sizh'an-ist), *n.* [< *precisian* + *-ist*.] One who adheres strictly to any doctrine, practice, or rule of conduct; a precisian.

Of course there are yet some *precisianists* that will not have it so; but the school is practically dead and buried. *N. and Q.*, 6th ser., XI. 302.

precision (prē-sizh'on), *n.* [= F. *précision* = Sp. *precision* = Pg. *precisão* = It. *precisione*, < L. *præcisio(n-)*, a cutting off, a cut, ML. precision, < *præcidere*, pp. *præcisus*, cut off: see *precise*.] 1. The quality or state of being precise, exact, or definite as to form or meaning; distinctness; accuracy.

What Lord Bacon blames in the schoolmen of his time is this, that they reasoned syllogistically on words which had not been defined with *precision*. *Macaulay*, Utilitarian Theory of Government.

We deprive ourselves of that remarkable and almost mysterious *precision* which is given to words when they are habitually used in discussions which are to issue directly in acts. *Maine*, Village Communities, p. 345.

2. In *logic*: (*a*) Freedom from inessential elements.

In the extensive quantity of distinctness absence of superfluity is called *precision*. Completeness and precision together constitute adequacy. *Kant*, Introd. to Logic (tr. by Abbott), viii.

There is a sin committed against logical purity or *precision* in assuming into the declaration qualities such as do not determinately designate what is defined. *Sir W. Hamilton*, Logic, xxiv.

(*b*) The separation from anything of extrinsic elements. [In this sense, probably introduced into Latin by Scotus, *precision* appears to be the abstract noun corresponding to the verb *prescind*, and is occasionally spelled *prescision*.]—**Arms of precision.** See *arm*².—**Instrument of precision**, an instrument suited for measurement of the highest degree of refinement and precision, as a circle for measuring angles to a second of an arc, or a comparator for measuring lengths to a micron.—**Mental precision**, separation in the mind.—**Negative precision**, the representation of one without the representation of the other.—**Positive precision**, the representation of one thing as separated from another thing.—**Real precision**, the separation of one thing from another in fact. =**Syn.** 1. *Propriety*, etc. (see *purity*), nicety, correctness, truth. See *accurate*.

precisionist (prē-sizh'on-ist), *n.* [< *precision* + *-ist*.] Same as *precisianist*.

Were a logical *precisionist* speaking, and speaking calmly and of aforethought, this would be of force. *N. and Q.*, 7th ser., VIII. 162.

precisionize (prē-sizh'on-īz), *v. t.*; pret. and pp. *precisionized*, ppr. *precisionizing*. [< *precision* + *-ize*.] To render precise; give precision to; state with precision or accuracy.

What a pity the same man does not . . . *precisionize* other questions of political morals! *Sir G. C. Lewis*, Letters (1847), p. 143. (*Davies*.)

precisive (prē-sī'siv), *a.* [= Sp. It. *precisivo*, < *precise* + *-ive*.] 1. Cutting off; amputative; eradicative.

At other times our church moderates her censure, . . . using a medicinal censure before a *precisive*; a less to prevent a greater excommunication. *T. Puller*, Moderation of Church of Eng., p. 369.

2. Pertaining to or resulting from the mental precision of one object from another.—**Precisive abstraction.** See the quotation, and *abstraction*.

Precisive abstraction is when we consider those things apart which cannot really exist apart, as when we consider mode without considering its substance and subject. *Watts*, Logic, I. vi. § 9.

preclare†, preclair† (prē-klãr'), *a.* [= Sp. Pg. It. *preclaro*, < L. *præclarus*, very bright or clear, splendid, noble, excellent, < *præ*, before, + *clarus*, shining, brilliant: see *clear*.] Illustrious; renowned.

Consider weill thow bene bot officiar,
And vassal to that King incomparabill,
Preis thow to pleis that puissant prince *preclair*.
Sir D. Lyndsay, Works (1592), p. 194. (*Jamieson*.)

preclassical (prē-klas'i-kal), *a.* [< *pre-* + *classical*¹.] Existing or occurring before classical times; prior to the classical.

He [Thoreau] seeks, at all risks, for perversity of thought, and revives the age of concetti while he fancies himself going back to a *preclassical* nature. *Lowell*, Study Windows, p. 202.

preclitellian (prē-kli-tel'i-an), *a.* [< L. *præ*, before, + NL. *clitellum*, q. v.] Having the ducts of the testes opening before and not behind or in the clitellum, as certain earthworms. Compare *postclitellian*.

precloacal (prē-klō-ā'kal), *a.* [< L. *præ*, before, + NL. *cloaca*: see *cloaca*, 3.] Of or pertaining to the front of the cloaca; situated in the fore part of the cloaca.—**Precloacal cartilage, precloacal ossicle**, the os cloacæ.

preclude (prē-klöd'), *v. t.*; pret. and pp. *precluded*, ppr. *precluding*. [= OF. *preclure* = It. *precludere*, < L. *præcludere*, shut up or off, < *præ*, before, + *claudere*, shut, close: see *close*¹. Cf. *conclude*, *exclude*, *include*, etc.] 1†. To close; stop up; shut; prevent access to.

Preclude your ears not against humble and honest petitioners. *Waterhouse*, Apol. for Learning, p. 187. (*Latham*.)

2. To shut out; hinder by excluding; prevent; impede.

Though the desires of his mind be granted, yet this *precludes* not the access of new desires to his mind. *Rev. T. Adams*, Works, II. 143.

To *preclude* the ambassadors of the neutral from egress and ingress into enemy's territory is unfriendly, although the enemy's envoys to the neutral may be seized except on neutral soil or ships. *Woolsey*, Introd. to Inter. Law, § 164.

3. To prevent by anticipative action; render ineffectual or unsuccessful; hinder the action of.

Shall I *preclude* my future by taking a high seat, and kindly adapting my conversation to the shape of heads? *Emerson*, Experience.

Smilie spoke against a system of precipitancy which would *preclude* deliberation on questions of the highest consequence. *Bancroft*, Hist. Const., II. 245.

=**Syn.** To prevent, bar, debar, prohibit.

preclusion (prē-klö'zhon), *n.* [< L. *præclusio(n-)*, a shutting up, < *præclusus*, pp. of *præcludere*, shut up or off: see *preclude*.] The act of precluding, or the state of being precluded, in any sense of that word.

It is St. Augustine's *preclusion* of all star-predictions out of this place. *Rev. T. Adams*, Works, I. 9.

preclusive (prē-klö'siv), *a.* [< L. *præclusus*, pp. of *præcludere*, shut up or off (see *preclude*), + *-ive*.] Tending to preclude; shutting out; preventive: generally followed by *of*.

Every act [of France] bespoke an intention *preclusive of* accommodation. *Burke*, Parliamentary Register, xxxiv. 482.

preclusively (prē-klö'siv-li), *adv.* In a preclusive manner; preventively.

precoce† (prē-kōs'), *a.* [In lit. sense, ME. *precox*, irreg. < L.; in second sense, < OF. *precoce*, F. *précoce* = Sp. *precoz* = Pg. It. *precoce*, < L. *præcox* (-coc-), *præcoquis*, *præcoquus*, ripe before time, early ripe, premature, < *præcoquere*, ripen beforehand, ripen fully, also boil beforehand, < *præ*, before, + *coquere*, cook, boil: see *cook*¹. Cf. *apricock*, *apricot*, from the same ult. source.] 1. Early ripe. [Rare.]

In places passyng colde it is moost sure
Precox [figs] to plaunte, her fruyte thai soone enhance
Er shoures come.
Palladius, Husbondrie (E. E. T. S.), p. 124.

2. Precocious.

An intellectus universalis, beyond all that we reade of Picus Mirandula, and other *precoce* witts, and yet withall a very humble child. *Evelyn*, Diary, July 6, 1679.

precoceness† (prē-kōs'nes), *n.* [Also *precoseness*; < *precoce* + *-ness*.] Precocity.

As to this extraordinary *precoseness*, the like is reported of a certain walnut-tree, as well as of the famous white-thorn of Glastonbury. *Evelyn*, Sylva.

precocial, præcocial (prē-kō'shial), *a.* [< *Præcoces* + *-ial*.] Of or pertaining to the *Præcoces*; having the characters of the *Præcoces*: opposed to *altricial*.

precocious (prē-kō'shus), *a.* [As *precoce* + *-ious*.] 1. Ripe before the natural time.

Many *precocious* trees, and such as have their spring in the winter, may be found in most parts of Europe. *Sir T. Browne*, Vulg. Err., ii. 6.

2. Ripe in understanding at an early period; prematurely developed; forward: as, a *precocious* child; *precocious* faculties.—3. Indicative of precocity; characteristic of early maturity; anticipative of greater age; premature.

'Tis superfluous to live unto gray hairs when in a *precocious* temper we anticipate the virtues of them. *Sir T. Browne*, To a Friend.

In the Italian States, as in many natural bodies, untimely decrepitude was the penalty of *precocious* maturity. *Macaulay*, Machiavelli.

4. In *bot.*, appearing before the leaves: said of flowers.

precociously (prē-kō'shus-li), *adv.* In a precocious manner; with premature ripeness or forwardness.

A man that 's fond *precociously* of stirring
Must be a spoon.
Hood, Morning Meditations.

precociousness (prē-kō'shus-nes), *n.* Same as *precocity*.

precocity (prē-kos'i-ti), *n.* [= F. *précocité* = Sp. *precosidad* = Pg. *precocidade* = It. *precocità*, < L. as if **præcocita(t-)s*, < *præcox*, early ripe: see *precoce*, *precocious*.] The state or character of being precocious; premature growth or development; early ripeness, especially of the mental powers.

Some . . . imputing the cause of it [his fall] to a *precocity* of spirit and valour in him.
Howell, Vocall Forrest, p. 77.

To the usual *precocity* of the girl, she added that early experience of struggle . . . which is the lot of every imaginative and passionate nature.
George Eliot, Mill on the Floss, iv. 2.

The term *precocity*, as applied by biologists to individuals, explains a similar phenomenon as applied to societies. Claude Bernard tells us that the force of development is greatest in the inferior animals, and that this *precocity* is an evidence of inferiority, and excludes longevity.
Science, III. 330.

precoëtaneant (prē-kō-ē-tā'nē-an), *n.* [< *pre-* + *coëtanean*.] One contemporary with, yet older than, another. [Rare.]

Indeed I read of Petrarch (the *pre-coetanean* of our Chaucer) that he was crowned with a laurel in the Capitol by the senate of Rome, an. 1341.
Fuller, General Worthies, ix.

precogitate (prē-koj'i-tāt), *v. t.*; pret. and pp. *precogitated*, ppr. *precogitating*. [< L. *præcogitatus*, pp. of *præcogitare* (> It. *precogitare*), ponder or consider in advance, < *præ*, before, + *cogitare*, think, consider: see *cogitate*.] To consider or contrive beforehand. [Rare.]

precogitation (prē-koj-i-tā'shon), *n.* [= It. *precogitazione*, < LL. *præcogitatio(n-)*, forethought, < L. *præcogitare*, think upon beforehand: see *precogitate*.] Previous thought or consideration.

precognition (prē-kog-nish'on), *n.* [= Sp. *precognicion* = It. *precognizione*, < LL. *præcognitio(n-)*, foreknowledge, < L. *præcognoscere*, foreknow: see *precognosce* and *cognition*.] **1.** Previous knowledge or cognition; antecedent examination.

When it is said our "righteousness must exceed that of the scribes and Pharisees," let us first take notice, by way of *precognition*, that it must at least be so much.
Jer. Taylor, Works (ed. 1835), II. 5.

2. A preliminary examination; specifically, in *Scots law*, a preliminary examination of a witness or of one likely to know something about a case, or the evidence taken down; especially, an examination of witnesses to a criminal act, before a judge, justice of the peace, or sheriff, by a procurator-fiscal, in order to know whether there is ground of trial, and to enable him to set forth the facts in the libel.

The ambassador, when he arrived at Sennaar, found it, in the first place, necessary to make a proces verbal, or what we call a *precognition*, in which the names of the authors, and substance of these reports, were mentioned.
Bruce, Source of the Nile, II. 503.

precognosce (prē-kog-nos'), *v. t.*; pret. and pp. *precognosced*, ppr. *precognoscing*. [= Sp. *precónocer* = It. *preconoscere*, < L. *præcognoscere*, foreknow, < *præ*, before, + *cognoscere*, become or be acquainted with, know: see *cognosce*.] In *Scots law*, to take the precognition of: as, to *precognosce* witnesses. See *precognition*.

precollection (prē-ko-lek'shon), *n.* [< *pre-* + *collection*.] A collection previously made. *Imp. Dict.*

pre-Columbian (prē-kō-lum'bi-an), *a.* [< *pre-* + *Columbian*.] Prior to the time of Christopher Columbus; occurring or existing before the discovery of America by Columbus: as, a *pre-Columbian* discovery of America.

Drawn wire, the manufacture of which it is not pretended the *pre-Columbian* native knew.
Pop. Sci. Mo., XXXI. 521.

precompose (prē-kom-pōz'), *v. t.*; pret. and pp. *precomposed*, ppr. *precomposing*. [< *pre-* + *compose*.] To compose beforehand.

In the latter part of his life he did not *pre-compose* his cursory sermons; but, having adjusted the heads, and sketched out some particulars, trusted for success to his extemporary powers.
Johnson, Watts.

preconceit (prē-kon-sēt'), *n.* [< *pre-* + *conceit*.] An opinion formed beforehand; a preconceived notion.

A thing in reason impossible, which notwithstanding through their misfashioned *preconceit* appeared unto them no less certain than if nature had written it in the very foreheads of all the creatures.
Hooker.

preconceited† (prē-kon-sē'ted), *a.* [< *pre-* + *conceited*.] Preconceived.

Faire blossomes, which of fairer fruites did bonst,
Were blasted in the flowers,
With eye-exacted showers,
Whose sweet supposed sowers
Of *preconceited* pleasures grieu'd me most.
Stirling, Aurora, ix.

preconceive (prē-kon-sēv'), *v. t.*; pret. and pp. *preconceived*, ppr. *preconceiving*. [< *pre-* + *conceive*.] To form a conception, notion, or idea of, in advance of actual knowledge.

In a dead plain the way seemeth the longer, because the eye hath *preconceived* it shorter than the truth. *Bacon.*

We do not form our opinions from it [fiction]; but we try it by our *preconceived* opinions. *Macaulay*, History.

preconception (prē-kon-sep'shon), *n.* [< *pre-* + *conception*.] A conception or opinion formed in advance of experience or actual knowledge; also, the influence of previous belief or states of mind in modifying the conceptions formed under the partial influence of experience.

Custom with most men prevails more than truth: according to the notions and *preconceptions* which it hath formed in our minds we shape the discourse of reason itself.
Hakewill, Apology, i. 1, § 6.

preconcert (prē-kon-sėrt'), *v. t.* [< *pre-* + *concert*, *v.*] To concert or arrange beforehand; constitute in advance.

Toro, . . . by a *preconcerted* agreement, was delivered into his hands by the Governor of the City.
Prescott, Ferd. and Isa., i. 5.

preconcert (prē-kon'sėrt), *n.* [< *pre-* + *concert*, *n.*] Previous arrangement; preconcerted action or agreement.

Much time may be required before a compact, organized majority can be thus formed; but formed it will be in time, even without *preconcert* or design, by the sure workings of that principle or constitution of our nature in which government itself originates. *Calhoun*, Works, I. 16.

preconcertedly (prē-kon-sėr'ted-li), *adv.* In a preconcerted manner; by preconcert.

preconcertedness (prē-kon-sėr'ted-nes), *n.* The state of being preconcerted.

preconcertion (prē-kon-sėr'shon), *n.* [< *pre-* + *concertion*.] The act of preconcerting, or concerting beforehand. *Dwight.* (*Imp. Dict.*)

precondemn (prē-kon-dem'), *v. t.* [< *pre-* + *condemn*.] To condemn beforehand.

They will quite reject and *precondemne* them ere they have once examined them.
Prynne, Histrio-Mastix, Ep. Ded., p. 8.

precondemnation (prē-kon-dem-nā'shon), *n.* [< *pre-* + *condemnation*.] The act of condemning, or the state of being condemned, beforehand.

precondition (prē-kon-dish'on), *n.* [< *pre-* + *condition*.] An antecedent condition; a condition requisite in advance; a prerequisite.

Up to 1763 he [Kant] had still maintained that the idea of God is the *precondition* of all thought and being.
E. Caird, Philos. of Kant, p. 165.

preconform (prē-kon-fôrm'), *v. t.* and *i.* [< *pre-* + *conform*.] To conform in anticipation. *De Quincey.*

preconformity (prē-kon-fôr'mi-ti), *n.* [< *pre-* + *conformity*.] Antecedent conformity. *Coleridge.*

preconizate† (prē-kon'i-zāt), *v. t.* [< ML. *præconizatus*, pp. of *præconizare*, proclaim: see *preconize*.] To proclaim; summon by proclamation.

The queen . . . incontinently departed out of the court; wherefore she was thrice *preconnisate*, and called eft-soons to return and appear.
Bp. Burnet, Records, ii. No. 28. The King's Letter, (June, 1529.

preconization (prē-kon-i-zā'shon), *n.* [= F. *préconisation* = Sp. *preconizacion* = Pg. *preconização* = It. *preconizzazione*, < ML. *præconizatio(n-)*, < *præconizare*, pp. *præconizatus*, proclaim: see *preconize*.] **1†.** A public proclamation or summons.

The time was when the minister, in a solemn *preconization*, called you either then to speak, or for ever after to hold your peace.
Bp. Hall, Cases of Conscience (Additional), iii.

2. Specifically, in the *Rom. Cath. Ch.*, the public confirmation by the Pope of the decision of the College of Cardinals to appoint a given ecclesiastic to a specified church dignity. This preconization is an essential part of an appointment to any of the higher ecclesiastical dignities, is the first public announcement of it, and is made in the presence of the College of Cardinals. The *bull of preconization* is the official letter of the Pope to an appointee announcing his preconization.

preconize, præconize (prē'kō-nīz), *v. t.*; pret. and pp. *preconized*, *præconized*, ppr. *preconizing*, *præconizing*. [= F. *préconiser* = Sp. *preconizar* = Pg. *preconisar* = It. *preconizzare*, < ML. *præconizare*, proclaim, < L. *præco(n-)*, a crier, herald.] **1.** To summon publicly; call upon as by a public crier.

The clergy are *præconized*, or summoned by name, to appear before the metropolitan or his commissary.
Encyc. Brit., VI. 329.

2. Specifically, in the *Rom. Cath. Ch.*, to confirm publicly or officially, as an ecclesiastical appointment: a prerogative of the Pope. See *preconization*, 2.

preconquer (prē-kong'kėr), *v. t.* [< *pre-* + *conquer*.] To conquer beforehand.

This kingdom . . . they had *preconquered* in their hopes.
Fuller, Worthies, Cornwall, I. 304.

preconscious (prē-kon'shus), *a.* [< *pre-* + *conscious*.] Pertaining to or involving a state anterior to consciousness.

preconsent (prē-kon-sent'), *n.* [< *pre-* + *consent*.] A previous consent. *Southey.*

preconsign (prē-kon-sīn'), *v. t.* [< *pre-* + *consign*.] **1†.** To consign beforehand; serve as a consignation or token of.

Therefore St. Cyril calls baptism . . . "the antitype of the passions of Christ." It does *preconsign* the death of Christ, and does the infancy of the work of grace.
Jer. Taylor, Works (ed. 1835), I. 118.

2. To make over in advance; make a previous consignment of: as, to *preconsign* one's property to another.

preconsolidated (prē-kon-sol'i-dā-ted), *a.* [< *pre-* + *consolidated*.] Consolidated beforehand.

preconstitute (prē-kon'sti-tūt), *v. t.*; pret. and pp. *preconstituted*, ppr. *preconstituting*. [< *pre-* + *constitute*. Cf. F. *préconstituer*.] To constitute or establish beforehand.

precontemporaneous (prē-kon-tem-pō-rā'nē-us), *a.* [< *pre-* + *contemporaneous*.] Prior to what is contemporaneous; antecedent; previous. [Rare.]

In discussing the *precontemporaneous* history of the subject, he defined the following epochs. *Science*, III. 57.

precontract (prē-kon'trakt, formerly also prē-kon-trakt'), *n.* [< *pre-* + *contract*.] A previous contract or engagement; especially, a previous betrothal or contract of marriage.

Gentle daughter, fear you not at all.
He is your husband on a *pre-contract*.
Shak., M. for M., iv. 1. 72.

Peter Gomera, thou hast lost thy wife;
Death pleads a *precontract*.
Beau. and Fl., Knight of Malta, i. 3.

precontract (prē-kon-trakt'), *v.* [< *precontract*, *n.*] **I.** *trans.* To contract beforehand; bind or make over by a previous contract; particularly, to betroth before something else.

This Lepida had been *pre-contracted* unto Metellus Scipio; but afterwards, the pre-contract being broken, he forsook her. *North*, tr. of Plutarch, p. 639.

II. *intrans.* To form a previous contract; come to a previous arrangement or agreement.

precontrive (prē-kon-trīv'), *v. t.* and *i.*; pret. and pp. *precontrived*, ppr. *precontriving*. [< *pre-* + *contrive*.] To contrive or plan beforehand.

Thus, for instance, when the mind had the will to raise the arm to the head, the body was so *precontrived* as to raise at that very moment the part required.
Warburton, On Pope's Essay on Man, iii. 295.

precoracoid, præcoracoid (prē-kor'a-koid), *a.* and *n.* [< *pre-* + *coracoid*.] **I.** *a.* Situated in front of the coracoid bone or cartilage; pertaining to the precoracoid. Also *precoracoidal*.

II. *n.* A precoracoidal bone or cartilage of the shoulder-girdle or pectoral arch of the lower vertebrates. See *coracoid*.

That region of the primitively cartilaginous pectoral arch . . . which lies on the ventral side [of the glenoid cavity] may present not only a coracoid, but a *precoracoid* and an epicoracoid. *Huxley*, Anat. Vert., p. 35.

precoracoidal (prē-kor-a-koi'dal), *a.* [< *precoracoid* + *-al*.] Same as *precoracoid*.

precordia, *n.* See *præcordia*.

precordial, præcordial (prē-kôr'di-al), *a.* and *n.* [= F. *précordial*, < ML. *præcordialis*, neut. pl. *præcordialia*, præcordia, < L. *præcordia*, præcordia: see *præcordia*.] **I.** *a.* Situated in front of the heart; pertaining to the præcordia.—**Precordial region**, the region of the heart, or the front of the chest over the heart; also, the epigastric region.

I am come to speak of the *præcordiall region* of the bodie. *Holland*, tr. of Pliny, xxx. 5.

II. *n. pl.* The precordial parts. [Rare.]

Wheras coulde is wantinge, the naturall heate is not dryuen frome the owtewarde partes into the inwarde partes and *precordials*, whereby digestion is much strengthened. *R. Eden*, tr. of Peter Martyr (First Books on America, [ed. Arber, p. 118).

precorneal, præcorneal (prē-kôr'nē-al), *a.* [< L. *præ*, before, + NL. *cornea*, cornea.] Situated on the front of the cornea of the eye.

precoseness†, *n.* See *precoceness*.

precourse (prę-kōrs'), *v. t.*; pret. and pp. *precoursed*, ppr. *precoursing*. [< *pre-* + *course*, *v.* Cf. *precurse*.] To go before as a herald or precursor; herald the approach of; announce; prognosticate. [Rare.]

The sea had strangely flattened; the weighty swells which had *precoursed* the growth of the storm had run away down the eastern waters. *W. C. Russell*, Death Ship, xl.

precritical (prē-krit'i-kal), *a.* [< *pre-* + *critical*.] Previous to the development of Kant's critical philosophy and to the publication of his "Critique of the Pure Reason."

The statement of the question carries one inevitably to the *precritical* philosophies, to Cartesianism. *Mind*, XII. 124.

The *precritical* period of Kant's development. *Encyc. Brit.*, XIII. 847.

precular (prek'ū-lär), *n.* [< L. *precari*, pray: see *pray*1. Cf. ML. *precula*, chaplet.] A prayerman; a beadsman; one bound to pray periodically for the founder or founders of the religious benefaction which he enjoys.

precuneal, præcuneal (prē-kū'nę-al), *a.* [< L. *præ*, before, + *cuneus*, wedge: see *cuneus* and *præcuneus*.] Situated in front of the cuneus of the brain: specifically noting the quadrate lobule, or præcuneus.

precuneus, *n.* See *præcuneus*.

precurrent (prę-kur'ent), *a.* [< L. *præcurren(t-)s*, ppr. of *præcurrere*, run before, < *præ*, before, + *currere*, run: see *current*1.] Running forward; specifically, in *zoöl.*, extending cephalad; antrorse: the opposite of *recurrent*.

precurrer† (prę-kėr'ėr), *n.* [< L. *præcurrere*, run before (see *precurrent*), + E. *-er*1.] A precursor; a forerunner.

Thou shrieking harbinger,
Foul *precurrer* of the fiend.
Shak., Phœnix and Turtle, l. 6.

precurse† (prę-kėrs'), *n.* [< L. *præcursus*, a coming or going before, < *præcurrere*, run before: see *precurrent*, and cf. *course*1.] A forerunning; a heralding; prognostication.

Even the like *precurse* of fierce events,
As harbingers preceding still the fates, . . .
Have heaven and earth together demonstrated
Unto our climatures and countrymen.
Shak., Hamlet, i. 1. 121.

precurser, *n.* See *precursor*.

precursive (prę-kėr'siv), *a.* [< *precurse* + *-ive*.] Preceding as a herald; prognosticative; predictive.

But soon a deep *precursive* sound moaned hollow.
Coleridge, Destiny of Nations.

precursor (prę-kėr'sor), *n.* [Also *precurser*; = F. *précurseur* = Sp. Pg. *precursor* = It. *precursore*, < L. *præcursor*, a forerunner, < *præcurrere*, run before: see *precurrent*.] A forerunner; also, that which precedes an event and indicates its approach.

Jove's lightnings, the *precursors*
O' the dreadful thunder-claps.
Shak., Tempest, i. 2. 201.

=**Syn.** Predecessor, herald, omen, sign.

precursory (prę-kėr'sō-ri), *a.* and *n.* [< L. *præcursorius*, precursory, < *præcursor*, a forerunner: see *precursor*.] **I.** *a.* Preceding as a herald; forerunning; introductory; indicative of something to follow.

We shall perceive more plainly the cosmopolite's fearful judgment if we take a *precursory* view of the parable's former passages. *Rev. T. Adams*, Works, II. 123.

Nations in a state of decay lose their idiom, which loss is always *precursory* to that of freedom. *Landor*, Demosthenes and Eubulides.

II.† *n.* A precursor; an introduction.

Virtue is the way to truth; purity of affections a necessary *precursory* to depth of knowledge. *Hammond*, Works, IV. 568.

predable (pred'a-bl), *a.* [< OF. **predable* (taken in active sense), < ML. *prædabilis*, in passive sense, that can be seized as prey, < L. *prædari*, seize as prey: see *prede*, *prey*2, *v.*] In *her.*, preying or carnivorous; raptorial: said of a bird.

predacean (prę-dā'sē-an), *n.* [< *predace-ous* + *-an*.] A carnivorous animal. *Kirby.* (*Imp. Dict.*)

predaceous (prę-dā'shius), *a.* [= It. *predace*, < L. as if **prædax*, given to preying, < *præda*, prey: see *prey*2.] Living by prey; disposed to prey or plunder; predatory.

predal† (prē'dal), *a.* [< L. *præda*, booty, spoil (see *prey*2), + *-al*.] Plundering; pillaging; predatory.

So England next the lustful Dane survey'd;
Allur'd, the *predal* raven took his flight,
Her coasts at first attempting to invade,
And violate her sweets with rude delight.
S. Boyse, The Olive, i.

predate (prē-dāt'), *v. t.*; pret. and pp. *predated*, ppr. *predating*. [< *pre-* + *date*1.] 1. To antedate; date before the actual time: as, to *predate* a bond.—2. To possess an earlier date than; precede in date.

The Bonnington, or Lawday, oak is not a boundary tree, but it *predates* the times of the Tudors. *N. and Q.*, 7th ser., VII. 480.

predation (prę-dā'shon), *n.* [< L. *prædatio(n-)*, a plundering, < *prædari*, pp. *prædatus*, plunder: see *prey*2, *v.*] The act of plundering or pillaging; robbery; predatory incursion.

For thei were charged with greate sommes of money to the kyng, and now this sodain visitacion or *predacion* cleane shaued them. *Hall*, Hen. IV., an. 17.

Predatores (pred-a-tō'rēz), *n. pl.* [NL., < L. *prædator*, a plunderer, < *prædari*, pp. *prædatus*, plunder: see *prey*2, *v.*] Swainson's name of a tribe of coleopterous insects, containing such as are predatory or adephagous and prey on other insects, including the families *Cicindelidæ*, *Carabidæ*, *Dytiscidæ*, *Silphidæ*, and *Staphylinidæ*.

predatorily (pred'a-tō-ri-li), *adv.* In a predatory manner; with pillaging or plundering.

predatoriness (pred'a-tō-ri-nes), *n.* The character of being predatory; inclination to prey or plunder.

predatorious† (pred-a-tō'ri-us), *a.* [< L. *prædatorius*, plundering: see *predatory*.] Predatory.

They become *predatorious* and adulterous, consumptionary and culinary, false and base fires. *Bp. Gauden*, Tears of the Church, p. 321. (*Davies.*)

predatory (pred'a-tō-ri), *a.* [= It. *predatorio*, < L. *prædatorius*, rapacious, plundering, *prædator*, a plunderer, < *prædari*, plunder: see *prey*2, *v.*] 1. Plundering; pillaging; living by rapine or preying.

Though the country was infested by *predatory* bands, a Protestant gentleman could scarcely obtain permission to keep a brace of pistols. *Macaulay*, Hist. Eng., vi.

The human race, though a gregarious race, has ever been, and still is, a *predatory* race. *H. Spencer*, Prin. of Psychol., § 510.

2. Characterized by rapine; spent in plundering; devoted to pillaging.

The position was already a very important one, for—according to the *predatory* system of warfare of the day—it was an excellent starting-point for those marauding expeditions. *Motley*, Hist. Netherlands, II. 363.

Human beings are cruel to one another in proportion as their habits are *predatory*. *H. Spencer*, Social Statics, p. 449.

3. In *zoöl.*, habitually preying upon other animals; carnivorous or insectivorous, as a mammal; rapacious or raptorial, as a bird; adephagous, as an insect.—4†. Hungry; ravenous.

The evils that come of exercise are . . . that it maketh the spirits more hot and *predatory*. *Bacon*, Nat. Hist., § 293.

prede†, *n.* [< L. *præda*, booty, plunder: see *prey*2, *n.*] Spoil; booty; plunder; pillage.

The gentleman, being nettled that his kinsman would seeme to rescue the *prede* of his deadlie fo, brake out in these cholerike words. *Stanihurst*, Descrip. of Ireland, iv.

prede†, *v. t.* [Also *preud*, *preid*; < L. *prædari*, plunder: see *prey*2, *v.*] To plunder; pillage; rob.

When the subjects were *preided*, you would be content to winke at their misery, so that your mouth were stopt with briberie. *Stanihurst*, Descrip. of Ireland, vi.

predecay† (prē-dę-kā'), *n.* [< *pre-* + *decay*.] Previous decay.

For (what we must confess unto relations of antiquity) some *pre-decay* [of oracles] is observable from that [passage] of Cicero, urged by Baronius. *Sir T. Browne*, Vulg. Err., vii. 12.

predecease (prē-dę-sēs'), *n.* [= F. *prédécès*; < L. *præ*, before, + *decessus*, departure.] Decease before another.

predecease (prē-dę-sēs'), *v. t.*; pret. and pp. *predeceased*, ppr. *predeceasing*. [< *predecease*, *n.*] To die before; precede in dying.

If children *pre-decease* progenitors,
We are their offspring, and they none of ours.
Shak., Lucrece, l. 1756.

The first is the only Stuart period on which a faint mark is left by Henry, Prince of Wales, who *predeceased* his father in 1612. *Edinburgh Rev.*, CLXIV. 406.

predecess (prē-dę-ses'), *v. t.* [< *predecessor*, taken as **predecess* + *-or*.] To precede; be the predecessor of. [Rare.]

Lord John Sackville *predecessed* me here. *Walpole*, Letters, II. 87.

predecessive (prē-dę-ses'iv), *a.* [< L. *præ*, before, + *decessus*, pp. of *decedere*, depart, withdraw (see *decease*), + *-ive*.] Going before; preceding; previous.

Our noble and wise prince has hit the law
That all our *predecessive* students
Have miss'd, unto their shame.
Middleton, Massinger, and Rowley, Old Law, i. 1.

predecessor (prē-dę-ses'or), *n.* [< OF. *predecessur*, F. *prédécesseur* = Sp. *predecesor* = Pg. *predecessor* = It. *predecessore*, < LL. *prædecessor*, one who has gone before, < L. *præ*, before, + *decessor*, a retiring officer, < *decedere*, pp. *decessus*, go away, depart: see *decease*. Cf. *antecessor* and *successor*.] One who goes before or precedes another. (*a*) One who precedes another in a given state, position, or office; a previous occupant of a position or office.

What know wee further of him [Leontius, Bishop of Magnesia] but that he might be as factious and false a Bishop as Leontius of Antioch, that was a hunderd yeares his *predecessor*? *Milton*, Prelatical Episcopacy.

(*b*†) An ancestor; a forefather.

Ross. Where is Duncan's body?
Macd. Carried to Colmekill,
The sacred storehouse of his *predecessors*,
And guardian of their bones.
Shak., Macbeth, ii. 4. 34.

predeclare (prē-dę-klãr'), *v. t.*; pret. and pp. *predeclared*, ppr. *predeclaring*. [< *pre-* + *declare*.] To declare beforehand; predict; foretell.

Though I write fifty odd, I do not carry
An almanack in my bones to *pre-declare*
What weather we shall have.
Massinger, Guardian, i. 1.

prededication (prē-ded-i-kā'shon), *n.* [< *pre-* + *dedication*.] A prior dedication; a dedication made beforehand or previously. *Webster's Dict.*

predefine (prē-dę-fīn'), *v. t.*; pret. and pp. *predefined*, ppr. *predefining*. [< OF. *predefinir* = Sp. Pg. *predefinir* = It. *predefinire*, < ML. **prædefinire*, predetermine, < L. *præ*, before, + *definire*, define: see *define*.] To define or limit beforehand; set a limit to previously; predetermine.

Daniel understood that the number of years which God had, in his word to Jeremiah the prophet, *predefined* for the continuance of the captivity of the Jews and the desolation of Jerusalem, viz. seventy years, were now near to their expiration. *Bp. Hall*, Hard Texts, Daniel, ix. 2.

predefinition (prē-def-i-nish'on), *n.* [Early mod. E. *prediffynycion*; = Sp. *predefinicion* = Pg. *predefinição* = It. *predefinizione*, < ML. **prædefinitio(n-)*, < **prædefinire*, predetermine: see *predefine*.] Definition in advance; predetermination.

Vntyl such tyme as the complete nomber of theyr constaunt fellowes and faithful bretherne . . . shoulde be fulfylled and whollye accomplyshed accordynge to the eternal *predyffynycion* of God. *Bp. Bale*, Image, i.

predeliberation (prē-dę-lib-e-rā'shon), *n.* [< *pre-* + *deliberation*.] Deliberation beforehand. *Roget.*

predelineation (prē-dę-lin-ę-ā'shon), *n.* [< *pre-* + *delineation*.] 1. Previous delineation.—2. The theory or doctrine of the animalculists of the last century, who considered the whole body of an individual to be preformed in a spermatozoön, and the figure to be predelineated in the head and other parts of the sperm-cells.

Leeuwenhoek, Hartsoeker, and Spallanzani were the chief defenders of this theory of *predelineation*. *Haeckel*, Evol. of Man (trans.), I. 37.

predella (prę-del'ä), *n.* [It. (ML. *prædella*), a stool, footstool, confessional.] Same as *gradino*.

predentary (prē-den'ta-ri), *a.* [< L. *præ*, before, + LL. *dentarius*, dentary: see *dentary*.] Situated in advance of the dentary element or bone of the lower jaw, as a bone of some reptiles. *Nature*, XL. 325.

predentate (prē-den'tāt), *a.* [< L. *præ*, before, + *dentatus*, toothed: see *dentate*.] In *Cetacea*, having teeth in the fore part of the upper jaw only. *Dewhurst*, 1834. [Rare.]

predesert (prē-dę-zėrt'), *n.* [< *pre-* + *desert*2.] Previous merit or desert.

Some good offices we do to friends, others to strangers, but those are the noblest that we do without *predesert*. *Sir R. L'Estrange*, tr. of Seneca's Morals, ii. (*Davies.*)

predesign (prē-dę-zīn'), *v. t.* [< LL. *prædesignare*, designate before, < L. *præ*, before, + *designare*, designate, design: see *pre-* and *design*, v.] To design or purpose beforehand; predetermine.

In artificial things we see many motions very orderly performed, and with a manifest tendency to particular and *predesigned* ends. *Boyle*, Free Inquiry.

predesignate (prē-des'ig-nāt), *v. t.*; pret. and pp. *predesignated*, ppr. *predesignating*. [< LL. *prædesignatus*, pp. of *prædesignare*, designate before: see *predesign*.] To determine upon in advance, as to settle upon the characters for which a collection is to be sampled in advance of the examination of the sample.

predesignate (prē-des'ig-nāt), *a.* [< LL. *prædesignatus*, pp. of *prædesignare*, predesignate: see *predesign*.] In *logic*: (*a*) Having the quantification of the subject distinctly expressed: said of a proposition. *Sir W. Hamilton.* (*b*) Designated in advance. Thus, it is a condition of valid induction that the characters for which a collection is sampled should be designated or determined in advance; and if this is done, these characters are *predesignate*.

predesignation (prē-des-ig-nā'shon), *n.* [< *predesignate* + *-ion*.] In *logic*: (*a*) A sign, symbol, or word expressing logical quantity.

He thinks that, in universal negation, the logicians employ the *predesignation* "all."
Sir W. Hamilton, Discussions, App. II., Logical (B).

(*b*) The act of predesignating.

Suppose we were to draw our inferences without the *predesignation* of the character [for which the class had been sampled]; then we might in every case find some recondite character in which those instances would all agree. *C. S. Peirce*, Theory of Probable Inference, viii.

predesignatory (prē-des'ig-nā-tō-ri), *a.* [< *predesignate* + *-ory*.] In *logic*, marking the logical quantity of a proposition.

Here the *predesignatory* words for universally affirmative and universally negative quantity are not the same.
Sir W. Hamilton, Discussions, App. II., Logical (B).

predestinarian (prē-des-ti-nā'ri-an), *a.* and *n.* [< *predestine* + *-arian*.] **I.** *a.* **1.** Believing in the doctrine of predestination.—**2.** Of or pertaining to predestination.

II. *n.* One who believes in the doctrine of predestination.

Why does the *predestinarian* so adventurously climb into heaven, to ransack the celestial Archives, read God's hidden decrees, when with less labour he may secure an authentic transcript within himself?
Decay of Christian Piety.

predestinarianism (prē-des-ti-nā'ri-an-izm), *n.* [< *predestinarian* + *-ism*.] The system or doctrines of the predestinarians.

Predestinarianism was in the first instance little more than a development of the doctrine of exclusive salvation.
Lecky, Rationalism, I. 385.

predestinary† (prē-des'ti-nā-ri), *a.* [< *predestine* + *-ary*.] Predestinarian. *Heylin*, Hist. Presbyterians, p. 21. (*Davies.*)

predestinate (prē-des'ti-nāt), *v. t.*; pret. and pp. *predestinated*, ppr. *predestinating*. [< L. *prædestinatus*, pp. of *prædestinare*, determine beforehand: see *predestine*.] To predetermine or foreordain; appoint or ordain beforehand by an unchangeable purpose.

Whom he did foreknow he also did *predestinate* to be conformed to the image of his Son. Rom. viii. 29.

By the decree of God, for the manifestation of his glory, some men and angels are *predestinated* unto everlasting life, and others foreordained to everlasting death. These angels and men, thus *predestinated* and foreordained, are particularly and unchangeably designed; and their number is so certain and definite that it cannot be either increased or diminished. *West. Conf. of Faith*, iii. 3, 4.

=**Syn.** *Predestinate, Foreordain, Predestine*, decree, foredoom. *Predestinate* and *foreordain* are exact words, applying only to the acts of God; *predestine* is used somewhat more freely.

predestinate (prē-des'ti-nāt), *a.* and *n.* [< ME. *predestinat*, < L. *prædestinatus*, pp.: see the verb.] **I.** *a.* Predestinated; foreordained; fated.

Of hevenes kyng thou art *predestinat*
To hele our soules of her seek estat.
Chaucer, Mother of God, l. 69.

Some gentleman or other shall 'scape a *predestinate* scratched face. *Shak.*, Much Ado, i. 1. 138.

The great good wizard, well beloved and well
Predestinate of heaven.
Swinburne, Tristram of Lyonesse, vi.

II. *n.* One who is predestinated or foreordained to a particular end.

We are taught to believe . . . that the promises are not the rewards of obedience, but graces pertaining only to a few *predestinates*. *Jer. Taylor*, Works (ed. 1835), II. 13.

predestination (prē-des-ti-nā'shon), *n.* [< F. *prédestination* = Sp. *predestinacion* = Pg. *predestinação* = It. *predestinazione*, < LL. *prædestinatio(n-)*, a determining beforehand, < *prædestinare*, determine beforehand: see *predestinate*.] The act of predestinating, or the state of being predestinated; fate; specifically, in *theol.*, the decree or purpose of God, by which he has from eternity immutably determined whatever comes to pass; in a more restricted sense, the decree by which men are destined to everlasting happiness or misery; in the most restricted sense, predestination to eternal life, or election (the correlative doctrine that God has predestined some to everlasting death is termed *reprobation*). See *predestinate*, *v. t.*

Predestination to Life is the everlasting purpose of God, whereby (before the foundations of the world were laid) he hath constantly decreed by His counsel, secret to us, to deliver from curse and damnation those whom he hath chosen in Christ out of mankind, and to bring them by Christ to everlasting salvation, as vessels made to honour.
Thirty-nine Articles of the Episcopal Church, Art. xvii.

As if *predestination* over-ruled
Their will, disposed by absolute decree
Or high foreknowledge. *Milton*, P. L., iii. 114.

Influenced by their belief in *predestination*, the men display, in times of distressing uncertainty, an exemplary patience. *E. W. Lane*, Modern Egyptians, I. 369.

=**Syn.** Foreordination, predetermination.

predestinative (prē-des'ti-nā-tiv), *a.* [= It. *predestinativo*; as *predestinate* + *-ive*.] Determining beforehand; foreordaining. *Coleridge.*

predestinator (prē-des'ti-nā-tor), *n.* [< F. *prédestinateur*; as *predestinate* + *-or*[1].] **1.** One who predestinates or foreordains.—**2.** One who believes in predestination; a predestinarian.

Let all *Predestinators* me produce,
Who struggle with Eternal Bonds in vain.
Cowley, The Mistress, My Fate.

predestine (prē-des'tin), *v. t.*; pret. and pp. *predestined*, ppr. *predestining*. [< F. *prédestiner* = Sp. Pg. *predestinar* = It. *predestinare*, < L. *prædestinare*, determine beforehand, < *præ*, beforehand, + *destinare*, determine: see *destine*.] To decree beforehand; predetermine; foreordain; predestinate.

At length he spoke, and, as the scheme was laid,
Doom'd to the slaughter my *predestin'd* head.
Pitt, Æneid, ii.

=**Syn.** See *predestinate*.

predestiny† (prē-des'ti-ni), *n.* [ME. *predesteyne*; as *pre-* + *destiny*. Cf. *predestine*.] Predestination.

Syn God seth every thynge, out of doutaunce, . . .
As they shul comen by *predesteyne*.
Chaucer, Troilus, iv. 966.

predeterminable (prē-dē-tėr'mi-na-bl), *a.* [< *predetermine* + *-able*.] Capable of being predetermined. *Coleridge.* (*Imp. Dict.*)

predeterminate (prē-dē-tėr'mi-nāt), *a.* [< LL. *prædeterminatus*, pp. of *prædeterminare*, determine beforehand: see *predetermine*.] Determined beforehand: as, the *predeterminate* counsel of God.

We cannot break through the bounds of God's providence and *predeterminate* purpose in the guidance of events.
Bp. Richardson, Obs. on the Old Testament, p. 313.

predetermination (prē-dē-tėr-mi-nā'shon), *n.* [= F. *prédétermination* = Sp. *predeterminacion* = Pg. *predeterminação* = It. *predeterminazione*, < LL. **prædeterminatio(n-)*, < *prædeterminare*, determine beforehand: see *predeterminate*.] **1.** The act of predetermining; preordination; previous determination to a given course or end.

This *predetermination* of God's own will is so far from being the determining of ours that it is distinctly the contrary. *Hammond*, Fundamentals.

2. The state of being previously determined; a state wherein each act or event is dependent upon antecedent conditions.

Our weary glance, as it strays over the outside of phenomena, meets nothing else than the whirl of impersonal substances, the blind conflict of unconscious forces, the drear necessity of inevitable *predetermination*.
Lotze, Microcosmus (trans.), I. 1.

predetermine (prē-dē-tėr'min), *v.*; pret. and pp. *predetermined*, ppr. *predetermining*. [= F. *prédéterminer* = Sp. Pg. *predeterminar* = It. *predeterminare*, < LL. *prædeterminare*, determine beforehand, < L. *præ*, before, + *determinare*, limit, determine: see *determine*.] **I.** *trans.* **1.** To determine beforehand; settle in purpose or counsel.

If God foresees events, he must have *predetermined* them.
Sir M. Hale.

The moment I cast my eyes upon him, I was *predetermined* not to give him a single sous.
Sterne, Sentimental Journey, p. 8.

2. To destine by previous decree.

So great was the love of God to mankind, that he prepared joys infinite and never ceasing for man before he had created him; but he did not *predetermine* him to any evil. *Jer. Taylor*, Sermons, I. ix.

II. *intrans.* To make a determination beforehand.

predeterminism (prē-dē-tėr'mi-nizm), *n.* [< *predetermine* + *-ism*.] Same as *determinism*. *Worcester.*

predevote (prē-dē-vōt'), *a.* [< *pre-* + *devote*, *a.*] Predestinate; foreordained.

The next Peter Bell was he
Predevote, like you and me,
To good or evil as may come.
Shelley, Peter Bell the Third, Prol.

predevour† (prē-dē-vour'), *v. t.* [< *pre-* + *devour*.] To consume beforehand; exhaust prematurely. *Fuller*, Worthies, II. 572.

predial (prē'di-al), *a.* and *n.* [Also *prædial* (after L.); < OF. *predial*, F. *prédial* = Sp. Pg. *predial* = It. *prediale*, a., < ML. *prædialis*, < L. *prædium*, a farm, an estate, for **præhedium*, < *præhendere*, *prehendere*, seize, take: see *prehend*. Cf. *præda*, booty: see *prey*[2].] **I.** *a.* **1.** Consisting of land or farms; real; landed.

By the civil law their *predial* estates are liable to fiscal payments and taxes. *Aylife*, Parergon.

2. Attached to farms or land; owing service as tenanting land.

The substitution of foreign-born *predial* slaves and disbanded soldiers, from every part of the ancient known world, for the native and aboriginal inhabitants of the soil [of Italy]. *G. P. Marsh*, Hist. Eng. Lang., p. 37.

3. Consequent upon tenanting farms or land; growing or issuing from farms or land: as, *predial* tithes.

Tithes . . . are defined to be the tenth part of the increase yearly arising and renewing from the profits of lands: . . . the first species being usually called *predial*, as of corn, grass, hops, and wood. *Blackstone*, Com., II. iii.

If there are reasons for thinking that some free village societies fell during the process [of feudalization] into the *predial* condition of villenage—whatever that condition may really have implied—a compensating process began at some unknown date, under which the base tenant made a steady approach to the level of the freeholder.
Maine, Village Communities, p. 141.

In France *predial* servitude existed down to the very days of the Revolution. *Westminster Rev.*, CXXVIII. 954.

The delinquent loseth all his right whatsoever, *prædial*, personal, and of privilege.
Jer. Taylor, Works (ed. 1835), II. 108.

Predial or real services, in the *law of servitudes*, such services as one estate owes unto another estate: as, because I am the owner of such a ground, I have the right of a way through the ground of another person. *Washburn.* —**Predial servitudes**, in *Scots law*, real servitudes affecting heritage.—**Predial tithes**, tithes of the produce of land, as corn, grass, hops, and wood.

II. *n.* A predial laborer or slave; one who owes service as a tenant of land.

These conditions were that the *prædials* should owe three fourths of the profits of their labor to their masters for six years, and the non-prædials for four years.
Emerson, Address, W. I. Emancipation.

prediastolic (prē-di-a-stol'ik), *a.* [< *pre-* + *diastolic*.] Just preceding the diastole of the heart.

predicability (pred"i-ka-bil'i-ti), *n.* [= F. *prédicabilité* = Pg. *predicabilidade*; as *predicable* + *-ity* (see *-bility*).] The quality of being predicable; capacity for being affirmed of or attributed to something.

predicable (pred'i-ka-bl), *a.* and *n.* [= F. *prédicable* = Sp. *predicable* = Pg. *predicavel* = It. *predicabile*, that may be affirmed, < ML. *prædicabilis*, predicable (neut. *prædicabile* (Petrus Hispanus), a predicable) (in L. *prædicabilis*, praiseworthy), < L. *prædicare*, declare, proclaim: see *predicate*.] **I.** *a.* Capable of being predicated or affirmed; assertable.

Of man, of life, of happiness, certain primordial truths are *predicable* which necessarily underlie all right conduct. *H. Spencer*, Social Statics, p. 508.

II. *n.* A logical term considered as capable of being universally predicated of another; usually, one of the five words, or five kinds of predicates, according to the Aristotelian logic, namely genus, species, difference, property, and accident. Thus, Petrus Hispanus says (in Latin, but it is equally true in English): "*Predicable* taken properly is the same as universal, only they differ in this, that *predicable* is defined by 'is said of' while universal is defined by 'is in.' For *predicable* is what is born apt to be said of many, and universal is what is born apt to be in many."

Thei be called *predicables*, because some one thing is spoken of another. And thei are (as a man would saie) markes or notes of woordes that are spoken of many, shewyng how and by what maner the same woordes are attributed to others. *Wilson*, Rule of Reason.

If any one takes the trouble to enumerate the *Predicables*, which he may easily derive from a good Ontology (e. g., Baumgarten's), and to arrange them in classes under the Categories, . . . he will . . . produce a purely analytic section of Metaphysic, which will not contain a single synthetic proposition.
E. Caird, Philos. of Kant, p. 309.

Predicables of the pure understanding, in the *Kantian terminology*, pure but derivative concepts of the understanding.

predicament (prẹ-dik'ạ-ment), *n.* [< OF. *predicament*, also *prediquement*, F. *prédicament* = Sp. Pg. It. *predicamento*, < LL. *prædicamentum*, that which is predicated, a predicament, category, ML. also a preaching, discourse, < L. *prædicare*, declare, proclaim, predicate: see *predicate*. Cf. *preachment*, from the same ult. source.] **1.** That which is predicated; specifically, in the *Aristotelian philos.*, one of the ten categories. See *category*, 1.

A *predicament* is nothing elles in Englishe but a shewyng or rehearsyng what wordes maie be truely ioyned together, or els a settyng foorth of the nature of euery thing, and also shewyng what maie be truely spoken and what not. *Wilson*, Rule of Reason.

2. A definite class, state, or condition.

Wee should apparauntly perceiue that we, beyng called reasonable creatures, and in that *predicament* compared and ioyned wyth angelles, bee more worthy to be nuncupate and demed persones vnreasonable. Hall, Edw. IV., an. 23.

If you have gained such a Place among the choicest Friends of mine, I hope you will put me somewhere amongst yours, though I but fetch up the Rear, being contented to be the infima [*sic*] species, the lowest in the *Predicament* of your Friends. *Howell*, Letters, I. i. 13.

Thou know'st it must be now thy only bent
To keep in compass of thy *predicament*.
Then quick about thy purposed business come.
Milton, Vacation Exercise, l. 56.

3. A dangerous or trying situation; an unpleasant position.

The offender's life lies in the mercy
Of the duke only, 'gainst all other voice.
In which *predicament*, I say, thou stand'st.
Shak., M. of V., iv. 1. 357.

God help good fellows when they cannot help themselves! slender relief in the *predicament* of privations and feigned habits. G. *Harvey*, Four Letters.

=**Syn.** 3. Position, plight, case.

predicamental (prẹ-dik-ạ-men'tạl), *a.* [= Sp. *predicamental*, < ML. *prædicamentalis* (John of Salisbury), < LL. *prædicamentum*, predicament: see *predicament*.] Of or pertaining to predicaments.

Old Cybele, the first in all
This human *predicamental* scale.
J. Hall, Poems (1646), p. 23.

Predicamental quantity, quantity properly so called; quantity in the sense in which it is one of the ten predicaments or categories: opposed to *intensive quantity*.—**Predicamental relates**, things named by relative terms, so that one has to be connoted in order completely to name the other: opposed to *transcendental relates*, which are so by their mode of being.

predicant (pred'i-kạnt), *a.* and *n.* [< OF. *predicant*, F. *prédicant* = Sp. It. *predicante*, < L. *prædican(t-)s*, ppr. of *prædicare*, declare, proclaim, LL. and ML. also preach: see *predicate*.] **I.** *a.* **1.** Predicating or affirming.—**2.** Preaching.

In spite of every opposition from the *predicant* friars and university of Cologne, the barbarous school-books were superseded. *Sir W. Hamilton.*

II. *n.* **1.** One who affirms anything.—**2.** One who preaches; specifically, a preaching friar; a black friar.

In this are not the people partakers neither, but only their *predicants* and their schoolmen. Hooker, Discourse of Justification, Habak. i. 4.

A Dutch *predicant*, holding precisely the same theological tenets [as a Scotch Presbyterian], will after morning service spend his Sunday afternoon in the Bosch at the Hague, listening to what his Scottish co-religionist would call godless music. *Nineteenth Century*, XXVI. 819.

predicate (pred'i-kāt), *v. t.*; pret. and pp. *predicated*, ppr. *predicating*. [< L. *prædicatus*, pp. of *prædicare*, declare, publish, proclaim, also praise, extol, LL. and ML. also preach, < *præ*, before, + *dicare*, declare, proclaim, < *dicere*, say, tell: see *diction*. Cf. *preach*, from the same L. verb.] **1.** To declare; assert; affirm; specifically, to affirm as an attribute or quality of something; attribute as a property or characteristic.

It is metaphorically *predicated* of God that he is a consuming fire. *Sir T. Browne*, Vulg. Err., v. 22.

It would have required . . . more elevation of soul than could fairly be *predicated* of any individual for Elizabeth in 1587 to pardon Mary. *Motley*, Hist. Netherlands, II. 190.

You cannot *predicate* rights where you cannot *predicate* duties. *Fortnightly Rev.*, N. S., XLIII. 75.

2. To assert, as a proposition or argument, upon given grounds or data; found; hence, to base, as an action, upon certain grounds or security: as, to *predicate* a loan. [U. S.]

His moroseness, his party spirit, and his personal vindictiveness are all *predicated* upon the Inferno, and upon a misapprehension or careless reading even of that. *Lowell*, Among my Books, 2d ser., p. 46.

The property represented by these notes must eventually pay all the loans *predicated* upon it. *Harper's Mag.*, LXXX. 464.

predicate (pred'i-kāt), *a.* and *n.* [= F. *prédicat* = Sp. Pg. *predicado* = It. *predicato* = D. *predikaat* = G. *prädicat*, *prädikat* = Sw. Dan. *predikat*, < L. *prædicatus*, pp., declared (neut. LL. *prædicatum*, a predicate): see the verb.] **I.** *a.* Predicated; belonging to a predicate; constituting a part of what is predicated or asserted of anything; made, through the instrumentality of a verb, to qualify its subject, or sometimes its direct object: thus, in the following sentences the italicized words are predicate: he is an *invalid*; he is *ill*; it made him *ill*; they elected him *captain*.

II. *n.* **1.** That which is predicated or said of a subject in a proposition; in *gram.*, the word or words in a proposition which express what is affirmed or denied of the subject; that part of the sentence which is not the subject. See *proposition*.

For *predicates*—qualities—are not mere patterns on the web of a subject; they are the threads of that web. *G. H. Lewes*, Probs. of Life and Mind, II. iii. § 25.

2. A class name; a title by which a person or thing may be known, in virtue of belonging to a class.

The noble author, head, I am given to understand, under the *predicate* of Aghrim, of the eldest branch of the once princely house of Imaney. *N. and Q.*, 7th ser., IV. 64.

Adverbial predicate, a word (adjective) that divides its qualifying force between a verb and its subject, or has the value partly of an adverb and partly of a predicate: as, he stands *firm*; they came *running*.—**First predicate** [*prædicatum primo*], a specific character belonging to the whole species, but not to the genus.—**Objective predicate**, a noun or an adjective made through a verb to qualify the object of the verb: as, she called him *her deliverer*; they found them *sleeping*. Sometimes, less properly, called *factitive object*.—**Quantification of the predicate.** See *quantification*.

predication (pred-i-kā'shon), *n.* [< ME. *predicacioun*, < OF. *predication*, F. *prédication* = Pr. *predicatio* = Sp. *predicacion* = It. *predicazione*, < L. *prædicatio(n-)*, a declaration, a proclamation, publication, < *prædicare*, pp. *prædicatus*, proclaim, declare: see *predicate*.] **1†.** The act of proclaiming publicly or preaching; hence, a sermon; a religious discourse.

If ye lakke oure *predicacioun*,
Thanne goth the world al to destruccioun.
Chaucer, Summoner's Tale, l. 401.

The day before were made many *predications* and sermons, and the last was in the church of S. Iohn Baptist. *Hakluyt's Voyages*, II. 78.

In the wonted *predication* of his own Vertues, he goes on to tell us that to Conquer he never desir'd, but onely to restore the Laws and Liberties of his people. *Milton*, Eikonoklastes, xix.

2. The act of predicating or affirming one thing of another; formation or expression of judgment; affirmation; assertion.

The most generally received notion of *predication* . . . is that it consists in referring something to a class, i. e. either placing an individual under a class or placing one class under another class. *J. S. Mill*, Logic, I. v.

In the Sophist Plato solved the problem, and gave an explanation of the nature of *predication* which, making allowances for the difference of Greek and English idiom, is substantially the same as that given in Mill's logic. *Amer. Jour. Philol.*, IX. 203.

Accidental predication, the predication of an accident not contained in the essence.—**Denominative predication**, the relation of the abstract name of a quality to the name of the subject in which it is said to inhere: opposed to *univocal predication*, by which the concrete is predicated instead of the abstract; also, the predication of anything of the nature of an accident of a subject.—**Direct predication.** See *direct*.—**Essential predication**, the predication concerning a subject of anything contained in its essence.—**Formal predication**, a predication by which it is asserted that what is denoted by the subject is denoted by the predicate.—**Indirect predication.** See direct *predication*.—**Material predication**, a predication in which the predicate is said to follow from or be otherwise related to the subject; in other words, a predication in which there is a material copula.—**Predication de omni**, the application of a predicate to the whole breadth of a subject.—**Predication in quid or in eo quod quid**, a predication answering a possible question "What is it?"; a predication of a species or genus.—**Predication in eo quod quale or in quale quid**, predication of the specific difference which distinguishes the subject from other things of the same genus.—**Predication in quale**, the predication of an inessential predicate.—**Signate predication**, a predication in which the usual copula is replaced by some phrase referring to the terms and not to the things signified, as when we say Man *is defined as* a rational animal, Man *belongs to the family of* Primates, To die *is a property of* man.—**Univocal predication.** See *denominative predication*.—**Usual predication** [*prædicatio exercita*], a predication in which the copula refers directly to the things or qualities signified by the subject and predicate.

predicative (pred'i-kā-tiv), *a.* [= F. *prédicatif* = Sp. Pg. It. *predicativo*, < LL. *prædicativus*, declaring, asserting, < L. *prædicare*, pp. *prædicatus*, declare: see *predicate*.] Predicating; affirming; asserting; expressing affirmation or predication: as, a *predicative* term.—**Predicative proposition**, in *logic*, same as *categorical proposition*. See *categorical*, 2.

predicatively (pred'i-kā-tiv-li), *adv.* In the manner of a predicate; like a predicate.

predicatory (pred'i-kạ-tọ-ri), *a.* [= Sp. *predicatorio*, a pulpit, = It. *predicatorio*, < LL. *prædicatorius*, only in sense of 'praising,' 'laudatory,' < L. *prædicator*, one who declares or proclaims, one who praises, LL. also a preacher, < *prædicare*, pp. *prædicatus*, declare, proclaim: see *predicate*.] **1†.** Pertaining to preaching; involving preaching.

Callings must be duly observed, whether in the schools, in a meer grammatical way, or in the church, in a *predicatory*. *Bp. Hall*, Cases of Conscience, iii. 10.

2. Affirmative; of the nature of a predicate: as, a *predicatory* statement.

predicrotic (prē-di-krot'ik), *a.* [< *pre-* + *dicrotic*.] Preceding the dicrotic.—**Predicrotic wave**, the wave next before the dicrotic wave. Sometimes called *first tidal wave*.

predict (prẹ-dikt'), *v. t.* [< L. *prædictus*, pp. of *prædicere*, say beforehand, premise, foretell, predict (> It. *predire* = Pg. *predizer* = Sp. *predecir* = F. *prédire*, foretell), < *præ*, before, + *dicere*, say, tell: see *diction*.] To foretell; prophesy; declare before the event happens; prognosticate; also, to declare before the fact is known by direct experience.

All things hitherto have happened accordingly to the very time that I *predicted* them. *Dryden*, To his Sons, Sept. 3, 1697.

=**Syn.** *Prophesy*, *Presage*, etc. (see *foretell*), foreshow, divine.

predict† (prẹ-dikt'), *n.* [< L. *prædictum*, a prediction, foretelling, neut. of *prædictus*, pp. of *prædicere*, foretell: see *predict*, *v.*] A prediction.

Nor can I fortune to brief minutes tell,
Pointing to each his thunder, rain, and wind,
Or say with princes if it shall go well,
By oft *predict* that I in heaven find.
Shak., Sonnets, xiv.

predictable (prẹ-dik'tạ-bl), *a.* [< *predict* + *-able*.] Capable of being predicted or foretold; admitting of prediction, or determination in advance.

At any particular place the direction of the [magnetic] needle is continually changing, these changes being, like the changes in the temperature of the air, in part regular and *predictable*, and partly lawless, so far as we can see. C. *A. Young*, The Sun, p. 151.

prediction (prẹ-dik'shọn), *n.* [< OF. *prediction*, F. *prédiction* = Sp. *prediccion* = Pg. *predicção* = It. *predizione*, prediction, < L. *prædictio(n-)*, a saying beforehand, premising, also a foretelling, prediction, < *prædicere*, pp. *prædictus*, say before, foretell: see *predict*.] The act of predicting or foretelling; a prophecy; declaration concerning future events.

I am thinking, brother, of a *prediction* I read this other day, what should follow these eclipses. *Shak.*, Lear, i. 2. 152.

Let me not rashly call in doubt
Divine *prediction*; what if all foretold
Had been fulfill'd but through mine own default,
Whom have I to complain of but myself?
Milton, S. A., l. 44.

=**Syn.** *Prediction*, *Prophecy*, *Divination*, *Prognostication*, augury, vaticination, soothsaying. *Prophecy* is the highest of these words, ordinarily expressing an inspired foretelling of future events, and only figuratively expressing anything else. It is the only one of them that expresses the power as well as the act: as, the gift of *prophecy*. *Prediction* may or may not be an inspired act; it is most commonly used of the foretelling of events in accordance with knowledge gained through scientific investigations or practical experience, and is thus the most general of these words. *Divination* is the act of an augur or an impostor. *Prognostication* is the interpretation of signs with reference to the future, especially as to the course of disease. See *foretell*, *prophet*, *inference*.

predictional (prẹ-dik'shọn-ạl), *a.* [< *prediction* + *-al*.] Of the nature of prediction; predictive; prophetic; indicative of later events.

The contests betwixt scholars and scholars . . . were observed *predictional*, as if their animosities were the index of the volume of the land. *Fuller*, Worthies, III. 8.

predictive (prẹ-dik'tiv), *a.* [< L. *prædictivus*, foretelling, < *prædicere*, pp. *prædictus*, foretell: see *predict*.] Prophetic; indicative of something future.

She slowly rose,
With bitter smile *predictive* of my woes.
Crabbe, Works, VII. 34.

The statements of Scripture which relate to judgment and heaven and hell are *predictive*, and therefore have the characteristics of prophetic teaching. *Progressive Orthodoxy*, p. 60.

predictively (prẹ-dik'tiv-li), *adv.* By way of prediction; prophetically.

predictor (prẹ-dik'tọr), *n.* [< ML. *prædictor*, one who foretells, < L. *prædicere*, foretell: see *predict.*] One who predicts or foretells; one who prophesies.

I thank my better stars I am alive to confront this false and audacious *predictor*. *Swift*, Bickerstaff Detected.

predictory (prẹ-dik'tọ-ri), *a.* [< *predict* + *-ory.*] Prophetic; predictive: as, *predictory* information. *J. Hervey*, Meditations, II. 63.

predigastric (prē-di-gas'trik), *a.* and *n.* **I.** *a.* Of or pertaining to the predigastricus.

II. *n.* The predigastricus.

predigastricus (prē-dī-gas'tri-kus), *n.*; pl. *predigastrici* (-si). [NL., < L. *præ*, before, + NL. *digastricus*, q. v.] The anterior belly of the digastricus, regarded as a distinct muscle. *Coues.*

predigest (prē-di-jest'), *v. t.* [< *pre-* + *digest.*] To digest more or less completely by artificial means before introduction into the body.

predigestion (prē-di-jes'chọn), *n.* [< *pre-* + *digestion.*] 1. Premature or overhasty digestion.

Affected dispatch . . . is like that which the physicians call *predigestion*, or hasty digestion, which is sure to fill the body full of crudities. *Bacon*, Dispatch (ed. 1887).

2. Previous digestion; artificial digestion, as of food by peptonization; digestion before eating.

predilatator (prē-dil'ạ-tā-tọr), *n.*; pl. *predilatatores* (prē-dil'ạ-tạ-tō'rēz). [< *pre-* + *dilatator.*] The anterior dilatator muscle of the nostril. *Coues.*

predilect (prē-di-lekt'), *v. t.* [< ML. *prædilectus*, pp. of *prædiligere*, love before, prefer, < L. *præ*, before, + *diligere*, love: see *dilection, diligent.*] To prefer; favor; choose.

Heav'n to its *predilected* children grants
The middle space 'twixt opulence and wants.
W. Harte, Eulogius.

predilection (prē-di-lek'shọn), *n.* [= F. *prédilection* = Sp. *predileccion* = Pg. *predilecção* = It. *predilezione*, < ML. **prædilectio(n-)*, preference, < *prædiligere*, prefer: see *predilect, dilection.*] A prepossession of the mind in favor of something; a preference.

For his sake I have a *predilection* for the whole corps of veterans. *Sterne*, Sentimental Journey, p. 56.

Temple had never sat in the English Parliament, and therefore regarded it with none of the *predilection* which men naturally feel for a body to which they belong. *Macaulay*, Sir William Temple.

=**Syn.** *Liking, Attachment*, etc. (see *love*), partiality, inclination (toward), preference.

prediscover (prē-dis-kuv'ėr), *v. t.* [< *pre-* + *discover.*] To discover beforehand; foresee.

These holy men did prudently *prediscover* that differences in judgements would unavoidably happen in the Church. *Fuller*, Ch. Hist., IX. i. 52. (*Davies.*)

prediscovery (prē-dis-kuv'ėr-i), *n.*; pl. *prediscoveries* (-iz). [< *pre-* + *discovery.*] A prior discovery.

It was a question between us and the court of Spain, touching the *pre-discovery* and consequently the right of dominion over certain islands in the South Seas. *Sir J. Hawkins*, Johnson, p. 464.

predisponency (prē-dis-pō'nẹn-si), *n.* [< *predisponen(t)* + *-cy.*] The state of being predisposed; predisposition. *Imp. Dict.*

predisponent (prē-dis-pō'nẹnt), *a.* and *n.* [= Pg. It. *predisponente*; as *pre-* + *disponent.*] **I.** *a.* Predisposing; creating an inclination or disposition toward something.

These graces and favours . . . are given to men irregularly, and without any order of *predisponent* causes. *Jer. Taylor*, Works (ed. 1835), I. 142.

II. *n.* That which predisposes; a predisposing cause.

predispose (prē-dis-pōz'), *v.*; pret. and pp. *predisposed*, ppr. *predisposing.* [< F. *prédisposer*; as *pre-* + *dispose.* Cf. Sp. *predisponer* = Pg. *predispôr* = It. *predisporre*, predispose.] **I.** *trans.* To incline beforehand; affect by a previous disposition or inclination; adapt beforehand; render susceptible or liable, either mentally or physically: as, to *predispose* the body to disease; to *predispose* the mind to anger.

Unless nature be *predisposed* to friendship by its own propensity, no arts of obligation shall be able to abate the secret hatreds of some persons towards others. *South.*

II. *intrans.* To create a previous disposition or inclination; cause a tendency in a particular direction.

It is . . . quite certain that the use of impure water of any kind *predisposes* to cholera. *Huxley and Youmans*, Physiol., § 413.

predisposing (prē-dis-pō'zing), *p. a.* [< *predispose* + *-ing*[2].] Inclining or disposing beforehand; making liable or susceptible.

A *predisposing* cause may . . . be defined to be anything whatever which has had such a previous influence upon the body as to have rendered it unusually susceptible to the exciting causes of the particular disease. *Sir T. Watson*, Lects. on Physic, vi.

predisposition (prē-dis-pọ̄-zish'ọn), *n.* [= F. *prédisposition* = Sp. *predisposicion* = Pg. *predisposição* = It. *predisposizione*; as *pre-* + *disposition.* Cf. L. *prædispositus*, prepared beforehand.] 1. The state of being previously disposed in a particular direction; previous tendency or inclination; mental or physical liability or susceptibility, as to a particular mode of thought or action.

The strong *predisposition* of Montaigne was to regard witchcraft as the result of natural causes. *Lecky*, Rationalism, I. 114.

The Indians showed a far greater natural *predisposition* for disfurnishing the outside of other people's heads than for furnishing the insides of their own. *Lowell*, Oration, Harvard, Nov. 8, 1886.

2. Specifically, in *med.*, a condition of body in which a slight exciting cause may produce disease.

predispositional (prē-dis-pō-zish'ọn-ạl), *a.* [< *predisposition* + *-al.*] Of the nature of or characterized by predisposition; belonging to or resulting from previous inclination or tendency.

Multitudes of Christian conversions . . . are only the restored activity and more fully developed results of some *predispositional* state. *H. Bushnell*, Christian Nurture, p. 247.

predominance (prẹ-dom'i-nạns), *n.* [= F. *prédominance* = Sp. Pg. *predominancia*, < ML. **prædominantia*, < *prædominan(t-)s*, predominant: see *predominant.*] 1. The quality of being predominant; prevalence over others; superiority in power, authority, or influence; domination; preponderance.

He who values Liberty confines
His zeal for her *predominance* within
No narrow bounds. *Cowper*, Task, v. 394.

2. In *astrol.*, the superior influence of a planet; ascendancy.

We make guilty of our disasters the sun, the moon, and the stars: as if we were . . . knaves, thieves, and treachers by spherical *predominance*. *Shak.*, Lear, i. 2. 134.

You're much inclin'd to melancholy, and that tells me
The sullen Saturn had *predominance*
At your nativity. *Fletcher*, Sea Voyage, iii. 1.

=**Syn.** 1. *Preëminence*, etc. (see *priority*), mastery.

predominancy (prẹ-dom'i-nạn-si), *n.* [As *predominance* (see *-cy*).] Same as *predominance.*

The *predominancy* of custom is everywhere visible. *Bacon*, Custom and Education (ed. 1887).

predominant (prẹ-dom'i-nạnt), *a.* [= F. *prédominant* = Sp. Pg. It. *predominante*, < ML. *prædominan(t-)s*, ppr. of *prædominare*, predominate: see *predominate.*] 1. Predominating; ruling; controlling; exerting power, authority, or influence; superior; ascendant.

His next precept is concerning our civil Liberties, which by his sole voice and *predominant* will must be circumscrib'd. *Milton*, Eikonoklastes, xxvii.

Alike in the European island and in the American continent, the English settlers were *predominant* in a world of their own. *E. A. Freeman*, Amer. Lects., p. 81.

2. In *her.*, occupying the whole field, to the exclusion of all bearings, as any tincture: thus, or *predominant* signifies a shield entirely gold, with no bearings of any description. [Rare.] — **Predominant branch**, a branch containing more than half the knots of a geometrical tree.— **Predominant nerve**, in *bot.*, the principal or main nerve, as in the leaves of mosses. =**Syn.** 1. *Prevailing, Ruling*, etc. (see *prevalent*), supreme, overruling, reigning, controlling, dominant, sovereign.

predominantly (prẹ-dom'i-nạnt-li), *adv.* In a predominant manner; with superior strength or influence.

predominate (prẹ-dom'i-nāt), *v.*; pret. and pp. *predominated*, ppr. *predominating.* [< ML. *prædominatus*, pp. of *prædominare* (> It. *predominare* = Sp. Pg. *predominar* = F. *prédominer*), predominate, < L. *præ*, before, + *dominari*, rule, dominate: see *dominate.*] **I.** *intrans.* To have or exert controlling power; surpass in authority or influence; be superior; preponderate.

Master Brook, thou shalt know I will *predominate* over the peasant. *Shak.*, M. W. of W., ii. 2. 294.

Men who are called in question for their opinions may be expected to under or over state them at such times, according as caution or temerity may *predominate* in their dispositions. *Southey*, Bunyan, p. 47.

=**Syn.** To prevail, preponderate.

II. *trans.* To overrule; master; prevail over.

Allure him, burn him up;
Let your close fire *predominate* his smoke.
Shak., T. of A., iv. 3. 142.

predominate (prẹ-dom'i-nāt), *a.* [< ML. *prædominatus*, pp.: see the verb.] Predominant; ruling.

They furiously rage, are tormented, and torn in pieces by their *predominate* affections. *Burton*, Anat. of Mel., p. 555.

predominatingly (prẹ-dom'i-nā-ting-li), *adv.* Predominantly.

predomination (prẹ-dom-i-nā'shọn), *n.* [= Sp. *predominacion* = Pg. *predominação* = It. *predominazione*, < ML. **prædominatio(n-)*, < *prædominare*, predominate: see *predominate.*] The act of predominating; ascendancy; superior power or influence; prevalence.

You would not trust to the *predomination* of right, which, you believe, is in your opinions. *Johnson*, in Boswell (ed. 1791), II. 453.

predomine†, *v. i.* [< OF. *predominer*, < ML. *prædominare*, predominate: see *predominate.*] To predominate.

So th' Element in Wine *predomining*,
It hot, and cold, and moist, and dry doth bring.
Sylvester, tr. of Du Bartas's Weeks, i. 21.

predone (prē-dun'), *a.* [< *pre-* + *done.*] Overdone; fordone; worn out; exhausted. [Rare.]

I am as one desperate and *predone* with various kinds of work at once. *Kingsley*, Life, II. 90. (*Davies.*)

predoom (prē-döm'), *v. t.* [< *pre-* + *doom*[1], *v.*] 1. To doom or pass sentence upon beforehand; condemn beforehand.

Some read the King's face, some the Queen's, and all
Had marvel what the maid might be, but most
Predoom'd her as unworthy.
Tennyson, Lancelot and Elaine.

Shall man, *predoomed*,
Cling to his sinking straw of consciousness?
R. Buchanan, N. A. Rev., CXL. 452.

2. To predestinate; foreordain.

The indwelling angel-guide, that oft
. . . shapes out Man's course
To the *predoomed* adventure.
Coleridge, Destiny of Nations.

predorsal (prē-dôr'sạl), *a.* [= F. *prédorsal*; < L. *præ*, before, + *dorsum*, back: see *dorsal.*] Situated in advance of the thoracic or dorsal region of the spine; cervical, as a vertebra.

predour†, *n.* [< OF. *predeur*, vernacularly *preeor*, etc., < L. *prædator*, a plunderer, < *prædari*, plunder: see *prey*[2], *prede*, *v.*, and cf. *preyer.*] A plunderer; a pillager.

The Earle with his band made hot-foot after, and, dogging still the tracke of the *predours*, he came to the place where the dart was hurled. *Stanihurst*, Descrip. of Ireland, iv.

predy† (prē'di), *a.* [Also *preedy, pready*; origin obscure.] *Naut.*, ready. *E. Phillips.*

pree (prē), *v. t.* [Also *prie*; a reduction of *prieve.*] To prove; test; try; especially, to prove by tasting; taste. [Scotch.]

According to De Quincey, "there was no one who had any talent, real or fancied, for thumping or being thumped, but he had experienced some *preeing* of his merits from Mr. Wilson." *Atlantic Monthly*, LVIII. 458.

To pree one's mouth, to kiss one.

Rab, stowlins, *prie'd her* bonnie *mou*
Fu' cozie in the neuk for 't,
Unseen that night. *Burns*, Halloween.

preef†, *n.* An obsolete variant of *proof.*

preëlect (prē-ẹ-lekt'), *v. t.* [< *pre-* + *elect.*] To choose or elect beforehand.

God . . . had chosen and *preelected* her before the worldes to be the mother of the Lorde. *Foxe*, Book of Martyrs, p. 733, an. 1509.

preëlection (prē-ẹ-lek'shọn), *n.* [< ML. *præelectio(n-)*, < *præeligere, præelegere*, choose before, < L. *præ*, before, + *eligere, elegere*, choose: see *elect.*] The act of choosing beforehand; an anticipative choice or election.

We shall satisfie his majesty with a *preelection*, and yours shall have my first nomination. *Sir H. Wotton*, Reliquiæ, p. 355.

To whatsoever degree of sobriety or austerity thy suffering condition did enforce thee, . . . do it now also by a *præ-election*. *Jer. Taylor*, Works, II. xi.

preëmbody (prē-em-bod'i), *v. t.*; pret. and pp. *preëmbodied*, ppr. *preëmbodying.* [< *pre-* + *embody.*] To embody previously; give form to beforehand. *T. Hill*, True Order of Studies, p. 157.

preëminence (prẹ-em'i-nẹns), *n.* [Early mod. E. also *preheminence*; < OF. *preeminence*, F. *prééminence* = Sp. Pg. *preeminencia* = It. *preeminenzia, preeminenza, preminenza*, < LL. *præeminentia*, < *præeminen(t-)s*, preëminent: see *preeminent.*] 1. The state or character of being preëminent; superiority; surpassing eminence; distinction; precedence.

And if your souerayne call you
With him to dyne or sup,
Giue him *preheminence* to begin,
Of meate and cake of Cup.
Babees Book (E. E. T. S.), p. 74.

Of these pleasures that the body ministereth, they give the *pre-eminence* to health.
Sir T. More, Utopia (tr. by Robinson), ii. 7.

Fathers in the ancient world did declare the *pre-eminence* of priority in birth by doubling the worldly portions of their first-born. *Hooker*, Eccles. Polity, v. 81.

He held it one of the prettiest attitudes of the feminine mind to adore a man's *preëminence* without too precise a knowledge of what it consisted in.
George Eliot, Middlemarch, xxvii.

2†. A prerogative; a privilege; a right; a power.

They of [the] Church where yͤ Body shalbe buried must have the *preeminence* to goe nearest the Corse within their juri[s]diction.
Booke of Precedence (E. E. T. S., extra ser.), i. 32.

All these *preeminences* no gentleman did inioy, but only such as were Citizens of Rome.
Guevara, Letters (tr. by Hellowes, 1577), p. 17.

I do invest you jointly with my power,
Pre-eminence, and all the large effects
That troop with majesty. *Shak.*, Lear, i. 1. 133.

=Syn. 1. *Precedence*, etc. See *priority*.

preëminency (prē-em'i-nen-si), *n.* [As *preëminence* (see -*cy*).] Same as *preëminence*.

preëminent (prē-em'i-nent), *a.* [< OF. *preeminent*, F. *prééminent* = Sp. Pg. *preeminente* = It. *preminente*, < LL. *præeminen(t-)s*, eminent before others, ppr. of *præeminere*, project forward, surpass, be preëminent, < L. *præ*, before, + *eminere*, project, be eminent: see *eminent*.] 1. Eminent above others; superior to or surpassing others; distinguished; remarkable; conspicuous, generally for a commendable quality or action.

Tell, if ye saw, how I came thus, how here?
Not of myself; by some great Maker then,
In goodness and in power *pre-eminent*.
Milton, P. L., viii. 279.

2. Superlative; extreme.

He possessed, as we have said, in a *pre-eminent* degree, the power of reasoning in verse. *Macaulay*, Dryden.

preëminently (prē-em'i-nent-li), *adv.* In a preëminent manner; with superiority or distinction above others; to a preëminent degree; especially: as, *preëminently* wise.

preëmploy (prē-em-ploi'), *v. t.* [< *pre-* + *employ*.] To employ previously or before others.

That false villain
Whom I employ'd was *pre-employ'd* by him.
Shak., W. T., ii. 1. 49.

preëmpt (prē-empt'), *v.* [< *preëmpt-ion*, *preëmpt-or*.] **I.** *trans.* To secure, as land, by preëmption; establish a claim to; appropriate. [U. S.]

Prospectors from adjoining camps thronged the settlement; the hillside for a mile on either side of Johnson's claim was staked out and *preempted*.
Bret Harte, Tales of the Argonauts, p. 59.

II. *intrans.* To take up land by preëmption. [U. S.]

As in our own western States, an unscrupulous "colonist" can often *preempt* in several places at the same time. *Science*, VI. 318.

preëmptible (prē-emp'ti-bl), *a.* [< *preëmpt* + *-ible*.] Open to preëmption; capable of being preëmpted.

Pre-emptible land recedes farther into the West.
N. A. Rev., CXLII. 54.

preëmption (prē-emp'shon), *n.* [= F. *préemption*, < ML. *præemptio(n-)*, a buying before, < L. *præ*, before, + *emptio(n-)*, a buying: see *emption*.] 1. The act of purchasing before others; also, the right of purchasing before others, as the right of a settler to a preference in the opportunity to buy land on or near which he has settled, or of an owner of the upland to buy lands under water in front of his shore, and, in England, the privilege once enjoyed by the king of buying provisions for his household at an appraisal, or in preference to others.

The profitable prerogative of purveyance and *pre-emption* . . . was a right enjoyed by the crown of buying up provisions and other necessaries, by the intervention of the king's purveyors, for the use of his royal household, at an appraised valuation, in preference to all others, and even without consent of the owner. *Blackstone*, Com., I. viii.

The *pre-emption* system was established, though at first the *pre-emption* claimant was stigmatized as a trespasser, and repulsed as a criminal.
T. H. Benton, Thirty Years, I. 102.

2. Specifically, in *international law*. See the quotation.

The harshness of the doctrine of occasional contraband brought into favor the rule of *preëmption*, which was a sort of compromise between the belligerents (if masters of the sea) and the neutrals. The former claimed that such articles may be confiscated, the latter that they should go free. Now, as the belligerent often wanted these articles, and at least could hurt his enemy by forestalling them, it came nearest to suiting both parties if, when they were intercepted on the ocean, the neutral was compensated by the payment of the market price and of a fair profit. *Woolsey*, Introd. to Inter. Law, § 182.

Clause of preëmption, in *Scots law*, a clause sometimes inserted in a feu-right, stipulating that if the vassal shall be inclined to sell the lands he shall give the superior the first offer, or that the superior shall have the lands at a certain price fixed in the clause.—**Preëmption Laws**, United States statutes of 1830, 1832, 1833 (4 Stat. 420, 603, 663), 1838, 1840, and 1841 (5 Stat. 251, 382, 453, consolidated in Rev. Stat. §§ 2257–88), which provide for vesting the title to parts of the public lands—not more than 160 acres to one person—in such settlers as inhabit and improve the same, upon payment of a nominal price.

preëmptive (prē-emp'tiv), *a.* [< *preëmpt* + *-ive*.] Pertaining to or of the nature of preëmption; preëmpting.

preëmptor (prē-emp'tor), *n.* [< LL. *præemptor*, one who buys before others, < L. *præ*, before, + *emptor*, a buyer: see *emption*.] One who preëmpts; especially, one who takes up land with the privilege of preëmption.

preen[1] (prēn), *n.* [Also dial. *prin*; < ME. *pren*, < AS. *preón*, a pin, brooch, clasp, bodkin (also in comp. *eár-preón*, ear-ring, *feax-preón*, hair-pin, *mentel-preón*, cloak-pin), = Icel. *prjönn*, a pin, knitting-needle, = Dan. *preen*, a bodkin, point of a graving-tool, = D. *priem* = MLG. *prēn*, *prēne*, LG. *preem*, a pin, spike, awl, = MHG. *pfrieme*, G. *pfriem*, an awl; cf. ML. dim. *premula*, an awl, appar. from the Teut.; ult. origin unknown.] 1. A pin. [Scotch.]

I thynk six pattryng is not worth twa *prenis*.
Sir D. Lyndsay, Monarchie.

My memory 's no worth a *preen*.
Burns, To William Simpson, Postscript.

2†. A bodkin; a brooch.

Othre ydeles brogt fro sichem,
Gol *prenes* and ringes with hem,
Diep he is dalf under an ooc.
Genesis and Exodus (E. E. T. S.), l. 1872.

3. A forked instrument used by clothiers in dressing cloth.

preen[1] (prēn), *v. t.* [< ME. *prenen*; < *preen*[1], *n.*] To pin; fasten. [Obsolete or Scotch.]

Hem lacked a lender the ludes to araie,
Hur Prince in the torme prese was *prened* to the erth.
Alisaunder of Macedoine (E. E. T. S.), l. 420.

preen[2] (prēn), *v. t.* [A variant of *prune*[2], 4.] 1. To prune or trim, as a tree. *Halliwell.* [Prov. Eng.]—2. To trim, dress, or fix with the beak, as a bird its plumage; plume. This habit is characteristic of birds, especially of water-fowl, the feathers being oiled with the unctuous substance of the rump-gland, as well as set in order. See *elæodochon*.

preëngage (prē-en-gāj'), *v. t.*; pret. and pp. *preëngaged*, ppr. *preëngaging*. [< *pre-* + *engage*.] 1. To engage by previous promise or agreement.

To Gipseus by his friends his suit he moved, . . .
But he was *pre-engaged* by former ties.
Dryden, Cym. and Iph., l. 246.

2. To engage or attach by previous influence; preoccupy; predispose: as, to *preëngage* one's attention.

The Lacedemonians, says Xenophon, . . . during war, put up their petitions very early in the morning, in order to be beforehand with their enemies, and, by being the first solicitors, *pre-engage* the gods in their favour.
Hume, Nat. Hist. of Religion, iv.

preëngagement (prē-en-gāj'ment), *n.* [< *pre-* + *engagement*.] 1. Prior engagement or agreement; a contract previously made.

Where neither . . . duty nor obedience to a lawful authority, nor the bond of an inviolable *pre-ingagement*, call you to the bar. *Bp. Hall*, Cases of Conscience, ii. 7.

2. A previous attachment; predisposition.

Had God but left it to mere reason, without this necessary *pre-engagement* of our natures, it would have been a matter of more doubt and difficulty than it is, whether this life should be loved and desired.
Baxter, Dying Thoughts.

My *pre-engagements* to other themes were not unknown to those for whom I was to write. *Boyle.*

preërect (prē-ē-rekt'), *v. t.* [< *pre-* + *erect*.] To erect beforehand; preëstablish. *Prynne*, Treachery and Disloyalty, i. 91.

preest, *v.* A Middle English form of *press*[1].

preësophageal, præesophageal (prē-ē-sō-faj'ē-al), *a.* [< L. *præ*, before, + NL. *œsophagus*, esophagus.] 1. Situated in front of the gullet.—2. Anterior with reference to the circumesophageal nerve-collar of an invertebrate.

Also *preœsophageal*, *præœsophageal*.

preëstablish (prē-es-tab'lish), *v. t.* [< *pre-* + *establish*.] To establish beforehand; ordain or settle previously.

They elected him for their King with unanimous consent, and, calling him unto them, showed him the lawes they had *pre-established*.
Prynne, Treachery and Disloyalty, p. 77, App.

Preëstablished harmony. See *harmony*.

preëstablishment (prē-es-tab'lish-ment), *n.* The act of preëstablishing, or the state of being preëstablished; settlement beforehand.

preëstival, preæstival (prē-es'ti-val), *a.* [< *pre-* + *estival*: see *estival*.] Occurring before midsummer: as, the *preëstival* plumage of a bird.

preëternity (prē-ē-tėr'ni-ti), *n.* [< *pre-* + *eternity*.] Infinite previous duration; time without a beginning.

He seemeth, with Ocellus, to maintain the world's *pre-eternity*. *Cudworth*, Intellectual System, p. 393.

preevet, *n.* An obsolete form of *proof*.

preevet, *v.* An obsolete form of *prove*.

preëvolutionist (prē-ev-ō-lū'shon-ist), *a.* [< *pre-* + *evolution* + *-ist*.] Existing or occurring before the theory of evolution became current. [Rare.]

Even this code of morals, Hartmann thinks, is a remnant of the false, *pre-evolutionist* individualism.
W. R. Sorley, Ethics of Naturalism, p. 170.

preëxamination (prē-eg-zam-i-nā'shon), *n.* [< *pre-* + *examination*.] Previous examination.

One of the inquisitors . . . would by no means proceed any farther without a *pre-examination* of the aforesaid Giovan Battista. *Sir H. Wotton*, Reliquiæ, p. 300.

preëxamine (prē-eg-zam'in), *v. t.*; pret. and pp. *preëxamined*, ppr. *preëxamining*. [< *pre-* + *examine*.] To examine beforehand.

preëxilic (prē-eg-zil'ik), *a.* [< *pre-* + *exile* + *-ic*.] Existing, done, etc., before the exile: said chiefly of certain Biblical writings supposed to have been written before the Jewish exile (about 586–537 B. C.).

Why must the 1st Book [of the Psalms], containing none but *pre-exilic* songs, date from the period after the exile?
Amer. Jour. Philol., I. 359.

The law in question [of the Nazarite vow] is not *pre-exilic*, and is plainly directed to the regulation of a known usage. *Encyc. Brit.*, XVII. 303.

preëxist (prē-eg-zist'), *v. i.* [= F. *préexister* = Sp. Pg. *preexistir* = It. *preesistere*; as *pre-* + *exist*.] 1. To exist before something else; have a prior existence.

Art *preëxists* in Nature, and Nature is reproduced in Art. *Longfellow*, Hyperion, iii. 5.

The new motion given to the parts of a moving equilibrium by a disturbing force must . . . be of such kind and amount that it cannot be dissipated before the *pre-existing* motions. *H. Spencer*, First Principles, § 170.

2. To exist in a previous state.

If thy *pre-existing* soul
Was form'd at first with myriads more,
It did through all the mighty poets roll.
Dryden, Ode to Mrs. Anne Killigrew, l. 29.

preëxistence (prē-eg-zis'tens), *n.* [= F. *préexistence* = Sp. Pg. *preexistencia* = It. *preesistenza*; as *pre-existen(t)* + *-ce*.] 1. Existence previous to something else.

Wisdom declares her antiquity and *pre-existence* to all the works of this earth. *T. Burnet*, Theory of the Earth.

2. Existence in a previous state; existence of the soul before its union with the body, or before the body is formed. Belief in it was a doctrine of the Pythagorean school, of Plato, and of other philosophers.

preëxistencist (prē-eg-zis'ten-sist), *n.* [< *preëxistence* + *-ist*.] One who believes in the doctrine of preëxistence. *Chambers's Encyc.* See *preëxistence*, 2.

preëxistency† (prē-eg-zis'ten-si), *n.* Same as *preëxistence*.

preëxistent (prē-eg-zis'tent), *a.* [= F. *préexistent* = Sp. Pg. *preexistente* = It. *preesistente*; as *pre-* + *existent*.] Existing beforehand; preceding.

What mortal knows his *pre-existent* state?
Pope, Dunciad, iii. 48.

preëxistimation (prē-eg-zis-ti-mā'shon), *n.* [< *pre-* + *existimation*.] Previous esteem.

Let not mere acquests in minor parts of learning gain thy *pre-existimation*. *Sir T. Browne*, Christ. Mor., ii. 4.

preëxpectation (prē-eks-pek-tā'shon), *n.* [< *pre-* + *expectation*.] Previous expectation. *Smart.*

pref. An abbreviation (*a*) of *preface*; (*b*) of *prefix*.

preface (pref'ās), *n.* [< OF. *preface*, F. *préface* = Sp. *prefacio* = Pg. *prefacio* = It. *prefazio*, < ML. **præfatium*, for LL. *præfatum*, what is said beforehand, a preface (cf. Sp. *prefacion* = Pg. *prefação* = It. *prefazione*, a preface, < L. *præfatio(n-)*, a saying beforehand, a formula of words, a preface, introduction), < *præfatus*, pp. of *præfari*, say beforehand, premise, < *præ*, before, + *fari*, say, speak: see *fate*.] 1. A statement or series of statements introducing a discourse, book, or other composition; a series of preliminary remarks, either written or spoken; a prelude. A *preface* is generally shorter than an *introduction*, which contains matter kindred in subject, and additional or leading up to what follows; while a *preface* is usually confined to particulars relating to the origin, history, scope, or aim of the work to which it is prefixed.

I thoughte it good to speake somewhat hereof, trusting yat the pleasaunt contemplacion of the thing it selfe shal make the length of this *preface* lesse tedious.
R. Eden, First Books on America, Ep. to Reader [(ed. Arber, p. 9).

Tush, my good lord, this superficial tale
Is but a *preface* of her worthy praise.
Shak., 1 Hen. VI., v. 5. 11.

How prologues into *prefaces* decay,
And these to notes are fritter'd quite away.
Pope, Dunciad, i. 277.

2. [*cap.* or *l. c.*] In *liturgics*, the introductory section of the anaphora; the solemn eucharistic thanksgiving and ascription of glory introducing the canon. The Preface is found of the same type in all liturgies. It begins with the Sursum Corda, generally preceded in early and Oriental forms by the apostolic (2 Cor. xiii. 14) or a similar benediction. After an exhortation to give thanks (Response: "It is meet and right . . ."), the Preface in the narrower sense begins with the affirmation (contestation) "It is very (truly) meet, etc., to give thanks . . ." The reason for thankfulness is given in the central division of the form. This in early and Oriental liturgies is invariable, and still retains much of its original character of an extended ascription of glory to God and rehearsal of his dealings with man from the Creation and Fall onward. In Western liturgies a number of *proper Prefaces* is provided, varying according to the day or season. Probably these were originally sections of the primitive Preface or of the earlier part of the Canon, selected as appropriate to the season or modeled on such sections. The Preface terminates with the Sanctus. Also, in Gallican uses, *contestation, illation, immolation.*

The *preface* is one of the most ancient, as it is one of the most universal, rites of the Church.
J. M. Neale, Eastern Church, i. 464.

3. A title; an introductory or explanatory epithet.

I say he is not worthy
The name of man, or any honest *preface*,
That dares report or credit such a slander.
Fletcher (and another), Love's Pilgrimage, v. 5.

preface (pref'ạs), *v.*; pret. and pp. *prefaced*, ppr. *prefacing*. [< *preface, n.*] **I.** *trans.* 1. To give a preface to; introduce by preliminary written or spoken remarks, or by an action significant of what is to follow.

He call'd his friend, and *prefaced* with a sigh
A lover's message. *Crabbe*, Works, II. 29.

Dinner, and frequently breakfast, is *prefaced* with a smörgås (butter-goose), consisting of anchovies, pickled herrings, cheese, and brandy.
B. Taylor, Northern Travel, p. 201.

2. To say as a preface; write or utter in view or explanation of what is to follow.

Before I enter upon the particular parts of her character, it is necessary to *preface* that she is the only child of a decrepit father, whose life is bound up in hers.
Steele, Spectator, No. 449.

3. To front; face; cover. [Rare.]

I love to wear clothes that are flush,
Not *prefacing* old rags with plush. *Cleaveland.*

II. *intrans.* To give a preface; speak, write, or do something preliminary to later action.

Our blessed Saviour, having *prefac'd* concerning prudence, adds to the integrity of the precept, and for the conduct of our religion, that we be simple as well as prudent, innocent as well as wary.
Jer. Taylor, Sermons, II. xxiii.

prefacer (pref'ạs-ėr), *n.* [< *preface* + *-er*[1].] One who prefaces; the writer of a preface.

The public will scarce be influenced in their judgment by an obscure *prefacer*.
Goldsmith, Pref. to Memoirs of a Protestant.

prefactor (prē-fak'tọr), *n.* The first or operative factor in a product of two factors.

prefatorial (pref-ạ-tō'ri-ạl), *a.* [< *prefatory* + *-al.*] Prefatory; introductory.

Much *prefatorial* matter also may arise, before we begin the discourse. *Gilpin*, Sermons, Pref.

prefatorily (pref'ạ-tọ-ri-li), *adv.* By way of preface.

prefatory (pref'ạ-tọ-ri), *a.* [< L. *præfatus*, pp. of *præfari*, say beforehand, premise (see *preface*), + *-ory.*] Belonging to a preface; serving as or resembling a preface; introductory.

Then, after somewhat more of *prefatory* matter, follow, in quick succession, the poems themselves.
Ticknor, Span. Lit., I. 72.

=**Syn.** Introductory, preliminary, precursory, preparatory. See *introduction*.

prefect (prē'fekt), *n.* [Also *præfect*; = F. *préfet* = Sp. *prefecto* = Pg. *prefecto*, *prefeito* = It. *prefetto*, < L. *præfectus*, an overseer, president, director, chief, prefect, prop. adj., *præfectus*, set over, pp. of *præficere*, set over, place in authority over, < *præ*, before, above, + *facere*, do, make: see *fact*.] 1. A governor, commander, chief magistrate, or superintendent. Specifically—(*a*) A name common to several officers, military and civil, in ancient Rome, who held particular commands or had charge of certain departments. Thus, the prefect or warden of the city at first exercised within the city the powers of the king or consuls during their absence; after 487 B. C., as a permanent elective magistrate, he was empowered to maintain peace and order in the city. After 246 B. C., when the first *prætor urbanus* was appointed, the importance of the prefect's office vanished; but its judicial functions were much enlarged by Augustus. Under Constantine the prefects were direct representatives of the emperor's person, civil governors of provinces or of chief cities. The title of *prefect* was also given to the commander of the fleet and to the commander of the pretorians, or troops who guarded the emperor's person, as well as to several other chief officials and magistrates. (*b*) The chief administrative official of a department of France; a préfet. The office dates from the year 1800; the prefect is appointed by the head of the state, and is the intermediary between the department and the central government; he is charged with the execution of the laws, with the superintendence of the police and of the administration, with the appointment of many minor officers, etc. He is assisted by the council of prefecture and the general council. (*c*) In China, a name given by foreigners to a chih-fu, or head of a department. See *chih-fu*.

2†. A director.

The psalm, thus composed by David, was committed to the *prefect* of his musick.
Hammond, Works, IV. 69. (*Latham.*)

3†. Tutelary divinity; presiding deity.

Venus . . . is *præfect* of marriage.
B. Jonson, Hue and Cry of Cupid.

Prefect of police, in France, the head of the police administration or prefecture of police, exercising especial authority in Paris and the region about Paris.

prefectoral (prẹ-fek'tọ-rạl), *a.* [< *prefect* + *-or* + *-al.*] Belonging or pertaining to a prefect; exercised by a prefect: as, *prefectoral* authority.

A few days since a company made propositions to the *prefectoral* administration with regard to the left bank of the Seine. *Electric Rev.* (Eng.), XXIV. 35.

It is proposed also to reduce the number of *prefectoral* councils [in France] from eighty-six to twenty-six.
Contemporary Rev., LII. 436.

prefectorial (prē-fek-tō'ri-ạl), *a.* [< *prefect* + *-or* + *-ial.*] Same as *prefectoral*.

prefectship (prē'fekt-ship), *n.* [< *prefect* + *-ship.*] Same as *prefecture*.

prefectural (prẹ-fek'ṭū-rạl), *a.* [< *prefecture* + *-al.*] Pertaining or belonging to a prefecture. *Encyc. Brit.*, XXIV. 722.

prefecturate (prẹ-fek'ṭū-rāt), *n.* [Irreg. < *prefecture* + *-ate*[1].] A prefecture. [Rare.]

The rumors that arose as to a *prefecturate* being offered him [Edmond About] proved unfounded.
Men of the Third Republic, p. 282.

prefecture (prē'fek-ṭūr), *n.* [Also *præfecture*; = F. *préfecture* = Sp. *prefectura* = Pg. *prefeitura* = It. *prefettura*, < L. *præfectura*, the office of a prefect, < *præfectus*, a prefect: see *prefect*.] 1. The office or jurisdiction of a prefect, chief magistrate, commander, or viceroy.

The army or its commanders becoming odious to the people, he [Cromwell] had sacrificed them to the hope of popularity, by abolishing the civil *prefectures* of the major-generals. *Hallam*, Hist. Eng., II. 255.

2. The district under the government of a prefect.

The arrangement of *præfectures* and dioceses, the crumbling into little bits of the older provinces, is practically the work of Diocletian. *The Academy*, Jan. 25, 1890, p. 67.

3. The official residence of a prefect.—4. A term often used by foreigners in and writers on China as equivalent to *fu*, an administrative division consisting of several districts called *hien* or *chow*. See *fu*.—**Council of prefecture**, a tribunal in each department of France, which is nominated by the executive and assists the prefect in his administration.

prefer (prẹ-fėr'), *v. t.*; pret. and pp. *preferred*, ppr. *preferring*. [< ME. *preferren*, < OF. *preferer*, F. *préférer* = Sp. Pg. *preferir* = It. *preferire*, < L. *præferre*, place or set before, < *præ*, before, + *ferre*, bear, place, = E. *bear*[1]. Cf. *confer*, *infer*, *refer*, etc.] 1. To bring or set before; present; proffer; offer.

He spake, and to her hand *preferr'd* the bowl. *Pope.*

2. To offer for consideration or decision; set forth; present in a conventional or formal manner, as a suit, prayer, or accusation.

To Mistress Dobson he *preferr'd* his suit;
There proved his service, there addressed his vows.
Crabbe, Works, I. 75.

Accusation was formally *preferred*, and retribution most signal was looked for. *Lamb*, Christ's Hospital.

Each *prefers* his separate claim.
Tennyson, In Memoriam, cii.

3†. To bring into notice or favor; recommend.

My father hauing some natural affection to me, when I was but xij yeares olde, did *prefer* me to the seruice of Captaine Jenkenson. *E. Webbe*, Travels (ed. Arber), p. 17.

You are most bound to the king,
Who lets go by no vantages that may
Prefer you to his daughter.
Shak., Cymbeline, ii. 3. 51.

She is a princess I *prefer* thee to.
Beau. and Fl., Philaster, ii. 1.

You would not *prefer* her to my acceptance, in the weighty consequence of marriage.
B. Jonson, Epicœne, ii. 3.

I *preferred* Mr. Philips (nephew of Milton) to the service of my Lord Chamberlaine. *Evelyn*, Diary, Sept. 18, 1677.

4. To bring forward or advance in dignity or office; raise; exalt.

For to conne it is an excellent thyng,
And cause of many mannys *preferring*.
Rom. of Partenay (E. E. T. S.), Int., l. 105.

Whom I would I abased, and *preferred* whom I thought good. *Hakluyt's Voyages*, II. 9.

What, those that were our fellow pages but now, so soon *preferred* to be yeomen of the bottles!
B. Jonson, Cynthia's Revels, ii. 1.

It is not honesty, learning, worth, wisdom, that *prefers* men. *Burton*, Anat. of Mel., p. 377.

5. To set before other things in estimation; hold in greater liking or esteem; choose; incline more toward.

The care of the sowle and sowles matters are to be *preferred* before the care of the body.
Spenser, State of Ireland.

He *preferrs* his love of Truth before his love of the People. *Milton*, Eikonoklastes, xi.

The husband, if he can conveniently so arrange, generally *prefers* that his mother should reside with him and his wife. *E. W. Lane*, Modern Egyptians, I. 219.

6. Specifically, in *law*, to give a preference to. See *preference*, 2.

There are certain debts in England, Scotland, and the United States which are said to be privileged—that is, such debts as the executor may pay before all others—for example, funeral expenses or servants' wages. In English law the term *preferred* rather than "privileged" is generally applied to such debts. *Encyc. Brit.*, XIX. 764.

7†. To outrank; be reckoned preferable to.

I graunte it wel, I have noon envie
Though maydenhede *preferre* bigamye.
Chaucer, Prol. to Wife of Bath's Tale, l. 96.

Preferred creditor. See *creditor*.—**Preferred stock**, preference shares (which see, under *preference*). =**Syn.** 5. *Elect*, *Select*, etc. See *choose*.

preferability (pref″ėr-ạ-bil'i-ti), *n.* [< *preferable* + *-ity* (see *-bility*).] The state or quality of being preferable. *J. S. Mill.*

preferable (pref'ėr-ạ-bl), *a.* and *n.* [= F. *préférable* (cf. Sp. *preferible* = Pg. *preferivel* = It. *preferibile*); as *prefer* + *-able.*] **I.** *a.* 1. Worthy to be preferred; more desirable.

Almost every man in our nation is a politician, and hath a scheme of his own which he thinks *preferable* to that of any other person. *Addison*, Freeholder, No. 48.

Sound sense, in my opinion, is *preferable* to bodiless, incomprehensible vagaries.
Landor, Chesterfield and Chatham.

2†. Preferring; exhibiting preference; arising from choice.

They will have it that I have a *preferable* regard for Mr. Lovelace. *Richardson*, Clarissa Harlowe, I. 171.

II. *n.* Something which is to be preferred; any object or course of action which is more desirable than others.

preferableness (pref'ėr-ạ-bl-nes), *n.* The character or state of being preferable.

My purpose is not to measure or weigh the *preferablenesse* of severall vocations.
W. Montague, Devoute Essays, I. x. 7.

preferably (pref'ėr-ạ-bli), *adv.* In or by preference; by choice of one thing rather than another; in a manner exhibiting preference.

To follow my own welfare *preferably* to those I love is indeed a new thing to me. *Pope*, To Mrs. B.

preference (pref'ėr-ẹns), *n.* [= F. *préférence* = Sp. Pg. *preferencia* = It. *preferenza*, < ML. *præferentia*, preference, < L. *præferen(t-)s*, ppr. of *præferre*, place or set before: see *prefer*.] 1. The act of preferring or choosing one thing rather than another, or the state of being preferred or chosen; estimation of one thing above another; choice.

Where then the *preference* shall we place,
Or how do justice in this case?
Cowper, Epistle to Robert Lloyd.

Jews had by that time earned the reputation, in Roman literature, of being credulous by *preference* amongst the children of earth. *De Quincey*, Secret Societies, ii.

That perfect state of mind at which we must aim, and which the Holy Spirit imparts, is a deliberate *preference* of God's service to everything else, a determined resolution to give up all for Him.
J. H. Newman, Parochial Sermons, i. 180.

Whatever be the variety in the sources of pleasure, whatever be the moral or conventional estimate of their worthiness, if a given state of consciousness is pleasant we seek to retain it, if painful to be rid of it: we prefer greater pleasure before less, less pain before greater. This is, in fact, the whole meaning of *preference* as a psychological term. *J. Ward*, Encyc. Brit., XX. 71.

2. Specifically, in *law*, the payment or right to have payment of one debt or class of debts made by a debtor or out of his estate, in full, before any of the assets are applied to unpreferred

debts: as, the debtor's assignment gave a *preference* to demands for borrowed money; the state has a *preference* for taxes.—3. The object of choice; a person, thing, or course of action chosen preferably to others.—4. In the game of boston, one of the two suits of the color of the card turned up, just after the first deal. The suit turned up is the *first preference*, and the other of the same color the *second preference*. These suits are more properly called *belle* and *petite*; but they are called *preference* because, of two players making equal offers, that one has the first preference who offers in belle, and that one the second preference who offers in petite.—**Fraudulent preference**, in *bankruptcy*, a transfer of money or other subject of value to a creditor, with the intention, on the part of the debtor, of preventing the operation of the law of bankruptcy in the distribution of his effects for the equal benefit of all his creditors.—**Preference shares** or **preference stock**, in *finance*, shares or stock on which dividends are payable before those on the original shares or common stock. In the United States called *preferred stock*.—**To have the preference**, to be preferred. = **Syn.** *Precedence*, etc. (see *priority*); *Choice*, *Election*, etc. (see *option*); selection.

preferential (pref-e̤-ren'shal), *a.* [< *preference* (ML. *præferentia*) + *-ial.*] Characterized by or having preference; such as to be preferred.

The King was allowed a *preferential* claim on the public revenue, to the amount of £10,000.
Stubbs, Const. Hist., § 323.

With the revival of Catholic feeling in the seventeenth century, and the continued cultus of the Blessed Virgin in this and the eighteenth, the Easter plays recovered their *preferential* position.
A. W. Ward, Eng. Dram. Lit., I. 27.

Retention in prose of words confined to earlier epic poetry . . . must not be tortured into conclusive evidence as to the place of origin of any portion of the Homeric text: it indicates rather the vigorous *preferential* uses of the Hellenic dialects. *Amer. Jour. Philol.*, VIII. 467.

preferentially (pref-e̤-ren'shal-i), *adv.* By preference; in a manner exhibiting preference or choice; preferably.

The same person . . . will, more likely than not, elect "is in preparation" *preferentially* to "is being prepared."
F. Hall, Mod. Eng., p. 351.

preferment (prē̤-fėr'ment), *n.* [= It. *preferimento*; as *prefer* + *-ment.*] 1. The act of preferring or esteeming more highly, or the state of being preferred; choice; preference; advancement; promotion.

For your *preferment* resorte
To such as may you vauntage.
Babees Book (E. E. T. S.), p. 86.

To get *preferment* who doth now intend,
He by a golden ladder must ascend.
Times' Whistle (E. E. T. S.), p. 47.

Nor is your firm resolve unknown to me,
In the *preferment* of the eldest sister.
Shak., T. of the S., ii. 1. 94.

Some trim fellows will not stick to maintain a brave paradox: that the opinion and semblance of things neither ever was, nor is now, inferior to the very things themselves, but in *preferment* and reputation many times superior. *G. Harvey*, Four Letters.

They that enter into the Ministry for *preferment* are like Judas that lockt after the Bag.
Selden, Table-Talk, p. 30.

Many Frenchmen, and even Italians, of whom nothing else is known, were enriched with English *preferment*.
Stubbs, Medieval and Modern Hist., p. 129.

2. A superior place or office, especially in the church.

I have a very small fortune, no *preferment*, nor any friends who are likely to give me any.
Sydney Smith, in Lady Holland, iv.

He was liable to be suspended from his office, to be ejected from it, to be pronounced incapable of holding any *preferment* in future. *Macaulay*, Hist. Eng., vi.

preferrer (prē̤-fėr'ėr), *n.* [< *prefer* + *-er*[1].] 1. One who prefers or sets forth an entreaty, a charge, an exhortation, or the like.

This admonition finding small entertainment, the authors or chief *preferrers* thereof being imprisoned, out cometh the second admonition.
Bp. Bancroft, Dangerous Proceedings, iii. 2. (*Latham.*)

2†. One who advances or promotes; a furtherer.

Doctor Stephens, secretary, and D. Foxe, almosiner, were the chiefe furtherers, *preferrers*, and defendors on the kings behalfe of the said cause.
Foxe, Martyrs, p. 1688, an. 1556.

prefident† (pref'i-de̤nt), *a.* [< L. *præfiden(t-)s*, trusting too much, taken in lit. sense 'trusting before' (hence prematurely), < *præ*, before, + *fiden(t-)s*, ppr. of *fidere*, trust: see *faith*. Cf. *confident.*] Trusting previously; overtrustful. *Baxter.* [Rare.]

prefigurate (prē̤-fig'ṳ̄-rāt), *v. t.*; pret. and pp. *prefigurated*, ppr. *prefigurating*. [< LL. *præfiguratus*, pp. of *præfigurare*, prefigure: see *prefigure.*] To show by antecedent representation; prefigure. [Rare.]

When from thy native soil love had thee driven
(Thy safe return *prefigurating*), a heaven
Of faltering hopes did in my fancy move.
W. Drummond, Death of Sir W. Alexander.

prefiguration (prē̤-fig-ū-rā'sho̤n), *n.* [< LL. *præfiguratio(n-)*, a figuring beforehand: see *prefigurate.*] The act of prefiguring, or the state of being prefigured; antecedent representation by similitude.

Most of the famous passages of providence (especially the signal afflictions of eminent persons representing our Saviour) do seem to have been *prefigurations* of or preludes to his passion. *Barrow*, Works, II. xxvii.

prefigurative (prē̤-fig'ṳ̄-rā-tiv), *a.* [< *prefigurate* + *-ive.*] Showing by previous figures, types, or similitude.

All the sacrifices of old instituted by God we may . . . affirm to have been chiefly preparatory unto, and *prefigurative* of, this most true and perfect sacrifice.
Barrow, Sermons, II. xxvii.

prefigure (prē̤-fig'ūr), *v. t.*; pret. and pp. *prefigured*, ppr. *prefiguring*. [= F. *préfigurer* = Sp. Pg. *prefigurar* = It. *prefigurare*, < LL. *præfigurare*, figure beforehand, < L. *præ*, before, + *figurare*, form, fashion: see *figure*, *v.*] To represent beforehand; show by previous types or figures; foreshow; presage.

By an oblation of the blood of beasts was *prefigured* the blood of that Lamb which should expiate all our sins.
Rev. T. Adams, Works, II. 3.

At her call, a waking dream
Prefigured to his sense the Egyptian Lady.
Wordsworth, The Egyptian Maid.

prefigurement (prē̤-fig'ūr-ment), *n.* [= It. *prefiguramento*; as *prefigure* + *-ment.*] The act of prefiguring; antecedent representation; presage; prognostication.

The two young women who constituted at Marmion his whole *prefigurement* of a social circle must, in such a locality as that, be taking a regular holiday.
H. James, Jr., The Century, XXXI. 91.

prefine[1]† (prē̤-fīn'), *v. t.* [< OF. *prefinir*, F. *préfinir* = Sp. Pg. *prefinir* = It. *prefinire*, < L. *præfinire*, determine or fix beforehand, < *præ*, before, + *finire*, finish, determine: see *finish*. Cf. *define*, etc.] To limit or define beforehand; assign beforehand as a limit.

He, in his immoderate desires, *prefined* unto himself three years, which the great monarchs of Rome could not perform in so many hundreds. *Knolles*, Hist. Turks.

prefine[2]† (prē'fīn), *n.* [< *pre-* + *fine*[2].] See *alienation-office*.

prefinite† (pref'i-nit), *a.* [< L. *præfinitus*, pp. of *præfinire*, determine or fix beforehand: see *prefine*[1].] Previously limited or defined; fixed beforehand: used with the force of a participle.

I thinke them no trewe Chrystian men that do not reioyce . . . for the deliuerie of these owre brootherne, . . . accordynge to the time *prefinite* by hym who . . . hath suffered the greate serpente of the sea Leuiathan to haue suche dominion in the Ocean.
R. Eden, First Books on America (ed. Arber), p. 50.

prefinition† (pref-i-nish'on), *n.* [= Sp. *prefinicion* = It. *prefinizione*, < LL. *præfinitio(n-)*, a determining or fixing beforehand, < L. *præfinire*, pp. *præfinitus*, determine or fix beforehand: see *prefine*[1].] Prior definition or limitation.

God hath encompassed all the kingdoms of the earth with a threefold restraint: to wit, a limitation of their powers; a circumscription of their bounds; and a *prefinition* of their periods. *Fotherby*, Atheomastix, p. 270.

prefix (prē̤-fiks'), *v. t.* [< OF. *prefixer*, F. *préfixer* = Sp. *prefijar* = Pg. *prefixar*, < ML. **præfixare*, < L. *præfixus*, pp. of *præfigere* (> It. *prefiggere*, prefix), set up in front, fix on the end of, prefix, < *præ*, before, in front, + *figere*, fix, attach: see *fix.*] 1. To fix or put before; place in front; put at the beginning.

I do now publish my Essays. . . . I thought it therefore agreeable to my affection and obligation to your Grace to *prefix* your name before them. *Bacon*, Essays, Ded.

2†. To fix beforehand; set or appoint in advance; settle beforehand.

And now he hath to her *prefixt* a day.
Spenser, F. Q., V. xi. 40.

The hour draws on
Prefix'd by Angelo. *Shak.*, M. for M., iv. 3. 83.

Or wert thou of the golden-winged host,
Who, having clad thyself in human weed,
To earth from thy *prefixed* seat didst post?
Milton, Death of a Fair Infant, l. 50.

Aganst the *prefixed* time, the women & children, with ye goods, were sent to ye place in a small barke.
Bradford, Plymouth Plantation, p. 13.

I would *prefix* some certain boundary between them.
Sir M. Hale, Hist. Com. Law of Eng.

prefix (prē'fiks), *n.* [= F. *préfixe* = Sp. *prefijo* = Pg. *prefixo* = It. *prefisso*, < NL. *præfixum*, a prefix, neut. of L. *præfixus*, pp. of *præfigere*, prefix: see *prefix*, *v.*] 1. A word or syllable, or a number of syllables, rarely more than two, and usually one (sometimes reduced to a single consonant not forming a syllable), affixed to the beginning of a word, to qualify its meaning or direct its application: opposed to *suffix* or *postfix*, a like addition at the end of a word. A prefix proper is an inseparable element, never used alone, as *pre-* in *prefix*, *con-* in *conjure*, *in-* in *inactive*, *un-* in *unseen*, etc.; but prepositions and primitive adverbs used in composition are usually accounted prefixes, as *fore-* in *forecast*, *down* in *downfall*, *in* in *income*, etc. By a looser use such recurring elements as *equi-*, *multi-*, *iso-*, *mono-*, *poly-*, etc., in compounds of Latin or Greek origin or formation, are called prefixes, though they are properly independent words in the original language. There is no hard and fast line between a prefix and the initial element of a compound.

2. The act of prefixing; prefixion.

The *prefix* of the definite article.
Roby, Latin Grammar, I. xviii.

Prefix language, a language which (like those of South Africa) makes its forms mainly by the use of prefixed rather than of suffixed elements.

prefixal (prē'fik-sa̤l), *a.* [< *prefix* + *-al.*] Of the nature of a prefix; characterized by prefixes.

The *prefixal* languages of Africa.
Jour. Anthrop. Inst., XVII. 170.

prefixation (prē-fik-sā'sho̤n), *n.* [< *prefix* + *-ation.*] The use of prefixes; prefixion. [Rare.]

By *prefixation* and suffixation a considerable number of tenses and modes are formed in the verb.
Amer. Antiquarian, XII. 121.

prefixion (prē̤-fik'sho̤n), *n.* [< *prefix* + *-ion.*] The act of prefixing.

prefixture (prē̤-fiks'tṳ̄r), *n.* [< *prefix* + *-ture*, after *fixture.*] Same as *prefixion*. *J. A. H. Murray*, 8th Ann. Address to Philol. Assoc., p. 41.

prefloration (prē-flō̤-rā'sho̤n), *n.* [Also *præfloration*; = F. *préfloraison*, < L. *præ*, before, + **floratio(n-)*, < *florare*, blossom, flower, < *flos* (*flor-*), a flower, a bloom: see *flower.*] In *bot.*, estivation.

prefoliation (prē-fō-li-ā'sho̤n), *n.* [< L. *præ*, before, + **foliatio(n-)*, < *foliare*, put forth leaves, < *folium*, leaf: see *foliation.*] In *bot.*, vernation.

prefool† (prē-föl'), *v. t.* [< *pre-* + *fool.*] To fool beforehand; anticipate in foolery.

I'll tell you a better project, wherein no courtier has *prefool'd* you. *Shirley*, Bird in a Cage, ii. 1.

preforceps (prē-fôr'seps), *n. pl.* [NL., < L. *præ*, before, + *forceps*, q. v.] Certain anterior fibers of the corpus callosum which curve forward into the frontal lobe of the cerebrum, and are likened to a pair of forceps in front of the callosum.

preform (prē-fôrm'), *v. t.* [= F. *préformer* = It. *preformare*, < L. *præformare*, form beforehand, prepare, < *præ*, before, + *formare*, shape, fashion: see *form.*] 1. To form beforehand; execute or create previously.

Why all these things change from their ordinance
Their natures and *preformed* faculties
To monstrous quality. *Shak.*, J. C., i. 3. 67.

2. In *biol.*, to determine beforehand the shape or form of; furnish the mold or model of (something afterward to take shape): as, bone *preformed* in cartilage; the fetal skeleton *preforms* that of the adult.

preformation (prē-fôr-mā'sho̤n), *n.* [= F. *préformation* = It. *preformazione*, < L. **præformatio(n-)*, < *præformare*, form beforehand: see *preform.*] Antecedent formation; shaping in advance.—**Theory of preformation**, a doctrine respecting generation or reproduction, prevalent down to and during the eighteenth century, according to which every individual is fully and completely preformed in the germ, the development of which consists in the growth and unfolding of preëxisting parts—that is to say, the perfect individual has always been there, and simply grows from microscopic to visible proportions, without developing any new parts. See *incasement*.

preformationist (prē-fôr-mā'sho̤n-ist), *n.* [< *preformation* + *-ist.*] A believer in the doctrine of preformation. *Encyc. Brit.*, XXIV. 815.

preformative (prē-fôr'mā̤-tiv), *a.* and *n.* [< L. *præformatus*, pp. of *præformare*, form or mold beforehand (see *preform*), + *-ive.*] I. *a.* Forming beforehand; pursuing a course of preformation; containing the essential germs of later development.

Furthermore, the apostolic Christianity is *preformative*, and contains the living germs of all the following periods, personages, and tendencies.
Schaff, Hist. Christ. Church, I. § 21.

II. *n.* In *philol.*, a formative letter or syllable at the beginning of a word; a prefix.

prefract† (prē̤-frakt'), *a.* [< L. *præfractus*, broken off, abrupt, stern, pp. of *præfringere*, break off before, < *præ*, before, + *frangere*, break: see *fraction.*] Obstinate; inflexible; refractory.

Thou . . . wast so *prefract* and stout in religion.
J. Bradford, Works (Parker Soc.), I. 474.

Yet still he stands *prefract* and insolent.
Chapman, Byron's Tragedy, iv. 1.

prefrontal (prē-fron'tal), *a.* and *n.* [Also *præfrontal*; < L. *præ*, before, + *fron(t-)s*, forehead: see *frontal*.] **I.** *a.* Of or pertaining to the fore part of the forehead, or to the part of the skull in which is the bone called the *prefrontal*.

II. *n.* A bone of the anterior region of the skull of sundry vertebrates, being a lateral ethmoidal or ante-orbital ossification, most distinct in vertebrates below birds.

prefulgency (prē-ful'jen-si), *n.* [< **prefulgen(t)* (= OF. *prefulgent*, < L. *præfulgen(t-)s*, ppr. of *præfulgere*, shine greatly, < *præ*, before, + *fulgere*, flash, gleam: see *fulgent*) + *-cy*.] Superior brightness or effulgency; surpassing glory. [Rare.]

If . . . by the *prefulgency* of his excellent worth and merit . . . St. Peter had the πρωτεῖα or first place.
Barrow, On the Pope's Supremacy.

pregage† (prē-gāj'), *v. t.* [< *pre-* + *gage*[1].] To preëngage; pledge beforehand.

The members of the Councell of Trent, both Bishops and Abbots, were by oath *pregaged* to the Pope to defend and maintain his authority against all the world.
Fuller, Ch. Hist., IX. i. 42.

pregeminal (prē-jem'i-nal), *a.* [< L. *præ*, before, + *geminus*, twin, + *-al*.] Pertaining to the anterior pair of the corpora quadrigemina of the brain.

pregeniculate, prægeniculate (prē-jē-nik'ū-lāt), *a.* Pertaining to the pregeniculum.

pregeniculatum, prægeniculatum (prē-jē-nik-ū-lā'tum), *n.*; pl. *pregeniculata, prægeniculata* (-tạ̈). [NL.] Same as *pregeniculum*.

pregeniculum (prē-jē-nik'ū-lum), *n.*; pl. *pregenicula* (-lạ̈). [NL., < L. *præ*, before, + *geniculum*, dim. of *genu*, a knee.] The external corpus geniculatum (which see, under *corpus*).

pregenital (prē-jen'i-tal), *a.* [< L. *præ*, before, + *genitalis*, belonging to generation: see *genital*.] In *entom.*, situated before the external opening of the oviduct, sting, or male intromittent organ.—**Pregenital segment**, the eighth primary abdominal ring, or the one immediately before the genital opening; in the perfect insect it may be partly or entirely hidden under other rings.

preglacial (prē-glā'shial), *a.* [< *pre-* + *glacial*.] In *geol.*, prior to the glacial or boulder-drift period.

preglenoid (prē-glē'noid), *a.* and *n.* [< *pre-* + *glenoid*.] **I.** *a.* Situated in advance or in front of the glenoid fossa of either the scapula or the temporal bone: as, a *preglenoid* process.

II. *n.* A preglenoid formation. In some animals, as badgers, both pre- and postglenoid processes of the temporal bone are so highly developed that the lower jaw is locked in its socket, and cannot be disarticulated even in the dry skull.

preglenoidal (prē-glē-noi'dal), *a.* [< *preglenoid* + *-al*.] Same as *preglenoid*.

pregnable (preg'na-bl), *a.* [With unorig. *g* (as also in *impregnable*), < OF. (and F.) *prenable*, that may be taken, < *prendre*, < L. *prendere*, seize, take: see *prender*, *prehend*.] **1.** Capable of being taken or won by force; expugnable.

Then yͤ marshall caused yͤ towne to be auewed, to see if it were *pregnable* or not.
Berners, tr. of Froissart's Chron., II. 51.

2. Capable of being moved, impressed, or convinced. [Rare.]

pregnance (preg'nans), *n.* [= It. *pregnanza*; as *pregnan(t)* + *-ce*.] Same as *pregnancy*.

pregnancy (preg'nan-si), *n.* [As *pregnance* (see *-cy*).] **1.** The state of being pregnant; the state of a female who has conceived or is with child; gestation; fetation.—**2.** Fruitfulness; fertility; fecundity; productiveness.

Famous for the judgment of Paris, and *pregnancy* in fountains, from whence descend four rivers.
Sandys, Travailes, p. 17.

3. Fullness, as of important contents; significance; suggestiveness.

The Diversions of the fallen Angels, with the particular Account of their Place of Habitation, are described with great *pregnancy* of Thought. *Addison*, Spectator, No. 309.

4†. Readiness of wit; shrewdness.

Pregnancy is made a tapster, and hath his quick wit wasted in giving reckonings. *Shak.*, 2 Hen. IV., i. 2. 192.

La-P. Do you think I am a dunce?
Lav. Not a dunce, captain; but you might give me leave to misdoubt that *pregnancy* in a soldier which is proper and hereditary to a courtier.
Beau. and Fl., Honest Man's Fortune, ii. 2.

He wants but three of fourscore, yet of a wonderful vigour and *pregnancy*. *Penn*, Travels in Holland, etc.

5†. A promising youth; a quick-witted person.

This was the fashion in his reign, to select yearly one or moe of the most promising *pregnancies* out of both universities, and to breed them beyond the seas on the king's exhibitions unto them. *Fuller*, Ch. Hist., VI. 340.

Extra-uterine pregnancy, gestation taking place in the abdomen outside the uterus.—**Fallopian pregnancy.** See *Fallopian*.—**Plea of pregnancy**, in *criminal law*, a plea to take advantage of the rule that, when a pregnant woman is capitally convicted, the execution of her sentence must be delayed until after the birth of the child.—**Tubal pregnancy.** Same as *Fallopian pregnancy*.

pregnant (preg'nant), *a.* and *n.* [In def. 8, ME. *preignant*, < OF. *preignant*, *pregnant*, pregnant, pithy, ready, capable, etc.; F. *prégnant* = It. *pregnante*, pregnant, < L. *prægnan(t-)s*, with child, pregnant, full, in form ppr. of a verb **prægnare*, < *præ*, before, + **gnare*, bear, pp. *gnatus*, *natus*, born: see *natal*[1]. In some Shaksperian uses *pregnant* has been referred to OF. *prenant*, ppr. of *prendre*, take (cf. *pregnable*, < OF. *prenable*); but all uses seem to be derivable from *pregnant* as above.] **I.** *a.* **1.** Being with young; big with child; gravid: as, a *pregnant* woman.

My womb,
Pregnant by thee, and now excessive grown.
Milton, P. L., ii. 779.

2. Impregnated; filled; big: generally followed by *with*.

These in their dark nativity the deep
Shall yield us, *pregnant with* infernal flame.
Milton, P. L., vi. 483.

Such the bard's prophetic words,
Pregnant with celestial fire.
Cowper, Boadicea.

Her eyes were *pregnant with* some tale
Of love and fear.
William Morris, Earthly Paradise, I. 422.

3. Heavily laden; freighted.

The elves present, to quench his thirst,
A pure seed-pearle of infant dew,
Brought and besweetened in a blew
And *pregnant* violet. *Herrick*, Oberon's Feast.

Whom the wing'd harpy, swift Podarge, bore,
By zephyr *pregnant* on the breezy shore.
Pope, Iliad, xvi. 185.

4. Full of meaning; giving food for thought; suggestive; significant; destined to develop important thought.

I fear no such thing of you, I have had such *pregnant* Proofs of your Ingenuity, and noble Inclinations to Virtue and Honour. *Howell*, Letters, I. iii. 2.

History yet points to the *pregnant* though brief text of Tacitus. *Story*, Discourse, Aug. 31, 1826.

He left home the next morning in that watchful state of mind which turns the most ordinary course of things into *pregnant* coincidences.
George Eliot, Mill on the Floss, v. 5.

5. Full of promise; of unusual capacity, ability, or wit; shrewd; witty; ingenious; expert.

The nature of our people,
Our city's institutions, and the terms
For common justice, you're as *pregnant* in
As art and practice hath enriched any
That we remember. *Shak.*, M. for M., i. 1. 12.

The famous Ptolemy . . . culled out a select number of his *pregnantest* young Nobles . . . to go to Greece, Italy, Carthage, and other Regions . . . to observe the Government. *Howell*, Forreine Travell, p. 72.

I went to Eton. . . . The school-master assur'd me there had not been for 20 yeares a more *pregnant* youth in that place than my grandson. *Evelyn*, Diary, April 23, 1696.

No one can read Goethe's recollections of his boyhood without feeling how, for example, the pageants of the empire which he witnessed at Frankfort helped to call out his *pregnant* sense of organic continuity.
B. Bosanquet, Mind, XIII. 363.

6. Characterized by readiness of wit; keen; apt; clever.

How *pregnant* sometimes his replies are! a happiness that often madness hits on. *Shak.*, Hamlet, ii. 2. 212.

If thou dost, [learned reader,] thy capacity is more *pregnant* then mine. *Coryat*, Crudities, I. 257.

7†. Ready; disposed; prompt; susceptible.

Glou. Now, good sir, what are you?
Edg. A most poor man, made tame to fortune's blows;
Who, by the art of known and feeling sorrows,
Am *pregnant* to good pity. *Shak.*, Lear, iv. 6. 227.

8†. Convincing; easily seen; clear; evident; probable in the highest degree.

This was hym a *preignant* argument,
That she was forth out of the world agon.
Chaucer, Troilus, iv. 1179.

Were't not that we stand up against them all,
'Twere *pregnant* they should square between themselves.
Shak., A. and C., ii. 1. 45.

9. In *logic*, requiring an explanation; exponible.—**Negative pregnant**, in *law*. See *negative*, *n.*—**Pregnant construction**, in *rhet.*, a construction in which more is implied than is said, as in "the beasts *trembled* forth (that is, came forth trembling) from their dens."—**Pregnant negative**, a negative proposition affected by a reduplicative, exceptive, or other expression requiring special treatment in logic: thus, "no man, qua man, ever sleeps" is a pregnant negative.

II. *n.* One who is pregnant, or with child. *Dunglison.*

pregnantly (preg'nant-li), *adv.* In a pregnant manner.

pregnantness (preg'nant-nes), *n.* Same as *pregnancy*. *Bailey*, 1727.

pregravate† (prē'grạ̈-vāt), *v. t.* [< L. *prægravatus*, pp. of *prægravare*, oppress with weight, < *præ*, before, + *gravare*, load, burden, < *gravis*, heavy: see *grave*[3].] To weigh heavily upon; bear down; depress.

The clog that the body brings with it cannot but *pregravate* and trouble the soul in all her performances.
Bp. Hall, Invisible World, ii. 1.

pregravitate† (prẹ̄-grav'i-tāt), *v. i.* [< *pre-* + *gravitate*.] To descend by gravity; sink.

Water does gravitate in water as well as out of it, though indeed it does not *prægravitate*, because it is counterballanced by an equal weight of collateral water, which keeps it from descending. *Boyle*, Free Inquiry, § 6.

pregustation (prē-gus-tā'shon), *n.* [< OF. *pregustation* = It. *pregustazione*, < L. as if **prægustatio(n-)*, < *prægustare*, pp. *prægustatus*, taste beforehand, < *præ*, before, + *gustare*, taste: see *gust*[2].] The act of tasting beforehand; foretaste; anticipation.

In the actual exercise of prayer, by which she so often anticipated heaven by *pregustation*.
Dr. Walker, Character of Lady Warwick, p. 117. (*Latham.*)

prehallux (prē-hal'uks), *n.*; pl. *prehalluces* (-ū-sēz). [NL. *præhallux*, < L. *præ*, before, + NL. *hallux*, q. v.] A kind of cartilaginous spur or calcar on the inner side of the foot of some batrachians, next to the hallux, commonly segmented in several pieces. It is inconstant in occurrence, and when present varies much in size, shape, and number of pieces. Its homology is not clear: it has been variously considered as a tarsal element, as a sixth digit, and as a supernumerary element of the foot.

That the *prehallux* takes on certain of the essential relationships of a digit is beyond dispute. That it really represents one is another question.
Proc. Zoöl. Soc. London, 1888, p. 150.

prehalter (prē-hal'tėr), *n.*; pl. *prehalteres* (-ēz). [< L. *præ*, before, + *halter*, q. v.] A small membranous scale behind the base of each wing and before the halter of dipterous insects; a prebalancer. Also called *tegula*.

pre-hemiplegic (prē-hem-i-plej'ik), *a.* [< *pre-* + *hemiplegia* + *-ic*.] Occurring previous to a hemiplegic attack.—**Pre-hemiplegic chorea**, choreic movements occurring previous to cerebral hemorrhage.

prehend† (prẹ̄-hend'), *v. t.* [< L. *prehendere*, contr. *prendere*, lay hold of, grasp, seize, take; prob. orig. **præhendere*, < *præ*, before, + *-hendere* (√ *hed*) = Gr. χανδάνειν (√ χαδ), seize, = E. *get*: see *get*[1]. Hence ult. *apprehend*, *comprehend*, *deprehend*, *reprehend*, etc., *prender*, *prehensile*, *prehension*, etc., *prize*[1], *prison*, etc.] To seize; take; apprehend.

They were greatly blamed that *prehended* hym and comitted hym.
Political Poems, etc. (ed. Furnivall), Pref., p. xv.

Is not that rebel Oliver, that traitor to my year,
Prehended yet?
Middleton (and another), Mayor of Queenborough, v. 1.

prehensible (prẹ̄-hen'si-bl), *a.* [= F. *préhensible*, < L. *prehensus*, pp. of *prehendere*, *prendere*, lay hold of, seize: see *prehend*.] Capable of being prehended, seized, or laid hold of.

prehensile (prẹ̄-hen'sil), *a.* [= F. *préhensile*, < L. *prehensus*, pp. of *prehendere*, lay hold of, seize: see *prehend*.] Seizing or grasping; taking and holding; adapted for prehension; especially, fitted for grasping or holding by folding, wrapping, or curving around the object prehended: as, the *prehensile* tail of a monkey or an opossum. Also *prehensory*. See cut above, and cuts at *Cebinæ*, *marmose*, *musk-cavy*, *opossum*, and *spider-monkey*.

Prehensile-tailed Porcupine (*Chætomys subspinosus*).

In the Hippocampidæ the caudal fin disappears, and the tail becomes a *prehensile* organ, by the aid of which the species lead a sedentary life.
E. D. Cope, Origin of the Fittest, p. 328.

prehension (prẹ̄-hen'shon), *n.* [= F. *préhension*, < L. *prehensio(n-)*, *prensio(n-)*, a seizing, < *prehendere*, *prendere*, pp. *prehensus*, lay hold of, take: see *prehend*. Cf. *prison*, a doublet of *prehension*.] 1. The act of prehending, seizing, or taking hold.

In a creature of low type the touch of food excites *prehension*. *H. Spencer*, Data of Ethics, § 41.

The trophi serve merely for the *prehension* of prey, and not for mastication. *Darwin*, Cirripedia, p. 40.

2. Apprehension; mental grasp.

In these experiments the span of *prehension* is measured by the number of letters and numerals that can be correctly repeated after twice hearing, the interval between them in the dictation being about one-half a second. *Amer. Jour. Psychol.*, I. 103.

prehensor (prẹ-hen'sọr), *n.* [= F. *préhenseur*, < NL. **prehensor*, one who seizes, < L. *prehendere*, *prendere*, pp. *prehensus*, lay hold of, seize, take: see *prehend*.] One who or that which prehends or lays hold of. [Rare.]

What was wanted is — a word that should signify to lay hold of. . . . *Prehensor* . . . does what is wanted, clear of everything that is not wanted. *Bentham*, Equity Dispatch Court Bill, i., § 7, 1, note.

prehensorium (prē-hen-sō'ri-um), *n.* [NL., neut. of **prehensorius*: see *prehensory*.] In *entom.*, a part or parts adapted for seizing or clasping: specifically applied to the posterior legs when the bases are very distant, the femora converging, and the tibiæ diverging and opposable, so that each leg forms an inward angle, generally armed with spines, as in certain *Arachnida*, etc.

prehensory (prẹ-hen'sọ-ri), *a.* [< NL. **prehensorius*, serving to seize, < L. *prehensor*, one who seizes: see *prehensor*.] Same as *prehensile*.

prehistoric (prē-his-tor'ik), *a.* [= F. *préhistorique*; as *pre-* + *historic*.] Existing in or relating to time antecedent to the beginning of recorded history: as, *prehistoric* races; the *prehistoric* period of a country.

prehistorical (prē-his-tor'i-kal), *a.* [< *pre-* + *historical*.] Same as *prehistoric*.

prehistorics (prē-his-tor'iks), *n.* [Pl. of *prehistoric* (see *-ics*).] The sum of knowledge relating to prehistoric times; knowledge which has been gained or recovered of epochs anterior to recorded history. [Rare.]

Chinese *prehistorics* have not as yet been sufficiently studied to decide which metal was the first to be wrought in that distant realm. *Science*, IV. 21.

prehistory (prē-his'tọ-ri), *n.* [< *pre-* + *history*.] History prior to recorded history.

In some districts of America history and *prehistory* lie far apart. *Pop. Sci. Mo.*, XXXIV. 686.

But the question of the original home of the Aryan nations is hardly the most important one connected with their *pre-history*. *New Princeton Rev.*, V. 2.

prehnite (pren'īt), *n.* [Named after Col. *Prehn*, who discovered the mineral at the Cape of Good Hope in the latter part of the eighteenth century.] A mineral, usually of a pale-green color and vitreous luster, commonly occurring in botryoidal or globular forms with crystalline surface. It is a hydrous silicate of aluminium and calcium, allied to the zeolites, and is found with them in veins and geodes, most frequently in rocks of the basaltic type. Also called *edelite*.

prehuman (prē-hū'man), *a.* [< *pre-* + *human*.] Occurring or existing before the appearance of man upon the earth; pertaining to times antecedent to human existence.

The forms which, on the theory of "development," must have connected the human root-stock with the *prehuman* root. *R. Proctor*, Nature Studies, p. 80.

preieret, *n.* An obsolete spelling of *prayer*[1].

preiff, *n.* Same as *prief* for *proof*.

Preignac (prā-nyak'), *n.* [< *Preignac*: see def.] A white wine of Bordeaux, unusually free from sweetness, but strong, and keeping for a long time. It is produced in the commune of Preignac, department of Gironde, France.

pre-incarnate (prē-in-kär'nāt), *a.* [< *pre-* + *incarnate*.] Previous to incarnation: said chiefly of Christ as existing before his assumption of human nature.

The *Pre-incarnate* Son was in the Form — the primal, essential Form — of God; the Incarnate Son appeared in the figure — the assumed, incidental figure — of a man. *G. D. Boardman*, Creative Week, p. 304.

preindesignate (prē-in-des'ig-nāt), *a.* [< *pre-* + *in-*[3] priv. + *designate*.] In *logic*, not having the quantity of the subject definitely expressed.

Propositions have either, as propositions, their quantity, determinate or indeterminate, marked out by a verbal sign, or they have not; such quantity being involved in every actual thought: they may be called in the one case (a) Predesignate; in the other (b) *Preindesignate*. *Sir W. Hamilton*, Lectures on Logic, xiii.

preindicate (prē-in'di-kāt), *v. t.*; pret. and pp. *preindicated*, ppr. *preindicating*. [< *pre-* + *indicate*.] To indicate beforehand; foreshow; prognosticate.

For how many centuries were the laws of electricity *pre indicated* by the single fact that a piece of amber, when rubbed, would attract light bodies! *Proc. Soc. Psych. Research*, I. 62.

preinstruct (prē-in-strukt'), *v. t.* [< *pre-* + *instruct*.] To instruct or direct beforehand.

As if Plato had been *preinstructed* by men of the same spirit with the Apostle. *Dr. H. More*, Def. of Moral Cabbala.

preintimation (prē-in-ti-mā'shọn), *n.* [< *pre-* + *intimation*.] Previous intimation; a suggestion beforehand.

preiset, *r.* and *n.* An obsolete spelling of *praise*.

prejacent† (prē-jā'sẹnt), *a.* [< L. *præjacen(t-)s*, ppr. of *præjacere*, lie before, < *præ*, before, + *jacere*, lie: see *jacent*.] Constituting a premise, especially of a logical conversion. [So Hamilton, following Scheibler. But Paulus Venetus uses the Latin word in a different sense.]

prejink (prē-jingk'), *a.* [Also *perjink*; appar. a loose variation of *prink*, simulating *pre-* or *per-* + *jink*[1].] Trim; finically dressed out; prinked. [Scotch.]

Mrs. Fenton, seeing the exposure that *prejink* Miss Peggy had made of herself, laughed for some time as if she was by herself. *Galt*, The Provost, p. 203.

prejudge (prē-juj'), *v. t.*; pret. and pp. *prejudged*, ppr. *prejudging*. [< F. *préjuger* = Sp. *prejuzgar* = Pg. *prejudicar* = It. *pregiudicare*, < L. *præjudicare*, judge or decide beforehand, < *præ*, before, + *judicare*, judge: see *judge*, *v.*] 1. To judge beforehand; decide in advance of thorough investigation; condemn unheard or in anticipation.

The expedition of Alexander into Asia . . . . at first was *prejudged* as a vast and impossible enterprise. *Bacon*, Advancement of Learning, i. 54.

And prays you'll not *prejudge* his play for ill
Because you mark it not, and sit not still.
B. Jonson, Staple of News, Prol.

2†. To anticipate in giving judgment; pass sentence before.

By this time suppose sentence given, Caiaphas *prejudging* all the sanhedrim; for he first declared Jesus to have spoken blasphemy, and the fact to be notorious, and then asked their votes. *Jer. Taylor*, Works (ed. 1835), I. 322.

3†. To prejudice; impair; overrule.

The saying of the father may no way *prejudge* the bishops' authority, but it excludes the assistance of laymen from their consistories. *Jer. Taylor*, Works (ed. 1835), II. 247.

prejudgment, prejudgement (prē-juj'mẹnt), *n.* [< F. *préjugement*; as *prejudge* + *-ment*.] The act of prejudging; judgment before full knowledge or examination of the case; decision or condemnation in advance.

It is not free and impartial inquiry that we deprecate, it is hasty and arrogant *prejudgement*. *Bp. W. Knox*, Two Sermons, p. 30.

I was not inclined to call your words raving. I listen that I may know, without *prejudgment*. *George Eliot*, Daniel Deronda, xl.

prejudicacy† (prẹ-jö'di-kạ-si), *n.* [< *prejudica(te)* + *-cy*.] Prejudice; prepossession.

But rather receive it from mine own eye, not dazzled with any affection, *prejudicacy*, or mist of education. *Blount*, Voyage to the Levant, p. 8. (*Latham.*)

prejudical (prẹ-jö'di-kal), *a.* [Irreg. < L. *præjudicare*, judge or decide beforehand (see *prejudicate*), + *-al*.] Pertaining to the determination of some matter not previously decided: as, a *prejudical* inquiry.

prejudicant† (prẹ-jö'di-kant), *a.* [< L. *præjudican(t-)s*, ppr. of *præjudicare*, judge or decide beforehand: see *prejudicate*.] Prejudging; prejudicative.

If we view him well, and hear him with not too hasty and *prejudicant* ears, we shall find no such terror in him. *Milton*, Tetrachordon.

prejudicate (prẹ-jö'di-kāt), *v.*; pret. and pp. *prejudicated*, ppr. *prejudicating*. [< L. *præjudicatus*, pp. of *præjudicare*, judge or decide beforehand: see *prejudge*.] I. *trans.* 1†. To prejudge; judge overhastily; condemn upon insufficient information; misjudge.

To *prejudicate* his determination is but a doubt of goodness in him who is nothing but goodness. *Sir P. Sidney*, Arcadia, iv.

Our dearest friend
Prejudicates the business, and would seem
To have us make denial. *Shak.*, All's Well, i. 2. 8.

Sir, you too much *prejudicate* my thoughts;
I must give due respect to men of honour.
Shirley, The Brothers, ii. 1.

Being ambitious to outdo the Earle of Sandwich, whom he had *prejudicated* as deficient in courage. *Evelyn*, Diary, June 6, 1666.

2†. To prejudice; injure; impair.

Item, no particular person to hinder or *preiudicate* the common stocke of the company, in sale or preferment of his own proper wares. *Hakluyt's Voyages*, I. 228.

II. *intrans.* To form overhasty judgments; pass judgment prematurely; give condemnation in advance of due examination.

I thinke, in a minde not preiudiced with a *preiudicating* humor, hee will be found in excellencie fruitefull. *Sir P. Sidney*, Apol. for Poetrie.

prejudicate† (prẹ-jö'di-kāt), *a.* [= It. *pregiudicato*; < L. *præjudicatus*, pp.: see the verb.] 1. Formed before due examination; prematurely conceived or entertained: as, a *prejudicate* opinion.

When I say men of letters, I would be understood to mean them who have contracted too great a familiarity with books, who are too much wedded to the *prejudicate* opinions of the Doctors. *J. Digby*, tr. of De Wicquefort, the Embassador (ed. 1750), [p. 60.

It is the rhetoric of Satan, and may pervert a loose or *prejudicate* belief. *Sir T. Browne*, Religio Medici, i. 20.

2. Prejudiced; biased.

Your link'd ears so loud
Sing with *prejudicate* winds, that nought is heard
Of all poor prisoners urge 'gainst your award.
Chapman, Byron's Tragedy, v. 1.

He that shall discourse Euclid's Elements to a swine . . . will as much prevail upon his assembly as St. Peter and St. Paul could do . . . upon the indisposed Greek, and *prejudicate* Jews. *Jer. Taylor*, Works (ed. 1835), I. 760.

prejudicately† (prẹ-jö'di-kāt-li), *adv.* In a prejudicate manner; with prejudice.

We are not too *prejudicately* to censure what has been produced for the proofs of their antiquity. *Evelyn*, Sylva, p. 504. (*Latham.*)

prejudication (prẹ-jö-di-kā'shọn), *n.* [< ML. *præjudicatio(n-)*, prejudice, damage (not found in lit. sense 'a judging beforehand'), < L. *præjudicare*, judge beforehand: see *prejudicate*.] 1. The act of prejudicating; prejudgment; a hasty or premature judgment.

Prejudications, having the force of a necessity, had blinded generation after generation of students. *De Quincey*, Herodotus.

2. In *Rom. law*: (*a*) A preceding judgment, sentence, or decision; a precedent. (*b*) A preliminary inquiry and determination about something that belonged to the matter in dispute.

prejudicative (prẹ-jö'di-kạ-tiv), *a.* [< *prejudicate* + *-ive*.] Forming an opinion or judgment without due examination; based on an opinion so formed.

A thing as ill beseeming philosophers as hasty *prejudicative* sentence political judges. *Dr. H. More*, Infinity of Worlds, Pref.

prejudice (prej'ọ̈-dis), *n.* [Early mod. E. also *prejudize*; < ME. *prejudice*, *prejudyse*, < OF. *prejudice*, also *prejuise*, a prejudgment, prejudice, F. *préjudice* = Pr. *prejudici* = Pg. *prejuizo* = Sp. *prejuicio*, *perjuicio* = It. *pregiudizio*, prejudice, < L. *præjudicium*, a preceding judgment, sentence, or decision, a precedent, a judicial examination before trial, damage, harm, prejudice, < *præ*, before, + *judicium*, a judgment, a judicial sentence, < *judex*, a judge: see *judge*. Cf. *prejudge*.] 1. An opinion or decision formed without due examination of the facts or arguments which are necessary to a just and impartial determination; a prejudgment; also, a state of mind which forms or induces prejudgment; bias or leaning, favorable or unfavorable; prepossession: when used absolutely, generally with an unfavorable meaning: as, a man of many *prejudices*; we should clear our minds of *prejudice*.

Nought mote hinder his quicke *prejudize*.
He had a sharpe foresight and working wit
That never idle was, ne once would rest a whit.
Spenser, F. Q., ii. 9. 49.

They who have already formed their judgment may justly stand suspected of *prejudice*. *Dryden*, Orig. and Prog. of Satire.

There is a *prejudice* in favour of the way of life to which a man has been educated. *Steele*, Spectator, No. 644.

Prejudice is the child of ignorance. *Sumner*, Hon. John Pickering.

2. Injury, as resulting from unfavorable prejudgment; detriment; hurt; damage.

Yis is here entent to make non ordinaunce in *prejudice* ne lettyng of ye comoun lawe. *English Gilds* (E. E. T. S.), p. 23.

My vengeance
Aim'd never at thy *prejudice*.
Ford, Broken Heart, v. 2.

In this cause no man's weakness is any *prejudice*; it has a thousand sons; if one man cannot speak, ten others can. *Emerson*, Address, W. I. Emancipation.

Legitimate prejudice. See *legitimate*.— **Without prejudice**, in *law*, without damage, namely to one's rights;

without detracting from one's rights or previous claims: a phrase used of overtures and communications between the parties to a controversy, importing that, should the negotiation fail, nothing that has passed shall be taken advantage of thereafter. Thus, should the defendant offer, *without prejudice*, to pay half the claim, the plaintiff cannot consider such offer as an admission of his having a right to some payment. =Syn. 2. Harm, detriment, disadvantage.

prejudice (prej'ǫ̈-dis), *v. t.*; pret. and pp. *prejudiced*, ppr. *prejudicing*. [< *prejudice*, *n.*] 1. To implant a prejudice in the mind of; bias; give an unfair bent to.

Who shall *prejudice* thy all-governing will?
Milton, On Def. of Humb. Remonst.

It is an irreparable injustice we are guilty of towards one another, when we are *prejudiced* by the looks and features of those whom we do not know. *Spectator*, No. 87.

2. To create a prejudice against; injure by prejudice; hurt, impair, or damage in any way.

In those parts wherein I have erred, I am sure I have not *prejudiced* the right by litigious arguments.
Bacon, Advancement of Learning, ii. 380.

From the beginning of January untill the midst of June, the egs being then most fit for that purpose, neither are they *prejudiced* by thunder. *Sandys*, Travailes, p. 98.

The power would be transferred from him that abused it to them that were *prejudiced* and injured by the abuse of it. *Milton*, Ans. to Salmasius.

Respect so far the holy laws of this fellowship as not to *prejudice* its perfect flower by your impatience for its opening. *Emerson*, Essays, 1st ser., p. 193.

=Syn. 1. To prepossess, warp.

prejudicial (prej-ǫ̈-dish'ạl), *a.* [< ME. *prejudiciall*, *prijudiciall*, < OF. *prejudicial*, *prejudiciel*, F. *préjudiciel* = Sp. Pg. *prejudicial* = It. *pregiudiziale*, harmful, < LL. *præjudicialis*, belonging to a previous judgment or examination, < L. *præjudicium*, a previous judgment or examination: see *prejudice*.] 1. Pertaining to prejudice or prejudgment; prejudiced; biased.

'Tis a sad irreverence, without due consideration, to look upon the actions of princes with a *prejudicial* eye.
Holyday.

2. Causing prejudice or injury; hurtful; detrimental; disadvantageous.

Provided alway that all theis articlis ne noone of them be noe wise deregatory, *prijudiciall*, ne contrary vnto the liberties and customys of the said Cite, and the comyn wele of the same. *English Gilds* (E. E. T. S.), p. 337.

The seate where the Syrens sit and chaunt their *preiudiciall* melodie.
Greene, Never too Late (Works, ed. Dyce, Int., p. xvii.).

Men of this temper are unserviceable and *prejudicial* in life. *Bacon*, Physical Fables, ii., Expl.

I must . . . continue to think those luxuries *prejudicial* to states by which so many vices are introduced.
Goldsmith, Des. Vil., Ded.

=Syn. 2. Deleterious, damaging.

prejudicial†, *v. t.* [< *prejudicial*, *a.*] To prejudice; injure; harm.

Take heed; the business,
If you defer, may *prejudicial* you
More than you think for.
B. Jonson, Tale of a Tub, ii. 1.

prejudicially (prej-ǫ̈-dish'ạl-i), *adv.* In a prejudicial manner; injuriously; disadvantageously.

prejudicialness (prej-ǫ̈-dish'ạl-nes), *n.* The state of being prejudicial; injuriousness.

prejudize†, *n.* An obsolete spelling of *prejudice*.

preke[1]†, *n.* and *v.* An obsolete form of *prick*.

preke[2] (prēk), *n.* A cuttlefish, the squid: same as *calamary*, 1.

preknowledge (prē-nol'ej), *n.* [< *pre-* + *knowledge*.] Prior knowledge; foreknowledge. *Coleridge*. (*Imp. Dict.*)

pre-Koranic (prē-kǭ-ran'ik), *a.* [< *pre-* + *Koran* + *-ic*.] Prior to the Koran.

An ancient title of the Deity among the *pre-Koranic* Arabs. *Cooper*, Archaic Dict., p. 30.

prelacy (prel'ạ̄-si), *n.*; pl. *prelacies* (-siz). [Early mod. E. *prelacie*, *prelasie*; < OF. *prelacie*, < ML. *prælatia*, the office or dignity of a prelate, < *prælatus*, a prelate: see *prelate*.] 1. The dignity or office of a prelate.

Lycomedes after enioyed that *Prelacie*, with foure Schœni of land added thereto. *Purchas*, Pilgrimage, p. 321.

Prelacies may be termed the greater benefices.
Ayliffe, Parergon.

Yet showed his meek and thoughtful eye
But little pride of *prelacy*. *Scott*, Marmion, vi. 11.

2. The system of church government by prelates, as distinguished from one in which all the clergy are on an equality.

Prelacy, . . . the ligament which tieth and connecteth the limbs of this body politic each to other, hath, instead of deserved honour, all extremity of disgrace.
Hooker, Eccles. Polity, vii. 18.

How many there are who call themselves Protestants who put *prelacy* and popery together as terms convertible!
Swift.

Sneer not at what *prelacy* holds the most pertinaciously of her doctrines.
Landor, William Penn and Lord Peterborough.

3. The order or rank of prelates; the body of prelates taken collectively.

Against the daie assigned, came the said archbishops, bishops, abbats, and other of the *prelacie*, both far and neere throughout all England.
Foxe, Martyrs, p. 241, an. 1220.

prelal† (prē'lạl), *a.* [< L. *prelum*, a press, a wine-press, < *premere*, press, bear down upon: see *press*[1].] Pertaining to printing; typographical: as, "*prelal* faults," *Fuller*. (*Imp. Dict.*)

prelate (prel'ạ̄t), *n.* [< ME. *prelate*, *prelat*, < OF. *prelat*, F. *prélat* = Sp. Pg. It. *prelato* = D. *prelaat* = MLG. *prelate* = MHG. *prêlâte*, *prêlât*, G. *prälat* = Sw. *prelat* = Dan. *prælat*, < ML. *prælatus*, a prelate, prop. adj., 'set over,' < L. *prælatus*, pp. of *præferre*, place or set before or above: see *prefer*.] An ecclesiastic of a higher order, having direct and not delegated authority over other ecclesiastics. Prelates include patriarchs, metropolitans, archbishops, bishops, and in the Roman Catholic Church also the heads of religious houses and certain other dignitaries.

A prioure that is a *prelate* of any churche Cathedralle
Above abbot or prioure with-in the diocise sitte he shalle.
Babees Book (E. E. T. S.), p. 103.

A *prelate* is that man, whosoever he be, that hath a flock to be taught of him. *Latimer*, Sermon of the Plough.

Hear him but reason in divinity, . . .
You would desire the king were made a *prelate*.
Shak., Hen. V., i. 1. 40.

prelate† (prel'ạ̄t), *v. i.* [< *prelate*, *n.*] To act as a prelate; perform the duties of a prelate.

Ye that be prelates, look well to your office; for right *prelating* is busy laboring, and not lording.
Latimer, Sermon of the Plough.

prelateity† (prel-ạ̄-tē'i-ti), *n.* [< *prelate* + *-e-ity*.] Prelacy; the theory or system of ecclesiastical government by prelates.

Whether Prelaty or *Prelateity* in abstract notion be this or that, it suffices me that I find it.
Milton, Church-Government, ii. 1.

prelately†, *a.* [< *prelate* + *-ly*[1].] Of a prelate; prelatical.

Their copes, perrours, and chasubles, when they be in their *prelately* pompous sacrifices.
Bp. Bale, Select Works, p. 526. (*Davies*.)

prelateship (prel'ạ̄t-ship), *n.* [< *prelate* + *-ship*.] The office or dignity of a prelate. *Foxe*, Martyrs, p. 280, an. 1118.

prelatess (prel'ạ̄t-es), *n.* [< *prelate* + *-ess*.] 1. A female prelate.

The adversary . . . raps up without pity the sage and rheumatick old *prelatess* with all her young Corinthian Laity to inquire for such a one.
Milton, Apology for Smectymnuus.

2. The wife of a prelate. [Humorous.]

"I cannot tell you how dreadfully indecent her conduct was." "Was it?" said the delighted countess. "Insufferable," said the *prelatess*.
Trollope, Barchester Towers, xxxvii.

prelatial (prē-lā'shạl), *a.* [< ML. *prælatia*, prelacy (see *prelacy*), + *-al*.] Prelatical; episcopal. [Rare.]

Servants came in bearing a large and magnificent portfolio; it was of morocco and of *prelatial* purple.
Disraeli, Lothair, xviii. (*Davies*.)

prelatic (prē-lat'ik), *a.* [< *prelate* + *-ic*.] Of or pertaining to prelacy or prelates; supporting prelacy.

Many on the *Prelatick* side, like the Church of Sardis, have a name to live, and yet are dead.
Milton, Church-Government, i. 6.

prelatical (prē-lat'i-kạl), *a.* [< *prelatic* + *-al*.] Same as *prelatic*.

We charge the *Prelatical* Clergy with Popery to make them odious. *Selden*, Table-Talk, p. 88.

We hold it [the Presbyterial government] no more to be the hedge and bulwark of religion than the Popish or *Prelatical* courts, or the Spanish Inquisition.
Milton, Articles of Peace with the Irish.

The *prelatical* party, which had endeavored again and again to colonize the coast, had tried only to fail.
Bancroft, Hist. U. S., I. 267.

prelatically (prē-lat'i-kạl-i), *adv.* As a prelate; with reference to prelacy.

prelation† (prē-lā'shon), *n.* [< ME. *prelacion*, < OF. *prelation*, *prelacion*, F. *prélation* = Sp. *prelacion* = Pg. *prelação* = It. *prelazione*, < LL. *prælatio(n-)*, a preferring, a preference, < L. *prælatus*, pp. of *præferre*, prefer: see *prelate*, *prefer*.] 1. The act of preferring or setting one thing above another; exaltation.

A direct preference or *prelation*, a preferring sin before grace. *Jer. Taylor*, Works (ed. 1835), I. 687.

2. The state of being preferred or exalted above others; preëminence; preferment.

Let, therefore, our life be moderate, our desires reasonable, our hopes little, our ends none in eminency and *prelation* above others. *Jer. Taylor*, Works (ed. 1835), I. 104.

prelatish† (prel'ạ̄t-ish), *a.* [< *prelate* + *-ish*[1].] Prelatical.

In any congregation of this island that hath not been altogether famished or wholly perverted with *prelatish* leaven, there will not want divers plain and solid men.
Milton, Apology for Smectymnuus, § viii.

prelatism (prel'ạ̄t-izm), *n.* [< *prelate* + *-ism*.] 1. Prelacy; episcopacy.

What doe wee suffer mis-shaped and enormous *Prelatisme*, as we do, thus to blanch and varnish her deformities with the faire colours, as before of Martyrdome, so now of Episcopacie? *Milton*, Reformation in Eng., i.

2. The belief in and advocacy of episcopacy: usually in an invidious sense.

The Councels themselves were foully corrupted with ungodly *Prelatisme*. *Milton*, Prelatical Episcopacy.

prelatist (prel'ạ̄t-ist), *n.* [< *prelate* + *-ist*.] An advocate of prelacy, or of the government of the church by bishops; an episcopalian.

Even the Grotian *prelatists* would wipe their mouths and speak me fairer if I could turn to them.
Baxter, Treatise of Self-denial, Pref.

The island now known as East Boston was occupied by Samuel Maverick, . . . himself a *prelatist*.
Bancroft, Hist. U. S., I. 266.

prelatize (prel'ạ̄t-īz), *v.*; pret. and pp. *prelatized*, ppr. *prelatizing*. [< *prelate* + *-ize*.] I.† *intrans.* To become prelatical; uphold or encourage prelacy; encourage or be imbued with episcopal doctrines and practices.

But being they are churchmen, we may rather suspect them for some *prelatizing* Spirits, that admire our bishopricks, not episcopacy. *Milton*, Reformation in Eng., ii.

As for Cyprians time, the cause was farre unlike; he indeed succeeded into an Episcopacy that began then to *Prelatize*. *Milton*, On Def. of Humb. Remonst.

II. *trans.* To bring under the influence and power of prelacy; influence toward prelacy.

Prelatizing the church of Scotland. *Palfrey*.

prelatry† (prel'ạ̄t-ri), *n.* [< *prelate* + *-ry*.] Prelacy.

The painted battlements and gaudy rottenness of *prelatry* . . . want but one puff of the king's to blow them down like a pasteboard house built of courtcards.
Milton, Reformation in Eng., ii.

prelature (prel'ạ̄-ṭūr), *n.* [< OF. *prelature*, F. *prélature* = Pr. Sp. Pg. *prelatura* = It. *prelatura* = G. *prälatur* = Sw. *prelatur*, < ML. *prælatura*, the office of a prelate, < *prælatus*, a prelate: see *prelate*.] 1. The state, dignity, or office of a prelate; also, the period during which the functions of a prelate are exercised.

Lycia . . . is chiefly celebrated for the holy Bishop S. Nicolas, whose praise is in all churches, though the time of his *prelature* is somewhat uncertain.
J. M. Neale, Eastern Church, i. 40.

2. Prelacy; the order of prelates.

The younger branches of the great princely families . . . by no means disdained the lofty titles, the dignity, the splendid and wealthy palaces of the *Prelature*.
Milman, Latin Christianity, xiv. 1.

prelaty† (prel'ạ̄-ti), *n.* [< OF. *prelatie*, *prelacie*, < ML. *prælatia*, prelacy: see *prelacy*.] 1. Prelacy; episcopacy.

It was not the prevention of schisme, but it was schisme it selfe, and the hatefull thirst of Lording in the Church, that first bestow'd a being upon *Prelaty*.
Milton, Church-Government, i. 6.

2. A prelatical office. [Rare.]

Laborious teaching is the most honourable *Prelaty* that one Minister can have above another in the Gospell.
Milton, Church-Government, i. 3.

prelect (prē-lekt'), *v.* [Also *prælect*; < L. *prælectus*, pp. of *prælegere*, read (anything) to or before (others), lecture upon, < *præ*, before, + *legere*, read: see *lection*, *legend*.] I. *trans.* To read publicly, as a lecture.

II. *intrans.* To read a lecture or discourse in public; hence, to discourse publicly; lecture.

I should seem not to have taken warning by the contempt which fell on that conceited Greek who had the vanity to *prelect* upon the military art before the conquerors of Asia. *Horsley*, Works, III. xxxix.

Spitting was shown to be a very difficult act, and publicly *prelected* upon about the same time, in the same great capital. *De Quincey*, Conversation.

prelection (prē-lek'shon), *n.* [Also *prælection*; < L. *prælectio(n-)*, a reading aloud to (others), < *prælegere*, pp. *prælectus*, read aloud: see *prelect*.] A lecture; a public discourse; a sermon.

You remember my last *prelection* of the division of the earth into parts real and imaginary?
Shirley, Witty Fair One, ii. 1.

An English ambassador, at the court of Philip II.'s viceroy, could indulge himself in imaginary *prelections* on the Æneid, in the last days of July, of the year of our Lord 1588! *Motley*, Hist. Netherlands, II. 403.

The counteraction of those errors by the *prelections* of godly and experienced ministers.
Hist. Anc. Merchants' Lecture.

prelector (prẹ-lek'tor), *n.* [Also *prælector*; < L. *prælector*, one who reads aloud to others, *prælegere*, read aloud: see *prelect*.] 1. A reader of discourses; a lecturer, particularly in a university.

> On the English "Odyssey" a criticism was published by Spence, at that time *Prelector* of Poetry at Oxford.
> *Johnson*, Pope.

2. Same as *father*, 12. *Dickens*, Dict. Oxf. and Camb.

preliation† (prē-li-ā'shọn), *n.* [< LL. *prœliatio(n-)*, fighting, < L. *prœliari*, join battle, fight, < *prœlium*, *prælium*, battle, fight.] Strife; contention.

> We have stirred the humors of the foolish inhabitants of the earth to insurrections, to warr and *præliation*.
> *Howell*, Parly of Beasts, p. 33. (*Davies*.)

prelibation (prē-li-bā'shọn), *n.* [= F. *prélibation* = Pg. *prelibação*, < LL. *prælibatio(n-)*, a tasting or taking away beforehand, < L. *prælibatus*, pp. of *prælibare*, taste beforehand, foretaste, < *præ*, before, + *libare*, take a little from, taste: see *libate*, *libation*.] 1. The act of tasting beforehand or by anticipation; a foretaste.

> In the first chapter of Genesis is also a *prelibation* of those illustrious truths which are more fully and circumstantially delivered in the second and third.
> *Dr. H. More*, Def. of Moral Cabbala, iv., App.

> *Prelibations*, as of some heavenly vintage, were inhaled by the Virgils of the day looking forward in the spirit of prophetic rapture. *De Quincey*, Philos. of Rom. Hist.

2. A previous libation; an offering made beforehand, as if in libation.

> The holy Jesus was circumcised, and shed the first fruits of his blood, offering them to God, like the *prelibation* of a sacrifice. *Jer. Taylor*, Works (ed. 1835), I. 51.

> There is Paradise that fears
> No forfeiture, and of its fruits he sends
> Large *prelibation* oft to saints below.
> *Cowper*, Task, v. 574.

preliminarily (prẹ-lim'i-nā̤-ri-li), *adv.* In a preliminary manner; as a preliminary; previously.

preliminary (prẹ-lim'i-nā̤-ri), *a.* and *n.* [= F. *préliminaire* = Sp. Pg. *preliminar* = It. *preliminare*, < ML. **præliminaris* (in adv. *præliminariter*), < L. *præ*, before, + *limen* (*limin-*), a threshold: see *limit*.] **I.** *a.* Preceding and leading up to something more important; introductory; preparatory; prefatory.

> I shall premise some *preliminary* considerations to prepare the way of holiness. *Jer. Taylor*, Works, III. iii.

> Swedish customs already appeared, in a *preliminary* decanter of lemon-colored brandy, a thimbleful of which was taken with a piece of bread and sausage, before the soup appeared. *B. Taylor*, Northern Travel, p. 14.

Preliminary injunction. See *ad interim injunction*, under *injunction*.—**Preliminary judgment.** See *judgment*. =**Syn.** *Preliminary*, *Preparatory*, *Introductory*, proemial. The first three agree in differing from the words compared under *previous*, in that they imply a necessary connection between that which precedes and that which follows, the latter being the essential thing. That which is *preliminary* literally brings one to the threshold of a discourse, contract, or the like; that which is *preparatory* prepares one, as to consider a proposition, subject, etc.; that which is *introductory* brings one inside the matter in question: as, a truce *preliminary* to a treaty; a disposition of troops *preparatory* to an attack; remarks *introductory* to the statement of one's theme.

II. *n.*; pl. *preliminaries* (-riz). Something which introduces or leads up to following matter or events; an introductory or preparatory statement, measure, action, etc.; a preface; a prelude.

> A serpent, which, as a *preliminary* to fascination, is said to fill the air with his peculiar odor.
> *Hawthorne*, Seven Gables, viii.

> On entering the abbey, she [Anne Boleyn] was led to the coronation chair, where she sat while the train fell into their places, and the *preliminaries* of the ceremonial were despatched. *Froude*, Sketches, p. 179.

prelingual (prē-ling'gwạl), *a.* [< *pre-* + *lingual*.] Preceding the acquisition of the power of speech; antecedent to the development of language.

> The first is the *prelingual* state, in which impressions of outward objects exist in the mind as inarticulate, voiceless concepts. *J. Owen*, Evenings with Skeptics, II. 364.

> Theoretical admirers of the *prelingual* period are, possibly, scattered here and there to this day.
> *F. Hall*, Mod. Eng., p. 334.

prelook†, *v. t.* [< *pre-* + *look*[1].] To look forward. [Rare.]

> It was the Lord that brake the bloody compackts of those
> That *preloked* on with yre, to slaughter me and myne.
> *Surrey*, Psalm lv.

prelude (prẹ-lūd' or prel'ūd), *v.*; pret. and pp. *preluded*, ppr. *preluding*. [< OF. *preluder*, F. *préluder* = It. *preludere*, prelude (in music) (cf. Sp. Pg. *preludiar*, prelude (in music); from the noun), < L. *præludere*, play beforehand by way of practice or rehearsal, sing beforehand, premise, preface, < *præ*, before, + *ludere*, play: see *ludicrous*. Cf. *allude*, *collude*, *elude*, *illude*. The E. verb is in part from the noun: see *prelude*, *n.*] **I.** *trans.* 1. To preface; prepare the way for; introduce as by a prelude; foreshadow.

> The literary change from alliteration to rhyme was mainly coeval with the Reformation; *preluded* by Chaucer a century and a half before.
> *E. Wadham*, Eng. Versification, p. 12.

> Here might be urged the necessity for *preluding* the study of moral science by the study of biological science.
> *H. Spencer*, Data of Ethics, § 38.

> Dan Chaucer, the first warbler, whose sweet breath
> *Preluded* those melodious bursts that fill
> The spacious times of great Elizabeth
> With sounds that echo still. *Tennyson*, Fair Women.

2. Specifically, in *music*, to play a prelude to; introduce by a musical prelude.

> And I—my harp would *prelude* woe—
> I cannot all command the strings;
> The glory of the sum of things
> Will flash across the chords and go.
> *Tennyson*, In Memoriam, lxxxviii.

3. To serve as a prelude to; precede as a musical prelude.

> Beneath the sky's triumphal arch
> This music sounded like a march,
> And with its chorus seemed to be
> *Preluding* some great tragedy.
> *Longfellow*, Occultation of Orion.

II. *intrans.* 1. To perform a prelude or introduction; give a preface to later action; especially, in *music*, to play a prelude, or introductory passage or movement, before beginning a principal composition.

> So Love, *preluding*, plays at first with Hearts,
> And after wounds with deeper piercing Darts.
> *Congreve*, tr. of Ovid's Art of Love, iii.

> She immediately rose and went to the piano—a somewhat worn instrument that seemed to get the better of its infirmities under the firm touch of her small fingers as she *preluded*. *George Eliot*, Daniel Deronda, xxxii.

2. To serve as a prelude or introduction; especially, to constitute a musical prelude.

> Sabbath of months! henceforth in him be blest,
> And *prelude* to the realm's perpetual rest!
> *Dryden*, Britannia Rediviva, l. 187.

> *Preluding* light, were strains of music heard.
> *Scott*, Vision of Don Roderick, The Vision, st. 33.

prelude (prē'lūd or prel'ūd), *n.* [Formerly also *preludium* (< ML.); < OF. *prelude*, F. *prélude* = Sp. Pg. It. *preludio*, < ML. **præludium*, a playing or performing beforehand, < L. *præludere*, play beforehand by way of practice or trial, premise, preface: see *prelude*, *v.*] 1. An introductory performance; a preliminary to an action, event, or work of broader scope and higher importance; a preface; presage; foreshadowing.

> A strange accident befell him, perchance not so worthy of memory for itself as for that it seemeth to have been a kind of *prelude* to his final period.
> *Sir H. Wotton*, Reliquiæ, p. 228.

> Maybe wildest dreams
> Are but the needful *preludes* of the truth.
> *Tennyson*, Princess, Conclusion.

2. In *music*, a prefatory or introductory piece, section, or movement, either extended and more or less independent, as in many elaborate fugues, in suites and sonatas, in oratorios and operas, or brief and strictly connected with what is to follow, as in various shorter works and at the opening of church services and before hymns. The organ prelude to a church service is often called a *voluntary*. Compare *intrada*, *introduction*, *overture*, *vorspiel*, etc.

> The title of *Prelude* has never been associated with any particular form in music, but is equally applicable to a phrase of a few bars or an extended composition in strict or free style. *Grove's Dict. Music*, III. 28.

=**Syn.** 1. *Preface*, etc. (see *introduction*), preliminary.—2. See *overture*, 4.

preluder (prē'lū-dėr or prel'ụ̄-dėr), *n.* [< *prelude* + *-er*[1].] One who preludes; one who plays a prelude.

> Invention, science, and execution Rousseau requires in a good *preluder*. *W. Mason*, Church Musick, p. 60.

preludial (prẹ-lū'di-ạl), *a.* [< *prelude* (ML. **præludium*) + *-i-al*.] Pertaining to a prelude; serving to introduce; introductory. *Edinburgh Rev.*

preludious (prẹ-lū'di-us), *a.* [< *prelude* (ML. **præludium*) + *-ous*.] Of the nature of a prelude; introductory. [Rare.]

> The office of Adam was *preludious* to and typical of the office of Christ.
> *Dr. H. More*, Phil. Writings, Gen. Pref., p. xxv.

preludium† (prẹ-lū'di-um), *n.* [< ML. **præludium*: see *prelude*.] An introduction; prefatory action or state; a prelude; a presage.

> This is a short *preludium* to a challenge.
> *Beau. and Fl.*, Captain, v. 1.

> Scared with some terrible apparition, . . . a presage and *preludium* of hell approaching, they cry out that they are damned. *Rev. S. Ward*, Sermons, p. 69.

prelumbar (prē-lum'bạ̈r), *a.* [< L. *præ*, before, + *lumbus*, loin: see *lumbar*[1].] In *anat.*, in front of the loins or of the lumbar vertebræ.

prelusion (prē-lū'zhọn), *n.* A prelude. [Rare.]

prelusive (prẹ-lū'siv), *a.* [< L. *prælusus*, pp. of *præludere*, play beforehand (see *prelude*), + *-ive*.] Serving as a prelude; introductory; indicative of the future; premonitory.

> This monarchy, before it was to settle in your majesty and your generations, . . . had these *prelusive* changes and varieties. *Bacon*, Advancement of Learning, ii. 132.

> Her foot pressed the strand,
> With step *prelusive* to a long array
> Of woes and degradations.
> *Wordsworth*, Mary Queen of Scots.

prelusively (prẹ-lū'siv-li), *adv.* Same as *prelusorily*.

prelusorily (prẹ-lū'sọ-ri-li), *adv.* By way of introduction or prelude; prefatorily; previously.

prelusory (prẹ-lū'sọ-ri), *a.* [< L. *prælusus*, pp. of *præludere*, play beforehand (see *prelude*), + *-ory*.] Introductory; prelusive.

> But the truth is, these are but the προπυγμαὶ or σκιαμαχίαι, the *prelusory* lighter brandishings of these swords.
> *Hammond*, Works, IV. 470.

premandibular (prē-man-dib'ụ̄-lạ̈r), *a.* [< L. *præ*, before, + NL. *mandibula*, mandible: see *mandibular*.] Situated in advance of the lower jaw, as a bone of some reptiles; predentary.

premaniacal (prē-mạ̄-nī'ạ-kạl), *a.* [< L. *præ*, before, + *mania*, madness (see *mania*), + *-ac-al*. Cf. *maniacal*.] Previous to insanity, or to an attack of mania.

> The *premaniacal* semblance of mental brilliancy.
> *Maudsley*, Body and Will, p. 297.

premature (prē-mạ̄-tūr'), *a.* [= Sp. Pg. It. *prematuro* (cf. F. *prématuré*, < L. as if **præmaturatus*), < L. *præmaturus*, early ripe, as fruit; hence very early, too early, untimely (said of actions, events, seasons, etc.), in ML. also very ripe in judgment, < *præ*, before, + *maturus*, ripe, mature: see *mature*.] Arriving too early at maturity; mature or ripe before the proper time; hence, coming into existence or occurring too soon; too early; untimely; overhasty.

> The report of our misfortunes might be malicious or *premature*. *Goldsmith*, Vicar, iii.

> Bashfulness and apathy are a tough husk, in which a delicate organization is protected from *premature* ripening. *Emerson*, Friendship.

Premature labor. See *labor*[1].

prematurely (prē-mạ̄-tūr'li), *adv.* In a premature manner; before the proper time; too early; overhastily.

prematureness (prē-mạ̄-tūr'nes), *n.* Prematurity.

prematurity (prē-mạ̄-tū'ri-ti), *n.* [= F. *prématurité* = Pg. *prematuridade*; as *premature* + *-ity*.] The state of being premature, or too early in development.

> It was the bewilderment and *prematurity* of the same instinct which restlessly impelled them to materialize the ideas of the Greek philosophers, and to render them practical by superstitious uses. *Coleridge*, The Friend, ii. 10.

premaxilla (prē-mak-sil'ạ̈), *n.*; pl. *premaxillæ* (-ē). [NL. *præmaxilla*, < L. *præ*, before, + *maxilla*, jaw-bone: see *maxilla*.] The intermaxillary or premaxillary bone. See *intermaxillary*.

premaxillary (prē-mak'si-lā̤-ri), *a.* and *n.*; pl. *premaxillaries* (-riz). [Also *præmaxillary*; < L. *præ*, before, + *maxilla*, jaw-bone: see *maxillary*.] **I.** *a.* Situated in front of or at the fore part of the maxilla; intermaxillary; pertaining to the premaxilla.

II. *n.* The premaxillary bone; the intermaxillary.

premaxillomaxillary (prē-mak-sil-ō-mak'si-lā̤-ri), *a.* Same as *maxillopremaxillary*. *Huxley*.

premet, *a.* A Middle English form of *prime*.

premediate (prẹ-mē'di-āt), *v. t.*; pret. and pp. *premediated*, ppr. *premediating*. [< *pre-* + *mediate*.] To advocate, as a cause. *Halliwell*. [Rare.]

premeditate (prẹ-med'i-tāt), *v.*; pret. and pp. *premeditated*, ppr. *premeditating*. [< L. *præmeditatus*, pp. of *præmeditari* (> It. *premeditare* = Sp. Pg. *premeditar* = F. *préméditer*), consider or think beforehand, < *præ*, before, + *meditari*, consider, meditate: see *meditate*.] **I.** *trans.* To meditate beforehand; think about and contrive previously; precogitate.

> Here, pale with fear, he doth *premeditate*
> The dangers of his loathsome enterprise.
> *Shak.*, Lucrece, l. 183.

> An express *premeditated* design to take away his life.
> *Blackstone*, Com., IV. iv. 196.

II. *intrans.* To meditate beforehand; deliberate upon future action.

They [the apostles] studied for no tongue, they spake with all; of themselves they were rude, and knew not so much as how to *premeditate*; the Spirit gave them speech and eloquent utterance. *Hooker*, Eccles. Polity, iii. 8.

Take no thought beforehand what ye shall speak, neither do ye *premeditate*. Mark xiii. 11.

premeditate† (prē-med'i-tāt), *a.* [< L. *præmeditatus*, pp.: see the verb.] **1.** Contrived by previous thought; premeditated.

Whatsoever a man shall have occasion to speak of, if he will take the pains, he may have it in effect *premeditate*, and handled "in thesi." *Bacon*, Advancement of Learning, ii. 219.

2. Using premeditation; disposed to premeditate.

A *premeditate* and resolute mind lightly shaketh off the heaviest crosses of malice. *G. Harvey*, Four Letters.

premeditatedly (prē-med'i-tā-ted-li), *adv.* Premeditately; deliberately.

Least of all could she dare *premeditatedly* a vague future in which the only certain condition was indignity. *George Eliot*, Daniel Deronda, xliv.

premeditatedness (prē-med'i-tā-ted-nes), *n.* The state or character of being premeditated, or planned beforehand.

premeditately (prē-med'i-tāt-li), *adv.* With premeditation; after previous deliberation; intentionally.

He that *premeditately* cozens one does not cozen all, but only because he cannot. *Feltham*, Resolves, ii. 62.

Accordingly, in all the number of laws passed with regard to the plantations, the words which distinguish revenue laws specifically as such were, I think, *premeditately* avoided. *Burke*, American Taxation.

premeditation (prē-med-i-tā'shon), *n.* [< OF. *premeditation*, F. *préméditation* = Sp. *premeditacion* = Pg. *premeditação* = It. *premeditazione*, < L. *præmeditatio(n-)*, a considering beforehand, < *præmeditari*, pp. *præmeditatus*, consider beforehand: see *premeditate*.] **1.** The act of premeditating; previous deliberation; forethought; precogitation.

Ye haue nowe hard what *premeditations* be expedient before that a man take on him the gouernance of a publyke weale. *Sir T. Elyot*, The Governour, ii. 1.

He [Pitt] spoke without *premeditation*; but his speech followed the course of his own thoughts, and not the course of the previous discussion. *Macaulay*, William Pitt.

2. Previous contrivance or design formed: as, the *premeditation* of a crime. In *law*, *premeditation* is by some authorities understood to mean previous deliberation, by others only previous intent, however sudden, and however quickly put into execution.

premeditative (prē-med'i-tā-tiv), *a.* [< *premeditate* + *-ive*.] Using premeditation; characterized by premeditation; showing thought for the future.

Every first thing accordingly shows some *premeditative* token of every last. *Bushnell*, Nature and the Supernat., p. 202.

premenstrual (prē-men'strọ̈-al), *a.* [< L. *præ*, before, + *menstrua*, menstrua, + *-al*.] Preceding menstruation.

premeridian (prē-mẹ-rid'i-an), *a.* [< L. *præ*, before, + *meridies*, midday: see *meridian*.] Immediately before midday; specifically [*cap.*], in *geol.*, according to Professor H. D. Rogers's nomenclature of the Paleozoic rocks, noting that part of the series which lies between the Meridian and the Scalent. It corresponds to part of the Lower Helderberg of the New York Survey.

premerit† (prẹ-mer'it), *v. t.* [< *pre-* + *merit*.] To merit or deserve beforehand.

They did not forgive Sir John Hotham, who had so much *premerited* of them. *Eikon Basilike*.

premial (prē'mi-al), *a.* [< LL. *præmialis*, used as a reward, < L. *præmium*, a reward: see *premium*.] Same as *premiant*.

premiant (prē'mi-ant), *a.* [< L. *præmian(t-)s*, ppr. of *præmiari*, stipulate for a reward: see *premiate*.] Serving to reward. *Baxter.* (*Webster.*)

premiate (prē'mi-āt), *v. t.*; pret. and pp. *premiated*, ppr. *premiating*. [< L. *præmiatus*, pp. of *præmiari*, stipulate for a reward, < *præmium*, a reward: see *premium*.] To reward with a premium: as, a *premiated* essay. [Rare.]

The ten *premiated* designs have been photographed. *Penn. Monthly*, Sept., 1873, p. 598.

premices† (prem'i-sez), *n. pl.* [< F. *prémices*, pl., = Sp. *primicia* = Pg. *primicias*, pl., = It. *primizia*, < L. *primitiæ*, *primiciæ*, first-fruits, < *primus*, first: see *prime*.] First-fruits. Also spelled *premice*.

A charger, or large platter, was yearly filled with all sorts of fruits, which were offered to the gods at their festivals as the *premices* or first gatherings. *Dryden*, Orig. and Prog. of Satire.

premier (prē'mi-ėr), *a.* and *n.* [< F. *premier*, first, chief, as a noun a chief, leader, < L. *primarius*, of the first rank, < *primus*, first: see *primary*.] **I.** *a.* **1.** First in importance; chief. [Rare.]

The Spaniard challengeth the *premier* place, in regard of his dominions. *Camden*, Remains.

Surely Canterbury, as the metropolitical city, and the seat of the primate of all England, ought to contain the *premier* parish church. *N. and Q.*, 7th ser., II. 168.

2. First in time; earliest in appearance or occurrence; specifically, in the English peerage, first in the order of precedence, which is now the order of date of creation.

Henry Beauchamp, son of Richard and Isabel, was at the age of nineteen created *premier* Earl of England, and three days after he was made Duke of Warwick, . . . a senseless jumble [*i. e.*, these creations and adjustments of precedence which followed], soon liquidated by a more egregious act of folly, the king [Henry VI.] with his own hand creating the young Duke of Warwick King of the Isle of Wight. *Walpole*, Anecdotes of Painting, I. ii.

The first opera of which we have any record is a translation of "Arsinoë," an Italian opera written by Stanzani of Bologna, for the theatre of that town, in 1677, and here is the *premier* advertisement of opera in England. *J. Ashton*, Social Life in Reign of Queen Anne, II. 28.

II. *n.* The first minister of state; the prime or premier minister.

Stand forth and tell yon *Premier* youth [Pitt]
The honest, open, naked truth.
Burns, Prayer to the Scotch Representatives.

A shout rose again, . . . a shout
More joyful than the city roar that hails
Premier or king! *Tennyson*, Princess, Conclusion.

premier (prē'mi-ėr), *v. i.* [< *premier*, *n.*] To govern as premier; serve as prime minister. [Rare.]

Nae sage North now, nor sager Sackville,
To watch and *premier* o'er the pack vile.
Burns, Address of Beelzebub.

première (prō-miãr'), *a.* and *n.* [F., fem. of *premier*, first: see *premier*.] **I.** *a.* First or foremost or chief, as said of women.

Five new *première* dancers, headed by Mlle. Lile from the Berlin Opera House, will arrive in the city the present week. *Music and Drama*, XI. vii. 7.

Première danseuse, the principal or leading female dancer in a ballet.

II. *n.* A woman who has a leading part to perform. Specifically—(*a*) In *theatrical representations*, a leading lady; the principal actress. (*b*) In *dancing*, a première danseuse. (*c*) In *dressmaking*, a forewoman.

premiership (prē'mi-ėr-ship), *n.* [< *premier* + *-ship*.] The state or dignity of being first or foremost; especially, the dignity or office of a prime minister.

On returning to England he [Wellesley] made one last bid for the *premiership*. *The Academy*, No. 900, p. 65.

premillenarian (prē-mil-e-nā'ri-an), *a.* and *n.* [< L. *præ*, before, + NL. *millennium*, millennium, + *-arian*. Cf. *millenarian*.] **I.** *a.* **1.** Of or pertaining to premillennialism.—**2.** Same as *premillennial*.

The rejection of the *pre-millenarian* advent has never been understood as required by our ordination vows. *Princeton Rev.*, March, 1879, p. 419.

II. *n.* A believer in the doctrine of premillennialism.

premillenarianism (prē-mil-e-nā'ri-an-izm), *n.* Same as *premillennialism*. *Andover Rev.*, VII. 201.

premillennial (prē-mi-len'i-al), *a.* [< L. *præ*, before, + NL. *millennium*, millennium, + *-al*. Cf. *millennial*.] Preceding the millennium; existing or occurring before the millennium.

The dogma of the *Pre-Millennial* Advent of Christ. *Princeton Rev.*, March, 1879, p. 415.

premillennialism (prē-mi-len'i-al-izm), *n.* [< *premillennial* + *-ism*.] The doctrine that the second coming of Christ will precede the millennium. See *millennium*, *millenarianism*.

premillennialist (prē-mi-len'i-al-ist), *n.* [< *premillennial* + *-ist*.] A premillenarian. *Bibliotheca Sacra*, XLV. 252.

premio†, *n.* [< Sp. Pg. It. *premio*, premium: see *premium*.] A premium.

It is just as if the ensurers brought in a catalogue of ensured ships lost, taking no notice of ships arrived and *premios*. *Roger North*, Examen, p. 490. (*Davies.*)

premisal (prẹ-mī'zal), *n.* [< *premise* + *-al*.] The act of premising; also, a prefatory statement; a premise. [Rare.]

And here, by way of *premisal*, it must be in a lawful and warrantable way. *Culverwell*, Mount Ebal, 90. (*Latham.*)

premise, premiss (prem'is), *n.* [More prop. *premiss*, but *premise* is the more common spelling; < ME. *premisse* (in pl. *premissis*), < OF. *premisse*, F. *prémisse*, usually in pl. *prémisses*, premises (in logic), = Sp. *premisa* = Pg. *premissa* = It. *premessa*, < ML. *præmissa*, sc. *propositio* or *conditio*, a premise, lit. 'a proposition or condition set forth beforehand,' fem. of L. *præmissus*, pp. of *præmittere*, send before, put or set before or in advance: see *premit*.] **1.** A judgment causing another judgment; a proposition belief in which leads to the belief in another proposition called a conclusion; a proposition from which, with or without others, something is inferred or concluded.

Passion violently snatches at the conclusion, but is inconsiderate and incurious concerning the *premises*. *Jer. Taylor*, Works (ed. 1835), I. 89.

He goes on building many faire and pious conclusions upon false and wicked *premises*, which deceave the common Reader not well discerning the antipathy of such connexions. *Milton*, Eikonoklastes, ii.

2†. A condition set forth; a supposition.

Iff forsoth the said maister, wardons, and theere successours, the *premissis*, as of there parti expressed and declared, hoold and trewly fulfill, . . . then the said writyng obligatorie of xx[li]. shalbe hadd for nought. *English Gilds* (E. E. T. S.), p. 320.

Here is my hand; the *premises* observed,
Thy will by my performance shall be served.
Shak., All's Well, ii. 1. 204.

The doctor happ'ly may persuade. Go to;
'Shalt give his worship a new damask suit
Upon the *premises*. *B. Jonson*, Alchemist, ii. 1.

3. *pl.* In *law*, what has been stated before or above (in a document); the aforesaid. (*a*) That part of the beginning of a deed or conveyance where the names of the parties, their additions, and the consideration and moving cause of the instrument are stated. (*b*) More commonly, that part of a deed or conveyance where the subject-matter of the grant is stated or described in full, afterward referred to collectively as the *premises*. Hence—**4.** *pl.* The subject of a conveyance; lands and houses or tenements; a house or building and the outhouses and places belonging to it.

During this period the family mansion had been consigned to the charge of a kinsman, who was allowed to make it his home for the time being, in consideration of keeping the *premises* in thorough repair. *Hawthorne*, Seven Gables, xiii.

In the premises, in relation to a subject which has been mentioned: as, he had no authority *in the premises*.—**Major premise.** See *major*, 5.—**Minor premise.** See *minor*.

premise (prẹ-mīz'), *v.*; pret. and pp. *premised*, ppr. *premising*. [< L. *præmissus*, pp. *præmittere*, send before or forward: see *premit*. For the form, cf. *premise*, *n.*, *demise*.] **I.** *trans.* **1.** To set forth or make known beforehand, as introductory to the main subject; offer previously, as something to explain or aid in understanding what follows; lay down as an antecedent proposition.

Foure only be of two times, and eight of three times, the rest compounds of the *premised* two sorts. *Puttenham*, Arte of Eng. Poesie, p. 92.

I shall *premise* some preliminary considerations. *Jer. Taylor*, Works (ed. 1835), II. 20.

Let me *premise*, twelve months have flown away,
Swiftly or sadly, since the happy day.
Crabbe, Works, VII. 202.

2†. To send before the time.

O let the vile world end,
And the *premised* flames of the last day
Knit earth and heaven together!
Shak., 2 Hen. VI., v. 2. 41.

II. *intrans.* To state premises; preface an argument or other discourse with premises.

I must *premise* with three circumstances. *Swift.*

premiss, *n.* See *premise*.

premit† (prẹ-mit'), *v. t.* [= OF. *premetre*, *premettre* = It. *premettere*, send forward, < L. *præmittere*, send forward, send in advance, despatch, < *præ*, before, + *mittere*, send: see *mission*. Cf. *admit*, *commit*, *demit*, etc. Hence (< L. *præmittere*) ult. E. *premise*, *n.*, *premise*, *v.*, etc.] To premise.

He doth, in this and the next verse, *premit* a general doctrine thereunto. *Hutcheson*, On John, p. 299. (*Jamieson.*)

premium (prē'mi-um), *n.* [Early mod. E. *premye* (q. v.), < OF. *premie* = Sp. Pg. It. *premio*, reward, premium; < L. *præmium*, profit derived from booty, booty, game, prey; in general (the usual sense), profit, advantage, and in particular, reward, recompense; contr. of **præimium*, < *præ*, before, + *emere*, take, buy: see *emption*, etc.] **1.** A reward; a recompense given for a particular action or line of conduct. Specifically—(*a*) A prize to be won by competition. (*b*) A bonus: an extra sum paid as an incentive; anything given as an inducement. (*c*) A fee paid for the privilege of being taught a trade or profession.

2. That which is given for the loan of money; interest.

Men never fail to bring in their money upon a land-tax when the *premium* or interest allowed them is suited to the hazard they run. *Addison*, Freeholder, No. 20.

3. In *insurance*, the amount paid or agreed to be paid in one sum or periodically to insurers as the consideration for a contract of insurance. See *insurance*, 2.—4. In *banking* and *currency*, the difference by which the value of one metallic currency exceeds that of another of the same denomination, or by which a metallic currency exceeds a paper currency of the same denomination in the same country; agio: the opposite of *discount*, or *disagio*, which is the amount by which the value of one currency has depreciated when compared with another. Thus, during the civil war in the United States, when $125 in paper currency was demanded for $100 in gold, the gold dollar was said to be *at a premium* of 25, as compared with paper, but it might more correctly be said that paper was *at a discount* of 20 per cent. as compared with gold.—5. In *stock-broking*, etc., the percentage of difference by which the market price of shares, stocks, bonds, etc., exceeds their face-value or the sum originally paid for them: thus, when stock originally issued at $100 per share sells at $140 per share, it is said to be *at a premium* of 40 per cent.—**At a premium**, above par; at a higher price than the original cost or normal value; hence, difficult to obtain; rare and valuable.—**Premium note**, a note given in place of payment of the whole or a part of an insurance premium.

Premna (prem'nä), *n.* [NL. (Linnæus, 1767), so called in allusion to the short stem or low tree-trunk; < Gr. πρέμνον, a stump.] A genus of gamopetalous shrubs and trees of the order *Verbenaceæ* and tribe *Viticeæ*. It is characterized by the four didynamous stamens included within the short, small, and nearly equally four-lobed corolla, and by the single four-celled drupe. There are about 42 species, natives of warm regions of the Old World. They bear opposite entire or toothed leaves and rather loose cymes of white or bluish flowers, in panicles or corymbs, or condensed into an elongated pyramidal inflorescence. *P. Taitensis* of the Fiji Islands, etc., there called *yaro*, affords wood for building, and its bark enters into the drug tonga. See *headache-tree* and *tonga*.

premolar (prē-mō'lär), *a.* and *n.* [Also *præmolar*; < L. *præ*, before, + *molaris*, molar: see *molar*[1].] **I.** *a.* Anterior in position, and prior in time, to a molar, as a tooth; situated in advance of molars; deciduous, as a molar; pertaining in any way to premolars: as, a *premolar* tooth; *premolar* dentition; the *premolar* part of a maxillary bone.

II. *n.* A milk-molar; a molar of the deciduous dentition; a tooth which in the permanent dentition replaces a milk-molar. Such teeth occur as a rule in mammals which have a diphyodont dentition. All the molars or grinders of the first set are technically premolars, and all those which succeed and replace them in the second set are also premolars, whatever their size, form, or number. They are usually smaller than true molars, and also less complicated in structure; but such distinctions do not hold in every case. Premolars are developed in an anterior part of the maxillary bone, and, when they coexist with true molars, are always situated in front of the latter. The first, foremost, or most anterior premolar is often specialized, and is then known as the *canine*. Excepting this tooth, the typical though not the most frequent number of premolars is three above and below on each side; there are rarely more than three, oftenest two, as in man; sometimes one or none, as in rodents. The two premolars of man are commonly called *bicuspids*. In dental formulæ the symbol of *premolar* is *pm* or *p*. The premolar formula of man is $pm. \frac{2-2}{2-2}$

premonarchical (prē-mō-när'ki-kal), *a.* [< *pre-* + *monarchical*.] Prior to monarchy; before adopting the monarchical form of government.

> *Premonarchical* Israel is represented as a hierocracy, and Samuel as its head. — *Encyc. Brit.*, XIII. 403.

premonish (prē-mon'ish), *v.* [Formerly also *præmonish*; < L. *præmonitus*, pp. of *præmonere* (> Pg. *premunir*), forward, < *præ*, before, + *monere*, remind, advise, warn: see *monish*. Cf. *præmunire*.] **I.** *trans.* To forewarn; caution beforehand; notify previously.

> Man cannot brook poor friends. This inconstant charity is hateful, as our English phrase *premonisheth*: "Love me little, and love me long." — *Rev. T. Adams*, Works, II. 418.

> We enter'd by the drawbridg, which has an invention to let one fall, if not *præmonished*. — *Evelyn*, Diary, May 2, 1644.

II. *intrans.* To give warning or advice beforehand; forebode.

> Your lordship doth very seasonably *premonish*. — *Chapman and Shirley*, Admiral of France, v.

> My love is virtuous; were it otherwise,
> I should elect, as you *premonish*, youth
> And prodigal blood. — *Shirley*, Love Tricks, ii. 2.

premonishment (prē-mon'ish-ment), *n.* [< *premonish* + *-ment*.] The act of premonishing; previous warning or admonition; previous information. [Rare.]

> After these *premonishments*, I will come to the compartition itself. — *Sir H. Wotton*, Reliquiæ, i. 40.

premonition (prē-mō-nish'on), *n.* [< OF. *premonition*, *premonicion* = It. *premonizione*, < LL. *præmonitio(n-)*, a forewarning, < L. *præmonere*, forewarn: see *premonish*.] The act of premonishing or forewarning; hence, a previous warning or notification of subsequent events; previous information.

> Such as haue not *premonition* hereof, and consideration of the causes alledged, would peradventure reproue and disgrace euery Romance or short historicall ditty, for that they be not written in long meeters or verses. — *Puttenham*, Arte of Eng. Poesie, p. 34.

> God hath sent all his servants, the prophets, and so done all that is necessary for *premonition*. — *Donne*, Sermons, vi.

premonitive (prē-mon'i-tiv), *a.* [< L. *præmonitus*, pp. of *præmonere*, forewarn (see *premonish*), + *-ive*.] Premonitory. *Imp. Dict.*

premonitor (prē-mon'i-tor), *n.* [< LL. *præmonitor*, a forewarner, < L. *præmonere*, forewarn: see *premonish*.] One who forewarns; a premonitory messenger or token.

> Some such like uncouth *premonitors* . . . God sends purposely to awaken our security. — *Bp. Hall*, Soliloquies, lxxix.

premonitorily (prē-mon'i-tō-ri-li), *adv.* By way of premonition.

premonitory (prē-mon'i-tō-ri), *a.* [= F. *prémonitoire*, < LL. *præmonitorius*, that gives previous warning (see *premonitor*), < L. *præmonere*, forewarn: see *premonish*.] Giving premonition; serving to warn or notify beforehand.

> In *premonitory* judgements God will take good words and sincere intents; but in peremptory, nothing but reall performances. — *N. Ward*, Simple Cobler, p. 46.

> All the signs and silences
> *Premonitory* of earthquake.
> — *Browning*, Ring and Book, I. 192.

Premonstrant (prē-mon'strant), *n.* [An accom. form (as if < L. *præmonstran(t-)s*, ppr. of *præmonstrare*, show beforehand, guide: see *premonstrate*) of F. *Prémontrés*, pl. (cf. Sp. *Premonstratense*, *Premostratense* = Pg. *Premonstratense* = It. *Premostratese* (?), < ML. *Præmonstratensis*, a Premonstrant), < *Prémontré*, near Laon, in France, where the order was founded (see def.). The name *Prémontré* is variously explained as orig. *pré montré*, < L. *pratum monstratum*, a meadow pointed out (sc. to the founder in a dream); or *près montré*, pointed out close at hand (*près*, near, close at hand); or < L. *præmonstratus*, pointed out beforehand: see *premonstrate*.] A member of a Roman Catholic religious order comprising monks and nuns, founded by St. Norbert at Prémontré near Laon, in France, 1119. The order was once very flourishing, but now numbers only a few houses, principally in the Austrian empire. The Premonstrants were also called *Norbertines*, and in England *White Canons* (from their garb). Also *Premonstratensian*.

premonstrate† (prē-mon'strāt), *v. t.* [< L. *præmonstratus*, pp. of *præmonstrare* (> It. *premostrare*), show beforehand, guide: see *Premonstrant*.] To foreshow; represent beforehand.

> This (text, Luke xii. 20) is the covetous man's scripture; and both (like an unflattering glass) presents his present condition, what he is, and (like a fatal book) *premonstrates* his future state, what he shall be. — *Rev. T. Adams*, Works, II. 123.

Premonstratensian (prē-mon-strā-ten'si-an), *a.* and *n.* [Also *Præmonstratensian*; < ML. *Premonstratensis*, a Premonstrant: see *Premonstrant*.] **I.** *a.* Of or relating to the Premonstrants: as, the *Premonstratensian* order.

> The *Præmonstratensian* Priory of Langdon. — *R. W. Dixon*, Hist. Church of Eng., v.

II. *n.* Same as *Premonstrant*.

> A procession of monks, Carmelites, Benedictines, *Premonstratencians*. — *The American*, VIII. 249.

premonstration† (prē-mon-strā'shon), *n.* [= It. *premostrazione*, < LL. *præmonstratio(n-)*, a showing beforehand: see *premonstrate*.] The act of premonstrating or foreshowing; indication or revelation of future events.

> If such demonstration was made for the beginning, then the like *premonstration* is to be looked for in the fulfilling. — *Shelford*, Learned Discourses, p. 323.

premonstrator† (prē-mon'strā-tor), *n.* [< L. *præmonstrator*, one who points out beforehand, a guide: see *premonstrate*.] One who or that which premonstrates, or shows beforehand. *Imp. Dict.*

premorse (prē-môrs'), *a.* [< L. *præmorsus*, pp. of *præmordere*, bite in front or at the end, < *præ*, before, + *mordere*, bite: see *mordant*.] 1. Bitten off.—2. In *bot.* and *entom.*, having the apex irregularly truncate, as if bitten or broken: as, a *premorse* leaf or root; *premorse* elytra; etc.

Premosaic (prē-mō-zā'ik), *a.* [< *pre-* + *Mosaic*.] Previous to the time of Moses; relating to times previous to the life and writings of Moses: as, *Premosaic* history.

premotion (prē-mō'shon), *n.* [< F. *prémotion* = Sp. *premocion* = Pg. *premoção*, < ML. **præmotio(n-)*, < L. *præmovere*, pp. *præmotus*, move beforehand: see *premove*.] Previous motion or excitement to action.

> It followeth . . . that no words or writings are of certain truth upon any account of God's inspiration or *premotion*, because God not only can, but doth, cause all the untruths that are spoken or written in the world; therefore no faith in God's revelation hath any sure foundation, . . . and so all religion is dashed out at a stroke. — *Baxter*, Divine Life, i. 10.

> Many Jesuit writers of note differ from Molina in almost all, save the one essential point of making the human will "a faculty that, even when all conditions of activity are present, is free either to act as it chooses or not to act at all." But this thesis is nothing more than the mere denial of "physical *premotion*." — *Mind*, XII. 266.

premove (prē-möv'), *v. t.*; pret. and pp. *premoved*, ppr. *premoving*. [< LL. *præmovere*, move beforehand, stir up, < L. *præ*, before, + *movere*, move: see *move*.] To incite or excite; effect by premotion.

> It followeth that we have no certainty when God *premoveth* an apostle or prophet to speak true, and when to speak falsely. — *Baxter*, Divine Life, i. 10.

premultiply (prē-mul'ti-plī), *v. t.*; pret. and pp. *premultiplied*, ppr. *premultiplying*. [< *pre-* + *multiply*.] To multiply by an operative factor written before the factor operated on.

premunire, *n.* and *v.* See *præmunire*.

premunite† (prē-mū-nīt'), *v. t.* [< L. *præmunitus*, pp. of *præmunire*, *præmœnire* (> It. *premunire* = F. *prémunir*), fortify or defend in front, < *præ*, before, + *munire*, *mœnire*, defend with a wall, fortify: see *munition*.] To fortify beforehand; guard or make secure in advance.

> For the better removing of the exception, which might minister any scruple, &c., I thought good to *premunite* the succeeding treatise with this preface. — *Fotherby*, Atheomastix, Pref. (*Latham.*)

premunition (prē-mū-nish'on), *n.* [= F. *prémunition*, < L. *præmunitio(n-)*, a fortifying or strengthening beforehand, < *præmunire*, pp. *præmunitus*, fortify or defend in front or in advance: see *premunite*.] The act of fortifying or guarding beforehand; a measure taken in advance to secure immunity from peril or objection.

> No: let me tell thee, prevision is the best prevention, and premonition the best *premunition*. — *Rev. S. Ward*, Sermons, p. 53.

premunitory (prē-mū'ni-tō-ri), *a.* [Also *præmunitory*; < *premunite* + *-ory*.] Belonging or relating to a præmunire.

> The clergy were summoned by the *premunitory* clause. — *Hody*, Hist. of Convocation, p. 402. (*Latham.*)

premye†, *n.* [< L. *præmium*, reward, recompense: see *premium*.] A gift.

> The cytie of London through his mere graunt and *premye*
> Was first privyleged to have both mayer and shryve,
> Where before hys tyme it had but baylyves onlye.
> — *Bale*, Kynge Johan, p. 85. (*Halliwell.*)

Prenanthes (prē-nan'thēz), *n.* [NL. (Vaillant, 1737), so called in allusion to the nodding flower-heads; < Gr. πρηνής, with the face downward, + ἄνθος, flower.] A genus of composite plants of the tribe *Cichoriaceæ* and subtribe *Lactuceæ*. It is characterized by nearly cylindrical or slightly compressed three- to five-angled achenes without beaks or ribs, and loosely panicled, nodding heads of ligulate flowers, with a peculiar cylindrical and slender involucre, having a few short bracts at its base, and mainly composed of from five to fourteen long and equal soft bracts in a single row, unchanged after blossoming. There are 20 species, natives of southern Europe, the Canary Islands, the East Indies, Japan, and North America. They are smooth and erect herbs, often tall and wand-like, or climbing (in a Himalayan species), with commonly whitish or yellowish flowers and copious pappus—a few American species being exceptional in their rough hairy inflorescence, or erect flowers. The leaves are alternate, and often of very peculiar shapes—arrow- or halberd-shaped, lyrate, or irregularly lobed, sometimes with great variation on the same plant. Three closely connected American species, *P. alba*, *P. serpentaria*, and *P. altissima*, are variously called *white lettuce*, *lion's-foot*, *rattlesnake-root*, and *gall-of-the-earth*—one, *P. serpentaria*, being locally reputed a cure for rattlesnake-bites. See *cancer-weed*, and cut under *rattlesnake-root*.

prenasal (prē-nā'zal), *a.* [< L. *præ*, before, + *nasus*, nose: see *nasal*.] Anterior with reference to the nose, nostrils, or nasal passages: as, the *prenasal* spine of the maxillary bone; a *prenasal* or rostral cartilage.

prenatal (prē-nā'tal), *a.* [< *pre-* + *natal*[1].] Previous to birth; of or pertaining to existence previous to birth.

> Plato assumed a *prenatal*, Malebranche a present intuition of the divine Being, as the source of the pure notions and principles of the understanding. — *E. Caird*, Philos. of Kant, p. 155.

prenatally (prē-nā'tal-i), *adv.* Before birth.

prender (pren'dėr), *n.* [< OF. *prendre*, a taking (inf. used as noun), prop. take, < L. *prendere*, *prehendere*, take, seize: see *prehend*, *v.*] In *law*, the power or right of taking a thing before it is offered.

prenet, *n.* and *v.* An obsolete form of *preen*[1].

prenomen, *n.* See *prænomen*.

prenominal, prænominal (prē-nom'i-nal), *a.* [< *prænomen* (*-nomin-*) + *-al*.] Of or pertaining to the prænomen; generic, as a name of an animal which precedes its specific name.

They deceived in the name of horse-radish, horse-mint, bull-rush, and many more; conceiving therein some *prenominal* consideration. *Sir T. Browne*, Vulg. Err., ii. 7.

prenominate† (prē-nom'i-nāt), *v. t.* [< L. *prænominatus*, pp. of *prænominare*, give a prænomen to, also name in advance, < *præ*, before, + *nominare*, name: see *nominate*.] To name beforehand; foretell.

Think'st thou to catch my life so pleasantly
As to *prenominate* in nice conjecture
Where thou wilt hit me dead?
Shak., T. and C., iv. 5. 250.

prenominate† (prē-nom'i-nāt), *a.* [< L. *prænominatus*, pp.: see the verb.] Forenamed; foretold; aforesaid.

Having ever seen in the *prenominate* crimes
The youth you breathe of guilty, be assured
He closes with you in this consequence.
Shak., Hamlet, ii. 1. 43.

prenomination† (prē-nom-i-nā'shon), *n.* [< L. as if **prænominatio*(*n-*), < *prænominare*, name in the first place or in advance, etc.: see *prenominate*.] The state or privilege of being named before others.

Moreover, if we concede that the animals of one element might bear the names of those in the other, yet in strict reason the watery productions should have the *prenomination*. *Sir T. Browne*, Vulg. Err., iii. 24.

prenominical, prænominical (prē-nō-min'i-kal), *a.* [< *prænomen* (*-nomin-*) + *-ic-al*.] Same as *prenominal*.

prenostic†, *n.* An obsolete form of *prognostic*. *Gower*.

prenote† (prē-nōt'), *v. t.* [< L. *prænotare*, mark or note before or beforehand, < *præ*, before, + *notare*, mark, designate: see *note*[1], *v.*] To note beforehand; designate or mention previously.

And this blind ignorance of that age, thus aboue *prenoted*, was the cause whie these kings builded so manie monasteries vpon zealous superstition.
Foxe, Martyrs, p. 120, an. 764.

prenotion (prē-nō'shon), *n.* [= F. *prénotion* = Sp. *prenocion* = Pg. *prenoção* = It. *prenozione*, < L. *prænotio*(*n-*), a previous notion, < *prænoscere*, pp. *prænotus*, learn or know beforehand, < *præ*, before, + *noscere*, come to know: see *know*[1].] Preconception; anticipation; a generalization from slight experience.

She had some *prenotion* or anticipation of them.
Bp. Berkeley, Siris, § 314.

prensation† (pren-sā'shon), *n.* [< L. *prensatio*(*n-*), a soliciting, < *prensatus*, *prehensatus*, pp. of *prensare*, *prehensare*, seize, lay hold of, freq. of *prendere*, *prehendere*, pp. *prensus*, *prehensus*, grasp, catch, take: see *prehend*.] The act of grasping; seizure.

That commonly by ambitious *prensations*, by simoniacal corruptions, by political bandyings, by popular factions, by all kinds of sinister ways, men crept into the place, doth appear by those many dismal schisms which gave the church many pretended heads, but not one certain one. *Barrow*, The Pope's Supremacy.

Prensiculantia (pren-sik-ū-lan'shi-ä), *n. pl.* [NL., neut. pl. of **prensiculan*(*t-*)*s*, ppr. of an assumed verb **prensiculare*, nibble, dim. or freq., < L. *prendere*, pp. *prensus*, take, seize: see *prender*, *prize*[1].] In Illiger's classification of mammals (1811), the fourth order, containing the rodents, and corresponding to the *Glires* or *Rodentia* of other authors. It was divided into 8 families, none constituted as in modern systems, the relationships of the rodents having been little understood at that time.

prent (prent), *v.* and *n.* An obsolete or dialectal (Scotch) form of *print*.

prentice (pren'tis), *n.* [< ME. *prentis*; by apheresis from *apprentice*.] An apprentice.

Alkynnes crafty men craven mede for here *prentis*;
Marchauntz and mede mote nede go togideres.
Piers Plowman (B), iii. 224.

I was bound *prentice* to a barber once,
But ran away i' the second year.
Middleton (*and others*), The Widow, iv. 2.

To put to prentice, to send to prentice, to apprentice; bind to an apprenticeship.

Sir Roger's kindness extends to their children's children; and this very morning he *sent* his coachman's grandson *to prentice*. *Steele*, Spectator, No. 107.

prenticehood (pren'tis-hůd), *n.* [Formerly also *prentisehood*; < ME. *prentishood*; < *prentice* + *-hood*.] Apprenticeship.

This jolly prentys with his maister bood,
Til he were ny out of his *prentishood*.
Chaucer, Cook's Tale, l. 36.

I serv'd no *prentisehood* to any Rod.
J. Beaumont, Psyche, ii. 43.

prentice-of-law† (pren'tis-ov-lâ'), *n.* A barrister. See *apprentice*, 3. *Halliwell*.

prenticeship (pren'tis-ship), *n.* [Formerly also *prentiship*; < *prentice* + *-ship*.] Apprenticeship.

While he [Moses] past his sacred *Prentiship*
(In Wildernes) of th' Hebrews Shepheardship.
Sylvester, tr. of Du Bartas's Weeks, ii., The Lawe.

prentist, *n.* An obsolete spelling of *prentice*.

prentisage† (pren'ti-sāj), *n.* [< *prentis*, *prentice*, + *-age*.] Apprenticeage; apprenticeship.

He was a gentleman to whom Amphialus that day had given armour and horse to try his valour, having never before been in any combat worthy remembrance. "Ah," said Phalautus, in a rage, "and must I be the exercise of your *prentisage*?" *Sir P. Sidney*, Arcadia, iii.

prenunciation† (prē-nun-si-ā'shon), *n.* [< LL. *prænuntiatio*(*n-*), a prediction, < L. *prænuntiare*, pp. *prænuntiatus*, announce beforehand, foretell, < *præ*, before, + *nuntiare*, announce, < *nuntius*, one who brings news, a messenger: see *nuncio*.] The act of telling before. *Bailey*.

prenuncious† (prē-nun'shus), *a.* [< L. *prænuntius*, *prænuncius*, that foretells or forebodes, < *præ*, before, + *nuntius*, one who brings news, a messenger: see *prenunciation*.] Announcing beforehand; presaging. *Blount*.

prenzie†, *a.* A dubious word in the following passage, probably an original error. Some conjecture it to be an error for *princelie* (*princely*) or for *priestlie* (*priestly*). Others conjecture Scotch *primsie*, prim, demure: but the existence of this word in Shakspere's time is not established, nor is it explained how Shakspere should come to use a colloquial Scotch diminutive term in this one place.

Claud. The *prenzie* Angelo!
Isab. O, 'tis the cunning livery of hell,
The damned'st body to invest and cover
In *prenzie* guards! *Shak.*, M. for M., iii. 1. 94.

preoblige (prē-ō-blīj'), *v. t.*; pret. and pp. *preobliged*, ppr. *preobliging*. [< *pre-* + *oblige*.] To bind by a previous obligation.

Nor was he *pre-obliged* by any kindness or benefit from us. *Tillotson*. (*Latham*.)

preobtain (prē-ob-tān'), *v. t.* and *i.* [< *pre-* + *obtain*.] To obtain beforehand. *Smart*.

preoccipital (prē-ok-sip'i-tal), *a.* [< *pre-* + *occipital*.] Placed in front of or in the anterior portion of the occipital lobe of the brain: as, the *preoccipital* fovea (a slight depression demarcating, in part, the occipital from the temporal lobe).—**Preoccipital fissure or notch**, a notch on the lower external surface of the cerebrum, marking the separation of the occipital and sphenotemporal lobes.

preoccupancy (prē-ok'ū-pan-si), *n.* [< *pre-* + *occupancy*.] 1. The act of taking possession before another; preoccupation: as, the *preoccupancy* of unoccupied land.

The *pre-occupancy* of the soil (prairies) by herbaceous vegetation, preventing or retarding the effective germination of the seeds of trees. *Science*, III. 442.

2. The right of taking possession before others: as, to have the *preoccupancy* of land by right of discovery.

preoccupant (prē-ok'ū-pant), *n.* [< L. *præoccupan*(*t-*)*s*, ppr. of *præoccupare*, seize or occupy beforehand: see *preoccupate*.] One who preoccupies; a prior occupant.

preoccupate† (prē-ok'ū-pāt), *v. t.* [< L. *præoccupatus*, pp. of *præoccupare*, seize or occupy beforehand: see *preoccupy*.] To take possession of before others; preoccupy; seize in advance.

Many worthy offices and places of high regarde in that vocation [the law] are now *pre-occupated* and usurped by ungentle and base stocke.
Ferne, Blazon of Gentrie (ed. 1586), p. 93.

I have propounded my opinions naked and unarmed, not seeking to *preoccupate* the liberty of men's judgments by confutations. *Bacon*, Advancement of Learning, ii.

preoccupation (prē-ok-ū-pā'shon), *n.* [= F. *préoccupation* = Sp. *preocupacion* = Pg. *preoccupação* = It. *preoccupazione*, < L. *præoccupatio*(*n-*), a seizing beforehand, an anticipation, < *præoccupare*, pp. *præoccupatus*, seize or occupy beforehand: see *preoccupate*.] 1. The act of preoccupying, or seizing beforehand; possession gained in advance.

More than three hundred men made a sudden break for the narrow gateway, struggled, fought, and crowded through it, and then burst into the kamens, in order to secure, by *preoccupation*, places on the sleeping-platforms. *The Century*, XXXVII. 40.

2†. The act of anticipating; anticipation.

To provide so tenderly by *preoccupation* as no spider may suck poison out of a rose.
Proceedings against Garnet. (*Latham*.)

As if, by way of *preoccupation*, he should have said: well, here you see your commission, this is your duty. *South*.

3. The state of being preoccupied; prior engrossment or absorption.

Preoccupation of mind is unfavourable to attention.
J. Sully, Outlines of Psychol., p. 88.

preoccupied (prē-ok'ū-pīd), *p. a.* [< *preoccupy*.] 1. Occupied previously; engrossed; hence, lost in thought; meditative; abstracted.

It is the beautiful *preoccupied* type of face which we find in his pictures that our modern Pre-Raphaelites reproduce, with their own modifications.
H. James, Jr., Trans. Sketches, p. 277.

2. In *zoöl.* and *bot.*, already used as a name for a genus, species, etc., and therefore, by the laws of priority, rejected for any other genus, species, etc., to which it has been applied.=**Syn.** 1. *Inattentive*, *Abstracted*, etc. See *absent*.

preoccupy (prē-ok'ū-pī), *v. t.*; pret. and pp. *preoccupied*, ppr. *preoccupying*. [= F. *préoccuper* = Sp. *preocupar* = Pg. *preoccupar* = It. *preoccupare*, < L. *præoccupare*, seize or occupy beforehand, < *præ*, before, + *occupare*, seize, take possession of: see *occupy*.] 1. To occupy before others; take possession of or appropriate for use in advance of others.

The tailor's wife . . . was wont to be *preoccupied* in all his customers' best clothes. *B. Jonson*, New Inn, Arg.

In the same publication the author . . . shows that the prior name, . . . being doubly *preoccupied* in insects, must give way to Acroculia. *Science*, III. 325.

2. To fill beforehand; cause to be occupied previously.

If field with corn ye fail *preoccupy*,
Darnel for wheat and thistle beards for grain . . .
Will grow apace in combination prompt.
Browning, Ring and Book, II. 156.

3. To occupy or engage the attention of beforehand; engross in advance of others; prepossess; preëngage.

Your minds,
Pre-occupied with what you rather must do
Than what you should, made you against the grain
To voice him consul. *Shak.*, Cor., ii. 3. 240.

preocular (prē-ok'ū-lär), *a.* and *n.* [< L. *præ*, before, + *oculus*, eye: see *ocular*.] I. *a.* Situated before the eye: specifically applied in herpetology to certain plates of the head.—**Preocular antennæ**, antennæ inserted on the genæ, close to the anterior borders of the eyes, as in many *Coleoptera*.

II. *n.* A preocular plate.

preœsophageal, *a.* See *preësophageal*.

preominate† (prē-om'i-nāt), *v. t.* [< *pre-* + *ominate*.] To be an omen of; betoken; foreshow; portend.

Because many Ravens were seene when Alexander entered Babylon, they were thought to *preominate* his death.
Sir T. Browne, Vulg. Err., v. 2.

preomosternal (prē-ō-mō-stėr'nal), *a.* [< *preomosternum* + *-al*.] Pertaining to the preomosternum.

preomosternum (prē-ō-mō-stėr'num), *n.*; pl. *preomosterna* (-nä). [NL., < L. *præ*, before, + NL. *omosternum*, q. v.] An anterior omosternum.

preopercle (prē-ō-pėr'kl), *n.* [< *præoperculum*.] The præoperculum.

preopercular, præopercular (prē-ō-pėr'kū-lär), *a.* [< *præopercul*(*um*) + *-ar*[3].] In *ichth.*, pertaining to or connected with the præoperculum. See *opercular*.

preoperculum, *n.* See *præoperculum*.

preopinion (prē-ō-pin'yon), *n.* [< *pre-* + *opinion*.] Opinion previously formed; prepossession.

The practice of diet doth hold no certain course nor solid rule of selection or confinement; some in an indistinct voracity eating almost any, others out of a timorous *preopinion* refraining very many.
Sir T. Browne, Vulg. Err., v. 21.

preoptic (prē-op'tik), *a.* [< *pre-* + *optic*.] Anterior with respect to optic lobes; pregeminal: specifically noting the anterior pair of the optic lobes or corpora quadrigemina of the brain.

preoption (prē-op'shon), *n.* [< *pre-* + *option*.] The right of first choice.

Agamemnon, as general, had the *preoption* of what part of the booty he pleased.
Stackhouse, Hist. Bible, I. 723. (*Latham*.)

preoral (prē-ō'ral), *a.* [< L. *præ*, before, + *os* (*or-*), the mouth: see *oral*.] Situated in front of or before the mouth. Specifically noting—(*a*) One of the visceral arches of the vertebrate embryo, in distinction from the several postoral arches. (*b*) A fringe of cilia in front of the mouth of certain infusorians, as the *Oxytrichidæ*.—**Preoral segments**, in the arthropods or articulated animals, hypothetical primitive rings, supposed to be anterior to those bearing the organs of the mouth and to be folded back, thus forming the top of the head: opposed to *postoral segments*. From these segments are developed the eyes, ocelli, antennæ, and antennules, which are therefore called *preoral* organs. Opinions differ as to the number of preoral segments; some writers believe that as many as four can be traced in insects, distinguishing them as the *antennary, ophthalmic, second ocellary*, and *first ocellary* segments, the last-named the most anterior, morphologically, of all.

preorally (prē-ō'ral-i), *adv.* In advance of the mouth.

There is reason to believe that these thirteen apparent ganglia really represent twenty pairs of primitive ganglia, one pair for each somite, the three anterior pairs having coalesced *preorally* to form the brain.
Huxley and Martin, Elementary Biology, p. 184.

preordain (prē-ôr-dān'), *v. t.* [= F. *préordonner* = Sp. *preordinar* = Pg. *preordenar* = It. *preordinare*, < LL. *præordinare*, order beforehand, < L. *præ*, before, + *ordinare*, order: see *ordain*.] To ordain or decree beforehand; predetermine.

May be this misery
Was *pre-ordainde* for thy felicity.
Times' Whistle (E. E. T. S.), p. 101.

If God *preordained* a Saviour for man before he had either made man or man marred himself, . . . then surely he meant that nothing should separate us from his eternal love in that Saviour. *Rev. T. Adams*, Works, III. 5.

preorder (prē-ôr'dėr), *v. t.* [< *pre-* + *order*.] To order or arrange beforehand; prearrange; foreordain.

The free acts of an indifferent are, morally and rationally, as worthless as the *preordered* passion of a determined will. *Sir W. Hamilton.*

preordinance (prē-ôr'di-nans), *n.* [< *pre-* + *ordinance*. Cf. L. *preordinate*.] An ordinance or rule previously established.

These couchings and these lowly courtesies
Might fire the blood of ordinary men,
And turn *pre-ordinance* and first decree
Into the law of children. *Shak.*, J. C., iii. 1. 38.

preordinate† (prē-ôr'di-nāt), *a.* [< LL. *præordinatus*, pp. of *præordinare*, order beforehand: see *ordinate*.] Foreordained; predetermined: used with the force of a participle.

Am I of that vertue that I may resiste agayne celestiall influence *preordinate* by prouidence diuine?
Sir T. Elyot, The Governour, ii. 12.

preordination (prē-ôr-di-nā'shon), *n.* [= F. *préordination* = Sp. *preordinacion* = Pg. *preordenação* = It. *preordinazione*; as *pre-* + *ordination*.] The act of preordaining; predetermination; foreordination.

The world did from everlasting hang in his [God's] foreknowledge and *preordination*.
Rev. T. Adams, Works, III. 165.

prep (prep), *n.* [Short for *preparatory*.] A student who is taking a preparatory course of study; especially, one who is preparing for college. [College slang, U. S.]

prep. An abbreviation of *preposition*.

Prepalæozoic, *a.* See *Prepaleozoic*.

prepalatal (prē-pal'ā-tal), *a.* [< L. *præ*, before, + *palatum*, palate, + *-al*.] In *anat.*, placed in front of the palate: as, the *prepalatal* aperture.

prepalatine (prē-pal'ā-tin), *a.* Same as *prepalatal*.

Prepaleozoic, Prepalæozoic (prē-pā"lē-ō-zō'-ik), *a.* [< *pre-* + *Paleozoic*.] Previous to the Paleozoic period.

preparable (prep'a-ra-bl), *a.* [= F. *préparable*; as *prepare* + *-able*.] Capable of being prepared.

If there be any such medicine *preparable* by art.
Boyle, Free Inquiry, § 7.

preparance† (prē-pār'ans), *n.* [< *prepare* + *-ance*.] Preparation.

I founde great tumultes among the people, and *preparance* for warres in Scotland.
Eden, tr. of Peter Martyr. (*Latham*.)

preparate†, *a.* [< ME. *preparat*, < L. *præparatus*, pp. of *præparare*, prepare: see *prepare*.] Prepared.

Sal tartre, alkaly, and sal *preparat*.
Chaucer, Prol. to Canon's Yeoman's Tale, l. 257.

Take that blood . . . and braie it with the .10. part of comen salt *preparate* to medicyns of men.
Book of Quintessence (ed. Furnivall), p. 11.

preparation (prep-a-rā'shon), *n.* [< OF. *preparation*, F. *préparation* = Sp. *preparacion* = Pg. *preparação* = It. *preparazione*, < L. *præparatio(n-)*, a making ready, < *præparare*, pp. *præparatus*, make ready beforehand: see *prepare*.] 1. The act of preparing or making ready; qualification for a particular use, service, or application; adaptation to an end; training; equipment.

Be yare in thy *preparation*, for thy assailant is quick, skilful, and deadly. *Shak.*, T. N., iii. 4. 245.

It is in and by freedom only, that adequate *preparation* for fuller freedom can be made.
Gladstone, Might of Right, p. 206.

2. Formation; composition; manufacture: as, the *preparation* of gunpowder; the *preparation* of glycerin.—3. A measure or means taken beforehand to secure a certain result; a preparatory proceeding or circumstance.

Defences, musters, *preparations*,
Should be maintain'd, assembled, and collected,
As were a war in expectation.
Shak., Hen. V., ii. 4. 18.

In the midst of these warlike *preparations*, however, they received the chilling news that the colony of Massachusetts refused to back them in this righteous war.
Irving, Knickerbocker, p. 304.

And the best *preparation* for a life of hard work, of trial, and difficulty, is to have a happy childhood and youth to look back to. *J. F. Clarke*, Self-Culture, Int., p. 21.

4. The state of being prepared or in readiness; preparedness.

Stand therefore, having . . . your feet shod with the *preparation* of the gospel of peace. Eph. vi. 15.

I wonder at the glory of this kingdom,
And the most bounteous *preparation*,
Still as I pass, they court me with.
Fletcher (*and another*), False One, iii. 4.

5†. That which is equipped or fitted out.

The Turkish *preparation* makes for Rhodes.
Shak., Othello, i. 3. 14.

6†. That which results from mental or moral training; qualification; accomplishment.

The *preparations* of the heart in man, and the answer of the tongue, is from the Lord. Prov. xvi. 1.

You are a gentleman of excellent breeding, . . . generally allowed for your many war-like, court-like, and learned *preparations*. *Shak.*, M. W. of W., ii. 2. 237.

7. That which is prepared, manufactured, or compounded: as, a chemical *preparation*; a *preparation* of oil and wax.

I wish the chymists had been more sparing who magnify their *preparations*. *Sir T. Browne.*

Free nations, for the sake of doing mischief to others, . . . have consented that a certain *preparation* of grain shall be interdicted in their families.
Landor, Kosciusko and Poniatowski.

8. In *anat.*, an animal body or any part of it prepared for anatomical purposes, or preserved to display parts already dissected. Preparations are roughly divided into *dry* and *wet*. A wet preparation is immersed in a preservative fluid, usually alcohol, often glycerin, sometimes chlorid of zinc. Dry preparations are of more varied character: a skeleton is a familiar example. Microscopic preparations are usually thin slices or sections permanently mounted on slides. All preparations are *specimens*, but a specimen may be a natural object upon which no work has been done, while *preparation* implies some special steps taken for display or preservation, or both. Models in wax and papier-maché are often called *preparations*.

9. In counterpoint and strict musical composition generally: (*a*) that treatment of the voice-parts whereby a dissonance in any chord is introduced as a consonance in the preceding chord, and simply held over into the dissonant chord by its own voice-part, while the others move; (*b*) a consonant tone in any voice-part which is thus about to become a dissonance. In early counterpoint no dissonances were permitted; later, they were admitted as suspensions (see *suspension*)—that is, consonances held over into chords with which they are at first dissonant; next, they were allowed whenever thus prepared or foreshadowed, whether resolved as suspensions or not. In free writing, dissonances are often abruptly introduced without previous sounding. *Preparation* is opposed to *percussion*, which is the actual sounding of the dissonance as such, and to *resolution*, which is the final merging of the dissonance into a consonant chord.

10. The day before the sabbath or any other Jewish feast-day. Also called *day of the preparation* (Mat. xxvii. 62). Compare *parascere*.

It was the *preparation*, that is, the day before the Sabbath. Mark xv. 42.

And it was the *preparation* of the passover, and about the sixth hour. John xix. 14.

11. *Eccles.*, devotions or prayers used by the celebrant or officiant, assistants, choristers, etc., before the eucharistic or other offices.

preparative (prē-par'a-tiv), *a.* and *n.* [< ME. **preparatif*, *preperatif*, < OF. (and F.) *preparatif* = Sp. Pg. It. *preparativo*; < ML. **præparativus*, serving to prepare, < L. *præparare*, prepare: see *prepare*.] **I.** *a.* Serving or tending to prepare or make ready; preparatory.

The work of reformation cannot be finished in a day, nor even begun before the *preparative* steps have been taken. *Goldsmith*, National Concord.

Wohler's synthetical method for *preparative* purposes usually assumes the following form.
Encyc. Brit., XXIV. 11.

Preparative meeting, in the Society of Friends: (*a*) a business meeting, or meeting for discipline, held before the monthly meeting, to which it is subordinate; (*b*) the organization which holds the meeting. Each monthly meeting has usually two or more preparative meetings connected with it.

II. *n.* That which is preparatory; something that prepares or paves the way; a preparatory measure or act.

Syghte riotours that wil no waryn spare,
Wythe-outen licens or eny liberte,
Tyl sodyn perel bryng hem yn the snare,
A *preperatif* that they shal neuer the.
Lydgate, Order of Fools, in Booke of Precedence
[(E. E. T. S., extra ser.), i. 83.

We . . . yet, after all these spirituall *preparatives* and purgations, have our earthly apprehensions so clamm'd and furr'd with the old levin.
Milton, On Def. of Humb. Remonst.

By all means they [the Jews] were resolv'd to endure a siege, and, as a *preparative* for that, they burnt up almost all the stores of provision which were among them.
Stillingfleet, Sermons, I. viii.

Their conversation is a kind of *preparative* for sleep.
Steele, Tatler, No. 132.

preparatively (prē-par'a-tiv-li), *adv.* In a preparative manner; by way of preparation.

It is *preparatively* necessary to many useful things in this life, as to make a man a good physician.
Sir M. Hale.

preparator (prē-par'a-tor), *n.* [= F. *préparateur* = It. *preparatore*, < LL. *præparator*, one who makes ready, < L. *præparare*, pp. *præparatus*, prepare: see *prepare*.] One who prepares or makes ready; a preparer; specifically, one who prepares anatomical subjects or specimens of natural history for study or exhibition; a prosector; a taxidermist.

The progress of the work upon the cast of the fin-back whale has been alluded to in connection with the work of the *preparators*. *Smithsonian Report*, 1881, p. 103.

While, however, the use of the photograph for outlines diminishes the labor of the artist about one-half, it increases that of the *preparator*. *Science*, III. 443.

preparatorily (prē-par'a-tō-ri-li), *adv.* Preparatively.

When we get the chromosphere agitated *preparatorily* to one of these tremendous outbursts—one of these metallic prominences, as they are called—the lines which we see are different from those in the table which I have given.
Nature, XXXIII. 540.

preparatory (prē-par'a-tō-ri), *a.* and *n.* [< ML. **præparatorius* (in neut. *præparatorium*, as a noun, apparatus), < L. *præparare*, prepare: see *prepare*.] **I.** *a.* 1. Preparing or serving to prepare the way for something to follow; antecedent; preparative; introductory: as, to adopt *preparatory* measures.

Rains were but *preparatory*; the violence of the deluge depended upon the disruption of the great abyss.
T. Burnet.

The Old Testament system was *preparatory* and prophetic. *C. Hodge*, On Rom. v. 14.

We were drinking coffee, *preparatory* to our leaving Metrahenny and beginning our voyage in earnest.
Bruce, Source of the Nile, I. 67.

After a *preparatory* hem! . . . the poetess began.
Barham, Ingoldsby Legends, I. 84.

The work most needed is not as yet pure criticism, but art-teaching as *preparatory* to it.
P. G. Hamerton, Thoughts about Art, xi.

2. In course of preparation; receiving preparative instruction or training: as, a *preparatory* student.—**Preparatory Committee**, in the Scottish Parliament, a committee of members which prepared legislation for the full body, or perhaps legislated in its place, in the fourteenth and fifteenth centuries. Subsequently called *Lords of the Articles*.—**Preparatory lecture** or **service**, in some churches, a week-day service preparatory to the communion. =**Syn.** 1. *Introductory*, etc. (see *preliminary*), prefatory.

II. *n.*; pl. *preparatories* (-riz). A preparative. [Rare.]

All this amazing majesty and formidable *preparatories* are for the passing of an eternal sentence upon us according to what we have done in the body.
Jer. Taylor, Works, I. iii.

prepare (prē-pār'), *v.*; pret. and pp. *prepared*, ppr. *preparing*. [< OF. *preparer*, F. *préparer* = Sp. Pg. *preparar* = It. *preparare*, < L. *præparare*, make ready beforehand, prepare, < *præ*, before, + *parare*, make ready: see *pare*[1].] **I.** *trans.* 1. To set in order or readiness for a particular end; make ready; provide; adapt by alteration or arrangement.

In fell motion,
With his *prepared* sword, he charges home
My unprovided body. *Shak.*, Lear, ii. 1. 53.

Do you know who dwells above, sir,
And what they have *prepar'd* for men turn'd devils?
Fletcher, Humorous Lieutenant, iv. 5.

Who would haue desired a better aduantage then such an aduertisement, to haue *prepared* the Fort for such an assault? Quoted in *Capt. John Smith's* Works, II. 90.

We ascended this first part of the hills, and stopped at a tent of Arabs, it being very hot weather; here they *prepared* for us eggs, and also sower milk.
Pococke, Description of the East, II. i. 75.

2. To bring into a particular mental state with reference to the future; fit by notification or

instruction for any definite action or direction of thought: as, to *prepare* a person for bad news; to *prepare* a boy for college.

> Go you to Juliet ere you go to bed,
> *Prepare* her, wife, against this wedding-day.
> *Shak.*, R. and J., iii. 4. 32.

> The Baptizing of Children with us does only *prepare* a Child, against he comes to be a man, to understand what Christianity means. *Selden*, Table-Talk, p. 19.

> The servant retired, found a priest, confessed himself, came back, and told his lord that he was now *prepared* to die. *Walpole*, Letters, II. 189.

> Still *prepared*,
> It seemed, to meet the worst his worn heart feared.
> *William Morris*, Earthly Paradise, II. 314.

3. To equip; fit out; provide with necessary means.

> Why, then, the champions are *prepared*, and stay
> For nothing but his majesty's approach.
> *Shak.*, Rich. II., i. 3. 5.

4. To provide or procure for future use; hence, to make; form; compound; manufacture.

> When the spirits are low, and nature sunk, the Muse, with sprightly and harmonious notes, gives an unexpected turn with a grain of poetry: which I *prepare* without the use of mercury. *Steele*, Tatler, No. 47.

> He *prepared* a circular letter to be sent to the different parts of the country. *Prescott*, Ferd. and Isa., ii. 17.

> Although the Chinese *prepare* their ink from the kernel of some amygdalaceous fruit, yet, by the aid of our present chemical appliances, we are able to produce a composition in no way inferior to the best China ink.
> *Ure*, Dict., IV. 436.

5. In *music*: (*a*) To lead up to by causing a dissonance to appear first as a consonance: as, the discord was carefully *prepared*. See *preparation*, 9. (*b*) To lead into (a tone or embellishment) by an appoggiatura or other prefatory tone or tones.—**Prepared trill**, a trill preceded by a turn or other embellishment.

II. *intrans.* 1. To make everything ready; put things in order beforehand.

> Boyet, *prepare*; I will away to-night.
> *Shak.*, L. L. L., v. 2. 737.

2. To make one's self ready; equip one's self mentally or materially for future action.

> *Prepare* to meet thy God, O Israel. Amos iv. 12.

> And now his voice, accordant to the string,
> *Prepares* our monarch's victories to sing.
> *Goldsmith*, Captivity, ii. 69.

prepare (prẹ-pãr'), *n.* [< *prepare*, *v.*] Preparation. [Obsolete or technical.]

> Go levy men, and make *prepare* for war.
> *Shak.*, 3 Hen. VI., iv. 1. 131.

> As *prepares* for steam-colours, all the antimonial compounds hitherto tried have shown themselves inferior to tin. *W. Crookes*, Dyeing and Calico-printing, p. 542.

preparedly (prẹ-pãr'ed-li), *adv.* With suitable preparation.

> The queen . . . desires instruction,
> That she *preparedly* may frame herself
> To the way she 's forced to.
> *Shak.*, A. and C., v. 1. 55.

preparedness (prẹ-pãr'ed-nes), *n.* The state of being prepared; readiness: as, *preparedness* for action or service.

> Besides actually doing a thing, we know what it is to be in an attitude or disposition of *preparedness* to act.
> *A. Bain*, Emotions and Will, p. 551.

preparement (prẹ-pãr'mẹnt), *n.* [= Sp. *preparamento*, *preparamiento* = It. *preparamento*, < ML. *præparamentum*, preparation, < L. *præparare*, make ready beforehand: see *prepare*.] Preparation. [Rare.]

> The soldier that dares not fight affords the enemy too much advantage for his *preparement*. *Feltham*, Resolves.

preparer (prẹ-pãr'ėr), *n.* [< *prepare* + *-er*[1].] One who prepares.

> They [teachers] will be led to require of the *preparers* of school-books a more conscientious performance of their tasks. *E. L. Youmans*, in Grove's Corr. of Forces, p. viii.

preparoccipital (prē-par-ok-sip'i-tạl), *a.* [< *pre-* + *paroccipital*.] Lying anteriorly in the paroccipital gyre of the brain: applied to a fissure.

prepatellar (prē-pat'e-lạ̈r), *a.* [< L. *præ*, before, + *patella*, patella.] Situated in front of or over the patella.—**Prepatellar bursa**, a subcutaneous bursa situated over the patella and upper part of the ligamentum patellæ.

prepay (prē-pā'), *v. t.*; pret. and pp. *prepaid*, ppr. *prepaying*. [< *pre-* + *pay*[1].] 1. To pay beforehand, as for an article before getting possession of it, or for service before it has been rendered: as, to *prepay* a subscription; to *prepay* postage or freight.—2. To pay the charge upon in advance: as, to *prepay* a letter or a telegram; to *prepay* an express parcel.

prepayment (prē-pā'mẹnt), *n.* [< *pre-* + *payment*.] The act of paying beforehand; payment in advance, as of postage or rent.

prepeduncle (prē-pẹ-dung'kl), *n.* [< NL. *præpedunculus*, < L. *præ*, before, + *pedunculus*, peduncle: see *peduncle*.] The superior peduncle of the cerebellum.

prepeduncular (prē-pẹ-dung'kụ̄-lạ̈r), *a.* [< *prepeduncle* (NL. *præpedunculus*) + *-ar*[3].] Pertaining to the prepeduncle.

prepedunculate (prē-pẹ-dung'kụ̄-lāt), *a.* [< *prepeduncle* (NL. *præpedunculus*) + *-ate*[1].] Pertaining to the prepeduncle.

prepelvisternal (prē-pel-vi-stėr'nạl), *a.* [< *præpelvisternum* + *-al*.] Pertaining to the præpelvisternum

prepelvisternum, *n.* See *præpelvisternum*.

prepense† (prẹ-pens'), *v.* [Formerly also *prepence*; < ME. *prepensen*, < OF. *prepenser* = It. *prepensare*, < ML. **præpensare*, think of beforehand, < L. *præ*, before, + *pensare*, think, consider, deliberate: see *poise*.] I. *trans.* 1. To consider beforehand; think upon in advance.

> All these thinges *prepensed*, . . . gathered together seriousely, and . . . iustely pondred.
> *Sir T. Elyot*, The Governour, i. 25.

> And ever in your noble hart *prepense*
> That all the sorrow in the world is lesse
> Then vertues might and values confidence.
> *Spenser*, F. Q., III. xi. 14.

> Certain penalties may and ought to be prescribed to capital crimes, although they may admit variable degrees of guilt: as in case of murder upon *prepensed* malice.
> *Winthrop*, Hist. New England, II. 252.

2. To plan or devise beforehand; contrive previously.

> The seid Duke of Suffolk, . . . *prepensing* that your seid grete enemeye and adversarie Charles schuld conquerr and gete be power and myght your seid realme, . . . councelled . . . your heighnesse to enlarge and deliver out of prison the same Duke of Orliaunce. *Paston Letters*, I. 100.

> I would not have the king to pardon a voluntary murder, a *prepensed* murder.
> *Latimer*, 5th Sermon bef. Edw. VI., 1549.

II. *intrans.* To reflect or meditate beforehand.

> To thinke, consydre, and *prepence*.
> *Sir T. Elyot*, The Governour, iii. 24.

prepense (prẹ-pens'), *a.* [With loss (in pronunciation) of the orig. accented final vowel (as in *costive* and other instances), < OF. *prepense*, < ML. **præpensatus*, pp. of **præpensare*, think of beforehand: see *prepense*, *v.*] Considered and planned beforehand; premeditated; purposed; intentional: generally in the phrase *malice prepense* (formerly also *prepensed malice*).

> From that period whatever resolution they took was deliberate and *prepense*. *Junius*, Letters, xxxix.

> The fashion of their eloquence is more deliberate and more *prepense*. *Swinburne*, Study of Shakespeare, p. 60.

Malice prepense. See *malice*.

prepensely (prẹ-pens'li), *adv.* Premeditately; deliberately; purposely; intentionally.

> Shakespeare . . . has set himself as if *prepensely* and on purpose to brutalise the type of Achilles and spiritualise the type of Ulysses.
> *Swinburne*, Study of Shakespeare, p. 201.

prepensive (prẹ-pen'siv), *a.* [< *prepense* + *-ive*.] Same as *prepense*.

> The carrying the penknife drawn into the room with you . . . seems to imply malice *prepensive*, as we call it in the law. *Fielding*, Amelia, i. 10.

preperception (prē-pėr-sep'shọn), *n.* [< *pre-* + *perception*.] A previous perception.

> Just as perceptions are modified by *pre-perceptions*, and the action of a stimulus is completed by the reaction of the Organism.
> *G. H. Lewes*, Probs. of Life and Mind, II. xi. § 28.

prepigmental (prē-pig'mẹn-tạl), *a.* [< *pre-* + *pigmental*.] Situated within the pigmented layer of the eye, as in some cuttlefishes.

prepituitary (prē-pit'ụ̄-i-tạ̄-ri), *a.* [< *pre-* + *pituitary*.] Situated in front of the pituitary fossa.

preplacental (prē-plạ̄-sen'tạl), *a.* [< *pre-* + *placental*.] Prior to the formation of a placenta; previous to the establishment of placental connection between the fetus and the parent. *Amer. Naturalist*, XXIII. 926.

prepollence (prẹ-pol'ẹns), *n.* [< *prepollen(t)* + *-ce*.] Prevalence; predominance; superiority in power or influence. [Rare.]

> The *prepollence* of evil in the world. *Warton.*

prepollency (prẹ-pol'ẹn-si), *n.* [As *prepollence* (see *-cy*).] Same as *prepollence*. [Rare.]

> Sometimes, in a more refined and highly philosophick sense, Osiris is the whole active force of the universe, considered as having a *prepollency* of good in its effects.
> *Coventry*, Philemon to Hydaspes, iii.

prepollent (prẹ-pol'ẹnt), *a.* [< L. *præpollen(t-)s*, ppr. of *præpollere*, surpass in power, be highly distinguished, < *præ*, before, + *pollere*, be powerful: see *pollent*.] Having superior power or influence; predominant. [Rare.]

> If the benefits are *prepollent*, . . . a rational, prudent, and moderate mind should be content to bear the disadvantages. *Bp. Huntingford*, To Lord Somers.

prepollex (prē-pol'eks), *n.*; pl. *prepollices* (-i-sēz). [NL. *præpollex*, < L. *præ*, before, + *pollex*, the thumb: see *pollex*.] A supernumerary bone or cartilage of the fore foot of some animals, corresponding to the prehallux of the hind foot. See *prehallux*.

> Prof. Bardeleben has discovered traces of a *prepollex* and a prehallux in certain Reptilia.
> *Amer. Naturalist*, XXIII. 921.

preponder† (prẹ-pon'dėr), *v. t.* [= Sp. Pg. *preponderar* = It. *preponderare*, < L. *præponderare*, be of greater weight, outweigh, be of more influence, < *præ*, before, beyond, + *ponderare*, weigh: see *ponder*.] To outweigh; preponderate.

> Though pillars by channeling be beseemingly ingrossed to our sight, yet they are truly weakened in themselves, and therefore ought perchance in sound reason not to be the more slender, but the more corpulent, unless apparences *preponder* truths. *Sir H. Wotton*, Reliquiæ, p. 27.

preponderance (prẹ-pon'dėr-ạns), *n.* [= F. *prépondérance* = Sp. Pg. *preponderancia* = It. *preponderanza*, < L. *præponderan(t-)s*, ppr. of *præponderare*, outweigh: see *preponderant*.] 1. The state or quality of preponderating or outweighing; superiority in weight: as, *preponderance* of metal.—2. Superiority in force, influence, quantity, or number; predominance.

> He did not find . . . that any other foreign powers than our own allies were likely to obtain a considerable *preponderance* in the scale. *Burke*, Army Estimates.

> In his speeches we are struck more by the general mental power they display than by the *preponderance* of any particular faculty. *Whipple*, Ess. and Rev., I. 185.

> There was a *preponderance* of women, as is apt to be the case in such resorts.
> *C. D. Warner*, Their Pilgrimage, p. 7.

3. In *gun.*, the excess of weight of that part of a gun which is to the rear of the trunnions over that in front of them. It is measured by the force, expressed in pounds, which must be applied under the rear end of the base-ring or neck of the cascabel in order to balance the gun exactly with the axis of the bore horizontal, when supported freely on knife-edges placed under the trunnions.

preponderancy (prẹ-pon'dėr-ạn-si), *n.* [As *preponderance* (see *-cy*).] Same as *preponderance*.

> A *preponderancy* of those circumstances which have a tendency to move the inclination.
> *Edwards*, On the Will, iii. 7.

preponderant (prẹ-pon'dėr-ạnt), *a.* [= F. *prépondérant* = Sp. Pg. It. *preponderante*, < L. *præponderan(t-)s*, ppr. of *præponderare*, outweigh: see *preponder*, *preponderate*.] Outweighing; preponderating; superior in weight, force, efficiency, or influence; predominant; prevalent.

> The *preponderant* scale must determine. *Reid.*

> The power of the House of Commons in the state had become so decidedly *preponderant* that no sovereign . . . could have imitated the example of James.
> *Macaulay*, Hist. Eng., vii.

> The *preponderant* benefits of law.
> *Bushnell*, Moral Uses of Dark Things, p. 54.

> No thoughtful person can have failed to observe, in any throng, the *preponderant* look of unrest and dissatisfaction in the human eye. *E. S. Phelps*, Beyond the Gates, p. 119.

preponderantly (prẹ-pon'dėr-ạnt-li), *adv.* In a preponderant manner or degree; so as to preponderate or outweigh.

preponderate (prẹ-pon'dėr-āt), *v.*; pret. and pp. *preponderated*, ppr. *preponderating*. [< L. *præponderatus*, pp. of *præponderare*, outweigh: see *preponder*.] I. *trans.* 1. To outweigh; surpass in weight, force, efficiency, or influence.

> An inconsiderable weight, by vertue of its distance from the centre of the ballance, will *preponderate* much greater magnitudes. *Glanville*, Vanity of Dogmatizing, xv.

> The triviallest thing, when a passion is cast into the scale with it, *preponderates* substantial blessings.
> *Government of the Tongue.*

2†. To cause to lean or incline in a particular direction; dispose; induce to a particular course of action or frame of mind.

> The desire to spare Christian blood *preponderates* him for peace. *Fuller.*

3†. To ponder or mentally weigh beforehand.

> How many things do they *preponderate*! how many at once comprehend! *Shaftesbury*, Moralists, ii. § 4.

II. *intrans.* 1. To exceed in weight; hence, to incline or droop, as the scale of a balance.

> That is no just balance wherein the heaviest side will not *preponderate*. *Bp. Wilkins.*

> I will assert nothing but what shall be reasonable, though not demonstrable, and far *preponderating* to whatever shall be alledged to the contrary.
> *Dr. H. More*, Immortal. of Soul, iii. 1.

Royalty, nobility, and state
Are such a dead *preponderating* weight,
That endless bliss (how strange soe'er it seem)
In counterpoise flies up and kicks the beam.
Cowper, Truth, l. 354.

2. To have superior power, influence, force, or efficiency; predominate; prevail.

Down to the very day and hour of the final vote, no one could predict, with any certainty, which side would *preponderate*. *D. Webster*, Speech at Pittsburg, July, 1833.

preponderatingly (prẹ̄-pon'dėr-ā-ting-li), *adv.* Preponderantly.

The book is *preponderatingly* full of herself. *W. R. Greg*, Misc. Ess., 1st ser., p. 178.

preponderation (prẹ̄-pon-dẹ-rā'shọn), *n.* [< L. *præponderatio(n-)*, an outweighing, < *præponderare*, pp. *præponderatus*, outweigh: see *preponder, preponderate*.] 1. The act or state of preponderating or outweighing; preponderance.

It is a *preponderation* of circumstantial arguments that must determine our actions in a thousand occurrences. *Watts*, Logic, ii. 5, § 3.

Choice and preference can no more be in a state of indifference than motion can be in a state of rest, or than the *preponderation* of the scale of a balance can be in a state of equilibrium. *Edwards*, On the Will, ii. 7.

2†. The act of pondering or mentally weighing beforehand.

preponderous (prẹ̄-pon'dėr-us), *a.* [< *preponder* + *-ous*. Cf. *ponderous*.] Preponderant; exceeding in quantity or amount: as, the *preponderous* constituents of a chemical solution.

prepontile (prē-pon'til), *a.* [< L. *præ*, before, + *pon(t-)s*, bridge: see *pontile*.] Situated in front of the pons Varolii: as, the *prepontile* recess: opposed to *postpontile*. See cut under *brain*.

preport† (prẹ̄-pōrt'), *v. t.* [< L. *præportare*, carry before, < *præ*, before, + *portare*, carry: see *port*[3].] To presage; forebode.

Pyraustæ gaudes gaudium: your inconstant joy *preports* annoy. *Withals*, Dict. (ed. 1634), p. 575. (*Nares*.)

prepose (prẹ̄-pōz'), *v. t.*; pret. and pp. *preposed*, ppr. *preposing*. [< OF. *preposer*, F. *préposer*, place before; as *pre-* + *pose*[2]. Cf. L. *præponere*, pp. *præpositus*, set before: see *preposition*.] To place before or in front of something else; prefix.

It is a word often read *preposed* before other words. *Bedwell*, Arabic Trudgman (1615), p. 90. (*Latham*.)

I did deem it most convenient to *prepose* mine epistle, only to beseech you to account of the poems as toys. *W. Percy*, Sonnets (1594), Pref. (*Latham*.)

preposition (prep-ọ̄-zish'ọn), *n.* [< ME. *preposicion*, < OF. *preposition*, F. *préposition* = Sp. *preposicion* = Pg. *preposição* = It. *preposizione*, < L. *præpositio(n-)*, a placing before, in gram. (translating Gr. πρόθεσις) a preposition, < *præponere*, pp. *præpositus*, set before, place first, < *præ*, before, + *ponere*, set, place: see *position*. Cf. *prepose*.] 1 (prē-pō-zish'ọn). The act of preposing, or placing before or in front of something else. [Rare.]

Mr. Herbert Spencer, in his Essay on the Philosophy of Style, contrasting the English *preposition* with the French postposition of the adjective, prefers the English usage. *Amer. Jour. Philol.*, VI. 346.

2. In *gram.*, something preposed; a prefixed element; a prefix; one of a body of elements (by origin, words of direction, having an adverbial character) in our family of languages often used as prefixes to verbs and verbal derivatives; especially, an indeclinable part of speech regularly placed before and governing a noun in an oblique case (or a member of the sentence having a substantive value), and showing its relation to a verb, or an adjective, or another noun, as *in, of, from, to, by*, etc. Abbreviated *prep.*—3†. A proposition; exposition; discourse.

He made a longe *preposicion* and oration concernynge ye allegiance which he exortyd his lordes to owe & bere to hym for ye terme of his lyfe. *Fabyan*, Chron., I. cxxxiii.

The said Sir John Bushe, in all his *prepositions* to the king, did not onely attribute to him worldly honours but diuine names. *Grafton*, Rich. II., an. 21.

Prayse made before a great man, or *preposition*, harengue. *Palsgrave*. (*Halliwell*.)

prepositional (prep-ọ̄-zish'ọn-al), *a.* [= F. *prépositionnel*; as *preposition* + *-al*.] Pertaining to or having the nature or function of a preposition: as, the *prepositional* use of a word. —**Prepositional phrase**, a phrase consisting of a noun with governing preposition, and having adjectival or adverbial value: as, a house *of wood*; he spoke *with haste*.

prepositionally (prep-ọ̄-zish'ọn-al-i), *adv.* In a prepositional manner: as, "concerning" is a participle used *prepositionally*.

prepositive (prẹ̄-poz'i-tiv), *a.* and *n.* [= F. *prépositif* = Pg. It. *prepositivo*, < LL. *præpositivus*, that is set before, < L. *præponere*, pp. *præpositus*, set before, prefer: see *preposition*.] I. *a.* Put before; prefixed: as, a *prepositive* particle.

These *prepositive* conjunctions, once separated from the others, soon gave birth to another subdivision. *Horne Tooke*, Diversions of Purley, I. ix.

II. *n.* A word or particle put before another word.

Grammarians were not ashamed to have a class of postpositive *prepositives*. *Horne Tooke*, Diversions of Purley, I. ix.

prepositor, præpositor (prẹ̄-poz'i-tọr), *n.* [< ML. *præpositor*, < L. *præponere*, pp. *præpositus*, set or place before: see *preposition*.] A scholar appointed to oversee or superintend other scholars, or hold them in discipline; a monitor. Also *prepostor, præpostor*.

While at Winchester, he [Sydney Smith] had been one year *Præpositor* of the College, and another *Præpositor* of the Hall. *Lady Holland*, Sydney Smith, i.

prepositure (prẹ̄-poz'i-tūr), *n.* [= Sp. Pg. It. *prepositura*, < LL. *præpositura*, the office of an overseer, < L. *præponere*, pp. *præpositus*, set or place before or over: see *preposition*.] The office or place of a provost; a provostship.

The king gave him the *prepositure* of Wells, with the probend annexed. *Bp. Lowth*, Wykeham, § 1.

The possessions conveyed are described as messuages and tenements in Carke and Howlker within the *prepositure* and manor of Cartmell.
Quoted in *Baines's* Hist. Lancashire, II. 679.

prepossess (prē-pọ-zes'), *v. t.* [< *pre-* + *possess*.] 1. To preoccupy, as ground or land; take previous possession of.

Wisedome, which being given alike to all Ages, cannot be *prepossest* by the Ancients. *Milton*, Reformation in Eng., i.

Permitting others of a later Extraction to *prepossess* that Place in Your Esteem. *Congreve*, Way of the World, Ded.

2. To preoccupy the mind or heart of; imbue beforehand with some opinion or estimate; bias; prejudice: as, his appearance and manners strongly *prepossessed* them in his favor. *Prepossess* is more frequently used in a good sense than *prejudice*, and the participial adjective *prepossessing* has always a good sense.

Master Montague is preparing to go to Paris as a Messenger of Honour, to *prepossess* the King and Council there with the Truth of Things. *Howell*, Letters, I. iv. 26.

They were so *prepossest* with this matter, and affected with ye same, as they commited Mr. Alden to prison. *Bradford*, Plymouth Plantation, p. 318.

Let not prejudice *prepossess* you. *I. Walton*, Complete Angler, p. 31.

To confess a truth, he has not *prepossessed* me in his favour. *Goldsmith*, Vicar, v.

prepossessing (prē-pọ-zes'ing), *p. a.* Predisposing the mind to favor; making a favorable impression; pleasing; attractive: as, a *prepossessing* address.

A young man of *prepossessing* appearance and gentlemanly deportment. *Barham*, Ingoldsby Legends, I. 190.

=**Syn.** Attractive, taking, winning.

prepossessingly (prē-pọ-zes'ing-li), *adv.* In a prepossessing manner; in such a way as to produce a favorable impression.

prepossession (prē-pọ-zesh'ọn), *n.* [< *pre-* + *possession*.] 1. The act of taking possession beforehand; preoccupation; prior possession.

God hath taken care to anticipate and prevent every man to give piety the *prepossession*, before other competitors should be able to pretend to him; and so to engage him in holiness first, and then in bliss. *Hammond*, Fundamentals.

2. The state of being prepossessed; predisposition; prejudice, usually of a favorable nature; hence, liking; favorable opinion.

They that were the hearers and spectators of what our Saviour said and did had mighty and inveterate *prepossessions* to struggle with. *Sharp*, Works, I. vi.

Such a hovering faith as this, which refuses to settle upon any determination, is absolutely necessary in a mind that is careful to avoid errors and *prepossessions*. *Addison*, Spectator, No. 117.

When you acknowledge her Merit, and own your *Prepossession* for another, at once, you gratify my Fondness, and cure my Jealousy. *Steele*, Conscious Lovers, ii. 1.

So long has general improvement to contend with the force of habit and the passion of *prepossession*. *I. D'Israeli*, Amen. of Lit., I. 148.

=**Syn. 2.** Bias, bent.

prepossessor (prẹ̄-pọ-zes'ọr), *n.* [< *pre-* + *possessor*.] One who prepossesses; one who possesses before another.

They signify only a bare *prepossessor*, one that possessed the land before the present possessor. *Brady*, Glossary.

preposter (prẹ̄-pos'tėr), *n.* Same as *prepostor*. See *prepositor*.

Intrusting more or less of the discipline to an aristocracy of the scholars themselves, whether under the name of prefects, monitors, or *preposters*. *Blackwood's Mag.*, I. 75.

preposterate† (prẹ̄-pos'tẹ-rāt), *v. t.* [< *preposterous* + *-ate*[1].] To invert; pervert; make preposterous.

I never saw thinge done by you which *preposterated* or perverted the good judgment that all the world esteemeth to shine in you. *Palace of Pleasure*, II., S. 7. b. (*Nares*.)

preposterous (prẹ̄-pos'tẹ-rus), *a.* [= Sp. *prepóstero* = Pg. It. *prepostero*, < L. *præposterus*, with the hinder part before, reversed, inverted, perverted, < *præ*, before, + *posterus*, coming after: see *posterity*.] 1†. Having that last which ought to be first; reversed in order or arrangement; inverted.

Ye haue another manner of disordered speach, when ye misplace your words or clauses and set that before which should be behind, & è conuerso: we call it, in English prouerbe, the cart before the horse; the Greeks call it Histeron proteron; we name it the *Preposterous*. *Puttenham*, Arte of Eng. Poesie, p. 141.

How backward! How *prepost'rous* is the motion
Of our ungain devotion! *Quarles*, Emblems, i. 13.

Gold and silver are heavy metals, and sink down in the balance; yet, by a *preposterous* inversion, they lift the heart of man upwards. *Rev. T. Adams*, Works, I. 52.

2. Contrary to nature, reason, or common sense; irrational; glaringly absurd; nonsensical.

"Good Gloucester" and "good devil" were alike,
And both *preposterous*. *Shak.*, 3 Hen. VI., v. 6. 5.

Great precisians of mean conditions and very illiterate, most part by a *preposterous* zeal, fasting, meditation, melancholy, are brought into those gross errors and inconveniences. *Burton*, Anat. of Mel., p. 627.

If a man cannot see a church, it is *preposterous* to take his opinion about its altar-piece or painted window. *Huxley*, Man's Place in Nature, p. 119.

3. Foolish; ridiculous; stupid; absurd.

Preposterous ass, that never read so far
To know the cause why music was ordain'd!
Shak., T. of the S., iii. 1. 9.

Man is the only *preposterous* creature alive who pursues the shadow of pleasure without temptation. *Goldsmith*, Richard Nash.

=**Syn. 2** and **3.** *Silly, Foolish*, etc. (see *absurd*), monstrous, crazy, mad, wild, ludicrous. See *foolish*.

preposterously (prẹ̄-pos'tẹ-rus-li), *adv.* 1†. In an inverted order or position; with the hind part foremost; with the bottom upward.

He gron'd, tumbl'd to the earth, and stay'd
A mightie while *preposterously*. *Chapman*, Iliad, v.

2. Irrationally; absurdly; stupidly.

The abbot [was] *preposterously* put to death, with two innocent vertuous monks with him.
Letter from Monks of Glastonbury (Bp. Burnet's Records, [II. ii. 305).

Wonder and doubt come wrongly into play,
Preposterously, at cross purposes.
Browning, An Epistle.

preposterousness (prẹ̄-pos'tẹ-rus-nes), *n.* The state or character of being preposterous; wrong order or method; unreasonableness; absurdity.

Preposterousness she counted it to wear
Her purse upon her back.
J. Beaumont, Psyche, xviii.

prepostor (prẹ̄-pos'tọr), *n.* Same as *prepositor*.

The master mounted into the high desk by the door, and one of the *præpostors* of the week stood by him on the steps. *T. Hughes*, Tom Brown at Rugby, i. 5.

prepotence (prẹ̄-pō'tẹns), *n.* [< OF. *prepotence*, F. *prépotence* = Sp. Pg. *prepotencia* = It. *prepotenza*, < LL. *præpotentia*, superior power, < L. *præpoten(t-)s*, very powerful: see *prepotent*.] Same as *prepotency*. *Landor*.

prepotency (prẹ̄-pō'tẹn-si), *n.* [As *prepotence* (see *-cy*).] The state or quality of being prepotent; superior power, influence, or efficiency; predominance; prevalence.

If there were a determinate *prepotency* in the right, . . . we might expect the same in other animals, whose parts are also differenced by dextrality. *Sir T. Browne*, Vulg. Err., iv. 5.

Scarcely any result from my experiments has surprised me so much as this of the *prepotency* of pollen from a distinct individual over each plant's own pollen. *Darwin*, Cross and Self Fertilisation, p. 397.

prepotent (prẹ̄-pō'tẹnt), *a.* [< OF. *prepotent* = Sp. Pg. It. *prepotente*, < L. *præpoten(t-)s*, ppr. of *præposse*, be very powerful, < *præ*, before, + *posse*, be powerful: see *potent*.] 1. Preëminent in power, influence, force, or efficiency; prevailing; predominant.

Here is no grace so *prepotent* but it may be disobeyed. *Plaifere*, Appendix to the Gospel, xiv.

If the influence of heauen be the most *prepotent* cause of this effecte, then it seemeth to me that it shuld woorke immediatly.
R. Eden, tr. of Biringuccio (First Books on America, ed. [Arber, p. 364).

No dragon does there need for thee
With quintessential sting to work alarms,
Prepotent guardian of thy fruitage fine,
Thou vegetable porcupine!
Southey, Gooseberry-pie.

When one parent alone displays some newly-acquired and generally inheritable character, and the offspring do not inherit it, the cause may lie in the other parent having the power of *prepotent* transmission.
Darwin, Var. of Animals and Plants, xiii.

2. Highly endued with potentiality or potential power.

It is by the operation of an insoluble mystery that life is evolved, species differentiated, and mind unfolded from their *prepotent* elements in the immeasurable past.
Tyndall.

prepotential (prē-pǭ-ten'shąl), *a.* and *n.* [< *pre-* + *potential.* Cf. *prepotent.*] **I.** *a.* Same as *prepotent.*

What a contrast between those days, when the "discretionary powers of a diplomatist" were duly recognised, and our times of "telegraphic ambassadors" and a *prepotential* "clerkery"!
The Academy, Nov. 24, 1888, p. 329.

II. *n.* A quantity similar to a potential and only differing therefrom in belonging to a force varying inversely as a power of the distance whose index is not one less than the number of dimensions of the space considered.

prepractise† (prē-prak'tis), *v. t.* [< *pre-* + *practise.*] To practise beforehand.

Making it necessary for others what voluntarily they had *prepractised* themselves.
Fuller, Ch. Hist., XI. iii. 14.

preprint (prē'print), *n.* [< *pre-* + *print.*] That which is printed in advance; an early issue, as of a paper that is to be published in a journal or as one of a series. [Rare.]

To issue these papers independently in a series of *preprints.*
The Academy, June 1, 1889, p. 385.

preproperation† (prę-prop-ę-rā'shǫn), *n.* [< LL. as if **præproperatio(n-)*, < *præproperare*, hasten greatly, < L. *præproperus*, very hasty: see *preproperous.*] Excessive haste; precipitancy; a rash measure.

I feare the importunity of some impatient, and subtlety of some malevolent mindes, will put both Parliament and Assembly upon some *preproperations.*
N. Ward, Simple Cobler, p. 41.

preproperous† (prę-prop'ę-rus), *a.* [< L. *præproperus*, very hasty, < *præ*, before, + *properus*, quick, speedy, hasty: see *properate.*] Over-hasty; precipitate. *Webster.*

preprovide (prē-prǭ-vīd'), *v. t.*; pret. and pp. *preprovided*, ppr. *preproviding.* [< *pre-* + *provide.*] To provide beforehand.

Before livings were actually void, he provisionally *preprovided* incumbents for them.
Fuller, Ch. Hist., III. ix. 25.

prepubic (prē-pū'bik), *a.* [< L. *præ*, before, + *pubis*, pubis.] In *zoöl.* and *anat.*, situated in front of, or on the fore part of, the pubis; of or pertaining to a prepubis.—**Prepubic angle**, the bend in the urethra of the pendent penis in front of the pubis.—**Prepubic bone**, the preacetabular part of the pubic bone of birds and reptiles. See cut under *pterodactyl.*—**Prepubic process**, in *Aves*, the pubis proper, or prepubis.

A large spatulate bone [in *Pterodactylus*] articulates with each pubis near the symphysis, and seems to be an exaggeration of the *pre-pubic process* of Lacertilia and Chelonia.
Huxley, Anat. Vert., p. 231.

prepubis (prē-pū'bis), *n.*; pl. *prepubes* (-bēz). [NL. *præpubis*, < L. *præ*, before, + *pubis*, pubis.] The front section or preacetabular part of the pubic bone, being the pubis proper of birds and reptiles, well developed in dinosaurs, small or rudimentary in birds. It is to the bone in birds that the word is usually applied, the same bone being called the *pubis* when well developed, as in dinosaurs.

prepuce (prē'pūs), *n.* [< F. *prépuce* = Sp. Pg. *prepucio* = It. *prepuzio*, < L. *præputium*, the foreskin, < *præ*, before, + **putium*, perhaps connected with Gr. πόσθιον, πόσθη, penis.] The fold of skin over the glans penis; the foreskin.—**Prepuce of the clitoris**, the folds of the nymphæ encircling the glans of the clitoris.

prepunctual (prę-pungk'tų̄-ąl), *a.* [< *pre-* + *punctual.*] 1. More than punctual; excessively prompt in action or movement.—2. Acting or occurring before a specified point of time.

prepunctuality (prę-pungk-tų̄-al'į-ti), *n.* [< *pre-* + *punctuality.*] Anticipative punctuality, as the habit of keeping an engagement somewhat before the time appointed; excessive punctuality.

In Mr. Arthur Helps' . . . "In Memoriam" in this month's "Macmillan," speaking of Charles Dickens's more than punctuality, he has happily described the quality by so characteristic a term, *prepunctuality*, that the word must henceforth assume a recognized place in our language.
N. and Q., 4th ser., VI. 25.

preputial (prę-pū'shąl), *a.* [Also *præputial*; = F. *préputial*, < L. *præputium*, the foreskin (see *prepuce*), + *-al.*] Of or pertaining to the prepuce: as, *preputial* folds of skin; *preputial* follicles or secretions.

The Musk Deer . . . is small and hornless, and the male has canine teeth in the upper jaw. The musk is contained in a *præputial* bag.
W. W. Greener, The Gun, p. 507.

Preputial crypts, follicles, or **glands**, small lenticular sebaceous glands situated upon the corona glandis and cervix of the penis, secreting the smegma. Also called *glands of Tyson* and *odoriferous glands.* The corresponding structures of some animals are highly developed, and yield commercial products, as musk and castoreum.

preputium, præputium (prę-pū'shi-um), *n.*; pl. *preputia, præputia* (-ạ̈). [L. *præputium*: see *prepuce.*] The prepuce or foreskin.

In most mammals the penis is inclosed in a sheath of integument, the *preputium.* *Huxley*, Anat. Vert., p. 99.

Frenum præputii. See *frenum.*

prepyloric (prē-pī-lor'ik), *a.* [< L. *præ*, before, + NL. *pylorus*: see *pyloric.*] Situated in front of the pylorus.—**Prepyloric ossicle**, in the stomach of the crawfish. See the quotation.

With this [urocardiac] process is articulated, posteriorly, a broad *prepyloric ossicle*, which . . . articulates with the anterior edge of the pyloric ossicle, thus forming a kind of elastic diagonal brace between the urocardiac process and the pyloric ossicle.
Huxley, Anat. Invert., p. 277.

Preraphaelism (prē-raf'ạ̈-el-izm), *n.* [= F. *préraphaélisme*; as *pre-* + *Raphael* + *-ism.*] Same as *Preraphaelitism.*

Preraphaelite (prē-raf'ạ̈-el-īt), *a.* and *n.* [= F. *préraphaélite*; as *pre-* + *Raphael* (It. *Raffaele*), Raphael (see def. of *Preraphaelitism*), + *-ite*[2].] **I.** *a.* Pertaining to or characteristic of Preraphaelitism: as, *Preraphaelite* theories; the *Preraphaelite* school of painting.

Every *Pre-Raphaelite* landscape background is painted to the last touch, in the open air, from the thing itself.
Ruskin, Lects. on Architecture and Painting, iv.

The *Pre-Raphaelite* movement is understood to have combined two very distinct aims: first, the intellectual elevation of art by the choice of noble and original subjects, and, secondly, its technical advancement by a new and minute analysis of nature.
P. G. Hamerton, Thoughts about Art, xiii.

II. *n.* One who practises or favors Preraphaelitism in art or poetry.

The principal ground on which the *Pre-Raphaelites* have been attacked is the charge that they wish to bring us back to a time of darkness and ignorance, when the principles of drawing, and of art in general, were comparatively unknown.
Ruskin, Lects. on Architecture and Painting, iv.

Preraphaelitish (prē-raf'ạ̈-el-ī-tish), *a.* [< *Preraphaelite* + *-ish*[1].] Inclining toward or influenced by Preraphaelitism; modeled upon Preraphaelite principles. *London Art Jour.*, No. 56, p. 222.

Preraphaelitism (prē-raf'ạ̈-el-ī-tizm), *n.* [= F. *préraphaélitisme*; as *Preraphaelite* + *-ism.*] The style of painting in vogue from the time of Giotto (died 1336) to that of Raphael (a celebrated Italian painter, 1483–1520); specifically, a modern revival of this style. The essential characteristic of the revived style is rigid adherence to natural form and effect, and consequent rejection of all effort to elevate or heighten the effect artificially, by modifications, whether in drawing, arrangement, or coloring, based on conventional rules. The name is also given to the application of similar principles in poetical composition, shown in attention to minute details.

Pre-Raphaelitism has but one principle, that of absolute uncompromising truth in all that it does, obtained by working everything, down to the most minute detail, from nature, and from nature only.
Ruskin, Lects. on Architecture and Painting, iv.

If *Preraphaelitism* is to be judged by its chief exponents, it will be seen to be primarily a protest, and not in itself a fixed creed.
W. Sharp, D. G. Rossetti, p. 61.

The father and mother of modern *Pre-Raphaelitism* were modern literary thought and modern scientific investigation of the facts of nature.
P. G. Hamerton, Thoughts about Art, xiii.

prerectal (prē-rek'tąl), *a.* [< L. *præ*, before, + NL. *rectum* + *-al.*] Placed in front of the rectum.

preregnant† (prę-reg'nąnt), *n.* [< *pre-* + *regnant.*] One who reigns before another; a predecessor in power.

Edward, king Harold's *preregnant*,
Of the same changes foretold.
Warner, Albion's England, v. 22.

preremote (prē-rę-mōt'), *a.* [< *pre-* + *remote.*] More remote in previous time or prior order. *Dr. E. Darwin.* (*Imp. Dict.*)

prerenal (prē-rē'nąl), *a.* [< L. *præ*, before, + *ren*, kidney: see *renal.*] Situated in advance of the kidney.

prerept†, *v. t.* [< L. *præreptus*, pp. of *præripere*, snatch away before another, seize beforehand, forestall, anticipate, < *præ*, before, + *rapere*, snatch: see *snatch.*] To forestall in seizing.

In vayne wept Esau aftir Jacob had *prerept* him his blyssinge.
Joye, Expos. of Daniel v.

prerequire (prē-rę-kwīr'), *v. t.*; pret. and pp. *prerequired*, ppr. *prerequiring.* [< *pre-* + *require.*] To require beforehand.

Some things are *pre-required* of us, to make us capable of the comfortable performance of so holy and heavenly a duty.
Bp. Hall, Devout Soul, iv. § 1.

The primitive church would admit no man to the superior orders of the clergy unless, among other *prerequired* dispositions, they could say all David's psalter by heart.
Jer. Taylor, Works (ed. 1835), II. 115.

prerequisite (prē-rek'wi-zit), *a.* and *n.* [< *pre-* + *requisite.*] **I.** *a.* Previously required; necessary as a condition of something following.

He only that hath the *prerequisite* qualifications shall have the crown.
Baxter, Saints' Rest, i. 3.

II. *n.* A condition required beforehand; a preliminary necessity.

This is but a *pre-requisite* to the main thing here required, . . . knowledge being but a step to this turret of happiness.
Rev. S. Ward, Sermons, p. 164.

How much more justly may I challenge that privilege to do it with the same *prerequisites*, from the best and most judicious of Latin writers.
Dryden, To Sir R. Howard.

We have just found that the *pre-requisite* to individual life is in a double sense the *pre-requisite* to social life.
H. Spencer, Man vs. State, p. 102.

preresolve (prē-rę-zolv'), *v. t.*; pret. and pp. *preresolved*, ppr. *preresolving.* [< *pre-* + *resolve.*] To resolve beforehand.

I will debarre mine eares, mine eyes from all the rest, because I detest their lewdnesse; no man goes thus *preresolved* to a play.
Prynne, Histrio-Mastix, II. iv. 2.

I am confident you are herein *preresolved* as I wish.
Sir E. Dering, Speeches, p. 143. (*Latham.*)

preretina, præretina (prē-ret'i-nạ̈), *n.*; pl. *preretinæ, præretinæ* (-nē). [NL. *præretina*, < L. *præ*, before, + NL. *retina*, retina.] The thin stratum of columnar nucleated cells continued forward from the ora serrata of the retina as far as the tips of the ciliary processes, where it gives place to the uveal pigment. Also called *pars ciliaris retinæ.*

preretinal (prē-ret'i-nąl), *a.* [< *preretina* + *-al.*] Of or pertaining to the preretina.

prerevolutionary (prē-rev-ǭ-lū'shǫn-ā-ri), *a.* [< *pre-* + *revolution* + *-ary.* Cf. *revolutionary.*] Prior to a revolution; specifically, prior to the American revolution.

prerima (prē-rī'mạ̈), *n.* [NL. *prærima*, < L. *præ*, before, + *rima*, a cleft, fissure: see *rima.*] An extension of the rima in advance of the porta in some animals, as dipnoans.

The rima (*prerima*) extends cephalad from the porta [in *Ceratodus*]. *Buck's Handbook of Med. Sciences*, VIII. 140.

prerimal (prē-rī'mąl), *a.* [< *prerima* + *-al.*] Of or pertaining to the prerima.

prerogative (prę-rog'ą-tiv), *a.* and *n.* [I. *a.* < L. *prærogativus*, that is asked before, < *prærogatus*, pp. of *prærogare*, ask before (another), < *præ*, before, + *rogare*, ask: see *rogation.* II. *n.* = F. *prérogative* = Sp. Pg. It. *prerogativa*, < L. *prærogativa*, f. (ML. also *prærogativum*, neut.), a previous choice or election, a sure sign or token, preference, privilege, prerogative; orig. *centuria prærogativa*, the tribe or century that was asked first for its opinion (according to lot, in the Roman vote by comitia); fem. of *prærogativus*, that is asked before: see above.] **I.** *a.* 1†. Called upon to vote first; having the right to vote first.

This foredome and choise of the *prerogative* centurie all the rest followed after, and by their suffrages confirme.
Holland, tr. of Livy, p. 601.

2†. Entitled to precedence; superior.

The affirmative hath the *prerogative* illation, and barbara engrosseth the powerful demonstration.
Sir T. Browne, Vulg. Err., i. 7.

3. Pertaining to, characteristic of, or held by prerogative or privileged right.

Why should we
Tax the *prerogative* pleasures of our prince,
Whom he shall grace, or where bestow his favours?
Beau. and Fl. (?), Faithful Friends, i. 1.

The abbot of Tavistock . . . was in the fifth year of Henry VIII. made a spiritual lord of parliament by letters patent. This is said to have been a unique exercise of *prerogative* power.
Stubbs, Const. Hist., § 430.

Prerogative court, in *Eng. law*, an ecclesiastical court established for the trial of all testamentary cases where the deceased possessed at death goods above the value of five pounds in each of two or more dioceses, and consequently where the diocesan courts could not possess jurisdiction. Such a court existed both in the province of Canterbury and in that of Armagh. This jurisdiction was transferred in 1857 to the court of probate.

The *Prerogative* Court and the consistory courts lived on the testamentary and matrimonial jurisdiction.
Stubbs, Medieval and Modern Hist., p. 324.

Prerogative writs, in *law*, process for the commencement of certain special or extraordinary proceedings, viz. *procedendo, mandamus, prohibition, quo warranto, habeas corpus, certiorari.*

II. *n.* 1†. The right of voting first; precedence in voting.

It hapned that the centurie of the younger sort was drawn out first by lot, and had the *prerogative*, and by their voices nominated T. Octacilius and M. Æmilius Regillus for consuls. *Holland*, tr. of Livy, p. 513.

2. A peculiar privilege; a characteristic right inhering in one's nature; a special property or quality.

Of the bresyle and mirobalane trees, with other innumerable *prerogatiues* and benefites whiche nature hath plentifully giuen to this blessed Iland, we haue spoken suffyciently in owr decades.
Peter Martyr (tr. in Eden's First Books on America, ed. [Arber, p. 190).

She's free as you or I am, and may have,
By that *prerogative*, a liberal choice
In the bestowing of her love.
Beau. and Fl., Captain, ii. 2.

Man, whose *prerogative* it is to be in a great degree a creature of his own making. *Burke*, Rev. in France.

Our fair one, in the playful exercise
Of her *prerogative* — the right divine
Of youth and beauty — bade us versify
The legend. *Whittier*, Bridal of Pennacook.

3. Specifically, a privilege inherent in one's office or position; an official right; an exclusive or sovereign privilege, in theory subject to no restriction or interference, but practically often limited by other similar rights or prerogatives; more specifically still, the royal prerogative.

As if those gifts had bin only his peculiar and *Prerogative*, intail'd upon him with his fortune to be a King.
Milton, Eikonoklastes, i.

The king hath a *prerogative* to coin money without consent of parliament; but he cannot compel the subject to take that money, except it be sterling gold or silver, because herein he is limited by law.
Swift, To the People of Ireland, iv.

A constitution where the prince is clothed with a *prerogative* that enables him to do all the good he hath a mind to. *Bp. Atterbury*, Sermons, I. vii.

Rutherford says, *prerogative* simply means a power or will which is discretionary and above and uncontrolled by any other will; the term is frequently used to express the uncontrolled will of the sovereign power in the State. It is applied not only to the king but also to the legislative and judicial branches of a government, as, "the royal *prerogatives*," the "*prerogatives* of parliament," the "*prerogatives* of the court," etc.
Halleck, International Law (new ed.), I. 125.

4†. Precedence; superiority in power, rank, or quality.

Then give me leave to have *prerogative*.
Shak., T. of the S., iii. 1. 6.

Within is a country that may haue the *prerogatiue* over the most pleasant places knowne, for large and pleasant navigable Rivers. *Capt. John Smith*, Works, I. 114.

5. In New Jersey, a court held by the chancellor sitting as ordinary in probate and similar causes.—**Royal prerogative**, that special preëminence which a sovereign has over all other persons, and out of the course of the common law, by right of regal dignity. In Great Britain the royal prerogative includes the right of sending and receiving ambassadors, of making treaties, and (theoretically) of making war and concluding peace, of summoning Parliament, and of refusing assent to a bill, with many other political, judicial, ecclesiastical, etc., privileges. The royal prerogative is usually exercised by delegation, and only in a few cases (as the conferring of honors) in person. =**Syn. 2** and **3**. *Immunity*, etc. See *privilege*.

prerogative (prẹ̄-rog′ạ-tiv), *v. t.*; pret. and pp. *prerogatived*, ppr. *prerogativing*. [< *prerogative*, *n.*] To endow with a prerogative.

Yet, 'tis the plague of great ones;
Prerogatived are they less than the base.
Shak., Othello, iii. 3. 274.

prerogatively (prẹ̄-rog′ạ-tiv-li), *adv.* By exclusive or peculiar privilege. *Imp. Dict.*

prest†, *n.* and *v.* A Middle English form of *press*[1].

pres. An abbreviation (*a*) of *present*; (*b*) [*cap.*] of *President*.

presa (prā′zạ), *n.* [It., a taking: see *prize*[1].] In a musical canon, a mark to indicate the point at which the successive voice-parts are to take up the theme; a lead. It has various shapes, as 𝄋, +, ※, etc.

presacral (prē-sā′kral), *a.* [< L. *præ*, before, + NL. *sacrum*: see *sacral*.] Preceding the sacrum in the spinal column; situated in front of the sacral vertebræ, as a vertebra; lumbar.

The lumbar region contains the *pre-sacral* group of vertebræ, which have only short ribs.
Gegenbaur, Comp. Anat. (trans.), p. 434.

presage (prẹ̄-sāj′), *v.*; pret. and pp. *presaged*, ppr. *presaging*. [< OF. *presagier* = Sp. Pg. *presagiar* (< ML. **præsagiare*, < L. *præsagium*, a presage) = It. *presagire*, < L. *præsagire*, feel or perceive beforehand, presage, foreshow (also LL. *præsagare*, < L. *præsagus*, foreshowing, presaging), < *præ*, before, + *sagire*, feel: see *sagacious*.] **I.** *trans.* **1.** To foreshow or foretoken; signify beforehand, as by an omen or prognostic; give warning of.

The o'erflowing Nilus *presageth* famine.
Shak., A. and C., i. 2. 49.

Hippocrates wisely considered dreams as they *presaged* alterations in the body. *Sir T. Browne*, To a Friend.

A sound in air *presag'd* approaching rain,
And beasts to covert scud across the plain.
Parnell, The Hermit.

The sharp heat-lightnings of her face
Presaging ill to him whom Fate
Condemned to share her love or hate.
Whittier, Snow-Bound.

2. To have a presentiment or prophetic impression of; forebode.

My mind *presageth* happy gain and conquest.
Shak., 3 Hen. VI., v. 1. 71.

"Dishonour!" then my soul is cleft with fear;
I half *presage* my misery; say on.
Ford, Love's Sacrifice, iii. 3.

With heavy hearts *presaging* nothing good.
William Morris, Earthly Paradise, II. 22.

3. To foretell; predict; calculate beforehand.

I see that come to pass which I *presaged* in the beginning. *B. Jonson*, Cynthia's Revels, v. 3.

Hear
What I *presage* with understanding clear.
Dekker and Ford, Sun's Darling, v. 1.

Lands he could measure, terms and tides *presage*.
Goldsmith, Des. Vil., l. 209.

4†. To point out.

Then seek this path that I to thee *presage*,
Which after all to heaven shall thee send.
Spenser, F. Q., I. x. 61.

=**Syn. 3**. *Predict*, *Prophesy*, etc. See *foretell*.

II. *intrans.* To have a presentiment of the future; have foreknowledge.

What power of mind,
Foreseeing or *presaging*, . . . could have fear'd
How such united force of gods, how such
As stood like these, could ever know repulse?
Milton, P. L., i. 627.

That by certain signs we may *presage*
Of heats and rains, and wind's impetuous rage.
Dryden, tr. of Virgil's Georgics, i. 463.

presage (pres′āj or prē′sāj; formerly also prẹ̄-sāj′), *n.* [< OF. *presage*, F. *présage* = Sp. Pg. It. *presagio*, < L. *præsagium*, a presentiment, a prognostic, < *præsagire*, feel or perceive beforehand: see *presage*, *v.*] **1.** Something which foreshows, portends, or gives warning of a future event; a prognostic; an omen.

Meteors, prodigies and signs,
Abortives, *presages*, and tongues of heaven,
Plainly denouncing vengeance upon John.
Shak., K. John, iii. 4. 158.

He had before him the sad *presage* of his ill success.
Milton, Eikonoklastes, v.

They [violent storms] give certain *Presages* of their being at hand several hours before they come.
Dampier, Voyages, II. iii. 60.

2. A foreboding; a presentiment; a feeling that something is to happen; a prophetic impression.

The sad augurs mock their own *presage*.
Shak., Sonnets, cvii.

She will call
That three-days-long presageful gloom of yours
No *presage*, but the same mistrustful mood
That makes you seem less noble than yourself.
Tennyson, Merlin and Vivien.

3. Foreknowledge; prescience.

If there be aught of *presage* in the mind,
This day will be remarkable in my life.
Milton, S. A., l. 1387.

Many a famous man and woman, town
And landskip, have I heard of, after seen
The dwarfs of *presage*. *Tennyson*, Princess, iv.

4. Prophetic significance or import.

This dreadful Conflict is of dire *Presage*;
Begone, and fly from Jove's impending Rage.
Congreve, Semele, i. 1.

=**Syn. 1**. *Sign*, *Augury*, etc. See *omen* and *foretell*.

presageful (pres′āj-fụl or prẹ̄-sāj′fụl), *a.* [< *presage*, *n.*, + *-ful*.] **1.** Full of presage; prophetic; ominous.

It comes to us like the first sounding of a *presageful* note of doom, repeated more than once before the final calamity.
E. Dowden, Shelley, I. 227.

2. Prophetic; foreknowing.

Ev'n such a wave, but not so pleasurable,
Dark in the glass of some *presageful* mood,
Had I for three days seen, ready to fall.
Tennyson, Merlin and Vivien.

Johnson had not that fine sensitiveness to the political atmosphere which made Burke *presageful* of coming tempest. *Lowell*, Among my Books, 1st ser., p. 353.

presagement (prẹ̄-sāj′ment), *n.* [< *presage*, *v.*, + *-ment*.] **1.** A foreboding; omen; presage.

I have spent some enquiry whether he had any ominous *presagement* before his end.
Sir H. Wotton, Reliquiæ, p. 234.

2. A foretelling; prediction.

presager (prẹ̄-sā′jėr), *n.* [< *presage*, *v.*, + *-er*[1].] One who presages or foretells; a prophet.

O, let my books be then the eloquence
And dumb *presagers* of my speaking breast.
Shak., Sonnets, xxiii.

presagie†, *n.* [< L. *præsagium*, a presage: see *presage*, *n.*] Same as *presage*.

Thinke thou this is a *presagie* of God's fearce wrath to thee,
If that thou cleave not to his woord, and eke repentant be.
Stubbes, Two Examples (1581). (*Nares*.)

presagious†, *a.* [< *presage* (L. *præsagium*) + *-ous*.] Ominous; presageful.

Some supernatural cause sent me strange visions, which being confirmed with *presagious* chances, I had gone to Delphos. *Sir P. Sidney*, Arcadia, ii.

presanctify (prẹ̄-sangk′ti-fī), *v. t.*; pret. and pp. *presanctified*, ppr. *presanctifying*. [< *pre-* + *sanctify*.] To consecrate beforehand.—**Liturgy or Mass of the Presanctified.** See *liturgy*.

presande†, *n.* A Middle English form of *present*[2].

presartorial (prē-sär-tō′ri-al), *a.* [< L. *præ*, before, + *sartor*, a tailor: see *sartorial*.] Before the age of tailoring; previous to the use of fashioned garments.

Bran had its prophets, and the *presartorial* simplicity of Adam its martyrs, tailored impromptu from the tar-pot of incensed neighbors, and sent forth to illustrate the "feathered Mercury" as defined by Webster and Worcester.
Lowell, Study Windows, p. 193.

presbyope (pres′bi-ōp), *n.* [< NL. *presbyopia*.] One who is affected with presbyopia; one who is long-sighted; a presbyte.

presbyopia (pres-bi-ō′pi-ạ), *n.* [NL., < Gr. πρέσβυς, old, + ὤψ, eye.] Diminished power of accommodation for near objects, incident to advancing years, and due to progressive loss of elasticity in the crystalline lens.

presbyopic (pres-bi-op′ik), *a.* [< *presbyopia* + *-ic*.] Pertaining to presbyopia; affected with presbyopia; old-sighted.

presbyopy (pres′bi-ō-pi), *n.* [< NL. *presbyopia*.] Same as *presbyopia*.

Presbypithecus (pres″bi-pi-thē′kus), *n.* [NL., < Gr. πρέσβυς, old, + πίθηκος, an ape.] A synonym of *Semnopithecus*. *Trouessart*, 1879.

presbyte (pres′bīt), *n.* [= F. *presbyte* = Sp. *présbita*, *présbete* = Pg. *presbyta* = It. *presbita*, *presbite*, < Gr. πρεσβύτης, an old man, < πρέσβυς, old. Cf. *presbyter*.] A person affected with presbyopia.

presbyter (pres′bi-tėr), *n.* [= F. *presbytère* = Sp. *presbitero* = Pg. *presbytero* = D. *presbyter*, < LL. *presbyter*, an older, esp. an elder or presbyter in the church, < Gr. πρεσβύτερος, an elder, prop. adj., older, compar. of πρέσβυς, old. Cf. *priest*, derived through AS., and *prester*[1], derived through OF., from the same ult. source.] **1.** An elder; a priest; specifically, in hierarchic churches, a minister of the second order, between the bishop and the deacon.

They that speak ingeniously of Bishops and *Presbyters* say that a Bishop is a great *Presbyter*, and, during the time of his being Bishop, above a *Presbyter*.
Selden, Table-Talk, p. 27.

Episcopacy, as it is taken for an Order in the Church above a *Presbyter*, or, as wee commonly name him, the Minister of a Congregation, is either of Divine constitution or of humane. *Milton*, Prelatical Episcopacy.

New *Presbyter* is but Old Priest writ large.
Milton, New Forcers of Conscience, l. 20.

2†. [*cap.*] A Presbyterian. [Rare.]

And *presbyters* have their jackpuddings too. *S. Butler*.

3. In *zoöl.*, a monkey of the genus *Presbytes*.

presbyteral (pres-bit′ėr-al), *a.* [= F. *presbytéral* = Sp. *presbiteral* = It. *presbiterale*, pertaining to the priesthood; as *presbyter* + *-al*.] Relating to a presbyter or presbytery; presbyterial.

There is no indication that he [Ignatius] is upholding the episcopal against any other form of Church government, as, for instance, the *presbyteral*.
Bp. Lightfoot, Apostolic Fathers, I. 390.

It is quite probable that the members of the *presbyteral* college distributed the various duties of their office among themselves according to their respective talents, taste, experience, and convenience.
Schaff, Hist. Christ. Church, I. § 61.

presbyterate (pres-bit′ėr-āt), *n.* [= Sp. *presbiterado*, *presbiterato* = Pg. *presbyterado*, *presbyterato* = It. *presbiterato*, < LL. *presbyteratus*, the office of a presbyter, < *presbyter*, a presbyter: see *presbyter*.] **1.** The office or station of a presbyter.

The *presbyterate*, as a distinct order from the ordinary office of apostleship, is not of Divine institution.
Jer. Taylor, Works (ed. 1835), II. 158.

2. A presbytery.

Meetings of the bishop and the *presbyterate* of every diocese, the oldest and simplest form of ecclesiastical organisation. *R. W. Dixon*, Hist. Church of Eng., xix.

presbyterated (pres-bit′ėr-ā-ted), *a.* [< *presbyterate* + *-ed*[2].] Organized with a government by elders or presbyters.

He asserts that a *presbyterated* society of the faithful hath within itself a compleat power of self-reformation, or, if you will, of self-preservation, and may within itself manage its own choices of officers and censures of delinquents. C. *Mather*, Mag. Chris., v. 2.

presbyteress (pres'bi-tėr-es), *n.* [‹ ML. *presbyterissa, presbiterissa*, fem. of L. *presbyter*, presbyter: see *presbyter* and *-ess*.] 1. In the *early church*, one of the elder women in the order of widows, presiding among these, and having authority to teach.—2. In the *early church*, and in the *medieval church*, a priest's wife, especially one living apart from her husband; a priest's widow; later, a priest's concubine.

Marianus sayth she was a *presbyteresse*, or a priestes leman. *Bp. Bale*, English Votaries, i.

presbyteria, *n.* Plural of *presbyterium*.

presbyterial (pres-bi-tē'ri-al), *a.* [‹ *presbytery* (ML. *presbyterium*) + *-al*.] Of or pertaining to presbyters or a presbytery; pertaining to government by presbyteries.

They have laboured . . . to advance the new fancied sceptre of lay *presbyterial* power. *Hooker*, Eccles. Polity, vi. 1.

About the manner and order of this government, whether it ought to be *Presbyteriall* or Prelaticall, such endlesse question, or rather uproare, is arisen in this land. *Milton*, Church-Government, Pref.

presbyterially (pres-bi-tē'ri-al-i), *adv.* After the manner of a presbytery; according to Presbyterianism.

Presbyterian (pres-bi-tē'ri-an), *a.* and *n.* [= F. *presbytérien* = Sp. It. *presbiteriano* = Pg. *presbyteriano* = G. Dan. *presbyterian-er* = Sw. *presbyterian*, ‹ NL. *presbyterianus*, pertaining to a presbytery or to presbyters, ‹ ML. *presbyterium*, a presbytery, LL. *presbyter*, a presbyter: see *presbytery*, *presbyter*.] I. *a.* Of or pertaining to ecclesiastical government by elders or by presbyteries. The word is specially used to note the various religious bodies which adopt the Presbyterian form of church government (see *Presbyterianism*), and hold a more or less modified form of Calvinism. Among the leading Presbyterian churches are the following: (1) The established Church of Scotland, formed in 1560 under the leadership of Knox; it prepared the First Book of Discipline in 1560, the Second Book of Discipline in 1581, and was formally established by the government in 1592. It was temporarily replaced by episcopacy during the period 1661–89. Later events were secessions leading to the formation of various bodies in the eighteenth century (Secession Church in 1733, Relief Church in 1761) and of the Free Church in 1843. See *Covenanter*, 2. (2) The Presbyterian Church in the United States. Its first presbytery was founded in 1705. After a temporary disruption, the first General Assembly met in 1789. In 1838 the church split on theology and the antislavery question. (See *New School* and *Old School*, etc., below.) The two wings were reunited in 1870. It numbers about 900,000 members. (3) The Presbyterian Church in the United States (Southern). This body seceded from the Old School Presbyterian Church in 1861 on the establishment of the Confederacy, and during the period 1861–5 it had the title of General Assembly of the Confederate States of America. It numbers about 200,000 members. Other bodies, besides the Free Church of Scotland (see *free*), and those mentioned below, are the Reformed Presbyterian Churches in the United States, the Welsh Presbyterian Church, the Presbyterian Churches of England, Canada, Ireland, etc. —**Cumberland Presbyterian Church**, a Presbyterian body which seceded from the Presbyterian Church in the United States, and was developed from the Cumberland presbytery in Kentucky and Tennessee in 1810. It numbers about 180,000 members.—**New School Presbyterian Church**, that wing of the Presbyterian Church in the United States which in 1838 separated from the other branch. It held pronounced views against slavery, and was regarded as less conservative in theology.—**Old School Presbyterian Church**, that wing of the Presbyterian Church in the United States which held more conservative views regarding slavery and Calvinism. The Southern Presbyterian Church seceded from it in 1861, and the remainder united with the New School Presbyterians in 1870.—**Reformed Presbyterian Church.** See *Cameronian*, n., 1, and *Covenanter*, 2.—**United Presbyterian Church.** (*a*) A Scottish church formed by the union of the United Secession Church and the Relief Church (see above) in 1847. It numbers over 180,000 members. (*b*) A church in the United States formed in 1858 by the coalition of various bodies. It numbers over 100,000 members.

II. *n.* One who holds to the system of Presbyterianism; a member of any of the Presbyterian churches.

Presbyterianism (pres-bi-tē'ri-an-izm), *n.* [= F. *presbytérianisme* = Sp. *presbiterianismo* = Pg. *presbyterianismo*; as *Presbyterian* + *-ism*.] The system of church government by elders or by presbyteries. The essential features of church government in Presbyterianism are—the equality of the clergy, the identification of the apostolic presbyter with the bishop, the division of elders into teaching elders (or ministers) and ruling or lay elders, the government of each local church by its session, composed of pastor and ruling elders, and the subordination of sessions to a presbytery, of presbyteries to a synod, and of synods to a general assembly. In the Dutch Reformed Church, which adopts Presbyterianism, the bodies corresponding to session, presbytery, synod, and general assembly are consistory, classis, synod, and general synod. This system of church government is opposed to episcopacy on one side and to congregationalism and independency on the other. It was developed in the sixteenth century by Calvin and other reformers, and was adopted in Geneva and by the reformers in France, Scotland, etc. It supplanted episcopacy for a short time in England, in the period of the Civil War and Commonwealth. Presbyterianism is the predominating form of church government in Scotland, and prevails extensively in the Netherlands, in the United States, and in Ireland and other parts of the British empire.

Presbyterianize (pres-bi-tē'ri-an-īz), *v. t.*; pret. and pp. *Presbyterianized*, ppr. *Presbyterianizing*. [‹ *Presbyterian* + *-ize*.] To render Presbyterian.

The Massachusetts churches . . . have always resisted the efforts . . . to *presbyterianize* them. *Andover Rev.*, VII. 536.

Presbyterianly (pres-bi-tē'ri-an-li), *adv.* After the manner of Presbyterians.

This person, tho' *presbyterianly* affected, yet he had the king's ear as much as any other person. *Wood*, Athenæ Oxon., II.

Presbyterism† (pres'bi-tėr-izm), *n.* [‹ *presbyter* + *-ism*.] Same as *Presbyterianism*.

It looks not at all like Popery that *Presbyterism* was disdained by the king; his father had taught him that it was a sect so perfidious that he found more faith among the Highlanders. *Bp. Hacket*, Abp. Williams, ii. 197. (*Davies.*)

presbyterium (pres-bi-tē'ri-um), *n.*; pl. *presbyteria* (-ä). [NL. (ML.), ‹ Gr. πρεσβυτέριον, a council of elders: see *presbytery*.] Same as *presbytery*, 5.

presbytership (pres'bi-tėr-ship), *n.* [‹ *presbyter* + *-ship*.] The office or rank of a presbyter.

presbytery (pres'bi-ter-i), *n.*; pl. *presbyteries* (-iz). [= F. *presbytère* = Sp. *presbiterio* = Pg. *presbyterio* = It. *presbiterio*, a presbytery, parsonage, ‹ ML. *presbyterium*, a council of elders, part of a church in which the elders sit, the function of a presbyter or priest, etc., ‹ Gr. πρεσβυτέριον, a body of elders, ‹ πρεσβύτερος, πρέσβυς, an elder: see *presbyter*.] 1. A body of presbyters or elders in the Christian church; the body or class of presbyters taken collectively.

Neglect not the gift that is in thee, which was given thee by prophecy, with the laying on of the hands of the *presbytery*. 1 Tim. iv. 14.

Strictly speaking, any body of elders is a *Presbytery*. *N. A. Rev.*, CXLII. 551.

2. In churches holding the Presbyterian form of government, a judicatory which ranks next above the session and below the synod. In the Presbyterian Church of the United States its composition and powers are thus defined in its Form of Government: "A presbytery consists of all ministers, and one ruling elder from each congregation, within a certain district. . . . The Presbytery has power to receive and issue appeals from church-sessions, and references brought before them in an orderly manner; to examine and license candidates for the holy ministry; to ordain, install, remove, and judge ministers; to examine and approve or censure the records of church-sessions; to resolve questions of doctrine or discipline seriously and reasonably proposed; to condemn erroneous opinions which injure the purity or peace of the church; to visit particular churches, for the purpose of inquiring into their state and redressing the evils that may have arisen in them; to unite or divide congregations, at the request of the people, or to form and receive new congregations; and, in general, to order whatever pertains to the spiritual welfare of the churches under their care."

3. The ecclesiastical district or division under the jurisdiction of a presbyter.—4. [*cap.*] The Presbyterian polity.

The question between Episcopacy and *Presbytery*. *Craik*, Hist. Eng. Lit., II. 60.

5. In *arch.*, the part of the church appropriated to the clergy; in the *early church*, and in the *Greek Church*, the space between the altar and apse, or the whole sanctuary; afterward, the space near the altar, or the sedilia; in later

Choir and Presbytery of Gloucester Cathedral, England, looking east.

medieval and modern use, the space in a cathedral or large church (often raised) between the choir and the altar; less strictly, the choir or chancel. Also *presbyterium*. See diagram under *cathedral*.

The enclosure of the choir was kept low, so as not to hide the view of the raised *presbytery*, or to prevent the congregation from witnessing the more sacred mysteries of the faith which were there performed by the higher order of clergy. *J. Fergusson*, Hist. Arch., I. 407.

6. A clergyman's house; a parsonage. [Roman Catholic use.]

Presbytes (pres-bī'tēz), *n.* [NL., ‹ Gr. πρεσβύτης, an old man: see *presbyte*.] A genus of semnopithecine or sacred monkeys: synonymous with *Semnopithecus*.

prescapula, præscapula (prē-skap'ū-lä), *n.*; pl. *prescapulæ, præscapulæ* (-lē). [NL. *præscapula*, ‹ L. *præ*, before, + *scapula*, shoulder-blade: see *scapular*.] That part of the scapula which is anterior to (cephalad of) its spine or median axis: opposed to *postscapula*. In man the prescapula corresponds to the supraspinatus fossa.

prescapular (prē-skap'ū-lär), *a.* and *n.* [‹ NL. *præscapularis*, ‹ *præscapula*: see *prescapula*.] I. *a.* Situated in front of the long axis of the shoulder-blade; noting a section of the scapula or shoulder-blade in advance of the spine; supraspinous, with reference to the scapula: the opposite of *postscapular*: as, the *prescapular* fossa. See cut under *omosternum*.

II. *n.* The prescapularis or supraspinatus muscle.

prescapularis (prē-skap-ū-lā'ris), *n.*; pl. *prescapulares* (-rēz). [NL. *præscapularis*: see *prescapular*.] The muscle of the prescapular or supraspinous aspect of the scapula; the supraspinatus. *Coues*.

prescene† (prē'sēn), *n.* [‹ L. *præ*, before, + *scena*, scene.] A preliminary scene; a prologue; an induction.

Profan'd with mischiefs, the *Pre-Scæne* of Hell
To cursed Creatures that 'gainst Heav'n rebell.
Sylvester, tr. of Du Bartas's Weeks, i. 6.

prescience (prē'shiens), *n.* [‹ ME. *prescience*, ‹ OF. *prescience*, F. *prescience* = Sp. Pg. *presciencia* = It. *prescienza*, ‹ LL. *præscientia*, foreknowledge, ‹ L. *præscien(t-)s*, ppr. of *præscire*, know beforehand: see *prescient*.] Foreknowledge; previous knowledge; knowledge of events before they take place; foresight.

And certes, if I hadde *prescience*
Your wil to know er ye your lust me tolde,
I wolde it doon withouten necligence.
Chaucer, Clerk's Tale, l. 603.

By my *prescience*
I find my zenith doth depend upon
A most auspicious star.
Shak., Tempest, i. 2. 180.

The most exact calculator has no *prescience* that somewhat incalculable may not balk the very next moment. *Emerson*, Essays, 1st ser., p. 244.

prescient (prē'shient), *a.* [‹ F. *prescient* = Pg. It. *presciente*, ‹ L. *præscien(t-)s*, ppr. of *præscire*, know beforehand, ‹ *præ*, before, + *scire*, know: see *scient*.] Foreknowing; having knowledge of events before they take place.

Governments rarely comprehend those *prescient* minds which anticipate wants posterity cannot always supply. *I. D'Israeli*, Amen. of Lit., II. 259.

prescientialt† (prē-shi-en'shal), *a.* [Also *præsciential*; ‹ LL. *præscientia*, prescience, + *-al*.] Prescient; foreknowing. [Rare.]

Love's of so quick a sight that he
Aforehand with his object is,
And into dark Futurity
With *præsciential* rays doth press.
Beaumont, Love's Eye.

prescientific (prē-sī-en-tif'ik), *a.* [‹ *pre-* + *scientific*.] Existing before the scientific age; belonging or relating to times prior to the reduction of knowledge in general, or of some special branch of it, to the form of science.

Even the intellects of men of science are haunted by *prescientific* survivals. *Littell's Living Age*, March 1, 1884, p. 523.

In the *prescientific* era of medicine, a brisk traffic took place in these prehistoric bone deposits, as in the analogous case of Egyptian mummies. *Sci. Amer.*, N. S., LIX. 247.

presciently (prē'shient-li), *adv.* In a prescient manner; with prescience.

On this memorable day a philosophical politician might have *presciently* marked the seed-plots of events which not many years afterwards were apparent to all men. *I. D'Israeli*, Curios. of Lit., IV. 380.

prescind (prē-sind'), *v.* [= OF. *prescinder* = Sp. Pg. *prescindir* = It. *prescindere*, ‹ L. *præscindere*, cut off in front, ‹ *præ*, before, + *scindere*, slit, cleave: see *scission*.] I. *trans.* To separate from other facts or ideas for special consideration; strip of extrinsic adjuncts, especially in conception.

The result of Attention, by concentrating the mind upon certain qualities, is . . . to withdraw or abstract it from all else. In technical language, we are said to *prescind* the phænomena which we exclusively consider. To *pre-*

scind, to attend, and to abstract are merely different but correlative names for the same process; and the first two are nearly convertible. When we are said to *prescind* a quality, we are merely supposed to attend to that quality exclusively. *Sir W. Hamilton*, Logic, vii.

If force be considered as *prescinded* from gravity and matter, and as existing only in points, or centers, what can this amount to but an abstract spiritual incorporeal force? *Berkeley*, Siris, § 225.

II. *intrans.* To withdraw the attention: usually with *from*.

Those things which Christianity, as it *prescinds from* the interest of the republic, hath introduced. *Jer. Taylor*, Works (ed. 1835), II. 210.

In what I am about to write I *prescind* entirely *from* all theological theories and religious symbols. *Fortnightly Rev.*, N. S., XLIII. 72.

prescindent (prẹ-sin′dent), *a.* [< L. *præscinden(t-)s*, ppr. of *præscindere*, cut off in front: see *prescind*.] Prescinding; abstracting.

We may, for one single act, abstract from a reward, which nobody who knows the *prescindent* faculties of the soul can deny. *G. Cheyne*, Philosophical Principles.

prescious† (prē′shi-us), *a.* [< L. *præscius*, foreknowing, < *præscire*, know beforehand: see *prescient*.] Prescient; foreknowing; having foreknowledge.

No *prescious* determination of our states to come. *Sir T. Browne*, Religio Medici, i. 11.

Prescious of ills. *Dryden*, Æneid, xi.

prescission (prẹ-sish′on), *n.* [< L. as if **præscissio(n-)*, < *præscindere*, cut off: see *prescind*. Cf. *scission*.] The act of prescinding. [Rare.]

prescribe (prẹ-skrīb′), *v.*; pret. and pp. *prescribed*, ppr. *prescribing*. [= F. *prescrire* = Sp. *prescribir* = Pg. *prescrever* = It. *prescrivere*, < L. *præscribere*, write before, prefix in writing, < *præ*, before, + *scribere*, write: see *scribe*.] **I.** *trans.* **1†.** To inscribe beforehand or in front.

Having heard your approbation of these in their presentment, I could not but *prescribe* them with your name. *Chapman*, Byron's Conspiracy and Tragedy, Ded.

2. To lay down beforehand, in writing or otherwise, as a rule of action; ordain; appoint; define authoritatively.

For her no other termes should ever tie
Then what *prescribed* were by lawes of chevalrie.
Spenser, F. Q., V. vii. 28.

Prescribe not us our duties. *Shak.*, Lear, i. 1. 279.

They may call back the sun as soon, stay time,
Prescribe a law to death, as we endure this.
Fletcher, Loyal Subject, v. 4.

Philosophers *prescribe* us Rules that they themselves, nor any Flesh and Blood, can observe. *Howell*, Letters, I. vi. 58.

Mankind in ways *prescribed* are found,
Like flocks that follow on a beaten ground.
Crabbe, Works, IV. 55.

The necessities which initiate government themselves *prescribe* the actions of government. *H. Spencer*, Data of Ethics, § 19.

3. Specifically, to advise, appoint, or designate as a remedy for disease.

Wrath-kindled gentlemen, be ruled by me;
Let's purge this choler without letting blood:
This we *prescribe*, though no physician.
Shak., Rich. II., i. 1. 154.

A druggist's assistant who . . . *prescribes* a sharp purgative and kills the patient is found guilty of manslaughter. *H. Spencer*, Man vs. State, p. 47.

4. In *law*, to render invalid through lapse of time or negative prescription.

"Could you not take up the action again?" said Mr. Mowbray.
"Whew! it 's been *prescribed* sax or seeven years sync."
Scott, St. Ronan's Well, viii.

=**Syn. 2.** To order, command, dictate, institute, establish.

II. *intrans.* **1.** To set rules; lay down the law; dictate.

The assuming an authority of dictating to others, and a forwardness to *prescribe* to their opinions, is a constant concomitant of this bias of our judgments. *Locke.* (*Johnson.*)

2. To give medical directions; designate the remedies to be used: as, to *prescribe* for a patient in a fever.

I will use the olive with my sword,
Make war breed peace, make peace stint war, make each
Prescribe to other as each other's leech.
Shak., T. of A., v. 4. 84.

3. In *law*: (*a*) To claim by prescription; claim a title to a thing by immemorial use and enjoyment: with *for*: as, to *prescribe for* a right of way, of common, or the like. (*b*) To become extinguished or of no validity through lapse of time, as a right, debt, obligation, and the like. See *prescription*, 3.

Under James VI. actions for servants' wages are to *prescribe* [applied to property when lost by the lapse of time] in three years, after which the debt can only be proved by writ or oath of the debtor (1579, c. 21). *Ribton-Turner*, Vagrants and Vagrancy, p. 362.

It [the action of spuilzie] must be brought within three years in order to entitle the pursuer to violent profits, otherwise it *prescribes* in forty years. *Encyc. Brit.*, XXIII. 589.

prescriber (prẹ-skrī′bėr), *n.* [< *prescribe* + *-er*[1].] One who prescribes; one who gives rules or directions, especially in medical treatment.

The phisicians of the bodyes haue practicioners and poticaries that doe minister theyr arte vnder them; and themselues are the *prescribers* and appoynters what it is that muste bee geuen to the sycke. *J. Udall*, On Luke, Pref.

God the *prescriber* of order. *Fotherby*, Atheomastix, p. 158.

prescript (prē′skript, formerly also prẹ-skript′), *a.* and *n.* [< OF. *prescript*, F. *prescrit* = Sp. Pg. *prescripto* = It. *prescritto*; < L. *præscriptus*, prescribed (neut. *præscriptum*, something prescribed, a copy, a precept, order, rule), pp. of *præscribere*, prescribe: see *prescribe*.] **I.** *a.* Prescribed; set down beforehand as a rule; ordained or appointed beforehand.

To the intent the *prescript* number of the citizens should neither decrease nor above measure increase. *Sir T. More*, Utopia (tr. by Robinson), ii. 5.

Baptism is given by the element of water, and that *prescript* form of words which the Church of Christ doth use. *Hooker*, Eccles. Polity, iv. 1.

I must apologize this to the reader, that I do not condemn all *prescript* penalties, although the argument seem to hold forth so much. *Winthrop*, Hist. New England, II. 257.

II. *n.* **1.** That which is prescribed; a regulation; direction; instruction; rule; law.

They [Utopians] define virtue to be life ordered according to the *prescript* of nature. *Sir T. More*, Utopia (tr. by Robinson), ii. 7.

Ne staid, till that he came with steep descent
Unto the place where his *prescript* did showe.
Spenser, Mother Hub. Tale, l. 1261.

Do not exceed
The *prescript* of this scroll.
Shak., A. and C., iii. 8. 5.

The Jews, by the *prescript* of their law, were to be merciful to all their nation and confederates in religion. *Jer. Taylor*, Works (ed. 1835), I. 196.

2†. Specifically, a medical direction; a prescription.

It is not a potion I send, but a *prescript* in paper, which the foolish patient did eat up when he read in it written, Take this. *Rev. T. Adams*, Memoir, p. xlvii. (Works, III.).

prescriptibility (prẹ-skrip-ti-bil′i-ti), *n.* [< *prescriptible* + *-ity* (see *-bility*).] The quality of being prescriptible. *Story.*

prescriptible (prẹ-skrip′ti-bl), *a.* [= F. *prescriptible* = Sp. *prescriptible* = Pg. *prescriptivel* = It. *prescrittibile*; as *prescript* + *-ible*.] Proper to be prescribed; depending on or derived from prescription.

If the matter were *prescriptible*. *Grafton*, Hen. VIII., an. 34.

prescription (prẹ-skrip′shon), *n.* [< F. *prescription* = Sp. *prescripcion* = Pg. *prescripção* = It. *prescrizione*, < L. *præscriptio(n-)*, a writing before or in front, a title, preface, pretext, precept, order, rule, law, exception, demurrer, ML. prescription, a prescriptive right, etc., < *præscribere*, pp. *præscriptus*, prescribe: see *prescribe*.] **1.** The act of prescribing or establishing by rules; that which is prescribed; direction; prescript.

I am thankful to you; and I'll go along
By your *prescription*. *Shak.*, Hen. VIII., i. 1. 151.

Men who could not be brought off from the *prescriptions* of gentilism to the seeming impossibilities of Christianity. *Jer. Taylor*, Works (ed. 1835), II. 181.

2. In *med.*, a statement, usually written, of the medicines or remedies to be used by a patient, and the manner of using them.

My reason, the physician to my love,
Angry that his *prescriptions* are not kept,
Hath left me. *Shak.*, Sonnets, cxlvii.

3. In *law*, a personal use or possession sufficiently long continued to secure to one or more persons a title or right as against others; the effect on rights of persons of the immemorial or long-continued and uninterrupted enjoyment of a thing, as a right of way or of common, by one person or class or succession of persons rather than by another or others: as, to acquire possession of a thing by *prescription*. After uninterrupted enjoyment for thirty, and in many cases for twenty years, a *prima facie* title arises by prescription to the thing enjoyed.

Those honours, and that worship, he has held in the Christian church by a *prescription* of fifteen, sixteen, or seventeen hundred years. *Waterland*, Works, II. 202.

Can any length of acquiescence turn a wrong thing into a right one; any length of *prescription* turn an abuse into a right? *Stubbs*, Medieval and Modern Hist., p. 22.

We are intolerant of everything that is not simple, unbiassed by *prescription*, liberal as the wind. *J. A. Symonds*, Italy and Greece, p. 297.

Hence, more specifically—(*a*) The acquisition of a right or title by such enjoyment, called sometimes *positive* or *acquisitive prescription*.

Some gentlemen doe hold that dignitie [nobility] by *prescription*, not hauing other proofe then that they and their ancestors were called Gentlemen time out of minde. *Segar*, Honor, p. 227.

When thou beginnest to sue him, he will plead *prescription*: . . . It is mine, it shall be mine, because it hath been mine. *Rev. T. Adams*, Works, II. 41.

The Lucquese plead *prescription* for hunting in one of the Duke's forests that lies upon their frontiers. *Addison*, Remarks on Italy (ed. Bohn), I. 493.

The institution called Usucapion or (in modern times) *Prescription*, the acquisition of ownership by continuous possession, lay at the root of the ancient Roman law, whether of persons or of things. *Maine*, Early Hist. of Institutions, p. 315.

(*b*) The loss of a right or title by suffering another to enjoy it, or by neglecting to assert it: called sometimes *negative prescription*.

And unless ye get your thumb-nail on them [poachers] in the very nick o' time, ye may dine on a dish of *prescription*, and sup upon an absolvitor. *Scott*, St. Ronan's Well, viii.

Barons by prescription. See *baron*, 1.—**Prescription Act** (sometimes called Lord *Tenterden's Act*), an English statute (2 and 3 William IV., c. 71) by which uninterrupted enjoyment of an easement for twenty years (forty at the most) under claim of right was made a bar to adverse claims, in lieu of requiring reference to immemorial usage.—**Title by prescription**, a title based solely on a showing that the claimant and those under whom he claims have immemorially been in the habit of enjoying that which he claims.

prescription-glass (prẹ-skrip′shon-glàs), *n.* **1.** A glass vessel with measures, as of a tablespoonful, teaspoonful, etc., marked on it.—**2.** A spectacle-glass or lens made according to an oculist's prescription.

The lens-grinding room . . . is devoted almost exclusively to making what are known as *prescription glasses*. *Sci. Amer.*, N. S., LVIII. 259.

prescriptionist (prẹ-skrip′shon-ist), *n.* [< *prescription* + *-ist*.] One who makes up or compounds a medical prescription.

The apparent deterioration was due to the dishonesty of the retail druggist or *prescriptionist*. *Sanitarian*, XVIII. 427.

prescriptive (prẹ-skrip′tiv), *a.* [= F. *prescriptif* = It. *prescrittivo*, < LL. *præscriptivus*, pertaining to a prescript, < L. *præscriptus*, pp. of *præscribere*, prescribe: see *prescribe*.] **1.** Arising from established usage or opinion; customary.

Emigrations for conquest, for gold, for very restlessness of spirit—if they grow towards an imperial issue, have all thus a *prescriptive* and recognized ingredient of heroism. *R. Choate*, Addresses, p. 90.

They were prepared to strip the church of its power, and royalty of its *prescriptive* sanctity. *Bancroft*, Hist. U. S., I. 383.

2. Specifically, in *law*, pertaining to, resulting from, or based upon prescription.

Yon tall Tower,
Whose cawing occupants with joy proclaim
Prescriptive title to the shattered pile.
Wordsworth, Sonnets, iii. 47.

It [the right of self-taxation] was in full exercise from the early years of Edward I., and accordingly was strong enough in *prescriptive* force to resist his attempts to incorporate the clergy as an estate of parliament. *Stubbs*, Const. Hist., § 306.

prescutal (prē-skū′tal), *a.* [< *præscutum* + *-al*.] Of or pertaining to the præscutum.

preset, *v.* and *n.* An obsolete variant of *press*[1].

preseance† (prē′sẹ-ans), *n.* [< OF. *preseance*, F. *préséance*, precedence, < ML. *præsidentia*, lit. a sitting before, < L. *præsidere*, sit before: see *presidence*. Cf. *séance*.] Privilege or priority of place in sitting.

The ghosts . . . may for their discreete judgement in precedence and *preseance* read a lesson to our ciuilest gentry. *R. Carew*, Survey of Cornwall, p. 71.

presee (prē-sē′), *v. t.*; pret. *presaw*, pp. *preseen*, ppr. *preseeing*. [< *pre-* + *see*[1].] To foresee.

You should have employed some other in the journey, which I had no reason to affect much, *preseeing* well enough how thankless it would be. *Motley*, Hist. Netherlands, I. 443, note 4.

preselect (prē-sẹ-lekt′), *v. t.* [< *pre-* + *select*.] To select beforehand.

presemilunar (prē-sem-i-lū′nạr), *a.* [< *pre-* + *semilunar*.] Anterior to the semilunar lobe of the cerebellum.—**Presemilunar lobe**, the posterosuperior lobe of the cerebellum.

preseminal (prē-sem′i-nal), *a.* [< *pre-* + *seminal*.] Prior to insemination or fecundation: as, the *preseminal* state of an ovum. Also *præseminal*.

presence (prez′ens), *n.* [< ME. *presence*, < OF. *presence*, F. *présence* = Sp. *presencia* = Pg. *presença* = It. *presenza*, *presenzia*, < L. *præsentia*, a being before, in view, or at hand, present, < *præsen(t-)s*, being before or at hand: see *present*.] 1. The state of being present; the state of being in a certain place, and not in some other place; being, continuance, or stay in a certain place: as, the *presence* of a planet in a particular part of its orbit; specifically, the state of being near the speaker or writer or in some place upon which his thought is directed.

The fields appeared covered with people and Baskets, to tempt vs on shore; but nothing was to be had without his *presence*. Quoted in *Capt. John Smith's* Works, I. 218.

Thy absence hath been very long in my conceit, and thy *presence* much desired. *Winthrop*, Hist. New England, I. 431.

The rich, . . . intent
On pleasure, haunt the capital, and thus
To all the violence of lawless hands
Resign the scenes their *presence* might protect.
Cowper, Task, iv. 592.

2. Companionship; attendance; company; society.

In all their affliction he was afflicted, and the angel of his *presence* saved them. Isa. lxiii. 9.

To-night we hold a solemn supper, sir,
And I'll request your *presence*.
Shak., Macbeth, iii. 1. 15.

If he see you himselfe, his *presence* is the worst visitation; for if he cannot heale your sicknes, he will bee sure to helpe it.
Bp. Earle, Micro-cosmographie, A Meere Dull Phisitian.

Phœbe's *presence*, and the contiguity of her fresh life to his blighted one, was usually all that he required.
Hawthorne, Seven Gables, ix.

3. Immediate neighborhood or vicinity; close proximity.

Full many a noble war-song had he sung
E'en in the *presence* of an enemy's fleet.
Tennyson, Guinevere.

4. The state of being face to face with a great personage or with a superior.

The shepherd Dorus answered with such a trembling voice . . . that it was some sport to the young ladies, thinking it want of education which made him so discountenanced with unwonted *presence*. *Sir P. Sidney*, Arcadia.

They rise to their husbands, and stand while they are in *presence*. *Purchas*, Pilgrimage, p. 293.

5. An assembly, particularly of persons of rank; a noble company.

Being so old a man, it was likely that he knew most of any man in that *presence* and company.
Latimer, Sermon bef. Edw. VI., 1550.

Here is like to be a good *presence* of Worthies.
Shak., L. L. L., v. 2. 536.

6. Personality; the sum of the qualities of an individual; personage.

Lord of thy *presence* and no land beside.
Shak., K. John, i. 1. 137.

Slowly passed that august *Presence*
Down the thronged and shouting street.
Whittier, The Sycamores.

7. Aspect; appearance; demeanor; mien; air.

Affable grace, speeche eloquent, and wise;
Stately *præsence*, suche as becometh one
Whoe seemes to rule realmes by her lookes alone.
Puttenham, Partheniades, viii.

Be, as thy *presence* is, gracious and kind.
Shak., Sonnets, x.

I am the neatliest-made gallant i' the company, and have the best *presence*. *B. Jonson*, Cynthia's Revels, iv. 1.

Nay, nay, God wot, so thou wert nobly born,
Thou hast a pleasant *presence*.
Tennyson, Gareth and Lynette.

8. An apparition; a vision; a specter.

A deadly silence step by step increased,
Until it seemed a horrid *presence* there,
And not a man but felt the terror in his hair.
Keats, Lamia, ii.

The only other time he was conscious of a *presence* was, he told me, one day when, coming out of one of the rooms on the upper lobby, he felt as if some person brushed closely by him, but he saw nothing.
Proc. Soc. Psych. Research, I. 111.

9. A presence-chamber.

Here lies Juliet, and her beauty makes
This vault a feasting *presence* full of light.
Shak., R. and J., v. 3. 86.

The next chamber within it, which is the *Presence*, is very faire. *Coryat*, Crudities, I. 32.

The rest of yᵉ apartments are rarely gilded and carv'd, wᵗʰ some good modern paintings. In the *presence* hang 3 huge branches of chrystal. *Evelyn*, Diary, Nov. 18, 1649.

Doctrine of the real presence, the doctrine that the body and blood of Christ are present in the eucharist. This view is held by the Roman Catholic and Greek Churches, and in a modified form by the Anglican Church. The Roman Catholic position is thus defined: "In the august sacrament of the holy Eucharist, after the consecration of the bread and wine, our Lord Jesus Christ, true God and man, is truly, really, and substantially contained under the species of those sensible things." (*Canons and Decrees of the Council of Trent*, Session XIII., Chap. I.) The High-church view is thus stated: "That the Body and Blood of Christ exist in those elements is as much the belief of the English Church as of the Latin and Greek Churches." (*Blunt*, Dict. Theol., p. 761.)

A sacramental or a hyperphysical change no English churchman who believes the *Real Presence* as his Church teaches could hesitate to accept. *Pusey*, Eirenicon, p. 33.

Doctrine of the virtual presence, the doctrine that Christ is present in the eucharist in such a manner that communicants receive the virtue or power and benefits of his body and blood, but not his real body and blood themselves.—**Hearing in presence.** See *hearing*.—**In presence of**, in *law*, being bodily so near another, who is conscious of the fact, as to be within the means of observation. If a person is sleeping, an act done in the same place is not considered as done in his presence.—**Presence of mind**, a calm, collected state of the mind, with its faculties ready at command, enabling a person to speak or act without disorder or embarrassment when taken by surprise; quickness in meeting the exigencies of sudden and trying occasions.

The—the—tremor of my passion entirely takes away my *presence of mind*. *Sheridan*, The Rivals, iv. 2.

As a soldier he [Charles I.] was feeble, dilatory, and miserably wanting, not in personal courage, but in the *presence of mind* which his station required.
Macaulay, Hallam's Const. Hist.

At the twelfth round the latter champion was all abroad, as the saying is, and had lost all *presence of mind* and power of attack or defence. *Thackeray*, Vanity Fair, v.

To be in presence, to be present.

If thou be fair, ther folk *ben in presence*,
Shew thou thy visage and thyn apparaille.
Chaucer, Clerk's Tale, l. 1151.

presence-chamber (prez'ẹns-chām″bėr), *n.* The room in which a great personage receives his guests, or those entitled to come before him; a hall of state.

The heaven of heavens, the *presence chamber* of God himself, expects the presence of our bodies.
Donne, Sermons, xii.

By the hands of these [silversmiths] . . . he finished his *presence-chamber* in a manner truly admirable.
Bruce, Source of the Nile, II. 633.

presence-room (prez'ẹns-röm), *n.* Same as *presence-chamber*.

That morning in the *presence* room I stood
With Cyril and with Florian, my two friends.
Tennyson, Princess, i.

presensation (prē-sen-sā'shọn), *n.* [< *pre-* + *sensation*.] A sensation anticipatory of a future sensation; a sensation due to imagining an object which is expected to produce a similar sensation through the channels of external sense. [Rare.]

That plenitude of happiness that has been reserved for future times, the presage and *presensation* of it, has in all ages been a very great joy and triumph to all holy men and prophets. *Dr. H. More*, Def. of Moral Cabbala, ii.

presension (prẹ̄-sen'shọn), *n.* [Also, erroneously, *presention*; < L. *præsensio(n-)*, a foreboding, < *præsensus*, pp. of *præsentire*, feel or perceive beforehand: see *presentient*.] 1. A direct perception of the future; a presentiment.

Natural [divination] is, when the mind hath a *presention* by an internal power, without the inducement of a sign.
Bacon, Advancement of Learning, ii. 203.

The hedgehog, whose *presention* of winds is so exact that it stoppeth the north or southern hole of its nest.
Sir T. Browne, Vulg. Err., iii. 10.

There is, saith Cicero, an ancient opinion . . . that there is among men a certain divination, which the Greeks call prophecy (or inspiration)—that is, a *presension* and knowledge of future things. *Barrow*, Works, II. ix.

2. An anticipation; a presensation.

We shall find ourselves in a heaven upon earth, and each act of virtue will be a *presention* and foretaste of the joys of a celestial life. *Scott*, Christian Life, i. 4.

I have a *prescension* of a grand royal meaning which some day will be revealed to me.
E. H. Sears, Fourth Gospel.

present[1] (prez'ẹnt), *a.* and *n.* [< ME. *present*, < OF. *present*, F. *présent* = Sp. Pg. It. *presente*, < L. *præsen(t-)s*, ppr. of *præesse*, be before, in view, or at hand, be present, < *præ*, before, + *esse*, be: see *essence*, *be*[1], and cf. *absent*.] I. *a.* 1. Being or abiding, as a person, in this or any specified place; being in view or immediately at hand: opposed to *absent*.

These things have I spoken unto you, being yet *present* with you. John xiv. 25.

So, either by thy picture or my love,
Thyself away art *present* still with me.
Shak., Sonnets, xlvii.

I will send word withynne a moneth day
Vnto your prince, where euer he be *present*,
All vtterly the fyne of myn entente.
Generydes (E. E. T. S.), l. 1757.

What could he advantage
Your fortune, were he *present*?
Shirley, Grateful Servant, i. 2.

The temple of the Greeks was the house of a *present* deity, its cell his chamber, its statue his reality.
J. A. Symonds, Italy and Greece, p. 217.

Present in this sense is often used in addressing a letter which is to be delivered to some one either actually present, or near at hand, as in the same neighborhood or town.
2. Now existing; being at this time; not past or future: as, the *present* session of Congress.

We apprehend them by memory, whereas the *present* time and things so swiftly passe away.
Puttenham, Arte of Eng. Poesie, p. 31.

We'll teach thee to forget, with *present* pleasures,
Thy late captivity.
Fletcher (*and another* ?), Prophetess, iv. 3.

The description also of Hermon, as a mountain of snow, agrees with its *present* appearance, being always covered with it. *Pococke*, Description of the East, II. i. 74.

If we compare the *present* state of France with the state in which she was forty years ago, how vast a change for the better has taken place! *Macaulay*, Mirabeau.

3. Being now in mind. (*a*) Under consideration.

I will not be negligent to put you always in remembrance of these things, though ye know them, and be established in the *present* truth. 2 Pet. i. 12.

The much greater part of them are not brought up so well, or accustomed to so much religion, as in the *present* instance. *Law.*

(*b*) Actually in consciousness.

They are never *present* in mind at what passes in discourse. *Swift*, On Conversation.

I call that clear which is *present* and manifest to the mind giving attention to it, just as we are said clearly to see objects when, being *present* to the eye looking on, they stimulate it with sufficient force, and it is disposed to regard them.
Quoted in *Veitch's* Int. to Descartes's Methods, p. lv.

4. Prompt or ready at need.

He oft finds *present* helpe who does his griefe impart.
Spenser, F. Q., II. i. 46.

Vouchsafe t' afford . . .
Some *present* speed to come and visit me.
Shak., Lucrece, l. 1307.

God is our refuge and strength, a very *present* help in trouble. Ps. xlvi. 1.

Nor could I hope, in any place but there,
To find a god so *present* to my prayer.
Dryden, tr. of Virgil's Eclogues, i. 59.

Present money. See *money*.—**Present tense**, in *gram.*, the tense of a verb which expresses action or being in the present time, as Latin *scribo*, English I *write*, or *do write*, or *am writing*. Abbreviated *pres.*

II. *n.* 1. Present time; time now passing.

And madness, thou hast forged at last
A night-long *Present* of the Past
In which we went thro' summer France.
Tennyson, In Memoriam, lxxi.

2. Present business; an affair in hand.

Shall I be charged no further than this *present*?
Must all determine here? *Shak.*, Cor., iii. 3. 42.

3†. The money or other property a person has on hand.

I'll make division of my *present* with you;
Hold, there's half my coffer. *Shak.*, T. N., iii. 4. 380.

4. *pl.* In *law*, a term used in a deed of conveyance, a lease, letter of attorney, or other document, to express the document itself; this present writing: as in the phrase "Know all men by these *presents*" (that is, by this very document, by the words here set down); hence, any writ or writing. [In this sense it is rarely used in the singular.]

Be it open and knowen apertiliche vn-to ȝow, be theis *presentes*, that we fulliche vndirstondend the lettres sent fro ȝour Chauncerye vn-to vs.
English Gilds (E. E. T. S.), p. 48.

King. What *present* hast thou there? . . .
Jaq. I beseech your grace, let this letter be read.
Shak., L. L. L., iv. 3. 189.

Romulus, after his death (as they report, or feign), sent a *present* to the Romans, that above all they should intend arms, and then they should prove the greatest empire of the world.
Bacon, True Greatness of Kingdoms and Estates (ed. 1887).

5. In *gram.*, the present tense.—**At present**, at this time; now.

Which not *at present* having time to do.
Pope, Epil. to Satires, ii. 156.

He is *at present* with his regiment.
Sheridan, The Rivals, i. 2.

These figures are of course between ourselves *at present*.
Forster, Dickens, ix.

Historical present (tense). See *historical*, 4.

On other points Hug disagrees with Hoffmann, especially with the latter's statement that the *historical present* was to the Romans simply a preterit.
Amer. Jour. Philol., X. 111.

That present, elliptically for *that present time*; the time being; then.

The wounds that this frost gave the commonwealth were for *that present* scarce felt.
The Great Frost (Arber's Eng. Garner, I. 91).

The present, an elliptical expression for *the present time*.

Men that set their hearts only upon *the present*.
Sir R. L'Estrange.

This present, elliptically for *this present time*; now.

We know your feare, and are in an agonie at *this present* lest you should lose that superfluity of riches and honour which your party usurp.
Milton, On Def. of Humb. Remonst.

present[1]† (prez'ẹnt), *adv.* [ME., < *present*[1], *a.*] At once; immediately; presently.

Let me dye *present* in this place.
Chaucer, Parliament of Fowls, l. 423.

present[2] (prē-zent'), *v.* [< ME. *presenten*, < OF. *presenter*, F. *présenter* = Sp. *presentar* = Pg. *presentear* = It. *presentare*, < L. *præsentare*, place before, show (lit. make present), exhibit, present, ML. also give, < *præsen(t-)s*, ppr. of *præesse*, be at hand: see *present*[1].] **I.** *trans.* **1.** To bring or introduce into the presence of some one, especially of a superior; recommend for acquaintance; make known: as, to *present* an envoy to the king; with a reflexive pronoun, to come into the presence of any one.

Now there was a day when the sons of God came to *present themselves* before the Lord. Job i. 6.

Let 's *present* him to the duke, like a Roman conqueror. *Shak.*, As you Like it, iv. 2. 3.

Ma'am, I'm an enthusiastic admirer of Darrell. You say he is a connection of yours? *Present* me to him. *Bulwer*, What will he Do with it?

2. To show; exhibit; demonstrate; reveal.

She went in perill, of each noyse affeard,
And of each shade that did it selfe *present*.
Spenser, F. Q., III. vii. 10.

Justly to your grave ears I'll *present*
How I did thrive in this fair lady's love.
Shak., Othello, i. 3. 124.

An exceedingly rich needle worke, interlaced very curiously with abundance of gold and silver, that *presents* a very goodly picture of Moyses. *Coryat*, Crudities, I. 110.

It is a degree towards the life of angels when we enjoy conversation wherein there is nothing *presented* but in its excellence. *Steele*, Spectator, No. 100.

3. To bring or lay before one for acceptance; offer as a gift, generally with formality; make an offer or expression of; hence, to bestow; give: as, to *present* a ring or a book to a friend; to *present* one's compliments.

Now goo, Sygrem, as fast as ye may spede,
To Auferius to *present* hym this stede.
Generydes (E. E. T. S.), l. 2394.

I pray *present* my most humble Service to my good Lady. *Howell*, Letters, I. v. 13.

Eight jousts had been, and still
Had Lancelot won the diamond of the year,
With purpose to *present* them to the Queen
When all were won. *Tennyson*, Lancelot and Elaine.

4. To approach with a gift or offering; give a present to; bestow a gift upon.

The Kyngdom of Cathay marchethe toward the West unto the Kyngdom of Tharse; the whiche was on of the Kinges that cam to *presente* our Lord in Betheleem. *Mandeville*, Travels, p. 255.

As matching to his youth and vanity,
I did *present* him with the Paris balls.
Shak., Hen. V., ii. 4. 131.

The skill is to be generous and seem not to know it of yourself, 'tis done with so much ease: but a liberal blockhead *presents* his mistress as he'd give an alms. *Steele*, Lying Lover, i. 1.

5. To hand over ceremoniously; give in charge or possession, as for use or service.

So ladies in romance assist their knight,
Present the spear, and arm him for the fight.
Pope, R. of the L., iii. 130.

6. *Eccles.*, to offer or recommend to the bishop or ordinary as a candidate for institution. See *presentation*[1], 5.

Any clerk may be *presented* to a parsonage or vicarage: that is, the patron to whom the advowson of the church belongs may offer his clerk to the bishop of the diocese to be instituted. *Blackstone*, Com., I. xi.

7. To nominate for support at a public school or other institution.

L's governor (so we called the patron who *presented* us to the foundation) lived in a manner under his paternal roof. *Lamb*, Christ's Hospital Five-and-Thirty Years Ago.

8†. To proffer; offer openly.

He . . . *presented* battle to the French navy, which they refused. *Sir J. Hayward.*

9. To lay before a judge, magistrate, or governing body for action or consideration; submit, as a petition, remonstrance, etc., for decision or settlement to the proper authorities.

That one talent which is death to hide
Lodged with me useless, though my soul more bent
To serve therewith my Maker, and *present*
My true account. *Milton*, Sonnets, xiv.

10. To accuse to the authorities; bring a charge against before those having authority to act upon it; lay before a court of judicature, as an object of inquiry; give notice of officially, as for a crime or offense.

You would *present* her at the leet,
Because she brought stone jugs and no seal'd quarts.
Shak., T. of the S., Ind., ii. 89.

Romanus keeps his monthly residence
At church, although against his conscience;
He would refraine (because he doth abhor it)
But that he feares to be *presented* for it.
Times' Whistle (E. E. T. S.), p. 102.

Being *presented* for this, and enjoined to suffer the child to be baptised, he still refusing, and disturbing the church, he was again brought to the court. *Winthrop*, Hist. New England, II. 213.

Persons who dredge or fish for oysters, not being free of the fishery, are called cable-bangers [at Rochester], and are *presented* and punished by the court. *Defoe*, Tour through Great Britain, I. 150.

11. To direct; point; level; aim, as a weapon or firearm: as, to *present* a loaded pistol.

According to Virgil, the Roman youth *presented* their lances towards their opponents in a menacing position. *Strutt*, Sports and Pastimes, p. 199.

12†. To represent; personate; act.

You, constable, are to *present* the prince's own person. *Shak.*, Much Ado, iii. 3. 79.

By sitting on the stage, you may, with small cost, . . . at any time know what particular part any of the infants *present*. *Dekker*, Gull's Hornbook, p. 141.

To **present arms** (*milit.*), to bring the piece to a perpendicular position in front of the body, as in saluting a superior officer. =**Syn.** 3. *Bestow, Grant*, etc. See *give*[1].

II. *intrans.* To make a presentation, particularly to an ecclesiastical office.

If . . . the true patron once waives this privilege of donation, and *presents* to the bishop, and his clerk is admitted and instituted, the advowson is now become forever presentative. *Blackstone*, Com., II. iii.

present[2] (prez'ent), *n.* [< ME. *present*, < OF. *present*, F. *présent* = Sp. Pg. It. *presente*, a gift, present; from the verb.] **1.** A thing presented or given; a gift.

So thanne ben the *presentes* of grettere plesance to him, and more benygnely he wil resceyven hem, than though he were presented with an 100 or 200. *Mandeville*, Travels, p. 228.

And for thei were so high astates and men of grete puyssaunce, he made hem riche *presentes*, and yaf hem grete yeftes and riche. *Merlin* (E. E. T. S.), i. 108.

His dog, . . . to-morrow, by his master's command, he must carry for a *present* to his lady. *Shak.*, T. G. of V., iv. 2. 80.

He told me I could not go to the pasha without making considerable *presents* of cloth, both to him and his Kiaia. *Pococke*, Description of the East, II. i. 127.

I can make no marriage *present*:
Little can I give my wife.
Tennyson, Lord of Burleigh.

2 (prē-zent'). [An elliptical use of the verb.] *Milit.*, the position from which a rifle or musket is fired.

"Who are you?" said she, with the musket ready for the *present*. *Marryat*, Privateersman, xvii.

=**Syn. 1.** *Present, Gift, Donation, Gratuity, Largess, Grant.* The difference between *present* and *gift* is felt in the fact that one may be willing to accept as a *present* that which he would not be willing to accept as a *gift*: a *gift* is to help the one receiving it; a *present* does him honor, or expresses friendly feeling toward him. A *present* is therefore ordinarily to an individual; but in law *gift* is used, to the exclusion of *present*, as including all transfers of property without consideration and for the benefit of the donee. A *donation* is of considerable value, and generally made to some public institution: as, a *donation* of books to a public library. *Gratuity* emphasizes the fact that the receiver has no legal claim to the gift; it is a gift to an inferior, as a fee to a servant, and generally a small sum: as, a self-respecting man will not expect a *gratuity* for every little service. *Largess* is an old word, representing a gift from a superior, especially one high in authority, generally shared by a considerable number. A *grant* is rarely the act of a private individual, but rather of a sovereign, legislature, or corporation: as, a *grant* of land to a company.

presentability (prē-zen-ta-bil'i-ti), *n.* [< *presentable* + *-ity* (see *-bility*).] The state or quality of being presentable.

People perversely wore their old boots, which had long passed the season of *presentability*. *Pop. Sci. Mo.*, XXXIII. 417.

presentable (prē-zen'ta-bl), *a.* [< *present*[2] + *-able*.] **1.** Capable of being presented; qualified or suitable for presentation. (*a*) Ready or suitable for introduction to others or into society; hence, in proper trim; fit to be seen.

Mrs. Lovell was informed that the baronet had been addressing his son, who was fresh from Paris, and not, in his own modest opinion, *presentable* before a lady. *G. Meredith*, Rhoda Fleming, xxxii.

(*b*) Capable of being offered for perception or understanding; capable of being made known: as, an idea *presentable* only in language.

If a key fits a lock, or a glove a hand, the relation of the things to one another is *presentable* to the perceptions. *H. Spencer*, Nineteenth Century, XIX. 750.

(*c*) Suitable for being offered as a gift.

2. *Eccles.*: (*a*) Capable of being presented to a church living: as, a *presentable* clerk. (*b*) Capable of receiving the presentation of a clerk: as, "churches *presentable*," *Ayliffe*, Parergon.

By the dissolution of religious houses, all appropriations had been *presentable* like other churches, if the statute of dissolution had not given them to the king. *Spelman*, On Tythes, xxix. 2.

presental (prē-zen'tal), *n.* [< *present*[2] + *-al*.] Same as *presentment*. [Rare.]

As illustrations of the author's *presental* of different sides of a subject, we give two extracts. *Chicago Advance*, Jan. 14, 1869.

presentaneous† (prez-en-tā'nē-us), *a.* [< L. *præsentaneus*, momentary, that operates quickly, < *præsen(t-)s*, present: see *present*[1].] Quick; prompt to act or take effect: as, "a *presentaneous* poison," *Harvey*.

presentary†, *a.* [ME., < L. *præsentarius*, that is at hand, ready, < *præsen(t-)s*, present: see *present*[1].] Present.

This like infynyt moevynge of temporel thinges folweth this *presentary* estat of lyf unmoevable. *Chaucer*, Boëthius, v. prose 6.

presentation[1] (prez-en-tā'shon), *n.* [< OF. *presentation*, F. *présentation* = Sp. *presentacion* = Pg. *presentação* = It. *presentazione*, < LL. *præsentatio(n-)*, a placing before, an exhibition, < L. *præsentare*, pp. *præsentatus*, place before, exhibit: see *present*[2], *v.*] **1.** The act, especially the ceremonious act, of presenting a gift, prize, trophy, donation, or the like: as, the *presentation* of a medal to a fireman; the *presentation* of a stand of colors to a regiment; the *presentation* of an organ to a church.—**2.** The act of presenting or offering as for recognition, acceptance, etc.

Prayers are sometimes a *presentation* of mere desires. *Hooker*, Eccles. Polity.

After the *presentation* of his letters of credence, it is then the duty of a minister, if accredited to a sovereign, to ask for *presentation* to the Queen or Empress. *E. Schuyler*, Amer. Diplomacy, p. 138.

3. That which is presented; a gift; an offering. [Rare.]

Aloft on the waters, the height or top of an olive tree did shew itself, whereof the dove brought a *presentation* to the good old man. *Time's Storehouse*, p. 154. (*Latham.*)

4. A representation; exhibition; appearance; show; semblance.

I call'd thee then poor shadow, painted queen;
The *presentation* of but what I was.
Shak., Rich. III., iv. 4. 84.

These *presentations* of fighting on the stage are necessary to produce the effects of an heroick play. *Dryden.*

5. (*a*) In *eccles. law*, a patron's act of offering to a bishop, presbytery, or other properly constituted authority a candidate for induction into a benefice. See *patronage*, 3.

It differs from nomination in this, that, while *presentation* signifies offering a clerk to the bishop for institution, nomination signifies offering a clerk to the patron in order that he may be presented. *Hook.*

Hence—(*b*) The nomination by one ecclesiastical authority of a candidate to be appointed by another. In the Protestant Episcopal Church the right of presentation to the bishop is lodged in the vestry or other parish authorities. (*c*) The right of presenting a clergyman.

If the bishop . . . admits the patron's *presentation*, the clerk so admitted is next to be instituted by him. *Blackstone*, Com., I. xi.

6. In *obstet.*, the appearance of a particular part of the fetus at the superior pelvic strait during labor. The most frequent form is *vertex presentation*, or presentation of the upper and back part of the fetal head. For each presentation there are several positions. See *position*, 10.

7. A cognitive modification of consciousness; an idea; a representation. This use of the word has recently been introduced to translate the German *vorstellung*, the term used by Wolff to translate the Latin *repræsentatio*. None of these words has ever been scientifically defined, and they are used, like their synonym *idea*, with vague variations of meaning. Of these, the following appear to be types: (*a*) An idea in general; any mental object subject to attention and association. Kant divides presentations (*vorstellungen*) in this sense into unconscious presentations and perceptions, the latter into sensations and cognitions, the latter again into intuitions and concepts, and the latter into empirical and pure concepts.

All that variety of mental facts which we speak of as sensations, perceptions, images, intuitions, concepts, notions, have two characteristics in common: (1) they admit of being more or less attended to, and (2) can be reproduced and associated together. It is here proposed to use the term *presentation* to connote such a mental fact, and as the best English equivalent for what Locke meant by idea and what Kant and Herbart called a Vorstellung. *J. Ward*, Encyc. Brit., XX. 41.

(*b*) A figurate conception; a product of the imagination.

The term *presentation* [German *vorstellung*], which Hegel employs to name these "picture-thoughts" or "figurate conceptions," corresponds to the facts of their nature. A *presentation* is one of two things: either a particular thing taken under general aspects, or a universal narrowed down to a particular thing. Thus, as it has been seen, a general name expresses a universal relation or attribute, but confines it to a particular object or class. *Wallace*, Prolegomena to Hegel's Logic, xii.

(*c*) A direct percept; a presentative cognition.

The percept involves the immediate assurance of the presence of the whole object. Hence, psychologists speak of percepts in their totality as *presentations*. *Sully*, Psychology, vi.

8. The process of formation of a presentation in sense 7.—**Bond of presentation**, in *Scots law*. See *bond*[1].—**Feast of the Presentation.** (*a*) *Of the Virgin Mary*, a festival in the Roman Catholic and Greek churches celebrated on November 21st. Also *Isodia*. (*b*) *Of Christ in the Temple*, a festival celebrated on February 2d, in the Greek, Roman Catholic, Anglican, and some other churches, commonly called the *Feast of the Purification*: same as *Candlemas*.—**Order of the Presentation of the Virgin Mary**, a Roman Catholic religious order of nuns, founded in Ireland in 1777. Religious instruction to poor girls is a specialty of the order.

presentation[2]†, *n.* [Irreg. < L. *præsentire*, perceive beforehand (see *presentient*), + *-ation*. The proper term is *presension*.] A direct perception of something in the future; presension.

> In sundry animals we deny not a kind of natural meteorology, or innate *presentation* both of wind and weather. — *Sir T. Browne*, Vulg. Err.

presentationism (prez-en-tā'shọn-izm), *n.* [< *presentation*[1] + *-ism*.] The doctrine that perception is an immediate cognition.

presentationist (prez-en-tā'shọn-ist), *n.* [< *presentation*[1] + *-ist*.] An adherent of the doctrine of presentationism.

presentative (prẹ̄-zen'tạ-tiv), *a.* [< ML. as if **præsentaticus*, < L. *præsentatus*, pp. of *præsentare*, place before, exhibit: see *present*[2].] 1. In *eccles. law*: (*a*) Having the right of presentation: as, advowsons are *presentative*, collative, or donative.

> An advowson *presentative* is where the patron hath a right of presentation to the bishop or ordinary. — *Blackstone*, Com., II. iii.

(*b*) Admitting the presentation of a clerk: as, a *presentative* parsonage.—2. In *metaph.*: (*a*) Consisting of or pertaining to immediate, proximate, or intuitive apprehension or cognition: opposed to *representative*.

> A thing known in itself is the (sole) *presentative* or intuitive object of knowledge, or the (sole) object of a *presentative* or intuitive knowledge. — *Sir W. Hamilton.*

(*b*) Cognitive; pertaining to knowledge.

presentee (prẹ̄-zen-tē'), *n.* [< *present*[2] + *-ee*[1].] One who is presented to a benefice.

> It is often very hard on the bishops to be obliged to institute the *presentees* of such men, . . . but the remedy is in their own hands, and the responsibility of its non-employment lies with themselves. — *The Churchman*, LIV. 402.

presenter (prẹ̄-zen'tėr), *n.* [< *present*[2], *v.*, + *-er*[1].] 1. One who presents or offers for acceptance; a giver.

> Such due fear
> As fits *presenters* of great works to Cæsar.
> — *B. Jonson*, Poetaster, v. 1.

> The thing was acceptable, but not the *presenter*. — *Sir R. L'Estrange.*

2†. An exhibitor; an actor.

> Seat ye;
> Are the *presenters* ready?
> — *Ford*, Perkin Warbeck, iii. 2.

presential (prẹ̄-zen'shạl), *a.* [< OF. *presencial* = It. *presenziale*, < ML. *præsentialis*, < L. *præsentia*, presence (see *presence*), + *-al*.] Having or implying actual presence; present.

> God, who was never visible to mortal eye, was pleased to make himself *presential* by substitution of his name. — *Jer. Taylor*, Works (ed. 1835), I. 154.

> To this grand vision, which the chosen three
> Were call'd before they tasted death to see,
> Was added proof to the astonish'd ear,
> That made *presential* Deity appear.
> — *Byron*, On Dr. Middleton's Exam. of Lord Bp. of London's Disc.

> What associating league to the imagination can there be between the seers and the seers not of a *presential* miracle? — *Lamb*, Barrenness of the Imaginative Faculty.

presentiality (prẹ̄-zen-shi-al'ị-ti), *n.* [< OF. *presencialite* = It. *presenzialità*, < ML. *præsentialita(t-)s*, < *præsentialis*, presential: see *presential*.] The state or quality of being presential; presentness; presence.

> A good is not barely to be measured by its immediate *presentiality*. — *South*, Sermons, VIII. vi.

> As if they knew not that terms of priority, and *presentiality*, and posteriority have not that significancy in or about eternity as they have with us. — *Baxter*, Divine Life, i. 5.

presentially (prẹ̄-zen'shạl-i), *adv.* In a presential manner; by actual presence; in person; with the notion of presence.

> It had been revealed to Simeon (whose words these are) that he should see Christ before he died; and actually and really, substantially, essentially, bodily, *presentially*, personally he does see him. — *Donne*, Sermons, iv.

> But he reigns in this place rather *presentially* by his grace; where his sceptre is a sceptre of righteousness, and his throne man's heart. — *Rev. T. Adams*, Works, II. 72.

presentialness (prẹ̄-zen'shạl-nes), *n.* The state of being immediately present to consciousness.

> If the *presentialness* of the object be necessary to the act of vision, the object perceived cannot possibly be external to us. — *A. Collier*, Clavis Universalis, I. i. § 2.

presentiate† (prẹ̄-zen'shi-āt), *v. t.* [< L. *præsentia*, presence (see *presence*), + *-ate*[2].] To make present or actual.

> The phancy may be so cleer and strong as to *presentiate* upon one theatre all that ever it took notice of in time past. — *N. Grew*, Cosmologia Sacra, iii. 4.

presentient (prē-sen'shient), *a.* [< L. *præsentien(t-)s*, ppr. of *præsentire*, feel or perceive beforehand, < *præ*, before, + *sentire*, feel: see *sentient*.] Perceiving beforehand; having a prophetic sense or impression.

presentific† (prez-en-tif'ik), *a.* [< L. *præsen(t-)s*, present, + *-ficus*, making (see *-fic*).] Making present.

> Adam had a sense of the divine presence; . . . notwithstanding that he found no want of any covering to hide himself from that *presentifick* sense of him. — *Dr. H. More*, Def. of Philosophic Cabbala, II.

presentifical† (prez-en-tif'i-kạl), *a.* [< *presentific* + *-al*.] Same as *presentific*.

presentificly† (prez-en-tif'ik-li), *adv.* In a presentific manner; in such a manner as to make present.

> The whole evolution of times and ages . . . is collectedly and *presentifickly* represented to God at once, as if all things and actions were at this very instant really present and existent before him. — *Dr. H. More.*

presentiment (prẹ̄-sen'ti-mẹnt), *n.* [< F. *pressentiment* = Sp. *presentimiento* = It. *presentimento*, < L. *præsentire*, feel or perceive beforehand: see *presentient*.] 1. A direct, though vague, perception of a future event, or a feeling which seems to be such a perception.

> A *presentiment* of what is to be hereafter. — *Butler*, Analogy of Religion, i. 6.

> Magic, and all that is ascribed to it, is a deep *presentiment* of the powers of science. — *Emerson*, History.

Specifically—2. An antecedent feeling or impression that some misfortune or calamity is about to happen; anticipation of impending evil; foreboding.

> A vague *presentiment* of impending doom . . .
> Haunted him day and night.
> — *Longfellow*, Wayside Inn, Torquemada.

presentimental (prẹ̄-sen-ti-men'tạl), *a.* [< *presentiment* + *-al*.] Relating to or in the nature of a presentiment: as, a *presentimental* anxiety.

presention† (prẹ̄-sen'shọn), *n.* A bad spelling of *presension*.

presentive (prẹ̄-zen'tiv), *a.* and *n.* [< *present*[2] + *-ive*.] I. *a.* 1. Causing to be presented directly to the mind, as a notion; presentative: contradistinguished from *representative* and *symbolical*.—2. In *gram.*, noting a class of words which present a definite conception of an object to the mind; not symbolic. *J. Earle*, Philology of the Eng. Tongue.

II. *n.* A presentive word.

presentiveness (prẹ̄-zen'tiv-nes), *n.* [< *presentive* + *-ness*.] The state or property of being presentive; the capability of a word to present a definite notion or conception of an object to the mind.

> The word shall offer a good example of the movement from *presentiveness* to symbolism. When it flourished as a presentive word, it signified to owe. — *J. Earle*, Philology of the Eng. Tongue.

presently (prez'ẹnt-li), *adv.* 1†. In presence; personally; actually.

> The glory of his Godhead is to be present and to fill all places at once essentially, *presently*, with his almighty power. — *Tyndale*, Ans. to Sir T. More, etc. (Parker Soc., 1850), [p. 282.

> I have a business
> Which much concerns you, *presently* concerns you.
> — *Beau. and Fl.*, Knight of Malta, ii. 1.

2†. At present; now; at the time spoken of.

> A childe will chose a sweeting because it is *presentlie* faire and pleasant. — *Ascham*, The Scholemaster, p. 36.

> The Irishmen and Scots fauoured not the race of the kings that *presentlie* reigned. — *Holinshed*, K. John, an. 1212.

> When God had created man, he was *presently* the owner of him. — *Baxter*, Treatise of Self-Denial, i. 1.

3. Immediately; by and by; in a little time; soon.

> I will serve process, *presently* and strongly,
> Upon your brother, and Octavio,
> Jacintha, and the boy.
> — *Fletcher*, Spanish Curate, iii. 1.

> Him therefore I hope to send *presently*, so soon as I shall see how it will go with me. — Phil. ii. 23.

> *Presently* after my arrival I was brought with the rest of my company to the Deputy Governor of the towne. — *Coryat*, Crudities, I. 2.

> I'm master of this house, which I'll sell *presently*;
> I'll clap up bills this evening.
> — *Middleton*, Chaste Maid, iii. 3.

presentment (prẹ̄-zent'mẹnt), *n.* [< OF. *presentement*, *presentment*, act of presenting, presentment, < *presenter*, present: see *present*[2].] 1. The act of presenting, or the state of being presented; presentation.

> To be his book-patron, with the appendant form of a ceremonious *presentment*, wil ever appeare among the judicious to be but an insulse and frigid affectation. — *Milton*, Apology for Smectymnuus.

> She was an honored guest at the *presentment* of a burlesque masque. — *Bancroft*, Hist. U. S., I. 116.

2. Anything presented or exhibited; appearance; likeness; representation.

> The counterfeit *presentment* of two brothers. — *Shak.*, Hamlet, iii. 4. 55.

> Thus I hurl
> My dazzling spells into the spungy air,
> Of power to cheat the eye with blear illusion,
> And give it false *presentments*.
> — *Milton*, Comus, l. 156.

> Oxford dropped the canon law decree altogether; Cambridge, by adopting a more general form, retained a shadowy *presentment* of the double honour. — *Stubbs*, Medieval and Modern Hist., p. 329.

3. In *law*: (*a*) A statement by a grand jury of an offense from their own knowledge or observation, without any bill of indictment laid before them: as, the *presentment* of a nuisance, a libel, or the like, on which the prosecuting officer must afterward frame an indictment, before the party presented can be put to answer it. In a more general sense, *presentment* comprehends inquisitions of office and indictments.

> As before, so after the Union, tithe-proctors with their remorseless exactions, and grand juries with road-jobbing *presentments*, came to shear the already shorn, and reduce their victims from misery to despair. — *E. Dowden*, Shelley, I. 237.

> In each of these baronies sessions—called presentment sessions—are held, where all *presentments* are introduced, to be submitted afterwards at the assizes to the grand jury. — *Fortnightly Rev.*, N. S., XL. 106.

(*b*) The formal information to the lord, by the tenants of a manor, of anything done out of court. (*c*) The presenting of a bill of exchange to the drawee for acceptance, or of a bill to the acceptor, or of a note to the maker, for payment.—4. *Eccles.*, a formal complaint made by the authorities of a parish to the bishop or archdeacon at his visitation.

> The Church-wardens should meet twice a yeere, to haue all the *presentments* made perfect against the Assises. — Quoted in *Capt. John Smith's* Works, II. 157.

Presentment of Englishry. See *Englishry*.

presentness (prez'ẹnt-nes), *n.* [< *present*[1] + *-ness*.] Same as *presence*.

> Goring had a much better understanding, . . . a much keener courage, and *presentness* of mind in danger. — *Clarendon*, Great Rebellion, viii.

presentoir (prez-en-twor'), *n.* [< F. *présentoir*, a form of cup, < *présenter*, present: see *present*[2].] 1. A utensil upon which things are

Presentoir of Japanese Lacquer-ware, with Bowl.

laid to be handed to the recipient; a tray or waiter; a salver. The name is also given to a Japanese stand, usually of lacquered wood, upon which a bowl is supported.

2. A cup-holder having three or more branches to support and inclose the cup, and often a ring-handle to carry the whole.

present-perfect (prez'ẹnt-pėr''fekt), *n.* In *gram.*, the perfect tense. *Academy*, Nov. 23, 1887, p. 343. [Rare.]

preservability (prẹ̄-zėr-vạ-bil'ị-ti), *n.* [< *preservable* + *-ity* (see *-bility*).] The property of being preservable; capability of being preserved.

> Securing safety, palatability, convenience, and *preservability* of drugs that had previously been administered in the form of huge boluses. — *Lancet*, No. 3426, p. 35 of adv'ts.

preservable (prẹ̄-zėr'vạ-bl), *a.* [< *preserve* + *-able*.] Capable of being preserved.

preservation (prez-ėr-vā'shọn), *n.* [< OF. *preservation*, F. *préservation* = Sp. *preservacion*

= Pg. *preservação* = It. *preservazione*, < ML. **præservatio(n-)*, < *præservare*, pp. *præservatus*, keep, preserve, LL. observe beforehand: see *preserve*.] 1. The act of preserving, or keeping safe or sound; the act of keeping from injury or decay: as, the *preservation* of life or of property.

We'll yet enlarge that man,
Though Cambridge, Scroop, and Grey, in their dear care
And tender *preservation* of our person,
Would have him punish'd. *Shak.*, Hen. V., ii. 2. 59.

Do not attempt to be more amusing and agreeable than is consistent with the *preservation* of respect. *Sydney Smith*, in Lady Holland, vi.

2. The state of being preserved from injury or decay; escape from destruction or danger: as, a building in good *preservation*.

Give us particulars of thy *preservation*. *Shak.*, Tempest, v. 1. 135.

Ev'ry senseless thing, by nature's light,
Doth *preservation* seek, destruction shun.
Sir J. Davies, Immortal. of Soul, xxx.

3. A means of security or escape.

It hapned, Master Argent had put his Bandileir of powder in his hat, which next God was all their *preseruations*. Quoted in *Capt. John Smith's* Works, II. 93.

Peace Preservation Acts. See *peace*.

preservative (prē̤-zėr'vạ-tiv), *a.* and *n.* [< OF. *preservatif*, F. *préservatif* = Sp. Pg. It. *preservativo*, < ML. **præservativus*, < *præservare*, pp. *præservatus*, preserve: see *preserve*.] I. *a.* Preserving; tending to keep safe, sound, or free from decay: as, the *preservative* quality of salt.

As above directed, the *preservative* bath contains about eight grains of nitrate of silver to the ounce. *Lea*, Photography, p. 350.

It will be, however, evident that a *preservative* society has a very uphill task. It has to war against the prejudices of the sexton and the immitis sapientia Grimthorpe. *Nineteenth Century*, XXII. 240.

II. *n.* That which preserves; anything which tends to keep safe and sound, or free from injury, corruption, or decay; a preventive of damage, decomposition, or waste.

Lyke as the phisitions call those diseases most peryllous against whom is founden no *preseruatiue*. *Sir T. Elyot*, The Governour, iii. 4.

Their [Druids'] druttenfuss, i. e., a pentagonal figure . . . which in Germany they reckon for a *preservative* against hobgoblins. *Selden*, Illustrations of Drayton's Polyolbion, ix. 417.

A heart in heaven will be a most excellent *preservative* against temptations. *Baxter*, Saints' Rest, iv. 3.

This ceremony of the sprinkling of salt is considered a *preservative*, for the child and mother, from the evil eye. *E. W. Lane*, Modern Egyptians, II. 276.

This facile adaptation was at once the symptom of perfect health and its best *preservative*. *Hawthorne*, Seven Gables, ix.

preservatory (prē̤-zėr'vạ-tọ̄-ri), *a.* and *n.* [< ML. **præservatorius* (cf. *præservator*, a preserver), < *præservare*, pp. *præservatus*, preserve: see *preserve*.] I. *a.* Tending to preserve; preservative.

The indeavours must be no other then *preservatory*, however it pleaseth God to order the events. *Bp. Hall*, Cases of Conscience, ii. 3.

II. *n.*; pl. *preservatories* (-riz). 1†. A preservative.

How many masters have some stately houses had, in the age of a small cottage, that hath, as it were, lived and died with her old master, both dropping down together! Such vain *preservatories* of us are our inheritances, even once removed. *Whitlock*, Manners of the English, p. 410. (*Latham.*)

2. An apparatus for preserving substances for food, or a building where the process of preserving food-products is carried on.

By all their hollow sides is made within a very large *preservatory*, cistern, or basin, fit to contain a pretty quantity of water. *Dr. Sloane*, in Ray's Works of Creation, p. 2.

preserve (prē̤-zėrv'), *v.*; pret. and pp. *preserved*, ppr. *preserving*. [< OF. *preserver*, F. *préserver* = Sp. Pg. *preservar* = It. *preservare*, keep, < LL. *præservare*, observe beforehand, ML. keep, preserve, < L. *præ*, before, + *servare*, save, preserve, protect. Cf. *conserve*, *reserve*.] I. *trans.* 1. To keep safe or free from harm; defend from injury or destruction; save.

God did send me before you to *preserve* life. Gen. xlv. 5.

Deliver me, O Lord, from the evil man; *preserve* me from the violent man. Ps. cxl. 1.

To *preserve* my sovereign from his foe,
Say but the word, and I will be his priest.
Shak., 2 Hen. VI., iii. 1. 271.

And could they have *preserved* the Magazine of Tobacco only, besides other Things in that Town, something might have been had to countervail the Charge of the Voyage. *Howell*, Letters, I. i. 4.

Preserve me from the thing I dread and hate,
A duel in the form of a debate.
Cowper, Conversation, l. 83.

2. To maintain; secure permanence to; keep in existence or alive; make lasting: as, to *preserve* one's good looks.

To worship God aright, and know his works
Not hid; nor those things last which might *preserve*
Freedom and peace to men. *Milton*, P. L., xi. 579.

The spectacle had allured Reynolds from that easel which has *preserved* to us the thoughtful foreheads of so many writers and statesmen, and the sweet smiles of so many noble matrons. *Macaulay*, Warren Hastings.

To such a name
Preserve a broad approach of fame,
And ever-echoing avenues of song.
Tennyson, Death of Wellington, v.

3. To keep possession of; retain.

Preserve your worth, and I'll *preserve* my money. *Beau. and Fl.*, Thierry and Theodoret, v. 1.

Only perchance some melancholy Stream
And some indignant Hills old names *preserve*,
When laws, and creeds, and people all are lost!
Wordsworth, Eccles. Sonnets, i. 12.

He can never *preserve* through a single paragraph either the calmness of a philosopher or the meekness of a Christian. *Macaulay*, Sadler's Ref. Refuted.

4. To prepare in such a manner as to resist decomposition or fermentation; prevent from spoiling by the use of preservative substances, with or without the agency of heat: as, to *preserve* meats or fruit; to *preserve* an anatomical specimen.

I ha' some quinces brought from our house i' th' country to *preserve*; when shall we have any good sugar come over? *Dekker and Webster*, Northward Ho, ii. 1.

Delectable dishes of *preserved* plums, and peaches, and pears, and quinces. *Irving*, Sketch-Book, p. 440.

5. To maintain and reserve for personal or special use in hunting or fishing. (*a*) To raise, provide for, and protect, as game, for use at certain seasons or by certain persons, as in hunting or fishing: as, to *preserve* quail; to *preserve* salmon. (*b*) To reserve and adapt to the protection and propagation of game designed for special use, as in hunting or fishing: as, *preserved* covers; a *preserved* stream. = Syn. 1 and 2. *Protect*, *Defend*, etc. (see *keep*), secure, shield, conserve, spare.

II. *intrans.* 1. To prepare decomposable substances, as meats or fruits, for preservation; make preserves.

Hast thou not learn'd me how
To make perfumes? distil? *preserve*?
Shak., Cymbeline, i. 5. 13.

2. To raise and protect game for special use, as in hunting or fishing.

Squire Thornhill . . . had taken the liberty to ask permission to shoot over Mr. Leslie's land, since Mr. Leslie did not *preserve*. *Bulwer*, My Novel, viii. 5.

preserve (prē̤-zėrv'), *n.* [< *preserve*, *v.*] 1†. That which preserves or saves.

Fetch balsamo, the kind *preserve* of life. *Greene and Lodge*, Looking Glass for Lond. and Eng.

Specifically — 2. *pl.* A kind of spectacles with colored glasses to protect the eyes from too strong light.

Preserves are used to conceal deformities or to protect the eyes in the many conditions where they cannot tolerate bright light. . . . They are made of bluish, "smoked," or almost black coloured glass, and are of very various shapes, according to the amount of obscuration necessary. *Encyc. Brit.*, XXII. 372.

3. That which is preserved, or prepared for keeping; especially, fruit, meats, etc., suitably seasoned and cooked to prevent fermentation or spoiling.

At this Treat I eat of a *Preserve* or Wet Sweetmeat, made of Orange Flowers, incomparable; and the Lady obliged me with the manner of making it. *Lister*, Journey to Paris, p. 190.

A female Dodson, when in "strange houses," always ate dry bread with her tea, and declined any sort of *preserves*, having no confidence in the butter, and thinking that the *preserves* had probably begun to ferment from want of due sugar and boiling. *George Eliot*, Mill on the Floss, i. 6.

4. A place where game is preserved; a place set apart for the protection and propagation of game intended for hunting or fishing.—5†. A thing preserved.

Wonderful indeed are the *preserves* of time, which openeth unto us mummies from crypts and pyramids. *Sir T. Browne*, Mummies.

preserve-jar (prē̤-zėrv'jär), *n.* A jar made to contain preserved meats, fruits, etc., so contrived that it may be tightly closed, to exclude the air and prevent evaporation.

preserver (prē̤-zėr'vėr), *n.* 1. A person or thing that preserves; one who or that which saves or guards from injury, destruction, or waste; a savior; a preservative.

What shall I do unto thee, O thou *preserver* of men? Job vii. 20.

Camillo,
Preserver of my father, now of me,
The medicine of our house, how shall we do?
Shak., W. T., iv. 4. 597.

"Tannin," says Poitevin, "is then a sensitizer, and must be considered as such, and not as a *preserver*." *Silver Sunbeam*, p. 354.

2. One who makes preserves, as of fruit, etc. —3. One who preserves game for sport.

preses (prē'sēz), *n.* [< L. *præses*, one who presides or guards, < *præsidere*, sit before or in front of: see *preside*.] One who presides over the deliberations of an organized society or the like; a president; the chairman of a meeting. [Scotch.]

preshow (prē-shō'), *v. t.* [< *pre-* + *show*.] To show beforehand; foreshow. *Roget*. [Rare.]

preside (prē̤-zīd'), *v. i.*; pret. and pp. *presided*, ppr. *presiding*. [< OF. *presider*, F. *présider* = Sp. Pg. *presidir* = It. *presidere*, *presiedere*, preside over, govern, < L. *præsidere*, guard, protect, defend, have the care or management of, superintend, direct, also lit. (LL.) sit before or in front of, < *præ*, before, + *sedere*, sit: see *sedentary*, etc., *sit*.] 1. To be set over others; have the place of authority, as a chairman or director; direct and control, as a chief officer: usually denoting temporary superintendence and direction: as, to *preside* over a society; to *preside* at a public meeting.

It is farther to be noted that, in these solemn assemblies for the churches service, there is no one *presides* among them, after the manner of the assemblies of other people. *Penn*, Rise and Progress of Quakers, iv.

Here comes the neighbouring justice, pleased to guide
His little club, and in the chair *preside*.
Crabbe, Works, I. 175.

Man now *presides*
In power, where once he trembled in his weakness.
Wordsworth, Sonnets, iii. 41.

I was glad to see my lord *presiding* at the democratical College. *Sydney Smith*, To the Countess Grey.

2. To exercise superintendence and direction; have a guiding or controlling influence: as, the fates *preside* over man's destiny.

The Holy Ghost, though it *presided* over the minds and pens of the apostles so far as to preserve them from error, yet doth not seem to have dictated to them what they were to say, word by word. *Bp. Atterbury*, Sermons, II. ix.

Who conquer'd nature should *preside* o'er wit.
Pope, Essay on Criticism, l. 652.

Those medicinal agents which possess the power of directly influencing the nervous mechanisms which *preside* over motion. *Buck's Handbook of Med. Sciences*, V. 27.

Presiding elder. See *elder*¹, 5 (*c*).—**Presiding judge.** See *judge*.

presidence (prez'i-dens), *n.* [< F. *présidence* = Pr. Sp. Pg. *presidencia* = It. *presidenza*, < ML. *præsidentia*, < L. *præsiden(t-)s*, ppr. of *præsidere*, preside: see *preside*. Cf. *prescance*.] Same as *presidency*. [Rare.]

The venerable pastor had come down
From his high pulpit, and assumed the seat
Of *presidence*. *J. G. Holland*, Kathrina, ii.

presidency (prez'i-den-si), *n.* [As *presidence* (see *-cy*).] 1. Superintendence and direction; controlling and directing influence, as of a president.

The primitive church, expressing the calling and offices of a bishop, did it in terms of *presidency* and authority. *Jer. Taylor*, Works (ed. 1835), II. 203.

For what account can be given of the determination of the growth and magnitude of plants from mechanical principles, of matter mov'd without the *presidency* and guidance of some superiour agent? *Ray*, Works of Creation, i.

2. The office of president: as, the *presidency* of a college or a railroad corporation; specifically [*cap.*], the office of President of the United States.

He [Grant] came to the *Presidency* a simple soldier, without many political ideas, or anything that could be called a political philosophy. *The Nation*, Sept. 7, 1882, p. 194.

3. The term during which a president holds office: as, the *presidency* of Lincoln, of Thiers, etc.—4. In British India, a chief administrative division. In the early history of British India there were three presidencies—Bengal, Bombay, and Madras; the last two are ruled by governors, and hence are sometimes called *governorships*; the former presidency of Bengal is now divided into several administrative territories, including the lieutenant-governorships of Bengal (or Lower Bengal), the Northwestern Provinces, etc. In the seventeenth century the chief of an important factory in India was popularly styled president, and in that sense the word is used in letters patent of the East India Company in 1661.—**First Presidency**, among the Mormons, a board of presiding officers, consisting of the head of the hierarchy with two counselors.

The second great power in the [Mormon] Church, next to the Prophet, is the *First Presidency*. This is composed of the Prophet and his two counsellors. The three together, known as the *First Presidency* or simply the Presidency, etc. *Fifteen Years among the Mormons*, p. 151.

president¹ (prez'i-dent), *a.* and *n.* [< ME. *president* (n.), < OF. *president*, F. *président* = Pr. *president* = Sp. Pg. It. *presidente* (= D. G. Sw. *president* = Dan. *præsident*, n.), < L. *præsiden(t-)s*, presiding, as a noun a director, ruler, president, ppr. of *præsidere*, direct, preside: see *preside*.] I. *a.* Presiding; directing; guiding; occupying the chief place or first rank. [Obsolete or archaic.]

Quid petitur sacris nisi tantum fama poetis, which, although it be oftentimes imprisoned in ladyes cask[et]s, and the *president* booke of such as cannot see without another man's spectacles, yet at length it breakes foorth in spight of his keepers.
Nashe, quoted in Int. to Pierce Penilesse, p. xxiii.

The prime and *president* zealot of the earth.
Middleton, Game at Chess, ii. 2.

Whence hast thou then thy truth,
But from him, or his angels *president*
In every province?
Milton, P. R., i. 447.

They [Israel] would be left in the same condition with other Gentile nations, who must therefore be supposed to be under the immediate conduct of *president* angels.
J. Scott, Christian Life, ii. 7.

II. *n.* 1†. One who presides; one who superintends and directs the proceedings of others; a ruler; a ruling spirit.

Commaunde as Romaines, and we shall obei as Hebrues; lene vs a *president* that is mercifull, and all our realme shal be obedient.
Golden Book, xi.

A charge we bear i' the war,
And, as the *president* of my kingdom, will
Appear there for a man.
Shak., A. and C., iii. 7. 18.

Thou wonder of all princes, *president*, and glory.
Middleton, The Phœnix, i. 1.

Happy is Rome, of all earth's other states,
To have so true and great a president
For her inferior spirits to imitate
As Cæsar is.
B. Jonson, Poetaster, v. 1.

2. An officer elected or appointed to preside over and control the proceedings of others. (*a*) The presiding officer of an assembly: as, the *president* of a convention.

For which delibered was by parlemente,
For Antenor to yelden out Cryseyde,
And it pronounced by the *president*.
Chaucer, Troilus, iv. 213.

Daughter to that good earl, once *President*
Of England's council and her treasury.
Milton, Sonnets, v.

(*b*) The chief officer of a corporation, company, or society: as, the *president* of a railway company, or of a bank.

They elected the *Presidents* (originally called Aldermen, afterwards Masters and Wardens) and other officials.
English Gilds (E. E. T. S.), Int., p. cxxv.

(*c*) The governing officer of a college or university. (*d*) The highest officer of state in a modern republic. The President of the United States is chosen once in four years by presidential electors, who are elected by the people of the several States, the electors in every State being equal in number to the senators and representatives of the State in Congress. The action of the electors is a mere formality, as they always vote for the nominees of the national conventions of their party. The President is commander-in-chief of the army and navy of the United States, and of the militia of the several States when called into the service of the United States. He is authorized to grant reprieves and pardons for violation of United States laws (except in cases of impeachment), to make treaties with the concurrence of two thirds of the Senate, to recommend legislation, and to see that the laws are faithfully executed. His powers of appointment to office are partly provided for in the Constitution and partly statutory; his chief appointments (requiring confirmation by the Senate) are—cabinet officers and heads of bureaus or subdivisions, diplomatic and consular agents, federal judges, officers of territories, postmasters of the first, second, and third classes, and the principal officers of the army and navy. His salary is $50,000 a year. *President* was the title of the chief executive magistrate in New Hampshire from 1784 to 1792 (*President of Council*, 1776–84), in Pennsylvania from 1776 to 1790, in Delaware from 1776 to 1792, and in South Carolina from 1776 to 1778. Subsequently these titles were exchanged for that of *governor*. The President of the French republic is elected for seven years by the Senate and Chamber of Deputies united in National Assembly. The President of the Swiss Confederation is elected for one year by the Federal Assembly, from among the members of the Federal Council. Abbreviated *Pres.*

3. A title given to the head of the Mormon hierarchy. He acts in conference with two counselors. It is his duty "to preside over the whole Church, and to be a Seer, a Revelator, a Translator, and a Prophet" (*Mormon Catechism*, p. 17).

4. A protector; a tutelary power; a patron. [Rare.]

Just Apollo, *president* of verse. *Waller*, At Pens-Hurst.

5. A kind of damask of silk, or silk and wool, used for upholstery.—**Lord President.** See *lord*.—**Lord President of the Council**, a cabinet officer of Great Britain, who must be a member of the House of Lords. He presides over the department of the privy council, and has special supervision of education; he also prepares minutes on matters which do not come to any other department, and has superintendence of the public health, quarantine, etc.—**President's freshman.** See *freshman*.—**Prince President.** See *prince*.

president[2]†, *n.* An erroneous spelling of *precedent*.

Presently obteyning two such auncient and famous champions, . . . by whose *presidents*, directions, and conductions I was forthwith deliuered of all perplexities.
E. Hellowes, Pref. to tr. of Guevara's Letters (1577), ii.

This *president* will much condemn
Your grace another day.
True Tale of Robin Hood (Child's Ballads, V. 366).

presidentess (prez'i-dent-es), *n.* [< *president*[1] + *-ess*.] A female president.

I became by that means the *presidentess* of the dinner and tea-table.
Mme. D'Arblay, Diary, III. 171.

The day on which I was there [at the Moravian establishment at Ebersdorf] was Sunday, and I . . . was introduced to the well-bred, accomplished *presidentess*, Fraulein Gerstendorf.
Henry Crabb Robinson, Diary, I. 59.

presidential (prez-i-den'shal), *a.* [= F. *présidentiel*, < ML. **præsidentialis*, pertaining to presidence (*præsidentialis magna curia*, a supreme council), < *præsidentia*, presidence, presidency: see *presidence*. *Presidential* means prop. 'relating to presidence or presidency'; for 'relating to a president,' the prop. form would be **presidental* (= F. *présidental* = Pg. *presidental*).] 1. Pertaining to presidency; having presidency; presiding.

This institution of these *Presidentiall* Courts was, at first, a very profitable ordinance, and much eased the people.
Heylin, Full Relation of Two Journeys, etc. (1656), p. 134.

Spoken [Jer. li. 9], as some of the learned ancients suppose, by the *presidential* angels.
Glanville, Discourses, iv.

2. Pertaining to a president, or relating to a presidency: as, the *presidential* chair; a *presidential* term.

The *presidential* fever, that typical disease which has proved fatal to the true glory of so many statesmen of the United States, permeated the very marrow of his bones.
H. von Holst, John C. Calhoun (trans.), p. 57.

They [the Democrats] will at the same time have before their eyes an unusually good chance of success at the next *Presidential* election.
The Nation, Nov. 16, 1882, p. 416.

Presidential electors. See *elector*.—**Presidential postmaster**, in the United States, a postmaster appointed by the President. See *postmaster*, 2.

presidentship (prez'i-dent-ship), *n.* [< *president*[1] + *-ship*.] 1. The office and dignity of president; presidency.

I wishe the newe prouision that his Maiestie hath bestowed vppon your honour for the *Presidentship* of this royall audience of Granado may be fortunate.
Guevara, Letters (tr. by Hellowes, 1577), p. 101.

In France the re-election of M. Grévy to the *Presidentship* has come and gone.
Fortnightly Rev., N. S., XXXIX. 288.

2. The term for which a president holds his office.

presider (prẹ-zī'dėr), *n.* [< *preside* + *-er*[1].] One who presides.

presidial (prẹ-sid'i-al), *a.* [< OF. *presidial*, F. *présidial* = Sp. Pg. *presidial*, < ML. **præsidialis*, pertaining to a garrison, < L. *præsidium*, defense, protection, a garrison, guard, post, fortification, < *præsidere*, keep guard: see *preside*. Cf. LL. *præsidalis*, *præsidialis*, belonging to the governor of a province, gubernatorial, < *præses* (*præsid-*), chief, governor: see *preses*.] 1. Of or pertaining to a garrison; having a garrison.

There are three *Presidial* Castles in this City.
Howell, Letters, I. i. 39.

2. Pertaining or belonging to a presidio.

A second class of pueblos, called, in the legal phrase of California's later days, "*Presidial* Pueblos," had originated in the settlement of the presidios.
The Century, XXVI. 203.

presidiary (prẹ-sid'i-ạ-ri), *a.* and *n.* [= Sp. Pg. *presidiario*, a criminal condemned to hard labor or banishment in a garrison; < L. *præsidiarius*, that serves for defense or protection, < *præsidium*, defense, protection, guard: see *preside*.] I. *a.* Same as *presidial*.

The *presidiary* souldiers . . . are all Spaniards.
Coryat, Crudities, I. 125.

The Protestants being so numerous, and having near upon fifty *presidiary* walled Towns in their Hands for Caution, they have Power to disturb France when they please.
Howell, Letters, I. ii. 25.

II. *n.*; pl. *presidiaries* (-riz). A guard.

Not one of those heavenly *presidiaries* struck a stroke for the prophet.
Bp. Hall, Cont., xix. 9. (*Davies.*)

presidio (prẹ-sid'i-ō), *n.* [Sp., < L. *præsidium*, a garrison, guard, post, fort: see *presidial*.] 1. A seat of government; especially, a place of military authority; a military post: used in the southwestern United States.

He referred me to the Mission and *Presidio* of San Ysabel, that had sent out the relief party, for further information.
Bret Harte, Gabriel Conroy, xi.

2. A place of deportation for criminals; a penitentiary.

The bulk of the prison population in Spain is still sent to *presidios*, or convict establishments, where general association both in the prison and at labour is the rule.
Encyc. Brit., XIX. 763.

presidy†, *n.* [< It. *presidio*, a fort, < L. *præsidium*, a fort: see *presidial*.] A fortress.

The French king hath ordained that seignour Renzio shall be in a *presidie*, between the army of Naples and the citie of Rome.
Foxe, Martyrs, p. 905, an. 1527.

presignification (prē-sig"ni-fi-kā'shon), *n.* [< LL. *præsignificatio(n-)*, a showing beforehand, < L. *præsignificare*, pp. *præsignificatus*, foreshow: see *presignify*.] The act of signifying or showing beforehand. [Rare.]

There, indeed, having scarce happened any considerable revolution in state or action in war whereof we do not find mentioned in history some *presignification* or prediction.
Barrow, Works, II. ix.

presignify (prē-sig'ni-fī), *v. t.*; pret. and pp. *presignified*, ppr. *presignifying*. [< L. *præsignificare*, foreshow, < *præ*, before, + *significare*, signify: see *signify*.] To signify or intimate beforehand. [Rare.]

Origen draws from this a mystical sense, and understands these two combatants to be within us; as if it had *presignified* what Paul affirmeth, Gal. v. 17: The flesh lusteth against the spirit, and the spirit against the flesh.
Rev. T. Adams, Works, I. 21.

presly†, *adv.* See *pressly*.

presphenoid (prē-sfē'noid), *a.* and *n.* [< *pre-* + *sphenoid*.] I. *a.* Situated in advance of the basisphenoid; forming an anterior median part of a compound sphenoid bone; pertaining to the presphenoid.

II. *n.* In *anat.*, a bone of the skull of vertebrates, situated before the basisphenoid, in the mid-line of the base of the skull, commonly blended with the basisphenoid and other sphenoidal elements. According to Owen, it is the centrum of the frontal cranial vertebra or prosencephalic cranial segment. According to others, who disregard the skull as representing vertebræ, it is the centrum or basis of the third from behind or frontal cranial segment, other parts of which are the orbitosphenoids and frontal bones. In man it is represented by the anterior part of the body of the sphenoid bone, bearing the lesser wings of the sphenoid, or processes of Ingrassias. At birth it is already ankylosed with the orbitosphenoids, yet totally distinct from both basi- and alisphenoids. See cuts under *Crotalus*, *Lepidosiren*, *Python*, *sphenoid*, and *Struthionidæ*.

presphenoidal (prē-sfẹ̄-noi'dal), *a.* [< *presphenoid* + *-al*.] Same as *presphenoid*.

prespinal (prē-spī'nal), *a.* [< L. *præ*, before, + *spina*, spine.] In *anat.*, situated in front (ventrad) of the spine; prevertebral.

press[1] (pres), *v.*; pret. and pp. *pressed*, sometimes *prest*, ppr. *pressing*. [Early mod. E. also *prease*, *preace*; < ME. *pressen*, *presen*, *precer*, < OF. *presser*, F. *presser* = Sp. *prensar*, *a-prensar* = Pg. *a-pressar* = It. *pressare*, press, = D. *pressen* = OHG. *pressōn*, *bressōn*, MHG. G. *pressen* = Sw. *prässa* = Dan. *presse*, < L. *pressare*, press, freq. of *premere*, pp. *pressus*, press, hold fast, cover, crowd, compress, contract, etc. (in a great variety of uses); no cognate forms found. From L. *premere* are also ult. *appress*, *compress*, *depress*, *express*, *impress*, *oppress*, *repress*, *suppress*, etc., *print*, *imprint*, etc., *imprimatur*, *reprimand*, *sprain*, etc., with numerous derivatives.] I. *trans.* 1. To exert weight or force against; bear down upon; act upon with weight or force; weigh heavily upon.

Good measure, *pressed* down, and shaken together, and running over, shall men give into your bosom.
Luke vi. 38.

Vile earth, to earth resign; end motion here;
And thou and Romeo *press* one heavy bier.
Shak., R. and J., iii. 2. 60.

The law which condemned a prisoner who refused to plead on a capital charge to be laid naked on his back in a dark room, while weights of stone or iron were placed on his breast till he was slowly *pressed* to death, was enforced in England in 1721 and in 1735, and in Ireland as late as 1740.
Lecky, Eng. in 18th Cent., iii.

2. To compress; squeeze: as, to *press* fruit for the purpose of extracting the juice.

I took the grapes, and *pressed* them into Pharaoh's cup.
Gen. xl. 11.

Thy monarchs . . . only in distress
Found thee a goodly sponge for Pow'r to *press*.
Cowper, Expostulation, l. 521.

3. To clasp; hold in an embrace.

She took her son, and *press'd*
Th' illustrious infant to her fragrant breast.
Dryden, Iliad, vi. 173.

Partakers of thy sad decline,
Thy hands their little force resign;
Yet, gently *press'd*, *press* gently mine.
Cowper, To Mary.

4. To reduce to a particular shape or form by pressure: as, to *press* cloth with an iron; to *press* a hat.—5. To drive or thrust by pressure; force in a certain direction: as, to *press* a crowd back.

The yoke of the Established Church was *pressed* down on the people till they would bear it no longer.
Macaulay, Burleigh.

Baby fingers, waxen touches, *press* me from the mother's breast.
Tennyson, Locksley Hall.

6†. To weigh upon; oppress; trouble.

A great and potent nobility . . . putteth life and spirit into the people, but presseth their fortune.
Bacon, Nobility (ed. 1887).

I'le somewhat *presse*
Thy irreligious minde.
Times' Whistle (E. E. T. S.), p. 6.

He turns from us;
Alas, he weeps too! something *presses* him
He would reveal, but dare not.—Sir, be comforted.
Fletcher, Pilgrim, i. 2.

7. To constrain or force to a certain end or result; urge strongly; impel.

Why should he stay, whom love doth *press* to go?
Shak., M. N. D., iii. 2. 184.

The two gentlemen who conducted me to the island were *pressed* by their private affairs to return in three days. *Swift*, Gulliver's Travels, iii. 8.

8. To hasten; bring to pass or execute hastily.

The posts that rode upon mules and camels went out, being hastened and *pressed* on by the king's commandment. Esther viii. 14.

You have Excess of Gallantry, Sir Rowland, and *press* Things to a Conclusion with a most prevailing Vehemence. *Congreve*, Way of the World, iv. 12.

Tressilian and his attendants *pressed* their route with all dispatch. *Scott*, Kenilworth, xiii.

9. To urge; beseech; entreat.

You *press* me far, and therefore I will yield.
Shak., M. of V., iv. 1. 425.

God heard their prayers, wherein they earnestly *pressed* him for the honor of his great name.
Winthrop, Hist. New England, II. 35.

And Lancelot ever *prest* upon the maid
That she should ask some goodly gift of him
For her own self or hers.
Tennyson, Lancelot and Elaine.

10. To seek earnestly; make request for; solicit.

It hath been earnestly *pressed* to have her go to Virginia for Mr. Maverick and his corn.
Winthrop, Hist. New England, I. 465.

Take heed what you *press*,
For beyond all Redress,
Should I grant what you wish, I shall harm ye.
Congreve, Semele, iii. 4.

11. To thrust upon others; enforce; impose.

Not to tolerate things meerly indifferent to weak consciences argues a conscience too strong; *pressed* uniformity in these causes much disunity.
N. Ward, Simple Cobler, p. 5.

Look at the Judge now! He is apparently conscious of having erred, in too energetically *pressing* his deeds of loving-kindness on persons unable to appreciate them.
Hawthorne, Seven Gables, viii.

He will not *press* the Statutes of Uses and Wills if they will agree that he shall forbid the paymen of annates.
Stubbs, Medieval and Modern Hist., p. 256.

12. To inculcate; impress upon the mind; urge as a doctrine, truth, fact, or rule of conduct.

That which they *pressed* was not notion, but experience; not formality, but godliness.
Penn, Rise and Progress of Quakers, ii.

[This] question did draw forth my heart to preach and *presse* the promise of pardon to all that were weary and sick of sinne.
T. Shepard, Clear Sunshine of the Gospel, p. 36.

13. To lay stress upon; attach special importance to; emphasize.

If we read but a very little, we naturally want to *press* it all; if we read a great deal, we are willing not to *press* the whole of what we read, and we learn what ought to be *pressed* and what not.
M. Arnold, Literature and Dogma, Pref.

14. To throng; fill with a crowd or press.

Where now the throng,
That *press'd* the beach, and, hasty to depart,
Look'd to the sea for safety? *Cowper*, Task, ii. 118.

15†. To print.

The discourse upon this conference . . . staid long before it could endure to be *pressed*.
Laud, in Heylin, p. 121. (*Davies*.)

Pressed brick, fuel, glass, loop, oil, etc. See the nouns.—**Pressing to death.** See *peine forte et dure*, under *peine*², and quotation from Lecky, under def. 1 above.—**To press sail.** Same as *to crowd sail* (which see, under *crowd*¹).

II. *intrans.* 1. To exert pressure or weight; specifically, to bear heavily.

Sometimes they swell and move,
Pressing up against the land,
With motions of the outer sea.
Tennyson, Eleänore.

A solid *presses* downwards only, but a fluid *presses* equally in all directions, upwards as well as downwards.
Huxley, Physiography, p. 88.

2. To strain or strive eagerly; advance with eagerness or energetic efforts; hasten.

Thanne thou3t y to frayne the first of this foure ordirs,
And *presede* to the prechoures to proven here wille.
Piers Plowman's Crede (E. E. T. S.), l. 154.

Whan Dorilas and Maglans thus hadde eche other ouerthrowen, bothe partees *pressed* to the rescu.
Merlin (E. E. T. S.), ii. 244.

The invader *presses* on to the fight.
Bacon, Political Fables, ix., Expl.

I *press* toward the mark for the prize of the high calling of God in Christ Jesus. Phil. iii. 14.

How on the faltering footsteps of decay
Youth *presses*. *Bryant*, Forest Hymn.

3. To crowd; throng.

Many mazed considerings did throng
And *press'd* in with this caution.
Shak., Hen. VIII., ii. 4. 186.

They *press* in from all the provinces,
And fill the hive. *Tennyson*, Princess, ii.

4. To advance with force; encroach.

On superior powers
Were we to *press*, inferior might on ours.
Pope, Essay on Man, i. 242.

5. To approach unseasonably or importunately; obtrude one's self.

Amonge the genteles gode & hende,
Prece thou not vp to hy3 for no thyng.
Babees Book (E. E. T. S.), p. 13.

Pardon me, madam, that so boldly
I *press* into your chamber.
Dekker and Webster, Sir Thomas Wyatt.

We need not fear to *press* into the farthest recesses of Christian antiquity, under any notion that we are prying into forbidden secrets. *De Quincey*, Essenes, i.

6†. To importune.

This your seruant *preaseth* with suche diligence for this letter that I shall be forced to aunswere more at large than I can, and much lesse than I would.
Guevara, Letters (tr. by Hellowes, 1577), p. 36.

7. To exert pressure, as by influence or moral force.

When arguments *press* equally in matters indifferent, the safest method is to give up ourselves to neither.
Addison.

To press upon, to act urgently or persistently upon; invade; attack at close quarters.

Patroclus *presses* upon Hector too boldly, and by obliging him to fight discovers it was not the true Achilles.
Pope.

press¹ (pres), *n.* [Early mod. E. also *presse*, *prese*, *prease*, *preace*; < ME. *presse*, *prese*, *prees*, *prees*, a throng, < OF. *presse*, a crowd, throng, etc., F. *presse*, a crowd, throng, urgency, a press (machine), a printing-press, the press (printing), etc., = Pr. Pg. It. *pressa* = Sp. *prensa* = OHG. *pressa*, MHG. G. *presse* = Sw. *präss* = Dan. *presse* (after F.), press, etc.; < ML. *pressa*, pressing (violence), fem. of L. *pressus*, pp. of *premere*, press: see *press*¹, *v.*] 1. The act of urging or pushing forward; a crowding or thronging.

In their throng and *press* to that last hold.
Shak., K. John, v. 7. 19.

On that superior height
Who sits is disencumbered from the *press*
Of near obstructions. *Wordsworth.*

2. A crowd; throng; multitude.

With mykull *prese* of pepull of prouynce aboute.
Destruction of Troy (E. E. T. S.), l. 2868.

Greet *prees* at market maketh deere ware.
Chaucer, Prol. to Wife of Bath's Tale, l. 522.

Cæs. Who is it in the *press* that calls on me? . . .
Cas. Fellow, come from the throng; look upon Cæsar.
Shak., J. C., i. 2. 15.

When didst thou thrust amid the mingled *preace*,
Content to bide the war aloof in peace?
Dryden, Iliad, i. 328.

That large-moulded man,
His visage all agrin as at a wake,
Made at me thro' the *press*.
Tennyson, Princess, v.

3†. Abundance; plenty.

Pas to that prouyns, *prese* to the londe,
And make puruiaunce plentie, while *prese* lasts.
Destruction of Troy (E. E. T. S.), l. 5183.

4†. Pressure; the exertion of force; compulsion.

Without *press* or compelling any man, beating up his drums, [he] levied so sufficient an army that with it he conquered all Spain.
Eng. Stratagem (Arber's Eng. Garner, I. 608).

5. A critical situation; a position of danger or embarrassment; the state of being beset.

In harde *presse* whan I was stedde,
Of my paynes 3e hadde pitee.
York Plays, p. 508.

6. Urgency; urgent demands of affairs: as, *press* of business.—7. An instrument or machine by which anything is subjected to pressure (especially if the pressure is great), as by the use of hand-levers, the screw, hydraulic agency, or steam-power. The object of the press may be to compress something into smaller compass, as a hay-press or cotton-press; to crush something and extract its juices, in which case it is named from the liquid produced, as a cider-press or wine-press; or to take a copy of something, with or without the use of a pigment, as a printing-press, a copying-press, or a seal-press.

Which wine houses doe serve for pressing of their grapes, and the making of their wine, having all things necessary therein for that purpose, as their wine *presses*.
Coryat, Crudities, I. 82.

8. In the Jacquard loom, the mechanism which actuates the cylinder or prism and its cards to press back the needles or wires which are not to act, so as to disengage them from the lifting-bar.—9. Specifically, a machine for printing; a printing-press; hence, collectively, the agencies employed in producing printed matter. Some writers limit the use of the word *press*, as defining a printing-apparatus, to the hand printing-press, moved by hand-power, and call any form of printing-press moved by steam or otherwise, not by hand-power, a *printing-machine*. See *printing-press*.

He will print them, out of doubt; for he cares not what he puts into the *press*. *Shak.*, M. W. of W., ii. 1. 80.

Lord Dorset is nobody's favourite but yours and Mr. Prior's, who has lately dedicated his book of poems to him, which is all the *press* has furnished us of any value since you went. *Swift*, Letter to Hunter, Jan. 12, 1708.

10. The art of printing; hence, those who are engaged in printing or publishing.

The liberty of the *press* is indeed essential to the nature of a free state; but this consists in laying no previous restraints upon publications, and not in freedom from censure for criminal matter when published.
Blackstone, Com., IV. xi.

11. That which is printed; the sum total of printed literature: specifically applied to newspapers and other periodical publications.

The *press*, an instrument neglected by the prosecutors, was used by Hastings and his friends with great effect.
Macaulay, Warren Hastings.

The *press* is destined, more than any other agency, to melt and mold the jarring and contending nations of the world into that one great brotherhood.
S. Bowles, in Merriam's Bowles, I. 99.

12. An upright case or cupboard in which clothes, books, china, or other articles are kept; specifically, in libraries, a bookcase, or a set of bookshelves.

His *presse* ycovered with a faldyng reed.
Chaucer, Miller's Tale, l. 26.

Large oaken *presses* filled with shelves of the same wood surrounded the room. *Scott*, Kenilworth, iv.

Press of Walnut-wood. (German, 15th century.)

13. In *photog.*, same as *printing-frame*.—**At press**, during or in the process of printing.

If the names were dropped *at press*, he could restore any speech in Shakespeare to the proper speaker.
R. L. Stevenson, Some Gentlemen in Fiction.

Autographic press, a small portable press for printing autographs from a lithographic stone or from an engraved plate.—**Bramah press, Bramah's press**, the hydraulic press, so called from its inventor, Mr. Bramah. See *hydraulic*.—**Cam-press**, a press in which the rotation of a cam communicates action to the punch or shear, as distinct from a *screw-*, *lever-*, or *pendulum-press*.—**Card-press.** (*a*) A small screw-press, used for keeping playing-cards flat when not in use. (*b*) A printing-press used for printing cards.—**Censorship of the press.** See *censorship*.—**Centripetal press.** See *centripetal*.—**Compound press**, a press in which the material is partially compressed by a light rapid movement, and the process completed by a more powerful and slower pressure.—**Correction of the press, corrector of the press.** See *correction*, *corrector*.—**Dry press**, in *printing*, a press for smoothing printed sheets.—**Hat-tip press**, a small hand-press used for printing the labels on the crown or inner lining of hats.—**Hunter's press**, a press worked by Hunter's screw (which see, under *screw*). [Not now in use.]—**Hydraulic or hydrostatic press.** See *hydraulic*.—**In press, in the press**, in process of being printed.—**Knee-joint press**, a toggle-press.—**Liberty of the press.** See *liberty*.—**Lithographic press.** See *lithographic*.—**Lying-press**, a small portable press of wood, used by bookbinders, in which pressure is given at the ends of two stout square blocks by two large wood-screws. When a cutting knife is attached, it is called a *binders' plow and press*.—**Minerva Press.** See *Minerva*.—**Napkin press**, a screw-press by means of which napkins are pressed flat after being dampened. Such a press is sometimes combined with a decorative piece of furniture, etc.—**Open-back press**, a press or punching-machine the standards of which are set apart so that the work to be punched can pass freely from front to rear through the opening.—**Pendulum press.** See *pendulum*.—**Platen press.** See *platen*.—**Plow and press**, in *bookbinding*, same as *cutting-press*, 2.—**Press-law**, a law in restraint of the liberty of the press; a law regulating or repressing the right of printing and publishing.—**Press of sail** (*naut.*), as much sail as the state of the wind, etc., will permit.—**Revolving press**, a form of baling-press in which the rotation of the box actuates the followers by means of a screw or screws working in stationary nuts.—**Rolling-cam press**, a press actuated by a roller which revolves between cam-wheels rising and falling between guides.—**Rolling-pressure press**, a press in which the follower is depressed by the pressure of a roller at the end of a pivoted extension-bar, which is caused by levers to traverse to and fro.—**Sewing-press**, a wooden frame in which books are sewed and prepared for binding. *Workshop Receipts*, Bookbinding, 4th ser.—**Standing-press**, a heavy press firmly attached to floor and ceiling, used by printers and bookbinders: so called to distinguish it from *portable presses*, such as are used by bookbinders.—**Stanhope press**, a form of printing-press invented by the Earl of Stanhope.—**Striking-up press**, a press used, in making cups or pots, to strike up the metal or raise it from the interior.—**To correct the press**, to correct proofs.

> Here comes . . . the proof of my East India speech from Hansard; so I must put my letter aside and *correct the press*.
> *Macaulay*, in Trevelyan, I. v.

Type-revolving press. See *cylinder-press*.

press[2] (pres), *v.* [A verb due to confusion of *press-* in *press-gang*, *press-money*, erroneously used for **prest-gang*, *prest-money*, etc., with *press*[1], force, etc. So *impress*, and F. *presser*, in like sense.] **I.** *trans.* To force into service, especially into military or naval service; impress.

> To the Tower, about shipping of some more *pressed* men.
> *Pepys*, Diary, II. 410.

> There are a couple of impudent fellows at an inn in Holborn who have affronted me, and you would oblige me infinitely by *pressing* them into his majesty's service.
> *Colman*, Jealous Wife, iii.

> She is rather an arbitrary writer too—for here are a great many poor words *pressed* into the service of this note that would get their habeas corpus from any court in Christendom.
> *Sheridan*, The Rivals, ii. 2.

II. *intrans.* To act as a press-gang; force persons into military or naval service.

> The legality of *pressing* is so fully established that it will not now admit of a doubt in any court of justice.
> *Christian*, Note on Blackstone's Com., I. xiii.

press[2] (pres), *n.* [< *press*[2], *v.*] An order or commission to impress men into public service, particularly into the army or navy.

> I have misused the king's *press* damnably. I have got, in exchange of a hundred and fifty soldiers, three hundred and odd pounds.
> *Shak.*, 1 Hen. IV., iv. 2. 13.

> They shrink like seamen when a *press* comes out.
> *Dryden*, Wild Gallant, Epil. (1667), l. 22.

press-agent (pres'ā"jent), *n.* A man employed to attend to newspaper advertising, and supply editors with news of changes of program, cast, etc. [Theatrical slang.]

press-beam (pres'bēm), *n.* A compression-beam.

press-bed (pres'bed), *n.* A bed inclosed in solid woodwork like a cupboard, or made to fold or turn up so as to be put in a cupboard.

> I was to sleep in a little *press-bed* in Dr. Johnson's room.
> *Boswell*, Tour to the Hebrides, p. 85.

press-blanket (pres'blang"ket), *n.* A flannel, cloth, or felt used on a printing-press to equalize the impression.

press-blocks (pres'bloks), *n. pl.* Clumps of wood used in a standing-press to fill up the space not occupied by paper or books.

press-boards (pres'bōrdz), *n. pl.* In *printing*, smooth and neatly jointed boards of wood between which printed sheets are pressed in the standing-press.

press-boy (pres'boi), *n.* Same as *machine-boy*.

press-cake (pres'kāk), *n.* In *gunpowder-manuf.*, incorporated cake, or mill-cake, ready for granulation. *E. H. Knight.*

presser (pres'ėr), *n.* [< ME. *pressour*; < OF. *presseur*, < *presser*, press: see *press*[1].] **1.** One who or that which presses. Especially—(*a*) One who presses garments for the purpose of renovating them, or who presses cloth after dyeing.

> I give the profits to dyers and *pressers*. *Swift.*

(*b*) One who works a press of any kind.

> But who in England cares about the singing in these fishing towns—singing which is only wilder and weirder than that of the cotton *pressers* of Louisiana?
> *Harper's Mag.*, LXXVII. 950.

(*c*) In *ceram.*, the workman who molds the handles, ears, and decorative reliefs to be applied to a pottery vessel before firing.

2. One who inculcates or enforces with argument or importunity.

> A common practiser and *presser* of the late illegal innovations.
> *J. White*, First Century of Malignant Priests (1623), p. 48. (*Latham.*)

3. In *mach.*: (*a*) In a knitting-machine, a bar which forces the barb of the needle into the groove of the shank to free the loop of yarn. (*b*) In a sewing-machine, the presser-foot which holds the fabric under the needle. See cut under *presser-foot*. (*c*) A form of ironing-machine. (*d*) In spinning, the pressure-roller of a drawing-frame, or the spring-finger of a bobbin-frame. *E. H. Knight.*

presser-bar (pres'ėr-bär), *n.* Same as *presser*, 3 (*a*).

presser-flyer (pres'ėr-flī"ėr), *n.* In *spinning*: (*a*) In a bobbin-frame, a flyer having a spring-arm or -finger (called *presser*) which presses against the bobbin to regulate the tension in winding on the yarn as it is spun. (*b*) A bobbin-frame on which presser-flyers are used.

presser-foot (pres'ėr-fůt), *n.* In a sewing-machine, a foot-plate by which the fabric is pressed against the face of the feed.

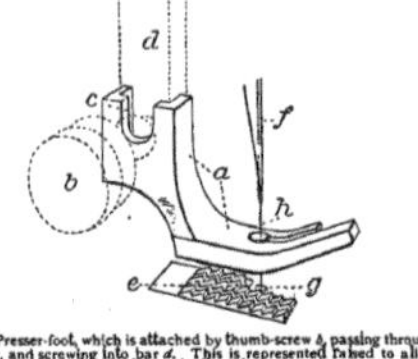

a, Presser-foot, which is attached by thumb-screw *b*, passing through slot *c*, and screwing into bar *d*. This is represented raised to allow the insertion of cloth under the inclined forward part of the foot. The bar and the foot are then lowered, pressing the cloth firmly upon the oscillating feed at *e*; *f* is the needle, which carries thread *h* through slot in foot and perforation *g* in throat-plate.

presser-frame (pres'ėr-frām), *n.* In *spinning*, a frame furnished with presser-flyers. *E. H. Knight.*

press-fat† (pres'fat), *n.* A vat belonging to an olive- or wine-press, used for the collection of the oil or wine.

> When one came to the *pressfat* for to draw out fifty vessels out of the press, there were but twenty. Hag. ii. 16.

press-gang (pres'gang), *n.* [< *press*[2], *prest*, + *gang*.] A detachment under the command of an officer empowered to impress men into the public service, especially the naval service.

> Last week a Lieutenant came hither with a *Press Gang*, and had so good Success that he soon Glean'd up a considerable number.
> Quoted in *Ashton's* Social Life in Reign of Queen Anne, [II. 208.

> Men were kidnapped, literally disappeared, and nothing was ever heard of them again. The street of a busy town was not safe from such *press-gang* captures.
> *Mrs. Gaskell*, Sylvia's Lovers, i.

press-gang (pres'gang), *v. i.* [< *press-gang*, *n.*] To act as a press-gang. [Rare.]

> There'll be no more *press-ganging* here a while.
> *Mrs. Gaskell*, Sylvia's Lovers, vii.

press-girthing (pres'gėr"thing), *n.* The belt of leather which moves the bed of a hand-press to and from impression.

pressing (pres'ing), *n.* [Verbal n. of *press*[1], *v.*] **1.** The act of one who presses; pressure.—**2.** What is expressed or squeezed out; what comes from a substance under pressure, as oil, juice, etc.

pressing (pres'ing), *p. a.* Requiring instant attention or action; urgent.

> An annuity for life of four thousand pounds was settled on Hastings; and, in order to enable him to meet *pressing* demands, he was to receive ten years annuity in advance.
> *Macaulay*, Warren Hastings.

> A *pressing* emergency required instant remedy.
> *W. M. Baker*, New Timothy, p. 125.

pressing-bag (pres'ing-bag), *n.* A bag of horse-hair to contain flaxseed from which oil is to be expressed, or to hold stearic acid under pressure, and for similar uses.

pressing-board (pres'ing-bōrd), *n.* **1.** One of the glazed millboards used by printers to put between printed sheets as resists to the impression these sheets receive in a standing-press.—**2.** One of the smoothly jointed boards of pine or cherry used in standing-presses.—**3.** An ironing-board.

pressing-iron (pres'ing-ī"ėrn), *n.* A flat-iron or smoothing-iron.

> Your *pressing-iron* will make no perfect courtier.
> Go stitch at home, and cozen your poor neighbours.
> *Fletcher and Rowley*, Maid in the Mill, iii. 2.

pressingly (pres'ing-li), *adv.* In a pressing manner; with force or urgency; closely.

pressingness (pres'ing-nes), *n.* Pressure; urgency.

> This consideration alone might apply itself with *pressingness* upon us. *R. Allestree*, Sermons, xviii. (*Latham.*)

pressing-plate (pres'ing-plāt), *n.* In an oil-press, one of the follower-boards which are alternated with bags of the material to be pressed.

pressing-roller (pres'ing-rō"lėr), *n.* In *paper-making*, a roller of iron, or of iron covered with brass, which squeezes out the water from the pulp or the felt. In England called *press-roll*. See *paper-making machine*.

pression (presh'on), *n.* [< F. *pression* = Sp. *presion* = Pg. *pressão* = It. *pressione*, < L. *pressio(n-)*, a pressing, pressure, < *premere*, pp. *pressus*, press: see *press*[1].] **1.** The act of pressing; pressure.

> Are not all my hypotheses erroneous in which light is supposed to consist in *pression* or motion propagated through a fluid medium? *Whewell.*

2. In *Cartesian philos.*, an endeavor to move.

pressiroster (pres-i-ros'tėr), *n.* [See *Pressirostres*.] A member of the *Pressirostres*.

pressirostral (pres-i-ros'tral), *a.* [< NL. *Pressirostres* + *-al*.] **1.** Pertaining to the *Pressirostres*.—**2.** Having a compressed bill shaped more or less like that of a plover.

Pressirostres (pres-i-ros'trēz), *n. pl.* [NL., < L. *pressus*, pp. of *premere*, press, compress, + *rostrum*, a beak: see *rostrum*.] In Cuvier's system of classification, a group of *Grallæ*, including the bustards, plovers, and some others, among them the cariama: so called from the compression or contraction of the bill of some of its members. It corresponds in the main to the *Charadriomorphæ* of later writers, or that large group of wading birds known as the *plover-snipe group*.

Bills of *Pressirostres*.
1. Lapwing (*Vanellus cristatus*). 2. Golden plover (*Charadrius dominicus*). 3. Turnstone (*Strepsilas interpres*).

pressitant† (pres'i-tant), *a.* [< ML. as if **pressitan(t-)s*, ppr. of **pressitare*, freq. of L. *pressare*, press down: see *press*[1], *v.*] Exerting pressure; gravitating; heavy.

> Neither the celestial matter of the vortices, nor the air, nor water are *pressitant* in their proper place.
> *Dr. H. More.*

pressive† (pres'iv), *a.* [< *press*[1] + *-ive*.] **1.** Pressing; requiring immediate attention and despatch.—**2.** Oppressive.

> How did he make silver to be in Jerusalem as stones, if the exactions were so *pressive*?
> *Bp. Hall*, Cont., xviii. 1. (*Latham.*)

press-ketch† (pres'kech), *n.* A ketch or small vessel used for patrolling harbors and for pressing seamen.

> Irish Letters of the 26th past say they continue to beat up for Soldiers at Dublin, where abundance list themselves, and that some *Press-Ketches* in that Harbour have pressed 400 Seamen within a few Days, and that a great many are voluntarily come in.
> Quoted in *Ashton's* Social Life in Reign of Queen Anne, [II. 208.

press-key (pres'kē), *n.* A small turn-screw used by book-sewers to tighten the cords of a sewing-press.

pressly† (pres'li), *adv.* [Appar. < **press*, *a.* (< L. *pressus*, pp., pressed), + *-ly*[2]. Cf. *pressness*.] Closely; compactly; concisely; succinctly.

> Though he may pursue his task *presly* and coherently, yet, because of the small importance of the matter debated of, his discourse must needs be both very tedious and not very profitable.
> *Parker*, Platonicke Philosophie (2d ed., 1667), p. 30.

> No man ever spake more neatly, more *pressly*, more weightily. *B. Jonson*, Works (ed. Gifford), p. 749.

pressman[1] (pres'man), *n.*; pl. *pressmen* (-men). [< *press*[1] + *man*.] **1.** One who is engaged in pressing; specifically, one who attends to a wine-press.

> One only path to all, by which the *pressemen* came
> In time of vintage. *Chapman*, Iliad, xviii.

2. One who operates or has charge of a printing-press; specifically, a printer who does press-work; one who runs a hand-press, or who manages a press or presses run by steam or other power.

> Watts, after some weeks, desiring to have me in the composing-room, I left the *pressmen*.
> *Franklin*, Autobiog., p. 147.

3. In *journalism*, sometimes, a man employed on the press; a writer or reporter for a newspaper.

pressman[2] (pres'man), *n.*; pl. *pressmen* (-men). [< *press*[2] + *man*.] **1.** One of a press-gang who aids in forcing men into military or naval service.—**2.** A man impressed into the public service, as the army or navy.

press-mark (pres'märk), *n.* [< *press*[1], *n.*, 12, + *mark*[1].] In libraries, a mark put upon a volume, generally by label or a writing upon a fly-leaf, indicating its location in the library. Thus, the press-mark "A, 8, 10," means "press A, shelf 8, tenth volume in order on the shelf." There are many systems of press-marking.

press-mark (pres'märk), *v. t.* and *i.* To place a press-mark on; also, to use press-marks.

press-master (pres'mȧs"tėr), *n.* The officer in command of a press-gang.

Are not our sailors paid and encouraged to that degree that there is hardly any need of *press-masters?*
Tom Brown, Works, IV. 123. (*Davies.*)

press-money (pres'mun"i), *n.* Same as *prest-money.*

This kiss shall be as good as *press-money*, to bind me to your service. *Shirley*, Maid's Revenge, ii. 1.

pressness† (pres'nes), *n.* [< **press*, *a.* (see *pressly*), + *-ness.*] The state of being pressed; closeness; compression; condensation of thought or language; terseness.

An excellent critic of our own commends Boileau's closeness, or, as he calls it, *pressness.*
Young, Love of Fame, Pref.

pressour†, *n.* An obsolete form of *presser.* *Piers Plowman* (A), v. 127.

press-pack (pres'pak), *v. t.* To compress by a hydraulic or other press: as, to *press-pack* bales of soft goods.

press-pile (pres'pīl), *n.* A pile or kench of fish. [Canada.]

The fish are put in a *press-pile*, in which they remain a week or more to sweat. *Perley.*

press-pin (pres'pin), *n.* In *bookbinding*, a bar of iron used as a lever for standing-presses. [Eng.]

press-plate (pres'plāt), *n.* One of a number of thin plates of sheet-iron which are placed between press-boards in a standing-press.

press-printing (pres'prin"ting), *n.* In *ceram.*, a variety of transfer-printing.

There are two distinct methods of printing in use for china and earthenware: one is transferred on the bisque, and is the method by which the ordinary printed ware is produced, and the other is transferred on the glaze. The first is called *press-printing* and the latter bat-printing.
Ure, Dict., III. 620.

press-proof (pres'prōf), *n.* The last proof examined before printed matter goes to press; the press-revise; a careful proof taken on the press, as distinguished from an ordinary rough proof.

press-room (pres'röm), *n.* 1. An apartment in which presses for any purpose are kept.— 2 In *printing*, a room where printing-presses are worked, as distinguished from a composing-room, etc.

press-stone (pres'stōn), *n.* The bed of a printing-press. *E. H. Knight.*

pressurage (presh'ụ̈r-āj), *n.* [< F. *pressurage;* as *pressure* + *-age.*] 1. The juice of the grape extracted by the press. *Imp. Dict.*—2. A fee paid to the owner of a wine-press for its use. *Imp. Dict.*

pressural (presh'ụ̈-ral), *a.* [< *pressure* + *-al.*] Of the nature of mechanical pressure.

pressure (presh'ụ̈r), *n.* [< OF. *pressure* = Sp. *presura* = It. *pressura*, < L. *pressura*, a pressing, a burden, < *premere*, pp. *pressus*, press: see *press*[1].] 1. The act of pressing; the exertion of force by pressing; the state of being pressed.

In my thoughts with scarce a sigh
I take the *pressure* of thine hand.
Tennyson, In Memoriam, cxix.

2. In *mech.*: (*a*) An equilibrated force.

Experience . . . showed that the *pressures* of a vault cannot be concentrated upon any single point, but only upon a line which extends over a considerable portion of the pier from the springing point upwards.
C. H. Moore, Gothic Architecture, p. 81.

(*b*) A force per unit area exerted over the surface of a body or part of a body, and toward the interior of the body. A force exerted upon a surface is necessarily equilibrated; otherwise, since the surface has no mass, it would produce infinite velocity until equilibrium ensued. A pressure can produce no motion, because it is a state of equilibrium; but a continuous variation of pressure in a given direction will tend to produce motion toward the places of less pressure. Thus, if a cylinder of liquid in a tube is under greater pressure per square inch at one end than at the other, there will be a tendency to motion toward the end where the pressure is less. (*c*) Stress in general, being either thrust, pull, or shearing stress. For *axis of pressure*, *conjugate pressure*, and other phrases where *pressure* means *stress*, see the latter word.

Boyle discovered a law about the dependence of the *pressure* of a gas upon its Volume, which showed that if you squeeze a gas into a smaller place it will press so much the more as the space has been diminished.
W. K. Clifford, Lectures, I. 180.

Uniform *pressure*, . . . such as the atmospheric, and, in a less degree, that of our bodily parts and of our clothes, produces no distinct consciousness.
J. Sully, Sensation and Intuition, p. 60.

3. The action of moral force; exertion of authority or influence; compulsion; a constraining influence or impulse.

The objections . . . are . . . rather like the intemperate talk of an angry child than *pressures* of reason or probability. *Jer. Taylor*, Works (ed. 1835), II. 250.

The convocation, which under the influence of Archbishop Bourchier was more amenable to royal *pressure*, was made to bestow a tenth in the following April.
Stubbs, Const. Hist., § 350.

The Preacher's contemporary, too, Malachi, felt the *pressure* of the same circumstances, had the same occasions of despondency. *M. Arnold*, Literature and Dogma, ii.

4. Weight upon the mind; burdensomeness; oppressiveness; also, burden; oppression.

Companions in grief sometimes diminish
And make the *pressure* easy.
Fletcher and Shirley, Night-Walker, iv. 6.

My own and my people's *pressures* are grievous.
Eikon Basilike.

The rulers augmented at the same time those public burdens the *pressure* of which is generally the immediate cause of revolutions. *Macaulay*, Mirabeau.

Days of difficulty and *pressure*. *Tennyson*, Enoch Arden.

5. Urgency; demand on one's time or energies; need for prompt or decisive action: as, the *pressure* of business.

Writing hastily and under *pressure*, his language is frequently involved and careless.
A. Dobson, Int. to Steele, p. xlvi.

6. Impression; stamp; character impressed.

I'll wipe away . . .
All saws of books, all forms, all *pressures* past.
Shak., Hamlet, i. 5. 100.

Absolute pressure. See *absolute.*—**Absolute steam pressure**, the total pressure computed from the zero of an absolute vacuum: distinguished from *relative pressure*, or from pressure indicated in pounds, kilograms, or other measure of weight above the ordinary atmospheric pressure at the sea-level. Ordinary steam-gages indicate pressure above that of the atmosphere. To the pressure so indicated the pressure of the atmosphere must be added to obtain the absolute steam pressure.—**Atmospheric pressure.** See *atmosphere*, 2.—**Center of pressure.** (*a*) In *physics*, that point of a body at which the whole amount of pressure may be applied with the same effect it would produce if distributed. (*b*) Specifically, in *hydros.*, that point of a plane, or of the side of a vessel containing a liquid, to which if a force were applied equal to the total pressure and in the opposite direction, it would exactly balance the total pressure.—**High pressure.** (*a*) Formerly, a phrase noting all steam-engines working at pressures materially higher than atmospheric pressure, but now merely a relative term. See *low pressure.* (*b*) Figuratively, a high degree of mental tension.

Miss Squeers . . . was . . . taken with one or two chokes and catchings of breath, indicative of feelings at a *high pressure.* *Dickens*, Nicholas Nickleby, xii.

Intensity of a pressure. See *intensity.*—**Low pressure**, in steam-engines, a phrase noting a motor using steam at a comparatively small pressure. The precise signification of the term is undetermined, but the standard of pressure is steadily rising, so that engines that were formerly considered high-pressure are now looked upon as low-pressure engines. The phrase formerly implied the presence of a condenser and pressure of not more than six pounds above atmospheric pressure, but it now has reference solely to the pressure, and describes that only relatively.—**Pressure myelitis**, myelitis due to compression of the spinal cord, as by a tumor.—**Pressure of atmosphere.** See *atmosphere*, 2.

pressure-bar (presh'ụ̈r-bär), *n.* In a planing-machine, a device for holding down lumber to be planed. *E. H. Knight.*

pressure-blower (presh'ụ̈r-blō"ėr), *n.* A blower in which a blast is produced by the direct pressure of pistons upon a definite and confined quantity of air, in contradistinction to the *fan-blower*, which produces a blast by centrifugal action.

pressure-figure (presh'ụ̈r-fig"ụ̈r), *n.* In *mineral.*, a figure produced in a section of some minerals by the pressure of a rather sharp point: thus, upon a sheet of mica the pressure-figure has the form of a six-rayed star, which is diagonal in position to the more easily obtained percussion-figure—that is, its rays are normal to edges of the prism and clinopinacoid.

pressure-filter (presh'ụ̈r-fil"tėr), *n.* A filter in which the liquid to be filtered is forced through filtering material by pressure greater than that of its own weight in the filter. Positive increase of the difference between the pressure on the liquid surface and against the discharge outlet is effected either by forcing air into an inclosed space over the liquid, by increasing the head through use of a standpipe, or by decreasing the atmospheric pressure upon the discharge outlet.

pressure-forging (presh'ụ̈r-fōr"jing), *n.* A method of shaping metal in dies in a forging-press by means of great pressure, usually hydraulic; hydraulic forging.

pressure-gage (presh'ụ̈r-gāj), *n.* 1. An apparatus or attachment for indicating the pressure of steam in a boiler.—2. In *gun.*, an instrument used to determine the pressure of powder-gas per square unit of area in the bore or chamber of a gun. The gas acts upon one end of a piston, whose opposite extremity is armed with a pyramidal or circular cutter, as in the Rodman gage; a conical cavity with a continuous spiral thread on its interior surface, as in the Woodbridge pressure-gage; or an anvil-head to compress a copper cylinder, as in the English "crusher" gage.

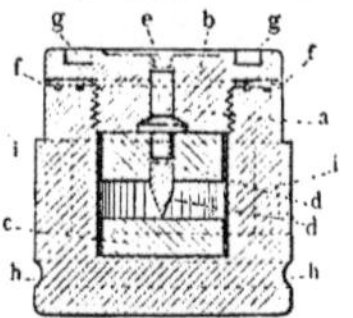

Pressure-gage.

a, piston; *i*, housing; *b*, screw-plug which closes the housing; *f*, gasket; *g*, recess for engagement of wrench with the plug; *d*, guide for cutting- or indenting-tool *d'*; *c*, register, a disk of copper, the indentation in which after discharge indicates the highest pressure attained in the gun during the combustion of the explosive; *e*, small copper cup or gas-check, which, while it transmits the pressure to the piston, prevents gas from entering the housing; *h*, groove for attaching the cartridge.

With the two cutter-gages, the lengths of the indentations in the soft copper disks are measured and compared with cuts of the same length made in the testing machine by the same cutters. From the tests in the machine, a table of lengths of cuts, with the pressures required to produce them, is made up. Hence, measuring the indentation in the disk taken from the pressure-gage, and turning to this table, the pressure exerted by the powder in the bore of the gun will be found opposite the measured length. The disks used in the pressure-gage and in the testing-machine should be taken from the same bar of copper, in order to secure a uniform density. In the "crusher" gage, the diminution in length of the copper cylinder is measured, and the pressure found by the testing-machine to produce an equal reduction in length of a cylinder from the same copper is assumed to be that exerted upon the bore of the gun. Pressure-gages may be placed either in a cavity in the walls of a gun or in the base of the cartridge-bag carrying the charge of powder.

pressure-note (presh'ụ̈r-nōt), *n.* In *music*, a note with a short crescendo upon it, as 𝅗𝅥, indicating a tone which is to be pressed into loudness as soon as sounded.

pressure-register (presh'ụ̈r-rej"is-tėr), *n.* An instrument which indicates and records the fluctuations of pressure of a fluid body, particularly an elastic fluid, as air, steam, or illuminating-gas. See *recording steam-gage*, under *steam-gage.*

pressure-screw (presh'ụ̈r-skrö), *n.* In *ordnance*, a screw used to hold parts in position by pressure. It is the analogue of the set-screw in general mechanism. See *set-screw.*

pressure-spot (presh'ụ̈r-spot), *n.* One of numerous minute spots or areas on the surface of the body, in which it appears from experimentation that the proper sensations of pressure reside, this sensation not being excitable in the intervening spaces.

The finest point, when it touches a *pressure-spot*, produces a sensation of pressure, and not one of being pricked. *G. T. Ladd*, Physiol. Psychology, p. 410.

presswork (pres'wėrk), *n.* 1. The working or management of a printing-press; also, any other work of a press-room relating to ink or impression on a press: in opposition to *composition*, or that branch of printing which is confined to preparing types for the press.—2. In *joinery*, cabinet-work of a number of successive veneers crossing grain, and united by glue, heat, and pressure. *E. H. Knight.*

press-yeast (pres'yēst), *n.* See *yeast.*

prest[1] (prest). An occasional preterit and past participle of *press*[1].

prest[2]† (prest), *v. t.* [< OF. *prester*, F. *prêter*, lend, ascribe, attribute, give rise to, afford, = Pr. Sp. Pg. *prestar* = It. *prestare*, < L. *præstare*, stand before, be surety for, execute, fulfil, discharge, < *præ*, before, + *stare*, stand: see *state.* Cf. *rest*[2].] To furnish; pay out; put out as a loan; lend.

To have *prested* and lent money to Kynge Henry for the arrayenge and settynge forth of a new armye against hym. *Hall*, Edw. IV., an. 10.

"I myself have *prested*," wrote the Earl to Burghley, "above 300*l.* among our men here since I came, and yet what need they be in . . . all the world doth see."
Motley, Hist. Netherlands, I. 523.

prest[2] (prest), *n.* [< OF. *prest*, F. *prêt* (= Pr. *prest* = It. *presto*), a loan, < OF. *prester*, lend: see *prest*[2], *v.*] 1†. A loan of money; hence, a loan in general; also, ready money.

The summe of expenses, as well of wages & *prests* as for the expenses of the kings houses.
Hakluyt's Voyages, I. 121.

2. Formerly, a duty in money paid by the sheriff on his account in the exchequer, or for money left or remaining in his hands. *Cowell.* —**To give in prest**, to give as prest-money; hence, to pay, give, or lend (money) in advance.

> He sent thyder three somers [baggage-horses] laden wt nobles of Castel and floreyns, to *gyue in prest* to knyghtes and squyers, for he knewe well otherwyse he sholde not haue them come out of theyr houses.
> *Berners*, tr. of Froissart's Chron., II. lxiv.

prest[3]† (prest), *a.* [< ME. *prest*, *prest*, < OF. *prest*, F. *prêt* = Pr. *prest* = Sp. Pg. It. *presto*, ready, < ML. *præstus*, ready, < L. *præsto*, adv., at hand, ready, present, here, < *præ*, before, + *stare*, stand. Cf. *prest*[2].] 1. Ready; prompt; quick.

> He is the *prestest* payer that pore men knoweth.
> *Piers Plowman* (B), v. 558.

> I am *prest* to fette hym when yow liste.
> *Chaucer*, Troilus, iii. 917.

> Cursed Dionyza hath
> The pregnant instrument of wrath
> *Prest* for this blow.
> *Shak.*, Pericles, iv., Prol., l. 45.

> Well, well, I'll meet ye anon, then tell you more, boys;
> However, stand prepar'd, *prest* for our journey.
> *Fletcher*, Wildgoose Chase, v. 2.

2. At hand; near.

> Set me vvhereas the sunne doth parch the greene,
> Or vvhere his beames do not dissolue the yce:
> In temperate heate vvhere he is felt and seene,
> In presence *prest* of people mad or vvise.
> *Puttenham*, Arte of Eng. Poesie, p. 186.

> Berdys ther sange on bowhes *prest*.
> *Robin Hood and the Potter* (Child's Ballads, V. 29).

3. Bold; valiant.

> Pausanias a pris King none *prester* ifounde.
> *Alisaunder of Macedoine* (E. E. T. S.), l. 1218.

4. Neat; comely; proper.

> More people, more handsome and *prest*,
> Where find ye? *Tusser.*

prest[3]† (prest), *adv.* [ME., < *prest*[3], *a.*] Quickly; promptly; immediately.

> Princes of this palys *prest* vndo the gates,
> For here cometh with coroune the kynge of alle glorie.
> *Piers Plowman* (C), xxi. 274.

prest[4]†, *n.* A Middle English form of *priest*.

prestable (pres'ta-bl), *a.* [< *prest*[2] + *-able*.] Payable; capable of being made good. [Scotch.]

prestant (pres'tant), *n.* [< L. *præstan(t-)s*, ppr. of *præstare*, stand before: see *prest*[2], *v.*] The open diapason of a pipe-organ.

prestation† (pres-tā'shon), *n.* [< F. *prestation* = Sp. *prestacion* = Pg. *prestação* = It. *prestazione*, < L. *præstatio(n-)*, a warranty, a payment of something due, < *præstare*, pp. *præstatus*, be surety for: see *prest*[2].] A presting or payment of money: sometimes used for *purveyance*. *Cowell.*

> Those grants be clogged with heavy feudal services and payments or *prestations* which no one dared refuse.
> *Russell*, Hist. Modern Europe, I. 290.

prester[1] (pres'tėr), *n.* [< ME. *prester*, < OF. *prestre*, F. *prêtre*, priest: see *priest*, *presbyter*.] A priest: often used in old writers as the title of a supposed Christian king and priest (*Prester* John) of a medieval kingdom. The belief in the existence of such a ruler in some undetermined part of Asia appeared in the twelfth century. From the fourteenth century the seat of the supposed Prester John was placed in Abyssinia, and this belief was held down to the close of the middle ages.

> In the East syde of Afrike, beneth the redde sea, dwelleth the greate and myghtye Emperour and Chrystian kynge *Prester* Iohan, well knowen to the Portugales in theyr vyages to Calicut.
> *R. Eden* (First Books on America, ed. Arber, p. 374).

> More than twenty years later, when the first book on Abyssinia was composed — that of Alvarez — the title constantly and as a matter of course designating the king of Abyssinia is "*Prester* John," or simply "the *Preste*."
> *Encyc. Brit.*, XIX. 718.

prester[2]† (pres'tėr), *n.* [< Gr. πρηστήρ, a meteor, a lightning-flash, < πρήθειν, blow up, blow up into flame.] A meteor.

presternal (prē-stėr'nal), *a.* [< *præsternum* + *-al*.] 1. Of or pertaining to the præsternum: as, *presternal* bone; *presternal* region.—2. In *entom.*, same as *prosternal*.—**Presternal muscle.** Same as *sternalis*.

presternum, *n.* See *præsternum*.

prestezza (pres-tet'sä), *n.* [It., quickness, < *presto*, quick: see *prest*[3] and *presto*.] In *music*, quickness of movement or execution; rapidity.

prestidigital (pres-ti-dij'i-tal), *a.* [< *prestidigit(ation)* + *-al* (after *digital*).] Engaged in prestidigitation; suited or qualified for legerdemain. [Rare.]

> The first his honest hard-working hand — the second his three-fingered Jack, his *prestidigital* hand.
> *C. Reade*, Never too Late to Mend, vi.

prestidigitation (pres-ti-dij-i-tā'shon), *n.* [< F. *prestidigitation*, an altered form (as if 'dexterous fingering,' < L. *præsto*, at hand, ready, + *digitus*, a finger, + *-ation*) of *prestigiation*: see *prestigiation*.] Legerdemain; sleight of hand; prestigiation; the performance of feats requiring dexterity and skill, particularly of the fingers; hence, juggling in general.

prestidigitator (pres-ti-dij'i-tā-tor), *n.* [< F. *prestidigitateur*; < *prestidigitat(ion)* + *-or*[1].] One who practises prestidigitation; a prestigiator; a juggler.

prestige (pres-tēzh' or pres'tij), *n.* [< F. *prestige* = Sp. Pg. *prestigio* = It. *prestigio*, *prestigia*, illusion, fascination, enchantment, prestige, < L. *præstigium*, a delusion, an illusion; cf. *præstigiæ*, deception, jugglers' tricks, < *præstinguere*, obscure, extinguish, < *præ*, before, + *stinguere*, extinguish: see *distinguish*, etc.] 1†. Illusion; juggling trick; fascination; charm; imposture.

> The sophisms of infidelity and the *prestiges* of imposture. *Warburton*, Works, IX. v.

2. An illusion as to one's personal merit or importance, particularly a flattering illusion; hence, a reputation for excellence, importance, or authority; weight or influence arising from reputation.

> Mr. Quincy had the moral firmness which enabled him to decline a duel without any loss of personal *prestige*.
> *Lowell*, Study Windows, p. 106.

> Unless a man can get the *prestige* and income of a Don, and write donnish books, it's hardly worth while for him to make a Greek and Latin machine of himself.
> *George Eliot*, Daniel Deronda, xvi.

prestigiate (pres-tij'i-āt), *v. t.* [< L. *præstigiatus*, pp. of *præstigiare*, deceive by juggling tricks, < *præstigiæ*, deceptions, jugglers' feats: see *prestige*.] To deceive as by an illusion or jugglers' trick. [Rare.]

> The wisest way, when all is said, is with all humility and feare to take Christ as himselfe hath revealed himselfe in his Gospel, and not as the Devill presents him to *prestigiated* phansies. *N. Ward*, Simple Cobler, p. 18.

prestigiation (pres-tij-i-ā'shon), *n.* [< F. **prestigiation* (later *prestidigitation*: see *prestidigitation*), < LL. *præstigiare*, pp. *præstigiatus*, deceive by juggling tricks: see *prestigiate*.] The playing of legerdemain tricks; a trick of legerdemain; juggling; sleight of hand. [Rare.]

> What a multitude of examples are there in good authentic authors of divers kinds of fascinations, incantations, *prestigiations!* *Howell*, Letters, iii. 23.

prestigiator (pres-tij'i-ā-tor), *n.* [< F. *prestigiateur* (Cotgrave), < L. *præstigiator*, a juggler, an impostor, < *præstigiare*, deceive by juggling tricks: see *prestigiate*. Cf. *prestidigitator*.] A juggler; a cheat.

> This cunning *prestigiator* [the devil] took the advantage of so high a place to set off his representations the more lively. *Dr. H. More*, Mystery of Godliness (1660), p. 105.

prestigiatory† (pres-tij'i-ā-tō-ri), *a.* [< *prestigiate* + *-ory*.] Juggling; consisting of tricks or impostures.

> We have an art call'd *præstigiatory*,
> That deals with spirits, and intelligences
> Of meaner office and condition.
> *T. Tomkis* (?), Albumazar, i. 7.

prestigious† (pres-tij'us), *a.* [< F. *prestigieux* = Sp. Pg. It. *prestigioso*, < LL. *præstigiosus*, full of deceitful tricks, delusive, < L. *præstigiæ*, jugglers' tricks, illusions: see *prestige*.] 1. Practising legerdemain; juggling; deluding.

> But, of all the preternatural things which befel these people, there were none more unaccountable than those wherein the *prestigious* dæmons would ever now and then cover the most corporeal things in the world with a fascinating mist of invisibility. *C. Mather*, Mag. Chris., ii. 13.

2. Performed by prestidigitation; illusory; deceptive.

> Who only sweld thee with vain-glorious pride,
> Devising strange *prestigious* tricks beside,
> Only to draw me from thee.
> *Heywood*, Dialogues (Works, ed. Pearson, 1874, VI. 180).

prestimony (pres'ti-mō-ni), *n.* [= F. *prestimonie* = Sp. Pg. *prestimonio*, < ML. *præstimonium*, an appropriated fund, < L. *præstare*, warrant, discharge: see *prest*[2].] In *canon law*, a fund for the support of a priest, appropriated by the founder, but not erected into any title or benefice, and not subject to the Pope or the ordinary, the patron being the collator. *Imp. Dict.*

prestissimo (pres-tis'i-mō), *adv.* [It., superl. of *presto*, q. v.] In *music*, very quickly; in the most rapid tempo.

prestly† (prest'li), *adv.* [< ME. *prestly*, *presteli*, *prestliche*, *pristly*; < *prest*[3] + *-ly*[2].] 1. Hastily; quickly; promptly; eagerly.

> *Prestili* with al that puple to Palerne thei went.
> *William of Palerne* (E. E. T. S.), l. 5309.

> Then [he] leues the lede, and of londe paste
> To Pelleus *pristly*.
> *Destruction of Troy* (E. E. T. S.), l. 1043.

2. Earnestly; firmly.

> Madame, mourne ȝe namore; ȝe mow wel seie
> That the prince of heuen ȝou hath *presli* in mynde,
> & socor sendeth ȝou sone.
> *William of Palerne* (E. E. T. S.), l. 2925.

> Now full *pristly* I pray to my prise goddes
> That I may see thee come sounde to this sale enys,
> And me comford of thy coursse, kepe I no more.
> *Destruction of Troy* (E. E. T. S.), l. 872.

> Therfore *pristly* I yow praye
> That ye will of youre talkyng blyn.
> *Thomas of Ersseldoune* (Child's Ballads, I. 97).

prest-money (prest'mun"i), *n.* Money paid to men when they enlist in the British service: so called because it binds those who receive it to be *prest* or ready at all times appointed. Also *press-money*. *Imp. Dict.*

presto (pres'tō), *adv.* [< It. *presto*, quick, quickly: see *prest*[3].] 1. Quickly; immediately; in haste.

> *Oni.* Well, you'll come?
> *Jun. Presto.* *B. Jonson*, Case is Altered, i. 1.

2. In *music*, quick; in rapid tempo.

presto (pres'tō), *n.* [< *presto*, *adv.*] In *music*, a passage in quick tempo.

prestomial (prē-stō'mi-al), *a.* [Also *præstomial*; < *præstomium* + *-al*.] Of or pertaining to the præstomium.

prestomium, *n.* See *præstomium*.

prestriction (prē-strik'shon), *n.* [< LL. *præstrictio(n-)*, a binding fast, < L. *præstringere*, pp. *præstrictus*, bind fast, tie up, also blind, obscure, < *præ*, before, + *stringere*, draw or tie tight: see *stringent*.] Blinding; blindness.

> 'Tis fear'd you have Balaams disease, a pearle in your eye, Mammons *Præstriction*.
> *Milton*, On Def. of Humb. Remonst.

prestudy (prē-stud'i), *v. t.*; pret. and pp. *prestudied*, ppr. *prestudying*. [< *pre-* + *study*.] To study beforehand.

> He . . . never broached what he had new brewed, but preached what he had *pre-studied* some competent time before. *Fuller*, Worthies, Cambridge, I. 240.

presultor (prē-sul'tor), *n.* [< LL. *præsultor*, one who dances before others, < L. **præsilire* (a false reading for *prosilire*), leap or dance before, < *præ*, before, + *salire*, leap, bound: see *salient*.] A leader or director of a dance. [Rare.]

> The Coryphæus of the world, or the precentor and *presultor* of it. *Cudworth*, Intellectual System, p. 307.

presumable (prē-zū'ma-bl), *a.* [< *presume* + *-able*.] Capable of being presumed or taken for granted; such as may be supposed to be true or entitled to belief without examination or direct evidence, or on probable evidence.

> It is now the *presumable* duty, imposed by law upon the Clergy, of themselves to alter their practice.
> *Gladstone*, Gleanings of Past Years, I. 90.

presumably (prē-zū'ma-bli), *adv.* As may be presumed or reasonably supposed; by or according to presumption; by legitimate inference from facts or circumstances.

presume (prē-zūm'), *v.*; pret. and pp. *presumed*, ppr. *presuming*. [< ME. *presumen*, < OF. *presumer*, F. *présumer* = Pr. Sp. Pg. *presumir* = It. *presumere*, < L. *præsumere*, take before or beforehand, take to oneself, anticipate, take for granted, presume, < *præ*, before, + *sumere*, take: see *assume*, and cf. *consume*, *resume*.] I. *trans.* 1. To take upon one's self; undertake; venture; dare: generally with an infinitive as object.

> He or they that *presumen* to doo the contrarie, as often tyme as they be founden in defaute, to paye xx. s.
> *English Gilds* (E. E. T. S.), p. 383.

> Death, I feel, *presumeth*
> To change this life of mine into a new.
> *Thomas Stukely* (Child's Ballads, VII. 312).

> Bold deed thou hast *presumed*, adventurous Eve.
> *Milton*, P. L., ix. 921.

> As soon as the sermon is finished, nobody *presumes* to stir till Sir Roger is gone out of the church.
> *Addison*, Sir Roger at Church.

> There was a time when I would have chastened your insolence, for *presuming* thus to appear before me.
> *Goldsmith*, Vicar, xxiv.

2. To believe or accept upon probable evidence; infer as probable; take for granted.

> *Presume* not that I am the thing I was.
> *Shak.*, 2 Hen. IV., v. 5. 60.

> Master Foxe mentioneth, in his Book of Martyrs, that one in the street crying "Fire, fire," the whole assembly in St. Mary's, in Oxford, at one Mallary's recantation, *presumed* it to be in the church.
> *Rev. T. Adams*, Works, III. 50.

Yet, sir, I *presume* you would not wish me to quit the army? *Sheridan*, The Rivals, ii. 1.

The business of farming . . . is assessed in respect of a *presumed* profit. *S. Dowell*, Taxes in England, III. 122.

=**Syn.** 2. *Surmise, Guess*, etc. (see *conjecture*), think, consider.

II. *intrans.* **1.** To be venturesome; especially, to venture beyond the limits of ordinary license or propriety; act or speak overboldly.

Neither boldness can make us *presume* as long as we are kept under with the sense of our own wretchedness. *Hooker*, Eccles. Polity, v. 47.

I found not what methought I wanted still;
And to the heavenly Vision thus *presumed*.
Milton, P. L., viii. 356.

2. To press forward presumptuously; be led by presumption; make one's way overconfidently into an unwarranted place or position.

Presume thou not to hye, I rid,
Least it turn thee to blame.
Babees Book (E. E. T. S.), p. 91.

Up-led by thee,
Into the heaven of heavens I have *presumed*,
An earthly guest. *Milton*, P. L., vii. 13.

To presume of†. Same as *to presume upon*.

They [the Waymoores] haue long haire, are without Townes or houses, and care not where they come, *presuming of* their swiftnesse. *Purchas*, Pilgrimage, p. 840.

To presume upon or **on**, to rely upon as a reason for boldness; hence, to act overboldly or arrogantly on the strength of, or on the supposition of.

Do not *presume* too much upon my love.
Shak., J. C., iv. 3. 63.

She, . . . *presuming on* the hire of her treason, deserted her Husband. *Milton*, Hist. Eng., ii.

presumedly (prē-zū'med-li), *adv.* By presumption; as one may suppose; presumably.

The matter was considerably simplified by the fact that these societies, *presumedly* from patriotic motives, send the persons they assist only to the Dominion of Canada. *Lancet*, No. 3412, p. 144.

presumer (prē-zū'mėr), *n.* [< *presume* + *-er*[1].] One who presumes; an arrogant or presumptuous person.

presuming (prē-zū'ming), *p. a.* Acting presumptuously; hence, overbold; forward; presumptuous.

presumingly (prē-zū'ming-li), *adv.* With presumption; overconfidently; arrogantly.

presumpt† (prē-zumpt'), *v. t.* [< L. *presumptus*, pp. of *presumere*, take beforehand: see *presume*.] To take inconsiderately or rashly.

The vow beynge *presumpted*, dyssembled, and fayned. *Bp. Bale*, Apology, fol. 10.

presumption (prē-zump'shon), *n.* [< OF. *presomption*, F. *présomption* = Sp. *presuncion* = Pg. *presumpção* = It. *presunzione*, < L. *præsumptio(n-)*, a taking beforehand, an anticipation, < *præsumere*, pp. *præsumptus*, presume: see *presume*.] **1.** The act of presuming, or taking upon one's self more than good sense and propriety warrant; excessive boldness or overconfidence in thought or conduct; presumptuousness; assurance; arrogance.

I could say much more of the king's majesty without flattery, did I not fear the imputation of *presumption*. *Raleigh*, Hist. World, Pref., p. 19.

We cannot tell what is a Judgment of God: 'tis *presumption* to take upon us to know. *Selden*, Table-Talk, p. 58.

If ye think ye may with a pious *presumption* strive to goe beyond God in mercy, I shall not be one now that would dissuade ye. *Milton*, Church-Government, ii., Con.

2. The act of presuming or probably inferring; hypothetical or inductive inference.

Most of those that believe a God and a judgment to come, and yet continue in sin, do it upon this *presumption*, that one time or other they shall leave their sins, and change the course of their lives before they go out of this world. *Stillingfleet*, Sermons, II. iii.

3. That which is presumed; that which is supposed to be true upon grounds of probability.

When we see any part or organ developed in a remarkable degree or manner in any species, the fair *presumption* is that it is of high importance to that species. *Darwin*, Origin of Species, p. 158.

4. A ground for presuming or believing; evidence or probability, as tending to establish an opinion.

There will always be a strong *presumption* against the sincerity of a conversion by which the convert is directly a gainer. *Macaulay*, Hist. Eng., vii.

The mere possibility of an event furnishes no *presumption*, not even the slightest, of its realization. *Mivart*, Nature and Thought, p. 113.

5. In *law*, an inference as to the existence of one fact from the existence of some other fact, founded upon a previous experience of their connection, or dictated by the policy of the law. Presumptions are generally inferences in accordance with the common experience of mankind and the established principles of logic; but, as they differ in cogency or convincing power, the term is used variously as signifying different degrees of certainty in the inference. (*a*) An inference which a jury, or a judge sitting in the place of a jury, may without error draw from a given state of facts, but is not bound to draw from them: called by way of distinction a *presumption of fact*. (*b*) An inference which, in absence of evidence to the contrary, the law draws, and a jury or judge cannot without error refuse to apply: called by way of distinction a *legal presumption* or a *presumption of law*; more specifically, a *rebuttable legal presumption*. (*c*) An inference which the law, usually for reasons of public policy, draws from a given state of facts, and refuses to allow evidence to countervail the inference: called a *conclusive presumption* or an *irrebuttable presumption*. (See *conclusive*.) Thus an infant under 7 is conclusively presumed incapable of criminal intent, and the law will not allow evidence to be received that he was precociously capable of it. An infant between 7 and 14 (by statute now in New York 12) is presumptively incapable of such intent, but this, though a presumption of law which cannot be disregarded in the absence of evidence, may be rebutted by evidence of actual capacity. An infant over that age shown to be untaught and dull of comprehension might be inferred to be without such capacity, but this inference (unless the evidence was clear) would be only a presumption of fact, which the jury alone could draw, and the court could not control.—**Philosophical** or **logical presumption.** See *philosophical*. =**Syn.** 1. *Pride, Arrogance, Presumption*, etc. (see *arrogance*), assurance, effrontery, forwardness. See *presumptuousness*.—2. *Surmise, Conjecture*, etc. See *inference*.—4. Likelihood, probability.

presumptive (prē-zump'tiv), *a.* [< F. *présomptif* = Sp. *presuntivo* = Pg. *presumptivo* = It. *presuntivo*, < LL. **præsumptivus* (in adv. *præsumptive*, boldly, presumptuously), < L. *præsumere*, pp. *præsumptus*, presume: see *presume*.] **1.** Based on presumption or probability; probable; grounded on probable evidence; proving circumstantially, not directly.

A strong *presumptive* proof that his interpretation of Scripture is not the true one. *Waterland*, Works, I. 321.

2†. Unreasonably confident; presumptuous; arrogant.

There being two opinions repugnant to each other, it may not be *presumptive* or sceptical to doubt of both.
Sir T. Browne.

Heir presumptive. See *heir*.—**Presumptive evidence.** See *evidence*. =**Syn.** 1. See *presumptuous*.

presumptively (prē-zump'tiv-li), *adv.* In a presumptive manner; by presumption or supposition grounded on probability; by previous supposition; presumably.

presumptuous (prē-zump'tū-us), *a.* [< ME. *presumptuous* (in adv.), < OF. *presumpcious*, *presumpticus*, *presompcieus*, etc., F. *présomptueux* = Sp. *presuntuoso* = Pg. *presumptuoso* = It. *presuntuoso*, < LL. *præsumptiosus*, *præsumptosus*, full of boldness, < L. *præsumptio(n-)*, boldness, presumption: see *presumption*.] Going beyond the limits of propriety or good sense in thought or conduct; exhibiting or marked by presumption; overbold; presuming; arrogant.

'Tis not thy southern power . . .
Which makes thee thus *presumptuous* and proud.
Shak., 3 Hen. VI., i. 1. 157.

Presumptuous man, see to what desperate end
Thy treachery hath brought thee!
Beau. and Fl., Knight of Burning Pestle, iii. 4.

Rash author, 'tis a vain *presumptuous* crime
To undertake the sacred art of rhyme.
Dryden and Soames, tr. of Boileau's Art of Poetry, i. 1.

=**Syn.** Forward, venturesome, foolhardy. *Presumptive* and *presumptuous* have no meanings in common. See *arrogance*.

presumptuously (prē-zump'tū-us-li), *adv.* [< ME. *presumptuowsly*; < *presumptuous* + *-ly*[2].] In a presumptuous manner; with rash confidence; overboldly; arrogantly.

Thou woldest konne that I can and carpen hit after,
Presumptuowsly, parauenture a-pose so manye,
That hit myȝthe turne me to tene and Theologie bothe.
Piers Plowman (A), xii. 8.

But I
God's counsel have not kept, his holy secret
Presumptuously have publish'd.
Milton, S. A., l. 498.

presumptuousness (prē-zump'tū-us-nes), *n.* The state or character of being presumptuous or rashly confident; groundless confidence; arrogance; irreverent boldness or forwardness. =**Syn.** *Presumptuousness* differs from *presumption* only in being simply a quality, while *presumption* may be either a quality or the conduct exhibiting the quality.

presupposal (prē-su-pō'zal), *n.* [< *pre-* + *supposal*.] Supposal formed beforehand; presupposition.

If our *presupposall* be true, . . . the Poet is of all other the most auncient Orator.
Puttenham, Arte of Eng. Poesie, p. 163.

presuppose (prē-su-pōz'), *v. t.*; pret. and pp. *presupposed*, ppr. *presupposing*. [< OF. *presupposer*, F. *présupposer*; as *pre-* + *suppose*. Cf. Sp. *presuponer* = Pg. *presuppôr* = It. *presupporre*.] **1.** To suppose beforehand; take for granted in advance of actual knowledge or experience.

Whatsoeuer the Philosopher sayth shoulde be doone, hee giueth a perfect picture of it in some one by whom hee *presupposeth* it was done. *Sir P. Sidney*, Apol. for Poetrie.

Men of corrupted minds *presuppose* that honesty groweth out of simplicity of manners.
Bacon, Advancement of Learning, ii. 282.

2. To assume beforehand; require or imply as an antecedent condition; necessitate the prior assumption of.

For a remembrance *presupposeth* the thyng to be absent; and therefore, if this be a remembraunce of hym, then can he not here be present. *Fryth*, Works, p. 121.

Those who attempt to reason us out of our follies begin at the wrong end, since the attempt naturally *presupposes* us capable of reason. *Goldsmith*, English Clergy.

Nutrition *presupposes* obtainment of food: food cannot be got without powers of prehension, and, usually, of locomotion. *H. Spencer*, Man vs. State, p. 95.

presupposition (prē-sup-ọ-zish'on), *n.* [< F. *présupposition* = Sp. *presuposicion* = Pg. *presupposição* = It. *presupposizione*; as *pre-* + *supposition*. Cf. *presuppose*.] **1.** Supposition in advance of experience or knowledge; surmise; conjecture.

There were many great conjectures and *presuppositions*, and many long circumstances to bring it to conclusion.
North, tr. of Plutarch, p. 383.

2. Postulation as of an antecedent condition; hence, that which is postulated as a necessary antecedent condition; a prerequisite.

Satan will be an adversary, man will be proud: a necessity upon *presupposition* of Satan's malice, and man's wickedness. *Rev. T. Adams*, Works, II. 304.

Self-directing agency is the *presupposition* of ethical science, and separates it by a sharp line from Physics.
New Princeton Rev., I. 183.

presuppositionless (prē-sup-ọ-zish'on-les), *a.* [< *presupposition* + *-less*.] Without or independent of presuppositions.

It has already been seen how the theory of knowledge, when it passed out of Kant's hands, and tried to make itself (*a*) complete and (*b*) *pre-suppositionless*, became for Hegel a logic that was in reality a metaphysic.
Encyc. Brit., XVIII. 795.

presurmise (prē-sėr-mīz'), *n.* [< *pre-* + *surmise*.] A surmise previously formed.

It was your *presurmise*
That, in the dole of blows, your son might drop.
Shak., 2 Hen. IV., i. 1. 168.

presylvian (prẹ-sil'vi-an), *a.* [< *pre-* + *Sylvian*.] Anterior, as a part of the Sylvian fissure: applied to the ascending branch of this fissure. See *postsylvian*.

presymphysial (prē-sim-fiz'i-al), *a.* [< L. *præ*, before, + NL. *symphysis*, symphysis: see *symphysial*.] Situated in advance of the symphysis menti. *Geol. Jour.*, XLIV. 146.

presystole (prē-sis'tọ-lē), *n.* [< L. *præ*, before, + NL. *systole*, systole.] The interval immediately prior to the systole.

A study of the sphincters of the cardiac and other veins, with remarks on their hermetic occlusion during the *presystole* state. *Nature*, XXX. 460.

presystolic (prē-sis-tol'ik), *a.* [< *presystole* + *-ic*.] Preceding the systole.—**Presystolic murmur**, a murmur at the close of diastole, immediately preceding systole.

pret. An abbreviation of *preterit*.

preteach† (prē-tēch'), *v. t.* [< *pre-* + *teach*.] To teach in advance. [Rare.]

He takes the oaths of allegiance and supremacy which he is *prætaught* to evade, or think null.
Amherst, Terræ Filius, No. 3.

pretence, *n.* See *pretense*.

pretend (prẹ-tend'), *v.* [< ME. *pretenden*, < OF. *pretendre*, F. *prétendre* = Sp. Pg. *pretender* = It. *pretendere*, < L. *prætendere*, stretch forth or forward, spread before, hold out, put forward as an excuse, allege, pretend, < *præ*, before, + *tendere*, stretch: see *tend*.] **I.** *trans.* **1†.** To hold out before one or in front; stretch forward; hence, to put before one for action, consideration, or acceptance; offer; present.

But Pastorella, wofull wretched Elfe,
Was by the Captaine all this while defended,
Who, minding more her safety than himselfe,
His target alwayes over her *pretended*.
Spenser, F. Q., VI. xi. 19.

All stood with their *pretended* spears prepar'd,
With broad steel heads the brandish'd weapons glar'd.
Dryden, tr. of Ovid's Meleager and Atalanta, l. 104.

I had not thought (courteous reader) to have *pretended* thus conspicuously in thy sight this rude and indigested chaos of conceites, the abortive issue of my vnfertile braine. *Times' Whistle* (E. E. T. S.), p. 110.

To that wench
I *pretend* honest love, and she deserves it.
Middleton and Rowley, Changeling, iv. 2.

From these Mahometan Sanctuaries, our Guide *pretended* to carry us to a Christian Church, about two furlongs out of Town on the South side.
Maundrell, Aleppo to Jerusalem, p. 15.

2. To put forward as a statement or an assertion; especially, to allege or declare falsely or with intent to deceive.

I examined every thing without any one to accompany me but my own servant, which they *pretended* was very dangerous. *Pococke*, Description of the East, II. ii. 110.

Then I *pretended* to be a musician; marry, I could not shew mine instrument, and that bred a discord.
B. *Jonson*, Love Restored.

In the vicinity of what was called the Lady Dudley's chamber, the domestics *pretended* to hear groans and screams, and other supernatural noises.
Scott, Kenilworth, xli.

His eulogists, unhappily, could not *pretend* that his morals had escaped untainted from the wide-spread contagion of that age. *Macaulay*, Hist. Eng., vi.

3. To put forward as a reason or excuse; use as a pretext; allege as a ground or reason; hence, to put forward a false appearance of; simulate; counterfeit; feign.

The queen, sir, very oft importuned me
To temper poisons for her, still *pretending*
The satisfaction of her knowledge only
In killing creatures vile, as cats and dogs.
Shak., Cymbeline, v. 5. 250.

Generally to *pretend* Conscience against Law is dangerous. *Selden*, Table-Talk, p. 39.

Lest that too heavenly form, *pretended*
To hellish falsehood, snare them!
Milton, P. L., x. 872.

This let him know,
Lest, wilfully transgressing, he *pretend*
Surprisal. *Milton*, P. L., v. 244.

No knave but boldly will *pretend*
The requisites that form a friend.
Cowper, Friendship, st. 3.

4. To lay claim to; assert as a right or possession; claim.

Why shall we fight, if you *pretend* no title?
Shak., 3 Hen. VI., iv. 7. 57.

The gentry *pretend* to have their victuals dressed and served up as nicely as if they were in London.
Beverley, Virginia, iv. ¶ 70.

5. To aspire to; attempt; undertake. [Obsolete or archaic.]

And those two brethren Gyauntes did defend
The walles so stoutly with their sturdie mayne,
That never entraunce any durst *pretend*.
Spenser, F. Q., II. xi. 15.

I will not *pretend* so much as to mention that chart on which is drawn the appearance of our blessed Lord after his resurrection. *Steele*, Spectator, No. 226.

Dost thou dare *pretend* to punish me
For not descrying sunshine at midnight?
Browning, Ring and Book, II. 222.

6†. To intend; design; plan; plot.

Marriage being the most holy conjunction that falls to mankind, . . . she had not only broken it, but broken it with death, and the most *pretended* death that might be.
Sir P. Sidney, Arcadia, v.

Reward not hospitality
With such black payment as thou hast *pretended*.
Shak., Lucrece, l. 576.

Harm not this young forrester;
Noe ill doth he *pretend*.
Robin Hood and the Tanner's Daughter (Child's Ballads, V. 337).

Get you and pray the gods
For success and return; omit not any thing
In the *pretended* celebration.
Fletcher (*and another*), Two Noble Kinsmen, i. 1.

7†. To presage; portend; forebode.

It plesith hem to dwelle in derk, and in blak, orrible, stynkynge placis, in heuynesse, wreche, and malencoly, and in tho thingis that *pretende* the coudicioun of helle.
Book of Quinte Essence (ed. Furnivall), p. 19.

Doth this churlish superscription
Pretend some alteration in good will?
Shak., 1 Hen. VI., iv. 1. 54.

II. *intrans.* 1. To stretch or reach forward; aim; aspire: often with *to*.

For *to* what fyn he wolde anon *pretende*,
That knowe I wel, and forthi yet I seye,
So lef this sorwe, or platly he wol dye.
Chaucer, Troilus, iv. 922.

I am content to go forward a little more in the madness of missing rather than not *pretend*; and rather wear out than rust. *Donne*, Letters, xxxvi.

2. To lay claim; assert a right of ownership or possession: generally followed by *to*.

A fellow that *pretends* only *to* learning, buys titles, and nothing else of books in him! B. *Jonson*, Epicœne, i. 1.

Men of those noble breedings you *pretend to*
Should scorn to lie, or get their food with falsehood.
Fletcher (*and another*), Sea Voyage, iv. 1.

The Book which I have to Answer *pretends to* reason, not *to* Autorities and quotations.
Milton, Eikonoklastes, v.

Merit is a claim, and may *pretend* justly *to* favour.
Steele, Lying Lover, i. 1.

3. To make pretense; make believe; counterfeit or feign.

pretendant, pretendent (prē-ten'dant, -dent), *n.* [< F. *prétendant* = Sp. *pretendiente* = Pg. It. *pretendente*, < L. *prætenden(t-)s*, ppr. of *prætendere*, pretend: see *pretend.*] A pretender; a claimant.

Neither the Confederation nor the duchies, nor all the *pretendents* to the succession, had acceded to the treaty.
Woolsey, Introd. to Inter. Law, App. ii., p. 428.

pretendedly (prē-ten'ded-li), *adv.* By or with pretense; by false representation; ostensibly.

An action . . . that came speciously and *pretendedly* out out of a Church. *Hammond*, Works, IV. 593. (*Latham.*)

He was also raising Forces in London, *pretendedly* to serve the Portugall, but with intent to seise the Tower.
Milton, Eikonoklastes, x.

pretendence† (prē-ten'dens), *n.* [< ML. *prætendentia*, pretense, claim, < L. *prætenden(t-)s*, claiming: see *pretendant.*] Pretension; claim.

Be it enough that God and men do scorn
Their projects, censures, vain *pretendences*.
Daniel, To the King's Majesty.

pretendent, *n.* See *pretendant*.

pretender (prē-ten'dėr), *n.* 1. One who pretends, or makes a false show, as of learning or of legal right.

The King
Pronounced a dismal sentence, meaning by it
To keep the list low and *pretenders* back.
Tennyson, Merlin and Vivien.

2. One who pretends, or puts forward a claim; a claimant; an aspirant.

You must know I am a *pretender* to the angle, and, doubtless, a Trout affords the most pleasure to the angler of any sort of fish whatever.
Cotton, in Walton's Angler, ii. 224.

There are no distinguishing qualities among men to which there are not false *pretenders*.
Steele, Tatler, No. 211.

3. Specifically, a claimant to a throne. In British history there have been several pretenders, especially "the Pretender," James Edward Stuart, son of James II., who in 1715 made an unsuccessful attempt to gain the English throne and supplant the reigning Hanoverian dynasty; another unsuccessful attempt was made in his behalf in 1745–6 by his son Charles Edward (often called "the Young Pretender").

God bless the king, I mean the faith's defender;
God bless—no harm in blessing—the *Pretender*;
But who pretender is, or who is king—
God bless us all!—that's quite another thing.
Byrom, To an Officer in the Army.

pretendership (prē-ten'dėr-ship), *n.* [< *pretender* + *-ship.*] The claim, character, or position of a pretender.

I am at a loss how to dispose of the Dauphine, if he happen to be king of France before the *pretendership* to Britain falls to his share. *Swift*, Public Spirit of the Whigs.

pretendingly (prē-ten'ding-li), *adv.* In a pretending manner; pretentiously.

I have a particular reason for looking a little *pretendingly* at present. *Jeremy Collier*, Pride.

pretense, pretence (prē-tens'), *n.* [< AF. **pretense*, *pretensse*, pretense, < ML. *prætensa*, fem. of *prætensus*, for L. *prætentus*, pp. of *prætendere*, pretend: see *pretend.*] 1†. An intention; a design; a purpose.

Put of your clothes in winter by the fire side, and cause your bed to bee heated with a warming panne, vnless your *pretence* bee to harden your members, and to apply your selfe vnto militarie discipline.
Babees Book (E. E. T. S.), p. 253.

I have perceived a most faint neglect of late; which I have rather blamed as mine own jealous curiosity than as a very *pretence* and purpose of unkindness.
Shak., Lear, i. 4. 75.

To Please, this Time, has been his sole *Pretence*.
Congreve, Way of the World, Prol.

2. The act of pretending, or putting forward something to conceal the true state of affairs, and thus to deceive; hence, the representation of that which does not exist; simulation; feigning; a false or hypocritical show; a sham.

He'll fill this land with arms,
And make *pretence* of wrong that I have done him.
Shak., Pericles, i. 2. 91.

Open violence
May bee avoided: but false *fair-pretense*
Is hardly 'scaped with much ieopardy.
Sylvester, tr. of Du Bartas's Triumph of Faith, ii. 32.

All zeal for a reform that gives offence
To peace and charity is mere *pretence*.
Cowper, Charity, l. 534.

3. That under cover of which an actual design or meaning is concealed; a pretext.

Charles the emperor,
Under *pretence* to see the queen his aunt—
For 'twas indeed his colour, but he came
To whisper Wolsey—here makes visitation.
Shak., Hen. VIII., i. 1. 177.

We told them that we came for a Trade with the Spaniards at Manila, and should be glad if they would carry a Letter to some Merchant there, which they promised to do. But this was only a *pretence* of ours, to get out of them what intelligence we could as to their Shipping, Strength, and the like. *Dampier*, Voyages, I. 383.

4. Pretension; aspiration; the putting forth of a claim, particularly to merit, dignity, or personal worth; pretentiousness.

Likewise, if I should disclose my *pretence* in loue, I would eyther make a strange discourse of some intollerable passion, or finde occasion to pleade by the example of some historie. *Gascoigne*, Steele Glas, etc. (ed. Arber), p. 32.

It has always been my endeavour to distinguish between realities and appearances, and separate true merit from the *pretence* to it. *Addison*, Sir Timothy Tittle.

You think him humble—God accounts him proud;
High in demand, though lowly in *pretence*.
Cowper, Truth, l. 93.

Mourn for the man of amplest influence,
Yet clearest of ambitious crime,
Our greatest yet with least *pretence*.
Tennyson, Death of Wellington, iv.

5. A claim; a right asserted, with or without foundation.

In the same time king Edward the iij., him selfe quartering the Armes of England and France, did discouer his *pretence* and clayme to the Crowne of Fraunce.
Puttenham, Arte of Eng. Poesie, p. 9.

Heard the complaints of the Jamaica merchants against the Spaniards for hindering them from cutting logwood on the main land, where they have no *pretence*.
Evelyn, Diary, April 19, 1672.

There breathes no being but has some *pretence*
To that fine instinct called poetic sense.
O. W. Holmes, Poetry.

Escutcheon of pretense. See *escutcheon*.—**False pretense**, a false representation as to a matter of fact, made in order to induce another to part with property, and with intent to cheat: commonly in the plural.—**Shield of pretense**, an inescutcheon borne to assert the owner's pretensions to an estate; an escutcheon of pretense.—**Statute of false pretenses.** See *statute*.=**Syn. 2.** *Pretense*, *Pretext*, *Pretension*, mask, color, excuse, simulation, affectation, cant, claptrap, subterfuge, evasion. A *pretense* is the holding forth of that which is false: as, his grief, admiration of a picture, piety, was all a *pretense*; selfish or ulterior purposes may be connected with the matter, but not necessarily so: as, to obtain money under false *pretenses*. A *pretext* has something else in view, and makes it seem right or natural, or hides it out of sight; the man whose friendship is mere *pretense* will trump up some *pretext* to escape from each claim upon him for help. That which is used as a *pretext* may or may not exist. A *pretension* is a claim advanced or asserted, or a holding out of an appearance: as, *pretensions* to wealth, learning, respectability. *Pretensions* generally go beyond fact or right, but not necessarily. *Pretense* and *pretext* of course ordinarily express that which is wrong; they may be lightly used of that which is proper.

Sincerity is impossible, unless it pervade the whole being, and the *pretence* of it saps the very foundation of character. *Lowell*, Study Windows, p. 399.

France and England, without seeking for any decent *pretext*, declared war against Holland.
Macaulay, Sir William Temple.

Without any considerable *pretensions* to literature in myself, I have aspired to the love of letters.
Burke, To a Noble Lord.

pretensed (prē-tenst'), *a.* [< L. *prætensus*, pp. of *prætendere*, pretend (see *pretense*), + *-ed*[2].] 1†. Intended; designed.

They can never be clerely extirpate or digged out of their rotten hartes, but that they wille with hande and fote, toothe and nayle, further if they can their *pretensed* enterprice. *Hall*, Henry VII., f. 6. (*Halliwell.*)

Wherupon Cesar, forasmuche as he made so great accompt of the Heduans, determyned by some meanes or other to brydle Dumnorix and to fear him from his *pretensed* purpose. *Golding*, tr. of Cæsar, fol. 112.

2. Pretended; feigned.

Protestants have had in England their *pretensed* synods and convocations.
Stapleton, Fortress of the Faith, fol. 140. (*Latham.*)

As for the sequestration of his fruits, he [Gardiner] protested that it was a *pretensed* decree, if indeed it existed.
R. W. Dixon, Hist. Church of Eng., xviii.

Pretensed right, in *law*, the right or title to land set up by one who is out of possession against the person in possession.

pretensedly† (prē-ten'sed-li), *adv.* Pretendedly; ostensibly.

The Parliament saw year after year their own statute of repeal traversed by these royal or *pretensedly* royal edicts.
R. W. Dixon, Hist. Church of Eng., xv.

pretenseless (prē-tens'les), *a.* [< *pretense* + *-less.*] Destitute of pretense or pretension.

What Rebellions, and those the basest, and most *pretenselesse*, have they not been chiefe in?
Milton, Reformation in Eng., ii.

pretension (prē-ten'shon), *n.* [Formerly also *pretention*; < OF. *pretention*, F. *prétention* = Sp. *pretension* = Pg. *pretenção* = It. *pretensione*, < ML. *prætentio(n-)*, < L. *prætendere*, pp. *prætentus* or *prætensus*, pretend: see *pretend.*] 1. The act of putting forth a claim (specifically, a false one), particularly to merit, dignity, or importance; pretentiousness.

Good without noise, without *pretension* great.
Pope, Epitaph on R. Digby.

Legates and delegates with pow'rs from hell,
Though heav'nly in *pretension*, fleec'd thee well.
Cowper, Expostulation, l. 515.

Another house
Of less *pretension* did he buy betimes,
The villa, meant for jaunts and jollity.
Browning, Ring and Book, I. 57.

2. Hence, a claim; an alleged or assumed right, not necessarily false.

The courtier, the trader, and the scholar should all have an equal *pretension* to the denomination of a gentleman.
Steele, Tatler, No. 207.

Let us from this moment give up all *pretensions* to gentility. *Goldsmith*, Vicar, iii.

Mind, I give up all my claim—I make no *pretensions* to anything in the world. *Sheridan*, The Rivals, v. 3.

3†. A false representation; a pretext; a sham.

This was but an invention and *pretension* given out by the Spaniards. *Bacon*, War with Spain.

He so much abhorr'd artifice and cunning that he had prejudice to all concealments and *pretensions*.
Bp. Fell, Hammond, p. 130.

4. An assertion; a proposition.

Miss Bird . . . declares all the viands of Japan to be uneatable—a staggering *pretension*.
R. L. Stevenson, The Foreigner at Home.

Arms of pretension, in *her.* See *arm*[2], 7 (*c*).=**Syn. 1** and **2**. *Pretext*, etc. See *pretense*.

pretentative† (prẹ-ten'tạ-tiv), *a.* [< L. *prætentatus*, pp. of *prætentare*, try beforehand, < *præ*, before, + *tentare*, try: see *tempt*.] Making previous trial; attempting to try or test beforehand.

This is but an exploratory and *pretentative* purpose between us; about the form whereof, and the matter, we shall consult tomorrow. *Sir H. Wotton*, Reliquiæ, p. 507.

pretention†, *n.* An obsolete form of *pretension*.

pretentious (prẹ-ten'shus), *a.* [< F. *prétentieux*, < *prétention*, pretension: see *pretension*.] **1.** Pretended; unfounded; false.

On the other hand, Mr. Chappell now says that Mallet, after Thomson's death, "put in a *pretentious* claim (to be the author of "Rule Britannia"), against all evidence."
N. and Q., 7th ser., II. 132.

2. Full of pretension, or claims to greater excellence or importance than the truth warrants; attempting to pass for more than the actual worth or importance; making an exaggerated outward show.

No *pretentious* work, from so great a pen, has less of the spirit of grace and comeliness.
E. C. Stedman, Vict. Poets, p. 336.

Most of the contributors to those yearly volumes, which took up such *pretentious* positions on the centre table, have shrunk into entire oblivion.
O. W. Holmes, A Mortal Antipathy, p. 7.

Pretentious poverty
At its wits' end to keep appearance up.
Browning, Ring and Book, I. 67.

pretentiously (prẹ-ten'shus-li), *adv.* In a pretentious manner.

pretentiousness (prẹ-ten'shus-nes), *n.* The quality of being pretentious; undue assumption of excellence, importance, or dignity.

preter†, **præter**† (prē'tėr), *a.* and *n.* [< *preter-*, prefix.] **I.** *a.* Past.

I had a crotchet in my head here to have given the raines to my pen, . . . and commented and paralogized on their condition in the present and in the *preter* tense.
Nashe, Lenten Stuffe (Harl. Misc., VI. 153).

II. *n.* The past; past time.

To come, when Micah wrote this, and in the future; but come, when St. Matthew cited it, and in the *præter*—"When Jesus was born at Bethlehem." But future and *præter* both are in time, so this His birth in time.
Bp. Andrews, Sermons, I. 162. (*Davies.*)

preter-. [Also *præter-*; < L. *præter-*, prefix, *præter*, adv. and prep., past, by, beyond, before, < *præ*, before, + demonstr. suffix *-ter*.] A prefix of Latin origin, meaning 'beyond,' 'over,' or 'by' in space or time, 'more than' in quantity or degree.

pretercanine (prē-tėr-kā-nīn'), *a.* [< *preter-* + *canine*.] More than canine. [Rare.]

A great dog . . . passed me, however, quietly enough; not staying to look up, with strange *pretercanine* eyes, in my face, as I half expected it would.
Charlotte Brontë, Jane Eyre, xii.

preterhuman (prē-tėr-hū'mạn), *a.* [< *preter-* + *human*.] More than human; beyond what is human. Also *præterhuman*.

All are essentially anthropomorphic, and cannot be regarded as supernatural or superhuman beings, but only *præterhuman*. *The Academy*, Jan. 28, 1888, p. 56.

preterient (prẹ-tē'ri-ẹnt), *a.* [< L. *præterien(t-)s*, ppr. of *præterire*, go by, go past: see *preterit*.] Going before; preceding; previous.

He told them his soul had passed through several antecedent forms, . . . with the faculty of remembering all the actions of its *preterient* states. *Observer*, No. 9.

preter-imperfect (prē'tėr-im-pėr'fekt), *n.* In *gram.*, a tense expressing time not perfectly past; the past imperfect: generally called simply *imperfect*. [Little used.]

preterist (pret'ẹ-rist), *n.* and *a.* [< *preter-* + *-ist*.] **I.** *n.* **1.** One whose chief interest is in the past; one who has regard principally to the past.—**2.** In *theol.*, one who believes that the prophecies of the Apocalypse have already been nearly or entirely fulfilled.

II. *a.* Relating to the preterists or their views.

preterit, preterite (pret'e-rit), *a.* and *n.* [Also sometimes *præterite*; < ME. *preterit*, < OF. *preterit*, F. *prétérit* = Pr. *preterit* = Sp. *pretérito* = Pg. It. *preterito*, < L. *præteritus*, gone by, past, past and gone (neut. *præteritum*, sc. *tempus*, in gram. the past or preterit tense), pp. of *præterire*, go by, go past, < *præter*, before, beyond, + *ire*, go.] **I.** *a.* **1.** Bygone; past.

Alle the infynyt spaces of tymes *preteritz* and futures.
Chaucer, Boëthius, v. prose 6.

The *præterite* and present dignity comprised in being a "widow well left" . . . made a flattering and conciliatory view of the future.
George Eliot, Mill on the Floss, i. 12.

Without leaving your elbow-chair, you shall go back with me thirty years, which will bring you among things and persons as thoroughly *preterite* as Romulus or Numa.
Lowell, Fireside Travels, p. 15.

2. In *gram.*, expressing past time; past: applied especially to the tense which expresses past action or existence simply, without further implication as to continuousness, etc.: as, *wrote* is the *preterit* tense of *write*.

II. *n.* **1**†. Time past; the past.

She wepeth the tyme that she hath wasted,
Compleyning of the *preterit*
And the present that not abit.
Rom. of the Rose, l. 5011.

2. In *gram.*, the tense which signifies past time, or which expresses action or being as simply past or finished. Abbreviated *pret.*

preteriteness, *n.* See *preteritness*.

preteritial (pret-ẹ-rish'ạl), *a.* [< *preterit* + *-ial*.] In *biol.*, having been active, but no longer being so: as, *preteritial* force—applied in biology to what is termed latent force or equilibrated energy.

preterition (pret-ẹ-rish'ọn), *n.* [Also *præterition*; = F. *prétérition* = Pr. Sp. *pretericion* = Pg. *preterição* = It. *preterizione*, < LL. *præteritio(n-)*, a passing over, an omission, < *præterire*, pp. *præteritus*, go by, go past: see *preterit*.] **1.** The act of passing over or by, or the state of being passed over or by.

He [Calvin] only held that God's purpose was indeed to deny grace to some, by way of *preterition*, or rather non-election. *Evelyn*, True Religion, II. 252.

The Israelites were never to eat the paschal lamb but they were recalled to the memory of that saving *preterition* of the angel. *Bp. Hall.*

Specifically—**2.** In *Calvinistic theol.*, the doctrine that God, having elected to everlasting life such as should be saved, passed over the others.—**3.** In *rhet.*, a figure by which a speaker, in pretending to pass over anything, makes a summary mention of it: as, "I will not say he is valiant, he is learned, he is just." Also *pretermission*.—**4.** In *law*, the passing over by a testator of one of his heirs otherwise entitled to a portion.

A reform effected by Justinian by his 115th Novel ought not to pass unnoticed; for it rendered superfluous all the old rules about disherison and *præterition* of a testator's children. *Encyc. Brit.*, XX. 714.

preteritive (prẹ-ter'i-tiv), *a.* [< *preterit* + *-ive*.] In *gram.*, expressing past time; also, limited to past tenses.

preteritness (pret'ẹ-rit-nes), *n.* The state of being past or bygone. Also *preteriteness*.

We cannot conceive a *præteriteness* (if I may say so) still backwards in infinitum that never was present, as we can an endless futurity that never will be present.
Bentley, Sermons, vi.

A valley in the moon could scarce have been lonelier, could scarce have suggested more strongly the feeling of *preteriteness* and extinction.
Lowell, Fireside Travels, p. 206.

preteritopresential (prẹ-ter'i-tō-prẹ-zen'shạl), *a.* [< NL. *præteritopræsen(t-)s*, preterit-present (< L. *præteritus*, preterit, + *præsen(t-)s*, present), + *-ial*.] Same as *preterit-present*. *Whitney*, Life and Growth of Lang., p. 93.

preterit-present (pret'ẹ-rit-prez'ẹnt), *a.* and *n.* **I.** *a.* Combining preterit form with present meaning: said of certain Germanic verbs, as *may*, *can*.

II. *n.* A verb combining preterit form with present meaning.

preterlapsed (prē-tėr-lapst'), *a.* [< L. *præterlapsus*, pp. of *præterlabi*, glide or flow by, < *præter*, by, + *labi*, glide, flow, lapse: see *lapse*.] Preterit; past; bygone. [Rare.]

We look with a superstitious reverence upon the accounts of *preterlapsed* ages.
Glanville, Vanity of Dogmatizing, xv.

preterlegal (prē-tėr-lē'gạl), *a.* [< *preter-* + *legal*.] Exceeding the limits of law; not legal. [Rare.]

I expected some evil customs *preterlegal*, and abuses personal, had been to be removed. *Eikon Basilike.*

preterminable†, *a.* [ME. *pretermynable*; appar. taken as equiv. to *interminable*; < L. *præ*, before, + LL. **terminabilis*, terminable: see *terminable*.] Eternal.

Thou quytez vchon as hys desserte,
Thou hyȝe kyng ay *pretermynable*.
Alliterative Poems (ed. Morris), i. 596.

pretermission (prē-tėr-mish'ọn), *n.* [= F. *prétermission* = Sp. *pretermision* = Pg. *pretermissão* = It. *pretermissione*, < L. *prætermissio(n-)*, an omission, a passing over, < *prætermittere*, pp. *prætermissus*, let pass, neglect: see *pretermit*.] **1.** The act of passing by; an omission.

A foul *pretermission* in the Author of this, whether Story or Fable: himself wearie, as seems, of his own tedious Tale. *Milton*, Hist. Eng., i.

2. In *rhet.*, same as *preterition*, 3.

pretermit (prē-tėr-mit'), *v. t.*; pret. and pp. *pretermitted*, ppr. *pretermitting*. [< OF. *pretermetre*, *pretermettre* = Sp. *pretermitir* = Pg. *pretermittir* = It. *pretermettere*, < L. *prætermittere*, pp. *prætermissus*, pass by, let pass, neglect, < *præter*, before, beyond, + *mittere*, send, let go: see *mission*.] **1**†. To let pass; permit to go by unused or not turned to account.

The Mariners, seeing a fit gale of winde for their purpose, wished Capnio to make no delayes, least (if they *pretermitted* this good Weather) they might stay long ere they had such a faire Winde. *Greene*, Pandosto.

Such an one as keeps the watch of his God, and *pretermits* no day without the forementioned duties, shall seldom or never fall into any foul slough.
Rev. S. Ward, Sermons, p. 29.

2. To omit; leave unnoticed or unmentioned; disregard; overlook.

I *pretermyt* also the ryche apparell of the pryncesse, the straunge fasshion of the Spanyshe nacion, the beautie of the Englishe ladyes. Hall, Hen. VII., f. 53. (*Halliwell.*)

I haue not thought good to *pretermitte* that which chaunced to Johannes Solysius, who, to searche the South syde of the supposed continent, departed with three shippes from porte Joppa.
Peter Martyr (tr. in Eden's First Books on America, ed. [Arber, p. 181).

The birth of a New Year is of an interest too wide to be *pretermitted* by king or cobbler. *Lamb*, New Year's Eve.

3. To leave undone; neglect to do, make, or perform.

We are infinitely averse from it [prayer], . . . weary of its length, glad of an occasion to *pretermit* our offices.
Jer. Taylor, Works (ed. 1835), I. 87.

4. To render ineffectual. [Rare.]

To *pretermit* the vigour and firmness of Phillippe le Bel, . . . Giovanni Buonacorsi of Lucca published, under the reign of Louis XII., a proposition that the pope was above the king in temporals.
Landor, King James I. and Isaac Casaubon.

pretermitter (prē-tėr-mit'ėr), *n.* One who pretermits.

[The poet] is himselfe partelye contented to be controwled by the stoick Damasip, as a sluggarde, and *pretermiter* of duetifull occasions.
Drant, tr. of Horace's Satires, ii. 3, Prol.

preternatural (prē-tėr-nat'ū-rạl), *a.* [= OF. *preternaturel* = Sp. Pg. *preternatural* = It. *preternaturale*; as *preter-* + *natural*.] Being beyond what is natural, or different from what is natural; extraordinary; being out of the regular or natural course of things: distinguished from *supernatural*, being above nature, and *unnatural*, being contrary to nature.

Any *preternatural* immutations in the elements, any strange concussations of the earth.
Bp. Hall, Invisible World, i. § 4.

Mr. Pickering was a widower—a fact which seemed to produce in him a sort of *preternatural* concentration of parental dignity. *H. James, Jr.*, Pass. Pilgrim, p. 191.

=**Syn.** *Miraculous*, etc. See *supernatural*.

preternaturalism (prē-tėr-nat'ū-rạl-izm), *n.* [< *preternatural* + *-ism*.] **1.** The tendency, habit, or system of ascribing preternatural qualities or powers to things which may be only natural; belief in the preternatural.

Camille's head, one of the clearest in France, has got itself . . . saturated through every fibre with *preternaturalism* of suspicion. *Carlyle*, French Rev., III. iii. 8.

2. Preternatural existence or existences.

Words cannot express the love and sorrow of my old memories, chiefly out of boyhood, as they occasionally rise upon me, and I have now no voice for them at all. One's heart becomes a grim Hades, peopled only with silent *preternaturalism*. *Carlyle*, in Froude, II. 19.

preternaturality (prē-tėr-naṭ-ṳ̄-ral′i̤-ti), *n.* [< *preternatural* + *-ity.*] Preternaturalness. [Rare.]

There is such an intricate mixture of naturality and *preternaturality* in age. *J. Smith*, Portrait of Old Age, p. 133. (*Latham.*)

preternaturally (prē-tėr-naṭ′ṳ̄-ra̤l-i), *adv.* In a preternatural manner; in a manner beyond or aside from the common order of nature.

preternaturalness (prē-tėr-naṭ′ṳ̄-ra̤l-nes), *n.* The state or character of being preternatural; a state or manner different from the common order of nature.

preternotorious (prē″tėr-nō̤-tō′ri-us), *a.* [< *preter-* + *notorious.*] Very notorious. [Rare.]

This professed cheating rogue was my master, and I confess myself a more *preternotorious* rogue than himself, in so long keeping his villanous counsel. *Fletcher (and another)*, Fair Maid of the Inn, iv. 2.

preternuptial (prē-tėr-nup′sha̤l), *a.* [< *preter-* + *nuptial.*] Beyond what is permitted by the nuptial or marriage tie; hence, euphemistically, adulterous.

Nay, poor woman, she by and by, we find, takes up with *preternuptial* persons. *Carlyle*, Misc., IV. 97. (*Davies.*)

preterperfect (prē-tėr-pėr′fekt), *a.* and *n.* [< *preter-* + *perfect.*] In *gram.*, past-perfect; perfect.

The same natural aversion to loquacity has of late made a considerable alteration in our language, by closing in one syllable the termination of our *preter-perfect* tense, as drown'd, walk'd, for drowned, walked. *Addison*, Spectator.

preter-pluperfect (prē″tėr-plö′pėr-fekt), *a.* and *n.* [< L. *præter*, beyond, + *plus*, more, + *perfectus*, perfect.] In *gram.*, past-pluperfect; pluperfect.

preterplurality (prē″tėr-plō̤-ral′i̤-ti), *n.* [< *preter-* + *plurality.*] Extraordinary number.

It is not easily credible what may be said of the *preterpluralities* of taylors in London. *N. Ward*, Simple Cobler, p. 31.

pretervection (prē-tėr-vek′sho̤n), *n.* [< L. *prætervectio(n-)*, a riding or passing by, < *prætervehi*, pp. *prætervectus*, be borne past, pass by, < *præter*, beyond, past, + *vehere*, carry, bear, pass, *vehi*, drive, ride: see *vehicle.*] The act of carrying past or beyond.

The *pretervection* of the body to some place. *Potter.*

pretex† (prē̤-teks′), *v. t.* [< L. *prætexere*, weave in front, fringe, edge, border, place before, allege as an excuse, pretend, < *præ*, before, + *texere*, weave: see *text.*] **1.** To frame; devise. *Knox.*—**2.** To cloak; conceal.

Ambition's pride
(Too oft *pretexed* with our country's good).
T. Edwards, Sonnets, l.

3. To pretend; allege.

Leste their rashnes (as thei *pretex* it) shuld confirme the enimies of the gospell. *Joye*, Expos. of Daniel xii.

pretext (prē′tekst or (formerly only) prē̤-tekst′), *n.* [< F. *prétexte* = Sp. Pg. *pretexto* = It. *pretesto*, < L. *prætextum*, an ornament, etc., wrought in front, a pretense, neut. of *prætextus*, pp. of *prætexere*, weave before, fringe or border, allege: see *pretex.*] That which is assumed as a cloak or means of concealment; something under cover of which a true purpose is hidden; an ostensible reason, motive, or occasion; a pretense.

I know it;
And my *pretext* to strike at him admits
A good construction. *Shak.*, Cor., v. 6. 20.

It either assumes the *pretext* of some virtue, or openly despises infamy. *Bacon*, Fable of Dionysius.

In almost all the little commonwealths of antiquity, liberty was used as a *pretext* for measures directed against everything which makes liberty valuable. *Macaulay*, History.

=**Syn.** *Pretension*, etc. See *pretense.*

pretext† (prē̤-tekst′), *v. t.* [< *pretext, n.*] To use as a pretext, or cloak or covering; assume as a means of concealment.

Such these are, who, under the abomination of luxury—nicely termed kindness—import the *pretexted* gloss of beauty's name. *Ford*, Honour Triumphant, iii.

pretexta, *n.* See *prætexta.*

pretexture (prē̤-teks′ṭṳ̄r), *n.* [< *pretext* + *-ure.*] A means of concealment; cloak; disguise; pretext.

Now we have studied both texture of words and *pretextures* of manners to shroud dishonesty. *Rev. T. Adams*, Works, II. 416.

prethoughtful (prē-thât′fu̇l), *a.* [< *pre-* + *thoughtful.*] Forethoughtful; prudent; considerate.

Prethoughtful of every chance. *Bulwer.*

pretibial (prē-tib′i-a̤l), *a.* [< L. *præ*, before, + *tibia*, tibia: see *tibial.*] Situated upon the front of the lower part of the leg: as, a *pretibial* muscle.

pretiosity†, *n.* An obsolete spelling of *preciosity.*

pretious†, *a.* An obsolete spelling of *precious.*

pretium affectionis (prē′shi-um a-fek-shi-ō′-nis). [L.: *pretium*, price (see *price*); *affectionis*, gen. of *affectio(n-)*, frame of mind, state of feeling, affection: see *affection.*] The value put upon a thing by the fancy of the owner, or by the regard in which he holds it, as distinguished from market or salable value.

pretonic (prē-ton′ik), *a.* [< L. *præ*, before, + Gr. τόνος, accent: see *tonic.*] Preceding the accent. *Amer. Jour. Philol.*, V. 499.

pretor, prætor (prē′tor), *n.* [= F. *préteur* = Pr. Sp. Pg. *pretor* = It. *pretore*, < L. *prætor*, a leader, chief, head, president, governor, general, commander, pretor; orig. **præitor*, one who goes before, < *præire*, go before, lead the way, < *præ*, before, + *ire*, go.] **1.** In *Rom. hist.*, a title which originally designated the consuls as the leaders of the armies of the state. Later (from about 367 B. C.) one and from about 242 B. C. two pretors were appointed as colleagues to the consuls, and specifically as judicial officers, one of whom (*prætor urbanus*) tried causes between Roman citizens, and the other (*prætor peregrinus*) causes between strangers, or between strangers and citizens. After the discharge of his judicial functions a pretor had often the administration of a province, with the title of propretor, or sometimes proconsul. When the dominions of Rome were extended beyond Italy, the number of pretorships was increased, and finally, under the empire, became eighteen, or even more. The *prætor urbanus* was the first in rank, and was specifically *the Pretor.*

Hence—**2.** A magistrate; a mayor. *Dryden.*

pretoria, *n.* Plural of *pretorium.*

pretorial, prætorial (prē̤-tō′ri-a̤l), *a.* [= OF. *pretorial* = Sp. Pg. *pretorial*, < L. *prætorius*, pertaining to a pretor (< *prætor*, a pretor, a leader: see *pretor*), + *-al.*] Same as *pretorian.* —**Pretorial court**†, in the colony of Maryland, a court erected for the trial of capital crimes, and consisting of the lord proprietor, or his lieutenant-general, and the council.

pretorian, prætorian (prē̤-tō′ri-a̤n), *a.* and *n.* [= F. *prétorien* = Sp. Pg. It. *pretoriano*, < LL. *prætorianus*, pertaining to a pretor, of pretorial rank, also of or belonging to the pretorium or imperial body-guard, < L. *prætor*, a pretor, *prætorium*, the imperial body-guard: see *pretor, pretorium.*] **I.** *a.* **1.** Of or pertaining to a pretor; exercised by a pretor; judicial: as, *pretorian* authority; also, of or pertaining to a pretorium.—**2.** Of or belonging to the body-guard of a Roman emperor.—**Pretorian gate**, that one of the four gates in a Roman camp which was nearest the enemy, or directly in front of the general's tent. See plan under *camp*[2] (at reference-letter *o*).—**Pretorian guard**, one of a body of troops originally formed by the emperor Augustus to protect his person and his power, and maintained by successive Roman emperors down to Constantine: so called as practically continuing the organization and functions of the *prætoria cohors*, or select troops which attended the person of the pretor or the general of the republic. These troops were under a special organization, and had special privileges of rank and pay, raising them above the ordinary soldiery. They soon acquired a dangerous power, and for a considerable time raised and deposed emperors at their pleasure.—**Pretorian pact.** See *pact.*—**Pretorian testament.** See *testament.*

II. *n.* A soldier of the pretorian guard.

pretorianism (prē̤-tō′ri-a̤n-izm), *n.* [< *pretorian* + *-ism.*] Venal military despotism.

Slavery, *pretorianism*, corruption of morals, and aversion to matrimony, decay of civic as also of military virtue. *Pop. Sci. Mo.*, July, 1878, p. 268.

pretorium (prē̤-tō′ri-um), *n.*; pl. *pretoria* (-ä̤). [L. *prætorium* (> Gr. πραιτώριον), a general's tent, a council of war, the official residence of a governor, a palace, the imperial body-guard, the pretorian guard, < *prætor*, a general, governor, pretor: see *pretor.* Cf. *pretory.*] **1.** That part of a Roman camp in which the general's tent stood. See plan under *camp*[2].—**2.** The official residence of a provincial governor among the ancient Romans; a hall of justice; a palace.

The soldiers led him away into the hall, called *Prætorium.* Mark xv. 16.

pretorship (prē′to̤r-ship), *n.* [< *pretor* + *-ship.*] The office or dignity of a pretor.

pretorture† (prē-tôr′ṭṳ̄r), *v. t.* [< *pre-* + *torture.*] To torture beforehand.

Remarkable was their cruelty in *pretorturing* of many whom afterwards they put to death. *Fuller*, Ch. Hist., VIII. ii. 27. (*Davies.*)

pretory†, *n.* [ME., also *pretorie*, < OF. *pretorie*, *pretoire*, F. *prétoire*, pretorian guard, = Sp. Pg. It. *pretorio*, < L. *prætorium*, pretorium: see *pretorium.*] **1.** Same as *pretorium*, 2.

Pilate up ros, and forth he yode
Out of the *pretory.*
Cursor Mundi. (*Halliwell.*)

2. The pretorian guard.

I took stryf ageins the provost of the *pretorie* for comune profit. *Chaucer*, Boëthius, i. prose 4.

prettify (prit′i-fī), *v. t.*; pret. and pp. *prettified*, ppr. *prettifying.* [< *pretty* + *-fy.*] To make pretty; embellish; especially, to make pretty in a petty, finical way, as by the excessive or fanciful use of ornament.

Sightly without being *prettified.* *W. M. Rossetti.*

He [Millet] would not stoop to alter facts and "*prettify* types" for all the critics in France. *Nineteenth Century*, XXIV. 431.

prettily (prit′i-li), *adv.* [< ME. *pratily*, *pratylych*; < *pretty* + *-ly*[2].] **1**†. In a cunning manner; cunningly; cleverly.

A bok hym is browt
Naylyd on a brede of tre,
That men callyt an abcce,
Pratylych I-wrout.
Political Poems, etc. (ed. Furnivall), p. 244.

2†. Excellently; well.

The profit of reading is singular, in that it serveth for a preparative unto sermons; it helpeth *prettily* towards the nourishment of faith which sermons have once engendered. *Hooker*, Eccles. Polity, v. 22.

3. In a pretty or pleasing manner; with neatness and taste; pleasingly; gracefully.

Still she entreats, and *prettily* entreats,
For to a pretty ear she tunes her tale.
Shak., Venus and Adonis, l. 73.

And here, below it, is the cipher too you spoke of; and 'tis *prettily* contrived. *Cotton*, in Walton's Angler, ii. 238.

prettiness (prit′i-nes), *n.* [Formerly also *prettinesse*; < *pretty* + *-ness.*] **1.** Pleasantness; agreeableness.

Thought and affliction, passion, hell itself,
She turns to favour and to *prettiness.*
Shak., Hamlet, iv. 5. 189.

He was all life, all *prettinesse*, far from morose, sullen, or childish in any thing he said or did. *Evelyn*, Diary, Jan. 27, 1658.

2. The state or quality of being pretty, or pleasing to the esthetic sense; especially, the effect of beauty in its slighter, more delicate, and more evanescent forms; the charm of grace, harmony, delicacy, or neatness, as presented to the sight or the hearing; diminutive or dainty beauty: as, the *prettiness* of a picture or a tune; the *prettiness* of a gesture, a dimple, or a lisp.

Majesty and stateliness, as in the lion, the horse, the eagle, and cock; . . . grave awfulness, as in your best bred mastiffs; or elegancy and *prettiness*, as in your lesser dogs and most sorts of birds, all which are several modes of beauty. *Dr. H. More*, Antidote against Atheism, ii. 9.

There [the squirrel] whisks his brush,
And perks his ears, and stamps, and cries aloud,
With all the *prettiness* of feigned alarm.
Cowper, Task, vi. 319.

There is much small art which has beauty, or at least that lower form of it which we call *prettiness*; yet the best art is both true and beautiful. *P. G. Hamerton*, Thoughts about Art, xviii.

3. Neatness and taste bestowed on small objects; hence, often, petty elegance; affected niceness; finicalness; foppishness.

A style . . . without sententious pretension or antithetical *prettiness.* *Jeffrey.*

4. That which is pretty; a pretty thing or person: generally in a depreciative sense, as suggesting pettiness.

A great affecter of wits and such *prettinesses*; and his company is costly to him, for he seldom ha's it but invited. *Bp. Earle*, Micro-cosmographie, A Weake Man.

Suburban villas, Belgrave terraces, and other such *prettinesses.* *Hawthorne*, Passages from Eng. Note Books, II. 306.

The painter . . . was forced by the fervour of his patrons, and his own desire for money, to perpetuate pious *prettinesses* long after he had ceased to feel them. *J. A. Symonds*, Italy and Greece, p. 76.

pretty (prit′i), *a.* [Early mod. E. also *prettie*, *pretie*; dial. also *pratty*; <ME. *prety*, *preti*, *praty*, *prati*, clever, cunning, pretty, elegant, < AS. *prættig*, also, with loss of *r*, *pætig*, *petig*, crafty, wily, astute (glossed by L. *callidus*, *astutus*, *sagax*, *gnarus*, *versipellis*), = Icel. *prettugr*, tricky, deceitful; associated with the noun, ME. *prat*, < AS. *præt*, *prætt*, craft, art, wile (glossed by L. *astu*, *ars*), = Icel. *prettr*, a trick (*pretta*, v., trick), = Norw. *pretta*, a trick (*pretta*, v., trick); cf. W. *praith*, an act, deed, Corn. *prat*, an act, deed, cunning trick; prob. < ML. *practicus*, skilled, cunning (glossed by *peritus*), < Gr. πρακτικός, skilled, versed in affairs: see *practic.* The noun, AS. *præt*, may be due to the adj., or, like the W. and Corn. words, it may be < ML. *practica*, practice: see *practice.* For the sense of 'cunning,' or 'sharp practice,' cf. *practice* in like association. For the development of *pretty* from 'cunning' or 'skilled' to 'cunning' or 'tricky' and thence to 'neat, fine, small, and beautiful,' cf. the histories of *cunning, fine, neat.* There is an unconscious sympathy with neat trickery, or a secret admiration of it, that imparts to words denoting it a quality of commendation: the epithets *cunning, shrewd, clever, sharp, smart, keen, cute,* etc., though they may insinuate dishonesty, are likely to be received with a secret complacency by those to whom they are applied.] 1. Crafty; cunning; clever; shrewd; keen. [Obsolete or archaic.]

It is great pitie that so *prettie* a fellow had not occupied his braynes in studies of more consequence.
Puttenham, Arte of Eng. Poesie, p. 258.

Meldritch, intending to make his passage perforce, was advised of a *pretty* stratagem by the English Smith.
Capt. John Smith, True Travels, I. 26.

Aboute some 3. or 4. years before this time ther came over one Captaine Wolastone (a man of *pretie* parts).
Bradford, Plymouth Plantation, p. 235.

Egad! ma'am, he has a *pretty* wit, and is a *pretty* poet too.
Sheridan, School for Scandal, i. 1.

2†. Strong and bold; warlike; accomplished in arms.

Euen before in the frunt of that faire yle
Was a prouynse of prise, & *praty* men in.
Destruction of Troy (E. E. T. S.), l. 10815.

Did yon ever see a *prettier* man
Than this Trumpeter of Fyvie?
Andrew Lammie (Child's Ballads, II. 192).

There is risen a rumour . . . that we would have broken the prison with such violence as, if master bailiffs had not played the *pretty* men, we should have made a scape.
Bp. Ridley, in Bradford's Letters (Parker Soc., 1853), II. 83.

He even mentioned the exact number of recruits who had joined Waverley's troop from his uncle's estate, and observed they were *pretty* men — meaning not handsome, but stout warlike fellows.
Scott, Waverley.

3. Comely; handsome; good-looking; hence, in later use, pleasing to the esthetic sense; attractive through grace, elegance, neatness, harmony of parts, or delicacy of outline or coloring; having delicate beauty; pleasing the eye or ear rather than impressing the mind: as, a *pretty* face; a *pretty* cottage; a *pretty* picture. In this use the word implies a certain slightness, limitation, or lack of power, and hence is easily made depreciative in cases where these attributes are out of place.

To-curte he came a *pratye* yong seruaunt.
Generydes (E. E. T. S.), l. 302.

So doth the earth seeme to dance, in little Hillocks and *pretie* Vallies, diuersifying the soile.
Purchas, Pilgrimage, p. 615.

That which is little can be but *pretty,* and by claiming dignity becomes ridiculous.
Johnson.

Beauties in vain their *pretty* eyes may roll;
Charms strike the sight, but merit wins the soul.
Pope, R. of the L.

Can any wife be *prettier* than an after dinner fancy, idle and yet vivid, can paint for you?
D. G. Mitchell, Reveries of a Bachelor, i.

It will be a sufficient word to the wise to say that it is a *pretty* book, and that it ends with a death.
The Academy, No. 891, p. 374.

Hence — 4. Affectedly neat or fastidious about one's personal appearance; finical; foppish.

I don't design you to personate a real Man, you are only to be a *pretty* Gentleman.
Steele, Tender Husband, i. 1.

The *pretty* gentleman must have his airs.
Steele, Guardian, No. 38.

5. Pleasing in general; pleasing to the mind; interesting; entertaining; gratifying.

Birds . . . that at sun-rising filled the wood with such a variety of notes as made the *prettiest* confusion imaginable.
Addison, Ancient Medals, iii.

'Tis *pretty* to observe how the King Disciplines this great City by small instances of Obedience.
Lister, Journey to Paris, p. 16.

It was *pretty* to see how easily the membranous cap of the rostellum [in *Epipactis Palustris*] came off.
Darwin, Fertil. of Orchids by Insects, p. 97.

6. Excellent; good; fine; nice: said loosely, like *fine* and *nice,* of almost any object or action as a general term of commendation, and also, like *fine* and *nice,* often used ironically, especially in exclamatory sentences.

Some speech may be whan it is spoken very vndecent, and yet the same, hauing afterward somewhat added to it, may become *prety* and decent.
Puttenham, Arte of Eng. Poesie, p. 230.

A *pretty* chandelier for a Christian Bishop to be chaining to the roof and lighting up for the glory of heathenism!
De Quincey, Secret Societies, i.

I had a *pretty* dinner for them: viz., a brace of stewed carps, six roasted chickens, and a jowle of salmon, hot, for the first course.
Pepys, Diary, I. 267.

The quarrel is a very *pretty* quarrel as it stands; we should only spoil it by trying to explain it.
Sheridan, The Rivals, iv. 3.

In the convent his news made a *pretty* to do.
Barham, Ingoldsby Legends, II. 316.

Yes, we have a *pretty* artillery of tools now in our social arrangements: we ride four times as fast as our fathers did; travel, grind, weave, forge, plant, till, and excavate better.
Emerson, Works and Days.

7. Good or sufficient; moderately large in quantity, number, extent, duration, etc.; considerable.

There were a *pretty* many of us upon the shore of Calais, who were carried thence in a chaloupe to a large ship.
N. Bailey, tr. of Colloquies of Erasmus, p. 300.

A *pretty* while these pretty creatures stand,
Like ivory conduits coral cisterns filling.
Shak., Lucrece, l. 1233.

It is a *pretty* way distant from the town.
Coryat, Crudities, I. 6.

They . . . call upon me to help them with tooles faster then I can get them, though I have now bought *pretty* store.
T. Shepard, Clear Sunshine of the Gospel, p. 42.

8. A term of endearment, supplying the place of a diminutive.

Piteous plainings of the *pretty* babes.
Shak., C. of E., i. 1. 73.

This *pretty,* puny, weakly little one.
Tennyson, Enoch Arden.

=Syn. 3. *Handsome, Fair,* etc. See *beautiful.*

pretty (prit'i), *adv.* [< *pretty, a.,* 7.] Moderately; reasonably; tolerably: expressing a degree less than *very:* as, a farm *pretty* well stocked; *pretty* good lodgings; I am *pretty* sure of the fact.

You are *pretty* near the business, for the bottom of all is for want of a change in their mind and will.
Bunyan, Pilgrim's Progress, p. 208.

We sat *pretty* late over our punch.
Addison, Tory Foxhunter.

I think your tricks are *pretty* well known.
Sheridan (?), The Camp, i. 1.

Pretty much, very nearly; in considerable degree.

The gallants of these times *pretty much* resembled the bloods of ours. *Goldsmith,* Reverie at Boar's-Head Tavern.

The trade to India . . . carried on *pretty much* in the same manner as it had been before the days of Alexander.
Bruce, Source of the Nile, I. 468.

pretty-grass (prit'i-gràs), *n.* [Tr. NL. *Calochortus.*] A plant of the genus *Calochortus.* These plants are grass-like below, but have large and beautiful flowers. Also called *butterfly-weed, mariposa-lily,* and *wild tulip.*

prettyism (prit'i-izm), *n.* [< *pretty* + *-ism.*] Affected prettiness of manner, style, or the like. *Edinburgh Rev.* (*Imp. Dict.*)

prettypretty (prit'i-prit"i), *n.*; pl. *prettypretties* (-iz). [< *pretty* + *pretty.*] A knickknack. [Colloq.]

My mother . . . had contrived to keep a certain number of *prettypretties* which were dear to her heart. They were not much; . . . some china and a little glass, a few books, and a very moderate supply of household silver.
Trollope, Autobiog., p. 21.

pretty-spoken (prit'i-spō"kn), *a.* Spoken or speaking prettily.

pretympanic (prē-tim-pan'ik), *a.* and *n.* [< L. *præ,* before, + NL. *tympanum.*] I. *a.* 1. In *anat.,* placed in advance of the tympanum of the ear: as, a *pretympanic* nerve.

A smaller *pretympanic,* which may represent the chorda tympani, and a larger post-tympanic or hyoid nerve.
Huxley and Martin, Elementary Biology, p. 29.

2. In *ichth.,* anterior with reference to the tympanic pedicle or suspensorium of the mandible; anterior among a set of bones composing this pedicle: correlated with *epi-, meso-,* and *hypotympanic.*

II. *n.* The pretympanic bone or cartilage of the suspensorium of the lower jaw of fishes, now generally called *metapterygoid,* under which name it is shown in the cut under *palatoquadrate.*

pretypify (prē-tip'i-fī), *v. t.*; pret. and pp. *pretypified,* ppr. *pretypifying.* [< *pre-* + *typify.*] To typify what is to come after in course of evolution, as an archetype; prefigure, forecast, or foreshadow.

Thus the session of the Messias was *pretypified.*
Bp. Pearson, Expos. of Creed, vi. (*Latham.*)

Paramœcium and its allies would thus appear to *pretypify* the Turbellarians. *W. S. Kent,* Man. Infus., p. 103.

pretzel (pret'sel), *n.* [< G. *pretzel,* var. of *bretzel,* formerly *brezel,* dial. *brestell, bretzen, brätzet,* < MHG. *brezel, prezel, brezile,* < OHG. *brizzilla, brezitella, prezitella,* also *brezita, precita* (MHG. *bræzte, breze*), a pretzel; cf. It. *bracciatello, bracciello,* a kind of cake or roll; appar. (with some variations of form) < ML. *bracellus,* also *brachiolum,* a kind of cake or roll, lit. 'an armlet' (OF. *bracel*): see *bracelet.*] A small brittle biscuit, usually baked in the form of a knot, and salted on the outside; a cracknel.

The German beer-houses, with their baskets of *pretzel,* are more frequent as we approach the commercial quarters.
Harper's Mag., LXXVIII. 692.

prevail (prẹ-vāl'), *v.* [Early mod. E. *prevayle,* < ME. *prevailen,* < OF. *prevaler, prevaloir,* F. *prévaloir* = OSp. *prevaler* = It. *prevalere* (cf. Sp. Pg. *prevalecer*), prevail, < L. *prævalere,* be very able or more able, be superior, prevail, < *præ,* before, + *valere,* be able or powerful: see *valid.*] I. *intrans.* 1. To be superior in strength; hence, to have or gain the advantage, as in a contest or matching of strength; be victorious; triumph; have the upper hand: often followed by *over* or *against.*

It came to pass, when Moses held up his hand, that Israel *prevailed;* and when he let down his hand, Amalek *prevailed.*
Ex. xvii. 11.

Meldritch, seeing there was no possibiliti long to *preuaile,* ioyned his small troopes in one body.
Capt. John Smith, True Travels, I. 28.

The disquiets of my mind *prevailed* over my weariness, and kept me awake. *Swift,* Gulliver's Travels, iii. 1.

2. To have or exert superior influence; have a controlling or overmastering authority; be predominant.

Barbarous climes, where violence *prevails,*
And strength is lord of all. *Cowper,* Task, i. 604.

Will he [man] not see, through all he miscalls accident, that Law *prevails* for ever and ever?
Emerson, Domestic Life.

3. To operate effectually; be effective; succeed, especially in persuading, inducing, or convincing.

If then
My words *preuailde* when they were wickednesse,
How much more now when they are just and good!
Tourneur, Revenger's Tragedy, iv. 4.

For when a world of men
Could not *prevail* with all their oratory,
Yet hath a woman's kindness over-ruled.
Shak., 1 Hen. VI., ii. 2. 49.

If Arguments *prevaile* not with such a one, force is well us'd. *Milton,* Eikonoklastes, vi.

4. To be in force; extend with power or effect; hence, to be prevalent or current.

It is plain from all history that two abominable practices, the one the eating of men, the other of sacrificing them to the devil, *prevailed* all over Africa.
Bruce, Source of the Nile, I. 303.

The Canarese alphabet *prevails* on the plateau of Mysore, in the western districts of the Nizam territory, and to a small extent in the Canara district on the Malabar coast. *Isaac Taylor,* The Alphabet, II. 355.

The morning comes; and thickening fogs *prevail,*
Hanging like curtains all the horizon round.
Jones Very, Poems, p. 90.

5†. To be currently received or believed; be established.

The second shock having happened exactly a month after the former, it *prevails* that there will be a third.
Walpole, Letters, II. 201.

6†. To avail; be of value or service.

What he shuld do he told hym euery thing,
That myght only to his wurchippe *preuaile.*
Generydes (E. E. T. S.), l. 1040.

For speech it selfe is artificiall and made by man, and the more pleasing it is the more it *preuaileth* to such purpose as it is intended for.
Puttenham, Arte of Eng. Poesie, p. 5.

II.† *trans.* To avail: used reflexively.

Prevail yourself of what occasion gives.
Dryden, Abs. and Achit., l. 461.

prevailing (prẹ-vā'ling), *p. a.* 1. Predominant; having superior influence or efficiency; controlling; moving.

The nightingale sings with more *prevailing* passion in Greece that we first heard her from the thickets of a Euripidean chorus. *Lowell,* Oration, Harvard, Nov. 8, 1886.

2. Prevalent; current; general; common.

Nothing sheds such light on the superstitions of an age as the *prevailing* interpretation and treatment of disease.
O. W. Holmes, Med. Essays, p. 314.

=Syn. 1. *Predominant, Ruling,* etc. (see *prevalent*), dominant, preponderating.—2. Received, established, ordinary, usual.

prevailingly (prẹ-vā'ling-li), *adv.* 1. With superior power or influence; so as to prevail.—2. Prevalently; currently; generally; for the most part.

prevailment (prẹ-vāl'mẹnt), *n.* [< *prevail* + *-ment.*] Prevailing influence; efficacy; ruling power. [Rare.]

Knacks, trifles, nosegays, sweetmeats, messengers
Of strong *prevailment* in unharden'd youth.
Shak., M. N. D., i. 1. 35.

prevalence (prev'ạ-lens), *n.* [< OF. *prevalence,* F. *prévalence* = It. *prevalenza,* < LL. *prævalentia,* superior force, < L. *prævalen(t-)s,* very strong: see *prevalent.*] The state or quality of being prevalent. (*a*) Superior strength, influence, or efficacy; predominance.

The absolute tyranny of the human will over a noble and powerful beast develops the instinct of personal *prevalence* and dominion. *O. W. Holmes,* Elsie Venner, xi.

Words and sense
Fall through the tune's imperious *prevalence.*
Swinburne, Two Dreams.

(*b*) General occurrence, practice, or reception; extensive existence or use: as, the *prevalence* of a custom or of a disease.

prevalency (prev'a̤-lẹn-si), *n.* [As *prevalence* (see *-cy*).] Same as *prevalence*.

It is not necessary to the *prevalency* of the prayer that the spirit actually accompany every clause or word.
Jer. Taylor, Works (ed. 1835), I. 231.

prevalent (prev'a̤-lẹnt), *a.* [= Sp. *prevalente* = Pg. *prevalecente* = It. *prevalente*, < L. *prævalen(t-)s*, very strong, superior in power, prevalent, ppr. of *prævalere*, be very able or more able: see *prevail*.] 1. Of such a character as to prevail; superior in power or might; controlling; ruling.

Brennus told the Roman Embassadors that *prevalent* arms were as good as any title. *Raleigh.*

Piety was so *prevalent* an ingredient in her constitution [that] . . . she no sooner became intimately acquainted, but she would endeavour to improve them, by insinuating something of religious. *Evelyn*, Diary, March 10, 1685.

The tribunes and people, having now subdued all competitors, began the last game of a *prevalent* populace.
Swift, Nobles and Commons, iii.

The *prevalent* wish to be better constitutes the being better. *T. H. Green*, Prolegomena to Ethics, § 110.

2. Influential; possessed of moral weight or authority.

Thus, my Lord, to perform your Commands, which are very *prevalent* with me, have I couched in this Letter what I could of the Condition of the Jews.
Howell, Letters, I. vi. 14.

The King, highly displeas'd, and instigated perhaps by her who was *prevalent* with him, not long after sent Dunstan into Banishment. *Milton*, Hist. Eng., v.

What art so *prevalent*, what proof so strong,
That will convince him his attempt is wrong?
Crabbe, Works, I. 154.

3. Effective; efficacious; productive of results, particularly of results desired.

A kind of Rue is here, . . . not onely a preservative against infection, but . . . *prevalent* against hurtfull spirits. *Sandys*, Travailes, p. 98.

4. Wide-spread; current; of wide extent, occurrence, practice, or acceptance: as, a *prevalent* belief; a *prevalent* custom.

His mind had not escaped the *prevalent* error of the primitive church, the belief, namely, that the second coming of Christ would shortly occur. *Emerson*, Misc., p. 20.

=**Syn.** 1 and 2. *Prevalent, Prevailing, Predominant, Ruling.* *Ruling* in this connection refers to moral ascendancy: as, a *ruling* fashion set by a reigning belle. *Prevalent* and *prevailing* are sometimes the same, and in two senses, that of exceeding in strength, as the *prevalent* (or *prevailing*) opinion was against action, and that of existing widely, as scarlet fever is a *prevalent* (or *prevailing*) distemper. The habitual is more likely to be expressed by *prevalent*; the present or actual, sometimes the temporary, by *prevailing*: as, the *prevailing* fashion. The words are weaker and less exact than *ruling*; *predominant* is the strongest of all. *Predominant* implies activity, and actual or figurative effort after leadership on the part of that which is predominated over: as, a *predominant* faction; a *predominant* opinion is one that seems to put down all others.—4. *Common, Prevalent*, etc. See *common*.

prevalently (prev'a̤-lẹnt-li), *adv.* 1. Prevailingly; powerfully; with predominance or superiority.—2. Currently; generally.

prevaly†, *adv.* A Middle English form of *privily*.

prevaricate (prẹ̄-var'i-kāt), *v.*; pret. and pp. *prevaricated*, ppr. *prevaricating*. [< L. *prævaricatus*, pp. of *prævaricari*, LL. also in active form *prævaricare* (> It. *prevaricare* = Pg. Sp. *prevaricar* = OF. *prevarier*, *prevariquer*, F. *prévariquer*), walk crookedly, collude, prevaricate, as an advocate, LL. also transgress, ML., in general, use deceit or concealment, etc., < L. *præ*, before, + *varicare*, straddle, < *varicus*, with feet spread apart, < *varus*, bent inward, awry: see *varicose*. Cf. *divaricate*.] **I.** *intrans.* 1†. To deviate; swerve from the normal or proper course; stray.

When these circumstants shall but live to see
The time that I *prevaricate* from thee.
Herrick, Welcome to Sack.

How widely they differ and *prevaricate* from the wholesome precepts and doctrine delivered from those Holy Oracles. *Evelyn*, True Religion, II. 305.

2. To swerve from the truth; act or speak evasively; quibble.

I would think better of himself than that he would wilfully *prevaricate*. *Stillingfleet.*

Prevaricate as often as you can defend the prevarication, being close pressed; but, my dear Canning, . . . never lie.
Landor, Mr. Pitt and Mr. Canning.

3†. In *law*: (*a*) To undertake a thing falsely and deceitfully, with the purpose of defeating or destroying the object which it is professed to promote. (*b*) To betray the cause of a client, and by collusion assist his opponent.

II.† *trans.* 1. To pervert; cause to deviate from the normal or proper path, application, or meaning.

If we consider only them [schismatics], better had it been for the English nation that it [the Bible] had still remained in the original Greek and Hebrew, or at least in the honest Latin of St. Jerome, than that several texts in it should have been *prevaricated* to the destruction of that government which put it into so ungrateful hands.
Dryden, Religio Laici, Pref.

2. To transgress; violate.

Men dare not *prevaricate* their duty, though they be tempted strongly. *Jer. Taylor*, Works (ed. 1835), I. 669.

prevarication (prẹ̄-var-i-kā'shọn), *n.* [= F. *prévarication* = Sp. *prevaricacion* = Pg. *prevaricação* = It. *prevaricazione*, < L. *prævaricatio(n-)*, a stepping out of the line (of duty or propriety), violation of duty, prevarication, < *prævaricari*, pp. *prævaricatus*, walk crookedly, prevaricate: see *prevaricate*.] 1. The act of prevaricating or deviating, especially from truth, honesty, or plain-dealing; evasion of truth or duty; quibbling or shuffling in words or conduct.

Th' august tribunal of the skies,
Where no *prevarication* shall avail,
Where eloquence and artifice shall fail.
Cowper, Retirement, l. 657.

The *prevarication* and white lies which a mind that keeps itself ambitiously pure is . . . uneasy under . . . are worn as lightly as mere trimmings when once the actions have become a lie. *George Eliot*, Silas Marner, xiii.

2†. Transgression; violation: as, the *prevarication* of a law.

In our *prevarications*, and easy betrayings, and surrendering of ourselves to the enemy of his [God's] kingdom, Satan, we are his enemies. *Donne*, Sermons, vii.

The *prevarications* of the natural law have also their portion of a special punishment, besides the scourge of an unquiet spirit.
Jer. Taylor, Works (ed. 1835), I. 10, Pref.

But on holi-dayes men every where runne to the alehouse, to playes, to enterludes, and dances, to the very derision of God's name, and the *prevarication* of the day.
Prynne, Histrio-Mastix, I., vi. 12.

3. A secret abuse in the exercise of a public office or commission.—4†. In *law*: (*a*) The conduct of an advocate who betrayed the cause of his client, and by collusion assisted his opponent. (*b*) The undertaking of a thing falsely, with intent to defeat the object which it was professed to promote. (*c*) The wilful concealment or misrepresentation of truth by giving evasive and equivocating evidence.=**Syn.** 1. *Equivocation, Shift*, etc. See *evasion*.

prevaricator (prẹ̄-var'i-kā-tọr), *n.* [= F. *prévaricateur* = Pr. Sp. Pg. *prevaricador* = It. *prevaricatore*, < L. *prævaricator*, one who violates his duty: see *prevaricate*.] 1. One who prevaricates; a shuffler; a quibbler.

This petty *prevaricator* of America, the zanie of Columbus (for so he must be till his worlds end), having rambl'd over the huge topography of his own vain thoughts, no marvell if he brought us home nothing but a meer tankard drollery. *Milton*, Apology for Smectymnuus.

2†. One who acts with unfaithfulness and want of probity; one who abuses a trust.

The law which is promulged against *prevaricators*.
Prynne, Treachery and Disloyalty, p. 160, App.

The Civilians define a *prevaricator* to be one that betrays his cause to the adversary and turns on the criminal's side, whom he ought to prosecute.
Kennet, Rom. Antiquities, II. iii. 18.

3. Formerly, at the University of Cambridge, England, the opponent of the inceptor at commencement. He delivered a prefatory oration, freely satirizing prominent individuals.

Was spent in hearing several exercises in the scholes, and after dinner ye Proctor opened ye Act at St. Marie's (according to custome), and ye *Prevaricators* their drolery.
Evelyn, Diary, July 8, 1654.

prevay†, *a.* A Middle English form of *privy*.

preve[1]†, *n.* and *v.* A Middle English form of *proof, prove*.

preve[2]†, *a.* A Middle English form of *privy*.

prevelache†, *n.* A Middle English form of *privilege*.

preveley†, *adv.* A Middle English form of *privily*.

prevenancy (prev'ẹ̄-nạn-si), *n.* [< F. *prévenance*, obliging thoughtfulness, < *prévenant*, ppr. of *prévenir*, anticipate, < L. *prævenire*, precede, come beforehand: see *prevene*.] Complaisance; prepossessing disposition or appearance; obliging manner. [Rare.]

La Fleur's *prevenancy* (for there was a passport in his very looks) soon set every servant in the kitchen at ease with him.
Sterne, Sentimental Journey, The Letter, Amiens.

prevene (prẹ̄-vēn'), *v.* [= F. *prévenir* = Pr. Sp. Pg. *prevenir* = It. *prevenire*, precede, arrive before, < L. *prævenire*, come before, anticipate, prevent, < *præ*, before, + *venire*, come.] **I.** *trans.* 1. To come or go before; precede. [Rare.]

Till our poor race has passed the tortuous years
That lie *prevening* the millennium.
J. G. Holland, Kathrina, ii.

2†. To hinder; prevent.

II.† *intrans.* To hinder; prevent.

If thy indulgent care
Had not *preven'd*, among unbody'd shades
I now had wandered. *J. Philips*, Cider, ii.

prevenience (prẹ̄-vē'niẹns), *n.* [< *prevenien(t)* + *-ce*. Cf. *prevenancy*.] The act of anticipating or going before; anticipation.

prevenient (prẹ̄-vē'niẹnt), *a.* [Also *prævenient*; < L. *prævenien(t-)s*, ppr. of *prævenire*, come before, anticipate: see *prevene*.] 1. Going before; precedent; anticipative of later events.

The Articles that Hooper used on this occasion resembled so closely in parts the great formulary of the faith with which, as we have seen, Cranmer was engaged, that they may be called a *prevenient* issue of some of the Forty-two Articles of Edward.
R. W. Dixon, Hist. Church of Eng., xx.

2. Preventive; hindering; restraining.—**Prevenient grace.** See *grace*.

From the mercy-seat above
Prevenient grace descending had removed
The stony from their hearts. *Milton*, P. L., xi. 3.

prevent (prẹ̄-vent'), *v.* [< L. *præventus*, pp. of *prævenire*, come before, anticipate, prevent: see *prevene*.] **I.** *trans.* 1. To go before; be earlier than; anticipate; forestall. [Obsolete or archaic.]

I *prevented* the dawning of the morning, and cried: I hoped in thy word. Ps. cxix. 147.

In this drought . . . the Lord *prevented* our prayers in sending us rain soon after, and before the day of humiliation came. *Winthrop*, Hist. New England, II. 264.

Lord, we pray thee that thy grace may always *prevent* and follow us. *Book of Common Prayer*, Collect for 17th [Sunday after Trinity.

Sweet Child, I hop'd to have *prevented* thee
In seeing Rachel thy deceased Mother:
But surely long behind I will not be.
J. Beaumont, Psyche, i. 139.

From the towers, *preventing* day,
With Wilfrid took his early way.
Scott, Rokeby, ii. 4.

2†. To take previous measures against; hence, to frustrate; disappoint; evade; escape.

I'll teach them to *prevent* wild Alcibiades' wrath.
Shak., T. of A., v. 1. 206.

Give my love fame faster than Time wastes life;
So thou *prevent'st* his scythe and crooked knife.
Shak., Sonnets, c.

Not too loud; the traitor
May hear, and by escape *prevent* our justice.
Shirley, The Traitor, i. 1.

3. To hinder from action by the opposition of obstacles; impede; restrain; check; preclude: generally followed by *from*.

I do at this hour joy o'er myself,
Prevented from a damned enterprise.
Shak., Hen. V., ii. 2. 164.

The natural affections which men have for their children often *prevent* them *from* entering upon any grand, noble, or meritorious enterprize for the public good.
Bacon, Physical Fables, iii., Expl.

4. To keep from existing or occurring; render impossible.

Mountains divide me from him! some kind hand
Prevent our fearful meeting!
Fletcher, Double Marriage, v. 3.

The Eternal, to *prevent* such horrid fray,
Hung forth in heaven his golden scales.
Milton, P. L., iv. 996.

As charity covers, so modesty *preventeth*, a multitude of sins. *Sir T. Browne*, Christ. Mor., i. 35.

=**Syn.** 3. To preclude, bar, debar.

II. *intrans.* 1†. To come beforehand; come before others, or before the usual time.

Strawberries watered now and then (as once in three days) with water wherein hath been steeped sheep's dung or pigeon's dung will *prevent* and come early.
Bacon, Nat. Hist., § 403.

2. To interpose a hindrance, especially an insurmountable obstacle; interpose an effectual check; hinder.

The climber-upward . . .
Looks in the clouds, scorning the base degrees
By which he did ascend. So Cæsar may.
Then, lest he may, *prevent*. *Shak.*, J. C., ii. 1. 28.

preventability (prẹ̄-ven-ta̤-bil'i-ti), *n.* [< *preventable* + *-ity* (see *-bility*).] The state of being preventable; the possibility of prevention.

As this conviction [of the communicability of consumption through articles of food or by personal contact] increases, the belief in the *preventability* of the disease will increase. *The Sanitarian*, XIV. 265.

preventable (prẹ̄-ven'ta̤-bl), *a.* [< *prevent* + *-able*.] That can be prevented or hindered; capable of being prevented.

The ignorance of the end is far more *preventable*, considering the helps we have to know it, than of the means.
Bp. Reynolds, Works, p. 771. (*Latham*.)

preventative (prẹ̄-ven'ta-tiv), *n.* [Irreg. and improp. < *prevent* + *-ative*. Cf. *preventitive*.] Same as *preventive*.

The powdered root [of deadly nightshade] has been given in doses of ten or more grains every other night, as a *preventative* after the bite of a mad dog.
Pilkington, View of Derbyshire (ed. 1789), I. 356.

preventer (prẹ̄-ven'tėr), *n.* 1†. One who goes before or takes the lead.

The archduke was the assailant, and the *preventer*, and had the fruit of his diligence and celerity.
Bacon, War with Spain.

2. One who prevents; a hinderer; that which hinders; a preventive. Specifically — 3. *Naut.*, an additional rope, chain, bolt, or spar employed to support any other when the latter suffers an unusual strain.

prevention (prẹ̄-ven'shọn), *n.* [< OF. *prevention*, F. *prévention* = Pr. *prevention* = Sp. *prevencion* = Pg. *prevenção* = It. *prevenzione*, < LL. *præventio(n-)*, a going before, an anticipating, < L. *prævenire*, pp. *præventus*, come before: see *prevent*.] 1†. The act of going before; the state of proceeding or being earlier; hence, an antecedent period of time.

The greater the distance the greater the *prevention*, as in thunder, where the lightning precedeth the crack a good space.
Bacon.

2†. The act of anticipating or forestalling; an anticipation; provision made in advance.

All other delights are the pleasures of beasts, or the sports of children; these are the antepasts and *preventions* of the full feasts and overflowings of eternity.
Jer. Taylor, Works (ed. 1835), I. 49.

God's *preventions*, cultivating our nature, and fitting us with capacities of his high donatives.
Hammond.

3. Precaution; a precautionary measure; a preventive.

Achievements, plots, orders, *preventions*,
Excitements to the field, or speech for truce,
Success or loss, what is or is not, serves
As stuff for these two to make paradoxes.
Shak., T. and C., i. 3. 181.

Not to procure health, but for safe *prevention*
Against a growing sickness. *Ford*, Lady's Trial, i. 1.

4. The act of hindering or rendering impossible by previous measures; effectual hindrance; restraint, as from an intended action; also, that which prevents; an obstacle; an obstruction or impediment.

Casca, be sudden, for we fear *prevention*.
Shak., J. C., iii. 1. 19.

Others, to make surer *prevention* against their sight of heaven, have rolled the whole earth betwixt that and their eyes.
Rev. T. Adams, Works, II. 386.

Forth stepping opposite, half-way he met
His daring foe, at this *prevention* more
Incensed.
Milton, P. L., vi. 129.

5†. Jurisdiction.

Your sayd Grace, by verteu off your legantine prerogative and *prevention*, conferr to hys chapleyn, Mr. Wilson, the vicarege of Thackstedd.
State Papers, i. 311. (*Halliwell.*)

6†. Prejudice; prepossession.

In reading what I have written, let them bring no particular gusto, or any *prevention* of mind, and that whatsoever judgment they make, it may be purely their own.
Dryden. (*Imp. Dict.*)

Corrupt and Illegal Practices Prevention Act. See *corrupt*.

preventional† (prẹ̄-ven'shọn-ạl), *a.* [< *prevention* + *-al*.] Tending to prevent; preventive. *Bailey*.

preventitive† (prẹ̄-ven'ti-tiv), *n.* Same as *preventive*. *Gregory*, Economy of Nature. (*Latham.*)

preventive (prẹ̄-ven'tiv), *a.* and *n.* [= F. *préventif* = Sp. Pg. It. *preventivo*, preventive, < L. *prævenire*, pp. *præventus*, come before: see *prevent*.] I. *a.* Serving to prevent or hinder; guarding against or warding off something, as disease, injustice, loss, etc.

There be multitude of Examples how *preventive* Wars have been practised from all Times.
Howell, Letters, I. vi. 18.

Preventive cautions are easier and safer then reprehensive corrosives.
Baxter, Life of Faith, i. 3.

Preventive service. See *coast-guard*.

II. *n.* 1†. That which goes before; an anticipation.

A certain anticipation of the gods, which he calls a prolepsis, a certain *preventive*, or foreconceived information of a thing in the mind.
J. Howe, Works, I. 22.

2. That which prevents; that which constitutes an effectual check or insurmountable obstacle.

As every event is naturally allied to its cause, so by parity of reason it is opposed to its *preventive*.
Harris, Hermes, ii. 2. (*Latham.*)

3. Specifically, something taken, used, or done beforehand to ward off disease.

He would persuade me, no doubt, that a squadron of horse on the low grounds is a *preventive* of agues, and a body of archers on the hills a specific for a fever.
Landor, Richard I. and the Abbot of Boxley.

Also *preventative*.

preventively (prẹ̄-ven'tiv-li), *adv.* In a preventive manner; by way of prevention; in a manner that tends to hinder.

It [the vicinage] is *preventively* the assertor of its own rights, or remedially their avenger.
Burke, A Regicide Peace, i.

preventiveness (prẹ̄-ven'tiv-nes), *n.* The quality of being preventive; capability of preventing or hindering.

prevermis (prē-vėr'mis), *n.*; pl. *prevermes* (-mēz). [NL. *prævermis*, < L. *præ*, before, + NL. *vermis*.] The anterior and prominent part of the vermis of the cerebellum, commonly called *vermis superior*: distinguished from the *postvermis*.

prevertebral (prē-vėr'tẹ̄-brạl), *a.* [Also *prævertebral*; < L. *præ*, before, + *vertebra*, vertebra.] 1. Situated in front of or before the vertebræ.— 2. Developing or appearing before the vertebræ.— **Prevertebral fascia**, a layer of fascia derived from the under surface of the cervical fascia, forming a sheath over the prevertebral muscles, and behind the carotid vessels, esophagus, and pharynx.— **Prevertebral muscles**, muscles which lie upon the front of the spinal column of man; especially, a group of such muscles in the neck, consisting of the longus colli, the rectus capitis anticus major and minor, and the three scaleni.— **Prevertebral plexuses.** See *plexus*.

prevesical (prē-ves'i-kạl), *a.* [< L. *præ*, before, + *vesica*, bladder.] Situated in front of or before the bladder.

preview (prē-vū'), *v. t.* [< *pre-* + *view*. Cf. F. *prévu*, pp. of *prévoir*, < L. *prævidere*, foresee.] To see beforehand. [Rare.]

Preview, but not prevent —
No mortall can — the miseries of life.
Marston, What you Will, v. 1.

previous (prē'vius), *a.* [= Sp. Pg. It. *previo*, < L. *prævius*, going before, < *præ*, before, + *via*, way, road.] Going before in time; being or occurring before something else; earlier; antecedent; prior.

The arrival of these chieftains must have been some years *previous*.
Haigh, Anglo-Saxon Sagas, p. 81.

Previous question. See *question*.— **Previous to.** (*a*) Being or occurring before; antecedent to, in any sense.

Something there is more needful than expense,
And something *previous* even *to* taste — 'tis sense.
Pope, Moral Essays, iv. 42.

(*b*) Previously to; before (*previous* being used adverbially, and with the preposition *to* equivalent to a simple preposition, *before*). Compare *prior to*, in a like loose use.

Previous to his embarkation Charles addressed a letter to his son.
Prescott, Philip II., i. 2.

=**Syn.** *Previous, Preceding, Precedent, Anterior, Prior, Former, Foregoing, Antecedent.* All these words have lost their original application to space, and now apply only to that which goes before in time, except *anterior*, which may apply also to space, as the *anterior* part of the brain, and *preceding*, which as a participle still primarily applies to space, but as an adjective generally expresses order in time. *Preceding* means immediately before; the others may mean the same. *Precedent* often applies to that which has to go before in order to the existence or validity of that which follows: as, a condition *precedent*. *Prior* often means superior by being earlier: as, a *prior* claim. *Anterior* is opposed to *posterior*, *prior* to *subsequent* or *subordinate*, *former* to *latter*, *foregoing* to *following*, *antecedent* to *subsequent*. See *preliminary*.

previously (prē'vius-li), *adv.* In time preceding; antecedently; beforehand: often followed by *to*.

In April . . . [Thoreau] went to live with Mr. Emerson, but had been on intimate terms with him *previously to* that time.
O. W. Holmes, Emerson, v.

=**Syn.** *Formerly, Previously.* See *formerly*.

previousness (prē'vius-nes), *n.* Previous occurrence; antecedence; priority in time.

previse (prẹ̄-vīz'), *v. t.*; pret. and pp. *prevised*, ppr. *prevising*. [< L. *prævisus*, pp. of *prævidere* (> It. *previdere* = Pg. Sp. *prever* = Pr. *prevezir* = OF. *preveoir*, F. *prévoir*), foresee, < *præ*, before, + *videre*, see: see *vision*. Cf. *advise*, *revise*.] 1. To foresee.— 2. To cause to foresee; forewarn; advise beforehand.

Mr. Pelham, it will be remembered, has *prevised* the reader that Lord Vincent was somewhat addicted to paradox.
Bulwer, Pelham, xv., note.

prevision (prẹ̄-vizh'ọn), *n.* [< F. *prévision* = Pr. *previzio*, *prevision* = Sp. *prevision* = Pg. *previsão* = It. *previsione*, < L. *prævidere*, pp. *prævisus*, foresee: see *previse*.] 1. The act of foreseeing; foresight; foreknowledge; prescience.

Prevision is the best prevention.
Rev. S. Ward, Sermons, p. 52.

On examination we see that the *prevision* might have been erroneous, and was not knowledge until experiment had verified it.
G. H. Lewes, Probs. of Life and Mind, II. 186.

2. A specific act of foresight or prescience.

Stella was quite right in her *previsions*. She saw from the very first what was going to happen.
Thackeray, English Humorists, Swift.

=**Syn.** See *inference*.

prevoyant (prẹ̄-voi'ant), *a.* [< F. *prévoyant*, ppr. of *prévoir*, foresee, < L. *prævidere*, foresee: see *previse*.] Foreseeing. [Rare.]

But Nature, *prevoyant*, tingled into his heart an inarticulate thrill of prophecy.
Mrs. Oliphant.

prewt, *n.* Same as *prow*[2].

prewarn (prē-wârn'), *v. t.* and *i.* [< *pre-* + *warn*.] To warn beforehand; give previous notice; forewarn.

Comets *prewarn*, whose havoc in vast field
Unearthed skulls proclaim.
Fletcher (*and another*), Two Noble Kinsmen, v. 1.

prex (preks), *n.* [A modified abbr. of *president*.] The president of a college. [U. S. college cant.]

prexy (prek'si), *n.* [Dim. of *prex*.] Same as *prex*. [U. S. college cant.]

prey[1]†, *v.* An obsolete form of *pray*[1].

prey[2] (prā), *n.* [Early mod. E. also *pray*; < ME. *preye*, *praye*, < OF. *preie*, *praie*, *proie*, F. *proie* = Pr. *preda* = OSp. *preda* = It. *preda*, prey, < L. *præda*, property taken in war, spoil, booty, plunder, also an animal taken in the chase, prey, game; prob. contr. from **præheda*, < **præhendere*, *prehendere*, contr. *prendere*, seize upon, take, < *præ*, before, + **hendere* (√ *hed*) = Gr. χανδάνειν (√ χαδ-), take, = E. *get*: see *prehend* and *get*[1]. Cf. *prede*, an obs. doublet of *prey*[2], and *predatory*, *depredate*, *prize*[1], etc., from the same ult. source.] 1. Goods taken by robbery or pillage; spoil; booty; plunder.

So thei entred in to the londe, and toke many *prayes*, and brent townes and vilages, and distroyed all the coutrees.
Merlin (E. E. T. S.), ii. 152.

The rascal people, thirsting after *prey*,
Join with the traitor, and they jointly swear
To spoil the city and your royal court.
Shak., 2 Hen. VI., iv. 4. 51.

2. That which is seized by any carnivorous animal to be devoured; quarry, as of a raptorial bird.

The Sparhauk and other Foules of Raveyne, whan thei fleen aftre here *praye*, and take it before men of Armes, it is a gode Signe; and zif he fayle of takynge his *praye*, it is an evylle sygne.
Mandeville, Travels, p. 160.

The old lion perisheth for lack of *prey*. Job iv. 11.

Stag, dog, and all, which from or towards flies,
Is paid with life or *prey*, or doing dies.
Donne, The Calm.

Hence — 3. That which is given into the power of another or others; a victim.

It may be men have now found out that God hath proposed the Christian clergy as a *prey* for all men freely to seize upon.
Hooker, Eccles. Polity, VII. 21.

I banish her my bed and company,
And give her as a *prey* to law and shame.
Shak., 2 Hen. VI., ii. 1. 198.

The great men, giv'n to gluttony and dissolute life, made a *prey* of the common people.
Milton, Hist. Eng., vi.

Both pined amidst their royal state, a *prey* to incurable despondency.
Prescott, Ferd. and Isa., ii. 16.

4. The act of preying or seizing upon anything. (*a*) Plundering; pillage; robbery; depredation.

To forage the countrey adioyning, and to liue vpon the spoyle of them that would not receiue their new doctrine, which they in many troupes, and with many *preyes*, accordingly performed.
Purchas, Pilgrimage, p. 359.

When his Soldiers had gotten great Spoils, and made *Prey* upon the innocent Countrey People, he commanded them to restore it all back again.
Baker, Chronicles, p. 11.

The whole little wood where I sit is a world of plunder and *prey*.
Tennyson, Maud, iv.

(*b*) The act of seizing in order to devour; seizure, as by a carnivorous animal of its Victim.

Yet dared not his victor to withstand,
But trembled like a lambe fled from the *pray*.
Spenser, F. Q., III. vii. 16.

Methought a serpent eat my heart away,
And you sat smiling at his cruel *prey*.
Shak., M. N. D., ii. 2. 150.

Animal or **beast of prey**, a carnivorous, predatory, or rapacious animal; one that feeds on the flesh of other animals.— **Bird of prey.** See *bird*[1] and *Raptores*.

Vulture, kite,
Raven, and gorcrow, all my *birds of prey*.
B. Jonson, Volpone, i. 1.

=**Syn.** 1. Booty, etc. (see *pillage*).— 4. Ravin.

prey[2] (prā), *v.* [Early mod. E. also *pray*, *preie*; < ME. *preyen*, *prayen*, < OF. *preier*, *preer*, *proier* = It. *predare*, < L. *prædari*, take booty, plunder, pillage, catch or take animals as game or prey, < *præda*, prey: see *prey*[2], *n.* Cf. *prede*, an obs. doublet of *prey*.] I. *intrans.* 1. To take booty; commit robbery or pillage; seize spoils: generally with *on* or *upon*.

They pray continually to their saint, the commonwealth — or rather, not pray to her, but *prey on* her.
Shak., 1 Hen. IV., ii. 1. 90.

A succession of ferocious invaders descended through the western passes, to *prey on* the defenceless wealth of Hindostan. *Macaulay*, Lord Clive.

2. To seize and devour an animal as prey: generally followed by *on* or *upon*.

Good morrow, masters; put your torches out;
The wolves have *prey'd*; and look, the gentle day . . .
Dapples the drowsy east with spots of grey.
Shak., Much Ado, v. 3. 25.

'Tis
The royal disposition of that beast [the lioness]
To *prey on* nothing that doth seem as dead.
Shak., As you Like it, iv. 3. 118.

3. To exert wasting or destroying power or influence; bring injury, decay, or destruction: generally followed by *on* or *upon*.

Language is too faint to show
His rage of love; it *preys upon* his life;
He pines, he sickens, he despairs, he dies.
Addison, Cato, iii. 2.

Some [critics] on the leaves of ancient authors *prey*,
Nor time nor moths e'er spoil'd so much as they.
Pope, Essay on Criticism, l. 112.

Keep his mind from *preying on* itself.
M. Arnold, Empedocles on Etna.

II.† *trans.* To ravage; pillage; make prey of.

Amongst the rest the which they then did *pray*,
They spoyld old Melibee of all he had.
Spenser, F. Q., VI. x. 40.

The said Justice *preied* the countrey Tirconnell.
Holland, tr. of Camden, II. 156. (*Davies.*)

preyer (prā'ėr), *n.* [Early mod. E. also *preier*; < ME. *preiour* (?), < OF. *preeor*, *preiour*, < L. *prædator*, a plunderer, < *prædari*, plunder: see *prey*[2]. Cf. doublet *predour*.] One who or that which preys; a plunderer; a waster; a devourer.

For, by hir owne procurement and intisings, she became and would needs be a preie vnto the *preier*.
Holinshed, Conquest of Ireland, i.

preyful† (prā'fůl), *a.* [< *prey*[2] + *-ful*.] 1. Prone to prey; savage.

The *preyful* brood of savage beasts.
Chapman, tr. of Homer's Hymns to Venus, l. 115.

2. Having much prey; killing much game. [Burlesque.]

The *preyful* princess pierced and prick'd a pretty pleasing pricket. *Shak.*, L. L. L., iv. 2. 58.

preyne†, *n.* An obsolete form of *preen*[1].

preyse†, *v.* and *n.* An obsolete variant of *praise*.

prezygapophysial (prē-zī″gap-ọ̄-fiz'i-al), *a.* [< *prezygapophysis* + *-al*.] Articulating anteriorly, as a vertebral process; having the character of or pertaining to a prezygapophysis.

prezygapophysis (prē-zi-ga-pof'i-sis), *n.*; pl. *prezygapophyses* (-sēz). [NL. *præzygapophysis*; < L. *præ*, before, + NL. *zygapophysis*, q. v.] An anterior or superior zygapophysis; in man, a superior oblique or articular process of a vertebra: opposed to *postzygapophysis*. See *zygapophysis*, and cuts under *dorsal*, *lumbar*, *sacrum*, *xenarthral*, *vertebra*, and *hypapophysis*.

Priacanthidæ (pri-a-kan'thi-dē), *n. pl.* [NL., < *Priacanthus* + *-idæ*.] A family of acanthopterygian fishes, represented by the genus *Priacanthus* alone, with about 20 species of tropical seas, known as *bigeyes*. They are of small size and carnivorous habits. See cut under *Priacanthus*.

Priacanthina (pri″a-kan-thi'nä), *n. pl.* [NL., < *Priacanthus* + *-ina*[2].] The *Priacanthidæ* as the fourth group of *Percidæ*. *Günther*.

priacanthine (pri-a-kan'thin), *a.* and *n.* [< *Priacanthus* + *-ine*.] **I.** *a.* Pertaining to the *Priacanthina* or *Priacanthidæ*, or having their characters.

II. *n.* A priacanthine fish; any member of the *Priacanthidæ*.

Priacanthus (pri-a-kan'thus), *n.* [NL. (Cuvier, 1817), so called from the serrated fin-spines; < Gr. πρίων, a saw, + ἄκανθα, spine.] In *ichth.*, the representative genus of *Priacanthidæ*. *P.*

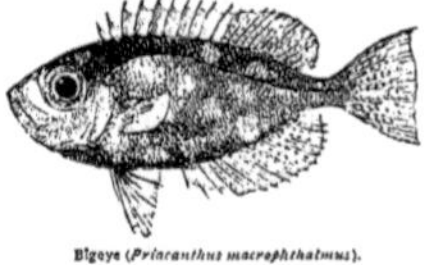

Bigeye (*Priacanthus macrophthalmus*).

macrophthalmus, the bigeye of the West Indies, occasional on the coast of the United States, is a characteristic example. *P. altus* is found on the New England coast.

prial† (pri'al), *n.* A corruption of *pair royal* (which see, under *pair*[1]).

But the annus mirabilis of his [Alexander the Great's] public life, the most effective and productive year throughout his oriental anabasis, was the year 333 before Christ. Here we have another *prial*, a *prial* of threes, for the locus of Alexander. *De Quincey*, Style, iii.

prian (pri'an), *n.* Same as *pryan*.

Priapean (pri-a-pē'an), *a.* and *n.* [< L. *Priapeius*, *Priapēus*, pertaining to Priapus (neut. pl. *Priapeia*, a collection of poems on Priapus), < Gr. Πριάπειος, < Πρίαπος, Priapus: see *Priapus*.] **I.** *a.* **1.** Of or pertaining to Priapus.—**2.** In *anc. pros.*, noting a certain verse or meter. See the noun.—**3.** [*l. c.*] Having a priapism.

II. *n.* In *anc. pros.*, a logaœdic meter consisting of a catalectic Glyconic and a Pherecratean. It assumes the following forms:

∠⏑⏑–⏑⏑–⏑– | ∠⏑⏑–⏑–
∠⏑–⏑⏑–⏑– | ∠⏑–⏑⏑–⏑
∠⏑–⏑⏑–⏑– | ∠⏑–⏑⏑–⏑
∠⏑–⏑⏑–⏑– | ∠⏑⏑–⏑⏑–⏑

The name was given by ancient writers to the second and third of these forms, but especially to the second with initial spondee in each colon. This was regarded by many as a variation of a dactylic hexameter with a spondee in the first, fourth, and sixth places, a diæresis being made after the third foot and the preceding syllable lengthened: thus,

– – | – ⏑ ⏑ | – ⏑ ⏑ | – – | – ⏑ ⏑ | – –.

See *Satyric*.

Priapic (pri-ap'ik), *a.* [< *Priapus* + *-ic*.] Of or relating to Priapus, or to the cult and myths concerning him; phallic.

The ithyphallic Hermes, represented after the fashion of the *Priapic* figures in paintings on the walls of caves among the Bushmen. *Encyc. Brit.*, XVII. 153.

priapism (pri'a-pizm), *n.* [= F. *priapisme* = Sp. Pg. It. *priapismo*, < L. *priapismus*, < Gr. πριαπισμός, priapism, lewdness, < πριαπίζειν, be lewd, < Πρίαπος, Priapus: see *Priapus*.] Morbidly persistent erection and rigidity of the penis.

Priapus (pri-ā'pus), *n.* [= F. *Priape*, < L. *Priapus*, < Gr. Πρίαπος, Priapus: see def.] **1.** The male generative power or function personified as a deity: originally an epithet or cognomen of Bacchus, then a personification of the phallus.

At Lampsacus, too, on the Hellespont, he [Bacchus] was venerated under a symbolical form adapted to a similar office [that of procreation], though with a title of a different signification, *Priapus*. . . . The Greeks, as usual, changed the personified attribute into a distinct deity called *Priapus*.
R. P. Knight, Anc. Art and Myth. (1876), pp. 10, 12.

2. [*l. c.*] A symbol or representation of the male generative organ; a phallus.—**3.** [*l. c.*] The male genitals; the virile organ in the state of erection.

pricasour†, *n.* [ME., also *prickasour*; origin obscure. Cf. *prick*, ride.] A hard rider.

A monk ther was, a fair for the maistrie,
An out-rydere, that loved venerye; . . .
Therfore he was a *pricasour* aright;
Greyhoundes he hadde as swifte as fowel in flight.
Of prikyng and of huntyng for the hare
Was al his lust, for no cost wolde he spare.
Chaucer, Gen. Prol. to C. T., l. 165–189.

price (prīs), *n.* [< ME. *price*, *pryce*, *pris*, *prys*, price, prize, value, excellence, = D. *prijs* = MHG. *prîs*, G. *preis*, praise, glory, price, reward, etc., < OF. *pris*, *preis*, F. *prix*, price, value, reward, prize, etc., = Pr. *pretz* = Sp. *precio* = Pg. *preço* = It. *prezzo*, price, value, < L. *pretium*, worth, price, money spent, wages, reward; prob. akin to Gr. περνάναι, sell; Skt. *pana* for **parna*, wages, price. Hence ult. (< L. *pretium*) E. *praise*, *prize*[2], *precious*, *appraise*, *apprize*[2], *appreciate*, *depreciate*, etc.] **1.** Worth; value; estimation; excellence.

Thei sette no *prys* be no richesse, but only of a precyous Ston that is amonges hem, that is of 60 coloures.
Mandeville, Travels, p. 196.

And how that freris folwed folke that was riche,
And folke that was pore at litel *prys* thei sette.
Piers Plowman (B), xiii. 8.

Who can find a virtuous woman? for her *price* is far above rubies. Prov. xxxi. 10.

I have ever loved the life removed,
And held in idle *price* to haunt assemblies.
Shak., M. for M., i. 3. 9.

O spare my youth, and for the breath I owe
Large gifts of *price* my father shall bestow.
Pope, Iliad, x. 450.

2. The sum or amount of money, or its equivalent, which a seller asks or obtains for his goods in market; the exchangeable value of a commodity; the equivalent in money for which something is bought or sold, or offered for sale; hence, figuratively, that which must be given or done in order to obtain a thing.

Come, buy wine and milk, without money and without *price*. Isa. lv. 1.

Poor fellow, never joyed since the *price* of oats rose; it was the death of him. *Shak.*, 1 Hen. IV., ii. 1. 14.

What then? is the reward of virtue bread?
That vice may merit; 'tis the *price* of toil;
The knave deserves it when he tills the soil.
Pope, Essay on Man, iv. 151.

The most accurate modern writers . . . have employed *Price* to express the value of a thing in relation to money; the quantity of money for which it will exchange.
J. S. Mill, Pol. Econ., III. i. § 2.

The *price* of a given article [in market] is the approximate mathematical expression of the rates, in terms of money, at which exchanges of the article for money were actually made at or about a given hour on a given day.
Encyc. Brit., XXII. 465.

3†. Esteem; high or highest reputation.

Ffor proude men in *price* haue playnly no fryndes,
But euery mon with enuy ertis hom skathe.
Destruction of Troy (E. E. T. S.), l. 4840.

The river Ladon . . . of all the rivers of Greece had the *price* for excellent pureness and sweetness.
Sir P. Sidney, Arcadia, ii.

4†. Prize; award.

Sche seyde, Y have welle sped
That soche a lorde hath me wedd,
That beryth the *pryce* in prees.
MS. Cantab. Ff. ii. 38, f. 82. (*Halliwell.*)

A price†, to approval; well.

Iob was a paynym and plesede God *a prys*.
Piers Plowman (C), xv. 194, note.

At Easter price†. See *Easter*[1].—**Famine prices.** See *famine*.—**Fiars' prices.** See *fiar*, 2.—**Making a price**, in *stock-broking*, a jobber's quotation of prices to a broker for buying and selling in the same security.—**Market price.** See *market*.—**Natural, normal, or average price**, in *polit. econ.*, the price which prevails in open market on the average for any length of time; the average of the market price for some length of time. See *value*.—**Price of money**, in *com.*, the price of credit; the rate of discount at which capital may be lent or borrowed.—**Without price**, beyond or above price; priceless.

A robe
Of samite *without price*, that more exprest
Than hid her, clung about her lissom limbs.
Tennyson, Merlin and Vivien.

=**Syn. 2.** *Price*, *Charge*, *Cost*, *Expense*, *Worth*, *Value*. For a given article these may all come to the same amount, but they are very likely to differ. The *price* of a shawl may be ten dollars, and that is then the dealer's *charge* for it, but he may finally make his *price* or *charge* nine dollars, and that will be the *cost* of it, or the *expense* of it to the buyer. Its *worth* or *value* may be what it will sell for, or what it ought to sell for, or what one would be willing to pay for it rather than go without it, the last being the highest sense.

price (prīs), *v. t.*; pret. and pp. *priced*, ppr. *pricing*. [In mod. use *price* is directly from the noun; in older use it is a var. of the verb *prize*, < ME. *prisen*, < OF. *priser*, value, esteem, etc.: see *prize*[2] and *praise*.] **1†.** To pay the price of.

The man that made Sansfoy to fall
Shall with his owne blood *price* that he hath spilt.
Spenser, F. Q., I. v. 26.

2. To put a price on; estimate the value of.—**3.** To ask the price of. [Colloq.]

If you *priced* such a one in a drawing-room here,
And was ask'd fifty pounds, you'd not say it was dear.
Barham, Ingoldsby Legends, II. 261.

price-current (prīs'kur″ent), *n.* [A sort of singular designating the printed paper, from *prices current*, the proper title of such a list itself.] In *com.*, a regularly published list of the prices at which merchandise has been sold for a day or other fixed period. See *price-list*.

priced (prīst), *a.* **1.** Having a (specified) price: used in composition: as, high-*priced*; low-*priced*.—**2.** Marked with the price or prices: as, a *priced* catalogue of machinery.

priceite (prī'sīt), *n.* [Named after Thomas *Price*, of San Francisco, Cal.] A hydrous borate of calcium, of a compact chalky appearance, often in rounded nodules, found in Oregon. Pandermite is similar to it, and both minerals are closely related to colemanite.

priceless (prīs'les), *a.* [< *price* + *-less*.] **1.** Too valuable to be priced; beyond price; invaluable.

What *priceless* wealth the heavens had him lent
In the possession of his beauteous mate.
Shak., Lucrece, l. 17.

2. Without value; worthless or unsalable. *Bp. Barlow*. (*Imp. Dict.*)=**Syn. 1.** Inestimable.

pricelessness (prīs'les-nes), *n.* The property or characteristic of being above price.

The *pricelessness* of water in a land where no rain falls during six months. *The Century*, XXVI. 804.

price-list (prīs'list), *n.* A list of the prices at which stocks, bonds, and other property and merchandise are offered for sale; a price-current.

pricement† (prīs'ment), *n.* [Var. of *prizement* for *apprizement*.] Valuation; appraisal. [Rare.]

Her yearly revenues did amount to 87*l.* 3*s.* 3*d.*, according to the *pricement* at the suppression.
Weever. (*Mason's Suppl. to Johnson's Dict.*)

pricer (prī'sėr), *n.* A person whose duty it is to regulate the prices of a market. *Halliwell.*

price-tag (prīs'tag), *n.* A tag or ticket on which the price of an article to which it is attached is marked.

Accordingly they attached "etiquettes," or *price-tags*, to their articles. *Chautauquan*, VIII. 422.

prick (prik), *n.* [< ME. *prik, pryk, prikke, prike, preke*, a point, a sting, < AS. *prica, pricu*, a sharp point, usually a minute mark, point, dot, a very small portion, prick, = MD. *prick*, D. *prik*, a prick, puncture, = MLG. *pricke*, LG. *prik*, a point, prick, spear, prickle, = G. *pricke*, *prick* = Icel. *prik* = Dan. *prik* = Sw. *prick*, a prick, dot, mark (cf. deriv. (partly dim.) *prickle*); perhaps akin (with loss of orig. initial *s*) to Ir. *sprichar*, a sting, Skt. *prishant*, speckled, also a dot, and so to E. *sprinkle*: see *sprinkle*. The OSp. *priego*, Pg. *prego*, a nail, are from the Teut.] **1.** A slender pointed instrument or other thing capable of puncturing; something sharp-pointed. (*a*) A thorn; spine; prickle.

Kynds of Whales, called Balene, . . . haue rough backes full of sharpe *prickes*.
R. Eden, tr. of Sebastian Munster (First Books on America, [ed. Arber, p. 22).

Hedgehogs which
Lie tumbling in my barefoot way, and mount
Their *pricks* at my footfall. *Shak.*, Tempest, ii. 2. 12.

The odoriferous & fragrant rose . . .
For fence itselfe with *prickes* doth round enclose.
Times' Whistle (E. E. T. S.), p. 128.

(*b*) A skewer.

Cornus, . . . the tree of the wood whereof butchers make their *pricks*. *Nomenclator.*

Bedlam beggars, who, with roaring voices,
Strike in their numb'd and mortified bare arms
Pins, wooden *pricks*, nails, sprigs of rosemary.
Shak., Lear, ii. 3. 16.

I know no use for them so meet
As to be pudding-*pricks*.
Robin Hood and the Beggar (Child's Ballads, V. 191).

(c) A goad. [Obsolete or prov. Eng.] (d) The penis. [Low.] (*e*) A kind of eel-spear. [Eng.]

The *prick* is constructed of four broad serrated blades or tines spread out like a fan, and the eel becomes wedged between them.
Day, Fishes of Great Britain and Ireland, II. 246.

(*f*) Same as *pricket*, 1.

Paid to Thomas Hope for *Pricks* that the Tappers [tapers] stand on, viiij d. Quoted in *Lee's Glossary.*

2. A point; dot; small mark. Specifically—(*a*†) A mark used in writing or printing, as a vowel-point or a comma.

Almost euery letter with his *pricke* or circumflexe signifieth a whole word. *Hakluyt's Voyages*, I. 394.

Martinius affirmeth That these Masorites inuented the *prickes* wherewith the Hebrew is now read, to supply the lacke of vowels. *Purchas*, Pilgrimage, p. 179.

(*b*) In *archery*, the point in the center of a target at which aim is taken; the white; also, the target itself, or, in the plural, a pair of targets, one at the top and the other at the bottom of the range.

And therfore every man judged as he thought, and named a sickness that he knew, shothing not nere the *pricke*, nor understanding the nature of the disease.
Hall, Hen. V., f. 50. (*Halliwell.*)

A pair of winding *pricks*, . . . things that hinder a man which looketh at his mark to shoot straight.
Ascham, Toxophilus, p. 161.

Off the marke he welde not fayle,
He cleffed the *preke* on thre.
Robin Hood and the Potter (Child's Ballads, V. 27).

Let the mark have a *prick* in 't, to mete at, if it may be.
Shak., L. L. L., iv. 1. 134.

(*c*†) A mark on a dial noting the hour; hence, a point of time.

Now Phaëthon hath tumbled from his car,
And made an evening at the noontide *prick*.
Shak., 3 Hen. VI., i. 4. 34.

(*d*†) A mark denoting degree; pitch; point.

There is no man koude brynge hire to that *prikke*.
Chaucer, Man of Law's Tale, l. 931.

Now ginnes that goodly frame of Temperaunce
Fayrely to rise, and her adorned hed
To *pricke* of highest prayse to advaunce.
Spenser, F. Q., II. xii. 1.

(*e*†) A mathematical point.

Arithmetic, geometry, and musicke do proceed
From one, a *pricke*, from divers sounds.
Warner, Albion's England, xiii. (*Nares.*)

(*f*†) In *music*, a note or point: so called from the dot or mark that formed its head.

3. The act or process of puncturing or pricking.

Gentlewomen that live honestly by the *prick* of their needles. *Shak.*, Hen. V., ii. 1. 36.

4. A puncture. (*a*) A minute wound, such as is made by a needle, thorn, or sting.

There were never any asps discovered in the place of her death. . . . only, it was said, two small and almost insensible *pricks* were found upon her arm.
Sir T. Browne, Vulg. Err., v. 12.

(*b*) The print of the foot of a hare or deer on the ground. (c) *pl.* In *tanning*, an appearance as of minute punctures in hides soaked in water until decomposition begins.

In . . . soaking the hides in clean water, *pricks*, pitted, frieze, and black spots originate. *C. T. Davis*, Leather, p. 238.

5. Figuratively, that which pierces, stings, goads, or incites the mind.

O werst of all wikke,
Of conscience whom no *prikke*
Male stere, lo what thou hast do!
Gower, Conf. Amant., v.

My conscience first received a tenderness,
Scruple, and *prick*, on certain speeches utter'd
By the Bishop of Bayonne. *Shak.*, Hen. VIII., ii. 4. 171.

This life is brief, and troubles die with it;
Where were the *prick* to soar up homeward else?
Browning, Ring and Book, I. 176.

6. A small roll: as, a *prick* of spun-yarn; a *prick* of tobacco.—**Prick and praise**†, the praise of excellence or success.

Are you so ignorant in the rules of courtship, to think any one man to bear all the *prick and praise*?
Middleton, Family of Love, ii. 4.

To kick against the pricks, to kick against the goads (said of plowing oxen); hence, to make ineffectual resistance to superior force.

It is hard for thee to *kick against the pricks*. Acts ix. 5.

prick (prik), *v.* [< ME. *pricken, prikken, prykien* (pret. *prikkede, pryghte*), < AS. *prician, priccan* = D. *prikken* = MLG. *pricken*, LG. *pricken, prikken, preken* = G. *pricken* = Icel. *prika* = Dan. *prikke* = Sw. *pricka* (cf. D. *prikkelen* = LG. *prickeln, prikkeln, prökeln* = G. *prickeln*), prick; from the noun.] **I.** *trans.* **1.** To pierce with a sharp point; puncture; wound.

With her beek hirselven . . . she *pryghte*.
Chaucer, Squire's Tale, l. 410.

I would your cambric were sensible as your finger, that you might leave *pricking* it for pity. *Shak.*, Cor., i. 3. 96.

A spear
Prick'd sharply his own cuirass.
Tennyson, Lancelot and Elaine.

2. To fix or insert by the point: as, to *prick* a knife into a board.—**3.** To transfix or impale.

And the ffirst good stroke John Steward stroke,
Child Maurice head he did cleeve,
And he *pricked* it on his swords poynt,
Went singing there beside.
Childe Maurice (Child's Ballads, II. 317).

4. To fasten by means of a pin or other pointed instrument; stick.

An old hat and 'the humour of forty fancies' *pricked* in 't for a feather. *Shak.*, T. of the S., iii. 2. 70.

5. To pick out with or as with a needle.

A round little worm
Prick'd from the lazy finger of a maid.
Shak., R. and J., i. 4. 66.

6. To spur, as a horse; hence, to stimulate to action; goad; incite; impel.

My duty *pricks* me on to utter that
Which else no worldly good should draw from me.
Shak., T. G. of V., iii. 1. 8.

Even as a Peacock, *prickt* with loues desire
To woo his Mistress, strowting stately by her.
Sylvester, tr. of Du Bartas's Weeks, i. 4.

Well, keep all things so in thy mind that they may be as a goad in thy sides, to *prick* thee forward in the way thou must go. *Bunyan*, Pilgrim's Progress, p. 108.

7. To affect with sharp pain; sting, as with remorse or sorrow.

O thing biseke I yow and warne also,
That ye ne *prikke* with no tormentinge
This tendre mayden, as ye han doon mo.
Chaucer, Clerk's Tale, l. 983.

When they heard this they were *pricked* in their heart.
Acts ii. 37.

8. To cause to point upward; erect: said chiefly of the ears, and primarily of the pointed ears of certain animals, as the horse: generally with *up*: hence, *to prick up the ears*, to listen with eager attention, or evince eager attention.

Then I beat my tabor,
At which, like unback'd colts, they *prick'd* their ears.
Shak., Tempest, iv. 1. 176.

The volunteers *prick'd up their ears.*
Battle of Tranent-Muir (Child's Ballads, VII. 169).

All ears were *prick'd* at once, all tongues were loosed.
Tennyson, Lancelot and Elaine.

9†. To stick upon by way of decoration; stick full, as of flowers or feathers; hence, to decorate; adorn; prink.

I *pricke* a cuppe or suche lyke thynge full of floures, je enfleure. *Palsgrave.* (*Halliwell.*)

I would they [women] would (as they have much *pricking*), when they put on their cap, I would they would have this meditation: "I am now putting on my power upon my head." If they had this thought in their minds, they would not make so much *pricking* up of themselves as they do now a days.
Latimer, Sermons and Remains (Parker Soc. ed.), I. 253. [(*Davies.*)

She [Nature] *prick'd* thee out for women's pleasure.
Shak., Sonnets, xx.

10. To place a point, dot, or similar mark upon; mark. (*a*†) To jot or set down in dots or marks, as music or words. See *counterpoint*[2] (etymology) and *pricksong*.

All that poites haue *pricket* of his prise dedis,
I haue no tome for to telle ne tary no lengur.
Destruction of Troy (E. E. T. S.), l. 306.

A faire rul'd singing hooke; the word
Perfect, if it were *prickt*.
Marston, Antonio and Mellida, I., v. 1.

He . . . did sing the whole from the words without any musique *prickt*, and played all along upon a harpsicon most admirably, and the composition most excellent.
Pepys, Diary, III. 41.

(*b*) To designate by a mark or dot; hence, to choose or select. Compare *pricking for sheriffs*, under *pricking*.

Oct. Your brother too must die; consent you, Lepidus?
Lep. I do consent.
Oct. *Prick* him down, Antony. . . .
Ant. He shall not live; look, with a spot I damn him.
Shak., J. C., iv. 1. 3.

Your husband, gentlewoman! why, he never was a soldier.
Ay, but a lady got him *prickt* for a captain.
Dekker and Webster, Northward Ho, v. 1.

11. To mark or trace by puncturing.

Has she a Bodkin and a Card?
She'll *prick* her Mind.
Prior, An English Padlock.

When, playing with thy vesture's tissu'd flowers, . . .
I *prick'd* them into paper with a pin.
Cowper, My Mother's Picture.

12. To trace or track by the marks or footsteps, as a hare.

Prick ye the fearful hare through cross-ways, sheepwalks. *Fletcher*, Beggars' Bush, iii. 4.

Send forth your woodmen then into the walks,
Or let them *prick* her footing hence.
B. *Jonson*, Sad Shepherd, ii. 2.

13. *Naut.*, to run a middle seam through the cloth of (a sail).—**Pricking-up coat**, in *building*, the first coating of plaster upon lath.

The first or *pricking-up* coat is of coarse stuff put on with a trowel to form a key behind the laths.
Workshop Receipts, 1st ser., p. 122.

Prick the garter. Same as *fast and loose* (*a*) (which see, under *fast*[1]).—**To prick a cartridge**, to pierce a hole leading into the chamber of the cartridge which contains the charge, in order to provide for the priming a clear passage to the powder.—**To prick out**, in *gardening*, to plant out, as seedlings from a greenhouse to an open border.

Shallow . . . wooden boxes . . . are very useful for seed-sowing, for *pricking out* seedlings, or for planting cuttings. *Encyc. Brit.*, XII. 240.

To prick the ship off, to mark the ship's position in latitude and longitude on a chart.—**To prick up**, in *plastering*, to plaster with the first of three coats.

The wall is first *pricked up* with a coat of lime and hair.
Workshop Receipts, 1st ser., p. 122.

II. *intrans.* **1**†. To aim, as at a point or mark.

The devil hath *pricked* at this mark, to frustrate the cross of Christ. *Latimer*, Sermon of the Plough.

Let Christ be your scope and mark to *prick* at; let him be your pattern to work by.
J. Bradford, Letters (Parker Soc., 1853), II. 80.

2. To give a sensation as of being pricked or punctured with a sharp point; also, to have such a sensation.

Have you no convulsions, *pricking* aches, sir?
Middleton (*and others*), The Widow, iv. 2.

When the blood creeps, and the nerves *prick*
And tingle. *Tennyson*, In Memoriam, l.

3. To spur on; ride rapidly; post; speed.

He *prikketh* thurgh a fair forest.
Chaucer, Sir Thopas, l. 43.

A gentle knight was *pricking* on the plaine.
Spenser, F. Q., I. i. 1.

Still at the gallop *prick'd* the knight:
His merry-men follow'd as they might.
Scott, L. of the L., v. 18.

4. To point upward; stand erect.

The spires
Prick'd with incredible pinnacles into heaven.
Tennyson, Holy Grail.

5. To dress one's self for show; prink. *Latimer.* —**6.** To germinate. *Halliwell.* [Prov. Eng.]

If beer which no longer *pricks* is pumped into another barrel without stirring up the sediment, it will again *prick* in the new barrel, a proof that it ferments more vigorously.
Thausing, Beer (trans.), p. 672.

7. To become acid or sour. Wine is said to be *pricked* when it is very slightly soured, as when the bottles have been kept in too warm a place.

It [salmon] is generally bought for 7*s.* a kit, a little bit *pricked*; but if good, the price is from 12*s.* to 18*s.*
Mayhew, London Labour and London Poor, I. 68.

Prick at the loop. Same as *fast and loose* (*a*) (which see, under *fast*[1]).—**To prick up**, to freshen, as the wind.

prickant† (prik'ant), *a.* [< ME. *prickand*; old ppr. of *prick*, *v.*] Pricking. (*a*) Pointing upward.

Without his door doth hang
A copper basin on a *prickant* spear.
Beau. and Fl., Knight of Burning Pestle, iii. 2.

(b) Spurring on; traveling; errant.

What knight is that, squire? ask him if he keep
The passage bound by love of lady fair,
Or else but *prickant*.
Beau. and Fl., Knight of Burning Pestle, ii. 5.

prick-eared (prik'ērd), *a.* Having pointed ears. [This epithet was commonly applied by the English Cavaliers to the Puritans, because, their hair being cut close all around, their ears stood out prominently.]

Pish for thee, Iceland dog! thou *prick-ear'd* cur of Iceland! *Shak.*, Hen. V., ii. 1. 44.

pricked (prikt), *p. a.* 1. In *ceram.*, ornamented with small indentations made by the end of a slender rod, or, for economy of time, with a sort of comb of from three to six teeth. The depressions, arranged in lines, zigzags, etc., and alternating with continuous lines drawn by a point, form often the sole decoration of simple pottery.
2. Same as *piqué*.

pricker (prik'ėr), *n.* [< ME. *priker, preker*; < *prick* + *-er*[1].] 1. That which pricks; a sharp-pointed instrument; a prickle. Specifically—(*a*) A saddlers' implement, usually a bifurcated tool for marking equidistant holes for stitching. (*b*) A needle used by draftsmen for marking points or measurements on drawing-paper, also for pricking through important points of a drawing, in order to locate such points on an underlaid sheet. (*c*) A slender iron rod, usually provided with a cross-handle at the top, used to sound the depths of bogs, or in searching for timber embedded in soft muck. (*d*) A spur or climbing-iron, either strapped to the boot or to the wrist, or grasped in the hand, for aid in climbing trees, telegraph-poles, flagstaffs, etc.

He had iron *prickers* to the hands and feet to aid in climbing lofty trees. *Annals of Phil. and Penn.*, II. 20.

(*e*) A small tool, resembling in form and use a fid or marlinespike, with a wooden handle, used by sail-makers. (*f*) A piercing implement used in a machine for manufacturing card-foundations. (*g*) A priming-needle of pointed copper wire, used in blasting. It is inserted in the charge of powder centrally with reference to the drilled hole, and the tamping is packed around it. On its withdrawal a hole is left, into which fine powder is poured, and a fuse is then connected with the top of the hole. (*h*) In *gun.*, a sharp wire introduced through the touch-hole of a gun to pierce the cartridge, thus opening a communication between the powder in the cartridge and the priming-powder when the gun is primed. (*i*) An implement for extracting primers from spent central-fire cartridges for small-arms, when the cases are to be reloaded. (*j*) A long iron rod with a sharp point, a kind of pointed crowbar, used in some of the English coal-mines for bringing down the coal from overhead, and for some other purposes.
2. One who pricks. Specifically—(*a*) A light horseman.

Send *prekers* to the price toune, and plaunte there my segge.
Bot if thay profre me the pece be processe of tyme.
Morte Arthure (E. E. T. S.), l. 355.

This sort of spur [consisting of only one point, but of an enormous length and thickness] was worn by a body of light horsemen in the reign of Henry VIII., thence called *prickers*. *Archæologia*, VIII. 113.

Northumbrian *prickers*, wild and rude.
Scott, Marmion, v. 17.

(*b*) One who tested whether women were witches by sticking pins into them; a witch-finder. *Imp. Dict.*
3. In *ichth.*, the basking-shark.

pricket (prik'et), *n.* [< ME. *priket, pryket*; < *prick* + *-et*.] 1. A sharp iron point upon which a candle may be stuck; hence, a candlestick, either separate or one of several connected together. Also *prick*.

Item, ij *prikettys* of silver.
Invent. of Sir John Fastolf's Goods, Paston Letters, I. 470.

Pricket. (From Viollet-le-Duc's "Dict. du Mobilier français.")

Hence—2. A wax taper.

To carry to the chaundrie all the remaine of . . . torches, . . . *prickets*, wholly and intirely.
Quoted in *Babees Book* (E. E. T. S.), ii. 108.

iiij. d. for ij. *pryketts* of wax barnyng to the same obett [funeral service]. *English Gilds* (E. E. T. S.), p. 326.

3. A buck in his second year: probably so called from his horns. See *spike*.

I went to raunge amydde the mazie thickette, . . .
And joyed oft to chace the trembling *Pricket*.
Spenser, Shep. Cal., December.

I said the deer was not a haud credo; 'twas a *pricket*.
Shak., L. L. L., iv. 2. 22.

4. The wall-pepper or biting stonecrop, *Sedum acre*. [Eng.]—**Pricket's sister**, the female of the fallow-deer in its second year. *W. W. Greener*, The Gun, p. 508.

pricking (prik'ing), *n.* [Verbal n. of *prick*, *v.*] 1. The act of piercing with a sharp point; a stinging or tingling sensation.

By the *pricking* of my thumbs,
Something wicked this way comes.
Shak., Macbeth, iv. 1. 44.

Specifically, in *farriery*: (*a*) The act of driving a nail into a horse's foot with the result of causing lameness. (*b*) The making of an incision at the root of a horse's tail to cause him to carry it higher. See *nick*[1], *v. t.*
2†. Musical notation.

Even in 1597 that learned theorist and composer, Thomas Morley, speaking of the notation found in ancient written music, said: "That order of *pricking* is gone out of vse now, so that wee vse the blacke voides as they vsed their black fulles, and the blacke fulles as they vsed the redde fulles." *York Plays*, p. 524.

3†. The prick or mark left by the foot of an animal, as a hare or deer; also, the act of tracking an animal by such marks.

Those [hounds] which cannot discerne the footings or *prickings* of the hare, yet will they runne speedily when they see her.
Topsell, Four-footed Beasts (1607), p. 152. (*Halliwell.*)

4. The condition of becoming sour, as wine. *Howell*.—5. *pl.* The slips of evergreens with which the churches are decorated from Christmas eve to the eve of Candlemas day. *Halliwell*. [Prov. Eng.]—**Pricking for sheriffs**, the ceremony of selecting one of three persons for each county in England and Wales to serve as sheriff for the ensuing year. The ceremony is so called from the circumstance that the appointment is made by marking the name with the prick of a point. See the quotation.

The Lord Lieutenant prepares a list of persons qualified to serve, and returns three names, which are read out in the Court of Queen's Bench upon the morrow of All Souls' Day, when the excuses of such as do not wish to serve are heard, and, if deemed sufficient, the objector is discharged. The list is then sent to the Sovereign, who, without looking at it, strikes a bodkin amongst the names, and he whose name is pierced is elected. This is called *pricking for sheriffs*. *A. Fonblanque, Jr.*, How we are Governed, ix.

Pricking up, in *building*, the first coating of plaster upon the lath.

pricking-note (prik'ing-nōt), *n.* A document delivered by a shipper of goods authorizing the receiving of them on board: so called from a practice of pricking holes in the paper corresponding with the number of packages counted into the ship.

pricking-wheel (prik'ing-hwēl), *n.* A tool used by saddlers to travel over the leather and mark the number of stitches to the inch; a stitch-wheel.

prickle (prik'l), *n.* [< ME. *prikel, prikil* (partly with loss of terminal *s*), < AS. *pricele, pricle, pricel*, also *pricels* (= D. *prikkel* = MLG. *prekel*, LG. *prickel, prikkel, prekkel* = G. *prickel*), a sharp point, < *prica, pricu*, a point: see *prick*.] 1. A little prick; a small sharp point; in *bot.*, a small sharp-pointed conical process growing from the bark only, as in the rose and blackberry, and thus distinguished from the spine or thorn, which is usually a modified branch or leaf growing from the wood of the plant.

The sweetest Rose hath his *prickell*.
Lyly, Euphues, Anat. of Wit, p. 33.

The leaf was darkish, and had *prickles* on it.
Milton, Comus, l. 631.

2. A sharp-pointed process or projection, as from the skin of an animal; a spine.—3. The sensation of being pricked or stung. [Colloq.]

All o' me thet wuzn't sore an' sendin' *prickles* thru me
Was jist the leg I parted with in lickin' Montezumy.
Lowell, Biglow Papers, 2d ser., i.

4. A kind of basket: still used in some trades. See the second quotation.

Well done, my pretty ones, rain roses still,
Until the last be dropt; then hence, and fill
Your fragrant *prickles* for a second shower.
B. *Jonson*, Pan's Anniversary.

The *prickle* is a brown willow basket in which walnuts are imported into this country from the Continent; they are about thirty inches deep, and in bulk rather larger than a gallon measure.
Mayhew, London Labour and London Poor, I. 27.

5. A sieve of filberts, containing about half of a hundredweight. *Simmonds*.

prickle (prik'l), *v.*; pret. and pp. *prickled*, ppr. *prickling*. [= LG. *prickeln, prikkeln, prokeln* = G. *prickeln*, prick: see *prickle, n., prick*.] I. *trans.* 1. To prick or puncture slightly; pierce with fine sharp points.—2. To cause a pricking sensation in: said of the skin.

I . . .
Felt a horror over me creep,
Prickle my skin and catch my breath.
Tennyson, Maud, xiv. 4.

3. To cover with pricks or points; dot.

Evening shadowed; the violet deepened and *prickled* itself with stars. *Harper's Mag.*, LXXVI. 753.

II. *intrans.* To be prickly.

The fragrant Eglantine did spred
His *prickling* armes, entrayld with roses red.
Spenser, F. Q., II. v. 29.

prickleback (prik'l-bak), *n.* The stickleback. Also *prickle-fish* and *pricklyback*.

prickle-cell (prik'l-sel), *n.* One of the rounded or polyhedral cells, marked on their surface with numerous ridges, furrows, or minute spines, which form the stratum spinosum of the epidermis.

prickled (prik'ld), *a.* [< *prickle* + *-ed*[2].] Furnished with prickles.

The *prickled* perch in every hollow creek
Hard by the bank and sandy shore is fed.
J. Dennys (Arber's Eng. Garner, I. 186).

prickle-fish (prik'l-fish), *n.* Same as *prickleback*.

prickle-layer (prik'l-lā″ėr), *n.* The lowest stratum of the epidermis; the stratum spinosum, next below the stratum granulosum. It is formed of prickle-cells, the lowest layer being prismatic, and resting on the corium.

prickle-yellow (prik'l-yel″ō), *n.* See *prickly yellowwood*, under *yellowwood*.

prickliness (prik'li-nes), *n.* The state of being prickly, or having many prickles.

pricklouse (prik'lous), *n.*; pl. *pricklice* (-līs). [< *prick, v.*, + obj. *louse*.] A tailor: so called in contempt. Also *prick-the-louse*.

A taylour and his wife quarrelling, the woman in contempt called her husband *pricklouse*. *Sir R. L'Estrange*.

prick-lugged (prik'lugd), *a.* Having erect ears; prick-eared. *Halliwell*.

prickly (prik'li), *a.* [< *prickle* + *-y*[1].] 1. Full of sharp points or prickles; armed with prickles: as, a *prickly* shrub.

The common, over-grown with fern, and rough
With *prickly* gorse. *Cowper*, Task, i. 527.

2. Pricking or stinging; noting the sensation of being pricked or stung.—**Prickly cat†**. See *cat*[1], 8.—**Prickly comfrey**. See *comfrey*.—**Prickly glasswort**. See *glasswort* and *kelpwort*.—**Prickly heat, lettuce, licorice**, etc. See the nouns.

prickly-ash (prik'li-ash'), *n.* A shrub or small tree, *Xanthoxylum Americanum*, with ash-like leaves, and branches armed with strong prickles. Its bark is an active stimulant, used in a fluid extract as a diaphoretic in chronic rheumatism, and popularly as a masticatory to cure toothache. Hence called *toothache-tree*, as is also the species *X. Clava-Herculis* (also called *prickly-ash*), which grows further south, and probably has similar properties.

pricklyback (prik'li-bak), *n.* 1. Same as *prickleback*.—2. The edible crab, *Callinectes hastatus*, when the new shell is only partially hardened; a shedder. [Long Island.]

prickly-broom (prik'li-bröm'), *n.* The furze, *Ulex Europæus*.

prickly-cedar (prik'li-sē'dạr), *n.* A juniper of southern Europe, *Juniperus Oxycedrus*.

prickly-grass (prik'li-gràs), *n.* Any grass of the old genus *Echinochloa*, now referred to *Panicum*.

prickly-pear (prik'li-pãr'), *n.* 1. The fruit of cacti of the genus *Opuntia*, a pear-shaped or ovoid berry, in many cases juicy and edible, armed with prickles or nearly smooth.—2. Any plant of this genus, primarily *O. vulgaris* (or *O. Rafinesquii*, which is not always distinguished from it). See *Opuntia*. These are native in barren ground on the eastern coast of the United States, the latter also in the upper Mississippi valley, the most northern species. With other members of the genus, they bear edible berries or pears. Some species support the cochineal-insect. (See *cochineal*.) Various species are available as uninflammable hedge-plants. *O. Tuna, O. vulgaris, O. Ficus-Indica*, and others are cultivated and more or less naturalized around the Mediterranean, etc., and their fruit is largely gathered for the market. Also called *Indian fig*.

prickly-pole (prik'li-pōl'), *n.* A West Indian palm, *Bactris Plumeriana*: so called from its slender trunks, which are ringed with long black prickles at intervals of half an inch. The stems grow in tufts, and are sometimes 40 feet high. The wood is said to be elastic, and suitable for bows and rammers.

prickly-spined (prik'li-spīnd), *a.* Acanthopterygious, as a fish or its fins.

prickly-withe (prik'li-with'), *n.* A cactaceous plant, *Cereus triangularis*, found in Mexico and Jamaica. It has climbing and rooting branches, which are three-cornered and armed with prickles.

prickmadam†, *n.* An old name of three species of stonecrop—*Sedum acre, S. album*, and *S. reflexum*.

prick-me-dainty, prick-ma-dainty (prik'mē-, prik'mạ-dān'ti), *a.* and *n.* I. *a.* Characterized by finical language or manners; finical; over-precise. [Scotch.]

"Nane of your doll's play-books for me," said she; "it's an ill warld since sic *prick-my-dainty* doings came in fashion." *Scott*, St. Ronan's Well, xii.

II. *n.* A finical, affected person. [Scotch.]

prick-post (prik'pōst), *n.* In *arch.*, same as *queen-post*.

prick-punch (prik'punch), *n.* Same as *center-punch*.

prick-shaft† (prik'shàft), *n.* An arrow used in shooting at a prick or target.

Who with her hellish courage, stout and hot,
Abides the brunt of many a *prickshaft* shot.
John Taylor, Works (1630). (*Nares.*)

I am sorry you are so bad an Archer, . . . to shoote at Buts when you shou'd use *prick-shafts*; short shooting will loose ye the game. *Rowley*, Match at Midnight, ii. 1.

prickshot (prik'shot), *n.* A bowshot; the space between an archer and the mark. *Davies.*

The tents, as I noted them, were divided into four several orders and rewes [rows] lying east and west, and a *prickshot* asunder. *Patten* (Arber's Eng. Garner, III. 99).

pricksong† (prik'sông), *n.* [< *prick* + *song*.] 1. Written music as distinguished from that which is extemporaneous.

He fights as you sing *pricksong*, keeps time, distance, and proportion; rests me his minim rest, one, two, and the third in your bosom. *Shak.*, R. and J., ii. 4. 21.

I can sing *pricksong*, lady, at first sight.
Chapman, Bussy D'Ambois, i. 1.

2. A descant or counterpoint as distinguished from a cantus firmus; contrapuntal music in general.

But yet, as I would have this sort of music decay among scholars, even so do I wish, from the bottom of my heart, that the laudable custom of England to teach children their plain song and *prick-song* were not so decayed throughout all the realm as it is.
Ascham, Toxophilus (ed. 1864), p. 29.

On the early morrow, Dirige, followed by two Masses, . . . the second . . . accompanied by the organ, and chanted in *prick-song*, or, as we would call it, florid music.
Rock, Church of our Fathers, ii. 503.

prick-spur (prik'spėr), *n.* A goad-spur.

prick-the-garter (prik'ᴛʜē-gär'tėr), *n.* Same as *fast and loose* (which see, under *fast*[1]).

Prick-spurs of the 13th century.

prick-the-louse (prik'ᴛʜē-lous'), *n.* Same as *pricklouse*.

Gae mind your seam, ye
prick-the-louse!
Burns, To a Tailor.

prick-timber (prik'tim'bėr), *n.* The spindle-tree, *Euonymus Europæus*; also, the European dogwood, *Cornus sanguinea*: so called because their stems are used to make skewers, goads, etc. Also *prickwood*.

prick-wand† (prik'wond), *n.* A wand set up for a mark to shoot arrows at. *Percy.* (*Halliwell.*)

prick-wheel (prik'hwēl), *n.* A rolling-stamp with sharp points which prick a row of dots or holes. It is used for marking out patterns, and is therefore also called a *pattern-wheel*.

prickwood (prik'wůd), *n.* Same as *prick-timber*.

pricky† (prik'i), *a.* [< *prick* + *-y*[1].] Prickly.

A *prickie* stalke it hath of the owne; . . . *prickie* moreouer it is like a thorne.
Holland, tr. of Pliny, xix. 3. (*Davies.*)

pride[1] (prīd), *n.* [ME. *pride*, *pryde*, *prude*, *pruide*, *pruyde*, *prute*, < AS. *prȳto* (= Icel. *prȳdhi* = Dan. *pryd*, ornament), pride, < *prūt*, *prȳt*, proud: see *proud*.] 1. The state or condition of being proud, or a feeling of elation or exultation on account of what one is or has or is connected with, in any sense. (*a*) Inordinate self-esteem; an unreasonable estimate of one's own superiority, which manifests itself in lofty airs, reserve, and often in contempt of others.

Pride goeth before destruction, and an haughty spirit before a fall. Prov. xvi. 18.

You sign your place and calling, in full seeming,
With meekness and humility; but your heart
Is cramm'd with arrogancy, spleen, and *pride*.
Shak., Hen. VIII., ii. 4. 110.

Pride relates more to our opinion of ourselves; vanity to what we would have others think of us.
Jane Austen, Pride and Prejudice, I. v.

(*b*) A becoming and dignified sense of what is due to one's personality, character, or position; firm self-respect.

He left his guests, and to his cottage turned,
And as he entered for a moment yearned
For the lost splendors of the days of old, . . .
And felt how bitter is the sting of *pride*,
By want embittered and intensified.
Longfellow, Wayside Inn, Student's Tale.

Gray's *pride* was not, as it sometimes is, allied to vanity; it was personal rather than social, if I may attempt a distinction which I feel but can hardly define.
Lowell, New Princeton Rev., I. 166.

(*c*) A reasonable feeling of elation or exultation in view of one's doings, achievements, or possessions, or those of a person or persons intimately connected with one.

Thus to relieve the wretched was his *pride*,
And e'en his failings leaned to virtue's side.
Goldsmith, Des. Vil., l. 163.

I felt a *pride*
In gaining riches for my destined bride.
Crabbe, Works, IV. 89.

We all take a *pride* in sharing the epidemic economy of the time. *O. W. Holmes*, Old Vol. of Life, p. 1.

Taking *pride* in her,
She look'd so sweet, he kiss'd her tenderly.
Tennyson, Aylmer's Field.

2. Haughty or arrogant bearing or conduct; overbearing treatment of others; insolent exultation; vainglorying.

For all that is in the world, the lust of the flesh, and the lust of the eyes, and the *pride* of life, is not of the Father. 1 John ii. 16.

Pride in their port, defiance in their eye,
I see the lords of humankind pass by.
Goldsmith, Traveller, l. 327.

3. Exuberance of animal spirits; warmth of temperament; mettle.

The colt that 's back'd and burden'd being young
Loseth his *pride* and never waxeth strong.
Shak., Venus and Adonis, l. 420.

His heart was warm, his *pride* was up,
Sweet Willie kentna fear.
Willie and May Margaret (Child's Ballads, II. 172).

Hence—4. Lust; sexual desire; especially, the excitement of the sexual appetite in a female animal.

As salt as wolves in *pride*. *Shak.*, Othello, iii. 3. 404.

5†. Wantonness; extravagance; excess; hence, impertinence; impudence.

He hath it when he cannot use it,
And leaves it to be master'd by his young;
Who in their *pride* do presently abuse it.
Shak., Lucrece, l. 864.

6. That which is or may be a cause of pride; that of which men are proud. (*a*) Any person, body of persons, or object possessed which causes others to delight or glory.

A hold peasantry, their country's *pride*,
When once destroyed, can never be supplied.
Goldsmith, Des. Vil., l. 55.

See yon pale stripling! when a boy,
A mother's *pride*, a father's joy!
Scott, Rokeby, iii. 15.

(*b*) Highest pitch; elevation; loftiness; the best or most admired part of a thing; the height; full force, extent, or quantity.

Now we have seen the *pride* of Nature's work,
We'll take our leave. *Marlowe*, Doctor Faustus, v. 3.

A falcon, towering in her *pride* of place,
Was by a mousing owl hawk'd at and kill'd.
Shak., Macbeth, ii. 4. 12.

Now may it please your highnesse to leaue your discontented passions, and take this morninge *pride* to hunt the Bore. *Chapman*, Blind Begger of Alexandria (Works, [1873), I. 17.

We are puppets, Man in his *pride*, and Beauty fair in her flower. *Tennyson*, Maud, iv. 5.

A fine roe at this season [December] makes better venison than either red or fallow deer; but when not in the *pride* of their grease their flesh is so much carrion.
W. W. Greener, The Gun, p. 513.

(*c*) Decoration; ornament; beauty displayed; specifically, in *her.*, a term applicable to the peacock, turkey-cock, and other birds which spread their tails in a circular form, and drop their wings: as, a peacock in his *pride*.

Whose loftie trees, yclad with sommers *pride*,
Did spred so broad that heavens light did hide.
Spenser, F. Q., I. i. 7.

The purple *pride*
Which on thy [the Violet's] soft cheek for complexion dwells. *Shak.*, Sonnets, xcix.

Be his this sword . . .
Whose ivory sheath, inwrought with curious *pride*,
Adds graceful terror to the wearer's side.
Pope, Odyssey, viii. 439.

(*d*) Splendid show; ostentation.

The madams too,
Not used to toil, did almost sweat to bear
The *pride* upon them. *Shak.*, Hen. VIII., i. 1. 25.

In this array, the war of either side
Through Athens pass'd with military *pride*.
Dryden, Pal. and Arc., iii. 102.

7†. A company or group (of lions).

When beasts went together in companies, there was said to be a *pride* of lions.
Strutt, Sports and Pastimes, p. 80.

8. Lameness; impediment. *Halliwell.* [Prov. Eng.] =**Syn.** 1. *Pride*, *Egotism*, *Vanity*, etc. (see *egotism*), self-exaltation, self-sufficiency, vainglory.—2. *Pride*, *Arrogance*, *Presumption*, etc. (see *arrogance*), lordliness, hauteur.—6. Ornament, glory, splendor.

pride[1] (prīd), *v.*; pret. and pp. *prided*, ppr. *priding*. [= Icel. *prȳdha* = Sw. *pryda* = Dan. *pryde*, adorn, ornament; from the noun.] I. *trans.* 1. To indulge in pride, elation, or self-esteem; value (one's self): used reflexively.

In the production whereof Prometheus had strangely and insufferably *prided himself*.
Bacon, Physical Fables, ii.

Many a man, instead of learning humility in practice, confesses himself a poor sinner, and next *prides himself* upon the confession.
J. H. Newman, Parochial Sermons, i. 28.

2. To spread, as a bird its tail-feathers.

Prideth her feathers, superbit pennis.
Hoole, Visible World, p. 26.

II. *intrans.* To be proud; exult; glory: sometimes with indefinite *it*.

Those who *pride* in being scholars. *Swift.*

Neither were the vain glories content to *pride it* upon success. *Bp. Hacket*, Abp. Williams, II. 203. (*Davies.*)

I regretted he was no more; he would so much have *prided* and rejoiced in showing his place.
Mme. D'Arblay, Diary, V. 30. (*Davies.*)

pride[2] (prīd), *n.* [Origin uncertain.] A kind of lamprey; especially, the mud-lamprey. See *Ammocœtes* and *lamprey*. Also *sand-pride* and *pride of the Isis*. [Local, Eng.]

Lumbrici are littell fysshes taken in small ryvers, whiche are lyke to lampurnes, but they be muche lesse, and somewhat yeolowe, and are called in Wilshyre *prides*.
Elyotes Dictionarie (fol., Lond., 1559). (*Halliwell.*)

We call it a lamperon; Plot calls it the *pride of the Isis*.
Hill, Hist. of Animals, p. 295.

Pride-gavel, a tax or tribute paid in certain places for the privilege of fishing for lampreys.

prideful (prīd'fůl), *a.* [< *pride*[1] + *-ful*.] Full of pride; insolent; scornful.

Then, thus indignant he accosts the foe
(While high disdain sat *prideful* on his brow).
P. Whitehead, The Gymnasiad, iii.

Then, in wrath,
Depart, he cried, perverse and *prideful* nymph.
W. Richardson.

pridefully (prīd'fůl-i), *adv.* In a prideful manner; scornfully.

pridefulness (prīd'fůl-nes), *n.* The state or condition of being prideful; scornfulness; also, vanity.

A white kirtle the wench wears—to hide the dust of the mill, no doubt—and a blue hood, that might weel be spared, for *pridefulness*. *Scott*, Monastery, viii.

prideless (prīd'les), *a.* [< *pride*[1] + *-less*.] Free from pride.

Discreet and *prydeles*, ay honurable.
Chaucer, Clerk's Tale, l. 874.

pride-of-Barbados (prīd'ọv-bär-bā'dōz), *n.* A shrub: same as *flower-fence*.

pride-of-China (prīd'ọv-chī'nạ̈), *n.* Same as *pride-of-India*. See *Melia*.

pride-of-Columbia (prīd'ọv-kọ̄-lum'bi-ạ̈), *n.* An ornamental plant, *Phlox speciosa*, of western North America.

pride-of-India (prīd'ọv-in'di-ạ̈), *n.* An ornamental tree, *Melia Azedarach*.

pride-of-London (prīd'ọv-lun'dun), *n.* Same as *London-pride*, 2.

pride-of-Ohio (prīd'ọv-ọ̄-hī'ō), *n.* An elegant plant, the shooting-star, *Dodecatheon Meadia*.

Pride's Purge. See *purge*.

pridian (prid'i-ạn), *a.* [< L. *pridianus*, < *prius*, before (see *prior*), + *dies*, day: see *dial*.] Pertaining or relating to the previous day; of yesterday.

Thrice a week at least does Gann breakfast in bed—sure sign of *pridian* intoxication.
Thackeray, Shabby Genteel Story, ii.

pridingly (prī'ding-li), *adv.* With pride; in pride of heart.

He *pridingly* doth set himself before all others.
Barrow, Pope's Supremacy.

pridy (prī'di), *a.* [< *pride*[1] + *-y*[1].] Proud. *Halliwell.* [Prov. Eng.]

prie[1]†, *v. i.* An obsolete form of *pry*[1].

prie[2], *v. t.* See *pree*.

prie[3]†, *n.* [Cf. *privet*.] A shrub, the common privet, *Ligustrum vulgare*.

prie-dieu (prē-diė'), *n.* [F., < *prier*, pray, + *dieu*, God.] 1. Same as *praying-desk*.

A great bedstead of carved oak, black with age, . . . flanked by a grimy *prie-dieu* and a wardrobe equally venerable. *The Century*, XXXVI. 239.

2. In *entom.*, a praying-mantis.

prief† (prēf), *n.* An obsolete form of *proof*.

prier (prī'ėr), *n.* One who pries; one who inquires narrowly; one who searches or scrutinizes. Also spelled *pryer*.

The moderation of the king . . . set the monks, the constant *pryers* into futurity, upon prophecying that the reign of this prince was to be equal in length to that of his father Yasous the Great.
Bruce, Source of the Nile, II. 577.

priest (prēst), *n.* [< ME. *preest*, *prest*, *prust*, *preost*, *pruest*, < AS. *preóst* = OS. *prēstre*, *priester* = OFries. *prēstere* = D. *priester* = MLG. *prēster* = OHG. *priestar*, MHG. G. *priester* = Icel. *prestr* = Sw. *prest* = Dan. *præst* = OF. *prestre* (> ME. *prester*, q. v.), F. *prêtre* = Sp. *preste* = OPg. *preste* = It. *prete*, a priest, < LL. *presbyter*, a presbyter, elder: see *presbyter*.] 1. One who is duly authorized to be a minister of sacred things; one whose stated duty it is to perform, on behalf of the community, certain public religious acts, particularly religious sacrifices.

And the *priest* shall make an atonement for them, and it shall be forgiven them. Lev. iv. 20.

On a seate of the same Chariot, a little more eleuate, sate Eunomia, the Virgine *Priest* of the Goddesse Honor. *Chapman*, Masque of the Middle Temple and Lincoln's Inn.

Prayers which in this golden censer, mix'd
With incense, I thy *priest* before thee bring.
Milton, P. L., xi. 25.

To what green altar, O mysterious *priest*,
Leadst thou that heifer lowing at the skies?
Keats, Grecian Urn.

2. One who is ordained to the pastoral or sacerdotal office; a presbyter; an elder. In Wyclif the word *priest* is used where in Tyndale and the authorized version the word *elder* is used; for example, "For this cause left I thee in Crete, that thou shouldest reforme the things that are wanting, and shouldest ordaine *priestes* (presbyters, πρεσβυτέρους; authorized version *elders*) by cities as I also appointed thee" (Titus i. 5).
3. Specifically, in hierarchical churches, the second in rank in the clerical orders, between bishop and deacon. Etymologically, the word *priest* is a derivative or modification of the word *presbyter*. As, however, the office of the presbyterate has been regarded in the Christian church from primitive or early times as a sacerdotal office in so far as it confers power to celebrate the eucharist and to confer absolution, and as no church officer below a presbyter can exercise these functions, and all above a presbyter continue to exercise them in virtue of their ordination as presbyters, the title of *presbyter* and that of *sacerdos* or ἱερεύς (sacrificing priest) soon came to be regarded as synonymous, and either one or the other of these titles to be preferred in popular use in different languages, to the exclusion of its synonym. The title of *priest* (ἱερεύς, *sacerdos*) was in the early church given by preëminence to the bishop (specifically the *high priest*) as ordinary celebrant of the eucharist in cities and the fountain of sacerdotal authority. The Roman Catholic Church teaches that it is the office of a priest "to offer, bless, rule, preach, and baptize." These same offices are assigned to priests in the Orthodox Greek and other Oriental churches and in the Anglican Church. In the church last named the form of ordination gives authority to forgive or retain sins and be a dispenser of the word and sacraments, and only priests (including bishops as in priest's orders) can give benediction, pronounce absolution, and consecrate the eucharist.

And xxvij Day of August, Decessyd Syr Thomas Toppe, a *prest* of the west countre.
Torkington, Diarie of Eng. Travell, p. 56.

It is evident unto all men, diligently reading Holy Scripture and ancient Authors, that from the Apostles' time there have been these orders of Ministers in Christ's Church — Bishops, Priests, and Deacons.
Book of Common Prayer, Preface to the Ordinal.

4. A breed of domestic pigeons, in four different color-varieties, black, blue, red, and yellow. —**5.** A mark composed of two concentric circles, used as a private stamp, a brand for cattle, and the like in England.—**Cardinal priest.** See *cardinal*, *n.*, 1.—**Chantry priest**, a priest employed to say mass in a chantry for the soul of the founder or other person, or for some specified intention. See *chantry*. —**High priest**, a chief priest. Specifically—(*a*) The chief ecclesiastical officer in the ancient Jewish church. He exercised certain judicial and quasi-political functions, as well as functions of a purely sacerdotal character; but his power varied at different periods of Jewish history. He alone entered the Holy of Holies in the temple; he was the arbiter in all religious matters, and to him lay the final appeal in all controversies. In later times he was the head of the Sanhedrim, and next in rank to the sovereign.

The priests went always into the first tabernacle. . . . But into the second went the *high priest* alone once every year. Heb. ix. 7.

(*b*) In the *early Christian church*, a bishop. (*c*) A member of an order in the Mormon Church ranking among the higher orders. See *Mormon*[2].—**Massing priest**†. See *mass*[1].—**Parish, penitentiary**, etc., **priest**. See the adjectives.—**Penitential priest**. Same as *penitentiary*, 1 and 2.—**Poor Priests**, an order of itinerant preaching clergy, founded by John Wyclif. They preached in different parts of England, in most places without ecclesiastical authority. They wore blue or russet gowns, went barefoot, and were dependent on the hospitality of their hearers for food and lodging. According to some authorities, laymen also were admitted among these preachers. The order was suppressed in 1381 or 1382, not long after its foundation. It had, however, succeeded in disseminating Wycliffite teachings widely throughout England. Also *Poor Preachers*, *Simple Priests*.—**Priest's bonnet**, in *fort.* See *bonnet à prêtre*, under *bonnet*.—**Seminary priest.** See *seminary*.—**The priest**, the celebrant of the eucharist, especially as distinguished from his assistants (deacon, subdeacon, etc.). = **Syn.** *Clergyman*, etc. See *minister*.

priest (prēst), *v.* [‹ *priest*, *n.*] **I.** *trans.* To ordain to the priesthood; make a priest of.

II. *intrans.* To hold the office or exercise the functions of a priest. [Rare.]

Honour God, and the bishop as high-priest, bearing the image of God according to his ruling, and of Christ according to his *priesting*. *Milton*, Prelatical Episcopacy.

priest-cap (prēst'kap), *n.* In *fort.*, an outwork with two salient and three reëntering angles.

Pains attacked with great vigor at what proved to be the strongest point of the whole work, the *priest-cap* near the Jackson road.
R. B. Irwin, in Battles and Leaders of the Civil War, [III. 595.

priestcraft (prēst'kràft), *n.* [‹ *priest* + *craft*.] Priestly policy or system of management based on temporal or material interest; the arts practised by selfish and ambitious priests to gain wealth and power, or to impose on the credulity of others.

From *priestcraft* happily set free,
Lo! every finish'd son returns to thee.
Pope, Dunciad, iv. 499.

Specimens of the *priestcraft* by which the greater part of Christendom had been fooled.
Macaulay, Hist. Eng., vi.

priestcrafty (prēst'kràf"ti), *a.* [‹ *priestcraft* + *-y*[1].] Relating to or characterized by priestcraft. *Worcester*. [Rare.]

priestery† (prēs'tėr-i), *n.* [‹ *priest* + *-cry*.] Priests collectively; the priesthood: in contempt. *Milton*.

priestess (prēs'tes), *n.* [‹ *priest* + *-ess*.] **1.** A woman who officiates in sacred rites.

She, as *priestess*, knows the rites
Wherein the God of earth delights.
Swift, Stella's Birthday, 1722.

2†. The wife or concubine of a priest.

priest-fish (prēst'fish), *n.* [Tr. F. *pêche-prêtre*.] The black rockfish of California, *Sebastichthys mystinus* or *melanops*. It is of a slaty-black color, paler below, and attains a length of a foot or more. It is the most abundant scorpænoid fish about San Francisco, and is found from Puget Sound to San Diego.

Priest-fish (*Sebastichthys mystinus*).

priesthood (prēst'hůd), *n.* [‹ ME. *preesthood*, *presthod*, ‹ AS. *preósthād*, ‹ *preóst*, priest, + *hād*, condition: see *priest* and *-hood*.] **1.** The office or character of a priest.

Chaplain, away! thy *priesthood* saves thy life.
Shak., 3 Hen. VI., i. 3. 3.

2. The order of men set apart for sacred offices; priests collectively.

priest-ill (prēst'il), *n.* The ague. *Halliwell*. [Prov. Eng.]

priestlike (prēst'līk), *a.* [‹ *priest* + *like*.] Resembling a priest, or that which belongs to priests; sacerdotal.

A *priestlike* habit of crimson and purple.
B. Jonson, Masque of Beauty.

The moving waters at their *priestlike* task
Of pure ablution round earth's human shores.
Keats, Last Sonnet.

priestliness (prēst'li-nes), *n.* The quality of being priestly; the appearance and manner of a priest.

priestly (prēst'li), *a.* [‹ ME. *prestly* (= D. *priesterlijk* = MLG. *prēsterlik*, *prēstlik* = OHG. *prēstarlīh*, MHG. *priesterlich*, G. *priesterlich* = Icel. *prestligr* = Sw. *presterlig* = Dan. *præstelig*; ‹ *priest* + *-ly*[1].] **1.** Of or pertaining to a priest or priests; sacerdotal: as, the *priestly* office.

The *priestly* brotherhood, devout, sincere.
Cowper, Expostulation, l. 438.

With . . . that fine piece of *priestly* needle-work she looked like some pious lay-member of a sisterhood.
H. James, Jr., Pass. Pilgrim, p. 297.

2. Befitting a priest: as, *priestly* sobriety and purity of life.

Hie thee, whiles I say
A *priestly* farewell to her.
Shak., Pericles, iii. 1. 70.

priest-monk (prēst'mungk), *n.* In the early church and in the Greek Church, a monk who is a priest; a hieromonach.

priestrid (prēst'rid), *a.* Same as *priestridden*.

Rome — not the toothless beldame of modern days, but the avenging divinity of *priest-rid* monarchs.
Motley, Hist. Netherlands, II. 341.

priestridden (prēst'rid"n), *a.* [‹ *priest* + *ridden*.] Managed or governed by priests; entirely swayed by priests.

That pusillanimity and manless subjugation which by many in our age scornfully is called *priestriddenness*, as I may so say: their term being *priestridden* when they express a man addicted to the clergy.
Waterhouse, Apol. for Learning (1653), p. 82. (*Latham*.)

priestriddenness (prēst'rid"n-nes), *n.* The state of being priestridden. See the quotation under *priestridden*. [Rare.]

priest's-crown (prēsts'kroun), *n.* The common dandelion: so called from its bald receptacle after the achenia are blown away, with allusion to the priestly tonsure. [Prov. Eng.]

Prestes crowne that flyeth about in somer, barbedieu.
Palsgrave. (*Halliwell*.)

prieve† (prēv), *v.* An obsolete form of *prove*.

prig[1] (prig), *v.*; pret. and pp. *prigged*, ppr. *prigging*. [Origin obscure. Cf. OF. *briguer*, steal purses on the highway, also solicit, canvas, intrigue, quarrel: see *brigue*, *brigand*.] **I.** *trans.* **1.** To filch or steal. [Slang.]

Higgen hath *prigg'd* the prancers in his days,
And sold good penny-worths.
Fletcher, Beggar's Bush, v. 2.

They can't find the ring!
And the Abbot declared that, "when nobody twigg'd it,
Some rascal or other had popp'd in and *prigg'd* it!"
Barham, Ingoldsby Legends, I. 211.

2. To cheapen; haggle about. [North. Eng. and Scotch.]

II. *intrans.* To plead hard; haggle. [Scotch.]

Men wha grew wise *priggin'* owre hops an' raisins.
Burns, Brigs of Ayr.

prig[1] (prig), *n.* [Cf. *prig*[1], *v.*] A thief. [Slang.]

Out upon him! *prig*, for my life, *prig*; he haunts wakes, fairs, and bear-baitings. *Shak.*, W. T., iv. 3. 108.

All sorts of villains, knaves, *prigs*, &c., are essential parts of the equipage of life. *De Quincey*.

prig[2] (prig), *n.* [Origin unknown; perhaps a later application of *prig*[1] in the general sense, among "the profession," of 'a smart fellow.'] **1.** A conceited, narrow-minded, pragmatical person; a dull, precise person.

Though swoln with vanity and pride,
You're but one driv'ler multiplied,
A *prig* — that proves himself by starts
As many dolts as there are arts.
Smart, Fables, i.

One of those conceited *prigs* who value nature only as it feeds and exhibits them. *Emerson*, Clubs.

A *prig* is a fellow who is always making you a present of his opinions. *George Eliot*, Middlemarch, xi.

2. A coxcomb; a dandy. [Now prov. Eng.]

A cane is part of the dress of a *prig*, and always worn upon a button, for fear he should be thought to have an occasion for it. *Steele*, Tatler, No. 77.

prig[3] (prig), *v. t.*; pret. and pp. *prigged*, ppr. *prigging*. [Cf. *prick* in like sense.] To dress up; adorn; prink. Compare *prick*, 9.

He's no more use than yer *prigged-up* creepers [vines].
S. Judd, Margaret, i. 4.

prig[4]† (prig), *v. t.* and *i.*; pret. and pp. *prigged*, ppr. *prigging*. [Cf. *prick* in like sense.] To ride. *Dekker*, Lanthorne and Candle-light, sig. C ii. (*Halliwell*.) [Old cant.]

prig[5] (prig), *n.* [Origin obscure. Cf. *pig*[2].] **1.** A small pitcher. *Halliwell*. [Prov. Eng.]—**2.** A small brass skillet. *Halliwell*. [Prov. Eng.]

prigger (prig'ėr), *n.* A thief. [Slang.]

He is commonly a stealer of Horses, which they terme a *Priggar* of Paulfreys. *Fraternity of Vagabonds* (1561).

priggery[1] (prig'ėr-i), *n.* [‹ *prig*[1] + *-ery*.] Thieving. [Slang.]

He said he was sorry to see any of his gang guilty of a breach of honour; that without honour *priggery* was at an end. *Fielding*, Jonathan Wild, iii. 6.

priggery[2] (prig'ėr-i), *n.* [‹ *prig*[2] + *-ery*.] The qualities of a prig; conceit; priggism.

priggish[1] (prig'ish), *a.* [‹ *prig*[1] + *-ish*[1].] Dishonest; thievish. [Slang.]

Every prig is a slave. His own *priggish* desires . . . betray him to the tyranny of others.
Fielding, Jonathan Wild, iv. 3.

priggish[2] (prig'ish), *a.* [‹ *prig*[2] + *-ish*[1].] Conceited; coxcombical; affected.

Trim sounds so very short and *priggish* — that my Name should be a Monosyllable! *Steele*, Grief A-la-Mode, iv. 1.

All but the very ignorant or the very *priggish* admit that the folk-lore of the people can teach us several things that are not to be learned in any other manner.
N. and Q., 7th ser., II. 438.

priggishly (prig'ish-li), *adv.* In a priggish manner; conceitedly; pertly.

priggishness (prig'ish-nes), *n.* The state or character of being priggish.

There is a deficiency, a littleness, a *priggishness*, a sort of vulgarity, observable about even the highest type of moral goodness attainable without it [a reverential spirit].
H. N. *Oxenham*, Short Studies, p. 150.

priggism[1] (prig'izm), *n.* [‹ *prig*[1] + *-ism*.] The condition, habits, or actions of a prig or thief; roguery. [Slang.]

How unhappy is the state of *priggism*! how impossible for human prudence to foresee and guard against every circumvention! *Fielding*, Jonathan Wild, ii. 4.

priggism[2] (prig'izm), *n.* [‹ *prig*[2] + *-ism*.] The manners of a prig.

Your great Mechanics' Institutes end in intellectual *priggism*. *T. Hughes*, Tom Brown at Rugby, i. 2.

prighte†. An obsolete preterit of *prick*. *Chaucer*.

prigman†, *n.* [Also *pridgeman*; < *prig*[1] + *man*.] A thief. *Halliwell.*

A *Prygman* goeth with a stycke in hys hand like an idle person. His propertye is to steale cloathes of the hedge, which they call storing of the Rogeman: or else filtch Poultry, carying them to the Alehouse, whych they call the Bowsyng In, & ther syt playing at cardes and dice, tyl that is spent which they haue so fylched.
Fraternity of Vagabonds (1561), quoted in Ribton Turner's [Vagrants and Vagrancy, p. 593.

A *pridgeman* from him pryuilie his money did purloyne.
Drant, tr. of Horace, To Julius Florus.

priket, *n.* A Middle English form of *prick*.

prilet, *v.* See *prill*[2].

prill[1]**†** (pril), *v. i.* [Perhaps a var. of *pirl*, *purl*: see *purl*[1]. The words spelled *prill* are scantly represented in literary use, and are more or less confused with one another.] To flow with a murmuring sound; purl.

An alabaster image of Diana, a woman for the most part naked, and water conveyed from the Thames *prilling* from her naked breast.
Whalley, Note to B. Jonson's Cynthia's Revels, i. 1.

prill[1] (pril), *n.* [< ME. *prille*, a whirligig; cf. *prill*[1], *v.*] 1. A child's whirligig.—2. A small stream of water. *Halliwell.* [Prov. Eng.]

Each siluer *prill* gliding on golden sand.
Davies, Microcosmos, p. 12. (*Davies.*)

prill[2]**†**, *v. t.* [ME. *prillen*, *prilen*, pierce; origin obscure.] To pierce.

Afterward they *prile* [var. *prill*] and pointen
The folk right to the bare boon.
Rom. of the Rose, l. 1058.

prill[3] (pril), *n.* Same as *brill*.

prill[4] (pril), *n.* [Origin obscure.] 1. A small bit or quantity. [Cornwall, Eng.]—2. In *mining*, the better parts of ore from which inferior pieces have been separated; a nugget of virgin metal.—3. A button or globule of metal obtained by assaying a specimen of ore in the cupel.—**Prill ore**, solid ore; large pieces and grains of solid dressed ore. *R. Hunt.* [Cornwall, Eng.]

prill[5] (pril), *v. i.* [Origin obscure.] 1. To turn sour. *Halliwell.* [Prov. Eng.]—2. To get tipsy. [Prov. Eng.]

prillon, prillion (pril'yon), *n.* [Cf. *prill*[4].] Tin extracted from the slag of a furnace.

prim[1] (prim), *a.* and *n.* [Not found in ME. use; appar. < OF. *prim*, m., *prime*, f., also *prime*, m. and f., first, also thin, slender, small, sharp, prime: see *prime*. The sense seems to have been affected by that of E. *prink*. Cf. *primp*.] I. *a.* Neat; formal; stiffly precise; affectedly nice; demure.

This hates the filthy creature, that the *prim*.
Young, Love of Fame, iii.

You could never laugh at her *prim* little curls, or her pink bows again, if you saw her as I have done.
Mrs. Gaskell, Cranford, ii.

The *prim* box path. Looker, A Garden Idyll.

II. *n.* A neat, pretty girl. *Halliwell.* [Prov. Eng.]

prim[1] (prim), *v.*; pret. and pp. *primmed*, ppr. *primming*. [< *prim*[1], *n.*] I. *trans.* To deck with great nicety; form or dispose with affected preciseness; prink; make prim.

When she was *primmed* out, down she came to him.
Richardson, Clarissa Harlowe, II. Let. 23.

Mark also the Abbé Maury: his broad, bold face, mouth accurately *primmed*. *Carlyle*, French Rev., I. iv. 4.

II. *intrans.* To make one's self prim or precise. [Rare.]

Tell dear Kitty not to *prim* up as if we had never met before. *Mme. D'Arblay*, Diary, ii. 108. (*Davies.*)

prim[2] (prim), *n.* [Perhaps < OF. *prim*, first, also thin, etc.: see *prim*[1].] The fry of the smelt. [Prov. Eng.]

prim[3] (prim), *n.* [Cf. *primprint* and *privet*.] The privet. See *Ligustrum*.

prim. An abbreviation of *primary*.

prima (prē'mä), *a.* [It., fem. of *primo*, first: see *prime*.] First.—**Prima buffa**, the first female singer in a comic opera.—**Prima donna** (first lady), the principal female singer in an opera.—**Prima vista**, in *music*, first sight: as, to play or sing *prima vista* (to play or sing from notes a composition the performer has never before seen or heard).—**Prima volta**, in *music*, first time, denotes that the measure or measures over which it is placed are to be played the first time a section is played, and when it is repeated are to be omitted, and those marked *seconda volta* are to be played instead. The abbreviations I[a] *volta*, II[a] *volta* are often used in modern music as merely I and II, the *volta* being omitted.

primacy (pri'ma-si), *n.* [< OF. *primacie*, *primatie*, also *primace*, F. *primatie* = Sp. *primacia* = Pg. It. *primazia*, < ML. *primatia*, the dignity of a primate, < LL. *primas* (*primat-*), principal, chief, ML. a primate: see *primate*.] 1. The condition of being prime or first in order, power, or importance.

It may be reasonable to allow St. Peter a *primacy* of order, such a one as the ringleader hath in a dance, as the primipilar centurion had in the legion.
Barrow, Works, VII. 70.

The king in the [early German] monarchic states does little more than represent the unity of race; he has a *primacy* of honour but not of power.
Stubbs, Const. Hist., § 19.

2. The rank, dignity, or office of an archbishop or other primate.

Let us grant that perpetuity of the *primacy* in the church was established in Peter, I would gladly learn why the seat of the *primacy* should be rather at Rome than elsewhere.
J. Bradford, Letters (Parker Soc., 1853), II. 144.

If any man say that it is not by the institution of our Lord Christ himself that St. Peter has perpetual successors in his *primacy* over the Universal Church, or that the Roman Pontiff is not by Divine right the successor of Peter in that same *primacy*, let him be anathema.
Draft of Dogmatical Decree submitted by Pius IX. to the [*Vatican Council*, July 18, 1870.

Making laws and ordinances
Against the Holy Father's *primacy*.
Tennyson, Queen Mary, iii. 3.

prima facie (pri'mä fā'shi-ē). [L.: *prima*, abl. of *primus*, first; *facie*, abl. of *facies*, form, shape, appearance: see *prime* and *face*[1].] At first view or appearance. See *at prime face*, under *prime*, *a.*—**Prima facie case**, in *law*: (*a*) A case which is established by sufficient evidence, and can be overthrown only by rebutting evidence adduced by the other side. (*b*) A case consisting of evidence sufficient to go to the jury: that is to say, one which raises a presumption of fact, and hence will justify a verdict, though it may not require one.—**Prima facie evidence**, in *law*, evidence which establishes a prima facie case. See *evidence*.

primage (pri'māj), *n.* [< F. *primage*; as *prime* + *-age*.] 1. A small sum of money formerly paid over and above the freight to the master of a ship for his care of the goods: now charged with the freight and retained by the ship-owner. Also called *hat-money*.

Primage is a small customary payment to the master for his care and trouble.
Bateman, Commercial Law, § 824.

2. The amount of water carried over in steam from a steam-boiler by foaming, lifting, and atomizing of the water. See *priming*. It is estimated, in relation to the amount of water evaporated or to the time of evaporation, usually as a percentage of the entire weight of water passed through the boiler: as, a *primage* of three per cent.

primal (pri'mal), *a.* [< ML. *primalis*, primary, < L. *primus*, first: see *prime*.] 1. Primary; first in time, order, or importance; original; primitive.

It hath the *primal*, eldest curse upon 't,
A brother's murder. *Shak.*, Hamlet, iii. 3. 37.

Step after step . . .
Have I climb'd back into the *primal* church.
Tennyson, Queen Mary, i. 2.

No great school ever yet existed which had not for *primal* aim the representation of some natural fact as truly as possible. *Ruskin.*

2. [*cap.*] In *geol.*, the earliest of H. D. Rogers's divisions of the Paleozoic series of Pennsylvania, equivalent to the Potsdam sandstone of the New York Survey.—3. In *nat. hist.*, specifically, of or pertaining to the kingdom *Primalia*.=**Syn. 1.** *Prime*, etc. See *primary*.

Primalia (pri-mā'li-ä), *n. pl.* [NL., neut. pl. of ML. *primalis*, primal: see *primal*.] A third and the lowest kingdom of organized beings, containing those which are neither true plants nor true animals: contrasted with *Vegetabilia* and *Animalia*. See *Protista*, *Protophyta*, *Protozoa*. The group has been defined and named as in the quotation.

A great group of organized beings of more simple structure than either vegetables or animals, which we regard as eminently and demonstrably a primary division or kingdom, and apply to it the name *Primalia*.
T. B. Wilson and *J. Cassin*, Proc. Acad. Nat. Sci. Phila., [May, 1863, p. 110.

primality (pri-mal'i-ti), *n.* [< *primal* + *-ity*.] The state of being primal. *Baxter.*

primaria[1] (pri-mā'ri-ä), *n.*; pl. *primariæ* (-ē). [NL., fem. sing. of L. *primarius*, primary: see *primary*.] A primary, or primary remex, of a bird's wing: generally in the plural.

Primaria[2] (pri-mā'ri-ä), *n. pl.* [NL., neut. pl. of L. *primarius*, primary: see *primary*.] A synonym of *Primates*, 2. *E. Blyth.*

primarian (pri-mā'ri-an), *n.* [< *primary* + *-ian*.] A pupil in a primary school.

As important for a *primarian* to develop a keen perception. *Education*, III. 637.

primaried (pri'ma-rid), *a.* [< *primary* + *-ed*.] In *ornith.*, having primaries (of the kind or to the number specified by a qualifying term): as, long-*primaried*; nine-*primaried*.

primarily (pri'ma-ri-li), *adv.* In the first or most important place; originally; in the first intention.

In fevers, where the heart *primarily* suffereth, we apply medicines unto the wrist.
Sir T. Browne, Vulg. Err., iv. 4.

primariness (pri'ma-ri-nes), *n.* The state of being primary, or first in time, act, or intention.

That which is peculiar must be taken from the *primariness* and secondariness of this perception. *Norris.*

primary (pri'mā-ri), *a.* and *n.* [= F. *primaire* = Sp. Pg. It. *primario*, < L. *primarius*, of the first, of the first rank, chief, principal, excellent, < *primus*, first: see *prime*. Cf. *primer*[1] and *premier*, from the same source.] I. *a.* 1. First or highest in rank, dignity, or importance; chief; principal.

As the six *primary* planets revolve about him, so the secondary ones are moved about them. *Bentley.*

The care of their children is the *primary* occupation of the ladies of Egypt. *E. W. Lane*, Modern Egyptians, I. 238.

The *primary* use of knowledge is for such guidance of conduct under all circumstances as shall make living complete. *H. Spencer*, Pop. Sci. Mo., XXII. 358.

The *primary* circuit or coil is the coil of comparatively thick wire which is connected with a battery and circuit-breaker. *T. D. Lockwood*, Elect., Mag., and Teleg., p. 82.

2. First in order of being, of thought, or of time; original; primitive; first.

The Church of Christ in its *primary* institution.
Bp. Pearson.

The three great and *primary* elements of all our knowledge are, firstly, the idea of our own individual existence, or of finite mind in general; secondly, the idea of nature; and, thirdly, the idea of the absolute and eternal, as manifested in the pure conceptions of our impersonal reason.
J. D. Morell, Hist. Mod. Philos. (2d ed.), I. 63.

3. First or lowest in order of growth or development; elementary; preparatory.

Education comprehends not merely the elementary branches of what on the Continent is called *primary* instruction. *Brougham.*

I am conscious is to me the first—the beginning alike of knowledge and being; and I can go no higher in the way of *primary* direct act.
Veitch, Int. to Descartes's Method, p. liii.

Military cooperation is that *primary* kind of coöperation which prepares the way for other kinds.
H. Spencer, Prin. of Sociol., § 451.

The seeing of colors is undoubtedly a far more simple and *primary* act than the seeing of colored objects as situated in relation to each other in objective space.
G. T. Ladd, Physiol. Psychology, p. 463.

4. First in use or intention; radical; original: as, the *primary* sense of a word.—5. In *ornith.*, of the first rank or order among the flight-feathers or remiges of the wing; situated upon the manus or pinion-bone, as a feather: correlated with *secondary* and *tertiary* or *tertial*. See II.—6. In *geol.*, lowest in the sequence of geological formations: said of rocks. It includes rocks previously denominated *primitive*, and, as generally used, the two terms are nearly or quite synonymous. See *primitive* and *Paleozoic*.

The strict propriety of the term primitive, as applied to granite and to the granitiform and associated rocks, thus became questionable, and the term *primary* was very generally substituted, as simply expressing the fact that the crystalline rocks, as a mass, were older than the secondary, or those which are unequivocally of a mechanical origin and contain organic remains.
Sir C. Lyell, Prin. of Geol. (4th ed., 1835), III. 340.

Primary accent, in *music*, the accent with which a measure begins: its place is indicated in written music by a bar.—**Primary assembly**, in *politics*, an assembly in which all the citizens have a right to be present and to speak, as distinguished from *representative parliaments*. *Imp. Dict.*—**Primary axis**, in *bot.*, the main stalk in a cluster of flowers.—**Primary coil**, in *elect.* See *induction*.—**Primary colors**, in *optics*. See *color*.—**Primary conveyances**, in *law*, original conveyances, consisting of feoffments, grants, gifts, leases, exchanges, partitions, etc., as distinguished from *mesne conveyances*.—**Primary coverts.** See *covert*, 6.—**Primary current, deviation, dial.** See the nouns.—**Primary elections**, elections, in primary assemblies of a section of a party, of nominees, delegates, or members of political committees.—**Primary evidence, factor, linkage, motion.** See the nouns.—**Primary meeting**, in *U. S. politics*, same as II., 4.—**Primary nerve or nerves**, the one or several principal veins or ribs of a leaf, from which the secondary anastomosing veins proceed. See *nervation*.—**Primary node**, in *bot.*, the first node that is developed in a plant.—**Primary number**, a complex integer congruent to unity to the modulus $2(1+i)$, where $i^2=-1$; or, more generally, one of a class of complex integers such that no one is equal to the product of another by a unit factor, but such that all the other integers of the system can be produced from these by multiplying them by unit factors.—**Primary olfactory pits**, two simple depressions which appear on the lower surface of the wall of the anterior cerebral vesicle before other parts of the face have yet been formed, and which later become the nasal fossæ. Also called *nasal pits*.—**Primary planets.** See *planet*, 1.—**Primary prime.** See *prime*.—**Primary qualities of bodies.** See *quality*.—**Primary quills**, in *ornith.*, the largest feathers of the wings of a bird; primaries.—**Primary root**, in *bot.*, the commonly single root which develops from the embryo itself, and in many plants persists as a tap-root: contrasted with *secondary* roots, which spring from other and later-developed parts of the plant, commonly nodes of the stem or branches.—**Primary tense, time.** See the nouns.=**Syn.** *Primary, Prime, Primitive, Pristine, Primeval, Primordial, Primal,* leading. All the italicized words go back by derivation to the idea of being or going before. *Primary* and *prime* mean first in time, and now especially first in order of importance: as, a *primary* class, definition, consideration, planet; *prime* mover, importance, idea (see definition of *prime*). *Primitive* means belonging to the beginning or origin, original, hence old-fashioned, having an old-fashioned simplicity: as, a *primitive* word, the *primitive* church, *primitive* purity, manners, unconventionality, dress. *Pristine* is essentially the same as *primitive*, except that it is never uncomplimentary; it is still more closely synonymous with *original*. *Primeval* means of the first or earliest ages, and nothing else. *Primordial* and *primal* are much the least common of these words; *primal* is poetic for *prime* or *primitive*; *primordial* pertains to that which is the first, but has or has had a history or development: as, *primordial* rocks; "a *primordial* leaf is that which is immediately developed from the cotyledon; in history or physiology we speak of the *primordial* condition of man, and in metaphysics of the '*primordial* facts of an intelligent nature' (Sir W. Hamilton)" (*C. J. Smith*, Synonyms Discriminated, p. 507). See *original*.

II. *n.*; pl. *primaries* (-riz). 1. That which stands first or highest in rank or importance, as opposed to *secondary*; that to which something else is subordinate.

The converters were banked on a wooden framework at a distance of some 30 yards from the dynamo, and their *primaries* were permanently secured to the dynamo circuit. *Elect. Rev.* (Amer.), XVI. vi. 9.

2. In *ornith.*, one of the remiges, flight-feathers, or large quills which are situated upon the manus, pinion-bone, or distal segment of the wing. Such feathers are commonly the largest or longest and strongest of the remiges, and some of them almost always enter into the formation of the point of the wing. They are collectively distinguished from the succeeding set, situated upon the forearm or cubit and known as *secondaries*. The primaries are enumerated from without inward, or toward the body, the *first* primary being the outermost remex. In most birds they are 10 in number; in many oscine passerine birds there are only 9; a few birds have 11. See cuts under *bird*, *covert*, and *emarginate*.

3. In *entom.*, one of the anterior or fore wings: used especially in descriptions of the *Lepidoptera*. See cut under *Cirrophanus*.

The *primaries* below are fulvous, with a single wavy brown line. *Saunders.*

4. In *U. S. politics*, a meeting of voters belonging to the same political party in a ward, township, or other election district, held for the purpose of nominating candidates for office, choosing delegates to a convention, etc. Theoretically every voter belonging to the party in a district has a right to attend the primary and vote, but in cities and large places only registered voters who have answered certain test questions relating to party adherence have that privilege. Compare *caucus*.

If the [election] district is not subdivided, its meeting is called a *Primary*. *Bryce*, Amer. Commonwealth, II. 52.

5. A planet in relation to its satellite or satellites: as, the earth is the *primary* of the moon.—**Lateral primaries**, in *bot.* See *nervation*.

primate (prī'māt), *n.* [< ME. *primate*, < OF. *primat*, F. *primat* = Pr. *primat* = Sp. Pg. *primado*, *primaz* = It. *primate*, < LL. *primas* (*primat-*), of the first, chief, excellent, ML. as a noun, a primate, < L. *primus*, first: see *prime*.] 1†. The first or chief person.

He [Daniel] schal be *prymate* & prynce of pure clergye [learning]. . . .
And of my reme the rychest to ryde wyth myseluen.
Alliterative Poems (ed. Morris), ii. 1570.

2. A bishop of a see ranking as first in a province or provinces; a metropolitan as presiding in his province, or one of several metropolitans as presiding over others. The title of *primate* did not come into ordinary use till the ninth century, after which it was given to metropolitans of certain sees as special representatives of the Pope. The term *primate* (πρωτεύων) has never been in regular use in the Greek Church. The title of *exarch* comes nearest to it. In the Roman Catholic Church a primate is a bishop or an archbishop to whom is delegated a certain jurisdiction as vicar of the Pope over the bishops of his province, or to whose see such authority has formerly been delegated. In the Church of England the Archbishop of Canterbury has the title *Primate* of all England, while the Archbishop of York is *Primate* of England. In the Church of Ireland the Archbishop of Armagh is *Primate* of all Ireland, and the Archbishop of Dublin *Primate* of Ireland.

It [Lyons] is the seat of an Archbishop, who is the *Primate* and Metropolitan of France.
Coryat, Crudities, I. 59.

Bishops in the chiefest mother churches were termed *primates*, and at the length, by way of excellency, patriarchs.
Hooker, Eccles. Polity, vii. 8.

In modern times those bishops only are properly called *primates* to whose see the dignity of vicar of the Holy See was formerly annexed. . . . Changed circumstances . . . have made the jurisdiction of *primates* almost a thing of the past. *Rom. Cath. Dict.*, p. 693.

3. In *zoöl.*, a member of the order *Primates*; a primatial or primatic mammal, as man.

Primates (prī-mā'tēz), *n. pl.* [NL., pl. of LL. *primas* (*primat-*), of the first or chief: see *primate*.] 1†. The first Linnean order of *Mammalia*, composed of the four genera *Homo*, *Simia*, *Lemur*, and *Vespertilio*, or man, monkeys, lemurs, and bats.—2. Now, the first or highest order of *Mammalia*, including man, monkeys, and lemurs. The brain has a relatively large cerebrum, overlapping much or all of the cerebellum and of the olfactory lobes, with usually a highly convoluted surface; there is a well-defined calcarine sulcus, and a hippocampus minor in the postcornu; the corpus callosum extends backward to the vertical of the hippocampal sulcus, and develops in front a well-marked recurved rostrum. The periotic and tympanic bones are normally joined to the squamosal. The pelvis and the posterior limbs are well developed, and the legs are exserted almost entirely beyond the common integument of the trunk. The first or inner digit of the foot, the great toe, is enlarged, provided with a nail (not a claw), and usually apposable to the other digits. Clavicles are present and perfect. There are teeth of three kinds, all enameled, and the molars have mostly two or three roots. The placenta is discoid and deciduate. The *Primates* correspond to the *Bimana* and *Quadrumana* together. They are divisible into two suborders, the *Anthropoidea* and *Prosimiæ*, the former represented by the families *Hominidæ*, *Simiidæ*, *Cynopithecidæ*, *Cebidæ*, and *Midadæ*, or man and all kinds of monkeys—the *Prosimiæ*, or lemurs and lemuroid animals, constituting the families *Lemuridæ*, *Tarsiidæ*, and *Daubentoniidæ*. Also *Primaria*.

primateship (prī'māt-ship), *n.* [< *primate* + *-ship*.] The office or dignity of primate.

primatial (prī-mā'shal), *a.* [< *primate* + *-i-al*.] 1. Of or pertaining to a primate. Also *primatical*.

Henry of Winchester pleaded hard at Rome that the ancient capital should be raised to *primatial* rank.
E. A. Freeman, Norman Conquest, V. 212.

2. Of or pertaining to the mammalian order *Primates*.

primatic (prī-mat'ik), *a.* [< *primate* + *-ic*.] Of or pertaining to the mammalian order *Primates*; primatial: as, *primatic* characters. *Huxley.*

primatical (prī-mat'i-kal), *a.* [< *primatic* + *-al*.] Same as *primatial*, 1.

The original and growth of metropolitical, *primatical*, and patriarchal jurisdiction. *Barrow*, Pope's Supremacy.

prima-vista (prē'mä-vis'tä), *n.* [It., < *prima*, fem. of *primo*, first, + *vista*, view, sight: see *vista*.] Same as *primero*.

The game at cards called primero or *prima-vista*.
Florio, p. 400. (*Halliwell.*)

prime (prīm), *a.* and *n.* [I. *a.* < OF. *prime*, *prim* = Pr. *prim* = Sp. Pg. It. *primo*, < L. *primus*, first, superl. (cf. *prior*, compar., former, prior), for **proimus*, < *pro*, forth, forward: see *pro-*. Cf. AS. *forma*, first: see *former*[1]. II. *n.* < F. *prime*, < L. *prima*, sc. *hora*, the first hour, fem. of *primus*, first: see above.] I. *a.* 1. First in order of time; primitive; original: as, the *prime* cost.

The most replenished sweet work of nature
That from the *prime* creation e'er she framed.
Shak., Rich. III., iv. 3. 19.

Those [words] which are derivative from others, with their *prime*, certaine, and natural signification.
Evelyn, To Sir Peter Wyche.

The mountains gemmed with morning dew,
In the *prime* hour of sweetest scents and airs.
Wordsworth, Excursion, vi.

While the *prime* swallow dips his wing.
Tennyson, Edwin Morris.

2. First in rank, degree, or importance; principal; chief: as, *prime* minister.

This invites
The *prime* men of the city to frequent
All places he resorts to.
Fletcher, Spanish Curate, i. 1.

Nor can I think that God, Creator-wise,
Though threatening, will in earnest so destroy
Us his *prime* creatures, dignified so high.
Milton, P. L., ix. 940.

Earnestly meting out the Lydian proconsular Asia, to make good the *prime* metropolis of Ephesus.
Milton, Church-Government, i., Pref.

They said all the *prime* People were against a War.
Steele, Grief A-la-Mode, iv. 1.

The *prime* utensil of the African savage is a gourd.
Sir S. W. Baker, Heart of Africa, p. 233.

3. Of the first excellence, value, or importance; first-rate; capital: as, *prime* wheat; *prime* quality; a *prime* joint of meat.

The last may prove the *prime* part of his life, and those his best days which he lived nearest heaven.
Sir T. Browne, Christ. Mor., iii. 22.

Your thorough French Courtier, whenever the fit he 's in,
Thinks it 's *prime* fun to astonish a citizen.
Barham, Ingoldsby Legends, ii. 8.

A flask of cider from his father's vats,
Prime, which I knew. *Tennyson*, Audley Court.

4. Relating to the period or the condition of early manhood and vigor; being in the best or most vigorous time of life. See *prime*, *n.*, 3.

His starry helm unbuckled showed him *prime*
In manhood, where youth ended.
Milton, P. L., xi. 245.

Since your garden is blasted, your vinedage ended. . . . your *prime* tyme finished, your youth passed, your old age come, it were much more conueniente to take order for amendement of old sinnes.
Guevara, Letters (tr. by Hellowes, 1577), p. 237.

5†. Ready; eager; bold.

As *prime* as goats. *Shak.*, Othello, iii. 3. 403.

6†. Fierce; strong.

Ther was no man yn hethyn londe
Myght sytte a dynte of hys honde,
The traytour was so *preme*.
MS. Cantab. Ff. ii. 38, f. 89. (*Halliwell.*)

7. In *math.*, indivisible without a remainder, except by unity; incapable of being separated into simpler factors. Two integers are said to be *prime together*, or *relatively prime*, when they have no common divisor except 1. (Thus, 1 alone of all numbers is *prime* to itself, and in the theory of numbers it must be so regarded.) One integer is said to be *prime* to a second with respect to a third when it does not contain the second with respect to the third. (See *contain*, 8.) One matrix is said to be *prime* to another when their determinants are relatively prime.—**At prime face**†, at first view; prima facie.

This accident so pitous was to here,
And ek so like a soth *at pryme face*.
Chaucer, Troilus, iii. 919.

Prime and ultimate ratios. See *ratio*.—**Prime circulator, conductor, factor.** See the nouns.—**Prime figure**, in *geom.*, a figure which cannot be separated into any figures more simple than itself, as a triangle or a pyramid.—**Prime matter**†. Same as *first matter* (which see, under *matter*).—**Prime meridian.** See *meridian*, and *longitude*, 2.—**Prime mess**, the second quality of pickled or salt pork, consisting of the hams, shoulders, and sides of the hog.—**Prime minister**, the leading minister of a government; the chief of the cabinet or ministry: commonly used with reference to countries which enjoy a representative government. The prime minister may hold one of various important portfolios, as that of foreign affairs, of war, of the interior, etc.; the British prime minister is usually First Lord of the Treasury. (Also called *premier*.) The office does not exist in the United States, although the Secretary of State is sometimes affectedly styled *premier*.—**Prime mover.** (*a*) The initial force which puts a machine in motion. (*b*) A machine which receives and modifies force as supplied by some natural source, as a water-wheel or a steam-engine.—**Prime number**, in *arith.*, a number not divisible without remainder by any number except itself and unity: such are 1, 2, 3, 5, 7, 11, 13, 17, 19, 23, 29, 31, 37, 41, 43, 47, 53, 59, 61, 67, 71, 73, 79, 83, 89, 97, 101, 103, 107, 109, 113, etc. See *law of reciprocity of prime numbers*, under *law*[1]. Also called *incomposite number*.—**Prime relation**, a relation not composite.—**Prime vertical**, in *astron.*, a celestial great circle passing through the east and west points and the zenith.—**Prime vertical dial**, a dial projected on the plane of the prime vertical circle, or on one parallel to it; a north-and-south dial.—**Prime vertical transit-instrument**, a transit-instrument the telescope of which revolves in the plane of the prime vertical, used for observing the transit of stars over this circle.=**Syn.** 1. *Pristine*, etc. See *primary*.—2 and 3. Chief, principal, best.

II. *n.* 1. The first period; the earliest stage or beginning; specifically, spring.

When comen was the tyme
Of Averil, whan clothed is the mede
With newe greene, of lusty Veer the *prime*.
Chaucer, Troilus, i. 157.

And brought him presents, flowers if it were *prime*,
Or mellow fruit if it were harvest time.
Spenser, Astrophel, l. 47.

We see how quickly sundry arts mechanical were found out, in the very *prime* of the world.
Hooker, Eccles. Polity, i. 10.

Awake: the morning shines, and the fresh field
Calls us: we lose the *prime*. *Milton*, P. L., v. 21.

Thee with the welcome Snowdrop I compare;
That child of winter, prompting thoughts that climb
From desolation toward the genial *prime*.
Wordsworth, Sonnets, iii. 17.

2. The first hour or period of the day. Specifically—(*a*) The first hour; the first twelfth of the time between sunrise and sunset. (*b*) In the early church, the Roman Catholic Church, the Greek Church, and in Anglican religious houses, etc., and in private devotion, one of the seven canonical hours; an office said, or originally intended to be said, at the first hour after sunrise. Prime follows next after matins and lauds. The psalms of the Greek office of prime (ἡ πρώτη, sc. ὥρα) are those already used in the fifth century (Psalms v., xc., ci.); in the Western Church they are Psalms xxii.-xxvi., liv., cxviii., cxix. 1–32 (with varying distribution according to the day and use). Among the principal features of the office are the hymn *Jam lucis orto sidere* (Now that the daylight fills the sky), the Athanasian Creed, Little Chapter, Lord's Prayer, Creed, Preces, Confession, Absolution, and Collects.

He made him to ben delyvered out of Presoun, and commanded that Psalm to ben seyd every day at *Pryme*.
Mandeville, Travels, p. 145.

Longe erst er *pryme* rong of any belle.
Chaucer, Pardoner's Tale, l. 200.

From *prime* to vespers will I chant thy praise.
Tennyson, Pelleas and Ettarre.

(*c*) In a more extended sense, from the fact that the lesser canonical hours followed at intervals of three hours, the first quarter of the time between sunrise and sunset, ending half-way between sunrise and midday.

The night has yielded to the morn,
And far the hours of *prime* are worn.
Scott, Rokeby, vi. 23.

3. The spring of life; youth; full health, strength, or beauty; hence, the highest or most perfect state or most flourishing condition of anything.

And will she yet debase her eyes on me,
That cropp'd the golden *prime* of this sweet prince?
Shak., Rich. III., i. 2. 248.

Ceres in her *prime*,
Yet virgin of Proserpina from Jove.
Milton, P. L., ix. 395.

The thyme it is wither'd, and the rue is in *prime*.
Farmer's Old Wife (Child's Ballads, VIII. 257).

It was in the golden *prime*
Of good Baroun Alraschid.
Tennyson, Arabian Nights.

Past my *prime* of life, and out of health.
Browning, Ring and Book, I. 202.

4. The best part; that which is best in quality; that which is of prime or high quality or grade, as fish, oysters, etc.; often, in the plural, a prime grade or quality.

Give no more to ev'ry guest
Than he's able to digest:
Give him always of the *prime*,
And but little at a time.
Swift, Verses on a Lady.

5. In *fencing*: (a) The first of eight parries or guards against thrusts in sword-play, afterward retained in exercise with the foils; the first guard a swordsman surprised by an attack could make, while drawing his weapon from the scabbard near his left thigh. It was followed by parries in *seconde, tierce, quarte*, up to *octave*, according as thrusts followed at the openings in the defense made by such guards. In prime guard the point remains low, the hand higher than the eyes, as in drawing the sword, and the knuckles are upward. It is the ordinary position of the German student "on guard," when fencing with the schläger. Hence—(b) Sometimes, the first and simplest thrust (and parry) which can be made after two fencers have crossed foils and are "on guard" with the left sides of their foils touching: used thus for the direct thrust. This is by some writers called *modern prime*, while the true prime is called *ancient* or *old prime*. In both *old* and *modern prime* the word *prime* is used to indicate the thrust as well as the parry or guard; but this comes from suppression of "in": thus, prime thrust, for thrust in *prime*. *Prime, seconde*, etc., represent numbered sections of an ideal chart covering such parts of a swordsman's trunk as are visible to his opponent, each of which sections is supposed to be guarded by the parry thus numbered. Hence the meaning of a "thrust in prime," etc.

6. In *chem.*, a number employed, in conformity with the doctrine of definite proportions, to express the ratios in which bodies enter into combination. Primes duly arranged in a table constitute a scale of chemical equivalents. They also express the ratios of atomic weights.

7. A prime number; an integer number not divisible without remainder by any number except itself and unity.—8†. (a) The game of primero.

To check at chesse, to heave at maw, . . . or set their rest at *prime*. *G. Turberville*, On Hawking. (*Nares.*)

(b) A term used in the playing of this game.—9. In *music*: (a) A tone on the same degree of the scale or staff with a given tone. (b) The interval between any tone and a tone on the same degree with it. (c) The simultaneous combination of two tones on the same degree. (d) In a scale, the first tone; the tonic or keynote. The typical interval of the prime is the unison, acoustically represented by the ratio 1:1; such a prime is called *perfect* or *major*. A prime in which one tone is a half-step above the other is called *augmented* or *superfluous*. The perfect prime is the most perfect of all consonances—so perfect, indeed, that in its ideal form it is better described as a unison than as a consonance. In harmony, the parallel motion of two voices in perfect primes is forbidden, except when a strictly melodic effect is desired: such primes are called *consecutive*. Compare *consecutive fifth* and *consecutive octave*, under *consecutive*.

10. One of the fractions into which a unit is immediately divided; a minute. It is generally $\frac{1}{60}$, but sometimes $\frac{1}{10}$. Hence, an accent as the symbol of such a fraction: thus b', in algebra, is read "*b prime*."

11. The footsteps of a deer. *Halliwell*.—**High prime†**, probably the close of prime—that is, 9 A. M. See def. 2 (c).

Att *hye pryme* Peers let the plouh stonde,
And ouer-seyh hem hym-self ho so best wrouhte.
Piers Plowman (C), ix. 119.

Then to Westmynster gate I presently went,
When the sonn was at *hyghe pryme*.
Lydgate, London Lickpeny (MS. Harl., 367).

Ideal prime, an ideal number that is prime. See *ideal*.—**Primary prime**, a complex prime number of the form $a\,b-1$ such that if of the two coefficients one is odd while the other is even then the number is congruent to unity on the modulus $2(1-i)$ (this definition includes $1-i$ as a primary prime, but some authors consider this as not of the class, because it is not a primary number); more generally, a complex prime number which is at the same time a primary number.—**Prime of the moon**, the new moon when it first appears after the change.

prime (prīm), *v.*; pret. and pp. *primed*, ppr. *priming*. [< *prime*, *a.*] **I.** *intrans.* 1†. To be as at first; be renewed.

Night's bashful empress, though she often wane,
As oft repeats her darkness, *primes* again.
Quarles, Emblems, iii. 1.

2. To insert a primer or priming-powder into the vent of a gun before firing.—3. In the steam-engine, to carry over hot water with the steam from the boiler into the cylinder: as, the engine *primes*. See *priming*, 2.

II. *trans.* 1. To perform the prime or first operation upon or with; prepare. Specifically—(a) To put into a condition for being fired; supply with powder for communicating fire to a charge: said of a gun, mine, etc.

We new *primed* all our Guns, and provided ourselves for an Enemy. *Dampier*, Voyages, I. 18.

Now, ere you sleep,
See that your polish'd arms be *prim'd* with care.
Cowper, Task, iv. 567.

(b) To cover with a ground or first color or coat in painting or plastering.

One of their faces has not the *priming* colour laid on yet. *B. Jonson*, Epicœne, ii. 4.

(c) To put in a fit state to act or endure; make ready; especially, to instruct or prepare (a person) beforehand in what he is to say or do; "post": as, to *prime* a person with a speech; to *prime* a witness.

Being always *primed* with politesse
For men of their appearance and address.
Cowper, Progress of Error, l. 387.

2. To trim or prune. [Obsolete or provincial.]

Showers, hails, snows, frosts, and two-edg'd winds that *prime*
The maiden blossoms; I provoke you all,
And dare expose this body to your sharpness.
Beau. and Fl., Coxcomb, iv. 2.

He has true fervor and dramatic insight, and all he needs is to *prime* down extravagances and modify excesses in voice and expression. *The American*, VII. 360.

Center-primed cartridge. See *center-fire cartridge*, under *cartridge*.—**To prime a match.** See *match*[2].—**To prime a pump**, to pour water down the tube of a pump, with the view of saturating the sucker, in order to cause it to swell, and thus act effectively in bringing up water.

primed (prīmd), *p. a.* 1. Intoxicated. [Slang.]—2. Spotted from disease. *Halliwell*. [Prov. Eng.]

primely (prīm'li), *adv.* 1†. At first; originally; primarily; in the first place, degree, or rank.

The creed hath in it all articles . . . *primely* and universally necessary. *Jer. Taylor*, Works (ed. 1835), II. 307.

Samson, being chief magistrate of the children of Israel, might destroy the Philistines, who were their enemies; and this was the thing *primely*, nay solely, intended by him, and not the taking away his own life.
South, Sermons, V. viii.

2. In a prime manner or degree; especially; also, excellently: as, venison *primely* cooked.

Though the natural law be always the same, yet some parts of it are *primely* necessary, others by supposition and accident. *Jer. Taylor*, Works (ed. 1835), I. 8, Pref.

primeness (prīm'nes), *n.* The state or quality of being prime or first; supreme excellence.

primer[1] (as adj., prī'mėr; as n., prim'ėr), *a.* and *n.* [Formerly also *primmer*; < ME. *primer*, *prymer*, n., < OF. *primer*, *primier*, *premier*, F. *premier* = Sp. *primero* = Pg. *primeiro* = It. *primiero*, first (cf. later F. *primaire* = Sp. Pg. It. *primario*, first, elementary), < L. *primarius*, of the first, primary: see *primary*. Cf. *premier*, doublet of *primer*[1].] **I.**† *a.* First; original; primary.

God had not depriv'd that *primer* season
The sacred lamp and light of learned Reason.
Sylvester, tr. of Du Bartas's Weeks, ii., Eden.

As when the *primer* church her councils pleas'd to call,
Great Britain's bishops there were not the least of all.
Drayton, Polyolbion, viii. 337.

He who from lusts vile bondage would be freed,
Its *primer* flames to suffocate must heed.
History of Joseph, 1691. (*Halliwell.*)

Primer fine, in *old Eng. law*, a payment to the crown (usually computed at one tenth of the annual value of the land) exacted from a plaintiff who commenced a suit for the recovery of lands known as a *fine*. See *fine*[1], *n.*, 3.

II. *n.* A first book; a small elementary book of instruction.

This litel child his litel book lerninge,
As he sat in the scole at his *prymer*.
Chaucer, Prioress's Tale, l. 72.

The New England *Primer*, which for a century and a half was in these parts the first book in religion and morals, as well as in learning and in literature.
N. and Q., 7th ser., IX. 64.

The New-England *Primer*, Improved for the more easy attaining the true reading of English.
New England Primer (ed. 1777), Title.

Specifically (*eccles.*), in England, both before and after the Reformation, a book of private devotions, especially one authorized by the church and partially or wholly in the vernacular, containing devotions for the hours, the Creed, the Lord's Prayer, the Ten Commandments, certain psalms, instruction as to elements of Christian knowledge, etc. Primers are extant dating from the fourteenth century and earlier. A reformed primer was set forth under Henry VIII. in 1545, and continued in use with alterations till 1575. A new series of primers began in 1553, and unauthorized primers were also often issued. Books of devotion closely resembling the old primers in contents and character are extensively used among Anglicans at the present day.

It was no more political feeling . . . that retained in the *Primer* down to the Reformation the prayers of the king [Henry VI.] who had perished for the sins of his fathers and of the nation. *Stubbs*, Const. Hist., § 341.

Another prayer to her is not only in the manual, but in the *primer* or office of the blessed Virgin. *Stillingfleet.*

Great primer, a printing-type, 18 points in size (see *point*[1], *n.*, 14).—**Long primer**, a size of printing-type about 7½ lines to the inch, intermediate between small pica (larger) and bourgeois (smaller). It is known as 10 point in the new system of sizes.

This is Long Primer type.

Two-line great primer, a size of printing-type about 25 lines to the foot, equal to 36 points in the new system of sizes.

primer[2] (prī'mėr), *n.* [< *prime*, *v.*, + *-er*[1].] 1. One who or that which primes. Specifically—(a) A tube, cap, wafer, or other device, containing a compound which may be exploded by percussion, friction, or other means, used for firing a charge of powder. (b) A utensil, formerly in use, for containing a small fixed amount of powder, and introducing it into the pan of a gun: sometimes combined with the spanner or key of the wheel-lock, as in the illustration.

Primer and Key for Wheel-lock.

a, barrel of primer; *b*, spring stopper; *c*, key fitted to the end of the pivot of the axle of the wheel (see *wheel-lock*). The primer is fitted to the key to increase the leverage of the latter.

2†. A small powder-horn containing fine powder used for priming.—**Friction-primer.** Same as *friction-tube*.

primero (pri-mē'rō), *n.* [< Sp. *primero*, first: see *primer*[1].] An old game of cards. It is not known precisely how the game was played. Each player seems to have held four cards; a flush was the best hand, and a *prime*, or one in which all four cards were of different suits, the next best.

I . . . left him at *primero*
With the Duke of Suffolk.
Shak., Hen. VIII., v. 1. 7.

Primero is reckoned among the most ancient games of cards known to have been played in England.
Strutt, Sports and Pastimes, p. 433.

primerole†, *n.* [ME., also *primerolle*, *prymerolle*; < OF. *primerole*, primrose, also privet; a quasi-dim. of *primule*, primrose, = Sp. *primula* = G. *primel*, < ML. *primula*, the primrose, also *primula veris* (OF. *primule de ver*, *primevere*, F. *primevère*, It. *fior de primavera*), 'the first little flower of spring'; fem. of L. *primulus*, dim. of *primus*, first: see *prime*. Cf. *primrose*.] A primrose.

The honysoucle, the froisshe *prymerollys*,
Ther levys splaye at Phebus up-rysyng.
Lydgate's Testament.

She was a *primerole*, a piggesnye.
Chaucer, Miller's Tale, l. 82.

primer-pouch (prī'mėr-pouch), *n.* *Milit.*, a leathern case for carrying primers, which forms a part of an artillery equipment.

primer-seizin (prī'mėr-sē'zin), *n.* Formerly, in English law, the payment due to the crown from a tenant who held in capite, if the heir succeeded by descent when of full age. Such a payment was one year's profits of the land if in possession, and half a year's profits if in reversion. It was abolished by 12 Car. II.

On the transmission of lay property in land, by the operation of the doctrine of wills and uses, the king lost his reliefs and *primer seisins*.
Stubbs, Medieval and Modern Hist., p. 280.

prime-staff (prīm'stȧf), *n.* Same as *clog-almanac*.

primet† (prim'et), *n.* [Appar. < *prim*, *primel*, + *-et*. Cf. *primprint*, *primrose*, *privet*.] 1. The primrose.—2. The privet.

primetemps†, *n.* [ME., < OF. *prim temps*, F. *printemps*, spring, < L. *primum*, neut. of *primus*, first, + *tempus*, time.] Spring.

Pryme temps fulle of frostes white,
And May devoid of al delite.
Rom. of the Rose, l. 4747.

primetide† (prīm'tīd), *n.* [ME.] 1. The time of prime.

Horn . . . cam to the kinge
At his uprisinge; . . .
Rigt at *prime tide*
Hi gunnen ut ride.
King Horn (E. E. T. S.), l. 849.

2. Spring.

primetime† (prīm'tīm), *n.* [ME.] Same as *primetide*, 2.

Certainely yf you had been taken as the floure for the herbe, if you had ben cut greene fro the tree, yf you had ben graffed in *primetime*. *Golden Book*, xi.

primeval (prī-mē'val), *a.* [< *primev-ous* + *-al.*] Of or belonging to the first ages; original; primal; primitive.

Remote from the polite, they still retained the *primeval* simplicity of manners. *Goldsmith*, Vicar, iv.

From Chaos and *primeval* Darkness came
Light. *Keats*, Hyperion. (*Latham.*)

This is the forest *primeval*. *Longfellow*, Evangeline.

=**Syn.** *Primitive*, etc. See *primary*.

primevally (prī-mē'val-i), *adv.* In a primeval manner; in the earliest times.

primevous (prī-mē'vus), *a.* [< L. *primævus*, in the first or earliest period of life, < *primus*, first, + *ævum*, time, age: see *prime* and *age*.] Primeval.

primi, *n.* Plural of *primus*.

Primianist (prim'i-an-ist), *n.* [< *Primianus* (see def.) + *-ist*.] One of the followers of Primianus, who became Donatist bishop of Carthage, A. D. 392. An opposite party among the Donatists were called *Maximianists*.

primigenal (prī-mij'e-nal), *a.* [Also erroneously *primogenial*; < *primigen-um* + *-al*.] Pertaining to the *Regnum primigenum*. *Hogg*, 1830.

primigenial (prī-mi-jē'ni-al), *a.* [< L. *primigenius*, first of its kind, primitive (see *primigenious*), + *-al*.] 1. First-born; original; primary. Also *primogenial*.

They recover themselves again to their condition of *primigenial* innocence. *Glanville*, Pre-existence of Souls, xiv.

2. Specifically applied to several animals of a primitive or early type after their kind, or to such a primitive type: as, the *primigenial* elephant (*Elephas primigenius*).

The *primigenial* elephant and rhinoceros. *Owen*, Anat., § 860.

primigenious (prī-mi-jē'ni-us), *a.* [< L. *primigenius*, first produced, primitive, < *primus*, first, + *genere*, *gignere*, beget, + *-al*.] First formed or generated; original.

Rutimeyer believes that these niatas cattle belong to the *primigenious* type. *Darwin*, Var. of Animals and Plants, iii.

primigenous (prī-mij'e-nus), *a.* [< L. *primigenus*, first produced, primitive, < *primus*, first, + *genere*, *gignere*, beget, produce.] Same as *primigenious*.

Primigenum (prī-mij'e-num), *n.* [NL., neut. of L. *primigenus*, first produced, primitive, original: see *primigenious*.] Hogg's name (1830) of a kingdom of nature, more fully called *Regnum primigenum*, the primigenal kingdom, composed of the same author's *Protoctista*, and corresponding to the *Primalia* of Wilson and Cassin, or the *Protista* of Haeckel.

primigravida (prī-mi-grav'i-dä), *n.*; pl. *primigravidæ* (-dē). [NL., < L. *primus*, first, + *gravidus*, pregnant: see *gravid*.] A woman pregnant for the first time.

priminary, *n.* See *priminery*.

primine (prī'min), *n.* [< L. *primus*, first (see *prime*), + *-ine*[2].] In *bot.*, the outer integument of an ovule when two are present, contrasted with the inner, or *secundine*. But since the inner coat appears first, this has by some authors been called *primine*, and the outer *secundine*. See *ovule*, 2.

priminery, priminary (pri-min'e-ri, -a-ri), *n.*; pl. *primineries*, *priminaries* (-riz). A difficulty; predicament. [Prov. Eng. and U. S.]

priming (prī'ming), *n.* [Verbal n. of *prime*, *v.*] 1. In *gun.* and *blasting*, the act of applying the powder, percussion-cap, or other material used to ignite the charge; hence, the powder or cap itself.

The one that escaped informed us that his and his companions' guns would not go off, the *priming* being wet with the rain. *Franklin*, Autobiog., p. 233.

2. Figuratively, anything as small relatively to something else as the gun-priming is relatively to the charge: as, his crop isn't a *priming* to mine. [Western U. S.]—3. In *painting*, the first layer of paint, size, or other material given to any surface as a ground. It may be of oil-color, and is then non-absorbent, or of chalk or plaster mixed with animal glue, and is then absorbent.

4. In steam-engines: (*a*) Hot water carried along by the steam from the boiler into the cylinder. (*b*) The carrying of such water from the boiler into the cylinder.—**Priming of the tides.** See *lagging of the tides*, under *lagging*.

priming-horn (prī'ming-hôrn), *n.* A miner's or quarryman's powder-horn.

priming-iron (prī'ming-ī"ėrn), *n.* In *gun.*, a pointed wire used through the vent of a cannon to prick the cartridge when it is home, and after discharge to extinguish any ignited particles. [Eng.] In the United States service called *priming-wire*.

priming-machine (prī'ming-ma-shēn"), *n.* A machine for putting fulminate into percussion-caps.

priming-powder (prī'ming-pou"dėr), *n.* 1. Detonating powder.—2. The train of powder connecting a fuse with a charge.

priming-tube (prī'ming-tūb), *n.* In *gun.*, same as *friction-tube*.

priming-wire (prī'ming-wīr), *n.* See *priming-iron*.

priminvariant (prim-in-vā'ri-ant), *n.* A fundamental asyzygetic invariant.

primipara (prī-mip'a-rä), *n.*; pl. *primiparæ* (-rē). [L.: see *primiparous*.] A woman who bears a child for the first time: correlated with *nullipara*, *multipara*.

primiparity (prī-mi-par'i-ti), *n.* [< *primipara* + *-ity*.] The state of being a primipara.

primiparous (prī-mip'a-rus), *a.* [< L. *primipara*, one that has brought forth for the first time, < *primus*, first, + *parere*, bring forth, bear.] Bearing a child for the first time.

primipilar (prī-mi-pī'lär), *a.* [< L. *primipilaris*, pertaining to the first maniple of the triarii, < *primipilus*, the chief centurion of the triarii, < *primus*, first, + *pilus*, the body of the triarii, < *pilum*, a heavy javelin: see *pile*[1].] Pertaining to the first maniple of the body of veterans (triarii) which formed a regular part of a Roman legion.

It may be reasonable to allow St. Peter a primacy of order, such a one as the ringleader hath in a dance, as the *primipilar* centurion had in the legion. *Barrow*, Works, VII. 70.

primitiæ (prī-mish'i-ē), *n. pl.* [L. (> F. *prémices*, > E. *premices*), the first things of their kind, first-fruits, < *primus*, first: see *prime*.] 1. The first-fruits of any production of the earth; specifically (*eccles.*), the first-fruits of an ecclesiastical benefice, payable to the Pope, the church, or other ecclesiastical authority: same as *annats*. See *annat*, 1.—2. In *obstet.*, the waters discharged before the extrusion of the fetus.

primitial (prī-mish'al), *a.* [< *primitiæ* + *-al*.] 1†. Being of the first production; primitive; original.—2. Pertaining to the primitiæ.

primitive (prim'i-tiv), *a.* and *n.* [< F. *primitif* = Sp. Pg. It. *primitivo*, < L. *primitivus*, first or earliest of its kind, < *primus*, first: see *prime*.] **I.** *a.* 1. Pertaining to the beginning or origin; original; especially, having something else of the same kind derived from it, but not itself derived from anything of the same kind; first: as, the *primitive* church; the *primitive* speech.

Sur. Did Adam write, sir, in High Dutch?
Mam. He did:
Which proves it was the *primitive* tongue.
B. Jonson, Alchemist, ii. 1.

Things translated into another Tongue lose of their *primitive* Vigour and Strength. *Howell*, Letters, ii. 47.

The power of thy grace is not past away with the *primitive* times, as fond and faithlesse men imagine.
Milton, On Def. of Humb. Remonst.

The settlers [in America] were driven to cast off many of the improvements or corruptions, as we may choose to call them, which had overshadowed the elder institutions of the mother-country, and largely to fall back on the *primitive* form of those institutions.
E. A. Freeman, Amer. Lects., p. 178.

2. Characterized by the simplicity of old times; old-fashioned; plain or rude: as, a *primitive* style of dress.

I should starve at their *primitive* banquet.
Lamb, Imperfect Sympathies.

3. In *gram.*, noting a word as related to another that is derived from it; noting that word from which a derivative is made, whether itself demonstrably derivative or not.—4. In *biol.*: (*a*) rudimentary; inceptive; primordial; beginning to take form or acquire recognizable existence: applicable to any part, organ, or structure in the first or a very early stage of its formation: as, the *primitive* cerebral vesicles (the rudiment of the brain, out of which the whole brain is to be formed). See cut at *protovertebra*. (*b*) Primary or first of its kind; temporary and soon to disappear: opposed to *definitive*: as, the *primitive* aorta.—5. In *bot.*, noting specific types, in opposition to forms resulting from hybridization. *Henslow.*—6. In *geol.*, of the earliest or supposed earliest formation: in the early history of geology noting the older crystalline rocks of which the age and stratigraphical relations were uncertain, and the fossils (where these had once been present) either entirely obliterated or rendered so indistinct by metamorphism of the strata in which they were embedded that their determination was a matter of doubt. Many of the rocks formerly called *primitive* are now known to be more or less thoroughly metamorphosed Paleozoic strata, and in the progress of geological investigation they have been referred to their place in the series of stratified formations. Other so-called *primitive* rocks belong to the azoic or archæan series (as this latter term was and still is used by Dana)—that is, they unmistakably underlie unconformably the oldest known fossiliferous strata. These azoic rocks are made up in part of eruptive masses, and in part of highly metamorphosed sedimentary deposits which, so far as can be determined from existing evidence, were deposited before the appearance of life on the earth. As there is much primitive rock of which the geological age has not as yet been fixed, it has been found convenient to designate this simply as *crystalline* or *metamorphic*; such rocks are, however, often called *archæan*; but this cannot be properly done until their infra-Silurian position has been established by observation.

These remarkable formations [granite, granitic schist, roofing-slate, etc.] have been called *primitive*, from their having been supposed to constitute the most ancient mineral productions of the globe, and from a notion that they originated before the earth was inhabited by living beings, and while yet the planet was in a nascent state.
Sir C. Lyell, Prin. of Geol. (4th ed., 1835), III. 336.

Primitive aorta. See *aorta*.—**Primitive axes of coordinates**, that system of axes to which the points of a magnitude are first referred with reference to a second set, to which they are afterward referred.—**Primitive carotid artery**, the common carotid artery.—**Primitive cerebral cleft.** See *cleft*[1].—**Primitive chord**, in *music*, a chord in its original position—that is, with its root in the lowest voice-part.—**Primitive circle**, in the stereographic projection of the sphere, the circle on the plane of which the projection is made.—**Primitive colors**, in *painting*, red, yellow, and blue: so called because it was erroneously believed that from mixtures of these all other colors could be obtained. In regard to mixtures of pigments, this very rudely approximates to the truth; in regard to true mixtures of colors, it is strikingly false. See *color*.—**Primitive contravariant, dislocation, equation.** See the nouns.—**Primitive curve, surface**, etc., that from which another is derived.—**Primitive fathers.** See *fathers of the church*, under *father*.—**Primitive fibrillæ**, the extremely fine filaments of which the axis-cylinder of a nerve-fiber is composed. Also called *nerve-fibrils*, *granular fibrils*.—**Primitive fire.** See *fire*.—**Primitive form**, in the theory of numbers, a form which is not equivalent to another form with smaller coefficients. Thus, the form

$$x^2 - 4xy + 2y^2,$$

by means of the transformation

$$x = \xi - 3\eta$$
$$y = 2\xi - 5\eta$$

(the determinant of which is unity), is shown to be equivalent to

$$\xi^2 - 2\xi\eta - \eta^2,$$

and this latter is evidently primitive.—**Primitive groove**, the first furrow which appears along the midline of the back of a vertebrate embryo, in the site of the future cerebrospinal axis. It is the very earliest characteristic mark or formation of a vertebrate, caused by a sinking in of a line of cells of the ectoblast, and a rising up of other cells of the same blastodermic layer to form right and left ridges or lips of the groove, which lips soon grow together and thus convert the groove into a tube, within which the cerebrospinal axis is developed. Also called *primitive furrow*, *streak*, and *trace*.—**Primitive group.** See *group*[1].—**Primitive Methodist Connection**, a Wesleyan denomination founded in 1810 by Hugh Bourne. In doctrine it is in substantial accord with other Methodist churches; in polity it is substantially Presbyterian. It is found principally in England, the British colonies, and the United States, and numbers about 185,000 members.—**Primitive Nth root of unity**, an imaginary root of unity which is not a root of unity of a lower order than *N*.—**Primitive plane**, in spherical projection, the plane upon which the projections are made, generally coinciding with some principal circle of the sphere.—**Primitive radii.** Same as *proportional radii* (which see, under *radius*).—**Primitive root of a prime number** *p*, a number whose *p*th power diminished by unity is the lowest power of it divisible by *p*.—**Primitive root of the binomial congruence appertaining to the exponent** *m*, a number which satisfies the congruence x^{l} (mod *p*) and no similar congruence of lower degree.—**Primitive sheath**, the membranous sheath of neurokeratin lying in medullated nerve-fibers outside of the white substance of Schwann. Also called *sheath of Schwann*, and *neurilemma*. =**Syn.** 1 and 2. *Pristine*, etc. See *primary*.

II. *n.* 1. An original or primary word; a word from which another is derived: opposed to *derivative*.—2†. An early Christian.

The zeal of the present age is stark cold, if compared to the fervours of the apostles and other holy *primitives*.
Jer. Taylor, Works (ed. 1835), I. 685.

3. In *math.*, a geometrical or algebraic form from which another is derived, especially an algebraic expression of which another is the derivative; an equation which satisfies a differential equation, or equation of differences, of which it is said to be the primitive (if it has the requisite number of arbitrary constants to form the solution of the differential equation, it is called the *complete primitive*: see *complete*); a curve of which another is the polar or reciprocal, etc.

primitively (prim'i-tiv-li), *adv.* 1. Originally; at first.

Tithers themselves have contributed to their own confutation by confessing that the Church liv'd *primitively* on Alms. *Milton*, Touching Hirelings.

Solemnities and ceremonies *primitively* enjoined were afterwards omitted, the occasion ceasing. *Sir T. Browne.*

2. Primarily; not derivatively.—3. According to the original rule or oldest practice; in the ancient or antique style.

The best, the purest, and most *primitively* ordered church in the world. *South*, Sermons, VI. 117.

primitiveness (prim'i-tiv-nes), *n.* The state of being primitive or original; antiquity; conformity to antiquity.

primitivity (prim-i-tiv'i-ti), *n.* [< *primitive* + *-ity.*] The character of being primitive: thus, in mathematics we speak of the *primitivity* of a form.

Oh! I can tell you, the age of George the Second is likely to be celebrated for more *primitivity* than the disinterestedness of Mr. Deard. *Walpole*, To Mann, Aug. 8, 1759.

primity† (prim'i-ti), *n.* [< L. *primus*, first, + *-ity.*] The state of being original or first; primitiveness.

This *primity* God requires to be attributed to himself. *Bp. Pearson*, Expos. of Creed, i.

primly (prim'li), *adv.* In a prim or precise manner; with primness.

primness (prim'nes), *n.* The state or condition of being prim or formal; affected niceness or preciseness.

The stiff unalterable *primness* of his long cravat. *Gentleman's Mag.*, 1745.

Primnoa (prim'nọ̄-ạ), *n.* [NL. (Lamarck, 1812).] The typical genus of *Primnoidæ*.

primnoid (prim'nọ̄-id), *n.* A polyp of the family *Primnoidæ*.

Primnoidæ (prim-nō'i-dē), *n. pl.* [NL., < *Primnoa* + *-idæ*.] A family of gorgoniaceous alcyonarian polyps, typified by the genus *Primnoa*.

Primnoa reseda. (One sixteenth natural size.)

primo (prē'mō). [It., < L. *primus*, first: see *prime*.] In *music*, a first or principal part, as in duets or trios.—**Tempo primo**, at the first or original tempo or pace: used after a passage in some other tempo than the first.

primogenial† (prī-mọ̄-jē'ni-ạl), *a.* An erroneous form of *primigenial*.

The *primogenial* light which at first was diffused over the face of the unfashion'd chaos. *Glanville*, Vanity of Dogmatizing, i.

Noon stands eternal here; here may thy sight
Drink in the rays of *primogenial* light.
Watts, Paradise.

primogenital (prī-mọ̄-jen'i-tạl), *a.* [< L. *primogenita*, the rights of the first-born (see *primogeniture*), + *-al*. Cf. LL. *primogenitalis*, original.] Primogenitary.

Those garments Rebecca put on Jacob, his sacerdotal vestment; but it was still the *primogenital* right, till a family separated. *Evelyn*, True Religion, II. 21.

Genesis, as a fundamental factor in evolution, may be more intelligently considered under some of its subordinate phases, as heredity, physiological selection, sexual selection, *primogenital* selection, sexual differentiation, including philoprogeneity, hybridity, etc. *Science*, XII. 124.

primogenitary (prī-mọ̄-jen'i-tạ̄-ri), *a.* [< L. *primogenita*, the rights of the first-born (see *primogeniture*), + *-ary*.] Of or belonging to primogeniture, or the rights of the first-born.

They do not explicitly condemn a limited monarchy, but evidently adopt his scheme of *primogenitary* right, which is perhaps almost incompatible with it. *Hallam.*

primogenitive (prī-mọ̄-jen'i-tiv), *a.* and *n.* [< L. *primogenita*, the rights of the first-born (see *primogeniture*), + *-ive*.] **I.** *a.* Relating to primogeniture.

II.† *n.* Primogeniture; right of primogeniture.

The *primogenitive* and due of birth. *Shak.*, T. and C., i. 3. 106.

primogenitor (prī-mọ̄-jen'i-tọr), *n.* [= Pg. *primogenitor* = It. *primogenitore*, primogenitor (cf. ML. *primogenitor*, first-born), < L. *primus*, first, + *genitor*, a parent, a father, < *genere*, *gignere*, beget, bring forth.] A forefather; an ancestor.

If your *primogenitors* be not belied, the general smutch you have was once of a deeper black, when they came from Mauritania into Spain. *Gayton*, Notes on Don Quixote.

Our *primogenitors* passed their days among trees. *Pennsylvania School Jour.*, XXXII. 382.

primogeniture (prī-mọ̄-jen'i-tūr), *n.* [= F. *primogéniture* = Pr. Sp. Pg. It. *primogenitura*, < ML. *primogenitura*, primogeniture, < L. *primogenita*, the rights of the first-born, birthright, neut. pl. of *primogenitus*, first-born, < *primo*, first, in the first place (abl. neut. of *primus*, first), + *genitus*, pp. of *gignere*, bring forth: see *geniture*.] **1.** The state of being the first-born among children of the same parents; seniority by birth.

Aristodemus . . . died leaving twin sons, Eurysthenes and Procles; their mother refusing to determine which had the right of *primogeniture*, it was agreed that both should succeed to the crown with equal authority. *J. Adams*, Works, IV. 549.

2. Descent to the eldest son; the principle or right by which (under the Norman law introduced into England) the oldest son of a family succeeds to the father's real estate in preference to, and to the absolute exclusion of, the younger sons and daughters. The ancient customs of gavelkind and borough-English form exceptions to the general rule of law as to primogeniture. (See *gavelkind* and *borough-English*.) In the modified form of the law of primogeniture now existing in England, the law, if left to operate, carries the land of a person dying to male heirs singly, in succession preferring the eldest, but to female heirs equally in common, and carries personalty to wife and children with no preference for the eldest son.

He was the first-born of the Almighty, and so, by the title of *primogeniture*, heir of all things. *South*, Sermons, IV. x.

The abolition of *primogeniture*, and equal partition of inheritances, removed the feudal and unnatural distinctions which made one member of every family rich and all the rest poor, substituting equal partition, the best of all agrarian laws. *Jefferson*, Autobiog., p. 40.

Primogeniture, as we know it in our law, had rather a political than a civil origin, and comes from the authority of the feudal lord and probably from that of the tribal chief; but here and there on the Continent there are traces of it as a civil institution, and in such cases the succession of the eldest son does not exclude provision for the younger sons by what are called appanages. *Maine*, Early Law and Custom, p. 261.

Representative primogeniture, the rule of feudal inheritance by which the issue of a deceased child were regarded as standing in the place of that child, subject to the same preference of males over females among them, and of elder over younger males among them, as obtained among children inheriting directly: so that, if an elder son died leaving sons and daughters, the eldest of the sons would take what his father, if living, would have taken.

primogenitureship (prī-mọ̄-jen'i-tūr-ship), *n.* [< *primogeniture* + *-ship*.] The state or right of a first-born son.

By the aristocratical law of *primogenitureship* in a family of six children, five are exposed. Aristocracy has never but one child. *Burke*, Appeal to the Old Whigs.

primordia, *n.* Plural of *primordium*.

primordial (prī-môr'di-ạl), *a.* and *n.* [< ME. *prymordiall* (n.), < OF. (also F.) *primordial* = Pr. Sp. Pg. *primordial* = It. *primordiale*, < ML. *primordialis*, < LL. *primordialis*, original, that is first of all, < L. *primordium*, pl. *primordia*, origin, beginnings: see *primordium*.] **I.** *a.* **1.** First in order; earliest; original; primitive; existing from the beginning.

The *primordial* state of our first parents. *Bp. Bull*, Works, III. 1102. (*Latham.*)

I have sometimes thought that the States in our system may be compared to the *primordial* particles of matter, . . . whose natural condition is to repel each other, or, at least, to exist in their own independent identity. *R. Choate*, Addresses, p. 401.

I should infer from analogy that probably all the organic beings which have ever lived on this earth have descended from some one *primordial* form, into which life was first breathed. *Darwin*, Origin of Species, p. 420.

2. In *anat.*, primitive; formative; in a rudimentary or embryonic state: opposed to *definitive*, or final, completed, or perfected: as, the *primordial* skull of man is partly membranous, partly cartilaginous.

Three pairs of segmental organs, which have only a temporary existence and have been regarded as *primordial* kidneys, are developed at the posterior end of the body. *Huxley*, Anat. Invert., p. 192.

3. In *bot.*, first formed: applied to the first true leaves formed by a young plant, also to the first fruit produced on a raceme or spike.—4. In *geol.*, containing the earliest traces of life.

Of all the results of geological and paleontological investigation during the past half-century, there is no one so remarkable as the revelation of the existence of the so-called *primordial* fauna. It is now clearly established that there was a time when life was represented by a few forms, which were essentially the same all over the globe. What has long been known to be true for Europe and America has been recently supplemented, for Asia, by the investigations of Richthofen in China, where the peculiar *primordial* fauna seems to be largely developed, bearing, as Professor Dames remarks, "an astonishing resemblance to that of North America and Scandinavia." *Whitney and Wadsworth*, The Azoic System, p. 546.

Primordial cell, in *bot.*, a cell of the simplest character, one which does not possess a cell-wall.—**Primordial utricle**, in *bot.*, the layer of somewhat denser protoplasm which lines the inner surface of the wall of a vacuolated cell.—**Primordial zone**, the name given by Barrande to certain strata in Bohemia which there contain the lowest fauna, pretty nearly the equivalent of the Potsdam sandstone of the New York Survey, and of the Cambrian of North Wales. In these various regions, as well as in other parts of the globe, as in China and the Cordilleras, the fauna of the primordial zone is strikingly similar, consisting largely of trilobites and brachiopods, certain genera of which appear to have had a world-wide distribution. = **Syn. 1.** *Prime*, etc. See *primary*.

II. *n.* A first principle or element.

The *primordials* of the world are not mechanical, but spermatical and vital. *Dr. H. More*, Divine Dialogues.

Primordialidæ (prī-môr-di-al'i-dē), *n. pl.* [NL., < LL. *primordialis*, primordial, + *-idæ*.] A family of goniatites, having smooth whorls with simple sutures and large divided ventral lobes. *Hyatt*, Proc. Bost. Soc. Nat. Hist., 1883, p. 315.

primordialism (prī-môr'di-ạl-izm), *n.* [< *primordial* + *-ism*.] Continuance or observance of primitive ceremonies or the like.

Yet another indication of *primordialism* may be named. This species of control [ceremonial observance] establishes itself anew with every fresh relation among individuals. *H. Spencer*, Prin. of Sociol., § 343.

primordiality (prī-môr-di-al'i-ti), *n.* [< *primordial* + *-ity*.] The character of being primordial, and therefore not derived from anything else.

primordially (prī-môr'di-ạl-i), *adv.* Under the first order of things: at the beginning.

primordiate (prī-môr'di-āt), *a.* [< L. *primordius*, original, + *-ate*[1].] Original; existing from the first.

Not every thing chymists will call salt, sulphur, or spirit, that needs always be a *primordiate* and ingenerable body. *Boyle.*

primordium (prī-môr'di-um), *n.*; pl. *primordia* (-ạ̈). [L., commonly in pl. *primordia*, the beginnings, < *primus*, first, + *ordiri*, begin. Cf. *exordium*.] **1.** Beginning; commencement; origin. *Quarterly Rev.* (*Worcester.*)—**2.** In *bot.*, the ultimate beginning of any structure.

primosity (prim-os'i-ti), *n.* [Irreg. < *prim*[1] + *-osity*, as in *pomposity*, etc.] Primness; prudery. [Rare.]

I should really like to know what excuse Lord A—— could offer for his *primosity* to us, when he was riding with such a Jezebel as Lady ——. *Memoirs of Lady Hester Stanhope*, xi.

primovant (prī-mō'vạnt), *n.* In *anc. astron.*, that sphere which was supposed to carry the fixed stars in their daily motions to which all the other orbs were attached. See *primum mobile*.

The motion of the *primovant* (or first equinoctial motion). *Dee*, Mathematicall Preface (1570).

primp (primp), *v.* [A form of *prink*, imitating *prim*.] **I.** *trans.* To dress or deck (one's self) in a formal and affected manner.

II. *intrans.* To be formal or affected. [Prov. Eng. and Scotch.]

primprint† (prim'print), *n.* [Also *primeprint*, *primprivet*; < *prim*, *prime*, + *primet*.] Same as *primet*.

That great bushy plant, usually termed privet, or *primprint*. *Topsell*, Historie of Serpents, p. 103. (*Halliwell.*)

primprivet†, *n.* Same as *primprint*. *Minsheu* (misprinted *prunprivet*).

primrose (prim'rōz), *n.* and *a.* [< ME. *primerose*, *prymerose*, < OF. *primerose*, primrose (according to Godefroy, same as *passerose*, hollyhock), as if < L. *prima rosa*, 'first rose,' but actually a substitution for OF. *primerole*, a primrose: see *primerole*. Cf. *tuberose*, which also simulates a connection with *rose*[2].] **I.** *n.* **1.** A plant of the genus *Primula*; especially, a variety of *Primula veris*, in which the flowers appear as if on separate peduncles, the short common stalk being hidden beneath the base of the leaves. Several of the best-known species and varieties, however, have independent names, as *auricula*, *cowslip*, *oxlip*, and *polyanthus*. See cut under *Primula*. See also the phrases below.

Thou seydest a ȝerd schulde sprynge
Oute of the rote of Ientill Iesse,
And schulde floure with florisschyng,
With *primeroses* greet plent.
Holy Rood (E. E. T. S.), p. 212.

The *primrose* placing first, because that in the spring
It is the first appears, then only flourishing.
Drayton, Polyolbion, xv. 149.

A *primrose* by a river's brim
A yellow *primrose* was to him,
And it was nothing more.
Wordsworth, Peter Bell, I.

2. One of a few other plants with some resemblance to the primrose. See the phrases below.—3†. The first or earliest flower; a spring flower.

With painted words tho gan this proude weede [the brier], . . .
Was I not planted of thine owne hand,
To be the *primrose* of all the land;
With flowring blossomes to furnish the prime?
Spenser, Shep. Cal., February.

4†. Figuratively, the first or choicest; the flower.

Two noble *Primeroses* of Nobilitie.
Ascham, The Scholemaster, p. 66.

She is the pride and *primrose* of the rest,
Made by the Maker selfe to be admired.
Spenser, Colin Clout, l. 560.

5. In *her.*, a quatrefoil used as a bearing.—6. A pale and somewhat greenish-yellow color.—7. A coal-tar color used in dyeing, being the potassium ethyl salt of tetrabrom-fluorescein. It is mostly used in silk-dyeing, producing pinkish-yellow shades.—**Bird's-eye primrose**, *Primula farinosa*, a pretty plant with silvery leaves in small rosettes, the flower-stalks 3 to 12 inches high, bearing compact umbels of lilac-purple yellow-eyed flowers. It is wild northward in both hemispheres.—**Cape primrose**, a plant of the genus *Streptocarpus*.—**Chinese primrose**, *Primula Sinensis*, a familiar house-plant.—**Evening primrose.** See *Œnothera*.—**Fairy primrose**, *Primula minima*, a species native in the mountains of southern Europe, only an inch or so high, but with flowers nearly an inch broad.—**Himalayan primrose**, *Primula Sikkimensis*, abounding in wet places of the Himalayas at high altitudes, also cultivated. It is the tallest described species, the scape often 2 feet high, the corollas of the numerous sweet-scented flowers funnel-shaped, with the limb concave.—**Japanese primrose**, *Primula Japonica*, one of the handsomest species, the flowers unfolding in successive whorls on the tall scape.—**Mistassinnie primrose**, *Primula Mistassinica*, of northern North America, named from a Canadian lake: a low, pretty plant, the flowers from one to eight, flesh-colored.—**Night primrose.** Same as *evening primrose*.—**Peerless primrose**, the primrose-peerless.—**Scotch primrose**, a variety of the bird's-eye primrose, *Primula farinosa*, var. *Scotica*.

II. *a.* 1. Of or belonging to a primrose; specifically, resembling a primrose in color; pale-yellow.

He had a buff waistcoat with coral buttons, a light coat, lavender trousers, white jean boots, and *primrose* kid gloves. *G. A. Sala*, Dutch Pictures. (*Latham.*)

2. Abounding with primroses; flowery; gay.

Himself the *primrose* path of dalliance treads.
Shak., Hamlet, i. 3. 50.

Primrose League. See *league*[1].

primrosed (prim'rōzd), *a.* [< *primrose* + *-ed*[2].] Covered or adorned with primroses.

Not one of your broad, level, dusty, glaring causeways, but a zig-zag, up-and-down *primrosed* by-road.
Savage, Reuben Medlicott, i. 1. (*Davies.*)

primrose-peerless (prim'rōz-pēr"les), *n.* A plant, *Narcissus biflorus*.

primrose-willow (prim'rōz-wil"ō), *n.* See *Jussiæa*.

primsie (prim'si), *a.* [< *prim* + *-sie*, equiv. to *-y*[1].] Prim; demure; precise. [Scotch.]

Primsie Mallie. *Burns*, Halloween.

Primula (prim'ū-lạ̈), *n.* [NL. (Malpighi, 1675), < ML. *primula*, primrose (so called in allusion to its early blooming), fem. of L. *primulus*, first, dim. of *primus*, first: see *prime*. Cf. *primerole*, *primrose*.] 1. A genus of gamopetalous plants, the primroses, type of the order *Primulaceæ* and the tribe *Primuleæ*, characterized by a conspicuous salver-shaped corolla, with five opposite stamens borne on its long tube, and by a roundish five-valved and one-celled capsule, containing many peltate seeds. There are about 130 species, mainly mountain-dwellers of Europe

Flowering Plant of *Primula Sinensis*.

and Asia, with 5 in the United States, 1 in extreme South America, and 1 in the mountains of Java. They are beautiful low-growing plants, with perennial rootstocks. The leaves are all radical, obovate or roundish, entire or toothed, and form a spreading tuft. The flowers are dimorphous, some having a short style and stamens borne high up on the tube, others opposite in both respects. They are white, pink, purple, or yellow in color, grouped in bracted umbels—in the true primrose, however, appearing as if on separate stalks. The common *P. veris* of Europe and northern Asia, elsewhere in gardens, with yellow or straw-colored flowers in early spring, has three varieties, often regarded as species, corresponding to the names *primrose* (*P. vulgaris*), *cowslip* or *pagle* (*P. veris*), and *oxlip* (*P. elatior*). It is, however, generally believed that *P. elatior* is a good species, indigenous, though rare, in England, called *Bardfield oxlip*; and, according to Darwin, *P. vulgaris* and *P. veris* are also distinct, while the common oxlip is a hybrid between them. (See the above common names, and *herb-peter* (*St.-Peter's-wort*), *lady-key*, *petty mullen* (under *mullen*), and *paleywort*.) Numerous other species are beautiful and more or less cultivated. See *auricula*, *baziers*, *bear's-ear*, *dusty-miller*, *French cowslip* (under *cowslip*), *polyanthus*, and *primrose*.

2. [*l. c.*] Any plant of the genus *Primula*.

Primulaceæ (prim-ū-lā'sē-ē), *n. pl.* [NL. (Ventenat, 1799), < *Primula* + *-aceæ*.] A very distinct order of gamopetalous herbs of the cohort *Primulales*, characterized by its five stamens opposite to the five lobes of the regular corolla, and the capsular ovary containing two or more ovules, a single style, and an undivided stigma; the primrose family. It includes about 315 species, classed under 4 tribes and 25 genera, natives of temperate regions and mainly alpine, rare in the southern hemisphere. They are herbs, growing usually from a perennial rootstock; the few that occur in the tropics become there annuals, an inversion of the usual effect of the tropics. They bear undivided or rarely lobed leaves, either all radical, or alternate, opposite, or whorled; and commonly racemed, umbeled, or long-stalked flowers. Very many of the most-prized flowers of cultivation belong to this family, as the primrose, cowslip, polyanthus, auricula, cyclamen, and soldanelle. For the best-known genera, see *Primula* (the type), *Lysimachia*, *Cyclamen*, *Trientalis*, *Glaux*, *Coris*, *Samolus*, *Soldanella*, *Dodecatheon*, and *Hottonia*.

primulaceous (prim-ū-lā'shius), *a.* Of or resembling the *Primulaceæ*.

Primulales (prim-ū-lā'lēz), *n. pl.* [NL. (Lindley, 1833), < *Primula*, q. v.] A cohort of gamopetalous plants of the series *Heteromeræ*, distinguished by a one-celled ovary with a central and basal placenta, and stamens opposite the regular corolla-lobes. It includes 3 orders, of which the *Myrsineæ*, mainly tropical trees, and the *Primulaceæ*, herbs of temperate regions, are alike in their simple style and stigma, whereas the *Plumbagineæ* are mainly maritime herbs, with five styles.

Primuleæ (pri-mū'lē-ē), *n. pl.* [NL. (Endlicher, 1836), < *Primula* + *-eæ*.] A tribe of plants of the order *Primulaceæ*, characterized by the regular imbricated corolla-lobes, stamens on the corolla, superior ovary, and half-anatropous ovules. It includes 12 genera, of which *Primula* is the type.

primulin (prim'ū-lin), *n.* [< NL. *Primula* + *-in*[2].] A crystallizable substance obtained from the root of the cowslip.

primum frigidum (prī'mum frij'i-dum). [L.: *primum*, neut. of *primus*, first; *frigidum*, neut. of *frigidus*, cold: see *prime* and *frigid*.] Pure cold: an elementary substance, according to the doctrine of Parmenides.

The first means of producing cold is that which nature presenteth us withal: namely, the expiring of cold out of the inward parts of the earth in winter, when the sun hath no power to overcome it, the earth being (as hath been noted by some) *primum frigidum*.
Bacon, Nat. Hist., i. 69.

The dispute which is the *primum frigidum* is very well known among naturalists; some contending for the earth, others for water, others for the air, and some of the moderns for nitre, but all seeming to agree that there is some body or other that is of its own nature supremely cold, and by participation of which all other bodies obtain that quality. But, for my part, I think that before men had so hotly disputed which is the *primum frigidum* they would have done well to inquire whether there be any such thing or no. *Boyle*, Experimental History of Cold, title xvii.

primum mobile (prī'mum mob'i-lē). [L.: *primum*, neut. of *primus*, first; *mobile*, neut. of *mobilis*, movable: see *prime* and *mobile*[1].] In the Ptolemaic system of astronomy, the tenth or outermost of the revolving spheres of the universe, which was supposed to revolve from east to west in twenty-four hours, and to carry the others along with it in its motion; hence, any great or first source of motion.

The motions of the greatest persons in a government ought to be as the motions of the planets under *primum mobile*, . . . carried swiftly by the highest motion, and softly in their own motion.
Bacon, Seditions and Troubles.

A star does not move more obediently from east to west than Bacon obeys, and appropriates as his own, the motion of his *primum mobile*, the King.
E. A. Abbott, Bacon, p. 249.

primus (prī'mus), *n.*; pl. *primi* (-mī). [L., first: see *prime*.] The first in dignity among the bishops of the Scottish Episcopal Church. He is chosen by the other bishops, presides at all their meetings, and has certain other privileges, but possesses no metropolitan authority.

primus inter pares (prī'mus in'tėr pā'rēz). [L.: *primus*, first; *inter*, among; *pares*, pl. of *par*, equal: see *prime*, *inter*[2], and *pair*[1].] A Latin phrase, meaning 'first among equals.'

primy† (prī'mi), *a.* [< *prime* + *-y*[1].] Early; blooming. [Rare.]

A violet in the youth of *primy* nature.
Shak., Hamlet, i. 3. 7.

prin[1] (prin), *n.* and *v.* A dialectal form of *preen*[1].

Wha will *prin* my sma' middle,
Wi' the short *prin* and the lang?
Sweet Willie and Fair Maisry (Child's Ballads, II. 334).

prin[2]† (prin), *a.* [< OF. *prin*, var. of *prim*, thin, slender: see *prim*[1].] Slender; thin.

Hee looks as gaunt and *prin* as he that spent
A tedious twelve years in an eager Lent.
Fletcher, Poems, p. 140. (*Halliwell.*)

prince (prins), *n.* [< ME. *prince*, *prynce* = D. *prins* = MLG. *prince*, *prinse* = MHG. *prinze*, G. *prinz* = Sw. Dan. *prins*, < OF. (and F.) *prince* = Pr. *princep*, *prince*, *prinsi* = Sp. Pg. It. *príncipe*, a prince; < L. *princeps* (*-cip-*), a first or chief person, a chief, superior, leader, ruler, sovereign, prince, prop. adj., first in time or order, < *primus*, prime, first, + *capere*, take, choose: see *capable*.] 1. A sovereign; a king; by extension, a royal personage of either sex.

As this noble *Prince* is endued with mercie, pacience, and moderation, so is she adourned with singuler beautie and chastitie. *Lyly*, Euphues and his England, p. 454.

Such duty as the subject owes the *prince*.
Shak., T. of the S., v. 2. 155.

"No one thing," sighed Walsingham, "doth more prognosticate an alteration of this estate than that a *prince* of her Majesty's judgment should neglect . . . the stopping of so dangerous a gap."
Motley, Hist. Netherlands, II. 329.

Some of the Mercian Kings were very powerful *Princes*.
E. A. Freeman, Old Eng. Hist., p. 39.

2. The title of the ruler of a principality: as, the *Prince* of Waldeck; the former *Princes* of Orange. Few such principalities now exist in Europe; they are either small in extent (as Montenegro and Monaco), or in certain relations subordinate in name or reality to a suzerain (as Bulgaria), or to a central government (as Lippe, Waldeck, and the other principalities of the German empire).

3. A title of nobility in certain countries on the continent, superior to *duke*: as, *Prince* Bismarck; *Prince* of Condé. There are, however, many exceptions in the relative standing of particular titles, owing to the fact that many princely designations are little more than courtesy titles, or to the circumstance that some princely titles are historically and intrinsically of comparatively small importance, while some ducal titles, on the contrary, are of the highest, sometimes even of sovereign dignity. *Prince* is the translation of the chief Russian title of nobility (*knyaz*).

4. A courtesy title given to non-regnant members of royal families, and often confined to the younger sons of the sovereign: as, *Prince* Arthur (of Great Britain); *Prince* Henry (of Prussia); the eldest sons are usually called *prince* with a territorial title (as *Prince* of Wales, in Great Britain; *Prince* of Naples, in Italy), *crown prince* (Greece), *prince imperial* (Austria, Germany, etc.), *prince royal* (Denmark, Sweden, etc.), or *duke* with a territorial title (as *Duke* of Sparta, in Greece; *Duke* of Brabant, in Belgium).

The empress and young *princes* of the blood of both sexes. *Swift*, Gulliver's Travels, i. 2.

Until he is created a peer, by the title of duke or other rank in the peerage, a member of the reigning family—even the sovereign's own younger son—though styled *prince* and royal highness, is in law but a commoner.
N. and Q., 7th ser., IV. 229.

5. A courtesy title given in some relations to dukes, marquises, and earls in Great Britain. See the quotation.

He [an earl, also a marquis] bears also the title, upon some occasions, of Most Noble and Puissant *Prince*.
Burke, Peerage, Int., p. lxxi.

6. One who is preëminent in his class or profession: as, a merchant *prince*; a *prince* of good fellows.

Hit semed as he myȝt
Be *prynce* with-outen pere,
In felde ther felle men fyȝt.
Sir Gawayne and the Green Knight (E. E. T. S.), l. 873.

Asclepius amongst the Ægines, Demosthenes amongst the Athenians, Æschines amongst the Rhodians, Cicero amongst the Romanes, were not only skilfull in Orations, but *Princes* of all other Oratours.
Guevara, Letters (tr. by Hellowes, 1577), p. 46.

These mentioned by their names were *princes* in their families. 1 Chron. iv. 38.

Brave Troilus! the *prince* of chivalry!
Shak., T. and C., i. 2. 249.

To use the words of the *prince* of learning hereupon, only in shallow and small boats they glide over the face of the Virgilian sea. *Peacham*, Poetry.

Christmas prince. See *Christmas*.—**Grand prince, or great prince.** (*a*) A title of various rulers or princes in Russia. See *grand duke* (*b*), under *grand*. (*b*) A title of the emperor of Austria (as Grand Prince of Transylvania).—**Merchant prince.** See *merchant*.—**Prince bishop,** formerly, a ruler who was at once the bishop of a diocese (or other spiritual ruler) and a sovereign prince; especially, such a prince and prelate of the German empire; also, in Montenegro, the chief ruler, or vladika, who was at the same time the head of the national church.

The eldest of these three persons was no other than Massalski, the *Prince-bishop* of Wilna in Lithuania.
Edinburgh Rev., CXLV. 2.

Prince consort. See *consort*[1].—**Prince Elector,** one of the electors of the former German empire.—**Prince imperial,** the eldest son of an emperor.—**Prince of Peace,** the Messiah; Christ.

For unto us a child is born: . . . and his name shall be called . . . The mighty God, The everlasting Father, The *Prince of Peace*.
Isa. ix. 6.

Prince of the Captivity, the title assumed by the head of the Mesopotamian community of the Jews subsequent to the destruction of Jerusalem.

Those [Jews] of the East were ruled by the *Prince of the Captivity*, who had his seat at Bagdad, which they called Babylon; and those of the West under the Patriarch of the West, who had his seat at Tiberias. The *Prince of the Captivity* was a secular ruler, and pretended to be a descendant of the royal house of David; the Patriarch of the West was an ecclesiastical ruler, of the sacerdotal tribe of Levi. The first *Prince of the Captivity* that we hear of was Huna, about the year 220. *N. and Q.*, 7th ser., II. 176.

Prince of the senate. See *princeps senatus*, under *princeps*.—**Prince of this world,** in *Scrip.*, Satan.

Now shall the *prince of this world* be cast out.
John xii. 31.

Prince of Wales, in England, the title given to the eldest son of the sovereign and heir apparent to the throne. The title is created in every case, and not hereditary. It dates from the reign of Edward III.—**Prince of Wales's feathers.** See *feather*.—**Prince President,** a title given to Prince Louis Napoleon while he was president of the French republic, 1848–52.—**Prince royal,** the eldest son of a king or queen; the heir apparent.—**Prince Rupert's drop.** Same as *detonating bulb* (which see, under *detonating*).—**Prince's metal, mixture,** etc. See *metal*, etc.—**The prince of darkness.** See *darkness*. =**Syn. 1-4.** *Prince, King, Sovereign, Monarch, Emperor.* *Prince* has a narrow and a broad meaning. It may indicate a son of the *sovereign*, or the grade of prescriptive rank next to that of the *sovereign*, or it may be a general word for *king*, etc., as often in Shakspere. A country not large enough to be ruled by a *king* may be ruled by a *prince*, as some of the states of Germany, and Montenegro. *Sovereign* is an impressive but somewhat general term, being applicable to a *king* or an *emperor*, and expressing a high degree of power and dignity. *Monarch* expresses the fact of ruling alone, and therefore is generally, though not necessarily, applied to one ruling autocratically and with splendid state, with similar figurative use. *Emperor* is sometimes affected, as a grander word than *king*, and seems to express more of absolute rule, but there have been kings of all degrees of absolutism and grandeur. Historically, *emperor* is especially associated with military command.

prince (prins), *v. i.*; pret. and pp. *princed*, ppr. *princing*. [< *prince*, *n.*] To play the prince; put on a stately arrogance: with a complementary *it*.

Nature prompts them
In simple and low things to *prince it* much
Beyond the trick of others.
Shak., Cymbeline, iii. 3. 85.

princeage (prin'sāj), *n.* [< *prince* + *-age*.] The body of princes. [Rare.] *Imp. Dict.*

princedom (prins'dum), *n.* [< *prince* + *-dom*.] 1. The rank, estate, or jurisdiction of a prince.

Next Archigald, who for his proud disdayne
Deposed was from *princedome* soverayne.
Spenser, F. Q., II. x. 44.

After that God against him war proclaim'd,
And Satan *princedom* of the earth had claim'd.
Sylvester, tr. of Du Bartas's Weeks, ii., Eden.

2. Same as *principality*, 5.

Under thee, as head supreme,
Thrones, *princedoms*, powers, dominions, I reduce.
Milton, P. L., iii. 320.

princehood (prins'hůd), *n.* [< *prince* + *-hood*.] The quality or rank of a prince.

Promysyng and behightyng by the faith of hys body and worde of his *princehode*. *Hall*, Hen. VI., an. 4.

A Prince might feel that he must maintain the principle which underlies his *princehood*.
New York Semi-weekly Tribune, Nov. 16, 1886.

Princeite (prin'sīt), *n.* [< *Prince* (see def.) + *-ite*[2].] A follower of Henry James Prince, who founded an association called Agapemone. See *Agapemone*.

princekin (prins'kin), *n.* [< *prince* + *-kin*.] A young or little prince; a petty or inferior prince.

The *princekins* of private life, who are flattered and worshipped. *Thackeray*, Newcomes, liii.

princeless (prins'les), *a.* [< *prince* + *-less*.] Without a prince.

This country is *Princeless*—I mean, affords no Royal natives. *Fuller*, Worthies, III. 38.

princelet (prins'let), *n.* [< *prince* + *-let*.] Same as *princekin*.

German *princelets* might sell their country piecemeal to French or Russian. *Kingsley*, Alton Locke, xxxii.

princelike (prins'līk), *a.* [< *prince* + *like*[2].] Befitting a prince; like a prince.

I euer set my fotestepps fre,
Princelike, where none had gone.
Drant, tr. of Horace's Ep., To Mæcenas.

The wrongs he did me
Were nothing *prince-like*.
Shak., Cymbeline, v. 5. 293.

princeliness (prins'li-nes), *n.* The quality of being princely.

princeling (prins'ling), *n.* [< *prince* + *-ling*[1].] Same as *princekin*.

The struggle in his own country has entirely deprived him of revenues as great as any forfeited by their Italian *princelings*. *Disraeli*, Lothair, xlix. (*Davies*.)

princely (prins'li), *a.* [= D. *prinselijk* = G. *prinzlich* = Dan. *prindselig*; as *prince* + *-ly*[1].] 1. Pertaining or belonging to a prince; having the rank of a prince; regal.

In Tarquin's likeness I did entertain thee. . . .
Thou wrong'st his honour, wound'st his *princely* name.
Shak., Lucrece, l. 599.

Princely dignities,
And powers that erst in heaven sat on thrones.
Milton, P. L., i. 359.

2. Resembling a prince; princelike; having the appearance or manner of one high-born; stately; magnanimous; noble.

He is as full of valour as of kindness:
Princely in both. *Shak.*, Hen. V., iv. 3. 16.

What sovereign was ever more *princely* in pardoning injuries, in conquering enemies, in extending the dominions and the renown of his people?
Macaulay, Conversation between Cowley and Milton.

She gazed upon the man
Of *princely* bearing, tho' in bonds.
Tennyson, Pelleas and Ettarre.

3. Befitting a prince; munificent; magnificent; regal: as, a *princely* gift; a *princely* banquet; a *princely* fortune.

There also my Lord did condole the Death of the late Queen, that Duke's Grandmother, and he received very *princely* Entertainment. *Howell*, Letters, I. vi. 5.

=**Syn. 2.** August, imperial.—**3.** Bounteous.

princely (prins'li), *adv.* [< *princely*, *a.*] In a princelike manner; royally.

Doth it not show vilely in me to desire small beer? . . .
Belike then my appetite was not *princely* got.
Shak., 2 Hen. IV., ii. 2. 12.

princeps (prin'seps), *a.* and *n.* [L., first, chief, prince: see *prince*.] **I.** *a.* First; original; hence, specifically, earliest printed; belonging to the first edition.

The *princeps* copy, clad in blue and gold.
J. Ferriar, Bibliomania, l. 6.

II. *n.*; pl. *principes* (prin'si-pēz). 1. One who is first or chief; a chief; specifically, in *early Teut. hist.*, a chief judicial officer or leader in a pagus or other division. Attached to him was a body of attendants called the *comitatus*.

Over each of their local divisions or pagi, at their own pleasure and on a plan which in their eyes was a prudent one, a single *princeps* or chieftain presided.
Stubbs, Const. Hist., § 22.

2. That which is first, foremost, original, or principal; especially, the first or original edition of a book: short for *princeps edition*, or *editio princeps*.—3. [*cap.*] [NL.] In *entom.*, a genus of lepidopterous insects. *Hübner*, 1806.—**Princeps cervicis,** a large branch of the occipital artery descending the neck to supply the trapezius, and anastomosing with the superficialis colli, vertebral, and superior intercostal arteries.—**Princeps pollicis,** a branch of the radial, at the beginning of the deep palmar arch, supplying the integument of the palmar surface of the thumb.—**Princeps senatus,** in ancient Rome, the senator first called in the roll of senators. He was usually of consular and censorian dignity.

prince's-feather (prin'sez-feтн"ėr), *n.* 1. A plant, *Amarantus hypochondriacus*. It is a showy garden annual from tropical America, sometimes 6 feet tall, bearing thick crowded spikes of small red flowers, the uppermost spike much longer and interrupted. The name sometimes extends to other species of the genus. Also *Prince-of-Wales's-feather*. 2. A taller garden annual, *Polygonum orientale*, in England called *tall persicaria*, bearing slender spikes on curving branches. Also called *ragged-sailor*.

prince's-pine (prin'sez-pīn), *n.* See *pine*[1].

princess (prin'ses), *n.* [< ME. *princesse* = D. *prinses* = G. *prinzesse*, *prinzess* = Sw. *prinsessa* = Dan. *prinsesse*, < OF. (and F.) *princesse* (= Pr. *princessa* = Sp. *princesa* = Pg. *princeza* = It. *principessa*), < ML. **principissa*, princess (found only as an abstract noun, principality, principate), fem. of L. *princeps*, prince: see *prince*.] 1. A female sovereign; a woman of princely rank.

How doth the city sit solitary, . . . she that was great among the nations, and a *princess* among the provinces!
Lam. i. 1.

So excellent a *princess* as the present queen. *Swift*.

2. The daughter of a sovereign: a female member of a royal family: in this sense a title of courtesy. Compare *prince*, 4.

I'll tell you who they were, this female pair,
Lest they should seem *princesses* in disguise.
Byron, Don Juan, ii. 124.

Their Majesties, the Prince of Wales, and the three eldest *princesses* went to the Chapel Royal.
Thackeray, Four Georges, George the Second.

3. The consort of a prince: as, the *Princess* of Wales.

Duke Victor [the hereditary prince] was fifty years of age, and his *princess* . . . was scarce three-and-twenty.
Thackeray, Barry Lyndon, x.

Such apparel as might well beseem
His [Geraint's] *princess*, or indeed the stately Queen.
Tennyson, Geraint.

4. A size of roofing-slate 24 inches long by 14 inches wide. Compare *duchess*, 2.—**Princess royal,** the eldest daughter of a king or queen.

princesse (prin-ses'), *a.* [< F. *princesse*, princess: see *princess*.] In *dressmaking*, noting the form and style of a long gown for women, made in one continuous piece without drapery, and fitting closely.—**Demi-princesse,** a gown of which a part only, as the back, is in one piece from top to bottom.

princessly (prin'ses-li), *a.* [< *princess* + *-ly*[1].] Princess-like; having the air or the pretensions of a princess. *Byron*. [Rare.]

The busy old tarpaulin uncle I make but my ambassador to Queen Annabella Howe, to engage her (for example-sake to her *princessly* daughter) to join in their cause.
Richardson, Clarissa Harlowe, I. 186. (*Davies*.)

princewood (prins'wůd), *n.* A light-veined brown West Indian wood, the product of *Cordia gerascanthoides* and *Hamelia ventricosa*—the latter also called *Spanish elm*.

principled (prin'si-fīd), *a.* [< *prince* + *-i-fy* + *-ed*[2].] Imitating a prince; ridiculously dignified.

The English girls . . . laughed at the *principled* airs which she gave herself from a very early age.
Thackeray, Virginians, v.

principal (prin'si-pal), *a.* and *n.* [< ME. *principal*, *prynsipall*, < OF. (and F.) *principal* = Sp. Pg. *principal* = It. *principale*, < L. *principalis*, first, original, chief, < *princeps* (*-cip-*), first, chief: see *prince*.] **I.** *a.* 1. Chief; highest in rank, authority, value, or importance; most considerable; main; first: as, the *principal* officers of a government; the *principal* points in an argument; the *principal* products of a country.

It is to large to vse at masse, but they use it in adhornynge the aulter at *pryncypall* tymes.
Sir R. Guylforde, Pylgrymage, p. 7.

Wisdom is the *principal* thing; therefore get wisdom.
Prov. iv. 7.

The *principal* men of the army meeting one evening at the tent of Sextus Tarquinius. *Shak.*, Lucrece, Arg.

Character is but one, though a *principal*, source of interest among several that are employed by the drama and the novel. *J. Sully*, Sensation and Intuition, p. 298.

2†. Of or pertaining to a prince; princely.

He, . . . by the great goodwill our Prince bears him, may soon obtain the use of his name and credit, which hath a *principal* sway, not only in his own Arcadia, but in all these countries of Peloponnesus.
Sir P. Sidney, Arcadia, i.

Center of principal curvature. See *center*[1].—**Principal axis,** in conic sections, the axis which passes through the two foci; in the parabola, the diameter passing through the focus.—**Principal brace.** See *brace*[1].—**Principal cells.** See *cell*.—**Principal challenge.** See *challenge*, 9.—**Principal chord,** a chord to a surface perpendicular to the plane through the middle points of all parallel chords.—**Principal close,** in *music*, same as *perfect cadence* (which see, under *cadence*).—**Principal end.** See *end*.—**Principal Factory Act.** See *Factory Acts*, under *factory*.—**Principal focus.** See *focus*, 1.—**Principal form, function, king-at-arms, part.** See the nouns.—**Principal points.** See *point*[1].—**Principal post,** the corner-post of a timber-framed house.—**Principal proposition,** a self-evident and undemonstrable maxim of proof.—**Principal rafter.** See *rafter*.—**Principal ray,** that ray which passes perpendicularly from the spectator's eye to the perspective plane or picture.—**Principal screw of inertia.** See *inertia*.—**Principal section,** in *optics*, any plane passing through the optical axis of a crystal.—**Principal subject or theme,** in *music*, one of the chief subjects of a movement in sonata form, as opposed to a subordinate theme.—**Principal tangent conic.** See *conic*.—**Principal value of a function,** the one real value. Thus, the logarithm of a real quantity is a real quality plus N times an imaginary quantity, and the value given by putting N = 0 is the *principal value*.—**The principal axes of inertia, of stress.** See *axis*[1]. =**Syn. 1.** Leading, great, capital, cardinal, supreme.

II. *n.* 1. A chief or head; one who takes a leading part; one primarily concerned in an action, and not an auxiliary, accessory, assistant, or agent: as, the *principals* in a duel.

Seconds in factions do many times, when the faction subdivideth, prove *principals*. *Bacon*, Faction.

It is devised that the Duke of Gloucester as *Principal*, and other Lords that crossed the King's Courses, should be invited to a supper in London, and there be murthered.
Baker, Chronicles, p. 142.

We engaged in this war as *principals*, when we ought to have acted only as auxiliaries.
Swift, Conduct of the Allies.

I thought you might be the young *principal* of a first-rate firm. *George Eliot*, Daniel Deronda, xxxiii.

2. A governor or presiding officer; one who is chief in authority. Specifically, the head of an institution of learning: a title used (*a*) in colleges or universities in Scotland, Canada, and other parts of the British empire; (*b*) in certain colleges (Brasenose, Jesus, etc.) and halls at Oxford; (*c*) in the public and in many private secondary schools in the United States; (*d*) in certain higher institutions of learning in the British empire.
3. In *law*: (*a*) A person who, being sui juris, and competent to do an act on his own account, employs another person to do it; the person from whom an agent's authority is derived. Compare *master*[1], 2.

The agent simply undertakes to execute a commission in the market; in that market he acts as though he were the *principal*. *Nineteenth Century*, XXVI. 845.

(*b*) A person for whom another becomes surety; one who is liable for a debt in the first instance. (*c*) In testamentary and administration law, the corpus or capital of the estate, in contradistinction to the income. Thus, under a gift of the income of stock to A for life, and on A's death the stock to B, it is often a contested question whether a stock dividend, as distinguished from a money dividend, is *income* or *principal*. (*d*) In criminal law, the actor in the commission of a crime; a person concerned in the commission of a crime, whether he directly commits the act constituting the offense or instigates or aids and abets in its commission. A *principal in the first degree* is the absolute perpetrator of the act which constitutes the crime, whether he does it with his own hand or by the hand of an innocent third person, the third person being ignorant of the character of the act perpetrated. A *principal in the second degree* is a person who, without actually participating in the act itself, is present, aiding and encouraging the person who commits the act. See *accessory*.

And before the coroner of Coventre, up on the sygth of the bodyes, ther ben endited, as *pryncipall* for the deth of Richard Stafford, Syr Robert Harcourt and the ij. men that ben dede. *Paston Letters*, I. 74.

By the Common Lawe, the accessoryes cannot be proceeded agaynst till the *principall* receave his tryall.
Spenser, State of Ireland.

4. In *com.*, money bearing interest; a capital sum lent on interest, due as a debt or used as a fund: so called in distinction to *interest* or *profits*.

Shall I not have barely my *principal*?
Shak., M. of V., iv. 1. 342.

5. In *organ-building*, a stop of the open diapason group, usually giving tones an octave above the pitch of the digitals used, like the octave. Such a stop is commonly the one in which the temperament is first set in tuning, and from which other stops are tuned. In Germany the open diapason is called the *principal*, and the octave is called the *octave principal*.
6. A musical instrument used in old orchestral music, especially that of Handel—a variety of trumpet, probably having a larger tube than the ordinary tromba.—7. In *music*: (*a*) The subject of a fugue: opposed to *answer*. (*b*) A soloist or other leading performer.—8. Same as *principal rafter*. See *rafter*.

Our lodgings . . . shook as the earth did quake;
The very *principals* did seem to rend,
And all-to topple. *Shak.*, Pericles, iii. 2. 16.

Thirty *principals*, made of great masts, being forty feet in length apiece, standing upright.
Stow (Arber's Eng. Garner, I. 477).

9. In the *fine arts*, the chief motive in a work of art, to which the rest are to be subordinate; also, an original painting or other work of art.

Another pretty piece of painting I saw, on which there was a great wager laid by young Pinkney and me whether it was a *principal* or a copy. *Pepys*, Diary, May 19, 1660.

10. One of the turrets or pinnacles of waxwork and tapers with which the posts and center of a hearse were formerly crowned. *Oxford Glossary*.

From these uprights [of a hearse of lights], technically called *principals*, as well as from the ribs which spanned the top and kept the whole together, sprouted out hundreds of gilt metal branches for wax tapers.
Rock, Church of our Fathers, ii. 496.

11†. An important personal belonging; an heirloom.

And also that my best horse shall be my *principal* [to be led at the funeral], without any armour or man armed, according to the custom of mean people.
Test. Vetust., p. 75. (*Halliwell.*)

In the district of Archenfield, near the Welsh border, the house and lands were divided between the sons on their father's death, but certain *principals* passed to the eldest as heirlooms, such as the best table and bed.
Encyc. Brit., XIX. 733.

12†. In *ornith.*, one of the primaries.

A bird whose *principals* be scarce grown out.
Spenser, Epist. to Maister Harvey.

principality (prin-si-pal'i-ti), *n.*; pl. *principalities* (-tiz). [< ME. *principalite*, < OF. *principalité*, also *principauté*, F. *principauté* = Sp. *principalidad* = Pg. *principalidade* = It. *principalità*, < L. *principalita(t-)s*, the first place, preeminence, < *principalis*, first, chief: see *principal*.] 1†. The state or condition of being principal or superior; priority or privilege; prerogative; predominance; preëminence.

In bevyn thow hast a *principalite*
Off worship and honowre.
Political Poems, etc. (ed. Furnivall), p. 145.

Charge him to go with her thro' all the courts of Greece, and with the challenge now made to give her beauty the *principality* over all other. *Sir P. Sidney*, Arcadia, i.

Moistenesse in aire houldes *principality*,
And heat is secundarie quality.
Times' Whistle (E. E. T. S.), p. 117.

If any mystery, rite, or sacrament be effective of any spiritual blessings, then this is much more, as having the prerogative and illustrious *principality* above everything else. *Jer. Taylor*, Worthy Communicant, i. § 3.

2. The authority of a prince; sovereignty; supreme power.

Nothing was given to King Henry . . . but only the bare name of a king; for all other absolute power of *principality* he had in himselfe before derived from many former kings. *Spenser*, State of Ireland.

The Bishops of Rome and Alexandria, who beyond their Priestly bounds now long agoe had stept into *principality*.
Milton, Reformation in Eng., ii.

3. The territory of a prince, or the country which gives title to a prince: as, the *principality* of Wales; the *principality* of Montenegro.

The *principality* is composed of two countries, Neuchatel and Valengin. *J. Adams*, Works, IV. 374.

The isle of Elba is given him [Napoleon] as his *principality*, with an annual revenue of two million francs, chargeable to France.
Woolsey, Introd. to Inter. Law, App. ii., p. 410.

The Danubian *Principalities* took their destiny into their own hands. *Fortnightly Rev.*, N. S., XXXIX. 148.

4. A prince; one invested with sovereignty.

Let her be a *principality*
Sovereign to all the creatures on the earth.
Shak., T. G. of V., ii. 4. 152.

5. *pl.* An order of angels. It was the seventh order in the celestial hierarchy of Dionysius. See *hierarchy*.

For we wrestle not against flesh and blood, but against *principalities*, against powers, . . . against spiritual wickedness in high places. Eph. vi. 12.

In the assembly next upstood
Nisroch, of *principalities* the prime.
Milton, P. L., vi. 447.

Danubian principalities. See *Danubian*.

principally (prin'si-pal-i), *adv.* In the principal or chief place; above all; chiefly: as, he was *principally* concerned about this.

Whereof the Aquæduct made by the Emperour Valentinian, and retaining his name, doth *principally* challeng remembrance. *Sandys*, Travailes, p. 26.

They wholly mistake the nature of criticism who think its business is *principally* to find fault. *Dryden.*

principalness (prin'si-pal-nes), *n.* The state of being principal or chief.

principalship (prin'si-pal-ship), *n.* [< *principal* + *-ship*.] The position or office of a principal.

principate (prin'si-pāt), *n.* [= OF. *principe*, *princie*, F. *principat* = Pr. *principat* = Sp. Pg. *principado* = It. *principato*, < L. *principatus*, the first place, preëminence, < *princeps* (*-cip-*), first, chief: see *prince*.] 1. The first or supreme place; primacy.

They proudely denye that the Romano churche obteyneth the *principate* and preeminent autoritie of all other.
R. Eden, tr. of Paolo Giovio (First Books on America, ed. [Arber, p. 315).

Of these words the sense is plain and obvious, that it be understood that under two metaphors the *principate* of the whole church was promised.
Barrow, Pope's Supremacy. (*Latham.*)

2. A principality.

All monarchies and best knowen Common weales or *principates*.
Sir H. Gilbert, Queen Elizabethes Achademy (E. E. T. S.), [extra ser., VIII. i. 3.

The Liukin [*i. e.*, Loochoo Islands] . . . constituted until lately a separate *principate* or Han.
J. J. Rein, Japan, p. 7.

3†. Same as *principality*, 5.

Which are called of Saint Paule *principates* and powers, lordes of the world. *Foxe*, Martyrs, p. 1609, an. 1555.

principes, *n.* Plural of *princeps*.

principia (prin-sip'i-ä), *n. pl.* [L., pl. of *principium*, a beginning: see *principle*.] First principles; elements. The word is most used as the contracted title of the "Philosophiæ Naturalis Principia Mathematica" of Newton; it is also used in the titles of elementary books, as "Principia Latina," etc.

principial (prin-sip'i-al), *a.* [< L. *principialis*, that is from the beginning, < *principium*, a beginning: see *principle*.] Elementary; initial. *Bacon.*

principiant (prin-sip'i-ant), *a.* and *n.* [< LL. *principian(t-)s*, ppr. of *principiare*, begin to speak, begin, < L. *principium*, beginning: see *principle*.] I. *a.* Relating to principles or beginnings.

Certain and known idolatry, or any other sort of practical impiety with its *principiant* doctrine, may be punished corporally. *Jer. Taylor*, Works (ed. 1835), II. 375.

II. *n.* A beginner; a tyro.

Do you think that I have not wit to distinguish a *principiant* in vice from a graduate?
Shirley, Grateful Servant, iii. 4.

principiate (prin-sip'i-āt), *v. t.*; pret. and pp. *principiated*, ppr. *principiating*. [< LL. *principiatus*, pp. of *principiare*, begin to speak, begin, < *principium*, beginning: see *principle*.] To begin; set in motion; initiate.

It imports the things or effects *principiated* or effected by the intelligent active principle.
Sir M. Hale, Orig. of Mankind.

principiate† (prin-sip'i-āt), *a.* [< LL. *principiatus*, pp.: see the verb.] Primitive; original.

Our eyes, that see other things, see not themselves; and those *principiate* foundations of knowledge are themselves unknown. *Glanville*, Vanity of Dogmatizing, iv.

principiation (prin-sip-i-ā'shon), *n.* [< *principiate* + *-ion*.] Analysis; reduction to constituent or elemental parts.

The separating of any metal into his original, or materia prima, or element, or call them what you will; which work we will call *principiation*. Bacon, Physiological Remains.

principium (prin-sip'i-um), *n.*; pl. *principia* (-ä). [L., beginning: see *principle*.] One of four solemn argumentations formerly held by every sententiary bachelor in theology, one upon each of the four books of Peter Lombard's "Sentences."

principle (prin'si-pl), *n.* [With unorig. *l* (as also in *participle*, *syllable*), < OF. (and F.) *principe* = Sp. Pg. It. *principio*, < L. *principium*, a beginning, < *princeps* (*-cip-*), first: see *prince*.] 1†. Beginning; commencement.

He gan to burne in rage, and friese in feare,
Doubting sad end of *principle* unsound.
Spenser, F. Q., V. xi. 2.

2. Cause, in the widest sense; that by which anything is in any way ultimately determined or regulated.

The Stoics could not but think that the fiery *principle* would wear out all the rest, and at last make an end of the world. *Sir T. Browne*, To a Friend.

What deep joy fills the mind of the philosopher when, throughout apparently inextricable confusion, he can trace some great *Principle* that governs all events, and that they all show forth. *Channing*, Perfect Life, p. 109.

Without entering on the various meanings of the term *Principle*, which Aristotle defines, in general, that from whence anything exists, is produced, or is known, it is sufficient to say that it is always used for that on which something else depends; and thus both for an original law and for an original element. In the former case it is a regulative, in the latter a constitutive, *principle*.
Sir W. Hamilton, Reid, Note A, § 5, Supplementary [Dissertations.

It is only by a very careful observation . . . that we are able from the singular and concrete operations to enunciate precisely the general law which is the expression of the regulative *principle*. *McCosh*, Locke's Theory, p. 5.

3. An original faculty or endowment of the mind: as, the *principle* of observation and comparison.

Under this title are comprehended all those active *principles* whose direct and ultimate object is the communication either of enjoyment or of suffering to any of our fellow-creatures. *D. Stewart*, Moral Powers, I. 3, § 1.

Active impulse comes under the dominion of the *principle* of habit. *J. Sully*, Outlines of Psychol., p. 585.

4. A truth which is evident and general; a truth comprehending many subordinate truths; a law on which others are founded, or from which others are derived: as, the *principles* of morality, of equity, of government, etc. In mathematical physics a *principle* commonly means a very widely useful theorem.

How doth Aristotle define *principles*? In this manner: *principles* be true propositions, having credit of themselves, and need no other proofs.
Blundeville, Logic (1619), vi. 18.

Doctrines . . . laid down for foundations of any science . . . [are] called *principles*.
Locke, Human Understanding, IV. xii. 1.

When a man attempts to combat the *principle* of utility, it is with reasons drawn, without his being aware of it, from that very *principle* itself.
Bentham, Introd. to Morals and Legislation, i. 13.

Many traces of this ancient theory [regarding the English common law as existing somewhere in the form of a symmetrical body of express rules, adjusted to definite *principles*] remain in the language of our judgments and forensic arguments, and among them we may perhaps place the singular use of the word *principle* in the sense of a legal proposition elicited from the precedents by comparison and induction.

Maine, Village Communities, p. 335.

5. That which is professed or accepted as a law of action or a rule of conduct; one of the fundamental doctrines or tenets of a system: as, the *principles* of the Stoics or of the Epicureans; hence, a right rule of conduct; in general, equity; uprightness: as, a man of *principle*.

If I had a thousand sons, the first humane *principle* I would teach them should be to forswear thin potations.

Shak., 2 Hen. IV., iv. 3. 133.

They dissolved themselves and turned Seekers, keeping that one *principle*, That every one should have liberty to worship God according to the light of their own consciences.

N. Morton, New England's Memorial, p. 154.

In all governments truly republican, men are nothing — *principle* is everything.

D. Webster, Speech at Salem, Mass., Aug. 7, 1834.

The party whose *principles* afforded him [James II.] no guarantee would be attached to him by interest. The party whose interests he attacked would be restrained from insurrection by *principle*.

Macaulay, Hist. Eng., vii.

The man of *principle* — that is, the man who, without any flourish of trumpets, titles of lordship, or train of guards, without any notice of his action abroad, expecting none, takes in solitude the right step uniformly, on his private choice, and disdaining consequences — does not yield, in my imagination, to any man.

Emerson, War.

6. In *chem.*: (*a*) A component part; an element: as, the constituent *principles* of bodies. (*b*) A substance on the presence of which certain qualities, common to a number of bodies, depend. See *proximate principles*, under *proximate*.

Confinement to a single alimentary *principle*, or to any one class of them alone, is sure to be followed by disease.

Huxley and Youmans, Physiol., § 429.

7. In *patent law*, a law of nature, or a general property of matter, a rule of abstract science. *George Ticknor Curtis*. A principle is not patentable, although a process for utilizing a principle may be. Compare *process*.

It is very difficult to distinguish it [the specification of the hot-blast furnace for throwing hot air into a furnace instead of coal, thereby increasing the intensity of the heat] from the specification of a patent for a *principle*, and this at first created in the minds of the court much difficulty; but, after full consideration, we think that the plaintiff does not merely claim a *principle*, but a machine embodying a *principle*, and a very valuable one. We think the case must be considered as if, the *principle* being well known, the plaintiff had first invented a mode of applying it by a mechanical apparatus to furnaces, and his invention then consists in this — by interposing a receptacle for heated air between the blowing apparatus and the furnace.

Baron Parke, 8 Meeson & W., 306.

A principle of human nature, a law of action in human beings; a constitutional propensity common to the human species.— **Archimedean principle.** See *Archimedean*.— **Bitter principles, commutative principle, constitutive principles.** See the adjectives.— **Carnot's principle**, a highly important principle of the theory of heat — namely, that the work done by an engine is proportional to the amount of heat used multiplied into the fall of temperature of that heat in the action of the engine. In the mechanical theory of heat, this principle is transformed into the second law of thermodynamics. It was discovered in 1824 by Sadi Carnot (1796–1832), son of the great war-minister Carnot.— **D'Alembert's principle**, an important principle of mechanics, to the effect that the forces impressed upon a mechanical system may be resolved into forces balancing one another perpendicular to the motions of the particles and of forces whose direct effects would be to make the particles move as they do move.— **Declination of principles.** See *declination*.— **Dirichlet's (or Dirichletian) principle**, a certain important proposition concerning the equation

$$\frac{\partial^2 P}{\partial x^2} + \frac{\partial^2 P}{\partial y^2} = 0.$$

Distributive principle. See *distributive*.— **Döppler's principle**, in *acoustics*, the phenomenon that, when a sound-body is rapidly approaching the ear, the pitch of the sound is raised, because more sound-waves reach the ear per second, and conversely if the sounding body recedes. This principle is also applied in optics, and the rapidity of relative approach or recession of the earth and some of the fixed stars has been deduced from it, by the change in the character of the light (as to wave-length), as shown by the spectroscope.— **Extractive principle.** Same as *extract*, 4.— **First principle**, one of the most general principles, not deducible from others.— **Fruitful principle.** See *fruitful*.— **General principle.** See *general*.— **Helmholtz's principle**, the proposition (enunciated by Helmholtz, a German physicist, born 1821) that if any source of light or of sound situated at any point will by the intervention of any system of reflectors or lenses produce any given intensity of illumination or of sound at any second point, then the same source being placed at the second point would produce the same intensity of radiation at the first point.— **Heterogeneous principle, heteronymous principles, immanent principle.** See the adjectives.— **Huygens's principle**, the proposition (enunciated by Christian Huygens in 1678) that any disturbance due to waves in any part of a medium at any instant is that due to the superposition of all the disturbances reaching it at that instant from the neighboring parts of the medium.— **Hypostatic principle**, a chemical element.— **Material principle.** See *material*.— **Organic principles.** Same as *proximate principles* (which see, under *proximate*).— **Principle of areas**, in *dynam.*, the proposition that, if all the external forces acting upon a moving system are directed toward an axis, the rotation-area for that axis will be described with a uniform motion.— **Principle of causality.** See *law of causation*, under *causation*.— **Principle of certainty, of coincidence.** See *certainty*, *coincidence*.— **Principle of conservation of number**, in *geom.*, the proposition that, if there is a finite number of figures of a given general description subject to certain conditions, then this number remains, if finite, of the same value, however the general description be specialized. For example, if we wish to know how many lines can cut four given lines, we take four special lines, say two cutting one another and two others cutting one another. Then there are evidently just two lines — namely the one through the two points of intersection and the one common to the planes of the two pairs — which cut all the four lines: and consequently the same will be true in all cases where the number remains finite.— **Principle of contradiction.** See *contradiction*.— **Principle of correspondence**, in *geom.*, the principle that, if the points on a line have an *m* to n correspondence with one another, there are *m* + *n* points which correspond to themselves. There is also an extension to the plane.— **Principle of duality, of homogeneity, of identity.** See *duality*, etc.— **Principle of least action, of least constraint.** See *action*, *constraint*.— **Principle of similitude**, in *dynam.*, proposition 32 of section 7 of the Second Book of Newton's "Principia," namely that, if two systems are geometrically similar, and have their corresponding masses proportional, and begin to move in the same way, in proportional times, they will continue to move in the same way, provided the forces are proportional to the masses and the linear dimensions, and are inversely as the squares of the times.— **Principle of sufficient reason.** See *reason*.— **Principle of the arithmetical mean**, the proposition that the mean of different results of direct observation of a quantity is the best way of combining them.— **Principle of the composition of rotations.** See *rotation*.— **Principle of the inclined plane**, in *mech.*, same as *principle of the parallelogram of forces* (which see, under *force*[1]).— **Principle of the last multiplier**, a certain principle used in the solution of dynamical equations.— **Principle of the lever**, in *mech.*, same as *Archimedean principle* (*a*) (which see, under *Archimedean*).— **Principle of the parallelogram of forces.** See *force*[1].— **Principle of translation**, in *math.*, the theorem that all the invariantive properties of a ternary form can be represented by the vanishing of invariants and the identical vanishing of covariants, contravariants, or mixed forms.— **Principle of virtual velocities.** See *velocity*.— **Reductive, regulative**, etc., **principle.** See the adjectives.— **Short-haul principle**, the principle that the charge for carrying freight should not be higher for a shorter than for a longer distance. See *long haul*, under *long*[1].— **The currency principle.** See *currency*.— **The principle of excluded middle or third.** See *middle*.— **Transcendental principle.** See *transcendental*. = **Syn.** 5. *Principle, Rule, Precept.* "There are no two words in the English language used so confusedly one for the other as the words *rule* and *principle*. . . . You can make a *rule*; you cannot make a *principle*; you can lay down a *rule*; you cannot, properly speaking, lay down a *principle*. It is laid down for you. You can establish a *rule*; you cannot, properly speaking, establish a *principle*. You can only declare it. *Rules* are within your power, *principles* are not. Yet the mass of mankind use the words as if they had exactly similar meanings, and choose one or the other as may best suit the rhythm of the sentence." (*Helps*.) A *principle* lies back of both *rules* and *precepts*; it is a general truth, needing interpretation and application to particular cases. From a *principle* we may deduce *rules* that we lay imperatively upon ourselves or upon others who are under our authority, and *precepts* that we lay upon those who look to us for instruction. It is a *principle* that "the Sabbath was made for man"; details as to the observance of the Sabbath would be not *principles*, but *rules*, maxims, or *precepts*. See *aphorism*.

Christianity is a spirit, not a law; it is a set of *principles*, not a set of *rules*. . . . Christianity consists of *principles*, but the application of those *principles* is left to every man's individual conscience.

F. W. Robertson, Sermons, Marriage and Celibacy.

Nations pay little regard to *rules* and maxims calculated in their very nature to run counter to the necessities of society.

A. Hamilton, The Federalist, No. 25.

Teachers best
Of moral prudence, with delight received
In brief sententious *precepts*, while they treat
Of fate, and chance, and change in human life.

Milton, P. R., iv. 264.

principle (prin'si-pl), *v. t.*; pret. and pp. *principled*, ppr. *principling*. [< *principle*, *n.*] To establish or fix in certain principles; impress with any tenet or belief, whether good or ill: used chiefly in the past participle.

Well did thir Disciples manifest themselves to bee no better *principl'd* then thir Teachers. *Milton*, Hist. Eng., iii.

A parliament so *principled* will sink
All antient schools of empire in disgrace.

Young, On Public Affairs.

We replied, we hoped he would distinguish and make a difference between the guilty and the innocent, and between those who were *principled* for fighting and those who were *principled* against it, which we were, and had been always known to be so.

T. Ellwood, Life (ed. Howells), p. 263.

princock† (pring'kok), *n.* [Also *princox*, *primecock*, etc.; < *prim*, *prime*, + *cock*[1].] A coxcomb; a conceited person.

Your proud university *princox* thinkes he is a man of such merit the world cannot sufficiently endow him with preferment. *Returne from Parnassus*, iii. 2.

A caualier of the first feather, a *princockes*, . . . all to be frenchified in his souldiour's sute.

Nashe, Pierce Penilesse, p. 52.

And thou, yong *Princox*, Puppet as thou art,
Shalt play no longer thy proud Kingling's Part
Vpon so rich a stage.

Sylvester, tr. of Du Bartas's Weeks, ii., The Decay.

princod (prin'kod), *n.* [< *prin*[1] + *cod*[1].] A pincushion; figuratively, a short thick-set woman. *Halliwell.* [Prov. Eng.]

princum† (pring'kum), *n.* [An arbitrary var. of *prink*, simulating a L. form. Cf. *prinkum-prankum*.] A scruple; a nice or affected notion.

My behaviour may not yoke
With the nice *princums* of that folk.

D'Urfey, Colin's Walk, i. (*Davies*.)

prine (prīn), *n.* [Cf. *prin*[1].] Same as *pick*[1], 5.

pringle† (pring'gl), *n.* A small silver coin, of about the value of a penny, formerly current in Scotland and in the northern parts of England. *Halliwell.*

Pringlea (pring'glē-ā), *n.* [NL. (J. D. Hooker, 1847), named after Sir John *Pringle* (1707–82), a British physician and natural philosopher.] A genus of plants of the order *Cruciferæ* and tribe *Alyssineæ*, characterized by its fruit, an oblong one-celled silicle, containing very many cordate seeds with their outer coat prolonged into a short beak, and by its growth from a thick rootstock with ample and compactly imbricated leaves. The only species, P. *antiscorbutica*, is a cabbage-like plant of Kerguelen Land, valuable as a preventive of scurvy. The thick round rootstock lies on the ground for 3 or 4 feet, and bears a single large ball of leaves which are loose and green outside, and form a dense white mass within. The flower-stalk grows out from below the head of leaves, and reaches 2 or 3 feet in height. An essential oil pervading the plant gives it a taste resembling a combination of mustard and cress.

Prinia (prin'i-ā), *n.* [NL. (Horsfield, 1820), < Javanese *prinya*, a native name.] A genus of grass-warblers or *Cisticolæ*, having a graduated tail of only ten rectrices and a long stout bill. The numerous species range through the Ethiopian and Indian regions. P. *familiaris* of Java and Sumatra is the type. Also called *Dasocharis* and *Drymoipus*.

prink[1] (pringk), *v. i.* [< ME. **prinken*, *preynken*; origin obscure.] To look; gaze. [Prov. Eng.]

Thanne Conscience curteisliche a contenaunce he made,
And *preynte* vpon Pacience to preie me to be stille.

Piers Plowman (B), xiii. 112.

prink[2] (pringk), *v.* [A weaker form of *prank*, to which it is related as *clink* to *clank*, etc.: see *prank*. Cf. *prick*, *v.*, in like sense.] I. *intrans.* 1. To prank; dress for show; adorn one's self.

Or womans wil (perhappes)
Enflamde hir haughtie harte
To get more grace by crummes of cost,
And *princke* it out hir parte.

Gascoigne, Philomene (ed. Arbor), p. 93.

They who *prink*, and pamper the Body, and neglect the Soul are like one who, having a Nightingale in his House, is more fond of the Wicker Cage than of the Bird.

Howell, Letters, iv. 21.

Hold a good wager she was every day longer *prinking* in the glass than you was. *Jane Collier.*

2. To strut; put on pompous airs; be pretentious or forward. [Prov. Eng.]

II. *trans.* To deck; adorn; dress ostentatiously or fantastically.

She *prink'd* hersell and prim'd hersell,
By the ae light of the moon.

The Young Tamlane (Child's Ballads, I. 118).

To gather kingcups in the yellow mead,
And *prink* their hair with daisies.

Cowper, Task, vi. 303.

Ay, prune thy feathers, and *prink* thyself gay.

Scott, Monastery, xxiv.

It is . . . a most perilous seduction for a popular poet like Burns to *prink* the unadorned simplicity of his ploughman's Muse with the glittering spangles and curious lacework of a highly polished literary style.

Prof. Blackie, Lang. and Lit. of Scottish Highlands, iii.

prinker (pring'kėr), *n.* One who prinks; one who dresses with much care.

prinkle (pring'kl), *v. i.*; pret. and pp. *prinkled*, ppr. *prinkling*. [Appar. a nasalized form of *prickle*.] To tingle or prickle. [Scotch.]

My blude ran *prinklin'* through my veins, . . .
As I beheld my dear, O.

Hogg, Mountain Bard, p. 200. (*Jamieson*.)

prinkle (pring'kl), *n.* The coalfish. [Local, Eng.]

prinkum-prankum (pring'kum-prang'kum), *n.* [A redupl. of *prink*[2] or *prank*, simulating a L. form. Cf. *princum*.] A kind of dance.

What dance?
No wanton jig, I hope: no dance is lawful
But *Prinkum-Prankum!*

Randolph, Muses Looking-glass, v. 1. (*Davies*.)

prinpriddle (prin'prid'l), *n.* The long-tailed titmouse, *Acredula rosea*. [Cornwall, Eng.]

print (print), *v.* [< ME. **printen*, *prenten*, *preenten*, print (= D. *prenten*, imprint, = MLG. *pren-*

ten, print, write, = Sw. *prenta*, write German letters, = Dan. *prente*, print), by apheresis from *emprinten*, *enprinten*, impress, imprint: see *imprint*, *v*. Cf. late OF. *printer*, press. See *print*, *n*.] **I.** *trans.* **1.** To press upon or into (something); impress; imprint.

In that Roche is *prented* the forme of his Body.
Mandeville, Travels, p. 62.

Think, when we talk of horses, that you see them
Printing their proud hoofs i' the receiving earth.
Shak., Hen. V., I., Prol., l. 27.

The murdred face lies *printed* in the mud.
Sylvester, tr. of Du Bartas's Weeks, ii., The Handy-Crafts.

And *print* on thy soft cheek a parent's kiss.
Byron, Childe Harold, iii. 116.

And hill and wood and field did *print*
The same sweet forms in either mind.
Tennyson, In Memoriam, lxxix.

2. To mark by pressing something upon; leave an imprint upon; as, to *print* butter.

On his fiery steed betimes he rode,
That scarcely *prints* the turf on which he trod.
Dryden, Pal. and Arc., ii. 46.

And little footsteps lightly *print* the ground.
Gray, Elegy (omitted stanza).

Where olives overhead
Print the blue sky with twig and leaf.
Browning, Old Pictures in Florence.

3. To make or form by pressure or impression of any kind; fashion or shape out by stamping, indentation, or delineation in general. [Obsolete or archaic in many applications.]

That god coueiteth nat the coygne that Crist hym-self *prentede*. *Piers Plowman* (C), xvii. 80.

Ye shall not make any cuttings in your flesh, . . . nor *print* any marks upon you. Lev. xix. 28.

Heaven guide thy pen to *print* thy sorrows plain.
Shak., Tit. And., iv. 1. 75.

Do not study
To *print* more wounds (for that were tyranny)
Upon a heart that is pierc'd through already.
Beau. and Fl., Knight of Malta, iii. 2.

Specifically—**4.** To stamp by direct pressure, as from the face of types, plates, or blocks covered with ink or pigments; impress with transferred characters or delineations by the exertion of force, as with a press or some other mechanical agency: as, to *print* a ream of paper; to *print* calico; to *print* pottery.

"Ye-ye-yes," sobbed the little boy, rubbing his face very hard with the Beggar's Petition in *printed* calico (a figured cotton handkerchief). *Dickens*, Nicholas Nickleby, iv.

But as for the cook, and as for that clever and willing lass, Maggie—well, I've bought each o' them a *printed* cotton gown. *W. Black*, In Far Lochaber, viii.

5. To copy by pressure; take an impression or impressions from or of: as, to *print* a form of type; to *print* an engraved plate or block; to *print* a pattern on paper, or on calico or some other fabric.—**6.** To make a copy or copies of by impression; produce by or issue from the press; put into print, as for publication: as, to *print* a book or a newspaper, an essay or a sermon; to *print* a picture.

In books, not authors, curious is my Lord; . . .
These Aldus *printed*, those Du Sueil has bound.
Pope, Moral Essays, iv. 136.

I . . . sought a Poet, roosted near the skies, . . .
Said nothing like his works was ever *printed*.
Burns, Address spoken by Miss Fontenelle on her Benefit [Night.

7. To cause to be printed; obtain the printing or publication of; publish.

Some said, "John, *print* it," others said, "Not so."
Some said, "It might do good," others said, "No."
Bunyan, Pilgrim's Progress, Apology.

A chiel's amang ye takin' notes,
An', faith, he'll *prent* it.
Burns, Captain Grose's Peregrinations.

8†. To form letters; write.

The hizest lessoun that man may lere . . .
Is playnli *printed* in Poulis booke.
Hymns to Virgin (1430) (E. E. T. S.), p. 114.

Loo! sir, this is a periurye
To *prente* vndir penne. *York Plays*, p. 222.

9. To form by imitation of printed characters; write in the style of print: as, the child has learned to *print* the letters of the alphabet.—**10.** To record, describe, or characterize in print as.

My safest way were to *print* myself a coward, with a discovery how I came by my credit, and clap it upon every post. *Beau. and Fl.*, King and No King, iii. 2.

Men . . .
Must now be named and *printed* Hereticks.
Milton, Forcers of Conscience.

11. In *photog.*: (*a*) To make a positive picture from (a negative) by contact. (*b*) To produce, as a positive from a negative, by transmitted light, as by the agency of a lens in an enlarging-camera.—**Printed carpet.** See *carpet*.—**Printed china, printed crockery**, porcelain or glazed pottery decorated with transfer-printing.—**Printed goods**, calicoes figured by printing from blocks or rollers.—**Printed ware**, a term applied to porcelain, queen's-ware, etc., decorated with printed designs.

II. *intrans.* **1.** To use or practise the art of taking impressions in a press.—**2.** To produce books or any form of printed work by means of a press; specifically, to publish books or writings.

Like Lee or Budgell, I will rhyme and *print*.
Pope, Imit. of Horace, II. i. 100.

3. To form imitations of printed characters; write in the style of print: as, the child can *print*, but has not learned to write yet.

print (print), *n.* [< ME. **print*, *prynt*, *printe*, *prente*, *preente*, *preynte* (= MD. *print*, D. *prent*, *print* = MLG. *prente* = Dan. *prent*), < OF. *preinte*, *prainte*, impression, print, by apheresis from *empreinte*, impression, print: see *imprint*, *n.* Cf. *print*, *v.*] **1.** A mark made by impression; any line, character, figure, or indentation made by the pressure of one body or thing on another; hence, figuratively, a mark, vestige, or impression of any kind; a stamp.

Your yeen hathe sette the *prynt* which that I feele
Withynne myne herte.
Political Poems, etc. (ed. Furnivall), p. 69.

Except I shall . . . put my finger into the *print* of the nails, . . . I will not believe. John xx. 25.

As when a seal in wax impression makes,
The *print* therein, but not itself, it leaves.
Sir J. Davies, Immortal. of Soul, xiii.

Sooner or later I too may passively take the *print*
Of the golden age. *Tennyson*, Maud, i.

2. Printed matter for reading; the state of being printed; character or style of printing, or size of the printed letters: as, to put a work into *print*; clear or blurred *print*.

Item, a Boke in *preente* off the Pleye off the [Chess].
Paston Letters, III. 300.

The small Geneva *print* referred to, we apprehend, was the type used in the common copies of the Geneva translation of the Bible. *Craik.*

A literary man—with a wooden leg—and all *print* is open to him. *Dickens*, Our Mutual Friend, I. v.

There has been established such an intimate association between truth and *print* upon paper that much of the reverence given to the one gathers round the other.
H. *Spencer*, Prin. of Psychol., § 389.

3†. An imprint; an edition.

When these two *pryntes* (there were of them bothe aboute v. thousand bokis printed) were al soulde more then a twelue moneth agoo [*i. e.*, before February, 1534] Tind[ale] was pricked forthe to take the testament in hande to priot it and correcke it.
George Joy, Apology to Tyndale (1535). (*Arber.*)

4. A printed publication, more especially a newspaper or other periodical.

What I have known
Shall be as public as a *print*.
Beau. and Fl., Philaster, ii. 4.

The *prints*, about three days after, were filled with the same terms. *Addison.*

5. A printed picture or design; an impression from engraved wood or metal taken in ink or other colored medium upon paper or any other suitable material.

That Bible, bought by sixpence weekly saved,
Has choicest *prints* by famous hands engraved.
Crabbe, Works, I. 38.

Conrad ab Uffenbach, a learned German, recreated his mind, after severe studies, with a collection of *prints* of eminent persons, methodically arranged.
I. D'Israeli, Curios. of Lit., I. 91.

6. Printed calico; a piece or length of cotton cloth stamped with designs: as, striped, black, colored, or figured *prints*.—**7.** (*a*) An impression of something having comparatively slight relief, such as to reproduce in reverse all the parts of the original. Hence, by extension—(*b*) A cast or impression from such a first impression, which reproduces exactly the original.—**8.** A pattern or device produced by stamping, as upon the surface of a piece of plate; hence, apparently by extension, the boss at the bottom of mazers and other vessels of the middle ages or later times, upon which are engraved or otherwise represented the arms of the owner or donor, or some other device.—**9.** Something bearing a figure or design to be impressed by stamping; a figured stamp: as, a butter-*print*. Specifically—(*a*) A mold for coin. *Halliwell.* (*b*) In *iron-working*, a swage; a mold sunk in metal from which an impression is taken.

10. In *photog.*, a positive picture made from a negative.—**Cotton prints.** See *cotton*1.—**In print.** (*a*) In a printed form; issued from the press; published; also, in a printed and published work.

I love a ballad *in print* o' life, for then we are sure they are true. *Shak.*, W. T., iv. 4. 264.

Margaret Fuller, less attractive *in print* than in conversation, did her part as a contributor as well as editor.
O. W. Holmes, Emerson, v.

(*b*) In stock: said of a book of which copies can be had of the publisher. Compare *out of print*. (c) In a formal method; with exactness; in a precise and perfect manner; to perfection.

P. jun. Fits my ruff well?
Lin. *In print.*
B. *Jonson*, Staple of News, i. 1.

He must speak *in print*, walk *in print*, eat and drink *in print*. Burton, Anat. of Mel., p. 539. (*Latham.*)

Jeypore print, a square of cotton cloth printed with an elaborate design in colors from small separate blocks. These squares are used as hangings and also for garments; they are of different sizes, sometimes as much as 8 or 9 feet square.—**Mezzotint print**, in *photog.* See *mezzotint*.—**Out of print**, no longer in stock: said of a book of which copies can no longer be supplied by its publisher.—**Solar print.** See *solar*.

print (print), *a.* [< *print*, *n.*] Clear and bright. *Halliwell.* [Prov. Eng.]

print-broker (print'brō"kėr), *n.* A broker in printed goods or figured calico. [Local, Eng.]

These are the *print-brokers*, who sell "gown-pieces" to the hawkers or street-traders.
Mayhew, London Labour and London Poor, I. 414.

print-cloth (print'klôth), *n.* Cotton cloth woven and finished suitably for printing.

Cloth of the kind called *print-cloth*, . . . which when printed becomes calico. *Pop. Sci. Mo.*, XXVIII. 480.

print-cutter (print'kut"ėr), *n.* A plain or a mechanical knife, such as a small knife-edged wheel mounted in a handle, for cutting photographic prints to shape and size. The prints are usually cut on a piece of glass, by means of a rule or a caliber of glass of the required size.

printer (prin'tėr), *n.* **1.** One who prints, impresses, or stamps by impression; a person whose business it is to produce copies or superficial transfers of anything by pressure, as in a press or the like, or by the agency of light on a sensitized surface, as in photography: usually distinguished, when not specific (def. 2), by an adjunct: as, a lithographic *printer*; a plate-*printer*; a calico-*printer*.—**2.** A person who practises or carries on the business of typographical printing; one who understands the mechanical process of producing printed matter for reading; specifically, as used of workmen, a compositor, or one who manipulates the types.—**3.** One who sells what he prints or procures the printing of; hence, a publisher of books or of a periodical. The early printers were generally also publishers, producing works on their own account; and the word *printer* long retained this extended meaning. Thus, most of the letters of Junius were addressed "To the *Printer* of the Public Advertiser"—the printer, Woodfall, being its proprietor, editor, and publisher. [Now nearly obsolete.]

Learning hath gained most by those books by which the *printers* have lost. *Fuller*, Books.

4. A telegraphic instrument which makes records in printed characters; a telegraphic printing instrument.

Edison's various devices in his old stock *printer* have formed the basis of all later variations on that sort of instrument. *Harper's Mag.*, LXXX. 432.

Mechanical printer, a type-writer.—**Motor printer.** See *motor*.—**Printers' Bible** a Bible printed prior to 1702, mentioned by Cotton Mather as containing the word *printers* in place of *princes* in Ps. cxix. 161: "*Printers* have persecuted me without a cause."—**Printer's devil.** See *devil*.—**Printer's flower**, an ornamental design at the end of a printed book; a tail-piece.—**Printer's imprint.** See *imprint*, 2.—**Printers' ink.** See *printing-ink*.—**Printer's mark**, an engraved device, sometimes a monogram or a rebus, used by printers as a trade-mark.—**Printers' ream**, or **printing ream**, the ordinary ream of 480 sheets, to which 1½ quires are added as an allowance for waste in printing, making 516 sheets: sometimes, but improperly, called a *perfect ream*. [Eng.]—**Printers' roller.** See *inking-roller*.—**Printers' varnish**, a varnish made of nut- or linseed-oil, black resin, and dry brown soap.—**Public printer**, an official of the United States government who has charge of the government printing-office at Washington. =**Syn.** *Compositor*, *Printer*. Before the introduction of power-presses both pressmen and compositors were called *printers*; but these classes are now nearly always distinct, and the term *printer* more especially, but less appropriately, designates the latter.

printery (prin'tėr-i), *n.*; pl. *printeries* (-iz). [< *print* + *-ery*.] **1.** An establishment for the printing of calico or the like.—**2.** A printing-office. [Rare.]

print-field (print'fēld), *n.* A print-works; an establishment for printing and bleaching calicoes.

print-holder (print'hōl"dėr), *n.* **1.** A small frame, standing like an easel by means of a support at the back, used to hold a photograph or an engraving.—**2.** In *photog.*, any device for holding a print flat, or in a desired position.

printing (prin'ting), *n.* [Verbal n. of *print*, *v.*] **1.** In general, the art or process of making copies or superficial transfers by impression; the reproduction of designs, characters, etc., on an impressible surface by means of an ink or a pigment (generally oily) applied to the solid surface on which they are engraved or otherwise formed. This sense is used specifically in typography of the actual taking of impressions by the operation of a press; in other uses, it is generally accompanied by some descriptive term; and in typography itself different methods are discriminated, as type, letterpress, or stereotype printing, color-printing, etc. Type or stereotype printing is done from a surface in high relief; lithographic printing, from the surface of a flat stone; copperplate printing, from inked lines engraved below the surface of a flat plate of copper or steel. The art of printing with ink from blocks of wood was practised in China at an early undetermined date. Silk and linen fabrics were printed from engraved hand-stamps in Europe in the twelfth century; playing-cards and prints of images were impressed on paper in the beginning of the fourteenth century. Calico-printing, oilcloth-printing, and carpet-printing are also distinct arts, each requiring specially made inks and machinery. Printing for the blind, in letters embossed in relief, is the only form of printing done without ink.

2. The art or process of producing printed matter for reading (including illustrations, etc.) by composition and imposition of types, and their subjection when inked to pressure upon paper in a printing-press; the typographic art; typography in the fullest sense. Although documents of a much earlier date exist, which show strong evidence of having been printed in some manner analogous to the modern practice, the history of printing properly begins with the first use of movable molded types, and is accredited to Gutenberg, with the aid of Schoeffer and Fust, of Mainz in Germany, in which city appeared the first book with an authenticated (written) date, 1456. Gutenberg's invention, however, is disputed in favor of his contemporary Coster, of Haarlem in Holland, from whom the former is said to have derived the process. Improvements have since been made in the speed of type-making and in the methods of type-setting, but there has been no radical change in their theory or process. The simple screw hand-press first used for printing from types received no considerable improvement before 1800. Since that date many inventions have been made in printing-machinery, and the collateral arts of stereotyping and electrotyping have been developed. Machines that print from 5,000 to 50,000 copies an hour are to be found in many large cities. The earliest Italian copperplate-print is by Maso Finiguerra, a goldsmith of Florence (1452). Lithography was invented by Aloys Senefelder, of Munich, about 1796; he made prints in 1798, and received a patent in 1800. Typography, also known as letterpress printing, obtains its greatest advantage from the mobility of its types of metal, which can be repeatedly used in endless combinations. Type-printing machinery permits the use, along with types, of engravings on wood, or of stereotype or electrotype plates. In all other kinds of printing, the use of an engraved design in a new combination is not practicable; it can be used only in its first state. Printing comprises two distinct trades — composition, or the art of arranging types, and presswork, or the art of getting impressions from composed types. See *compositor*, *pressman*[1], and *printer*, 2.

3. In *photog.*, the act or art of obtaining a positive photographic picture from a negative, or a picture in which the lights and shades are true to nature from one in which they are reversed. When based upon the properties of a salt of silver, such printing is called *silver-printing*, and similarly with other salts.—4. In *ceram.*, the art of decorating pottery by means of transfers, either by paper printed with mineral colors or by sheets of gelatin printed in oil. By the first plan, the paper is pressed, printed side down, on the ware to make the transfer, and afterward removed by softening in water. By the other plan, the gelatin film or bat simply transfers the oil to the ware, when it can be removed and used again, the oil-print being then dusted with mineral colors.

5. Advertising-bills, posters, dodgers, window-bills, and the like. [Theat. slang.]—**Anastatic printing.** See *anastatic*.—**Artificial** or **artistic printing.** See *artificial*.—**Bureau of Engraving and Printing.** See *bureau*.—**Chromatic printing.** See *chromatic*.—**Lithographic printing.** See *lithography*.—**Logographic printing**, printing with types bearing whole words or syllables. See *logography*.—**Natural printing**, the taking of an impression from an etched plate as it comes from the bath, for the purpose of showing its exact state. See also *nature-printing*.—**Polychrome printing.** See *polychrome*.—**Solar printing**, in *photog.*, the process or operation of printing or enlarging from a negative by the use of the solar camera. See *copying camera*, under *camera*.

printing-body (prin'ting-bod"i), *n.* A piece of ceramic ware ready for printing.

printing-frame (prin'ting-frām), *n.* In *photog.*, a quadrangular frame in which sensitized paper is placed beneath a negative held firmly in position and exposed to the direct rays of light. Also called *pressure-frame* and *press*.

printing-house (prin'ting-hous), *n.* A house or office where letterpress printing is done.

printing-ink (prin'ting-ingk), *n.* Ink used in typographical printing. Its composition, generally speaking, is linseed-oil boiled to a varnish, with coloring matter added to it.

printing-machine (prin'ting-ma-shēn"), *n.* An apparatus for printing with types or typographic forms, more elaborate than a hand-press; a printing-press adapted for operation at greater speed, and commonly with larger areas of type, than a hand-press; a power-press (properly so called, although with some of the smaller forms manual power may be used). See *printing-press*. Many such machines have been invented. Platen-machines are provided with flat beds for the types, which are impressed by flat platens. Favorite styles of platen-machines for book-work are the Adams press of America and the Napier press of England; for job-work, the Gordon press of America and the Cropper press of England. Cylinder-machines are provided with flat sliding bed-plates for the type-forms, which at intervals are impressed by a rotating cylinder. (See *cylinder-press*.) Rotary machines are provided with cylinders on the curved surface of which the types or plates are fixed, and which are impressed by another rotating cylinder. In some styles of rotary press the central cylinder containing the type is impressed by two or more impression-cylinders, which make a corresponding number of impressions at every rotation. All forms of platen- and cylinder-machines receive, by hand-feeding, cut sheets of paper which are delivered printed usually on one side only, and not folded. Some forms of cylinder-machines are provided with two cylinders for printing a sheet on both sides or in two colors. Web-machines (so called because they use paper in a web-roll, which may be two or more miles long) are provided with cylinders on the curved surface of which the plates are fastened, and which are impressed by other cylinders on both sides. All of these machines are complex, and have an apparatus for cutting and folding sheets and pasting in supplementary single or double leaves, and are largely used for printing daily newspapers. Their performance varies, according to the size of the sheet and other conditions, from 5,000 to 70,000 copies an hour. Nicholson of England received a patent for a cylinder printing-machine in 1790, but his invention was never perfected. Koenig and Bauer in 1811 did the first practical work on their machine, which in 1814 was used to print the London "Times." Early forms of cylinder-machines have been largely improved by Napier of London and Hoe of New York. The web-machine was introduced in 1853, and has received many improvements from Applegath of London, Marinoni of Paris, Hoe of New York, and others.—**Cradle printing-machine.** See *cradle*.

Hand-press.

a, frame; *b*, bed, containing a four-page form, *c*; *d*, platen; *e*, bar that moves compound lever; *f*, compound lever; *g*, platen-springs; *h*, one of two ribs on which the bed slides on its way to the platen; *j*, rounce, with handle, attached to girths that pull the bed to and from the platen; *k*, tympan, with its drawer; *l*, frisket.

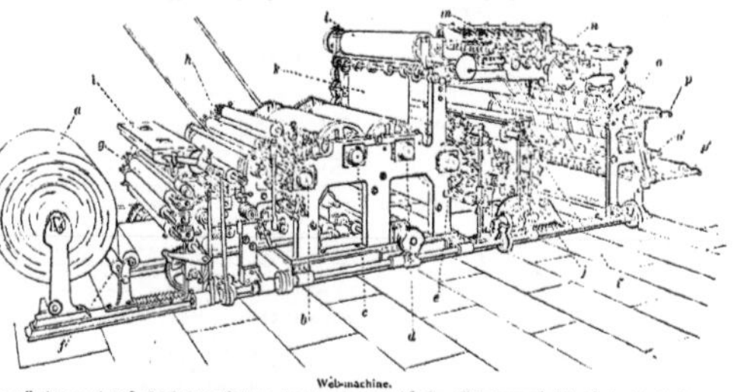

Web-machine.

a, roll of paper; *b*, shaft of first plate-cylinder; *c*, shaft of first impression-cylinder; *d*, shaft of second printing-cylinder; *e*, shaft of second plate-cylinder; *f*, perforated steam-pipe for steaming the paper as it unwinds; *g*, ink-distributing rollers; *h*, inking-rollers for first plate-cylinder; *i*, first ink-fountain; *i'*, second ink-fountain; *j*, ink-distributing rollers for second plate-cylinder; *k*, web of paper, printed on both sides, on its way to the first cutting-cylinder; *l*, cutting-cylinder; *m*, insetting-apparatus; *n*, folding-apparatus; *o*, *o'*, delivering-cylinders with transverse cutters; *p*, *p'*, tables on which the cut and printed sheets are delivered.

Stop-cylinder Machine.

a, bed and side frames; *b*, driving-pulley; *c*, impression-cylinder; *d*, feed-table; *e*, delivery-cylinder; *f*, bed on which the form of type is laid; *g*, inking-rollers; *h*, ink-fountain; *i*, ink-table; *k*, distributing-rollers; *l*, wheel-and-axle movement which moves the sliding bed; *m*, the fly, working on a rocking shaft, which takes the paper from the delivery-cylinder and lays it on the delivery-board; *n*, delivery-board; *o*, steps on which the feeder stands; *p*, guides against which the sheets of paper are fed; *q*, grippers in impression-cylinder which take the sheets; *r*, two cams which bring the impression-cylinder to a stop after each impression; *s*, cam which operates the fly.

printing-office (prin'ting-of"is), *n.* An office where typographic printing is done.

printing-paper (prin'ting-pā"pėr), *n.* See *paper*.

printing-press (prin'ting-pres), *n.* A machine for taking impressions from an inked surface upon paper. A press that prints from stone is always specified as a lithographic press; a press that prints from etched or engraved copperplates, as a copperplate-press. Presses for typographic printing are broadly divided into three classes — hand-presses, job-presses, and power-presses. Those of the last class are treated under *printing-machine*. The early hand-press was largely of wood. A stone was provided as a bed for the form of types, and iron for minor pieces only. Impression was made by the direct action of a screw on the platen or pressing surface, which covered only one half of the bed-plate of stone. The first notable improvement was that of Stanhope of England, who in 1798 made a hand-press entirely of iron, with a platen that fully covered the bed-plate. Many improvements have followed. The hand-presses now preferred are those in which impression is given by compound levers, and the descent and return of the platen are controlled by coiled springs instead of the screw. Presses of various forms have been devised for special kinds of printing, as in different colors at the same time. The prevalent style of job-presses, for the printing of cards and small sheets, has the type secured to a bed-plate which stands vertically, and the platen swings to and from it on a rocking shaft, or is brought to it by means of a side-lever. They are often worked by a treadle, and hence are also called *treadle-presses*. Their prototype is the Gordon press, invented by George P. Gordon in 1850.—**Chromatic printing-press.** See *chromatic*.—**Copperplate printing-press**, a roller-press used in printing from plates engraved or etched in sunken lines. The original form, still in use, was invented in 1545. It consists of a bed moving on rollers and supporting the plate which is to be printed from. The requisite pressure is obtained by means of a roller above the bed, having a vertical adjustment by means of screws attached to its journal-boxes. The bed is rolled forward to bring the plate and the sheet upon which the drawing is to be transferred beneath the pressing-roll. The pressure is adjusted by means of the screws, and the roll turned by a lever-arm attached to its axis, causing the plate and its bed to roll forward beneath it, so as to subject the whole surface of the plate and the sheet which covers it to its action.—**Multicolor printing-press**, a chromatic printing-press for printing simultaneously in bands or stripes of different colors: distinguished from a *chromolithographic press*, which prints in overlaid colors by successive operations.

printing-telegraph (prin'ting-tel"ē-grȧf), *n.* Any form of automatic self-recording telegraph, as the "ticker" of a stock-reporting telegraph. See *telegraph*.

printing-type (prin'ting-tīp), *n.* Letterpress-type. See *type*.

printing-wheel (prin'ting-hwēl), *n.* A wheel having letters or figures on its periphery, used in paging- or numbering-machines, or in ticket-printing machines.

printless (print'les), *a.* [< *print* + *-less.*] Without a print. (*a*) Receiving or bearing no print or impression.

> Lighting on the *printless* verdure.
> *Keats*, Lamia, i.
>
> Free as air, o'er *printless* sands we march.
> *Wordsworth*, Excursion, iv.

(*b*) Making no print or impression.

> Thus I set my *printless* feet
> O'er the cowslip's velvet head.
> *Milton*, Comus, l. 897.
>
> With golden undulations such as greet
> The *printless* summer-sandals of the moon.
> *Lowell*, Bon Voyage!

print-room (print'röm), *n.* An apartment containing a collection of prints or engravings.

print-seller (print'sel'ėr), *n.* One who sells prints or engravings.

> Any *printsellers* who have folios of old drawings or facsimiles of them. *Ruskin*, Elem. of Drawing, ii.

print-shop (print'shop), *n.* A shop where prints or engravings are sold.

> I picked up in a *print-shop* the other day some superb views of the suburbs of Chowringhee.
> *Macaulay*, in Trevelyan, I. 309.

print-works (print'wėrks), *n. sing.* and *pl.* An establishment where machine- or block-printing is carried on; a place for printing calicoes or paper-hangings.

> There were for many years extensive calico *print-works* at Primrose, but these are now converted into paper-mills.
> *Baines*, Hist. Lancashire, II. 21.

Priodon (prī'ǫ-don), *n.* [NL.] Same as *Prionodon.*

Priodontes (prī-ǫ-don'tēz), *n.* [NL.] Same as *Prionodon.*

Prion (prī'on), *n.* [NL. (Lacépède, 1800–1), < Gr. πρίων, a saw, < πρίειν, saw.] A genus of *Procellariidæ*, having the bill expanded and strongly beset along the cutting edges with lamellæ like the teeth of a saw; the saw-billed petrels. *P. vittata* is a blue-and-white petrel inhabiting southern seas. Also *Pachyptila.*

Prioneæ (prī-ō'nẹ-ē), *n. pl.* [NL., < *Prion* + *-eæ.*] A section of *Procellariinæ* established by Coues in 1866, having the bill lamellate, and containing the genera *Prion*, *Pseudoprion*, and *Halobæna*; the saw-billed petrels.

Prionidæ (prī-on'i-dē), *n. pl.* [NL. (Leach, 1819), < NL. *Prion* + *-idæ.*] A family of longicorn beetles, typified by the genus *Prionus*, related to the *Cerambycidæ*, having the sides of the prothorax sharply delineated and often serrate or spinous.

Prionidus (prī-ǫ-nī'dus), *n.* [NL. (Uhler, 1886), < Gr. πρίων, a saw, + εἶδος, form.] A genus of reduvioid bugs, replacing *Prionotus* of Laporte, 1833, which is preoccupied in ichthyology. It includes many strange tropical and semi-tropical forms, as *P. cristatus*, the wheel-bug, useful in destroying willow-slugs and many other noxious insects.

Prioninæ (prī-ō-nī'nē), *n. pl.* [NL., < *Prion* + *-inæ.*] The *Prionidæ* as a subfamily of *Cerambycidæ*, distinguished by the margined prothorax and the connate labrum. The species are of large size and of brown or black color, and some of them are the longest beetles known. They stridulate by rubbing the hind femora against the edge of the elytra. *Prionus imbricornis* is a common North American species. *Orthosoma cylindricum* is also a striking example of this group. It is found in the West Indies and all through North America, feeding in the larva state in decaying stumps of oak, walnut, pine, and hemlock.

Orthosoma cylindricum, one of the *Prioninæ*. (Natural size.)

Prionites (prī-ǫ-nī'tēz), *n.* [< NL., < Gr. πρίων, a saw: see *Prion.*] In *ornith.*, a genus of motmots: same as *Momotus. Illiger*, 1811.

Prionitidæ (prī-ǫ-nit'i-dē), *n. pl.* [NL., < *Prionites* + *-idæ.*] Same as *Momotidæ. Bonaparte*, 1849.

Prionitinæ (prī″ǫ-ni-tī'nē), *n. pl.* [NL., < *Prionites* + *-inæ.*] Same as *Momotinæ*, 1. *Cabanis*, 1847.

Prioniturus (prī″ǫ-ni-tū'rus), *n.* [NL. (Wagler, 1830), < *Prionites* + Gr. οὐρά, tail.] A genus of *Psittacidæ*, having the central rectrices spatulate, as in the motmots of the genus *Prionites* (or *Momotus*), whence the name; the racket-tailed parrakeets. Several species inhabit Celebes and the Philippines, as *P. platurus*, *P. discurus*, and *P. spatuliger.*

Racket-tailed Parrakeet (*Prioniturus discurus*).

Prionium (prī-ō'ni-um), *n.* [NL. (E. Meyer, 1832), so called in allusion to the sharply saw-toothed leaves; < Gr. πρίων, a saw.] A genus of monocotyledonous plants of the order *Juncaceæ* and tribe *Eujunceæ.* It is distinguished from *Juncus*, the rushes, which it closely resembles in structure, by the three-celled ovary with a few seeds in the lower half of each cell, the large club-shaped embryo, and the three separate styles. The only species, *P. Palmita*, is a native of South Africa, known as *palmet* or *palmiet*, and *palmite.* See *palmite.*

Prionodesmacea (prī″ǫ-nǫ-des-mā'sẹ-ạ̈), *n. pl.* [NL., < Gr. πρίωνια, saw, + δέσμας, band, ligature.] An order or group of bivalve shells with the hinge primitively transversely plicated or prionodont. It includes the *Nuculacea*, *Arcacea*, *Trigoniacea*, *Naiadacea*, and *Monomyaria.*

Prionodon (prī-on'ǫ-don), *n.* [NL., < Gr. πρίων, a saw, + ὀδούς (ὀδοντ-) = E. *tooth.*] In *zoöl.*, a generic name variously used. (*a*) In *mammal.*: (1) The emended form of *Priodon* or *Priodontes*, a genus of giant armadillos of South America, the only species of which is the kabalassou, *P. gigas.* (2) A genus of Malayan viverrine quadrupeds of the subfamily *Prionodontinæ*, containing such as *P. gracilis*, which is white with broad black crossbands; the linsangs. This genus was founded by Horsfield in 1823. See cut under *delundung.* (*b*) In *ichth.*, a genus of sharks or subgenus of *Carcharias* or *Carcharinus. Müller and Henle*, 1841.

prionodont (prī-on'ǫ-dont), *a.* and *n.* [< Gr. πρίων, a saw, + ὀδούς (ὀδοντ-) = E. *tooth.*] I. *a.* Having teeth set like a saw; having serrated teeth. Specifically—(*a*) Having very numerous teeth, 20 or 25 above and below on each side, as an armadillo of the genus *Prionodon.* (*b*) Having the tubercular molars reduced to one on each side above and below, as a civet-cat of the genus *Prionodon.* (*c*) In *conch.*, transversely plicated, as the hinge of the *Prionodesmacea.*

II. *n.* 1. An armadillo of the subfamily *Prionodontinæ.*—2. A linsang of the subfamily *Prionodontinæ.*

Prionodontinæ (prī-on″ō-don-tī'nē), *n. pl.* [NL., < *Prionodon* (*-odont-*) + *-inæ.*] 1. A subfamily of *Viverridæ*, named from the genus *Prionodon* of Horsfield, having the body slender and elongate, and the tubercular molars reduced to one above and below on each side; the linsangs.—2. A South American subfamily of *Dasypodidæ*, having from 20 to 25 teeth above and below on each side, a greater number than in any other land-animal; the kabalassous, grand tatous, or giant armadillos. It is named from the genus *Prionodon* (emended from *Priodon* or *Priodontes* of F. Cuvier).

prionodontine (prī-on-ǫ-don'tin), *a.* and *n.* [< *prionodont* + *-ine*[1].] Same as *prionodont.*

Prionurus (prī-ǫ-nū'rus), *n.* [NL. (Ehrenberg, 1829), < Gr. πρίων, a saw, + οὐρά, tail.] 1. A genus of scorpions: same as *Androctonus* of the same author and date.—2. In *ichth.*, a genus of *Teuthididæ.*

Prionus (prī'ǫ-nus), *n.* [NL. (Geoffroy, 1762), < Gr. πρίων, a saw.] A genus of large longicorn beetles, of the broad-bodied series of *Cerambycidæ*, typical of the family *Prionidæ*, having the antennæ imbricated or pectinated in the male. It is wide-spread and has about 30 species, of which 9 inhabit North America, *P. laticollis* and *P. imbricornis* being among the commonest of the latter. The larvæ of both of these feed upon the roots of the grape. *P. coriarius* is European. *P. brevicornis* is destructive to orchard and other trees in North America. *P. cervicornis* is a South American staghorn beetle, whose larvæ are eaten by the natives. See also cut under *Phytophaga.*

Prionus imbricornis, male. (Natural size.)

prior (prī'ǫr), *a.* [< L. *prior* (neut. *prius*), former, earlier, previous (pl. *priores*, forefathers, ancestors, the ancients), superior, better, used as the comparative of *primus*, first: see *prime*, and cf. *pristine.*] 1. Preceding, as in the order of time, of thought, of origin, of dignity, or of importance; in *law*, senior in point of time: as, a prior and a junior incumbrance.

> Sche seyde thou semyste a man of honour,
> And therfore thou schalt be *pryowre.*
> *MS. Cantab.* Ff. ii. 38, f. 110. (*Halliwell.*)
>
> The thought is always *prior* to the fact; all the facts of history preëxist in the mind as laws. *Emerson*, History.

2. Previous: used adverbially, followed by *to*, like *previous.* See *previous*, *a.*

> At the close of the Republican era, and *prior to* the reconstruction of society under the Emperors, skepticism had widely spread.
> *G. P. Fisher*, Begin. of Christianity, p. 133.
>
> What I propose to do is merely to consider a little Burke's life *prior to* his obtaining a seat in Parliament.
> *Contemporary Rev.*, L. 28.

Prior Analytics of Aristotle. See *analytics*, 1.=**Syn.** See *previous.*

prior (prī'ǫr), *n.* [< ME. *priour*, *preyour* = D. *prioor* = MLG. *prior*, *prier* = MHG. *prior*, G. *prior* = Sw. Dan. *prior*, < OF. *priour*, *prieur*, F. *prieur* = Sp. Pg. *prior* = It. *priore*, < ML. *prior*, a prior, lit. superior, < L. *prior*, former, superior: see *prior*, *a.*] A superior officer; a superior. Specifically—(*a*) *Eccles.*, an official in the monastic orders next in dignity and rank to an abbot. Before the thirteenth century he seems to have been called *provost* (præpositus) or *prelate* (prælatus), and *prior* seems to have meant any superior or senior. If in an abbey, and an assistant of the abbot, he is called a *claustral prior*; if the superior of a priory—that is, of a monastery of lower than abbatial rank—he is called a *conventical* or *conventual prior.* The superiors of the houses of regular canons were always called *priors*, and the commandants of the priories of the military orders of St. John of Jerusalem, of Malta, and of the Templars were called *grand priors.* See *hegumen.*

> The *prior* of Durham, modest as the name might sound, was a greater personage than most abbots.
> *Rom. Cath. Dict.*

(*b*) Formerly, in Italy, a chief magistrate, as in the medieval republic of Florence.

> The *Priors* of the [Florentine] Arts.
> *C. E. Norton*, Church-building in Middle Ages, p. 193.
>
> In 1300 we find him [Dante] elected one of the *priors* of the city. *Lowell*, Among my Books, 2d ser., p. 10.

=**Syn.** *Abbot*, *Prior.* See def. (*a*).

priorate (prī'ǫr-ạ̄t), *n.* [= F. *prieuré* = Sp. *priorato* = Pg. *priorado*, *priorato* = It. *priorato* = D. *prioraat* = G. Sw. Dan. *priorat*, < ML. *prioratus*, the office of a prior, < *prior*, a prior: see *prior*, *n.*] 1. The rank, office, or dignity of prior, in any sense of that word.

> Dante entered on his office as one of the priors of the city; and in that *priorate*, he himself declared, all the ills and calamities of his after-years had their occasion and beginning.
> *C. E. Norton*, Church-building in Middle Ages, p. 194.

2. The period during which a prior holds office; priorship.

> An eulogy on Walkelin, bishop of Winchester, and a Norman, who built great part of his stately cathedral, as it now stands, and was bishop there during Godfrey's *priorate.* *T. Warton*, Hist. Eng. Poetry, Dis. ii.

prioress (prī'ǫr-es), *n.* [< ME. *prioresse* = D. *priores*, < OF. *prioresse* = Pg. *prioreza* = MLG. *priorisse*, *priorsche*, *priersche*, < ML. *priorissa*, a prioress, fem. of *prior*, prior: see *prior*, *n.*] A female prior, having charge of a religious house; a woman who is the coadjutor of and next in rank to an abbess.

Yon shrouded figure, as I guess,
By her proud mien and flowing dress,
Is Tynemouth's haughty *Prioress*.
Scott, Marmion, ii. 19.

prioristic (prī-ọ-ris'tik), *a.* [< *prior* + *-istic.*] Of or belonging to the Prior Analytics of Aristotle. See *posterioristic*.

priority (prī-or'i-ti), *n.* [< F. *priorité* = Sp. *prioridad* = Pg. *prioridade* = It. *priorità*, < ML. *priorita(t-)s*, < L. *prior*, former: see *prior*, *a.*] 1. The state of being prior or antecedent, or of preceding something else: as, *priority* of birth: opposed to *posteriority*.

As there is order and *priority* in matter, so is there in time. *Bacon*, Advancement of Learning, ii. 345.

2. Precedence in place or rank; the having of certain rights before another.

Follow Cominius; we must follow you;
Right worthy you *priority*. *Shak.*, Cor., i. 1. 251.

After his [Austin's] decease there should be equalitie of honour betwixt London and Yorke, without all distinction of *prioritie*. *Foxe*, Martyrs, p. 156, an. 1070.

It was our Saviour's will that these, our four fishermen, should have a *priority* of nomination. *I. Walton*, Complete Angler, p. 48.

Under these the scholars and pupils had their places or formes, with titles and *priority* according to their proficiency. *Evelyn*, Diary, Oct. 5, 1641.

3. In *law*, a precedence or preference, as when one debt is paid in *priority* to others, or when an execution is said to lose its *priority* by the neglect of the party to enforce it.—4. Apriority. = **Syn.** *Priority, Antecedence, Precedence, Preëminence, Predominance, Preference, Superiority, Supremacy.* *Priority* is the state or fact of coming first in order of time; what little use it has beyond this meaning is only a figurative extension. *Antecedence* is strictly *priority*, without any proper figurative use. *Precedence* may mean *priority*, but generally means the right to go or come first, the privilege of going before another: as, the question of *precedence* among sovereigns or ambassadors makes great trouble, because the dignity of the nations represented is supposed to be at stake. *Preëminence* is, figuratively, height by nature above all others, generally in some one respect: as, the *preëminence* of Shakspere as a dramatist. *Predominance* is superior and dominating power or influence: as, the *predominance* of a certain faction; figuratively, the *predominance* of light or shade or a particular color in a certain picture. *Preference* is the putting forward of a person or thing by choice, on the ground of worthiness, or on account of the taste, fancy, or arbitrary will of the one preferring: as, to give the *preference* to Milton over Dante. *Superiority* may refer to nature or to given or achieved position over others; it differs from *supremacy* as the comparative differs from the superlative degree: as, the *superiority* of the appearance of certain troops; the *superiority* of the dairy-products of a certain region; *superiority* to one's circumstances; *supremacy* on the land and *supremacy* on the sea do not always go together. See *previous*.

priorly (prī'ọr-li), *adv.* [< *prior*, *a.*, + *-ly*[2].] Antecedently.

Whether *priorly* to that æra it had ever been inhabited, or lain till then in its chaotic state, is a question which it would be rash to decide. *Geddes*, tr. of Bible, I., Pref.

priorship (prī'ọr-ship), *n.* [< *prior*, *n.*, + *-ship.*] The office of prior; a priorate.

The archbishop, prouoked the more by that, deposed him from the *priorship*. *Foxe*, Martyrs, p. 214, an. 1190.

priory (prī'ọr-i), *n.*; pl. *priories* (-iz). [< ME. *priorie*, < OF. *priorie*, *prioree*, *prieurce* (= It. *prioria*), f., a priory (cf. ML. *prioria*, the office of a prior, a priory), a later form for OF. *priore*, *prieure*, < ML. *prioratus*, the office of a prior, < *prior*, a prior: see *prior*, *n.*, and cf. *priorate*.] A religious house next in dignity below an abbey, and often, but not necessarily, dependent upon an abbey. Its superior is called a *prior* or *prioress*.

Our abbeys and our *priories* shall pay
This expedition's charge. *Shak.*, K. John, i. 1. 48.

Alien priory, a cell or small religious house dependent upon a large monastery in another country.

And [the parliament] showed no reluctance to confiscate the property of the *alien priories* which Henry had restored in the previous year. *Stubbs*, Const. Hist. of Eng., § 306.

pripri (prē'prē), *n.* [S. Amer.] In French Guiana, a marshy belt occurring immediately behind the mangrove or submerged belt of the coast. It can easily be drained and made into good meadow-land.

prist, *n.* A Middle English form of *price*. *Chaucer*.

prisage (prī'zāj), *n.* [< OF. *prisage*, prizing, rating, valuing, < *priser*, estimate; in def. 2, rather < OF. *prise*, a taking: see *prize*[1].] 1†. A prizing; rating; valuing. *Cotgrave*.—2. In *early Eng. and French law*, a seizure or asserted right of seizure by way of exaction or requisition for the use of the crown. More specifically—(a) A right which once belonged to the English crown, of taking two tuns of wine from every ship importing twenty tuns or more. This by charter of Edward I. was commuted into a duty of two shillings for every tun imported by merchant strangers, and called *butlerage*, because paid to the king's butler. (b) The share of merchandise taken as lawful prize at sea which belongs to the crown—usually one tenth.

prisal† (prī'zal), *n.* [Also *prizall*; by abbr. from *reprisal*.] A taking; a capture.

They complain of two ships taken on the coast of Portugal. . . . They of Zeland did send unto Holl[and] to let them know of these *prisals*. *Sir P. Sidney*, quoted in Motley's Hist. Netherlands, [III. 174, note.

priscan (pris'kan), *a.* [< L. *priscus*, primitive, + *-an*.] Primitive. [Rare.]

We seem to hear in the songs and dances of the savage Indians the echoes of our own *priscan* history. *Smithsonian Report*, 1881, p. 506.

Priscian (prish'ian), *n.* [So called from *Priscian* (LL. *Priscianus*), a Latin grammarian (about A. D. 500).] A grammarian. Compare the phrase *to break Priscian's head*, under *break*.

But thus it is when petty *Priscians*
Will needs step up to be censorians.
Marston, Satires, iv. 104.

Priscillianism (pri-sil'yan-izm), *n.* [< *Priscillian-ist* + *-ism*.] The doctrines of the Priscillianists.

Priscillianist (pri-sil'yan-ist), *n.* [< *Priscillian* or *Priscilla* (see defs.) + *-ist*.] 1. One of a sect, followers of Priscillian, a Spanish heretic of the fourth century. The sect, which originated in Spain, held various Gnostic and Manichean doctrines. The Priscillianists considered it allowable to conceal their tenets by dissimulation; they were accused of gross immorality, and were severely persecuted by the emperor Maximus.
2. A name given to the Montanists (see *Montanist*), from their alleged prophetess Priscilla.

prise[1]†, *n.* and *v.* An obsolete form of *prize*[1].

prise[1]†, *a.* [ME., also *pryse*, *pris*, < OF. *pris*, taken, received, accepted, etc. (used in various adj. senses), pp. of *prendre*, take, receive, accept: see *prise*[1], *prize*[1], *n.* and *v.*] Choice; excellent; noble.

I bid that ye buske, and no bode make;
Pas into Payone there *prise* knightes dwellis,
Doughty of dede, derfe men in Armys.
Destruction of Troy (E. E. T. S.), l. 2568.

So dide wele thoo *prise* knyghtes in her companye, and also the knyghtes of the rounde table, that ne ought not to be for-yeten. *Merlin* (E. E. T. S.), ii. 220.

I haue a *pris* present; to plese with thi hert.
William of Palerne (E. E. T. S.), l. 411.

prise[2]†, *v.* and *n.* A variant of *prize*[2].

prise[3], *n.* and *v.* See *prize*[3].

prisehead†, *n.* [ME. *prishede*; < *prise*[1], *a.*, + *-head*.] Excellence; worthiness.

The *prishede* of Parys was praisit so mekyll,
With ferly of his fairnes, & his fre buernes.
Destruction of Troy (E. E. T. S.), l. 2907.

priser†, *n.* An obsolete form of *prizer*.

prism (prizm), *n.* [= F. *prisme* = Sp. Pg. It. *prisma* = D. G. Sw. Dan. *prisma*, < LL. *prisma*, a prism (in geom.), < Gr. πρίσμα, a prism (in geom.), lit. something sawed (as a block of wood), also sawdust, < πρίειν, πρίζειν, saw.] 1. In *geom.*, a solid whose bases or ends are any similar, equal, and parallel plane polygons, and whose sides are parallelograms. Prisms are triangular, square, pentagonal, etc., according as the figures of their ends are triangles, squares, pentagons, etc.

When the mirror is entirely inlaid with large pieces of Marble, some of which are found to rise above the others, or to be detached from them, they are forced down again with a quadrangular wooden *prism*. *Marble-Worker*, § 152.

Triangular Prism.

Specifically—2. An optical instrument consisting of a transparent medium so arranged that the surfaces which receive and transmit light form an angle with each other: usually of a triangular form with well-polished sides, which meet in three parallel lines, and made of glass, rock-salt, or quartz, or a liquid, as carbon disulphid, contained in a prismatic receptacle formed of plates of glass. A ray of light falling upon one of the sides of a prism is refracted (see *refraction*) or bent from its original direction at an angle depending upon its own wave-length, the angle of incidence, the angle of the prism, and the material of which the prism is made. This angle of deviation, as it is called, has a definite minimum (minimum deviation) value when the angle of incidence is equal to the angle of emergence.

Glass Prism upon Adjustable Stand.

The angle of deviation increases as the wave-length of the light-ray diminishes; consequently, if a pencil of white light falls upon the prism, the different rays are separated or dispersed, and a spectrum is the result. (See *spectrum*.) Prisms are hence used in spectrum analysis to decompose light, so that the rays of which it is made up may be examined.

The beams that thro' the Oriel shine
Make *prisms* in every carven glass.
Tennyson, Day-Dream, The Sleeping Palace.

3. In *crystal.*, a form consisting of planes, usually four, six, eight, or twelve, which are parallel to the vertical axis. If the planes intersect the lateral axes at the assumed unit distances for the given species, it is called a *unit prism*; otherwise it may be described, according to the position of the planes, as a *macroprism*, *brachyprism*, *orthoprism*, or *clinoprism*. In the triclinic system the form includes two planes only, and it is hence called a *hemiprism*. In the tetragonal system the unit prism is sometimes called a *protoprism*, or prism of the first order, and the diametral prism, whose planes are parallel to a lateral axis, a *deuteroprism*, or prism of the second order; these names are also used in an analogous manner in the hexagonal system.

4. In canals, a part of the water-space in a straight section of a canal, considered as a parallelopiped.—5. In *weaving*, same as *pattern-box* (*b*).—**Achromatic prism**, a prism through which an incident beam of light is refracted into a new direction without color. It consists of a combination of two prisms, made of two different transparent substances of unequal dispersive powers, as flint-glass and crown-glass.—**Amici's prism**, in *microscopy*, a form of illuminator consisting of a prism having one plane and two lenticular surfaces, so that it serves at once to concentrate the rays and to reflect them obliquely upon the object. It is supported upon an adjustable stand.—**Bisulphid prism.** See *bisulphid*.—**Diametral prism.** See *diametral planes*, under *diametral*.—**Diatom prism**, a prism used as an attachment to a microscope to give the oblique illumination favorable for observing very fine lines or markings, as those on the shells of diatoms.—**Double-image prism**, in *optics*, a prism of Iceland spar which yields two images of like intensity, but polarized in planes at right angles to each other.—**Equilateral prism**, a prism having equal sides, used as an attachment to a microscope to illuminate the object. It acts on the principle of total reflection.—**Erecting prism**, a prism placed between the two lenses of the eyepiece, and serving to erect the inverted image of a compound microscope.—**Natchet's prism.** (*a*) In *microscopy*, an erecting prism. (*b*) A form of illuminator consisting of a prism with two convex surfaces, by which the light is brought to a focus upon the object.—**Nicol prism**, or *nicol*, a prism of Iceland spar (calcite), used when polarized light is required: named from its inventor, William Nicol, of Edinburgh, who first described it in 1828. The common form is constructed from an oblong cleavage piece, first by grinding two new faces at the ends (as *pp'*) inclined about 68° to the vertical edges, and then cementing the halves together by Canada balsam in the line *AB*. The ordinary ray now suffers total reflection at c, and is absorbed by the blackened sides at *g*, while the extraordinary ray, polarized with vibrations parallel to the shorter diagonal of the cross-section, emerges at c. Modified forms of the prism, accomplishing the same end, have been devised in recent years (often called *nicols* also), which are much shorter, and hence have the advantages of giving a larger field in the microscope and less loss of light by absorption, together with an important saving of the material; one of these is the Razumovsky prism.—**Prism battery**, a Leclanché battery in which a pair of compressed prisms, containing all the materials commonly used in the porous cup, is employed in place of the latter.—**Reversing prism**, a small obtuse-angled isosceles prism (*p* in the cut) of flint-glass, placed between the eye-lens of a positive eyepiece *e* and the eye, with its longest side parallel to the optical axis of the eyepiece. It inverts the image viewed through the eyepiece, and when it is made to rotate around the optical axis the image also appears to turn, so that any line in it can be made vertical or horizontal at pleasure. This enables the observer to avoid, or to eliminate, certain errors of measurement which depend upon the apparent position of the object.—**Right-angle prism**, a prism attached to a microscope-stand to throw light upon an object. It is so made that it can rotate on a horizontal or vertical axis, so as to throw light as required.—**Wenham prism**, in a binocular microscope, a quadrilateral prism used to retract part of the light-rays from the object up the second tube to its eyepiece.

Vertical and Transverse Sections of a Nicol Prism.
pp', direction of terminal face of prism; *AB*, direction of surface by which the parts are cemented together; *bcg*, path of ordinary ray; *bdef*, path of extraordinary ray; *vv'*, direction of vibration plane in shorter diagonal of transverse section (*pp'* being longer diagonal, cf. above).

Reversing Prism.
The prism can be rotated on the optical axis *ef*.

prismatic (priz-mat'ik), *a.* [= F. *prismatique* = Sp. *prismático* = Pg. It. *prismatico*, < Gr. πρίσμα(τ-), a prism: see *prism*.] 1. Of or pertaining to a prism; having the form of a prism.

False eloquence, like the *prismatic* glass,
Its gaudy colours spreads on every place.
Pope, Essay on Criticism, l. 311.

2. Separated or distributed by, or as if by, a transparent prism; formed by a prism; varied

in color: as, a *prismatic* spectrum; *prismatic* colors.

> He talks of light and the *prismatic* hues.
> Cowper, Charity, l. 391.

Prismatic cleavage, cleavage parallel to the planes of a prism.—**Prismatic colors**, the colors into which ordinary white light is decomposed by a prism, from the red to the violet. See *color* and *spectrum*.—**Prismatic compass**, a compass held in the hand when used, and so arranged that by means of a prism the graduations can be read off at the same time that the object sighted is seen through the sight-vane. It is used for taking bearings in sketching ground for military purposes, and for filling in the interior details of rough surveys.—**Prismatic crystal**, a crystal having a prismatic form.—**Prismatic planes**, in *crystal.*, planes parallel to the vertical axis of the crystal.—**Prismatic powder.** See *powder*.

Prismatic Compass.

a, floating card beginning at the N. point and numbered entirely around the circle, 360°; *b*, vertical sight-vane with central vertical wire *d*; *c*, prism. On applying the eye at *c*, and causing the wire *d* to bisect any object, the division on the card coinciding with the wire and reflected to the eye will show the angle formed with the meridian by the object sighted.

prismatical (priz-mat'i-kal), *a.* [< *prismatic* + *-al.*] Same as *prismatic*.

prismatically (priz-mat'i-kal-i), *adv.* In the form or manner of a prism; by means of a prism.

> What addition or decrement . . . befalls the body of the glass by being *prismatically* figured?
> Boyle, Works, I. 556.

prismatoid (priz'ma-toid), *n.* [< Gr. πρίσμα(τ-), a prism, + εἶδος, form.] A solid having two parallel polygonal bases connected by triangular faces. If A and C are the areas of the bases of a prismatoid, and B that of the section half-way between them, then, *h* being the altitude, August's formula for the solid contents is $\frac{1}{6}h(A + 4B + C)$.

Prismatoid.

prismatoidal (priz-ma-toi'dal), *a.* In the form of or connected with a prismatoid.

prismenchyma† (priz-meng'ki-mä), *n.* [< Gr. πρίσμα, a prism, + NL. (*par*)*enchyma*.] In *bot.*, cellular tissue in which the cells are of a prismatic form.

prismoid (priz'moid), *n.* [< Gr. πρίσμα, prism, + εἶδος, form.] A body that approaches to the form of a prism; a prismatoid.

prismoidal (priz-moi'dal), *a.* [< *prismoid* + *-al.*] 1. Having or relating to the form of a prismoid.—2. In *entom.*, noting long bodies when they have more than four faces: as, *prismoidal* joints of the antennæ. *Kirby.*—**Prismoidal formula**, a formula based on the consideration of a solid as composed of prismoids.

prism-train (prizm'trān), *n.* A series of prisms used with the spectroscope to give increased dispersion. See *spectroscope*.

> Instruments [spectroscopes] in which the *prism-train* is replaced by a diffraction-grating are still more powerful.
> C. A. Young, The Sun, p. 191.

prismy (priz'mi), *a.* [< *prism* + *-y*[1].] Pertaining to or like a prism; prismatic in color.

> The mighty ministers
> Unfurled their *prismy* wings.
> Shelley, Demon of the World.

> The *prismy* hues in thin spray showers.
> Whittier, Tent on the Beach.

prison (priz'n), *n.* [< ME. *prison*, *prisoun*, *prisun*, *pryson*, *prysoun*, *prysun*, *preson*, late AS. *prisun*, < OF. *prison*, *prisoun*, *prisun*, a prison, a prisoner, F. *prison*, a prison, imprisonment, = Pr. *preiso* = Sp. *prision* = Pg. *prisão* = It. *prigione*, a prison (ML. reflex *prisio*(*n-*), captivity, prison), < L. *prensio*(*n-*), a taking, seizing, arresting, contr. of *prehensio*(*n-*) (found only in the sense of a machine for raising or screwing up anything, a jackscrew), < *prehendere*, *prendere*, take, seize: see *prehend*, and cf. *prehension* (a doublet of *prison*) and *prize*[1], etc.] 1. A place of confinement or involuntary restraint; especially, a public building for the confinement or safe custody of criminals and others committed by process of law; a jail.

> The jailor . . . thrust them into the inner *prison*, and made their feet fast in the stocks. Acts xvi. 24.

> Each heart would quit its *prison* in the breast,
> And flow in free communion with the rest.
> Cowper, Charity, l. 610.

2†. A prisoner.

> Mi lord the king was ther cauȝt in kene stoure,
> & ȝour sone also, and are *prisons* bothe.
> William of Palerne (E. E. T. S.), l. 4215.

> "Consummatum est," quod Cryst, and comsed forto swowe
> Pitousliche and pale as a *prisoun* that deyeth.
> Piers Plowman (B), xviii. 59.

Fleet Prison. See *fleet*[3].—**Keeper of the Queen's prison.** See *marshal of the King's Bench*, under *marshal*.—**Limits of a prison, prison bounds**, jail liberties (which see, under *jail*).—**Prison-breach** or **-breaking**, in *law*, a breaking and going out of prison by one lawfully confined therein. (*Bishop.*) Breaking into a prison to set a prisoner at large is commonly called *rescue*.—**Prison rustic ashler.** See *ashler*, 3.—**Rules of a prison.** See *rule*.—**State prison.** (*a*) A jail for political offenders only. (*b*) A public prison or penitentiary. [U. S.]—**To break prison.** See *to break jail*, under *break*.—**To go out of prison by baston.** See *baston*, 3.

prison (priz'n), *v. t.* [< ME. *prisonen*; < *prison*, *n.*] To shut up in a prison; restrain from liberty; imprison, literally or figuratively.

> Sir William Crispyn with the duke was led,
> Togidder *prisoned*. Rob. of Brunne, p. 101.

> Her tears began to turn their tide,
> Being *prison'd* in her eye like pearls in glass.
> Shak., Venus and Adonis, l. 980.

> He groped; I arrested his wandering hand, and *prisoned* it in both mine. Charlotte Brontë, Jane Eyre, xxxvii.

prison-bars (priz'n-bärz), *n. pl.* 1. The bars or grates of a prison; hence, whatever confines or restrains.

> Even through the body's *prison-bars*,
> His soul possessed the sun and stars.
> D. G. Rossetti, Dante at Verona.

2. Same as *prisoners' base* (which see, under *prisoner*).

prison-base (priz'n-bās), *n.* Same as *prisoners' base* (which see, under *prisoner*).

prisoner (priz'n-ėr), *n.* [< ME. *prisoner*, *prisuner*, *prysoner*, < AF. *prisuner*, OF. *prisonier*, F. *prisonnier* (= Sp. *prisionero* = Pg. *prisioneiro*), a prisoner, < *prison*, prison: see *prison*.] 1†. One who keeps a prison; a jailer.

> He bad [Joseph] ben sperd fast dun,
> And holden herde in prisun.
> An litel stund, quhile he was ther,
> So gan him luuen the *prisuner*.
> Genesis and Exodus (E. E. T. S.), l. 2042.

2. One who is confined in a prison by legal arrest or warrant.

> She leteth passe *prisoneres* and payeth for hem ofte,
> And gyueth the gailers golde.
> Piers Plowman (B), iii. 136.

> The High Priest and the Elders with their eloquent Tertullus were forced to return as they came, and leave St. Paul under the name of a *Prisoner*, but enjoying the conveniencies of liberty. Stillingfleet, Sermons, II. i.

3. A person under arrest or in custody of the law, whether in prison or not: as, a *prisoner* at the bar of a court.

> The jury, passing on the *prisoner's* life.
> Shak., M. for M., ii. 1. 19.

4. A captive; one taken by an enemy in war.

> He yielded on my word;
> And, as my *prisoner*, I restore his sword.
> Dryden, Indian Emperor, iii. 4.

5. One who or that which is deprived of liberty or kept in restraint.

> Most souls, 'tis true, but peep out once an age,
> Dull, sullen *prisoners* in the body's cage.
> Pope, To the Memory of an Unfortunate Lady.

> If the person sent to relieve his confederate [in prisoners' base] be touched by an antagonist before he reaches him, he also becomes a *prisoner*, and stands in equal need of deliverance. Strutt, Sports and Pastimes, p. 145.

Prisoners' bars. Same as *prisoners' base*.—**Prisoners' base**, a children's game in which one player strives to touch the others as they run from one goal or base to another: when one player is thus touched, he too stands between the bases and tries to touch the rest, and so on till all are caught. There are many other ways of playing the game. Also called *prisoners' bars*, *prison-base*, and *prison-bars*.—**Prisoner's-bolt**, in *her.*, same as *shackle-bolt*.—**State prisoner**, one confined for a political offense. =**Syn.** *Prisoner, Captive.* See *captive*.

prison-fever (priz'n-fē'vėr), *n.* Typhus fever (which see, under *fever*[1]). Also called *jail-fever*.

prison-house (priz'n-hous), *n.* A house in which prisoners are kept; a jail; a place of confinement.

> I am forbid
> To tell the secrets of my *prison-house*.
> Shak., Hamlet, i. 5. 14.

> That I may fetch thee
> From forth this loathsome *prison-house*.
> Milton, S. A., l. 922.

prisonment (priz'n-ment), *n.* [< *prison* + *-ment*.] Confinement in a prison; imprisonment.

> Item, the *presonment* of John Porter of Blykelyng.
> Paston Letters, I. 189.

> 'Tis *prisonment* enough to be a maid;
> But to be mew'd up too, that case is hard.
> Middleton, More Dissemblers besides Women, ii. 3.

prison-ship (priz'n-ship), *n.* A ship fitted up for receiving and detaining prisoners.

> They saw themselves melting away like slaves in a *prison-ship*. Prescott, Ferd. and Isa., ii. 14.

prison-van (priz'n-van), *n.* A close carriage for conveying prisoners.

pristav (pris'tav), *n.* [< Russ. *pristavŭ*.] In Russia, an overseer, police official, commissioner, commissary, or inspector.

> He was styled the grand *pristaw*, or great commissioner, and was universally known amongst the Tartar tribes by this title. De Quincey, Flight of a Tartar Tribe.

> I have in my possession the original report of a Russian police *pristav*, written upon a printed form.
> George Kennan, The Century, XXXVII. 893.

Pristidæ (pris'ti-dē), *n. pl.* [NL., < *Pristis* + *-idæ*.] A family of selachians or plagiostomous fishes, typified by the genus *Pristis*, having the snout enormously prolonged into a flattened beak, armed with a row of saw-like teeth on each side; the saw-fishes. (*a*) In Gray's system the *Pristidæ* included the *Pristiophoridæ*. (*b*) In Günther's system, a family of *Batoidei*, including only the saw-fishes proper. They chiefly inhabit tropical seas. See cuts under *Pristis* and *saw-fish*.

pristinate† (pris'ti-nāt), *a.* [< *pristine* + *-ate*[1].] Original; pristine.

> But as it [health] hath recovered the *pristinate* strength, which thing only in all the fight it coveted, shall it incontinent be astonished? Sir T. More, Utopia (trans.), ii. 7.

> I thynke, yea and doubt not, but your line shalbe again restored to the *pristinate* estate and degree.
> Hall, Rich. III., f. 13. (Halliwell.)

> Beside the only name of Christ, and externall contempt of their *pristinate* idolatrye, he taught them nothing at all.
> Holinshed, Chron., I., B. 3, col. 2, b. (Nares.)

pristine (pris'tin), *a.* [Formerly *pristin*; < OF. *pristin* = Sp. *prístino* = Pg. It. *pristino*, < L. *pristinus*, early, original, primitive, also just past (of yesterday); akin to *priscus*, former, ancient, antique, and to *prior*, former: see *prior*, *prime*.] Of or belonging to a primitive or early state or period; original; primitive: as, *pristine* innocence; the *pristine* manners of a people.

> Find her disease,
> And purge it to a sound and *pristine* health.
> Shak., Macbeth, v. 3. 52.

> Adam's self, if now he liv'd anew,
> Could scant vnwinde the knotty snarled clew
> Of double doubts and questions intricate
> That Schools dispute about this *pristin* state.
> Sylvester, tr. of Du Bartas's Weeks, ii., Eden.

> After all their labour, [they] at last return to their *pristine* ignorance. Goldsmith, Citizen of the World, xxxvii.

=**Syn.** *Primitive*, etc. See *primary*.

Pristiophoridæ (pris'ti-ō-for'i-dē), *n. pl.* [NL., < *Pristiophorus* + *-idæ*.] A family of plagiostomous fishes, typified by the genus *Pristiophorus*. They are anarthrous sharks, having the snout much produced and armed with lateral saw-like teeth. They thus resemble the true saw-fishes, but have lateral branchial apertures like other sharks, and do not attain such size. The species are confined to tropical Pacific waters.

Pristiophorus (pris-ti-of'ō-rus), *n.* [NL., < Gr. πρίστης, a saw, + φέρειν = E. *bear*[1].] The typical

Pristiophorus cirratus.

genus of *Pristiophoridæ*, including such forms as *P. cirratus*. *Müller and Henle*, 1837.

Pristis (pris'tis), *n.* [NL., < Gr. πρίστις, a large fish of the whale kind, formerly supposed to be a saw-fish, < πρίειν, saw.] The only genus of *Pristidæ*, having the form elongate, with the

Sword of *Pristis pectinatus.*

snout prolonged into a toothed sword. The European saw-fish is known as *P. antiquorum*. The common American species is *P. pectinatus*, whose weapon (figured above) is about three feet long. See also cut under *saw-fish*.

pritch (prich), *n.* [An assibilated form of *prick*, *n.*] 1. Any sharp-pointed instrument. *Halliwell.*—2†. Pique; offense taken.

> The least word uttered awry, the least conceit taken, or *pritch*, . . . is enough to make suits, and they will be revenged. D. Rogers, Naaman the Syrian, p. 270.

pritch (prich), *v. t.* [An assibilated form of *prick*, *v.*] To pierce or make holes in. *Halliwell.* [Prov. Eng.]

Pritchardia (pri-chär'di-ä), *n.* [NL. (Seeman and Wendland, 1862), named after W. T. *Pritchard*, British consul in Fiji.] A genus of palms of the tribe *Corypheæ*, remarkable among palms for its persistent corolla-tube, from which the lobes fall away. It is characterized by the valvate corolla-lobes and three-angled or three-lobed ovary, attenuated into a robust style. There are 3 or 4 species, natives of the Friendly and the Hawaiian Islands. They are moderate-sized or low palms, the trunk clad above with the sheathing bases of the leaves, and ringed below with their annular scars. They bear large terminal rounded or fan-shaped leaves, often whitened below with a mealy dust, cut into shallow and slender two-lobed segments, bearing projecting fibers on their margins. Their flowers are rather large, with a bell-shaped three-toothed calyx, and a tubular corolla bearing three thick, rigid, ovate lobes. The flowers are scattered on the stiff ascending branchlets of a long-stalked spadix, inclosed in a large, thick, and coriaceous spathe, which is tubular below and dusted over with silvery particles. In the Hawaiian Islands the leaves of *P. Gaudichaudii* afford fans and hats, and its fruit-kernels, called *hawane*, are eaten unripe. The leaves of *P. Pacifica* in the Fijis are four feet long by three wide, and make fans and umbrellas, their use being confined to the chiefs. Some authors have proposed to unite with this genus the American palm *Washingtonia*.

pritchel (prich'el), *n.* [An assibilated form of *prickle*. Cf. *pritch*.] 1. In *farriery*, a punch employed for making or enlarging the nail-holes in a horseshoe, or for temporary insertion into a nail-hole to form a means of handling the shoe. *E. H. Knight.*—2. An iron share fixed to a thick staff, used for making holes in the ground. *Halliwell.* [Prov. Eng.]

prithee (priṫн'ē). [Formerly also *prythee*, *pree-thee*; a weakened form of (*I*) *pray thee*.] A corruption of *pray thee*; I pray thee.

My soules deer Soule, take in good part (I *pree-thee*)
This pretty Present that I gladly giue thee.
Sylvester, tr. of Du Bartas's Weeks, ii., The Handy-Crafts.

I *prithee* let me go;
I shall do best without thee; I am well.
Beau. and Fl., Philaster, iv. 3.

Prithee, be forgiven, and I *prithee* forgive me too.
Fletcher, Pilgrim, v. 6.

My Love, my Life, said I, explain
This Change of Humour; *prythee* tell;
That falling Tear—what does it mean?
Prior, The Garland, st. 6.

prittle† (prit'l), *v. t.* [A weakened form of *prattle*, as in *prittle-prattle*.] To chatter.

Awe man, you *prittle* and prattle nothing but leasings and untruths.
Heywood, Royal King (Works, ed. Pearson, 1874, VI. 9).

prittle-prattle (prit'l-prat"l), *n.* [A varied reduplication of *prattle*.] Empty or idle talk; trifling loquacity. [Colloq.]

Cianfrogna [It.], gibrish, pedlars french, roguish language, fustian toong, *prittle prattle*. *Florio.*

It is plain *prittle-prattle*, and ought to be valued no more than the shadow of an ass.
Abp. Bramhall, Church of Eng. Defended (1659), p. 46. (*Latham*.)

prius (prī'us), *n.* [< L. *prius*, neut. of *prior*, being before, prior: see *prior*.] That which necessarily goes before; a precondition.

priv. An abbreviation of *privative*.

Priva (prī'vạ̈), *n.* [NL. (Adanson, 1763); origin unknown.] A genus of erect herbs of the order *Verbenaceæ* and tribe *Verbeneæ*. It is characterized by a fruit of two nutlets, each two-celled and two-seeded, a long spike with small bracts and interrupted at the base, and an enlarged fruiting-calyx tightly including the fruit within its closed apex. The 9 species are natives of warm regions of both hemispheres. They bear opposite toothed leaves, slender spikes terminal or long-stalked in the axils, and small and somewhat two-lipped flowers which have five lobes and four short didynamous stamens. *P. echinata* of Brazil, the West Indies, southern Florida, etc., is called *styptic-* or *velvet-bur*, its fruiting-calyx being bristly with small hooked hairs. *P. lævis* of Chili and the Argentine Republic yields small edible tubers.

privacy (prī'vạ̈-si or priv'a-si), *n.*; pl. *privacies* (-siz). [< *priva*(*te*) + *-cy*.] 1. A state of being private, or in retirement from the company or from the knowledge or observation of others; seclusion.

In the closet, where *privacy* and silence befriend our inquiries. *Bp. Atterbury*, Sermons, I. x.

The housemates sit
Around the radiant fireplace, enclosed
In a tumultuous *privacy* of storm.
Emerson, The Snow-Storm.

2. A place of seclusion from company or observation; retreat; solitude; retirement.

Her sacred *privacies* all open lie. *Rowe.*

3†. Joint knowledge; privity. See *privity*.

You see Frog is religiously true to his bargain, scorns to hearken to any composition without your *privacy*.
Arbuthnot, Hist. John Bull.

4†. Taciturnity. *Ainsworth.*—5. Secrecy; concealment of what is said or done.

Of this my *privacy*
I have strong reasons.
Shak., T. and C., iii. 3. 190.

There was no affectation of *privacy* in what they [Christ and his apostles] said or did; their doctrines were preached, and their miracles wrought, in broad day-light, and in the face of the world! *Bp. Atterbury*, Sermons, II. i.

6. A private or personal matter, circumstance, or relation.

What concernes it us to hear a Husband divulge his Household *privacies*, extolling to others the vertues of his Wife? *Milton*, Eikonoklastes, vii.

In all my Acquaintance and utmost *Privacies* with her.
Steele, Conscious Lovers, i. 2.

privado† (pri-vä'dō), *n.* [Sp., = E. *private*: see *private*.] 1. A private or intimate friend; a court favorite.

The modern languages give unto such persons the name of favourites, or *privadoes*. *Bacon*, Friendship (ed. 1887).

The Duke of Lerma was the greatest *Privado*, the greatest Favourite, that ever was in Spain since Don Alvaro de Luna. *Howell*, Letters, I. iii. 11.

Lat. May I desire one favour?
Y. Book. What can I deny thee, my *privado*?
Steele, Lying Lover, ii. 1.

2. A private soldier or inferior (non-commissioned) officer.

Lantz *privadoes*, who are Corporals' Lieutenants.
Ranks in British Army (Arber's Eng. Garner, I. 463).

privant (prī'vạnt), *a.* [< L. *privan*(*t-*)*s*, ppr. of *privare*, deprive: see *private*.] Noting privative opposites. See *privative*.

privat-docent (prē-vät'dō-tsent'), *n.* [G., < L. *privatus*, private, + *docen*(*t-*)*s*, ppr. of *docere*, teach: see *private* and *docent*.] In the universities of Germany and some other countries of Europe, a teacher of the third rank: unlike professors, he has no part in the government of the university, and receives no compensation from the university, but is remunerated by fees.

private (prī'vạ̄t), *a.* and *n.* [= F. *privé* = Sp. Pg. *privado* = It. *privato* = D. *privaat* = G. Sw. Dan. *privat*, private, < L. *privatus*, apart from what is public, pertaining to an individual, private, pp. of *privare*, separate, deprive, release, < *privus*, single, every, one's own, private, prob. for orig. **praivus*, < *prai*, older form of *præ*, before: see *pre-*. Cf. *privy*. Hence also ult. *deprive*.] I. *a.* 1. Peculiar to, belonging to, or concerning an individual only; respecting particular individuals; personal.

Why should the *private* pleasure of some one
Become the public plague of many moe?
Shak., Lucrece, l. 1478.

When was public virtue to be found,
Where *private* was not? *Cowper*, Task, v. 503.

That he [Buckingham] should think more about those who were bound to him by *private* ties than about the public interest . . . was perfectly natural.
Macaulay, Lord Bacon.

This [the peace policy] is not to be carried by public opinion, but by *private* opinion, by *private* conviction, by *private*, dear, and earnest love. *Emerson*, War.

The expression . . . sounded more harshly as pronounced in a public lecture than as read in a *private* letter.
O. W. Holmes, Emerson, v.

2. Kept or removed from public view; not known; not open; not accessible to people in general; secret.

O unfelt sore! crest-wounding, *private* scar!
Shak., Lucrece, l. 828.

The poor slave that lies *private* has his liberty
As amply as his master in that tomb.
Fletcher, Wife for a Month, ii. 2.

Reason . . . then retires
Into her *private* cell, when nature rests.
Milton, P. L., v. 109.

The Rais gave the captain of the port a *private* hint to take care what they did, for they might lose their lives.
Bruce, Source of the Nile, I. 249.

3. Not holding public office or employment; not having a public or official character: as, a *private* citizen; *private* life; *private* schools.

"Prayers made for the use of the 'idiotæ' or *private* persons," as the word is, contradistinguished from the rulers of the church. *Jer. Taylor*, Works (ed. 1835), II. 282.

Christ and his Apostles, being to civil affairs but *privat* men, contended not with Magistrates.
Milton, Eikonoklastes, xiii.

Any *private* person . . . that is present when a felony is committed is bound by the law to arrest the felon.
Blackstone, Com., IV. xxi.

4. Noting a common soldier, or one of the ordinary rank and file.

I cannot put him to a *private* soldier that is the leader of so many thousands. *Shak.*, 2 Hen. IV., iii. 2. 177.

5. Being in privacy; retired from company; secluded.

Away from light steals home my heavy son,
And *private* in his chamber pens himself.
Shak., R. and J., i. 1. 144.

Cæsar is *private* now; you may not enter.
B. Jonson, Poetaster, v. 1.

I came home to be *private* a little, not at all affecting the life and hurry of Court. *Evelyn*, Diary, Jan. 18, 1662.

Sir, we are *private* with our women here.
Tennyson, Queen Mary, v. 5.

6†. Privy; informed of what is not generally known.

She knew them [her sister's council of state] adverse to her religion . . . and *private* to her troubles and imprisonment. *Sir R. Naunton*, Fragmenta Regalia.

7. Keeping privacy or confidence; secretive; reticent.

You know I am *private* as your secret wishes,
Ready to fling my soul upon your service.
Fletcher, Wife for a Month, i. 1.

Let these persons march here [with] a charge to be *private* and silent in the business till they see it effected.
Winthrop, Hist. New England, II. 470.

8†. Intimate; confidential.

If Dauid, beeing a king, a Prophet, a Sainct, and with God so *priuate*, understoode not what to present unto God, . . . what shall we doe?
Guevara, Letters (tr. by Hellowes, 1577), p. 2.

What makes the Jew and Lodowick so *private*?
Marlowe, Jew of Malta, ii. 2.

9. Particular; individual; special: opposed to *general*.

No prophecy of the scripture is of any *private* interpretation. 2 Pet. i. 20.

Who cries out on pride,
That can therein tax any *private* party? . . .
Who can come in and say that I mean her,
When such a one as she such is her neighbour?
Shak., As you Like it, ii. 7. 71.

Private acts, bills, or statutes, those acts, etc., which concern private interests—that is, the interests of particular persons—as distinguished from measures of public policy in which the community is interested. See *bill*[3].—**Private attorney.** See *attorney*[1], 2.—**Private bank.** See *bank*[2], 4.—**Private baptism.** See *baptism*.—**Private carrier.** See *carrier*[1], 2.—**Private chapel**, a chapel attached to a private residence.—**Private corporations**, corporations created for private as distinguished from purely public purposes. Such corporations are not, in contemplation of law, public merely because it may have been supposed by the legislature that their establishment would promote, either directly or consequentially, the public interest. (*Dillon.*) Thus, a railroad company is a *private corporation*, although it takes property for public use. See *corporation*.—**Private detective.** See *detective*.—**Private international law.** See *international*.—**Private judgment**, in *theol.*, the judgment of an individual as to doctrine or interpretation of Scripture, in contradistinction to the judgment of the church.—**Private law**, that branch of the law which deals with the rights and duties of persons considered in their private or individual capacity, as distinguished from the rights and duties which are possessed by and incumbent on persons or bodies of persons considered as filling public positions or offices, or which have relation to the whole political community, or to its magistrates and officers. *Kenelm Edward Digby*, Hist. of Law of Real Prop., p. 255.—**Private legislation**, legislation affecting the interests of particular persons, as distinguished from measures of public policy in which the community is interested.—**Private mass.** See *mass*[1].—**Private nuisance.** See *nuisance*, 5.—**Private parts**, the organs of sex.—**Private person**, one not having or not for the time being acting in a public official capacity.—**Private property, private rights**, the property and rights of persons, natural or artificial, in their individual, personal, or private capacity, as distinguished from the rights of the state or public vested in a body politic or a public officer or board as such and for public use. Thus, if a city owns a building which it leases for obtaining a revenue, the property and its rights in respect thereto are deemed the *private property* of the city, as distinguished from parks, etc., and buildings in municipal use.—**Private rights of way, or private ways**, rights which belong to a particular individual only, or to a body of individuals exclusively, either for the purpose of passing generally or for the purpose of passing from a particular tenement of which they are possessed. *Goddard.*—**Private trusts**, those trusts in the maintenance of which the public have no interest.

Private Trusts are those wherein the beneficial interest is vested absolutely in one or more individuals, who are, or within a certain time may be, definitely ascertained, and to whom, therefore, collectively, unless under some legal disability, it is competent to control, modify, or determine the trust. *Bispham*, Principles of Equity, § 58.

Private war, a war carried on by individuals, without the authority or sanction of the state of which they are subjects. *Halleck.*—**Private wrong**, a civil injury; an infringement or privation of some civil right which belongs to a person considered in his private capacity. =**Syn.** 2. *Latent, Covert*, etc. (see *secret*), retired, secluded, isolated, sequestered.

II. *n.* 1†. A person not in public life or office.

And what have kings that *privates* have not too,
Save ceremony? *Shak.*, Hen. V., iv. 1. 255.

2. A common soldier; one of the rank and file of an army.—3†. A secret message; private intimation.

Pem. Who brought that letter from the cardinal?
Sal. The Count Melun, a noble lord of France;
Whose *private* with me of the Dauphin's love
Is much more general than these lines import.
Shak., K. John, iv. 3. 16.

4†. Personal interest or use; particular business.

My lords, this strikes at every Roman's *private*.
B. Jonson, Sejanus, iii. 1.

Our President . . . ingrossing to his *private* Oatmeale, Sacke, Oyle, Aquavitæ, Beefe, Egges, or what not.
Quoted in *Capt. John Smith's* Works, I. 154.

5†. Privacy; retirement.

Go off! . . . let me enjoy my *private*.
Shak., T. N., iii. 4. 100

In our *private* towards God being as holy and devout as if we prayed in public.
Jer. Taylor, Works (ed. 1835), I. 888.

6. *pl.* The private parts of the body.—7. In some colleges, a private admonition.—**In private**, privately; in secret; not publicly.

They do desire some speech with you *in private*.
B. Jonson, Catiline, iv. 5.

The private, private life of individuals, or what relates to private life: opposed to and suggested by the phrase *the public*. [Rare.]

I long to see you a history painter. You have already done enough for *the private*; do something for the public.
Pope, To Jervas, Nov. 29, 1716.

private† (prī'vāt), *v. t.* [< L. *privatus*, pp. of *privare*, strip, deprive: see *private, a.* Cf. *prive.*] To deprive.

They woulde not onelye lese their worldely substaunce, but also be *pryvated* of their lives and worldly felycytie, rather then to suffre Kynge Rycharde, that tyraunt, lenger to rule and reygne over them.
Hall, Rich. III., f. 17. (*Halliwell.*)

privateer (prī-vạ-tēr'), *n.* [< *private* + *-eer*.] 1. An armed vessel owned and officered by private persons, but acting under a commission from the state usually called letters of marque. It answers to a company on land raised and commanded by private persons, but acting under regulations emanating from the supreme authority, rather than to one raised and acting without license, which would resemble a privateer without commission. (*Woolsey*, Introd. to Inter. Law, § 121.)

He is at no charge for a fleet farther than providing *privateers*, wherewith his subjects carry on a piratical war at their own expense.
Swift, Conduct of the Allies.

2. The commander of, or a man serving on board of, a privateer.

Meeting with divers Disappointments, and being out of hopes to obtain a Trade in these Seas, his Men forced him to entertain a Company of *Privateers* which he met with near Nicoya.
Dampier, Voyages, I. 137.

privateer (prī-vạ-tēr'), *v. i.* [< *privateer*, *n.*] To cruise in a privateer for the purpose of seizing an enemy's ships or annoying his commerce. Privateering was abolished by the treaty of Paris of 1856, and this article has been assented to by nearly all civilized nations; the most prominent exception is the United States.

In 1797 the United States passed a law to prevent citizens of the United States from *privateering* against nations in amity with or against citizens of the United States.
Schuyler, Amer. Diplomacy, p. 383.

privateering (prī-vạ-tēr'ing), *n.* [Verbal n. of *privateer*, *v.*] The act or practice of cruising in a privateer for hostile purposes.

Many have felt it to be desirable that *privateering* should be placed under the ban of international law, and the feeling is on the increase, in our age of humanity, that the system ought to come to an end.
Woolsey, Introd. to Inter. Law, § 122.

privateerism (prī-vạ-tēr'izm), *n.* [< *privateer* + *-ism*.] *Naut.*, disorderly conduct, or anything out of man-of-war rules. Also called *privateer practice*. *Admiral Smyth.* [Rare.]

privateersman (prī-vạ-tērz'man), *n.*; pl. *privateersmen* (-men). [< *privateer's*, poss. of *privateer*, + *man*.] An officer or seaman of a privateer.

Marquis Santa Cruz, lord high admiral of Spain, . . . looked on, mortified and amazed, but offering no combat, while the Plymouth *privateersman* [Drake] swept the harbour of the great monarch of the world.
Motley, Hist. Netherlands, II. 283.

privately (prī'vạt-li), *adv.* 1. In a private or secret manner; not openly or publicly.

And as he sat upon the mount of Olives the disciples came unto him *privately*.
Mat. xxiv. 3.

2. In a manner affecting an individual; personally: as, he is not *privately* benefited.

privateness (prī'vạt-nes), *n.* 1. Secrecy; privacy.

Knew theye how guiltless and how free I were from prying into *privateness*.
Marston, End of Scourge of Villanie, To him that hath [perused me.

2. Retirement; seclusion from company or society.

A man's nature is best perceived in *privateness*, for there is no affectation.
Bacon, Nature in Men (ed. 1887).

3. The state of an individual in the rank of a common citizen, or not invested with office.

Men cannot retire when they would, neither will they when it were reason, but are impatient of *privateness*, even in age and sickness, which require the shadow.
Bacon, Great Place (ed. 1887).

privation (prī-vā'shọn), *n.* [< ME. *privacion*, < OF. (and F.) *privation* = Sp. *privacion* = Pg. *privação* = It. *privazione*, < L. *privatio(n-)*, a taking away, < *privare*, pp. *privatus*, deprive: see *private*.] 1. The state of being deprived; particularly, deprivation or absence of what is necessary for comfort; destitution; want.

Pains of *privation* are the pains that may result from the thought of not possessing in the time present any of the several kinds of pleasures.
Bentham, Introd. to Morals and Legislation, v. 17.

Maggie's sense of loneliness and utter *privation* of joy had deepened with the brightness of advancing spring.
George Eliot, Mill on the Floss, iv. 3.

2. The act of removing something possessed; the removal or destruction of any thing or any property; deprivation.

Kyng Richard had bene in greate ieopardie either of *priuacion* of his realme, or losse of his life, or both.
Hall, Rich. III., an. 3.

3. In *logic*, a particular kind of negation consisting in the absence from a subject of a habit which ought to be, might be, or generally is in that subject or others like it.

Privation sometimes signifies the absence of the form which may be introduced upon the subject: so the *privation* of the soul may be said to be in the seed, of heat in cold water; sometimes the absence of the form which ought to be in the subject. That is a physical privation, and is numbered among the principles of generation; this is a logical.
Burgersdicius, tr. by a Gentleman, i. 22.

Whether this comparative specifying foundation be a *privation* or a mode is a philosophical controversy.
Baxter, Divine Life, i. 10.

4. The act of degrading from rank or office.

If part of the people or estate be somewhat in the election, you cannot make them nulls or cyphers in the *privation* or translation.
Bacon.

5. Technically, in the *Rom. Cath. Ch.*, the suspension of an ecclesiastic from his office, stipend, ecclesiastical functions, or jurisdiction.—**Logical privation.** See *logical*.=**Syn.** 1. Need, penury, poverty, necessity, distress.

privative (priv'ạ-tiv), *a.* and *n.* [= F. *privatif* = Sp. Pg. It. *privativo*, < LL. *privativus*, denoting privation, negative, < L. *privare*, pp. *privatus*, deprive: see *private, v.*] I. *a.* 1. Causing privation or destitution.

We may add that negative or *privative* will, also, whereby he withholdeth his graces from some.
Hooker, Eccles. Polity, v., App. 1.

2. Depending on or consisting in privation in the logical sense.

The very *privative* blessings, the blessings of immunity, safeguard, liberty, and integrity, which we all enjoy, deserve the thanksgiving of a whole life.
Jer. Taylor, Holy Living, ii. 6.

Descartes is driven by the necessary logic of his thought to conceive all limits and differences as purely *privative* —i. e. as mere absence or defect of existence.
E. Caird, Philos. of Kant, p. 42.

3. In *gram.*: (*a*) Changing the sense of a word from positive to negative: as, a *privative* prefix; *ȧ-* or *ȧν- privative*. (*b*) Predicating negation: as, a *privative* word.—**Privative connotative term**, an adjective noting some privation, as "blind."—**Privative jurisdiction.** In *Scots law*, a court is said to have *privative jurisdiction* in a particular class of causes when it is the only court entitled to adjudicate in such causes. *Imp. Dict.*—**Privative nothing.** See *nothing*.—**Privative opposites**, a habit and its privation.—**Privative proposition**, a proposition declaring a privation.

II. *n.* 1. That which depends on, or of which the essence is, the absence of something else, as silence, which exists by the absence of sound.

Blackness and darkness are indeed but *privatives*, and therefore have little or no activity.
Bacon, Nat. Hist., § 873.

2. In *gram.*: (*a*) A prefix to a word which changes its signification and gives it a contrary sense, as *un-* in *unwise*, *in-* in *inhuman*, *an-* in *anarchy*, *a-* in *achromatic*. (*b*) A word which not only predicates negation of a quality in an object, but also involves the notion that the absent quality is naturally inherent in it, and is absent through loss or some other privative cause.

privatively (priv'ạ-tiv-li), *adv.* 1. In a privative manner; in the manner or with the force of a privative.—2†. By the absence of something; negatively. [Rare.]

The duty of the new covenant is set down first *privatively*.
Hammond.

privativeness (priv'ạ-tiv-nes), *n.* The condition of being privative. [Rare.]

privet†, *v. t.* [< ME. *priven*, < OF. *priver* = Sp. Pg. *privar* = It. *privare*, < L. *privare*, separate, deprive: see *private, v.* Cf. *deprive*.] To deprive.

Temple devout, ther God hath his woninge,
Fro which these misbileved *priced* [var. *deprived*] been.
Chaucer, A. B. C., l. 146.

For what can be said worse of slepe, if it, *priving* you of all pleasures, do not suffer you to feele any thing at all?
Barker, Fearful Fancies, P 1 b. (*Nares.*)

priveet†, privet†, *a.* Middle English forms of *privy*.

privet (priv'et), *n.* [Formerly also *privie*; appar. a corruption of *primet*. Cf. *prie*[3].] 1. A shrub, *Ligustrum vulgare*, of the northern Old World, planted and somewhat naturalized in North America; the common or garden privet. The name extends also to the other members of the genus.—2. In the southern United States, a small oleaceous tree of wet grounds, *Forestiera acuminata*.—**Barren privet**, the alaternus. See *Rhamnus*.—**California privet**, the Japanese privet, sometimes misnamed *Ligustrum Californicum*.—**Egyptian privet.** See *Lawsonia*.—**Japanese privet**, *Ligustrum Japonicum* (including *L. ovalifolium*).—**Mock privet**, the jasmine box. See *Phillyrea*.

priveteet, *n.* A Middle English spelling of *privity*.

privet-hawkmoth (priv'et-hâk"môth), *n.* A sphinx, *Sphinx ligustri*, so called from its ovipositing on privet, on which its larva feeds.

priviet, *n.* An obsolete form of *privet*.

The borders round about are set with *priuie* sweet.
Breton, Daffodils and Primroses, p. 3. (*Davies.*)

privilege (priv'i-lej), *n.* [Formerly also *priviledge*; < ME. *privilege*, *prevelache*, < OF. *privilege*, F. *privilège* = Sp. Pg. It. *privilegio*, < L. *privilegium*, an ordinance in favor of an individual, prerogative, < *privus*, one's own, private, peculiar, + *lex*, law: see *private* and *legal*.] 1. An ordinance in favor of an individual.

Be ye our help and our proteccioun,
Syn for meryt of your virginitee
The *privilege* of his deleccioun
In yow confermed God upon a tree
Hanging.
Chaucer, Mother of God, l. 122.

Privilege, in Roman jurisprudence, means the exemption of one individual from the operation of a law.
Mackintosh, Study of the Law of Nature, p. 50, note.

2. A right, immunity, benefit, or advantage enjoyed by a person or body of persons beyond the common advantages of other individuals; the enjoyment of some desirable right, or an exemption from some evil or burden; a private or personal favor enjoyed; a peculiar advantage.

As under *privilege* of age to brag
What I have done being young.
Shak., Much Ado, v. 1. 60.

It hath been an accustom'd liberty
To spend this day in mirth, and they will choose
Rather their Soules then *priviledges* loose.
Times' Whistle (E. E. T. S.), p. 20.

Pastures, wood-lots, mill-sites, with the *privileges*,
Rights, and appurtenances which make up
A Yankee Paradise.
Whittier, Bridal of Pennacook.

Specifically—(*a*) In the *Rom. Cath. Ch.*, an exemption or license granted by the Pope. It differs from a *dispensation* and from a *grace* in that it never refers to a single act, but presupposes and legalizes many acts done in pursuance of it, and confers on its possessor immunity in regard to every act so privileged. (*b*) Special immunity or advantage granted to persons in authority or in office, as the freedom of speech, freedom from arrest, etc., enjoyed by members of Parliament or of Congress. Compare *breach of privilege*, below.

The Parliament-men are as great Princes as any in the World, when whatsoever they please is *Priviledge* of Parliament.
Selden, Table-Talk, p. 81.

3†. An advantage yielded; superiority.

Compassion of the king commands me stoop,
Or I would see his heart out, ere the priest
Should ever get that *privilege* of me.
Shak., 1 Hen. VI., iii. 1. 121.

4. In *law*: (*a*) A special and exclusive right conferred by law on particular persons or classes of persons, and ordinarily in derogation of the common right. Such grants were often sought to be justified on grounds of public utility, but were, to a greater or less extent, really intended to benefit the privileged person or persons.

If the printer haue any great dealings with thee, he were best get a *priuiledge* betimes, ad imprimendum solum, forbidding all other to sell waste paper but himselfe.
Nashe, Pierce Penilesse, p. 46.

Our King, in lieu of Money, among other Acts of Grace, gave them a *Privilege* to pay but 1 per Cent.
Howell, Letters, I. vi. 3.

(*b*) The law, rule, or grant conferring such a right. (*c*) In the civil law, a lien or priority of right of payment, such as the artisans' privilege, corresponding to the common-law lien of a bailee or the lien under mechanics' lien-laws, carriers' privilege, inn-keepers' privilege, etc. In this sense the word is more appropriately applicable to a preference secured by law, and not to one granted by special agreement. (*d*) In some of the United States, the right of a licensee in a vocation which is forbidden except to licensees. (*e*) In modern times (since all have become generally equal before the law), one of the more sacred and vital rights common to all citizens: as, the *privilege* of the writ of habeas corpus; the *privileges* of a citizen of the United States.—5. A speculative contract covering a "put" or a "call," or both a put and a call (that is, a "straddle"). See *call*[1], *n.*, 15, *put*[1], *n.*, 6, and *straddle*, *n.*—**Breach of privilege**, violation of the privileges specially possessed by members of legislative bodies. See the quotation.

Breaches of privilege may be summarized as disobedience to any orders or rules of the House, indignities offered to its character or proceedings, assaults, insults, or libels upon members, or interference with officers of the House in discharge of their duty, or tampering with witnesses. *Sir T. Erskine May*, Encyc. Brit., XVIII. 311.

Conservator of the apostolic privileges. See *conservator*.—**Exclusive privilege.** See *exclusive*.—**Mixed privilege**, a privilege granted to classes of persons.—**Personal privilege**, a privilege primarily and directly granted to some person, regarded as an individual.—**Question of privilege**, in *parliamentary law*, a question arising upon the privileges or rights of an assembly or of a member of an assembly. It takes precedence of all questions except a motion to adjourn.—**Real privilege**, a privilege granted to some thing (building, place, or benefice), although indirectly extended to the persons by whom the thing is owned or enjoyed.—**Writ of privilege**, a writ to deliver a privileged person from custody when arrested in a civil suit. =**Syn.** 2. *Privilege, Prerogative, Exemption, Immunity, Franchise.* *Privilege* is a right to do or a right to be excused or spared from doing or bearing, this right being possessed by one or more, but not by all. *Privilege* is also more loosely used for any special advantage: as, the *privilege* of intimacy with people of noble character. *Prerogative* is a right of precedence, an exclusive privilege, an official right, a right indefeasible on account of one's character or position: as, the Stuart kings were continually asserting the royal *prerogative*, but Parliament resisted any infringement upon its *privileges*. (See definition of *prerogative*.) An *exemption* is an exception or excuse from what would otherwise be required: as, *exemption* from military service, or from submitting to examination; figuratively, *exemption* from care, from disease. *Immunity* is the same as *exemption*, except that *exemption* more often expresses the act of authority, and *immunity* expresses more of the idea of safety: as, *immunity* from harm. A *franchise* is a sort of freedom; the word has very exact senses, covering certain *privileges*, *exemptions*, or *immunities*.

privilege (priv'i-lej), *v. t.*; pret. and pp. *privileged*, ppr. *privileging*. [Formerly also *priviledge*; < OF. *privelegir*, F. *privilégier* = Sp. Pg. *privilegiar* = It. *privilegiare*, < ML. *privilegiare*, privilege, approve, < L. *privilegium*, privilege: see *privilege*, *n.*] 1. To grant some privilege to; bestow some particular right or exemption on; invest with a peculiar right or immunity; exempt from censure or danger: as, to *privilege* diplomatic representatives from arrest; the *privileged* classes.

Your Dignity does not *Priviledge* you to do me an Injury. *Selden*, Table-Talk, p. 45.

Ther. Peace, fool! I have not done.
Achil. He is a *privileged* man. Proceed, Thersites.
Shak., T. and C., ii. 3. 61.

This freedom from the oppressive superiority of a *privileged* order was peculiar to England.
Hallam, Middle Ages, viii. 3.

Gentilhomme in France was the name of a well-defined and *privileged* class. *E. A. Freeman*, Amer. Lects., p. 307.

2. To exempt in any way; free: with *from*.

He took this place for sanctuary,
And it shall *privilege* him *from* your hands.
Shak., C. of E., v. 1. 95.

It was not a Jewish ephod, it is not a Romish cowl, that can *privilege* an evil-doer *from* punishment.
Rev. T. Adams, Works, II. 289.

3. To authorize; license.

Wilt thou be glass wherein it shall discern
Authority for sin, warrant for blame,
To *privilege* dishonour in thy name?
Shak., Lucrece, l. 621.

A poet's or a painter's licence is a poor security to *privilege* debt or defamation. *G. Harvey*, Four Letters.

Privileged altar, communication, debt. See the nouns.—**Privileged deeds**, in *Scots law*, holograph deeds, which are exempted from the statute that requires other deeds to be signed before witnesses.—**Privileged summonses**, in *Scots law*, a class of summonses in which, from the nature of the cause of action, the ordinary induciæ are shortened.—**Privileged villeinage.** See *villeinage*.

privily (priv'i-li), *adv.* [< ME. *privily*, *prevely*, *prevaly*, etc.; < *privy* + *-ly*[2].] In a privy manner; privately; secretly.

Sir, a kynge ought not to go so *prevely*, but to haue his moyne a-boute hym. *Merlin* (E. E. T. S.), i. 51.

There shall be false teachers among you, who *privily* shall bring in damnable heresies. 2 Pet. ii. 1.

privity (priv'i-ti), *n.*; pl. *privities* (-tiz). [< ME. *privitee*, *privetee*, *privete*, *pryvete*, etc., < OF. *privete*, < ML. **privita(t-)s*, privacy, < L. *privus*, one's own, private: see *private*.] 1†. Privacy; secrecy; confidence.

Ther shallow fynde
A thyng that I have hyd in *privitee*.
Chaucer, Summoner's Tale, l. 443.

I will to you, in *privity*, discover the drift of my purpose. *Spenser*, State of Ireland.

2†. Private life; privacy; seclusion.

Then Pirrus with pyne put hym to serche
Of Polexena the pert, in *priuete* holdyn,
That was cause of the cumbranse of his kynd fadur.
Destruction of Troy (E. E. T. S.), l. 12078.

For all his dayes he drownes in *privitie*,
Yet has full large to live and spend at libertie.
Spenser, F. Q., III. ix. 3.

3†. Intimate relation; intimacy.

With the praise of armes and chevalrie
The prize of beautie still hath joyned beene;
And that for reasons speciall *privitie*,
For either doth on other much relie.
Spenser, F. Q., IV. v. 1.

4†. That which is to be kept privy or private; a secret; a private matter.

Blamed hymself for he
Hadde told to me so greet a *privitee*.
Chaucer, Prol. to Wife of Bath's Tale, l. 542.

To signify unto your grace, besides our common letters, also with these my private letters the *privities* of my heart and conscience in that matter.
Bp. Ridley, in Bradford's Works (Parker Soc., 1853), II. 370.

5. Private knowledge; joint knowledge with another of a private concern, which is often supposed to imply consent or concurrence.

I had heard of his intending to steal a marriage without the *privity* of us his intimate friends and acquaintance.
Steele, Spectator, No. 133.

This marriage . . . brought upon Garcilasso, in consequence of his *privity*, the displeasure of the Emperor.
Ticknor, Span. Lit., I. 448.

6†. *pl.* The private parts. *Abp. Abbot.*—7. In *law*: (*a*) That relation between different interests of several persons in the same lands which arises under feudal tenures. All the various estates, less than a fee simple absolute, were regarded as so many parts of entire title, and the persons among whom such partial interests were distributed were said to stand in privity or in privity of estate to each other. If the interests belonging to one of such persons devolved either by act of law, as in the case of his death intestate, or by act of the parties, as in the case of a conveyance, upon a third person, that person was thereby brought into privity with him and the others. In the former case he was said to be *privy in law*, in the latter case *privy in deed*, each of these being only species of *privies in estate*. Upon the same principle, whenever several lesser estates were carved out of a larger, as by grant of a qualified interest or life estate leaving a remainder or reversion in the grantor, the parties were termed *privies*. (*b*) More loosely, since the abrogation of tenure, any joint, separate, or successive interest affecting the same realty is deemed to constitute a privity between the parties in interest. Thus, if B inherits land from A, there is privity of estate between them, and if C inherits the same land from B, the privity extends to him, so that B and C may be both bound in respect to the land by whatever bound A. (*c*) In the law of obligations, the mutual relationships between contractor and contractee, and either of them and a third person claiming under the contract, which result from the existence of the contract. Thus, if A gives his note to B, and B separately gives his note to C, there is privity of contract between A and B, and also between B and C, but none between A and C. But if A gives his note to B, and B indorses it over to C, there is privity of contract among all. (*d*) In the law of contracts and torts, the legal relation consequent on joint or common knowledge and concurrence, particularly in respect to a breach of contract, a tort, or a wrong.—**Privity of tenure**, the relation subsisting between a lord and his immediate tenant.

privy (priv'i), *a.* and *n.* [< ME. *privy*, *privee*, *prive*, *privei*, *pryve*, *prevy*, *preve*, < OF. *prive*, F. *privé* = Sp. Pg. It. *privado*, private, < L. *privatus*, apart from the public, private: see *private*, *a.*, of which *privy* is a doublet.] I. *a.* 1. Private; pertaining to some person exclusively; assigned to private uses; not public: as, the *privy* purse.

The other half
Comes to the *privy* coffer of the state.
Shak., M. of V., iv. 1. 354.

2. Secret; not seen openly; not made known in public.

A counsail sall I tel to the,
The whilk I will you hald *priué*.
Holy Rood (E. E. T. S.), p. 92.

This drudge, or diviner, . . . told me what *privy* marks I had about me. *Shak.*, C. of E., iii. 2. 146.

The Seas breaking their sandie barres, and breaking vp by secret vnderminings the *priuie* pores and passages in the earth. *Purchas*, Pilgrimage, p. 40.

Place and occasion are two *privy* thieves.
B. Jonson, Cynthia's Revels, v. 3.

3. Private; appropriated to retirement; sequestered; retired.

If your Lordship shall commaund to chastise or to whip any page or seruant, prouide that it be done in a place *priuie* and secrete.
Guevara, Letters (tr. by Hellowes, 1577), p. 161.

It is the sword of the great men that are slain, which entereth into their *privy* chambers. Ezek. xxi. 14.

4. Privately knowing; admitted to the participation with another in knowledge of a secret transaction: generally with *to*.

And couth remove from the seid French kynge the *preryest* man of heis Councell yf he wold.
Paston Letters, I. 104.

His wife also being *privy* to it. Acts v. 2.

Myself am one made *privy* to the plot.
Shak., T. G. of V., iii. 1. 12.

Our mortal eyes
Pierce not the secrets of your heart: the gods
Are only *privy to* them. *Ford*, Broken Heart, iii. 1.

This sudden change was much observed by some, who were *privy* that Mr. Wilson had professed as much before.
Winthrop, Hist. New England, I. 282.

5†. Intimate; familiar; on confidential terms; well known.

And two knyghtes that hen moste *privy* with hym, that noon ne knoweth so moche of his counselle.
Merlin (E. E. T. S.), i. 76.

Gentlemen ushers of the privy chamber, four functionaries in the lord chamberlain's department of the royal household in Great Britain, who attend various ceremonies of court.—**Privy chamber**, in Great Britain, a private apartment in a royal residence.—**Privy coat**, a light coat or defense of mail concealed under the ordinary dress.—**Privy council.** See *council*.—**Privy councilor**, a member of the privy council. Abbreviated *P. C.*—**Privy purse, seal**, etc. See the nouns.—**Privy verdict**, a verdict given to the judge out of court. =**Syn.** 1. Individual, special, personal, peculiar, particular.—4. Cognizant (of), acquainted (with).

II. *n.*; pl. *privies* (-iz). 1. In *law*, one standing in a relation of privity to another. See *privity*, 7. (*a*) A partaker: a person having a joint or common knowledge, right, or responsibility. More specifically—(*b*) One bound by an obligation irrespective of his being a party to it; one bound or entitled in respect to an estate irrespective of his having been a party to the transaction by which it was created. The term *privy* is properly used in distinction from *party*; but *privies to a contract* is used to mean the parties themselves. *Stimson.*

2†. A secret friend.—3. A necessary.

privy-fly (priv'i-fli), *n.* A fly of the family *Anthomyiidæ*, *Homalomyia scalaris*, whose larva is usually found in human excrement. It is probably indigenous in Europe, though also found in North America. See cut under *Homalomyia*.

prix (prē), *n.* [F.: see *price*.] A premium; a prize; specifically, the stakes or cup in a French horse-race or other sporting event: used by English writers in such phrases as *grand prix* and *prix de Rome* (in French national competitions in the fine arts).

prizable (prī'zạ-bl), *a.* [< *prize*[2] + *-able*.] Valuable; worthy of being prized. Also spelled *prizeable*.

The courage of the tongue
Is truly, like the courage of the hand,
Discreetly used, a *prizeable* possession.
Sir H. Taylor, St. Clement's Eve, i. 1.

prizage†, *n.* See *prisage*.

prizall†, *n.* See *prisal*.

prize[1] (prīz), *n.* and *a.* [Formerly also *prise*; < ME. *prise*, < OF. *prise*, a taking, capture, a seizure, a thing seized, a prize, booty, also hold, purchase (= It. *presa*), < F. *prise*, < *pris*, pp. of *prendre*, take, capture, < L. *prendere*, *prehendere*, take, seize: see *prehend*. Cf. *prize*[3], *prison*, etc., *apprise*, *comprise*, *enterprise*, *purprise*, *reprisal*, *surprise*, etc. *Prize*[1] and *prize*[2] have been in some senses more or less confused.] I. *n.* 1. A taking or capture, as of the property of an enemy in war.

His leg, through his late luckelesse *prise*,
Was crackt in twaine. *Spenser*, F. Q., VI. viii. 25.

2. In *hunting*, the note of the horn blown at the capture or death of the game.

Syr Eglamour hase done to dede
A grete herte, and tane the hede;
The *pryse* he blowe fulle schille.
MS. Lincoln A. i. 17, f. 140. (*Halliwell.*)

Aim'd well, the Chieftain's lance has flown;
Struggling in blood the savage lies;
His roar is sunk in hollow groan—
Sound, merry huntsman! sound the *pryse*!
Scott, Cadyow Castle.

3. That which is taken from an enemy in war; any species of goods or property seized by force as spoil or plunder; that which is taken in combat, particularly a ship with the property taken in it. The law as to prizes is regulated by the general law of nations. Prizes taken in war are condemned (that is, sentence is passed that the thing captured is lawful prize) by the proper judicature in the courts of the captors, called *prize*-courts.

And when the saisnes were thus disconfited and fledde, the kynge Vrien and his peple gedered vp that was lefte therof . . . grete richesse, . . . the richest *prise* that euer was sein. *Merlin* (E. E. T. S.), ii. 240.

I have made, mother,
A fortunate voyage, and brought home rich *prize*
In a few hours. *Fletcher*, Spanish Curate, i. 2.

The distinction between a *prize* and booty consists in this, that the former is taken at sea and the latter on land.
Bouvier.

4. In *early Eng. law*, a seizure or the asserted right of seizure of money or chattels by way of exaction or requisition for the use of the crown; more specifically, a toll of that nature exacted on merchandise in a commercial town.—5. That which is obtained or offered as the re-

ward of exertion or contest: as, a *prize* for Latin verses.

> I'll never wrestle for the *prize* more.
> *Shak.*, As you Like it, i. 1. 168.

> At every shot the *prize* he got,
> For he was both sure and dead.
> *Robin Hood and the* Golden *Arrow* (Child's Ballads, V. 386).

> You love
> The metaphysics! read and earn our *prize*,
> A golden brooch. *Tennyson*, Princess, iii.

6. That which is won in a lottery, or in any similar way.

> The word lottery . . . may be applied to any process of determining *prizes* by lot. *Encyc. Brit.*, XV. 11.

7. A possession or acquisition which is prized; any gain or advantage; privilege.

> It is war's *prize* to take all vantages.
> *Shak.*, 3 Hen. VI., i. 4. 59.

> The lock, obtain'd with guilt, and kept with pain,
> In every place is sought, but sought in vain;
> With such a *prize* no mortal must be blest.
> *Pope*, R. of the L., v. 111.

8†. A contest for a reward; a competition.

> Like one of two contending in a *prize*.
> *Shak.*, M. of V., iii. 2. 142.

> And now, as it were, a *Prize* began to be played between the two Swords, the Spiritual and the Temporal.
> *Baker*, Chronicles, p. 73.

Maritime prize, a prize taken by capture on the high seas.—**To play prizes**†, to fight publicly for a prize; hence, figuratively, to contend only for show.

> He is my brother that *plays the prizes*.
> *B. Jonson*, Cynthia's Revels, v. 2.

> By their endless disputes and wranglings about words and terms of art, they [the philosophers] made the people suspect they did but *play prizes* before them.
> *Stillingfleet*, Sermons, II. iii.

II. *a.* 1. Worthy of a prize; that has gained a prize.

> A lord of fat *prize* oxen and of sheep.
> *Tennyson*, Princess, Conclusion.

2. Given or awarded as a prize: as, a *prize* cup.

prize[1] (priz), *v. t.*; pret. and pp. *prized*, ppr. *prizing*. [< *prize*[1], *n.*] 1†. To risk or venture. *Davies.*

> Thou 'rt worthy of the title of a squire,
> That durst, for proof of thy affection,
> And for thy mistress' favour, *prize* thy blood.
> *Greene*, Friar Bacon, p. 175.

2. To make a prize of; capture; seize.

> In the British House of Commons it was explained that the David J. Adams was *prized* for concealing her name and her sailing-port. *The American*, XII. 67.

prize[2] (priz), *v. t.*; pret. and pp. *prized*, ppr. *prizing*. [< ME. *prysen*, < OF. (and F.) *priser*, set a price or value on, esteem, value, < *pris*, price, < L. *pretium*, price, value: see *price*. Cf. *praise*, *appraise*, *apprize*[2].] 1. To set or estimate the value of; rate.

> Having so swift and excellent a wit
> As she is *prized* to have.
> *Shak.*, Much Ado, iii. 1. 90.

2. To value highly; regard as of great worth; esteem.

> Whoe'er excels in what we *prize*
> Appears a hero in our eyes.
> *Swift*, Cadenus and Vanessa, l. 733.

> Gold is called gold, and dross called dross, i' the Book;
> Gold you let lie, and dross pick up and *prize!*
> *Browning*, Ring and Book, II. 254.

3. To favor or ease (an affected limb), as a horse. *Halliwell.* [Prov. Eng.] = **Syn. 1.** To appraise.—**2.** *Value, Esteem*, etc. See *appreciate*.

prize[2]† (priz), *n.* [< *prize*[2], *v.* Cf. *price*, *n.*] Estimation; valuation; appraisement.

> Cæsar's no merchant, to make *prize* with you
> Of things that merchants sold.
> *Shak.*, A. and C., v. 2. 183.

prize[3] (prīz), *n.* [Also *prise*; < F. *prise*, a hold, grasp, purchase: see *prize*[1].] 1. The hold of a lever; purchase.—2. A lever. *Halliwell.* [Prov. Eng.]

prize[3] (prīz), *v. t.*; pret. and pp. *prized*, ppr. *prizing*. [Also *prise*; < *prize*[3], *n.* Hence, by confusion, *pry*[2].] To force or press, especially force open by means of a lever, as a door, etc.

> Taking a marling-spike hitch over a marling-spike, and with the point *prizing* it against the rope until the service is taut. *Luce*, Seamanship, p. 48.

> When I gently *prised* up the anther-case at its base or on one side, the pollinium was ejected.
> *Darwin*, Fertil. of Orchids by Insects, p. 216.

prizeable, *a.* See *prizable*.

prize-bolt (priz'bōlt), *n.* A projection on a gun-carriage for a handspike to hold by in raising the breech. [Eng.]

prize-court (priz'kōrt), *n.* A court whose function it is to adjudicate on captures made at sea.

prize-fight (priz'fīt), *n.* A pugilistic encounter or boxing-match for a prize or wager.

prize-fighter (priz'fī"tėr), *n.* One who fights another with his fists for a wager or reward; a professional pugilist or boxer.

prize-fighting (priz'fī"ting), *n.* Fighting, especially boxing, in public for a reward or stake. It prevails in Great Britain, the United States, and in the British possessions; in most of its forms and in most localities it is illegal. Prize-fighting is conducted generally under one of two codes of rules—the London prize-ring rules and the Marquis of Queensberry rules. The fighting is either with bare knuckles or with light gloves.

prizeless† (priz'les), *a.* [< *prize*[2] + *-less*. Cf. *priceless*.] Inestimable; priceless.

> Oh, mediocrity,
> Thou *prizeless* jewel only mean men have,
> But cannot value.
> *Fletcher (and another)*, Queen of Corinth, iii. 1.

prize-list (priz'list), *n.* 1. A detailed list of the winners in any competition for prizes, as a school examination or a flower-show.—2. *Naut.*, a return of all the persons on board entitled to receive prize-money at the time a capture is made.

prizeman (priz'man), *n.*; pl. *prizemen* (-men). [< *prize*[1] + *man*.] The winner of a prize.

prize-master (priz'mås"tėr), *n.* A person put in command of a ship that has been made a prize.

prize-money (priz'mun"i), *n.* Money paid to the captors of a ship or place where booty has been obtained, in certain proportions according to rank, the money divided being realized from the sale of the prize or booty.

prizer (prī'zėr), *n.* [Formerly also *priser*; < *prize*[2], *v.*, + *-er*[1].] 1. One who estimates or determines the value of a thing; an appraiser.

> But value dwells not in particular will;
> It holds his estimate and dignity
> As well wherein 'tis precious of itself
> As in the *prizer*. *Shak.*, T. and C., ii. 2. 56.

2. One who competes for a prize, as a prize-fighter, a wrestler, etc.

> Why would you be so fond to overcome
> The bonny *priser* of the humorous duke?
> *Shak.*, As you Like it, ii. 3. 8.

> Appeareth no man yet to answer the *prizer?*
> *B. Jonson*, Cynthia's Revels, v. 2.

> As if a cloud enveloped him while fought
> Under its shade grim *prizers*, thought with thought
> At dead-lock. *Browning*, Sordello.

prize-ring (prīz'ring), *n.* A ring or inclosed place for prize-fighting; also, sometimes, the practice itself. The ring has now become an area eight yards square, inclosed by poles and ropes. It probably derived its name from the fact that the combatants originally fought in a ring formed by the onlookers.

> It was lately remarked . . . that we take our point of honour from the *prize-ring*; but we do worse—we take our point of honour from beasts.
> *H. Spencer*, Study of Sociol., p. 188.

p. r. n. An abbreviation of the Latin phrase *pro re nata*, as occasion may require.

pro (prō). [L. *pro*, before, in front of, for, etc.: see *pro-*.] A Latin preposition occurring in several phrases used in English.—**Pro and con.**, for Latin (New Latin) *pro et con.*, abbreviation of *pro et contra*, for and against; hence, as a quasi-noun, in plural *pros and cons*, the arguments or reasons for and against a proposition or opinion; and (rarely) as a verb, to weigh or consider impartially.

> Grand and famous scholars often
> Have argu'd *pro and con*, and left it doubtful.
> *Ford*, Fancies, iii. 3.

> A man in soliloquy reasons with himself, and *pro's and con's*, and weighs all his designs.
> *Congreve*, Double Dealer, Ep. Ded.

> My father's resolution of putting me into breeches . . . had . . . been *pro'd and con'd*, and judicially talked over betwixt him and my mother, about a month before.
> *Sterne*, Tristram Shandy, vi. 16.

> They do not decide large questions by casting up two columns of *pros and cons*, and striking a balance.
> *Nat. Rev.*

pro-. [1. F. Sp. Pg. It. *pro-*, < L. *pro-* (*prō-* or *prŏ-*), prefix, *prō*, adv. and prep., before, in front of, in favor of, for the benefit of, in place of, for, in proportion, in conformity with, etc., = Gr. πρό, before, for, etc., προ- prefix, = Skt. *pra*, before; cf. L. *por-*, *po-*, collateral forms; Gr. πρός, before, forth, from, etc. (see *pros-*); akin to E. *for-*[1], *fore-*[1], q. v. 2. F., etc., *pro-*, < L. *pro-*, < Gr. προ- prefix, before, etc., like the cognate L. *pro-*: see above.] A prefix of Latin or Greek origin, meaning 'before,' 'in front,' 'fore,' 'forth,' 'forward.' In some words, as *proconsul*, *proprætor*, *pronoun*, etc., it is properly the preposition (L. *pro*, for, instead of).

proa (prō'ä), *n.* [Also *prau*, *prahu*, and formerly *proe*, *prow*, also *praw* (as Malay); < Malay *prāu*, a proa (a general term for all vessels between a canoe and a square-rigged vessel).] A kind of Malay vessel remarkable for swiftness, formerly much used by pirates in the Eastern Archipelago. Proas are found chiefly within the region of the trade-winds, to which by their construction they are peculiarly adapted; for, being formed with stem and stern equally sharp, they never require to be turned round in order to change their course, but sail equally well in either

Proa, with Outrigger.

direction. The lee side is flat and in a straight line from stem to stern, and acts as a lee-board or center-board; but the weather side is rounded as in other vessels. This shape, with their small breadth, would render them very liable to heel over, were it not for the outrigger, which is used on either side or on both. The proa is fastened together with coir yarns, is extremely light, and carries an enormous triangular sail. Also called *flying proa*.

> They [the Dutch] have *Procs* of a particular neatness and curiosity. We call them Half-moon *Proes*, for they turn up so much at each end from the water that they much resemble a Half-moon with the Horns upwards.
> *Dampier*, Voyages, II. i. 5.

> I spied, where she pointed, the reedy booms and buoyant out-riggers of freebooting *proas* lurking in cunning coves.
> *J. W. Palmer*, Up and Down the Irrawaddi, p. 29.

proach† (prōch), *v. i.* [Early mod. E. *proch*; < OF. *prochier*, come near: see *approach*.] To approach.

> Ffriday, the v Day of ffebruarii, *proched* nye the Cyte of Corfew. *Torkington*, Diarie of Eng. Travell, p. 61.

proal (prō'al), *a.* [< Gr. πρό, before, + *-al*.] Directed or moved forward, as the lower jaw in the act of chewing: as, the *proal* mode of mastication, in which the food is acted on as the lower jaw pushes forward: opposed to *palinal*. See *propalinal*. *E. D. Cope.*

pro-amnion (prŏ-am'ni-on), *n.* [< Gr. πρό, before, + E. *amnion*.] The primitive amnion of some animals, succeeded by the definitive amnion in a later stage of the embryo.

pro-amniotic (prō-am-ni-ot'ik), *a.* Of or pertaining to the pro-amnion; characterized by or provided with a pro-amnion.

> Long after the true amnion has been quite completed the head gradually emerges from this *pro-amniotic* pit.
> *Micros. Sci.*, N. S., XXX. iii. 290.

proanaphoral (prō-an-af'ọ-rạl), *a.* [< Gr. πρό, before, + ἀναφορά, anaphora: see *anaphora*, 3.] *Eccles.*, in liturgics, preceding the anaphora (which see): applied to so much of the eucharistic office as precedes the Sursum Corda.

> In every Liturgical family there is one Liturgy (or at most two) which supplies the former or *proanaphoral* portion to all the others.
> *J. M. Neale*, Eastern Church, i. 319.

pro and con. See *pro*.

proangiosperm (prō-an'ji-ọ-spėrm), *n.* [< Gr. πρό, before, + E. *angiosperm*.] An archaic or ancestral angiosperm; the ancestral form or forms from which the modern angiosperms are supposed to have been developed. They may be known only in the fossil state, or may be manifested by rudiments of once functional organs or parts in living angiosperms.

> The ancestral *pro-angiosperms* are supposed to have borne leaves such as are found diminished or marked in so many of their existing descendants.
> *Nature*, XXXIII. 389.

proangiospermic (prō-an"ji-ọ-spėr'mik), *a.* [< *proangiosperm* + *-ic*.] In *bot.*, pertaining to or resembling a proangiosperm.

> Plants in their *pro-angiospermic* stage.
> *Nature*, XXXIII. 389.

Proarthri (prō-är'thrī), *n. pl.* [NL., < Gr. πρό, before, + ἄρθρον, joint.] One of four suborders of existing *Squali*, or sharks, represented only by the *Heterodontidæ*, having the palatoquadrate apparatus articulated by an extensive surface with the preorbital region of the skull: correlated with *Opistharthri*, *Anarthri*, and *Rhinæ*. *T. Gill.*

proarthrous (prō-är'thrus), *a.* In *ichth.*, pertaining to the *Proarthri*, or having their characters.

proatlas (prō-at'las), *n.* [NL., < L. *pro*, before, + NL. *atlas*: see *atlas*, 3.] A rudimentary vertebra which in some animals precedes the atlas proper. *Encyc. Brit.*, XX. 447. [Rare.]

proaulion (prō-â'li-on), *n.* [< Gr. προαύλιον, a court, a vestibule, < πρό, before, + αὐλή, a court, a hall, a chamber: see *aula*.] In the early church and in the Greek Church, the porch of a church. In Greek churches the proaulion is a porch at the west end of a church, open on three sides and of the same width as the narthex, into which it opens.

The *Proaulion*, or porch, is . . . sometimes a lean-to against the west end of the narthex, but oftener it forms with the narthex one lean-to against the west end of the nave. *J. M. Neale*, Eastern Church, i. 215.

probabiliorism (prob-a-bil'i-ọr-izm), *n.* [< NL. **probabiliorismus*, < L. *probabilior*, compar. of *probabilis*, probable: see *probable*.] In *Rom. Cath. theol.*, the doctrine that it is lawful to act in a certain manner only when there is a more probable opinion in favor of such action than against it, so that when there are two equally probable opinions, one for and the other against liberty of action, it is not lawful to accept the former opinion and follow one's inclinations. See *probabilism*, *probabilist*.

probabiliorist (prob-a-bil'i-ọr-ist), *n.* [< NL. **probabiliorista*, < L. *probabilior*, compar. of *probabilis*, probable: see *probable*.] One who holds to the doctrine of probabiliorism.

Probabiliorists, who hold that the law is always to be obeyed unless an opinion clearly very probable (probabilior) is opposed to it. *Encyc. Brit.*, XIV. 636.

probabilis causa (prọ-bab'i-lis kâ'zạ). [L.: see *probable* and *cause*.] A probable cause.—**Probabilis causa litigandi**, in *Scots law*, plausible ground of action or defense.

probabilism (prob'a-bil-izm), *n.* [= F. *probabilisme* = Sp. Pg. It. *probabilismo* = G. *probabilismus*, < NL. *probabilismus*, < L. *probabilis*, probable: see *probable*.] In *Rom. Cath. theol.*, the doctrine that when there are two probable opinions, each resting on apparent reason, one in favor of and the other opposed to one's inclinations, it is lawful to follow the probable opinion which favors one's inclination. See *probabiliorism*, *probabilist*.

The working of the principle known as *Probabilism*. The meaning of this principle . . . is simply this: when a doubt arises as to the binding force of some divine or human precept in any given case, it is permissible to abandon the opinion in favour of obedience to the law—technically known as "safe" (tuta) opinion—for that which favours non-compliance, provided this laxer opinion be "probable." And by "probable" is meant any judgment or opinion based on some reasonable grounds, though with some doubt that the opposite view is perhaps the true one (Gury, Theol. Mor., I. n. 51). *Encyc. Brit.*, XIV. 636.

probabilist (prob'a-bil-ist), *n.* [= F. *probabiliste* = Sp. Pg. It. *probabilista* = G. *probabilist*, < NL. *probabilista*, < L. *probabilis*, probable: see *probable*.] 1. One who holds the doctrine of probabilism.—2. One who maintains that certainty is impossible, and that probability alone is to govern faith and practice.

probability (prob-a-bil'i-ti), *n.*; pl. *probabilities* (-tiz). [= F. *probabilité* = Sp. *probabilidad* = Pg. *probabilidade* = It. *probabilità*, < L. *probabilita(t-)s*, probability, credibility, < *probabilis*, probable, credible: see *probable*.] 1. The state or character of being probable; likelihood; appearance of truth; that state of a case or question of fact which results from superior evidence or preponderation of argument on one side, inclining the mind to receive that as the truth, but leaving some room for doubt.

Thus, first traditions were a proof alone,
Could we be certain such they were, so known;
But, since some flaws in long descent may be,
They make not truth, but *probability*.
Dryden, Religio Laici, l. 345.

Probability is nothing but the appearance of such an agreement or disagreement, by the intervention of proofs whose connection is not constant, . . . but is or appears for the most part to be so. . . . In which case the foundation of his assent is the *probability* of the thing, the proof being such as for the most part carries truth with it. . . . So that that which causes his assent to this proposition is the wonted veracity of the speaker in other cases. *Locke*, Human Understanding, IV. xv. § 1.

2. Quantitatively, that character of an argument or proposition of doubtful truth which consists in the frequency with which like propositions or arguments are found true in the course of experience. Thus, if a die be thrown, the probability that it will turn up ace is the frequency with which an ace would be turned up in an indefinitely long succession of throws. It is conceivable that there should be no definite probability: thus, the proportion of aces might so fluctuate that their frequency in the long run would be represented by a diverging series. Yet even so, there would be approximate probabilities for short periods of time. All the essential features of probability are exhibited in the case of putting into a bag some black beans and some white ones, then shaking them well, and finally drawing out one or several at random. The beans must first be shaken up, so as to assimilate or generalize the contents of the bag; and a similar result must be attained in any case in which probability is to have any real significance. Next, a sample of the beans must be drawn out at random—that is, so as not to be voluntarily subjected to any general conditions additional to those of the course of experience of which they form a part. Thus, out-of-the-way ones or uppermost ones must not be particularly chosen. This random choice may be effected by machinery, if desired. If, now, a great number of single beans are so taken out and replaced successively, the following phenomenon will be found approximately true, or, if not, a prolongation of the series of drawings will render it so: namely, that if the whole series be separated into parts of two fixed numbers of drawings, say into series of 100 and of 10,000 alternately, then the average proportion of white beans among the sets of 100 will be nearly the same as the average proportion among the sets of 10,000. This is the fundamental proposition of the theory of probabilities—we might say of logic—since the security of all real inference rests upon it. The greater the frequency with which a specific event occurs in the long run, the stronger is the expectation that it will occur in a particular case. Hence, probability has been defined as the degree of belief which ought to be accorded to a problematical judgment; but this *conceptualistic probability*, as it is termed, is strictly not probability, but a sense of probability. Probability may be measured in different ways. The conceptualistic measure is the degree of confidence to which a reason is entitled; it is used in the mental process of balancing reasons pro and con. The conceptualistic measure is the logarithm of another measure called the *odds*—that is, the ratio of the number of favorable to the number of unfavorable cases. But the measure which is most easily guarded against the fallacies which beset the calculation of probabilities is the ratio of the number of favorable cases to the whole number of equally possible cases, or the ratio of the number of occurrences of the event to the total number of occasions in the course of experience. This ratio is called the *probability* or chance of the event. Thus, the probability that a die will turn up ace is $\frac{1}{6}$. Probability *zero* represents impossibility; probability *unity*, certainty. The fundamental rules for the calculation of probabilities are two, as follows: *Rule I.* The probability that one or the other of two mutually exclusive propositions is true is the sum of the probabilities that one and the other are true. Thus, if $\frac{1}{6}$ is the probability that a die will turn up ace, and $\frac{1}{2}$ is the probability that it will turn up an even number, then, since it cannot turn up at once an ace and an even number, the probability that one or other will be turned up is $\frac{1}{6} + \frac{1}{2} = \frac{2}{3}$. It follows that if p is the probability that any event will happen, $1 - p$ is the probability that it will not happen. *Rule II.* The probability of an event multiplied by the probability, if that event happens, that another will happen, gives as product the probability that both will happen. Thus, if a die is so thrown that the probability of its not being found is $\frac{1}{2}$, then the probability of its being found ace up is $\frac{1}{2} \times \frac{1}{6} = \frac{1}{12}$. If the probability that a certain man will reach the age of forty is p, and the probability, when he is forty, that he will then reach sixty is q, then the probability now that he will reach sixty is pq. If two events A and B are such that the probability of A is the same whether B does or does not happen, then, also, the probability of B is the same whether A does or does not happen, and the events are said to be *independent*. The probability of the concurrence of two independent events is the product of their separate probabilities. The probability that a general event, whose probability on each one of n occasions is p, should occur just k times among these n occasions, is equal to the term containing p^k in the development of $(p+q)^k$, where $q = 1 - p$. Thus, suppose the event is the appearance of head when a coin is tossed up, so that $p = q = \frac{1}{2}$, and the coin be tossed up six times. Then the probabilities of 0, 1, 2, 3, 4, 5, 6 heads respectively are $\frac{1}{64}$, $\frac{6}{64}$, $\frac{15}{64}$, $\frac{20}{64}$, $\frac{15}{64}$, $\frac{6}{64}$, $\frac{1}{64}$. The most probable value of k is that whole number next less than $(n+1)p$, unless this be itself a whole number, when it is equally probable. When the number of trials is large, the probabilities of the different numbers of occurrences of the given event are proportional to areas included between the so-called probability curve, its asymptote, and ordinates at successive distances equal to $1/\sqrt{2npq}$. This probability curve, whose equation is $y = \varpi^{-\frac{1}{2}}\epsilon^{-x^2}$ (where ϖ is the circumference for unit diameter, and ϵ is the Napierian base), is represented in the figure, where the approximate straightness

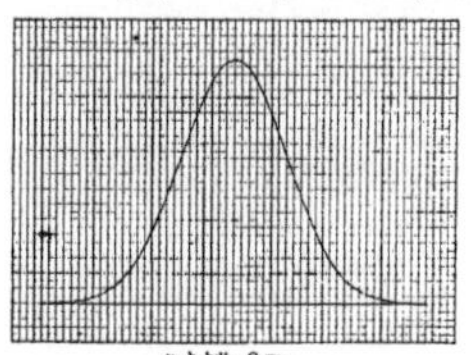

Probability Curve.

of the slope will be remarked. If it is desired to ascertain the probability of the occurrence from k_1 to k_2 times inclusive in n trials of an event whose probable occurrence at each trial is p, the approximate value is the area included between the probability curve, the asymptote, and the two ordinates, for which

$$x = \frac{k_1 - (n+1)p}{\sqrt{2npq}} \text{ and } x = \frac{k_2 + 1 - (n+1)p}{\sqrt{2npq}}.$$

Twice the quadratures of the areas are given in treatises on probabilities as tables of the theta function of probabilities. The chief practical application of probability is to insurance; and its only significance lies in an assurance as to the average result in the long run. The theory of probability is to be regarded as the logic of the physical sciences.

3. Anything that has the appearance of reality or truth.

Both the rocks and the earth are so splendent to behold that better iudgements then ours might haue beene perswaded they contained more then *probabilities*. Quoted in *Capt. John Smith's* Works, I. 115.

4. A statement of what is likely to happen; a forecast: applied in the plural by Cleveland Abbe to his daily weather-predictions in Cincinnati in 1869, and subsequently adopted by General Myer to designate the official weather-forecasts of the United States Signal Service. The same term had been similarly used by Leverrier in Paris since 1859.

The whole system [of meteorological predictions] is excellently organized and very extensive; the official publications embrace the *probabilities* and the so-called weather-maps. *Pop. Sci. Mo.*, XXIX. 546.

Antecedent probability. See *antecedent*.—**Balance of probabilities.** See *balance*.—**Calculus of probability**, a branch of mathematics teaching how to calculate probabilities by general methods.—**Curve of probability.** See above.—**Inverse probability**, the probability of a hypothesis as deduced from the comparison of its consequences with observation. Thus, the following is a familiar problem of inverse probability: Suppose a bag contains a series of tickets numbered consecutively from 1 up. Suppose a ticket is drawn at random, and its number is 13, what is the most probable number of tickets in the bag? The best opinion concerning inverse probability seems to be that it is altogether fallacious, unless the antecedent probability of the hypothesis is known. Some writers hold that the probability of a proposition about which we are completely ignorant is $\frac{1}{2}$; others hold that it is indeterminate.—**Local probability.** See *local*.—**Old Probabilities.** See *old*.

probable (prob'a-bl), *a.* and *n.* [< F. *probable* = Sp. *probable* = Pg. *provavel* = It. *probabile*, < L. *probabilis*, that may be proved, credible, < *probare*, test, examine: see *probe*, *prove*.] **I.** *a.* 1†. Capable of being proved; provable.

It is doubtlessly *probable* that women are nature's pride, virtue's ornaments. Ford, Honour Triumphant.

It ought to be a total fast from all things during the solemnity, unless a *probable* necessity intervene. *Jer. Taylor*, Holy Living, iv. 5.

No man . . . is properly a heretic . . . but he who maintains traditions or opinions not *probable* by scripture. *Milton*, Civil Power.

2. Having more evidence for than against, or evidence which inclines the mind to belief, but leaves some room for doubt; likely.

I do not say that the principles of religion are merely *probable*, I have before asserted them to be morally certain. *Bp. Wilkins.*

That is accounted *probable* which has better arguments producible for it than can be brought against it. *South.*

I made up a story as short and *probable* as I could, but concealed the greatest part. *Swift*, Gulliver's Travels, iii. 11.

Chaucer . . . makes it possible, and even *probable*, that his motley characters should meet on a common footing. *Lowell*, Study Windows, p. 284.

3. Rendering something likely, or showing it to be likely: as, *probable* evidence; a *probable* presumption. *Blackstone*.—4†. Plausible; specious; colorable.

Make this haste as your own good proceeding,
Strengthen'd with what apology you think
May make it *probable* need.
Shak., All's Well, ii. 4. 52.

Probable cause. See *cause*.—**Probable error**, in *astron.* and *physics*. When the value of any quantity or element has been determined by means of a number of independent observations every one liable to a small amount of accidental error, the determination will also be liable to some uncertainty, and the *probable error* is the quantity which is such that there is the same probability of the difference between the determination and the true absolute value of the thing to be determined exceeding or falling short of it. But it is to be remarked that, as so defined, the constant error belonging to all observations of the given series is not included in the probable error.—**Probable evidence**, evidence distinguished from demonstrative evidence in that it admits of degrees, and of all variety of them, from the highest moral certainty to the very lowest presumption.—**Probable inference.** See *inference*.—**Probable proposition.** See *proposition*.
=**Syn.** 2. Presumable, credible, reasonable.

II. *n.* A probable opinion; an opinion resting upon good but not sufficient grounds.

The casuists' doctrine of *probables*, in virtue of which a man may be probabiliter obligatus and probabiliter deobligatus at the same time. *Lowell*, Among my Books, 2d ser., p. 264.

probably (prob'a-bli), *adv.* 1. With probability; in a probable manner; in all likelihood; with the appearance of truth or reality; likely: as, the story is *probably* true; the account is *probably* correct.

Distinguish betwixt what may possibly and what will *probably* be done. *Sir R. L'Estrange.*

2†. Plausibly; with verisimilitude.

Those that held religion was the difference of man from beasts have spoken *probably*.
Sir T. Browne, Religio Medici, i. 20.

Call this a Mede, and that a Parthian youth;
Talk *probably*; no matter for the truth.
Dryden, tr. of Ovid's Art of Love, l. 260.

probal† (prō'bal), *a.* [< LL. *proba*, proof, + *-al.*] Probable.

This advice is free I give, and honest,
Probal to thinking, and indeed the course
To win the Moor again. *Shak.*, Othello, ii. 3. 344.

probality† (prọ̄-bal'i-ti), *n.* [Appar. < *probal* + *-ity*; but prob. an error for *probability*.] Probability.

[After describing a far-fetched derivation for the name *Brigantes*.] But if such a conjecture may take place, others might with as great *probality* derive them from the Brigantes of Britaine.
Holland, tr. of Camden, II. 84. (*Davies.*)

probang (prō'bang), *n.* In *surg.*, a long and slender elastic rod of whalebone, with a piece of sponge attached to one end, or other similar instrument, for introduction into the esophagus or larynx, as for the application of remedies or the removal of foreign bodies.

probate (prō'bāt), *a.* and *n.* [< L. *probatus*, pp. of *probare*, test, examine, judge of: see *probe*, *prove.*] I. *a.* 1†. Proved; approved.

The veray true & *probate* assercyons of hystoryal men touchynge and concernynge thantyquytes of thonourable monastery of oure lady in Glastenburye.
Joseph of Arimathie (E. E. T. S.), p. 27.

2. Relating to the proof or establishment of wills and testaments: as, *probate* duties.—**Probate Act**, an English statute, also called the *Court of Probate Act*, 1857 (20 and 21 Vict., c. 77), abolishing the jurisdiction of ecclesiastical and other courts in matters of probate of wills and administration, and vesting it in a new Court of Probate, whose authority was increased by the Confirmation and Probate Act, 1858 (21 and 22 Vict., c. 56), and the Court of Probate Act, 1858 (id., c. 95).—**Probate courts**, the general name given in American law to courts having jurisdiction of probate and administration. Often more specifically called *orphans' courts*, *surrogates' courts*, etc.—**Probate judge.** See *judge*.

II. *n.* 1†. Proof.

Macrobius, that did treate
Of Scipion's dreme what was the treu *probate*.
Skelton, Garland of Laurel, l. 368.

2. In *law*, official proof of a will. (*a*) The determination of the court before which a will is propounded that the paper is the last will and testament of the deceased, and its admission thereupon to record as such. It determines or implies that the instrument is genuine, and regular in form and execution, and that the testator was competent to make a will, but not usually that the provisions of the will are valid. (*b*) A copy of the will so proved, authenticated by the court, usually under its seal, and with a certificate that it has been proved, etc.—**Probate in common form**, a summary probate granted in some jurisdictions on production of the will with an affidavit, when there is no contest: as distinguished from *probate in solemn form*, or by litigation on issues or opportunity for contest.

probate-duty (prō'bāt-dū"ti), *n.* A tax on property passing by will.

probation (prọ̄-bā'shọn), *n.* [< F. *probation* = Pr. *proazo*, *probatio* = Sp. *probacion* = Pg. *proração* = It. *probazione*, < L. *probatio(n-)*, a trying, inspection, examination, < *probare*, pp. *probatus*, test, examine: see *probate*, *probe*, *prove.*] 1. The act of proving; proof.

And what he with his oath
And all *probation* will make up full clear.
Shak., M. for M., v. 1. 157.

He that must eat an hour before his time gives *probation* of his intemperance or his weakness.
Jer. Taylor, Works (ed. 1835), I. 35.

2. Any proceeding designed to ascertain truth, character, qualifications, or the like; trial; examination.

Let us buy our entrance to this guild [friendship] by a long *probation*. *Emerson*, Friendship.

Life is *probation*, and this earth no goal,
But starting-point of man.
Browning, Ring and Book, II. 211.

Specifically—(*a*) *Eccles.*, the trial of a candidate for church membership, holy orders, or other ecclesiastical position and functions, preparatory to his final admission thereto. (*b*) In *theol.*, moral trial; a state of life affording an opportunity to test moral character.

3. Any period of trial. Specifically—(*a*) In religious houses, the period for the trial of a novice before he or she takes the vows of the monastic order.

I, in *probation* of a sisterhood,
Was sent to by my brother.
Shak., M. for M., v. 1. 72.

She . . . may be a nun without *probation*.
Beau. and Fl., Philaster, ii. 20.

(*b*) In the *Meth. Epis. Ch.*, a period, usually six months, at the end of which a candidate for admission to the church determines whether he will unite with the church, and the church decides whether he should be admitted to membership.—**The doctrine of future probation**, the doctrine that the gospel will be preached in another life, either (*a*) to all who die unregenerate, or (*b*) to those to whom it was never preached, or who never apprehended it, in this life, particularly to the heathen and to those dying in infancy. In this latter and more common form it is entertained by members of various Protestant denominations. This doctrine is distinguishable from the doctrine of purgatory, or future disciplinary sufferings for the faithful, supposed to be necessary for their purification, and from the various forms of universalism, which holds that in a future probation all men will sooner or later accept the gospel.

probational (prọ̄-bā'shọn-al), *a.* [< *probation* + *-al.*] Serving for trial or probation.

Their afflictions are not penal, but medicinal, or *probational*. *Bp. Richardson*, Obs. on the Old Testament, p. 278.

probationary (prọ̄-bā'shọn-ā-ri), *a.* [< *probation* + *-ary.*] Pertaining to probation; embracing or serving for trial or probation.

Like Eden's dread *probationary* tree,
Knowledge of good and evil is from Thee.
Cowper, Progress of Error, l. 468.

That the present life is a sufficient period of *probationary* existence to the Righteous will be readily acknowledged by all men. *Timothy Dwight*, Sermons, clxiii.

probationer (prọ̄-bā'shọn-ėr), *n.* [< *probation* + *-er*[1].] One who is on probation or trial; one who is placed so that he may give proof of certain qualifications for a place or state.

Every day gain to their college some new *probationer*.
B. Jonson, Epicœne, i. 1.

While yet a young *probationer*
And candidate for heaven.
Dryden, To the Memory of Mrs. Anne Killigrew, l. 21.

Specifically—(*a*) A novice.

A stripling divine or two of those newly-fledged *probationers* that usually come scouting from the university, and lie here no lame legers to pop into the Bethesda of some knight's chaplainship. *Milton*, Colasterion.

Green *probationers* in mischief. *Lamb*, Old Actors.

(*b*) In the Presbyterian churches in Scotland, one who has been licensed to preach, but who has not been ordained or does not hold a pastoral charge.

How do they expect a *probationer* to become a capable teacher if they never give him the chance of a pulpit?
W. Black, In Far Lochaber, viii.

(*c*) In the *Meth. Epis. Ch.*, a candidate for membership received for a specified period on trial before final admission.

probationership (prọ̄-bā'shọn-ėr-ship), *n.* [< *probationer* + *-ship.*] The condition or state of being a probationer.

He has afforded us the twilight of probability, suitable to that state of mediocrity and *probationership*. *Locke.*

probationism (prọ̄-bā'shọn-izm), *n.* [< *probation* + *-ism.*] Views or beliefs as to human probation in relation to the future state. *Religious Herald*, July 15, 1886.

probationist (prọ̄-bā'shọn-ist), *n.* [< *probation* + *-ist.*] A probationer.

What portion of the *probationists* uniting with the M. E. church become full members?
The Congregationalist, May 14, 1885.

probationship (prọ̄-bā'shọn-ship), *n.* [< *probation* + *-ship.*] A state of probation; novitiate; probation. [Rare.]

Before the end of these ladies' *probationship* and matriculation, his majesty charged the cathedral doctors to dismiss them out of the university.
Translation of Boccalini (1626), p. 202. (*Latham.*)

probative (prō'bā-tiv), *a.* [< *probate* + *-ive.*] 1. Serving to test or prove.

Some are only *probative*, and designed to try and stir up those virtues which before lay dormant in the soul.
South, Sermons, IV. ix.

2. Pertaining to proof or demonstration: as, the *probative* force of evidence.

probator (prọ̄-bā'tọr), *n.* [< L. *probator*, examiner, approver, < *probare*, test, examine, prove: see *probate*, *prove.*] 1. An examiner.—2†. In *law*, one who turns king's (queen's) evidence; an approver.

probatory (prō'bā-tọ̄-ri), *a.* and *n.* [< ML. **probatorius*, adj. (neut. *probatorium*, a house for novices), < L. *probare*, pp. *probatus*, test, examine, prove: see *probate.*] I. *a.* 1. Serving for trial; being a proof or test.

Job's afflictions were no Vindicatory punishments, but *probatory* chastisements to make trial of his graces.
Abp. Bramhall.

2. Pertaining to or serving for proof.

His other heap of arguments are assertory, not *probatory*.
Jer. Taylor (?), Artif. Handsomeness, p. 126.

II. *n.*; pl. *probatories* (-riz). A house for novices.

In the same yeere Christian, Bishop of Lismore, . . . and Pope Eugenius, a venerable man, with whom he was in the *Probatorie* at Clarevall, who also ordained him to be the Legate in Ireland. . . . departed to Christ.
Holland, tr. of Camden, II. 151. (*Davies.*)

probatum est (prọ̄-bā'tum est). [L.: *probatum*, neut. of *probatus*, pp. of *probare*, test, examine; *est*, 3d pers. sing. pres. ind. of *esse*, be.] It has been tried or proved: often appended to recipes or prescriptions.

Take, . . . if your point be rest,
Lettuce and cowslip wine; *Probatum est.*
Pope, Imit. of Horace, II. i. 18.

probe (prōb), *v. t.*; pret. and pp. *probed*, ppr. *probing.* [< L. *probare*, test, examine, prove, < *probus*, good: see *prove*, an older form from the same L. verb. The verb *probe* is partly from the noun.] 1. To examine with or as with a probe; explore, as a wound or other cavity, especially of the body: often used of searching for some extraneous object in a part or organ by means of an instrument thrust into it.

Yet durst she not too deeply *probe* the wound.
Dryden, Hind and Panther, iii.

Thither too the woodcock led her brood, to *probe* the mud for worms. *Thoreau*, Walden, p. 24¢.

2. Figuratively, to search to the bottom; scrutinize; examine thoroughly into.

The late discussions in parliament, and the growing disposition to *probe* the legality of all acts of the crown, rendered the merchants more discontented than ever.
Hallam.

Why do I seek to *probe* my fellow's sin?
William Morris, Earthly Paradise, II. 170.

3. To prick, as a sealed can, so as to allow the compressed air or gas within to escape.

probe (prōb), *n.* [< LL. *proba*, a proof, < *probare*, test, examine, prove: see *probe*, *v.*, and *proof*, *n.* Cf. Sp. *tienta*, a surgeon's probe, < *tentar*, try, test: see *tempt.*] 1. A proof; a trial; a test.

We who believe life's bases rest
Beyond the *probe* of chemic test. *Lowell.*

2†. A printer's proof.

The thanksgiving for the queen's majesty's preservation I have inserted into the collect, which was apter place in my opinion than in the psalm; ye shall see in the *probe* of the print, and after judge.
Abp. Grindal, Remains, p. 268. (*Davies.*)

3. In *surg.*, a slender flexible rod of silver or other substance for examining the conditions of a wound or other cavity, or the direction of a sinus.—**Nélaton's probe**, a probe tipped with unglazed porcelain, used in feeling for bullets. The lead, if touched, leaves a mark upon the porcelain.

probe-pointed (prōb'poin"ted), *a.* Having a blunt end, like that of a probe; not sharp-pointed: as, *probe-pointed* scissors; a *probe-pointed* bistoury.

probe-scissors (prōb'siz"ọrz), *n. pl.* Scissors used to open wounds, the blade of which, to admit of being thrust into the orifice, has a button at the end.

probing-awl (prō'bing-âl), *n.* A steel prod or awl, used to pierce the brain in killing fish for the table.

probity (prob'i-ti), *n.* [< F. *probité* = Sp. *probidad* = Pg. *probidade* = It. *probità*, < L. *probita(t-)s*, uprightness, honesty, < *probus*, good, excellent, honest: see *probe*, *prove.*] Tried virtue or integrity; strict honesty; virtue; sincerity; high principle.

So near approach we their celestial kind
By justice, truth, and *probity* of mind. *Pope.*

A minister [Walpole] . . . who had seen so much perfidy and meanness that he had become sceptical as to the existence of *probity*. *Macaulay*, Lord Holland.

Let the reign of the good Stuyvesant show . . . how frankness, *probity*, and high-souled courage will command respect, and secure honor, even where success is unattainable. *Irving*, Knickerbocker, p. 469.

=**Syn.** *Integrity*, *Uprightness*, etc. (see *honesty*), worth, trustworthiness, trustiness, incorruptibility.

problem (prob'lem), *n.* [< ME. *probleme*, < OF. *probleme*, F. *problème* = Sp. Pg. It. *problema* = D. *probleem*, *problema* = G. Sw. Dan. *problem*, < L. *problema*, < Gr. πρόβλημα, a question proposed for solution, < προβάλλειν, throw or lay before, < πρό, before, + βάλλειν, throw, put: see *ball*[2], *ballista*, etc., and cf. *emblem.*] 1. A question proposed for decision or discussion; a matter for examination; any question involving doubt, uncertainty, or difficulty; also, a question with a discussion of it.

Although in general one understood colours, yet were it not an easy *problem* to resolve why grass is green.
Sir T. Browne.

The Conclusion is the *Problem* (problema), question (quæstio, quæsitio), which was originally asked, stated now as a decision. The *Problem* is usually omitted in the expression of a syllogism, but is one of its essential parts.
Sir W. Hamilton, Logic, xv.

Few researches can be conducted in any one line of inquiry without sooner or later abutting on some metaphysical *problem*, were it only that of Force, Matter, or Cause.
G. H. Lewes, Probs. of Life and Mind, I. i. § 8.

Specifically—2. In *geom.*, a proposition requiring some operation to be performed or construction to be executed, as to bisect a line, and the like. It differs from a *theorem* in that the latter requires something to be proved, a relation or identity to be shown or established. The Greek word is used in this sense by Pappus, in the third century after Christ.

3†. In English universities, a public disputation. —**Absolute problem.** See *absolute*.—**Alhazen's problem**, the problem from two given points in the plane of a given circle to draw lines intersecting on the circumference and making equal angles with the tangent at the point of intersection.—**Apollonius's problem**, the problem to draw a circle tangent to three given circles in a plane. This celebrated problem was proposed, according to Pappus, by Apollonius in his work on contacts.—**Busschop's problems**, the following problems: (1) to cut a square into eight pieces which will fit together to make two squares, one twice as large as the other; (2) to cut a regular hexagon into five parts which will make a square; (3) to cut a regular pentagon into seven parts which will make a square.—**Characteristic problem.** See *characteristic*.—**Chess problem**, a given position of chess pieces in which it is required that one side mate the other (or sometimes compel the other to give mate) in a stipulated number of moves.—**Comparative problem**, a question in regard to the degree of any quality possessed by any subject.—**Crown, Delian, determinate problem.** See the qualifying words.—**Fermat's problem**, given two media separated by a plane and the velocities of light in them, to find the path of quickest transmission between two given points.—**Florentine, goniometrical, imperial, indeterminate, inverse problem.** See the adjectives.—**Gergonne's problem**, the problem to cut a cube so that the section shall enter at a diagonal of one face and emerge at the non-parallel diagonal of the opposite face, making the surface of section the smallest possible.—**Huygens's problem**, a problem proposed by Christian Huygens in 1669, to this effect: a given number of perfectly elastic spheres lie in one straight line; the masses of the first and last are known; the first strikes the second with a given velocity; what must the masses of the intermediate ones be to make the velocity imparted to the last a maximum? This was solved by Huygens for three bodies, by Lagrange in 1750 for five, and by Picart in 1874 completely.—**Isoperimetrical problem**, a problem relating to a maximum or minimum condition to be fulfilled by the form of a function: so called because the earliest problems of this kind were of isoperimetry in the narrower sense.—**Kepler's problem**, the problem from a given point on the diameter of a semicircle to draw a line dividing the area in a given proportion; to solve the equation $a = x - b \sin x$; to find the position of a planet at a given time from its elements. This problem, of capital importance, was proposed by Kepler in 1609.—**L'Huilier's problems**, the following problems: (1) to cut a given triangular prism so that the plane section shall be equal to a given triangle; (2) on a given triangle as base to erect an oblique prism so that the perpendicular section shall be similar to a given triangle.—**Limited problem**, in *math.*, a problem that has but one solution, or some determinate number of solutions.—**Linear, local, notional problem.** See the adjectives.—**Malfatti's problem**, a problem of elementary geometry, mentioned by Pappus about 300, but first solved by Gianfrancesco Malfatti (1731–1807) in 1788: namely, to inscribe in a given triangle three circles, each touching two sides of the triangle, and all tangent to one another. The best construction was given by Steiner in 1826.—**Mechanical solution of a problem.** See *mechanical*.—**Nonius's problem**, the problem to find the day of shortest twilight for a given latitude.—**Pappus's problem**, in a given circle to inscribe a triangle whose sides produced shall contain three given points. —**Pell's problem**, the problem to solve the equation $x^2 - Ay^2 = \pm B$.—**Petersburg problem**, a celebrated problem in probabilities, to determine how much ought to be paid for the assurance of being paid \$2^m, where *m* is the number of times that a coin will be tossed up without coming up head: so called because mentioned by Daniel Bernoulli in the Memoirs of the St. Petersburg Academy, but already treated by Nicolas Bernoulli the first in 1713. —**Pfaff's problem**, the problem to transform an expression $X_1 dx_1 + X_2 dx_2 + \ldots$ into another of similar form with a given number of terms, and to determine the smallest possible number of terms.—**Pothenot's problem**, to find a point from which two given segments are seen under given angles.—**Problem of duration of play**, to find the probability that one player will ruin another within a given number of bets, and the probable number of bets before he is ruined.—**Problem of squaring the circle.** See *squaring*.—**Problem of the couriers.** See *courier*.—**Problem of the duplication.** See *duplication*.—**Problem of the inscription of the heptagon**, the impossible problem to inscribe a regular heptagon in a circle with a rule and compass.—**Problem of the school-girls**, the problem to show how fifteen school-girls might walk out in ranks of three every day for a week, without any one walking a second time in the same rank with any other.—**Problem of three bodies**, the problem to determine the motions of three mutually gravitating particles.—**Sursolid problem**, in *math.*, a problem which cannot be resolved but by curves of a higher kind than the conic sections.—**Viviani's problem**, to pierce a hemispherical dome with four equal windows so that the rest of the surface shall be quadrable.

problematic (prob-le-mat'ik), *a.* [= F. *problématique* = Sp. *problemático* = Pg. It. *problematico*, < L. *problematicus*, < Gr. προβληματικός, pertaining to a problem, < πρόβλημα(τ-), a problem: see *problem*.] 1. Of the nature of a problem; questionable; uncertain; unsettled; disputable; doubtful.

The probability of foreign rivalry was not believed in, or was treated as at least distant and *problematic*.
W. R. Greg, Misc. Essays, 1st ser., p. 8.

2. In *logic*, of the nature of a question, possible or doubtful.

I call a concept *problematic* if it is not self-contradictory, and if, as limiting other concepts, it is connected with other kinds of knowledge, while its objective reality cannot be known in any way. . . . The concept of a noumenon is problematical—that is, the representation of a thing of which we can neither say that it is possible nor that it is impossible, because we have no conception of any kind of intuition but that of our senses, or of any kind of concepts but of our categories, neither of them being applicable to any extrasensuous object.
Kant, Critique of Pure Reason (tr. by Müller), iii.

Problematic proposition. See *proposition*.

problematical (prob-le-mat'i-kal), *a.* [< *problematic* + *-al*.] Same as *problematic*.

Wagers are laid in the city about our success, which is yet, as the French call it, *problematical*.
Johnson, to Mrs. Thrale, Nov. 1, 1777.

problematically (prob-le-mat'i-kal-i), *adv.* [< *problematical* + *-ly*[2].] In a problematic manner; doubtfully; dubiously; uncertainly.

problematist (prob'lem-a-tist), *n.* [< Gr. πρόβλημα(τ-), a problem, + *-ist*.] One who proposes problems. [Rare.]

This learned *problematist*.
Evelyn, To Dr. Beale, Aug. 27, 1668.

problematize (prob'lem-a-tīz), *v. i.*; pret. and pp. *problematized*, ppr. *problematizing*. [< Gr. πρόβλημα(τ-), a problem, + *-ize*.] To propose problems.

Tip. Hear him *problematize*.
Pru. Bless us, what's that?
Tip. Or syllogize, elenchize. B. *Jonson*, New Inn, ii. 2.

pro bono publico (prō bō'nō pub'li-kō). [L.: *pro*, for; *bono*, abl. of *bonum*, good; *publico*, abl. of *publicus*, public: see *pro*, *bona*, *public*.] For the public good.

Proboscidæ (prọ-bos'i-dē), *n. pl.* [NL., for **Proboscididæ*, < Gr. προβοσκίς (-κιδ-), proboscis, + *-idæ*.] The family of the elephants: now called *Elephantidæ*.

proboscidal (prọ-bos'i-dal), *a.* [< L. *proboscis* (*-cid-*), < Gr. προβοσκίς (-κιδ-), proboscis, + *-al*.] Same as *proboscidiform*.

A *proboscidal* prolongation of the oral organs. *Shuckard.*

proboscidate (prọ-bos'i-dāt), *a.* [< L. *proboscis* (*-cid-*), < Gr. προβοσκίς (-κιδ-), proboscis, + *-ate*[1].] Having a proboscis; proboscidean.—**Proboscidate insect**, an insect having a proboscidate mouth.—**Proboscidate mouth**, in *entom.*, a haustellate mouth; a mouth in which the organs are modified to form a proboscis, as in most flies. See cut under *house-fly*.

proboscide (prọ-bos'id), *n.* [< F. *proboscide*, < L. *proboscis*, proboscis: see *proboscis*.] In *her.*, the trunk of an elephant used as a bearing or part of a bearing.

Proboscidea (prō-bo-sid'ẹ-ạ̈), *n. pl.* [NL. (Illiger, 1811), < L. *proboscis* (*-cid-*), < Gr. προβοσκίς (-κιδ-), proboscis: see *proboscis*.] 1. An order of *Mammalia* having a long flexible proboscis or trunk. It now contains only the elephants and their allies, as the mammoths and mastodons. The legs are mostly exserted beyond the common integument of the trunk, and all their joints are extensible in a right line. The teeth are enameled; the incisors are—in the living elephants two above and none below, in some extinct *Proboscidea* none above and two below, or two above and below, any of which may be developed into long tusks curving out of the mouth. The feet are all five-toed, so far as is known, incased in broad shallow hoofs, one to each digit, and the palmar and plantar surfaces are padded. The carpal bones are broad and short, in two separate, not interlocking, rows; the scaphoid and lunar are separate from each other; the cuneiform is broad, extended inward, and attached to the ulna; the unciform is directly in front of the cuneiform, and the magnum in front of the lunar; in the hind foot the astragulus articulates in front only with the navicular. The placenta is deciduate, zonary. The *Proboscidea* belong to the higher or educabilian series of placental mammals. Their nearest living relatives are the *Hyracoidea*. There are 2 families—*Elephantidæ*, containing the elephants, mammoths, and mastodons, and *Dinotheriidæ*, the dinotheres, the latter all extinct, the former now represented by only 2 living species. See cuts under *Dinotherium*, *elephant*, *Elephantinæ*, and *Mastodontinæ*.
2. A class of corticate protozoans, also called *Rhynchoflagellata*, represented by the noctilucans. *E. R. Lankester.*

proboscidean (prō-bo-sid'ẹ-an), *a.* and *n.* [< L. *proboscis* (*-cid-*), < Gr. προβοσκίς (-κιδ-), proboscis, + *-e-an*.] I. *a.* 1. Having a proboscis or trunk; proboscidate or proboscidiferous; belonging to the mammalian order *Proboscidea*.—2. Of or pertaining to a proboscis: as, "the *proboscidean* sheath of the Nemertines," *Encyc. Brit.*, XXIV. 184.
Also *proboscidial*, *proboscoid*.
Proboscidean flukes, the trematoids of the family *Tetrarhynchidæ*.
II. *n.* A mammal of the order *Proboscidea*; an elephantid or dinotheriid.
Also *proboscidian*.

proboscideous (prō-bo-sid'ẹ-us), *a.* [< L. *proboscis* (*-cid-*), < Gr. προβοσκίς (-κιδ-), proboscis, + *-eous*.] In *bot.*, having a hard terminal horn, as the fruit of *Martynia*. *Treasury of Botany.*

proboscides, *n.* Latin plural of *proboscis*.

proboscidial (prō-bo-sid'i-al), *a.* [< L. *proboscis* (*-cid-*), < Gr. προβοσκίς (-κιδ-), proboscis, + *-ial*.] Same as *proboscidean*.

proboscidian (prō-bo-sid'i-an), *a.* and *n.* [< L. *proboscis* (*-cid-*), < Gr. προβοσκίς (-κιδ-), proboscis, + *-ian*.] Same as *proboscidean*.

Proboscidifera (prọ-bos-i-dif'ẹ-rạ̈), *n. pl.* [NL., neut. pl. of *proboscidifer*: see *proboscidiferous*.] A division of pectinibranchiate gastropods with a small head, a proboscis retractile under the base of the tentacles, and variable teeth on a long cartilaginous lingual ribbon. It includes a large number of carnivorous gastropods, among the best-known of which are the *Muricidæ* and the *Buccinidæ*. Contrasted with *Rostrifera*.

proboscidiferous (prọ-bos-i-dif'ẹ-rus), *a.* [< NL. *proboscidifer*, < L. *proboscis* (*-cid-*), proboscis, + *ferre* = E. *bear*[1].] 1. Having a proboscis.—2. In *conch.*, pertaining to the *Proboscidifera*.

proboscidiform (prọ-bos'i-di-fôrm), *a.* [< L. *proboscis* (*-cid-*), proboscis, + *forma*, form.] Proboscis-like. Also *proboscidal*, *probosciform*, *probosciformed*.

probosciform (prọ-bos'i-fôrm), *a.* [< L. *proboscis*, proboscis, + *forma*, form.] Same as *proboscidiform*. *Encyc. Dict.*

probosciformed (prọ-bos'i-fôrmd), *a.* [< *probosciform* + *-ed*[2].] Same as *proboscidiform*.

The surface of the *probosciformed* mouth, facing the first pair of cirri, has a deep central longitudinal fold.
Darwin, Cirripedia, p. 176.

Probosciger (prọ-bos'i-jėr), *n.* [NL. (Kuhl, 1820), < L. *proboscis*, proboscis, + *gerere*, carry.] A genus of black cockatoos: synonymous with *Microglossa*.

proboscigerous (prō-bo-sij'ẹ-rus), *a.* [< L. *proboscis*, proboscis, + *gerere*, carry.] Having a proboscis; proboscidiferous.

proboscis (prọ-bos'is), *n.*; pl. *proboscides* (-i-dēz). [= F. *proboscide* = Sp. *probóscide* = Pg. *proboscis* = It. *proboscide*, proboscis, < L. *proboscis*, < Gr. προβοσκίς (-κιδ-), the trunk or proboscis of an elephant, the proboscis of a fly, an arm of a cuttlefish, < πρό, before, + βόσκειν, feed, graze.] 1. An elephant's trunk; hence, a long flexible snout, as the tapir's, or the nose of the proboscis-monkey. See cut under *Nasalis*.

The unwieldy elephant,
To make them mirth, used all his might, and wreathed
His lithe *proboscis*. *Milton*, P. L., iv. 347.

2. Any proboscidiform part or organ; anything that sticks out in front of an animal like an elephant's trunk. See cut under *Cystophorinæ*. (*a*) The human nose, especially when very large. [Humorous.] (*b*) In *entom.*: (1) The rostrum or beak of a rhynchophorous beetle, or snout-beetle. (2) The long coiled haustellate organ of lepidopterous insects; an antlia. See cut under *haustellum*. (3) The sucking-mouth of a fly, a cylindrical membranous or fleshy organ terminating in a dilated portion which is applied to the substance to be sucked up. (See *promuscis*, and cut under *house-fly*.) (4) The extensible mouth-organs of a bee, consisting of the labium and lingua with their various divisions, and the maxillæ, united at their bases with the labium. (*c*) In *Vermes*, a diversiform buccal, oral, or pharyngeal organ of many worms, as errant annelids, gephyreans, turbellarians, and nemerteans. In the last the proboscis is a tubular invaginated eversible organ opening in the anterior part of the body above the mouth, formed by a differentiation of the integument; it is variable in details of structure: it may be divided, coiled, glandulous, and furnished with stylets, a retractor muscle, etc. (For various proboscides of this kind, see cuts under *Acanthocephala*, *Balanoglossus*, *Cestoides*, *Nereis*, *Proctucha*, *Rhabdocœla*, and *Rhynchocœla*.) (*d*) In *conch.*, the tongue of certain gastropods, such as shell-snails, when it is so long as to be capable of being protruded for some distance from the mouth, in which case it is used for boring the shells of other testaceans, and for destroying by suction the soft parts of the inhabitant: distinguished from *rostrum*. (*e*) In polyps, the central polypite of a medusan. (*f*) In gregarines, the epimerite.

proboscis-monkey (prō-bos'is-mung″ki), *n.* A semnopithecine ape, *Nasalis larvatus*; a kahau: so called from the elongated and flexible snout, which resembles the human nose in size and shape. See cut under *Nasalis*.

proboscis-rat (prọ-bos'is-rat), *n.* Same as *elephant-shrew*.

proboscoid (prọ-bos'koid), *a.* [< Gr. προβοσκίς, proboscis, + εἶδος, form.] Same as *proboscidean*.

probouleutic (prō-bọ̈-lū'tik), *a.* [< Gr. προβούλευσις (-λευτ-), previous deliberation (cf. MGr. προβουλευτής, one who deliberates before), < προβουλεύειν, contrive before, < πρό, before, + βουλεύειν, take counsel, deliberate: see *boule*[2].] Concerned with the preparation of measures for action: noting specifically the Senate, or Council of Five Hundred, in the ancient Athenian constitution.

A misapprehension as to the powers of the Roman Senate, which is represented as being a *probouleutic* body, like that of Athens, which prepared business for the Assembly.
W. F. Allen, Penn. Monthly, Feb., 1879, p. 124.

procacious (prọ̄-kā'shus), *a.* [= OF. *procace* = It. *procace*, < L. *procax* (*-ac-*), forward, bold, shameless, impudent, < *procare*, ask, demand, akin to *precari*, pray: see *pray*[1].] Pert; petulant; saucy.

I confess these [personal comeliness and beauty] are commonly but the temptations of women and *procacious* youth. *Baxter*, Self-Denial, xliv.

Now abating a *procacious* youth, now heartening a shy homely one. *Dr. J. Brown*, Spare Hours, 3d ser., p. 297.

procacity (prọ̄-kas'i-ti), *n.* [= OF. *procacite* = Sp. *procacidad* = Pg. *procacidade* = It. *procacità*, < L. *procacita(t-)s*, forwardness, impudence, < *procax* (*-ac-*), forward, bold: see *procacious*.] Impudence; petulance.

In vaine are all your knaveries,
Delights, deceipts, *procacities*.
Burton, Anat. of Mel., p. 541.

procambial (prọ̄-kam'bi-al), *a.* [< *procambium* + *-al*.] In *bot.*, pertaining to or resembling the procambium.

A *procambial* bundle being first formed. *Encyc. Brit.*, IV. 105.

procambium (prō-kam'bi-um), *n.* [NL., < L. *pro*, before, + NL. *cambium*: see *cambium*[2].] In *bot.*, a long-celled initial strand of a vascular bundle; a similar or homogeneous formative cell of a bundle. Compare *cambium*[2].

This mass [of elongated cells] is termed the *procambium* of the fibro-vascular bundle. *Encyc. Brit.*, IV. 93.

procardium (prō-kär'di-um), *n.*; pl. *procardia* (-ạ̈). [NL., < Gr. πρό, before, + καρδία = E. *heart*.] The pit of the stomach; the scrobiculus cordis.

procarp (prō'kärp), *n.* [< NL. *procarpium*, < Gr. πρό, before, + καρπός, a fruit.] In *bot.*, in certain algæ and fungi, a unicellular or pluricellular female sexual organ, which consists of a filamentous receptive part called the *trichogyne* and a dilated part called the *carpogonium*. The protoplasm is not rounded off to form an oösphere, but is excited by fertilization to a process of growth which results in a sporocarp.

In the Florideæ it is the procarpium (*procarp*), which consists of a single cell or a small cell-group. *De Bary*, Fungi (trans.), p. 121.

procarpium (prọ̄-kär'pi-um), *n.*; pl. *procarpia* (-ạ̈). [NL.: see *procarp*.] Same as *procarp*.

procatalectic (prō-kat-a-lek'tik), *a.* [< Gr. πρό, before, + καταληκτικός, leaving off: see *catalectic*. Cf. προκαταλήγειν, leave off beforehand.] In *anc. pros.*, catalectic at the beginning; wanting the arsis (metrically unaccented part) of the first foot. Thus, the following colon in an iambic period is procatalectic: ∠ ⏑ ∠ ⏑ ∠ ⏑ ∠ (for ⏑ ∠ ⏑ ∠ ⏑ ∠ ⏑ ∠).

procatarctic† (prō-ka-tärk'tik), *a.* [< Gr. προκαταρκτικός, beginning beforehand, being the immediate cause, < προκατάρχειν, begin first, < πρό, before, + κατάρχειν, begin upon, < κατά, upon, + ἄρχειν, be first, begin.] Being the immediate cause; in *med.*, noting a cause which immediately kindles a disease into action when there exists a predisposition to it. The procatarctic cause is often denominated the exciting cause. See *efficient cause*, under *efficient*.

procatarctical† (prō-ka-tärk'ti-kal), *a.* [< *procatarctic* + *-al*.] Same as *procatarctic*.

The *procatarctical* and proegumenal causes are of great use in physick; for the physicians reduce almost all diseases to three causes: *procatarctical*, proegumenal, and synectical or containing. The *procatarctical* is with them the external and evident cause. . . . For example: The *procatarctical* cause of the fever is either cold or the astringent bathes. *Burgeredicius*, tr. by a Gentleman, i. 17.

procatarxis† (prō-ka-tärk'sis), *n.* [< Gr. προκάταρξις, a first beginning, < προκατάρχειν, begin first: see *procatarctic*.] In *med.*, the kindling of a disease into action by a procatarctic cause, when a predisposition exists; also, the procatarctic cause of a disease.

procathedral (prō-ka-thē'dral), *n.* [< L. *pro*, for, + ML. *cathedralis*, a cathedral: see *cathedral*.] A church used temporarily as a cathedral.

procede†, *v. i.* An obsolete spelling of *proceed*.

procedendo (prō-sẹ-den'dō), *n.* [L., abl. sing. gerundive of *procedere*, go forward, proceed: see *proceed*.] In *law*, a writ which formerly issued out of the English Court of Chancery in the exercise of its common-law jurisdiction, when judges of any subordinate court wrongfully delayed the parties, and would not give judgment either on the one side or on the other. It commanded the judges to proceed to give judgment, without specifying any particular judgment to be given. A writ of procedendo also lay where an action had been removed from an inferior to a superior court, and it appeared to the superior court that it was removed on insufficient grounds.

procedure (prọ̄-sē'dụ̄r), *n.* [< OF. *procedure*, F. *procédure* = It. *procedura*, < L. *procedere*, go forward, proceed: see *proceed*.] 1†. The act of proceeding or moving forward; progress.

He overcame the difficulty in defiance of all such pretences as were made even from religion itself to obstruct the better *procedure* of real and material religion. *Jer. Taylor*, Works, III. vii.

2. Manner of proceeding or acting; a course or mode of action; conduct.

Those more complex intellectual *procedures* which acute thinkers have ever employed. *H. Spencer*, Prin. of Psychol.

He would learn if they
Connive at Pym's *procedure*!
Browning, Strafford.

3. A step taken; an act performed; a proceeding.—4†. That which proceeds from something; product.

No known substance but earth, and the *procedures* of earth, as tile and stone. *Bacon.*

5. The modes, collectively, of conducting business, especially deliberative business; specifically, in *law*, the modes of conduct of litigation and judicial business, as distinguished from that branch of the law which gives or defines rights. It includes practice, pleading, and evidence.

By itself indeed the lately revealed Irish law would carry us a very little way. Its great peculiarity is the extraordinary prominence it gives to *Procedure*. *Maine*, Early Law and Custom, p. 374.

Civil *procedure* . . . is chiefly intended to realize and enforce the legalized interests or "rights" of individuals. *Polit. Sci. Quarterly*, II. 123.

Common-law procedure acts. See *common*.—**New** or **reformed procedure.** See *equity*, 2 (*b*).=**Syn. 2.** *Proceeding, Operation*, etc. See *process*.

proceed (prọ̄-sēd'), *v. i.* [Early mod. E. also *procede*; < ME. *proceden*, < OF. *proceder*, F. *procéder* = Sp. Pg. *proceder* = It. *procedere*, < L. *procedere*, go forth, go forward, advance, come forth, issue, go on, result, proceed, < *pro*, forth, + *cedere*, go: see *cede*.] 1. To move, pass, or go forward or onward; continue or renew motion or progress; advance; go on, literally or figuratively: as, to *proceed* on one's journey; the vessel touched at Queenstown, and then *proceeded* on her voyage.

Come, cite them, Crites, first, and then *proceed*. *B. Jonson*, Cynthia's Revels, v. 3.

Hadst thou . . . *proceeded*
The sweet degrees that this brief world affords.
Shak., T. of A., iv. 3. 252.

Proceeding the space of a flight-shoot, they finde another Arch, like vnto the first. *Purchas*, Pilgrimage, p. 269.

I shall . . . *proceed* to more complex ideas. *Locke*, Human Understanding. II. xviii. 2.

Having already mentioned those Speeches which are assigned to the Persons in this Poem, I *proceed* to the Description which the Poet gives us of Raphael. *Addison*, Spectator, No. 327.

2. To issue or come, as from an origin, source, or fountain; go forth: with *from*.

Excuse me that I am so free with you; what I write *proceeds from* the clear Current of a pure Affection. *Howell*, Letters, I. v. 11.

From the death of the old the new *proceeds*. *Whittier*, The Preacher.

3. To carry on some series of actions; set one's self at work and go on in a certain way and for some particular purpose; act according to some method.

If you promise vs peace, we will beleeue you; if you *proceed* in revenge we will abandon the Country. Quoted in *Capt. John Smith's* Works, I. 225.

From them I will not hide
My judgments, how with mankind I *proceed*.
Milton, P. L., xi. 69.

He that *proceeds* on other principles in his inquiry into any sciences posts himself in a party. *Locke.*

But how severely with themselves *proceed*
The men who write such verse as we can read!
Pope, Imit. of Hor., II. ii. 157.

4†. To be transacted or carried on; be done; pass; go on.

He will, after his sour fashion, tell you
What hath *proceeded* worthy note to-day.
Shak., J. C., i. 2. 180.

5. To begin and carry on a legal action; take any step in the course of procedure: as, to *proceed* against an offender.—6. To come into effect or action. [Rare.]

This rule only *proceeds* and takes place when a person cannot of common law condemn another by his sentence. *Ayliffe*, Parergon.

7. To take an academic degree: now used only in the universities of Great Britain and Ireland. "To *proceed* master" is an abbreviated form of "to *proceed* to the degree of master."

Ignorance in stilts . . .
With parrot tongue perform'd the scholar's part,
Proceeding soon a graduated dunce.
Cowper, Task, ii. 739.

The oldest [surviving graduate] *proceeded* Bachelor of Arts the very Commencement at which Dr. Stiles was elected to the Presidency. *Woolsey*, Discourse, Yale Coll., Aug. 14, 1850, p. 38. [(*College Words*.)

=**Syn. 2.** To arise, emanate, flow, accrue, result, be derived.

proceed (prō'sēd), *n.* [Early mod. E. also *procede*; < *proceed*, *v.*] The amount proceeding or accruing from some possession or transaction; especially, the sum derived from the sale of goods: now used only in the plural: as, the consignee was directed to sell the goods forwarded and invest the *proceeds* in coffee.

The only *Procede* (that I may use the mercantile Term) you can expect is Thanks, and this Way shall not be wanting to make you rich Returns. *Howell*, Letters, I. i. 29.

Net proceeds. See *net*[2].—**Proceeds of a cargo**, in general, the return or substituted cargo, acquired by sale or exchange of the goods originally shipped. *Dow v. Hope Ins. Co.*, 1 Hall, 166.

proceeder (prō-sē'dėr), *n.* 1. One who proceeds or goes forward; one who makes a progress.

Let him not set himself too great nor too small tasks; for the first will make him dejected by often failing, and the second will make him a small *proceeder*, though by often prevailing. *Bacon*, Nature in Men (ed. 1887).

Specifically—2. One who takes an academic degree.

A little before the Reformation, the greatest part of the *proceeders* in divinity at Oxford were monks and Regular canons. *Tanner*, quoted in Forewords to Babees Book, p. xxxvi.

proceeding (prọ̄-sē'ding), *n.* [Verbal n. of *proceed*, *v.*] 1. A going forward; a procession; the act of one who proceeds; especially, a measure or step taken; a doing; a transaction: as, an illegal *proceeding*; a cautious *proceeding*; a violent *proceeding*. In the plural the term is specifically applied to suits and judicial actions of all kinds involving rights of persons or of property, as well as to the course of steps or measures in the prosecution of actions at law: as, to institute *proceedings* against a person.

The *proceeding* was thus ordered: viz., First the City Marshal, to follow in the rear of His Majesty's Life Guards. *England's Joy* (Arber's Eng. Garner, I. 29).

The clerk . . . should keep a record of the *proceedings*. *Robert*, Rules of Order, § 51.

We have learned some of us to approve, and more perhaps to acquiesce in, *proceedings* which our fathers looked on as in the last degree unrighteous and intolerable. *Stubbs*, Medieval and Modern Hist., p. 3.

2†. Advancement.

My dear dear love
To your *proceeding* bids me tell you this.
Shak., J. C., ii. 2. 103.

3. *pl.* A record or account of the transactions of a society: as, the *Proceedings* of the American Philological Association. The *proceedings* of this and other societies differ from the *transactions*, in that the *proceedings* are the record of all the business done, with mere abstracts of the papers read, while the *transactions* consist of the papers themselves.—**Collateral proceeding.** See *collateral*.—**Dispossess proceedings.** See *dispossess*.—**Proceeding via executiva**, in *civil law*, executory process (which see, under *executory*).—**Special proceeding**, a judicial proceeding other than an action, as a writ of mandamus, a petition to appoint a trustee, etc.—**Stay of proceedings.** See *stay*.—**Summary proceedings**, in *law*, certain legal remedies authorized by statute to be taken without the formal bringing of an action by process and pleading—an affidavit laid before a magistrate under warrant issued thereon being usually substituted; more specifically, such proceedings taken to dispossess a tenant for non-payment of rent, or for holding over, etc.—**Supplementary proceedings**, sometimes called **supplemental proceedings**, proceedings supplementary to judgment and execution for the enforcement thereof, when the execution remains unsatisfied. Courts of equity have given such a remedy by bill compelling examination of a debtor under oath, and by injunction against disposing of his assets; and the codes of procedure have added as an alternative remedy, at the option of the creditor, a supplementary proceeding, either entitled in the original cause or a special proceeding issuing out of it, by which, on affidavit, an order is granted compelling the debtor, or a third person holding his assets or indebted to him, to appear for examination, and forbidding disposal of assets meanwhile; and, if assets are discovered, a receiver can be appointed.=**Syn. 1.** *Procedure, Operation*, etc. (see *process*), measure, performance, step.

proceleusmatic (pros″e-lūs-mat'ik), *a.* and *n.* [< LL. *proceleusmaticus*, < Gr. προκελευσματικός (sc. πούς), a foot consisting of four short syllables, lit. 'pertaining to incitement,' < *προκέλευσμα, < προκελεύειν, arouse to action beforehand, incite before, < πρό, before, + κελεύειν, order, < κέλλειν, urge, drive on, incite.] I. *a.* 1. Inciting; animating; encouraging.

The ancient *proceleusmatick* song, by which the rowers of Gallies were animated, may be supposed to have been of this kind. *Johnson*, Jour. to Western Isles, p. 140.

2. In *pros.*, consisting, as a metrical foot, of four short syllables; of or pertaining to feet so constituted.

II. *n.* In *anc. pros.*, a foot consisting of four short times or syllables. The proceleusmatic (⏑ ⏑ | ⏑ ⏑) is tetrasemic and isorrhythmic.

Procellaria (pros-e-lā'ri-ä), *n.* [NL., < L. *procella*, a storm, a hurricane: see *procellous*.] A Linnean genus of *Procellariidæ*, or petrels, formerly conterminous with the family, later variously restricted, now usually confined to the very small black-and-white species known as *Mother Carey's chickens*, as *P. pelagica*, the stormy petrel: in this restricted sense synonymous with *Thalassidroma* of Vigors. See cut under *petrel*.

procellarian (pros-e-lā'ri-an), *a.* and *n.* [< *Procellaria* + *-an*.] I. *a.* Of or pertaining to the genus *Procellaria*, in any sense; resembling or related to a petrel; belonging to the family *Procellariidæ*.

II. *n.* A member of the genus *Procellaria* or family *Procellariidæ*; a petrel of any kind.

Procellariidæ (pros″e-lā-ri'i-dē), *n. pl.* [NL., < *Procellaria* + *-idæ*.] A family of oceanic or pelagic natatorial birds, named from the genus *Procellaria*, belonging to the order *Longipennes* and suborder *Tubinares*, having tubular nostrils, epignathous bill with discontinuous horny covering, and webbed feet with very small, elevated, functionless or rudimentary hallux, if any; the petrels. The *Procellariidæ* are birds of the high seas, of unsurpassed volitorial powers, of all birds the most nearly independent of land. They abound on all seas. There are probably about 90 species, of numerous modern genera, divisible into three subfamilies — *Diomedeinæ*, albatrosses; *Procellariinæ*; and *Halodrominæ*, sea-runners: to which is to be added *Oceanitinæ*, if the so-called *Oceanitidæ* are referred back to this family. Also *Procellariadæ*, *Procellaridæ*.

Procellariinæ (pros-e-lā-ri-ī'nē), *n. pl.* [NL., < *Procellaria* + *-inæ*.] The largest and leading subfamily of *Procellariidæ*; this family, divested of the albatrosses and sea-runners; the petrels proper. They are characterized by the union of the nostrils in one double-barreled tube lying horizontally on the base of the culmen, and the presence of a hallux, however minute. There are five groups of species — the fulmars; the petrels of the genus *Œstrelata* and its relatives; the stormy petrels; the shearwaters or hagdens; and the saw-billed petrels. The genus *Oceanites* and three others, usually ranged with the stormy petrels, are sometimes detached as type of a family *Oceanitidæ*. Also *Procellarinæ*. See cuts under *Daption*, *fulmar*, *hagden*, *Œstrelata*, *petrel*, and *shearwater*.

procellas (prō-sel'as), *n.* [Origin unknown.] In *glass-blowing*, a jaw-tool for pinching in the neck of a bottle, or giving to it some peculiar shape, as it is revolved on the extremity of the pontil. Also called *pucellas*. *E. H. Knight.*

procellous† (prō-sel'us), *a.* [= OF. *procelleux* = Sp. *proceloso* = Pg. It. *procelloso*, < L. *procellosus*, tempestuous, boisterous, < *procella*, a storm, a hurricane (by which things are prostrated), < *procellere*, throw down, prostrate, < *pro*, forward, + **cellere*, drive, urge: see *excel*, *celerity*.] Stormy. *Bailey*, 1731.

procephalic (prō-se-fal'ik or prō-sef'a-lik), *a.* [< Gr. πρό, before, + κεφαλή, head.] 1. Of or pertaining to the fore part of the head.—2. In *Crustacea*, specifically noting certain lobes or processes which form an anterior part of the wall of the head. See the quotation.

> Two flat calcified plates, which appear to lie in the interior of the head (though they are really situated in its front and upper wall) on each side of the base of the rostrum, and are called the *procephalic* processes.
> *Huxley*, Crayfish, p. 160.

3. In *anc. pros.*, same as *macrocephalic*.—**Procephalic lobe**, one of a pair of rounded expansions, developed on the anterior end of the ventral aspect of the embryo of arthropods, which becomes one side and part of the front of the head.

> The neural face of the embryo is fashioned first, and its anterior end terminates in two rounded expansions — the *procephalic lobes*. *Huxley*, Anat. Invert., p. 219.

proception† (prō-sep'shon), *n.* [< L. as if **proceptio(n-)*, < *pro*, before, + *capere*, pp. *captus* (in comp. *-ceptus*), take: see *capable*. Cf. *conception*, *inception*, *perception*, etc.] The act of taking or seizing something beforehand; preoccupation. [Rare.]

> Having so little power to offend others that I have none to preserve what is mine own from their *proception*.
> *Eikon Basilike.*

procere† (prō-sēr'), *a.* [= Sp. *prócer*, *procero* = Pg. It. *procero*, < L. *procerus*, high, tall, long, < *pro*, for, before, + √*cer-* as in *creare*, create: see *create*.] High; tall; lofty. Also *procerous*.

> Such lignous and woody plants as are hard of substance, *procere* of stature. *Evelyn*, Sylva, Int., § iii.

procerebral (prō-ser'ē-bral), *a.* [< *procerebrum* + *-al*.] Pertaining to the fore-brain or procerebrum; prosencephalic.

procerebrum (prō-ser'ē-brum), *n.* [NL., < L. *pro*, before, + *cerebrum*, the brain.] The fore-brain, comprising the cerebral hemispheres, corpora striata, and olfactory lobes; the prosencephalon.

proceres (pros'e-rēz), *n. pl.* [L., pl. of *procer*, rarely *procus*, a chief, noble, magnate; cf. *procerus*, high: see *procere*, *a.*] 1. The nobles or magnates of a country.

> In 1328 it was with the counsel and consent of the prelates and *proceres*, earls, barons, and commons, that Edward resigned his claims on Scotland.
> *Stubbs*, Const. Hist., § 294.

2. [*cap.*] [NL.] In Sundevall's system, an order of birds: same as the *Proceri* of Illiger.

Proceri (prō-sē'rī), *n. pl.* [NL., pl. of L. *procerus*, high: see *procere*.] In *ornith.*, in Illiger's system of classification, a group of birds, the same as *Ratitæ* of Merrem, embracing the struthious birds, or ostriches and their allies: so called from their procere or tall stature.

Proceridæ (prō-ser'i-dē), *n. pl.* [NL., < *Procerus* + *-idæ*.] A family of coleopterous insects, named by Laporte in 1834 from the genus *Procerus*, and now merged with the *Carabidæ*.

procerite (pros'e-rīt), *n.* [< Gr. πρό, before, + κέρας, horn, + *-ite*[2].] In *Crustacea*, the long many-jointed filament which terminates the antenna or feeler of many species, as lobsters and crawfish. It constitutes nearly the whole length of the organ in such cases, the several other named joints of the feeler being short and close to the base. It is the last one of a series of joints named *coxocerite*, *basicerite*, *scaphocerite*, *ischiocerite*, *merocerite*, *carpocerite*, and *procerite*, and is an excellent illustration of an organ with so many joints (technically *subjoints*) that they are not taken into separate morphological consideration. See cuts under *antenna*, *Astacus*, *lobster*, and *Palinurus*.

proceritic (pros-e-rit'ik), *a.* [< *procerite* + *-ic*.] Pertaining to the procerite of a crustacean.

procerity (prō-ser'i-ti), *n.* [< OF. *procerite*, F. *procérité* = Sp. *proceridad* = Pg. *proceridade* = It. *procerità*, < L. *proceritas*, height, tallness, < *procerus*, high, tall: see *procere*.] Tallness; loftiness.

> They were giants for their cruelty and covetous oppression, and not in stature or *procerity* of body.
> *Latimer*, Sermon bef. Edw. VI, 1550.

> Experiments in consort touching the *procerity*, and lowness, and artificiall dwarfing of trees.
> *Bacon*, Nat. Hist., § 532, note.

> His insufferable *procerity* of stature, and uncorresponding dwarfishness of observation.
> *Lamb*, Popular Fallacies, xiii.

procerous (prō-sē'rus), *a.* [< L. *procerus*, high, tall: see *procere*.] 1†. Same as *procere*.

> The compasse about the wall of this new mount is five hundreth foot, . . . and the *procerous* stature of it, so embailing and girdling in this mount, twentie foot and sixe inches. *Nashe*, Lenten Stuffe (Harl. Misc., VI. 153).

2. Tall, as a bird; belonging to the *Proceres* or *Proceri*.

Procerus (pros'e-rus), *n.* [NL. (Megerle, 1821), < Gr. πρό, before, + κέρας, horn.] 1. A genus of beetles, giving name to the family *Proceridæ*, containing a number of east European and west Asiatic species, found on forest-covered mountain-slopes. These beetles resemble *Carabus*, but differ in having the anterior tarsi simple in both sexes.—2. [*l. c.*; pl. *proceri* (-rī).] A pyramidal muscle on the bridge of the nose, more fully called *procerus nasi* and *pyramidalis nasi*. See *pyramidalis*.

Procervulus (prō-sėr'vū-lus), *n.* [NL. (Gaudry, 1878), < L. *pro*, before, + NL. *cervulus*, q. v.] A Miocene genus of *Cervidæ*.

process (pros'es), *n.* [Early mod. E. also *proces*, *processe*; < ME. *processe*, *proces*, *proses*, < OF. *proces*, F. *procès* = Sp. *proceso* = Pg. It. *processo*, < L. *processus*, a going forward, progress, an appearance, an attack, a projection, lapse of time, < *procedere*, pp. *processus*, go forward, advance, proceed: see *proceed*.] 1. A proceeding or moving forward; progressive movement; gradual advance; continuous proceeding.

> So multeply ȝe sall
> Ay furth in fayre *processe*.
> *York Plays*, p. 13.

> That there is somewhat higher than either of these two no other proof doth need than the very *process* of man's desire. *Hooker.*

> The whole vast sweep of our surrounding prospect lay answering in a myriad fleeting shades the cloudy *process* of the tremendous sky. *H. James, Jr.*, Pass. Pilgrim, p. 41.

2. Course; lapse; a passing or elapsing; passage, as of time.

> And therfor we muste abide, and wirke be *processe* of tyme. *Hampole*, Prose Treatises (E. E. T. S.), p. 20.

> By *proces*, as ye knowen everichoon,
> Men may so longe graven in a stoon
> Til some figure therinne emprented be.
> *Chaucer*, Franklin's Tale, l. 101.

> Swich fire by *processe* shal of kynde colden.
> *Chaucer*, Troilus, iv. 418.

> Three beauteous springs to yellow autumn turn'd
> In *process* of the seasons have I seen.
> *Shak.*, Sonnets, civ.

> The thoughts of men are widen'd with the *process* of the suns. *Tennyson*, Locksley Hall.

3. Manner of proceeding or happening; way in which something goes on; course or order of events.

> Now I pas will to Pirrus by *proses* agayne.
> *Destruction of Troy* (E. E. T. S.), l. 13670.

> Commend me to your honourable wife;
> Tell her the *process* of Antonio's end.
> *Shak.*, M. of V., iv. 1. 274.

> Our parts that are the spectators, or should hear a comedy, are to await the *process* and events of things.
> *B. Jonson*, Magnetick Lady, iv. 2.

> Saturnian Juno now with double care
> Attends the fatal *process* of the war.
> *Dryden*, Æneid, vii.

4. An action, operation, or method of treatment applied to something; a series of actions or experiments: as, a chemical *process*; a manufacturing *process*; mental *process*.

> When the result or effect is produced by chemical action, or by the application of some element or power of nature, or of one substance to another, such modes, methods, or operations are called *processes*.
> *Piper v. Brown*, 3 Fish. Pat. Cas., 175.

> Cable-car lines are in *process* of construction.
> *Appleton's Ann. Cyc.*, 1886, p. 184.

5. Series of motions or changes going on, as in growth, decay, etc.: as, the *process* of vegetation; the *process* of decomposition.

> He who knows the properties, the changes, and the *processes* of matter must, of necessity, understand the effects.
> *Bacon*, Physical Fables, vii., Expl.

> To him was given
> Full many a glimpse . . . of Nature's *processes*
> Upon the exalted hills.
> *Wordsworth*, On the Side of the Mountain of Black Comb.

6. In *law*: (*a*) The summons, mandate, or command by which a defendant or a thing is brought before the court for litigation: so called as being the primary part of the proceedings, by which the rest is directed. Formerly the superior common-law courts of England, in the case of personal actions, differed greatly in their modes of process; but since the passing of the Process Uniformity Act personal actions in general, except replevin, are begun in the same way in all the English courts — namely, by a writ of summons. In chancery the ordinary process was a writ of subpœna. The mode common in probate and ecclesiastical courts is by a citation or summons. In criminal cases, if the accused is not already in custody, the process is usually a writ or warrant.

> The Abbot of S. Isidor is of my acquaintance and my great friend, . . . and now of late there hath beene *processe* against him to appear in this your audience.
> *Guevara*, Letters (tr. by Hellowes, 1577), p. 202.

> I'll get out *process*, and attach 'em all.
> *Middleton (and others)*, The Widow, ii. 1.

> The next step for carrying on the suit, after suing out the original, is called the *process*; being the means of compelling the defendant to appear in court.
> *Blackstone*, Com., III. xix.

> They [the bishops] regarded the *processes* against heretics as the most distressing part of their office.
> *R. W. Dixon*, Hist. Church of Eng., iii.

(*b*) The whole course of proceedings in a cause, real or personal, civil or criminal, from the original writ to the end of the suit. Hence —7†. A relation; narrative; story; detailed account.

> But hennes forth I wol my *proces* holde
> To speke of aventures and of batailles.
> *Chaucer*, Squire's Tale, l. 650.

> To teche chylder curtasy is myne entent,
> And thus forth my *proces* I purpos to be-gynne.
> *Boke of Precedence* (E. E. T. S., extra ser.), l. 56.

> In brief, to set the needless *process* by,
> How I persuaded, how I pray'd, and kneel'd,
> How he refell'd me, and how I replied.
> *Shak.*, M. for M., v. 1. 92.

8†. Proclamation.

> When Pelleus his *proses* hade publishit on highe,
> And all soburly said with a sad wille,
> Jason was Joly of his Juste wordes,
> That in presens of the pepull tho profers were made,
> And mony stythe of astate stonding aboute.
> *Destruction of Troy* (E. E. T. S.), l. 247.

9. In *anat.* and *zoöl.*, a processus; an outgrowth or outgrowing part; a protuberance; a prominence; a projection: used in the widest sense, specific application being made by some qualifying term: as, coracoid *process*.

> A third comes out with the important discovery of some new *process* in the skeleton of a mole.
> *Goldsmith*, Citizen of the World, lxxxix.

10. In *bot.*, a projection from a surface; specifically, in mosses, one of the principal divisions or segments of the inner peristome.—11. Same as *photo-process*: commonly used attributively:

as, *process* blocks, *process* cuts, *process* pictures, etc.

The bare floor was clean, and the walls were hung with cheap prints of the kind known as *process* pictures. *The Standard*, VII. 12.

Abating process. See *abate.*—**Abuse of process.** See *abuse.*—**Accessory process.** Same as *anapophysis.*—**Acromial or acromion process.** See *acromion.*—**Actinic process.** See *actinic.*—**Alar processes,** two small wing-like processes proceeding from the crista galli in front against the frontal bone, and partially including the foramen cæcum.—**Albumin process,** in *photog.* See *albumin.*—**Alinasal, alveolar, angular processes.** See the adjectives.—**Ammonia ore process.** See *ammonia.*—**Anconeus process.** Same as *olecranon.*—**Annular, anteorbital, auditory, autographic process.** See the adjectives.—**Articular process of the lower jaw.** See *articular.*—**Augustin's process,** a method of extracting silver from the ground chloridized ores of that metal, by the use of a solution of common salt. The silver chlorid, formed in the chloridizing roasting, is soluble in the saline solution, a double chlorid of silver and sodium being formed. From this solution the silver is precipitated by means of copper.—**Barff's process,** a method of protecting the surface of iron from rust by forming upon it a thin film of magnetic oxid. It is done by subjecting it at a red heat to the action of superheated steam.—**Basic process.** See *basic.*—**Basilar process.** See *basilar.*—**Basipterygoid processes.** See *basipterygoid.*—**Beer process,** in *photog.* See *beer*[1].—**Bessemer process,** a method, invented by Bessemer, of decarburizing cast-iron. It is of great importance, since by this process steel can now be made much more cheaply than was formerly possible. See *steel.*—**Bethell process,** a process for preserving wood, consisting in its impregnation with tar, oil of tar, and carbolic acid: this mixture is commercially known as *gallatin*, and is obtained by the distillation of coal.—**Bird's-head process,** one of the avicularia of a polyzoan, which are shaped and have a snapping motion like the beak of a bird.—**Bitumen process,** in *photog.* See *bitumen.*—**Boucherie's process,** the injection of a solution of sulphate of copper into the pores of wood.—**Burnettizing process,** the introduction of zinc chlorid into the pores of wood.—**Capitular, carbon, Carinthian process.** See the qualifying words.—**Cazo process** [Sp. *cazo*, a pan], in *metal.*, the treatment of silver ores in the moist way, with the aid of heat, which in the patio process is not used. See *patio process.*—**Chenot process,** a process, invented by the French metallurgist Chenot, for producing cast-steel. Wrought-iron in the form of a metallic sponge is first obtained directly from the ore by cementation with charcoal. This iron is then carburized by being impregnated with some liquid substance rich in carbon, then torrified, and finally melted in crucibles, as in the ordinary method of manufacturing cast-steel.—**Chlorination, chlorin, ciliary, clay, clinoid, cochleariform process.** See the qualifying words.—**Collodion process,** in *photog.* See *collodion.*—**Condyloid process.** Same as *articular process of the lower jaw.*—**Coracoid, coronoid, costal process.** See the adjectives.—**Corduriè's process,** a method of dezincification, by the use of superheated steam, of lead from which the silver has been separated by the Parkes process.—**Creosoting process,** the application of creosote to wood (especially telegraph-poles) for its preservation.—**Direct process.** See *bloomery.*—**Dry process.** (*a*) In *photog.*, the use of dry plates or films; specifically, the use of gelatinobromide emulsions as a sensitive coating for plates or films which are used in a dry state. See *photography.* (*b*) In *fish-culture*, a process of fecundating spawn, invented by V. P. Vrasski. It differs from the *moist process* by requiring two vessels, one for the spawn, which is placed in it without water, and the other for the milt, to which water is added to moisten the eggs. By the dry process, scarcely one per cent. of the eggs escape fecundation, while in the moist method ten or twelve per cent. of the spawn may be lost. (*c*) In *assaying.* See *assaying.*—**Due process of law.** See *due*1.—**Eckart's process,** a method of preserving meats, game, fish, etc., by means of a solution of 1,240 parts salt, 10 parts saltpeter, and 25 parts salicylic acid in 8,725 parts of clean water, applied under a pressure of 180 to 200 pounds per square inch.—**Ensiform process.** Same as *metasternum.*—**Ethmoidal process,** a small projection on the posterior superior border of the turbinate bone for articulation with the uncinate process of the ethmoid.—**Executory process.** See *executory.*—**Falciform process.** Same as *falx cerebri* (which see, under *falx*).—**Fallacy of an illicit process.** See *fallacy.*—**Final process,** the writ of execution used to carry the judgment into effect.—**Floccular process,** the flocculus.—**Foreign Process Acts.** See *foreign.*—**Fox-Talbot process.** Same as *Fox-type*, 1.—**Frontonasal, galvanoplastic, gelatin, geniculate, Ingrassian process.** See the qualifying words.—**Hamular process.** (*a*) Of the lacrymal bone, a hook-like projection at the lower extremity, curving forward in the lacrymal notch of the maxilla. (*b*) Of the sphenoid, the inferior hook-like extremity of the internal pterygoid plate, under which the tendon of the tensor palati plays.—**Heliotype process.** See *heliotype.*—**Intercoxal, jugal, jugular process.** See the adjectives.—**Iron-reduction process,** a method of smelting lead in which metallic iron is employed as an accessory agent of desulphurization, or else some oxidized compound of iron, which during the process will yield metallic iron. This process has been extensively experimented with at Tarnowitz in Silesia, and in the Harz, and there abandoned. It has also been tried in other localities, and is (or was recently) in use to some extent in Japan. Also called *precipitation process*, a translation of the German name for it (*niederschlagarbeit*).—**Jugular process,** in man, a thickened part of the occipital bone to the back and outer side of the jugular fossa, articulating with the mastoid part of the temporal.—**Kenogenetic process.** See *kenogenetic.*—**Kyanizing process.** See *kyanizing.*—**Lacrymal process,** a small projection on the upper anterior border of the turbinate bone for articulation with the lacrymal bone.—**Le Blanc process.** See *soda.*—**Lenticular process.** See *incus* (*a*).—**Long process of the malleus,** a slender process received in the Glaserian fissure. Also called *processus gracilis, longus, tenuis, folianus, anterior,* and *tertius.* See cut under *hyoid.*—**Malar process,** a thick triangular projection of the maxilla for articulation with the malar bone.—**Mammillary, mastoid, mesne process.** See the adjectives.—**Martin process.** See *steel.*—**Maxillary process.** (*a*) Of the palate-bone, a tongue-shaped projection on the anterior border of the vertical plate, overlapping the orifice of the antrum of Highmore in the articulated skull. (*b*) Of the turbinate bone, a flattened plate descending from the attached margin, forming, when articulated, a part of the inner wall of the antrum below the entrance.—**Monteith's process,** the discharging of color from mordanted cotton cloth by the direct application of chlorin.—**Morphine or morphia process.** See *morphine.*—**Nasal process.** (*a*) The slender tapering process on the anterior superior part of the maxilla articulating with the frontal above. (*b*) Same as *lacrymal process.* (*c*) Same as *nasal spine* (which see, under *nasal*).—**Nutant process.** See *nutant.*—**Oblique processes of the vertebræ.** See *oblique.*—**Obliterate, odontoid, orbital process.** See the adjectives.—**Olivary process.** Same as *olivary eminence* (which see, under *olivary*).—**Orbicular process.** See *incus* (*a*).—**Palatal or palatine process,** any marked outgrowth of a palate-bone, especially the flat horizontal plate of that bone which meets its fellow in mid-line, the pair together forming the hinder part of the hard palate or bony roof of the mouth.—**Palingenetic process.** See *palingenetic.*—**Paramastoid process,** in man, an obtuse projection of the under surface of the jugular process, at the insertion of the rectus capitis lateralis muscle, corresponding to a prominent process present in many mammals, especially the ungulates and rodents. Also called *paracondyloid process.*—**Parkes process,** a method of separating silver from lead by fusion with metallic zinc. When a molten mixture of these two metals is allowed to cool, the zinc separates and solidifies first, forming a crust on the other metal. If the lead contains silver, this is concentrated in the solidified crust of zinc, from which it may afterward be separated by distillation.—**Parotic process.** See *parotic.*—**Patera process.** See *Von Patera process*, below.—**Patio process** [Sp. *patio*, an open space], in *metal.*, a method of obtaining the silver from argentiferous ores by amalgamation, extensively practised in Mexico and South America. It is suited for ores in which the silver is present in the form of simple or complex sulphids, without a large percentage of blende or galena, or more than three or four per cent. of copper pyrites. In this process the ore, ground by arrastres, is mixed with common salt, roasted copper pyrites (called *magistral*), and quicksilver. The whole mass is thoroughly mixed, usually by being trodden by mules, the result being that the silver becomes amalgamated with the quicksilver, and can then be easily separated. The mixing (as indicated by the name) takes place on large level floors in the open air.—**Pattinson process,** in *metal.*, a method of desilverizing lead, in general use in the treatment of argentiferous lead, and capable of being profitably employed even when the precious metal is present in the lead in so small quantity as two or three ounces to the ton of the baser metal. The process depends on the fact that melted lead containing silver solidifies gradually in cooling, small particles like crystals separating from the liquid mass, which latter is much richer in silver than the other part—the part which solidifies or crystallizes first yielding up a large part of its silver to that part of the lead which remains fluid. By several repetitions of the operation, the remaining lead becomes at last so enriched with silver that this metal can be easily and profitably separated. The process, which is one of great importance in the metallurgic treatment of argentiferous galena, was the invention of Hugh Lee Pattinson of Alston in Cumberland, and was first applied on a scale of some magnitude in 1833. Before this invention silver had always been separated from lead (these two metals being almost always found associated together in nature) by cupellation, through which process a proportion of silver less than about eight ounces to the ton of lead could not be separated with profit. The process is sometimes called *pattinsonization.*—**Pectineal, phalangeal, photolithographic process.** See the adjectives.—**Photogelatin process,** in *photog.*, any process in which gelatin plays an important part, as in the ordinary gelatinobromide dry plates and films.—**Plaster process.** See *plaster.*—**Plattner's process,** a method of separating gold from pyrites by the employment of chlorin gas, by which the gold is converted into a soluble chlorid, which can then be washed out with water, and precipitated by sulphureted hydrogen in the form of a sulphuret, from which combination the precious metal is easily obtained. See *chlorination.*—**Polychromatic, postauditory, postfrontal, post-tympanic, prepubic process.** See the adjectives.—**Precipitation process.** Same as *iron-reduction process.*—**Process acts,** United States statutes of 1789 and 1792 (1 Stat. 93, 275), the first requiring the writs, executions, and other processes of the United States courts in suits at law to conform to those used in the supreme courts of the several States where such courts were held, except as to their style and teste. The second, in effect, reënacted the first, but allowed the courts or the Supreme Court of the United States by rule to make such alterations or additions as might seem expedient, and regulated the fees of court-officers, etc.—**Process caption.** See *caption.*—**Process of augmentation.** See *augmentation.*—**Process work,** any form of relief-printing plate made by photographic or etching processes, and not by cutting with a graver. See *photo-process.*—**Prosternal, pterygoid, etc., process.** See the adjectives.—**Pyramidal process.** Same as *tuberosity of the palate-bone.*—**Russell's process,** a modification of the Von Patera process for the separation of silver from its ores. The peculiarity of the process depends on the fact that a solution of thiosulphate of copper and soda has a powerful decomposing influence on the sulphureted, antimoniureted, and arseniureted combinations of silver. The roasted ore is first lixiviated with sodium thiosulphate to dissolve the silver chlorid, and afterward with copper thiosulphate. This latter solvent is called the "extra solution," and by its use an additional amount of silver is saved, which would otherwise have been lost in the tailings.—**Short process of malleus,** a small conical eminence at the root of the manubrium. Also called *processus brevis, obtusus, externus, conoideus,* or *secundus,* or *tuberculum mallei.*—**Siemens-Martin process.** See *steel.*—**Siemens process.** See *steel.*—**Solvay process.** See *soda.*—**Sphenoidal process,** the posterior of the two processes surmounting the vertical plate of the palate-bone. It curves inward and backward on the under surface of the body of the sphenoid bone.—**Spinous process.** See *spinous.*—**Styloid process.** (*a*) A conical eminence at the upper extremity of the fibula. (*b*) A short, stout, pyramidal process projecting downward from the outer part of the distal extremity of the radius. (*c*) A short cylindrical eminence at the inner and back part of the distal extremity of the ulna. (*d*) A long, slender, tapering process projecting downward and forward from the outer part of the under surface of the petrous portion of the temporal bone: it is developed from independent centers of ossification, corresponding to the tympanohyal and stylohyal bones.—**Supracondylar process,** a small hook-like process, with its point directed downward, not unfrequently found in front of the internal condylar ridge of the humerus in man. It represents a part of the bone inclosing a foramen in carnivorous animals.—**Thomas-Gilchrist process.** Same as *basic process.*—**To obstruct process.** See *obstruct.*—**Trustee process.** See *garnishment*, 2 (*b*).—**Turbinate process.** (*a*) Superior, a short sharp margin of the ethmoid overhanging the superior meatus. (*b*) Inferior, the folded margin of the sphenoid overhanging the middle meatus. Also called *superior* and *middle spongy bones.*—**Uchatius process,** a method of making steel which has been tried in various places, but is not in general use. It consists in decarburizing pig-iron by fusing it with a material which will give up oxygen, especially iron peroxid or roasted spathic ore.—**Uncinate process.** See *processus uncinatus*, under *processus.*—**Vaginal process.** (*a*) Of the sphenoid, a slightly raised edge at the base of the internal plate of the pterygoid, articulating with the everted margin of the vomer. (*b*) Of the temporal, a flattened plate of bone on the under surface of the petrous portion, immediately back of the glenoid fossa, and partly surrounding the styloid process at its base.—**Vermiform process,** the elevated median portion or lobe between the hemispheres of the cerebellum—that portion on the upper surface being known as the *superior*, that on the under surface the *inferior.*—**Von Patera process,** a method of separating silver from its ores, after a chloridizing roasting, by means of a solution of hypophosphite of soda or lime, which takes up the chlorid of silver, from which solution the metal can be precipitated by an alkaline sulphuret.—**Washoe process,** in *metal.* See *pan*[1], 3.—**Wet process,** in *photog.*, the collodion process.—**Ziervogel's process,** the separation of silver from the sulphate by lixiviation with hot water containing some sulphuric acid. It is used in the treatment of argentiferous copper mattes in which the silver has been transformed into the sulphate by a peculiar kind of roasting. This process is one of very limited application, as great skill is required for the management of the roasting, and but few silver ores can be profitably treated by the method.—**Zygomatic process,** a horizontal bar, directed forward from the squamous part of the temporal bone, and articulating in front with the malar. Also called *zygoma.* =**Syn.** *Process, Proceeding, Procedure, Operation.* In this connection *process* applies to a way of doing something by rule or established method: as, the Bessemer *process*; the *process* of drilling an artesian well; a legal *process*. *Proceeding* expresses a complex action making a whole: as, it was a very strange *proceeding*. Jefferson and Cushing, in their manuals of parliamentary *procedure*, use *proceeding*, perhaps as a participial noun, where *procedure*, being more exact, would be the better word. *Procedure* applies to a way of doing things formally; a legal *proceeding* is a thing done legally; a legal *process* is a legal form gone through for the attainment of a definite purpose; legal *procedure* is the way of doing things in the administration of law, as in the courtroom; a legal *procedure* is a less desirable form of expression for a legal *proceeding*. *Operation* may be used for the way in which a thing works or operates: as, the *operation* of a nail-making machine; it is rarely used thus of personal activity, except in a bad sense: as, the *operations* of a gang of thieves. See *act*, *v. t.*

process (pros'es), *v. t.* [< *process*, *n.*] **1.** To proceed against by legal process; summon in a court of law.

He was at the quarter-sessions, *processing* his brother for tin and tinpence, hay-money. *Miss Edgeworth*, Ennui, viii.

If a man *processes* a neighbour for debt, he is in danger of being paid with a full ounce of lead. *Fortnightly Rev.*, N. S., XL. 430.

2. To reproduce, as a drawing, etc., by any mechanical process, especially by a photographic process. See *photo-process*. [Recent.]

Of course all American readers saw at once that every cut in Mr. Pyle's admirable book was *processed*—to use a new verb invented to fit a new thing. *New York Evening Post*, Jan. 28, 1884.

Both [books], we should say, are rather well illustrated, Lady J——'s with heliogravure portraits . . . and Capt. B——'s with copies (also *processed* in some way) of drawings. *Athenæum*, No. 3251, p. 207.

processal (pros'es-al), *a.* [< *process* + *-al.*] Pertaining to or involving a process. [Rare.]

All Sorts of Damages, and *processal* Charges, come to above two hunderd and fifty thousand Crowns. *Howell*, Letters, I. iii. 8.

procession (prō-sesh'on), *n.* [< ME. *processioun*, *processiun* = D. *processie* = G. Sw. Dan. *procession*, < OF. *procession*, F. *procession* = Sp. *procesion* = Pg. *procissão*, *processão* = It. *processione*, < L. *processio(n-)*, a marching forward, an advance, LL. a religious procession, < *procedere*, pp. *processus*, move forward, advance, proceed: see *proceed*. Cf. *process*.] **1.** The act of proceeding or issuing forth or from anything.

The Greek churches deny the *procession* of the Holy Ghost from the Son. *Jer. Taylor*, Works (ed. 1835), II. 299.

In the *procession* of the soul from within outward, it enlarges its circles ever, like . . . the light proceeding from an orb. *Emerson*, Essays, 1st ser., p. 166.

It is obvious that the Effect is always the *Procession* of its Cause, the dynamical aspect of the statistical conditions. *G. H. Lewes*, Probs. of Life and Mind, I. ii. 87.

2. A succession of persons walking, or riding on horseback or in vehicles, in a formal march, or moving with ceremonious solemnity.

Goth with faire *processioun*
To Ierusalem thorwe the toun.
King Horn (E. E. T. S.), p. 91.

All the priests and friars in my realm
Shall in *procession* sing her endless praise.
Shak., 1 Hen. VI., i. 6. 20.

The whole body, clothed in rich vestments, with candles in their hands, went in *procession* three times round the holy sepulchre. *Pococke*, Description of the East, II. i. 18.

Let the long, long *procession* go,
And let the sorrowing crowd about it grow.
Tennyson, Death of Wellington, iii.

3. An office, form of worship, hymn, litany, etc., said or sung by a number of persons advancing with a measured and uniform movement.—**Procession of the Holy Ghost**, in *theol.*, the emanation or proceeding of the Holy Ghost either from the Father (*single procession*) or from the Father and the Son (*double procession*). See *Filioque*, and *Nicene Creed* (under *Nicene*).—**Procession week.** Same as *Rogation week* (which see, under *rogation*).—**To go procession†**, to take part in a procession of parishioners, led by the parish priest or the patron of the church, making the round of the parish, and invoking blessings on the fruits, with thanksgiving.

Bury me
Under that holy-oke or gospel-tree,
Where, though thou see'st not, thou may'st think upon
Me when thou yeerly *go'st procession*.
Herrick, To Anthea.

procession (prǫ-sesh'ǫn), *v.* [= It. *processionare*, < ML. *processionare*, go in procession; from the noun.] **I.** *intrans.* To go in procession.

There is eating, and drinking, and *processioning*, and masquerading. *Colman*, Man and Wife, i. (*Davies.*)

Two weary hours of *processioning* about the town, and the inevitable collation.
Josiah Quincy, Figures of the Past, p. 368.

II. *trans.* **1.** To treat or beset with processions. [Rare.]

When theyr feastfull dayes come, they are . . . with no small solemnitye matteused, massed, candeled, lyghted, *processioned*, censed, etc. *Bp. Bale*, English Votaries, i.

2. In some of the American colonies, to go about in order to settle the boundaries of, as land. The term is still used in North Carolina and Tennessee. Compare *to beat the bounds*, under *bound*1.

Once in every four years [in the Virginia colony] the vestry, by order of the county court, divided the parish into precincts, and appointed two persons in each precinct to *procession* the lands. These surveyors, assisted by the neighbors, examined and renewed, by blazing trees or by other artificial devices, the old landmarks of the fathers, and reported the result to the vestry, who recorded the same in the parish books.
Johns Hopkins Hist. Studies, III. 64.

processional (prǫ-sesh'ǫn-al), *a.* and *n.* [< ME. *processyonal* (n.), < OF. *processional*, F. *processional* = Sp. *procesional* = Pg. *processional* = It. **processionale* (in adv. *processionalmente*), < ML. **processionalis*, in neut. *processionale*, a processional (book), < L. *processio(n-)*, procession: see *procession*.] **I.** *a.* Pertaining to a procession; consisting in, having the movement of, or used in a procession: as, a *processional* hymn.—**Processional cross.** See *cross*1.

II. *n.* **1.** An office-book containing the offices with their antiphons, hymns, rubrical directions, etc., for use in processional litanies and other religious processions.

The ancient service books, . . . the Antiphoners, Missals, Grailes, *Processionals*, . . . in Latin or English, written or printed. *R. W. Dixon*, Hist. Church of Eng., xvi.

2. A hymn sung during a religious procession, particularly during the entry of the clergy and choir into the church before divine service.

processionalist (prǫ-sesh'ǫn-al-ist), *n.* [< *processional* + *-ist*.] One who walks in a procession; a processionist.

processionally (prǫ-sesh'ǫn-al-i), *adv.* In the manner of a procession; in solemn or formal march.

Henry [V.] himself rode between long glittering rows of clergy who had come *processionally* forth to bring him into Rouen by its principal gate.
Rock, Church of our Fathers, III. i. 305.

processionary (prǫ-sesh'ǫn-ā-ri), *a.* and *n.* [< ME. *processionary*, n.; = F. *processionnaire* = Sp. *procesionario* = Pg. *processionario*, < ML. *processionarius*, pertaining to a procession, < L. *processio(n-)*, procession: see *procession*.] **I.** *a.* **1.** Consisting in formal or solemn procession. *Hooker*, Eccles. Polity, v. § 41.—**2.** In *entom.*, specifically, forming and moving in a procession: said of certain caterpillars.—**Processionary caterpillar**, the larva of the European bombycid moth *Cnethocampa processionea*, which travels up and down the trunks of trees in single, double, or quadruple file. The name is also extended to other larvæ of similar habit. See the quotation.

You will see one caterpillar come out and explore the ground with care; a second immediately follows, a third following the second, and after these come two which touch each other and the one that precedes them; these are followed by three; then comes a row of four, then a row of five, then a row of six, all these following with precision the movements of the leader. From this circumstance is derived their name of *processionary caterpillar*.
S. G. Goodrich, in H. J. Johnson's Nat. Hist.

II. *n.* Same as *processioner*, 2.

processioner (prǫ-sesh'ǫn-ėr), *n.* [< ME. *processyonare* (def. 2), < OF. *processionaire*, F. *processionnaire*, < ML. *processionarius*, pertaining to a procession, neut. *processionarium*, a processional (book): see *processionary*.] **1.** One who goes in a procession. [Rare.]

The *processioners*, seeing them running towards them, and with them the troopers of the holy brotherhood with their cross-bows, began to fear some evil accident.
Jarvis, tr. of Don Quixote, I. iv. 25. (*Davies.*)

2. A county officer in North Carolina and Tennessee charged with the duty of surveying lands at the request of an occupant claiming to be owner.

procession-flower, *n.* See *milkwort*, 1.

processioning (prǫ-sesh'ǫn-ing), *n.* [Verbal n. of *procession*, *v.*] A survey and inspection of boundaries periodically performed in some of the American colonies by the local authorities, for the purpose of ascertaining and perpetuating correct boundaries of the various landowners. It was analogous in part to the perambulations practised in England (see *perambulation*, 4), and was superseded by the introduction of the practice of accurate surveying and of recording. The term is still used of some official surveys in North Carolina and Tennessee.

processionist (prǫ-sesh'ǫn-ist), *n.* [< *procession* + *-ist*.] One who takes part in a procession.

A few roughs may have thrown stones; and certainly the *processionists* gave provocation, attacking and wrecking the houses of Protestants, especially at the Broadway.
Fortnightly Rev., N. S., XL. 259.

processive (prǫ-ses'iv), *a.* [= F. *processif* = It. *processivo*, < ML. **processivus* (in adv. *processive*), < L. *procedere*, pp. *processus*, go forward: see *proceed*, *process*.] Going forward; advancing. *Coleridge.*

process-server (pros'es-sėr"vėr), *n.* One who processes or summonses; a sheriff's officer; a bailiff.

He hath been . . . a *process-server*, a bailiff.
Shak., W. T., iv. 3. 102.

processual (prǫ-ses'ų̈-al), *a.* [< L. *processus*, process (see *process*), + *-al*.] In *civil law*, relating to legal process or proceedings: as, *processual* agency (the peculiar agency of a cognitor appointed in court by a party to act in his place, or of a procurator appearing instead of an absent party to take his place in the cause).

processum continuando (prǫ-ses'um kǫn-tin-ų̈-an'dō). [L.: *processum*, accus. sing. of *processus*, process; *continuando*, abl. gerund. of *continuare*, continue: see *continue*.] In *Eng. law*, a writ for the continuance of process after the death of the chief justice or other justices in the commission of oyer and terminer.

processus (prǫ-ses'us), *n.*; pl. *processus*. [NL., < L. *processus*, a process: see *process*.] In *anat.*, a process; an outgrowth; a part that proceeds to or toward another part.—**Processus a cerebello ad cerebrum**, the anterior peduncles of the cerebellum. See *peduncle*.—**Processus a cerebello ad testes**, the anterior peduncles of the cerebellum. See *peduncle*.—**Processus ad medullam**, the inferior peduncles of the cerebellum. See *peduncle*.—**Processus ad pontem**, the middle peduncles of the cerebellum. See *peduncle*.—**Processus anonymus**, an obtuse tubercular projection on either side of the cerebral surface of the basilar process, in front of the orifice of the precondylar foramen.—**Processus brevis**, the short process of the malleus. Also called *processus conoideus externus*, *obtusus*, and *secundus*.—**Processus caudatus**, the tail of the anthelix of the ear. See second cut under *ear*1.—**Processus clavatus**, the clava or superior enlargement of the funiculus gracilis.—**Processus cochleariformis**, a thin lamina of bone above the Eustachian canal in the petrous section of the temporal bone, separating that canal from the canal for the tensor tympani muscle.—**Processus costarius.** (*a*) The ventral root of a cervical transverse process. (*b*) A transverse process of a lumbar vertebra.—**Processus cuneatus**, the tuberculum cuneatum, or slight superior enlargement of the funiculus cuneatus.—**Processus e cerebello ad cerebrum**, the superior peduncle of the cerebellum. See *peduncle*.—**Processus e cerebello ad medullam oblongatam**, the inferior peduncle of the cerebellum.—**Processus e cerebello ad pontem**, the middle peduncle of the cerebellum.—**Processus e cerebello ad testes**, the superior peduncle of the cerebellum.—**Processus falciformis**, the falciform process of the eye of a fish.—**Processus folianus, gracilis, longus, tenuis**, etc. See *long process of the malleus*, under *process*.—**Processus interjugularis**, a process from the occipital bone uniting with the petrous part of the temporal, and dividing the jugular inclosure into two foramina, a large outer, and smaller inner one.—**Processus lenticularis**, the lenticular process.—**Processus muscularis**, the projection at the external angle of the arytenoid cartilage, where the posterior and lateral crico-arytenoid muscles are inserted.—**Processus reticularis**, a reticulated offset of gray matter near the middle of the outer surface of the gray crescents of the spinal cord. See figure under *spinal cord*.—**Processus uncinatus**, the hooked process of a rib, as of a bird, which is articulated with and projects backward from the rib, overlying the next rib or several ribs; an epipleura. See cut under *epipleura*.

The vertebral pieces are distinguished by backwardly direct processes (*processus uncinati*), which are applied to the body of the succeeding rib.
Gegenbaur, Comp. Anat. (trans.), p. 440.

Processus vaginalis peritonei, a pouch of peritoneum extending into the scrotum during the descent of the testicle. Afterward the upper part becomes obliterated, leaving the lower part as a closed sac, which is known as the *tunica vaginalis*.—**Processus vocalis**, the horizontal projection at the anterior angle of the base of the arytenoid cartilage, for the insertion of the true vocal cord.

procès verbal (pro-sā' ver-bal'). [F., a minute, an authenticated statement in writing: *procès*, a process; *verbal*, verbal: see *verbal*.] In *French law*, a detailed authenticated account of an official act or proceeding; a statement of facts, especially in a criminal charge; also, the minutes drawn up by the secretary or other officer of the proceedings of an assembly.

prochein, *a.* [F. *prochain*, next, neighboring, < L. *proximus*, near: see *proximate*.] Next; nearest: used in the law phrase *prochein amy* (or *ami*), the next friend, a person who undertakes to assist an infant or minor in prosecuting his or her rights.—**Prochein avoidance**, in *law*, a power to present a minister to a church when it shall become void.

prochilous (prǫ-kī'lus), *a.* [< Gr. πρόχειλος, with prominent lips, < πρό, before, forward, + χεῖλος, lip, snout.] Having protuberant or protrusile lips. *Coues.*

prochlorite (prǫ-klō'rīt), *n.* [< *pro-* + *chlorite*.] In *mineral.*, a kind of chlorite occurring in foliated or granular masses of a green color: it contains less silica and more iron than the allied species clinochlore and ripidolite.

prochoanite (prǫ-kō'ạ-nīt), *a.* and *n.* **I.** *a.* Belonging to the *Prochoanites*.

II. *n.* A cephalopod of the group *Prochoanites*.

Prochoanites (prǫ-kō-ạ-nī'tēz), *n. pl.* [NL., < Gr. πρό, before, + χοάνη, a funnel: see *choana*, *choanite*.] A group of holochoanoid nautiloid cephalopods whose septal funnels are turned forward: contrasted with *Metachoanites*. *Hyatt*, Proc. Bost. Soc. Nat. Hist., 1883, p. 260.

prochondral (prō-kon'drạl), *a.* [< Gr. πρό, before, + χόνδρος, cartilage: see *chondral*.] Prior to the formation of cartilage; about to become cartilage.

prochoös (prō'kǫ-os), *n.*; pl. *prochoöi* (-oi). [< Gr. πρόχοος, πρόχους (see def.), < προχεῖν, pour forth.] In *Gr. antiq.*, a small vase of elegant form, resembling the oinochoë, but in general more slender, and with a handle rising higher above the rim: used especially to pour water on the hands before meals were served.

The holding the *prochus* up high (ἄρδην) is often observed in those who pour out for a libation.
C. O. *Müller*, Manual of Archæol. (trans.), § 298.

Greek Prochoös with black-figured decoration.

prochorion (prǫ-kō'ri-on), *n.*; pl. *prochoria* (-ạ̈). [NL., < L. *pro*, before, + NL. *chorion*, q. v.] The primitive chorion; the outer envelop of an ovum: in man and some other animals specially known as the *zona pellucida*. It is the yolk-sac or vitelline membrane, not entering into the formative changes which go on within it during the germination and maturation of the ovum, but in the course of development becoming the chorion proper, and forming the outermost of the membranes which envelop the fetus.

prochorionic (prǫ-kō-ri-on'ik), *a.* [< *prochorion* + *-ic*.] Of or pertaining to the prochorion.

prochronism (prō'krǫn-izm), *n.* [= Pg. *prochronismo* = Sp. It. *procronismo*; < Gr. πρόχρονος, preceding in time, previous (< πρό, before, + *χρόνος*, time), + *-ism.*] An error in chronology consisting in antedating something; the dating of an event before the time when it happened, or the representing of something as existing before it really did.

The *prochronisms* in these [Towneley] Mysteries are very remarkable. *Archæologia*, XXVII. 252. (*Davies.*)

"Puffed with wonderful skill" he [Lord Macaulay] introduces with the half-apology "to use the modern phrase"; and that though he had put the verb, and without *prochronism*, into the mouth of Osborne, the bookseller knocked down by Dr. Johnson. *F. Hall*, Mod. Eng., p. 130.

procidence (pros'i-dens), *n.* [= F. *procidence* = Sp. Pg. *procidencia* = It. *procidenza*, < L. *procidentia*, a falling down or forward, < *prociden(t-)s*, ppr. of *procidere*, fall forward or prostrate: see *procident.*] A falling down; in *pathol.*, a prolapsus.

procident (pros'i-dent), *a.* [< L. *prociden(t-)s*, ppr. of *procidere*, fall forward or prostrate, < *pro*, forward, + *cadere*, fall: see *cadent.*] Falling or fallen; in *pathol.*, affected by prolapsus.

procidentia (pros-i-den'shi-ä), *n.* [L.: see *procidence.*] In *pathol.*, a falling downward or forward; prolapsus.—**Procidentia iridis**, prolapse of the iris.—**Procidentia recti**, the descent of the upper part of the rectum, in its whole thickness, or all its coats, through the anus.—**Procidentia uteri**, complete prolapsus of the uterus, with inversion of the vagina, and extrusion of the uterus through the vulva.

prociduous (prō-sid'ū-us), *a.* [< L. *prociduus*, fallen down, prostrate, < *procidere*, fall forward or prostrate: see *procidence*. Cf. *deciduous.*] Falling from its proper place. *Imp. Dict.*

procinct (prō-singkt'), *n.* [= Sp. It. *procinto*, < L. *procinctus*, preparation or readiness for battle, < *procinctus*, pp. of *procingere*, gird up, prepare, equip, < *pro*, before, + *cingere*, gird, encircle: see *cincture.*] Preparation or readiness, especially for battle.—**In procinct** or **procincts** [L. *in procinctu*], at hand; ready: a Latinism.

He stood *in procinct*, ready with oil in his lamp, watching till his Lord should call. *Jer. Taylor*, Works (ed. 1835), II. 141.

War he perceived, war *in procinct*. *Milton*, P. L., vi. 19.

proclaim (prō-klām'), *v. t.* [< ME. *proclaymen*, < OF. *proclamer*, F. *proclamer* = Sp. Pg. *proclamar* = It. *proclamare*, < L. *proclamare*, call out, < *pro*, before, + *clamare*, call, cry: see *claim*[1].] 1. To make known by public announcement; promulgate; announce; publish.

The pardon that the legat hadde graunted and *proclaymed* thourgh all cristindom. *Merlin* (E. E. T. S.), iii. 577.

He hath sent me to . . . *proclaim* liberty to the captives. Isa. lxi. 1.

The countenance *proclaims* the heart and inclinations. *Sir T. Browne*, Christ. Mor., ii. 9.

The schoolhouse porch, the heavenward pointing spire,
Proclaim, in letters every eye can read,
Knowledge and Faith, the new world's simple creed.
Holmes, A Family Record.

2. To make announcement concerning; publish; advertise, as by herald or crier: said of persons.

I heard myself *proclaim'd*;
And by the happy hollow of a tree
Escaped the hunt. *Shak.*, Lear, ii. 3. 1.

You should have us'd us nobly,
And, for our doing well, as well *proclaim'd* us,
To the world's eye have shew'd and sainted us.
Fletcher, Loyal Subject, ii. 1.

3. To apply prohibition to by a proclamation.—**Proclaimed district**, any county or other district in Ireland in which the provisions of the Peace Preservation Acts are for the time being in force by virtue of official proclamation.=**Syn. 1.** *Declare, Publish, Announce, Proclaim*, etc. (see *announce*), blaze abroad, trumpet, blazon.

proclaim (prō-klām'), *n.* [= Sp. Pg. It. *proclama*, proclaim; from the verb.] A calling or crying out; proclamation. [Rare.]

Hymns of festival, . . .
Voices of soft *proclaim*, and silver stir
Of strings in hollow shells. *Keats*, Hyperion, i.

proclaimant (prō-klā'mant), *n.* [< *proclaim* + *-ant.*] A proclaimer.

I was spared the pain of being the first *proclaimant* of her flight. *E. Brontë*, Wuthering Heights, xii.

proclaimer (prō-klā'mėr), *n.* One who proclaims or publishes; one who announces or makes publicly known.

proclamation (prok-lā-mā'shon), *n.* [< F. *proclamation* = Sp. *proclamacion* = Pg. *proclamação* = It. *proclamazione*, < LL. *proclamatio(n-)*, a calling or crying out, < L. *proclamare*, pp. *proclamatus*, cry out: see *proclaim.*] 1. The act of proclaiming, or making publicly known; publication; official or general notice given to the public.

King Asa made a *proclamation* throughout all Judah. 1 Ki. xv. 22.

2. That which is put forth by way of public notice; an official public announcement or declaration; a published ordinance.

The Prince and his Lordship of Rochester passed many hours of this day composing *Proclamations* and Addresses to the Country, to the Scots, . . . to the People of London and England. *Thackeray*, Henry Esmond, iii. 11.

The deacon began to say to the minister, of a Sunday, "I suppose it 's about time for the Thanksgiving *proclamation*." H. B. *Stowe*, Oldtown, p. 337.

3. Open declaration; manifestation; putting in evidence, whether favorably or unfavorably.

Upon that day that the gentleman doth begin to hourde vp money, from thence forth he putteth his fame [reputation] in *proclamation*. *Guevara*, Letters (tr. by Hellowes, 1577), p. 153.

You love my son; invention is ashamed,
Against the *proclamation* of thy passion,
To say thou dost not. *Shak.*, All's Well, i. 3. 180.

4. In *law*: (*a*) A writ once issued to warn a defendant in outlawry, or one failing to appear in chancery. (*b*) In modern public law, usually, if not always, an executive act in writing and duly authenticated, promulgating a command or prohibition which the executive has discretionary power to issue, or a notification of the executive intent in reference to the execution of the laws. In early English history positive laws were to some extent made by proclamation, which were usually allowed the force of statutes. The opinion of some that a proclamation usually ceased to operate on a demise of the crown does not seem to be well founded.—**Case of proclamations**, a noted case in English constitutional history, decided in 1610 (2 How. St. Tr., 723, and 12 Coke, 74), upon questions submitted by the lord chancellor and others, wherein it was held "that the king by his proclamation cannot create any offense which was not an offense before"; "that the king hath no prerogative but that which the law of the land allows him"; and that, "if the offense be not punishable in the star-chamber, the prohibition of it by proclamation cannot make it punishable there."—**Emancipation proclamation.** See *emancipation*.—**Fine with proclamations.** See *fine*[1].—**Proclamation Act**, an English statute of 1539 (31 Hen. VIII., c. 8), enacting that proclamations made by the king and council which did not prejudice estates, offices, liberties, etc., should be obeyed as if made by act of Parliament, and providing for the prosecution and punishment of those who refused to observe such proclamations.—**Proclamation of a fine**, at *common law*, the public notice repeatedly to be given of a fine of lands.—**Proclamation of neutrality.** See *neutrality*.

proclamator (prok'lā-mā-tor), *n.* [= F. *proclamateur* = Pg. *proclamador* = It. *proclamatore*, < L. *proclamator*, a crier, < *proclamatus*, pp. of *proclamare*, cry out: see *proclaim.*] In *Eng. law*, an officer of the Court of Common Pleas.

procline (prō-klīn'), *v. i.*; pret. and pp. *proclined*, ppr. *proclining*. [< L. *proclinare*, lean forward, < *pro*, forward, + *clinare*, lean: see *cline.*] To lean forward.

Inclining dials . . . were further distinguished as . . . *proclining* when leaning forwards. *Encyc. Brit.*, VII. 155.

proclitic (prō-klit'ik), *a.* and *n.* [= F. *proclitique*, < NL. *procliticus*, < Gr. *προκλίνειν*, lean forward, < *πρό*, forward, + *κλίνειν*, lean, bend: see *cline*. Cf. *enclitic.*] I. *a.* In *Gr. gram.*, dependent in accent upon the following word: noting certain monosyllabic words so closely attached to the word following as to have no accent.

II. *n.* In *Gr. gram.*, a monosyllabic word which leans upon or is so closely attached to a following word as to have no independent accent. The proclitics are certain forms of the article, certain prepositions and conjunctions, and the negative *οὐ*. Compare *atonic*.

proclive† (prō-klīv'), *a.* [< OF. *proclif*, m., *proclive*, f., = Sp. It. *proclive*, < L. *proclivis*, *proclivus*, sloping downward, < *pro*, forward, + *clivus*, a declivity or slope: see *clivus*, *clivous.*] Inclined; prone; disposed; proclivous.

A woman is fraile, and *proclive* unto all evils. *Latimer*, 1st Sermon bef. Edw. VI.

The world knows a foolish fellow somewhat *proclive* and hasty. B. *Jonson*, Case is Altered, i. 2.

proclive (prō-klīv'), *v.*; pret. and pp. *proclived*, ppr. *procliving*. [< *proclive*, *a.*] I. *trans.* To incline; make prone or disposed.

That guilt *proclives* us to any impiety. *Rev. T. Adams*, Works, III. 190.

II. *intrans.* To be prone. *Halliwell.*

proclivity (prō-kliv'i-ti), *n.* [< F. *proclivité* = Sp. *proclividad* = It. *proclività*, < L. *proclivita(t-)s*, a declivity, a propensity, < *proclivus*, sloping, disposed to: see *proclive.*] 1. Inclination; propensity; proneness; tendency.

And still retain'd a natural *proclivity* to ruin. *Fletcher*, Purple Island, i.

Mr. Adams' *proclivity* to grumble appears early. *T. Parker*, Historic Americans, John Adams, i.

When we pass from vegetal organisms to unconscious animal organisms, we see a like connexion between *proclivity* and advantage. *H. Spencer*, Data of Ethics, § 32.

2. Readiness; facility of learning.

He had such a dexterous *proclivity* that his teachers were fain to restrain his forwardness. *Sir H. Wotton.*

"Ventilate" and "*proclivity*," after having been half-forgotten, have come again into brisk circulation; and a comparison of the literature of the seventeenth, eighteenth, and nineteenth centuries will show multitudes of words common to the first and last of these periods, but which were little used in the second. *G. P. Marsh*, Lects. on Eng. Lang., xii., note.

=**Syn. 1.** Bent, bias, predisposition, aptitude, turn (for).

proclivous (prō-klī'vus), *a.* [< L. *proclivis*, *proclivus*, sloping downward: see *proclive.*] Inclined; slanting or inclined forward and upward or downward: as, *proclivous* teeth.

proclivousness (prō-klī'vus-nes), *n.* Inclination downward; propensity. *Bailey*, 1727.

Procne (prok'nē), *n.* Same as *Progne*.

Procnias (prok'ni-as), *n.* [NL. (Illiger, 1811), < L. *Procne*, *Progne*, < Gr. *Πρόκνη*, in myth., daughter of Pandion, transformed into a swallow. Cf. *Progne.*] A notable genus of tanagers,

Procnias tersa.

type of the subfamily *Procniatinæ*. *P. tersa*, the only species, inhabits the Neotropical region. Also called *Tersa* and *Tersina*.

Procniatinæ (prok″ni-a-tī'nē), *n. pl.* [NL. (P. L. Sclater), < *Procnias* (*Procniat-*) + *-inæ.*] A subfamily of oscine passerine birds of the family *Tanagridæ*, representing an aberrant form with a short fissirostral bill, notched upper mandible, long wings, and moderate emarginate tail, typified by the genus *Procnias*: formerly referred to the *Cotingidæ*.

procœlia[1] (prō-sē'li-ä), *n.*; pl. *procœliæ* (-ē). [NL. (Wilder), < Gr. *πρό*, before, + *κοιλία*, a hollow: see *cœlia.*] A prosencephalic ventricle; either lateral ventricle of the brain.

Procœlia[2] (prō-sē'li-ä), *n. pl.* [NL., < Gr. *πρό*, before, + *κοῖλος*, hollow.] A suborder of Crocodilia; crocodiles with procœlous vertebræ, as distinguished from *Amphicœlia*. All the living crocodiles, alligators, and gavials, and extinct ones down to the Chalk, are *Procœlia*. Also called *Eucrocodilia*.

procœlian (prō-sē'li-an), *a.* and *n.* [As *procœl-ous*, *procœlia*[1], + *-an.*] I. *a.* 1. Hollowed or cupped in front, as the centrum or body of a vertebra: correlated with *amphicœlian*, *opisthocœlian*, and *heterocœlian*.—2. Having procœlian vertebræ, as a crocodile; belonging to the *Procœlia*.—3. Hollowed by a ventricle, as the prosencephalon; of or pertaining to the procœliæ of the brain.

II. *n.* A member of the suborder *Procœlia*.

procœlous (prō-sē'lus), *a.* [< Gr. *πρό*, before, + *κοῖλος*, hollow (cf. *procœlia*[1]).] Same as *procœlian*. *Huxley*, Lay Sermons, p. 224.

pro confesso (prō kon-fes'ō). [L.: *pro*, for, in place of; *confesso*, abl. sing. neut. of *confessus*, pp. of *confiteri*, confess: see *confess.*] In *law*, held as confessed or admitted. For example, if a defendant in chancery did not file an answer, the matter contained in the bill was taken *pro confesso*—that is, as though it had been confessed.

proconsul (prō-kon'sul), *n.* [= F. Sp. Pg. *proconsul* = It. *proconsole*, < L. *proconsul*, a proconsul, orig. as two words, *pro consule*, one who acts in place of a consul: *pro*, for, in place of; *consule*, abl. of *consul*, a consul: see *consul.*] In ancient Rome, an officer who discharged the duties and had, outside of Rome itself, most of the authority of a consul, without holding the office of consul. The proconsuls were almost invariably persons who had been consuls, so that the proconsulship was a continuation, in a modified form, of the consulship. They were appointed to conduct a war in or to administer the affairs of some province. The duration of the office was one year.

> Prætors, *proconsuls* to their provinces
> Hasting, or on return, in robes of state.
> *Milton*, P. R., iv. 63.

proconsular (prọ̄-kon′ṣū-lạ̈r), *a.* [= F. *proconsulaire* = Sp. Pg. *proconsular* = It. *proconsolare*, < L. *proconsularis*, pertaining to a proconsul, < *proconsul*, a proconsul: see *proconsul*.] 1. Of or pertaining to a proconsul or his position or authority: as, *proconsular* rule.

> Beyond the capital the *proconsular* power was vested in him [Augustus] without local limitations.
> *W. W. Capes*, The Early Empire, i.

> The *proconsular* status of Achaia under Gallio.
> *Schaff*, Hist. Christ. Church, I. § 85.

2. Under the government of a proconsul: as, a *proconsular* province.

proconsulary (prọ̄-kon′ṣū-lạ̄-ri), *a.* [< L. *proconsularis*, proconsular: see *proconsular*.] Proconsular.

> *Proconsularie* authority, election to be consull, and other steps to mount to the empire were procured.
> *Greneway*, tr. Tacitus's Annales, xiii. 5.

proconsulate (prọ̄-kon′ṣū-lạ̄t), *n.* [= F. *proconsulat* = Sp. Pg. *proconsulado* = It. *proconsulato*, < L. *proconsulatus*, the office of a proconsul, < *proconsul*, a proconsul: see *proconsul*.] The office of a proconsul, or the term of his office.

proconsulship (prọ̄-kon′sul-ship), *n.* [< *proconsul* + *-ship*.] Same as *proconsulate*.

> R. fixes on 158 A. D. as the date of the *proconsulship* of Claudius Maximus. *Amer. Jour. Philol.*, X. 106.

procrastinate (prọ̄-kras′ti-nāt), *v.*; pret. and pp. *procrastinated*, ppr. *procrastinating*. [< L. *procrastinatus*, pp. of *procrastinare*, put off till the morrow, < *pro*, for, + *crastinus*, pertaining to the morrow, < *cras*, to-morrow. Cf. *crastination*, *procrastine*.] I. *trans.* To put off till another day, or from day to day; delay; defer to a future time.

> Hopeless and helpless doth Ægeon wend,
> But to *procrastinate* his lifeless end.
> *Shak.*, C. of E., i. 1. 159.

> Gonsalvo still *procrastinated* his return on various pretexts. *Prescott*, Ferd. and Isa., ii. 19.

=**Syn.** To postpone, adjourn, defer, retard, protract, prolong.

II. *intrans.* To delay; be dilatory.

> I *procrastinate* more than I did twenty years ago.
> *Swift*, To Pope.

procrastination (prọ̄-kras-ti-nā′shọn), *n.* [< OF. *procrastination* = Pg. *procrastinação* = It. *procrastinazione*, < L. *procrastinatio(n-)*, a putting off till the morrow, < *procrastinatus*, pp. of *procrastinare*, put off till the morrow: see *procrastinate*.] The act or habit of procrastinating; a putting off to a future time; delay; dilatoriness.

> *Procrastination* in temporals is always dangerous, but in spirituals it is often damnable. *South*, Sermons, XI. x.

> *Procrastination* is the thief of time.
> *Young*, Night Thoughts, i. 393.

procrastinative (prọ̄-kras′ti-nạ̄-tiv), *a.* [< *procrastinate* + *-ive*.] Given to procrastination; dilatory.

> I was too *procrastinative* and inert while you were still in my neighborhood. *The Critic*, XI. 140.

procrastinator (prọ̄-kras′ti-nā-tọr), *n.* [= Pg. *procrastinador* = It. *procrastinatore*; as *procrastinate* + *-or*[1].] One who procrastinates, or defers the performance of anything to a future time.

procrastinatory (prọ̄-kras′ti-nạ̄-tọ̄-ri), *a.* [< *procrastinate* + *-ory*.] Pertaining to or implying procrastination. *Imp. Dict.*

procrastine† (prọ̄-kras′tin), *v. t.* [< OF. *procrastiner* = Pg. *procrastinar* = It. *procrastinare*, < L. *procrastinare*, put off till the morrow: see *procrastinate*.] To procrastinate.

> Thinkyng that if that pardon were any lenger space *procrastened* or prolonged that in the meane ceason, etc.
> Hall, Hen. VII., an. 1.

procreant (prō′krẹ̄-ạnt), *a.* and *n.* [= Sp. It. *procreante*, < L. *procrean(t-)s*, ppr. of *procreare*, bring forth, beget: see *procreate*.] I. *a.* Procreating; producing young; related to or connected with reproduction.

> No jutty, frieze,
> Buttress, nor coign of vantage, but this bird [the martlet]
> Hath made his pendent bed and *procreant* cradle.
> *Shak.*, Macbeth, i. 6. 8.

> But the loss of liberty is not the whole of what the *procreant* bird suffers. *Paley*, Nat. Theol., xviii.

> Her *procreant* vigils Nature keeps
> Amid the unfathomable deeps.
> *Wordsworth*, Vernal Ode.

Procreant cause. See *conservant*.

II. *n.* One who or that which procreates or generates.

> Those imperfect and putrid creatures that receive a crawling life from two most unlike *procreants*, the Sun and mudde. *Milton*, On Def. of Humb. Remonst.

procreate (prō′krẹ̄-āt), *v. t.*; pret. and pp. *procreated*, ppr. *procreating*. [< L. *procreatus*, pp. of *procreare* (> It. *procreare* = Sp. Pg. *procrear* = F. *procréer*), bring forth, beget, < *pro*, before, + *creare*, produce, create: see *create*.] To beget; generate; engender; produce: as, to *procreate* children.

> He was lineally descended, and naturally *procreated*, of the noble stocke and familie of Lancaster.
> Hall, Edw. IV., an. 9.

> Since the earth retains her fruitful power
> To *procreate* plants, the forest to restore.
> *Sir R. Blackmore.*

procreation (prō-krẹ̄-ā′shọn), *n.* [< OF. *procreation*, F. *procréation* = Sp. *procreacion* = Pg. *procreação* = It. *procreazione*, < L. *procreatio(n-)*, generation, < *procreare*, pp. *procreatus*, bring forth, beget: see *procreate*.] The act of procreating or begetting; generation and production of young.

> 'Tis onlie incident
> To man to cause the bodies *procreation*;
> The soule 's infusde by heavenly operation.
> *Times' Whistle* (E. E. T. S.), p. 7.

> Uncleanness is an unlawful gratification of the appetite of *procreation*. *South.*

procreative (prō′krẹ̄-ạ̄-tiv), *a.* [< *procreate* + *-ive*.] Having the power or function of procreating; reproductive; generative; having the power to beget.

> The ordinary period of the human *procreative* faculty in males is sixty-five, in females forty-five. *Sir M. Hale.*

procreativeness (prō′krẹ̄-ạ̄-tiv-nes), *n.* [< *procreative* + *-ness*.] The state or quality of being procreative; the power of generating.

> These have the accurst privilege of propagating and not expiring, and have reconciled the *procreativeness* of corporeal with the duration of incorporeal substances.
> *Decay of Christian Piety.*

procreator (prō′krẹ̄-ā-tọr), *n.* [< OF. *procreateur*, F. *procréateur* = Sp. Pg. *procreador* = It. *procreatore*, < L. *procreator*, a begetter, a producer, < *procreare*, pp. *procreatus*, bring forth, generate: see *procreate*.] One who begets; a generator; a father or sire.

> He is vnkynd and vnnaturall that wil not cherishe hys natural parentes and *procreators*. *Hall*, Edw. IV., an. 8.

procreatrix (prō′krẹ̄-ā-triks), *n.* [= F. *procréatrice*, < L. *procreatrix*, fem. of *procreator*, procreator: see *procreator*.] A mother. *Cotgrave.*

Procris (prok′ris), *n.* [NL. (Fabricius, 1808), < L. *Procris*, < Gr. Πρόκρις, a daughter of Erechtheus.] In *entom.*: (*a*) A genus of zygænid moths, having the fore wings blue, the hind brown, antennæ sublinear, in the male bipectinate, palpi slender, wings maculate, and larvæ ovate, contracted, delicately pilose. It is wide spread, of 20 or 30 species, represented in Europe, Africa, Australia, and both Americas. *P. americana* is very destructive to the grape in the United States, its larvæ feeding gregariously on the under side of the leaves, and often entirely defoliating the vine. There are two annual generations, and the pupæ hibernate in tough oblong oval cocoons spun in some sheltered spot or crevice. The best remedy is underspraying with Paris green. *P. statice* is known as the *forester-moth*. (*b*) A genus of butterflies. *Herrich-Schäffer*, 1864.

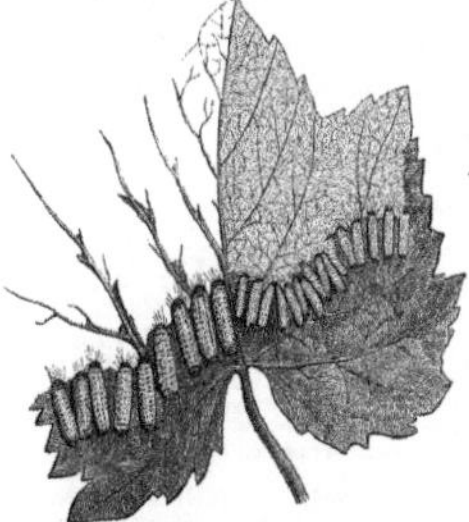

Larvæ of *Procris americana* feeding on grape-leaf.

Procrustean (prọ̄-krus′tẹ̄-ạn), *a.* [< L. *Procrustes*, < Gr. Προκρούστης, Procrustes (see def.).] 1. Of, pertaining to, or resembling Procrustes, a robber of ancient Greece, who, according to the tradition, tortured his victims by placing them on a certain bed, and stretching them or lopping off their legs to adapt the body to its length; resembling this mode of torture. Hence —2. Reducing by violence to strict conformity to a measure or model; producing uniformity by deforming or injurious force or by mutilation.

> When a story or argument undergoes contortion or mutilation, it is said to go through a *procrustean* process.
> *Sir J. Davies.*

> He stretches his favorite characters on a *Procrustean* bed, while he subordinates his plot and his episodes to conflicting calculations. *Fortnightly Rev.*, N. S., XL. 30.

procrusteanize (prọ̄-krus′tẹ̄-ạn-īz), *v. t.*; pret. and pp. *procrusteanized*, ppr. *procrusteanizing*. [< *Procrustean* + *-ize*.] To stretch or contract to a given or required extent or size.

Procrustesian (prō-krus-tē′si-ạn), *a.* [Irreg. < *Procrustes* (see *Procrustean*) + *-ian*.] Same as *Procrustean*. *Quarterly Rev.* (*Imp. Dict.*)

Proctacanthus (prok-ta-kan′thus), *n.* [NL. (Macquart, 1838), < Gr. πρωκτός, the anus, + ἄκανθα, a thorn.] A genus of dipterous insects of the family *Asilidæ*. They are among those known as *robber-flies* and *hawk-flies*. *P. milberti* is the Missouri bee-killer. See cut under *hawk-fly*.

proctagra (prok-tag′rạ̈), *n.* [NL., < Gr. πρωκτός, the anus, + ἄγρα, a taking; cf. *podagra*.] Same as *proctalgia*.

proctalgia (prok-tal′ji-ạ̈), *n.* [NL., < Gr. πρωκτός, the anus, + ἄλγος, pain.] Pain of the anus or rectum.

proctatresia (prok-ta-trē′si-ạ̈), *n.* [NL., < Gr. πρωκτός, the anus, + ἄτρητος, not perforated: see *atresia*.] The condition of having an imperforate anus.

procter†, *n.* An obsolete form of *proctor*.

proctitis (prok-tī′tis), *n.* [NL., < Gr. πρωκτός, the anus, + *-itis*.] Inflammation of the rectum or anus.

proctocele (prok′tọ̄-sēl), *n.* [< Gr. πρωκτός, the anus, + κήλη, a tumor.] In *pathol.*, inversion and prolapse of the rectum, from relaxation of the sphincter.

proctocystotomy (prok″tọ̄-sis-tot′ọ̄-mi), *n.* [< Gr. πρωκτός, the anus, + E. *cystotomy*.] Cystotomy performed through the rectum.

proctodæum (prok-tọ̄-dē′um), *n.*; pl. *proctodæa* (-ạ̈). [NL., < Gr. πρωκτός, the anus, + ὁδαῖος, by the way, < ὁδός, way.] A posterior section of the alimentary canal or digestive tract, being so much of the whole intestine or enteric tube as is formed at the aboral end by an ingrowth of the ectoderm: correlated with *stomodæum*, which is derived from the ectoderm at the oral end—both being distinguished from *enteron* proper, which is of endodermal origin. Also *proctodeum*.

> The anal opening forms at a late period by a very short ingrowth or *proctodæum*, coinciding with the blind termination of the rectal peduncle. *Encyc. Brit.*, XVI. 682.

proctodeal (prok-tọ̄-dē′ạl), *a.* [< *proctodæ-um* + *-al*.] Pertaining to the proctodæum.

> The terminal section of the intestine is formed by the *proctodæal* invagination. *Encyc. Brit.*, XXIV. 680.

proctodeum, *n.* See *proctodæum*.

proctodynia (prok-tọ̄-din′i-ạ̈), *n.* [NL., < Gr. πρωκτός, the anus, + ὀδύνη, pain.] Proctalgia.

Proctonotidæ (prok-tọ̄-not′i-dē), *n. pl.* [NL., < *Proctonotus* + *-idæ*.] A family of polybranchiate nudibranchiates, typified by the genus *Proctonotus*. They have a distinct mantle, non-retractile rhinophoria, and dorsal papillæ without cnidophorous pouches around the mantle and passing forward under the head. The jaws are corneous, and the teeth of the radula are multiserial.

Proctonotus (prok-tọ̄-nō′tus), *n.* [NL., < Gr. πρωκτός, the anus, + νῶτος, back.] A genus of nudibranchiates, typical of the family *Proctonotidæ*. The species occur in the European seas.

Proctonotus mucroniferus. (Line shows natural size.)

proctoparalysis (prok″tọ̄-pa-ral′i-sis), *n.* [NL., < Gr. πρωκτός, the anus, + παράλυσις, paralysis: see *paralysis*.] Paralysis of the sphincter ani.

proctoptoma (prok-top-tō′mạ̈), *n.* [NL., < Gr. πρωκτός, the anus, + πτῶμα, fall, < πίπτειν, fall.] Prolapse of the rectum.

proctor (prok'tor), *n.* [Early mod. E. also *procter, proctour;* < ME. *prokture, proketour, proketowre,* abbr. of OF. *procurator,* < L. *procurator,* a manager, agent: see *procurator.* Cf. *proxy,* contr. of *procuracy.*] 1. One who is employed to manage the affairs of another; a procurator.

Where the sayde mariage was by writinges and instrumentes couenaunted, condiscended, and agreed, and affiances made and taken by *procters* and deputies on bothe parties. *Hall,* Rich. III., an. 3.

The most clamorous for this pretended reformation are either atheists or else *proctors* suborned by atheists. *Hooker.*

2. Specifically, a person employed to manage another's cause in a court of civil or ecclesiastical law, as in the court of admiralty or a spiritual court. Proctors discharged duties similar to those of solicitors and attorneys in other courts. The term is also used in some American courts for practitioners performing functions in admiralty and in probate corresponding to those of attorneys at law.

"What is a *proctor,* Steerforth?" said I. "Why, he is a sort of monkish attorney," replied Steerforth. "He is to some faded courts held in Doctors' Commons — a lazy old nook near St. Paul's Churchyard — what solicitors are to the courts of law and equity." *Dickens,* David Copperfield, xxiii.

During the whole of Stafford's primacy the pope filled up the sees by provision, the council nominated their candidates; at Rome the *proctors* of the parties contrived a compromise. *Stubbs,* Const. Hist., § 386.

3. One of the representatives of the clergy in the Convocations of the two provinces of Canterbury and York in the Church of England. They are elected by the cathedral chapters and the clergy of a diocese or an archdeaconry.

The clerical *proctors* . . . were originally summoned to complete the representation of the spiritual estate, with an especial view to the taxation of spiritual property; and in that summons they had standing-ground from which they might have secured a permanent position in the legislature. By adhering to their ecclesiastical organisation in the convocations they lost their opportunity, and, almost as soon as it was offered them, forfeited their chance of becoming an active part of parliament. *Stubbs,* Const. Hist., § 432.

4. An official in a university or college whose function it is to see that good order is kept. In the universities of Oxford and Cambridge the proctors are two officers chosen from among the masters of arts.

It is the *Proctors'* duty to look after the business of the University, to be assessors of the Chancellor or Vice-Chancellor in the causes heard in the University, to count the votes in the Houses of Convocation and Congregation, . . . and to exact fines and other penalties for breaches of University discipline among Undergraduates. *Dickens,* Dict. Oxford, p. 95.

We, unworthier, told
Of college: he had climb'd across the spikes, . . .
And he had breath'd the *Proctor's* dogs.
Tennyson, Princess, Prol.

5. A keeper of a spital-house; a liar. *Harman,* Caveat for Cursetors, p. 115.—6†. One who collected alms for lepers or others unable to beg in person. [Cant.]

According to Kennett, beggars of any kind were called *proctors.* The Fraternitye of Vacabondes, 1575, has the following notice:—"*Proctour* is he that wil tary long, and bring a lye, when his maister sendeth him on his errand." *Halliwell.*

Proctors' dogs, proctors' men, proctors' servants. Same as *bulldog,* 3.

proctor (prok'tor), *v. t.* [< *proctor, n.*] 1. To manage as an attorney or pleader.

I cannot *proctor* my own cause so well
To make it clear.
Warburton, On Shakespeare's Antony and Cleopatra. [(*Latham.*)

2†. To hector; swagger; bully. *Forby,* quoted in Halliwell.

proctorage (prok'tor-āj), *n.* [< *proctor* + *-age.*] Management by a proctor or other agent; hence, management or superintendence in general.

As for the fogging *proctorage* of money, with such an eye as strooke Gehezi with Leprosy, and Simon Magus with a curse, so does she [excommunication] looke. *Milton,* Reformation in Eng., ii.

proctorial (prok-tō'ri-al), *a.* [< *proctor* + *-i-al.*] Relating or pertaining to a proctor, especially a university proctor. [Rare.]

proctorical (prok-tor'i-kal), *a.* [< *proctor* + *-ic-al.*] Proctorial.

Every tutor, for the better discharging of his duty, shall have *proctorical* authority over his pupils. *Prideaux,* Life, p. 231.

proctorize (prok'tor-īz), *v. t.*; pret. and pp. *proctorized,* ppr. *proctorizing.* [< *proctor* + *-ize.*] To summon before a proctor, as for reprimand. [Eng. university slang.]

One don't like to go in while there's any chance of a real row, as you call it, and so gets *proctorized* in one's old age for one's patriotism. *T. Hughes,* Tom Brown at Oxford, I. xii.

proctorrhagia (prok-tō-rā'ji-ä), *n.* [NL., < Gr. πρωκτός, the anus, + -ραγία, < ῥηγνύναι, break, burst.] Hemorrhage from the anus.

proctorrhea, proctorrhœa (prok-tō-rē'ä), *n.* [NL. *proctorrhœa,* < Gr. πρωκτός, the anus, + ῥοία, a flowing, < ῥεῖν, flow.] A morbid discharge from the anus.

proctorship (prok'tor-ship), *n.* [< *proctor* + *-ship.*] The office of a proctor; management or procuratorship; specifically, the position of the proctor of a university.

The *proctorship* for science, justly assumed for matters within his province as a student, is rather hastily extended to matters which he himself declares to be beyond it. *Pop. Sci. Mo.,* XXVIII. 615.

proctotomy (prok-tot'ō-mi), *n.* [< Gr. πρωκτός, the anus, + -τομία, < τέμνειν, ταμεῖν, cut.] In *surg.,* a cutting of the rectum, as in the division of a stricture or for the cure of a fistula.

proctotrete (prok'tō-trēt), *n.* A lizard of the genus *Proctotretus.*

Proctotretus (prok-tō-trē'tus), *n.* [NL., < Gr. πρωκτός, the anus, + τρητός, perforated.] A genus of South American iguanoid lizards, as *P. multimaculatus,* of southern South America.

Proctotrupes, etc. See *Proctotrypes,* etc.

Proctotrypes (prok-tō-trī'pēz), *n.* [NL. (Latreille, 1796, in the form *Proctotrupes*), < Gr. πρωκτός, the anus, + τρυπᾶν, bore, pierce through.] The typical genus of *Proctotrypidæ.* They are small black insects, often with reddish abdomen, having edentate mandibles and single-spurred fore tibiæ. About 50 species of this wide-spread genus have been described. They are mainly parasitic upon the larvæ of dipterous insects which infest fungi.

Proctotrypidæ (prok-tō-trip'i-dē), *n. pl.* [NL. (Stephens, 1829, in the form *Proctotrupidæ*), < *Proctotrypes* + *-idæ.*] A notable family of parasitic entomophagous hymenopterous insects, typified by the genus *Proctotrypes,* of minute size and usually somber colors, having the hind margin of the prothorax reaching the tegulæ, and the ovipositor issuing from the tip of the abdomen. The group is very large and of universal distribution. Over 800 species of 120 genera are known in Europe alone. The 11 subfamilies are *Dryininæ, Emboliminæ, Bethylinæ, Ceraphroninæ, Proctotrypinæ, Scelioninæ, Platygasterinæ, Mymarinæ, Diapriinæ, Belytinæ,* and *Helorinæ.* See cut under *Platygaster.*

Proctucha (prok-tū'kä), *n. pl.* [NL., neut. pl. of *proctuchus:* see *proctuchous.*] One of two divisions of the *Turbellaria* (the other being *Aprocta*), in which there is an anal aperture of the alimentary cavity. They are the rhynchocœlous turbellarians or nemertean worms; some of them differ little from the aproctous rhabdocœlous turbellarians, save in having an anus; but there is generally a frontal proboscis without a buccal proboscis, eyes and ciliated fossæ on the head, and sexual distinctness. See also cuts under *Rhynchocœla* and *Pilidium.*

A Proctuchous Turbellarian (*Tetrastemma*).

a, a, central nervous ganglia; *b, b,* ciliated fossæ; *c,* orifice for protrusion of the frontal proboscis; *d,* anterior part of the proboscis; *e,* posterior muscular part of same, fixed to the parietes at *f*; *g,* intestine; *h,* anus; *i,* water-vessels; *k,* rhythmically contractile vessels.

proctuchous (prok-tū'kus), *a.* [< NL. *proctuchus,* < Gr. πρωκτός, the anus, + ἔχειν, have.] Having an anus: said of the *Proctucha,* in distinction from the *Aprocta.*

procumbent (prō-kum'bent), *a.* [< L. *procumben(t-)s,* ppr. of *procumbere,* fall forward or prostrate, < *pro,* forward, + **cumbere, cubare,* lie: see *cumbent.*] 1. Lying down or on the face; prone.

Procumbent each obeyed. *Cowper.* (*Imp. Dict.*)

2. In *bot.,* trailing; prostrate; unable to support itself, and therefore lying on the ground, but without putting forth roots: as, a *procumbent* stem.

procurable (prō-kūr'a-bl), *a.* [< *procure* + *-able.*] That may be procured; obtainable: as, an article readily *procurable.*

It [syrup of violets] is a far more common and *procurable* liquor. *Boyle,* Works, I. 744.

procuracy (prok'ū-rā-si), *n.* [< ME. *procuracie,* < OF. **procuracie,* < ML. *procuratia, procuracia,* a caring for, charge: see *procuration.* Cf. *proxy,* contr. of *procuracy.*] 1. The office or service of a procurator; the management of an affair for another.—2†. A proxy or procuration.

The seyd priour hath sent also to yow, and to Mayster William Swan, whiche longe hathe be his procurator, a *procuracie* for my person, and v. marcz of moneye onward. *Paston Letters,* I. 21.

The legat assembled a synod of the clergie at London, vpon the last of Julie, in the which he demanded *procuracies.* *Holinshed,* Hen. III., an. 1239.

procuration (prok-ū-rā'shon), *n.* [< ME. *procuracioun,* < OF. (and F.) *procuration* = Pr. *procuration* = Sp. *procuracion* = Pg. *procuração* = It. *procurazione,* < L. *procuratio(n-)* (ML. also *procuratia*), a caring for, charge, administration, procuration, < *procurare,* pp. *procuratus,* take care of, manage, administer: see *procure.*] 1†. Care; management.

Eke plauntes have this *procuracioun*
Unto thaire greet multiplicacion;
That first is doone the seede with moold & dounge
In skeppes [baskets] under lande to rere up yonge.
Palladius, Husbondrie (E. E. T. S.), p. 214.

2. The management of another's affairs; the being intrusted with such management.

I take not upon me either their *procuration* or their patronage. *Bp. Hall,* Remains, p. 370. (*Latham.*)

It were well to be wished that persons of eminence would cease to make themselves representatives of the people of England without a letter of attorney, or any other act of *procuration.* *Burke,* A Regicide Peace, iii.

3. A document by which a person is empowered to transact the affairs of another. See *mandate,* 4 (*b*).—4. *Eccles.*: (*a*) Formerly, provision of the necessary expenses for visitation, due from a church, monastery, or incumbent, etc., to the bishop or archdeacon upon his visitation. (*b*) In modern usage, the sum of money paid to a bishop or archdeacon as a commutation for the above provision.—**Procuration-fee, or procuration-money,** a sum of money taken by scriveners on effecting loans of money.

procurator (prok'ū-rā-tor), *n.* [Early mod. E. *procuratour,* < ME. *procurator, procuratour, prokeratour,* < OF. *procurator,* F. *procurateur* = Sp. Pg. *procurador* = It. *procuratore,* < L. *procurator,* a manager, agent, administrator, deputy, steward, bailiff, < *procurare,* pp. *procuratus,* take care of, manage: see *procure.* Cf. *proctor,* contr. of *procurator.*] 1. The manager of another's affairs; one who acts for or instead of another, and under his authority; especially, one who undertakes the care of any legal proceedings for another, and stands in his place; a proctor; an agent; in Scotland, one who represents a party in the inferior courts.

May I not axe a libel, sire somonour,
And answere ther by my *procuratour*
To swich thyng as men wole apposen me?
Chaucer, Friar's Tale, l. 298.

The speaker of the commons, . . . in addition to the general superintendence of business and his authority as *procurator* and prolocutor of the house, had also to maintain order. *Stubbs,* Const. Hist., § 435.

2. In *Rom. hist.,* a financial agent or manager in an imperial province, corresponding to the questor in a senatorial province; also, an administrator of the imperial fiscus, or treasury, or one of certain other personal agents or representatives of the emperor.

Pilate, . . . the fifth Roman *procurator* . . . of Judæa, Samaria, and Idumæa. *Encyc. Brit.,* XIX. 89.

Procurator fiscal, in Scotland, a public prosecutor.

The public prosecutor for counties is the *procurator-fiscal,* who takes the initiative in cases of suspected death. *Encyc. Brit.,* XXI. 535.

procuratorial (prok"ū-rā-tō'ri-al), *a.* [< *procurator* + *-i-al.*] Of or pertaining to a procurator or proctor; made or done by a proctor.

All *procuratorial* exceptions ought to be made before contestation of suit, and not afterwards, as being dilatory exceptions, if a proctor was then made and constituted. *Ayliffe,* Parergon.

Procuratorial cycle, in English universities, a fixed rotation in which proctors are selected from certain colleges and halls.

In the old *procuratorial cycle,* in the University Statutes, it [Queen's College] is styled "Collegium Reginense." *N. and Q.,* 7th ser., III. 392.

procuratorship (prok'ū-rā-tor-ship), *n.* [< *procurator* + *-ship.*] The office of a procurator.

The office which Pilate bore was the *procuratorship* of Judæa. *Bp. Pearson,* Expos. of Creed, iv.

procuratory (prok'ū-rā-tō-ri), *a.* and *n.* [< LL. *procuratorius,* pertaining to a manager or agent, < L. *procurator,* a manager: see *procurator.*] I. *a.* Pertaining to procuration.

II. *n.* The instrument by which any person constitutes or appoints his procurator to represent him in any court or cause.

procure (prō-kūr'), *v.*; pret. and pp. *procured,* ppr. *procuring.* [< ME. *procuren,* < OF. *procurer,* F. *procurer* = Sp. Pg. *procurar* = It. *procurare,* < L. *procurare,* take care of, care for, look after, manage, administer, be a procurator, also make expiation, < *pro,* for, before, + *curare,* care for, look after, < *cura,* care: see *cure.*] I. *trans.* 1†. To care for; give attention to; look after.

By all means it is to be *procured* . . . that the natural subjects of the crown or state bear a sufficient proportion to the strange subjects.
Bacon, True Greatness of Kingdoms.

2. To bring about by care and pains; effect; contrive and effect; induce; cause: as, he *procured* a law to be passed.

The traytor Antenor hade truly no cause
Ffor to *procur* his payne, and his pale harme.
Destruction of Troy (E. E. T. S.), l. 11614.

By all means possible they *procure* to have gold and silver among them in reproach and infamy.
Sir T. More, Utopia (tr. by Robinson), ii. 6.

Proceed, Solinus, to *procure* my fall.
Shak., C. of E., i. 1. 1.

No sought relief
By all our studies can *procure* his peace.
B. *Jonson*, Sad Shepherd, i. 2.

I *procured*
That rumour to be spread.
Shirley, Grateful Servant, i. 2.

Subornation of perjury is the offence of *procuring* another to take such a false oath as constitutes perjury in the principal. *Blackstone*, Com., IV. x.

3. To obtain, as by request, loan, effort, labor, or purchase; get; gain; come into possession of.

Procure vnto your self suche faithfull frendes as will rather staie yow from fallinge.
Booke of Precedence (E. E. T. S., extra ser.), i. 74.

You desired me lately to *procure* you Dr. Davies's Welsh Grammar, to add to those many you have.
Howell, Letters, I. v. 26.

Go; for yourself *procure* renown; . . .
An' for your lawful King his crown.
Burns, Highland Laddie.

4†. To prevail with unto some end; lead; bring.

Is it my lady mother? . . .
What unaccustom'd cause *procures* her hither?
Shak., R. and J., iii. 5. 68.

Yonder is a pleasant arbour, *procure* him thither.
Shirley, Love Tricks, iv. 2.

5†. To solicit; urge earnestly.

The famous Briton prince and Faery knight . . .
Of the faire Alma greatly were *procur'd*
To make there lenger sojourne and abode.
Spenser, F. Q., III. i. 1.

=**Syn.** 2. To provide, furnish, secure, compass.—3. *Obtain*, etc. See *attain*.

II. *intrans.* To pander; pimp.

How doth my dear morsel, thy mistress? *Procures* she still, ha? *Shak.*, M. for M., iii. 2. 58.

procurement (prọ̄-kūr'mẹnt), *n.* [< OF. *procurement*, < ML. *procuramentum*, procurement, solicitation, < L. *procurare*, procure: see *procure*.] 1. The act of bringing about, or causing to be effected.

A second Baiazeth, who in his fathers life, by *procurement* of the Janissayres, and in the hope of their ayde, purposed to vsurpe the State and Empyre to him selfe.
Guevara, Letters (tr. by Hellowes, 1577), p. 333.

They think it done
By her *procurement* to advance her son.
Dryden, Aurengzebe, ii. 1.

The king sends for the Count, but finds him dead, probably by the royal *procurement*.
Ticknor, Span. Lit., I. 150.

2. The act of procuring or obtaining; obtainment.

Shalt not engage thee on a work so much
Impossible as *procurement* of her love.
Shirley, Bird in a Cage, i. 1.

procurer (prọ̄-kūr'ėr), *n.* 1. One who procures or obtains; that which brings on or causes to be done.

Be you rather a hearer and bearer away of other men's talk than a beginner or *procurer* of speech.
Sir H. Sidney (Arber's Eng. Garner, I. 42).

If the *procurers* of . . . [a new law] have betrayed a conduct that confesses by-ends and private motives, the disgust to the circumstances disposes us . . . to an irreverence of the law itself. *Goldsmith*, The Bee, No. 7.

2†. One who uses means to bring anything about, especially one who does so secretly and corruptly.

You are to inquire of wilful and corrupt perjury in any of the king's courts: and that as well of the actors as of the *procurers* and suborners.
Bacon, Charge at Session of the Verge.

3. One who procures for another the gratification of his lust; a pimp; a pander.

Strumpets in their youth turn *procurers* in their age.
South, Sermons, II. 183.

procuress (prọ̄-kūr'es), *n.* [< *procure* + *-ess*.] A female pimp; a bawd.

Hold thou the good: define it well:
For fear divine Philosophy
Should push beyond her mark, and be
Procuress to the Lords of Hell.
Tennyson, In Memoriam, liii.

procureur (prọ̄-kü-rėr'), *n.* [F. (> G. *procureur* = Russ. *prokurorŭ*), < L. *procurator*, procurator: see *procurator* and *proctor*.] A procurator; especially, in some countries, an attorney; in *French law*, the public prosecutor (*procureur du roi* or *de la république*), corresponding in a general way to a district or county attorney in the United States.

Chudnofski . . . was put into a strait-jacket in the same bastion in the spring of 1878 for insisting upon his legal right to have pen and paper for the purpose of writing a letter of complaint to the *Procureur*.
G. *Kennan*, The Century, XXXV. 527.

Procureur général, in *French law*, the public prosecutor-in-chief, corresponding in a general way to the attorney-general in American law, but having supervision over the *procureurs du roi* or *de la république*.

procursive (prọ̄-kėr'siv), *a.* [< L. *procursus*, pp. of *procurrere*, run forth (< *pro*, forth, + *currere*, run: see *current*[1]), + *-ive*.] Running forward.—**Procursive epilepsy**, epilepsy in which the fits begin with or consist of a purposeless running forward.

procurvation (prō-kėr-vā'shọn), *n.* [< L. *procurvare*, pp. *procurvatus*, bend or curve forward, < *pro*, forward, + *curvare*, bend, curve: see *curve*.] A bending forward.

Procyon (prō'si-on), *n.* [NL., < L. *Procyon*, < Gr. Προκύων, the name of a star, or of a constellation, rising a little before the dog-star, < πρό, before, + κύων, dog: see *hound*.] 1. (*a*) An ancient constellation: same as *Canis Minor*. See *Canis*. (*b*) The principal star of the constellation Canis Minor, the eighth brightest in the heavens.—2. In *zoöl.*, the typical genus of the family *Procyonidæ*, and the only genus of the subfamily *Procyoninæ*, founded by Storr in 1784, containing the racoons. See cut under *racoon*.

Procyonidæ (prō-si-on'i-dē), *n. pl.* [NL., < *Procyon* (see *Procyon*, 2) + *-idæ*.] An American family of plantigrade carnivorous mammals of the arctoid series of fissiped *Feræ*, represented by the genera *Procyon* and *Nasua*, respectively the types of its two subfamilies, *Procyoninæ* and *Nasuinæ*, or the racoons and coatis. The family was formerly defined with latitude enough to include other procyoniform animals, as the kinkajou and bassaris. It is now restricted to forms having 40 teeth, of which the last upper premolar and first lower molar are tubercular, and the lower jaw moderate or slender, with short symphysis, recurved coronoid process, and mandibular angle near the condyle. See cuts under *coati* and *racoon*.

procyoniform (prō-si-on'i-fôrm), *a.* [< *Procyon* (see *Procyon*, 2) + L. *forma*, form.] Racoon-like in structure and affinity; belonging to or resembling the *Procyoniformia*.

Procyoniformia (prō-si-on-i-fôr'mi-ạ̈), *n. pl.* [NL.: see *procyoniform*.] A section of the arctoid series of fissiped *Feræ*, contrasted with the ursiform and musteliform sections of *Arctoidea*. They have two true lower molars, the last upper molar more or less transverse, the carotid canal not behind the middle of the inner wall of the auditory bulla, and the foramen lacerum posterius antrorse from the postero-internal angle of the tympanic bone. There are 4 families, *Æluridæ* of the Old World, and the American *Cercoleptidæ*, *Procyonidæ*, and *Bassarididæ*.

Procyoninæ (prō'si-ọ̄-nī'nē), *n. pl.* [NL., < *Procyon* + *-inæ*.] A subfamily of *Procyonidæ*, represented by the genus *Procyon* alone, having the snout short in comparison with *Nasuinæ*, and large mastoid processes and auditory bullæ. See cut under *racoon*.

procyonine (prō'si-ọ̄-nin), *a.* Racoon-like; of or pertaining to the *Procyonidæ* or *Procyoniformia*: as, the *procyonine* type.

prod (prod), *n.* [Formerly also *prodd*; perhaps a var. of *brod*, *brad*.] 1. A pointed (often blunt-pointed) weapon or instrument, as a goad or an awl.—2. A long wooden pin used to secure thatch upon a roof. See the quotation.

A *prod* [used in thatching amongst North Lancashire people] is a wooden pin pointed fine, and is used for putting straight into the thatch. It may be a foot or fifteen inches long, or even more. *N. and Q.*, 6th ser., X. 193.

3†. A crossbow used for throwing balls of metal or stone. Compare *stone-bow*.—4. [< *prod*, *v.*] A prick or punch with a pointed or somewhat blunt instrument; a poke.

If a child tittered at going under the confessional tent, its mother gave it a rear *prod* with admonishing hand.
The Century, XXXVII. 265.

prod (prod), *v. t.*; pret. and pp. *prodded*, ppr. *prodding*. [< *prod*, *n.*] To prick or punch with a pointed instrument; goad; poke.

The lady has *prodded* little spirting holes in the damp sand before her with her parasol.
Dickens, Our Mutual Friend, i. 10.

Hungarian soldiers—who may have soon afterward *prodded* their Danish fellow-beings all the more effectively for that day's training. *Howells*, Venetian Life, xv.

prodatary (prọ̄-dā'tạ-ri), *n.*; pl. *prodataries* (-riz). [< NL. *prodatarius*, < L. *pro*, for, + ML. *datarius*, a datary: see *datary*[1].] The title borne by the officer who presides over the office of the datary at Rome, when of the rank of a cardinal.

proddt, *n.* An obsolete form of *prod*.

prodder (prod'ėr), *n.* One who prods.

Prodenia (prọ̄-dē'ni-ạ̈), *n.* [NL. (Guenée, 1852).] A genus of noctuid moths of the subfamily *Xylophasinæ*, having the palpi ascending,

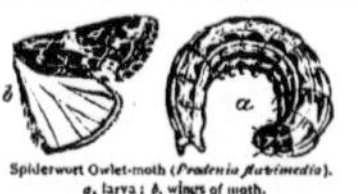

Spiderwort Owlet-moth (*Prodenia flavimedia*).
a, larva; *b*, wings of moth.

the third joint long-conical, and the posterior wings semi-hyaline. It is a wide-spread genus, with some 30 species of Europe, southern Asia, the Malay archipelago, Australia, and both Americas. *P. flavimedia* is common in the United States; its larva feeds, like a cutworm, on various succulent vegetables. See also cut under *owlet-moth*.

Prodician (prō-dish'iạn), *n.* [< L. *Prodicus*, < Gr. Πρόδικος, Prodicus: see def.] A member of a Gnostic sect founded by Prodicus in the second century.

Prodidomidæ (prod-i-dom'i-dē), *n. pl.* [NL. (Marx, 1890), < *Prodidomus* + *-idæ*.] A family of spiders, closely allied to the *Drassidæ*, and standing between the superfamilies *Retitelariæ* and *Tubitelariæ*. It contains 3 genera, among them the North American genus *Prodidomus*.

Prodidomus (prọ̄-did'ọ̄-mus), *n.* [NL. (Hentz, 1849).] A genus of spiders, typical of the family *Prodidomidæ*, confined to North America. The type-species was found in an old cellar.

prodigt, *a.* [= F. *prodigue* = Sp. Pg. It. *prodigo*, < L. *prodigus*, lavish, wasteful, prodigal, < *prodigere*, consume, squander, drive forth, < *pro(d-)*, before, forward, + *agere*, drive.] Same as *prodigal*. [Rare.]

In a goodly Garden's alleys smooth,
Where *prodig* Nature sets abroad her booth
Of richest beauties.
Sylvester, tr. of Du Bartas's Weeks, ii., Eden.

prodigal (prod'i-gạl), *a.* and *n.* [< LL. (ML.) *prodigalis*, wasteful, < L. *prodigus*, wasteful: see *prodig*.] I. *a.* 1. Given to extravagant expenditure; expending money or other property without necessity; profuse; lavish; wasteful: said of persons: as, a *prodigal* man; the *prodigal* son.

If I would be *prodigal* of my time and your patience, what might not I say? *I. Walton*, Complete Angler, p. 30.

Free livers on a small scale, who are *prodigal* within the compass of a guinea. *Irving*, The Stout Gentleman.

Your wild, wicked, witty *prodigal* son is to a spiritual huntsman an attractive mark.
H. B. *Stowe*, Oldtown, p. 492.

2. Profuse; lavish; wasteful: said of things: as, a *prodigal* expenditure of money.

Or spendthrift's *prodigal* excess.
Cowper, In Memory of John Thornton.

3. Very liberal; lavishly bountiful: as, nature is *prodigal* of her gifts.

The chariest maid is *prodigal* enough
If she unmask her beauty to the moon.
Shak., Hamlet, i. 3. 36.

Realms of upland, *prodigal* in oil,
And hoary to the wind.
Tennyson, Palace of Art.

4. Proud. *Halliwell.* [Prov. Eng.] =**Syn.** *Lavish*, *Profuse*, etc. See *extravagant*.

II. *n.* One who expends money extravagantly or without necessity; one who is profuse or lavish; a waster; a spendthrift. With the definite article, *the prodigal*, the term, taken from the ordinary chapter-heading, is used to designate the younger son in Christ's parable, Luke xv. 11–32.

A bankrupt, a *prodigal*, who dare scarce show his head on the Rialto. *Shak.*, M. of V., iii. 1. 47.

prodigalise, *v.* See *prodigalize*.

prodigality (prod-i-gal'i-ti), *n.* [= F. *prodigalité* = Pr. *prodigalitat* = Sp. *prodigalidad* = Pg. *prodigalidade* = It. *prodigalità*, < LL. *prodigalita(t-)s*, wastefulness, < (ML.) *prodigalis*, wasteful, lavish: see *prodigal*.] 1. The quality of being prodigal; extravagance in expenditure, particularly of money; profusion; waste.

It is not always so obvious to distinguish between an act of liberality and an act of *prodigality*. *South.*

If a man by notorious *prodigality* was in danger of wasting his estate, he was looked upon as non compos, and committed to the care of curators or tutors by the prætor. *Blackstone*, Com., I. viii.

2. Excessive or profuse liberality.

A sweeter and a lovelier gentleman,
Framed in the *prodigality* of nature.
Shak., Rich. III., i. 2. 244.

=**Syn.** 1. Wastefulness, lavishness, squandering. See *extravagant*.

prodigalize (prod'i-gal-īz), *v.*; pret. and pp. *prodigalized*, ppr. *prodigalizing*. [< OF. *prodigaliser* = Pg. *prodigalizar* = It. *prodigalizzare*; as *prodigal* + *-ize*.] I. *trans*. To spend or give with prodigality or profuseness; lavish; prodigate.

Major MacBlarney *prodigalises* his offers of service in every conceivable department of life.
Bulwer, Caxtons, xvii. 1. (*Davies*.)

II. *intrans*. To be extravagant in expenditure: with an indefinite *it*. *Cotgrave*.

Also spelled *prodigalise*.

prodigally (prod'i-gal-i), *adv*. [< *prodigal* + *-ly*[2].] In a prodigal manner. (*a*) With profusion of expenses; extravagantly; lavishly; wastefully: as, an estate *prodigally* dissipated.

The next in place and punishment are they
Who *prodigally* throw their souls away.
Dryden, Æneid, vi. 587.

(*b*) With liberal abundance; profusely.

The fields,
With ripening harvest *prodigally* fair,
In brightest sunshine bask.
Wordsworth, Sonnets, ii. 13.

prodigate (prod'i-gāt), *v. t.*; pret. and pp. *prodigated*, ppr. *prodigating*. [< ML. *prodigatus*, pp. of *prodigare* (> Sp. *prodigar*), consume, squander, freq. of L. *prodigere*, consume, squander: see *prodigal*.] To squander prodigally; lavish.

His gold is *prodigated* in every direction which his foolish menaces fail to frighten. *Thackeray*.

prodigence† (prod'i-jens), *n*. [< L. *prodigentia*, extravagance, profusion, < *prodigen(t-)s*, ppr. of *prodigere*, consume, squander: see *prodigal*.] Waste; profusion; prodigality.

There is no proportion in this remuneration; this is not bounty, it is *prodigence*. *Bp. Hall*, John Baptist Beheaded.

prodigious (prǭ-dij'us), *a*. [< F. *prodigieux* = Sp. Pg. It. *prodigioso*, < L. *prodigiosus*, unnatural, strange, wonderful, marvelous, < *prodigium*, an omen, portent, monster: see *prodigy*.] 1†. Having the character or partaking of the nature of a prodigy; portentous.

Super. The Diuill ouer-take thee!
Amb. O fatall!
Super. O *prodigious* to our blouds!
Tourneur, Revenger's Tragedy, ii. 6.

I never see him but methinks his face
Is more *prodigious* than a fiery comet.
Beau. and Fl. (?), Faithful Friends, i. 3.

Hang all the sky with your *prodigious* signs.
B. Jonson, Sejanus, v. 6.

2. Wonderfully large; very great in size, quantity, or extent; monstrous; immense; huge; enormous.

His head is like a huge spherical chamber, containing a *prodigious* mass of soft brains.
Irving, Knickerbocker, p. 157.

Instead of the redress of such injuries, they saw a new and *prodigious* tax laid on the realm by the legislature.
R. W. Dixon, Hist. Church of Eng., xv.

3. Very great in degree; excessive; extreme.

I had much discourse with my Lord Winchelsea, a *prodigious* talker. *Evelyn*, Diary, Aug. 4, 1669.

For so small a man, his strength was *prodigious*.
Barham, Ingoldsby Legends, I. 77.

They tell me I'm a *prodigious* favourite, and that he talks of leaving me every thing.
Sheridan, School for Scandal, iii. 3.

These optical splendours, together with the *prodigious* enthusiasm of the people, composed a picture at once scenical and affecting, theatrical and holy. *De Quincey*.

=Syn. Monstrous, marvelous, amazing, astonishing, astounding, extraordinary.

prodigiously (prǭ-dij'us-li), *adv*. In a prodigious manner. (*a*†) In the manner of a prodigy or portent; ominously; portentously.

And Hyæna's and Wolues, *prodigiously* entering their Cities, seemed to howle their Funerall obsequies.
Purchas, Pilgrimage, p. 157.

(*b*) Wonderfully; astonishingly; enormously: as, a number *prodigiously* great. (*c*) Excessively; immensely; extremely. [Colloq.]

I am *prodigiously* pleased with this joint volume. *Pope*.

prodigiousness (prǭ-dij'us-nes), *n*. The state or quality of being prodigious; enormousness; the state of having qualities that excite wonder or astonishment.

prodigy (prod'i-ji), *n*.; pl. *prodigies* (-jiz). [Formerly also *prodige*; = F. *prodige* = Sp. Pg. It. *prodigio*, < L. *prodigium*, a prophetic sign, token, omen, portent, prob. for **prodicium*, < *prodicere*, say beforehand, foretell, < *pro*, before, + *dicere*, say: see *diction*. Otherwise < *prod-*, older form of *pro*, before, + **agium*, a saying, as in *adagium*, a saying: see *adage*.] 1. Something extraordinary from which omens are drawn; a portent.

Think the easiest temptations a porpoise before a tempest, smoke before fire, signs and *prodiges* of a fearful conflict to come. *Rev. T. Adams*, Works, II. 164.

So many terrours, voices, *prodigies*,
May warn thee, as a sure foregoing sign.
Milton, P. R., iv. 482.

2. A person or thing so extraordinary as to excite great wonder or astonishment.

The Churches are many and very fayre; in one of them lyes interr'd that *prodigy* of learning, the noble and illustrious Joseph Scaliger. *Evelyn*, Diary, Aug. 19, 1641.

Ay, but her beauty will affect you — she is, though I say it who am her father, a very *prodigy*.
Sheridan, The Duenna, ii. 1.

3. A monster; an animal or other production out of the ordinary course of nature.

Most of mankind, through their own sluggishness, become nature's *prodigies*, not her children. *B. Jonson*.

=Syn. 1. Sign, wonder, miracle.—2. Marvel.

prodition† (prǭ-dish'ǫn), *n*. [< OF. (and F.) *prodition* = Sp. *prodicion* = Pg. *prodição* = It. *prodizione*, < L. *proditio(n-)*, discovery, betrayal, < *prodere*, bring forth, betray, < *pro*, forth, + *dare*, give: see *date*[1]. Cf. *treason*, which contains the same radical element.] Treachery; treason.

Certes, it had bene better for thee not to haue accused the king of this *prodition*. *Grafton*, Hen. II., an. 18.

Prodition is the rankling tooth that follows her [iniquity's] ravishing kisses. *Rev. T. Adams*, Works, I. 222.

proditor† (prod'i-tǫr), *n*. [< OF. *proditeur* = Pg. *proditor* = It. *proditore*, < L. *proditor*, a traitor, < *prodere*, pp. *proditus*, bring forth, betray: see *prodition*. Cf. *traitor*, which contains the same radical element.] A traitor.

Thou most usurping *proditor*,
And not protector, of the king or realm.
Shak., 1 Hen. VI., i. 3. 31.

proditorious† (prod-i-tō'ri-us), *a*. [< ML. *proditorius*, traitorous: see *proditory*.] 1. Treacherous; perfidious; traitorous.

Now, *proditorious* wretch! what hast thou done,
To make this barbarous base assassinate? *Daniel*.

2. Apt to disclose or make known.

Those more solid and conclusive characters . . . which oftentimes do start out of children when themselves least think of it; for, let me tell you, nature is *proditorious*.
Sir H. Wotton, Reliquiæ, p. 82.

proditoriously† (prod-i-tō'ri-us-li), *adv*. In a proditorious or perfidious manner; with treachery.

proditory† (prod'i-tǭ-ri), *a*. [= F. *proditoire* = Sp. Pg. It. *proditorio*, < ML. *proditorius*, traitorous, < L. *proditor*, a traitor: see *proditor*.] Treacherous; perfidious.

If this were that touch of conscience which he bore with greater regrett, then for any other sin committed in his life, whether it were that *proditory* Aid sent to Rochel and Religion abroad, or that prodigality of shedding blood at home, to a million of his Subjects lives not valu'd in comparison of one Strafford, we may consider yet at last what true sense and feeling could be in that conscience.
Milton, Eikonoklastes, ii.

prodromal (prod'rǭ-mal), *a*. [< *prodrome* + *-al*.] In *pathol.*, preliminary; pertaining to or of the nature of prodromata. Also *prodromous*.

In most insanities a "period of incubation" is observed, generally spoken of as the *prodromal* or initial period.
Encyc. Brit., XIII. 108.

prodromata (prǭ-drom'a-tä), *n. pl*. [NL., < Gr. πρόδρομος, running before: see *prodromus*.] Minor symptoms preceding the well-marked outbreak of a disease; prodromal symptoms.

The severity of the *prodromata* serves as a guide.
Quain, Med. Dict., p. 1390.

prodromatic (prod-rǭ-mat'ik), *a*. [< *prodromata* + *-ic*.] Of or pertaining to prodromata; prodromal.

prodrome (prō'drōm), *n*. [< Gr. προδρομή, a running forward: see *prodromus*.] 1†. A forerunner.

Sober morality, conscientiously kept to, is like the morning light reflected from the higher clouds, and a certain *prodrome* of the Sun of Righteousness itself.
Dr. H. More, cited in Ward's Life, p. 53. (*Latham*.)

2. Any prodromal symptom.—3. A precursory or preliminary treatise; a prodromus (which see).

prodromic (prǭ-drom'ik), *a*. [< Gr. προδρομικός, ready to run forward, < πρόδρομος, running forward: see *prodromous*.] Precursory; pertaining to prodromata.

The eruption was fully out. It . . . closely resembled the *prodromic* exanthem of variola.
Medical News, LII. 545.

prodromous (prod'rǭ-mus), *a*. [< Gr. πρόδρομος, running forward, < προδραμεῖν, run forward, < πρό, forward, + δραμεῖν, run.] Same as *prodromal*.

prodromus (prod'rǭ-mus), *n*.; pl. *prodromi* (-mī). [< L. *prodromus*, < Gr. πρόδρομος, running before: see *prodromous*.] Same as *prodrome*; especially, a preliminary treatise upon a subject respecting which a subsequent more elaborate work is intended. This was formerly a very common name of minor treatises composed in Latin, and survives, especially as English *prodrome*, for books of this class. [This word seems to be used by Bacon for 'prophecy, anticipation, to be afterward verified.' See the quotation.]

Bacon arranged his writings for the "Instauratio Magna" into six divisions: . . . 5. The *Prodromi*; or, the Anticipations of the Second Philosophy — provisional anticipations, founded on experience, which the investigator needs as starting-points in his research.
Henry Morley, First Sketch of Eng. Lit., viii. § 22.

prodromy (prod'rǭ-mi), *n*. [< Gr. προδρομή, a running forward: see *prodrome*.] A sign of something in the future; a presage.

produce (prǭ-dūs'), *v.*; pret. and pp. *produced*, ppr. *producing*. [= F. *produire* = Pr. *produire* = Sp. *producir* = Pg. *produzir* = It. *producere*, < L. *producere*, lead forth or forward, bring forward, draw or stretch out, extend, prolong, conduct, etc., bring forth, bear, etc., < *pro*, forth, forward, + *ducere*, lead, bring: see *duct*.] I. *trans*. 1. To lead or place forward or in front. [Rare.]

Hed. O, his leg was too much *produced*.
Ana. And his hat was carried scurvily.
B. *Jonson*, Cynthia's Revels, v. 2.

2. To lengthen out; extend; prolong.

In which great work, perhaps our stay will be
Beyond our will *produced*. B. *Jonson*, Sejanus, iii. 3.

An insect with the extremity of its abdomen *produced* into a sharp point alights on the flower.
Darwin, Fertil. of Orchids by Insects, p. 169.

Straight lines exist which have the property that any one of them may be *produced* both ways without limit.
Encyc. Brit., X. 377.

3. To bring forward; bring or offer to view or notice; exhibit.

I . . . am moreover suitor that I may
Produce his body to the market-place.
Shak., J. C., iii. 1. 228.

He is on fire to succour the oppressed, to *produce* the merit of the one, and confront the impudence of the other.
Steele, Tatler, No. 242.

Where is no door, I but *produce*
My key to find it of no use.
Lowell, Credidimus Jovem Regnare.

4. To bring forth; generate; bear; furnish; yield.

All things in common nature should *produce*
Without sweat or endeavour.
Shak., Tempest, ii. 1. 159.

Many plants are known which regularly *produce* at the same time differently-constructed flowers.
Darwin, Origin of Species, p. 182.

The infelicitous wife who had *produced* nothing but daughters. *George Eliot*, Daniel Deronda, xxxvi.

The Greeks had the very largest ideas upon the training of man, and *produced* specimens of our kind with gifts that have never been surpassed.
Gladstone, Might of Right, p. 15.

5. To cause; effect; bring about.

The agitations and struggling motions of matter first *produced* certain imperfect and ill-joined compositions of things. *Bacon*, Physical Fables, i., Expl.

Competition has *produced* activity where monopoly would have *produced* sluggishness. *Macaulay*, History.

It is not trial by jury that *produces* justice, but it is the sentiment of justice that *produces* trial by jury.
H. *Spencer*, Social Statics, p. 289.

6. To make; bring into being or form: as, to *produce* wares.

The jongleurs *produced* chansons de geste full of tales of battle and combat. *Encyc. Brit.*, XIX. 873.

7. To yield; make accrue: as, money *produces* interest; capital *produces* profit. =Syn. 3. To show.—4. To breed, beget, engender, propagate.—6. To afford, impart, give, occasion, furnish, supply.

II. *intrans*. 1. To bring forth or yield appropriate offspring, products, or consequences: as, this tree *produces* well.—2. In *polit. econ.*, to create value; make anything valuable; bring goods, crops, manufactures, etc., into a state in which they will command a price.

Capitalists will not go on permanently *producing* at a loss. *J. S. Mill*, Pol. Econ., III. iii. § 1.

produce (prod'ūs), *n*. [< *produce*, *v*.] That which is produced; a product, of either natural growth, bodily yield, labor, or capital: as, the *produce* of the soil, of the flock, of the factory, etc.

In an open country too, of which the principal *produce* is corn, a well-inclosed piece of grass will frequently rent higher than any corn-field in its neighbourhood.
Adam Smith, Wealth of Nations, i. 11.

To give the pole the *produce* of the sun,
And knit th' unsocial climates into one.
Cowper, Charity, l. 125.

The value of mining *produce* is determined generally in the same way as that of agricultural *produce*.
Encyc. Brit., XXIV. 51.

Is it not the case that Satan has so composed and dressed out what is the mere natural *produce* of the human heart under certain circumstances as to serve his purposes as the counterfeit of the Truth?
J. H. Newman, Parochial Sermons, i. 313.

Specifically—(*a*) The total yield or outcome: as, the *produce* of the county for the past year has been very large.

In Staffordshire, after their lands are marled, they sow it with barley, allowing three bushels to an acre. Its common *produce* is thirty bushels. *Mortimer*, Husbandry.

(*b*) In *com.*, agricultural products, as grain, lard, hops, etc., and other articles, as petroleum, which are bought and sold with them on the same exchange. (*c*) In *metal.*, the assay percentage of copper ore. [This use of the word is limited to Cornwall, England.]

The assays [of copper] are made by units and eighths per cent., which result of percentage is called the *produce*.
Phillips, Explorers' Companion, p. 395.

=**Syn.** *Product*, etc. See *production*.

produce-broker (prod'ūs-brō"kėr), *n.* A dealer in produce, as grain, groceries, or dyestuffs, usually acting as agent or on commission.

produced (prọ̄-dūst'), *p. a.* In *zoöl.*, drawn out; elongated; extended; protrusive or protuberant: as, the *produced* jaws of a garpike.

produce-exchange (prod'ūs-eks-chānj"), *n.* An exchange where produce is bought and sold. See *produce* (*b*).

producement† (prọ̄-dūs'ment), *n.* [< *produce* + *-ment*.] Production.

Which repulse only, given to the Prelats, . . . was the *producement* of . . . glorious effects and consequences in the Church. *Milton*, Apology for Smectymnuus.

produce-merchant (prod'ūs-mėr"chant), *n.* Same as *produce-broker*.

producent (prọ̄-dū'sent), *n.* [< L. *producen(t-)s*, ppr. of *producere*, bring forth or forward: see *produce*.] One who or that which produces, brings forth, exhibits, or effects.

These species are made a medium between body and spirit, . . . and the supposition infers a creative energie in the object their *producent*, which allows not to creature efficients. *Glanville*, Vanity of Dogmatizing, iv.

If an instrument be produced with a protestation in favour of the *producent*, and the adverse party does not contradict, it shall be construed to the advantage of the *producent*. *Aylife*, Parergon.

producer (prọ̄-dū'sėr), *n.* One who or that which produces or generates: as, an agricultural *producer* (farmer); a gas-*producer* (apparatus); specifically, in *polit. econ.*, one who causes any article to have an exchangeable value: the opposite of *consumer*.

The divine will is absolute; it is its own reason; it is both the *producer* and the ground of all its acts.
South, Sermons, VIII. x.

Now wages and profits will be in proportion to the sacrifices undergone wherever, and only as far as, competition prevails among *producers*. *Cairnes*, Pol. Econ., I. iii. § 5.

The hands are the *producers*, and the aim of the masters was to regard the *producers* as so many machines.
W. Besant, Fifty Years Ago, p. 225.

producibility (prọ̄-dū-si-bil'į-ti), *n.* [< *producible* + *-ity* (see *-bility*).] The capability of being produced.

There being nothing contained in the notion of substance inconsistent with such a *producibility*.
Barrow, Works, II. xii.

producible (prọ̄-dū'si-bl), *a.* [< *produce* + *-ible*.] 1. Capable of being produced or brought into view or notice, or of being exhibited.

Many warm expressions of the fathers are *producible* in this case. *Decay of Christian Piety.*

Certain sleeping accommodations *producible* from recesses in the front and back counting-houses.
Charlotte Brontë, Shirley, iv.

2. Capable of being produced or brought into being; able to be generated or made.

Mischief *producible* by the ravages of noxious animals, such as beasts of prey, locusts.
Bentham, Introd. to Morals and Legislation, xvi. 33, note.

producibleness (prọ̄-dū'si-bl-nes), *n.* [< *producible* + *-ness*.] The state or quality of being producible.

That alone will suffice to destroy the universality and intireness of their hypothesis, and besides give cause to suspect that by further industry the *producibleness* of other principles also may be discovered.
Boyle, Works, I. 661.

product (prọ̄-dukt'), *v. t.* [< L. *productus*, pp. of *producere*, lead forth, produce: see *produce*.] 1†. To bring forward; produce.

Beeing *producted* to his last examination before the said bish. yᵉ xv day of January. *Foxe*, Martyrs, an. 1556.

Great plentie of fine amber, . . . which is *producted* by the working of the sea upon those coasts.
Holinshed, Descrip. of Britain, x.

It seemes not meete, nor wholesome to my place,
To be *producted* (as, if I stay, I shall)
Against the Moore.
Shak., Othello (folio 1623), i. 1. 147.

2. In *entom.*, to draw out; lengthen.—**Producted pronotum**, a pronotum terminated behind in a long process extending over the mesothorax, metathorax, and part of the abdomen, as in certain grasshoppers.

product (prod'ukt), *n.* [= F. *produit* = Sp. Pg. *producto* = It. *prodotto*, *produtto* = D. G. Sw. Dan. *produkt*, product, < L. *productum*, neut. of *productus*, pp. of *producere*, lead forth, produce: see *produce*.] That which is produced; a production. (*a*) A thing which is produced by nature, as fruits or grain-crops; what is yielded by the soil: as, the agricultural *products* of a country.

Fetch uncontrolled each labour of the sun,
And make the *product* of the world our own.
Addison, To the King.

See thy bright altars throng'd with prostrate kings,
And heap'd with *products* of Sabean springs!
Pope, Messiah, l. 94.

(*b*) Offspring. [Rare.]

To whom thus Michael: These are the *product*
Of those ill-mated marriages thou saw'st.
Milton, P. L., xi. 683.

(*c*) That which is formed or produced by labor, usually by physical labor.

The centres of this organization of trade were the cloth-halls, to which the masters brought their *products* to market. *English Gilds* (E. E. T. S.), Int., p. clxxi.

Most of those books which have obtained great reputation in the world are the *products* of great and wise men.
Watts, Improvement of the Mind, i. 2.

Some of the richest land in England lies in the fen country, and that land is as much the *product* of engineering skill and prolonged labour as Portland Harbour or Menai Bridge. *Rae*, Contemporary Socialism, p. 446.

(*d*) Effect; result; something resulting as a consequence.

He, with all his capacities, and desires, and beliefs, is not an accident, but a *product* of the time.
H. Spencer, Social Statics, p. 517.

[Show me]
What thy life last put heart and soul into;
There shall I taste thy *product*.
Browning, Ring and Book, II. 178.

(*e*) In *math.*, the result of multiplying one quantity or expression by another. Thus, 72 is the *product* of 8 multiplied by 9; and *dy/dx* is the *product* of *y* multiplied by the operator *d/dx*. The quantities multiplied together are usually termed *factors*. *Product* results from *multiplication*, as *sum* does from *addition*. (*f*) In *chem.*, a compound not previously existing in a body, but formed during decomposition: as, the *products* of destructive distillation: contradistinguished from *educt*.—**Direct, genital, organic, etc., products.** See the adjectives.—**Homogeneous product**, a product of abstract numbers or quantities of one kind.—**Product of inertia.** See *inertia*.—**Resolvent product**, the product $f\omega . f\omega^2 . f\omega^3 . f\omega^4$, where ω is a fifth root of unity and $f\omega = x_1 + \omega x_2 + \omega^2 x_3 + \omega^3 x_4 + \omega^4 x_5$, the *x*'s being roots of a quintic equation.—**Skew product**, the product of the tensors of two vectors into the sine of the angle between them, and the whole multiplied by a unit vector perpendicular to the two vectors and directed in the way in which the revolution from the first factor to the second appears counter-clockwise.

productibility (prọ̄-duk-ti-bil'į-ti), *n.* [< *productible* + *-ity* (see *-bility*).] Capability of being produced. [Rare.]

No produce ever maintains a consistent rate of *productibility*. *Ruskin*, Unto This Last, p. 53, note.

productible (prọ̄-duk'ti-bl), *a.* [< L. *productus*, pp. of *producere*, lead forth, produce (see *product*), + *-ible*.] Capable of being produced; producible. [Rare.]

productile (prọ̄-duk'til), *a.* [< L. *productilis*, that may be drawn out, < *productus*, pp. of *producere*, lead forth, draw out, product: see *produce*, *product*.] Capable of being extended in length.

production (prọ̄-duk'shọn), *n.* [< F. *production* = Sp. *produccion* = Pg. *producção* = It. *produzione*, < L. *productio(n-)*, a prolonging, lengthening, < *producere*, pp. *productus*, lead forth, prolong, produce: see *produce*, *product*.] 1. The act or process of producing. (*a*) The act of bringing forward or adducing.

Public documents in general must be proved either by the *production* of the original or by the official copies.
Encyc. Brit., VIII. 742.

(*b*) The act of making or creating.

It can also be shown that the *production* of the two sorts of flowers by the same plant has been effected by finely-graduated steps. *Darwin*, Origin of Species, p. 182.

Certain it is that hate and destruction are just as necessary agents as love and *production* in nature.
Maudsley, Body and Will, xi. p. 239.

The component elements of *production* are labour and capital, acting by natural forces upon raw material.
Encyc. Brit., XXIV. 48.

(*c*) In *polit. econ.*, the creation of values; the producing of articles having an exchangeable value.

Besides the primary and universal requisites of *production*, labour and natural agents, there is another requisite, . . . namely, a stock, previously accumulated, of the products of former labour. *J. S. Mill*, Pol. Econ., I. iv. § 1.

2. That which is produced or made; a product of physical or mental labor; specifically, a work of literature or art.

The Lion and the Leviathan are two of the noblest *Productions* in this World of living Creatures.
Addison, Spectator, No. 339.

We have had our names prefixed at length to whole Volumes of mean *productions*. *Swift.*

So one, whose story serves at least to show
Men loved their own *productions* long ago,
Woo'd an unfeeling statue for his wife.
Cowper, Progress of Error, l. 527.

3. In *zoöl.* and *anat.*, the act of drawing forth or out; the state of being produced (see *produced*, *p. a.*); extension; protrusion: as, the *production* of the pike's jaws.—4. *pl.* In *Scots law*, in judicial proceedings, written documents or other things produced in process in support of the action or defense.—**Interdict for production.** See *interdict*, 2.=**Syn.** 1. Work, performance.—1 and 2. *Produce*, *Product*, *Production*. Of these only *production* may mean the act of producing. As standing for the thing or things produced, *produce* applies now almost exclusively to the raw *products* or yield of land: as, to bring fresh *produce* to market. Where Jonathan Edwards spoke of regarding "all free actions as the *produce* of free choice," we should speak now of regarding them as the *products* of free choice, or, better, as its effects. There is a lingering use of *produce* in such expressions as "the *produce* of a tax," but better now the *product*, or, still better, the proceeds. The word is always collective; we do not speak of *a produce*. *Product* and *production*, on the other hand, are particular. *Product* is the most general of the three words, but expresses the result of some operation, generally, but not necessarily, physical: as, the apple is especially an American *product*; Great Britain exports chiefly manufactured *products*. Thus, the word may apply to almost anything where emphasis is laid upon the fact of its being produced by some cause, especially by some cause that is named; but, apart from this, the word is applied chiefly to things having a material value, covering *produce*, manufactures, etc. *Production* applies now almost exclusively to the visible results of the operation of mind or the handiwork of art, as a book, a poem, an oration, a statue, a painting, a piece of needlework—the act or fact of producing being only subordinate in mind. *Product* is also a technical word of mathematics, but the others are not.

productive (prọ̄-duk'tiv), *a.* [= F. *productif* = Sp. Pg. *productivo* = It. *produttivo*, < L. *productivus*, serving to produce or prolong, < *producere*, pp. *productus*, lead forth, produce: see *produce*, *product*.] 1. Serving to produce; having the power of producing: as, an age *productive* of great men.

Productive in herb, plant, and nobler birth
Of creatures animate with gradual life.
Milton, P. L., ix. 111.

Chaste as cold Cynthia's virgin light,
Productive as the Sun.
Pope, Choruses to Brutus, ii.

Heav'n would sure grow weary of a world
Productive only of a race like ours.
Cowper, Task, ii. 584.

2. Fertile; producing abundant crops: as, a *productive* soil.

Fruitful vales so *productive* of that grain. *Swift.*

3. In *polit. econ.*, causing or tending to cause an increase in the quantity or quality of things of value; causing commodities to possess exchangeable value: as, *productive* labor.

The business of transporting merchandise or passengers by land or by sea is as much a *productive* industry as the raising of wheat, the spinning of fibres, or the smelting or forging of iron.
D. A. Wells, Our Merchant Marine, p. 35.

Productive imagination. See *imagination*, 1.=**Syn.** 1 and 2. *Prolific*, etc. See *fruitful*.

productively (prọ̄-duk'tiv-li), *adv.* [< *productive* + *-ly*[2].] In a productive manner; by production; with abundant produce.

productiveness (prō-duk'tiv-nes), *n.* [< *productive* + *-ness*.] The character of being productive: as, the *productiveness* of land or labor.

productivity (prō-duk-tiv'į-ti), *n.* [< *productive* + *-ity*.] The power of producing; productiveness.

They have reinforced their own *productivity* by the creation of that marvellous machinery which differences this age from any other age. *Emerson*, Eng. Traits, x.

Labourers who do not possess the average *productivity* are turned off on the ground that they are unable to do a minimum day's work.
Rae, Contemporary Socialism, p. 166.

productress (prọ̄-duk'tres), *n.* [< **productor* (< LL. *productor*, one who leads away, one who produces, < L. *producere*, pp. *productus*, lead forth, produce: see *produce*, *product*) + *-ess*.] A female who produces.

proegumenal† (prō-ē-gū'me-nạl), *a.* [< Gr. προηγούμενος, ppr. of προηγεῖσθαι, go first, lead the way, < πρό, before, + ἡγεῖσθαι, lead: see *hegemony*.] In *med.*, serving to predispose; predisposing; preceding: as, a *proegumenal* cause of disease. See quotation under *procatarctical*.

proem (prō'em), *n.* [Formerly also *proeme*; < ME. *proeme*, *proem*, *proheme*, < OF. *proeme*, *proesme*, F. *proème* = Sp. Pg. It. *proemio*, < L. *proœmium*, < Gr. προοίμιον, Attic φροίμιον, an opening, an introduction, < πρό, before, + οἶμος, a path, road.] A preface; introduction; preamble; preliminary observations prefixed to a book or writing.

> In the *proheim* off hys notabile boke.
> *Rom. of Partenay* (E. E. T. S.), Int., l. 30.

> So glozed the tempter, and his *proem* tuned.
> *Milton*, P. L., ix. 549.

> Thus much may serve by way of *proem;*
> Proceed we therefore to our poem.
> *Swift*, Death of Dr. Swift.

> The *proeme*, or preamble, is often called in to help the construction of an act of parliament.
> *Blackstone*, Com., I., Int., ii.

proem† (prō'em), *v. t.* [< *proem*, *n.*] To preface. [Rare.]

> Moses might here very well *proeme* the repetition of the covenant upbraiding reprehension.
> *South*, Sermons, VIII. xiii.

proembryo (prō-em'bri-ō), *n.* [< Gr. πρό, before, + ἔμβρυον, embryo: see *embryo*.] In *bot.*: (*a*) In *Characeæ*, the product of the development and division of the oöspore, upon which the characeous plant develops as a lateral bud. (*b*) In *Archegoniatæ*, the product of the development and division of the oöspore before the differentiation of the embryo. *Goebel.* (*c*) In phanerogams, same as *suspensor*.

proembryonic (prō-em-bri-on'ik), *a.* [< *proembryo*(*n*-) + -*ic*.] In *bot.*, of or relating to the proembryo. *Vines*, Physiol. of Plants, p. 599.—**Proembryonic branch**, in the *Characeæ*, a propagative body, with the structure of a proembryo, which springs from a node of the stem.

proemial (prǫ-ē'mi-ạl), *a.* [< *proem* + -*ial*.] Having the character of a proem; introductory; prefatory; preliminary.

> This contempt of the world may be a piece of *proemial* piety, an usher or Baptist to repentance.
> *Hammond*, Works, IV. 492.

proemptosis (prō-emp-tō'sis), *n.* [< Gr. as if *προέμπτωσις, < προεμπίπτειν, fall or push in before, < πρό, before, + ἐμπίπτειν, fall upon (> ἔμπτωσις, a falling upon), < ἐν, in, upon, + πίπτειν, fall.] In *chron.*, an anticipation, or occurrence of a natural event sooner than the time given by a rule; especially, the falling of the new moon earlier than the nineteen-year period would make it, amounting to one day in 312½ years according to Clavius and the constructors of the Gregorian calendar (really 310 years), in consequence of which a lunar correction is introduced into the tables for calculating Easter; also, the effect of the precession of the equinoxes in making these come before the sun has performed his circuit among the stars. See *metemptosis*.

proëpimeral (prō-ep-i-mē'rạl), *a.* [< *proëpimer-on* + -*al*.] Of or pertaining to the proëpimeron.

proëpimeron (prō-ep-i-mē'ron), *n.*; pl. *proëpimera* (-rạ̈). [NL., < L. *pro*, before, + NL. *epimeron*, q. v.] The epimeron of the prothorax; the epimeral sclerite of the propleuron.

proëpisternal (prō-ep-i-stėr'nạl), *a.* [< *proëpisternum* + -*al*.] Of or pertaining to the proëpisternum.

proëpisternum (prō-ep-i-stėr'num), *n.*; pl. *proëpisterna* (-nạ̈). [NL., < L. *pro*, before, + NL. *episternum*, q. v.] The prothoracic episternum; the episternal sclerite of the propleuron.

proëthnic (prō-eth'nik), *a.* [< Gr. πρό, before, + ἐθνικός, ethnic: see *ethnic*.] Prior to division into separate races: said of an original prehistoric stock, for example, Indo-European or Aryan.

proeupolyzoön (prō-ū-pol-i-zō'on), *n.* [NL., < L. *pro*, before, + NL. *Eupolyzoa*, q. v.] The hypothetical ancestral form of the *Eupolyzoa*. *E. R. Lankester.* [Rare.]

profacet, *interj.* [< OF. *prou face*, *prou fasse*: *prou*, profit (see *prow*[2]); *face*, *faice*, *fasse*, 3d pers. sing. pres. subj. of *faire*, do: see *fact*.] Much good may it do you! an old exclamation of welcome.

> The cardinall came in, booted and spurred, all sodainly amongst them—and bade them *proface*.
> *Stow*, Chron., p. 528.

> Sweet sir, sit. . . . *Proface!* What you want in meat we'll have in drink. *Shak.*, 2 Hen. IV., v. 3. 30.

profanate† (prof'ạ-nāt), *v. t.* and *i.* [< L. *profanatus*, pp. of *profanare*, consecrate, desecrate: see *profane*.] To profane.

> And there, in a certaine chappell not hallowed, or rather in a prophane cottage, hath in contempt of the keyes presumed of his owne rashnesse to celebrate, nay rather to *prophanate*. *Foxe*, Martyrs, p. 430, an. 1391.

profanation (prof-ạ-nā'shọn), *n.* [Formerly also *prophanation*; < OF. *profanation*, *prophanation*, F. *profanation* = Sp. *profanacion* = Pg. *profanação* = It. *profanazione*, < LL. *profanatio*(*n*-), profanation, < L. *profanare*, pp. *profanatus*, desecrate, also consecrate: see *profane*.] 1. The act of violating sacred things, or of treating them with contempt or irreverence; desecration: as, the *profanation* of the Lord's day; the *profanation* of a sanctuary.

> Here I observed a great *prophanation* of the Lord's supper. *Coryat*, Crudities, I. 3.

> I held it no *Profanation* of this Sunday-evening . . . to employ some Hours to meditate on you, and send you this friendly Salute. *Howell*, Letters, I. v. 11.

2. The act of treating with too little reserve or delicacy, or of making common.

> 'Twere *profanation* of our joys
> To tell the laity our love.
> *Donne*, Valediction Forbidding Mourning.

> Distorted from its [poetry's] use and just design,
> To make the pitiful possessor shine, . . .
> Is *profanation* of the basest kind.
> *Cowper*, Table-Talk, l. 758.

=**Syn.** 1. *Profanation, Desecration, Sacrilege*, pollution. The first three words express offenses, amounting almost or quite to outrages, against the religious sentiment, in connection with places, days, etc., taking off their sacred character. They are in the order of strength. *Profanation* is perhaps most distinctly a matter of irreverence. *Sacrilege* seems most directly an invasion of the rights of God.

> Great men may jest with saints; 'tis wit in them,
> But in the less, foul *profanation*.
> *Shak.*, M. for M., ii. 2. 128.

> O double *sacrilege* on things divine,
> To rob the relic, and deface the shrine!
> *Dryden*, To the Memory of Mrs. Anne Killigrew, l. 160.

profanatory (prǫ-fan'ạ-tǫ-ri), *a.* [< *profane* + -*atory*.] Profaning or desecrating; destructive to sacred character or nature; apt to produce irreverence, contempt, or the like.

> Every one now had tasted the wassail-cup except Paulina, whose pas de fée ou de fantaisie nobody thought of interrupting to offer so *profanatory* a draught.
> *Charlotte Brontë*, Villette, xxv.

profane (prǫ-fān'), *a.* [Formerly also *prophane*; < OF. *profane*, *prophane*, F. *profane* = Sp. Pg. It. *profano* = D. *profaan* = G. Sw. Dan. *profan*, < L. *profanus*, ML. also often *prophanus*, not sacred, unholy, profane; of persons, not initiated (whence, in LL., ignorant, unlearned), also wicked, impious; appar. orig. 'before, or outside of, the temple,' < *pro*, before, + *fanum*, temple: see *fane*[2].] 1. Not sacred, or not devoted to sacred purposes; not possessing any peculiar sanctity; unconsecrated; secular: as, a *profane* place; *profane* history (that is, history other than Biblical); *profane* authors.

> In a certaine chappell not hallowed, or rather in a *prophane* cottage. *Foxe*, Martyrs, p. 430, an. 1391.

> Our holy lives must win a new world's crown,
> Which our *profane* hours here have stricken down.
> *Shak.*, Rich. II., v. 1. 25.

> There is met in your majesty a rare conjunction, as well of divine and sacred literature as of *profane* and human.
> *Bacon*, Advancement of Learning, i. 5.

> The seven *Profane* Sciences begin at the right hand as you face the fresco, the seven Theological at the left.
> *The Century*, XXXVII. 672.

2. Irreverent toward God or holy things; speaking or spoken, acting or acted, in manifest or implied contempt of sacred things; blasphemous: as, *profane* language; *profane* swearing.

> Then was the Sacred Bible sought out of the dusty corners where *prophane* Falsehood and Neglect had throwne it. *Milton*, Reformation in Eng., i.

> I din'd with ye Treas', where was ye Earle of Rochester, a very *prophane* wit. *Evelyn*, Diary, Nov. 24, 1670.

3. Not initiated into certain religious rites; hence, of less dignity or standing; inferior; common.

> Hence, ye *profane*, I hate you all,
> Both the great vulgar and the small.
> *Cowley*, tr. of Horace's Odes, iii. 1.

> "Far hence be souls *prophane*,"
> The Sibyl cryed, "and from the grove abstain."
> *Dryden*, Æneid, vi. 368.

=**Syn.** 1. Temporal, unhallowed, unholy.—2. *Impious, Atheistic*, etc. (see *irreligious*); irreverent, sacrilegious.

profane (prǫ-fān'), *v.*; pret. and pp. *profaned*, ppr. *profaning*. [Formerly also *prophane*; < F. *profaner* = Sp. Pg. *profanar* = It. *profanare*, < L. *profanare*, ML. also often *prophanare*, desecrate, profane, also consecrate, < *profanus*, profane: see *profane*, *a.*] I. *trans.* 1. To treat as if not sacred or deserving reverence; violate, as anything sacred; treat with irreverence, impiety, or contempt; pollute; desecrate.

> They *profaned* my holy name. Ezek. xxxvi. 20.

> Wonder of nature, let it not *profane* thee
> My rude hand touch thy beauty.
> *Fletcher (and others)*, Bloody Brother, v. 2.

> How by her patient Victor Death was slain,
> And Earth *prophan'd*, yet bless'd, with Deicide.
> *Prior*, I am that I am, st. 8.

> The temple and its holy rites *profaned*.
> *Cowper*, Expostulation, l. 145.

2. To put to a wrong use; employ basely or unworthily.

> I feel me much to blame,
> So idly to *profane* the precious time.
> *Shak.*, 2 Hen. IV., ii. 4. 391.

> One word is too often *profaned*
> For me to *profane* it. *Shelley*, To ——.

3†. To make known; make common: said of something confined to an initiated few. [Rare.]

> Wisdom is not *profaned* unto the world, and 'tis the privilege of a few to be virtuous.
> *Sir T. Browne*, Religio Medici, ii. 4.

II. *intrans.* To speak or behave blasphemously or profanely.

> They grew very troublesome to the better sort of people, and furnished the looser with an occasion to *profane*.
> *Penn*, Rise and Progress of Quakers, i.

profanely (prǫ-fān'li), *adv.* In a profane manner; with irreverence to sacred things or names; impiously; with abuse or contempt for anything venerable: as, to speak *profanely* of God or sacred things.

profaneness (prǫ-fān'nes), *n.* The state or character of being profane; irreverence toward sacred things; particularly, the use of language which manifests or implies irreverence toward God; the taking of God's name in vain.

profaner (prǫ-fā'nėr), *n.* 1. One who profanes, or who by words or actions treats sacred things with irreverence; a user of profane language.

> There are a lighter ludicrous sort of *profaners*, who use Scripture to furnish out their jests.
> *Government of the Tongue.*

2. A polluter; a defiler.

> Rebellious subjects, enemies to peace,
> *Profaners* of this neighbour-stained steel.
> *Shak.*, R. and J., i. 1. 89.

profanism†, *n.* [Also *prophanisme*; < *profane* + -*ism*.] Profaneness; profanity. [Rare.]

> Bee it spoken without *prophanisme*.
> *Marston*, What you Will, iv. 1.

profanity (prǫ-fan'i-ti), *n.* [< OF. *profanité*, *prophanité* = Sp. *profanidad* = Pg. *profanidade* = It. *profanità*, < LL. *profanita*(*t*-)*s*, profaneness, < L. *profanus*, profane: see *profane*.] 1. Profaneness; the quality of being profane.—2. That which is profane; profane language or conduct.

> In a revel of debauchery, amid the brisk interchange of *profanity* and folly, religion might appear a dumb, unsocial intruder. *Buckminster*. (*Webster*, 1848.)

=**Syn.** *Blasphemy, Profanity.* See *blasphemy*.

profect†, *n.* [< L. *profectus*, profit: see *profit*.] Profit.

> This shall (I truste) be consecrated to Apollo and the Muses, to theire no small *profecte* and your good contentation and pleasure.
> Quoted in *Babees Book* (E. E. T. S.), p. xxi.

profection† (prǫ-fek'shọn), *n.* [< OF. *profection*, < L. *profectio*(*n*-), a setting forth, departure, < *proficisci*, pp. *profectus*, set forth, proceed, set out, depart, < *pro*, forth, forward, + *facere*, make, do.] A setting forth; departure.

> The time of the yeere hasting the *profection* and departure of the Ambassador. *Hakluyt's Voyages*, I. 288.

profectitious (prō-fek-tish'us), *a.* [< LL. *profecticius*, *profectitius*, that proceeds from some one, < L. *proficisci*, pp. *profectus*, proceed: see *profection*.] Proceeding forth, as from a father; derived from an ancestor or ancestors. [Rare.]

> The threefold distinction of *profectitious*, adventitious, and professional was ascertained.
> *Gibbon*, Decline and Fall, VIII. xliv.

profecyet, *n.* A Middle English form of *prophecy*.

profert, *v.* and *n.* An obsolete form of *proffer*.

profert (prō'fėrt), *n.* [The first word of the L. phrase *profert in curia*, he produces in court: *profert*, 3d pers. sing. of *proferre*, bring forward, produce: see *proffer*.] In *law*, an exhibition of a record or paper in open court. At common law, a party who alleged a deed was generally obliged to make profert of such deed—that is, to produce it in court simultaneously with the pleading in which it was alleged. According to present usage this profert consists of a formal allegation that he shows the deed in court, it being, in fact, retained in his own custody.

profess (prǫ-fes'), *v.* [< ME. *professen* (first in pp. *professed*, after OF. *profes*, professed), < OF. (and F.) *professer* = Sp. *profesar* = Pg. *professar* = It. *professare*, < ML. *professare*, profess, receive on profession, < L. *professus*, pp. of *profiteri*, declare publicly, acknowledge, profess, confess, ‹ *pro*, forth, + *fateri*, confess. Cf. *confess*.] I. *trans.* 1. To declare openly; make open declaration of; avow or acknowledge; own freely; affirm.

And then will I *profess* unto them, I never knew you: depart from me, ye that work iniquity. Mat. vii. 23.

Is it sin
Still to *profess* I love you, still to vow
I shall do ever?
Beau. and Fl., Knight of Malta, v. 1.

We *profess*
Ourselves to be the slaves of chance.
Shak., W. T., iv. 4. 550.

Many things which they did were by the Apostles themselves *profest* to be done only for the present.
Milton, Reformation in Eng., i.

Rodolph would not consecrate Thurstane unless he would *profess* Obedience. Baker, Chronicles, p. 41.

2. To acknowledge or own publicly; also, to lay claim openly to the character of.

I first discover'd
Her bloody purposes, which she made good,
And openly *profess'd* 'em.
Fletcher, Double Marriage, v. 2.

But Purbeck (as *profess'd*, a huntress and a nun)
The wide and wealthy sea, nor all his pow'r respects.
Drayton, Polyolbion, ii. 92.

3. To affirm faith in or allegiance to: as, to *profess* Christianity.

By the saint whom I *profess*, I will plead against it with my life. Shak., M. for M., iv. 2. 192.

We sometimes find men loud in their admiration of truths which they never *profess*.
J. H. Newman, Gram. of Assent, p. 159.

4. To make a show of; make protestations of; make a pretense of; pretend.

The wretched man gan then avise too late
That love is not where most it is *profest*.
Spenser, F. Q., II. x. 31.

Wee *professe* to decide our controversies only by the Scriptures. Milton, On Def. of Humb. Remonst.

5. To announce publicly one's skill in, as a science or a profession; declare one's self versed in: as, to *profess* surgery.

I thank him that he cuts me from my tale;
For I *profess* not talking. Shak., 1 Hen. IV., v. 2. 92.

The severall Schooles wherein the seven liberall sciences are *professed*. Coryat, Crudities, I. 67.

Medicine is a science which hath been, as we have said, more *professed* than laboured.
Bacon, Advancement of Learning, ii. 193.

6. In the *Rom. Cath.* and *Anglican churches*, to receive into a religious order by profession.

I prey yow wyt al my herte, and as I evere may do yow service, that it lyke to your grace to graunte of your charite, by yowr worthy lettres to the priour of Thetford in Norfolk, of the seyde ordre of Clunye, autorite and power as your ministre and depute to *professe* in dwe forme the seyd monkes of Bromholm unprofessed.
Paston Letters, I. 30.

Neither a slave nor a married person (without the consent of the other spouse) . . . can be validly *professed*.
Rom. Cath. Dict., p. 699.

7. To present the appearance of. [Rare.]

Yet did her face and former parts *professe*
A faire young Mayden, full of comely glee.
Spenser, F. Q., VI. vi. 10.

=**Syn. 1** and **2**. To declare, allege, aver, avouch.—**4**. To lay claim to.

II. *intrans.* 1. To declare openly; make any declaration or assertion.—2. To enter into the religious state by public declaration or profession.

They [Calamarians] cannot *profess* before they are twenty-five years old; and they may take the vow after that age without probation.
Pococke, Description of the East, II. ii. 4.

3†. To declare or pretend friendship.

As he does conceive
He is dishonour'd by a man which ever
Profess'd to him, why, his revenges must
In that be made more bitter.
Shak., W. T., i. 2. 456.

professed (prǫ-fest'), *p. a.* [Pp. of *profess*, *v.*] Avowed; declared; pledged by profession; professional: as, a *professed* woman-hater; a *professed* nun; a *professed* cook.

Use well our father;
To your *professed* bosoms I commit him.
Shak., Lear, i. 1. 275.

Mr. Simpkinson from Bath was a *professed* antiquary, and one of the first water.
Barham, Ingoldsby Legends, I. 26.

The *professed* beauties, who are a people almost as insufferable as the *professed* wits. Steele, Spectator, No. 33.

Though not *Professed* but Plain, still her [the cook's] wages should be a sufficient object to her.
Dickens, Edwin Drood, xxii.

Monk (or **nun**) **professed**, one who by promise freely made and accepted has, after a year of probation, been received in and bound to a religious order.

Thare come the prior of the plas, and *professide monnkes*.
Morte Arthure (E. E. T. S.), l. 4014.

professedly (prǫ-fes'ed-li), *adv.* [‹ *professed* + *-ly*[2].] By profession; avowedly; by open declaration or avowal.

profession (prǫ-fesh'ǫn), *n.* [‹ ME. *professioun*, *professiun*, ‹ OF. *profession*, F. *profession* = Sp. *profesion* = Pg. *profissão* = It. *professione*, ‹ L. *professio(n-)*, a public acknowledgment or expression, ‹ *profiteri*, pp. *professus*, declare publicly: see *profess*.] 1. The act of professing; open declaration; public avowal or acknowledgment of one's sentiments or belief.

Grant unto all those who are admitted into the fellowship of Christ's Religion that they may avoid those things that are contrary to their *profession*.
Book of Common Prayer, Collect for Third Sunday after [Easter.

I hold it [christening] a good and gracious woorke, for the generall *profession* which they then take upon them of the Cross and faythe of Christ.
Spenser, State of Ireland.

2. That which is professed; a declaration; a representation or protestation; pretense; specifically, an open and formal avowal of Christian faith and purpose.

It is natural in absence to make *professions* of an inviolable constancy. Steele, Tatler, No. 104.

Perhaps, though by *profession* ghostly pure,
He too [the priest] may have his vice.
Cowper, Task, iv. 603.

What would he [Balaam] have given if words and feelings might have passed for deeds! See how religious he was so far as *profession* goes!
J. H. Newman, Parochial Sermons, i. 169.

3. The calling or occupation which one professes to understand and to follow; vocation; specifically, a vocation in which a professed knowledge of some department of science or learning is used by its practical application to affairs of others, either in advising, guiding, or teaching them, or in serving their interests or welfare in the practice of an art founded on it. Formerly theology, law, and medicine were specifically known as *the professions*; but, as the applications of science and learning are extended to other departments of affairs, other vocations also receive the name. The word implies professed attainments in special knowledge, as distinguished from mere skill; a practical dealing with affairs, as distinguished from mere study or investigation; and an application of such knowledge to uses for others as a vocation, as distinguished from its pursuit for one's own purposes. In professions strictly so called a preliminary examination as to qualifications is usually demanded by law or usage, and a license or other official authority founded thereon required. In law the significance of the word has been contested under statutes imposing taxes on persons pursuing any "occupation, trade, or profession," and under statutes authorizing arrest in civil actions for misconduct in a "professional employment"; and it has been, in the former use, held clearly to include the vocation of an attorney, and upon the same principle would doubtless include physicians, unless the mention of trade, etc., in the same clause of the statute be ground for interpreting the statute as relating only to business vocations. Professional employment, in statutes allowing arrest, is regarded as not including a private agency like that of a factor or a real-estate broker, which can be taken up and laid down at pleasure.

Being mechanical, you ought not walk
Upon a labouring day without the sign
Of your *profession*. Speak, what trade art thou?
Shak., J. C., i. 1. 5.

I hold every man a debtor to his *profession*.
Bacon, Maxims of the Law, Pref.

New *professions* have come into existence, and the old *professions* are more esteemed. It was formerly a poor and beggarly thing to belong to any other than the three learned *professions*. W. Besant, Fifty Years Ago, p. 262.

4. The collective body of persons engaged in a calling: as, practices disgraceful to the *profession*; to be at the head of one's *profession*.—5. The act by which a novice enters into a religious order and takes its vows. In the Roman Catholic Church he or she must be at least sixteen years of age and must have completed a year of probation.

He . . . yalt [yieldeth himself] into somme covente [convent] . . .
If he there make his mansioun [abiding-place]
For to abide *professioun*. Rom. of the Rose, l. 4910.

A religious or regular *profession* is "a promise freely made and lawfully accepted, whereby a person of the full age required, after the completion of a year of probation, binds him- (or her-) self to a particular religious institute approved by the Church." Rom. Cath. Dict.

6†. Character; nature.

And shortte to sai—so the *profession*
Of every vyne, and wherin thai myscheve
As counter it by goode discrecion.
Palladius, Husbondrie (E. E. T. S.), p. 63.

=**Syn. 3.** *Vocation*, *Business*, etc. See *occupation*.

professional (prǫ-fesh'on-al), *a.* and *n.* [‹ *profession* + *-al*.] I. *a.* 1. Pertaining or appropriate to a profession or calling: as, *professional* studies; *professional* skill.

With his quick *professional* eye, he [an Italian organ-boy] took note of the two faces watching him from the arched window, and, opening his instrument, began to scatter its melodies abroad. Hawthorne, Seven Gables, xi.

His brother,
Pale from long pulpit studies. . . . alternating between
A decent and *professional* gravity
And an irreverent mirthfulness.
Whittier, Bridal of Pennacook, Int.

2. Engaged in a profession; being such by profession.

Such marks of confidence must be very gratifying to a *professional* man. Dickens, Pickwick, iv.

The economic resistance to militant action, . . . leading to . . . fixed money payments in place of personal services, results in the growth of a revenue which serves to pay *professional* soldiers.
H. Spencer, Prin. of Sociol., § 520.

There has been a great upward movement of the *professional* class. W. Besant, Fifty Years Ago, p. 262.

The modern schoolmaster should change his name, for he has become a kind of standing or *professional* parent.
J. R. Seeley, Nat. Religion, p. 128.

3. Undertaken or engaged in for money or as a means of subsistence: opposed to *amateur*: said of sports and amusements: as, a *professional* base-ball match; a *professional* performance of a play.—**Professional education.** See *education*, 1.

II. *n.* 1. One who regularly pursues any profession or art.—2. Specifically, a person who makes his living by an art, game, or sport in which amateurs are accustomed to engage for amusement or recreation. The term thus more specifically designates professional musicians, actors, ball-players, oarsmen, boxers, etc.

"Try . . . cricket, for instance. The players generally beat the gentlemen, don't they?" "Yes; but they are *professionals*." T. Hughes, Tom Brown at Oxford, I. xii.

professionalism (prǫ-fesh'ǫn-al-izm), *n.* [‹ *professional* + *-ism*.] The characteristics, ideas, or methods of professional persons; that which savors of a professional, especially when so marked as to become objectionable or offensive: specifically used of athletic sports, etc., opposed to the methods or work of amateurs.

We need more manhood and less *professionalism*.
H. W. Beecher, Yale Lectures on Preaching, 1st ser., p. 40.

Professionalism in cricket . . . is divested of any obnoxious influences that may surround it in other amusements. Philadelphia Times, May 17, 1886.

professionalist (prǭ-fesh'ǫn-al-ist), *n.* [‹ *professional* + *-ist*.] One who practises or belongs to some profession; a professional. [Rare.] *Imp. Dict.*

professionality (prǭ-fesh-ǫn-al'i-ti), *n.* [‹ *professional* + *-ity*.] The state or property of being professional; adherence to professional standards. [Rare.]

There is one characteristic in which it is well for every country to imitate France: that is, the honesty and *professionality*, if I may invent such a word, of its work.
The Century, XXXI. 399.

professionalize (prǭ-fesh'ǫn-al-iz), *v.*; pret. and pp. *professionalized*, ppr. *professionalizing*. [‹ *professional* + *-ize*.] I. *trans.* To render professional. [Rare.]

They belittle where they should mature, or else they *professionalize* where they should humanize.
Andover Rev., VII. 1.

II. *intrans.* To become professional; behave or proceed in a professional manner. [Rare.]

professionally (prǭ-fesh'ǫn-al-i), *adv.* [‹ *professional* + *-ly*[2].] In a professional manner; by or in the way of one's profession or calling.

professor (prǭ-fes'ǫr), *n.* [= F. *professeur* = Sp. *profesor* = Pg. *professor* = It. *professore* = D. G. Sw. Dan. *professor*, ‹ L. *professor*, one who makes instruction in any branch his business, a public teacher, ‹ *profiteri*, pp. *professus*, declare publicly: see *profess*.] 1. One who professes; one who openly declares or makes profession of specific belief or views, of adherence to a certain course of action or way of life, or of knowledge or skill in any particular calling.

Q. Kath. [to Wolsey]. Ye turn me into nothing: woe upon ye
And all such false *professors*!
Shak., Hen. VIII., iii. 1. 115.

Whereas the more constant and devoted kind of *professors* of any science ought to propound to themselves to make some additions to their science, they convert their labours to aspire to certain second prizes.
Bacon, Advancement of Learning, i. 58.

2. One who makes open profession of religious faith and conversion, and attaches himself to some religious denomination. This use, probably originating among the English Puritans, is chiefly confined to English and Scottish nonconformists and their descendants.

Then the name of a *professor* was odious.
Bunyan, Pilgrim's Progress, ii., House of Mnason.

A mere *professor*, though a decent one, looks on the Bible as a dull book, and peruseth it with such indifference as you would read the title-deeds belonging to another man's estate. Berridge.

"As he was a *professor*, he would drive a nail for no man on the Sabbath, or kirk-fast, unless it were in a case of absolute necessity, for which he always charged sixpence each shoe." . . . The hearer . . . wondered what college this veterinary professor belonged to—not aware that the word was used to denote any person who pretended to uncommon sanctity of faith and manner. *Scott*, Waverley, xxx.

I'm a *professor*, and I ain't ashamed of it, week-days nor Sundays neither. *S. O. Jewett*, Deephaven, p. 197.

3. A public teacher in a university, especially one to whom this title has been formally granted. The title, now the highest that a teacher can receive, appears to have originated in the Italian universities. In Oxford and Cambridge, the professors, and the instruction which they convey by lectures, are only auxiliary instead of principal agents, the routine work of instruction being carried on by the tutors connected with the several colleges. In the universities of Scotland and Germany, on the other hand, the professors are at once the governing body and principal functionaries for the purposes of education. In American universities there is generally a professor at the head of each department of instruction, having often other professors and assistant professors under him. The title is often given, also, to teachers of special branches in secondary schools, and locally to principals of common schools (a use derived from the French).

At the present moment we want a *Professor* of Later Ecclesiastical History, to take up the subject at the point at which the department assigned to the Regius *Professor* comes to an end. *Stubbs*, Medieval and Modern Hist., p. 43.

4. In a loose use, any one who publicly teaches or exercises an art or occupation for pay, as a dancing-master, phrenologist, balloonist, juggler, acrobat, boxer, etc.

There be manie *professors* of the science of defence, and very skilful men in teaching the best and most offensive and defensive use of verie many weapons. *The Third University of England*, quoted in Strutt's Sports [and Pastimes, p. 355.

Ordinary professor, in German and some other European universities, an instructor of the highest grade, above an extraordinary professor.—**Professor emeritus.** See *emeritus*.—**Professor extraordinary.** See *extraordinary*, *a.*, 3.—**Regius professor.** See *regius*.

professorate (prǫ-fes'ǫr-āt), *n.* [= D. *professoraat* = G. Sw. Dan. *professorat* = F. *professorat* = Sp. *profesorado* = Pg. *professorado*, < ML. **professoratus*, < L. *professor*, a professor: see *professor*.] 1. The office or state of a professor or public teacher.—2. The period of time during which a professor occupies his office.

The sainted Bishop of Nola, who had been a favorite pupil of the poet during the *professorate* of the latter at Bordeaux. *The Atlantic*, LXV. 157.

3. A body of professors; the teaching staff of professors in a college or a university.

A complex organization for the higher education, with a regular *professorate*. *Encyc. Brit.*, XI. 64.

professoress (prǫ-fes'ǫr-es), *n.* [< *professor* + *-ess*.] A woman who is a professor. [Rare.]

If I had children to educate, I would at ten or twelve years of age have a professor, or *professoress*, of whist for them. *Thackeray*, Roundabout Papers, Autour de mon Chapeau.

professorial (prō-fe-sō'ri-al), *a.* [= F. *professorial* = It. *professoriale*, < L. *professorius*, pertaining to a public teacher, < *professor*, a public teacher: see *professor*.] Of or pertaining to a professor: as, a *professorial* chair.

I . . . will claim it as a *professorial* right to be allowed to utter truisms. *Stubbs*, Medieval and Modern Hist., p. 72.

Professorial socialist, socialism, etc. Same as *socialist*, *socialism*, etc., *of the chair*. See *socialist*, *socialism*, etc.

professorialism (prō-fe-sō'ri-al-izm), *n.* [< *professorial* + *-ism*.] The character or prevailing mode of thinking or acting of university or college professors. [Rare.]

professorially (prō-fe-sō'ri-al-i), *adv.* In the manner of a professor; as befits a professor.

professoriate (prō-fe-sō'ri-āt), *n.* An improper form of *professorate*.

The University [Oxford] will have to supply a large part of the teaching power, now provided by the colleges, in the shape of an increased *professoriate* or sub-*professoriate*. *Stubbs*, Medieval and Modern Hist., p. 43.

professorship (prǫ-fes'ǫr-ship), *n.* [< *professor* + *-ship*.] The state or office of a professor or public teacher, as of a college.

professory (prǫ-fes'ǫ-ri), *a.* [= Pg. *professorio*, < L. *professorius*, pertaining to a public teacher, < *professor*, a public teacher: see *professor*.] Of or pertaining to professors; professorial.

This dedicating of foundations and donations to *professory* learning hath . . . had a malign aspect. *Bacon*, Advancement of Learning, ii. 110.

profet[1]†, *n.* and *v.* A Middle English form of *profit*.

profet[2]†, *n.* A Middle English form of *prophet*.

proffer (prof'ėr), *v.* [< ME. *profren*, *profren*, < OF. *proferer*, F. *proférer* = Sp. Pg. *proferir* = It. *profferire*, *proferire*, bring forward, produce, allege, < L. *proferre*, bring forth, < *pro*, forth, + *ferre*, bring, = E. *bear*[1]. Cf. *prolate*.] I. *trans.* 1†. To bring or put forward; hold forth.

The paume is the pith of the honde, and *profreth* forth the fyngres
To mynystre and to make. *Piers Plowman* (C), xx. 116.

2. To hold forth so that a person may take; offer for acceptance: as, to *proffer* a gift; to *proffer* services; to *proffer* friendship.

Thanne come oon & stood ful stille,
And his seruice *profride* he.
Hymns to Virgin, etc. (E. E. T. S.), p. 59.

Ye hous of Zachei, in the whiche our Sauyoure *proferde* hymself to be lodged. *Sir R. Guylforde*, Pylgrymage, p. 41.

He *proffers* his defence, in tones subdued. *Browning*, Ring and Book, I. 36.

=**Syn.** 2. To tender, volunteer, propose.

II. *intrans.* To dodge. *Halliwell.* [Prov. Eng.]

proffer (prof'ėr), *n.* [< ME. *profer*, *profur*; < *proffer*, *v.*] 1. An offer made; something proposed for acceptance by another: as, *proffers* of peace or friendship.

And yet the kynges *profer* myght not agree the lady, and also hir frendes, thei hadde saf condite to returne to Tintagel. *Merlin* (E. E. T. S.), i. 82.

She to Paris made
Proffer of royal power, ample rule. *Tennyson*, Œnone.

2. In *law*, an offer or endeavor to proceed in an action.—3†. An essay; an attempt.

It is done with time, and by little and little, and with many essays and *proffers*. *Bacon.*

Y'are but a bad Fencer, for you never make a *proffer* against another mans weaknesse. *Milton*, On Def. of Humb. Remonst.

4. A rabbit-burrow. *Halliwell.* [Prov. Eng.]

The conies in making *profers* and holes to breed in have scraped them out of the ground in verie great abundance. *Holinshed*, Descrip. of England, ii. 24.

=**Syn.** 1. Tender, proposal.

profferer (prof'ėr-ėr), *n.* One who proffers; one who offers anything for acceptance.

Since maids, in modesty, say no to that
Which they would have the *profferer* construe ay.
Shak., T. G. of V., i. 2. 56.

proffet†, *n.* A Middle English form of *profit*.

proficiat† (prǫ-fish'i-at), *n.* [< OF. *proficiat*, a fee or benevolence (see def.), also congratulation, < ML. *proficium*, for *proficuum*, fee, emolument, profit, neut. of *proficuus*, profitable, < L. *proficere*, profit: see *profit*.] A fee or benevolence bestowed on bishops, in the manner of a welcome, immediately after their instalment. *Cotgrave.*

[He] would have caused him to be burnt alive, had it not been for Morgante, who for his *proficiat* and other small fees gave him nine tuns of beer. *Urquhart*, tr. of Rabelais, ii. 30. (*Davies.*)

proficience (prǫ-fish'ens), *n.* [= Pg. *proficiencia*; as *proficien(t)* + *-ce*.] Same as *proficiency*.

Let me endeavour an endless progress, or *proficience* in both. *Bacon*, Advancement of Learning, i. 13.

One Peckitt, at York, began the same business, and has made good *proficience*. *Walpole*, Anecdotes of Painting, II. i.

proficiency (prǫ-fish'en-si), *n.* [As *proficience* (see *-cy*).] 1†. Advancement; progress.

Though the Scriptures are read every day in our churches, . . . yet we make but slow *proficiency* towards a true taste, and a clear discernment, of those high truths which are contained in them. *Bp. Atterbury*, Sermons, II. ii.

2. The state of being proficient; the degree of advancement attained in any branch of knowledge; advance in the acquisition of any art, science, or knowledge; improvement: as, to attain great *proficiency* in Greek or in music.

Persons of riper years who flocked into the church during the three first centuries were obliged to pass through instructions, and give account of their *proficiency*. *Addison.*

All training is founded on the principle that culture must precede *proficiency*. *H. Spencer*, Social Statics, p. 205.

=**Syn.** 2. *Advance*, etc. (see *progress*), skill.

proficient (prǫ-fish'ent), *a.* and *n.* [= OF. *proficient* = Sp. Pg. It. *proficiente*, < L. *proficien(t-)s*, ppr. of *proficere*, go forward, advance, make progress, succeed, be profitable or useful, < *pro*, forth, forward, + *facere*, make, do: see *fact*. Cf. *profit*.] I. *a.* Well versed in any business, art, science, or branch of learning; skilled; qualified; competent: as, a *proficient* architect.

Proficient in all craft and stealthiness. *Browning*, Ring and Book, I. 132.

II. *n.* One who has made considerable advance in any business, art, science, or branch of learning; an adept; an expert: as, a *proficient* in a trade or occupation.

I am so good a *proficient* in one quarter of an hour that I can drink with any tinker in his own language. *Shak.*, 1 Hen. IV., ii. 4. 19.

We are such considerable *proficients* in politics that we can form rebellions within rebellions. *Walpole*, Letters, II. 6.

proficiently (prǫ-fish'ent-li), *adv.* [< *proficient* + *-ly*[2].] In a proficient manner; with proficiency.

proficuous (prǫ-fik'ū-us), *a.* [= Sp. *proficuo* = Pg. It. *proficuo*, < LL. *proficuus*, advantageous, beneficial, < L. *proficere*, advance, go forward: see *proficient*.] Profitable; advantageous; useful. [Rare.]

It is very *proficuous* to take a good large dose. *Harvey.*

proficy†, *v.* A Middle English form of *prophesy*.

profile (prō'fēl or -fil), *n.* [Formerly also *profil* (= D. *profil*, *profiel* = G. Sw. Dan. *profil*), < F. *profil*, a profile, < It. *profilo*, a border, later also *proffilo*, a side-face, profile, < *pro-*, < L. *pro*, before, + *filo*, a line, stroke, thread, < L. *filum*, a thread: see *file*[3]. Cf. *purfle*, from the same L. source.] 1. An outline or contour; specifically, the largest contour or outline of anything, usually seen in or represented by a vertical longitudinal section or side view. For example, nearly all the fishes, butterflies, etc., figured in this dictionary are drawn in *profile*. Hence—2. (*a*) The outline of the human face in a section through the median line; a side view; the side-face or half-face: as, a Greek *profile*.

Till about the end of the third century, when there was a general decay in all the arts of designing, I do not remember to have seen the head of a Roman emperor drawn with a full face. They always appear in *profil*, to use a French term of art. *Addison*, Ancient Medals, iii.

I'll break your faces till you haven't a *profile* between you. *Dickens*, Old Curiosity Shop, vi.

(*b*) A representation of the face in side view: as, *profiles* cut in black paper are called silhouettes.

Two *profile* heads in medal of William and Mary. *Walpole*, Anecdotes of Painting, V. 171.

(*c*) In *arch.*, the outline or contour of anything, such as a building, a figure, a molding, as shown by a section through it.

It is true that the *Profil* or Draught of Cambalu, which the Portuguese have at Lisbon in the Custom-House, differs from that of Peking, which the Hollanders brought along with them. *Hist.*, *Geog.*, etc., *Dict.*, ed. Collier, 2d [ed. (1701), s. v. Cambalu.

(*d*) In *engin.* and *surv.*, a vertical section through a work or a section of country, to show the elevations and depressions.

An article on the actual status of the Panama Canal, . . . accompanied by a progress *profile*, showing the amount of work done and undone to January 1st of the present year. *Jour. Franklin Inst.*, CXXVI. 341.

(*e*) In *fort.*, a light wooden frame set up to guide workmen in throwing up a parapet. (*f*) The outline of a vertical section made through any part of a fortification in a direction perpendicular to its principal bounding lines. *Mahan.* (*g*) In *ceram.*, a thin plate, as of zinc, in which is cut the outline of half of an object. The mass of clay being revolved on the potters' wheel and the profile applied to it, the exterior form is given. =**Syn.** 1. *Contour*, etc. See *outline*.

profile (prō'fēl or -fil), *v. t.*; pret. and pp. *profiled*, ppr. *profiling*. [< F. *profiler*, draw in outline, < *profil*, an outline: see *profile*, *n.*] 1. To draw with a side view; outline (any object or objects) so as to show a section as if cut perpendicularly from top to bottom.

Had they [Gothic architects] carefully *profiled* and ornamented the exterior of the stone roofs . . . *J. Fergusson*, Hist. Arch., I. 450.

2. In *mech.*, to impart by means of a tool or tools a definite prescribed form to (pieces of wood or metal) by chiseling, milling, filing, or like operations.—3. *Theat.*, to cut (the edge of wings or set pieces) into irregular shapes to represent trees, rocks, etc.

profile-board (prō'fēl-bōrd), *n.* A thin plate or board having its edge so cut as to delineate the outline of an object: used to prove the models of the breech and other exterior parts of a gun.

profile-cutter (prō'fēl-kut"ėr), *n.* In *wood-working*, a knife with an irregular or curved cutting edge corresponding to the shape to be cut; in *metal-working*, a circular milling-cutter.

profile-paper (prō'fēl-pā"pėr), *n.* Paper ruled with horizontal and vertical lines for convenience in drawing profiles of engineering works.

profile-piece (prō'fēl-pēs), *n.* *Theat.*, a strip of scenery that has been profiled.

profiling-machine (prō'fēl-ing-ma-shēn"), *n.* A form of milling-machine for cutting out small parts of machinery, etc., from a pattern or templet; an edging-machine. The cutter is guided by the movement of a guide-pin around the edge or profile of the pattern. Such machines are largely used to make the parts of such machinery as has to be turned out in large quantity with interchangeable parts, as locomotives, fire-arms, watches, etc.

profilist (prō'fēl-ist or -fil-ist), *n.* [< *profile* + *-ist.*] One who takes or makes profiles.

profilograph (prō-fil'ō-gråf), *n.* [< E. *profile* + Gr. γράφειν, write.] An instrument used for making an automatic record of the profile of the ground over which it moves. It consists of a light four-wheeled vehicle so arranged that as it advances a band of paper is moved mechanically over a table on top of the machine a distance corresponding to the distance traveled according to a prearranged scale of distances. Beneath the machine is suspended a pendulum always hanging vertically, and serving to actuate a pencil the point of which rests on the paper and leaves a trace upon it. Any inequality of the surface causes the machine to incline from the level, and produces a corresponding deviation from a straight line in the mark traced by the pencil. The data obtained from these indications are sufficient for reproduction to scale of the profile traversed.

profit (prof'it), *n.* [< ME. *profit, profet, proffit, proffet, prophete* = D. *profijt* = G. Sw. Dan. *profit*, < OF. *profit*, F. *profit* = It. *profitto*, advantage, profit, < L. *profectus*, advance, progress, growth, increase, profit, < *proficere*, pp. *profectus*, go forward, advance, make progress, be profitable or useful: see *proficient*. Cf. *profect*, directly from the L. The Sp. *provecho* = Pg. *proveito*, profit, is < LL. *provectus*, advancement, < L. *provehere*, pp. *provectus*, carry forward, advance: see *provection*.] 1†. Advancement; improvement.

My brother Jaques he keeps at school, and report speaks goldenly of his *profit*. *Shak.*, As you Like it, i. 1. 7.

2. Any advantage; accession of good from labor or exertion; the acquisition of anything valuable, corporeal or intellectual, temporal or spiritual.

All the grete of the grekes gedrit hym somyn
To a counsell to come for the comyn *profet*.
Destruction of Troy (E. E. T. S.), l. 9320.

Wisdom is good with an inheritance; and by it there is *profit* to them that see the sun. Eccl. vii. 11.

What neither yields us *profit* nor delight
Is like a nurse's lullaby at night.
Cowper, Conversation, l. 241.

3. Specifically, the advantage or gain resulting to the owner of capital from its employment in any undertaking; the excess of the selling price over the original cost of anything; acquisition beyond expenditure; pecuniary gain in any action or occupation; gain; emolument: in commerce commonly used in the plural. As used in political economy, *profit* means what is left of the product of industry after deducting the wages, the price of raw materials, and the rent paid in the production, and is considered as being composed of three parts—interest, risk or insurance, and wages of superintendence. *Profits* in the law of real property designate rights of taking something off or out of the land, as, for instance, the right of common, as distinguished from *easements*, such as ways and access of air and light, which do not involve taking anything from the land.

Ne alle the *prophete* of the lond that the prince owed [owned] . . .
Myзte not areche . . . to paie the pore peple.
Richard the Redeles (ed. Skeat), iv. 10.

In Italy they make great *profit* of the spawn of Carps, by selling it to the Jews, who make it into red caviare. *I. Walton*, Complete Angler, p. 145.

The revenue derived from labour is called wages; that derived from stock, by the person who manages or employs it, is called *profit*. *Adam Smith*, Wealth of Nations, i. 7.

The gross *profit* from capital . . . must afford a sufficient equivalent for abstinence, indemnity for risk, and remuneration for the labour and skill required for superintendence. *J. S. Mill*, Pol. Econ., II. xv. § 1.

Action of mesne profits, trespass for mesne profits, the action brought after successful ejectment, or the claim made in an action of ejectment, to compel the disseizor to account for and pay over the mesne profits.—**Mesne profits.** See *mesne*.—**Net profits.** See *net*2.—**Profit and loss**, the gain or loss arising from the buying or selling of goods, or from other commercial transactions. In bookkeeping gains and losses are spoken of jointly as *profit and loss*, but the former are placed on the creditor and the latter on the debtor side in the accounts. *Profit and loss* is also the name of a rule in arithmetic which teaches how to calculate the gains or losses on mercantile transactions.—**Rate of profit**, the proportion which the amount of profit derived from an undertaking bears to the capital employed in it. =**Syn.** 2. *Benefit, Utility*, etc. (see *advantage*), service, welfare, behalf, behoof, weal, good.—3. *Revenue*, etc. (see *income*), return, avails.

profit (prof'it), *v.* [< ME. *profiten, profyten, proffeten, prophiten*, < OF. *profiter*, F. *profiter*, profit; from the noun.] **I.** *trans.* To benefit; advantage; be of service to; help on; improve; advance.

If any man chyde thee with cause, be thou assured that he doeth *profyte* thee. *Babees Book* (E. E. T. S.), p. 106.

'Tis a great means of *profiting* yourself, to copy diligently excellent pieces and beautiful designs. *Dryden.*

II. *intrans.* 1. To make improvement; improve; grow better; make progress, intellectually or morally: as, to *profit* by reading or by experience.

My son *profits* nothing in the world at his book. *Shak.*, M. W. of W., iv. 1. 15.

No man *profits* by a sermon that hears with pain or weariness. *Donne*, Sermons, v.

2. To gain in a material sense; become better off or richer: as, to *profit* by trade or manufactures.

The Romans, though possessed of their ports, did not *profit* much by trade. *Arbuthnot*, Ancient Coins.

An animal of a predatory kind, which has prey that can be caught and killed without help, *profits* by living alone. *H. Spencer*, Prin. of Psychol., § 503.

3. To be of use or advantage; bring good.

Riches *profit* not in the day of wrath. Prov. xi. 4.

What the world teaches *profits* to the world,
What the soul teaches *profits* to the soul.
Lowell, Parting of the Ways.

profitable (prof'i-ta-bl), *a.* [< ME. *profitable, proffitable, prophitable*, < OF. *profitable*, F. *profitable* (= Pr. *profechable, profichable, proficitable* = It. *profittabile, profittabole*), advantageous, < *profit*, advantage: see *profit*.] Useful; advantageous; yielding or bringing profit or gain; gainful; lucrative: as, a *profitable* trade; *profitable* business.

Yf we take this full tite, and tary no lengur,
Bothe pepull and pilage, and put [them] into ship,
Hit is a *profitable* pray of persons me thinke.
Destruction of Troy (E. E. T. S.), l. 3106.

"Bi seint Poul!" quod Pers, "theos beoth *prophitable* wordes!
This is a louell lesson; vr lord hit the for-зelde!"
Piers Plowman (A), vii. 262.

A pound of man's flesh taken from a man
Is not so estimable, *profitable* neither,
As flesh of muttons, beefs, or goats.
Shak., M. of V., i. 3. 167.

To tell you my dream . . . was pleasant to me, and *profitable* to you. *Bunyan*, Pilgrim's Progress, p. 227.

=**Syn.** Remunerative, productive, beneficial.

profitableness (prof'i-ta-bl-nes), *n.* [< *profitable* + *-ness*.] The quality of being profitable; gainfulness; usefulness; advantageousness: as, the *profitableness* of trade.

profitably (prof'i-ta-bli), *adv.* [< *profitable* + *-ly*2.] In a profitable manner; with gain; gainfully; usefully; advantageously.

profitet, *n.* A Middle English form of *prophet*.

profiter (prof'i-tėr), *n.* One who profits.

A wonderful *profiter* by opportunities. *Nineteenth Century*, XXIV. 473.

profitless (prof'it-les), *a.* [< *profit* + *-less*.] Void of profit, gain, or advantage.

Profitless usurer, why dost thou use
So great a sum of sums, yet canst not live?
Shak., Sonnets, iv.

profitlessly (prof'it-les-li), *adv.* [< *profitless* + *-ly*2.] In a profitless manner; without profit.

profit-sharing (prof'it-shãr"ing), *n.* The fact or principle of the division of realized profits between the capitalist, the employer, and the employee, in addition to regular interest, salary, and wages. *N. P. Gilman*, Profit Sharing, x.

profligacy (prof'li-gā-si), *n.* [< *profliga(te)* + *-cy*.] The character or condition of being profligate; a profligate or very vicious course of life; abandoned conduct; shameless dissipation.

Hitherto it has been thought the highest pitch of *profligacy* to own instead of concealing crimes, and to take pride in them instead of being ashamed of them. *Bolingbroke*, Idea of a Patriot King.

The fatal consequences which must flow from *profligacy* and licentiousness. *Bp. Barrington*, Letter to his Clergy, 1789.

=**Syn.** Shamelessness. See *abandoned*.

profligate† (prof'li-gāt), *v. t.* [< L. *profligatus*, pp. of *profligare* (> Sp. Pg. *profligar*), dash to the ground, overthrow, ruin, destroy, < *pro*, forth, forward, + *fligere*, strike, dash: see *blow*3.] To drive away; disperse; discomfit; overcome.

In the which I doubt not but God will rather aid us, yea, and fight for us, than see us vanquished and *profligated*. *Hall's Union* (1548). (*Halliwell.*)

You have not yet *profligated* the Pope quite, till the second and third . . . Part of your Book of his Supremacy come out. *Milton*, Answer to Salmasius, viii. 194.

profligate (prof'li-gāt), *a.* and *n.* [< L. *profligatus*, overthrown, abandoned, wretched, vile, pp. of *profligare*, overthrow, ruin: see *profligate, v.*] **I.** *a.* 1†. Overthrown; conquered; defeated.

We once more, as conquerors,
Have both the field and honour won;
The foe is *profligate*, and run.
S. Butler, Hudibras, I. iii. 728.

2. Ruined in morals; abandoned to vice; lost to principle, virtue, or decency; extremely vicious; shamelessly wicked.

Made prostitute and *profligate* the muse,
Debased to each obscene and impious use.
Dryden, To the Memory of Mrs. Anne Killigrew, l. 58.

No absolutely *profligate* king could have got into the miserable abyss in which we find Henry VIII. struggling during the latter half of his reign. *Stubbs*, Medieval and Modern Hist., p. 290.

=**Syn.** 2. *Profligate, Abandoned, Reprobate*, etc. See *abandoned* and *wicked*.

II. *n.* An abandoned person; one who has lost all regard for good principles, virtue, or decency.

How could such a *profligate* as Antony, or a boy of eighteen like Octavius, ever dare to dream of giving law to such an empire? *Swift.*

profligately (prof'li-gāt-li), *adv.* [< *profligate* + *-ly*2.] In a profligate manner; without principle or shame; in a course of extreme viciousness.

profligateness (prof'li-gāt-nes), *n.* [< *profligate* + *-ness*.] The character of being profligate; profligacy.

He was of opinion that, "if this country could be preserved from utter *profligateness* and ruin, it must be by their [the clergy's] means." *Bp. Porteous*, Abp. Secker.

profligation† (prof-li-gā'shon), *n.* [< LL. *profligatio(n-)*, ruin, destruction, < L. *profligare*, overthrow, ruin, destroy: see *profligate, v.*] Defeat; rout.

The braying of Silenus's ass conduced much to the *profligation* of the giants. *Bacon*, Wisdom of the Ancients, Pref.

profluence† (prof'lö-ens), *n.* [< L. *profluentia*, a flowing forth, < *profluen(t-)s*, flowing forth: see *profluent*.] The act or quality of being profluent; a forward progress or course.

The *profluence* or proceedings of their fortunes. *Sir H. Wotton*, Reliquiæ, p. 164.

profluent† (prof'lö-ent), *a.* [< L. *profluen(t-)s*, ppr. of *profluere*, flow forth or along, < *pro*, forth, + *fluere*, flow: see *fluent*.] Flowing forth or forward.

Baptizing in the *profluent* stream. *Milton*, P. L., xii. 442.

pro forma (prō fôr'mä). [L.: *pro*, for; *formā*, abl. of *forma*, form.] As a matter of form.

During his [Foote's] continuance in the Temple he was seen there *pro forma*, . . . eating his way (via commons) to the profession of the law. *W. Cooke*, Memoirs of S. Foote, I. 16.

Pro forma invoice, a statement in the form of an invoice which may be presented at the custom-house by an owner or importer who cannot furnish an invoice, and if duly verified is allowed as a substitute.

profound (prō-found'), *a.* and *n.* [< ME. *profound, profunde*, < OF. *profond, profund*, F. *profond* = Sp. Pg. *profundo* = It. *profondo*, < L. *profundus*, deep, vast, < *pro*, forth, forward, + *fundus*, bottom: see *fund*1.] **I.** *a.* 1. Deep; descending or being far below the surface, or far below the adjacent places; having great depth.

The diches *profunde*. *Rom. of Partenay* (E. E. T. S.), l. 1180.

All . . . the *profound* seas hide
In unknown fathoms. *Shak.*, W. T., iv. 4. 501.

A gulf *profound* as that Serbonian bog. *Milton*, P. L., ii. 592.

Specifically—(*a*) In *anat.*, deep-seated; not superficial: specifically applied to several structures, as arteries and muscles. See *profunda*. (*b*) In *entom.*, strongly impressed; very deep and distinct: as, *profound* punctures, striæ, or indentations. (*c*) Coming from a great depth; deep-fetched.

He raised a sigh so piteous and *profound*
As it did seem to shatter all his bulk,
And end his being. *Shak.*, Hamlet, ii. 1. 94.

(*d*) Bending low; hence, lowly; humble; exhibiting or expressing deep humility: as, a *profound* bow.

2. Intellectually deep; entering deeply into subjects; not superficial or obvious; deep in knowledge or skill; penetrating.

A head for thought *profound* and clear unmatch'd. *Burns*, On William Smellie.

A sparrow fluttering about the church is an antagonist which the most *profound* theologian in Europe is wholly unable to overcome. *Sydney Smith*, in Lady Holland, iii.

3. Characterized by magnitude or intensity; deep-felt; intense; great.

I do love
My country's good with a respect more tender,
More holy and *profound*, than mine own life.
Shak., Cor., iii. 3. 113.

They treat themselves with most *profound* respect. *Pope*, Imit. of Horace, II. ii. 154.

The members rose and uncovered their heads in *profound* silence, and the King took his seat in the chair. *Macaulay*, Nugent's Hampden.

With a general sigh
At matrimony the *profound* mistake.
Browning, Ring and Book, I. 130

If God exists, no injustice can be so excessive, no error can be so *profound*, as to fail in uttering the deepest adoration and greatest praise our minds can conceive or our actions express. *Mivart*, Nature and Thought, p. 231.

4. Deep-seated; thorough; complete.

Which of your hips has the most *profound* sciatica? *Shak.*, M. for M., i. 2. 59.

5. Deep in skill or contrivance. [Rare.]

The revolters are *profound* to make slaughter. Hos. v. 2.

6. Having hidden qualities; obscure; abstruse.

Upon the corner of the moon
There hangs a vaporous drop *profound*.
Shak., Macbeth, iii. 5. 24.

II. *n.* **1.** A deep, immeasurable space; an abyss.

Sinking from thought to thought, a vast *profound!* *Pope*, Dunciad, i. 118.

From the curved horizon's bound
To the point of heaven's *profound*.
Shelley, Written among the Euganean Hills.

And we shout so adeep down creation's *profound*,
We are deaf to God's voice.
Mrs. Browning, Rhapsody on Life's Progress.

2. The deep; the sea; the ocean: with the definite article.

Now I die absent, in *the* vast *profound;*
And me without myself the seas have drowned.
Dryden, tr. of Ovid's Metamorph., xi. 423.

Between where Samos wide his forests spreads
And rocky Imbrus lifts its pointed heads,
Down plung'd the maid (the parted waves resound);
She plung'd, and instant shot *the* dark *profound*.
Pope, Iliad, xxiv. 106.

profound† (prọ̄-found'), *v.* [< OF. *profonder*, sound the depths of, plunge into, penetrate, < *profond*, deep, profound: see *profound, a.*] **I.** *trans.* **1.** To cause to sink deeply; cause to penetrate far down.—**2.** To penetrate.

There is no danger to *profound* these mysteries. *Sir T. Browne*, Religio Medici, i. 13.

II. *intrans.* To dive; penetrate.

We cannot *profound* into the hidden things of nature. *Glanville.*

profoundly (prọ̄-found'li), *adv.* In a profound manner; deeply; with deep penetration; with deep knowledge or insight; thoroughly; extremely; very.

Why sigh you so *profoundly?* *Shak.*, T. and C., iv. 2. 83.

Domenichino was *profoundly* skilled in all the parts of painting. *Dryden.*

There are other forms of culture besides physical science; and I should be *profoundly* sorry to see the fact forgotten. *Huxley*, Lay Sermons, p. 62.

profoundness (prọ̄-found'nes), *n.* Depth; profundity.

Let any gentle apprehension that can distinguish learned pains from unlearned drudgery imagin what pleasure or *profoundnesse* can be in this. *Milton*, Church-Government, ii., Int.

Perhaps he required to take a deep, deep plunge into the ocean of human life, and to sink down and be covered by its *profoundness*. *Hawthorne*, Seven Gables, xi.

profulgent (prọ̄-ful'jẹnt), *a.* [< L. *pro*, forth, + *fulgen(t-)s*, ppr. of *fulgere*, flash, shine: see *fulgent.*] Shining forth; effulgent.

Profulgent in preciousnes, O Sinope the quene. *The Nine Ladies Worthy*, l. 1.

profund† (prọ̄-fund'), *v. t.* [< L. *profundere*, pour forth, pour out, < *pro*, forth, + *fundere*, pour: see *found*[3]. Cf. *profuse.*] To lavish.

For the exchewing of great expences, whiche shuld be *profunded* and consumed in the said interview. *State Papers*, i. 251. (*Halliwell.*)

profunda (prọ̄-fun'dạ̈), *n.*; pl. *profundæ* (-dē). [NL. (sc. *arteria*), fem. of L. *profundus*, deep: see *profound.*] A deep-seated or profound artery, as of the arm, neck, or leg: more fully called *arteria profunda.*—**Profunda artery.** (*a*) *Inferior of the arm*, a small branch of the brachial, arising about the middle of the arm, more fully called *profunda brachii inferior.* (*b*) *Superior of the arm*, the largest branch of the brachial, arising near its beginning, and winding round the humerus in the musculospiral groove, more fully called *profunda brachii superior.* (*c*) *Of the clitoris* or *of the penis*, the artery of the corpus cavernosum, a branch of the pudic. (*d*) *Of the thigh*, the principal branch of the femoral, arising below Poupart's ligament, and descending deeply on the adductor magnus. It gives off the circumflex and perforating arteries. Also called *profunda femoris, deep femoral artery.*—**Profunda cervicis**, the deep artery of the neck, a branch of the superior intercostal which anastomoses with the principal branch of the occipital artery.

profundipalmar (prọ̄-fun-di-pal'mạ̈r), *a.* [< L. *profundus*, deep, + *palma*, the palm of the hand: see *palmar.*] Deep or profound, as the palmar flexor tendons; pertaining to the deep-seated flexor tendons of the palm. *Coues.*

profundiplantar (prọ̄-fun-di-plan'tạ̈r), *a.* [< L. *profundus*, deep, + *planta*, the sole of the foot: see *plantar.*] Deep or profound, as the plantar tendons; pertaining to the deep-seated flexor tendons of the planta or sole.

The tendons of *profundiplantar* mys. *Coues*, The Auk, Jan., 1888, p. 105.

profunditude† (prọ̄-fun'di-tūd), *n.* [< L. *profundus*, deep, + *-itude* as in *altitude*, etc.] Profundity.

The body three dimensions doth include,
And they are these, length, bredth, *profunditude*.
Times' Whistle (E. E. T. S.), p. 149.

'Tis reported of that *profunditude* in the middle that it is botomelesse. *Evelyn*, Diary, Feb. 7, 1645.

profundity (prọ̄-fun'dị-ti), *n.* [= OF. *profondité, profundité* = Sp. *profundidad* = Pg. *profundidade* = It. *profondità*, < LL. *profunditu(t-)s*, depth, intensity, < L. *profundus*, deep, vast: see *profound.*] **1.** The character or condition of being profound; depth, as of place, of knowledge, of science, of feeling, etc.

Seek not for *profundity* in shallowness, or fertility in a wilderness. *Sir T. Browne*, Christ. Mor., iii. 11.

She had been trying to fathom the *profundity* and appositeness of this concluding apothegm. *Hawthorne*, Seven Gables, x.

2. That which is profound; depth; abyss.

He took the golden compasses, prepared; . . .
One foot he centred, and the other turn'd
Round through the vast *profundity* obscure.
Milton, P. L., vii. 229.

profuse† (prọ̄-fūz'), *v. t.* [< L. *profusus*, pp. of *profundere*, pour forth, pour out: see *profund.*] To pour out; dispense liberally; lavish; squander.

Thy helpe hath beene *profused*
Euer with most grace in consorts of trauailers distresst.
Chapman.

If I had laid out that which I *profused* in luxury and wantonness in acts of generosity or charity. *Steele*, Spectator, No. 260.

profuse (prọ̄-fūs'), *a.* [= Sp. Pg. It. *profuso*, < L. *profusus*, liberal, lavish, pp. of *profundere*, pour forth: see *profuse, v.*] **1.** Liberal to excess; extravagant; lavish; prodigal: as, *profuse* hospitality; *profuse* expenditure.

Profuse to many unworthy applicants, the ministers were niggardly to him [Temple] alone. *Macaulay*, Sir William Temple.

He indulged in a *profuse* magnificence in his apparel, equipage, and general style of living. *Prescott*, Ferd. and Isa., ii. 2.

2. Abundant; exuberant; bountiful; copious: as, *profuse* ornament; *profuse* compliment.

Returning loaden with the shining Stores
Which lie *profuse* on either India's Shores.
Prior, Carmen Seculare (1700), st. 36.

That ye may garnish your *profuse* regales
With summer fruits brought forth by wintry suns.
Cowper, Task, iii. 551.

Flattering superlatives and expressions of devotion are less *profuse* here than abroad. H. *Spencer*, Prin. of Sociol., § 398.

=**Syn.** **1.** *Lavish*, etc. See *extravagant.*

profusely (prọ̄-fūs'li), *adv.* In a profuse manner; exuberantly; lavishly; prodigally; with rich abundance.

Then spring the living herbs *profusely* wild. *Thomson*, Spring, l. 221.

profuseness (prọ̄-fūs'nes), *n.* [< *profuse* + *-ness.*] The state, quality, or habit of being profuse; profusion; prodigality.

Be the sums never so vast we pay away, their being due, in spight of their being great, makes the disbursement too much an act of justice to be one of *profuseness*. *Boyle*, Works, I. 255.

profuser (prọ̄-fū'zėr), *n.* One who pours out or lavishes. [Rare.]

Fortune's a blind *profuser* of her own;
Too much she gives to some, enough to none.
Herrick, Fortune.

profusion (prọ̄-fū'zhọn), *n.* [< F. *profusion* = Sp. *profusion* = Pg. *profusão* = It. *profusione*, < L. *profusio(n-)*, a pouring out, shedding, effusion, prodigality, profusion, < *profusus*, pp. of *profundere*, pour forth: see *profuse.*] **1.** Profuse or extravagant expenditure; prodigality; lavishment; waste.

He was desirous to avoid not only *profusion*, but the least effusion of Christian blood. *Sir J. Hayward.*

Upon these *Profusions*, a Consultation is had for new Supplies, and no Way thought so fit as by Parliament. *Baker*, Chronicles, p. 81.

Mary Magdalen having been reproved by Judas for spending ointment upon Jesus's feet, it being so unaccustomed and large a *profusion*. *Jer. Taylor*, Works (ed. 1835), I. 290.

They now found that, in enterprises like theirs, parsimony is the worst *profusion*. *Macaulay*, Hallam's Const. Hist.

2. Abundance; lavish supply; superfluity.

To have furnished out so many glorious palaces with such a *profusion* of pictures, statues, and the like ornaments. *Addison*, Remarks on Italy (ed. Bohn), I. 421.

Curls became her, and she possessed them in picturesque *profusion*. *Charlotte Brontë*, Shirley, vi.

=**Syn.** **2.** *Abundance, Exuberance*, etc. (see *plenty*), lavishness, superabundance.

profusive† (prọ̄-fū'siv), *a.* [< *profuse* + *-ive.*] Profuse; lavish; prodigal. *Evelyn.*

prog (prog), *v.*; pret. and pp. *progged*, ppr. *progging*. [Formerly also *proag, progue;* a var. of *proke:* see *proke*, and cf. *prowl.*] **I.** *trans.* To poke; prod. [Scotch.]

II. *intrans.* **1.** To go prowling about, as for pickings or plunder; prowl; filch; forage; especially, to go a-begging.

That man in the gown, in my opinion,
Looks like a *proguing* knave.
Fletcher, Spanish Curate, iii. 3.

Pandulf, an Italian and pope's legate, a perfect artist in *progging* for money. *Fuller.*

Excommunication servs for nothing with them but to *prog* and pandar for fees, or to display their pride and sharpen their revenge. *Milton*, Reformation in Eng., ii.

You are the lion; I have been endeavouring to *prog* for you. *Burke.*

2. To search carelessly or aimlessly, as for oysters, clams, etc., along the shore in a rambling way. [U. S.]

prog (prog), *n.* [< *prog, v.*] **1.** A pointed instrument for poking or prodding.

The Cooks . . . prick it [mutton] on a *prog* of iron, and hang it in a furnace. *Sandys*, Travailes, p. 21.

2. A poke; a prod. [Scotch.]

But I was not so kittly as she thought, and could thole her *progs* and jokes with the greatest pleasure and composure. *Galt*, The Steam-Boat, p. 155. (*Jamieson.*)

3. Victuals got by begging; hence, victuals in general; food. [Colloq.]

The Abbot also every Saturday was to visit their beds, to see if they had not . . . purloyned some *progge* for themselves. *Fuller*, Ch. Hist., V. 290. (*Davies.*)

You can junket together at nights upon your own *prog*, when the rest of the house are a-bed. *Swift*, Directions to Servants, ii.

Livin' on hard-tack an' salt *prog*. *The Century*, XXXV. 621.

4. One who goes from place to place begging for victuals. *Imp. Dict.*

progametange (prō-gam'e-tanj), *n.* [< NL. *progametangium.*] Same as *progametangium.*

progametangium (prō-gam"e-tan-ji'um), *n.*; pl. *progametangia* (-ạ̈). [NL., < L. *pro*, before, + NL. *gametangium.*] In *bot.*, an immature or resting gametangium, as that which occurs in the development of *Protomyces macrosporus*. See *gametangium.*

progenerate† (prọ̄-jen'ẹ-rāt), *v. t.* [< L. *progeneratus*, pp. of *progenerare* (> It. *progenerare*), beget, < *pro*, forth, + *generare*, beget, produce: see *generate.*] To beget; propagate.

They were all *progenerated* colonies from a Scythian or Tartar race. *Archæologia* (1773), II. 250. (*Davies.*)

What then, I pray thee, is there dead? . . . Surely not he who is yet to *progenerate* a more numerous and far better race. *Landor*, Imaginary Conversations.

progeneration† (prọ̄-jen-ẹ-rā'shọn), *n.* [< LL. *progeneratio(n-)*, a begetting, < L. *progenerare*, pp. *progeneratus*, beget: see *progenerate.*] The act of begetting; propagation.

progenial† (prọ̄-jē'niạl), *a.* [< L. *progenies*, descent, progeny (see *progeny*), + *-al.*] Pertaining to descent or lineage.

Whether [the intellectual Soul is] immediately produced, without any *progenial* traduction or radiation. *Evelyn*, True Religion, I. 159.

progenitiveness (prọ̄-jen'i-tiv-nes), *n.* [Irreg. < L. *progenies*, progeny, + *-itive* + *-ness.* Cf. *philoprogenitiveness.*] Philoprogenitiveness, in a modified biological sense. [Rare.]

There is another difficulty in the way of accepting metaphysical peculiarity or *progenitiveness* as isolating species. It is marked often strongly in races or varieties which no one pretends to have had distinct origin. *E. D. Cope*, Origin of the Fittest, p. 111.

progenitor (prọ̄-jen'i-tọr), *n.* [Early mod. E. *progenitour*, < OF. *progeniteur* = Sp. Pg. *progenitor* = It. *progenitore*, < L. *progenitor*, the founder of a family, an ancestor, < *progignere*, pp. *progenitus*, beget, bring forth, < *pro*, forth, + *gignere*, beget, produce: see *genitor.*] An ancestor in the direct line; a forefather; a parent.

If children pre-decease *progenitors*,
We are their offspring, and they none of ours.
Shak., Lucrece, l. 1756.

Ah! whither shall we go?
Down to the grave, down to those happy shades below,
Where all our brave *progenitors* are blest
With endless triumph and eternal rest.
Pomfret, A Prospect of Death.

By the term fresh stock I mean a non-related plant the *progenitors* of which have been raised during some generations in another garden. *Darwin*, Cross and Self Fertilisation, p. 257.

progenitorial (prọ̄-jen-i-tō'ri-ạl), *a.* [< *progenitor* + *-ial.*] Pertaining to or constituting a progenitor.

Some abnormal growth, like and unlike the species to which the *progenitorial* germ belonged.
The Congregationalist, Oct. 29, 1879.

progenitress (prǭ-jen'i-tres), *n.* [< *progenitor* + *-ess*.] A female progenitor or parent; an ancestress.

Yet she was a worthy *progenitress* of a long line of most charming women novelists. *The Century*, XXVI. 291.

progenitrix (prǭ-jen'i-triks), *n.* Same as *progenitress*.

progeniture (prǭ-jen'i-tūr), *n.* [< F. *progéniture* = Sp. Pg. *progenitura*, < L. *progenitus*, pp. of *progignere*, beget, bring forth: see *progenitor*.] A begetting or birth. [Rare.]

progenity†, *n.* [Irreg. < *progen-y* + *-ity*.] Descent; lineage; extraction. [Rare.]

Barrys of the old house of Lancaster; and that *progenity* do I loue. *Heywood*, 1 Edw. IV. (Works, I. 45).

progeny (proj'e-ni), *n.* [< ME. *progenie*, *progenye*, < OF. *progenie* = Sp. Pg. *progenie* = It. *progenie*, *progenia*, progeny, < L. *progenies*, descent, lineage, race, offspring, family, < *progignere*, beget, bring forth: see *progenitor*.] 1†. Descent; lineage; family; ancestry.

All French and France exclaims on thee,
Doubting thy birth and lawful *progeny*.
Shak., 1 Hen. VI., iii. 3. 61.

Now show thy *progeny*; if not to stand,
Cast thyself down; safely, if Son of God.
Milton, P. R., iv. 554.

2. Children; offspring, whether of the human kind or of the lower animals; descendants.

Did ever joyful Mother see
So bright, so brave a *Progeny*?
Steele, Tender Husband (song).

What idle *progeny* succeed
To chase the rolling circle's speed,
Or urge the flying ball?
Gray, Prospect of Eton College.

Around this fort a *progeny* of little Dutch-built houses, with tiled roofs and weathercocks, soon sprang up, nestling themselves under its walls for protection.
Irving, Knickerbocker, p. 132.

=**Syn. 2.** *Issue*, *Posterity*, etc. See *offspring*.

progermination (prǭ-jėr-mi-nā'shǫn), *n.* [< LL. as if **progerminatio(n-)*, < L. *progerminare*, shoot forth, germinate, < *pro*, forth, + *germinare*, germinate: see *germinate*.] Origin; birth; issue.

Ignoble births which shame the stem
That gave *progermination* unto them.
Herrick, To Sir John Berkeley.

progger (prog'ėr), *n.* One who progs; a rambling or aimless searcher; specifically, one who progs for clams, oysters, etc., alongshore; a pot-fisherman. [Eastern U. S.]

The class of men who get them [quahaugs] and the soft clams mainly are a miserable set who help the oystermen in winter and "go clamming" in summer. They are locally known as *proggers*. *Fisheries of U. S.*, V. ii. 604.

proglottic (prǭ-glot'ik), *a.* [< *proglott-is* + *-ic*.] Of or pertaining to a proglottis. Also *proglottidean*.

proglottid (prǭ-glot'id), *n.* [< *proglottis* (*-id-*).] One of the detached sexually mature segments of a tapeworm or tænia; a proglottis.

In this way the Tænia-chain is formed, the last metameres of which (the so-called *proglottids*) break off at a certain stage of development, and form more or less independent individuals.
Gegenbaur, Comp. Anat. (trans.), p. 129.

proglottidean (prō-glo-tid'ẹ̄-ạn), *a.* [< *proglottid* + *-e-an*.] Same as *proglottic*.

proglottis (prō-glot'is), *n.*; pl. *proglottides* (-i-dēz). [NL., < Gr. *προγλωττίς, προγλωσσίς, the point of the tongue, < πρό, before, + γλῶσσα, tongue.] A detachable sexually mature segment of a cestoid worm; one of the zoöids of the *Scolecida*, propagated by gemmation from a scolex, which in their turn produce ova; a proglottid, or generative joint. The joints of a tapeworm, for example, are p g es. This is what makes tapeworms such formidabidqatdsites and so difficult to eradicate. For they are continually budded off from the scolex or "head" (really the whole worm), to the number sometimes of hundreds, like successive links of a chain; each such link or "joint" contains all the sexual elements, and is thus capable itself of starting a new series of the parasites in the eggs it produces. See cut under *Cestoidea*.

Each segment [of a tapeworm] is eventually found to contain a set of male and female organs. . . . At the extreme end of the body the segments become detached, and may for some time retain an independent vitality. In this condition each segment is termed a *proglottis*, and its uterus is full of ova. *Huxley*, Anat. Invert., p. 184.

prognathic (prog-nath'ik), *a.* [< *prognath-ous* + *-ic*.] Having protrusive jaws; characterized by or exhibiting prognathism. Also *prognathous*.

The relative large size of the jaws and lower parts of the face we see in the negro races, especially, as compared with our own, and to this type we give the name *prognathic*.
Pop. Sci. Mo., XIII. 432.

prognathism (prog'nạ̄-thizm), *n.* [< *prognath-ous* + *-ism*.] The prognathic state or condition; the quality of being prognathic; the condition of having a small facial or a large craniofacial angle. See *orthognathous*.

This [a large craniofacial angle] is the fundamental condition of *prognathism*. *Huxley*, Anat. Vert., p. 420.

Alveolosubnasal prognathism. See *alveolosubnasal*.

prognathous (prog'nạ̄-thus), *a.* [< Gr. πρό, before, forward, + γνάθος, jaw, mouth.] Same as *prognathic*; opposed to *opisthognathous* and *orthognathous*.

The lower race had long snouty noses, *prognathous* mouths, and retreating foreheads.
Harper's Mag., LXXVII. 290.

prognathy (prog'nạ̄-thi), *n.* Same as *prognathism*.

Progne (prog'nē), *n.* [Also *Procne*; < L. *Progne*, *Procne*, < Gr. Πρόκνη, in myth. the daughter of Pandion, transformed into a swallow; hence poet., in L., a swallow.] 1. [*l. c.*] A swallow. *Dryden*.—2. An American genus of *Hirundinidæ* or swallows, containing several species of large size, robust form, and dark coloration, some of which are known as *purple martins*, as

Purple Martin (*Progne subis*).

P. subis or *P. purpurea*, the very common and familiar purple martin of the United States. This bird is deep lustrous steel-blue, with black bill and blackish wings, tail, and feet, about 7½ inches long and 15½ in extent of wings. The female is greenish-brown glossed with steel-blue, the under parts whitish shaded with gray. It is a sociable loquacious bird, which breeds naturally in holes of trees, and now, in populous districts, often in boxes provided for its accommodation. The eggs are pure white. It is migratory and insectivorous, like other swallows. There are several other species in the warmer parts of America.

prognosis (prog-nō'sis), *n.* [= F. *prognose* = It. *prognosi*, < L. *prognosis*, < Gr. πρόγνωσις, foreknowledge, forecast, < προγιγνώσκειν, know beforehand, < πρό, before, + γιγνώσκειν, know, perceive: see *know*[1], *gnosis*.] 1. A foreknowing of the course of events; forecast.

An intimate knowledge of the domestic history of nations is therefore absolutely necessary to the *prognosis* of political events. *Macaulay*, History.

2. A forecast of the probable course and termination of a case of disease; also, what is thus forecast.

In a fever, great prostration, high temperature, and rapid pulse . . . must lead to the formation of an unfavourable *prognosis*. *Quain*, Med. Dict., p. 392.

prognostic (prog-nos'tik), *a.* and *n.* [I. *a.* < F. *prognostique* = Pg. *pronostico*, *prognostico*, < NL. **prognosticus*, < Gr. προγνωστικός, adj., < προγιγνώσκειν, see or know beforehand: see *prognosis*. II. *n.* First in E. as a noun, < ME. *pronostique*, *prenostik*, < OF. *pronostique*, *prognostique*, m., F. *prognostic*, usually *pronostic*, m., = Sp. *pronóstico* = Pg. *pronostico*, *prognostico* = It. *pronostico*, *prognostico*, < L. *prognosticon*, *prognosticum*, < Gr. προγνωστικόν, a token of the future, a prognostic, neut. of προγνωστικός, adj.: see above.] I. *a.* Foreshowing; indicating something in the future by signs or symptoms: as, the *prognostic* indications of a disease.

It will become a gentleman to have some knowledge in medicine, especially the diagnostic part, whereby he may take timely notice of a disease, and by that means timely prevent it, as also the *prognostic* part, whereby he may judge of the symptoms either increasing or decreasing in the disease, as also concerning the crisis or indiction thereof. Lord *Herbert of Cherbury*, Life (ed. Howells), p. 44.

II. *n.* 1. That which prognosticates or foretells; a sign by which a future event may be known or foreshown; an omen; a token.

The negardye in kepynge hyr rychesse
Prenostik is thou wolt hir towr assayle.
Chaucer, Fortune, l. 54.

He saith for suche a *prenostike*
Most of an bounde was to him like.
Gower, Conf. Amant., ii.

Therefore [I] believe that those many prodigies and ominous *prognostics* which forerun the ruins of states, princes, and private persons are the charitable premonitions of good angels. *Sir T. Browne*, Religio Medici, i. 31.

Careful observers may foretell the hour
(By sure *prognostics*) when to dread a shower.
Swift, Descrip. of a City Shower.

2. A prediction; a foretelling.

Though your *prognosticks* run too fast,
They must be verified at last.
Swift, Death of Dr. Swift.

=**Syn.** *Sign*, *Presage*, etc. See *omen*, and *foretell*, *v. i.*

prognostic†(prog-nos'tik), *v. t.* [< OF. *prognostiquer* = Sp. *pronosticar* = Pg. *pronosticar*, *prognosticar* = It. *pronosticar*, *prognosticare*, < ML. *prognosticare*, prognosticate: see *prognosticate*.] To prognosticate.

When the sun shines waterishly and *prognosticks* rain.
Dr. H. More, Immortal. of Soul, III. iii. 5.

I never dreamed that ministers should be compelled to impugn ministers; the adversaries have good sport betwixt themselves to *prognostick* the likelyhood.
Bp. Burnet, Records, II. iii., No. 8, Parker's Answer.

prognosticable (prog-nos'ti-kạ-bl), *a.* [< *prognostic(ate)* + *-able*.] Capable of being prognosticated, foreknown, or foretold.

The causes of this inundation cannot indeed be regular, and, therefore, their effects not *prognosticable* like eclipses.
Sir T. Browne, Vulg. Err., vi. 8.

prognosticate (prog-nos'ti-kāt), *v.*; pret. and pp. *prognosticated*, ppr. *prognosticating*. [< ML. *prognosticatus*, pp. of *prognosticare*, foretell, prognosticate, < L. *prognosticon*, a prognostic: see *prognostic*.] I. *trans.* 1. To foretell by means of present signs; predict.

I neither will nor can *prognosticate*
To the young gaping heir his father's fate.
Dryden, tr. of Juvenal's Satires, iii.

Cassandra-like, *prognosticating* woe.
Longfellow, Birds of Killingworth.

2. To foreshow or betoken; presage.

The other [top of Vesuvius] towards the South aspireth more high, which when hid in clouds *prognosticates* raine to the Neapolitans. *Sandys*, Travailes, p. 203.

The death of a monarch or prince of some corner of the world, *prognosticated* by an eclipse or comet.
Jer. Taylor, Works (ed. 1835), I. 371.

=**Syn. 1** and **2.** *Predict*, *Presage*, etc. See *foretell*.—**2.** To betoken.

II. *intrans.* To judge or pronounce from presage or foreknowledge.

If any man's father be sick, the son straight goes vnto the sooth-saying or *prognosticating* priest, requesting him to demand of his God whether his father shall recouer of that or no. *Hakluyt's Voyages*, II. 58.

prognostication (prog-nos-ti-kā'shǫn), *n.* [< ME. *prenosticacioun*, < OF. (and F.) *pronostication* = Sp. *pronosticacion* = Pg. *pronosticação* = It. *pronosticazione*, < ML. *prognosticatio(n-)*, < *prognosticare*, prognosticate: see *prognosticate*.] 1. The act of prognosticating, foretelling, or foreshowing future events by present signs; a presage; a prediction.

Be the flyenge of Foules, thei wolde telle us the *prenosticaciouns* of thinges that felle aftre.
Mandeville, Travels, p. 167.

In this Year, through Books of *Prognostications* foreshewing much Hurt to come by Waters and Floods, many Persons withdrew themselves to high Grounds, for Fear of drowning. *Baker*, Chronicles, p. 272.

The doctor's *prognostication* in reference to the weather was speedily verified. *Dickens*, Martin Chuzzlewit, xiii.

2. That which foreshows or foretells; a sign.

The whole inhabitants of Italy were wonderfully afraid, and judged that it was some sign and *prognostication* of some wonderfull thing to come.
North, tr. of Plutarch, p. 114.

If an oily palm be not a fruitful *prognostication*, I cannot scratch mine ear. *Shak.*, A. and C., i. 2. 54.

The meteors afford him *prognostications* of the weather.
Bacon, Physical Fables, ii., Expl.

=**Syn. 1.** *Prophecy*, etc. See *prediction*.

prognosticative (prog-nos'ti-kạ̄-tiv), *a.* [< OF. *pronosticatif*, < ML. *prognosticativus*, predictive, < *prognosticare*, predict, prognosticate: see *prognosticate*.] Having the character of a prognostic; predictive.

prognosticator (prog-nos'ti-kā-tọr), *n.* [= Sp. *pronosticador* = Pg. *pronosticador*, *prognosticador* = It. *pronosticatore*, < ML. **prognosticator*, < *prognosticare*, prognosticate: see *prognosticate*.] A foreknower or foreteller of future events by present signs; a soothsayer.

Let now the astrologers, the stargazers, the monthly *prognosticators*, stand up, and save thee from these things that shall come upon thee. Isa. xlvii. 13.

Trismegistus, the later Ptolemy, and the everlasting *prognosticator*, old Erra Pater.
Massinger, City Madam, ii. 2.

Progonochelys (prog-ọ̄-nok'e-lis), *n.* [NL., < Gr. πρόγονος, born before, also a forefather, ancestor, + χέλυς, a tortoise.] A genus of fossil turtles from the Triassic of Würtemberg, the oldest known representative of the *Chelonia*.

program, programme (prō'gram), *n.* [Formerly, as LL., *programma*; < F. *programme* =

Sp. *programa* = Pg. It. *programma* = D. *programma* = G. *programm* = Sw. Dan. *program*, < LL. *programma*, a proclamation, edict, < Gr. πρόγραμμα, a written public notice, an edict, < προγράφειν, write beforehand, < πρό, before, + γράφειν, write.] 1. A written or printed list of the pieces or selections which constitute a musical, theatrical, or other performance or entertainment, set down in the order of their performance or exhibition. The titles, authors, and performers of musical pieces are ordinarily given, often with the addition of descriptive or explanatory remarks.

Scraps of regular Memoir, College-Exercises, *Programs*, Professional Testimoniums.
Carlyle, Sartor Resartus, ii. 3.

Hence—2. The collection of such pieces or selections. The several pieces are often called *numbers*.—3. A method of operation or line of procedure prepared or announced beforehand; an outline or abstract of something to be done or carried out: as, the *program* of the new administration; the *program* of a school or university.

Well, here surely is an Evangel of Freedom, and real *Program* of a new Era.
Carlyle, Latter Day Pamphlets, Model Prisons.

A series of impudent shams have been palmed off on the country as a *programme* for general reform.
Nineteenth Century, XXVI. 745.

The *programme* of the inaugural is already modified.
The Century, XXXV. 720.

4. A preface; prolegomena; a preliminary or introductory statement or announcement.

He (Guilelmus Christ) admires greatly Hermann's *program* on "Interpolations in Homer."
Amer. Jour. Philol., V. 504.

Program music. See *music*.

programma (prǭ-gram'ạ̈), *n.*; pl. *programmata* (-ạ-tạ̈). [< LL. *programma*, < Gr. πρόγραμμα, a public notice: see *program*.] 1. A public notice; an edict.

A *programma* stuck up in every college hall, under the vice-chancellor's hand, that no scholars abuse the soldiers.
Life of A. Wood. (*Latham.*)

2. A preface; prolegomena.

His (Dr. Bathurst's) *programma* on preaching, instead of a dry formal remonstrance, is an agreeable and lively piece of writing.
T. Warton, Life of Bathurst, p. 218. (*Latham.*)

The peculiar features of the arrangement of his (Euthalius's) text are prefaces, *programmata*, lists of quotations, with reference to the authors, sacred and profane, from whom they come.
J. Rendel Harris, Amer. Jour. Philol., IV. 315.

programme, *n.* See *program*.

programmer (prō'gram-ėr), *n.* One who makes up a program: as, the official *programmer* of the Jockey Club.

Progresista (prō-gre-sis'tạ̈), *n.* [Sp., = E. *progressist*.] Same as *Progressist* (*a*).

progress (prog'res), *n.* [< OF. *progres*, *progrez*, F. *progrès* = Sp. *progreso* = Pg. It. *progresso* = G. *progress*, < L. *progressus*, an advance, < *progredi*, pp. *progressus*, go forward, advance, proceed, < *pro*, forth, before, + *gradi*, walk, go. Cf. *congress*, *ingress*, *egress*, *regress*, etc.] 1. A going onward; a moving or proceeding forward; advance: as, to make slow or rapid *progress* on a journey; to hinder one's *progress*.

Thou by thy dial's shady stealth mayst know
Time's thievish *progress* to eternity.
Shak., Sonnets, lxxvii.

Our *progress* was often delay'd
By the nightingale warbling nigh.
Cowper, Catharina.

We trace his *progress* (that of one of Shakspere's characters) from the first dawning of unlawful ambition to the cynical melancholy of his impenitent remorse.
Macaulay, Dryden.

2. A passage from place to place; a journey; wayfaring.

So forth they forth yfere make their *progresse*,
And march not past the mountenaunce of a shott
Till they arriv'd whereas their purpose they did plott.
Spenser, F. Q., III. xi. 20.

It was my fortune, with some others moe,
One summer day a *progresse* for to goe
Into the countrie.
Times' Whistle (E. E. T. S.), p. 82.

Bass. My Penthea, miserable soul,
Was starved to death.
Cal. She 's happy; she hath finish'd
A long and painful *progress*. *Ford*, Broken Heart, v. 2.

In summer they leave them, beginning their *progresse* in Aprill, with their wives, children, and slaves, in their carted houses. *Capt. John Smith*, True Travels, I. 36.

Specifically—3. A journey or circuit of state: as, a royal *progress*.

It was now the seventh year of Queen Elizabeth, when, making a *Progress*, she went to see Cambridge.
Baker, Chronicles, p. 333.

I . . . met the archbishop of Ægina, . . . who was making a *progress* to collect charity for his church.
Pococke, Description of the East, II. ii. 160.

The royal *progresses* were diligently carried on, when the king (Cnut), with his following of counsellors and scribes, administered justice and redressed wrong as Eadgar and Ælfred had done before him.
J. R. Green, Conq. of Eng., p. 409.

The king . . . spent the autumn in a royal *progress*, the object of which was to reconcile all parties.
Stubbs, Const. Hist., § 348.

4. Advancement of any kind; growth; development; improvement: as, the *progress* of a negotiation; the *progress* of a plant; the *progress* of a patient toward recovery; the *progress* of a scholar in his studies; the *progress* of the arts and sciences.

Growth is *progress*; and all *progress* designs and tends to the acquisition of something which the growing person is not yet possessed of. *South*, Sermons, III. vi.

How swift and strange a *progress* the Gospel made at and after its first setting out from Jerusalem!
Bp. Atterbury, Sermons, I. iii.

Physiologically as well as morphologically, development is a *progress* from the general to the special.
Huxley, Anat. Invert., p. 30.

A new stage of intellectual *progress* began with the Augustan age, as it did with our own Elizabethan era.
Maine, Village Communities, p. 380.

Progress of titles, in *Scots law*, such a series of title-deeds as constitute a valid feudal title to heritable property.—**State of progress** (tr. of Gr. προκοπή), a state which the Stoical and other philosophies claim to confer of becoming constantly wiser and better, without danger of relapse. =**Syn.** 1-4. *Progress, Progression, Advance, Advancement*, and *Proficiency* agree in expressing the idea of a forward movement, literally or figuratively. *Proficiency* applies only to a person; the rest to a person or thing. *Progress* is a lively word for continued improvement in any respect, or it may mean simply a course, whether good or evil: as, "The Rake's Progress" (*Hogarth*). *Progression* is less common and not general; it emphasizes the act of moving. *Progress* and *advance* are high words for the promotion of human knowledge, character, and general welfare. *Advancement* is essentially synonymous with *advance*, but is not so general; the word applies chiefly to things mental: as, "The *Advancement* of Learning" (*Bacon*); but we speak also of the *advancement* of human welfare: here the word suggests the help given by men, viewing it as external, and thus is essentially synonymous with *promotion*. *Advance* and *progress* seem figurative when not physical. *Proficiency* is the state resulting from having made *progress* in acquiring either knowledge or skill: as, *proficiency* in Latin or in music.

Human *progress* is gradual, by slow degrees, evil by degrees yielding to good, the spiritual succeeding the natural by almost imperceptible processes of amelioration.
O. B. Frothingham, George Ripley, p. 188.

This mode of *progression* requires some muscular exertion. *The Century*, XXVI. 925.

It is only by perpetual aspiration after what has been hitherto beyond our reach that *advance* is made.
H. Spencer, Social Statics, p. 506.

Tom had always possessed the honesty and fearless candor that belonged to his idea of a gentleman, and had never thought of questioning his father's *proficiency* in the same virtues. *J. Hawthorne*, Dust, p. 187.

progress (prǫ-gres', formerly prog'res), *v.* [= Sp. *progresar*; < L. *progressus*, pp. of *progredi*, go forward, advance: see *progress*, *n.* The verb is in part from the noun.] I. *intrans.* 1. To move forward or onward in space; proceed; pass; go.

Let me wipe off this honourable dew
That silverly doth *progress* on thy cheeks.
Shak., K. John, v. 2. 46.

Although the popular blast . . .
Hath rear'd thy name up to bestride a cloud,
Or *progress* in the chariot of the sun.
Ford, Broken Heart, iii. 2.

We travel sea and soil, we pry, we prowl,
We *progress* and we prog from pole to pole.
Quarles, Emblems, ii. 2.

Thou may'st to Court, and *Progress* to and fro;
Oh, that thy captiv'd Master could do so.
Howell, Letters, I. vi. 60.

Like the hare, if the fore-leg is injured, deer cannot *progress*. *The Century*, XXXVI. 810.

2. To continue onward in course; proceed or advance.

After the war had *progressed* for some time.
Marshall, Washington.

As the great ship *progresses* towards completion.
Times (London), April 30, 1857.

3. To move toward something better; advance on the line of development or improvement.

From the lowest to the highest creatures, intelligence *progresses* by acts of discrimination; and it continues so to *progress* among men, from the most ignorant to the most cultured. *H. Spencer*, Man vs. State, p. 5.

The growth of the concept *progresses* step by step with the extension of the name to new objects.
J. Sully, Outlines of Psychol., p. 346.

4. Specifically, in *music*, of a voice-part, to advance from one tone to another, or, of the harmony in general, from one chord to another. =**Syn.** 1-3. To go or get on, ahead, forward, or along; make haste.—3. To make headway.

II. *trans.* 1†. To pass over or through; make the tour or circuit of.

So, when my soul had *progress'd* ev'ry place
That love and dear affection could contrive,
I threw me on my couch. *Quarles*, Emblems, iv. 12.

2. To cause to advance or pass; push forward.

The heavier portion (of ore) is *progressed* across the table, and passed into an ore bin. *Ure*, Dict., II. 131.

Urging that the bills . . . be *progressed* as rapidly as possible. *New York Tribune*, March 7, 1887.

progression (prǫ-gresh'ǫn), *n.* [= F. *progression* = Sp. *progresion* = Pg. *progressão* = It. *progressione*, < L. *progressio(n-)*, a going forward, advancement, < *progredi*, pp. *progressus*, go forward: see *progress*, *n.*] 1. The act or state of progressing, advancing, or moving forward; a proceeding in a course; advance: as, a slow method of *progression*.

The experimental sciences are generally in a state of *progression*. *Macaulay*, History.

Nature's great *progression*, from the formless to the formed—from the inorganic to the organic.
Huxley, Man's Place in Nature, p. 128.

There is a *progression*—I cannot call it a progress—in his work toward a more and more strictly prosaic level.
R. L. Stevenson, Thoreau, iii.

2. Lapse or process of time; course; passage. *Evelyn.* (*Imp. Dict.*)—3. In *math.*, a series of quantities of which every one intermediate between the first and the last is a mean of some constant kind between those which immediately precede and follow it. Arithmetical, geometrical, harmonic, arithmetico-geometrical, and quadratic progressions are progressions depending on means so named. 4. In *philol.*, the increase or strengthening of a vowel under the accent. [Rare.]—5. In *music*: (*a*) The act, process, or result of advancing from one tone to another (of a particular voice-part), or from one chord to another (of the harmony in general); motion. *Progression* in either of these senses may be regular or irregular, correct or false. See *motion*, 14. (*b*) Same as *sequence*.

To read chords and *progressions* of chords by means of letters is somewhat fatiguing.
The Academy, Sept. 29, 1888, p. 213.

Arithmetical, conjunct, diatonic, harmonic progression. See the adjectives.—**Geometrical progression**, a series of numbers each derived from the preceding by multiplication by a constant factor, as 2, 6, 18, 54, 162, etc. —**Musical progression.** Same as *harmonic progression*. —**Progression of parts**, in *music*, usually the progression of two or more voice-parts relatively to each other. See *motion*.—**Progression with *n* ratios**, a series of quantities whose ratios (of each to the preceding) pass through a cycle of *n* values, as 2, 1, 3, $1\frac{1}{2}$, $4\frac{1}{2}$, $2\frac{1}{4}$, $6\frac{3}{4}$, etc. =**Syn.** 1. *Advancement*, etc. See *progress*, *n.*

progressional (prǫ-gresh'ǫn-ạl), *a.* [< *progression* + *-al*.] Pertaining to progression, advance, or improvement.

To tell him . . . that there is no further state to come, unto which this seemes *progressional*, and otherwise made in vain. *Sir T. Browne*, Urn-burial, iv.

The "inventive powers of the human mind"—powers which exemplify and embody the "*progressional* force" of civilization. *Amer. Anthropologist*, I. 9.

progressionist (prǫ-gresh'ǫn-ist), *n.* [< *progression* + *-ist*.] 1. One who believes in or advocates progress in society or politics.

The enforced opening of the country [Korea] . . . had given rise to two new, all-embracing and all-engrossing, antagonistic parties. These two parties were named by the Japanese the *progressionists* and the seclusionists.
The Atlantic, LVIII. 603.

2. One who maintains the doctrine that society is in a state of progress toward perfection, and that it will ultimately attain it. [Rare.]—3. One who holds that the existing species of animals and plants were not originally created, but were gradually developed from one simple form.

Were the geological record complete, or did it, as both Uniformitarians and *Progressionists* have habitually assumed, give us traces of the earliest organic forms, the evidence hence derived, for or against, would have had more weight than any other evidence.
H. Spencer, Prin. of Biol., § 140.

progressist (prog'res-ist), *n.* [= Sp. *progresista* = It. *progressista*; as *progress* + *-ist*.] One who holds to a belief in progress; a progressionist.

The most plausible objection raised against resistance to conventions is grounded on its impolicy, considered even from the *progressist's* point of view.
H. Spencer, Universal Progress, p. 98.

Specifically [*cap.*]—(*a*) In *mod. Span. hist.*, a member of a political party holding advanced liberal views. The Progressists and Moderados were the two parties into which the Christinos (adherents of the queen regent Christina) separated about 1835. (*b*) A member of a liberal political party in Germany (Fortschrittspartei), formed in 1861. From it was formed, a few years later, the National Liberal party. The remnant in 1884 united with the Liberal Union to form the German Liberal party (Deutsch-Freisinnige).

The workmen's unions which had grown so rapidly in Germany in the years following 1860, and which had first been patronized by the *Progressist* party.
Encyc. Brit., XXII. 214.

progressive (prǫ-gres'iv), *a.* and *n.* [< F. *progressif* = Sp. *progresivo* = Pg. It. *progressivo*, < L. *progressus*, pp. of *progredi*, go forward, advance: see *progress*.] **I.** *a.* **1.** Going forward; moving onward; advancing; making progress, in any sense: as, *progressive* motion or course.

Their wandering course, now high, now low, then hid,
Progressive, retrograde, or standing still.
Milton, P. L., viii. 127.

At first *progressive* as a stream, they [the sheep] seek
The middle field; but, scatter'd by degrees,
Each to his choice, soon whiten all the land.
Cowper, Task, i. 292.

Science in its contemplation of the method of nature is *progressive*, and continually changing its point of view.
Dawson, Nature and the Bible, p. 12.

The deification of the Emperors was a suitable climax to the *progressive* degradation of the religion of Rome.
G. P. Fisher, Beginnings of Christianity, p. 125.

2. Favoring progress; using one's influence or directing one's efforts in the line of advancement or improvement: as, to be *progressive* in one's ideas about education; a *progressive* age. —**3.** Indicative of progress.

Ecker, for reasons which are not quite clear, considers that unusual length [of the index-finger] is a *progressive* character.
Amer. Anthropologist, I. 71.

Progressive bulbar paralysis. See *paralysis*.—**Progressive euchre, metamorphosis, method.** See the nouns.—**Progressive Friends.** See *friend*.—**Progressive locomotor ataxia.** See *ataxia*.—**Progressive muscular atrophy**, a progressive atrophy of the voluntary muscles. Two entirely distinct torms are recognized —(*a*) a neuropathic form, in which the myo-atrophy is the result of the degeneration of ganglion-cells in the anterior horns of the spinal cord (this form is related to amyotrophic lateral sclerosis and to bulbar paralysis); and (*b*) a myopathic form, related to pseudohypertrophic paralysis. —**Progressive muscular sclerosis.** Same as *pseudohypertrophic paralysis* (which see, under *paralysis*).—**Progressive Orthodoxy**, that body of Christian doctrine which is held by its supporters to preserve the essential features of historic Christian theology, while modified to meet the requirements of modern thought. The name is especially applied to the views of the advanced wing of theologians in the Congregational, Presbyterian, and other American churches.—**Progressive paralysis.** See *paralysis*.—**Progressive pernicious anemia.** Same as *idiopathic anemia* (which see, under *anemia*).

II. *n.* One who is in favor of progress; one who promotes or commends reforms or changes: opposed to *conservative*.

Some are conservatives, others *progressives*, still others may be called radicals.
H. White, Pop. Sci. Mo., XXXVI. 400.

We are forced to take sides on it, either as *progressives* or conservatives. *S. Thurber*, in Education, III. 619.

progressively (prǫ-gres'iv-li), *adv.* In a progressive manner; by gradual or regular steps or advances.

Lost and confus'd, *progressively* they fade,
Not fall precipitate from light to shade.
W. Mason, tr. of Dufresnoy's Art of Painting, l. 375.

What was the commerce that, *progressively*, laid the foundation of all that immense grandeur of the east?
Bruce, Source of the Nile, I. 370.

progressiveness (prǫ-gres'iv-nes), *n.* The state or character of being progressive; a condition of advance or improvement: as, the *progressiveness* of science or of taste.

There is nothing in the nature of art to exempt it from that character of *progressiveness* which belongs to science and philosophy, and in general to all spheres of intellectual activity. *J. Caird.*

progressor (prǫ-gres'or), *n.* [< LL. *progressor*, one who advances, < L. *progredi*, pp. *progressus*, go forward, advance: see *progress*.] **1.** One who goes or travels; one who makes a journey or progress.

Being a great *progressor* through all the Roman empire, whenever he [Adrian] found any decays of bridges or highways, or cuts of rivers and sewers, . . . or the like, he gave substantial order for their repair.
Bacon, Offer of a Digest of Laws.

2. One who makes progress or advances.

proguet, *v.* and *n.* An obsolete spelling of *prog*.

progymnasium (prō-jim-nā'zi-um), *n.*; pl. *progymnasia* (-ä). [< Gr. πρό, before, + γυμνάσιον, gymnasium. Cf. Gr. προγυμνασία, previous exercise.] A kind of classical school in Germany in which the higher classes are wanting; a school preparatory to a gymnasium.

The classical schools proper [in Prussia] consist of Gymnasia and *Progymnasia*, the latter being simply gymnasia wanting the higher classes. *Encyc. Brit.*, XX. 17.

progymnosperm (prō-jim'nǫ-spėrm), *n.* [< Gr. πρό, before, + E. *gymnosperm*.] An archaic or ancestral gymnosperm; the ancestral form from which later gymnosperms are supposed to have been developed.

progymnospermic (prō-jim-nǫ-spėr'mik), *a.* [< *progymnosperm* + *-ic*.] Of or relating to a progymnosperm.

In the remote past, before even the seasons were well defined, the cambium layer may have existed in an irregular or fugitive manner in the pro-angiospermic as it did in the *pro-gymnospermic* stem. *Nature*, XXXIII. 389.

prohemet, *n.* An obsolete form of *proem*.

prohibit (prǫ-hib'it), *v. t.* [< L. *prohibitus*, pp. of *prohibere* (> It. *proibire* = Pg. Sp. *prohibir* = F. *prohiber*), hold back, forbid, < *pro*, before, + *habere*, have, hold: see *habit*. Cf. *inhibit*, *exhibit*.] **1.** To forbid; interdict by authority: as, to *prohibit* a person from doing a thing; to *prohibit* the doing of a thing.

So of degenerate and revolted spirits, the conversing with them or the employment of them is *prohibited*.
Bacon, Advancement of Learning, ii. 154.

To this day, in France, the exportation of corn is almost always *prohibited*. *Hume*, Essays, ii. 5.

South Carolina has *prohibited* the importation of slaves for three years; which is a step towards a perpetual prohibition. *Jefferson*, Correspondence, II. 161.

2. To hinder; debar; prevent; preclude.

And [the Britons], folowyng after wyth al the rest of theyr power, *prohibited* our men to take land.
Golding, tr. of Cæsar, fol. 99.

Soodenly a tempest of contrary wynde *prohibited* theym to take lande, and droue them backewarde to Cozumella.
Peter Martyr (tr. in Eden's First Books on America, [ed. Arber, p. 192).

Gates of burning adamant,
Barr'd over us, *prohibit* all egress.
Milton, P. L., ii. 437.

Prohibited degrees. See *degree*. =**Syn. 1.** *Interdict*, etc. See *forbid*.

prohibiter (prǫ-hib'i-tėr), *n.* [< *prohibit* + *-er*[1].] One who prohibits or forbids; an interdicter.

Cecilia . . . cast her eyes round in the church, with no other view than that of seeing from what corner the *prohibiter* would start. *Miss Burney*, Cecilia, ix. 8.

prohibition (prō-hi-bish'ǫn), *n.* [Early mod. E. *prohybycyon*; < OF. (and F.) *prohibition* = Sp. *prohibicion* = Pg. *prohibição* = It. *proibizione*, < L. *prohibitio(n-)*, a hindering or forbidding, prohibition, < *prohibere*, pp. *prohibitus*, hold back, forbid: see *prohibit*.] **1.** The act of prohibiting, forbidding, or interdicting; an edict or a decree to forbid or debar.

In Iherico also is yet shewed the place where ye blynde man, notwithstondynge the *prohybycyon* and rebukes of the people, cryed incessauntly.
Sir R. Guylforde, Pylgrymage, p. 41.

God's commandments or *prohibitions* were not the originals of good and evil.
Bacon, Advancement of Learning, i. 63.

He said the Prophet never forbade aquavitæ, only the drinking of wine; and the *prohibition* could not be intended for Egypt, for there was no wine in it.
Bruce, Source of the Nile, I. 76.

She made a repelling gesture with her hand, and stood, a perfect picture of *prohibition*, at full length, in the dark frame of the doorway. *Hawthorne*, Seven Gables, viii.

2. In a restricted sense, the interdiction by law of the manufacture and sale of alcoholic drinks, except for medicinal or sacramental uses.—**Prohibition of light**, in *astrol.*, the supposed effect of two neighboring planets in annihilating the influence of one between them.—**Prohibition party**, in *U. S. politics*, a political party which aims to secure by legislation the prohibition of the manufacture and sale of alcoholic drinks, except for medicinal or sacramental uses. Such measures have at times been supported by a considerable section of one or the other of the two great parties, and such legislation has been enacted by certain States, as Maine, Kansas, and Iowa. The Prohibitionists were organized as a distinct national party in 1869, and since 1872 they have nominated candidates for the office of President.—**Training to Arms Prohibition Act**, an English statute of 1819 (60 Geo. III. and 1 Geo. IV., c. 1) prohibiting meetings for the purpose of practising military exercises.—**Writ of prohibition.** (*a*) In *law*, a writ issuing from a superior tribunal to prohibit or prevent an inferior court or a suitor therein, or both, from proceeding in a suit or matter, upon suggestion that such court is proceeding or about to proceed beyond its jurisdiction or in an illegal manner. (*b*) In *Scots law*, a technical clause in a deed of entail prohibiting the heir from selling the estate, contracting debt, altering the order of succession, etc. =**Syn. 1.** Interdiction, inhibition, embargo. See *prohibit*.

Prohibitionism (prō-hi-bish'ǫn-izm), *n.* [< *prohibition* + *-ism*.] The doctrine and methods of the Prohibitionists.

In Macmillan's for March Goldwin Smith has a timely paper on "*Prohibitionism* in Canada and the United States."
Literary World, XX. 116.

prohibitionist (prō-hi-bish'ǫn-ist), *n.* and *a.* [< *prohibition* + *-ist*.] **I.** *n.* One who is in favor of prohibition, especially the prohibition by law of the manufacture and sale of alcoholic drinks, except for medicinal or sacramental uses; specifically [*cap.*], in *U. S. politics*, a member of the Prohibition party.

II. *a.* Favoring such prohibition.

If the growing *prohibitionist* party should ever get its way in Victoria, the strange spectacle will be presented of one of the chief wine-producing countries being under the control of an electorate which is opposed to the manufacture and sale of wine.
Sir C. W. Dilke, Probs. of Greater Britain, ii. 1.

prohibitive (prǫ-hib'i-tiv), *a.* [= F. *prohibitif* = Sp. Pg. *prohibitivo* = It. *proibitivo*; as *prohibit* + *-ive*.] Same as *prohibitory*.

The *prohibitive* Commandement of stealing is of greater force, and more bindeth. *Purchas*, Pilgrimage, p. 23.

The cab-rates are *prohibitive*—more than half the people who in England would use cabs must in America use the horse-cars. *M. Arnold*, Civilization in the U. S., iv.

prohibitively (prǫ-hib'i-tiv-li), *adv.* In a prohibitive manner; with prohibition; so as to prohibit: as, prices were *prohibitively* high.

I waved my hand *prohibitively*.
Carlyle, in Froude, Life in London, xxviii.

prohibitor (prǫ-hib'i-tǫr), *n.* [= OF. *prohibeur* = Pg. *prohibidor* = It. *proibitore*, < LL. *prohibitor*, a withholder, < L. *prohibere*, prohibit: see *prohibit*.] One who prohibits or interdicts.

A sharp and severe *prohibitor*.
Hooker, Works (ed. Appleton, 1877), II. 43.

prohibitory (prǫ-hib'i-tǫ-ri), *a.* [= Sp. Pg. *prohibitorio*, < L. *prohibitorius*, restraining, prohibiting, < *prohibere*, pp. *prohibitus*, prohibit: see *prohibit*.] Serving to prohibit, forbid, or interdict; implying prohibition: as, *prohibitory* duties on imports.

A prohibition will lie on this statute, notwithstanding the penalty annexed, because it has words *prohibitory* as well as a penalty annexed. *Ayliffe*, Parergon.

It is of the nature and essence of law to have penal sanctions. Without them, all laws are vain, especially *prohibitory* laws.
Warburton, Julian's Attempt to Rebuild the Temple, ii. 4.

In 1777, North repealed the customs duties on imported materials for the making of glass, and laid duties professedly *prohibitory* upon the importation of wrought or manufactured glass. *S. Dowell*, Taxes in England, IV. 308.

proin, proiner. Obsolete or dialectal forms of *prune*[2], *pruner*.

pro indiviso (prō in-di-vī'sō). [L.: *pro*, for, in manner of; *indiviso*, abl. sing. neut. of *indivisus*, not divided or cleft, < *in-* priv. + *divisus*, pp. of *dividere*, separate, divide: see *divide*.] In *law*, a term applied to rights held by two or more persons undivided, and otherwise termed *indivisible rights*.

project (prǫ-jekt'), *v.* [< OF. *projecter*, *projeter*, F. *projeter* = Sp. *proyectar* = Pg. *projectar*, project, < LL. *projectare*, thrust forth, L. reproach, accuse, freq. of L. *projicere*, *proicere*, pp. *projectus*, throw before, thrust out, < *pro*, forth, before, + *jacere*, throw, cast: see *jet*[1]. Cf. *abject*, *deject*, *eject*, *inject*, *object*, etc.] **I.** *trans.* **1.** To throw out or forth; cast or shoot forward.

Before his feet her selfe she did *project*.
Spenser, F. Q., VI. i. 45.

The ascending villas on my side
Project long shadows o'er the crystal tide.
Pope, Windsor Forest, l. 376.

A ball once *projected* will fly on to all eternity with undiminished velocity, unless something checks.
Macaulay, Utilitarian Theory of Government.

2. To cast forward in the mind; scheme; contrive; devise; plan.

This end I never did *project*,
To hang upon a tree.
Macpherson's Rant (Child's Ballads, VI. 266).

What sit we then *projecting* peace and war?
Milton, P. L., ii. 329.

A world which has Alla for its contriver is much more wisely formed than that which has been *projected* by Mahomet. *Goldsmith*, Asem.

3. In *geom.*: (*a*) To throw forward in rays or straight lines, especially from a center; draw such rays through every point of.

To *project* from a fixed point, S (the centre of projection), a figure ABCD . . . *abcd*, . . . composed of points and straight lines, is to construct the straight lines or projecting rays SA, SB, SC, SD, . . . and the projecting planes Sa, Sb, Sc, Sd. . . . We thus obtain a new figure composed of straight lines and planes which all pass through S.
Cremona, Projective Geometry, § 2.

(*b*) To throw forward (lines) from a center through every point of the figure said to be projected, and then cut these with a surface upon which the figure is said to be projected. (*c*) To delineate according to any system of correspondence between the points of a figure and the points of the surface on which the delineation is made.—**4.** To throw, as it were, from the mind into the objective world; give an objective or real seeming to (something subjective).

Thoughts became things, and ideas were *projected* from her vivid fancy upon the empty air around her.
J. A. Symonds, Italy and Greece, p. 58.

5. To set forth; set out. [Rare.]

I cannot *project* mine own cause so well
To make it clear, but do confess I have
Been laden with . . . frailties.
Shak., A. and C., v. 2. 121.

II. *intrans.* **1.** To shoot forward; extend beyond something else; jut; be prominent: as, a cornice or a promontory *projects*. The rays thrown forward in geometrical projection are said to *project* in this sense.

The craggy Rock *projects* above the sky.
Prior, Solomon, i.

As the boughs all temptingly *project*.
Burns, Address spoken by Miss Fontenelle.

2†. To form a scheme or project. *Fuller.*—**3†.** In *alchemy*, to make projection—that is, to throw philosopher's stone into a crucible of melted metal, and thus convert the latter into silver, gold, or the philosopher's stone.

My only care is
Where to get stuff enough now to *project* on.
B. Jonson, Alchemist, ii. 1.

=**Syn. 1.** To protrude, bulge (out), stand out.

project (proj'ekt), *n.* [< OF. *project*, *projet*, F. *projet* = Sp. *proyecto* = Pg. *projecto* = It. *progetto*, a project, purpose, < L. *projectum*, a projection, jutty, something thrust out, neut. of *projectus*, pp. of *projicere*, *proicere*, throw forth, thrust out: see *project*, *v.*] That which is projected or devised; a plan; a scheme; a design: as, *projects* of happiness.

Amo. What say you to a masque?
Hed. Nothing better, if the *project* were new and rare.
B. Jonson, Cynthia's Revels, iv. 1.

Here this mad fickle Crew were upon new *Projects* again.
Dampier, Voyages, I. 507.

I have a *project* of publishing in the spring a pamphlet, which I think of calling "Common-Sense for 1810."
Sydney Smith, To Lord Holland.

=**Syn.** *Scheme*, *Design*, etc. See *plan*.

projectile (prọ̄-jek'til), *a.* and *n.* [< F. *projectile* = Sp. *proyectil* = Pg. *projectil* = It. *projettile*; as *project* + *-ile*.] **I.** *a.* **1.** Impelling, throwing, driving, or shooting forward: as, a *projectile* force.

The planets are constantly acted upon by two different forces, viz. gravity or attraction, and the *projectile* force.
G. Cheyne, On Regimen, v.

2. Caused by impulse; impelled or driven forward.

Good blood, and a due *projectile* motion or circulation, are necessary to convert the aliment into laudible animal juices.
Arbuthnot, Aliments, p. 35.

3. In *zoöl.*, capable of being thrust forward or protruded, as the jaws of a fish; protrusile.

II. *n.* **1.** A body projected, or impelled forward by force, particularly through the air. Thus, a stone thrown from the hand or a sling, an arrow shot from a bow, and a ball discharged from a cannon are projectiles. The path of a projectile, or its trajectory (neglecting the effect of air-resistance), is a parabola.

The motion of a *projectile*—that is to say, of a body thrown in any direction and falling under the influence of gravity—was investigated by Galileo.
W. K. Clifford, Lectures, II. 13.

2. Specifically, a missile intended to be projected from a cannon by the explosive force of gunpowder or some similar agent. Projectiles used in smooth-bore guns are usually spherical, though sometimes oblong, as is the case in the Manby, Parrott, and Lyle life-saving projectiles. Projectiles for rifled guns are oblong, the cylindroconoidal form being generally adopted. It is essential for the range and accuracy of such a projectile that it should pass through the air in the direction of its longer axis, and the only certain method of effecting this is to give it a rapid rotary motion about this axis. To this end the projectile must be so prepared that it will engage and follow grooves in the bore of the gun. This is done in several ways: (*a*) By the *flange system*, in which the projectile is provided with flanges, studs, or buttons made of a soft metal, as copper, zinc, or brass, which fit into the grooves of the bore. (*b*) By the *expansion method*, often called the *American system*, in which the projectile is fitted with an expanding device made of softer material, such as brass, copper, or papier-maché, which is wedged into the grooves by the explosive force of the charge. This system requires more and shallower grooves than the flange system. Both the preceding methods are applicable to muzzle-loaders. (*c*) By the *compressive system*, in which the projectile is surrounded by a soft metal band or jacket, the diameter of which is greater than that of the bore without the grooves, the projectile being forced into and through the rifled part of the bore by the explosive force of the charge. The bands in the bore cut grooves in the encircling bands, which center and give rotation to the projectile. The rifling is polygroove and shallow, sometimes narrowing toward the muzzle. This system is in use in breech-loading guns.—**Amplitude of the range of a projectile.** See *amplitude*.—**Deviation of a projectile.** See *deviation*.—**Horizontal range of a projectile.** See *horizontal*.—**Subcaliber projectile**, a projectile made of less diameter than that of the bore of the piece from which it is fired, but having a cup or disk large enough to fill the bore, allowing the ordinary windage; or it may have a cup or disk capable of being forced out to fill the bore when the gun is discharged. A high initial velocity is obtainable in subcaliber projectiles, for while their weight and hence inertia are much less than those of the full-sized shot, the area acted upon by the expanding gases is the same.—**Theory of projectiles**, that branch of mechanics which treats of the motion of bodies thrown or driven by an impelling force from the surface of the earth, and affected by gravity and the resistance of the air, as the motion of a cannon- or rifle-ball, or of a jet of water, etc.

projecting (prọ̄-jek'ting), *p. a.* Inventive; enterprising. [Rare.]

Christopher Columbus, . . . being a man of *projecting* wit, excellently skilled in astronomy and navigation, strongly conceited that some lands must needs lie in the portion of the circle which should make up the world into a globe.
S. Clarke, Geog. Description (1671), p. 257.

projectingly (prọ̄-jek'ting-li), *adv.* In the manner of something that juts out or projects.

A . . . hat . . . *projectingly* and out of all proportion cocked before.
Annals of Phil. and Penn., I. 381.

projection (prọ̄-jek'shọn), *n.* [< F. *projection* = Sp. *proyeccion* = Pg. *projecção* = It. *projezione*, < L. *projectio(n-)*, a throwing forward, a stretching out, < *projicere*, *proicere*, pp. *projectus*, throw forth: see *project*.] **1.** The act of projecting, throwing, or shooting forward: as, the *projection* of a shadow upon a bright surface; hence, the act or process of throwing, as it were, something that is subjective into the objective world; the act of giving objective or seeming reality to what is subjective: as, the *projection* of a sensation of color into space as the quality of an object (a colored thing).—**2.** That image or figure which results from the act of projecting an idea or a sensation.

Soon or late to all our dwellings come the spectres of the mind,
Doubts and fears and dread forebodings, in the darkness undefined;
Round us throng the grim *projections* of the heart and of the brain.
Whittier, Garrison of Cape Ann.

3. That which projects; a part projecting or jutting out, as of a building extending beyond the surface of the wall; a prominence.

The main peculiarity in the outside [of the amphitheater at Pola] is to be found in four tower-like *projections*.
E. A. Freeman, Venice, p. 117.

4. The act of projecting, or scheming or planning: as, he undertook the *projection* of a new enterprise.

Which, of a weak and niggardly *projection*,
Doth, like a miser, spoil his coat with scanting
A little cloth.
Shak., Hen. V., ii. 4. 46.

5. (*a*) In *geom.*, the act or result of constructing rays or right lines through every point of a figure, according to certain rules. These rays are called *projecting rays*. In *central projection*, often called *projection* simply, the projecting rays all pass through one point called the *center of projection*. In this way a point is projected into a ray, a straight line into a plane. In *axial projection*, a plane, called a *projecting plane*, is passed through every point of the figure, all these planes containing one line called the *axis of projection*. (*b*) The act or result of constructing rays through every point of a figure, all passing through one point, and cutting these rays by a plane or other surface, so as to form a section on that surface which corresponds point for point with the original figure. (*c*) In *chartography*, the act or result of constructing a figure upon a plane or other surface, which corresponds point by point with a sphere, spheroid, or other figure; a map-projection (which see, below).—**6.** The mental operation in consequence of which objects of the imagination or retinal impressions appear to be seen external to us.

What we call the field of view is naught else than the external *projection* into space of retinal states.
Le Conte, Sight, p. 71.

7. In *alchemy*, the act of throwing anything into a crucible or other vessel, especially the throwing of a portion of philosopher's stone, upon a metal in fusion with the result of transmuting it; hence, the act or result of transmutation of metals; humorously, the crisis of any process, especially of a culinary process.

The red ferment
Has done his office; three hours hence prepare you
To see *projection*.
B. Jonson, Alchemist, ii. 1.

At the same time a ring was shewed to the King, pretended to be a *projection* of mercury.
Evelyn, Diary, June 1, 1667.

It is indeed the great business of her life to watch the skillet on the fire, to see it simmer with the due degree of heat, and to snatch it off at the moment of *projection*.
Johnson, Rambler, No. 51.

Had he not had *projection*, think you? Saw you no ingots in the crucibles?
Scott, Kenilworth, xli.

Center of projection. See def. 5 (*a*).—**Central projection.** See *central* and def. 5 (*a*).—**Cylindrical projection.** See *map-projection*.—**Gauche projection.** See *gauche*.—**Geometric projection**, a parallel perspective projection equally inclined to the three principal axes of the body to be represented, as a machine.—**Homolographic, horizontal, imaginary, isometric, loxodromic projection.** See the adjectives.—**Globular projection.** See *map-projection*.—**Map-projection**, a system of continuous correspondence between the points of a spherical or spheroidal surface and those of a plane, this correspondence determining what points on a map represent given points on the earth, and conversely. Of the systems in use, only a small number are perspective representations (or rather perversions of such representations), so that the word *projection* must here be understood in a peculiar technical sense, not implying any simple geometrical relation between the sphere and the plane. The theory of projections is in itself one of the most scientific branches of applied mathematics; it may, indeed, be said to be simply the theory of functions viewed under the strong perspective of a practical standpoint. But only certain parts of the subject, such as the theory of orthomorphic projections, have as yet taken scientific shape. No satisfactory classification of map-projections is known; but orthomorphic, equivalent, zenithal (including the perspective), meridional, and conical projections are some of the main kinds. The following are the more important: *Airy's map-projection.* See *map-projection by balance of errors*.—*Albers's map-projection*, an equivalent map-projection in which the entire sphere appears as the space bounded by two lines and by two arcs of circles having their center at the intersections of these lines, these two arcs representing the infinitesimal parallels about the poles. The other parallels are concentric arcs having the same boundaries, and the meridians are straight lines radiating from the center. This map-projection was invented by H. C. Albers in 1805, and has been used for the map of Europe by Reichard.—*Apianus's map-projection*, a discontinuous map-projection in which the equator is represented by a limited straight line, and one of the meridians by a circle whose center bisects that line, while its circumference bisects each half formed by the first bisection; then, the semi-meridians toward the center are represented by arcs of circles cutting the equator orthogonally at equidistances, and bisecting the first circle at the points most distant from the equator; but the semi-meridians more distant from the center are represented by semicircles of the same radius as the full circle, and cutting the equator orthogonally at the same distances as the inner meridians; and the parallels are represented by equidistant straight lines parallel to the equator. This map-projection was much used in the sixteenth century, having been introduced by Peter Bennewitz or Apianus in 1524.—*Arago's map-projection*, a map-projection in which one of the meridians is a circle, and the parallels are parallel straight lines dividing the circumference of this circle into equal arcs, while the other meridians are ellipses dividing the parallels into equal parts. This projection was invented by the French astronomer Arago in 1834.—*Arrowsmith's map-projection.* See *globular map-projection* (*b*).—*Babinet's map-projection.* See *homolographic map-projection*.—*Bennewitz's map-projection.* Same as *Apianus's map-projection*.—*Bonne's map-projection*, an equivalent map-projection in which all the parallels are represented by concentric and equidistant arcs of circles, and the central meridian by a straight line, the central parallel being cut orthogonally by all meridians. The entire spheroid appears in a kidney shape. This map-projection was invented by Ptolemy, and described in his geography, although his rules for drawing it did not contemplate a degree of precision which the geographical knowledge of his time would not warrant. It was extensively used during the sixteenth century. It bears the name of the French geodesist Bonne, who improved the theory of it. It has been employed in several of the government maps of European countries. Also called *modified Flamsteed's map-projection*.—*Boole's map-projection.* Same as *Lagrange's map-projection*.—*Broken map-projection.* Same as *discontinuous map-projection*.—*Cassini's map-projection*, an equivalent map-projection, the development of a cylinder tangent to the sphere along a meridian, upon which cylinder the sphere has been orthogonally projected from the axis of the cylinder. This projection was used for Cassini de Thury's great map of France, of which the publication was begun in 1745.—*Central equivalent map-projection.* Same as *isomeric map-projection*. It was proposed by J. H. Lambert.—*Central map-projection.* (*a*) Same as *gnomonic map-projection*. (*b*) Same as *zenithal map-projection*.—*Clarke's map-projection*, a perspective map-projection in which the distance of the eye from the center of the sphere is 1.368 times the radius. This projection was invented by the English geodesist Colonel A. R. Clarke.—*Collignon's map-projection.* (*a*) The quadrilateral map-projection. (*b*) The central equivalent projection.—*Conform map-projection.* Same as *orthomorphic map-projection*.—*Conical map-projection.* (*a*) Properly, a map-projection the development of a tangent or secant cone upon which the sphere is conceived to have been projected by lines of projection perpendicular to its axis. (*b*) Any projection which may naturally be regarded as the development of a projection upon a cone.—*Cylindrical map-projection.* (*a*) A parallelogrammatic or square map-projection. (*b*) A map-projection showing the earth in repeated stripes, as Mercator's. (*c*) A perspective or central projection in which the center is at infinity.—*Delisle's map-projection*, the secant conical projection proposed by Mercator, and applied by J. N. Delisle to the great map of Russia.—*Discontinuous map-projection*, a map-projection which follows one law in one part, and another in another part. Also called *broken map-projection*, *irregular map-projection*.—*English map-projection.* Same as *globular map-projection* (*b*).—*Equidistant map-projection*, a zenithal map-projection in which the radius of each almucantar is equal to its angular distance from the zenith. This map-projection, invented by the French mathematician Postel in the sixteenth century, is frequently employed for star-maps, etc.—*Equivalent map-projection*, a map-projection which represents all equal surfaces on the spheroid by equal areas on the map. Also called *equal-surface map-projection*.—*Equivalent stereographic map-projection*, an equiv-

Bonne's Projection.

alent map-projection in which the parallels are represented by parallel straight lines at distances from the equator proportional to the tangents of half the latitudes. This projection was proposed in 1862 by M. de Prépetit Foucaut.—*Flamsteed's map-projection.* Same as *sinusoidal map-projection.*—*Foucaut's map-projection*, the equivalent stereographic map-projection.—*Fournier's map-projection.* (*a*) A meridional map-projection in which the meridians are equidistant ellipses, while the parallels are circular arcs equally dividing the central and extreme meridians. (*b*) A map-projection in which the meridians are as in (*a*), but the parallels are straight lines as in the meridional orthogonal projection. These map-projections were proposed in 1646 by the French geographer Fournier.—*Gauss's map-projection.* Same as *Lagrange's map-projection.*—*Glareanus's map-projection*, a discontinuous map-projection differing from that of Apianus only in setting the parallels at the same distances as in the meridional orthographic map-projection. It was invented by the Swiss mathematician Loriti or Glareanus, and published in 1527.—*Globular map-projection.* (*a*) Any projection of a hemisphere with curvilinear meridians and parallels. (*b*) A meridional hemispherical map-projection in which the equator is a straight line, the semimeridians are circular arcs dividing the equator into equal parts, and the parallels are circular arcs dividing the extreme and central meridians into equal parts. This projection, invented in 1660 by the Italian Nicolosi, has been extensively employed ever since. (*c*) La Hire's map-projection.—*Gnomonic map-projection.* (*a*) A perspective map-projection from the center of the sphere. All great circles are represented by straight lines. Hence, by extension—(*b*) Any map-projection

Gnomonic Projection.

representing all great circles by straight lines. Such a projection can contain but one half of the sphere on an infinite plane. This system is probably ancient.—*Harding's map-projection.* Same as *Lagrange's map-projection.*—*Herschel's map-projection.* Same as *Lagrange's map-projection.*—*Homalographic* (or *homolographic*) *map-projection*, an equivalent map-projection in which the meridians are ellipses meeting at the poles, and the parallels and equator are parallel straight lines: invented by the German mathematician Mollweide in 1805. It has been considerably used.—*Intermediary map-projection*, a zenithal map-projection in which, z being the zenith distance of an almucantar, r its radius on the map, and n a constant,

$$r = n \tan z/n.$$

This projection was invented by A. Germain.—*Irregular map-projection.* Same as *discontinuous map-projection.*—*Isocylindric map-projection*, an equivalent map-projection the development of a cylinder upon which the sphere has been orthogonally projected. It was invented by the German mathematical philosopher J. H. Lambert.—*Isomeric map-projection*, the zenithal equivalent map-projection, invented by J. H. Lambert, and the best of the equivalent projections.—*Isospherical map-projection.* Same as *isomeric map-projection.*—*Jaeger's map-projection*, a discontinuous projection in the shape of an eight-pointed star. It was proposed by Jaeger in 1865, and was modified by Petermann.—*James's map-projection*, a perspective map-projection in which the center of projection is distant from that of the sphere by 1.5 times the radius. It was invented by the English geodesist Sir Henry James.—*Lagrange's map-projection*, an orthomorphic map-projection in which the sphere is shown a finite number of times on a finite number of sheets, but in which all the north poles (or zeniths) coincide, as well as all the south poles (or nadirs). The projection was invented by J. H. Lambert, and has been called by many names. It has been used in a government map of Russia.—*La Hire's map-projection*, a perspective projection having the center of projection at a distance from the center of the sphere equal to 1.707 times the radius. This projection, proposed by the French geodesist La Hire in 1701, has been frequently used.—*Littrow's map-projection*, an orthomorphic projection in which the meridians are hyperbolas and the parallels ellipses, all these conics being confocal. This projection has two north and two south poles, all four coincident at infinity, and shows the sphere twice on two sheets, which are merely perversions of each other. It has many remarkable properties. It was invented by the Bohemian astronomer Littrow in 1833.—*Lorgna's map-projection.* Same as *isomeric map-projection.*—*Map-projection by balance of errors*, that zenithal projection which makes the "misrepresentation" a minimum, as determined by least squares. If r is the radius of an almucantar on the chart, z its zenith distance, and Z that of the limit of the chart, which cannot exceed 126° 24′ 53″, then

$$r = \cot \tfrac{1}{2}z \log \sec \tfrac{1}{2}z + \tan \tfrac{1}{2}z \cot^2 \tfrac{1}{2}Z \log \sec \tfrac{1}{2}Z.$$

Map-projection by development, a projection upon a developable surface which is then developed into a plane.—*Mercator's map-projection*, an orthomorphic map-projection in which the whole sphere is shown in equal repeating stripes. The point at infinity represents the whole sphere, and the zenith and nadir do not elsewhere appear. As ordinarily used, the poles are taken as these points, when the meridians appear as equidistant parallel lines, and the parallels as parallel lines cutting them at distances from the equator proportional to log tan ½ latitude. This has the advantage that the points of the compass preserve the same directions all over the map.

Mercator's Projection.

This projection, invented by the Flemish cosmographer Mercator in 1550, is the most useful of all.—*Meridional map-projection*, a map-projection which seems to be projected upon the plane of a meridian, showing the poles at the extremities of a central meridian.—*Modified Flamsteed's map-projection.* Same as *Bonne's map-projection.*—*Mollweide's map-projection.* Same as *homolographic map-projection.*—*Murdoch's map-projection*, one of three conical map-projections in which the part of the cone of which the map is a reduced development is equal to the spherical zone represented. These were invented by Patrick Murdoch in 1758.—*Orthographic map-projection*, a perspective map-projection from an infinitely distant center.—*Orthomorphic map-projection*, a map-projection which preserves all angles—that is, the shapes of all infinitesimal portions of the sphere. When one such map-projection has been obtained, say the polar stereographic, which is the simplest, all others may be derived from this by a transformation of the plane. Let r and θ be the polar coördinates of any point on the polar stereographic projection, let i denote the imaginary whose square is -1, and let F denote any function having a differential coefficient. If, then, $F(r \cos \theta + r \sin \theta . i)$ be put into the form $x + yi$, x and y will be the rectangular coördinates of the corresponding point on another orthomorphic projection. Also called *conform map-projection.*—*Parallelogrammatic map-projection*, a map-projection in which the parallels are represented by equidistant straight lines, and the meridians by equidistant straight lines perpendicular to the parallels. This is an ancient projection. Also called *rectangular map-projection.*—*Parent's map-projection*, one of two perspective map-projections. In Parent's first map-projection the center of projection is distant from the center of the sphere 1.595 times the radius. In his second this distance is 1.732.—*Perspective map-projection*, a true projection of the sphere by straight lines from a center of projection intersecting the plane of the map.—*Petermann's map-projection*, a discontinuous map-projection showing the sphere in the form of an eight-pointed star. It is used to decorate the title-page of Stieler's atlas.—*Polar map-projection*, a map-projection showing one of the poles in the center.—*Polyconic map-projection*, a map-projection in which the surface of the earth is cut into an infinite number of zones parallel to the equator; a central meridian is then developed into a straight line, and then each zone is developed separately. This projection, invented by Hassler, superintendent of the United States Coast Survey, is used in all government maps of the United States.—*Quadrilateral map-projection*, a broken equivalent projection in which one meridian has the form of a square, of which another meridian and the equator are the diagonals. It was invented by Collignon.—*Quincuncial map-projection*, an orthomorphic pro-

The World on a Quincuncial Projection.

jection of the earth into repeating squares, invented by C. S. Peirce in 1876.—*Rectangular map-projection.* Same as *parallelogrammatic map-projection.*—*Ruysch's map-projection*, a conical projection in which the cone cuts the equator and has its vertex at one pole, and the sphere is projected upon the cone by lines perpendicular to the axis. It was invented by Ruysch in 1508.—*Sanson's map-projection.* Same as *sinusoidal map-projection.*—*Schmidt's map-projection*, a meridional map-projection in which the meridians are represented by ellipses cut at equal distances by the parallels. It was proposed by the physicist G. G. Schmidt in 1801.—*Sinusoidal map-projection*, an equivalent map-projection in which the parallels are equidistant straight lines to which the central meridian is perpendicular. This projection (so called from the form of the meridians) was first used by the French chartographer Sanson in 1650.—*Square map-projection*, the projection of a map which the successive meridians and parallels cut up into squares.—*Stenoterous map-projection*, an equivalent projection which represents the whole earth on the sector of a circle, the pole being at the center and the parallels concentric circles. It was invented by J. H. Lambert.—*Stereographic map-projection*, the simplest of all projections, representing the whole sphere once on one infinite plane, the parts at infinity being considered as a point. All circles on the sphere

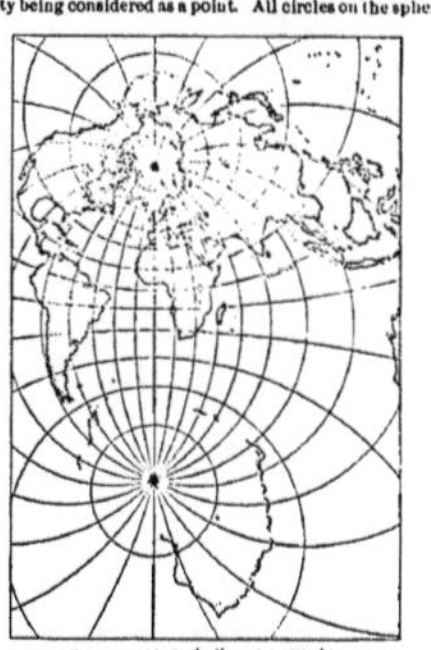
Stereographic Projection of the World.

are represented circles, and the angles are preserved. The stereographic projection of the sphere is a perspective projection, a point on the surface being the center of projection; but the stereographic map-projection of the spheroid is not a perspective projection. The stereographic projection was known to the ancients, and has always been employed for special purposes.—*Textor's map-projection*, a modification of the isocylindrical map, by J. C. von Textor, 1808.—*Transverse map-projection*, a meridional map-projection.—*Trapeziform map-projection*, a map-projection in which the space between two meridians and two parallels is represented by a trapezoid, the sides of which are divided proportionally to determine other straight lines representing meridians and parallels.—*Werner's map-projection*, that equivalent map-projection which has the parallels concentric and equidistant arcs of circles, with the north pole at the center. The whole sphere has a heart shape. This was invented by Johann Werner, 1514.—*Zenithal map-projection*, a map-projection which is symmetrical about a central point, the almucantars being represented by concentric circles.—**Mercator's projection.** See *Mercator's chart* (under *chart*) and *Mercator's map-projection* (above).—**Natural projection**, a perspective delineation of a surface on a given plane. *Stormonth.*—**Oblique projection**, a cylindrical projection upon a plane not at right angles to the sides of the cylinder.—**Orthogonal projection**, a projection by means of rays all perpendicular to the plane of projection.—**Orthographic projection.** See under *map-projection*, above.—**Parallel projection**, a perspective projection in which the center is at infinity.—**Plane of projection.** Same as *perspective plane* (which see, under *perspective*).—**Powder of projection**, in *alchemy*, a powder added to base metals in a molten state, and supposed to have the power of transmuting them into gold or silver.—**Stereoscopic projection**, a double perspective projection adapted to be viewed one part by one eye, the other by the other.

projective (prǭ-jek'tiv), *a.* [< *project* + *-ive.*] 1. Produced by projection.—2. In *geom.*, relating to incidences and coincidences; not metrical: as, a *projective* theorem or property.—3. Capable, as two plane figures, of being derived from one another by a number of projections and sections. Thus, let the plane pencil OABCD be cut by the line AD in the points A, B, C, D, and from the center P let these points be projected into the rays AE, BF, CG, DH, and let these be cut by the line EH in the points E, F, G, H. Then, the range of points EFGH is projective with the plane pencil OABCD.—**Projective geometry.** See *geometry.*

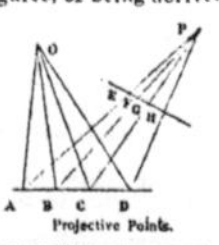

Projective Points.

projectivity (prǭ-jek-tiv'i-ti), *n.* [< *projective* + *-ity.*] The character of being projective, as two plane figures.

projectment† (prǭ-jekt'ment), *n.* [< *project* + *-ment.*] Projection; design; contrivance. [Rare.]

> She never doubted but that men that were never so dishonest in their *projectments* of each other's confusion might agree in their allegiance to her.
> *Clarendon*, Great Rebellion.

projector (prǭ-jek'tọr), *n.* [< NL. *projector, < L. *projicere*, *proicere*, pp. *projectus*, project: see *project.*] 1. One who forms projects; one who forms a scheme or design; a schemer.

Fitz. But what is a *projector?*
I would conceive.
Eng. Why, one, sir, that projects
Ways to enrich men, or to make them great
By suits, by marriages, by undertakings.
B. Jonson, Devil is an Ass, i. 3.

Well, Sir, how fadges the new Design? have you not the Luck of all your Brother *Projectors*, to deceive only yourself at last? *Wycherley*, Country Wife, iv. 1.

Sir Gilbert Heathcote, who was one of the *projectors* of the Bank of England. *N. and Q.*, 7th ser., II. 102.

2. That which projects; specifically, a parabolic mirror, or a lens or combination of lenses, used for projecting a beam of light. The source of light is usually arranged in relation to the projector so that the beam is composed of rays nearly parallel.

The search-light *projector*, which is hung in a cage over the ship's bow. *Engineer*, LXVI. 313.

On May 4th there were placed in position two electric *projectors*, which from the Eiffel Tower will throw their powerful rays of light over Paris. *Electric Rev.* (Eng.), XXIV. 540.

3. A camera for throwing an image on a screen by means of electric, magnesium, oxyhydrogen, or other suitable light.—4. The square of the area of a plane triangle divided by the continued product of the sides.

projectrix (prǫ-jek'triks), *n.* A curve derived from another curve by composition of projections.

projecture (prǫ-jek'tūr), *n.* [‹ F. *projecture* = Sp. *proyectura* = Pg. *projectura* = It. *projettura*, ‹ L. *projectura*, something jutting out, ‹ *projicere, proicere*, pp. *projectus*, thrust forth or forward: see *project.*] A jutting or standing out beyond the line or surface of something else; projection.

projet (prǫ-zhā'), *n.* [F.: see *project.*] Scheme; plan; design; specifically, in *international law*, the draft of a proposed treaty or convention.

proke (prōk), *v. t.*; pret. and pp. *proked*, ppr. *proking*. [‹ W. *procio*, poke, thrust, stab. Cf. *prog* and *prowl.*] To poke; stir; goad; urge. [Now only prov. Eng.]

The queene ever at his elbowe to pricke and *proke* him forward. *Holland*, tr. of Ammianus (1609). (*Nares.*)

prokecyet, *n.* A Middle English form of *proxy*. *Prompt. Parv.*, p. 414.

prokeimenon (prǫ-ki'me-non), *n.* [‹ Gr. προκείμενον, neut. ppr. of πρόκειμαι, be placed before, ‹ πρό, before, + κεῖμαι, lie, be placed.] In the *Gr. Ch.*, a short anthem preceding the epistle, consisting of two verses, generally from the psalms. There is also a prokeimenon at Sunday lauds and at vespers.

proker (prō'kėr), *n.* That which prokes or pokes; particularly, a poker. [Prov. Eng.]

Before the antique Hall's turf fire
Was stretch'd the Porter, Con Maguire,
Who, at stout Usquebaugh's command,
Snor'd with his *proker* in his hand.
Colman, Poetical Vagaries, p. 46. (*Davies.*)

The *prokers* are not half so hot, or so long,
By an inch or two, either in handle or prong.
Barham, Ingoldsby Legends, II. 227.

prokeratourt, *n.* A Middle English form of *procurator*. *Prompt. Parv.*, p. 414.

proketowret, *n.* A Middle English form of *proctor*. *Prompt. Parv.*, p. 414.

proking-spitt (prō'king-spit), *n.* A sword used for thrusting or poking; a rapier; a weapon. [Humorous.]

Piping hote, puffes toward the pointed plaine
With a broad Scot, or *proking-spit* of Spaine.
Bp. Hall, Satires, IV. iv. 57.

prokket, *v. t.* and *i.* [ME.; cf. Dan. *prukke* = Sw. *pracka*, go a-begging, = G. *prachen*, *prachern*, beg; perhaps ‹ L. *procare, procari*, ask. Cf. *proke, prog.*] To beg.

Prokkyn or styfly askyn, *procor*, *procito*. *Prompt. Parv.*, p. 414.

prolabial (prō-lā'bi-al), *a.* [‹ *prolabium* + *-al.*] Of or relating to the prolabia. *Lancet*, No. 3465, p. 182.

prolabium (prō-lā'bi-um), *n.*; pl. *prolabia* (-ä). [NL., ‹ L. *pro*, before, + *labium*, lip: see *labium.*] One of the oral margins of the lips, forming the red exposed part.

prolapse (prǫ-laps'), *v. i.*; pret. and pp. *prolapsed*, ppr. *prolapsing*. [‹ L. *prolapsus*, pp. of *prolabi*, fall or slide forward, ‹ *pro*, before, + *labi*, fall: see *lapse.*] To fall down or out: chiefly a medical term. See *prolapse, n.*

prolapse (prǫ-laps'), *n.* [‹ L. *prolapsus*, a falling, ‹ *prolabi*, pp. *prolapsus*, fall or slide forward: see *prolapse, v.*] In *pathol.*, a falling down of some part of the body, as the uterus or rectum, from the position which it normally occupies.

prolapsion (prǫ-lap'shon), *n.* [‹ L. *prolapsio(n-)*, a slipping or falling forward, ‹ *prolabi*, fall forward: see *prolapse, v.*] Prolapse. [Rare.]

prolapsus (prǫ-lap'sus), *n.*; pl. *prolapsus*. [LL.: see *prolapse, n.*] In *pathol.*, prolapse.

prolatet (prǫ-lāt'), *v. t.* [‹ L. *prolatus*, pp. of *proferre*, bring forward, carry out or forth, produce: see *proffer.*] To utter, especially in a drawling manner; lengthen in pronunciation or sound.

The pressures of war have somewhat cowed their spirits, as may be gathered from the accent of their words, which they *prolate* in a whining querulous tone, as if still complaining and crest-fallen. *Howell.*

For the sake of what was deemed solemnity, every note was *prolated* into one uniform mode of intonation.
W. Mason, Eng. Church Musick, p. 261. (*Latham.*)

prolate (prō'lāt), *a.* [‹ L. *prolatus*, brought forward, pp. of *proferre*, bring forward, produce: see *prolate, v.*] Lengthened along one direction. A *prolate spheroid* is produced by the revolution of a semi-ellipse about its larger diameter. See *oblate.*—**Prolate cycloid.** See *cycloid*, 1.

prolateness (prō'lāt-nes), *n.* The condition or character of being prolate.

prolationt (prǫ-lā'shon), *n.* [‹ ME. *prolacioun*, ‹ OF. (and F.) *prolation* = Sp. *prolacion* = Pg. *prolação* = It. *prolazione*, ‹ L. *prolatio(n-)*, a bringing forward or putting forth, ‹ *prolatus*, pp. of *proferre*, bring out or forth: see *prolate.*] 1. Bringing forth; utterance; pronunciation.

S is a most easy and gentle letter, and softly hisseth against the teeth in the *prolation*.
B. Jonson, Eng. Grammar, i. 4.

2. Delivery; measure; tune.

With rethorice com forth musice, a damoisel of oure hous, that syngeth now lyghter moedes or *prolaciouns* (var. *probasyons*), now hevyer. *Chaucer*, Boëthius, ii. prose 1.

3. The act of deferring; delay.—4. In *mediæval music*, a method of subdividing the semibreve into minims—that is, rhythmical subdivision. Two varieties were recognized—the greater or perfect, which was triple, and the less or imperfect, which was duple.

prolectationt, *n.* [‹ OF. *prolectation* = Sp. *prolectacion* = It. *prolettazione*, ‹ L. as if **prolectatio(n-)*, ‹ *prolectare*, allure, entice, freq. of *prolicere*, allure, entice, ‹ *pro*, forth, + *lacere*, allure: see *allect.*] Enticement; allurement. *Minsheu.*

proleg (prō'leg), *n.* [‹ L. *pro*, for, + E. *leg.*] In *entom.*, a false leg; a proped; one of the abdominal limbs or ambulatory processes of the

Larva of Milkweed Butterfly (*Anosia plexippus*).

larvæ of insects, usually fleshy and always distinct from the true thoracic legs. The ten posterior legs of a caterpillar of ordinary form are prolegs. Also called *prop-leg*. See also cut under *Amara.*—**Coronate prolegs.** See *coronate*.

prolegate (prō-leg'āt), *n.* [‹ L. *prolegatus*, the substitute of a legate or lieutenant-governor, ‹ *pro*, for, + *legatus*, legate: see *legate.*] A deputy legate.

prolegomenary (prō-le-gom'e-nā-ri), *a.* [‹ *prolegomenon* + *-ary.*] Having the character of prolegomena; preliminary; introductory; containing prefixed explanations. *Imp. Dict.*

prolegomenon (prō-le-gom'e-non), *n.*; pl. *prolegomena* (-nä). [NL., ‹ Gr. προλεγόμενον, neut. of προλεγόμενος, ppr. pass. of προλέγειν, say before, foretell, ‹ πρό, before, + λέγειν, tell, speak: see *legend, Logos.*] A preliminary observation: chiefly used in the plural, and applied to an introductory discourse prefixed to a book or treatise.

"'Tis a pithy *prolegomenon*," quoth I—and so read on.
Sterne, Tristram Shandy, vii. 38.

The mention of the Venetian scholia leads us at once to the Homeric controversy; for the immortal *Prolegomena* of Wolf appeared a few years after Villoison's publication.
Encyc. Brit., XII. 115.

prolegomenous (prō-le-gom'e-nus), *a.* [‹ *prolegomen-on* + *-ous.*] 1. Preliminary; introductory; prefatory.

The *prolegomenous* or introductory chapter.
Fielding, Tom Jones, viii. 1.

2. Given to making long exordiums or prefatory remarks.

While the curt, pithy speaker misses the point entirely, a wordy, *prolegomenous* babbler will often add three new offences in the process of excusing one.
R. L. Stevenson, Virginibus Puerisque, iv.

prolepsis (prǫ-lep'sis), *n.* [‹ L. *prolepsis*, ‹ Gr. πρόληψις, an anticipating, ‹ προλαμβάνειν, take beforehand, receive in advance, ‹ πρό, before, + λαμβάνειν, λαβεῖν, take, receive.] Anticipation. (*a*) In the *Stoic philos.*, a common notion, axiom, or instinctive belief which is not irresistible, and which may be in conflict with the truth. (*b*) In the *Epicurean philos.*, a general conception based on sense-experience.

A certain anticipation of the gods, which he calls a *prolepsis*, a certain preventive, or foreconceived information of a thing in the mind. *J. Howe*, Works, I. 22.

(c) In *rhet.*: (1) A name sometimes applied to the use of an adjective (or a noun) as objective predicate (see *predicate*), as if implying an anticipation of the result of the verb's action. (2) A figure consisting in anticipation of an opponent's objections and arguments in order to preclude his use of them, answer them in advance, or prepare the reader to receive them unfavorably. This figure is most frequently used in the exordium. Also called *procatalepsis*. (*d*) An error in chronology, consisting in dating an event before the actual time of its occurrence; an anachronism.

Mr. Errington, called Lord Errington in the dispatches, by a *prolepsis* we suppose. *The American*, VI. 87.

proleptic (prǫ-lep'tik), *a.* [‹ Gr. προληπτικός, anticipating, ‹ πρόληψις, an anticipation: see *prolepsis.*] 1. Pertaining to prolepsis or anticipation; anticipatory; antecedent.

Far different and far nobler was the hard simplicity and noble self-denial of the Baptist. It is by no idle fancy that the mediæval painters represent him as emaciated by a *proleptic* asceticism. *Farrar*, Life of Christ, viii.

Specifically—(*a*) In *med.*: (1) Anticipating the usual time: noting a periodical disease whose paroxysm returns at an earlier hour at every recurrence. (2) Prognostic. (*b*) In *rhet.*, implying prolepsis.

2. Axiomatic; of the nature of prolepsis.

To lead him by induction through a series of propositions depending upon and orderly deduced from your first *proleptick* principles. *Parker*, Platonic Philosophy.

proleptical (prǫ-lep'ti-kal), *a.* [‹ *proleptic* + *-al.*] Same as *proleptic*.

So that our knowledge here is not after singular bodies, or secondarily or derivatively from them; but in order of nature, before them, and *proleptical* to them.
Cudworth, Intellectual System, p. 732.

proleptically (prǫ-lep'ti-kal-i), *adv.* [‹ *proleptical* + *-ly*[2].] By prolepsis; in a proleptic manner; by way of anticipation.

The particle has also the power of indicating *proleptically* in the subordinate clause that the principal one will spring from it. *Amer. Jour. Philol.*, VI. 46.

proleptics (prǫ-lep'tiks), *n.* [Pl. of *proleptic* (see *-ics*).] The art or science of prognosticating in medicine. *Imp. Dict.*

proles (prō'lēz), *n.* [L., offspring, progeny, ‹ *pro*, forth, forward, + √ *al* in *alere*, nourish (see *aliment*), or *olere*, grow (see *adolescent*).] Progeny; offspring.

proletaire (prō-le-tãr'), *a.* and *n.* [‹ F. *prolétaire*: see *proletary.*] Same as *proletarian*.

These ancestors of Roman prelates were poor dirty *proletaires*, without distinction, without manners.
E. Renan, Hibbert Lectures, 1880 (tr. by C. Beard), ii.

The plant is the ideal *prolétaire* of the living world, the worker who produces. *Huxley*, An. and Veg. Kingdoms.

proletairism (prō-le-tãr'izm), *n.* [‹ *proletaire* + *-ism.*] Same as *proletarianism*.

proletaneous (prō-le-tā'nẹ-us), *a.* [‹ L. *proletaneus*, equiv. to *proletarius*: see *proletary.*] Having a numerous offspring. [Rare.]

proletarian (prō-le-tā'ri-an), *a.* and *n.* [‹ *proletary* + *-an.*] I. *a.* Of or belonging to the lower classes; hence, mean; vile; vulgar.

Low *proletarian* tything men.
S. Butler, Hudibras, I. i. 720.

II. *n.* A member of the poorest class of a community; one who is without capital or regular employment.

We have considered the forcible creation of a class of outlawed *proletarians*, the bloody discipline that turned them into wage-labourers. *Marx*, Capital (trans.), xxix.

A *proletarian* is a person who is possessed of labour-force, and of nothing else. *Westminster Rev.*, CXXVI. 221.

Also *proletaire*.

proletarianism (prō-le-tā'ri-an-izm), *n.* [‹ *proletarian* + *-ism.*] The condition, or the political influence, of the lower classes of the community. Also *proletairism*.

The bourgeoisie had played a most revolutionary part in history. They had overturned feudalism, and now they had created *proletarianism*, which would soon swamp themselves. *Rae*, Contemp. Socialism, p. 129.

proletarianize (prō-le-tā'ri-an-īz), *v. t.*; pret. and pp. *proletarianized*, ppr. *proletarianizing*. [‹ *proletarian* + *-ize.*] To make proletarian; reduce to a state of proletarianism.

The largesses pauperized and *proletarianized* the populace of the great city. *Pop. Sci. Mo.*, XXX. 293.

proletariat (prō-le-tā'ri-at), *n.* Same as *proletariate*[2].

proletariate[1] (prō-le-tā'ri-āt), *a.* [‹ *proletary* + *-ate*[1]. Cf. *proletariate*[2].] Of or pertaining to the proletariate; relating to the proletarians; proletarian.

The very efforts of philanthropy at the improvement of the *proletariate* classes.
The Academy, June 29, 1889, p. 441.

proletariate[2], **proletariat** (prō-le-tā'ri-āt, -at), *n.* [< F. *prolétariat*, the state or condition of a proletary, < L. *proletarius*, a proletary: see *proletary* and *-ate*.] Proletarians collectively; a body of proletarians; the class of wage-workers dependent for support on daily or casual employment; the lowest and poorest class in the community.

The *proletariat*, as the agitators delighted to call the standing class of operatives: meaning, by this Roman term for the lowest class in that republic, those who had only hands to work with and no laid-up capital.
Woolsey, Communism and Socialism, iv. § 1.

These [socialistic] doctrines had in the west [of Europe] been bred among the *proletariate*, the large class of society who had no property, no stable source of income, no steady employment, and no sure hope for the morrow.
Rae, Contemp. Socialism, p. 268.

proletary (prō'le-tā-ri), *a.* and *n.* [= F. *prolétaire* = Sp. Pg. It. *proletario*, < L. *proletarius*, according to a division of the state traditionally ascribed to Servius Tullius, a citizen of the lowest class, without property, and regarded as useful to the state only as the parent of children, < *proles*, offspring, progeny: see *proles*.] **I.** *a.* Of or belonging to the lowest or poorest class of people; pertaining to those who are dependent on daily or casual employment for support; proletarian.

II. *n.*; pl. *proletaries* (-riz). A common person; one belonging to the lower orders.

Of 15,000 *proletaries* slain in a battel, scarce fifteen are recorded in history.
Burton, Anat. of Mel., To the Reader, p. 33.

prolicide (prō'li-sīd), *n.* [< L. *proles*, offspring, + *-cidium*, < *cædere*, kill.] The crime of destroying one's offspring, either before or after birth; feticide or infanticide.

proliferate (prō-lif'e-rāt), *v.*; pret. and pp. *proliferated*, ppr. *proliferating*. [< L. *proles*, offspring, + *ferre* = E. *bear*[1], + *-ate*[2].] **I.** *intrans.* **1.** To reproduce; grow by multiplication of elementary parts.

All the cells of the body possess a latent capacity which enables them, under various stimuli, to *proliferate* and form new tissue. *Electric Rev.* (Eng.), XXIV. 498.

2. Specifically, in *zoöl.*, to generate or reproduce by the act of proliferation; bear generative persons or zoöids, as distinguished from nutritive persons, as is the usual process in the hydroid polyps.

The annual stock is . . . composed of nutritive and *proliferating* persons, the latter again bearing the buds or generative persons. . . . The *proliferating* persons of a colony present various degrees of degeneration.
Gegenbaur, Comp. Anat. (trans.), p. 95.

II. *trans.* To bear; form by reproduction.

The mesoblast is completed ventrally by the downgrowth on each side of the mesoblastic plates. These *proliferate* cells at their edge.
A. E. Shipley, Proc. Roy. Soc., XXXIX. 246.

proliferation (prō-lif-e-rā'shon), *n.* [< *proliferous* + *-ation*.] **1.** In *zoöl.*, the origination and development of generative zoöids, as in the formation of medusa-buds (planoblasts or hedrioblasts) by a polyp. See *planoblast*.—**2.** In *bot.*, same as *prolification*.—**Entogastric proliferation.** See *entogastric*.

proliferative (prō-lif'e-rā-tiv), *a.* [< *proliferate* + *-ive*.] Reproductive; budding or sprouting into new similar forms.

Ulceration may be attended with *proliferative* vegetations which may occlude the air-passages.
Med. News, LIII. 507.

proliferous (prō-lif'e-rus), *a.* [= F. *prolifère* = Sp. *prolifero* = Pg. *prolifero*, < L. *proles*, offspring, progeny, + *ferre* = E. *bear*[1].] Bearing offspring. (*a*) In *bot.*, subject to or affected by prolification. See *prolification*, 2. Also *prolific*, *proligerous*. (*b*) In *zoöl.*, proliferating; bearing generative persons; producing medusa-buds, as a polyp.

The *proliferous* Polyps develop generative buds on their walls. *Claus*, Zoölogy (trans.), p. 237.

Proliferous cyst, in *pathol.*, a cyst producing highly organized and even vascular structures.

proliferously (prō-lif'e-rus-li), *adv.* [< *proliferous* + *-ly*[2].] In a proliferous manner.

Fronds originating *proliferously* from other fronds sometimes, when mature, disconnect themselves from their parents. *H. Spencer*, Prin. of Biol., § 192.

prolific (prō-lif'ik), *a.* [< F. *prolifique* = Sp. *prolifico* = Pg. It. *prolifico*, < ML. **prolificus*, producing offspring, < L. *proles*, offspring, + *facere*, make, produce: see *-fic*. Cf. *prolify*.] **1.** Producing young or fruit, especially in abundance; fruitful; fertile; productive in general: as, a *prolific* female; a *prolific* tree; *prolific* seed.

The branches, sturdy to his utmost wish,
Prolific all, and harbingers of more.
Cowper, Task, iii. 531.

That in the capital, and in great manufacturing towns, marriages are less *prolific* than in the open country, we admit, and Mr. Malthus admits.
Macaulay, Sadler's Ref. Refuted.

2. Serving to give rise or origin; having the quality of generating; as, a controversy *prolific* of evil consequences; a *prolific* brain.

With warm
Prolific humour softening all her globe.
Milton, P. L., vii. 280.

The extant remains of the literary work of the period are so great that, if we suppose them to bear the ordinary proportion to the lost works of the same age, they would prove it to be enormously *prolific*.
Stubbs, Medieval and Modern Hist., p. 150.

3. Same as *proliferous* (*a*).=**Syn. 1 and 2.** *Productive*, etc. See *fruitful*.

prolificacy (prō-lif'i-kā-si), *n.* [< *prolific* + *-acy*.] Fruitfulness; great productiveness.

With plants like carrots, cabbages, and asparagus, which are not valued for their *prolificacy*, selection can have played only a subordinate part.
Darwin, Var. of Animals and Plants, xvi. 9.

prolifical† (prō-lif'i-kal), *a.* [< *prolific* + *-al*.] Same as *prolific*.

Every dispute in religion grew *prolifical*, and in ventilating one question many new ones were started.
Decay of Christian Piety.

prolifically (prō-lif'i-kal-i), *adv.* [< *prolifical* + *-ly*[2].] In a prolific manner; fruitfully; with great increase. *Imp. Dict.*

prolificate (prō-lif'i-kāt), *v. t.*; pret. and pp. *prolificated*, ppr. *prolificating*. [< ML. *prolificatus*, pp. of *prolificare*, beget: see *prolify*.] To impregnate; make prolific. *Sir T. Browne.*

prolification (prō-lif-i-kā'shon), *n.* [= OF. (and F.) *prolification* = Pg. *prolificação*, < ML. *prolificatio(n-)*, < *prolificare*, produce offspring: see *prolificate*, *prolify*.] **1.** The generation of young animals or plants.—**2.** In *bot.*, the development of an organ or a shoot from an organ which is itself normally ultimate, as a shoot or new flower from the midst of a flower, a frond from a frond, etc. Thus, a rose not unfrequently gives birth to a second from its center, a pear bears a leafy shoot on its summit, and species of *Juncus* and *Scirpus* emit small sprouts from their flower-heads. This is often a case of morphological reversion, the axis whose leaves were altered to make the flower resuming its onward and foliating tendency. Also *proliferation*. Compare *proliferous*.

Abundant nutrition will abbreviate the intervals between the successive *prolifications*; so that eventually, while each frond is yet imperfectly formed, the rudiment of the next will begin to show itself.
H. Spencer, Prin. of Biol., § 194.

prolificness (prō-lif'ik-nes), *n.* [< *prolific* + *-ness*.] The character or state of being prolific.

If there are classes of creatures that expend very little for self-support in comparison with allied creatures, a relatively extreme *prolificness* may be expected of them.
H. Spencer, Prin. of Biol., § 356.

prolified (prō'li-fīd), *a.* [< *prolify* + *-ed*[2].] In *bot.*, developed proliferously. [Rare.]

This plant [the water-avens] is frequently found in a *prolified* state, that is, with a branch or a second flower in the center of the original one. *Treasury of Bot.*, p. 530.

prolify (prō'li-fī), *v. i.*; pret. and pp. *prolified*, ppr. *prolifying*. [< OF. **prolifier* = Pg. *prolificar*, < ML. *prolificare*, produce offspring, beget (cf. **prolificus*, producing offspring), < L. *proles*, offspring, + *facere*, make, produce: see *-fy*. Cf. *prolific*.] To bring forth offspring.

There remained in the heart of such some piece of ill-temper unreformed, which in time *prolified*, and sent out great and wasting sins.
Bp. Sanderson, Works, V. 338. (*Davies*.)

proligerous (prō-lij'e-rus), *a.* [< NL. *proligerus*, **proliger*, < L. *proles*, offspring, + *gerere*, bear.] **1.** Producing progeny; bearing offspring; especially, germinating, as an ovum; entering into the formation of an embryo.—**2.** Specifically, noting the film, pellicle, or membrane of infusions, as the supposed origin or source of the infusorial animalcules which appear in such infusions. See *pseudovary*, 2.—**3.** In *bot.*, same as *proliferous*.—**Proligerous disk** or **layer** [NL. *discus proligerus*], in *embryol.*, the mass of cells upon the outside of an ovum, derived from the inside of a Graafian follicle, wrongly supposed to be germinative, or to enter into the formation of an embryo. The real germinative area of an ovum is of course within its cell-wall.

prolix (prō'liks or prō-liks'), *a.* [< F. *prolixe* = Sp. *prolijo* = Pg. *prolixo* = It. *prolisso*, < L. *prolixus*, stretched out, extended (as the hair, neck, tail, trees, tunic, etc.), LL. also prolix in speech, comprehension; also favorable, fortunate, courteous, etc.; prob. orig. 'overflowing,' < *pro*, forth, + **lixus*, orig. pp. of *liqui*, flow; cf. *elixus*, thoroughly soaked, boiled; *lix*, lye: see *liquid*. The second element cannot be *laxus*, loose, wide: see *lax*[1].] **1**†. Long; extended.

She had also a most *prolix* beard, and moustachios.
Evelyn, Diary, Sept. 15, 1657.

With wig *prolix*, down flowing to his waist.
Cowper, Tirocinium, l. 361.

2†. Of long duration.

If the appellant appoints a term too *prolix*, the judge may then assign a competent term. *Aylife*, Parergon.

3. Long and wordy; extending to a great length; diffuse: as, a *prolix* oration or sermon.

If they [philosophers] had consulted with nature, they had made their doctrines less *prolix* and more profound.
Bacon, Advancement of Learning, ii. 265.

He [Bunsen] is about to publish a book about ancient and modern Rome, which, from what I hear, will be too minute and *prolix*. *Greville*, Memoirs, April 9, 1830.

4. Indulging in lengthy discourse; discussing at great length; tedious: as, a *prolix* speaker or writer.

We shall not be more *prolix*, but refer the substantial, perfect, and assured handling hereof to your circumspections, fidelities, and diligences. *Burnet*, Records, I. ii.

=**Syn. 3.** Long, lengthy, wordy, long-winded, spun out, prolonged.—**4.** Tiresome, wearisome.

prolixious† (prō-lik'shius), *a.* [< *prolix* + *-i-ous*.] Dilatory; intended to delay or put off; causing delay; prolix.

Your Lordship commanded me to be large, and I take licence to be *prolixious*, and shalbe peraduenture tedious.
Hakluyt's Voyages, I. 217.

Lay by all nicety and *prolixious* blushes.
Shak., M. for M., ii. 4. 162.

prolixity (prō-lik'si-ti), *n.* [< ME. *prolixitee*, < OF. *prolixite*, F. *prolixité* = Pr. *prolixitat* = Sp. *prolijidad* = Pg. *prolixidade* = It. *prolissità*, < LL. *prolixita(t-)s*, great length or extension, < L. *prolixus*, stretched out: see *prolix*.] The state of being prolix; extension; length. (*a*) Length in a material sense. [Rare.]

Our fathers . . . in their shaded walks
And long protracted bow'rs enjoyed at noon
The gloom and coolness of declining day.
Thanks to Benevolus—he spares me yet . . .
The obsolete *prolixity* of shade.
Cowper, Task, i. 265.

The monkey, meanwhile, with a thick tail curling out into preposterous *prolixity* from beneath his tartans, took his station at the Italian's feet.
Hawthorne, Seven Gables, xi.

(*b*) Lengthiness; minute and superfluous detail; tediousness.

I might expatiate in a large description of the several holy places which this Church (as a Cabinet) contains in it. But this would be a superfluous *prolixity*, so many Pilgrims having discharg'd this office with so much exactness already. *Maundrell*, Aleppo to Jerusalem, p. 68.

The minuteness of Zurita's investigations has laid him open to the charge of *prolixity*.
Prescott, Ferd. and Isa., ii. 1, note.

prolixly (prō'liks-li or prō-liks'li), *adv.* [< *prolix* + *-ly*[2].] In a prolix manner; at great length.

That we have in the former chapters hitherto extended our discourse so *prolixly*, none ought to wonder.
Evelyn, True Religion, I. 253.

prolixness (prō'liks-nes or prō-liks'nes), *n.* [< *prolix* + *-ness*.] The character of being prolix; prolixity.

The *prolixness*, constraint, and monotony of modern languages.
Adam Smith, On the Formation of Languages. (*Latham*.)

proll†, *v.* An obsolete form of *prowl*.

proller†, *n.* An obsolete form of *prowler*.

prolocutor (prō-lok'ū-tor or prō'lō-kū-tor), *n.* [Formerly *prolocutour*; < OF. *prolocuteur*, < L. *prolocutor*, *proloquutor*, a pleader, an advocate, < *proloqui*, speak out, utter, declare, < *pro*, for, before, + *loqui*, pp. *locutus*, speak: see *locution*.] **1.** One who speaks for another or for others. [Rare.]

Olivia undertook to be our *prolocutor*, and delivered the whole in a summary way. *Goldsmith*, Vicar, xi.

The silence of records cannot be held to prove that an organised assembly like that of the commons could ever have dispensed with a recognised *prolocutor* or foreman.
Stubbs, Const. Hist., § 435.

2. The speaker or chairman of the lower house of the Convocation. (See *convocation*, 3.) He is elected by the lower house, subject to the approval of the metropolitan.

As for the convocation, the queen thought fit to prorogue it, though at the expence of Dr. Atterbury's displeasure, who was designed their *prolocutor*.
Swift, Letter, Jan. 12, 1708-9.

prolocutorship (prō-lok'ū-tor-ship or prō'lō-kū-tor-ship), *n.* [< *prolocutor* + *-ship*.] The office or station of a prolocutor.

prolocutrix (prọ̄-lok'ū̧-triks or prō'lọ̄-kū-triks), *n.* [< L. *prolocutrix, fem. of prolocutor, an advocate: see *prolocutor*.] A woman who speaks for others.

Lady Countesse, hath the Lords made you a charter, and sent you (for that you are an eloquent speaker) to be their aduccate and *prolocutrix?* *Daniel*, Hist. Eng., p. 141. (*Davies.*)

prologize, *v. i.* See *prologuize*.

prologue, prolog (prō'log), *n.* [< ME. *prologue, prologe*, < OF. *prologue*, F. *prologue* = Pr. *prologue, prologre* = Sp. *prólogo* = Pg. It. *prologo*, < L. *prologus*, < Gr. πρόλογος, a preface or introduction, < πρό, before, + λόγος, a saying or speaking: see *Logos*.] 1. The preface or introduction to a discourse or performance; specifically, a discourse or poem spoken before a dramatic performance or play begins; hence, that whi precedes or leads up to any act or event. ch

Jerom in hise twei *prologis* on Matheu seith this. *Wyclif*, Prolog (on Matthew).

Think'st thou that mirth and vain delights,
High feed, and shadow-short'ning nights, . . .
Are proper *prologues* to a crown? *Quarles*, Emblems, ii. 11.

How this vile World is chang'd! In former Days *Prologues* were serious Speeches before Plays. *Congreve*, Old Batchelor, Prol.

I'll read you the whole, from beginning to end, with the *prologue* and epilogue, and allow time for the music between the acts. *Sheridan*, The Critic, i. 1.

2. The speaker of a prologue on the stage.

It is not the fashion to see the lady the epilogue; but it is no more unhandsome than to see the lord the *prologue*. *Shak.*, As you Like it, Epil.

The duke is entering; set your faces right,
And bow like country *prologues*. *Fletcher (and another)*, Noble Gentleman, iii. 2.

=**Syn.** 1. *Preface, Preamble*, etc. See *introduction*.

prologue (prō'log), *v. t.*; pret. and pp. *prologued*, ppr. *prologuing*. [< *prologue*, *n.*] To introduce with a formal prologue or preface; preface.

Thus he his special nothing ever *prologues*. *Shak.*, All's Well, ii. 1. 95.

prologuize, prologize (prō'log-īz), *v. i.*; pret. and pp. *prologuized, prologized*, ppr. *prologuizing, prologizing*. [< *prologue* + *-ize*.] To deliver a prologue.

There may *prologize* the spirit of Philip, Herod's brother. *Milton*, Plan of a Tragedy called Baptistes.

Artemis *Prologuizes*. *Browning*, Dramatic Romances and Lyrics (subtitle).

prologuizer (prō'log-ī-zėr), *n.* [< *prologuize* + *-er*[1].] One who makes or delivers a prologue. [Rare.]

Till, decent sables on his back
(Your *prologuizers* all wear black),
The prologue comes; and, if it's mine,
It's very good, and very fine. *Lloyd*, To George Colman.

prolong (prọ̄-lông'), *v.* [< ME. *prolongen* (also *purlongen*), < OF. (and F.) *prolonger* = Pr. *prolonguar* = Sp. Pg. *prolongar* = It. *prolongare, prolungare*, < LL. *prolongare*, lengthen, extend, < L. *pro*, forth, + *longus*, long: see *long*[1]. Cf. *purloin*, ult. from the same L. verb.] **I.** *trans.* 1. To lengthen in time; extend the duration of; lengthen out.

I fly not death, nor would *prolong*
Life much. *Milton*, P. L., xi. 547.

And frequent cups *prolong* the rich repast. *Pope*, R. of the L., iii. 112.

2. To put off to a future time; postpone.

This wedding-day
Perhaps is but *prolong'd*; have patience and endure. *Shak.*, Much Ado, iv. 1. 256.

3. To extend in space or length: as, to *prolong* a straight line.

On each side, the countless arches *prolong* themselves. *Ruskin.*

=**Syn.** 1 and 3. To protract, extend, continue, draw out.

II. *intrans.* To lengthen out; extend. [Rare.]

This page, which from my reveries I feed,
Until it seems *prolonging* without end. *Byron*, Childe Harold, iii. 109.

prolongable (prọ̄-lông'ạ-bl), *a.* [< *prolong* + *-able*.] Capable of being prolonged, extended, or lengthened.

Had the rod been really indefinitely *prolongable*. *Philosophical Mag.*, XXVII. 14.

prolongate† (prọ̄-lông'gāt), *v. t.* [< LL. *prolongatus*, pp. of *prolongare*, lengthen, extend: see *prolong*.] To prolong; lengthen.

His *prolongated* nose
Should guard his grinning mouth from blows. *W. Combe*, Dr. Syntax, iii. 2. (*Davies.*)

prolongation (prọ̄-lông-gā'shọn), *n.* [< F. *prolongation* = Pr. *prolongacio* = Sp. *prolongacion* = Pg. *prolongação* = It. *prolongazione, prolungazione*, ML. **prolongatio(n-)*, < LL. *prolongare*, pp. *prolongatus*, lengthen, extend: see *prolong*.] 1. The act of prolonging, or lengthening in time or space: as, the *prolongation* of a line.

Nourishment in living creatures is for the *prolongation* of life. *Bacon*, Nat. Hist.

If we begin to die when we live, and long life be but a *prolongation* of death, our life is a sad composition. *Sir T. Browne*, Urn-burial, v.

2. A part prolonged; an extension: as, the *prolongation* of a mountain-range.

Two remarkable processes or *prolongations* of the bones of the leg. *Paley*, Nat. Theol., viii.

Sofas resembling a *prolongation* of uneasy chairs. *George Eliot*, Middlemarch, xvii.

3. Extension of time by delay or postponement.

This ambassage concerned only the *prolongation* of days for payment of monies. *Bacon*, Hist. Hen. VII.

prolonge (prọ̄-lonj'), *n.* [< F. *prolonge*, a binding-rope, < *prolonger*, prolong: see *prolong*.] *Milit.*, a hempen rope composed of three pieces joined by two open rings, and having a hook at one end and a toggle at the other. It is usually about nine yards long. It is used to draw a gun-carriage without the limber in a retreat or advance through a narrow street or defile, or for temporarily attaching the gun to the limber when it is not desired to limber up. It is also employed in getting guns across ditches, for righting overturned gun-carriages, and for any other purpose in which such a rope can be made useful. The prolonge can be shortened by looping it back, and engaging either the terminal hook or toggle in one of the intermediate rings. When not in use, it is wound about and carried on the prolonge-hooks on the trail of the gun. See cut under *gun-carriage*.—**Prolonge-knot** (*naut.*), a useful as well as ornamental knot, sometimes called a *capstan-knot*, formerly known by gunners as a *delay-knot*.

Prolonge- or Capstan-knot.

prolonger (prọ̄-lông'ėr), *n.* One who or that which prolongs, or lengthens in time or space.

O! . . . Temperance! Thou *Prolonger* of Life! *W. Hay*, Fugitive Pieces, I. 106.

prolongment (prọ̄-lông'mẹnt), *n.* [< *prolong* + *-ment*.] The act of prolonging, or the state of being prolonged; prolongation.

Tho he himself may have been so weak as earnestly to decline Death, and endeavour the utmost *Prolongment* of his own un-eligible State. *Shaftesbury*, Characteristics, II. 141.

prolusion (prọ̄-lū'zhọn), *n.* [= Sp. *prolusion* = It. *prolusione*, < L. *prolusio(n-)*, a prelude, < *proludere*, pp. *prolusus*, play or practise beforehand, < *pro*, before, + *ludere*, play: see *ludicrous*.] 1. A prelude to a game, performance, or entertainment; hence, a prelude, introduction, or preliminary in general.

The . . . noble soul must be vigilant, go continually armed, and be ready to encounter every thought and imagination of reluctant sense, and the first *prolusions* of the enemy. *Evelyn*, True Religion, I. 227.

But why such long *prolusion* and display,
Such turning and adjustment of the harp? *Browning*, Transcendentalism.

2. An essay or preparatory exercise in which the writer tries his own strength, or throws out some preliminary remarks on a subject which he intends to treat more profoundly.

Ambition which might have devastated mankind with *Prolusions* on the Pentateuch. *Lowell*, Fireside Travels, p. 62.

As literary supports . . . came two remarkable *prolusions* of Visconti before the Paris Academy. *Edinburgh Rev.*, CLXIV. 508.

promachos (prom'ạ-kos), *n.* [< Gr. πρόμαχος, fighting in front or as a champion; as a noun, a defender, a champion, a defending deity; < πρό, before, + μάχεσθαι, fight.] In *Gr. myth.* and *archæol.*, a deity who fights before some person, army, or state, as a protector or guardian: said especially of Athene and Apollo. In art and archæology the type is distinguished by the attitude of combat, often with upraised shield and the spear or other weapon extended threateningly.

Promachos.—Athene the Defender. (Marble from Herculaneum, in the Museo Nazionale, Naples.)

Promachus (prom'ạ-kus), *n.* [NL. (Loew, 1848), < Gr. πρόμαχος, fighting in front: see *promachos*.] A genus of robber-flies or *Asilidæ*, having the abdomen longer than the wings, the body thinly pilose, and the wings with three submarginal cells. *P. fitchi* is an enemy of the honey-bee in the United States.

Promachus fitchi.

promammal (prō-mam'ạl), *n.* One of the *Promammalia*.

Promammalia (prō-ma-mā'li-ạ̈), *n. pl.* [NL., < L. *pro*, before, + NL. *Mammalia*, q. v.] The unknown hypothetical ancestors of mammals; a supposed primitive type of *Mammalia*, of which the existing monotremes are the nearest relatives or descendants. Compare *Prototheria*.

The unknown extinct Primary Mammals, or *Promammalia*, . . . probably possessed a very highly developed jaw. *Haeckel*, Hist. Creat. (trans.), II. 235.

promammalian (prō-ma-mā'liạn), *a.* and *n.* **I.** *a.* Pertaining to the *Promammalia*.

II. *n.* A promammal.

promanation (prom-ạ-nā'shọn), *n.* [< L. *pro*, before, + *manatio(n-)*, a flowing, < *manare*, pp. *manatus*, flow, drip.] The act of flowing forth; emanation.

Promanation . . . of the rays of light. *Dr. H. More*, Def. of Philosophical Cabbala, viii., App.

promenade (prom-e-näd'), *n.* [< F. *promenade*, a walking, walk, airing, drive, a public walk, < *promener*, take out (animals), conduct, take (one) out for a walk, ride, or drive, < LL. *prominare*, drive forward, < *pro*, forward, + *minare*, drive (animals): see *mine*[2], *mien*.] 1. A walk for pleasure or display, or for exercise.—2. A place for walking.

No unpleasant walk or *promenade* for the unconfined portion of some solitary prisoner. *W. Montague*, Devoute Essays, I. xix. 6.

Moored opposite Whitehall was a very large barge with a saloon, and *promenade* on the top, called the Folly. *J. Ashton*, Social Life in Reign of Queen Anne, II. 149.

Promenade concert, a musical entertainment in which the audience promenades or dances during the music, instead of remaining seated.

promenade (prom-e-näd'), *v. i.*; pret. and pp. *promenaded*, ppr. *promenading*. [< *promenade*, *n.*] To walk about or up and down for amusement, display, or exercise; also, recently, to take exercise in carriage, saddle, or boat.

The poplars, in long order due,
With cypress *promenaded*. *Tennyson*, Amphion.

The grandes dames, in their splendid toilets, *promenaded* in their gilded phaetons on the magnificent Avenue of the Champs Elysées. *E. B. Washburne*, Recollections of a Minister, I. 3.

promenader (prom-e-nä'dėr), *n.* [< *promenade* + *-er*[1].] One who promenades.

The Riva degli Schiavoni catches the warm afternoon sun in its whole extent, and is then thronged with *promenaders* of every class, condition, age, and sex. *Howells*, Venetian Life, iii.

Promephitis (prō-mẹ̄-fī'tis), *n.* [NL. (Gaudry, 1861), < L. *pro*, before, + *Mephitis*, q. v.] A genus of musteline carnivorous quadrupeds from the Upper Miocene.

promerit† (prọ̄-mer'it), *v. t.* [< L. *promeritus*, pp. of *promerere*, be deserving of, < *pro*, for, + *merere*, deserve, be worthy of: see *merit*.] 1. To deserve; procure by merit.

From him [Christ] then, and from him alone, must we expect Salvation, acknowledging and confessing freely there is nothing in ourselves which can effect or deserve it from us, nothing in any other creature which can *promerit* or procure it to us. *Bp. Pearson*, Expos. of Creed, ii.

2. To befriend; confer a favor on.

He loves not God: no, not whiles He *promerits* him with His favours. *Bp. Hall*, Sermon on Jas. iv. 8.

promeritor† (prọ̄-mer'i-tọr), *n.* [< *promerit* + *-or*[1].] One who deserves or merits, whether good or evil.

Whatsoever mischiefs befall them or their posterity, though many ages after the decease of the *promeritors*, were inflicted upon them in revenge. *Christian Religion's Appeal.* (*Latham.*)

promerope (prom'ẹ-rōp), *n.* A bird of the genus *Promerops*, in any sense.

Promeropidæ (prom-ẹ-rop'i-dē), *n. pl.* [NL., < *Promerops* + *-idæ*.] A family of tenuirostral insessorial birds, named by Vigors in 1825 from the genus *Promerops*: synonymous with *Nectariniidæ*, and still sometimes used in that sense, as by G. R. Gray, 1869.

Promeropinæ (prom″e-rọ̄-pī′nē), *n. pl.* [NL., ‹ *Promerops* + *-inæ*.] A subfamily of birds, named from the genus *Promerops* by G. R. Gray in 1847. It has included heterogeneous elements, and is little used. In 1869 Gray made it the second subfamily of *Nectariniidæ*, containing *Promerops*, *Æthopyga*, etc., thus embracing birds now referred to two different families, *Meliphagidæ* and *Nectariniidæ*. It was called *Ptiloturinæ* by Cabanis, 1850.

Promerops (prom′e-rops), *n.* [NL. (Brisson, 1760), ‹ Gr. πρό, before, + μέροψ, a bird, the bee-eater: see *Merops*.] **1.** In *ornith.*, a generic name variously used. (*a*) Applied to many different tenuirostral or slender-billed birds of the passerine families *Paradiseidæ*, *Meliphagidæ*, and *Nectariniidæ*, and of the picarian family *Upupidæ*, as of the genera *Epimachus*, *Cinnyris*, *Irrisor*, and others not specially related. (*b*) Properly restricted to an African genus of oscine passerine birds of the family *Meliphagidæ* and subfamily *Meliphaginæ*, having a slender curved bill about twice as long as the head and not bristled, unfeathered operculated nostrils, scutellate tarsi, and extremely long tail. The type is the Cape promerops, *P. cafer*, of South Africa; there is a second species, *P. gurneyi*. Also called *Falcinellus*, and *Ptiloturus* or *Pilurus*.

Cape Promerops (*Promerops cafer*).

2. [*l. c.*] A species of the genus *Promerops*, in any sense; a promerope.

promesset, *v.* A Middle English form of *promise*.

promethea (prọ̄-mē′thē-ạ̈), *n.* [NL.: see *Prometheus*.] In *entom.*, same as *prometheus*.

Promethean (prọ̄-mē′thē-an), *a.* and *n.* [‹ L. *Prometheus*, of or pertaining to Prometheus, ‹ *Prometheus*, ‹ Gr. Προμηθεύς, Prometheus, lit., according to the usual explanation, 'Forethinker' (brother to Ἐπιμηθεύς, Epimetheus, 'Afterthinker'), cf. προμηθής, forethinking, provident, ‹ πρό, before, + μαθεῖν, pres. μανθάνειν, learn, find out (or, as commonly supposed, μῆδος, counsel, providence, μήδεσθαι, intend, devise, μῆτις, counsel, all ult. ‹ √ μα, think). In another view this is merely popular etymology, the name being compared with Skt. *pramantha*, a stick which by friction produces fire.] **I.** *a.* **1.** Of, pertaining to, or resembling Prometheus in Greek mythology, who showed men various arts, including the use of fire, and by the will of Zeus was chained to a rock and tortured by a vulture.

> These vultures in my breast
> Gripe my *Promethean* heart both night and day.
> *Quarles*, Emblems, iv. 14.

> I know not where is that *Promethean* heat
> That can thy light relume. *Shak.*, Othello, v. 2. 12.

> *Promethean* fire
> Is quite extinct in them; yea, vse of sence
> Hath within them noe place of residence.
> *Times' Whistle* (E. E. T. S.), p. 67.

2. [*l. c.*] In *entom.*, of or pertaining to the prometheus; being or known as the prometheus: as, a *promethean* silkworm.

II. *n.* [*l. c.*] A small glass tube containing sulphuric acid, and surrounded by an inflammable mixture which it ignited on being pressed: formerly used for affording a ready light.

prometheus (prọ̄-mē′thūs), *n.* [NL., ‹ L. *Prometheus*, ‹ Gr. Προμηθεύς, Prometheus: see *Promethean*.] **1.** In *entom.*: (*a*) The popular name and also the technical specific name of a large silk-spinning moth, *Attacus prometheus*, or *Telea* or *Callosamia promethea*. The male moth is of a dark rich smoky or amber brown, the female of a lighter rusty or reddish brown. In both sexes the wings are crossed by a wavy whitish line near the middle, and have a wide clay-colored border. Near the tips of the fore wings there is an eye-like spot within a bluish-white crescent, and in the female there is an angular reddish-white spot, edged with black, near the middle of each wing. The eggs are laid in little clusters of five or six upon twigs in the spring. The larva or worm is delicate bluish-white with a faint pruinescence, with four black tubercles on the thorax. It feeds on ash, sassafras, wild cherry, lilac, maple, plum, poplar, birch, and other trees. The cocoon is oblong, dense, gray, and remarkable for the long tough band of silk which suspends it and which is securely wrapped around the supporting twig. Also *promethea*, *promethia*.

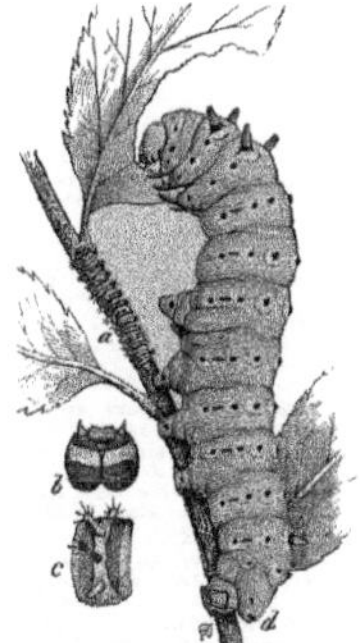

Promethean Silkworm (*Attacus prometheus*).
a, larva of third stage, natural size; *b*, head of larva of fourth stage, enlarged; *c*, side view of segment of larva of fourth stage, enlarged; *d*, full-grown larva, natural size.

(*b*) [*cap.*] A genus of moths. *Hübner*, 1826.— **2.** In *ornith.*, the Blackburnian warbler, *Dendrœca blackburniæ*: so named by Coues from the flame color of the breast.

prominence (prom′i-nens), *n.* [‹ OF. *prominence* = Sp. Pg. *prominencia* = It. *prominenza*, ‹ L. *prominentia*, a projection, ‹ *prominen(t-)s*, ppr. of *prominere*, jut out: see *prominent*.] **1.** The property of being prominent; a standing or jutting out from the surface of something; also, that which juts out; protuberance: as, the *prominence* of a joint; the *prominence* of a rock or cliff; the *prominences* of the face.

> It shows the nose and eye-brows, with the several *prominences* and fallings in of the features.
> *Addison*, Ancient Medals, iii.

2. The state of being conspicuous; conspicuousness; distinction; notoriety.—**Canine, mental, etc., prominence.** See the adjectives.—**Prominence of Doyère.** Same as *eminence of Doyère* (which see, under *eminence*).—**Solar prominence**, one of the great clouds of incandescent hydrogen seen during a total eclipse on the edge of the sun's disk, and at other times observable with the spectroscope.=**Syn. 1.** Projection, bulge, process, eminence.

prominency (prom′i-nen-si), *n.* [As *prominence* (see *-cy*).] Same as *prominence*.

prominent (prom′i-nent), *a.* and *n.* [‹ OF. *prominent* = Sp. Pg. It. *prominente*, ‹ L. *prominen(t-)s*, ppr. of *prominere*, project, jut out, ‹ *pro*, forth, + **minere*, project, jut. Cf. *eminent*, *imminent*.] **I.** *a.* **1.** Standing out beyond the line or surface of something; jutting; protuberant; in high relief: as, a *prominent* figure on a vase.

> It compresses hard
> The *prominent* and most unsightly bones,
> And binds the shoulders flat.
> *Cowper*, Task, ii. 588.

2. In *entom.*: (*a*) Raised above the general surface: as, *prominent* eyes. (*b*) Projecting horizontally: as, *prominent* angles of the prothorax. The head of an insect is said to be *prominent* when its upper surface is horizontal and continuous with that of the thorax.

3. Standing out so as to be easily seen; most visible or striking to the eye; conspicuous: as, the figure of a man is *prominent* in the picture.

> The side of things which is most *prominent* when they are looked at from European soil may not always be the most *prominent* when they are looked at from American soil. *E. A. Freeman*, Amer. Lects., p. 8.

4. Standing out from among the multitude; distinguished above others: as, a *prominent* citizen.=**Syn. 1.** Projecting, bulging.—**4.** Eminent, leading.

II. *n.* **1†.** A promontory.

> (The winds asleepe) he freely poutes, till highest *Prominents*,
> Hill tops, low meddowes, and the fields, that crowne with most contents
> The toiles of men, sea-ports, and shores, are hid.
> *Chapman*, Iliad, xii.

2. One of certain bombycid moths; a tooth-back or pebble. The American red-humped prominent is *Notodonta concinna*; the European coxcomb prominent is *N. camelina*. See cut under *Notodonta*.

prominently (prom′i-nent-li), *adv.* In a prominent manner; so as to stand out beyond the other parts; eminently; in a striking manner; conspicuously.

promiscuity (prō-mis-kū′i-ti), *n.* [= F. *promiscuité* = Pg. *promiscuidade* = It. *promiscuità*, ‹ L. *promiscuus*, mixed, not separated: see *promiscuous*.] **1.** Promiscuousness; confusion; indiscriminate mixture.

> The God-abstractions of the modern polytheism are nearly in as sad a state of perplexity and *promiscuity* as were the more substantial deities of the Greeks.
> *Poe*, Marginalia, lxxv. (*Davies*.)

> Lady Charlotte . . . was fond of flooding the domestic hearth with all the people possessed of any sort of a name. . . . Mr. Wynnstay loathed such *promiscuity*.
> *Mrs. Humphry Ward*, Robert Elsmere, xvii.

2. Promiscuous sexual union, as among some races of people.

> *Promiscuity* may be called indefinite polyandry joined with indefinite polygyny: and one mode of advance is by a diminution of the indefiniteness.
> *H. Spencer*, Prin. of Sociol., § 297.

promiscuous (prọ̄-mis′kū-us), *a.* [= OF. *promiscue* = Sp. Pg. It. *promiscuo*, ‹ L. *promiscuus*, mixed, not separated, ‹ *pro*, forth, + *miscere*, mix: see *mix*[1].] **1.** Consisting of parts or individuals grouped together without order; mingled indiscriminately; confused.

> Distinction in *promiscuous* Noise is drown'd.
> *Congreve*, On the Taking of Namure.

> In rushed at once a rude *promiscuous* crowd.
> *Dryden*, Pal. and Arc., iii. 551.

> He went on contentedly enough, picking up a *promiscuous* education chiefly from things that were not intended for education at all. *George Eliot*, Mill on the Floss, i. 4.

2. Forming part of a mingled or confused crowd or mass.

> This, like the public inn, provides a treat
> Where each *promiscuous* guest sits down to eat.
> *Crabbe*, The Newspaper.

3. Distributed or applied without order or discrimination; common; indiscriminate; not restricted to one individual: as, *promiscuous* sexual intercourse.

> Heaps on heaps expire;
> Nations with nations mixed confusedly die,
> And lost in one *promiscuous* carnage lie.
> *Addison*, The Campaign.

4. Casual; accidental. [Prov. Eng.]

> I walked in, gentlemen, just to say good mornin', and went, in a *permiscuous* manner, up stairs, and into the back room. *Dickens*, Pickwick Papers, xxxiv.

=**Syn. 1.** *Promiscuous*, *Miscellaneous*. *Promiscuous* emphasizes the complete lack of arrangement; *miscellaneous* the throwing together of different kinds. Hence we speak of *promiscuous*, but not of *miscellaneous*, confusion; of *miscellaneous*, not *promiscuous*, articles in a magazine. A work-bag contains a *miscellaneous* collection of things, which should never be allowed to become *promiscuous*.

> It is an argument of a loose and ungoverned mind to be affected with the *promiscuous* approbation of the generality of mankind. *Steele*, Spectator, No. 188.

> What the people but a herd confused,
> A *miscellaneous* rabble? *Milton*, P. R., iii. 50.

promiscuously (prọ̄-mis′kū-us-li), *adv.* In a promiscuous manner; in a crowd or mass without order; with confused mixture; indiscriminately; without distinction of kinds or individuals.

> Like beasts and birds *promiscuously* they join. *Pope*.

promiscuousness (prọ̄-mis′kū-us-nes), *n.* The state or character of being promiscuous, or of being mixed without selection, order, or distinction.

promise (prom′is), *n.* [Early mod. E. also *promys*, *promes*; ‹ ME. *promys*, *promesse*, ‹ OF. *promesse*, F. *promesse* = Sp. *promesa* = Pg. It. *promessa*, ‹ ML. *promissa*, f., L. *promissum*, neut., a promise, fem. and neut. of L. *promissus*, pp. of *promittere*, send or put forth, let go forward, say beforehand, promise: see *promit*.] **1.** A declaration in reference to the future, whether written or verbal, made by one person to another, purporting to assure the latter that the former will do or forbear from a specified act, or cause it to be done or refrained from; a declaration intended to give to the person to whom it is made assurance of his right to expect from the promisor the thing promised; especially, a declaration that something shall be done or given for the benefit of the promisee or another. In law, a promise is not binding in such sense as to be directly enforceable through the courts, unless made upon a consideration good or valuable; in which case the promise and the consideration together form a contract or agreement (if under seal, termed a *covenant*) which binds the promisor, and it may be his legal representatives, and gives the promisee, and in some cases a third person for whose benefit the promise was made, the right to enforce it by suit, or to recover damages for its breach.

Also, no Straungere comethe before him but that he makethe him sum *Promys* and Graunt, of that the Straungere askethe resonabely. *Mandeville*, Travels, p. 40.

O Rome, I make thee *promise;*
If the redress will follow, thou receivest
Thy full petition at the hand of Brutus!
Shak., J. C., ii. 1. 56.

Statesman, yet friend to Truth! of soul sincere, . . .
Who broke no *promise*, served no private end.
Pope, To Addison, l. 69.

2. Ground or basis of expectation; earnest; pledge.

There buds the *promise* of celestial worth!
Young, The Last Day, iii.

Thy [Friendship's] blossoms deck our unsuspecting years;
The *promise* of delicious fruit appears.
Cowper, Valediction.

3. That which affords a ground or basis for hope or for expectation of future excellence or distinction: as, a youth of great *promise*.

You have an unspeakable comfort of your young prince Mamillius; it is a gentleman of the greatest *promise* that ever came into my note. *Shak.*, W. T., i. 1. 39.

O, I see the crescent *promise* of my spirit hath not set.
Tennyson, Locksley Hall.

4. That which is promised; fulfilment or grant of what is promised.

And . . . commanded them that they should not depart from Jerusalem, but wait for the *promise* of the Father.
Acts i. 4.

Glou. Look, when I am king, claim thou of me
The earldom of Hereford. . . .
Buck. I'll claim that *promise* at your grace's hands.
Shak., Rich. III., iii. 1. 197.

Absolute promise, a promise which pledges fulfilment at all events; a promise unqualified by a condition.—**Breach of promise.** See *breach*.—**Conditional promise**, a promise the obligation to fulfil which depends on the performance of a condition, or on a contingent or yet unknown event.—**Express promise**, a promise expressed orally or in writing.—**Implied promise**, a promise which the law implies from conduct, as when one employs a man to perform a day's labor, without any express promise to pay him. The law then presumes a promise on the employer's part to give the man a reasonable reward, and it will enforce such implied promise.—**Land of Promise**, Canaan: so called because promised by God to Abraham in Haran; figuratively, heaven. Also called *The Promised Land.*

By faith he [Abraham] sojourned in the *land of promise*, . . . dwelling in tabernacles with Isaac and Jacob.
Heb. xi. 9.

Mesmeric promise, mutual promises, new promise. See the adjectives.—**Parole promise.** (*a*) A promise made orally. (*b*) A promise made without seal, either orally or in writing, as distinguished from one made under seal, which is technically called a *covenant*.—**Promise and offer.** In *Scots law*, an *offer* is a proposal made to give or to do something, either gratuitously or on an onerous consideration; a *promise* is an offer of such a nature that the promisor takes the other party's assent for granted. An *offer* is not binding till it is accepted; a *promise* is binding as soon as it is known by the party it is made to.—**Special promise**, an actual promise as distinguished from an implied promise.—**The Promise**, according to the account given in the Bible, the assurance given by God to Abraham that his descendants should become the chosen people, and that in him all the families of the earth should be blessed.

"So help me *the promise*, fair sirs," said Isaac, . . .
"as no such sounds ever crossed my lips!"
Scott, Ivanhoe, xxxii.

To give a lick and a promise of better. See *lick*. =**Syn. 1.** *Assurance, Promise, Engagement, Pledge, Covenant.* These words are arranged in the order of strength; it would be dishonorable to fail to keep what even the weakest of them expresses. The formality and solemnity of each are proportioned to its strength. A *covenant* is a mutual obligation; the others are not. Each of them may be either spoken or written, but the written is generally more formal, and may have greater legal obligation.

promise (prom'is), *v.*; pret. and pp. *promised*, ppr. *promising*. [< ME. *promysen, promyssen;* < *promise, n.*] **I.** *trans.* **1.** To make a promise of; engage to do, give, grant, or procure for some one; especially, to engage that some benefit shall be conferred.

Thei hym *promyseden* that thei sholde kepe well the Citee while there life myght endure.
Merlin (E. E. T. S.), ii. 296.

I was *promised* them [ribbons] against the feast.
Shak., W. T., iv. 4. 237.

You said that your Sponsors did *promise* for you that you should keep God's commandments.
Book of Common Prayer, Catechism.

2. To afford reason to expect: as, the year *promises* a good harvest; the clouds *promise* rain.

Surely this seemeth a plott of great reason and small difficultye, which *promiseth* hope of a shorte end.
Spenser, State of Ireland.

Seeing the old castle of the state,
That *promis'd* once more firmness, so assail'd.
Cowper, Task, v. 526.

3. To assure. [Colloq.]

And what that euer be withynne this place,
That wolle for the entrete in eny wise,
He shall not spede, I yow *promysse.*
Generydes (E. E. T. S.), l. 1603.

I do not like thy look, I *promise* thee.
Shak., Much Ado, iv. 2. 47.

I *promise* you I don't think near so ill of you as I did.
Sheridan, School for Scandal, iv. 3.

4. To make as promisor; be the promisor in. [Rare trade use.]

These notes were *promised* by S. and S.
Boston Traveller, Jan. 24, 1880.

The Promised Land. Same as *Land of Promise* (which see, under *promise, n.*).—**To be promised**†, to have an engagement.

Cassius. Will you sup with me to-night, Casca?
Casca. No, *I am promised* forth. *Shak.*, J. C., i. 2. 293.

=**Syn. 1.** To assure, engage, covenant. See the noun.

II. *intrans.* **1.** To assure one by a promise or binding declaration.

Tho' fickle fortune has deceiv'd me,
She *promis'd* fair, and perform'd but ill.
Burns, I Dream'd I Lay.

2. To afford hopes or expectations; give ground for expecting satisfactory or agreeable results.

A . . . son of the last Archbishop, who *promises* very greatly. *Walpole*, Letters, II. 96.

The day was named, the weather *promised* well.
Miss Edgeworth, Helen, xvii.

3. To stand sponsor. [Rare.]

There were those who knew him near the king
And *promised* for him; and Arthur made him knight.
Tennyson, Pelleas and Ettarre.

promise-breach (prom'is-brēch), *n.* Failure to perform what is promised. [Rare.]

Since miserie hath daunted all my mirth,
And I am quite vndone through *promise-breach.*
Nashe, Pierce Penilesse, p. 6.

In double violation
Of sacred chastity and of *promise-breach*
Thereon dependent. *Shak.*, M. for M., v. 1. 410.

promise-breaker (prom'is-brā"kėr), *n.* One who breaks or fails to make good his promises.

He's a most notable coward, an infinite and endless liar, an hourly *promise-breaker*. *Shak.*, All's Well, iii. 6. 12.

promise-crammed (prom'is-kramd), *a.* Crammed or stuffed with promises. [Rare.]

I eat the air, *promise-crammed.* *Shak.*, Hamlet, iii. 2. 99.

promisee (prom-i-sē'), *n.* [< *promise* + *-ee*[1].] The person to whom a promise is made.

Where things promised in a treaty are incompatible, the *promisee* may choose which he will demand the performance of. *Woolsey*, Introd. to Inter. Law, § 109.

promiseful (prom'is-fůl), *a.* [< *promise* + *-ful.*] Full of promise; promising.

So som he wins with *promise-full* intreats,
With presents som, and som with rougher threats.
Sylvester, tr. of Du Bartas's Weeks, ii., Babylon.

promiser (prom'i-sėr), *n.* [< *promise* + *-er*[1].] One who promises; one who engages, assures, stipulates, or covenants: in legal use *promisor.*

He was a subtyle deceiuer, a fayer false *promiser*.
Joye, Expos. of Daniel xi.

Though the expectation which is raised by impertinent *promisers* is thus barren, their confidence, even after failures, is so great that they subsist by still promising on.
Steele, Spectator, No. 448.

promising (prom'i-sing), *p. a.* [Ppr. of *promise, v.*] Giving promise; affording just expectations of good; affording reasonable ground of hope for the future; looking as if likely to turn out well: as, a *promising* youth; a *promising* prospect.

A course more *promising*
Than a wild dedication of yourselves
To unpath'd waters, undream'd shores.
Shak., W. T., iv. 4. 576.

promisingly (prom'i-sing-li), *adv.* [< *promising* + *-ly*[2].] In a promising manner.

promisor (prom'i-sọr), *n.* [< *promise* + *-or*[1]. Cf. L. *promissor*, a promiser.] In *law*, one who promises.

promiss†, *a.* [< L. *promissus*, hanging down, long, pp. of *promittere*, send or put forth, let go forward, let hang down, etc., see *promise, promit.*] Hanging down; long.

I know him by his *promisse* beard,
And beetle browes.
Heywood, Dialogues (Works, ed. Pearson, 1874, VI. 190).

promission† (prọ̄-mish'ọn), *n.* [< ME. *promissioun*, < L. *promissio(n-)*, promise, < *promittere*, pp. *promissus*, promise: see *promise.*] Promise.

The Holy Land, that Men callen the Lond of *Promyssioun*, or of Beheste. *Mandeville*, Travels, p. 1.

Isaac, that was the child of *Promission*, although God kept his life that was vnlooked for.
Sir T. More, Cumfort against Tribulation (1573), fol. 37.

promissive (prọ̄-mis'iv), *a.* [< L. *promissivus*, promising, < *promittere*, pp. *promissus*, promise: see *promise.*] Making or implying a promise. [Rare.]

promissorily (prom'i-sọ̄-ri-li), *adv.* By way of promise. *Sir T. Browne.*

promissory (prom'i-sọ̄-ri), *a.* [< L. *promissor*, a promiser, < *promittere*, pp. *promissus*, promise: see *promise.*] Containing a promise, or binding declaration of something to be done or forborne.

As the preceptive part enjoins the most exact virtue, so is it most advantageously enforced by the *promissory*.
Decay of Christian Piety.

Promissory note, in *law*, an absolute promise in writing, signed but not sealed, to pay a specified sum at a time therein limited, or on demand, or at sight, to a person therein named or designated, or to his order, or to the bearer. *Byles.* See *negotiable*.—**Promissory oath.** See *oath*.

promit†, *v. t.* [ME. *promytten* = OF. *promettre, prometre*, F. *promettre* = Sp. *prometer* = It. *promettere*, promise, < L. *promittere*, send or put forth, let go forward, say beforehand, promise, < *pro*, forth, + *mittere*, send: see *mission*. Cf. *admit, commit, permit*, etc.] **1.** To send forth; let go.

Commaunded hym he sholde *promytte* and suffre the seruauntes of almyghty god to passe out of pryson and to be at lyberte. *Joseph of Arimathie* (E. E. T. S.), p. 32.

2. To disclose; make known.

Promising . . . frank and free pardon of all offences and crimes *promitted*.
Hall, Chron. Hen. VII., fol. 33. (*Encyc. Dict.*)

3. To promise.

It like, therfore, to my Lord of Gloucestre, and to alle the Lordes of the Kinges Counsail, to *promitte* to the said Erle and assure him that thei shul fermely and trewely assisten him in the excercise of the charge and occupacion that he hathe aboute the Kinges persone.
Paston Letters, I. 33.

promont†, *n.* [< *promont-ory*, as if directly < L. *pro*, forth, + *mon(t-)s*, hill: see *mount*[1].] A promontory. [Rare.]

A *promont* jutting out into the dropping South.
Drayton, Polyolbion, i. 151.

promontorious (prom-ọn-tō'ri-us), *a.* [< *promontor-y* + *-ous.*] Resembling a promontory; high; projecting; conspicuous.

The ambitious man's mountain is his honour: and who dares find fault with so *promontorious* a celsitude?
Rev. T. Adams, Works, II. 497.

promontorium (prom-ọn-tō'ri-um), *n.*; pl. *promontoria* (-ạ̈). [< L. *promonturium*, a mountain-ridge, a headland: see *promontory.*] In *anat.*, a promontory.

promontory (prom'ọn-tọ̄-ri), *n.* and *a.* [= F. *promontoire* = Sp. Pg. It. *promontorio*, < ML. *promontorium*, L. *promonturium, promunturium*, a mountain-ridge, a headland, appar. < *pro*, forth, + *mon(t-)s*, mountain (see *mount*[1]), but prob. < *prominere* (pp. as if **prominitus*, **prominlus*, **promuntus*), project, jut out, < *pro*, forth, + **minere*, project, jut, akin to *mon(t-)s*, mountain: see *prominent.*] **I.** *n.*; pl. *promontories* (-riz). **1.** A high point of land or rock projecting into the sea beyond the line of coast; a headland.

Like one that stands upon a *promontory*,
And spies a far-off shore where he would tread.
Shak., 3 Hen. VI., iii. 2. 135.

The city Ragusa occupied a peninsula, sheltered on the one hand by the mainland, on the other by another *promontory* forming the outer horn of a small bay.
E. A. Freeman, Venice, p. 235.

2. In *anat.*, a prominent or protuberant part; a prominence, eminence, or protuberance. (*a*) Of the sacrum, the bold salient angle between the first sacral and last lumbar vertebra, bounding the brim of the true pelvis posteriorly, and especially pronounced in man. (*b*) Of the tympanum, a rounded hollow protuberance of the inner wall of the tympanic cavity, expressing the projection of the first whorl of the cochlea. It is situated between the fenestræ, and its surface is furrowed by branches of the tympanic plexus of nerves.

II.† *a.* Resembling a promontory; high; projecting.

He found his flockes grazing vpon the *Promontorie* Mountaines. *Greene*, Menaphon, p. 23. (*Davies.*)

Who sees not that the clambering goats get upon rocks and *promontory* places, whiles the humble sheep feed in the bottoms and dejected valleys?
Rev. T. Adams, Works, I. 428.

promorph (prō'môrf), *n.* [< Gr. πρό, before, + μορφή, form.] In *biol.*, a fundamental type of form; a form promorphologically considered as to its fundamental character, without regard to its actual modifications: as, a vertebrate, a molluscan, or an articulate *promorph.* *Nature*, XXXIX. 409.

promorphological (prọ̄-môr-fọ̄-loj'i-kạl), *a.* [< *promorpholog-y* + *-ic-al.*] Pertaining to promorphology; mathematically or stereometrically morphological.

The idea of the antimere is omitted, as being essentially a *promorphological* conception.
Encyc. Brit., XVI. 843.

promorphologically (prǫ-mòr-fǭ-loj'i-kal-i), *adv.* Upon considerations of or according to promorphology.

promorphologist (prō-mòr-fol'ǭ-jist), *n.* [< *promorphology* + *-ist.*] One who is versed in or understands promorphology. *Encyc. Brit.*, XVI. 845.

promorphology (prō-mòr-fol'ǭ-ji), *n.* [As *promorph* + *-ology* (cf. *morphology*).] In *biol.*, stereometric morphology; the morphology of organic forms considered with reference to mathematical figures or to a few fundamental types of structure; the mathematical conception or geometrical treatment of organic form.

> *Promorphology* develops the crystallography of organic form. *Encyc. Brit.*, XVI. 843, note.

promote (prǭ-mōt'), *v.*; pret. and pp. *promoted*, ppr. *promoting*. [< OF. *promoter*, < L. *promotus*, pp. of *promovere*, move forward, push onward, advance, bring to pass, reveal: see *promove.*] **I.** *trans.* **1.** To contribute to the establishment, growth, enlargement, or improvement of, as of anything valuable, or to the development, increase, or influence of, as of anything evil; forward; advance.

> Mr. John Jenny . . . was always a leading man in *promoting* the general interest of the colony. *N. Morton*, New England's Memorial, p. 102.

> Those friendships which once *promoted* literary fame seem now to be discontinued. *Goldsmith*, The Bee, No. 5.

2. To exalt, or raise to a higher post or position; prefer in rank or honor: as, to *promote* a captain to a majority.

> I will *promote* thee unto very great honour. Num. xxii. 17.

> Did I solicit thee
> From darkness to *promote* me, or here place
> In this delicious garden? *Milton*, P. L., x. 745.

3†. To inform against.

> There lack men to *promote* the king's officers when they do amiss, and to *promote* all offenders. *Latimer*, 2d Sermon bef. Edw. VI., 1550.

=**Syn. 1.** To further, help, encourage, assist.

II.† *intrans.* To give information; be an informer.

> Steps in this false spy, this *promoting* wretch;
> Closely betrays him that he gives to each. *Drayton*, The Owl.

promote†, *pp.* [ME., < L. *promotus*, pp.: see *promote, v.*] Promoted.

> For where a lover thinketh him *promote*,
> Envy will grucche, repining at his wele. *Court of Love*, l. 1261.

promotement† (prǭ-mōt'ment), *n.* [< *promote* + *-ment.*] Promotion. *Evelyn.*

promoter (prǭ-mō'tėr), *n.* [< F. *promoteur* = Sp. Pg. *promotor* = It. *promotore*, < ML. *promotor*, a promoter, < L. *promovere*, promote: see *promove, promote.*] **1.** One who or that which promotes, forwards, or advances; an encourager: as, a *promoter* of charity.

> We are no more justified in treating what we take to be untrue theories of morals as positive *promoters* of vice than in treating what we deem truer theories as positive *promoters* of virtue. *T. H. Green*, Prolegomena to Ethics, § 336.

2. One who aids in promoting some financial undertaking; one engaged in getting up a joint-stock company; one who makes it his business to assist in the organization and capitalizing of corporations.

> It is notorious that some of the [rail]roads have been robbed to the extent of thirty, forty, and even more per cent. by *promoters* and syndicates, who have placed in their own pockets such large proportions of the sums subscribed. *Fortnightly Rev.*, N. S., XLIII. 858.

3†. An informer; specifically, a person who prosecuted offenders as an informer in his own name and the king's, receiving in reward part of the fines or penalties.

> These be accusers, *promoters*, and slanderers. *Latimer*, Misc. Selections.

> Came sneaking to my house like a *promoter* to spye flesh in the Lent. *Marston and Barksted*, Insatiate Countess, iv.

promotion (prǭ-mō'shǫn), *n.* [< ME. *promocyon*, < OF. (and F.) *promotion* = Pr. *promotio* = Sp. *promocion* = Pg. *promoção* = It. *promozione*, < LL. *promotio(n-)*, advancement, < L. *promovere*, pp. *promotus*, move forward, promote: see *promove, promote.*] **1.** The act of promoting; advancement; encouragement: as, the *promotion* of virtue or morals; the *promotion* of peace or of discord.—**2.** Advancement in rank or honor; preferment.

> The highest *promotion* that God can bring his unto in this life is to suffer for his truth. *Latimer*, Misc. Selections.

> Many fair *promotions*
> Are daily given to ennoble those
> That scarce, some two days since, were worth a noble. *Shak.*, Rich. III., i. 3. 80.

3†. The act of informing; the laying of an information against any one.

> Covetousness and *promotion* and such like. *Tyndale*, Expos. of Matthew vi. (*Encyc. Dict.*)

To be on one's promotion. (*a*) To be in the line of promotion; have the prospect or right of promotion in case of vacancy. (*b*) To be on good behavior or diligent in duty with a view to recommending one's self for promotion.

> "You want to smoke those filthy cigars," replied Mrs. Rawdon. "I remember when you liked 'em, though," answered the husband. . . . "That was when I was *on my promotion*, Goosey," she said. *Thackeray*, Vanity Fair, xliv.

=**Syn.** See *progress.*

promotive (prǭ-mō'tiv), *a.* [< *promote* + *-ive.*] Tending to promote, advance, or encourage.

> In the government of Ireland, his [Strafford's] administration had been equally *promotive* of his master's interest and that of the subjects committed to his care. *Hume*, Hist. Eng., liv.

promoval† (prǭ-mö'val), *n.* [< *promove* + *-al.*] Advancement; promotion.

> Tell me if my recommendation can in anything be steadable for the *promoval* of the good of that youth. *Urquhart*, tr. of Rabelais, iii. 29. (*Davies.*)

promove† (prǭ-möv'), *v. t.* [< F. *promouvoir* = Pr. Sp. Pg. *promover* = It. *promuovere*, < L. *promovere*, move forward, push onward, advance, bring to pass, enlarge, increase, extend, reveal, < *pro*, forth, forward, + *movere*, move: see *move*. Cf. *promote.*] **1.** To promote; forward; advance.

> Th' increase
> Of trades and tillage, under laws and peace,
> Begun by him, but settled and *promoved*
> By the third hero of his name. *B. Jonson*, Prince Henry's Barriers.

> Without Christ we can do just nothing but lie becalmed and unable to move or *promove*. *Rev. S. Ward*, Sermons and Treatises, p. 171.

2. To incite; encourage.

> Those works of ours are greatest in the sight of God that . . . conduce most to the *promoving* of others to glorify God. *Donne*, Sermons, viii.

promovent† (prǭ-mö'vent), *n.* [< L. *promoven(t-)s*, ppr. of *promovere*, move forward: see *promove.*] The plaintiff in the instance court of the admiralty.

promover† (prǭ-mö'vėr), *n.* [< *promove* + *-er*[1].] A promoter.

> For bokis & heresies, as they call goddis worde, be prohibited, pressed downe, & burned with all the *promouers* thereof. *Joye*, Expos. of Daniel vii.

prompt (prompt), *a.* [< ME. **prompt*, < OF. (and F.) *prompt* = Sp. *pronto* = Pg. *prompto* = It. *pronto*, < L. *promptus*, *promtus*, visible, apparent, evident, at hand, prepared, ready, quick, prompt, inclined, disposed, pp. of *promere*, take or bring out or forth, produce, bring to light, < *pro*, forth, forward, + *emere*, take, acquire, buy: see *emption.*] **1.** Ready; quick to act as occasion demands; acting with cheerful alacrity; ready and willing: as, *prompt* in obedience or compliance.

> Very discerning and *prompt* in giving orders. *Clarendon*, Great Rebellion.

> Good temper; spirits *prompt* to undertake,
> And not soon spent, though in an arduous task. *Cowper*, Task, i. 400.

> Hundreds *prompt* for blows and blood. *Scott*, L. of the L., iii. 24.

2. Given or performed without delay; quick; ready; not delayed.

> I do agnize
> A natural and *prompt* alacrity
> I find in hardness. *Shak.*, Othello, i. 3. 233.

> But chief myself I will enjoin,
> Awake at duty's call,
> To show a love as *prompt* as thine. *Cowper*, Dog and Water-lily.

3. Hasty; forward; abrupt.

> I was too hasty to condemn unheard;
> And you, perhaps, too *prompt* in your replies. *Dryden.*

4†. Inclined or disposed.

> Fair virtues all,
> To which the Grecians are most *prompt* and pregnant. *Shak.*, T. and C., iv. 4. 90.

=**Syn.** Early, timely, punctual.

prompt (prompt), *v. t.* [< ME. *prompten*; < *prompt, a.*] **1.** To move or excite to action; incite; instigate.

> Murderer, do the worst
> Thy base unnoble thoughts dare *prompt* thee to!
> I am above thee, slave! *Beau. and Fl.*, Woman-Hater, v. 5.

> His wish and mine both *prompt* me to retire. *Cowper*, Retirement, l. 390.

2. To assist (a learner or speaker) by suggesting something forgotten or imperfectly learned or known, or by pronouncing the words next in order: as, to *prompt* a pupil; to *prompt* an actor.

> Let him translate it into Latin againe, abiding in soch place where no other scholer may *prompe* him. *Ascham*, The Scholemaster, p. 89.

> They whisper: — sever them quickly, I say, officers! why do you let them *prompt* one another? *Beau. and Fl.*, Coxcomb, v. 3.

> If she shou'd flag in her part, I will not fail to *prompt* her. *Congreve*, Way of the World, iii. 18.

3. To dictate; suggest to the mind; inspire.

> And whisp'ring angels *prompt* her golden dreams. *Pope*, Eloisa to Abelard, l. 210.

> By these Steps I strive to climb up to Heaven, and my Soul *prompts* me I shall go thither. *Howell*, Letters, I. vi. 32.

4†. To remind; put (one) in mind.

> Soft and delicate desires,
> All *prompting* me how fair young Hero is,
> Saying I liked her ere I went to wars. *Shak.*, Much Ado, i. 1. 306.

=**Syn. 1.** *Actuate, Impel, Induce*, etc. (see *actuate*), incline, dispose, suggest to. See list under *impel*.

prompt (prompt), *n.* [< *prompt, v.*] **1.** In *com.*, a limit of time given for payment for merchandise purchased, the limit being stated on a note of reminder called a *prompt-note*.

> He does pay in money — that is, he gives his acceptance at two or three months or whatever *prompt* is customary in the trade, and when the bill falls due he pays it. *Nineteenth Century*, XIX. 392.

2. Information suggested or prompted.

> Few [children in schools] will not give, and not many will not take *prompts*, or peep in their books. *G. S. Hall*, Amer. Jour. Psychol., III. 63.

prompt-book (prompt'bu̇k), *n.* A copy of a play prepared for the prompter's use, and containing the text as cut and altered for representation, with all the stage business and other directions required for performance.

prompt-center (prompt'sen"tėr), *n.* See *stage.*

prompter (promp'tėr), *n.* [< ME. *promptere*, *promptare*, *promptowre*; < *prompt* + *-er*[1].] **1.** One who or that which prompts, or admonishes or incites to action.

> We understand our duty without a teacher, and acquit ourselves as we ought to do without a *prompter*. *Sir R. L'Estrange.*

> We find in ourselves some *prompter* called a desire; and, the more essential the action, the more powerful is the impulse to its performance. *H. Spencer*, Social Statics, p. 30.

Specifically—**2.** A person stationed behind the scenes or in a covered box at the front of the stage in a theater, for the purpose of assisting the actors when they are at a loss by repeating to them the first words of a sentence; also, any person who aids a public speaker, etc., by suggesting words he may be at a loss for.

> No without-book prologue, faintly spoke
> After the *prompter*, for our entrance. *Shak.*, R. and J., i. 4. 8.

> The play is done; the curtain drops,
> Slow falling to the *prompter's* bell. *Thackeray*, The End of the Play.

prompting (promp'ting), *n.* [Verbal n. of *prompt, v.*] **1.** The act of inciting, instigating, suggesting, or reminding.—**2.** An incitement or impulse, especially from inner desires or motives: as, the *promptings* of affection.

> Many sane persons have experienced horrid *promptings* when standing looking over a precipice. *Pop. Sci. Mo.*, XXXVI. 83.

> The later the date the more likely that he [the architect] built his arcade according to the *promptings* of his own genius. *E. A. Freeman*, Venice, p. 254.

promptitude (promp'ti-tūd), *n.* [< F. *promptitude* = Sp. *prontitud* = It. *prontitudine*, < LL. *promptitudo*, promptitude, < L. *promptus*, ready, prompt: see *prompt.*] **1.** Promptness; readiness; quickness of decision or action when occasion demands; cheerful alacrity.

> Much will depend on the *promptitude* with which these means can be brought into activity. *Jefferson*, Works, VIII. 69.

2. Prompting.

> Those who were contented to live without reproach, and had no *promptitude* in their minds towards glory. *Steele*, Spectator, No. 407.

promptly (prompt'li), *adv.* [< *prompt* + *-ly*[2].] In a prompt manner; readily; quickly; expeditiously; cheerfully.

promptness (prompt'nes), *n.* [< *prompt* + *-ness.*] The state or quality of being prompt; readiness; quickness of decision or action; especially, quickness of action in executing a decision; cheerful willingness; alacrity.

> Cassius alone, of all the conspirators, acted with *promptness* and energy in providing for the war which he foresaw the death of Cæsar would kindle. *Ames*, Works, II. 271.

> A good judgment combines *promptness* with deliberateness. *J. Sully*, Outlines of Psychol., p. 409.

They seemed desirous to prove their title to them by their thorough discipline and by their *promptness* to execute the most dangerous and difficult services. *Prescott.*

prompt-note (prompt'nōt), *n.* In *com.*, a note of reminder of the day of payment and sum due, etc., given to a purchaser at a sale of merchandise. See *prompt, n.*

prompt-side (prompt'sīd), *n.* See *stage.*

promptuary (promp'tū-ā-ri), *n.*; pl. *promptuaries* (-riz). [= F. *promptuaire* = Sp. *prontuario* = Pg. *promptuario*, ‹ LL. *promptuarium*, *promtuarium*, a repository, storehouse, store-room, hence in ML. used (like E. *magazine*) for a repository of information, handbook (in this sense also irreg. *promptorium*, *promptorius*), as in *Promptuarium Parvulorum Clericorum* or *Promptorium Parvulorum*, 'the little scholars' handbook,' or *Promptorius Puerorum*, 'the boys' handbook,' the name of an English-Latin dictionary of the 15th century; ‹ L. *promptus*, *promtus*, pp. of *promere*, produce, bring out: see *prompt*.] That from which supplies are drawn; a storehouse; a magazine; a repository.

History, that great treasury of time and *promptuary* of heroique actions. *Howell*, Forreine Travell, p. 22.

Bid Naddo think, at Mantua, he had but
To look into his *promptuary*, put
Finger on a set thought in a set speech.
Browning, Sordello.

prompture (promp'tūr), *n.* [‹ *prompt* + *-ure.*] Suggestion; incitement; instigation.

I'll to my brother;
Though he hath fall'n by *prompture* of the blood.
Shak., M. for M., ii. 4. 178.

promulgate (prọ-mul'gāt), *v. t.*; pret. and pp. *promulgated*, ppr. *promulgating.* [‹ L. *promulgatus*, pp. of *promulgare*, make known, publish, ‹ *pro*, forth, + *-mulgare*, of uncertain origin. Cf. *promulge.*] To make known by open declaration, as laws, decrees, or tidings; publish; announce; proclaim.

'Tis yet to know—
Which, when I know that boasting is an honour,
I shall *promulgate*—I fetch my life and being
From men of royal siege. *Shak.*, Othello, i. 2. 21.

The Statute of Uses was delayed until 1536, and the Statute of Wills until 1540, but both statutes were *promulgated* in 1532. *Stubbs*, Medieval and Modern Hist., p. 255.

=**Syn.** *Declare, Announce, Proclaim*, etc. See *announce.*

promulgation (prō-mul-gā'shon), *n.* [= F. *promulgation* = Sp. *promulgacion* = Pg. *promulgação* = It. *promulgazione*, ‹ L. *promulgatio(n-)*, a proclamation, a publication, ‹ *promulgare*, pp. *promulgatus*, publish, make known: see *promulgate.*] 1. The act of promulgating; publication; open declaration.

The stream and current of this rule hath gone as far, it hath continued as long, as the very *promulgation* of the gospel. *Hooker*, Eccles. Polity. (*Latham.*)

The doctrine of evolution at the present time rests upon exactly as secure a foundation as the Copernican theory of the motions of the heavenly bodies did at the time of its *promulgation*. *Huxley*, Amer. Addresses, p. 90.

2. In *law*: (*a*) The first official publication of a law which has been passed, or of an ordinance or a proclamation. (*b*) More strictly, the final order of the sovereign power which puts an enacted law into execution. *Clark.*

promulgator (prō'mul-gā-tor), *n.* [= F. *promulgateur* = Sp. Pg. *promulgador* = It. *promulgatore*, ‹ L. *promulgator*, one who publishes or proclaims, ‹ *promulgare*, pp. *promulgatus*, publish, make known: see *promulgate.*] One who promulgates or publishes; one who makes known or teaches publicly.

An old legacy to the *promulgators* of the law of liberty. *Warburton*, Sermons, xi. (*Latham.*)

promulge (prọ-mulj'), *v. t.*; pret. and pp. *promulged*, ppr. *promulging.* [= F. *promulguer* = Sp. Pg. *promulgar* = It. *promulgare*, ‹ L. *promulgare*, publish, make known: see *promulgate.*] To promulgate; publish; teach publicly.

Extraordinary doctrines these for the age in which they were *promulged*. *Prescott.* (*Webster.*)

Considering his Highness's wisdom, . . . they would henceforth make, *promulge*, or execute no such constitutions without his consent.
R. W. Dixon, Hist. Church of Eng., ii.

promulger (prọ-mul'jėr), *n.* Same as *promulgator.*

Its [the gospel's] *promulgers* delivered it not out by parcels, as is the way of cunning and designing men, but offered the whole of it to be altogether examined and compared. *Bp. Atterbury*, Sermons, I. iii.

promuscidate (prọ-mus'i-dāt), *a.* [‹ *promuscis* (*-muscid-*) + *-ate*[1].] In *entom.*: (*a*) Having the form of a promuscis: as, a *promuscidate* mouth. (*b*) Furnished with a promuscis: as, a *promuscidate* insect.

promuscis (prọ-mus'is), *n.*; pl. *promuscides* (-i-dēz). [NL., ‹ L. *promuscis*, a corrupt form for *proboscis*, proboscis: see *proboscis*.] In *entom.*, a proboscis; a beak or rostrum of various insects: originally applied by Illiger (1806) to the mouth-parts of bees; applied by Kirby and Spence (1818) and subsequent authors to the oral instrument of hemipterous insects, in which the ordinary trophi are replaced by a sheath containing four hair-like lancets or scalpella.

Punctures the cuticle with a proboscis (a very short three-jointed *promuscis*) springing as it were from the breast, but capable of being gently porrected.
E. P. Wright, Anim. Life, p. 472.

promycele (prō-mi-sēl'), *n.* [‹ NL. *promycelium.*] In *bot.*, same as *promycelium.*

promycelial (prō-mi-sē'li-al), *a.* [‹ *promycelium* + *-al.*] In *bot.*, of or pertaining to the promycelium.

The *promycelial* tube is divided by transverse walls into a series of two or more short cells.
De Bary, Fungi (trans.), p. 177.

promycelium (prō-mi-sē'li-um), *n.* [NL., ‹ L. *pro*, before, + NL. *mycelium*, q. v.] In *bot.*, a short and short-lived filamentous product of the germination of a spore, which bears sporidia and then dies. Also *promycele.*

pron. An abbreviation of (*a*) *pronoun*; (*b*) *pronounced*; (*c*) *pronunciation.*

pronaos (prō-nā'os), *n.* [‹ Gr. πρόναος, also neut. πρόναον, a porch before a temple, prop. adj., πρόναος, προναῖος, Attic πρόνεως, before a temple, ‹ πρό, before, + ναός, a temple, a cella: see *naos*.] In *arch.*: (*a*) An open vestibule or

Pronaos.—Heroum adjoining the baths at Assos in the Troad, as discovered and restored by the Archæological Institute of America, 1881-3.

portico in front of the naos or cella of a temple. See *naos*, 2.

The temple . . . consists of a *pronaos* or vestibulum . . . and of the naos proper. *Schliemann*, Troja, p. 79.

(*b*) Same as *narthex*, 1. [This use is not to be recommended.]

pronate (prō'nāt), *v. t.*; pret. and pp. *pronated*, ppr. *pronating.* [‹ LL. *pronatus*, pp. of *pronare*, bend forward, bow, ‹ L. *pronus*, bent: see *prone.*] To render prone; specifically, to rotate (the hand) so that its palmar surface faces in the same direction as the posterior surface of the ulna.

pronation (prọ-nā'shon), *n.* [= F. *pronation* = Sp. *pronacion* = Pg. *pronação* = It. *pronazione*, ‹ LL. *pronare*, pp. *pronatus*, bend forward, bow: see *pronate.*] The act or result of pronating; the prone position of the fore limb, in which the bones of the forearm are more or less crossed, and the palm of the hand is turned downward: the opposite of *supination*. Pronation and its reverse movement, supination, are free and perfect in man and in some other mammals which use their fore paws as hands. In pronation the bones of the forearm are crossed: in supination they lie parallel to each other. The fore limbs of most quadrupeds are permanently fixed in the state of pronation, with the palmar surface or sole of the fore foot downward or backward, and the knuckles or convexities of the joints of the digits upward or forward; supination is absent, and the ulna is often reduced to a mere appendage of the radius, ankylosed at the upper end of the latter.

pronator (prọ-nā'tor), *n.*; pl. *pronatores*, *pronators* (prō-nā-tō'rēz, prō-nā'torz). [= F. *pronateur* = Sp. Pg. *pronador* = It. *pronatore*, ‹ LL. *pronare*, pp. *pronatus*, bend forward, bow: see *pronation.*] A muscle of the forearm whose action pronates the hand or assists in pronation: opposed to *supinator*.—**Pronator quadratus**, a flat muscle on the lower part of the forearm in front, passing from the ulna to the radius. Also called *cubitoradialis*, *quadrate pronator*, and more fully *pronator radii quadratus*.—**Pronator radii teres**, a pronator and flexor of the forearm. It arises chiefly from the inner condyle of the humerus, and passes across obliquely in front, to be inserted in the outer side of the radius near its middle. Also called *pronator teres*, and *round* or *terete pronator*. See cut under *muscle*.

prone (prōn), *a.* [‹ F. *prone* = Sp. Pg. It. *prono*, ‹ L. *pronus*, bent, leaning forward, ‹ *pro*, forward: see *pro-*.] 1. Bending forward with the face downward; inclined; lying flat; not erect.

A creature who, not *prone*
And brute as other creatures, but endued
With sanctity of reason, might erect
His stature. *Milton*, P. L., vii. 508.

Ancient tow'rs,
And roofs embattled high, . . .
Fall *prone*. *Cowper*, Task, ii. 125.

2. Lying with the face or front downward.

The lamb *prone*,
The serpent towering and triumphant.
Browning, Ring and Book, II. 56.

Specifically, in *anat.*: (*a*) Lying face downward; stretched at full length on the belly. (*b*) Lying with the palm downward; pronated, as the hand. In both senses, the opposite of *supine*.

3. Moving or sloping downward; descending; inclined.

The sun,
Declined, was hasting now with *prone* career
To the ocean isles. *Milton*, P. L., iv. 353.

Prone down the rock the whitening sheet descends.
Burns, Written by the Fall of Fyers.

Since the floods demand
For their descent a *prone* and sinking land,
Does not this due declivity declare
A wise director's providential care?
Sir R. Blackmore.

Just where the *prone* edge of the wood began
To feather toward the hollow.
Tennyson, Enoch Arden.

4. Inclined by disposition or natural tendency; propense; disposed: usually in an ill sense.

He is . . . as *prone* to mischief
As able to perform 't. *Shak.*, Hen. VIII., i. 1. 160.

Anna's mighty Mind,
To Mercy and soft Pity *prone*.
Congreve, Pindaric Odes, i.

Prone mouth, a mouth which lies entirely on the lower surface of the head, owing to the fact that the head itself forms a right angle with the thorax, as in the grasshoppers.—**Prone surface**, the lower surface.=**Syn.** 1 and 2. See *prostrate*.

pronely (prōn'li), *adv.* In a prone manner or position; so as to bend downward.

proneness (prōn'nes), *n.* The state of being prone. (*a*) The state of bending downward: as, the *proneness* of beasts that look downward: opposed to the *erectness* of man. (*b*) The state of lying with the face or front downward: contrary to *supineness*. (*c*) Descent; declivity: as, the *proneness* of a hill. (*d*) Inclination of mind, heart, or temper; propensity; disposition: as, *proneness* to self-gratification or to self-justification.=**Syn.** (*d*) *Tendency*, *Disposition*, etc. See *bent*[1].

pronephron (prō-nef'ron), *n.*; pl. *pronephra* (-rä). [NL., ‹ L. *pro*, before, + Gr. νεφρός, a kidney.] A part of the primitive kidney of the lower vertebrates, which appears at the most anterior end of the archinephric duct before the rest of the kidney and at some distance from it. It consists of a number of coiled tubuli, beginning with ciliated infundibula or nephrostomata: its duct is the Müllerian duct. See *mesonephron*.

pronephros (prō-nef'ros), *n.* Same as *pronephron*.

prong[1]† (prông), *n.* [ME., also *pronge*, *prange*, a pang: see *pang*[1], which is an altered form of the same word.] A pang. *Prompt. Parv.*, pp. 415, 493.

prong[2] (prông), *n.* [Early mod. E. also *prongue*; cf. *prog*, thrust, *proke*, thrust.] 1. A sharp point or a pointed instrument; especially, one of several points which together make up a larger object: as, the *prong* of a fork; the *prong* of a deer's antler.

I dine with forks that have but two *prongs*.
Swift, to Gay, March 19, 1729.

The *prongs* of rock rose spectral on every side.
N. Y. Semi-weekly Tribune, Sept. 28, 1878.

2. A hay-fork. *Halliwell.* [Prov. Eng.]

Would not sell me,
But, being his domesticke friend, expell me
With forks and *prongs*, as one insenc'd with ire.
Heywood, Dialogues (Works, ed. Pearson, 1874, VI. 164).

3. A fork or branch of a stream or inlet. [Southern U. S.]—4. A prawn (?).

They speed their way through the liquid waste;
Some are rapidly borne along
On the mailed shrimp or the prickly *prong*.
J. R. Drake, Culprit Fay, p. 29.

prong[2] (prông), *v. t.* [‹ *prong*[2], *n.*] To stab with or as with a fork. [Humorous.]

Dear brethren, let us tremble before those august portals. I fancy them guarded by grooms of the chamber with flaming silver forks with which they *prong* all those who have not the right of the entrée.
Thackeray, Vanity Fair, li.

prongbuck (prông'buk), *n.* The American antelope or pronghorn, *Antilocapra americana.*

prong-chuck (prông'chuk), *n.* A burnishing-chuck with a steel prong. *E. H. Knight.*

prongdoe (prông'dō), *n.* The female of the prongbuck.

prong-hoe (prông'hō), *n.* A hoe with prongs to break the earth.

pronghorn (prông'hôrn), *a.* and *n.* **I.** *a.* Having horns with a prong or snag, as the prongbuck: as, the *pronghorn* antelope.

II. *n.* The prongbuck or cabrit. This remarkable animal is an isolated American type, like the saiga of the Old World; it has no near relatives living, and is supposed to be in the line of descent from some stock more or less like the fossil *Sivatherium* of India. It is not an antelope in any proper sense, though universally so called in the regions it inhabits—the first literary use of the name dating about 1812. The pronghorn was first scientifically described from material furnished by Lewis and Clarke to George Ord, who called it *Antilope americana* in 1815, but very soon instituted the genus *Antilocapra* (which see, and *Antilocapridæ*, for technical characters). The male stands about 3 feet high at the croup and withers; the limbs are very slender; the general form is that of a deer, but rather stouter (contrary to a general impression); the eyes are extremely large and full, and placed directly under the base of the horns; these in the male are from 6 or 8 inches to a foot in length, curved variously, but always with the characteristic prong or snag—in the female mere hairy cones tipped with a horny thimble an inch long. The horns are shed annually, late in the fall or early in winter. The pelage is close, without any flowing tufts, but coarse and brittle, and nearly worthless; the hide makes a valuable buckskin when dressed. The venison is excellent, resembling mutton rather than deer-meat. There is an extensive set of cutaneous sebaceous glands, eleven in number, which during the rut exhale a strong hircine odor. The prongdoe regularly drops twins, usually late in spring or early in summer, and the kids are not spotted (as the young of *Cervidæ* usually are), but resemble their parents. The bucks and does are alike of a tawny or yellowish-brown color, with a large white disk on the buttocks, a white crescent and triangle on the fore part of the neck, and the under parts and inner sides of the limbs white; the forehead, muzzle, a spot on the neck over the gland, and the horns and hoofs are mostly black or blackish. During most of the year the animals go in bands, sometimes numbering thousands, but oftener of much less extent. They range over all the region of the great plains, from British America far into Mexico, excepting where they have of late years been driven off by the settlement of the country. Unlike the bison, the pronghorn does not appear to have ever ranged east of the Mississippi. It is noted for its fleetness, and for a singular mixture of timidity and curiosity, which renders it susceptible of being "flagged," or decoyed within rifle-range by the exhibition of any unusual object, as a handkerchief tied to a pole. The gait is buoyant and easy, and when bounding at full speed the animal is probably the fleetest of any American game. But it lacks bottom, and its astonishing bursts of speed cannot be long sustained. Almost any pack of hounds can overtake it, if the game has not too much advantage at the start. The pronghorn is subject to an epidemic disease of unknown character, which in some years has destroyed many thousands. This fact, together with the incessant persecution it suffers, has very appreciably diminished its numbers as well as contracted its range of late years, though it appears to be still very far from the point of extermination.

pronity† (prō'ni-ti), *n.* [= It. *pronità* (cf. Sp. *proneidad* = Pg. *proneidade*), < L. *pronita(t-)s*, inclination, < *pronus*, bent, inclined: see *prone.*] Same as *proneness.*

Saint Paule in hys Pistle to ye Rom. speketh of the *pronity* and mocions in the fleshe remaining as the reliques of original sinne. *Sir T. More*, Works, p. 550.

pronominal (prǫ-nom'i-nal), *a.* [= F. Sp. Pg. *pronominal* = It. *pronominale*, < L. *pronominalis*, pertaining to a pronoun, < *pronomen*, a pronoun: see *pronoun.*] Belonging to or of the nature of a pronoun: as, a *pronominal* root.

In Siam, when asking the king's commands, the *pronominal* form is, as much as possible, evaded. *H. Spencer*, Prin. of Sociol., § 397.

pronominally (prǫ-nom'i-nal-i), *adv.* With the effect or force of a pronoun; by means of a pronoun.

"What was that notion of his"—they usually spoke of the minister *pronominally.* *Howells*, Annie Kilburn, xxx.

pronotal (prō-nō'tal), *a.* [< *pronotum* + *-al.*] Situated on the pronotum; of or pertaining to the pronotum.

pronotary, *n.* Same as *prothonotary.*

And I knew you a *Pronotaries* boy,
That wrote Indentures at the toune house doore.
Daniel, Queen's Arcadia, iii. 1.

pronotum (prō-nō'tum), *n.*; pl. *pronota* (-tạ̈). [NL., < Gr. πρό, before, + νῶτος, back: see *notum.*] The anterior one of the three divisions of the notum of an insect, preceding the mesonotum; the dorsal or tergal section of the prothorax; the upper part of the first thoracic segment or prothoracic tergum. It is typically divided into four sclerites (the præscutum, scutum, scutellum, and postscutellum), which sclerites are, however, usually more or less consolidated and therefore indistinguishable. See cut under *Insecta.*—**Cruciate, emarginate, obvolvent, pulvinate,** etc., **pronotum.** See the adjectives.—**Producted pronotum.** See *product.*

pronoun (prō'noun), *n.* [Not found in ME.; appar. altered (to suit the earlier *noun*) < F. *pronom* = Sp. *pronombre* = Pg. *pronome* = It. *pronome*, < L. *pronomen*, a word standing in place of a noun, < *pro*, for, + *nomen*, a noun: see *noun.*] In *gram.*, a word used instead of a noun to avoid the repetition of it; a demonstrative word, pointing to a person or thing, but not describing it otherwise than by designating position, direction, relation to the speaker, or the like; one of a small body of words, in Indo-European and other families of language, coming from a few roots, different from those from which come in general verbs and nouns, and having the office of designating rather than describing: they are believed to have borne an important part in the development of inflective structure in language. They are divided into various classes: *personal* (doubtless originally demonstrative), as *I, thou, he*, etc.; *possessive*, which are the adjective forms of the personal, as *my, thy, his*, etc.; *demonstrative*, as *this, that*, etc.; *interrogative*, as *who, what*, etc.; *relative* (which are always either demonstratives or interrogatives with changed office, implying an antecedent to which they refer or relate), as *that, which, who*, etc.; and *indefinite*, which are of various meaning, and shade off into ordinary nouns, as *each, either, some, any, such*, etc. Abbreviated *pr., pron.*

pronounce (prǫ-nouns'), *v.*; pret. and pp. *pronounced*, ppr. *pronouncing.* [< ME. *pronouncen*, < OF. *prononcer*, F. *prononcer* = Sp. Pg. *pronunciar* = It. *pronunciare, pronunziare*, < L. *pronuntiare*, proclaim, publish, < *pro*, forth, + *nuntiare*, announce, < *nuntius*, that makes known: see *nuncio.* Cf. *announce, denounce, enounce, renounce.*] **I.** *trans.* **1**†. To declare; make known; announce; proclaim.

I will *pronounce* this bloudie deede,
And blotte thine honor so.
Gascoigne, Philomene, p. 100. (*Arber.*)

2. To form or articulate by the organs of speech; utter articulately; speak; utter; specifically, to give a word its due recognized sound in uttering it.

Then said they unto him, Say now Shibboleth: and he said Sibboleth: for he could not frame to *pronounce* it right. Judges xii. 6.

Yet sometime "Tarquin" was *pronounced* plain,
But through his teeth, as if the name he tore.
Shak., Lucrece, l. 1786.

3. To utter formally, officially, or solemnly.

I do beseech your lordship, for the wrongs
This man hath done me, let me *pronounce* his punishment!
Beau. and Fl., Woman-Hater, v. 5.

An Idol in the form of a Dog or Wolf, which was worshipped, and is said to have *pronounc'd* Oracles at this place. *Maundrell*, Aleppo to Jerusalem, p. 36.

4. To speak or utter rhetorically; deliver: as, to *pronounce* an oration.

The things that mount the rostrum with a skip,
And then skip down again; *pronounce* a text . . .
Cowper, Task, ii. 410.

5. To declare or affirm.

O gentle Romeo,
If thou dost love, *pronounce* it faithfully.
Shak., R. and J., ii. 2. 94.

I dare not *pronounce* you will be a just monarch.
Ford, Broken Heart, iv. 3.

An author who laughs at the public which *pronounces* him a dunce. *Goldsmith*, The Bee, No. 2.

=**Syn.** *Enunciate, Deliver*, etc. See *utter.*

II. *intrans.* **1.** To speak with confidence or authority; make declaration; utter an opinion; declare one's self.

Nor can [I] *pronounce* upon it
. . . whether
The habit, hat, and feather,
Or the frock and gipsy bonnet,
Be the neater and completer.
Tennyson, Maud, xx. 1.

Asked what she most desired, she *pronounced* for a special providence of tea and sugar.
First Year of a Silken Reign, p. 22.

Among the Irish peerage there are more than a dozen who have either *pronounced* for the principle of Home Rule or are not hostile to it if a fair scheme be devised.
Contemporary Rev., LII. 314.

2. To utter words; specifically, to articulate words correctly.

pronounce† (prǫ-nouns'), *n.* Pronunciation; declaration.

That all controversie may end in the finall *pronounce* or canon of one Arch-primat.
Milton, Church-Government, i. 6.

pronounceable (prǫ-noun'sa-bl), *a.* [< *pronounce* + *-able.* Cf. *pronunciable.*] Capable of being pronounced or uttered.

Its first syllable, "Pen,"
Is *pronounceable*; then
Come two LLs and two HHs, two FFs and an N.
Barham, Ingoldsby Legends, I. 65.

pronounced (prǫ-nounst'), *p. a.* [Pp. of *pronounce, v.*] Strongly marked or defined; decided.

Our friend's views became every day more *pronounced.* *Thackeray.*

The outline of the tower is not unlike that of the Parasuramcswara temple, . . . but the central belt is more *pronounced.* *J. Fergusson*, Hist. Indian Arch., p. 438.

Wolsey was too great a man, and More too good a man, to be tools of Henry, especially after the inclination towards tyrannic caprice became more *pronounced.*
Stubbs, Medieval and Modern Hist., p. 248.

pronouncedly (prǫ-noun'sed-li), *adv.* In a pronounced manner; markedly.

"Fatal Water," the most *pronouncedly* pathetic of the tales. *The Academy*, Feb. 8, 1890, p. 93.

pronouncement (prǫ-nouns'ment), *n.* [< F. *prononcement* = Pr. *prononciamen* = Sp. *pronunciamiento* = It. *pronunziamento*; < ML. *pronunciamentum*, < L. *pronuntiare*, pronounce: see *pronounce.*] The act of pronouncing; a proclamation; a formal announcement.

The law is apprehended by ocular inspection, audible *pronouncement*, and other like natural ways of cognition. *Bushnell*, Forgiveness and Law, p. 114.

pronouncer (prǫ-noun'sėr), *n.* One who pronounces, or utters or declares.

pronouncing (prǫ-noun'sing), *p. a.* [Ppr. of *pronounce, v.*] Pertaining to, indicating, or teaching pronunciation: as, a *pronouncing* dictionary.

pronubial (prǫ-nū'bi-al), *a.* [< L. *pronubus*, pertaining to marriage, < *pro*, for, + *nubere*, marry, wed: see *nubile.*] Presiding over marriage. *Congreve.* [Rare.]

pronuclear (prō-nū'klẹ-ạ̈r), *a.* [< *pronucle-us* + *-ar*[3].] Pertaining to a pronucleus, or having its character.

pronucleate (prō-nū'klẹ-āt), *a.* [< *pronucle-us* + *-ate*[1].] Having a pronucleus or pronuclei.

pronucleus (prō-nū'klẹ-us), *n.*; pl. *pronuclei* (-ī). [< L. *pro*, before, + *nucleus*, nucleus.] **1.** A primitive nucleus; the nucleus of an ovum or of a spermatozoön before these have united to form the definitive nucleus of an impregnated ovum. That of the ovum is the *female*, that of the spermatozoön the *male* pronucleus. The formation of the female pronucleus commonly occurs in a ripe ovum after the extrusion of the particles of yolk known as the *polar globules of Robin*, and it is that part of the original germinal vesicle which remains behind after such extrusion, receding from the surface of the ovum and assuming a spherical form. The male pronucleus is simply the head of a spermatozoön buried in the yolk, and about to blend its substance with that of the female pronucleus. See *feminonucleus, masculonucleus.*

2. In *bot.*, the nucleus of a conjugating gamete, which on coalescing with another pronucleus forms the germ-nucleus. *Goebel.*

pronunciable† (prǫ-nun'si-a-bl), *a.* [= It. *pronunziabile*, < L. *pronuntiare, pronunciare*, pronounce (see *pronounce*), + *-able.*] Pronounceable.

Vowels *pronunciable* by the intertexture of a consonant.
Jer. Taylor, Works (ed. 1835), I. 54.

pronuncial (prǫ-nun'sial), *a.* [< L. *pronuntiare, pronunciare*, pronounce (see *pronounce*), + *-al.*] Pertaining to pronunciation.

pronunciamento (prǫ-nun'si-a-men'tō), *n.* Same as *pronunciamiento.*

pronunciamiento (Sp. pron. prō-nön-thē-ä-mien'tō), *n.* [Sp., = E. *pronouncement.*] A manifesto or proclamation; a formal announcement or declaration: often applied to the declarations of insurrectionists. Also *pronunciamento.*

They [the people of Suez] are, according to all accounts, a turbulent and somewhat fanatic set, fond of quarrels, and slightly addicted to *pronunciamentos.*
R. F. Burton, El-Medinah, p. 118.

pronunciation (prǫ-nun-si-ā'shon), *n.* [< F. *prononciation* = Sp. *pronunciacion* = Pg. *pronunciação* = It. *pronunciazione*, < L. *pronuntiatio(n-), pronunciatio(n-)*, a proclamation, a publication, < *pronuntiare, pronunciare*, proclaim, announce: see *pronounce.*] **1.** The act of pronouncing, or uttering with articulation; the manner of uttering words or letters; specifically, the manner of uttering words which is held to be correct, as based on the practice of the best speakers: as, the *pronunciation* of a name; distinct or indistinct *pronunciation.* Abbreviated *pron.*

The standard of *pronunciation* is not the authority of any dictionary, or of any orthoepist; but it is the present usage of literary and well-bred society.
Nuttall, quoted in N. and Q., 7th ser., VII. 174.

2. The art or manner of uttering a discourse with euphony and grace: now called *delivery.*

Well-placing of words for the sweetness of *pronunciation* was not known till Mr. Waller introduced it.
Dryden, Def. of Epil. to second part of Conq. of Granada, ii.

Pronunciation of Greek and Latin. (*a*) *Continental pronunciation* or *system of pronunciation*, a system of pronunciation of Latin or Greek conforming or approximating to that in use on the continent of Europe, especially in the vowel-sounds. As each of the principal nations in western Europe pronounces Latin, and the most of them Greek also, in the main after the analogy of its own language, it is only in their chief points of agreement that a usage which can justify this epithet *continental* exists. The system of pronunciation known as *continental* retains, for the most part, the English sounds of the consonants, and pronounces the vowels as in German or Italian. There is a stricter form of continental pronunciation of Latin, approaching the Roman, and a modified form, approaching the English. The continental system of pronouncing Greek is often called *Erasmian*, as closely resembling the modified or modern Erasmian pronunciation used in Germany. (*b*) *Eclectic pronunciation* (*of Greek*), a system of pronunciation of ancient Greek which seeks to approximate to the actual ancient pronunciation. It agrees on the whole with the stricter continental system, and pronounces the diphthongs so that each element can be heard separately. (*c*) *English pronunciation* (*of Greek*), a system of pronouncing Greek with the English sounds of the corresponding Latin letters. This system is now little used in the United States. (*d*) *English pronunciation* (*of Latin*), a system of pronouncing Latin which follows, with some exceptions, the general analogy of the modern pronunciation of English. The Latin rule of accentuation determines the place of the accent; but the vowels are given their long or short English sounds without regard to their Latin quantity. The English long sounds are used at the end of a word (but final *a* is usually obscure, as in *conna*), before another vowel, and at the end of an accented penult or of any unaccented syllable (except penultimate *i*). The English short sounds are used in a syllable ending with a consonant (except final *es*, *os*), before two consonants (not a mute and liquid) and *x* (= *cs*), and (excepting *u*) in an accented antepenult before a single consonant, if not followed by two vowels the former of which is *e*, *i*, or *y*. C, *s*, and *t*, succeeding the accent, are equivalent to sh, and *x* is sounded like ksh, before two vowels the former of which is an unaccented *i* or *y*, unless *s*, *t*, or *x* precedes. Initial *x* is pronounced *z*. If the second of two initial consonants is not *h*, *l*, or *r*, the first (if not *s*) is silent. Initial *chth* and *phth* are pronounced th. There are no silent vowels. Different authorities vary these rules somewhat, or acknowledge various exceptions to them. The English system of pronunciation of Latin regulates the pronunciation in English of all proper names which have not altered their Latin spelling, and of all Latin words and phrases which have become Anglicized. (*e*) *Erasmian pronunciation* (*of Greek*), a system the earliest champion of which was Erasmus in his treatise "De Recta Latini Græcique Sermonis Pronunciatione" (Basel, 1528). The pronunciation universally in use at that time was the modern Greek as used in the middle ages and supported by Byzantine scholars at the time of the revival of letters. Investigation led to a general conviction among scholars in the west of Europe that the Erasmian theory of the ancient pronunciation was correct; and by the end of the sixteenth century—after considerable controversy, embittered by the fact that the traditional or modern pronunciation was favored by supporters of the papacy, and the Erasmian system by the Reformers—the Erasmian system had come into general use, and the Byzantine method of pronouncing Greek as a living language—also called the *Reuchlinian*, from Johann Reuchlin, the first great representative of Greek scholarship in Germany—became obsolete in the western schools. In its original form the Erasmian pronunciation was distinguished from the Reuchlinian by giving most of the vowels the sounds which they have in Latin as pronounced by most of the western nations, the Italians, Germans, etc., and by pronouncing the diphthongs so that each vowel in them should preserve its own sound. As, however, this pronunciation closely approached that of the modern western languages in the sixteenth century, it became practically the usage that every nation should pronounce Greek after the analogy of its own language, and, as this has gradually changed in each country, the pronunciation of Greek has varied with it. In England, in the time of Henry VIII., the pronunciation of Vowels was nearly the same as in continental languages. This is evident from the fact that the relation of the Greek vowels, as pronounced by the Erasmian system, to those in the Latin alphabet, as used in the vernacular, is treated by writers of that time as identical in England and on the continent. In England, accordingly, the Erasmian system of pronunciation was insensibly transformed into what is now called the *English pronunciation* of Greek. The system known as the *continental* is a partial revision of the Erasmian; that designated as the *eclectic* restores the Erasmian with some alterations. (*f*) *Modern Greek pronunciation*, the pronunciation of Greek, ancient and modern, actually in use in Greece at the present day. The change from the ancient to the present pronunciation was very gradual. The first signs of its prevalence are found in the Bœotian dialect and among Hellenists. Confusion of ει with ι became general about 200–100 B. C., but good speakers still made some difference between these sounds till after 200 A. D. The vowel η began to be frequently confounded with ι about 250–150 B. C., but persons of culture retained the sound of a Latin *ē* (English *ā*) for it till 500 A. D. or later. The diphthong αι became identical in sound with ε about 150–200 A. D., and somewhat later οι was pronounced like υ (ü). The vowel υ was distinguished from ι till late Byzantine times. After about 150–200 A. D. αυ, ευ came to be sounded as av, ev, and later as af, ef before surds. During the Roman imperial period distinctions of quantity fell more and more into disuse, and merely accentual poetry began as early as the fourth century. In Egypt and other countries outside of Greece these changes of pronunciation began very early, and even the older manuscripts are accordingly full of their effects (*iotacisms*). This system of pronunciation prevailed throughout the middle ages not only in the East, but in the West till the time of the Reformation. Also called *iotacism*, *itacism*, *Reuchlinian pronunciation*. (*g*) *Reuchlinian pronunciation* (*of Greek*). Same as (*f*). See (*e*). (*h*) *Roman pronunciation* (*of Latin*), a system of pronunciation of Latin which seeks to approximate to the actual ancient pronunciation. It differs from the stricter continental system chiefly in the sounds given to *æ*, *œ*, *c*, and *v*, and in having only one sound for each vowel. In the ancient pronunciation *e* and *o* varied in sound, and there are indications that the short vowels in general differed somewhat in quality from the long vowels. The following tables exhibit the leading systems described above.

PRONUNCIATION OF GREEK.

	Continental.	English.	Modern Greek.
ᾰ	ă	a	ă
ᾱ	ä	â	ä
αι	ī (*or* äē)	ī	ā *or* e
ᾳ	ä	â	ä
αυ	ou (*or* äō)	au	äv *or* äf
β	b	b	v
γ[1]	g	g	gh *or* y
γ[2]	ng	ng	ng
δ	d	d	dh = TH
ε	e	e	e *or* ā
ει	ī (*or* ĕē, ā)	ī	ē
ευ	ū (*or* ĕö)	ū	ev *or* ef
ζ	dz *or* z	z	z
η	ā (*or* ā)	ē	ē
η	ā	ē	ē
ηυ	ū (*or* äö, äö)	ū	ēv *or* ēf
θ	th	th	th
ῐ	i	i	ē
ῑ	ē	ī	ē
ξ	ks	ks	ks
ο	o (ô)	o	ô
οι	oi	oi	ē
ου	ö	ou	ö
ῠ	ü (ŭ)	ū	ē
ῡ	ü (ü)	ū	ē
υι, υi	wē, whē (üē, hüē)	wi, whi	ē
χ	k (ch)	k	ch
ω	ō	ō	ô
ψ	ō	ō	ô
ωυ	ö (ōö)	ou	ôv *or* ôf
Rough breathing (ʽ)	h	h	Silent.

In all these systems κ, λ, μ, ν, π, ρ, σ, τ, φ, and ψ respectively have the same sounds as *k*, *l*, *m*, *n*, *p*, r, *s*, *t*, *f*, and *ps*. The sounds given in parentheses represent the stricter continental pronunciation. γ^2 is γ before γ, κ, ξ, χ (γ^1 being γ elsewhere); gh represents the corresponding sonant to ch (nearly as German *g* in *Wagen* as pronounced by most Germans). In the Modern Greek system χ is ch as in German *ich*, and γ is y before ā and ē sounds (ε, ι, etc.); γκ is ngg, μπ is mb, and ντ is nd. The strict continental system and the Modern Greek pronounce by the written accent, while the English and the modified continental accent Greek by the rule for accent in Latin. The two last-named systems generally make α and ι long in open syllables and short in closed syllables (the English pronunciation treating them as *a* and *i* in Latin), but υ is always long.

PRONUNCIATION OF LATIN.

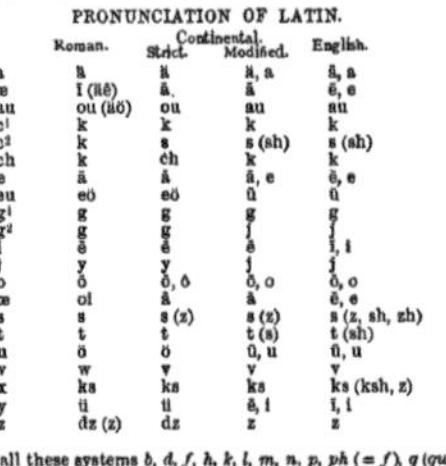

	Roman.	Continental. Strict.	Continental. Modified.	English.
a	ä	ä	ä, a	ā, a
æ	ī (äē)	ā	ā	ē, e
au	ou (äö)	ou	au	au
c[1]	k	k	k	k
c[2]	k	s	s (sh)	s (sh)
ch	k	ch	k	k
e	ā	ā	ā, e	ē, e
eu	eö	eö	ū	ū
g[1]	g	g	g	g
g[2]	g	g	j	j
i	ē	ē	ē	ī, i
j	y	y	j	j
o	ō	ō, ô	ō, o	ō, o
œ	oi	ā	ā	ē, e
s	s	s (z)	s (z)	s (z, sh, zh)
t	t	t	t (s)	t (sh)
u	ö	ö	ū, u	ū, u
v	w	v	v	v
x	ks	ks	ks	ks (ksh, z)
y	ü	ü	ē, i	ī, i
z	dz (z)	dz	z	z

In all these systems *b*, *d*, *f*, *h*, *k*, *l*, *m*, *n*, *p*, *ph* (= *f*), *q* (*qu* = *kw*), r, t, *th* (in *thin*), have their ordinary English sounds. C^2 and g^2 represent c and *g* before *e*, *æ*, *œ*, *i*, and *y*; c^1 and g^1 represent c and *g* before other letters than these. The short Vowel-sounds are used in the English and in the modified continental system in closed syllables, and the long vowel-sounds in open syllables, regardless of the ancient quantity. The Roman system gives the same quality of sound to a short vowel as to a long, but makes it more rapid in pronunciation. In continental pronunciation *s* is by some pronounced *z* between two vowels, and in the modified system final *ēs* is pronounced āz, and final *ōs* ōs. For the pronunciation of c, *s*, and t as sh, and of *x* as ksh or *z*, see (*d*). Pronounce *ü* as in German, or as French *u*.

pronunciative (prọ̄-nun′ṣi-ā̤-tiv), *a.* [= It. *pronunziativo*, < L. *pronuntiativus*, *pronunciativus*, declarative, enunciative, < *pronuntiare*, *pronunciare*, proclaim, enounce: see *pronounce*.] 1. Of or pertaining to pronunciation; pronunciatory.—2†. Uttering confidently; dogmatical.

> The confident and *pronunciative* school of Aristotle.
> *Bacon*, Prometheus.

pronunciator (prọ̄-nun′ṣi-ā-tọr), *n.* [= Sp. Pg. *pronunciador* = It. *pronunziatore*, < L. *pronuntiator*, *pronunciator*, a reciter, a relater, < *pronuntiare*, *pronunciare*, publish, proclaim: see *pronounce*.] One who pronounces.

pronunciatory (prọ̄-nun′ṣi-ā̤-tọ̄-ri), *a.* [< *pronunciator* + *-y*[1].] Relating to pronunciation.

Prony's dynamometer. A dynamometer, named after its inventor, much used for obtaining data for computing the power delivered by turbines and other water-wheels, or from the fly-wheel of an engine, or transmitted by shafting. The principle of this apparatus is the same in all of its forms. In the accompanying illustration, which represents a form of the apparatus used in laboratories, *e* is a shaft provided with a winch c, and supported in bearings d in a frame *h*; *j* is a lever having a scale-pan suspended from the point *m* near the extremity of the longer arm as shown at *b*, on which, when in use, a weight or weights *i* are placed; *a* is a counterpoise; *f* is a chain connected at its ends to tightening-bolts *k*, *k′*; *l* indi-

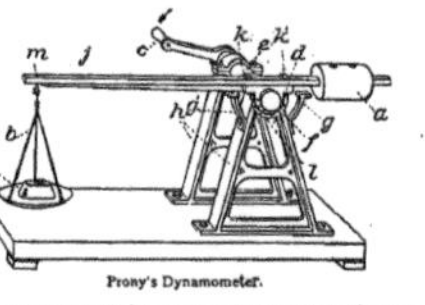

Prony's Dynamometer.

cates wooden brake-shoes, which, by tightening the chain *f*, can be made to press strongly against the projecting end of the shaft *e*; *g*, *g′* are stop-rests, which limit the motion of the lever, used only for convenience in applying the brake, and not essential to its action. In the determination of the power transmitted through the shaft *e*, moving in the direction shown by the arrow, the counterpoise is first adjusted to counterbalance the long arm of the lever and the empty scale-pan. The chain *f* is then tightened and the scale-pan loaded, so that at a given velocity the lever is by the friction of the brake held away from the rest *g′*, but not in contact with *g*. Under conditions so established, if L = the perpendicular distance in feet of the point l from the axis of *e*, S = the weight in pounds placed in the pan, r = the radius in feet or fractions of a foot of the shaft *e*, and M = the moment of torsion in pounds, then will $LS/r = M$, and $2\pi rM$ = the power transmitted in foot-pounds during each turn of the winch. Also called *Prony's brake*.

proœmiac (prọ̄-ē′mi-ak), *a.* [< *proœmium* + *-ac*.] Relating to or constituting a proœmium or preface.

> The 104th [Psalm] is the *Proœmiac*, because it commences Vespers. *J. M. Neale*, Eastern Church, i. 856.

proœmium, proœmion (prọ̄-ē′mi-um, -on), *n.* [L. *proœmium*, < Gr. προοίμιον, an opening: see *proem*.] 1. Same as *proem*.

> Forgetful how my rich *proœmion* makes
> Thy glory fly along the Italian field,
> In lays that will outlast thy Deity.
> *Tennyson*, Lucretius.

> In his *proœmium* he plainly intimates that he is putting forth a kind of commonplace book of historical anecdotes.
> *Encyc. Brit.*, XXIV. 41.

2. In *rhet.*, the exordium.

proof (pröf), *n.* and *a.* [Early mod. E. *proofe*, *profe*, < ME. *proof*, *prouff*, *profe*, also (whence early mod. E. *prief*, *preef*) *preef*, *preeve*, *preve*, *preove*, < OF. *prove*, *proeve*, *preuve*, F. *preuve* = Pr. *prova*, *proa*, a proof, < LL. *proba*, a proof, < L. *probare*, prove: see *prove*.] I. *n.* 1. Any effort, act, or operation made for the purpose of ascertaining any truth or fact; a test; a trial: as, to make *proof* of a person's trustworthiness or courage.

> The verray *preeve* sheweth it indede.
> *Chaucer*, Nun's Priest's Tale, l. 163.

> Here and se, and sey thou nought,
> Than schall thou not to *profe* be brought.
> *Babees Book* (E. E. T. S.), p. 23.

> Madam, you may make *Proof* of him, and if your Ladyship find him too saucy or wasteful, you may return him whence you had him. *Howell*, Letters, I. v. 36.

> Let there be
> Once every year a joust for one of these;
> For so by nine years' *proof* we needs must learn
> Which is our mightiest.
> *Tennyson*, Lancelot and Elaine.

2. Evidence and argumentation putting the conclusion beyond reasonable doubt; demonstration, perfect or imperfect.

> Trifles light as air
> Are to the jealous confirmations strong
> As *proofs* of holy writ. *Shak.*, Othello, iii. 3. 324.

> They [miracles] are not private, but public *proofs*; not things to be done in a corner, for the sake of single persons, but before multitudes, and in the face of the sun.
> *Bp. Atterbury*, Sermons, I. xii.

> Credulous enough
> To swallow much upon much weaker *proof*.
> *Cowper*, Conversation, l. 722.

3†. A thing proved or tried; truth or knowledge gathered by experience; experience.

> Out of your *proof* you speak; we, poor unfledged,
> Have never wing'd from view o' the nest, nor know not
> What air 's from home. *Shak.*, Cymbeline, iii. 3. 27.

4. The state of having been tested and approved; firmness, hardness, or impenetrability: specifically applied to arms or armor of defense, to note that they have been duly tested and are impenetrable.

There died of his hand Sarpedon, Plistonax, Strophilus, and Hippolytus, men of great *proof* in wars.
Sir P. Sidney, Arcadia, iii.

She hath Dian's wit;
And, in strong *proof* of chastity well arm'd,
From love's weak childish bow she lives unharm'd.
Shak., R. and J., i. 1. 216.

They harnessed him from head to foot with what was of *proof*, lest perhaps he should meet with assaults in the way. *Bunyan*, Pilgrim's Progress, p. 124.

5. In *law:* (*a*) The convincing effect of evidence; the manifestation of the truth of a proposition by presenting the reasons for assenting to it; such an array of evidence as should determine the judgment of the tribunal in regard to a matter of fact. In criminal cases, to be effectual as proof, the evidence must satisfy beyond a reasonable doubt. In civil cases it is enough that the evidence preponderates.

Evidence is the medium of *proof; proof* is the effect of evidence. *Judge Danforth*, 108 N. Y., 73.

(*b*) *pl.* In equity practice, the instruments of evidence in their documentary form, as depositions, deeds, etc., received in a cause. (*c*) The presentation of sufficient evidence: as, the burden of *proof* lies with the plaintiff. *Proof* is either written or parole. The former consists of records, deeds, or other writings; the latter of the testimony of witnesses personally appearing in court or before a proper officer, and, as a rule, sworn to the truth of what they depose. In this sense the word is used to designate either the task of going forward with the giving of evidence at the trial or the task of satisfying the minds of the jury. Owing to the different functions of the judge and the jury, the distinction is of great practical importance, because when the plaintiff has given evidence which would entitle him if unanswered to go to the jury, it is proper for him to tell counsel that the burden of proof is on defendant, meaning that if the defendant adduces no evidence the plaintiff will be entitled to have the case submitted to the jury; but it is error for him thereupon, whether defendant offers evidence or not, to tell the jury that the burden of proof is on defendant to contradict plaintiff's case, for, considered as a task of satisfying the jury, the burden of proof remains upon the plaintiff throughout. The burden of proof is never on the defendant in this sense, except in respect to an affirmative defense in avoidance as distinguished from a denial. (*d*) In Scots law, the taking of evidence by a judge upon an issue framed in pleading. Sometimes disputed facts may be sent to a jury, but, except in actions of damages, a proof is almost invariably the course adopted. . . . The evidence as the proof is taken down in shorthand, and counsel are heard at the close. *Henry Goudy.*

6. A test applied to manufactured articles or to natural substances prepared for use; hence, the state of that which has undergone this test, or is capable of undergoing it satisfactorily. Compare *armor of proof.*—7. In alcoholic liquors, the degree of strength which gives a specific gravity of 0.920. See II., 2. Liquors lighter than this are said to be *above proof*, and heavier liquors are *below proof*. See *overproof* and *underproof*.

The expressions "20 per cent over proof," "20 per cent under proof," mean that the liquor contains 20 volumes of water for every 100 volumes over or under this fixed quantity, and that, in order to reduce the spirit to *proof*, 20 per cent of water by volume must be subtracted or added as the case may be. *Spons' Encyc. Manuf.*, I. 215.

8. In *printing*, a trial impression from composed type, taken for correction. Generally a number of successive proofs are read before the matter is ready for the press, corrections being made first in the printing-office until what is technically called a *clean proof* can be submitted to the author. The final proof is called a *press-proof* or a *foundry-proof*, the first being used of letterpress work, and the latter of plate-work.

Lap. What says my printer now?
Gal. Here 's your last *proof*, sir. [Giving proof-sheet.]
You shall have perfect books now in a twinkling.
Fletcher (*and another?*), Nice Valour, iv. 1 (circa 1625).

9. In *engraving* and *etching*, an impression taken from an engraved plate to show its state during the progress of executing it; also, an early and superior impression, or one of a limited number, taken before the title or inscription is engraved on the plate, and known as *proof before letter.* There may be first, second, and third proofs, marking successive states of the work. See also *artist's proof*, *India proof*, *proof with open letters*, and *proof with remarque*, below.

10. In *numis.*, any early impression struck at the mint from a coin-die used for producing the current coins of the realm. Proofs are often distinguished from the coins struck off for actual currency by having their edges left plain instead of being milled or inscribed. They are also often struck in a metal of greater or less value than that which is proper to the current coin: thus, there are gold, silver, and bronze *proofs* of the English copper farthing issued by George III. in 1799. Compare *pattern*, 8.

11. In *bookbinding*, the rough uncut edges of the shorter leaves of a trimmed book, which prove that the book has not been cut down too much. —12. In *arith.*, an operation serving to check the accuracy of the calculation.—**Acroamatic proof.** See *acroamatic*.—**A priori proof.** (*a*) Proof deduced from principles. (*b*) Proof independent of experience.—**Armor of proof**, armor which has been proved trustworthy, or which is known to be trustworthy, as against ordinary weapons.—**Artist's proof**, in *engraving*, a first impression taken from an engraved plate or block after its completion.—**Burden of proof.** See *burden*1 and def. 5 (*c*).—**Composite proof, direct proof.** See the adjectives.—**Dogmatic or discursive proof.** Same as *acroamatic proof*.—**Empirical proof**, proof from actual experience.—**Foul proof, imperfect proof.** See the adjectives.—**India proof.** See *India*.—**Indirect proof**, in *logic*, same as *apagoge*, 1 (*b*).—**Irregular proof**, a proof the external form of which is different from the standard form of logic.—**Making proof**, under United States land laws, furnishing to the proper officer the requisite affidavits of actual residence, etc., to entitle a settler to a patent for his land.—**Marked proof.** See *marked*.—**Mathematical proof**, proof from construction of concepts, from a diagram or its equivalent.—**Mixed proof**, a proof partly analytic and partly synthetic.—**Monosyllogistic proof**, a proof consisting of a single syllogism.—**Ontological, ostensive, positive proof.** See the adjectives.—**Proof before letter**, an early proof of a plate taken before the title or explanatory lettering has been engraved.—**Proof by notoriety.** Same as *judicial notice* (which see, under *notice*).—**Proof of gunpowder**, a test of strength, one ounce of powder being used with a 24-pound ball, which must be driven a distance of not less than 250 yards.—**Proof of ordnance and small-arms**, tests by means of hydraulic pressure and the firing of heavy charges.—**Proof with open letters**, or **open-letter proof**, an early proof of an engraving, on which the title is engraved in letters that are merely outlined.—**Proof with remark**, or **remark proof**, a proof of an engraving or etching in which the early state is denoted by one or more croquis or fanciful marks traced on the margin, or by the absence of certain lines in different parts of the plate. These remarks are sometimes used to denote the different states of the plate up to the point of completion.—**Pure proof.** See *pure*1.—**To the proof**†, to the quick; so as to touch a vital part.

But now I'll speak, and *to the proof*, I hope.
Marlowe, Edward II., i. 1.

We must be patient: I am vex'd *to the proof* too.
Fletcher, Wildgoose Chase, iii. 1.

=**Syn. 1.** Experiment, essay, ordeal.—**2.** *Testimony*, etc. (see *evidence* and *inference*), demonstration, certification.

II. *a.* [Elliptical for *of proof:* see *proof*, *n.*, 4.] 1. Impenetrable; able to resist, physically or morally: as, water-*proof*, fire-*proof*, shot-*proof*, bribe-*proof:* often followed by *to* or *against* before the thing resisted.

Now put your shields before your hearts, and fight,
With hearts more *proof* than shields.
Shak., Cor., i. 4. 25.

Now am I high *proof*
For any action; now could I fight bravely,
And charge into a wildfire.
Beau. and Fl., Captain, iv. 2.

I . . . have found thee
Proof against all temptation.
Milton, P. R., iv. 533.

I do not know . . . a task so difficult in human life as to be *proof against* the importunities of a woman a man loves. *Steele*, Spectator, No. 510.

If James had not been *proof to* all warnings, these events would have sufficed to warn him.
Macaulay, Hist. Eng., vi.

2. Noting alcoholic liquors which have the specific gravity 0.91984, usually considered as 0.920, which is sufficiently accurate for practical purposes. Such spirits contain 0.495 of their weight, or 0.5727 of their volume, of absolute alcohol. The strength is usually determined by a hydrometer. See *alcoholometry*, *overproof*, and *underproof*.

3. Of excellent quality: said of land. *Halliwell.* [Prov. Eng.]—**Proof strength.** See the quotation.

The *proof strength* is the load required to produce the greatest strain of a specific kind consistent with safety.
Rankine, Steam Engine, § 58.

proof-arm†, *v. t.* [< *proof* + *arm*2.] To arm as with proof; make secure.

Men. She is a handsome wench.
Leu. A delicate, and knows it;
And out of that *proof-arms* herself.
Fletcher, Humorous Lieutenant, ii. 3.

proof-armor (prōf'är"mor), *n.* Same as *armor of proof* (which see, under *proof*).

proofed (prōft), *a.* [< *proof* + *-ed*2.] Made proof; specifically, made water-proof: as, *proofed* silk. [Trade term.]

proof-ful† (prōf'fůl), *a.* [< *proof* + *-ful.*] Conveying proof; bearing testimony.

Had you been so blest
To give such honour to your captains' counsels
As their alacrities did long to merit
With *proofful* action. *Chapman*, Cæsar and Pompey.

proof-galley (prōf'gal"i), *n.* In *printing*, a brass galley flanged at one end and on both sides. The type to be proved is held in position by a sidestick secured by quoins. See *galley*, 5.

proof-glass (prōf'glås), *n.* A cylindrical glass vessel very deep in proportion to its diameter, and having a foot and a lip for pouring out liquids; a hydrometer-glass. It is principally used for holding liquids while testing their densities or specific gravities by the use of a hydrometer. See cut under *hydrometer*.

proof-house (prōf'hous), *n.* In *gun-manuf.*, a building in which gun-barrels are proved or tested for flaws or defects by firing them with critical test-charges of a definite weight of a standard powder, and also by hydraulic pressure. See *proof*, *n.*, 6. In London a proof-house is established by law, to which gun-barrels of different makers can be sent for proof. Gun-barrels which meet the test are then stamped with authorized proof-marks.

proof-leaf (prōf'lēf), *n.* A proof; a proof-sheet.

They appear printed in a few *proof-leaves* of it in my possession. *Boswell*, Johnson, I. 204.

proofless (prōf'les), *a.* [< *proof* + *-less.*] Lacking sufficient evidence to constitute proof; not proved.

Such questionable, not to say altogether *proof-less* conceits. *Boyle*, Works, II. 290.

prooflessly (prōf'les-li), *adv.* Without proof.

The maxim . . . Locus conservat locatum . . . has been *proof-lessly* asserted. *Boyle*, Works, IV. 390.

proof-mark (prōf'märk), *n.* In *gun-making*, a mark stamped in the metal of a gun-barrel to show that it has been tested and found good.

proof-plane (prōf'plān), *n.* In *elect.*, a small thin metallic disk, insulated on a non-conducting handle, by which electricity may be carried from one place to another. It is used in experiments on the distribution of electricity on conductors. When it is laid against the surface whose electric density it is intended to measure, it forms, as it were, a part of the surface, and takes the charge due to the area which it covers, which charge may be carried to an electrometer and measured.

proof-press (prōf'pres), *n.* A printing-press used exclusively for taking proofs.

proof-print (prōf'print), *n.* An early impression of an engraving, taken with greater care than an ordinary print; a proof.

proof-printer (prōf'prin"tėr), *n.* In *engraving*, a skilled workman whose especial province is the printing of proofs from engraved or etched plates.

proof-reader (prōf'rē"dėr), *n.* A person who reads printers' proofs for correction; one whose occupation is to discover errors in proofs and note on them the necessary changes. A *critical* or *editorial proof-reader* is one who not only corrects the compositors' errors, but notes or points out the lapses of the original text, or makes or indicates changes for its improvement. Proof-readers were originally called *correctors of the press*, and that phrase still remains in literary or formal use, especially for those who read proofs for criticism as well as for correction.

proof-reading (prōf'rē"ding), *n.* The correction of errors in printers' proofs. See *proof-reader.* In marking a proof, the places in the text where changes are to be made are indicated in the following modes. A caret (‸) is inserted in the bottom of a line at a point where something is to be put in or a new paragraph is to be made; a line is drawn through anything to be taken out or changed for something else, and under anything to be changed to different type; the mark ⌈ is made to the left of a word to be shifted in that direction, and ⌋ to the right; and letters or parts of a word improperly separated are connected by a curve or curves (‿ or ⊂). In the last two cases the same marking is repeated in the margin. The other indicative marks or signs made in the margin (besides a few strictly technical ones, which admit of much variation) are the following: ₰ or ₰ (*dele-mark*), representing *d* (δ) for *dele*, take out; ꝗ (*turn-mark*), for turning an inverted letter; # (*space-mark*), for inserting a space, or more space; ⊥, for putting down space; □, for inserting an em-quadrat, or increasing the space to that amount; ¶ (*paragraph-mark*), for making a new paragraph; ×, for a broken or imperfect letter; *stet* (let it stand), for something that is to remain after being crossed out, a row of dots being made under the erasure; *tr.* for *transpose*; *w. f.* for *wrong font* (meaning a letter or letters of different size or face from the others); *ital.* for *italic*, and *rom.* for *roman*; *cap.* or *caps.* for *capital* or *capitals*; *s. c.* for *small capitals*; *l. c.* for *lower-case*. In the last five cases, where only a single letter is involved, proof-readers usually write the letter itself in the margin, in the form desired, or with the proper underscoring. In underscoring, italics are indicated by a single line, small capitals by two lines, and capitals by three lines. A single letter written as a capital does not usually need to be underscored. Where two paragraphs in the text are to be joined or "run in," a line curving at the ends is drawn between them, and "No ¶" written in the margin. A marginal correction should always be written as nearly as possible opposite the place affected in the text; and where the connection cannot thus be made clear, a line should be drawn between the place and the correction.

proof-sheet (prōf'shēt), *n.* A printers' proof.

Mr. Arthur Pendennis having written his article, . . . reviewed it approvingly as it lay before him in its wet *proof-sheet* at the office of the paper.
Thackeray, Pendennis, xlvi.

She recognized the name as that of a distinguished publisher, and the packet as a roll of *proof-sheets*.
H. James, Jr., Harper's Mag., LXXVII. 106.

proof-spirit (prōf'spir"it), *n.* In *com.*, an alcoholic liquor which has a specific gravity of 0.920, and contains 0.495 of its weight, or 0.5727 of its volume, of absolute alcohol.

proof-staff (prōf'stȧf), *n.* A metallic straight-edge used as a standard to correct a wooden staff made for ordinary service.

proof-stick (prōf'stik), *n.* In *sugar-manuf.*, a rod of wood for dipping in boiling syrup to test its condition by the rapidity and character of the crystallization. *E. H. Knight.*

proof-text (prōf'tekst), *n.* A passage of Scripture brought forward to prove a special doctrine.

It is not a legitimate use of the Old Testament to seek in it *proof-texts* for all the doctrines that are found in the New Testament. *Bibliotheca Sacra*, XLIII. 563.

proof-valiant† (prōf'val'yant), *a.* Of tried courage.

Believe me, captain, such distemper'd spirits,
Once out of motion, though they be *proof-valiant*,
If they appear thus violent and fiery,
Breed but their own disgraces.
Beau. and Fl., Captain, ii. 1.

proöstracal (prō-os'tra-kal), *a.* [< *proöstracum* + *-al.*] Forming or formed by the proöstracum; of or pertaining to a proöstracum.

proöstracum (prō-os'tra-kum), *n.* [NL., < Gr. πρό, before, + ὄστρακον, shell: see *Ostracea.*] The broad and projecting lamella of the thick covering of the phragmacone of a cephalopod, extending beyond the base of the phragmacone, and being a continuation of the wall of the most anterior chamber of the shell; the foremost part of the guard or rostrum of a fossil cephalopod of the belemnite group. It is variously shaped, usually lamellate, and with the rostrum represents the pen of the squids. See cuts under *belemnite*, *Belemnitidæ*, and *calamary*.

The genus Acanthoteuthis, . . . in which the guard is almost rudimentary, while the *pro-ostracum* is large and penlike. *Huxley*, Anat. Invert., p. 465.

proötic (prō-ō'tik), *a.* and *n.* [< Gr. πρό, before, + οὖς (ὠτ-), ear, + *-ic.*] **I.** *a.* Anterior with reference to the otic capsule or among otic bones; of or pertaining to the proötic: correlated with *opisthotic*, etc. See II., and *otic.*

II. *n.* In *zoöl.* and *anat.*, a bone of the ear, an anterior ossification of the periotic capsule, forming with the epiotic and opisthotic the petrosal or petromastoid bone, developed in especial relation with the anterior vertical semicircular canal of the bony labyrinth of the ear. It frequently remains distinct from the other otic bones; in man it assists the opisthotic in the formation of the mastoid as well as the petrous part of the temporal bone. See cuts under *Crocodilia*, *Gallinæ*, and *periotic*.

The *pro-otic* is, in fact, one of the most constant bones of the skull in the lower Vertebrata, though it is commonly mistaken on the one hand for the alisphenoid, and on the other for the entire petro-mastoid.
Huxley, Anat. Vert., p. 26.

prop[1] (prop), *n.* [Early mod. E. *proppe*, < ME. *proppe*, a prop; = MD. *proppe*, a prop, support; cf. MD. *proppe*, *prop*, a stopple, D. *prop*, a stopple, cork, plug, wad, pellet, = MLG. *prop*, *proppe*, LG. *propp* = G. *propf*, *propfen*, a stopple, cork (not found before the 19th century), = Sw. *propp* = Dan. *prop*, a cork, stopple, plug. The origin of these words is uncertain; some compare G. *pfropf*, *propfen*, a graft, MHG. *pfropfen*, OHG. **pfropfo*, *pfroffo*, a set, slip, < L. *propago*, a set, slip, layer of a plant: see *propago*, *propagate*, etc. The Gael. *prop*, Ir. *propa*, a prop, support, are prob. borrowed from E.] **1.** A stick, staff, pole, rod, beam, or other rigid thing used to sustain an incumbent weight; that on which anything rests for support; a support; a stay; a fulcrum: usually applied to something not forming a part of the object supported: as, a *prop* for vines; a *prop* for an old wall.

Proppe, longe (staffe), contus. *Prompt. Parv.*, p. 415.

You take my house when you do take the *prop*
That doth sustain my house.
Shak., M. of V., iv. 1. 375.

Justice and religion are the two chief *props* and supporters of a well-governed commonwealth.
Burton, Anat. of Mel., p. 603.

But wit's like a luxuriant vine,
Unless to virtue's *prop* it join,
Firm and erect towards heaven bound.
Cowley, Death of Mrs. C. Philips.

They are the *props* of national wealth and prosperity, not the foundations of them.
D. Webster, Speech, House of Representatives, Jan. 2, 1815.

2. In *bot.*, same as *fulcrum*, 3.—**3.** *pl.* Legs. *Halliwell.* [Prov. Eng.] = **Syn. 1.** See *staff*.

prop[1] (prop), *v.*; pret. and pp. *propped*, ppr. *propping.* [Early mod. E. *proppe*; = MD. *proppen*, prop, stay, or bear up (cf. MLG. *proppen* = G. *propfen* = Sw. *proppa* = Dan. *proppe*, stop up, cork); appar. from the noun, but the verb may possibly be older: see *prop*, *n.*] **I.** *trans.* **1.** To support or prevent from falling by placing something under or against: as, to *prop* a roof or wall.

Here wee saw certain great Serraglios, exceeding high, and *propt* up by buttresses. *Sandys*, Travailes, p. 106.

What shalt thou expect,
To be depender on a thing that leans,
Who cannot be new built, nor has no friends,
So much as but to *prop* him?
Shak., Cymbeline, i. 5. 60.

He was *propped* up on a bed-rest, and always had his gold-headed stick lying by him.
George Eliot, Middlemarch, xxxii.

2. To support by standing under or against: as, a pillar *props* a roof; beams *prop* a wall.

He whose Arms alone sustain'd the Toil,
And *propp'd* the nodding Frame of Britain's Isle.
Congreve, Birth of the Muse.

Eternal snows the growing mass supply,
Till the bright mountains *prop* th' incumbent sky.
Pope, Temple of Fame, l. 58.

But build a castle on his head,
His skull will *prop* it under.
Burns, Epigram on a Coxcomb.

3. To support or sustain in a general sense: as, to *prop* a failing cause.

Wise men must be had to *prop* the republic.
Fletcher (and another?), Prophetess, i. 3.

It behoved our Merchants to get an Interest here to *prop* up their declining Trade. *Dampier*, Voyages, II. i. 182.

To *prop* fair Liberty's declining Cause,
And fix the jarring World with equal Laws.
Prior, To Boileau Despreaux (1704).

4. To help; assist. *Halliwell.* [Prov. Eng.]

II. *intrans.* To stop or pull up suddenly; balk: said of a horse or other beast. *Douglas Sladen.* [Australia.]

prop[2] (prop), *n.* A shell used in the game of props. See *props*[1].

prop. An abbreviation of (*a*) *proposition*; (*b*) *properly*.

propædeutic (prō-pē-dū'tik), *a.* and *n.* [< Gr. προπαιδεύειν, teach beforehand, < πρό, before, + παιδεύειν, teach, bring up or rear: see *pædeutics*.] **I.** *a.* Pertaining to propædeutics, or the introduction to any art or science; relating to preliminary instruction; instructing beforehand.

The conceptual suppositions, which are taken for assured premises and are in truth erroneous, and at best *propædeutic*, but are dragged unnoticed into the conclusion.
Westminster Rev., CXXVI. 475.

II. *n.* A branch of knowledge introductory to a particular art or science; a subject to be mastered as a preliminary to some other subject.

It [logic] is a *propædeutic* to all other sciences.
Atwater, Logic, p. 37.

That study [physical geography] which Kant justly termed the "*propædeutic* of natural knowledge."
Huxley, Physiography, Pref., p. vi.

propædeutical (prō-pē-dū'ti-kal), *a.* [< *propædeutic* + *-al.*] Same as *propædeutic*.

propædeutics (prō-pē-dū'tiks), *n.* [Pl. of *propædeutic* (see *-ics*).] The preliminary body of knowledge and of rules necessary for the study of some particular art, science, etc.; the introduction to an art or a science.

It [our secular life] is not a mere instrumentality for the purpose of silencing the beast of the body, but rather is it the *propædeutics* of human combination and communication, wherein spiritual life becomes a reality.
A. B. Alcott, Table-Talk, p. 114.

propagable (prop'a-ga-bl), *a.* [= It. *propagabile*, < L. as if **propagabilis*, < *propagare*, propagate: see *propagate*.] **1.** Capable of being propagated, or of being continued or multiplied by natural generation or production.

Such creatures as are produced each by its peculiar seed constitute a distinct *propagable* sort of creatures. *Boyle.*

2. Capable of being spread or extended by any means, as tenets, doctrines, or principles.

propagand (prop'a-gand), *n.* [< F. *propagande*: see *propaganda*.] Same as *propaganda*.

A grand scheme for the union of Protestant Christendom, and his [Hartlib's] *propagand* of Comenius's school-reform. *Mark Pattison*, Life of Milton, p. 33.

propaganda (prop-a-gan'dä), *n.* [= F. *propagande* = Sp. Pg. It. *propaganda*; short for L. (ML.) *congregatio de propaganda fide*, association for propagating the faith (see def.): *propaganda*, abl. fem. gerundive of *propagare*, propagate: see *propagate*.] **1.** A committee of cardinals (Congregation *de Propaganda Fide*, 'for propagating the faith') which has the supervision of foreign missions in the Roman Catholic Church. It was founded by Pope Gregory XV. in 1622. One of its chief instrumentalities is the Propaganda College in Rome. See *congregation*, 6 (*a*), 10. Hence—**2.** Any kind of institution or organization for propagating a new doctrine or system of doctrines, or for proselyting.

The first attempts at a *propaganda* of liberty, and the first attempts at a *propaganda* of nationality, were marked by great excesses and great mistakes.
Stubbs, Medieval and Modern Hist., p. 237.

The rules of the association [the National Secular Society] inform us that it is the duty of an "active member" to promote the circulation of secular literature, and generally to aid the Free-thought *propaganda* of his neighbourhood. *Saturday Rev.*

propagandic (prop-a-gan'dik), *a.* [< *propaganda* + *-ic.*] Pertaining to a propaganda or to propagandism.

propagandism (prop-a-gan'dizm), *n.* [= F. *propagandisme* = Pg. *propagandismo*; as *propaganda* + *-ism.*] The system or practice of propagating tenets or principles; zealous dissemination of doctrines; proselytism.

We have attempted no *propagandism*, and acknowledged no revolution. *Lincoln*, in Raymond, p. 309.

What were the causes which made his [Mohammed's] disciples the leaders of a successful armed *propagandism*?
Stillé, Stud. Med. Hist., p. 102.

propagandist (prop-a-gan'dist), *n.* and *a.* [= F. *propagandiste* = Pg. *propagandista*; as *propaganda* + *-ist.*] **I.** *n.* One who devotes himself to the propagation or spread of any system of principles.

Bonaparte selected a body to compose his Sanhedrim of political *propagandists*. *R. Walsh.*

The eager *propagandists* who prowl about for souls.
Hawthorne, Marble Faun, xx.

II. *a.* Pledged to or employed in such propagation; given to proselyting.

On the second day after Kullmann's murderous attempt, the authorities had been ordered to deal with the Catholic Press, and with *propagandist* societies under the influence of the Jesuits, according to the utmost rigour of the law. *Lowe*, Bismarck, II. 321.

propagate (prop'a-gāt), *v. t.*; pret. and pp. *propagated*, ppr. *propagating.* [< L. *propagatus*, pp. of *propagare* (> It. *propagare* = Pg. Sp. *propagar* = F. *propager*), peg down (a layer), set (slips or cuttings), propagate, extend, continue (cf. *propago*, a layer of a plant, a set, slip, shoot, hence offspring, progeny), < *pro*, forth, + *pangere* (√ *pag*), fasten, set: see *pact*. Hence ult. *proin*, *prune*[1].] **I.** *trans.* **1.** To multiply or continue by natural generation or reproduction; cause to reproduce itself: applied to plants and animals: as, to *propagate* fruit-trees; to *propagate* a breed of horses or sheep.

I sought the purchase of a glorious beauty,
From whence an issue I might *propagate*.
Shak., Pericles, i. 2. 73.

The wriggling fry soon fill the creeks around, . . .
The *propagated* myriads spread.
Cowper, Progress of Error, l. 484.

But cockle, spurge, according to their law,
Might *propagate* their kind with none to awe.
Browning, Childe Roland.

2. To transmit or spread from person to person or from place to place; carry forward or onward; diffuse; extend: as, to *propagate* a report; to *propagate* the Christian religion.

I first upon the mountains high built altars to thy name,
And grav'd it on the rocks thereby to *propagate* thy fame.
Drayton, Quest of Cynthia.

By newspaper reports, any great effect in one assise town, or electoral town, has been *propagated* to the rest of the empire. *De Quincey*, Style, i.

The idle writers of the day continued to *propagate* dulness through a series of heavy tomes.
Prescott, Ferd. and Isa., i. 18.

Throw a stone into the stream, and the circles that *propagate* themselves are the beautiful type of all influence.
Emerson, Nature.

3†. To promote; augment; increase.

Griefs of mine own lie heavy in my breast,
Which thou wilt *propagate*, to have it prest
With more of thine. *Shak.*, R. and J., i. 1. 193.

While tender airs and lovely dames inspire
Soft melting thoughts, and *propagate* desire.
Addison, The Greatest English Poets.

4†. To produce; originate; invent.

Thence to visit honest and learned Mr. Hartlib, a public spirited and ingenious person, who had *propagated* many usefull things and arts. *Evelyn*, Diary, Nov. 27, 1655.

For the greatest part of the Island of Sumatra *propagates* this Plant [pepper], and the Natives would readily comply with any who would come to Trade with them.
Dampier, Voyages, II. i. 116.

5. To scatter; disperse. [Rare.]

This short harangue *propagated* the Juncto, and put an end to their resolves; however, they took care of their fee, but then left all concern for the lady behind them.
Gentleman Instructed, p. 544. (*Davies.*)

= **Syn. 1.** To increase, spread, disseminate.

II. *intrans.* To be multiplied or reproduced by generation, or by new shoots or plants; bear young.

Fix'd like a plant on his peculiar spot,
To draw nutrition, *propagate*, and rot.
Pope, Essay on Man, ii. 64.

Every thread of silk in the rich vestments seems only a provision from the worms that spin, for the behoof of worms that *propagate* in sepulchres.
Dickens, Pictures from Italy, ix.

propagating-bench (prop'a-gā-ting-bench), *n.* In *hort.*, a stationary shallow box, usually filled with fine sand, but sometimes with earth, which is kept moist, and into which cuttings or slips are inserted until they have taken root. The propagating-bench is usually so placed that heat can be applied beneath it.

propagating-box (prop'a-gā-ting-boks), *n.* In *hort.*, a shallow wooden box or pan, properly movable (compare *propagating-bench*), for holding slips and cuttings in sand. It is usually placed over the hot flues or water-pipes in a shady part of a plant-house, or on the sand-bed in a propagating-house. Sometimes the cuttings in the box are covered with a propagating-glass.

propagating-glass (prop'a-gā-ting-glås), *n.* In *hort.*, a bell-glass used to cover cuttings or seedlings in a hotbed, nursery, or garden.

propagating-house (prop'a-gā-ting-hous), *n.* In *hort.*, etc., any greenhouse especially adapted or used for the propagation or increase of plants from cuttings, or for growing them from the seeds.

propagation (prop-a-gā'shon), *n.* [< ME. *propagacion*, < OF. *propagation*, *propagacion*, F. *propagation* = Sp. *propagacion* = Pg. *propagação* = It. *propagazione*, < L. *propagatio(n-)*, a propagating, an extension, < *propagare*, pp. *propagatus*, propagate: see *propagate*.] 1. The act of propagating; the multiplication or continuance of the kind or species by natural generation or reproduction: as, the *propagation* of plants or animals. In the greater number of flowering plants propagation is effected naturally by means of seeds: but many plants are also propagated by the production of runners or lateral shoots, which spread along the surface of the soil, and root at the joints, from which they send up new stems. Plants are also propagated by suckers rising from rootstocks, and by various other natural means. Propagation may be effected artificially by cuttings, grafting, budding, inarching, etc.

In September the *propagacion*,
In landes suche as tolde is of before,
Is best to sette in occupacion.
Palladius, Husbondrie (E. E. T. S.), p. 189.

How is it that in the *propagation* of the race such a marvel is repeated as that . . . every germ of a bodily organism receives the quickening breath of its spirit?
Lotze, Microcosmus (trans.), I. 370.

There is not in nature any spontaneous generation, but all come by *propagation*. *Ray*, Works of Creation.

2. The spreading or extension of anything; diffusion: as, the *propagation* of Christianity; the *propagation* of socialistic ideas.

The Apostle [Paul] did act like a prudent Governour, and in such a manner as he thought did most tend to the *propagation* of the Gospel. *Stillingfleet*, Sermons, II. vi.

It [speech] may be used for the *propagation* of slander.
H. Spencer, Social Statics, p. 166.

3†. Increase; augmentation; enlargement; aggrandizement.

For *propagation* of a dower
Remaining in the coffer of her friends.
Shak., M. for M., i. 2. 154.

The spoil and waste they [the Jews] had made upon all nations round about them for the *propagation* of their empire, which they were still enlarging as their desires.
South, Sermons, XI. ii.

4. Transmission from one point to another, as of sound by waves of condensation and rarefaction in the air, and of radiant heat and light by undulations in the ether. See *sound*[5], *heat*, *light*[1], and *radiant energy* (under *energy*).

To account for the enormous velocity of *propagation* of light, the substance which transmits it is assumed to be both of extreme elasticity and of extreme tenuity.
Tyndall, Light and Elect., p. 60.

=Syn. 1. Increase, generation, procreation, breeding.—2. Dissemination.

propagative (prop'a-gā-tiv), *a.* [= Sp. Pg. *propagativo*; as *propagate* + *-ive*.] Having the power of propagation; propagating.

Every man owes more of his being to Almighty God than to his natural parents, whose very *propagative* faculty was at first given to the human nature by the only virtue, efficacy, and energy of the divine commission and institution. *Sir M. Hale*, Origin of Mankind, p. 354. (*Latham.*)

A church without *propagative* power in the world cannot be other than a calamity to all within its borders.
H. *Drummond*, Natural Law in the Spiritual World, [p. 356.

propagator (prop'a-gā-tor), *n.* [= F. *propagateur* = Sp. Pg. *propagador* = It. *propagatore*, < L. *propagator*, a propagator, enlarger, extender, < *propagare*, pp. *propagatus*, generate, increase: see *propagate*.] One who propagates; one who continues by generation or successive production; one who causes something to extend or spread; a promoter; a diffuser: as, a *propagator* of heresies. The name is given to one whose business is the propagation of plants in nurseries, etc., by budding, grafting, etc.

The Author then of Originall Sinne is the *propagator* of our Nature. *Purchas*, Pilgrimage, p. 29.

Socrates, . . . the greatest *propagator* of morality.
Addison, Freeholder, No. 45.

Jacobus Baradæus, a Syrian, who was a chief *propagator* of the Eutychian doctrines.
E. W. Lane, Modern Egyptians, II. 312.

propagatorium (prop'a-gā-tō'ri-um), *n.*; pl. *propagatoria* (-ä). [NL., neut. *propagatorius*, propagatory: see *propagator*.] In *biol.*, the reproductive apparatus; the entire physical mechanism of reproduction; the organs of generation of either sex, consisting essentially of a sexual gland producing ova or spermatozoa, passages for the conveyance of the product, or for detaining it until mature in the body, and, usually, organs of sexual congress. Compare *nutritorium*, *locomotorium*, *sensorium*.

propagatory (prop'a-gā-tō-ri), *a.* [< NL. *propagatorius*, < L. *propagator*, propagator: see *propagator*.] Serving to accomplish propagation, as the organs of generation; reproductive, as a system of physical organs.

propago (prō-pā'gō), *n.*; pl. *propagines* (prō-paj'i-nēz). [L., < *propagare*, propagate: see *propagate*.] 1. In *hort.*, a branch laid down in the process of layering.—2. In *bot.*, same as *bulblet*.

propagule (prō-pag'ūl), *n.* [< NL. *propagulum*, q. v.] In *bot.*, same as *propagulum*.

propagulum (prō-pag'ū-lum), *n.*; pl. *propagula* (-lä). [NL., dim. of *propago*.] In *bot.*: (*a*) A shoot, such as a runner or sucker, which may serve for propagation. (*b*) In algæ, a modified branch by which non-sexual reproduction is effected. (*c*†) One of the powder-like grains which form the soredia of lichens.

Propalæotherium (prō-pā″lē-ō-thē'ri-um), *n.* [NL., < Gr. πρό, before, + παλαιός, ancient, + θηρίον, a wild beast: see *Palæotherium*.] A genus of fossil tapiroid mammals from the Eocene of Europe.

propale (prō-pāl'), *v. t.*; pret. and pp. *propaled*, ppr. *propaling*. [= Sp. Pg. *propalar* = It. *propalare*, < LL. *propalare*, make public, divulge, < L. *propalam*, openly, publicly, < *pro*, forth, + *palam*, openly.] To publish; disclose. *Scott.*

propalinal (prō-pal'i-nal), *a.* [< Gr. πρό, before, + πάλιν, back, backward, + *-al*.] Moving forward and backward; relating to forward and backward movement; protracted and retracted, as the lower jaw when it moves forth and back in the act of chewing: as, the *propalinal* movement in mastication.

The *propalinal* mastication is to be distinguished into the proal, from behind forwards, . . . and the palinal, from before backwards. *Cope*, Amer. Nat., XXII. 7.

proparapteral (prō-pa-rap'te-ral), *a.* [< *proparapteron* + *-al*.] Of or pertaining to the proparapteron.

proparapteron (prō-pa-rap'te-ron), *n.*; pl. *proparaptera* (-rä). [NL., < Gr. πρό, before, + NL. *parapteron*.] In *entom.*, the parapteron of the prothoracic segment; the third sclerite of the propleuron.

proparent (prō-pãr'ent), *n.* [< L. *pro*, for, + *paren(t-)s*, parent.] One who stands in the place of a parent. *Imp. Dict.*

proparoxytone (prō-par-ok'si-tōn), *a.* and *n.* [< Gr. προπαροξύτονος (see def.), < πρό, before, + παροξύτονος, paroxytone: see *paroxytone*.] I. *a.* In *Gr. gram.*, having or characterized by the acute accent on the antepenultimate: sometimes applied to words in English and other languages to signify that they have the tonic accent on the antepenultimate.

II. In Gr. *gram.*, a word which has the acute accent on the antepenultimate.

proparoxytone (prō-par-ok'si-tōn), *v. t.*; pret. and pp. *proparoxytoned*, ppr. *proparoxytoning*. [< Gr. προπαροξυτονεῖν, < προπαροξύτονος, proparoxytone: see *proparoxytone*, *a.*] In *Gr. gram.*, to write or pronounce (a word) with the acute accent on the antepenultimate.

proparoxytonic (prō-par-ok-si-ton'ik), *a.* [< *proparoxytone* + *-ic*.] Accented on the antepenult; proparoxytone.

propassion (prō-pash'on), *n.* [< ML. *propassio(n-)*, < L. *pro*, before, + *passio(n-)*, passion: see *passion*.] A feeling antecedent to passion; an inchoate passion; the first stir of passion.

The philosopher calls it [anger] the whetstone to fortitude, a spur intended to set forward virtue. This is simply rather a *propassion* than a passion.
Rev. T. Adams, Works, I. 476.

Not the first motions [of anger] are forbidden: the twinklings of the eye, as the philosophers call them, the *propassions* and sudden and irresistible alterations.
Jer. Taylor, Works (ed. 1835), I. 211.

propatagial (prō-pat-ā-jī'al), *a.* and *n.* [< NL. *propatagialis*, < *propatagium*, q. v.] I. *a.* Of or pertaining to the propatagium; as, a *propatagial* fold of integument; a *propatagial* muscle.

II. *n.* A propatagialis.

propatagialis (prō-pat″ā-ji-ā'lis), *n.*; pl. *propatagiales* (-lēz). [NL.: see *propatagial*.] A tensor muscle of the propatagium, of which there are two, long and short.—**Propatagialis brevis**, the short propatagial muscle, also called *tensor propatagii brevis*.—**Propatagialis longus**, the long propatagial muscle, also called *tensor propatagii longus*.

propatagian (prō-pat-ā-jī'an), *a.* [< *propatagium* + *-an*.] Same as *propatagial*.

The *propatagian* muscles of the swallows.
Science, X. 71.

propatagium (prō-pat-ā-jī'um), *n.*; pl. *propatagia* (-ä). [NL., < Gr. πρό, before, + NL. *patagium*, q. v.] The so-called patagium of a bird's wing: the more precise name of the fold of skin in front of the upper arm and of the forearm which fills up the reëntrance between these parts, and so forms the smooth fore-border of the wing from the shoulder to the carpal angle.

pro patria (prō pā'tri-ä). [L.: *pro*, for; *patriā*, abl. of *patria*, one's native land: see *patria*.] For one's native land.

proped (prō'ped), *n.* [< L. *prō*, for, + *pes* (*ped-*) = E. *foot*.] In *entom.*, a proleg. *Kirby.* See cut under *proleg*.

propedal (prō'ped-al), *a.* [< *proped* + *-al*.] Of the nature of or pertaining to a proped: as, a *propedal* process.

propel (prō-pel'), *v. t.*; pret. and pp. *propelled*, ppr. *propelling*. [< ME. *propellen*, < L. *propellere*, drive or push forward, < *pro*, forward, + *pellere*, drive, push: see *pulse*[1]. Cf. *expel*, *impel*, *repel*, etc.] To drive forward; move or cause to move on; urge or press onward by force.

Ferre awaie *propelle*
Horrend odoure of kychen, bath, gutters.
Palladius, Husbondrie (E. E. T. S.), p. 38.

That overplus of motion would be too feeble and languid to *propel* so vast and ponderous a body with that prodigious velocity. *Bentley.*

The rate of succession may be retarded by insisting upon one object, and *propelled* by dismissing another before its time. *Kames*, Elem. of Criticism, ix.

propellant (prō-pel'ant), *n.* [Erroneous form of *propellent*.] That which propels or drives forward; a propelling agent.

Though not as a military *propellant*, it [guncotton] has been used with great success in sporting cartridges.
The Engineer, LXIX. 117.

In all saloon rifles and pistols the *propellant* is fulminating powder contained in a small copper case.
W. W. Greener, The Gun, p. 368.

propellent (prō-pel'ent), *a.* [< L. *propellen(t-)s*, ppr. of *propellere*, drive or push forward: see *propel*.] Driving forward; propelling.

propeller (prō-pel'ėr), *n.* [< *propel* + *-er*[1].] 1. One who or that which propels; in *marine engin.*, broadly, any contrivance or appliance, as a sail, paddle, oar, paddle-wheel, screw, etc., used for moving vessels floating upon the surface of water, or under the surface; in a more restricted and more generally accepted sense, any instrument or appliance, and especially a screw, used for marine propulsion and actuated by machinery (usually a steam-engine called a *marine engine*) carried by the vessel so propelled. A principle common to all this class of propellers is that a vessel is moved forward by the reaction on the propeller of the water thrown rearward, the propelling machinery being at some part or parts rigidly attached to the ship. The net propelling power is therefore determined by the mass of water thrown rearward multiplied into the square of the velocity with which it is thrown, allowance being made for prejudicial resistances.
2. A boat or vessel driven by a propeller.—3. In *fishing*, a kind of trolling-hook with artificial bait, fitted with wings or flanges to make it spin in the water; a spinning-bait.—**Archimedean, fish-tail, screw**, etc., **propeller**. See the qualifying words.

propeller-engine (prō-pel'ėr-en″jin), *n.* A marine engine for driving a screw propeller.

propeller-mower (prō-pel'ėr-mō″ėr), *n.* Same as *front-cut mower* (which see, under *mower*[1]).

propeller-pump (prō-pel'ėr-pump), *n.* A form of rotary pump with helical blades inclosed in a casing and submerged in the water.

propeller-shaft (prō-pel'ėr-shȧft), *n.* The rigid metallic shaft which carries the propeller of a marine engine.

propeller-well (prǫ-pel'ėr-wel), *n.* A vertical aperture over the screw in the stern of a ship which has a hoisting propeller. When it is desired to proceed under sail, the screw, a two-bladed one, is hoisted off the end of the shaft into the propeller-well, so that it may not retard the ship by dragging in the water.

propeller-wheel (prǫ-pel'ėr-hwēl), *n.* A marine propeller or screw; a screw propeller.

propelment (prǫ-pel'mẹnt), *n.* [< *propel* + *-ment.*] 1. The act of propelling.—2. In clockwork, electrical recording-instruments, calculating-machines, etc., the propelling mechanism; more particularly, an escapement mechanism in which the primary propulsive power is applied to the escapement, and the pallets of the escapement drive the scape-wheel, instead of the latter operating the escapement, as in ordinary clocks.

propend† (prǫ-pend'), *v. i.* [= OF. *porpendre, pourpendre,* < L. *propendere,* hang forward or down, be inclined or disposed, < *pro,* forward, + *pendere,* hang: see *pendent.*] To lean forward; incline; be propense or disposed in favor of anything.

Ne'ertheless,
My spritely brethren, I *propend* to you
In resolution to keep Helen still.
Shak., T. and C., ii. 2. 190.

His eyes are like a balance, apt to *propend* each way.
Burton, Anat. of Mel., p. 454.

propendency† (prǫ-pen'dẹn-si), *n.* [< *propenden(t)* + *-cy.*] 1. A leaning toward anything; inclination; tendency of desire to anything.—2. Attentive deliberation. [Rare.]

An act above the animal actings, which are transient, and admit not of that attention and *propendency* of actions. *Sir M. Hale.*

propendent (prǫ-pen'dẹnt), *a.* [< L. *propenden(t-)s,* ppr. of *propendere,* hang forward or down: see *propend.*] 1†. Inclining forward or toward anything. *South.* (*Imp. Dict.*)—2. In *bot.*, hanging forward and downward. *Paxton.*

propense (prǫ-pens'), *a.* [< L. *propensus,* pp. of *propendere,* hang forward or down, be inclined: see *propend.*] Leaning toward anything, in a moral sense; inclined; disposed, whether to good or evil; prone.

God is more *propense* to rewards than to punishments.
Jer. Taylor, Works (ed. 1835), II. 40.

Our agents shall discern the mind of the parliament towards us, which if it be *propense* and favorable, there may be a fit season to procure . . . countenance of our proceedings. *Winthrop*, Hist. New England, II. 345.

propensely (prǫ-pens'li), *adv.* In a propense manner; with natural tendency.

Others . . . looked upon it, on the contrary, as a real and substantial oath *propensely* formed against Yorick.
Sterne, Tristram Shandy, iv. 27.

propenseness (prǫ-pens'nes), *n.* The state of being propense; natural tendency.

A *propenseness* to diseases in the body.
Donne, Devotions, p. 573.

propension (prǫ-pen'shọn), *n.* [< F. *propension* = Sp. *propension* = Pg. *propensão* = It. *propensione,* < L. *propensio(n-),* inclination, propensity, < *propendere,* pp. *propensus,* hang forward or down: see *propend.*] 1. The state of being propense; propensity.

I ever had a greater zeal to sadness,
A natural *propension.*
Middleton, Massinger, and Rowley, Old Law, iv. 2.

Such by-words as reaction and progress are but the political slang which each side uses to express their aversions and their *propensions.*
Stubbs, Medieval and Modern Hist., p. 18.

2. The state or condition of tending to move in a certain direction.

In natural motions this impetuosity continually increases, by the continued action of the cause—namely, the *propension* of going to the place assigned it by nature.
Whewell.

propensitude† (prǫ-pen'si-tūd), *n.* [< *propense* + *-itude,* as in *attitude,* etc.] Propensity. [Rare.]

T'abandon naturall *propensitudes.*
Marston, What you Will, ii. 1.

propensity (prǫ-pen'si-ti), *n.* [= It. *propensità;* as *propense* + *-ity.*] A bent of mind, natural or acquired; inclination; natural tendency; disposition to anything good or evil, particularly to evil: as, a *propensity* to gamble.

He that learns it [angling] must not onely bring an enquiring, searching, and discerning wit, but he must bring also that patience you talk of, and a love and *propensity* to the art itself.
I. Walton, Complete Angler (rep. of 1653), p. 11.

Let there be but *propensity* and bent of will to religion.
South.

=**Syn.** Bias, *Inclination*, etc. See *bent*1.

propensive† (prǫ-pen'siv), *a.* [< *propense* + *-ive.*] Inclined; disposed; favorable.

This Edward the Thirde, of his *propensive* minde towardes them, united to Yarmouth Kirtleyroad, from it seaven mile vacant.
Nashe, Lenten Stuffe (Harl. Misc., VI. 152). (*Davies.*)

propenyl (prop'e-nil), *n.* [< *prop(ionic)* + *-en-* + *-yl.*] Same as *glyceryl.*

propeptone (prō-pep'tōn), *n.* [< *pro-* + *peptone.*] One of the first products of peptic and tryptic digestion: same as *hemialbumose.*

propeptonuria (prō-pep-tō-nū'ri-ä), *n.* [NL., < *propeptone* + Gr. οὖρον, urine.] The presence of propeptone in the urine.

proper (prop'ėr), *a.* and *n.* [< ME. *propre,* < OF. *propre,* F. *propre* = Sp. Pg. It. *proprio,* < L. *proprius,* special, proper, one's own, personal, also lasting: no certain connections. From L. *proprius* are also ult. *propriety, property, propriate, appropriate, expropriate,* etc.] I. *a.* 1. Special; peculiar; belonging to a species or individual and to nothing else; springing from the peculiar nature of a given species or individual; particularly suited to or befitting one's nature; natural; original.

Vexed I am
Of late with passions of some difference,
Conceptions only *proper* to myself,
Which give some soil perhaps to my behaviours.
Shak., J. C., i. 2. 41.

They have a *proper* saint almost for every peculiar infirmity. *Burton*, Anat. of Mel., p. 274.

But first he casts to change his *proper* shape,
Which else might work him danger or delay.
Milton, P. L., iii. 634.

He knew how to adapt every plant to its *proper* soil.
Addison, Hilpah and Shalum.

A neatness that seemed less the result of care and plan than a something as *proper* to the man as whiteness to the lily. *Lowell*, Cambridge Thirty Years Ago.

2. Belonging to one; one's own.

For if they sholde abyde longe with vs they shuld vndo vs all and ete vs lyke as they do their owne *propre* folke.
R. Eden, tr. of Amerigo Vespucci (First Books on America, ed. Arber, p. xxxiii.).

Here at my house and at my *proper* cost.
Shak., T. N., v. 1. 327.

The waiter's hands that reach
To each his perfect pint of stout,
His *proper* chop to each.
Tennyson, Will Waterproof.

3. Fit; suitable; appropriate.

'Tis *proper* I obey him, but not now.
Shak., Othello, v. 2. 196.

A middle estate is most *proper* to the office of teaching.
Milton, Apology for Smectymnuus.

To sit with her in sight was happiness, and the *proper* happiness for early morning—serene, incomplete, but progressive. *Charlotte Brontë*, Shirley, xxxvi.

Unhappily, you are in a situation in which it is *proper* for you to do what it would be improper in me to endure.
Macaulay, in Trevelyan, I. 185.

The *proper* function of authority is to enlarge, not to contract, our horizon. *Gladstone*, Might of Right, p. 196.

4. According to recognized usage; correct; just: as, a *proper* word; a *proper* expression.

Those parts of nature into which the chaos was divided they signified by dark names which we have expressed in their plain and *proper* terms.
T. Burnet, Theory of the Earth.

No dawn—no dusk—no *proper* time of day!
Hood, November.

5. Rightly so called, named, or described; taken in a strict sense: in this sense usually following the noun: as, the apes *proper* belong to the Old World; no shell-fish are fishes *proper.*

This elevation descended . . . into what might be called the garden *proper.* *Scott*, Waverley, ix.

It is safe to assert that no Government *proper* ever had a provision in its organic law for its own termination.
Lincoln, in Raymond, p. 114.

6. Decent; correct in behavior; respectable; such as should be: as, *proper* conduct.

That is an advertisement to a *proper* maid in Florence, one Diana. *Shak.*, All's Well, iv. 3. 240.

Under the most exciting circumstances, Titia was such an exceedingly *proper* child.
Mrs. D. M. Craik, Christian's Mistake, ii.

7. Well-formed; good-looking; personable; handsome; also, physically strong or active. [Now only prov. Eng.]

There is not among us al one
That dare medle with that potter, man for man.
I felt his handes not long agone. . . .
He is as *propre* a man as ever you medle withal.
Playe of Robyn Hode (Child's Ballads, V. 425).

I am a *proper* fellow of my hands.
Shak., 2 Hen. IV., ii. 2. 72.

A comely, *proper* woman, though not handsome.
Pepys, Diary, I. 98.

And still my delight is in *proper* young men.
Burns, Jolly Beggars.

8. In *her.*, having its natural color or colors: said of any object used as a bearing: thus, a coil of rope *proper* is represented brown, and the spiral lines of the cordage are indicated.—9. In *liturgics*, used only on a particular day or festival, or during a particular octave or season: as, the *proper* introit; a *proper* preface; *proper* psalms.—10. Fine; pretty: said ironically of what is absurd or objectionable.

Talk with a man out at a window! a *proper* saying.
Shak., Much Ado, iv. 1. 312.

Expect. They two help him to a wife.
Mirth. Ay, she is a *proper* piece that such creatures can broke for. *B. Jonson*, Staple of News, i. 2.

11. Becoming; deserved. *Halliwell.* [Prov. Eng.]—**Definition proper,** a definition by means of the genus and specific difference.—**Proper adjunct,** an adjunct which belongs to the whole of a species, and always, and to nothing else.—**Proper chant,** an old name for the key of C major. *Stainer and Barrett.*—**Proper cognition**†. See *cognition.*—**Proper conversion,** in *logic.* See *conversion,* 2.—**Proper difference,** an inseparable accident distinguishing two things.—**Proper exciple.** See *exciple.*—**Proper feud,** in *law,* an original and genuine feud held by pure military service.—**Proper fraction.** See *fraction,* 4.—**Proper jurisdiction.** See *jurisdiction.*—**Proper motion,** in *astron.* See *motion.*—**Proper noun** or **name,** a name given to an individual member of a class, for distinction from other members of the same class, as *Shakspere, Cæsar, London, April, Tuesday, Tray, Eclipse,* etc.: opposed to *common* or *appellative noun.*—**Proper object,** an object that is object to but one subject.—**Proper preface.** See *preface.*—**Proper quantity.** Same as *extensive quantity* (which see, under *extensive*).—**Proper syllogism,** the Ramist name for a syllogism having an individual middle: as, Hobbes was a genius; Hobbes showed no early bent in the direction in which he afterward distinguished himself; hence, it is possible for a man of genius to show no early bent in the direction in which he will afterward distinguish himself. =**Syn.** 1. Particular, individual, specific.—3 and 4. Fitting, befitting, meet, seemly, becoming, legitimate.

II. *n.* 1. That which is set apart to special or individual use. [Rare.] Specifically, in *liturgics*, a special office or special parts of an office appointed for a particular day or time: as, the *proper* of the day; the *proper* of Whitsunday.

2†. A property in the logical sense.

Propers either flow immediately from the essence of the subject . . . or by the mediation of some other property.
Burgersdicius, tr. by a Gentleman.

In proper†, individually; privately.

The princes found they could not have that *in proper* which God made to be common.
Jer. Taylor, Holy Living, iii. 3.

Proper of saints, the variable parts of an office appointed for use on the festival of an individual saint. Compare *Common of the saints,* under *common.*—**Proper of the mass,** the proper of the season for the mass.—**Proper of the season,** in *liturgics*, the variable parts of an office appointed for use on a Sunday or other day (not celebrated as a saint's day), at a certain festival, etc., or during a certain octave or season.

proper (prop'ėr), *adv.* [< *proper, a.*] Properly; very; exceedingly. [Vulgar.]

"Isn't it lovely, Mrs. Flint?" "*Proper* pretty," replied Celyndy. *Jane G. Austen*, The Desmond Hundred, vi.

proper† (prop'ėr), *v. t.* [< OF. *proprier,* < L. *propriare,* take as one's own, appropriate, < *proprius,* one's own: see *proper, a.*] 1. To appropriate. *Palsgrave.* (*Halliwell.*)—2. To make proper; adorn. *Halliwell.*

properate† (prop'ẹ-rāt), *v. i.* [< L. *properatus,* pp. of *properare,* hasten, quicken, < *properus,* quick, speedy, < *pro,* forward, forth, + √ *par-,* make.] To hasten.

And, as last helps, hurle them down on their pates,
Awhile to keep off death, which *properates.*
Vicars, tr. of Virgil. (*Nares.*)

properation† (prop-ẹ-rā'shọn), *n.* [< L. *properatio(n-),* quickness, a hastening, < *properare,* pp. *properatus,* hasten: see *properate.*] The act of properating or hastening; haste; speed.

There is great preparation of this banquet, *properation* to it, participation of it; all is carried with joy and jouisance. *Rev. T. Adams*, Works, I. 216.

properispome (prō-per'i-spōm), *n.* and *a.* [< NL. *properispomenon,* q. v.] I. *n.* In *Gr. gram.*, a word which has the circumflex accent on the penultimate.

II. *a.* In *Gr. gram.*, having or characterized by the circumflex accent on the penultimate.

properispome (prō-per'i-spōm), *v. t.*; pret. and pp. *properispomed,* ppr. *properispoming.* [< *properispome, n.*] In *Gr. gram.*, to write or pronounce with the circumflex accent on the penultimate.

properispomenon (prō-per-i-spom'e-non), *n.* [NL., < Gr. προπερισπώμενον, a word with the circumflex accent on the penult, neut. of προπερισπώμενος, ppr. of προπερισπᾶν, draw around before, < πρό, before, + περισπᾶν, draw around, strip off: see *perispomenon.*] Same as *properispome.*

properistoma (prō-pe-ris'tǫ-mä), *n.*; pl. *properistomata* (prō-per-i-stō'mạ-tä). [NL., < L. *pro,* before, + NL. *peristoma:* see *peristome.*]

The lip of the primitive mouth of a gastrula. Also *properistome*.

At the thickened edges of the gastrula, the primitive . . . *properistoma*, the endoderm and the exoderm pass into each other. *Haeckel*, Evol. Anim. (trans.), I. 220.

properistomal (prō-per'i-stō-mal), *a.* [< *properistoma* + *-al*.] Pertaining to a properistoma.

properistome (prō-per'i-stōm), *n.* [< NL. *properistoma*, q. v.] Same as *properistoma*.

properly (prop'ėr-li), *adv.* [< ME. *properly*, *proprely*, *propreliche*; < *proper* + *-ly*[2].] 1†. In one's own manner, speech, action, etc.

Ne though I speke here wordes *properly*.
Chaucer, Gen. Prol. to C. T., l. 729.

2. In a proper manner; with propriety; fitly; suitably; correctly: as, a word *properly* applied; a dress *properly* adjusted.

"Parfay," quath Pacience, "*propreliche* to telle
In English, hit is ful harde."
Piers Plowman (C), xvii. 119.

Ignorance of forms cannot *properly* be styled ill manners.
Swift, Good Manners.

3. To a high degree; quite; entirely; exceedingly; extremely. [Colloq.]

All which I did assure my lord was most *properly* false, and nothing like it true. *Pepys*, Diary, July 14, 1664.

Father . . . gave me a wipe . . . on the side of my face that knocked me over and hurt me *properly*.
Haliburton, Sam Slick in England, xxvi. (*Bartlett*.)

Abbreviated *prop*.

Properly speaking. (*a*) In the correct or strict sense. (*b*) Speaking without qualification.

properness (prop'ėr-nes), *n.* [< *proper* + *-ness*.] The character of being proper, in any sense of that word.

'Slight, sir! yonder is a lady veil'd,
For *properness* beyond comparison,
And, sure, her face is like the rest; we'll see 't.
Fletcher (and another) Love's Pilgrimage, iv. 1.

propertied (prop'ėr-tid), *a.* [< *property* + *-ed*[2].] Possessed of property.

An institution devoted . . . to the *propertied* and satisfied classes generally.
M. Arnold, Last Essays, Church of England.

The loyal and *propertied* part of the community.
Gladstone, Nineteenth Century, XXII. 458.

property (prop'ėr-ti), *n.*; pl. *properties* (-tiz). [< ME. *propertee*, *properte*, *proprete*, *propirte*, *propurte*, < OF. *properte*, propriety, fitness, property, < L. *proprieta(t-)s*, a peculiarity, peculiar nature or quality, right or fact of possession, property, < *proprius*, special, particular, one's own: see *proper*. Cf. *propriety*, a doublet of *property*.] 1. Any character always present in an individual or a class; an essential attribute; a peculiar quality; loosely, any quality or characteristic.

It is the *propertie* of a wyse buylder to vse such tooles as the woorke requireth.
R. Eden (First Books on America, ed. Arber, p. 57).

Delectable and pleasant conversation, whose *property* is to move a kindly delight. *B. Jonson*, Cynthia's Revels, v. 3.

But Thou art the same Lord, Whose *property* is always to have mercy.
Book of Common Prayer, Communion Office, Prayer of [Humble Access.

Property is correctly a synonym for peculiar quality; but it is frequently used as co-extensive with quality in general. *Sir W. Hamilton*.

Strictly speaking, we ought to confine the term *property* to Bodies, not to Matter; for an abstraction can have no *properties*; and it is the bodies which severally manifest the qualities.
G. H. Lewes, Probs. of Life and Mind, II. iv. § 42.

Soft iron loses almost all magnetic *properties* at a red heat. *Atkinson*, tr. of Mascart and Joubert, I. 384.

2. In *logic*, a character which belongs to the whole of a species, and to nothing else, but not to the essence or definition.

Propretie is a naturall promenesse and maner of dooyng whiche agreeth to one kinde and to the same onely and that evermore. *Wilson*, Rule of Reason (1551).

What is *propertie?* It is a natural inclination or *property*, incident to one special kind; which is to be understood foure manner of waies. First, it is called proprium, which is proper to one onely kind, as to be a poet or musician is proper to man, but not to every man: secondly, it is called proper that belongeth to all the kind, but not to that kind alone: thirdly, it is said to be proper when it belongeth to one onely kind and to all that kind, but yet not alwayes, as to be bare-headed or bald is proper to man in old age, but yet not alwaies: fourthly, it is said to be proper, or rather most proper, which is incident to one kind alone, to all that kind, and alwaies, as to have a natural aptnesse to laugh or to speake is proper to man onely, to every man, and alwaies, and therefore this kind of *property* is said to be convertible with the kind whereunto it belongeth, as whatsoever hath naturally power to speake or laugh the same is man, and whatsoever is man the same hath power to speake or laugh. *Blundeville*, Arte of Logicke, i. 4.

3. The right to the use or enjoyment or the beneficial right of disposal of anything that can be the subject of ownership; ownership; estate; especially, ownership of tangible things. In the broader sense, a right of action is *property*; so is a mere right to use or possess. If it be a right as against the general owner, but is usually termed *special property*, to distinguish it from the right of the general owner, which is termed the *general property*. The *entire property* is the exclusive right of possessing, enjoying, and disposing of a thing. See *bailment*, and *lien*[2], 1.

Ne truste no wight to finden in Fortune
Ay *properte*; hir giftes ben comune.
Chaucer, Troilus, iv. 392.

Jack has an unresisting good nature, which makes him incapable of having a *property* in any thing.
Steele, Spectator, No. 82.

The idea of *property* being a right to any thing.
Locke, Human Understanding, IV. iii. 18.

Property . . . denotes in every state of society the largest powers of exclusive use or exclusive control over things (and sometimes, unfortunately, over persons) which the law accords, or which custom, in that state of society, recognizes. *J. S. Mill*, Socialism, p. 129.

4. A thing or things subject to ownership; anything that may be exclusively possessed and enjoyed; chattels and land; possessions.

The King has also appropriated the Queen's jewels to himself, and conceives that they are his undoubted private *property*. *Greville*, Memoirs, Jan. 8, 1823.

It was the misfortune of my friend . . . to have embarked his *property* in large speculations.
Irving, Sketch-Book, p. 36.

English political economy and English popular notions are very deeply and extensively pervaded by the assumption that all *property* has been acquired through an original transaction of purchase, and that, whatever be the disadvantages of the form it takes, they were allowed for in the consideration for the original sale.
Maine, Early Law and Custom, p. 325.

5. A thing required for some peculiar or specific use, as a tool; an accessory; specifically, in theaters, a stage requisite, as any article of costume or furniture, or other appointment, necessary to be produced in a scene (in this specific sense used also attributively).

This devil Photinus
Employs me as a *property*, and, grown useless,
Will shake me off again.
Fletcher (and another), False One, v. 3.

To hire some of our *properties*: as a sceptre and crown for Jove; and a caduceus for Mercury.
B. *Jonson*, Poetaster, iv. 2.

Not to be of any Use or Consequence in the World as to your self, but merely as a *Property* to others.
Steele, Tender Husband, i. 1.

I had seen many rehearsals, and sometimes got a peep at the play, having been taken on "in arms" as a *property* child in groups of happy peasantry.
J. Jefferson, Autobiog., i.

6†. Propriety.

Our poets excel in grandity and gravity, smoothness and *property*, in quickness and briefness. *Camden*.

7. Individuality; that which constitutes an individual. [Rare.]

Property was thus appalled
That the self was not the same.
Shak., Phœnix and Turtle, l. 37.

8. A cloak or disguise. *Halliwell*. [Prov. Eng.]

Hadst thou so cheap opinion of my birth,
My breeding, or my fortunes, that none else
Could serve for *property* of your lust but I?
Shirley, Wedding, i. 3.

Anharmonic, community, corporeal, descriptive property. See the qualifying words.—**Cotes's properties of the circle.** See *circle*.—**De Moivre's property of the circle.** See *circle*.—**Discussion of property.** See *discussion*.—**Focal, individual, etc., property.** See the adjectives.—**Mixed subjects of property.** See *mixed*[1].—**Movable property.** Same as *personal property*.—**Perishable, personal, private property.** See the adjectives.—**Property in action,** ownership without possession, but with the present right of possession enforceable by action. In the broadest sense the term may include any right of action for money or other property. Compare *chose in action*, under *chose*[2].—**Property qualification.** See *qualification*.—**Qualified property,** a limited right of ownership. (*a*) Such right as a man has in wild animals which he has reclaimed. Also called *special property*. (*b*) Such right as a bailee has in the chattel transferred to him by the bailment.—**Real property.** See *real*.—**Special property.** Same as *qualified property* (*a*).=**Syn. 1.** *Attribute, Characteristic*, etc. See *quality*.—**4.** *Property, Effects, Chattels, Goods, Wares, Commodities, Merchandise*, possessions, wealth. *Property* is the general word for those material things which are one's own, whether for sale or not. *Effects* applies to personal property, viewed as including the things even of least value. *Chattels* comprises every kind of property except freehold. (See the definitions of the classes *real* and *personal*, under *chattel*.) *Goods* includes a merchant's stock-in-trade, or one's movable property of any sort. *Wares* are manufactured articles, especially of the heavier sort, as earthenware, woodenware. *Commodities* are such movable articles as are necessities of life, and have a money value. *Merchandise* is the general word for articles of trade.

property† (prop'ėr-ti), *v. t.* [< *property*, *n.*] 1. To invest with (certain) properties or qualities.

His voice was *propertied*
As all the tuned spheres. *Shak.*, A. and C., v. 2. 83.

2. To make a property or tool of; appropriate.

I am too high-born to be *propertied*,
To be a secondary at control,
Or useful serving-man and instrument.
Shak., K. John, v. 2. 79.

property-man (prop'ėr-ti-man), *n.* A person employed in a theater and having the charge of stage properties.

At the death of Peer, the *property man* at this theatre, the Guardian extracted much fun from a catalogue of articles under his care.
Ashton, Social Life in Reign of Queen Anne, II. 16.

property-master (prop'ėr-ti-mås'tėr), *n.* In a theater, a person who superintends the making, storage, and use of stage properties; a head property-man.

While the *property-master* and his men were fashioning the god Talepulka, the scenic artist had sketched and modelled the scenery of the opera.
Scribner's Mag., IV. 440.

property-plot (prop'ėr-ti-plot), *n.* In a theater, a list of the accessories required in the production of a play.

property-room (prop'ėr-ti-röm), *n.* The room in a theater in which the stage properties are kept.

property-tax (prop'ėr-ti-taks), *n.* A direct tax imposed on the property of individuals, amounting to a certain percentage on the estimated value of their property.

prophane†, **prophanely**†, etc. Obsolete spellings of *profane*, etc.

prophasis (prof'ạ-sis), *n.* [NL., < Gr. πρόφασις, that which appears, a motive, a pretext, < προφαίνειν, show forth, manifest, < πρό, forth, + φαίνειν, show, φαίνεσθαι, appear: see *phase*.] In *med.*, prognosis; foreknowledge of the course of a disease.

prophecy (prof'e-si), *n.*; pl. *prophecies* (-siz). [< ME. *prophecy*, *prophecie*, *profecye*, < OF. *prophecie*, *prophetie*, F. *prophétie* = Sp. *profecia* = Pg. *prophecia* = It. *profezia*, < LL. *prophetia* (ML. also *prophecia*), < Gr. προφητεία, the gift of interpreting the will of the gods, in N. T. inspired discourse, prediction (see def. 2), < προφητεύειν, prophesy, predict, < προφήτης, a prophet: see *prophet*.] 1. Inspired discourse; specifically, in *Christian theol.*, discourse flowing from the revelation and impulse of the Holy Spirit.

Sone a Iew stode vp in hy,
And thus he said thurgh *prophecy*.
Holy Rood (E. E. T. S.), p. 83.

The rest of the acts of Solomon, . . . are they not written in the book of Nathan the prophet, and in the *prophecy* of Ahijah? 2 Chron. ix. 29.

For the *prophecy* came not in old time by the will of man, but holy men of God spake as they were moved by the Holy Ghost. 2 Pet. i. 21.

2. A prediction; declaration of something to come; especially, a foretelling under divine inspiration.

In them is fulfilled the *prophecy* of Esaias. Mat. xiii. 14.

A *prophecy*, which says that G
Of Edward's heirs the murderer shall be.
Shak., Rich. III., i. 1. 39.

3†. Interpretation of Scripture; religious exhortation or instruction.

The words of king Lemuel, the *prophecy* that his mother taught him. Prov. xxxi. 1.

Mr. Wilson, praying and exhorting the congregation to love, &c., commended to them the exercise of *prophecy* in his absence. *Winthrop*, Hist. New England, I. 60.

4. In *liturgics*: (*a*) A lection from the Old Testament, especially a eucharistic or missal lection; also, a lection in the Mozarabic daily office, and in the Greek Church at sabbath vespers on certain festivals. (*b*) The canticle Benedictus (Luke i. 68–79) as sung in the Gallican liturgy, afterward displaced by the Gloria in Excelsis.=**Syn. 1.** *Divination*, etc. See *prediction*.

prophecy-monger (prof'e-si-mung'gėr), *n.* One who deals in prophecies: so called in contempt.

The English [are] observed by forrainers to be the greatest *prophecy-mongers*, and, whilst the Devil knows their diet, they shall never want a dish to please the palate.
Fuller, Ch. Hist., IV. ii. 46. (*Davies*.)

prophesier (prof'e-si-ėr), *n.* [< *prophesy* + *-er*[1].] One who prophesies or predicts.

Saynt Dauyd of Wales, the great archebishop of Mencuia, had many *prophesiers* and manye angels sent afore to geue warning of his comming . . . yeares ere he was borne.
Bp. Bale, English Votaries, i.

The counterfeit module has deceived me, like a double-meaning *prophesier*. *Shak.*, All's Well, iv. 3. 115.

prophesy (prof'e-si), *v.*; pret. and pp. *prophesied*, ppr. *prophesying*. [Formerly also *prophecy*, < late ME. *prophecie*, *proficy*; < *prophecy*, *n*. The orig. long final syllable, having retained its accent, though now secondary, has undergone the usual change of long accented ME. *i*, as in *pacify*, *multiply*, etc.] **I.** *trans.* To predict; foretell; foreshow. See *prophet.*

> Methought thy very gait did *prophesy*
> A royal nobleness. *Shak.*, Lear, v. 3. 176.

Amongst many other dignities which this letter hath by being received and seen by you, it is not the least that it was *prophesied* of before it was born. *Donne*, Letters, xxv.

One of his [Clive's] masters . . . was sagacious enough to *prophesy* that the idle lad would make a great figure in the world. *Macaulay*, Lord Clive.

> For by the warning of the Holy Ghost
> I *prophesy* that I shall die to-night.
> *Tennyson*, St. Simeon Stylites.

II. *intrans.* **1.** To speak by divine inspiration; utter or tell as prophet.

Again he said unto me, *Prophesy* upon these bones, and say unto them, O ye dry bones, hear the word of the Lord. Ezek. xxxvii. 4.

The prophets . . . *prophesied* of the grace that should come unto you. 1 Pet. i. 10.

2. To utter predictions; foretell future events.

Prophesy not in the name of the Lord, that thou die not by our hand. Jer. xi. 21.

3†. To interpret or explain Scripture or religious subjects; preach; exhort.

In the afternoon, Mr. Roger Williams (according to their custom) propounded a question, to which the pastor, Mr. Smith, spake briefly; then Mr. Williams *prophesied*. *Winthrop*, Hist. New England, I. 109.

They also allowed greater liberty to *prophesy* than those before them; for they admitted any member to speak and pray as well as their pastor. *Penn*, Rise and Progress of Quakers, i.

prophesying (prof'e-si-ing), *n.* [Verbal n. of *prophesy, v.*] **1†.** Preaching; religious exhortation; the act of speaking on religious subjects.

The Liberty of *Prophesying*. [Title.] *Jer. Taylor.*

The Puritans maintained frequent religious exercises, in which texts of Scripture were interpreted or discussed, one speaking to the subject after another, in an orderly method. This was called *prophesying*, in reference to 1 Corin. xiv. 31: Ye may all prophesy, that all may learn, and all may be comforted. *Neal*, in New England's Memorial, p. 171, note.

2. The act of foretelling.

prophet (prof'et), *n.* [< ME. *prophete*, *profett*, *profite*, < OF. *prophete*, *profete*, F. *prophète* = Pr. Pg. *propheta* = Sp. It. *profeta* = OFries. *propheta* = D. *profeet* = MLG. *prophēte* = MHG. *prophēte*, G. *prophet* = Sw. Dan. *profet*, < LL. *propheta*, *prophetes* = Goth. *praufētēs*, *praufētus*, < Gr. προφήτης, Doric προφάτης, one who speaks for a god, an interpreter (as Tiresias was of Zeus, Orpheus of Bacchus, Apollo of Zeus, the Pythia of Apollo), expounder (as those who interpreted the words of the inspired seers), proclaimer, harbinger (as the bowl is of mirth, or the cicada of summer), in the Septuagint an interpreter, spokesman, usually an inspired prophet, also a revealer of the future, in N. T. and eccl. an interpreter of Scripture, a preacher, < προφάναι, say before or beforehand, < πρό, before, in public, + φάναι, speak, say: see *fable*, *fame*[1], *fate*.] **1.** One who speaks by a divine inspiration as the interpreter through whom a divinity declares himself. In the times of the Old Testament there was an order of prophets, for the duties of whose office men were trained in colleges called *schools of the prophets*. The members of these schools acted as public religious teachers, and the prophets in the stricter sense (inspired teachers) generally belonged to this order. In the New Testament, Christian prophets were recognized in the church as possessing a charism distinct from that of mere teachers, and as uttering special revelations and predictions. They are often mentioned with apostles, and next after them in order.

> Ihesus that sprong of Iesse roote,
> As us hath prechid thi *prophete*.
> *Hymns to Virgin*, etc. (E. E. T. S.), p. 12.

The word *prophet* (προφήτης) was derived in the first instance from the interpreters of the will of the gods (see Pindar, N., i. 91); later and especially it was applied to those who expounded the unintelligible oracles of the Pythoness of Delphi, or the rustling of the leaves of Dodona. In a metaphorical sense it was used of poets, as of interpreters of the gods or Muses. It was then adopted by the Septuagint as the best equivalent of the *nabi* or *prophet* of the Old Testament. . . . In all these cases (Acts ii. 17, 18; xiii. 1; xv. 32; Rev. i. 3; xi. 3, 6, 10, 18; xvi. 6; xviii. 20, 24; xix. 10; xxii. 6, 7, 9, 10, 18), in the New Testament as in the Old, and it may be added in the Koran, the prominent idea is not that of prediction, but of delivering inspired messages of warning, exhortation, and instruction; building up, exhorting, and comforting; convincing, judging, and making manifest the secrets of the heart (1 Cor. xiv. 3, 24, 25). The ancient classical and Hebrew sense prevails everywhere. Epimenides and Mahomet on the one hand, Elijah and Paul on the other, are called *prophets*, not because they foretold the future, but because they enlightened the present. *A. P. Stanley*, Com. on Corinthians, p. 243.

2. One who foretells future events; a predicter; a foreteller; especially, a person inspired to announce future events.

As he spake by the mouth of his holy *prophets*, which have been since the world began: That we should be saved from our enemies, and from the hand of all that hate us. Luke i. 70.

Polybius was of the best sort of *prophets*, who predict from natural causes those events which must naturally proceed from them. *Dryden*, Character of Polybius.

> I do rest
> A *prophet* certain of my prophecy,
> That never shadow of mistrust can cross
> Between us. *Tennyson*, Geraint.

3. An orthopterous insect of the family *Mantidæ*. [Local, U. S.]—**French prophets**, a name sometimes given in England to the Camisards.—**Major prophets**, Isaiah, Jeremiah, Ezekiel, and Daniel; also, the books of their prophecies in the Old Testament.—**Minor prophets**, the writers of the Old Testament from Hosea to Malachi inclusive; also, their books. The distinction between *major* and *minor* relates to the size of the books.—**School of the prophets**, among the ancient Jews, a school or college in which young men were educated and qualified to be public teachers. One elderly or leading prophet presided over them, called their *father* or *master*; hence the students were called *sons of the prophets*. Their chief subject of study was the law and its interpretation, but music and sacred poetry were subsidiary branches of instruction.—**The Prophets**, those books of the Old Testament which are largely composed of prophecies, or which were written or compiled by members of the order of prophets. The ancient Jews sometimes divided the Old Testament into the Law (Pentateuch) and the Prophets, and sometimes (as still in Hebrew Bibles) into Law, Prophets, and Hagiographa. In Hebrew Bibles the *Former Prophets* are Joshua, Judges, I. and II. Samuel, and I. and II. Kings; the *Latter Prophets* are the books from Isaiah to Malachi inclusive, with the exception of Lamentations and Daniel, which are placed in the Hagiographa.

On these two commandments hang all the law and *the prophets*. Mat. xxii. 40.

=**Syn.** 1. *Prophet, Seer, Soothsayer.* A *prophet* is properly one who discloses or speaks forth to others the will of God; a *seer* is one who has himself learned God's will by a vision. Both titles were applied in the Old Testament to the same class of men, but at different times. The extra-Biblical uses of the words correspond to the Biblical. The word *prophet* is sometimes used in the Bible of a candidate for the prophetic office, or of an inspired preacher or interpreter. *Soothsayer*, as used in the Bible, implies imposture, and in other literature its standing is little better.

Beforetime, in Israel, when a man went to enquire of God, thus he spake, Come, and let us go to the *seer*: for he that is now called a *Prophet* was beforetime called a *Seer*. 1 Sam. ix. 9.

They had with them inspired men, *Prophets*, and it were not sober to say they did ought of moment without divine intimation. *Milton*, Church-Government, i. 2.

The secret which the king hath demanded cannot . . . the *soothsayers* shew unto the king. Dan. ii. 27.

prophet† (prof'et), *v. i.* [< *prophet*, *n.*] To prophesy. [Rare.]

> Nor *propheting* Helenus, when he foretold dangerous hard haps,
> Forspake this burial mourning.
> *Stanihurst*, Æneid, iii. 727. (*Davies.*)

prophetet, *n.* A Middle English form of *profit.*

prophetess (prof'et-es), *n.* [< F. *prophétesse* = Pg. *prophetiza* = Sp. *profetisa* = It. *profetessa*, < LL. *prophetissa*, a prophetess, < *propheta*, a prophet: see *prophet.*] A female prophet; a woman who speaks with inspiration or foretells future events.

> Ourself have often tried
> Valkyrian hymns, or into rhythm have dash'd
> The passion of the *prophetess*.
> *Tennyson*, Princess, iv.

prophet-flower (prof'et-flou"ėr), *n.* A boraginaceous herb, *Arnebia Griffithii*, found in northwest India, etc., and somewhat cultivated for its interesting flowers. The corolla is funnel-shaped, of a bright primrose-yellow, the limb at opening marked with five dark spots which fade away as the day advances. The flowers are racemed, the plant hairy. The name is of Mussulman origin, probably suggested by the somewhat crescent-shaped spots.

prophethood (prof'et-hụd), *n.* [< *prophet* + *-hood.*] The quality or condition, or the position or office, of a prophet.

His environment and rural *prophethood* has hurt him [Wordsworth] much. *Carlyle*, in Froude, I. 27.

prophetic (prọ-fet'ik), *a.* [< F. *prophétique* = Pg. *prophetico* = Sp. *profético* = It. *profetico* (cf. D. *profetisch* = G. *prophetisch* = Sw. Dan. *profetisk*), < LL. *propheticus*, < Gr. προφητικός, pertaining to a prophet or to prophecy, < προφήτης, a prophet: see *prophet.*] **1.** Pertaining or relating to a prophet or to prophecy; having the character of prophecy; containing prophecy: as, *prophetic* writings.

> Till old experience do attain
> To something like *prophetick* strain.
> *Milton*, Il Penseroso, l. 174.

It was with something of quite true *prophetic* fervour that each of these [Byron and Shelley] . . . denounced the hypocrisies which they believed they saw around them. *J. C. Shairp*, Aspects of Poetry, p. 119.

2. Presageful; predictive: with *of* before the thing foretold.

> And fears are oft *prophetic of* the event.
> *Dryden*, tr. of Ovid's Metamorph., x. 46.

3. Anticipative; having or tending to a presentiment or an intuitive discernment of the future.

> O my *prophetic* soul! my uncle!
> *Shak.*, Hamlet, i. 5. 40.

prophetical (prọ-fet'i-kạl), *a.* [< *prophetic* + *-al.*] Same as *prophetic.*

God hath endued us . . . with the heavenly support of *prophetical* revelation, which doth open those hidden mysteries that reason could never have been able to find out. *Hooker*, Eccles. Polity, i. 15.

propheticality (prọ-fet-i-kal'ị-ti), *n.* [< *prophetical* + *-i-ty.*] Propheticalness. *Coleridge.* [Rare.]

prophetically (prọ-fet'i-kạl-i), *adv.* [< *prophetical* + *-ly*[2].] In a prophetic manner; by way of prediction; in the manner of prophecy.

They *prophetically* did fore-signify all such sects to be avoided. *Jer. Taylor*, Works (ed. 1835), I. 883.

propheticalness (prọ-fet'i-kạl-nes), *n.* [< *prophetical* + *-ness.*] The character of being prophetical. [Rare.]

prophetism (prof'et-izm), *n.* [< *prophet* + *-ism.*] The system, practice, or doctrine of inspired teaching. *The American*, XIII. 59.

prophetize† (prof'et-īz), *v. i.* [< F. *prophétiser* = Sp. *profetizar* = Pg. *prophetizar* = It. *profetizzare*, < LL. *prophetizare*, < Gr. προφητίζειν, be a prophet, prophesy, < προφήτης, a prophet: see *prophet.*] To utter predictions; prophesy.

> Nor, thrild with bodkins, raues in frantik-wise,
> And in a furie seems to *prophetize*.
> *Sylvester*, tr. of Du Bartas's Weeks, ii., The Schisme.

> Nature . . . so doth warning send
> By *prophetizing* dreams. *Daniel*, Civil Wars, iii.

prophetship (prof'et-ship), *n.* [< *prophet* + *-ship.*] Same as *prophethood.*

To deny Mahomet's *prophetship* would excite a violent antagonism. *B. Taylor*, Lands of the Saracen, p. 24.

prophitet, *n.* A Middle English form of *profit.*

prophloëm (prō-flō'em), *n.* [< *pro-* + *phloëm.*] A tissue in the sporophore of mosses, resembling the phloëm of ordinary stems in microscopic structure, and corresponding to it in position.

prophoric† (prọ-for'ik), *a.* [< Gr. προφορικός, pertaining to utterance, < προφορά, a bringing forward, utterance, < προφέρειν, bring forward, < πρό, forward, + φέρειν, bring, bear, = E. *bear*[1].] Enunciative. *Wright.*

prophragma (prō-frag'mạ̈), *n.*; pl. *prophragmata* (-ma-tạ̈). [< Gr. πρό, before, + φράγμα, fence, partition: see *phragma.*] In *entom.*, a transverse internal plate which, in many *Coleoptera*, descends from the anterior margin of the mesoscutellum, between the mesothorax and the metathorax, serving for the attachment of internal organs. It probably corresponds to the mesoscutum.

prophylactic (prof-i-lak'tik), *a.* and *n.* [= F. *prophylactique* = Sp. *profiláctico* = Pg. *prophylactico*, < Gr. προφυλακτικός, pertaining to guarding, precautionary, < προφυλάσσειν, keep guard before, < πρό, before, + φυλάσσειν, Attic φυλάττειν, watch, guard: see *phylactery.*] **I.** *a.* In *med.*, preventive; defending from disease: as, *prophylactic* doses of quinine.

His ears had needed no *prophylactic* wax to pass the Sirens' isle. *Lowell*, Fireside Travels, p. 77.

Notwithstanding the directions issued for *prophylactic* treatment, and the system of domiciliary visits, the cholera carried off a greater number than before. *H. Spencer*, Social Statics, p. 425.

II. *n.* **1.** Anything, as a medicine, which defends against disease; a preventive of disease.

Inventive persons have from time to time thought that they had secured a sure cure, if not an unfailing *prophylactic* [for consumption]. *Pop. Sci. Mo.*, XXVIII. 669.

2. Same as *prophylaxis.*

Medicine is distributed into *prophylactick*, or the art of preserving health, and therapeutick, or the art of restoring health. *Watts*, Logic, I. vi. § 10.

prophylactical (prof-i-lak'ti-kạl), *a.* [< *prophylactic* + *-al.*] Same as *prophylactic.*

Dieteticall and *prophylacticall* receipts of wholesome caution. *Bp. Hall*, Sermon preached to the Lords.

prophylaxis (prof-i-lak'sis), *n.* [NL., < Gr. as if *προφύλαξις, < προφυλάσσειν, keep guard before: see *prophylactic.*] In *med.*, the guarding against the attack of some disease. Also *prophylactic*, *prophylaxy.*

The germs do not appear to be very tenacious of life, so that an efficient *prophylaxis* can be readily exercised. *Science*, III. 557.

prophylaxy (prof'i-lak-si), *n.* [< NL. *prophylaxis*, q. v.] Same as *prophylaxis.*

The discussion on the *prophylaxy* of tuberculosis was then resumed. *Lancet*, No. 3465, p. 218.

prophyllum (prō-fil'um), *n.* [< Gr. πρό, before, + φύλλον, leaf.] A primary leaf; one of the first leaves of a branch or axis.

propice†, *a.* [Also *propise*; < OF. *propice*, < L. *propitius*, propitious: see *propitious*.] Propitious.

> Of that mater . . . I wyll traicte more amply in a place more *propise* for that purpose. *Sir T. Elyot*, The Governour, ii. 7.

> [The wind] veered to the South and South South West, so apt and *propice* for our journey. *Exped. in Scotland* (Arber's Eng. Garner, I. 115).

> This place [where the Cherubim were in the Tabernacle] was called the Propitiatory, because in that place the Lord God did manifest him selfe more *propise* and neere. *Guevara*, Letters (tr. by Hellowes, 1577), p. 352.

propination (prop-i-nā'shon), *n.* [= OF. *propination*, absorption, = Pg. *propinação*, < L. *propinatio(n-)*, a drinking to one's health, < *propinare*, pp. *propinatus*, drink to one's health: see *propine*.] The act of drinking with another, or together, in fellowship; the act of drinking a pledge or a health.

> This *propination* was carried about towards the right-hand, where the superiour quality of some of the guests did not oblige them to alter that method. *Abp. Potter*, Antiq. of Greece, iv. 20.

propine (prọ-pīn'), *v. t.*; pret. and pp. *propined*, ppr. *propining*. [< OF. *propiner* = Sp. Pg. *propinar* = It. *propinare*, < L. *propinare*, drink to one's health, give one to drink, give to eat, give, present, offer, furnish, < Gr. προπίνειν, drink before another or to his health, < πρό, before, + πίνειν, drink: see *potation*.] **1.** To pledge in drinking; drink to; wish for in behalf of some one while drinking to him.

> The lovely sorceress mixed, and to the prince
> Health, joy, and peace *propined*.
> *C. Smart*, The Hop-Garden.

2†. To present; offer; guarantee.

> It [the doctrine of Jesus Christ] *propines* to us the noblest, the highest, and the bravest pleasures of the world. *Jer. Taylor*, Moral Demonstration of the Christian Religion (1660).

> The priests of a neighbouring convent, in expectation of the ample donation, or soul-scat, which Cedric had *propined*, attended upon the [funeral] car. *Scott*, Ivanhoe, xxxii.

> Unless we would *propine* both ourselves and our cause unto open and just derision. *Fotherby*, Atheomastix, p. 11. (*Latham*.)

propine† (prọ-pīn'), *n.* [< OF. *propine*, drink-money, present; from the verb: see *propine*, *v.*] **1.** Money given as drink-money, or any gift, favor, or loving pledge.

> For no rewarde, gyft, nor *propyne*,
> Thole none of thir twois causis tyne.
> *Lauder*, Dewtie of Kyngis (E. E. T. S.), l. 499.

> And a' that he gied me to my *propine*
> Was a pair of green gloves and a gay gold ring.
> *Bothwell* (Child's Ballads, I. 160).

> There was never sic a braw *propine* as this sent to a yerl. *Scott*, Abbot, xxvii.

2. The power of giving.

> And if I were thine, and in thy *propine*,
> O what wad ye do to me?
> *Lady Anne* (Child's Ballads, II. 264).

propinquate (prọ-ping'kwāt), *v. i.*; pret. and pp. *propinquated*, ppr. *propinquating*. [< L. *propinquatus*, pp. of *propinquare*, bring near, hasten, < *propinquus*, near: see *propinquity*. Cf. *appropinque*.] To approach; be near. *Imp. Dict.*

propinque (prọ-pingk'), *a.* [= Sp. *propincuo* = Pg. It. *propinquo*, < L. *propinquus*, near, < *prope*, near.] Near; contiguous. *Swan*, Speculum Mundi, p. 81. (*Latham*.)

propinquity (prọ-ping'kwi-ti), *n.* [< ME. *propinquitee*, < OF. *propinquite* = Sp. *propincuidad* = Pg. *propinquidade* = It. *propinquità*, < L. *propinquita(t-)s*, vicinity, nearness, < *propinquus*, near: see *propinquate*.] **1.** Nearness in place; neighborhood.

> It was delightful to see . . . his pure joy in her *propinquity*; he asked nothing, sought nothing, save to be near the beloved object. *Hawthorne*, Marble Faun, ix.

2. Nearness in time.

> Thereby was declared the *propinquity* of their desolations, and that their tranquillity was of no longer duration than those soon decaying fruits of summer. *Sir T. Browne*.

3. Nearness of blood; kindred.

> Here I disclaim all my paternal care,
> *Propinquity*, and property of blood.
> *Shak.*, Lear, i. 1. 116.

> They may love other individuals far better than their relatives, . . . but yet, in view of death, the strong prejudice of *propinquity* revives, and impels the testator to send down his estate in the line marked out by custom so immemorial that it looks like nature. *Hawthorne*, Seven Gables, i.

propiolic (prō-pi-ol'ik), *a.* [< *propi(onic)* + *-ol* + *-ic*.] Noting an acid derived from a monovalent radical C_3H_3.—**Propiolic acid**, the abbreviated commercial name for ortho-nitrophenyl-propiolic acid, one of the coal-tar derivatives, which, although colorless in itself, may be converted in calico-printing into indigo blue on the fiber. It is a very close approach both chemically and physically to natural indigo. In its application borax is used as a solvent, xanthate of soda as a reducing agent, and starch as a thickening.

propionate (prō'pi-ọ-nāt), *n.* [< *propionic* + *-ate*[1].] In *chem.*, a compound of propionic acid and a base. See *propionic*.

propionic (prō-pi-on'ik), *a.* [< Gr. πρῶ(τος), first, + πίων, fat, + *-ic*.] Noting an acid ($C_3H_6O_2$), the third substance in the monatomic fatty series.—**Propionic acid**, a colorless liquid, with a pungent odor like that of acetic acid, found in perspiration, the juices of the stomach, the blossoms of milfoil, etc. It is monobasic, forming salts called *propionates*, which have a fatty feel, whence the name.

propise†, *a.* See *propice*.

Propithecus (prō-pi-thē'kus), *n.* [NL. (Bennett, 1832), < Gr. πρό, before, + πίθηκος, an ape: see *Pithecus*.] A genus of lemuroid animals of Madagascar, of the family *Lemuridæ* and subfamily *Indrisinæ*, established upon the *Propithecus diadema*, the diadem-lemur.

propitiable (prọ-pish'i-a-bl), *a.* [< OF. *propitiable*, *propiciable*, < L. *propitiabilis*, easy to be appeased, < *propitiare*, appease: see *propitiate*.] Capable of being propitiated; that may be made propitious.

> It could never enter into my mind that he [God] was either irritable or *propitiable* by the omitting or performing of any mean and insignificant services. *Dr. H. More*, Gen. Pref. to Philos. Writings, p. x.

propitiate (prọ-pish'i-āt), *v.*; pret. and pp. *propitiated*, ppr. *propitiating*. [< L. *propitiatus*, pp. of *propitiare* (> It. *propiziare* = Pg. Sp. *propiciar* = F. *propitier*), appease, < *propitius*, favorable, well-disposed: see *propitious*.] **I.** *trans.* To appease and render favorable; make propitious; conciliate.

> Let fierce Achilles, dreadful in his rage,
> The god *propitiate* and the pest asswage.
> *Pope*, Iliad, i. 192.

> He [Frederic William] could always be *propitiated* by a present of a grenadier of six feet four or six feet five. *Macaulay*, Frederic the Great.

II. *intrans.* To make propitiation or atonement.

propitiation (prọ-pish-i-ā'shọn), *n.* [< F. *propitiation* = Sp. *propiciacion* = Pg. *propiciação* = It. *propiziazione*, < LL. *propitiatio(n-)*, an appeasing, an atonement, < L. *propitiare*, pp. *propitiatus*, appease: see *propitiate*.] **1.** The act of propitiating; the act of making propitious.—**2.** That which propitiates or appeases; that which furnishes a reason for not executing a punishment justly due for wrong-doing; specifically, in the New Testament, Christ himself, because his life and death furnish a ground for the forgiveness of sins.

> And he is the *propitiation* for our sins; and not for ours only, but also for the sins of the whole world. 1 John ii. 2.

=**Syn.** *Atonement*, *Reconciliation*, *Propitiation*, *Expiation*, *Satisfaction*. By derivation and by Biblical usage *atonement* and *reconciliation* are essentially the same: two that were alienated are made at one, or put back into friendship. *Atonement*, however, is not now applied to the relation of man to man, except in its extra-Biblical extension, by which it means also the making of full and satisfactory amends (*satisfaction*) or the enduring of proper penalties (*expiation*) for a great wrong: as, there could be no *atonement* for such an outrage. As applied to the relations of God and man, *atonement* has been lifted into much greater dignity than any other word in the list; it is now the august, chosen, and only endeared word for the effect of the life and especially of the death of Christ in establishing right relations between God and man; *reconcile* and *reconciliation* are the principal words for this in the New Testament, *atonement* being used only once, and *atone* not at all. *Propitiation* is the only one of these words having exclusive reference to the feelings or purposes of the person or being offended; it is a severe word, implying slowness to relent, and is, in regard to the attitude of God toward man, chiefly a theological term. *Expiation* regards the guilt of the offense; it is the suffering of the penalty proper for an act (as, to make *expiation* for one's crime upon the scaffold), or of an adequate substituted pain. The word is general, and only barely Biblical (Num. xxxv. 33, margin, and revised version), although the fact is by the mass of Christians believed to lie in some form in the sufferings of Christ. *Satisfaction* in this connection means adequate amends: as, *satisfaction* for an insult or for damage; the word has been taken by a school in theology to express the sufficiency of the sufferings of Christ to meet the demands of the retributive justice of God.

> The *atonement* has for its object to restore that relation of man to God which sin had disturbed, and to reconcile the sinner to God. *Ullmann*, Sinlessness of Jesus (trans.), IV. ii. § 2.

> The doctrine of *Reconciliation* has not escaped the fate of other Christian truths; it has done and is doing its work in converting the world, and consoling many a crushed heart; but at the same time the terms in which it should be set forth have been disputed, and sometimes the doctrine itself denied. *W. Thomson*, in Aids to Faith, Essay viii., Int.

> We may have it as our privilege, I think, when our mind recoils from the tremendous difficulty of *propitiation* itself, to carry the whole matter up above the ranges of time, and look on him who stands there "in the midst of the throne, as it had been a Lamb slain from the foundation of the world." *H. Bushnell*, Forgiveness and Law, i. 4.

> In the great tragic poet Æschylus is a striking instance of λύτρον in the sense of an *expiation* or *atonement* for murder. The chorus of mourning women, bewailing the untimely end of Agamemnon, exclaim, "What *atonement* is there for blood that has fallen on the ground? . . . All the rivers moving in one channel would flow in vain to purify murder." *J. P. Thompson*, Theology of Christ, v.

> *Satisfaction* expresses the relation which the work of Christ sustains to the demands of God's law and justice. *A. A. Hodge*, Outlines of Theology, xxii. 2.

propitiator (prọ-pish'i-ā-tọr), *n.* [< F. *propitiateur* = Sp. Pg. *propiciador* = It. *propiziatore*, < LL. *propitiator*, a peacemaker, < L. *propitiare*, pp. *propitiatus*, appease: see *propitiate*.] One who propitiates. *Johnson.*

propitiatorily (prọ-pish'i-ạ-tọ-ri-li), *adv.* [< *propitiatory* + *-ly*[2].] By way of propitiation.

propitiatory (prọ-pish'i-ạ-tọ-ri), *a.* and *n.* [= F. *propitiatoire* = Sp. Pg. *propiciatorio* = It. *propiziatorio*, < LL. *propitiatorius*, atoning, reconciling, < L. *propitiatus*, pp. of *propitiare*, appease: see *propitiate*.] **I.** *a.* Having the power to make propitious; effecting or intended to effect propitiation: as, a *propitiatory* sacrifice.

> Christ's sacrifice on the cross was the only perfect and all-sufficient *propitiatory* sacrifice "for the sins of the world." *J. Bradford*, Works (Parker Soc., 1853), II. 285.

> When the predominance of the chief has become so decided that he is feared, he begins to receive *propitiatory* presents. *H. Spencer*, Prin. of Sociol., § 542.

II.† *n.* **1.** In *Jewish antiq.*, the mercy-seat; the lid or cover of the ark of the covenant, lined within and without with plates of gold.

> But nowe hath God declared Christe to be unto all people the very *propitiatory*, mercie table, and sacrifice. *J. Udall*, On Rom. iii.

> They [Joseph and Mary], like the two cherubims about the *propitiatory*, took the Child between them. *Jer. Taylor*, Works (ed. 1835), I. 76.

2. A propitiation.

> God hath set forth Christ to be the *propitiatory* in his blood. *Locke*, On Rom. iii. 25.

propitious (prọ-pish'us), *a.* [= OF. *propice* (> obs. E. *propice*) = Sp. Pg. *propicio* = It. *propizio*, < L. *propitius*, favorable, well-disposed, kind (usually said of deities); origin unknown. Some conjecture it to have been orig. a term in augury with ref. to the flying of birds, < L. *pro*, forward, + *petere*, seek, orig. fly (see *petition*); according to another view, < L. *prope*, near.] **1.** Favorably disposed; ready to grant a favor or indulgence; kind; disposed to be gracious or merciful; ready to forgive and bestow favors.

> My Maker, be *propitious* while I speak!
> *Milton*, P. L., viii. 380.

> Would but thy sister Marcia be *propitious*
> To thy friend's vows.
> *Addison*, Cato, i. 2.

> As *propitious* Heav'n might send
> What once I valu'd and could boast, a friend.
> *Cowper*, Retirement, l. 377.

2. Affording favorable conditions or circumstances; favorable: as, a *propitious* season.

> That diet which is most *propitious* to one is often pernicious to another. *Burton*, Anat. of Mel., p. 284.

> No time could be more *propitious* than the present. *D. Webster*, Speech, June 17, 1825.

=**Syn.** 1. Gracious, benign.—2. *Auspicious*, *Propitious*, promising. *Auspicious* cannot be safely used in any meaning beyond that of giving omen or indication of success; an *auspicious* event is one that seems an omen of prosperity for that which follows. *Auspicious* could be applied to a person only by a highly figurative use of the word. The earlier tendency to use the word outside of the limits here indicated is not now sanctioned by good usage. *Propitious* applies primarily to persons, but may be freely extended by figure to things. *Propitious* goes beyond *auspicious* in representing a benign disposition and manner, leading one to expect a kind reception and help.

> *Auspicious* omens from the past and present cheer us for the future. *Sumner*, Orations, I. 109.

> And now t' asswage the force of this new flame,
> And make thee more *propitious* in my need,
> I meane to sing the praises of thy name.
> *Spenser*, Hymne in Honour of Love, l. 9.

> Sure some *propitious* planet then did smile,
> When first you were conducted to this isle.
> *Dryden*, To Sir Godfrey Kneller, l. 133.

propitiously (prọ-pish'us-li), *adv.* In a propitious manner; favorably; kindly.

propitiousness (prọ-pish'us-nes), *n.* The state or character of being propitious, in any sense of that word.

The *propitiousness* of climate to that sort of tree.
Sir W. Temple, Anc. and Mod. Learning.

prop-joint (prop'joint), *n.* In *carriage-making*, a jointed bar which spreads the bows of a calash-top. *E. H. Knight.* Compare *rule-joint.*

proplasm (prō'plazm), *n.* [< Gr. πρόπλασμα, a model, < πρό, for, before, + πλάσσειν, form, mold, shape: see *plasm.*] A mold; a matrix.

Those shells serving as *proplasms* or moulds to the matter which so filled them.
Woodward, Essay towards a Nat. Hist. of the Earth.

We gather that the mysterious Spirit is merely the noumenon or *proplasm* of physical and psychical phenomena. Now it is surely far simpler and better to speak of this *proplasm* as Matter, and thus avoid the very equivocal term Spirit. *Lond. Jour. of Sci.*, No. cxxiv. 242.

proplastic (prō-plas'tik), *a.* [< Gr. πρό, for, before, + πλαστικός, pertaining to molding or modeling: see *plastic.*] Forming a mold or cast.

proplastics (prọ̄-plas'tiks), *n.* [Pl. of *proplastic* (see *-ics*).] The art of making molds for castings, etc.

prop-leg (prop'leg), *n.* In *entom.*, same as *proleg.*

propleural (prō-plö'rạl), *a.* [< *propleuron* + *-al.*] Anterior and lateral or pleural, as a part of the prothorax; of or pertaining to the propleura.

propleuron (prō-plö'ron), *n.*; pl. *propleura* (-rạ̈). [NL., < Gr. πρό, before, + πλευρά, side: see *pleuron.*] The lateral part of the prothorax; a prothoracic pleuron. There are two propleura, right and left; and each propleuron is typically divided into three sclerites—an episternum, an epimeron, and a parapteron.

proplex (prō'pleks), *n.* [< NL. *proplexus*, q. v.] Same as *proplexus.*

proplexus (prō-plek'sus), *n.*; pl. *proplexus* or *proplexuses.* [NL., < L. *pro*, before, + *plexus*, a braiding: see *plexus.*] The plexus of the procœlia; the choroid plexus of either lateral ventricle of the brain. *Wilder and Gage*, Anat. Tech., p. 485.

propodeum (prọ̄-pō'dẹ̄-um), *n.*; pl. *propodea* (-ạ̈). [NL., irreg. < L. *pro*, before, + *pod(ex)*, fundament.] In *entom.*, a part of the thorax immediately over and partly surrounding the insertion of the abdomen, seen principally in the *Hymenoptera.* It is originally the first abdominal segment, which, during the development of the larva and pupa, becomes transferred to the thorax, and so intimately joined with it that it appears to be a part of the last thoracic ring.

propodia, *n.* Plural of *propodium.*

propodial (prọ̄-pō'di-ạl), *a.* and *n.* [< *propodium* + *-al.*] **I.** *a.* **1.** Of or pertaining to the propodium of a mollusk.—**2.** Of or pertaining to the propodialia.

II. *n.* Same as *propodium.*

Limbs consisting of one basal element, two *propodials*, and metapodials and digits. *Amer. Nat.*, XXIII. 852.

propodialia (prọ̄-pō-di-ā'li-ạ̈), *n. pl.* [NL., < Gr. προπόδιος, before the feet: see *propodium.*] The bones of the proximal segment of both fore and hind limbs (that is, the humerus and femur) taken together or considered as corresponding to each other. See *epipodialia.*

propodite (prop'ọ̄-dīt), *n.* [< Gr. πρό, before, + πούς (ποδ-), = E. *foot*, + *-ite*[1].] In *Crustacea*, the sixth (penultimate) joint of a developed endopodite, between the carpopodite and the dactylopodite. In a lobster, for example, it is the joint which with the movable dactylopodite makes the nipper or chelate claw. *Milne-Edwards*; *Huxley.* Also *propodos.* See cut under *endopodite.*

propoditic (prop-ọ̄-dit'ik), *a.* [< *propodite* + *-ic.*] Of or pertaining to the propodite of the limb of a crustacean.

propodium (prọ̄-pō'di-um), *n.*; pl. *propodia* (-ạ̈). [NL., < Gr. προπόδιος, before the feet, < πρό, for, before, + πούς (ποδ-) = E. *foot.*] The anterior one of the three median parts into which the foot of some mollusks may be divided: correlated with *mesopodium* and *metapodium.* Also *propodial.* Compare *epipodium.*

propodos (prop'ọ̄-dos), *n.* Same as *propodite.*

propolis (prop'ọ̄-lis), *n.* [< L. *propolis*, < Gr. πρόπολις, the substance with which bees line and fence their hives, the suburb or outer part of a city, < πρό, for, before, + πόλις, city.] A red, resinous, odorous substance having some resemblance to wax and smelling like storax. It is collected by bees from the viscid buds of various trees, and used to stop the holes and crevices in their hives to prevent the entrance of cold air, to strengthen the cells, etc. Also called *bee-glue.*

Speaking of the honey-bee reminds me that the subtle and sleight-of-hand manner in which it fills its baskets with pollen and *propolis* is characteristic of much of nature's doings. *The Century*, XXV. 678.

propolize (prop'ọ̄-līz), *v. t.*; pret. and pp. *propolized*, ppr. *propolizing.* [< *propol-is* + *-ize.*] To cover with propolis. *Phin*, Dict. Apicul-ture, p. 55.

propone (prọ̄-pōn'), *v. t.*; pret. and pp. *proponed*, ppr. *proponing.* [= Sp. *proponer* = Pg. *propôr* = It. *proporre*, *proponere*, < L. *proponere*, set forth, place before, < *pro*, forth, before, + *ponere*, set, place: see *ponent.* Cf. *propound*, a doublet of *propone.*] **1.** To put forward; propose; propound.

He [Aristotle] . . . neuer *propones* any allegation, or makes any surmise, but he yeelds a reason or cause to fortifie and proue it. *Puttenham*, Arte of Eng. Poesie, p. 191.

He *proponed* vnto me sundry questions, both touching religion, and also the state of our countreys.
Hakluyt's Voyages, I. 346.

2. In *Scots law*, to bring forward; state.

Denlyng fiersly al the other new invencions alleged and *proponed* to his charge.
Hall's Union (1548). (*Halliwell.*)

Pleas proponed and repelled, in *Scots law*, pleas stated in court, and overruled before decree.

proponent (prọ̄-pō'nẹnt), *a.* and *n.* [= Sp. Pg. It. *proponente*, < L. *proponen(t-)s*, ppr. of *proponere*, set forth, place before: see *propone.*] **I.** *a.* Making proposals; proposing.

For mysterious things of faith rely
On the *proponent* Heaven's authority.
Dryden, Hind and Panther, i. 121.

II. *n.* **1.** One who makes a proposal, or lays down a proposition.—**2.** In *law*, one who propounds a will for probate.

propons (prō'ponz), *n.* [< L. *pro*, before, + *pons*, bridge: see *pons.*] In *anat.*, a small bundle of transverse fibers just below the pons, crossing the proximal end of the pyramid. Also called *ponticulus.*

proport†, *v. t.* An obsolete form of *purport.*

proportion (prọ̄-pōr'shọn), *n.* [< ME. *proporcion*, *proporcioun*, < OF. *proportion*, *proporcion*, F. *proportion* = Sp. *proporcion* = Pg. *proporção* = It. *proporzione*, < L. *proportio(n-)*, comparative relation, proportion, symmetry, analogy, < *pro*, for, before, + *portio(n-)*, share, part: see *portion.*] **1.** The relation of one thing to another in respect to size, quantity, magnitude of corresponding parts, capacity, or degree.

He must be little skilled in the world who thinks that men's talking much or little shall hold *proportion* only to their knowledge. *Locke.*

Every thing must bear a *proportion* with the outward value that is set upon it. *Steele*, Tatler, No. 171.

In *proportion* as men know more and think more, they look less at individuals and more at classes.
Macaulay, Milton.

Justice can be well administered only in *proportion* as men become just. *H. Spencer*, Social Statics, p. 289.

2. Specifically, the relation of one part to another or to the whole with respect to magnitude; the relative size and arrangement of parts: as, the *proportion* of the parts of an edifice, or of the human body. Commonly in the plural.

The system of definite *proportion* which the Greeks employed in the design of their temples was another cause of the effect they produce even on uneducated minds.
J. Fergusson, Hist. Arch., I. 251.

The three vast recesses [of the façade of Peterborough Cathedral: see cut under *portal*] have not, as they have at Lincoln, any correspondence with the *proportions* of the nave and aisles which they terminate. Being of equal height, and the narrow one being in front of the wide central aisle while the wide ones fall in front of the narrow side aisles, they wholly contradict these *proportions.*
Moore, Gothic Architecture, p. 165.

3. Symmetrical arrangement, distribution, or adjustment; the proper relation of parts in a whole; symmetry or harmony.

Hee commeth to you with words sent in delightfull *proportion*, either accompanied with or prepared for the well inchaunting skill of Musicke.
Sir P. Sidney, Apol. for Poetrie, p. 40.

Statues which are placed on high are made greater than the life, that they may descend to the sight in their just *proportion.* *Dryden*, Essay on Dram. Poesy.

[We,] your guilty Subjects, . . . have held pace and *proportion* with you in our evill wayes.
N. Ward, Simple Cobler, p. 63.

4. That which falls to one's lot when a whole is divided according to a rule or principle; just or proper share; in general, portion; lot.

Wee were all constrained to liue onely on that Smith had onely for his owne Companie, for the rest had consumed their *porportions.*
Quoted in *Capt. John Smith's* Works, II. 1.

I have received my *proportion*, like the prodigious son.
Shak., T. G. of V., ii. 3. 3.

5†. Form; shape; figure.

I thought King Henry had resembled thee
In courage, courtship, and *proportion.*
Shak., 2 Hen. VI., i. 3. 57.

Look: here 's a face now of another making,
Another mould; here 's a divine *proportion.*
Fletcher (and another?), Prophetess, iii. 3.

The people . . . [are] generally tall and straight, of a comely *proportion.* *Capt. John Smith*, Works, I. 129.

6. In *math.*, the equality of ratios or relations; analogy. Complicated and difficult definitions of this word were given by Euclid and the old mathematicians, because they were unwilling to regard a ratio as a quantity capable of equality; but it is now recognized that such generalizations are at once the most profound and the most intelligible way throughout mathematics.

When he badde founde his firste mansioun [in astrology],
He knew the remenaunt by *proporcioun.*
Chaucer, Franklin's Tale, l. 558.

7. In *music*: (*a*) The ratio between the vibration-numbers of two tones. (*b*) Same as *rhythm* or *meter.*—**8.** In *arith.*, the rule of three; that rule which, according to the theory of proportion, enables us to find a fourth proportional to three given numbers—that is, a number to which the third bears the same ratio as the first does to the second.—**Academic proportions.** See *figure of academic proportions*, under *academic.*—**Alternate proportion.** See *alternate.*—**Combining proportions.** Same as *definite proportions.*—**Composition of proportion.** See *composition.*—**Compound proportion**, the equality of the ratio of two quantities to another ratio, the antecedent and consequent of which are respectively the products of the antecedents and consequents of two or more ratios.—**Continued proportion**, a succession of several equal ratios the consequent of each of which is identical with the antecedent of that which follows, as 8 : 12 = 12 : 18 = 18 : 27, etc.—**Contra-arithmetical proportion, contraharmonical mean and proportion, definite proportions.** See the adjectives.—**Conversion of proportions.** See *conversion.*—**Direct proportion.** See *direct ratio*, under *ratio.*—**Discrete proportion.** See *discrete*, 2.—**Duplicate, geometrical, harmonic, inordinate proportion.** See the adjectives.—**Gunter's proportion.** Same as *Gunter's line* (*a*) (which see, under *line*[2]).—**Inverse proportion.** See *reciprocal proportion.*—**Law of multiple proportion.** See *multiple.*—**Mixed ratio or proportion.** See *mixed*[1].—**Musical proportion.** Same as *harmonic proportion.*—**Reciprocal or inverse proportion**, an equality between a direct and a reciprocal ratio, or a proportion in which two of the quantities are taken inversely: thus, the ratio of 4 to 2 is that of 3 to 6 taken inversely, or 4 : 2 = ⅓ : ⅙.—**Simple proportion**, the equality of the ratio of two quantities to that of two other quantities.=**Syn.** 3. See *symmetry.*

proportion (prọ̄-pōr'shọn), *v. t.* [< ME. *proporcionen*, *porporciounen*, < OF. *proportionner*, *proporcionner*, F. *proportionner* = Sp. Pg. *proporcionar* = It. *proporzionare*; from the noun.] **1.** To adjust in suitable relations; adapt harmoniously to something else as regards dimensions or extent: as, to *proportion* the size of a building to its height, or the thickness of a thing to its length; to *proportion* expenditure to income.

He . . . [advises] men to live within Bounds, and to *proportion* their Inclinations to the Extent of their Fortune. *Congreve*, tr. of Juvenal's Satires, xi., Arg.

Fortunately, the Sphinx proposes her conundrums to us one at a time, and at intervals *proportioned* to our wits.
Lowell, Address at Harvard Anniversary.

2. To form with symmetry; give a symmetrical form to.

Sir, zeff thow wilt wrappe thy soueraynes bred stately,
Thow must square & *porporcioun* thy bred clene and evenly. *Babees Book* (E. E. T. S.), p. 130.

Nature had *proportioned* her without any fault quickly to be discovered by the senses. *Sir P. Sidney.*

3. To bear proportion or adequate relation to; correspond to.

Bid him therefore consider of his ransom, which must *proportion* the losses we have borne.
Shak., Hen. V, iii. 6. 134.

4†. To divide into portions; allot; apportion.

Next, for your monthly pains, to shew my thanks,
I do *proportion* out some twenty ducats.
Fletcher, Spanish Curate, ii. 2.

Here are my commodities, whereof take your choice, the rest I will *proportion* fit bargains for your people.
Quoted in *Capt. John Smith's* Works, I. 214.

5. To compare; estimate the relative proportions of.

Now, Penshurst, they that will *proportion* thee
With other edifices, when they see
Those proud ambitious heaps, and nothing else,
May say their lords have built, but thy lord dwells.
B. Jonson, The Forest.

Fond earth! *proportion* not my seeming love
To my long stay. *Quarles*, Emblems, iv. 2.

6. In *type-manuf.*, to adjust (a font of type) so that it shall contain the proper number of each letter, point, etc.

proportionable (prọ̄-pōr'shọn-ạ-bl), *a.* [< OF. *proportionable*, *proportionnable* = Sp. *proporcionable* = Pg. *proporcionavel* = It. *proporzionabile*, < LL. **proportionabilis* (in adv. *proportionabiliter*), < L. *proportio(n-)*, proportion: see *proportion.*] Capable of being proportioned or made proportional; also, being in due proportion; having a due comparative relation; proportional; corresponding.

For us to levy power
Proportionable to the enemy
Is all unpossible. *Shak.*, Rich. II., ii. 2. 125.

My encouragement in the Navy alone being in no wise *proportionable* to my pains or deserts. *Pepys*, Diary, II. 317.

Such eloquence may exist without a *proportionable* degree of wisdom. *Burke.*

proportionableness (prǭ-pōr'shǫn-a̤-bl-nes), *n.* The state of being proportionable.

Because there will be a *proportionableness* of the parts of our perfection; and therefore, as our love to God and his works will be there perfected, so will be our knowledge. *Baxter*, Dying Thoughts.

proportionably (prǭ-pōr'shǫn-a̤-bli), *adv.* [< *proportionable* + *-ly*².] Proportionally.

As he approached nearer home, his good humour *proportionably* seemed to increase. *Goldsmith*, Citizen of the World, lii.

proportional (prǭ-pōr'shǫn-a̤l), *a.* and *n.* [< ME. *proporcionel*, n., < OF. *proportionel*, *proporcionel*, F. *proportionnel* = Sp. Pg. *proporcional* = It. *proporzionale*, < LL. *proportionalis*, pertaining to proportion, < L. *proportio(n-)*, proportion: see *proportion*.] **I.** *a.* **1.** Based upon proportion; pertaining to or having proportion.

Relations depending on the equality and excess of the same simple idea in several subjects may be called . . . *proportional*. *Locke*, Human Understanding, II. xxviii. 1.

2. According to or having a due proportion; being in suitable proportion or degree.

The conquerors were contented to share the conquered country, usually according to a strictly defined *proportional* division, with its previous occupants. *Craik*, Hist. Eng. Lit., I. 62.

They see a great amount of wealth in the country, and they think that their share is not *proportional* to their deserts. *New Princeton Rev.*, II. 52.

3. In *math.*, having the same or a constant ratio: as, *proportional* quantities.—**Directly proportional**, in *math.*, noting proportional quantities when the proportion is according to the order of the terms (that is, one thing is greater in the same ratio that another is greater): in contradistinction to *inversely* or *reciprocally proportional*, when the proportion is contrary to the order of the terms (that is, one thing is less in the same ratio that another is greater, and vice versa).

We may assume that the elastic force of the luminiferous medium called into play by a displacement is *directly proportional* to the displacement. *Tait*, Light, § 281.

Proportional compasses, compasses with a pair of legs at each end, turning on a common pivot. The pivot is secured in a slide which is adjustable in the slots of the legs so as to vary in any required proportion the relative distances of the points at the respective ends. The legs are provided with marks by which the ratio of proportion of the respective ends may be arranged or determined. The instrument is used in reducing or enlarging drawings, etc.—**Proportional parts**, parts of magnitudes such that the corresponding ones, taken in their order, are proportional—that is, the first part of the first is to the first part of the second as the second part of the first is to the second part of the second, and so on.—**Proportional radii.** See *radius*.—**Proportional representation.** See *representation*.—**Proportional scale.** (*a*) A scale on which are marked parts proportional to the logarithms of the natural numbers; a logarithmic scale. (*b*) A scale for preserving the proportions of drawings or parts when changing their size.

II. *n.* **1.** A quantity in proportion. Specifically—(*a*) In *chem.*, in the theory of definite proportions, the weight of an atom or prime. See *prime*, *n.*, 6. (*b*) In *math.*, one of the terms of a proportion: of these the first and last are called the *extremes*, and the intermediate the *means*, or, when the proportion consists of only three terms, the *mean*. See *mean*³.

2†. A table of proportional parts.

Hise *proporcioneles* convenientz
For hise equacions in every thyng.
Chaucer, Franklin's Tale, l. 550.

Continued proportionals. See *continued*.

proportionality (prǭ-pōr-shǫ-nal'i̤-ti), *n.* [< F. *proportionnalité* = Sp. *proporcionalidad* = Pg. *proporcionalidade* = It. *proporzionalità*, < LL. *proportionalita(t-)s*, proportion, < *proportionalis*, proportional: see *proportional*.] The character or state of being in proportion.

The principle of *proportionality* of cause and effect is suspended, the smallest causes producing, if need be, the largest effects. *A. Bain*, Mind, XII. 178.

proportionally (prǭ-pōr'shǫn-a̤l-i), *adv.* In proportion; in due degree; with suitable comparative relation.

If these circles, whilst their centres keep their distances and positions, could be made less in diameter, their interfering one with another . . . would be *proportionally* diminished. *Newton.*

proportionary†, *n.* [ME. *proporcynary*, < ML. *proportionarius*, proportional, < L. *proportio(n-)*, proportion: see *proportion*.] Proportion.

And so to werke it, after his *proporcynary*,
That it may appere to all that shall it se
A thyng ryght parfyte and wel in eche degre.
Fabyan, Chron., I., Prol., p. 3.

proportionate (prǭ-pōr'shǫn-ạt), *a.* [= F. *proportionné* = Sp. Pg. *proporcionado* = It. *proporzionato*, < LL. *proportionatus*, proportioned, < L. *proportio(n-)*, proportion, symmetry, analogy: see *proportion*.] Having proportion, or due proportion; adjusted to something else according to a certain rate or comparative relation; proportional.

In the state of nature, one man comes by no absolute power to use a criminal according to the passion or heats of his own will, but only to retribute to him . . . what is *proportionate* to his transgression. *Locke.*

Is such effect *proportionate* to cause?
Browning, Ring and Book, II. 214.

If the demand for increase of power in some particular faculty is great and unceasing, development will go on with *proportionate* speed. *H. Spencer*, Social Statics, p. 452.

proportionate (prǭ-pōr'shǫn-āt), *v. t.*; pret. and pp. *proportionated*, ppr. *proportionating*. [< *proportionate*, *a.*] To make proportional; adjust according to a settled rate or to due comparative relation or proportion: as, to *proportionate* punishments to crimes.

Every single particle hath an innate gravitation towards all others, *proportionated* by matter and distance. *Bentley*, Sermons.

proportionately (prǭ-pōr'shǫn-ạt-li), *adv.* In a proportionate manner or degree; with due proportion; according to a settled or suitable rate or degree.

To this internal perfection is added a *proportionately* happy condition. *Bp. Pearson*, Expos. of Creed, xii.

proportionateness (prǭ-pōr'shǫn-ạt-nes), *n.* The character or state of being proportionate.

proportioning (prǭ-pōr'shǫn-ing), *n.* [Verbal n. of *proportion*, *v.*] Relation of size, height, etc.; adjustment of proportions.

The vertical *proportioning* [of the interior of Durham Cathedral] is quite unlike what we have seen in the eastern districts; the main arcade is much higher, and the triforium arcade relatively lower. *The Century*, XXXV. 228.

proportionment (prǭ-pōr'shǫn-mẹnt), *n.* [< OF. *proportionnement*, < *proportionner*, proportion: see *proportion*.] The act of proportioning, or the state of being proportioned.

A regard to the *proportionment* of the projective motion to the vis centripeta. *Molyneux*, To Locke, July 26, 1697.

propos (prǭ-pō'), *n.* [F.: see *purpose*.] A proposition; statement.

John the Saint,
Who maketh oft *Propos* full queint.
Prior, Earl Robert's Mice.

proposal (prǭ-pō'za̤l), *n.* [< *propose* + *-al*.] **1.** A proposition, plan, or scheme offered for acceptance; a scheme or design; in the plural, terms or conditions proposed: as, to make *proposals* for a treaty of peace; to make a *proposal* of marriage.

When we . . . propounded terms
Of composition, straight they changed their minds. . . .
If our *proposals* once again were heard,
We should compel them to a quick result.
Milton, P. L., vi. 618.

2. Offer or presentation to the mind; statement.

The *proposal* of an agreeable object. *South.*

The truth is not likely to be entertained readily upon the first *proposal*. *Bp. Atterbury.*

3. In *law*, a statement in writing of some special matter submitted to the consideration of a master in Chancery, pursuant to an order made upon an application ex parte, or a decretal order of the court. *Imp. Dict.*—**Sealed proposals**, competitive offers to furnish supplies or perform work, made as bids for a contract to be awarded therefor, each offer being inclosed in a sealed envelop when presented, and all to be opened simultaneously, so as to prevent later bidders from learning the terms offered by earlier bidders in time to underbid.=**Syn. 1.** *Proposal, Proposition, Overture.* A *proposal* is something proposed to be done, which the person addressed may accept or reject: as, a *proposal* of marriage. A *proposition* may be something proposed for discussion, with a view to ascertaining the truth or the wisdom of it: as, a *proposition* in Euclid; few now refuse assent to the *proposition* that the earth is round. *Proposition* is likely to be applied to a *proposal* which is deliberated upon, discussion and deliberation being associated with the word *proposition*, and action with the word *proposal*: as, a *proposition* to build a new dam, if it will not cost too much; a *proposal* to build it for $10,000. Both these words imply some exactness, completeness, or formality, whereas an *overture* may be of a tentative sort. By derivation, an *overture* opens negotiation or business: as, an *overture* from an inferior to a superior ecclesiastical body; an *overture* of peace from one of two estranged friends or neighbors. An *overture*, if not rejected, may be followed by a definite *proposal*.

propose (prǭ-pōz'), *v.*; pret. and pp. *proposed*, ppr. *proposing*. [< ME. *proposen*, < OF. *proposer*, F. *proposer*, propose, purpose, taking the place of L. *proponere*, pp. *propositus*, set forth, place before (< *pro*, forth, before, + *ponere*, set, place: see *propone*), as with similar words: see *pose*².] **I.** *trans.* **1.** To put forward or offer for consideration, discussion, acceptance, admission, or adoption: as, to *propose* a bill or resolution to a legislative body; to *propose* a question or subject for discussion; to *propose* one as a member of a club.

Sphinx is said to *propose* various difficult questions and riddles to men. *Bacon*, Physical Fables, x., Expl.

It is hard to find a whole age to imitate, or what century to *propose* for example. *Sir T. Browne*, Christ. Mor., iii. 1.

2. To place before as something to be done, attained, or striven after; form or declare as an intention or design.

What to ourselves in passion we *propose*,
The passion ending, doth the purpose lose.
Shak., Hamlet, iii. 2. 204.

But ere we could arrive the point *proposed*,
Cæsar cried, "Help me, Cassius, or I sink!"
Shak., J. C., i. 2. 110.

And then come to town till I begin my journey to Ireland, which I *propose* the middle of August.
Swift, Letter, July 8, 1726.

3†. To set or place forth; place out; state.

Milton has *proposed* the Subject of his Poem in the following Verses. *Addison*, Spectator, No. 303.

4†. To place one's self before; face; confront.

Aaron, a thousand deaths
Would I *propose* to achieve her whom I love.
Shak., Tit. And., ii. 1. 80.

5†. To speak; utter; discourse.

Of hyr lenger wold I haue spoke sure,
Iff more of wryting therof founde myght be; . . .
And sin more ther-of I can noght *propose*,
Offors moste I here take rest and repose.
Rom. of Partenay (E. E. T. S.), l. 6404.

Euery one gaue his consent with Surius, yeelding the choyce of that nights pastime to the discretion of the Ladie Flauia, who thus *proposed* her mind.
Lyly, Euphues and his England (ed. Arber), p. 40.

Where I stand kneel thou,
Whilst I *propose* the selfsame words to thee
Which, traitor, thou would have me answer to.
Shak., 3 Hen. VI., v. 5. 20.

=**Syn. 1.** To propound, present, suggest, recommend, move, enounce.—**2.** To intend, mean, design.

II. *intrans.* **1.** To form or declare an intention or design.

Man *proposes*, but God disposes.
Chron. of Battle Abbey (Lower's trans.), p. 27.

2. To offer; specifically, to make an offer of marriage.

Why don't the men *propose*, mamma?
T. Haynes Bayly, Why Don't the Men *Propose*?

3†. To converse; discourse.

Run thee into the parlour;
There shalt thou find my cousin Beatrice
Proposing with the Prince and Claudio.
Shak., Much Ado, iii. 1. 3.

propose† (prǭ-pōz'), *n.* [< *propose*, *v.*; cf. *purpose*, *n.*] Talk; discourse.

There will she hide her,
To listen our *propose*.
Shak., Much Ado, iii. 1. 12.

proposedly† (prǭ-pō'zed-li), *adv.* Designedly; purposely.

They had been *proposedly* planned and pointed against him. *Sterne*, Tristram Shandy, i. 117.

proposer (prǭ-pō'zėr), *n.* [< *propose* + *-er*¹.] **1.** One who proposes; one who offers anything for consideration or adoption.

He [Nicholas Briot] was the inventor, or at least one of the first *proposers*, of coining money by a press, instead of the former manner of hammering.
Walpole, Anecdotes of Painting, II. i.

The candidates should be nominated by means of a paper containing the names of a *proposer* and seconder and eight assentors. *J. McCarthy*, Hist. Own Times, lix.

2†. A speaker; an orator.

Let me conjure you, . . . by what more dear a better *proposer* could charge you withal, be even and direct with me. *Shak.*, Hamlet, ii. 2. 297.

proposita, *n.* Plural of *propositum*.

proposition (prop-ǭ-zish'ǫn), *n.* [< ME. *proposicioun*, < OF. *proposition*, F. *proposition* = Sp. *proposicion* = Pg. *proposição* = It. *proposizione*, < L. *propositio(n-)*, a setting forth, a representation, < *proponere*, pp. *propositus*, propose: see *propone*, *propose*.] **1.** The act of placing or setting forth; the act of offering.

The ample *proposition* that hope makes
In all designs begun on earth below
Fails in the promised largeness.
Shak., T. and C., i. 3. 3.

Gums fit for incense, and oblations for the altar of *proposition*. *Jer. Taylor*, Works (ed. 1835), I. 677.

2. That which is proposed; that which is offered for consideration, acceptance, or adoption; a proposal; offer of terms: commonly in the plural: as, *propositions* of peace.

The Governour and council of Plimouth returned answerable courteous acceptance of their loving *propositions*
N. Morton, New England's Memorial, p. 133.

The enemy sent *propositions*, such as upon delivery of a strong fortified town, after a handsome defence, are usually granted. *Clarendon*, Great Rebellion.

3. A representation in thought or language of an act of the mind in thinking a quality or general sign, termed a *predicate*, to be applicable to something indicated, and termed a *subject*. This connecting of predicate and subject may range from a mental necessity to a mere impulse to look at a certain possibility. These differences are called differences in the *mode*, or *modality*, of the proposition, according to which, as ordinarily stated, propositions are either *de inesse* (that is, the mode is not considered) or *modal*, and in this case *problematical*, *contingent*, or *apodictic*. The modality may properly be said to affect the copula, or form of junction of the predicate and subject. The predicate, logically speaking, embraces the whole representation of the quality of the fact. Thus, in the proposition "Elijah was caught up to heaven," the grammatical predicate is "was caught up to heaven"; but the logical predicate includes the whole picture which the sentence conveys—that of a man caught up to heaven. The predicate, however, is not a mere picture; it views the fact represented analytically, and distinguishes certain objects as identical with the subjects. There may be only one subject, or, if the predicate expresses a relation, there may be several. These subjects cannot be sufficiently indicated by any general description, but only by a real junction with experience, as by a finger-pointing. In ordinary language they are for the most part but imperfectly expressed. In whatever way they are represented, they can commonly (in the last analysis always) be set forth in classes only; from such a class the subject meant is to be taken in one or other of three ways: first, by a suitable selection, so as to render the proposition true; secondly, by taking any one, no matter which; thirdly, by taking no matter what one among a selected proportion of those which present themselves in experience. The first mode of selection gives a particular proposition, as "An object can be selected which is a man caught up to heaven"; the second mode gives a universal proposition, as "Take any object you please in this world, and it is not a man caught up to heaven"; the third mode gives a statistical proposition, as "Half the human beings in the world are women." If there are several subjects, the order of their selection is often important. Thus, it is one thing to say that having taken any man you please a woman can be found who was his mother, and quite another to say that a woman can be found such that, whatever man you select, that woman was that man's mother. Several of the distinctions between propositions found in the old treatises are based on distinctions between the different categories (or, in modern logical language, *universes*) from which the subjects are understood to be drawn. Such is the distinction between a *categorical proposition*, whose subject is denoted by a noun, and a *hypothetical proposition*, whose subject is a hypothetical state of things denoted by a sentence. Such is also the distinction between a *synthetical proposition*, whose subject is drawn from the world of real experience, and may suitably be denoted by a concrete noun, and an *analytic proposition*, whose subject is drawn from a world of ideas, and may suitably be denoted by an abstract noun. Propositions are further distinguished according to the forms of their predicates; but these distinctions, unlike those already noticed, merely concern the form under which the proposition happens to be thought or expressed, and do not concern its substance. The predicates of propositions are either simple, negative, or compound; and in the latter case they may conveniently be considered (by a slight fiction) as either disjunctive or conjunctive.

A *proposicion* is a perfeicte sentence spoken by the indicative mode, signifying either a true thing or a false without al ambiguite or doubtfulnesse. *Wilson*, Rule of Reason.

Verbal *propositions*, which are words, the signs of our ideas, put together or separated in affirmative or negative sentences. *Locke*, Human Understanding, IV. v. 5.

All that is necessary to constitute a *proposition* is that it should imply inclusion or exclusion, attribution or non-attribution. *Veitch*, Int. to Descartes's Method, p. xxxv.

4. In *math.*, a statement in terms of either a truth to be demonstrated or an operation to be performed. It is called a *theorem* when it is something to be proved, and a *problem* when it is an operation to be done. Abbreviated *prop.*

Ros. What said he? How looked he? Wherein went he? . . .
Cel. It is as easy to count atomies as to resolve the *propositions* of a lover. *Shak.*, As you Like it, iii. 2. 246.

5. In *rhet.*, that which is offered or affirmed as the subject of the discourse; anything stated or affirmed for discussion or illustration; the first part of a poem, in which the author states the subject or matter of it: as, Horace recommends modesty and simplicity in the *proposition* of a poem.

It is very disproportionable for a man to persecute another certainly for a *proposition* that, if he were wise, he would know is not certain. *Jer. Taylor*, Works (ed. 1835), II. 376.

Though that *proposition* had many degrees of truth in the beginning of the law, yet the case is now altered: God hath established its contradictory. *Jer. Taylor*, Works (ed. 1835), I. 806.

6. In *music*: (*a*) The act or process of enunciating or giving out a theme or subject. Specifically—(*b*) The subject of a fugue, as distinguished from the *answer*.—**Absolute, adversative, affirmative, ampliative, analytical, apodictic, assertory, binary, categorical, causal, cognate proposition.** See the adjectives.—**Composite proposition**, a proposition consisting of several propositions all asserted at once.—**Compound proposition**, a proposition consisting of two or more propositions, associated copulatively, disjunctively, conditionally, or otherwise.—**Comprehensive proposition**, a proposition in which the subject is regarded as a whole of logical comprehension including the predicate as a part.—**Conditional, conflictive, contradictory, contrary proposition.** See the adjectives.—**Contrariety of propositions.** See *contrariety*.—**Converted proposition, converting proposition.** See *convert*.—**Copulative proposition**, a proposition consisting of parts united by a copulative conjunction; a composite proposition.—**Correlative proposition.** See *correlative*.—**Cumulative proposition**, a proposition regarded as a compound of singular propositions, united conjunctively or disjunctively. Thus, "every man is mortal" is cumulative, as implying the first, the second, the third, etc., man to be, each of them, mortal.—**Descriptive proposition.** See *descriptive*.—**Dialectic proposition.** (*a*) A probable interrogation; a problem suitable for discussion. (*b*) An assumption of what appears likely.—**Dilemmatic, discretive, disjunct, disjunctive, divided proposition.** See the adjectives.—**Dual proposition.** Same as *binary proposition*. See *binary enunciation*, under *binary*.—**Elementary, equal, exceptive, exclusive, exemplar, explicative, explicatory, explicit, exponent, exponible, extensive, false proposition.** See the adjectives.—**Finite proposition**, a proposition whose predicate is not an infinitated term.—**Form of a proposition.** See *form*.—**Fundamental, hypothetical, hypothetico-disjunctive, identical, incident proposition.** See the adjectives.—**Impossible proposition**, a proposition which cannot be true.—**Indefinite proposition.** See *indefinite*.—**Infinite proposition**, a proposition whose predicate, affirmed of its subject, has the form of a negative: as, Every devil is non-human.—**Intensive proposition.** See *intensive*.—**Inventive proposition**, a proposition de inesse.—**Loaves of proposition†**, in *Jewish antiq.*, the showbread.

Under this fair heauen . . . there was the holy table, vppon whiche was set the holy bread, called the *loaves of proposition*.
Guevara, Letters (tr. by Hellowes, 1577), p. 351.

Local proposition. See *local*.—**Major proposition**, a major premise.—**Minor proposition**, a minor premise.—**Modal, necessary, negative proposition.** See the adjectives.—**Numerically definite proposition**, a proposition which states how many objects, at least, there are of a given description.—**Obligistic proposition**, a proposition which has to be admitted in disputation owing to institution, petition, position, deposition, dubitation, or truth.—**Opposite propositions**, propositions having the same terms but not identical: as, Some woman is mother of some man; Some woman is mother of each man; Some woman is mother of every man; Every woman is mother of some man; All women are mothers of one man; Every woman is mother of every man.—**Particular, perfect, practical, principal, privative proposition.** See the adjectives.—**Possible proposition.** Same as *problematic proposition*.—**Predicative proposition.** Same as *categorical proposition*.—**Probable proposition**, a proposition stating with more or less determinacy how often within a certain genus of events a certain specific event would be found to occur, in a given range of experience.—**Problematic proposition**, a proposition asserting something to be possible in some sense.—**Proposition de inesse.** See def. 3.—**Proposition de necessario**, a proposition thought to be necessary. Such propositions were divided by the old logicians into (*a*) propositions *de necessario conditionali*, which stated something to be necessarily true, provided a certain condition held; (*b*) propositions *de necessario quando*, which stated something to be necessarily true at specified times; and (*c*) propositions *de necessario simpliciter*, or categorical apodictic propositions. The latter were further divided into propositions *de necessario simpliciter pro nunc*, or propositions stating something to be necessarily true now, and propositions *de necessario simpliciter pro semper*, stating something to be always necessarily true.—**Proposition de omni**, a universal proposition.—**Proposition in sensu composito**, a proposition in which the expression of the mode is attached to the subject or predicate. Such a proposition, as remarked by Scotus, is not, properly speaking, a modal but an ordinary proposition concerning possibility.—**Proposition in sensu diviso**, a proposition in which the expression of the mode is attached to the copula.—**Proposition per se**, a proposition which asserts something to be essentially true—that is, the universe is a universe of essences, not of existences. Four modes of such propositions are recognized by Aristotle: first, where the predicate is involved in the idea of the subject; second, where the subject is involved in the idea of the predicate; while the third and fourth modes are respectively modes of existing and of causing.—**Propositions of second adjacent, of third adjacent.** See *adjacent*.—**Pure proposition**, a proposition not modal.—**Pythagorean proposition.** See *Pythagorean*.—**Quantified proposition**, a proposition in which the manner of selecting the subject is fully expressed.—**Rational proposition**, a hypothetical proposition in which several categoricals are united by a causal conjunction.—**Reciprocating proposition**, one which asserts two terms to be coextensive: as, "Man" is identical with "rational animal."—**Relative proposition**, a proposition whose predicate is a relative term.—**Remotive proposition.** See *remotive*.—**Restrictive proposition**, a proposition with a restrictive clause: as, Christ, in his divine nature, is omnipresent.—**Simple proposition.** (*a*) Properly, a proposition whose predicate is simple: as, There is a man. (*b*) Usually, a categorical proposition, or one expressed by means of a noun and a verb, as contradistinguished from a *conditional proposition*.—**Singular proposition**, a proposition whose subjects are single individuals: as, Cain killed Abel.—**Spurious proposition**, a proposition one of the subjects of which is a character designated as one of those which belong to a given group. Thus, from the premises, Every European wants some character of Americans, and Every nobleman possesses some character other than those that are common to Americans, we can infer, first, that every European wants some character different from some character common to noblemen, and that every nobleman possesses a character different from some character wanting to every European. These are spurious propositions.—**Statistical proposition**, a proposition which states how many objects of one kind there are in connection with each one of another kind, in the average of a certain line of experience.—**Subaltern proposition**, a proposition asserting a part, and only a part, of what is asserted in another proposition.—**Subcontrary propositions**, propositions which have the same terms and may be true together but cannot be false together.—**Syllogistic proposition**, a proposition forming part of a syllogism.—**Synthetic proposition.** See *synthetic judgment*, under *synthetic*.—**Temporal proposition**, a proposition consisting of two categoricals united by a temporal adverb.—**Ternal** or **trinary proposition**, a proposition of third adjacent.—**Theoretical proposition**, a proposition concerning the fact, not concerning what ought to be done.—**True proposition.** See *true*.—**Universal proposition**, a proposition whose subject is any object whatever in the universe of discourse: as, Take any object you please, you will find it not a griffin. Every such proposition states the non-existence of something. If, in addition, it asserts the existence of something, it should be regarded as a composite proposition, partly universal and partly particular. But many logicians divide universal propositions into different species according as they do or do not assert the existence of their subjects. The result of this mode of treating the subject is a highly complicated doctrine.—**Unquantified proposition**, an indefinite proposition. = **Syn. 2.** *Overture*, etc. See *proposal*.—3 and 5. Position, thesis, statement, declaration, dictum, doctrine. *Proposition* differs from the words compared under *subject*, in that it is the technical word in rhetoric for the indication of the theme of a discourse.

The *proposition* is that part of a discourse by which its subject is defined. It includes, therefore, but is not restricted to, that which is termed *proposition* in the nomenclature of logic. It embraces all varieties of rhetorical form by which a *subject* is indicated to the audience. An interrogative may be in rhetorical dialect the *proposition*.
A. Phelps, Theory of Preaching, xx. § 1.

propositional (prop-ǭ-zish'ǫn-ạl), *a.* [< *proposition* + *-al*.] Pertaining to or constituting a proposition; considered as a proposition.

If a proposition ascribing the nature of things has an indefinite subject, it is generally to be esteemed universal, in its *propositional* sense. *Watts*, Logic, II. ii. § 1.

In theology truth is *propositional*—tied up in neat parcels, systematized, and arranged in logical order.
H. Drummond, Natural Law in the Spiritual World, p. 362.

Propositional quantity. See *quantity*.

propositionally (prop-ǭ-zish'ǫn-ạl-i), *adv.* In the manner of a proposition.

If he only uttered them [propositions] at random, or if they were only signs of emotion, they would not serve *propositionally*. *Lancet*, No. 3476, p. 787.

propositionize (prop-ǭ-zish'ǫn-īz), *v. i.*; pret. and pp. *propositionized*; ppr. *propositionizing*. [< *proposition* + *-ize*.] To make a proposition.

To speak is not merely to utter words, but to *propositionize*. *Lancet*, No. 3476, p. 787.

propositum (prǭ-poz'i-tum), *n.* [ML., < L. *propositum*, the first premise of a syllogism, an argument, neut. of *propositus*, pp. of *proponere*, set forth: see *propose*, *v.*, and *purpose*, *n.*] In medieval universities, a disputation concerning the canon law, which had to be performed by every bachelor in law.

propostscutellar (prō-pōst-skū'te-lạ̈r), *a.* [< *propostscutell-um* + *-ar*[3].] Of or pertaining to the propostscutellum.

propostscutellum (prō-pōst-skụ̄-tel'um), *n.*; pl. *propostscutella* (-ạ̈). [NL., < L. *pro*, before, + NL. *postscutellum*, q. v.] In *entom.*, the postscutellum of the pronotum; the postscutellar sclerite of the prothorax.

propound (prǭ-pound'), *v. t.* [With unorig. *-d*, for earlier *propoune*, var. of *propone*, < L. *proponere*, set forth, place before: see *propone*. Cf. *compound*, *expound*.] 1. To put forward; offer for consideration; offer; put or set, as a question; propose.

If then he [the offender] appear not, they banish him, and *propound* a reward according to the greatness of the offence. *Sandys*, Travailes, p. 6.

Give me leave to *propound* to you a second question.
Bunyan, Pilgrim's Progress, p. 150.

2. Among Congregationalists, to propose or name as a candidate for admission to membership in a church.

He was . . . (with his wife) *propounded* to be admitted a member. *Winthrop*, Hist. New England, I. 131.

propounder (prǭ-poun'dėr), *n.* [< *propound* + *-er*[1].] 1. One who propounds; one who proposes or offers for consideration.

The point of the sword thrust from him both the propositions and the *propounders*. *Milton*, Eikonoklastes, § 11.

Some deny the infallibility of the present church, and only make the tradition of all ages the infallible *propounder*. *Chillingworth*, Works, I. 119.

2. A monopolist. *Blount.* (*Halliwell.*)

proppage (prop'ạ̄j), *n.* [< *prop* + *-age*.] That which props or supports; materials for propping.

Hat and stick were his *proppage* and balance-wheel.
Carlyle.

propræscutal, *a.* See *proprescutal.*

propræscutum (prō-prē-skū'tum), *n.*; pl. *propræscuta* (-tạ̈). [NL., ‹ L. *pro*, before, + NL. *præscutum*, q. v.] In *entom.*, the præscutum of the pronotum; the prescutal sclerite of the prothorax.

propprætor, propprætorial. See *propretor, propretorial.*

propret†, propretet†. Middle English forms of *proper, property.*

proprescutal, propræscutal (prō-prē-skū'tạl), *a.* [‹ *propræscut-um* + *-al.*] Of or pertaining to the propræscutum.

propretor, proprætor (prō-prē'tọr), *n.* [‹ L. *proprætor*, ‹ *pro*, for, + *prætor*, pretor.] In *Rom. antiq.*, a magistrate filling the office and exercising the authority of a pretor, but not holding the titular rank; one who, having discharged the office of pretor at home, was sent into a province to command there with pretorial authority; also, an officer sent extraordinarily into the provinces to conduct the government with the authority of a pretor.

propretorial, proprætorial (prō-prē-tō'ri-ạl), *a.* [‹ *propretor, proprætor*, + *-ial.*] Of or relating to a propretor or the office of propretor.

Thus the distinction between consular (or proconsular) and prætorial (or *proprætorial*) provinces varied from year to year with the military exigencies of different parts of the empire. *Encyc. Brit.*, XIX. 885.

propriate (prō'pri-āt), *a.* [Appar. by apheresis for *appropriate* (?); otherwise ‹ L. *propriatus*, pp. of *propriare*, appropriate: see *proper, v.*] Peculiar; specific. [Rare.]

> But any simple Tom will tell ye,
> The source of life is in the belly,
> From whence are sent out those supplies
> Without whose *propriate* sympathies
> We should be neither strong nor wise.
> *W. Combe*, Dr. Syntax, ii. 7. (*Davies.*)

propriest, *n.* [‹ L. *propria*, neut. pl. of *proprius*, proper, own: see *proper.*] Possessions; property. *Halliwell.*

proprietarian (prọ̄-pri-e-tā'ri-ạn), *n.* [‹ *propriet-y* + *-arian.*] A stickler for the proprieties; a formal and precise person. [Rare.]

The conversazioni of the rigid *proprietarians*, where people sit down to a kind of hopeless whist, at a soldo the point, and say nothing. *Howells*, Venetian Life, xxi.

proprietary (prọ̄-prī'e-tā-ri), *a.* and *n.* [= F. *propriétaire* = Sp. *propietario* = Pg. It. *proprietario*, ‹ LL. *proprietarius*, pertaining to a property-holder; as a noun, an owner; ‹ L. *proprieta(t-)s*, property: see *propriety, property.*] I. *a.* Belonging to a proprietor or owner; of or pertaining to property or ownership: as, *proprietary* rights.

Though sheep which are *proprietary* are seldom marked, yet they are not apt to straggle. *N. Grew*, Cosmologia Sacra.

The recognition by kings that, if they do not recognise the *proprietary* rights of the weaker, then the stronger will not consider theirs. *Stubbs*, Medieval and Modern Hist., p. 214.

Proprietary colony. See II., 1.—**Proprietary medicine**, a medicine the manufacture or sale of which is restricted through patent of the drug or combination of drugs, of the label, or of the name, or otherwise, or a medicine concerning which the person making it claims a private formula.—**Proprietary right**, the right of a proprietor; specifically, in the theatrical profession, the common-law right of the author of a drama to control exclusively its production or representation so long as the drama remains unpublished: also applied to the right when protected by copyright after publication.

II. *n.*; pl. *proprietaries* (-riz). 1. One who has exclusive title; one who possesses or holds the title to a thing in his own right; an owner; a proprietor; specifically, in *Amer. colonial hist.*, the grantee or owner, or one of the owners, of one of those colonies called *proprietary colonies* (in distinction from charter colonies and royal colonies or provinces). See *colony*, 1.

'Tis a mistake to think ourselves stewards in some of God's gifts and *proprietaries* in others. *Government of the Tongue.*

To the *proprietaries* of Carolina the respect of the revolution [of 1688] for vested rights secured their possessions. *Bancroft*, Hist. U. S. (12th ed.), III. 13.

2. A body of proprietors collectively: as, the *proprietary* of a county.

The influence of a monopolist middleman—such as the corporate *proprietary* of a railway virtually constitute—is placed in a new light. *The Academy*, July 27, 1889, p. 53.

3. The right of proprietor; ownership.

Peasant *proprietary* or occupying ownership, which are the names European economists give to that system of ownership which we have regarded as typically American, may exist for a long while among a population whose natural increase is restrained, where emigration is not thought of. *N. A. Rev.*, CXLII. 395.

4. In monasteries, a monk who had reserved goods and effects to himself, notwithstanding his renunciation of all at the time of his profession. *Imp. Dict.*

proprietor (prọ̄-prī'e-tọr), *n.* [An accom. form, with substituted suffix *-or*, for **proprieter*, ‹ OF. *proprietaire*, an owner: see *proprietary, n.*] One who has the legal right or exclusive title to something; an owner: as, the *proprietor* of a farm or of a mill.

French . . . was at any rate the only language spoken for some ages after the Conquest by our kings, and not only by nearly all the nobility, but by a large proportion even of the inferior landed *proprietors*. *Craik*, Hist. Eng. Lit., I. 98. (*Latham.*)

Lord proprietor, in *Amer. colonial hist.*, same as *proprietary*, 1.

Charleston became the principal town; and to it the whole political power of the colony [South Carolina] was exclusively confined during the government of the Lords *Proprietors*. *Calhoun*, Works, I. 401.

Peasant proprietor. See *peasant.*

proprietorial (prọ̄-pri-e-tō'ri-ạl), *a.* [‹ *proprietor* + *-i-al.*] Proprietary.

Proprietorial rights. *N. A. Rev.*, CXLII. 56.

proprietorship (prọ̄-prī'e-tọr-ship), *n.* [‹ *proprietor* + *-ship.*] The state or right of a proprietor; the condition of being a proprietor.

If you think she has anything to do with the *proprietorship* of this place, you had better abandon that idea. *Dickens*, Martin Chuzzlewit, xxxvi.

proprietress (prọ̄-prī'e-tres), *n.* [‹ *proprietor* + *-ess.*] A female proprietor.

> Are castles shadows? Three of them? Is she
> The sweet *proprietress* a shadow?
> *Tennyson*, Princess, ii.

proprietrix (prọ̄-prī'e-triks), *n.* [Fem. of *proprietor.*] A proprietress.

propriety (prọ̄-prī'e-ti), *n.*; pl. *proprieties* (-tiz). [‹ OF. *propriete*, later form of the vernacular *proprete* (› E. *property*), F. *propriété* = Pr. Sp. *propiedad* = Pg. *propriedade* = It. *proprietà*, ‹ L. *proprieta(t-)s*, peculiarity, property: see *property.*] 1†. Peculiar or exclusive right of possession; ownership; possession; property.

Why hath not a man as true *propriety* in his estate as in his life? *Bp. Hall*, Cases of Conscience.

So are the *proprieties* of a wife to be disposed of by her lord; and yet all are for her provisions, it being a part of his need to refresh and supply hers. *Jer. Taylor*, Works (ed. 1835), I. 710.

The reasons annexed to the second commandment are God's sovereignty over us, his *propriety* in us, and the zeal he hath to his own worship. *Shorter Catechism*, ans. to qu. 52.

Pensylvania. . . . The *Propriety* and Goverment of this Country was given by King Charles II. to William Pen, Esq. *Hist., Geog.*, etc., *Dict.*, ed. Collier, 2d ed. (1701).

2†. That which is proper or peculiar; property; peculiarity.

Man did give names unto other creatures in Paradise, as they were brought before him, according unto their *proprieties*. *Bacon*, Advancement of Learning, i.

A court which, if you will give me leave to use a term of logick, is only an adjunct, not a *propriety* of happiness. *Dryden*, Aurengzebe, Ded.

3†. An estate; a holding.

The splitting the colony into *proprieties*, contrary to the original charters. *Beverley*, Virginia, i. ¶ 92.

4. Suitableness to an acknowledged or correct standard or rule; consonance with established principles, rules, or customs; fitness; justness; correctness.

> *Propriety's* cold, cautious rules
> Warm Fervour may o'erlook.
> *Burns*, Apologetic, to Mrs. Lawrie.

Miss Temple had always something of serenity in her air, of state in her mien, of refined *propriety* in her language. *Charlotte Brontë*, Jane Eyre, viii.

After all his [Daniel Webster's] talents have been described, there remains that perfect *propriety* which animated all the details of the action or speech with the character of the whole, so that his beauties of detail are endless. *Emerson*, Fugitive Slave Law.

5†. Individuality; particular or proper state.

> Alas! it is the baseness of thy fear
> That makes thee strangle thy *propriety* [*i. e.*, makes thee disavow thyself].
> *Shak.*, T. N., v. 1. 150.

> Silence that dreadful bell: it frights the isle
> From her *propriety* [*i. e.*, out of herself].
> *Shak.*, Othello, ii. 3. 176.

The proprieties, the standards of conduct and behavior adopted and approved by society; conventional customs. =**Syn.** 4. *Precision*, etc. (see *purity*); appropriateness, seemliness.

proprium (prō'pri-um), *n.* [L., neut. of *proprius*, special, peculiar, own: see *proper.*] In *Swedenborgianism*, what is one's own; selfhood.

You will find that the will of man is his *proprium*, and that this from nativity is evil, and that thence is the false in the understanding. *Swedenborg*, True Christian Religion (trans.), iv.

Their character is the majestic *proprium* of their personality. *Bushnell*, Nature and the Supernat., ii.

Religion has had but one legitimate spiritual aim, namely, the softening of the selfhood or *proprium* which man derives from nature. *H. James*, Subs. and Shad., p. 256.

proproctor (prō-prok'tọr), *n.* [‹ *pro-* + *proctor.*] In English universities, an assistant proctor.

props[1] (props), *n. pl.* 1. A gambling game in vogue about 1850–60, especially in Boston. It was, in effect, a crude sort of dice-throwing. Small shells were partially ground down and their hollows filled with sealing-wax. Four of these shells were shaken in the hand and thrown on a table, the stake being won or lost according to the number of red or white sides coming up. 2. The shells used in this game.

Shells used in the Game of Props.

props[2] (props), *n.* [Short for *properties(-man).*] The property-man of a theater. [Theatrical slang.]

The property-man, or, as he is always called, *props* for short. *New York Tribune*, July 14, 1889.

prop-stay (prop'stā), *n.* In *steam* and *pneumatic engin.*, a stay used to strengthen tubes, water-spaces in steam-boilers, or large tubes and annular spaces in air-tanks, and resist pressure tending to collapse or rupture after the manner of a strut, instead of acting by tensile strength after the manner of a tie-rod. Where such stays pass through flues of steam-boilers, they are usually made tubular, thus permitting water to flow through them as a protection from overheating, while at the same time their exteriors become more or less effective heating-surfaces. The so-called Galloway boiler is a good example of the use of tubular prop-stays.

propterygial (prō-tẹ-rij'i-ạl), *a.* [‹ *propterygium* + *-al.*] Of or pertaining to the propterygium: as, the *propterygial* basale.

propterygium (prō-tẹ-rij'i-um), *n.*; pl. *propterygia* (-ạ̈). [NL. (Gegenbaur), ‹ L. *pro*, before, + NL. *pterygium*, q. v.] In *ichth.*, the foremost one of three basal cartilages which the pterygium of a fish, as an elasmobranch, may present. See *pterygium.*

The peculiar form of the [pectoral] fin in the Ray is due to the great development of the *propterygium*. *Gegenbaur*, Comp. Anat. (trans.), p. 478.

proptosed (prop'tōst), *a.* [‹ **proptose*, *v.* (‹ *proptosis*), + *-ed*[2].] Prolapsed. [Rare.]

A small portion of the bladder wall was *proptosed* through the deficient neck. *Lancet*, No. 3466, p. 246.

proptosis (prop-tō'sis), *n.* [NL., ‹ Gr. πρόπτωσις, a fall forward, ‹ προπίπτειν, fall forward, ‹ πρό, before, + πίπτειν, fall.] Prolapse or protrusion, as of the eyeball.

propugn† (prọ̄-pūn'), *v. t.* [‹ OF. **propugner* = Pg. *propugnar* = It. *propugnare*, ‹ L. *propugnare*, go forth to fight, fight for, defend, ‹ *pro*, forth, before, + *pugnare*, fight: see *pugnacious*. Cf. *expugn, impugn, oppugn.*] To fight for; defend; vindicate.

Thankfulness is our meet tribute to those sacred champions for *propugning* of our faith. *Hammond.*

propugnacle† (prō'pug-nạ̄-kl), *n.* [‹ OF. *propugnacle*, also *propugnacule* = Sp. *propugnáculo* = Pg. *propugnaculo* = It. *propugnacolo*, *propugnaculo*, ‹ L. *propugnaculum*, a bulwark, rampart, defense, ‹ *propugnare*, fight or contend for: see *propugn.*] Same as *propugnaculum.*

Rochel [La Rochelle] was the chiefest *Propugnacle* of the Protestants there. *Howell*, Letters, I. v. 8.

propugnaculum (prō-pug-nak'ụ̄-lum), *n.*; pl. *propugnacula* (-lạ̈). [L.: see *propugnacle.*] A bulwark; a defense.

The Roman colonies were thus not merely valuable as *propugnacula* of the state. *Encyc. Brit.*, VI. 158.

propugnation† (prō-pug-nā'shọn), *n.* [= It. *propugnazione*, ‹ L. *propugnatio(n-)*, a defense, vindication, ‹ *propugnare*, pp. *propugnatus*, fight or contend for: see *propugn.*] Defense.

> What *propugnation* is in one man's valour,
> To stand the push and enmity of those
> This quarrel would excite?
> *Shak.*, T. and C., ii. 2. 136.

propugner† (prọ̄-pū'nėr), *n.* [Also *propugnor*; ‹ OF. **propugneor*, also *propugnateur*, ‹ L. *propugnator*, a defender, ‹ *propugnare*, defend: see *propugn.*] A defender; a vindicator.

Zealous *propugners* are they of their native creed.
Government of the Tongue.

He [Plutarch] was an earnest *propugnor* of another third principle. *Cudworth*, Intellectual System, p. 216.

propulsation† (prō-pul-sā'shon), *n.* [< L. *propulsatio(n-)*, a driving forth, a repulse, < *propulsare*, pp. *propulsatus*, drive forth, ward off: see *propulse*.] The act of driving away or repelling; the keeping at a distance.

The just cause of war is the *propulsation* of public injuries. *Bp. Hall*, Cases of Conscience, iii. 8.

propulse† (prọ̄-puls'), *v. t.* [= Pg. *propulsar* = It. *propulsare*, < L. *propulsare*, drive forth, ward off, freq. of *propellere*, pp. *propulsus*, drive forth, push before, < *pro*, forward, before, + *pellere*, drive: see *pulse*[1].] To repel; drive off; keep away.

Perceavyng that all succours were clerely estopped and *propulsed* from them, and so brought into utter despaire of aide or comfort. *Hall*, Hen. VII., f. 23. (*Halliwell.*)

propulsion (prọ̄-pul'shon), *n.* [< F. *propulsion* = Sp. *propulsion* = Pg. *propulsão*, < ML. **propulsio(n-)*, < L. *propellere*, pp. *propulsus*, drive forth: see *propulse*, *propel*.] 1. The act of propelling or driving forward; impulse given.

The reasonable soul and all its faculties are in children, will and understanding, passions, and powers of attraction and *propulsion*. *Jer. Taylor*, Works (ed. 1835), I. 131.

God works in all things; all obey
His first *propulsion*. *Whittier.*

2. In *pathol.*, same as *paralysis festinans*.—**Modulus of propulsion.** See *modulus*.

propulsity (prọ̄-pul'si-ti), *n.* [< L. *propulsus*, pp. of *propellere*, propel (see *propulse*), + *-ity*.] Propulsion; motive power.

It euer was; that was ere Time had roome
To stirre itselfe by Heau'n's *propulsity*.
Davies, Summa Totalis, p. 10. (*Davies.*)

propulsive (prọ̄-pul'siv), *a.* [< *propulse* + *-ive*.] Tending or having power to propel; driving or urging on.

The *propulsive* movement of the verse. *Coleridge.*

Two *propulsive* forces, which appear to have overcome the body's inertia, and to have imparted to it a rapid motion. *J. Sully*, Sensation and Intuition, p. 24.

propulsory (prọ̄-pul'sọ̄-ri), *a.* [< *propulse* + *-ory*.] Same as *propulsive*.

propupa (prō-pū'pạ̈), *n.* [NL., < L. *pro*, before, + NL. *pupa*.] A stage of development of certain insects, intermediate between the larva and the pupa. Also called *semipupa*.

prop-wood (prop'wụd), *n.* 1. Saplings and copse-wood suitable for cutting into props.—2. Short stout lengths of fir and other wood used for propping up the roofs of collieries.

propygidium (prō-pi-jid'i-um), *n.*; pl. *propygidia* (-ạ̈). [NL., < Gr. πρό, before, + πυγή, rump, + dim. -ίδιον. Cf. *pygidium*.] In *entom.*, the penultimate or subterminal dorsal segment of the abdomen: especially used in describing those beetles whose elytra do not reach to the end of the abdomen.

propylæum (prop-i-lē'um), *n.*; pl. *propylæa* (-ạ̈). [L., also *propylæon*, < Gr. προπύλαιον, usually in pl. προπύλαια, a gateway, an entrance, neut. of προπύλαιος, before a gate, < πρό, before, + πύλη, a gate.] An important architectural vestibule or entrance to a sacred inclosure or other precinct, as that of the Acropolis of Athens, or that of the sanctuary of Eleusis: usually in the plural. In its origin it was a strongly fortified gateway, but it became developed into an ornamental structure, often elaborate and magnificent, with which were combined gates of more or less defensive strength.

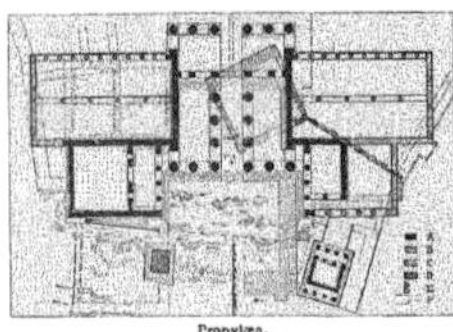
Propylæa.
A, plan of the propylæa of the Acropolis of Athens and Temple of Nike Apteros, as they stood in Pericles's time; B, wings, never completed, which formed part of the original project of Mnesicles; C, the earlier propylæa of Cimon, removed by Pericles; D, Roman pedestal of Agrippa; E, ancient Pelasgic wall of the primitive fortification of the Acropolis; F, ramparts of the Periclean citadel.

propylene (prop'i-lēn), *n.* [< *prop(ionic)* + *-yl* + *-ene*.] A gaseous hydrocarbon (C_3H_6), belonging to the series of olefines. It is one of the products of the destructive distillation of organic matters, and is produced artificially by the action of phosphorus iodide on glycerin, and in other ways.

propylite (prop'i-līt), *n.* [So called because supposed to have opened a new era in volcanic geology, or to have opened the Tertiary volcanic epoch; < Gr. πρόπυλον, a gateway (see *propylon*), + *-ite*[2].] In *lithol.*, the name given by Richthofen to a volcanic rock occurring in and considered by him as characteristic of various important silver-mining regions, especially those of Washoe (in Nevada) and Hungary. It is a considerably altered form of andesite, or of some igneous rock more or less nearly related to it. The metamorphism which was displayed in the formation of the metalliferous deposits of these regions was also attended by great changes in the inclosing and associated rocks. Also called *greenstone trachyte*.

I hope shortly to be able to describe some of the chief types of these rocks, . . . their altered forms (the *propylites*), and their Plutonic representatives (diorites and quartz-diorites). *Quart. Jour. Geol. Soc.*, XLV. 201.

propylitic (prop-i-lit'ik), *a.* [< *propylite* + *-ic*.] Related to or characteristic of propylite.

These rocks . . . may be traced undergoing certain changes due to both deep-seated and surface action, and also exhibiting interesting examples of the so-called *propylitic* modification. *Quart. Jour. Geol. Soc.*, XLV. 179.

propylon (prop'i-lon), *n.* [L., < Gr. πρόπυλον, a gateway, a vestibule, < πρό, before, + πύλη, gate. Cf. *propylæum*.] In *anc. Egypt. arch.*, a monumental gateway, usually between two towers in outline like truncated pyramids, of which one or a series stood before the actual entrance or pylon of most temples or other important buildings.

Propylon at Karnak, Egypt.

At Essabua, Girsheh, and Dandour, the cells of the temple have been excavated from the rock, but their courts and *propylons* are structural buildings added in front.
J. Fergusson, Hist. Arch., I. 126.

prora (prō'rạ̈), *n.*; pl. *proræ* (-rē). [NL., < L. *prora*, the fore part of a ship: see *prore*.] The prow or point of a cymba, or C-shaped sponge-spicule. When lobed or alate, the proræ are called *pteres*. See *ptere*. *Sollas.*

proral (prō'ral), *a.* [< *prora* + *-al*.] Of or pertaining to the proræ of a cymba: as, *proral* pteres. *Sollas.*

pro rata (prō rā'tạ̈). [ML.: L. *pro*, for, in accordance with; ML. *ratā*, abl. sing. of *rata*, rate: see *rate*[2].] In proportion.

pro-ratable (prō-rā'ta-bl), *a.* [< *pro-rate* + *-able*.] Capable of being pro-rated. [U. S.]

pro-rate (prō-rāt'), *v.* [< *pro rata*.] I. *trans.* To assess pro rata; distribute proportionally. [U. S.]

II. *intrans.* To make arrangement or agreement on a basis of proportional distribution.

A general circular was issued from the Santa Fe headquarters yesterday giving notice to all lines doing business between the Missouri River and St. Louis that it will hereafter refuse to *prorate* with them on shipments of grain and live stock. *New York Tribune*, June 6, 1890.

prore (prōr), *n.* [< L. *prora*, < Gr. πρῷρα, the prow of a ship, < πρό, before, in front. Cf. *prow*[2], a doublet of *prore*.] The prow or fore part of a ship. [Poetical and rare.]

There no vessel with vermilion *prore*,
Or bark of traffic, glides from shore to shore.
Pope, Odyssey, ix. 145.

The tall ship, whose lofty *prore*
Shall never stem the billows more.
Scott, L. of the L., vi. 13.

prorector (prō-rek'tor), *n.* [< L. *pro*, for, instead of, + *rector*, a governor, a ruler: see *rector*.] An officer in a German university who represents the rector, or who is next in authority to the directing officer.

prorectorate (prō-rek'tor-āt), *n.* [< *prorector* + *-ate*[3].] The office of a prorector.

prorenal (prō-rē'nal), *a.* [< L. *pro*, for, before, + *renes*, the kidneys: see *renal*.] Existing or acting instead of or prior to the definite formation of a kidney; of or pertaining to the segmental organ, or primitive kidney.

The *pro-renal* (segmental) duct; a conspicuous thick-walled tube seen, on either side, lying within the somatic mesoblast. *Huxley and Martin*, Elementary Biology, p. 109.

pro re nata (prō rē nā'tạ̈). [L.: *pro*, for, according to; *re*, abl. sing. of *res*, thing, affair, circumstance; *natā*, abl. sing. fem. of *natus*, pp. of *nasci*, be born, arise, originate: see *natal*[1].] For some contingency that arises unexpectedly or out of due course. A pro re nata meeting, for instance, is one called not at the stated time of meeting, but on account of the emergence of some occurrence or circumstance requiring it.

proreption† (prọ̄-rep'shon), *n.* [< L. *proreptus*, pp. of *prorepere*, creep forth, come out, < *pro*, forward, before, + *repere*, creep, crawl: see *repent*[2], *reptile*.] A creeping on. *Imp. Dict.*

prorex (prō'reks), *n.* [< L. *pro*, for, instead of, + *rex*, king: see *rex*.] A viceroy. [Rare.]

Create him *Pro-rex* of all Africa.
Marlowe, Tamburlaine, I., i. 1.

proritation†, *n.* [< L. as if **proritatio(n-)*, < *proritare*, provoke, < *pro*, forth, + **ritare*, as in *irritare*, excite, provoke, irritate: see *irritate*[1].] Provocation; challenging.

Your Maimonides, after all your *proritation*, holds no other than fair terms with our Samaritan Chronicle.
Bp. Hall, Works, X. 399. (*Davies.*)

Prorodon (prō'rọ̄-don), *n.* [NL. (Ehrenberg), < Gr. πρῷρα, prow (see *prore*), + ὀδούς (ὀδοντ-) = E. *tooth*.] The typical genus of the family *Prorodontidæ*, with terminal mouth and armed pharynx. There are many species, mostly of fresh water, as *P. niveus*; *P. marinus* is found in salt water.

Prorodontidæ (prō-rọ̄-don'ti-dē), *n. pl.* [NL., < *Prorodon* (*-dont-*) + *-idæ*.] A family of holotrichous ciliate infusorians, named from the genus *Prorodon*, of symmetrical oval or cylindric figure, with lateral or terminal mouth and a distinct pharynx, usually plicate or armed with rod-like teeth. It corresponds to Perty's *Decteria*, but is more restricted. *W. S. Kent.*

prorogate (prō'rọ̄-gāt), *v. t.*; pret. and pp. *prorogated*, ppr. *prorogating*. [< L. *prorogatus*, pp. of *prorogare*, prolong, extend, defer: see *prorogue*.] To prorogue; put off. *Brougham.*

prorogation (prō-rọ̄-gā'shon), *n.* [< F. *prorogation* = Sp. *prorogacion* = Pg. *prorogação* = It. *prorogazione*, < L. *prorogatio(n-)*, an extension, a putting off, < *prorogare*, pp. *prorogatus*, prolong, extend: see *prorogue*.] 1. The act of continuing, prolonging, or protracting; continuance in time or duration; a lengthening out to a distant time; prolongation; the delaying of action upon anything.

When they preferred another law for the *prorogation* of the provinces and armies which Cæsar demanded, Cato would speak no more to the people to hinder it.
North, tr. of Plutarch, p. 651.

Patriarchal *prorogations* of existence.
Lowell, Among my Books, 2d ser., p. 253.

2. The act of proroguing; more specifically, the right which belongs to the British crown, exercised by its ministers, of terminating a session of Parliament; also, the exercise of that right.

But it now seems to be allowed that a *prorogation* must be expressly made in order to determine the session.
Blackstone, Com., I. ii.

The power of *prorogation* either before or after the day of meeting rested with the king.
Stubbs, Hist. Eng., § 296.

Prorogation of a judge's jurisdiction, a judge's adjudication by consent of parties on matters properly outside his jurisdiction.—**Prorogation of a lease**, the extension of a lease. = **Syn. 2.** *Recess*, *Dissolution*, etc. See *adjournment*.

prorogue (prọ̄-rōg'), *v. t.*; pret. and pp. *prorogued*, ppr. *proroguing*. [Early mod. E. *proroge*; < OF. *proroguer*, F. *pr r ger* = Sp. Pg. *prorogar* = It. *prorogare*, < L. *prorogare*, prolong, protract, extend, continue, defer, < *pro*, forth, + *rogare*, ask: see *rogation*.] 1†. To prolong; protract.

We'll *prorogue* his expectation, then, a little.
B. Jonson, Every Man in his Humour, iii. 1.

Mirth *prorogues* life. *Burton.*

2†. To defer; put off; delay.

To promise better at the next we bring
Prorogues disgrace, commends not anything.
B. Jonson, Cynthia's Revels, Epil.

The king's journey into Scotland must be *prorogued* until another year, notwithstanding the gestes thereof be already set down. *Court and Times of Charles I.*, II. 207.

3. To discontinue meetings of for a time, usually for a period of time not expressly stated: used specifically of the British Parliament. Parliament is prorogued from session to session by the sovereign's authority, either by the lord chancellor in the royal presence, or by commission, or by proclamation. See *parliament* and *adjournment*.

The Parliament is *prorogued* till Michaelmas Term.
Howell, Letters, I. v. 6.

prorsad (prôr'sad), *adv.* [< L. *prorsum*, forward, + *-ad*³.] In *anat.*, forward; so as to be to or toward the front; antrorsely; cephalad: opposed to *retrad*.

prorsal (prôr'sal), *a.* [< L. *prorsum*, forward, + *-al.*] In *anat.*, forward; anterior: the opposite of *retral*.

prorumpt (prǫ-rump'), *v. i.* [= OF. *prorompre*, *prorumpre* = Sp. *prorumpir* = Pg. *proromper* = It. *prorompere*, < L. *prorumpere*, pp. *proruptus*, break forth, burst out, < *pro*, forth, + *rumpere*, break: see *rupture*.] To break forth; burst out. [Rare.]

What a noise it made! as if his spirit would have *prorumpt* with it. *B. Jonson*, Poetaster, v. 1.

proruption (prǫ-rup'shon), *n.* [< LL. *proruptio(n-)*, a breaking or bursting forth, < L. *prorumpere*, pp. *proruptus*, break or rush forth: see *prorump*.] The act of bursting forth; a bursting out. [Rare.]

Excluding but one day, the latter brood, impatient, by a forcible *proruption* anticipate their period of exclusion.
Sir T. Browne, Vulg. Err., iii. 16.

pros. An abbreviation of *prosody*.

pros-. [L., etc., *pros-*, < Gr. προς-, prefix, πρός, prep., from forth, from (one point) toward (another), toward, before, in presence of, hard by, near, etc.; earlier προτί, ποτί, = Skt. *prati*, toward, against, = OBulg. *proti* (cf. with ποτί the Zend *paiti*); with a formative *-ti*, from the base of πρό, forth, before: see *pro-*.] A prefix in words of Greek origin or formation, meaning 'to,' 'toward,' 'before,' etc.

prosaic (prǫ-zā'ik), *a.* [= F. *prosaïque* = Sp. *prosáico* = Pg. It. *prosaico* (cf. D. *prozaïsch* = G. *prosaisch* = Sw. Dan. *prosaisk*), < LL. *prosaicus*, pertaining to prose, in prose, < L. *prosa*, prose: see *prose*.] 1†. Pertaining to prose; resembling prose; in the form of prose.

In modern rhythm, . . . be it *prosaic* or poetic, he [the reader] must expect to find it governed for the greater part by accent. *Harris*, Philol. Inquiries, ii. 3.

2. Ordinary or commonplace in style or expression; uninteresting; dull; of persons, commonplace in thought; lacking imagination; literal.

These *prosaic* lines, this spiritless eulogy, are much below the merit of the critic whom they are intended to celebrate. *J. Warton*, Essay on Pope. (*Latham.*)

The danger of the *prosaic* type of mind lies in the stolid sense of superiority which blinds it to everything ideal.
Lowell, Study Windows, p. 250.

=**Syn.** 2. Vapid, flat, bald, tame, humdrum, stupid.

prosaical (prǫ-zā'i-kal), *a.* [< *prosaic* + *-al.*] Same as *prosaic*.

The first *prosaical* work with which Rastell's ponderous folio opens is called "The Life of John Picus."
Int. to *Sir T. More's* Utopia, p. lxxiii.

All manner of Greek writers, both metrical and *prosaical*. *Cudworth*, Intellectual System, p. 261.

prosaically (prǫ-zā'i-kal-i), *adv.* In a dull or prosaic manner.

prosaicism (prǫ-zā'i-sizm), *n.* [< *prosaic* + *-ism.*] A prosaic style or quality.

Through this species of *prosaicism*, Cowper, with scarcely any of the higher poetical elements, came very near making his age fancy him the equal of Pope.
Poe, Marginalia, xxviii. (*Davies.*)

prosaicness (prǫ-zā'ik-nes), *n.* The quality or character of being prosaic.

The vulgarity and *prosaicness* of these people.
Athenæum, No. 3254, p. 303.

prosaism (prō'zā-izm), *n.* [= F. *prosaïsme*; as L. *prosa*, prose, + *-ism.*] A prose idiom; a prosaic phrase. *Coleridge.*

prosaist (prō'zā-ist), *n.* [< L. *prosa*, prose, + *-ist.*] 1. A writer of prose.

There is no other *prosaist* who possesses anything like Milton's command over the resources of language.
Mark Pattison, Milton, l. 46.

2. A prosaic or commonplace person; one destitute of poetic thought or feeling.

Thou thyself, O cultivated reader, who too probably art no Psalmist, but a *Prosaist*, knowing God only by tradition. *Carlyle*, Sartor Resartus, i. 11.

prosal† (prō'zal), *a.* [< OF. *prosal*, < ML. as if **prosalis*, < L. *prosa*, prose: see *prose*.] In the form of prose.

The priest not always composed his *prosal* raptures into verse. *Sir T. Browne*, Misc., p. 177.

prosapie†, *n.* [< OF. *prosapie* = Sp. Pg. It. *prosapia*, < L. *prosapia*, also *prosapies*, a stock, race, family.] A stock; race. [Rare.]

My harte abhorreth that I should so
In a woman's kirtle my self disguise,
Beyng a manne, and begotten to
Of a mannes *prosapie*, in manly wise.
Udall, tr. of Apophthegms of Erasmus, p. 69. (*Davies.*)

prosar (prō'zär), *n.* [< ML. *prosarium*, a book containing the proses, < L. *prosa*, prose: see *prose*.] A service-book containing the proses. See *prose*, 3.

proscapula (prō-skap'ū-lä), *n.*; pl. *proscapulæ* (-lē). [NL., < L. *pro*, before, + *scapula*, shoulder-blade.] In *ichth.*, the principal and outer element of the scapular arch, generally carried forward and downward to articulate with its fellow of the opposite side, and supporting on its inner surface the cartilage or the bones which in turn bear the pectoral fin. It was called by Cuvier *humeral*, by Owen *coracoid*, and by later writers *clavicle*.

proscapular (prō-skap'ū-lär), *a.* [< *proscapula* + *-ar*³.] In *ichth.*, relating to the proscapula, or having its character.

proscenium (prǫ-sē'ni-um), *n.*; pl. *proscenia* (-ä). [< L. *proscænium*, *proscenium*, < Gr. προσκήνιον, the place in front of the scene or scenery, the stage, also the fore part or entrance of a tent, < πρό, before, in front of, + σκηνή, a tent, scene: see *scene*.] 1. In the ancient theater, the stage before the scene or back wall.

During his time, from the *Proscenium* ta'en,
Thalia and Melpomene both vanish'd.
Colman, Poetical Vagaries, p. 16. (*Davies.*)

In Asia Minor some of the theatres have their *proscenia* adorned with niches and columns, and friezes of great richness. *J. Fergusson*, Hist. Arch., I. 271.

2. In the modern theater, that part of the house which lies between the curtain or drop-scene and the orchestra: often used also to mean the curtain and the arch or framework which holds it.

proscenium-arch (prǫ-sē'ni-um-ärch), *n.* An arch or archway or any equivalent opening in the wall, which, except for this opening, is usually built solid as a precaution in case of fire between the stage and the auditorium of a modern theater.

proscenium-box (prǫ-sē'ni-um-boks), *n.* A stage-box; a box in the proscenium-arch.

proscenium-grooves (prǫ-sē'ni-um-grövz), *n. pl.* The scenery-grooves nearest the proscenium.

proscind† (prǫ-sind'), *v. t.* [< L. *proscindere*, tear open in front, rend, < *pro*, before, + *scindere*, cut, tear: see *scission*. Cf. *exscind*, *prescind*.] To rend in front.

They did too much *proscind* and prostitute (as it were) the Imperial purple.
Bp. Gauden, Tears of the Church, p. 573. (*Davies.*)

proscolecine (prō-skol'e-sin), *a.* [< *proscolex* (*-ec-*) + *-ine*¹.] Pertaining to a proscolex, or having its character.

proscolex (prō-skō'leks), *n.*; pl. *proscolices* (-li-sēz). [NL., < Gr. πρό, before, + σκώληξ, a worm: see *scolex*.] The first embryonic stage of a cestoid, as a tapeworm, when it has been liberated from the egg and is a minute vesicular body provided with hooks or horny processes for adhering to and working its way into the tissues of the host. Compare *deutoscolex* and *proglottis*. See cut under *Tænia*.

The *proscolex*, or six-hooked embryo, which gives rise to the bladder-worm. *Encyc. Brit.*, XXIII. 52.

proscolla (pros-kol'ä), *n.*; pl. *proscollæ* (-ē). [NL., < Gr. πρός, before, + κόλλα, glue.] In *bot.*, a viscid gland on the upper side of the stigma of orchids, to which the pollen-masses become attached. *Treas. of Bot.*

proscribe (prǫ-skrīb'), *v. t.*; pret. and pp. *proscribed*, ppr. *proscribing*. [= F. *proscrire* = Sp. *proscribir* = Pg. *proscrever* = It. *proscrivere*, < L. *proscribere*, write before, publish, advertise, publish as having forfeited one's property, confiscate the property of, outlaw, proscribe, < *pro*, before, + *scribere*, write.] 1. To publish the name of, as condemned to death and liable to confiscation of property.

Sylla and the triumvirs never *proscribed* so many men to die as they do by their ignorant edicts.
Bacon, Advancement of Learning, ii. 196.

2. To put out of the protection of the law; banish; outlaw; exile.

Robert Vere, Earl of Oxford, was . . . banished the realm and *proscribed*. *Spenser*, State of Ireland.

3. To denounce and condemn as dangerous; reject utterly; interdict; prohibit.

In the year 325 . . . the Arian doctrines were *proscribed* and anathematized in the famous council of Nice.
Waterland.

That he who dares, when she [Fashion] forbids, be grave,
Shall stand *proscrib'd* a madman or a knave.
Cowper, Conversation, l. 476.

The king told Rochester to choose any ministers of the Established Church, with two exceptions. The *proscribed* persons were Tillotson and Stillingfleet.
Macaulay, Hist. Eng., vi.

=**Syn.** 1. To doom.—3. To forbid.

proscriber (prǫ-skrī'bėr), *n.* One who denounces; one who dooms to destruction.

The triumvir and *proscriber* had descended to us in a more hideous form than they now appear, if the Emperour had not taken care to make friends of him and Horace.
Dryden, Æneid, Ded.

proscript (prō'skript), *n.* [< OF. *proscript*, F. *proscrit* = Sp. Pg. *proscripto* = It. *proscritto*, < L. *proscriptus*, pp. of *proscribere*, write before, etc.: see *proscribe*.] 1. A proscribed person. —2. A prohibition; an interdict.

For whatsoeuer he were which for the diminution of the liberties of the church were excommunicat, and so continued a yeeres space, then he should be within the danger of this *proscript*. *Foxe*, Martyrs, p. 271, an. 1250.

[Rare in both uses.]

proscription (prǫ-skrip'shon), *n.* [< F. *proscription* = Sp. *proscripcion* = Pg. *proscripção* = It. *proscrizione*, < L. *proscriptio(n-)*, public notice, advertisement, proscription, < *proscribere*, pp. *proscriptus*, publish, proscribe: see *proscribe*.] The act of proscribing; outlawry; denunciation; prohibition; exclusion; specifically, the dooming of citizens to death as public enemies, and the confiscation of their goods. The two great proscriptions in Roman history were that by Sulla about 82 B. C., and that by the second triumvirate 43 B. C.

By *proscription* and bills of outlawry,
Octavius, Antony, and Lepidus
Have put to death an hundred senators.
Shak., J. C., iv. 3. 173.

proscriptive (prǫ-skrip'tiv), *a.* [< L. *proscriptus*, pp. of *proscribere*, publish, proscribe: see *proscribe*.] Pertaining to or consisting in proscription; proscribing; disposed to proscribe.

The Imperial ministers pursued with *proscriptive* laws and ineffectual arms the rebels whom they had made.
Gibbon, Decline and Fall, xxxv.

People frequently acquire in such confederacies a narrow, bigoted, and *proscriptive* spirit.
Burke, Present Discontents.

proscriptively (prǫ-skrip'tiv-li), *adv.* In a proscriptive manner.

proscutal (prō-skū'tal), *a.* [< *proscut-um* + *-al.*] Of or pertaining to the proscutum.

proscutellar (prō-skū'te-lär), *a.* [< *proscutellum* + *-ar*³.] Of or pertaining to the proscutellum.

proscutellum (prō-skū-tel'um), *n.*; pl. *proscutella* (-ä). [NL., < L. *pro*, before, + NL. *scutellum*, q. v.] In *entom.*, the scutellum of the pronotum; the scutellar sclerite of the prothorax.

proscutum (prō-skū'tum), *n.*; pl. *proscuta* (-tä). [NL., < L. *pro*, before, + NL. *scutum*, q. v.] In *entom.*, the scutum of the pronotum; the scutal sclerite of the prothorax.

prose (prōz), *n.* and *a.* [< ME. *prose*, < OF. *prose*, F. *prose* = Sp. Pg. It. *prosa* = D. *proza* = OHG. *prōsa*, MHG. *prōse*, G. *prosa* = Icel. *prōsa* = Sw. Dan. *prosa*, < L. *prosa*, prose, short for *prosa oratio*, straightforward or direct speech (i. e. without transpositions or ornamental variations as in verse): *prosa*, fem. of *prosus*, contr. of *prorsus*, straightforward, direct, contr. of **proversus*, < *pro*, forth, + *versus*, turned, pp. of *vertere*, turn (> *versus* (*versu-*), a turning, a line, verse): see *verse*. The element *vers-* is thus contained, though in different applications, in both *verse* and *prose*. Cf. Gr. πεζὸς λόγος or πεζὴ λέξις, L. *pedestris oratio*, prose, lit. 'speech afoot' (not 'mounted' or elevated).] I. *n.* 1. The ordinary written or spoken language of man; language not conformed to poetical measure, as opposed to verse or metrical composition. See *poetry*.

"Sire, at o word, thou shalt no lenger ryme." . . .
"I wol yow telle a litel thyng in *prose*
That oghte liken yow, as I suppose."
Chaucer, Prol. to Tale of Melibeus, l. 19.

Prompt eloquence
Flow'd from their lips, in *prose* or numerous verse.
Milton, P. L., v. 149.

Well, on the whole, plain *prose* must be my fate: . . .
I'll e'en leave verses to the boys at school.
Pope, Imit. of Horace, II. ii. 198.

Prose, however fervid and emotional it may become, must always be directed, or seem to be directed, by the reins of logic. *Encyc. Brit.*, XIX. 261.

Hence—2. Commonplace ideas or discourse. *Goodrich*.—3. In *liturgics*, a hymn sung after the gradual, originating from a practice of setting words to the jubilatio of the alleluia. Such hymns were originally either in the vernacular or in rimed Latin, with rhythms depending, as in modern verse, upon the accent: hence they were called *prosæ*, proses, in distinction from *versus*, verses, this latter term being applied only to poetry written in meters depending on quantity as in the ancient classic poets. See *sequence*.

Hymns or *proses* full of idolatry.
Harmar, tr. of Beza (1587), p. 267.

On all higher festivals, besides this sequence, the rhythm called the *prose*, which generally consisted of between twenty and thirty verses, was likewise chanted.
Rock, Church of our Fathers, III. ii. 21.

4†. An oration; a story.

Whethur long, othir littull, list me not tell,
Ffor no mynd is there made in our mene bokes,
Ne noght put in our *proses* by poiettes of old.
Destruction of Troy (E. E. T. S.), l. 9075.

II. *a*. Relating to or consisting of prose; prosaic; not poetic; hence, plain; commonplace. *Thackeray*.

There you have the poetic reverie, . . . and the dull *prose* commentary. *Longfellow*, Hyperion, ii. 7.

prose (prōz), *v.*; pret. and pp. *prosed*, ppr. *prosing*. [< ME. *prosen*; < *prose*, *n*.] I. *trans*. To write or compose in prose: as, a fable *prosed* or versified.

But alle shul passe that men *prose* or ryme;
Take every man hys turn as for his tyme.
Chaucer, Scogan, l. 41.

And if ye winna mak' it clink,
By Jove I'll *prose* it!
Burns, Second Epistle to Lapraik.

II. *intrans*. 1. To write or compose in prose.

It was found . . . that whether ought was impos'd me by them that had the overlooking, or betak'n to of mine own choise in English or other tongue, *prosing* or versing, but chiefly this latter, the stile by certain vital signes it had was likely to live.
Milton, Church-Government, ii., Int.

"To prose" is now to talk or to write heavily, tediously, without spirit and without animation; but "to *prose*" was once the antithesis of to versify, and "proser" of a writer in metre. *Trench*, Select Glossary.

2. To write or speak in a dull or tedious manner.

When much he speaks, he finds that ears are closed,
And certain signs inform him when he's *prosed*.
Crabbe, Works, II. 158.

"My very good sir," said the little quarto, yawning most drearily in my face, "excuse my interrupting you, but I perceive you are rather given to *prose*."
Irving, Sketch-Book, p. 168.

The wither'd Misses! how they *prose*
O'er books of travell'd seamen.
Tennyson, Amphion.

prosect (prǫ-sekt'), *v*. [< L. *prosectus*, pp. of *prosecare*, cut off from before (taken in sense of 'dissect beforehand'), < *pro*, before, + *secare*, cut: see *section*.] I. *trans*. To dissect (a subject) beforehand; prepare (a cadaver) for anatomical demonstration by a professor.

II. *intrans*. To fill the office or perform the duties of a prosector: as, to *prosect* for anatomical lectures.

prosection (prǫ-sek'shǫn), *n*. [< LL. *prosectio(n-)*, a cutting off, < L. *prosecare*, pp. *prosectus*, cut off from before: see *prosect*.] The act or process of prosecting; dissection practised by a prosector.

prosector (prǫ-sek'tǫr), *n*. [< LL. *prosector*, one who cuts in pieces, < L. *prosecare*, pp. *prosectus*, cut off from before: see *prosect*.] One who prosects; one who dissects the parts of a cadaver for the illustration of anatomical lectures; a dissector who assists a lecturer by preparing the anatomical parts to be described by the latter. The office of prosector in a medical college ranks nearly with that of demonstrator.

A competent *prosector* attached to our zoölogical garden—one who combined the qualities of an artist, an author, and a general anatomist—would soon demonstrate the high importance of his work, and contribute the most efficient aid to animal taxonomy. *Science*, VII. 505.

prosectorial (prō-sek-tō'ri-ạl), *a*. [< *prosector* + *-ial*.] Of or pertaining to a prosector or prosection; fitted for prosecting: as, *prosectorial* duties; a *prosectorial* office.

Often small species can be at once consigned to alcohol, for the future use of the *prosectorial* department.
Pop. Sci. Mo., XXXIV. 790.

prosectorship (prǫ-sek'tǫr-ship), *n*. [< *prosector* + *-ship*.] The office or position of a prosector.

During his tenure of this *Prosectorship* he [Henle] published three anatomical monographs on previously undescribed species of animals.
Proc. Roy. Soc., XXXIX. No. 239, p. iv.

prosecutable (pros'ę-kū-tạ-bl), *a*. [< *prosecute* + *-able*.] Capable of being prosecuted; liable to prosecution. *Quarterly Rev.*

prosecute (pros'ę-kūt), *v.*; pret. and pp. *prosecuted*, ppr. *prosecuting*. [Formerly also *prosequute*; < OF. *prosecuter*, < L. *prosecutus*, *prosequutus*, pp. of *prosequi* (> It. *proseguire* = Pg. Sp. *proseguir* = OF. *prosequer*, vernacularly *porsuir*, *poursuivre*, > E. *pursue*), follow after or up, pursue, < *pro*, for, forth, + *sequi*, follow: see *sequent*. Cf. *execute*, *persecute*, etc., and see *pursue*, from the same L. verb.] I. *trans*. 1. To follow up; pursue with a view to attain or obtain; continue endeavors to accomplish or complete; pursue with continued purpose; carry on; follow up: as, to *prosecute* a scheme; to *prosecute* an undertaking.

So forth she rose, and through the purest sky
To Joves high Palace straight cast to ascend,
To *prosecute* her plot. *Spenser*, F. Q., VII. vi. 23.

I am beloved of beauteous Hermia;
Why should not I then *prosecute* my right?
Shak., M. N. D., i. 1. 105.

In the yeare 1596, there were sent other two shippes, to *prosequute* this Discouerie. *Purchas*, Pilgrimage, p. 434.

This intelligence put a stop to my travels, which I had *prosecuted* with much satisfaction.
Addison, Coffee House Politicians.

The very inhabitants discourage each other from *prosecuting* their own internal advantages.
Goldsmith, Citizen of the World, lxiii.

2. In *law*: (*a*) To seek to obtain by legal process: as, to *prosecute* a claim in a court of law. (*b*) To arraign before a court of justice for some crime or wrong; pursue for redress or punishment before a legal tribunal: as, to *prosecute* a man for trespass or for fraud. A person instituting civil proceedings is said to *prosecute* his action or suit; a person instituting criminal proceedings, or civil proceedings for damages for a wrong, is said to *prosecute* the party charged. (*c*†) To proceed against or pursue by law: said of crimes.

What they will inform,
Merely in hate, 'gainst any of us all,
That will the king severely *prosecute*
'Gainst us, our lives, our children, and our heirs.
Shak., Rich. II., ii. 1. 244.

=Syn. 1. To follow out, persevere in.—2 (*b*). To arraign.

II. *intrans*. To carry on a legal prosecution; act as a prosecutor before a legal tribunal.

Faith, in such case, if you should *prosecute*,
I think Sir Godfrey should decide the suit.
Pope, Imit. of Horace, II. ii. 23.

He [the king] is therefore the proper person to *prosecute* for all public offences and breaches of the peace, being the person injured in the eye of the law.
Blackstone, Com., I. vii.

prosecution (pros-ę-kū'shǫn), *n*. [< OF. *prosecution*, *prosecucion* = Sp. *prosecucion* = Pg. *prosecução* = It. *prosecuzione*, < LL. *prosecutio(n-)*, a following or accompanying, < L. *prosequi*, pp. *prosecutus*, follow after, pursue: see *prosecute*.] 1†. A following after; a pursuing; pursuit.

When I should see behind me
The inevitable *prosecution* of
Disgrace and horror. *Shak.*, A. and C., iv. 14. 65.

Let us therefore press after Jesus, as Elisha did after his master, with an inseparable *prosecution*, even whithersoever he goes. *Jer. Taylor*, Works (ed. 1835), I. 25.

2. The act or process of prosecuting, or pursuing with the object of obtaining or accomplishing something; pursuit by endeavor of body or mind; the carrying on or following up of any matter in hand: as, the *prosecution* of a scheme or undertaking; the *prosecution* of war or of commerce; the *prosecution* of a work, argument, or inquiry.

It is a pursuit in the power of every man, and is only a regular *prosecution* of what he himself approves.
Steele, Tatler, No. 202.

3. (*a*) The institution and carrying on of a suit in a court of law or equity to obtain some right or to redress and punish some wrong: as, the *prosecution* of a claim in chancery. (*b*) The institution and continuance of a criminal suit; the process of exhibiting formal charges or accusations before a legal tribunal and the pressing of them: as, *prosecutions* by the crown or by the state.—4. The party by whom proceedings are instituted: as, such a course was adopted by the *prosecution*.—**Criminal, malicious, etc., prosecution.** See the adjectives.—**Prosecution of Offenses Act**, an English statute of 1879 (42 and 43 Vict., c. 22) which established the office of director of public prosecutions for the purpose of instituting and carrying on criminal proceedings under the superintendence of the attorney-general, giving advice to police authorities, etc.

prosecutor (pros'ę-kū-tǫr), *n*. [< LL. *prosecutor*, *prosequutor*, prosecutor, < L. *prosequi*, pp. *prosecutus*, *prosequutus*, follow after, pursue: see *prosecute*.] 1. One who prosecutes; one who pursues or carries on any purpose, plan, enterprise, or undertaking.

The lord Cromwell was conceived to be the principal mover and *prosecutor* thereof.
Spelman, Hist. Sacrilege. (*Latham.*)

2. In *law*, the person who institutes and carries on any proceedings in a court of justice, whether civil or criminal: generally applied to a complainant who institutes criminal proceedings.

In criminal proceedings, or prosecutions for offences, it would still be a higher absurdity if the king personally sat in judgment; because in regard to these he appears in another capacity, that of *prosecutor*.
Blackstone, Com., I. vii.

Public prosecutor, an officer charged with the conduct of criminal prosecutions in the interests of the public, as a district attorney and in Scotland a procurator fiscal.

prosecutrix (pros'ę-kū-triks), *n*. [NL., fem. of LL. *prosecutor*, prosecutor: see *prosecutor*.] A female prosecutor.

proselachian (prō-se-lā'ki-ạn), *n*. [< NL. *Proselachius* + *-an*.] A hypothetical primitive selachian of the imaginary genus *Proselachius*.

Proselachius (prō-se-lā'ki-us), *n*. [NL., < L. *pro*, before, + NL. *selachius*, q. v.] A hypothetical genus of primitive selachians, "closely related to the existing sharks, and hypothetical ancestors of man" (*Haeckel*).

proselyte (pros'ę-līt), *n*. [Formerly also *proselite*; < ME. *proselite*, < OF. *proselite*, F. *prosélyte* = Sp. *prosélito* = Pg. *proselyto* = It. *proselito*, < LL. *proselytus*, < Gr. προσήλυτος, a convert, proselyte, lit. one who has come over to a party, < προσέρχεσθαι (2d aor. προσῆλθον), come to, < πρός, to, toward, + ἔρχεσθαι (2d aor. ἐλθεῖν), come.] 1. One who changes from one opinion, creed, sect, or party to another, with or without a real change in purpose and principle: chiefly used in a religious sense. Often accompanied with an adjective indicating the religion to which the change is made: as, a Jewish *proselyte* (that is, a proselyte to Judaism). See *convert*.

Ye compass sea and land to make one *proselyte*.
Mat. xxiii. 15.

False teachers commonly make use of base, and low, and temporal considerations, of little tricks and devices, to make disciples and gain *proselytes*. *Tillotson*.

Fresh confidence the speculatist takes
From ev'ry hair-brain'd *proselyte* he makes.
Cowper, Progress of Error, l. 491.

It is not to make *proselytes* to one system of politics or another that the work of education is to be directed.
Stubbs, Medieval and Modern Hist., p. 19.

2. Specifically, in *Jewish hist.*, one who became detached from the heathen and joined a Jewish community.

Many of the Jews and religious *proselytes* followed Paul.
Acts xiii. 43.

Proselytes of righteousness, in *rabbinical lit.*, those proselytes who were circumcised and adopted into the body of the Israelites.—**Proselytes of the gate**, in *rabbinical lit.*, those proselytes who were not compelled to submit to the regulations of the Mosaic law.

At the last Passover, we read in John's Gospel, certain Greeks—who were not Jews, but heathen, probably *proselytes of the gate*—who had come up to the festival to worship, came to Philip, one of the twelve, and expressed their wish to see Jesus (John xii. 20).
The Century, XXXIX. 538.

=Syn. 1. *Neophyte, Convert, Proselyte*, etc. (see *convert*), catechumen.

proselyte (pros'ę-līt), *v. t.*; pret. and pp. *proselyted*, ppr. *proselyting*. [< *proselyte*, *n*.] To induce to become the adherent of some given doctrine, creed, sect, or party; proselytize: as, "a *proselyted* Jew," *South*, Sermons, XI. 108.

There dwells a noble pathos in the skies,
Which warms our passions, *proselytes* our hearts.
Young, Night Thoughts, ix.

I have no wish to *proselyte* any reluctant mind.
Emerson, Free Religious Associations.

proselytise, proselytiser. See *proselytize*, *proselytizer*.

proselytism (pros'ę-li-tizm), *n*. [= F. *prosélytisme* = Pg. *proselytismo*; as *proselyte* + *-ism*.] 1. The act or practice of making proselytes or converts to a religion or to any doctrine, creed, system, sect, or party.

They were possessed of a spirit of *proselytism* in the most fanatical degree. *Burke*.

2. Conversion to a system or creed.

Spiritual *proselytism*, to which the Jew was wont to be wash'd, as the Christian is baptized.
Hammond, Works, IV. 500.

proselytist (pros'ę-li-tist), *n.* [< *proselyte* + *-ist.*] A proselytizer.

The Mormon *proselytists* report unusual success in their missionary work. *New York Evangelist*, June 22, 1876.

proselytize (pros'ę-li-tiz), *v.*; pret. and pp. *proselytized*, ppr. *proselytizing*. [< *proselyte* + *-ize.*] **I.** *trans.* To make a proselyte of; induce to become the adherent of some religion, doctrine, sect, or party; convert.

If his grace be one of these whom they endeavour to *proselytize*, he ought to be aware of the character of the sect whose doctrines he is invited to embrace. *Burke*, To a Noble Lord.

II. *intrans.* To make proselytes or converts.

As he was zealously *proselytizing* at Medina, news came that Abusophian Ben-Hareth was going into Syria. *L. Addison*, Mahomet (1679), p. 71.

Man is emphatically a *proselytizing* creature. *Carlyle*, Sartor Resartus, i. 2.

The egoism of the Englishman is self-contained. He does not seek to *proselytise*. *R. L. Stevenson*, The Foreigner at Home.

Also spelled *proselytise*.

proselytizer (pros'ę-li-ti-zėr), *n.* One who makes or endeavors to make proselytes. Also spelled *proselytiser*.

There is no help for it; the faithful *proselytizer*, if she cannot convince by argument, bursts into tears. *Thackeray*, Vanity Fair, xxxiii.

prose-man (prōz'man), *n.* A writer of prose; a proser.

All broken poets, all *prose-men* that are fallen from small sense to mere letters. *Beau. and Fl.*, Woman-Hater, iv. 2.

Verse-man or *prose-man*, term me which you will. *Pope*, Imit. of Horace, II. i. 64.

Let them rally their heroes, send forth all their powers, Their verse-men and *prose-men*, then match them with ours. *Garrick*, quoted in Boswell's Johnson, II. 53.

proseminary (prō-sem'i-nā-ri), *n.*; pl. *proseminaries* (-riz). [< *pro-*, before, + *seminary*.] A preparatory seminary; a school which prepares students to enter a higher school or seminary.

Merchant Taylors' School in London was then just founded as a *proseminary* for Saint John's College, Oxford, in a house called the Manour of the Rose. *T. Warton*, Hist. Eng. Poetry.

proseminate (prō-sem'i-nāt), *v. t.*; pret. and pp. *proseminated*, ppr. *proseminating*. [< L. *proseminatus*, pp. of *proseminare*, sow, scatter about, < *pro*, forward, + *seminare*, sow: see *seminate*.] To sow; scatter abroad, as seed.

Not only to oppose, but corrupt the heavenly doctrine, and to *proseminate* his curious cockles, dissensions, and factions. *Evelyn*, True Religion, II. 222.

prosemination (prō-sem-i-nā'shon), *n.* [< *proseminate* + *-ion*.] Propagation by seed.

We are not, therefore, presently to conclude every vegetable sponte natum, because we see not its *prosemination*. *Sir M. Hale*, Orig. of Mankind, p. 268.

prosencephalic (pros"en-sę-fal'ik or pros-en-sef'a-lik), *a.* [< *prosencephalon* + *-ic*.] **1.** Pertaining to the prosencephalon or fore-brain.—**2.** Pertaining to the forehead or fore part of the head; frontal: applied to the next to the first one of four cranial vertebræ or segments of the skull. *Owen.*

prosencephalon (pros-en-sef'a-lon), *n.* [NL., < Gr. πρός, before, + ἐγκέφαλος, the brain.] **1.** (*a*) The fore-brain; the cerebral hemispheres, together with the callosum, striate bodies, and fornix. It may also include the rhinencephalon. (*b*) All of the parts developed from the anterior of the three primary cerebral vesicles, including, in addition to those of (*a*), the thalamencephalon. Also called *procerebrum*.—**2.** The second cranial segment, counting from before backward, of the four of which the head has been theoretically assumed to be composed. See cuts under *encephalon* and *Petromyzontidæ*.

prosenchyma (pros-eng'ki-mā), *n.* [NL., < Gr. πρός, to, toward, + ἔγχυμα(τ-), that which is poured in, an infusion: see *enchymatous* and *parenchyma*.] In *bot.*, the fibrovascular system or tissue of plants; the cells and modified cells which constitute the framework of plants, as distinguished from *parenchyma*, or the cells which constitute the soft tissues of plants. See *parenchyma*. In most of the lower plants it is barely if at all developed, but in the higher plants it exists as a skeleton which brings all the parts into closer relation. The solid wood of trunks and the veins of leaves are familiar examples. As in parenchyma, the cells composing this tissue are very various in form, size, etc., and have been minutely classified, yet they may be reduced to a few comparatively simple types. These cells, which are normally of considerable length in proportion to the transverse diameter, are generally more or less sharply pointed, and are divided into typical wood-cells and woody fibers (including libriform cells and secondary wood-cells) and vasiform wood-cells or tracheïds. The most important modification is that in which cells belonging to this system unite to form long rows in which the terminal partitions are nearly or quite obliterated, throwing the cavities into one, forming a duct. These ducts or vessels may be dotted, spirally marked, annular, reticulated, or trabecular. A modification in a different direction produces bast-cells, bast-fibers, or liber-fibers. See also *wood-cell*, *libriform cells* (under *libriform*), *duct*, 2 (*b*), *bast*[1], 2, *liber*[1], 1.

prosenchymatous (pros-eng-kim'a-tus), *a.* [< *prosenchyma*(*t-*) + *-ous*.] In *bot.*, like or belonging to prosenchyma.

According to the amount of surface-growth and thickening of the cell-wall, various forms of parenchymatous and *prosenchymatous* tissue result. *Encyc. Brit.*, IV. 85.

proser (prō'zėr), *n.* [< *prose* + *-er*[1].] **1†.** A writer of prose.

And surely Nashe, though he a *proser* were,
A branch of laurel yet deserves to bear.
Drayton, Poets and Poesy.

[See also second quotation under *prose*, *v. t.*, 1.]

2. One who proses or makes a tedious narration of uninteresting matters.

But Saddletree, like other *prosers*, was blessed with a happy obtuseness of perception concerning the unfavourable impression which he sometimes made on his auditors. *Scott*, Heart of Mid-Lothian, xxvii.

Proserpina (pros-ėr-pī'nā), *n.* [NL., < L. *Proserpina*: see *Proserpine*.] A genus of gastropods, typical of the family *Proserpinidæ*.

Proserpinaca (pros"ėr-pi-nā'kā), *n.* [NL. (Linnæus, 1753), so called because of its partly prostrate habit; < L. *proserpinaca*, a plant, *Polygonum aviculare*, < *proserpere*, creep forward, creep along, < *pro*, forward, + *serpere*, creep: see *serpent*.] A genus of polypetalous water-plants of the order *Halorageæ*. It is characterized by the absence of petals, and by the numerical symmetry in threes, having usually a three-sided calyx-tube, three calyx-lobes, three stamens, three stigmas, and for fruit a three-angled three-seeded nutlet. There are but 2 species, natives of North America, including the West Indies. They are smooth and low-growing aquatics, bearing alternate lanceolate leaves, pectinately toothed or cut, and minute sessile axillary flowers. They are named *mermaid-weed*, doubtless from their comb-like leaves and growth in water.

Proserpine (pros'ėr-pin), *n.* [= F. *Proserpine*, < L. *Proserpina*, OL. *Prosepna*, corrupted from Gr. Περσεφόνη, also Περσεφόνεια, Proserpine (see def.), traditionally explained as 'bringer of death,' < φέρειν, bring (see *bear*[1]), + φόνος, death (see *bane*[1]); but this explanation, untenable in itself, fails to apply to the equiv. Περσέφασσα, Περσέφαττα; these forms, if not adaptations of some antecedent name, are appar. < περσε-, a form in comp. of πέρθειν, destroy; the second element -φονη may be connected with φόνος, death, -φασσα with √ φα, shine.] In *Rom. myth.*, one of the greater goddesses, the Greek Persephone or

Proserpine.
Relief of Ceres (Demeter), Iacchus or Triptolemus, and Proserpine (Persephone or Kora), found at Eleusis, Attica.

Kora, daughter of Ceres, wife of Pluto, and queen of the infernal regions. She passed six months of the year in Olympus with her mother, during which time she was considered as an amiable and propitious divinity; but during the six months passed in Hades she was stern and terrible. She was essentially a personification of the changes in the seasons, in spring and summer bringing fresh vegetation and fruits to man, and in winter harsh and causing suffering. She was intimately connected with such mysteries as those of Eleusis. The Roman goddess was practically identical with the Greek. Compare cuts under *Pluto* and *modius*.

Proserpinidæ (pros-ėr-pin'i-dē), *n. pl.* [NL., < *Proserpina* + *-idæ*.] A family of rhipidoglossate gastropods, typified by the genus *Proserpina*. The animal has a foot truncated in front and acute behind, without appendages, and a pulmonary pouch. The shell is heliciform, with a semilunar aperture, the columella plicated or truncated at the base, and the interior is absorbed with advancing age. The operculum is wanting. The species are inhabitants of middle America and the West Indies.

prosest†, *n.* An obsolete (Middle English) spelling of *process*.

prosethmoid (pros-eth'moid), *n.* [< Gr. πρός, toward, + E. *ethmoid*.] In *ichth.*, the foremost upper bone of the cranium of typical fishes, generally regarded as homologous with the ethmoid of the higher vertebrates.

proseuche, proseucha (pros-ū'kē, -kā), *n.*; pl. *proseuchæ* (-kē). [< LGr. προσευχή, prayer, place of prayer, < προσεύχεσθαι, pray, offer up vows, < πρός, toward, + εὔχεσθαι, pray.] A place of prayer; specifically, among the Jews, one that was not a synagogue, in distinction from the temple. These proseuchæ were usually outside the town, near some river or the sea, and built in the form of a theater, unroofed.

A *Proseucha* among the Hebrew people was simply an oratory or place of retirement and devotion. *E. H. Sears*, The Fourth Gospel the Heart of Christ, [p. 271, note.

prose-writer (prōz'rī"tėr), *n.* A writer of prose; a prosaist.

A poet lets you into the knowledge of a device better than a *prose-writer*. *Addison.*

prosiliency (prǫ-sil'i-en-si), *n.* [< L. *prosilien(t-)s*, ppr. of *prosilire*, leap forth, spring up, < *pro*, forth, forward, + *salire*, ppr. *salien(t-)s*, leap, bound: see *salient*.] The act of leaping forward; hence, a standing out. [Rare.]

Such *prosiliency* of relief. *Coleridge.* (*Imp. Dict.*)

prosily (prō'zi-li), *adv.* In a prosy manner; tediously; tiresomely.

prosimetrical (prō-zi-met'ri-kal), *a.* [< L. *prosa*, prose, + *metrum*, meter, + *-ic-al* (cf. *metrical*[2]).] Consisting of both prose and verse.

Prosimia (prǫ-sim'i-ā), *n.* [NL., < L. *pro*, before, + *simia*, an ape.] A genus of lemurs: same as *Lemur*. *Brisson*, 1764.

Prosimiæ (prǫ-sim'i-ē), *n. pl.* [NL., pl. of *Prosimia*.] A group of primatial quadrumanous mammals, founded by Storr in 1780 on the genus *Prosimia* of Brisson, later called *Strepsirrhini* and *Lemuroidea*; the lemurs. It is now regarded as one of two suborders of the order *Primates*, including all the lemurine or lemuroid quadrupeds. The cerebrum leaves much of the cerebellum uncovered. The lacrymal foramen is extra-orbital, and the orbits are open behind. The ears are more or less lengthened and pointed, without a lobule. The uterus is two-horned, the clitoris is perforated by the urethra, and the mammæ are variable. There are three families, *Lemuridæ*, *Tarsiidæ*, and *Daubentoniidæ*. See cut under *Lemur*.

prosimian (prǫ-sim'i-an), *a.* and *n.* [< *Prosimia* + *-an*.] **I.** *a.* Lemurine or lemuroid; strepsirrhine, as a lemur; of or pertaining to the *Prosimiæ*.

II. *n.* A member of the *Prosimiæ*; a lemuroid, lemurine, or lemur.

prosiness (prō'zi-nes), *n.* [< *prosy* + *-ness*.] The character or quality of being prosy.

His garrulity is true to nature, yielding unconsciously to the *prosiness* of dotage. *Noctes Ambrosianæ*, Feb., 1832.

prosing (prō'zing), *n.* [Verbal n. of *prose*, *v.*] Dullness or tediousness in speech or writing.

He . . . employed himself rather in the task of anticipating the nature of the reception he was about to meet with . . . from two beautiful young women, than with the *prosing* of an old one, however wisely she might prove that small-beer was more wholesome than strong ale. *Scott*, Pirate, xii.

prosingly (prō'zing-li), *adv.* In a prosing manner; prosily.

prosiphon (prō-sī'fon), *n.* [< *pro-* + *siphon*.] The predecessor of the protosiphon in the *Ammonites*, consisting of a kind of ligament united to the wall of the initial chamber, or protoconch.

prosiphonal (prō-sī'fon-al), *a.* [< *prosiphon* + *-al*.] Of or pertaining to the prosiphon.

Prosiphonata (prō-si-fǫ-nā'tā), *n. pl.* [NL.: see *prosiphonate*.] A primary group of camerate cephalopods, having the siphonal funnel directed forward, or in the direction of growth. (*a*) In the *Nautiloidea* the group is represented only by the extinct *Nothoceratidæ*. (*b*) In the *Ammonitoidea* the corresponding group includes all except the family *Goniatitidæ*.

prosiphonate (prō-sī'fon-āt), *a.* [< L. *pro*, before, + NL. *siphon*: see *siphon*, 2.] Having the siphonal region of the partitions convex forward, or in the direction of growth: applied to various cephalopodous shells so distinguished.

prosit (prō'sit). [L., 3d pers. sing. pres. subj. of *prodesse* (ind. pres. 1st pers. *prosum*, 3d pers. *prodest*), be of use or advantage, do good, < *pro*, for, + *esse*, be.] Good luck to you: a salutation used in drinking healths and otherwise among Germans and Scandinavians, especially among university students.

There were students from different Universities. . . . There was jesting, singing, . . . some questioning, some answering, . . . *prosit!* luck be with you! Adieu! C. G. *Leland*, tr. of Heine's Pictures of Travel, The Hartz [Journey.

proslambanomenos (pros-lam-ba-nom'e-nos), *n.* [< Gr. προσλαμβανόμενος (sc. τόνος), < προσλαμβάνειν, take or receive besides, add, < πρός, before, + λαμβάνειν, take.] In *Byzantine music*, the lowest tone of the recognized system of tones: so called because it was added below the lowest tetrachord. Its pitch is supposed to have corresponded to that of the second A below middle C.

pro-slavery (prō-slā'vėr-i), *a.* [< L. *pro*, for, + E. *slavery*.] In *U. S. hist.*, favoring the principles and continuance of the institution of slavery, or opposed to national interference therewith: as, a *pro-slavery* Whig; *pro-slavery* resolutions.

The majority in the Senate was not merely Democratic, of the Lecompton or extreme *pro-Slavery* caste; it was especially hostile to Senator Douglas. H. *Greeley*, Amer. Conflict, I. 306.

proslepsis (pros-lep'sis), *n.* [NL., < Gr. πρόσληψις, an assumption, < προσλαμβάνειν, take besides, assume besides, < πρός, before, + λαμβάνειν, λαβεῖν, take, assume (> λῆψις, an assumption).] In *Stoic philos.*, a premise, the minor premise of a modus ponens or tollens.

prosne†, *n.* [< OF. *prosne*, *prone*, "the publication made or notice given by a priest unto his parishioners (when service is almost ended) of the holy days and fasting days of the week following, of goods lost or strayed," etc. (Cotgrave).] A homily.

I will conclude this point with a saying, not out of Calvin or Beza, who may be thought partial, but out of a *prosne* or homily made . . . two hundred years ago. *Bp. Hacket*, Abp. Williams, ii. 56. (*Davies.*)

prosneusis (pros-nū'sis), *n.* [NL., < Gr. πρόσνευσις, a tendency, direction of a falling body, < προσνεύειν, incline toward, nod to, < πρός, before, + νεύειν (= L. *nuere*), nod, incline (> νεῦσις, inclination).] The position-angle of the part of the moon first eclipsed.

prosobranch (pros'ǫ-brangk), *a.* and *n.* Same as *prosobranchiate*.

Prosobranchiata (pros-ǫ-brang-ki-ā'tä), *n. pl.* [NL.: see *prosobranchiate*.] An order or subclass of gastropods, having the gills anterior to the heart, generally breathing water, more or less completely inclosed in a univalve shell, and sexually distinct: opposed to *Opisthobranchiata*.

prosobranchiate (pros-ǫ-brang'ki-āt), *a.* and *n.* [< NL. *prosobranchiatus*, < Gr. πρόσω, later Attic also πόρρω (= L. *porro*), forward, further, further on, in advance, + βράγχια, gills: see *branchiate*.] I. *a.* Having the gills in front of the heart, as a gastropod; of or pertaining to the *Prosobranchiata*.

II. *n.* A member of the *Prosobranchiata*.

prosobranchism (pros'ǫ-brang-kizm), *n.* [< *prosobranch* + *-ism*.] Disposition of the gills of a gastropod before the heart; the character of a prosobranchiate.

prosodal (pros'ǫ-dal), *a.* [< *prosodus* + *-al*.] Incurrent or adital, as an opening in a sponge; of the nature of or pertaining to a prosodus.

prosodiac¹ (prǫ-sō'di-ak), *a.* [< LL. *prosodiacus*, < Gr. προσῳδιακός, pertaining to accentuation, < προσῳδία, accentuation: see *prosody*.] Same as *prosodic*.

prosodiac² (prǫ-sō'di-ak), *a.* and *n.* [< *prosodion* + *-ac*.] I. *a.* Used in prosodia (see *prosodion*); hence, constituting or pertaining to a variety of anapestic verse, named from its use in prosodia. See II.

II. *n.* In *anc. pros.*, an anapestic tripody with admission of an (anapestic) spondee or an iambus in the first place.—**Hyporchematic prosodiac.** See *hyporchematic*.

prosodial¹ (prǫ-sō'di-al), *a.* [< L. *prosodia*, accentuation (see *prosody*), + *-al*.] Same as *prosodic*.

Chapleted youths singing the praise of Pallas in *prosodial* hymns. *J. A. Symonds*, Italy and Greece, p. 215.

prosodial² (prǫ-sō'di-al), *a.* Same as *prosodiac²*.

prosodian (prǫ-sō'di-an), *n.* [< L. *prosodia*, accentuation (see *prosody*), + *-an*.] One who is skilled in prosody, or in the rules of metrical composition.

Some have been so bad *prosodians* as from thence to derive the Latine word malum, because that fruit [apple] was the first occasion of evil. *Sir T. Browne*, Vulg. Err., vii. 1.

Each writer still claiming in more or less indirect methods to be the first *prosodian* among us. *S. Lanier*, Science of English Verse, p. viii.

prosodic (prǫ-sod'ik), *a.* [= F. *prosodique* = Sp. *prosódico* = Pg. *prosodico*, < Gr. προσῳδικός, pertaining to accentuation, < προσῳδία, accentuation: see *prosody*.] Pertaining to prosody, or to quantity and versification.

The normal instrumental ending â, preserved for *prosodic* reasons. *Encyc. Brit.*, XXI. 270.

prosodical (prǫ-sod'i-kal), *a.* [< *prosodic* + *-al*.] Same as *prosodic*.

prosodically (prǫ-sod'i-kal-i), *adv.* As regards prosody.

prosodiencephal (pros-ǫ-di-en-sef'al), *n.* [< Gr. πρόσω, forward, + NL. *diencephalon*, q. v.] The prosencephalon and the diencephalon taken together.

prosodiencephalic (pros-ǫ-di″en-se-fal'ik or -sef'a-lik), *a.* [< *prosodiencephal* + *-ic*.] Pertaining to the prosodiencephal.

prosodion (prǫ-sō'di-on), *n.*; pl. *prosodia* (-ä). [< Gr. προσόδιον, neut. of προσόδιος, belonging to processions, processional, < πρόσοδος, a procession, < πρός, from, + ὁδός, way, expedition.] In *anc. Gr. lit.*, a song or hymn sung by a procession approaching a temple or altar before a sacrifice.

prosodist (pros'ǫ-dist), *n.* [< *prosod-y* + *-ist*.] One who understands prosody; a prosodian.

The exact *prosodist* will find the line of swiftness by one time longer than that of tardiness. *Johnson*, Pope.

prosodus (pros'ǫ-dus), *n.*; pl. *prosodi* (-dī). [NL., < Gr. πρός, to, + ὁδός, a way, road.] An incurrent opening or passageway in a sponge; an aditus. *Encyc. Brit.*, XXII. 415.

prosody (pros'ǫ-di), *n.* [= F. *prosodie* = Sp. Pg. It. *prosodia*, < L. *prosodia*, < Gr. προσῳδία, a song with accompaniment, modulation of voice, especially tone or accentuation, mark of pronunciation, < πρός, to, + ᾠδή, a song: see *ode*.] The science of the quantity of syllables and of pronunciation as affecting versification; in a wider sense, metrics, or the elements of metrics, considered as a part of grammar (see *metrics*², 2).

[The modern sense of *prosody* (*prosodia*) seems to have originated from the fact that the marks of quantity were among the ten signs called προσῳδίαι.]

Prosody and orthography are not parts of grammar, but diffused like the blood and spirits through the whole. *B. Jonson*, English Grammar, i.

prosogaster (pros-ǫ-gas'tėr), *n.* [NL., < Gr. πρόσω, forward, + γαστήρ, stomach.] An anterior section of the peptogaster, extending from the pharynx to the pylorus, and including the esophagus or gullet, with the stomach in all its subdivisions, from the cardiac to the pyloric orifice—the fore-gut of some writers.

prosognathous (prǫ-sog'nạ-thus), *a.* Same as *prognathic*.

prosoma (prō-sō'mä), *n.* [NL., < Gr. πρό, before, + σῶμα, body.] 1. The anterior or cephalic section of the body of a cephalopod, bearing the rays or arms; the head or anterior part of any mollusk, in advance of the mesosoma.—2. In dimyarian lamellibranchs, a region of the body in which is the anterior adductor muscle, and which is situated in front of the mouth: it is succeeded by the mesosoma.—3. In *Cirripedia*, the wide part of the body, preceding the thoracic segments: in the barnacle, for example, that part which is situated immediately behind the point of attachment of the body to the shell on the rostral side. *Darwin*. See cuts under *Balanus* and *Lepadidæ*.

prosomal (prō-sō'mal), *a.* [< *prosoma* + *-al*.] Same as *prosomatic*.

prosomatic (prō-sǫ-mat'ik), *a.* [< *prosoma* (*-somat-*) + *-ic*.] Anterior, as a part of the body; pertaining to the prosoma.

prosome (prō'sōm), *n.* [< NL. *prosoma*.] Same as *prosoma*.

prosonomasia (pros-on-ǫ-mā'si-ä), *n.* [< Gr. προσονομασία, a naming, < προσονομάζειν, call by a name, < πρός, to, + ὀνομάζειν, name, < ὄνομα, name.] In *rhet.*, a figure wherein allusion is made to the likeness of a sound in two or more names or words; a kind of pun.

A iesting frier that wrate against Erasmus called him, by resemblance to his own name, Errans mus, and [is] . . . mainteined by this figure *Prosonomasia*, or the Nicknamer. *Puttenham*, Arte of Eng. Poesie, p. 169.

prosopalgia (pros-ǫ-pal'ji-ä), *n.* [NL., < Gr. πρόσωπον, face, + ἄλγος, pain.] Facial neuralgia.

prosopalgic (pros-ǫ-pal'jik), *a.* [< *prosopalgia* + *-ic*.] Pertaining to or affected with facial neuralgia, or tic-douloureux.

Prosopis (prǫ-sō'pis), *n.* [NL. (Linnæus, 1767), < Gr. προσωπίς, an unidentified plant, < πρόσωπον, face.] 1. A genus of leguminous trees and shrubs of the suborder *Mimoseæ* and tribe *Adenanthereæ*, characterized by the cylindrical spikes, and by the pod, which is nearly cylindrical, straight or curved or twisted, coriaceous or hard and spongy, indehiscent, and commonly filled with a pulpy or fleshy substance between the seeds. There are about 16 species, scattered through tropical and subtropical regions, often prickly, thorny, or both, bearing broad and short twice-pinnate leaves, and small green or yellow flowers in axillary spikes, rarely shortened into globose heads. Each flower has a bell-shaped calyx, five petals often united below, and ten separate stamens, their anthers crowned with glands. *P. juliflora* is the mesquit, also called *honey-pod* and *honey-locust* in the southwestern United States, *cashaw* and *July-flower* in Jamaica, and *pacay* in Peru: see *mesquit²*, *algarroba*, 2, *algarrobilla*, *honey-mesquit*, and *mesquit-gum* (under *gum²*). For *P. pubescens*, the tornilla or tornillo, see *screw-pod mesquit* (under *mesquit²*), and *screw-bean* (under *bean¹*).

Branch of Mesquit (*Prosopis juliflora*), with Flowers and Leaves. *a*, a flower; *b*, a pod.

2. In *zoöl.*: (*a*) A genus of obtusilingual solitary bees of the family *Andrenidæ*. *Fabricius*, 1804. (*b*) A section or subgenus of *Trochatella*, a genus of *Helicinidæ*.

prosopite (pros'ǫ-pīt), *n.* [< Gr. προσωπ(εῖον), a mask (< πρόσωπον, face), + *-ite²*.] A hydrous fluoride of aluminium and calcium occurring in colorless monoclinic crystals in the tin-mines of Bohemia, and also found in Colorado.

Prosopocephala (prǫ-sō-pǫ-sef'a-lä), *n. pl.* [NL., < Gr. πρόσωπον, face, + κεφαλή, head.] The tooth-shells, or *Dentaliidæ*, as an order of gastropods: synonymous with *Cirribranchiata*, *Scaphopoda*, and *Solenoconchæ*. See cut under *tooth-shell*.

prosopography (pros-ǫ-pog'ra-fi), *n.* [< Gr. πρόσωπον, face, + -γραφία, < γράφειν, write.] In *rhet.*, the description of any one's personal appearance.

First touching the *prosopographie* or description of his person. *Holinshed*, Stephan, an. 1154.

The reader that is inquisitive after the *prosopography* of this great man [Mr. Cotton] may be informed that he was a clear, fair, sanguine complexion, and, like David, of a "ruddy countenance." *C. Mather*, Mag. Chris., iii. 1.

prosopolepsy† (prǫ-sō'pǫ-lep-si), *n.* [< Gr. προσωποληψία, respect of persons, < πρόσωπον, face, countenance, + λαμβάνειν, λαβεῖν, take.] Respect of persons; especially, an opinion or a prejudice formed merely from a person's appearance. [Rare.]

There can be no reason given why there might not be as well other ranks and orders of souls superior to those of men, without the injustice of *prosopolepsie*. *Cudworth*, Intellectual System, p. 567.

prosopology (pros-ǫ-pol'ǫ-ji), *n.* [< Gr. πρόσωπον, face, + -λογία, < λέγειν, speak: see *-ology*.] Physiognomy.

Prosoponiscus (prǫ-sō-pǫ-nis'kus), *n.* [NL. (Kirby, 1857), < Gr. πρόσωπον, face, + ὀνίσκος, a wood-louse, dim. of ὄνος, ass: see *Oniscus*.] A genus of supposed amphipod crustaceans, a species of which, *P. problematicus*, occurs in the Permian of England.

prosopopeia, prosopopœia (prǫ-sō-pǫ-pē'yä), *n.* [= F. *prosopopée* = Sp. *prosopopeya* = Pg. *prosopopea*, *prosopopeia* = It. *prosopopea*, *prosopopeja*, < L. *prosopopœia*, < Gr. προσωποποιία, personification, a dramatizing, < προσωποποιεῖν, personify, dramatize, < πρόσωπον, face, person, a dramatic character, + ποιεῖν, make, form, do.] Literally, making (that is, inventing or imagining) a person; in *rhet.*, originally, introduction, in a discourse or composition, of a pretended speaker, whether a person absent or deceased, or an abstraction or inanimate object: in modern usage generally limited to the latter sense, and accordingly equivalent to *personification*.

The first species [of representative figures] is *prosopopœia*, in which the speaker personates another: as where Milo is introduced by Cicero as speaking through his lips. . . . Sometimes this figure takes the form of a colloquy or a dialogue. This was the ancient sermocinatio.
H. N. Day, Art of Discourse, § 344.

prosopopey†, *n.* [< F. *prosopopée*, < L. *prosopopœia*: see *prosopopeia*.] Same as *prosopopeia*.

The witlessly malicious *prosopopey*, wherein my Refuter brings in the Reverend and Peerless Bishop of London pleading for his wife to the Metropolitan, becomes well the mouth of a scurril Mass-priest.
Bp. Hall, Honor of Married Clergy, ii. § 7.

prosopopœia, *n.* See *prosopopeia*.

prosoposternodymia (prǫ-sō-pǫ-stėr-nǫ-dim′-i-ạ̈), *n.* [NL., < Gr. πρόσωπον, face, + στέρνον, breast, + δίδυμος, double: see *didymous*.] In *teratol.*, a double monstrosity, with union of faces from forehead to sternum.

prosopotocia (prǫ-sō-pǫ-tō′ṣiạ̈), *n.* [NL., < Gr. πρόσωπον, face, + τόκος, parturition.] Parturition with face-presentation.

Prosopulmonata (pros-ǫ-pul-mǫ-nā′tạ̈), *n. pl.* [NL.: see *prosopulmonate*.] Those air-breathing gastropods whose pulmonary sac occupies an anterior position.

prosopulmonate (pros-ǫ-pul′mǫ-nāt), *a.* [< Gr. πρόσω, forward, + L. *pulmo*, lung: see *pulmonate*.] Having anterior pulmonary organs: applied to those pulmonates or pulmoniferous gastropods in which the pallial region is large, and gives to a visceral sac, with the concomitant forward position of the pulmonary chamber, an inclination of the auricle of the heart forward and to the right, and of the ventricle backward and to the left.

prosopylar (pros′ǫ-pī-lạ̈r), *a.* [< *prosopyle* + *-ar*³.] Of or pertaining to a prosopyle; provided with a prosopyle; incurrent, as an orifice of an endodermal chamber of a sponge.

prosopyle (pros′ǫ-pīl), *n.* [< Gr. πρόσω, forward, + πύλη, a gate.] In sponges, the incurrent aperture by which an endodermal chamber communicates with the exterior.

Returning to the ancestral form of sponge, Olynthus, let us conceive the endoderm growing out into a number of approximately spherical chambers, each of which communicates with the exterior by a *prosopyle* and with the paragastric cavity by a comparatively large aperture, which we may term for distinction an apopyle.
W. J. Sollas, Encyc. Brit., XXII. 414.

prosothoracopagus (pros-ǫ-thō-rạ-kop′ạ-gus), *n.* [NL., < Gr. πρόσω, forward, + θώραξ (-ακ-), thorax, + πάγος, that which is fixed or firmly set, < πηγνύναι, stick, fix in.] In *teratol.*, a double monster with the thoraces fused together in front.

prospect (prǫ-spekt′), *v.* [< L. *prospectare*, look forward, look out, look toward, foresee, freq. of *prospicere*, pp. *prospectus*, look forward or into the distance, look out, foresee, < *pro*, forth, + *specere*, look; in signification I., 2, from the n.] **I.** *intrans.* 1†. To look forward; have a view or outlook; face.

This poynte . . . *prospectethe* towarde that parte of Aphrike whiche the portugales caule Caput Bonæ Sperantiæ. *Peter Martyr* (tr. in Eden's First Books on America, [ed. Arber, p. 129).

Like Carpenters, within a Wood they choose
Sixteen fair Trees that never leaues do loose,
Whose equall front in quadran form *prospected*,
As if of purpose Nature them erected.
Sylvester, tr. of Du Bartas's Weeks, ii., The Handy-Crafts.

2 (pros′pekt). In *mining*, to make a search; explore: as, to *prospect* for a place which may be profitably worked for precious metal.

II. *trans.* 1. To look forward toward; have a view of.

He tooke the capitaine by the hand and brought him with certeine of his familiars to the highest towre of his palaice, from whense they myght *prospecte* the mayne sea. *Peter Martyr* (tr. in Eden's First Books on America, [ed. Arber, p. 179).

2 (pros′pekt). In *mining*: (*a*) To explore for unworked deposits of ore, as a mining region. (*b*) To do experimental work upon, as a new mining claim, for the purpose of ascertaining its probable value: as, he is *prospecting* a claim. [Pacific States.]

prospect (pros′pekt), *n.* [< F. *prospect* = Sp. Pg. *prospecto* = It. *prospetto*, < L. *prospectus*, a lookout, a distant view, < *prospicere*, pp. *prospectus*, look forward or into the distance: see *prospect*, *v.*] 1. The view of things within the reach of the eye; sight; survey.

Who was the lord of house or land, that stood
Within the *prospect* of your covetous eye?
Fletcher, Beggars' Bush, i. 2.

The streets are strait, yeelding *prospect* from one gate to another. *Purchas*, Pilgrimage, p. 436.

Eden, and all the coast, in *prospect* lay.
Milton, P. L., x. 89.

2. That which is presented to the eye; scene; view.

There is a most pleasant *prospect* from that walke ouer the railes into the Tuillerie garden.
Coryat, Crudities, I. 35, sig. D.

Up to a hill anon his steps he rear'd,
From whose high top to ken the *prospect* round.
Milton, P. R., ii. 286.

What a goodly *prospect* spreads around,
Of hills, and dales, and woods, and lawns, and spires!
Thomson, Summer.

There was nothing in particular in the *prospect* to charm; it was an average French view.
H. James, Jr., Little Tour, p. 95.

3†. A view or representation in perspective; a perspective; a landscape.

I went to Putney and other places on yᵉ Thames to take *prospects* in crayon to carry into France, where I thought to have them engrav'd. *Evelyn*, Diary, June 20, 1649.

The Domes or Cupolas have a marvellous effect in *prospect*, though they are not many.
Lister, Journey to Paris, p. 8.

The last Scene does present Noah and his Family coming out of the Ark, with all the Beasts two by two, and all the Fowls of the Air seen in a *Prospect* sitting upon the Trees. Quoted in *Ashton's* Social Life in Reign of Queen [Anne, I. 257.

4. An object of observation or contemplation.

Man to himself
Is a large *prospect*.
Sir J. Denham, The Sophy, v. 1.

The Survey of the whole Creation, and of every thing that is transacted in it, is a *Prospect* worthy of Omniscience. *Addison*, Spectator, No. 315.

5†. A place which affords an extensive view.

People may from that place as from a most delectable *prospect* contemplate and view the parts of the City round about them. *Coryat*, Crudities, I. 205.

Him God beholding from his *prospect* high.
Milton, P. L., iii. 77.

6. A wide, long, straight street or avenue: as, the Ascension *Prospect* in St. Petersburg. [A Russian use.]—7. Direction of the front of a building, window, or other object, especially in relation to the points of the compass; aspect; outlook; exposure: as, a *prospect* toward the south or north.

Without the inner gate were the chambers of the singers; . . . and their *prospect* was toward the south; one at the side of the east gate having the *prospect* toward the north. Ezek. xl. 44.

8. A looking forward; anticipation; foresight.

Is he a prudent man as to his temporal estate who lays designs only for a day, without any *prospect* to or provision for the remaining part of life? *Tillotson*.

9. Expectation, or ground of expectation, especially expectation of advantage (often so used in the plural): as, a *prospect* of a good harvest; a *prospect* of preferment; his *prospects* are good.

I had here also a *prospect* of advancing a profitable Trade for Ambergrease with these People, and of gaining a considerable Fortune to my self.
Dampier, Voyages, I. 481.

For present joys are more to flesh and blood
Than a dull *prospect* of a distant good.
Dryden, Hind and Panther, iii. 365.

Without any reasonable hope or *prospect* of enjoying them. *Bp. Atterbury*, On Mat. xxvii. 25.

I came down as soon as I thought there was a *prospect* of breakfast. *Charlotte Brontë*, Jane Eyre, xxxvii.

Over and over again did he [Cellini] ruin excellent *prospects* by some piece of madcap folly.
Fortnightly Rev., N. S., XL. 75.

10. In *mining*, any appearance, especially a surface appearance, which seems to indicate a chance for successful mining. Sometimes used as a synonym of *color* in panning out auriferous sand, or more often for the entire amount of metal obtained in panning or vanning.

11. In *her.*, a view of any sort used as a bearing: as, the *prospect* of a ruined temple.=**Syn.** 1-3. *Scene, Landscape*, etc. See *view*, *n.*—9. Promise, presumption, hope.

prospecter, *n.* See *prospector*.

prospection (prǫ-spek′shǫn), *n.* [< *prospect* + *-ion*.] The act of looking forward, or of providing for future wants; providence.

What does all this prove, but that the *prospection*, which must be somewhere, is not in the animal, but in the Creator? *Paley*, Nat. Theol., xviii.

prospective (prǫ-spek′tiv), *a.* and *n.* [< ME. *prospectyve*, n., < OF. *prospectif*, a. (as a noun, *prospective*, f.), = It. *prospettivo*, < LL. *prospectivus*, pertaining to a prospect or to looking forward, < L. *prospicere*, pp. *prospectus*, look forward, look into the distance: see *prospect*.] **I.** *a.* 1†. Suitable for viewing at a distance; perspective.

In time's long and dark *prospective* glass
Foresaw what future days should bring to pass.
Milton, Vacation Exercise, l. 71.

This is the *prospective* glass of the Christian, by which he can see from earth to heaven.
Baxter, Saints' Rest, iv. 8.

2. Looking forward in time; characterized by foresight; of things, having reference to the future.

The French king and king of Sweden are circumspect, industrious, and *prospective* too in this affair. *Sir J. Child*.

A large, liberal, and *prospective* view of the interests of states. *Burke*, A Regicide Peace.

Nothing could have been more proper than to pass a *prospective* statute tying up in strict entail the little which still remained of the Crown property.
Macaulay, Hist. Eng., xxiii.

3. Being in prospect or expectation; looked forward to; expected: as, *prospective* advantages; a *prospective* appointment.

II. *n.* 1. Outlook; prospect; view.

A quarter past eleven, and ne'er a nymph in *prospective*. *B. Jonson*, Cynthia's Revels, ii. 1.

Men, standing according to the *prospective* of their own humour, seem to see the self same things to appear otherwise to them than either they do to other, or are indeed in themselves. *Daniel*, Defence of Rhyme.

The reports of millions in ore, and millions in *prospective*. *Boston Traveller*, Jan. 24, 1880.

2†. The future scene of action.

Howsoever, the whole scene of affairs was changed from Spain to France; there now lay the *prospective*.
Sir H. Wotton, Reliquiæ, p. 219.

3†. A perspective glass; a telescope.

They speken of Alocen and Vitulon,
And Aristotle, that writen in her lyves
Of queynte mirours and of *prospectyves*.
Chaucer, Squire's Tale, l. 226.

It is a ridiculous thing, and fit for a satire to persons of judgment, to see what shifts these formalists have, and what *prospectives* to make superficies to seem body that hath depth and bulk. *Bacon*, Seeming Wise (ed. 1887).

What doth that glass present before thine eye? . . .
And is this all? doth thy *prospective* please
Th' abused fancy with no shapes but these?
Quarles, Emblems, iii. 14.

4†. A lookout; a watch.

Be ther placd
A *prospective* vpon the top o' th' mast, . . .
And straight give notice when he doth descrie
The force and comming of the enemie.
Times' Whistle (E. E. T. S.), p. 145.

5. In *her.*, perspective: as, a pavement paly barry in *prospective*.

prospectively (prǫ-spek′tiv-li), *adv.* [< *prospective* + *-ly*².] In a prospective manner; with reference to the future.

prospectiveness (prǫ-spek′tiv-nes), *n.* [< *prospective* + *-ness*.] The state of being prospective; the act or habit of regarding the future; foresight.

If we did not already possess the idea of design, we could not recognize contrivance and *prospectiveness* in such instances as we have referred to. *Whewell*.

prospectivewise (prǫ-spek′tiv-wīz), *adv.* In *her.*, in prospective. See *prospective*, 5.

prospector, prospecter (pros′pek-tǫr, -tėr), *n.* [< *prospect* + *-or*¹, *-er*¹.] In *mining*, one who explores or searches for valuable minerals or ores of any kind as preliminary to regular or continuous operations. Compare *fossicker*.

A large number of *prospectors* have crossed over the divide to the British head waters of the Yukon, in search of the rich diggings found by a lucky few last year.
Science, VIII. 179.

On all diggings there is a class of men, impatient of steady constant labour, who devote themselves to the exploring of hitherto unworked and untrodden ground: these men are distinguished by the name of *prospectors*.
A. C. Grant, Bush Life in Queensland, II. 253.

prospectus (prǫ-spek′tus), *n.* [< L. *prospectus*, a lookout, prospect: see *prospect*.] A printed sketch or plan issued for the purpose of making known the chief features of some proposed enterprise. A prospectus may announce the subject and plan of a literary work, and the manner and terms of publication, etc., or the proposals of a new company, joint-stock association, or other undertaking.

prosper (pros′pėr), *v.* [< F. *prospérer* = Sp. Pg. *prosperar* = It. *prosperare*, < L. *prosperare*, cause to succeed, render happy, < *prosper*, *prosperus*, favorable, fortunate: see *prosperous*.] **I.** *intrans.* 1. To be prosperous or successful; succeed; thrive; advance or improve in any good thing: said of persons.

They, in their earthly Canaan placed,
Long time shall dwell and *prosper*.
Milton, P. L., xii. 316.

Enoch . . . so *prosper'd* that at last
A luckier or a bolder fisherman,
A carefuller in peril, did not breathe.
Tennyson, Enoch Arden.

2. To be in a successful state: turn out fortunately or happily: said of affairs, business, and the like.

The Lord made all that he did to *prosper* in his hand.
Gen. xxxix. 3.

All things do *prosper* best when they are advanced to the better; a nursery of stocks ought to be in a more barren ground than that whereunto you remove them. *Bacon*.

I never heard of any thing that *prospered* which, being once designed for the Honour of God, was alienated from that Use. *Howell*, Letters, I. v. 8.

Well did all things *prosper* in his hand,
Nor was there such another in the land
For strength or goodliness.
William Morris, Earthly Paradise, III. 112.

3†. To increase in size; grow.

Black cherry-trees *prosper* ever to considerable timber. *Evelyn.*

II. *trans.* To make prosperous; favor; promote the success of.

Let every one of you lay by him in store as God hath *prospered* him. 1 Cor. xvi. 2.

We have so bright and benign a star as your majesty to conduct and *prosper* us.
Bacon, Advancement of Learning, ii. 103.

All things concur to *prosper* our design. *Dryden.*

prosperation (pros-pe-rā'shon), *n.* [< OF. *prosperation*, < LL. *prosperatio(n-)*, prosperity, < L. *prosperare*, prosper: see *prosper*.] Prosperity. *Halliwell.* [Obsolete or provincial.]

I bethink me of much ill-luck turned to *prosperation*.
Amelia E. Barr, Friend Olivia, vi.

prosperity (pros-per'i-ti), *n.* [< ME. *prosperitie*, < OF. *prosperite*, *prosprete*, F. *prospérité* = Sp. *prosperidad* = Pg. *prosperidade* = It. *prosperità*, < L. *prosperita(t-)s*, good fortune, < *prosper*, favorable, fortunate: see *prosperous*.] The state of being prosperous; good fortune in any business or enterprise; success in respect of anything good or desirable: as, agricultural or commercial *prosperity*; national *prosperity*.

Prosperity doth best discover vice, but adversity doth best discover virtue. *Bacon*, Adversity.

Prosperity hath the true Nature of an Opiate, for it stupefies and pleases at the same time.
Stillingfleet, Sermons, III. xiii.

He . . . would . . . return
In such a sunlight of *prosperity*
He should not be rejected.
Tennyson, Aylmer's Field.

=Syn. Good fortune, weal, welfare, well-being. See *prosperous*.

prosperous (pros'pėr-us), *a.* [< ME. **prosperous*, < AF. *prosperous*, *prospereus*, prosperous, an extended form of OF. *prospere*, F. *prospère* = Sp. Pg. It. *prospero*, < L. *prosperus*, *prosper*, favorable, fortunate, lit. 'according to one's hope,' < *pro*, for, according to, + *spes*, hope (> *sperare*, hope). Cf. *despair*, *desperate*.] 1. Making good progress in the pursuit of anything desirable; having continued good fortune; successful; thriving: as, a *prosperous* trade; a *prosperous* voyage; a *prosperous* citizen.

The seed shall be *prosperous*; the vine shall give her fruit. Zech. viii. 12.

Count all the advantage *prosperous* vice attains;
'Tis but what virtue flies from and disdains.
Pope, Essay on Man, iv. 89.

There the vain youth who made the world his prize,
That *prosperous* robber, Alexander, lies.
Rowe, tr. of Lucan's Pharsalia, x.

2. Favorable; benignant; propitious: as, a *prosperous* wind.

A calmer voyage now
Will waft me; and the way, found *prosperous* once,
Induces best to hope of like success.
Milton, P. R., i. 104.

A favourable speed
Ruffle thy mirror'd mast, and lead
Thro' *prosperous* floods his holy urn.
Tennyson, In Memoriam, ix.

=Syn. 1. *Successful*, etc. (see *fortunate*), flourishing, well-off, well-to-do.—2. Propitious, auspicious.

prosperously (pros'pėr-us-li), *adv.* In a prosperous manner; with success or good fortune.

Consider that he liue at his hartes ease *prosperously* in this worlde to his liues end.
Bp. Gardiner, True Obedience, To the Reader.

prosperousness (pros'pėr-us-nes), *n.* The state of being prosperous; prosperity.

prosphysis (pros'fi-sis), *n.*; pl. *prosphyses* (-sēz). [NL., < Gr. πρόσφυσις, a growing to something, a joining, < προσφύειν, make to grow to, fasten, pass. προσφύεσθαι, grow to or upon, < πρός, to, + φύειν, cause to grow, pass. φύεσθαι, grow.] In *pathol.*, adhesion; a growing together.

prospicience (prō-spish'ens), *n.* [< L. *prospicien(t-)s*, ppr. of *prospicere*, look forward, look out: see *prospect*.] The act of looking forward.

prosporangium (prō-spō-ran'ji-um), *n.*; pl. *prosporangia* (-ä). [NL., < L. *pro*, before, + NL. *sporangium*, q. v.] A vesicular cell in the *Chytridieæ*, the protoplasm of which passes into an outgrowth of itself, the sporangium, and becomes divided into swarm-spores. *De Bary.*

pross[1] (pros), *n.* [Appar. a dial. form of *prose* in like sense.] Talk; conversation. *Halliwell.* [Prov. Eng.]

pross[2]† (pros), *n.* [In pl. *prosses*, as if pl. of *pross*, but appar. orig. sing., same as *process*: see *process*.] A process or projection, as of or on a horn. [Rare.]

They have onely three speers or *prosses*, and the two lower turne awry, but the uppermost groweth upright to heaven. *Topsell's* Four-Footed Beasts, p. 327. (*Halliwell.*)

Prostanthera (pros-tan-thē'rä), *n.* [NL. (Labillardière, 1806), so called in allusion to the spurred anthers; irreg. < Gr. προστιθέναι, add (< πρός, to, besides, + τιθέναι, put), + NL. *anthera*, anther.] A genus of shrubs of the order *Labiatæ*, type of the tribe *Prostanthereæ*. It is characterized by a two-lipped calyx with the lips entire or one minutely notched, and by completely two-celled anthers, usually with the back of the connective spurred, but the base not prolonged. The 38 species are all Australian. They are resinous, glandular, and powerfully odorous shrubs or undershrubs, with usually small leaves, and with white or red flowers solitary in the axils, sometimes forming a terminal raceme. They are known as *mint-tree*, *mint-bush*, or *Australian lilac*; and *P. lasianthos*, the largest species, sometimes reaching 30 feet, is also called the *Victorian dogwood*.

Prostanthereæ (pros-tan-thē'rē-ē), *n. pl.* [NL. (Bentham, 1836), < *Prostanthera* + *-eæ*.] A tribe of Australian shrubs of the order *Labiatæ*. It is characterized by a ten- to thirteen-nerved equal or two-lipped calyx, four stamens with two-celled or one-celled anthers, a two-lipped corolla with broad throat and broad flattish upper lip, an ovary but slightly four-lobed, and obovoid reticulated nutlets, fixed by a broad lateral scar. It includes about 98 species in 7 genera, of which *Prostanthera* is the type.

prostata (pros'tā-tā), *n.*; pl. *prostatæ* (-tē). [NL., < Gr. προστάτης, one who stands before: see *prostate*.] The prostatic gland, or prostate: chiefly in the phrase *levator prostatæ*, a part of the levator ani muscle in special relation with the prostate. Also *prostatica*.

prostatalgia (pros-tā-tal'ji-ä), *n.* [NL., < *prostata*, q. v., + ἄλγος, pain.] Pain, most properly neuralgia, in the prostate gland.

prostate (pros'tāt), *a.* and *n.* [< Gr. προστάτης, one who stands before, < προιστάναι, stand before, < πρό, before, + ἱστάναι, stand.] I. *a.* Standing before or in front of something; prostatic: specifically noting the gland known as the *prostate*.—**Prostate body** or **gland.** Same as II.—**Prostate concretions**, calculi of the prostate gland.

II. *n.* The prostate gland; a large glandular body which embraces the urethra immediately in front of the mouth of the bladder, whence the name. In man the prostate is of the size and shape of a horse-chestnut, surrounding the first section of the course of the urethra. It is a pale firm body, placed in the pelvis behind and below the symphysis of the pubis, posterior to the deep perineal fascia, and resting upon the rectum, through the walls of which it may easily be felt, especially when enlarged. It is held in place by the puboprostatic ligaments, by the posterior layer of deep perineal fascia, and by a part of the levator ani muscle called on this account *levator prostatæ*. It measures about 1½ inches in greatest width, 1¼ inches in length, and 1 inch in depth, and weighs about 6 drams. It is partially divided into a median and two lateral lobes. The prostate is inclosed in a firm fibrous capsule, and consists of both muscular and glandular tissue. The latter is composed of numerous racemose follicles whose ducts unite to form from 12 to 20 large excretory ducts, which pour their secretion into the prostatic part of the urethra.

prostatectomy (pros-tā-tek'tō-mi), *n.* [< NL. *prostata*, q. v., + Gr. ἐκτομή, a cutting out.] Excision of more or less of the prostate gland.

prostatic (pros-tat'ik), *a.* [< Gr. προστατικός, pertaining to one who stands before, < προστάτης, one who stands before: see *prostate*.] Of or pertaining to the prostate gland: as, the *prostatic* fluid, the secretion of this gland; *prostatic* urethra, the part of the urethra embraced by the prostate; *prostatic* concretions, calculi of the prostate.—**Prostatic ducts**, twelve to twenty short ducts which open upon the floor of the urethra, chiefly in the prostatic sinuses.—**Prostatic plexus.** See *plexus*.—**Prostatic sinus**, a longitudinal groove in the floor of the urethra, on either side of the crest, into which the prostatic ducts open.—**Prostatic vesicle**, a small cul-de-sac, from a quarter to a half of an inch in its greatest diameter, situated at the middle of the highest part of the crest of the urethra. It corresponds with the uterus of the female. Also called *sinus pocularis*, *utricle*, and *uterus masculinus*.

prostatica (pros-tat'i-kä), *n.*; pl. *prostaticæ* (-sē). [NL.: see *prostatic*.] The prostate gland: more fully called *glandula prostatica*.

prostatitic (pros-tā-tit'ik), *a.* [< NL. *prostatitis* + *-ic*.] Affected with prostatitis.

prostatitis (pros-tā-tī'tis), *n.* [NL., < *prostata*, q. v., + *-itis*.] Inflammation of the prostate.

prostatocystitis (pros'tā-tō-sis-tī'tis), *n.* [NL., < *prostata*, q. v., + Gr. κύστις, bladder, + *-itis*. Cf. *cystitis*.] Inflammation of the prostate and the bladder.

prostatolithus (pros-tā-tol'i-thus), *n.* [NL., < *prostata*, q. v., + Gr. λίθος, stone.] A calculus of the prostate gland.

prostatorrhœa, prostatorrhea (pros'tā-tō-rē'ä), *n.* [NL., < *prostata*, q. v., + Gr. ῥοία, a flow, < ῥεῖν, flow.] Excessive or morbid discharge from the prostate gland.

prostatotomy (pros-tā-tot'ō-mi), *n.* [< NL. *prostata*, q. v., + Gr. -τομία, < τέμνειν, ταμεῖν, cut.] In *surg.*, incision into the prostate.

prosternal (prō-stėr'nal), *a.* [< *prosternum* + *-al*.] Of or pertaining to the prosternum; prothoracic and sternal or ventral, as a sclerite of an insect's thorax.—**Prosternal epimera and episterna**, the pleuræ or side pieces of the prothorax, adjoining the prosternum.—**Prosternal groove** or **canal**, a hollow extending between the front coxæ: it is found in many *Rhynchophora*, serving for the reception of the rostrum in repose.—**Prosternal lobe**, a central prolongation of the front of the prosternum, more or less completely concealing the mouth when the head is in repose, as in the *Elateridæ* and *Histeridæ*.—**Prosternal process**, a posterior process of the prosternum, between the anterior coxæ.—**Prosternal sutures**, the impressed lines separating the side-pieces from the prosternum.

prosternation† (pros-tėr-nā'shon), *n.* [< F. *prosternation* = Sp. *prosternacion* = Pg. *prosternação* = It. *prosternazione*, < L. *prosternere*, throw to the ground, overthrow: see *prostrate*. Cf. *consternation*.] The state of being cast down; prostration; depression.

While we think we are borne aloft, and apprehend no hazzard, the failing floor sinks under us, and with it we descend to ruine. There is a *prosternation* in assaults unlookt for. *Feltham*, Resolves, ii. 60.

Fever, watching, and *prosternation* of spirits.
Wiseman, Surgery.

prosternum (prō-stėr'num), *n.*; pl. *prosterna* (-nä). [NL., < L. *pro*, before, + NL. *sternum*, q. v.] 1. In *entom.*, the ventral or sternal sclerite of the prothorax; the under side of the prothoracic somite; the middle piece of the antepectus. Also *præsternum*.—2. [*cap.*] A genus of coleopterous insects. Also *Prosternon*.—**Lobed prosternum.** See *lobed*.

prosthaphæresis† (pros-tha-fer'e-sis), *n.* [NL., < Gr. προσθαφαίρεσις, previous subtraction, < πρόσθεν, before, + ἀφαίρεσις, a taking away: see *aphæresis*.] 1. The reduction to bring the apparent place of a planet or moving point to the mean place.—2. A method of computing by means of a table of natural trigonometrical functions, without multiplying. It was invented by a pupil of Tycho Brahe, named Wittig, but was entirely superseded by logarithms.

prostheca (pros-thē'kä), *n.*; pl. *prosthecæ* (-sē). [NL., < Gr. προσθήκη, an addition, appendage, < προστιθέναι, put to, add: see *prosthesis*.] A somewhat gristly or subcartilaginous process of the inner side, near the base, of the mandibles of some coleopterous insects, as the rove-beetles or *Staphylinidæ*.

prosthecal (pros-thē'kal), *a.* [< *prostheca* + *-al*.] Of or pertaining to the prostheca.

prosthema (pros'the-mä), *n.*; pl. *prosthemata* (pros-them'a-tä). [NL., < Gr. πρόσθεμα, an addition, appendage, < προστιθέναι, put to, add: see *prostheca*.] A nose-leaf; the leafy appendage of the snout of a bat. See cut under *Phyllorhina*.

prosthencephalon (pros-then-sef'a-lon), *n.* [NL., < Gr. πρόσθεν, before, in front, + ἐγκέφαλος, the brain.] A segment of the brain consisting essentially of the cerebellum and medulla oblongata. *Spitzka.*

prosthenic (pros-then'ik), *a.* [< Gr. πρό, before, + σθένος, strength.] Strong in the fore parts; having the fore parts preponderating in strength.

prosthesis (pros'the-sis), *n.* [< LL. *prosthesis*, < Gr. πρόσθεσις, a putting to, an addition, < προστιθέναι, put to, add, < πρός, to, + τιθέναι, put, place: see *thesis*.] Addition; affixion; appendage. Specifically—(*a*) In *gram.*, the addition of one or more sounds or letters to a word; especially, such addition at the beginning. (*b*) In *anc. pros.*, a disemic pause. (c) In *surg.*, the addition of an artificial part to supply a defect of the body, as a wooden leg, etc.; also, a flesh-growth filling up an ulcer or fistula. Also *prothesis*.

prosthetic (pros-thet'ik), *a.* [< Gr. πρόσθετος, added or fitted to, < προστιθέναι, put to, add: see *prosthesis*.] Exhibiting or pertaining to prosthesis; added; especially, prefixed.

The *prosthetic* initial sound for words beginning with vowels is now (the infant learning to articulate is twenty months old) zh, or an aspirated y. *Pop. Sci. Mo.*, XIII. 593.

Prosthobranchia (pros-thō-brang'ki-ä), *n. pl.* [NL., < Gr. πρόσθεν, before, + βράγχια, gills.] Same as *Prosobranchiata*.

prostibulous† (pros-tib'ū-lus), *a.* [< L. *prostibulum*, *prostibula*, *prostibilis*, a prostitute, < *prostare*, stand forth, stand in a public place, < *pro*, forth, before, + *stare*, stand: see *stable*.] Pertaining to prostitutes; hence, meretricious.

Prostibulouse prelates and priestes. *Bp. Bale*, Image, iii.

prostitute (pros'ti-tūt), *v. t.*; pret. and pp. *prostituted*, ppr. *prostituting*. [< L. *prostitutus*, pp. of *prostituere* (> It. *prostituire* = Sp. Pg. *prostituir* = F. *prostituer*), place before or in front, expose publicly, < *pro*, forth, before, + *statuere*, cause to stand, set up: see *statue*, *statute*. Cf. *constitute*, *institute*, etc.] 1. To offer to a lewd use, or to indiscriminate lewdness, for hire.

Do not *prostitute* thy daughter, to cause her to be a whore. Lev. xix. 29.

For many went to Corinth, in respect of the multitude of Harlots *prostituted* or consecrated to Venus. *Purchas*, Pilgrimage, p. 321.

2. To surrender to any vile or infamous purpose; devote to anything base; sell or hire to the service of wickedness.

Shall I abuse this consecrated gift
Of strength, . . . and add a greater sin,
By *prostituting* holy things to idols?
Milton, S. A., l. 1358.

I pity from my soul unhappy men
Compell'd by want to *prostitute* their pen.
Roscommon, Translated Verse.

The title [of esquire] has, however, become so basely *prostituted* as to be worthless. *N. and Q.*, 7th ser., V. 478.

prostitute (pros'ti-tūt), *a.* and *n.* [I. *a.* < L. *prostitutus*, exposed publicly, prostituted, pp. of *prostituere*, expose publicly: see *prostitute*, *v.* II. *n.* = Sp. Pg. It. *prostituta*, < L. *prostituta*, a prostitute, fem. of *prostitutus*, exposed publicly: see I.] I. *a.* 1. Openly devoted to lewdness for gain.

Made bold by want, and *prostitute* for bread.
Prior, Henry and Emma.

2. Sold for base or infamous purposes; infamous; mercenary; base.

I found how the world had been misled by *prostitute* writers to ascribe the greatest exploits in war to cowards. *Swift*, Gulliver's Travels, iii. 8.

So shameless and so *prostitute* an attempt to impose on the citizens of America. *A. Hamilton*, The Federalist, No. lxv.

II. *n.* 1. A woman given to indiscriminate lewdness for gain; a strumpet; a harlot. In criminal law it has been held that the element of gain is not essential or may be presumed.

Dread no dearth of *prostitutes* at Rome. *Dryden*.

2. A base hireling; a mercenary; one who engages in infamous employments for hire.

No hireling she, no *prostitute* to praise.
Pope, Ep. to Harley, l. 36.

prostitution (pros-ti-tū'shon), *n.* [< F. *prostitution* = Sp. *prostitucion* = Pg. *prostituição* = It. *prostituzione*, < L. *prostitutio*(*n*-), prostitution, < *prostituere*, pp. *prostitutus*, expose publicly: see *prostitute*.] 1. The act or practice of prostituting, or offering the body to indiscriminate sexual intercourse for hire.

Till *prostitution* elbows us aside
In all our crowded streets.
Cowper, Task, iii. 60.

2. The act of offering or devoting to a base or infamous use: as, the *prostitution* of talents or abilities.

When a country (one that I could name)
In *prostitution* sinks the sense of shame,
When infamous Venality, grown bold,
Writes on his bosom "to be let or sold."
Cowper, Table-Talk, l. 415.

I hate the *prostitution* of the name of friendship to signify modish and worldly alliances. *Emerson*, Friendship.

prostitutor (pros'ti-tū-tor), *n.* [= F. *prostituteur* = Pg. *prostituidor*, < L. *prostitutor*, a prostitutor, pander, violator, < *prostituere*, pp. *prostitutus*, expose publicly: see *prostitute*, *v.*] One who prostitutes; one who submits one's self or offers another to vile purposes; one who degrades anything to a base purpose.

This sermon would be as seasonable a reproof of the Methodists as the other was of the *prostitutors* of the Lord's supper. *Bp. Hurd*, To Warburton, Let. cl.

prostomial (prọ-stō'mi-ạl), *a.* [< *prostomi-um* + *-al*.] Preoral; situated in advance of the mouth; pertaining to the prostomium.

The Mollusca are sharply divided into two great lines of descent or branches, according as the *prostomial* region is atrophied on the one hand or largely developed on the other. *E. R. Lankester*, Encyc. Brit., XVI. 639.

prostomiate (prọ-stō'mi-āt), *a.* [< *prostomium* + *-ate*[1].] Provided with a prostomium.

prostomium (prọ-stō'mi-um), *n.*; pl. *prostomia* (-ạ̈). [NL., < Gr. πρό, before, + στόμα, mouth.] The region in front of the mouth in the embryos of the *Cœlomata*; the preoral part of the head: said chiefly of invertebrates, as mollusks and worms. This is the essential part of the head, and is connected with the faculty of forward locomotion in a definite direction and the steady carriage of the body, as opposed to rotation of the body on its long axis. As a result the *Cœlomata* present, in the first instance, the general condition of the body known as bilateral symmetry.

Prostomum (pros'tọ-mum), *n.* [NL., < Gr. πρό, before, + στόμα, mouth.] A genus of aproctous rhabdocœlous *Turbellaria*, having a second or frontal in addition to the usual buccal proboscis. Also *Prostoma*.

prostrate (pros'trāt), *v. t.*; pret. and pp. *prostrated*, ppr. *prostrating*. [< L. *prostratus*, pp. of *prosternere* (> It. *prosternere*, *prosternare* = Sp. Pg. *prosternar* = F. *prosterner*), strew in front of, throw down, overthrow, < *pro*, before, in front of, + *sternere*, spread out, extend, strew: see *stratus*, *strew*.] 1. To lay flat; throw down: as, to *prostrate* the body.—2. To throw down; overthrow; demolish; ruin: as, to *prostrate* a government; to *prostrate* the honor of a nation.

In the streets many they slew, and fired divers places, *prostrating* two parishes almost entirely. *Sir J. Hayward*.

3. To throw (one's self) down, in humility or adoration; bow with the face to the ground: used reflexively.

All the spectators *prostrated themselves* most humbly upon their knees. *Coryat*, Crudities, I. 39, sig. D.

I *prostrate myself* in the humblest and decentest way of genuflection I can imagine. *Howell*, Letters, I. vi. 32.

4. To present submissively; submit in reverence.

We cannot be
Ambitious of a lady, in your own
Dominion, to whom we shall more willingly
Prostrate our duties.
Shirley, Grateful Servant, i. 1.

5. In *med.*, to make to sink totally; reduce extremely; cause to succumb: as, to *prostrate* a person's strength.

prostrate (pros'trāt), *a.* [< ME. *prostrat* = OF. *prostré*, < L. *prostratus*, pp. of *prosternere*, strew in front of: see *prostrate*, *v.*] 1. Lying at length, or with the body extended on the ground or other surface.

Well ny so half hour she lay, this swet wight,
Prostrat to the erth.
Rom. of Partenay (E. E. T. S.), l. 3569.

Mother Jourdain, be you *prostrate*, and grovel on the earth. *Shak.*, 2 Hen. VI., i. 4. 13.

Havoc and devastation in the van,
It [Etna's eruption] marches o'er the *prostrate* work of man.
Cowper, Heroism, l. 22.

2. Lying at mercy, as a suppliant or one who is overcome in fight: as, a *prostrate* foe.

Look gracious on thy *prostrate* thrall.
Shak., 1 Hen. VI., i. 2. 117.

3. Lying or bowed low in the posture of humility or adoration.

O'er shields, and helms, and helmed heads he rode
Of thrones and mighty seraphim *prostrate*.
Milton, P. L., vi. 841.

See thy bright altars throng'd with *prostrate* kings.
Pope, Messiah, l. 93.

4. In *bot.*, lying flat and spreading on the ground without taking root; procumbent.—5. In *zoöl.*, closely appressed to the surface; lying flat: as, *prostrate* hairs.=**Syn.** 1. *Prostrate*, *Supine*, *Prone*. He who lies *prostrate* may be either *supine* (that is, with his face up) or *prone* (that is, with his face down).

prostration (pros-trā'shọn), *n.* [< F. *prostration* = Sp. *postracion* = Pg. *prostração* = It. *prostrazione*, < LL. *prostratio*(*n*-), an overthrowing, a subverting, < L. *prosternere*, pp. *prostratus*, overthrow, prostrate: see *prostrate*.] 1. The act of prostrating, throwing down, or laying flat.

Though the loss of power to resist which *prostration* on the face implies does not reach the utter defencelessness implied by *prostration* on the back, yet it is great enough to make it a sign of profound homage. *H. Spencer*, Prin. of Sociol., § 384.

2. The act of falling down, or the act of bowing, in humility or adoration; primarily, the act of falling on the face, but the word is now used also for kneeling or bowing in reverence and worship.

The comely *Prostrations* of the Body, with Genuflection, and other Acts of Humility in time of divine Service, are very Exemplary. *Howell*, Letters, iv. 36.

How they can change their noble Words and Actions, heretofore so becoming the majesty of a free People, into the base necessity of Court-flatteries and *Prostrations*, is not only strange and admirable, but lamentable to think on. *Milton*, Free Commonwealth.

Lying at the feet of their blessed Lord, with the humblest attention of scholars, and the lowest *prostration* of subjects. *South*, Sermons, IV. i.

3. Great depression; dejection: as, a *prostration* of spirits.—4. In *med.*, a great loss of strength, which may involve both voluntary and involuntary functions.

A sudden *prostration* of strength, or weakness, attends this collick. *Arbuthnot*.

A condition of *prostration*, whose quickly consummated debility puzzled all who witnessed it. *Charlotte Brontë*, Shirley, xxiv.

Nervous prostration. See *nervous*.

prostrator (pros'trā-tor), *n.* [< LL. *prostrator*, prostrator, < L. *prosternere*, pp. *prostratus*, overthrow: see *prostrate*.] One who prostrates, overturns, or lays low.

Common people . . . are the great and infallible *prostrators* of all religion, vertue, honour, order, peace, civility, and humanity, if left to themselves. *Bp. Gauden*, Tears of the Church, p. 189. (*Davies*.)

prostyle (prō'stīl), *a.* [< L. *prostylos*, < Gr. πρόστυλος, having columns in front, < πρό, in front, + στῦλος, column.] In *arch.*, noting a portico in which the columns stand out entirely in front of the walls of the building to which it is attached; also, noting a temple or other structure having columns in front only, but across the whole front, as distinguished from a portico *in antis*, or a structure characterized by such a portico. See *amphiprostyle*, *anta*[1], and *portico*.

Plan of Prostyle Temple.

The next step [in the development of a temple plan] was the removal of these side walls [antæ], . . . columns taking their place in the corners, . . . and the *prostyle* temple was thus obtained. *Reber*, Ancient Art (tr. by Clarke), p. 200.

prosy (prō'zi), *a.* [< *prose* + *-y*[1].] Like prose; prosaic; hence, dull; tedious; tiresome.

Poets are *prosy* in their common talk,
As the fast trotters, for the most part, walk.
O. W. Holmes, The Banker's Dinner.

They tell us we have fallen on *prosy* days.
Lowell, Under the Willows.

prosyllogism (prō-sil'ọ-jizm), *n.* [= F. *prosyllogisme* = Pg. *prosillogismo*, < Gr. προσυλλογισμός, a syllogism of which the conclusion forms the major premise of another, < πρό, before, in front of, + συλλογισμός, a conclusion, a consequence: see *syllogism*.] A syllogism of which the conclusion is a premise of another.

A *prosyllogism* is then when two syllogisms are so contained in five propositions as that the conclusion of the first becomes the major or minor of the following. *Burgersdicius*, tr. by a Gentleman, ii. 13.

Epicheirema denotes a syllogism which has a *prosyllogism* to establish each of its premises. *Atwater*, Logic, p. 157.

Prot. An abbreviation of *Protestant*.

protactic (prọ-tak'tik), *a.* [< Gr. προτακτικός, placing before, < προτάσσειν, place before, < πρό, before, in front, + τάσσειν, place, arrange: see *tactic*.] Being placed at the beginning; previous.

protagon (prō'tạ-gon), *n.* [NL., < Gr. πρῶτος, first, + ἄγων, ppr. of ἄγειν, lead, act: see *agent*.] A phosphureted, fatty, crystalline substance, which forms a chief constituent of nervous tissue. Its composition has been represented by the formula $C_{160}H_{308}N_5PO_{35}$.

Now it has recently been discovered that white or fibrous nerve-tissue is chemically distinguished from gray or vesicular nerve-tissue by the presence in large quantity of a substance called *protagon*. *H. Spencer*, Prin. of Psychol., § 34, note.

protagonist (prọ-tag'ọ-nist), *n.* [< Gr. πρωταγωνιστής, a chief actor, < πρῶτος, first, + ἀγωνιστής, a combatant, pleader, actor: see *agonist*.] In the *Gr. drama*, the leading character or actor in a play; hence, in general, any leading character.

Tis charged upon me that I make debauched persons (such as they say my Astrologer and Gamester are) my *protagonists*, or the chief persons of the drama. *Dryden*, Mock Astrologer, Pref.

It is impossible to read the books of the older prophets, and especially of their *protagonist* Amos, without seeing that the new thing which they are compelled to speak is not Jehovah's grace, but His inexorable and righteous wrath. *Encyc. Brit.*, XIX. 818.

Protalcyonaria (prọ-tal'si-ọ-nā'ri-ạ̈), *n. pl.* [NL., < Gr. πρῶτος, first, + NL. *Alcyonaria*, q. v.] In some systems, an order of alcyonarian polyps.

protamnion (prọ-tam'ni-on), *n.* [NL., < Gr. πρῶτος, first, + ἀμνίον, amnion: see *amnion*.] A hypothetical primitive amniotic animal, the supposed ancestor or common parent-form of the *Amniota*, or those vertebrates which are provided with an amnion.

In external appearance the *protamnion* was probably an intermediate form between the salamanders and the lizards. *Haeckel*, Evol. of Man (trans.), II. 134.

Protamœba (prō-ta-mē'bä), *n.* [NL., < Gr. πρῶτος, first, + NL. *Amœba*.] A genus of *Monera*, or myxopodous *Protozoa*, with lobate, not filamentous, pseudopods. See *Protogenes*.

It is open to doubt, however, whether either *Protamœba*, Protogenes, or Myxodictyum is anything but one stage of a cycle of forms which are more completely, though perhaps not yet wholly, represented by some other very interesting Monera. *Huxley*, Anat. Invert., p. 75.

protamœban (prō-ta-mē'ban), *a.* and *n.* **I.** *a.* Having the characters of *Protamœba*.

II. *n.* A member of the genus *Protamœba*.

protamphirhine (prō-tam'fi-rin), *n.* [< Gr. πρῶτος, first, + NL. *amphirhinus*: see *amphirhine*.] The hypothetical primitive ancestral form of vertebrates having paired nostrils. See *amphirhine*, *monorhine*.

From this *Protamphirhine* were developed, in divergent lines, the true Sharks, Rays, and Chimæræ; the Ganoids, and the Dipneusta. *Huxley*, Critiques and Addresses, p. 284.

protandric (prō-tan'drik), *a.* [As *protandr-y* + *-ic*.] In *bot.*, same as *protandrous*.

protandrous (prō-tan'drus), *a.* [As *protandr-y* + *-ous*.] In *bot.*, same as *proterandrous*.

protandry (prō-tan'dri), *n.* [< Gr. πρῶτος, first, + ἀνήρ (ἀνδρ-), male (in mod. bot. stamen).] In *bot.*, same as *proterandry*.

The terms *protandry* and protogyny used by Hildebrand to express, in the one case the development of the stamens before the pistils, in the other case the development of the pistils before the stamens, are so convenient and expressive that they have been adopted in this paper. *Nature*.

pro tanto (prō tan'tō). [L.: *pro*, for, so far as; *tanto*, abl. sing. neut. of *tantus*, so much.] For so much; to that extent.

protarch (prō'tärk), *n.* [< Gr. πρῶτος, first, + ἄρχειν, rule.] A chief ruler.

In the age of the Apostles and the age next succeeding, the highest order in the church under the Apostles were national *protarchs* or patriarchs. *Abp. Bramhall*, Works, II. 149. (*Davies.*)

protarsus (prō-tär'sus), *n.*; pl. *protarsi* (-sī). [NL., < Gr. πρό, before, + ταρσός, > NL. *tarsus*.] In *entom.*, the whole tarsus of the first or fore leg of a six-footed insect, in front of the mesotarsus, which in turn is succeeded by the metatarsus.

protasis (prot'ạ-sis), *n.* [< L. *protasis*, < Gr. πρότασις, a stretching forward, a proposition, < προτείνειν, stretch forward, < πρό, forward, + τείνειν, stretch, extend: see *tend*.] **1.** A proposition; a maxim. *Johnson*. [Rare.]—**2.** In *gram.* and *rhet.*, the first clause of a conditional sentence, being the condition on which the main term (*apodosis*) depends, or notwithstanding which it takes place: as, if we run (*protasis*), we shall be in time (*apodosis*); although he was incompetent (*protasis*), he was elected (*apodosis*). See *apodosis*.—**3.** In the ancient drama, the first part of a play, in which the several persons are shown, their characters intimated, and the subject proposed and entered on: opposed to *epitasis*.

I will . . . returne to thee, gentle reader, because thou shalt be both the *protasis* and catastrophe of my epistle. *Times' Whistle* (E. E. T. S.), p. 111.

Now, gentlemen, what censure you of our *protasis*, or first act? *B. Jonson*, Magnetick Lady, i. 1.

4. In *anc. pros.*, the first colon of a dicolic verse or period.

protastacine (prō-tas'tạ-sin), *a.* [< *Protastacus* + *-ine*[1].] Having the character of *Protastacus*; primitive or ancestral as regards crawfishes.

The common *protastacine* form is to be sought in the Trias. *Huxley*, Crayfish, vi.

Protastacus (prō-tas'tạ-kus), *n.* [NL., < Gr. πρῶτος, first, + ἀστακός, a lobster.] A hypothetical ancestral marine form from which the existing fluviatile *Potamobiidæ* and *Parastacidæ* may have been developed. *Huxley*, 1878.

protatic (prō-tat'ik), *a.* [< L. *protaticus*, < Gr. προτατικός, pertaining to a protasis, < πρότασις, a protasis: see *protasis*.] Of or pertaining to a protasis; introductory.

There are indeed some *protatick* persons in the ancients whom they make use of in their plays either to hear or give the relation. *Dryden*, Essay on Dram. Poesy.

Protaxonia (prō-tak-sō'ni-ä), *n. pl.* [NL., < Gr. πρῶτος, first, + ἄξων, axis.] In *morphology*, axonial organic forms all of whose parts are arranged round a main axis: correlated with *Homaxonia*. The *Protaxonia* are divided into *Monaxonia* and *Stauraxonia*.

protaxonial (prō-tak-sō'ni-al), *a.* [< *Protaxonia* + *-al*.] Having all parts arranged round a main axis; of or pertaining to *Protaxonia*.

Protea (prō'tē-ä), *n.* [NL. (Linnæus, 1737), so called in allusion to the numerous forms naturally taken by these shrubs, and especially the many new forms and the loss of satiny surfaces when first cultivated; < Gr. Πρωτεύς, Proteus, a sea-god fabled to change himself into any shape he wished: see *Proteus*.] A genus of apetalous shrubs, the type of the order *Proteaceæ* and tribe *Proteeæ*. It is characterized by a slender two-lipped and prolonged calyx, with the narrow upper segment separate to the base at flowering, and the three others forming an entire or toothed broader lower lip, by the four sessile anthers borne on the calyx and tipped with a prolonged connective, and by the fruit, a hairy nut tipped with the smooth persistent style. There are about 60 species, natives of South Africa, one or two extending north into Abyssinia. They bear alternate or scattered rigid entire leaves, of many shapes in the different species, and flowers in large dense round or cone-like heads, with numerous overlapping scales between, which are sometimes conspicuous and colored, especially red or purple. *P. cynaroides* is known

Branch of *Protea mellifera*, with inflorescence.
a, a flower; *b*, the hairy nut with the persistent style.

as the *Cape artichoke-flower*, and *P. mellifera* as the *Cape honeysuckle*, *honey-flower*, or *sugar-bush*. The latter contains in its flower-cup an abundant sweet watery liquor, valued as a remedy for coughs.

Proteaceæ (prō-tē-ā'sē-ē), *n. pl.* [NL. (R. Brown, 1809), < *Protea* + *-aceæ*.] A large and very distinct order of apetalous plants of the series *Daphnales*, characterized by the four valvate calyx-lobes, four opposite stamens, one-celled ovary and one or two ovules, and further distinguished from the nearly related laurel family by its anthers opening, not by a valve, but by a longitudinal line. It includes about 960 species and 52 genera, mainly South African or Australian shrubs or trees, with some in South America, Asia, and the South Pacific. They are classed in two series, *Nucumentaceæ*, with four tribes, bearing a nut or drupe, and *Folliculares*, with three, bearing a follicle or capsule. Nearly all bear alternate or scattered coriaceous leaves, often polymorphous and entire, toothed, or dissected on the same plant. The flowers are usually in a head, spike, or raceme, set with numerous bracts, which often harden into an imbricated cone in fruit. For important genera, see *Protea* (the type), *Petrophila*, *Persoonia*, *Banksia*, *Grevillea*, and *Hakea*.

proteaceous (prō-tē-ā'shius), *a.* [< NL. *Protea* + *-aceous*.] Of or pertaining to the *Proteaceæ*.

Protean (prō'tē-an), *a.* and *n.* [< *Proteus* (see def.) + *-an*.] **I.** *a.* **1.** Pertaining to Proteus, a sea-god of classical mythology, who could change his shape at will; hence, readily assuming different shapes; exceedingly variable.

Your *Protean* turnings cannot change my purpose. *Beau. and Fl.*, Thierry and Theodoret, iv. 2.

All the *Protean* transformations of nature, which happen continually. *Cudworth*, Intellectual System, p. 32.

2. [*l. c.*] In *zoöl.*, changeable in form; executing movements involving shifting of shape, as an animalcule; amœbiform or amœboid; amœban; of or pertaining to a proteus-animalcule. Also *proteiform*.—**Protean animalcules**, *Amœbæ*.—**Protean stone**, a kind of semi-translucent artificial stone prepared from gypsum.

II. *n.* [*l. c.*] **1.** An actor who plays a number of parts in one piece. [Theatrical slang.]—**2.** A salamander of the family *Proteidæ*; a proteid.

Proteana (prō-tē-ā'nä), *n. pl.* [NL.: see *Protean*.] Same as *Proteomyxa*. *E. R. Lankester*.

Proteanly (prō'tē-an-li), *adv.* In a Protean manner; with assumption of different shapes.

Which matter of the universe is alwaies substantially the same, and neither more nor less, but only *Proteanly* transformed into different shapes. *Cudworth*, Intellectual System, p. 26.

protect (prō-tekt'), *v. t.* [< OF. *protecter*, < L. *protectus*, pp. of *protegere* (> It. *proteggere* = Sp. Pg. *proteger* = F. *protéger*), protect, defend, cover before or over, < *pro*, before, in front of, + *tegere*, cover, roof: see *tegument*.] **1.** To cover or shield from danger, harm, damage, trespass, exposure, insult, temptation, or the like; defend; guard; preserve in safety: applied with a wide range, both literally and figuratively, actively and passively.

The gods of Greece *protect* you! *Shak.*, Pericles, i. 4. 97.

Captain, or Colonel, or Knight in arms,
Whose chance on these defenceless doors may seize, . . .
Guard them, and him within *protect* from harms. *Milton*, Sonnets, iii.

As the good shepherd tends his fleecy care, . . .
By day o'ersees them, and by night *protects*. *Pope*, Messiah, l. 52.

It is plain, as a matter of fact, that the great mass of men are *protected* from gross sin by the forms of society. *J. H. Newman*, Parochial Sermons, i. 131.

Six fresh plants were *protected* [from insects] by separate nets in the year 1870. Two of these proved almost completely self-sterile. *Darwin*, Cross and Self Fertilisation, p. 338.

2. To act as protector or regent for. Compare *protector*, 2 (*a*).

Car. He will be found a dangerous protector.
Buck. Why should he, then, *protect* our sovereign, . . .
He being of age to govern of himself? *Shak.*, 2 Hen. VI., i. 1. 165.

3. Specifically, in *polit. econ.*, to guard or strengthen against foreign competition by means of a protective duty.

Whatever increased profits our manufacturers of *protected* articles get, or whatever increased wages they pay their workmen, must come from other classes—the consumers of their products. *The Nation*, XLVII. 454.

=**Syn. 1.** *Defend*, *Shelter*, etc. (see *keep*), screen, secure.

protectee (prō-tek-tē'), *n.* [< *protect* + *-ee*[1].] A person protected; a protégé. [Rare.]

Your *protectee*, White, was clerk to my cousin. *W. Taylor*, of Norwich, 1807 (Memoirs, II. 198). (*Davies.*)

protecter, *n.* See *protector*.

protectingly (prō-tek'ting-li), *adv.* [< *protecting*, ppr. of *protect*, *v.*, + *-ly*[2].] In a protecting manner; by way of protection; so as to protect.

The straw-roofed Cottages, . . . all hidden and *protectingly* folded up in the valley-folds. *Carlyle*, Sartor Resartus, ii. 9.

protection (prō-tek'shon), *n.* [< F. *protection* = Sp. *proteccion* = Pg. *protecção* = It. *protezione*, < L. *protectio(n-)*, a covering over, < *protegere*, pp. *protectus*, cover over or in front: see *protect*.] **1.** The act of protecting, or the state of being protected; defense; shelter or preservation from loss, injury, or any form of harm or evil: as, the *protection* of good laws; divine *protection*.

To your *protection* I commend me, gods! *Shak.*, Cymbeline, ii. 2. 8.

O happy islands, if you know your bliss!
Strong by the sea's *protection*, safe by his. *Roscommon*, A Prologue.

Beauty of that tender and beseeching kind which looks for fondness and *protection*. *Irving*, Alhambra, p. 327.

2. That which protects or shields from harm; something that preserves from injury: as, camphor serves as a *protection* against moths.

Let them rise up and help you, and be your *protection*. Deut. xxxii. 38.

3. A writing that guarantees protection; a passport, safe-conduct, or other writing which secures the bearer from molestation; especially, a certificate of nationality issued by the customs authorities of the United States to seamen who are American citizens.

The party who procured the commission, one George Cleves, brought also a *protection* under the privy signet for searching out the great lake of Iracoyce. *Winthrop*, Hist. New England, I. 276.

They [boats] generally belong to Greek masters, who have a *protection* from the convent for twelve mariners, and cannot be taken by the Maltese within eighty leagues of the Holy Land. *Pococke*, Description of the East, II. i. 51.

He had a *protection* during the rebellion. *Johnson*.

4. In *polit. econ.*, the theory, doctrine, or system of fostering or developing the industries of a country by means of imposts on products of the industries imported into that country; the discouragement of foreign competition with the industries of a country by imposing import duties, granting monopolies of commerce, etc. The system of protection was little known in antiquity, but prevailed extensively in the middle ages, and has flourished widely since. A strong influence in favor of free trade was exerted in the eighteenth century by the physiocrats and by the writings of Adam Smith. Great Britain adopted a system of practical free trade by the abolition of the corn-laws in 1846 and later years, followed by the removal of duties on nearly all imported articles. On the continent of Europe the general tendency in recent years has been in the direction of increased protection. In the United States the policy of protection has, especially in later history, formed one of the leading national questions. See *tariff* and *revenue*.—**Animals' Protection Acts.** See *animal*.—**Flag of protection.** See *flag*[2].—**Game protection.** See *game*[1].—**Writ of protection.** (*a*) A writ, very rarely granted, whereby the sovereign's protection is guaranteed. (*b*) A writ issued to a person required to attend court as witness, juror, etc., to secure him from arrest for a certain time.=**Syn. 2.** Guard, refuge, security.

protectional (prǫ-tek'shǫn-al), *a.* [< *protection* + *-al*.] Pertaining to protection.

protectionism (prǫ-tek'shǫn-izm), *n.* [= F. *protectionnisme* = Sp. *proteccionismo*; as *protection* + *-ism*.] The doctrine of the protectionists; the system of protection. See *protection*, 4.

I do not speak . . . of the friendly controversy . . . between the leanings of America to *protectionism* and the more daring reliance of the old country upon free and unrestricted intercourse with all the world.
Gladstone, N. A. Rev., CXXVII. 179.

protectionist (prǫ-tek'shǫn-ist), *n.* and *a.* [= F. *protectionniste* = Sp. *proteccionista*; as *protection* + *-ist*.] **I.** *n.* One who favors the protection of some branch of industry, or of native industries generally, from foreign competition, by imposing duties on imports and by other means.

Polk was accused of having gone over, bag and baggage, to the camp of the *protectionists*.
H. von Holst, John C. Calhoun, p. 217.

II. *a.* Favoring or supporting the economic doctrine of protection.

Pennsylvania has always been a *Protectionist* State.
Westminster Rev., CXXVIII. 832.

protective (prǫ-tek'tiv), *a.* and *n.* [= Pg. *protectivo*; < *protect* + *-ive*.] **I.** *a.* **1.** Affording protection; sheltering; defensive.

The favour of a *protective* Providence.
Feltham, Resolves, ii. 58.

There is not a single white land-bird or quadruped in Europe, except the few arctic or Alpine species, to which white is a *protective* colour.
A. R. Wallace, Nat. Select., p. 65.

Law is the necessary check upon crime, and gives to the standard of public morality a *protective* sanction which it sorely needs. *H. N. Oxenham*, Short Studies, p. 37.

2. Adapted or intended to afford protection: as, a *protective* measure; affording protection to commodities of home production: as, a *protective* tariff; *protective* taxes.—**Protective mimicry.** See *mimicry*, 3.—**Protective paper**, paper so made that anything printed or written upon it cannot be tampered with without leaving traces. Water-marks, the incorporation of a special fiber, and a peculiar texture produced in the manufacture are devices employed for this purpose, as well as the printing of the surface with fine lines, and various chemical treatment of the paper.—**Protective person**, in *zoöl.*, that part of a compound organism which specially functions as a protection to other parts or persons of a cormus, as the hydrophyllium of a hydroid polyp.—**Protective sheath**, in *bot.* See *sheath*.

II. *n.* **1.** That which protects; something adapted to afford protection.

Fur coats are the grand *protective* on the journey.
Nineteenth Century, XXIV. 60.

2. In *surg.*, carbolized oiled silk applied over wounds for the exclusion of pathogenic bacteria.

protectively (prǫ-tek'tiv-li), *adv.* In a manner adapted to give protection; so as to protect: as, insects *protectively* colored.

The markings . . . about the muzzle, ears, and throat of antelope, deer, hares, and other mammals, whether *protectively* colored or not. *Amer. Nat.*, XXII. 203.

protectiveness (prǫ-tek'tiv-nes), *n.* A disposition to protect or guard; the quality of being protective.

Shelley's affection for his young wife had strengthened with his growing sense of *protectiveness* towards her.
E. Dowden, Shelley, I. 196.

protector (prǫ-tek'tǫr), *n.* [Also *protecter*; = F. *protecteur* = Sp. Pg. *protector* = It. *protettore*, < LL. *protector*, a protector, < L. *protegere*, pp. *protectus*, cover before or over: see *protect*.] **1.** One who or that which protects, defends, or shields from injury or any evil; a defender; a guardian; a patron: as, a child's natural *protectors*.

As for me, tell them I will henceforth be their God, *protector*, and patron, and they shall call me Quirinus.
North, tr. of Plutarch, p. 29.

I hither fled,
Under the covering of a careful night,
Who seem'd my good *protector*.
Shak., Pericles, i. 2. 82.

What farther relates to Charles I. as *protector* of the arts will be found in the subsequent pages, under the articles of the different professors whom he countenanced.
Walpole, Anecdotes of Painting, II. ii.

But Vivien . . . clung to him and hugg'd him close;
And call'd him dear *protector* in her fright.
Tennyson, Merlin and Vivien.

2. In *Eng. hist.*: (*a*) One who had the care of the kingdom during the king's minority or incapacity; a regent: as, the Duke of Somerset was *protector* in the reign of Edward VI.

Go in peace, Humphrey, no less beloved
Than when thou wert *protector* to thy king.
Shak., 2 Hen. VI., ii. 3. 27.

The council . . . would have preferred to adopt the system which had been adopted in the early days of Henry VI., and to have governed the kingdom in the King's name, with Gloucester as president or *protector*.
Stubbs, Const. Hist., § 360.

(*b*) [*cap.*] The title (in full *Lord Protector*) of the head of the executive during part of the period of the Commonwealth: it was held by Oliver Cromwell 1653–8, and by Richard Cromwell 1658–9.—**3.** In *weaving*, a stop-motion attached to a power-loom, which immediately stops the loom when the shuttle fails to enter the box.—**Cardinal protector**, a cardinal who represents at Rome the interests of a nation or of several nations; also, a cardinal who represents the interests of a religious order, etc.—**Lord Protector.** Same as *protector*, 2 (*b*).—**Protector of the settlement**, in *law*, the person whose consent is necessary under a settlement to enable the tenant in tail to cut off the entail. He is usually the tenant for life in possession, but the settler of the lands may appoint in his place any number of persons, not exceeding three, to be together protector during the continuance of the estate preceding the estate tail. *Digby.*

protectoral (prǫ-tek'tǫr-al), *a.* [< *protector* + *-al*.] Relating to a protector; protectorial.

The contention of the representative system and the *protectoral* power. *Godwin*, Mandeville, I. 225. (*Davies.*)

protectorate (prǫ-tek'tǫr-āt), *n.* [= F. *protectorat* = Sp. Pg. *protectorado* = It. *protettorato*, < NL. **protectoratus*, the office of a protector, < LL. *protector*, protector: see *protector*.] **1.** Government by a protector; also, the rank or position of a protector, or the period of his rule: specifically [*cap.*] used with reference to the period in English history during which Oliver and Richard Cromwell held the title of Lord Protector.

Richard Cromwell . . . being designed to be his Father's Successor in the *Protectorate*, was, about the time that this honour was done to him, sworn a Privy Counsellor.
Wood, Fasti Oxon., II. 119.

His well-known loyalty [was] evinced by secret services to the Royal cause during the *Protectorate*.
Barham, Ingoldsby Legends, I. 208.

The arrival of a governor of course put an end to the *protectorate* of Olotie the Dreamer.
Irving, Knickerbocker, p. 147.

2. A relation assumed by a strong nation toward a weak one, whereby the former protects the latter from hostile invasion or dictation, and interferes more or less in its domestic concerns.

The seven Ionian islands—their consent being given through their parliament, and Great Britain's abandonment of her *protectorate* having been accepted—are to form a part of the Greek monarchy.
Woolsey, Introd. to Inter. Law, App. ii., p. 422.

In summing up what we have discovered with regard to our new *protectorates* and our recent annexations, we have then to note that until about 1884 we had for some time almost consistently refused offers of territory which had been pressed upon us.
Sir C. W. Dilke, Probs. of Greater Britain, v. 1.

protectorial (prō-tek-tō'ri-al), *a.* [< LL. *protectorius*, pertaining to a protector (see *protectory*), + *-al*.] Relating to a protector; protectoral.

protectorian (prō-tek-tō'ri-an), *a.* [< LL. *protectorius*, pertaining to a protector, + *-an*.] Same as *protectorial*; specifically [*cap.*], relating to the Protectorate in English history.

This Lord . . . during the tyranny of the *Protectorian* times kept his secret Loyalty to his Sovereign.
Fuller, Worthies, Herefordshire, II. 95.

protectorless (prǫ-tek'tǫr-les), *a.* [< *protector* + *-less*.] Having no protector.

protectorship (prǫ-tek'tǫr-ship), *n.* [< *protector* + *-ship*.] The office of a protector or regent; a protectorate; the period during which a protector governs.

And did he not, in his *protectorship*,
Levy great sums of money through the realm?
Shak., 2 Hen. VI., iii. 1. 60.

The duke of York, when he accepted the *protectorship* in 1455, insisted on the payment of the council.
Stubbs, Const. Hist., § 367.

protectory (prǫ-tek'tǫ-ri), *n.*; pl. *protectories* (-riz). [= Sp. *protectorio*, a., < LL. *protectorius*, pertaining to a protector (ML. *protectorium*, n., a safe-conduct), < *protector*, protector: see *protector*.] An institution for the protection and training of destitute, vagrant, truant, or vicious children: the specific name of a Roman Catholic institution in New York city.

protectress (prǫ-tek'tres), *n.* [< F. *protectrice* = Sp. *protectriz* = It. *protettrice*, < LL. *protectrix*, fem. of *protector*, a protector: see *protector*.] A woman who protects.

All things should be guided by her direction, as the sovereign patroness and *protectress* of the enterprize.
Bacon.

protectrix (prǫ-tek'triks), *n.* [< LL. *protectrix*, fem. of *protector*, protector: see *protectress*.] Same as *protectress*.

Queene Katharine, *protectrixe* of kyng Iohn her son, while he was yet in his nonage.
Peter Martyr (tr. in Eden's First Books on America, ed. [Arber, p. 65).

Proteeæ (prǫ-tē'ẹ-ē), *n. pl.* [NL. (A. de Candolle, 1856), < *Protea* + *-eæ*.] A tribe of plants of the order *Proteaceæ* and series *Nucumentaceæ*. It is characterized by its dry nut, single ovule, and anthers seated on the base of the calyx-lobes at the summit of the tube, and usually all perfect. It includes 14 genera, of which *Protea* is the type.

protégé (prǫ-tā-zhā'), *n.* [F., pp. of *protéger*, protect, < L. *protegere*, protect: see *protect*.] One who is under the care and protection of another.

protégée (prǫ-tā-zhā'), *n.* [F., fem. of *protégé*, q. v.] A girl or woman who is under the care and protection of another person.

proteid[1] (prō'tẹ-id), *n.* [< *proto(in)* + *-id*[1].] A substance formerly supposed to contain protein as an essential ingredient. The term is now applied to a considerable number of nitrogenous bodies which make up the substance of the soft tissues of the body and of the blood, and are also widely distributed in the vegetable kingdom. They are amorphous solids, having certain general features in common, but differing widely in solubility and in their decomposition products. The gluten of flour, egg, albumin, the fibrin of the blood, syntonin, and casein are examples of proteids. Gelatin and chondrin Huxley calls outlying members of the same group. Also called *albuminoid*.

Food-stuffs have been divided into heat-producers and tissue-formers—the amyloids and fats constituting the former division, the *proteids* the latter. But this is a very misleading classification, inasmuch as it implies on the one hand that the oxidation of the *proteids* does not develop heat, and on the other that the amyloids and fats, as they oxidize, subserve only the production of heat. *Proteids* are tissue-formers, inasmuch as no tissue can be produced without them; but they are also heat-producers, not only directly, but because, as we have seen, . . . they are competent to give rise to amyloids by chemical metamorphosis within the body.
Huxley and Youmans, Physiol. (1875), § 176.

proteid[2] (prō'tẹ-id), *n.* [< *Proteid-æ*.] In *zoöl.*, an amphibian of the family *Proteidæ*.

Proteida (prǫ-tē'i-dạ̈), *n. pl.* [NL., < *Proteus* + *-ida*.] In *zoöl.*, an order or suborder of tailed amphibians, conterminous with the family *Proteidæ*.

Proteidæ (prǫ-tē'i-dē), *n. pl.* [NL., < *Proteus* + *-idæ*.] A family of gradient or tailed amphibians, typified by the genus *Proteus*, with external gills persistent throughout life, maxillaries absent, intermaxillaries and mandible toothed, palatine and pterygoid bones developed, and orbitosphenoid elongate and not entering into the palate. The American representative of this family is the menobranch. See cut under *Menobranchus*. *Menobranchidæ* is a synonym.

Proteidea (prō-tẹ-id'ẹ-ạ̈), *n. pl.* [NL.: see *Proteidæ*.] A division of saurobatrachian or urodele *Amphibia*, having the external branchiæ or gill-clefts persistent, or disappearing only in old age, no eyelids, amphicœlous vertebræ, and cartilaginous carpus and tarsus: synonymous with *Proteida*, and contrasted with the *Salamandridea*.

proteidean (prō-tẹ-id'ẹ-an), *a.* [< *Proteidæ* + *-an*.] Of or pertaining to the *Proteidea*.

proteiform (prō'tẹ-i-fôrm), *a.* [< NL. *Proteus* (see *Proteus*, 2) + L. *forma*, form.] Same as *protean*, 2. *Encyc. Brit.*, IX. 376.

protein (prō'tẹ-in), *n.* [< Gr. πρῶτος, first, + *-e-in*[2].] A hypothetical substance formerly believed to be the essential nitrogenous constituent of food, and to exist in animal and vegetable albumin, fibrin, casein, and other bodies. This view has been abandoned, and at present the word is chiefly used as the first element in compounds.—**Protein-bodies.** Same as *proteids*. See *proteid*.—**Protein-granules.** Same as *aleurone*.

Proteina (prō-tẹ-ī'nạ̈), *n. pl.* [NL. (Wallich), < *Proteus* + *-ina*[2].] A group of protean or amœbiform rhizopods, having a nucleus and contractile vacuole: divided into *Actinophryna* and *Amœbina*, respectively characterized by their monomorphous and polymorphous pseudopods. Sun-animalcules and ordinary proteus-animalcules illustrate the two divisions. See cut under *amœba*.

proteinaceous (prō″tē-i-nā′shius), *a.* [< *protein* + *-aceous*.] Resembling, containing, or consisting of protein. Also *proteinous*.

Digestion—that is, solution of the *proteinaceous* and other nutritive matters contained in food.
Huxley and Martin, Elem. Biology, xi.

Proteininæ (prō″tē-i-nī′nē), *n. pl.* [NL., < *Proteinus* + *-inæ*.] A subfamily of *Staphylinidæ* or rove-beetles, typified by the genus *Proteinus*. Also *Proteinina*, *Proteinini*.

proteinous (prō′tē-i-nus), *a.* [< *protein* + *-ous*.] Same as *proteinaceous*.

Proteinus (prō-tē-ī′nus), *n.* [NL. (Latreille, 1796).] The typical genus of the subfamily *Proteininæ*, having the elytra mostly covering the abdomen, and somewhat perfoliate antennæ inserted before the eyes.

Proteles (prot′e-lēz), *n.* [NL. (Geoffroy,), irreg. so called as having five toes on the fore feet, lit. 'complete in front,' < Gr. πρό, before, in front, + τέλος, end. Cf. *Ateles*, *Brachyteles*, words of like formation.] The only genus of the family *Protelidæ*, containing one species, the aardwolf or earthwolf of South Africa, *P. lalandi*. See cut under *aardwolf*.

Protelidæ (prō-tel′i-dē), *n. pl.* [NL., < *Proteles* + *-idæ*.] A family of hyeniform æluroid carnivorous quadrupeds, of the order *Feræ*, typified by the genus *Proteles*, having 32 teeth, very small and distant molars, no functional-ized sectorial molars, the feet digitigrade, and the fore feet five-toed.

pro tem. An abbreviation of *pro tempore*.

protembryo (prō-tem′bri-ō), *n.* [NL., < Gr. πρῶτος, first, + ἔμβρυον, embryo.] A stage of the ova of metazoic animals which is parallel with the adult colonies of certain protozoans: the *monoplast* of Lankester, or *amphimorula* of Haeckel, including the *monoplacula* and *diploplacula* of Hyatt. *Hyatt*, Proc. Bost. Soc. Nat. Hist., Nov. 16, 1887.

protembryonic (prō-tem-bri-on′ik), *a.* [< *protembryo(n-)* + *-ic*.] Of or pertaining to a protembryo.

Protemnodon (prō-tem′nō-don), *n.* [NL. (Owen, 1874), < Gr. προτέμνειν, cut short, + ὀδούς (ὀδοντ-) = E. *tooth*.] A genus of fossil diprotodont marsupials from the late Tertiary of Australia.

pro tempore (prō tem′pō-rē). [L.: *pro*, for; *tempore*, abl. sing. of *tempus*, time: see *temporal*[1].] For the time being; temporary: as, a secretary *pro tempore*. Abbreviated *pro tem.*

protencephalon (prō-ten-sef′a-lon), *n.*; pl. *protencephala* (-lä). [NL., < Gr. πρῶτος, first, + ἐγκέφαλος, the brain.] The fore-brain: divided into *protencephalon primarium*, the fore-brain proper, or prosencephalon, and *protencephalon secundarium*, the thalamencephalon or diencephalon. *Rabl-Ruckard*, 1884. See cuts under *encephalon* and *Petromyzontidæ*.

protenchyma (prō-teng′ki-mä), *n.* [NL., < Gr. πρῶτος, first, + ἔγχυμα, an infusion (see *parenchyma*).] In *bot.*, a term used by Nägeli for all tissues except the fibrovascular (epenchyma)—including, therefore, the primary meristem, epidermal tissue, and fundamental tissue of Sachs. See *fundamental cells*, under *fundamental*.

The *protenchyma* of Nägeli therefore splits up, according to me, into three kinds of equal value with his epenchyma.
Sachs, Botany (trans.), p. 103.

protend (prō-tend′), *v. t.* [= It. *protendere*, < L. *protendere*, stretch forth or out, < *pro*, forth, forward, + *tendere*, stretch, extend: see *tend*. Cf. *portend*.] To hold out; stretch forth; extend forward: used especially of a spear.

He spoke no more, but hasten'd, void of fear,
And threaten'd with his long *protended* spear.
Dryden, Æneid, x.

Thy fate was next, O Phaestus! doom'd to feel
The great Idomeneus' *protended* steel.
Pope, Iliad, v. 58.

From hill to hill he hies,
His staff *protending* like a hunter's spear,
Or by its aid leaping from crag to crag.
Wordsworth, Prelude, viii.

protense† (prō-tens′), *n.* [Irreg. for *protension*, q. v.] Extension; drawing out. [Rare.]

Begin, O Clio! and recount from hence
My glorious Soveraines goodly ancestrye,
Till that by dew degrees, and long *protense*,
Thou have it lastly brought unto her Excellence.
Spenser, F. Q., III. iii. 4.

protension (prō-ten′shon), *n.* [< L. *protensio(n-)*, a stretching out, < *protendere*, pp. *protensus*, stretch forth or out: see *protend*.] Temporal extension; duration.

Time, *protension*, or protensive quantity, called likewise duration, is a necessary condition of thought.
Sir W. Hamilton, Discussions, Appendix I. (A).

protensity (prō-ten′si-ti), *n.* [< L. *protensus*, pp. of *protendere*, stretch forth or out (see *protend*), + *-ity*.] The character of being protensive or of taking up time.

protensive (prō-ten′siv), *a.* [< L. *protensus*, pp. of *protendere*, stretch forth or out (see *protend*), + *-ive*.] Drawn out in one dimension; extended; stretching forward.

Examples of this sudden effort, and of this instantaneous desisting from the attempt, are manifested in the extensive sublime of space, and in the *protensive* sublime of time.
Sir W. Hamilton, Metaph., xlvi.

Protensive quantity. See *quantity*.

Proteolepadidæ (prō″tē-ō-le-pad′i-dē), *n. pl.* [NL., < *Proteolepas* (*-ad-*) + *-idæ*.] A family of apodal cirripeds, represented by the genus *Proteolepas*.

Proteolepas (prō-tē-ol′e-pas), *n.* [NL., < *Proteus* (see *Proteus*, 3) + Gr. λεπάς, a limpet: see *Lepas*.] The single known genus of the cirriped group *Apoda*. *P. bivincta* is about one fifth of an inch long, and resembles the larva of an insect. It is a parasite of another cirriped, *Alepas cornuta*.

Proteolepas bivincta. *m*, mouth; *g*, *h*, peduncle and antennæ; *i*, *k*, vesicula seminalis and penis.

proteolysis (prō-tē-ol′i-sis), *n.* [NL., < *prote(id)* + Gr. λύσις, dissolving.] The change effected in proteids during their digestion.

proteolytic (prō″tē-ō-lit′ik), *a.* [< *proteolysis* (*-lyt-*) + *-ic*.] Pertaining to proteolysis, or the digestion of proteids.

Proteomyxa (prō″tē-ō-mik′sä), *n. pl.* [NL., < Gr. Πρωτεύς, Proteus, + μύξα, slime, mucus: see *mucus*.] Lankester's name of a so-called class of gymnomyxine *Protozoa*, containing a great many of the lowest protozoans, of negative characters, insufficiently known, or not satisfactorily referred to any definable group. The name is a formal expression of ignorance upon the subject. Many of the so-called *Proteomyxa* are usually referred to other and more definite groups, especially the *Mycetozoa*. The *Monera* of Haeckel, in so far as they are proper persons at all, come under this head. The group is also called *Proteana*.

proter (prō′tėr), *n.* [Appar. a var. of *proker*, by confusion with *poter*, < *pote*, poke.] A poker. *Halliwell*. [Prov. Eng.]

proterandrous (prot-e-ran′drus), *a.* [< *proterandr-y* + *-ous*.] In *bot.* and *zoöl.*, exhibiting or characterized by proterandry. Also *protandrous*.

Certain individuals mature their pollen before the female flowers on the same plant are ready for fertilization, and are called *proterandrous*; whilst conversely other individuals, called proterogynous, have their stigmas mature before their pollen is ready.
Darwin, Different Forms of Flowers, p. 10.

proterandry (prot-e-ran′dri), *n.* [< Gr. πρότερος, being before, fore, former, + ἀνήρ (ἀνδρ-), male (in mod. bot. stamen).] 1. In *bot.*, the maturation of the anthers and the discharge of the pollen in a hermaphrodite flower before the stigmas of that flower are receptive of pollen: an adaptation for cross-fertilization. Compare *proterogyny*, and see *dichogamy* and *heteracmy*.—2. In *zoöl.*, development of male parts or maturation of male products in hermaphrodite animals before the development or maturation of those of the opposite sex.

If the polypides are unisexual, then the *proterandry* refers only to the colony as a whole.
W. A. Herdman, Nature, XXXVII. 213.

Also *protandry*.

proteranthous (prot-e-ran′thus), *a.* [< Gr. πρότερος, fore, + ἄνθος, flower.] In *bot.*, noting a plant whose flowers appear before the leaves. *Asa Gray*.

proterobase (prot′e-rō-bās), *n.* [< Gr. πρότερος, fore, + βάσις, base.] The name given by Gümbel to a Paleozoic eruptive rock resembling diabase in composition, but being in a somewhat more advanced stage of alteration than are the varieties of the rock ordinarily designated by that name. The term *proterobase* has also been used by other lithologists, generally with reference to rocks of the diabasic type, but in a highly altered condition.

Proteroglossa (prot′e-rō-glos′ä), *n. pl.* [NL., < Gr. πρότερος, fore, + γλῶσσα, tongue: see *gloss*[2].] In Günther's classification, one of three prime divisions of salient batrachians, having the tongue free in front, represented by the family *Rhinophrynidæ*: correlated with *Aglossa* and *Opisthoglossa*.

proteroglossate (prot″e-rō-glos′āt), *a.* [< *Proteroglossa* + *-ate*[1].] Having the tongue free in front, as a batrachian; pertaining to the *Proteroglossa*, or having their characters.

proteroglyph (prot′e-rō-glif), *n.* A venomous serpent of the group *Proteroglypha*.

Proteroglypha (prot-e-rog′li-fä), *n. pl.* [NL. (F. *Protéroglyphes*, Duméril and Bibron), < Gr. πρότερος, fore, + γλύφειν, carve.] A suborder or other division of *Ophidia*, containing venomous cobriform serpents whose anterior maxillary teeth are grooved or perforate and succeeded by smooth solid teeth, and whose maxillary bones are horizontal and do not reach the premaxillaries: thus contrasted with the crotaliform venomous snakes, or *Solenoglypha*. Though the general aspect of these snakes is colubrine, or like that of harmless serpents, they are all poisonous, and some of them are among the most deadly of all thanatophidians. The families *Elapidæ*, *Najidæ*, *Dendraspididæ*, and *Hydrophidæ* compose the *Proteroglypha*. Also *Proteroglyphia*.

proteroglyphic (prot″e-rō-glif′ik), *a.* [< *Proteroglypha* + *-ic*.] Of or pertaining to the *Proteroglypha*.

proterogynous (prot-e-roj′i-nus), *a.* [< *proterogyn-y* + *-ous*.] In *bot.*, exhibiting or characterized by proterogyny. See extract under *proterandrous*.

proterogyny (prot-e-roj′i-ni), *n.* [< Gr. πρότερος, fore, + γυνή, female (in mod. bot. pistil).] In *bot.*, the maturation of the stigmas in a hermaphrodite flower before the anthers in that flower have matured their pollen. It is an adaptation for cross-fertilization. Compare *proterandry*, and see *dichogamy*.

proterosaur (prot′e-rō-sâr), *n.* A reptile of the family *Proterosauridæ*.

Proterosauria (prot″e-rō-sâ′ri-ä), *n. pl.* [NL., see *Proterosaurus*.] One of the major divisions of the *Lacertilia*, a fossil group consisting of some of the oldest known reptiles, whose remains occur in rocks of the Permian formation in Thuringia and in those of corresponding age in England: no later representatives of the group are known. It is typified by the genus *Proterosaurus*, based upon the Thuringian lizard, which attained a length of 6 or 7 feet.

proterosaurian (prot″e-rō-sâ′ri-an), *a.* and *n.* I. *a.* Of or pertaining to the *Proterosauria*.

II. *n.* A member of the *Proterosauria*; a proterosaur.

Proterosauridæ (prot″e-rō-sâ′ri-dē), *n. pl.* [NL., < *Proterosaurus* + *-idæ*.] A family of fossil saurians, based on the genus *Proterosaurus*.

Proterosaurus (prot″e-rō-sâ′rus), *n.* [NL., < Gr. πρότερος, fore, + σαῦρος, lizard.] The genus represented by the fossil monitor of Thuringia, which also occurs in the Durham Permian rocks. It was long the earliest known fossil reptile.

Proterospongia (prot″e-rō-spon′ji-ä), *n.* [NL., < Gr. πρότερος, fore, + σπογγιά, a sponge.] A genus of choanoflagellate animalcules, founded by Saville Kent on the form *Protospongia*, placed by him in a family *Phalansteriidæ*, and regarded as furnishing a stock-form from which, by the process of evolution, all sponges might have been derived. A species is named *P. haeckeli*.

protervity (prō-tėr′vi-ti), *n.*; pl. *protervities* (-tiz). [< OF. *protervite* = Sp. *protervidad* = It. *protervità*, < L. *protervita(t-)s*, boldness, impudence, < *protervus* (> It. Sp. Pg. *protervo* = OF. *proterve*), violent, wanton, prob. < *proterere*, trample down, overthrow, < *pro*, forth, + *terere*, rub, bruise: see *trite*.] Peevishness; petulance; wantonness.

Companion to T. Becket in his exile, but no partner in his *protervity* against his Prince.
Fuller, Worthies, Wilts, II. 442. (*Davies*.)

In his [Victor Hugo's] poems and plays there are the same unaccountable *protervities* that have already astonished us in the romances.
R. L. Stevenson, Victor Hugo's Romances.

protest (prō-test′), *v.* [< F. *protester* = Sp. Pg. *protestar* = It. *protestare*, < L. *protestari*, *protestare*, declare in public, bear witness, < *pro*, before, forth, + *testari*, bear witness, < *testis*, a witness, one who attests: see *test*[2].] I. *trans.* 1. To make a solemn declaration or affirmation of; bear witness or testimony to; assert; asseverate; declare: as, to *protest* one's innocence.

Verily he [D. Barnes] *protested* openly at St. Mary's spital, the Tuesday in Easter week, that he was never of that mind.
Coverdale, Remains (Parker Soc.), p. 341.

To think upon her woes I do *protest*
That I have wept a hundred several times.
Shak., T. G. of V., iv. 4. 149.

Their own guilty carriage *protests* they doe feare.
Milton, Church-Government, i. 5.

"I *protest*, Charles," cried my wife, "this is the way you always damp my girls and me when we are in spirits."
Goldsmith, Vicar, v.

2. To call as a witness in affirming or denying, or to prove an affirmation; appeal to. [Rare.]

Fiercely opposed
My journey strange, with clamorous uproar
Protesting fate supreme. *Milton*, P. L., x. 480.

3†. To declare publicly; publish; make known.

I will make it good how you dare, with what you dare, and when you dare.—Do me right, or I will *protest* your cowardice. *Shak.*, Much Ado, v. 1. 149.

Thou wouldst not willingly
Live a *protested* coward, or be call'd one?
Beau. and Fl., Little French Lawyer, i. 1.

4†. To promise solemnly; vow.

On Diana's altar to *protest*
For aye austerity and single life.
Shak., M. N. D., i. 1. 89.

5. To declare formally to be insufficiently provided for by deposit or payment: said of a note or bill of exchange, and also, figuratively, of personal credit, statements, etc. See *protest*, *n.*, 3.

Turn country bankrupt
In mine own town, upon the market day,
And be *protested* for my butter and eggs,
To the last bodge of oats and bottle of hay.
B. *Jonson*, New Inn, i. 1.

The bill lies for payment at Dollar's and Co., in Birchin-lane, and if not taken up this afternoon will be *protested*.
Colman, The Spleen, i. (*Davies.*)

"I said—I did nothing," cried Lady Cecilia. . . . An appealing look to Helen was, however, *protested*. "To the best of my recollection at least," Lady Cecilia immediately added. *Miss Edgeworth*, Helen, vi. (*Davies.*)

The moral market had the usual chills
Of Virtue suffering from *protested* bills.
O. W. Holmes, The Banker's Dinner.

=**Syn.** 1. *Protest* differs from the words compared under *assert* (*aver*, *asseverate*, etc.) in being more solemn and earnest, and in implying more of previous contradiction or expectation of contradiction (see the quotations above); like them, it is used to make the statement seem certainly true.

II. *intrans.* 1. To bear testimony; affirm with solemnity; make a solemn declaration of a fact or an opinion; asseverate.

The man did solemnly *protest* unto us, saying, Ye shall not see my face, except your brother be with you.
Gen. xliii. 3.

The lady doth *protest* too much, methinks.
Shak., Hamlet, iii. 2. 240.

2. To make a solemn or formal declaration (often in writing) in condemnation of an act or measure proposed or accomplished: often with *against*.

Now therefore hearken unto their voice: howbeit yet *protest* solemnly unto them, and shew them the manner of the king that shall reign over them. 1 Sam. viii. 9.

When they say the Bishops did antiently *protest*, it was only dissenting, and that in the case of the Pope.
Selden, Table-Talk, p. 68.

Warham, as an old lawyer, *protested* in a formal document *against* all legislation which might be enacted against ecclesiastical or papal power.
Stubbs, Medieval and Modern Hist., p. 279.

protest (prō'test, formerly also prọ-test'), *n.* [< ME. *protest* (= D. G. Sw. Dan. *protest*), < OF. *protest* (F. *protêt*), m., *proteste*, f., = Sp. *protesto*, m., *protesta*, f., = Pg. It. *protesto*, m. (ML. *protestum*, neut.), a protest (mostly in the commercial sense); from the verb.] 1. The act of protesting, or that which is protested; an affirmation; asseveration; protestation: now restricted for the most part to a solemn or formal declaration against some act or course of action, by which a person declares (and sometimes has his declaration recorded) that he refuses, or only conditionally yields, his consent to some act to which he might otherwise be assumed to have yielded an unconditional assent: as, to submit under *protest*; a *protest* against the action of a committee.

Swear me, Kate, like a lady as thou art,
A good mouth-filling oath, and leave "in sooth,"
And such *protest* of pepper-gingerbread,
To velvet-guards. *Shak.*, 1 Hen. IV., iii. 1. 260.

He [Spenser] is a standing *protest* against the tyranny of Commonplace. *Lowell*, Among my Books, 2d ser., p. 199.

He took away the reproach of silent consent that would otherwise have lain against the indignant minority, by uttering, in the hour and place wherein these outrages were done, the stern *protest*. *Emerson*, Theodore Parker.

Two *protests* of peers against the proceedings of the ministers were expunged from the records of the House of Lords. *Lecky*, Eng. in 18th Cent., i.

2. In *law*: (*a*) In a popular sense, all the steps taken to fix the liability of a drawer or indorser of commercial paper when the paper is dishonored. (*b*) Technically, the solemn declaration on the part of the holder of a bill or note against any loss to be sustained by him by reason of the non-acceptance or non-payment, as the case may be, of the bill or note in question, and the calling of a notary to witness that due steps have been taken to prevent such loss. (*c*) The document authenticating this act. (*d*) A written declaration, usually by the master of a ship, attested by a justice of the peace or a consul, stating the circumstances under which any injury has happened to the ship or cargo, or other circumstances calculated to affect the liability of the owners, officers, crew, etc.—**Acceptance supra protest.** See *acceptance*, 1.—**Acceptor supra protest.** See *acceptor*.—**Protest of Spires (Speyer)**, a protest of Lutherans against the decision of the Diet of Spires in 1529, which had denounced the Reformation. The essential principles involved in the protest against this decree were—(*a*) that the Roman Catholic Church could not judge the Reformed churches, because they were no longer in communion with her; (*b*) that the authority of the Bible is supreme, and above that of councils and bishops; and (*c*) that the Bible is not to be interpreted according to tradition, but is to be interpreted by means of itself.

Protestancy (prot'es-tạn-si), *n.* [< *Protestan(t)* + *-cy*.] Protestantism.

Protestancy is called to the bar, and though not sentenced by you to death without mercy, yet arraigned of so much natural malignity (if not corrected by ignorance or contrition) as to be in itself destructive of salvation.
Chillingworth, Religion of Protestants, i. 1.

protestando (prō-tes-tan'dō), *n.* [L., abl. sing. gerund. of *protestari*, declare in public, bear witness: see *protest*.] In *law*, a protestation. See *protestation*, 3.

protestant (prot'es-tạnt), *a.* and *n.* [< F. *protestant* = Sp. Pg. It. *protestante* = D. G. Dan. Sw. *protestant* = Russ. *protestantŭ*, < L. *protestan(t-)s*, ppr. of *protestari*, declare in public, bear witness: see *protest*.] I. *a.* 1. Protesting; making a protest. [In this use also pronounced distinctively prọ-tes'tạnt.]

A private *protestant* tribunal [conscience], where personal moral convictions preside, and which alone enables men to adapt themselves to new ethical situations or environments. *G. S. Hall*, Amer. Jour. Psychol., III. 61.

2. [*cap.*] Of or pertaining to Protestants or their doctrines or forms of religion.

All sound *Protestant* writers. *Milton*, Civil Power.

Protestant Friends. Same as *Free Congregations* (which see, under *congregation*).

II. *n.* 1. One who protests; one who makes protestation. [In this use also pronounced distinctively prọ-tes'tạnt.]

Bid me to live, and I will live
Thy *protestant* to be;
Or bid me love, and I will give
A loving heart to thee.
Herrick, To Anthea.

If consistency were a matter of great concern to partizans, it might also be pertinent to suggest that no great moral value can be attached to a protest against evil-doing at which the *protestant* has connived.
The Century, XXX. 328.

2. [*cap.*] A member or an adherent of one of those Christian bodies which are descended from the Reformation of the sixteenth century; in general language, opposed to *Roman Catholic* and *Greek*. The name, first applied to the Lutherans who protested at the Diet of Spires in 1529, came to be applied to Lutherans generally, and afterward was extended to Calvinists and other opponents of the papacy in countries where the papacy had formerly been in power. (See *protest of Spires*, under *protest*.) The Protestants gained a strong foothold in some countries, as France, in which they are now numerically weak. They are in the majority in Great Britain and many of its possessions, in Germany, the Netherlands, Switzerland, the Scandinavian countries, and the United States.

What Gerson and Panormitanus write, which were ancient fathers, and not new *Protestants*.
Bp. Pilkington, Works (ed. Parker Soc., 1562), p. 532.

One of these tracts [printed about 1570] has the following title: Ane prettie Mirrour, or Conference betuix the Faithfull *Protestant* and the Dissemblit false Hypocreit.
Lauder, Dewtie of Kyngis (E. E. T. S.), Pref., p. ix.

Queen Elizabeth, finding how fickle the French *Protestants* had carried themselves towards her, intended to make a Peace. *Baker*, Chronicles, p. 332.

Papist or *Protestant*, or both between,
Like good Erasmus, in an honest mean.
Pope, Imit. of Horace, II. i. 65.

Protestantical† (prot-es-tan'ti-kạl), *a.* [< *Protestant* + *-ic-al*.] Protestant. [Rare.]

The *protestantical* Church of England.
Bacon, Obs. on a Libel.

Protestantism (prot'es-tạn-tizm), *n.* [= F. *protestantisme* = Sp. Pg. *protestantismo*; as *Protestant* + *-ism*.] The state of being a Protestant; the religious principles of Protestants; the religious and other tendencies fostered by the Protestant movement. See *protest of Spires*, under *protest*.

The liberal genius of *Protestantism* had perfected its work. *T. Warton*, Hist. Eng. Poetry, II. 461. (*Latham.*)

The *Protestantism* of a great number of the Anglican clergy is supposed to be but languid.
M. Arnold, A Persian Passion Play.

Protestantize (prot'es-tạn-tiz), *v. t.*; pret. and pp. *Protestantized*, ppr. *Protestantizing*. [< *Protestant* + *-ize*.] To render Protestant; convert to Protestantism.

To *Protestantize* Ireland. *Disraeli.*

Protestantly† (prot'es-tạnt-li), *adv.* [< *Protestant* + *-ly*².] In conformity to Protestantism or the Protestants.

To protestants . . . nothing can with more conscience, more equitie, nothing more *protestantly* can be permitted then a free and lawful debate at all times . . . of what opinion soever, disputable by scripture.
Milton, Civil Power.

protestation (prot-es-tā'shọn), *n.* [< ME. *protestacioun*, < OF. *protestation*, F. *protestation* = Sp. *protestacion* = Pg. *protestação* = It. *protestazione*, *protestagione*, < LL. *protestatio(n-)*, a declaration, < L. *protestari*, pp. *protestatus*, declare in public, bear witness: see *protest*.] 1. A solemn or formal declaration of a fact, opinion, or resolution; an asseveration: as, *protestations* of friendship or of amendment.

But first I make a *protestacioun*
That I am dronke, I knowe it by my soun.
Chaucer, Prol. to Miller's Tale, l. 29.

Whereas ye write the day and year of D. Barnes' death, it increaseth your own confusion, and shall be a clear testimony against yourself for resisting those good words of his *protestation*, if ye forsake not your heresy in time.
Coverdale, Remains (Parker Soc.), p. 328.

You are welcome too, sir;
'Tis spoken from the heart, and therefore needs not
Much *protestation*.
Beau. and Fl., Custom of the Country, iii. 5.

Hear but some vows I make to you;
Hear but the *protestations* of a true love.
Fletcher and Rowley, Maid in the Mill, i. 3.

2. A solemn or formal declaration of dissent; a protest.

Which *protestation*, made by the first public reformers of our religion against the imperial edicts of Charles the fifth imposing church-traditions without Scripture, gave first beginning to the name of Protestant.
Milton, Civil Power.

I hear at once
Hubbub of *protestation*!
Browning, Ring and Book, II. 215.

3. In *law*, a declaration in pleading, by which the party interposed an oblique allegation or denial of some fact, by protesting that it did or did not exist, and at the same time avoiding a direct affirmation or denial, the object being to admit it for the purpose of the present action only, and reserve the right to deny it in a future action—"an exclusion of a conclusion." *Coke.* In *Scots law*, a proceeding taken by a defender, where the pursuer neglects to proceed, to compel him either to proceed or to suffer the action to fall. =**Syn.** 1. Affirmation, averment. See *protest*, *v. t.*

protestator (prot'es-tā-tọr), *n.* [= Pg. *protestador* = It. *protestatore*, < NL. *protestator*, < L. *protestari*, pp. *protestatus*, declare in public, bear witness: see *protest*.] One who protests; a protestor.

protested (prọ-tes'ted), *p. a.* Having made a protest. [Rare.]

In this age, Britons, God hath reformed his church after many hundred years of popish corruption; . . . in this age he hath renewed our protestation against all those yet remaining dregs of superstition. Let us all go, every true *protested* Briton, throughout the three kingdoms, and render thanks to God. *Milton*, Animadversions.

protester (prọ-tes'tėr), *n.* [< *protest* + *-er*¹.] 1. One who protests; one who utters a solemn or formal declaration.

Were I a common laugher, or did use
To stale with ordinary oaths my love
To every new *protester*. *Shak.*, J. C., i. 2. 74.

A Protestant, a *protester*, belonging nearly always to an extreme minority, is inevitably disliked—sometimes feared, but always disliked. *Sharp*, D. G. Rossetti, ii.

2. One who protests a bill of exchange, etc.—3. [*cap.*] Specifically, in *Scottish hist.*, a member of a party which protested against the union of the Royalists with the Presbyterians in 1650. Also spelled *Protestor*.

After having been long comrades, they had parted in some unkindness, at the time when the Kingdom of Scotland was divided into Resolutioners and *Protesters*: the former of whom adhered to Charles II. after his father's death upon the scaffold, while the *Protesters* inclined rather to a union with the triumphant republicans.
Scott, Old Mortality, v.

protestingly (prọ-tes'ting-li), *adv.* [< *protesting*, ppr. of *protest*, *v.*, + *-ly*².] In a protesting manner; by way of protesting.

Protestor (prọ-tes'tọr), *n.* Same as *Protester*, 3.

Proteus (prō'tūs or -tē-us), *n.* [L., < Gr. Πρωτεύς, the name of a sea-god: see def.] 1. In *classical myth.*, a sea-god, the son of Oceanus and Tethys, who had the power of assuming different shapes.—2. [NL.] A genus of tailed amphibians, typical of the family *Proteidæ*,

Proteus anguinus.

established by Laurenti in 1768.—3†. [NL.] In *Protozoa*, a genus of animalcules, based as such by O. F. Müller in 1786 upon the proteus or protean animalcule of earlier writers, as Rösel, 1755. The genus is the same as *Amœba*, a common species of which is named *Amœba proteus.* This generic name is untenable, because antedated in the binomial system by the amphibian genus *Proteus* of Laurenti, for, although the name *proteus* was first applied to these animalcules, it was given at a time when genera, in the modern sense of the term, had not been established in zoölogy. See cut under *Amœba*.
4†. [*l. c.*] An animalcule of the genus *Proteus* (or *Amœba*); an amœba.

proteus-animalcule† (prō'tūs-an-i-mal″kūl), *n.* Same as *proteus*, 4.

protevangelium (prō-tē-van-jel'i-um), *n.* [< Gr. πρῶτος, first, + εὐαγγέλιον, gospel: see *evangel.*] The earliest announcement of the gospel: referring to Gen. iii. 15. Also called *protogospel*.

The Messianic promises and hopes which run like a golden thread from the *protevangelium* in paradise lost to the voice of John the Baptist.
Schaff, Hist. Christ. Church, I. § 17.

protext (prō'tekst), *n.* [< L. *pro*, before, + *textus*, text. Cf. *context.*] That part of a discourse or writing which precedes some other part referred to or quoted.

See Baring-Gould's "Curious Myths of the Middle Ages," p. 600 (ed. London, 1881), and the *protext*.
N. and Q., 7th ser., II. 279.

prothalamium, prothalamion (prō-tha-lā'mi-um, -on), *n.* [< Gr. πρό, before, + θάλαμος, a bride-chamber: see *thalamus*. Cf. *epithalamium.*] A piece written to celebrate a marriage; an epithalamium.

Prothalamion, or a Spousall Verse, made by Edmund Spenser. *Spenser*, Prothalamion (Title).

When *prothalamions* prais'd that happy day
Wherein great Dudley match'd with noble Gray.
Drayton, Lady Jane Gray to Lord Dudley.

prothalli, *n.* Plural of *prothallus*.

prothallia, *n.* Plural of *prothallium*.

prothallic (prọ̄-thal'ik), *a.* [< *prothalli-um* + *-ic.*] In *bot.*, of or relating to the prothallium.

prothalline (prọ̄-thal'in), *a.* [< *prothall-ium* + *-ine*[1].] In *bot.*, similar to, characteristic of, or belonging to a prothallium.

Their [spermatia's] fecundating influence is . . . exercised on the *prothalline* elements of the growing thallus.
Encyc. Brit., XIV. 555.

prothallium (prọ̄-thal'i-um), *n.*; pl. *prothallia* (-ạ̈). [NL., < L. *pro*, before, + NL. *thallus.*] In *bot.*, a thalloid oöphyte or its homologue; a little thalloid structure resembling a lichen or *Marchantia*, which is produced by the germination of

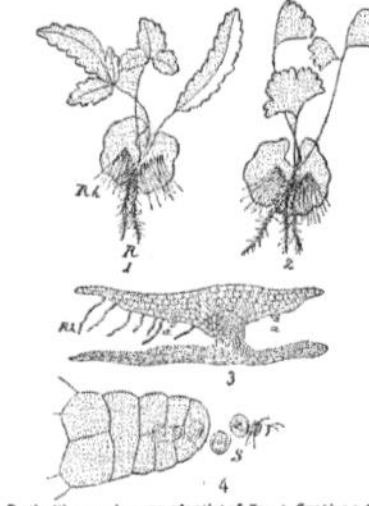

1. Prothallium and young plantlet of *Pteris Cretica*: *Rh*, the rhizoids; *R*, the roots. 2. *Adiantum cuneatum*. 3. Vertical section of the same, but the plantlet very young (magnified): *Rh*, the rhizoids; *a*, archegonia. 4. The antheridium of the same: *S*, the escaping antherozoids (highly magnified).

the spore in the higher cryptogams, and which bears the sexual organs (antheridia and archegonia). It is rarely more than one tenth of an inch in length, is composed of cellular tissue, and bears the antheridia and archegonia on its under surface. After fertilization the oösphere remains for a time within the archegonium, and proceeds to grow by the ordinary processes of cell-multiplication, until finally it breaks through the walls of the archegonium differentiated into its first root and leaf. The young plant continues to draw its nourishment for a time from the prothallium, but it soon develops root-hairs which extend into the soil and render it independent of the prothallium, which, having accomplished its purpose, withers away. See *fern*[1], *Musci*, *Ophioglossaceæ*. Also *prothallus*, *protothallus*.

prothalloid (prọ̄-thal'oid), *a.* [< *prothall-ium* + *-oid.*] In *bot.*, resembling a prothallium.—**Prothalloid branch.** Same as *proëmbryonic branch* (which see, under *proembryonic*).

prothallus (prọ̄-thal'us), *n.*; pl. *prothalli* (-ī). [NL., < L. *pro*, before, + NL. *thallus.*] Same as *prothallium*.

prothelminth (prọ̄-thel'minth), *n.* [< Gr. πρῶτος, first, + ἕλμινς (ἑλμινθ-), a worm: see *helminth.*] A ciliate or flagellate infusorian; any member of the *Prothelmintha*, regarded as representing an ancestral type of worms.

Prothelmintha (prō-thel-min'thạ̈), *n. pl.* [NL.: see *prothelminth.*] An order of protozoan animalcules named by K. M. Diesing (1865) as foreshadowing or pretypifying the lowest worms of the metazoic series, as the turbellarians. The term regarded more especially the holotrichous ciliate infusorians, but included all the ciliate and flagellate forms, excepting *Vorticellidæ* and *Stentoridæ*, and is thus nearly synonymous with *Infusoria*. See cut under *Paramecium*.

prothelminthic (prō-thel-min'thik), *a.* [< *prothelminth* + *-ic.*] Having the character of an archetypal worm; of or pertaining to the *Prothelmintha*.

prothelmis (prọ̄-thel'mis), *n.* [NL., < Gr. πρῶτος, first, + ἕλμις, a worm.] A hypothetical primitive worm, the entire body of which is supposed to have permanently consisted of four layers corresponding to those of the four-layered germ of most animals. *Haeckel*.

prothesis (proth'e-sis), *n.* [< LL. *prothesis*, < Gr. πρόθεσις, a putting before, proposition, purpose, preposition, < προτιθέναι, put before, < πρό, before, + τιθέναι, put, place: see *thesis*. Cf. *prosthesis.*] 1. In the *Gr. Ch.*: (*a*) The preparation and preliminary oblation of the eucharistic elements before the liturgy: more fully called the *office of prothesis*. This office is said responsively by priest and deacon. The priest signs an oblate with the holy lance, thrusts the lance into the right, left, upper, and lower sides of the holy lamb, lifts this off, cuts it crosswise, and stabs it. He then blesses the chalice which the deacon has prepared (mixed). Appropriate prayers and verses of Scripture accompany these rites. He then takes from the remainder of this and other oblates pyramidal pieces called *portions* of the Virgin Mary, apostles, martyrs, etc., the living and the dead, commemorating these classes, and arranging the portions in a prescribed manner on the disk (paten). Incense is then offered, the asterisk and veils placed over the elements, and the prayer of prothesis said. The elements are left in the chapel of prothesis till taken to the altar at the Great Entrance. (*b*) The table on which this preparation is made (the table or altar of prothesis). It answers to the Western credence-table. (c) The apartment or the part of the bema or sanctuary in which this table is situated and the office used (the chapel of prothesis). See *bema* and the cut there given.—2. In *gram.*, addition of one or more sounds or letters at the beginning of a word. Some Latin writers use this form for the Greek πρόσθεσις (see *prosthesis*) apparently through misapprehension, and some modern writers prefer it as more specific.
3. In *surg.*, prosthesis.

prothetic (prọ̄-thet'ik), *a.* [< *prothesis* (*-thet-*) + *-ic.*] Pertaining to or exhibiting prothesis.

prothetically (prọ̄-thet'i-kạl-i), *adv.* By prothesis.

Letters added *prothetically*.
Trans. Amer. Philol. Ass., XVI. App. p. xxxiii.

prothonotarial (prọ̄-thon-ọ̄-tā'ri-ạl), *a.* [< *prothonotary* + *-al.*] Pertaining or belonging to a prothonotary.

prothonotariat (prọ̄-thon-ọ̄-tā'ri-at), *n.* [Also prop. *protonotariat*, < OF. **prothonotariat*, < ML. *protonotarius*, prothonotary: see *prothonotary.*] The college constituted by the twelve apostolical prothonotaries in Rome.

prothonotary, protonotary (prọ̄-thon'ọ̄-tạ̄-ri, prọ̄-ton'ọ̄-tạ̄-ri), *n.*; pl. *prothonotaries, protonotaries* (-riz). [Prop. *protonotary*, formerly *protonotarie*; < OF. *prothonotaire*, F. *protonotaire* = Sp. Pg. It. *protonotario*, < ML. *protonotarius*, a chief notary or scribe, < Gr. πρῶτος, first, + L. *notarius*, notary: see *notary.*] A chief notary or clerk.

Can I not sin but thou wilt be
My private *protonotarie*?
Herrick, To his Conscience.

Specifically—(*a*) Originally, the chief of the notaries; now, in the *Rom. Cath. Ch.*, one of a college of twelve (formerly seven) ecclesiastics charged with the registry of acts, proceedings relating to canonization, etc. (*b*) In the *Gr. Ch.*, the chief secretary of the patriarch of Constantinople, who superintends the secular work of the provinces. (c) In *law*, a chief clerk of court; formerly, a chief clerk in the Court of Common Pleas and in the King's Bench.—**Prothonotary warbler**, *Protonotaria citrea*, a small migratory insectivorous bird of North America belonging to the family *Sylvicolidæ* or *Mniotiltidæ*. It is a beautiful warbler, of a rich yellow color, passing by degrees through olivaceous to bluish tints on the rump, wings, and tail,

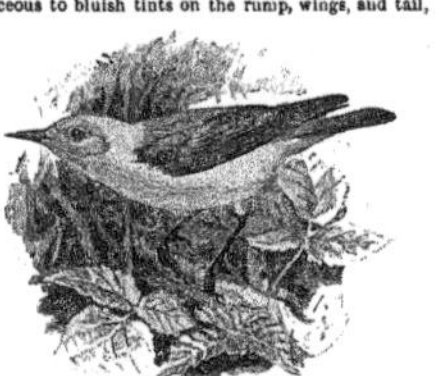

Prothonotary Warbler (*Protonotaria citrea*).

the last blotched with white; the bill is comparatively large, half an inch long, and black; the length is 5½ inches, the extent 9¼. It inhabits swamps, thickets, and tangle, nests on or near the ground in holes or other sheltered cavities in trees, stumps, or logs, and lays four or five creamy-white profusely speckled eggs.

prothonotaryship (prọ̄-thon'ọ̄-tạ̄-ri-ship), *n.* [< *prothonotary* + *-ship.*] The office of a prothonotary.

prothoracic (prō-thọ̄-ras'ik), *a.* [< *prothorax* (*-thorac-*) + *-ic.*] In *entom.*, of or pertaining to the prothorax.—**Prothoracic case**, that part of the integument of a pupa which covers the prothorax.—**Prothoracic epipleura.** See *epipleura*, 3.—**Prothoracic legs**, the first or anterior pair of legs, sometimes aborted, as in certain butterflies.—**Prothoracic shoulder-lobes**, lobes of the prothorax which cover the anterior corners of the mesothorax, as in certain *Diptera*: when they show no apparent separation from the mesothorax they are called *shoulder-callosities*.

prothoracotheca (prō-thō″rạ-kọ̄-thē'kạ̈), *n.*; pl. *prothoracothecæ* (-sē). [NL., < Gr. πρό, before, + θώραξ (θωρακ-), breast, + θήκη, a case, box.] In *entom.*, the prothoracic case, or that part of the integument of a pupa covering the prothorax.

prothorax (prō-thō'raks), *n.* [NL., < Gr. πρό, before, + θώραξ, breast: see *thorax.*] In *Insecta*, the first one of the three thoracic somites, which succeeds the head, is succeeded by the mesothorax, and bears the first pair of legs. In descriptions of *Coleoptera* and *Hemiptera* the term is often restricted to the broad shield, or pronotum, forming the part of the thorax seen from above. In the *Hymenoptera*, *Diptera*, and *Lepidoptera* the prothorax is generally so small as to be hardly distinguishable. See cuts under *Coleoptera*, *Insecta*, *mesothorax*, and *metathorax*.—**Cruciate, emarginate, lobed**, etc., **prothorax**. See the adjectives.

prothyalosoma (prọ̄-thī″ạ-lọ̄-sō'mạ̈), *n.*; pl. *prothyalosomata* (-mạ-tạ̈). [NL., < Gr. πρῶτος, first, + ὕαλος, glass, + σῶμα, body.] Van Beneden's name (1883) of an investing portion or spherical envelop of the nucleolus of the nucleus of an ovum.

prothyalosomal (prọ̄-thī″ạ-lọ̄-sō'mạl), *a.* [< *prothyalosoma* + *-al.*] Of or pertaining to the prothyalosoma.

prothysteron (prọ̄-this'tẹ-ron), *n.* [< Gr. πρωθύστερον, < πρῶτος, first, + ὕστερος, last. Cf. *hysteron-proteron.*] In *rhet.*, same as *hysteron-proteron*, 1.

protichnite (prọ̄-tik'nīt), *n.* [< Gr. πρῶτος, first, + ἴχνος, a track, trace, footstep, + *-ite*[2].] A fossil track or trace occurring in the Potsdam sandstone of Canada, supposed to have been made by trilobites, or some related animals, as eurypterids.

protist (prō'tist), *a.* and *n.* [< *Protista.*] **I.** *a.* Pertaining to the *Protista*, or having their characters.
II. *n.* Any member of the *Protista*.

Protista (prọ̄-tis'tạ̈), *n. pl.* [< Gr. πρώτιστα, neut. pl. of πρώτιστος, the very first, superl. of πρῶτος, first, < πρό, before, first. Cf. *former*[1] and *first*[1].] One of the kingdoms of animated nature, which Haeckel proposed (1868) to include the *Protozoa* and the *Protophyta*, or the lowest animals and plants as collectively distinguished from other organisms. The proposition to recognize this alleged "third kingdom" had been several times made before, and the unicellular plants and animals had been grouped together under various names, as *Protoctista* of Hogg (1830), and *Primalia* of Wilson and Cassin (1863).

protistan (prō-tis'tạn), *a.* and *n.* [< *Protista* + *-an.*] **I.** *a.* Of or pertaining to the *Protista.*

II. *n.* A member of the *Protista;* any unicellular organism not definitely regarded as a plant or an animal.

protistic (prō-tis'tik), *a.* [< *Protista* + *-ic.*] Of or pertaining to the *Protista.*

Protium (prō'shi-um), *n.* [NL. (Wight and Arnott, 1834); perhaps from a native name in Java.] A genus of polypetalous trees of the order *Burseraceæ* and tribe *Bursereæ.* It is characterized by a free cup-shaped four- to six-cleft calyx, a cup-like disk bearing the four to six long narrow petals, and the eight to twelve unequal erect stamens on its margin, and a globose drupe, the fleshy outside splitting into four valves and the stone consisting of from one to four bony one-seeded nutlets, at first united together but finally free. There are about 50 species, natives of the tropics of both hemispheres. They are small trees, exuding a balsamic resin, and bearing pinnate leaves toward the end of the branchlets, composed of three or more large stalked leaflets. The small slender-pedicelled flowers form branching panicles borne on long stalks. *P. Guianense* is the hyawa or incense-tree of British Guiana, and *P. altissimum* is there known as white cedar. Some of the species have formerly been classed under *Icica* (*Aublet,* 1775). They produce many valuable gum-resins, for which see *elemi, acouchi-resin, caranna, conima,* and *hyawa gum* (under *gum*[2]).

proto-. [< Gr. πρῶτος, first, superl., < πρό, before, first, in advance of.] An element in compound words of Greek origin, meaning 'first,' and denoting precedence in time, rank, or degree. Besides its frequent use in scientific names, it is common in compounds having a historical reference, as *proto-Arabic, proto-Medic,* etc. Compare *proto-compound.*

proto-abbacy† (prō-tō-ab'ạ-ti), *n.* [< Gr. πρῶτος, first, + ML. *abbatia,* abbacy: see *abbacy.*] A first or principal abbacy.

Dunstan . . . was the first abbot of England, not in time, but in honour, Glastonbury being the *proto-abbacy* then and many years after.
Fuller, Worthies, Somersetshire, III. 92.

proto-apostate (prō"tō-ạ-pos'tāt), *n.* [< Gr. πρῶτος, first, + ἀποστάτης, apostate: see *apostate.*] A first or original apostate.

Sir James Montgomery, the false and fickle *proto-apostate* of whiggism. *Hallam,* Const. Hist., III. 127, note.

protoblastic (prō-tọ-blas'tik), *a.* [< Gr. πρῶτος, first, + βλαστός, germ.] Same as *holoblastic.*

The eggs of mammals are, as embryologists would say, regularly *protoblastic.* *Amer. Nat.,* XVIII. 1270.

protocanonical (prō"tō-kạ-non'i-kạl), *a.* [< ML. *protocanonicus,* < Gr. πρῶτος, first, + κανονικός, canonical: see *canonic.*] Of the first or original canon. See *deuterocanonical.*

From the perpetual and universal tradition and practice of the whole church from the apostles' time to ours, we may have a human persuasion, and that certain and infallible, of the divine and canonical authority of those books which were still undoubted, or which some call the *protocanonical.* *Baxter,* Saints' Rest, ii., Pref.

Protocaulidæ (prō-tō-kâ'li-dē), *n. pl.* [NL., < *Protocaulon* + *-idæ.*] A family of spicateous pennatuloid polyps, typified by the genus *Protocaulon.* They are of small size, without cells or rachial pinnules, and with sessile polypites on both sides of the rachis in a single series or in indistinct rows.

Protocaulon (prō-tō-kâ'lon), *n.* [NL., < Gr. πρῶτος, first, + καυλός, the stalk of a plant.] The typical genus of *Protocaulidæ.*

protocercal (prō-tọ-sėr'kạl), *a.* [< Gr. πρῶτος, first, + κέρκος, tail: see *cercal.*] Having a primitive tail-fin: noting the embryonic stage of the vertical fins and tail of a fish, when these consist of a continuous skinfold along both upper and under sides of the body and around its tail-end. *Jeffries Wyman.*

protocere (prō'tọ-sēr), *n.* [< Gr. πρῶτος, first, + κέρας, horn.] The rudiment of the antler of a deer, or that process of the antler which is best developed in the second year.

protocerebral (prō-tọ-ser'ẹ-brạl), *a.* [< *protocerebrum* + *-al.*] Of or pertaining to the protocerebrum.

protocerebrum (prō-tọ-ser'ẹ-brum), *n.* [NL., < Gr. πρῶτος, first, + L. *cerebrum,* the brain: see *cerebrum.*] The primitive anterior cerebral vesicle or rudiment of the cerebrum proper. *N. Y. Med. Jour.,* March 28, 1885, p. 354.

protochlorid, protochloride (prō-tọ-klō'rid), *n.* [< Gr. πρῶτος, first, + E. *chlorid, chloride.*] A chlorid whose molecule contains a single chlorin atom, or one in which the ratio of chlorin atoms to basic atoms is the smallest. —**Protochlorid of mercury.** Same as *calomel.*

Protococcaceæ (prō"tọ-ko-kā'sẹ-ē), *n. pl.* [NL., < *Protococcus* + *-aceæ.*] An order of unicellular algæ of the class *Protococcoideæ,* typified by the genus *Protococcus.* It includes a number of organisms of very simple structure, many of which occur both in a free-swimming and in a resting condition.

protococcoid (prō-tọ-kok'oid), *a.* [< *Protococcus* + *-oid.*] In *bot.,* resembling *Protococcus.*

Protococcoideæ (prō"tọ-ko-koi'dẹ-ē), *n. pl.* [NL., < *Protococcus* + *-oideæ.*] A class of minute plants belonging to the group *Schizophyceæ,* taking its name from the genus *Protococcus.* It includes those simplest forms of vegetable life in which the endochrome consists of pure chlorophyl of its natural green color, sometimes replaced, to a greater or less extent, by a red pigment, but never possessing in the cell-sap a soluble blue coloring matter. They are of microscopic size, and may occur in both the resting and the motile condition. They multiply very rapidly by bipartition and also by means of swarm-spores. This class is a purely provisional one, and probably includes many forms that are nothing more than stages in the development of algæ of greater complexity and belonging to widely separated families. The *Protococcoideæ* embrace two orders, the *Eremobieæ* and *Protococcaceæ.* See *Schizophyceæ.*

Protococcus (prō-tọ-kok'us), *n.* [NL. (Agardh), < Gr. πρῶτος, first, + κόκκος, a berry: see *coccus.*] A genus of algæ, typical of the order *Protococcaceæ* and class *Protococcoideæ.* They are in the strictest sense unicellular plants, being spherical, unbranched, and single, or gathered into irregular groups or clusters. They are primarily always filled with chlorophyl-green cytioplasm, which often changes to red by exposure or other circumstances. They multiply rapidly by repeated bipartition of the cell-contents. *P. viridis* is exceedingly abundant everywhere, forming broadly expanded strata of yellowish- or darker-green color on trunks of trees, moist rocks, walls, timbers of shaded buildings, old fences, etc. *P. nivalis* is the well-known "red snow" which frequently covers large tracts of snow in arctic or alpine regions in a very short time.

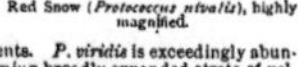

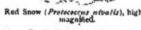

Red Snow (*Protococcus nivalis*), highly magnified.

Protocœlomata (prō"tọ-sẹ-lō'mạ-tạ̈), *n. pl.* [NL., < Gr. πρῶτος, first, + κοίλωμα(τ-), a hollow, cavity: see *cœloma.*] Animals which have a primitive archenteron with simple cœlomic sacs or branching diverticula, as most sponges: more fully called *Metazoa protocœlomata.* *A. Hyatt,* Proc. Bost. Soc. Nat. Hist., 1884, p. 113.

protocœlomate (prọ"tọ-sẹ-lọ'māt), *n.* One of the *Protocœlomata.*

protocœlomatic (prō-tọ-sē-lọ-mat'ik), *a.* [< *Protocœlomata* + *-ic.*] Of or pertaining to the *Protocœlomata.*

protocol (prō'tọ-kol), *n.* [< OF. *protocole, prothocole, protecole,* F. *protocole* = Pr. *prothcolle* = Sp. *protocolo* = Pg. It. *protocollo* = D. *protokol* = G. *protocoll, protokoll* = Sw. *protokoll* = Dan. *protokol,* < ML. *protocollum,* corruptly *prothocollum,* a draft of a document, a minute, a public register, a paper confirmed by a seal, < MGr. πρωτόκολλον, a protocol, orig. a leaf or sheet glued in front of a manuscript, on which to enter particulars as to the administration under which the manuscript was written, the writer's name, etc., < Gr. πρῶτος, first, + κολλᾶν, glue, < κόλλα, glue: see *collodion,* etc.] **1**†. The original of any writing.

An original is styled the *protocol,* or scriptural matrix; and if the *protocol,* which is the root and foundation of the instrument, does not appear, the instrument is not valid.
Aylife, Parergon.

2. In *diplomacy,* the minutes or rough draft of an instrument or a transaction; hence, the original copy of any despatch, treaty, or other document; a document serving as a preliminary to or opening of any diplomatic transaction; also, a diplomatic document or minute of proceedings signed by friendly powers in order to secure certain diplomatic ends by peaceful means.

The next day the Doctor [Dale], by agreement, brought a most able *protocol* of demands in the name of all the commissioners of her Majesty [Elizabeth].
Motley, Hist. Netherlands, II. 406.

3. A record or registry; in *law,* a notary's record of copies of his acts.

The *protocol* here is admirable, taken on the spot by Mr. B—— and printed in full, and Mr. G—— is very positive in stating that there were a large number of complete successes [in experiments]. *Amer. Jour. Psychol.,* I. 136.

4. In the parts of the United States acquired from Mexico, the original record of the transfer of land. Under Spanish laws the parties to a deed, or other instrument affecting land, appeared before a *regidor,* a sort of notary or alderman, accompanied by their neighbors as "instrumental witnesses," and stated the terms of their agreement. That officer made a minute of the terms and entered the formal agreement in a book. This entry was called the *protocol* or *matrix,* and remained with the officer, the parties receiving from him a similar document called a *testimonio.*

protocol (prō'tọ-kol), *v.;* pret. and pp. *protocoled,* ppr. *protocoling.* [< *protocol, n.*] **I.** *intrans.* To form protocols or first drafts; issue protocols.

Serene Highnesses who sit there *protocolling,* and manifestoing, and consoling mankind.
Carlyle, French Rev., II. vi. 3. (*Davies.*)

Nevertheless, both in Holland and England, there had been other work than *protocolling.*
Motley, Hist. Netherlands, II. 445.

II. *trans.* To make a protocol of.

protocol-book (prō'tọ-kol-bůk), *n.* A book for the purpose of entering records; a register.

A second person sitting at the other side of the table reads off and records in the *protocol-book* the distance of each excursion. *Mind,* IX. 103.

protocolist (prō'tọ-kol-ist), *n.* [= G. *protocollist* = Sw. Dan. *protokollist* = Russ. *protokolistŭ;* as *protocol* + *-ist.*] A register or clerk.

The *protocolists,* or secretaries.
Harper's Monthly, LXIV. 275.

protocolize (prō'tọ-kol-īz), *v. i.;* pret. and pp. *protocolized,* ppr. *protocolizing.* [< *protocol* + *-ize.*] To write or draw up protocols.

Kept *protocolizing* with soft promises and delusive delays. *Mahony,* Father Prout, p. 35, note. (*Encyc. Dict.*)

proto-compound (prō'tō-kom"pound), *n.* In *chem.,* originally, the first of a series of binary compounds arranged according to the number of atoms of the electronegative element. At present the term is most commonly used, in contradistinction to *per-compounds,* to designate those compounds of an element which contain relatively less of the electronegative radical. Thus, two chlorids of iron are known, $FeCl_2$ and Fe_2Cl_6; the former is called *protochlorid,* the latter *perchlorid.* [The name is less usual now than it was some years ago.]

protoconch (prō'tọ-kongk), *n.* [< Gr. πρῶτος, first, + κόγχη, a mussel, shell: see *conch.*] The embryonal or primitive shell of an ammonoid cephalopod. *Owen.* Also called *embryo-sac, ovicell,* and *ovisac.*

The position was taken that the scar of the Nautiloides showed that a *protoconch* had existed in the embryo of Nautilus, but had disappeared during the growth of the shell, the scar being uncovered by its removal.
A. Hyatt, Proc. Amer. Assoc. Adv. Sci., 1884, p. 325.

protoconchal (prō'tọ-kong-kạl), *a.* [< *protoconch* + *-al.*] Pertaining to the protoconch.

Protodermiaceæ (prō-tọ-dėr-mi-ā'sẹ-ē), *n. pl.* [NL. (Rostafinski), < *Protodermium* + *-aceæ.*] A family of *Myxomycetes* of the order *Protodermieæ,* containing the monotypic genus *Protodermium.* It has the characters of the order.

Protodermieæ (prō"tọ-dėr-mī'ẹ-ē), *n. pl.* [NL., < *Protodermium* + *-eæ.*] An order of *Myxomycetes,* embracing the single family *Protodermiaceæ.* The peridium is simple, of regular shape, and destitute of capitulum; the spores are violet.

Protodermium (prō-tọ-dėr'mi-um), *n.* [NL. (Rostafinski, 1875), < Gr. πρῶτος, first, + δέρμα, skin.] A monotypic genus of myxomycetous fungi, typical of the family *Protodermiaceæ* and order *Protodermieæ.* *P. presillum,* the only species, is found on decaying wood.

protodipnoan (prō-tọ-dip'nọ-ạn), *n.* [< Gr. πρῶτος, first, + E. *dipnoan.*] A primitive dipnoan; a supposititious representative of the stock from which the dipnoans sprang.

Protodonata (prọ-tō-dō-nā'tạ̈), *n. pl.* [NL., < Gr. πρῶτος, first, + NL. *Odonata,* q. v.] A group of fossil pseudoneuropterous insects of the coal period, containing forms resembling the *Odonata* or dragon-flies of the present day.

Proto-Doric (prō-tō-dor'ik), *a.* and *n.* [< Gr. πρῶτος, first, + Δωρικός, Doric.] **I.** *a.* In *arch.,* primitively Doric; noting any style, member, etc., as a column or capital, which exhibits the rudiments of the later-developed Grecian Doric, or is considered as having contributed to the evolution of the Grecian Doric.

II. *n.* In *arch.,* primitive or rudimentary Doric. See cut under *hypogeum.*

protogaster (prō-tọ-gas'tėr), *n.* [< Gr. πρῶτος, first, + γαστήρ, stomach.] In *embryol.,* the central cavity of a gastrula; the primitive intestinal cavity of a two-layered germ; the hollow of the archenteron of a germ-cup, inclosed by the hypoblastic blastodermic membrane or endoderm, and communicating with the exterior by the protostoma or archæostoma, which is the orifice of invagination of the antecedent blastula.

protogastric (prō-tǫ-gas'trik), *a.* [< *protogaster* + *-ic.*] 1. Of or pertaining to the protogaster.—2. In brachyurous *Crustacea*, noting an anterolateral subdivision of the gastric lobe of the carapace. See cut under *Brachyura*.

protogenal (prǫ-toj'e-nal), *a.* [< Gr. πρῶτος, first, + -γενής, produced (see *-gen*), + *-al.*] First-born; primitive or original, as organized matter.

Sarcode or the *protogenal* jelly-speck.
Owen, Comp. Anat. (1868), III. 817.

Protogenes (prǫ-toj'e-nēz), *n.* [NL., < Gr. πρῶτος, first, + -γενής, produced: see *-gen.*] A genus of amœbiform mastigopodous protozoans, referred by Haeckel to the *Lobosa*, by Lankester to the *Proteomyxa*, having filamentous, ramified, and anastomosing pseudopodia.

In the *Protogenes* of Professor Haeckel, there has been reached a type distinguishable from a fragment of albumen only by its finely-granular character.
H. Spencer, Prin. of Psychol., § 55.

protogenesis (prō-tǫ-jen'e-sis), *n.* [< Gr. πρῶτος, first, + γένεσις, generation.] The origination of living from not-living matter; abiogenesis. It is a logical inference that protogenesis has occurred at some time, but we have no knowledge of the fact.

protogenetic (prō"tǫ-ję-net'ik), *a.* [As *protogenic*, with term. as in *genetic.*] Same as *protogenic*.

protogenic (prō-tǫ-jen'ik), *a.* [< Gr. πρῶτος, first, + -γενής, produced (see *-gen*), + *-ic.*] 1. In *geol.*, noting crystalline or fire-formed rocks, in contradistinction to *deuterogenic*, which notes those formed from them by mechanical action. —2. In *bot.*, noting those intercellular spaces of plants which are formed when the tissues begin to differentiate. Compare *hysterogenic*, *lysigenous*, *schizogenic*.

protogine (prō'tǫ-jēn), *n.* [Irreg. < Gr. πρῶτος, first, + γίνεσθαι, γίγνεσθαι, become, be.] A variety of granite occurring in the Alps. This was formerly considered a peculiar rock, the light-colored mica which it contains having been mistaken for talc. Some varieties of the Alpine granite do contain talc or chlorite, but these minerals do not appear to be essential to its constitution. Formerly written sometimes by French geologists *protogyne*. Also called *Alpine granite* and *protogine granite*.

protogospel (prō-tǫ-gos'pel), *n.* [< Gr. πρῶτος, first, + E. *gospel.*] Same as *protevangelium*. *Schaff.*

protograph (prō'tǫ-gràf), *n.* [< Gr. πρῶτος, first, + γράφειν, write.] A preliminary draft or proposed statement.

protogynous (prǫ-toj'i-nus), *a.* [< *protogyn-y* + *-ous.*] 1. Of or pertaining to protogyny; characterized or affected by protogyny.—2. In *bot.*, same as *proterogynous*.

In *protogynous* flowers the stigma is receptive before the anthers in the same flower are mature.
Sachs, Botany (trans.), p. 813.

protogyny (prǫ-toj'i-ni), *n.* [< Gr. πρῶτος, first, + γυνή, female (in mod. bot. a pistil).] In *bot.*, same as *proterogyny*. See the quotation under *protandry*.

Protohippus (prō-tǫ-hip'us), *n.* [NL., < Gr. πρῶτος, first, + ἵππος, horse.] A genus of fossil horses of the family *Equidæ*, founded by Leidy in 1858 upon remains from the early Pliocene of North America.

proto-historic (prō"tǫ-his-tor'ik), *a.* [< Gr. πρῶτος, first, + ἱστορικός, historic.] Belonging or relating to the dawn or very beginnings of recorded history.

The discourse of Signor Vilanova is on pre-historic or *proto-historic* Spain. *The Academy*, No. 897, p. 28.

Protohydra (prō-tǫ-hī'drä), *n.* [NL., < Gr. πρῶτος, first, + NL. *Hydra*: see *Hydra*, 4.] A genus of eleutheroblastic hydroids resembling *Hydra*, but of still simpler form, as they lack tentacles.

Proto-Ionic (prō"tō-ī-on'ik), *a.* [< Gr. πρῶτος, first, + Ἰωνικός, Ionic.] In *arch.*, primitively

Proto-Ionic Capital, discovered in the Troad by the Archæological Institute of America.

Ionic; exhibiting or containing the germs of Ionic.

protomala (prō-tǫ-mā'lä), *n.*; pl. *protomalæ* (-lē). [NL. (Packard, 1883), < Gr. πρῶτος, first, + L. *mala*, mandible.] The mandible of a myriapod, the morphological equivalent of that of a hexapodous insect, but not structurally homologous therewith, rather resembling the lacinia of the maxilla of the hexapods. See the quotation, and cut under *epilabrum*.

The *protomala* consists of two portions, the cardo and stipes, while the hexapodous mandible is invariably composed of but one piece, to which the muscles are directly attached, and which corresponds to the stipes of the myriapodous *protomala*.
A. S. Packard, Proc. Amer. Philos. Soc., June, 1883, p. 198.

protomalal (prō-tǫ-mā'lal), *a.* [< *protomala* + *-al.*] Of or pertaining to the protomala of a myriapod. *Packard.*

protomalar (prō-tǫ-mā'lär), *a.* [< *protomala* + *-ar*³.] In *Myriapoda*, same as *protomalal*.

protomartyr (prō-tǫ-mär'tėr), *n.* [Formerly also *prothomartyr*; = F. *protomartyr* = Sp. *protomártir* = Pg. *protomartyr* = It. *protomartire*, < ML. *protomartyr*, < MGr. πρωτόμαρτυρ, first martyr, < Gr. πρῶτος, first, + μάρτυρ, martyr: see *martyr.*] The first martyr; the first of any series of martyrs; the first who suffers or is sacrificed in any cause; specifically, Stephen, the earliest Christian martyr.

In the honoure of that holy *prothomartyr*, seynt Albon.
Fabyan, Chron., I. cxviii.

That *Proto-Martyr*, the yong faithfull Steven,
Whom th' hatefull Iews with hellish rage did stone.
Sylvester, tr. of Du Bartas's Triumph of Faith, iii. 28.

Myself were like enough, O girls,
To unfurl the maiden banner of our rights,
And clad in iron burst the ranks of war,
Or, falling, *protomartyr* of our cause,
Die. *Tennyson*, Princess, iv.

protomeristem (prō-tǫ-mer'is-tem), *n.* [< Gr. πρῶτος, first, + E. *meristem.*] In *bot.*, primary meristem—that is, young and imperfectly developed meristem which forms the first foundation or beginning of an organ or a tissue. See *meristem*.

protomerite (prǫ-tom'ę-rīt), *n.* [< Gr. πρῶτος, first, + μέρος, a part, + *-ite*².] The smaller anterior one of the two cells of a dicystidan or septate gregarine. It may bear the epimerite, or proboscis serving for the attachment of the parasite to its host, in which case the gregarine is called a *cephalont*. The protomerite is distinguished from the larger posterior *deutomerite*.

protomeritic (prō"tǫ-me-rit'ik), *a.* [< *protomerite* + *-ic.*] Pertaining to the protomerite of a gregarine.

Protomeryx (prō-tǫ-mē'riks), *n.* [NL., < Gr. πρῶτος, first, + μήρυξ, a ruminating mammal.] A genus of fossil camels of the family *Camelidæ*, named by Leidy in 1856 from remains of Miocene age of North America.

protomesal (prō-tǫ-mes'al), *a.* [< Gr. πρῶτος, first, + μέσος, middle: see *mesal.*] In *entom.*, noting a series of wing-cells or areolets in hymenopterous insects, between the pterostigma or the costal cells and the apical margin. *Kirby.* There may be as many as three of these cells, distinguished as upper, middle, and lower. They correspond to the second, third, and fourth submarginal or cubital cells of modern entomologists.

Protomonas (prǫ-tom'ǫ-nas), *n.* [NL., < Gr. πρῶτος, first, + μόνος, single: see *monad.*] A genus of *Monera*, or myxopodous *Protozoa*, characterized by the production, after becoming encysted and rupturing, of free mastigopodous germs, which swim by means of a long vibratile flagellum, like flagellate infusorians. In this free state the germs are mastigopods, but they afterward withdraw their filamentous pseudopodia, and become myxopods, which creep about by means of lobate pseudopodia. See cut under *Protomyxa*.

protomorphic (prō-tǫ-mōr'fik), *a.* [< Gr. πρῶτος, first, + μορφή, form.] Being in the first, most primitive, or simplest form or shape; having a primitive character or structure; not metamorphic: as, "a *protomorphic* layer" [of tissue], *H. Spencer*, Prin. of Biol., § 290.

Protomyces (prǫ-tom'i-sēz), *n.* [NL., < Gr. πρῶτος, first, + μύκης, a mushroom.] A small genus of zygomycetous fungi, type of the order *Protomycetaceæ*. They are mostly parasitic upon the *Umbelliferæ*, inhabiting the intercellular spaces of the leaf-stem, petiole, flower-stalk, and pericarp. They have a branching septate mycelium, upon which are formed at irregular intervals large oval resting progametangia. When the mycelium dies they persist and hibernate, and are liberated when the tissues of the host decay.

Protomycetaceæ (prō-tǫ-mī-sę-tā'sę-ē), *n. pl.* [< *Protomyces* (*-et-*) + *-aceæ.*] An order of zygomycetous fungi, typified by the genus *Protomyces*.

Protomyxa (prō-tǫ-mik'sä), *n.* [NL. (Haeckel, 1868), < Gr. πρῶτος, first, + μύξα, mucus.] A genus of *Monera*, represented by an organism which consists of a number of myxopods run together into an active plasmodium, which, becoming quiescent and encysted, undergoes fis-

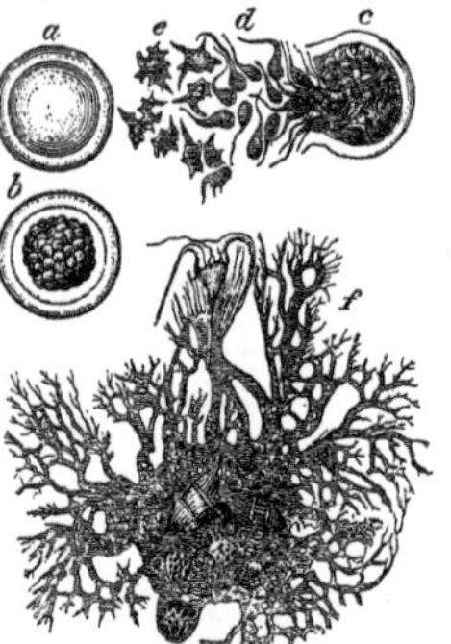

Protomyxa aurantiaca.
a, quiescent, encysted; *b*, dividing in the cyst; *c*, cyst burst, giving exit to mastigopods resembling monads or flagellate infusorians (*d*), which after a while become amœbiform myxopods (*e*), a number of which then unite into a single active plasmodium (*f*), which grows and feeds, as upon the infusorians and the diatoms figured in its substance (these are a peridinium above, next two isthmiæ, below three dictyocystæ).

sive multiplication within the cyst, and gives rise to a number of germs which alternate between the myxopod and the mastigopod state.

There is no means of knowing whether the cycle of forms represented by Protomonas and *Protomyxa* is complete, or whether some term of the series is still wanting.
Huxley, Anat. Invert., p. 77.

protomyxoid (prō-tǫ-mik'soid), *a.* [< *Protomyxa* + *-oid.*] Resembling, relating to, or belonging to the genus *Protomyxa*.

The writer has attempted to explain the forms of free and united cells as specializations of a (*protomyxoid*) cycle in which variations of functional activity are accompanied by the assumption of corresponding forms, the whole series of changes depending upon the properties of protoplasm under the variations in the supply of energy from the environment.
Encyc. Brit., XVI. 846.

protonema (prō-tǫ-nē'mä), *n.* [NL., < Gr. πρῶτος, first, + νῆμα, a thread.] In *Muscineæ*, a pluricellular, confervoid or filamentous, usually chlorophyllose, structure upon which the leafy plant which bears the sexual organs arises as a lateral or terminal shoot. Also *protoneme*.

protonemal (prō-tǫ-nē'mal), *a.* [< *protonema* + *-al.*] In *bot.*, belonging to a protonema.

protonematoid (prō-tǫ-nem'a-toid), *a.* [< *protonema*(*t-*) + *-oid.*] In *bot.*, resembling or having the character of a protonema.

protoneme (prō'tǫ-nēm), *n.* [< NL. *protonema*, q. v.] In *bot.*, same as *protonema*.

protonephric (prō-tǫ-nef'rik), *a.* [< *protonephron* + *-ic.*] Pertaining to the protonephron, or having its character.

protonephron (prō-tǫ-nef'ron), *n.*; pl. *protonephra* (-rä). [NL., < Gr. πρῶτος, first, + νεφρός, a kidney.] A primitive kidney or segmental organ; the original renal organ of an embryo; a Wolffian body, later absorbed or modified into some other part of the urogenital system, and thus giving place to the permanent functional kidney. In some of the lower vertebrates the renal organ is regarded as a persistent Wolffian body, and therefore as a definitive protonephron. A protonephron is divisible into three recognizable structures, called *pronephron*, *mesonephron*, and *metanephron*. See these words.

protonic (prō-ton'ik), *a.* [< Gr. πρό, before, + τόνος, accent: see *tonic.*] Preceding the tone or accent.

Protonopsidæ (prō-tō-nop'si-dē), *n. pl.* [NL., < *Protonopsis* + *-idæ.*] A family of gradient or tailed amphibians, typified by the genus *Protonopsis*, without eyelids, with teeth on the anterior margin of the palatine bones, no dentigerous plates on the parasphenoid, vertebræ amphicœlian, no anterior axial cranial bone, the parietals and prefrontals prolonged, meeting and embracing the frontals, the wall of the vestibule membranous internally, premaxillaries separated, the occipital condyles sessile, and well-developed limbs. Also called *Menopomidæ*.

Protonopsis (prō-tǫ-nop'sis), *n.* [NL., irreg. < Gr. Πρωτεύς (see *Proteus*) + ὄψις, view.] A genus of tailed amphibians, typical of the family *Protonopsidæ*: synonymous with *Menopoma*. See cut under *hellbender*.

protonotariat, protonotary (prǫ-ton-ǫ-tā'ri-at, prǫ-ton'ǫ-tā-ri), *n.* See *prothonotariat, prothonotary*.

Protonucleata (prō-tǫ-nū-klę-ā'tạ̈), *n. pl.* [NL.: see *protonucleate*.] A hypothetical ancestral stock of protonucleate protozoans, derived from homogeneous protoplasm, and giving rise to all other animals.

protonucleate (prō-tǫ-nū'klę-āt), *a.* [< Gr. πρῶτος, first, + L. *nucleatus*, having a kernel: see *nucleate*.] Exhibiting the first signs of nucleation; having a primitive or primordial nucleus; of or pertaining to the *Protonucleata*.

proto-organism (prō-tō-ôr'gan-izm), *n.* [< Gr. πρῶτος, first, + E. *organism*.] A micro-organism, whether animal or vegetal; a protozoan or protophyte; a protist.

protopapas (prō-tǫ-pap'as), *n.* [= ML. *protopapa, prothopapus*, < MGr. πρωτοπαπᾶς, a chief priest, < Gr. πρῶτος, first, + LGr. παπᾶς, a bishop, priest: see *papa*[2].] In the *Gr. Ch.*, a chief priest; a priest of superior rank, corresponding nearly to a dean or an archdeacon.

protoparent (prō-tǫ-pār'ent), *n.* [< Gr. πρῶτος, first, + L. *paren(t-)s*, parent.] A first parent. *Davies*, Microcosmos, p. 23.

protopathia (prō-tǫ-path'i-ạ̈), *n.* [NL., < Gr. πρῶτος, first, + πάθος, disease.] Primary disease.

protopathic (prō-tǫ-path'ik), *a.* [< *protopathia* + *-ic*.] Pertaining to the original lesion of a disease; primary.

protopepsia (prō-tǫ-pep'siạ̈), *n.* [NL., < Gr. πρῶτος, first, + πέψις, digestion: see *pepsin*.] Primary digestion; digestion proper as it occurs in the cavity of the alimentary tract, and as distinguished from any further elaboration of the products effected in the walls of the intestine, the liver, or elsewhere.

protophloëm (prō-tǫ-flō'em), *n.* [< Gr. πρῶτος, first, + E. *phloëm*.] In *bot.*, the first formed elements of phloëm in a vascular bundle.

Protophyta (prō-tof'i-tạ̈), *n. pl.* [NL., pl. of *protophytum*: see *protophyte*.] One of the primary groups or divisions of the vegetable kingdom, containing the lowest and simplest plants, and corresponding to the *Protozoa* of the animal kingdom. They are usually exceedingly minute plants, requiring the highest powers of the microscope for their study. The cells are in general poorly developed; the nucleus is wanting in many cases, and frequently there is either no cell-wall or an imperfectly developed one. They multiply most commonly by fission, the sexual organs being unknown or only very slightly differentiated. According to the classification of Bennett and Murray, the *Protophyta* embrace two groups — the chlorophyllous group, or *Schizophyceæ*, and the non-chlorophyllous group, or *Schizomycetes*. The first group includes the classes *Protococcoideæ*, *Diatomaceæ*, and *Cyanophyceæ*; the second includes the *Bacteria*. See *Schizophyceæ* and *Schizomycetes*.

protophyte (prō'tǫ-fīt), *n.* [< NL. *protophytum*, < Gr. πρωτόφυτος, first-produced, < πρῶτος, first, + φυτόν, a plant.] A plant of the group *Protophyta*.

protophytic (prō-tǫ-fit'ik), *a.* [< *Protophyta* + *-ic*.] Of or pertaining to the *Protophyta*, or having their characters.

protoplasm (prō'tǫ-plazm), *n.* [< NL. *protoplasma*, protoplasm, < ML. *protoplasma*, the first creation, the first creature or thing made (*protoplasmus*, the first man made), < MGr. πρωτόπλασμα, < Gr. πρῶτος, first, + πλάσμα, anything formed or molded: see *plasm*.] An albuminoid substance, ordinarily resembling the white of an egg, consisting of carbon, oxygen, nitrogen, and hydrogen in extremely complex and unstable molecular combination, and capable, under proper conditions, of manifesting certain vital phenomena, as spontaneous motion, sensation, assimilation, and reproduction, thus constituting the physical basis of life of all plants and animals; sarcode. It is essential to the nature of protoplasm that this substance consist chemically of the four elements named (with or without a trace of some other elements); but the molecule is so highly compounded that these elements may be present in somewhat different proportions in different cases, so that the chemical formula is not always the same. The name has also been somewhat loosely applied to albuminous substances widely different in some physical properties, as density or fluidity. Thus the hard material of so-called vegetable ivory and the soft body of an amœba are both protoplasmic. The physiological activities of protoplasm are manifested in its irritability, or ready response to external stimuli, as well as its inherent capacity of spontaneous movement and other indications of life; so that the least particle of this substance may be observed to go through the whole cycle of vital functions. Protoplasm builds up every vegetable and animal fabric, yet is itself devoid of discernible histological structure. It is ordinarily colorless and transparent, or nearly so, and of glairy or viscid semifluid consistency, as is well seen in the bodies of foraminifers, amœbæ, and other of the lowest forms of animal life. Such protoplasm (originally named *sarcode*), when not confined by an investing membrane, has the power of extension in any direction in the form of temporary processes (see *pseudopodium*) capable of being withdrawn again; and it has also the characteristic property of streaming in minute masses through closed membranes without the loss of the identity of such masses. An individuated mass of protoplasm, generally of microscopic size, and with or without a nucleus and a wall, constitutes a *cell*, which may be the whole body of an organism, or the structural unit of aggregation of a multicellular animal or plant. The ovum of any creature consists of protoplasm, and all the tissues of the most complex living organisms result from the multiplication, differentiation, and specialization of such protoplasmic cell-units. The life of the organism as a whole consists in the continuous waste and repair of the protoplasmic material of its cells. No animal, however, can elaborate protoplasm directly from the chemical elements of that substance. The manufacture of protoplasm is a function of the vegetable kingdom. Plants make it directly from mineral compounds and from the atmosphere under the influence of the sun's light and heat, thus becoming the storehouse of food-stuff for the animal kingdom. Protoplasm appears to have been first recognizably described by Rösel, in or about 1755, in his account of the proteus-animalcule. It was observed, not named, seventeen years later by Corti, in the cells of *Chara*. Like motions of protoplasm were noticed by Meyen in 1827 in *Vallisneria*, and by R. Brown in 1831 in his discovery of the cyclosis in the filaments of *Tradescantia*. In 1835 Dujardin called attention to a "primary animal substance" in the cells of foraminifers, described as "a sort of slime" endowed with the property of spontaneous motion and contractility, and called it *sarcode*. The word *protoplasm* was first used (in the form *protoplasma*) by Hugo von Mohl, in 1846, with reference to the slimy granular semi-fluid contents of vegetable cells. The identity of this vegetable "protoplasm" with animal "sarcode," suggested in 1850 by Cohn, who regarded this common substance as "the prime seat of almost all vital activity," was confirmed by Schultze in 1861; Virchow had in 1858 abandoned the idea that a cell-wall is necessary to the integrity of a cell, holding that a nucleus surrounded by a molecular blastema (that is, protoplasm) constitutes a cell, and Schultze defined the cell as protoplasm surrounding a nucleus, which since that time the term has come into universal use. Also called *bioplasm*, *cytoplasm* or *cytioplasm*, and *plasmogen*. See these words, and cuts under *amœba* and *cell*, 5.

Hence this substance, known in Vegetable Physiology as *protoplasm*, but often referred to by zoölogists as sarcode, has been appropriately designated by Prof. Huxley "the Physical Basis of Life." *W. B. Carpenter*, Micros., § 219.

For the whole living world, then, it results that the morphological unit — the primary and fundamental form of life — is merely an individual mass of *protoplasm*, in which no further structure is discernible. *Huxley*, Anat. Invert., p. 18.

protoplasma (prō-tǫ-plas'mạ̈), *n.* [NL.: see *protoplasm*.] Protoplasm. *Hugo von Mohl*, 1846.

protoplasmal (prō-tǫ-plaz'mal), *a.* [< *protoplasm* + *-al*.] Protoplasmic.

protoplasmatic (prō-tǫ-plaz-mat'ik), *a.* [< *protoplasm* + *-atic*[2].] Same as *protoplasmic*.

Part of its *protoplasmatic* matter has undergone resorption and served nutritory purposes. *Quart. Jour. of Micros. Sci.*, N. S., XXX. 345.

protoplasmic (prō-tǫ-plaz'mik), *a.* [< *protoplasm* + *-ic*.] 1. First-formed, as a constituent of organized beings; primitive or primordial, as a cause or result of organization; of or pertaining in any way to protoplasm: as, a *protoplasmic* substance; a *protoplasmic* process; a *protoplasmic* theory.

In the young state of the cell, the whole cavity is occupied by the *protoplasmic* substance. *W. B. Carpenter*, Micros., § 224.

2. Consisting of, formed or derived from, or containing protoplasm; bioplasmic; sarcodous. — 3. Resembling protoplasm in chemical composition or in vital activities; protoplastic; plastic; germinative or formative. — **Protoplasmic processes of Deiters**, the thickly branched processes of the large central ganglion-cells: distinguished from the *axis-cylinder process of Deiters*.

protoplast (prō'tǫ-plast), *n.* [< ML. *protoplastus*, the first man made, the first creation, < Gr. πρωτόπλαστος, formed or created first, < πρῶτος, first, + πλαστός, formed, molded: see *plastic*. Cf. *protoplasm*.] 1. That which or one who is first formed; the original, type, or model of some organic being; especially, the hypothetical first individual or one of the supposed first pair of the human race; a protoparent.

The consumption was the primitive disease which put a period to our *protoplasts*, Adam and Eve. *Harvey*.

Adam was set up as our great *protoplast* and representative. *Glanville*, Pre-existence of Souls, Pref.

Fresh from the *Protoplast*,
Furnished for ages to come, when a kindlier wind should blow,
Lured now to begin and live. *Browning*, Abt Vogler, st. 5.

2. A protozoan; a simple unicellular organism; specifically, a member of the *Protoplasta*.

Protoplasta (prō-tǫ-plas'tạ̈), *n. pl.* [NL.: see *protoplast*.] An order of rhizopods; unicellular organisms in general; those *Protozoa*, *Protista*, or *Plastidizoa* the organization of which has the morphological valence of a simple cell.

protoplastic (prō-tǫ-plas'tik), *a.* [< *protoplast* + *-ic*.] 1. Protoplasmic; pertaining to or having the character of a protoplast.

Our *protoplastick* sire
Lost paradise.
Howell, Lexicon Tetraglotton (1660).

A return to the condition of Lord Monboddo's *protoplastic* baboon even the Carlylists . . . might find it irksome to realize with equanimity. *F. Hall*, Mod. Eng., p. 30.

2. Specifically, belonging to the *Protoplasta*.

Protopoda (prǫ-top'ǫ-dạ̈), *n. pl.* [NL., < Gr. πρῶτος, first, + πούς (ποδ-) = E. *foot*.] A group of tænioglossate gastropods, with the foot rudimentary, including the *Vermetidæ*.

protopodia, *n.* Plural of *protopodium*.

protopodial (prō-tǫ-pō'di-al), *a.* [< *protopodium* + *-al*.] Of or pertaining to the protopodium, or having its character.

protopodite (prǫ-top'ǫ-dīt), *n.* [< Gr. πρῶτος, first, + πούς (ποδ-), = E. *foot*, + *-ite*[2].] In *Crustacea*, the first or basal division of an appendage of a segment, by which such appendage articulates with its somite; the root or first joint of a limb, which may bear an endopodite or an exopodite, or both of these. See *endopodite*, and cut under *chela*[1].

Each appendage consists of three divisions . . . supported on a *protopodite*, or basal division. *Huxley*, Anat. Invert., p. 244.

Probably the coxo- and basipodite [of the ambulatory leg of a crawfish] together answer to the *protopodite* of the abdominal appendages, the remaining joints representing the endopodite. *Huxley*, Anat. Invert., p. 269, note.

protopoditic (prō"tǫ-pǫ-dit'ik), *a.* [< *protopodite* + *-ic*.] Of or pertaining to a protopodite.

protopodium (prō-tǫ-pō'di-um), *n.*; pl. *protopodia* (-ạ̈). [NL., < Gr. πρῶτος, first, + NL. *podium*, q. v.] In *Mollusca*, the primitive or typical podium; the foot proper, irrespective of its various modifications.

The valve of the siphon [in cephalopods] is a true foot, or *protopodium*, and the two lateral folds are pteropodia. *Gill*, Smithsonian Report, 1880, p. 361.

protopope (prō'tǫ-pōp), *n.* [< Russ. *protopopŭ*, < MGr. πρωτοπαπᾶς, a chief priest: see *protopapas*, and cf. *pope*[1].] Same as *protopapas*.

protopresbyter (prō-tǫ-pres'bi-tėr), *n.* [< Gr. πρῶτος, first, + πρεσβύτερος, presbyter: see *presbyter*.] Same as *protopope*.

protoprism (prō'tǫ-prizm), *n.* [< Gr. πρῶτος, first, + πρίσμα, prism: see *prism*.] See *prism*, 3.

protopsyche (prō-tǫ-sī'kē), *n.* [< Gr. πρῶτος, first, + ψυχή, soul: see *Psyche*.] See *psyche*, 4 (c). *Haeckel*.

protopteran (prǫ-top'tę-ran), *a.* and *n.* **I.** *a.* Same as *protopterous*.

II. *n.* A member of the *Protopteri*.

protoptere (prǫ-top'tėr), *n.* A fish of the order *Protopteri*. *Sir J. Richardson*.

Protopteri (prǫ-top'tę-rī), *n. pl.* [NL., pl. of *Protopterus*.] In Owen's classification, an order of cold-blooded vertebrates transitional between the fishes and the amphibians: same as *Sirenoidei* and *Dipnoi*.

Protopteridæ (prō-top-ter'i-dē), *n. pl.* [NL., < *Protopterus* + *-idæ*.] A family of dipnoans, typified by the genus *Protopterus*: same as *Lepidosirenidæ*.

protopterous (prǫ-top'tę-rus), *a.* [< NL. *protopterus*, < Gr. πρῶτος, first, + πτερόν, wing, = E. *feather*.] Having a simple or primitive type of limb, as a protopterus; of or pertaining to the *Protopteri*.

Protopterus (prǫ-top'tę-rus), *n.* [NL. (Owen, 1837): see *protopterous*.] 1. The typical genus of *Protopteridæ*, containing the African mudfish, *P. annectens*. In this dipnoöus fish the pectorals and ventrals are reduced to long filaments with fringes containing rudimentary rays. See *Lepidosiren*, and cut under *mudfish*.

2. [*l. c.*] A member of this genus.

protopyramid (prǫ-tǫ-pir'a-mid), *n.* In *crystal.* See *pyramid*, 3.

Protornis (prǫ-tôr'nis), *n.* [NL., < Gr. πρῶτος, first, + ὄρνις, bird.] A genus of birds, founded by Von Meyer upon remains from the Lower Eocene of Glaris. *P. glariensis* is regarded as the oldest known passerine bird.

protosalt (prō'tǫ-sâlt), *n.* [< Gr. πρῶτος, first, + E. *salt*[1].] In *chem.*, that one of two or more compounds of the same metal with the same acid which contains relatively the least quantity of metal.

protosiphon (prō-tō-sī'fon), *n.* [< Gr. πρῶτος, first, + E. *siphon.*] The representative or origin of the siphuncle in the protoconch of ammonitoid cephalopods.

protosomite (prō-tō-sō'mīt), *n.* [< Gr. πρῶτος, first, + E. *somite.*] One of the primitive or rudimentary somites or segments of an embryonic worm or arthropod.

Generally, the development of the *protosomites*, as these segments might be called, does not occur [in annelids] until some time after the embryo has been hatched. *Huxley*, Anat. Invert., p. 243.

protosomitic (prō"tō-sō-mit'ik), *a.* [< *protosomite* + *-ic.*] Primitively segmented; of or pertaining to a protosomite.

protospasm (prō'tō-spazm), *n.* [< Gr. πρῶτος, first, + σπασμός, spasm: see *spasm.*] See *Jacksonian epilepsy*, under *Jacksonian.*

protospermatoblast (prō-tō-spėr'ma-tō-blast), *n.* [< Gr. πρῶτος, first, + E. *spermatoblast.*] A cellular blastema in which spermatozoa originate. See *spermatoblast.*

The spermatozoa of the decapods studied by him [Sabatier] arise in large cells, the *protospermatoblasts*, and are homologous with the epithelial cells of the Graafian follicle. *Micros. Sci.*, N. S., No. cxix., XXX. iii. 251.

Protospongia (prō-tō-spon'ji-ạ̈), *n.* [NL. (Salter), < Gr. πρῶτος, first, + σπογγιά, a sponge.] A genus of lyssacine hexactinellidan sponges, including the oldest known forms of fossil sponge, from the Menevian beds of the Lower Cambrian of Wales, as *P. fenestrata.*

protospongian (prō-tō-spon'ji-ạn), *a.* Primitive, as a stage in the evolution of sponges or in the development of a sponge. *Haeckel.*

We have not been able to separate the *Protospongian* stage of Haeckel from the ascula, and think it should be merged in the latter. *Hyatt*, Proc. Bost. Soc. Nat. Hist., XXIII. 86.

protospore (prō'tō-spōr), *n.* [< Gr. πρῶτος, first, + σπόρος, seed.] In *bot.*, one of the primary or apparent spores of certain fungi, corresponding to the prothallus of the higher cryptogams.

Protostapedifera (prō-tō-stap-e-dif'e-rạ̈), *n. pl.* [NL., < Gr. πρῶτος, first, + NL. *Stapedifera*, q. v.] A hypothetical form from which the *Stapedifera* are supposed to have originated. See *Stapedifera.* *Thacher*, 1877.

Protostigma (prō-tō-stig'mạ̈), *n. pl.* [NL. (Lesquereux, 1877), < Gr. πρῶτος, first, + στίγμα, a spot, mark.] A name provisionally given to certain doubtful plant remains, consisting of fragments of stems found in rocks of the Hudson River (Cincinnati) group, near Cincinnati, and considered by the author of the name to be related to *Sigillaria* and other types of vegetation of the Devonian and Carboniferous. The specimens found are very obscure, and are referred by some paleobotanists to the sponges or other low forms of marine life.

protostoma (prọ-tos'tō-mạ̈), *n.*; pl. *protostomata* (prō-tos-tō'ma-tạ̈). [NL., < Gr. πρῶτος, first, + στόμα, mouth.] The archæostoma or primitive mouth-opening of a gastrula, by which the protogaster or cavity of the archenteron communicates with the exterior. It is the original orifice of that invagination whereby a blastula is converted into a gastrula, and is mouth and anus in one. In some kinds of gastrulæ the protostoma is also called *anus of Rusconi*; in others, a *blastulapore*. *Haeckel*, Evol. of Man (trans.), I. 194.

Protosymphyla (prō"tō-sim-fī'lạ̈), *n. pl.* [NL., < Gr. πρῶτος, first, + NL. *Symphyla*, q. v.] A term applied by Erich Haase to a hypothetical group, from which he supposed the orders *Symphyla*, *Thysanura*, and *Chilopoda* to have been derived by evolution: its existence in nature is disputed or denied.

protosymphylar (prō"tō-sim-fī'lạ̈r), *a.* [< *Protosymphyla* + *-ar*³.] Of or pertaining to the *Protosymphyla.*

Protosyngnatha (prō-tō-sing'nạ̈-thạ̈), *n. pl.* [NL., < Gr. πρῶτος, first, + σύν, along with, + γνάθος, jaw.] A group of fossil myriapods of Carboniferous age, represented by the genus *Palæocampa*, resembling the extant chilopods in having but one pair of legs to each segment of the body. Also called *Protosygnatha.*

protosyngnathous (prō-tō-sing'nạ̈-thus), *a.* [< *Protosyngnatha* + *-ous.*] Of or pertaining to the *Protosyngnatha*, or having their characters.

prototergite (prō-tō-tėr'jīt), *n.* [< Gr. πρῶτος, first, + L. *tergum*, back.] In *entom.*, the first dorsal segment of the abdomen.

protothallus (prō-tō-thal'us), *n.*; pl. *protothalli* (-ī). [NL., < Gr. πρῶτος, first, + θαλλός, a young shoot.] In *bot.*: (*a*) Same as *prothallium.* (*b*) Same as *hypothallus.*

protothere (prō'tō-thēr), *n.* A mammal of the group *Prototheria*; any prototherian.

Prototheria (prō-tō-thē'ri-ạ̈), *n. pl.* [NL., < Gr. πρῶτος, first, + θήρ, a wild beast.] 1. A name proposed by Gill in 1872 for one of the major groups of the *Mammalia*, consisting of the *Monotremata* alone, as distinguished from the *Eutheria*: coextensive with *Ornithodelphia.*—2. Those unknown primitive mammals which are the hypothetical ancestors of the monotremes: synonymous with *Promammalia.*

It will be convenient to have a distinct name, *Prototheria*, for the group which includes the at present hypothetical embodiments of that lowest stage of mammalian type of which the existing monotremes are the only known representatives. *Huxley*, Proc. Zoöl. Soc., 1880, p. 653.

prototherian (prō-tō-thē'ri-ạn), *a.* and *n.* [< *Prototheria* + *-an.*] I. *a.* Primitively mammalian; primeval or ancestral, as a mammal; of or pertaining to the *Prototheria* in either sense.

II. *n.* A member of the *Prototheria*, hypothetical or actual.

protothorax (prō-tō-thō'raks), *n.* [< Gr. πρῶτος, first, + θώραξ, thorax.] Same as *prothorax.*

Prototracheata (prō-tō-trā-kẹ-ā'tạ̈), *n. pl.* [NL., < Gr. πρῶτος, first, + τραχεῖα, trachea, + *-ata*².] Same as *Protracheata.*

prototypal (prō'tō-tī-pạl), *a.* [< *prototyp-e* + *-al.*] Pertaining to a prototype; forming or constituting a prototype or primitive form; archetypical. Also *prototypical.*

Survivors of that *prototypal* flora to which I have already referred. *Dawson*, Geol. Hist. of Plants, p. 24.

prototype (prō'tō-tīp), *n.* [< F. *prototype* = Sp. It. *prototipo* = Pg. *prototypo*, a prototype; LL. *prototypus*, original, primitive; < Gr. πρωτότυπος, in the first form, original, neut. πρωτότυπον, a first or primitive form, < πρῶτος, first, + τύπος, impression, model, type: see *type.*] A primitive form; an original or model after which anything is formed; the pattern of anything to be engraved, cast, etc.; an exemplar; an archetype; especially, in *metrology*, an original standard, to which others must conform, and which, though it may be imitated from something else, is not required to conform to anything else, but itself serves as the ultimate definition of a unit. Thus, the *mètre des archives* is a prototype, and so is the new international meter at Breteuil, although the latter is imitated from the former. But the *mètre du conservatoire* and the meters distributed by the International Bureau are not prototypes, since they have no authority except from the evidence that they conform to other measures.

In many respects [he] deserves to be enriched, as a *prototype* for all writers, of voluminous works at least. *Sterne*, Tristram Shandy, iii. 38.

The square or circular altar, or place of worship, may easily be considered as the *prototype* of the Sikra surrounded by cells of the Jains. *J. Fergusson*, Hist. Indian Arch., p. 208.

prototypembryo (prō"tō-tīp-em'bri-ō), *n.* [< *prototype* + *embryo.*] A later stage of the embryo, which exhibits the essential characters of the division of animals to which it belongs. Thus, the veliger of a mollusk, the nauplius of a crustacean, and the notochordal stage of a vertebrate are respectively *prototypembryos* of the *Mollusca*, *Crustacea*, and *Vertebrata*. *Hyatt.* [Rare.]

prototypembryonic (prō"tō-tīp-em-bri-on'ik), *a.* [< *prototypembryo(n-)* + *-ic.*] Having the character of a prototypembryo. [Rare.]

prototypical (prō-tō-tip'i-kạl), *a.* [< *prototype* + *-ic-al.*] Same as *prototypal.*

Their [the Maruts'] coming to the fight must be taken as *prototypical* of the coming of the Greek heroes to the great fields of battle. *Keary*, Prim. Belief, p. 152.

protova, *n.* Plural of *protovum.*

protovertebra (prō-tō-vėr'-tē-brạ̈), *n.*; pl. *protovertebræ* (-brē). [NL., < Gr. πρῶτος, first, + L. *vertebra*, vertebra.] 1†. In Carus's nomenclature (1828), a rib regarded as a vertebral element developed to contain and protect the viscera, or organs of vegetative life: correlated with *deutovertebra* and *tritovertebra.*—2. A primitive, temporary vertebra; one of the series of segments which appear in pairs in the early embryo along the course of the notochord, and from or about which the permanent vertebræ are developed. They soon disappear, being replaced by definitive vertebræ.

Vertebrate Embryo (chick, second day of incubation).
a, cephalic end; *b*, caudal end; *c*, primitive groove, over which *d*, the dorsal laminæ, have closed for the greater part of its length; *e*, numerous protovertebræ; *f*, rudiment of an omphalomesaraic vein.

protovertebral (prō-tō-vėr'tē-brạl), *a.* [< *protovertebra* + *-al.*] Having the character of a protovertebra; pertaining to protovertebræ: as, a *protovertebral* segment; a *protovertebral* portion of the notochord.

Protovertebrata (prō-tō-vėr-tē-brā'tạ̈), *n. pl.* [NL.: see *protovertebrate.*] A hypothetical group of animals, assumed to have been the ancestral forms of the *Vertebrata.*

protovertebrate (prō-tō-vėr'tē-brāt), *a.* [< NL. **protovertebratus*, < *protovertebra*, q. v.] 1. Provided with or characterized by the presence of protovertebræ: as, the *protovertebrate* stage of a vertebrate embryo.—2. Of or pertaining to the *Protovertebrata.*

protovestiary† (prō-tō-ves'ti-ā-ri), *n.* [< ML. *protovestiarius*, < Gr. πρῶτος, first, + ML. *vestiarius*, the keeper of a wardrobe: see *vestiary.*] The head keeper of a wardrobe.

Protovestiary, or wardrobe keeper of the palace of Antiochus at Constantinople. *T. Warton*, Hist. Eng. Poetry, I. 132.

protovum (prọ-tō'vum), *n.*; pl. *protova* (-vạ̈). [NL., < Gr. πρῶτος, first, + L. *ovum*, egg: see *ovum.*] An original or primitive egg; an ovum or ovule in its first state, as when still in its Graafian follicle, or, in general, before its impregnation, when it becomes a cytula or parent-cell by fecundation with sperm; or, in the case of meroblastic eggs, an undifferentiated female egg-cell before it acquires the mass of non-formative food-yolk which converts it into a metovum.

protoxid, protoxide (prọ-tok'sid), *n.* [< Gr. πρῶτος, first, + E. *oxid.*] That member of a series of oxids which contains a single oxygen atom combined with a single bivalent atom or with two univalent atoms: applied only to oxids which are not strongly basic or acid.

protoxylem (prō-tō-zī'lem), *n.* [< Gr. πρῶτος, first, + E. *xylem.*] In *bot.*, the first-formed elements of the xylem of a vascular bundle.

Protozoa (prō-tō-zō'ạ̈), *n. pl.* [NL., pl. of *Protozoön.*] Primordial or first-formed animals, or cell-animals; protozoans: a subkingdom of *Animalia* or prime division of animals, contrasted with *Metazoa*, or all other animals collectively. The *Protozoa* are animal organisms consisting of a single cell, or of several cells not differentiated into tissues. This is the essential distinction between protozoan and metazoan animals, though no hard and fast line can be drawn around *Protozoa* to distinguish them on the one hand from *Protophyta*, and on the other from *Metazoa*. The name *Protozoa* was first used by Goldfuss (1809) to include microscopic animals and also the polyps and medusæ. Siebold and Stannius first used it in its modern signification as comprising and limited to the infusorians and rhizopods. Owen (1859) used the term *Protozoa* for a kingdom including diatoms, etc., and therefore synonymous with *Protista*. The sponges, in the view (as held by W. Saville Kent, for example) that they consist essentially of an aggregate of choanoflagellate infusorians, are often brought under *Protozoa*, though they have not only an ectoderm and an endoderm, but also a mesoderm, and are therefore tissue-animals as distinguished from cell-animals. Excluding sponges, *Protozoa* may be characterized as animals composed of a simple nearly structureless jelly-like substance called *sarcode*, a kind of protoplasm, devoid of permanent distinction or separation of parts resulting from tissue-formation or histogenesis (though they may have very evident organs as parts of a single cell), without a permanent definitive body-cavity or any trace of a nervous system, no permanent differentiated alimentary system except in a most rudimentary state, and no multicellular membranes or tissues. Nevertheless, there is really a wide range of variation or gradation of structure in these seemingly structureless animalcules. Some of the lowest forms are mere microscopic specks of homogeneous sarcode, of any or no definite shape. Such are moners, or representatives of a division *Monera* or *Proteomyxa*; but it is not certain that all such objects are either individuals or species in a usual sense of these words. Among the lowest protozoans of which species and genera can be definitely predicated are the amœbiform organisms, which have a nucleus, and locomotory organs in the form of pseudopods, temporarily protruded from any part of the body, and which ingest and egest foreign substance from any part of the body. Vast numbers of protozoans are of this grade of complexity, and with the simpler forms constitute a class, *Rhizopoda*, including the normal amœboids and the foraminifers and radiolarians. For, though both these latter may have very complicated shells, tests, or skeletons, their sarcodous substance remains of a low and simple type. It is an advance in organization when a protozoan becomes *corticate* — that is, assumes a form in which an outer harder ectoplasm and an inner softer endoplasm are distinguishable — since this confines the sarcodous mass and gives it definite shape or form. This advance in organization is often marked by the appearance of a nucleolus or endoplastule, besides the nucleus or endoplast which most protozoans possess, by the presence of definite and permanent locomotory organs in the form of cilia or flagella, and finally by the fixation of a specialized oral or ingestive area or mouth, in place of the one or several temporary vacuoles which serve as stomachs in lower forms. Protozoans of this higher grade occur under various forms. The class *Gregarinida* represents parasitic forms, one- or two-celled, essentially like the ova of *Metazoa*. The class *Infusoria* comprehends an enormous number of minute, nearly always microscopic, animalcules, found in infusions, inhabiting both fresh and salt water, sometimes parasitic, but mostly leading an independent fixed or free life. There are many groups of these, as the ciliate, flagellate, choanoflagellate, and suctorial infusorians, among them the most complex organisms which are commonly included under *Protozoa*, as the *Noctiluca*, for example. With or without some of the lowest disputed forms, and with or without the sponges, *Protozoa* have been very variously subdivided, almost every author having his own arrangement. A so-called moner, an amœba, a foraminifer, a radiolarian, a gregarine, and an infusorian respectively exemplify as many leading types of *Protozoa*. One division is into *Astomata* and *Stomatoda*, according to the absence or presence of a mouth. Another is into *Monera* and *Endoplastica*, according to the absence or presence of a nucleus, the latter being again distinguished as *Myxopoda* and *Mastigopoda*, according to whether the locomotory organs are temporary pseudopods or permanent cilia or flagella. A third is into *Gymnomyxa* and *Corticata*, according to the absence or presence of a distinguishable ectoplasm. (1) The *Gymnomyxa* are separated into 7 classes: *Proteomyxa* (indefinable), *Mycetozoa* (often regarded as plants), *Lobosa* (ordinary amœbiforms), *Labyrinthulidea*, *Heliozoa* (sun-animalcules), *Reticularia* (the foraminifers), and *Radiolaria*. (2) The *Corticata* are divided into 6 classes: *Sporozoa* (gregarines and many others), *Flagellata*, *Dinoflagellata*, *Rhynchoflagellata*, *Ciliata*, and *Acinetaria*, the last five being as many classes of infusorians. This is the classification presented in the latest edition of the Encyclopædia Britannica. By Saville Kent the *Protozoa* (including sponges) are divided into 4 prime "evolutionary series," not exactly coincident, however, with any recognized zoölogical groups, called *Pantostomata*, *Discostomata*, *Eustomata*, and *Polystomata*. (See these words.) Also called *Hypozoa*, *Oözoa*, *Plastidozoa*. Compare *Primalia*, *Protista*, *Protophyta*. See cuts under *Actinosphærium*, *amœba*, *Euglena*, *Foraminifera*, *Globigerinidæ*, *Gregarinidæ*, *Infusoria*, *Noctiluca*, *Paramecium*, *radiolarian*, and *sun-animalcule*.

protozoal (prō-tọ̄-zō'ạl), *a.* [< *protozoön* + *-al.*] Same as *protozoan*.

Bütschli's classification of these *protozoal* forms.
Lancet, No. 3467, p. 308.

protozoan (prō-tọ̄-zō'an), *a.* and *n.* [< *protozoön* + *-an.*] **I.** *a.* First, lowest, simplest, or most primitive, as an animal; of or pertaining to the *Protozoa*.

II. *n.* A member of the *Protozoa*; a protozoön.

protozoanal (prō-tọ̄-zō'ạn-ạl), *a.* [Irreg. < *protozoan* + *-al.*] Of or pertaining to a protozoan. [An improper form.]

The individualized *protozoanal* stage has become confined to the earliest periods of existence.
Stand. Nat. Hist., I. 60.

protozoary (prō-tọ̄-zō'ạ-ri), *n.*; pl. *protozoaries* (-riz). [< F. *protozoaire*, < Gr. πρῶτος, first, + ζῴάριον, dim. of ζῷον, an animal.] A protozoan.

protozoic (prō-tọ̄-zō'ik), *a.* [< *protozoön* + *-ic.*] **1.** In *zoöl.*, same as *protozoan*.

They exhibit the rhythmically contracting vacuoles which are specially characteristic of *protozoic* organisms.
W. B. Carpenter, Micros., § 225.

2. In *geol.*, containing the earliest traces of life. — **Protozoic schists**, the name given by Barrande to the lowest division of the fossiliferous rocks of Bohemia. See *primordial*.

protozoön, protozoum (prō-tọ̄-zō'on, -um), *n.*; pl. *protozoa* (-ạ̈). [NL., < Gr. πρῶτος, first, + ζῷον, animal.] An individual or a species of *Protozoa*; a protozoan.

protozoönal (prō-tọ̄-zō'ọn-ạl), *a.* [< *protozoön* + *-al.*] Pertaining to a protozoön: as, *protozoönal* collars and flagella. *Hyatt.*

protozoum, *n.* See *protozoön*.

Protracheata (prọ̄-trā-kẹ̄-ā'tạ̈), *n. pl.* [NL., < L. *pro*, before, + *Tracheata*, q. v.] In Gegenbaur's system, one of three prime series into which all arthropods are divided (the others being *Branchiata*, or *Crustacea* in a wide sense, and *Tracheata*, or insects in the widest sense), established for the reception of the single genus *Peripatus*: thus conterminous with *Malacopoda*, *Onychophora*, and *Peripatidea*.

More exact investigations into the organization of Peripatus show that this animal, which as yet has been generally placed with the Vermes, is the representative of a special class of Arthropoda which must be placed before the Tracheata [that is, *Protracheata*].
Gegenbaur, Comp. Anat. (trans.), p. 230.

protracheate (prọ̄-trā'kẹ̄-āt), *a.* Of or pertaining to the *Protracheata*; malacopodous; onychophorous; peripatidean.

protract (prọ̄-trakt'), *v. t.* [< L. *protractus*, pp. of *protrahere* (> It. *protraere*, *protrarre* = OF. *pourtraire*), draw forth, lengthen out, < *pro*, forth, + *trahere*, draw: see *tract*. Cf. *portray*, *portrait*, from the same source.] **1.** To draw out or lengthen in time; prolong: now chiefly in the past participle.

The Galles were now weary with long *protracting* of the war.
Golding, tr. of Cæsar, fol. 32.

Doubtless he shrives this woman to her smock,
Else ne'er could he so long *protract* his speech.
Shak., 1 Hen. VI., i. 2. 120.

You shall *protract* no time, only I give you a bowl of rich wine to the health of your general.
B. Jonson, Case is Altered, iii. 1.

Her spirit seemed hastening to live within a very brief span as much as many live during a *protracted* existence.
Charlotte Brontë, Jane Eyre, viii.

2. To lengthen out in space; extend in general. [Rare.]

Their shaded walks
And long *protracted* bowers.
Cowper, Task, i. 257.

Many a ramble, far
And wide *protracted*, through the tamer ground
Of these our unimaginative days.
Wordsworth.

3. To delay; defer; put off to a distant time.

Let us bury him,
And not *protract* with admiration what
Is now due debt. To the grave!
Shak., Cymbeline, iv. 2. 232.

4. In *surv.*, to draw to a scale; lay down, by means of a scale and protractor, the lines and angles of, as a piece of land; plot.—**5.** In *anat.*, to draw forward (a part or an organ); extend (a part) anteriorly; have the action or effect of a protractor upon.—**Protracted meeting**, a revival meeting continued or protracted; a series of meetings of unusual importance, often lasting for several days and attended by large numbers: chiefly used by Congregationalists, Methodists, and Baptists. [New Eng.]

protract† (prọ̄-trakt'), *n.* [< LL. *protractus*, a prolonging, < L. *protrahere*, pp. *protractus*, prolong: see *protract*.] A lengthening out; delay; putting off.

And wisdome willed me without *protract*,
In speedie wise, to put the same in ure.
Norton and Sackville, Ferrex and Porrex, iv. 2.

Many long weary dayes I have outworne;
And many nights, that slowly seemd to move
Theyr sad *protract* from evening untill morne.
Spenser, Sonnets, lxxxvi.

protractedly (prọ̄-trak'ted-li), *adv.* [< *protracted*, pp. of *protract*, *v.*, + *-ly*[2].] In a protracted or prolonged manner; tediously.

protracter (prọ̄-trak'tėr), *n.* [< *protract* + *-er*[1].] One who protracts, or lengthens in time. Also *protractor*.

protractile (prọ̄-trak'til), *a.* [< *protract* + *-ile.*] Susceptible of being drawn forward or thrust out, as the tongue of a woodpecker; protrusile: correlated with *retractile*, that which is one being also the other.

protracting-bevel (prọ̄-trak'ting-bev"el), *n.* A combined sector, rule, straight-edge, and bevel used in plotting plans and other drawings.

protraction (prọ̄-trak'shọn), *n.* [< F. *protraction* = It. *protrazione*, < LL. *protractio(n-)*, a drawing out or lengthening, < L. *protrahere*, pp. *protractus*, draw forth, drag out: see *protract*.] **1.** The act of drawing out or prolonging; the act of delaying: as, the *protraction* of a debate.

If this grand Business of State, the Match, suffer such *Protractions* and Puttings off, you need not wonder that private Negotiations, as mine is, should be subject to the same Inconveniencies.
Howell, Letters, I. iii. 24.

2. In *surv.*: (*a*) The act of plotting or laying down on paper the dimensions of a field, etc. (*b*) That which is protracted or plotted on paper.—**3.** The action of a protractor in sense (*b*).—**4.** In *anc. pros.*, the treatment as metrically long of a syllable usually measured as a short: opposed to *correption*.

protractive (prọ̄-trak'tiv), *a.* [< *protract* + *-ive.*] Drawing out or lengthening in time; prolonging; continuing; delaying.

The *protractive* trials of great Jove
To find persistive constancy in men.
Shak., T. and C., i. 3. 20.

He saw, but suffered their *protractive* arts.
Dryden, Hind and Panther, iii. 1103.

protractor (prọ̄-trak'tọr), *n.* [< NL. *protractor* (cf. ML. *protractor*, one who calls or drags another into court); < L. *protrahere*, pp. *protractus*, draw or drag forth: see *protract*.] One who or that which protracts. As applied to persons, also *protracter*. Specifically—(*a*) In *surv.*, an instrument for laying down and measuring angles on paper. It is of various forms—semicircular, rectangular, or circular. See also cut under *bevel-protractor*.

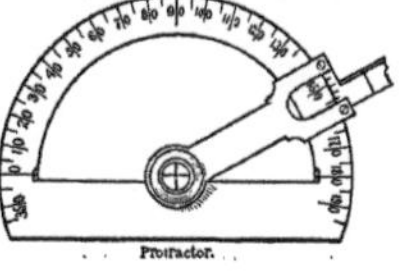
Protractor.

This parallelogram is not, as Mr. Sheres would the other day have persuaded me, the same as a *protractor*, which do so much the more make me value it, but of itself it is a most useful instrument.
Pepys, Diary, Feb. 4, 1668.

(*b*) In *anat.*, a muscle which protracts, or extends or draws a part forward: the opposite of *retractor*. See diagram under *Echinoidea*.

The psoas minor . . . is a *protractor* of the pelvis.
Huxley, Anat. Vert., p. 47.

(*c*) An adjustable pattern, agreeing in proportion with particular measurements, used by tailors in cutting out garments.

protreptical (prọ̄-trep'ti-kạl), *a.* [< Gr. προτρεπτικός, fitted for urging on, exhorting, < προτρέπειν, turn toward, < πρό, forth, forward, + τρέπειν, turn: see *trope*.] Intended or adapted to persuade; persuasive; hortatory.

The means used are partly didactical and *protreptical*.
Bp. Ward, Infidelity.

protriæne (prō-trī'ēn), *n.* [< Gr. πρό, before, + τρίαινα, a trident: see *triæne*.] In the nomenclature of sponge-spicules, a triæne with porrect cladi. It is a simple spicule of the rhabdus type, bearing at one end a cladome of three cladi or rays which project forward. *Sollas.*

protrite† (prō'trīt), *a.* [< L. *protritus*, pp. of *proterere*, drive forth, wear away, < *pro*, forth, + *terere*, pp. *tritus*, rub: see *trite*.] Common; trite.

They are but old and rotten errors, *protrite* and putid opinions of the ancient Gnosticks.
Bp. Gauden, Tears of the Church, p. 195. (*Davies.*)

Whereuppon grew that *protrite* distinction of a triple appetite, naturall, sensitive, and reasonable.
T. Wright, Passions of the Minde (1601), i. 7.

protrudable (prọ̄-trö'dạ-bl), *a.* [< *protrude* + *-able.*] Protrusible or protrusile; protractile.

The *protrudable* trunk or proboscis of other annelids.
Darwin, Vegetable Mould, i.

protrude (prọ̄-tröd'), *v.*; pret. and pp. *protruded*, ppr. *protruding*. [< L. *protrudere*, thrust forth, protrude, < *pro*, forth, forward, + *trudere*, thrust, push: see *threat*. Cf. *extrude*, *intrude*, etc.] **I.** *trans.* **1.** To thrust forward or onward; drive or force along.

The sea's being *protruded* forwards . . . by the mud or earth discharged into it by rivers.
Woodward.

2. To shoot or thrust forth; project; cause to project; thrust out as from confinement; cause to come forth: as, a snail *protrudes* its horns.

Spring *protrudes* the bursting gems. *Thomson*, Autumn.

II. *intrans.* To shoot forward; be thrust forward; project beyond something.

The parts *protrude* beyond the skin. *Bacon.*

With that lean head-stalk, that *protruding* chin,
Wear standing collars, were they made of tin!
O. W. Holmes, A Rhymed Lesson.

=**Syn.** To project, jut (out), bulge (out).

protrusible (prọ̄-trö'si-bl), *a.* [< L. *protrusus*, pp. of *protrudere*, thrust forth (see *protrude*), + *-ible.*] Capable of being protruded; protrusile.

In many the oral aperture is surrounded by a flexible muscular lip, which sometimes takes on the form of a *protrusible* proboscis.
Huxley, Anat. Invert., p. 157.

protrusile (prọ̄-trö'sil), *a.* [< L. *protrusus*, pp. of *protrudere*, thrust forth (see *protrude*), + *-ile.*] Capable of being protruded; protrudable; protrusible; protractile.

protrusion (prọ̄-trö'zhọn), *n.* [< L. as if **protrusio(n-)*, < L. *protrudere*, pp. *protrusus*, thrust forth: see *protrude*.] **1.** The act of protruding or thrusting forth, or the state of being protruded.

Some sudden *protrusion* to good; . . . a mere actual, momentary, transient conduction.
Bp. Hall, Sermon on Rom. viii. 14.

Without either resistance or *protrusion*. *Locke.*

We see adaptation to the wind in the incoherence of the pollen, . . . in the *protrusion* of the stigmas at the period of fertilisation.
Darwin, Different Forms of Flowers, p. 94.

2. That which stands out beyond something adjacent; that which protrudes or projects.

The only features of the enormous structure are the blank, sombre stretches and *protrusions* of wall, the effect of which, on so large a scale, is strange and striking.
H. James, Jr., Little Tour, p. 98.

protrusive (prọ̄-trö'siv), *a.* [< L. *protrusus*, pp. of *protrudere*, thrust forth (see *protrude*), + *-ive.*] Thrusting or impelling forward; obtrusive; protruding: as, *protrusive* motion.

The chin *protrusive*, and the cervical vertebræ a trifle more curved.
George Eliot, Daniel Deronda, vii.

protrusively (prọ̄-trö'siv-li), *adv.* [< *protrusive* + *-ly*[2].] In a protrusive manner; obtrusively.

protrusiveness (prọ̄-trö'siv-nes), *n.* Tending to protrude or to be protrusive; obtrusiveness.

prott-goose (prot'gōs), *n.* [< *prott* (said to be imitative) + *goose*.] The brent- or brant-goose, *Bernicla brenta*.

protuberance (prọ̄-tū'be̤-rans), *n.* [< F. *protubérance* = Sp. Pg. *protuberancia* = It. *protuberanza*, < NL. **protuberantia*, < LL. *protuberan(t-)s*, protuberant: see *protuberant*.] A swelling or tumor on the body; a prominence; a bunch or knob; anything swelled or pushed beyond the surrounding or adjacent surface; on the surface of the earth, a hill, knoll, or other elevation; specifically, in *anat.* and *zoöl.*, a protuberant part; a projection or prominence; a tuberosity: as, a bony *protuberance*. See cut under *conjugation*.

Mountains, that seem but so many wens and unnatural *protuberances* upon the face of the earth.
Dr. H. More, Antidote against Atheism, I. ii. 3.

He had a little round abdominal *protuberance*, which an inch and a half added to the heels of his boots hardly enabled him to carry off as well as he could have wished.
Trollope, Doctor Thorne, xii.

Annular protuberance of the brain. See *annular*.—**Occipital, parietal**, etc., **protuberance.** See the adjectives.

protuberancy (prọ̄-tū'be̤-ran-si), *n.* [As *protuberance* (see *-cy*).] Same as *protuberance*.

protuberant (prọ̄-tū'be̤-rant), *a.* [< F. *protubérant*, < LL. *protuberan(t-)s*, ppr. of *protuberare*, swell, grow forth: see *protuberate*.] Swelling; prominent beyond the surrounding surface.

Though the eye seems round, in reality the iris is *protuberant* above the white. *Ray.*

Those large brown *protuberant* eyes in Silas Marner's pale face. *George Eliot*, Silas Marner, i.

protuberantly (prọ̄-tū'be̤-rant-li), *adv.* [< *protuberant* + *-ly*2.] In a protuberant manner; in the way of protuberance.

protuberate (prọ̄-tū'be̤-rāt), *v. i.*; pret. and pp. *protuberated*, ppr. *protuberating*. [< LL. *protuberatus*, pp. of *protuberare*, swell out, grow forth, < L. *pro*, forth, forward, + **tuberare*, swell, < *tuber*, a bump, swelling, tumor: see *tuber*.] To swell beyond the adjacent surface; be prominent; bulge out.

If the navel *protuberates*, make a small puncture with a lancet through the skin. *Sharpe*, Surgery.

protuberation (prọ̄-tū-be̤-rā'shọn), *n.* [< *protuberate* + *-ion*.] The act of swelling beyond the surrounding surface.

protuberous† (prọ̄-tū'be̤-rus), *a.* [< LL. *protuberare*, swell out, grow forth (see *protuberate*), + *-ous*. Cf. *tuberous*.] Protuberant. [Rare.]

The one being *protuberous*, rough, crusty, and hard; the other round, smooth, spongy, and soft. *J. Smith*, Portrait of Old Age, p. 183.

Protula (prọ̄-tū'lạ̈), *n.* [NL. (Risso), prob. < Gr. πρό, before, + τύλος, a knot or knob.] A genus of cephalobranchiate tubicolous worms of the family *Serpulidæ*. *P. dysteri* is an example. Also called *Apomatus*.

Protula dysteri, a tubicolous polychætous annelid: anterior part of the body, cut off at *d*, the stomach, and seen in longitudinal section; *c*, mouth; *b*, hood-like expansion; *a*, branchial plumes or branchiæ.

Protungulata (prọ̄-tung-gū-lā'tạ̈), *n. pl.* [NL., < Gr. πρῶτος, first, + NL. *Ungulata*, q. v.] A group of Cretaceous hoofed mammals regarded as the probable ancestral stock of all subsequent ungulates.

protureter (prō-tụ̄-rē'tėr), *n.* [NL., < Gr. πρῶτος, first, + NL. *ureter*.] A primitive ureter, or excretory duct of a protonephron.

protutor (prō-tū'tọr), *n.* [= F. *protuteur* = Sp. *protutor*, < ML. *protutor*, < L. *pro*, for, + *tutor*, guardian: see *tutor*.] In *Scots law*, one who acts as tutor to a minor without having a regular title to the office.

protyle (prọ̄-tī'lē), *n.* [NL., < Gr. πρῶτος, first, + ὕλη, matter: see *Hyla*.] An imagined supersensible, imponderable, indifferent, or primal substance, from which all forms of living matter are supposed to be derived by modification, differentiation, or specialization. *W. Crookes.* Also called variously *biod*, *biogen*, *zoëther*, *psychoplasm*, etc.

proud (proud), *a.* [< ME. *proud*, *prowd*, *prud*, earlier *prout*, *prut*, < AS. *prūt*, proud (very rare); cf. deriv. *prūtung* (verbal n.), pride, *prȳte*, pride (> E. *pride*1); root unknown. The Icel. *prūdhr*, proud, Dan. *prud*, stately, magnificent, are appar. from the AS.] **1.** Having or cherishing a high opinion of one's own merits; showing great or lofty self-esteem; expecting great deference or consideration; haughty; full of pride. Specifically—(*a*) Having undue or inordinate pride; arrogant; haughty; supercilious; presumptuous.

Better is it to beate a *prowde* man
Then for to rebuke him;
For he thinkes in his own conceyte
He is wyse and very trim.
Babees Book (E. E. T. S.), p. 96.

We have heard of the pride of Moab; he is very *proud*: even of his haughtiness, and his pride, and wrath.
Isa. xvi. 6.

Norfolk rides foremostly, his crest well known,
Proud as if all our heads were now his own.
Webster and Dekker, Sir Thomas Wyatt.

And was so *proud* that, should he meet
The twelve apostles in the street,
He'd turn his nose up at them all,
And shove his Saviour from the wall. *Churchill.*

Knowledge is *proud* that he has learn'd so much;
Wisdom is humble that he knows no more.
Cowper, Task, vi. 96.

(*b*) Having a worthy and becoming sense of what is due to one's self; self-respecting: as, too *proud* to beg.

F. You're strangely *proud*.
P. So *proud*, I am no slave.
Pope, Epil. to Satires, ii. 205.

Too poor for a bribe, and too *proud* to importune,
He had not the method of making a fortune.
Gray, On Himself.

Lady Clara Vere de Vere,
I know you proud to bear your name.
Your pride is yet no mate for mine,
Too *proud* to care from whence I came.
Tennyson, Lady Clara Vere de Vere.

(*c*) Priding one's self; having high satisfaction; elated: as, *proud* to serve a cause.

What satisfaction can their deaths bring to you,
That are prepar'd and *proud* to die, and willingly?
Fletcher, Wife for a Month, ii. 3.

A divine ambition and a zeal
The boldest patriot might be *proud* to feel.
Cowper, Charity, l. 308.

He'll be a credit till us a'—
We'll a' be *proud* o' Robin.
Burns, There was a Lad was born in Kyle.

2. Proceeding from pride; daring; dignified.

As choice a copy of Verses as any we have heard since we met together; and that is a *proud* word, for we have heard very good ones. *I. Walton*, Complete Angler, p. 188.

But higher far my *proud* pretensions rise.
Cowper, On the Receipt of his Mother's Picture.

3. Of fearless or untamable spirit; full of vigor or mettle.

I have dogs, my lord,
Will rouse the *proudest* panther in the chase.
Shak., Tit. And., ii. 2. 21.

The fiend replied not, overcome with rage;
But, like a *proud* steed rein'd, went haughty on.
Milton, P. L., iv. 858.

Like a *proud* swan, conqu'ring the stream by force.
Cowper, Table-Talk, l. 523.

4. Giving reason or occasion for pride, congratulation, or boasting; suggesting or exciting pride; ostentatious; grand; gorgeous; magnificent.

One is higher in authority, better clad or fed, hath a *prouder* coat or a softer bed.
Ep. Pilkington, Works (Parker Soc., 1842), p. 124.

I better brook the loss of brittle life
Than those *proud* titles thou hast won of me.
Shak., 1 Hen. IV., v. 4. 79.

Storms of stones from the *proud* temple's height
Pour down, and on our batter'd helms alight.
Dryden, Æneid, ii. 553.

The *proudest* memory in the later history of the island is the defeat of the Turks in 1716.
E. A. Freeman, Venice, p. 359.

5. Full; high; swelled. *Halliwell.* [Prov. Eng.]

The wind was loud, the stream was *proud*,
And wi' the stream gaed Willie.
Willie's Drowned in Gamery (Child's Ballads, II. 183).

Proud flesh. See *flesh*.—**Proud stomach.** See *stomach*.—**To do one proud.** See *do*1.=**Syn. 1.** Lofty, lordly.—**4.** Stately, noble. See references under *pride*.

proud† (proud), *v.* [< ME. *prouden*, *pruden*, *prouten*, < AS. **prūtian* (in verbal n. *prūtung*), *prȳtian*, be proud, < *prūt*, proud: see *proud*, *a*. Cf. *pride*1, *v*.] **I.** *intrans.* **1.** To be proud or haughty.

There *proudeth* Power, Heer Prowess brighter shines.
Sylvester, tr. of P. Mathieu's Henry the Great, l. 117.

2. To be full of spirit or animation; be gay.

Yong man wereth jolif,
And than *proudeth* man and wiif.
Arthour and Merlin, p. 11. (*Halliwell.*)

3. To be excited by sexual desire.

II. *trans.* To make or render proud.

Sister *proudes* Sister, Brother hardens Brother,
And one Companion doth corrupt another.
Sylvester, tr. of Du Bartas's Weeks, ii., The Trophies.

proudfall†, *n.* [ME., < *proud* + *fall*; a dubious formation.] The front hair which falls or is folded over the forehead; forelock.

Streght as a strike, straght thurgh the myddes [of her hair]
Depertid the *proudfall* pertly in two,
Atiret in tressis trusset full faire.
Destruction of Troy (E. E. T. S.), l. 3025.

proud-hearted (proud'här″ted), *a.* Arrogant; haughty; proud.

And so, *proud-hearted* Warwick, I defy thee.
Shak., 3 Hen. VI., v. 1. 98.

proudling† (proud'ling), *n.* [< *proud* + *-ling*1.] One who is proud: used in rebuke or contempt.

Milde to the Meek, to *Proudlings* sterne and strict.
Sylvester, tr. of P. Mathieu's Henry the Great, l. 152.

proudly (proud'li), *adv.* [< ME. *prudly*, *proudliche*, *prudliche*, < AS. *prūtlice*, < *prūt*, proud: see *proud*.] In a proud manner; with inordinate self-esteem; haughtily; ostentatiously; with lofty mien or airs; with vigor or mettle.

And past furth *prudly* his pray for to wyn.
Destruction of Troy (E. E. T. S.), l. 855.

Question her *proudly*, let thy looks be stern.
Shak., 1 Hen. VI., i. 2. 62.

proudness (proud'nes), *n.* [< *proud* + *-ness*.] The state or quality of being proud; pride.

Set aside all arrogancy and *proudness*.
Latimer, Sermons on the Lord's Prayer, ii.

proud-pied (proud'pīd), *a.* Gorgeously variegated. [Rare.]

Proud-pied April dress'd in all his trim.
Shak., Sonnets, xcviii.

proud-stomached (proud'stum″ạkt), *a.* Of a haughty spirit; self-asserting; arrogant; high-tempered.

If you get a parcel of *proud-stomached* teachers that set the young dogs a rebelling, what else can you look for?
Dickens, Nicholas Nickleby, xiii.

proustite (prös'tīt), *n.* [Named after J. L. *Proust*, a French chemist.] A native sulphid of arsenic and silver, occurring in rhombohedral and scalenohedral crystals and also massive. It has a beautiful cochineal-red color, and is hence called *ruby silver*, or *light-red silver ore*; the latter name is given to distinguish it from the other form of ruby silver, pyrargyrite, which is dark-red or nearly black, and is called *dark-red silver ore*. Magnificent specimens of proustite are obtained from the mines of Chañarcillo in Chili.

prov. An abbreviation of (*a*) *proverb*; (*b*) *proverbially*; (*c*) *provincial*; (*d*) *provost*; (*e*) [*cap.*] *Provençal*.

provable (prö'vạ-bl), *a.* [< ME. *provable*, < OF. *provable*, *prouvable*, provable, certain, < L. *probabilis*, that may be proved, probable: see *probable*. In mod. use as if directly < *prove* + *-able*.] Capable of being proved or demonstrated.

And if thee thynke it is doutable,
It is thurgh argument *provable*.
Rom. of the Rose, l. 5414.

The crime was a suspicion, *provable* only by actions capable of divers constructions.
Jer. Taylor, Works (ed. 1835), II. 316.

Proof supposes something *provable*, which must be a Proposition or Assertion. *J. S. Mill*, Logic, I. iii. § 1.

Provable debt, a debt of such a class that it may be proved against the estate of a bankrupt.

provableness (prö'vạ-bl-nes), *n.* The state or quality of being provable; capability of being proved.

provably (prö'vạ-bli), *adv.* In a manner capable of proof.

If thou knowe any man of that maners and upright lyuinge that no faulte can *prouably* be layed to him.
J. Udall, On Tit. i.

provand†, **provend**† (prov'ạnd, -ẹnd), *n.* and *a.* [Also *provant*, *provent*; < ME. *provande*, *provende*, *promande*, < OF. *provende*, *prouvende* (also with unorig. r, *provendre*, > ME. *provendre*, E. *provender*), an allowance of food, also a prebend, < LL. *præbenda*, a payment, ML. also an allowance of food and drink, pittance, also a prebend: see *prebend*.] **I.** *n.* **1.** A regular allowance of food; provender; especially, the food or forage supplied to an army or to its horses and beasts of burden.

The Aueyner schalle ordeyn *prouande* good won
For tho lordys horsis euerychon.
Babees Book (E. E. T. S.), p. 319.

These sea-sick soldiers rang hills, woods, and vallies,
Seeking *provant* to fill their empty bellies.
Legend of Captain Jones (1659). (*Halliwell.*)

Camels in the war, who have their *provand*
Only for bearing burdens. *Shak.*, Cor., ii. 1. 267.

I say unto thee, one pease was a soldier's *provant* a whole day at the destruction of Jerusalem.
Fletcher (*and another*), Love's Cure, ii. 1.

2. A prebend. [In this sense only *provend*.]

Cathedral chirches that han *prouendis* appropried to hem. *Wyclif*, Tracts (ed. Matthew), p. 419.

II. *a.* Belonging to a regular allowance; such as was provided for the common soldiers; hence, of common or inferior quality.

In the yeare 1543 the weather was so cold that the provant wine ordained for the army, being frozen, was divided with hatchets, and by the souldiers carried away in baskets. *Hakewill*, Apology, II. vii. § 1.

The good wheaten loaves of the Flemings were better than the *provant* rye-bread of the Swede. *Scott*, Legend of Montrose, ii.

provand†, provend† (prov'ąnd, -ęnd), *v. t.* [Also *provant, provent* (?); < OF. *provender*, supply with provisions, < *provende*, provision, provender: see *provand, provend, n.*] To supply with provender, provisions, or forage.

Do throughly *provend* well your horse, for they must bide the brunt. *Hall*, Homer (1581), p. 30. (*Nares.*)

Should . . . *provant* and victuall moreover this monstrous army of strangers. *Nashe*, Lenten Stuffe (Harl. Misc., VI. 149).

provant-master†, *n.* An officer who served out provisions, etc., to soldiers. *Barnaby Rich*, Fruites of Long Experience (1604), p. 19. (*Halliwell.*)

prove (pröv), *v.*; pret. *proved*, pp. *proved* (sometimes incorrectly *proven*), ppr. *proving*. [< ME. *proven* (partly < AS. *prōfian*), also *preven* (> early mod. E. *prieve, preeve*), < OF. *prover, prouver, pruver, preuver*, F. *prouver* = Pr. *provar* = Sp. *probar* = Pg. *provar* = It. *probare* = AS. *prōfian*, test, try, prove, = LG. *proven, pröven* = MHG. *pruoven, prüeven*, G. *prüfen* (also *proben* and *probieren*) = Icel. *prōfa, prōva* = Sw. *pröfva* (also *probera*) = Dan. *pröve* (also *probere*), < L. *probare*, test, try, examine, approve, show to be good or fit, prove, < *probus*, good, excellent. Cf. *probe, probity, proof*, etc., and cf. *approve, disprove, improve, reprove*, etc., *approbate, reprobate*, etc., *approbation, probation*, etc.] **I.** *trans.* **1.** To try by experiment, or by a test or standard; test; make trial of; put to the test: as, to *prove* the strength of gunpowder; to *prove* the contents of a vessel by comparing it with a standard measure.

I bad Thougt tho be mene bitwene,
And put forth somme purpos to *prouen* his wittes.
Piers Plowman (B), viii. 120.

Ne would I it have ween'd, had I not late it *prieved*.
Spenser, F. Q., V. iv. 33.

Ye'll say that I've ridden but into the wood,
To *prieve* gin my horse and hounds are good.
Sir Oluf and the Elf-King's Daughter (Child's Ballads, [I. 300).

And another said, I have bought five yoke of oxen, and I go to *prove* them. Luke xiv. 19.

I have *proved* thee, thou art never destitute of that which is convenient. *Bunyan*, Pilgrim's Progress, p. 302.

He felt happy, and yet feared to *prove*
His new-born bliss, lest it should fade from him.
William Morris, Earthly Paradise, III. 342.

2. To render certain; put out of doubt (as a proposition) by adducing evidence and argumentation; show; demonstrate.

That pitee renneth sone in gentil herte . . .
Is *preved* al day, as men may it see,
As wel by werk as by auctoritee.
Chaucer, Squire's Tale, l. 473.

Give me the ocular proof; . . .
Make me to see 't; or, at the least, so *prove* it
That the probation bear no hinge nor loop
To hang a doubt on. *Shak.*, Othello, iii. 3. 360.

The wise man . . . hath condescended to *prove* as well as assert it, and to back the severe rule he hath laid down with very convincing reasons. *Bp. Atterbury*, Sermons, I. vi.

Reduc'd to practice, his beloved rule
Would only *prove* him a consummate fool.
Cowper, Conversation, l. 140.

3. To establish the authenticity or validity of; obtain probate of: as, to *prove* a will. See *probate*.

The holy crosse was *provyd* by resyng of a Dede man whanne they wer in Dowte whiche it was of the thre. *Torkington*, Diarie of Eng. Travell, p. 41.

4. To have personal experience of; experience; enjoy or suffer.

But I did enter, and enjoy
What happy lovers *prove*.
Carew, Deposition from Love. (*Nares.*)

Let him in arms the power of Turnus *prove*.
Dryden, Æneid, vii. 610.

Such feebleness of limbs thou *prov'st*
That now at every step thou mov'st
Upheld by two. *Cowper*, To Mary (1793).

5. In *arith.*, to ascertain or demonstrate the correctness of (an operation or result) by a calculation in the nature of a check: as, to *prove* a sum. Thus, in subtraction, if the difference between two numbers added to the lesser number makes a sum equal to the greater, the correctness of the subtraction is *proved*.
6. In *printing*, to take a proof of.—**To prove masteries†**, to make trial of skill; contend for the mastery.

He would often run, leape, or *prove masteries* with his chiefe courtiers. *Knolles*, Hist. Turks, 516, I. (*Nares.*)

=**Syn. 2.** To verify, justify, confirm, substantiate, make good, manifest.

II. *intrans.* **1.** To make trial; essay.

It is a pur pardoners craft; *proue* and assaye!
Piers Plowman's Crede (E. E. T. S.), l. 247.

2. To be found or ascertained to be by experience or trial; be ascertained or shown by the event or something subsequent; turn out to be: as, the report *proves* to be true; to *prove* useful or wholesome; to *prove* faithful or treacherous.

That *proved* [var. *preved*] wel, for overal ther he cam,
At wrastlynge he wolde have alwey the ram.
Chaucer, Gen. Prol. to C. T., l. 547.

If springing things be any jot diminish'd,
They wither in their prime, *prove* nothing worth.
Shak., Venus and Adonis, l. 418.

If his children *prove* vicious or degenerous, . . . we account the man miserable. *Jer. Taylor* (ed. 1835), Works, I. 717.

He knows
His end with mine involved; and knows that I
Should *prove* a bitter morsel, and his bane,
Whenever that shall be. *Milton*, P. L., ii. 808.

When the two processes of deduction *prove* to be identical, we have no choice but to abide by the result, and to assume that the one inference is equally authoritative with the other. *H. Spencer*, Social Statics, p. 191.

Hence—**3.** To become; be.

Tell him, in hope he'll *prove* a widower shortly;
I'll wear the willow garland for his sake.
Shak., 3 Hen. VI., iii. 3. 227.

4†. To succeed; turn out well.

If the experiment *proved* not, it might be pretended that the beasts were not killed in the due time. *Bacon.*

5. To thrive; be with young: generally said of cattle. *Halliwell.*—**To fend and prove†.** See *fend*[1].—**To prove up**, to show that the requirements of the law for taking up government land have been fulfilled, so that a patent for the same may be issued. [U. S.]

Under these laws the settler is obliged to pay the government two hundred dollars for his claim, whether he *proves up* after a six months' residence, or waits the full limit of his time for making proof—thirty-three months. *Harper's Mag.*, LXXVII. 238.

prove†, *n.* An obsolete form of *proof*.

provect† (prọ-vekt'), *a.* [= OF. *provect*, a man advanced in years; < L. *provectus*, advanced (of time), pp. of *provehere*, carry forward, advance, < *pro*, forth, + *vehere*, carry: see *vehicle*.] Advanced.

We haue in daily experience that little infantes assayeth to folowe . . . the wordes . . . of them that be *prouecte* in yeres. *Sir T. Elyot*, The Governour, i. 4.

provectant (prọ-vek'tąnt), *n.* [< L. *provehere*, pp. *provectus*, carry forward, advance (see *provect*), + *-ant*.] A covariant considered as produced by the operation of a provector on a contravariant.

provection (prọ-vek'shọn), *n.* [< LL. *provectio(n-)*, a carrying forward, an advancement, promotion, < L. *provehere*, pp. *provectus*, carry forward, advance: see *provect*.] In *philol.*, the carrying of a terminal letter from a word to the next succeeding one, when it begins with a vowel, as *the tone* for *that one*, *the tother* for *that other*. [Rare.]

provector (prọ-vek'tọr), *n.* [NL., < L. *provehere*, pp. *provectus*, carry forward, advance: see *provect*.] The contravariant operator $(a, b, \ldots \between \partial_\xi, \partial_\eta, \ldots)^m$, where ∂_ξ, ∂_η, etc., replace x, y, etc., in the quantic $(a, b, \ldots \between x, y, \ldots)^m$, or any contravariant operator resulting from a similar substitution in any covariant of the original quantic.

proveditor† (prọ-ved'i-tọr), *n.* [Also *proveditore, providitore*; < It. *proveditore* (= Sp. *proveedor* = Pg. *provedor*), a provider, purveyor, < *provedere*, provide, purvey: see *provide*. Cf. *provedor* and *purveyor*.] **1.** A purveyor; one employed to procure supplies; a provider.

Thrice was he made,
In dangerous armes, Venice *providetore*.
Marston, What you Will, i. 1.

The entertainment that St. John's *proveditóre*, the angel, gave him was such as the wilderness did afford. *Jer. Taylor*, Works (ed. 1835), I. 82.

Ready money in open market . . . being found upon experience to be the best *proveditor* of any. *Blackstone*, Com., I. viii.

2. An overseer; a governor.

When they have any great Expedition to make, they have always a Stranger for their General, but he is supervis'd by two *Proveditors*, without whom he cannot attempt any thing. *Howell*, Letters, I. i. 35.

provedor, provedore (prov'e-dôr, -dōr), *n.* [Also *providore*; < Sp. *proveedor* = Pg. *provedor*, provider, purveyor: see *proveditor* and *purveyor*.] A purveyor; one who provides necessaries and supplies; a proveditor.

When the famous Beefsteak Club was first instituted, he [Richard Estcourt] had the office of *providore* assigned him. *W. King*, Art of Cookery, note on l. 519 (Chalmers's [English Poets).

I was much amused in watching our *provedor*, as he went about collecting things by ones and twos, until he had piled a little cart quite full. *Lady Brassey*, Voyage of Sunbeam, I. xiv.

proven (prö'vn), *pp.* [An improper form of *proved*, with *-en*[1], suffix of strong participles, for orig. *-ed*[2].] Proved: an improper form, lately growing in frequency, by imitation of the Scotch use in "not proven."

The evidence is voluminous and conclusive, and by common consent a verdict of *proven* is returned. *H. Spencer*, Social Statics, p. 422.

Not proven, in *Scots law*, a verdict rendered by a jury in a criminal case when the evidence is insufficient to justify conviction, yet strong enough to warrant grave suspicion of guilt.

provenance (prov'ẹ-nąns), *n.* [< F. *provenance*, origin, production: see *provenience*.] Origin; source or quarter from which anything comes; provenience: especially in the sense of 'place of manufacture, production, or discovery.' [A French term, better in the English form *provenience*.]

[Well-tombs] in which we have the use of metallic chisels clearly and indisputably indicated, and the presence of bronze work of Oriental *provenance*. *The Nation*, XLVIII. 203.

Style of art, historical probability, and the *provenance* of the coins themselves, all seem to indicate a Spanish origin. *B. V. Head*, Historia Numorum, p. 4.

Provençal (F. pron. prọ-voṅ-sal'), *a.* and *n.* [< F. *Provençal* (< L. *Provincialis*), < *Provincia* (> F. *Provence*), a former province of southeastern France, < L. *provincia*, a province, a Roman government outside of Italy: see *province*.] **I.** *a.* Pertaining or belonging to Provence in France, or to its old language.

II. *n.* **1.** A native of Provence.—**2.** The Romance tongue of Provence. It is the *langue d'oc*, and was the dialect used by the Troubadours. See *langue d'oc*.

Abbreviated *Pr.* or *Prov.*

Provence oil. See *oil*.

Provence rose. [A misnomer for *Provins rose*.] Same as *cabbage-rose*.

Provencial (prọ-ven'shąl), *a.* [= F. *Provençal*; < *Provence* + *-ial*.] Same as *Provençal*.

provend†, provende†, *n.* and *a.* See *provand*.

provend†, *v. t.* See *provand*.

provender (prov'en-dėr), *n.* [< ME. *provendre*, < OF. *provendre*, var. of *provende*, allowance, provision: see *provand*.] **1.** Food; provisions; especially, dry food for beasts, as hay, straw, or corn; fodder.

I tynde payne for the pope and *prouendre* for his palfrey. *Piers Plowman* (B), xiii. 243.

Shall we go send them dinners and fresh suits,
And give their fasting horses *provender*,
And after fight with them? *Shak.*, Hen. V., iv. 2. 58.

In the connivance of his [the prodigal's] security, harlots and sycophants rifle his estate, and then send him to rob the hogs of their *provender*, Jove's nuts, acorns. *Rev. T. Adams*, Works, I. 497.

2†. A prebend.

And porchace ȝow *prouendres* while ȝoure pans lasteth,
And bigge ȝow benefices pluralite to haue.
Piers Plowman (C), iv. 32.

=**Syn. 1.** Fodder, etc. See *feed, n.*

provender (prov'en-dėr), *v. t.* [< *provender, n.* Cf. *provand, v.*] To feed; fodder, as a horse.

His horses (quatenus horses) are *provendered* as epicurely. *Nashe*, Lenten Stuffe (Harl. Misc., VI. 179). (*Davies.*)

provendre[1]†, *n.* A Middle English form of *provender*.

provendre[2]†, *n.* [ME., < OF. *provendier*, < ML. *præbendarius*, a prebendary: see *prebendary*.] A prebendary.

provenience (prọ-vē'niẹns), *n.* [= F. *provenance* (> E. *provenance*) = It. *provenienza*, < NL. **provenientia*, origin, < L. *provenire*, come forth, appear, originate, < *pro*, forth, + *venire*, come.] Origin; the place from which something comes or is derived; the place of production or derivation of an object, especially in the fine arts and in archæology. Compare *provenance*.

Wherever the place in which an object was found, or—to use a convenient word already borrowed by German archæologists from the Italians and French—its *provenience*, is stated. *A. D. Savage*, The Century, XXIV. 632.

The surface of the marble [of a statue found at Sicyon]—the *provenience* of which I am unable to state—is somewhat corroded. *Amer. Jour. Archæol*, V. (1889) 293.

provent†, *n.* Same as *provand*.

proventricular (prọ-ven-trik'ū-lär), *a.* [< *proventriculus* + *-ar*[3].] Pertaining to the proventriculus: as, *proventricular* glands; *proventricular* digestion.

proventriculus (prọ-ven-trik'ū-lus), *n.*; pl. *proventriculi* (-lī). [NL., < L. *pro*, before, + *ventriculus*, dim. of *venter*, stomach: see *ventricle*.]

1. In *ornith.*, the glandular stomach; a second dilatation of the esophagus, succeeding the crop or craw, and succeeded by the gizzard, gigerium, or muscular stomach. It is the true stomach of a bird, or place where digestion is chiefly carried on, and corresponds to the cardiac end or division of the stomach of a mammal. It is situated at the lower end of the gullet, next to the gizzard, and is always recognized by the gastric follicles which form a zone or belt of variously disposed patches upon its mucous surface. Also called *ventriculus glandulosus.* **2.** In insects, the first stomach, the ingluvies or crop, being merely an expansion of the esophagus. It generally has thick muscular walls, and is often armed interiorly with horny plates or teeth of various forms. The proventriculus lies wholly or partly in the abdomen, and is generally absent in haustellate insects. See cut under *Blattidæ.* **3.** In worms, a muscular crop.

provenue† (prov'e-nū), *n.* [< OF. *provenu, prouvenu,* produce, revenue, < *provenu,* pp. of *provenir,* < L. *provenire,* come forth, appear: see *provenience.* Cf. *revenue.*] Produce.

Our liberal Creator hath thought good to furnish our tables with . . . the rich and dainty *provenues* of our gardens and orchards.
Bp. Hall, Christian Moderation, i. 1, § 2.

prover (prö'vėr), *n.* [< *prove* + *-er*[1].] **1.** One who or that which proves or tries.

Patr. Why am I a fool?
Ther. Make that demand of the *prover.*
Shak., T. and C., ii. 3. 72.

2. A skilled workman employed to strike off proofs from engraved plates.

From two to six men, . . . whose duty it is to print proof impressions only; they are called *provers.*
Ure, Dict., II. 289.

proverb (prov'ėrb), *n.* [< ME. *proverbe,* < OF. (and F.) *proverbe* = Sp. Pg. It. *proverbio,* < L. *proverbium,* a common saying, saw, adage, a proverb, later also byword, < *pro,* before, forth, + *verbum,* a word: see *verb.*] **1.** A short pithy sentence, often repeated colloquially, expressing a well-known truth or a common fact ascertained by experience or observation; a popular saying which briefly and forcibly expresses some practical precept; an adage; a wise saw: often set forth in the guise of metaphor and in the form of rime, and sometimes alliterative.

And trewe is the *proverbe* that the wise man seith, that "who is fer from his iye is soone foryeten."
Merlin (E. E. T. S.), iii. 693.

They said they were an-hungry; sigh'd forth *proverbs,*
That hunger broke stone walls, that dogs must eat,
That meat was made for mouths. *Shak.*, Cor., i. 1. 209.

What is a *proverb* but the experience and observation of several ages gathered and summed up into one expression?
South, Sermons (ed. 1823), I. 437.

The pithy quaintness of old Howell has admirably described the ingredients of an exquisite *proverb* to be sense, shortness, and salt. *I. D'Israeli*, Curios. of Lit., III. 359.

2. A byword; a reproach; an object of scorn or derision.

I will deliver them . . . to be a reproach and a *proverb,* a taunt and a curse, in all places whither I shall drive them.
Jer. xxiv. 9.

Salisbury was foolish to a *proverb.*
Macaulay, Hist. Eng., vii.

3. In *Scrip.*, an enigmatical utterance; a mysterious or oracular saying that requires interpretation.

To understand a *proverb,* and the interpretation; the words of the wise, and their dark sayings. Prov. i. 6.

4. *pl.* [*cap.*] One of the books of the Old Testament, following the Book of Psalms. The full title is Proverbs of Solomon (i. 1). It is a collection of the sayings of the sages of Israel, taking its full title from the chief among them, though it is by no means certain that he is the author of a majority of them. The original meaning of *mashal,* the Hebrew word translated 'proverb,' seems to be 'a comparison.' The term is sometimes translated 'parable' in our English Bible; but, as such comparisons were commonly made in the East by short and pithy sayings, the word came to be applied to these chiefly, though not exclusively. They formed one of the most characteristic features of Eastern literature.

5. A dramatic composition in which some proverb or popular saying is taken as the foundation of the plot. Good examples are—"A Door must be either Open or Shut," *Alfred de Musset;* "Still Water Runs Deep," *Dion Boucicault.* When such dramas are extemporized, as in private theatricals, the proverb employed is often withheld, to be guessed by the audience after the representation.—**To cap proverbs.** See *cap*[1]. =**Syn. 1.** *Axiom, Maxim,* etc. See *aphorism.*

proverb (prov'ėrb), *v.* [< ME. *proverben;* < *proverb, n.*] **I.** *trans.* **1.** To utter in the form of a proverb; speak of proverbially; make a byword of.

For which this wise clerkes that ben dede
Han evere this *proverbed* to us yonge:
That firste vertu is to kepe tonge.
Chaucer, Troilus, iii. 293.

Am I not sung and *proverb'd* for a fool
In every street? *Milton*, S. A., l. 203.

2. To provide with a proverb.

I am *proverb'd* with a grandsire phrase.
Shak., R. and J., i. 4. 37.

II. *intrans.* To utter proverbs.

All their pains taken to seem so wise in *proverbing* serve but to conclude them downright slaves; and the edge of their own proverb falls reverse upon themselves.
Milton, Articles of Peace with the Irish.

proverbial (prǫ-vėr'bi-al), *a.* [< F. *proverbial* = Sp. Pg. *proverbial* = It. *proverbiale,* < LL. *proverbialis,* < L. *proverbium,* proverb: see *proverb.*] **1.** Pertaining to proverbs; resembling or characteristic of a proverb: as, to express one's self with *proverbial* brevity.

This river whose head being unknown, and drawn to a *proverbial* obscurity, the opinion thereof became without bounds. *Sir T. Browne*, Vulg. Err., vi. 8.

2. Mentioned in a proverb; used or current as a proverb: as, a *proverbial* saying; hence, commonly spoken of; well-known; notorious.

In case of excesses, I take the German *proverbial* cure, by a hair of the same beast, to be the worst in the world.
Sir W. Temple.

That *proverbial* feather which has the credit or discredit of breaking the camel's back.
George Eliot, Mill on the Floss, ii. 2.

Equally *proverbial* was the hospitality of the Virginians.
Bancroft, Hist. U. S., I. 177.

proverbialism (prǫ-vėr'bi-al-izm), *n.* [< *proverbial* + *-ism.*] A proverbial phrase or saying.

proverbialist (prǫ-vėr'bi-al-ist), *n.* [< *proverbial* + *-ist.*] A composer, collector, or user of proverbs.

proverbialize (prǫ-vėr'bi-al-īz), *v.;* pret. and pp. *proverbialized,* ppr. *proverbializing.* [< *proverbial* + *-ize.*] **I.** *trans.* To make into a proverb; turn into a proverb, or use proverbially; speak of in a proverb. [Rare.]

II. *intrans.* To use proverbs. *Davies.*

But I forbear from any further *proverbializing,* lest I should be thought to have rifled my Erasmus's adages.
Kennet, tr. of Erasmus's Praise of Folly, p. 135.

proverbially (prǫ-vėr'bi-al-i), *adv.* In a proverbial manner or style; by way of proverb; as a proverb.

So are slow-worms accounted blind, and the like we affirm *proverbially* of the beetle, although their eyes be evident, and they will flye against lights, like many other insects. *Sir T. Browne*, Vulg. Err., ii. 18.

proverbize (prov'ėrb-īz), *v. t.* and *i.;* pret. and pp. *proverbized,* ppr. *proverbizing.* [< *proverb* + *-ize.*] Same as *proverbialize.* [Rare.]

For House-hold Rules, read not the learned Writs
Of the Stagirian (glory of good wits);
Nor his whom, for his hony-steeped stile,
They *Proverbiz'd* the Attick Muse yer-while.
Sylvester, tr. of Du Bartas's Weeks, i. 7.

proviant†, *n.* and *a.* [A corrupt form of *provand, provant,* appar. simulating *proviaunce.*] Same as *provand.*

providable (prǫ-vī'da-bl), *a.* [< *provide* + *-able.*] That may be provided; capable of being provided.

I have no deeper wish than that bread for me were *providable* elsewhere. *Carlyle.*

provide (prǫ-vīd'), *v.;* pret. and pp. *provided,* ppr. *providing.* [= F. *pourvoir,* OF. *pourvoir, pourveir* (> E. *purvey*) = Pr. *provezir* = Sp. *proveer* = Pg. *prover,* < It. *provedere, provvedere,* < L. *providere,* see forward, act with foresight, take care, provide, < *pro,* forward, + *videre,* see: see *vision.* Cf. *purvey,* from the same source, through OF.] **I.** *trans.* **1**†. To foresee; look forward to.

Severe and wise patriots. . . . *providing* the hurts these licentious spirits may do in a state.
B. Jonson, Volpone, Ded.

2. To procure beforehand; get, collect, or make ready for future use; prepare.

God will *provide* himself a lamb for a burnt-offering.
Gen. xxii. 8.

A small spare mast,
Such as seafaring men *provide* for storms.
Shak., C. of E., i. 1. 81.

There are very good Laws *provided* against Scandal and Calumny. *Steele*, Tender Husband, v. 1.

3. To furnish; supply: now often followed by *with,* but formerly also by *of.*

And I know you well *provided of* Christian, and learned, and brave defences against all human accidents.
Donne, Letters, cxxiii.

Rome, by the care of the magistrates, was well *provided with* corn. *Arbuthnot*, Ancient Coins.

4. To make ready; prepare.

I shall expect thee next summer (if the Lord please), and by that time I hope to be *provided* for thy comfortable entertainment. *Winthrop*, Hist. New England, I. 447.

They . . . told vs, We were welcome if wee came to fight, for they were *prouided* for vs.
Quoted in *Capt. John Smith's* Works, II. 15.

5. To make or lay down as a previous arrangement, guaranty, or provision; make a previous condition, supposition, or understanding: as, the agreement *provides* that the party shall incur no loss.

We also *provided* to send one hundred and sixty [men] more . . . to prosecute the war.
Winthrop, Hist. New England, I. 265.

The Constitution *provides,* and all the States have accepted the provision, that "the United States shall guarantee to every State in this Union a republican form of Government." *Lincoln*, in Raymond, p. 150.

6. *Eccles.*, to grant the right to be in future presented to a benefice which is not vacant at the time of the grant. See *provision,* 8.

Robert Waucop, "the blind Scot," who had just been *provided* by the Pope to the vacancy of Armagh.
R. W. Dixon, Hist. Church of Eng., xix.

II. *intrans.* **1.** To procure or furnish supplies, means of defense, or the like: as, to *provide* liberally for the table.

They say Nature brings forth none but she *provides* for them; I'll try her liberality.
Beau. and Fl., Scornful Lady, i. 1.

O Thou who kindly dost *provide*
For every creature's want! *Burns*, A Grace.

The cross housekeeper was gone; . . . her successor, who had been matron at the Lowton Dispensary, unused to the ways of her new abode, *provided* with comparative liberality. *Charlotte Brontë*, Jane Eyre, ix.

2. To take measures for counteracting or escaping something: often followed by *against* or *for.*

This gaue vs cause to *prouide for* the worst.
Quoted in *Capt. John Smith's* Works, I. 190.

Providing against the inclemency of the weather.
Sir M. Hale.

3†. To make ready; prepare.

A hunting he *provides* to go;
Straight they were ready all.
The Cruel Black (Child's Ballads, III. 371).

When they sawe their desire and hope of the arriuall of the rest of the shippes to be euery day more and more frustrated, they *prouided* to sea againe.
Hakluyt's Voyages, I. 246.

provided (prǫ-vī'ded), *pp.* and *quasi-conj.* [Tr. of L. *proviso* in similar use, 'it being provided' (that . . .); prop. pp. absolute. See *proviso.*] This (or it) being understood, conceded, or established; on (this) condition; on these terms: in this sense always introducing a clause of condition or exception, and followed by *that* (expressed or understood).

I take your offer, and will live with you,
Provided that you do no outrages
On silly women or poor passengers.
Shak., T. G. of V., iv. 1. 71.

This man loves to eat good meat—always *provided* he do not pay for it himself.
Beau. and Fl., Woman-Hater, i. 3.

providence (prov'i-dens), *n.* [< ME. *providence,* < OF. *providence,* F. *providence* = Pr. *providentia* = Sp. Pg. *providencia* = It. *providenza,* < L. *providentia,* < *providen(t-)s,* ppr. of *providere,* foresee, provide: see *provident.* Cf. *prudence* and *purveyance.*] **1.** Foresight; timely care or preparation.

These Zemes, they beleue to . . . haue the cure and *prouidence* of the sea, wooddes, and sprynges and fountaynes, assigninge to euery thynge theyr peculier goddes.
Peter Martyr (tr. in Eden's First Books on America, ed. Arber, p. 101).

Alas, how shall this bloody deed be answer'd?
It will be laid to us, whose *providence*
Should have . . . restrain'd . . .
This mad young man. *Shak.*, Hamlet, iv. 1. 17.

2. Frugality; prudence in the management of one's concerns; economy.

My heart shall be my own; my vast expense
Reduced to bounds by timely *providence.*
Dryden, Theodore and Honoria, l. 242.

3. The care and guardianship of God over his creatures; divine supervision. The doctrine of divine providence is the doctrine that God both possesses and exercises absolute power over all the works of his hands; it thus differs from the doctrine of omnipotence, which only attributes to him the power, but does not necessarily imply that he uses it; and it is opposed to the doctrine of naturalism, or that nature is governed wholly by natural laws with which God never interferes.

It is a part of the Divine *Providence* of the World that the Strong shall influence the Weak.
Ascham, The Scholemaster, p. 3.

God, in his ordinary *providence,* maketh use of means, yet is free to work without, above, and against them, at his pleasure. *Westminster Confession of Faith*, v.

That to the highth of this great argument
I may assert eternal *Providence,*
And justify the ways of God to men.
Milton, P. L., i. 25.

Hence—**4.** [*cap.*] God, regarded as exercising forecast, care, and direction for and over his creatures; the divine power and direction.

The world was all before them, where to choose
Their place of rest, and *Providence* their guide.
Milton, P. L., xii. 647.

Who finds not *Providence* all good and wise,
Alike in what it gives, and what denies?
Pope, Essay on Man, i. 87.

5. Something due to an act of providential intervention; an act or event in which the care of God is directly exhibited.

A remarkable *providence* appeared in a case which was tried at the last court of assistants.
Winthrop, Hist. New England, I. 330.

Special providence, the special intervention in or administration of the laws of nature and life by God, for special ends; specifically, a particular act of divine interposition in favor of one or more individuals.

There 's a *special providence* in the fall of a sparrow.
Shak., Hamlet, v. 2. 231.

=**Syn.** 1 and 2. *Prudence, Discretion*, etc. See *wisdom*.

provident (prov'i-dent), *a.* [< F. *provident* = Sp. Pg. *providente*, < L. *providen(t-)s*, ppr. of *providere*, foresee, provide: see *provide*. Cf. *prudent*, of same ult. formation.] 1. Foreseeing wants and making provision to supply them; forecasting; cautious; prudent in preparing for future exigencies; having an anticipatory perception of something: sometimes followed by *of*.

First crept
The parsimonious emmet, *provident*
Of future. *Milton*, P. L., vii. 485.

A Parent who, whilst *provident of* his whole family, watches over every particular child.
Channing, Perfect Life, p. 83.

The little Maid again, *provident of* her domestic destiny, takes with preference to Dolls. *Carlyle*, Sartor Resartus.

Suppose your savings had to be made, not, as now, out of surplus income, but out of wages already insufficient for necessaries; and then consider whether to be *provident* would be as easy as you at present find it.
H. Spencer, Social Statics, p. 252.

2. Frugal; economical.—**Provident societies.** Same as *friendly societies*.

While the Briton does not make as a rule those sacrifices for the benefit of all those about him which are made by the poorly-paid Hindoo, who, in a country of low wages in which a poor law is unknown, invariably provides for his old people and keeps them in greater comfort than he keeps himself, Englishmen and colonists alike are remarkable for the extent to which they have carried the system of *provident societies*.
Sir C. W. Dilke, Probs. of Greater Britain, vi. 2.

providential (prov-i-den'shal), *a.* [< F. *providentiel* = Sp. Pg. *providencial*, < L. *providentia*, foresight: see *providence*.] Effected by the providence of God; proceeding from divine direction; referable to divine providence.

This thin, this soft contexture of the air,
Shows the wise author's *providential* care.
Sir R. Blackmore.

I claim for ancient Greece a marked, appropriated, distinctive place in the *providential* order of the world.
Gladstone, Might of Right, p. 107.

providentially (prov-i-den'shal-i), *adv.* In a providential manner; by means of God's providence.

providently (prov'i-dent-li), *adv.* In a provident manner; with prudent foresight; with wise precaution in preparing for the future.

He that doth the ravens feed,
Yea, *providently* caters for the sparrow,
Be comfort to my age!
Shak., As you Like it, ii. 3. 44.

providentness (prov'i-dent-nes), *n.* The quality of being provident; foresight; carefulness; prudence; providence.

Companions of shootings be *providentness*, good heede geving, true meetinge, honest comparison, which thinges agree with vertue verye well. *Ascham*, Toxophilus, i.

provider (prō-vī'dėr), *n.* One who provides, furnishes, or supplies.

Here 's money for my meat;
I would have left it on the board so soon
As I had made my meal, and parted
With prayers for the *provider*.
Shak., Cymbeline, iii. 6. 53.

A good provider, one who is liberal in supplying provisions, etc., for his family. [Colloq.]—**Lion's provider.** See *lion*.

providore†, *n.* Same as *proveditor*.

providore (prov'i-dōr), *n.* Same as *provedor*.

province (prov'ins), *n.* [< ME. *provynce*, < OF. *province*, F. *province* = Pr. *proensa, prohensa* = Sp. Pg. *provincia* = It. *provincia* = D. MLG. *provincie* = G. *provintzie, provintz*, now *provinz* = Sw. Dan. *provins*, a province, < L. *provincia*, a territory outside of Italy brought (chiefly by conquest) under Roman dominion, also official duty, office, charge, province, < *pro*, before, in front of, + *vincere*, conquer.] 1. Originally, a country of considerable extent which, being reduced under Roman dominion, was remodeled, subjected to the rule of a governor sent from Rome, and charged with such taxes and contributions as the Romans saw fit to impose. The earliest Roman province was Sicily.

Judea now, and all the Promised Land,
Reduced a *province* under Roman yoke,
Obeys Tiberius. *Milton*, P. R., iii. 158.

A *province*, in the Roman system, was a subject land, a land beyond the bounds of Italy, a land of which the Roman People was the corporate sovereign.
E. A. Freeman, Amer. Lects., p. 320.

2. (*a*) An administrative division of a country: as, the *provinces* of Spain; the former *provinces* of France; more loosely, any important administrative unit, as one of the governments of Russia or of the crownlands of Austria.

Galilee is one of the *Provynces* of the Holy Lond; and in that *Provynce* is the Cytee of Naym and Capharnaum and Chorosaym and Bethsayde.
Mandeville, Travels, p. 110.

Over each *province* is placed a Governor, who is assisted in his duties by a Vice-Governor and a small council.
D. M. Wallace, Russia, p. 199.

(*b*) A part of a country or state as distinguished from the capital or the larger cities; the country: usually in the plural: as, an actor who is starring in the *provinces*. (*c*) *Eccles.*, the territory within which an archbishop or a metropolitan exercises jurisdiction: as, the *province* of Canterbury; the *province* of Illinois. (*d*) In the *Rom. Cath. Ch.*, one of the territorial divisions of an ecclesiastical order, as of the Franciscans, or of the Propaganda. (*e*) A region of country; a tract; a large extent.

Over many a tract
Of heaven they march'd, and many a *province* wide.
Milton, P. L., vi. 77.

3. The proper duty, office, or business of a person; sphere of action; function.

I have taken all knowledge to be my *province*.
Bacon, Advancement of Learning, Pref., p. iv.

The family is the proper *province* for private women to shine in. *Addison*, Party Patches.

The most difficult *province* in friendship is the letting a man see his faults and errors. *Budgell*, Spectator, No. 385.

Within the region of religious activity itself there are *provinces* which demand varying degrees of distinctness in definition and graduation of discipline.
Stubbs, Medieval and Modern Hist., p. 293.

4. A division in any department of knowledge or activity; a department.

Their understandings are . . . cooped up in narrow bounds, so that they never look abroad into other *provinces* of the intellectual world.
Watts, Improvement of Mind, I. xiv. § 10.

5. In *zoöl.*, a prime division of animals; a phylum; a subkingdom; a branch; a type: as, in Owen's classification, the four *provinces*—*Vertebrata, Articulata, Mollusca*, and *Radiata*. The prime divisions of a province are called *subprovinces*.—6. In *zoögeog.*, a subregion; a faunal area less extensive than a region. Thus, the Nearctic or North American region is zoölogically divided into the eastern, middle, and western *provinces*.—**Boreal province, Illyrian provinces, Peruvian province.** See the adjectives.—**Province of distribution.** See *distribution*.

province-rose (prov'ins-rōz), *n.* An erroneous form of *Provins rose*, the cabbage-rose.

provincial[1] (prō-vin'shal), *a.* and *n.* [< ME. *provinciall* (n.); < OF. *provincial*, F. *provincial* = Pr. Sp. Pg. *provincial* = It. *provinciale*, < L. *provincialis*, pertaining to a province, < *provincia*, a province: see *province*.] I. *a.* 1. Of or pertaining to a province; existing in a province; characteristic of a province: as, a *provincial* government; a *provincial* dialect.

A nobleman of Picardy, . . . a man of considerable *provincial* distinction, sought and obtained a commission as lord of the unknown Norimbega.
Bancroft, Hist. U. S., I. 16.

Already he [the king] had assembled *provincial* councils formed of representatives from cities, boroughs, and market-towns, that he might ask them for votes of money.
H. Spencer, Prin. of Sociol., § 501.

2. Forming a province or territory appendant to a principal kingdom or state: as, *provincial* territory.—3. Pertaining to an ecclesiastical province, or to the jurisdiction of an archbishop; not ecumenical: as, a *provincial* council.

Since the Conquest most of the archbishops had held *provincial* synods and issued *provincial* canons.
Stubbs, Medieval and Modern Hist., p. 307.

4. Exhibiting the manners of a province; characteristic of the inhabitants of a province, or of the country as distinguished from the metropolis or larger cities; countrified; rustic; hence, not polished; narrow; unenlightened.

Fond of exhibiting *provincial* airs and graces. *Macaulay*.

A society perfectly *provincial*, with no thought, with no hope, beyond its narrow horizon.
J. H. Shorthouse, Countess Eve, i.

5. Restricted to a province; local.

His [Shakespeare's] patriotism was too national to be *provincial*. *Swinburne*, Shakespeare, p. 113.

Provincial congresses. See *congress*.—**Provincial Letters**, the name by which a celebrated collection of letters written in French by Blaise Pascal in 1656–7, in condemnation of the Jesuits, is ordinarily known. The phrase, which appears as the title of English translations of the letters, representing the popular French *Provinciales*, is a misnomer—the actual title being *Letters to a Provincial*.

II. *n.* 1. A person belonging to a province; one from any part of the country except the metropolis or one of the larger cities. The name *Provincials* was often applied to the inhabitants of the American colonies before the revolution, especially to their contingents engaged in military service.

The land law of the Gracchi was well intended, but it bore hard on many of the leading *provincials*, who had seen their estates parcelled out. *Froude*, Cæsar, p. 58.

Vulgarized by the constant influx of non-Italian *provincials* into Rome. *Encyc. Brit.*, XIV. 333.

2. In some religious orders, a monastic superior who has the general superintendence of his fraternity in a given district called a province.

Oure *prouinciall* hath power to assoilen
Alle sustren & bretheren that beth of our order.
Piers Plowman's Crede (E. E. T. S.), l. 328.

Two years after this event, he was elected *provincial* of his order in Castile, which placed him at the head of its numerous religious establishments.
Prescott, Ferd. and Isa., ii. 5.

Provincial[2] (prō-vin'shal), *a.* [< ML. *Provincialis*, Provençal: see *Provençal*.] Pertaining to Provence; Provençal.

Provyncial of is dyvers kynde of vynys.
Palladius, Husbondrie (E. E. T. S.), p. 69.

Provincial rose. (*a*) The cabbage-rose. (*b*) A rosette of ribbons formerly worn on a shoe; a shoe-rose.

With two *Provincial roses* on my razed shoes.
Shak., Hamlet, iii. 2. 288.

provincialism (prō-vin'shal-izm), *n.* [< F. *provincialisme* = Sp. Pg. It. *provincialismo*; as *provincial*[1] + *-ism*.] 1. That which characterizes a province or a provincial person; a certain narrowness or localism of thought or interest, or rudeness of manners, characteristic of the inhabitants of a province as distinguished from the metropolis, or of the smaller cities and towns as distinguished from the larger; lack of polish or enlightenment.

But *provincialism* is relative, and where it has a flavor of its own, as in Scotland, it is often agreeable in proportion to its very intensity. *Lowell*, Study Windows, p. 94.

2. Specifically, a word or manner of speaking peculiar to a province; a local or dialectal term or expression.

The inestimable treasure which lies hidden in the ancient inscriptions might be of singular service, particularly in explaining the *provincialisms*.
H. Marsh, tr. of Michaelis (1793).

provincialist (prō-vin'shal-ist), *n.* [< *provincial*[1] + *-ist*.] 1. An inhabitant of a province; a provincial. *Imp. Dict.*—2. One who uses provincialisms. *Imp. Dict.*

provinciality (prō-vin-shi-al'i-ti), *n.* [< *provincial*[1] + *-i-ty*.] The character of being provincial.

That circumstance must have added greatly to the *provinciality* and . . . the unintelligibility of the poem.
T. Warton, Enquiry into the Authenticity of the Poems [attributed to Thomas Rowley, p. 46.

provincialize (prō-vin'shal-īz), *v. t.*; pret. and pp. *provincialized*, ppr. *provincializing*. [< *provincial*[1] + *-ize*.] To render provincial.

provincially (prō-vin'shal-i), *adv.* In a provincial manner.

provincialship (prō-vin'shal-ship), *n.* [< *provincial*[1] + *-ship*.] The post or dignity of a provincial. See *provincial*[1], *n.*, 2.

In the said generalship or *provincialship* he [Rich. Brynckley] succeeded Dr. Henry Standish.
Wood, Fasti Oxon., I. 38.

provinciate† (prō-vin'shi-āt), *v. t.* [< *province* (L. *provincia*) + *-ate*[2].] To convert into a province.

There was a design to *provinciate* the whole kingdom.
Howell, Vocall Forrest.

provine (prō-vīn'), *v. i.* [< F. *provigner*, lay a stock or branch of a vine, < *provin*, < L. *propago* (*-gin-*), the layer of a vine: see *prune*[2]. The F. form *provigner* simulates *vigne*, a vine.] To bury a stock or branch of a vine in the ground and bring up the end at a distance from the root, to form a bearing plant for the next season. This system is extensively practised in the viticulture of several regions of France.

proving (prö'ving), *n.* [Verbal n. of *prove*, *v.*] 1. Testing or trying in any way.—2. In *law*, probation; leading of proof.—**Action of proving the tenor**, in *Scots law*, an action, peculiar to the Court of Session, by which the terms of a deed which has been lost or destroyed may be proved.

proving-ground (prö′ving-ground), *n.* A ground or place used for firing proof charges in cannon, for testing powder, and for making ballistic experiments.

proving-hut (prö′ving-hut), *n.* Same as *proof-house. E. H. Knight.*

proving-press (prö′ving-pres), *n.* A press for testing the strength of iron girders, etc.

proving-pump (prö′ving-pump), *n.* A special form of force-pump combined with a pressure-gage for testing the strength of boilers, tubes, etc., by means of water-pressure.

Provins rose. The cabbage-rose. Also *Provincial rose.* See *provincial*[2].

provision (prǫ̈-vizh′ǫn), *n.* [‹ F. *provision* = Pr. *provisio* = Sp. *provision* = Pg. *provisão* = It. *provisione*, ‹ L. *provisio(n-)*, a foreseeing, foresight, purveying, ‹ *providere*, pp. *provisus*, foresee, provide: see *provide.*] 1†. Foreseeing; foresight.

> The direful spectacle of the wreck . . .
> I have with such *provision* in mine art
> So safely ordered. *Shak.*, Tempest, i. 2. 28.

2. The act of providing, or making previous preparation.

> Five days we do allot thee, for *provision*
> To shield thee from diseases of the world.
> *Shak.*, Lear, i. 1. 176.

3. A measure taken beforehand; something arranged or prepared in advance; a preparation; provident care.

> For great and horrible punishments be appointed for thieves, whereas, much rather, *provision* should have been made that there were some means whereby they might get their living. *Sir T. More*, Utopia (tr. by Robinson), i.

> To be ignorant of evils to come, and forgetful of evils past, is a merciful *provision* in nature. *Sir T. Browne*, Urn-burial, v.

> Marriage had always been her object; it was the only honourable *provision* for well-educated young women of small fortune. *Jane Austen*, Pride and Prejudice, xxii.

4. Accumulation of stores or materials beforehand; a store or stock provided.

> There is a store house in the Citadell, wherein is kept *provision* of corne, oyle, and other things. *Coryat*, Crudities, I. 124.

5. Specifically, a stock of food provided; hence, victuals; food; provender: usually in the plural.

> *Provisions* laid in large
> For man and beast. *Milton*, P. L., xi. 732.

> This first day I had not taken care to have any *provisions* brought, and desiring the man that was sent with me to bring me some bread, he went and brought me of such fare as they have, and I dined in the temple. *Pococke*, Description of the East, I. 90.

> I had furnished the stranger Turks with water and *provision* at my own expence, when crossing the desert. *Bruce*, Source of the Nile, I. 191.

6. In *law*, a stipulation; a rule provided; a distinct clause in an instrument or statute; a rule or principle to be referred to for guidance: as, the *provisions* of law; the *provisions* of the constitution. It is sometimes used of unwritten as well as of written laws and constitutions.

> Such persons would be within the general pardoning power, and also the special *provision* for pardon and amnesty contained in this act. *Lincoln*, in Raymond, p. 202.

> All the three [archdeacons] had, by the *provisions* of the cathedral statutes, dispensation from residence whilst they were away at the schools. *Stubbs*, Medieval and Modern Hist., p. 140.

7. *pl.* Certain early or medieval English statutes. See phrases below.—8. In *eccles. law*, promotion to office by an ecclesiastical superior; especially, appointment by the Pope to a see or benefice in advance of the next vacancy, setting aside the regular patron's right of nomination. Canonical provision consists of designation, collation or institution, and installation. In the thirteenth and fourteenth centuries the Pope made frequent provisions to bishoprics and livings in England, but these acts were strenuously resisted. See *Statute of Provisors*, under *provisor*.

> The weakness of Edward II. and the exigencies of the papacy emboldened Clement V. and his successors to apply to the episcopal sees the system of *provision* and reservation. *Stubbs*, Const. Hist., § 384.

Provisions made in the Exchequer. See *Statute of Rutland*, under *statute*.—**Provisions of Merton**, an English statute of 1235–6 (20 Hen. III.), so called because made at Merton, relating to bastardy, dower, common of pasture, appearance by attorney in local courts, etc. Also called *statute of Merton*.—**Provisions of Oxford**, in *Eng. hist.*, certain articles enacted by the Parliament at Oxford in 1258. See *Mad Parliament*, under *mad*[1].—**Provisions of the Barons, or Provisions of Westminster**, in *Eng. hist.*, certain ordinances issued by the barons in 1259, which provided for the reform of various abuses. =**Syn. 2.** *Providence, Prudence.* See *wisdom.*

provision (prǫ̈-vizh′ǫn), *v. t.* [‹ *provision*, *n.*] To provide with things necessary; especially, to supply with a store of food.

> It was also resolved to notify the Governor of South Carolina that he might expect an attempt would be made to *provision* the fort. *Lincoln*, in Raymond, p. 140.

provisional (prǫ̈-vizh′ǫn-al), *a.* [= F. *provisionnel* = Sp. Pg. *provisional* = It. *provisionale*; as *provision* + *-al.*] Provided for present need or for the occasion; temporarily established; temporary: as, a *provisional* regulation; a *provisional* treaty.

> It was . . . agreed to name a *provisional* council, or regency, who should carry on the government, and provide for the tranquillity of the kingdom. *Prescott*, Ferd. and Isa., ii. 19.

Provisional concession, in the parts of the United States acquired from Mexico, the first act of Mexican authorities in granting land. It was subject to further action, notably the definite location of the property, which was generally accomplished by the "extension of title" or "delivery of juridical possession."—**Provisional injunction.** Same as *ad interim injunction* (which see, under *injunction*).—**Provisional judgment**, a conclusion admitted for the time being, though affected with doubt which it is expected may be cleared up.—**Provisional remedy**, in *law*, a remedy, as arrest, attachment, temporary injunction, and receiver, intended to restrain the person of the debtor or property in question until judgment.

provisionally (prǫ̈-vizh′ǫn-al-i), *adv.* In a provisional manner; by way of provision; temporarily; for a present exigency.

> The abbot of St. Martin . . . was born, . . . was baptised, and declared a man *provisionally* [till time should show what he would prove]. *Menage*, quoted in Locke, Human Understanding, III. vi. [§ 26.

provisionary (prǫ̈-vizh′ǫn-ā-ri), *a.* [‹ ML. *provisionarius*, n., ‹ L. *provisio(n-)*, provision: see *provision.*] 1. Provident; making provision for the occasion. *Shaftesbury.*

> Public forms of prayer, . . . whose design is of universal extent, and *provisionary* for all public, probable, feared, or foreseen events. *Jer. Taylor*, Works (ed. 1835), II. 274.

2. Containing a provision; giving details of provisions.

> The preamble of this law, standing as it now stands, has the lie direct given to it by the *provisionary* part of the act. *Burke*, American Taxation.

3. Provisional; provided for the occasion; not permanent.

provision-car (prǫ̈-vizh′ǫn-kär), *n.* A railroad-car provided with refrigerating apparatus for the preservation of perishable products during transportation. Cold air caused to circulate over ice and over the articles to be kept cool is usually the means employed for cooling the substances. The interiors of the cars are kept tightly closed, and are protected from external heat by non-conducting materials.

provision-dealer (prǫ̈-vizh′ǫn-dē″lėr), *n.* Same as *provision-merchant.*

provisioner (prǫ̈-vizh′ǫn-ėr), *n.* One who furnishes provisions or supplies.

> Among other *provisioners* who come to your house in Venice are those ancient peasant-women who bring fresh milk in bottles. *Howells*, Venetian Life, vii.

provision-merchant (prǫ̈-vizh′ǫn-mėr″chant), *n.* A general dealer in articles of food, as hams, butter, cheese, and eggs.

proviso (prǫ̈-vī′zō), *n.* [So called from its being usually introduced in the original Latin wording by the word *proviso*, 'it being provided'; L., abl. sing. neut. of *provisus*, pp. of *providere*, provide: see *provide*. Cf. *provided.*] 1. A clause making what precedes conditional on what follows; a provision or article in a statute, contract, or other writing, by which a condition is introduced; a conditional stipulation that affects an agreement, law, grant, etc.

> He doth deny his prisoners,
> But with *proviso* and exception,
> That we at our own charge shall ransom straight
> His brother-in-law, the foolish Mortimer.
> *Shak.*, 1 Hen. IV., i. 3. 78.

> I was to be the young gentleman's governor, but with a *proviso* that he should always be permitted to govern himself. *Goldsmith*, Vicar, xx.

2. *Naut.*, a stern-fast or hawser carried to the shore, to steady a ship.—**Trial by proviso**, in *law*, a trial at the instance of the defendant in a case in which the plaintiff, after issue joined, does not proceed to trial, when by the practice of the court he ought to have done so. *Imp. Dict.*—**Wilmot proviso**, in *U. S. hist.*, an amendment to a bill which appropriated money for the purchase of territory from Mexico during the course of the Mexican war. This amendment was introduced in the House of Representatives in 1846 by Mr. Wilmot of Pennsylvania, and provided that slavery should never exist in any part of such territory. It played a prominent part in subsequent discussions.

provisor (prǫ̈-vī′zǫr), *n.* [‹ ME. *provisour*, ‹ OF. *provisour*, *proviseur*, F. *proviseur* = Sp. Pg. *provisor* = It. *provvisore*, ‹ L. *provisor*, a foreseer, a provider, ‹ *providere*, pp. *provisus*, provide: see *provide.*] 1†. One who provides; a purveyor; a provider.

> The chief *provisor* of our horse. *Ford.*

2. A person who has the right, gained by mandate of the Pope, to be in future presented to a benefice which is not vacant at the time of the grant. See *provide*, 6. In England, the appointment of provisors was restrained by statutes of Richard II. and Henry IV.

> Symonye and Cyuyle seiden and sworen
> That prestes and *prouisours* sholde prelates seruen.
> *Piers Plowman* (C), iii. 182.

> *Provisor* . . . here has the usual sense in which it is employed in our statutes, viz. one that sued to the Court of Rome for a provision. A provision meant the providing of a bishop or any other person with an ecclesiastical living by the pope before the death of the actual incumbent. *Piers Plowman* (ed. Skeat), II. 38, notes.

> Whoever disturbs any patron in the presentation to a living by virtue of any papal provision, such *provisor* shall pay fine and ransom to the king at his will, and be imprisoned till he renounces such provision. *Blackstone*, Com., IV. viii.

Statute of Provisors, an English statute of 1351, designed to prevent the Pope from exercising the right of provision in England. Subsequent statutes of 1390 and other years, in furtherance of the same design, are known by the same name.

provisorily (prǫ̈-vī′zǫr-i-li), *adv.* In a provisory manner; conditionally.

> This doctrine . . . can only, therefore, be admitted *provisorily*. *Sir W. Hamilton.*

provisorship† (prǫ̈-vī′zǫr-ship), *n.* [‹ *provisor* + *-ship.*] The office of provisor.

> A worthy fellow h' is; pray let me entreat for
> The *provisorship* of your horse.
> *Webster*, Duchess of Malfi, i. 2.

provisory (prǫ̈-vī′zǫr-i), *a.* [= F. *provisoire* = Sp. Pg. *provisorio* = It. *provvisorio*, ‹ L. as if **provisorius*, ‹ *providere*, provide (› *provisor*, a provider): see *provide*, *provisor.*] 1. Serving to provide for the time; temporary; provisional.

> A new omnipotent unknown of democracy was coming into being, in presence of which no Versailles Government either could or should, except in a *provisory* character, continue extant. *Carlyle*, French Rev., I. iv. 1.

2. Containing a proviso or condition; conditional.—**Provisory hoop.** See *hoop*[1].

provocable (prǫ̈-vō′kạ-bl), *a.* [‹ LL. *provocabilis*, excitable, ‹ L. *provocare*, call forth, excite: see *provoke.*] Same as *provokable.*

provocation (prov-ǫ̈-kā′shǫn), *n.* [‹ ME. *provocacion*, ‹ OF. *provocation*, *provocacion*, F. *provocation* = Sp. *provocacion* = Pg. *provocação* = It. *provocazione*, ‹ L. *provocatio(n-)*, a calling forth, a challenge, summoning, citation, ‹ *provocatus*, pp. of *provocare*, call forth, call out: see *provoke.*] 1. The act of provoking or exciting anger or vexation.

> The unjust *provocation* by a wife of her husband, in consequence of which she suffers from his ill-usage, will not entitle her to a divorce on the ground of cruelty. *Bouvier.*

2. Anything that excites anger; a cause of anger or resentment.

> By meanes of *prouocacion* on eyther party vsed, the Romaynes issued oute of the cytie and gaue batayl to the Brytons. *Fabyan*, Chron., I. lxiv.

> For when I had brought them into the land, . . . there they presented the *provocation* of their offering [i. e., to false gods]. Ezek. xx. 28.

> O the enormous crime
> Caused by no *provocation* in the world!
> *Browning*, Ring and Book, I. 199.

3†. An appeal to a court or judge.

> Nought with stondyng that I herde nevere of this matier no maner lykly ne credible evidence unto that I sey your lettre and the instrument, yet I made an appell and a procuracie, and also a *provocacion*, at London, longe biforn Cristemasse. *Paston Letters*, I. 25.

> A *provocation* is every act whereby the office of the judge or his assistance is asked: a *provocation* including both a judicial and an extrajudicial appeal. *Aylife*, Parergon.

4. Incitement; stimulus.

> I thought it but my duty to add some further spur of *provocation* to them that run well already. *John Robinson*, in New England's Memorial, p. 25.

> It is worth the expense of youthful days and costly hours if you learn only some words of an ancient language, which are raised out of the trivialness of the street to be perpetual suggestions and *provocations*. *Thoreau*, Walden, p. 110.

The provocation, the time of the Jews' wanderings in the wilderness, when they roused the anger of God by their sins.

> Harden not your hearts, as in *the provocation*, and as in the day of temptation in the wilderness, when your fathers tempted me. Ps. xcv. 8, 9.

provocative (prǫ̈-vok′ạ-tiv), *a.* and *n.* [= F. *provocatif* = Pr. *provocatiu* = Sp. Pg. It. *provocativo*, ‹ LL. *provocativus*, called forth, elicited, ‹ L. *provocare*, pp. *provocatus*, call forth, call out: see *provoke.*] I. *a.* Serving or tending to provoke, excite, or stimulate; exciting; apt to incense or enrage: as, *provocative* threats.

> Not to be hasty, rash, *provocative*, or upbraiding in our language. *Jer. Taylor*, Works (ed. 1835), I. 197.

> In the humorous line I am thought to have a very pretty way with me: and as for pathos, I am as *provocative* of tears as an onion. *Hawthorne*, Seven Gables, xii.

II. *n.* Anything that tends to excite appetite or passion; a stimulant.

> *Provocatives* to stir vp appetite
> To brutish lust & sensuall delight
> Must not be wanting.
> *Times' Whistle* (E. E. T. S.), p. 87.

On a superficial view it might be supposed that so eager-seeming a personality was unsuited to the publican's business; but in fact it was a great *provocative* to drinking. *George Eliot*, Felix Holt, xi.

provocativeness (prọ̄-vok'ạ-tiv-nes), *n.* The quality of being provocative or stimulating. *Bailey*, 1727.

provocatory† (prọ̄-vok'ạ-tọ̄-ri), *n.* [< L. *provocatorius*, pertaining to a challenge or challenger, < *provocator*, a challenger, an exciter, < *provocatus*, pp. of *provocare*, call forth or out: see *provoke*.] A challenge.

provokable (prọ̄-vō'kạ-bl), *a.* [< *provoke* + *-able*. Cf. *provocable*.] Capable of being provoked.

Irascible, and therefore *provokable*. *Cudworth*, Intellectual System, p. 188.

provoke (prọ̄-vōk'), *v.*; pret. and pp. *provoked*, ppr. *provoking*. [< ME. *provoken*, < OF. (and F.) *provoquer* = Sp. Pg. *provocar* = It. *provocare*, < L. *provocare*, call forth, call out, challenge, summon, appeal, incite, excite, provoke, < *pro*, forth, + *vocare*, call, summon, convoke: see *vocation*. Cf. *avoke, convoke, evoke, invoke, revoke*.] **I.** *trans.* **1**†. To call forth or out; challenge; summon.

This lenity, this long-forbearing and holding of his hand, *provoketh* us to repent and amend. *Latimer*, Sermon bef. Edw. VI., 1550.

> He, sitting me beside in that same shade,
> *Provoked* me to plaie some pleasant fit.
> *Spenser*, Colin Clout, l. 69.

> He now *provokes* the sea-gods from the shore.
> *Dryden*, Æneid, vi.

2. To stimulate to action; move; excite; arouse.

Let us consider one another to *provoke* unto love and to good works. Heb. x. 24.

> Beauty *provoketh* thieves sooner than gold.
> *Shak.*, As you Like it, i. 3. 112.

> Be ever near his watches, cheer his labours,
> And, where his hope stands fair, *provoke* his valour.
> *Fletcher*, Humorous Lieutenant, i. 1.

> Mine [shadow], spindling into longitude immense, . . .
> *Provokes* me to a smile. *Cowper*, Task, v. 14.

In solid and molten bodies a certain amplitude cannot be surpassed without the introduction of periods of vibration which *provoke* the sense of vision. *Tyndall*, Radiation, § 10.

3. To call forth; cause; occasion; instigate.

> Let my presumption not *provoke* thy wrath.
> *Shak.*, 1 Hen. VI., ii. 3. 70.

Cant is good to *provoke* common sense. *Emerson*, Fortunes of the Republic.

4. To excite to anger or passion; exasperate; irritate; enrage.

Charity . . . is not easily *provoked*. 1 Cor. xiii. 5.

> Take heed you laugh not at me;
> *Provoke* me not; take heed.
> *Fletcher*, Wildgoose Chase, iii. 1.

I am a little *provok'd* at you. I have something to be angry with you for. *N. Bailey*, tr. of Colloquies of Erasmus, I. 117.

=**Syn. 2** and **3.** To stir up, rouse, awake, induce, incite, impel, kindle.—**4.** *Irritate, Incense*, etc. (see *exasperate*), offend, anger, chafe, nettle, gall.

II. *intrans.* **1**†. To appeal.

> Even Arius and Pelagius durst *provoke*
> To what the centuries preceding spoke.
> *Dryden*, Religio Laici, l. 346.

2. To produce anger or irritation. Compare *provoking*.

provokement† (prọ̄-vōk'ment), *n.* [< *provoke* + *-ment*.] Provocation.

> Whose sharpe *provokement* them incenst so sore
> That both were bent t' avenge his usage base.
> *Spenser*, F. Q., IV. iv. 4.

provoker (prọ̄-vō'kėr), *n.* One who or that which provokes, excites, promotes, or stirs up; one who stirs up anger or other passion.

> In the mene whyle mine enemies still encrease;
> And my *provokers* hereby doo augmente,
> That without cause to hurt me do not cease.
> *Wyatt*, Ps. xxxviii.

Drink, sir, is a great *provoker* of three things, . . . nose-painting, sleep, and urine. *Shak.*, Macbeth, ii. 3. 27.

As common perturbers of the quyet people, and capytaines and *provokers* of trayterous ruffilngs. *Grafton*, Hen. VIII., an. 17.

As in all civil insurrections, the ringleader is looked on with a peculiar severity, so, in this case, the first *provoker* has double portion of the guilt. *Government of the Tongue.*

provoking (prọ̄-vō'king), *p. a.* Having the power or quality of exciting resentment; tending to stir up passion; irritating; vexatious: as, *provoking* words; *provoking* treatment.

> One, his equal in athletic frame,
> Or, more *provoking* still, of nobler name.
> *Cowper*, Hope, l. 192.

provokingly (prọ̄-vō'king-li), *adv.* In a provoking manner; so as to excite anger or annoyance.

This erudite but *provokingly* fragmentary edition of a true poet. *A. B. Grosart*, Biog. Sketch of Bp. John King, in King on Jonah, p. 5.

provost (prov'ọst), *n.* [< ME. *provost, provest*, partly < AS. *prāfost, prāfest, praūost, profost* (= OFries. *progost, provest* = MD. *proost*, D. *prost* = MLG. *provest, prōst* = OHG. *probast, probist, provost, probasto, prubesto*, MHG. *probest, provist, probst, brobest, brobst*, G. *probst* = Icel. *prōfastr* = Sw. *prost* = Dan. *provst*, provost, dean), and partly < OF. *provost, prevost*, F. *prévôt* = Pr. *prebost* = Sp. Pg. *preboste* = It. *prevosto, preposto*, < L. *præpositus*, a principal, president, chief, provost, pp. of *præponere*, put or set before, set over as chief, < *præ*, before, + *ponere*, set, place: see *ponent, posit*. Cf. *prepositor, prepostor*.] **1.** One who is appointed to superintend or preside over something; the chief or head of certain bodies. (*a*) The head of one of certain colleges (as of Oriel, Queen's, etc., in the university of Oxford, of King's College, Cambridge, Eton College, etc.): equivalent to *principal* in other colleges. (*b*) *Eccles.*, the chief dignitary of a cathedral or collegiate church; in monastic orders, a second in authority under an abbot or the head of a subordinate house. (*c*) In the Scotch burghs, the chief magistrate, corresponding to the English mayor. The chief magistrates of Edinburgh, Glasgow, Aberdeen, Perth, and Dundee are styled *lord provost*. The title *provost* was formerly given to the heads of corporations in England.

> My trusty *provost*, tried and tight,
> Stand forward for the Good Town's right.
> *Scott*, Carle, Now the King's Come.

(*d*) The keeper of a prison; a chief jailer.

The kyng commaunded hym and sayd: *Prouost*, get you men togyther well horsed, and pursewe that traytour syr Peter of Craon. *Berners*, tr. of Froissart's Chron., II. clxxv.

> The *provost* hath
> A warrant for his execution.
> *Shak.*, M. for M., i. 4. 73.

(*e*†) Formerly, one holding a position in the English schools of fence higher than that of scholar and lower than that of master.

2. A temporary prison in which the military police confine prisoners until they are disposed of.—**Provost marshal.** (*a*) In the army, an officer who acts as the head of police of any district, town, or camp, for the preservation of order, and to bring to punishment all offenders against military discipline. He is responsible for all prisoners confined on charges of a general nature under the articles of war, and in the field his power is summary. (*b*) In the navy, an officer who is charged with the safe-keeping of a prisoner, pending his trial by a court martial, and who is responsible for his production before the court whenever his presence is required. [Also pronounced prō-vọ̄ mär'shal, in partial imitation of the modern F. *prévôt*.]—**Provost sergeant**, a sergeant who has charge of the military police, and also, in the British service, of the custody of prisoners in the cells.

provostal†, *a.* [< OF. *prevostal*, F. *prévôtal*, < *prevost*, provost: see *provost*.] Pertaining to a provost. *Cotgrave.*

provoster†, *n.* [< *provost* + *-er*[1]; ult. a var. of *prepostor*.] Same as *provost*, 1 (*e*).

For of fence, almost in everye towne, there is not only maisters to teach it, with his *provosters*, ushers, scholars . . . *Ascham*, Toxophilus, i.

provostry (prov'ọst-ri), *n.* [< ME. *provostrye*, < OF. *prevosterie*, the office of a provost, < *prevost*, provost: see *provost*.] **1**†. Provostship; the office of provost or chief magistrate.

Certes the dignite of the *provostrye* of Rome was whylom a gret power. *Chaucer*, Boëthius, iii. prose 4.

2. A district or town under the jurisdiction of a provost, or an ecclesiastical or monastic foundation of which a provost is the head. [Scotch.]

The *Provostry* of Abernethie. *Spottiswoode*, Hist Scotland.

We likewise make, constitute and ordain, and perpetually establish the *Provostry* of the said Collegiate Church of the Holy Trinity near Edinburgh, upon the following Fruits and Appointments, as hereafter limited and modified. *Charter of Trin. Coll. Church*, 1574 (Maitland, [Hist. Edinburgh, p. 207).

provostship (prov'ọst-ship), *n.* [< *provost* + *-ship*.] The office of a provost.

What an enormity is this in a Christian realm, to serve in a civility, having the profit of a *provostship*, and a deanery, and a parsonage! *Latimer*, 2d Sermon bef. [Edw. VI., 1549.

prow[1] (prou), *n.* [< OF. *proue*, F. *proue* = Pr. Sp. Pg. *proa* = It. *prua*, < L. *prora*, < Gr. πρῷρα, the bow of a ship, < πρό, before. Cf. *prore*.] **1.** The fore part of a ship; the bow; the beak.

Prow of French Ship of War of about 1680.

With that they bid vs amaine English dogs, and came vpon our quarter starboard; and, giuing vs fiue cast pieces out of her *prowe*, they sought to lay vs aboord. *Hakluyt's Voyages*, III. 566.

> Turn thy curved *prow* ashore,
> And in our green isle rest forevermore.
> *Lowell*, The Sirens.

2. In *zoöl.*, a prora.

prow[2]† (prou), *n.* [< ME. *prow*, < OF. *prou*, *prod*, profit, advantage: origin uncertain. Cf. *prowess*.] Profit; advantage; benefit.

> All thynges is mayd, man, for thy *prowe*,
> All creatours shall to the bowe
> That here is mayd erthly. *York Plays*, p. 20.

> So ye lyve al in lest,
> Ye lovers, for the konnyngest of yow,
> That serveth most ententifliche and best,
> Hym tyt als often harme there of as *prowe*.
> *Chaucer*, Troilus, i. 333.

prow[2] (prou), *a.* [ME. **prow* (not found), < OF. *prou, prod, prude, pros, proz*, fem. *prode, prude*, good, excellent, brave, F. *preux* = Pr. *proz* = It. *prode*, brave, valiant, doughty. Cf. *prow*[2], *n.*, and *prude*.] Valiant. [Now rare and archaic.]

> They be two the *prowest* knights on grownd.
> *Spenser*, F. Q., II. iii. 15.

> From prime to vespers will I chant thy praise
> As *prowest* knight and truest lover.
> *Tennyson*, Pelleas and Ettarre.

prow[3]†, *n.* An obsolete form of *proa*.

prowess (prou'es), *n.* [Early mod. E. also *prowes, proues, prowse*; < ME. *prowess, prowesse*, < OF. *prouesse*, goodness, excellence, bravery, F. *prouesse* (= Pr. Sp. Pg. *proeza* = It. *prodezza*), bravery, < *prou*, good, excellent, brave: see *prow*[2].] **1**†. Excellence; virtue; goodness; integrity.

> Ful selde up riseth by his branches smale
> *Prowesse* of man, for God of his goodnesse
> Wol that of hym we clayme oure gentilesse.
> *Chaucer*, Wife of Bath's Tale, l. 273.

2. Bravery; valor; particularly, military bravery combined with skill; gallantry; daring.

And thei were noble knyghtes and hardy, and full of high *prowess*. *Merlin* (E. E. T. S.), i. 117.

> Your self his *prowesse* prov'd, and found him fiers and bold.
> *Spenser*, F. Q., II. viii. 13.

Proofs of *prowess* are above all things treasured by the savage. H. *Spencer*, Prin. of Sociol., § 286.

3†. A feat or deed of valor; a valiant act.

Kyng Codogan . . . remembrede alle the *prowesses* that he hadde sein hym do, and so sadly he sat in that thought that alle thei were troubled, and lefte theire mete. *Merlin* (E. E. T. S.), ii. 226.

prowessful† (prou'es-fůl), *a.* [< *prowess* + *-ful*.] Bold; fearless; daring. [Rare.]

> Nimrod usurps: his *prowes-full* Policy
> To gain himself the Goal of Soueraintу.
> *Sylvester*, tr. of Du Bartas's Weeks, ii., Babylon (Arg.).

prowl (proul), *v.* [Formerly also *proul*, var. of earlier *proll, prole*, < ME. *prollen, prolen*, search about; perhaps a contr. freq. form, < *proke*, in like sense: see *proke*, and cf. *prog*.] **I.** *trans.* **1.** To rove or wander over in a stealthy manner: as, to *prowl* the woods or the streets.

> He *prowls* each place, still in new colours deck'd.
> *Sir P. Sidney.*

2†. To collect by plunder.

By how many tricks did he *proll* money from all parts of Christendom? *Barrow*, Pope's Supremacy.

II. *intrans.* **1.** To rove or wander stealthily, as one in search of prey or plunder; search carefully, and in a quiet or secretive manner.

> Though ye *prolle* ay, ye shul it never fynde.
> *Chaucer*, Canon's Yeoman's Tale, l. 401.

> We travel sea and soil, we pry, we *prowl*,
> We progress, and we prog from pole to pole.
> *Quarles*, Emblems, ii. 2.

Wild and savage insurrection quitted the woods, and *prowled* about our streets in the name of reform. *Burke*, To a Noble Lord.

He walked to the railway station and *prowled* all about, with a forlorn sort of hope that she might have missed her train. *Mrs. Oliphant*, Poor Gentleman, xxxvi.

2†. To plunder; prey; foray.

prowl (proul), *n.* [< *prowl*, *v.*] The act of prowling; a roving as for prey: as, to be on the *prowl*. [Colloq.]

> The bar-girl that waits, the bailiff on the *prowl*.
> *Thackeray*, Four Georges, p. 216.

prowler (prou'lėr), *n.* One who prowls or roves, as for prey.

> Such run-about *prowlers*, by night and by day,
> See punished justly, for prowling away.
> *Tusser*, Husbandry, September.

Suttle *Prowlers*, Pastors in Name, but indeed Wolves. *Milton*, Hist. Eng., iii.

> On church-yards drear (inhuman to relate!)
> The disappointed *prowlers* fall, and dig
> The shrouded body from the grave.
> *Thomson*, Winter.

prowlery† (prou'lėr-i), *n.* [< *prowl* + *-ery.*] Prowling; pillage.

Thirty-seven monopolies, with other sharking *prowleries*, were decry'd in one proclamation. *Bp. Hacket*, Abp. Williams, i. 51. (*Davies.*)

prowlingly (prou'ling-li), *adv.* In a prowling manner.

prowor†, *n.* A Middle English form of *purveyor.*

My *prowor* and my plowman Piers shal ben on erthe,
And for to tulye treuthe a teme shal he haue.
Piers Plowman (B), xix. 255.

prox (proks), *n.* [Abbr. of *proxy.*] In Rhode Island, a list of candidates for election; a ticket or ballot containing such a list.

Such of the colony as could not attend the General Assembly had the right to send their votes for these officers by some other persons; hence the origin of the terms *prox*, and proxy votes, as applied to the present mode of voting for state officers in Rhode Island. *Staples*, Annals of Providence, Coll. R. I. Hist. Soc., V. 64.

prox. An abbreviation of *proximo.*

proxenet (prok'se-net), *n.* [< Gr. προξενητής, an agent or broker, < προξενεῖν, be a protector, patron, or agent, < πρόξενος, a protector, patron, public friend: see *proxenus.*] A negotiator; a go-between. [Rare.]

The common *proxenet* or contractor of all natural matches and marriages betwixt forms and matter. *Dr. H. More*, Immortal. of Soul, III. iii. 13.

proxenus (prok'se-nus), *n.*; pl. *proxeni* (-nī). [< Gr. πρόξενος, a public guest or friend, a patron, protector, < πρό, before, + ξένος, guest, friend.] In *Gr. antiq.*, a citizen who was appointed by a foreign state to represent its interests and to protect its travelers in his native country. The office corresponded closely to that of a modern consul.

The good understanding between Greek States must have been promoted by this habit of appealing to arbitration, and also by the institution of *proxeni*, whose office was in many respects analogous to that of a modern consul. *C. T. Newton*, Art and Archæol., p. 121.

proximad (prok'si-mad), *adv.* [< L. *proximus*, nearest (see *proxime*), + *-ad*3.] Toward the proximal part, or point of attachment or insertion.

For example, the shoulder is *proximad* of the elbow, but the elbow is *proximad* of the wrist. *Buck's Handbook of Med. Sciences*, VIII. 536.

proximal (prok'si-mal), *a.* and *n.* [= OF. *proximal*; < L. *proximus*, nearest: see *proxime.*] **I.** *a.* Proximate; nearest; next. In anatomy, zoölogy, and botany, noting that end of a bone, limb, or organ which is nearest the point of attachment or insertion: opposed to *distal* and *extremital.* Thus, of the two rows of carpal or tarsal bones, the one next to the arm or leg is *proximal*, and the other is *distal*; of the humerus or femur the head of the bone is *proximal*, and its condyles are *distal*. See cuts under *Artiodactyla* and *carpus.*

In the province of Ise one often sees a brace or bracket made out of an unhewed piece of timber, generally the *proximal* portion of some big branch. *Pop. Sci. Mo.*, XXVIII. 650.

II. *n.* In *zoöl.*, the comparatively fixed or basal extremity of a limb or of an organism.

proximally (prok'si-mal-i), *adv.* In *zoöl.*, toward the proximal end of a part or organ; proximad.

The quadrate bone loosely articulated with adjacent elements, and only *proximally*. *Amer. Nat.*, XXIII. 863.

proximate (prok'si-māt), *a.* [< LL. *proximatus*, pp. of *proximare*, draw near, approach, < L. *proximus*, nearest: see *proxime.* Cf. *approximate.*] Next; immediate; without the intervention of a third.

The general truth that pursuit of *proximate* satisfactions is, under one aspect, inferior to pursuit of ultimate satisfactions has led to the belief that *proximate* satisfactions must not be valued. *H. Spencer*, Data of Ethics, § 43.

The enormous consumption of petroleum and natural gas frequently raises the question as to the probability of the *proximate* exhaustion of the supply. *Science*, XIV. 228.

Internal proximate cause. See *internal.*—**Proximate analysis**, in *chem.*, the separation of a complex substance into its constituent compounds.—**Proximate cause**, that cause which immediately precedes and directly produces an effect, as distinguished from a *remote, mediate*, or *predisposing cause.*—**Proximate matter**, the matter of anything in the last degree of elaboration before that thing was formed.—**Proximate object**, immediate object; that object without the existence of which it would be logically impossible for the cognition to exist.—**Proximate principles**, organic compounds which are the constituents of more complex organizations, and exist ready formed in animals and vegetables, such as albumen, gelatin, and fat in the former, and sugar, gum, starch, and resins in the latter. Also called *organic principles.*

proximately (prok'si-māt-li), *adv.* In a proximate position, time, or relation; immediately; directly; by direct relation.

They know it immediately or *proximately* from their proper guides or other instructors, who in the last resort learn it from the ancients. *Waterland*, Works, V. 287.

Proximately, the source of the Thames and other rivers is to be found in springs; but ultimately it must be traced to rain. *Huxley*, Physiography, p. 38.

proxime† (prok'sim), *a.* [= Sp. *próximo* = Pg. *proximo* = It. *prossimo*, < L. *proximus*, nearest, superl. of *prope*, near.] Nearest; immediate; proximate.

The three terms [of the propositions] are called the remote matter of a syllogism; and the three propositions the *proxime* or immediate matter of it. *Watts*, Logic, iii. 1.

proximious† (prok-sim'i-us), *a.* An erroneous form of *proximous.* [Rare.]

This righteousness is the *proximious* cause operating to Salvation. *Dean Tucker.* (*Worcester.*)

proximity (prok-sim'i-ti), *n.* [< OF. *proximite*, F. *proximite* = Sp. *proximidad* = Pg. *proximidade* = It. *prossimità*, < L. *proximita(t-)s*, nearness, vicinity, < *proximus*, nearest: see *proxime.*] The state of being proximate; nearness in place, time, or relation.

We would muche rather haue remitted these iniuries in respect of *proximitie* of bloud to our nephieu, than we did heretofore yᵉ inuasion of his father. *Hall*, Hen. VIII., an. 34.

For the *proximity* of blood, he is the more stirred to have special eye and regard to our surety and good education in this our said minority. *Bp. Burnet*, Records, II. i. 6.

Always after a time came the hour . . . when he could endure *proximity* without oneness no longer, and would suddenly announce his departure. *George MacDonald*, What's Mine's Mine, vii.

=**Syn.** *Vicinity*, etc. (see *neighborhood*), adjacency.

proximo (prok'si-mō), *adv.* [L., abl. sing. (sc. *mense*, month) of *proximus*, nearest, next: see *proxime.*] In or of the next or coming month; noting a day of the coming month: as, the 1st *proximo.* Often abbreviated to *prox.*

proximocephalic (prok″si-mō-se-fal'ik or -sef'a-lik), *a.* [< L. *proximus*, nearest, + Gr. κεφαλή, head.] Nearest the head.

In numbering the individual elements [of the carpus] the first is the most *proximocephalic*, that is the scaphoid. *Buck's Handbook of Med. Sciences*, VIII. 536.

proximous† (prok'si-mus), *a.* [< L. *proximus*, nearest, next: see *proxime.*] Nearest.

proxy (prok'si), *n.*; pl. *proxies* (-siz). [Early mod. E. *prockesy*, < ME. *prokecye* (as if **procʹacy*), contr. of *procuracy*: see *procuracy.* Cf. *proctor*, similarly contracted from *procurator.*] **1.** The agency of a substitute; the office or authority of one who is deputed to act for another.

In the upper house they giue their assent and dissent each man seuerally and by himselfe, first for himselfe, and then for so many as he hath *proxie.* *Sir T. Smith*, Commonwealth of Eng., ii. 3.

We cannot be punished unto amendment by *proxy.* *Sir T. Browne*, Christ. Mor., ii. 11.

Upon my conscience, a pretty way this of working at second-hand! I wish myself could do a little by *proxy.* *Sheridan* (?), The Camp, i. 1.

The twelve archons met in a general assembly, sometimes in person, and sometimes by *proxy.* *J. Adams*, Works, IV. 500.

One of the reasons of non-attendance of the members of the House of Lords in former times was their special privilege of voting by *proxy*, which has now, however, fallen into disuse. *Encyc. Brit.*, VIII. 259.

2. One who is deputed to represent or act for another; a deputy.

The King replied That, since his Highness was resolved upon so sudden a Departure, he would please to leave a *Proxy* behind to finish the Marriage, and he would take it for a Favour if he would depute Him to personate him. *Howell*, Letters, I. iii. 23.

I am oblig'd to you, that you would make me your *Proxy* in this Affair. *Congreve*, Way of the World, iv. 2.

Another privilege is that every peer, by license obtained from the king, may make another lord of parliament his *proxy*, to vote for him in his absence. A privilege which a member of the other house can by no means have, as he is himself but a *proxy* for a multitude of other people. *Blackstone*, Com., I. ii.

Will not one
Of thine harmonious sisters keep in tune
Thy spheres, and as thy silver *proxy* shine?
Keats, Lamia, i. 267.

3. A document authorizing one person to act as substitute or deputy for another; a written authorization to exercise the powers and prerogatives of others.

A copy of the *proxy* sent to the Duke of Chevreuse to marry the queen in the name of our king, and another, of my lord duke's commission to bring her majesty into England, I shall have time enough to send you the next week. *Court and Times of Charles I.*, I. 27.

Under no circumstances should a *proxy* be executed in favor of an officer or director of a company that will enable him to vote upon it in approval of his own acts, or to perpetuate his own power. *N. A. Rev.*, CXXXIX. 538.

4. That which takes the place of something else; a substitute.

Talents are admirable when not made to stand *proxy* for virtues. *Mrs. H. More.*

In the Picture Gallery are quantities of portraits; but in general they are not only not so much as copies, but *proxies*—so totally unlike they are to the persons they pretend to represent. *Walpole*, Letters, II. 356.

5. *Eccles.*, same as *procuration*, 4.

The other fifty must go in a curate and visitation charges and poxes—*proxies*, I mean. *Swift*, Letter, June 28, 1725.

6. An election, or a day of election. [Connecticut.]

proxy (prok'si), *v. i.*; pret. and pp. *proxied*, ppr. *proxying.* [< *proxy, n.*] To vote or act by proxy, or by the agency of another.

Proxys (prok'sis), *n.* [NL. (Spinola, 1837).] A genus of heteropterous insects of the family *Pentatomidæ.* The species are few in number, and are confined to tropical and subtropical America. *P. punctulatus* is common in the southern United States, and is said to be both carnivorous and phytophagous.

Proxys punctulatus.

proxyship (prok'si-ship), *n.* [< *proxy* + *-ship.*] The office or agency of a proxy.

The two cases are so like: . . . the same correspondency and *proxiship* between these spirits and their images. *Brevint*, Saul and Samuel at Endor, p. 394.

proxy-wedded (prok'si-wed″ed), *a.* Wedded by proxy.

She to me
Was *proxy-wedded* with a bootless calf
At eight years old. *Tennyson*, Princess, i.

proÿmnion (prō-im'ni-on), *n.*; pl. *proÿmnia* (-ä). [NL., < Gr. προύμνιον, < πρό, before, + ὕμνος, hymn: see *hymn.*] In *anc. pros.*, a short colon preceding a system, strophe, or antistrophe, especially in a hymn. See *ephymnium, mesymnion, methymnion.*

proyn†, *v.* An obsolete spelling of *prune*2.

prozoösporange (prō-zō-ǫ-spō'ranj), *n.* [< Gr. πρό, before, + ζῷον, animal, + σπόρος, seed, + ἀγγεῖον, vessel.] In *bot.*, a stage in the reproduction of certain fungi which is to develop zoöspores. From the prozoösporange there grows out a thick, cylindrical, thin-walled process, into which all the protoplasm passes and within which it breaks up into zoöspores.

prozygapophysis (prō-zi-ga-pof'i-sis), *n.*; pl. *prozygapophyses* (-sēz). [NL., < Gr. πρό, before, + ζυγόν, yoke, + ἀπόφυσις, process.] Same as *prezygapophysis.* [Rare.]

A prominence is developed from each *prozygapophysis.* *Mivart*, Elem. Anat., p. 46.

Prozymite (proz'i-mīt), *n.* [< Gr. προζυμίτης, one who uses leavened bread, < προζύμη, leavened bread, < πρό, for, + ζύμη, leaven.] One who uses leavened bread in the eucharist: applied, especially in the eleventh century, by Latin controversialists to members of the Greek Church. See *Azymite.*

Pruce† (prös), *n.* [< OF. *Pruce*, < ML. *Prussia*, Prussia: see *Prussian.* Cf. *spruce.*] An obsolete form of *Prussia*: erroneously defined as "Prussian leather" by Johnson and Ash.

Ful ofte tyme he hadde the bord bygonne [sat at the head of the table]
Aboven alle naciouns in *Pruce.*
Chaucer (ed. Morris), Prol. to C. T., l. 53.

Some for defence would leathern bucklers use
Of folded hides, and others shields of *Pruce.*
Dryden, Pal. and Arc., iii. 31.

prud†, *a.* A Middle English form of *proud.*

prude (pröd), *n.* [< F. *prude*, OF. *prude, prode*, fem. of *prou, prod, prud*, good, excellent, brave: see *prow*2.] A woman who affects rigid correctness in conduct and thought; one who exhibits extreme propriety or coyness in behavior: occasionally applied also to a man.

Another customer happened to be a famous *prude*; her elbows were rivetted to her sides, and her whole person so ordered as to inform every body that she was afraid they should touch her. *Tatler*, No. 5.

Let the *prude* at the name or sight of man
Pretend to rail severely.
Sheridan (?), The Camp, i. 2.

With *prudes* for proctors, dowagers for deans,
And sweet girl-graduates in their golden hair.
Tennyson, Princess, Prol.

prudence (prö'dens), *n.* [< ME. *prudence, prudens*, < OF. (and F.) *prudence* = Pr. *prudenza* = Sp. Pg. *prudencia* = It. *prudenzia, prudenza*, < L. *prudentia*, a foreseeing, sagacity, prudence, < *pruden(t-)s*, foreseeing, prudent: see *prudent.* Cf. *providence* and *purveyance*, ult. doublets of *prudence.*] **1.** The quality of being prudent. (*a*) Practical wisdom; discretion; good judgment; sagacity.

Prudens, allas! oon of thyn eyen thre
Me lakked alwey, er that I com here:
On tyme ypassed wel remembred me,
And present tyme ek koude I wel ysee;
But future tyme, er I was in the snare,
Koude I not sen; that causeth now my care.
Chaucer, Troilus, v. 744.

He [Hesiod] was wonderfully grave, discreet, and frugal; he lived altogether in the country, and was probably for his great *prudence* the oracle of the whole neighbourhood.
Addison, On Virgil's Georgics.

Lafayette, who commanded the American forces in the province, appears to have shown skill and *prudence* in baffling the attempts of Cornwallis to bring on a general action.
Lecky, Eng. in 18th Cent., xiv.

(*b*) Regard for self-interest; worldly wisdom; policy.

Is it your *prudence* to be inraged with your best friends, for adventuring their lives to rescue you from your worst enemies?
N. Ward, Simple Cobler, p. 58.

All the virtues range themselves on the side of *prudence*, or the art of securing a present well-being.
Emerson, Essays, 1st ser., p. 218.

There is then a Duty of seeking one's own happiness, commonly known as the Duty of *Prudence*.
H. Sidgwick, Methods of Ethics, p. 304.

2. Knowledge; science. Compare *jurisprudence*.

In his [Mr. Webster's] profession of politics, nothing, I think, worthy of attention had escaped him; nothing of the ancient or modern *prudence*.
R. Choate, Addresses, p. 285.

= Syn. 1. *Discretion*, *Providence*, etc. (see *wisdom*), judiciousness, care, considerateness, caution, circumspection, judgment, wariness.

prudency† (prö'dẹn-si), *n.* [As *prudence* (see *-cy*).] Same as *prudence*.

O maruellous politicall, & princely *prudencie*, in time of peace to foresee and preuent . . . all possible malice!
Hakluyt's Voyages, I. 7.

prudent (prö'dẹnt), *a.* [< ME. *prudent*, < OF. *prudent*, F. *prudent* = Sp. Pg. It. *prudente*, < L. *pruden(t-)s*, foreseeing, prudent, contr. from *providen(t-)s*, foreseeing, provident: see *provident*.] 1. Thoughtful; judicious; sagacious; sensible.

A Polititian very *prudent*, and much inured with the priuat and publique affaires.
Puttenham, Arte of Eng. Poesie, p. 2.

But that he hath the gift of a coward to allay the gust he hath in quarrelling, 'tis thought among the *prudent* he would quickly have the gift of a grave.
Shak., T. N., i. 3. 34.

The age in which we live claims, and in some respects deserves, the praise of being active, *prudent*, and practical.
Gladstone, Might of Right, p. 297.

2. Careful of self-interest; provident; politic; worldly-wise.

The *prudent* man looketh well to his going.
Prov. xiv. 15.

So steers the *prudent* crane
Her annual voyage, borne on winds.
Milton, P. L., vii. 430.

3. Discreet; circumspect; decorous.

Friend Pope! be *prudent*, let your Muse take breath,
And never gallop Pegasus to death.
Pope, Imit. of Horace, I. i. 13.

To wish thee fairer is no need,
More *prudent*, or more sprightly.
Cowper, Poet's New-Year's Gift.

The *prudent* partner of his blood
Lean'd on him, faithful, gentle, good,
Wearing the rose of womanhood.
Tennyson, Two Voices.

4. Judicious; wise; prudential.

A Life which, if not fenc'd by *prudent* Fears
And Jealousies, its own self overthrows.
J. Beaumont, Psyche, iv. 6.

According as his conduct tended to self-conservation or the reverse it might be termed *prudent* or imprudent, but a wicked or righteous act would be impossible.
C. Mercier, Mind, X. 7.

= Syn. Careful, circumspect, etc. See *cautious*.

prudential (prọ̈-den'shạl), *a.* and *n.* [= Sp. Pg. *prudencial* = It. *prudenziale*, < L. *prudentia*, prudence: see *prudence*.] I. *a.* 1. Involving prudence; characterized or prescribed by prudence: as, *prudential* motives; *prudential* considerations.

My resentment . . . was by this time pretty much cooled, and restrained by *prudential* reasons so effectually that I never so much as thought of obtaining satisfaction for the injuries he had done me.
Smollett, Roderick Random, vii.

Considering things in a *prudential* light, perhaps I was mistaken.
Goldsmith, The Bee, No. 4.

His great excellence was his sound understanding and solid judgment in *prudential* matters, both in private and public affairs.
B. Franklin, Autobiog., p. 15.

There may be . . . a *prudential* genius, as well as a mathematical or a musical genius; the fact of intense persistence in idea of the characteristic impressions of the department being common to all.
A. Bain, Emotions and Will, p. 477.

2. Exercising prudence; hence, advisory; discretionary: as, a *prudential* committee (a committee having discretionary charge of various affairs of a society).—3. Instructed; scientific.

Such in kind . . . is the additional power you give to labor by improving the intellectual and *prudential* character which informs and guides it.
R. Choate, Addresses, p. 121.

II. *n.* That which demands the exercise of prudence; a matter for prudence.

Many stanzas in poetic measures contain rules relating to common *prudentials*, as well as to religion. *Watts*.

prudentialist (prọ̈-den'shạl-ist), *n.* [< *prudential* + *-ist*.] One who acts from or is governed by prudential motives. *Coleridge*. (*Imp. Dict.*)

prudentiality (prọ̈-den-shi-al'ị-ti), *n.* [< *prudential* + *-ity*.] The quality of being prudential, or characterized by prudence.

Being uncapable . . . rightly to judge the *prudentiality* of affairs, they onely gaze upon the visible success.
Sir T. Browne, Vulg. Err., i. 3.

prudentially (prọ̈-den'shạl-i), *adv.* In conformity with prudence; prudently.

I know not how any honest man can charge his conscience in *prudentially* coniuiving at such falsities.
Dr. H. More, Enthusiasm, ii. 47.

prudently (prö'dẹnt-li), *adv.* In a prudent manner; with prudence or discretion; judiciously.

Accordingly Virgil has *prudently* joined these two together, accounting him happy who knows the causes of things, and has conquered all his fears.
Bacon, Physical Fables, ii., Expl.

prudery (prö'dẹ-ri), *n.* [< F. *pruderie*, prudery, < *prude*, a prude: see *prude*.] The quality or character of being prudish; extreme propriety in behavior; affected coyness or modesty; primness.

Mrs. Lov. The world begins to see your *prudery*.
Mrs. Prim. *Prudery!* What! do they invent new words as well as new fashions? Ah! poor fantastick age, I pity thee.
Mrs. Centlivre, Bold Stroke for a Wife, ii.

What is *prudery?* 'Tis a beldam
Seen with wit and beauty seldom. *Pope*.

I would send to my friend Clara, but that I doubt her *prudery* would condemn me. *Sheridan*, The Duenna, i. 5.

A Frenchman, whatever be his talents, has no sort of *prudery* in showing them.
Sterne, Sentimental Journey, p. 45.

They thanked God in their hearts that they had a country to sell; they were determined to sell it at the highest figure; but reserve was decent and profitable, and *prudery* haggled for its price. *Westminster Rev.*, CXXVIII. 812.

prud'homme (prü-dom'), *n.* [F., < OF. *preudhom*, *prodhom*, *prodhoem*, *prodom*, *proddom*, *preudon*, *preudomme*, *preudome*, *prodomme*, etc., pl. *preudomes*, *preudeshomes*, *proudes homes*, etc., a good or discreet man, a skilful or expert man, < *preu*, *prud*, *prod*, etc., good, excellent (see *prow*²), + *home*, *homme*, man, < L. *homo*, man: see *Homo*. Cf. OF. *preudefemme*, a good or discreet woman.] A discreet man; specifically, in France, a member of a tribunal composed of masters and workmen, especially charged with the arbitration of trade disputes. Such tribunals existed from the time of the later middle ages, and have been reorganized in the present century. Such a council was constituted at Lyons in 1806, and several others have been created since.

The *prudhommes* were arrayed at every election, at every hustings, against the lesser folk.
W. J. Loftie, Hist. London, v.

prudish (prö'dish), *a.* [< *prude* + *-ish*¹.] 1. Having the character or manner of a prude; affecting extreme propriety of behavior; also, characteristic of a prude; prim.

I know you all expect, from seeing me,
Some formal lecture, spoke with *prudish* face.
Garrick, Prologue.

The moon, whether *prudish* or complaisant,
Has fled to her bower. *Keats*, Song.

2. Excessively formal or precise; rigid; stiff; severe.

There was a parlor in the house, a room
To make you shudder with its *prudish* gloom.
Lowell, Fitz Adam's Story.

A verse not fettered in its movements, or *prudish* in its expressions, but Protean in the forms it can assume, passing naturally from grave to gay.
Edinburgh Rev., CLXIII. 133.

prudishly (prö'dish-li), *adv.* In a prudish manner.

prudishness (prö'dish-nes), *n.* Same as *prudery*.

pruinate (prö'i-nāt), *a.* [< L. *pruina*, hoarfrost, rime, also snow, + *-ate*¹.] Same as *pruinose*.

pruinescence (prö-i-nes'ẹns), *n.* [< L. *pruina*, hoar-frost, + *-escence*.] In *zoöl.*, hoariness; the quality or condition of being pruinose.

pruinose (prö'i-nōs), *a.* [= It. *pruinoso*, < L. *pruinosus*, frosty, rimy, < *pruina*, hoar-frost.] Covered with a bloom or powder so as to appear as if frosted: said of some plant-surfaces dusted with a fine granular secretion.

pruinous (prö'i-nus), *a.* Same as *pruinose*.

prune¹ (prön), *n.* [< F. *prune* = Sp. Pg. *pruno* = It. *pruno*, < L. *prunum*, a plum, *prunus*, plum-tree, < Gr. προῦνον, a plum, προῦνος, plum-tree, earlier προῦμνον, plum, προύμνη, plum-tree: see *plum*¹.] 1. A plum; in recent usage (especially in the western United States), a plum suitable to be dried as a prune.

The damask *prune* rather bindeth than lowseth, and is more commodious vnto the stomake.
Sir T. Elyot, Castle of Health, ii. 27. (*Richardson*.)

2. The dried fruit of one of several varieties of the common plum-tree. The most highly reputed prunes are produced in the valley of the Loire, from the St. Julien and other varieties of plum, the very finest being known as *French plums*. There is a large and increasing production of prunes in California, the variety of plum chiefly grown for that purpose being identical or nearly so with that employed in France, while the myrobalan variety is the accepted grafting stock. Prunes are produced also in Spain and Portugal. German prunes are largely produced, though of second quality. Bosnia and Servia export large quantities. Prunes are stewed as a sauce, or otherwise prepared, and are valued for their nutritious, demulcent, and laxative properties.

I must have saffron to colour the warden pies; . . . four pound of *prunes*, and as many of raisins o' the sun.
Shak., W. T., iv. 3. 51.

Wild prune. See *Pappea*.

prune² (prön), *v.*; pret. and pp. *pruned*, ppr. *pruning*. [Early mod. E. also *proin*, *proyn*; also *preen* (prob. due in part to confusion with *preen*¹); < ME. *prunen*, *proinen*, *proynen*, trim or adorn oneself, prob. also in the sense of 'trim trees,' 'take a cutting from a vine,' < OF. *proignier*, *proognier*, *prougner*, *progner*, *preugner*, *prooingnier*, contr. of *provigner*, F. *provigner* (> E. *provine*), lay (a slip or cutting of a vine), layer, propagate, multiply, < *provin*, *provain*, F. *provin* = It. *propaggine*, a slip or cutting of a vine, a layer, sucker, < L. *propago* (*propagin-*), a layer, sucker: see *propago*, *propagate*. Cf. *provine*.] I. *trans.* 1. To lop superfluous twigs or branches from (a vine, bush, or tree); trim with a knife.

What Vine, if it be not *proyned*, bringeth foorth Grapes?
Lyly, Euphues, Anat. of Wit, p. 127.

But, poor old man, thou *prunest* a rotten tree,
That cannot so much as a blossom yield
In lieu of all thy pains and husbandry.
Shak., As you Like it, ii. 3. 63.

2. To lop off as superfluous or injurious; remove by cutting.

Do men *proine*
The straight young boughs that blush with thousand blossoms,
Because they may be rotten?
Fletcher (*and another*), Two Noble Kinsmen, iii. 6.

3. To clear from anything superfluous; remove what is superfluous or objectionable from.

Laws . . . are to be *pruned* and reformed from time to time. *Bacon*, Advancement of Learning, ii.

4. To dress or trim, as birds their feathers; preen: also used figuratively.

Ne dare she *proin* hir plumes againe,
But feares a second flight.
Gascoigne, Philomene (ed. Arber), p. 98.

His royal bird
Prunes the immortal wing, and cloys his beak.
Shak., Cymbeline, v. 4. 118.

Where I sit and *proyne* my wings
After flight. *B. Jonson*, Underwoods, v.

Neither doe I know anything wherein a man may more improue the reuenues of his learning, or make greater show with a little, decking and *pruning* himselfe with borrowed feathers, than in this matter of the Creation.
Purchas, Pilgrimage, p. 6.

II. *intrans.* 1. To lop off superfluous twigs or branches, as from a vine, bush, or tree.

A good husbandman is ever *proyning* and stirring in his vineyard; he ever findeth somewhat to do. *Bacon*.

With plenty where they waste, some others touch'd with want;
Here set, and there they sow; here *proin*, and there they plant. *Drayton*, Polyolbion, iii. 358.

2. To arrange or dress the feathers with the bill: said of birds, and also used figuratively.

And, efter this, the birdis everichone
Take up ane other sang full loud and clere;
We *proyne* and play without dout and dangere,
All clothit in a soyte full fresch and newe.
King's Quair, ii. 45. (*Jamieson*.)

A hawk *proines* when she fetches oil with her beak over her tail. *Markham*. (*Halliwell*.)

Every scribbling man
. . . grows a fop as fast as e'er he can,
Prunes up, and asks his oracle the glass,
If pink or purple best become his face.
Dryden, All for Love, Epil., l. 13.

Pruneæ (prö'nẹ-ē), *n. pl.* [NL. (Bentham and Hooker, 1865), < *Prunus* + *-eæ*.] A tribe of rosaceous plants, characterized by the drupaceous fruit, numerous stamens in a complete ring, and a single pistil with one subterminal style and two pendulous ovules. It includes 5 genera, of which *Prunus* is the type. (See also *Nuttallia*.) They are trees and shrubs, natives chiefly of northern temperate regions, including most of the drupes among the edible fruits, and sometimes known as the plum family, sometimes as the almond family. Also called *Drupaceæ* (A. P. de Candolle, 1805) and *Amygdaleæ* (Jussieu, 1789). See cuts under *almond-tree*, *Prunus*, *apricot*, and *corymb*.

prunell (prọ̈-nel'), *n.* Same as *prunella*².

prunelet (prön'let), *n.* [< *prune*[1] + dim. *-let.*] A liquor made from sloes or wild plums. *Simmonds.*

prunell (prö-nel'), *n.* [< F. *prunelle,* prunella: see *prunella*[4].] A milled cashmere. Compare *prunella*[4].

prunella[1]† (prö-nel'ä), *n.* [< ML. *prunella* (Kilian), a disorder of the throat, < MHG. *briune,* G. *bräune,* sore throat, quinsy, lit. browness, < *brun* (> ML. *brunus*), brown: see *brown.*] In *pathol.*: (*a*) Sore throat. (*b*) Thrush. (*c*) Angina pectoris.

prunella[2] (prö-nel'ä), *n.* [Also *prunello,* formerly *prunel, prunello* (= G. *prunelle,* formerly *braunelle* = Dan. *prunel*); < F. *prunelle, brunelle* = Sp. *brunela,* self-heal, = It. *prunella,* wall-wort, < ML. *prunella,* the plant self-heal, said to have been named from the disease prunella, which it was reputed to cure: see *prunella*[1].] 1†. A plant of the genus *Prunella.* Also *brunel.* —2. [*cap.*] [NL. (Linnæus, 1737; earlier *Brunella,* Tournefort, 1700).] A genus of plants, now known as *Brunella,* belonging to the order *Labiatæ,* tribe *Stachydeæ,* and subtribe *Scutellarieæ,* characterized by a two-lipped calyx with three lobes in the upper and two in the lower lip, anthers with two divaricate cells, and both style and filaments two-toothed at the apex. There are two or three species, widely dispersed throughout temperate regions and on mountains in the tropics. They are perennial herbs, partially erect from a decumbent base, with opposite and entire toothed or pinnatifid leaves, a flattened and truncate ten-nerved calyx, and purplish, blue, red, or white flowers, six in a verticillaster, and crowded in a dense terminal spike with broad rounded bracts between. *P.* (*Brunella*) *grandiflora* and other species are cultivated for the beauty of their flowers. *P.* (*Brunella*) *vulgaris,* the self-heal, widely distributed over the world (except Africa) and remarkable for the intense violet of its flower-buds, has also the old or provincial names *allheal, brunel, carpenter-grass, herb-carpenter, heart-of-the-earth, hookheal, hookweed, sicklewort.* (See *heal-all* and *carpenter's-herb,* and cut under *self-heal.*) The decoction of its leaves and stem is still in domestic use for healing wounds, for which it was once in the highest esteem.

prunella[3] (prö-nel'ä), *n.* [NL. *prunella,* < F. *prunelle,* the ball of the eye, lit. a plum, < ML. *prunellum,* a plum (*prunellus,* plum-tree), dim. of L. *prunum,* a plum: see *prune*[1].] A preparation of purified niter or potassium nitrate molded into cakes or balls. Also called *prunella salt* and *sal prunella.*

prunella[4] (prö-nel'ä), *n.* [Also *prunello;* = G. *prunell* = Dan. *prunel,* < F. *prunelle,* a stuff so called, supposed to be so named from its color, < *prunelle,* plum: see *prunella*[3].] A kind of lasting of which clergymen's gowns were once made, now rarely used except for the uppers of women's shoes. Also called *everlasting.*

> Worth makes the man, and want of it the fellow;
> The rest is all but leather or *prunella.*
> *Pope,* Essay on Man, iv. 204.

> The finest lawn makes common cause with any linen bands—the silken apron shrinks not from poor *prunella.*
> *D. Jerrold,* Men of Character, John Applejohn, viii.

> You know the sort of man—a linen duster for a coat, *prunella* shoes, always smiling and hopeful—a great deal about "Brethren." *Harper's Mag.,* LXXVII. 845.

Prunella[5] (prö-nel'ä), *n.* [NL.] In *ornith.,* a genus of birds: same as *Accentor.* *Vieillot,* 1816.

prunello[1] (prö-nel'ō), *n.* Same as *prunella*[1].

prunello[2] (prö-nel'ō), *n.* Same as *prunella*[2]

prunello[3] (prö-nel'ō), *n.* [< F. *prunelle,* a plum, = It. *prunello,* blackthorn: see *prunella*[3].] A prune of the finest grade, prepared from the green gage and the St. Catherine varieties of plum. The skin and stone are removed.

prune-purple (prön'pėr"pl), *n.* A maroon or dark and rather reddish purple color, like the stain of prunes. A color-disk mixture of artificial ultramarine 7 parts, intense red 8 parts, and black 85 parts gives a prune-purple.

pruner (prö'nėr), *n.* [Formerly also *proiner;* < *prune*[2] + *-er*[1].] One who prunes, or removes what is superfluous.

> His father was
> An honest *proiner* of our country vines.
> *Machin,* Dumb Knight, iii.

prune-tree (prön'trē), *n.* 1. A plum-tree. Specifically—2. *Prunus occidentalis,* an excellent timber-tree of the West Indies. See *Prunus.*

pruniferous (prö-nif'e-rus), *a.* [< L. *prunum,* a plum, + *ferre* = E. *bear*[1].] Bearing plums. *E. Phillips,* 1706.

pruniform (prö'ni-fôrm), *a.* [< L. *prunum,* a plum, + *forma,* form.] Having the appearance of a plum; plum-shaped. *Thomas,* Med. Dict.

pruning (prö'ning), *n.* [Verbal n. of *prune*[2], *v.*] 1. The act of trimming or lopping off what is superfluous; specifically, the act of cutting off branches or parts of trees and shrubs with a view to the strengthening of those that remain, or to the bringing of the tree or plant into a desired shape. Root-pruning is also practised with a spade or otherwise in order to control size, promote fruitfulness, or secure a growth of fibrous roots near the stem prior to transplanting. Compare *lopping,* 1, and *pollard,* 1. 2†. In *falconry,* what is cast off by a bird when it prunes itself; hence, refuse. *Beau. and Fl.*

pruning-chisel (prö'ning-chiz"el), *n.* A chisel used for pruning trees. It is often made with a concave cutting edge, as a safeguard against slipping.

pruning-hook (prö'ning-hůk), *n.* A knife with a hooked blade, used for pruning trees, vines, etc.

> They shall beat their swords into plowshares, and their spears into *pruninghooks.* Isa. ii. 4.

pruning-knife (prö'ning-nīf), *n.* A knife used for pruning; a cutting-tool with a curved blade for pruning; a pruning-hook.

pruning-saw (prö'ning-sâ), *n.* A saw similar to a table- or compass-saw, but with larger, thicker, and keener teeth. Some pruning-saws are made with double teeth and the back and cutting edge of the blade nearly parallel, but with the back only half as thick as the tooth-edge.

pruning-shears (prö'ning-shērz), *n. pl.* Shears for pruning shrubs. One form has one of the blades moving on a pivot, which works in an oblong opening instead of a circular one, by which means a draw-cut is produced similar to that of a knife, instead of the crushing cut produced by common shears.

Prunus (prö'nus), *n.* [NL. (Tournefort, 1700), < L. *prunus,* plum-tree: see *prune*[1].] A genus of rosaceous trees, the type of the tribe *Pruneæ.* It is characterized by a five-lobed calyx, five petals, commonly broad, large, and showy, numerous stamens, and a single ovary, becoming in fruit a fleshy drupe with a hard, smooth, or roughened bony stone, containing a single pendulous seed with two thick seed-leaves. There are about 96 species, mainly natives of north temperate regions, also numerous in tropical America, rare in tropical Asia, and elsewhere entirely lacking. They are usually

Wild Yellow or Red Plum (*Prunus Americana*).
1. Branch with flowers. 2. Branch with leaves and fruit.

small trees, sometimes shrubs, bearing alternate undivided leaves, usually finely toothed and folded lengthwise by the midrib (conduplicate) in the bud. The white, pink, or rose-colored flowers are in umbel-like clusters or racemes, or sometimes solitary. Many of the most valuable fruit-trees belong to this genus, including the peach, apricot, cherry, and plum. Many are used as febrifuges or for other medicinal properties. A gum exudes from their bark, especially in the cherry. Nearly all parts contain the elements of prussic acid, rendering the kernels and bark of some species poisonous if eaten freely, particularly the wilted leaves and young branches of some cherries. One fourth of the known species are American, of which 14 are found east and 6 west of the Rocky Mountains. Mexico is the home of a remarkable group of 6 species (section *Empectocladus,* Torrey), extending to Utah and California, with velvety fruit, smooth stone, and solitary or twin flowers appearing with the leaves, somewhat akin to the almond. The section or former genus *Amygdalus* has a downy fruit, rough and wrinkled stone, conduplicate vernation, and flowers preceding the leaves, and includes about 10 species, natives of warmer Europe and Asia, of which the type is *P. Amygdalus* (*A. communis*), the almond. (See *almond, almond-tree, Amygdalus,* and *amygdalin.*) Its variety *amara,* the bitter almond, is the source of a well-known essence. *P. Persica,* the peach, is now placed in this section also. (See *peach*[1], *nectarine, clingstone,* and *Persica.*) The apricot section, *Armeniaca* (Tournefort, 1700), is similar in its downy drupe and flowers preceding the leaves, but differs in its smooth stone and convolute vernation. It includes *P. Armeniaca,* the apricot; *P. Sibirica,* the Siberian apricot, valued for its earlier and ornamental flowers; *P. dasycarpa,* the black apricot, also Siberian; and *P. Brigantiaca* from Briançon in France, known as the *marmottes-oil tree,* from the oil expressed from its kernels and used like olive-oil. The section *Prunus* proper, including the plums of the Old World, has a short calyx, smooth fruit, usually with a bloom, a flattened stone, and solitary or twin flowers preceding or accompanying the leaves, which are convolute in the bud, as in *P. domestica,* the cultivated plum, and its probable original, *P. spinosa,* the sloe or blackthorn. (See *plum*[1].) The related *P. cocomilia* of Calabria is valued in Italy as a remedy for fever. The plums of the New World differ in their conduplicate vernation, fruit with little or no bloom, and in some species very turgid stones, approaching those of the cherry, as in *P. Americana,* the red or yellow plum of the Atlantic States (also called *Canada plum* and *horse-plum*); *P. maritima,* the beach-plum; *P. subcordata,* the wild plum of California; and *P. angustifolia* (*P. Chicasa*), the Chickasaw plum, or hog-plum. The cherry section, *Cerasus,* known by its smooth fruit without a bloom, conduplicate vernation, and solitary clustered or umbeled flowers preceding or accompanying the leaves, includes about 20 species, of which *P. Cerasus* is the parent of the red and many other garden cherries. (See *cherry*[1], *Cerasus, bigaroon,* and *morello.* For *P. avium,* also called *mazard* and *merry,* see *gean* and *hedgeberry;* also *kirsch-wasser, marasca, maraschino,* and *ratafia.* For *P. Mahaleb,* see *mahaleb,* and cut under *corymb.* For *P. Chamæcerasus,* see *ground-cherry.*) Two related species belong to the eastern United States, the dwarf *P. pumila,* or sand-cherry, and *P. Pennsylvanica,* the wild red cherry, pin-cherry, or pigeon-cherry. (See *pin-cherry.*) The section *Padus* contains cherries with racemed flowers following the leaves, and smaller, less edible fruit, as *P. Padus* of Europe, known as *bird-cherry,* and 4 American species, *P. Capuli* and *P. demissa,* the wild cherries, respectively, of Texas and the Rocky Mountains; *P. serotina,* the black cherry, rum-cherry, or cabinet-cherry (see *rum-cherry*); and *P. Virginiana,* the choke-cherry. Another section, *Laurocerasus,* suggests the true laurel in its evergreen leaves, and has racemed flowers with a short obconical calyx, a conduplicate vernation, and a small, smooth, inedible berry-like fruit. It includes about 30 species, both temperate and tropical, mainly American, as *P. occidentalis,* the West Indian laurel or prune-tree; the Californian *P. ilicifolia,* the islay, also called *holly-laurel;* and *P. Caroliniana,* the Carolina cherry-laurel, also known as *wild orange* and *wild peach.* (See *orange*[1] and *peach-brake.*) For the long-cultivated *P. Laurocerasus,* type of this section, also known as *cherry-bay, laurel-cherry,* and *date of Trebizond,* see *cherry-laurel,* also *laurel-water.* The Versailles laurel of gardens is a variety of this. *P. Lusitanica* is the Portugal laurel. A species similarly valued for the beauty of both its leaves and flowers is *P. Pseudocerasus,* the sakura of Japan, also called *Chinese cherry,* used in Japanese wood-engraving.

prurience (prö'ri-ens), *n.* [< *prurien(t)* + *-ce.*] Same as *pruriency.*

> There is a *prurience* in the speech of some,
> Wrath stays him, or else God would strike them dumb.
> *Cowper,* Conversation, l. 31.

pruriency (prö'ri-en-si), *n.* [As *prurience* (see *-cy*).] The character or state of being prurient. (*a*) An itching or longing after something; an eager desire or appetite.

> This selfsame vile *pruriency* for fresh adventure in all things has got . . . strongly into our habits and humours.
> *Sterne,* Tristram Shandy, i. 20.

> The bustling insignificance of Maximilian, cursed with an impotent *pruriency* for renown. *Macaulay,* Machiavelli.

(*b*) A tendency toward, or a habit of, lascivious thought; sensuality.

> Between prudery and *pruriency* in such matters there is a wide debatable ground, and it is not always easy to draw the line which separates what is permissible from what is not. *The American,* XVII. 110.

prurient (prö'ri-ent), *a.* [= Pg. *pruriente,* < L. *prurien(t-)s,* ppr. of *prurire,* itch.] 1. Itching; having an eager desire or longing for something.

> There was always in the generality of mankind a *prurient* desire and hankering after the knowledge of future events. *Culverwell,* Light of Nature. (Ord MS.)

> Love
> Should have some rest and pleasure in himself,
> Not ever be too curious for a boon,
> Too *prurient* for a proof against the grain
> Of him ye say ye love. *Tennyson,* Merlin and Vivien.

2. Inclined to lascivious thought; of an unclean habit of mind; sensual.

> The eye of the vain and *prurient* is darting from object to object of illicit attraction. *Isaac Taylor.*

pruriently (prö'ri-ent-li), *adv.* In a prurient manner; with a longing or lascivious desire.

pruriginous (prö-rij'i-nus), *a.* [= F. *prurigineux* = Sp. Pg. It. *pruriginoso,* < L. *pruriginosus,* having the itch, scabby, < *prurigo* (*-gin-*), an itching, < *prurire,* itch: see *prurient.*] Affected by prurigo; caused by or of the nature of prurigo.

> Their blood becoming *pruriginous,* and exalted by the salt and corrupt diet, as it often does, produces mange, scabs, and leprosies.
> *Greenhill,* Art of Embalming (1705), p. 164.

prurigo (prö-rī'gō), *n.* [L., an itching, < *prurire,* itch: see *prurient.*] An itching; specifically, a papular eruption of the skin in which the papules vary in size from a millet-seed to a small pea, are discrete, often in great numbers and close set, irregular in distribution, nearly of the color of the cuticle, and usually intolerably itchy.

pruritus (prö-rī'tus), *n.* [L., an itching, < *prurire,* itch: see *prurient.*] An itching; more specifically, a functional affection of the skin characterized by simple itching without structural change.

If there be a *pruritus*, or itch of talking, let it be in matters of religion. *Jer. Taylor*, Works (ed. 1835), I. 740.

Pruritus hiemalis, a form of pruritus in which the skin is dry and harsh, with smarting and burning sensations. It occurs chiefly in winter, and affects especially the inner sides of the thighs, the popliteal spaces, and the calves.

prusiano (prö-si-ä'nō), *n.* [Sp.: see *Prussian*.] The western nonpareil, *Passerina versicolor*, a beautiful finch of southwestern parts of the United States and Mexico, related to the nonpareil, lazuli-finch, and indigo-bird, of a Prussian-blue color varied with purplish tints.

Prussian (prush'an), *a.* and *n.* [< F. *Prussien* = Sp. *Prusiano* = Pg. It. *Prussiano*, < ML. **Prussianus*, < ML. *Prussia*, *Prusia*, *Prucia*, *Prutia*, *Borussia*, *Brussia*, etc., G. *Preussen*, etc., Prussia. Cf. *pruce*, *spruce*.] **I.** *a.* Of or pertaining to Prussia—(*a*) a former duchy near the southeastern angle of the Baltic, which, after its union with the Mark of Brandenburg, formed the nucleus of the Prussian monarchy; or, (*b*) a kingdom of northern Germany, now the chief state in the reconstituted German empire.—**Native Prussian blue.** Same as *blue ocher* (which see, under *ocher*).—**Prussian asparagus.** See *asparagus*.—**Prussian binding**, a kind of twilled binding having a silk face and a cotton back.—**Prussian blue, brown, carp, green,** etc. See the nouns.

II. *n.* 1. A native or an inhabitant of Prussia.—2. A language belonging to the Lettish division of the Slavo-Lettic branch of the Aryan family, and usually called *Old Prussian*. It was spoken in the region between the lower Vistula and the Niemen; it became extinct in the sixteenth or seventeenth century, being replaced largely by German.

Prussianize (prush'an-īz), *v. t.*; pret. and pp. *Prussianized*, ppr. *Prussianizing*. [< *Prussian* + *-ize*.] To render Prussian in character, institutions, laws, etc.

The first step taken by the Emperor Paul after his accession to the throne was to march his little *Prussianized* army from Gatchina to St. Petersburg.
Westminster Rev., CXXVIII. 580.

prussiate (prus'i-āt), *n.* [< *pruss(ic)* + *-i-ate*.] A common name for the ferrocyanides and ferricyanides: thus, potassium ferrocyanide is commonly called yellow prussiate of potash, potassium ferricyanide red prussiate of potash, etc.—**Prussiate cake**, in the manufacture of Prussian blue, the solid cake produced by calcining potassium carbonate, iron-borings, -filings, or -clippings, and animal matter, such as dried blood, horn, leather-clippings, etc. This cake, when broken up, is leached, and the liquor concentrated to crystallization. The crystals are purified by re-crystallization.

prussic (prus'ik), *a.* [< *Pruss-ian* (with ref. to *Prussian blue*) + *-ic*.] In *chem.*, related to Prussian blue, which was the first cyanogen compound isolated.—**Prussic acid**, the common name of *hydrocyanic acid*. See *hydrocyanic*.

prussine (prus'in), *n.* [< *pruss-ic* + *-ine*[2].] Cyanogen.

prut[1]†, *a.* A Middle English form of *proud*.

prut[2] (prut), *interj.* [ME. *prut*, *ptrot*, *ptrupt*, also *trut*, < OF. *trut*, an exclamation of contempt or indignation. Cf. *trut*, *tut*.] An exclamation of contempt or indignation.

And setteth hym ryȝt at the lefte,
And scyth *prut* for thy cursyng prest.
MS. Harl. 1701, f. 20. (*Halliwell.*)

Prutenic (prö-ten'ik), *a.* [< ML. *Prutenus*, *Prutinus*, *Pruxenus*, etc., a Prussian: see *Prussian*.] Prussian: noting certain planetary tables by Erasmus Reinhold in 1551, and so called by the author in allusion to the liberality of his patron, Albert, Duke of Prussia. They were the first application of the Copernican system.

I trust anon, by the help of an infallible guide, to perfect such *Prutenic* tables as shall mend the astronomy of our wide expositors. *Milton*, Divorce, i. 1. (*Davies.*)

prutten†, *v. i.* [< *prut*[1], obs. form of *proud*.] To be proud; hold up the head in pride or disdain. *Halliwell.* [Prov. Eng.]

pry[1] (prī), *v.*; pret. and pp. *pried*, ppr. *prying*. [< ME. *pryen*, *prien*, peep, peer; supposed to be a transposed form of *piren*, peer: see *peer*[1]. Transposition of this kind (of r in second syllable before a vowel to the first syllable before the first vowel) is peculiar; transposition as in *brid* to *bird* is in the other direction.] **I.** *intrans.* To look closely or with scrutinizing curiosity; hence, to search curiously or impertinently into any matter; peer; peep.

So ferde another clerk with astromye;
He walked in the feeldes, for to *prye*
Upon the sterres, what ther sholde bifalle,
Til he was in a marie put yfalle;
He saugh nat that. *Chaucer*, Miller's Tale, l. 272.

O eye of eyes,
Why *pry'st* thou through my window? leave thy peeping.
Shak., Lucrece, l. 1089.

Woe to the vassal who durst *pry*
Into Lord Marmion's privacy!
Scott, Marmion, iii. 15.

II. *trans.* To observe; note.

Pandarus, that gan ful faste *prye*
That al was wel. *Chaucer*, Troilus, ii. 1710.

pry[1] (prī), *n.*; pl. *pries* (prīz). [< *pry*[1], *v.*] 1. A peeping glance; peering; curious or narrow inspection. [Rare.]

From the sun and from the show'r
Haste we to you boxen bow'r,
Secluded from the teasing *pry*
Of Argus' curiosity. *C. Smart*, A Noon-piece.

They seldom meet the eye
Of the little loves that fly
Round about with eager *pry*.
Keats, To ——.

2. One who pries; a prier; an inquisitive, intrusive person (with allusion to Paul *Pry*, a fictitious name which, in its turn, was evidently suggested by this sense of the word).

We in our silence could hear and smile at the busy cackle of the "*Prys*" outside the door.
Harper's Mag., LXXVIII. 82.

pry[2] (prī), *n.*; pl. *pries* (prīz). [Appar. for *prize*[3], taken erroneously as a plural: see *prize*[3].] A large lever employed to raise or move heavy substances; a prize.

A dozen strong wooden poles served us as *pries* over many a lake and river bar of sand, gravel, and mud.
Science, III. 226.

pry[2] (prī), *v. t.*; pret. and pp. *pried*, ppr. *prying*. [< *pry*[2], *n.*] To raise or move by means of a pry; prize; bring into a desired position or condition by means of a pry: as, to *pry* a box open.

pryan (prī'an), *n.* [Corn. *pryan*, *prian*, clayey ground.] Clay. [Cornwall, Eng.]

pryany (prī'an-i), *a.* [< *pryan* + *-y*[1].] Containing pryan, or mixed with pryan.—**Pryany lode**, a lode in which the masses, bunches, or stones of ore occur mixed with more or less flucan and gossan. [Cornwall, Eng.]

pryde†, *n.* An obsolete spelling of *pride*[1].

pryer, *n.* See *prier*.

pryghte†. An obsolete preterit of *prick*. *Chaucer.*

prying (prī'ing), *p. a.* Peeping; peering; looking closely into anything; hence, inquisitive; curious.

Many have been *prying* and inquisitive into this matter, hoping to know something more particularly of it.
Waterland, Works, I. 227.

Prying eyes the fire-blast seldom lack.
William Morris, Earthly Paradise, III. 13.

=**Syn.** *Inquisitive*, etc. See *curious*.

pryingly (prī'ing-li), *adv.* In a prying manner; with close inspection or impertinent curiosity.

To those who peer *pryingly* into all corners the little fun of the place will suggest some memories of a very modern history. *E. A. Freeman*, Venice, p. 236.

pryk†, **pryke**†, *v.* Middle English spellings of *prick*.

pryme†, *a.* and *n.* A Middle English spelling of *prime*.

prymer†, *n.* An obsolete form of *primer*[1].

pryst, *n.* A Middle English spelling of *price*.

pryse†, *v. t.* An obsolete spelling of *prize*[2].

prytaneum (prit-a-nē'um), *n.*; pl. *prytanea* (-ä). [L., < Gr. πρυτανεῖον, the meeting-place or official house of the prytanes, < πρύτανις, a presiding magistrate: see *prytanis*.] A public hall in ancient Greek states and cities, housing and typifying the common ritual or official hearth of the community. That of Athens is especially famous. In it the city extended hospitality both to her honored citizens and to strangers. The prytanes, or presidents of the senate, were entertained in it at the public charge, together with those who, on account of personal or ancestral services, were entitled to this honor.

prytanis (prit'a-nis), *n.*; pl. *prytanes* (-nēz). [L., < Gr. πρύτανις, dial. πρότανις, a chief lord, prince, ruler, a presiding magistrate, president (see def.); prob. < πρό, before.] In ancient Greece: (*a*) A chief magistrate or priest in several states, as Rhodes, Lycia, and Miletus. (*b*) A member, during the term of presidency of his section, of one of the ten sections of fifty each into which the Senate of Five Hundred was divided at Athens. These sections constituted standing committees, every one of which, in rotation, represented the full senate in minor matters, and had charge of routine business. See the quotations.

The *prytanes* were by turns presidents, had the custody of the seal, and the keys of the treasury and citadel, for one day. *J. Adams*, Works, IV. 480.

The principal functions of the state itself grew out of the care which was bestowed on the tribal fire. The men who attended it in Hellas were called the *Prytanes*.
Encyc. Brit., IX. 229.

prytanize (prit'a-nīz), *v. i.*; pret. and pp. *prytanized*, ppr. *prytanizing*. [< *prytan-y* + *-ize*.] In *Gr. antiq.*, to exercise the prytany: said of a state or tribe, or of an individual legislator.

The order of the ten tribes in line of battle, beginning from the right wing, was conformable to their order in *prytanizing*, as drawn by lot for the year.
Grote, Hist. Greece, IV. 300.

prytany (prit'a-ni), *n.* [< Gr. πρυτανεία, a presidency, the term of office or authority of a prytanis, < πρύτανις, a presiding magistrate: see *prytanis*.] In ancient Greece, a presidency or direction; the office or dignity of a prytanis; especially, in ancient Athens, the period during which the presidency of the senate belonged to the prytanes of one section.

If Schömann's older view is correct, the presiding officer in the Senate and the Assembly must always belong to the tribe which holds the *prytany* at the time.
Trans. Amer. Philol. Ass., XVI. 169.

prythee†. An obsolete spelling of *prithee*.

P. S. An abbreviation (*a*) of *postscript*; (*b*) (*theat.*) of *prompt-side*.

psallenda (sa-len'dä), *n.*; pl. *psallendæ* (-dē). [L., fem. sing. gerund. of *psallere*, play on a stringed instrument, LL. sing the Psalms: see *psalm*.] In the Ambrosian office, one of two proper antiphons sung at lauds and vespers on Sundays and certain saints' days.

psalloid (sal'oid), *a.* [< NL. *psalloides*, irreg. < Gr. ψάλλειν, play on a stringed instrument, + εἶδος, form.] Lyriform; like the lyra, or corpus psalloides, of the brain.

psalm (säm), *n.* [< ME. *psalme*, *psaume*, *salm*; partly (*a*) < AS. *sealm* = D. *psalm* = MLG. *salme* = OHG. *psalmo*, *salmo*, *salm*, MHG. *psalme*, *psalm*, *salme*, *salm*, G. *psalm* = Sw. *psalm* = Dan. *psalme*; partly (*b*) < OF. *psaume*, F. *psaume* = Pr. *psalm*, *psalme*, *salme* = Sp. It. *salmo* = Pg. *salmo*, *psalmo*; < LL. *psalmus* = Goth. *psalma*, *psalmō*, < Gr. ψαλμός, a song sung to the harp, a song, psalm, the sound of the cithara or harp, a pulling or twitching with the fingers (cf. ψάλμα, a tune played on a cithara or harp, > LL. *psalma*, a psalm), < ψάλλειν, touch, twitch, play on a stringed instrument (> L. *psallere*, play on a stringed instrument, LL. sing the Psalms). Cf. *psalter*, *psaltery*.] 1. A sacred poem or song, especially one in which expressions of praise and thanksgiving are prominent: usually restricted either to those contained in the Book of Psalms, or to the versifications of these composed for the use of churches, as the *Psalms* of Tate and Brady, of Watts, etc.

"This Dragon of Dissait, that thou derfly hath fourmet:"
So sethe in the sauter the *Salme* to the end.
Destruction of Troy (E. E. T. S.), l. 4436.

Euen the name *Psalmes* will speake for mee, which, being interpreted, is nothing but songes.
Sir P. Sidney, Apol. for Poetrie.

They do no more adhere and keep place together than the Hundredth *Psalm* to the tune of "Green Sleeves."
Shak., M. W. of W., ii. 1. 63.

The great organ . . . rolling thro' the court
A long melodious thunder to the sound
Of solemn *psalms*, and silver litanies.
Tennyson, Princess, ii.

2. *pl.* [*cap.*] A book of the Old Testament which follows Job and precedes Proverbs, and contains 150 psalms and hymns; more fully, the Book of Psalms. The authorship of a large number of the psalms is ascribed traditionally to David. Many of them, however, are supposed to date from the time of the exile or later.

3. *pl.* Among the ancient Jews, the Hagiographa: so called because the Psalms constitute the first book in it. Luke xxiv. 44.—**Abecedarian, gradual, penitential,** etc., **psalms.** See the adjectives.—**Psalms of commendation.** See *commendation*, 5.—**Psalms of degrees.** Same as *gradual psalms* (see *gradual*).

psalm (säm), *v.* [ME. **psalmen*, *salmen*; < *psalm*, *n.*] **I.**† *intrans.* To sing psalms.

II. *trans.* To celebrate in psalms; hymn.

That we her Subjects, whom He blesseth by her,
Psalming His praise, may sound the same the higher.
Sylvester, tr. of Du Bartas's Weeks, ii., The Handy-Crafts.

psalm-book (säm'bůk), *n.* [< ME. **salmbok*, *salmboc*, < AS. *sealmbōc* (= D. *psalmboek* = MLG. *salmbōk* = G. *psalmbuch* = Sw. *psalmbok* = Dan. *psalmebog*), < *sealm*, psalm, + *bōc*, book: see *psalm* and *book*.] 1. A collection of metrical translations of the Psalms prepared for liturgical use; a Psalter.—2. Any collection of sacred poems or songs for liturgical use, with or without music.

psalmist (sä'mist or sal'mist), *n.* [= F. *psalmiste* = Pr. *psalmista*, *salmista* = Sp. It. *salmista*, < LL. *psalmista*, < LGr. *ψαλμιστής, a composer or singer of psalms, < Gr. ψαλμός, a psalm: see *psalm*.] 1. A writer or composer of psalms; especially, one of the authors of the psalms in the Bible; specifically, David.

David, . . . the anointed of the God of Jacob, and the sweet *psalmist* of Israel. 2 Sam. xxiii. 1.

She tun'd to pious notes the *psalmist's* lyre.
J. Hughes, Divine Poetry.

2. In *early Christian music*, a cantor or other official of the minor clergy charged with the singing of church music.

psalmister (sä'mis-tėr or sal'mis-tėr), *n.* [< *psalmist* + *-er*1.] Same as *psalmist*, 2.

psalmistry (sä'mis-tri or sal'mis-tri), *n.* [< *psalmist* + *-ry.*] The art, act, or practice of singing psalms; psalmody.

He who, from such a kind of *psalmistry*, or any other verbal devotion, . . . can be persuaded of a zeal and true righteousness in the person, hath much yet to learn. *Milton*, Works, I. 408. (*Jodrell.*)

psalm-melodicon (säm'me-lod″i-kon), *n.* A musical instrument of the wood wind group, having several finger-holes and keys and a compass of four octaves, and so constructed that from four to six tones could be produced at once. It was invented by S. Weinrich in 1828, and improved by L. Schmidt in 1832. Also called *apollolyra*.

psalmodic (sal-mod'ik), *a.* [< *psalmod-y* + *-ic.*] Belonging or relating to psalmody.

That glorious body of *psalmodic* literature or hymnology which constitutes the Book of Psalms. *J. A. Alexander*, On the Psalms, II. 294.

psalmodical (sal-mod'i-kal), *a.* [< *psalmodic* + *-al.*] Same as *psalmodic*.

If Queen Elizabeth patronized cathedral musick exclusively, she did not interdict *psalmodical*. *W. Mason*, Church Music, p. 170.

psalmodist (sal'mǫ-dist or sä'mǫ-dist), *n.* [< *psalmod-y* + *-ist.*] One who composes or sings psalms or sacred songs.

It will be thought as fit for our lips and hearts as for our ears to turn *psalmodists*. *Hammond*, On the Psalms, Pref. (*Latham.*)

Prophet in some parts of the Scripture seems to imply little more than a mere poet, or *psalmodist*, who sung extempore verses to the sound of an instrument. *Dr. Burney*, Hist. Music, I. 230.

psalmodize (sal'mǫ-dīz or sä'mǫ-dīz), *v. i.*; pret. and pp. *psalmodized*, ppr. *psalmodizing*. [< *psalmod-y* + *-ize.*] To practise psalmody.

In short, the bird perform'd his part
In all the *psalmodising* art.
J. G. Cooper, Ver-Vert, ii.

psalmody (sal'mǫ-di or sä'mǫ-di), *n.* [< ME. *psalmody*, < OF. (and F.) *psalmodie* = Pr. *psalmodia* = Sp. *salmodia* = It. *salmodia* = Pg. *psalmodia*, < ML. *psalmodia*, < Gr. ψαλμῳδία, a singing to the harp, < (MGr.) ψαλμῳδεῖν, sing to the harp, < ψαλμός, a song (see *psalm*), + ἀείδειν, ᾄδειν, sing: see *ode*1.] 1. The art, act, or practice of singing psalms or hymns as a part of worship.

As touching that is laide to our charge in *psalmodies* and songs, wherewith our slaunderers do fray the simple, I haue thus to say. *Foxe*, Martyrs, p. 1921, an. 1588.

Calvin, who had certainly less music in his soul than the other [Luther], rejected both vocal and instrumental harmony, and admitted only unisonous *psalmody*. *W. Mason*, Church Music, iii.

He was also an expert in *psalmody*, having in his youth been the pride of the village singing-school. *H. B. Stowe*, Oldtown, p. 34.

2. Psalms collectively, especially in the form of metrical versions prepared for liturgical use.

psalmody (sal'mǫ-di or sä'mǫ-di), *v. t.*; pret. and pp. *psalmodied*, ppr. *psalmodying*. [< *psalmody*, *n.*] To hymn; celebrate in psalms.

It is an event which can be looked on; which may still be execrated, still be celebrated and *psalmodied*; but which it were better now to begin understanding. *Carlyle*, Misc., iv. 119. (*Davies.*)

psalmograph† (sal'mǫ-gräf), *n.* [< LL. *psalmographus*, < Gr. ψαλμογράφος, a psalm-writer, < ψαλμός, a psalm, + γράφειν, write.] Same as *psalmographer*.

That great King-Prophet, Poet, Conqueror,
Sweet *Psalmograph*.
Sylvester, tr. of Du Bartas's Triumph of Faith, iii. 10.

This, the most sweet and sacred *psalmograph*. *Middleton*, World Tost at Tennis.

psalmographer (sal-mog'ra-fėr), *n.* [< *psalmograph* + *-er*1.] A writer of psalms or sacred songs.

Therefore our *Psalmographer*, ver. 15 [Ps. cxviii.], having shewed that "the voice of rejoicing and salvation is in the tabernacles of the righteous," he adds, "The right hand of the Lord hath done valiantly." *Rev. T. Adams*, Works, I. 119.

psalmographist (sal-mog'ra-fist), *n.* [< *psalmograph* + *-ist.*] Same as *psalmographer*.

psalmography (sal-mog'ra-fi), *n.* [< Gr. ψαλμός, song, + -γραφία, < γράφειν, write. Cf. *psalmograph*.] The art or practice of writing psalms or sacred songs.

psalm-singer (säm'sing″ėr), *n.* One who sings psalms; especially, one who holds that the congregational singing of psalms is a necessary part of all church worship.

psalm-singing (säm'sing″ing), *n.* The act or practice of singing psalms or similar sacred poems as a part of church worship.

psalm-tone (säm'tōn), *n.* In *medieval music*, a melody or tone to which a portion of the Psalter was habitually sung.

psaloid (sä'loid), *a.* [< Gr. ψαλίς, an arch, vault, + εἶδος, form.] Resembling an arch. *Thomas*, Med. Dict.

psalter (sâl'tėr), *n.* [< ME. *psauter*, *psautere*, *sauter*, *sautre*, < OF. *psaultier*, *sautier*, F. *psautier* = Pr. *psalteri*, *salteri*, *sauteri* = Sp. *salterio* = Pg. *psalterio* = It. *saltero*, *salterio*, < L. *psalterium*, a song sung to the psaltery, LL. the psalms of David, < Gr. ψαλτήριον, a psaltery, LGr. the Psalter, Book of Psalms: see *psaltery*.] 1. [*cap.*] The Book of Psalms, considered as a separate book of the Old Testament: usually restricted to those versions of or compends from it which are arranged especially for the services of the church, such as the version of the Psalms in the Book of Common Prayer. The translation of the Psalter in the Book of Common Prayer is not that of the authorized version, but that of the earlier version of Cranmer's Bible.

The prophete his payn eet in penaunce and wepyng;
As the *psauter* vs seith, so dude moni othere.
Piers Plowman (A), viii. 107.

As David scythe in the *Psautere*, Quoniam persequebatur unus mille, & duo fugarent decem milia. *Mandeville*, Travels, p. 261.

2. In *liturgics*, that portion of the Psalms appointed for a given day or service.

And [let] each brother of common condition [sing] two *psalters* of psalms, one for the living and one for the dead. Quoted in *English Gilds* (E. E. T. S.), Int., p. xviii.

3. In the *Rom. Cath. Ch.*: (*a*) A series of devout utterances or aspirations, 150 in number, in honor of certain mysteries, as the sufferings of Christ.

Euery brother and sister shal payen, of ye commoun catel, a peny to a *sauter* for ye dedes soule. *English Gilds* (E. E. T. S.), p. 26.

(*b*) A large chaplet or rosary, consisting of 150 beads, corresponding to the number of the Psalms.

psalterial (sal-tē'ri-al), *a.* [< *psalterium* + *-al.*] In *zoöl.*, of or pertaining to the psalterium: as, the *psalterial* aperture of the reticulum; the *psalterial* laminæ.

psalterian (sal-tē'ri-an), *a.* [< *psaltery* + *-an.*] Pertaining to a psaltery; resembling the music of a psaltery; musical.

Then once again the charmed God began
An oath, and through the serpent's ears it ran
Warm, tremulous, devout, *psalterian*.
Keats, Lamia, i.

psalterion (sal-tē'ri-on), *n.*; pl. *psalteria* (-ä). [< Gr. ψαλτήριον: see *psalterium*.] Same as *psaltery*, 1.

He was driven, for revenge and his own defence, to answer with great and stout words, saying that indeed he had no skill to tune a harp, nor a viol, nor to play on a *psalterion*. *North*, tr. of Plutarch, p. 96.

psalterium (sal-tē'ri-um), *n.*; pl. *psalteria* (-ä). [L.: see *psalter*, *psaltery*.] 1. Same as *psalter*.—2. Same as *psaltery*, 1.

The *psalterium* was a kind of lyre of an oblong square shape; . . . it was played with a rather large plectrum. *South Kensington Art Handbook*, No. v., p. 35.

3. In *zoöl.*, the third division of the stomach of a typical ruminant, between the reticulum or honeycomb and the abomasum; the omasum: also called *manyplies*, from the numerous folds of mucous membrane which nearly fill the interior. It is reduced to a mere tube, without folds, in the less typical ruminants, as the *Tragulidæ*. See cut under *ruminant*.

When this portion of the stomach is slit open longitudinally, the lamellæ fall apart like the leaves of a book, whence it has received the fanciful name of the *Psalterium* from anatomists, while butchers give it that of Manyplies. *Huxley*, Anat. Vert., p. 323.

4. In *anat.*: (*a*) The lyra of the fornix. (*b*) The pectunculus.

Psaltery of the 12th century.

psaltery (sâl'tėr-i), *n.*; pl. *psalteries* (-iz). [< ME. *psalterie*, *sautrie*, < OF. *psalterie*, < L. *psalterium*, psaltery, also a psalter, < Gr. ψαλτήριον, a stringed instrument, a psaltery, also the Psalms of David, the Psalter, < ψάλλειν, touch, twitch, play on a stringed instrument: see *psalm*.] 1. A musical instrument of the zither group, having several or many strings variously tuned, which are sounded by the finger with or without the aid of a plectrum. Its use has been extensive, beginning in Biblical times, and continuing to the seventeenth century. It is similar to the dulcimer, except that its tone is produced by twitching or picking instead of by striking. It differs from the harp proper in having a sound-board behind and parallel with the strings. In some cases two or three strings tuned in unison were provided for a single tone.

And al above ther lay a gay *sautrie*,
On which he made a nyghtes melodie,
So swetely that al the chambre rong.
Chaucer, Miller's Tale, l. 27.

Praise the Lord with harp; sing to him with the *psaltery*, and an instrument of ten strings. Ps. xxxiii. 2.

Deep roh'd in white, he made the Levites stand
With cymbals, harps, and *psalteries* in their hand.
Parnell, Gift of Poetry.

2. Same as *psalter*.

She knew all the *Psaltery* by heart, ay, and a great part of the Testament besides. *Lamb*, Dream-Children. (*Davies.*)

psaltress (sâl'tres), *n.* [< Gr. *ψαλτρίς, equiv. to ψάλτης, a harper (< ψάλλειν, play on a stringed instrument), + *-ess.*] A woman who plays upon the psaltery.

Earth is a wintry clod;
But spring-wind, like a dancing *psaltress*, passes
Over its breast to waken it.
Browning, Paracelsus.

Psaltria (sal'tri-ä), *n.* [NL. (Temminck, 1832), < L. *psaltria*, < Gr. ψάλτρια, fem. of ψαλτής, a harper: see *psaltress*, *Psaltriparus*.] A genus of *Paridæ*, the type of which is *P. exilis*, a very small Javan titmouse: extended to various American species. See *Psaltriparus*.

Psaltriparus (sal-trip'a-rus), *n.* [NL. (Bonaparte, 1851), < Gr. ψάλτρια, fem. of *ψαλτήρ, a harper, + L. *parus*, a titmouse.] An American genus of *Paridæ*, containing several species of diminutive tits, with long tails, building very large pensile nests and laying pure-white eggs; the bush-tits. *P. melanotis*, *P. minimus*, and *P. plumbeus* are three species found in western parts of the United States, respectively known as the *black-eared*, *least*, and *plumbeous bush-tit*. See cut under *bush-tit*.

Psamma† (sam'ä), *n.* [NL. (P. de Beauvois, 1812), < Gr. ψάμμος, sand.] A former genus of grasses: same as *Ammophila*, 1.

Psamminæ (sa-mī'nē), *n. pl.* [NL., < Gr. ψάμμος, sand, + *-inæ.*] A subfamily of *Spongillidæ*, without flesh-spicules, the skeleton consisting of foreign bodies cemented by indistinct spongin.

psammismus (sa-mis'mus), *n.* [NL., < Gr. ψάμμος, sand. Cf. Gr. ψαμμισμός, a burying in the sand.] In *pathol.*, the passage of gravel in the urine.

psammite (sam'īt), *n.* [< F. *psammite*, < Gr. ψαμμίτης, of sand, sandy, < ψάμμος, sand.] Sandstone; gritstone. [Little used by American geologists.]

psammitic (sa-mit'ik), *a.* [< *psammite* + *-ic.*] In *geol.*, having a structure like that of sandstone made up of rounded grains of sand. If the grains are sharp, the structure is called *gritty*, and the rock a *grit* or *gritstone*.

psammocarcinoma (sam-ǫ-kär-si-nō'mä), *n.* [NL., < Gr. ψάμμος, sand, + NL. *carcinoma*.] A carcinoma with a calcareous deposit.

psammoma (sa-mō'mä), *n.* [NL., < Gr. ψάμμος, sand, + *-oma.*] A tumor containing abundant calcareous deposit, usually growing from the membranes of the brain, and most frequently a myxoma or fibroma.

Psammonemata (sam-ǫ-nē'ma-tä), *n. pl.* [NL., < Gr. ψάμμος, sand, + νῆμα (νηματ-), thread.] A group of horny or fibrous sponges, having sand or other foreign substance in the axis of the spongin. The common bath-sponge is an example.

Psammophidæ (sa-mof'i-dē), *n. pl.* [NL., < *Psammophis* + *-idæ.*] A family of harmless colubrine *Ophidia*, typified by the genus *Psammophis*, now reduced to a subfamily of *Colubridæ*; the sand-snakes. In Günther's classification it contained four genera, represented chiefly by African and Indian species. Also *Psammophididæ*.

Psammophinæ (sam-ǫ-fī'nē), *n. pl.* [NL., < *Psammophis* + *-inæ.*] A subfamily of *Colubridæ*, represented by three genera, *Psammophis*, *Psammodynastes*, and *Mimophis*; the sand-snakes or desert-snakes. They have the head distinct, the body moderately slender, not compressed, the middle teeth elongated, and the posterior ones grooved. The species are all tropical. Also *Psammophidinæ*. *E. D. Cope.*

Psammophis (sam'ǫ-fis), *n.* [NL. (Wagler), < Gr. ψάμμος, sand, + ὄφις, a serpent.] The typical genus of *Psammophidæ*, having a loral plate and divided anal gastrostege. There are numerous African and Asiatic species, as P. *condanarus*, frequenting sandy places.

Psaris (sā'ris), *n.* [NL. (Cuvier, 1817), < Gr. ψάρ, a starling.] A genus of tityrine birds, now called *Tityra*.

Psarocolius (sar-ọ̄-kō'li-us), *n.* [NL., < Gr. ψαρός, speckled, + κολιός, a woodpecker.] A very extensive genus of *Icteridæ*, under which Wagler in 1829 included a number of dissimilar generic types: inexactly synonymous with *Cacicus* and *Icterus* in a broad sense.

Psaronius (sā-rō'ni-us), *n.* [NL., < L. *psaronius*, < Gr. *ψαρώνιος, an unidentified precious stone, < ψαρός, speckled, < ψάρ, a starling.] In *fossil bot.*, a genus of petrified tree-ferns. They have been found chiefly in the Permian, but also in the coal-measures. Portions of these petrified trunks have been cut and polished for ornamental purposes, and called by the name of *staarstein* in German, and *star-* or *starry-stone* in English.

psautert, *n.* A Middle English form of *psalter*.

psautriet, *n.* A Middle English form of *psaltery*.

pschem, *n.* Same as *pshem*.

pschent (psḗhent), *n.* [Egypt.] In *archæol.*, the sovereign crown of all Egypt, composed of the tall pointed miter, or white crown, of southern

Pschent.—From reliefs of the temple-court of Edfou, Egypt.

Egypt, combined with the red crown, square in front and rising to a point behind, of northern Egypt. The two kingdoms were united by Menes, who founded the greatness of the Egyptian monarchy and restrained the power of the priests, at the dawn of recorded history.

Pselaphi (sel'a-fī), *n. pl.* [NL., pl. of *Pselaphus*, q. v.] In Latreille's classification, the third family of trimerous *Coleoptera*, containing *Pselaphus* and *Claviger* as leading genera. It corresponds to the modern family *Pselaphidæ*, but was differently located in the system.

pselaphid (sel'a-fid), *a.* and *n.* I. *a.* Of or pertaining to the *Pselaphidæ*.

II. *n.* Any beetle of this family.

Pselaphidæ (sē-laf'i-dē), *n. pl.* [NL. (Leach, 1817), < *Pselaphus* + *-idæ*.] An anomalous family of *Coleoptera*, typified by the genus *Pselaphus*. They have been variously located in the *Palpicornia* or *Clavicornia*, and are now classed with the latter suborder. The tarsi are trimerous, the dorsal abdominal segments are entirely corneous, and the abdomen is fixed, unappendaged, and of five or six segments. They are very small brownish beetles, more or less pubescent, found in most countries in moss and ants' nests and under stones. The family is rich in genera and species; of the former, 29 are represented in the United States.

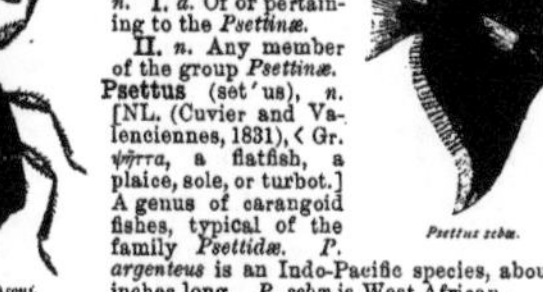

Pselaphus erichsoni.
(Cross shows natural size.)

pselaphotheca (sel″a-fọ̄-thē'kä), *n.*; pl. *pselaphothecæ* (-sē). [NL., < Gr. ψηλαφᾶν, feel about, + θήκη, a box, chest.] In *entom.*, one of the two conical processes on the anterior extremity of many butterfly pupæ, in which the palpi are developed.

Pselaphus (sel'a-fus), *n.* [NL. (Herbst, 1792), < Gr. ψηλαφᾶν, feel or grope about.] The typical genus of *Pselaphidæ*, having the tarsi single-clawed, and the maxillary palpi extremely long, the last joint club-shaped. It is wide-spread, but the species are not numerous, less than 30 being described. Only two, P. *erichsoni* and P. *longiclavus*, are found in North America north of Mexico.

psellism (sel'izm), *n.* [< NL. *psellismus*, < Gr. ψελλισμός, a stammering, < ψελλίζειν, stammer, pronounce indistinctly, < ψελλός, faltering in speech, stammering.] A defect in enunciation; misenunciation. Psellism may consist in lisping, stammering, burring, hesitation, etc. It also designates defective enunciation due to a hare-lip or defect of lip.

psellismus (se-lis'mus), *n.* [NL.] Same as *psellism*.

Psephenidæ (sē-fen'i-dē), *n. pl.* [NL., < *Psephenus* + *-idæ*.] A family of coleopterous insects, named by Le Conte in 1861 from the genus *Psephenus*: now merged in *Parnidæ*.

Psephenus (sẹ̄-fē'nus), *n.* [NL. (Haldeman, 1853), < Gr. ψεφηνός, dark, obscure.] The typical genus of *Psephenidæ*. Two species only are known, both of the United States.

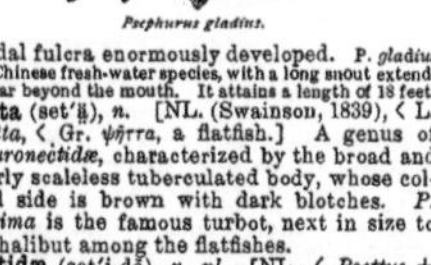

Psephenus lecontei.
(Cross shows natural size.)

psephism (sē'fizm), *n.* [< L. *psephisma*, < Gr. ψήφισμα, an ordinance of a deliberative assembly, < ψηφίζειν, count, reckon with pebbles or counters, < ψῆφος, also ψηφίς, a pebble, a smooth stone, < ψάειν, rub.] In *Gr. antiq.*, a public vote of an assembly, specifically of an assembly of the Athenian people; a decree or statute enacted by such a vote.

psephomancy (sē'fọ̄-man-si), *n.* [< Gr. ψῆφος, a pebble, + μαντεία, divination.] Divination by means of pebbles drawn from a heap. *Roget.*

Psephurus (sẹ̄-fū'rus), *n.* [NL. (Günther, 1873), < Gr. ψῆφος, pebble, + οὐρά, tail.] A genus of polyodont fishes, having six upper

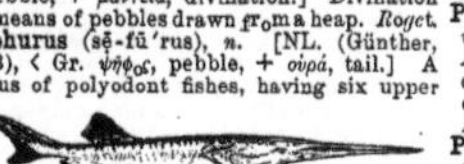

Psephurus gladius.

caudal fulcra enormously developed. P. *gladius* is a Chinese fresh-water species, with a long snout extending far beyond the mouth. It attains a length of 18 feet.

Psetta (set'ä), *n.* [NL. (Swainson, 1839), < L. *psetta*, < Gr. ψῆττα, a flatfish.] A genus of *Pleuronectidæ*, characterized by the broad and nearly scaleless tuberculated body, whose colored side is brown with dark blotches. *P. maxima* is the famous turbot, next in size to the halibut among the flatfishes.

Psettidæ (set'i-dē), *n. pl.* [NL., < *Psettus* + *-idæ*.] A family of acanthopterygian fishes, typified by the genus *Psettus* (or *Monodactylus*). The body is much compressed and elevated, the vertical fins are covered with scales, the dorsal has seven or eight spines and the anal three, and the ventrals are rudimentary. The few species are inhabitants of the Pacific and African coasts. See cut under *Psettus*.

Psettinæ (se-tī'nē), *n. pl.* [NL., < *Psetta* + *-inæ*.] A subfamily of *Pleuronectidæ*, typified by the genus *Psetta*. They have a nearly symmetrical and generally large mouth, and the ventral fins unsymmetrical, that of the eyed side having an extended base on the ridge of the abdomen, while the other is narrower and lateral. The eyes are on the left side. It includes the turbot, brill, whiff, topknot, scaldfish, and many other flatfishes.

psettine (set'in), *a.* and *n.* I. *a.* Of or pertaining to the *Psettinæ*.

II. *n.* Any member of the group *Psettinæ*.

Psettus (set'us), *n.* [NL. (Cuvier and Valenciennes, 1831), < Gr. ψῆττα, a flatfish, a plaice, sole, or turbot.] A genus of carangoid fishes, typical of the family *Psettidæ*. *P. argenteus* is an Indo-Pacific species, about 10 inches long. *P. sebæ* is West African.

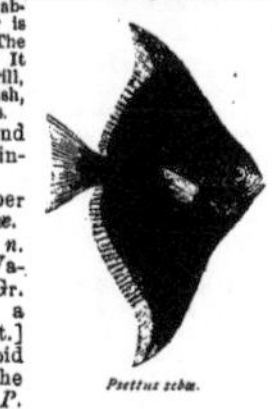

Psettus sebæ.

pseud-. See *pseudo-*.

pseudaconitine (sū-da-kon'i-tin), *n.* Same as *pseudo-aconitine*.

pseudacusis (sū-dạ-kū'sis), *n.* [NL., < Gr. ψευδής, false, + ἄκουσις, a hearing.] False hearing.

pseudæsthesia (sū-des-thē'si-ạ̈), *n.* [NL., < Gr. ψευδής, false, + αἴσθησις, feeling: see *æsthesia*.] Imaginary or false feeling; imaginary sense of touch in organs that have been removed, as when pain is felt as if in the fingers or toes of an amputated limb. Also spelled *pseudesthesia*.

Pseudalopex (sū-da-lō'peks), *n.* [NL. (Burmeister, 1856), < Gr. ψευδής, false, + ἀλώπηξ, a fox.] A genus or subgenus of South American *Canidæ*, related to *Lycalopex*, but further resembling foxes in having the pupil of the eye elliptical when contracted, as in *P. azaræ*, *P. magellanicus*, etc.

pseudambulacral (sū-dam-bụ̄-lā'kral), *a.* Simulating ambulacra or ambulacral areas, as certain spaces observed in blastoid crinoids.

pseudaphia (sū-dā'fi-ạ̈), *n.* [< Gr. ψευδής, false, + ἀφή, a touch: see *paraphia*.] Paraphia.

pseudapostle (sūd-a-pos'l), *n.* [< LL. *pseudapostolus*, < LGr. ψευδαπόστολος, a false apostle, < ψευδής, false, + ἀπόστολος, apostle: see *apostle*.] A false or pretended apostle. Also *pseudo-apostle*.

For these Philippian *pseudapostles*, two ways were they enemies to the crosse of Christ: in their doctrines, in their practice. *Bp. Hall*, Sermon on Phil. iii. 18, 19.

Pseudarachnæ (sū″da-rak'nē), *n. pl.* [NL., < Gr. ψευδής, false, + ἀράχνη, a spider: see *Arachnida*.] A group of arthropod animals composed by Haeckel to contain the sea-spiders, or *Pycnogonida*, and the water-bears, or *Arctisca*. In Gegenbaur's system the *Pseudarachnæ* are one of two prime divisions of *Arachnida*, the other being *Autarachnæ*. Also called *Pseudarachna*. See cuts under *Arctisca* and *Pycnogonida*.

pseudarthrosis (sū-där-thrō'sis), *n.* A condition in which, after fracture, there is failure of bony union, and there remains an actual joint or a fibrous union with slight movement.

Pseudastacus (sū-das'tạ-kus), *n.* [NL., < Gr. ψευδής, false, + ἀστακός, a lobster, crawfish: see *Astacus*.] A genus of fossil decapod crustaceans, from the Solenhofen slates of Bavaria, containing such species as *P. pustulosus*. Also *Pseudo-astacus*.

Pseudecheneis (sū-dek-e-nē'is), *n.* [NL. (Blyth, 1860), < Gr. ψευδής, false, + NL. *Echeneis*.] A genus of Asiatic catfishes of the family *Siluridæ*: so called from the adhesive apparatus or sucking-disk formed by plaits of skin between the pectorals, enabling the fish to cling to stones in the mountain streams which it inhabits.

pseudelephant (sū-del'ẹ̄-fạnt), *n.* A mastodon. *Coues.*

pseudelminth (sū-del'minth), *n.* [< Gr. ψευδής, false, + ἕλμινς (ἑλμινθ-), a worm: see *helminth*.] A supposed entoparasitic worm which proves to be something else. Also *pseudhelminth*.

Sometimes the *pseudelminths* are really so worm-like that a mere naked-eye examination is insufficient to determine their nature.
T. S. Cobbold, Tapeworms (1866), p. 9.

pseudelytrum, pseudelytron (sū-del'i-trum, -tron), *n.*; pl. *pseudelytra* (-trạ̈). A false elytrum; a spurious or degenerate wing-cover or fore wing, as the small twisted process of a stylops. See *Strepsiptera* and *Stylopidæ*.

pseudembryo (sū-dem'bri-ō), *n.* [< Gr. ψευδής, false, + ἔμβρυον, embryo.] A false embryo: applied to various larval forms after the egg stage. (*a*) The echinopædium of a sea-urchin. *Wyville Thomson.* (*b*) The bipinnaria or brachiolaria of a starfish. (*c*) The swarm-gemmule of a sponge, or so-called sponge-embryo. *W. S. Kent.*

pseudembryonic (sū-dem-bri-on'ik), *a.* [< *pseudembryo*(*n-*) + *-ic*.] Pertaining to a pseudembryo, or having its character; echinopædic.

Pseudemydæ (sū-dem'i-dē), *n. pl.* [NL., < *Pseudemys* (*-emyd-*) + *-æ*.] A family of cryptodirous tortoises, named from the genus *Pseudemys*, now merged in the family *Clemmyidæ* or *Testudinidæ*. *J. E. Gray.*

Pseudemys (sū'de-mis), *n.* [NL. (J. E. Gray, 1856), < Gr. ψευδής, false, + NL. *Emys*.] A genus of tortoises of the family *Emydidæ*, sometimes giving name to the *Pseudemydæ*. It contains chiefly North American turtles, among them *P. rugosa* or *rubriventris* (the potter, slider, or red-bellied terrapin), *P. concinna*, *P. mobiliensis*, etc.

pseudencephalus (sūd-en-sef'a-lus), *n.*; pl. *pseudencephali* (-lī). [NL., < Gr. ψευδής, false, + ἐγκέφαλος, the brain.] In *teratol.*, a monster in which the brain is replaced by a vascular tumor derived from the pia mater.

pseudepigrapha (sū-de-pig'ra-fạ̈), *n. pl.* [NL., < Gr. ψευδεπίγραφα, neut. pl. of ψευδεπίγραφος, falsely inscribed or ascribed: see *pseudepigraphous*.]

Spurious writings; specifically, those writings which profess to be Biblical in character and inspired in authorship, but are not adjudged genuine by the general consent of scholars; those professedly Biblical books which are regarded as neither canonical nor inspired, and from their character are not worthy of use in religious worship. Biblical literature is divided into three classes: (a) The canonical and inspired; (b) the non-canonical and uninspired, but on account of their character worthy of use in the services of the church; (c) those which, though Biblical in form, so vary from the Biblical writings in spirit that they are not deemed worthy of any place in religious use. The second constitute the apocrypha, the third the pseudepigrapha. Thus, what is sometimes known as the New Testament Apocrypha, being not considered worthy of regard by any branch of the Christian church, properly consists of pseudepigrapha.

pseudepigraphic (sū-dep-i-graf'ik), *a.* [< *pseudepigraph-ous* + *-ic.*] Inscribed with a false name: specifically, pertaining to the Jewish pseudepigrapha.

Of these *pseudepigraphic* Hermetic writings some have come down to us in the original Greek. *Encyc. Brit.*, XI. 751.

pseudepigraphical (sū-dep-i-graf'i-kal), *a.* [< *pseudepigraphic* + *-al.*] Same as *pseudepigraphic.*

Pseudepigraphical writings, which ought not only to be rejected but condemned. *Encyc. Brit.*, V. 12.

pseudepigraphous (sū-de-pig'ra-fus), *a.* [< Gr. ψευδεπίγραφος, falsely inscribed or ascribed, not genuine, < ψευδής, false, + ἐπιγράφειν, inscribe: see *epigraph.*] Same as *pseudepigraphic.*

Herodotus . . . seemed . . . to conclude the Orphick poems to have been *pseudepigraphous.* *Cudworth*, Intellectual System, p. 296.

pseudepigraphy (sū-de-pig'ra-fi), *n.* [< *pseudepigraph-ous* + *-y.* Cf. *epigraphy.*] The false ascription of a particular authorship to works.

pseudepiploic (sū″dep-i-plō'ik), *a.* [< *pseudepiploön* + *-ic.*] Of or pertaining to the pseudepiploön.

pseudepiploön (sū-de-pip'lō-on), *n.* A kind of omentum found in birds.

The *pseudepiploon* [of the flamingo] was also shown to differ from that of Lamellirostres, and to agree with that of storks, in extending back to the cloaca. *Athenæum*, No. 2931, p. 870.

pseudepiscopacy (sū-dē-pis'kō-pā-si), *n.* False or pretended episcopacy. Also *pseudepiscopy, pseudo-episcopacy.* [Rare.]

A long usurpation and convicted *pseudepiscopy* of prelates. *Milton*, On Def. of Humb. Remonst., Pref.

pseudesthesia, *n.* See *pseudæsthesia.*

pseudhæmal (sūd-hē'mal), *a.* Same as *pseudohemal.*

pseudhelminth, *n.* Same as *pseudelminth.*

pseudimaginal (sū-di-maj'i-nal), *a.* Pertaining to or having the character of a pseudimago; subimaginal.

pseudimago (sū-di-mā'gō), *n.*; pl. *pseudimagines* (sū-di-maj'i-nēz). A false imago: same as *subimago.*

Pseudis (sū'dis), *n.* [NL. (Wagler, about 1830), < Gr. ψεῦδις, var. of ψευδής, false: see *pseudo-.*] A genus of arciferous batrachians of the family *Cystignathidæ*, containing frogs the webs of whose hind toes extend up between the metatarsals, and whose tadpoles acquire legs and reach the size of the adults before losing their tails. The jakie, *P. paradoxa*, is an example, inhabiting South America.

pseudisodomon (sū-di-sod'ō-mon), *n.* [< Gr. ψευδισόδομος, built of stones of unequal size, < ψευδής, false, + ἰσόδομος, built alike, i. e. in equal courses: see *isodomon.*] In *arch.*, a type of masonry in which the courses differ as to the height, length, or thickness of their stones, the stones of any one course, however, being alike: opposed to *isodomon.* In the form characteristic of Greek masonry, in which, however, the pseudisodomon is usually earlier or (especially) later than the best time, the courses are alternately thick and thin, all the thick courses being of the same thickness, and so with all the thin courses. Masonry of this kind is frequent in Roman work.

Pseudisodomon.

pseudo-. [Before a vowel sometimes *pseud-*; < Gr. ψευδο-, ψευδ-, combining form of ψευδής, false, sham, deceitful, ψεῦδος, a falsehood — or rather of the orig. verb, ψεύδειν, lie, cheat, deceive.] An element, a quasi-prefix, in compounds of Greek origin, meaning 'false,' 'counterfeit,' 'spurious,' 'sham.' It is freely used as an English prefix, with words of any origin, and by no means all the compounds made with it are given below. In scientific compounds it implies something deceptive in appearance, function, or relation. Thus, in crystallography, it is used in such compounds as *pseudo*-isometric, *pseudo*-tetragonal, etc., to describe crystals which appear to belong to the isometric, tetragonal, etc., systems, but in fact belong to a system of lower grade of symmetry. (See *pseudosymmetry.*) In biology it is much used (like *quasi-*) to indicate deceptive likeness of things really quite unlike; but it frequently implies a real resemblance so close as to obscure or hide actual difference.

pseudo-aconitine (sū″dō-a-kon'i-tin), *n.* A crystalline alkaloid ($C_{36}H_{49}NO_{12}$) derived from *Aconitum ferox.* Also *pseudaconitine.*

pseudo-angle (sū-dō-ang'gl), *n.* An angle in non-Euclidean geometry.

pseudo-annulus (sū-dō-an'ū-lus), *n.* In *Musci*, an apparent annulus or ring of non-vesicular cells.

pseudo-apostle (sū″dō-a-pos'l), *n.* Same as *pseudapostle.*

pseudo-aquatic (sū″dō-a-kwat'ik), *a.* Growing in very moist places, yet not strictly aquatic.

pseudo-archaic (sū″dō-är-kā'ik), *a.* Same as *archaistic:* used especially in the fine arts.

It is possibly a *pseudo-archaic* work of the fifteenth century. *C. C. Perkins*, Italian Sculpture, p. 344, note.

pseudo-articulation (sū″dō-är-tik-ū-lā'shon), *n.* In *entom.*: (*a*) A deep impressed line or constriction surrounding a part, and resembling a true joint. (*b*) A pseudo-joint, or part resembling a true joint, but not really jointed.

pseudo-ascetic (sū″dō-a-set'ik), *n.* A pretended ascetic.

These may be termed a set of *pseudo-asceticks*, who can have no real converse either with themselves or with heaven. *Shaftesbury*, Advice to an Author, i. § 1.

pseudo-axis (sū-dō-ak'sis), *n.* In *bot.*, same as *sympodium.*

pseudobacterium (sū″dō-bak-tē'ri-um), *n.*; pl. *pseudobacteria* (-ä). A corpuscle resembling or mistaken for a bacterium.

It was simply *pseudo-bacteria*, or broken blood corpuscles. *Science*, III. 739.

pseudobasidia (sū″dō-bā-sid'i-ä), *n. pl.* In *bot.*, false basidia: bodies with the form and appearance of basidia and produced with them. See *basidium.*

pseudo-Bible (sū-dō-bī'bl), *n.* A false or pretended Bible.

The work which the reader has now the privilege of perusing is as justly entitled to the name of the Koran as the so-called *pseudo-bible* itself, because the word signifies "that which ought to be read." *Southey*, The Doctor, Interchapter ix. (*Davies.*)

pseudoblepsia (sū-dō-blep'si-ä), *n.* [NL.: see *pseudoblepsis.*] Same as *pseudoblepsis.*

pseudoblepsis (sū-dō-blep'sis), *n.* [< Gr. ψευδής, false, + βλέψις, vision, < βλέπειν, look, see.] Parablepsia; visual illusion or hallucination.

Pseudobombus (sū-dō-bom'bus), *n.* [NL., < Gr. ψευδής, false, + NL. *Bombus:* see *Bombus*, 2.] In *entom.*: (*a*) An alternative generic name of bees of the genus *Apathus*, which closely resemble the species of *Bombus* proper and live parasitically in their nests. (*b*) [*l. c.*] A bee of this genus.

Pseudobombyces (sū″dō-bom-bī'sēz), *n. pl.* [NL., < Gr. ψευδής, false, + βόμβυξ, a silkworm: see *Bombyx.*] In Latreille's classification, a division of nocturnal *Lepidoptera*, approximately corresponding to the modern families *Arctiidæ, Lithosiidæ*, and *Psychidæ.* Also *Pseudobombycini.*

pseudobombycine (sū-dō-bom'bi-sin), *a.* Pertaining to the *Pseudobombyces.*

Pseudobombycini (sū-dō-bom-bi-sī'nī), *n. pl.* [NL., as *Pseudobombyces* + *-ini.*] Same as *Pseudobombyces. Boisduval.*

pseudobrachial (sū-dō-brā'ki-al), *a.* Pertaining to the pseudobrachium.

pseudobrachium (sū-dō-brā'ki-um), *n.*; pl. *pseudobrachia* (-ä). A kind of false arm formed by the actinosts of the pectoral fin of pediculate fishes. *Gill.*

pseudobranch (sū'dō-brangk), *n.* A false or spiracular gill. *Stand. Nat. Hist.*, III. 43.

pseudobranchia[1] (sū-dō-brang'ki-ä), *n.*; pl. *pseudobranchiæ* (-ē). [< Gr. ψευδής, false, + βράγχια, gills.] A false gill. See the quotation.

The anterior branchial vein [in fishes] gives off the hyoidean artery, which ascends along the hyoidean arch, and very generally terminates by one branch in the cephalic circle, and by another enters a rete mirabile which lies in the inner side of the hyomandibular bone, and sometimes has the form of a gill. This is the *pseudobranchia.* *Huxley*, Anat. Vert., p. 140.

Pseudobranchia[2] (sū-dō-brang'ki-ä), *n. pl.* [NL.: see *pseudobranchia*[1].] A suborder of scutibranchiate gastropods, with the gills developed as a branching vessel on the inner surface of the mantle, the body and shell spiral, the lateral central teeth of the odontophore large and irregular, and no operculum. The group was instituted by J. E. Gray for terrestrial forms belonging to the family *Proserpinidæ.*

pseudobranchial (sū-dō-brang'ki-al), *a.* [< *pseudobranchia*[1] + *-al.*] Of or pertaining to a pseudobranch or to pseudobranchiæ.

pseudobranchiate (sū-dō-brang'ki-āt), *a.* [< *pseudobranchia*[1] + *-ate*[1].] Provided with pseudobranchiæ.

pseudobrookite (sū-dō-brůk'īt), *n.* A mineral occurring in minute rectangular tables in cavities in some volcanic rocks, as andesite. It resembles brookite, and is related to it in composition, consisting of the oxids of titanium and iron.

pseudobulb (sū'dō-bulb), *n.* A fleshy enlargement of the base of the stem in many epiphytic orchids, having the appearance of a bulb, but solid in structure: nearly allied to the corm, but not subterranean.

pseudobulbar (sū-dō-bul'bär), *a.* Noting a kind of paralysis. See *pseudobulbar paralysis*, under *paralysis.*

pseudobulbil (sū-dō-bul'bil), *n.* In *bot.*, an oöphytic outgrowth sometimes replacing ordinary sporangia in ferns, and producing antheridia and archegonia.

pseudobulbous (sū-dō-bul'bus), *a.* Having the character of, or marked by the presence of, a pseudobulb.

pseudocarcinoid (sū-dō-kär'si-noid), *a.* and *n.* I. *a.* Being macrurous and simulating a brachyurous crustacean; looking like a crab without being one.

II. *n.* A pseudocarcinoid crustacean, as a member of the genus *Thenus* or *Ibacus. Huxley.*

pseudocarp (sū'dō-kärp), *n.* [< NL. *pseudocarpus*, < Gr. ψευδής, false, + καρπός, fruit.] That part of an anthocarpous fruit which does not belong to the pericarp. Also called *anthocarp* or *anthocarpium.* See *anthocarpous.*

pseudocarpous (sū-dō-kär'pus), *a.* [< NL. *pseudocarpus:* see *pseudocarp.*] In *bot.*, same as *anthocarpous.*

pseudo-Christ (sū'dō-krīst), *n.* [< LL. *pseudochristus*, < Gr. ψευδόχριστος, a false Christ, < ψευδής, false, + Χριστός, Christ.] One who falsely claims to be the Christ.

Be on your guard against the seductions of the *pseudo-Christs.* *Lange*, Com. on Mark xiii. 5–13 (trans.).

pseudo-Christianity (sū-dō-kris-ti-an'i-ti), *n.* The religion or doctrines of a false or pretended Christ; counterfeit Christianity.

Pseudo-Christs, *pseudo-Christianities*, false prophets. *Lange*, Com. on Mark xiii. 5–13 (trans.).

pseudo-Christology (sū″dō-kris-tol'ō-ji), *n.* An erroneous doctrine or system of doctrines regarding the nature of Christ.

The latter [modern evangelical theology] has to vindicate . . . the true divinity and historicity of Christ against the mythical, legendary, and humanitarian *pseudo-Christologies* of the nineteenth century. *P. Schaff*, Christ and Christianity, p. 172.

pseudochromia (sū-dō-krō'mi-ä), *n.* [NL., < Gr. ψευδής, false, + χρῶμα, color.] False perception of color.

Pseudochromidæ (sū-dō-krom'i-dē), *n. pl.* [NL.] Same as *Pseudochromididæ. J. Richardson*, 1856.

Pseudochromides (sū-dō-krom'i-dēz), *n. pl.* [NL., pl. of *Pseudochromis*, q. v.] A group of acanthopterygian trachinoid fishes, having the dorsal fin continuous and the lateral line interrupted, typified by the genus *Pseudochromis*, and corresponding to the family *Pseudochromididæ.* In Günther's classification it was the fourth group of *Trachinidæ. Müller and Troschel*, 1849.

Pseudochromididæ (sū″dō-krō-mid'i-dē), *n. pl.* [NL., < *Pseudochromis* (*-mid-*) + *-idæ.*] A family of acanthopterygian fishes, typified by the genus *Pseudochromis.* The body is oblong, the lateral line interrupted, the head convex forward, and the pharyngeal lines distinct. The species are mostly inhabitants of the Indo-Pacific ocean. They have a superficial resemblance to pomacentrids, but the distinct lower pharyngeals distinguish them. Also *Pseudochromidæ, Pseudochromides*, and *Pseudochromidoidei.* See *Plesiopidæ*, and cut under *Plesiops.*

pseudochromidoid (sū-dō-krom'i-doid), *a.* and *n.* I. *a.* Of or pertaining to the *Pseudochromididæ.*

II. *n.* A member of the *Pseudochromididæ.*

Pseudochromidoidei (sū-dǫ-krom-i-doi′dẹ-ī), *n. pl.* [NL.] Same as *Pseudochromididæ*. *Bleeker*, 1859.

Pseudochromis (sū-dok′rǫ-mis), *n.* [NL. (Rüppell, 1837), < Gr. ψευδής, false, + χρόμις, a kind of sea-fish.] The typical genus of the family *Pseudochromididæ*.

pseudochrysalis (sū-dǫ-kris′a̤-lis), *n.* Same as *pseudopupa*.

pseudo-citizen (sū-dō-sit′i-zn), *n.* One who falsely lays claim to the right of citizenship.

Some indeed hold that he who is unjustly a citizen is a *pseudocitizen*, a mere counterfeit.
Gillies, tr. of Aristotle, II. 195. (*Jodrell.*)

pseudo-classicism (sū-dō-klas′i-sizm), *n.* A false or affected classicism.

An increasing number of persons were perverse enough to feel [a difficulty in reading] . . . the productions of a *pseudo-classicism*, the classicism of red heels and periwigs.
Lowell, Study Windows, p. 391.

pseudocœle (sū′dǫ-sēl), *n.* [< Gr. ψευδής, false, + κοῖλος, hollow.] In *zoöl.*, a certain cavity of some invertebrates: better called *pseudocœlom*.

The adult body cavity comes entirely from *pseudocœle*.
Adam Sedgwick, Micros. Science, XXVII. 491.

pseudocœlic (sū-dǫ-sē′lik), *a.* Of or pertaining to the pseudocœle.

This statement applies also to the heart and pericardium. These are both *pseudocœlic*.
Adam Sedgwick, Micros. Science, XXVII. 491.

pseudocœlom (sū-dǫ-sē′lom), *n.* [< Gr. ψευδής, false, + κοίλωμα, a hollow, cavity: see *cœloma*.] Same as *pseudocœle*.

pseudocolumella (sū-dǫ-kol-ụ̄-mel′ä̤), *n.*; pl. *pseudocolumellæ* (-ē). In corals, a kind of false columella formed by the twisting together of the inner ends of septa; a parietal or septal columella.

The more prominent septa extend to the centre of the corallite, and then either unite evenly by their free inner margins or curve round each other to a slight extent, thus forming a structure to which the name of *pseudocolumella* has been given.
Quart. Jour. Geol. Soc., XLIV. 210.

pseudocolumellar (sū″dǫ-kol-ụ̄-mel′ä̤r), *a.* Pertaining to a pseudocolumella.

pseudocommissura (sū-dǫ-kom-i-sū′rä̤), *n.*; pl. *pseudocommissuræ* (-rē). Same as *pseudocommissure*. *Wilder and Gage*, Anat. Tech., p. 420.

pseudocommissural (sū-dǫ-kǫ-mis′ụ̄-ra̤l), *a.* Of or pertaining to a pseudocommissure: as, *pseudocommissural* fibers.

pseudocommissure (sū-dǫ-kom′i-sūr), *n.* A sort of commissure, formed of connective tissue, between the olfactory lobes of some batrachians, as the frog. Also *pseudocommissura*.

pseudoconcha (sū-dǫ-kong′kä̤), *n.*; pl. *pseudoconchæ* (-kē). [NL., < Gr. ψευδής, false, + κόγχη, a shell: see *conch*.] An alinasal turbinated structure in the nose of birds, in front of and below the turbinal proper, connected with the internasal septum, and separating the vestibule of the nose from the internal nasal cavity. *Gegenbaur*, Comp. Anat. (trans.), p. 547.

pseudocorneous (sū-dǫ-kôr′nẹ-us), *a.* Partly or somewhat horny, as the mass of agglutinated hairs of the deciduous horns of the American antelope, which form the base of the horn-sheath and gradually change into true horn toward the tip of those organs.

pseudocortex (sū-dǫ-kôr′teks), *n.* [NL., < Gr. ψευδής, false, + L. *cortex*, bark.] In *bot.*, an agglomeration of secondary branches in the *Florideæ*, originating at the nodes, and closely adpressed to the main or axial branch of a frond, forming a false cortex.

pseudocosta (sū-dǫ-kos′tä̤), *n.*; pl. *pseudocostæ* (-tē). [< Gr. ψευδής, false, + L. *costa*, rib.] One of the flattened or rounded interspaces which stand out in slight relief between the septa of some corals. *Quart. Jour. Geol. Soc.*, XLIV. 213.

pseudocostate (sū-dǫ-kos′tāt), *a.* [< Gr. ψευδής, false, + L. *costa*, rib: see *costa*, *costate*.] 1. In *bot.*, false-ribbed: said of leaves in which the true veins are confluent into a marginal or intramarginal rib or vein, as in many *Myrtaceæ*. —2. In *zoöl.*, having pseudocostæ, as a coral.

pseudocotyledon† (sū-dǫ-kot-i-lē′dǫn), *n.* In *bot.*, one of the germinating threads of the spores of cryptogams. The name was formerly so employed on the supposition that these threads were in a measure analogous to the cotyledons of phanerogams, but is not now in use.

pseudocrisis (sū-dǫ-krī′sis), *n.*; pl. *pseudocrises* (-sēz). In *pathol.*, a sudden remission of temperature, resembling a crisis, but followed immediately by a return to the previous fever, as may occur in croupous pneumonia.

pseudo-critic (sū-dō-krit′ik), *n.* A pretended or would-be critic.

The greatest hurt those poetasters and *pseudo-criticks* did him was pretending to fix things on him of which he was not author. *Ayre*, Pope (ed. 1754), I. 247. (*Jodrell.*)

pseudo-croup (sū′dō-kröp), *n.* False croup; laryngismus stridulus.

pseudocyclosis (sū″dǫ-sī-klō′sis), *n.* The apparent circulation of food in an amœba, superficially resembling cyclosis. *Wallich.*

pseudocyesis (sū″dǫ-sī-ē′sis), *n.* Spurious pregnancy.

pseudocyst (sū′dǫ-sist), *n.* [< Gr. ψευδής, false, + κύστις, a bladder: see *cyst*.] In *bot.*, one of many more or less imperfectly spherical bodies produced by the breaking up of the protoplasm of the filaments in certain of the *Protophyta*.

pseudodeltidium (sū″dǫ-del-tid′i-um), *n.*; pl. *pseudodeltidia* (-ä̤). In *Brachiopoda*, a false deltidium, such as occurs in a spirifer.

pseudodipteral (sū-dǫ-dip′tẹ-ra̤l), *a.* [< L. *pseudodipteros*, < Gr. ψευδοδίπτερος, < ψευδής, false, + δίπτερος, two-winged: see *dipteral*.] In *classical arch.*, noting a disposition in the plan of a columnar structure resembling that of a dipteral building in the wide space left between the peristyle and the cella, but with the inner row of columns omitted, or, a disposition of plan like that of the Parthenon, in which there is an inner portico of six columns within the peristyle before both pronaos and opisthodomos, but no such secondary range on the flanks.

pseudodipterally (sū-dǫ-dip′tẹ-ra̤l-i), *adv.* In a pseudodipteral manner or style. *Encyc. Brit.*, II. 471.

pseudodistance (sū-dǫ-dis′ta̤ns), *n.* The distance in non-Euclidean geometry.

pseudodont (sū′dǫ-dont), *a.* [< Gr. ψευδής, false, + ὀδούς (ὀδοντ-) = E. *tooth*.] Having false teeth, as a monotreme.

pseudodox (sū′dǫ-doks), *a.* and *n.* [< Gr. ψευδόδοξος, holding a false opinion, < ψευδής, false, + δόξα, a notion, an opinion, < δοκεῖν, think. Cf. *orthodox*.] I. *a.* False; not true in opinion. [Rare.]

II. *n.* A false but common opinion.

Mad. He's a rare fellow, without question! but
He holds some paradoxes.
Alm. Ay, and *pseudodoxes*.
B. Jonson, Staple of News, iii. 1.

The Romists stick not, as once the Valentinian heretics veritatis ignorantiam cognitionem vocare, by a paradox, *pseudodox*, to call the ignorance of the truth the true knowledge thereof. *Rev. T. Adams*, Works, I. 412.

The counterpart of false and absurd paradox is what is called the vulgar error, the *pseudodox*.
De Morgan, Budget of Paradoxes, p. 23.

pseudodoxal (sū′dǫ-dok-sa̤l), *a.* [< *pseudodox* + *-al*.] Of the nature of a pseudodox or false opinion; falsely believed; untrue or mistaken in opinion. [Rare.]

Orosia is much degenerated from what she was by the Gherionian sectaries, who have infected the inhabitants with so many *pseudodoxall* and gingling opinions.
Howell, Parly of Beasts, p. 122. (*Davies.*)

pseudo-episcopacy (sū″dǫ-ẹ̄-pis′kǫ-pā̤-si), *n.* Same as *pseudepiscopacy*.

pseudofilaria (sū″dǫ-fi-lā′ri-ä̤), *n.*; pl. *pseudofilariæ* (-ē). [NL., < Gr. ψευδής, false, + L. *filum*, thread: see *filar*.] A stage in the development of a gregarina, supervening upon the finishing of the early embryonic condition of a pseudonavicella, and passing into the condition of the adult. See *pseudonavicella*. *E. Van Beneden.*

pseudofilarian (sū″dǫ-fi-lā′ri-a̤n), *a.* and *n.* [< *pseudofilaria* + *-an*.] I. *a.* Pertaining to a pseudofilaria, or having its character.

II. *n.* A pseudofilaria.

pseudofoliaceous (sū-dǫ-fō-li-ā′shius), *a.* [< Gr. ψευδής, false, + L. *foliaceus*, leafy: see *foliaceous*.] In *bot.*, provided with lobes or expansions resembling leaves: said of a thallus or stem.

Pseudo-foliaceous forms, in which the thallus is lobed, the lobes assuming leaf-like forms.
Underwood, Bull. of Ill. State Laboratory, II. 6.

pseudogalena (sū″dǫ-gā-lē′nä̤), *n.* False galena. See *black-jack*, 3, and *blende*.

pseudogastrula (sū-dǫ-gas′trǫ-lä̤), *n.* A false gastrula; that embryonic stage or state in which an organism resembles a gastrula without having undergone a proper gastrulation. *Jour. Micros. Sci.*, XXVIII. 348.

pseudogeneral (sū-dǫ-jen′ẹ-ra̤l), *a.* Noting a kind of paralysis. See *pseudogeneral paralysis*, under *paralysis*. The *pseudo-* here really qualifies not *general*, but *general paralysis*.

pseudogeneric (sū″dǫ-jẹ-ner′ik), *a.* Spurious or merely nominal as a genus; of the character of a pseudogenus: as, a *pseudogeneric* form; *pseudogeneric* names.

pseudogenus (sū-dǫ-jē′nus), *n.*; pl. *pseudogenera* (-jen′ẹ-rä̤). [NL., < Gr. ψευδής, false, + L. *genus*, birth: see *genus*.] 1. In *bot.*, a form-genus; a genus based upon apparent species which are really only stages in the life-cycle of species of other genera. Many of the so-called genera of fungi, bacteria, etc., are *pseudo-* or *form-genera*. See *form-genus*, and compare *form-species*.—2. In *zoöl.*, a spurious genus.

Pseudogenera, or pseudogeneric names, may be due to (*a*) the imagination, as when hypothetical or supposititious ancestral forms, of which nothing is actually known, are named as genera (see several cases among words beginning in *Pro-*, *Proto-*); (*b*) defect or error of observation, particularly of microscopic objects liable to look different when differently manipulated; (*c*) defective or mutilated specimens accurately described but mistaken for normal examples of their kind; (*d*) natural monstrosities not recognized as such; (*e*) normal stages of growth or development of any organism mistaken for a different organism. Many pseudogenera of class (*e*) have been named among animals which undergo marked or peculiar transformations from the embryo to the adult, not understood by the observer at the time, as many cœlenterates, echinoderms, crustaceans, etc., and even some vertebrates, as fishes and batrachians. Pseudogenera in the above senses are all foreign to the question of what degree of difference shall be accounted generic, and also of any question of priority or other nomenclatural rule. Those of class (*a*) have such standing as one may choose to allow them. Those of class (*b*) can have no standing. In classes (*c*) and (*d*) pseudogeneric names may hold if they can be identified and properly recharacterized (and are not obnoxious to any rule of nomenclature). The large class (*e*) of cases based upon literally "larval" or masked forms of organisms whose adults are already named generically has no claim to recognition among New Latin genera properly so called. But many such pseudogeneric words are conveniently retained in a modified sense as English names of the objects which they designate. See, for examples, *Bipinnaria*, *Brachiolaria*, *Cysticercus*, *Leptocephalus*, *Megalops*, *Nauplius*, *Phyllosoma*, *Zœa*.

pseudogeusia (sū-dǫ-gū′si-ä̤), *n.* [NL., < Gr. ψευδής, false, + γεῦσις, sense of taste, < γεύεσθαι, taste: see *gust*².] False taste-perception.

pseudogeustia (sū-dǫ-gūs′ti-ä̤), *n.* [NL., < Gr. ψευδής, false, + γευστός, verbal adj. of γεύεσθαι, taste.] Same as *pseudogeusia*.

pseudograph (sū′dǫ-gràf), *n.* A false writing. See *pseudography*.

pseudographeme (sū-dog′ra̤-fēm), *n.* [< Gr. ψευδογράφημα, that which is untruly drawn, < ψευδής, false, + γράφειν, write.] A fallacy imitating an apodictic syllogism.

pseudographize (sū-dog′ra̤-fīz), *v. t.*; pret. and pp. *pseudographized*, ppr. *pseudographizing*. [< *pseudograph-y* + *-ize*.] To write wrongly; present a word, etc., in an incorrect form by writing, printing, or any other method of graphic representation. [Rare.]

If we account this error typographical, there must have been a widespread conspiracy among old printers to *pseudographize*. *F. Hall*, Mod. Eng., p. 159.

pseudography (sū-dog′ra̤-fi), *n.* [< Gr. ψευδογραφία, a false drawing of a line, < ψευδογραφεῖν, draw falsely, < ψευδής, false, + γράφειν, write.] An incorrect system or method of graphic representation; bad spelling.

"Gh" is only a piece of ill writing with us, . . . for the g sounds just nothing in "trough," "cough," "might," "night," &c. Only the writer was at leisure to add a superfluous Letter, as there are too many in our *pseudography*. *B. Jonson*, Eng. Grammar, i. 4.

I do not intend to pursue the many *pseudographys* in use, . . . but to shew of how great concern the emphasis were, if rightly used. *Holder*, Elements of Speech, p. 104.

Pseudogryphus (sū-dog′ri-fus), *n.* [NL. (Ridgway, 1874), < Gr. ψευδής, false, + LL. *gryphus*, a griffin: see *Gryphæa*.] A genus of *Cathartidæ*, or American vultures, of which the California condor, *P. californianus*, is the only species, having no caruncles on the head, and the plumage of the under parts of peculiar texture. See cut under *condor*.

pseudogyne (sū′dǫ-jīn), *n.* [< Gr. ψευδής, false, + γυνή, female.] One of the agamic or asexual females of plant-lice and some other insects which reproduce without union with the male.

With the *Aphididæ*, coition of males and true females results in the winter egg, from which hatches a pseudogyne, which gives birth to a number of generations of pseudogynes. Lichtenstein and others use the term especially for a member of the first-winged or migrant generation of plant-lice, as distinguished from one of the pupiferous or return migrant generation.

A gall-making aphis, the foundress *pseudogyne*.
Nature, XXX. 69.

pseudogynous (sū-doj′i-nus), *a.* [< *pseudogyne* + *-ous*.] Pertaining to a pseudogyne, or having its character.

pseudogyrate (sū-dǫ-jī′rāt), *a.* [< Gr. ψευδής, false, + L. *gyratus*, pp., turned round: see *gy-*

rate.] • In *bot.*, falsely ringed, as when an elastic ring is confined to the vertex of the spore-cases of ferns. *Treasury of Botany.*

pseudo-heart (sū-dō-härt'), *n.* In brachiopods, one of several tubular infundibuliform organs by which the perivisceral cavity communicates with the pallial chamber, and which were described by Owen as hearts. See cut under *Waldheimia.*

It is probable that these *pseudo-hearts* subserve the function both of renal organs and of genital ducts; and that they are the homologues of the organs of Bojanus of other mollusks, and of the segmental organs of worms. *Huxley*, Anat. Invert., p. 400.

pseudohemal (sū-dō-hē'mal), *a.* [< Gr. ψευδής, false, + αἷμα, blood: see *hemal.*] Like or analogous to blood without being blood: noting various fluids which circulate in the bodies of some invertebrates, especially annelids, and the structures which provide for the circulation of such fluids; water-vascular; chylaqueous; aquiferous. Also *pseudhæmal.*

In the Arthropoda no segmental organs or *pseud-hæmal* vessels are known. *Huxley*, Anat. Invert., p. 57.

pseudohermaphrodite (sū'dō-hėr-maf'rọ-dīt), *a.* Apparently hermaphrodite, though sexed; affected by pseudohermaphroditism.

pseudohermaphroditism (sū"dō-hėr-maf'rọ-di-tizm), *n.* False hermaphroditism; an appearance of hermaphroditism resulting from a monstrous conformation of the external genitals in sexed individuals. The usual conditions are extensive hypospadia of the male organs, or hypertrophy of the clitoris of the female.

pseudohexagonal (sū"dō-hek-sag'ọ-nąl), *a.* In *crystal.*, falsely hexagonal; appearing to be hexagonal, though not really so. Twins of orthorhombic aragonite resembling hexagonal crystals are said to be *pseudohexagonal*; some of the micas are *pseudohexagonal*, because they approximate to the hexagonal system closely in angle.

pseudohypertrophic (sū-dō-hī-pėr-trof'ik), *a.* Pertaining to or of the nature of pseudohypertrophy.—**Pseudohypertrophic paralysis.** See *paralysis.*

pseudohypertrophy (sū"dō-hī-pėr'trọ-fi), *n.* The enlargement of an organ without increase of its proper tissue, as when in muscular pseudohypertrophy there is increase of fat and connective tissue while the muscle-fibers are atrophied.—**Muscular pseudohypertrophy.** Same as *pseudohypertrophic paralysis.*

pseudo-Isidorian Decretals. See *False Decretals*, under *decretal.*

pseudolabial (sū-dō-lā'bi-ąl), *a.* [< *pseudolabi-um* + *-al.*] Of or pertaining to the pseudolabium of a myriapod.

pseudolabium (sū-dō-lā'bi-um), *n.*; pl. *pseudolabia* (-ä). [NL. (Packard, 1883), < Gr. ψευδής, false, + L. *labium*, lip.] In chilopodous *Myriapoda*, the sternite of the subbasilar plate, being the part called *labium* by Newport: usually a large plate, with a median indentation in front and teeth on each side.

It may for convenience in descriptive zoölogy be termed the *pseudolabium.* *A. S. Packard*, Proc. Amer. Philos. Soc., June, 1883, p. 201.

Pseudolarix (sū-dol'a-riks), *n.* [NL. (Gordon, 1858), < Gr. ψευδής, false, + λάριξ, larch: see *Larix.*] A genus of coniferous trees of the tribe *Abietineæ.* By some it is included in the genus *Larix*, the larch, from which it differs in its cones, their pointed scales falling away with the seeds, and in its leaves, which resemble those of *Cedrus*, the cedar, but are deciduous like those of the larch. The only species, *P. Kæmpferi*, is a native of China, and is known as *golden larch*, from the color to which the light-green leaves turn in autumn. It bears pendulous cones about 3 inches long, broad and conical, falling asunder when ripe, except as long woody threads, passing out of the base of the scales, bind them in masses. See *larch.*

pseudolateral (sū-dō-lat'ẹ-rąl), *a.* In *bot.*, having a tendency to become lateral when it is normally terminal, as the fruit of certain *Hepaticæ.*

pseudoleucemia (sū"dō-lū-sē'mi-ä), *n.* [NL. *pseudoleucæmia*, < Gr. ψευδής, false, + λευκός, white, + αἷμα, blood. Cf. *leucemia.*] A disease characterized by progressive hyperplasia of the lymph-glands, sometimes of the spleen, with anemia and the development of secondary lymphatic growth in various parts of the body, but without leucocytosis. Also called *Hodgkin's disease, lymphadenoma, malignant lymphoma, lymphosarcoma, anemia lymphatica*, etc.

pseudoleucocythemia (sū-dō-lū"kō-si-thē'mi-ä), *n.* [NL. *pseudoleucocythæmia*, < Gr. ψευδής, false, + λευκός, white, + κύτος, cell, + αἷμα, blood. Cf. *leucemia.*] Same as *pseudoleucemia.*

pseudolichen (sū-dō-lī'ken), *n.* A so-called lichen which does not possess the one mark of a true lichen—that is, the presence of algæ in the thallus. These plants are simply ascomycetous fungi parasitic upon a true lichen-thallus or other plant. See *lichen.*

Pseudoliva (sū-dol'i-vä), *n.* [NL., < Gr. ψευδής, false, + NL. *Oliva*, q. v.] In *conch.*, the typical genus of *Pseudolivinæ.* *Swainson.* Also *Gastridium.*

Pseudolivinæ (sū-dol-i-vī'nē), *n. pl.* [NL., < *Pseudoliva* + *-inæ.*] A subfamily of *Buccinidæ*, typified by the genus *Pseudoliva.* The shell is bucciniform, and the operculum has a lateral nucleus. The typical species is the existing *Pseudoliva plumbea* of the Atlantic coast of Africa, but most of the species are extinct.

Pseudoliva plumbea.

Pseudolmedia (sū-dol-mē'di-ä), *n.* [NL. (Trécul, 1847), < Gr. ψευδής, false, + NL. *Olmedia*, a related genus of plants.] A genus of apetalous trees and shrubs of the order *Urticaceæ*, tribe *Artocarpeæ*, and subtribe *Olmedieæ*, characterized by receptacles containing numerous staminate flowers mixed with scales and without distinct perianths, and by pistillate flowers solitary in their receptacles. There are 5 species, natives of tropical America and the West Indies. They bear shining entire alternate short-stalked leaves, which are feather-veined and thin but coriaceous. The ovoid fruit is inclosed in a persistent and enlarged fleshy perianth, and the whole forms in *P. spuria* of Jamaica an edible red drupe-like fruit. See *bastard bread-nut* (under *bread-nut*), and *milkwood.*

pseudologist† (sū-dol'ọ-jist), *n.* [< Gr. ψευδολογιστής, one who speaks falsely, a liar, < ψευδολόγος, speaking falsely: see *pseudology.*] A retailer of falsehoods; a liar.

pseudology† (sū-dol'ọ-ji), *n.* [< Gr. ψευδολογία, falsehood, < ψευδολόγος, speaking falsely, < ψευδής, false, + λέγειν, speak: see *-ology.*] The science of lying; falsehood of speech; mendacity; lying.

Not according to the sound rules of *pseudology.* *Arbuthnot.*

pseudomalachite (sū-dō-mal'ạ-kīt), *n.* A hydrous phosphate of copper occurring ordinarily in massive forms of a bright-green color, much resembling malachite. It is closely related to dihydrite and ehlite.

Pseudomelania (sū-dō-mẹ-lā'ni-ä), *n.* [NL., < Gr. ψευδής, false, + NL. *Melania*, q. v.] An extinct genus of shells superficially resembling a melanian, typical of the family *Pseudomelaniidæ.*

Pseudomelaniidæ (sū-dō-mel-ạ-nī'i-dē), *n. pl.* [NL., < *Pseudomelania* + *-idæ.*] A family of tænioglossate gastropods, typified by the genus *Pseudomelania.* They had elongated turreted shells with the aperture oral and the columella simple or plicated forward. The species inhabited the seas of the Paleozoic to the Tertiary epochs, and are entirely extinct.

pseudomembrane (sū-dō-mem'brān), *n.* A false membrane. See *membrane.*

pseudomembranous (sū-dō-mem'brạ-nus), *a.* Of, pertaining to, or of the nature of a pseudomembrane.—**Pseudomembranous bronchitis**, bronchitis with the formation of a false membrane lining the bronchial tubes. It may be due to diphtheria, to the inhalation of hot steam, or to other causes.—**Pseudomembranous enteritis**, a non-febrile affection of the intestinal mucous membrane, characterized by the periodical formation of viscous, shreddy, or tubular exudates composed mainly of mucin.—**Pseudomembranous laryngitis**, a laryngitis characterized by the formation on and in the mucous membrane of a croupous pseudomembrane; true croup.—**Pseudomembranous tracheitis**, an inflammation of the mucous membrane of the trachea accompanied by the formation of a pseudomembrane.

pseudometallic (sū"dō-me-tal'ik), *a.* Falsely or imperfectly metallic: specifically applied to a kind of luster closely resembling that of metals.

pseudomonocotyledonous (sū-dō-mon-ọ-kot-i-lē'dō-nus), *a.* In *bot.*, having two or more cotyledons consolidated into a single mass, as in the horse-chestnut.

pseudomorph (sū'dō-môrf), *n.* [< Gr. ψευδής, false, + μορφή, form.] A deceptive, irregular, or false form; specifically, in *mineral.*, a mineral having a definite form belonging, not to the substance of which it consists, but to some other substance which has wholly or partially disappeared. Sometimes quartz is found in the form of fluor-spar crystals, the fluor-spar having been changed by a process of substitution into quartz. Such crystals are pseudomorphs by substitution; another illustration is that of tinstone, cassiterite, after orthoclase feldspar. A more common and important class of pseudomorphs includes those formed by the chemical alteration of the original mineral: these are illustrated by pseudomorphs of native copper after the oxid cuprite, where there has been a simple loss of one ingredient, in this case oxygen; also, of gypsum after anhydrite, where the anhydrous calcium sulphate has been changed by assumption of water to the hydrous sulphate; or, still more important, where there has been a more or less complete exchange of constituents, as of the lead carbonate cerusite after the lead sulphid galena, or of serpentine after chrysolite, or of kaolin after feldspar, etc. Pseudomorphs are also formed by molecular change without change of chemical substance, as of calcite after aragonite, or rutile after brookite; these last are also called *paramorphs.* (See *paramorphism.*) Pseudomorphs very commonly have a non-crystalline waxy structure, but this is not necessarily the case.

pseudomorphia (sū-dọ-môr'fi-ä), *n.* [NL., < Gr. ψευδής, false, + NL. *morphia.*] One of the alkaloids of opium, $C_{17}H_{19}NO_4$. Also called *phormia, oxymorphia.*

pseudomorphic (sū-dẹ-môr'fik), *a.* [< *pseudomorph* + *-ic.*] Same as *pseudomorphous.*

pseudomorphine (sū-dọ-môr'fin), *n.* [< Gr. ψευδής, false, + NL. *morphina*, morphine.] Same as *pseudomorphia.*

pseudomorphism (sū-dō-môr'fizm), *n.* [< *pseudomorph* + *-ism.*] The state of having a form, usually crystalline, different from that proper to the mineral; the process by which this state is brought about. See *pseudomorph.*

pseudomorphosis (sū"dọ-môr-fō'sis), *n.* [NL., < Gr. ψευδής, false, + μόρφωσις, a shaping, < μορφοῦν, form, shape, < μορφή, form.] Same as *pseudomorphism.*

pseudomorphous (sū-dō-môr'fus), *a.* [< *pseudomorph* + *-ous.*] Not having the true form; characterized by or exhibiting pseudomorphism; in *mineral.*, noting substances having an external form, usually crystalline, which does not properly belong to themselves. See *pseudomorph.*

pseudomorula (sū-dọ-mor'ọ-lä), *n.*; pl. *pseudomorulæ* (-lē). A false morula: applied by W. S. Kent to a collection or aggregate of cells or spores of distinctly unicellular animals, resembling a morula, but of a different morphological character. See *morula.*

pseudomorular (sū-dọ-mor'ọ-lär), *a.* [< *pseudomorula* + *-ar*[3].] Having the character of a pseudomorula.

pseudonavicella (sū-dō-nav-i-sel'ä), *n.*; pl. *pseudonavicellæ* (-ē). [NL., < Gr. ψευδής, false, + LL. *navicella*, a small boat, dim. of *navis*, a ship: see *nave*[2].] The embryonic form of a gregarine; one of a number of minute bodies into which the substance of an adult encysted gregarine breaks up in reproduction. Pseudonavicellæ are so called from their resemblance to the navicellæ or naviculæ of diatoms. On the rupture of the cyst of the adult gregarine these bodies escape; and on rupture of the pseudonavicellæ themselves the embryo proper is similarly set free. See *pseudofilaria*, and cut under *Gregarinidæ.* Also *pseudonavicula.*

pseudonavicellar (sū-dō-nav-i-sel'är), *a.* [< *pseudonavicella* + *-ar*[3].] Pertaining to a pseudonavicella, or having its character, as the spores of *Sporozoa.* Also *pseudonavicular.*

pseudonavicula (sū"dọ-nạ-vik'ụ-lä), *n.*; pl. *pseudonaviculæ* (-lē). [NL., < Gr. ψευδής, false, + L. *navicula*, a small boat, dim. of *navis*, a ship.] Same as *pseudonavicella.*

pseudonavicular (sū"dọ-nạ-vik'ụ-lär), *a.* [< *pseudonavicula* + *-ar*[3].] Same as *pseudonavicellar.*

pseudoneuropter (sū"dọ-nụ-rop'tėr), *n.* [< *Pseudoneuroptera.*] A pseudoneuropterous insect.

Pseudoneuroptera (sū"dọ-nụ-rop'tẹ-rä), *n. pl.* [NL., < Gr. ψευδής, false, + NL. *Neuroptera*, q. v.] An order of *Insecta*, proposed by Erichson in 1840 to contain those neuropterous insects which have the metamorphosis incomplete, four membranous wings usually many-veined, and mandibulate mouth-parts (except in one family, *Ephemeridæ*). The order thus defined has been divided into three suborders: (1) *Platyptera*, including the *Perlidæ, Psocidæ, Embiidæ*, and *Termitidæ*; (2) *Odonata* or dragon-flies; and (3) *Ephemerina* or May-flies. Brauer, however, dismembers the *Pseudoneuroptera*, and distributes its components in his second, third, fourth, and sixth orders—*Ephemerida, Odonata, Plecoptera*, and *Corrodentia*—his *Plecoptera* including the perlids, and his *Corrodentia* the termites and *Psocidæ.*

pseudoneuropterous (sū"dō-nụ-rop'tẹ-rus), *a.* [< *Pseudoneuropter-a* + *-ous.*] Pertaining to the *Pseudoneuroptera*, or having their characters.

pseudo-nipple (sū'dō-nip"l), *n.* A false nipple of the mammary gland, produced by the elevation of the non-glandular part around a depression at the bottom of which the ducts open.

Pseudoniscidæ (sū-dō-nis'i-dē), *n. pl.* [NL., < *Pseudoniscus* + *-idæ.*] A family of synziphosurous merostomatous crustaceans of Carboniferous age, typified by the genus *Pseudoniscus.* They had an oval body, short head, large compound eyes, and abdomen with seven segments besides the telson.

Pseudoniscus (sū-dō-nis'kus), *n.* [NL., < Gr. ψευδής, false, + NL. *Oniscus*, q. v.] The typical genus of *Pseudoniscidæ*.

pseudonomania (sū"don-ō-mā'ni-ạ), *n.* [Irreg. < Gr. ψεύδειν (ppr. ψεύδων), belie, mid. ψεύδεσθαι, lie (see *pseudo-*), + μανία, madness.] A morbid propensity to lie.

pseudonucleolus (sū"dō-nū-klē'ō-lus), *n.*; pl. *pseudonucleoli* (-lī). [NL., < Gr. ψευδής, false, + L. *nucleolus*, dim. of *nucleus*, a little nut: see *nucleolus*.] An accessory or supplementary nucleus of some ova.

pseudonychium (sū-dō-nik'i-um), *n.*; pl. *pseudonychia* (-ạ̈). [NL., < Gr. ψευδής, false, + NL. *onychium*, q. v.] In *entom.*, the onychium or spurious claw between the true tarsal claws. See *empodium* and *onychium*, and compare *paronychium*.

pseudonym (sū'dō-nim), *n.* [Also *pseudonyme*; < F. *pseudonyme*, < Gr. ψευδώνυμος, having a false name, < ψευδής, false, + ὄνυμα, ὄνομα, name.] 1. A false name; especially, a fictitious name assumed by an author in order to conceal or veil his identity.

The [Brontë] sisters adopted the *pseudonyms* Currer, Ellis, and Acton Bell, corresponding to their initials.
L. Stephen, Dict. National Biog., VI. 410.

2. In *nat. hist.*, the vernacular name of a species or other group of animals or plants, as distinguished from its tenable technical name: thus, *robin* is the *pseudonym* of *Turdus migratorius*. *Coues*, The Auk, I. 321 (1884).

pseudonymal (sū-don'i-mạl), *a.* [< *pseudonym* + *-al*.] In *zoöl.*, vernacular; not technical nor tenable, as the name of an animal; not having the character of an onym. *Coues.*

pseudonymity (sū-dō-nim'ị-ti), *n.* [< *pseudonym* + *-ity*.] The state of being pseudonymous, or of bearing a false name or signature; the act or practice of writing under an assumed name. *Contemporary Rev.* (*Imp. Dict.*)

pseudonymous (sụ̄-don'i-mus), *a.* [< Gr. ψευδώνυμος, having a false name: see *pseudonym*.] Bearing a pseudonym, or false name: applied to an author who publishes a work under a false or feigned name, or to a work thus published.

In the primitive age of publication, before there existed "a reading public," literary productions were often anonymous; or . . . they wore the mask of a fictitious name, and were *pseudonymous*.
I. D'Israeli, Amen. of Lit., II. 346.

pseudonymously (sụ̄-don'i-mus-li), *adv.* In a pseudonymous manner; under a pseudonym, or fictitious or false name.

That vile concoction of camomile which you so *pseudonymously* dignify with the title of "Bitter Ale."
Barham, Ingoldsby Legends, II., Pref.

pseudoparalysis (sū"dō-pạ-ral'i-sis), *n.* An affection resembling paralysis, but regarded as distinct from ordinary forms.—**Spastic pseudoparalysis.** Same as *spastic spinal paralysis* (which see, under *paralysis*).

pseudoparaplegia (sū-dō-par-ạ-plē'ji-ạ̈), *n.* An affection like paraplegia, but regarded as essentially distinct.—**Tetanoid pseudoparaplegia.** Same as *spastic spinal paralysis* (which see, under *paralysis*).

pseudo-parasite (sū-dō-par'ạ-sīt), *n.* An apparent parasite; a commensal or inquiline; also, a plant which attacks vegetable tissues, but only when they are dead.

pseudoparasitic (sū-dō-par-ạ-sit'ik), *a.* Parasitic apparently but not really; commensal; inquiline.

pseudoparenchyma (sū"dō-pa-reng'ki-mạ̈), *n.* In *mycol.*, a tissue resembling parenchyma, but of far different origin, being produced from united and transformed hyphæ.

pseudoparenchymatous (sū-dō-par-eng-kim'ạ-tus), *a.* In *bot.*, belonging to or resembling pseudoparenchyma.

pseudoparenchyme (sū"dō-pa-reng'kim), *n.* Same as *pseudoparenchyma*.

pseudoparesis (sū-dō-par'ē-sis), *n.* An affection resembling paresis, but regarded as distinct from ordinary forms.—**Spastic pseudoparesis.** Same as *spastic spinal paralysis* (which see, under *paralysis*).

pseudoparthenogenesis (sū-dō-pär"the-nō-jen'e-sis), *n.* That mode of reproduction which is intermediate between metagenesis and parthenogenesis proper. *Spencer*, Prin. of Biol., I. 214.

pseudo-patron (sū-dō-pā'trọn), *n.* A pretended or would-be patron. [Rare.]

Disturbers of a right of advowson may therefore be these three persons—the *pseudo-patron*, his clerk, and the ordinary.
Blackstone, Com., III. xvi.

pseudopediform (sū-dō-ped'i-fôrm), *a.* [< Gr. ψευδής, false, + L. *pes* (*ped-*), = E. *foot*, + *forma*, form.] Having the character of a pseudopod; pseudopodial.

Body ciliated, . . . without *pseudopediform* prolongations.
Arthur Adams, Man. Nat. Hist., p. 370.

pseudopercular (sū-dō-pėr'kū-lạ̈r), *a.* [< *pseudopercul-um* + *-ar*3.] False or secondary, as an operculum; pertaining to a pseudoperculum.

pseudoperculate (sū-dō-pėr'kū-lāt), *a.* [< *pseudopercul-um* + *-ate*1.] Provided with a pseudoperculum; having the aperture closed by a pseudoperculum.

pseudoperculum (sū-dō-pėr'kū-lum), *n.*; pl. *pseudopercula* (-lạ̈). [NL., < Gr. ψευδής, false, + L. *operculum*, a lid, cover: see *opercle*.] A false opercle; a kind of secondary lid closing the aperture of the shell of some pulmonate gastropods. See *clausilium*. Also called *hibernaculum*.

pseudoperidium (sū"dō-pe-rid'i-um), *n.* In *mycol.*, a false peridium: a name given to the membranous cup inclosing the spores in *Æcidium*. See *peridium* and *Æcidium*.

pseudoperiodic (sū-dō-pē-ri-od'ik), *a.* Quasi-periodic.

pseudoperipteral (sū"dō-pe-rip'te-rạl), *a.* In *arch.*, falsely peripteral: noting a temple with a portico in front, or porticos in front and rear,

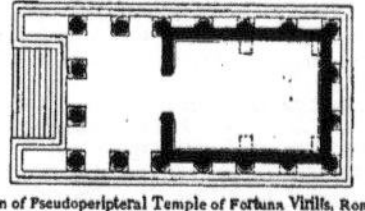

Plan of Pseudoperipteral Temple of Fortuna Virilis, Rome.

but with the columns on its flanks engaged in the walls, instead of standing free. Compare plan under *opisthodomos*.

There are but two known examples of Greek antiquity of a *pseudo-peripteral* structure—the gigantic fane of Jupiter Olympius at Agrigentum, and the nine-columned edifice at Pæstum.
Encyc. Brit., II. 410.

pseudoperipteros (sū"dō-pe-rip'te-ros), *n.* [L., < Gr. ψευδοπερίπτερος, with a false peristyle, < ψευδής, false, + περίπτερος, with a single row of columns all around: see *peripteros*.] A pseudoperipteral structure.

It would be difficult to decide whether this peculiar *pseudo-peripteros* [temple of Zeus at Agrigentum] owed its conformation to the building-stone at disposal, . . . or whether other considerations led to this abnormal negation of the fundamental principles of columnar architecture.
Reber, Ancient Art (tr. by Clarke), p. 219.

Pseudophallia (sū-dō-fal'i-ạ̈), *n. pl.* [NL., < Gr. ψευδής, false, + φαλλός, phallus.] In Mörch's system, a class of gastropods characterized by the supposed absence of an intromittent male organ, comprising the orders *Rhipidoglossa* and *Docoglossa*. Also called *Exocephala*.

Pseudophidia (sū-dō-fid'i-ạ̈), *n. pl.* [NL., < Gr. ψευδής, false, + ὀφίδιον, dim. of ὄφις, a serpent: see *Ophidia*.] In De Blainville's system of classification, an order of *Amphibia*, characterized by the limbless serpentiform body (whence the name); the cæcilians, or *Ophiomorpha*. See *Cæciliidæ*.

pseudophidian (sū-dō-fid'i-an), *a.* and *n.* [< *Pseudophidia* + *-an*.] **I.** *a.* Having the appearance of an ophidian, as an amphibian; belonging to the *Pseudophidia*.

II. *n.* A member of the *Pseudophidia*.

pseudophone (sū'dō-fōn), *n.* [< Gr. ψευδής, false, + φωνή, voice.] An instrument for the study of the perception of direction of sounds by the human ear. By it sound may be made to appear as coming from any direction other than the true one. Ear-pieces fastened to the head by straps, and carrying adjustable tin-plate mirrors—the latter producing the effects—constitute the instrument.

Pseudophyllidea (sū"dō-fi-lid'ē-ạ̈), *n. pl.* [NL., < Gr. ψευδής, false, + φύλλον, leaf, + *-idea*.] A group of the *Cestoidea*, or cestoid worms, including those tapeworms which, when mature, have neither suckers nor lobes on the head, but a deep groove on each side. The group includes tapes found in various fishes, amphibians, and water-birds, as well as *Bothriocephalus latus*, the broad tapeworm, occasionally infesting the human body.

Pseudopneumona (sū-dō-nū'mō-nạ̈), *n. pl.* [NL., < Gr. ψευδής, false, + πνεύμων, lung.] A group of rostriferous gastropods, with the gills in very numerous cross-rows on the inner surface of the mantle, eyes in front of the bases of the tentacles, and operculum spiral. It included the families *Littorinidæ*, *Lacunidæ*, and *Truncatellidæ*. *J. E. Gray.*

pseudopod (sū'dō-pod), *n.* [< Gr. ψευδής, false, + πούς (ποδ-) = E. *foot*.] 1. A member of the *Pseudopoda*, as an amœba; any protozoan which is provided with pseudopodia, or has the power of protruding diversiform parts of its sarcode in the form of pseudopodia, serving as temporary organs of locomotion; a rhizopod; a myxopod.—2. A pseudopodium.

Pseudopoda (sụ̄-dop'ō-dạ̈), *n. pl.* [NL.: see *pseudopod*.] In Ehrenberg's system of classification (1836), a division of anenterous infusorians, containing those called *root-footed*, or the *Amœbæa*, *Arcellina*, and *Bacillaria*. The term is disused, but is the origin of the very common words *pseudopod* and *pseudopodium*.

pseudopodal (sụ̄-dop'ō-dạl), *a.* [< *pseudopod* + *-al*.] 1. Provided with pseudopods; furnished with false feet; of or pertaining to the *Pseudopoda*; rhizopod; myxopod.—2. Pertaining to pseudopodia; pseudopodial.

pseudopode (sū'dẹ̄-pōd), *n.* [< *pseudopodium*.] Same as *pseudopodium*.

pseudopodia, *n.* Plural of *pseudopodium*.

pseudopodial (sū-dō-pō'di-ạl), *a.* [< *pseudopodium* + *-al*.] Pertaining to pseudopodia; forming or formed by pseudopodia: as, a *pseudopodial* process; *pseudopodial* movement; the *pseudopodial* aperture for the protrusion of pseudopodia in the test of a foraminifer.

pseudopodian (sū-dō-pō'di-ạn), *a.* [< *pseudopodium* + *-an*.] Same as *pseudopodial*.

pseudopodic (sū-dō-pod'ik), *a.* [< *pseudopod* + *-ic*.] Same as *pseudopodal*. *W. S. Kent.*

pseudopodium (sū-dō-pō'di-um), *n.*; pl. *pseudopodia* (-ạ̈). [NL., < Gr. ψευδής, false, + πούς (ποδ-) = E. *foot*.] 1. In *Protozoa*, as pseudopods, rhizopods, or myxopods, a temporary diversiform prolongation or protrusion of the sarcode or body-substance of the animalcule, to any extent or in any shape, capable of being withdrawn or reabsorbed into the general mass of the body, and serving as an organ of locomotion, prehension, or ingestion; a pseudopod, or false foot: generally in the plural. The term is very comprehensive in its application to foot-like, finger-like, or ray-like processes of the body of protozoans; but it is the essential character of a pseudopodium to be soft, diversiform, or variable in shape, and temporary, or subject to reabsorption—in which respects the organ differs from the fixed or constant processes of many protozoans, as cilia or flagella. Pseudopodia are highly characteristic of the lower or non-corticate protozoans, the myxopods or rhizopods proper, as all the amœbiforms, the heliozoans, the foraminifers, etc. They may be broad and lobate processes of sarcode, or slender filamentous rays. When lobate the pseudopodia remain distinct from one another, their margins are clear and transparent, and the granules which they may contain plainly flow into their interior from the more fluid central part of the body; or the whole body of the animalcule may flow into such a pseudopod, thus effecting a peculiar kind of locomotion. But when they are filiform they are very apt to run into one another, and give rise to networks, the constituent filaments of which, however, readily separate and regain their previous form; and, whether they do this or not, the surfaces of these pseudopodia are beset by minute granules, which are in incessant motion. See cuts under *Actinosphærium*, *Amœba*, and *Rotalia*.

2. In *Rotifera*, the aboral region, caudal extremity, or tail-end of a wheel-animalcule. It varies much in size, form, and function, and may be absent. When best developed, it is a considerable muscular organ, serving as a sucker-like means of attachment or as a fin-like organ for swimming. It is sometimes a pair of tails, like styles or flaps.

3. In *bot.*: (*a*) In *Musci*, a false pedicel, or elongation of the extremity of a branch of the oöphyte, in the form of a stalk, supporting a sporogonium or capsule.

In Sphagnum, the sporogonium is fully developed within the epigonal leaves, and when complete the axis beneath it elongates, forming the *pseudopodium*.
Encyc. Brit., IV. 116.

(*b*) In *Mycetozoa*, a protrusion of the protoplasm of an amœboid body, which may be drawn in, or into which the whole body may move.

pseudoproct (sū'dō-prokt), *n.* [< Gr. ψευδής, false, + πρωκτός, anus.] 1. The anus or anal opening of the pseudembryo or echinopædium of an echinoderm.—2. The false oscule, or pseudostome, of a sponge. *W. J. Sollas.*

The faulty use of the term oscule for what is neither functionally nor morphologically a mouth is here obvious, for in one sense the oscule is always a pseudostome; it would be better if the term *pseudoproct* could be substituted.
Encyc. Brit., XXII. 416.

pseudoproctous (sū-dō-prok'tus), *a.* [< *pseudoproct* + *-ous*.] Provided with a pseudoproct.

pseudoprostyle (sū-dō-prō stīl), *a.* [< Gr. ψευδής, false, + πρόστυλος, prostyle.] Noting a portico the projection of which from the wall is less than the width of its intercolumniation. *Hosking.*

pseudopsia (sū-dop'si-ạ̈), *n.* [NL., < Gr. ψευδής, false, + ὄψις, sight.] False sight-perception.

pseudopupa (sū-dọ̄-pū'pạ̈), *n.*; pl. *pseudopupæ* (-pē). [NL., < Gr. ψευδής, false, + NL. *pupa*, q. v.] A false pupa: applied to the fifth stage, or coarctate pupa, of those insects which undergo hypermetamorphosis. Also called *semipupa*. See *coarctate*, and cut under *Sitaris*.

pseudopupal (sū-dọ̄-pū'pạl), *a.* [< *pseudopupa* + *-al.*] Pertaining to a pseudopupa, or having its characters.

Pseudopus (sū'dọ̄-pus), *n.* [NL. (Merrem, 1820), < Gr. ψευδής, false, + πούς (ποδ-) = E. *foot.*] A genus of lizards of the family *Zonuridæ*, having rudimentary hind limbs and traces of shoulder-girdles. *P. pallasi* is an example.

pseudoramose (sū-dọ̄-rā'mōs), *n.* [< Gr. ψευδής, false, + L. *ramus*, a branch: see *ramus*, *ramose.*] In *bot.*, forming false branches. See *pseudoramulus*.

pseudoramulus (sū-dọ̄-ram'ụ̄-lus), *n.*; pl. *pseudoramuli* (-lī). [NL., < Gr. ψευδής, false, + L. *ramulus*, dim. of *ramus*, a branch.] In *bot.*, a false branch: applied to the filaments of the *Rivulariaceæ* and other algæ, in which the terminal part of the filament detaches itself and applies itself laterally to an enlarged part of the filament called the heterocyst. See *heterocyst*.

pseudo-ray (sū'dọ̄-rā), *n.* A straight line or ray in non-Euclidean geometry.

Pseudorca (sū-dôr'kạ̈), *n.* [NL., < Gr. ψευδής, false, + L. *orca*, a kind of whale: see *Orca*[1].] A genus of cetaceans, established for the reception of the *Phocæna crassidens* of Owen, discovered subfossil in England, and afterward found living, related to *Orca*, but having only about 40 teeth and 50 vertebræ, the cervicals mostly ankylosed, the lumbars half as long again as they are broad. The animal is black, and attains a length of 14 feet.

Pseudoscines (sụ̄-dos'i-nēz), *n. pl.* [NL., < Gr. ψευδής, false, + L. *oscen* (*oscin-*), a singing bird: see *Oscines*.] In *ornith.*, in Sclater's arrangement of 1880, a suborder of *Passeres*, including the *Acromyodi abnormales* of Garrod and Forbes, or the genera *Menura* and *Atrichia* of Australia, as together distinguished from *Oscines*, or normal acromyodian *Passeres*.

pseudoscinine (sū-dos'i-nin), *a.* Anomalously oscinine, as the lyre-birds and scrub-birds of Australia; belonging to the *Pseudoscines*.

pseudosclerosis (sū"dọ̄-sklē-rō'sis), *n.* A case resembling clinically multiple sclerosis, but not presenting the characteristic lesions post mortem.

pseudoscope (sū'dọ̄-skōp), *n.* [< Gr. ψευδής, false, + σκοπεῖν, view.] A kind of stereoscope that makes concave parts appear convex, and convex parts concave. Wheatstone's pseudoscope produces these effects by the use of two hint-glass rectangular prisms, which reflect the light coming from the object viewed from their inner surfaces, the latter being, with reference to the eye of the observer, at the angle of total reflection.

> Hence, too, the obstinacy with which human faces and forms, and other extremely familiar convex objects, refuse to appear hollow when viewed through Wheatstone's *pseudoscope*. *W. James*, Mind, XII. 528.

pseudoscopic (sū-dọ̄-skop'ik), *a.* [< *pseudoscope* + *-ic.*] Pertaining to the pseudoscope, or to the class of optical phenomena which it presents, in which false impressions of visual objects are conveyed to the mind.

> By *pseudoscopic* vision we mean that "conversion of relief" which is produced by the combination of two reversed perspective projections. *W. B. Carpenter*, Micros., § 31.

> The second [group of illusions] relates to the instability of our judgments of relative distance and size by the eye, and includes especially what are known as *pseudoscopic* illusions. *W. James*, Mind, XII. 524.

pseudoscopically (sū-dọ̄-skop'i-kạl-i), *adv.* In a pseudoscopic manner; as in a pseudoscope.

> When mounted *pseudoscopically*, at first it [a photograph] is very unsatisfactory. *Jour. Franklin Inst.*, CXXIII. 428.

pseudoscopy (sū'dọ̄-skō-pi), *n.* [< *pseudoscope* + *-y*[3].] The use of the pseudoscope, or the production of effects similar to those exhibited by it.

pseudoscorpion (sū-dọ̄-skôr'pi-ọn), *n.* [< NL. *pseudoscorpio(n-)*, < Gr. ψευδής, false, + σκορπίος, L. *scorpio(n-)*, a scorpion.] A false scorpion; a member of the *Pseudoscorpiones* or *Cheliferidæ*. See cut in next column.

Pseudoscorpiones (sū"dọ̄-skôr-pi-ọ̄'nēz), *n. pl.* [NL., pl. of *pseudoscorpio(n-)*: see *pseudoscorpion.*] An order of tracheate arachnidans, with segmented abdomen not distinctly separated from the cephalothorax, didactyl or chelate maxillary palps, two or four eyes, and no postabdomen nor poison-glands; the false scorpions, of the families *Cheliferidæ* and *Obisiidæ*. Also called *Cheliferidea*. Also *Pseudoscorpionina*, and as a family *Pseudoscorpionidæ*.

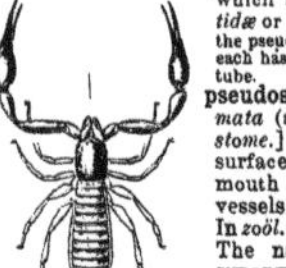

Pseudoscorpion (*Chelifer obisium*). (Hair-line shows natural size.)

pseudoseptate (sū-dọ̄-sep'tāt), *a.* 1. In *bot.*, having the appearance of being septate, as many spores.—2. In *zoöl.*, having pseudosepta, as corals.

pseudoseptum (sū-dọ̄-sep'tum), *n.*; pl. *pseudosepta* (-tạ̈). In corals, a false septum; a septum not homologous with the regular septa of corals—that is, not identified as a calcified mesentery. Thus, in *Heliopora*, with eight mesenteries only, there are twelve pseudosepta.

pseudosiphon (sū-dọ̄-sī'fọn), *n.* [NL., < Gr. ψευδής, false, + σίφων, siphon: see *siphon.*] A false siphon; the vertical trace in the external solid plug of the truncated shell of certain cephalopods, as orthoceratites, continuous with the true siphon. *A. Hyatt*, Proc. Bost. Soc. Nat. Hist., XXII. 258.

pseudosiphonal (sū-dọ̄-sī'fọ̄-nạl), *a.* [< *pseudosiphon* + *-al.*] Of, pertaining to, or resembling the pseudosiphon of cephalopods.

pseudosiphuncle (sū-dọ̄-sī'fung-kl), *n.* [< Gr. ψευδής, false, + E. *siphuncle.*] A pseudosiphon. *A. Hyatt.*

pseudosmia (sū-dos'mi-ạ̈), *n.* [NL., < Gr. ψευδής, false, + ὀσμή, odor.] False smell-perception.

Pseudosolaneæ (sū"dọ̄-sọ̄-lā'nẹ̄-ē), *n. pl.* [NL. (Bentham and Hooker, 1876), < Gr. ψευδής, false, + NL. *Solaneæ.*] A series or suborder of gamopetalous plants of the order *Scrophularineæ*, having some relationship with the order *Solanaceæ*, and characterized by alternate leaves, uniformly centripetal inflorescence, a five-lobed corolla with the two upper lobes exterior, and four, sometimes five, perfect stamens. It includes 9 genera and 3 tribes, of which the *Verbasceæ*, or the mullen tribe, is the chief. They are herbs or shrubs, the flowers with a broad corolla-tube bearing rather flat and spreading lobes.

pseudospermic (sū-dọ̄-spėr'mik), *a.* [< *pseudospermium* + *-ic.*] In *bot.*, forming or pertaining to a pseudospermium.

pseudospermium (sū-dọ̄-spėr'mi-um), *n.* [NL., < Gr. ψευδής, false, + σπέρμα, seed.] In *bot.*, any one-seeded indehiscent fruit in which the pericarp so closely invests the seed that the whole appears as merely a seed—for example, an achenium.

pseudospermous (sū-dọ̄-spėr'mus), *a.* [As *pseudosperm-ic* + *-ous.*] Same as *pseudospermic*.

pseudosphere (sū'dọ̄-sfēr), *n.* 1. A surface of constant negative curvature.—2. A sphere in non-Euclidean geometry.

pseudospherical (sū-dọ̄-sfer'i-kạl), *a.* Having a constant negative curvature.

> Were space really *pseudospherical*, then stars would exhibit a real parallax even if they were infinitely distant. *Encyc. Brit.*, XV. 664.

Pseudospherical surface, a surface like that generated by the rotation on its axis of the curve

$$x + \sqrt{r^2 - y^2} = r \log \frac{r - \sqrt{r^2 - y^2}}{y}.$$

Pseudospora (sụ̄-dos'pọ̄-rạ̈), *n.* [NL., < Gr. ψευδής, false, + σπόρος, seed.] A genus of myxomycetous fungi, typical of the family *Pseudosporeæ*, with plasmodium wanting, or at least unknown.

pseudospore (sū'dọ̄-spōr), *n.* [< Gr. ψευδής, false, + σπόρος, seed.] In *mycol.*, same as *teleutospore*.

Pseudosporeæ (sū-dọ̄-spō'rẹ̄-ē), *n. pl.* [NL. (Zopf), < *Pseudospora* + *-eæ.*] A family of myxomycetous fungi of the class *Monadineæ*, typified by the genus *Pseudospora*.

pseudostella (sū-dọ̄-stel'ạ̈), *n.* [NL., < Gr. ψευδής, false, + L. *stella*, star.] A meteor or phenomenon of any kind resembling a star in the heavens.

pseudostigma (sū-dọ̄-stig'mạ̈), *n.*; pl. *pseudostigmata* (-mạ-tạ̈). A kind of false stigma with which some tracheate acarines, as the *Oribatidæ* or beetle-mites, are provided. In these mites the pseudostigmata are conspicuous, dorsal, tubular, and each has a filament projecting from the interior of the tube.

pseudostoma (sụ̄-dos'tọ̄-mạ̈), *n.*; pl. *pseudostomata* (sū-dọ̄-stō'mạ-tạ̈). [NL.: see *pseudostome.*] 1. In *anat.*, a supposed opening on the surface of a serous membrane, regarded as the mouth of one of the absorbents or lymphatic vessels which begin in such membranes.—2. In *zoöl.*: (*a*) Same as *pseudostome*, 2. (*b*†) [*cap.*] The name-giving genus of *Pseudostomidæ*: synonymous with *Geomys*. *Thomas Say*, 1823. Also called *Diplostoma*, *Saccophorus*, and *Ascomys*.

pseudostomatous (sū-dọ̄-stom'ạ-tus), *a.* [< *pseudostoma(t-)* + *-ous.*] Provided with pseudostomata, as a serous surface; of or pertaining to a pseudostoma.

pseudostome (sū'dọ̄-stōm), *n.* [< NL. *pseudostoma* (cf. Gr. ψευδόστομα, the false or blind mouth of a river), < Gr. ψευδής, false, + στόμα, mouth.] 1. The mouth or oral orifice of the pseudembryo or echinopædium of an echinoderm; a pseudostoma: correlated with *pseudoproct*.—2. The false osculum or secondary opening replacing an original, oscule of a sponge. Also called *pseudoproct*.

> Secondary canals or cavities, which may be incurrent (vestibular) or excurrent (cloacal), the opening of the latter to the exterior being termed a false oscule or *pseudostome*. *W. J. Sollas*, Encyc. Brit., XXII. 416.

3. A pouched rat, or pocket-gopher, of North America, as *Geomys bursarius*. See *Pseudostoma*, 2 (*b*).

Pseudostomidæ (sū-dọ̄-stom'i-dē), *n. pl.* [NL. (Gervais, 1848), < *Pseudostoma* + *-idæ.*] A family of American rodents, with external cheek-pouches, named from the genus *Pseudostoma*; the pocket-rats and pocket-mice, now dissociated in the two families *Geomyidæ* and *Saccomyidæ*; the pseudostomes.

pseudostomine (sū-dọ̄-stō'min), *a.* [< *pseudostome* + *-ine*[1].] Having external cheek-pouches, as a pocket-rat or pocket-mouse; saccomyine.

pseudostomosis (sū"dọ̄-stọ̄-mō'sis), *n.* [NL., < *pseudostome* + *-osis.*] The formation or existence of a pseudostome, or false oscule, as that of a sponge. *W. J. Sollas*, Encyc. Brit., XXII. 416.

pseudostomotic (sū"dọ̄-stọ̄-mot'ik), *a.* [< *pseudostomosis* (*-ot-*) + *-ic.*] Characterized by or exhibiting pseudostomosis; provided with pseudostomes or false oscules, as a sponge.

pseudostomous (sụ̄-dos'tọ̄-mus), *a.* [< *pseudostome* + *-ous.*] Having pseudostomes, as a sponge; of or pertaining to pseudostomes.

pseudostroma (sū-dọ̄-strō'mạ̈), *n.* In *mycol.*, a false stroma; a cellular body resembling a stroma, as that produced in certain lichens. See *stroma*.

pseudosymmetry (sū-dọ̄-sim'e-tri), *n.* In *crystal.*, false symmetry; the appearance of having a higher degree of symmetry than is actually the case, usually produced through twinning. See *twin*.

Pseudotetramera (sū"dọ̄-te-tram'ẹ-rạ̈), *n. pl.* [NL. (Westwood, 1839): see *pseudotetramerous.*] In Westwood's system of classification, one of the four prime divisions of *Coleoptera*, including those beetles in which the tarsi are five-jointed, but the fourth joint is minute and concealed between the lobes of the preceding. It is equivalent to the *Cryptopentamera* of Burmeister and the *Subpentamera* of Latreille. It includes the large and important groups *Rhynchophora*, *Longicornia*, and *Phytophaga*.

pseudotetramerous (sū"dọ̄-te-tram'ẹ-rus), *a.* [< Gr. ψευδής, false, + τέτταρες (τετρα-), four, + μέρος, part.] Having apparently four-jointed but actually five-jointed tarsi, as a beetle; of or pertaining to the *Pseudotetramera*.

pseudotinea (sū-dọ̄-tin'ẹ̄-ạ̈), *n.* [< Gr. ψευδής, false, + L. *tinea*, a worm.] The larva of certain pyralid moths, as the bee-moth, *Galeria cereana*, which feeds on wax, and is a terrible enemy to bees. They sometimes infold the cells in their webs to such an extent as to destroy the community. See *Galeria*, and cut under *bee-moth*.

Pseudotrimera (sū-dọ̄-trim'ẹ-rạ̈), *n. pl.* [NL. (Westwood, 1839): see *pseudotrimerous.*] In Westwood's system of classification, one of the four prime divisions of *Coleoptera*, including those beetles in which the tarsi are four-jointed, the third joint being very diminutive and concealed between the lobes of the preceding. It is equivalent to the *Cryptotetramera* of Burmeister and to the *Subtetramera* and *Trimera* of Latreille. It includes the three families *Erotylidæ*, *Endomychidæ*, and *Coccinellidæ*.

pseudotrimerous (sū-dǫ-trim'ẹ-rus), *a.* [< Gr. ψευδής, false, + τρεῖς (τρι-), three, + μέρος, part.] Having apparently only three, but actually four tarsal joints, as a beetle; of or pertaining to the *Pseudotrimera*.

Pseudotsuga (sū-dot-sū'gä), *n.* [NL. (Carrière, 1867), < Gr. ψευδής, false, + NL. *Tsuga*, q. v.] A genus of coniferous trees of the tribe *Abietineæ*. By Eichler, Bugler, and others it is united with the related genus *Tsuga*, the hemlock-spruce, from which it has been distinguished by the absence of resin-vesicles in the seeds, by the smooth branchlets, and by cones fringed with conspicuous sharply two-lobed bracts much longer than the scales, with their midribs prolonged into a spine or bristle. There is but one species, *P. Douglasii*, discovered by the Scotch botanist David Douglas, in Oregon, in 1825, the most widely distributed timber-tree of the Pacific States, known as *red* or *yellow fir*, *Oregon pine*, *Douglas fir*, *Douglas spruce*, and *Douglas pine*. (See *Oregon pine*, under *pine*[1].) The wood is unlike that of any related conifer in its abundance of spirally marked wood-cells. The trees are at first pyramidal and spruce-like, afterward more spreading, with very thick and rough brown bark. They bear flat and very narrow linear leaves, spirally inserted, but spreading somewhat in two ranks by a twist at the base, and handsome pendulous cones, which are nearly cylindrical, 2 or 3 inches long, and are matured the first year. In the variety *macrocarpa*, the hemlock of the San Bernardino Mountains, a smaller tree, about 50 feet in height, the cones reach 7 inches long, and the larger seeds contain as many as from nine to twelve seed-leaves.

Pseudoturbinolidæ (sū-dǫ-tėr-bi-nol'i-dē), *n. pl.* [NL., < Gr. ψευδής, false, + NL. *Turbinolidæ*.] A family of extinct aporose sclerodermatous corals, resembling *Turbinolidæ*, but with septa each composed of three laminæ free internally, externally united by a single costa. The genus *Dasmia* is an example. Also called *Dasmiidæ*. *Edwards and Haime*, 1850.

pseudova, *n.* Plural of *pseudovum*.

pseudoval (sū-dō'vạl), *a.* [< *pseudovum* + *-al*.] Of or pertaining to a pseudovum or metovum. *Huxley*, Anat. Invert., p. 331.

pseudovarian (sū-dǫ-vā'ri-ạn), *a.* [< *pseudovar-y* + *-ian*.] Of or pertaining to a pseudovary: as, a *pseudovarian* tubule; a *pseudovarian* ovum.

> The terminal or anterior chamber of each *pseudovarian* tube is lined by an epithelium, which incloses a number of nucleated cells. *Huxley*, Anat. Invert., p. 385.

pseudovarium (sū-dǫ-vā'ri-um), *n.* [NL.: see *pseudovary*.] Same as *pseudovary*.

> A portion of the cells . . . becomes converted into a *pseudovarium*, and the development of new pseudova commences before the young leaves the body of its parent. It is obvious that this operation is comparable to a kind of budding. *Huxley*, Anat. Invert., p. 447.

pseudovary (sū-dō'vạ-ri), *n.*; pl. *pseudovaries* (-riz). [< NL. *pseudovarium*, < Gr. ψευδής, false, + NL. *ovarium*, ovary: see *ovary*[1].] 1. The ovary of a viviparous insect, as an aphis, in which are developed the kind of ova called pseudova.

> The young are developed within organs which resemble the ovarioles of the true females in their disposition, and may be termed *pseudovaries*. *Huxley*, Anat. Invert., p. 385.

2. The filmy pellicle or so-called proligerous membrane of infusions of hay, etc., out of which infusorial animalcules were supposed to be produced by the heterogenists, or believers in spontaneous generation.

pseudovelar (sū-dǫ-vē'lär), *a.* [< *pseudovelum* + *-ar*[3].] Vascular, as the velum of a scyphomedusan; having the character or quality of a pseudovelum.

pseudovelum (sū-dǫ-vē'lum), *n.*; pl. *pseudovela* (-lạ). [NL., < Gr. ψευδής, false, + NL. *velum*.] The vascular velum of some hydrozoans, as the *Scyphomedusæ*, containing enteric vessels, and regarded as morphologically distinct from the true velum of the *Hydromedusæ*. See *velum*.

Pseudoviperæ (sū-dǫ-vī'pẹ-rē), *n. pl.* [NL. (Oppel, 1811), < Gr. ψευδής, false, + L. *vipera*, viper.] The wart-snakes (genera *Acrochordus* and *Erpeton*).

pseudoviperine (sū-dǫ-vī'pẹ-rin), *a.* [As *Pseudoviper-æ* + *-ine*[1].] Having the appearance of a viper or other venomous serpent, but harmless, as a wart-snake; pertaining to the *Pseudoviperæ*.

pseudo-volcanic (sū"dō-vol-kan'ik), *a.* Pertaining to or produced by a pseudo-volcano.

pseudo-volcano (sū"dō-vol-kā'nō), *n.* A volcano that, when in a state of activity, emits smoke and sometimes flame, but no lava; also, a burning mine of coal.

Pseudovomer (sū-dǫ-vō'mėr), *n.* [NL., < Gr. ψευδής, false, + L. *vomer*, plowshare: see *vomer*.] A genus of fossil carangoid fishes of Miocene age.

pseudovum (sū-dō'vum), *n.*; pl. *pseudova* (-vạ). [NL., < Gr. ψευδής, false, + L. *ovum*, egg.] A pseudovarian ovum; the egg produced in a pseudovary; a false egg, or the germ of an individual, as an aphid, produced agamogenetically and parthenogenetically. The unimpregnated eggs laid by a virgin aphis are pseudova. The delicate investing membrane or cell-wall is ruptured immediately by the active embryos.

> One of the hindermost of these cells enlarges and becomes detached from the rest as a *pseudovum*. It then divides and gives rise to a cellular mass, distinguishable into a peripheral layer of clear cells and a central more granular substance, which becomes surrounded by a structureless cuticula. It is this cellular mass which gradually becomes fashioned into the body of a larval aphis. *Huxley*, Anat. Invert., p. 385.

> The ova which originate in it [pseudovary] and are incapable of fertilization [it will be convenient to call] the *pseudova*. *Claus*, Zoölogy (trans.), p. 544.

pseudoxanthin (sū-dok-san'thin), *n.* [< Gr. ψευδής, false, + ξανθός, yellow, + *-in*[2].] A leucomaïne found in muscular tissue.

psha, pshah (shä or pshä), *interj.* See *pshaw*.

pshaw (shâ or pshâ), *interj.* [Also *psha*, *pshah*; a mere exclamation, of no definite formation, but suggesting *pish* and *sho*, accom. to *ah*, *aw*.] An exclamation implying contempt, disdain, impatience, or a sense of absurdity.

> *Pshaw, Pshaw!* you fib, you Baggage, you do understand. *Congreve*, Double-Dealer, iv. 3.

> *Pshaw!* Sure I must know better than you whether he's come or not. *Sheridan*, School for Scandal, iii. 3.

> You will say that the story is not probable. *Psha!* Is n't it written in a book? *Thackeray*, Bluebeard's Ghost.

pshaw (shâ or pshâ), *v. i.* [< *pshaw*, *interj.*] To utter the interjection *pshaw*; evince contempt or impatience by such interjections as *pshaw*.

> My father travelled homewards . . . in none of the best of moods, *pshaw-ing* and pish-ing all the way down. *Sterne*, Tristram Shandy, I. xvii.

Pshem.

pshem (pshem), *n.* A head-dress for women, derived from the East, probably the Levant, and adopted in Spain in the thirteenth century. It was practically an upright and nearly cylindrical hat.

psi (psē or sī), *n.* A Greek letter, Ψ, ψ. It belongs to the Ionic alphabet, and stands for *ps* or *phs*. The character may be a modification of Φ, φ.

Psidium (sid'i-um), *n.* [NL. (Linnæus, 1737), said to have been so called in allusion to the succulent fruit; irreg. < Gr. ψίζειν, ψίειν, feed on pap, + dim. -ίδιον.] A genus of polypetalous trees and shrubs of the order *Myrtaceæ* and tribe *Myrteæ*. It is characterized by a broad calyx-tube bearing four or five lobes which are closed in the bud and become separated on flowering, four or five spreading petals, an ovary commonly with four or five cells, and numerous many-ranked ovules containing a curved and ring-like embryo. There are over 100 species, all American, except one in Asia, and all tropical or subtropical. They are commonly hairy or woolly, and bear opposite feather-veined leaves, rather large cymose flowers, and roundish or pear-shaped berries, sometimes crowned with the calyx-lobes, often edible, and known as *guava*. See *guava* (with cut).

Psila (sī'lạ), *n.* [NL. (Meigen, 1803), < Gr. ψιλός, bare, naked, smooth, blank, mere.] A notable genus of dipterous insects, typical of the family *Psilidæ*, containing shining-black or rust-colored flies, the larvæ of which feed on the roots of plants. *P. rosæ* of Europe is a pest of the carrot and cabbage. See cut under *Psilidæ*.

psilanthropic (sī-lan-throp'ik), *a.* [< *psilanthrop-y* + *-ic*.] Of, pertaining to, or embodying psilanthropism. *Coleridge*. (*Imp. Dict.*)

psilanthropism (sī-lan'thrǫ-pizm), *n.* [< *psilanthrop-y* + *-ism*.] The doctrine or belief of the mere human existence of Christ. [Rare.]

psilanthropist (sī-lan'thrǫ-pist), *n.* [< *psilanthrop-y* + *-ist*.] One who believes that Christ was a mere man; a humanitarian.

> The schoolmen would perhaps have called you Unicists: but your proper name is *Psilanthropists* — believers in the mere human nature of Christ. *Coleridge*, Table-Talk, April 4, 1832.

psilanthropy (sī-lan'thrǫ-pi), *n.* [< LGr. ψιλάνθρωπος, merely human, < ψιλός, bare, mere, + ἄνθρωπος, man.] Same as *psilanthropism*.

Psilidæ (sil'i-dē), *n. pl.* [NL. (Loew), < *Psila* + *-idæ*.] A family of acalyptrate *Muscidæ*,

Loxocera cylindrica (much enlarged), one of the *Psilinæ*.

comprising a few small forms distributed in a half-dozen genera, of which *Psila* and *Loxocera* are the most notable.

Psilocephalinæ (sī-lǫ-sef-ạ-lī'nē), *n. pl.* [NL., < *Psilocephalus* + *-inæ*.] In Gill's classification, a subfamily of *Balistidæ*, with the vertebræ increased to 29 or 30, the anterior dorsal represented by a weak spine over the frontal region, and the branchial apertures in advance of the eyes. The only species is from East Indian seas.

Psilocephalus (sī-lǫ-sef'ạ-lus), *n.* [NL. (Swainson, 1839), < Gr. ψιλός, bare, + κεφαλή, head.] 1. The typical genus of *Psilocephalinæ*, contain-

Psilocephalus barbatus.

ing the fish otherwise known as *Anacanthus barbatus*.—2. In *entom.*: (*a*) A genus of dipterous insects. *Zetterstedt*, 1842. (*b*) A genus of coleopterous insects of the family *Pselaphidæ*. *Raffray*, 1877.

Psiloceras (sī-los'ẹ-ras), *n.* [NL. (Hyatt, 1868), < Gr. ψιλός, bare, + κέρας, horn.] A genus of Jurassic ammonites of the family *Arietidæ*, to which, according to Hyatt, all the forms of true ammonites may be traced. *P. planorbis* is an example.

psiloceratite (sī-lǫ-ser'ạ-tit), *n.* [< *Psiloceras* (*-cerat-*) + *-ite*[1].] A fossil cephalopod of the genus *Psiloceras*.

Psilodermata (sī-lǫ-dėr'mạ-tạ), *n. pl.* Same as *Amphibia*, 2 (c).

psilodermatous (sī-lǫ-dėr'mạ-tus), *a.* [< Gr. ψιλός, bare, + δέρμα, skin.] Having the skin naked (that is, not scaly), as an amphibian; of or pertaining to the *Psilodermata*.

psilology (sī-lol'ǫ-ji), *n.* [< Gr. ψιλός, bare, mere, + -λογία, < λέγειν, speak: see *-ology*.] Love of idle talk. *Coleridge*. [Rare.] *Imp. Dict.*

psilomelan (sī-lom'e-lan), *n.* Same as *psilomelane*. *Encyc. Brit.*, XV. 479.

psilomelane (sī-lom'e-lān), *n.* [< Gr. ψιλός, bare, + μέλας (μελαν-), black.] A hydrous oxid of manganese occurring in smooth botryoidal and stalactitic forms and massive, and having a color iron-black to steel-gray.

psilomelanic (sī"lǫ-me-lan'ik), *a.* [< *psilomelane* + *-ic*.] Pertaining to or consisting of psilomelane.

> The writer found in one of these [manganese nodules] . . . a total of 21.04 per cent. of the *psilomelanic* par. *Encyc. Brit.*, XVI. 479.

Psilonotidæ (sī-lǫ-not'i-dē), *n. pl.* [NL., < *Psilonotus* + *-idæ*.] In Gill's system of classification, a family of gymnodont plectognath fishes, represented by the genus *Psilonotus*. They are among the smallest plectognaths, and inhabit tropical seas. The frontals are separated from the supraoccipital by the intervention of the postfrontals, which are connected together and laterally expanded but short; the ethmoid is prominent above, enlarged and narrow forward; the vertebræ are few, about 8 + 9; the head is compressed, with a projecting attenuate snout, and the dorsal and anal fins are short and pauciradiate.

Psilonotus (sī-lǫ-nō'tus), *n.* [NL., < Gr. ψιλός, bare, + νῶτος, back.] The typical genus of *Psilonotidæ*.

Psilopædes (sī-lǫ-pē'dēz), *n. pl.* [< Gr. ψιλός, bare, naked, + παῖς (παιδ-), pl. παῖδες, child.] In *ornith.*, in Sundevall's system (1872), a primary group of birds, embracing those which are hatched naked and require to be fed in the nest by the parent. The term is nearly conterminous with *Altrices*, but of more exact signification. The antithesis is *Ptilopædes* or *Dasypædes*. Also called *Gymnopædes*.

psilopædic (sī-lọ-pē'dik), *a.* [< *Psilopæd-es* + *-ic.*] Of or pertaining to the *Psilopædes*: opposed to *ptilopædic* and *hesthogenous*. Also *gymnopædic*.

Psilophyton (sī-lof'i-ton), *n.* [NL., < Gr. ψιλός, bare, smooth, + φυτόν, a plant: see *phyton*.] A genus of fossil plants considered by Dawson as being a connecting-link between the rhizocarps and lycopods, and so named by him in consequence of its partial resemblance to certain parasitic lycopods placed in the modern genus *Psilotum*. This plant is abundant in the Devonian of Gaspé Bay, Canada. Remains of plants referred to this genus by Lesquereux are also said to have been found in both Ohio and Michigan: in the former case, in rocks of Lower Silurian age; in the latter, of Upper Silurian. The plant has also been found in the Devonian of England and Germany.

Psiloptera (sī-lop'tẹ-rạ̈), *n.* [NL. (Solier, 1833), < Gr. ψιλός, bare, naked, + πτερόν, wing, = E. *feather*.] An important genus of buprestid beetles, comprising more than a hundred species, extremely variable in form, and found mainly in Africa and South America.

Psilorhinus (sī-lọ-rī'nus), *n.* [NL. (Rüppell, 1831), < Gr. ψιλός, bare, + ῥίς (ῥιν-), nose.] An American genus of *Corvidæ*, containing large magpie-like jays, of dark coloration, with very long graduated tail, crestless head, a stout bill, and naked nostrils; the smoky pies. There are several species, as the brown jay, *P. morio*. This bird inhabits Texas and Mexico, is smoky-brown, paler below, with bluish gloss on the wings and tail, the bill black or yellow, the length 16 inches, of which the tail is about one half.

Psilosomata (sī-lọ-sō'ma-tạ̈), *n. pl.* [NL., < Gr. ψιλός, bare, + σῶμα, body: see *Psila*.] In De Blainville's classification (1825), a family of his *Aporobranchiata*, consisting of the genus *Phyllirhoë* alone. It was one of three families of pteropods, contrasting with *Thecosomata* and *Gymnosomata*. It is now generally called *Phyllirhoidæ* and referred to the nudibranchiates. See cut under *Phyllirhoë*.

psilosopher (sī-los'ọ̄-fėr), *n.* [< Gr. ψιλός, bare, mere, + σοφός, wise.] A would-be or pretended philosopher; a sham sage; an incompetent or mean pretender to philosophy. [Rare.] *Imp. Dict.*

Psittaci (sit'ạ-sī), *n. pl.* [NL., pl. of *Psittacus*.] An order of birds, having the bill hooked and cered, and the feet yoke-toed; the parrots, or the parrot tribe. This is one of the most natural and well-marked groups in ornithology, formerly referred to an "order" *Scansores*. The feet are permanently zygodactyl by reversion of the fourth toe, and covered with rugose or granular scales or plates. The wings have ten primaries, and the tail has ten rectrices. The bill is strongly epignathous, and furnished with a naked or feathered cere. The tongue is thick and fleshy, sometimes peculiarly brushy, and may be used as an organ of taction or prehension; the upper mandible is peculiarly movable, and the beak is habitually employed in progression. The symphysis of the lower jaw is short and obtuse. The bony orbits of the eyes are often completed by union of the lacrymal with the postorbital process. The sternum is entire or simply fenestrated behind, and the clavicles are weak, sometimes defective or wanting. The lower larynx or syrinx is peculiarly constructed, with three pairs of intrinsic muscles. The plumage is aftershafted; the oil-gland is absent, or present and tufted; there are no cæca and no gall-bladder; the carotid arteries are variable; the ambiens muscle is present, variable, or absent; the femorocaudal, semitendinosus, and its accessory are present; the accessory femorocaudal is absent. The *Psittaci* are considered to represent only one family, *Psittacidæ*; or two families, *Stringopidæ* and *Psittacidæ* (Sclater); or two families, *Palæornithidæ* and *Psittacidæ* (Garrod, Coues); or three families, *Psittacidæ*, *Cacatuidæ*, and *Strigopidæ* (Gray); or nine families, *Stringopidæ*, *Plissolophidæ*, *Platycercidæ*, *Micropsittacidæ*, *Trichoglossidæ*, *Palæornithidæ*, *Psittacidæ*, *Conuridæ*, and *Pionidæ*. There are upward of 400 species, inhabiting all tropical regions, but poorly represented in the temperate zones. They are chiefly frugivorous, and are sometimes called *frugivorous Raptores*. See the family names, and *cockatoo*, *lory*, *lorikeet*, *love-bird*, *macaw*, *owl-parrot*, *parrakeet*, and *parrot*. Also called *Psittacinæ*, *Psittacini*, and *Psittacomorphæ*.

psittacid (sit'ạ-sid), *n.* and *a.* I. *n.* A parrot, as a member of the *Psittacidæ* in any sense.

II. *a.* Same as *psittacine*.

Psittacidæ (si-tas'i-dē), *n. pl.* [NL., < *Psittacus* + *-idæ*.] A family of *Psittaci*; the parrots. (*a*) The only family, conterminous with the order. In this sense the *Psittacidæ* are divided by Finsch into 5 subfamilies: *Stringopinæ*, owl-parrots; *Plictolophinæ*, cockatoos; *Sittacinæ*, with numerous genera, both American and Old World; *Psittacinæ*; and *Trichoglossinæ*, the lories. See cuts under *owl-parrot*, *parrot*, *parrakeet*, *Prioniturus*. (*b*†) Restricted by exclusion of the owl-parrots and cockatoos, and divided into *Pezoporinæ*, *Arinæ*, *Loriinæ*, *Trichoglossinæ*, *Nestorinæ*, and *Psittacinæ*. *G. R. Gray*. (*c*) Restricted by exclusion of the *Palæornithinæ* to *Psittaci* with two carotids, of which the left is normal, and divided into *Arinæ*, *Pyrrhurinæ*, *Platycercinæ*, and *Chrysotinæ*. *Garrod*; *Coues*. (*d*) Restricted to the gray African parrots of the genera *Psittacus* and *Coracopsis*. *Reichenow*.

psittacine (sit'ạ-sin), *a.* [< LL. *psittacinus*, of or pertaining to a parrot, < *psittacus*, a parrot: see *Psittacus*.] Parrot-like; resembling or related to parrots; of or pertaining to the *Psittaci* or *Psittacidæ* in any sense; psittacomorphic. Also *psittacean*, *psittaceous*, *psittacid*.

Psittacini (sit-ạ-sī'ni), *n. pl.* [NL., < *Psittacus* + *-ini*.] Same as *Psittaci*.

psittacinite (sit'ạ-si-nīt), *n.* [< *psittacine* + *-ite*[2].] A vanadate of lead and copper from Montana, occurring in thin crusts of a siskin or parrot-green color.

Psittacirostra (sit"ạ-si-ros'trạ̈), *n.* [NL., < L. *psittacus* (< Gr. ψιττακός), a parrot, + *rostrum*, beak.] A remarkable genus of Hawaiian birds of the family *Dicæidæ*, having a stout festooned bill. The only species is the parrot-billed grosbeak, *P. psittacea*. Originally *Psittirostra*. *Temminck*, 1820. Also called *Psittacopis*, *Psittacina*.

Psittacomorphæ (sit"ạ-kọ-môr'fē), *n. pl.* [NL. (Huxley, 1867), < Gr. ψιττακός, a parrot, + μορφή, form.] A superfamily of desmognathous carinate birds, established by Huxley in 1867, corresponding to the order *Psittaci*. The technical characters used in defining the group are the arched and hooked rostrum, regularly articulated with the skull; no basipterygoid processes; movable, vertically elongated palatines; spongy maxillopalatines; lacrymal and postorbital processes approximated or united; quadrate bone with a small orbital and single mandibular facet; mandibular rami deep, with rounded truncate symphysis; sternum unnotched or single fenestrate; clavicles weak and separate, or wanting; tarsometatarsus short, broad, with two articular facets on its outer distal end, for jointing with the reversed fourth digit; syringeal muscles three pairs; contour-feathers aftershafted, and oil-gland with a circlet of feathers when present.

psittacomorphic (sit"ạ-kọ-môr'fik), *a.* [< *Psittacomorph-æ* + *-ic*.] Having the structure of a parrot; belonging to the *Psittacomorphæ*; psittacine.

Psittacula (si-tak'ụ̄-lạ̈), *n.* [NL. (Brisson, 1760), dim. of *Psittacus*, q. v.] A genus of *Psittacidæ*, sometimes made the type of a subfamily *Psittaculinæ*, containing the pygmy parrots of various countries, some of which are commonly known as *love-birds*, and including in its different applications a large number of small species with short tail and mostly green coloration. (*a*) American parrots, such as *P. passerina* and sundry other small species. *Illiger*, 1811. (*b*) African species of small size, as *P. pullaria* or *P. roseicollis*, now placed in *Agapornis*. These are the love-birds proper. (*c*) Various small Indian, Philippine, Papuan, and Australian parrots, among them species of *Loriculus* and *Nasiterna*.

Psittaculinæ (si-tak-ụ̄-lī'nē), *n. pl.* [NL., < *Psittacula* + *-inæ*.] A subfamily of *Psittacidæ*, named from the genus *Psittacula*.

Psittaculus (si-tak'ụ̄-lus), *n.* [NL., dim. of *Psittacus*, q. v.] 1. Same as *Psittacula* (*a*). *Spix*, 1824.—2. Same as *Psittacula* (c), or *Loriculus*. *Swainson*, 1837.

Psittacus (sit'ạ-kus), *n.* [NL., < L. *psittacus*, < Gr. ψιττακός, also ψιττάκη (also βίττακος, σιττάκη), a parrot; prob. of foreign origin.] A Linnean genus of *Psittaci*, formerly conterminous with the order, subsequently variously restricted, now usually confined to the gray African parrots, or jackos (as *P. erithacus*, in which the plumage is grayish, with a short square red tail), which are among the commonest cage-birds. See cut under *parrot*.

psittaket†, *n.* [ME. *psitake*; < L. *psittacus*, < Gr. ψιττακός, a parrot: see *Psittacus*.] A parrot.

> And there ben manye Popegayes, that thei clepen *Psitakes* in hire Langage. *Mandeville*, Travels, p. 274.

Psittirostra (sit-i-ros'trạ̈), *n.* [NL.] Same as *Psittacirostra*.

psoadic (sọ̄-ad'ik), *a.* [< *psoas* (assumed stem *psoad-*) + *-ic*.] Of or pertaining to the psoas muscles; psoatic: as, the *psoadic* plexus. *Owen*.

psoas (sō'as), *n.* [NL., prop. *psoa* (the form *psoas* being perhaps due to a genitive *psoas*), < Gr. ψόα, also ψύα, usually in pl. ψόαι, ψύαι, a muscle of the loins.] A muscle of the loins and pelvis; the tenderloin.—**Psoas abscess**, a burrowing abscess formed by caries of the spine, and confined by the sheath of the psoas magnus muscle.—**Psoas magnus**, a large fusiform muscle situated within the abdomen at the side of the bodies of the lumbar vertebræ, from which it takes its origin, and inserted with the iliacus into the trochanter minor of the femur. It helps to form the iliopsoas. Also called *psoas major lumbaris*, and *magnipsoas*. See cut 3, c, under *muscle*, and *tenderloin*.—**Psoas major**. Same as *psoas magnus*.—**Psoas parvus**, a small muscle, frequently absent in man, lying on the front and inner side of the psoas magnus, and inserted into the brim of the pelvis by a long tendon. Also called *parvipsoas*.

psoatic (sọ̄-at'ik), *a.* [< *psoas* (assumed stem *psoat-*) + *-ic*.] Of or pertaining to the psoas muscles; psoadic.

Psocidæ (sos'i-dē), *n. pl.* [NL. (Stephens, 1836), < *Psocus* + *-idæ*.] An important family of pseudoneuropterous insects, typified by the genus *Psocus*, having an oval body, a free head, and a small prothorax. The wings when present are of unequal size, the hind pair being smaller. The tarsi are two- or three-jointed. It comprises two subfamilies, the *Atropinæ* and *Psocinæ*. The former contains wingless species, such as *Atropos divinatoria*, the common book-louse, and *Clothilla pulsatoria* (formerly *Atropos pulsatorius*), the death-watch, while the latter contains a host of small winged forms which feed upon lichens, fungi, and decaying vegetation. Also *Psocina*. See cut under *death-watch*.

psocine (sō'sin), *a.* [< *Psocus* + *-ine*[1].] Of or pertaining to the *Psocidæ* or *Psocina*, especially to the subfamily *Psocinæ*.

Psocus (sō'kus), *n.* [NL. (Latreille, 1797), appar. for **Psochus*, < Gr. ψώχειν, rub in pieces (cf. deriv. ψῶχος, dust, sand); cf. *ψώειν, collat. form of ψᾶν, rub away, grind.] A large and wide-spread genus of pseudoneuropterous insects, typical of the family *Psocidæ*. The species have ocelli, and the wings are well developed. *P. venosus* is often found in decaying cotton-bolls in the southern United States.

psoitis (sọ̄-ī'tis), *n.* [NL., < *psoas* + *-itis*.] Inflammation of the psoas muscle.

Psolidæ (sol'i-dē), *n. pl.* [NL. (Forbes, 1841), < *Psolus* + *-idæ*.] A family of dendrochirotous dipneumonous holothurians, typified by the genus *Psolus*, having branching tentacles, a pair of water-lungs, polar mouth and anus, uniserial pedicels, separate sexes, and Cuvierian organs.

Psolus (sō'lus), *n.* [NL. (Oken), < Gr. ψωλός, circumcised.] The typical genus of *Psolidæ*, having the dorsal ambulacra atrophied.

Psophia (sō'fi-ạ̈), *n.* [NL., < Gr. ψόφος, any inarticulate noise.] The only genus of *Psophiidæ*, containing several species, the best-known of which is *P. crepitans*, the trumpeter, agami, or yakamik. See cut under *agami*.

Psophiidæ (sọ̄-fī'i-dē), *n. pl.* [NL., < *Psophia* + *-idæ*.] A family of gruiform or geranomorphic grallatorial birds, represented by the genus *Psophia*; the trumpeters or agamis. They are confined to South America. The family is isolated, to some extent combining the characters of cranes and rails, and having some relationship with the seriema and kagu. The *Psophiidæ* share with tinamous the remarkable character of a chain of suborbital bones. The sternum is entire; the pterylosis is crane-like; the legs are long, and the bill is stout, shaped somewhat as in gallinaceous birds; the plumage of the head and neck is short and velvety, that of the rump long and flowing. Also *Psophidæ*.

psora (sō'rạ̈), *n.* [NL., < L. *psora*, < Gr. ψώρα, the itch, mange, < *ψώειν, ψᾶν, rub.] Same as *scabies*.

Psoralea (sọ̄-rā'lẹ̄-ạ̈), *n.* [NL. (Linnæus, 1753), so called in allusion to the glands or dots sprinkled over their surface; < Gr. ψωραλέος, scurfy, scabby, mangy, < ψώρα, the itch, mange: see *psora*.] A genus of leguminous herbs and shrubs of the tribe *Galegeæ*, the type of the subtribe *Psoralieæ*, characterized by an ovary with one ovule, an indehiscent pod with its seed adherent, and entire calyx-lobes which are unchanged in fruit. There are about 105 species—over 40 in South Africa, 30 in North America, and others in both tropical and temperate regions. They are peculiar in their glandular-dotted herbage, and bear compound leaves usually of three leaflets, and purple, blue, red, or white flowers, in heads or spikes, or variously clustered. Many species have been cultivated on account of their flowers, both for the lawn and for the greenhouse. *P. esculenta*, of the plains from the Saskatchewan to Texas, yields an edible tuberous root, known as *pomme-de-prairie*, *pomme-blanche*, *prairie-turnip*, *prairie-apple*, *Cree potato*, or *Missouri bread-root*. Its introduction into Europe as an esculent was unsuccessfully attempted at the time of the potato-rot. It is a rough-hairy plant with palmate leaves and dense oblong spikes of purplish flowers, and once yielded a great part of the food of the Indians. *P. Lupinellus* is the small lupine of southern pine-barrens, a slender plant with violet flowers. *P. bituminosa* is the bitumen-trefoil, an evergreen shrub of the south of Europe. *P. glandulosa* is the Jesuit's tea or Mexican tea, known in Chili as *culen*, and there used to form a medicinal drink, also as a purgative and for poultices. For *P. corylifolia*, see *bawchan-seed*.

psoriasis (sọ̄-rī'ạ-sis), *n.* [NL., < Gr. ψωρίασις, the itch, < ψωριᾶν, have the itch, < ψώρα, the itch, mange: see *psora*.] A chronic non-contagious skin-disease, characterized by reddish, slightly elevated, dry patches of varying size, shape, and number, covered with whitish or grayish imbricated scales. The upper stratum and papillæ of the corium become infiltrated with leucocytes, the lower part of the epidermis becomes overgrown, cornification of the surface is interfered with, and the cells become loosened. Psoriasis is found chiefly on extensor surfaces—elbows, knees, back, and scalp—not on mucous surfaces.—**Psoriasis annularis** or **circinata**, patches of psoriasis which have healed in the center, but are progressing at the edges.—**Psoriasis diffusa**, patches of psoriasis of very irregular shapes.—**Psoriasis guttata**, psoriasis with drop-like nodules, of the size of peas.—**Psoriasis gyrata**, patches similar to psoriasis circinata, except that the edges take on a wavy, festooned, or figured shape.—**Psoriasis linguæ**. Same as *leucoplacia*.—**Psoriasis nummularis**, patches of psoriasis of the size and shape of small coins.—**Psoriasis palmaris**, psoriasis affecting the palms of the hands.—**Psoriasis punctata**, an early stage of psoriasis, with a small pinhead eruption.

psoric (sō'rik), *a.* and *n.* [< Gr. ψωρικός, itchy, mangy, < ψώρα, the itch, mange: see *psora.*] **I.** *a.* Pertaining to psora or scabies.

If the *Psoric* theory has led to no proper schism, the reason is to be found in the fact that it is almost without any influence in practice.
Quoted in *O. W. Holmes's* Med. Essays, p. 83.

II. *n.* A remedy for the itch.

psoroid (sō'roid), *a.* [< Gr. ψωροειδής, ψωρώδης, like the itch, < ψώρα, the itch, mange, + εἶδος, form: see *psora.*] Similar to, or relating to, psora or scabies.

psorophthalmia (sō-rof-thal'mi-ä), *n.* [NL., < Gr. ψώρα, the itch, mange, + ὀφθαλμία, a disease of the eyes: see *ophthalmia.*] Inflammation of the eyelids, especially along the margins.

psorophthalmic (sō-rof-thal'mik), *a.* [< *psorophthalmi-a* + *-ic.*] Pertaining to or affected with psorophthalmia.

psorosperm (sō'rō-spėrm), *n.* One of the psorospermiæ.

The *psorosperms* of J. Müller are the spores of Myxosporidia. *E. R. Lankester,* Encyc. Brit., XIX. 855.

psorospermiæ (sō-rō-spėr'mi-ē), *n. pl.* [NL., < Gr. ψωρός, itchy, mangy (< ψώρα, the itch, mange), + σπέρμα, seed.] Certain vesicular, usually caudate, bodies that occur as parasites in the bodies of various animals. Their nature is questionable; some are probably embryonic *Gregarinidæ;* others may be different organisms.

psorospermial (sō-rō-spėr'mi-al), *a.* [< *psorospermiæ* + *-al.*] Same as *psorospermic.*

psorospermic (sō-rō-spėr'mik), *a.* [< *psorospermiæ* + *-ic.*] Of the nature of psorospermiæ; composed of psorospermiæ.

psorous (sō'rus), *a.* [< Gr. ψωρός, itchy, mangy: see *psora.*] Affected by psora or the itch.

psychal (sī'kal), *a.* [< *psyche*, 2, + *-al.*] Pertaining to the soul; spiritual; psychic. [Rare.]

All excitements are, through a *psychal* necessity, transient. *Poe,* The Poetic Principle.

psychalgia (sī-kal'ji-ä), *n.* [NL., < Gr. ψυχή, soul, + ἄλγος, pain.] The painful feeling attending mental action observed in melancholia.

Psyche (sī'kē), *n.* [< L. *Psyche* (in myth.), < Gr. ψυχή, breath, spirit, life, the spirit, soul, mind, etc., a departed spirit, ghost, etc., also a butterfly or moth as the symbol of the soul, < ψύχειν, breathe, blow.] **1.** In *classical myth.*, the personified and deified soul or spirit, the beloved of Eros, by whom she was alternately caressed and tormented. She was considered as a fair young girl, often with the wings of a butterfly, and the butterfly was her symbol.

Cupid (Eros) and Psyche.—Capitoline Museum, Rome.

2. [*l. c.*] The human soul or spirit or mind.

Psychology is the science of the *psyche* or soul.
New Princeton Rev., V. 272.

3. The 16th planetoid, discovered by De Gasparis at Naples in 1852.—**4.** In *zoöl.*: (*a*) In *entom.*, a genus of bombycid moths, erected by Schrank in 1801 (after Linnæus, 1735), and typical of the family *Psychidæ.* They have wingless females, and males with wings which scarcely reach beyond the tip of the abdomen. About 70 species are known, nearly all of which are European, one belonging to Australia and one to Ceylon. (*b*) In *conch.*, a genus of gymnosomatous pteropods of the family *Eurybiidæ.* Also called *Halopsyche.*—**5.** [*l. c.*] In *anat.*, the cerebrospinal nervous system: in Haeckel's vocabulary applied to the brain and spinal cord as the physiological center of the nervous system, in the activities of which he supposed the soul or spirit to subsist. In this use of the term, the psyche is divided into *protopsyche* (forebrain), *deutopsyche* ('tween-brain), *mesopsyche* (midbrain), *metapsyche* (hindbrain), *epipsyche* (afterbrain, or medulla oblongata), and *notopsyche* (the spinal cord).
6. [*l. c.*] A large mirror, in which the whole person can be seen, usually hung on pivots at the sides, the whole being supported in a movable frame.

psyche-glass (sī'kē-glȧs), *n.* Same as *psyche*, 6.

psycheometry (sī-kē-om'e-tri), *n.* [< NL. *psycheometria* (Wolf), irreg. < Gr. ψυχή, soul, mind, + -μετρία, < μέτρον, measure. Cf. *psychometry.*] The mathematical theory of mental phenomena.

psychiater (sī-kī'a-tėr), *n.* [< Gr. ψυχή, soul, mind, + ἰατρός, a physician, < ἰᾶσθαι, cure, heal: see *iatric.*] One who treats diseases of the mind; an alienist.

psychiatria (sī-ki-ā'tri-ä), *n.* [NL.: see *psychiatry.*] Same as *psychiatry.*

psychiatric (sī-ki-at'rik), *a.* [< *psychiatr-y* + *-ic.*] Of or pertaining to or connected with psychiatry.

psychiatrical (sī-ki-at'ri-kal), *a.* [< *psychiatric* + *-al.*] Same as *psychiatric.* *Alien. and Neurol.*, IX. 449.

psychiatrist (sī-kī'a-trist), *n.* [< *psychiatr-y* + *-ist.*] One who practises psychiatry; a psychiater.

psychiatry (sī-kī'a-tri), *n.* [< NL. *psychiatria*, < Gr. ψυχή, soul, + ἰατρεία, a healing, < ἰατρεύειν, heal, < ἰατρός, a healer, physician.] The treatment of mental diseases.

psychic (sī'kik), *a.* and *n.* [= F. *psychique*, < Gr. ψυχικός, pertaining to the soul or to life, also (> LL. *psychicus*), pertaining to mere animal life, carnal, < ψυχή, soul, life, mind: see *Psyche.*] **I.** *a.* **1.** Of or belonging to the human soul or mind; mental; spiritual; psychological.

A good third of our *psychic* life consists in these rapid premonitory perspective views of schemes of thought not yet articulate. *W. James,* Mind, ix. 15.

2. Pertaining to the science of mind: opposed to *physical:* as, *psychic* force.—**3.** Pertaining to the class of extraordinary and obscure phenomena, such as thought-reading, which are not ordinarily treated by psychologists: as, *psychic* research.—**4.** Pertaining to the lower soul, or animal principle, and not to the spirit, or higher soul.

The *psychic*, or animal, man is the natural man of this present age. *Bibliotheca Sacra,* XLVI. 399.

Psychic force, a supposed power or influence, not physical or mechanical, exhibiting intelligence or volition, and capable of causing certain so-called spiritualistic phenomena: so named by William Crookes in 1871.

II. *n.* A person specially susceptible of psychic impressions, or subject to psychic force; a medium; a sensitive. [Recent.]

psychical (sī'ki-kal), *a.* [< *psychic* + *-al.*] Same as *psychic.*

Hence the right discussion of the nature of price is a very high metaphysical and *psychical* problem. *Ruskin.*

Psychical excitation, an idea considered as the cause of another idea by virtue of an association: so called to express the hypothesis that there is some scientific analogy between this phenomenon and the excitation of a peripheral nerve by a physical excitation.—**Psychical research,** experimental and observational research into alleged phenomena apparently implying a connection with another world, or faculties unknown to psychologists.

psychically (sī'ki-kal-i), *adv.* In a psychical manner; with reference to the mind; in connection with or by effect upon the mind: opposed to *physically.*

psychics (sī'kiks), *n.* [Pl. of *psychic* (see *-ics*).] The science of psychology, or the investigation of mind; especially, the doctrine of those who reject the methods of the psychophysicists and favor those of the advocates of psychical research.—**Mathematical psychics,** the application of mathematics to the moral sciences.

Psychidæ (sī'ki-dē), *n. pl.* [NL. (Boisduval, 1829), < *Psyche*, 4 (*a*), + *-idæ.*] A family of bombycid moths, including forms which have case-bearing larvæ and wingless females. It is not a well-defined group, and its genera may be divided among several other families. As at present accepted, the family is of wide distribution, and comprises about 20 genera. The common bag-worm of the United States, *Thyridopteryx ephemeræformis*, is a representative form. See cut under *bag-worm.*

psychism (sī'kizm), *n.* [< Gr. ψυχή, soul, + *-ism.*] **1.** The doctrine that there is a fluid diffused throughout all nature, animating equally all living and organized beings, and that the difference which appears in their actions comes of their particular organization. *Fleming.*—**2.** The character of being psychic or mental.

There can be no question that the world-object furnishes overwhelming proof of *psychism.* *Contemporary Rev.*, L. 54.

psychist (sī'kist), *n.* [< *Psyche* (see *psyche*, 2) + *-ist.*] One who engages in psychical research; especially, one who holds the doctrines of psychics or of psychic force in any form.

psychoblast (sī'kō-blȧst), *n.* [< Gr. ψυχή, soul, mind, + βλαστός, a germ.] The germ from which a soul is developed.

Instead of the association of mental atoms, we are coming to the idea of segmentation of a *psychoblast*, if we may invent such a term. *Athenæum,* No. 3193, p. 12.

Psychoda (sī-kō'dä), *n.* [NL. (Latreille, 1796), < Gr. ψυχή, a butterfly (see *Psyche*), + εἶδος, form.] A genus of dipterous insects, typical of the family *Psychodidæ*, comprising small light-colored flies which live as larvæ in dung and decaying vegetation, as *P. phalænoides.* Only a few species are known, two of which inhabit North America.

psychodectic (sī-kō-dek'tik), *a.* [< Gr. ψυχοδαίκτης, destroying the soul, < ψυχή, soul, + δαίκτης, < δαΐζειν, cleave, slay.] Soul-destroying.

Psychodidæ (sī-kod'i-dē), *n. pl.* [NL. (Zetterstedt, 1842), < *Psychoda* + *-idæ.*] A small family of nemocerous dipterous insects, allied to the *Tipulidæ*, represented in Europe by ten small genera, and in North America by only two species of the typical genus *Psychoda.*

psychodometer (sī-kō-dom'e-tėr), *n.* [< Gr. ψυχή, soul, mind, + ὁδός, way, process, + μέτρον, measure.] An instrument for measuring the duration of mental processes.

psychodynamic (sī"kō-dī-nam'ik), *a.* [< Gr. ψυχή, soul, mind, + δύναμις, power: see *dynamic.*] Pertaining to psychodynamics.

psychodynamics (sī"kō-dī-nam'iks), *n.* [Pl. of *psychodynamic* (see *-ics*).] The science of the laws of mental action.

psycho-ethical (sī-kō-eth'i-kal), *a.* [< Gr. ψυχή, soul, mind, + ἠθικός, ethical: see *ethic, ethical.*] Of or pertaining to inborn moral notions.

psychogenesis (sī-kō-jen'e-sis), *n.* [NL., < Gr. ψυχή, soul, mind, + γένεσις, origin.] **1.** The origination and development of the soul, or psychic organism.

Psychogenesis . . . teaches that instinct is organized experience, i. e. undiscursive intelligence.
G. H. Lewes, Probs. of Life and Mind, I. i. § 21.

It interests the psychologist as an important chapter in the study of mind, its *psychogenesis.* *Science,* VI. 435.

2. Generation or reproduction by means of or due to the activity of the inmost life or vitality of an organism; biogenesis referred to the operation of higher than vital forces.

Specific change must be, above all, due to the action of an organism's innermost life: that is to say, it must be a result of a process of *psychogenesis.*
Mivart, The Forum, VII. 102.

psychogenetical (sī"kō-jē-net'i-kal), *a.* [< *psychogenesis*, after *genetical.*] Pertaining to the formation of the mind by development.

psychogenetically (sī"kō-jē-net'i-kal-i), *adv.* In reference to the theory of the origin of the mind.

psychogeny (sī-koj'e-ni), *n.* [< Gr. ψυχή, soul, mind, + -γένεια, < -γενής, producing: see *-geny.*] **1.** The development of mind.—**2.** The theory of the development of mind.

Psychogeny will show us that color, heat, etc., are, from one point of view, both in the objects and in us.
G. H. Lewes, Probs. of Life and Mind, I. ii. § 82.

psychogonic (sī-kō-gon'ik), *a.* [< *psychogon-y* + *-ic.*] Same as *psychogenetical.*

psychogonical (sī-kō-gon'i-kal), *a.* [< *psychogony* + *-ic-al.*] Same as *psychogenetical.*

The controversy between the *psychogonical* and introspective methods of studying mind.
H. Sidgwick, Mind, XI. 211.

psychogony (sī-kog'ō-ni), *n.* [< Gr. ψυχογονία, the generation of the soul, < ψυχή, soul, mind, + -γονία, < -γονος, generation: see *-gony.*] The doctrine of the development of mind.

Psychogony . . . endeavors to interpret the genesis of intellectual faculties and emotional feelings in the race, and their slow modifications throughout countless generations. *J. Fiske,* Cosmic Philos., I. 221.

It deals rather with *psychogony*, or how mind came to be what it is, than with psychology, or the description of mind as it is. *Athenæum,* No. 3069, p. 235.

psychograph (sī'kō-grȧf), *n.* [< Gr. ψυχή, soul, mind, + γράφειν, write.] An instrument or machine used in psychography. Several kinds are in use. A common one consists of a light, freely movable bar or pointer pivoted on a board upon which the letters of the alphabet are printed in a circle, the movement of the pointer spelling out words. The planchette is a kind of psychograph.

psychographic (sī-kō-graf'ik), *a.* [< *psychograph-y* + *-ic.*] Of or pertaining to psychography.

psychography (sī-kog'ra-fi), *n.* [< Gr. ψυχή, soul, mind, + -γραφία, < γράφειν, write.] **1.** The natural history of mind; the description of the phenomena of mind: a branch of psychology.—**2.** Supposed "spirit-writing" by the hand of a medium; the supposed transmission of a spirit's thought in writing by the hand of a medium, either directly or by means of an instrument.

psychol. An abbreviation of *psychology*.

psychologic (sī-kō-loj'ik), *a.* [= F. *psychologique* = Sp. *psicológico*; as *psycholog-y* + *-ic*.] Same as *psychological*.

psychological (sī-kō-loj'i-kal), *a.* [< *psychologic* + *-al*.] Of or pertaining to psychology; of the nature of psychology; of, or pertaining to the mind as the subject of psychology.

Shakspeare was pursuing two Methods at once; and, besides the *Psychological* Method, he had also to attend to the Poetical. . . . We beg pardon for the use of this insolens verbum; but it is one of which our Language stands in great need. We have no single term to express the Philosophy of the Human Mind, and, what is worse, the Principles of that Philosophy are commonly called Metaphysical, a word of very different meaning.
Coleridge, Method, § 2.

Doubt of it [personal identity] in a sane person is a *psychological* impossibility.
H. B. *Smith*, Christian Theology, p. 171.

Psychological materialism, the doctrine that intelligence is a consequent of matter.

psychologically (sī-kō-loj'i-kal-i), *adv.* [< *psychological* + *-ly*[2].] In a psychological manner; from a psychological point of view; by psychological methods.

psychologics (sī-kō-loj'iks), *n.* [Pl. of *psychologic* (see *-ics*).] Psychology; metaphysics.

Five thousand crammed octavo pages
Of German *psychologics*.
Shelley, Peter Bell the Third, vi. 14.

psychologist (sī-kol'ō-jist), *n.* [= F. *psychologiste*; as *psycholog-y* + *-ist*.] One who studies, writes on, or is versed in psychology.

psychologize (sī-kol'ō-jīz), *v.*; pret. and pp. *psychologized*, ppr. *psychologizing*. [< *psychology* + *-ize*.] **I.** *intrans.* To make psychological speculations; investigate or reason psychologically.

Why, since the feeling has no proper subjective name of its own, should we hesitate to *psychologize* about it as "the feeling of that relation"?
W. James, Mind, ix. 5.

II. *trans.* To hypnotize or mesmerize. [Recent.]

Is the non-concurrence of the obstinate juryman in a righteous verdict owing to an honest conviction, or has he been unconsciously *psychologized* by the lawyer who has the biggest fee in his pocket?
Atlantic Monthly, LVIII. 592.

psychologue (sī'kō-log), *n.* [< F. *psychologue* = Sp. *psicólogo*, < Gr. ψυχή, soul, mind, + -λογος, < λέγειν, speak: see *-ology*.] A psychologist.

psychology (sī-kol'ō-ji), *n.* [= F. *psychologie* = Sp. *psicologia*, *sicologia* = Pg. *psychologia* = It. *psicologia* = G. *psychologie*, < NL. *psychologia* (Melanchthon), < Gr. ψυχή, soul, mind, + -λογία, < λέγειν, say, speak: see *-ology*.] The science of the phenomena of mind; mental science. It is said to have originated with Pythagoras. Aristotle greatly improved it, and stated its most important principle, that of the association of ideas. It has, however, only recently taken the position of a universally acknowledged science; and its methods are still in dispute. Some psychologists hold that we know the mind by direct intuition in consciousness; others, distinguishing between consciousness and self-consciousness, hold that the former involves no recognition of the mind, while the latter is not an original power, but only acquired knowledge. But, though such inward vision be denied, most psychologists still consider the observation of what passes within us as the main foundation for psychology. Others regard introspection as too deceptive to be of much use, and some deny its possibility. A few psychologists only, since Descartes, have held that the distinctions we naturally draw about mental functions—as, for example, between thinking and willing—have, in good part at least, a real significance. The great majority have denied this, explaining that the faculties are nothing in the soul (which itself has no parts), but are mere conveniences of description. Nevertheless, these writers are accused by many modern psychologists of practically assuming that our natural ideas of mind are in some approximate harmony with the facts of mind, just as physicists assume that among the conceptions which appear simple and natural to man are likely to be found those that are embodied in laws of nature. The prevalent school of modern psychologists attributes great importance to systematic experimentation by one person upon another, especially to quantitative determinations, as of the time occupied in different mental processes, the force required to produce sensations of given intensity, and the like; yet some of the older generation predict that the utility of this method will be found to have narrow limits. Psychology has also been pursued by means of extensive observations upon persons in abnormal mental states, upon persons having some mental peculiarity, upon the development of the minds of children, upon the languages, institutions, mythology, and arts of different races, and by means of the comparative study of biography. Psychology has often been divided into psychography, psychonomy, and psychosophy. See the somewhat deceptive quotation from Coleridge, 1817, under *psychological*, and the first quotation below.

Under the general term [physiology] I also comprehend natural theology and *psychology*, which in my opinion have been most unnaturally disjoined by philosophers.
G. *Campbell*, Philos. of Rhet. (1776), I. v. 2.

Psychology, or the Philosophy of the Human Mind, strictly so denominated, is the science conversant about the phænomena, or modifications, or states of the Mind, or Conscious-Subject, or Soul, or Spirit, or Self, or Ego.
Sir W. Hamilton, Metaphysics, viii.

Abstract psychology, the account of the general phenomena of the human mind, their classification, and laws.—**Comparative psychology**, the study of mental phenomena in different kinds of animals, including man.—**Criminal psychology**, the study of psychology in relation to crime.—**Empirical psychology**, psychology studied by means of observation.—**Evolutional psychology**, the account of the development of mind.—**Experimental psychology**, psychology studied largely by the method of experiment.—**Infant-psychology**, the study of the development of mind in children.—**Introspective psychology**, psychology resting mainly on self-observation.—**Mathematical, nomological psychology**. See the adjectives.—**Objective psychology**, psychology resting mainly upon observations of minds other than that of the observer.—**Physiological psychology**, the physiology of psychical functions.—**Rational psychology**, the deduction of certain characters of the mind from certain others assumed as axiomatic.—**Scientific psychology**, psychology based on well-considered methods in harmony with those of the physical sciences.

psychomachy (sī-kom'a-ki), *n.* [< Gr. ψυχομαχία, desperate fighting, < ψυχομαχεῖν, fight to the death, < ψυχή, soul, life, + μάχεσθαι, fight.] A conflict of the soul with the body.

psychomancy (sī'kō-man-si), *n.* [< Gr. ψυχή, soul, mind, + μαντεία, divination. Cf. ψυχομαντεῖον, a place where the souls of the dead were conjured up.] **1.** Divination by consulting the souls of the dead; necromancy.—**2.** A mysterious influence of one soul upon another.

psychomantic (sī-kō-man'tik), *a.* [< *psychomancy* (*-mant-*) + *-ic*.] Of or pertaining to psychomancy.

psychometric (sī-kō-met'rik), *a.* [< *psychometr-y* + *-ic*.] Pertaining to psychometry.

psychometrical (sī-kō-met'ri-kal), *a.* Same as *psychometric*.

psychometrize (sī-kom'e-trīz), *v. t.*; pret. and pp. *psychometrized*, ppr. *psychometrizing*. [< *psychometr-y* + *-ize*.] To practise psychometry on, as a letter or photograph.

psychometry (sī-kom'et-ri), *n.* [< Gr. ψυχή, soul, mind, + -μετρία, < μέτρον, measure.] **1.** The power, fancied to be possessed by some sensitive persons, of catching impressions from contact which enable them to describe the properties of medicines, the vital forces of any part of the human constitution, the character, physiological condition, etc., of persons whose autographs or photographs are touched, and the scenes associated with any substance investigated. *J. R. Buchanan*, 1842.—**2.** The measurement of the duration of psychic processes.

Psychomorpha (sī-kō-mor'fä), *n.* [NL. (Harris, 1839), < Gr. ψυχή, butterfly (see *Psyche*), + μορφή, form.] A genus of bombycid moths of the family *Lithosiidæ*, having the body slender, and pilose at the apex, palpi porrect, antennæ simple in the female, shortly pectinate in the male. The sole species is *P. epimenis*, of North America, commonly called the *grape-vine epimenis*, of considerable economic importance from the damage its larva does in drawing together and destroying the terminal shoots of the vine in early summer. The moth is velvety-black, with a white patch on the front wings, and an orange or brick-red blotch on the hind wings.

Grape-vine Epimenis (*Psychomorpha epimenis*), natural size.

Grape-vine Epimenis (*Psychomorpha epimenis*).
a, larva; *b*, side view of one segment, enlarged; *c*, hump on eleventh joint, enlarged.

psychomotor (sī'kō-mō-tor), *a.* [< Gr. ψυχή, soul, mind, + L. *motor*, mover.] Pertaining to such mental action as induces muscular contraction.—**Psychomotor centers**, the areas of the cortex about the central fissure immediately related to muscular action.—**Psychomotor nerve-fibers**, the fibers passing downward from the psychomotor centers to the points of origin of the motor nerves.

psychoneurology (sī"kō-nū-rol'ō-ji), *n.* [< Gr. ψυχή, soul, mind, + νεῦρον, nerve, + -λογία, < λέγειν, speak: see *-ology*.] That part of neurology which deals with mental action.

psychoneurosis (sī'kō-nū-rō'sis), *n.* [NL., < Gr. ψυχή, soul, + NL. *neurosis*, q. v.] Mental disease without recognizable anatomical lesion, and without evidence and history of preceding chronic mental degeneration. Under this head come melancholia, mania, primary acute dementia, and mania hallucinatoria. These cases issue in recovery, or in secondary dementia or imbecility of various grades.

psychonomy (sī-kon'ō-mi), *n.* [< Gr. ψυχή, soul, mind, + ὄνομα, name.] The science of the laws of mental action: one of the branches of psychology in many of the older systems.

psychonosology (sī"kō-nō-sol'ō-ji), *n.* [< Gr. ψυχή, soul, mind, + νόσος, disease, + -λογία, < λέγειν, speak: see *-ology*.] That branch of medical science which treats of the nature and classification of mental disease.

psychopannychism (sī-kō-pan'i-kizm), *n.* [< Gr. ψυχή, soul, mind, + παννύχιος, all night long (< πᾶς, πᾶν, all, + νύξ (νυκτ-), night), + *-ism*.] The theological doctrine that at death the soul falls asleep, and does not awake till the resurrection of the body.

psychopannychist (sī-kō-pan'i-kist), *n.* [< *psychopannych-ism* + *-ist*.] One who holds to the doctrine of psychopannychism.

The Saducees might deny and overthrow the resurrection against Christ, or the *Psychopannuchists* the soul's immortality.
Bp. Gauden, Tears of the Church, p. 283. (*Davies.*)

psychoparesis (sī-kō-par'e-sis), *n.* [NL., < Gr. ψυχή, soul, mind, + πάρεσις, paralysis: see *paresis*.] Mental weakness.

psychopath (sī'kō-path), *n.* [< *psychopath-ic*.] A morally irresponsible person.

psychopathic (sī-kō-path'ik), *a.* and *n.* [< *psychopath-y* + *-ic*.] **I.** *a.* **1.** Pertaining to or of the nature of psychopathy.—**2.** Pertaining to the cure of the sick by psychic means.

II. *n.* An insane or nearly insane patient.

psychopathist (sī-kop'a-thist), *n.* [< *psychopath-y* + *-ist*.] A physician for psychopathy; an alienist.

psychopathy (sī-kop'a-thi), *n.* [< Gr. ψυχή, soul, mind, + πάθος, disease.] **1.** Derangement of the mental functions. This is a slightly more extensive word than *insanity*, as the latter is not usually applied to idiocy, and is often reserved for disorder of a certain considerable grade of intensity.
2. The cure of the sick by psychical influence.

psychophysic (sī-kō-fiz'ik), *a.* [< Gr. ψυχή, soul, mind, + φυσικός, physical: see *physic*.] Same as *psychophysical*.

psychophysical (sī-kō-fiz'i-kal), *a.* [< *psychophysic* + *-al*.] Of or pertaining to psychophysics.—**Fechner's psychophysical law.** See *law*[1].—**Psychophysical time**, that part of the reaction-time which is occupied with brain-action. See *reaction-time*.

psychophysicist (sī-kō-fiz'i-sist), *n.* and *a.* [< *psychophysic* + *-ist*.] **I.** *n.* A student of psychology who relies mainly or extensively upon quantitative experiments made by one person upon another.

II. *a.* Pertaining to or composed of psychophysicists.

psychophysics (sī-kō-fiz'iks), *n.* [Pl. of *psychophysic* (see *-ics*).] The science of the relations between stimuli and the sensations which they evoke.

psychophysiological (sī-kō-fiz"i-ō-loj'i-kal), *a.* [< *psychophysiolog-y* + *-ic-al*.] Of or pertaining to psychophysiology.

psychophysiology (sī-kō-fiz-i-ol'ō-ji), *n.* [< Gr. ψυχή, soul, mind, + φυσιολογία, physiology.] Physiological psychology. See *psychology*.

psychoplasm (sī'kō-plazm), *n.* [< Gr. ψυχή, soul, mind, + πλάσμα, anything formed: see *plasm*.] The material medium or physical basis of consciousness: same as *protyle*. See the quotation.

The vital organism is evolved from the bioplasm, and we can now see how the psychical organism is evolved from what may be analogically called the *psychoplasm*. . . . We may represent the molecular movements of the bioplasm by the neural tremors of the *psychoplasm*; these tremors are what I call neural units—the raw material of Consciousness. The movements of the bioplasm constitute vitality; the movements of the *psychoplasm* constitute sensibility. We may say that the sentient material out of which all the forms of consciousness are evolved is the *psychoplasm*, incessantly fluctuating, incessantly renewed.
G. H. *Lewes*, Probs. of Life and Mind, I. 100.

psychoplasmic (sī-kō-plaz'mik), *a.* [< *psychoplasm* + *-ic*.] Of or pertaining to psychoplasm; composed of or subsisting in psychoplasm.

psychopomp (sī'kō-pomp), *n.* [< Gr. ψυχοπομπός, conductor of souls, < ψυχή, soul, + πομπός, conductor, < πέμπειν, send, conduct: see *pomp*.] A guide or conductor of spirits or souls to the other world: a special title of Hermes.

A kind of *psychopomp* or leader of departed souls.
J. Fiske, Myths and Mythmakers, p. 102.

psychoscope (sī'kō-skōp), *n.* [< Gr. ψυχή, soul, mind, + σκοπεῖν, view.] A means of observing the mind.

Somnambulism, double-consciousness, epilepsy, insanity itself, are all of them natural *psychoscopes*.
Proc. Soc. Psych. Research, III. 61.

psychosensorial (sī″kọ̄-sen-sō′ri-al), *a.* [< *psychosensor-y* + *-al.*] Of the nature of percepts, but not produced by any real action on the senses at the time. Thus, a person who sees an object which is not really present, and does not merely have an ordinary imagination of it, though he may be able to distinguish it from real perception, has a *psychosensorial* hallucination.

psychosensory (sī-kọ̄-sen′sọ̄-ri), *a.* [< Gr. ψυχή, soul, mind, + E. *sensory*.] Same as *psychosensorial*. *Amer. Jour. Psychol.*, 1887.

psychosis (sī-kō′sis), *n.*; pl. *psychoses* (-sēz). [< Gr. ψύχωσις, a giving of life or soul, animating, < ψυχοῦν, give life or soul to, animate, < ψυχή, soul, life, mind: see *Psyche*.] 1. Mental constitution or condition.

It is, in fact, attended with some peculiar difficulty, because not only are we unable to make brute *psychosis* a part of our own consciousness, but we are also debarred from learning it by a process similar to that which enables us to enter into the minds of our fellow-men — namely, rational speech. *Mivart.*

2. A change in the field of consciousness.

This conception of the relation of states of consciousness with molecular changes in the brain — of *psychoses* with neuroses — does not prevent us from ascribing freewill to brutes. *Huxley*, Animal Automatism.

3. In *pathol.*, any mental disorder; any form of insanity.

psychosomatic (sī″kọ̄-sọ̄-mat′ik), *a.* [< Gr. ψυχή, soul, mind, + σῶμα, body: see *somatic*.] Relating to both soul and body.

psychosophy (sī-kos′ọ̄-fi), *n.* [< Gr. ψυχή, soul, mind, + σοφία, skill, knowledge.] The metaphysics of mind: one of the branches of psychology in the older systems.

psychostasia (sī-kọ̄-stā′si-ạ̈), *n.* [NL., < Gr. ψυχοστασία, weighing of souls, < ψυχή, soul, + στάσις, weighing.] The weighing of souls: an ancient belief that during a combat the souls of the combatants were weighed against one another, and that he whose soul was overbalanced was slain.

psychostasy (sī′kọ̄-stā-si), *n.* [< NL. *psychostasia*, q. v.] Same as *psychostasia*.

psychostatic (sī-kọ̄-stat′ik), *a.* [< Gr. ψυχή, soul, mind, + στατικός, causing to stand: see *static*.] Pertaining to psychostatics.

psychostatical (sī-kọ̄-stat′i-kal), *a.* [< *psychostatic* + *-al.*] Same as *psychostatic*.

But the feelings registered are *psychostatical* elements.
G. H. Lewes, Probs. of Life and Mind, I. 195.

psychostatically (sī-kọ̄-stat′i-kal-i), *adv.* In a psychostatic manner.

psychostatics (sī-kọ̄-stat′iks), *n.* [Pl. of *psychostatic* (see *-ics*).] The theory of the conditions of the phenomena of mind.

To those who . . . have adopted the view that mind is only one of the forms of life, and that life is not an entity but an abstraction expressing the generalities of organic phenomena, it is obvious that psychology must endeavour to ascertain the conditions of these phenomena, both general and special. These may be classed (by a serviceable extension of the term statics) under the heads of biostatics and *psychostatics*.
G. H. Lewes, Probs. of Life and Mind, I. ii. § 3.

psychotheism (sī′kọ̄-thē-izm), *n.* [< Gr. ψυχή, soul, spirit, + θεός, God: see *theism*.] The doctrine that God is pure spirit.

psychotherapeutic (sī-kọ̄-ther-a-pū′tik), *a.* [< Gr. ψυχή, soul, + θεραπευτικός, pertaining to medical treatment: see *therapeutic*.] Pertaining to psychotherapeutics.

psychotherapeutics (sī-kọ̄-ther-a-pū′tiks), *n.* [Pl. of *psychotherapeutic* (see *-ics*).] The art of curing mental disease.

psychotherapy (sī-kọ̄-ther′a-pi), *n.* [< Gr. ψυχή, soul, mind, + θεραπεία, medical treatment: see *therapy*.] Same as *psychotherapeutics*.

Psychotria (sī-kot′ri-ạ̈), *n.* [NL. (Linnæus, 1767), said to refer to the medicinal qualities of some of the species; < Gr. ψυχώτρια, vivifying, animating, < ψυχοῦν, give life to, animate: see *psychosis*.] A genus of gamopetalous plants of the order *Rubiaceæ*, type of the tribe *Psychotrieæ*. It is characterized by corymbose or panicled flowers with a five-lobed valvate corolla, a short calyx-tube having a small five-toothed border, linear or oblong-obtuse anthers fixed by their back near the base, entire and membranaceous stipules, and a drupaceous fruit with two plano-convex nutlets. It is a vast and polymorphous genus, one of the largest among plants, containing about 425 species, all tropical and especially American. They are shrubs or small trees, rarely perennial herbs, either erect, climbing, or twining. They bear opposite entire and sometimes whorled leaves, and stipules within the petioles, often twin and united into a sheath. The small flowers are white, green, red, or yellow. Most of the species have handsome leaves, but are inconspicuous in flower. *P. parasitica*, a red-berried, fleshy-leafed species of the West Indies, is there known as *climbing-vine*. *P. daphnoides*, a small evergreen, is the *brushland sage-tree* of Australia. *P. emetica* yields the drug striated ipecacuanha (see *ipecacuanha*), and some other species furnish a dyestuff.

Psychotrieæ (sī-kọ̄-trī′ẹ̄-ē), *n. pl.* [NL. (Bentham and Hooker, 1873), < *Psychotria* + *-eæ*.] A large tribe of plants of the order *Rubiaceæ*, the madder family. It is characterized by an ovary with two or many cells, each with a single basilar erect anatropous ovule and inferior radicle; a valvate corolla bearing the stamens on its throat; a stigma entire or nearly so; and an indehiscent fruit, commonly with two nutlets, corneous albumen, and curved embryo. It includes about 1,084 species of 32 genera, mostly tropical trees or shrubs. *Psychotria* (the type) with 425 species, *Palicourea* with 135, *Rudgea* with 92, and *Uragoga* (*Cephaëlis*) with 120, are large genera mainly of America, and *Lasianthus* with 80 species is principally Asiatic.

psychovital (sī-kọ̄-vī′tal), *a.* [< Gr. ψυχή, soul, mind, + L. *vita*, life, + *-al*: see *vital*.] Psychical and vital; pertaining at once to mind and to life.

psychozoic (sī-kọ̄-zō′ik), *a.* [< Gr. ψυχή, soul, mind, + ζωή, life, + *-ic*.] Same as *psychovital*.

psychrometer (sī-krom′e-tėr), *n.* [< Gr. ψυχρός, cold, chill (< ψύχειν, blow, make cool or cold), + μέτρον, a measure.] An instrument for determining the tension of the aqueous vapor in the air or the relative humidity. It consists of two thermometers, commonly called the *dry-bulb* and the *wet-bulb*. The dry-bulb thermometer gives the temperature of the air. The wet-bulb thermometer, whose bulb is covered with muslin wetted at the time of observation, cools below the air-temperature, and indicates what is known as the temperature of evaporation. From the combined readings of the two thermometers, along with that of the barometer at the time, the pressure of the vapor in the air is obtained by means of an empirical formula, or more conveniently from specially constructed tables.

Psychrometer.

psychrometric (sī-krọ̄-met′rik), *a.* [< *psychrometer* + *-ic*.] Of or pertaining to a psychrometer; hygrometrical.

psychrometrical (sī-krọ̄-met′ri-kal), *a.* [< *psychrometric* + *-al.*] Same as *psychrometric*.

psychrometry (sī-krom′et-ri), *n.* [< Gr. ψυχρός, cold, + -μετρία, < μέτρον, measure.] The theory and art of determining by means of a psychrometer the tension of the aqueous vapor in the atmosphere.

psychrophobia (sī-krọ̄-fō′bi-ạ̈), *n.* [< Gr. ψυχροφόβος, dreading cold or cold water, < ψυχρός, cold, + φοβεῖσθαι, fear, < φόβος, fear.] A dread of anything cold, especially cold water; impressibility to cold. *Dunglison.*

psychrophore (sī′krọ̄-fōr), *n.* [< Gr. ψυχροφόρος, carrying cold water, < ψυχρός, cold, + φέρειν = E. *bear*[1].] In *surg.*, a sound with double bore through which a current of cold water is made to flow for applying cold to the urethra.

psydracium (sī-drā′si-um), *n.*; pl. *psydracia* (-ạ̈). [NL., < Gr. ψυδράκιον, dim. of ψύδραξ (ψυδρακ-), a white blister on the tip of the tongue, feigned to be caused by one's telling a lie, < ψυδρός, lying, < ψεύδειν, lie: see *pseudo-*.] A small pustule without inflammatory base.

Psykter in red-figured pottery: style of the artist Euthymides, 5th century, B. C.

psykter (sik′tėr), *n.* [< Gr. ψυκτήρ, a vase for cooling wine (see def.), < ψύχειν, blow, make cool.] In *Gr. antiq.* and *archæol.*, a type of vase used for cooling wine. The body is of conoid form, with short cylindrical neck and a somewhat tall cylindrical foot, adapted in form for insertion in the crater, and for standing on the table. It was sometimes supported on a tripod. See cut in preceding column.

Psylla (sil′ạ̈), *n.* [NL. (Geoffroy, 1764), < Gr. ψύλλα, a flea; cf. L. *pulex*, a flea.] A genus of homopterous insects, typical of the family *Psyllidæ*, having a pointed, bent front, highly arched scutum, and strongly developed scutellum, the body smooth, naked, or finely pilose, and the extreme tip of the wing falling between the radius and the fourth vein. It is a large group, represented in all parts of the world. *P. pyri* is a common pest of the pear in Europe and North America, producing two or more summer generations of naked young. From the damage it does to young blossoms in the spring, it is sometimes called the *bud-blight insect*, though more commonly known as the *flea-louse of the pear*.

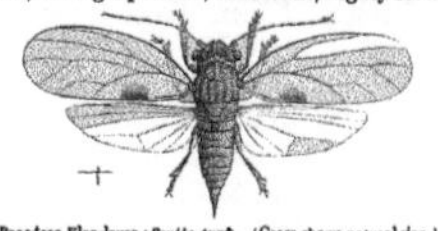

Pear-tree Flea-louse (*Psylla pyri*). (Cross shows natural size.)

Psyllidæ (sil′i-dē), *n. pl.* [NL. (Latreille, 1807), < *Psylla* + *-idæ*.] A notable family of hemipterous insects, typified by the genus *Psylla*, comprising the flea-lice or jumping plant-lice. They are small insects, resembling plant-lice, having stout legs, the hinder pair fitted for jumping, antennæ nine- or ten-jointed and armed at the tip with one or two bristles. They live on the juices of plants, and many of them form galls. The principal subfamilies are *Liviinæ*, *Aphalarinæ*, *Psyllinæ*, and *Triozinæ*. See cuts under *flea-louse* and *Psylla*.

psylly† (sil′i), *n.* [< Gr. ψύλλα, a flea: see *Psylla*.] The fleawort, *Plantago Psyllium*. See quotation under *fleawort*.

pt. An abbreviation (*a*) of *part*; (*b*) of *pint*.

Pt. The chemical symbol of *platinum*.

Ptæroxylon (tē-rok′si-lon), *n.* [NL. (Ecklon and Zeyher, 1834), so called in allusion to the effect on those working with its wood; < Gr. πταίρειν, sneeze, + ξύλον, wood.] A genus of polypetalous trees of the order *Sapindaceæ*, characterized by four small erect and finally recurved petals, and by the fleshy annular disk, four-parted coriaceous two-celled capsule, and the two long compressed, broadly winged seeds. The only species, *P. utile*, the sneezewood of South Africa, is a tree with bitter bark, opposite pinnate leaves, and flowers in small panicles shorter than the leaves. See *sneezewood*.

Ptah (ptā), *n.* [Egyptian.] An Egyptian divinity of high rank, worshiped especially at Memphis, and reverenced as the creative force.

ptarmic (tär′mik), *n.* [< Gr. πταρμικός, causing to sneeze, < πταρμός, a sneezing, < πταίρειν, Attic πτάρνυσθαι (√ πταρ), sneeze, akin to L. *sternuere*, sneeze: see *sternutation*.] A medicine which excites sneezing; a sternutatory.

Ptarmica (tär′mi-kạ̈), *n.* [NL. (Necker, 1791), < Gr. πταρμική, a plant, yarrow or milfoil; prop. fem. of πταρμικός, causing to sneeze: see *ptarmic*.] A former genus of plants, now united with *Achillea*.

ptarmigan (tär′mi-gan), *n.* [With unorig. initial *p* (appar. first in F. *ptarmigan*, so spelled

Rock Ptarmigan (*Lagopus rupestris*), in winter plumage.

prob. because assumed to be of Gr. origin), for **tarmigan*, formerly *termigant*, *termagant*, < Gael. *tarmachan* = Ir. *tarmochan*, also *tarmonach*, the ptarmigan.] A bird of the family *Tetraonidæ* and genus *Lagopus*, having feathered feet. The name was originally applied, in Scotland, to L. *mutus* or *alpinus*, a bird which formerly inhabited England and Wales as well as Scotland, and is also found in Russia, Scandinavia, the Alps, Pyrenees, etc., and is represented in Iceland, Greenland, Siberia, and North America by a closely allied species, L. *rupestris*. This bird turns white in winter, like all of the genus *Lagopus*, excepting L. *scoticus*, the red grouse, moor-fowl, or moor-game of Great Britain. The willow-grouse, L. *albus* or *saliceti*, of subarctic distribution in Europe, Asia, and America, L. *hemileucurus* of Spitzbergen, and L. *leucurus* of alpine regions in western North America are other ptarmigans. See *Lagopus*, and cut under *grouse*.

Ptelea (tē'lē-ä), *n.* [NL. (Linnæus, 1737), so called from the similarity of the fruit to that of the elm; < Gr. πτελέα, the elm.] A genus of polypetalous shrubs and trees of the order *Rutaceæ* and tribe *Toddalieæ*. It is characterized by having four or five imbricated petals, as many stamens, and for fruit a broadly winged orbicular samara with two or three cells, each one-seeded. The 8 species are all natives of North America. They are shrubs or small trees, with bitter bark, bearing alternate compound leaves of two or rarely five leaflets, which are broad and punctate with pellucid dots. The yellowish-green flowers are followed by rather large clusters of dry and flat disk-like fruit, with veiny wings. P. *trifoliata* is the hop-tree, known also as *wingseed* (from the fruit), *wafer-ash*, and *shrubby trefoil*. See *hop-tree*.

Ptenoglossa (tē-nō-glos'ä), *n. pl.* [NL., < Gr. πτηνός, feathered, + γλῶσσα, the tongue.] A division or suborder of pectinibranchiate gastropods, whose odontophore has numerous similar acuminate admedian teeth in each transverse row. It comprises the families *Ianthinidæ*, *Scalariidæ*, *Eulimidæ*, and *Pyramidellidæ*.

ptenoglossate (tē-nō-glos'āt), *a.* [< Gr. πτηνός, feathered, + γλῶσσα, tongue: see *glossate*.] In *Mollusca*, having on the radula or lingual ribbon, in any one cross-row, no median tooth, but an indefinitely large number of lateral teeth. The term is correlated with *rachiglossate*, *rhipidoglossate*, etc.

Ptenopleura† (tē-nō-plö'rä), *n. pl.* [NL., < Gr. πτηνός, feathered, + πλευρά, the side.] One of the divisions of the *Prosimiæ* or lemurine animals, represented by the so-called flying-lemurs: now classed with the *Insectivora*. See *Galeopithecus*.

ptenopleural (tē-nō-plö'ral), *a.* [< Gr. πτηνός, feathered, + πλευρά, the side, + *-al*.] Having the sides of the body winged or alate; having a parachute or flying-membrane; belonging to the *Ptenopleura*.

Pteranodon (te-ran'ō-don), *n.* [NL., < *Pter*(*odactylus*) + Gr. ἀνόδους (ἀνοδοντ-), toothless: see *Anodon*.] The typical genus of *Pteranodontidæ*.

pteranodont (te-ran'ō-dont), *a.* Of or pertaining to the *Pteranodontidæ*.

Pteranodontia (te-ran-ō-don'shi-ä), *n. pl.* [NL., < *Pter*(*odactylus*) + Gr. ἀνόδους (ἀνοδοντ-), toothless: see *Anodon*.] The toothless pterodactyls, a division of *Pterosauria*, represented by the family *Pteranodontidæ*, by some ranked as a peculiar order.

Pteranodontidæ (te-ran-ō-don'ti-dē), *n. pl.* [NL., < *Pteranodon*(*t*-) + *-idæ*.] A family of pterodactyls of the order *Pterosauria*, or giving name to the *Pteranodontia*, having toothless jaws and the coracoid bone solidly united with the scapula. Their remains occur in the Cretaceous. Some species have a spread of wing of 20 feet.

Pteraspis (te-ras'pis), *n.* [< Gr. πτερόν, wing, + ἀσπίς, shield.] A fossil genus of fishes, the remains of which are found in the Middle Devonian and the Lower Ludlow.

ptere (tēr), *n.* [< Gr. πτερόν, feather, wing, usually in pl., feathers, wings, plumes, plumage, foliage, also a fan, oar, side-row of columns, side-wall, etc., = E. *feather*: see *feather*.] In *zoöl.*, an alate or wing-like part or organ; specifically, one of the lobes of the prora of a cymba. A ptere resulting from the broadening or lobation of the prora itself is known as a *proral ptere*; a lateral lobe, between the prora and the tropis, is called a *pleural ptere*; additional pteres, resulting from lateral outgrowths of the tropis or keel, are *tropidial pteres*.

pteria, *n.* Plural of *pterion*.

Pterichthyidæ (ter-ik-thī'i-dē), *n. pl.* [NL., < *Pterichthys* + *-idæ*.] A family of fishes of uncertain relations, typified by the genus *Pterichthys*. It had a cephalic shield with dorsal eyes separated by a movable plate, a dorsal buckler and a flattish abdominal one, long pectoral appendages of two pieces, incased in armor, and a caudal portion destitute of a fin and covered with polygonal scales. The jaws were small and armed with confluent denticles. The organization of the species indicates that they could not have progressed by swimming, and that they probably crawled by the use of the finless pectoral members. They inhabited the Devonian seas. Their pertinence to the class of fishes has been disputed, and they have even been referred to the tunicates in an order called *Antiarcha*.

Pterichthys (te-rik'this), *n.* [NL., < Gr. πτερόν, wing, + ἰχθύς, a fish.] A genus of fishes, typical of the family *Pterichthyidæ*.

Pterideæ (te-rid'ē-ē), *n. pl.* [NL., < *Pteris* (*-id-*) + *-eæ*.] A tribe of polypodiaceous ferns, typified by the genus *Pteris*. The sori are marginal or intramarginal, provided with an indusium formed of the reflexed margin of the frond, and opening inward.

pteridium (te-rid'i-um), *n.* [NL., < Gr. πτερόν, wing, + dim. *-ίδιον*.] A key-fruit or samara. Also *pterodium*.

pteridologist (ter-i-dol'ō-jist), *n.* [< *pteridology* + *-ist*.] One who is versed in the study of ferns.

pteridology (ter-i-dol'ō-ji), *n.* [< Gr. πτερίς (πτεριδ-), fern (see *Pteris*), + -λογία, < λέγειν, speak: see *-ology*.] The science of ferns; a treatise on ferns.

pteridomania (ter″i-dō-mā'ni-ä), *n.* [NL., < Gr. πτερίς (πτεριδ-), fern, + μανία, madness.] A mania or excessive enthusiasm in regard to ferns. [Rare.]

Your daughters, perhaps, have the prevailing *pteridomania*, and are collecting and buying ferns. *Kingsley.*

Pteridophyta (ter-i-dof'i-tä), *n. pl.* [NL., pl. of *pteridophytum*: see *pteridophyte*.] A division of the vegetable kingdom including the ferns and their allies; the vascular cryptogams. See *Cryptogamia*, and compare *Bryophyta*.

pteridophyte (ter'i-dō-fīt), *n.* [< NL. *pteridophytum*, < Gr. πτερίς (πτεριδ-), fern, + φυτόν, plant.] One of the *Pteridophyta*.

pterigraphy (te-rig'ra-fi), *n.* [Irreg. for **pteridography*, < Gr. πτερίς (πτεριδ-), fern, + γράφειν, write.] In *bot.*, a description of ferns.

Pteriidæ (te-rī'i-dē), *n. pl.* [NL., < *Pteria* + *-idæ*.] A family of bivalve mollusks, typified by the genus *Pteria*; the wing-shells. Now called *Aviculidæ*. Also *Margaritidæ*, *Malleidæ*.

pterion (tē'ri-on), *n.*; pl. *pteria* (-ä). [NL., < Gr. πτερόν, feather, wing: see *ptere*.] In *craniom.*, the region where the frontal, squamosal, parietal, and sphenoid bones meet or approach one another. The squamosal is usually cut off from the frontal by a short line of sphenoparietal articulation, where the lower anterior corner of the parietal joins the tip of the alisphenoid; but in some cases this line is reduced to nothing, and then the frontal and squamosal come into contact. See cut under *craniometry*.

In the region of the *pterion* in the male, the squamosal articulates with the frontal on the right side for a space of 4 mm. *Anthropological Jour.*, XVIII. 7.

pteriplegistic (ter-i-plē-jis'tik), *a.* Same as *pteroplegistic*. *Webster.*

Pteris (tē'ris), *n.* [NL. (Linnæus, 1737), < Gr. πτερίς (πτεριδ-), also πτέρις (πτερε-), a kind of fern, so called from its feathery leaves, < πτερόν, a feather: see *ptere*.] A cosmopolitan genus of ferns, typical of the tribe *Pterideæ*; the brakes. It includes plants of almost every kind of venation and division. The sporangia are in a continuous slender line occupying the entire margins of the fertile frond, and covered by its narrow reflexed edge, which forms a continuous membranaceous indusium. Of the more than 100 species known, only 4 are found in North America. P. *aquilina*, the common brake, is very abundant in rocky thickets, dry fields, etc. See *brake*⁶, *bracken*, *adder-spit*, and cut under *prothallium*.

Pteris aquilina.
a, a pinnule on larger scale, showing the revolute margin.

pterna (tėr'nä), *n.*; pl. *pternæ* (-nē). [< Gr. πτέρνα, the heel.] In *ornith.*, the heel-pad; the sole of the foot, at the place where the toes dispart.

Pterobranchia (ter-ō-brang'ki-ä), *n. pl.* [NL., < Gr. πτερόν, wing, + βράγχια, gills.] 1. In J. E. Gray's classification (1821), one of two orders of pteropods (the other being *Dactyliobranchia*): same as *Gymnosomata*.—2. In Lankester's classification of molluscoids, the second section of the third class of a phylum *Podaxonia*, composed of two genera, *Rhabdopleura* and *Cephalodiscus*: called by others *Podostomata* and *Aspidophora*. *Encyc. Brit.*, XIX. 430.

pterobranchiate (ter-ō-brang'ki-āt), *a.* [< *Pterobranchia* + *-ate*¹.] Of or pertaining to the *Pterobranchia*.

pterocardiac (ter-ō-kär'di-ak), *a.* [< Gr. πτερόν, wing, + E. *cardiac*.] Alate, or wing-like, and cardiac: used specifically by Huxley to note an ossicle in the stomach of the crawfish, which articulates with the cardiac ossicle. See cut under *Astacidæ*.

pterocarpous (ter-ō-kar'pus), *a.* [< Gr. πτερόν, wing, + καρπός, fruit.] In *bot.*, having winged fruit.

Pterocarpus (ter-ō-kär'pus), *n.* [NL. (Linnæus, 1767), < Gr. πτερόν, wing, + καρπός, fruit.] A genus of leguminous trees of the tribe *Dalbergieæ*, type of the subtribe *Pterocarpeæ*. It is characterized by a broad or nearly orbicular and oblique pod, which is tipped by a lateral style, is flattened around the edges into a thin coriaceous or membranous wing, and contains in its hard thickened center one, two, or three seeds separated by woody partitions. The 18 species are all tropical, and natives of Asia, Africa, and America. They are large thornless trees, bearing alternate pinnate leaves, and yellow papilionaceous flowers, often showy and sometimes variegated with white or violet, forming racemes or loose panicles. In general they produce hard and valuable timber, and also gum-resins, some very important. For P. *Marsupium*, the bija or bastard teak or Amboyna kino-tree, see *kino* and under *teak*. For P. *Indicus*, the padouk, lingo-tree, Burmese rosewood, or Andaman redwood, see *kiabooca-wood* and under *redwood*. P. *erinaceus* is the molompi, Gambia kino-tree, cornwood, or African rosewood. For P. *Draco*, see *dragon's-blood*. P. *santalinus* is the red sandalwood, red sanders-wood, rubywood, or East Indian redwood, affording an important dyestuff.

Pterocaulon (ter-ō-kâ'lon), *n.* [NL. (Elliott, 1824), < Gr. πτερόν, wing, + καυλός, stem.] A genus of composite plants of the tribe *Inuloideæ* and subtribe *Plucheineæ*. It is characterized by its small flower-heads massed in dense clusters which are spiked or scattered, and by the slender capillary pappus, and stem winged by the decurrent leaves. The 9 species are nearly equally divided between America and the Old World, and are principally natives of warm climates. They are herbs, or sometimes shrubby at the base, commonly whitened with a dense wool, and bearing alternate leaves and numerous small white or yellow flowers. Two species are found in the southern United States, P. *pycnostachyum* (see *black-root*, 2), and P. *virgatum*, a plant of Texas, Mexico, and the West Indies, known in Jamaica as *golden-locks* and *golden-tuft*. See *golden cudweed*, under *cudweed*.

Pterocephala (ter-ō-sef'a-lä), *n. pl.* [NL., < Gr. πτερόν, wing, + κεφαλή, head.] Thecosomatous pteropods: a synonym of *Thecosomata*. *Wagner*, 1885.

Pterocles (ter'ō-klēz), *n.* [NL. (Temminck, 1809), < Gr. πτερόν, wing, feather, + κλείς, key, bolt, tongue of a buckle.] The typical genus of *Pteroclidæ*. There are 12 or 14 species, mostly African. Three are Asiatic—P. *arenaria*, the common sand-grouse (see *sand-grouse*), P. *fasciata*, and P. *alchata*; the first and last of these also occur in Europe, and the last is sometimes placed in a different genus, *Pteroclurus*. See also cut under *ganga*.

Sand-grouse (*Pterocles arenaria*).

Pteroclidæ (te-rok'li-dē), *n. pl.* [NL., < *Pterocles* + *-idæ*.] A family of sand-grouse, alone representing the *Pteroclomorphæ*, and composed of the subfamilies *Pteroclinæ* and *Syrrhaptinæ*. They are essentially terrestrial columbine birds, modified for a grouse-like life; the digestive system resembles that of gallinaceous birds, but the pterylosis and many osteological characters are like those of pigeons.

Pteroclomorphæ (ter″ō-klō-môr'fē), *n. pl.* [NL., < *Pterocles* + Gr. μορφή, form.] In Huxley's classification of birds, a superfamily group consisting of the sand-grouse, considered to be intermediate between the *Columbæ* and the *Gallinæ*.

pteroclomorphic (ter″ō-klō-môr'fik), *a.* [< *Pteroclomorphæ* + *-ic*.] Having the structure and affinities of the *Pteroclidæ*; belonging to the *Pteroclomorphæ*.

pterocymba (ter-ō-sim'bä), *n.* [NL., < Gr. πτερόν, wing, + NL. *cymba*, q. v.] A cymba, or cymbate flesh-spicule of a sponge, whose proræ are alate, or widened into proral and pleural pteres, whence a figure resembling an anchor results. *W. J. Sollas*, Encyc. Brit., XXII. 418.

pterocymbate (ter-ō-sim'bāt), *a.* [< *pterocymba* + *-ate*¹.] Alate, as a cymba; having the form or character of a pterocymba.

Pterocynes (te-ros'i-nēz), *n. pl.* [NL., < Gr. πτερόν, wing, + κύων (κυν-), dog.] In some systems, a division of the mammalian order *Chiroptera*, including the frugivorous bats, or flying-foxes, as distinguished from all the rest of the order, then collectively called *Nycterides*. The two divisions correspond respectively to the terms *Frugivora* and *Animalivora*, which are more frequently used.

pterodactyl, pterodactyle (ter-ō-dak'til), *n.* [< NL. *Pterodactylus*.] An extinct reptile of the genus *Pterodactylus* or order *Pterosauria*; a pterosaurian; an ornithosaurian; a flying-dragon. Also *pterodactylian*.

Skeleton of Pterodactyl.

Pterodactyli (ter-ō-dak'ti-lī), *n. pl.* [NL., pl. of *Pterodactylus*.] The pterodactyls as a group of extinct flying-dragons, typified by the genus *Pterodactylus*: same as *Pterosauria*.

pterodactylian (ter″ō-dak-til'i-an), *n.* [< *pterodactyl* + *-ian*.] Same as *pterodactyl*.

Pterodactylidæ (ter″ō-dak-til'i-dē), *n. pl.* [NL., < *Pterodactylus* + *-idæ*.] A family of pterodactyls, typified by the genus *Pterodactylus*. See *Pterosauridæ*. *Bonaparte*, 1841.

pterodactylous (ter-ō-dak'ti-lus), *a.* [< NL. *pterodactylus*, < Gr. πτερόν, wing, + δάκτυλος, finger, digit.] Adapted for flight by having one digit of the fore limb much enlarged and webbed, as a pterodactyl; specifically, pertaining to pterodactyls, or having their characters; pterosaurian; ornithosaurian.

Pterodactylus (ter-ō-dak'ti-lus), *n.* [NL. (Oken, 1816), < Gr. πτερόν, wing, + δάκτυλος, finger, digit.] The leading genus of the order *Pterosauria*. It was formerly conterminous with the group *Pterodactyli*, but now gives name to the family *Pterodactylidæ*, and is restricted to species having the usual four joints in the ulnar digit, a very short flexible tail, the metacarpus usually more than half as long as the forearm, and the strong pointed jaws furnished with teeth to their tips. (Compare *Rhamphorhynchus*.) There are several species, extending from the Jura to the Chalk. See cut under *pterodactyl*.

Pterodicera (ter-ō-dis'e-rä), *n. pl.* [NL. (Latreille, 1806), < Gr. πτερόν, feather, wing, + δίκερος, a double horn: see *dicerous*.] In Latreille's classification, one of the two main divisions of the class *Insecta*, including all the winged orders. The other division is *Aptera*.

Pterodina (ter-ō-dī'nä), *n.* [NL. (Ehrenberg), < Gr. πτερόν, feather, + δῖνος, wheel, ring.] A genus of rotifers, typical of the family *Pterodinidæ*.

Pterodinidæ (ter-ō-din'i-dē), *n. pl.* [NL., < *Pterodina* + *-idæ*.] A family of rotifers, typified by the genus *Pterodina*. They have a trochal disk of two transverse circular lobes, the wreath on each being double; the trophi are malleoramate; and the foot is transversely wrinkled, wholly retractile, and ends in a ciliate cup.

pterodium (te-rō'di-um), *n.* Same as *pteridium*.

Pterodon (ter'ō-don), *n.* [NL. (De Blainville, 1841), < Gr. πτερόν, wing, + ὀδούς (ὀδοντ-) = E. *tooth*.] A genus of fossil carnivorous quadrupeds, closely related to *Hyænodon*, based upon remains of Eocene age found in France.

pteroglossine (ter-ō-glos'in), *a.* [< Gr. πτερόν, feather, + γλῶσσα, tongue (see *Pteroglossus*), + *-ine*[1].] Having a feathery or brushy tongue: specifically applied to the aracaris.

Pteroglossus (ter-ō-glos'us), *n.* [NL., < Gr. πτερόν, feather, + γλῶσσα, tongue.] 1. In *ornith.*, a genus of *Rhamphastidæ*, including those toucans known as *aracaris*. *Illiger*, 1811. See cut under *aracari*.—2. In *entom.*, a genus of coleopterous insects of the family *Carabidæ*. *Chaudoir*, 1847. Also called *Oödius*.

pterographer (te-rog'ra-fėr), *n.* [< *pterograph-y* + *-er*[1].] A writer of pterography; the author of a pterographic treatise.

pterographic (ter-ō-graf'ik), *a.* [< *pterograph-y* + *-ic*.] Of or pertaining to pterography.

pterographical (ter-ō-graf'i-kal), *a.* [< *pterographic* + *-al*.] Same as *pterographic*.

pterography (te-rog'ra-fi), *n.* [< Gr. πτερόν, feather, + γράφειν, write.] The description of feathers; a treatise on plumage: a term of wider sense than *pterylography*, which it includes.

pteroid[1] (tē'roid), *n.* [< Gr. πτερόν, wing (see *ptere*), + εἶδος, form.] A slender bone of some pterodactyls extending from the carpal region in the direction of the humerus. Some consider it as an ossification of a tendon corresponding with one which is found in a similar position in birds, while others regard it as a rudimentary first digit, modified to support the edge of the patagium.

pteroid[2] (tē'roid), *a.* [< Gr. πτερίς, fern (see *Pteris*), + εἶδος, form.] In *bot.*, fern-like; resembling a fern; filicoid.

pterological (ter-ō-loj'i-kal), *a.* [< *pterolog-y* + *-ic-al*.] Of or pertaining to pterology; founded on pterology: as, *pterological* characters; the *pterological* description of an insect.

pterology (te-rol'ō-ji), *n.* [< Gr. πτερόν, wing, + -λογία, < λέγειν, speak: see *-ology*.] In *entom.*, the science of insects' wings; the description of the neuration or venation and other characteristics of the wing-structure.

pteroma (te-rō'mä), *n.*; pl. *pteromata* (-ma-tä). [L., < Gr. πτέρωμα, a 'wing' of a temple (see def.), also a feathered arrow, < πτεροῦν, furnish with feathers or wings, < πτερόν, feather, wing: see *ptere*.] In *arch.*, the space between the wall of the cella of a classical temple or any similar columnar structure and the pteron, or the columns of the peristyle.

Pteromalidæ (ter-ō-mal'i-dē), *n. pl.* [NL. (Walker, 1831), < *Pteromalus* + *-idæ*.] 1. The *Pteromalinæ* considered as a separate family. —2. A family of parasitic *Hymenoptera*: used by Dalman as the equivalent of and superseding the family *Chalcididæ*.

Pteromalinæ (ter″ō-ma-lī'nē), *n. pl.* [NL. (Walker), < *Pteromalus* + *-inæ*.] One of the largest subfamilies of *Chalcididæ*, named from the genus *Pteromalus*, comprising about 1,000 species of several tribes and many genera, having thirteen-jointed antennæ with a three-jointed club and two ring-joints. They are small, usually metallic insects, parasitic generally upon lepidopterous, dipterous, or coleopterous larvæ. The group has 8 tribes, and nearly 100 genera besides *Pteromalus*.

pteromaline (te-rom'a-lin), *a.* Of or pertaining to the *Pteromalidæ* or *Pteromalinæ*.

Pteromalus (te-rom'a-lus), *n.* [NL. (Swederus, 1795), < Gr. πτερόν, wing, + ὁμαλός, even.] A genus of chalcidid hymenopterous insects, giving name to the subfamily *Pteromalinæ*. It is characterized by the one-spurred hind tibiæ; antennal club not clavate; head with the vertex sometimes medially acute; eyes occasionally hairy; mandibles fourdentate; ring-joints of antennæ plain; metathorax carinate; and abdomen never produced at the apex. It is a large unwieldy genus, universally distributed, parasitic upon insects of several different orders. *P. puparum* lives upon several lepidopterous larvæ, notably that of *Pieris rapæ*.

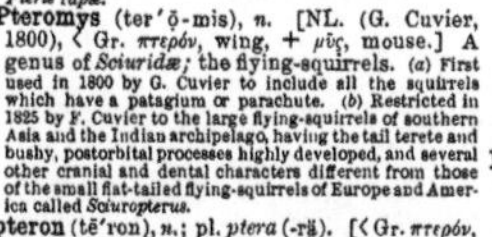

Pteromalus puparum. *a*, male; *b*, female. (Lines show natural sizes.)

Pteromys (ter'ō-mis), *n.* [NL. (G. Cuvier, 1800), < Gr. πτερόν, wing, + μῦς, mouse.] A genus of *Sciuridæ*; the flying-squirrels. (*a*) First used in 1800 by G. Cuvier to include all the squirrels which have a patagium or parachute. (*b*) Restricted in 1825 by F. Cuvier to the large flying-squirrels of southern Asia and the Indian archipelago, having the tail terete and bushy, postorbital processes highly developed, and several other cranial and dental characters different from those of the small flat-tailed flying-squirrels of Europe and America called *Sciuropterus*.

pteron (tē'ron), *n.*; pl. *ptera* (-rä). [< Gr. πτερόν, wing, side-row of columns: see *ptere*.] In *Gr. arch.* and *archæol.*, a range of columns; a portico.

Pteronura (ter-ō-nū'rä), *n.* [NL. (J. E. Gray, 1837), prop. *Pterura*, < Gr. πτερόν, wing, + οὐρά, tail.] A South American genus of otters of the family *Mustelidæ* and subfamily *Lutrinæ*, having the tail alate, or margined with a flange-like fold or ridge on each side. The type is *P. sandbachi*, known as the *margin-tailed otter*. Also *Pterura*.

Pteropædes (ter-ō-pē'dēz), *n. pl.* [NL., < Gr. πτερόν, feather, wing, + παῖς (παιδ-), child.] Those birds which are fledged and able to fly when hatched, as the mound-birds. Compare *Ptilopædes*.

pteropædic (ter-ō-pē'dik), *a.* [< *Pteropæd-es* + *-ic*.] Having the characters of the *Pteropædes*.

Pteropappi (ter-ō-pap'ī), *n. pl.* [NL., < Gr. πτερόν, feather, wing, + πάππος, down: see *pappus*.] A rare synonym of *Odontotormæ*.

pterope (ter'ōp), *n.* [< NL. *Pteropus*, q. v.] A fruit-bat or flying-fox; a member of the genus *Pteropus* in a broad sense.

pteropegal (ter-ō-pē'gal), *a.* [< *pteropeg-um* + *-al*.] Pertaining to the pteropegum, or having its character.

pteropegum (ter-ō-pē'gum), *n.*; pl. *pteropega* (-gä). [NL., < Gr. πτερόν, feather, wing, + πηγός, lit. fastened, < πηγνύναι, fasten: see *pact*.] In *entom.*, the socket on the side of the thorax in which a wing is articulated.

Pterophora (te-rof'ō-rä), *n. pl.* [NL. (Clairville, 1798), < Gr. πτεροφόρος, having wings: see *Pterophorus*.] In Clairville's system, one of the prime divisions of *Insecta*, including all hexapodous insects except *Aptera*: same as *Ptilota*, *Pterodicera*, and *Pterygota*.

Pterophoridæ (ter-ō-for'i-dē), *n. pl.* [NL. (Zeller, 1841), < *Pterophorus* + *-idæ*.] A family of lepidopterous insects, typified by the genus *Pterophorus*, including the plume-moths. They have long slim bodies and legs, and most of them are remarkable for having their wings divided into lobes or feathers. The larvæ are fusiform, sixteen-legged, and furnished with irregular protuberances and tubular hairs, and some of them resemble small bundles of dried leaves. The species are not numerous, although the family is of wide distribution. Also called *Alucitidæ*. See *Fissipennæ*, and cut under *plume-moth*.

Pterophorina (te-rof-ō-rī'nä), *n. pl.* [NL., < *Pterophorus* + *-ina*.] A division of moths, represented by the family *Pterophoridæ*.

Pterophorus (te-rof'ō-rus), *n.* [NL. (Geoffroy, 1764), < Gr. πτεροφόρος, bearing feathers, feathered, winged, < πτερόν, feather, wing, + -φόρος, < φέρειν = E. *bear*[1].] A genus of lepidopterous insects, type of the *Pterophoridæ*. *P. monodactylus* occurs in Europe, western Asia, and all parts of North America. Its larva feeds on *Convolvulus* and *Chenopodium*. See cut under *plume-moth*.

Pterophyllum (ter-ō-fil'um), *n.* [NL. (Brongniart, 1828), < Gr. πτερόν, feather, wing, + φύλλον, a leaf.] 1. A genus of cycadaceous fossil plants, with linear leaves attached to the rachis by the full width of their bases, and at right angles to it; the nervation is simple and parallel to the length of the leaf. This genus is first seen in the upper part of the coal-measures, attains its greatest development in the Trias, and finally disappears at the close of the Jurassic.
2. A genus of fishes of the family *Cichlidæ*.

Pteropidæ, etc. See *Pteropodidæ*, etc.

Pteroplatea (ter-ō-plā'tē-ä), *n.* [NL., < Gr. πτερόν, wing (fin), + πλατύς (fem. πλατεῖα), broad.] A genus of sting-rays, typical of the subfamily *Pteroplateinæ*. *P. maclura* is an eastern and *P. marmorata* a western American species.

Pteroplateinæ (ter-ō-plā-tē-ī'nē), *n. pl.* [NL., < *Pteroplatea* + *-inæ*.] A subfamily of trygonoid sting-rays, typified by the genus *Pteroplatea*. They have a very broad disk, the pectoral fins extending far sideways, and the tail short.

pteropod (ter'ō-pod), *a.* and *n.* [< NL. *pteropus* (*-pod-*), < Gr. πτερόπους (-ποδ-), wing-footed (as Hermes), < πτερόν, wing, + πούς (ποδ-) = E. *foot*.] I. *a.* Having an alate podium, or wing-like expansions of the foot, as a mollusk; of or pertaining to the *Pteropoda*. Also *pteropodous*.

II. *n.* A mollusk of the class *Pteropoda*. The shell-bearing pteropods are the *Thecosomata*; the naked pteropods are the *Gymnosomata*; spiny pteropods belong to the family *Cavoliniidæ*, and spiral pteropods to the *Limacinidæ*; slipper-pteropods are *Cymbuliidæ*. Also *pteropode*.

Pteropoda (te-rop'ō-dä), *n. pl.* [NL., neut. pl. of *pteropus* (*-pod-*), wing-footed: see *pteropod*.] 1. A division of *Mollusca*, having the mesopodium or middle part of the podium or foot expanded into a pair of large alate lobes like wings or flippers, and used as such to swim with; the pteropods. The ctenidia are abortive, the nephridium is single, and the general configuration is more or less unsymmetrical, somewhat as in gastropods. The propodium may be produced into tentaculiform organs. There are otidia or otocysts, and one osphradium. The pteropods are hermaphroditic or monœcious; there are organs of copulation and a single genital pore. According to the presence or absence of a mantle-skirt and shell, the *Pteropoda* are *Thecosomata* and *Gymnosomata*. All are oceanic. They originally formed the second class of Cuvier's branch *Mollusca*, under the French name *Ptéropodes*. By most conchologists this view has been accepted, but others have united the pteropods with the cephalopods, and still others with the gastropods. By several anatomists they have been approximated to the tectibranchiates, and even supposed to be derived from different stocks of that order—the thecosomes from the *Cephalaspidea*, and the gymnosomes from the *Anaspidea*. Also called *Coponautæ*. See cuts under *Cavoliniidæ* and *Pneumodermon*.

2. In De Blainville's classification (1825), one of two families of his fifth order, *Nucleobranchiata* (the other being *Nectopoda*), composed of the genera *Atlanta*, *Spiratella*, and *Argonauta*. It is thus a highly artificial group, comprising a part of the heteropods together with some cephalopods, etc.

pteropodan (te-rop'ǫ-dạn), *a.* and *n.* [< *pteropod* + *-an*.] Same as *pteropod*.

pteropode (ter'ǫ-pōd), *n.* [< NL. *Pteropus* (*-pod-*).] 1. An animal of the genus *Pteropus*; a fruit-bat or flying-fox; a pterope.—2. Same as *pteropod*.

pteropodia, *n.* Plural of *pteropodium*.

pteropodial (ter-ǫ-pō'di-ạl), *a.* [< *pteropodium* + *-al*.] Of or pertaining to a pteropodium: as, the *pteropodial* fins or wings of a pteropod.

Pteropodidæ (ter-ǫ-pod'i-dē), *n. pl.* [NL., < *Pteropus* (*-pod-*) + *-idæ*.] A family of *Megachi-*

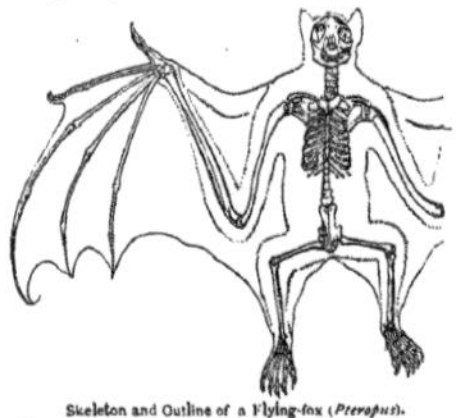

Skeleton and Outline of a Flying-fox (*Pteropus*).

roptera, *Frugivora*, or fruit-eating bats, of the tropical and subtropical parts of the Old World. They are generally of large size, with the tail excluded from the interfemoral membrane when present, little or no spigelian lobe of the liver but a large caudate lobe, the cardiac end of the stomach generally elongated, the index-finger with three phalanges and usually a claw, and the molar crowns smooth. The family contains about 8 genera, of which the best-known are *Pteropus*, *Epomophorus*, and *Harpyia*. It is sometimes divided into *Pteropi* and *Macroglossi*. Also called *Pteropidæ*. See also cut under *Pteropus*.

pteropodium (ter-ǫ-pō'di-um), *n.*; pl. *pteropodia* (-ạ̈). [NL., < Gr. πτερόν, wing, + πόδιον, dim. of πούς = E. *foot*: see *podium*.] The peculiar podium or foot of a pteropod.

pteropodous (te-rop'ǫ-dus), *a.* [< *pteropod* + *-ous*.] Same as *pteropod*.

Pteroptochidæ (ter-op-tok'i-dē), *n. pl.* [NL., < *Pteroptochus* + *-idæ*.] A South American family of formicarioid passerine birds, typified by the genus *Pteroptochus*, with tracheophonous mesomyodian syrinx, taxaspidean tarsi, operculate nostrils, and ten primaries; the rock-wrens. They are small wren-like birds of skulking habits, especially characteristic of Chili and Patagonia. There are about 24 species, leading genera of which, besides the type genus, are *Hylactes*, *Scytalopus*, and *Rhinocrypta*. Some of them are known as *barking-birds*.

Pteroptochus (ter-op-tō'kus), *n.* [NL. (Kittlitz, 1830, in the form *Pteroptochos*), < Gr. πτερόν, wing, + πτωχός, one who crouches or cringes.] The typical genus of *Pteroptochidæ*. *P. rubecula* and *P. albicollis* inhabit Chili.

Fruit-bat (*Pteropus edulis*).

Pteropus (ter'ǫ-pus), *n.* [NL. (Brisson, 1756), < Gr. πτερόπους, wing-footed: see *pteropod*.] The typical genus of the flying-foxes, or large fruit-bats of the family *Pteropodidæ*. It includes some 40 species, or more than half the family, chiefly of the Malay archipelago and Australia, having no tail, a pointed muzzle like a fox's, woolly fur on the neck, and the dental formula 2 incisors, 1 canine, and 3 premolars in each upper and lower half-jaw, and 2 molars above and 3 below on each side. *P. edulis* of Java, one of the best-known species, is the largest, measuring five feet in extent of wings. See also cuts under *Pteropodidæ* and *flying-fox*.

Pterorhina (ter-ǫ-rī'nạ̈), *n. pl.* [NL., prop. **Pterorrhina*, neut. pl. of **pterorrhinus*: see *pterorhine*.] A division of *Alcidæ*, including those whose nostrils are feathered, as typical auks, murres, and guillemots.

pterorhine (ter'ǫ-rin), *a.* [Prop. **pterorrhine*, < NL. **pterorrhinus*, < Gr. πτερόν, feather, wing, + ῥίς (ῥιν-), nose.] Having feathered nostrils, as an auk; belonging to the *Pterorhina*.

pterosaur (ter'ǫ-sâr), *n.* [< *Pterosaur-ia*.] A member of the *Pterosauria*; a pterodactyl.

Pterosauria (ter-ǫ-sâ'ri-ạ̈), *n. pl.* [NL., < Gr. πτερόν, wing, + σαῦρος, a lizard.] 1. An order of extinct Mesozoic *Reptilia* adapted for flight; the pterosaurians, pterodactyls, ornithosaurians, or flying-dragons. The whole fore limb is modified to support a flying-membrane somewhat like that of bats, and the rest of the skeleton is conformable with this modification. The vertebræ are comparatively few, procœlous, those of the neck very large, and from three to six of the pelvic ones are united to form a sacrum. The anterior ribs have bifurcated heads. The skull is of great size, with long heavy jaws and large eye-sockets including a circlet of sclerotic ossifications. The sternum is broad and carinate, the scapula and coracoid are slender, and clavicles are wanting. The phalanges of the ulnar digit are extremely long and strong, and support the parachute. The hind limbs are smaller than the fore limbs, and comparatively weak. The order contains the families *Pterosauridæ* and *Pteranodontidæ*. They lived from the Lias to the Chalk. See cut under *pterodactyl*. Also called *Ornithosauria*, *Pterodactyli*.
2. Same as *Pterosauridæ*.

pterosaurian (ter-ǫ-sâ'ri-ạn), *a.* and *n.* **I.** *a.* Of or pertaining to the *Pterosauria*; ornithosaurian.

II. *n.* A pterosaur, pterodactyl, or ornithosaur.

Pterosauridæ (ter-ǫ-sâ'ri-dē), *n. pl.* [NL., < *Pterosauria* + *-idæ*.] A family of pterodactyls, of the order *Pterosauria*, with teeth and separate scapula and coracoid bones. It is represented by such genera as *Pterodactylus*, *Rhamphorhynchus*, and *Dimorphodon*, from the Jurassic formation. Also *Pterosauria*.

Pterospermum (ter-ǫ-spėr'mum), *n.* [NL. (Schreber, 1789), < Gr. πτερόν, wing, + σπέρμα, seed.] A genus of polypetalous trees and shrubs of the order *Sterculiaceæ* and tribe *Helictereæ*. It is characterized by stalked anthers, with parallel linear cells, woody round or five-angled five-valved capsules, and winged seeds. The 16 species are all natives of tropical Asia. They are commonly clothed with stellate hairs, and bear oblique coriaceous leaves, and elongated flowers, which are axillary and nearly or quite solitary, and consist of a tubular five-cleft calyx with five obovate petals and a prominent column of united stamens. The flowers are usually white, fragrant, and several inches in length. *P. acerifolium* and *P. suberifolium* are trees of the East Indies, sometimes cultivated under the name of *wingseed*. *P. Javanicum* is the bayur of Java.

Pterospora (te-ros'pǫ-rạ̈), *n.* [NL. (Nuttall, 1818), < Gr. πτερόν, wing, + σπόρος, seed.] A genus of root-parasitic plants belonging to the order *Monotropeæ*. It is characterized by a gamopetalous urn-shaped corolla with five short recurving lobes, five persistent sepals, ten stamens with pendulous anthers facing inward and two-spurred on the back, and a five-lobed and five-celled capsule filled with minute seeds which terminate in a large and broad hyaline reticulated wing. The only species, *P. andromedea*, known as *pine-drops*, is a slender, purplish-brown, clammy-hairy, and scaly herb, growing 1 or 2 feet high, leafless like most parasites, and with roots consisting of a mass of coral-like thickened fibers. The white nodding flowers are borne in a long raceme. It is a rare plant, found on hard clay soil under pines from Vermont and Pennsylvania northward and westward across the continent. From its early discovery near Albany, and its resemblance to beech-drops, it is also known as *Albany beech-drops*.

pterostigma (ter-ǫ-stig'mạ̈), *n.*; pl. *pterostigmata* (-mạ-tạ̈). [NL., < Gr. πτερόν, feather, wing, + στίγμα, a spot, mark: see *stigma*.] The carpus or stigma, a peculiar mark or spot on the wings of some insects. It is a dark-colored triangular or quadrate space on the anterior border of the fore wings of hymenopters, and on both fore and hind wings of dragon-flies. It corresponds to that one of the costal cells which is thickened to strengthen the costal border. —**Fenestrate pterostigma.** See *fenestrate*.

pterostigmal (ter-ǫ-stig'mạl), *a.* [< *pterostigma* + *-al*.] Pertaining to a pterostigma or having its character; pterostigmatic: as, a *pterostigmal* cell or spot.

pterostigmatic (ter″ǫ-stig-mat'ik), *a.* [< *pterostigma(t-)* + *-ic*.] Having a pterostigma, as an insect's wing; provided with pterostigmata, as an insect; pterostigmal.

pterostigmatical (ter″ǫ-stig-mat'i-kạl), *a.* [< *pterostigmatic* + *-al*.] Same as *pterostigmatic*. *Hagen*.

pterotheca (ter-ǫ-thē'kạ̈), *n.*; pl. *pterothecæ* (-sē). [NL., < Gr. πτερόν, wing, + θήκη, case: see *theca*.] In *entom.*, a wing-case, or that part of the integument of a pupa on which is outlined the undeveloped wing beneath it.

pterotic (te-rot'ik), *a.* and *n.* [< Gr. πτερόν, feather, wing, + οὖς (ὠτ-), = E. *ear*, + *-ic*.] **I.** *a.* In *zoöl.* and *anat.*, noting an ossification of the periotic capsule or petrosal bone, distinct from the proötic, epiotic, and opisthotic, which occurs in some vertebrates between the proötic and the epiotic.

II. *n.* A pterotic ossification. See first cut under *teleost* and cut under *Esox*.

Pterotrachea (ter″ǫ-trạ-kē'ạ̈), *n.* [NL. (Forskål), < Gr. πτερόν, wing, + τραχύς, fem. τραχεῖα, rough: see *trachea*.] The typical genus of *Pterotracheidæ*. Also called *Firola*.

Pterotracheacea (ter-ǫ-trā-kẹ-ā'sẹ-ạ̈), *n. pl.* [NL., < *Pterotrachea* + *-acea*.] The *Pterotracheidæ* considered as a suborder of heteropods.

Pterotracheidæ (ter″ǫ-trạ-kē'i-dē), *n. pl.* [NL. (J. E. Gray, 1840), < *Pterotrachea* + *-idæ*.] A family of shell-less heteropods, typified by the genus *Pterotrachea*. Different limits have been assigned to it. By some it is extended to all the heteropods with the branchiæ carried in a dorsal peduncle and protected by a small or no shell, and the mesopodium lamelliform. By others it is limited to *Pterotrachea* and *Firoloides*, having the visceral hump, reduced to a mere oval sac, embedded in the posterior region of the body, no shell, and a cylindrical slug-like form. Also called *Firolidæ* and, as a suborder, *Pterotracheacea*.

Pterotrachea pedunculata.

Pterozamites (ter-ǫ-zam'i-tēz), *n.* [NL. (Schimper, 1870), < Gr. πτερόν, feather, + *Zamites*, q. v.] A genus of fossil cycadaceous plants, differing from other genera chiefly in having only the stronger veins fork at base. It embraces about 5 or 6 species, found in the Rhetic, Lias, and Oölite of Europe.

Pterura (te-rö'rạ̈), *n.* Same as *Pteronura*.

pterygial (te-rij'i-ạl), *a.* [< *pterygium* + *-al*.] Of or pertaining to a pterygium.

pterygium (te-rij'i-um), *n.*; pl. *pterygia* (-ạ̈). [NL., also *pterygion*; cf. L. *pterygium*, < Gr. πτερύγιον, a little wing, a fin, projection, film over the eye, growth of flesh over the nails, dim. of πτέρυξ (πτερυγ-), wing, < πτερόν, wing, feather: see *ptere*.] 1. In *zoöl.* and *anat.*, a limb or member of one of the vertebrates, as a fish, in the most general sense, without reference to its specialization in any given instance. A hypothetical pterygium, whence other pterygia are supposed to have been evolved, is an *archipterygium*; the ichthyic modification is an *ichthyopterygium*; the air-breathers' modification is a *chiropterygium*. Parts of the pterygium of an elasmobranchiate fish have been called *mesopterygium*, *metapterygium*, *propterygium*, bearing basalia and radialia, as in the accompanying figure.
2. In *pathol.*, a more or less triangular patch of hypertrophied conjunctiva and subconjunctival tissue with its apex at the edge of the cornea or upon the cornea.—3. In *entom.*, one of the two lateral expansions at the end of the rostrum of certain weevils. They lie above and partly conceal the scrobes or grooves in which the antennæ are concealed.

Pterygium, or (right) Pectoral Limb of the Monkfish (*Squatina*). *p*, propterygium; *ms*, mesopterygium; *mt*, metapterygium—bearing respectively the propterygial, mesopterygial, and metapterygial basalia and radialia.

pterygoblast (ter'i-gǫ-blast), *n.* [< Gr. πτέρυξ (πτερυγ-), wing, + βλαστός, germ.] A germinal fin-ray; the histological element from which the embryonic fin-rays of fishes are developed. *J. A. Ryder*.

pterygobranchiate (ter″i-gǫ-brang'ki-āt), *a.* [< Gr. πτέρυξ (πτερυγ-), feather, + βράγχια, gills.] Having feathery gills: noting a section of isopods, in distinction from *phytobranchiate*.

pterygoda (ter-i-gō'dạ̈), *n. pl.* [NL., < Gr. πτερυγώδης, wing-like: see *pterygoid*.] In *entom.*, the tegulæ, a pair of small movable scales or epaulets attached to the mesothorax of *Lepidoptera*, near the insertion of the first legs.

In front of the fore wings . . . are a pair of *pterygoda*, a kind of epaulettes, which extend backwards.
Latreille, in Cuvier's Règne Animal (trans.), ed. 1849, [p. 476.

pterygode (ter'i-gōd), *n.* One of the pterygoda. Also *pterygoid.* *J. O. Westwood.*

pterygofaceting (ter″i-gō-fas'et-ing), *n.* [< *pterygo(id)* + *facet*[1] + *-ing*[1].] The formation of an articulate facet for the pterygoid bone on the rostrum of a bird's skull. *Coues.*

pterygoid (ter'i-goid), *a.* and *n.* [< Gr. πτερυγοειδής (contr. πτερυγώδης), wing-like, feathery, < πτέρυξ (πτερυγ-), a wing, + εἶδος, form.] **I.** *a.* Wing-like or wing-shaped; aliform or alate: specifically applied in anatomy to certain bones or bony processes and associate parts. —**Pterygoid artery**, a branch of the internal maxillary, from the second or pterygoid section of that vessel, supplying the pterygoid muscles.—**Pterygoid bones**, the pterygoids.—**Pterygoid canal.** Same as *Vidian canal* (which see, under *canal*).—**Pterygoid fossa.** See *fossa*[1]. —**Pterygoid muscles**, the pterygoidei, or muscles which arise from the pterygoid bones or pterygoid processes of the sphenoid. In man the *external* pterygoid muscle arises from the external pterygoid process of the sphenoid and the part of the alisphenoid below the pterygoid ridge, and extends nearly horizontally outward to be inserted into the condyloid section of the lower jaw-bone: it is also called *ectopterygoid*. The *internal* pterygoid muscle arises from the pterygoid fossa and palate-bone, and passes downward and outward to be inserted into the inner surface of the ascending ramus and angle of the lower jaw-bone: it is also called *entopterygoid* and *internal masseter*. The pterygoid muscles effect the lateral and forward and backward movements of the jaw, and the internal maxillary raises it.—**Pterygoid nerves**, two branches of the inferior maxillary to the internal and external pterygoid muscles.—**Pterygoid notch.** See *notch*.—**Pterygoid plate**, a pterygoid process.—**Pterygoid plexus.** See *plexus*.—**Pterygoid process.** (*a*) Either one of two parts of the compound sphenoid bone of mammals. (1) The *external* pterygoid process is a process or extension of the alisphenoid, or great wing of the sphenoid bone, having no independent center of ossification, and never being a distinct part. (2) The *internal* pterygoid process, on the other hand, is a distinct bone, the pterygoid proper, having its own center of ossification, and representing the freely articulated pterygoid bone of lower vertebrates. These processes are also distinguished as *ectopterygoid* and *entopterygoid*. (*b*) The combined internal and external pterygoid processes, the two parts being distinguished as the *internal* and *external pterygoid plates*. (*c*) The pyramidal process, or tuberosity of the palate.—**Pterygoid ridge**, a ridge traversing the outer surface of the alisphenoid, or great wing of the sphenoid bone, delimiting the respective attachments of the temporal and external pterygoid muscles, and also serving to distinguish the temporal from the zygomatic fossa.

II. *n.* In *zoöl.* and *anat.*: (*a*) A bone of the facial part of the skull, forming a part of the hard palate, or pterygopalatal bar, commonly a horizontal rod-like bone, one of a pair on each side of the median line intervening between the palatal and the quadrate bone, or suspensorium of the mandible, and movably articulated with both, frequently also articulating with the basisphenoidal rostrum of the skull: in any mammal, detached from its posterior connection with the suspensorium, and commonly immovably sutured with the palatal and ankylosed with the sphenoid, when it forms the part known in human anatomy as the internal pterygoid process of the sphenoid. In fishes there are several different pterygoid bones, entering into the formation of the pterygopalatal bar or palatoquadrate arch, and distinguished as *entopterygoid*, *ectopterygoid*, and *metapterygoid*: see these words, and cut under *palatoquadrate*. See also cuts under *desmognathous*, *dromæognathous*, *periotic*, *Petromyzon*, *Physeter*, *poison-fang*, *Python*, and *temporomastoid*. (*b*) A pterygoid muscle.—**2.** *pl.* In *entom.*, same as *pterygoda*.

pterygoideus (ter-i-goi'dḗ-us), *n.*; pl. *pterygoidei* (-ī). [NL.: see *pterygoid*.] A pterygoid muscle.—**Pterygoideus externus** or **minor** and **pterygoideus internus** or **major**, two stout muscles of mastication; the pterygoid muscles (which see, under *pterygoid*).—**Pterygoideus proprius**, a small occasional muscle of man, passing from the alisphenoid to the outer plate or tuberosity of the palate.

pterygomaxillary (ter″i-gō-mak'si-lā-ri), *a.* [< *pterygo(id)* + *maxillary*.] Pertaining to a pterygoid process or the pterygoid bone and to either the superior or inferior maxillary bone: specifically applied in anatomy to several parts. —**Pterygomaxillary fissure.** See *fissure*.—**Pterygomaxillary fold**, the fold formed by the pterygomaxillary ligament in the mouth, back of the last molar tooth. —**Pterygomaxillary ligament**, a tendinous band passing from the apex of the internal pterygoid plate to the posterior extremity of the internal oblique line of the lower jaw.

pterygopalatal (ter″i-gō-pal'ā-tal), *a.* [< *pterygo(id)* + *palatal*.] Same as *pterygopalatine*.—**Pterygopalatal bar**, the movable series of bones which connect the upper jaw of vertebrates below mammals with the suspensorium of the lower jaw. No such bar occurs in mammals, in which the lower jaw has no suspensorium, and the pterygoids are entirely cut off from connections behind. In birds the bar is always a single and simple pterygoid bone, movably articulated behind with a quadrate and in front with a palate-bone. The case becomes complicated in lower vertebrates by the presence of more than one pterygoid, and in fishes with several pterygoids, variously disposed, the arrangement is more commonly called the *palatoquadrate arch*. See cut under *palatoquadrate*.

pterygopalatine (ter″i-gō-pal'ā-tin), *a.* [< *pterygo(id)* + *palatine*[2].] Pertaining to the pterygoid process of the sphenoid, or to the pterygoid bone, and to the palate or palate-bone: as, the *pterygopalatine* branch of the internal maxillary artery.—**Pterygopalatine artery**, a small branch of the internal maxillary, which passes through the pterygopalatine canal to the pharynx, nasal fossa, and sphenoidal sinus. Also called *pharyngeal artery*.—**Pterygopalatine canal.** (*a*) The canaliculus pharyngeus. (*b*) The posterior palatine canal.—**Pterygopalatine foramen.** See *foramen*.—**Pterygopalatine nerve**, a small branch of Meckel's ganglion that passes through the canal of the same name to the pharynx.

pterygo-pharyngeus (ter″i-gō-far-in-jē'us), *n.* [NL., < *pterygo(id)* + *pharyngeus*.] That part of the superior constrictor of the pharynx which arises from the internal pterygoid process.—**Pterygo-pharyngeus externus**, a small supernumerary muscle arising from the hamular process and inserted into the wall of the pharynx.

pterygoquadrate (ter″i-gō-kwod'rāt), *a.* [< *pterygo(id)* + *quadrate*.] **1.** Pertaining to the pterygoid bone proper and to the quadrate bone, or suspensorium of the lower jaw, as in a vertebrate below mammals: as, the *pterygoquadrate* articulation.—**2.** Combining elements of the pterygoid and quadrate bones: as, the *pterygoquadrate* cartilage of a shark.

pterygosphenoid (ter″i-gō-sfē'noid), *a.* [< *pterygo(id)* + *sphenoid*.] Same as *sphenopterygoid*.

pterygospinosus (ter″i-gō-spī-nō'sus), *n.*; pl. *pterygospinosi* (-sī). [NL.: see *pterygospinous*.] A muscular slip, occasionally seen in man, arising from the sphenoidal spine and inserted into the external pterygoid plate.

pterygospinous (ter″i-gō-spī'nus), *a.* [< NL. *pterygospinosus*, < E. *pterygo(id)* + L. *spinosus*, spinous.] Pertaining to a pterygoid process and to the spine of the sphenoid.—**Pterygospinous ligament**, a fibrous band running from the spine of the sphenoid to the posterior margin of the outer pterygoid plate.

pterygostaphylinus (ter″i-gō-staf-i-lī'nus), *n.*; pl. *pterygostaphylini* (-nī). [NL., < Gr. πτέρυξ (πτερυγ-), wing, + σταφυλή, uvula.] Same as *tensor palati*.

pterygostium (ter-i-gos'ti-um), *n.*; pl. *pterygostia* (-ā). [Also *pterygosteum*; NL. (Leach, 1829), < Gr. πτέρυξ (πτερυγ-), wing, + L. *ostium*, mouth.] One of the nervures or veins of an insect's wing. They are thickenings of the two surfaces of the upper and lower wing-membranes exactly opposed to each other, the inner surfaces being grooved so as to allow the circulation of fluids and the entrance of tracheæ.

pterygostomial (ter″i-gō-stō'mi-al), *a.* [< Gr. πτέρυξ (πτερυγ-), wing, + στόμα, mouth, + *-ial*.] In *zoöl.*, noting the flaring anterior edges of the carapace of crustaceans, when these turn forward in front of the bases of the limbs, parallel with each other and with the axis of the body. *Milne-Edwards.*—**Pterygostomial plates**, those parts of the carapace of the brachyurous crustaceans which run forward parallel with the axis of the body. *Huxley*, Anat. Invert., p. 295.

pterygostomian (ter″i-gō-stō'mi-an), *a.* [< *pterygostomi-al* + *-an*.] Same as *pterygostomial*. [Rare.]

Epistome longer than wide, and the *pterygostomian* regions rudimentary. *Eng. Cyc.*, Nat. Hist., III. 575.

Pterygota (ter-i-gō'tā), *n. pl.* [NL., neut. pl. of *Pterygotus*: see *pterygote*.] One of the prime divisions of *Insecta*, containing all hexapodous insects except *Aptera*. *Gegenbaur.* They are normally winged (wingless only as an adaptive specialized modification), and metabolous—that is, they undergo a more or less complete metamorphosis. Also called *Pterodicera*, *Pterophora*, and *Ptilota*.

pterygote (ter'i-gōt), *a.* [< NL. *Pterygotus*, < Gr. πτερυγωτός, winged, < πτέρυξ (πτερυγ-), wing: see *pterygium*.] Winged; alate; having wings or wing-like parts; specifically, belonging to the *Pterygota*.

pterygotrabecular (ter″i-gō-trā-bek'ū-lār), *a.* [< *pterygo(id)* + *trabecular*.] Pertaining to the pterygoid bone and the trabecular region of the skull.

A well developed *pterygo-trabecular* process—homologous . . . with the pedicle of the tadpole's suspensorium.
A. S. Woodward, Proc. Zoöl. Soc., 1886, p. 221.

Pterygotus (ter-i-gō'tus), *n.* [NL., < Gr. πτερυγωτός, winged: see *pterygote*.] A genus of extinct crustaceans of the Silurian period, belonging to the group *Eurypterida*, occurring chiefly in the passage-beds between the Silurian and the Devonian system. It has a long lobster-like form, composed in the main of a cephalothorax, an abdominal division of several segments, and a somewhat oval telson or tail-plate. The organs of locomotion, three or four pairs in number, are all attached to the under side of the carapace, as in the king-crab. *P. anglicus* is a species sometimes called *seraphim*.

Pterygura (ter-i-gū'rā), *n. pl.* [NL., < Gr. πτέρυξ (πτερυγ-), feather, wing, + οὐρά, tail.] A division of anomurous decapod crustaceans.

pterygurous (ter-i-gū'rus), *a.* Of or pertaining to the *Pterygura*.

pteryla (ter'i-lā), *n.*; pl. *pterylæ* (-lē). [NL., < Gr. πτερόν, feather, wing, + ὕλη, wood.] A feather-tract; one of the sets or clumps of feathers which are inserted in definite tracts or areas in the skin of a bird, separated by apteria, or places where no feathers grow. The fact that birds' feathers are seldom implanted uniformly over the whole skin, but usually grow in definite patches, had been known long before the publication of Nitzsch's "System of Pterylography" in 1840; but it remained for this author to define the principal pterylæ and point out the taxonomic significance of pterylosis. The most constant pterylæ are eight: (1) *Pteryla spinalis*, the spinal or dorsal tract, from the nape of the neck to the tail, subject to much modification. (2) *Pteryla humeralis*, the humeral tract, on each wing, running from the shoulder obliquely backward, parallel with the scapula. (3) *Pteryla femoralis*, the femoral tract, a similar oblique strip on each thigh. (4) *Pteryla ventralis*, the ventral tract, forming most of the plumage of the under parts, and presenting numerous modifications. (5) *Pteryla capitalis*, the head-tract. (6) *Pteryla alaris*, the wing-tract. (7) *Pteryla caudalis*, the tail-tract. (8) *Pteryla cruralis*, the lower leg-tract.

pterylographic (ter″i-lō-graf'ik), *a.* [< *pterylograph-y* + *-ic*.] Of or pertaining to pterylography; descriptive of pterylæ or pterylosis.

pterylographical (ter″i-lō-graf'i-kal), *a.* [< *pterylographic* + *-al*.] Same as *pterylographic*.

pterylographically (ter″i-lō-graf'i-kal-i), *adv.* With reference to pterylography; upon pterylographical principles.

pterylography (ter-i-log'ra-fi), *n.* [< NL. *pteryla* + Gr. -γραφία, < γράφειν, write.] The description of pterylæ, or a treatise on pterylosis: a science which had its origin in the "System der Pterylographie" of Nitzsch, 1833–40.

pterylosis (ter-i-lō'sis), *n.* [NL., < *pteryla* + *-osis*.] The arrangement or disposition of ptilosis; the plumage of a bird, considered with reference to the manner in which the feathers are implanted in the skin in definite pterylæ; the mode of feathering; the distribution of the feathers in tracts. It differs from *ptilosis* in that the latter relates to the character of the plumage itself, not to its disposition upon the body.

Ptilichthyidæ (til-ik-thī'i-dē), *n. pl.* [NL., < *Ptilichthys* + *-idæ*.] A family of acanthopterygian fishes, typified by the genus *Ptilichthys*. The body is very elongated and anguilliform, the head small, the mouth oblique with the lower jaw projecting, branchial apertures restricted, dorsal very long and with about 90 spines and 145 rays, anal long, and ventrals absent. Only one species is known.

Ptilichthys (ti-lik'this), *n.* [NL., < Gr. πτίλον, feather, + ἰχθύς, fish.] A genus of fishes, typical of the family *Ptilichthyidæ*. The only known species is *P. goodei* of Bering Sea.

Spiny-back Eel (*Ptilichthys goodei*).

Ptilocercus (til-ō-sėr'kus), *n.* [NL. (J. E. Gray, 1848), < Gr. πτίλον, feather, + κέρκος, tail.] A

Pentail (*Ptilocercus lowei*).

genus of *Tupaiidæ* or elephant-shrews, containing a single species, *P. lowei*, of Borneo, having a long tail furnished with distichous hairs toward the end, like a pen or feather, whence the name; the pentails.

Ptilogonatinæ (til-ō-gon-a-tī'nē), *n. pl.* [NL., < *Ptilogonys* (*-gonat-*) + *-inæ*.] A subfamily of oscine passerine birds, typified by the genus *Ptilogonys*, referred to the conventional family *Ampelidæ*. The bill is slenderer than in *Ampelis*, with naked nasal scale and slightly bristled rictus; the tarsus is scutellate anteriorly and sometimes also on the sides; the wings are rounded, with ten primaries, of which the first is spurious; the tail is variable, and the head crested. The few species are confined to western North America, Mexico, and Central America. Also *Ptilogonydinæ*.

Ptilogonys (ti-log'ō-nis), *n.* [NL. (Swainson, 1824), also in the forms *Ptiligonys*, *Ptilogonys*, and *Ptiliogonatus*; < Gr. πτίλον, wing, + γόνυ (γονατ-), knee, joint. Cf. *gonys*.] 1. The typical genus of *Ptilogonatinæ* or *Ptilogonydinæ*. The type is *P. cinereus* of Mexico.—2†. Extended to birds of the genus *Myiadestes* and others.—3. [*l. c.*] A bird of the genus *Ptilogonys* in any sense. Townsend's ptilogonys is *Myiadestes townsendi*. The black ptilogonys is *Phainopepla nitens*. See cut under *fly-snapper*.

ptilolite (til'ō-līt), *n.* [< Gr. πτίλον, wing, + λίθος, stone.] A zeolitic mineral, occurring in white tufts or spongy masses of minute acicular crystals, found in cavities in augite-andesite in Jefferson county, Colorado. It is a hydrous silicate of aluminium, calcium, and potassium, and is remarkable for its high percentage of silica.

Ptilonopinæ (til''ō-nō-pī'nē), *n. pl.* [NL., < *Ptilonopus* + *-inæ*.] A subfamily of *Columbidæ*, named from the genus *Ptilonopus*. *P. J. Selby*, 1835. See *Treroninæ*.

Ptilonopus (ti-lon'ō-pus), *n.* [NL. (Swainson, 1837), prop. *Ptilopus*, < Gr. πτίλον, feather, + πούς = E. *foot*.] An extensive genus of pigeons of the family *Columbidæ*, giving name to the *Ptilonopinæ*. Also *Ptilinopus* (*Swainson*, 1825) and *Ptilopus* (*Strickland*, 1841).

Ptilopædes (til-ō-pē'dēz), *n. pl.* [< Gr. πτίλον, down, + παῖς (παιδ-), child.] In *ornith.*, in Sundevall's classification, a primary group of birds, embracing such as are clothed at birth with down (which sprouts not only from pterylæ, but also from parts of the skin which form apteria when the true plumage is acquired), and are generally able to run about and feed themselves when hatched: opposed to *Psilopædes*: nearly equivalent to *Præcoces*, but of more exact signification. Also called *Dasypædes*, *Autophagi*.

ptilopædic (til-ō-pē'dik), *a.* [< *Ptilopæd-es* + *-ic*.] Of or pertaining to the *Ptilopædes*; præcocial: opposed to *psilopædic*.

Ptilophyton (ti-lof'i-ton), *n.* [NL. (Dawson, 1878), < Gr. πτίλον, feather, + φυτόν, a plant.] A plant of very uncertain affinities, so called by Dawson and supposed by him to be aquatic, and more likely to have been allied to rhizocarps than to any other group. It consists of beautiful feathery fronds, bearing on parts of the main stem or petiole small rounded sporocarps. It is found in the Devonian and Lower Carboniferous of New York, in Nova Scotia, and in Scotland.

Ptilopteri (tī-lop'te-rī), *n. pl.* [NL., < Gr. πτίλον, feather, + πτερόν, wing.] The penguins as an order of birds: conterminous with *Impennes*, *Squamipennes*, *Sphenisci*, and *Spheniscomorphæ*.

Ptilorhis (til'ō-ris), *n.* [NL. (Swainson, 1825), erroneously *Ptilornis* and *Ptiloris*, prop. **Ptilorrhis*, < Gr. πτίλον, soft feather, + ῥίς (ῥιν-), nose.] A genus of *Paradiseidæ*, belonging to the subfamily *Epimachinæ*, or slender-billed birds of paradise, having the tail not longer than the body, and a jugular shield of metallic plumes. The nostrils are feathered, whence the name. Four species of these beautiful birds inhabit Australia and New Guinea—*P. paradisea*, the rifle-bird, *P. victoriæ*, *P. alberti*, and *P. (Craspedophora) magnifica*. See cut under *rifle-bird*.

ptilosis (tī-lō'sis), *n.* [NL., < Gr. πτίλωσις, plumage, also a disease of the eyelids resulting in loss of the eyelashes, < πτιλοῦσθαι, be winged (or feathered), < πτίλον, feather, wing.] 1. In *ornith.*, plumage; the feathering of a bird, considered with reference to the texture or other character of the feathers themselves. Compare *pterylosis*.—2. In *med.*, loss of the eyelashes.

Ptilota (tī-lō'tạ), *n. pl.* [NL. (Macleay, 1821), < Gr. πτιλωτός, winged, verbal adj. of πτιλοῦσθαι, be winged: see *ptilosis*.] In Macleay's classification, one of the prime divisions of the class *Insecta*, distinguished from *Aptera*, corresponding to Latreille's *Pterodicera*, and divided primarily into *Mandibulata* and *Haustellata*. See *Pterygota*.

Ptilotis (ti-lō'tis), *n.* [NL. (Swainson, 1837), < Gr. πτίλον, feather, + οὖς (ὠτ-) = E. *ear*.] A very extensive genus of meliphagine birds. It includes nearly 40 species, ranging through the Austromalayan, Australian, and Polynesian regions, mostly of plain dull olivaceous and yellowish colors, with the skin of the sides of the head often bare and wattled, or the parotic feathers (ear-coverts) stiffened and usually white or yellow, forming a conspicuous mark, whence the name. *P. chrysotis* and *P. carunculata* are examples.

Ptinidæ (tin'i-dē), *n. pl.* [NL. (Leach, 1819), < *Ptinus* + *-idæ*.] A large family of serricorn coleopterous insects, containing beetles of small size, having the antennæ with from nine to eleven joints, the head retractile, and the elytra entire. Both larvæ and beetles feed mostly on dead animal and vegetable matter. The larvæ eat drugs, even pepper and tobacco. Some 44 genera and 150 species are recognized in the United States. *Lasioderma serricorne* is known in the United States as the *cigarette-beetle*, on account of the damage it does to cigarettes. *Sitodrepa panicea* is a wide-spread museum-pest, and is found in many drugs. Members of the genus *Anobium* are known as *death-watches*. Many of the species are cosmopolitan. See cut under *book-worm*.

Ptinus (tī'nus), *n.* [NL. (Linnæus, 1767), irreg. < Gr. φθίνειν, φθίειν, decay, waste, destroy: see *phthisis*.] A large and wide-spread genus of beetles, typical of the family *Ptinidæ*, of which about 80 species are known, 6 inhabiting the United States. A number of them occur both in Europe and in North America. *P. fur* is cosmopolitan and a well-known museum-pest. See cut under *book-worm*.

ptisan (tiz'an), *n.* [Also *ptisane*, formerly *ptysane*, *tisan*; = F. *tisane* = Pr. *tizana*, *tipsana* = Sp. Pg. It. *tisana*, < L. *ptisana*, < Gr. πτισάνη, peeled barley, also a drink made from it, < πτίσσειν, peel, husk.] 1. A mild harmless drink, or one having a slight medicinal quality, as barley-water or herb-tea.

> For what auncient phisition is there that in his workes commendeth not *ptysane*, whiche is none other than pure barley braied in a morter and sodden in water?
> *Sir T. Elyot*, Castle of Health, ii. 21.

2. Grape-juice allowed to drain on the slab, without pressure. *R. F. Burton*, Arabian Nights, V. 158, note.

P. T. O. An abbreviation of *Please turn over*: a direction, usually at the foot of a page, to call attention to matter on the other side of the leaf.

ptochocracy (tō-kok'rạ-si), *n.* [< Gr. πτωχός, a beggar (< πτώσσειν, crouch or cower from fear), + -κρατία, < κρατεῖν, rule.] Government by beggars; the rule of paupers: the opposite of *plutocracy*. [Rare.]

> It [the opposition to the extension of the county franchise] alleges the risks we run from the old and the rich, the danger of a gerontocracy and a ploutocracy; whereas, to make its argument good, it should have shown the imminence of a *ptochocracy*.
> *Gladstone*, Gleanings of Past Years, I. 182.

ptochogony (tō-kog'ō-ni), *n.* [< Gr. πτωχός, a beggar, + -γονία, generation: see *-gony*.] The production of beggars; pauperization. [Rare.]

> The whole plan of the Bishop of London is a *ptochogony*—a generation of beggars.
> *Sydney Smith*, To Archdeacon Singleton, iii.

Ptolemæan (tol-e-mē'an), *a.* [< L. *Ptolemæus*, *Ptolemæius*, of Ptolemy, < *Ptolemæus*, < Gr. Πτολεμαῖος, Ptolemy.] Same as *Ptolemaic*. *Max Müller*, Sci. of Lang., p. 27.

Ptolemaic (tol-e-mā'ik), *a.* [< Gr. Πτολεμαϊκός, pertaining to Ptolemy, < Πτολεμαῖος, Ptolemy: see def.] Of or pertaining to Ptolemy; (*a*) relating to one or all of the line of Ptolemies, rulers of Egypt from the end of the fourth to the first century B. C.; (*b*) relating to the Alexandrian geographer and astronomer Ptolemy (see below).—**Ptolemaic chart.** See *Bonne's map-projection*, under *projection*.—**Ptolemaic system**, the structure of the heavens according to Ptolemy, an Egyptian-Greek astronomer, whose recorded observations extend from 127 to 151 A. D. His "Treatise of Mathematics" (Μαθηματικὴ σύνταξις), commonly called the "Almagest," is mainly devoted to an investigation of the movements of the heavenly bodies. Ptolemy holds that the earth is stationary, because there is no appearance of variation in the perspective of the fixed stars. He admits it would simplify astronomy to suppose it rotated daily on its axis, but thinks that refuted by physical considerations, while, regarding the stars as devoid of weight, he sees no objection to supposing them to move with immense velocity. But these two errors of denying the motion of the earth both in translation and in rotation were not incompatible with a correct representation of the motions of the planets relatively to the earth. The figure shows his theory of Mars, which was exactly like that of Jupiter and Saturn. He supposed that about a circular deferent, which was really nearly similar and similarly placed to the true orbit of the planet about the sun, moved an epicycle, which was really of nearly the same proportionate size as the earth's true orbit and parallel to it—this epicycle carrying the planet on its circumference. In the figure, T is the earth; XDIYJ, the orbit, deferent, or eccentric of Mars; C, the center of the orbit; GH, the equant; E, its center; AKPL, the epicycle; D, its center; ♂, Mars; IJ, the line of nodes of the orbit; KL, the line of nodes of the eccentric (which is parallel to the ecliptic) upon the plane of the orbit. Mars revolves upon the epicycle so as to move uniformly relatively to P, the perigee of the epicycle, which it reaches so as to be then in opposition to the mean sun. The center D of the epicycle moves about the orbit so as to describe in equal times equal angles about E, the center of the equant. C, the center of the orbit, bisects the eccentricity ET. The essential errors in his representation were as follows. (1) He represented the deferent by the circle, thus giving it a breadth too great. This circle remained in an eccentric position, whence it was called the *eccentric*, as well as the *deferent* and the *orbit*. (2) Instead of supposing the moving radius, TD, to describe equal areas in equal times, he drew a line to D, the attachment of the epicycle with the deferent, from E, really corresponding to the empty focus of the ellipse, but called by him the *center of the equant*, and he supposed this line ED to turn with an equable motion so as to describe equal angles in equal times. This made an observable error only in the case of Mars. It made a tolerable approximation to the elliptic motion, which excited the admiration of Kepler, and it shows that Ptolemy aimed at something much better than a mere harmonic analysis of the motions of the planets. (3) He not only made the epicycle circular, but he placed its center upon the deferent, thus virtually neglecting the eccentricity as well as the ellipticity of the earth's orbit in its effects on the apparent places of the exterior planets. (4) He made the planet revolve in its epicycle so as to describe in equal times equal arcs measured from the perigee of the epicycle, as if the earth's motion were affected by the eccentricity of the orbit of the other planet. And (5) he made the planet come to the perigee of its epicycle when it was just opposite the mean place of the sun, instead of the true place. Other still more serious falsities affected his theories of the inferior planets and of the moon. Yet, notwithstanding all these errors, Ptolemy's theory satisfied pretty closely, in the cases of all the planets except Mercury and the moon, such observations as could be made in his time. In his phrase, it "saved appearances." The Ptolemaic theory continued in vogue until Copernicus (in 1543) explained the relations between the motions of the planets and that of the sun, and thus supplied a method for determining the relative magnitudes of the different planetary orbits. But the system of Copernicus did not in itself represent the phenomena any better than that of Ptolemy; and it was not until the great work of Kepler on the motions of Mars, published in 1609, that the real truth was known. The Almagest remains, however, a model of scientific investigation, most admirable for the genius with which it manages not only the astronomical problems attacked, but also those of pure mathematics.

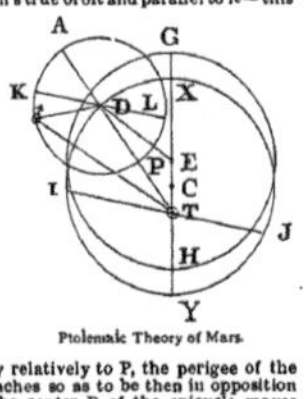

Ptolemaic Theory of Mars.

Ptolemaist (tol-e-mā'ist), *n.* [< *Ptolema-ic* + *-ist*.] A believer in the Ptolemaic system of astronomy.

ptomaine, ptomain (tō'ma-in), *n.* [Irreg. < Gr. πτῶμα, a corpse (prop. that which is fallen, < πίπτειν, fall), + *-ine*[2].] A generic name of alkaloid bodies formed from animal or vegetable tissues during putrefaction, and the similar bodies produced by pathogenic bacteria. Some of them are poisonous.

ptosis (tō'sis), *n.* [< Gr. πτῶσις, a fall, a falling, < πίπτειν (perf. πέπτωκα, verbal adj. πτωτός), fall, = L. *petere*, fall upon, attack, seek, etc.: see *petition*.] A falling of the upper eyelid, or inability to raise it, due to paralysis of the levator palpebræ. Slight ptosis may be due to paralysis of Müller's muscle innervated through the cervical sympathetic. Also called *blepharoptosis*, *blepharoplegia*.

ptotic (tō'tik), *a.* [< *ptosis* (*ptot-*) + *-ic*.] Pertaining to, characterized by, or affected with ptosis.

ptyalin, ptyaline (tī'a-lin), *n.* [< Gr. πτύαλον, spittle, < πτύειν, spit: see *spew*.] The peculiar principle of saliva, believed to be a proteid body, which acts as a ferment on starch, rapidly converting it into dextrose.

ptyalism (tī'a-lizm), *n.* [< Gr. πτυαλισμός, a spitting, < πτυαλίζειν, spit much: see *ptyalize*.] In *med.*, salivation; a morbid and copious excretion of saliva.

ptyalize (tī'a-līz), *v. i.*; pret. and pp. *ptyalized*, ppr. *ptyalizing*. [< Gr. πτυαλίζειν, spit much, < πτύαλον, spittle, < πτύειν, spit: see *ptyalin*.] To salivate.

ptyalogogic (tī''a-lō-goj'ik), *a.* [< *ptyalogogue* + *-ic*.] Promoting a flow of saliva.

ptyalogogue (tī-al'ō-gog), *n.* [< Gr. πτύαλον, spittle, + ἀγωγός, leading, < ἄγειν, do, bring.] A medicine which causes salivation, or a flow of saliva.

Ptyas (tī'as), *n.* [NL., ‹ Gr. πτυάς, a kind of serpent, lit. 'spitter,' ‹ πτύειν, spit.] A genus of *Colubrinæ* or snakes. They have the posterior maxillary teeth not abruptly longer than the preceding ones, rostral plate narrow and free laterally, one median dorsal row of scales, internasals separate from nasals, several lorals, and two or more preoculars. *P. mucosus* is known as the *rat-snake*.

ptychodont (tī'kō-dont), *a.* [‹ Gr. πτύξ (πτυχ-), πτυχή, a fold, + ὀδούς (ὀδοντ-) = E. *tooth*.] In *odontol.*, having the crowns of the molar teeth folded.

Ptychodus (tī'kō-dus), *n.* [NL. (Agassiz, 1837), ‹ Gr. πτύξ (πτυχ-), πτυχή, a fold, + ὀδούς (ὀδοντ-) = E. *tooth*.] A genus of fossil selachians, of the Cretaceous age: so called from the transverse or radiating plications on the large square teeth. It was formerly supposed to be related to the cestraciont sharks, but is now referred to or near the family *Myliobatidæ*.

Ptychopleura (tī-kō-plö'rạ̈), *n. pl.* [NL., ‹ Gr. πτύξ (πτυχ-), πτυχή, a fold, + πλευρά, the side.] A group of lizards: same as *Cyclosaura*. Also *Ptychopleuri*.

ptychopleural (ti-kō-plö'ral), *a.* [‹ *Ptychopleura* + *-al*.] Of or pertaining to the *Ptychopleura*.

Ptychopteris (ti-kop'te-ris), *n.* [NL., ‹ Gr. πτύξ (πτυχ-), πτυχή, a fold, + πτερίς, fern.] In *fossil bot.*, a genus of fossil ferns, known chiefly from the form of the leaf-scars. These are elongated-oval or elliptic in form; of their details but little has been made out. The fern-stems which have been placed in this genus are said by Schimper to bear a close resemblance in external appearance to the living *Cyathea* and *Alsophila*. They are found in abundance in the Carboniferous, especially in the St. Etienne (France) coal-field, where they occur associated with leaves of *Pecopteris*, to which they may belong.

Ptychosperma (tī-kō-spėr'mạ̈), *n.* [NL. (Labillardière, 1808), ‹ Gr. πτύξ (πτυχ-), πτυχή, a fold, + σπέρμα, seed.] A genus of palms of the tribe *Arecew*, type of the subtribe *Ptychospermeæ*. It is characterized by monœcious flowers, both sexes within the same spadix, the staminate flowers having orbicular concave broadly imbricated and heeled sepals, acute petals as many as the sepals, and from twenty to thirty stamens—the pistillate flowers being smaller, nearly globose, and having a single ovary which becomes a one-celled fruit whose thick fibrous pericarp contains a single erect seed with ruminate albumen and a smooth or deeply five-grooved surface. The 11 species are natives of the Malay archipelago, Papua, Australia, and the islands of the Pacific. They are thornless palms, with a tall trunk marked by annular scars, and terminal pinnately divided leaves with the segments commonly dilated to the broad apex and there erose, or appearing as if eaten off. The flowers are small, and are borne in clusters on the slender spreading branches of a spadix inclosed by two spathes. The species are of little known industrial use, but rank among the most elegant of decorative palms. Those in greenhouse cultivation are sometimes called in general *feather-palms*, and very often *Seaforthia* (R. Brown, 1810), from Lord Seaforth, a patron of botany. *P. Seemani*, a beautiful dwarf species, produces a stem only about one inch in diameter and very strong and straight. Most of the species reach a commanding height: among them *P. Alexandræ*, the Alexandra palm, is remarkable as the tallest palm of Australia, exceeding 100 feet in height; *P. Cunninghamii*, the Illawarra palm, as found further south than almost any other palm; and *P.* (*Seaforthia*) *elegans*, the bangalow palm, as the most common in cultivation, and one of the most beautiful of all palms. The trunk of the last-named species is a smooth cylindrical shaft, swollen at the base and crowned by drooping feather-like leaves of a bright and intense green. Each leaf-stalk is dilated at the base into a smooth bright-green sheath completely inclosing the upper part of the trunk for 5 feet or more, below which the trunk is variegated by the broad deep-brown ring-like scars left by the preceding similar sheaths. This palm occurs in the coast forests of tropical Australia and to 35° south. See *palm*[2], and under it *Alexandra palm*, *bangalow palm*, and *feather-palm*.

Ptychozoön (tī-kō-zō'on), *n.* [‹ Gr. πτύξ (πτυχ-), πτυχή, a fold, + ζῷον, an animal.] A genus of

Flying-gecko (*Ptychozoön homalocephalum*).

gecko lizards, containing the flying-gecko of India and the East Indian archipelago, *P. homalocephalum*, about 7 inches long, having alate folds of the integument, whence the name.

ptygodere (tī'gō-dēr), *n.* A lizard of the genus *Ptygoderus*.

Ptygoderus (ti-god'e-rus), *n.* [NL., irreg. ‹ Gr. πτύξ (πτυχ-), πτυχή, a fold, + δέρος, skin, hide.] A genus of iguanoid lizards, having a crest of keeled scales on each side, as *P. pectinatus*.

Ptynx (tingks), *n.* [NL., ‹ Gr. πτύγξ, the eagle-owl.] 1†. An old generic name of the darters: same as *Plotus*. *Moehring*, 1752.—2. A genus of smooth-headed owls, so named by Blyth in 1840. The type is *Ptynx uralensis*, commonly called *Syrnium uralense*.

Ptyobranchina (tī"ō-brang-kī'nạ̈), *n. pl.* [NL., ‹ *Ptyobranchus* + *-ina*[2].] In Günther's system, a group of *Murænidæ platyschistæ*, with the tail much shorter than the trunk, and the heart situated at a great distance behind the gills: same as the family *Moringuidæ*.

ptysmagogue (tis'ma-gog), *n.* [‹ Gr. πτύσμα, saliva (‹ πτύειν, spit), + ἀγωγός, leading, ‹ ἄγειν, lead, bring.] A medicine that promotes discharges of saliva; a sialogogue.

ptyxis (tik'sis), *n.* [NL., ‹ Gr. πτύξις, a folding, ‹ πτύσσειν, fold.] In *bot.*, the folding or configuration of a single part in a leaf- or flower-bud: opposed to *vernation* and *estivation*, the disposition of the parts conjointly.

pu' (pù), *v.* A Scotch form of *pull*.

> Why *pu'* ye the rose, Janet?
> What gars ye break the tree?
> *The Young Tamlane* (Child's Ballads, I. 116).

pua (pö'ạ̈), *n.* [Hawaiian.] A Hawaiian musical instrument, made of a gourd or a joint of bamboo. It has three holes, two of which are finger-holes. It is blown by putting the third hole to the player's nose. When made of gourd, it resembles the ocarina; and when of bamboo, it is a variety of nose-flute.

puant†, *a.* [‹ OF. *puant*, ‹ L. *puten(t-)s*, ppr. of *putere*, stink: see *putid*.] Stinking. *Skelton.* (*Halliwell.*)

pub (pub), *n.* [Abbr. of *public*, *n.*, 2.] A public house; a tavern. *Athenæum*, No. 3198, p. 177. [Slang, Eng.]

pub. An abbreviation of *public*, *publish*, or *publisher*.

pubble† (pub'l), *a.* [Origin obscure.] Fat; plump. [Prov. Eng.]

> Thou shalt Me fynde fat and well fed,
> As *pubble* as may be.
> *Drant*, tr. of Horace's Ep. to Tibullus.

pub. doc. An abbreviation of *public document*.

puberal (pū'be-ral), *a.* [‹ L. *pubes*, *puber*, adult (see *puberty*), + *-al*.] Pertaining to puberty. *Dunglison.* [Rare.]

puberty (pū'bėr-ti), *n.* [‹ OF. *puberte*, F. *puberté* = Pr. *pubertat* = Sp. *pubertad* = Pg. *puberdade* = It. *pubertà*, ‹ L. *puberta(t-)s*, the age of maturity, manhood, ‹ *pubes*, *puber*, grown up, of mature age, adult; of plants, downy, pubescent; ‹ √ *pu*, beget.] 1. The condition of being able to reproduce; sexual maturity in the human race. In males this is usually developed between the ages of thirteen and sixteen, and in females somewhat earlier; and it appears that in very warm climates puberty is reached somewhat sooner than elsewhere. At common law the age of puberty is conclusively presumed to be fourteen in the male and twelve in the female.

2. In *bot.*, the period when a plant begins to bear flowers.

puberulent (pū̦-ber'ō̦-lent), *a.* [‹ L. *pubes*, *puber*, downy, pubescent, + *-ulent*.] 1. Finely and softly pubescent; downy.—2. In *bot.*, covered with fine, short down; minutely pubescent.

pubes (pū'bēz), *n.* [‹ L. *pubes*, the hair which appears on the body at the age of puberty, the genitals, ‹ *pubes*, *puber*, grown up, of mature age; of plants, downy, pubescent: see *puberty*.] 1†. The pubescence or hairiness of the genitals, which appears at puberty. Hence—2. (*a*) The place where hair grows at puberty; the suprapubic or hypogastric region, at the middle of the lowest part of the abdomen: in women known as the *mons*, or *mons Veneris*. (*b*) The pubic bones, or bony framework of the pubes; the underlying skeleton of the pubic region, more fully called *os pubis*. There being a pair of pubic bones, right and left, each is now called *os pubis*, plural *ossa pubis*, or, more frequently, *pubis*, in the plural *pubes*. See *pubis*.

3. In *bot.*, same as *pubescence*, 3.—4. Plural of *pubis*.

pubescence (pū̦-bes'ens), *n.* [‹ *pubescen(t)* + *-ce*.] 1. The coming of puberty, or attaining to puberty; the state of being pubescent; puberty.

> In the first [septenary] is dedentition or falling of teeth; in the second *pubescence*. *Sir T. Browne*, Vulg. Err., iv. 12.

2. Hairiness; especially, the fine soft hairs of various insects, etc.; lanugo.—3. In *bot.*: (*a*) The condition or character of being pubescent. (*b*) The down or hair which grows on many plant-surfaces. See *pubescent*.

pubescency (pū̦-bes'en-si), *n.* [As *pubescence* (see *-cy*).] Pubescence.

> From crude *pubescency* unto perfection.
> *Sir T. Browne*, Garden of Cyrus, iii.

pubescent (pū̦-bes'ent), *a.* [‹ L. *pubescen(t-)s*, reach the age of puberty, become downy, ‹ *pubes*, *puber*, of mature age, downy: see *pubes*.] 1. Arriving at puberty.—2. Covered with pubescence, or fine short hair; downy.—3. In *bot.*, covered or sprinkled with down or hairs: a general term, including *villous*, *hirsute*, *strigose*, *lanate*, etc., but when used alone in specific description denoting a soft or downy and short pubescence.

pubic (pū'bik), *a.* [‹ *pub-is* + *-ic*.] Of or pertaining to the pubes or pubis: as, the *pubic* bones; the *pubic* symphysis, ramus, spine, ligament, artery, etc.—**Pubic angle**, the angle formed by the pubic crest and the inner border of the pubis.—**Pubic arch**, the arch formed by the inferior ramus of each pubis converging to the pubic symphysis. In the male it is narrower and more acute-angled than in the female, being in the former case like a letter V inverted. It represents a great part of the inferior outlet of the pelvis. Also called *arch of the pubis*, sometimes *subpubic arch*.—**Pubic crest**, the crista pubis (which see, under *crista*).—**Pubic ligaments**, certain ligaments uniting the two pubic bones: an anterior, a superior, an inferior, and a posterior are distinguished, respectively specifically called *prepubic*, *suprapubic*, *infrapubic*, and *postpubic*.—**Pubic ramus**, one of the two branches of which each pubis chiefly consists in man and some other animals. In man the two rami are (*a*) the superior or horizontal, forming much of the true brim of the pelvis, and ankylosed with the ilium, and (*b*) the inferior, oblique, or descending ramus, forming each half of the pubic arch, partly circumscribing the obturator foramen, and ankylosed with the ischium.—**Pubic spine**, a prominent tubercle on the upper border of the horizontal ramus of the pubis of man, about an inch from the symphysis. Poupart's ligament is inserted into it. Also called *tuberculum pubis* or *tuberculum pubicum*.—**Pubic symphysis**, or **symphysis pubis**, the coming or growing together of the right and left pubic bones at the median line of the pubes. It may be a simple apposition or articulation of the bones, or complete ankylosis. In man the bones are commonly articulated but not ankylosed, forming in any case an immovable joint.—**Pubic vein**, a tributary to the external iliac vein from the obturator vein.

pubigerous (pū̦-bij'e̦-rus), *a.* [‹ L. *pubes*, the hair which appears on the body at the age of puberty (see *pubes*), + *gerere*, carry.] Bearing down or downy hairs; pubescent.

pubiotomy (pū-bi-ot'ō̦-mi), *n.* [‹ L. *pubis* (see *pubis*) + Gr. τομία, ‹ τέμνειν, ταμεῖν, cut.] In *surg.*, a section of the pubic symphysis.

pubis (pū'bis), *n.*; pl. *pubes* (-bēz). [NL., for *os pubis*: *os*, bone; *pubis*, gen. of *pubes*, pubes: see *pubes*.] In *anat.* and *zoöl.*, a pubic bone, or bone of the pubes (os pubis); a distal inferior and anterior division of the pelvic arch, forming a part of the os innominatum or haunch-bone by ankylosis at the acetabulum with the ilium and ischium, and often, as in man and most mammals, united also with the ischium to circumscribe the obturator foramen, and, with its fellow of the opposite side, forming the pubic symphysis. In man each pubis is united to its fellow in the median line at the pubic symphysis, and the two circumscribe the brim of the pelvis in front by their bodies and horizontal rami, their descending rami becoming ankylosed with the ischium to circumscribe the obturator foramen, furnishing bony support to the genitals, and forming part of the inferior strait or outlet of the pelvis. In a few mammals, and in all birds excepting the ostrich, there is no pubic symphysis. See *epipubis*, *prepubis*, and cuts under *Dromæus*, *epipleura*, *ligament*, *Ornithoscelida*, *pelvis*, *sacrarium*, and *marsupial*.—**Angle, arch,** etc., **of the pubis.** See *pubic*.

public (pub'lik), *a.* and *n.* [Formerly *publick*, earlier *publique*, *publike*, *publyke*; ‹ OF. (and F.) *public*, m., F. *publique*, m. and f., = Sp. *público* = Pg. *publico* = It. *pubblico*, *publico*, ‹ L. *publicus*, in inscriptions also *poblicus*, *poplicus*, pertaining to the people, contr. from **populicus*, ‹ *populus*, people: see *people*.] I. *a.* 1. Of or belonging to the people at large; relating to or affecting the whole people of a state, nation, or community: opposed to *private*: as, the *public* good; *public* affairs; the *public* service; a *public* calamity; *public* opinion.

> *Publike* toke his begynnyng of people, whiche in latin is Populus, in whiche worde is conteyned all the inhabitantes of a realme or citie, of what astate or condition so euer they be. *Sir T. Elyot*, The Governour, i. 1.

> That here was an Vniuersitie, the Students whereof were maintained at *publique* charge, of which number himselfe was one. *Purchas*, Pilgrimage, p. 74.

> Many springs are gathered together . . . into an ample cistern, . . . and . . . from thence by conduits conducted unto their *publique* uses. *Sandys*, Travailes, p. 26.

To the *publick* good
Private respects must yield. *Milton*, S. A., l. 867.

2. Open to all the people; shared in or to be shared or participated in or enjoyed by people at large; not limited or restricted to any particular class of the community: as, a *public* meeting; *public* worship; a *public* subscription; a *public* road; a *public* house; *public* baths.

The church, by her *publick* reading of the book of God, preached only as a witness; now the principal thing required in a witness is fidelity. *Hooker*, Eccles. Polity.

I saw her once
Hop forty paces through the *public* street.
Shak., A. and C., ii. 2. 234.

And this was observed both for their *publique* and private prayers. *Purchas*, Pilgrimage, p. 119.

There are also divers Convents, which have spacious and well kept Gardens, which are always open and *publick* to People of any Note. *Lister*, Journey to Paris, p. 185.

We leave the narrow lanes behind, and dare
Th' unequal combat in the *public* square.
Dryden, Æneid, ii.

3. Open to the view or knowledge of all; notorious: as, a *public* exposure; *public* scandal.

Of this ordynaunce and bondes there were made instrumentes *publikes* and letters patentes.
Berners, tr. of Froissart's Chron., I. clxxiii.

Joseph her husband, being a just man, and not willing to make her a *public* example, was minded to put her away privily. Mat. i. 19.

4. Regarding or directed to the interests of the community at large, and not limited or confined to private, personal, or selfish matters or interests: as, *public* spirit; a *public* benefaction.

Every true member of the church hath a *public* spirit, preferring the church's interest to his own, and suffering with fellow-members in their suffering, and having a care of one another, 1 Cor. xii. 25, 26. *Baxter*, Self-Denial, ii.

In the public line, engaged in keeping a public house or tavern. [Colloq., Great Britain.]

Mysell being *in the public line*,
I look for howfs I kenn'd lang syne,
Whar gentles used to drink gude wine.
Scott, Epil. (spoken by Meg Dods) to Drama founded on [St. Ronan's Well.

Notary public. See *notary*[1].—**Public acts, bills, laws, legislation, statutes**, such acts, bills, etc., as concern the community at large, or the state or its municipalities, as distinguished from *private acts*, etc. (see *private*), one important result of the distinction being in the rule that the courts take judicial notice of public acts, but a private act must be alleged and proved by him who relies upon it.—**Public administrator, corporation, credit, document, domain, enemy**, etc. See the nouns.—**Public funds.** See *fund*[1].—**Public holiday.** Same as *legal holiday* (which see, under *holiday*).—**Public house.** (*a*) An inn or tavern; in England, especially, one which rarely accommodates lodgers, and which has for its chief business the selling of beer and other liquors. [In the United States rare and used in a general sense.] (*b*) *Public house* and *public place* are used in numerous statutes against immoral practices, gaming, prostitution, etc., with varying limitations of meaning, but generally implying a place to which any one may have access without trespassing.—**Public indecency.** See *indecency*.—**Public institution**, an establishment of an educational, charitable, reformatory, or sanitary character, maintained and conducted for the use and benefit of the public, and usually at the public expense.

Education, shorter hours of labour, sanitary homes, and *public institutions* to take the place of the public house.
Nineteenth Century, XXVI. 741.

Public lands, lands belonging to government, especially such as are open to sale, grant, or other method of disposal to whosoever will comply with the conditions prescribed by law.—**Public law**, international law. See *international, a.*—**Public loan.** See *loan*[1].—**Public nuisance.** See *nuisance*, 5.—**Public office.** See *office*, 4.—**Public opinion.** See *opinion*.—**Public orator.** See *orator*, 6.—**Public policy**, the policy, or general purpose and spirit, of the law: thus, contracts calculated to defeat justice or to hinder wholesome competition in trade are held void, as against *public policy*, or against the policy of the law, even when there is no positive statutory prohibition. See *policy of the law*, under *law*[1].—**Public printer, prosecutor, records**, etc. See the nouns.—**Public right**, in *Scots feudal law*, the technical name given to a heritable right granted by a vassal to be held, not of himself, but of his superior.—**Public school.** See *school*.—**Public spirit.** See *spirit*.—**Public stores.** (*a*) Naval and military stores, equipment, etc. (*b*) Warehouses to which dutiable goods are sent for appraisement; bonded warehouses, or stores in which goods are held under bond for duty until sold or exported. [U. S.]—**Public trust**, a trust constituted for the benefit either of the public at large or of some considerable part of it answering to a particular description. See *private*.—**Public use.** (*a*) In the constitutional provisions authorizing the taking by the state or nation of private property for the use of the people at large on making compensation, a use directly subservient to public necessity or convenience, as for a park, a highway, a railroad, etc., as distinguished from uses for private interest, though incidentally beneficial to the public, as for a mill or factory: thus, the supplying of water to a town is a *public use* for which it may constitutionally be authorized to condemn the rights of private owners in watercourses. (*b*) A use so intimately allied to or affecting the public welfare or convenience that the state may regulate it as to the management or charges: thus, the great grain-elevators of modern commerce, standing between the wharves of lake or ocean navigation and the termini of trunk lines of railway, have been held to be so affected with a *public use* that the state may regulate by law the rates of charges. (*c*) In *patent law*, use without restriction by one or more members of the community, as distinguished from use by the inventor: thus, an inventor of a secret spring who should allow its use by others without patenting it might be deemed to allow its *public use*, although, from its peculiarities of structure and relation, its use could not be seen by the public.—**Public war.** See *war*.—**Public waters**, waters which are deemed navigable at common law. See *navigable*.—**Public works**, all fixed works constructed for public use, as railways, docks, canals, water-works, roads, etc.; more strictly, military and civil engineering works constructed at the public cost.

II. *n.* 1. The general body of people constituting a nation, state, or community; the people, indefinitely: with *the*.

God made man in his own image; but *the public* is made by newspapers, members of parliament, excise officers, poor-law guardians. *Disraeli*, Coningsby, iii. 1.

That . . . the nobler, and what are vulgarly called the higher classes of society, are insufficient in their number, their power, and co-operation of sentiment to support any particular theatre, or piece, independent of *the public*; and that it is only the great mass of the people that can finally establish the fate of any theatrical representation.
W. Cooke, Memoirs of S. Foote, I. 64.

2. A public house. [Colloq., Eng.]

It 's so far from the world, as a man may say; not a decent *public* within a mile and a half, where one can hear a bit of news of an evening.
Mrs. Gaskell, Sylvia's Lovers, xli.

In every little comfortable *public* within a circle of thirty miles' diameter, the home-brewed quivers in the glasses on the open tables. *The Atlantic*, LVIII. 458.

In public, in open view; before the people at large; not in private or secretly.

In private grieve: but, with a careless scorn,
In public seem to triumph, not to mourn.
Granville.

publican (pub'li-kạn), *n.* [< ME. *publican*, < OF. *publicain, publican, puplicain, popelican*, etc., F. *publicain* = Sp. Pg. It. *publicano*, a publican, < L. *publicanus*, pertaining to the public revenues, or to their farming out or collection; as a noun, a farmer-general of the public revenue, a tax-gatherer; < *publicus*, public: see *public*.] 1. In ancient Rome, one who farmed the public revenues; a tax-gatherer. On account of their oppressive exactions, especially in the conquered provinces, the publicans were commonly regarded with detestation.

As Jesus sat at meat in the house, behold, many *publicans* and sinners came and sat down with him and his disciples. Mat. ix. 10.

How like a fawning *publican* he looks!
Shak., M. of V., i. 3. 42.

Hence—2. Any collector of toll, tribute, customs, or the like.

The custom-house of certain *publicans* that have the tonnaging and poundaging of all spoken truth.
Milton, Areopagitica.

3. The keeper of a public house or other such place of entertainment. In law, under the term *publicans* are included innkeepers, hotel-keepers, keepers of ale-houses, wine-vaults, etc. *Wharton.* [Great Britain.]

The *publican* can . . . profitably combine the business of a bookmaker with the equally profitable business of selling intoxicant fluids. *Nineteenth Century*, XXVI. 849.

publicate† (pub'li-kāt), *v. t.* [< L. *publicatus*, pp. of *publicare*, publish: see *publish*.] To publish. [Rare.]

Little sins in them [the clergy], if *publicated*, grow great by their scandall and contagion.
Bp. Gauden, Tears of the Church, p. 115. (*Davies.*)

publication (pub-li-kā'shọn), *n.* [< F. *publication* = Sp. *publicacion* = Pg. *publicação* = It. *pubblicazione*, < L. *publicatio(n-)*, a making public, an adjudging to the public treasury, < *publicare*, pp. *publicatus*, make public: see *publicate, publish*.] 1. The act of publishing, or bringing to public notice; notification to people at large, by speech, writing, or printing; proclamation; promulgation; announcement: as, the *publication* of statutes; *publication* of banns. In law, the publication of defamation consists in communicating it to any third person; the publication of a will is that act of a testator in which he declares to the subscribing witnesses that the instrument he asks them to attest is his will; in chancery proceedings, opening to the inspection of the parties depositions that have been taken and returned under seal to the court or clerk is *publication*.

The communication of a libel to any one person is a *publication* in the eye of the law. *Blackstone*, Com., IV. xi.

On the third *publication* they [betrothed persons] are said to be asked out. *Dickens*, David Copperfield.

2. The act of offering a book, map, print, piece of music, or the like, to the public by sale or by gratuitous distribution.

An imperfect copy having been offered to a bookseller, you consented to the *publication* of one more correct.
Pope.

3. A work printed and published; any book, pamphlet, or periodical offered for sale to the public: as, a monthly *publication*; an illustrated *publication*.—4†. Appearance in public; public appearance. [Rare.]

His jealousy . . . attends the business, the recreations, the *publications*, and retirements of every man.
Jer. Taylor, Works (ed. 1835), I. 772.

Obscene publication. See *obscene*.—**To pass publication**, to reach the stage of a cause in chancery when the time for examining witnesses has expired, and the depositions kept secret may be disclosed on the application of either party.

public-hearted (pub'lik-här"ted), *a.* Having the interests of the people at heart; public-spirited.

They were *public-hearted* men; as they paid all taxes, so they gave up all their time to their country's service, without any reward. *Clarendon*, Great Rebellion.

publicist (pub'li-sist), *n.* [= F. *publiciste* = Sp. Pg. *publicista* = It. *pubblicista*; as *public* + *-ist*.] 1. A writer on the law of nature or the laws of nations; one who is versed in public or international law; one who treats of the rights and mutual obligations of nations.

The methodized reasonings of the great *publicists* and jurists form the digest and jurisprudence of the Christian world. *Burke*, A Regicide Peace, ii.

The mixed systems of jurisprudence and morals constructed by the *publicists* of the Low Countries appear to have been much studied by English lawyers.
Maine, Ancient Law, p. 45.

Many *publicists* still view the allowance of transit [to belligerents] as reconcilable with the notion of neutrality, and a number of treaties have expressly granted it to certain states. *Woolsey*, Introd. to Inter. Law, § 160.

2. One who is versed in or who writes upon the current political topics of the time.

This eminent *publicist*, . . . Mr. Arthur Pendennis.
Thackeray, Pendennis, xxxvi.

"Slow and sure" is not the motto of either reader or writer in these days. Public and *publicist* are acceptable to each other in proportion as they are ready to conform to the electric influences of the times.
Nineteenth Century, XX. 515.

publicity (pub-lis'ị-ti), *n.* [< F. *publicité* = Sp. *publicidad* = Pg. *publicidade* = It. *pubblicità*; as *public* + *-ity*.] The state of being public, or open to the observation or inquiry of a community; notoriety: as, to give *publicity* to a private communication.

publicly (pub'lik-li), *adv.* In a public manner. (*a*) Openly; without reserve or privacy.

Sometimes also it may be private, communicating to the judges some things not fit to be *publicly* delivered.
Bacon.

When Socrates reproved Plato at a feast, Plato told him "it had been better he had told him his fault in private, for to speak it *publicly* is indecency."
Jer. Taylor, Works, V. 378.

But he so much scorned their charitie, and *publikely* defied the vttermost of their crueltie, he wisely prevented their policies. Quoted in *Capt. John Smith's* Works, I. 152.

(*b*) In the name of the community; with general consent.

This has been so sensibly known by trading nations that great rewards are *publicly* offered for its supply. *Addison.*

public-minded (pub'lik-mīn"ded), *a.* Disposed to promote the public interest; public-spirited.

public-mindedness (pub'lik-mīn"ded-nes), *n.* A disposition to promote the public interest; public spirit.

All nations that grew great out of little or nothing did so merely by the *public-mindedness* of particular persons.
South.

publicness (pub'lik-nes), *n.* 1. The character of common possession or interest; joint holding: as, the *publicness* of property.

The vast multitude of partners does detract nothing from each private share, nor does the *publickness* of it lessen propriety in it. *Boyle*, Works, I.

2. Openness or exposure to the notice or knowledge of the community or of people at large; notoriety: as, the *publicness* of a resort; the *publicness* of a scandal.

The *publickness* of a sin is an aggravation of it; makes it more scandalous, and so more criminous also.
Hammond, Works, I. 218. (*Latham.*)

public-spirited (pub"lik-spir'i-ted), *a.* 1. Having or exercising a disposition to promote the interest or advantage of the community; disposed to make private sacrifices for the public good: as, a *public-spirited* citizen.

At Geyra I went to the house of the aga, a venerable old man, who was one of those *public-spirited* Turks that entertains all strangers.
Pococke, Description of the East, II. ii. 71.

It was generous and *public-spirited* in you to be of the kingdom's side in this dispute. *Swift.*

2. Dictated by or based on regard for the public good: as, a *public-spirited* measure.

Another *public-spirited* project, which the common enemy could not foresee, might set King Charles on the throne. *Addison.*

public-spiritedly (pub"lik-spir'i-ted-li), *adv.* With public spirit.

public-spiritedness (pub"lik-spir'i-ted-nes), *n.* The quality or character of being public-spirited; a disposition to act with energy for the public interest or advantage; a willingness to make sacrifices of private interest for the public good.

The spirit of charity, the old word for *public-spiritedness*. *Whitlock*, Manners of Eng. People, p. 382.

publish (pub'lish), *v. t.* [< ME. *publischen*, *puplischen*, *pupplischen*; with term. *-ish*², after the analogy of words like *abolish*, *polish*, etc.; < OF. *publier*, F. *publier* = Pr. *publicar*, *publiar* = Sp. Pg. *publicar* = It. *publicare*, *pubblicare*, < L. *publicare*, make public, show or tell to the people, make known, declare, also (and earlier) confiscate for public use, < *publicus*, pertaining to the people, public: see *public*.] 1. To make public; make known to people in general; promulgate or proclaim, as a law or edict.

For he that wil *pupplische* ony thing to make it openly knowen, he wil make it to ben cryed and pronounced in the myddel place of a Town. *Mandeville*, Travels, p. 2.

Publish it that she is dead indeed;
Maintain a mourning ostentation.
Shak., Much Ado, iv. 1. 206.

Mahomet hauing with Word and Sword *published* his Alcoran (as you haue heard), his followers after his death, succeeding in his place, exceeded him in tyrannie. *Purchas*, Pilgrimage, p. 273.

Nay, the Royal Society have found and *published* lately that there be thirty-and-three kinds of spiders; and yet all, for aught I know, go under that one general name of spider. *I. Walton*, Complete Angler, p. 76.

2. To exhibit, display, disclose, or reveal.

Fut. Stand by, then, without noise, a while, brave Don,
And let her only view your parts; they'll take her.
Gus. I'll *publish* them in silence.
Ford, Lady's Trial, iv. 2.

The unwearied sun, from day to day,
Does his Creator's power display,
And *publishes* to every land
The work of an Almighty hand.
Addison, Paraphrase of Psalm xix.

3. To utter, or put in circulation, as counterfeit paper; communicate to another person, as a libel or slander.—4. To cause to be printed and offered for sale; issue from the press; put in circulation: as, to *publish* a book, map, print, periodical, piece of music, or the like.

Books were not *published* then so soon as they were written, but lay most commonly dormient many years. *Abp. Bramhall*, Works, II. 142.

5. To introduce to public notice; offer or advertise to the public. [Obsolete or rare.]

The gentleman that gave fifty pounds for the box set with diamonds may show it until Sunday night, provided he goes to church; but not after that time, there being one to be *published* on Monday which will cost fourscore guineas. *Steele*, Tatler, No. 142.

I have a small bust of the Duke of York. It is of silver gilt, measuring with the pedestal about three inches in height. On the back are engraved the words "*Published* by T. Hamlet, Aug. 16, 1824." *N. and Q.*, 7th ser., VI. 207.

=**Syn.** 1. *Declare, Proclaim*, etc. (see *announce*), disclose, divulge, reveal, spread abroad. See list under *proclaim*.

publishable (pub'lish-a-bl), *a.* [< *publish* + *-able*.] Capable of being published; fit for publication.

publisher (pub'lish-ėr), *n.* One who publishes. (*a*) One who makes known what was before private or unknown; one who divulges, declares, proclaims, or promulgates.

Use all the best means and ways ye can, in the diligent examining and searching out, from man to man, the authors and *publishers* of these vain prophesies and untrue bruits. *Bp. Burnet*, Records, II. ii. 14.

The many *publishers*, . . . in a short time, the Lord had raised to declare his salvation to the people. *Penn*, Rise and Progress of Quakers, v.

The mob uniformly cheers the *publisher*, and not the inventor. *Emerson*, Success.

(*b*) One who, as the first source of supply, issues books and other literary works, maps, engravings, musical compositions, or the like for sale; one who prints and offers a book, pamphlet, engraving, etc., for sale to dealers or to the public.

Most of the *publishers* had absolutely refused to look at his manuscripts; one or two had good-naturedly glanced over and returned them at once. *Bulwer*, My Novel, vi. 14.

(*c*) One who utters or passes counterfeit paper, or puts it in circulation.—**Publisher's imprint.** See *imprint*, 2.

publishment (pub'lish-ment), *n.* [< *publish* + *-ment*.] 1. The act of publishing or proclaiming; public exposure.

Ye cardinall . . . rebuked them by open *publysshement* and otherwyse. *Fabyan*, Chron., I. ccix.

2. An official notice made by a town clerk or other civil or clerical official of an intended marriage; a publishing of the banns of marriage. [U. S.]

pubococcygeal (pū"bō-kok-sij'ē-al), *a.* [< *pubococcygeus* + *-al*.] Of or pertaining to the pubis and the coccyx: as, the *pubococcygeal* muscle.

pubococcygeus (pū"bō-kok-sij'ē-us), *n.*; pl. *pubococcygei* (-ī). [< NL. *pubis*, pubis, + *coccyx* (*coccyg-*), coccyx.] That part of the levator ani which arises from the pubis.

pubofemoral (pū-bō-fem'ọ-ral), *a.* [< NL. *pubis*, pubis, + *femur* (*femor-*), thigh-bone, + *-al*.] Common to the pubis and the thigh-bone: as, the *pubofemoral* fascia or ligament.—**Pubofemoral ligament**, an accessory bundle of fibers entering into the formation of the capsule of the hip-joint.

pubo-iliac (pū-bō-il'i-ak), *a.* [< NL. *pubis*, pubis, + *ilium*, ilium, + *-ac*.] Common to the pubis and the ilium: as, the *pubo-iliac* suture.

pubo-ischiac (pū-bō-is'ki-ak), *a.* [< NL. *pubis*, pubis, + *ischium*, ischium, + *-ac*.] Common to the pubis and the ischium; pertaining to the pubo-ischium; ischiopubic.

pubo-ischium (pū-bō-is'ki-um), *n.* [NL., < *pubis*, pubis, + *ischium*, ischium.] The ischiopubic bone. See *ischiopubic*, 2.

pubo-peritonealis (pū-bō-per-ị-tō-nẹ-ā'lis), *n.* Same as *pubo-transversalis*.

puboprostatic (pū"bō-pros-tat'ik), *a.* [< NL. *pubis*, pubis, + *prostata*, prostate gland, + *-ic*.] Common to the pubis and the prostate gland: as, the *puboprostatic* ligament.—**Puboprostatic ligament**, one of the two anterior ligaments of the bladder, running from the back of the pubis over the upper surface of the prostate gland to the front of the neck of the bladder.

pubotibial (pū-bō-tib'i-al), *a.* [< NL. *pubis*, pubis, + *tibia*, tibia, + *-al*.] Common to the pubis and the tibia: as, a *pubotibial* muscle.

pubo-transversalis (pū-bō-trans-vėr-sā'lis), *n.* A thin muscular slip arising from the upper margin of the superior pubic ramus and inserted into the transversalis fascia.

pubo-urethral (pū"bō-ụ-rē'thral), *a.* [< NL. *pubis*, pubis, + *urethra*, urethra, + *-al*.] Passing from the pubis to the urethra: noting an occasional muscle of man.—**Pubo-urethral muscle**, fibers passing from the back part of the pubis to the prostate gland, or to the base of the bladder in the female.

pubovesical (pū-bō-ves'i-kal), *a.* [< NL. *pubis*, pubis, + L. *vesica*, bladder, + *-al*.] Common to the pubis and the bladder, as a muscle or ligament.—**Pubovesical ligament.** Same as *puboprostatic ligament* (which see, under *puboprostatic*).—**Pubovesical muscles**, the fibers of the external longitudinal muscular layer of the bladder which arise from the posterior surface of the body of the pubis.

Puccianite (pö'chi-an-īt), *n.* [< *Pucci* (see def.) + *-an* + *-ite*².] One of a body of Universalists, followers of Francesco Pucci, an Italian theologian of the sixteenth century.

Puccinia (puk-sin'i-ä), *n.* [NL. (Persoon, 1797), named after T. *Puccini*, an Italian anatomist.] 1. A genus of parasitic fungi of the class *Uredineæ*; the rusts. Plants of this genus exhibit the phenomenon of heterœcism—that is, they pass through different stages of their life-history upon different host-plants. *P. graminis*, one of the commonest and most destructive species, may be taken as a type. It appears in the spring on the leaves of *Berberis vulgaris*, constituting what is known as *barberry-rust* or *barberry cluster-cups*. This is the æcidial stage, and received the name of *Æcidium Berberidis* be-

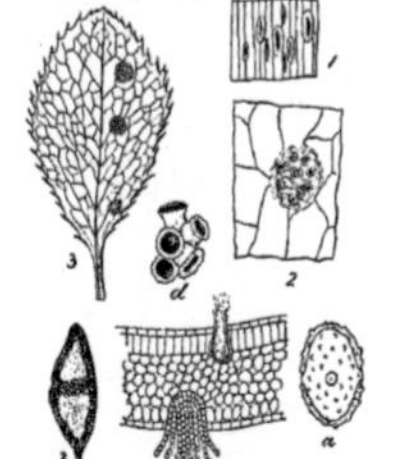

Puccinia graminis and *Æcidium Berberidis*.

1, puccinia on the leaf of a grass; *a*, one of the uredo-spores; *b*, one of the teleutospores; 2, part of the superior face of the leaf of *Berberis vulgaris*, showing the spermogonia; 3, leaf of *Berberis vulgaris*, inferior face, showing the æcidia; *c*, transverse section of the leaf of *Berberis vulgaris*, showing the spermogonia on the superior and the æcidia on the inferior face; *d*, the cupules, forming the groups of æcidia.

fore the heterœcism was suspected. Later in the season the uredo stage makes its appearance on the leaves and stems of the cultivated oats, wheat, etc., appearing as pale-yellowish or whitish spots on the leaves. Soon the tissues are ruptured, and the long lines of orange-red uredo-spores are exposed, now constituting the red rust of oats, etc. By the rapid germination of the uredo-spores the disease is quickly spread, and may involve the entire plant. In the fall, just before cold weather, the black teleutospores are produced. This is known as the black rust, and is designed to carry the fungus over the winter, when it again begins its life-cycle on the barberry. About 450 species of *Puccinia* are known, not a few of which are serious pests to the agriculturist or horticulturist. See *heterœcism*, *barberry-fungus*, *rust*, *Uredineæ*.

2. A plant of this genus.

puccoon (pu-kön'), *n.* [Also *poccoon*; Amer. Ind. (?).] 1. The bloodroot, *Sanguinaria Canadensis*: called *red puccoon*. See *bloodroot*, 2.—2. One of three or four American species of *Lithospermum*, with bright golden-yellow nearly salver-shaped flowers, and hairy surfaces. *L. canescens*, the hoary puccoon, is the puccoon of the Indians. *L. hirtum*, a rougher plant, is the hairy puccoon.—**Yellow puccoon.** See *Hydrastis*, and *Indian paint* (under *paint*).

puce (pūs), *a.* [< F. *puce*, puce, flea-colored, < OF. *pulce*, a flea, < L. *pulex* (*pulic-*), a flea: see *Pulex*.] Purple-brown; reddish-brown; of a flea-color.

pucel†, *n.* Same as *pucelle*.

pucelage (pū'se-lạj), *n.* [< F. *pucelage*, virginity, < *pucelle*, a virgin: see *pucelle*.] A state of virginity. [Rare.]

The examen of *pucelage*, the waters of jealousy, &c., were very strict; and, to the same end, municipal. *R. Robinson*, Eudoxa (1658), p. 37. (*Latham*.)

pucellas (pụ-sel'as), *n.* In *glass-blowing*, same as *procellas*.

pucelle† (pū-sel'), *n.* [Early mod. E. also *pucel*, *pucell*; < ME. *pucelle*, < OF. *pucelle*, *pulcelle*, F. *pucelle* = Pr. *piucela*, *pieucela* = OSp. *puncella* = It. *pulcella*, *pulzella*, a virgin, maid, girl, < ML. as if **pullicella*, dim. fem. of L. *pullus*, a young animal, a chick: see *pullet*.] 1. A maid; a virgin: specifically applied in history to Joan of Arc, the Maid of Orleans.—2. A wanton girl; a harlot.

Does the Court *Pucelle* then so censure me,
And thinks I dare her not? . . .
For bawd'ry, 'tis her language, and not mine.
B. Jonson, Underwoods, lxvii.

Pucherania (pū-ke-rā'ni-ä), *n.* [NL.] In *ornith.*, same as *Pachycephala*¹, 1.

pucherite (pö'chėr-īt), *n.* [< *Pucher* (see def.) + *-ite*².] A vanadate of bismuth, occurring in reddish-brown orthorhombic crystals in the Pucher mine in Schneeberg, Saxony.

puchero (pọ-chā'rō), *n.* [S. Amer. (?).] A fleshy plant, *Talinum patens*, of tropical American shores. It is used as a vegetable like purslane.

puck (puk), *n.* [Early mod. E. also *pouk*, *pouke*; < ME. *pouke*, *puke*, a fairy, elf, sprite, devil (cf. AS. *pucel*, a demon: see *puckle*), < Ir. *puca*, an elf, sprite, = W. *pwca*, *pwci*, a goblin, fiend; cf. Icel. *pūki*, a devil, imp. The G. *spuk* (> E. *spook*), a hobgoblin, is prob. a diff. word. Cf. *pug*¹, a var. of *puck*. Cf. also *puckle*, *puckrel*, also *pixy* and *poker*², and *bug*¹, *bog*², *bogy*, *bogle*.] 1. A fairy; elf; sprite.

Ne let the *Pouks*, nor other evill sprights, . . .
Fray us with things that be not.
Spenser, Epithalamion, l. 341.

And so likewise those . . . which (saith Lavater) draw men out of the way, and lead them all night a by-way, or quite barre them of their way: these have severall names in severall places; we commonly call them *Pucks*. *Burton*, Anat. of Mel., p. 30.

Ne let hobgoblin ne the *pouk* [read *pouk*] profane
With shadowy glare the light, and mad the bursting brain. *W. Thompson*, Hymn to May, st. 33.

Specifically—2. [*cap.*] A fairy of high repute, who was also known by the names of *Robin Goodfellow* and *Friar Rush*. His character and attributes are depicted in Shakspere's "Midsummer Night's Dream." He was the chief of the domestic tribe of fairies, or brownies as they are called in Scotland.

He meeteth *Puck*, which most men call
Hobgoblin. *Drayton*, Nymphidia, st. 36.

3†. The devil; Satan.

Fro the *poukes* poundfalde no maynprise may ous fecche,
Till he come that ich carpe of, Crist is hus name.
Piers Plowman (C), xix. 282.

pucka (puk'ạ̈), *a.* [Hind. *pakkā*, ripe, cooked, strong, firm, adept, etc.] Solid; substantial; real; permanent; lasting: as, a *pucka* wall; a *pucka* road: opposed to *cutcha*. [Anglo-Ind.]

My Parsee neighbor, the amiable Gheber, . . . in the *pucka* house that adjoined my own in Cossitollah. *J. W. Palmer*, The New and the Old, p. 271.

puck-ball (puk'bâl), *n.* Same as *puffball*.

pucker (puk'ėr), *v.* [A freq. form, < *poke*², a bag or pocket. Cf. *purse*, *v.*, wrinkle, < *purse*, *n.*; It. *saccolare*, puckėr, < *sacco*, a bag, sack.] I. *trans.* To draw up or contract into irregular folds or wrinkles; specifically, in *sewing*, to gather: often followed by *up*: as, to *pucker* cloth in sewing.

I saw an hideous spectre; his eyes were sunk into his head, his face pale and withered, and his skin *puckered up* in wrinkles. *Spectator*.

It is forgotten now; and the first mention of it *puckers* thy sweet countenance into a sneer. *Carlyle.*

The flowers on the potato plants, saucer-shaped by day, are now perchance nodding with their open rim *puckered* in gathers around the central stamens — a common caprice of these flowers, but dependent upon some whim which I have not yet solved. *Harper's Mag.*, LXXVIII. 143.

II. *intrans.* To become irregularly ridged or wrinkled: as, his face *puckered* up into a smile; the mouth *puckers* on eating choke-cherries.

pucker (puk'ėr), *n.* [< *pucker*, *v.*] 1. A drawing or gathering into folds or wrinkles; an irregular folding or wrinkling; a collection of irregularly converging ridges or wrinkles.

Ruff, Anything collected into *puckers* or corrugations. *Johnson.*

Held from rolling off the seat only by the steady hold of her mother in the *puckers* of her dress during the rest. *W. M. Baker*, New Timothy, p. 22.

The cloth to be stitched, being placed close up to the cog-wheels on the opposite side of where the needle point rests, is dragged in *puckers* into the latter, by turning the winch handle. *Spons' Encyc. Manuf.*, I. 471.

2. A state of flutter, agitation, or confusion. [Colloq.]

Well to be sure, the whole parish was in a *pucker*: some thought the French had landed. *Smollett*, Peregrine Pickle (2d ed.), ii.

I told William when we first missed her this mornin', and he was in such a *pucker* about her, I bet anything he was a mind to that the child had gone back to Miss Kilburn's. *Howells*, Annie Kilburn, xxix.

puckerer (puk'ėr-ėr), *n.* One who or that which puckers.

puckeridge (puk'ėr-ij), *n.* [Origin obscure.] 1. The night-jar, *Caprimulgus europæus*. *Montagu.*— 2. A fatal distemper of cattle. *Gilbert White.* [Prov. Eng. in both uses.]

puckery (puk'ėr-i), *a.* [< *pucker* + *-y*¹.] 1. Producing or tending to produce puckers: as, a *puckery* taste (that is, a bitter or astringent taste such as may cause the mouth to pucker).

Some of these wildings [apples] are acrid and *puckery*, genuine verjuice. *Thoreau*, Excursions, p. 291.

There are plenty [of American proverbs] that have a more native and *puckery* flavor, seedlings from the old stock often, and yet new varieties. *Lowell*, Biglow Papers, 2d ser., Int.

2. Inclined to become puckered or wrinkled; full of puckers or wrinkles: said especially of a textile fabric.

pucket (puk'et), *n.* [Origin obscure.] A nest of caterpillars. *Halliwell.* [Prov. Eng.]

puckfist† (puk'fist), *n.* [Also *puckfoist*; cf. LG. *pukfust*, a fist doubled up, < *pukken*, strike, poke, + *fust*, fist.] 1. A niggardly or close-fisted person.

O, they are pinching *puckfists!* B. *Jonson*, New Inn, iii. 1.

Petrarch was a dunce, Dante a jig-maker,
Sanazzar a goose, and Ariosto a *puck-fist* to me!
Ford, Love's Sacrifice, ii. 1.

For those are pinching *puckfoists*, and suspicious.
Fletcher (and another), Love's Pilgrimage, i. 1.

2. In *bot.*, a puffball.

puckfoist† (puk'foist), *n.* Same as *puckfist*.

puckish (puk'ish), *a.* [< *puck* + *-ish*¹.] Resembling the fairy Puck; like what Puck might do; merry. *J. R. Green.*

puckle (puk'l), *n.* [Prob. < ME. **poukel*, **pukel* (not found), < AS. *pūcel*, a demon (found once, in acc. pl. *pucelas*, glossed by *piiapos*): see *puck*.] Same as *puck*. [Obsolete or provincial.]

The spoorne, the mare, the man in the oke, the hell waine, the fierdrake, the *puckle*, Tom thombe, hobgoblin, etc. *R. Scot*, Discoverie of Witchcraft (ed. 1584), vii. 153.

The scene of fairy revels, . . . the haunt of bulbeggars, witches, . . . [and] the *puckle*. *S. Judd*, Margaret, i. 5.

puckrel†, *n.* Same as *puckle*. *Halliwell.*

pucras (pū'kras), *n.* [Native name.] A pheasant of the genus *Pucrasia*. *P. L. Sclater.*

Pucrasia (pū-krā'si-ä), *n.* [NL. (G. R. Gray, 1841), < *pucras*, a native name.] A beautiful genus of pheasants of the family *Phasianidæ* and subfamily *Lophophorinæ*, having the head crested, the nostrils feathered, the tail long and cuneate, the wings short and rounded, inhabiting Asia in the Himalayan region, China, and parts of India. The common pucras is *P. macrolopha*; the buff-spotted is *P. xanthospila*; *P. duvauceli* is a third species.

pud¹ (pud), *n.* [Perhaps orig. a slang form of D. *poot*, paw: see *paw*¹.] A paw; fist; hand. [Colloq.]

The kangaroos — your Aborigines — do they keep their primitive simplicity un-Europe-tainted, with those little short fore *puds*, looking like a lesson framed by nature to the pickpocket? *Lamb*, Distant Correspondents.

pud² (pöd), *n.* Same as *pood*.

puddening (pùd'ning), *n.* [So called as making as it were a pudding, i. e. a thick soft mass around the rope; < *pudden*, a dial. form of *pudding* (see *pudding*, 3, in same sense), + *-ing*¹.] A thick pad of rope-yarns, oakum, etc., covered with a mat or canvas, and tapering from the middle toward the ends, used as a fender on the bow of a boat. When rope cables were used, the covering of soft rope and canvas on the ring of an anchor was so called. Also called *pudding*.

pudder (pud'ėr), *v.* [Also *putter*; dial. form of *potter*² or *pother*.] I. *intrans.* To make a tumult, bustle, or stir; potter.

Such as are least able are most busie to *pudder* in the rubbish, and to raise dust. *N. Ward*, Simple Cobler, p. 2.

Some [fishes] almost alwayes *pudder* in the mud
Of sleepy Pools.
Sylvester, tr. of Du Bartas's Weeks, i. 5.

II. *trans.* To perplex; embarrass; confuse; bother.

He that will improve every matter of fact into a maxim will abound in contrary observations, that can be of no other use but to perplex and *pudder* him if he compares them. *Locke*, Conduct of Understanding, § 13.

[Obsolete or dialectal in both uses.]

pudder (pud'ėr), *n.* [< *pudder*, *v.*] A tumult; a confused noise; a bustle; pother.

Some fellows would have cried now, and have curs'd thee,
And faln out with their meat, and kept a *pudder*;
But all this helps not. *Beau. and Fl.*, Scornful Lady, ii. 2.

What a *pudder* and racket . . . in the schools of the learned about power and about spirit!
Sterne, Tristram Shandy, ii. 2.

Parkin's Pints has been makin' a great *pudder* over to England. *S. Judd*, Margaret, i. 16.

pudding (pùd'ing), *n.* [Also dial. *puddin*, *pudden*; early mod. E. also *poding*; < ME. *puddyng*, *poding*; appar., with accom. suffix, < Ir. *putog* = Gael. *putag*, a pudding; cf. (with diff. term.) W. *poten*, a paunch, pudding; cf. also W. *pwtyn*, a short round body, Corn. *pot*, a bag, pudding, Gael. *put*, an inflated skin, a large buoy. The E. word may have been in part confused with F. *boudin*, black-pudding, blood-pudding, roller-pudding (naut.), etc., ult. < L. *botulus*, sausage. The F. *pouding* = D. *pudding*, *podding* = LG. *pudding*, *pudden*, *budden* = G. Sw. *pudding* = Dan. *budding*, pudding, are all < E.] 1. Minced meat, or blood, properly seasoned, stuffed into an intestine, and cooked by boiling.

As sure as his guts are made of *puddings*.
Shak., M. W. of W., ii. 1. 32.

And first they ate the white *puddings*,
And syne they ate the black.
Get up and Bar the Door (Child's Ballads, VIII. 126).

They make better *puddings* of their horses then of their hogs, which they eate being new made.
Hakluyt's Voyages, I. 97.

2. A dish consisting of flour or other farinaceous substance with suet, or milk, eggs, etc., sometimes enriched with fruit, as raisins, etc., originally boiled in a bag to a moderately hard consistence, but now made in many other ways.

ȝe han harmed vs two in that ȝe eten the *puddyng*,
Mortrewes, and other mete, and we no morsel hade!
Piers Plowman (B), xiii. 106.

Then to their supper were they set orderlye,
With hot bag-*puddings*, and good apple-pyes.
King and Miller of Mansfield (Child's Ballads, VIII. 36).

When I was a young man, we used to keep strictly to my father's rule, "No broth, no ball; no ball, no beef"; and always began dinner with broth. Then we had suet-*puddings*, boiled in the broth with the beef; and then the meat itself. *Mrs. Gaskell*, Cranford, iv.

3. *Naut.*, same as *puddening*.— **Dundee pudding**, a sailors' dish, commonly called *dandyfunk*.— **Indian pudding**. See *Indian*.— **Pudding pipe-tree**. See *pipe-tree*. (See also *black-pudding* (also called *blood-pudding*), *cap-pudding*, *hasty-pudding*, *hog's-pudding*, *white-pudding*.)

pudding-bag (pùd'ing-bag), *n.* 1. A bag in which a pudding is boiled: usually not sewed in any way, but a cloth gathered around the uncooked pudding and tied with a string.

About half a yard long, of the breadth of a *pudding-bag*.
Letter dated 1626. (*Nares.*)

2. The long-tailed titmouse: same as *feather-poke*. [Norfolk, Eng.]

pudding-cloth (pùd'ing-klôth), *n.* The cloth in which a pudding is boiled.

pudding-faced (pùd'ing-fāst), *a.* Having a fat, round, smooth face; having a face suggestive of a pudding.

Stupid, *pudding-faced* as he looks and is, there is still a vulpine astucity in him. *Carlyle*, Cagliostro.

pudding-fish (pùd'ing-fish), *n.* A labroid fish of West Indian waters, *Platyglossus radiatus*, the bluefish or doncella.

pudding-grass (pùd'ing-gràs), *n.* The pennyroyal, *Mentha Pulegium*: so called from its use in seasoning puddings. Also *pudding-herb*. [Old and provincial.]

pudding-head (pùd'ing-hed), *n.* A dull, stupid person.

pudding-headed (pùd'ing-hed″ed), *a.* Dull; stupid. [Colloq.]

A purse-proud, *pudding-headed*, fat-gutted, lean-brained Southron. *Scott*, Fortunes of Nigel, xxvi.

pudding-heart† (pùd'ing-härt), *n.* A coward. [Rare.]

Go, *pudding-heart!*
Take thy huge offal and white liver hence.
Sir H. Taylor, Ph. van Artevelde, II., iii. 1. (*Davies.*)

pudding-house† (pùd'ing-hous), *n.* The paunch; belly. [Slang.]

He . . . thrust him downe his *pudding-house* at a gobbe.
Nashe, Lenten Stuffe (Harl. Misc., VI. 166). (*Davies.*)

pudding-pie (pùd'ing-pī), *n.* A pudding with meat baked in it.

Three well larded *pudding-pyes* he hath at one time put to foyle. *John Taylor*, Works (1630). (*Nares.*)

Some cried the Covenant, instead
Of *pudding-pies* and gingerbread.
S. Butler, Hudibras, I. ii. 546.

pudding-prick†, *n.* A skewer used to fasten a pudding-bag.

His mighty arguments prove not the value of a *poding-prick*.
Tyndale, Ans. to Sir T. More, etc. (Parker Soc., 1850), [p. 141.

pudding-sleeve (pùd'ing-slēv), *n.* A large, loose sleeve; especially, in England, a sleeve of the black gown of a clergyman.

He sees, yet hardly can believe,
About each arm a *pudding-sleeve*;
His waistcoat to a cassock grew.
Swift, Baucis and Philemon.

pudding-stone (pùd'ing-stōn), *n.* A rock made up of rounded and water-worn debris of other rocks, a considerable proportion of the pieces being large enough to be called pebbles or cobbles. Detrital rocks made up of finer materials are called sandstones, shales, or mudstones. *Pudding-stone* is a synonym of *conglomerate*. See cut under *conglomerate*.

pudding-time (pùd'ing-tīm), *n.* 1. The time for pudding — that is, dinner-time.— 2†. The nick of time; critical time.

I came in season — as they say, in *pudding time*, tempore veni. *Withals' Dictionarie* (ed. 1608), p. 3. (*Nares.*)

But Mars, that still protects the stout,
In *pudding-time* came to his aid.
S. Butler, Hudibras, I. ii. 865.

When George in *pudding-time* came o'er,
And moderate men looked big, sir,
My principles I changed once more,
And so became a Whig, sir. *Vicar of Bray.*

pudding-tobacco† (pùd'ing-tọ̄-bak″ō), *n.* Tobacco made up in rolls like puddings.

Never kneels but to pledge healths, nor prays but for a pipe of *pudding-tobacco*. B. *Jonson*, Cynthia's Revels, ii. 1.

pudding-wife (pùd'ing-wīf), *n.* A labroid fish, *Platyglossus radiatus*, with a long body, large scales, and the color bluish or bronze, with wavy sky-blue spots, a stripe from snout to nape, and blue stripes in the fins. It occurs from the Florida Keys to Brazil.

puddingy (pùd'ing-i), *a.* [< *pudding* + *-y*¹.] Resembling or suggestive of a pudding. [Colloq.]

A limpness and roundness of limb which give the form a *puddingy* appearance.
Mayhew, London Labour and London Poor, III. 65.

puddle¹ (pud'l), *n.* [Early mod. E. also *puddel*; < ME. *podel*, a pool; origin obscure. Cf. AS. *pudd* (rare), a ditch or furrow (glossed by L. *sulcus*); E. dial. *pudge*, a ditch. The W. *pwdel*, a puddle, is prob. < E.] 1. A small pool of water, especially of dirty rain-water; a muddy plash.

Ther's not a *Puddle* (though it strangely stink)
But dry they draw 't, Sea-Water 's dainty Drink.
Sylvester, tr. of Du Bartas's Weeks, ii., The Schisme.

The Lucrine lake is but a *puddle* in comparison of what it once was, its springs having been sunk in an earthquake. *Addison*, Remarks on Italy (ed. Bohn), I. 432.

2. Clay to which a little water has been added and which has then been tempered, so as to make it homogeneous and increase its plasticity. It is used in a great variety of ways when a water-tight stopping is required. It is also called *puddling*.

puddle¹ (pud'l), *v.*; pret. and pp. *puddled*, ppr. *puddling*. [Early mod. E. also *poodle*; appar. from the noun, but prob. in part a var. of *paddle*¹ and *pudder* in similar senses. In the technical sense, def. 3, the verb has been adopted into other tongues (F. *puddler*, etc.).] I. *trans.* 1. To make foul or muddy; stir up the mud or sediment in; hence, to befoul in a figurative sense.

Something . . . hath *puddled* his clear spirit.
Shak., Othello, iii. 4. 143.

But such extremes, I told her, well might harm
The woman's cause. "Not more than now," she said,
"So *puddled* as it is with favouritism."
Tennyson, Princess, iii.

2. To work puddle into; render water-tight by means of puddle. See *puddle*[1], *n.*, 2.—3. To convert (pig-iron) into wrought-iron by stirring while subjected to intense heat, in order to expel the oxygen and carbon. See *puddling*, *n.*, 2. **II.** *intrans.* To make a stir, as in a pool.

Indeed I were very simple, if with Crabronius I should *poodle* in a wasp's nest, and think to purchase ease by it! *Junius*, Sin Stigmatized (1639), Pref. (*Latham.*)

puddle[2] (pud'l), *n.* [Cf. LG. **puddel*, *purrel*, something short and thick (*puddel-rund*, *purrel-rund*, short, thick, and round), *puddig*, thick, *puddeln*, *pudeln*, waddle, *pudel*, a thick-haired dog (see *poodle*).] A pudgy, ill-shaped, awkward person.

I remember when I was quite a boy hearing her called a limping old *puddle*.
Miss Burney, Cecilia, vii. 5. (*Davies.*)

A foot which a *puddle* of a maid scalded three weeks ago. *Carlyle*, in Froude, Life in London, I. 16.

puddle-ball (pud'l-bâl), *n.* In *iron-manuf.*, a lump of red-hot iron taken from the puddling-furnace in a pasty state to be hammered or rolled.

puddle-bar (pud'l-bär), *n.* Bar-iron as it comes from the puddle-rolls (see that word).—**Puddle-bar train.** See *muck-rolls*.

puddle-duck (pud'l-duk), *n.* The common domestic duck: so called from its characteristic habit of puddling water.

puddle-poet (pud'l-pō″et), *n.* A low, mean poet. [Rare.]

The *puddle-poet* did hope that the jingling of his rhyme would drown the sound of his false quantity.
Fuller, Ch. Hist., I. iii. 1. (*Davies.*)

puddler (pud'lėr), *n.* One who or that which puddles; specifically, one who is employed in the process of converting cast-iron into wrought-iron.—**Rotary puddler**, in *metal-working*, a mechanical puddler in which the treatment of the molten metal is effected by the rotation of the furnace. See *Danks rotary furnace*, under *furnace*.

puddle-rolls (pud'l-rōlz), *n. pl.* In *iron-manuf.*, a pair of heavy iron rollers with grooved surfaces, between which the lumps of iron taken from the puddling-furnace, after being subjected to a preliminary forging, are passed so as to be converted into rough bars.

puddling (pud'ling), *n.* [Verbal n. of *puddle*[1], *v.*] 1. In *hydraul. engin.*, the operation of working plastic clay behind piling in a coffer-dam, the lining of a canal, or in other situation, to prevent the penetration of water; also, the clay or other material used in this operation.—2. The operation of transforming pig-iron into wrought-iron in a reverberatory furnace. The object of puddling is to remove the carbon in the pig-iron; and this is effected partly by the direct action of the oxygen of the air at the high temperature employed, and partly by the action of the cinder formed, or the oxidized compounds of iron added during the process. After the iron "comes to nature" in the furnace, it is made up into balls for convenient handling; these are "shingled" by hammering or squeezing, and passed between rolls, by which the metal is made to assume any desired form. There are two methods of puddling: the process as originally performed is called *dry puddling*; that which is now most generally followed is known as *wet puddling*, but is oftener called *pig-boiling*. In the older process only white or refined iron could be used; in the newer unrefined iron is employed, and this melts more perfectly and boils up more freely than is the case when refined iron is used, which remains in a more or less pasty condition during the process; hence the name *pig-boiling*. The puddling process was invented in England by Henry Cort, about 1784, and he was also the inventor of the method of finishing iron by passing it through grooved rolls—processes of immense importance as determining the long-maintained supremacy of England in the iron-manufacturing business. The invention of what is known as "Bessemer steel" has considerably diminished, and is likely still further to diminish, the relative importance of the puddling process.—**Mechanical puddling**, the substitution for hand-labor of some one of the various mechanical contrivances which have been invented to make the operation of puddling less fatiguing for the workmen. Various methods of mechanical puddling have within the past few years come more or less extensively into use: one is to arrange the tools so as to imitate manual rabbling (see *rabble*[3]) as nearly as possible; in the other method some form of rotating or oscillating hearth is employed, the motion of which replaces the operation of rabbling. See *Danks rotary furnace*, under *furnace*; also (under the same heading) *Pernot furnace*, a form which has been employed for puddling iron as well as for making steel.

puddling-furnace (pud'ling-fėr″nās), *n.* A kind of reverberatory furnace in which iron is puddled. See *puddling*, 2 (*a*), and cut in next column.

puddling-machine (pud'ling-ma-shēn″), *n.* See *puddling*, 2 (*a*).

puddling-rolls (pud'ling-rōlz), *n. pl.* Same as *forge-train*.

Puddling-furnace.
a, Fire-chamber; *b*, iron-chamber; *c*, hearth; *d*, stock-hole; *e*, throat; *f*, neck; *g*, bridge; *h*, stack; *i*, velvet-tree; *k*, grate; *l*, roof; *m*, tap-hole; *n*, stopper-hole.

puddly (pud'li), *a.* [< *puddle*[1] + *-y*[1].] Like the water of a puddle; muddy; foul; dirty.

For He (I hope) who, no less good then wise,
First stirr'd vs vp to this great Enterprise, . . .
Will change the Pebbles of our *puddly* thought
To Orient Pearls, most bright and bravely wrought.
Sylvester, tr. of Du Bartas's Weeks, ii., The Vocation.

Limy or thick *puddly* water killeth them. *Carew.*

puddock[1] (pud'ok), *n.* A variant of *paddock*[1]. [Scotch.]

puddock[2] (pud'ok), *n.* [Var. of *paddock*[2]. Cf. equiv. *purrock*, var. of *parrock*.] A small inclosure; a paddock. [Prov. Eng.]

puddock[3] (pud'ok), *n.* A variant of *puttock*. [Prov. Eng.]

puddy (pud'i), *a.* Same as *pudgy*.

Their little *puddy* fingers. *Albert Smith.*

pudency† (pū'den-si), *n.* [< L. *puden(t-)s*, bashful, modest, ppr. of *pudere*, be ashamed, feel shame.] Modesty; shamefacedness.

Women have their bashfulness and *pudency* given them for a guard of their weakness and frailties.
W. Montague, Devoute Essays, i.

I observe that tender readers have a great *pudency* in showing their books to a stranger. *Emerson*, Books.

pudenda, *n.* Plural of *pudendum*.

pudendal (pū-den'dal), *a.* [< *pudendum* + *-al*.] Of or pertaining to the pudendum; connected with or relating to the pudenda; pudic: as, the *pudendal* vessels, nerves, etc.—**Common pudendal nerve.** Same as *pudic nerve* (which see, under *pudic*).—**Inferior pudendal nerve**, a branch of the small sciatic distributed to the skin of the upper and back part of the thigh and of the outer surface of the scrotum or of the labium.—**Pudendal hematocele**, a collection of blood in the labium.—**Pudendal hernia**, a hernia into the lower part of the labium, by the side of the vagina. Also called *labial hernia*.—**Pudendal plexus.** See *plexus*.

pudendohemorrhoidal (pū-den″dō-hem-ō-roi'dal), *a.* [< L. *pudendum*, pudendum, + E. *hemorrhoid* + *-al*.] Pertaining to the pudendum and the lower part of the rectum where hemorrhoids occur.—**Pudendohemorrhoidal nerve.** Same as *pudic nerve* (which see, under *pudic*).

pudendous (pū-den'dus), *a.* [= Sp. Pg. *pudendo*, < L. *pudendus*, participial adj. of *pudere*, feel shame.] Shameful; disgraceful. [Rare.]

A feeling laughable in a priestess, *pudendous* in a priest.
Sydney Smith, Peter Plymley's Letters, ii. (*Latham.*)

pudendum (pū-den'dum), *n.*; pl. *pudenda* (-dā). [L., gerund. of *pudere*, feel shame: see *pudency*.] 1. In *anat.*: (*a*) The region of the private parts; the pubes and perineum, together or indiscriminately. (*b*) Specifically, the vulva.—2. *pl.* The private parts; the genitals.

pudge (puj), *n.* [Cf. *puddle*[1].] A ditch or gap. *Halliwell.* [Prov. Eng.]

pudgy (puj'i), *a.* [Also *podgy*, *pudsy*, *pudsey*, *puddy*; origin obscure.] Fat and short; thick; fleshy. [Colloq.]

The vestry-clerk, as every body knows, is a short, *pudgy* little man. *Dickens*, Sketches, i.

A blond and disorderly mass of tow-like hair, a *podgy* and sanguine countenance.
M. Arnold, Friendship's Garland, v.

She was caught now under the mistletoe . . . by little fellows with *pudgy* arms, who covered her all over with kisses. *Harper's Mag.*, LXXVIII. 156.

pudic (pū'dik), *a.* [= F. *pudique* = Sp. *púdico* = Pg. It. *pudico*, < L. *pudicus*, shamefaced, bashful, modest, < *pudere*, feel shame.] In *anat.*, pudendal.—**Pudic artery.** (*a*) *External*, one of two (a deep and a superficial) branches of the femoral artery, supplying parts of the pudenda. (*b*) *Internal*, a large and surgically very important branch of the anterior trunk of the internal iliac artery, the principal source of the blood-supply of the external genitals. It leaves the pelvis by the greater sciatic foramen, winds around the ischiac spine, reënters the pelvis by the lesser sciatic foramen, courses along the inner side of the rami of the ischium and pubis, gives off inferior hemorrhoidal and superficial and transverse perineal branches, and divides into three penial arteries—of the bulb and cavernous body and dorsum of the penis.—**Pudic nerve**, the smaller terminal division of the sacral plexus. It issues from the pelvis through the greater and reënters through the lesser sciatic foramen, and afterward divides into the perineal and dorsalis penis. It also gives off the inferior hemorrhoidal. Also called *common pudendal*, *pudendohemorrhoidal nerve*.—**Pudic vein.** (*a*) *External*, a tributary of the external saphenous, collecting blood from the genitals and inner part of the thigh. (*b*) *Internal*, a vein corresponding to the internal pudic artery, except that it does not receive the blood from the dorsal vein of the penis.

pudical (pū'di-kal), *a.* [< *pudic* + *-al*.] Same as *pudic*.

pudicity (pū-dis'i-ti), *n.* [= F. *pudicité*, < L. *pudicitia*, modesty, chastity, < *pudicus*, bashful, modest: see *pudic*.] Modesty; chastity.

It sheweth much granitie & also *pudicitie*, hiding euery member of the body which had not bin pleasant to behold.
Puttenham, Arte of Eng. Poesie, p. 237.

pudsy (pud'zi), *a.* Same as *pudgy*.

pudu (pö'dö), *n.* [S. Amer.] The venada, *Cervus pudu* or *Pudua humilis*, a Chilian deer.

pudworm (pud'wėrm), *n.* The piddock, *Pholas dactylus*. [Local, Eng.]

pue[1]†, *n.* An obsolete form of *pew*[1].

pue[2]† (pū), *v. i.* [Also *pew*; an imitative word; cf. *pule*.] To chirp or cry like a bird; make a sound like this word.

The birds likewise with chirps and *puing*.
Sir P. Sidney. (*Richardson.*)

pueblo (pöeb'lō), *n.* [Sp., a town, village, people, < L. *populus*, people: see *people*.] 1. In Spanish America, a municipality; a town or village; any inhabited place. In the parts of the United States acquired from Mexico it is used in the sense of the English word *town*. It has the indefiniteness of that term, and, like it, it sometimes applies to a mere collection of individuals residing at a particular place, a settlement or village, as well as to a regularly organized municipality.

In its special significance, a *pueblo* means a corporate town, with certain rights of jurisdiction and administration. In Spain the term lugar was usually applied to towns of this nature, but the Spanish Americans have preferred and persistently used the term *pueblo*.
Johns Hopkins Univ. Studies, 8th ser., IV. 48.

2. [*cap.*] A Pueblo Indian.—**Pueblo Indians**, a body of Indians in New Mexico and Arizona, who dwell in communal villages (pueblos). They are partly civilized and self-governing. Among the best-known of them are the Zuñis.

puer (pū'ėr), *n.* An erroneous spelling of *pure*[2]. *Simmonds.*

puerile (pū'e-ril), *a.* [= F. *puéril* = Pr. Sp. Pg. *pueril* = It. *puerile*, < L. *puerilis*, pertaining to a boy or child, boyish, childish, < *puer*, boy, child, < √*pu-*, beget, whence also *pupus*, a boy, *pupa*, a girl, etc.: see *pupa*, *pupil*[1], etc.] 1. Of or pertaining to a boy or child; boyish; childish; juvenile.

Franciscus Junius . . . was born at Heidelberg, a famous city and university in Germany, an. 1589, educated in *puerile* Learning at Leyden in Holland.
Wood, Athenæ Oxon., II. 602.

Hence—2. Merely childish; lacking intellectual force; trivial: as, a *puerile* criticism.

It was therefore useless, almost *puerile*, to deny facts which were quite as much within the knowledge of the Netherlanders as of himself.
Motley, Hist. Netherlands, II. 288.

Puerile respiration, the respiratory murmur as heard in (healthy) children, louder and less vesicular than in healthy adults.

Puerile respiration in the lung of an adult is generally a sign of disease. *Sir T. Watson*, Lectures on Physic, xlvii.

=**Syn.** 1. *Juvenile*, *Boyish*, etc. (see *youthful*).—2. Weak, foolish, silly.

puerilely (pū'e-ril-li), *adv.* In a puerile manner; boyishly; triflingly.

puerileness (pū'e-ril-nes), *n.* The state or character of being puerile; puerility.

puerility (pū-e-ril'i-ti), *n.*; pl. *puerilities* (-tiz). [= F. *puérilité* = Sp. *puerilidad* = Pg. *puerilidade* = It. *puerilità*, < L. *puerilita(t-)s*, boyhood, childhood, < *puerilis*, pertaining to a boy or child: see *puerile*.] 1. A puerile character or condition; boyishness; childishness.

A reserve of *puerility* . . . not shaken off from school.
Sir T. Browne, Vulg. Err., i. 7.

2. The time of childhood; specifically, in *civil law*, the period of life from the age of seven years to that of fourteen.—3. That which is puerile; what is characteristic of or done in boyhood; hence, a childish or silly act, thought, or expression.

Of the learned *puerilities* of Cowley there is no doubt, since a volume of his poems was not only written, but printed, in his thirteenth year. *Johnson*, Cowley.

One God would not suffice
For senile *puerility*; thou framedst
A tale to suit thy dotage.
Shelley, Queen Mab, vi.

Even amid the affectation and love of anagrams and *puerilities* which sullied her later years, Elizabeth remained a lover of letters and of all that was greatest and purest in letters. *J. R. Green*, Hist. Eng. People, vi. 2.

puerperal (pū-ėr'pe-ral), *a.* [= F. *puerpéral* = Pg. *puerperal* = It. *puerperale*, < NL. *puerperalis*, < L. *puerpera*, f., bringing forth, a parturient woman, < *puer*, a child, + *parere*, bring forth, bear.] Of or pertaining to childbirth.—**Puerperal convulsions**, epileptiform attacks occurring im-

4. To praise with exaggeration; give undue or servile praise to.

> This starving public then — through the medium of posters, newspaper advertisements, men in cardboard extinguishers, and other modes of legitimate *puffing* — had been informed that its cravings were at last to be satisfied, in a grand, new, original melodrama called Pope Clement, or the Cardinal's Collapse.
> *Whyte Melville*, White Rose, II. xxviii.

> A man may be *puffed* and belauded, envied, ridiculed, counted upon as a tool, and fallen in love with, or at least selected as a future husband, and yet remain virtually unknown.
> *George Eliot*, Middlemarch, xv.

> Steele *puffed* him [Estcourt] in the Spectator, and wept over his decease in the same periodical.
> *Ashton*, Social Life in Reign of Queen Anne, II. 19.

puff (puf), *n.* [< ME. *puf* = D. *pof*, *bof* = MLG. *puf* = G. *puff* = Sw. Dan. *puf*, a puff; OF. *pouf*, F. *pouf*, a kind of head-dress, a low seat or ottoman, a puff (advertisement); W. *pwff*, a puff; ult. imitative: see *puff*, *v.*] **1.** A sharp, forcible blast; a whiff; a sudden emission, as of air from the mouth, or smoke from the stack of an engine; also, as much as is suddenly so emitted at one time.

> For not one *puffe* of winde there did appeare.
> *Spenser*, F. Q., II. xii. 22.

> The young Cardinal of Guise died, being struck down by the *Puff* of a Cannon-bullet, which put him in a burning Fever.
> *Howell*, Letters, I. iii. 5.

> At length a *puff* of northern wind
> Did blow him to the land.
> *Young Bearwell* (Child's Ballads, IV. 303).

2. A puffball.—**3.** An inflated, swollen, light, fluffy, or porous thing or part. (*a*) In *dressmaking*, a strip of some fabric gathered and sewed down on both edges, but left full in the middle.

> Long *Puffes* of Yellow and Blewe Sarcenet rising vp betwixt the Panes, besides Codpieces of the like colours.
> *Coryat*, Crudities, I. 41, sig. E.

> The duchess wears a fine gauze dress, trimmed with *puffs* and rosettes of satin.
> *The Century*, XXXIX. 265.

(*b*) A light, porous, spongy, or friable cake, generally filled with preserve or the like: as, cream-*puffs*; jam-*puffs*.

> "Tom," said Maggie, as they sat on the boughs of the elder-tree, eating their jam-*puffs*, "shall you run away to-morrow?"
> *George Eliot*, Mill on the Floss, i. 6.

4. An implement consisting of swan's down or a wad of flossy or loose texture, used for applying powder to the hair or skin. See *powder-puff*.—**5.** Exaggerated or undue praise uttered or written from an interested point of view; especially, a written commendation of a book, an actor's or a singer's performance, a tradesman's goods, or the like.

> My American *puffs* I would willingly burn all
> (They're all from one source, monthly, weekly, diurnal)
> To get but a kick from a transmarine journal!
> *Lowell*, Fable for Critics.

6. One who is puffed up; an inflated, conceited person.

> The other, a strange arrogating *puff*,
> Both impudent and ignorant enough.
> B. *Jonson*, Cynthia's Revels, iii. 2.

> A very *puff*, a weak animal. *Shirley*, Love Tricks, ii. 2.

7. One who writes puffs.—**8.** A small vessel with minute openings for scattering liquid perfumes. *Rev. George Ormsby*, Jour. Brit. Archæol. Ass., XXII. 404.

puff (puf), *interj.* [See *puff*, *v.*] An exclamation of contempt or impatience.

> *Puff!* did not I take him nobly?
> *Beau. and Fl.*, King and No King, i. 1.

puff-adder (puf'ad"ėr), *n.* The largest and most venomous African serpent of the family *Viperidæ*, *Clotho arietans*. It lies with its body partly immersed in the sand, its head only being exposed, so that pedestrians are liable to tread on it. It is sluggish in its nature, and the Bushman will fearlessly put his foot on its neck, and then cut off its head for the sake of its venom, with which he poisons his arrows. It is, when full-grown, from 4 to 5 feet long, and as thick as a man's arm. It is named from its habit of puffing up the upper part of its body when irritated. See cut under *Viperidæ*. Compare *puffing-adder*.

puffball (puf'bâl), *n.* Any one of various gasteromycetous fungi, especially of the genus *Lycoperdon*: so called from their habit of puffing or suddenly discharging a cloud of spores when they are shaken or squeezed after the chamber in which the spores develop breaks

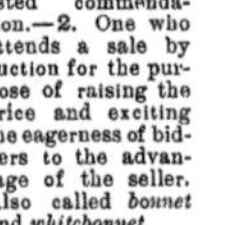

Puff-bird (*Malacoptila fusca*).

open. See *Fungi*, *Gasteromycetes*, and *Lycoperdon*; see also *fist-ball*[2], *foist*[1], *fuzzball*, *earthpuff*, *Bovista* (with cut), *blind-Harry*, *blindman's-buff*, *deil's snuff-box* (under *deil*), *devil's snuff-box* (under *devil*), and cut under *basidium*.—**Giant puffball**, a fungus, *Lycoperdon giganteum*, which often grows to a large size, having been known to attain a diameter of 5 feet. It is edible when young, and the mature dry spores may be used to stanch slight wounds.

puff-bird (puf'bėrd), *n.* Any fissirostral barbet of the American family *Bucconidæ*: so called from its habit of puffing up the plumage. See cut in preceding column, also *barbet*[2], *Bucco*, and cut under *nun-bird*.

puff-box (puf'boks), *n.* A box designed to contain toilet-powder and a puff. It is often made an ornamental article for the toilet-table.

puffed (puft), *a.* [< *puff* + *-ed*[2].] In *costume*, gathered up into rounded ridges, as a sleeve, or one leg of a pair of hose.—**Puffed and slashed armor**, armor of the middle of the sixteenth century, in which the peculiar stuffed forms of the puffed and slashed dresses of the time are imitated.

Puffed and Slashed Costume.

puffer (puf'ėr), *n.* [< *puff* + *-er*[1].] **1.** One who puffs; one who praises with exaggerated and interested commendation.—**2.** One who attends a sale by auction for the purpose of raising the price and exciting the eagerness of bidders to the advantage of the seller. Also called *bonnet* and *whitebonnet*.

> Upon the suspicion that the plaintiff was a *puffer*, the question was put whether any *puffers* were present.
> *Lord Chan. Eldon* (1806), Mason v. Armitage, 13 Ves. [25, 37.

> Puffing, it has been said, is illegal, even if there be only one *puffer*.
> *Encyc. Brit.*, III. 60.

3. A fish that swells or puffs up; specifically, any member of either of the plectognath families *Tetrodontidæ* and *Diodontidæ*, all of whose species, some eighty in number, have the habit of inflating themselves with air which they swallow; a swell-fish or globe-fish; a blower. The common puffer or swell-fish, *Sphæroides maculatus* or *Tetrodon turgidus*, is a good example. The tambor or smooth puffer is *Lagocephalus lævigatus*. The rough puffer is *Chilomycterus schœpfi* or *geometricus*. See cuts under *Diodon*, *swell-fish*, and *Tetrodontidæ*.

4. A porpoise or puffing-pig.—**5.** In *weaving*, a vat in which linen and cotton cloth is cleansed by boiling; a bucking-keir.

puffer-pipe (puf'ėr-pīp), *n.* In *weaving*, the central pipe of a bucking-keir, from the top of which water is discharged over the cloth.

puffery (puf'ėr-i), *n.* [< *puff* + *-ery*.] Systematic puffing; extravagant praise.

> I have reviewed myself incessantly,
> Nay, made a contract with a kindred spirit
> For mutual interchange of *puffery*.
> Gods! how we blew each other!
> *W. E. Aytoun*, Firmilian.

puff-fish (puf'fish), *n.* A puffer or swell-fish.

puffily (puf'i-li), *adv.* In a puffy manner.

puffin (puf'in), *n.* [Said to be so called from its puffed-out beak; < *puff* + *-in*, appar. a dim. termination. The NL. *Puffinus*, also *Puphinus*, is from E.] **1.** A sea-parrot, colter-neb, or bottle-

Common Puffin (*Fratercula arctica*).

nosed auk; a bird of the family *Alcidæ* and genus *Fratercula* or *Lunda*. See these words. There are several species. The common puffin is *F. arc-*

tica, which abounds on both coasts of the North Atlantic, nesting in holes in the ground. It is about 12 inches long, of a blackish color above, white below, with a black collar and gray face; the bill is very curious — bright-red, blue, and yellow, extremely high, narrow, and furrowed; the feet are small, placed far back, red; the eyelids are carunculate; the wings and tail are short. The bird flies swiftly and dives well. The whole horny covering of the beak and the caruncles of the eyelids are regularly molted. *F. glacialis* and *F. corniculata* are closely related; the latter has the fleshy process of the eyelid elongated into a

Head of Tufted Puffin (*Lunda cirrata*).

horn. *Lunda cirrata* is the tufted puffin, quite different, inhabiting the North Pacific, with a long tuft of yellow plumes on each side of the head, the coloration mostly blackish, with white face, and the beak peculiar in shape.

What shall we do with this same *puffin* here,
Now he 's on the spit? B. Jonson, Alchemist, iii. 2.

2. A kind of fungus; a fuzzball; a puffball. —**Crested puffin**, the tufted puffin.—**Manx puffin†**, or **puffin of the Isle of Man†**, the manx shearwater, *Puffinus anglorum*. *Willughby*.

puffin-apple†, *n.* A variety of apple. *B. Jonson.*

Puffineæ (pu-fin'ē-ē), *n. pl.* [NL., < *Puffinus* + *-eæ*.] A division of *Procellariinæ*, represented by the genus *Puffinus* in a broad sense; the shearwaters.

puffiness (puf'i-nes), *n.* A puffy or turgid character or state.

Some of Voltaire's pieces are so swelled with this presumptuous *puffiness* that I was forced into abatements of the disposition I once felt to look upon him as a generous thinker. A. Hill.

puffing (puf'ing), *n.* [Verbal n. of *puff*, *v.*] 1. The practice of writing or publishing puffs, or uncritical or venal praises of another person's productions or wares.

Puffing is of various sorts: the principal are the puff direct, the puff preliminary, the puff collateral, the puff collusive, and the puff oblique, or puff by implication. These all assume, as circumstances require, the various forms of letter to the editor, occasional anecdote, impartial critique, observation from correspondent, or advertisement from the party. Sheridan, Critic, i. 2.

2. In *costume*, one or more ridges or ribs intended for ornament; ornamentation by means of such ridges. See *puffed*.—3. In gasteromycetous fungi, the sudden discharging of a cloud of spores. See *puffball*.

puffing-adder (puf'ing-ad"ėr), *n.* A hog-nosed snake or blowing viper; any one of several species of the genus *Heterodon* (which see). They are ugly snakes of threatening aspect, but quite harmless. [Local, U. S.]

puffingly (puf'ing-li), *adv.* In a puffing manner.

puffing-pig (puf'ing-pig), *n.* A porpoise: so called from its blowing or puffing as it comes to the surface of the water.

Puffinuria (puf-i-nū'ri-ä), *n.* [NL. (Lesson, 1828), < *Puffinus* + *Uria*.] In *ornith.*, same as *Pelecanoides*.

Puffinus (puf'i-nus), *n.* [NL. (Brisson, 1760, after Gesner, etc.), < E. *puffin*: see *puffin*.] A genus of *Procellariidæ*, characterized by the short low nasal tubes obliquely truncate at the end, and with a thick septum, a long, comparatively slender, and much-hooked beak, thin pointed wings, very short tail, and large feet; the shearwaters. There are numerous species, found on all seas, some of them known as *hags* or *hagdens*. The greater shearwater is *P. major*, widely distributed over the Atlantic; the cinereous shearwater is *P. kuhli* of the Mediterranean. The Manx shearwater is *P. anglorum*; the dusky, *P. obscurus*; the sooty, *P. fuliginosus*. See cut under *hagden*.

puffkin† (puf'kin), *n.* [< *puff* + *-kin*.] A fungous excrescence; a worthless dustball; hence, a light, worthless person.

And now and then too, when the fit 's come on 'em,
Will prove themselves but flirts and tirliry-*puffkins*.
Ford, Lady's Trial, iii. 1.

puffleg (puf'leg), *n.* A humming-bird of the genus *Eriocnemis*: so called from the white fleecy tufts or puffs about the legs. See cut under *Eriocnemis*.

puff-netting (puf'net"ing), *n.* Same as *leaf-netting*.

puff-paste (puf'pāst), *n.* In *cookery*, a rich dough for making the light friable covers of tarts, etc.

puffroar†, *n.* A noisy blast. [Rare.]

East, weast, and South-wynd with *puffroare* mightelye ramping. Stanihurst, Æneid, ii.

puff-wig† (puf'wig), *n.* A fluffy kind of wig.

Here, sirrah, here 's ten guineas for thee; get thyself a drugget suit and a *puff-wig*, and so I dub thee gentleman-usher. Farquhar, The Inconstant, i. 1.

puff-wing† (puf'wing), *n.* A puffed-up part of a dress, rising from the shoulders, and resembling a wing.

You shall see them flock about you with their *puff-wings*, and ask you where you bought your lawn. B. Jonson, Poetaster, iv. 1.

puffy (puf'i), *a.* [< *puff* + *-y*1.] 1. Swollen, as with air or some soft substance; puffed up; tumid; soft: as, a *puffy* tumor.

A very stout *puffy* man in buckskins and Hessian boots. Thackeray, Vanity Fair, iii.

2. Tumid; turgid; bombastic: as, a *puffy* style.

He lives at a high sail, that the *puffy* praises of his neighbours may blow him into the enchanted island, vainglory. Rev. T. Adams, Works, I. 486.

Nor [could] the tickling sense of applause and vaine-glory [make me stoop so low as] to affect the *puffy* name and title of an Orator. Dr. H. More, Immortal. of Soul, Ep. Ded.

There is a man, . . .
Better than you, or all your *puffy* race,
That better would become the great battalion.
Dryden, Duke of Guise, ii. 2.

3. Coming in puffs; characterized by puffs; gusty.

We were running wing and wing before a very fresh and *puffy* wind. The Century, XXVIII. 106.

pug1 (pug), *n.* [A var. of *puck*. Cf. *bug*1. As applied to a monkey, fox, or little dog, it means 'a little imp': so called in allusion to its pert, ugly face.] 1†. An elf; fairy; goblin; sprite: same as *puck*, 1.

In John Milesius any man may reade
Of Divels in Sarmatia honored
Call'd Kottri or Kibaldi; such as wee
Pugs and hobgoblins call. Their dwellings bee
In corners of old houses least frequented,
Or beneath stacks of wood; and these convented
Make fearfull noise in buttries and in dairies.
Robin good-fellows some, some call them fairies.
Heywood, Hierarchy of Angels, ix. 574. (Nares.)

2. A monkey.

Poor *pug* was caught; to town convey'd;
There sold. How envy'd was his doom,
Made captive in a lady's room! Gay, Fables, i. 14.

3. A fox.

Some well-known haunts of *pug*. Kingsley, Yeast, i.

4. A dwarf variety of dog; a pug-dog.

All at once a score of *pugs*
And poodles yell'd within.
Tennyson, Edwin Morris.

5. A term of familiarity or endearment, like *duck*, etc.

Good *pugge*, give me some capon.
Marston, Antonio and Mellida, I., ii. 1.

The first I called sweet duck; the second, deare heart; the third, prettie *pugge*.
Marston, Antonio and Mellida, II., iii. 4.

6. A three-year-old salmon. *Halliwell.* [Prov. Eng.]—7. One of certain small geometrid moths: an English collectors' name. The netted pug is *Eupithecia venosata*; the foxglove-pug is *E. pulchellata*.—8†. A short cloak worn by ladies about the middle of the eighteenth century.

pug2 (pug), *n.* [Abbr. of *pug-nose*.] A pug-nose; the form or turn of a pug-nose: as, a decided *pug*. [Colloq.]

pug3 (pug), *v. t.*; pret. and pp. *pugged*, ppr. *pugging*. [A var. of *poke*.] 1. To thrust; strike. *Halliwell.* [Prov. Eng.]—2. In *building*: (*a*) To tamp with clay, or stop with puddle; clay. (*b*) To line (spaces between floor-joists) or cover (partition-walls) with coarse mortar, felt, sawdust, or any other material to impede the passage of sound; deaden; deafen.—3. In *pottery-* and *brick-manuf.*, to grind, as clay, with water in order to render it plastic.

The mixing and *pugging* apparatus is 23.6 inches in diameter at the feed end, and diminishes to 20.7 inches at the delivery end. Ure, Dict., IV. 531.

pug3 (pug), *n.* [See *pug*3, *v.*] 1. Clay ground and worked or kneaded with water, and sometimes with other substances, into consistency for molding, as into bricks, etc.—2. A pug-mill.

pug4† (pug), *n.* [ME. *pugge*; origin obscure.] Chaff; refuse of grain.

Mast, chastene, yeve hem *pugges* of thi corne.
Palladius, Husbondrie (E. E. T. S.), p. 99.

It can not abide rank mucke, but contenteth itselfe with rotten chaffe or *pugs*, and such like plain mullock.
Holland, tr. of Pliny, xix. 5. (Davies.)

pug5 (pug), *n.* [Hind. *pag*, foot.] The print of a foot; a footmark. See *puggi*.

pugaree (pug'a-rē), *n.* See *pugree*.

pug-dog (pug'dog), *n.* A small dog which bears a resemblance in miniature to the bulldog. It is characterized by timidity and gentleness, is often very affectionate and good-natured, and is kept only as a pet or curiosity. It is very liable to disease, from being pampered and from lack of exercise and proper food. There are different varieties of pug-dogs, some characterized by an extreme peculiarity of the jaws and teeth. Commonly called *pug*. See *Dysodus*.

pug-faced (pug'fāst), *a.* [< *pug*1 + *face* + *-ed*2.] Having a monkey-like face.

puggard†, *n.* [Perhaps an orig. misprint for **priggard*, < *prig*1 + *-ard*. Cf. *pugging*2.] A thief.

Cheators, lifters, nips, foists, *puggards*, curbers,
With all the devil's black-guard.
Middleton and Dekker, Roaring Girl, v. 1.

puggered†, *a.* An obsolete variant of *puckered*, past participle of *pucker*.

Nor are we to cavil at the red *pugger'd* attire of the turkey. Dr. H. More, Antidote against Atheism, II. xi. 1.

puggery (pug'ėr-i), *n.*; pl. *puggeries* (-iz). Same as *pugree*.

puggi (pug'i), *n.* [Hind. *pagī*, < *pag*, foot: see *pug*5.] In India, a tracker; one whose occupation is to trace thieves, etc., by their footprints.

pugging1 (pug'ing), *n.* [Verbal n. of *pug*3, *v.* In def. 1 perhaps an altered form (by some confusion) of *puddling*.] 1. The process of mixing and working clay for bricks, etc.—2. In *arch.*, any composition laid under the boards of a floor, or on partition-walls, to prevent the transmission of sound. Also called *deadening* or *deafening*.

pugging2†, *a.* [Perhaps an orig. misprint for *prigging*, < *prig*1, *v.*] Thieving.

The white sheete bleaching on the hedge,
With hey the sweet birds, O how they sing;
Doth set my *pugging* tooth an edge.
Shak., W. T., iv. 3. 7 (1623).

puggle (pug'l), *v. t.* [Freq. of *pug*3, *v.*] To stir (the fire). *Halliwell.* [Prov. Eng.]

puggree, puggry, *n.* Same as *pugree*.

pugh (pö or pûh), *interj.* [Also *puh*; a mere exclamation; cf. *phew*, *pooh*, etc.] An exclamation of contempt, disdain, or disgust.

pugil1 (pū'jil), *n.* [= Sp. *púgil* = Pg. *pugil* = It. *pugile*, a boxer, < L. *pugil*, a boxer, one who fights with the fists, < *pugnus* (√ *pug*), fist. Cf. *pugil*2, *pugnacious*, etc.] A boxer; a pugilist.

He was no little one, but saginati corporis bellus, as Curtius says of Dioxippus the *pugil*.
Bp. Hacket, Abp. Williams, i. 37. (Davies.)

pugil2 (pū'jil), *n.* [= It. *pugillo*, a pinch, < L. *pugillus*, *pugillum*, a handful, dim., < *pugnus* (√ *pug*), fist: see *pugil*1.] As much as can be taken up between the thumb and the first two fingers; a pinch. [Obsolete or archaic.]

Take violets, and infuse a good *pugill* of them in a quart of vinegar. Bacon, Nat. Hist., § 17.

The old gentleman . . . at last extracted an ample round snuff-box. I looked as he opened it and felt for the wonted *pugil*. O. W. Holmes, Autocrat, iv.

pugilism (pū'ji-lizm), *n.* [< *pugil*1 + *-ism*.] The art or practice of boxing or fighting with the fists.

The writing is a kind of *pugilism* — the strokes being made straight out from the shoulder.
Howells, Venetian Life, vii.

pugilist (pū'ji-list), *n.* [= F. *pugiliste* = Pg. *pugilista*; as *pugil*1 + *-ist*.] A boxer; one who fights with his fists.

pugilistic (pū-ji-lis'tik), *a.* [< *pugilist* + *-ic*.] Of or pertaining to pugilists or pugilism; relating to boxing or fighting with the fists.

Gentlemen of the *pugilistic* profession are exceedingly apt to keep their vital fire burning with the blower up.
O. W. Holmes, Autocrat, vi.

pugilistically (pū-ji-lis'ti-kal-i), *adv.* In a pugilistic manner; with reference to pugilism.

The record of these gentlemen, like my own, proves that we are, *pugilistically* speaking, men of peace.
The Century, XXXIX. 655.

pugillares (pū-ji-lā'rēz), *n. pl.* [L. *pugillares* (sc. *libelli*), or *pugillaria*, neut. pl., tablets; also *ceræ pugillares*, waxen tablets; pl. of *pugillaris*, that can be held in the hand: see *pugillaris*.] In *Rom. antiq.*, writing-tablets. See *triptych*.

pugillaria, *n. pl.* See *pugillares*.

pugillaris (pū-ji-lā'ris), *n.*; pl. *pugillares* (-rēz). [ML., < L. *pugillaris*, that can be held in the hand, < *pugillus*, a handful: see *pugil*2.] The eucharistic calamus or fistula. See *calamus*, 4.

pugioniform (pū-ji-on'i-fôrm), *a.* [< L. *pugio(n-)*, a dagger (< *pugnus* (√ *pug*), fist: see *poniard*), + *forma*, form.] In *bot.*, having the shape of a dagger.

pug-mill (pug'mil), *n.* A machine for mixing and tempering clay. A common form consists of a hollow iron cylinder, generally set upright, with a revolving shaft in the line of its axis, carrying several knives arranged in a spiral manner round the shaft, with their edges somewhat depressed. The clay is thrown in at the top of the cylinder, cut and kneaded by the knives in its downward progress, and finally forced out through a hole in the bottom of the cylinder.

Pugnaces (pug-nā'sēz), *n. pl.* [NL., pl. of L. *pugnax* (*pugnac-*), combative: see *pugnacious*.] An old division of domestic dogs, including those notable for their fighting qualities, as mastiffs and bulldogs: distinguished from *Celeres* and *Sagaces*.

pugnacious (pug-nā'shus), *a.* [< L. *pugnax* (*pugnac-*), combative, < *pugnare*, fight, < *pugnus*, fist. Cf. *pugil*[1], *pugil*[2].] Disposed to fight; quarrelsome; given to fighting: as, a *pugnacious* fellow; a *pugnacious* disposition.

A furious, *pugnacious* pope, as Julius II.
Barrow, Pope's Supremacy.

The mistress of the *pugnacious* quadruped entered to the rescue. *Barham*, Ingoldsby Legends, I. 33.

=**Syn.** Contentious.

pugnaciously (pug-nā'shus-li), *adv.* [< *pugnacious* + *-ly*[2].] In a pugnacious manner.

pugnaciousness (pug-nā'shus-nes), *n.* [< *pugnacious* + *-ness*.] Pugnacity. [Rare.]

pugnacity (pug-nas'i-ti), *n.* [= F. *pugnacité* = Sp. *pugnacidad* = Pg. *pugnacidade*, < L. *pugnacita(t-)s*, combativeness, quarrelsomeness, < *pugnax* (*pugnac-*), combative: see *pugnacious*.] The quality of being pugnacious; disposition to fight; quarrelsomeness.

I like better that entry of truth which cometh peaceably . . . than that which cometh with *pugnacity* and contention. *Bacon*, Advancement of Learning, ii. 177.

Keeping alive a natural *pugnacity* of character. *Motley*.

pug-nose (pug'nōz'), *n.* [< *pug*[1], *pug*[2], + *nose*.] 1. A nose turned upward at the tip like that of the pug-dog; a snub-nose.

Then half arose,
From beside his toes,
His little pug-dog with his little *pug-nose*.
Barham, Ingoldsby Legends, I. 55.

2. The pug-nosed eel. See *eel* and *Simenchelys*.

pug-nosed (pug'nōzd), *a.* [< *pug*[1] + *nose* + *-ed*[2].] Having a pug-nose.—**Pug-nosed eel.** See *eel*.

pug-piles (pug'pīlz), *n. pl.* Piles mortised into one another by a dovetail-joint. Also called *dovetailed piles*.

pug-piling (pug'pī"ling), *n.* Dovetailed piling.

pugree (pug'rē), *n.* [Also *puggree*, *puggery*, *pugaree*, etc.; < Hind. *pagri*, a turban.] A scarf of cotton or silk wound round the hat or helmet like a turban to protect the head from the sun. [Anglo-Indian.]

With a little pulling and wrenching, and the help of my long, tough turban-cloth, a real native *pugree*, we set and bound the arm as best we could.
F. M. Crawford, Mr. Isaacs, x.

puh†, *interj.* Same as *pooh*. *Shak.*, Hamlet (folio 1623), i. 3.

I am careless what the fusty world speaks of me. *Puh!*
B. Jonson, Every Man out of his Humour, iii. 1.

puisne (pū'ne), *a.* and *n.* [An archaic form of *puny*, retained in legal use: see *puny*[1].] **I.** *a.* 1. In *law*, younger or inferior in rank.

An old gentleman . . . declaiming against the times, and treating them and their *puisny* advocate with more contempt than either one or the other seemed to deserve.
Observer, No. 82.

2†. Later.

If he undergo any alteration, it must be in time, or of a *puisne* date to eternity. *Sir M. Hale*.

3†. Same as *puny*[1], 2.—**Mulier puisne.** See *mulier*[2].—**Puisne judge.** See *judge*. [Eng.]

II. *n.* A junior; an inferior; specifically, in *law*, a judge of inferior rank.

Each odd *puisne* of the lawyer's inn,
Each barmy-froth, that last day did begin
To read his little, or his ne'er a whit.
Marston, Scourge of Villanie, To the Reader.

This 'tis for a *puisne*
In policy's Protean school to try conclusions
With one that hath commenced, and gone out doctor.
Massinger, Duke of Milan, iv. 1.

If still this privilege were ordinarily left in the Church, it were not a work for *puisnes* and novices, but for the greatest masters, and most learned and eminently holy doctors, which the times can possibly yield.
Bp. Hall, Invisible World, iii. § 9.

Lord Chief Justice Coke did not pass sentence on Mrs. Turner; that grim office was performed by his *puisne*, Croke, J. *N. and Q.*, 7th ser., IX. 263.

puisny†, *a.* Same as *puisne*, *puny*[1]. [Rare.]

puissance (pū'i-sans), *n.* [< ME. *puyssance*, *puyssaunce*, < OF. *puissance*, *poissance*, F. *puissance*, power, < *puissant*, powerful: see *puissant*.] 1. Power; strength; force; vigor.

Thei were moche peple and riche lordes of grete *puyssance*, and ther-to were thei well horsed.
Merlin (E. E. T. S.), ii. 232.

With what help and aid the virtues resist and overcome the *puissance* of the vices.
Sir T. More, Utopia (tr. by Robinson), ii. 4.

Commonly ciuil and popular warres decay in *puisance*, preuaile sildome, and may not indure.
Guevara, Letters (tr. by Hellowes, 1577), p. 248.

His hart did earne
To prove his *puissance* in battell brave.
Spenser, F. Q., I. i. 3.

Leave your England, as dead midnight still,
Guarded with grandsires, babies, and old women,
Either past or not arrived to pith and *puissance*.
Shak., Hen. V., iii., Prol., l. 21.

Still from time to time
Came murmurs of her beauty from the South,
And of her brethren, youths of *puissance*.
Tennyson, Princess, i.

2†. Jurisdiction; power; control.

The educacion of childeren should not altogeather be vnder the *puissaunce* of their fathers, but vnder the publique power and aucthority, becawse the publique haue therein more Intereste then their parentes.
Booke of Precedence (E. E. T. S., extra ser.), i. 11.

3†. Armed force.

Than, with the firste *puyssaunce* that we may make, lete vs distroye the vitaile fro them thourgh the contreye, and lete vs sette in eche garuyson as moche peple as we may.
Merlin (E. E. T. S.), ii. 174.

All the *puyssance* that was sent by Kyng Philyppe . . . they were all discomfytted and slayne.
Berners, tr. of Froissart's Chron., I. 731.

Cousin, go draw our *puissance* together.
Shak., K. John, iii. 1. 339.

puissant (pū'i-sant), *a.* [< ME. *puyssant*, *puysaunt*, *pusant*, < OF. *puissant*, *poissant*, F. *puissant* = It. *possente*, powerful, < ML. as if **possen(t-)s*, for L. *poten(t-)s*, ppr. of *posse*, be able: see *potent*.] Powerful; mighty; strong; vigorous; forcible: as, a *puissant* prince or empire.

Which fele letters brought with breffes many
Of Anthony hys part, a *pusant* man tho.
Rom. of Partenay (E. E. T. S.), l. 2683.

The flemynges were beyond the ryuer *puyssaunt* ynough . . . to kepe the passage.
Berners, tr. of Froissart's Chron., I. 721.

I will be *puissant*,
And mighty in my talk to her.
B. Jonson, Alchemist, v. 1.

Puissant is the Danish king, and strong
In all the sinews of approved force.
Ford, Honour Triumphant, Monarchs' Meeting.

Lofn is as *puissant* a divinity in the Norse Edda as Camadeva in the red vault of India, Eros in the Greek, or Cupid in the Latin heaven. *Emerson*, Success.

puissantly (pū'i-sant-li), *adv.* In a puissant manner; powerfully; potently.

Mahomet, a man subtile in witte, of valiant hearte, and fortunate in exployt of war, as he manifested most *puissantly* by obteyning more honour than any other in the campe. *Guevara*, Letters (tr. by Hellowes, 1577), p. 326.

puissantness (pū'i-sant-nes), *n.* Puissance; power; strength.

The emperour . . . hath bene driuen to extreme shiftes, and that by the pollicie of mean men who were thought to be hys frendes, and not by the *puissantnes* of others who were knowne to be his open enemys.
Ascham, Affairs of Germany, p. 3.

puist, puistie (püst, pūs'ti), *a.* [< *poust*, *n.*] In easy circumstances; well-to-do: said of persons of the lower classes who have made money. [Scotch.]

puit[1] (pū'it), *n.* Same as *pewit* (*b*). [Eng.]

puit[2]† (püt), *n.* [< F. *puits* = Pr. *potz*, *poutz* = Sp. *pozo* = Pg. *poço* = It. *pozzo*, < L. *puteus*, a well: see *pit*[1].] A spring; a fountain; a well; a rill.

The *puits* flowing from the fountains of life.
Jer. Taylor.

puka-puka (pö'kä-pö'kä), *n.* [New Zealand.] A small branching composite tree, *Senecio Forsteri*, of New Zealand. Its leaves are very large, sometimes a foot long, and used by the natives as paper, whence *puka-puka* has become the native word for common paper.

puke[1] (pūk), *v.*; pret. and pp. *puked*, ppr. *puking*. [Origin obscure; perhaps for **spuke* or **speuk*, extended form of *spew*. Cf. G. *spucken*, spit.] **I.** *intrans.* 1. To vomit; eject the contents of the stomach.

The infant
Mewling and *puking* in the nurse's arms.
Shak., As you Like it, ii. 7. 144.

2. To sicken; be overcome with loathing.

As one of Woodward's patients, sick and sore,
I *puke*, I nauseate—yet he thrusts in more.
Pope, Satires of Donne, iv. 153.

II. *trans.* 1. To vomit; throw up; eject from the stomach: generally with *up*.—2. To cause to puke or vomit.

puke[1] (pūk), *n.* [< *puke*[1], *v.*] 1. Vomit; a vomiting; that which is vomited.—2. An emetic.—3. A disgusting person. [Low.]—4. [*cap.*] An inhabitant of the State of Missouri. [Vulgar, U. S.]

puke[2]† (pūk), *a.* and *n.* [Formerly also *pewke*; < ME. *puke*; appar. an unassibilated form of *puce*.] **I.** *a.* Of a dark color, said to be reddish brown.

The coulour of this camell is for the most part browne, or *puke*. *Topsell*, Four-footed Beasts. (*Halliwell*.)

II. *n.* A dark color between russet and black; puce.

I wolde in alle hast possible have that same gowne of *puke* ffurryd with whyght lambe. *Paston Letters*, III. 153.

You shall doe well to send fiue or sixe broad clothes, some blackes, *pukes*, or other sad colours.
Hakluyt's Voyages, I. 357.

puker (pū'kėr), *n.* 1. One who pukes or vomits.—2†. A medicine which causes vomiting; an emetic.

The griper senna, and the *puker* rue,
The sweetener sassafras, are added too.
Garth, Dispensary, iii.

puke-stocking† (pūk'stok'ing), *a.* Wearing puke-colored stockings. [Rare.]

Wilt thou rob this leathern jerkin, crystal-button, notpated, agate-ring, *puke-stocking*, caddis-garter?
Shak., 1 Hen. IV., ii. 4. 78.

puke-weed (pūk'wēd), *n.* The officinal lobelia, *Lobelia inflata*, once much employed as an emetic.

puking-fever (pū'king-fē"vėr), *n.* Same as *milk-sickness*.

pukish† (pū'kish), *a.* [< *puke*[2] + *-ish*[1].] Of the color called puke.

I saw my selfe old Ganadie,
About twelve of the clocke,
Bare foote, hyr lockes about her heade,
Ytuckde in *pukishe* pocke.
Drant, tr. of Horace's Satires, viii.

pulas (pu-las'), *n.* [Hind. *palāsh*, *palās*.] An East Indian tree, *Butea frondosa*; also, *B. superba*, which differs chiefly in its climbing habit. Also *palas*, and *pulas-tree*. See *Butea* and *kino*[1].

pulas-oil (pu-las'oil), *n.* Same as *moodooga-oil*.

pulas-tree (pu-las'trē), *n.* Same as *pulas*.

pulchrious†, *a.* [ME. *pulcrious*, < L. *pulcher*, *pulcer*, beautiful, + *-ious*.] Beauteous; beautiful; fair.

The seffe child Ffromont that time callyd was,
Of stature of persone hie, gret, and long,
Inly wel formed, *pulcrious* of face,
Sage, subtile, wel taught, myghty and stronge.
Rom. of Partenay (E. E. T. S.), l. 1263.

pulchritude (pul'kri-tūd), *n.* [< ME. *pulcritude*, < OF. **pulcritude* = Sp. *pulcritud* = Pg. *pulchritude*, < L. *pulchritudo*, *pulcritudo*, beauty, < *pulcher*, *pulcer*, OL. *polcer*, beautiful.] Beauty; comeliness; handsomeness.

Persing our hartes with thi *pulcritude*.
Court of Love, l. 613.

Themistius . . . maintain'd an Opinion that . . . the *Pulchritude* and Preservation of the World consisted in Varieties and Dissimilitudes. *Howell*, Letters, iii. 20.

The queen, when she had view'd
The strange eye-dazzling admirable sight,
Fain would have prais'd the state and *pulchritude*.
Sir J. Davies, Dancing.

What more than heavenly *pulchritude* is this?
B. Jonson, Every Man out of his Humour, ii. 1.

puldron†, *n.* An obsolete form of *pauldron*.

pule (pūl), *v.*; pret. and pp. *puled*, ppr. *puling*. [Formerly also *pewl*, *peule*; < OF. *piuler*, *pioler*, *piauler*, < F. *piauler*, chirp, pule; cf. It. *pigolare*, chirp, moan; imitative words; cf. *pipe*[1], *peep*[1], etc., *pue*[2], etc.] **I.** *intrans.* 1. To peep or pipe plaintively, as a chick.—2. To cry as a complaining child; whine; whimper.

The poore silly Soules *pewling* out of Purgatory.
Sir T. More, Tracts (Utopia, Int., p. xcvii.).

A wretched *puling* fool. *Shak.*, R. and J., iii. 5. 185.

Thou 'rt such a *puling* thing! wipe your eyes and rise; go your ways. *Beau. and Fl.*, Coxcomb, iv. 7.

Wherefore should I *pule*, and, like a girl,
Put finger in the eye? *Ford*, Broken Heart, v. 2.

All the wisdom of the ages will avail it nothing if it *pule* in discontent and fret in nervous sickness.
N. A. Rev., CXLII. 145.

II.† *trans.* To utter in a whining or querulous manner: with *out*.

I say "You love"; you *peule* me out a No.
Drayton, Ideas, v.

puler (pū'lėr), *n.* One who pules or whines; a sickly, complaining person.

If she be pale of complexion, she will prove but a *puler*; is she high coloured, an ill cognizance.
The Man in the Moone (1609), sig. G. (*Halliwell*.)

Pulex (pū'leks), *n.* [NL. (Linnæus, 1735), < L. *pulex*, a flea.] 1. A notable genus of insects, typical of the *Pulicidæ*, or flea family. They lead a semi-parasitic life upon man and other animals. The larvæ feed on refuse, and are slender and whitish. Many species are known. *P. irritans* is the common flea which infests man. *P. canis* is found upon the cat and the dog. See cut under *flea*[1].

2. [*l. c.*] A flea, or some similar creature.—**Pulex arborescens**†, arborescent flea, an old name of any water-flea with branched horns—that is, of any cladocerous crustacean.

puliall†, *n.* See *puliol.*

puliall-mountain†, *n.* Same as *pella-mountain.*

pulic (pū'lik), *n.* [Shortened from NL. *Pulicaria.*] In *bot.*, a plant of the genus *Pulicaria*; fleabane.

Pulicaria (pū-li-kā'ri-ä), *n.* [NL. (Gärtner, 1791), < LL. *pulicaria*, a plant, also called *psyllion* (from the supposed power of the smoke of *P. dysenterica* to drive away fleas), < L. *pulex*, a flea.] A genus of composite herbs of the tribe *Inuloideæ* and subtribe *Euinuleæ.* It is characterized by a long inner pappus of one row of bristles, a very short outer pappus more or less united into a crown or a fringed cup, a broad involucre of narrow bracts in but few rows, yellow ray-flowers in one or two rows, and either smooth or ribbed achenes. Some species have the appearance of *Inula*, the elecampane, which is distinguished by its nearly uniform pappus. There are about 30 species, natives of Europe, Africa, and Asia, especially in the Mediterranean region. They are hairy annuals or perennials, with alternate sessile leaves, and flower-heads solitary at the summits of the branches. *P. (Inula) dysenterica*, the fleabane, was once supposed to destroy fleas, and has sometimes been used to cure dysentery. Old names of the plant are *fleabane-mullet* and *herb-christopher.*

pulicat, *n.* See *pullicat.*

pulicene (pū'li-sēn), *a.* [Irreg. for **pulicine*, < L. *pulex* (*pulic-*), a flea, + *-ine*[1].] Relating to fleas; pulicous.

Pulicidæ (pū-lis'i-dē), *n. pl.* [NL. (Stephens, 1829), < *Pulex* (*Pulic-*) + *-idæ.*] The flea family, considered as either a family of *Diptera*, or the sole family of an order called *Aphaniptera* or *Siphonaptera.* Several genera are known, the principal ones being *Pulex* and *Sarcopsylla.* Insects of this family are minute, wingless, with the antennæ from three- to fourteen-jointed, mandibles long and serrate, body ovate and much compressed, two simple eyes, no compound eyes, and edges of the head and prothorax armed with stout spines directed backward. See cuts under *flea*[1] and *chigoe.*

pulicose† (pū'li-kōs), *a.* [< L. *pulicosus*, full of fleas, < *pulex* (*pulic-*), a flea.] Abounding with fleas.

pulicous† (pū'li-kus), *a.* Same as *pulicose.*

puling (pū'ling), *n.* [Verbal n. of *pule*, *v.*] A plaintive piping, as of a chicken; a whining complaint.

> Let the songs be loud and cheerful, and not chirpings or *pulings.* — Bacon, Masques and Triumphs (ed. 1887).

> What 's the news from London, sirrah? My young mistress keeps such a *puling* for a lover. — *Yorkshire Tragedy*, i. 1.

puling (pū'ling), *p. a.* Complaining; whining; crying; childish; weak.

> Come, look up bravely; put this *puling* passion
> Out of your mind.
> — *Beau. and Fl.*, Knight of Malta, ii. 3.

> Where be those *puling* fears of death, just now expressed or affected? — Lamb, New Year's Eve.

pulingly (pū'ling-li), *adv.* In a puling manner; with whining or complaint.

> I do not long to have
> My sleep ta'en from me, and go *pulingly*,
> Like a poor wench had lost her market-money.
> — *Beau. and Fl.*, Captain, iii. 1.

puliol†, *n.* [Also *pulioll*, *pulial*, *puliall*, ult. < L. *puleium*, *pulegium*, fleabane, pennyroyal, < *pulex* (*pulic-*), a flea: see *Pulex.*] Same as *pennyroyal*, 1.

puliol-royal†, *n.* [Also *puliall royal*; < ME. *puliall real*, < ML. *puleium regale*, equiv. to L. *puleium regium*, royal fleabane: see *puliol* and *royal.* Hence, by corruption, *pennyroyal.*] Same as *pennyroyal*, 1.

pulish (pū'lish), *n.* [Native name (?).] The Angola ant-thrush, *Pitta angolensis.*

pulk[1] (pulk), *n.* [Appar. a contracted dim. of *pool*[1].] A pool; a pond. [Prov. Eng.]

pulk[2], **pulkha** (pulk, pul'kä), *n.* [Lappish.] A Laplanders' traveling-sledge. It is built in the

Lapland Pulk. (From an original in the possession of the American Geographical Society.)

form of a boat, of light materials, covered with reindeer-skin. It is drawn by a single reindeer, and is used in journeying over the snow in winter.

> These *pulks* are shaped very much like a canoe; they are about five feet long, one foot deep, and eighteen inches wide, with a sharp bow and a square stern. You sit upright against the stern-board, with your legs stretched out in the bottom. — *B. Taylor*, Northern Travel, p. 103.

pulk-hole (pulk'hōl), *n.* Same as *pulk*[1].

> This underwood, with the turf in the *pulk hole* or bog lands, . . . constituted absolutely the only fuel at the beginning of the century. — *A. Jessopp*, Arcady, ii.

pull (pùl), *v.* [< ME. *pullen*, < AS. *pullian*, pull (also in comp. *āpullian*, pull), = LG. *pulen*, pick, pluck, pull, tear; cf. MD. *pullen*, drink; root unknown.] **I.** *trans.* **1.** To draw or try to draw forcibly or with effort; drag; haul; tug: opposed to *push*: generally with an adverb of direction, as *up*, *down*, *on*, *off*, *out*, *back*, etc.: as, to *pull* a chair *back*; to *pull down* a flag; to *pull* a bucket *out* of a well; to *pull off* one's coat.

> This Arcite, with ful despitous herte
> Whan he him knew, and hadde his tale herd,
> As fers as leoun *pullede out* a swerd.
> — *Chaucer*, Knight's Tale, l. 740.

> So hangs, and lolls, and weeps upon me; so hales, and *pulls* me. — *Shak.*, Othello, iv. 1. 144.

> O Night, thou *pullest* the proud Mask *away*
> Where-with vaine Actors, in this Worlds great Play,
> By Day disguise them.
> — *Sylvester*, tr. of Du Bartas's Weeks, i.

> *Pull off*, *pull off* the broach of gold,
> And fling the diamond necklace by.
> — *Tennyson*, Lady Clare.

2. To pluck; gather by hand: as, to *pull* flax; to *pull* flowers.

> He joys to *pull* the ripened pear.
> — *Dryden*, tr. of Horace's Epodes, ii.

3. To draw in such a way as to rend or tear; draw apart; rip; rend: followed by some qualifying word or phrase, such as *asunder*, *in pieces*, *apart*: also used figuratively.

> Fearing lest Paul should have been *pulled in pieces.* — Acts xxiii. 10.

> It is hardly possible to come into company where you do not find them *pulling* one another *to pieces.* — *Steele*, Spectator, No. 348.

4. To extract; draw, as a tooth or a cork.—**5.** To agitate, move, or propel by tugging, rowing, etc.: as, to *pull* a bell; to *pull* a boat.

> I have *pulled* a whale boat in the Pacific, and paddled a canoe on Lake Huron. — *Whyte Melville*, White Rose, II. vii.

> May bend the bow or *pull* the oar.
> — *Whittier*, Mogg Megone, ii.

6. To transport by rowing: as, to *pull* a passenger across the bay.

> To *pull* Lady Cramly and her daughter down the river. — *T. Hook*, Fathers and Sons, xvii.

7. In *printing*, to produce on a printing-press worked by hand; hence, to take or obtain by impression in any way: as, to *pull* a proof.

> The "copy" was quickly put in type, a proof was *pulled*, and at 10h. 50m. it was placed in my hands, exactly an hour after the observations had been made at a station nearly 3000 miles away. — *The Century*, XXXVIII. 605.

8†. To bring down; reduce; abate.

> His rank flesh shall be *pull'd* with daily fasting.
> — *Fletcher*, Wife for a Month, v. 3.

9†. To pluck; fleece; cheat.

> What plover 's that
> They have brought to *pull*?
> — *B. Jonson*, Staple of News, ii. 1.

10. In *tanning*, to remove the wool from (sheepskins), or the hair from (hides). A pulling-knife, made of steel with a rather blunt edge, is used, acting much on the principle of a scraper. It engages the hair without cutting it off, and pulls it out. The skin is spread, with the hair or wool side uppermost, on an inclined support during the process.

11. To steal; filch. [Thieves' slang.]

> We lived by thieving, and I do still—by *pulling* flesh (stealing meat). — *Mayhew*, London Labour and London Poor, I. 460.

12. To make a descent upon for the purpose of breaking up; raid; seize: as, to *pull* a gambling-house: said of police. [Slang.]—**13.** In *horse-racing*, to check or hold back (a horse) in order to keep it from winning: as, the jockey was suspected of *pulling* the horse. [Slang.]—**To pull a face**, to draw the countenance into a particular expression; grimace: as, to *pull a* long *face* (that is, to look very serious).

> The Prior and the learned *pulled a face.*
> — *Browning*, Fra Lippo Lippi.

To pull a finch†. See *finch*[1].—**To pull down.** (*a*) To take down or apart; demolish by separating and removing the parts: as, to *pull down* a house.

> *Pull* not *down* my palace towers, that are
> So lightly, beautifully built.
> — *Tennyson*, Palace of Art.

(*b*) To subvert; overthrow; demolish.

> In politicall affairs, as well as mechanical, it is farre easier to *pull down* then build up. — *Howell*, Vocall Forrest, p. 104.

> The world is full of institutions which, though they never ought to have been set up, yet, having been set up, ought not to be rudely *pulled down.* — *Macaulay*, Gladstone on Church and State.

(*c*) To abase; humble; degrade.

> Nothing *pulleth downe* a mans heart so much as aduersitie and lacke. — *Puttenham*, Arte of Eng. Poesie, p. 34.

> He *pulleth downe*, he setteth up on hy;
> He gives to this, from that he takes away.
> — *Spenser*, F. Q., V. ii. 41.

> To raise the wretched and *pull down* the proud.
> — *Roscommon*, tr. of Horace's Art of Poetry.

> The feind no sooner Jesus there did read,
> But Guilt *pull'd down* his eyes, and fear his head.
> — *J. Beaumont*, Psyche, ii. 122.

To pull down the side†, to cause the defeat of the party or side on which a person plays.

> If I hold your cards I shall *pull down the side*;
> I am not good at the game.
> — *Massinger*, Great Duke of Florence, iv. 2.

To pull in one's horns. See *horn.*—**To pull one through**, to extricate one from a difficulty.

> I am very hopeful of your regiment arriving in time to *pull us through.* — *Phantom Piquet*, Cornhill Mag., Oct., 1888.

To pull the dead horse. See *horse*[1].—**To pull the long-bow.** See *longbow.*—**To pull up.** (*a*) To pluck up; tear up, as by the roots; hence, to extirpate; eradicate; destroy.

> They shall no more be *pulled up* out of their land which I have given them. — Amos ix. 15.

> I observed that they reap their corn in these parts, whereas about Damascus they *pull* it *up* by the roots. — *Pococke*, Description of the East, II. i. 142.

(*b*) To take to task; administer reproof or admonition to; put a check upon. [Colloq.] (*c*) To arrest and take before a court of justice. [Colloq.] (*d*) To bring to a stop by means of the reins: as, to *pull up* a horse when driving or riding. Hence—(*e*) To stop or arrest in any course of conduct, especially in a bad course.=**Syn.** 1. To drag.—2. To gather.

II. *intrans.* To give a pull; tug; draw with strength and force: as, to *pull* at a rope.

> I haf gerned & ȝat ȝokkez of oxen,
> & for my hyȝes hem boȝt, to bowe haue I mester,
> To see hem *pulle* in the plow aproche me byhouez.
> — *Alliterative Poems* (ed. Morris), ii. 68.

To pull apart, to separate or break by pulling: as, a rope will *pull apart.*—**To pull for**, to row toward: as, they *pulled for* the ship or the shore.—**To pull through**, to get through any undertaking with difficulty. [Colloq.]

> I shall be all right! I shall *pull through*, my dear!
> — *Dickens*, Bleak House, xxxvii.

To pull up, to stop in riding or driving by drawing the reins; halt; stop.

> The Slogger *pulls up* at last for a moment, fairly blown.
> — *T. Hughes*, Tom Brown at Rugby, i. 5.

> Mr. Kearney *pulled up* at the outskirts of the town in front of a small general store. — *The Century*, XXXVII. 602.

pull (pùl), *n.* [< ME. *pul*; < *pull*, *v.*] **1.** The exercise of drawing power; effort exerted in hauling; a tug; drawing power or action; force expended in drawing.

> The husbandman, whose costs and pain,
> Whose hopes and helps lie buried in his grain,
> Waiting a happy Spring to ripen full
> His long'd-for harvest to the reapers' *pull.*
> — *Beau. and Fl.*, Four Plays in One, Epil.

> Particles . . . arranging themselves under the influence of the *pull* or gravity of the earth. — *Pop. Sci. Mo.*, XXIX. 46.

> An iron bar, . . . one inch square, cooled through 80° Fahr., contracts with a *pull* of fifty tons. — *W. L. Carpenter*, Energy in Nature (1st ed.), p. 46.

2. Exercise in rowing; an excursion in a row-boat: as, to have a *pull* after dinner. [Colloq.]—**3**†. A contest; a struggle.

> This wrastling *pull* between Corineus and Gogmagog.
> — *R. Carew*, Survey of Cornwall, p. 2.

4. That which is pulled. Specifically—(*a*) The lever of a counter-pump or beer-pull. (*b*) The knob and stem of a door-bell; a bell-pull.

5. Influence; advantageous hold or claim on some one who has influence: as, to have a *pull* with the police; he has a *pull* on the governor. [Slang.]

> A good feature of the ordinance is the power given to the city engineer, . . . who is too often handicapped by politicians and contractors who have a *pull* on the City Fathers. — *The Engineer*, LXV. 392.

6. A favorable chance; an advantage: as, to have the *pull* over one. [Slang.]

> Do you know, it 's a great *pull* not having married young.
> — *Whyte Melville*, White Rose, II. xxiv.

> The great *pull* that men have over us [women] is that they are supposed to do only one thing at a time.
> — *Nineteenth Century*, XXVI. 782.

7. A drink; a swig: as, to have a *pull* at the brandy-bottle. [Colloq.]

> The other hiccoughed, and sucked in a long *pull* of his hot coffee. — *Whyte Melville*, White Rose, II. ii.

> "Bre'r Torm," he said, after a long *pull* at the pitcher of persimmon beer. — *The Century*, XXXVIII. 88.

8. In *printing*, a single impression made by one pull of the bar of a hand-press.—**Candy-pull.** See *candy*[1].—**Dead pull**, in *mech.*, total pressure; impressed force.

pullaile†, *n.* [ME., < OF. *poulaille*, F. *poulaille*, poultry, < *poule*, hen, < L. *pullus*, a young animal, a chicken: see *pullet.*] Poultry.

With caleweis or with *pullayle*,
With conynges or with fyne vitaille.
Rom. of the Rose, l. 7043.

Pullastræ (pu-las'trē), *n. pl.* [NL., pl. of L. *pullastra*, a young hen, a pullet, dim. of *pullus*, a young fowl: see *pullet*.] An artificial assemblage of birds, in which those gallinaceous birds which are peristeropod or pigeon-toed, as the *Cracidæ* and *Megapodidæ*, are grouped with the true pigeons, or *Columbæ*, including the dodos.

pullastriform (pu-las'tri-fôrm), *a.* [< L. *pullastra*, a young hen, a pullet, + *forma*, form.] Same as *pullastrine*.

Pullastriform and Struthious Birds.
E. D. Cope, Origin of the Fittest, p. 122.

pullastrine (pu-las'trin), *a.* [< *Pullastræ* + *-ine*².] Pertaining to the *Pullastræ*, or having their characters.

The *Pullastrine* birds are a generalized group.
E. D. Cope, Origin of the Fittest, p. 114.

pull-back (pùl'bak), *n.* [< *pull* + *back*¹, *adv.*] 1. That which keeps one back or restrains; a drawback.

I appeal to the mind of every particular person that hears me whether he has not often found a struggle within himself, and a kind of *pullback* from the sin that he has been about to engage in. *South*, Sermons, VII. xi.

2. In modern costume for women, a contrivance by which the folds of the skirt behind were held together closely, so that the skirt in front was drawn tightly and hung straight down. It was in fashion about 1885.

pull-cock (pùl'kok), *n.* A faucet of which the lever is vertical when the outlet is closed, and is pulled forward 90° in a vertical plane to open the passage fully.

pull-devil (pùl'dev'l), *n.* A device for catching fish, made of several hooks fastened back to back, to be dragged or jerked through the water.

pulldoo (pùl'dö), *n.* [< F. *poule d'eau*, 'water-hen': *poule*, hen (see *pullet*); *de*, of (see *de*²); *eau*, water (see *ewe*²).] The American coot, *Fulica americana*. [Local, U. S.]

pull-down (pùl'doun), *n.* In *organ-building*, the wire whereby a pallet or valve is opened when its digital is depressed; a pallet-wire.

pullen† (pùl'en), *n.* [Also *pullein*, *pullain*, *pullin*, < OF. *poulain*, *puleyn*, *polan*, F. *poulain* (cf. Pr. *pollin*, *polli* = Sp. *pollino* = It. *pollino*), the young of any animal, esp. a foal, colt, < ML. *pullanus*, also, after Rom., *pullenus*, *polinus*, m., **pullana*, *pulina*, f., a foal, colt, filly, < L. *pullus*, a young animal: see *pullet*.] Poultry.

They bring up a great multitude of *pullein*, and that by a marvellous policy; for the hens do not sit upon the eggs; but by keeping them in a certain equal heat they bring life into them, and hatch them.
Sir T. More, Utopia (tr. by Robinson), ii. 1.

A false theefe
That came like a false foxe my *pullain* to kil and mischeefe. *Bp. Still*, Gammer Gurton's Needle, v. 2.

To see how pitifully the *pullen* will look, it makes me after relent, and turn my anger into a quick fire to roast 'em. *Middleton*, Your Five Gallants, ii. 1.

Luss. What, three and twenty years in law?
Vind. I haue knowne those that haue beene fiue and fifty, and all about Pullin and Pigges.
C. Tourneur, Revenger's Tragedy, iv. 2.

puller (pùl'ėr), *n.* [< *pull* + *-er*¹.] One who or that which pulls.

Peace, impudent and shameless Warwick, peace,
Proud setter up and *puller* down of kings!
Shak., 3 Hen. VI., iii. 3. 157.

Puller off, in a press or punching-machine, a forked piece which is so adjusted as to be almost in contact with the work to be stamped or punched, which it prevents from rising when the die or punch is drawn back.

pullet (pùl'et), *n.* [ME. *pulette*, *polete*, < OF. *polete*, *poulette*, F. *poulette*, a chick, young hen, dim. of *poule*, a hen, < ML. *pulla* (> OF. and F. *poule*), a young hen, fem. of L. *pullus*, a young animal, young, esp. of domestic fowls, a young fowl, a chicken, a young sprout, = E. *foal*, q. v. Cf. *poult*.] 1. A young hen.

And in this maner, ye that be auncient teachynge vs, and wee obedient, as old fathers and young *pullettes*, beeyng in the nest of the Senate. *Golden Boke*, viii.

2. A bivalve, *Tapes pullastra*, of the family *Veneridæ*, abundant in European seas, chiefly in muddy sand or sandy bottoms near tide-mark. It also occupies deserted holes, and is then apt to show distortion of the shell, which in growing adapts itself to its surroundings. When not malformed, the shell is oblong, and the valves are covered with concentric striæ becoming coarser and more wavy toward the ends, and crossed by diverging striæ.

pullet-sperm† (pùl'et-spėrm), *n.* The treadle or chalaza of an egg: so called because formerly supposed to be the sperm of the egg.

I'll no *pullet-sperm* in my brewage.
Shak., M. W. of W., iii. 5. 32.

pulley (pùl'i), *n.* [Formerly also *pully*, *pullie*; < (*a*) late ME. *polley* (= MD. *poleye* = Sp. *polea* = Pg. *polé* = It. *puleggia*, formerly also *puleggio*) (ML. *polea*, *polegia*, *polegium*), < OF. *poulie*, a pulley (Cotgrave), F. *poulie*, a pulley, block, sheave; cf. OF. *poulie*, *poullie*, a place to hang out clothes; origin uncertain; by some connected with AS. *pullian*, E. *pull*. (*b*) Cf. ME. *police*, appar., with accom. term. *-ive*, of like origin with the above. (*c*) ME. *poleyne*, a pulley, < OF. *poulain* (ML. *polanus*), a pulley-rope, a particular use of *poulain*, a colt: see *pullen*. The transfer of sense from 'colt' to 'a support' is paralleled in the use of *horse* and *easel* (lit. 'ass'), and of F. *poutre*, 'filly,' also 'beam,' *chèvre*, 'goat,' also 'crane,' and of E. *crane* itself; also by Gr. ὄνος, ass, crane, pulley.] 1. (*a*) Properly, a simple machine consisting of a wheel having a grooved rim for carrying a rope or other line, and turning in a frame, which, when movable, is termed a *pulley-block*. (*b*) A block containing several grooved wheels. (*c*) A tackle or apparatus consisting of one or more pulley-blocks with a rope or ropes reeved through them for use in hoisting. The pulley serves to balance a great force against a small one; its sole use is to produce equilibrium; it does not save work, unless indirectly in some unmechanical way. The pulley is a lever with equal arms; but when it turns, the attachments of the forces are moved. Fig. 1 shows a fixed pulley. The equal weights *d* and *e* are in equilibrium, because they hang from the equal arms of the lever *ab*, having its fulcrum at *c*. Fig. 2 illustrates the principle of the movable pulley. The equal-armed lever, with fulcrum at *c*, has on one arm the weight *d* and on the other the force of the stretched string *be*. If there is equilibrium, this force must be equal to the weight of *d*. Thus, the total downward pull on *f*, one arm of the equal-armed lever *fg*, with fulcrum at *h*, is twice the weight of *d*, which must, therefore, be the weight of *i* to keep it in balance. We may also use the axiom that when a cord is free to move along its length it must be under equal stress in all its parts. Consequently, when a movable block is supported by a number of parallel parts of the same cord,

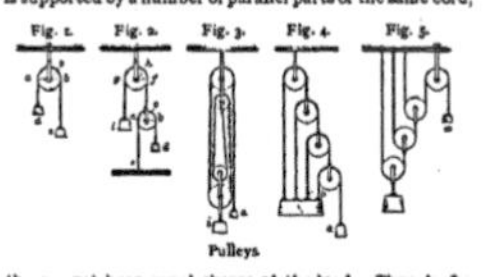

Pulleys.

these must bear equal shares of the load. Thus, in fig. 3, the lower block with the weight *b* brings equal strains upon four stretches of the cord, one of which is balanced by *a*. Consequently, the weight of *b* is four times that of *a*. But the effects of friction and of the stiffness of the cord are of great importance in the calculation of the advantages of pulleys. There is a great mechanical advantage in having separate blocks for all the movable pulleys, as in figs. 4 and 5. Thus, in fig. 4, the weight *a* is balanced over the lowest pulley by the pull on *b*, and the sum of these forces drawing down the lowest pulley is balanced over the second pulley by the pull on *c*, which is therefore double the weight at *b*. Thus, by means of four pulleys *a* balances $a + 2a + 4a + 8a = a(2^4 - 1)$, or fifteen times instead of (as by the arrangement of fig. 3) only four times its own weight. Another arrangement is shown in fig. 5. Here, by means of four pulleys, *a* balances eight times its own weight.

2. In *anat.*: (*a*) A trochlea, or trochlear surface of an articulation. (*b*) A ligamentous loop which confines or changes the direction of the tendon of a muscle passing through it: as, the digastric muscle of the chin and the superior oblique of the eye both pass through a *pulley*. See cuts under *muscle* and *eye*¹.—**Compound pulley**, a system of pulleys by which the power to raise heavy weights or overcome resistances is gained at the expense of velocity. See def. 1 (*c*).—**Conical pulley**, a cone-pulley.—**Crowning pulley**, a pulley with a convex rim, much used where from various causes belts are in danger of slipping off—the centrifugal force keeping the belt on the convexity.—**Dead pulley.** Same as *loose pulley*. [Local, Eng.]—**Differential pulley**, a peculiar machine operating upon the principle of the lever. Let AD (fig. 1) be a lever, having its fulcrum at C, half-way between A and D. From D and B (a point on AC) cords are attached to the equal arms of the lever EF, with fulcrum at G. Then, if weights are placed on A and G so as to balance one another, G is practically supported at the point half-way between B and D. The ratio of the weight at G to that at A is therefore AC:(CD − BC). The differential pulley has above one solid wheel with two grooved rims, the lower one being furnished with spikes to enter the links of a chain and prevent it from running over the wheel (see fig. 2). An endless chain is reeved upon this and upon a pulley below, as shown in fig. 3. The lettering corresponds to that in fig. 1, and serves to show the principle. Fig. 4 shows the machine in action. Here *a a* is the triangular frame of the

Crowning Pulley.

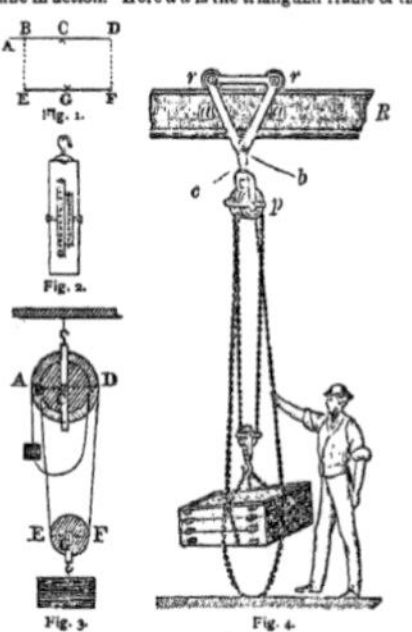

Differential Pulley.

traveler, *b* a link with which the hook *c* of the differential pulley *p* engages, and *r*, *r* rollers which support the frame on the rail R.—**Double-speed pulley**, a combination of two loose pulleys (see *loose pulley*) and toothed gearing with one fast-driven pulley, whereby two different speeds of rotation may be obtained with pulleys of the same diameter by shifting the band from the fast pulley to one of the loose pulleys. Also called *two-speed pulley*.—**Driven pulley**, in *mech.*, a pulley which receives its motion through a belt or band from another pulley called the *driving pulley*.—**Driving pulley**, a pulley which, by means of a belt or band, transmits its motion to another pulley. A wide-faced pulley is often both a driven and a driving pulley.—**Fast-and-loose pulleys.** See *fast*¹.—**Fast pulley**, a pulley firmly attached to the shaft from which it receives or to which it communicates motion.—**Flat-rope pulley**, a pulley with a sheave having in its perimeter a rectangular or nearly rectangular groove, instead of the usual semicircular score.—**Frame pulley**, a pulley which has, instead of a block, a sort of frame of iron in which the sheave or sheaves are pivoted.—**Loose pulley**, a pulley fitted loosely on a shaft and placed near a fast pulley to receive and support the belt when it is thrown off in order to disconnect the shaft. It is practically an idle-wheel.—**Parting pulley**, a pulley or belt-wheel that can be separated into two parts so that a shaft need not be dismounted in order to receive it.—**Scored pulley**, a pulley having a semicircular groove about its perimeter to receive a band of circular section, or a rope. *E. H. Knight.*—**Side pulley**, a pulley the block of which has laterally or vertically extending lugs, with holes therein, by which it may be bolted to a wall or post.—**Sliding pulley**, a pulley with a clutch mechanism placed so as to slide backward and forward on a shaft: used for coupling and disengaging machinery, and also as a pulley.—**Tug pulley**, in a well-boring rig, the pulley which, by means of the bull-rope acting as a crossed band, imparts motion to the bull-wheel of an oil-derrick. See *oil-derrick*.

Flat-rope Pulley for transmitting power by means of a band or rope. *f*, face of pulley; *q*, flanges.

pulley (pùl'i), *v. t.* [< *pulley*, *n.* Cf. F. *poulier*, raise with a pulley, < *poulie*, a pulley.] To raise or hoist with a pulley. [Rare.]

A Mine of white Stone was discovered hard by, which runs in a continued Vein of Earth, and is digged out with Ease, being soft, and is between a white Clay and Chalk at first; but being *pulleyed* up with [into?] the open Air, it receives a crusty kind of hardness, and so becomes perfect Freestone. *Howell*, Letters, I. i. 16.

pulley-block (pùl'i-blok), *n.* A shell containing one or more sheaves, the whole forming a pulley.

pulley-box (pùl'i-boks), *n.* In a draw-loom, a frame containing the pulleys for guiding the tail-cords. *E. H. Knight.*

pulley-check (pùl'i-chek), *n.* An automatic clutch or locking device designed to prevent a rope from running backward through a pulley-block.

pulley-clutch (pùl'i-kluch), *n.* An automatic device, in the form of a grappling-tongs, for fastening a hoisting-pulley to a beam or rafter.

pulley-drum (pùl'i-drum), *n.* A pulley-shell or pulley-block.

pulley-frame (pùl'i-frām), *n.* In *mining*, same as *head-frame*, *poppet-head*, etc.

pulley-mortise (pùl'i-môr'tis), *n.* Same as *chase-mortise*.

pulley-sheave (pùl'i-shēv), *n.* The grooved roller over which a rope runs in a pulley-block.

pulley-shell (pùl'i-shel), *n.* The outer part or casing of a pulley-block.

pulley-stand (pùl'i-stand), *n.* A hanger on which pulleys can be adjusted as to height and angle of axis, so as to make them suit the belting, which may reach them at angles varying with the stem of the hanger. *E. H. Knight.*

pulley-stone (pùl'i-stōn), *n.* In *geol.*, a name familiarly given to the silicious pulley-like casts or molds of the joints and stems of encrinites.

pulley-wheel (pùl'i-hwēl), *n.* A pulley-sheave.

pullicat, pulicat (pul'i-kat), *n.* A cotton check handkerchief of real or imitation Indian make. *Balfour.*

pullin†, *n.* See *pullen.*

pulling-jack (pùl'ing-jak), *n.* A hydraulic jack which has a pulling instead of a pushing action.

pulling-out (pùl'ing-out'), *n.*; pl. *pullings-out* (-ingz-out'). The lining worn with a slashed garment and drawn partly through the slash, so as to project loosely.

pull-iron (pùl'ī'ėrn), *n.* 1. In a railroad-car, an eye-bolt or lug to which a chain may be attached when the car is to be moved by horses. —2. A hook or ring at the back end of the tongue of a horse-car, for attaching it to the car.

pullish†, *v.* An obsolete form of *polish*1.

pullock (pùl'ọk), *n.* A putlog. *E. H. Knight.*

pull-off (pùl'ôf), *n.* In *gun-making*, the power required to be applied to the trigger to discharge a gun.

pull-over (pùl'ō'vėr), *n.* In *hat-manuf.*, a cap of silk or felted fur drawn over a hat-body to form the napping; also, a hat so made.

pull-piece (pùl'pēs), *n.* In a clock, a wire or string which, when pulled, causes the clock to strike: used, if necessary, to bring the striking-mechanism into accord with the hands.

pull-pipes (pùl'pīps), *n.* [A corruption of *pool-pipes.*] Various species of *Equisetum*: so called from their hollow stems and growth in wet places. [North. Eng.]

pull-to (pùl'tö), *n.* In *weaving*, same as *lay-cap.*

pullulate (pul'ū-lāt), *v. i.*; pret. and pp. *pullulated*, ppr. *pullulating.* [< L. *pullulatus*, pp. of *pullulare* (> It. *pullulare, pollolare* = Sp. *pulular* = Pg. *pullular* = F. *pulluler*), put forth, sprout forth, < *pullulus*, a young animal, a sprout, dim. of *pullus*, a young animal, a chick: see *pullet.*] To germinate; bud.

> Money is but as drugs and lenitive ointments, to mitigate the swellings and diseases of the body, whose root remaineth still within, and *pullulateth* again, after the same or some other manner. *Grainger*, On Ecclesiastes (1621), p. 175.

> Instead of repairing the mistake, and restoring religious liberty, which would have stifled this *pullulating* evil in the seed by affording it no further nourishment, they took the other course. *Warburton*, Divine Legation, ii. 6.

> Ovisacs or bulbules naked, bud like, *pullulating* from the bases of the tentacula. *Johnston*, British Zoophytes.

pullulation (pul-ū-lā'shọn), *n.* [= F. *pullulation* = Pg. *pullulação* = It. *pullulazione*, < L. as if **pullulatio(n-)*, < *pullulare*, pp. *pullulatus*, pullulate: see *pullulate.*] 1. The act of germinating or budding.

> These were the Generations or *Pullulations* of the Heavenly and Earthly Nature. *Dr. H. More*, Moral Cabbala, ii.

2\. Specifically, in *bot.*, a mode of cell-multiplication in which a cell forms a slight protuberance on one side, which afterward increases to the size of the parent-cell, and is cut off from it by the formation of a dividing wall at the narrow point of junction: same as *sprouting.* This mode of multiplication is especially characteristic of the yeast-plant and its allies.

pullus (pul'us), *n.* [NL., < L. *pullus*, a young animal.] 1. In *ornith.*, a chick; a very young bird; a nestling: applied to any bird in the down, or before it has acquired its first full feathering. Hence—2. In *zoöl.*, the young (embryonic or larval) condition of any animal.

> Craven has . . . subsequently acknowledged that his Sinusigera perversa (from the Indian Ocean) is only a *pullus* of Triforis. *P. Pelseneer*, Challenger Reports, XXIII., Zoöl., part lxv., [Report on Thecosomata, p. 40.

pulment†, *n.* Same as *polment.*

Pulmobranchia (pul-mọ-brang'ki-ạ̈), *n. pl.* [NL., < L. *pulmo(n-)*, lung, + *branchiæ*, gills. In this and following compounds, *pulmo-* is short for *pulmono-*, prop. *pulmoni-.*] Same as *Pulmobranchiata.*

pulmobranchiæ (pul-mọ-brang'ki-ē), *n. pl.* [NL., < L. *pulmo(n-)*, lung, + *branchiæ*, gills.] Gills or branchiæ modified into organs of aërial respiration; the respiratory apparatus peculiar to certain animals. (*a*) The lung-sacs of air-breathing mollusks, as snails. See cut under *Pulmonata.* (*b*) The lung-sacs of certain arachnidans, as spiders; the pulmotracheæ. See cuts under *pulmonary* and *Scorpionidæ.*

pulmobranchial (pul-mọ-brang'ki-ạl), *a.* [< *Pulmobranchia* + *-al.*] 1. In *conch.*, breathing by means of pulmobranchiæ or lung-sacs; pertaining to pulmobranchiæ; pulmonate, pulmoniferous, or pulmonary, as a snail.—2. In *entom.*, breathing by means of pulmotracheæ; pertaining to pulmotracheæ; pulmonary, as a spider. = **Syn.** *Pulmobranchial*, etc. In application to those arachnidans which have lung-sacs by which they breathe, as well as by tracheæ, the terms *pulmonary, pulmonate, pulmobranchial, pulmobranchiate, pulmotracheal, pulmotracheate*, and *pulmotracheary* mean the same, the first two terms being the least specific, since they are applied to other animals, the two middle terms being less specific, as shared by certain mollusks, the last three being specific and precise, since they apply only to these arachnidans. In application to mollusks, *pulmonary, pulmonate, pulmoniferous, pulmobranchial, pulmobranchiate*, and *pulmogasteropod* are a parallel series of words, the first three shared by any other animals which have lungs, the fourth and fifth by arachnidans, the sixth being specific and precise.

Pulmobranchiata (pul-mō-brang-ki-ā'tạ̈), *n. pl.* [NL., neut. pl. of *pulmobranchiatus*: see *pulmobranchiate.*] In De Blainville's classification (1825), the first one of three orders of his *Paracephalophora monoica asymmetrica*, containing the three families *Limnacea, Auriculacea*, and *Limacinea*, or the pulmonary gastropods, as snails, slugs, etc., both aquatic and terrestrial. Also *Pulmobranchia.* Now commonly called *Pulmonata* or *Pulmonifera.*

pulmobranchiate (pul-mọ-brang'ki-āt), *a.* [< NL. *pulmobranchiatus*, < *pulmobranchiæ*, q. v.] Provided with pulmobranchiæ. (*a*) Breathing by lung-sacs or pulmobranchiæ, as mollusks; of or pertaining to the *Pulmobranchiata.* (*b*) Breathing by lung-sacs or pulmotracheæ, as spiders; pulmotracheate. = **Syn.** See *pulmobranchial.*

pulmocutaneous (pul″mō-kụ̄-tā'nẹ̄-us), *a.* [< L. *pulmo(n-)*, lung, + *cutis*, skin: see *cutaneous.*] Of or pertaining to the lungs and skin: said of the hindmost one of three passages into which each of the two aortic trunks of the adult frog is divided, which ends in pulmonary and cutaneous arteries.

pulmogasteropod, pulmogastropod (pul-mọ-gas-tėr'ọ-pod, -gas'trọ-pod), *a.* and *n.* [< L. *pulmo(n-)*, lung, + Gr. γαστήρ, stomach, + πούς (ποδ-) = E. *foot.*] **I.** *a.* Pulmonate or pulmoniferous, as a gastropod; of or pertaining to the *Pulmogasteropoda.*

II. *n.* A pulmonate gastropod; any member of the *Pulmogasteropoda.*

Also *pulmonogasteropod.*

Pulmogasteropoda (pul-mọ-gas-tẹ-rop'ọ-dạ̈), *n. pl.* [NL.] Same as *Pulmonata*, 1 (*a*).

Pulmograda (pul-mog'rạ̄-dạ̈), *n. pl.* [NL., neut. pl. of *pulmogradus*: see *pulmograde.*] De Blainville's name of a group of acalephs, approximately the same as *Discophora.*

pulmograde (pul'mọ-grād), *a.* and *n.* [< NL. *pulmogradus*, < L. *pulmo(n-)*, a lung, + *gradi*, walk.] **I.** *a.* Having the characters of the *Pulmograda*; swimming by means of alternate contraction and expansion of the body, as if by a kind of respiration, as a jellyfish.

II. *n.* An acaleph of the group *Pulmograda*; a discophorous hydrozoan.

pulmometer (pul-mom'e-tėr), *n.* [< L. *pulmo(n-)*, lung, + Gr. μέτρον, measure.] An instrument for measuring the capacity of the lungs; a spirometer.

pulmometry (pul-mom'e-tri), *n.* [< L. *pulmo(n-)*, lung, + Gr. -μετρία, < μέτρον, measure.] The measurement of the capacity of the lungs; spirometry.

Pulmonacea (pul-mọ-nā'shiạ̈), *n. pl.* [< L. *pulmo(n-)*, lung, + *-acea.*] In *conch.*, same as *Pulmonata*, 1.

pulmonar (pul'mọ-nạ̈r), *a.* [= F. *pulmonaire*: see *pulmonary.*] Having lungs or lung-like organs; pulmonate or pulmonary; specifically, belonging to the arachnidan order *Pulmonaria.*

Pulmonaria1 (pul-mọ-nā'ri-ạ̈), *n.* [NL. (Tournefort, 1700), so called from its reputation and former use; fem. of *pulmonarius*, pertaining to the lungs, as a pulmonary remedy: see *pulmonary.*] A genus of gamopetalous plants of the order *Boragineæ*, tribe *Borageæ*, and subtribe *Anchuseæ.* It is characterized by a five-lobed funnel-shaped corolla without scales in the throat, a five-cleft calyx enlarged in fruit, and four broad erect nutlets with an elevated and slightly concave basilar scar which is without a surrounding ring. There are 5 or 6 species, natives of Europe and Asia, especially of western Asia. They are erect perennial hairy herbs, bearing large petioled radical leaves and a few small alternate stem-leaves, and terminal two-parted cymes of blue or purplish flowers. They are generally known as *lungwort* (which see), especially *P. officinalis*, which is the common English species, having also the old or local names of *spotted comfrey, bugloss cowslip, Jerusalem cowslip, beggar's-basket*, etc. See also *Joseph-and-Mary.*

Pulmonaria2 (pul-mọ-nā'ri-ạ̈), *n. pl.* [NL., neut. pl. of L. *pulmonarius*, pertaining to the lungs: see *pulmonary.*] 1. In *conch.*, same as *Pulmonata*, 1.—2. In *entom.*, the pulmonary arachnidans, as spiders and scorpions. In Latreille's system of classification they were one of two orders of *Arachnida*, the other being *Trachearia.* Also called *Pulmonariæ* and *Pulmonata.*

pulmonaria3, *n.* Plural of *pulmonarium.*

Pulmonariæ (pul-mọ-nā'ri-ē), *n. pl.* Same as *Pulmonaria*2, 2.

pulmonarious (pul-mọ-nā'ri-us), *a.* [< L. *pulmonarius*, diseased in the lungs: see *pulmonary.*] Diseased in the lungs; affected with pulmonary disease.

pulmonarium (pul-mọ-nā'ri-um), *n.*; pl. *pulmonaria* (-ạ̈). [NL., neut. of L. *pulmonarius*, pertaining to the lungs: see *pulmonary.*] In *entom.*, the lateral membrane often separating the dorsal and ventral abdominal segments, and containing stigmata or breathing-holes. *Kirby.*

pulmonary (pul'mọ-nạ̄-ri), *a.* and *n.* [= F. *pulmonaire* = Sp. Pg. *pulmonar* = It. *pulmonare, pulmonario*, < L. *pulmonarius*, pertaining to the lungs, affecting the lungs, < *pulmo(n-)*, lung, = Gr. πλεύμων, usually πνεύμων, lung: see *pneumonia.*] **I.** *a.* 1. Of or pertaining to the lungs, in the widest sense; respiratory: as, *pulmonary* organs.

> The force of the air upon the *pulmonary* artery is but small in respect to that of the heart. *Arbuthnot.*

2\. Affecting the lungs: as, *pulmonary* disease. —3. Remedial of affections of the lungs; pulmonic: as, *pulmonary* medicine.—4. Done by means of lungs; aërial, as a mode of breathing: opposed to *branchial* or *tracheal*: as, *pulmonary* respiration.—5. Having lungs, lung-sacs, or lung-like organs; able to breathe air; pulmobranchiate, pulmonate, or pulmoniferous: distinguished from *branchiate*: as, a *pulmonary* mollusk.—6. Of or having the characteristics of the *Pulmonaria*: distinguished from *trachcary*: as, a *pulmonary* arachnidan.—**Pulmonary alveoli**, air-cells. See *alveolus*, *b*).—**Pulmonary artery**, any artery conveying blood directly from the heart to the lungs: in man, a large vessel, about two inches in length, conveying venous blood from the right cardiac ventricle. It divides into two branches, called the right and the left pulmonary artery, for the respective lungs. See cuts under *lung* and *thorax.*—**Pulmonary branchiæ**, of spiders and other arachnidans, peculiar breathing-organs or gills, situated in the abdomen and consisting of many membranous folds, appearing like the leaves of a book or porte-monnaie. The air enters these folds from the exterior orifice, and passes through the membrane to the blood which circulates between them. See cut below.—**Pulmonary calculus.** See *calculus*, 2.—**Pulmonary cartilage**, the second costal cartilage of the left side.—**Pulmonary circulation**, the lesser circulation of the blood, from the right cardiac ventricle through the pulmonary artery, pulmonary capillaries, and pulmonary veins, back to the left auricle. See cut under *circulation.*—**Pulmonary consumption**, phthisis.—**Pulmonary lobules**, small sections of lung-tissue, each receiving a bronchiole, and separated from one another by connective-tissue septa in which vessels ramify.—**Pulmonary nerves**, a variable number of branches of the pneumogastric, distributed to the root of the lungs.—**Pulmonary pleura**, the pleura pulmonalis.—**Pulmonary plexuses.** See *plexus.*—**Pulmonary sac**, in *entom.*, a special form of respiratory organ found only in some arachnidans (spiders), being an involution of the integument, the walls of which are so folded as to expose a large surface to the air, which is alternately inspired and expired, the blood being brought to the sacs by venous channels.—**Pulmonary sinuses**, the sinuses of Valsalva in the pulmonary artery.—**Pulmonary valves**, the semilunar valves of the right cardiac ventricle.—**Pulmonary veins**, any veins which bring blood direct from the lungs to the heart; in man, four veins, two from each lung, which convey arterial blood to the left auricle of the heart. See cuts under *lung* and *thorax.*—**Pulmonary vesicles**, air-cells. = **Syn.** See *pulmobranchial.*

Pulmonary Sac of a Spider (*Mygale cæmentaria*). *p*, the leaflets or lamellæ; *s*, stigma or breathing-hole.

II. *n.*; pl. *pulmonaries* (-riz). 1. A pulmonary arachnidan, as a spider or scorpion; a member of the *Pulmonaria.*—2. Lungwort.

Pulmonata (pul-mọ-nā'tạ̈), *n. pl.* [NL., neut. pl. of *pulmonatus*, having lungs: see *pulmonate.*] 1. In *conch.*: (*a*) An order or subclass of *Gasteropoda*, air-breathing and adapted to a terrestrial life; the true pulmonate or pulmoniferous gastropods, as snails and slugs, having the pallial cavity or mantle-chamber converted into a lung-sac, no ctenidia or true gills, and generally no true operculum to the shell. Some other gastropods are pulmonate in the sense that they breathe air, but are otherwise structurally related to the pectinibranchiate or to the rhipidoglossate gastropods. The *Pulmonata* are hermaphrodite, with highly developed copulatory and other sexual organs in every individual, and well-formed odontophore. A shell is usually present, sometimes small or wanting; its aperture is closed in some cases by a pseudoperculum. They are divided into *Basommatophora* and *Stylommatophora*. There are more than

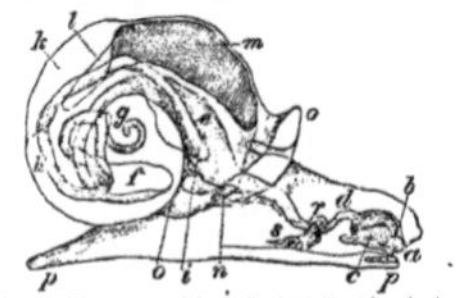

Diagram of the Anatomy of the Snail (*Helix*), illustrating structure of *Pulmonata*.

a, mouth; *b*, tooth; *c*, odontophore; *d*, gullet; *e*, crop; *f*, stomach; *g*, coiled end of the visceral mass; *h*, rectum; *i*, anus; *k*, renal sac; *l*, heart; *m*, lung-sac, or modified pallial chamber; *n*, its external opening; *o*, thick edge of mantle; *p*, *p*, extent of the foot; *r*, *s*, nervous ganglia round the esophagus.

6,000 species. By Férussac and many later conchologists the order was extended to include the operculate tænioglossate and rhipidoglossate terrestrial gastropods, the true *Pulmonata* being then called *P. inoperculata*, and the others *P. operculata*. This use of the word was long prevalent, but is now obsolete. Also called *Pulmonea*, *Pulmonifera*, *Pulmonogasteropoda*, and *Pulmogasteropoda*. (*b*) A section of rhipidoglossate gastropods, characterized by adaptation for aërial respiration, and including the families *Helicinidæ*, *Hydrocenidæ*, and *Proserpinidæ*. *Fischer*.—2. In *entom.*, the pulmonary arachnidans: same as *Pulmonaria*[2], 2.

pulmonate (pul'mọ̄-nāt), *a.* and *n.* [< NL. *pulmonatus*, < L. *pulmo(n-)*, lung: see *pulmonary*.] I. *a.* Having lungs, lung-sacs, or lung-like organs; pulmonary or pulmoniferous, as a mollusk or an arachnidan; pulmonated, as a vertebrate: distinguished from *branchiate* and *tracheate*. = Syn. See *pulmobranchial*.

II. *n.* A member of the *Pulmonata* in either sense, as a snail or a spider.

pulmonated (pul'mọ̄-nā-ted), *a.* [< *pulmonate* + *-ed*[2].] Same as *pulmonate*.

In the lower *pulmonated* Vertebrata, the sacculation is more marked near the entrance of the bronchus. *Huxley*, Anat. Vert., p. 92.

Pulmonea (pul-mō'nẹ̄-ạ̈), *n. pl.* [NL., < L. *pulmo(n-)*, lung: see *pulmonate*.] In Latreille's classification, an order of *Gasteropoda*: now called *Pulmonata* or *Pulmonifera*.

pulmonian (pul-mō'ni-ạn), *n.* [< L. *pulmo(n-)*, lung, + *-ian*.] A pulmonate gastropod, as a snail.

Pulmonibranchiata (pul"mọ̄-ni-brang-ki-ā'tạ̈), *n. pl.* [NL.] The more correct form of *Pulmobranchiata*.

pulmonibranchiate (pul"mọ̄-ni-brang'ki-āt), *a.* The more correct form of *pulmobranchiate*.

pulmonic (pul-mon'ik), *a.* and *n.* [= F. *pulmonique* = Pg. *pulmonico* (cf. Sp. *pulmoniaco*), < L. *pulmo(n-)*, lung: see *pulmonary*.] I. *a.* Of or pertaining to the lungs.

An ulcer of the lungs may be a cause of *pulmonick* consumption, or consumption of the lungs. *Harvey*, Consumptions.

Pulmonic circulation. Same as *pulmonary circulation* (which see, under *pulmonary*).

II. *n.* 1. A medicine for diseases of the lungs. *Dunglison*.—2. One who is affected with a disease of the lungs.

Pulmonicks are subject to consumptions, and the old to asthmas. *Arbuthnot*.

pulmonifer (pul-mon'i-fėr), *n.* [< NL. *Pulmonifera*.] A pulmonate gastropod, as a snail; any member of the *Pulmonifera*.

Pulmonifera (pul-mọ̄-nif'e-rạ̈), *n. pl.* [NL., neut. pl. of *pulmonifer*, having lungs: see *pulmoniferous*.] In *conch.*: (*a*) Same as *Pulmonata*, 1 (*a*). (*b*) The *Pulmonata* considered as a subclass of gastropods, *Pulmonata* then being reserved as the ordinal name. (*c*) A section of tænioglossate pectinibranchiate gastropods, characterized by a modification of the respiratory apparatus as a lung for aërial respiration. It includes the families *Cyclostomidæ*, *Pomatiidæ*, *Cyclophoridæ*, and *Aciculidæ*. *Fischer*. *Adelopneumona* is a synonym.

pulmoniferous (pul-mọ̄-nif'e-rus), *a.* [< NL. *pulmonifer*, < L. *pulmo(n-)*, lung, + *ferre* = E. *bear*[1].] 1. Provided with lungs, as an animal; pulmonary or pulmonate, as a mollusk; of or pertaining to the *Pulmonifera*.—2. Containing the lungs, as a part of the body: as, the *pulmoniferous* somites of an arachnidan.

Pulmonigrada (pul-mọ̄-nig'rạ̄-dạ̈), *n. pl.* [NL., neut. pl. of *pulmonigradus*: see *pulmonigrade*.] Same as *Pulmograda*.

pulmonigrade (pul-mon'i-grād), *a.* and *n.* [< NL. *pulmonigradus*, < L. *pulmo(n-)*, lung, + *gradi*, walk.] Same as *pulmograde*.

pulmonobranchous (pul"mọ̄-nọ̄-brang'kus), *a.* [< L. *pulmo(n-)*, lung, + Gr. βράγχια, gills.] Pulmonate, as a gastropod; pulmonibranchiate. [Rare.]

Affording a good character for dividing the land *pulmonobranchous* Mollusca into two families. *Eng. Cyc.*, Nat. Hist., III. 65.

pulmonogasteropod (pul"mọ̄-nọ̄-gas'tėr-ọ̄-pod), *a.* and *n.* Same as *pulmogasteropod*.

Pulmonogasteropoda (pul"mọ̄-nọ̄-gas-tẹ-rop'ọ̄-dạ̈), *n. pl.* [NL., < L. *pulmo(n-)*, lung, + NL. *Gasteropoda*.] Same as *Pulmonata*, 1 (*a*).

pulmotracheal (pul-mọ̄-trā'kẹ̄-ạl), *a.* [< L. *pulmo(n-)*, lung, + NL. *trachea*, windpipe, + *-al*.] In *entom.*, pulmobranchial; pertaining to or done by means of pulmotracheæ: as, *pulmotracheal* respiration.

Pulmotrachearia (pul-mọ̄-trā-kẹ̄-ā'ri-ạ̈), *n. pl.* [NL., < L. *pulmo(n-)*, lung, + NL. *trachea*, windpipe.] A group of pulmobranchiate or pulmotracheate arachnidans; an order of *Arachnida*, containing those arachnidans which have pulmonary sacs as well as tracheæ, as spiders and scorpions. See cut under *Scorpionidæ*.

pulmotracheary (pul-mọ̄-trā'kẹ̄-ạ̄-ri), *a.* and *n.* I. *a.* Of or pertaining to the *Pulmotrachearia*.

II. *n.*; pl. *pulmotrachearies* (-riz). A pulmotracheate arachnidan.

pulmotracheate (pul-mọ̄-trā'kẹ̄-āt), *a.* [< L. *pulmo(n-)*, lung, + *trachea*, windpipe, + *-ate*[1].] Pulmobranchiate, as a spider; of or pertaining to the *Pulmotrachearia*.

pulp (pulp), *n.* [= F. *pulpe* = Sp. *pulpa* = Pg. It. *polpa*, < L. *pulpa*, the fleshy part of an animal body, etc., solid flesh, the pulp of fruit, etc.] A moist, slightly cohering mass, consisting of soft undissolved animal or vegetable matter. Specifically—(*a*) The soft, succulent part of fruit: as, the *pulp* of an orange, or of a grape. In the American grape of the *Vitis Labrusca* varieties (as Concord, etc.) the pulp is a distinct portion of the berry inclosing the seeds, and is characteristically tough and sour. It is inclosed in a sweet and well-flavored layer formed beneath the skin.

The savoury *pulp* they chew, and in the rind,
Still as they thirsted, scoop the brimming stream.
Milton, P. L., iv. 335.

(*b*) The material from which paper is manufactured after it is reduced to a soft uniform mass. (*c*) Chyme; the pulpified mass of food after chymification and before chylification. (*d*) The soft pulpy core of a tooth, consisting chiefly of the nerve accompanied by its vessels and connective tissue; a tooth-pulp. (*e*) The soft elastic fibrocartilage forming much of the substance of the intervertebral disks. It chiefly occupies the interior of these disks, whose periphery is more fibrous and tougher. To the compressibility and elasticity of this pulp is mainly due the action of the disks in serving as buffers to diminish concussion of the spine. The pulp is compressible enough to account also for the fact that a man may be appreciably taller in the morning after lying all night than in the evening after a day spent on the feet. (*f*) In *mining*, slimes; ore pulverized and mixed with water.

In the case of silver the ore is frequently pulverized by stamps, and the resulting *pulp* amalgamated in pans or barrels. *Encyc. Brit.*, XVI. 465.

Blue, dental, etc., **pulp.** See the adjectives.—**Persistent pulps.** See *dental pulp* (*b*).—**Pulp-colors.** See *color*.

pulp (pulp), *v.* [< *pulp*, *n.*] I. *trans.* 1. To make into pulp, in any sense; reduce to pulp: as, to *pulp* wood-fiber for paper; to *pulp* old papers.—2. To deprive of the surrounding pulp or pulpy substance: as, to *pulp* coffee-beans.

The other mode is to *pulp* the coffee immediately as it comes from the tree. By a simple machine a man will *pulp* a bushel in a minute. *Bryan Edwards*.

II. *intrans.* To be or to become ripe and juicy like the pulp of fruit.

A kiss should bud upon the tree of love,
And *pulp* and ripen richer every hour. *Keats*.

The buried seed begins to pulp and swell
In Earth's warm bosom. *R. H. Stoddard*, Ode.

pulpamenta† (pul-pạ-men'tạ̈), *n. pl.* [L., pl. of *pulpamentum*, meat, pulp, < *pulpa*, meat, pulp: see *pulp*.] Delicacies; tidbits.

What, Friday night, and in affliction, too, and yet your *pulpamenta*, your delicate morsels! *B. Jonson*, Every Man out of his Humour, v. 7.

pulpatoon†, *n.* [Origin obscure.] A kind of confection or cake, supposed to be made of the pulp of fruits.

With a French troop of *pulpatoons*, mackaroons, kickshaws, grand and excellent. *Nabbes*, Microcosmus, iii.

pulp-boiler (pulp'boi"lėr), *n.* Same as *pulp-digester*.

pulp-cavity (pulp'kav"i̥-ti), *n.* The hollow interior of a tooth which contains the pulp. Also called *nerve-canal*. See cut under *tooth*.

pulp-digester (pulp'di-jes"tėr), *n.* In *paper-manuf.*, a machine for digesting straw, wood, bamboo, and other materials, to free the fibrous matter from gluten, gum, starch, and other extraneous matters. Such machines are essentially boilers, in which the paper-stock is cooked with various chemicals under more or less steam-pressure. In some digesters the boilers are stationary and are provided with a stirring-mechanism; in others the boilers are made to rotate. Also called *pulp-boiler*.

pulp-dresser (pulp'dres"ėr), *n.* In *paper-manuf.*, an apparatus for clearing paper-pulp from impurities, and freeing it from lumps and knots.

pulp-engine (pulp'en"jin), *n.* In *paper-manuf.*, a machine for converting paper-rags, esparto,

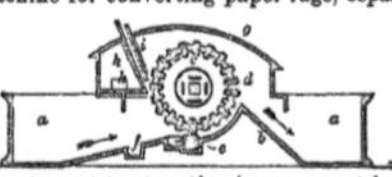

Pulp-engine, consisting of an oblong iron vat *a*, rounded at the ends and divided by a partition *b*, over which is journaled a cylinder *c*, having grooves into which chisel-edged blades *d* are inserted in sets of three, generally to the number of sixty; beneath these, and set at an angle therewith, other blades *e* are fixed in the bottom of the vat; the distance between the two may be adjusted by raising or lowering the cylinder *c*. The part *e* of the bottom is sloping, and has a recess *f* for the reception of grit. A hood *g* prevents the pulp from being thrown out of the machine, and one side of this is a sieve *h*, with a removable cover *i*, through which the foul water expelled from the pulp passes and is discharged through the opening *k*.

and other materials into a pulp with water. Also called *pulper*, *pulp-machine*, *pulping engine*, and *pulp-mill*.

pulper (pul'pėr), *n.* 1. A machine for reducing roots, as turnips, mangel-wurzel, etc., to a pulp; a root-pulper.—2. A machine for removing the fleshy pulp of coffee-berries.—3. A pulp-digester, pulp-grinder, or pulp-engine.

pulpet†, *n.* A Middle English form of *pulpit*.

pulp-grinder (pulp'grīn"dėr), *n.* In *paper-manuf.*, a form of grinding-mill for crushing, disintegrating, and grinding partially made paper-pulp, or for grinding wood to form paper-stock.

pulpifier (pul'pi-fī'ėr), *n.* An apparatus for grinding up fresh meat, and converting it into an almost jelly-like pulp as an aid to digestion for dyspeptics. Also called *meat-pulpifier* and *meat-pulverizer*.

pulpify (pul'pi-fī), *v. t.*; pret. and pp. *pulpified*, ppr. *pulpifying*. [< *pulp* + *-ify*.] To render pulpy; make into pulp.

These actions [of rumination] are repeated until the greater portion of the grass which has been cropped is *pulpified*. *Huxley*, Anat. Vert., p. 324.

pulpiness (pul'pi-nes), *n.* A pulpy character or consistency.

pulping-machine (pul'ping-mạ-shēn"), *n.* In *agri.*, a pulper or root-pulper.

pulpit (pu̇l'pit), *n.* and *a.* [< ME. *pulpit*, *pulpet*, < OF. *pulpite*, F. *pupitre*, dial. *pulpite* = Sp. *púlpito* = Pg. It. *pulpito*, < L. *pulpitum*, a staging, stage, platform, scaffold.] I. *n.* 1. A rostrum or elevated platform from which a

Pulpit of Niccolò Pisano, in the Baptistery at Pisa, Italy.

speaker addresses an audience or delivers an oration; specifically, in the Christian church, an elevated and more or less inclosed platform from which the preacher delivers his sermon and, in churches of many denominations, conducts the service.

And Ezra the scribe stood upon a *pulpit* of wood, which they had made for the purpose. Neh. viii. 4.

Produce his body to the market-place,
And in the *pulpit*, as becomes a friend,
Speak in the order of his funeral.
Shak., J. C., iii. 1. 229.

And the reader droned from the *pulpit*,
Like the murmur of many bees.
Longfellow, King Witlaf's Drinking-Horn.

2. A bow of iron lashed to the end of the bowsprit of a whaling-vessel, and forming a support for the waist of the harpooner, to insure his safety.—**The pulpit**, preachers collectively, or what they preach.

By *the pulpit* are adumbrated the writings of our modern saints in Great Britain. *Swift*, Tale of a Tub, i.

II. *a.* Of or pertaining to the pulpit or preachers and their teaching: as, *pulpit* eloquence; *pulpit* utterances.

pulpit (pụl'pit), *v. t.* [< *pulpit, n.*] To place in or supply with a pulpit. [Rare.]

Certainly it is not necessary to the attainment of Christian knowledge that men should sit all their life long at the feet of a *pulpited* divine. *Milton*, Touching Hirelings.

pulpitarian† (pụl-pi-tā'ri-an), *n.* [< *pulpit* + *-arian.*] A preacher. [Rare.]

The Scottish brethren were acquainted by common intercourse with these directions that had settled the aggrieved *pulpitarians*. *Bp. Hacket*, Abp. Williams, i. 90. (*Davies.*)

pulpiteer (pụl-pi-tēr'), *n.* [< *pulpit* + *-eer.*] A preacher: a contemptuous term.

Then it was under the name of puritans and round-heads, and now it is openly as ministers, under the name of priests, and blackcoats, and presbyters, and *pulpiteers* [that many servants of the Lord are reviled]. *Baxter*, Self-Denial, Epistle Monitory.

To chapel; where a heated *pulpiteer*,
Not preaching simple Christ to simple men,
Announced the coming doom, and fulminated
Against the scarlet woman and her creed.
Tennyson, Sea Dreams.

pulpiter† (pụl'pi-tėr), *n.* [< *pulpit* + *-er*1.] One who preaches from a pulpit; a preacher.

O most gentle *pulpiter!* what tedious homily of love have you wearied your parishioners withal! *Shak.*, As you Like it, iii. 2. 163.

pulpitical (pụl-pit'i-kal), *a.* [< *pulpit* + *-ic-al.*] Of or pertaining to the pulpit; suited to the pulpit. [Rare.] *Imp. Dict.*

pulpitically (pụl-pit'i-kal-i), *adv.* In a manner suited to the pulpit. [Rare.]

To proceed then regularly and *pulpitically*. *Lord Chesterfield*, Letters. (*Latham.*)

pulpitish (pụl'pi-tish), *a.* [< *pulpit* + *-ish*1.] Smacking of the pulpit; like a pulpit performance.

pulpitman† (pụl'pit-man), *n.* A preacher.

Grew a fine *pulpitman*, and was beneficed. *Massinger*, Duke of Milan, iii. 2.

Dr. Hooper preached. . . . This is one of the first rank of *pulpit men* in the nation. *Evelyn*, Diary, Nov. 5, 1681.

pulpitry (pụl'pit-ri), *n.* [< *pulpit* + *-ry.*] Teaching such as that given from the pulpit; preaching.

They teach not that to govern well is to train up a nation in true wisdom and virtue, . . . and that this is the true flourishing of a land, other things follow as the shadow does the substance; to teach thus were mere *pulpitry* to them. *Milton*, Reformation in Eng., ii. (*Davies.*)

pulpless (pulp'les), *a.* [< *pulp* + *-less.*] Lacking or deficient in pulp; free from pulp.

There is a greater interest manifested by the masses of the dental profession in the retention of *pulpless* teeth. *Science*, XI. 216.

pulp-machine (pulp'ma-shēn"), *n.* Same as *pulp-engine.*

pulp-meter (pulp'mē"tėr), *n.* A device for regulating the quantity of pulp supplied to a paper-machine, that the quantity may be adjusted to the required width and weight of the sheet.

pulp-mill (pulp'mil), *n.* A pulp-grinder, pulping-machine, or pulper.

pulpous (pul'pus), *a.* [= F. *pulpeux* = Sp. Pg. *pulposo* = It. *polposo*, pulpy, < L. *pulposus*, fleshy, < *pulpa*, the fleshy portion of a body, solid flesh: see *pulp.*] Consisting of or resembling pulp; pulpy.

The redstreak, . . . whose *pulpous* fruit
With gold irradiate and vermilion, shines
Tempting. *J. Philips*, Cider, i.

pulpousness (pul'pus-nes), *n.* The state or quality of being pulpous; softness and moistness. *Imp. Dict.*

pulp-strainer (pulp'strā"nėr), *n.* A sieve for straining pulp; specifically, a sieve for this purpose used in paper-making.

pulp-washer (pulp'wosh"ėr), *n.* A machine for cleansing paper-pulp from dirt and foreign matter; a pulp-dresser. It has a screen to retain grain, stones, etc., and devices for carrying off dirty water and admitting a fresh supply.

pulpy (pul'pi), *a.* [< *pulp* + *-y*1.] Like pulp; soft; fleshy; pultaceous; succulent: as, the *pulpy* covering of a nut; the *pulpy* substance of a peach or cherry.

Long'st thou for Butter? bite the *poulpy* part,
And neuer better came to any Mart.
Sylvester, tr. of Du Bartas's Weeks, i. 3.

In lupins these *pulpy* sides [of the bean] do sometimes arise with the stalk in a resemblance of two fat leaves. *Sir T. Browne*, Urn-burial, iii.

Pulpy disease of the synovial membrane, Brodie's disease. See *disease.*

pulque (pụl'ke), *n.* [Sp., < Mex. *pulque.*] A fermented drink made in Mexico and some countries of Central America from the juice of the agave or maguey, *Agave Americana.* The sap, which abounds in sugar and mucilage when the plant is about to flower, is at that time drawn into a cavity formed by cutting out the bud and upper leaves. The yield may be as much as two gallons a day for several months. The juice is fermented in reservoirs of rawhide, and early in the process is pleasant, resembling spruce-beer, but at the end acquires the putrid odor of the animal matter contained in the hides. It is, however, a favorite beverage with the Mexicans.

pulque-brandy (pụl'ke-bran"di), *n.* A strong spirituous liquor produced in Mexico by distilling pulque, the larger part of which is so consumed; aguardiente; mescal.

pulsate (pul'sāt), *v. i.*; pret. and pp. *pulsated*, ppr. *pulsating.* [< L. *pulsatus*, pp. of *pulsare*, beat, strike, push, drive: see *pulse*1.] To beat or throb, as the heart or a blood-vessel; contract and dilate in alternation or rhythmically, as the heart in systole and diastole, the disk of a jellyfish in swimming, the vacuoles in some protozoans, etc.

The heart of a viper or frog will continue to *pulsate* long after it is taken from the body. *Darwin.*

pulsatile (pul'sa-til), *a.* and *n.* [= F. *pulsatile* = Sp. *pulsátil* = Pg. *pulsatil* = It. *pulsatile*, < ML. *pulsatilis*, beating, striking, throbbing (neut. *pulsatile*, a sieve), < L. *pulsare*, pp. *pulsatus*, beat, strike: see *pulsate, pulse*1.] I. *a.* 1. Capable of pulsating; pulsating or pulsatory; throbbing; beating.—2. Requiring to be struck in order to produce sound; in *music*, noting an instrument the tone of which is produced by blows, as of a hammer, as a drum, tambourine, cymbals, or a bell. The epithet is not commonly used with reference to stringed instruments, like the dulcimer or the pianoforte, though it properly belongs to them. Compare *percussive.*

II. *n.* A musical instrument which is sounded by means of blows.

pulsatilla (pul-sa-til'ä), *n.* [ML. *pulsatilla*, pulsatilis, dim., < L. *pulsare*, pp. *pulsatus*, beat, strike: see *pulsate, pulsatile.*] The pasque-flower, *Anemone Pulsatilla*; also, in *pharmacography*, *A. pratensis* and *A. patens* (var. *Nuttalliana*). These plants have medicinal properties. Also *pulsatill.* See *pasque-flower.*

pulsation (pul-sā'shon), *n.* [= F. *pulsation* = Pr. *pulsacio* = Sp. *pulsacion* = Pg. *pulsação* = It. *pulsazione*, < L. *pulsatio(n-)*, a beating, a striking, < *pulsare*, pp. *pulsatus*, strike, beat: see *pulsate, pulse*1.] 1. The act or process of pulsating, or beating or throbbing: as, the *pulsation* of the heart, of an artery, of a tumor.—2. A single beat of the heart or a blood-vessel.—3. A beat or stroke by which some medium is affected, as in the propagation of sound. See *beat*1, *n.*, 2.—4. In *law*, a beating without pain.

The Cornelian law "de injuriis" prohibited *pulsation* as well as verberation, distinguishing verberation, which was accompanied with pain, from *pulsation*, which was attended with none. *Blackstone*, Com., III. viii.

pulsative (pul'sa-tiv), *a.* [= F. *pulsatif* = Sp. Pg. *pulsativo*; as *pulsate* + *-ive.*] Same as *pulsatile.*

pulsator (pul-sā'tor), *n.* [< L. *pulsator*, one who beats or strikes, < *pulsare*, pp. *pulsatus*, beat, strike: see *pulsate.*] 1. A beater; a striker.—2. The pulsometer pump.—3. A small gravitating machine or shaker, used in diamond-mining in South Africa and elsewhere. It works on the same principle as the jigger.

Pulsatoria (pul-sa-tō'ri-ä), *n. pl.* [NL.: see *pulsator.*] A group of parasitic *Infusoria*, called a subclass, framed for the reception of *Pulsatella convolutæ*, a rhythmically pulsatile organism without cilia and with a differentiated contractile vesicle, found in the mesoderm of a planarian worm, *Convoluta schulzei.*

pulsatory (pul'sa-tọ-ri), *a.* [= Sp. Pg. *pulsatorio*, < L. *pulsare*, beat, strike: see *pulse*1.] Same as *pulsatile.*

An inward, pungent, and *pulsatory* ache within the skull. *Sir H. Wotton*, Reliquiæ, p. 418.

Pulsatory current, in *elect.*, a current rapidly and regularly intermitted.

The *pulsatory* current is one which results from sudden or instantaneous changes in the intensity of a continuous current. *Jour. Franklin Inst.*, CXXI. 34.

pulse1 (puls), *n.* [Now accom. to L. spelling; in ME. *poulce, pouse, pous*, < OF. *pouls, pous, poux*, a beat, stroke, pulse, F. *pouls*, pulse, = Pr. *pols* = Sp. Pg. *pulso* = It. *polso* = D. *pols* = MLG. *puls* = G. Sw. Dan. *puls*, pulse, < L. *pulsus*, a beating, striking, pushing (*pulsus venarum*, 'the beating of the veins,' the pulse), < *pellere*, pp. *pulsus*, strike, drive, push. Cf. *pulse*1, *v.*] 1. A beat; a stroke; especially, a measured, regular, or rhythmical beat; a short, quick motion regularly repeated, as in a medium of the transmission of light, sound, etc.; a pulsation; a vibration.

The vibrations or *pulses* of this medium, that they may cause the alternate fits of easy transmission and easy reflexion, must be swifter than light, and by consequence above 700,000 times swifter than sounds. *Newton.*

I . . . caught once more the distant shout,
The measured *pulse* of racing oars
Among the willows.
Tennyson, In Memoriam, lxxxvii.

2. Specifically, in *physiol.*, the series of rhythmically recurring maxima of fluid tension in any blood-vessel, consequent on the contractions of the heart. These may be perceived by palpation, and recorded by the sphygmograph, and often produce a visible effect in dilating the vessel, or causing a lateral movement of it. The pulse is for the most part confined to the arteries, but a venous pulse occurs (see below). There is one arterial pulse for each ventricular systole; but in disease a ventricular systole may be too feeble to produce a sensible pulsation in a distant artery, as at the wrist, or again each pulsation may be double. (See *dicrotic pulse.*) The features of the pulse are the times between successive pulsations, the maxima and minima of pressure, and the way in which the tension changes from maximum to minimum and to maximum again, represented in the form of the sphygmographic tracing. The normal pulse exhibits approximately equal and equidistant maxima, the rate being in adults between 70 and 80 (see *pulse-rate*); the rise of pressure is sharp, the fall slow with only a slight dicrotic wave; the extent of change (amplitude) is not excessive; and the tension of the blood in the vessel is neither too high nor too low. As taken with Basch's sphygonomanometer, the radial (maximum) tension in health usually lies between 135 and 165 millimeters mercury.

He perceyuede by his *pous* he was in peril to deye,
And bote he hadde recouer the rather that rise sholde he neuere.
Piers Plowman (C), xx. 66.

His *pous* [var. *pows, poulce*] and pawmes of his hondes.
Chaucer, Troilus, iii. 1120.

Yet she 's warm, her *pulses* beat,
'Tis a sign of life and heat.
Fletcher, Faithful Shepherdess, iii. 1.

Stir not a *Pulse*; and let my Blood,
That turbulent, unruly Flood,
Be softly staid.
Congreve, On Mrs. Hunt.

3. In *music*, same as *beat* or *accent.*—4. Figuratively, feeling; sentiment; general opinion, drift, tendency, or movement, private or public: as, the *pulse* of an occasion; the *pulse* of the community.—**Anacrotic pulse**, a pulse in which the first wave is not the highest, so that the ascending limb of the pulse-curve is notched.—**Bounding pulse**, a large, more or less frequent pulse.—**Corrigan's pulse**, the typical pulse of aortic regurgitation: a large, quick, suddenly collapsing pulse.—**Dicrotic pulse**, a pulse in which the dicrotic wave is excessive; a double pulse.—**Entoptic pulse**, pulsation of the retinal arteries, as revealed by the ophthalmoscope or by Purkinje's method.—**Filiform pulse**, a thready pulse; the pulse when the artery is contracted and the pulsations are feeble.—**Frequent pulse**, a pulse in which the number of beats per minute is excessive. Also called *rapid* and sometimes *quick pulse.*—**Full pulse**, a large pulse, the artery not being contracted.—**Hard pulse**, a pulse where the artery is not easily compressed, the blood-tension being high; pulsus durus.—**Hyperdicrotic pulse**, a very marked dicrotic pulse.—**Infrequent pulse**, a pulse in which the number of pulsations per minute is abnormally low; pulsus rarus. Sometimes called *slow pulse.*—**Irregular pulse**, a pulse in which the pulsations are of unequal strength or recur at unequal intervals, or which is abnormal in both these respects.—**Large pulse**, a pulse in which the amplitude or difference between the maximum and minimum of tension is great; pulsus magnus.—**Monocrotic pulse**, a pulse with only one distinguishable wave.—**Polycrotic pulse**, a pulse where there are several secondary waves.—**Postdicrotic pulse**, a pulse in which the postdicrotic wave is well marked.—**Predicrotic pulse**, a pulse in which there is a large predicrotic wave.—**Quick pulse.** (*a*) A pulse in which the rise of tension is very rapid, or in which the time occupied by the rise and the greater part of the fall is very short; pulsus celer. (*b*) A frequent pulse.—**Recurrent pulse**, the reappearance of a pulse in an artery beyond the point where it is compressed, due to distal anastomosis.—**Slow pulse.** (*a*) A pulse in which the rise of tension is very slow, or in which the time occupied by the rise and the greater part of the fall is unusually long; pulsus tardus. (*b*) An infrequent pulse.—**Small pulse**, a pulse

in which the amplitude or difference between maximum and minimum of tension is small; pulsus parvus.—**Soft pulse**, a pulse where the artery is easily compressed; pulsus mollis. The individual pulsations may be well marked.—**Thready pulse**, a very small, frequent pulse in a contracted artery.—**To feel one's pulse**, figuratively, to sound one's opinion; try or know one's mind.—**Wiry pulse**, a small, frequent pulse in a contracted artery.

pulse[1] (puls), *v.*; pret. and pp. *pulsed*, ppr. *pulsing*. [< L. *pulsare*, beat, strike, push, drive, freq. of *pellere*, pp. *pulsus*, beat, strike, push, drive. Cf. *push*[1], ult. < L. *pulsare*, and see *compel*, *expel*, *impel*, *propel*, *repel*, *appulse*, *compulse*, *expulse*, *impulse*, etc.: see also *pulsate*, and *pulse*[1], *n.*] **I.** *trans.* **1**†. To drive.

And I [my sunne] thy noble name with foule reproch have stain'd,
Puls forth through spyte from princely throne, and place where father rain'd.
Phaer, Æneid.

2. To drive by a pulsation of the heart. [Rare.]

II. *intrans.* To beat, as the arteries or heart.

Faint panting *puls* his loynts, and tier'd with pains his entrails beat. *Phaer*, Æneid, x.

The heart, when separated wholly from the body, in some animals, continues still to *pulse* for a considerable time. *Ray.*

pulse[2] (puls), *n.* [< ME. *puls*, also *pouse*, < OF. *pouls*, *pols*, *pous*, < L. *puls* (*pult-*) = Gr. πόλτος, pottage of beans, peas, etc., porridge. Cf. *poultice*.] **1.** The esculent seeds of leguminous plants cultivated as field or garden crops, as peas, beans, lentils, etc.

With Elijah he partook,
Or as a guest with Daniel, at his *pulse*.
Milton, P. R., ii. 278.

2. One of the plants producing pulse.

Every *puls*,
There lande is colde, is hervest nowe to huls.
Palladius, Husbondrie (E. E. T. S.), p. 160.

High climb his *pulse* in many an even row,
Deep strike the ponderous roots in soil below.
Crabbe, Works, I. 41.

pulse-curve (puls'kėrv), *n.* The sphygmographic tracing of a pulse-wave.

pulse-glass (puls'glàs), *n.* An instrument intended to exhibit the ebullition of liquid at low temperatures, constructed like a cryophorus. The bulbs are connected by a slender stem, and partially charged with water, ether, or alcohol, the supernatant air having been expelled by boiling, and the opening hermetically sealed by a blowpipe. If one of the bulbs is grasped, the heat of the hand will cause the formation of vapor and drive the liquid into the other bulb, producing a violent ebullition in the latter. *E. H. Knight.*

Pulse-glass.

pulseless (puls'les), *a.* [< *pulse* + *-less*.] Having no pulse or pulsation.

He lay a full half-hour on the sofa, death-cold, and almost *pulseless*. *Kingsley*, Two Years Ago, xi.

pulselessness (puls'les-nes), *n.* Failure or cessation of the pulse.

pulsellum (pul-sel'um), *n.*; pl. *pulsella* (-ä). [NL., dim. of L. *pulsus*, a beating: see *pulse*[1].] A propulsive filament or flagelliform appendage, as the tail of a spermatozoan, which by its lashing motions propels the body to which it is attached. It is a modified form of flagellum chiefly characteristic of spermatozoa, but possessed by some few flagellate infusorians, whose action serves to drive the animalcule backward through the water. *E. R. Lankester; W. S. Kent.* Compare *flagellum*, *gubernaculum*, *tractellum*.

The flagellum of the Flagellata is totally distinct from the *pulsellum* of the Bacteria. *Encyc. Brit.*, XIX. 859.

pulse-rate (puls'rāt), *n.* The number of pulsations of an artery in a minute. The normal pulse-rate of man in adult life, reclining, and undisturbed by exertion, averages, for the time between breakfast and retiring at night, about 72. There is a large diurnal variation, the rate falling to 60 or below during the night, and rising to 75 or more at noon or some other time during the day. The rate is from 140 to 120 or less during the first year of life, falls in the next year to 100, and reaches the adult rate shortly after puberty; after 60 years of age there is a slight increase. The pulse-rate of woman is 8 to 5 beats higher than that of man. Height of stature diminishes pulse-rate. The rate during health varies greatly, from unknown causes, in different persons—some rates being 40 or less, and others 100 or more, without inconvenience or other derangement of health. The pulse-rate is higher in a standing than in a sitting, or, still more, in a recumbent posture. It is raised by excitement, by exertion, by pyrexia, by various drugs and diseases.

pulse-warmer (puls'wâr″mėr), *n.* A wristlet. [Colloq.]

pulse-wave (puls'wāv), *n.* The wave of raised tension and arterial expansion which starts from the aorta with each ventricular systole, and travels to the capillaries. Its velocity varies greatly, but in most cases lies between 4 and 12 meters per second.—**Fundamental or primary pulse-wave**, the wave resulting from the primary or ventricular impulse; the wave indicated by the initial upward stroke of the pulse-curve.—**Secondary pulse-wave**, a wave following the primary wave, and due to the elastic nature of the arterial walls; a wave indicated by an elevation following the initial upward stroke of the pulse-curve. See *pulse*[1], 2.

pulsific (pul-sif'ik), *a.* [< *pulse* + *-i-fic*.] Exciting the pulse; causing pulsation. [Rare.]

To make [the muscular constriction of the heart] nothing but a *pulsifick* corporeal quality in the substance of the heart itself is very unphilosophical and absurd.
Cudworth, Intellectual System, p. 161.

pulsimeter (pul-sim'e-tėr), *n.* [Also *pulsometer*; < L. *pulsus*, pulse, + Gr. μέτρον, measure.] An instrument for measuring the strength or quickness of the pulse.

pulsion (pul'shon), *n.* [< LL. *pulsio(n-)*, a beating, a striking, < L. *pellere*, pp. *pulsus*, beat, strike, drive: see *pulse*[1].] The act of driving forward: opposed to *suction* or *traction*.

How general and ancient soever the common opinion may be that attraction is a kind of motion quite differing from *pulsion*, if not also opposite to it, yet I confess I concur in opinion . . . with some modern naturalists that think attraction a species of *pulsion*.
Boyle, Cause of Attraction by Suction, i.

The operation of nature is different from mechanism, it doing not its work by trusion or *pulsion*, by knockings or thrustings, as if it were without that which it wrought upon. *Cudworth*, Intellectual System, p. 156.

pulsive (pul'siv), *a.* [< L. *pulsus*, pp. of *pellere*, beat, strike, drive (see *pulse*[1]), + *-ive*.] **1.** Constraining; compulsory. [Rare.]

The *pulsive* strain of conscience. *Marston.*

2. Impulsive. *Nares.*

In end my *pulsive* braine no art affoords
To mint, or stamp, or forge new coyned words.
John Taylor, Works (1630).

pulsometer (pul-som'e-tėr), *n.* [< L. *pulsus*, a beating, + Gr. μέτρον, measure.] **1.** Same as *pulsimeter*.—**2.** In *mech.*, a kind of steam-condensing pump acting on the principle of a vacuum-pump. By interposing a stratum of air between the steam and the water it forms a far more economical machine than the old style of vacuum-pump. In the illustration *a* and *a'* are bottle-shaped chambers; *b* is the bonnet with steam passages; *c* is a spherical valve which excludes the steam from one chamber while permitting it to flow into the other. Steam enters at *s*; *d* is an induction-passage for water; *e* and *e'* are vulcanized rubber valves; *f* and *f'*, valve-seats; *h*, the delivery passage, shown (with other parts) in dotted outline; *g* and *g'*, eduction-valves for water; *i* and *i'*, valve guards; *j*, an air-chamber; *k* and *k'*, bonnets covering openings whereby the valves may be reached for adjustment or repair; *l* and *l'*, rods which hold the induction-valves and their attachments in place; *n* and *n'*, brass socket-headed bolts which secure the valves *g* and *g'* and their attachments in their places. Into the neck of each of the chambers *a* and *a'* is screwed a small inlet air-valve (not shown). A similar valve is fitted to the chamber *j*. Steam entering chamber *a* expels its contents, and then, condensing, forms a partial vacuum. The valve then closes the opening into that chamber, and admits steam into the other. Water then rises to fill the vacuous chamber; also a little air enters through the minute air-valve in the neck. By this time the contents of the other chamber are expelled, the steam condenses therein, and other events follow as described for the first chamber. The small quantity of air admitted, being heavier than steam, forms a film over the upper surface of the water, and, being a non-conductor of heat, prevents wasteful condensation of steam, which would otherwise arise from the direct contact of the steam with the water. The machine derives its name from the pulsatory action of the steam ejected, and the analogy of its form, with its interior valves, to the construction of the heart. Also called *aquameter*.

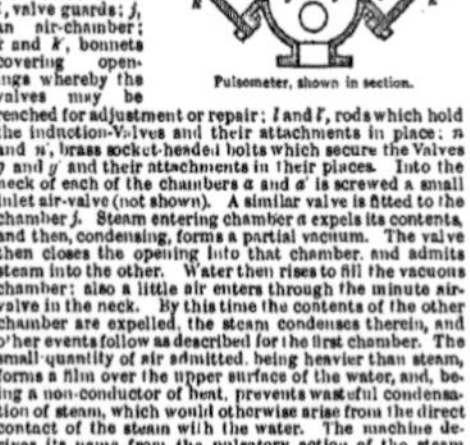

Pulsometer, shown in section.

pulsus (pul'sus), *n.* [L.: see *pulse*[1].] The pulse.—**Pulsus alternans**, a pulse in which alternate beats are strong and weak.—**Pulsus bigeminus**, a pulse made up of cycles consisting of two beats followed by a pause.—**Pulsus celer**, a quick pulse. See *pulse*.—**Pulsus dicrotus**, a dicrotic pulse. See *pulse*.—**Pulsus differens**, a pulse unequal in strength, or dissimilar in form in the two radials.—**Pulsus durus**, a hard pulse. See *pulse*.—**Pulsus filiformis**, a filiform pulse. See *pulse*.—**Pulsus hyperdicrotus**, a hyperdicrotic pulse. See *pulse*.—**Pulsus intercurrens**, a pulse in which there is an extra beat intercalated in a normal series.—**Pulsus intermittens**, an intermittent pulse. See *pulse*.—**Pulsus magnus**, a large pulse. See *pulse*.—**Pulsus mollis**, a soft pulse. See *pulse*.—**Pulsus monocrotus**, a monocrotic pulse.—**Pulsus myurus**, a pulse which becomes feebler and then stronger in alternate series.—**Pulsus paradoxus**, a pulse which for the most part or entirely disappears during inspiration, returning with expiration. It occurs in some cases when the aorta is compressed during inspiration by cicatricial bands produced by pericarditis or mediastinitis, in some cases of adherent pericardium, and in some of stenosis of the trachea or larynx.—**Pulsus parvus**, a small pulse. See *pulse*.—**Pulsus quadrigeminus**, a pulse in which there is a longer pause after every four beats.—**Pulsus tardus**, a slow pulse. See *pulse*.—**Pulsus tremulus**, a very feeble pulse just perceptible at the wrist as a faint fluttering sensation.—**Pulsus trigeminus**, a pulse with a longer pause after every three beats.—**Pulsus venosus**, the alternating expansion and contraction of a vein or veins, either due to the contractions of the heart acting backward through the large veins, or constituting a direct centripetal pulse due to arterial relaxation.

pult†, *v.* A Middle English form of *pelt*[1].

pultaceous (pul-tā'shius), *a.* [< L. *puls* (*pult-*), pottage, porridge (see *pulse*[2]), + *-aceous*.] **1.** Soft or semi-fluid, as the substance of a poultice; pulpy.—**2.** Macerated; pulpified; partly digested: as, a *pultaceous* mass of food in the stomach.

Pultenæa (pul-te-nē'ä), *n.* [NL. (Sir J. E. Smith, 1793), named after Richard *Pulteney* (1730–1801), an English botanist.] A genus of leguminous shrubs of the tribe *Podalyrieæ*. It is characterized by united keel-petals, a large banner-petal, two ovules, an ovate two-valved pod, persistent bractlets closely investing the calyx, and dry or thread-like stipules. The 75 species are all Australian. They bear undivided and alternate or rarely whorled flat or concave leaves, and brownish stipules often enlarged to form an involucre under the yellow or orange flowers, which are solitary in the axils or crowded in terminal heads. They are dwarf and ornamental evergreens, usually from 1 to 3 feet high, cultivated chiefly under the name *Pultenæa*; one, *P. daphnoides*, which reaches 8 feet, is known in Victoria as *wall-flower*. See *Viminaria*.

pulter†, *n.* An obsolete form of *poulterer*.

pultesse†, **pultise**†, *n.* Obsolete forms of *poultice*.

pultrie†, *n.* An obsolete form of *poultry*.

pulture, *n.* See *puture*.

pulu (pö'lö), *n.* [Hawaiian.] A fine silky yellowish fiber obtained in the Hawaiian Islands from tree-ferns of the genus *Cibotium*, the bases of whose leafstalks it densely covers. It is exported in considerable quantity, chiefly to San Francisco, for use in stuffing mattresses, etc. A species of the genus, *C. Barometz*, of tropical Asia and the Malayan islands, yields (as do also species of *Dicksonia*) a like product, used for the same purpose, and also employed in surgery as a mechanical styptic.

pulv. An abbreviation of Latin *pulvis*, powder: used in medical prescriptions.

pulverable (pul've-ra-bl), *a.* [< L. *pulverare*, cover with dust, reduce to powder (< *pulvis* (*pulver-*), dust, powder), + *-able*.] Capable of being pulverized, or reduced to fine powder. [Rare.]

In . . . the Indies he furnished himself with some liquid substances afforded by wounded plants, that as soon as he came near Europe, and not before, turned into consistent and *pulverable* bodies. *Boyle*, Works, I. 636.

pulveraceous (pul-ve-rā'shius), *a.* [< L. *pulvis* (*pulver-*), dust, powder, + *-aceous*.] In *bot.* and *zoöl.*, having a dusty or powdery surface; pulverulent.

pulverain† (pul've-rān), *n.* [= F. *pulvérin*, < It. *polverino*, < *polvere*, powder: see *powder*.] A powder-horn, especially one for fine priming-powder.

pulverate (pul've-rāt), *v. t.*; pret. and pp. *pulverated*, ppr. *pulverating*. [< L. *pulveratus*, pp. of *pulverare* (> It. *polverare*), cover with dust, reduce to powder, < *pulvis* (*pulver-*), dust, powder: see *powder*.] To beat or reduce to powder or dust; pulverize. [Rare.]

They litter them [their horses] in their own dung, first dryed in the Sun and *pulverated*. *Sandys*, Travailes, p. 51.

Pulveratores (pul″ve-rā-tō'rēz), *n. pl.* [NL., pl. of *pulverator*, < L. *pulverare*, pp. *pulveratus*, reduce to powder: see *pulverate*.] Birds which habitually roll themselves in the dust, as the *Rasores*.

pulver-day† (pul'vėr-dā), *n.* Same as *Pulver-Wednesday*.

pulver-dish† (pul'vėr-dish), *n.* [< L. *pulvis* (*pulver-*), dust, ashes, + E. *dish*.] A vessel in which were placed the ashes which were to be sprinkled upon the faithful on Ash Wednesday.

pulvereous (pul-vē'rē-us), *a.* [< L. *pulvereus*, containing dust, < *pulvis* (*pulver-*), dust, ashes: see *powder*.] Powdery or dusty; pulverulent.

pulverin, **pulverine** (pul've-rin), *n.* [< L. *pulvis* (*pulver-*), dust, ashes, + *-in*[2], *-ine*[2].] Ashes of barilla.

pulverizable (pul've-ri-za-bl), *a.* [= F. *pulvérisable* = Sp. *pulverizable* = It. *polverizzabile*; as *pulverize* + *-able*.] Capable of being pulverized. Also spelled *pulverisable*.

pulverization (pul″ve-ri-zā'shon), *n.* [= F. *pulvérisation* = Sp. *pulverizacion* = Pg. *pulve-*

rização = It. *polverizzazione;* as *pulverize* + *-ation.*] The act of pulverizing, or reducing to dust or powder. Also spelled *pulverisation.*

pulverize (pul'vẹ-rīz), *v.*; pret. and pp. *pulverized*, ppr. *pulverizing.* [= F. *pulvériser* = Pr. *polverizar* = Sp. Pg. *pulverizar* = It. *polverizzare, polverezzare,* < LL. *pulverizare*, reduce to dust, < L. *pulvis* (*pulver-*), dust, powder: see *powder.*] **I.** *trans.* To reduce to fine powder, as by pounding, grinding, etc.

> The zealous Prophet, with lust fury moov'd,
> 'Fore all the Host, his Brother sharp reproov'd,
> And *pulveriz'd* their Idol.
> *Sylvester*, tr. of Du Bartas's Weeks, ii., The Lawe.

II. *intrans.* 1. To become reduced to fine powder; fall to dust.—2. In *ornith.*, to roll or wallow in the dust; take a sand- or dust-bath, as a hen or partridge.

Also spelled *pulverise.*

pulverizer (pul'vẹ-rī-zėr), *n.* 1. One who or that which pulverizes; especially, a machine for breaking the soil, crushing stone, grinding grain, etc.—2. In *ornith.*, a bird that habitually rolls or wallows in the dust or takes sand-baths; one of the *Pulveratores.*

> The singularity of manners . . . peculiar to a few species, by some called *pulverizers.*
> *J. Rennie*, in Montagu's Ornith. Dict.

Also spelled *pulveriser.*

pulverizing-mill (pul'vẹ-rī-zing-mil), *n.* An apparatus for reducing the ingredients of gunpowder separately to an impalpable powder before they are combined in the incorporating-mill.

pulverous (pul'vẹ-rus), *a.* [< L. *pulvis* (*pulver-*), dust, powder: see *powder.*] Consisting of dust or powder; like powder. *Smart.*

pulverulence (pul-ver'ọ̈-lens), *n.* [< *pulverulen(t)* + *-ce.*] Dustiness; powder; the state of being dusted over, powdery, or pulverulent.

pulverulent (pul-ver'ọ̈-lent), *a.* [= F. *pulvérulent* = Sp. Pg. *pulverulento*, < L. *pulverulentus*, full of dust, covered with dust, < *pulvis* (*pulver-*), dust, powder: see *powder.*] 1. Dusty; consisting of fine powder; powdery: as, calcareous stone is sometimes found in the *pulverulent* form.—2. In *zoöl.*, finely powdery or dusty, as a surface; especially, covered as if powdered with very minute scales, as an insect.—3. In *bot.*: (*a*) Covered as if with powder or dust; pulveraceous: said of surfaces. (*b*) Of very slight cohesion: said of tissues.

> The "thallus," which increases in thickness by the formation of new layers upon its tree surface, has no very defined limit, and, in consequence of the slight adhesion of its components, is said to be "*pulverulent.*"
> *W. B. Carpenter*, Micros., § 325.

4. Addicted to lying and rolling in the dust, as fowls.

Pulver-Wednesday† (pul'vėr-wenz"dā̤), *n.* [< L. *pulvis* (*pulver-*), dust, ashes (see *powder*), + *Wednesday.*] Same as *Ash Wednesday.*

pulvil† (pul'vil), *n.* [Also *pulville* and *pulvillo*, *pulvillio*, *pulvilio;* < It. *polviglio*, < L. *pulvillus*, a little cushion, contr. from *pulvinulus*, < *pulvinus*, a cushion, an elevation.] A little bag of perfumed powder; a sachet.

> There stands the Toilette, Nursery of Charms,
> Completely furnish'd with bright Beauty's Arms;
> The Patch, the Powder Box, *Pulville*, Perfumes,
> Pins, Paint, a flattering Glass, and Black lead Combs.
> *Gay*, The Fan, i. 129.

pulvil† (pul'vil), *v. t.* [< *pulvil*, *n.*] To sprinkle with pulvil or a perfumed powder.

> Have you *pulvill'd* the Coachman and Postilion, that they may not stink of the Stable?
> *Congreve*, Way of the World, iv. 1.

pulvil-case† (pul'vil-kās), *n.* A receptacle for perfumed powder and other articles of the toilet, as combs, etc.

pulvilio†, *n.* Same as *pulvil.*

> It was easy for the porter in Farquhar to pass for Beau Clincher, by borrowing his lace and his *pulvilio.*
> *Macaulay*, Petrarch.

pulvillar (pul'vi-lạ̈r), *a.* [< L. *pulvillus* + *-ar*[2].] Cushion-like or pad-like, as a process on an insect's tarsus between the claws; of or pertaining to a pulvillus.

pulville†, *n.* Same as *pulvil.*

pulvilli, *n.* Plural of *pulvillus.*

pulvilliform (pul-vil'i-fôrm), *a.* [< L. *pulvillus*, a little cushion, + *forma*, form.] In *entom.*, resembling a pulvillus; cushion-like: as, a *pulvilliform* empodium.

pulvillio†, **pulvillo**†, *n.* Same as *pulvil.*

> The flowers perfumed the air with smells of incense, ambergris, and *pulvillios*, and were so interwoven with one another that they grew up in pieces of embroidery.
> *Addison*, Spectator, No. 63.

pulvillus (pul-vil'us), *n.*; pl. *pulvilli* (-ī). [L., a little cushion: see *pulvil.*] In *entom.*, a little process, like a cushion, pad, or sucker, between the clavi or claws of the apical or terminal tarsal joint of an insect's leg; a foot-pad. A pulvillus is a modified plantula, onychium, or empodium, forming a pad often furnished with tubular hairs which secrete an adhesive substance, enabling the insect to walk on smooth surfaces. The cushion of a fly's foot is an example. Also *pulvinulus.*

pulvinar (pul-vī'nạ̈r), *a.* and *n.* [< L. *pulvinaris*, of or belonging to a cushion or pillow; *pulvinarium*, usually *pulvinar*, a couch made of cushions; < *pulvinus*, a cushion, bolster, pillow, elevation: see *pillow.*] **I.** *a.* Padded or pad-like; cushiony; pillowy: as, the *pulvinar* prominence of the brain.

II. *n.* 1. A pillow or cushion; a medicated cushion.—2. The posterior inner part of the optic thalamus, forming a prominence on its upper surface. Also called *posterior tubercle.*—3. The cushion of fat filling up the non-articular part of the acetabulum.

Pulvinaria (pul-vi-nā'ri-ạ̈), *n.* [NL. (Targioni-Tozzetti, 1868), < L. *pulvinus*, a cushion: see *pulvinus.*] A notable genus of bark-lice or scale-insects of the homopterous family *Coccidæ.* The females are large, circular, and flat, with a dense white, cushion-shaped, and waxy egg-mass. They are very injurious to trees and plants. *P. vitis* damages grape-vines in Europe, and *P. innumerabilis* is a great pest to maple shade-trees in the United States, where it is known as the *cottony maple-scale.*

pulvinate (pul'vi-nāt), *a.* [< L. *pulvinatus*, cushion-shaped, having a swelling or elevation, < *pulvinus*, a cushion, an elevation: see *pillow.*] 1. Pulvinar; cushiony; pillowy; pad-like.—2. In *bot.*, cushion-shaped.

Also *pulviniform.*

Pulvinate prothorax or **pronotum**, in *entom.*, a prothorax or pronotum which is depressed in one place and appears to be puffed out in others, giving a fanciful resemblance to a cushion or pillow that has been pressed down in any part. *Kirby.*

pulvinated (pul'vi-nā-ted), *a.* [< *pulvinate* + *-ed*[2].] In *arch.*, noting a swelling or bulging out in any part of an order, or any member so characterized, as some friezes. Also called *pillowed.*

pulvinately (pul'vi-nāt-li), *adv.* In *bot.*, in a pulvinate manner.

pulvini, *n.* Plural of *pulvinus.*

pulviniform (pul-vin'i-fôrm), *a.* [< L. *pulvinus*, a cushion, an elevation, + *forma*, form.] Same as *pulvinate.*

pulvinulus (pul-vin'ụ̈-lus), *n.*; pl. *pulvinuli* (-lī). [NL., < L. *pulvinulus*, a little cushion, a little bank of earth, dim. of *pulvinus*, a cushion, an elevation.] In *entom.*, same as *pulvillus.*

pulvinus (pul-vī'nus), *n.*; pl. *pulvini* (-nī). [NL., < L. *pulvinus*, a cushion, bolster, pillow, elevation: see *pillow.*] In *bot.*, same as *cushion*, 2 (*j*).

pulviplume (pul'vi-plöm), *n.* [< NL. *pulvipluma*, < L. *pulvis*, dust, powder, + *pluma*, a feather.] Same as *powder-down.*

pulwar (pul'wär), *n.* [Also *pulwar;* E. Ind.] A light, keelless, neatly built boat used on the Ganges.

pulza-oil (pûl'zạ̈-oil), *n.* [Origin uncertain.] A fixed oil yielded by the seeds of the physic-nut, *Jatropha Curcas*, used medicinally and for general purposes. The seed is produced largely in the Cape Verd Islands, and exported to Lisbon, where chiefly the oil is expressed. Also called *jatropha-oil* (see *Jatropha*), *seed-oil*, and *purgueira-oil.*

puma (pū'mạ̈), *n.* [< Peruv. *puma*, a puma.] 1. Same as *cougar.*—2. [*cap.*] [NL.] A genus of *Felidæ*, such as the cougar. *Sir W. Jardine.*

pumelo, *n.* See *pomelo.*

pumey†, *n.* Same as *pumice.*

> Thetis in her bower
> Of *pumey* and tralucent pebble stones
> Receives the weary bridegroom of the sea.
> *Peele*, England's Holidays.

pumicate (pū'mi-kāt), *v. t.*; pret. and pp. *pumicated*, ppr. *pumicating.* [< L. *pumicatus*, pp. of *pumicare*, rub smooth with pumice, < *pumex* (*pumic-*), a pumice-stone: see *pumice.*] To make smooth with pumice. [Rare.]

pumice (pum'is or pū'mis), *n.* [Early mod. E. also *pumish*, also *pumicy*, *pumic(-stone)*; < ME. *pomyce*, *pomys*, *pomeys*, *pomayse*, *pomege*, < OF. **pomice* (?), vernacularly *ponce* (> E. *pounce*[2]) = Sp. *pómez* = Pg. *pomes* = It. *pomice* = AS. *pumic(stān)* = D. *puim(steen)* = OHG. *bumez*, MHG. *bumez*, *bimz*, G. *bims*, *bims(stein)* = Sw. *pim(sten)* = Dan. *pimp(sten)*, pumice, < L. *pumex* (*pumic-*), pumice-stone, any light porous stone; perhaps orig. **spumex*, < *spuma*, foam: see *spume.* Cf. doublet *pounce*[2].] Lava having a loose, spongy or cellular structure; lava from which gas or steam has escaped in large quantities while it was becoming consolidated. Pumice is usually a form of obsidian, and contains from 67 to 75 per cent. of silica. It is often so porous as to float on water for a considerable time after being ejected from a Volcano. After its pores become filled with water it sinks to the bottom, its specific gravity being nearly two and a half times that of water.

> Planted in rude and uncultivated places, amongst rocks and dry *pumices.* *Evelyn*, Silva.

> Like as a swarm of bees that in an hollow *pumice* pend.
> *Phaer*, Æneid, xii.

pumice (pum'is or pū'mis), *v. t.*; pret. and pp. *pumiced*, ppr. *pumicing.* [< *pumice*, *n.*] To polish, rub, or otherwise treat with pumice-stone; especially, in *silver-plating*, to clean with pumice and water, as the surface of an article to be plated.

> We who have ragged beards are cruel by prescription and acclamation; while they who have *pumiced* faces and perfumed hair are called cruel only in the moments of tenderness, and in the pauses of irritation.
> *Landor*, Diogenes and Plato.

> The box being finished, the outside is *pumiced* and polished, and any applications of gilding can be made.
> *Workshop Receipts*, 1st ser., p. 389.

pumiceous (pụ̈-mish'ius), *a.* [< L. *pumiceus*, of or pertaining to pumice, < *pumex* (*pumic-*), pumice: see *pumice.*] Pertaining to pumice; consisting of pumice, or resembling pumice: as, *pumiceous* structure.

> Minute angular fragments of *pumiceous* glass, such as is thrown high in the air during violent eruptions.
> *Science*, VII. 373.

pumice-stone (pum'is-stōn), *n.* [Formerly also *pumic-stone*, *pumy-stone;* < *pumice* + *stone.* Cf. AS. *pumic-stān.*] Same as *pumice.*

> Fire, fall'n from Heav'n, or else by Art incited, . . .
> Or from som Mountains burning bowels throw'n,
> Replent with Sulphur, Pitch, and *Pumy stone*,
> With sparkling fury spreads.
> *Sylvester*, tr. of Du Bartas's Weeks, ii., The Furies.

> This mountain, and indeed the whole island, is evidently of volcanic origin, and formed of lava, tufo, and *pumice stone.* *Eustace*, Italy, III. i.

> *Pumic stones* I hastly hent
> And threwe. *Spenser*, Shep. Cal., March.

pumiciform (pum'i-si-fôrm), *a.* [< L. *pumex* (*pumic-*), pumice, + *forma*, form.] Resembling pumice: specifically applied in geology to certain light spongy rocks having the texture of pumice.

pumicose (pum'i-kōs), *a.* [= It. *pumicoso*, *pomicoso*, < L. *pumicosus*, like pumice, porous, < *pumex* (*pumic-*), pumice: see *pumice.*] Consisting of or resembling pumice.

> The cavity of the sinus was almost entirely occupied by a *pumicose* deposit. *Sir W. Hamilton.*

pumic-stone†, *n.* Same as *pumice-stone.*

pummace†, *n.* An obsolete form of *pomace.*

pummel, *n.* and *v.* See *pommel.*

pummelo, *n.* See *pomelo.*

pump[1] (pump), *n.* [< ME. *pumpe*, < OF. *pompe*, F. *pompe* (> Russ. *pompa*) = Cat. Sp. Pg. *bomba*, pump; cf. D. *pomp* = MLG. LG. *pumpe* = G. *pumpe* = Sw. *pump* = Dan. *pumpe*, a pump; also in another form, G. *plumpe*, a pump; cf. G. *plumpen* = E. dial. *plump*, *v.*, pump, forms simulating *plump*[2], or more prob. original, and connected with *plump*[2], and thus ult., like *plunge*, < L. *plumbum*, lead: see *plump*[2]. The relations of the forms are difficult to determine, owing in part to the imitative intent appar. present in them.] 1. One of several kinds of hydraulic and pneumatic machines. (*a*) A hydraulic machine for raising liquids from a lower to a higher level through a pipe or passage by means of one or more pistons or plungers (with or without valves), or analogues of these devices, working in, or in correlation with, one or more pump-barrels, pump-stocks, chambers, or confined spaces. Of this class the common single-acting house-pump, the details of which are shown in the cut, is a familiar example. (*b*) A hydraulic machine for forcing liquids under pressure through one or more pipes or passages, in any direction, by means of one or more pistons or plungers, or analogues of these devices, working in one or more cylinders, trunks, pump-barrels, pump-stocks, chambers, or confined spaces. See *force-pump.* (*c*) A pneumatic machine for forcing aëriform fluids or vapors in any direction through a pipe or passage by means of one or more pistons, or their analogues or equivalents, working in one or more chambers, cylinders, pump-barrels, or pump-stocks. See *air-pump* and *mercury air-pump.* (In the *diaphragm-pump*, a reciprocating diaphragm performs the function of a

Single-acting Cast-iron House-pump.

a, lever; *b*, plunger or piston; *c*, fulcrum; *d*, cylinder or barrel; *e*, lower valve, or foot-valve; *f*, base, supporting all other parts.

piston. In the *chain-pump*, the "buttons" on the chain are substantially pistons of a lifting-pump. In the *spiral-pump*, which forces water through a spiral passage, as the Archimedean screw, the portions of the walls of the passage lying behind the liquid are the analogues of pistons. In *rotary pumps*, acting by direct pressure or by centrifugal force, or having a turbinate form, the analogues of pistons are the rotating vanes, buckets, etc. In *propeller-pumps*, the blades of the propeller-wheel represent the pistons. In pumps of the *monte-jus* variety, including steam vacuum-pumps, the pulsometer, etc., the representation of the piston is a volume of steam which first presses upon the liquid, and is then condensed and replaced by an equal volume of liquid, which in its turn is displaced by another volume of steam. In *jet-pumps*, the analogue of the piston is either a liquid column moving at high velocity to force other portions of liquid or vapor forward, or a column of air, gas, or vapor, which, in the steam injector and ejector, is steam that is condensed to a liquid during its movement without much reduction in its velocity.] 2. [< *pump*[1], *v.*] An artful effort to extract or elicit information, as by indirect question or remark. [Colloq.]

> I was the easier indeed because, for all her *pumps*, she gave no hints of the key and the door, &c., which, had he communicated to her, she would not have forborne giving me a touch of. *Richardson*, Pamela, I. 171.

Atmospheric, centrifugal, centripetal pump. See the adjectives.—**Circulating pump**, the pump employed to move a current of cold water through a surface-condenser. In a marine engine the water is taken from the sea, made to circulate through the condenser, and then thrown overboard.—**Dental pump**, a device for freeing the mouth from saliva during dental operations. Also called *saliva-pump*.—**Differential pump.** See *differential*.—**Double-acting pump**, a pump which, instead of discharging and inducting liquid in its outward stroke only, both inducts and discharges at each stroke. An inlet- and an outlet-valve is arranged at each end of the pump; the piston is solid and valveless; an induction branch-pipe or passage leads to each inlet-valve; and a discharge branch-pipe or passage leads from each outlet-valve.—**Eccentric pump**, a cylinder in which revolve a hub and axis arranged eccentrically. The water enters by one opening and escapes by another, expelled by flaps upon the hub, which serve as pistons in the space between the hub and case.—**Jack-head pump**, a pump having its delivery-pipe attached to the pump-barrel or -cylinder by a gooseneck connection. This form of attachment is used especially in lifting-pumps for raising water from deep shafts or borings.—**Mercurial pump.** See *mercury air-pump*, under *mercury*.—**Oscillating pump**, a form of pump in which a vessel incloses two valved sectors or vibrating chambers that oscillate upon a pivot under the control of a handle or lever. It operates by the oscillation of the sector-shaped pistons, which alternately suck water into and discharge it from the inclosing vessel.—**Pendulum pump.** See *pendulum*.—**Pump-joint machine**, a machine for fitting together the joints of pump-stocks, by boring out and turning down the joining ends to form a socket-joint.—**Rotary pump**, any pump that acts by the rotary motion of the part or parts that force the liquid forward. See cut under *centrifugal*.—**Saliva-pump.** Same as *dental pump*.—**Single-acting pump**, in contradistinction to *double-acting pump*, a pump that inducts and discharges during one stroke only—the outward stroke. Compare *stroke*.—**Spiral-pump.** Same as *Archimedean screw* (which see, under *Archimedean*).—**Steam jet-pump**, a jet-pump in which water is driven by steam. In the case of the injector this form of pump is used to feed water to the boiler. See *injector* and *ejector*, which are special names for steam jet-pumps.—**Steam vacuum-pump.** See *vacuum-pump*.—**Submerged pump**, a pump the barrel and valves of which are submerged, while its pump-rod and discharge-pipe extend above the surface of the water in which the pump-barrel is placed. The principal advantage pertaining to submerged pumps is that their working parts are not liable to be obstructed by the formation of ice (called *freezing up*), as is the case with pumps exposed to effects of very cold air.—**To fetch a pump.** See *fetch*[1].—**To prime a pump.** See *prime*. (See also *air-pump*, *chain-pump*, *filter-pump*, *force-pump*, *jet-pump*.)

Oscillating Pump.

The body of the pump is made in two sections, *a* and *b*, flanged and bolted together. The induction-chamber *c* has upwardly opening valves *d*, *d*, through which water is drawn by oscillating the handle *B*, causing corresponding oscillation of the piston *f*, *f*, which turns upon *f* as a center, and is provided with valves *i*, *i*, opening upwardly into the chamber *l*, into which the water is forced at each successive oscillation, and discharged therefrom through the eduction-opening *k*.

pump[1] (pump), *v.* [= D. *pompen* = G. *pumpen* = Sw. *pumpa* = Dan. *pumpe*; from the noun. Cf. E. dial. *plump* = G. *plumpen*, pump.] **I.** *intrans.* To work a pump; raise water or other liquid with a pump.

> Not so, oh Charon, wanting to defray,
> Thou hast my paines, I *pumpt* part of the way,
> Then tug'd at th' oare, being that only soule
> Who in thy barge did neither mourne nor houle.
> *Heywood*, Dialogues (Works, ed. Pearson, 1874, VI. 233).

> Mariners, . . . while they pour out their vows to their saviour gods, at the same time fall lustily to their tackle, and *pump* without intermission. *Warburton*, Divine Legation, iii. 6.

Pumping of the barometer, the oscillation of the mercury in the tube of a barometer, resulting from sudden movements of the instrument, or sometimes from the mechanical influence of blasts of air in compressing or rarefying the air when the barometer is placed near an obstruction. At sea, where the barometer is subject to the pitching and rolling of the vessel, pumping is especially troublesome, and, in order to diminish it, marine barometers are constructed with the tube contracted for a considerable part of its length.

II. *trans.* 1. To raise with a pump: as, to *pump* water.—2. To free from water or other fluid by means of a pump or pumps: as, to *pump* a ship.—3. To elicit or draw out by or as by artful interrogation: as, to *pump* out secrets.

> I'll stand aside whilst thou *pump'st* out of him
> His business. *B. Jonson*, Tale of a Tub, iv. 3.

4. To subject to a pumping process for the purpose of extracting, procuring, or obtaining something, such as money, information, or secrets.

> Here—'tis too little, but 'tis all my store;
> I'll to *pump* my dad, and fetch thee more.
> *Randolph*, Muses Looking Glass, ii. 4.

> Not to rove, and *pump* one's Fancy
> For Popish Similes beyond Sea.
> *Prior*, To Fleetwood Shephard.

> I am going to *pump* Mr. Bentley for designs.
> *Walpole*, Letters, II. 264.

> He . . . finally made a motion with his arm as if he were working an imaginary pump-handle, thereby intimating that he (Mr. Trotter) considered himself as undergoing the process of being *pumped* by Mr. Samuel Weller.
> *Dickens*, Pickwick, xvi.

To pump ship, to urinate. [Low.]

pump[2] (pump), *n.* [Prob. < F. *pompe*, pomp, ornament, show (> LG. *pump*, pomp, show); cf. G. *pumphosen*, wide pantaloons, < (LG.) *pump*, pomp, show, + *hosen*, hose; *pumpstiefel*, a large, clumsy boot, < (LG.) *pump*, pomp, show, + *stiefel*, boot: see *pomp*. For the form, cf. *pumpet* for *pompet*.] A low shoe or slipper, with a single unwelted sole, and without a heel, or with a very low heel, worn chiefly for dancing.

> Thy *pumps*, as white as was the milk,
> And yet thou wouldst not love me.
> *Greensleeves* (Child's Ballads, IV. 242).

> Thou shalt not need to travel with thy *pumps* full of gravel any more, after a blind jade and a hamper.
> *B. Jonson*, Poetaster, iii. 1.

> The usual attire of a gentleman, viz. *pumps*, a gold waistcoat, a crush hat, a sham frill, and a white choker.
> *Thackeray*, Book of Snobs, i.

pumpage (pum'pāj), *n.* [< *pump*[1] + *-age*.] The amount pumped; the quantity or amount raised by pumping.

> The *pumpage* for the year averaged 69,658,969 gallons per day. *Sanitarian*, XVII. 119.

pump-barrel (pump'bar″el), *n.* The wooden or metal cylinder or tube which forms the body of a pump, and in which the piston moves.

pump-bit (pump'bit), *n.* Same as *nose-bit*.

pump-bob (pump'bob), *n.* In a steam-engine, a form of bell-crank lever serving to convert rotary motion into reciprocating motion, for operating a pump-piston.

pump-bolt (pump'bōlt), *n.* A toggle-pin used on fishing-vessels. [Massachusetts, U. S.]

pump-box (pump'boks), *n.* 1. The piston of the common pump, having a valve opening upward.—2. The casing or cap of a pump.—**Lower pump-box**, the casing of the lower valve of a pump.—**Upper pump-box**, the casing of the upper valve.

pump-brake (pump'brāk), *n.* The arm or handle of a pump, more particularly that form which has a horizontal hand-piece at the end of a lever. See *brake*[3].

pump-cart (pump'kärt), *n.* A vehicle carrying a pump and reservoir, used for watering and irrigating. *E. H. Knight.*

pump-chain (pump'chān), *n.* The chain of a chain-pump. See *chain-pump*.

pump-cistern (pump'sis″tėrn), *n.* 1. *Naut.*, a cistern over the head of a chain-pump to receive the water, whence it is conveyed through the ship's side by the pump-dales.—2. A contrivance to prevent chips and other matters from getting to and fouling the chain-pumps.

pump-coat (pump'kōt), *n.* *Naut.*, a canvas cover fastened about a pump, and nailed to the partners, to prevent water from running down its sides.

pump-dale (pump'dāl), *n.* The discharge-spout (originally and still commonly a trough) of a pump, which directs the flow; specifically, a long detachable hose or tube used on board ship to conduct water from a pump across the ship and over the side. Pump-dales are also used in tanneries to convey tan-liquor pumped from one vat into another. Also called *dale*.

pumped[1] (pumpt), *p. a.* [< *pump*[1] + *-ed*[2].] Out of breath; panting; breathless: sometimes with *out*. [Colloq. or slang.]

> Darkness began to set in, the artillery horses were *pumped out*, and orders were given to retire.
> *W. H. Russell*, Diary in India, II. 370.

pumped[2] (pumpt), *a.* [< *pump*[2] + *-ed*[2].] Provided with pumps; wearing pumps or low dress shoes. [Rare.]

> All the young gentlemen tightly cravatted, curled, and *pumped*. *Dickens*, Dombey and Son, xiv.

pumper (pum'pėr), *n.* [= G. *pumper*; as *pump*[1] + *-er*[1].] 1. One who or that which pumps.

> The flame lasted about two minutes from the time the *pumper* began to draw out the air. *Boyle*, Works, I. 26.

2. A mineral-oil well from which the oil must be pumped up, as distinguished from one from which the oil issues in a natural jet.

pumpernickel (pum'pėr-nik″el), *n.* [< G. *pumpernickel*, formerly also *pompernickel*, orig. a heavy, blockish fellow, hence applied to a coarse, heavy bread; < *pumper*, the noise of a heavy fall (< *pumpen*, fall, plump: see *plump* and *pump*[1]), + *Nickel*, a popular abbr. of the common personal name *Nicolaus*, Nicholas: see *Nick*[4], *nickel*.] A kind of coarse bread made from unbolted rye, used especially in Westphalia. It has a little acidity, but is agreeable to the taste, though not very nourishing. Also called *bombernickel*.

pumpet†, *n.* See *pompet*.

pump-gear (pump'gēr), *n.* *Naut.*, apparatus employed in pumping.

pump-handle (pump'han″dl), *n.* The handle or lever attached to the piston-rod of a pump for moving the piston up and down.

> She 's five and forty. She 's red hair. She 's a nose like a *pump-handle*. *Thackeray*, Book of Snobs, xi.

pump-head (pump'hed), *n.* The cap or top of a chain-pump, which serves to guide the water into the discharge-spout, and as a cover for the pump and well; a pump-hood.

pump-hood (pump'hůd), *n.* A semicylindrical frame covering the upper wheel of a chain-pump; a pump-head. It directs the water into the discharge-spout, and prevents the throwing out of part of it by centrifugal force.

pump-house (pump'hous), *n.* Same as *pump-room*.

> It is customary to begin the morning [Bath, 1766] by bathing, which continues from six till about nine; the company then repair to the *pump-house*, some to drink the hot waters, but more for pastime, as they are here amused by a band of music, which fills up the intervals of wit and pleasantry. *Life of Quin* (reprint 1887), p. 50.

pumping-engine (pump'ing-en″jin), *n.* Any form of motor for operating a pump. While pumping-engines of many types are merely large steam-pumps, a distinction appears to obtain between the terms. Pumping-engines are among the largest engines constructed. They are often built as beam-engines, as at the water-works of Louisville in Kentucky, and also as horizontal engines directly connected with horizontal pumps, as in the common steam-pump.

pumping-shaft (pum'ping-shȧft), *n.* See *shaft*.

pumpion (pum'pi̦on), *n.* [Also *pompion*, *pompeon*, *poumpion*, *pompon*; < OF. *pompon*, a melon, a variant (simulating a reduplicated form) of earlier *pepon* (> ME. *pepon*), < L. *pepo(n-)*, < Gr. πέπων, a kind of melon: see *pepo*. Cf. *pippin*[1]. Hence *pumpkin*, q. v.] A pumpkin. [Obsolete or archaic.]

> Herbes of the bygger sorte, as gourdes, melones, cucumers, *pompons*, citrons, and suche other, coome to their perfection in the space of thirtie dayes.
> *Peter Martyr* (tr. in Eden's First Books on America, [ed. Arber, p. 168).

> All manner of strange fruits, as pomegranates, oranges, *pompions*. *Stow* (Arber's Eng. Garner, I. 477).

> We'll use this unwholesome humidity, this gross watery *pumpion*; we'll teach him to know turtles from jays.
> *Shak.*, M. W. of W., iii. 3. 43.

> Indian *pompeons*, the water melon, and the musk-mellon. *S. Clarke*, Four Plantations in America (1670), p. 26.

> Observe a *pompion*-twine afloat;
> Pluck me one cup from off the castle-moat!
> Along with cup you raise leaf, stalk, and root,
> The entire surface of the pool to boot.
> *Browning*, Sordello, ii.

pump-kettle (pump'ket″l), *n.* A convex perforated diaphragm fixed at the bottom of a pump-tube to prevent the entrance of foreign matters; a strainer. *E. H. Knight.*

pumpkin (pump'kin), *n.* [Formerly also *pumkin* (and in popular use, though spelled *pumpkin*, now generally pronounced pung'kin, as if written *punkin*); an altered form, simulating the term. *-kin*, of *pumpion*.] The fruit of a variety of *Cucurbita Pepo*; also, the plant which produces it. The plant is a coarse decumbent vine, often many feet long; the leaves are heart-shaped and somewhat lobed, nearly a foot across, and rough and almost prickly, as are also their hollow stalks. The gourd-like fruit is nearly globular or somewhat oblong, flattened at the ends, a foot or more in length, and of a deep orange-yellow color when ripe. Inside it is partly filled with a dryish stringy pulp containing the seeds; the esculent part is a fleshy layer an inch or two thick beneath the rind. The pumpkin is of supposed Asiatic origin, and is cultivated in many countries; in England it has been cultivated either as a curiosity or for food since 1570. It is thought to have been known to the American aborigines, and to have been planted by them among their maize. In America it has been largely given as food to cattle, and is also used on the table, especially in pumpkin-pie; but in culinary use it is now largely superseded by the squash, and is less grown for other purposes than formerly. The pumpkin has various subvarieties, and is closely related to the vegetable marrow. (See *marrow*1.) The name is sometimes wrongly applied to forms of the squash. In England occasionally called *gourd* or *pumpkin-gourd*. See *Cucurbita*.

We had an entertainment of boiled wheat with meat in it, and a dish of the *pumkin* kind, dressed after their way.
Pococke, Description of the East, II. i. 181.

pumpkin-head (pump'kin-hed), *n.* A stupid fellow; a dolt. [Colloq., U. S.]

pumpkin-seed (pump'kin-sēd), *n.* **1.** The seed of the pumpkin.—**2.** One of many small centrarchoid fishes of the genus *Lepomis* or *Pomotis*, especially the common sunfish of the eastern United States, *L. gibbosus*: so called from the shape. Also *tobacco-box*. See cut under *sunfish*. [U. S.]—**3.** A type of yacht-built boat, broad and cat- or sloop-rigged. It is a very wet sailor. *Henshall.* [Florida.]—**4.** A very flat, wide row-boat, of the shape of a pumpkin-seed, used in water that is shallow or encumbered with weeds or grass. [U. S.]

pumpkin-vine (pump'kin-vīn), *n.* The pumpkin-plant.

pump-lug (pump'lug), *n.* A lug cast upon the cross-head of a locomotive, to which the pump-plunger is attached, and which imparts a reciprocating motion to the plunger.

pump-piston (pump'pis'ton), *n.* The plunger, cup, or bucket, reciprocating in a cylinder, by means of which the function of a pump is performed.

pump-plunger (pump'plun'jėr), *n.* **1.** The solid piston of a plunger-pump: used to distinguish this class of pump-piston from those which contain a valve.—**2.** A pump-piston of which the part that operates in the pump-barrel also extends out through the stuffing-box, and is either itself the piston-rod or plunger-rod, or is connected with a piston-rod or plunger-rod exteriorly to the stuffing-box.

pump-room (pump'röm), *n.* A room connected with a mineral spring, in which the waters are drunk.

Her first resolution . . . [was to seek Miss Tilney] in the *Pump Room* at noon. In the *Pump Room* one so newly arrived in Bath must be met with.
Jane Austen, Northanger Abbey, ix.

pump-scraper (pump'skrā'pėr), *n.* A circular plate used for cleaning out a pump-barrel.

pump-spear (pump'spēr), *n.* The rod connecting the handle and the valve of a pump.

pump-staff (pump'staf), *n.* The pump-spear or piston-rod of a pump.

pump-stock (pump'stok), *n.* The body of a pump.

pump-stopper (pump'stop'ėr), *n.* *Naut.*, a plug.

pump-thunder (pump'thun'dėr), *n.* [So called in allusion to its booming cry; < **pump*, var. of *bump*1, + *thunder*.] The American bittern, *Botaurus mugitans* or *lentiginosus*. Also called *thunder-pumper*. [Local; U. S.]

pump-well (pump'wel), *n.* **1.** A well from which water or other fluid is raised by means of a pump.—**2.** *Naut.*, a compartment formed by bulkheads round the pumps on shipboard, to keep them clear of obstructions, to protect them from injury, and to afford ready admittance for examining their condition.

pumy†, *n.* [A quasi-sing. form of *pumice*, taken as plural: see *pumice*. Cf. *pumice-stone*.] A pebble; a stone. [Rare.]

And oft the *pumies* latched.
Spenser, Shep. Cal., March.

pun1 (pun), *v. t.*; pret. and pp. *punned*, ppr. *punning*. [< ME. **punen*, < AS. *punian*, beat, pound: see *pound*3, the same word in diff. form.] To beat; strike with force; ram; pound, as in a mortar; reduce to powder. [Obsolete or prov. Eng.]

He would *pun* thee into shivers with his fist, as a sailor breaks a biscuit. *Shak.*, T. and C., ii. 1. 42.

The roots must be first sliced and dried in the sunne, or by the fire, and then, being *punned* into floure, will make good bread. *Hakluyt's Voyages*, III. 272.

Yea sometimes in the winter season, when he was in the country, he refused not to cleave wood, and to *punne* barley, and to doe other country works only for the exercise of his body. *Goghan's* Haven of Health, p. 225.

Too much stress cannot be laid upon good sound *punning*. The earth, as it is thrown in, should be thoroughly well *punned* at every stage.
Preece and Sivewright, Telegraphy, p. 196.

pun2 (pun), *v.*; pret. and pp. *punned*, ppr. *punning*. [Usually explained as a particular use of *pun*1, pound, as if to pound or beat words, as it were into new shapes (cf. *twist*, *wrest*, as used of words; *clench*, *clinch*, a pun); but this explanation requires the verb to have been orig. transitive, 'to pound' (sc. words); evidence of such a use is lacking, and it is not certain that the verb precedes the noun.] **I.** *intrans.* To make puns.

Who dealt in doggrel, or who *punned* in prose.
Dryden, tr. of Juvenal, x. 180.

II. *trans.* To affect by a pun.

The sermons of Bishop Andrews and the tragedies of Shakspeare are full of them [puns]. The sinner was *punned* into repentance by the former, as in the latter nothing is more usual than to see a hero weeping and quibbling for a dozen lines together.
Addison, Spectator, No. 61.

pun2 (pun), *n.* [See *pun*2, *v.*] An expression in which the use of a word in two different applications, or the use of two different words pronounced alike or nearly alike, presents an odd or ludicrous idea; a play on words that are alike or nearly alike in sound but differ in meaning; a kind of verbal quibble.

A *pun* can be no more engraven than it can be translated. When the word is construed into its idea, the double meaning vanishes. *Addison*, Ancient Medals, ii.

A better *pun* on this word [gay] was made on the Beggar's Opera, which, it was said, made Gay rich, and Rich gay. *Walpole*, Anecdotes of Painting, V. 92, note.

=**Syn.** *Pun*, *Paronomasia*, *Assonance*. *Pun* and *paronomasia* are often confounded, but are in strictness distinct in form and effect. A *pun* is a play upon two senses of the same word or sound, and its effect is to excite a sense of the ludicrous: as,

They went and told the sexton, and
The sexton toll'd the bell.
Hood, Sally Brown.

Even when taken into sober discourse, the *pun* has an effect at least of oddity: as,

For *Suffolk's* duke, may he be *suffocate*.
Shak., 2 Hen. VI., i. 1. 124.

Hence modern taste excludes puns from serious writing and speaking. *Paronomasia* is rather the use of words that are nearly but not quite alike in sound, and it heightens the effect of what is said without suggesting the ludicrous: as, "Per *angusta* ad *augusta*"; "And catch with his *surcease success*," *Shak.*, Macbeth, i. 7. 4;

To begirt the almighty throne
Beseeching or *besieging*. *Milton*, P. L., v. 869.

As in these examples, it is most likely to be used where the words thus near in sound are far apart in meaning. It is very common in the original languages of the Bible, especially in the Old Testament, as in Isa. v. 7. An attempt to imitate it may be found in Mat. xxi. 41, revised version. *Assonance* is the bare fact of resemblance of sound, being generally accidental, and in the majority of cases disagreeable to the ear: as, *unfold old* truths, *our power, if of, is as, and Andrew drew, the then* condition. For the technical meaning of *assonance*, see def. 2 under that word.

puna (pö'nä), *n.* [Peruv.] In the Peruvian Andes, nearly the same as *paramo*.

Tschudi says that by the name of *puna* is designated the high table-land in Peru and Bolivia lying between the two great chains of the Cordillera, beginning at an elevation of about 10,500 feet above the sea-level, and extending to the regions of eternal snow.
J. D. Whitney, Names and Places, p. 196.

punatoo (pun-a-tö'), *n.* [Cingalese.] In Ceylon, the preserved pulp of the fruit of the palmyra-palm. It is the chief food of the poorer classes of the peninsula of Jaffna for several months of the year, and is used in soups, etc.

puna-wind (pö'nä-wind), *n.* A cold and remarkably dry wind which blows from the Cordilleras across the table-land called the Puna, in Peru.

punch1 (punch), *v. t.* [< ME. *punchen* = Sp. *punchar* (< ML. *punctare*), *punzar* = Pg. *punçar* (< ML. **punctiare*, *punctuare*), pierce, prick, punch, sting, < ML. *punctuare*, *puncture*, pierce, prick, punch, < L. *punctum*, *punctus*, a point: see *point*1, *n.* and *v.* The E. form is in part due to the related noun *puncheon* (see *puncheon*1), and has been in part confused with ME. *punchen*, var. of *punischen*, punish (see *punch*2), also with ME. *bunchen*, beat, strike (see *bunch*2).] **1.** To make a hole or holes in with a punch or some similar instrument; pierce; perforate: as, to *punch* a metal plate.

When I was mortal, my anointed body
By thee was *punched* full of deadly holes.
Shak., Rich. III., v. 3. 125.

2. To make with or as with a punch: as, to *punch* a hole in something.—**Punching-and-shearing machine**, a machine having both punches and shearing-plates connected with the same standard or bed, and with the same driving pulley or motor.—**Punching-press**, a die-press constructed like an ordinary punching-machine.

punch1 (punch), *n.* [< *punch*1, *v.*; in part prob. abbr. of *puncheon*1, q. v.] **1.** A tool the working end of which is pointed, blunt, a continuous edge inclosing an area, or a pattern in relief or intaglio, and which acts either by pressure or percussion (applied in the direction of its longitudinal axis) to perforate or indent a solid material, or to drive out or in objects inserted in previously formed perforations or cavities. The pointed punch may be regarded as a chisel with a very narrow edge, cutting, therefore, in one point only, and forcing adjacent parts of the material asunder by a wedge-like action. The action of a punch with a continuous edge inclosing an area is also analogous to the action of a chisel. The action of a flat-nosed punch, when used with a die to which it is fitted, is that of a shear-blade, the parts of the material operated upon being separated by sliding over each other, instead of being wedged apart, as is the operation of the pointed punch. Hardened and tempered steel is the usual material of which punches are made. Solid punches with engraved faces are used for stamping-dies, as in coining, and with plain flat faces are used in connection with accurately fitted dies for making clean-cut holes in metal plates, and also for punching out blanks for buttons, coins, small gear-wheels, etc. Hollow punches, or punches having continuous edges inclosing an area, are principally used for cutting either very thin, soft sheet-metal, as tin, brass, or copper plates, or other soft flexible substances, as leather, paper, or cloth. The pointed punch is used for marking centers in the operation of turning, or for punching holes in thin materials where clean cutting is of no importance, as in punching holes in sheet-zinc or -tin for the reception of nails in nailing such sheets to wood.

Punch.

a, piece to be punched; *p*, punch; *h*, handle; *s*, support for *a*; *t*, tongs. The punch is operated by striking with a hammer or sledge at *m*. The tongs are usually held in the left hand of the smith, and the handle of the punch in his right hand, his assistant delivering the blows.

2. A tool used to force nail-heads below the surface.—**3.** A stone-masons' chipping-tool; a puncheon.—**4.** In *surg.*, an instrument used for extracting the stumps of teeth.—**5.** In *decorative art*, a tool in the form of a bar, sometimes fitted with a handle and engraved at the end in a cross, concentric ring, or other device. It is used for impressing ornamental patterns upon clay or other plastic materials.—**6.** The engraved model of a printing-type on the end of a steel rod: so called from its being punched in a copper bar which makes the matrix, or a reversed impression of the model.—**7.** In *carp.*, studding by which a roof is supported.—**8.** In *hydraul. engin.*, a short length placed on the top of a pile to permit the monkey of a pile-driver to bear upon it when it has been driven too low to be struck directly; a dolly.—**9.** In *coal-mining*, same as *pout*4. [North. Eng.]—**Centering punch**, a pointed steel punch with parallel sides, sliding freely in the stem of an inverted funnel or centering cone. *C. P. B. Shelley*, Workshop Appliances, p. 166.—**Coopers' punch**, a punch operated by a lever and making two holes at once. It is used to punch rivet-holes in iron hoops.—**Duplex punch.** (*a*) A punch which has a counter-die on the opposite pan, as in a ticket-punch. (*b*) A punch operated by the rolling action of two levers on one fulcrum, forming a toggle.—**Hollow punch.** See def. 1.

punch2 (punch), *v. t.* [< ME. *punchen*, a syncopated form of *punischen*, punish (cf. similar syncopated ME. forms of *polish*, *vanish*, and the reverse in ME. *perishen*, var. of *perchen*, *percen*, pierce: see *pierce*). *Punch* in this sense has been confused with *punch*1, with which it is now practically identified: see *punch*1, and cf. *bunch*2.] **1**†. Same as *punish*.

Punchyn, or chastysen, punysshen, punio, castigo.
Prompt. Parv., p. 416.

For ȝour errours on erthe . . .
ȝe schulle be *punched*.
Alexander and Dindimus, l. 747.

2. To give a blow, dig, or thrust to; beat with blows of the fist: as, to *punch* one on the head, or to *punch* one's head. [Colloq.]

With a goade he *puncht* each furious dame,
And made them every one cast downe their greene and leavie speares. *Chapman*, Iliad, vi.

Smart chap that cabman—handled his fives well; but if I'd been your friend in the green jemmy— . . . punch his head—'cod I would. *Dickens*, Pickwick Papers, ii.

Wou't you please *punch* that fire, and give us more blaze? *C. D. Warner*, Backlog studies, p. 155.

punch[2] (punch), *n.* [< *punch*[2], *v.*] A blow, dig, or thrust, as with the fist, elbow, or knee: as, to give one a *punch* in the ribs or a *punch* on the head. [Colloq.]

punch[3] (punch), *a.* and *n.* [Perhaps a var. of *bunch*[1]; cf. *punchy* with *bunchy*.] **I.** *a.* Short and fat. [Prov. Eng.]

II. *n.* 1. A short, fat fellow.

I . . . did hear them call their fat child *punch*, which pleased me mightily, that word being become a word of common use for all that is thick and short. *Pepys*, Diary, April 30, 1669.

2. A short-legged, barrel-bodied horse, of an English draft-breed.

A stout Suffolk *punch*, about thirteen hands and a half in height. *Barham*, Ingoldsby Legends, I. 119.

Punch[4] (punch), *n.* [Abbr. of *Punchinello*, by conformation with *punch*[3].] A short hump-backed hook-nosed puppet, with a squeaking voice, the chief character in a street puppet-show called "Punch and Judy," who strangles his child, beats his wife (Judy) to death, belabors a policeman, and does other tragical and outrageous things in a comical way.

punch[5] (punch), *n.* [Formerly also *pounche*, *punce* (= D. *pons* = G. Sw. Dan. *punsch* = F. *punch*, *ponche* = Sp. Pg. *poncho* = It. *punchio*, *ponchio*, < E.); so called from its five ingredients, < Hind. *panch*, five, < Skt. *pancha*, five, = E. *five*: see *five*. The Hind. *punch* does not seem to occur alone in the sense of 'punch,' but it is much used in composition to denote various mixtures of five things, as *panch-āmrit*, a mixture of milk, curds, sugar, glue, and honey, *panch-bhadra*, a sauce of five ingredients, *panch-pallav*, a medical preparation from the sprouts of five trees, etc., or sets of five things, as *panch-pir*, five saints, *panch-gavya*, the five things yielded by the cow, etc.; also alone for an assembly of five men, or any council (cf. *punchayet*).] A drink commonly made with wine or spirits, and either water or some substitute, as a decoction of tea, and flavored with lemon-juice or lemon-peel and sugar. Punch is usually named from the alcoholic liquor which it contains, as brandy-*punch*, claret-*punch*, rum-*punch*, but sometimes also from other ingredients, as milk-*punch*, tea-*punch*, or from some person or circumstance, as Regent's *punch*, Swedish *punch*, Webster *punch*.

E'en now the godlike Brutus views his score
Scroll'd on the bar-board, swinging with the door;
Where, tippling *punch*, grave Cato's self you see,
And Amor Patriæ vending smuggled tea.
Crabbe, Works, I. 186.

Punch had begun to make its appearance, but it was a simple liquor to what afterwards became known by that name. *J. Ashton*, Social Life in Reign of Queen Anne, I. 202.

Cobbler's punch. See *cobbler*[1].—**Roman punch.** See *Roman*.

punchayet (pun-chī'et), *n.* [Hind. *panchāyat*, contr. *panchāt*, a court of arbitration consisting of five or more members, a council; cf. *panch*, a council of five, < *punch*, five: see *punch*[5].] In the village communities of Hindustan, a committee of five men sitting as a jury to try offenses against caste, etc., or as an administrative council or the like.

Bigamy is a Parsee abomination, . . . and the unfortunate Jemshedjee was excommunicated by the honorable *punchayet*. *J. W. Palmer*, The New and the Old, p. 274.

punch-bowl (punch'bōl), *n.* [= Sw. *punschbål* = Dan. *punschebolle*; as *punch*[5] + *bowl*[1].] A bowl in which the ingredients of punch are mixed, and from which it is served by means of a ladle. See cut under *monteith*.

They hae gard [caused] fill up ae *punch-bowl*. *Jock o' the Side* (Child's Ballads, VI. 88).

Take, for instance, the *punch-bowl*. . . . It was a thing to be brought forth and filled with a fragrant mixture of rum, brandy, and curaçoa, lemon, hot water, sugar, grated nutmeg, cloves, and cinnamon. *W. Besant*, Fifty Years Ago, p. 170.

punch-check (punch'chek), *n.* Same as *bell-punch*.

punch-cutter (punch'kut"ėr), *n.* The engraver on punches of letters for a type-foundry.

puncheon[1] (pun'chon), *n.* [Formerly also *punchion*, *punchin*; < ME. *punchon*, *punsoun*, < OF. *poinchon*, *poinson*, F. *poinçon* = Sp. *punzon* = Pg. *punção* = It. *punzone*, a sharp instrument, a bodkin, dagger, < L. *punctio(n-)*, a pricking, puncture, < *pungere*, pp. *punctus*, prick, punch: see *punch*[1] and *point*[1]. Cf. doublet *punction*.] 1. A perforating- or stamping-tool; a punch. (*a*) An iron instrument with a sharp steel point used in marble-working: as, a dog's-tooth or gradin *puncheon*; a stone-cutters' *puncheon*. *E. H. Knight*. (*b*) A tool by which a plate-mark is put upon silverware or the like.

That other signet of gold w' my *puncheon* of ivory and silver, I geue and bequeath unto Robert my secunde sone. *Fabyan*, Chron., I., Pref., p. vii.

2. In *carp.*: (*a*) A short upright piece of timber in framing; a dwarf post, stud, or quarter. (*b*) A slab of split timber with the face smoothed with an adz or ax, sometimes used for flooring or bridge-boards in the absence of sawed boards. [U. S.]

The house was constructed of logs, and the floor was of *puncheons*—a term which in Georgia means split logs with their faces a little smoothed with the axe or hatchet. *Georgia Scenes*, p. 12.

He had danced on *puncheon* floors before, but never on one that rattled so loudly. *The Century*, XXXIX. 286.

(*c*) One of the small quarters of a partition above the head of a door. *E. H. Knight*.

puncheon[2] (pun'chon), *n.* [Formerly also *punchion*; ME. not found; < OF. *poinson*, *ponçon*, F. *poinçon*, a wine-vessel, = It. *punzone*, a wine-vessel; perhaps so called orig. with ref. to the stamp or print impressed on the cask by a puncheon or stamping-tool, and so a transferred use of *puncheon*[1] (cf. *hogshead*, a cask). The OF. *poçon*, *posson*, a small measure, quarter of a pint, can hardly be related. The G. dial. (Bav.) *punzen*, *ponzen*, a cask, is perhaps of F. origin.] A cask; a liquid measure of from 72 to 120 gallons: as, a *puncheon* of wine. The puncheon of beer in London contained 72 beer-gallons; that of wine, 84 wine-gallons. The latter Value was legalized in 1423.

And he 's sew'd up the bloody hide,
A *puncheon* o' wine put in.
King Henry (Child's Ballads, I. 149).

puncher (pun'chėr), *n.* [< *punch*[1] + *-er*[1].] One who or that which punches, perforates, or stamps.

He was a rival of the former, who used puncheons for his graving, which Johnson never did, calling Simon a *puncher*, not a graver. *Walpole*, Anecdotes of Painting, II. 250.

punch-glass (punch'glȧs), *n.* A small tumbler or ornamental mug with a handle, made of glass and used for punch and similar drinks: usually forming part of a set, as with a tray, or a tray and punch-bowl.

punch-gut†, *a.* Pot-bellied.

O swinish, *punch-gut* God, say they, that smells rank of the sty he was sowed up in. *Kennet*, tr. of Erasmus's Praise of Folly, p. 19. (*Davies*.)

punch-house (punch'hous), *n.* In India, an inn or tavern; specifically, in the Presidency towns, a boarding-house or house of entertainment for seamen.

Sailors, British and American, Malay and Lascar, [belong] to Flag Street, the quarter of *punch-houses*. *J. W. Palmer*, The New and the Old, p. 264.

punchin†, *n.* An obsolete variant of *puncheon*[1].

Punchinello (pun-chi-nel'ō), *n.* [Formerly also *Punchanello*, *Punchionello*; = F. *Polichinelle*, < It. *pulcinello*, a clown, buffoon, prop. a puppet, dim. of *pulcino*, formerly also *polcino*, a young chicken, a child; cf. *pulcella*, f., a young girl, maiden, = F. *pucelle* (see *pucelle*); ult. < L. *pullus*, the young of an animal, a chicken: see *pullet*. Cf. *Punch*[4].] 1†. [*l. c.*] A puppet; specifically, a popular puppet of Italian origin, the prototype of Punch. See *Punch*[4]. [In the first quotation the name is applied to an exhibitor of puppets.]

1666, March 29. Rec. of *Punchinello*, the Itallian popet player, for his booth at Charing Cross, £2 12*s.* 6*d.* *Overseer's Books of the Parish of St. Martin's in the Fields*, [London. (*Nares*.)

'Twas then, when August near was spent,
That Bat, the grilliado'd saint,
Had usher'd in his Smithfield-revels,
Where *punchionelloes*, popes, and devils
Are by authority allow'd,
To please the giddy gaping crowd.
Hudibras Redivivus (1707). (*Nares*.)

2. Any grotesque or absurd personage, likened to the familiar character of the popular comedy in Italy.

Being told that Gilbert Cooper called him [Johnson] the Caliban of literature: "Well," said he, "I must dub him the *Punchinello*." *Boswell*, Johnson, ætat. 61.

punching-bag (pun'ching-bag), *n.* A bag, generally large and heavy, suspended from the ceiling, to be punched by an athlete, especially a boxer, for the sake of exercise.

punching-bear (pun'ching-bãr), *n.* A punching-machine, operated by hydraulic power or by ordinary lever-power, for punching holes in bars or sheets of metal.—**Close-mouthed punching-bear**, a punching-bear which has a central opening through the body of the machine, into which metal bars are thrust and brought into position for the action of the punch.—**Open-mouthed punching-bear**, a punching-bear which has in its side an opening or slot for the insertion of the margin of a metallic sheet or plate to be punched. See cut under *bear*[2], 9.

punching-machine (pun'ching-ma-shēn"), *n.* A power-punch for making rivet-holes in plates, tubes, and other work in wrought-iron. Such machines are operated by means of cams with steam or other power. They are often combined with shearing-machines.

punchion†, *n.* An obsolete form of *puncheon*[1].

punch-jug (punch'jug), *n.* A jug, usually of pottery, formed in a grotesque shape like Punch.

punch-ladle (punch'lā"dl), *n.* A ladle of medium size, the bowl of which has two spouts, one on each side, used for filling glasses from a punch-bowl.

punch-pliers (punch'plī"ėrz), *n. pl.* A tool with two jaws, one bearing a hollow punch, and the other constituting a flat die against which the punch works. Punches of this nature are used by shoemakers, railroad and street-car conductors, etc.

punch-prop (punch'prop), *n.* In *coal-mining*, a short prop of timber used to support the coal in holing or undercutting; a punch. Also called *sprag*.

punchy (pun'chi), *a.* [< *punch*[3] + *-y*[1]; prob. in part a var. of *paunchy*, < *paunch* + *-y*[1].] Paunchy; pot-bellied; short, squat, and fat. [Colloq.]

A fat, little, *punchy* concern of sixteen. *Barham*, Ingoldsby Legends, II. 124.

punct† (pungkt), *n.* [< L. *punctum*, a point: see *point*[1].] A point.

And neuerthelesse at the same instant and *punct* of time it maketh day and high noone in one place, and nyght and mydnyght on the opposite part. *R. Eden* (First Books on America, ed. Arber, p. xliii.).

punct† (pungkt), *v. t.* [< ML. *punctare*, pierce, punch: see *punch*[1], *point*[1].] To pierce; puncture. *Halliwell*.

puncta, *n.* Plural of *punctum*.

Punctaria (pungk-tā'ri-ạ̈), *n.* [NL. (Greville), so called in allusion to the dots formed by the sporangia and hairs; < L. *punctum*, point, dot: see *point*[1].] A genus of olive-brown seaweeds, with a simple membranaceous frond which is composed of from two to six layers of cuboidal cells. The unilocular sporangia, which are immersed in the frond, are formed from the superficial cells; the plurilocular sporangia also are collected in spots and immersed, except at the apex. There are 5 or 6 widely distributed species.

Punctariaceæ (pungk-tā-ri-ā'sẹ̄-ē), *n. pl.* [NL., < *Punctaria* + *-aceæ*.] An order of marine algæ of the class *Phæosporeæ*, taking its name from the genus *Punctaria*; a family of fucoid algæ. The root is a minute naked disk. The frond is cylindrical or flat, unbranched, and cellular. The fructification consists of sori scattered all over the fronds in minute distinct dots, composed of roundish sporangia, producing zoöspores.

punctate (pungk'tāt), *a.* [< ML. *punctatus*, marked with dots (NL. *punctatus*, pointed), pp. of *punctare*, mark with dots, mark, point, < L. *punctum*, point, dot: see *point*[1].] 1. Having a point or points; pointed.—2. In *math.*, having an acnode, or point separate from the rest of the locus spoken of. *Newton*, 1706.—3. In *bot.* and *zoöl.*, having dots scattered over the surface; studded with points, as of color, shape, texture, etc.; dotted; pitted.

punctated (pungk'tā-ted), *a.* [< *punctate* + *-ed*[2].] Punctate; dotted; finely pitted.

Nearly allied to this is the genus Bacillaria; . . . its valves have a longitudinal *punctated* keel. *W. B. Carpenter*, Micros., § 285.

Punctated curve, a curve with an acnode, or separate point.

punctate-striate (pungk'tāt-strī'āt), *a.* In *entom.*, having striæ or impressed lines with punctures in them at more or less regular intervals. Also *punctatostriate*.

punctate-sulcate (pungk'tāt-sul'kāt), *a.* In *entom.*, sulcate or grooved, with punctures in the grooves. Also *punctatosulcate*.

punctation (pungk-tā'shọn), *n.* [< ML. *punctatio(n-)*, < *punctare*, mark, dot: see *punctate*.] 1. The state or condition of being punctate, in any of the senses of that word.

The absence of *punctation* in the test is referred to metamorphism, as in C. Guerangeri all stages were discovered, from impunctate to completely punctate. *Science*, III. 325.

2. In *civil law*, a document made between the parties before the contract to which it refers has binding force, generally merely with the object of putting clearly before them the principal points discussed. *Goudsmit*.—**Punctation of Ems**, a document prepared at Bad Ems, Germany, in 1786, by representatives of the Roman Catholic archbishops of Co-

logne, Treves, Mainz, and Salzburg, in which episcopal rights were maintained against the pretensions of the papal see.

punctator (pungk-tā'tor), *n.* [< ML. *punctator*, one who marks with dots (applied to one who so marked the names of persons absent from service), < *punctare*, mark with dots: see *punctate*.] One who marks with dots: specifically applied to the Masorites, who invented the Hebrew vowel-points. See *masoretic*.

punctatostriate (pungk-tā'tō-strī'āt), *a.* Same as *punctate-striate*.

punctatosulcate (pungk-tā'tō-sul'kāt), *a.* Same as *punctate-sulcate*.

puncticular (pungk-tik'ū-lär), *a.* [< NL. **puncticulum*, dim. of L. *punctum*, point: see *point*[1].] Comprised in a point; being a mere point as to size. [Rare.]

The *puncticular* originals of periwinkles and gnats. *Sir T. Browne*, Urn-burial, iii.

puncticulate (pungk-tik'ū-lāt), *a.* [< NL. **puncticulatus*, < **puncticulum*, dim. of L. *punctum*, point: see *point*[1].] Minutely punctate; punctulate.

Punctidæ (pungk'ti-dē), *n. pl.* [NL., < *Punctum* + *-idæ*.] A family of geophilous pulmonate gastropods, typified by the genus *Punctum*, having the shell heliciform, the mantle submedian, the jaw disintegrated into many separate pieces, and the teeth peculiarly modified, represented only by medians and laterals, having the bases of attachment longer than wide, and the free parts narrowed and reflected. It contains a few minute species, such as the *Punctum pygmæum* of Europe and *P. minutissimum* of North America.

punctiform (pungk'ti-fôrm), *a.* [< L. *punctum*, point, + *forma*, form.] Like a point or dot; having the character of a point; located in a point.

A *punctiform* sensation of cold is experienced. *Science*, VII. 450.

punctigerous (pungk-tij'e-rus), *a.* [< L. *punctum*, point, + *gerere*, carry.] Having a small simple eye or eye-spot, without a lens: opposed to *lentigerous*. *Encyc. Brit.*, XVI. 680.

punctilio (pungk-til'iō), *n.* [Formerly also *punctillo*; < Sp. *puntillo* = It. *puntiglio*, a small point, punctilio, < LL. *punctillum*, a small point, a dot, dim. of L. *punctum*, point: see *point*[1]. Cf. *puncto*.] 1†. A small point. *B. Jonson.*

In that *punctilio* of time wherein the bullets struck him . . . he is in an instant disanimated. *The Unhappy Marksman*, 1659 (Harl. Misc., IV. 4). (*Davies.*)

2. A nice point, especially in conduct, ceremony, or proceeding; also, particularity or exactness in the observance of forms.

Where reputation is almost every thing becometh; but where that is not, it must be supplied by *punctilios* and compliments. *Bacon*, Advancement of Learning, ii. 308.

'Sdeath! to trifle with me at such a juncture as this—now to stand on *punctilios*—love me! I don't believe she ever did. *Sheridan*, The Duenna, i. 2.

Societies
Polished in arts, and in *punctilio* versed.
Wordsworth, Prelude, ix.

punctilious (pungk-til'ius), *a.* [< *punctilio* + *-ous*.] Attentive to punctilios; very nice or precise in behavior, ceremony, or intercourse; exact (sometimes, to excess) in the observance of rules or forms prescribed by law or custom.

Fletcher's whole soul was possessed by a sore, jealous, *punctilious* patriotism. *Macaulay*, Hist. Eng., xxiv.

The courtiers, in emulation of their master, made frequent entertainments, at which he [Columbus] was treated with the *punctilious* deference paid to a noble of the highest class. *Prescott*, Ferd. and Isa., i. 18.

=**Syn.** Particular, precise, scrupulous.

punctiliously (pungk-til'ius-li), *adv.* In a punctilious manner; with exactness or great nicety.

I have thus *punctiliously* and minutely pursued this disquisition. *Johnson*, False Alarm.

punctiliousness (pungk-til'ius-nes), *n.* The quality of being punctilious; exactness in the observance of forms or rules; attention to nice points of behavior or ceremony.

punction (pungk'shon), *n.* [Early mod. E. also *puncion*; < OF. *ponction*, F. *ponction* = Pr. *punccio*, *puncio* = Sp. *puncion* = Pg. *punção* = It. *punzione*, < L. *punctio(n-)*, a pricking, < *pungere*, pp. *punctus*, pierce, prick: see *point*[1], *punch*[1]. Cf. doublet *puncheon*[1].] A pricking; puncture.

But I thynke this was no dreame, but a *puncion* and pricke of hys synfull conscyence. *Hall*, Rich. III., an. 3.

punctist (pungk'tist), *n.* [< L. *punctum*, a point (see *punct*), + *-ist*.] Same as *punctator*.

puncto (pungk'tō), *n.* [< Sp. and It. *punto*, < L. *punctum*, a point: see *punct*, *point*[1]. Cf. *punctilio*.] 1†. A nice point of form or ceremony; a punctilio.

All the particularities and religious *punctos* and ceremonies. *Bacon*, Hist. Hen. VII., p. 165.

2. In *fencing*, the point of the sword or foil; also, a blow with the point. See *point*.

punctual (pungk'tū-al), *a.* [= F. *ponctuel* = Pr. *punctal* = Sp. *puntual* = Pg. *pontual* = It. *puntuale*, < ML. **punctualis* (in adv. *punctualiter*), < L. *punctus*, a point: see *point*[1].] 1. Consisting of a point; being a point.

To officiate light
Round this opacous earth, this *punctual* spot,
One day and night. *Milton*, P. L., viii. 23.

2. Exact; precise; nice.

No doubt, many may be well seen in the passages of government and policy which are to seek in little and *punctual* occasions. *Bacon*, Advancement of Learning, i. 35.

I hope the adversaries of episcopacy, that are so *punctual* to pitch all upon Scripture ground, will be sure to produce clear Scripture. *Jer. Taylor*, Works (ed. 1835), II. 149.

Must he therefore believe himself well because he cannot tell the *punctual* time when he fell sick? *Stillingfleet*, Sermons, II. i.

Upon his [St. John's] examination upon oath, he made a clear, full, and *punctual* declaration. *Court and Times of Charles I.*, II. 39.

We should search in vain for its *punctual* equivalent. *F. Hall*, Mod. Eng., p. 307.

3. Exact or prompt in action or in the observance of time, the keeping of appointments, engagements, etc.

Punctual be thou in Payments. *Steele*, Grief A-la-Mode, v. 1.

4. Prompt; at the exact or stipulated time: as, *punctual* payment.

She enjoins the *punctual* discharge of all her personal debts within a year. *Prescott*, Ferd. and Isa., ii. 16.

Punctual coördinate. Same as *point-coördinate*.

punctualist† (pungk'tū-al-ist), *n.* [< *punctual* + *-ist*.] One who is very exact in observing forms and ceremonies.

Bilson hath decipher'd us all the galanteries of Signore and Monsignore, and Monsieur, as circumstantially as any *punctualist* of Casteel, Naples, or Fountain-Bleau could have don. *Milton*, Church-Government, ii. 1.

punctuality (pungk-tū-al'i-ti), *n.* [= F. *ponctualité*; as *punctual* + *-ity*.] The state or character of being punctual. (*a*) Scrupulous exactness with regard to matters of fact or detail; exactness; nicety.

I have in a table
With curious *punctuality* set down,
To a hair's breadth, how low a new-stamped courtier
May vail to a country gentleman.
Massinger, Emperor of the East, i. 2.

Who teaches you the mimic posture of your body, the *punctuality* of your beard, the formality of your pace? *Shirley*, Witty Fair One, ii. 1.

(*b*) Adherence to the exact time of meeting one's obligations or performing one's duties; especially, the fact or habit of promptness in attendance or in fulfilling appointments.

We were not a little displeased to find that, in the first promise of *punctuality* our Rais had made, he had disappointed us by absenting himself from the boat. *Bruce*, Source of the Nile, I. 47.

(*c*) The character of being, or existence in, a point.

A state of rest in our own body or in external things, the perception of any defined and static form whatever, and most of all the very possibility of unspeciality or *punctuality*, must be subsequently inferred as negative instances from indeterminate extension and movement. *G. S. Hall*, German Culture, p. 230.

punctually (pungk'tū-al-i), *adv.* [< *punctual* + *-ly*[2].] In a punctual manner. (*a*) With attention or reference to minute points or particulars; nicely; exactly; precisely.

In imitation of what I have seene my Father do, I began to observe matters more *punctualy*, which I did use to set down in a blanke almanac. *Evelyn*, Diary (1631), p. 9.

What did you with it?—tell me *punctually*;
I look for a strict accompt.
Massinger, Emperor of the East, iv. 5.

It [the gift of reading] consists, first of all, in a vast intellectual endowment, . . . by which a man rises to understand that he is not *punctually* right, nor those from whom he differs absolutely wrong. *R. L. Stevenson*, Books which have Influenced me, p. 14.

(*b*) With scrupulous exactness or promptness in regard to the fulfilling of obligations, duties, appointments, etc.: as, to pay debts or rent *punctually*.

punctualness (pungk'tū-al-nes), *n.* [< *punctual* + *-ness*.] Exactness; punctuality; promptness.

Yet I can obey those wherein I think power is unguided by prudence with no less *punctualness* and fidelity. *Boyle*, Works, II. 413.

punctuate (pungk'tū-āt), *v. t.*; pret. and pp. *punctuated*, ppr. *punctuating*. [< ML. *punctuare* (> F. *ponctuer*), mark with points, < L. *punctus*, a point: see *point*[1], *n.*, and cf. *point*[1], *v.*, *punch*[1], *v.*, and *punctate*.] 1. In *writing* and *printing*, to mark with points in some significant manner; specifically, to divide into sentences and parts of sentences by the conventional signs called points or marks of punctuation: as, to *punctuate* one's letters carefully. See *punctuation*.—2. Figuratively, to emphasize by some significant or forcible action; enforce the important parts or points of in some special manner: as, to *punctuate* one's remarks by gestures. [Colloq.]

punctuate (pungk'tū-āt), *a.* [< ML. *punctuatus*, pp.: see the verb.] In *entom.*, same as *punctured*.

punctuated (pungk'tū-ā-ted), *a.* [< *punctuate* + *-ed*[2].] In *zoöl.*, same as *punctate*.

punctuatim (pungk-tū-ā'tim), *adv.* [NL., formed in imitation of *verbatim* and *literatim*, < L. *punctus*, a point: see *punctuate*.] Point for point; with respect to every point or mark of punctuation: in the phrase *verbatim, literatim, et punctuatim*, word for word, letter for letter, and point for point.

punctuation (pungk-tū-ā'shon), *n.* [= F. *ponctuation*, < ML. *punctuatio(n-)*, a marking with points, a writing, agreement, < *punctuare*, mark with points, settle: see *punctuate*.] 1. In *writing* and *printing*, a pointing off or separation of one part from another by arbitrary marks; specifically, the division of a composition into sentences and parts of sentences by the use of marks indicating intended differences of effect by differences of form. The points used for punctuation exclusively are the period or full-stop, the colon, the semicolon, and the comma. (See *point*[1], *n.*, 11 (*a*).) The interrogation- and exclamation-points serve also for punctuation in the place of one or another of these, while having a special rhetorical effect of their own; and the dash is also used, either alone or in conjunction with one of the preceding marks, in some cases where the sense or the nature of the pause required can thereby be more clearly indicated. (See *parenthesis*.) The modern system of punctuation was gradually developed after the introduction of printing, primarily through the efforts of Aldus Manutius and his family. In ancient writing the words were at first run together continuously; afterward they were separated by spaces, and sometimes by dots or other marks, which were made to serve some of the purposes of modern punctuation, and were retained in early printing. Long after the use of the present points became established, they were so indiscriminately employed that, if closely followed, they are often a hindrance rather than an aid in reading and understanding the text. There is still much uncertainty and arbitrariness in punctuation, but its chief office is now generally understood to be that of facilitating a clear comprehension of the sense. *Close punctuation*, characterized especially by the use of many commas, was common in English in the eighteenth century, and is the rule in present French usage; but *open punctuation*, characterized by the avoidance of all pointing not clearly required by the construction, now prevails in the best English usage. In some cases, as in certain legal papers, title-pages, etc., punctuation is wholly omitted.

The principles of *punctuation* are subtle, and an exact logical training is requisite for the just application of them. *G. P. Marsh*, Lects. on Eng. Lang., xix.

2. In *zoöl.*, the punctures of a punctate surface.

The very fine and close *punctuation* of the head, etc. *Waterhouse*, in Trans. Entom. Soc. of London.

punctuative (pungk'tū-ā-tiv), *a.* [< *punctuate* + *-ive*.] Pertaining or relating to punctuation.

punctuator (pungk'tū-ā-tor), *n.* [< *punctuate* + *-or*[1].] One who punctuates.

punctula, *n.* Plural of *punctulum*.

punctulate (pungk'tū-lāt), *a.* [< NL. *punctulatus*, < L. *punctulum*, a slight prick, a small point (dim. of *punctus*, a pricking, a point), + *-ate*[2].] Minutely punctate; studded with very small pits or dots.

punctulated (pungk'tū-lā-ted), *a.* Same as *punctulate*.

The studs have their surface *punctulated*, as if set all over with other studs infinitely lesser. *Woodward*, Fossils.

punctulation (pungk-tū-lā'shon), *n.* [< *punctulate* + *-ion*.] The state of being punctulate; a set of punctules; minute or fine puncturation.

punctule (pŭngk'tūl), *n.* [< LL. *punctulum*, dim. of L. *punctum*, a point: see *point*[1].] In *entom.*, a very small puncture or impressed dot.

punctulum (pungk'tū-lum), *n.*; pl. *punctula* (-lä). [NL.: see *punctule*.] Same as *punctule*.

punctum (pungk'tum), *n.*; pl. *puncta* (-tä). [L., a point, dot: see *point*[1].] 1. In *zoöl.* and *anat.*, a point; a dot; a pit; a papilla; some little place, as if a mere point, in any way distinguished.—2. [*cap.*] [NL.] In *conch.*, a genus of geophilous pulmonate gastropods, type of the family *Punctidæ*: so called on account of its minute size. *E. S. Morse*, 1864.—**Puncta vasculosa**, numerous small red spots observed on a section of the

Punctum minutissimum, magnified. (The mark below shows natural size.)

brain, due to the escape of blood from the vessels divided in the operation.—**Punctum cæcum**, the blind spot in the eye; the optic papilla, where the nerve enters the eyeball.—**Punctum lacrymale**, the lacrymal punctum; the minute aperture of the lacrymal canal at the summit of a lacrymal papilla.—**Punctum luteum**, the yellow spot.—**Punctum proximum**, the nearest point which a given eye can bring to focus upon its retina; the near point.—**Punctum remotum**, the furthest point which a given eye can bring to focus upon its retina; the far point.—**Punctum saliens**, a salient point; an initial point of a movement or procedure; hence, a starting-point of anything; specifically, in *embryol.*, the first trace of the embryonic heart, as a pulsating point or vesicle of a primitive blood-vessel.—**Punctum vegetationis**, in *bot.*, the growing-point or vegetating-point of an organ.

puncturation (pungk-tū-rā'shon), *n.* [< LL. *punctura*, a prick, a puncture, + *-ation*.] 1. In *surg.*, the act of puncturing.—2. In *zoöl.*, the state of being punctured, dotted, or pitted; a set of punctures.

puncture (pungk'tūr), *n.* [= Sp. It. *puntura* = Pg. *punctura*, *puntura*, < LL. *punctura*, a pricking, a puncture, < L. *pungere*, pp. *punctus*, pierce, prick: see *pungent*, *point*[1].] 1. The act of perforating or pricking, as with a pointed instrument, or a small hole so made; a small wound, as one made by a needle, prickle, or sting: as, the *puncture* of a lancet, nail, or pin.

When prick'd by a sharp-pointed weapon, which kind of wound is call'd a *puncture*, they are much to be regarded.
Wiseman, Surgery, v. 3.

A lion may perish by the *puncture* of an asp.
Johnson, Rambler.

2. In *zoöl.*, a depressed point or dot, as if punctured; a small depression, as if pricked into a surface; a punctum. See cut under *Coscinoptera*.—**Confluent, dilated, distinct, dorsal, obliterate, ocellate, etc., punctures.** See the adjectives.

puncture (pungk'tūr), *v. t.*; pret. and pp. *punctured*, ppr. *puncturing*. [< *puncture*, *n.*] To prick; pierce with a sharp point of any kind: as, to *puncture* the skin.

With that he drew a lancet in his rage
To *puncture* the still supplicating sage.
Garth, Dispensary, vi.

Punctured work, in *masonry*, a kind of rustic stonework in which the face is ornamented with series of holes.

punctureless (pungk'tūr-les), *a.* [< *puncture* + *-less*.] In *entom.*, without punctures; smooth.

punctus (pungk'tus), *n.*; pl. *punctus*. [ML., < L. *punctus*, a point: see *point*[1].] In *medieval musical notation*: (*a*) A note. (*b*) A dot or point, however used.

pund (pund), *n.* A dialectal variant of *pound*[1]. [Scotch and North. Eng.]

pundert, *n.* An obsolete variant of *pinder*[1].

pundit (pun'dit), *n.* [Also *pandit* (the Hind. *a* being pronounced like E. *u*); < Hind. *pandit*, *pandat*, a learned man, master, teacher, an honorary title equiv. to *doctor* or *professor*; also a Hindu law-officer, jurist; < Skt. *pandita*, a learned man, scholar, as adj. learned.] A learned Brahman; one versed in the Sanskrit language, and in the science, laws, and religion of India: as, formerly, the *Pundits* of the supreme court; by extension, any learned man.

[An Anglo-Indian child] calls a learned *Pundit* "asal ulu," an egregious owl.
J. W. Palmer, The New and the Old, p. 342.

The young *pandit*, then, is expected to master the system of Hindu Grammar, and to govern his Sanskrit speech and writing by it. *Whitney*, Amer. Jour. Philol., V. 281.

It behooved the squire himself to . . . see certain learned *pundits* . . . at various dingy dismal chambers in Lincoln's Inn Fields, the Temple, and Gray's Inn Lane.
Trollope, Doctor Thorne, xliv.

pundlet (pun'dl), *n.* [Origin obscure; cf. *punch*[3] and *bundle*.] A short, fat woman. *Imp. Dict.*

pundonor (pun'do-nôr'), *n.* [Sp., contraction of *punto de honor* = F. *point d'honneur*, point of honor: see *point*[1], *de*[2], *honor*.] Point of honor.

They stood not much upon the *pundonor*, the high punctilio, and rarely drew the stiletto in their disputes.
Irving, Granada, p. 256.

The Spaniard fights, or rather fought, for religion and the *Pundonor*, and the Irishman fights for the fun of fighting. *R. F. Burton*, El-Medinah, p. 325.

pundum (pun'dum), *n.* Same as *piny resin* (which see, under *piny*[1]).

puneset, *n.* See *punice*[2].

pung (pung), *n.* [Origin obscure.] A rude form of sleigh consisting of a box-like body placed on runners; any low box-sleigh. [New Eng.]

pungar (pung'gär), *n.* A crab. *Halliwell*. [Local, Eng.]

pungence (pun'jens), *n.* [< *pungen(t)* + *-ce*.] Pungency.

Around the whole rise cloudy wreaths, and far
Bear the warm *pungence* of o'er-boiling tar.
Crabbe, Works, II. 6.

pungency (pun'jen-si), *n.* [As *pungence* (see *-cy*).] Pungent character or quality; the power of sharply affecting the taste or smell; keenness; sharpness; tartness; causticity.

The *pungency* of forbidden lust is truly a thorn in the flesh. *Jer. Taylor*, Great Exemplar, Pref., p. 10.

This unsavory rebuke, which probably lost nothing of its *pungency* from the tone in which it was delivered, so incensed the pope that he attempted to seize the paper and tear it in pieces. *Prescott*, Ferd. and Isa., ii. 10.

=**Syn.** Poignancy, acriduess, pointedness.

pungent (pun'jent), *a.* [= Sp. Pg. It. *pungente*, < L. *pungen(t-)s*, ppr. of *pungere*, pierce, prick, sting, penetrate: see *point*[1]. From L. *pungere* are also E. *punch*[1], *punction*, *puncheon*[1] (and prob. *puncheon*[2]), *point*[1], *punct*, *punctule*, *punctilio*, *punctilious*, etc., *punctual*, *punctuate*, etc., *puncture*, *compunction*, *expunge*, *pounce*[1], *poignant* (doublet of *pungent*), etc.] 1. Piercing; sharp.

A rush which now your heels do lie on here
Was whilome used for a *pungent* spear.
Chapman, Gentleman Usher, ii. 1.

Specifically—(*a*) In *bot.*, terminating gradually in a hard sharp point, as the lobes of the holly-leaf. (*b*) In *entom.*, fitted for piercing or penetrating: as, a *pungent* ovipositor.

2. Sharp and painful; poignant.

We also may make our thorns, which are in themselves *pungent* and dolorous, to be a crown.
Jer. Taylor, Works (ed. 1835), I. 325.

3. Affecting the tongue like small sharp points; stinging; acrid.

Among simple tastes, such as sweet, sour, bitter, hot, *pungent*, there are some which are intrinsically grateful.
D. Stewart, Philos. Essays, i. 5.

And herbs of potent smell and *pungent* taste
Give a warm relish to the night's repast.
Crabbe, Works, I. 41.

4. Sharply affecting the sense of smell: as, *pungent* snuff.

The *pungent* grains of titillating dust.
Pope, R. of the L., v. 84.

5. Hence, sharply affecting the mind; curt and expressive; caustic; racy; biting.

A sharp and *pungent* manner of speech. *Dryden*.

She could only tell me amusing stories, and reciprocate any racy and *pungent* gossip I chose to indulge in.
Charlotte Brontë, Jane Eyre, ix.

The attention of the reader is continually provoked by the *pungent* stimulants which are mixed in the composition of almost every sentence.
Whipple, Ess. and Rev., I. 14.

=**Syn.** Sharp, stinging, keen, peppery, acrid, caustic. *Piquant, Pungent, Poignant.* That which is *piquant* is just tart enough to be agreeable; that which is *pungent* is so tart that, if it were more so, it would be positively disagreeable; that which is *poignant* is likely to prove actually disagreeable to most persons. *Pungent* is manifestly figurative when not applied to the sense of taste, or, less often, of smell; *piquant* is similar, but less forcible; *poignant* is now used chiefly of mental states, etc., as *poignant* grief, or of things affecting the mind, as *poignant* wit.

pungently (pun'jent-li), *adv.* With pungency; sharply.

pungi (pöng'gē), *n.* [Hind. *pūngī*.] A Hindu pipe or nose-flute composed of a gourd or nutshell into which two wooden pipes or reeds are inserted. It emits a droning or humming sound, and is the instrument commonly used by snake-charmers.

pungled (pung'gld), *a.* [Origin obscure.] Shriveled; shrunken: applied specifically to grain whose juices have been extracted by the insect *Thrips cerealium*. *Halliwell*. [Prov. Eng.]

pungy (pung'i), *n.*; pl. *pungies* (-iz). [Origin obscure.] 1. A small boat like a sharpey. [Massachusetts.]—2. A kind of schooner peculiar to the oyster-trade of Chesapeake Bay, sailing fast, and holding from 300 to 600 bushels of oysters. *Brooa*.—**Canoe pungy**, a canoe like a pungy, used in oyster-dredging. [Chesapeake Bay.]

Punic (pū'nik), *a.* and *n.* [< L. *Punicus*, *Pœnicus*, Carthaginian, < *Pœnus*, a Carthaginian, a Phenician, akin to Gr. Φοῖνιξ, a Phenician: see *Phenician*.] **I.** *a.* Of, pertaining to, or characteristic of the Carthaginians, who were characterized by the Romans as being unworthy of trust; hence, faithless; treacherous; deceitful.

Yes, yes; his faith attesting nations own;
'Tis *Punic* all, and to a proverb known!
Brooke, tr. of Tasso's Jerusalem Delivered, ii.

Punic apple, the pomegranate.

But the territorie of Carthage chalengeth to itselfe the *punicke apple*; some call it the pomegranat [granatum], and they have made severall kindes thereof.
Holland, tr. of Pliny, xiii. 19.

Punic faith. See *faith*.—**Punic wars**, in *Rom. hist.*, the three wars waged by Rome against Carthage, 264–241, 218–201, and 149–146 B. C. They resulted in the overthrow of Carthage and its annexation to Rome.

II. *n.* The language of the Carthaginians, which belongs to the Canaanitish branch of the Semitic tongues, and is an offshoot of Phenician, and allied to Hebrew.

Punica (pū'ni-kä), *n.* [NL. (Tournefort, 1700), < L. *punicum*, sc. *malum*, the pomegranate, lit. 'Carthaginian apple,' < L. *punicus*, Carthaginian: see *Punic*.] A monotypic genus of plants of the polypetalous order *Lythrarieæ*, formerly classed in the *Myrtaceæ*, or myrtle family, and by many constituted into a separate order, *Granateæ* (Don, 1826). It is anomalous in its ovary, which is inferior and consists of two circles of cells, a lower set of three or four and an upper circle of from five to ten, each with many ovules crowded in numerous rows on enlarged fleshy placentas, which become united to the membranous partitions and walls. It is also characterized by very numerous stamens in many rows, ovate versatile anthers on slender incurved filaments, leaf-like, spirally rolled seed-leaves with two auricles at their bases, and a persistent flexuous style with swollen base and capitate stigma. The only species, *P. granatum*, the pomegranate, is a native of western Asia to northwestern India, growing in the Himalayas to the altitude of 6,000 feet, long naturalized throughout the Mediterranean countries, and now widely cultivated in subtropical regions, including, in the United States, chiefly Louisiana, Texas, and Florida. (See *pomegranate*, *balausta*, and *balaustine*.) Of ornamental varieties may be mentioned especially the variety *nana*, the dwarf pomegranate, a favorite double-flowered lawn and greenhouse plant, native of the East Indies, and now naturalized in places in the southern United States and West Indies.

punice[1]†, *v. t.* An obsolete form of *punish*.

punice[2]†, **puneset**, *n.* [Also *puny* (see *puny*[2]); < F. *punaise*, a bedbug, fem. of *punais*, stinking, ult. < L. *putere*, stink.] A bedbug.

His flea, his morpion, and *punese*,
He 'ad gotten for his proper ease.
S. Butler, Hudibras, III. i. 433.

puniceous (pū-nish'ius), *a.* [< L. *puniceus*, reddish, purple, < *Punicus*, Carthaginian, Phenician. Cf. Gr. φοῖνιξ, red, purple: see *Phenician*.] In *entom.*, purplish-red or crimson; having the color of a pomegranate.

punieshipt, *n.* See *punyship*.

puniness (pū'ni-nes), *n.* [< *puny*[1] + *-ness*.] The state or character of being puny; littleness; pettiness; smallness with feebleness.

punish (pun'ish), *v. t.* [< ME. *punischen*, *punisshen*, *punicen*, *punchen*, < OF. *puniss-*, stem of certain parts of *punir*, F. *punir* = Pr. Sp. Pg. *punir* = It. *punire*, < L. *punire*, *pœnire*, inflict punishment upon, < *pœna*, punishment, penalty: see *pain*[1]. Cf. *pain*[1], *pine*[2], from the same ult. source, and *punch*[2], a contracted form of *punish*.] 1. To inflict a penalty on; visit judicially with pain, loss, confinement, death, or other penalty; castigate; chastise.

The spirits perverse
With easy intercourse pass to and fro,
To tempt or *punish* mortals.
Milton, P. L., ii. 1032.

2. To reward or visit with pain or suffering inflicted on the offender: applied to the crime or offense: as, to *punish* murder or theft.

By an Act of Parliament, or rather by a Synod of Bishops holden at London, he [Henry I.] was authorized to *punish* Marriage and Incontinency of Priests.
Baker, Chronicles, p. 40.

Our Supreme Foe in time may much remit
His anger; and perhaps thus far removed
Not mind us not offending; satisfied
With what is *punish'd*. *Milton*, P. L., ii. 213.

3. To handle severely: as, to *punish* an opponent in a boxing-match or a pitcher in a base-ball game; to *punish* (that is, to stimulate by whip or spur) a horse in running a race. [Colloq.]—4. To make a considerable inroad on; make away with a good quantity of. [Colloq.]

He *punished* my champagne.
Thackeray, Vanity Fair, liii.

=**Syn. 1.** *Chasten*, etc. (see *chastise*), scourge, whip, lash, correct, discipline.

punishability (pun'ish-a-bil'i-ti), *n.* [= F. *punissabilité*.] The quality of being punishable; liability to punishment.

The vexed question of *punishability* is raised by certain forms of insanity. *A. Bain*, Emotions and Will, p. 522.

punishable (pun'ish-a-bl), *a.* [< OF. *punissable*, F. *punissable*; as *punish* + *-able*.] Deserving punishment; liable to punishment; capable of being punished by right or law: applied to persons or conduct.

That time was when to be a Protestant, to be a Christian, was by Law as *punishable* as to be a traitor.
Milton, Eikonoklastes, xi.

Dangerous tumults and seditions were *punishable* by death. *Bancroft*, Hist. U. S., I. 97.

punishableness (pun'ish-a-bl-nes), *n.* The character of being punishable.

punisher (pun'ish-er), *n.* One who punishes; one who inflicts pain, loss, or other evil for a crime or offense.

For he [the Sultan] is of no bloody disposition, . . . yet he is an unrelenting *punisher* of offences, even in his own houshold. *Sandys*, Travailes, p. 57.

So should I purchase dear
Short intermission bought with double smart.
This knows my *Punisher*. *Milton*, P. L., iv. 103.

punishment (pun'ish-ment), *n.* [< *punish* + *-ment.*] 1. The act of punishing; the infliction of pain or chastisement.

How many sorts of fears possess a sinner's mind? fears of disappointments, fears of discovery, and fears of *punishment*. *Stillingfleet*, Sermons, I. x.

We now come to speak of *punishment*: which, in the sense in which it is here considered, is an artificial consequence, annexed by political authority to an offensive act in one instance; in the view of putting a stop to the production of events similar to the obnoxious part of its natural consequences in other instances.
Bentham, Introd. to Morals and Legislation, xii. 36.

Crime and *punishment* grow out of one stem. *Punishment* is a fruit that unsuspected ripens within the flower of the pleasure which concealed it.
Emerson, Compensation.

It is impossible to separate that moral indignation which expresses itself in *punishment* from the spirit of self-redress for wrongs. *Woolsey*, Introd. to Inter. Law, § 20 a.

2. Pain, suffering, loss, confinement, or other penalty inflicted on a person for a crime or offense, by the authority to which the offender is subject; a penalty imposed in the enforcement or application of law.

Whatsoever hath been said or written on the other side, all the late statutes, which inflict capital *punishment* upon extollers of the Pope's supremacy, . . . have for their principal scope, not the punishment of the error of conscience, but the repressing of the peril of the state.
Bacon, Charge upon the Commission for the Verge.

So this Prophet [Amos] tells us that the true account of all Gods *punishments* is to be fetched from the sins of the people. *Stillingfleet*, Sermons, I. i.

I proceed, in the next place, to consider the general nature of *punishments*, which are evils or inconveniences consequent upon crimes and misdemeanours; being devised, denounced, and inflicted, by human laws, in consequence of disobedience or misbehaviour in those to regulate whose conduct such laws were respectively made.
Blackstone, Com., IV. i.

3. Pain or injury inflicted, in a general sense; especially, in colloquial use, the pain inflicted by one pugilist on another in a prize-fight.

Tom Sayers could not take *punishment* more gaily.
Thackeray, Philip, iv.

Canonical punishments. See *canonical*. =**Syn. 2.** Chastisement, correction, discipline. See *chastise*.

punition† (pū-nish'on), *n.* [< ME. *punicion*, *punyssyon* = F. *punition* = Pr. *punicio* = Sp. *punicion* = Pg. *punição* = It. *punizione*, < LL. *punitio(n-)*, a punishment, < L. *punire*, pp. *punitus*, punish: see *punish.*] Punishment.

The dole that thou haste for Gaffray thy sone,
That the monkes brende so disordinaitly,
Knowith thys, that it was for *punicion*
Taken vppon tho of religion hy.
Rom. of Partenay (E. E. T. S.), l. 3671.

The translation of kingdoms and governments by such wonderful methods and means, for the *punition* of tyrants and the vices of men, of which history abounds with examples [is the decree of a most admirable disposer].
Evelyn, True Religion, I. 85.

punitive (pū'ni-tiv), *a.* [< OF. *punitif* = Pg. It. *punitivo*, < L. *punire*, pp. *punitus*, punish: see *punish.*] Pertaining to or involving punishment; awarding or inflicting punishment: as, *punitive* law or justice.

The *punitive* part of repentance is resolved on, and begun, and put forward into good degrees of progress.
Jer. Taylor, Works (ed. 1835), I. 70.

The penal code then would consist principally of *punitive* laws, involving the imperative matter of the whole number of civil laws: along with which would probably also be found various masses of expository matter, appertaining, not to the civil, but to the punitory laws.
Bentham, Introd. to Morals and Legislation, xvii. 29, note.

Punitive damages. Same as *exemplary damages* (which see, under *damage*).

punitory (pū'ni-tō-ri), *a.* [< LL. as if **punitorius*, < *punitor*, a punisher, < L. *punire*, pp. *punitus*, punish: see *punish.*] Punishing, or tending to punishment; punitive.

"Let no man steal," and "Let the judge cause whoever is convicted of stealing to be hanged." . . . The former might be styled a simple imperative law; the other a *punitory*; but the *punitory*, if it commands the punishment to be inflicted, and does not merely permit it, is as truly imperative as the other; only it is *punitory* besides, which the other is not.
Bentham, Introd. to Morals and Legislation, xix. 2, note.

Punjabee, Punjabi (pun-jä'bē), *n.* [< Hind. Pers. *Panjābī*, < Pers. *panj*, five, + *āb*, water, river.] 1. A native or an inhabitant of the Punjab (or Panjab), literally the country of the five rivers, in extreme northwestern British India.

He was clad in the white dress of a *Punjabee*.
Proc. Soc. Psych. Research (London), IX. 368.

2. The dialect of the Punjab, a variety of Hindi.

punjum (pun'jum), *n.* [E. Ind.] Same as *panjam*.

punk (pungk), *n.* [Appar. reduced from *spunk*. Cf. *funk*[1], rotten wood.] 1. Wood decayed through the influence of a fungus or otherwise, and used like tinder; touchwood.—2. Tinder made from certain fungi. See *amadou* and *fungus-tinder*.—3. A prostitute; a courtezan.

This *punk* is one of Cupid's carriers.
Shak., M. W. of W., ii. 2. 141.

punka (pung'kä), *n.* [Also *punkah*; < Hind. *pankha*, a fan (cf. Pers. *pankan*, a fan), akin to *pankha*, a wing, feather, and to *paksha* (< Skt. *paksha*), a wing.] In the East Indies, a fan of any kind; specifically, a swinging screen consisting of cloth stretched on a rectangular frame, hung from the ceiling and kept in motion by a servant, or in some cases by machinery, by means of which the air of an apartment is agitated.

The cool season was just closing. *Punka* fans were coming into play again.
J. W. Palmer, The New and the Old, p. 401.

The day following I was engaged to pull a *punkah* in the house of an English lawyer.
F. M. Crawford, Mr. Isaacs, i.

punk-fist (pungk'fist), *n.* Same as *puckfist*.

punkin (pung'kin), *n.* A dialectal or colloquial form of *pumpkin*.

punkish† (pung'kish), *a.* [< *punk* + *-ish*[1].] Meretricious.

The credit of a good house is made not to consist in inward hospitality, but in outward walls. These *punkish* outsiders beguile the needy traveller; he thinks there cannot be so many rooms in a house and never a one to harbour a poor stranger. *Rev. T. Adams*, Works, I. 28.

punkling† (pungk'ling), *n.* [< *punk* + *-ling*[1].] A little or young punk. See *punk*, 3.

And then earn'd your royal a day by squiring punks and *punklings* up and down the city?
Fletcher (*and another*), Love's Cure, ii. 1.

punk-oak (pungk'ōk), *n.* The water-oak, *Quercus aquatica*.

punky (pung'ki), *n.*; pl. *punkies* (-kiz). [Origin obscure.] A minute dipterous insect common in the Adirondack region of New York and in the Maine woods, which bites severely and is a great nuisance to travelers and sportsmen. It has not been determined entomologically, but is probably a midge of the genus *Ceratopogon*.

Sandy beaches or gravelly points are liable to swarm with midges or *punkies*. *Sportsman's Gazetteer*, p. 642.

punnage (pun'āj), *n.* [< *pun*[2] + *-age.*] Punning. [Rare.]

The man who maintains that he derives gratification from any such chapters of *punnage* as Hood was in the daily practice of committing to paper should not be credited upon oath. *Poe*, Marginalia, clxxvii. (*Davies.*)

punner[1] (pun'ėr), *n.* [< *pun*[1] + *-er*[1].] One who or that which puns or rams earth into a hole; specifically, a tool for ramming earth. [Eng.]

The hole should not be hastily filled up, but ample time be given to the *punners* to do their share of the work.
Preece and Sivewright, Telegraphy, p. 196.

punner[2] (pun'ėr), *n.* [< *pun*[2] + *-er*[1].] One who makes puns; a punster. *Swift.*

punnet (pun'et), *n.* A small but broad shallow basket for displaying fruit or flowers.

punning (pun'ing), *n.* [Verbal n. of *pun*[2], *v.*] The practice of making puns.

Several worthy gentlemen and critics have applied to me to give my censure of an enormity which has been reviv'd after being long suppressed, and is call'd *punning*.
Steele, Tatler, No. 32.

punning (pun'ing), *p. a.* [Ppr. of *pun*[2], *v.*] Given to making puns; exhibiting a pun or play on words: as, a *punning* reply.—**Punning arms**, in *her.*, same as *allusive arms* (which see, under *arm*[2]).

punnology (pu-nol'ō-ji), *n.* [Irreg. < *pun*[2] + *-ology.*] The art of punning. [Rare.]

He might have been better instructed in the Greek *punnology*. *Pope.* (*Jodrell.*)

punquetto†, *n.* [< *punk* + It. dim. *-etto.*] Same as *punk*, 3. [Slang.]

Marry, to his cockatrice, or *punquetto*, half a dozen taffata gowns or satin kirtles in a pair or two of months—why, they are nothing. *B. Jonson*, Cynthia's Revels, ii. 1.

punster (pun'stėr), *n.* [< *pun*[2] + *-ster.*] One who puns or is skilled in punning; a quibbler on words.

Whatever were the bons mots of Cicero, of which few have come down to us, it is certain that Cicero was an inveterate *punster*; and he seems to have been more ready with them than with repartees.
I. D'Israeli, Curios. of Lit., I. 126.

punt[1] (punt), *n.* [< ME. **punt*, < AS. *punt* = D. *ponte*, *pont* = MLG. *punte*, a punt, ferry-boat, pontoon, < L. *ponto(n-)*, a punt, a pontoon: see *pontoon.*] 1. A flat-bottomed, square-ended, mastless boat of varying size and use. The smaller punts are used in fishing, and by sportsmen in shooting wild fowl; larger ones are often used as ferry-boats across shallow streams, and still larger ones are used as lighters and scows.

As for Pamphilus, . . . of his making is the picture of Vlysses in a *punt* or small bottom.
Holland, tr. of Pliny, xxxv. 10.

They came on a wicked old gentleman breaking the laws of his country, and catching perch in close time out of a *punt*. *H. Kingsley*, Ravenshoe, lxiv.

2. [< *punt*[1], *v.*, 3.] In *foot-ball*, a kick of the ball as it is dropped from the hands and before it strikes the ground.

punt[1] (punt), *v.* [< *punt*[1], *n.*] **I.** *trans.* 1. To convey in a punt: as, he was *punted* across the river. Hence—2. To propel as a punt is usually propelled, by pushing with a pole against the bed of the water; force along by pushing: as, to *punt* a boat.—3. In *foot-ball*, to kick, as the ball, when it is dropped from the hands, and before it touches the ground; give a punt to.—4. In general, to knock; hit.

Punting.

To see a stout Flamand of fifty or thereabouts solemnly *punting*, by the aid of a small tambourine, a minute india-rubber ball to another burgher of similar aspect, which is the favourite way in which all ages and sexes take exercise on the digue, is enough to restore one's faith in human nature. *Contemporary Rev.*, XLIX. 52.

II. *intrans.* To hunt for aquatic game in a punt and with a punt-gun (which see).

punt[2] (punt), *n.* [= F. *ponte*, a punt, < Sp. *punto*, a point, a pip at cards, < L. *punctum*, a point: see *point.*] A point in the game of basset.

punt[2] (punt), *v. i.* [< F. *ponter*, punt (at cards), < *ponte*, punt: see *punt*[2], *n.*] To play at basset or ombre.

Another is for setting up an assembly for basset, where none shall be admitted to *punt* that have not taken the oaths. *Addison*, Freeholder, No. 8.

Wretch that I was! how often have I swore,
When Winnall tally'd, I would *punt* no more!
Pope, The Basset Table.

He was tired of hawking, and fishing, and hunting,
Of billiards, short-whist, chicken-hazard, and *punting*.
Barham, Ingoldsby Legends, II. 252.

punt[3] (punt), *n.* Same as *punty*, *pontil*.

puntee (pun'tē), *n.* Same as *punty*, *pontil*.

punter[1] (pun'tėr), *n.* [< *punt*[1] + *-er*[1].] 1. One who fishes or hunts in a punt.

He . . . caught more fish in an hour than all the rest of the *punters* did in three. *T. Hook*, Gilbert Gurney, iii.

2. One who punts a boat.

Wherever you go, you see the long, straight boat with its passengers luxuriously outstretched on the cushions in the stern, the *punter* walking from the bow and pushing on his long pole. *The Century*, XXXVIII. 488.

punter[2] (pun'tėr), *n.* [< *punt*[2] + *-er*[1].] One who marks the points in the game of basset; a marker.

There used to be grown men in London who loved . . . to accompany lads to the gaming-table, and perhaps have an understanding with the *punters*.
Thackeray, Virginians, xxx. (*Davies.*)

Some of the *punters* are professional gamblers, others are mere general swindlers.
Fortnightly Rev., N. S., XXXIX. 324.

punt-fishing (punt'fish"ing), *n.* Fishing from a punt or boat on a pond, river, or lake.

punt-gun (punt'gun), *n.* A heavy gun of large caliber (usually 1½ inches) and long range, used with large shot for killing water-fowl from a punt (which see).

puntil (pun'til), *n.* Same as *pontil*.

puntilla (pun-til'ä), *n.* [Sp., dim. of *punto*, point: see *point*[1].] Lacework; hence, in *decorative art*, decoration in color or relief in slender lines or points resembling lace: applied especially to such work of Spanish origin.

punto (pun'tō), *n.* [< Sp. It. *punto*, < L. *punctum*, a point: see *point*[1]. Cf. *puncto*.] 1. A point; specifically, in *music*, a dot or point.

This cannot be any way offensive to your own, and is expected to the utmost *punto* by that other nation. *Bp. Hacket*, Abp. Williams, I. 150. (*Davies.*)

2†. One of the old forms given to the beard.

I have yet
No ague. I can look upon your buff,
And *punto* beard, yet call for no strong-water.
Shirley, Honoria and Mammon, i. 2.

3. A thrust or pass in fencing; a point.

I would teach these nineteen the special rules, as your *punto*, your reverso, your stoccata, your imbroccato, your passada, your montanto. *B. Jonson*, Every Man in his Humour, iv. 5.

4. A stitch or method of work with the needle or the loom: same as *point*[1], 18.—5. Same as *pontil*.

A solid iron rod tipped with melted glass, called a *punto*. *Ure*, Dict., II. 657.

Punto dritto, a direct point or hit.

Your dagger commanding his rapier, you may give him a *punta*, either *dritta*, or *riversa*. *Saviolo*, On the Duello, K2. (*Nares.*)

Punto riverso, a back-handed stroke.

Ah, the immortal passado! the *punto reverso!* *Shak.*, R. and J., ii. 4. 27.

puntsman (punts'man), *n.*; pl. *puntsmen* (-men). [< *punt's*, poss. of *punt*[1], + *man*.] A sportsman who uses a punt.

It being the desire of *puntsmen* to pot as many birds as possible by one shot. *W. W. Greener*, The Gun, p. 531.

punty (pun'ti), *n.*; pl. *punties* (-tiz). [Also *puntee*, *ponty*, etc.: see *pontil*.] 1. Same as *pontil*.

Now the glass globe is fastened to two bars, the *punty* and the blow-pipe. *Harper's Mag.*, LXXIX. 254.

2. An oval or circular dot or depression: a kind of ornamentation employed in glass-cutting.

punty-rod (pun'ti-rod), *n.* Same as *pontil*.

puny[1] (pū'ni), *a.* and *n.* [Formerly also *puney*, *punie*, *punny*, also *puisne*, *puisny*, the form *puisne* being still retained archaically in legal use; < OF. *puisne*, F. *puîné*, < ML. *postnatus*, later-born, younger, < L. *post*, after, + *natus*, born: see *postnate*.] **I.** *a.* **1†.** Later-born; younger; junior. See *puisne*, 1.—2. Small and weak; inferior or imperfectly developed in size or strength; feeble; petty; insignificant.

How the young whelp of Talbot's, raging-wood,
Did flesh his *puny* sword in Frenchmen's blood!
Shak., 1 Hen. VI., iv. 7. 36.

I do but ask my month,
Which every petty, *puisne* devil has.
B. Jonson, Devil is an Ass, i. 1.

He is a *puny* soul who, feeling pain,
Finds ease because another feels it too.
Wordsworth, The Borderers, iii.

=**Syn. 2.** Little, diminutive, stunted, starveling.

II.† *n.*; pl. *punies* (-niz). A young, inexperienced person; a junior; a novice.

Nay, then, I see thou 'rt but a *puny* in the subtill Mistery of a woman. *Tourneur*, Revenger's Tragedy, i. 3.

There is only in the anity of women an estate for will, and every *puny* knows that is no certain inheritance. *Dekker and Webster*, Westward Ho, i. 2.

He . . . must appear in Print like a *punie* with his guardian and his censors hand on the back of his title to be his bayl and surety that he is no idiot or seducer. *Milton*, Areopagitica, p. 31.

Others to make sporte withall; of this last sorte were they whom they call freshmen, *punies* of the first yeare. *Christmas Prince at St. John's Coll.*, p. 1. (*Nares.*)

puny[2]†, *n.* [Adapted as a sing. from the supposed plural *punice*, *punese*, < F. *punaise*, a bedbug: see *punice*[2].] A bedbug: same as *punice*[2]. *Cotgrave.*

punyship† (pū'ni-ship), *n.* [< *puny* + *-ship*.] The state of a puny, junior, or novice; nonage. [Rare.]

In the *punieship* or nonage of Cerdicke Sandes . . . the best houses and walles there were of mudde. *Nashe*, Lenten Stuffe (Harl. Misc., VI. 171). (*Davies.*)

pup (pup), *n.* [Abbr. from *puppy*, erroneously regarded as a dim. of *pup*.] Same as *puppy*, 2.—**To be in pup**, to be pregnant, or heavy with young: said of dogs. [Colloq.]

pup (pup), *v. i.*; pret. and pp. *pupped*, ppr. *pupping*. [< *pup*, *n.*] To bring forth pups, as a bitch; whelp, as a carnivorous quadruped.

pupa (pū'pạ), *n.*; pl. *pupæ* (-pē). [< NL. *pupa*, a pupa, chrysalis, < L. *pupa*, *puppa*, a girl, a doll, puppet, fem. of *pupus*, a boy, child; cf. *puer*, a boy, child, *pusus*, a boy, < √ *pu*, beget. From L. *pupus*, *pupa*, are also ult. *pupe*, *pupil*[1], *pupil*[2], etc., *puppet*, *puppy*, *pup*, etc.] 1. The third and usually quiescent stage of those insects which undergo complete metamorphosis, intervening between the larval and the imaginal stage. It is usually called the second stage, the egg not being counted. Some pupæ, as those of mosquitoes, are active. The pupa of some insects is called a *puparium*, and of others a *nymph* or *chrysalis*. See these words. See also cuts under *beetle*, *Carpocapsa*, *chinch-bug*, *Erotylus*, and *house-fly*. 2. A stage in the development of some other arthropods, as cirripeds. See *locomotive pupa*, below.—3. [*cap.*] [NL.] In *conch.*, the typical genus of *Pupidæ*; the chrysalis-shells.—**Coarctate pupa, conical pupæ, exarate pupæ, inert pupa.** See the adjectives.—**Incased pupa.** See *incase*.—**Locomotive pupa**, in *Cirripedia*, the third stage of the larva, the first being a nauplius, the second resembling *Daphnia* or *Cypris*. In this stage little is visible externally but the carapace, the limbs being hidden. There are, however, large lateral eyes and six pairs of legs, and the gut-formed gland is well developed. After swimming awhile the pupa becomes attached to some object, at first only by its suctorial disks, soon, however, becoming permanently fixed to the spot by the secretion of a cement. See cut under *Cirripedia*.

Pupa of *Prionus laticollis*.

This *locomotive pupa* . . . is unable to feed; . . . other important alterations take place during the passage of the *locomotive pupa* into the fixed young Cirripede. *Huxley*, Anat. Invert., p. 250.

Mature, naked, obtected, etc., **pupa.** See the adjectives.—**Pupa coarctata**, a coarctate pupa.

The pupa, in the majority of Diptera, is merely the larva with a hard case (*pupæ coarctatæ*). *Pascoe*, Class. Anim., p. 122.

Pupa obtecta, an obtected pupa.

Pupacea (pụ-pā'sẹ-ạ̈), *n. pl.* [NL., < *Pupa* + *-acea*.] Same as *Pupidæ*.

pupal (pū'pạl), *a.* [< *pupa* + *-al*.] Of or pertaining to a pupa; nymphal; chrysalid; pupiform.

puparial (pụ-pā'ri-ạl), *a.* [< *puparium* + *-al*.] Of or pertaining to a puparium, or dipterous pupa.

puparium (pụ-pā'ri-um), *n.*; pl. *puparia* (-ạ̈). [NL., < *pupa*, a pupa: see *pupa*.] A pupa included within the last larval skin; a coarctate pupa; a larva pupigera, as in all dipterous insects of the division *Cyclorhapha* and in many of the *Orthorhapha*. See cut under *Pipiza*.

pupate (pū'pāt), *v. i.*; pret. and pp. *pupated*, ppr. *pupating*. [< *pupa* + *-ate*[2].] To become a pupa; enter upon the pupal state; undergo transformation from the state of the grub or larva to that of the perfect insect or imago: as, to *pupate* under ground; to *pupate* in winter.

pupation (pụ-pā'shọn), *n.* [< *pupate* + *-ion*.] The act of pupating, or the state of being a pupa; the pupal condition; the time during which an insect is a pupa.

pupe (pūp), *n.* [< F. *pupe*, < NL. *pupa*, a pupa: see *pupa*.] Same as *pupa*. *Wright.*

pupelo (pū'pe-lō), *n.* [Perhaps a corrupted form, ult. < F. *pomme*, apple. Cf. *pomperkin*.] Cider-brandy. [New Eng.]

In Livingston there were five distilleries for the manufacture of cider-brandy, or what was familiarly known as *pupelo*. *S. Judd*, Margaret, i. 7.

Pupidæ (pū'pi-dē), *n. pl.* [NL., < *Pupa* + *-idæ*.] A family of geophilous pulmonate gastropods, typified by the genus *Pupa*. The animal has a nearly smooth jaw and teeth like those of *Helicidæ*; the shell is generally pupiform, but sometimes conic or cylindric, and has usually a contracted aperture and teeth or lamellæ on the lips. The species are mostly of small size. By many they are united with the *Helicidæ*. Also called *Pupacea*.

pupifera (pụ-pif'ẹ-rạ̈), *n. pl.* [NL. (Lichtenstein), < *pupa*, a pupa, + L. *ferre* = E. *bear*[1].] The return migrant generation of plant-lice, or the last winged generation, which gives birth agamically to the true sexual generation. See *pseudogyne*.

pupiform (pū'pi-fôrm), *a.* [< NL. *pupa*, pupa, + L. *forma*, form.] 1. In *entom.*, having the form or character of a pupa; pupal; puparial: as, a *pupiform* larva.—2. In *conch.*, shaped like a shell of the genus *Pupa*; resembling one of the *Pupidæ* in the form of the shell.

pupigenous (pụ-pij'e-nus), *a.* [< NL. *pupa*, pupa, + *-genus*, producing: see *-genous*.] Same as *pupiparous*.

pupigerous (pū-pij'ẹ-rus), *a.* [< NL. *pupa*, pupa, + L. *gerere*, carry.] Having the pupa contained within the last larval skin; forming a puparium, as most dipterous insects; coarctate, as a pupa. See *larva pupigera*, under *larva*.

In the other group [of dipterous insects], which are always *pupigerous*, the perfect insect escapes from the larval skin through a more or less circular opening. *Stand. Nat. Hist.*, II. 406.

pupil[1] (pū'pil), *n.* and *a.* [Formerly *pupill*; < OF. *pupile*, *pupille*, F. *pupille*, m. and f., = Pr. *pupilli* = Sp. *pupilo*, m., *pupila*, f., = Pg. It. *pupillo*, m., *pupilla*, f., a ward, < L. *pupillus*, m., *pupilla*, f., an orphan child, a ward or minor, dim. of *pupus*, a boy, *pupa*, a girl: see *pupa*.] **I.** *n.* 1. A youth or any person of either sex under the care of an instructor or tutor; in general, a scholar; a disciple.

Tutors should behave reverently before their *pupils*. *Sir R. L'Estrange.*

2†. A ward; a youth or person under the care of a guardian.

What, shall King Henry be a *pupil* still
Under the surly Gloucester's governance?
Shak., 2 Hen. VI., i. 3. 49.

3. In *civil law*, a person under puberty (fourteen for males, twelve for females), over whom a guardian has been appointed.

II. *a.* Under age; in a state of pupilage or nonage; minor.

The custody of his *pupil* children. *Westminster Rev.*, CXXVIII. 703.

pupil[2] (pū'pil), *n.* [Formerly also *pupill*; < F. *pupille*, f., = Pr. *pupilla* = Sp. *pupila* = Pg. It. *pupilla* = D. *pupil* = G. *pupille* = Sw. *pupill* = Dan. *pupil*, < L. *pupilla*, the pupil of the eye, a particular use (as a 'baby' in the eye: see *baby*) of *pupilla*, an orphan girl, a ward or minor, dim. fem. of *pupa*, a girl: see *pupil*[1].] 1. The orifice of the iris; the hole or opening in the iris through which light passes. The pupil appears usually as a black spot in the middle of the colored part of the eye, this appearance being due to the darkness of the back of the eye. The pupil contracts when the retina is stimulated, as by light, on accommodation for near distances and on convergence of the visual axes; pain may cause a dilatation. The size of the pupil is determined by the circular and radiating muscular fibers of the iris. It may also be influenced by drugs. Thus, opium contracts and belladonna dilates the pupil. The same consequences may result from disease or injury. The shape of the pupil in most animals is circular, as the expression of the uniform action of the contractile fibers of the iris; but in many animals it is oval, elliptical, or slit-like. Thus, the pupil of the cat contracts to a mere chink in the sunlight and dilates to a circle in the dark. The pupil of the horse is a broad, nearly parallel-sided fissure obtusely rounded at each end. The variability of the pupil in size is not less remarkable in owls than in cats, but in these birds it keeps its circular figure, changing in size from a mere point to a disk which leaves the iris a mere rim. The pupil sometimes gives zoölogical characters, as in distinguishing foxes from wolves or dogs. See *iris*, 6, and cuts under *eye*[1]. 2. In *zoöl.*: (*a*) The central dark part of an ocellated spot. See *ocellus*, 4. (*b*) A dark, apparently interior, spot seen in the compound eyes of certain insects, and changing in position as it is viewed from different sides.—**Argyll-Robertson pupil**, a pupil which does not contract from light, but does with accommodation for short distances. It is a frequent symptom in locomotor ataxia.—**Exclusion of the pupil.** See *exclusion*.—**Occlusion of the pupil**, the filling up of the pupil with inflammatory material.—**Pinhole pupil**, the pupil when so contracted, as it sometimes is, as to resemble a pinhole.

pupilability† (pū"pi-lạ-bil'ị-ti), *n.* [< *pupil*[1] + *-able* + *-ity* (see *-bility*).] Pupilary nature; confidential character. [Rare.]

What can he mean by the lambent *pupilability* of slow, low, dry chat, five notes below the natural tone? *Sterne*, Tristram Shandy, iv. 1.

pupilage, pupillage (pū'pi-lạ̄j), *n.* [= Sp. *pupilaje* = Pg. *pupillagem*; as *pupil*[1] + *-age*.] 1. The state of being a pupil or scholar, or the period during which one is a pupil.

Most Noble Lord, the pillor of my life
And Patrone of my Muses *pupillage*.
Spenser, To Lord Grey of Wilton.

The severity of the father's brow, . . . whilst they [the children] are under the discipline and government of *pupilage*, I think . . . should be relaxed as fast as their age, discretion, and good behaviour could allow it. *Locke*, Education, § 95.

2. The state or period of being a ward or minor.

Three sones he dying left, all under age,
By meanes whereof their uncle Vortigere
Usurpt the crowne during their *pupillage*.
Spenser, F. Q., II. x. 64.

There, there, drop my wardship,
My *pupillage* and vassalage together.
B. Jonson, Staple of News, i. 1.

That they themselves might confine the Monarch to a kind of *Pupillage* under their Hierarchy. *Milton*, Reformation in Eng., ii.

pupilar, pupillar (pū'pi-lạ̈r), *a.* Same as *pupilary*[1].

pupilarity, pupillarity (pū-pi-lar'ị-ti), *n.* [= F. *pupillarité* = Pr. *pupillaretat*, < ML. **pupillarita(t-)s*, *pupillarieta(t-)s*, < L. *pupillaris*, pupilary: see *pupilary*[1].] In *Scots law*, the interval from birth to the age of fourteen in males and twelve in females; pupilage.

It's a fatherless bairn, . . . and a motherless: . . . we are in loco parentis to him during his years o' *pupillarity*. *Scott*, Heart of Mid-Lothian, v.

pupilary[1], **pupillary**[1] (pū'pi-lā-ri), *a.* [= F. *pupillaire* = Pr. *pupilari* = Sp. *pupilar* = Pg. *pupillar* = It. *pupillare*, < L. *pupillaris*, pertaining to an orphan or ward, < *pupillus*, an orphan, a ward: see *pupil*[1].] Pertaining to a pupil or ward.

pupilary[2], **pupillary**[2] (pū'pi-lā-ri), *a.* [< *pupil*[2] + *-ary*. Cf. *pupilary*[1].] Of or pertaining to the pupil of the eye.

Now it becomes an interesting question, When the axial and focal adjustments are thus dissociated, with which one does the *pupillary* contraction ally itself? I answer, it allies itself with the focal adjustment. *Le Conte*, Sight, p. 118.

Pupillary membrane. See *membrane*.

pupilate, pupillate (pū'pi-lāt), *a.* [< NL. *pupillatus*, < L. *pupilla*, pupil: see *pupil*[2].] In *zoöl.*, having a central spot of another and generally darker color; noting marks so characterized.

pupiled, pupilled (pū'pild), *a.* [< *pupil*[2] + *-ed*[2].] In *entom.*, furnished with a central dark spot; pupilate: as, a white spot *pupiled* with blue: used especially of ocellated spots.

pupilize, pupillize (pū'pi-līz), *v. i.*; pret. and pp. *pupilized*, *pupillized*, ppr. *pupilizing*, *pupillizing*. [< *pupil*[1] + *-ize*.] To take pupils; teach; tutor.

When the student takes his degree, he obtains by *pupilizing* enough to render further assistance unnecessary. *C. A. Bristed*, English University, p. 111.

pupilla (pū-pil'ạ̈), *n.*; pl. *pupillæ* (-ē). [L.: see *pupil*[2].] In *anat.*, the pupil of the eye.

pupillage, pupillar, etc. See *pupilage*, etc.

pupillometer (pū-pi-lom'e-tėr), *n.* [< L. *pupilla*, pupil, + Gr. μετρον, measure.] An instrument for measuring the size of the pupil of the eye.

pupil-monger† (pū'pil-mung"gėr), *n.* One who takes or teaches pupils; a tutor or schoolmaster. [Rare.]

John Preston . . . was the greatest *pupil-monger* in England in man's memory, having sixteen fellow commoners . . . admitted in one year in Queen's College, and provided convenient accommodations for them. *Fuller*, Worthies, Northampton, II. 517.

pupil-teacher (pū'pil-tē"chėr), *n.* One who is both a pupil and a teacher. In Great Britain pupil-teachers are apprenticed for five years under a certificated master or mistress, receive daily instruction out of school-hours, and assist in the regular school-work during school-hours. Their subsequent training consists of a course of two years at a normal college and training-school.

The large towns, which are the almost only nurseries of *pupil-teachers*, are mostly working on the centre-system, which makes the *pupil-teacher* merely a kind of inferior assistant, not a pupil at all, to the teacher under whom he is apprenticed. *The Academy*, June 1, 1889, p. 370.

Pupina (pū-pī'nạ̈), *n.* [NL. (Ehrenberg, 1831), < *Pupa*, the shell so called, + *-ina*.] The typical genus of *Pupinidæ*. The species are of a lustrous brown or mahogany color, and inhabit India, China, Australia, and islands of the Pacific ocean. *P. bicanicu-lata* is an example.

Pupinacea (pū-pi-nā'sẹ̄-ạ̈), *n. pl.* [NL., < *Pupina* + *-acea*.] Same as *Pupinidæ*.

Pupinæ (pū-pī'nē), *n. pl.* [NL., < *Pupa* + *-inæ*.] The *Pupidæ* considered as a subfamily of *Helicidæ*.

Pupinidæ (pū-pin'i-dē), *n. pl.* [NL., < *Pupina* + *-idæ*.] A family of terrestrial pectinibranchiate gastropods, typified by the genus *Pupina*. They are closely related to the *Cyclophoridæ*, and are by many referred to that family, but are distinguished by a pupiform shell. The species are confined to tropical countries. *Pupina* and *Megalomastoma* are the principal genera.

Pupininæ (pū-pi-nī'nē), *n. pl.* [NL., < *Pupina* + *-inæ*.] A subfamily of *Cyclophoridæ*, typified by the genus *Pupina*: same as *Pupinidæ*.

Pupipara (pū-pip'ạ-rạ̈), *n. pl.* [NL. (Nitzsch, 1818), < *pupa*, pupa, + L. *parere*, bring forth.] A division of dipterous insects in which the eggs are hatched and the larval state is passed within the body of the parent, the young being born ready to become pupæ. The head is closely connected with the body, and the proboscis is strong and adapted for piercing. Certain genera are wingless. The pupiparous *Diptera* are of the three families *Hippoboscidæ*, *Nycteribiidæ*, and *Braulidæ*. The first family includes the well-known horse-tick, sheep-tick, and bird-ticks, the second the bat-ticks, and the third the bee-lice. Sometimes called *Nymphipara*.

Pupiparia (pū-pi-pā'ri-ạ̈), *n. pl.* [NL.] Same as *Pupipara*.

pupiparous (pū-pip'ạ-rus), *a.* [< NL. *pupa*, pupa, + L. *parere*, bring forth.] Bringing forth pupæ; giving birth to larvæ which are already advanced to the pupal state; of or pertaining to the *Pupipara*. Also *pupigenous*.

Pupivora (pū-piv'ọ-rạ̈), *n. pl.* [NL., < NL. *pupa*, pupa, + L. *vorare*, devour.] A division of *Hymenoptera* characterized by the petiolate or stalked abdomen, the female armed with an extensile ovipositor, the larvæ footless, and having the habit of ovipositing in the larvæ or pupæ of other insects (often however in plants, as in the gall-insects), upon which the young feed when they hatch, whence the name; the pupivorous, entomophagous, or spiculiferous hymenopterous insects. In Latreille's system of classification the *Pupivora* formed the second family of *Hymenoptera*, divided into six tribes, *Evaniades*, *Ichneumonidæ*, *Gallicolæ*, *Chalcidiæ*, *Oxyuri*, and *Chrysides*, respectively corresponding to the modern families *Evaniidæ*, *Ichneumonidæ* (with *Braconidæ*), *Cynipidæ*, *Chalcididæ*, *Proctotrypidæ*, and *Chrysididæ*. The *Pupivora*, slightly modified, are also called *Entomophaga*, and by Westwood *Spiculifera*.

pupivore (pū'pi-vōr), *n.* A pupivorous insect; a member of the *Pupivora*.

pupivorous (pū-piv'ọ-rus), *a.* [< NL. *pupa*, pupa, + L. *vorare*, devour.] Devouring the pupæ of other insects, as an insect; parasitic on pupæ; belonging to the *Pupivora*. See cut under *Pimpla*.

puplet, *n.* A Middle English form of *people*.

pupoid (pū'poid), *a.* [< NL. *pupa*, pupa, + Gr. εἶδος, form.] In *conch.*, pupiform; resembling or related to the *Pupidæ*.

puppet (pup'et), *n.* [Also *poppet*; early mod. E. *popet*, < ME. *popet*, < OF. *poupette*, a doll, puppet, dim. of **poupe*, < L. *pupa*, a doll, puppet, a girl: see *pupa*. Cf. *puppy*.] **1**†. A doll.

This were a *popet* in an arm tenbrace
For any woman, smal and fair of face.
Chaucer, Prol. to Sir Thopas, l. 11.

2. A little figure of a person, moved by the fingers, or by cords or wires, in a mock drama; a marionette.

Neither can any man marvel at the play of *puppets* that goeth behind the curtain, and adviseth well of the motion. *Bacon*, Advancement of Learning, i. 94.

Hence—**3.** One who is actuated by the will of another; a tool: used in contempt.

Puppet to a father's threat, and servile to a shrewish tongue. *Tennyson*, Locksley Hall.

4†. *pl.* Toys; trinkets.

A maid makes conscience
Of half-a-crown a-week for pins and *puppets*.
Fletcher, Wit without Money, ii. 2.

5. The head-stock or the tail-stock of a lathe. See *lathe*.

puppet† (pup'et), *v. t.* [< *puppet*, *n.*] To dress as a doll; bedeck with finery.

Behold thy darling, whom thy soul affects
So dearly; whom thy fond indulgence decks
And *puppets* up in soft, in silken weeds.
Quarles, Emblems, v. 8.

puppet-head (pup'et-hed), *n.* A sliding piece on the upper part of the lathe-bed of a lathe or boring-machine, to hold and adjust the back-center.

puppetish (pup'et-ish), *a.* [Early mod. E. *popetish*; < *puppet* + *-ish*[1].] Pertaining to or resembling puppets or puppetry.

Ne lesse also doth he that setteth menne to open penaunce at Paules Crosse, for holye water makyng, for procession and sensinge, wyth other *popetishe* gaudes, constrayninge them to promise the adnauncement of the old faith of holy church by such fantasticall popperyes. *Bp. Bale*, Image, ii.

puppetly† (pup'et-li), *a.* [< *puppet* + *-ly*[1].] Like a puppet. [Rare.]

Puppetly idols, lately consecrated to vulgar adoration. *Bp. Gauden*, Hieraspistes (1653), p. 448.

puppetman (pup'et-man), *n.*; pl. *puppetmen* (-men). Same as *puppet-player*.

From yonder *puppet-man* enquire,
Who wisely hides his wood and wire. *Swift.*

puppet-master (pup'et-mas"tėr), *n.* The master or manager of a puppet-show.

Host. Of whom the tale went to turn *puppet-master*.
Lov. And travel with young Goose, the motion-man.
B. Jonson, New Inn, i. 1.

puppet-play (pup'et-plā), *n.* **1.** A dramatic performance with puppets, with or without a dialogue spoken by concealed persons.—**2.** That kind of performance which is carried on by means of puppets; entertainment by means of marionettes.

puppet-player (pup'et-plā"ėr), *n.* One who manages the motions of puppets.

puppetry (pup'et-ri), *n.* [Formerly also *puppetry*, *popetry*; < *puppet* + *-ry*.] **1.** Finery, as that of a doll or puppet; outward show; affectation.

Rave, talk idly, as 'twere some deity,
Adoring female painted *puppetry*.
Marston, Scourge of Villanie (ed. 1599), viii. 204.

Your dainty ten-times-drest buff, with this language,
Bold man of arms, shall win upon her, doubt not,
Beyond all silken *puppetry*. *Ford*, Lady's Trial, ii. 1.

The theatre seems to me almost as bad as the church; it is all *puppetry* alike. *S. Judd*, Margaret, ii. 11.

2. The exhibition of puppets or puppet-shows; a puppet-show.

How outragiously are their preistes and chirches orned and gorgiously garnisshed in their *popetry*, passe tymes, and apes playe. *Joye*, Expos. of Dan. vii.

Thou profane professor of *puppetry*, little better than poetry. *B. Jonson*, Bartholomew Fair, v. 3.

A grave proficient in amusive feats
Of *puppetry*. *Wordsworth*, Excursion, v.

puppet-show (pup'et-shō), *n.* Same as *puppet-play*, 1.

A man who seldom rides needs only to get into a coach and traverse his own town, to turn the street into a *puppet-show*. *Emerson*, Misc., p. 47.

puppet-valve (pup'et-valv), *n.* A valve which, in opening, is lifted bodily from its seat instead of being hinged at one side.

puppify (pup'i-fī), *v. t.*; pret. and pp. *puppified*, ppr. *puppifying*. [< *puppy* + *-fy*.] To make a puppy of; assimilate to a puppy or puppies. [Rare.]

Concerning the peeple, I verily believe ther were never any so far degenerated since the Devill had to do with mankind, never any who did fool and *puppifie* themselfs into such a perfect slavery and confusion. *Howell*, Parly of Beasts, p. 29. (*Davies.*)

puppily (pup'i-li), *a.* [< *puppy* + *-ly*[1].] Puppy-like. [Rare.]

This impertinent heart is more troublesome to me than my conscience, I think. I shall be obliged to hoarsen my voice and roughen my character, to keep up with its *puppily* dancings. . . *Richardson*, Clarissa Harlowe, V. 79. (*Davies.*)

pupping†, *n.* An obsolete form of *pippin*[2]. *Minsheu.*

Puppis (pup'is), *n.* [NL., < L. *puppis*, a ship, the stern of a ship: see *poop*[1].] A subdivision of the constellation Argo, introduced by Baily in the British Association Catalogue.

puppy (pup'i), *n.*; pl. *puppies* (-iz). [Early mod. E. *puppie*; < OF. *poupee*, F. *poupée*, a doll, puppet, < ML. as if **pupata*, < L. *pupa*, a doll, puppet: see *pupa*, *puppet*. A little dog appears to have been called *puppy* because petted as a doll or puppet. Hence, by abbr., *pup*.] **1**†. A doll; a puppet. *Halliwell.*—**2.** A young dog; a whelp; also, by extension, a young seal or other young carnivore.

A bitch's blind *puppies*, fifteen i' the litter.
Shak., M. W. of W., iii. 5. 11.

3. A conceited, frivolous, and impertinent man; a silly young fop or coxcomb: used in contempt.

Go, bid your lady seek some fool to fawn on her,
Some unexperienc'd *puppy* to make sport with;
I have been her mirth too long.
Beau. and Fl., Little French Lawyer, ii. 3.

You busy *Puppy*, what have you to do with our Laws? *Milton*, Answer to Salmasius, Pref., p. 15.

I am by no means such a *puppy* as to tell you I am upon sure ground; however, perseverance. *Miss Burney*, Evelina, lxxvi.

4. A white bowl or buoy used in the herring-fisheries to mark the position of the net nearest the fishing-boat. [Eng.]

puppy (pup'i), *v. i.*; pret. and pp. *puppied*, ppr. *puppying*. [< *puppy*, *n.*] To bring forth puppies; whelp. Also *pup*.

puppy-dog (pup'i-dog), *n.* A pup or puppy. [Colloq.]

Talks as familiarly of roaring lions
As maids of thirteen do of *puppy dogs!*
Shak., K. John, ii. 1. 460.

puppy-fish (pup'i-fish), *n.* A selachian, the angel-fish, *Squatina angelus*. See cuts under *angel-fish* and *Squatina*.

puppy-headed (pup'i-hed"ed), *a.* Stupid.

I shall laugh myself to death at this *puppy-headed* monster. *Shak.*, Tempest, ii. 2. 159.

puppyhood (pup'i-hụd), *n.* [< *puppy* + *-hood*.] The condition of being a puppy, or the period during which this condition lasts.

Large dogs "are still in their *puppyhood* at this time [one year old]." *Darwin*, Var. of Animals and Plants, i.

puppyism (pup'i-izm), *n.* [< *puppy* + *-ism*.] Conduct becoming a puppy; silly, conceited foppishness; empty-headed affectation.

It is surely more tolerable than precocious *puppyism* in the Quadrant, whiskered dandyism in Regent-street and Pall-mall, or gallantry in its dotage anywhere. *Dickens*, Sketches, Characters, i.

puppy-snatch†, *n.* Apparently, a snare. *Davies.*

It seem'd indifferent to him
Whether he did or sink or swim;
So he by either means might catch
Us Trojans in a *Puppy-snatch*.
Cotton, Scarronides, p. 10.

pur[1], *v.* and *n.* See *purr*[1].

pur[2]†, **purr**[2]†, *n.* A term of unknown meaning used in the game of post and pair.

Some, having lost their double Pare and Post,
Make their advantage on the *Purrs* they haue;
Whereby the Winners winnings all are lost,
Although, at best, the other's but a knaue.
Sir J. Davies, Wittes Pilgrimage, quoted in Masque of [Christmas, by B. Jonson.

Post and Pair, with a pair-royal of aces in his hat; his garment all done over with pairs and *purs*. *B. Jonson*, Masque of Christmas.

pur[3]†, *a.* and *adv.* A Middle English form of *pure*.

Purana (pö-rä'nä), *n.* [Skt. *purāna*, things of the past, tale of old times, prop. adj., past, former, ancient, < *purā*, formerly, before; akin to E. *fore*: see *fore*[1].] One of a class of sacred poetical writings in the Sanskrit tongue, which treat chiefly of the creation, destruction, and renovation of worlds, the genealogy and deeds of gods, heroes, and princes, the reigns of the Manus, etc.

The *Puranas*, though comparatively modern, make up a body of doctrine mixed with mythology and tradition such as few nations can boast of. *J. Fergusson*, Hist. Indian Arch., p. 7.

Puranic (pö-ran'ik), *a.* [< *Purana* + *-ic*.] Pertaining to the Puranas.

Purbeck beds. In *geol.* See *bed*[1].

Purbeck marble. A gray marble obtained from the upper Purbeck strata. See *Purbeck beds*, under *bed*[1]. It is made up chiefly of specimens of *Paludina*. This marble has been worked for more than 700 years, and used especially for slender shafts in medieval architecture, "but the introduction of foreign marbles has decreased the demand for it" (*Woodward*).

purblind (pėr'blīnd), *a.* [Formerly also *perblind* (simulating L. *per*, through, as if 'thoroughly blind'), *poreblind*, *poarblind* (simulating *pore*[1], as if 'so nearly blind that one must pore or read close'), *poorblind* (simulating *poor*, as if 'having poor sight—almost blind'); < ME. *purblynde*, *pur blind*, quite blind, later merely dim-sighted (tr. by L. *luscus*); orig. two words: *pur*, *pure*, adv., quite; *blind*, blind. The use of the adv. *pure* becoming obs. or dial., the meaning of *pur-* became obscure; hence the variations noted.] 1†. Quite blind; entirely blind.

Me ssolde pulte oute bothe hys eye, and make hym *pur blynd*. *Rob. of Gloucester*, p. 376.

A gouty Briareus, many hands and no use, or *purblind* Argus, all eyes and no sight. *Shak.*, T. and C., i. 2. 31.

2. Nearly blind; dim-sighted; seeing dimly or obscurely.

Thy dignitie or auctoritie, wherein thou only differeth from other, is (as it were) but a weyghty or heuy cloke, freshely glitteryng in the eyen of them that be *poreblind*. *Sir T. Elyot*, The Governour, ii. 3.

Pore-blind men see best in the dimmer lights, and likewise have their sight stronger near hand than those that are not *pore-blind*. *Bacon*, Works (ed. 1826), IV. 470.

O *purblind* race of miserable men!
Tennyson, Geraint.

purblindly (pėr'blīnd-li), *adv.* In a purblind manner.

purblindness (pėr'blīnd-nes), *n.* The state of being purblind; shortness of sight; near-sightedness; dimness of vision.

The Professor's keen philosophic perspicacity is somewhat marred by a certain mixture of almost owlish *purblindness*. *Carlyle*, Sartor Resartus, iii. 10.

purcatorye†, *n.* A Middle English form of *purgatory*.

purchasable (pėr'chā-sa-bl), *a.* [Also *purchaseable*; < *purchase* + *-able*.] Capable of being bought, purchased, or obtained for a consideration.

Money being the counterbalance to all things *purchaseable* by it. *Locke*, Lowering of Interest.

purchase (pėr'chās), *v.*; pret. and pp. *purchased*, ppr. *purchasing*. [< ME. *purchasen*, *purchacen*, *purchesen*, *porchacyen*, < OF. *porchacier*, *purchasier*, *porchacer*, *porchaser*, *purcacer*, etc., F. *pourchasser* (= Pr. *percassar* = It. *procacciare*), seek out, acquire, get, < *pur-* (< L. *pro*), forth, + *chacier*, *chaser*, *chasser*, pursue: see *chase*[1].] I. *trans.* 1. To gain, obtain, or acquire; secure, procure, or obtain in any way other than by inheritance or by payment of money or its equivalent; especially, to secure or obtain by effort, labor, risk, sacrifice, etc.: as, to *purchase* peace by concessions; to *purchase* favor with flattery.

The Monstre answerde him, and seyde he was a dedly Creature, suche as God hadde formed, and duelled in tho Desertes, in *purchasynge* his Sustynance. *Mandeville*, Travels, p. 47.

So it Renyth in my Rememberaunce
That dayly, nyghtly, tyde, tyme, and owre,
Hit is my will to *purches* youre fauoure.
Political Poems, etc. (ed. Furnivall), p. 43.

By reproving faults they *purchased* unto themselves with the multitude a name to be virtuous. *Hooker*, Eccles. Polity, Pref., iii.

Lest it make you choleric and *purchase* me another dry basting. *Shak.*, C. of E., ii. 2. 63.

I think I must be enforced to *purchase* me another page. *B. Jonson*, Cynthia's Revels, ii. 1.

Would that my life could *purchase* thine!
Shelley, The Cenci, v. 1.

2. To secure, procure, or obtain by expenditure of money or its equivalent; buy: as, to *purchase* provisions, lands, or houses.

The field which Abraham *purchased* of the sons of Heth. Gen. xxv. 10.

'Twill *purchase* the whole bench of aldermanity. *B. Jonson*, Magnetick Lady, v. 5.

The Pasha grants a licence to one person, generally a Jew, to buy all the senna, who is obliged to take all that is brought to Cairo, and no one else can *purchase* it. *Pococke*, Description of the East, I. 122.

3†. To expiate or recompense by a fine or forfeit.

I will be deaf to pleading and excuses,
Nor tears nor prayers shall *purchase* out abuses.
Shak., R. and J., iii. 1. 198.

4. [< *purchase*, *n.*, 10.] To apply a purchase to; raise or move by mechanical power: as, to *purchase* an anchor.—5†. To steal. *Imp. Dict.*

II. *intrans.* 1†. To put forth efforts to obtain anything; strive.

Duke John of Brabant *purchased* greatly that the Earl of Flanders should have his daughter in marriage. *Berners.*

2†. To bring something about; manage.

On that other side this Claudas hath so *purchased* that he hath be at Rome, and he and the kynge of Gaule hane take theire londes to the Emperoure be soche covenaunt that the Emperour Iulius shall sende hym socour. *Merlin* (E. E. T. S.), ii. 203.

3†. To acquire wealth.

Were all of his mind, to entertain no suits
But such they thought were honest, sure our lawyers
Would not *purchase* half so fast.
Webster, Devil's Law-Case, iv. 1.

4. *Naut.*, to draw in the cable: as, the capstan *purchases* apace.

purchase (pėr'chās), *n.* [Early mod. E. also *purchas*; < ME. *purchase*, *purchas*, *porchas*, < OF. *porchas*, purchase; from the verb.] 1. Acquisition; the obtaining or procuring of something by effort, labor, sacrifice, work, conquest, art, etc., or by the payment of money or its equivalent; procurement; acquirement.

And sent yow here a stede of his *purchase*;
Of kyng Ruben he wanne hym for certayn.
Generydes (E. E. T. S.), l. 2812.

Say I should marry her, she'll get more money
Than all my usury, put my knavery to it:
She appears the most infallible way of *purchase*.
Fletcher, Rule a Wife, iii. 5.

For on his backe a heavy load he bare,
Of nightly stelths, and pillage severall,
Which he had got abroad by *purchas* criminall.
Spenser, F. Q., I. iii. 16.

I glory
More in the cunning *purchase* of my wealth
Than in the glad possession.
B. Jonson, Volpone, i. 1.

2. That which is acquired or obtained otherwise than by inheritance; gain; acquisitions; winnings; specifically, that which is obtained by the payment of money or its equivalent.

& he gan of her *porchas* largeliche hom hede.
Rob. of Gloucester, p. 34.

A beauty-waning and distressed widow, . . .
Made prize and *purchase* of his lustful eye.
Shak., Rich. III., iii. 7. 187.

Our lives are almost expired before we become estated in our *purchases*. *Jer. Taylor*, Works (ed. 1835), I. 861.

3†. Prey; booty; plunder; hence, ill-gotten gain or wealth.

That has fray'd many a tall thief from a rich *purchase*!
Middleton (*and others*), Widow, iii. 1.

Rod. Who are out now?
Fourth Out. Good fellows, sir, that, if there be any *purchase* stirring,
Will strike it dead. *Fletcher*, Pilgrim, ii. 2.

Do you two pack up all the goods and *purchase*
That we can carry in the two trunks.
B. Jonson, Alchemist, iv. 4.

Tailors in France they grow to great
Abominable *purchase*, and become great officers.
Webster, Devil's Law-Case, ii. 1.

4†. Means of acquisition or gain; occupation.

Thou hast no land;
Stealing 's thy only *purchase*.
Fletcher and Shirley, Night-Walker, i. 1.

5. In *law*: (*a*) The act of obtaining or acquiring an estate in lands, etc., in any manner other than by inheritance or escheat. (*b*) The acquisition of property by contract. (*c*) The acquisition of property by contract for a valuable consideration. (*d*) The suing out and obtaining of a writ.—6. Value; advantage; worth: as, to buy an estate at twenty years' *purchase* (that is, at a price equal to twenty times its annual value, or the total return from it for twenty years).

A monarch might receive from her, not give,
Though she were his crown's *purchase*.
Fletcher, Beggars' Bush, v. 2.

Some fall in love with . . . popular fame and applause, supposing they are things of great *purchase*; when in many cases they are but matters of envy, peril, and impediment. *Bacon*, Advancement of Learning, ii. 344.

One report affirmed that Moore dared not come to Yorkshire; he knew that his life was not worth an hour's *purchase* if he did. *Charlotte Brontë*, Shirley, xxx.

7†. Attempt; endeavor.

I'll sit down by thee,
And, when thou wak'st, either get meat to save thee,
Or lose my life i' the *purchase*. *Fletcher*, Bonduca, v. 3.

8†. Course; way; departure.

For whan she died that was my maistresse,
Alle my weelfare made than the same *purchas*.
Political Poems, etc. (ed. Furnivall), p. 54.

9. The acquisition of position, promotion, etc., by the payment of money. See *purchase system*, below.

He abolished *purchase* in the army.
N. A. Rev., CXLII. 590.

10. Firm or advantageous hold by which power may be exerted; specifically, any mechanical power, force, or contrivance which may be advantageously used in moving, raising, or removing heavy bodies; in nautical use, a tackle of any kind for multiplying power.

The head of an ox or a horse is a heavy weight acting at the end of a long lever (consequently with a great *purchase*), and in a direction nearly perpendicular to the joints of the supporting neck. *Paley*, Nat. Theol.

A politician, to do great things, looks for a power, what our workmen call a *purchase*; and if he finds that power in politicks as in mechanicks, he cannot be at a loss to apply it. *Burke*, Rev. in France.

The last screw of the rack having been turned so often that its *purchase* crumbled, and it now turned and turned with nothing to bite. *Dickens*, Tale of Two Cities, ii. 23.

11. A knob or raised thumb-piece, allowing the hand which holds the handle to throw back the hinged cover of a tankard, beer-mug, or similar vessel.—**Bell purchase** (*naut.*), a kind of burton, consisting of four single blocks and a fall, frequently used for topsail-halyards of small vessels in the United States: so called from the name of the inventor.—**Gadsden purchase**, a territory purchased by the United States from Mexico in 1853 for $10,000,000, and included in the southern part of New Mexico and Arizona: so called from James Gadsden, United States minister to Mexico, who negotiated the treaty.—**Griolet purchase**, an arrangement of blocks and falls for mounting and dismounting heavy guns on the deck of a man-of-war.—**Gun-tackle purchase.** See *gun-tackle*. 2.—**Louisiana purchase**, the territory which the United States in 1803, under Jefferson's administration, acquired by purchase from France, then under the government of Bonaparte as first consul. The price was $15,000,000. The purchase consisted of New Orleans and a vast tract extending westward from the Mississippi river to the Rocky Mountains, and from the Gulf of Mexico to British America. The United States claimed West Florida and the extreme northwest, including Idaho, Oregon, and Washington as parts of the purchase; but it appears that they were wrong in so doing. Texas, which was part of the purchase, was ceded to Spain in 1819 by the treaty by which Florida was acquired. In 1845 it again became a part of the United States.—**Peak-purchase.** See *peak*[1].—**Purchase of Land Act.** See *land*[1].—**Purchase system**, the system under which commissions in the British army were formerly purchased. By this system nearly all the first appointments and a large proportion of the subsequent promotions of officers were effected. The regulation prices of commissions varied from £450 for an ensigncy to £7,250 for a lieutenant-colonelcy in the Life Guards, the highest commission purchasable. The system was abolished in 1871.—**Rolling purchase**†. Same as *cranequin*, 1.—**To raise a purchase.** See *raise*[1].

purchaseable, *a.* See *purchasable*.

purchase-block (pėr'chās-blok), *n.* *Naut.* See *block*[1].

purchase-fall (pėr'chās-fâl), *n.* The rope rove through a purchase-block.

purchase-money (pėr'chās-mun″i), *n.* The money paid or contracted to be paid for anything bought.

Whether ten thousand pounds, well laid out, might not build a decent college, fit to contain two hundred persons; and whether the *purchase-money* of the chambers would not go a good way towards defraying the expense? *Bp. Berkeley*, Querist, § 189.

purchaser (pėr'chā-sėr), *n.* [< ME. *purchasour*, < OF. *porchaceor*, *pourchasseur*, one who acquires or purchases, < *porchacier*, *pourchaser*, etc., acquire, purchase: see *purchase*.] 1†. An acquirer; a money-maker.

> So gret a *purchasour* was nowher noon.
> *Chaucer*, Gen. Prol. to C. T., l. 318.

2. One who obtains or acquires the property of anything by purchase; a buyer. Specifically, in *law*: (*a*) One who acquires property by the payment of a consideration.

> What supports and employs productive labour is the capital expended in setting it to work, and not the demand of *purchasers* for the produce of the labour when completed. *J. S. Mill.*

(*b*) One who acquires or obtains by conquest or by deed of gift, or in any manner other than by inheritance or escheat. Thus, a devisee or a donee in a deed of gift is technically a purchaser.—**Bona-fide purchaser.** See *bona fide*.—**First purchaser,** in the *law of inheritance*, the one who first among the family acquired the estate, whether by gift, buying, or bequest, to which others have succeeded; the earliest person in a line of descent.

purchase-shears (pėr′chās-shērz), *n. pl.* A very powerful form of shears, the cutters of which are rectangular steel bars inserted in grooves, so that they can be readily removed for sharpening or renewal. They have usually at the back of the blade a strong spring or backstay to hold the two edges in contact, and a stop to regulate the size of the pieces to be sheared off.

purcy†, *a.* A Middle English form of *pursy*.

purcyvauntet†, *n.* A Middle English form of *pursuivant*.

purdah (pėr′dā̤), *n.* [Also *pardah*; < Hind. *parda*, a curtain, screen, privacy, Pers. *parda*, a curtain.] In India, a curtain. (*a*) A curtain serving as a screen in an audience-hall or room of state.

> The guns are kept loaded inside the *purdah* at the hall-door. *W. H. Russell*, Diary in India, II. 103.

(*b*) A curtain screening women of superior rank from the sight of men and from contact with strangers.

> The doctor is permitted to approach the *purdah*, and put the hand through a small aperture . . . in order to feel the patient's pulse.
> *Williamson*, East India Vade Mecum, I. 130.
> [(*Yule and Burnell.*)

Hence—(*c*) The kind of seclusion in which such women live, constituting a mark of rank. (*d*) The material of which the curtain is made; especially, a fine kind of matting, or a cotton cloth woven in white and blue stripes.

purdahed (pėr′dā̤d), *a.* [< *purdah* + *-ed*[2].] Screened by a purdah or curtain: said of a Moslem woman of rank.

> The hour is passed in lively dialogues with the several *purdahed* dames.
> *Mrs. Meer Ali*, Observations on Mussalmans of India.

pure (pūr), *a.* and *n.* [< ME. *pure*, *pur*, < OF. (and F.) *pur*, m., *pure*, f., = Sp. Pg. It. *puro*, < L. *purus*, clean, free from dirt or filth, hence free from extraneous matter, plain, unadorned, unwrought, unoccupied, also free from fault or taint, as speech or morals, in law free from conditions, unconditional; akin to *putus*, clear (see *pute*), and to Skt. √ *pu*, purify. From L. *purus* are also ult. *purity*, *puritan*, *purify*, *depure*, *depurate*, etc., *purge*, *purgation*, etc., *expurgate*, *spurge*, etc.] **I.** *a.* **1.** Free from extraneous matter; separate from matter of another kind; free from mixture; unmixed; clear; especially, free from matter that impairs or pollutes: said of physical substances.

> Lastly I saw an Arke of *purest* golde
> Upon a brazen pillour standing hie.
> *Spenser*, Ruines of Time, l. 659.

> In *pure* white robes,
> Like very sanctity, she did approach
> My cabin. *Shak.*, W. T., iii. 3. 22.

2. Bare; mere; sheer; absolute; very: as, it was done out of *pure* spite; a *pure* villain.

> And cum wightly therwith the weghes hom selfe,
> To a place that was playne on the *pure* ground.
> *Destruction of Troy* (E. E. T. S.), l. 4794.

> For the meschief and the meschaunce amonges men of Sodome
> Wex therw plente of payn and of *pure* sleuthe.
> *Piers Plowman* (B), xiv. 76.

> The *pure* wyse of hire mevynge
> Shewede wel that men myghte in hire gesse
> Honor, estate, and womanly noblesse.
> *Chaucer*, Troilus, l. 285.

> Alas, sir, we did it for *pure* need.
> *Shak.*, 2 Hen. VI., ii. 1. 157.

> And half his blood burst forth, and down he sank
> For the *pure* pain, and wholly swoon'd away.
> *Tennyson*, Lancelot and Elaine.

3†. Sole; only.

> More feruent in faith thi falle I dessyre,
> Ffor Patroclus, my *pure* felow, thou put vnto dethe.
> *Destruction of Troy* (E. E. T. S.), l. 7934.

4†. Whole; thorough; complete.

> Ac hor nother, as me may ise, in *pur* righte nas.
> *Rob. of Gloucester*, l. 174.

> And Paris, that is prinsipall of our *pure* hate,
> If hit happe vs to hent, hongit shalbe
> As a felon falsest foundyn with thefte.
> *Destruction of Troy* (E. E. T. S.), l. 3634.

5†. Fine; nice.

> Venus the worthy, that wemen ay pleayn;
> And Palades, with *pure* wit that passes all other;
> And Jono, a iustis of loyes in erthe.
> *Destruction of Troy* (E. E. T. S.), l. 2384.

> Nay, I confess I was quiet enough, till my Husband told me what *pure* Lives the London Ladies live abroad, with their Dancing, Meetings, and Junquetings.
> *Wycherley*, Country Wife, iii. 1.

> You are a *pure* Fellow for a Father. This is always your Tricks, to make a great Fool of one before Company.
> *Steele*, Tender Husband, i. 1.

6. Figuratively, free from mixture with things of another kind; homogeneous.

> Howsoeuer, in the time of Elisa or Dido, the Phœnicean or Punike, which she carried into Africa, was *pure* Hebrew, as was also their letters. *Purchas*, Pilgrimage, p. 47.

> Although very much more modern in date, and consequently less *pure* in style, the ruins at Pollonarua are scarcely less interesting than those of the northern capital to which it succeeded.
> *J. Fergusson*, Hist. Indian Arch., p. 199.

7. Free from mixture with that which contaminates, stains, debases, or blemishes. (*a*) Free from moral defilement or guilt; innocent; guileless; spotless; chaste: applied to persons.

> Unto the *pure* all things are *pure*. Tit. i. 15.

> I have been made to believe a man of honour a villain, and the best and *purest* of creatures a false profligate.
> *Scott*, Kenilworth, xxxix.

> Who would against thine own eye-witness fain
> Have all men true and leal, all women *pure*.
> *Tennyson*, Merlin and Vivien.

(*b*) Ritually or ceremonially clean; unpolluted.

> All of them were *pure*, and killed the passover.
> Ezra vi. 20.

(*c*) Free from that which vitiates, pollutes, or degrades; unadulterated; genuine; stainless; sincere: said of thoughts, actions, motives, etc.

> *Pure* religion, and undefiled. Jas. i. 27.

> In their looks divine
> The image of their glorious Maker shone,
> Truth, wisdom, sanctitude severe and *pure*.
> *Milton*, P. L., iv. 293.

> A friendship as warm and as *pure* as any that ancient or modern history records. *Macaulay.*

8. In *music*: (*a*) Of intervals, intonation, and harmony, mathematically correct or perfect: opposed to *tempered*. (*b*) Of tones, without discordant quality. (*c*) Of style of composition or of a particular work, correct; regular; finished. —9. In *metaph.*, of the nature of form; untainted; in the Kantian terminology, not depending on experience; non-sensuous.—**Predicables of the pure understanding.** See *predicable*.—**Pure act, algebra, apperception, being.** See the nouns.—**Pure beauty,** a judgment of taste unmixed with other emotions. *Kant.*—**Pure body,** the first and simplest form united to the first and simplest matter.—**Pure categorical, cognition, color.** See the nouns.—**Pure concept of the understanding,** a concept which expresses universally and adequately the formal objective condition of experience. *Kant.*—**Pure conversion,** in *logic*, simple conversion. See *conversion*, 2.—**Pure culture, enunciation, equation, forest.** See the nouns.—**Pure ethics,** the science of the necessary moral laws of a free will.—**Pure harmony.** See *harmony*, 2 (*d*).—**Pure hyperbola,** a hyperbola without cusp, node, or acnode.—**Pure intellect.** See *intellect*, 1.—**Pure interval** or **intonation,** in *music*, an interval or intonation mathematically correct: opposed to *tempered interval* or *intonation*.—**Pure intuition,** the pure form of sensibility, not derived from experience, and virtually preceding all actual intuition; pure space and time.—**Pure knowledge** (NL. *cognitio pura*), knowledge unmixed with any sensuous element; with the Cartesians and Leibnitzians, that knowledge in which there is no mixture of sensible images, it being purely intellectual. Using the term *intellect* less precisely than the Aristotelians, the Cartesians found it necessary to employ, in ordinary, for the sake of discrimination, the expression *pure intellect* (L. *intellectus purus*) in contrast to *sense* and *imagination*. This phrase was, however, borrowed from the schools, who again borrowed it, through the medium of St. Augustine, from the Platonists. *Sir W. Hamilton*, Reid, note A, § 5, Supplementary Dissertations.—**Pure logic.** (*a*) See *logic*. (*b*) Logic based solely on a priori principles; a canon of the understanding and of the reason in reference to the formal element. *Kant.*—**Pure mathematics.** See *mathematics*.—**Pure natural science,** the science of the a priori laws of nature, such as "substance is permanent," and "every event is completely determined by causes." *Kant.*—**Pure obligation,** in *Scots law*. See *obligation*.—**Pure power.** See *power*[1].—**Pure proof,** an a priori proof, drawing nothing from experience.—**Pure proposition,** a non-modal proposition in which the predicate is applied to the subject without qualification.—**Pure reason.** See *reason*[1].—**Pure representation,** a representation which contains no matter of experience. *Kant.*—**Pure scarlet.** See *scarlet*.—**Pure syllogism,** in the *scholastic logic*, a non-modal syllogism composed of pure propositions; in the *Kantian logic*, one which involves no immediate inference; direct syllogism.—**Pure synthesis,** one whose manifold is given a priori. *Kant.*—**Pure truth,** absolutely a priori truth.—**Pure villeinage.** See *villeinage*.—**The pure ego.** See *ego*.=**Syn.** 7. Uncorrupted, incorrupt, unsullied, untainted, untarnished, unstained, clean, fair, unspotted, unpolluted, undefiled, immaculate, guiltless, holy.

II. *n.* **1.** Purity. [Rare.]

> Here are snakes within the grass;
> And you methinks, O Vivien, save ye fear
> The monkish manhood, and the mask of *pure*
> Worn by this court, can stir them till they sting.
> *Tennyson*, Merlin and Vivien.

2. In *tanning*, a bate of dog's dung, used for counteracting the action of the lime on the skins in the process of unhairing.

> There are about 30 tanyards, large and small, in Bermondsey, and these all have their regular *Pure* collectors from whom they obtain the article.
> *Mayhew*, London Labour and London Poor, II. 158.

pure (pūr), *adv.* [< ME. *pure*, *pur*, < OF. *pur* (in the phrase *a pur*, purely, absolutely), = Pr. *pur*, quite, = It. *pure*, *pur*, however, nevertheless, though, < L. *pure*, purely, plainly, simply, unconditionally, absolutely, < *purus*, pure, simple, unconditional: see *pure*, *a.* This adverb exists unrecognized in *purblind*.] Quite; very; absolutely; perfectly. [Now only prov. Eng.]

> Natheless there is gode Londe in sum place; but it is *pure* litille, as men seyn. *Mandeville*, Travels, p. 130.

> Godes pyne and hus passion is *pure* selde in my thouhte.
> *Piers Plowman* (C), viii. 20.

> His countess, a bouncing kind of lady-mayoress, looks *pure* awkward amongst so much good company.
> *Walpole*, Letters, II. 207.

pure (pūr), *v. t.*; pret. and pp. *pured*, ppr. *puring*. [< ME. *puren*, < OF. *purer*, < LL. *purare*, make pure, purify (by religious rites), < L. *purus*, pure: see *pure*, *a.*] 1. To purify; cleanse; refine.

> Allas! that I bihighte
> Of *pured* gold a thousand pound of wighte
> Unto this philosophre.
> *Chaucer*, Franklin's Tale, l. 832.

> If we had their peace and good will
> To myne and fine, and metal for to *pure*,
> In wilde Irish might we finde the cure.
> *Hakluyt's Voyages*, I. 199.

> If you be unclean, mistress, you may *pure* yourself.
> *Middleton*, Family of Love, iii. 3.

Specifically—2. In *tanning*, to cleanse with a bate of dog's dung.

> They [calf-skins] are then unhaired and fleshed in the usual manner, *pured* with a bate of dog's dung.
> *Workshop Receipts*, 2d ser., p. 366.

purée (pü-rā′), *n.* [F., a thick soup or porridge prepared from vegetables: see *porrey*.] A kind of broth or soup consisting of meat, fish, or vegetables boiled to a pulp, and passed through a sieve. The ordinary pea-soup is a familiar example.

purely (pūr′li), *adv.* [< ME. *purely*, *pureliche*, *purli*; < *pure* + *-ly*[2].] 1. Without admixture or blemish; in such a way or to such a degree as to be free from anything that is heterogeneous or tends to impair.—2. Entirely; wholly; completely; thoroughly; absolutely; quite: as, the whole thing was *purely* accidental.

> Neuer-more for no man mowe be deliuered,
> Ne pult out [of] prison but *purli* thourh 3our help.
> *William of Palerne* (E. E. T. S.), l. 4219.

> And I will turn my hand upon thee, and *purely* purge away thy dross, and take away all thy tin. Isa. i. 25.

> With these powers were combined others of a *purely* judicial character. *Prescott*, Ferd. and Isa., ii. 9.

3. Very; wonderfully; remarkably: as, *purely* well. [Obsolete or prov. Eng.]

> *Purely* jealous I would have her.
> *B. Jonson*, Poetaster, ii. 1.

> He is *purely* happy, because he knowes no euill, nor hath made meanes by sinne to bee acquainted with misery. *Bp. Earle*, Micro-cosmographie, A Childe.

4. Innocently; without guilt or sin; chastely.

purely (pūr′li), *a.* [An elliptical use of *purely*, *adv.*] Very or wonderfully well; having good health. [Prov. Eng.]

> So, Mr. Reynolds, if the ladies' prayers are of any avail, you ought to be *purely*.
> *Miss Edgeworth*, Absentee, xvi. (*Davies.*)

> "Lawk a' massey, Mr. Benjamin," cries a stout motherly woman in a red cloak, as they enter the field, "be that you? Well I never! you do look *purely*."
> *T. Hughes*, Tom Brown at Rugby, i. 2.

pureness (pūr′nes), *n.* The state or quality of being pure; purity. (*a*) An unmixed state; separation or freedom from any heterogeneous or foreign matter: as, the *pureness* of water or other liquor; the *pureness* of a metal; the *pureness* of air. (*b*) Freedom from improper words, phrases, or modes of speech: as, *pureness* of style. (*c*) Freedom from moral turpitude or guilt; moral cleanness; innocence.

> He was all *pureness*, and his outward part
> But represents the picture of his heart.
> *Cowley*, Death of John Littleton.

purfilet†, *v.* and *n.* An obsolete form of *purfle*.

purfle (pėr′fl), *v.*; pret. and pp. *purfled*, ppr. *purfling*. [Early mod. E. also *purfile*, *pourfill*; < ME. *purfilen*, *purfylen*, < OF. *pourfiler*, *porfiler*, F. *pourfiler*, also *parfiler* = It. *profilare*, embroider, border, < L. *pro*, before, + *filum*, thread: see *pro-* and *file*[3], and cf. *profile*, from the same ult. source. Hence, by contr., *purl*[3].] **I.** *trans.* **1.** To ornament or decorate with a wrought or flowered border; border. Specifically—(*a*) To embroider on the edge or margin.

Hue was *purfild* with peloure non purere in erthe,
And coroned with a corone the kynge hath no betere.
Piers Plowman (C), iii. 10.

A goodly lady clad in scarlot red,
Purfled with gold and pearle of rich assay.
Spenser, F. Q., I. ii. 13.

After they have wash'd the Body . . . they put it on a Flannel Shirt, which has commonly a Sleeve *purfled* about the Wrists.
Quoted in *Ashton's* Social Life in Reign of Queen Anne, [I. 54.

The unburnt end o' the very candle, Sirs,
Purfled with paint so prettily round and round,
He carried in such state last Peter's day.
Browning, Ring and Book, I. 211.

And on his brows a *purfled* purple hood.
Swinburne, St. Dorothy.

(*b*) To edge with fur. (*c*) To line with fur: as, a mantling *purfled* and bordered vair. (*d*) In *her.*, to decorate with gold mountings, such as the studs or bosses in armor, as in the phrase "a leg in armor proper, *purfled* or." (*e*) In *arch.*, to decorate richly, as with sculpture.

To this chest [shrine] the goldsmith, whose work it always was, gave an architectural form: it had its flying buttresses, its windows filled in with tracery, its pinnacles ribbed with crockets as light and thin and crispy as leaves upon a bough, and its tall crest *purfled* with knobs of sparkling jewels to run along the ridge of its steeply-pitched roof. *Rock*, Church of our Fathers, III. i. 390.

(*f*) In *viol-making*, to decorate (the edges of the body of an instrument) with a wavy inlay of valuable wood.

2. To mark or draw in profile.

She [the daughter of Dibutades] used ordinarily to marke upon the wall the shadow of her lover's face by candle light, and to *pourfil* the same afterward deeper, that so shee might enjoy his visage yet in his absence.
Holland, tr. of Pliny, xxxv. 12.

II. *intrans.* To hem a border.

purfle (pėr'fl), *n.* [Early mod. E. *purfyll*, *purful* (also *purflew*); < ME. *purfyle*, *purfoyl*, *porfil*, *porfyl*; from the verb.] A decorated or wrought border; a border of embroidered work.

Of precios perle in *porfyl* pyzte.
Alliterative Poems (ed. Morris), i. 216.

He preizede Pernel hire *porfil* to leue,
And kepen hit in hire cofre for catel at neode.
Piers Plowman (A), v. 26.

Many a riche stone
Was set on the *purfles*, out of doute,
Of colors, sleves and traines round aboute.
Flower and Leaf, l. 146.

Specifically, in *her.*, a border of one of the furs: not common, for a border *purfle* ermine means no more than a border ermine. An attempt has been made to discriminate the number of rows of the bells of the fur by the terms *purfled*, *counter-purfled*, and *vair*, for one, two, and three rows. It is not usual.

purflew†, *n.* Same as *purfle*.

purfling (pėr'fling), *n.* [Verbal n. of *purfle*, *v.*] An ornamental border, generally composed of ebony and maple or sycamore, inlaid in the edges of violins and similar instruments.

purfly (pėr'fli), *a.* [< *purfle* + *-y*[1].] Wrinkled; seamed: as, a large, *purfly*, flabby man. *Carlyle*, in Froude.

purgament† (pėr'ga-ment), *n.* [= It. *purgamento*, < L. *purgamentum*, what is swept or washed off, offscourings, < *purgare*, cleanse: see *purge*.] 1. A cathartic; a purge.—2. That which is excreted from anything; excretion.

The humours . . . are commonly passed over in anatomies as *purgaments*.
Bacon, Advancement of Learning, ii. 195.

purgation (pėr-gā'shon), *n.* [< ME. *purgacion*, < OF. *purgation*, F. *purgation* = Pr. Sp. *purgacion* = Pg. *purgação* = It. *purgazione*, < L. *purgatio(n-)*, a cleansing, < *purgare*, pp. *purgatus*, cleanse: see *purge*.] 1. The act of purging; clearing, cleansing, or purifying by separating and carrying away impurities or whatever is extraneous or superfluous; purification; specifically, evacuation of the intestines by purgatives.

Or that haue studied Phisicke so longe that he or they can giue his Masters purse a *Purgacion*, or his Chist, shoppe, and Countinghouse a strong vomit.
Babees Book (E. E. T. S.), p. 241.

Let the physician apply himself more to *purgation* than to alteration, because the offence is in quantity. *Bacon.*

We do not suppose the separation . . . finished before the *purgation* of the air began.
T. Burnet, Theory of the Earth.

2. The act of cleansing from the imputation of guilt; specifically, in *old law*, the clearing of one's self from a crime of which one has been publicly suspected and accused. It was either *canonical* (that is, prescribed by the canon law, the form whereof used in the spiritual court was that the person suspected took his oath that he was clear of the facts objected against him, and brought his honest neighbors with him to make oath that they believed he swore truly) or *vulgar* (that is, by fire or water ordeal, or by combat). See *ordeal*.

She was always an honest, civil woman; her neighbours would have gone on her *purgation* a great way.
Latimer, 5th Sermon bef. Edw. VI., 1549.

The inquisitors had a discretion to allow the accused to make the canonical *purgation* by oath instead of undergoing corporal torture, but the rule which allows this to be done at the same time discountenances it as fallacious.
Encyc. Brit., XXIII. 463.

purgative (pėr'ga-tiv), *a.* and *n.* [< F. *purgatif* = Pr. *purgatiu* = Sp. Pg. It. *purgativo*, < LL. *purgativus*, cleansing, cathartic, < L. *purgare*, pp. *purgatus*, cleanse: see *purge*.] I. *a.* 1. Having the power of cleansing; usually, having the power of evacuating the intestines; cathartic.

Purging medicines . . . have their *purgative* virtue in a fine spirit. *Bacon*, Nat. Hist., § 20.

They had not yet analysed these *purgative* waters, and consequently "Epsom salts" were unknown, so that people, did they wish for them, must either go to Epsom or buy the water in London.
Ashton, Social Life in Reign of Queen Anne, II. 113.

2. Having the property, as judicial torture in some cases, of invalidating the evidence against an accused person, when he, under torture, satisfactorily answered the questions of the judges.

II. *n.* A medicine that evacuates the intestines, producing more or less abundant and watery stools.—**Cholagogue purgative**, a purgative which increases the flow of bile into the intestine.—**Drastic purgative**, a violent purgative.—**Hydragogue purgative**, a purgative causing profuse watery stools.—**Laxative purgative**, a gentle purgative.

purgatively (pėr'ga-tiv-li), *adv.* In a purgative manner; cleansingly; cathartically.

purgatorial (pėr-ga-tō'ri-al), *a.* [< *purgatory* + *-al*.] Of or pertaining to purgatory; expiatory.

The sculptured dead on each side seem to freeze,
Emprison'd in black, *purgatorial* rails.
Keats, Eve of St. Agnes, ii.

The idea of *purgatorial* suffering, which hardly seems to have entered the minds of the lower races, expands in immense vigour in the great Aryan religions of Asia.
E. B. Tylor, Prim. Culture, II. 88.

purgatorian (pėr-ga-tō'ri-an), *a.* and *n.* [< *purgatory* + *-an*.] I. *a.* Same as *purgatorial*.

The delusions of purgatory, with all the apparitions of *purgatorian* ghosts.
J. Mede, Apostacy of Latter Times (1641), p. 45.

II. *n.* A believer in purgatory.

Boswell. We see in Scripture that Dives still retained an anxious concern about his brethren.
Johnson. Why, sir, we must either suppose that passage to be metaphorical, or hold, with many divines and all *Purgatorians*, that departed souls do not all at once arrive at the utmost perfection of which they are capable.
Boswell, Life of Johnson, iii. 193. (*Davies.*)

purgatorious (pėr-ga-tō'ri-us), *a.* [< L. *purgatorius*, cleansing: see *purgatory*.] Having the nature of or connected with purgatory.

Purgatorious and superstitious uses.
Milton, Touching Hirelings.

purgatory (pėr'ga-tọ-ri), *a.* and *n.* [< ME. *purgatorye*, *purcatorye*, *purcatorie*, n., = F. *purgatoire* = Pr. *purgatori*, *porguatori* = Sp. Pg. It. *purgatorio*, < LL. *purgatorius*, cleansing, purgative (ML. *purgatorium*, neut., a place of purgation, purgatory, also a wash-house, laundry), < L. *purgare*, pp. *purgatus*, cleanse: see *purge*.] I. *a.* Tending to cleanse; cleansing; expiatory.

This *purgatory* interval is not unfavourable to a faithless representative, who may be as good a canvasser as he was a bad governor. *Burke*, Rev. in France.

II. *n.*; pl. *purgatories* (-riz). 1. In the belief of Roman Catholics and others, a place of purgation in which the souls of those dying penitent are purified from venial sins, or undergo the temporal punishment which, after the guilt of mortal sin has been remitted, still remains to be endured by the sinner. It is not considered as a place of probation; for the ultimate salvation of those in purgatory is assured, and the impenitent are not received into purgatory. The souls in purgatory are supposed, however, to receive relief through the prayers of the faithful and through the sacrifice of the mass. The common belief in the Latin Church is that the purgatorial suffering is by fire; the Greek Church, however, does not determine its nature.

A robbere had remission rathere thanne thei alle,
Withoute penaunce of *purcatorie* to haue paradis for euere.
Piers Plowman (A), xi. 278.

How many men have been miserably afflicted by this fiction of *purgatory*! *Burton*, Anat. of Mel., p. 609.

2. Any place or state of temporary suffering or oblivion.

Any subject that was not to their palat they either condemn'd in a prohibition, or had it straight into the new *Purgatory* of an Index. *Milton*, Areopagitica, p. 10.

3. A gorge or cleft between perpendicular or steeply inclined walls of rock. [New Eng.] It is nearly the same as *flume* (used as a topographical word), except that localities called *flumes* in New England always have a stream of water running through them, which the *purgatories* have not.

The best-known localities bearing the name of *purgatories* are those at Sutton and Great Barrington, Mass., and there is one on the sea-shore at Newport, R. I.
J. D. Whitney, Names and Places, p. 160.

Purgatory hammer, one of the ancient and prehistoric perforated axes found in Scotland. This implement was so named as being supposed to have been buried with its owner in order that he might have the wherewithal "to thunder at the gates of Purgatory till the heavenly janitor appeared" (*Wilson*, Prehist. Ann. of Scotland, I. 191).

As we find the little flint arrow-head associated with Scottish folk-lore as the Elfin's bolt, so the stone hammer of the same period was adapted to the creed of the middle ages. The name by which it was popularly known in Scotland almost till the close of last century was that of the *Purgatory Hammer*.
Wilson, Arch. and Prehist. Ann. of Scotland, p. 135.

St. Patrick's Purgatory, a cavern in an island in Lough Derg, county Donegal, Ireland, to which pilgrimages are made, where Christ is said to have appeared to St. Patrick and showed him a deep pit, telling him that whoever remained in it a day and a night should be purified from his sins and behold both the torments of the damned and the joys of the blessed. A person of the name of Owen is said to have done this in the above cavern, formerly also called *Owen's cave*.

He satte all heavie and glommyng, as if he had come lately from Troponius' cave, or *Saint Patrick's purgatory*.
Erasmus, Praise of Folie, sig. A. (*Nares.*)

purge (pėrj), *v.*; pret. and pp. *purged*, ppr. *purging*. [Early mod. E. also *pourge*; < ME. *purgen*, < OF. (and F.) *purger* = Pr. Sp. Pg. *purgar* = It. *purgare*, < L. *purgare*, make pure, cleanse, < *purus*, clean, pure, + *agere*, make, do.] I. *trans.* 1. To cleanse or purify by separating and carrying off whatever is impure, heterogeneous, foreign, or superfluous; cleanse; clean, or clean out.

Nowe *purge* upp broke and diche.
Palladius, Husbondrie (E. E. T. S.), p. 190.

The people doe eftsoones adde their owne industry to clense and *purge* them [the streets].
Coryat, Crudities, I. 213.

Nor have we yet quite *purg'd* the Christian Land;
Still Idols here, like Calves at Bethel, stand.
Cowley, Death of Crashaw.

Thy chill persistent rain has *purged* our streets
Of gossipry. *Browning*, Ring and Book, II. 177.

2. To remove by some cleansing or purifying process or operation; clear or wash away: often followed by *away* and *off*.

Purge away our sins, for thy name's sake. Ps. lxxix. 9.

I am thy father's spirit,
Doom'd for a certain term to walk the night,
And for the day confined to fast in fires,
Till the foul crimes done in my days of nature
Are burnt and *purged away*. *Shak.*, Hamlet, i. 5. 13.

The ethereal mould,
Incapable of stain, would soon expel
Her mischief, and *purge off* the baser fire,
Victorious. *Milton*, P. L., ii. 141.

National corruptions were to be *purged* by national calamities. *Goldsmith*, Bolingbroke.

3. To clear from moral defilement or guilt: in this and next sense often followed by *of* or *from*.

My heart is *purged from* grudging hate.
Shak., Rich. III., ii. 1. 9.

4. To clear from accusation of a crime, as by ordeal, or from charge of contempt, as by oath showing that there was no wrong intent; free from taint or suspicion of crime.

He [Richard III.] sent to the Queen, being still in Sanctuary, divers Messengers, who should first excuse and *purge* him *of* all Things formerly attempted and done against her.
Baker, Chronicles, p. 231.

As usual, the first charge gave rise to a large number of informations. Thomas Mowbray, the earl-marshal, was unable to deny that he had some inkling of the plot, and archbishop Arundel had to *purge* himself *from* a like suspicion. *Stubbs*, Const. Hist., § 312.

5. To clarify; defecate, as liquors.—6. To operate on by or as by means of a cathartic.

He *purged* him with salt water. *Arbuthnot.*

7†. To void.

The satirical rogue says . . . that old men have grey beards, that their faces are wrinkled, their eyes *purging* thick amber and plum-tree gum. *Shak.*, Hamlet, ii. 2. 200.

8†. To trim.

Care the ground well, dresse the vines, *purge* the trees, and alway haue memorie of the Goddesse Ceres.
Guevara, Letters (tr. by Hellowes, 1577), p. 73.

Every branch that beareth fruit, he *purgeth* [in the revised version *cleanseth*] it, that it may bring forth more fruit. John xv. 2.

II. *intrans.* 1. To become pure by clarification.—2. To take a purge; produce evacuations from the intestines by means of a cathartic.

I'll *purge*, and leave sack, and live cleanly, as a nobleman should do. *Shak.*, 1 Hen. IV., v. 4. 168.

3. To be cleansed or purified by the escape of certain gases, as a lake or river. See *purging*, 2.

purge (pėrj), *n.* [< *purge*, *v.*] 1. The act of purging; purgation.

The preparative for the *purge* of paganism out of the kingdoms of Northumberland. *Fuller.*

2. Anything that purges; specifically, a medicine that evacuates the intestines; a cathartic. —**Pride's Purge**, in *Eng. hist.*, a forcible reduction, December 6th, 1648, of the membership of the Long Parliament, effected by troops under the command of Colonel Pride, who excluded all persons suspected of Royalist or Presbyterian sympathies. The diminished Parliament was known as the *Rump*, and consisted of about 60 to 80 members.

purge-cock (pėrj'kok), *n.* A purging-cock.

When it becomes necessary to empty the receiver, use is made of a *purge-cock*. *Sci. Amer. Supp.*, p. 8897.

purger (pėr'jėr), *n.* [< *purge* + *-er*¹.] 1. A person or thing that purges or cleanses.

We shall be call'd *purgers*, and not murderers. *Shak.*, J. C., ii. 1. 180.

Faith is a great *purger* and purifier of the soul. *Jer. Taylor*, Works (ed. 1835), II. 22.

2. A cathartic.

It is of good use in physic if you can retain the purging vertue and take away the unpleasant taste of the *purger*. *Bacon*, Nat. Hist., § 20.

purgery (pėr'jėr-i), *n.*; pl. *purgeries* (-iz). [= F. *purgerie*; as *purge* + *-ery*.] The part of a sugar-house where the sugar from the coolers is placed in hogsheads or in cones, and allowed to drain off its molasses or imperfectly crystallized cane-juice. *E. H. Knight.*

purging (pėr'jing), *n.* [Verbal n. of *purge*, *v.*] 1. Any purifying process.—2. A diarrhea or dysentery: looseness of the bowels.

purging-agaric (pėr'jing-ag'a-rik), *n.* The white or "female" agaric, *Polyporus officinalis*, a fungus growing upon the larch of the Old World. It is more or less employed in Europe as a cathartic.

purging-cassia (pėr'jing-kash'iä), *n.* The plant *Cassia fistula*, or its fruit. See *Cassia*.

purging-cock (pėr'jing-kok), *n.* The mud-cock or discharge-valve of a steam-boiler. *E. H. Knight.*

purging-flax (pėr'jing-flaks), *n.* An Old World plant, *Linum catharticum*, a decoction of which is used as a cathartic and diuretic.

purging-nut (pėr'jing-nut), *n.* See *Jatropha*.

purification (pū'ri-fi-kā'shọn), *n.* [< F. *purification* = Sp. *purificacion* = Pg. *purificação* = It. *purificazione*, < L. *purificatio(n-)*, a purifying, < *purificare*, pp. *purificatus*, make clean: see *purify*.] 1. The act of purifying; the act of freeing from impurities, or from whatever is heterogeneous or foreign; as, the *purification* of liquors or of metals.—2. The act or process of cleansing ceremonially; a ritual observance by which the person or thing subjected to it is cleansed from a ceremonial uncleanness, as a symbol of a spiritual cleansing. Ceremonial purification by washing or by other means was common to the Hebrews, Greeks, Romans, and other peoples, and is still practised by the Mohammedans, Greeks, and Roman Catholics, as well as by Hindus and other Orientals. In the Jewish ceremonial law the use of water was essential to purification, and it was often accompanied by sacrifices. The purifications of the Mosaic law fall under several heads, among which are those for defilement arising from secretions, those for leprosy, those for pollution from corpses, and those for defilement from eating the flesh of certain animals.

3. A cleansing of the soul from guilt; the extinguishment of evil desire as something which does not belong to the children of God.

Water is the symbol of *purification* of the soul from sin. *Jer. Taylor*, Worthy Communicant, i. § 3.

4. In the Roman Catholic and Anglican churches, the pouring of wine into the chalice to rinse it after communion, the wine being then drunk by the priest.—**Purification of St. Mary the Virgin**, a feast observed in the Roman Catholic and some other liturgical churches on February 2d, in commemoration of the purification of the Virgin Mary, according to the Jewish ceremonial, forty days after the birth of Christ. Also called *Candlemas*, *Hypapante*, *Presentation of Christ in the Temple*, and *Purification of Our Lady*.

Tewysday, the ij Day of Februarii, that was the *Purificacon of our lady*, the wynde made well for us. *Torkington*, Diarie of Eng. Travell, p. 61.

purification-flower (pū"ri-fi-kā'shọn-flou"ėr), *n.* The European snowdrop, *Galanthus nivalis*, which blossoms at about the time of the feast of the Purification, when maidens in white formerly walked in procession. Compare *fair-maids-of-February*.

purificative (pū'ri-fi-kā-tiv), *a.* [< F. *purificatif* = Pr. *purificatiu* = It. *purificativo*, < L. *purificare*, pp. *purificatus*, purify, make clean: see *purify*.] Having power to purify; tending to cleanse. *Johnson.*

purificator (pū'ri-fi-kā-tọr), *n.* [Also *purificatory*; < ML. *purificatorium*, < L. *purificare*, pp. *purificatus*, make clean: see *purify*.] In the Roman Catholic and Anglican churches, a cloth or napkin used to wipe the chalice before the mixture (krasis) and oblation, and the celebrant's fingers and mouth and the holy vessels after the ablutions. Before celebration and until the offertory, and after celebration, it covers the chalice, and the paten rests on it covered by the pall and veil. Also called *mundatory*.

purificatory (pū'ri-fi-kā-tọ-ri), *a.* and *n.* [= F. *purificatoire* = Sp. Pg. *purificatorio* = It. *purificatojo*, n., < LL. *purificatorius*, cleansing, < L. *purificare*, pp. *purificatus*, make clean: see *purify*.] I. *a.* Purificative. *Johnson.*

II. *n.* Same as *purificator*.

purifier (pū'ri-fī-ėr), *n.* 1. One who or that which purifies or cleanses; a cleanser; a refiner; specifically, a purificator.

He shall sit as a refiner and *purifier* of silver. Mal. iii. 3.

2. In *milling*, an apparatus for separating bran-scales and flour from grits or middlings.—**Dry-lime purifier, wet-lime purifier.** See *gas-purifier*.

puriform (pū'ri-fôrm), *a.* [< L. *pus* (*pur-*), pus, + *forma*, form.] Pus-like; resembling pus.

purify (pū'ri-fī), *v.*; pret. and pp. *purified*, ppr. *purifying*. [< ME. *puryfyen*, < OF. *purifier*, F. *purifier* = Sp. Pg. *purificar* = It. *purificare*, < L. *purificare*, make clean or pure, < *purus*, clean, pure, + *facere*, make.] I. *trans.* 1. To make pure or clear; free from contamination or extraneous admixture: as, to *purify* liquors or metals; to *purify* the blood; to *purify* the air. —2. To make ceremonially clean; cleanse or free from whatever pollutes or renders ceremonially unclean and unfit for sacred service.

Whosoever hath killed any person, and whosoever hath touched any slain, *purify* both yourselves and your captives on the third day, and on the seventh day. Num. xxxi. 19.

3. To free from guilt, or the defilement of sin; free from whatever is sinful, vile, or base.

Who gave himself for us, that he might redeem us from all iniquity, and *purify* unto himself a peculiar people, zealous of good works. Tit. ii. 14.

Thy soul from all guilt will we *purify*,
And sure no heavy curse shall lie on thee.
William Morris, Earthly Paradise, III. 93.

4. To elevate and free from barbarisms or inelegances: as, to *purify* a language.

II. *intrans.* To grow or become pure or clear.

We do not suppose the separation of these two liquors wholly finished before the purgation of the air began, though let them begin to *purify* at the same time. *T. Burnet*, Theory of the Earth.

Purim (pū'rim), *n.* [Heb.] An annual festival observed by the Jews on the 14th and 15th of the month Adar (about the 1st of March). It is preceded by the Fast of Esther on the 13th. These three days commemorate the deliverance of the Jews by Esther from the massacre planned by Haman, as related in the book of Esther.

Wherefore they called these days *Purim* after the name of Pur. Esther ix. 26.

puriri (pọ̈-rē'rē), *n.* [Maori.] A New Zealand tree, *Vitex littoralis*, 50 or 60 feet high, with robust spreading branches. It yields a very hard, heavy, and durable timber, of a brown color, in short lengths, often curved, suitable for ships' frames and many other purposes.

purism (pūr'izm), *n.* [= F. *purisme* = Sp. Pg. It. *purismo*; as *pure* + *-ism*.] The exclusion of admixture of any kind; the affectation of rigid purity, as in language, style, etc.; specifically, excessive nicety as to the choice of words.

The English language, however, it may be observed, had even already become too thoroughly and essentially a mixed tongue for this doctrine of *purism* to be admitted to the letter. *Craik*, Hist. Eng. Lit., I. 419.

Orthographic *purism* is of all kinds of *purism* the lowest and the cheapest, as is verbal criticism of all kinds of criticism, and word-faith of all kinds of orthodoxy. *Whitney*, Linguistic Studies, 2d ser., p. 192.

purist (pūr'ist), *n.* [= F. *puriste* = Sp. Pg. It. *purista*; as *pure* + *-ist*.] 1. One who aims scrupulously at purity, particularly in the choice of language; one who is a rigorous critic of purity in literary style.

He [Fox] was so nervously apprehensive of sliding into some colloquial incorrectness . . . that he ran into the opposite error, and purified his vocabulary with a scrupulosity unknown to any *purist*. *Macaulay*, Sir James Mackintosh.

2. One who maintains that the New Testament was written in pure Greek. *M. Stuart.* [Rare.]

puristic (pụ̄-ris'tik), *a.* [< *purist* + *-ic*.] Pertaining or relating to purism; characteristic of a purist. *Maurice.*

puristical (pụ̄-ris'ti-kạl), *a.* [< *puristic* + *-al*.] Same as *puristic*.

puritan (pū'ri-tạn), *n.* and *a.* [Irreg. < L. *purita(t-)s*, purity, + *-an*. The F. *Puritain* and Sp. Pg. It. *Puritano* are from E. The noun precedes the adj. in use.] I. *n.* 1. One who is very strict and serious in his religious life, or who pretends to great purity of life: first used about 1564, and applied to certain Anabaptists: frequently a term of contempt.

About that tyme were many congregations of the Anabaptysts in London, who cawlyd themselves *Puritans* or Unspotted Lambs of the Lord. *Stow*, Memoranda (Three Fifteenth-Century Chronicles, [Camden Soc., p. 143).

She would make a *puritan* of the devil, if he should cheapen a kiss of her. *Shak.*, Pericles, iv. 6. 9.

2. [*cap.*] One of a class of Protestants which arose in England in the sixteenth century. The Puritans maintained a strict Calvinism in doctrine, and demanded, in opposition to those who desired a reform of the church service, the substitution of one from which should be banished all resemblance whatever to the forms of the Roman Catholic Church. Large numbers of them were found both in and out of the Church of England, and various repressive measures were directed against them by the sovereigns and by the prelates Parker, Whitgift, Bancroft, Laud, and others. In the reign of Charles I. the Puritans developed into a political party and gradually gained the ascendancy, but lost it on Cromwell's death, and after the Restoration ceased to be prominent in history. During their early struggles many of them emigrated to New England, especially to the Massachusetts Bay Colony. One band of Puritans who separated entirely from the Church were called *Separatists* or *Brownists*, and from them came the founders of the Plymouth Colony, often called *Pilgrim Fathers* or *Pilgrims*.

Now as solemn as a traveller, and as grave as a *Puritan's* ruff. *Marston*, Antonio and Mellida, I., Ind.

From that time followed nothing but Imprisonments, troubles, disgraces on all those that found fault with the Decrees of the Convocation, and strait were they branded with the Name of *Puritans*. *Milton*, Reformation in Eng., i.

The extreme *Puritan* was at once known from other men by his gait, his garb, his lank hair, the sour solemnity of his face, the upturned white of his eyes, the nasal twang with which he spoke, and above all by his peculiar dialect. *Macaulay.*

=**Syn.** *Puritan*, *Pilgrim*. Careful distinction should be made between the *Pilgrims* or *Pilgrim Fathers*, who settled at Plymouth in 1620, and the *Puritans*, who in 1628–30 founded the colony of Massachusetts Bay at Salem and Boston.

II. *a.* [*cap.*] Of, pertaining to, or characteristic of the Puritans.

Hee's gone; I'll after him
And know his trespasse, seeme to beare a part
In all his ills, but with a *Puritane* heart.
Tourneur, Revenger's Tragedy, ii. 2.

Mr. Pyncheon's long residence abroad, and intercourse with men of wit and fashion—courtiers, worldlings, and free-thinkers—had done much toward obliterating the grim *Puritan* superstitions which no man of New England birth, at that early period, could entirely escape. *Hawthorne*, House of Seven Gables, xiii.

Gathering still, as he went, the May-flowers blooming around him; . . .
"*Puritan* flowers," he said, "and the type of *Puritan* maidens,
Modest and simple and sweet, the very type of Priscilla!"
Longfellow, Miles Standish, iii.

=**Syn.** *Puritan*, *Puritanic*. *Puritanic* (or *puritanical*) is now generally used in a depreciative sense; *Puritan* in a commendatory or a neutral sense.

puritanic (pū-ri-tan'ik), *a.* [< *puritan* + *-ic*.] 1. Pertaining to the Puritans or their doctrines and practice. Hence—2. Very scrupulous in religious matters; exact; rigid: often used in contempt or reproach.

Too dark a stole
Was o'er religion's decent features drawn
By *puritanic* zeal. *W. Mason*, English Garden, iv.

=**Syn.** See *Puritan*, *a*.

puritanical (pū-ri-tan'i-kạl), *a.* [< *puritanic* + *-al*.] Same as *puritanic*.

Wearing feathers in thy hair, whose length before the vigorous edge of any *puritanical* pair of scissors should shorten the breadth of a finger, let the three housewifely spinsters of destiny rather curtail the thread of thy life. *Dekker*, Gull's Hornbook, p. 83.

Puritanical and superstitious principles. *I. Walton.*

It is quite certain that Bunyan was, at eighteen, what, in any but the most austerely *puritanical* circles, would have been considered as a young man of singular gravity and innocence. *Macaulay*, Encyc. Brit., IV. 526.

puritanically (pū-ri-tan'i-kạl-i), *adv.* In a puritanical manner; with the exact or rigid notions or manners of the Puritans.

puritanism (pū'ri-tạn-izm), *n.* [= F. *puritanisme* = Sp. Pg. *puritanismo*; as *puritan* + *-ism*.] 1. Strictness of religious life; puritanic strictness in religious matters.—2. The principles and practices of the Puritans.

How resplendent and superb was the poetry that lay at the heart of *Puritanism* was seen by the sightless eyes of John Milton, whose great epic is indeed the epic of *Puritanism*. *M. C. Tyler*, Hist. Amer. Lit., I. 206.

puritanize (pū'ri-tạn-īz), *v. i.*; pret. and pp. *puritanized*, ppr. *puritanizing*. [< *puritan* + *-ize*.] To conform to the opinions of Puritans; affect or teach puritanism.

purity (pū'ri-ti), *n.* [< ME. *purete*, < OF. *purete*, F. *pureté* = Sp. *puridad* = Pg. *puridade* = It. *purità*, < LL. *purita(t-)s*, cleanness, pureness, < L. *purus*, clean, pure: see *pure*.] The condition or quality of being pure. (*a*) Freedom from foreign admixture of heterogeneous matter: as, the *purity* of water, of wine, of spirit; the *purity* of drugs; the *purity* of metals.

> The *pureté* of the quinte essencie schal be sublymed aboue, and the grosté schal abide bynethe in the botme.
> *Book of Quinte Essence* (ed. Furnivall), p. 5.

> The slight touch of Renaissance in some of the capitals of the palace in no sort takes away from the general *purity* of the style.
> *E. A. Freeman*, Venice, p. 257.

(*b*) Cleanness; freedom from foulness or dirt: as, the *purity* of a garment. (*c*) Freedom from guilt or the defilement of sin; innocence: as, *purity* of heart or life.

> If we describe *purity* by reference to contrasts, then it is a character opposite to all sin.
> *Bushnell*, Sermons for New Life, p. 264.

(*d*) Freedom from lust, or moral contamination by illicit sexual connection; chastity.

> So bold is Lust that she
> Dares hope to find a Blot in *Purity*.
> *J. Beaumont*, Psyche, ii. 207.

(*e*) Freedom from sinister or improper views; sincerity: as, *purity* of motives or designs.

> Princes have vouchsafed grace to trifles offered from a *purity* of devotion.
> *Ford*, 'Tis Pity, Ded.

(*f*) Freedom from foreign idioms, or from barbarous or improper words or phrases: as, *purity* of style or language.

> After Cæsar and Cicero's Time, the Latin Tongue continued in Rome and Italy in her *Purity* 400 Years together.
> *Howell*, Letters, ii. 58.

=**Syn.** (*c*) and (*d*) Immaculateness, guilelessness, honesty, integrity, virtue, modesty. (*f*) *Purity, Propriety, Precision.* As a quality of style, "*Purity* . . . relates to three things, viz. the form of words [etymology], the construction of words in continuous discourse [syntax], and the meaning of words and phrases [lexicography]." (*A. Phelps*, Eng. Style, p. 9.) "*Propriety* . . . relates to the signification of language as fixed by usage." (*A. Phelps*, Eng. Style, p. 79.) "The offences against the usage of the English language are . . . *improprieties*, words or phrases used in a sense not English." (*A. S. Hill*, Rhet., p. 19.) "An author's diction is pure when he uses such words only as belong to the idiom of the language, in opposition to words that are foreign, obsolete, newly coined, or without proper authority. . . . A violation of *purity* is called a barbarism. . . . But another question arises. . . . Is the word used correctly in the sentence in which it occurs? . . . A writer who fails in this respect offends against *propriety*." (*J. S. Hart*, Comp. and Rhet., pp. 68, 74.) "*Precision* includes all that is essential to the expression of no more, no less, and no other than the meaning which the writer purposes to express." (*A. Phelps*, Eng. Style, p. 6.)

> Parsons may be ranked among the earliest writers of our vernacular diction in its *purity* and pristine vigor, without ornament or polish.
> *I. D'Israeli*, Amen. of Lit., II. 85.

> In our own tongue we may err egregiously against *propriety*, and consequently against *purity*, though all the words we employ be English, and though they be construed in the English idiom. The reason is evident: they may be misapplied; they may be employed as signs of things to which use hath not affixed them. This fault may be committed either in single words or in phrases.
> *G. Campbell*, Philosophy of Rhetoric, II. iii. § 3.

> Our verse . . . had become lax and trivial, and we needed to be recalled to *precision* and moral vigor.
> *E. Gosse*, From Shakespeare to Pope, p. 131.

Purkinjean (pėr-kin′jē-an), *a.* [< *Purkinje* (see def.) + *-an.*] Pertaining to or named after the Bohemian physiologist Purkinje (1787–1869): as, the *Purkinjean* vesicle, discovered by him in 1825. See *germinal vesicle*, under *germinal*.

Purkinje's cells. See *cells of Purkinje*, under *cell*.

Purkinje's fibers. Large beaded and reticulated fibers found in the subendocardial tissue of some animals, and occasionally in man.

Purkinje's figures. See *figure*.

Purkinje's vesicle. See *germinal vesicle*, under *germinal*.

purl[1] (pėrl), *v. i.* [Formerly also *pirl*; < Sw. *porla*, purl, bubble, as a stream; cf. D. *borrelen*, bubble; a freq. form from the imitative base seen in *pirr* and *purr*[1]. It is partly confused with *pirl*, *prill*[1], whirl.] To flow with a rippling or murmuring sound, as a shallow stream over or among stones or other obstructions; ripple along in eddying and bubbling swirls.

> From dry Rocks abundant Rivers *purl'd*.
> *Sylvester*, tr. of Du Bartas's Weeks, i. 3.

> The brooks run *purling* down with silver waves.
> *Parnell*, Health.

> Swift o'er the rolling pebbles, down the hills,
> Louder and louder *purl* the falling rills.
> *Pope*, Iliad, xxi. 207.

> See from the weedy earth a rivulet break,
> And *purl* along the untrodden wilderness.
> *Bryant*, The Path.

purl[1] (pėrl), *n.* [Formerly also *pirl*; < *purl*[1], *v.*] 1. A continued murmuring sound, as of a shallow stream of water running over small stones: as, the *purl* of a brook.—2†. A murmuring brook or rippling stream of water.

> A broket or *pirle* of water.
> *Leland's Itinerary* (1769), iii. 132. (*Halliwell.*)

purl[2] (pėrl), *v.* [Formerly also *pirl*; < ME. *pyrlen*, whirl, throw; cf. *purl*[1].] **I.** *intrans.* 1. To curl or swirl; move in rippling or eddying swirls.

> From his lips did fly
> Thin winding breath, which *purl'd* up to the sky.
> *Shak.*, Lucrece, l. 1407.

> A *purling* wind that flies
> Off from the shore each morning, driving up
> The billows far to sea.
> *Chapman*, Cæsar and Pompey, ii. 1.

2. To upset; overturn; capsize. [Slang.] See the quotation under II., 2.

II. *trans.* 1. To whirl about; cause to rotate: as, the wind *purls* a snow-drift.—2. To upset; overturn; also, specifically, as a hunting term, to unseat or unhorse. [Slang.]

> They commonly paddle in companies of three; so then, whenever one is *purled* the other two come on each side of him, each takes a hand and with amazing skill and delicacy they reseat him in his cocked hat, which never sinks, only *purls*.
> *C. Reade*, Never too Late, xxxviii. (*Davies.*)

3. To wind, as thread, upon a reel or spindle.

> I *pyrle* wyre of golde or syluer, I wynde it vpon a whele as sylke women do.
> *Palsgrave.* (*Jamieson.*)

purl[2] (pėrl), *n.* [< *purl*[2], *v.* Cf. *purl*[1], *n.*] 1. A circle or curl made by the motion of water; a ripple; an eddy.

> Whose stream an easie breath doth seem to blow,
> Which on the sparkling gravel runs in *purles*,
> As though the waves had been of silver curles.
> *Drayton*, Mortimeriados, l. 1596. (*Richardson.*)

> So have I seen the little *purls* of a spring sweat through the bottom of a bank, and intenerate the stubborn pavement.
> *Jer. Taylor*, Works (ed. 1835), I. 849.

purl[3] (pėrl), *v. t.* [Contr. of *purfle.*] 1. To ornament with a decorative border of any sort; decorate with fringe or embroidery; purfle.

> For all the copes and vestementes wer but of one pece, so wouen for the purpose, cloth of tissue and poudered with redde roses *purled* with fine gold.
> *Hall*, Hen. VIII., an. 12.

> Is thy skin whole? art thou not *purl'd* with scabs?
> *Fletcher (and another)*, Sea Voyage, i. 3.

2. To invert, as a stitch in knitting; turn over and knit the other way; seam.

purl[3] (pėrl), *n.* [Contr. of *purfle.*] 1. A border of embroidery or perhaps of lace, or gold lace or galloon. Throughout the fifteenth, sixteenth, and seventeenth centuries the term is in use, and evidently with different significations, but always as an ornamental adjunct, an edging or the like to a garment. Also *pearl*.

Embroidered Border. *a*, the purl.

> Himself came in next after a triumphant chariot made of carnation velvet, enriched with *purl* and pearl.
> *Sir P. Sidney.*

> How many puffs and *purls* lay in a miserable case for want of stiffening [starch]!
> *Middleton*, Father Hubbard's Tales.

> My lord, one of the *purls* of your band is, without all discipline, fallen out of his rank.
> *Massinger and Field*, Fatal Dowry, ii. 2.

2. A spiral of gold or silver wire, used in lace-work.—3. An inversion of the stitches in knitting, which gives to parts of the work an appearance different from the general surface, such as the ribbed appearance of those parts where great elasticity is required.—4. A plait or fold, as in an article of dress.—5. In *lace-making*, a kind of lace in common use in the sixteenth century, and often of great value. The term is used in the general sense as indicating the fabric spoken of, and also as denoting a certain quantity of it: as, so many shillings the *purl*.

purl[4] (pėrl), *n.* [Appar. another spelling of *pearl*, so called with ref. to the bubbles on the surface, < *pearl*, *v.*] A drink, of which beer is the principal ingredient, defined about 1815 as hot beer mixed with gin: same as *dog's-nose*; in later times, a stimulating mixture of beer, gin, sugar, and ginger. It was, before coffee and tea were used, commonly made to be drunk in the morning, and hence the liquor is called *early purl*.

> Early in the morning I set my books . . . in order. Thence, forth to Mr. Harper's to drink a draft of *purle*.
> *Pepys*, Diary, Feb. 19, 1660.

> My lord duke would have a double mug of *purl*.
> *Steele*, Spectator, No. 88.

> Mr. Swiveller . . . had by this time taken quite as much to drink as promised to be good for his constitution (*purl* being a rather strong and heady compound).
> *Dickens*, Old Curiosity Shop, lviii.

> Again, there was *purl*—*early purl*. Once there was a club in the neighbourhood of Covent Garden which existed for the purpose of arising betimes and drinking *purl* before breakfast.
> *W. Besant*, Fifty Years Ago, p. 170.

purl[5]†, *v.* A Middle English form of *prowl*. *Prompt. Parv.*, p. 417.

purl[6] (pėrl), *n.* [Imitative, like *purr*[3], etc.] The common tern, or sea-swallow. [Norfolk, Eng.]

purley†, *n.* An obsolete form of *purlieu*.

purl-goods (pėrl′gůdz), *n. pl.* English machine-made lace.

> The *Purl-goods* . . . in imitation of the hand-made laces of France.
> *Artisan's Report*, p. 150.

purl-house (pėrl′hous), *n.* A place where purl is sold and drunk.

> There were lower depths yet: there were the *purl houses*, where "Tradesmen flock in their Morning gowns, by Seven, to cool their Plucks."
> *J. Ashton*, Social Life in Reign of Queen Anne, I. 234.

purlicue (pėr′li-kū), *v. t.* Same as *parlecue*.

purlie†, *n.* An obsolete form of *purlieu*.

purlieu (pėr′lū), *n.* [Formerly also *purlue*, *purluy*; an altered form, simulating F. *lieu*, a place (see *lieu*), of *purlie*, *purly*, *purley*, prop. land which, having been part of a royal forest, has been severed from it by perambulation or survey, < OF. *pourallee*, *puralee*, a going through or about, perambulation, < *pour-*, *pur-* (< L. *pro-*), used for *per-*, *par-* (< L. *per*), through, + *alee*, a going: see *alley*[1].] 1†. Land added to a royal forest by unlawful encroachment, but afterward disafforested, and restored to the former owners, its bounds and extent being settled by perambulation.

> With all amercements due
> To such as hunt in *purley*; this is something,
> With mine own game reserved.
> *Randolph*, Muses' Looking-glass, iv. 3.

> As a *purly* hunter, I have hitherto beaten about the circuit of the forest of this microcosm.
> *Burton*, Anat. of Mel., p. 227.

> Th' infernal Nimrod's halloo?
> The lawless *purlieus*? and the game they follow? . . .
> These *purlieu* men are devils; and the hounds . . .
> Temptations.
> *Quarles*, Emblems, iii. 9.

> Land which had . . . been once forest land and was afterwards disafforested was known as *purlieu*.
> *Encyc. Brit.*, IX. 400.

2. *pl.* The borders or environs of any place; the outskirts; outlying places: as, the *purlieus* of Paris.

> Pray you, if you know,
> Where in the *purlieus* of this forest stands
> A sheep-cote fenced about with olive trees?
> *Shak.*, As you Like it, iv. 3. 77.

> A party next of glittering dames,
> From round the *purlieus* of St. James,
> Came early.
> *Swift*, Cadenus and Vanessa.

> Fresh from brawling courts
> And dusty *purlieus* of the law.
> *Tennyson*, In Memoriam, lxxxix.

Purlieu men, in *old forest law*, men who had ground within the border of a forest, and were licensed to hunt within their own purlieus. *Manwood*, Forest Laws, xx. § 8.

purlin, purline (pėr′lin), *n.* [Origin obscure.] In *carp.*, a piece of timber laid horizontally upon the principal rafters of a roof to support the common rafters on which the covering is laid. Also called *side timber* or *side waver*. See cut under *roof*.

purlin-post (pėr′lin-pōst), *n.* In *carp.*, one of the struts by which a purlin is supported to prevent it from sagging.

purlman (pėrl′man), *n.*; pl. *purlmen* (-men). A seller of the liquor called purl.

> There is yet another class of itinerant dealers, . . . the river beer-sellers, or *purlmen* as they are more commonly called.
> *Mayhew*, London Labour and London Poor, II. 107.

purloin (pėr-loin′), *v.* [< ME. *purloynen*, *perloynen*, *purlongen*, < OF. *purloignier*, *porloignier*, prolong, retard, delay, < LL. *prolongare*, prolong: see *prolong*. Cf. *eloin*, *eloign*.] **I.** *trans.* 1†. To put off; prolong; delay. *Prompt. Parv.*, pp. 394, 417.—2†. To set back or aside; put away; remove.

> Who that youre perceptis pertely *perloyned*,
> With drede in to dede schall ye dryffe hym.
> *York Plays*, p. 271.

3. To remove, carry off, or take for one's self; hence, to take by theft; filch; steal.

> Vast Quantities of Stores did he
> Embezzle and *purloin*.
> *Prior*, The Viceroy, st. 25.

> Your butler *purloins* your liquor, and the brewer sells your hog-wash.
> *Arbuthnot*, Hist. John Bull.

> If rigid honesty permit
> That I for once *purloin* the wit
> Of him, who, were we all to steal,
> Is much too rich the theft to feel.
> *Churchill*, Ghost, iv.

> Perverts the Prophets and *purloins* the Psalms.
> *Byron*, Eng. Bards and Scotch Reviewers.

> A certain document of the last importance has been *purloined* from the royal apartments.
> *Poe*, Prose Tales, I. 264.

II. *intrans.* To practise theft.

> Not *purloining*, but shewing all good fidelity. Tit. ii. 10.

purloiner (pėr-loi′nėr), *n.* One who purloins; a thief.

> The only reason why these *purloiners* of the public cause such a clutter to be made about their reputations.
> *Swift*, Examiner, No. 28.

purlong†, *v.* A Middle English form of *purloin*.
purly†, *n.* An obsolete form of *purlieu*, 1.
purpart† (pėr′pärt), *n.* Same as *purparty*.
purparty† (pėr′pär-ti), *n.*; pl. *purparties* (-tiz). [Also *pourparty*; < ME. *purpartie*, < AF. *purpartie*, OF. *porpartie* (cf. ML. *propars*, *perpars*), share of an estate, < *por*, *pur* (< L. *pro*), for, + *partie*, part: see *party*[1].] In *law*, an allotment; the share or portion of an estate allotted to a coparcener by partition.

> Through which the grounde by *purpartiez*
> Departed is in thre parties,
> That is Asie, Affrike, Europe.
> *Gower*, Conf. Amant., vii.

purpeys†, *n.* A Middle English form of *porpoise*.
purple (pėr′pl), *n.* and *a.* [< ME. *purpul*, earlier *purpre*, *pourpre*, also *purpur*, *purpure*, *purpour* (cf. AS. *purpure*, a purple garment, *purpuren*, purple), < OF. *porpre*, *pourpre*, *pouple*, *pople*, AF. also *purpille*, F. *pourpre* = Pr. *porpra*, *polpra* = Sp. *púrpura* = Pg. *purpura* = It. *porpora* = D. *purper* = MLG. *purper*, *purpur* = OHG. *purpura*, MHG. *purper*, G. *purpur* = Icel. *purpuri* = Sw. Dan. *purpur* = Goth. *paurpaura*, *paurpura*, purple, < L. *purpura*, the purple-fish, purple dye, < Gr. *πορφύρα*, the purple-fish; cf. *πορφύρεος* (later also poet. *πόρφυρος*), purple, orig. applied to the surging sea, dark, prob. redupl. of *φύρειν*, mix up, mingle, confound, = L. *furere*, rage: see *fury*. Cf. *porphyry*, from the same Gr. source.] **I.** *n.* **1.** A color formed by the mixture of blue and red, including the violet of the spectrum above wave-length 0.417 micron, which is nearly a violet-blue, and extending to but not including crimson. The following color-disk formulæ will serve to identify several purples. The red used is the most intense procurable, so that mixed with 7 per cent. of blue it gives a good carmine.

	Red.	Blue.	Black.	White.
Auricula purple	17	28	55	0
Dahlia purple	14	7	79	0
Heliotrope purple	25	25	25	25
Indian purple	20	31	40	0
Magenta	67	33	0	0
Mauve	37	50	0	13
Plum purple	5	25	70	0
Pomegranate purple	50	10	40	0
Royal purple	55	12	33	0
Solferino	83	17	0	0
Wine purple	50	17	33	0

Of the various colors called *purple* at any time, the Tyrian dye (which was properly a crimson) was anciently the most celebrated. This color was produced from an animal juice found in a shell-fish called *murex* or *conchylium* by the ancients. See *Purpura*, 2.

> Musidorus . . . had upon him a long cloak . . . made of purple satin; not that *purple* which we now have and is but a counterfeit of the Getulian *purple*, which yet was far the meaner in price and estimation, but of the right Tyrian *purple*, which was nearest to a colour betwixt our murrey [a dark-reddish brown] and scarlet.
> *Sir P. Sidney*, Arcadia, v.

> Great part of the colouring yet remains upon the stones: red, in all its shades, especially that dark dusky colour called Tyrian *purple*. *Bruce*, Source of the Nile, I. 105.

> *Purple* is very seldom used in English heraldry. It is nonsense, however, to say it is improper to use it, as it is quite good heraldry.
> *Booke of Precedence* (E. E. T. S., extra ser.), i. 96, note 1.

2. A cloth robe, dress, or mantle of this hue, formerly the distinguishing dress of emperors, kings, or princes: as, to wear the *purple*.

> "Hi ham clotheth," he zayth, "mid *pourpre* and mid uayre robes." *Ayenbite of Inwyt* (E. E. T. S.), p. 229.

> The 3 thousand is clothed in Clothes of Silk, of *Purpre*, or of Ynde. *Mandeville*, Travels, p. 233.

> How uneasy must the leather and frieze sit upon the shoulder that used to shine with the *purple* and the ermin! *South*, Sermons, III. viii.

> This spectacle of the discrowned queen with her *purple* in the dust, and her sceptre fallen from her hand, was one that nearly broke his heart to see. *Cornhill Mag.*

Hence—**3.** Imperial or regal power; the office or dignity of an emperor or king.

> And hurid him from the Scepter to the Spade;
> Turn'd him out of his *purple*, here to sweat
> And hardly carne his meat before he eat.
> *Heywood*, Dialogues (Works, ed. Pearson, 1874, VI. 161).

> That which raised him [Vespasian] to the *purple*, that which suggested him to men's minds, was his military eminence. *De Quincey*, Essenes, ii.

4. A cardinalate: so called in allusion to the red or scarlet hat and robes worn officially by cardinals.

> The cardinal . . . is old and infirm, and could never be induced to resign his *purple*.
> *Addison*, Remarks on Italy (ed. Bohn), I. 500.

> Cardinal de Tencin . . . had been recommended to the *purple* by the Chevalier de St. George.
> *Smollett*, Hist. Eng., ii. 8.

5†. A gastropod yielding a purple fluid for dyeing, as a murex. *Holland*, tr. of Pliny.—**6.** A shell of the genus *Purpura*.—**7.** A purple fluid secreted by certain shell-fish, more fully called *purple of Mollusca*.—**8.** *pl.* See *purples*.—**Alizarin purple**, a shade of purple or lilac obtained by treating fabrics with alizarin and sulphate of iron.—**Aniline purple.** Same as *mauve*.—**Ethyl purple**, a coal-tar color used in dyeing, being the hexa-ethyl-para-rosaniline producing the bluest shade of violet.—**Field's purple.** Same as *madder purple*.—**French purple**, a color obtained from archil, *Roccella tinctoria*, and used for dyeing purples and mauves on silk and wool.—**Indian purple**, an artists' pigment prepared by precipitating cochineal-extract with copper sulphate. It is a deep-toned purple which is apt to blacken on exposure to light, and is now little used.—**London purple**, a residue from the manufacture of aniline dyes, which consists of calcium arsenite with some coloring matter. It is largely used as an insecticide.

> The supply of powder can be regulated to such a nicety that Mr. Leggett claims he can make half a pound of *London purple* cover an acre. *Science*, XIII. 394.

Madder purple, a very deep rich lake, of great body and intensity, prepared from madder. The color, though not brilliant, is transparent and durable. Also called *purple rubiate* and *Field's purple*.—**Mineral purple.** Same as *Mars violet* (which see, under *violet*). Also called *purple ocher*.—**Orchil purple**, a dye-color obtained from several varieties of seaweed. It is very beautiful, but not durable, and is little used since the introduction of tar-colors.—**Perkins's purple.** Same as *mauve*.—**Purple of Amorgos**, a celebrated dye obtained from the Grecian island Amorgos, believed to have been a kind of orchil.—**Purple of Cassius** [named from the Danish physician Andreas *Cassius*, died 1673], a compound oxid precipitated when solutions of the chlorids of gold and tin are mixed. It is a rich and powerful color, not bright but very durable, and varies in hue from deep crimson to a murrey or dark purple. Used mostly in miniature-painting.—**Purple of Mollusca**, a viscid liquor secreted by certain gastropods of the families *Muricidæ* and *Purpuridæ*, as *Purpura lapillus*, which dyes wool, etc., of a purple color.—**Regina purple**, a coal-tar color used in dyeing, being the hydrochlorid of diphenyl rosaniline, producing a dull violet shade.—**Tyrian purple.** See def. 1.

II. *a.* **1.** Of a hue or color composed of red and blue blended.

> Feed him with apricocks and dewberries,
> With *purple* grapes, green figs, and mulberries.
> *Shak.*, M. N. D., iii. 1. 170.

> A *purple* lion was borne by the De Lacy family, Earls of Lincoln, and is (accordingly) the arms of Lincoln's Inn.
> *Booke of Precedence* (E. E. T. S., extra ser.), i. 96, note 1.

> Here comes a middle-aged gentleman who looks almost like a coachman in his coat with many capes and his *purple* cheeks. *W. Besant*, Fifty Years Ago, p. 50.

2. Imperial; regal; of the conventional color of imperial robes.—**Purple avens.** See *avens*.—**Purple azalea** or **honeysuckle.** Same as *pinkster-flower*.—**Purple beech**, a variety of the European beech, *Fagus sylvatica*, with deep reddish-brown or purplish leaves; copper beech.—**Purple birch.** See *birch*, 1.—**Purple brown.** See *brown*.—**Purple bullfinch.** Same as *purple finch*.—**Purple clover**, the red or meadow clover, *Trifolium pratense*.—**Purple cone-flower.** See *cone-flower*.—**Purple copper.** Same as *bornite*.—**Purple crow, emperor, fever, finch, fringe-tree.** See the nouns.—**Purple gland**, the purpuriparous adrectal gland of some gastropods.—**Purple grackle.** See *grackle*, 2.—**Purple haw.** Same as *bluewood*.—**Purple heron**, a European heron, *Ardea purpurea*, resembling the common heron, but darker in coloration, and in some places purplish.—**Purple jacobæa, lake, laver.** See the nouns.—**Purple lily.** (*a*) Same as *martagon*. (*b*) See *Patersonia*.—**Purple loosestrife, madder, maroon, medic**, etc. See the nouns.—**Purple martin**, a large blue-black swallow of the United States, *Progne subis* or *P. purpurea*, without a trace of purple: the name originated in a wrongly colored figure given by Catesby. See cut under *Progne*.—**Purple melic-grass, purple moor-grass.** See *Molinia*.—**Purple ocher.** Same as *Mars violet* (which see, under *violet*).—**Purple ragwort.** See *ragwort*.—**Purple rubiate.** Same as *madder purple*. See I.

purple (pėr′pl), *v.*; pret. and pp. *purpled*, ppr. *purpling*. [< *purple*, *a.*] **I.** *trans.* To tinge or stain with purple; impart a purplish hue to.

> Like a jolly troop of huntsmen come
> Our lusty English, all with *purpled* hands,
> Dyed in the dying slaughter of their foes.
> *Shak.*, K. John, ii. 1. 322.

> Aurora had but newly chas'd the night,
> And *purpled* o'er the sky with blushing light.
> *Dryden*, Pal. and Arc., i. 187.

II. *intrans.* To become purple; assume a purplish hue.

> From the *purpling* east departs
> The star that led the dawn.
> *Wordsworth*, Ode Composed on May Morning.

> Rapidly the glow crimsoned—shadows *purpled*; and night spread swiftly from the east—black-violet and full of stars. *L. Hearn*, Youma, xii.

purple-egg (pėr′pl-eg), *n.* A common sea-urchin, *Strongylocentrotus drobachiensis*: so called from the shape and tint of the test.
purple-fish (pėr′pl-fish), *n.* A shell-fish of the genus *Purpura* or some allied genus.
purple-grass† (pėr′pl-gràs), *n.* A cultivated variety of the common red clover, *Trifolium pratense*, with dark-brown or purplish foliage. Also *purplewort*. *Britten and Holland*, Eng. Plant Names.
purple-heart (pėr′pl-härt), *n.* The heart-wood of *Copaifera Martii*, var. *pubiflora*, and of *C. bracteata* of Guiana, or the trees themselves. Also called *purple-wood*.
purplelip (pėr′pl-lip), *n.* A West Indian climbing orchid, *Vanilla claviculata*.
purple-marbled (pėr′pl-mär′bled), *n.* A British moth, *Micra ostrina*.
purples (pėr′plz), *n. pl.* [< ME. *purpyls*; pl. of *purple*.] **1.** In *med.*, petechiæ, or spots of livid red on the body, such as appear in certain diseases; purpura.

> All the myracles to shewe it were to longe;
> There is many mo full great that I do not reherse,
> As pestylence, *purpyls*, and agonys strong.
> *Joseph of Arimathie* (E. E. T. S.), p. 48.

> There is a fresh Report blown over that Laines is lately dead in the Army of the Plague, some say of the *Purples*, the next Cousin-german to it. *Howell*, Letters, I. iii. 5.

2. A disease of wheat caused by a nematoid worm of the family *Anguillulidæ*, *Tylenchus scandens* or *T. tritici*. Also called *car-cockle*. *Curtis*, Farm Insects, p. 297.—**3.** An early purple-flowered orchid, *Orchis mascula*, common in Europe and part of Asia.

> With fantastic garlands did she come
> Of crow-flowers, nettles, daisies, and long *purples*,
> That liberal shepherds give a grosser name.
> *Shak.*, Hamlet, iv. 7. 170.

purple-wood (pėr′pl-wůd), *n.* Same as *purple-heart*.
purplewort (pėr′pl-wėrt), *n.* Same as *purple-grass*.
purple-wreath (pėr′pl-rēth), *n.* See *Petrea*.
purpoint† (pėr′point), *n.* See *pourpoint*.
purport (pėr′pōrt or pėr-pōrt′), *v. t.* [< ME. **purporten*, *proporten*, OF. *pourporter*, *purporter*, *porporter*, *proporter*, intend, < *pour-* (< L. *pro*), forth, + *porter*, bear, carry: see *port*[3], and cf. *import*.] To convey to the mind as the meaning or thing intended; imply; mean, or seem to mean: as, the document *purported* to be official.

> Sable, goulis, asur, vert; perpure
> The[r]-with wnproper, as *proportis* the text.
> *Booke of Precedence* (E. E. T. S., extra ser.), i. 96.

> In this Treatie there was an expresse article against the reception of the rebels of either prince by other; *purporting* that, if any such rebell should bee required by the prince whose rebell hee was of the prince confederate, that forthwith the prince confederate should by proclamation command him to auoid the countrie.
> *Bacon*, Hist. Hen. VII, p. 162.

> I do not believe there ever was put upon record more depravation of Man, and more despicable frivolity of thought and aim in Woman, than in the novels which *purport* to give the picture of English fashionable life.
> *Marg. Fuller*, Woman in 19th Cent., p. 139.

> Christianity *purports* to be not a system of moral teaching only, but, in vital union therewith, a system of revealed facts concerning the nature of God, and his dispensations towards mankind. *Gladstone*, Might of Right, p. 77.

purport (pėr′pōrt, formerly also pėr-pōrt′), *n.* [< OF. *pourport*, *purport*, *porport*, intent, purport, < *pourporter*, *purporter*, intend: see *purport*, *v.*] **1.** Meaning; tenor; import; nature: as, the *purport* of a letter.

> Thus there he stood, whylest high over his head
> There written was the *purport* of his sin,
> In cyphers strange, that few could rightly read.
> *Spenser*, F. Q., V. ix. 26.

> With a look so piteous in *purport*
> As if he had been loosed out of hell
> To speak of horrors. *Shak.*, Hamlet, ii. 1. 82.

> Mr. Pyncheon heard a half-uttered exclamation from his daughter, . . . very faint and low; so indistinct that there seemed but half a will to shape out the words, and too undefined a *purport* to be intelligible.
> *Hawthorne*, Seven Gables, xiii.

2†. Pretext; disguise; covering.

> For shee her sexe under that strange *purport*
> Did use to hide. *Spenser*, F. Q., III. i. 52.

=**Syn. 1.** Gist, drift, sense, signification.
purportless (pėr′pōrt-les), *a.* [< *purport* + *-less*.] Without purport, meaning, or design. *Southey*.
purpos†, *n.* A Middle English form of *purpose*.
purpose (pėr′pọs), *v.*; pret. and pp. *purposed*, ppr. *purposing*. [< ME. *purposen*, < OF. *purposer*, var. of *proposer*, propose: see *propose*, of which *purpose* is a doublet. The verb should prop. be accented on the last syllable (as in *propose*, *compose*, etc.), but it has conformed to the noun, which is wholly from the L. (see *purpose*, *n.*), whereas the verb (OF. *purposer*) is partly of different origin (see *pose*[2]).] **I.** *trans.* **1.** To propose; intend; design; mean: generally with an infinitive.

> And alle the disciplis *purposiden* after that ech hadde for to sende in to mynysterie to britheren that dwelliden in Iudee. *Wyclif*, Acts xi. 29.

> I have possess'd your grace of what I *purpose*.
> *Shak.*, M. of V., iv. 1. 35.

> He sav'd my life, though he *purpos'd* to destroy me.
> *Fletcher*, Wife for a Month, v. 3.

The ship a naked helpless hull is left;
Forc'd round and round, she quits her *purpos'd* way,
And bounds uncertain o'er the swelling sea.
Rowe, tr. of Lucan's Pharsalia, ix.

2. To resolve; determine, or determine on.

Because you look not to hear of your well-doing of man, I am *purposed* to pass it over with silence.
J. Bradford, Letters (Parker Soc., 1853), II. 52.

Reg. For his particular, I'll receive him gladly,
But not one follower.
Gon. So am I *purposed*.
Shak., Lear, ii. 4. 296.

=**Syn.** 1. To mean, meditate.

II. *intrans.* 1. To have intention or design; intend; mean.

Upon my soul,
You may believe him; nor did he e'er *purpose*
To me but nobly.
Fletcher (and another ?), Prophetess, iv. 1.

2†. To discourse.

Although it serve you to *purpose* with the ignorant and vulgar sort, who measure by tale and not by weight.
Hooker, Eccles. Polity, Pref., iv.

She in merry sort
Them gan to bord, and *purpose* diversly.
Spenser, F. Q., II. xii. 16.

purpose (pėr'pǫs), *n.* [< ME. *purpose, porpose, purpos, porpos*; < OF. *pourpos, purpose, porpos*, a var. of *propos, propost*, F. *propos*, a purpose, aim, end, < L. *propositum*, a thing proposed or intended, neut. of *propositus*, pp. of *proponere*, set forth, place before: see *propose, propound*. Cf. *purpose*, *v.*] 1. A thing proposed or intended; an object to be kept in view or subserved in any operation or course of action; end proposed; aim.

True it is, that the kingdom of God must be the first thing in our *purposes* and desires.
Hooker, Eccles. Polity, i. 10.

I wondred to what *purpose* they built Castles so near.
Coryat, Crudities, I. 93.

When they had environed and beset the fields in this manner, they thought their *purpose* sure.
Quoted in *Capt. John Smith's* Works, I. 218.

Those great number of Oriental Books he had most from his Nephew, whom he sent abroad for that *purpose*.
Lister, Journey to Paris, p. 102.

This man . . . had made a vow that, every Lent, he would spend the whole forty days in some part of the Abyssinian kingdom; and to this *purpose* he had raised, at his own expence, a small body of veteran troops, whom he inspired with the same spirit and resolution.
Bruce, Source of the Nile, II. 115.

Nothing can make ritual safe except the strict observance of its *purpose*, namely that it shall supply wings to the human soul in its callow efforts at upward flight.
Gladstone, Might of Right, p. 222.

2†. Proposition; proposal; point to be considered or acted upon.

As I bad Thouȝt tho be mene bitwene,
And put forth somme *purpos* to prouen his wittes.
Piers Plowman (B), viii. 120.

And therefore have we
Our written *purposes* before us sent;
Which, if thou hast consider'd, let us know
If 'twill tie up thy discontented sword.
Shak., A. and C., ii. 6. 4.

Hence—3. Intended or desired effect; practical advantage or result; use; subject or matter in hand; question at issue: as, to speak to the *purpose*.

He was wont to speak plain and to the *purpose*, like an honest man and a soldier. *Shak.*, Much Ado, ii. 3. 20.

He would answer me quite from the *purpose*.
B. *Jonson*, Volpone, iii. 2.

It is to small *purpose* to have an erected face towards heaven, and a perpetual grovelling spirit upon earth.
Bacon, Advancement of Learning, ii. 351.

The speech he made was so little to the *purpose* that I shall not trouble my readers with an account of it.
Addison, Sir Roger at the Assizes.

4. Intention; design; resolve; resolution; determination.

Full long agoo I was in this *purpose*,
Butt theme I myght not telle yow what I ment.
Generydes (E. E. T. S.), l. 484.

I schall do my part as feythfully as I can to lett Wyndhamys *porpose* tyl ye come home. *Paston Letters*, I. 250.

Infirm of *purpose*!
Give me the daggers. *Shak.*, Macbeth, ii. 2. 52.

At this Time Intelligence was given to the Lords that Richard, King of the Romans, had a *Purpose* to come into England. *Baker*, Chronicles, p. 86.

The *purpose* firm is equal to the deed:
Who does the best his circumstance allows
Does well, acts nobly; angels could no more.
Young, Night Thoughts, ii. 1. 90.

A certain hot fellness of *purpose*, which annihilated everything but itself. *Hawthorne*, Seven Gables, viii.

5. Import; meaning; purport; intent.

The intent and *purpose* of the law
Hath full relation to the penalty,
Which here appeareth due upon the bond.
Shak., M. of V., iv. 1. 247.

With words to this *purpose*, he [Ambrose] put back the Emperor as inferior to himself.
Milton, Ans. to Salmasius.

6†. Discourse; conversation.

For she in pleasaunt *purpose* did abound,
And greatly joyed merry tales to faine.
Spenser, F. Q., II. vi. 6.

7†. Instance; example.

'Tis common for double dealers to be taken in their own snares, as, for the *purpose*, in the matter of power.
Sir R. L'Estrange.

8†. *pl.* A sort of conversational game. Compare *cross-purpose*, 2.

Oft *purposes*, oft riddles he devysd,
And thousands like which flowed in his braine.
Spenser, F. Q., III. x. 8.

For sport's sake let 's have some Riddles or *Purposes* ho!
B. *Jonson*, Cynthia's Revels, iv. 1.

9†. A dance resembling a cotillion, a characteristic feature of which was the introduction of confidential or coquettish conversation.

The *Purpose* was so called because the figure exacted that at stated intervals the couples should dance together through the doorway into an adjoining room, and, having made the circuit of that apartment, should return, unbosomed of any secrets they might have had to interchange, to the rest of the laughing company. It was a figure obviously adopted for the triumph of coquetry and the discomfiture of mankind.
Whyte Melville, Queen's Maries, xvi.

Of purpose, on purpose, purposely; intentionally; with design: as, to do a thing *on purpose*; the door was left open *of purpose*.

Wherefore we must thinke he did it *of purpose*, by the odde sillable to giue greater grace to his meeter.
Puttenham, Arte of Eng. Poesie, p. 108.

Nature herself seemed to have studied *of purpose* how to make herself there admired. *Howell*, Letters, I. i. 39.

Her father, a hale and hearty man, died, *on purpose*, I believe, for the pleasure of plaguing me with the care of his daughter. *Sheridan*, School for Scandal, iii. 1.

To all intents and purposes. See *intent*.—**To be in purpose**†, to be resolved; intend.

I *am in purpos* to passe perilous wayes,
To kaire with my kene mene, to conquere gone landes.
Morte Arthure (E. E. T. S.), l. 641.

purposedly† (pėr'pǫst-li), *adv.* [< *purposed*, pp. of *purpose*, *v.*, + *-ly*[2]. Cf. *purposely*.] Intentionally; designedly; purposely. *North*, tr. of Plutarch, p. 615.

purposeful (pėr'pǫs-fůl), *a.* [< *purpose* + *-ful*.] 1. Characterized by purpose or definite aim; having an object in view; full of purpose or meaning; of serious import or significance: opposed to *aimless*.

The group of mother and child on page 89 is sincere, *purposeful*, downright drawing.
The Nation, Dec. 16, 1869, p. 539.

The funeral offerings of food, clothing, weapons, &c., to the dead are absolutely intelligible and *purposeful* among savage races, who believe that the souls of the departed are ethereal beings, capable of consuming food.
E. B. Tylor, Encyc. Brit., II. 122.

Hence—2. Intended; made or introduced on purpose.

The angles [were] all measured, and the *purposeful* variation of width in the border therefore admits of no dispute.
Ruskin.

purposefully (pėr'pǫs-fůl-i), *adv.* With full purpose or design; of set purpose.

You may indeed perhaps think . . . that it is much more pardonable to slay needlessly than *purposefully*.
Ruskin.

purposefulness (pėr'pǫs-fůl-nes), *n.* Purposeful character or quality; adaptation to a purpose: as, the *purposefulness* of an architectural design.

The *purposefulness* of the process of evolution.
Encyc. Brit., VIII. 769.

purposeless (pėr'pǫs-les), *a.* [< *purpose* + *-less*.] Lacking purpose or use; without practical advantage; aimless; useless.

purposelessly (pėr'pǫs-les-li), *adv.* In a purposeless manner; aimlessly; without apparent object.

purposelessness (pėr'pǫs-les-nes), *n.* 1. Lack of definite or practical purpose or aim.—2. The state or quality of being purposeless, and therefore without design or final cause. See *dysteleology*.

purpose-like (pėr'pǫs-lik), *a.* 1. Having a definite purpose or object to be subserved: as, a *purpose-like* person or action.—2. Having the appearance of being fit for a purpose.

Cuddie soon returned, assuring the stranger . . . that the gudewife should make a bed up for him at the house, mair *purpose-like* and comfortable than the like o' them could gie him. *Scott*, Old Mortality, xxxviii.

purposely (pėr'pǫs-li), *adv.* [A reduction of *purposedly*; as if *purpose* + *-ly*[2].] Intentionally; designedly; on purpose.

purposer (pėr'pǫs-ėr), *n.* [< *purpose* + *-er*[1].] 1. One who purposes, resolves, or determines on any particular course of action; one who forms a resolution.—2. One who proposes or sets forth anything.

purposive (pėr'pǫs-iv), *a.* [< *purpose* + *-ive*.] 1. Having an aim or purpose; having an end in view; purposeful. [Rare.]

We want a word to express the adaptation of means to an end, whether involving consciousness or not; the word purpose will do very well, and the adjective *purposive* has already been used in this sense.
W. K. Clifford, Lectures, II. 168.

To ascertain the origin and progress of *purposive* action it seems, then, that we must look to the effects of pain rather than to those of pleasure. *Encyc. Brit.*, XX. 73.

2. Accomplishing some end; functional; useful in animal or vegetable economy: applied in biology to parts and organs which are not rudimentary or vestigial, and may therefore be regarded as teleological.

purposiveness (pėr'pǫs-iv-nes), *n.* The quality or character of being purposive, or designed for an end. [Rare.]

Its movements, instead of being wholly at random, show more and more signs of *purposiveness*. *Contemporary Rev.*

purpoynt†, *n.* An obsolete form of *pourpoint*.

purpre†, *n.* and *a.* An obsolete variant of *purple*. *Chaucer.*

purpresture (pėr-pres'tūr), *n.* [Also *pourpresture*; < OF. *porpresture, pourpresture, purpresture* (ML. *purprestura, porprestura, proprestura*), an encroachment, purpresture, a fee paid by villeins for the privilege of inclosing land; a variant of *pourpresure, porpresure, pourprissure*, an inclosure, space occupied, < *pourprise, porprise, purprise, pourprinse*, an inclosure: see *purprise*.] In *law*, a nuisance consisting in an inclosure of or encroachment on something that belongs to another person or to the public, as the shutting up or obstruction of a highway or of navigable waters. Encroachments other than against the public are no longer termed *purprestures*.

The offence of *purpresture* . . . was an encroachment on the forest rights, by building a house within the forest, and it made no difference whether the land belonged to the builder or not. *Encyc. Brit.*, IX. 409.

purprise (pėr-prīz'), *n.* [Early mod. E. also *pourprise*; < ME. *purprise*, < OF. *pourprise, porprise, purprise*, an inclosure, < *pourpris, porpris, purpris*, pp. of *pourprendre, porprendre, purprendre*, seize upon, occupy, encroach upon, invest, surround, inclose, < *pour-, por-, pur-*, < L. *pro*, before, + *prendere*, take: see *prehend* and *prize*[1], *surprise*, etc. Cf. *purpresture*.] A close or inclosure; also, the whole compass of a manor.

And eke amydde this *purprise*
Was maad a tour of gret maistrise.
Rom. of the Rose, l. 4171.

The place of justice is a hallowed place; and therefore not only the bench, but the footpace and precincts and *purprise* thereof ought to be preserved without scandal and corruption. *Bacon*, Judicature (ed. 1887).

purpul†, *a.* A Middle English form of *purple*.

purpura (pėr'pū-rä), *n.* [NL., < L. *purpura*, < Gr. πορφύρα, the purple-fish, a purple dye or color: see *purple*.] 1. In *med.*, an eruption of small purple spots and patches, caused by extravasation of blood in the skin; the purples.—2. [*cap.*] A genus of gastropods, typical of the family *Purpuridæ*. The animal has a purpurigenous gland, and secretes a purplish fluid which has given name to the genus. The shell is generally oblong-ovate, its surface usually being rather rough with spines or tubercles. The species are numerous, and are divided in various subgenera, considered by some as genera. *P. lapillus* is an abundant northern species, common to both shores of the Atlantic. See also cut under *operculum*.—**Malignant purpura**, cerebrospinal fever.—**Purpura hemorrhagica**, purpura attended with hemorrhage into and from mucous membranes, and often into serous membranes and cavities. Pyrexia may be present or absent. Also called *morbus maculosus Werlhofii*.—**Purpura nautica**, scurvy.—**Purpura nervosa**, purpura with rheumatoid pains, with colic and vomiting, sometimes hemorrhage from the bowels, and frequently cutaneous edema. It occurs mostly in children. The specific name refers to a supposed dependence on the sympathetic nervous system.—**Purpura papulosa**, purpura in which the ecchymoses are interspersed with livid papules. Also called *lichen lividus*.—**Purpura rheumatica**, a disease characterized by a purpuric eruption, often with some fever, nausea, colicky pains, diarrhea, or constipation, and with rheumatoid pains and often swelling and redness in certain joints.—**Purpura simplex**, a disease characterized by a purpuric eruption, with slight general symptoms such as languor and loss of appetite. The spots come out in successive crops, each lasting a week or ten days; there may be a number of such recurrent eruptions.—**Purpura**

Purpura lapillus.

symptomatica, a purpuric eruption occurring as a symptom of some distinct disease, as smallpox, cholera, measles, or scarlet fever.—**Purpura urticans**, a variety of purpura simplex in which the eruption is raised into wheals, which may or may not be accompanied by itching.

Purpuracea (pėr-pū̦-rā'sē-ā̤), *n. pl.* [NL., < *Purpura* + *-acea*.] Same as *Purpuridæ*. *Menke*, 1828.

purpuracean (pėr-pū̦-rā'sē̦-a̤n), *a.* and *n.* **I.** *a.* Same as *purpuraceous*.

II. *n.* A member of the *Purpuracea*.

purpuraceous (pėr-pū̦-rā'shius), *a.* [< L. *purpura*, purple, + *-aceous*.] Of a purple color; of or pertaining to the *Purpuracea*; purpurate.

purpurate[1] (pėr'pū̦-rāt), *a.* [< L. *purpuratus*, purpled, clad in purple, pp. of *purpurare*, make purple, < *purpura*, purple: see *purple*.] Of a purple color.

purpurate[1] (pėr'pū̦-rāt), *n.* [< *purpur(ic)* + *-ate*[1].] A salt of purpuric acid.

purpurate[2] (pėr'pū̦-rāt), *a.* [< *purpura* + *-ate*[1].] Of or pertaining to purpura; purpuric.

purpure (pėr'pūr), *n.* and *a.* [< ME. *purpure*, *purpur*, *purpour*, < OF. *purpure*, vernacularly *purpre*, purple: see *purple*.] Purple: represented in heraldry by diagonal lines from the sinister base of the shield to the dexter chief. [Obsolete except in heraldic use.]

> The whit cote that hade sem none,
> And the *purpure* that layd both upon one,
> They be my sokur and my helping,
> That my bodi hath usid soft cloging.
> *Holy Rood* (E. E. T. S.), p. 178.

> The ground that erst was yellow, greene, and blew
> Is overcled with blood in *purpure* hew.
> *Hudson*, tr. of Du Bartas's Judith, v.

purpureal (pėr-pū'rē̦-a̤l), *a.* [< L. *purpureus* (< Gr. πορφύρεος), purple-colored, < *purpura*, purple: see *purple*.] Purple.

> More pellucid streams,
> An ampler ether, a diviner air,
> And fields invested with *purpureal* gleams.
> *Wordsworth*, Laodamia.

purpurescent (pėr-pū̦-res'e̦nt), *a.* [< L. *purpura*, purple, + *-escent*.] In *zoöl.*, purplish; tinged with purple.

purpuresse†, *n.* [ME., < *purpure* + *-ess*.] A woman who sells purple. *Wyclif*.

purpuric[1] (pėr-pū'rik), *a.* [< L. *purpura*, purple, + *-ic*.] Having a purple color; also, producing a purple color; specifically, in *chem.*, noting an acid produced by the action of nitric acid upon uric acid. It forms deep-red or purple compounds with most bases, whence the name. It cannot be obtained except in combination. Also *isopurpuric*.

purpuric[2] (pėr-pū'rik), *a.* [< *purpura* + *-ic*.] Of the nature of or pertaining to purpura.—**Malignant purpuric fever.** See *fever*[1].

Purpuridæ (pėr-pū'ri-dē), *n. pl.* [NL., < *Purpura* + *-idæ*.] A family of gastropods, typified by the genus *Purpura*: same as the subfamily *Purpurinæ*.

Purpurifera (pėr-pū̦-rif'e̦-rā̤), *n. pl.* [NL.: see *purpuriferous*.] In Lamarck's system, a family of trachelipodous gastropods containing species producing a purple fluid, and others supposed to resemble them. It included the *Purpurinæ* (but not the *Muricinæ*) and various incongruous genera referred by modern authors to different families and even suborders.

purpuriferous (pėr-pū̦-rif'e̦-rus), *a.* [< L. *purpura*, purple, + *ferre*, bear.] Purpuriparous; belonging to the *Purpurifera*.

purpuriform (pėr'pū̦-ri-fôrm), *a.* [< NL. *Purpura*, q. v., + L. *forma*, form.] Resembling a shell of the genus *Purpura*; related or belonging to the *Purpuridæ*. Also *purpuroid*.

purpurigenous (pėr-pū̦-rij'e-nus), *a.* [< L. *purpura*, purple, + *gignere*, *genere*, bear: see *-genous*.] Producing purple.—**Purpurigenous gland**, a gland, especially developed in the gastropods of the family *Muricidæ*, secreting a liquid of a purplish color.

purpurin, purpurine (pėr'pū̦-rin), *n.* [< L. *purpura*, purple, + *-in*[2], *-ine*[2].] A red coloring matter, $C_{14}H_5O_2(OH)_3$, used in dyeing, extracted from madder and prepared artificially by the oxidation of artificial alizarin. Its application in dyeing is similar to that of alizarin. In commerce it is known as *alizarin, yellow shade* (of red), the true alizarin giving blue shades of red.

Purpurinæ (pėr-pū̦-rī'nē), *n. pl.* [NL., < *Purpura* + *-inæ*.] A subfamily of *Muricidæ*, characterized by having an operculum with a lateral nucleus. It includes the genera *Purpura*, *Acanthina*, *Pentadactylus*, *Concholepas*, and others.

purpuriparous (pėr-pū̦-rip'a̦-rus), *a.* [< L. *purpura*, purple, + *parere*, bring forth, bear.] Producing or secreting a purple substance: as, the *purpuriparous* glands of the sea-hare.

purpuroid (pėr'pū̦-roid), *a.* [< L. *purpura*, purple, + Gr. εἶδος, form.] Same as *purpuriform*.

purr[1], **pur**[1] (pėr), *v.* [Imitative; cf. *pirr*, *purl*[1], and *puss*.] **I.** *intrans.* To utter a low murmuring sound expressive of satisfaction or pleasure, as a cat. The sound is made by throwing the vocal cords into vibration measured and regulated by the respiration; and this vibration is strong enough to make the whole larynx tremble, so that it may be felt or seen from the outside. Purring is highly characteristic of the cat tribe, though probably not confined to it.

> I know somebody to whose knee that black cat loves to climb; against whose shoulder and cheek it likes to *purr*.
> *Charlotte Brontë*, Shirley, xii.

> Sitting drowsy in the fire-light, winked and *purred* the mottled cat.
> *Whittier*, Mary Garvin.

Purring thrill, a thrill or fremitus, or sense of fine vibration, perceptible to the hand, as sometimes over an aneurism, or over the heart in some cases of valvular lesion. It resembles the sensation which the back of a purring cat yields to the hand. Also called *purring tremor*, *purring fremitus*, and, in French, *frémissement cataire*.

II. *trans.* To express or signify by purring.

> Her ears of jet and emerald eyes
> She saw, and *purr'd* applause.
> *Gray*, Death of a Favourite Cat.

[Figuratively of persons in both uses.]

purr[1], **pur**[1] (pėr), *n.* [< *purr*[1], *v.*] The sound made by a cat in purring.

> [She] thrills the hand that smooths her glossy fur
> With the light tremor of her grateful *purr*.
> *O. W. Holmes*, Terpsichore.

purr[2]†, *n.* See *pur*[2].

purr[3], **purre**[1] (pėr), *n.* [Also *pirr*; perhaps ult. < AS. *pur*, occurring in two glosses, as a synonym of *rāradumbla*, a bittern (glossed by L. *onocrotalus*, a pelican), or of *hæferblǣte*, appar. a snipe (E. dial. *hammerbleat*).] A sandpiper, *Tringa alpina*, commonly called *dunlin*.

purr[4] (pėr), *n.* [Origin obscure.] A bivalve of the family *Veneridæ*, *Tapes decussata*. It inhabits chiefly the European coasts on sandy or gravelly bottoms between tide-marks. It burrows in the ground, and is usually indicated by two little holes about an inch apart, made by the siphons. The purrs are held in some esteem for food, being considered better than cockles. Also called *butter-fish*.

purre[1], *n.* See *purr*[3].

purre[2]†, *n.* An obsolete form of *perry*[1].

purree, purrhee (pur'ē), *n.* A yellow coloring matter. See *euxanthin*. Also called *Indian yellow*.

purreic (pu-rē'ik), *a.* [< *purree* + *-ic*.] Pertaining to or derived from purree.—**Purreic acid.** Same as *euxanthic acid* (which see, under *euxanthic*).

purrelt, *n.* [Perhaps a form of *purl*[3] for *purfle*, border.] A list ordained to be at the end of kerseys to prevent deceit in diminishing their length. *Halliwell*.

purre-maw (pėr'mâ), *n.* The roseate tern. [Prov. Eng.]

purrock (pur'o̦k), *n.* [A var. of *parrock*, as equiv. *puddock*[2] of *paddock*[2].] Same as *paddock*[2].

purse (pėrs), *n.* [< ME. *purse*, *purs*, *pors*, an altered form of *burs*, *bors*, < OF. *borse*, *bourse*, F. *bourse* = It. *borsa*, < ML. *bursa*, *byrsa*, < Gr. βύρσα, a hide or skin. Cf. *burse*, *bourse*.] **1.** A bag or pouch; specifically, a small bag or case in which money is contained or carried.

Belt-purse or Sporran, 17th century.

> Her girdle was greene, and at that hung a large leather *purse*.
> *Greene* (?), Vision.

> A pouch with many parts and *purses* thin,
> To carry all your tools and trinkets in.
> *J. Dennys* (Arber's Eng. Garner, I. 154).

> Out has he ta'en a *purse* o' gowd,
> Was a' fou to the string.
> *Brown Adam* (Child's Ballads, IV. 62).

2. Figuratively, money; means; resources.

> Had men beene as forward to adventure their *purses*, and performe the conditions they promised mee, as to crop the fruits of my labours, thousands ere this had beene bettered by these designes. *Capt. John Smith*, Works, II. 241.

> But here attir'd beyond our *purse* we go,
> For useless ornament and flaunting show.
> *Dryden*, tr. of Juvenal's Satires, iii. 230.

> He needs his *purse*, and knows how to make use on it.
> *Fletcher*, Spanish Curate, i. 1.

> You never refused your *purse* and credit to the service and support of learned or ingenious men.
> *Swift*, Improving English Tongue.

3. A treasury; finances: as, to exhaust a nation's *purse*, or the public *purse*. *Shak.*, T. of A., i. 2. 200.—**4.** A purseful of money; a sum of money offered as a prize or collected as a present: as, to win the *purse* in a horse-race; to make up a *purse* as a present.—**5.** A specific sum of money. In Turkey large accounts are often set down in purses of 500 Medjidie piasters, equivalent to 4 pounds 10 shillings of English money, or about $22.

> The Greeks have three churches, and their bishop resides here, who has an income of about four *purses* a year.
> *Pococke*, Description of the East, II. ii. 24.

> A Turkish merchant residing in Cairo died leaving property to the amount of six thousand *purses*.
> *E. W. Lane*, Modern Egyptians, I. 136.

6. In *zoöl.* and *anat.*, some kind of a pouch, bursa, marsupium, or ovicapsule.—**A light purse, or an empty purse**, poverty, or want of resources.—**A long purse, or a heavy purse**, wealth; riches.—**Cold purse.** See *cold*.—**Halfpenny-purse**, a small purse worn at the side: the name probably implies its use for the smallest coins, as, perhaps, the silver halfpence of the middle ages down to the seventeenth century.—**Maundy purse.** See *maundy*.—**Mermaid's purse.** See *mermaid's-purse*.—**Privy purse.** (*a*) An allowance for the private expenses of the British sovereign, forming part of the civil list. (*b*) An officer of the British royal household charged with the payment of the sovereign's private expenses. His official title is *keeper of the privy purse*.—**Purse of state**, in *her.*, a bag or pouch resembling an aumônière, bearing the arms of the sovereign or state on the side, and having cords fashioned into an elaborate knot or plaiting.—**Sword and purse**, the military power and wealth of a nation.

purse (pėrs), *v. t.*; pret. and pp. *pursed*, ppr. *pursing*. [< ME. *pursen*, *porsen*; < *purse*, *n.* For the sense 'wrinkle,' 'pucker' (like the mouth of a purse drawn together with a gathering-string), cf. *pucker*, as related to *poke*[2], a bag, sack, pocket.] **I.** *trans.* **1.** To put in a purse.

> 3eue poure peuple the pans; ther-of *porse* thow none,
> Ac 3eue hem forth to poure folke that for my loue hit askketh.
> *Piers Plowman* (C), xiii. 164.

> I will go and *purse* the ducats. *Shak.*, M. of V., i. 3. 175.

> The benefits you have done me are not lost,
> Nor cast away; they are *purs'd* here in my heart.
> *Massinger and Field*, Fatal Dowry, ii. 2.

2. To contract into folds or wrinkles; knit; pucker: frequently with *up*.

> Thou criedst "Indeed!"
> And didst contract and *purse* thy brow together.
> *Shak.*, Othello, iii. 3. 113.

> Was this a story to *purse up* people's hearts and pennies against giving an alms to the blind?
> *Lamb*, Decay of Beggars.

> O moralist, frown not so dark,
> *Purse* not thy lip severe.
> *Harper's Mag.*, LXXIX. 972.

II.† *intrans.* To take purses; rob.

> I'll *purse*; if that raise me not, I'll bet at bowling alleys.
> *Beau. and Fl.*, Scornful Lady, i. 1.

purse-bearer (pėrs'bãr'ėr), *n.* One who carries or guards the purse of another.

> I'll be your *purse-bearer*, and leave you
> For an hour. *Shak.*, T. N., iii. 3. 47.

purse-bearing (pėrs'bãr'ing), *a.* Pouched or marsupiate: an epithet formerly used to note the marsupials, as *purse-bearing* animals, translating Scaliger's phrase *Animalia crumenata*.

purse-boat (pėrs'bōt), *n.* A boat 28 feet long, 6 feet wide, and 2 feet deep, from which the seine is worked in the menhaden-fishery. The captain of a gang has charge of this boat.

purse-clasp (pėrs'klásp), *n.* A metal frame of a large medieval purse or aumônière, often very elaborate and richly decorated, and an object of curiosity when the bag of the purse has perished. Sometimes a pistol is concealed in the frame, and would be discharged by an unskilful attempt to open it. Also *purse-snap*.

purse-crab (pėrs'krab), *n.* A short-tailed ten-footed crustacean of the genus *Birgus*, as *B. latro*, the cocoanut-crab, found in Mauritius and the more eastern islands of the Indian Ocean, and one of the largest crustaceans. It resides on land, often burrowing under the roots of trees, lines its hole with the fibers of the cocoanut-husk, and lives on the nuts, which it procures by climbing the trees, breaking the shells with great ingenuity.

purse-crew (pėrs'krö), *n.* The crew or gang of a purse-net; a purse-gang.

purse-cutter (pėrs'kut'ėr), *n.* A thief who steals purses; a cutpurse.

> It is a gentle admonition, you must know, sir, both to the *purse-cutter* and the purse-bearer.
> *B. Jonson*, Bartholomew Fair, iii. 1.

purse-davit (pėrs'dav'it), *n.* A short, strong davit attached to the gunwale and a thwart of a boat, supporting the pursing-blocks of a purse-seine.

purseful[1] (pėrs'fůl), *a.* [< *purse* + *-ful*, 1.] Rich.

> Dr. Percy's next difficulty was how to supply the *purseful* and purse-proud citizen with motive and occupation.
> *Miss Edgeworth*, Patronage, xix. (*Davies.*)

purseful[2] (pėrs'fůl), *n.* [< *purse* + *-ful*, 2.] As much as a purse will hold. *Dryden*.

purse-gang (pėrs'gang), *n.* A purse-crew.

purse-gill (pėrs'gil), *n.* A marsipobranchiate fish: one of the *Marsipobranchii*.

purse-gilled (pėrs'gild), *a.* Marsipobranchiate.

purse-leech (pėrs'lēch), *n.* One who grasps at money; a grasping person. [Rare.]

> Whilst the king and his faithfuls retained their places of dominion, we enjoyed such golden days of peace and plenty

as we must never see again, so long as you harpyes, you sucking *purse-leeches*, and your implements be our masters.
British Belman, 1648 (Harl. Misc., VII. 625.) (*Davies.*)

purse-line (pėrs'līn), *n.* The line by means of which a purse-seine is pursed.

purse-milking† (pėrs'mil"king), *a.* Making frequent or heavy demands upon one's purse; extortionate; expensive. [Rare.]

Purse-milking nation.
Burton, Anat. of Mel., To the Reader, p. 49. (*Davies.*)

purse-mouth (pėrs'mouth), *n.* A prim or pursed-up mouth. [Rare.]

Maud with her sweet *purse-mouth* when my father dangled the grapes. *Tennyson*, Maud, i. 18.

purse-net (pėrs'net), *n.* A net the mouth of which may be drawn close with cords, or closed quickly in any way. See cut under *purse-seine*.

We shopkeepers, when all 's done, are sure to have 'em in our *pursenets* at length.
Middleton and Dekker, Roaring Girl, iv. 2.

Conies are taken by *pursenets* in their burrows.
Mortimer, Husbandry.

pursenet-fish (pėrs'net-fish), *n.* Same as *basket-fish*. *John Winthrop.*

purse-pinched (pėrs'pincht), *a.* Impecunious; poor.

Ladies and Lords, *purse-pinchèd* and soule-pain'd.
Davies, Microcosmos, p. 14. (*Davies.*)

purse-pride (pėrs'prīd), *n.* Pride of wealth; insolence proceeding from consciousness of the possession of wealth.

Even *purse-pride* is quarrellous, domineering over the humble neighbourhood, and raising quarrels out of trifles.
Bp. Hall, Superuumeraries, § 4.

purse-proud (pėrs'proud), *a.* Proud of wealth; puffed up with the possession of money or riches.

This person was . . . a noisy, *purseproud*, illiterate demagogue, whose Cockney English and scraps of mispronounced Latin were the jest of the newspapers, Alderman Beckford. *Macaulay*, Earl of Chatham.

purser (pėr'sėr), *n.* [< *purse* + *-er*[1]. Cf. *bursar*.] **1.** An official charged with the keeping of accounts and the disbursing of money; specifically, an officer who keeps the accounts of a ship, and has charge of the provisions, pay, etc.: now called in the navy *paymaster*.

And this order to be seene and kept euery voyage orderly, by the *pursers* of the companie's owne ship, in any wise.
Hakluyt's Voyages, I. 273.

2. In *mining*, the paymaster or cashier of a mine, and the official to whom notices of transfer are sent for registration in the cost-book. [Cornwall, Eng.]

purse-ring (pėrs'ring), *n.* A metal ring attached to the bridle-rope on the foot of a purse-seine, for the pursing-line to run through.

purse-rope (pėrs'rōp), *n.* Same as *purse-line*.

pursership (pėr'sėr-ship), *n.* [< *purser* + *-ship*.] The office of purser.

purses (pėr'sez), *n. pl.* A seaweed, *Alaria esculenta*. [Prov. Eng.]

purse-seine (pėrs'sān), *n.* A seine which may be pursed or drawn into the shape of a bag.

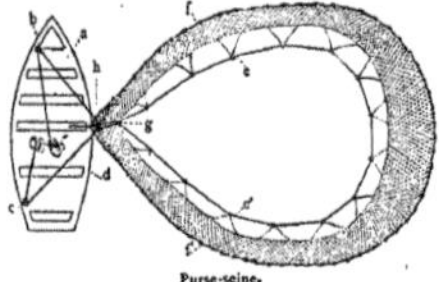

Purse-seine.

a, boat; *b* and *c*, blocks; *d*, gunwale of boat; *e*, purse-line or bridle; *f*, *f*, corks or floats; *g*, sheave; *h*, pursing-blocks attached to purse-davit. See cut under *pursing-block*.

Mackerel purse-seines range from 120 to 220 fathoms long by 20 to 30 fathoms deep, having 750 to 1,000 meshes of depth. The average mesh is 2¼ inches. The pursing weight varies from 150 to 200 pounds. The seines are made of fine Sea Island cotton twine.

The *purse-seine* first came into general use in 1850.
Nature, XLI. 180.

purse-seiner (pėrs'sā"nėr), *n.* A vessel employed in the menhaden or the mackerel purse-seine fishery.

purse-silk (pėrs'silk), *n.* A stout silk thread used for knitting purses, and also for embroidery with the needle. Also *purse-twist*.

purse-snap (pėrs'snap), *n.* Same as *purse-clasp*.

purse-spider (pėrs'spī"dėr), *n.* A spider, *Atypus niger*, which spins a close web of varying shape and size against the bark of trees at the surface of the ground. [Southern U. S.]

purse-strings (pėrs'stringz), *n. pl.* The strings by means of which a purse is fastened or unfastened.

The merchants, frightened by Drake's successes, and appalled by the ruin all around them, drew their *purse-strings* inexorably. *Motley*, Hist. Netherlands, II. 18.

purset† (pėr'set), *n.* [< *purse* + *-et*.] A purse or bag. [Rare.]

The blood of the frog and the bone in his back
I have been getting; and made of his skin
A *purset* to keep Sir Cranion in.
B. *Jonson*, Masque of Queens.

purse-taking (pėrs'tā"king), *n.* The act of stealing a purse; robbing.

I see a good amendment of life in thee; from praying to *purse-taking*. *Shak.*, 1 Hen. IV., i. 2. 115.

purse-twist (pėrs'twist), *n.* Same as *purse-silk*.

pursevant†, *n.* An obsolete form of *pursuivant*.

purse-weight (pėrs'wāt), *n.* The weight or sinker of a purse-seine concerned in drawing the net. In a menhaden-seine it weighs about 35 pounds; in a mackerel-seine, 200 pounds or more.

pursey†, *a.* See *pursy*[2].

pursif†, *a.* An obsolete form of *pursy*. *Levins.*

pursiness (pėr'si-nes), *n.* [Early mod. E. also *pursiveness*, *pursifness*; < ME. *pursynes*, **pursifnes*; < *pursif*, pursy: see *pursy*[1] and *-ness*.] The state of being pursy; the state of being short-winded; shortness of breath.

pursing-block (pėr'sing-blok), *n.* A block used in hauling in the pursing-line or bridle of a purse-seine. Two of these are attached to the purse-davit by hooks, as shown in the cut.

Pursing-block.

a, *a'*, pursing-blocks; *b*, *b'*, hooks which engage eyes in the upper extremity of the purse-davit *c*; *g*, gunwale; *d*, brace fastened to gunwale and also bolted at *e* to the thwart *f*.

pursing-gear (pėr'sing-gēr), *n.* The gear by which a seine is pursed.

pursive† (pėr'siv), *a.* An obsolete form of *pursy*. *Holland.*

pursiveness† (pėr'siv-nes), *n.* An obsolete form of *pursiness*. *Bailey*, 1727.

purslane (pėrs'lān), *n.* [Also *purslain*; early mod. E. *pourslane*, *purseline*; < ME. *purslane*, < OF. *porcelaine*, *pourcelaine* = It. *porcellana*, purslane, with accom. term., < ML. **porcilana*; cf. OHG. *purzella*, MHG. *purzel*, G. *burzel*, < L. *porcilaca*, var. of *portulaca*, purslane, portulaca: see *Portulaca*.] A herbaceous plant, *Portulaca oleracea*, widely distributed through warm and temperate climates. It is a prostrate annual of a reddish-green aspect, with fleshy stems and leaves, and small yellow flowers. Purslane is used, now less than formerly, in salads, as a pot-herb, in pickles, and for garnishing, and is cultivated in Europe in several varieties for these purposes. In America it is regarded chiefly as a weed, and is rather troublesome in gardens, from its abundance and persistent vitality. In the United States vulgarly *pussly* (or *pusley*) or *pussly-weed*.

Pourslane dothe mitigate the great heat in al the inward partes of the bodye, semblably of the head and eyes.
Sir T. Elyot, Castle of Health, ii. 15.

Black purslane, a kind of spurge, *Euphorbia Preslii* (*E. hypericifolia*), a common weed of the United States, somewhat resembling purslane in habit, but not fleshy.—**Milk-purslane**, the spotted spurge, *Euphorbia maculata*, a prostrate weed having a milky juice.—**Mud-purslane**, a waterwort, *Elatine Americana*.—**Sea-purslane**. (*a*) In Great Britain, *Atriplex portulacoides*, the purslane orach, a low straggling sea-shore shrub. (*b*) In America, *Sesuvium Portulacastrum*, of the warmer Atlantic shores and the saline or alkaline valleys of the southwestern United States, a prostrate fleshy plant, forming mats sometimes 6 feet broad; also, *S. pentandrum*, sometimes erect, reaching north to New Jersey.—**Water-purslane**. (*a*) *Peplis Portula*. (*b*) *Ludwigia palustris*. (*c*) An American aquatic or sometimes terrestrial herb, *Didiplis linearis*, of the *Lythrarieæ*, with opposite linear leaves and very small greenish flowers.—**Wild purslane**, a European species, *Euphorbia Peplis*, with prostrate leafless flowering branches which fork repeatedly, forming mats on maritime sands.

purslane-tree (pėrs'lān-trē), *n.* The African shrub *Portulacaria Afra*.

purslane-worm (pėrs'lān-wėrm), *n.* The larva of a zygænid moth, *Copidryas gloveri*, which feeds in enormous numbers on the wild purslane. [Western U. S.]

pursuable (pėr-sū'a-bl), *a.* [< *pursue* + *-able*.] Capable of being, or fit to be, pursued, followed, or prosecuted.

pursual (pėr-sū'al), *n.* [< *pursue* + *-al*.] The act of pursuing; pursuit: as, "quick *pursual*," *Southey*. [Rare.]

pursuance (pėr-sū'ans), *n.* [< *pursuan(t)* + *-ce*.] The act of following or pursuing; pursuit; prosecution: as, the *pursuance* of some design; in *pursuance* of orders.

He being in *pursuance* of the imperial army, the next morning, in a sudden fog that fell, the cavalry on both sides being engaged, he was killed in the midst of the troops. *Howell*, Letters, i. 6. (*Latham.*)

Whether he [Samson] acted in *pursuance* of a Command from Heaven, or was prompted by his own Valour only, or whatsoever inducement he had, he did not put to death one, but many that tyrannized over his Countrey.
Milton, Ans. to Salmasius, iv. 104.

George was to depart for town the next day, to secure his commission, in *pursuance* of his generous patron's directions. *Goldsmith*, Vicar, xxi.

=**Syn.** See *pursuit*.

pursuant (pėr-sū'ant), *a.* and *n.* [< ME. **pursuant*, *persewend*, < OF. *pursuiant*, *poursuiant*, ppr. of *pursuir*, pursue: see *pursue*. Cf. *pursuivant*.] **I.** *a.* Done in consequence of or in the prosecution of something.

You may perceive that which I now desire to be *pursuant* thereupon.
Bacon, Advancement of Learning, Pref., p. ix.

II.† *n.* A pursuivant.

Ye poore people were so vexed with apparators, & *pursuants*, & ye comissarie courts, as truly their affliction was not smale. *Bradford*, Plymouth Plantation, p. 8.

pursuant (pėr-sū'ant), *adv.* [< *pursuant*, *a.*] According; agreeably: with *to*.—**Pursuant to**, following; according to; in accordance with: as, *pursuant to* orders, passage was denied.

Mr. President: I rise, Sir, *pursuant to* notice, to ask leave to bring in a bill.
D. Webster, Senate, March 18, 1834.

pursuantly (pėr-sū'ant-li), *adv.* [< *pursuant* + *-ly*[2].] Pursuant; agreeably; conformably.

pursue (pėr-sū'), *v.*; pret. and pp. *pursued*, ppr. *pursuing*. [Early mod. E. also *pursew*, *persue*, *persew*, < ME. *pursuen*, *pursuwen*, *porsuen*, *porsewen*, < OF. *pursuer*, *poursuier*, *poursuiver*, *porsuiver*, also *porsuir*, *porsuivir*, *poursuir*, *poursuivir*, also *poursuivre*, *poursevre*, *porsevre*, F. *poursuivre* = Sp. Pg. *proseguir* = It. *proseguire*, < L. *prosequi*, follow forth, follow after, pursue, prosecute, < *pro*, forth, + *sequi*, follow: see *sequent*. Cf. *prosecute*, from the same L. verb; and cf. *sue*, *ensue*.] **I.** *trans.* **1.** To follow; proceed along; follow in action.

There are those who *pursue* their own way out of a sourness and spirit of contradiction. *Steele*, Spectator, No. 264.

Wilfrid a safer path *pursued*. *Scott*, Rokeby, ii. 16.

It will not be necessary to *pursue* his course further than to notice a single occurrence of most extraordinary nature. *Prescott*, Ferd. and Isa., II. 8.

2. To follow with the view of overtaking; follow with haste; chase; hunt: as, to *pursue* a hare; to *pursue* a fleeing enemy.

And Pouerte *pursuwede* me and putte me to be lowe,
And flittynge fond ich the frere that me confessede.
Piers Plowman (C), xiii. 15.

Then they fled
Into this abbey, whither we *pursued* them.
Shak., C. of E., v. 1. 155.

Each creature returned to its own nature, and *pursued* and preyed upon its fellow. *Bacon*, Physical Fables, iii.

They fled
This way and that, *pursued* by nought but dread.
William Morris, Earthly Paradise, III. 322.

3. To seek; seek to obtain: as, to *pursue* a remedy at law; to *pursue* pleasure.

Quod the child, "y come poore the world withinne
To *pursue* a wondirful eritage."
Hymns to Virgin, etc. (E. E. T. S.), p. 59.

Too hard a Censure they *pursue*
Who charge on all the Failings of a few.
Congreve, tr. of Ovid's Art of Love.

They who most passionately *pursue* pleasure seldomest arrive at it. *Steele*, Spectator, No. 544.

4. To follow close upon; attend; be present with; accompany.

Fortune *pursue* thee! *Shak.*, A. and C., iii. 12. 25.

Both here and hence *pursue* me lasting strife,
If, once a widow, ever I be wife!
Shak., Hamlet, iii. 2. 232.

5†. To follow vindictively or with enmity; persecute; treat with hostility; seek to injure.

For a cursed Emperour of Persie, that highte Saures, *pursuede* alle Cristene men, to destroye hem, and to compelle hem to make Sacrifise to his Ydoles.
Mandeville, Travels, p. 260.

I will to death *pursue* him with revenge.
Beau. and Fl., Maid's Tragedy, iii. 2.

Will you the knights
Shall to the edge of all extremity
Pursue each other?
Shak., T. and C., iv. 5. 69.

6. To follow as a principle of action, profession, trade, or occupation; prosecute; practise systematically; carry on.

Men must *pursue* things which are just in present, and leave the future to the divine Providence.
Bacon, Advancement of Learning, ii. 284.

The . . . measures which are now *pursued* tend to strengthen and aggrandize . . . absolute monarchy.
Goldsmith, Seven Years' War, ii.

Both Foote and Fielding *pursued* the law until the law pursued them.
Jon Bee, Essay on Samuel Foote.

The principle of asceticism never was, nor ever can be, consistently *pursued* by any living creature.
Bentham, Introd. to Morals and Legislation, ii. 10.

7. To follow up; continue; proceed with.

Thus far, with rough and all-unable pen,
Our bending author hath *pursued* the story.
Shak., Hen. V., Epil.

Be slow to stir inquiries which you do not mean particularly to *pursue* to their proper end.
Gladstone, Might of Right, p. 245.

8†. To endeavor; try.

Men fyndeth that Makamede was a man yerystned,
And a cardinal of court a gret clerk with-alle,
And *porsuede* to haue be pope, pryns of holychurche;
And for he was lyke a Lussheborgh ich leyue oure lord
hym lette.
Piers Plowman (C), xviii. 167.

=Syn. 2. To track, hound.—3. To strive for.—6. To conduct, keep up, persist in.

II. *intrans.* 1†. To give chase; charge.

Therfore, wende well Caherlos he hadde be slayn; and, therfore, he *pursude* vpon hym with swerde drawen, as fiercely as a wilde boor.
Merlin (E. E. T. S.), ii. 194.

2†. To seek; endeavor; try.

The dede of Andromaca duli thai told,
And how Elynus egerly ertid the lordis
To *pursu* for the pes to the pure Grekis.
Destruction of Troy (E. E. T. S.), l. 12050.

Quod enule, "thi foote thou holde;
And *pursue* for to passe the beest."
Hymns to Virgin, etc. (E. E. T. S.), p. 62.

3. To go on; continue; proceed.

I have, *pursues* Carneades, wondered chemists should not consider, etc.
Boyle.

4. To sue; act as prosecutor; take legal steps as plaintiff or prosecutor.

And, ofyr yat, yei shul *pursu* for her Catelle in qwat cowrte yat hem liste.
English Gilds (E. E. T. S.), p. 71.

pursue†, *n.* [Early mod. E. also *persue*; < *pursue*, *v.*] Pursuit.

By the great *persue* which she there perceav'd,
Well hoped shee the beast engor'd had beene.
Spenser, F. Q., III. v. 28.

pursuement† (pėr-sū'ment), *n.* [Early mod. E. also *pursument*; < *pursue* + *-ment*.] Pursuit.

The Spachies are horsemen, weaponed for the most part at once with bow, masc, lance, harquebush, and cymiter; whereof they haue the seuerall vses, agreeing with their fights, their flights, or *pursuments*.
Sandys, Travels, p. 48. (*Davies.*)

pursuer (pėr-sū'ėr), *n.* [< ME. *pursuwer*; < *pursue* + *-er*[1].] 1. One who pursues or follows; one who chases; one who follows in haste with a view to overtake.—2†. One who follows vindictively or with enmity; a persecutor.

I first was a blasphemer and *pursuwer*.
Wyclif, 1 Tim. i. 13. (*Trench.*)

If God leave them in this hardness of heart, they may prove as desperate opposites and *pursuers* of all grace, of Christ and Christians, as the most horrible open swine, as we see in Saul and Julian.
D. Rogers, Naaman the Syrian, p. 106. (*Trench.*)

3. In *Scots law*, the plaintiff; the party who institutes and insists in an ordinary action.

pursuit (pėr-sūt'), *n.* [Early mod. E. *pursute*; < ME. *pursute*, < OF. *porsuit*, *poursuit*, m., *poursieute*, *poursiute*, *poursuite*, F. *poursuite*, a following, chase, < *porsuir*, etc., *poursuivre*, pursue: see *pursue*.] 1. The act of pursuing, or of following briskly for the purpose of overtaking; a following hastily, either for sport or in hostility; the chase, or a chasing: as, the *pursuit* of game, or of an enemy.

In his earnestness to expedite the *pursuit*, Uncas had left himself nearly alone.
J. F. Cooper, Last of Mohicans, xxxii.

The *pursuit* was kept up for some three miles beyond the point where the picket guard had been captured.
U. S. Grant, Personal Memoirs, I. 333.

2. The act of following with a view to reach, accomplish, or obtain; the endeavor to attain to or gain: as, the *pursuit* of happiness.

It ys lyke that grete labour and speciall *pursute* shall be made to the Lord Scalys that he wolle meynteyn the said Tuddenham and Heydon in all he can or may, and thus I have herd sey.
Paston Letters, I. 172.

Paris should ne'er retract what he hath done,
Nor faint in the *pursuit*.
Shak., T. and C., ii. 2. 142.

A man in *pursuit* of greatness feels no little wants.
Emerson, Conduct of Life.

3. The object of one's endeavors or continued exertions or application; that which one systematically engages in or follows as a recreation, occupation, profession, or trade, or with some similar end in view; course of occupation or employment: as, literary *pursuits*; mercantile *pursuits*.

He lived where gallantry was the capital *pursuit*.
Goldsmith, Richard Nash, Pref.

I judge of the value of human *pursuits* by their bearing upon human interests.
Huxley, Amer. Addresses, p. 142.

4. A following up or out; a carrying out; prosecution: as, the *pursuit* of a design.

Æneas and that noble reste of Troye,
In martial moodes Lucane did singe the chaunce,
End, and *pursute* of that lamented warre.
Puttenham, Partheniades, ii.

5†. Persecution.

And thei pursueth the pouere & passeth [go beyond] *pursutes*, . . .
First to brenne [burn] the bodye in a bale of fijr,
And sythen the sely soule slen [slay] & senden hyre to helle!
Piers Plowman's Crede (E. E. T. S.), l. 664.

Curve of pursuit. See *curve*.—**Fresh pursuit**, in *law*. See *fresh*. =**Syn.** 1 and 2. *Pursuit, Pursuance*. *Pursuit* is free in either physical or moral uses: as, the *pursuit* of a tiger, a profession, an ambition. *Pursuance* is not now used except in the moral sense, and then generally in the sense of following out: as, *pursuance* of his original intention; in *pursuance* of a peculiar theory. We speak of the *pursuit* of pleasure.

Say, in *pursuit* of profit or delight,
Who risk the most—that take wrong means, or right?
Pope, Essay on Man, iv. 85.

George was to depart for town the next day, to secure his commission, in *pursuance* of his generous patron's directions.
Goldsmith, Vicar, xxi.

3. *Calling, Employment*, etc. See *occupation*.

pursuivant (pėr'swi-vant), *n.* [Formerly also *poursuivant*, *pursevant*; < ME. *pursivaunt*, *purcyvaunt*, < OF. (and F.) *poursuivant*, a follower, prop. ppr. of *poursuivre*, pursue: see *pursue*. Cf. *pursuant*.] 1. A follower, attendant, or messenger; especially, one who attended the king in his wars.

In respecte of the office of Harold, *Pursuivant*, Messenger, or Interpreter, they [the Readers] always beare with patience . . . all actions, both of woord and deede, apperteining vnto his office.
Guevara, Letters (tr. by Hellowes, 1577), To the Reader.

How oft do they with golden pineons cleave
The flitting skyes, like flying *Pursuivant*,
Against fowle feendes to ayd us militant!
Spenser, F. Q., II. viii. 2.

Swift insects shine, thy hovering *pursuivants*.
Wordsworth, Sonnets, ii. 33.

2. A state messenger; an officer who executes warrants.

That great man [Dr. Goodwin] lay wind-bound in hourly suspicions that the *pursevants* would stop his voyage, and seize his person, before the wind would favour his getting away for Holland.
C. Mather, Mag. Chris., iii. 5.

One *pursuivant* who attempted to execute a warrant there was murdered.
Macaulay.

3. One of the third and lowest order of heraldic officers. There are four pursuivants belonging to the English College of Arms, named *Rouge Croix*, *Blue Mantle*, *Portcullis*, and *Rouge Dragon*. In the court of the Lyon King-of-Arms in Scotland there are three pursuivants, *Unicorn*, *Carrick*, *Bute*. In the court of the Ulster King-of-Arms in Ireland there are four pursuivants, *Athlone* and *St. Patrick* Nos. 1, 2, and 3.

The *pursevants* came next, in number more;
And like the heralds each his scutcheon bore.
Dryden, Flower and Leaf, l. 250.

pursuivant† (pėr'swi-vant), *v. t.* [< *pursuivant*, *n.*] To pursue; follow after; chase. [Rare.]

Their navy was *pursuivanted*.
Fuller.

pursument†, *n.* See *pursuement*.

pursy (pėr'si), *a.* and *n.* [Early mod. E. also *pursie*, *pursive*, *pursif*, *purcif*, *purseyf*; mod. dial. *pussy*; < ME. *pursy*, *purcy*, earlier *purcyf*, < OF. *pourcif*, var. of *poulsif*, *poussif*, F. *poussif*, short-winded, < OF. *poulser*, *pousser*, F. *pousser*, beat, pant, gasp, also push, < L. *pulsare*, beat, push: see *push*, *pulse*[1].] I. *a.* Short-winded; asthmatic; now, usually, fat and short-winded.

As in hem that haue the pirre and styffles and ben *purseyf* and thikke brethid.
Trevisa, tr. Barthol. de Proprietatibus Rerum, iii. 15 (Cath. Ang., p. 294).

When I grew somewhat *pursy*, I grew then
In men's opinions too and confidences.
Beau. and Fl., Wit at Several Weapons, i. 1.

I had a start out, and by chance set upon a fat steward, thinking his purse had been as *pursy* as his body.
Middleton (?), The Puritan, i. 4.

Slothful and *pursy*, insolent and mean,
Were every bishop, prebendary, dean.
Crabbe, Works, IV. 12.

A short *pursy* man, stooping and laboring at a bass-viol, so as to show nothing but the top of a round bald head.
Irving, Sketch-Book, p. 264.

II.† *n.* See the quotation.

Pursy is a desease in an horses bodye, and maketh hym to blow shorte, and appereth at his nosethrilles, and commeth of colde, and may be well mended.
Fitzherbert, Husbandry (Cath. Ang., p. 294).

purtenance (pėr'te-nans), *n.* [< ME. *purtenance*, *purtenaunce*, *portenaunce*, *portinaunce*; by apheresis from *appurtenance*.] Appurtenance; pertinents; belongings; the inwards or intestines of an animal: especially applied to the pluck, or the heart, liver, and lungs.

With al the *portinaunce* of purgatorye and the payne of helle.
Piers Plowman (C), iii. 108.

Kydde roste with ye heed & the *portenaunce* on lambe & pygges fete, with vinegre & percely theron.
Babees Book (E. E. T. S.), p. 275.

Roast with fire; his head with his legs, and with the *purtenance* thereof.
Ex. xii. 9.

How she can dress and dish up—lordly dish
Fit for a duke, lamb's head and *purtenance*—
With her proud hands.
Browning, Ring and Book, I. 204.

purtray†, **purtrey**†, *v.* Middle English forms of *portray*.

purulence (pū'rö-lens), *n.* [= F. *purulence* = Sp. Pg. *purulencia* = It. *purulenza*, < LL. *purulentia*, an accumulation of pus, < L. *purulentus*, full of pus, festering: see *purulent*.] The state of being purulent; the generation of pus or matter; pus, or its presence; suppuration.

purulency (pū'rö-len-si), *n.* [As *purulence* (see *-cy*).] Same as *purulence*.

purulent (pū'rö-lent), *a.* [= F. *purulent* = Sp. Pg. It. *purulento*, < L. *purulentus*, full of pus, festering, < *pus* (*pur-*), pus: see *pus*.] Consisting of pus or matter; full of, resembling, or of the nature of pus; suppurating.—**Purulent pleurisy**, empyema.

purulently (pū'rö-lent-li), *adv.* [< *purulent* + *-ly*[2].] In a purulent manner; as pus.

puruloid (pū'rö-loid), *a.* [< *puru*(*lent*) + *-oid*.] Resembling pus.

purvey (pėr-vā'), *v.* [Early mod. E. also *pourvey*; < ME. *purveyen*, *purvayen*, *purveien*, *porveyen*, < OF. *porveier*, *purveier*, *porveer*, *porveoir*, *porvoir*, *pourvoir*, F. *pourvoir* = Sp. *proveer* = Pg. *prover* = It. *provedere*, < L. *providere*, provide: see *provide*, of which *purvey* is a doublet.] I. *trans.* 1†. To foresee.

What myght I wene, and I badde swich a thoght,
But that God *purveieth* thynge that is to come.
Chaucer, Troilus, iv. 1066.

2. To provide; supply; furnish; especially (in modern use), to provide or supply provisions or other necessaries for (a number of persons).

The thinges thet byeth to comene he deth *poruay* and ordayny.
Ayenbite of Inwyt (E. E. T. S.), p. 152.

He chees hym for to wende
And come agayn right at the yeres ende
With swich answere as God wolde hym *purveye*.
Chaucer, Wife of Bath's Tale, l. 61.

Whenne yee answere or speke, yee shulle be *purveyde*
What yee shalle say.
Babees Book (E. E. T. S.), p. 3.

And the seid grevaunces shewed also here amongs the Kyng and the Lordz, it ys verrayly to thynk that they shall be *purveyed* of a remedie.
Paston Letters, I. 173.

Get thy wounds healed, *purvey* thee a better horse, and it may be I will hold it worth my while to scourge out of thee this boyish spirit of bravado.
Scott, Ivanhoe, xliv.

II. *intrans.* 1. To provide; make provision; purchase or supply provisions, especially for a number.

And as for the remenant of the assizes, he shall *purvey* to be ther by water.
Paston Letters, I. 50.

And therfore the Patron of the Galye and euery man *purueyed* to be redy as defensyble as myght be.
Sir R. Guylforde, Pylgrymage, p. 11.

The meane time that the repaires and trauerses were made with all diligence, Sir Gabriel Martiningo neuer ceased going to euery place to *puruey* for all things.
Hakluyt's Voyages, II. 86.

2. To pander: with *to*.

Their turpitude *purveys to* their malice.
Burke.

purveyance (pėr-vā'ans), *n.* [Early mod. E. also *purveyaunce*, *pourveyance*; < ME. *purveyance*, *purveiance*, *purveiaunce*, *porveance*, *porveaunce*, *purvyans*, < OF. *porveiance*, *porveance*, *pourveiance*, *purveiaunce*, etc., foresight, provision, < L. *providentia*, foresight: see *providence*, of which *purveyance* is a doublet, as *purvey* is of *provide*.] 1†. Foresight; providence.

Eterne God, that thurgh thy *purveiaunce*
Ledest the world by certein governaunce,
In ydel, as men seyn, ye no thyng make.
Chaucer, Franklin's Tale, l. 137.

Who wol do *perveaunce* in worldes longe
The palmes forto sette he must have mynde,
Palladius, Husbondrie (E. E. T. S.), p. 198.

2. The act of purveying, providing, furnishing, or procuring; supply; specifically, the procuring of provisions or victuals for a number of persons.

> The *purueaunce* therof lith you vppon,
> Auaunce you now, for hys loue in trinite,
> So that thys contre well purueyed be.
> *Rom. of Partenay* (E. E. T. S.), l. 2376.

The Commons have their Commodities daily taken from them for the *Purveyance* of the King's Houshold, for which they are not paid. *Baker*, Chronicles, p. 190.

3. That which is purveyed or prepared, as provision, supplies, etc.

> Philip for that may mad *purueiance* redy,
> With folk of gode aray to Douer com in hy.
> *Rob. of Brunne*, p. 307.

Therfore alle the *purveyance* that he hadde ordeyned to make the Temple with, he toke it Salomon his Sone; and he made it. *Mandeville*, Travels, p. 87.

> Of vitaille and of other *purveiaunce*.
> *Chaucer*, Franklin's Tale, l. 176.

> And ofter to his Pallace he them bringes, . . .
> Whence, mounting up, they fynd *purveyaunce* meet
> Of all that royall Princes court became.
> *Spenser*, F. Q., I. xii. 13.

4†. Preparation.

Folks ben rytȝ sore afred that they wel don moche harm this somer, but if ther be made rytȝ grett *pureyans* aȝens hem. *Paston Letters*, I. 116.

5. In *law*, the royal prerogative or right of preemption, by which the king was privileged to buy provisions and necessaries for the use of his household at an appraised value, in preference to all his subjects, and even without the consent of the owner; also, the right of impressing horses and carriages and the enforcement of personal labor, etc., for the use of the sovereign—a right abolished by the statute 12 Charles II., c. 24.

The treasurer, . . . by the exercise of the right of *purveyance*, . . . drew down popular hatred on the cause which was reduced to such expedients. *Stubbs*, Const. Hist., § 353.

purveyor (pėr-vā'ọr), *n.* [Early mod. E. also *pourveyor*; ‹ ME. *purveour*, ‹ OF. *porveor*, *porveour*, *purveour*, *pourveur*, F. *pourvoyeur* (= Sp. *proveedor* = Pg. *provedor* = It. *provveditore*), a provider, purveyor, ‹ *porveir*, etc., purvey: see *purvey*. Cf. *proveditor*, *provedor*.] 1. One who purveys or provides; specifically, one who purveys victuals, or whose business it is to make provision for the table; one who supplies eatables for a number of persons; a caterer.

Our *purveyors* are herein said to have their provision from the popish shambles. *Hooker*, Eccles. Polity, viii. 4.

> I love the sea; she is my fellow-creature,
> My careful *purveyor*; she provides me store.
> *Quarles*, Emblems, v. 6.

2. An officer who formerly provided or exacted provision for the king's household.

The statute of Edward III. was ordered to be enforced on the royal *purveyors*. *Stubbs*, Const. Hist., § 340.

3. One who provides the means of gratifying lust; a procurer or procuress; a pimp; a bawd.

This stranger, ravished at his good fortune, is introduced to some imaginary title; for this *purveyor* has her representatives of some of the finest ladies. *Addison*.

purview (pėr'vū), *n.* [‹ OF. *pourvieu*, purview, ‹ *pourveu*, F. *pourvu*, provided, pp. of *pourvoir*, provide, purvey: see *purvey*.] 1. A condition, provision, or disposition; in *law*, that part of a statute which begins with the words "Be it enacted," as distinguished from the preamble, and hence the whole body of provisions.—2. Field, scope, sphere, or limits of anything, as of a law, authority, etc.: as, the *purview* of science; facts that come under the *purview* of consciousness.

If any fair or market have been kept in any church-yard, these are profanations within the *purview* of several statutes; and those you are to present.
Bacon, Charge upon the Commission for the Verge.

The phenomena he describes fortunately fall within the *purview* of the association over whose deliberations you preside. *Science*, VII. 166.

All nations of all past ages have confessedly founded their states upon their religions. This is true of Egypt, Greece, and Rome, of China, Japan, and all else within the *purview* of history.
A. A. Hodge, in New Princeton Rev, III. 37.

It is only by becoming familiar with forms so utterly dissimilar from those we have hitherto been conversant with, that we perceive how narrow is the *purview* that is content with one form or one passing fashion.
J. Fergusson, Hist. Indian Arch., p. 404.

pus (pus), *n.* [= F. Sp. Pg. It. *pus*, ‹ L. *pus* (*pur-*) = Gr. πύον = Skt. *pûya*, matter, pus, ‹ √ *pu* (Skt. √ *puy*) in L. *putere*, stink. From L. *pus* are also ult. *purulent*, *suppurate*, etc.; and from the same root are *puant*, *putid*, *putrid*; etc.] An inflammatory exudation composed of modified white blood-cells (pus-corpuscles), with more or less of the debris and of the proliferating cells of the solid tissues of the part, and a liquid plasma. The formation of pus is called *suppuration*. A collection of pus within the solid tissues is called an *abscess*. A suppurating open sore is an *ulcer*.—**Ichorous pus.** Same as *ichor*.—**Laudable pus**, thick, creamy pus such as may be formed in the progressing repair of wounds.—**Pus-cells** or **-corpuscles**, the leucocytes of pus.—**Pus-disease**, pyemia.—**Sanious pus**, a somewhat thin, often ill-smelling, greenish or reddish pus, as discharged from an ill-conditioned ulcer.

pusant†, **pusane†**, *n.* Same as *pisan*².

Puseyism (pū'zi-izm), *n.* [‹ *Pusey* (see def.) + *-ism*.] The principles and teachings characteristic of a High-church party in the Church of England, originating in Oxford University in the early part of the nineteenth century: so called from one of the leaders in this so-called Oxford movement, Dr. E. B. Pusey, professor of Hebrew in the university. See *Tractarianism*, *ritualism*.

Ecclesiastical sentiment, which, in a morbidly exaggerated condition, forms one of the principal elements of *Puseyism*. *Ruskin*, Elements of Drawing, iii., note.

Puseyistic (pū-zi-is'tik), *a.* [‹ *Puseyist* + *-ic*.] Of or pertaining to Puseyism or Tractarianism.

Puseyistical (pū-zi-is'ti-kal), *a.* [‹ *Puseyistic* + *-al*.] Same as *Puseyistic*.

Puseyite (pū'zi-īt), *n.* [‹ *Pusey* (see *Puseyism*) + *-ite*².] An adherent of the Oxford movement as advocated by Pusey (see *Puseyism*); hence, a ritualist.

Puseyites and ritualists, aiming to reinforce ecclesiasticism, betray a decided leaning towards archaic print as well as archaic ornaments.
H. Spencer, Study of Sociol., p. 107.

When I go into a house where there is a pretty engraving of surpliced choristers, with an inscription in red letters underneath—probably a scrap of Latin—I know that the master of the house, or its mistress, is a *Puseyite*.
P. G. Hamerton, Thoughts about Art, ix.

push[1] (push), *v.* [Early mod. E. also *posse*; ‹ ME. *pussen*, *possen*, ‹ OF. *pousser*, *poulser*, F. *pousser* = Pr. *pulsar* = Sp. Pg. *pulsar* = It. *pulsare*, ‹ L. *pulsare*, strike, beat, drive, push, freq. of *pellere*, pp. *pulsus*, strike, drive, push: see *pulse*[1].] **I.** *trans.* 1. To strike with a thrusting motion; thrust, as with a sword; thrust or gore, as with the horns.

If the ox shall *push* a manservant or maidservant, . . . the ox shall be stoned. Ex. xxi. 32.

2. To thrust forcibly against for the purpose of moving or impelling in a direction other than that from which the pressure is applied; exert a thrusting, driving, or impelling pressure upon; drive or impel by pressure; shove: opposed to *draw*: as, to *push* a hand-cart; to *push* a thing up, down, away, etc.

> The see by nyghte as any torche brende
> For wode, and *posseth* hym now up now doun.
> *Chaucer*, Good Women, l. 2420.

Push him out of doors. *Shak.*, As you Like it, iii. 1. 15.

> Waters forcing way
> Sidelong had *push'd* a mountain from his seat.
> *Milton*, P. L., vi. 197.

They walked out, or drove out, or were *pushed* about in bath-chairs. *Dickens*, Pickwick, xxxvi.

3. To impel in general; drive; urge.

We are solicited so powerfully by evil objects without, and *pushed* on so violently by evil inclinations within, that it is impossible but that both these should now and then prevail. *Bp. Atterbury*, Sermons, II. iv.

4. To press or urge; advance or extend by persistent or diligent effort or exertion: as, to *push* on a work.

He had a true British determination to *push* his way in the world. *George Eliot*, Mill on the Floss, ii. 1.

I had intended to *push* my excursion further, but, not being quite well, I was compelled to return.
Darwin, Voyage of Beagle, I. 171.

To say at the end of the second year of the war the line dividing the contestants at the East was *pushed* north of Maryland . . . would have been discouraging indeed.
U. S. Grant, Personal Memoirs, I. 406.

5. To prosecute or carry on with energy or enterprise; use every means to extend and advance: as, to *push* one's business; to *push* the sale of a commodity.

We may *push* the commerce, but the *pushing* must be done in South America, not in Washington.
The Century, XL. 318.

6. To press hard.

We are *pushed* for an answer. *Swift*.

=**Syn.** 1. To hustle, jostle, elbow, crowd, force. See *thrust*.

II. *intrans.* 1. To thrust, as with the horns or with a sword; hence, to make an attack.

At the time of the end shall the king of the south *push* at him. Dan. xi. 40.

> None shall dare
> With shortened sword to stab in closer war, . . .
> Nor *push* with biting point.
> *Dryden*, Pal. and Arc., iii. 511.

2. To exercise or put forth a thrusting or impelling pressure; use steady force in moving something in a direction the opposite of that implied in the word *draw*: as, to *push* with all one's might.—3. To advance or proceed with persistence or unflagging effort; force one's way; press eagerly or persistently; hasten; usually with *on*, *forward*, etc.: as, to *push on* at a rapid pace.

> The se bigan to *posse*
> Riȝt in to Westernesse.
> Hi strike seil and maste
> And ankere gunne caste.
> *King Horn* (E. E. T. S.), l. 1011.

Deserted, surrounded, outnumbered, and with everything at stake, he [Clive] did not even deign to stand on the defensive, but *pushed* boldly *forward* to the attack.
Macaulay, Lord Clive.

4. To sit abaft an oar and propel a boat with forward strokes: as, to *push* down a stream.

push[1] (push), *n.* [Early mod. E. also *poushe*; ‹ *push*[1], *v.* In sense 6 the word is appar. the same (an 'eruption'); it cannot be, as some suggest, connected with *pustule*, or with F. *poche*, a pocket.] 1. A thrust; the exercise of a driving or impelling thrust; the application of pressure intended to overturn or set in motion in the direction in which the force or pressure is applied; a shove: as, to give a thing or a person a *push*.

> Yet so great was the puissance of his *push*
> That from his sadle quite he did him beare.
> *Spenser*, F. Q., I. iii. 35.

Notwithstanding, with an incredible courage they advanced to the *push* of the Pike with the defendants.
Capt. John Smith, True Travels, I. 19.

> I'm pleased with my own work; Jove was not more
> With infant nature, when his spacious hand
> Had rounded this huge ball of earth and seas
> To give it the first *push*, and see it roll
> Along the vast abyss. *Dryden*, Cleomenes, i. 1.

2. An assault or attack; a forcible onset; a vigorous effort; a stroke; a blow.

Through the prowesse of our owne souldiours practysed in former conflicts, they were not able to abyde one *pushe* of us, but by and by tourned their backs.
Golding, tr. of Cæsar, fol. 78.

Here might you see the strong walls shaking and falling with the *pushes* of the yron ramme.
Purchas, Pilgrimage, p. 156.

Exact reformation is not perfected at the first *push*.
Milton, Reformation in Eng., i.

3. An emergency; a trial; an extremity.

> This honest chambermaid,
> That help'd all at a *push*.
> *Middleton*, Chaste Maid, v. 4.

'Tis common to talk of dying for a friend, but when it comes to the *push*, it is no more than talk.
Sir R. L'Estrange.

4. Persevering energy; enterprise. [Colloq.]

Bysshe Shelley was a gentleman of the old school, with a dash of New World cleverness, *push*, and mammon-worship. *E. Dowden*, Shelley, I. 2.

Where every one recognizes that it is either money or *push* which secured the place that should have been awarded to merit. *The Century*, XXXVIII. 156.

5. A button, pin, or similar contrivance to be pushed in conveying pressure: as, the electric bell-*push*.

The spring *push*, which was secured higher up on the door, was too much of a toy affair, and could be tampered with by patients so inclined. *Sci. Amer.*, N. S., LX. 313.

6. A pustule; a pimple. [Obs. or prov. Eng.]

Some tyme blacke *poushes* or boyles, with inflammation and moch peyne. *Sir T. Elyot*, Castle of Health, iii. 7.

It was a proverb amongst the Grecians, that "He that was praised to his hurt should have a *push* rise upon his nose." *Bacon*, Praise (ed. 1887).

Push of an arch. Same as *thrust of an arch* (which see, under *thrust*).

push[2]† (push), *interj.* Same as *pish*.

> *Push!* I take 't, unkindly, i' faith.
> *Middleton*, Your Five Gallants, ii. 1.

push-a-pike† (push'a-pik), *n.* An old game.

> Since only those at kick and cuff
> Are beat that cry they have enough;
> But when at *push a pike* we play
> With beauty, who shall win the day?
> *Hudibras Redivivus* (1707). (*Nares.*)

push-button (push'but"n), *n.* See *button*, 4 (*c*).

push-car (push'kär), *n.* 1. A light four-wheeled platform-car used on railways by track-repairers in moving tools and materials.—2. A car used at a ferry-slip to connect an engine with a train on a ferry-boat. [U. S.]

pusher (push'ėr), *n.* 1. One who or that which pushes; one who drives forward.—2. In *mech.*, a stem or rod, usually with a button on the outer end, by which, from the outside of an inclosed space, some movement or result is accomplished within the space by pressing upon the button or outer extremity of the rod to push it toward the interior: as, the *pusher* of an electric signal or a system of electric bells, whereby an electric circuit is completed or broken.—3. One of the levers of a type-setting machine, which, when touched on the keyboard, dislodges and pushes out a type.

push-hoe (pu̇sh'hō), *n.* See *hoe*[1].

push-hole (pu̇sh'hōl), *n.* In *glass-making*, a hole in a flattening furnace for annealing and flattening plate-glass. *E. H. Knight.*

pushing (pu̇sh'ing), *p. a.* [Ppr. of *push*[1], *v.*] Pressing forward in business; putting one's self forward; self-assertive.

An intriguing, *pushing* Irishman named White.
Macaulay, Hist. Eng., vi.

pushing-jack (pu̇sh'ing-jak), *n.* An implement for moving a large and heavy object, such as a railroad-car, for a short distance. In one form it is a toggle-bar, one end of which is put against a tie, and the other against the car, which is moved by the action of the lever.

pushingly (pu̇sh'ing-li), *adv.* In a pushing, vigorous, energetic manner.

pushm, *n.* [Pers. Hind. *pashm*, wool, fur, hair, down.] Same as *pashm*.

pushmina (push-mē'nạ̈), *n.* [Pers. Hind. *pashmina*, woolen cloth.] Woolen cloth: used attributively: as, a *pushmina* shawl. The word is applied to true Cashmere shawls of fine quality, as distinguished from imitations or inferior manufactures. Also *pashmina*.

push-pick (pu̇sh'pik), *n.* A tool with a short handle and a heart-shaped blade, used in military mining for loosening the earth behind the cases of galleries preparatory to inserting new cases. See cut under *pick*[1].

push-pin (pu̇sh'pin), *n.* [< *push*[1], *v.*, + obj. *pin*[1].] A children's play in which pins are pushed alternately. Also *put-pin*.

Lol. Once more and you shall go play, Tony.
Ant. Ay, play at *push-pin*, cousin.
Middleton and Rowley, Changeling, i. 2.

Push-pin is a very silly sport, being nothing more than simply pushing one pin across another.
Strutt, Sports and Pastimes, p. 506.

pushti (push'ti), *n.* [Pers. *pushti*, a support (for the back), cf. *pushta*, a bundle, load, hillock, < *pusht*, the back.] A square of material, often embroidered silk, used in Persia and the East to cover the wall where a sofa touches it, so that a person seated leans against it.

Pushtu, Pushtoo (push'tö), *n.* [Also *Pushto*, *Pashto*; Afghan.] The language of the Afghans: it belongs to the Iranian group of the Indo-European languages.

pusil† (pū'sil), *a.* [= It. *pusillo*, < L. *pusillus*, very little, petty, insignificant, dim. of *pusus*, a boy, a little boy; cf. *pupus*, a boy, *puer*, boy, child: see *pupil*[1].] Very little. *Bacon.*

pusillanimity (pū"si-la-nim'i-ti), *n.* [< F. *pusillanimité* = Pr. *pusillanimitat* = Sp. *pusilanimidad* = Pg. *pusillanimidade* = It. *pusillanimità*, < LL. *pusillanimita(t-)s*, faint-heartedness, < *pusillanimis*, faint-hearted, timid: see *pusillanimous*.] The state or condition of being pusillanimous; lack of that spirit which constitutes courage or fortitude; cowardliness; timidity.

The liver white and pale, which is the badge of *pusillanimity* and cowardice. *Shak.*, 2 Hen. IV., iv. 3. 114.

There may be a *pusillanimity* even towards God; a man may over-clog his own conscience, and belie himself in his confessions, out of a distempered jealousy.
Donne, Sermons, xi.

=**Syn.** Poltroonery. See *coward*, *n.*

pusillanimous (pū-si-lan'i-mus), *a.* [= F. *pusillanime* = Sp. *pusilánime* = Pg. *pusillanime* = It. *pusillanime*, *pusillanimo*, < LL. *pusillanimis*, faint-hearted, timid, < L. *pusillus*, very little, + *animus*, mind, heart: see *pusil* and *animus*.] 1. Lacking strength and firmness of mind; wanting in courage and fortitude; being of weak courage; faint-hearted; mean-spirited; cowardly.

The dangers which he avoided with a caution almost *pusillanimous* never confused his perceptions.
Macaulay, Machiavelli.

Pow'r usurp'd
Is weakness when oppos'd; conscious of wrong,
'Tis *pusillanimous* and prone to flight.
Cowper, Task, v. 373.

He was a man of incurably commonplace intellect, and of no character but a hollow, blustery, *pusillanimous*, and unsound one. *Carlyle*, Sterling, iii. 5.

2. Proceeding from lack of courage; indicating timidity.

An argument fit for great and mighty princes, . . . that, neither, by over-measuring their forces, they lose themselves in vain enterprises; nor, on the other side, by undervaluing them, descend to fearful and *pusillanimous* counsels.
Bacon, True Greatness of Kingdoms and Estates (ed. 1887).

He is slow and full of Wariness, and not without a Mixture of Fear: I do not mean a *pusillanimous*, but politic Fear. *Howell*, Letters, I. i. 10.

=**Syn. 1.** *Poltroon*, *Dastard*, etc. See *coward*.—1 and 2. Weak, feeble, timorous, spiritless, effeminate, dastardly.

pusillanimously (pū-si-lan'i-mus-li), *adv.* In a pusillanimous manner; mean-spiritedly; with want of courage.

The rebels, *pusillanimously* opposing that new torrent of destruction, gaze awhile. *Sir T. Herbert*, Travels, p. 86.

pusillanimousness (pū-si-lan'i-mus-nes), *n.* Pusillanimous character; pusillanimity.

pusio, *n.*; pl. *pusiones*. Same as *pisan*[2].

pusley (pus'li), *n.* See *pussly*.

puson†, *n.* and *v.* A late Middle English form of *poison*. *Cath. Ang.*, p. 295.

puss (pu̇s), *n.* [= D. *poes* = LG. *pus*, *bus* (in comp. *puskatte*) = Dan. *pus* = Sw. dial. *pus* = Norw. *puse*, a cat, = Ir. *pus*, a cat, = Gael. *puis*, Ir. dim. *puisin*, a kitten; similar forms are found in some remote tongues, and the word is supposed to have been orig. imitative, perhaps of the noise made by the cat when "spitting." Cf. Hind. *fish*, *fish*, popularly *phis*, *phis*, 'puss! puss!' used in calling a cat.] 1. A cat; a pussy or pussy-cat.

Thus Dorset, purring like a thoughtful cat,
Married, but wiser *puss* ne'er thought of that.
Dryden, Essay upon Satire, l. 179.

2. A hare or rabbit.

Thou shalt not give *Puss* a hint to steal away — we must catch her in her form. *Scott*, Kenilworth, xxix.

3. A puss-moth.—4. A pet name for a child or young woman.

Gone! what a pox had I just run her down, and is the little *puss* stole away at last? *Colman*, Jealous Wife, ii. 3.

The little *puss* seems already to have airs enough to make a husband as miserable as it's a law of nature for a quiet man to be when he marries a beauty.
George Eliot, Adam Bede, ix.

Puss-in-the-corner, a children's game. "A certain number of boys or girls stand singly at different distances; suppose we say for instance one at each of the four corners of a room, a fifth is then placed in the middle; the business of those who occupy the corners is to keep changing their positions in a regular succession, and of the outplayer to gain one of the corners vacated by the change before the successor can reach it; if done, he retains it, and the loser takes his place in the middle." (*Strutt*, Sports and Pastimes, p. 488.)

puss-clover (pu̇s'klō"vėr), *n.* The rabbit's-foot or stone-clover, *Trifolium arvense*: so named from its silky heads.

pussel (pus'el), *n.* The large scallop, *Pecten magellanicus*. [Local, Labrador.]

puss-gentleman (pu̇s'jen"tl-man), *n.* An effeminate dandy. [Rare.]

A fine *puss-gentleman* that's all perfume.
Cowper, Conversation, l. 284.

pussly (pus'li), *n.* A corruption of *purslane*. Also written *pusley*. [U. S.]

When asked to select the most offensive among the worst weeds, the task becomes an exceedingly difficult one. Among the annuals, especially in gardens, the purslane or *pusley* perhaps takes the lead.
Amer. Nat., XXII. 778.

puss-moth (pu̇s'mōth), *n.* A moth of the genus *Cerura*. *C.* (or *Dicranura*) *vinula* is a handsome large-bodied bombycid moth of Europe, of a whitish color with black spots. The larva, which feeds on poplars and willows, is blackish when young, pale-green when full-grown, and provided with two long anal projections; it ejects an acrid fluid when irritated. See cut under *Cerura*.

pusstail (pu̇s'tāl), *n.* A common grass of the genus *Setaria*: so called on account of the bristly cylindrical spikes. More often called *foxtail*.

pussy[1] (pu̇s'i), *n.*; pl. *pussies* (-iz). [< *puss* + dim. *-y*.] A diminutive of *puss*.

pussy[2] (pus'i), *a.* [< *pus*[1] + *-y*[1].] Filled with pus.

The most *pussy* gland ruptured during extrication.
Med. News, LIII. 695.

pussy[3] (pus'i), *a.* A dialectal form of *pursy*.

pussy-cat (pu̇s'i-kat), *n.* [= LG. *pusekatte*; < *pussy*[1] + *cat*[1].] 1. A puss or cat.—2. The silky catkin of various willows, in England chiefly of *Salix Caprea*, the common sallow. Also applied to the catkins of *Populus alba*.

pussy-willow (pu̇s'i-wil"ō), *n.* A common American willow, *Salix discolor*, producing in earliest spring catkins that are very silky when young. It is a shrub or small tree with glaucous leaves, growing in moist ground. The name is also applied to other willows whose young catkins are silvery. Sometimes called *glaucous willow*, and *swamp-willow*.

In his dreams he hunts for *pussy-willows*, as he did when a boy. *Harper's Mag.*, LXXVII. 924.

pustular (pus'tū-lär), *a.* [< *pustule* + *-ar*[3].] 1. Of the nature of a pustule; proceeding from pustules, or characterized by their presence: as, a *pustular* disease.—2. In *bot.* and *zoöl.*, having low elevations like blisters. Also *pustulate*, *pustulose*.

pustulate (pus'tū-lāt), *v. i.*; pret. and pp. *pustulated*, ppr. *pustulating*. [< L. *pustulatus*, pp. of *pustulare*, blister, < *pustula*, a blister, pimple: see *pustule*.] To form pustules.

The blanes [of Job] *pustulated* to afflict his body.
Stackhouse, Hist. Bible, I. 364.

pustulate (pus'tū-lāt), *a.* [< L. *pustulatus*, pp.: see the verb.] 1. In *bot.*, same as *pustular*, 2. —2. In *entom.*, covered with small spots, or with slight rounded elevations less distinct and regular than those of a granulated surface.

pustulation (pus-tū-lā'shon), *n.* [< LL. *pustulatio(n-)*, a breaking out into pustules, < L. *pustulare*, pp. *pustulatus*, blister: see *pustulate*.] The formation or breaking out of pustules.

pustulatous (pus'tū-lā-tus), *a.* [< *pustulate* + *-ous*.] Pustulate.—**Pustulatous moss**, a commercial name of certain lichens of the genera *Lecanora* and *Parmelia*, used in the preparation of archil. *Lindsay*, British Lichens.

pustule (pus'tūl), *n.* [= F. *pustule* = Sp. *pústula* = Pg. *pustula* = It. *pustula*, *pustola*, < L. *pustula*, a blister, pimple, pustule; cf. *pusula*, a bubble, blister, pimple; perhaps akin to Gr. φυσαλίς, φυσαλλίς, a bladder: see *physalis*.] 1. In *med.*, a small inflammatory tumor containing pus; a small pimple containing pus.—2. In *bot.*, a slight elevation like a pimple or little blister.—3. In *zoöl.*: (*a*) A small rounded elevation of surface, like a blister; a papule or pimple. (*b*) A spot of color larger than a dot, and suggestive of a blister.—**Malignant pustule**, a pustule forming the initial lesion of anthrax. See *malignant anthrax*, under *anthrax*.—**Pustules of the sea**, a sailors' name of sessile barnacles or acorn-shells. Also called *sea-thorns*.

pustuliform (pus'tū-li-fôrm), *a.* [< L. *pustula*, a blister, pustule, + *forma*, form.] In *bot.* and *zoöl.*, having the form of a pustule.

pustulocrustaceous (pus"tū-lō-krus-tā'shius), *a.* [< L. *pustula*, a blister, pustule, + *crusta*, crust: see *crustaceous*.] Pertaining to pustules which, discharging, form more or less extensive crusts; having or characterized by such pustules.

pustulose (pus'tū-lōs), *a.* [< L. *pustulosus*: see *pustulous*.] In *bot.*, same as *pustular*, 2.

pustulous (pus'tū-lus), *a.* [= F. *pustuleux* = Pr. *pustulos* = Pg. *pustuloso*, < L. *pustulosus*, full of pustules, < *pustula*, a blister, pustule: see *pustule*.] Full of or covered with pustules; resembling a pustule or pustules; pustular.

put[1] (pu̇t), *v.*; pret. and pp. *put*, ppr. *putting*. [Formerly also *putt* (dial. *pit*); < ME. *putten*, *puten*, a secondary form or variant of *poten*, < AS. *potian*, push, thrust; cf. Dan. *putte* (< E. ?), put; prob. of Celtic origin: < W. *pwtio* = Corn. *poot* = Gael. *put*, push, thrust. Cf. *pote*.] I. *trans.* 1. To push; thrust: literally or figuratively.

Ther as the mene peple were fledde in to caves for socour, thei *putt* in fier, and brent hem ther-ynne.
Merlin (E. E. T. S.), ii. 236.

Seem you but sorry for what you haue done,
And straight shele *put* the finger in the eye,
With comfort now, since it cannot be helpt.
Heywood, 1 Edw. IV. (Works, ed. Pearson, 1874, I. 5).

2. To cast; throw; particularly, to throw with an upward and forward motion of the arm: as, to *put* the stone; to *put* the shot. Compare *putt*. [In this sense pronounced put in Scotland.]

In the square are wooden benches for looking on at the tossing of the caber, *putting* the stone, and other Highland games. *W. Black*, In Far Lochaber, ii.

The sports will include a 100-yard dash, running broad jump, 220-yard hurdle (low), *putting* sixteen-pound shot, running high jump, and a one-mile run.
New York Tribune, May 11, 1890.

3. To drive; impel; force, either literally or figuratively; hence, to oblige; constrain; compel.

A-bove alle other was Sir Gawein comended, ffor thourgh his prowesse thei were *putte* bakke and chaced to the town. *Merlin* (E. E. T. S.), iii. 460.

Rashly I thought her false, and *put* her from me.
Fletcher, Loyal Subject, v. 2.

Shee *put* him soone after to his choyce, whether he would enioy what he had seene, and the Kingdome for dowrie, without other ioynture then Candaules blood, or would there himselfe be slaine. *Purchas*, Pilgrimage, p. 330.

He espied two ships more riding by them, *put* in by the storm. *Capt. John Smith*, True Travels, I. 5.

That trick
Was well *put* home.
B. Jonson, Sejanus, ii. 2.

They all agreed to censure him, and *put* him from that employment. *Winthrop*, Hist. New England, I. 375.

I shall be *put* unwillingly to molest the publick View with the vindication of a private name.
Milton, Apology for Smectymnuus.

4. To place, set, lay, deposit, bring, or cause to be in any position, place, or situation.

Sume *putten* Wax in Oyle of the Wode of the fruyt of Bawme, and seyn that it is Bawme.
Mandeville, Travels, p. 51.

Caduce if that the fruyte be, cleef the roote,
And *putte* in hit a stoone.
Palladius, Husbondrie (E. E. T. S.), p. 92.

And the Lord God planted a garden eastward in Eden; and there he *put* the man whom he had formed.
Gen. ii. 8.

You *put* sharp weapons in a madman's hands.
Shak., 2 Hen. VI., iii. 1. 347.

The aquavitæ was *put* aboard by my brother Peter's order, without my appointment.
Winthrop, Hist. New England, I. 467.

I went to the Sheik's house, and carried the letter I had from the Sheik of Furshout. When he knew who it was from, he kiss'd the letter and *put* it to his forehead, which is a mark of great respect.
Pococke, Description of the East, I. 113.

But sit beside my bed, mother, and *put* your hand in mine.
Tennyson, May Queen, Conclusion.

5. To set in some particular way or course; instigate; urge; incite; entice.

If your Majesty be not Popish, as you professe, and I am very willing to beleeve, why doe you *put* the Parliament to resume the Sacrament of the Altar?
N. Ward, Simple Cobler, p. 59.

It might have *put* him upon some dangerous design of surprising our ships.
Winthrop, Hist. New England, II. 135.

6. To cause, or cause to be; bring or place in some specified state or condition: as, to *put* one in mind; to *put* to shame; to *put* to death; to *put* one out of pain; to *put* in motion; to *put* in order; to *put* to inconvenience.

It is playnly your purpos to *put* you to dethe,
With suche fyndes to fight till ye fay worthe.
Destruction of Troy (E. E. T. S.), l. 597.

Put me in a surety with thee.
Job xvii. 3.

But as we were allowed of God to be *put* in trust with the gospel, even so we speak.
1 Thes. ii. 4.

This question ask'd
Puts me in doubt.
Milton, P. L., iv. 888.

This last Storm *put* our Men quite out of heart.
Dampier, Voyages, I. 439.

Recently, he had been a public lecturer on Mesmerism, for which science (as he assured Phœbe, and, indeed, satisfactorily proved by *putting* Chanticleer, who happened to be scratching near by, to sleep) he had very remarkable endowments.
Hawthorne, Seven Gables, xii.

"Yes, sir," murmured Polly, *put* to blush by the apparition.
Harper's Mag., LXXIX. 929.

7. To assign; set, as to a task or the doing of something: as, to *put* men to work.

And for my curtesie I was *put* to the Soudenys house & was made vssher of halle.
Political Poems, etc. (ed. Furnivall), p. 13.

The women, as the weaker sort, be *put* to the easier crafts: as to work wool and flax.
Sir T. More, Utopia (tr. by Robinson), ii. 4.

It was not till the yeare 1628 that I was *put* to learne my Latine rudiments, and to write of one Citolin, a Frenchman, in Lewes.
Evelyn, Diary, p. 8.

8. To set or propose for consideration, deliberation, judgment, reply, acceptance, or rejection; propound; propose; offer; state as a hypothesis or proposition: as, to *put* a case (see phrases below); to *put* a question; to *put* it to one to say.

I *put* it to the common sense of all of you . . . whether any great body of the conquered people could have lived on in their former dwelling-places through such a conquest as this.
E. A. Freeman, Amer. Lects., p. 131.

The questions which the Indians *put* betray their reason and their ignorance.
Emerson, Hist. Discourse at Concord.

9. To state; express; phrase.

Stupidly *put*! Inane is the response.
Browning, Ring and Book, II. 69.

A thought 's his who kindles new youth in it,
Or so *puts* it as makes it more true.
Lowell, Franciscus de Verulamio.

The old Hydrous appears as a Greek colony, placed, as one of the old geographers happily *puts* it, on the mouth either of the Hadriatic or of the Ionian sea.
E. A. Freeman, Venice, p. 313.

10. To render; do; turn; translate.

I have *put* this Boke out of Latyn into Frensche, and translated it azen out of Frensche into Englyssche.
Mandeville, Travels, p. 5.

So did euery scholer & secular clerke or versifier, when he wrote any short poeme or matter of good lesson, *put* it in ryme.
Puttenham, Arte of Eng. Poesie, p. 10.

11†. To posit; affirm.

The true faith *putteth* the resurrection, which we be warned to look for every hour. The heathen philosophers, denying that, did *put* that the souls did ever live.
Tyndale, Ans. to Sir T. More, etc. (Parker Soc., 1850), p. 180.

12. To apply; use.

And the comoun Peple, that wolde *putte* here Bodyes and here Catelle for to conquere oure Heritage, thei may not don it withouten the Lordes.
Mandeville, Travels, p. 3.

The Mayor, &c. [of Bristol], approve the ordinances [of fullers], and *put* thereto the Common Seal of the City, in September, 1406.
English Gilds (E. E. T. S.), p. 286.

The great difference in the notions of mankind is from the different use they *put* their faculties to.
Locke.

In truth it is rare for me to *put* pen to paper for private correspondence, so much is my time and attention engrossed by public business.
George Washington, To Col. Sam'l Washington, quoted [in N. A. Rev., CXLIII. 482.

13†. To lay down; give up; surrender.

No man hath more loue than this, that a man *putte* his lyf for hise frendis.
Wyclif, John xv. 13.

Put it in assay†. See *assay*.—**Put the case**, elliptically **put case**, suppose the case to be; suppose.

But *put the case*, in travel I may meet
Some gorgeous structure, a brave frontispiece,
Shall I stay captive in the outer court?
B. Jonson, New Inn, iii. 2.

Put case our author should, once more,
Swear that his play were good.
B. Jonson, Poetaster, Ind.

Put the case, I was a gentleman (which, thank God, no one can say of me); well—my honour makes me quarrel with another gentleman of my acquaintance.
Sheridan, The Rivals, iv. 1.

To **be put to it**, to be hard pressed or tried; be driven to extremities; be embarrassed; be hampered.

Others of them were worse *put to it*, wher they were faine to eate doggs, toads, and dead men, and so dyed almost all.
Bradford, Plymouth Plantation, p. 137.

The pathway was here also exceeding narrow, and therefore good Christian *was* the more *put to it*; for when he sought in the dark to shun the ditch on the one hand, he was ready to tip over into the mire on the other.
Bunyan, Pilgrim's Progress, p. 132.

To be put to one's trumps, to be driven to one's resources or endeavor.—To **put a bone in any one's hood†**. See *bone*1.—To **put about**. (*a*) *Naut.*, to reverse the course of. (*b*) To put to inconvenience, trouble, annoyance, bewilderment, or embarrassment: as, he was much *put about* by that occurrence.

"Nay," pleaded Jeremiah. "Thee art sorry for what thee said; thee were sore *put about*, or thee wouldn't have said it."
Mrs. Gaskell, Sylvia's Lovers, xxxvi.

(*c*) To publish; declare; circulate. [Colloq.]

Put it *about* in the right quarter that you'll buy queer bills by the lump.
Dickens, Our Mutual Friend, ii. 5.

To put all one's eggs into one basket, a nail in one's coffin, an ape in one's hood†. See *egg*1, *coffin*, *ape*.—To **put an end to.** See *end*.—**To put a stop to.** See *stop*.—**To put away.** (*a*†) To drive away; remove; expel.

This oyle, that is to seie quinta essencia of gold, hath the mooste swetnes and Vertu to a-swage and *putte awei* the ache of woundis.
Book of Quinte Essence (ed. Furnivall), p. 10.

Henry the Fifth *put away* the Friars, Aliens, and seiz'd to himself 100,000*l.* a year.
Selden, Table-Talk, p. 18.

(*b*) To renounce; discard.

Put away the gods which your fathers served.
Josh. xxiv. 14.

(c) To divorce.

Is it lawful for a man to *put away* his wife? . . . Moses suffered to write a bill of divorcement, and to *put* her *away*.
Mark x. 2, 4.

(*d*†) To dispose of.

He took two skins and a half, . . . which he carried to Mr. Cutting's ship, and *put* it *away* there for twenty-four shillings.
Winthrop, Hist. New England, II. 426.

By reason some Hollanders, and others, had bin there lately before him, who carried away with them all the Tobacco, he was forced to *put away* all his commodities upon trust till the next crop.
Quoted in *Capt. John Smith's* Works, II. 271.

To put back. (*a*) To hinder; delay. (*b*) To restore to the original place. (*c*) To set, as the hands of a clock, to an earlier time. (*d*) To refuse; say nay to.

Coming from thee, I could not *put* him *back*.
Shak., Lucrece, l. 843.

To **put by.** (*a*) To turn away; divert.

Watch and resist the devil: his chief designs are to hinder thy desire in good, to *put* thee *by* from thy spiritual employment.
Jer. Taylor.

(*b*) To set or thrust aside.

Just God, *put by* th' unnatural blow.
Cowley, Davideis, iii.

The chancellor, sedate and vain,
In courteous words return'd reply,
But dallied with his golden chain,
And, smiling, *put* the question *by*.
Tennyson, Day-Dream, The Revival.

(*c*) To place in safe keeping; save or store up: as, "to *put by* something for a rainy day."—To **put down.** (*a*) To repress; crush; suppress.

The great feast at Whitehall was on Tuesday, where is unspeakable bravery; but the Duke of Chevreuse *put down* ours.
Court and Times of Charles I., I. 37.

Sir Peter is such an enemy to scandal, I believe he would have it *put down* by parliament.
Sheridan, School for Scandal, ii. 2.

(*b*) To degrade; deprive of authority, power, or place. (c) To defeat; put to rout; overcome; excel.

The Spaniards, notwithstanding they are the Masters of the Staple of Jewels, stood astonished at the Beauty of these, and confessed themselves to be *put down*.
Howell, Letters, I. iv. 1.

(*d*†) To bring into disuse.

Sugar hath *put down* the use of honey.
Bacon.

Here is no trading; carriers from most places *put downe*; nor no receiving of any money, though long due.
Sherley, quoted in Bradford's Plymouth Plantation, p. 345.

(*e*) To confute; silence.

Mark now, how a plain tale shall *put* you *down*.
Shak., 1 Hen. IV., ii. 4. 281.

As I live, madam, you *put* them all *down*
With your mere strength of judgment.
B. Jonson, Catiline, ii. 1.

(*f*) To write, as in a subscription-list or in a program: as, to *put* one's name *down* for a handsome sum; to *put* one *down* for a toast or a speech. (*g*) To give up; do without. [Eng.]

He had set himself not only to *put down* his carriage, but . . . to order the whole establishment on the sparest footing possible.
George Eliot, Daniel Deronda, xxiv.

To put forth. (*a*) To stretch out; reach.

He *put forth* his hand, and took her.
Gen. viii. 9.

(*b*) To shoot out; send forth or out, as a sprout.

A standard of a damask rose with the root on was set . . . upright in an earthen pan full of fair water without any mixture: . . . within the space of ten days the standard did *put forth* a fair green leaf.
Bacon, Nat. Hist., § 407.

(c) To exert; bring into action.

Virgil *putteth* himself *forth* to attribute to Augustus Cæsar the best of human honours.
Bacon, Advancement of Learning, i. 97.

In honouring God, *put forth* all thy strength.
Jer. Taylor.

(*d*) To propose; offer.

Samson said unto them, I will now *put forth* a riddle unto you.
Judges xiv. 12.

At their request he *put forth* him selfe to make a triall . . . of his skill.
Bradford, Plymouth Plantation, p. 211.

(*e*) To issue; publish.

I am not yet fully determined with myself whether I will *put forth* my book or no.
Sir T. More, Utopia, Ded. to Peter Giles, p. 11.

The proposed Congress, commonly called the "Stamp-Act Congress," . . . also *put forth* a declaration of colonial rights, acknowledging allegiance to the crown, and claiming "all the inherent rights and privileges of natural-born subjects within the kingdom of Great Britain."
A. Johnston, Encyc. Brit., XXIII. 738.

To **put forth one's hand against.** See *hand*.—To **put heads together.** See *to lay heads together*, under *lay*1.—**To put in.** (*a*) To hand in; present.

He is to *put in* his answer the 13th of January.
Walpole, Letters, II. 69.

(*b*) To introduce among others; interpose.

Give me leave to *put in* a word, to tell you that I am glad you allow us different degrees of worth.
Jeremy Collier.

(c) To insert: as, to *put in* a passage or clause; to *put in* a scion. (*d*) To appoint to an office.

The archbishop is *put in* by the patriarch of Constantinople, and the metropolitan makes the bishops, who *put in* the parish priests.
Pococke, Description of the East, II. i. 267.

To put in an appearance, to put in or **into commission, to put in mind, to put in pledge, to put in practice.** See the nouns.—**To put in the pin.** See *pin*1.

He had two or three times resolved to better himself and to *put in the pin*, meaning he had made a vow to refrain from drinking.
Mayhew, London Labour and London Poor, I. 345.

To **put off.** (*a*) To push off from land; push out into the water.

Two of them going out of the boat, he caused the boatsmen to *put off* the boat.
Winthrop, Hist. New England, I. 376.

(*b*) To palm off; pass fraudulently; foist.

The Natives are for *putting off* bad Money, if possibly they can.
Dampier, Voyages, II. i. 131.

It is the hardest case in the world that Mr. Steele should take up the artificial reports of his own faction, and then *put* them *off* upon the world as "additional tears of a popish successor."
Swift, Public Spirit of the Whigs.

(*c*†) To dispose of, as by barter or sale; sell.

In ye midds of these distractions, they of Leyden, who had *put of* their estats, and laid out their moneys, were brought into a greate streight.
Bradford, Plymouth Plantation, p. 45.

These ships, by reason of their short passage, had store of provisions left, which they *put off* at easy rates, viz. biscuit at 20*s.* the hundred; beef at £6 the hogshead, etc.
Winthrop, Hist. New England, I. 159.

(*d*) To take off or lay aside; doff.

None of us *put off* our clothes.
Neh. iv. 23.

Hell about me,
Behind me, and before me; yet I dare not,
Still fearing worse, *put off* my wretched being.
Beau. and Fl., Knight of Malta, iv. 1.

Could hee *put off* his body with his little Coate, he had got eternitie without a burthen, and exchang'd but one Heauen for another.
Bp. Earle, Micro-cosmographie, A Childe.

(*e*) To dismiss; discard.

The kyng to the komyns carpit agayne;
To *put of* that purpos he paynet hym sore.
Destruction of Troy (E. E. T. S.), l. 11416.

The clothiers all . . . *put off*
The spinsters, carders, fullers, weavers.
Shak., Hen. VIII., i. 2. 32.

I do not send you George, because they are speaking of *putting off* servants. *Winthrop*, Hist. New England, I. 471.

(*f*) To defer; postpone; delay: as, to *put off* something to a more convenient season; to *put off* one's departure for a week.

The promised collection was long *put off* under various pretexts. *Macaulay*, Hist. Eng., vi.

(*g*) To defeat or baffle, as by delay, artifice, plausible excuse, etc.

Do men in good earnest think that God will be *put off* so? or that the law of God will be baffled with a lie clothed in a scoff? *South.*

When I ask, I am not to be *put off*, Madam. No, no, I take my friend by the button. *Goldsmith*, Good-natured Man, ii.

Hastings, who wanted money and not excuses, was not to be *put off* by the ordinary artifices of Eastern negotiation. *Macaulay*, Warren Hastings.

To put on or **upon.** (*a*) [*On*, adv.] (1) To clothe, cover, or invest the person, or some part of it, with; assume as a covering, or as something to be worn: as, to *put on* one's clothes; to *put on* a new pair of gloves.

He's *pitten on* his cork-heel'd shoon,
And fast awa rade he.
Burd Ellen (Child's Ballads, III. 213).

Fresh was Phœbe, moreover, and airy and sweet in her apparel; as if nothing that she wore . . . had ever been *put on* before; or, if worn, were all the fresher for it, and with a fragrance as if they had lain among the rosebuds. *Hawthorne*, Seven Gables, xi.

Hence—(2) To assume; assume the garb or appearance of; show externally; exhibit: as, to *put on* a solemn countenance, or a show of interest; to *put on* airs.

We made love, and contemn'd love; now seem'd holy,
With such a reverent *put-on* reservation
Which could not miss, according to your principles.
Fletcher, Wildgoose Chase, iii. 1.

Putting off the Courtier, he now *puts on* the Philosopher. *Milton*, Eikonoklastes, vi.

Mal. Now all in tears, now smiling, and at parting.
Guise. Dissembled, for she told me this before;
'Twas all *put on* that I might hear and rave.
Dryden, Duke of Guise, iii. 1.

(3) To turn or let on; turn or bring into action: as, to *put on* more steam. (4) To forward; promote.

This came handsomely to *put on* the peace. *Bacon*, Hist. Hen. VII.

(5) To instigate; incite.

You protect this course, and *put it on*
By your allowance. *Shak.*, Lear, i. 4. 227.

These two, as the king conceived, *put* him *on* to that foul practise and illusion of Sathans. *Apothegms of King James* (1660). (*Nares.*)

(6) To deceive; impose upon; cheat; trick: as, I will not be *put upon*.

The stork found he was *put upon*, but set a good face, however, upon his entertainment. *Sir R. L'Estrange.*

(*b*) [*On*, prep.] (1) To impose upon; inflict upon.

That which thou *puttest on* me, will I bear. 2 Ki. xviii. 14.

Sir, I must have you know
That you are and shall be at our pleasure, what
Fashion we will *put upon* you.
Beau. and Fl., Philaster, i. 1.

(2) To lay on; impute to: as, *to put* the blame *on* somebody else.

I'll try you for his Murder, which I find you'd *put on* me, thou hellish Engine! *Steele*, Grief A-la-Mode, v. 1.

(3) To impel to; instigate to; incite to.

Ambition often *puts* men *upon* doing the meanest offices. *Swift*, Thoughts on Various Subjects.

But pray, Mr. *Puff*, what first *put you on* exercising your talents in this way? *Sheridan*, The Critic, i. 2.

(4) To ascribe to.

Thus the priests of elder time have *put upon* them many incredible conceits. *Sir T. Browne*, Vulg. Err.

In faith, in faith,
You do not fair to *put* these things *upon* me,
Which can in no sort be.
B. *Jonson*, Sad Shepherd, i. 2.

(5) To foist upon; palm off on.

My Lady Townshend has picked up a little stable-boy in the Tower, which the warders have *put upon* her for a natural son of Lord Kilmarnock's. *Walpole*, Letters, II. 81.

(6) In *law*, to rest on; rest one's case in; submit to: as, the defendant *puts* himself *upon* the country (that is, he pleads not guilty, and will go to trial).—**To put one in a hole, to put one on** or **to his mettle, to put one's back up.** See the nouns.—**To put one's best foot forward, to put one's foot in it, to put one's foot into.** See *foot*.—**To put one's hand to.** See *hand*.—**To put one's hand to the plow.** See *plow*.—**To put one's head into the lion's mouth, one's nose out of joint, one's nose to the grindstone, one's oar in.** See *lion, joint, grindstone, oar*.—To **put one to the door.** See *door*.—**To put on trial.** See *trial*.—To **put out.** (*a*) To thrust out. (1) To destroy, so as to blind: said of the eyes.

But now with a most inhumane cruelty they who have *put out* the peoples eyes reproach them of their blindnesse. *Milton*, Apology for Smectymnuus.

(2) To extend; reach out; protrude.

It came to pass, when she travailed, that the one *put out* his hand. Gen. xxxviii. 28.

(*b*) To extinguish.

Is the light of thy Vnderstanding now cleane *put out?* *Dekker*, Seven Deadly Sins, p. 24.

(*c*) To shoot forth, as a bud or sprout: as, to *put out* leaves.
(*d*) To exert; use.

Let us all set ourselves in good earnest to resist all manner of temptations: let us *put out* all the strength which we naturally have to this purpose, and beg of God supernaturally to supply us with what we have not. *Bp. Atterbury*, Sermons, II. iv.

(*e*) To expel; eject; drive out; dismiss: as, to *put out* an intruder; to be *put out* of office.

The same Day that he [Adam] was putt in Paradys, the same Day he was *put outt*. *Mandeville*, Travels, p. 67.

Whanne nature hath sett in you plente
Of alle goodnesse, by vertu and bi grace,
He neuere assembled hem, as semeth me,
To *put* pyte *owte* of his dwellyng place.
Political Poems, etc. (ed. Furnivall), p. 67.

They should *put out* four of the magistrates from that power and trust which the freeman had committed to them. *Winthrop*, Hist. New England, II. 205.

(*f*) To publish; make public; issue: as, to *put out* a pamphlet.

I was surprized at the Impudence of a Booth, which *put out* the Pictures of some Indian Beasts with hard Names; and of four that were Painted I found but two. *Lister*, Journey to Paris, p. 177.

They were *putting out* very curious stamps of the several edifices which are most famous for their beauty. *Addison*, Works (ed. Bohn), I. 388.

Every case in which copies of the original letters can be compared with the revised editions *put out* by the writers. *Stubbs*, Medieval and Modern Hist., p. 127.

(*g*) To confuse; disconcert.

My Aunt is here, and she will *put* me *out*: you know I cannot dance before her. *Wycherley*, Gentleman Dancing-Master, iv. 1.

Something has gone wrong, Miss Fanny, I'm afraid. You seem *put out*, and it's very becoming, I give you my honour. *Whyte Melville*, White Rose, I. viii.

(*h*) To offend.

You're a good old brick to be serious, and not *put out* with me. *T. Hughes*, Tom Brown at Rugby, ii. 7.

(*i*) To lay out. (1) To expend; spend: as, to *put out* money. (2) To invest; place at interest.

He called his money in,
But the prevailing love of pelf
Soon split him on the former shelf:
He *put it out* again.
Dryden, tr. of Horace's Epodes, ii.

(*j*) To dislocate: as, to *put out* one's ankle.—**To put out of sight.** See *sight*.—**To put over.** (*a*) [*Over*, adv.] (1) To refer; send.

For the certain knowledge of that truth
I *put* you *o'er* to heaven and to my mother.
Shak., K. John, i. 1. 62.

(2) To defer; postpone: as, the court *put over* the cause to the next term. (3†) To transfer; make over; assign.

If he intends to come hither, it were good he sold his land, and paid his sister her £100, which he promised when I *put over* his land to him. *Winthrop*, Hist. New England, I. 458.

(4) To knock over; kill. [Australia.]

"I wouldn't lose that pistol for five pounds," he said, "No—nor more. I should never have one like it again. I've *put over* a parrot at twenty yards with it." *H. Kingsley*, Geoffry Hamlyn, p. 412.

(*b*) [*Over*, prep.] (1) To place in authority over. (2) To transport across; ferry or carry across.

Cattle . . . which came late, and could not be *put over* the river, lived very well all the winter without any hay. *Winthrop*, Hist. New England, I. 210.

To put the ax in the helve, the boot on the wrong leg, the cart before the horse. See *ax*[1], *boot*[2], cart.—**To put the case.** See *case*[1], and *put the case*, above.—**To put the change on** or **upon†.** See *change*.—To **put the fool on** or **upon†.** See *fool*[1].—**To put the hand to** (or **unto**). (*a*) To take hold of; begin; undertake.

Ye shall rejoice in all that ye *put your hand unto*. Deut. xii. 7.

(*b*) To take or seize, as in theft; steal.

If the thief be not found, then the master of the house shall be brought unto the judges, to see whether he have *put his hand unto* his neighbour's goods. Ex. xxii. 8.

To put the helm down. See *helm*[1].—**To put the last** or **finishing hand to.** See *hand*.—**To put this and that together,** to draw a conclusion from certain circumstances; think of two related facts and form an opinion thereon; infer from given premises.

Putting this and that together—combining under the head "this" present appearances, . . . and ranging under the head "that" the visit to his sister—the watchman reported to Miss *Peecher* his strong suspicions. *Dickens*, Our Mutual Friend, ii. 11.

To **put through,** to carry or conduct to a successful termination: as, the measure was *put through* without hesitation.

That was the way he *put* her *through*—
"There!" said the Deacon, "naow she'll dew!"
O. W. Holmes, The Deacon's Masterpiece.

To put to (or **unto**). (*a*) [*To*, adv.] (1) To add; unite.

I muste a-bide al manere aventure,
For I may not *put too*, nor take away.
Political Poems, etc. (ed. Furnivall), p. 70.

(2) To put forth; apply; use.

If the iron be blunt, and he do not whet the edge, then must he *put to* more strength. Eccl. x. 10.

Who shall *put-to* his power
To draw those virtues out of a flood of humours
Where they are drown'd, and make 'em shine again?
Beau. and Fl., King and no King, iv. 2.

(*b*) [*To*, prep.] (1) To add to; unite with.

Whatsoever God doeth, it shall be for ever; nothing can be *put to* it, nor any thing taken from it. Eccl. iii. 14.

(2) To drive; force; impel: as, to be *put to* one's shift.
(3) To send, bring, or consign to.

Such as were taken on either side were *put to* the sword or *to* the halter. *Clarendon*, Great Rebellion.

They *put* him *to* the cudgel fiercely.
S. *Butler*, Hudibras, III. i. 1148.

(4) To expose to; refer to.

Having lost two of their bravest commanders at sea, they durst not *put* it *to* a battle at sea. *Bacon.*

When our universal state
Was *put to* hazard.
Dryden, tr. of Ovid's Metamorph., i.

(5) To limit or confine to.

If there be twenty ways to some poor village,
'Tis strange that virtue should be *put to* one.
Middleton, Game at Chess, ii. 1.

To put to a stand, to death, to earth, to prentice. See the nouns.—**To put together,** to unite; place in juxtaposition or combination.—**To put to rights.** See *right*.—**To put to the blush, to (the) foil†, to the horn, to the rack, to trial,** etc. See the nouns.—To **put two and two together.** Same as to *put this and that together*.—To **put up.** (*a*†) To bear or suffer without protest or resentment; pass unnoticed or unavenged; overlook: now, *to put up with*.

Take my armour off quickly, 'twill make him swoon, I fear; he is not fit to look on 't that will *put up* a blow. B. *Jonson*, Every Man in his Humour, v. 1.

Every body tells me I am the properest gentleman in the town, and I *put* it *up;* for the truth is, I dare not give any one the lie. *Shirley*, Love Tricks, ii. 1.

(*b*†) To send forth or shoot up, as plants.

Hartshorn . . . mixed with dung and watered *putteth up* mushrooms. *Bacon.*

(*c*) To offer.

I cannot see how he will escape that heathenish Battologie of multiplying words which Christ himselfe, that has the *putting up* of our Praiers, told us would not be acceptable in heaven. *Milton*, On Def. of Humb. Remonst.

The itinerant bookseller evades, or endeavours to evade, the payment of an auctioneer's licence, by *putting-up* his books at a high price, and himself decreasing the terms. *Mayhew*, London Labour and London Poor, I. 323.

(*d*) To start from a cover: as, to *put up* a hare.

In town, whilst I am following one character, I am crossed in my way by another, and *put up* such a variety of odd creatures in both sexes that they foil the scent of one another, and puzzle the chase. *Addison*, Spectator.

I started off on a walk through the country—a short one—incited thereto by the possibility of *putting up* a deer, or slaying a jackal. *W. H. Russell*, Diary in India, I. 160.

(*e*) To hoard.

Himself never *put up* any of the rent. *Spelman.*

(*f*) To pack; store up, as for preservation: as, to *put up* beef or pork in casks.

Not any of them would eate a bit with him, but *put up* all the remainder in Baskets. Quoted in *Capt. John Smith*'s Works, I. 161.

(*g*) To put into its ordinary place when not in use, as a sword in its scabbard, or a purse in the pocket.

Faith, we may *put up* our p pe , and be gone. *Shaks*, R. and J., iv. 5. 96.

Put thy sword *up*, traitor. *Shak.*, Tempest, i. 2. 469.

She *put up* her spectacles, shut the Bible, and pushed her chair back from the table. *Charlotte Brontë*, Jane Eyre, xxiv.

(*h*) To accommodate with lodging: as, I can *put* you *up* for a night.

I'se warrant ye'll be weel *put up;* for they never turn awa' naebody frae the door. *Scott*, Guy Mannering, i.

(*i*) To post as a candidate; nominate for election.

Soon after this debate Pitt's name was *put up* by Fox at Brookes's. *Macaulay*, William Pitt.

To put upon. See *to put on*.—**To put up** to, to give information respecting; make acquainted with; explain; teach: as, he *put* me *up to* a thing or two; we were *put up to* the trick or dodge. [Slang.]=**Syn.** *Put, Set, Lay, Place. Put* is a very indefinite word, with a wide range of idiomatic uses. *Set* has also a wide range; it suggests fixedness, especially of something upright: as, to *set* a vase or lamp on the table, or a chair by the table. *Lay* suggests a horizontal position: as, to *lay* one's self down; to *lay* a knife or book on the table. *Place* suggests definiteness of location: as, to *place* one's finger on the spot.

II. *intrans.* 1. To go or move; especially, to go quickly; hasten.

In fibrous [roots] . . . the sap delighteth more in the earth, and therefore *putteth* downward. *Bacon*, Nat. Hist., § 6, vi.

Stay in your place, know your own strength, and *put* not Beyond the sphere of your activity. B. *Jonson*, Devil is an Ass, i. 1.

2. To direct one's course; turn.

His fury thus appeased, he *puts* to land.
Dryden, Æneid, vi. 554.

3†. To make an effort; try; endeavor.

If it be possible
That an arch-villain may ever be recover'd,
This penitent rascal will *put* hard.
Fletcher (*and another*), False One, iv. 3.

4†. To put the case; suppose.

Lat us now *putte* that ye han leve.
Chaucer, Tale of Melibeus.

To put about, to go about; turn back; change or reverse one's course.—**To put at,** to throw with an upward and forward motion of the arm.

O it fell anes upon a time
They *putted at* the stane;
And seven foot ayond them a'
Brown Robin's gar'd it gang.
Rose the Red and White Lilly (Child's Ballads, V. 176).

To put away for (*naut.*), to start to go to: as, to *put away for* home after a cruise.—**To put fair**, to bid fair.

And he had *put fair* for it, had not death prevented him, by which his life and projects were cut off together.
Heylin, Hist. Presbyterians, p. 130. (*Davies.*)

To put for, to start for; especially, to get in resolute motion toward with decided purpose and vigorous action: as, to *put for* home; to *put for* the shore.—**To put forth.** (*a*) To shoot; bud; germinate.

Take earth from under walls where nettles *put forth*.
Bacon, Nat. Hist.

Then the flowers *put forth* and spring, and then the Sunne shall scatter the mists.
Milton, Church-Government, i. 6.

(*b*) To set out; depart.

Order for sea is given;
They have *put forth* the haven.
Shak., A. and C., iv. 10. 7.

To put forward†, to hasten on.

I am willing *to put forward* as fast as my beast will give me leave, though I fear nothing in your company.
Cotton, in Walton's Angler, ii. 228.

To put in. (*a*) *Naut.*, to enter a port or harbor; especially, to deviate from the regular course to seek shelter from storms, or to refit, procure provisions, etc.: as, the ship *put in* to Charleston.

We sailed for Mytilene, but *put in* the first evening at Cardamills in Scio, where I pitched my tent, and lay all night, and the next evening arrived at the port of Mytilene.
Pococke, Description of the East, II. ii. 14.

(*b*) To call at and enter a place, as a house of refreshment.

We took horse, and got early to Baldwick, where there was a fair, and we *put in*, and eat a mouthfull of porke, which they made us pay 14*d.* for, which vexed me much.
Pepys, Diary, I. 220.

(*c*) To dash into covert for safety, as a bird when hard pressed by a hawk. (*d*) To interpose.

He has . . . kicked me three or four times about the tiring-house . . . for but offering to *put in* with my experience.
B. Jonson, Bartholomew Fair, Ind.

And although astrology may here *put in*, and plead the secrett influence of this star [the dog-star] . . .
Sir T. Browne, Vulg. Err., iv. 13.

To put in for, to put in a claim for; make application for; seek to obtain.

Jacob had suffered patiently the direction of those that governed him, so long as the excuse of his minority was a good one. But, being now arrived at the age of 17, he began to *put in* by degrees *for* his share in the direction of affairs.
Bruce, Source of the Nile, II. 241.

Many most unfit persons are now *putting in for* that place.
Abp. Usher, Letters, cxvi.

To put off, to leave land; sail off.

Let me cut the cable,
And, when we are *put off*, fall to their throats.
Shak., A. and C., ii. 7. 78.

To put on, to move or hasten on.

So *put on*, my brave boy, and make the best of thy way to Boulogne.
Sterne, Tristram Shandy, vii. 6.

We *put on* pretty fast; the janizary, and guide to whom the horses belonged, frequently looking back in the utmost consternation, lest they should send after us, and injure us some way or other.
Pococke, Description of the East, II. ii. 65.

To put out. (*a*) *Naut.*, to start; sail. (*b*) To leave suddenly; be off; get out. (*c*) In tanning morocco leather, to remove small fragments of flesh still adhering to the flesh-side of the tanned skins, and at the same time to stretch and smooth the skins. Formerly done almost exclusively by hand-labor, this operation is now largely performed by putting-out machines.—**To put over.** (*a*) To sail over or across. (*b*) To remove her meat from the gorge into the stomach: said of a hawk.—**To put up.** (*a*) To take lodgings; lodge. (*b*) To offer one's self as a candidate.

The beasts met to chuse a king, when several *put up*.
Sir R. L'Estrange.

(*c*) To sheath the sword; cease from further contest.

Troth, I'll *put up* at all adventures, master:
It comes off very fair yet.
Middleton (*and others*), The Widow, i. 2.

(*d*) To pay down or stake money. [Slang, U. S.]—**To put up to**, to advance to; approach. [Rare.]

With this he *put up to* my lord;
The courtiers kept their distance due. *Swift.*

To put up with, to bear without resentment or repining; tolerate: as, to *put up with* many annoyances; to *put up with* injury; to *put up with* bad fare.

It would no more repay us for all the insolence that we have *put up with* than does the infliction of a forty-shilling fine on the cabman recompense the gentleman whom he has blackguarded for an hour in a crowded thoroughfare.
Blackwood's Mag., XLVI. 198.

put[1] (put), *n.* [Formerly also *putt*; < ME. *put*, < *put*[1], *v.*] **1.** A thrust; a push.

The dear creature, I doubted not, wanted to instruct me how to answer the captain's home *put*.
Richardson, Clarissa Harlowe, IV. 316. (*Davies.*)

2. A cast or throw; specifically, a throw made by an upward and forward motion of the arm, as in putting the stone. [Pronounced in Scotland put.]

The *put* of the stoon thou maist not reche,
To lilil mygte is in thi sloue.
Hymns to Virgin, etc. (E. E. T. S.), p. 73.

3†. An attempt; particularly, an attempt to avoid something, as when a bird or beast of chase, hard pressed, seeks safety under cover.

The stag's was a forced *put*, and a chance rather than a choice.
Sir R. L'Estrange.

4. A game at cards, played generally by two people, but sometimes by three, and often four. The whole pack is used in playing, but only three cards are dealt out at a time. Whoever gains at least two tricks out of the three counts five points, which make game.

There are some playing at back-gammon, some at trick-track, some at picket, some at cribidge, and, perhaps, at a by-table in a corner, four or five harmless fellows at *put* and all-foures.
Country Gentleman's Vade Mecum (1699), [p. 75. (*Halliwell.*)

He had heard an old tailor say that in his youth, fifty years ago, *put* was a common public-house game.
Mayhew, London Labour and London Poor, I. 267.

5. A contract by which the party signing or making the same agrees, in consideration usually of a certain sum of money, that he will accept and pay for specified securities or commodities which the party named therein, or the bearer of the contract, at or within a time named, shall, at the option of the latter, offer to sell the former at a specified price. It is used chiefly in the stock-market, for speculative purposes, and if the intent of the parties is to settle the difference of price in money, it is illegal.

Gran. And all this out of Change-Alley?
Wit. Every Shilling, Sir; all out of Stocks,
Putts, Bulls, Rams, Bears, and Bubbles.
Cibber, Refusal, i.

A *put* is an option to deliver, or not deliver, at a future day.
Bisbee and Simonds, Law Prod. Ex., p. 50.

put[2] (put), *n.* [Also *putt*; perhaps < W. *pwt*, any short thing; cf. *pwtan*, *pwtog*, a squat woman.] A rustic; a clown; a silly fellow; a simpleton; an oddity. [Eng.]

As he gave the good-night to two or three young fellows a little before our landing, one of them, instead of returning the civility, asked us what queer old *put* we had in the boat.
Addison, Sir Roger at Vauxhall.

What Letacre said to you upon that occasion you ought to have borne with more decency . . . than to have called him country *put*.
Steele, Spectator, No. 263.

put[3]† (put), *n.* [< OF. *pute*, *puite* (= Pr. Sp. Pg. *puta* = It. *putta*), a prostitute, fem. of *put*, *puit*, *pout*, *pot* (= Sp. Pg. *puto* = It. *putto*), foul, bad, wicked.] A strumpet; a prostitute.

put[4]†, *n.* An obsolete form of *pit*[1].

putage (pū'tāj), *n.* [< OF. *putage* (ML. *putagium*), fornication, prostitution, < *pute*, a prostitute: see *put*[3].] In *law*, prostitution or fornication on the part of a woman.

If any heir female under guardianship were guilty of *putage*, she forfeited her part to her coheirs.
Jacob, Law Dict.

putaile†, *n.* A variant form of *pitaile*.

putamen (pū-tā'men), *n.*; pl. *putamina* (pū-tam'i-nä). [< L. *putamen*, a trimming or clipping, waste, husk, < *putare*, cleanse, trim, prune: see *putation*.] **1.** In *bot.*, the endocarp of a fruit when hard and stony; the shell of a nut, or the stone of a stone-fruit or drupe; also, one of the pyrenæ or apparent seeds of some drupes. See *drupe* and *endocarp*, and cut under *drupe*.—**2.** In *ornith.*, the soft shell of an egg; a last layer of tough tenacious albumen deposited upon the soft white of the egg, forming a membrane in and upon which the hard shell is deposited.—**3.** In *anat.*, the outer zone of gray matter of the lenticular part of the corpus striatum of the brain. The claustrum separates the putamen from the cortex of the brain.

putaminous (pū-tam'i-nus), *a.* [< *putamen* (*-min-*) + *-ous.*] Of or pertaining to the putamen: as, a *putaminous* envelop or membrane.

putanism (pū'tạ-nizm), *n.* [< F. *putanisme* (= Sp. *putanismo*, *putaismo* = It. *puttanismo*), prostitution, < *putain* (= It. *puttana*), a prostitute, < *pute*, a prostitute: see *put*[3].] Customary lewdness or prostitution in a female. *Bailey.*

putation (pū-tā'shọn), *n.* [< ME. *putacion*, < OF. *putation*, < L. *putatio(n-)*, a pruning, lopping, also (LL.) a reckoning, computing, considering, < *putare*, pp. *putatus*, cleanse, trim, prune, fig. adjust, settle (*rationem* or *rationes*) accounts; hence reckon, count, compute, value, estimate, esteem, consider, think, suppose, believe; < *putus*, clean, clear: see *pute*.] **1.** A lopping or pruning, as of trees; pruning.

Eke thai be apte unto *putacion*
Of bowes drie or foule elacion.
Palladius, Husbondrie (E. E. T. S.), p. 91.

2. The act of considering, deeming, or supposing; supposition; estimation.

If we were not the actors and sufferers, it is not possible that we should be made the natural subjects of the accidents of another's body, by any *putation*, estimation, or misjudging whatsoever.
Baxter, Life of Faith, iii. 8.

putative (pū'tạ-tiv), *a.* [< F. *putatif* = Sp. Pg. *putativo*, < LL. *putativus*, supposed, < L. *putare*, pp. *putatus*, think, suppose: see *putation*.] Supposed; reputed; commonly thought or deemed: as, the *putative* father of a child.

Thus things indifferent, being esteem'd useful or pious, became customary, and then came for reverence into a *putative* and usurp'd authority.
Jer. Taylor, Dissuasive from Popery, II. i. § 3.

Her *putative* parents had impressed,
On their departure, their enjoinment.
Browning, Ring and Book, I. 175.

Putative marriage, in *canon law*, a marriage contracted in violation of an impediment, but in good faith on the part of at least one party.

put-by† (put'bī), *n.* An excuse for setting aside or ignoring. See quotation under *put-off*.

put-case† (put'kās), *n.* [< *put*[1], *v.*, + obj. *case*[1], *n.*] A propounder of hypotheses, or hypothetical cases.

He used to say that no man could be a good lawyer that was not a *put-case*.
Roger North, Lord Guilford, I. 20. (*Davies.*)

putchuk, putchock (pu-chuk', pu-chok'), *n.* [E. Ind.] In India, the costus-root.—**Green** or **native green putchuk**, the Chinese *Aristolochia recurvilabra*: so called from some resemblance of its rootstock to the putchuk imported from India. It is used as a remedy for burns and indigestion, and, like many other species of *Aristolochia*, is regarded as an antidote to snake-poison. Physicians, however, now credit these plants with the virtues of diaphoretics, stimulant tonics, and emmenagogues only. The drug is obtained chiefly from cultivation, and is at Ningpo a large article of commerce.

pute† (pūt), *a.* [< L. *putus*, cleansed, clean, clear, pure, unmixed (usually joined with *purus*, pure: *purus putus*, or *purus ac putus*), orig. pp., < √ *pu*, in *purus*, pure, clean: see *pure*. From this adj. are also ult. E. *putamen*, *putation*, *putative*, *compute*, *count*[1], *account*, *dispute*, *repute*, etc.] Clear; pure; mere.

Arminius . . . acknowledges faith to be the pure *pute* gift of God.
Bp. Hall, Via Media (trans.), v. (*Davies.*)

Generally pure *pute* Italians, preferred in England, transmitted the gain they got . . . into their own country.
Fuller, Worthies, York, III. 464. (*Davies.*)

That cause . . . was pure and *pute* factions.
Roger North, Examen, p. 527. (*Davies.*)

puteal (pū'tẹ-ạl), *n.* [L., a stone curb surrounding the mouth of a well, < *puteus*, a well: see *pit*[1].] An inclosure surrounding a well to prevent persons from falling into it; a well-curb. Sculptured examples of both antiquity and the middle ages occur, among which are works of art of high excellence. See cut under *pozzo*.

puteli (put'e-li), *n.* [E. Ind.] A broad flat-bottomed boat, used for transporting the products of India down the Ganges. It is from 40 to 65 feet long, lightly made, and capable of conveying a heavy cargo. The puteli is surmounted by a large flat-topped shed, nearly as long as the boat, and carries a single large square sail.

Puteli of the Ganges.

puterie†, *n.* [ME., < OF. *puterie* (= Sp. *puteria*; ML. reflex *puteria*), prostitution, < *pute*, a prostitute: see *put*[3].] Prostitution. *Chaucer.*

putid† (pū'tid), *a.* [< L. *putidus*, stinking, fetid, < *putere*, stink, be rotten, < √ *pu*, = Skt. √ *pūy*, stink. Cf. *putrid*.] **1.** Stinking; rotten.

This Mother of divinest Love, as pure
As is that other *putid*!
J. Beaumont, Psyche, ii. 220.

2. Mean; low; worthless; foul; dirty; disgusting.

Putid fables and ridiculous fictions.
Jer. Taylor (?), Artif. Handsomeness, p. 126.

putidity† (pū-tid'i-ti), *n.* [< *putid* + *-ity*.] The quality of being putid; foulness; vileness; meanness.

putidness† (pū'tid-nes), *n.* [< *putid* + *-ness*.] The quality of being putid; rottenness; putidity.

High-tasted sawces made with garlick or onions, purposely applied to tainted meats, to make their *putidness* less perceptible. *Bp. Gauden*, Tears of the Church, p. 199. (*Davies.*)

putlog (put'log), *n.* [< *put*[1] (?) + *log*[1].] In *carp.*, one of a number of short pieces of timber used in building to carry the floor of a scaffold. They are placed at right angles to the wall, one end resting on the ledgers of the scaffold, and the other in holes left in the wall, called *putlog-holes*.

a, putlog; *b*, *b*, putlog-holes; *c*, ledger.

putlog-hole (put'log-hōl), *n.* One of a series of small holes left in a wall, to admit the ends of putlogs.

put-off (put'ôf), *n.* An excuse; a shift for evasion or delay.

There be so many *put-offs*, so many put-byes, so many respects and considerations of worldly wisdom. *Latimer*, Sermon of the Plough.

"We want t' man who came here for hiding last night; t' man called John Whitehead." "He came not here last night." "That's a *put-off*. He came this morning—then." *A. E. Barr*, Friend Olivia, iii.

putois (F. pron. pü-two'), *n.* [F. *putois* (ML. *putacius*), a polecat, its fur, a brush made of its fur, < L. *putere*, stink: see *putid*.] A brush supposed to be made of the hair of the polecat, used by painters of ceramic ware.

putoo (put'ö), *n.* [Cingalese.] A dish made from flour or meal from the germinal shoots of the palmyra-nut, scraped cocoanut, and jackfruit, much esteemed by the Cingalese.

Putorius (pū-tō'ri-us), *n.* [NL., < L. *putor*, a stench, < *putere*, stink: see *putid*.] An extensive genus of *Mustelidæ*, belonging to the subfamily *Mustelinæ*, having 34 teeth, instead of 38 as in *Mustela*, and containing the animals known as *weasels*, *stoats*, *ermines*, *polecats*, *ferrets*, and *minks*. They are related to the martens and sables, but are smaller, with much slenderer body and tail, and very short limbs. They inhabit nearly all countries. They are often destructive to poultry, but are beneficial in destroying rats, mice, and other vermin. Species inhabiting cold countries turn white in winter, the tip of the tail remaining black. Such furnish a highly prized fur, known as *ermine*. The common weasel, *Putorius vulgaris*, is one of the smallest species, 6 or 8 inches long, with a short tail. *P. erminea* is the common stoat or ermine. *P. fœtidus* is the polecat, of which a variety, *P. furo*, commonly an albino with pink eyes, is the domesticated ferret. The spotted polecat is *P. sarmaticus*. (See *sarmatier*.) The black-footed ferret of the western prairies of the United States is *P.* (*Cynomyonax*) *nigripes*. The bridled weasel of South America is *P. frenatus*. A Siberian form, *P. sibiricus*, is the red sable, chorok, or kolinsky (which see). An aquatic species, somewhat otter-like, is *P. lutreola*, the European mink. The American mink is *P. vison*. See cuts under *Cynomyonax*, *ermine*, *ferret*, *mink*, *polecat*, and *weasel*.

putour†, *n.* [ME., < OF. *pute*, a prostitute: see *put*[3].] A pimp; a procurer; a keeper of a brothel. *Chaucer.*

put-pin (put'pin), *n.* [< *put*[1], *v.*, + obj. *pin*[1].] Same as *push-pin*.

Playing at *put-pin*, doting on some glass
(Which, breath'd but on, his falsed gloss doth pass).
Marston, Scourge of Villanie, viii. 205.

Putranjiva (put-ran-jī'vä), *n.* [NL. (Wallich, 1824), from a native name in India, < Skt. *putra*, son, + *jīva*, living.] A genus of apetalous trees of the order *Euphorbiaceæ* and tribe *Phyllantheæ*. It is characterized by numerous staminate flowers in dense heads at the nodes, each with a slender unequally five-lobed calyx and two or three stamens; pistillate flowers with three short spreading styles expanded into broad fleshy papillose branches; and an ovary of three carpels each with two ovules, becoming in fruit an ovoid drupe with one cell and one seed. The two species are natives of the mountains of central and southern India, and are large timber-trees with close-grained and very hard wood, bearing rigid and entire veiny alternate leaves, and axillary flowers, the staminate numerous and short-stalked and the pistillate one or few and long-stalked. *P. Roxburghii* is known in India as *wild olive*.

putredinous (pū-tred'i-nus), *a.* [< OF. *putredineux* = Pg. It. *putredinoso*, < LL. *putredo* (*-din-*), rottenness, < L. *putrere*, be putrid: see *putrid*.] Proceeding from putrefaction, or partaking of the putrefactive process; having an offensive smell.

A *putredinous* ferment coagulates all humours, as milk with rennet is turned. *Floyer*, Animal Humours.

putrefacient (pū-trē-fā'shient), *a.* and *n.* [= Pg. *putrefaciente*, < L. *putrefacien(t-)s*, ppr. of *putrefacere*, putrefy: see *putrefy*.] **I.** *a.* Same as *putrefactive*.

Putrefacient action on the blood and tissues after the lapse of some hours. *Alien. and Neurol.*, IX. 303.

II. *n.* An agent or a substance that produces putrefaction.

putrefacted† (pū'trē-fak-ted), *a.* [Also *putrifacted*; < L. *putrefactus*, pp. of *putrefacere*, putrefy, + *-ed*[2].] Putrid; putrefied.

Vermine bred of *putrifacted* slime.
Marston, Antonio and Mellida, II., iv. 4.

putrefaction (pū-trē-fak'shon), *n.* [Also *putrifaction*; < ME. *putrifaccioun*, < OF. *putrefaction*, F. *putréfaction* = Pr. *putrefaccio* = Sp. *putrefaccion* = Pg. *putrefacção* = It. *putrefazione*, < LL. *putrefactio(n-)*, < L. *putrefacere*, pp. *putrefactus*, putrefy: see *putrefy*.] **1.** The act or process of putrefying; the decomposition of animal and vegetable substances, attended by the evolution of fetid gases. Putrefaction is at present believed to be a result of the activity of organisms of the simplest form—the *Schizomycetes*. It can therefore take place only when the conditions are favorable for the life and growth of these organisms. A temperature of from 60° to 80° F., a moderate degree of humidity, and limited access of air are the conditions most favorable to putrefaction. Extremes of heat and cold, salt, sugar, vinegar, carbolic acid, corrosive sublimate, and other antiseptics prevent putrefaction by destroying or rendering inactive the organisms which induce it. The chemical changes in a putrefying body are most complex. From proteid bodies are formed leucin, tyrosin, a considerable number of alkaloids, the ptomaïnes, compound ammonias, hydrogen sulphid, and many other solid and gaseous products. See *fermentation*, and *germ theory* (under *germ*).

Alle philosophoris seyn that the feuere contynuele is gendrid of *putrifaccioun* of blood and of corrupcioun of humouris. *Book of Quinte Essence* (ed. Furnivall), p. 21.

All creatures that have breath in their nostrils must suddenly return to *putrefaction*. *I. Walton*, Complete Angler, p. 31.

Pasteur proved that in the special fermentation which bears the name of *putrefaction* the primum movens of the *putrefaction* resides in microscopic vibrios of absolutely the same order as those which compose the butyric ferment. *Life of Pasteur* (trans.), p. 57.

2. Putrefied matter.

putrefactious† (pū-trē-fak'shus), *a.* [< *putrefacti(on)* + *-ous*.] Putrefying; putrid.

Drunkennesse, whose *putrefactious* slime
Darkens the splendour of our common wealth.
Times' Whistle (E. E. T. S.), p. 70.

putrefactive (pū-trē-fak'tiv), *a.* [Also *putrifactive*; = F. *putréfactif* = Sp. Pg. *putrefactivo* = It. *putrefattivo*, < L. *putrefactus*, pp. of *putrefacere*, putrefy: see *putrefy*.] **1.** Pertaining to putrefaction: as, the *putrefactive* smell or process, or the *putrefactive* fermentation.

If the bone be corrupted, the *putrefactive* smell will discover it. *Wiseman*, Surgery.

There were small signs yet of the acetous and *putrefactive* stages which were to follow in the victory and decline of Puritanism. *Lowell*, Among my Books, 1st ser., p. 154.

2. Causing putrefaction.

The vessels of the living body, whether of man or animals, are sealed up beyond the reach of *putrefactive* germs so long as they are in a sound and healthy state. *S. B. Herrick*, Wonders of Plant Life, p. 77.

putrefactiveness (pū-trē-fak'tiv-nes), *n.* Putrefactive character, quality, or condition. Also *putrifactiveness*.

putrefiable (pū'trē-fī-a-bl), *a.* [Also *putrifiable*; < *putrefy* + *-able*.] Liable to putrefy; subject to or causing putrefaction.

For absorption of *putrefiable* materials Esmarch has used with great satisfaction turf enclosed in gauze bags. *W. T. Belfield*, Rel. of Micro-Org. to Disease, p. 60.

putrefier (pū'trē-fī-ėr), *n.* A putrefacient. Also *putrifier*.

An account of a series of experiments upon *putrefiers* and antiseptics. *Workshop Receipts*, 2d ser., p. 196.

putrefy (pū'trē-fī), *v.*; pret. and pp. *putrefied*, ppr. *putrefying*. [Also *putrify*; < ME. *putrefien*, < OF. *putrefier*, F. *putréfier* = Sp. Pg. *putrificar* (< ML. **putreficare*) = It. *putrefare*, < L. *putrefacere*, cause to rot, putrefy, *putrefieri*, rot, putrefy, < *putrere*, be rotten (see *putrid*), + *fieri*, pass. of *facere*, make, do.] **I.** *trans.* **1.** To render putrid; cause to decay with an offensive odor; cause to become fetid by rotting. See *putrefaction*.—**2.** To make carious or gangrenous.

A wound was so *putrefied* as to endanger the bone. *Sir W. Temple.*

3. To corrupt; make foul or offensive. [Rare.]

They would but stink and *putrefy* the air.
Shak., 1 Hen. VI., iv. 7. 90.

II. *intrans.* To become putrid; decay with a fetid smell. See *putrefaction*.

Wounds and bruises, and *putrifying* sores. *Isa.* i. 6.

Whenne they shewe uppe thaire fertilitee,
So turne hem with the plough to *putrifie*;
And after that thi lande shal multiplie.
Palladius, Husbondrie (E. E. T. S.), p. 182.

Many substances in nature which are solid do *putrify* and corrupt into worms. *Bacon*, Advancement of Learning, i. 43.

=**Syn.** *Decay*, *Corrupt*, etc. See *rot*.

putrescence (pū-tres'ens), *n.* [< F. *putrescence* = It. *putrescenza*; as *putrescen(t)* + *-ce*.] Putrescent character or condition; tendency to putridity or decay; a putrid state.

We must confess in the common *putrescence* it may promote elevation, which the breaking of the bladder of gall, so small a part in man, cannot considerably advantage. *Sir T. Browne*, Vulg. Err., iv. 6.

In attempting to sterilize a putrescible solution by means of cold, it was found that, though in some cases *putrescence* was delayed, in no case were the organisms completely destroyed. *Science*, VI. 393.

putrescent (pū-tres'ent), *a.* [< OF. *putrescent* = It. *putrescente*, < L. *putrescen(t-)s*, ppr. of *putrescere*, grow rotten, decay, freq. from *putrere*, be rotten or putrid: see *putrid*.] **1.** Becoming or growing putrid, or fetidly rotten; in course of putrefying; tainted with putrefaction or decay: as, *putrescent* flesh.

Stately, externally powerful, although undermined and *putrescent* at the core, the death-stricken empire still dashed back the assaults of its barbarous enemies. *Motley*, Dutch Republic, I. 18.

If from the hospitals . . .
All the diseases in one moat were gathered,
Such was it here, and such a stench came from it
As from *putrescent* limbs is wont to issue.
Longfellow, tr. of Dante's Inferno, xxix. 51.

2. Of or pertaining to the process of putrefaction: as, a *putrescent* smell.

putrescible (pū-tres'i-bl), *a.* [< OF. (and F.) *putrescible* = It. *putrescibile*, < L. *putrescere*, grow rotten, + *-ible*.] Subject to putrefaction; liable to become putrid: as, *putrescible* substances.

It does not appear to be *putrescible*. *Philosophical Transactions* (1798), I. § 2.

Finely divided charcoal is usually stated to have strong antiseptic powers. It certainly has a remarkable action upon *putrescible* substances. *W. A. Miller*, Elem. of Chem., § 355.

putrid (pū'trid), *a.* [< F. *putride* = Sp. *pútrido* = Pg. It. *putrido*, < L. *putridus*, rotten, corrupt, < *putrere*, be rotten, *putris*, rotten; cf. *putere*, be rotten, Ir. *putar*, stinking, L. *pus*, matter, etc.: see *putid* and *pus*.] **1.** In a state of decay or putrefaction; exhibiting putrefaction; corrupt; fetid from rottenness; stinking: said of animal and vegetable bodies: as, *putrid* flesh.

The wine to *putrid* blood converted flows. *Waller*, Æneid, iv.

A wide and melancholy waste
Of *putrid* marshes. *Shelley*, Alastor.

2. Indicating a state of putrefaction; proceeding from or pertaining to putrefaction: as, a *putrid* scent.—**Putrid fever.** See *fever*[1].—**Putrid sore throat**, gangrenous pharyngitis.

putridity (pū-trid'i-ti), *n.* [= F. *putridité* = It. *putridità*; as *putrid* + *-ity*.] **1.** The state of being putrid; corruption; fetid rottenness.—**2.** Putrid matter.

A hundred and thirty corpses of men, nay of women and even children, . . . lie heaped in that glacière: putrid under *putridities*. *Carlyle*, French Rev., II. v. 3.

putridness (pū'trid-nes), *n.* Putrid character or condition.

putrifacted†, **putrifaction**, etc. See *putrefacted*, etc.

putrification (pū"tri-fi-kā'shon), *n.* [< *putrefy* + *-ation* (see *-fy*).] Putrefaction.

Putrification must nedes be in a bodye. *Confutation of N. Shaxton* (1546).

putrify, *v.* See *putrefy*.

putry[1]† (pū'tri), *a.* [< L. *putris*, *putridus*, rotten: see *putrid*.] Putrid.

Howl not, thou *putry* mould! groan not, ye graves! *Marston*, Antonio and Mellida, II. (*Richardson.*)

putry[2]†, *n.* Same as *puterie*.

putt[1] (put), *v. i.* [A spelling of *put*[1]; obsolete in the general sense.] In *golf-playing*, to play with a putter; play when the ball lies at a short distance from the hole.

putt[1] (put), *n.* [< *putt*[1], *v.*] In *golf-playing*, a stroke made with a putter, or made in attempting to hole a ball.

putt[2], *n.* See *put*[2].

puttah, *n.* Same as *patah*.

putter[1] (put'ėr), *n.* [< *put*[1] + *-er*[1].] **1.** One who puts or places: as, a *putter* of obstacles in one's way.—**2.** One who puts or hauls coal from the place where it is mined to the point from which it is raised to the surface; one who transports coal on any underground road. Also called *haulier*, *drawer*, and *trammer*. [Little, if at all, used in the United States.]—3. One who puts or throws, especially a stone: as, he is but a poor *putter*. [In this sense pronounced put'ėr in Scotland.]

> Fame saying that Troy trains vp approvèd sons
> In deeds of arms, braue *putters*-off of shafts,
> For winging lances, masters of their crafts.
> *Chapman*, Odyssey, xviii. 379.

4 (put'ėr). In *golf-playing*, a club with a stiff and comparatively short shaft, generally used when the ball is on the putting-green.—**Putter on.** (*a*) One who urges, instigates, or incites; an instigator or inciter.

> They vent reproaches
> Most bitterly on you, as *putter on*
> Of these exactions. *Shak.*, Hen. VIII., i. 2. 24.

(*b*) One who puts or places something on something else.—**Putter out**, formerly, one who deposited money on going abroad, on condition of receiving a very much larger sum on his return, the money being forfeited in case of his non-return. This mode of gambling was practised in the reigns of Elizabeth and James I. On dangerous expeditions the money received was sometimes as much as five pounds for every pound deposited.

> Or that there were such men
> Whose heads stood in their breasts? which now we find
> Each *putter-out* of five for one will bring us
> Good warrant of. *Shak.*, Tempest, iii. 3. 48.

putter[2] (put'ėr), *v. i.* A variant of *potter*[2].

> Lies abed Sunday morning, and gets up late to *putter* with the furnace. *The Century*, XXVI. 635.

putti (pût'ti), *n. pl.* [It., pl. of *putto*, a little child, < L. *putus*, a boy, child: see *pupil*[1].] Representations of Cupid-like nude children common in the art of the fifteenth and following centuries, especially in Italy.

puttier (put'i-ėr), *n.* [< *putty*, *v.*, + *-er*[1].] One who putties; one who fills up or cements with putty, as a glazier.

> Cracked old houses where the painters and plumbers and *puttyers* are always at work.
> *Thackeray*, Lovel the Widower, ii.

putting-green (put'ing-grēn), *n.* That part of a golfing-ground which surrounds a hole: it is usually carefully prepared and preserved.

> Some of the *putting-greens* [at St. Andrews] are not what they should be, . . . but others, again, are things of beauty. The green of the "hole o' cross" is probably the best in all the world of golf.
> *Golf* (Badminton Library), p. 313.

putting-stone (put'ing-stōn), *n.* In Scotland, a heavy stone to be thrown with the hand, raised and thrust forward from the shoulder: chiefly used in gymnastic exercises or athletic sports.

> She lifted the heavy *putting-stane*,
> And gave a sad "Ohon!"
> *Rose the Red and White Lilly* (Child's Ballads, V. 177).

putto, *n.* See *puttoo*.

puttock (put'ok), *n.* [< ME. *puttok*, *potok*; origin uncertain.] A kind of hawk. (*a*) The kite or glede, *Milvus regalis*. (*b*) The common buzzard, *Buteo vulgaris*.

> The Hen which when the *Puttocke* hath caught hir Chekin beginneth to cackle.
> *Lyly*, Euphues, Anat. of Wit, p. 92.

> Who finds the partridge in the *puttock's* nest
> But may imagine how the bird was dead,
> Although the kite soar with unbloodied beak?
> *Shak.*, 2 Hen. VI., iii. 2. 191.

puttoo (put'ö), *n.* [Also *putto*; < Hind. *pattū*.] A fabric made in Cashmere and neighboring countries of the longer and coarser wool of the goat, after the fine and soft undergrowth has been separated from it. See *cashmere shawl*, under *cashmere*. Also called *Cashgar cloth*.

putty (put'i), *n.* [< OF. *potee*, brass, copper, tin, etc., calcined, also a potful, F. *potée*, powdered tin, oxid, putty, also a potful, < *pot*, a pot: see *pot*[1]. Cf. *potin*, *pottain*, *pot-metal*.] 1. A kind of paste or cement compounded of whiting, or soft carbonate of lime, and linseed-oil, mixed to the consistence of dough. In this state it is used by glaziers for fixing the panes of glass in window-sashes, etc., and also by house-painters to stop up holes and cavities in woodwork before painting. It is often tinted with various pigments to make it agree in color with the surface on which it is used. 2. A powder of oxid of tin, used in polishing glass and steel: sometimes called *jewelers' putty*.—3. A very fine cement, used by plasterers and stone-masons, made of lime only. See the quotation.

> Fine stuff [mortar made of fine white lime] very carefully prepared, and so completely macerated as to be held in solution in water, which is allowed to evaporate till it is of sufficient consistence for working, is called *putty*, plasterers' *putty*. *Workshop Receipts*, 1st ser., p. 121.

4. A mixture of ground materials in which in potteries earthenware is dipped for glazing.—5. A mixture of clay and horse-dung used in making molds in foundries.—**Glycerin putty**, a kind of putty, more properly a cement, made of glycerin and litharge.

putty (put'i), *v. t.*; pret. and pp. *puttied*, ppr. *puttying*. [< *putty*, *n.*] To cement with putty; fill up with putty.

putty-eye (put'i-ī), *n.* A name given by pigeon-fanciers to the eyes of pigeons which have a thick orbit of a fleshy character.

putty-faced (put'i-fāst), *a.* Having a face resembling putty in pastiness or color.

putty-knife (put'i-nīf), *n.* A knife with a blunt, flexible blade, used by glaziers for laying on putty; a stopping-knife.

Putty-knives.

putty-powder (put'i-pou"dėr), *n.* An artificially prepared oxid of tin (SnO_2), sometimes mixed with oxid of lead (PbO), used for polishing glass and other substances.

puttyroot (put'i-röt), *n.* An American orchid, *Aplectrum hiemale*, producing every year on a slender rootstock a corm an inch in diameter, filled with an extremely glutinous matter, which has been used as a cement, whence the name.

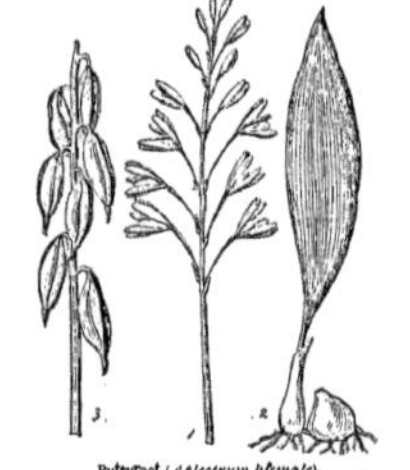

Puttyroot (*Aplectrum hiemale*).
1, upper part of flowering scape; 2, a leaf from a bulb of the season, showing attachment to bulb of preceding season; 3, fruiting scape.

Each corm persists till there are three or four horizontally connected. The newest sends up, late in summer, a single much-veined and plaited leaf, which lasts through the winter, and in spring a scape a foot or more high, with a loose raceme of brownish flowers. Also called *Adam and Eve*.

putty-work (put'i-wėrk), *n.* Decoration by means of a composition in which ornaments are modeled while it is soft, and which grows very hard. Coffers, picture-frames, shrines, etc., were elaborately decorated in this material in Italy in the sixteenth and seventeenth centuries, color being often added to the ornaments in relief.

put-up (pût'up), *a.* Concocted or planned by intimates or insiders, but so as to appear to emanate from or be the work of others; speciously conceived, planned, or carried out: as, a *put-up* job. [Colloq.]

> "Well, master," said Blathers, . . . "this warn't a *put-up* thing." "And what the devil 's a *put-up* thing?" demanded the doctor impatiently. "We call it a *put-up* robbery, ladies," said Blathers, turning to them as if he pitied their ignorance, but had a contempt for the doctor's, "when the servants is in it."
> *Dickens*, Oliver Twist, xxxi. (*Davies.*)

puture, pulture (pū'tūr, pul'tūr), *n.* [< OF. *peuture*, *puture*, *pouture*, *poture*, *pulture*, food, nourishment, < ML. **pultura*, *putura*, food, pottage, < L. *puls* (*pult-*), a thick broth or pottage: see *pulse*[2].] A custom claimed by keepers in forests, and sometimes by bailiffs of hundreds, to take food for man, horse, and dog from the tenants and inhabitants within the perambulation of the forest, hundred, etc.

> In 6 Henry VIII. (1514) *puture* was paid for the forest which was reclaimed towards the close of that reign.
> *Baines*, Hist. Lancashire, II. 25.

puxi (puk'si), *n.* [Mex. Ind.] The larvæ of the various dipterous insects of the genus *Ephydra*, which inhabit the alkali lakes of western North America, and are made into edible cakes: so called by Mexican Indians and Spanish Americans. See *Ephydra*, *ahuatle*, and *koochahbee*.

Puxi Fly (*Ephydra californica*).
(Line shows natural size.)

puy[1], *n.* Same as *poy*.

puy[2] (pwē), *n.* [F. *puy*: see *poy*, *pew*[2].] One of the small volcanic cones which are common in Auvergne, central France.

> It is a most striking sight to see the small cones or *Puys* of the later date, of which there are not fewer than 230, still looking as fresh and perfect as though they had been in eruption within the present century.
> *Prestwich*, Geol., I. 363.

Puya[1] (pū'yä), *n.* [NL. (Molina, 1782), from a native name in Chili.] A genus of monocotyledonous plants of the order *Bromeliaceæ*, unlike the rest of its tribe *Pitcairnieæ* in its loculicidal, not septicidal, dehiscence, and otherwise characterized by a filiform style, three-valved capsule, and numerous seeds surrounded by a wing. There are 3 or 4 species, natives of Peru and Chili. They bear narrow spiny leaves crowded at the base or apex of the unbranched and sometimes arborescent stem, and a terminal simple or pyramidally compound raceme, with a single showy flower under each bract. Several species are in cultivation under glass, sometimes under the former name *Pourretia*, including white and yellow, and less often blue, pink, and green flowering varieties. See *chagual gum*, under *gum*[2].

puya[2] (pū'yä), *n.* 1. See *pooa*.—2. A textile fiber yielded by the pooa.

puyssance†, puyssant†. Middle English forms of *puissance*, *puissant*.

puzzel†, *n.* [Appar. < OF. *pucelle*, a girl, maid: see *pucelle*. Some compare It. *puzzolente*, filthy.] A dirty drab.

> Pucelle or *puzzel*, dolphin or dogfish.
> *Shak.*, 1 Hen. VI., i. 4. 107.

> No, nor yet any droyle or *puzzel* in the country but will carry a nosegay in her hand.
> *Stubbes*, Anat. of Abuses. (*Nares.*)

puzzle (puz'l), *n.* [By apheresis, as if **pozel*, **posal*, from early mod. E. *opposal*, *opposelle*, *apposelle*, < ME. *opposayle*, a question put, < *opposen*, *apposen*, E. *oppose*, by apheresis *pose*, question: see *oppose* and *pose*[3].] 1. A difficult question or problem; specifically, a riddle, or a toy or contrivance which is designed to try one's ingenuity.

> Keep it like a *puzzle*, chest in chest,
> With each chest lock'd and padlock'd thirty-fold, . . .
> I yet should strike upon a sudden means
> To dig, pick, open, find, and read the charm.
> *Tennyson*, Merlin and Vivien.

2. Embarrassment; perplexity: as, to be in a *puzzle*, or in a state of *puzzle*.

puzzle (puz'l), *v.*; pret. and pp. *puzzled*, ppr. *puzzling*. [< *puzzle*, *n.*] I. *trans.* 1. To perplex or pose with or as with difficult points, problems, or questions; put to a stand; gravel.

> My Thoughts are now *puzzled* about my Voyage to the Baltic Sea upon the King's Service, otherwise I would have ventured upon an Epithalamium.
> *Howell*, Letters, ii. 72.

> A very shrewd disputant in those points is dexterous in *puzzling* others. *Dr. H. More*, Divine Dialogues.

> You meet him under that name incognito; then, if an accident should happen, both you and she may be safe, and *puzzle* the truth. *Steele*, Lying Lover, ii. 1.

2. To entangle; make intricate.

> The ways of heaven are dark and intricate,
> *Puzzled* in mazes and perplex'd with error.
> *Addison*, Cato, i. 1.

> They disentangle from the *puzzled* skein . . .
> The threads of politic and shrewd design
> That ran through all his purposes.
> *Cowper*, Task, iii. 145.

3. To resolve or discover by long cogitation or careful investigation; make out by mental labor; cogitate: with *out*.

> He endeavoured to *puzzle* its principle *out* for himself.
> *Gladstone*.

The bloodhound has a much more delicate nose than any other known breed of hound, and can *puzzle out* a cold scent under the most adverse conditions.
The Century, XXXVIII. 190.

=Syn. 1. *Perplex*, etc. (see *embarrass*), pose, nonplus, bewilder, stagger.

II. *intrans.* To be bewildered; be perplexed or posed.

"And now," he cried, "I shall be pleased to get
Beyond the Bible—there I *puzzle* yet." *Crabbe.*

puzzle-cup (puz'l-kup), *n.* Same as *surprise-cup.*

A two-handled *puzzle-cup* painted with flowers.
Hamilton Sale Catalogue, 1882, No. 806.

puzzledom (puz'l-dum), *n.* [< *puzzle* + *-dom.*] A puzzled or perplexed condition; bewilderment. [Colloq.]

I was resolved to travel with him into the land of *puzzledom.* *Richardson*, Clarissa Harlowe, VI. 367. (*Davies.*)

The wonderful interior of the double basilica opens upon us. The first feeling is simply *puzzledom.*
E. A. Freeman, Venice, p. 79.

puzzlehead (puz'l-hed), *n.* One who puzzles over matters that are plain and intelligible; a person of confused notions.

"All this theistic philosophy of yours only means so much grist to their mill in the end." "They don't see it in that light themselves," said Robert, smiling. "No," returned the Squire, "because most men are *puzzleheads.*"
Mrs. Humphry Ward, Robert Elsmere, xli.

puzzle-headed (puz'l-hed″ed), *a.* Given to puzzling over matters that are plain and intelligible; also, characteristic of puzzleheads.

He [Maittaire] seems to have been a *puzzle-headed* man, with a large share of scholarship, but with little geometry or logick in his head, without method, and possessed of little genius. *Johnson*, in Boswell, an. 1780.

puzzle-headedness (puz'l-hed″ed-nes), *n.* The state of being puzzle-headed or a puzzlehead. *The Academy*, April 26, 1890, p. 291.

puzzle-jug (puz'l-jug), *n.* A surprise-cup.

puzzle-lock (puz'l-lok), *n.* See *lock*[1].

At one time it used to be supposed that locks which could only be opened by setting a number of rings or disks to a particular combination of letters could not possibly be opened by anybody who was not in possession of the secret; and hence they were also called *puzzle-locks.*
Encyc. Brit., XIV. 746.

puzzlement (puz'l-ment), *n.* [< *puzzle* + *-ment.*] The state of being puzzled; bewilderment.

"I have heard of a wedding very often," said Fanny, with a pretty look of *puzzlement* and doubt, "but I don't know exactly what it means."
Bulwer, Night and Morning, v. 6.

A delightful air of *puzzlement* came over her face.
W. C. Russell, Jack's Courtship, xxviii.

puzzle-monkey (puz'l-mung″ki), *n.* [< *puzzle*, *v.*, + obj. *monkey.*] Same as *monkey-puzzle.* See *Araucaria.*

puzzle-peg (puz'l-peg), *n.* A short piece of board fastened under the lower jaw of a dog, and projecting a few inches beyond it, to prevent him from putting his nose close to the ground.

puzzler (puz'lėr), *n.* [< *puzzle* + *-er*[1].] One who or that which puzzles or perplexes.

Hebrew, the general *puzzler* of old heads.
A. Brome, Elegy on his Schoolmaster.

puzzle-ring (puz'l-ring), *n.* A number of small rings intertwined with one another so that they cannot be separated, the puzzle being to bring them together in the form of a single ring or in some other combination, as a sort of knot.

puzzling (puz'ling), *p. a.* [Ppr. of *puzzle*, *v.*] 1. Perplexing; embarrassing; bewildering.—2. Evidencing bewilderment or perplexity; easily bewildered or perplexed.

The servant is a *puzzling* fool, that heeds nothing.
Sir R. L'Estrange.

puzzlingly (puz'ling-li), *adv.* In a puzzling manner; perplexingly.

puzzolana, puzzolano (puz-ọ-lä'nạ̈, puz-ọ-lä'nō), *n.* Same as *pozzuolana.*

puzzolite (puz'ọ-lit), *n.* [< *puzzol(ana)* + *-ite*[2].] Same as *pozzuolana.*

pwys, *n.* [W., a state of rest, weight, a weight.] A Welsh weight of wool, about two pounds.

pxt. A contraction of the Latin *pinxit*, '(He) painted (it).'

pyæmia, pyæmic. See *pyemia*, *pyemic.*

Pyanepsia (pi-a̤-nep'si-ạ̈), *n. pl.* [< Gr. Πυανέψια (sc. ἱερά), an Athenian festival (see def.), said to be so called from a dish of beans which was then cooked and eaten, < πύανος, a bean, + ἕψειν, boil.] In ancient Athens, an annual festival of Apollo, celebrated on the 7th of the month Pyanepsion (October–November). It had the character of a harvest-feast.

pyarthrosis (pī-är-thrō'sis), *n.* [NL., < Gr. πύον, pus (see *pus*), + ἄρθρωσις, a jointing: see *arthrosis.*] The presence of pus in a joint.

pyat, *n.* See *piet.*

Pycnanthemum (pik-nan'thē-mum), *n.* [NL. (F. A. Michaux, 1803), so called in allusion to the dense inflorescence; < Gr. πυκνός, thick, dense, + ἄνθεμον, blossom.] A genus of gamopetalous plants of the order *Labiatæ*, tribe *Satureineæ*, and subtribe *Menthoideæ*. It is characterized by its four nearly equal straight and divergent stamens, a calyx sometimes two-lipped, with five teeth and about thirteen nerves, and a somewhat two-lipped corolla, with five ovate lobes, the flowers in dense verticillasters, involucrate with crowded bracts, and commonly corymbosely panicled. The 13 species, known as *mountain-mint*, and sometimes as *American basil* (see *basil*), are North American, and all but one are natives of the eastern or southern United States. They are erect and rigid perennial herbs, warmly aromatic and odorous, often hoary with minute down, and with flat-topped inflorescence, frequently conspicuous by reason of large whitened floral leaves. The flowers are whitish or purple and purple-dotted. They are commonly dimorphous in having in different flowers their stamens either exserted or included. The *P. lanceolatum* is sometimes known as *Virginian thyme* or *prairie-hyssop.* See cut under *linear.*

Pycnaspideæ (pik-nas-pid'ẹ̄-ē), *n. pl.* [NL., < Gr. πυκνός, thick, dense, + ἀσπίς (ἀσπιδ-), a round shield.] In Sundevall's system of classification, the fourth cohort of scutelliplantar *Passeres*, including a heterogeneous group of chiefly Neotropical birds, such as those of the genera *Rupicola*, *Chasmorhynchus*, *Cephalopterus*, *Tityra*, and *Lipaugus*, to which are added the East Indian genera *Calyptomena*, *Eurylæmus*, and others.

pycnaspidean (pik-nas-pid'ẹ̄-an), *a.* [< *Pycnaspideæ* + *-an.*] In *ornith.*, having the planta, or back of the tarsus, studded with many small irregular scales or plates, as a modification of the scutelliplantar tarsus.

pycnaster (pik-nas'tėr), *n.* [< Gr. πυκνός, thick, dense, + ἀστήρ, a star.] A kind of sponge-spicule. *Sollas.*

pycnid, pycnide (pik'nid), *n.* Same as *pycnidium*, 1.

pycnides, *n.* Plural of *pycnis.*

pycnidia, *n.* Plural of *pycnidium.*

pycnidial (pik-nid'i-al), *a.* [< *pycnidi-um* + *-al.*] Relating to a pycnidium, or having its character.

pycnidiophore (pik-nid'i-ọ-fōr), *n.* [< NL. *pycnidium*, q. v., + Gr. φέρειν = E. *bear*[1].] In *bot.*, a compound sporophore bearing pycnidia.

pycnidiospore (pik-nid'i-ọ-spōr), *n.* [< NL. *pycnidium* + Gr. σπόρος, seed.] In *bot.*, same as *stylospore.*

pycnidium (pik-nid'i-um), *n.*; pl. *pycnidia* (-ạ̈). [NL., < Gr. πυκνός, thick, dense, + dim. -ίδιον.] 1. In *bot.*, a receptacle in ascomycetous fungi, resembling a perithecium, in which stylospores or pycnospores are produced: same as *clinosporangium.* See *stylospore.* Also *pycnid*, *pycnide.*—2. [*cap.*] [NL.] In *entom.*, a genus of coleopterous insects of the family *Tenebrionidæ.* Also called *Oochrotus.* *Erichson*, 1846.

pycnis (pik'nis), *n.*; pl. *pycnides* (pik'ni-dēz). [NL., < Gr. πυκνός, thick, dense, compact.] In *bot.*, the same or nearly the same as *clinosporangium.*

pycnite (pik'nīt), *n.* [< Gr. πυκνός, thick, dense, compact, + *-ite*[2].] A compact columnar variety of topaz, from the tin-mines of Saxony and Bohemia.

Pycnocoma (pik-nok'ọ-mạ̈), *n.* [NL. (Bentham, 1849), < Gr. πυκνός, thick, + κόμη, hair (alluding to the stamens).] A genus of apetalous shrubs of the order *Euphorbiaceæ*, tribe *Crotoneæ*, and subtribe *Plukenetieæ.* It is characterized by numerous stamens which are often flexuous in the bud, small terminal anthers, and a long columnar style. The 8 species are equally divided in nativity between tropical Africa and the Mascarene Islands. They are shrubs, sometimes becoming small trees, bearing large entire leaves crowded at the end of the branches, and monœcious flowers in racemes in the upper axils, remarkable for the large number of the elongated stamens, often over fifty, borne on an elevated receptacle and intermixed with glands. See *bomah-nut.*

pycnoconidium (pik″nō-kō-nid'i-um), *n.*; pl. *pycnoconidia* (-ạ̈). [NL., < Gr. πυκνός, thick, + NL. *conidium*, q. v.] In *mycol.*, an asexually produced spore or conidium the character of which has recently (1888) been demonstrated. It is what has been called a *spermatium* in certain lichens, and was thought to be a fertilizing organ, but on being sown on a proper medium it immediately germinated and produced a thallus.

pycnodont (pik'nō-dont), *a.* and *n.* I. *a.* Pertaining to the *Pycnodontidæ*, or having their characters

II. *n.* A fossil fish of the family *Pycnodontidæ.*

Pycnodontes (pik-nọ-don'tēz), *n. pl.* [NL., pl. of *Pycnodus* (*-odont-*).] Same as *Pycnodontidæ.*

Pycnodontidæ (pik-nọ-don'ti-dē), *n. pl.* [NL., < *Pycnodus* (*-odont-*) + *-idæ.*] A family or suborder of ganoid fishes, typified by the genus *Pycnodus.* The tail is homocercal; the neural arches and ribs are ossified; the roots of the ribs are but little expanded in the older genera, but enlarged in the later ones, so as to simulate vertebræ; the paired fins are not lobate; the teeth on the palate and on the sides of the mandible are obtuse; the intermaxillary teeth are incisiform; and none of the fins are fulcrate. These fishes are characteristic of the Mesozoic and Tertiary; all are extinct.

Pycnodontini (pik″nọ-don-tī'ni), *n. pl.* [NL., < *Pycnodus* (*-odont-*) + *-ini.*] Same as *Pycnodontoidei.*

pycnodontoid (pik-nọ-don'toid), *a.* and *n.* I. *a.* Resembling or related to a pycnodont; belonging to the *Pycnodontoidei.*

II. *n.* A member of the *Pycnodontoidei.*

Pycnodontoidei (pik″nọ-don-toi'dẹ-ī), *n. pl.* [NL., < *Pycnodus* (*-odont-*) + *-oidei.*] A suborder of ganoid fishes, characterized by a persistent notochord, rhombic scales in pleurolepidal rows, paired fins without axial skeleton, and effulcrate and branchiostegal rays. The principal family is that of the *Pycnodontidæ.*

Pycnodus (pik'nō-dus), *n.* [NL. (Agassiz, 1833), < Gr. πυκνός, thick, + ὀδούς (ὀδοντ-) = E. *tooth.*] The typical genus of *Pycnodontidæ.*

Pycnogonata (pik-nọ-gon'a̤-tạ̈), *n. pl.* [NL., < Gr. πυκνός, thick, + γόνυ (γονατ-), knee, joint.] Same as *Pycnogonida.*

Pycnogonida (pik-nọ-gon'i-dạ̈), *n. pl.* [NL., < *Pycnogonum* + *-ida.*] A group of marine arthropod articulate animals, combining some characters of both *Crustacea* and *Arachnida* with others of neither of these classes; the sea-spiders. They have a four-segmented cephalothorax bearing four pairs of many-jointed legs ending in claws, and in the female a pair of additional appendages

Ammothea pycnogonoides, one of the *Pycnogonida*—female.
a, esophagus; *b*, stomach, prolonged into the limbs *e* and antennæ *d*; *c*, rectum.

between the anterior legs; a rudimentary unsegmented abdomen; a tubular or proboscis-like mouth, simple or appendaged; four ocelli; no respiratory organs; and the sexes distinct. The palpi when present have from five to nine joints and end in a claw. The group has been variously rated as a family, suborder, order, subclass, and class, and has been called or placed in *Arachnopoda*, *Araneiformia*, *Apotobranchia*, *Lævigrada*, *Nymphonacea*, *Pantopoda*, *Podosomata*, *Polygonopoda*, *Pseudarachna*, *Pycnogonata*, *Pycnogonidæ*, *Pycnogonidea*, and *Pycnogonides.* Some are parasitic, others are found moving sluggishly among seaweeds. Leading genera are *Pycnogonum*, *Phoxichilus*, *Nymphon*, and *Ammothea.* See also cut under *Nymphon.*

Pycnogonidæ (pik-nọ-gon'i-dē), *n. pl.* [NL., < *Pycnogonum* + *-idæ.*] 1. A family of *Pycnogonida*, typified by the genus *Pycnogonum*, containing parasites of comparatively stout form, with relatively short and knotty legs, and tubular mouth without either mandibles or palpi.—2†. Same as the group *Pycnogonida.*

Pycnogonidea (pik″nọ-gọ-nid'ẹ̄-ạ̈), *n. pl.* [NL.] Same as *Pycnogonida.*

Pycnogonides (pik-nọ-gon'i-dēz), *n. pl.* [NL.] Same as *Pycnogonida.*

pycnogonidium (pik″nọ-gọ-nid'i-um), *n.*; pl. *pycnogonidia* (-ạ̈). [NL., < Gr. πυκνός, thick, + NL. *gonidium.*] In *bot.*, same as *stylospore.*

pycnogonoid (pik-nog'ọ-noid), *a.* and *n.* I. *a.* Resembling a sea-spider; of or pertaining to the *Pycnogonida.*

II. *n.* Any member of the *Pycnogonida*.

Pycnogonum (pik-nog'ọ̄-num), *n.* [NL., < Gr. πυκνός, thick, + γόνυ, knee, joint.] The typical genus of *Pycnogonidæ*. *P. littorale* is a parasite of cetaceans, and is half an inch long.

Pycnogonum littorale, 1½ times natural size.

pycnometer (pik-nom'e-tėr), *n.* [< Gr. πυκνός, thick, dense, + μέτρον, measure.] An instrument for determining the relative density or specific gravity of solid bodies; a specific-gravity flask. It consists of a glass flask with a long tubular stopper. The flask, when filled with distilled water, and when the stopper is pressed in till the water overflows through the tubule of the stopper, will at any given temperature hold a specific volume and therefore a specific weight of the liquid. The combined weight of the flask and its stopper, and the weight of water it contains when the stopper is pressed in, having been ascertained, and also the total weight of the flask and its contents after the solid body has been placed in it, the then unfilled space refilled with distilled water, and the stopper again pressed in, the weight of the solid body in air and the weight of the water displaced by it when it is put in the pycnometer can be easily determined. These are the data necessary to compute the relative density or specific gravity of the body—a unit of mass of distilled water at 4° C. divided by its apparent volume at the same temperature being the usual unit of density. This unit is written "1.000" in specific-gravity tables in which the specific gravity of bodies lighter than water is expressed in three places of decimals. See *density*, *densimeter*, *specific gravity* (under *gravity*), *volume*, and *mass*[2].

Pycnometers.

pycnometochia (pik"nọ̄-me-tō'ki-ạ̈), *n.* [NL., < Gr. πυκνός, thick, close, crowded, + μετοχή, a participle.] Use of participles or participial clauses at short intervals; close succession of participles. Compare *oligometochia*.

pycnometochic (pik"nọ̄-me-tō'kik), *a.* [< *pycnometochia* + *-ic*.] Characterized by using or containing participles in close succession.

pycnon (pik'non), *n.* [Also *pyknon*; < Gr. πυκνόν, neut. of πυκνός, thick, dense, close, compact.] 1. In *anc. Gr. music*, one of the short intervals in the chromatic or euharmonic scales, usually about equivalent to a quarter-step.— 2. In *medieval music*, a half-step or semitone.

Pycnonotidæ (pik-nọ̄-not'i-dē), *n. pl.* [NL., < *Pycnonotus* + *-idæ*.] The bulbuls, rock-thrushes, or *Pycnonotinæ* rated as a family of *Passeres*.

Pycnonotinæ (pik"nọ̄-nọ̄-tī'nē), *n. pl.* [NL., < *Pycnonotus* + *-inæ*.] A subfamily of turdiform or thrush-like oscine passerine birds, placed in the family *Turdidæ*, or merged in the subfamily

White-eared Bulbul (*Pycnonotus leucotis*).

Brachypodinæ; the bulbuls or rock-thrushes, typified by the genus *Pycnonotus*.

pycnonotine (pik-nọ̄-nō'tin), *a.* Resembling or related to *Pycnonotus*; belonging to the *Pycnonotinæ*.

Pycnonotus (pik-nọ̄-nō'tus), *n.* [NL. (Kuhl, 1826), < Gr. πυκνός, thick, + νῶτος, the back.] An extensive genus of Old World thrush-like passerine birds, typical of the subfamily *Pycnonotinæ* or family *Pycnonotidæ*. It contains about fifty kinds of bulbuls, ranging from Persia and Palestine to South Africa. Also spelled *Piconotus*. See cut in preceding column.

pycnospore (pik'nọ̄-spōr), *n.* [< Gr. πυκνός, close, + σπόρος, seed.] Same as *stylospore*. *De Bary*.

pycnostyle (pik'nọ̄-stīl), *a.* [< Gr. πυκνός, thick, close, compact, + στῦλος, column.] In *classical columnar arch.*, according to the Vitruvian system, noting a conventional intercolumniation, less than that usually employed. It is commonly reckoned at one diameter and a half.

pyet, *n.* See *pie*[1], *pie*[2], etc.

pyebald†, *a.* An obsolete form of *piebald*.

pyedema (pī-ẹ̄-dē'mạ̈), *n.* [NL., < Gr. πύον, pus (see *pus*), + οἴδημα, a swelling, tumor.] Infiltration with pus.

pyelitic (pī-e-lit'ik), *a.* [< *pyelitis* + *-ic*.] Of or pertaining to pyelitis; affected with pyelitis.

pyelitis (pī-e-lī'tis), *n.* [NL., < Gr. πύελος, a trough or pan, hence the pelvis, + *-itis*.] Inflammation of the pelvis of the kidney. Also called *endonephritis*.

pyelocystitis (pī"e-lọ̄-sis-tī'tis), *n.* [NL., < Gr. πύελος, pelvis, + κύστις, bladder, + *-itis*.] Inflammation of the renal pelvis and of the urinary bladder.

pyelonephritic (pī"e-lọ̄-nef-rit'ik), *a.* [< *pyelonephritis* + *-ic*.] Of, pertaining to, or affected with pyelonephritis.

pyelonephritis (pī"e-lọ̄-nef-rī'tis), *n.* [NL., < Gr. πύελος, pelvis, + νεφρός, kidney, + *-itis*.] Inflammation of the kidney and the renal pelvis.

pyemia, pyæmia (pī-ē'mi-ạ̈), *n.* [NL. *pyæmia*, < Gr. πύον, pus (see *pus*), + αἷμα, blood.] In *pathol.*, a febrile disease caused by the absorption of pus, or certain of its constituents, or of its bacteria, with the formation of metastatic abscesses.

pyemic, pyæmic (pī-ē'mik), *a.* [< *pyemia*, *pyæmia* + *-ic*.] Of, pertaining to, or characterized by pyemia; of the nature of pyemia; affected with pyemia.

pyengadu (pī-eng'gạ-dö), *n.* [E. Ind.] An acacia-like tree, *Xylia dolabriformis*, one of the ironwoods, found in considerable quantities in India, Burma, etc. It rises 70 or 80 feet without branches, and furnishes a reddish-brown timber in large sizes and of remarkable quality. It is heavier than water, and so hard that the Burmese work it only before seasoning. It resists decay even better than teak, and its heart-wood is proof against white ants and teredo. From its power of resisting shocks, it is valued for gun-carriages, but it is also used for numerous other purposes requiring strength, hardness, and durability. Also *pynkado*.

pye-powder†, *n.* An old spelling of *piepowder*.

pyet, *n.* A variant of *piet*.

Pygæra (pī-jē'rạ̈), *n.* [NL. (Ochsenheimer, 1810), < Gr. πυγή, rump, + αἴρειν, raise, lift up.] A genus of lepidopterous insects of the bombycid family *Notodontidæ*, occurring in Europe and Asia; the buff-tips. *P. bucephala* is an example.

pygal (pī'gạl), *a.* and *n.* [< Gr. πυγή, rump, + *-al*.] **I.** *a.* In *zoöl.*, of or pertaining to the rump or posterior part of an animal.—**Pygal plate** or **shield**, in *herpet.*, one of the posterior median pieces of the carapace of a turtle. See *pygidium*, *uropygium*, and cuts under *carapace* and *Chelonia*.

II. *n.* The posterior median or supracaudal plate of the carapace of a tortoise; a pygal shield.

pygarg (pī'gärg), *n.* [< L. *pygargus*, a kind of antelope, also a kind of eagle, < Gr. πύγαργος, a kind of antelope, also the white-tailed eagle, *Falco albicilla*, also a kind of sandpiper, *Totanus ochropus*, lit. 'white-rumped,' < πυγή, rump, + ἀργός, shining, white.] 1†. A kind of antelope, perhaps the addax.

> The hart, and the roebuck, and the fallow deer, and the wild goat, and the *pygarg* [marg. or, bison; Heb. *dishon*], and the wild ox, and the chamois. Deut. xiv. 5.

2. The osprey, sea-eagle, or fish-hawk.

pygargue, *n.* Same as *pygarg*, 2.

pygargus (pī-gär'gus), *n.*; pl. *pygargi* (-jī). [NL.: see *pygarg*.] 1. Same as *pygarg*, 2.— 2. [*cap.*] [NL.] A genus of hawks: same as *Circus*. *Koch*, 1816.

pyght†. Same as *pight*, an obsolete past participle of *pitch*[1].

pygidial (pī-jid'i-ạl), *a.* [< *pygidium* + *-al*.] Of or pertaining to the pygidium; caudal; anal; cercal.

Pygidiidæ (pī-ji-dī'i-dē), *n. pl.* [NL., < *Pygidium* + *-idæ*.] A family of nematognathous fishes, typified by the genus *Pygidium*. They have a naked body, air-bladder confined in a capsule formed by the lateral processes of the anterior vertebræ only, the dorsal generally posterior, and no adipose fin. The species, about 40, are confined to the fresh waters of South America. Also called *Trichomycteridæ*.

pygidium (pī-jid'i-um), *n.*; pl. *pygidia* (-ạ̈). [NL., < Gr. πυγή, rump, + dim. -ίδιον.] 1. A posterior part of the body, in any way distinguished; an

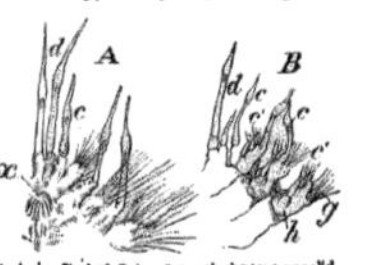

Posterior End of *Polynoë*, a polychætous annelid.
A, from above, *B*, from below, showing pygidium, etc.: *c*, *c'*, notopodial and neuropodial cirri of last true somite of the body; *d*, cirri of pygidium; *g*, setæ; *h*, inferior tubercle; *x*, anus.

anal, caudal, or pygal part or organ: said chiefly of insects, crustaceans, and worms. (*a*) In *entom.*, the last dorsabdominal segment, when modified or specialized, as into an ovipositor, sting, anal forceps or cerci, etc. The term is much used in the classification of coleopters, hymenopters, and some of the homopters. In *Coleoptera*, the term generally applies to any part of the dorsabdominal segments which may be visible beyond the ends of the closed elytra. This is usually harder than the part covered by the elytra. When more than one segment is thus exposed, *pygidium* may be restricted to the last one, the next preceding being distinguished as *propygidium*. (*b*) The terminal division of the body of a trilobite. See cut under *Trilobita*. (*c*) The terminal segment of a worm. 2. [*cap.*] A genus of nematognaths, typical of the family *Pygidiidæ*. Later called *Trichomycterus*.—**Divided pygidium.** See *divided*.

pygmean, pigmean (pig-mē'ạn), *a.* [< L. *pygmæus*, < Gr. πυγμαῖος, dwarfish: see *pygmy*, *pigmy*.] Pertaining to a pygmy or dwarf; very small; dwarfish.

> Throng numberless, like that *pygmean* race
> Beyond the Indian mount. *Milton*, P. L., i. 780.

pygmy, pigmy (pig'mi), *n.* and *a.* [Early mod. E. also *pigmie*, *pigmey*, *pigmee*; < ME. *pigmey*, *pygmey*, *pygme* = OF. *pigme*, *pygme*, F. *pygmée* = Sp. *pigmeo* = Pg. *pigmeo*, *pygmeo* = It. *pigmeo* = G. *pygmäe* = Sw. *pygmé* = Dan. *pygmæ* = Russ. *pigmeĭ*, < L. *Pygmæus*, a Pygmy, dwarf, as adj. dwarfish, < Gr. Πυγμαῖος, in pl. Πυγμαῖοι, a Pygmy, a dwarf, adj. dwarfish, lit. long or tall as a πυγμή, < πυγμή, a measure of length, the distance from the elbow to the knuckles, equal to 18 δάκτυλοι ('fingers') or about 13½ inches, a particular use of πυγμή, a fist, akin to L. *pugnus*, the fist: see *pugil*[1], *pugnacious*.] **I.** *n.*; pl. *pygmies* (-miz). 1. [*cap.*] One of a fabulous race of dwarfs, mentioned by various ancient authors. The Pygmies (Pygmæi, with an eponymic ancestor Pygmæus) of Greek fable were represented by Homer as dwelling on the southern shores of Ocean, and as being warred upon by the cranes in their annual migrations. Later writers placed them in India and elsewhere. The African Pygmies described by Herodotus, and hitherto supposed to be equally fabulous, were apparently the same as the remarkable race or races of dwarfs found by recent explorers in various parts of equatorial Africa, especially those discovered by Stanley (1888) in the forests of the upper Congo region.

Hence—2. A little or dwarfish person; a dwarf; also, anything very small of its kind.

> In another Yle ther ben litylle folk, as Dwerghes; and thei ben to so meche as the *Pygmeyes*, and thei han no Mouthe, but in stede of hire Mouthe thei han a lytylle round hole. *Mandeville*, Travels, p. 205.

> Thy God raigns in his Ark, and I on Earth:
> I Chalenge Him, Him (if he dare come forth),
> Not Thee, base *Pigmee*.
> *Sylvester*, tr. of Du Bartas's Weeks, ii., The Trophies.

> *Pygmies* are *pygmies* still though perch'd on Alps,
> And pyramids are pyramids in vales.
> *Young*, Night Thoughts, vi.

3. The chimpanzee: perhaps as the supposed original of the fabled Pygmies.

II. *a.* 1. Belonging to or resembling a pygmy; pygmean; dwarfish; very small of its kind; little.

> Behold the Child among his new-born blisses,
> A six years' Darling of a *pigmy* size.
> *Wordsworth*, Ode to Immortality.

2. In *zoöl.*, very small of its kind; dwarfish or dwarf: applied to many animals.

pygmy, pigmy (pig'mi), *v. t.*; pret. and pp. *pygmied, pigmied*, ppr. *pygmying, pigmying*. [< *pygmy, n.*] To make like a pygmy; dwarf. [Rare.]

> Stand off, thou poetaster, from thy press,
> Who *pygmiest* martyrs with thy dwarf-like verse.
> *Wood*, Fasti Oxon. (1st ed.), II. 799. (*Latham.*)

pygmy-weed (pig'mi-wēd), *n.* A plant, *Tillæa simplex*, a tufted annual an inch or two high, found on muddy banks from Nantucket to Maryland.

Pygobranchia (pī-gō-brang'ki-ä), *n. pl.* [NL., < Gr. πυγή, rump, + βράγχια, gills.] In J. E. Gray's classification (1821), one of two orders (the other being *Polybranchia*) of gymnobranchiate gastropods, having plumose or branching gills surrounding the anus on the middle of the hinder part of the back, and the skin more or less spiculous. It was framed to receive the families *Onchidoridæ, Dorididæ, Goniodoridæ, Polyceridæ, Triopidæ*, and *Ceratosomidæ*. *Anthobranchia* is a synonym.

Pygobranchiata (pī-gō-brang-ki-ā'tä), *n. pl.* [NL., neut. pl. of *pygobranchiatus*: see *pygobranchiate*.] Same as *Pygobranchia*.

pygobranchiate (pī-gō-brang'ki-āt), *a.* [< NL. *pygobranchiatus*, < Gr. πυγή, rump, + βράγχια, gills: see *branchiate*.] Having gills around the anus; of or pertaining to the *Pygobranchiata*.

pygodidymus (pī-gō-did'i-mus), *n.*; pl. *pygodidymi* (-mī). [NL., < Gr. πυγή, rump, + δίδυμος, double, twofold, twin.] Same as *dipygus*.

pygopagus (pī-gop'a-gus), *n.*; pl. *pygopagi* (-jī). [NL., < Gr. πυγή, rump, + πάγος, that which is fixed or firmly set, < πηγνύναι, make fast, make solid.] In *teratol.*, a double monster with union at the buttocks.

pygoparasiticus (pī-gō-par-a-sit'i-kus), *n.*; pl. *pygoparasitici* (-sī). [NL., < Gr. πυγή, rump, + παρασιτικός, parasitic.] In *teratol.*, a pygopagus where one fetus is a parasite.

pygope (pī'gōp), *n.* A lizard of the family *Pygopodidæ*; a pygopod.

Pygopidæ (pī-gop'i-dē), *n. pl.* [NL.] Same as *Pygopodidæ*.

pygopod (pī'gō-pod), *a.* and *n.* [< Gr. πυγή, rump, + πούς (ποδ-) = E. *foot*.] **I.** *a.* **1.** In *ornith.*, rump-footed, as an auk, loon, or grebe; having the legs inserted far back, appearing close by the rump; of or pertaining to the *Pygopodes*.—**2.** In *herpet.*, of or pertaining to the *Pygopodidæ*.

II. *n.* In *herpet.*, a lizard of the family *Pygopodidæ*.

Pygopodes (pī-gop'ō-dēz), *n. pl.* [NL.: see *pygopod*.] An order of swimming and diving birds, the rump-footed birds, having the legs inserted very far back, and buried in the common integument of the body nearly to the heel. Its limits have varied with different writers, but it is now generally considered to include the loons, grebes, and auks, and to exclude the penguins, which, though pygopodous, are otherwise very different in important respects. It then consists of the families *Colymbidæ, Podicipedidæ*, and *Alcidæ*. In consequence of the position of the legs, these birds can hardly walk, and when on land they assume a more or less nearly upright attitude. See cuts under *Alca, grebe*, and *loon*.

Pygopodidæ (pī-gō-pod'i-dē), *n. pl.* [NL., < *Pygopodes* + *-idæ*.] An Australian family of eriglossate lacertilians, typified by the genus *Pygopus*, alone representing the superfamily *Pygopodoidea*, having the frontal bone excluded from the orbit, the prefrontal and postfrontal bones being extended and contiguous. Also *Pygopidæ*.

Pygopodoidea (pī"gō-pō-doi'dē-ä), *n. pl.* [NL., < *Pygopodes* + *-oidea*.] A superfamily of eriglossate lacertilians, represented by the family *Pygopodidæ* alone, having concavo-convex vertebræ, the clavicle not dilated and loop-shaped proximally, and no postorbital or postfrontal squamosal arches. *T. Gill*, Smithsonian Report, 1885.

Pygopus lepidopodus. *a*, rudiment of hind leg.

pygopodous (pī-gop'ō-dus), *a.* [< *pygopod* + *-ous*.] In *ornith.*, rump-footed; specifically, of or pertaining to the *Pygopodes*, or having the characters of that group of birds: also applied to some birds, as cormorants and penguins, which do not belong to the *Pygopodes*.

Pygopus (pī'gō-pus), *n.* [NL. (Merrem, 1820), < Gr. πυγή, rump, + πούς = E. *foot*.] A genus of lizards, typical of the family *Pygopodidæ*, having a pair of rudimentary hind limbs. *P. lepidopodus*, the only species, inhabits Australia; it is about 2 feet long. See cut in preceding column.

Pygoscelis (pī-gos'e-lis), *n.* [NL. (Wagler, 1832), < Gr. πυγή, rump, + σκέλος, leg.] A genus of penguins, of which the gentoo or so-called Papuan penguin, *P. papua* or *P. tæniata*, is the type. It is one of those commonly called *johnny* by sailors. See *gentoo*[2].

Gentoo (*Pygoscelis tæniata*).

pygostyle (pī'gō-stīl), *n.* [< Gr. πυγή, rump, + στῦλος, column.] In *ornith.*, the vomer or plowshare bone of a bird's tail, consisting of a number of caudal vertebræ ankylosed together for the support of the tail-feathers, and possessed by nearly all birds. Since the oldest known birds (of Jurassic age) had no pygostyle, but a long tapering tail like a lizard's with a pair of large feathers to each vertebra (see cut under *Archæopteryx*), and since all modern birds have a pygostyle, upon which feathers are bunched in several pairs, it follows that, theoretically, a pygostyle includes or represents as many coalesced caudal vertebræ as there are pairs of feathers in the tail—namely, five or six in most birds, up to twelve or more in some. But this view does not rest upon observation. Whatever its morphological character, the pygostyle is always the last bone of the tail, and always conspicuous in size; in shape it is very variable in different birds.

Pygostyle.—Eight caudal vertebræ of an eagle (*Haliaetus leucocephalus*), of which the last, *p*, is the pygostyle. (Two thirds natural size.)

pygostyled (pī'gō-stīld), *a.* [< *pygostyle* + *-ed*[2].] Furnished with a pygostyle; forming or converted into a pygostyle.

> Tail short as to its vertebræ, which are *pygostyled*.
> *Coues*, Key to N. A. Birds, p. 238.

pyic (pī'ik), *a.* [< Gr. πύον, pus, + *-ic*.] Of or belonging to pus; purulent.

pyjamas, *n. pl.* Same as *pajamas*.

pykt, pyket, *n.* and *v.* Obsolete spellings of *pike*[1].

pykedt, *a.* A Middle English form of *piked*.

pykeyst, *n.* A Middle English form of *pickax*. *Prompt. Parv.*

pyknometer, *n.* Same as *pycnometer*.

pyknon, *n.* See *pycnon*.

pyla (pī'lä), *n.*; pl. *pylæ* (-lē). [NL., < Gr. πύλη, a gate.] The orifice by which each paraqueduct or optic ventricle of the brain communicates with the aqueduct of Sylvius.

pylagoras (pi-lag'ō-ras), *n.*; pl. *pylagorai* (-rī). [< Gr. Πυλαγόρας (see def.), < Πύλαι, the Pass of Thermopylæ (pl. of πύλη, gate, pass), + ἀγείρειν, collect, gather: see *agora*.] In ancient Greece, an elected delegate or representative of a constituent state in the Amphictyonic Council. The pylagorai were secondary to the delegates entitled *hieromnemones* (see *hieromnemon*), and had their name from the older place of assembly of the Pythian Amphictyony, at Pylai (Thermopylæ).

pylagore (pī'la-gōr), *n.* [< Gr. Πυλαγόρας: see *pylagoras*.] Same as *pylagoras*.

pylangial (pī-lan'ji-al), *a.* [< *pylangi-um* + *-al*.] Pertaining to the pylangium.

pylangium (pī-lan-jī'um), *n.*; pl. *pylangia* (-ä). [NL., < Gr. πύλη, a gate, + ἀγγεῖον, a vessel.] The first section of the arterial trunk (truncus arteriosus) of the lower vertebrates. See *truncus*.

pylar (pī'lär), *a.* [< *pyle*[3] + *-ar*[3].] Of or pertaining to a pyle; specifically, pertaining to the pylæ of the brain.

pylchet, *n.* A Middle English form of *pilch*[1].

pyle[1]**t**, *n.* A Middle English form of *pile*[1], etc.

pyle[2] (pīl), *n.* [Perhaps a use of *pyle*[1] = *pile*[1].] A single grain of chaff. *Burns*, To the Unco Guid. [Scotch.]

pyle[3] (pīl), *n.* [< Gr. πύλη, a gate.] A pore or other orifice or opening of small size, as a micropyle. *Coues.*

pylemphraxis (pī-lem-frak'sis), *n.* [NL., < Gr. πύλη, a gate, + ἔμφραξις, a stopping: see *emphractic*.] Obstruction of the portal vein.

pylephlebitis (pī-lef-lē-bī'tis), *n.* [NL., < Gr. πύλη, a gate, + φλέψ (φλεβ-), a vein, + *-itis*. Cf. *phlebitis*.] Inflammation of the portal vein and its branches.

pylethrombosis (pī-leth-rom-bō'sis), *n.* [NL., < Gr. πύλη, a gate, + NL. *thrombosis*, q. v.] Thrombosis of the portal vein.

pylgrimt, *n.* A Middle English form of *pilgrim*.

pylon (pī'lon), *n.* [< Gr. πυλών, a gateway, < πύλη, a gate, a gateway.] In *arch.*, a monumental gateway to an Egyptian temple, or other important building. The pylon was sometimes a single structure, in outline resembling a truncated pyramid, through which the passage for the gate was pierced, but was more typically a combination of two such truncated pyramidal structures, connected by a lower architectural member, in which was the gate proper. They were usually covered with elaborate decoration in sculpture, together with hieroglyphic inscriptions. Often used synonymously with *propylon*. (Compare *propylon*.) Various forms of the pylon are used as hieroglyphic symbols. That shown in the cut stands for *On*, the Greek Heliopolis.

Pylon.—Temple of Edfou, Egypt.

Hieroglyphic Pylon.

pylorectomy (pī-lō-rek'tō-mi), *n.* [< NL. *pylorus* + Gr. ἐκτομή, a cutting out.] Excision of the pylorus, as for cancer.

pyloric (pī-lor'ik), *a.* and *n.* [< NL. *pylorus* + *-ic*.] **I.** *a.* In *anat.*, of or pertaining to the pylorus: opposed to *cardiac*: as, *pyloric* valve; *pyloric* orifice; *pyloric* compartment of the stomach. See cuts under *Dibranchiata, ink-bag*, and *intestine*.

> In the darter, which has a *pyloric* division or compartment of the gizzard, this is nearly filled with a mass of matted hairs, a peculiar modification of the epithelial lining, serving to guard the *pyloric* orifice.
> *Coues*, Key to N. A. Birds, p. 213.

Pyloric artery, a branch of the hepatic artery, distributed to the pyloric extremity and lesser curvature of the stomach. The name is sometimes restricted to the small branch given off to the pylorus only.—**Pyloric cæca.** (*a*) In *ichth.*, more or less numerous cæcal diverticula which are generally found about the beginning of the small intestine of fishes. (*b*) In *entom.*, the cæcal diverticula with which the chylific ventricle of an insect may be provided. See cut under *Blattidæ*.—**Pyloric glands.** See *gland*.—**Pyloric orifice.** Same as *pylorus*, 1 (*a*).—**Pyloric ossicle**, a transverse, partly calcified plate situated in the root of the pyloric part of the stomach of some crustaceans, as crawfish, and connected with the pterocardiac by the zygocardiac ossicle.—**Pyloric plexus.** See *plexus*.—**Pyloric sacs**, in echinoderms, dilatations of the alimentary canal, as of a starfish, on the aboral side of the cardiac sacs, separated by a constriction from the latter, and provided with tubular processes along the aboral aspect of a ray or arm.—**Pyloric tube**, a narrowed or tubular part of the stomach of a fish.—**Pyloric vein**, a small vein accompanying the pyloric artery and emptying into the portal vein.

II. *n. pl.* The pyloric cæca of a fish.

> When ascending into fresh water with their ova nearly ready for extrusion, their *pylorics* are loaded with fat.
> *The Field* (London), Dec. 26, 1885.

Pylorideat (pī-lō-rid'ē-ä), *n. pl.* [NL., < Gr. πυλωρός, also πυλουρός, a gate-keeper (see *pylorus*), + *-idea*.] In De Blainville's classification, the tenth family of bivalve mollusks, characterized by gaping shells with deep pallial emargination. It contains a number of genera now dissociated in several different families, especially *Myidæ, Solenidæ, Saxicavidæ*, and *Gastrochænidæ*.

pyloridean (pī-lō̤-rid′ē̤-an), *a.* and *n.* [< NL. *Pyloridea* + *-an.*] I. *a.* Gaping, as a bivalve mollusk; of or pertaining to the *Pyloridea*.

II. *n.* A member of the *Pyloridea*.

pyloristenosis (pī-lō̤-ris-te-nō′sis), *n.* [NL., < Gr. πυλωρός, pylorus, + στένωσις, a narrowing, straitening, < στενοῦν, narrow, straiten, στενός, narrow, strait.] Morbid contraction of the pylorus.

pylorochesis (pī-lō-rō̤-kē′sis), *n.* [NL., < Gr. πυλωρός, pylorus, + ὄχησις, a carrying, driving (taken in sense of 'holding'), < ὀχεῖν, bear, carry, drive, < ἔχειν, hold, have.] Obstruction of the pylorus.

pylorus (pī-lō′rus), *n.*; pl. *pylori* (-rī). [NL., < LL. *pylorus*, < Gr. πυλωρός, also πυλουρός, a gatekeeper, also the lower orifice of the stomach, < πύλη, a gate, a pass, + ὤρα, Ionic ὤρη, care, heed, or οὖρος, a watcher or warder, < ὁρᾶν, see.] 1. In the *early church*, a doorkeeper; an ostiary (which see).—2. In *anat.*: (*a*) The orifice of communication between the stomach and the intestine, by which the contents of the stomach pass into the intestine. It is usually situated on the right-hand side, opposite the cardiac or esophageal orifice, but may closely approximate or be adjoined to the latter. See cut under *stomach*. (*b*) The fold of mucous membrane, containing muscular fibers, which guards the pyloric orifice, or other contrivance for retarding or opposing the passage of food from the stomach into the intestine. (*c*) The pyloric end or division of the stomach.—3. In *Hydrozoa*, a valvular structure which separates the gastric from the somatic cavity in the siphonophorous hydrozoans.—**Antrum pylori.** See *antrum*.—**Sphincter pylori**, a bundle of unstriped muscular fibers encircling the pyloric end of the stomach.

pymma (pim′ạ̈), *n.* Same as *bloodwood*, 4.

pympert, *v. t.* An obsolete variant (or misprint) of *pamper*.

> Good mistress Statham, . . . seeing what case I was in, hath fetched me home to her own house, and doth *pymper* me up with all diligence, for I fear a consumption.
> *Latimer*, Sermons and Remains (Parker Soc.), p. 386. [(*Davies*.)

pynaclet, *n.* A Middle English form of *pinnacle*.

pyncht, *v.* An obsolete spelling of *pinch*.

pyndt, **pyndert**. Middle English forms of *pind*, *pinder*.

pynet, *n.* and *v.* A Middle English spelling of *pine*[2].

pynnet, *n.* and *v.* A Middle English form of *pin*[1].

pyoblennorrhœa (pī-ō̤-blen-ō̤-rē′ạ̈), *n.* [NL., < Gr. πύον, pus, + βλέννος, mucus, + ῥοία, a flow, < ῥεῖν, flow. Cf. *blennorrhea*.] Muco-purulent discharge.

pyochezia (pī-ō̤-kē′zi-ạ̈), *n.* [NL., < Gr. πύον, pus, + χέζειν, ease oneself.] The condition in which pus is discharged by the intestine.

pyocœlia (pī-ō̤-sē′li-ạ̈), *n.* [NL., < Gr. πύον, pus, + κοιλία, a cavity: see *cœlia*.] The presence of pus in the abdominal cavity.

pyocolpos (pī-ō̤-kol′pos), *n.* [NL., < Gr. πύον, pus, + κόλπος, womb.] The presence of pus in the vagina.

pyocystis (pī-ō̤-sis′tis), *n.* [NL., < Gr. πύον, pus, + κύστις, bladder: see *cystis*.] An encysted collection of pus.

pyogenesis (pī-ō̤-jen′e-sis), *n.* [NL., < Gr. πύον, pus, + γένεσις, origin, source: see *genesis*.] The generation of pus; the theory or process of the formation of pus. Also *pyogenia*.

pyogenetic (pī″ō̤-jē̤-net′ik), *a.* [< *pyogenesis*, after *genetic*.] Pertaining to pyogenesis; pyogenic.

pyogenia (pī-ō̤-jē′ni-ạ̈), *n.* [NL., < Gr. πύον, pus, + -γένεια, < -γενής, producing.] Same as *pyogenesis*.

pyogenic (pī-ō̤-jen′ik), *a.* [< Gr. πύον, pus, + -γενής, producing, + *-ic*.] Having relation to the formation of pus; producing or generating pus.—**Pyogenic fever**, pyemia.

pyohemothorax (pī-ō̤-hē-mō̤-thō′raks), *n.* [NL., irreg. < Gr. πύον, pus, + αἷμα, blood, + θώραξ, thorax.] The presence of pus and blood in the pleural cavity.

pyoid (pī′oid), *a.* [< Gr. πυοειδής, like pus, < πύον, pus, + εἶδος, form.] Having the nature of or resembling pus; purulent.

pyolymph (pī′ō̤-limf), *n.* [< Gr. πύον, pus, + NL. *lympha*, lymph: see *lymph*.] Lymph somewhat turbid with pus-corpuscles.

pyometra (pī-ō̤-mē′trạ̈), *n.* [NL., < Gr. πύον, pus, + μήτρα, uterus.] The presence of pus in the uterus.

pyonephritis (pī″ō̤-nef-rī′tis), *n.* [NL., < Gr. πύον, pus, + NL. *nephritis*, q. v.] Suppurative inflammation of the kidney.

pyonephrosis (pī″ō̤-nef-rō′sis), *n.* [NL., < Gr. πύον, pus, + νεφρός, kidney, + *-osis*.] The presence of pus in the kidney and its pelvis.

pyonephrotic (pī″ō̤-nef-rot′ik), *a.* [< *pyonephrosis* (*-ot-*) + *-ic*.] Pertaining to pyonephrosis.

pyoningt, *n.* See *pioning*.

pyonyt, *n.* An obsolete form of *piony*, *peony*.

pyopericardium (pī-ō̤-per-i-kär′di-um), *n.* [NL., < Gr. πύον, pus, + NL. *pericardium*: see *pericardium*.] The presence of pus in the pericardial sac.

pyoperitonitis (pī-ō̤-per″i-tō̤-nī′tis), *n.* [NL., < Gr. πύον, pus, + NL. *peritonitis*, q. v.] Suppurative peritonitis.

pyophthalmia (pī-of-thal′mi-ạ̈), *n.* [NL., < Gr. πύον, pus, + ὀφθαλμία, a disease of the eyes: see *ophthalmia*.] Production of pus in the eye.

pyopneumothorax (pī-ō̤-nū-mō̤-thō′raks), *n.* [NL., < Gr. πύον, pus, + πνεύμων, lung, + θώραξ, thorax.] Same as *pneumopyothorax*.

pyopoësis (pī″ō̤-pō̤-ē′sis), *n.* Same as *pyopoiesis*.

pyopoiesis (pī″ō̤-poi-ē′sis), *n.* [NL., < Gr. πύον, pus, + ποίησις, production, < ποιεῖν, make.] Suppuration; production of pus; pyosis. Also *pyopoësis*.

pyoptysis (pī-op′ti-sis), *n.* [NL., < Gr. πύον, pus, + πτύσις, a spitting, < πτύειν, spit.] Expectoration of pus.

pyorrhea, **pyorrhœa** (pī-ō̤-rē′ạ̈), *n.* [NL. *pyorrhœa*, < Gr. πύον, pus, + ῥοία, a flow, < ῥεῖν, flow.] Purulent discharge.—**Pyorrhœa alveolaris**, an alveolar abscess.

pyosalpingitis (pī-ō̤-sal-pin-jī′tis), *n.* [NL., < Gr. πύον, pus, + σάλπιγξ (σαλπιγγ-), a tube, + *-itis*.] Purulent inflammation of a Fallopian tube.

pyosalpinx (pī-ō̤-sal′pingks), *n.* [NL., < Gr. πύον, pus, + σάλπιγξ, a tube.] The presence of pus in a Fallopian tube.

> The difficulty of accurate diagnosis between a *pyosalpinx* and a hydrosalpinx . . . must here be taken into account.
> *Lancet*, No. 3477, p. 837.

pyosapremia (pī″ō̤-sap-rē′mi-ạ̈), *n.* [NL., < Gr. πύον, pus, + σαπρός, rotten, + αἷμα, blood.] The infection of the blood with a purulent exudate, as pus.

pyoscope (pī′ō̤-skōp), *n.* [< Gr. πύον, pus, + σκοπεῖν, view.] An instrument for the determination of the amount of fat in milk.

pyosis (pī-ō′sis), *n.* [< Gr. πύωσις, suppuration, < πυοῦν, cause to suppurate, < πύον, pus: see *pus*.] The progress or formation of pus.

pyott, *n.* See *piet*.

pyothorax (pī-ō̤-thō′raks), *n.* [NL., < Gr. πύον, pus, + θώραξ, thorax.] The presence of pus in a pleural cavity; empyema.

> He had seen the rapid formation of an abscess follow an exploratory puncture in a case of tuberculous *pyothorax*.
> *Lancet*, No. 3479, p. 989.

pyracanth (pir′ạ̈-kanth), *n.* [< Gr. πυράκανθα, a variety of thorn, < πῦρ, fire, + ἄκανθος, a prickly tree, a thorn.] A thorn, *Cratægus Pyracantha*, found in the south of Europe.

pyracid (pī-ras′id), *n.* Same as *pyro-acid*.

pyral (pī′ral̤), *a.* [< *pyre* + *-al*.] Of or pertaining to a pyre.

> Whether unto eight or ten bodies of men to adde one of a woman, as being more inflammable, and unctuously constituted for the better *pyrall* combustion, were any rational practise.
> *Sir T. Browne*, Urn-burial, iv.

> In connection with each house supposed by Mr. Cushing to be the house of a clan or one of the sociological divisions, such as are found among the Pueblo Indians, was what the explorer calls a *pyral* mound. On this the bodies and effects of the dead were consigned to fire.
> *Science*, XII. 40.

pyralid (pir′ạ̈-lid), *a.* and *n.* I. *a.* Resembling a moth of the family *Pyralidæ*; belonging to this family; pyralideous.

II. *n.* A pyralid moth; any member of the *Pyralidæ* or *Pyralidina*.

Also *pyralidine*.

Pyralidæ (pī-ral′i-dē), *n. pl.* [NL. (Leach, 1819), < *Pyralis* + *-idæ*.] A heterogeneous family of moths, of uncertain limits and characters. They are generally of medium size or small, with slender bodies and long legs, and with both maxillary and labial palpi. The family has in fact for many years been a resting-place for genera which do not find place in the other, better defined, families. Also *Pyralidina*, and preferably *Pyralididæ*. See cut under *bee-moth*.

pyralideous (pir-ạ̈-lid′ē̤-us), *a.* [< *pyralid* + *-eous*.] Pyralid; of or pertaining to the *Pyralidina*: as, "the *pyralideous* group," *Stainton*.

Pyralididæ (pir-ạ̈-lid′i-dē), *n. pl.* [NL.] Same as *Pyralidæ*.

pyralidiform (pir-ạ̈-lid′i-fôrm), *a.* [< NL. *Pyralis* (*-id-*) + L. *forma*, form.] Having the form or structure of a pyralid moth; pyralidine or pyralideous; belonging to the *Pyralidiformia*.

Pyralidiformia (pir-ạ̈-lid-i-fôr′mi-ạ̈), *n. pl.* [NL.: see *pyralidiform*.] A group of pyralidiform or pyralideous moths. *Schrank*, 1802.

Pyralidina (pir″ạ̈-li-dī′nạ̈), *n. pl.* [NL., < *Pyralis* (*-id-*) + *-ina*[2].] Same as *Pyralidæ*.

pyralidine (pī-ral′i-din), *a.* and *n.* Same as *pyralid*.

Pyralis (pir′ạ̈-lis), *n.* [NL. (Schrank, 1801), < L. *pyralis*, < Gr. πυραλίς, πυρραλίς, a winged insect supposed to live on fire, < πῦρ, fire: see *pyre*.] A genus of moths, typical of the family *Pyralidæ*, having a conspicuous proboscis and ascending palpi. About a dozen species are known, mainly European. *P. farinalis* is a cosmopolitan flour-pest.

pyrallolite (pī-ral′ō̤-lit), *n.* [So called as taking another color; < Gr. πῦρ, fire, + ἄλλος, other, + λίθος, stone.] A white or greenish altered variety of pyroxene, found in Finland.

pyramid (pir′ạ̈-mid), *n.* [Formerly also, as L., *pyramis*, pl. *pyramides*; = F. *pyramide*, formerly *piramide* = Sp. *pirámide* = Pg. *piramide*, *pyramide* = It. *piramide* = D. *piramiede* = G. *pyramide* = Sw. *pyramid* = Dan. *pyramide*, < L. *pyramis* (*-mid-*), < Gr. πυραμίς (-μιδ-), a pyramid, perhaps < Egypt. *pir-em-us*, the slanting edge of a pyramid. Some have imagined a connection with Gr. πῦρ, fire, as if named from the resemblance to a tapering flame.] 1. A massive structure of polygonal, usually square plan, the sides of which slope, each usually in one plane, to a common apex. Pyramids have been erected in different parts of the world, especially in Egypt, where there are numerous groups in different styles of execution and states of preservation. By far the most interesting of these groups is that of Ghizeh, near Cairo, where there are three pyramids of large size, and several smaller ones. All the Egyptian pyramids were built for tombs, and certainly in most cases, if not in all, for royal personages. They are remarkable not only for the great size of many of them, but for the manner in which they were hermetically sealed, there being no external opening of any kind, nor any indication of the place in which the mummy had been deposited; on the contrary, some of them exhibit very ingenious arrangements intended to lead astray those search-

The Pyramids of Ghizeh, Egypt.

ing for the sepulchral chamber. Everything was planned in their construction to insure permanence, concealment, and security from violation. Of the three great pyramids at Ghizeh, the largest and by far the most important and interesting is the so-called Great Pyramid, in regard to which a very extensive literature exists, and which has frequently been measured and elaborately described. It is the largest work of man's hands in the world, having been originally 481 feet in height, and each of the sides of its very nearly square base measuring on the average nearly 756 feet (9068.8 in., Petrie). It is the only one remaining of the "seven wonders of the world." Its interior structure is more elaborate than that of any of the other pyramids, and some of the features which it displays are peculiar, and remarkable as showing the desire of the builders that at least one geometrical fact of fundamental importance should be incorporated into the structure. Thus the height of the Great Pyramid bears, with remarkable precision, the same relation to the total length of the four sides of its base that the radius of a circle has to its circumference, and other indications of the π ratio exist in its interior. This and other interesting peculiarities of this pyramid have led various persons, some of whom have been eminent in science, to adopt the view that it was a divinely inspired building, and that the so-called "coffer" contained within the principal sepulchral chamber was intended to serve as a standard of weights and measures and a record of various fundamental facts in geophysics, and not for a sarcophagus. Of the manner in which the huge stones of which this pyramid is built were raised to their present position but little is definitely known, but it is inferred that the work was done without the aid of complicated machinery; that they were shaped — to a very considerable extent at least — by the use of saws of bronze, the teeth of which were gems or hard stones, has been clearly shown by the most recent investigations. The date of the Great Pyramid, which is believed to have been built by or for King Shufu (Cheops) of the fourth dynasty, is variously fixed by Egyptologists at from 2450 to 4235 B. C. The latter is the date assigned by Mariette.

2. In *geom.*, a solid contained by a plane polygon as base and other planes meeting in a point. This point is called the vertex of the pyramid; and the planes which meet in the vertex are called the

sides, which are necessarily all triangles, having for their bases the sides of the base of the pyramid. Any pyramid is in volume one third of a prism that has the same base and altitude. Pyramids are denominated from the figures of their bases, being triangular, square, pentagonal, etc., according as the base is a triangle, a square, a pentagon, etc.

Knowledges are as *pyramids*, whereof history is the basis. *Bacon*, Advancement of Learning, ii. 165.

3. In *crystal.*, a form, in any system but the isometric, bounded by eight, twelve, sixteen, or twenty-four planes, and consisting of two four-, six-, eight-, or twelve-sided pyramids placed base to base. The name is also extended to embrace any form the planes of which intersect all three of the axes; in the monoclinic system it includes only four, and in the triclinic only two planes, being in each case an open form. If the planes intersect the lateral axes at the assumed unit distances, the pyramid is called a *unit pyramid*; other forms are designated *macropyramids*, *clinopyramids*, etc. (see these terms), according to their position. In the tetragonal system a unit pyramid is also called a *protopyramid*, or pyramid of the first order or series, and a square octahedron formed by pyramidal planes parallel to one of the lateral axes is in distinction called a *deuteropyramid* or *diametral pyramid*, or one of the second order or series. These terms are also used in an analogous manner in the hexagonal system.
4. In *zoöl.* and *anat.*, a pyramidal or conical part, structure, or organ; specifically, a mass of longitudinal fibers on each side of the anterior median fissure of the oblongata. See cut under *Elasmobranchii*.—5. The pile of five or six triangular valves covering an opening on the oral surface of the body of a cystic crinoid. The structure is variously interpreted as ovarian or oro-anal.—6. In *medieval arch.*, a pinnacle of quadrangular plan, most commonly

Pyramids.—Apsidal Buttresses of Rheims Cathedral, France.

acutely pyramidal in form; hence, any similar feature. Compare *pyramidion*.

Accordingly at Amiens this weight is set . . . in the form of an upright square mass of masonry crowned by a steep *pyramid*, and the Gothic pinnacle stands forth in essential completeness. *C. H. Moore*, Gothic Architecture, p. 84.

7. The American columbo, or Indian lettuce, *Frasera Carolinensis*.—**Decussation of the pyramids**, the crossing over of the crossed pyramidal tract of one side to join the direct pyramidal tract of the other, revealed externally by bundles crossing the anterior median fissure of the oblongata a little below the olivary bodies.—**Double pyramid group.** See *group*[1].—**Malpighian pyramids.** See *Malpighian*.—**Posterior pyramid**, a funiculus gracilis. (Rare.)—**Pyramid of the cerebellum**, a lobe of the vermis interior of the cerebellum, behind the uvula. It is connected laterally with the digastric lobes.—**Pyramid of the thyroid gland**, an occasional conical third lobe of the thyroid gland.—**Pyramid of the tympanum**, a small conical bony prominence on the posterior wall of the tympanic cavity, behind the fenestra ovalis, containing the stapedius muscle in its interior, and transmitting the tendon of that muscle through a foramen at its apex.—**Pyramid of the vestibule**, a prominence on the inner wall of the vestibular cavity, behind the fovea hemispherica.—**Pyramid of Wistar**, the sphenoturbinal bone.—**Pyramid pool.** See *pool*[2], *n.*, 2 (*a*).—**Pyramids of Ferrein**, a name given to the bundles of straight renal tubules which constitute the medullary rays. These bundles as they approach the cortical margin become smaller and more conical from the diminution of the number of tubules, whence the name.—**Pyramids of the medulla oblongata**, *anterior* and *posterior*. See def. 4, and *posterior pyramid*, above.—**Pyramids of the spine**, a name given to the anteriorly projecting parts of the spinal column. The *upper pyramid* is formed by all the vertebræ from the second cervical to the last lumbar, and this is again subdivided into three lesser pyramids; the *lower pyramid* is composed of the sacrum and coccyx.

pyramidal (pi-ram'i-dal), *a.* [= F. *pyramidal* = Sp. *piramidal* = Pg. *pyramidal* = It. *piramidale* = D. *piramiedaal*, < ML. *pyramidalis*, pertaining to a pyramid, < L. *pyramis* (*-mid-*), a pyramid: see *pyramid*.] 1. Pertaining to a pyramid, or having its form. Also *pyramidical*.

He [Plato] would compound the earth of cubical and fire of *pyramidal* atoms, and the like. *Cudworth*, Intellectual System, p. 53.

These meadows are planted with mulberry trees, and adorned by the *pyramidal* tomb of Caius Cestius. *Eustace*, Italy, I. xi.

2. In *bot.*, *anat.*, and *zoöl.*, shaped more or less like a pyramid; conical; pyriform.—**Pyramidal bell-flower**, an ornamental plant, *Campanula pyramidalis*. Also called *chimney-plant*.—**Pyramidal bone**, the cuneiform bone of the carpus; the pyramidale.—**Pyramidal column.** Same as *fasciculus gracilis*.—**Pyramidal hemihedrism.** See *hemihedrism*.—**Pyramidal muscle**, the pyramidalis.—**Pyramidal numbers**, the third order of figurate numbers. See *figurate*.—**Pyramidal plane**, in *crystal.*, one of the faces of a pyramidal crystal. See *pyramid*, 3.—**Pyramidal tract**, a system of nerve-fibers which originate in the cortex, in the region of the central fissure, pass down in the posterior limb of the internal capsule and the central section of the crusta, form the pyramids in the oblongata, and divide into the direct and crossed pyramidal tracts, to terminate in the immediate vicinity of and in close physiological connection with the origins of motor nerves in the anterior columns of the spinal cord. Some few fibers may pass to the lateral pyramidal tract without crossing, and a few may cross and re-cross in the cord to the original side. (Also called *peduncular tract*.) *The pyramidal tract crossed* is that part of the pyramidal fibers which crosses in the oblongata to pass downward in the posterior part of the lateral column of the opposite side of the cord. *The pyramidal tract direct* is that part of the pyramidal fibers which descends the cord without crossing over to the contralateral side. It lies close to the anterior median fissure, and is sometimes called the *column of Türck*.

pyramidale (pi-ram-i-dā'lē), *n.*; pl. *pyramidalia* (pir'a-mi-dā'li-ä). [NL., neut. of *pyramidalis*, q. v.] The cuneiform bone of the carpus, more fully called *os pyramidale*.

pyramidalis (pi-ram-i-dā'lis), *n.*; pl. *pyramidales* (-lēz). [NL., sc. *musculus*, muscle: see *pyramidal*.] One of several different pyramidal or pyriform muscles. (*a*) In *human anat.*: (1) The external rectus muscle of the abdomen, a small triangular muscle, two or three inches long, arising from the os pubis in front of the rectus, and inserted into the linea alba below the navel. More fully called *pyramidalis abdominis*, and also *rectus externus*. It is comparatively small and vestigial, and often absent, in man, representing a large muscle which in some animals reaches from the pubes to the clavicles. (2) A slip from the occipitofrontalis, lying upon the nose, more fully called *pyramidalis nasi*. Also called *dorsalis narium*, *procerus nasi*, and *procerus*. (*b*) In *ornith.*, one of the two muscles of the nictitating membrane, situated upon the back of the eyeball, of a pyramidal or pyriform shape, cooperating with the quadratus in movements of the third eyelid. See third cut under *eye*[1].—**Pyramidalis abdominis.** See def. (*a*) (1).—**Pyramidalis femoris.** Same as *pyriformis*.—**Pyramidalis narium.** Same as *levator labii superioris alæque nasi* (which see, under *levator*). See also *sneering-muscle*, under *muscle*[1].—**Pyramidalis nasi.** See def. (*a*) (2).

pyramidalism (pi-ram'i-dal-izm), *n.* [< *pyramidal* + *-ism*.] The body of facts or beliefs respecting the pyramids of Ghizeh. C. *Piazzi Smyth*.

pyramidalist (pi-ram'i-dal-ist), *n.* [< *pyramidal* + *-ist*.] A pyramidist.

pyramidally (pi-ram'i-dal-i), *adv.* In the form of a pyramid: as, a part *pyramidally* produced; in a loose sense, so as to form a high, angular elevation; hence, extremely.

If, according unto his [Aristotle's] own ethicks, sense is not essential unto felicity, but a man may be happy without the apprehension thereof, surely in that sense he is *pyramidally* happy. *Sir T. Browne*, Vulg. Err., vii. 13.

pyramidate (pi-ram'i-dāt), *a.* [< *pyramid* + *-ate*[1].] In *entom.*, pyramidal; jutting out into a prominent angle: as, a *pyramidate* fascia.

Pyramidella (pir"a-mi-del'ä), *n.* [NL. (Lamarck, 1796), dim. of L. *pyramis* (*-mid-*), a pyramid: see *pyramid*.] The typical genus of *Pyramidellidæ*.

Pyramidella (*Obeliscus*) *dolabrata*.

Pyramidellacea (pir-a-mid-e-lā'sē-ä), *n. pl.* [NL., < *Pyramidella* + *-acea*.] Same as *Pyramidellidæ*.

Pyramidellidæ (pir"a-mi-del'i-dē), *n. pl.* [NL., < *Pyramidella* + *-idæ*.] A family of gymnoglossate holostomatous pectinibranchiate gastropods, typified by the genus *Pyramidella*. The animal has flattened auriform tentacles, eyes sessile on the tentacles behind, a long retractile proboscis, and a mentum below the mouth. The shell is turreted or conic, with the nucleus sinistral and the rest of the shell dextral, aperture entire, and columellar lip plicated or simple. Species are distributed in all temperate and warm seas.

pyramides, *n.* Plural of *pyramis*.

pyramidia, *n.* Plural of *pyramidion*.

pyramidic (pir-a-mid'ik), *a.* [< *pyramid* + *-ic*.] Having the form of a pyramid; pyramidal.

Their gold in *pyramidic* plenty piled. *Shenstone*, Elegies, xix.

pyramidical (pir-a-mid'i-kal), *a.* [< *pyramidic* + *-al*.] Same as *pyramidic*.

The contrivance of nature is singular in the opening and shutting of bindweeds, performed by five inflexures, distinguishable by *pyramidical* figures, and also different colours. *Sir T. Browne*, Garden of Cyrus, iii.

This bounding line [of a building] from top to bottom may either be inclined inwards, and the mass therefore *pyramidical*; or vertical, and the mass form one grand cliff; or inclined outwards, as in the advancing fronts of old houses. *Ruskin*, Seven Lamps of Architecture, iii. § 6.

pyramidically (pir-a-mid'i-kal-i), *adv.* In a pyramidical manner; in the form of a pyramid.

Pelion, being the least, is placed above Ossa, and thus they rise *pyramidically*. *Pope*, Odyssey, xi., note.

pyramidicalness (pir-a-mid'i-kal-nes), *n.* The character of being pyramidic. *Bailey*, 1727.

pyramidion (pir-a-mid'i-on), *n.*; pl. *pyramidia* (-ä). [NL., < Gr. *πυραμίδιον, dim. of πυραμίς, a pyramid: see *pyramid*.] In *arch.*, the apex in the shape of a small pyramid which often terminates the top of an obelisk, and was very commonly sheathed with a cap of metal: often applied to any comparatively small structure or member of pyramidal shape.

pyramidist (pir'a-mid-ist), *n.* [< *pyramid* + *-ist*.] One who makes a special study of the pyramids of Egypt, or is versed in their structure and history.

pyramidoid (pi-ram'i-doid), *n.* [< Gr. πυραμίς (-μιδ-), pyramid, + εἶδος, form. Cf. *pyramoid*.] A parabolic spindle. Also *pyramoid*. *Bailey*, 1727.

pyramidoidal (pir-a-mi-doid'al), *a.* [< *pyramidoid* + *-al*.] Having the shape of a pyramidoid.

pyramidon (pi-ram'i-don), *n.* [< *pyramid* + *-on*, as in *harmonicon*, *accordion*, etc.] In *organ-building*, a stop having wooden pipes in the form of an inverted pyramid, about four times as large at the top as below, and giving very deep tones somewhat like those of a stopped diapason.

pyramid-shell (pir'a-mid-shel), *n.* Any member of the *Pyramidellidæ*.

pyramis (pir'a-mis), *n.*; pl. *pyramides* (pi-ram'i-dēz). [L., a pyramid: see *pyramid*.] A pyramid. Formerly also *piramis*.

Make
My country's high *pyramides* my gibbet,
And hang me up in chains!
Shak., A. and C., v. 2. 61.

Place me, some god, upon a *pyramis*
Higher than hills of earth, and lend a voice
Loud as your thunder to me.
Beau. and Fl., Philaster, iv. 4.

At the end of this Labyrinth there stood a square *Pyramis* of a marvellous breadth and answerable altitude. *Sandys*, Travailes, p. 88.

Pyramis vestibuli, the pyramidal eminence of the vestibule.

pyramoid (pir'a-moid), *n.* [< Gr. πυραμοειδής, like a pyramid, < πυραμίς (-μιδ-), a pyramid, + εἶδος, form.] Same as *pyramidoid*.

pyramoidal (pir-a-moi'dal), *a.* [< *pyramoid* + *-al*.] Same as *pyramidoidal*.

Pyranga, *n.* See *Piranga*. *Vieillot*, 1816.

pyrargyrite (pī-rär'ji-rīt), *n.* [< Gr. πῦρ, fire, + ἄργυρος, silver, + *-ite*[2].] An important ore of silver, consisting of the sulphid of silver and antimony. It occurs in crystals belonging to the rhombohedral system, often highly complex, and also in massive forms. When transparent it has a deep ruby-red color by transmitted light, though on the surface it is nearly black with a metallic adamantine luster; the streak has a cochineal-red color. Also called *ruby silver*, or, in distinction from proustite, *dark-red silver ore*. The common Spanish name in Mexico and South America is *rosicler oscuro*, or sometimes *petlanque*. See *proustite*.

pyrate†, *n.* and *v.* An obsolete spelling of *pirate*.

pyre (pīr), *n.* [= Sp. *pira* = Pg. *pyra* = It. *pira* (cf. F. *pyrée*), < L. *pyra*, < Gr. πυρά, Ionic πυρή, a hearth, the place of a funeral fire, a funeral pile, a mound raised on the place of a pyre, < πῦρ = E. *fire*: see *fire*.] A pile or heap of wood or other combustible materials for burning a dead body; a funeral pile.

For nine long nights, through all the dusky air,
The *pyres* thick flaming shot a dismal glare.
Pope, Iliad, i. 72. (*Richardson.*)

Apollo's upward fire
Made every eastern cloud a silvery *pyre*
Of brightness. *Keats*, Endymion, i.

pyrena (pī-rē'nä), *n.*; pl. *pyrenæ* (-nē). [NL.: see *pyrene*[1].] Same as *pyrene*[1].

Pyrenæmata (pir-ẹ̄-nē'ma-tạ̈), *n. pl.* [NL., neut. pl. of *pyrenæmatus*: see *pyrenematous*.] Those animals which are pyrenematous, as a lower series of vertebrates. See *Apyrenæmata*.

pyrenarium (pī-rẹ̄-nā'ri-um), *n.*; pl. *pyrenaria* (-ạ̈). [NL., < *pyrena*, stone of a fruit, + *-arium*.] A pome; properly, a drupaceous pome—that is, one containing pyrenes, as that of the medlar and of *Cratægus*. [Rare.]

pyrene[1] (pī'rēn), *n.* [< NL. *pyrena*, < Gr. πυρήν, the stone of a fruit, as of a date or olive.] A stone or putamen, properly when there are several in a single fruit, as in the huckleberry and other berry-like drupes, and in some pomes with a stony endocarp, as those of the hawthorn and medlar; a nutlet. Also *ossiculus*.

pyrene[2] (pī'rēn), *n.* [< Gr. πῦρ, fire, + *-ene*.] A hydrocarbon ($C_{15}H_{12}$) obtained from coal-tar.—**Pyrene-oil.** See *olive-oil*.

Pyrenean (pir-ẹ̄-nē'ạn), *a.* [= F. *Pyrénéen*, < L. *Pyrenæi*, sc. *montes*, the Pyrenees, < *Pyrene*, < Gr. Πυρήνη, the Pyrenees.] Of or pertaining to the Pyrenees, a range of mountains between France and Spain.

> Till o'er the hills her eagles flew
> Beyond the *Pyrenean* pines.
> *Tennyson*, Death of Wellington, vi.

pyreneite (pir-ẹ̄-nē'īt), *n.* [< *Pyrenees* (see def.) + *-ite*[2].] A variety of garnet of a grayish-black color, found in the Pyrenees.

pyrenematous (pir-ẹ̄-nem'ạ-tus), *a.* [< NL. *pyrenæmatus*, < Gr. πυρήν, the stone of a fruit, + αἷμα (αἱματ-), blood.] Having nucleated blood-corpuscles: distinguished from *apyrenematous*. *Gulliver*.

Pyrenestes (pir-ẹ̄-nes'tēz), *n.* [NL. (Swainson, 1837), also erron. *Pirenestes*; irreg. < Gr. πυρήν, the stone of a fruit, + ἐσθίειν, eat (cf. *Chondestes*).] A leading genus of *Spermestinæ*, including a number of African spermestine birds, as *P. ostrina* (or *sanguinea*) and *P. coccinea*.

pyrenin (pī-rē'nin), *n.* [< *pyrene*[2] + *-in*[2].] In *biol.*, according to F. Schwartz, the chemical substance composing the nucleoli of a cell—the nuclear membrane being accordingly termed *amphipyrenin*.

pyrenium (pī-rē'ni-um), *n.*; pl. *pyrenia* (-ạ̈). [NL., < Gr. πυρήνιον, dim. of πυρήν, the stone of a fruit: see *pyrene*[1].] In *bot.*, the hypothecium of a nucleiform or angiocarpous apothecium. *Encyc. Brit.*

pyrenocarp (pī-rē'nọ̄-kärp), *n.* [< Gr. πυρήν, the stone of a fruit, + καρπός, fruit.] In *bot.*: (*a*) Any drupaceous fruit. (*b*) In *mycol.*, same as *perithecium*.

pyrenocarpous (pī-rē-nọ̄-kär'pus), *a.* [< *pyrenocarp* + *-ous*.] In *bot.*, resembling, belonging to, or possessing a pyrenocarp.

pyrenodean (pī-rẹ̄-nō'dẹ̄-ạn), *a.* [< *pyrenodeous* + *-an*.] In *bot.*, pyrenodeous; specifically, having the character of a pyrenium.

pyrenodeine (pī-rẹ̄-nō'dẹ̄-in), *a.* [< *pyrenodeous* + *-ine*[1].] In *bot.*, same as *pyrenoid*.

pyrenodeous (pī-rẹ̄-nō'dẹ̄-us), *a.* [< Gr. πυρήν, the stone of a fruit, + εἶδος, form, + *-eous*.] In *bot.*, same as *pyrenoid*.

pyrenoid (pī-rē'noid), *a.* and *n.* [< Gr. πυρήν, the stone of a fruit, + εἶδος, form.] **I.** *a.* Resembling in form the stone of a fruit; globular; nucleiform; of excrescent bodies, wart-like.

II. *n.* A small colorless mass of proteid substance of a crystalline form, usually appearing hexagonal in optical section. *Huxley and Martin*, Elementary Biology, p. 398.

Pyrenolichenes (pī-rē″nọ̄-lī-kē'nēz), *n. pl.* [NL., < *Pyreno*(*mycetes*) + *Lichenes*.] A division of lichens in which the fungus which enters into the composition of the lichen belongs to the *Pyrenomycetes*.

pyrenomycete (pī-rē-nọ̄-mī'sēt), *n.* [< *Pyrenomycetes*.] In *bot.*, a member of the *Pyrenomycetes*.

Pyrenomycetes (pī-rē″nọ̄-mī-sē'tēz), *n. pl.* [NL., < Gr. πυρήν, the stone of a fruit, + μύκης, pl. μύκητες, mushroom.] An order of ascomycetous fungi of parasitic or saprophytic habit, with the tissues usually hard and somewhat coriaceous. The asci are long and club-shaped, usually containing eight spores, and are produced in deep flask-shaped cavities or perithecia. This order includes a large number of exceedingly injurious fungi which attack and destroy plants and also insects. The ergot, *Claviceps purpurea*, and the black-knot, *Sphæria morbosa* of cherry- and plum-trees, are familiar examples. The most destructive diseases of the grape are also due to members of this order, such as the black-rot, *Physalospora Bidwellii*, and the powdery grape-mildew, *Uncinula spiralis* or *Oïdium Tuckeri*. See *ergot*[1], for cut and description; also *black-knot*, *Sphæria* and *Valsa*, *grape-mildew*, *Phoma*, *Uncinula*, *Oïdium*, *Phyllosticta*.

pyrenomycetous (pī-rē″nọ̄-mī-sē'tus), *a.* [< *Pyrenomycetes* + *-ous*.] In *bot.*, belonging to, similar to, or characteristic of the *Pyrenomycetes*.

> Certain *pyrenomycetous* fungi. *Encyc. Brit.*, XIV. 559.

pyrenous (pī-rē'nus), *a.* [< *pyrene*[1] + *-ous*.] In *bot.*, containing pyrenes: used only in composition with a numeral: as, 2-*pyrenous*, 5-*pyrenous*, etc.

pyrethrum (pir'e-thrum), *n.* [NL. (Gärtner, 1791), < L. *pyrethrum*, < Gr. πύρεθρον, a plant, *Anacyclus Pyrethrum*, so called from the hot spicy taste of the root, < πῦρ, fire.] **1.** A plant of the genus *Pyrethrum*; feverfew.—**2.** [*cap.*] A former genus of composite plants of the tribe *Anthemideæ*, now included as part of the section *Pyrethra* in the genus *Chrysanthemum*, from which it was distinguished by achenes nearly equally from five- to ten-ribbed and crowned with a pappus, characters now known to vary in the same species. The most common species is now called *Chrysanthemum Parthenium* (for which see *feverfew*, 1, *pellitory*, 2, and *bertram*). Its variety *aureum* is the golden-feather of the gardens, used for edging.
3. A powdered preparation of pyrethrum, used as an insectifuge. Also called *pyrethrum-powder*. See *insect-powder* and *buhach*.—**4.** In *phar.*, the *Anacyclus Pyrethrum*, or pellitory-of-Spain.

pyretic (pī-ret'ik), *a.* and *n.* [Irreg. < Gr. πυρεκτικός, feverish, < πυρέσσειν, be feverish, < πυρετός, burning heat, fever, < πῦρ, fire: see *fire*.] **I.** *a.* Characterized by or affected with pyrexia or fever; feverish.

> Antipyrin, however, was continued night and morning in doses of gr. xv. throughout the *pyretic* period.
> *Medical News*, XLIX. 40.

II. *n.* A remedy for fever.

pyretogenesia (pir″e-tọ̄-je-nē'si-ạ̈), *n.* [NL.: see *pyretogenesis*.] Same as *pyretogenesis*.

pyretogenesis (pir″e-tọ̄-jen'e-sis), *n.* [NL., < Gr. πυρετός, fever, + γένεσις, origin: see *genesis*.] The genesis of pyrexia.

pyretology (pir-e-tol'ọ̄-ji), *n.* [< Gr. πυρετός, fever, + -λογία, < λέγειν, speak: see *-ology*.] The branch of medical science which treats of fevers.

pyrexia (pī-rek'si-ạ̈), *n.* [NL., < Gr. πύρεξις, feverishness, < πυρέσσειν, be feverish, < πυρετός, fever: see *pyretic*.] A higher bodily temperature than is normal; fever.

pyrexial (pī-rek'si-ạl), *a.* [< *pyrexia* + *-al*.] Of or pertaining to pyrexia.

pyrexic (pī-rek'sik), *a.* [Irreg. < *pyrexy* + *-ic*.] Same as *pyrexial*.

pyrexical (pī-rek'si-kạl), *a.* [< *pyrexic* + *-al*.] Same as *pyrexial*.

pyrexy (pir'ek-si), *n.* [< NL. *pyrexia*, q. v.] Same as *pyrexia*.

Pyrgita (pėr-jī'tạ̈), *n.* [NL., < Gr. πυργίτης, of a tower (cf. στρουθὸς πυργίτης, a house-sparrow), < πύργος, a tower.] A genus of fringilline birds, the sparrows, now usually placed in the genus *Passer*: so called because the common house-sparrow often builds its nest in towers.

pyrgoidal (pėr-goi'dạl), *a.* [< *pyrgoid (< Gr. πυργοειδής, like a tower, < πύργος, a tower, + εἶδος, form) + *-al*.] Tower-shaped; of the form of a prism having at one end a pyramid on the same base.—**Pyrgoidal number,** a number of the form

$$\tfrac{1}{6}(m-2)r^3 - \tfrac{1}{2}(2m-7)r^2 + \tfrac{1}{6}(2m-7)r.$$

pyrheliometer (pėr-hē-li-om'e-tėr), *n.* [< Gr. πῦρ, fire, + ἥλιος, sun, + μέτρον, measure.] An instrument devised by M. Pouillet for measuring the intensity of the heat of the sun. It consists of a shallow cylindrical vessel of thin silver or copper, containing water or mercury in which a thermometer is plunged. The upper surface of the vessel is covered with lampblack, so as to make it absorb as much heat as possible, and the vessel is attached to a support in such a way that the upper surface can always be made to receive the rays of the sun perpendicularly. The actual amount of heat absorbed by the instrument is calculated by ordinary calorimetrical means: the area of the exposed blackened surface is known, and the amount of water or mercury which has been raised through a certain number of thermometric degrees is known, and thus the absolute heating effect of the sun, acting upon a given area under the conditions of the experiment, can be readily found. Also *pyroheliometer*.

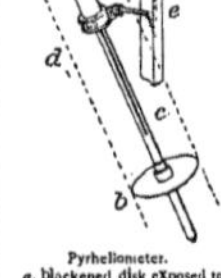

Pyrheliometer.
a, blackened disk exposed to sun's rays, the direction of which is indicated by dotted lines, as *ab*; *c*, column of delicate thermometer whose bulb is inserted in the box beneath *a*; *e*, place of support.

> The *pyrheliometer* and actinometer measure for us the outflow of solar heat, and show us that the blaze is at least seven or eight times as intense as that of any furnace known to art. *C. A. Young*, The Sun, p. 18.

pyrheliometric (pėr-hē″li-ọ̄-met'rik), *a.* [< *pyrheliometer* + *-ic*.] Of or pertaining to, or recorded or indicated by, the pyrheliometer: as, *pyrheliometric* observations.

pyridia, *n.* Plural of *pyridium*.

pyridine (pir'i-din), *n.* [< Gr. πῦρ, fire, + *-id* + *-ine*[2].] A colorless liquid (C_5H_5N) of pungent odor, derived from coal-tar, and useful in allaying asthmatic paroxysms.

pyridium (pī-rid'i-um), *n.*; pl. *pyridia* (-ạ̈). [NL., < L. *pyrum*, prop. *pirum*, a pear, + Gr. dim. -ίδιον.] In *bot.*, same as *pome*.

pyriform (pir'i-fôrm), *a.* and *n.* [Prop. *piriform*; < L. *pyrum*, prop. *pirum*, a pear (see *pear*[1]), + *forma*, form.] **I.** *a.* Pear-shaped; having the general shape of a pear; obconic; differing from egg-shaped or oviform in having a slight constriction running around it, or, in section, a reverse or concave curve between the convex curves of the two ends: as, a *pyriform* vase. See cut of egg under *plover*.

II. *n.* In *anat.*, the pyriformis.

pyriformis (pir-i-fôr'mis), *n.*; pl. *pyriformes* (-mēz). [NL., sc. *musculus*, muscle: see *pyriform*.] A flat triangular muscle situated partly within and partly without the pelvis. It arises chiefly from the anterior surface of the sacrum, and, after passing through the sacrosciatic foramen, is inserted into the upper fore part of the great trochanter of the femur. It is one of a group of six muscles collectively known as *rotatores femoris*. The character of the muscle varies much in different animals. Also called *pyramidalis femoris* and *iliacus externus*.—**Fascia of the pyriformis.** See *fascia*.

pyritaceous (pir-i-tā'shius), *a.* [< *pyrites* + *-aceous*.] Of or pertaining to pyrites. See *pyritic*.

pyrite (pī'rīt), *n.* [Formerly also *pyrit*; < L. *pyrites*, < Gr. πυρίτης, a flint, millstone, pyrite, prop. adj., pertaining to fire (πυρίτης λίθος, a mineral which strikes fire), < πῦρ, fire: see *pyre*. Cf. *pyrites*.] Native iron disulphid (FeS_2), a very common mineral, occurring in isometric crystals, cubes, octahedrons, pyritohedrons, etc., and also, and more often, massive. It has a pale brass-yellow color and brilliant metallic luster, and is very hard. It is used in large quantities in the manufacture of sulphuric acid and of sulphur. It is commonly called *iron pyrites*, which term, however, also includes the related orthorhombic species marcasite, as well as the magnetic pyrites, or pyrrhotine. Compare *marcasite*, 1.

> Like the *pyrit* stone, that is fier without and frost within. *Greene*, Never too Late (Works, ed. Dyce, Int., p. xii.).

> Hence sable coal his massy couch extends,
> And stars of gold the sparkling *pyrite* blends.
> *Dr. E. Darwin*, Botanic Garden, I. ii. 350.

pyritegium (pir-i-tē'ji-um), *n.*; pl. *pyritegia* (-ạ̈). [ML., < Gr. πῦρ, = E. *fire*, + L. *tegere*, cover. Cf. equiv. ML. *ignitegium*.] The curfew-bell: so called in medieval Latin. See *curfew*.

pyrites (pi-rī'tēz), *n.* [NL., < L. *pyrites*, < Gr. πυρίτης, a flint, millstone, pyrite.] Either of the common sulphids of iron, pyrite and marcasite, but also the yellow sulphid of copper and iron, chalcopyrite: the former are called distinctively *iron pyrites*, while the latter is known as *copper pyrites*. The name is also extended to other related sulphids and arsenides of iron, cobalt, nickel, etc.: as, pyrrhotine or *magnetic pyrites*, arsenopyrite or *arsenical pyrites*, linnæite or *cobalt pyrites*, millerite or *capillary pyrites*, etc.—**Cockscomb pyrites, spear pyrites, white iron pyrites.** See *marcasite*, 2.—**Hepatic pyrites.** See *hepatic*.

pyritic (pi-rit'ik), *a.* [< NL. *pyrites* + *-ic*.] Pertaining to pyrites; consisting of or resembling pyrites.

pyritical (pi-rit'i-kạl), *a.* [< *pyritic* + *-al*.] Same as *pyritic*.

pyritiferous (pir-i-tif'ẹ-rus), *a.* [< NL. *pyrites* + L. *ferre* = E. *bear*[1].] Containing or producing pyrites.

pyritization (pir″i-ti-zā'shọn), *n.* [< *pyritize* + *-ation*.] Conversion into pyrites.

> Prof. T. Rupert Jones commented on the rarity of fossil Radiolaria. Some few have been found in the Chalk. Their *pyritization* would tend to their ready destruction.
> *Quart. Jour. Geol. Soc.*, XLV. 124.

pyritize (pir'i-tīz), *v. t.*; pret. and pp. *pyritized*, ppr. *pyritizing*. [< NL. *pyrites* + *-ize*.] To convert into pyrites.

pyritohedral (pi-ri-tọ̄-hē'dral), *a.* [< *pyritohedron* + *-al*.] Pertaining to the pyritohedron, or belonging to the class of hemihedral forms of which it is the type.

It is very curious that in the treatment with aqua regia the cube and octahedron faces remain unattacked, while the acids exert a decided action upon the *pyritohedral* (pentagonal dodecahedral) faces, entirely destroying their power of reflecting light. *Sci. Amer.*, N. S., LX. 162.

Pyritohedral hemihedrism, in *crystal*. See *hemihedrism*.

pyritohedron (pi-ri-tō-hē'dron), *n.* [NL., < Gr. πυρίτης, pyrites, + ἕδρα, a seat, base.] In *crystal.*, a pentagonal dodecahedron (see *dodecahedron*); a solid contained by twelve pentagons: a common form with pyrite, whence the name. It is the hemihedral form of the tetrahexahedron.

Pyritohedron.

pyritology (pir-i-tol'ō-ji), *n.* [< Gr. πυρίτης, pyrites, + -λογία, < λέγειν, speak: see *-ology*.] **1.** Facts or information relating to pyrites.—**2.** A system of or treatise on blowpipe analysis.

pyritous (pir'i-tus), *a.* [< NL. *pyrites* + *-ous*.] Consisting of pyrites.

pyro- (pī'rō- or pir'ō-). [L., etc., < Gr. πυρο-, combining form of πῦρ, fire, = E. *fire*: see *fire*.] An element in many words of Greek origin or formation, meaning 'fire.'

pyro-acetic (pī-rō-a-set'ik), *a.* [< Gr. πῦρ, fire, + E. *acetic*.] Pertaining to or obtained from acetic acid when subjected to the action of heat.—**Pyro-acetic spirit.** Same as *acetone*.

pyro-acid (pī-rō-as'id), *n.* [< Gr. πῦρ, fire, + E. *acid*.] A product obtained by subjecting certain organic acids to heat. Also *pyracid*.

pyroballogy (pī-rō-bal'ō-ji), *n.* [< Gr. πῦρ, fire, + βάλλειν, throw, hurl (see *ballista*), + -λογία, < λέγειν, speak: see *-ology*.] The art of throwing fire; the science of artillery, or a work on artillery. [Rare.]

He was enabled, by the help of some marginal documents, . . . together with Gobesius's military architecture and *pyroballogy*, translated from the Flemish, to form his discourse with passable perspicuity.
Sterne, Tristram Shandy, ii. 3.

Pyrocephalus (pī-rō-sef'a-lus), *n.* [NL. (J. Gould, 1838), < Gr. πῦρ, fire, + κεφαλή, head.] A genus of *Tyrannidæ*; the vermilion flycatchers, which have in the male sex a full globular

Vermilion Flycatcher (*Pyrocephalus rubineus*), male.

crest and the whole under parts flaming-red, the back, wings, and tail dusky-brown. *P. rubineus* is about six inches long. A variety of this is found in Mexico and the southwestern parts of the United States. There are several others.

pyrochlore (pī'rō-klōr), *n.* [< Gr. πῦρ, fire, + χλωρός, yellowish-green: see *chlorin*.] A niobo-titanate of calcium, cerium, and other bases, occurring in isometric crystals, commonly octahedrons, of a brownish color and resinous luster. It turns yellowish-green under the blowpipe, whence the name.

Pyrochroa (pī-rok'rō-ä), *n.* [NL. (Geoffroy, 1762), < Gr. πῦρ, fire, + χρόα, color.] A genus of heteromerous beetles, typical of the family *Pyrochroidæ*, and comprising about a dozen species, of which 2 are found in North America, 1 in Japan, and the rest in Europe. *P. coccinea* and *P. rubens* are known as *cardinal beetles*, from their red color.

pyrochroid (pī-rok'rō-id), *a.* and *n.* **I.** *a.* Of or pertaining to the *Pyrochroidæ*.

II. *n.* A beetle of the family *Pyrochroidæ*.

Pyrochroidæ (pī-rō-krō'i-dē), *n. pl.* [NL. (Leach, 1817), < *Pyrochroa* + *-idæ*.] A small family of heteromerous beetles of moderate size, with broad depressed bodies and elytra

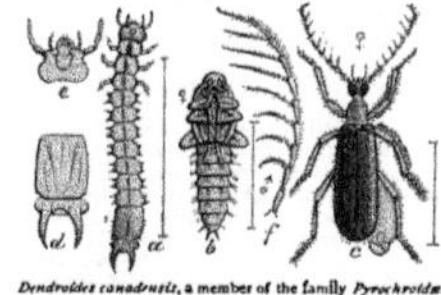

Dendroides canadensis, a member of the family *Pyrochroidæ*.
a, larva; *b*, pupa; *c*, beetle (female); *d*, enlarged anal horns; *e*, enlarged head of larva; *f*, antenna of male beetle, magnified. (Lines show natural sizes of *a*, *b*, *c*.)

broadening behind, and remarkable for their relative size. They live in all stages under the half-decayed bark of many trees. Five genera and about 20 species are known, represented in Europe, Asia, North America, and Australia. *Dendroides canadensis* is a common North American member of this family.

pyrochroite (pī-rok'rō-īt), *n.* [< Gr. πῦρ, fire, + χρόα, color, + *-ite*[2].] Manganese hydrate, a mineral occurring in foliated forms with pearly luster, resembling brucite. It is white when fresh, but changes to bronze and black upon exposure.

pyrocitric (pī-rō-sit'rik), *a.* [< Gr. πῦρ, fire, + E. *citric*.] Obtained by subjecting citric acid to the action of heat.—**Pyrocitric acid.** Same as *citraconic acid* (which see, under *citraconic*).

pyroclastic (pī-rō-klas'tik), *a.* [< Gr. πῦρ, fire, + κλαστός, broken: see *clastic*.] Formed by volcanic agencies, or in the process of being erupted: applied to volcanic breccia or to any angular or comminuted material of igneous origin.

It is asserted that there is an absence of masses of *pyroclastic* materials (tuffs and dust) such as we should expect to find around great volcanic centres.
Quart. Jour. Geol. Soc., XLV. 204.

Pyroderinæ (pī-rod-e-rī'nē), *n. pl.* [NL., < *Pyroderus* + *-inæ*.] A subfamily named from the genus *Pyroderus*. See *Gymnoderinæ*.

Pyroderus (pī-rod'e-rus), *n.* [NL. (G. R. Gray, 1840), < Gr. πῦρ, fire, + δέρη, neck.] A genus of South American fruit-crows belonging to the subfamily *Gymnoderinæ*, giving name to the *Pyroderinæ*. There are 3 species, *P. scutatus*, *P. orinocensis*, and *P. granadensis*, inhabiting tropical parts of South America.

pyrodin (pī'rō-din), *n.* [< Gr. πυρώδης, like fire (< πῦρ, fire, + εἶδος, form), + *-in*[2].] An antipyretic, acetyl-phenyl hydrazine, $C_6H_5.C_2H_3O.N_2H_2$. Also called *phenacethydrazine*.

pyro-electric (pī'rō-ē-lek'trik), *a.* and *n.* [< Gr. πῦρ, fire, + E. *electric*.] **I.** *a.* Relating to pyro-electricity; having the property of becoming electropolar when heated, as certain crystals; thermo-electric.

There are certain crystals which, while being heated or cooled, exhibit electrical charges at certain regions or poles. Crystals thus electrified by heating or cooling are said to be *pyro-electric*. *S. P. Thompson*, Elect. and Mag., p. 64.

II. *n.* A substance which becomes electrified when heated.

pyro-electricity (pī'rō-ē-lek-tris'i-ti), *n.* [< Gr. πῦρ, fire, + E. *electricity*.] That branch of electricity which considers the production of a state of electrification in certain crystallized bodies by change of temperature alone. Thus, when a prismatic crystal of tourmalin is slightly heated, positive electricity is found to be developed at one extremity (called the *analogous pole*) and negative at the other (the *antilogous pole*). If the crystal is cooled, similar properties are developed, but the poles are reversed. Many other crystals show the same property, especially those whose molecular structure differs at the opposite extremities of the same crystallographic axis (like tourmalin)—that is, which are hemimorphic or hemihedral. The unlike parts of a compound (twin) crystal of quartz become dissimilarly electrified by change of temperature. This can be well shown by shaking over a heated section of such a crystal a mixture of red lead and sulphur: the former collects on the parts which are negatively, the latter on those which are positively electrified. The phenomenon is closely related to the variations in stress which occur in the crystal when its temperature is altered. By some writers *pyro-electricity* is used to include also the phenomena of thermo-electricity, which, however, are totally different in character.

pyrogallate (pī-rō-gal'āt), *n.* [< Gr. πῦρ, fire, + E. *gallate*.] A salt of pyrogallic acid.

pyrogallic (pī-rō-gal'ik), *a.* [< Gr. πῦρ, fire, + E. *gallic*[2].] Obtained from gallic acid by the action of heat: noting an acid, or more properly a phenol ($C_6H_3(OH)_3$), which forms colorless crystalline plates or needles, soluble in water and poisonous. In the presence of alkalis it rapidly absorbs oxygen, and it is used in chemical processes for that purpose. Pyrogallic acid rapidly reduces salts of mercury, silver, and gold, precipitating the metals, and from its property of reducing silver salts is one of the most efficient and most extensively used of photographic developing agents.

pyrogen (pī'rō-jen), *n.* [< Gr. πῦρ, fire, + -γενής, producing: see *-gen*.] **1.** Any substance which, introduced into the blood, causes pyrexia or fever.—**2.** The electric fluid.

pyrogenesia (pī'rō-je-nē'si-ä), *n.* [NL.] Same as *pyrogenesis*.

pyrogenesis (pī-rō-jen'e-sis), *n.* [< Gr. πῦρ, fire, + γένεσις, generation: see *genesis*.] Production of fire or heat.

pyrogenetic (pī'rō-jē-net'ik), *a.* [< *pyrogenesis*, after *genetic*.] Heat-producing.

The actual rise of temperature that follows upon stripping in a cold atmosphere or upon first entering into a cold bath is not one of the least curious phenomena of the regulative function of the *pyrogenetic* mechanism.
Arc. Cruise of the Corwin, 1881, p. 12.

pyrogenic (pī-rō-jen'ik), *a.* [< Gr. πῦρ, fire, + -γενής, producing: see *-gen*, *-genous*.] Producing fever.

pyrogenous (pī-roj'e-nus), *a.* [< Gr. πῦρ, fire, + -γενής, producing: see *-genous*.] **1.** Producing or concerned in the production of fire or heat: as, *pyrogenous* action in the blood.—**2.** Produced by fire; igneous.

pyrognomic (pī-rog-nom'ik), *a.* [< Gr. πῦρ, fire, + γνώμων, index, mark: see *gnomon*.] Exhibiting an incandescent glow when heated to a certain degree: specifically noting certain minerals.

pyrognostic (pī-rog-nos'tik), *a.* [< Gr. πῦρ, fire, + γνωστικός, knowing: see *gnostic*.] Pertaining to fire or heat: specifically noting those characters of a mineral which are observed by means of the blowpipe.

pyrognostics (pī-rog-nos'tiks), *n.* [Pl. of *pyrognostic* (see *-ics*).] Those properties of a mineral which it exhibits when heated, alone or with fluxes, in the blowpipe-flame or in the flame of a Bunsen burner, as the fusibility, intumescence, or other phenomena of fusion, flame-coloration, etc.

pyrography (pī-rog'ra-fi), *n.* [< Gr. πῦρ, fire, + γράφειν, write.] A method of reproducing a design or an inscription on wood by the application under pressure of heated metallic plates or cylinders, the surfaces or peripheries of which bear dies or matrices in relief.

pyrogravure (pī'rō-grā-vūr'), *n.* [< Gr. πῦρ, fire, + F. *gravure*, engraving, < *graver*, grave: see *grave*[1].] A method of engraving on wood by the use of a red-hot metallic point; also, a picture produced by this method.

Pyrogravure is a new method of engraving in black, reddish brown, bister, etc., by the use of a red hot metallic point. *Sci. Amer.*, N. S., LVIII. 353.

pyroheliometer (pī-rō-hē-li-om'e-tėr), *n.* Same as *pyrheliometer*.

Pyrola (pir'ō-lä), *n.* [NL. (Tournefort, 1700), so called from the resemblance of the shining leaves to those of the pear-tree; prop. *Pirola*; dim. of L. *pirus*, improp. *pyrus*, a pear-tree: see *Pyrus*.] **1.** A genus of dicotyledonous plants of the order *Ericaceæ*, the heath family, type of the tribe *Pyroleæ*, characterized by racemed flowers with five converging petals, ten stamens with peculiar four-celled inverted anthers opening by pores, and a capsule opening from the base upward, with cobwebby margins. The 16 species are natives of the northern hemisphere, including 8 in the United States. They are smooth perennial herbs, sending out subterranean runners, and bearing radical or alternate long-stalked evergreen leaves, commonly entire and rounded, and an erect scape of bracted nodding flowers, which are white, yellowish, rose-colored, or purple. Several species are known in England and among American writers as *wintergreen* or *false wintergreen*. *P. rotundifolia*, the larger wintergreen, is the most conspicuous species, a plant of both hemispheres, with thickish veiny round leaves, and commonly pure-white flowers, the stalk 6 to 12 inches high. It has been called *Indian lettuce* and *canker-lettuce*. *P. elliptica*, a smaller American plant with thin elliptical leaves, is called *shinleaf*, a name also extended to the genus.

2. [*l. c.*] Any plant of the above genus.—**One-flowered pyrola**, *Moneses grandiflora*, a plant once included in the genus *Pyrola*.

Pyrolaceæ (pir-ō-lā'sē-ē), *n. pl.* [NL. (Lindley, 1836), < *Pyrola* + *-aceæ*.] Same as *Pyroleæ*.

pyrolater (pī-rol'a-tėr), *n.* [< *pyrolatry* (cf. *idolater*).] A fire-worshiper. [Rare.]

The fires [were rejected] . . . as having too near an analogy to the religion of the *pyrolators*.
Southey, Thalaba, viii., note.

pyrolatry (pī-rol'ạ-tri), *n.* [< Gr. πῦρ, fire, + λατρεία, worship.] The worship of fire; fire-worship.

Pyroleæ (pī-rō'lẹ̄-ē), *n. pl.* [NL. (Lindley, 1821), < *Pyrola* + *-eæ*.] A tribe of plants of the gamopetalous order *Ericaceæ*, the heath family, unlike the rest of the order in its polypetalous corolla and herbaceous habit, and also characterized by a loculicidal capsule, five imbricated deciduous petals, and a perennial creeping rhizome. It includes about 21 species in the three genera *Pyrola*, *Moneses*, and *Chimaphila*, all small, smooth, shining evergreen herbs of northern temperate regions, and well represented in the United States. See the above genera, and compare *Ericaceæ*. Also *Pyrolaceæ*.

pyroleter (pī-rol'e-tėr), *n.* [< Gr. πῦρ, fire, + ὀλετήρ, destroyer, < ὀλλύναι, destroy.] An apparatus for the extinction of fire, especially on board ships, by which hydrochloric acid and sodium bicarbonate, partly dissolved and partly suspended in water, are pumped into a cylinder, and the carbonic acid there generated is projected on the fire.

The *pyroleter* is a small double pump worked by hand, which sucks up from tubes on either side muriatic acid and a solution of carbonate of soda. These mingle in a generator forming part of the pump. The carbonic acid gas formed and the solution of salt and acid pass at once down a metal pipe to the hold; along the keelson of the ship runs a perforated wooden box, which admits the dry carbonic acid gas amongst the burning materials.
Ure, Dict., IV. 712.

pyroligneous (pī-rọ̄-lig'nẹ̄-us), *a.* [< Gr. πῦρ, fire, + L. *ligneus*, of wood: see *ligneous*.] Generated or procured by the distillation of wood. Also *pyrolignous*.—**Pyroligneous acid**, impure acetic acid obtained by the distillation of wood.—**Pyroligneous alcohol**, methylic alcohol.—**Pyroligneous vinegar**, wood-vinegar.

pyrolignic (pī-rọ̄-lig'nik), *a.* [< Gr. πῦρ, fire, + L. *lignum*, wood, + *-ic*.] Same as *pyroligneous*.

pyrolignite (pī-rọ̄-lig'nīt), *n.* [< *pyrolign(ic)* + *-ite*[2].] A salt of pyroligneous acid.

pyrolignous (pī-rọ̄-lig'nus), *a.* [< Gr. πῦρ, fire, + L. *lignosus*, like wood: see *lignous*.] Same as *pyroligneous*.

pyrolithic (pī-rọ̄-lith'ik), *a.* [< Gr. πῦρ, fire, + λίθος, stone.] In *chem.*, same as *cyanuric*.

pyrologist (pī-rol'ọ̄-jist), *n.* [< *pyrolog-y* + *-ist*.] One who is versed in the doctrines of heat; an investigator of the laws of heat.

pyrology (pī-rol'ọ̄-ji), *n.* [< Gr. πῦρ, fire, + -λογία, < λέγειν, speak: see *-ology*.] The science of heat, latent and sensible.

pyrolusite (pī-rọ̄-lū'sīt), *n.* [< Gr. πῦρ, fire, + λοῦσις, a washing (< λούειν, wash), + *-ite*[2].] Native manganese dioxid (MnO_2), a common ore of manganese, occurring crystallized and massive, of a gray color and metallic luster. It parts with a portion of its oxygen at a red heat, and is on this account used to discharge the brown or green tints of glass, whence its name. When crystallized it has often the form of manganite, from which it has been, at least in many cases, derived by alteration. It is very soft, and is readily distinguished by this property from the other form of manganese dioxid, called polianite.

pyromagnetic (pī"rọ̄-mag-net'ik), *a.* [< Gr. πῦρ, fire, + E. *magnetic*.] Relating to magnetism as modified by heat: noting a dynamo and motor of novel construction, devised by Edison, the operation of which depends on the fact that the intensity of magnetization of iron diminishes as the temperature increases.

pyromancy (pī'rọ̄-man-si), *n.* [< ME. **piromancie*, *perimancie*, < OF. **piromancie*, *piromance*, *pyromance*, < ML. *pyromantia*, *pyromancia*, < Gr. πυρομαντεία, divination by fire, < πῦρ, fire, + μαντεία, divination.] Divination by fire, or by the forms appearing in fire.

Nigromancye and *perimancie* the pouke to rise maketh;
gif thou thenne Dowel dele with hem neuere.
Piers Plowman (A), xi. 158.

Amphiaraus was the first that had knowledge of *Pyromancie*, and gathered signs by speculations of fire.
Holland, tr. of Pliny, vii. 56.

pyromania (pī-rọ̄-mā'ni-ạ̈), *n.* [< Gr. πῦρ, fire, + μανία, madness.] A mania for destroying things by fire; a form of insanity marked by a mania for setting things on fire.

pyromaniac (pī-rọ̄-mā'ni-ak), *a.* and *n.* [< *pyromania* + *-ac*.] **I.** *a.* Of, pertaining to, characterized by, or affected with pyromania.

II. *n.* A person possessed of a mania or irresistible impulse to burn things.

As *pyromaniacs* rarely incriminate themselves, it becomes the more important to study the many indications by which the diagnosis can be made by indirect examinations.
Amer. Jour. Psychol., I. 191.

pyromaniacal (pī"rọ̄-mạ̄-nī'ạ-kạl), *a.* [< *pyromaniac* + *-al*.] **1.** Affected with or having a tendency to pyromania: as, *pyromaniacal* persons.—**2.** Caused by pyromaniacs: as, *pyromaniacal* fires.

pyromantic (pī-rọ̄-man'tik), *a.* and *n.* [< *pyromancy* (*-mant-*) + *-ic*.] **I.** *a.* Pertaining to pyromancy.

II. *n.* One who pretends to divine by means of fire.

pyrometamorphism (pī-rọ̄-met-ạ-môr'fizm), *n.* [< Gr. πῦρ, fire, + E. *metamorphism*.] Metamorphism resulting from the action of heat, as distinguished from hydrometamorphism, that produced by water. See *metamorphism*.

pyrometer (pī-rom'e-tėr), *n.* [< Gr. πῦρ, fire, + μέτρον, measure.] An instrument, in the form of a simple metallic bar, employed by Muschenbroek, about 1730, for measuring the changes produced in the dimensions of solid bodies by the application of heat. The name is now applied, however, to any instrument the object of which is to measure all gradations of temperature above those that can be indicated by the mercurial thermometer. Wedgwood's pyrometer, the first which came into extensive use, was employed by him for testing the heat of his pottery- and porcelain-kilns, and depended on the property of clay to contract on exposure to heat. Many different modes have been proposed or actually employed for measuring high temperatures: as (*a*) by contraction, as in Wedgwood's; (*b*) by the expansion of bars of different metals; (*c*) by change of pressure in confined gases, as in Lamy's instrument, or by the expansion of gases, as in the air-thermometer; (*d*) by the amount of heat imparted to a cold mass, as in Siemens's instrument; (*e*) by the fusing-point of solids; (*f*) by conduction and radiation of heat (see *pyroscope*); (*g*) by color, as red and white heat; (*h*) by change in the velocity of sound; (*i*) by the resolution of chemical compounds; (*j*) by generation of electricity, as in Becquerel's thermo-electric pyrometer; and (*k*) by change in resistance to electricity, as in the instrument invented by Siemens, which may be adapted to measuring either high or low temperatures.

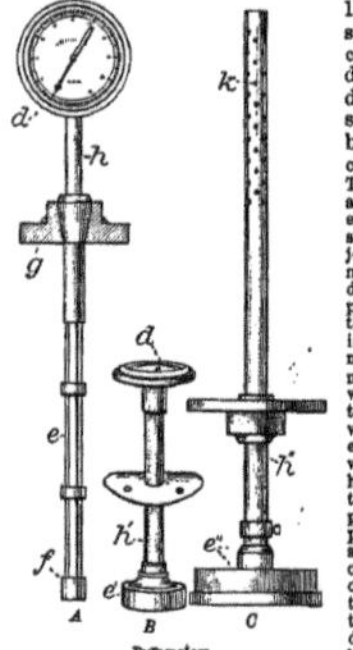

Pyrometers.

A, pyrometer (Gauntlett's) in which the pointer of dial *d* is turned by the unequal expansion of rods *e*, which are made fast at *f*: *e* consists of three brass or copper rods surrounding one of iron which connects with dial through tube *h* supported at *g*. *B*, pyrometer in which the motive power is a coil of wire inside *e'*, the connecting rods passing through tube *k'* to dial at *d'*. *C*, pyrometer with screw-shaped metallic coil within the tube *hh''* which, when heated, moves the pointer of dial at *e''*.

pyrometric (pī-rẹ̄-met'rik), *a.* [As *pyrometer* + *-ic*.] Pertaining to the pyrometer, or to its use; ascertained or shown by means of the pyrometer.

pyrometrical (pī-rẹ̄-met'ri-kạl), *a.* [< *pyrometric* + *-al*.] Same as *pyrometric*.

pyrometrically (pī-rọ̄-met'ri-kạl-i), *adv.* In a pyrometric manner; with or by means of the use of the pyrometer.

pyrometry (pī-rom'e-tri), *n.* [< Gr. πῦρ, fire, + -μετρία, < μέτρον, a measure.] That branch of science which treats of the measurement of heat; the act or art of measuring amounts or degrees of heat.

pyromorphite (pī-rọ̄-môr'fīt), *n.* [So called in allusion to the peculiar crystalline form which a fused globule assumes on cooling; < Gr. πῦρ, fire, + μορφή, form, + *-ite*[2].] Native phosphate of lead with lead chlorid. It is a mineral of a green, yellow, or brown color, crystallizing in hexagonal prisms, and isomorphous with apatite, mimetite, and vanadinite. It also occurs massive in globular, reniform, fibrous, moss-like, granular, or earthy forms. Often called *green lead ore*.

pyromorphous (pī-rọ̄-môr'fus), *a.* [< Gr. πῦρ, fire, + μορφή, form, + *-ous*.] In *mineral.*, having the property of being crystallizable upon fusion.

pyronaphtha (pī-rọ̄-naf'thạ̈), *n.* [< Gr. πῦρ, fire, + νάφθα, naphtha: see *naphtha*.] An illuminating agent which has been prepared in Russia from the waste products of the distillation of Baku petroleum. It burns with a bright light.

pyronomics (pī-rọ̄-nom'iks), *n.* [< Gr. πῦρ, fire, + νόμος, law.] The science of the properties and action of heat. [Rare.]

pyrope (pī'rōp), *n.* [< Gr. πυρωπός, a kind of red bronze, prop. adj., fire-eyed, fiery, < πῦρ, fire, + ὤψ, eye.] Fire-garnet, or Bohemian garnet, a dark-red variety of garnet, sometimes used as a gem, found embedded in serpentine at Budweis in Bohemia and elsewhere. It belongs to the magnesia-alumina variety of the species, and often contains also some chromium. See *garnet*[1].

pyrophane (pī'rọ̄-fān), *n.* [< Gr. πῦρ, fire, + φαίνειν, show.] A kind of opal (hydrophane) which by the absorption of melted wax is rendered translucent so long as it is hot, but becomes opaque again on cooling.

pyrophanous (pī-rof'ạ-nus), *a.* [< Gr. πῦρ, fire, + φαίνειν, show.] Rendered transparent or translucent by heat.

Pyrophila (pī-rof'i-lạ̈), *n.* [NL. (Stephens, 1829), < Gr. πῦρ, fire, + φιλεῖν, love.] A genus of noctuid moths, containing a number of species which are destructive in their larval states. *P. pyramidoides* is the pyramidal grape-vine worm of the United States, which damages grape-vines, and also raspberry, poplar, and red-bud (*Cercis*).

Pyramidal Grape-vine Moth and Worm (*Pyrophila pyramidoides*).

pyrophobia (pī-rọ̄-fō'bi-ạ̈), *n.* [< Gr. πῦρ, fire, + -φοβία, < φόβος, fear.] A morbid dread of fire.

pyrophone (pī'rọ̄-fōn), *n.* [< Gr. πῦρ, fire, + φωνή, sound, tone.] A musical instrument in which the tones are produced by means of burning jets of hydrogen inclosed in graduated glass tubes. It was invented about 1875 by Frederic Kastner. Sometimes called *chemical harmonicon*.

pyrophor (pī'rọ̄-fôr), *n.* [< Gr. πυροφόρος, fire-bearing: see *pyrophore*.] A name sometimes given to the stirrup-lantern.

pyrophore (pī'rọ̄-fōr), *n.* [< Gr. πυροφόρος, fire-bearing, < πῦρ, fire, + φέρειν = E. *bear*[1].] **1.** A body which will become ignited if exposed to air or water, such as self-lighting logs intended for use at sea in facilitating the rescue of a person who is overboard.—**2.** A composition or an apparatus for kindling fire.

pyrophoric (pī-rọ̄-for'ik), *a.* [< NL. *pyrophor(us)* + *-ic*.] Same as *pyrophorous*.

pyrophorous (pī-rof'ọ̄-rus), *a.* [< NL. *pyrophor(us)* + *-ous*.] Pertaining to or resembling pyrophorus.

pyrophorus (pī-rof'ọ̄-rus), *n.* [NL., < Gr. πυροφόρος, fire-bearing: see *pyrophore*.] **1.** A substance which takes fire on exposure to air. Many metals (iron, lead, etc.), when exposed to the air in a very finely divided condition, combine so rapidly with oxygen as to cause an evolution of light.
2. [*cap.*] [NL. (Illiger, 1809).] A notable genus of elaterid beetles, comprising nearly a hundred species, confined to tropical and subtropical America, and containing the most brilliant forms of luminous insects. The light is given out from two oval spots in the pronotum near each basal angle, and from a point beneath, between the thorax and the abdomen. These beetles fly in a nearly direct line, and the light is more intense and sustained than that of the *Lampyridæ*. In many countries of tropical America they are used as toilet ornaments and form an article of trade. *P. noctilucus* is a large West Indian species, often brought alive to the United States. See also cut under *antenna*.

Pyrophorus noctilucus.

3. [*cap.*] A genus of arachnidans. *Koch*, 1837.

pyrophosphate (pī-rọ̄-fos'fāt), *n.* [< *pyrophosph(oric)* + *-ate*[1].] A salt of pyrophosphoric acid. See *pyrophosphoric*.

pyrophosphoric (pī″rọ̄-fos-for′ik), *a.* [< Gr. πῦρ, fire, + E. *phosphoric.*] Formed by heating phosphoric acid: noting an acid ($H_4P_2O_7$) produced by exposing concentrated phosphoric acid to a temperature of 415° F. Pyrophosphoric acid is tetrabasic—that is, capable of forming four distinct classes of salts according as one, two, or three atoms or the whole of the hydrogen is replaced by a metal. The pyrophosphates, especially that of iron, are used in medicine.

pyrophotography (pī″rọ̄-fọ̄-tog′ra-fi), *n.* [< Gr. πῦρ, fire, + E. *photography.*] Certain photographic processes in which heat is used to fix the picture.

pyrophyllite (pī-rọ̄-fil′īt), *n.* [So called in allusion to its exfoliation before the blowpipe; < Gr. πῦρ, fire, + φύλλον, leaf, + *-ite*².] A hydrated aluminium silicate, occurring in foliated talc-like subtransparent masses having a white, green, or yellow color and pearly luster.

pyrophysalite (pī-rọ̄-fis′a-līt), *n.* [< Gr. πῦρ, fire, + E. *physalite.*] See *physalite.*

pyropuncture (pī-rọ̄-pungk′tūr), *n.* [< Gr. πῦρ, fire, + E. *puncture.*] Puncturing with hot needles; also, a puncture so made.

pyroracemate (pī-rọ̄-ras′e-māt), *n.* [< *pyroracem(ic)* + *-ate*¹.] A salt formed by the union of pyroracemic acid with a base.

pyroracemic (pī″rọ̄-ra-sem′ik), *a.* [< Gr. πῦρ, fire, + E. *racemic.*] Produced by the distillation of tartaric and racemic acids: as, *pyroracemic* acid ($C_3H_4O_3$).

pyroschist (pī′rọ̄-shist), *n.* [< Gr. πῦρ, fire, + E. *schist.*] Schist or shale containing sufficient bituminous matter (hydrocarbons) to burn with a bright flame, or yielding volatile hydrocarbon or inflammable gas when heated.

pyrosclerite (pī-rọ̄-sklē′rīt), *n.* [< Gr. πῦρ, fire, + σκληρός, hard, + *-ite*².] An emerald-green mineral allied to the chlorites, occurring in serpentine in the island of Elba, Italy.

pyroscope (pī′rọ̄-skōp), *n.* [< Gr. πῦρ, fire, + σκοπεῖν, view.] An instrument for measuring the intensity of radiating heat or cold. It resembles a differential thermometer, having one bulb covered with quicksilver-leaf, while the other is bare.

pyrosilver (pī-rọ̄-sil′vėr), *n.* [< Gr. πῦρ, fire, + E. *silver.*] A trade-name for electroplated wares which, after they are taken from the bath, are subjected to heat. This treatment seems to cause the metal to sink into the pores of the plated base metal and adhere to it much more firmly and durably. The process is technically called *burning-in.*

pyrosis (pī-rō′sis), *n.* [< Gr. πύρωσις, a burning, a kindling, < πυροῦν, set on fire, burn, < πῦρ, fire: see *fire.*] In *pathol.*, the eructation of watery fluid, usually insipid, but sometimes acrid, attended with more or less burning pain in the epigastrium. It is commonly called *water-brash.*

pyrosmalite (pī-ros′ma-līt), *n.* [< Gr. πῦρ, fire, + ὀσμή, a smell, an object of smell, + λίθος, stone.] A mineral of a liver-brown color, or pistachio-green, occurring in six-sided prisms, with perfect basal cleavage, found in Sweden. It is a silicate of iron and manganese, containing chlorin, the odor of which it exhales when heated.

Pyrosoma (pī-rọ̄-sō′mạ̈), *n.* [NL. (Péron), < Gr. πῦρ, fire, + σῶμα, body.] The typical genus of *Pyrosomatidæ:* so called from their phosphorescence. They inhabit the Mediterranean and Atlantic. They unite in great numbers, forming a large hollow cylinder, open at one end and closed at the other, swimming in the ocean by the alternate contraction and dilatation of its component individual animals. See cut under *cyathozoöid.*

Pyrosomatidæ (pī″rọ̄-sọ̄-mat′i-dē), *n. pl.* [NL., < *Pyrosoma* (*-somat-*) + *-idæ.*] A family of compound or aggregate ascidians of the class *Tunicata*, typified by the genus *Pyrosoma*, sometimes representing an order or suborder *Dactyliobranchia;* the firebodies. They are free-swimming pelagic organisms, highly luminous, united together in hollow chains or rods several inches long, one end of each individual fitting into the cavity of the next, somewhat like a set of thimbles. Also *Pyrosomidæ, Pyrosomiidæ.*

pyrosome (pī′rọ̄-sōm), *n.* [< NL. *Pyrosoma.*] A member or individual of the genus *Pyrosoma;* a firebody.

Pyrosomidæ (pī-rọ̄-som′i-dē), *n. pl.* [NL., < *Pyrosoma* + *-idæ.*] Same as *Pyrosomatidæ.*

Pyrosomiidea (pī-rọ̄-sō-mi-id′ẹ̄-ạ̈), *n. pl.* [NL.] A false form of *Pyrosomatidæ* or *Pyrosomidæ*, taken as the name of an order of ascidians which that family is supposed to represent. *E. R. Lankester.*

pyrostat (pī′rọ̄-stat), *n.* [< Gr. πῦρ, fire, + στατός, < ἱστάναι, set up, stand: see *static.*] An automatic draft-regulator for chimneys, smoke-pipes, and smoke-stacks. See *draft-regulator*, under *regulator.*

pyrostereotype (pī-rọ̄-ster′ẹ̄-ọ̄-tīp), *n.* [< Gr. πῦρ, fire, + E. *stereotype.*] A process by which a mold for casting a printing relief-plate is obtained by burning an intaglio to a definite depth in the face of a wood block by means of heated steel dies and a special apparatus. It is used for printing music, etc.

pyrostilpnite (pī-rọ̄-stilp′nīt), *n.* [< Gr. πῦρ, fire, + στιλπνός, glistening, + *-ite*².] A rare mineral, occurring in minute tabular monoclinic crystals. It is a sulphid of arsenic and silver, near proustite in composition. Also called *fireblende.*

pyrosulphuric (pī″rọ̄-sul-fū′rik), *a.* [< Gr. πῦρ, fire, + E. *sulphuric.*] Obtained from sulphuric acid by the action of heat.—**Pyrosulphuric acid.** Same as *disulphuric acid* (which see, under *disulphuric*).

pyrotartaric (pī″rọ̄-tär-tar′ik), *a.* [< Gr. πῦρ, fire, + E. *tartaric.*] Obtained by heating tartaric acid in a close vessel: as, *pyrotartaric* acid ($C_5H_8O_4$).

pyrotartrate (pī-rọ̄-tär′trāt), *n.* [< Gr. πῦρ, fire, + E. *tartrate.*] A salt of pyrotartaric acid.

pyrotechnian (pī-rọ̄-tek′ni-ạn), *n.* [< *pyrotechny* + *-an.*] A pyrotechnist.

pyrotechnic (pī-rọ̄-tek′nik), *a.* [< *pyrotechn-y* + *-ic.*] Of or pertaining to fireworks or the art of making them.

pyrotechnical (pī-rọ̄-tek′ni-kạl), *a.* [< *pyrotechnic* + *-al.*] Same as *pyrotechnic.*—**Pyrotechnical sponge.** Same as *amadou.*

pyrotechnician (pī″rọ̄-tek-nish′ạn), *n.* [< *pyrotechnic* + *-i-an.*] A pyrotechnist.

pyrotechnics (pī-rọ̄-tek′niks), *n.* [Pl. of *pyrotechnic* (see *-ics*).] The art of making fireworks; the composition, structure, and use of fireworks. See *firework*, 2.

pyrotechnist (pī-rọ̄-tek′nist), *n.* [< *pyrotechn-y* + *-ist.*] One who is skilled in pyrotechny; a manufacturer of fireworks.

pyrotechny (pī′rọ̄-tek-ni), *n.* [< Gr. πῦρ, fire, + τέχνη, art.] 1. The management and mechanical application of fire.

> Does man go thus far by his skill in *pyrotechny*, and shall not God do more, who is the Cosmotect?
>
> *Evelyn*, True Religion, I. 190.

2. The fabrication of fireworks for military and ornamental purposes (see *firework*, 2); the composition and scientific use of combustible substances employed as signals, as destructive agents, or for purposes of display.

pyrothonide (pī-roth′ọ̄-nīd), *n.* [< Gr. πῦρ, fire, + ὀθόνη, fine linen, + *-ide*¹.] A kind of empyreumatic oil produced by the combustion of textures of hemp, linen, or cotton in a copper vessel, formerly used in medicine. *Dunglison.*

pyrotic (pī-rot′ik), *a.* and *n.* [< Gr. πυρωτικός, burning, heating, < πυροῦν, set on fire, < πῦρ, fire: see *pyrosis.*] I. *a.* Caustic.

II. *n.* A caustic medicine.

pyro-uric (pī-rō-ū′rik), *a.* [< Gr. πῦρ, fire, + οὖρον, urine, + *-ic.*] In *chem.*, same as *cyanuric.*

pyroxanthine, pyroxanthin (pī-rok-san′thin), *n.* [< Gr. πῦρ, fire, + ξανθός, yellow, + *-ine*², *-in*².] A yellow crystalline substance found in crude wood-spirit. Also called *eblanin.*

pyroxene (pī′rok-sēn), *n.* [< Gr. πῦρ, fire, + ξένος, a guest.] An important mineral species, embracing many varieties differing in appearance and chemical composition. It occurs in monoclinic crystals, often short prismatic in habit, and with an angle in front of nearly 90°, so that these crystals resemble square prisms. Granular forms are common, and also massive varieties, the latter being usually coarsely laminated in structure, rarely fibrous or columnar. The color varies from white to gray, green, brown, and black, and the composition from the simple metasilicate of calcium and magnesium to kinds containing, with calcium or magnesium, or both, iron, manganese, and aluminium. The different varieties are usually divided into two groups, the non-aluminous and the aluminous. Of the former the prominent kinds are—diopside or malacolite, which contains only calcium and magnesium, and is white to gray or light-green in color, with the subvarieties called alalite or mussite (the diopside proper, from the Mussa Alp in the Ala valley in Piedmont, occurring in beautiful slender crystals), traversellite, canaanite, and white granular coccolite, and those containing iron, namely the grayish-green to deep-green or black salite, occurring in laminated masses, the crystallized baikalite, the granular green coccolite, and the deep-green diallage, which is characterized by a distinct parting parallel to the orthopinacoid plane and often by a pearly to metalloidal luster on this surface; also the lime-iron variety, hedenbergite, and the manganesian schefferite. The aluminous kinds include fassaite, which is light- to dark-green in color, and the common augite, which is dark-green to black and contains considerable iron. Augite is characteristic of many eruptive rocks, especially those of a basic character, as diabase, basalt, etc. Diallage is an essential constituent of the gabbros, of norite, etc. Besides the above varieties or subspecies belonging to pyroxene proper, the pyroxene group includes the related species enstatite or bronzite and hypersthene, which are orthorhombic in crystallization (hence called *rhombic pyroxenes*); also the monoclinic species wollastonite, ægirite and acmite, spodumene, and the triclinic rhodonite and babingtonite. Jadeite probably also belongs here. All these are characterized by the same prismatic angle of 87°. This group is closely related to the analogous amphibole (or hornblende) group, the species of which are characterized by a prismatic angle of 124½°; and several of the kinds under the two groups correspond exactly in composition—for example, diopside to tremolite, etc. A change of pyroxene to hornblende by a process of paramorphism is often observed, especially in certain igneous rocks. See *uralite* and *uralitization.*

pyroxenic (pī-rok-sen′ik), *a.* [< *pyroxene* + *-ic.*] Pertaining to pyroxene, or partaking of its qualities; composed of or containing pyroxene.

pyroxyle (pī-rok′sil), *n.* [< Gr. πῦρ, fire, + ξύλον, wood.] Same as *pyroxylin.*

pyroxylic (pī-rok-sil′ik), *a.* [< Gr. πῦρ, fire, + ξύλον, wood (cf. *pyroxyle*), + *-ic.*] Obtained by distilling wood.—**Pyroxylic spirit**, methylic alcohol; a product of the distillation of wood. It constitutes about one tenth of the watery products after separation of the tar, and is obtained from these products by re-distillation. Rectification is partially effected by first heating it with slaked lime, which frees a large quantity of ammonia, next neutralizing the remainder of the ammonia and precipitating the remaining traces of tar by sulphuric acid, then again distilling and passing it several times over quicklime. The product is the crude wood-spirit of commerce, which still contains many impurities: these are removed by chemically combining it with calcium chlorid and heating the compound over a water-bath to 100° C., which drives off volatile impurities. It is then distilled with water, which breaks up the combination and sets free the pyroxylic spirit diluted with water. The latter is then removed to get the desired strength by treatment with quicklime. Also called *wood-spirit* and *wood-alcohol.*

pyroxylin, pyroxyline (pī-rok′si-lin), *n.* [< *pyroxyle* + *-in*², *-ine*².] Guncotton or a similar substance obtained by immersing vegetable fiber in nitric or nitrosulphuric acid, and then suffering it to dry. Such substances are nitro-derivatives of cellulose. Also *pyroxyle.*—**Soluble pyroxylin.** Same as *dinitrocellulose.*

pyrrhic[1] (pir′ik), *n.* and *a.* [< L. *pyrrhicha, pyrrhiche*, < Gr. πυρρίχη, a kind of war-dance, said to be named from Pyrrhichus, the inventor, < Πύρριχος, Pyrrhichus.] I. *n.* An ancient Grecian warlike dance, in quick and light measure, accompanied by the flute. It consisted chiefly in adroit and nimble steps and motions of the body, intended to represent the attempt to avoid strokes of an enemy in battle and to inflict injury upon him. It was performed under arms, and the movements and practice necessary were looked upon as training for service in the field.

II. *a.* Of or pertaining to the Greek martial dance called a pyrrhic.

> You have the *Pyrrhic* dance as yet;
> Where is the Pyrrhic phalanx gone?
>
> *Byron*, Don Juan, iii. 86 (song).

pyrrhic[2] (pir′ik), *a.* and *n.* [< L. *pyrrhichius*, < Gr. πυρρίχιος, of or belonging to the pyrrhic (dance) (πούς πυρρίχιος, a pyrrhic foot), < πυρρίχη, a pyrrhic: see *pyrrhic*[1].] I. *a.* In *pros.*, consisting of two short times or syllables: as, a *pyrrhic* foot; composed of or pertaining to feet so constituted: as, *pyrrhic* verse; *pyrrhic* rhythm.

II. *n.* In *anc. pros.*, a foot consisting of two short times or syllables. A pyrrhic is apparently a disemic isorrhythmic foot (⏑́ | ⏑ or ⏑ | ⏑́). The earlier and better ancient authorities (the rhythmicians), however, did not acknowledge the existence of a disemic foot, and it seems to have been first introduced into metrical analysis by the grammarians and later metricians. An apparent pyrrhic (⏑ ⏑) can occur—(*a*) at the end of an iambic line (⏑ ⏑ for ⏑ –); (*b*) as part of proceleusmatics (⏑ ⏑ ⏑ ⏑), Ionics (⏑ ⏑ – – or – – ⏑ ⏑), or pæons (– ⏑ ⏑ ⏑, ⏑ – ⏑ ⏑, ⏑ ⏑ – ⏑, ⏑ ⏑ ⏑ –), regarded by later writers as compound feet; and (*c*) in the so-called basis or polyschematist foot of a logaœdic series. Wherever it occurs as a separate foot, it is accordingly a representative of a trisemic foot (– ⏑ or ⏑ –). Pyrrhics in continuous composition would constitute proceleusmatic verse, and, although there is little trace of the actual existence of such a meter, it may have been used in single lines or short systems to accompany or suggest the more rapid movements of the war-dance (*pyrrhic*[1]) from which it probably takes its name. Also called *dibrach* (Latin *dibrachys* or *bibrevis*), *pariambus*, and (*single* or *disemic*) *proceleusmatic.* The name ἡγεμών or *hegemon* (leader), often given to the pyrrhic in ancient writers, was apparently suggested by its being placed first in the accepted list of feet. Also *pyrrhichius.*

> A verse made up of *pyrrhics* in immediate succession.
>
> *J. Hadley*, Essays, p. 99.

Pyrrhic[3] (pir′ik), *a.* [< L. *Pyrrhus*, < Gr. Πύρρος, Pyrrhus (see def.), < πυρρός, red-haired, reddish: see *burrel.*] Pertaining to Pyrrhus, especially to Pyrrhus, King of Epirus (see phrase below).—**Pyrrhic victory**, a success obtained at too great a cost: in allusion to the reputed exclamation of Pyrrhus, King of Epirus, after the battle of Asculum against the Romans (279 B. C.), "Another such victory and we are lost!"

pyrrhicist (pir′i-sist), *n.* [< Gr. πυρριχιστής, one who danced the pyrrhic, < πυρριχίζειν, dance the pyrrhic, < πυρρίχη, the pyrrhic: see *pyrrhic*[1].] One who danced in the pyrrhic. *Imp. Dict.*

pyrrhichius (pi-rik′i-us), *n.*; pl. *pyrrhichii* (-ī). [L.: see *pyrrhic*[2].] Same as *pyrrhic*[2].

This word [rénêt] hauing both sillables sliding and slipper make the foote *Pirrichius*, because if he be truly vttered, he beares in maner no sharper accent vpõ the one then the other sillable, but be in effect egall in time and tune, as is also the Spondeus.
Puttenham, Arte of Eng. Poesie, p. 102.

pyrrhite (pir'īt), *n.* [< Gr. πυρρός, reddish (see *burrel*), + *-ite*².] A rare mineral, occurring in minute regular reddish-yellow octahedrons. Its composition is not certainly known, but it is supposed to be related to the niobate pyrochlore.

pyrrhoarsenite (pir-ǭ-är'se-nit), *n.* [< Gr. πυρρός, reddish, + E. *arsenite*.] An arseniate of calcium, magnesium, and manganese, in which the arsenic is in part replaced by antimony. It occurs in embedded grains of a deep yellowish-red color in Sweden.

Pyrrhocoracinæ (pir-ǭ-kor-a-sī'nē), *n. pl.* [NL., < *Pyrrhocorax* (*-corac-*) + *-inæ*.] A subfamily of *Corvidæ*, named in 1846 by G. R. Gray from the genus *Pyrrhocorax*; the choughs. Also called *Fregilinæ*.

pyrrhocoracine (pir-ǭ-kor'a-sin), *a.* Of or pertaining to the *Pyrrhocoracinæ*.

Pyrrhocorax (pi-rok'ǭ-raks), *n.* [NL. (Vieillot, 1816), < Gr. πυρρός, reddish, + κόραξ, a raven.] A genus of *Corvidæ*, typical of the *Pyrrhocoracinæ*: the choughs. *P.* or *Fregilus graculus* is the common chough, with red bill and feet (see cut under *chough*); *P. alpinus* is the alpine chough. The genus is sometimes restricted to the latter, and then distinguished from *Fregilus*.

Pyrrhocoridæ (pir-ǭ-kor'i-dē), *n. pl.* [NL., < *Pyrrhocoris* + *-idæ*.] A family of heteropterous insects, consisting of large, stout bugs, usually marked with red and black, and containing many tropical and subtropical species. The cotton-stainer of the West Indies and southern United States, *Dysdercus suturellus*, is an example.

Pyrrhocoris (pi-rok'ǭ-ris), *n.* [NL. (Fallen, 1841), < Gr. πυρρός, reddish, + κόρις, a bug.] A genus of true bugs, typical of the family *Pyrrhocoridæ*.

Pyrrhonean (pi-rō'nē-an), *a.* [< L. *Pyrrhoneus* (< Gr. Πύρρων, Pyrrho: see *Pyrrhonic*) + *-an*.] Pyrrhonic.

Pyrrhonian (pi-rō'ni-an), *a.* [< Gr. Πύρρων, Pyrrho, + *-i-an*.] Same as *Pyrrhonist*.

Pyrrhonic (pi-ron'ik), *a.* [< Gr. Πύρρων, Pyrrho, + *-ic*.] Of or pertaining to Pyrrho (about 360–270 B. C.), a philosopher of Elis, and disciple of Anaxarchus; of or pertaining to Pyrrhonism or skepticism: as, the *Pyrrhonic* form of doubt. The doctrine of Pyrrho was that there is just as much to be said for as against any opinion whatever; that neither the senses nor the reason are to be trusted in the least; and that when we are once convinced we can know nothing, we cease to care, and in this way alone can attain happiness. It is said that Pyrrho would take no ordinary practical precautions, such as getting out of the way of vehicles.

Pyrrhonism (pir'ǭ-nizm), *n.* [< Gr. Πύρρων, Pyrrho, + *-ism*.] The doctrines of Pyrrho and his followers; absolute skepticism; universal doubt.

And thus, O circular philosopher, . . . you have arrived at a fine *Pyrrhonism*, at an equivalence and indifferency of all actions. *Emerson*.

Pyrrhonist (pir'ǭ-nist), *n.* [< Gr. Πύρρων, Pyrrho, + *-ist*.] A follower of Pyrrho; an adherent of Pyrrhonism; one who doubts everything.

Pyrrhopappus (pir-ǭ-pap'us), *n.* [NL. (A. P. de Candolle, 1838), < Gr. πυρρός, reddish, + πάππος, taken in mod. sense 'pappus': see *pappus*.] A genus of composite plants of the tribe *Cichoriaceæ* and subtribe *Lactuceæ*. It is characterized by its smooth habit, and its nearly cylindrical beaked achenes, covered with many rough and muricate ridges and bearing a reddish pappus which is either persistent or in falling carries with it a disk from which it grows. There are 3 or, according to some authors, 4 species, all natives of the United States or Mexico. They are annual or perennial herbs, with radical leaves or with alternate stem-leaves, and both entire and deeply cut on the same stem. The yellow flower-heads terminate long erect stalks, and resemble those of the common dandelion, which, however, are readily distinguished by their white pappus. See *false dandelion*, under *dandelion*.

pyrrhotine (pir'ǭ-tin), *n.* [< Gr. πυρρός, reddish, + *-t-* + *-ine*².] Native iron sulphid, a mineral crystallizing in hexagonal prisms and occurring also massive, of a bronze color and metallic luster. It is generally slightly magnetic, and is hence called *magnetic pyrites*. In composition it conforms to the general formula Fe_nS_{n+1}, but varying from Fe_7S_8 to $Fe_{11}S_{12}$. The mineral troilite, common in nodules in meteoric iron, may be the same mineral, although to this the formula FeS is generally ascribed.

pyrrhotite (pir'ǭ-tīt), *n.* [As *pyrrhot-ine* + *-ite*².] Same as *pyrrhotine*.

pyrrhous (pir'us), *a.* [< Gr. πυρρός, flame-colored, yellowish-red, reddish, red-haired, < πῦρ, fire. Cf. *burrel*.] Reddish.

Pyrrhula (pir'ǭ-lä), *n.* [NL. (Brisson, 1760), dim. < Gr. πυρρός, reddish: see *pyrrhous*.] A genus of *Fringillidæ*, giving name to the *Pyrrhulinæ*, characterized by the very short stout turgid bill; the bullfinches. See cut under *bullfinch*¹.

Pyrrhulinæ (pir-ǭ-lī'nē), *n. pl.* [NL., < *Pyrrhula* + *-inæ*.] An undefinable subfamily of *Fringillidæ*, named by Swainson in 1837 from the genus *Pyrrhula*; the bullfinches.

pyrrhuline (pir'ǭ-lin), *a.* [< *Pyrrhula* + *-ine*¹.] Resembling a bullfinch, especially in the form of the bill: said of various birds.

Pyrrhuloxia (pir-ǭ-lok'si-ä), *n.* [NL. (Bonaparte, 1850), < *Pyrrhula* + *Loxia*: see *Pyrrhula*, and *Loxia*, 2.] A genus of *Fringillidæ*, closely related to *Cardinalis*, but having a very short stout turgid bill, like a bullfinch's; the Texas cardinals. The species is *P. sinuata*, having the size and form of the common cardinal, but the plumage gray, beautifully varied with carmine red.

Pyrrhura (pi-rö'rä), *n.* [NL. (Bonaparte, 1856), < Gr. πυρρός, reddish, + οὐρά, tail.] A genus of parrots, giving name to the *Pyrrhurinæ*. *P. cruentatus* of South America is an example.

Pyrrhurinæ (pir-ǭ-rī'nē), *n. pl.* [NL., < *Pyrrhura* + *-inæ*.] A subfamily of *Psittacidæ*, named by Garrod from the genus *Pyrrhura*, resembling *Arinæ*, but having no ambiens.

pyrry†, *n.* An obsolete form of *pirry*.

Pyrula (pir'ǭ-lä), *n.* [NL. (Lamarck, 1799), < L. *pirum*, improp. *pyrum*, a pear: see *pear*. Cf. *Pyrola*.] A genus of gastropods having a pyriform shell, whence the name; the fig-shells or pear-shells. (See cut under *fig-shell*.) Very different limits have been assigned to it. (*a*) Originally it was named in connection with *P. ficus* only. (*b*) Subsequently it was used for many species agreeing with *P. ficus* in general form, but radically differing in other characters, and consequently afterward generically differentiated. (*c*) Later it was restricted to the genus now generally called *Fulgur* and related forms, *P. ficus* then being called *Ficula* or *Sycotypus*. (*d*) By recent authors it is restricted to *P. ficus* and closely related species. Also spelled *Pirula*.

Pyrularia (pir-ǭ-lā'ri-ä), *n.* [NL. (F. A. Michaux, 1803), so called with ref. to the small pear-shaped fruit; < L. *pirum*, improp. *pyrum*, a pear: see *Pyrula*.] A genus of apetalous shrubs of the order *Santalaceæ*, the sandalwood family, and of the tribe *Osyrideæ*. It is characterized by partly diœcious flowers, with parallel anther-cells, and a disk with scale-shaped lobes alternating with the five stamens, the small clusters of staminate flowers racemed toward the ends of the branches, and the pistillate flowers terminal, and few or single. The two species are shrubs or small trees, with thin and veiny alternate short-stalked and minutely pellucid-dotted leaves, small greenish flowers with a short columnar style and capitate stigma, and an inferior one-celled ovary, with two or three ovules hanging from the apex of a free central placenta. The rather large obovoid fruit is a fleshy drupe, with a hard thin-shelled spherical stone, containing a globose seed with fleshy and very oily albumen. One of the species is North American, for which see *oil-nut* (*b*); the other, *P. edulis*, is found in India, a large tree, yielding an edible fruit.

Pyrulidæ (pī-rö'li-dē), *n. pl.* [NL., < *Pyrula* + *-idæ*.] A family of tænioglossate gastropods, typified by the genus *Pyrula* (*d*) or *Ficula*. The animal has a narrow long head with subulate tentacles and eyes at their external bases, mantle with large lobes reflected over the shell, and a large foot. The shell is pyriform, thin, and generally sculptured with transverse and longitudinal lines. The species are inhabitants of tropical or warm seas. Also *Pirulidæ*, *Ficulidæ*, and *Sycotypidæ*.

Pyrulinæ (pir-ǭ-lī'nē), *n. pl.* [< *Pyrula* + *-inæ*.] 1. The *Pyrulidæ* as a subfamily of *Doliidæ*.—2. A subfamily restricted to *Pyrula* as represented by species of *Fulgur* and related forms. They are known as *fig-shells* and *pear-shells*.

pyruline (pir'ǭ-lin), *a.* Pertaining to the *Pyrulinæ*, or having their characters.

pyruric (pī-rö'rik), *a.* [< Gr. πῦρ, fire, + οὖρον, urine. Cf. *pyro-uric*.] In *chem.*, same as *cyanuric*.

Pyrus (pī'rus), *n.* [NL. (Tournefort, 1700), prop. *Pirus*, < L. *pirus*, improp. *pyrus*, a pear-tree: see *pear*¹.] A genus of rosaceous trees and shrubs, including the apple and pear, the type of the tribe *Pomeæ*, which takes its name from the pome, the characteristic fruit of this genus. It is characterized by an urn-shaped superior calyx, of which the limb is deciduous or persistent, and by an ovary of from two to five mostly two-ovuled cells, which in fruit are two- or one-seeded, separated, cartilaginous-walled, and immediately invested by a fleshy expansion of the disk, the whole being surrounded by the thickened calyx. There are about 50 species, natives of northern temperate regions and extending into the mountains of India. They bear alternate petioled and usually toothed leaves, deciduous stipules, and numerous cymes of snowy-white or pink flowers, each with five roundish petals and numerous stamens, terminating short spur-like branches. The numerous sections are strikingly different in habit, and several were long received as distinct genera. The typical section *Pyrophorum* (De Candolle, 1825) includes the pear and the wild pear or choke-pear and allied species. (See *pear*1.) The section *Malus* (Tournefort, 1700), the apple, distinguished by a fruit hollowed in at the base, includes *P. Malus*, for which see *apple*, *apple-tree*, and *crab*². To the section *Aria* (De Candolle, 1825), having only two or three styles and ovate leaves whitened beneath, belongs *P. Aria*, the beam-tree, with several varieties, including *P. intermedia*, the Swedish beam-tree. To the section *Torminaria* (De Candolle, 1825), with pinnately lobed leaves and somewhat obconical fruit, belongs *P. torminalis*, the wild service-tree (see *service-tree*). In the section *Sorbus* (Tournefort, 1700), with compound cymes and pinnate leaves, are included *P. domestica* (formerly *Sorbus domestica*), for which see *service-tree*; *P. Americana* and *P. aucuparia*, for which see *mountain-ash*. Another section, *Adenorhachis* (De Candolle, 1825), with berry-like fruit, but undivided leaves and glandular petioles, includes *P. arbutifolia*, for which see *chokeberry*, and cut under *inflorescence*. To the section *Cydonia* (Tournefort, 1700) belong the quinces. (See *Cydonia* and *quince*1.) The genus *Mespilus* was also made by Bentham and Hooker a section of *Pyrus*. See *Mespilus* and *medlar*. Also *Pirus*.

pyry†, *n.* An obsolete form of *pirry*.

pysa (pī'sä), *n.* Same as *pice*.

pysane†¹, *n.* Same as *pisan*².

pyt†, **pytte**†, *n.* Obsolete forms of *pit*¹.

Pythagorean (pi-thag-ǭ-rē'an), *a.* and *n.* [< L. *Pythagoreus*, < Gr. Πυθαγόρειος, pertaining to Pythagoras, < Πυθαγόρας, Pythagoras.] **I.** *a.* Of or pertaining to Pythagoras, a Greek philosopher (perhaps 532 B. C.), or the school founded at Crotona (modern Cotrone), in Italy. All testimony concerning this school is of a late date, and the substance of it is rejected by many critics either as improbable, or as probable, and "on that account all the more indemonstrable" (*Zeller*). The stories are, however, very consistent. The higher grade of the school is represented as a strict monastic community, the doctrine being kept secret, and all betrayals terribly punished, for the purpose of maintaining political ascendancy. Pythagoras is said to have traveled to Egypt and Babylon; and many circumstances are accounted for by supposing that he did so. From those countries he might have brought, as it is said he did, a superior knowledge of mathematics. This knowledge, if kept secret, might have supplied revenues to the school, by calculations and surveys made for citizens. It is difficult to doubt that mathematical science was much advanced within the school. All writers upon ancient mathematics attribute to Pythagoras the Pythagorean proposition and a rule for finding Pythagorean triangles. The importance attached to the pentagram in the school shows that the Pythagoreans were acquainted with its geometrical construction, which is very difficult. They knew the regular or cosmical bodies. They were in possession of many propositions in the theory of numbers, including the doctrine of the arithmetical, geometrical, and harmonical proportions. It is not impossible that they may have had an abacus, little inferior to the Arabic system of arithmetical notation. It is not known how long the society lasted, perhaps for many centuries; as long as it retained any valuable secret it would continue to exist. The Pythagorean philosophy has never been comprehended. The substances of things were held to be abstract numbers; they were in some sense the elements of the universe. Each number, therefore, had its virtue. One was the number of the origin, of reason. Two was the number of matter, of brute force, of evil. Three was the number of mediation, four of justice, five of reproduction, etc. Ten governed the world. In the Pythagorean oath, Pythagoras is called the revealer of the quaternary number—that is, ten—as if something decimal were what he chiefly taught. Something fundamental was also found in odd and even, in square numbers, and the like. Harmony, or music, consists in number. The soul is the harmony, or number, of the body. The universe has also a soul. The remainder of the prominent Pythagorean teachings with which we are acquainted are apparently religious. Pythagoras taught the transmigration of souls. Spirits, both ghosts and demigods, were an object of Pythagorean belief. The brotherhood celebrated certain mysterious rites connected with a view of life as a process of purification. About the time of Augustus, perhaps earlier, Pythagoreanism became mixed with Platonism.—**Pythagorean bean.** See *bean*¹.—**Pythagorean comma.** See *comma*, 5 (*a*).—**Pythagorean dyad.** See *dyad*.—**Pythagorean letter,** the letter Y, so called because its Greek original represented the sacred triad, formed by the duad proceeding from the monad.—**Pythagorean lyre,** a lyre of eight strings, said to have been invented by Pythagoras.—**Pythagorean proposition,** the 47th proposition of the first book of Euclid's "Elements," that the sum of the squares on the legs of a right-angled triangle is equal to the square on the hypotenuse: said to have been discovered by Pythagoras.—**Pythagorean semitone.** Same as *limma*, 1.—**Pythagorean system,** in *astron.*, the astronomical system of Copernicus, erroneously attributed to the Pythagoreans.—**Pythagorean table,** the multiplication-table. But this appellation is due to a corruption in the text of Boethius. The table originally referred to was an abacus.—**Pythagorean triangle,** a triad of whole numbers proportional to the sides of a right-angled triangle—the square of one being equal to the sum of the squares of the other two: as, 3, 4, 5; 12, 35, 37.—**Pythagorean tuning,** in *music*, a system of tuning in which the tones of the scale are fixed by tuning upward in perfect fifths, and back in octaves. The major third thus obtained was long considered the true one, and its recognition as a consonance correspondingly delayed.

II. *n.* A follower of Pythagoras, the founder of the Italic sect of philosophers.

Not that I wanted beans to eat, for I am by nature a *Pythagorean*, so far as beans are concerned.
Thoreau, Walden, p. 175.

Pythagoreanism (pi-thag-ǭ-rē'an-izm), *n.* [< *Pythagorean* + *-ism*.] Same as *Pythagorism*.

Pythagoreanize (pi-thag-ǭ-rē'an-īz), *v. i.* [< *Pythagorean* + *-ize*.] Same as *Pythagorize*.

Pythagoric (pith-ạ-gor'ik), *a.* [< L. *Pythagoricus*, < Gr. Πυθαγορικός, pertaining to Pythagoras, < Πυθαγόρας, Pythagoras: see *Pythagorean.*] Pythagorean. *Imp. Dict.*

Pythagorical (pith-ạ-gor'i-kạl), *a.* [< *Pythagoric* + *-al.*] Same as *Pythagoric.*

That *Pythagorical* rascal! in a gentleman's suit to-day, in a knight's to-morrow.
Middleton, Your Five Gallants, v. 1.

Breeches *Pythagorical*, by reason of their transmigration into several shapes. *B. Jonson*, Cynthia's Revels, iv. 1.

Pythagorism (pi-thag'ọ-rizm), *n.* [< Gr. Πυθαγορισμός, adherence to the principles laid down by Pythagoras, < Πυθαγόρας, Pythagoras: see *Pythagorean.*] The doctrines or philosophy of Pythagoras or of the Pythagoreans. Also *Pythagoreanism.*

Pythagorize (pi-thag'ọ-rīz), *v. i.*; pret. and pp. *Pythagorized*, ppr. *Pythagorizing.* [< Gr. Πυθαγορίζειν, be a disciple of Pythagoras, < Πυθαγόρας, Pythagoras: see *Pythagorean.*] To speculate after the manner of Pythagoras or his followers; tend toward or become imbued with Pythagorism.

Pythia (pith'i-ạ̈), *n.* [< Gr. Πυθία (sc. ἱέρεια, a priestess), the Pythia, priestess of Apollo at Delphi: see *Pythian.*] 1. In *Gr. antiq.*, the priestess who held communion with Apollo and received his oracles in the inner sanctuary of the great temple at Delphi, throughout historic antiquity. See *oracle.*—2. [NL.] In *conch.*: (*a*) A genus of gastropods of the family *Auriculidæ*, generally called *Scarabus. Bolton*, 1798. (*b*) A genus of bulimiform shells, comprising species of *Achatina, Bulimus, Glandina*, etc. *Oken*, 1815.

The Pythia Seated on the Oracular Tripod. (From a Greek red-figured vase.)

pythiad (pith'i-ad), *n.* [< Gr. πυθιάς (-αδ-), a period of four years between two consecutive celebrations of the Pythian games, < Πύθια (sc. ἱερά), the Pythian games: see *Pythian.*] The period of four years intervening between one celebration of the Pythian games and the succeeding.

Pythiambic (pith-i-am'bik), *a.* [As *Pythian* + *iambic.*] In *anc. pros.*, constituting an episynthetic meter consisting of a dactylic hexameter (*Pythian verse*) followed by an iambic colon. The *first Pythiambic system* (*stanza* or *strophe*) subjoins an iambic dimeter and the *second Pythiambic system* (*stanza* or *strophe*) an iambic trimeter to the hexameter.

Pythian (pith'i-ạn), *a.* [< L. *Pythius*, < Gr. Πύθιος, pertaining to Delphi, or to the Delphic Apollo, < Πυθώ, also Πυθών, the older name of Delphi and the surrounding region.] Pertaining to Delphi, or to the priestess of Apollo at Delphi, who there delivered oracles.—**Pythian Apollo.** See *Apollo.*—**Pythian games**, one of the four great national festivals of Greece, celebrated once in four years in honor of Apollo at Delphi.—**Pythian meter, Pythian verse**, the dactylic hexameter: probably so called from its use in the oracles delivered by the Pythia, or, according to ancient writers, from the first song of triumph to Apollo for his victory over the Python, a triple ἰη παιάν (– – | – – | – – | – – | – – | – –).

Pythidæ (pith'i-dē), *n. pl.* [NL., < *Pytho* + *-idæ.*] A small family of heteromerous coleopterous insects, typified by the genus *Pytho.* They have the anterior coxal cavities open behind, the antennæ free, the thorax not margined at the sides, and its disk not impressed at the base. Ten genera are known, distributed in Europe and North America, a single species only occurring elsewhere. They are found under bark and stones.

Pytho (pī'thō), *n.* [NL. (Latreille, 1796): see *Pythian.*] A genus of coleopterous insects, typical of the family *Pythidæ*, comprising forms with very depressed body, striate elytra, and one-toothed mandibles. A half-dozen species are known, 3 from North America, and the others from Europe. They live under the bark of trees.

pythogenesis (pī-thọ-jen'e-sis), *n.* [< Gr. πύθειν, rot, become putrid, + γένεσις, origin: see *genesis.*] Production by means of filth. See *pythogenic.*

pythogenic (pī-thọ-jen'ik), *a.* [< Gr. πύθειν, rot, + -γενής, producing: see *-genous.*] Produced by filth: specifically applied to a class of diseases, as typhoid, the occurrence of which is favored by filth, especially by a vitiated atmosphere.

Cause and effect were for the first time connected in the public mind, which was thus enlightened for the first time as to the nature of what we now call *pythogenic* or filth-born maladies. *Pall Mall Gazette.*

Pythogenic fever. See *fever*[1].

pythometric (pi-thọ-met'rik), *a.* [Improp. for *pithometric, < Gr. πίθος, a wine-jar, + μέτρον, measure: see *metric.*] Pertaining to the gaging of casks.

Python (pī'thon), *n.* [< L. *Python*, < Gr. Πύθων, Python (see def. 1). Cf. Πυθώ, Πυθών, the earlier name of Delphi, and see *Pythian.*] 1. In classical antiquities and in the New Testament, a soothsaying spirit or demon; hence, also, a person possessed by such a spirit; especially, a ventriloquist. Some ancient writers speak of the serpent Python as having delivered oracles at Delphi before the coming of Apollo, and during the Roman imperial period we find the name often given to soothsayers. The spirit was supposed to speak from the belly of the soothsayer, who was accordingly called ἐγγαστρίμυθος, a ventriloquist, a word used in the Septuagint to represent the Hebrew *'ôbh* (see *ob*[1]), often rendered *python* in the Vulgate. In Acts xvi. 16 the usual reading is 'a spirit of Python,' while some manuscripts read 'a spirit, a Python.'

A certain maid having a spirit of divination [margin: Gr. a spirit, a *Python*] met us.
Acts xvi. 16 (revised version).

Like thee [the Sun], the Hero does his Arms employ
The raging *Python* to destroy.
Prior, Hymn to the Sun, st. 3.

2. [*l. c.*] Any very large serpent, as a rock-snake: loosely used, like *boa* and *anaconda*, but properly applicable only to the large Old World non-venomous serpents of the family *Pythonidæ.*—3. [NL.] The typical genus of *Pythonidæ:* formerly conterminous with the family, now restricted to species having premaxillary teeth, labial plates of both jaws fossate, and scuta extending to between the orbits. These are the rock-snakes proper, as *P. molurus* and *P. reticulatus.* See cut under *Pythonidæ*, also cuts under *Ophidia, zygantrum*, and *zygosphene.*

Python (*Python molurus*).

pythoness (pith'ọ-nes), *n.* [Also, as ML., *Pythonissa;* < ME. *Phitonesse, Phitonisse*, etc., < OF. *Pythonesse*, etc., < ML. *Pythonissa*, < MGr. πυθώνισσα, fem. of Gr. πύθων, a ventriloquist, also prob. a diviner (cf. πνεῦμα πύθωνος, a spirit of divination), < Πυθώ, Πυθών, the older name of Delphi: see *Pythian.*] The Pythia or especial priestess of Apollo at his temple at Delphi, who was supposed to be inspired to give his oracular answers; hence, any woman supposed to have a spirit of divination; a witch.

Magiciens and tregetours,
And *phitonisses*, charmeresses,
Olde wyches, sorceresses.
Chaucer, House of Fame, l. 1261.

Saith the *Pythonissa* to Saul, "To-morrow thou and thy sons shall be with me." *Bacon*, Prophecies (ed. 1887).

She stood a moment as a *Pythoness*
Stands on her tripod.
Byron, Don Juan, vi. 107.

pythonic[1] (pi-thon'ik), *a.* [< Gr. Πυθωνικός, pertaining to Pytho, < Πυθώ, Πυθών, the older name of Delphi: see *Pythian.*] Oracular; pertaining to the prediction of future events; prophetic.

pythonic[2] (pī-thon'ik), *a.* [< *python* + *-ic.*] Of or pertaining to a python or the pythons; resembling a python.

I got from the cretaceous deposit of my neighborhood enough fossil material to diagnose a new species of reptile, which, although with powerful paddles, was almost *pythonic* in structure. *Science*, VII. 242.

Pythonidæ (pi-thon'i-dē), *n. pl.* [NL., < *Python* (see *Python*, 3) + *-idæ.*] An Old World family of peropodous colubriform *Ophidia*, having rudiments of posterior extremities, a coronoid bone, supraorbital and postorbital bones, and premaxillary teeth, with or without maxillary teeth; the rock-snakes. There are several genera, as *Python, Morelia, Liasis, Nardoa, Aspidiotes, Loxocemus, Chondropython*, and *Aspidopython.*

Skull of a Python, left side and in longitudinal section.

BO, basioccipital; *BS*, basisphenoid; *Cm*, columella of ear, or stapes (not the columella of the skull); *EO*, exoccipital; *EpO*, epiotic; *Fr*, frontal; *FO*, fenestra ovalis; *L*, lacrymal; *Na*, nasal; *OpO*, opisthotic; *Pa*, parietal; *Pl*, palatine; *Pmx*, premaxilla; *PrO*, prootic; *PS*, presphenoid; *Pt*, pterygoid; *Ptf*, postfrontal; *Qu*, quadrate; *SO*, supraoccipital; *SOr*, supraorbital; *Sq*, squamosal; *Tt*, turbinal; *Tr*, transverse bone; *V*, *VII*, *VIII*, exits of fifth, seventh, and eighth nerves; *Vo*, vomer. The teeth show the aglyphodont dentition.

pythoniform (pi'thon-i-fôrm), *a.* [< NL. *Python*, q. v., + L. *forma*, form.] Resembling or related to a python, boa, or rock-snake; pythonoid; peropodous, as a serpent.

Pythoninæ (pī-thọ-nī'nē), *n. pl.* [NL., < *Python* + *-inæ.*] A subfamily of pythonoid serpents, typified by the genus *Python*, having premaxillary teeth. They chiefly inhabit the tropics of Africa and Asia, and some of them are among the largest of snakes.

pythonine (pī'thọ-nin), *a.* and *n.* I. *a.* Of or pertaining to the *Pythoninæ* or *Pythonidæ;* pythoniform.

II. *n.* A python or member of the *Pythonidæ.*

pythonism (pith'ọ-nizm), *n.* [< Gr. Πυθώ, Pytho, the older name of Delphi (see *Pythian, Python*), + *-ism.*] The art of foretelling future events after the manner of the Delphic oracle.

pythonist† (pith'ọ-nist), *n.* [Also *pithonist;* < Gr. Πυθώ, Πυθών, Pytho, the older name of Delphi (see *Pythian, Python*), + *-ist.* Cf. *pythoness.*] A conjurer.

See the conjuring, proud, remorceless Priest
Rend in full rage (too like a furious fiend)
The pompous vestures of this *Pithonist*,
When Christ doth (vrg'd) aright His cause defend.
Davies, Holy Roode, p. 7. (*Davies.*)

pythonoid (pī'thọ-noid), *a.* and *n.* [< L. *Python*, q. v., + Gr. εἶδος, form.] I. *a.* Resembling or related to a python; belonging to the *Pythonoidea;* pythoniform.

II. *n.* A member of the *Pythonoidea.*

Pythonoidea (pī-thọ-noi'dẹ-ạ̈), *n. pl.* [NL.: see *pythonoid.*] A suborder of *Ophidia;* the peropodous ophidians, having no trace of a pelvis, but almost invariably rudiments of hind limbs in the form of anal spurs. They are not poisonous, but are for the most part of great size, and often have great powers of constriction. They are the rock-snakes, pythons, boas, and anacondas, of the families *Pythonidæ, Boidæ*, and *Charinidæ.*

pythonomorph (pī'thọ-nọ-môrf), *n.* Any member of the *Pythonomorpha.*

Pythonomorpha (pī'thọ-nọ-môr'fạ̈), *n. pl.* [NL., < *Python*, q. v., + Gr. μορφή, form.] In Cope's classification (1871), an order of fossil streptostylic reptiles: same as *Mosasauria.*

pythonomorphic (pī'thọ-nọ-môr'fik), *a.* [< *pythonomorph* + *-ic.*] Same as *pythonomorphous.*

pythonomorphous (pī'thọ-nọ-môr'fus), *a.* [< *Python* + Gr. μορφή, form.] Pertaining to the *Pythonomorpha*, or having their characters; mosasaurian.

The two orders of Ophidians and Lacertilians are nearly allied; the former is probably merely a specialized descendant of the latter or of the *pythonomorphous* reptiles, or perhaps of both. *Günther*, Encyc. Brit., XXII. 180.

pyuria (pī-ū'ri-ạ̈), *n.* [NL., < Gr. πύον, pus, + οὖρον, urine.] The presence of pus in the urine.

pyx (piks), *n.* [Formerly also *pix;* < L. *pyxis, puxis*, < Gr. πυξίς (-ιδ-), a box, orig. one of boxwood, < πύξος, the box-tree, boxwood: see *box*[1].] 1. In the *Rom. Cath. Ch.*, the vase or vessel in which the reserved eucharist is kept. The name *pyx* (*pyxis*) for this vessel seems to have come into use in the ninth century. In earlier times the reserved sacrament was kept in an arca, columba, or turris (see *reservation*). In the Greek Church the vessel in which the sacrament is reserved is called the *artophorion*, *pyxion*, or *pyxis*. The pyx has also been used for unconsecrated altar-breads. It has generally been made cylindrical in shape, with a foot like that of a chalice, and has sometimes had a conical cover. In modern usage it is much smaller than formerly, and is often made round and flat like a watch-case, for convenience, especially in carrying the sacrament to the sick. For public exposition of the sacrament a monstrance or ostensory is used instead.

Pyx for holding the Consecrated Host, 12th century.

The King marched towards Calais, so strictly observing his Proclamation against Church-robbing that, when one was complained of for having taken a Silver *Pixe* out of a Church, he not only caused the same to be restored, but the Soldier also to be hanged. *Baker*, Chronicles, p. 170.

2. A box or chest in which specimen coins are deposited at the British mint.—3. *Naut.*, the metallic box in which the nautical compass-card is suspended.—4. In *anat.*, the acetabulum of the hip-bone; the cotyloid cavity; the pyxis.—**Trial of the pyx**, the final trial by weight and assay of the gold and silver coins of the United Kingdom, one coin being deposited in the pyx from every fifteen pounds of gold and one from every sixty pounds of silver coined. The trial is conducted periodically by a jury of goldsmiths under the direction of the queen's remembrancer, and constitutes a public attestation of the standard purity of the coin. The phrase is also applied to the assaying of gold and silver plate which takes place at the different assay-offices.

pyx (piks), *v. t.* [‹ *pyx*, *n.*] To test by weight and assay, as the coins deposited in the pyx at the British mint. See *trial of the pyx*, above.

pyx-cloth (piks'klôth), *n.* A cloth of silk or other material in which it was formerly customary to wrap or veil the pyx. Also *Corpus Christi cloth*, *pyx-kerchief*, *pyx-veil*.

Pyxicola (pik-sik'ọ-lạ̈), *n.* [NL., ‹ Gr. πυξίς, a box (see *pyx*), + L. *colere*, inhabit.] A genus of vaginicolous *Vorticellinidæ*, in which the animalcules are attached behind to a lorica which can be closed by a discoidal operculum like the lid of a box, whence the name.

Pyxidanthera (pik″si-dan-thē'rạ̈), *n.* [NL. (F. A. Michaux, 1803), so called in allusion to the lid-like opening of the anthers; ‹ Gr. πυξίς, a box, + NL. *anthera*, anther.] A genus of gamopetalous plants of the order *Diapensiaceæ*. It is characterized by a persistent sessile corolla with short bell-shaped tube and five flat roundish lobes, five stamens fixed in the notches between the lobes, no staminodes, a three-celled ovary with many ovules, and globose anther-cells which are transversely two-valved and awn-pointed at the base. The only species, P. *barbulata*, is a dwarf and trailing shrubby evergreen, found in sands under pines from New Jersey southward to North Carolina; it is eagerly sought as a highly ornamental early spring-flowering plant, being covered with a profusion of small starry blossoms. It is known as the *pine-barren beauty*, and *flowering moss* (which see, under *moss*[1]), and also, locally, by contraction of its generic name, as *pyxie*. It bears crowded awl-shaped dark-green leaves covering the short erect branches, or alternate on the longer creeping ones, and somewhat hairy or bearded near the base, whence the specific name.

pyxidate (pik'si-dāt), *a.* [‹ *pyxis* (*-id-*) + *-ate*[1].] In *bot.*, having the character of a pyxis.

pyxidium (pik-sid'i-um), *n.*; pl. *pyxidia* (-ạ̈). [‹ Gr. πυξίδιον, a writing-tablet, dim. of πυξίς, a box: see *pyx*.] 1. In *bot.*, same as *pyxis*, 9.—2. [*cap.*] [NL.] In *zoöl.*, a genus of *Vorticellinidæ*.

Greek Pyxis of red-figured pottery, 4th century B. C.

Pyxinei, Pyxineæ (pik-sin'ẹ̄-ī, -ē), *n. pl.* [NL., ‹ L. *pyxis*, ‹ Gr. πυξίς, a box, + *-in-* + *-ei*, *-eæ*.] A natural order of lichens, comprising those known in the arctic regions as *tripe de roche*. The order is characterized by a horizontal foliaceous thallus, mostly fixed by the center, and an orbicular disk, with the exciple distinct from the thallus, and at first closed.

pyxis (pik'sis), *n.*; pl. *pyxides* (-si-dēz). [L., also *puxis*, ‹ Gr. πυξίς, a box: see *pyx*.] 1. In *Gr. antiq.* and *archæol.*, a type of cylindrical vase or box with a cover, used especially by women, as for the toilet. See cut in preceding column.—2. A box; a jewel-case.—3. In *anat.*, the cotyloid cavity, or acetabulum of the hip-joint.—4. [*cap.*] [NL.] A genus of brachiopods. *Chemnitz*, 1784.—5. [*cap.*] [NL.] In *conch.*, a genus of gastropods. *Humphreys*, 1797.—6. [*cap.*] [NL.] A genus of land-tortoises of the family *Testudinidæ*, having the anterior part of the plastron so movable that it can be shut like the lid of a pyxis. *T. Bell*, 1827.—7. A tortoise of this genus, the only known species, *Pyxis arachnoidea*, of Madagascar and Mauritius. Its shell is yellow, with broad black bands radiating from the center of the dorsal shields.—8. [*cap.*] [NL.] In *entom.*, a genus of coleopterous insects. *Dejean*, 1834.—9. In *bot.*: (*a*) A seed-vessel, commonly a capsule, with a circumscissile dehiscence, the top falling away like a lid, as in the common purslane and plantain, and in the fruit known as monkey-pots. See *Lecythis*, and cut under *circumscissile*. (*b*) The theca of mosses. Also *pyxidium*.—**Pyxis Nautica**, a southern constellation introduced by Lacaille, representing a ship's compass or binnacle. It seems no longer to be in use.

Pyxis arachnoidea.

pyx-kerchief (piks'kėr″chif), *n.* Same as *pyx-cloth*.

pyx-veil (piks'vāl), *n.* Same as *pyx-cloth*.

1. The seventeenth letter and thirteenth consonant in the English alphabet. It had a corresponding position in the early Greek and in the Latin alphabet, as also in the Phenician, where it was the nineteenth character. Its value in Phenician was that of a deeper or more guttural *k;* and a like distinction of two *k's*, less and more guttural (*kaf* and *qof*), is still made in the Semitic languages generally. But in Greek and Latin there was no such distinction to be maintained; hence the sign was abandoned in Greek (being retained only as an episemon, or sign of number, in its old place between π and ρ, and called *koppa*); while in Latin, on the other hand, it was kept, though without a value different from that of *k*, in the combination *qu*, equivalent to our *kw;* and so we have it also in English as a superfluous letter, simply because it existed in Phenician with a real office. The comparative table of early forms (as given for the other letters: see especially *A*) is as follows:

Egyptian. Hieroglyphic.	Hieratic.	Phenician.	Early Greek and Latin.

Q occurs in English, as in Latin, only before a *u* that is followed by another vowel. The combination *qu* is pronounced either as *kw* (for example, *quinquennial*), or, the *u* being silent, as *k* simply (for example, *pique*). The words containing it are nearly all of Latin or French origin; but there are a few common words (as *queen, queer, quench, quick, quoth*) in which *qu* has been substituted for the equivalent Anglo-Saxon *cw* or Teutonic *kw*, and a number of other words (Asiatic, African, American, etc.) in which *qu* represents a like combination. In the transliteration of some Oriental alphabets (Arabic, Persian, Turkish, etc.), *q* represents the more guttural form of *k*. See *qu*.

2. As a medieval Roman numeral, 500.—3. An abbreviation: (*a*) [*l. c.*] of *quadrans* (a farthing); (*b*) [*l. c.*] of *query;* (*c*) [*l. c.*] of *question;* (*d*) of *queen;* (*e*) [*l. c.*] in a ship's log-book, of *squalls;* (*f*) in *Rom. lit.* and *inscriptions*, of *Quintus*.—4†. A half-farthing: same as *cue*[2], 2 (*a*).

> Rather pray there be no fall of money, for thou wilt then go for a *q*. *Lyly*, Mother Bombie, iv. 2. (*Nares.*)

To mind one's p's and q's. See *mind*[1].

qabbalah, *n.* See *cabala*.

Q. B. An abbreviation of *Queen's Bench*.

Q. C. An abbreviation: (*a*) of *Queen's Council* or *Queen's Counsel;* (*b*) of *Queen's College*.

Q. d., or **q. d.** An abbreviation of the Latin phrase *quasi dicat*, as if he should say.

qd. An old contraction for *quod* or *quoth*. *Halliwell.*

Q. e., or **q. e.** An abbreviation of the Latin phrase *quod est*, which is.

Q. E. D. An abbreviation of the Latin phrase *quod erat demonstrandum*, which was to be demonstrated.

Q. E. F. An abbreviation of the Latin phrase *quod erat faciendum*, which was to be done.

Q. E. I. An abbreviation of the Latin phrase *quod erat inveniendum*, which was to be found out.

Q. M. An abbreviation of *quartermaster*.

Qm., or **qm.** An abbreviation of the Latin word *quomodo*, by what means.

Q. M. G. An abbreviation of *quartermaster-general*.

Qr., or **qr.** An abbreviation: (*a*) of *quarter* (28 pounds); (*b*) of *quadrans* (farthing); (*c*) of *quire*.

Q. S. An abbreviation of *quarter-sessions*.

Q. s., or **q. s.** An abbreviation: (*a*) of *quarter-section;* (*b*) of the Latin phrase *quantum sufficit*.

Qt., or **qt.** An abbreviation: (*a*) of *quart;* (*b*) of *quantity*.

qu†, *n.* An obsolete spelling of *queue* or *cue*[1].

> In 1724 the peruke-makers advertised "full-bottom tyes, . . . *qu* perukes, and bagg wiggs" among the variety of artificial head-gear which they supplied. *Encyc. Brit.*, XXIV. 560.

qu. [(1) ‹ ME. *qu-, gw-*, ‹ OF. *qu-*, F. *qu-* = Sp. *cu-* = Pg. *cu-*, *qu-* = It. *qu-*, ‹ L. *qu-* = Gr. κ- (κϝ), sometimes π = Skt. *kv-, k-*, etc. (2) ‹ ME. *qu-, qw-, kw-, ku-, cu-, cw-*, ‹ AS. *cw-* = OS. *kw-* = OFries. *kw-* = D. *kw-* = OHG. *kw-, cw-*, MHG. *kw-, qu-*, G. *qu-* = Icel. *kv-* = Sw. *kv-*, *qu-* = Dan. *kv-* = Goth. *kw-* (by Germans often written *kv-*, also rendered by *q-* or *qu-*; the Goth. character being single, namely, ų—the resemblance to the Roman u being accidental). (3) ‹ ME. *qu-, qw-, quw-, quh-, wh-, hw-*, ‹ AS. *hw-* = OS. OFries. *hw-* = D. *w-* = G. *w-* = Icel. Sw. Dan. *hv-*, etc.: see *wh-*. (4) Of various origin, ult. due to *c-* or *k-* or *ch-*.] 1. An initial and medial sequence in words of Latin origin, as in *quarrel*[1], *quarrel*[2], *quadrant, query*, etc.—2. An initial sequence in some words of Anglo-Saxon (or other Teutonic) origin, properly written *kw-*, or as originally *cw-*, but altered in the Middle English period to *qu-* in conformity with the spelling of French and Latin words with *qu-* (see 1). It occurs in *quail*[1], *quake, qualm, queen, quell, quick*, etc. It does not occur medially except in composition.—3. An initial sequence in some Middle English or modern dialectal (Scotch) variants of words regularly spelled with *wh-*, as in *qual, qwaylle*, qu*hal*, for *whale; quhilk* for *whilk* (which), *quhyp* for *whip*, etc.—4. An initial sequence of various origin other than the above, as in *quaint, quassia, quay, quince, quip, quire*[1], *quire*[2], *quiver*[2], *quoin, quoit*, etc. See the etymology of these words.

qu. An abbreviation: (*a*) of *queen, quarterly;* (*b*) of *question*, or *quære*, query.

qua[1]**†**, *pron.* An old Scotch form of *who*.

> *Qua* herd ever a warr auntur,
> That he that noght hadd bot of him
> Agayn him suld becum sua grim?
> *MS. Cott. Vespas.* (A), iii. f. 4. (*Halliwell.*)

qua[2] (kwä), *adv.* [L. *quā* (often written *quâ*), as far as, so far as, as, at or in which place, in what manner, how, orig. abl. fem. of *qui*, who, which: see *who*.] As being; so far as.

> I know what that man's mind, *quâ* mind, is, well enough. *M. Arnold*, Friendship's Garland, vi.

> The first thing to notice about this position is, that the Darwinian, *quâ* Darwinian, has nothing to do with it. *Nature*, XXXVII. 291.

qua[3] (kwä), *n.* [Appar. a var. of *quad*[2], *quod*[2].] A jail; quod. *Tufts's Glossary of Thieves' Jargon*, 1798. [Thieves' jargon.]

quab[1], **quob** (kwob), *v. i.* [Var. of the earlier *quap, quop:* see *quap*[1], *quop*[1], and cf. *quave*.] To shake; tremble; quiver; throb; flutter.

> After whan the storme ys al ago,
> Yet wol the watir *quappe* a day or two.
> *Chaucer*, Good Women, l. 1767.

> But, zealous sir, what say to a touch at praier?
> How *quops* the spirit? In what garb or ayre?
> *Fletcher*, Poems, p. 203. (*Halliwell.*)

> O, my eyes grow dim! my heart *quabs*, and my back acheth. *Dryden*, Limberham, iii. 2.

quab[1], **quob** (kwob), *n.* [‹ *quab*[1], *v.* Cf. *quavemire*.] A bog or quagmire. *Halliwell.*

quab[2]**†** (kwob), *n.* [Early mod. E. *quabbe;* ‹ MD. *quabbe, quappe*, D. *kwab, kwabbe* = OLG. *quappa*, MLG. *quappe*, LG. *quabbe, quappe*, an eel-pout, = G. *quabbe, quappe*, an eel-pout, tadpole, = Sw. *qvabba* = Dan. *krabbe*, a burbot; so called from its active motions; from the verb represented by *quab*[1], *quap*[1]. Cf. *quap*[2].] 1. A fish, the eel-pout or miller's-thumb. *Minsheu.*—2. A gudgeon. Also *quabling* and *quap*.

> A quabling or little *quabbe*, a fish, . . . gouión. *Minsheu.*

quab[3]**†** (kwob), *n.* [‹ *quab*[1], *v.*, as *squab*[2] ‹ *squab*[1], *v.*] 1. A squab, or other unfledged young bird. See *squab*[2].—2. Something immature or crude.

> A trifle of mine own brain, . . . a scholar's fancy,
> A *quab*—'tis nothing else—a very *quab*.
> *Ford*, Lover's Melancholy, iii. 3.

qua-bird (kwä'bėrd), *n.* [‹ *qua* (imitative, like equiv. *quark, quawk*) + *bird*[1].] The American night-heron, *Nyctiardea grisea nævia*.

quacha (kwä'chạ̈), *n.* Same as *quagga*. *Imp. Dict.*

quachi, *n.* Same as *coati*.

quachil, *n.* [Native name.] A large pocket-gopher, *Geomys hispidus* (formerly *Saccophorus quachil*). It inhabits Central America and some parts of Mexico, and is larger than any of the United States species, being nearly or quite a foot long, with the tail three inches more; the tail and feet are nearly naked; the pelage is harsh and lusterless, of a uniform dull chocolate-brown, merely paler or grayer below; the upper incisors have each one deep furrow lying wholly in the inner half of the tooth. Its nearest relative is the Mexican tucan, *G. mexicanus*.

quack[1] (kwak), *v. i.* [‹ ME. **quakken* (?), *queken* = MD. *quacken, queken*, croak, quack, cry as a frog, goose, or quail, later *kwakken, kwaaken*, D. *kwaken*, croak, as a frog, = MLG. *quaken* = G. *quacken, quaken*, quack, croak, babble, *quäcken, quäken*, cry, scream, = Icel. *kraka* = Sw. *qväka* = Dan. *kvakke*, croak, quack; cf. L. *coaxare*, croak, Gr. κοάξ, a quacking (see *coaxation*); all imitative words. Hence freq. *quackle*[1], and ult. *quail*[3].] 1. To utter a harsh, flat, croaking sound or cry, as a goose or duck; croak; now, usually, to cry as a duck.

> He toke a gose fast by the nek,
> And the goose thoo begann to *quek*.
> *Rel. Antiq.*, i. 4. (*Halliwell.*)

> There were thirteen ducks, and . . . they all *quacked* very movingly. *R. D. Blackmore*, Lorna Doone, x.

2. To make an outcry: said of persons. [Prov. Eng.]

> He slew the captain where he stood,
> The rest they did *quack* an' roar.
> *Willie Wallace* (Child's Ballads, VI. 235).

quack[1] (kwak), *n.* [‹ ME. *quakke, queke* = G. *quack, quak* = Dan. *kvak;* from the verb.] 1. A harsh, croaking sound.

> He speketh thurgh the nose,
> As he were on the *quakke* or on the pose.
> *Chaucer*, Reeve's Tale, l. 232.

2. The cry of a duck; a quacking.

> He gave me a look from his one little eye, . . . and then a loud *quack* to second it. *R. D. Blackmore*, Lorna Doone, x.

quack[2] (kwak), *v.* [A particular use of *quack*[1], now associated with *quack*[2], *n.*, which is in part an abbr. of *quacksalver*.] **I.** *intrans.* 1. To talk noisily and ostentatiously; make vain and loud pretensions.

> Seek out for plants with signatures,
> To *quack* of universal cures.
> *S. Butler*, Hudibras, III. i. 328.

2. To play the quack; practise arts of quackery, as a pretender to medical skill.

> Hitherto I had only *quack'd* with myself, and the highest I consulted was our apothecary. *B. Mandeville*, Hypochondrical Disorders (1730), p. 7. (*Latham.*)

II. *trans.* 1. To treat in the manner of a quack; play the quack with.

> If he [Monro] has any skill in *quacking* madmen, his art may perhaps be of service now in the Pretender's court. *Walpole*, Letters, II. 6.

> Quackery, and the love of being *quacked*, are in human nature as weeds are in our fields. *Dr. J. Brown*, Spare Hours, 3d ser., Int., p. 32.

2. To tamper with dishonestly; use fraudulently.

> *Mallet.* My third Son . . . has an admirable knack at *quacking* Titles. . . . They tell me, when he gets an old good-for-nothing Book, he claps a new Title to it, and sells off the whole Impression in a Week. *Mrs. Centlivre*, Gotham Election, i. 1.

quack[2] (kwak), *n.* and *a.* [Partly ‹ *quack*[2], *v.*, partly an abbr. of *quacksalver*, q. v.] **I.** *n.* 1. An impudent and fraudulent pretender to medical skill; a mountebank; a knavish practitioner of medicine.

> *Quacks* in their Bills, and Poets in the Titles of their Plays, do not more disappoint us than Gallants with their Promises. *Wycherley*, Love in a Wood, iii.

> A potent *quack*, long versed in human ills,
> Who first insults the victim whom he kills.
> *Crabbe*, Works, I. 14.

These, like *quacks* in medicine, excite the malady to profit by the cure, and retard the cure to augment the fees. *Irving*, Knickerbocker, p. 229.

Hence — 2. One who pretends to skill or knowledge of any kind which he does not possess; an ignorant and impudent pretender; a charlatan.

Men that go mincing, grimacing, with plausible speech and brushed raiment; hollow within! *quacks* political; *quacks* scientific, academical. *Carlyle*, French Rev., II. iii. 2.

=**Syn.** *Quack, Empiric, Mountebank, Charlatan.* A *quack* is, by derivation, one who talks much without wisdom, and, specifically, talks of his own power to heal; hence, any ignorant pretender to medical knowledge or skill. *Empiric* is a more elevated term for one who goes by mere experience in the trial of remedies, and is without knowledge of the medical sciences or of the clinical observations and opinions of others; hence, an incompetent, self-confident practitioner. A *mountebank* is generally a *quack*, but may be a pretender in any line. *Charlatan* (literally 'chatterer') is primarily applied, not to a person belonging to any particular profession or occupation, but to a pretentious cheat of any sort.

II. *a.* Pertaining to or characterized by quackery of any kind; specifically, falsely pretending to cure disease, or ignorantly or fraudulently set forth as remedies: as, a *quack* doctor; *quack* medicines.

If all understood medicine, there would be none to take his *quack* medicine. *Whately.*

The attractive head
Of some *quack*-doctor, famous in his day.
Wordsworth, Prelude, vii.

In the eighteenth century men worshipped the things that seemed; it was a *quack* century.
Caroline Fox, Journal, p. 111.

They're set to the doing of *quack* work, and paid wages for dishonesty. *New Princeton Rev.*, II. 7.

quackened (kwak'nd), *a.* [Var. of *querkened*, accom. to **quack, quackle*².] See *querken*.] Almost choked. [Prov. Eng.]

quackery (kwak'ėr-i), *n.*; pl. *quackeries* (-iz). [< *quack*² + *-ery*.] The boastful pretensions or knavish practice of a quack, particularly in medicine; empiricism; charlatanry; humbug.

Such *quackery* is unworthy any person who pretends to learning. *Porson*, Letters to Travis, p. 41, note.

An epoch when puffery and *quackery* have reached a height unexampled in the annals of mankind.
Carlyle, Sartor Resartus, i. 2.

quack-grass (kwak'gràs), *n.* Same as *quick-grass, quitch-grass*.

quackhood (kwak'hůd), *n.* [< *quack*² + *-hood*.] Quackery. *Carlyle*, Past and Present, iii. 13. [Rare.]

quacking-cheat† (kwak'ing-chēt), *n.* [< *quacking*, ppr. of *quack*¹, *v.*, + *cheat*³.] A duck. *Dekker* (1616). (*Halliwell.*) [Old slang.]

quackish (kwak'ish), *a.* [< *quack*² + *-ish*¹.] Like a quack or charlatan; dealing in quackery; humbugging.

The last *quackish* address of the National Assembly to the people of France.
Burke, To a Member of the Nat. Assembly, note.

quackism (kwak'izm), *n.* [< *quack*² + *-ism*.] The practice of quackery. *Carlyle*, Cagliostro.

quackle¹ (kwak'l), *v. i.*; pret. and pp. *quackled*, ppr. *quackling*. [Freq. of *quack*¹.] To quack; croak. [Prov. Eng.]

Simple ducks in those royal waters *quackle* for crumbs from young royal fingers.
Carlyle, French Rev., XI. i. 1. (*Davies.*)

quackle² (kwak'l), *v. t.*; pret. and pp. *quackled*, ppr. *quackling*. [Freq. of **quack*, imitative, like *choke*¹, of the sound of choking. Cf. *quackened*.] To suffocate; strangle; choke. [Prov. Eng.]

As he was drinking, the drink, or something in the cup, *quackled* him, stuck so in his throat that he could not get it up nor down, but strangled him presently.
Rev. S. Ward, Sermons, p. 153.

quacksalve† (kwak'säv), *n.* [< **quacksalve* (D. *kwakzalven*), a verb assumed from *quacksalver*.] A quacksalver.

A *quacksalve*,
A fellow that does deal with drugs.
Massinger, Parliament of Love, iv. 5.

quacksalver (kwak'sal-vėr), *n.* [< D. *kwakzalver* (= LG. *quaksalver*, > G. *quacksalber* = Sw. *qvacksalvare* = Dan. *kvaksalver*), a quacksalver, < *kwaken*, quack, + *zalver*, salver: see *salver*¹.] One who boasts of his skill in medicines and salves, or of the efficacy of his nostrums; a charlatan; a quack.

And of a Physitian, That he is a *Quack-salver*, which signifieth a Quick Healer, yet for the common acception adjudged actionable. *Jos. Keble* (1685), Reports, I. 62.

They are *quacksalvers*,
Fellows that live by venting oils and drugs.
B. Jonson, Volpone, ii. 1.

These are not physicians indeed, but Italian *quack-salvers*, that, having drunk poison themselves, minister it to the people. *Rev. T. Adams*, Works, I. 390.

quacksalving (kwak'sal-ving), *a.* [Ppr. of **quacksalve*, v., implied in *quacksalve*, *n.*, and *quacksalver*.] Quackish; humbugging.

Tut, man, any *quacksalving* terms will serve for this purpose. *Middleton*, Mad World, ii. 6.

quad¹†, *a.* and *n.* See *qued*.

quad² (kwod), *n.* [Abbr. of *quadrangle*.] **1.** A quadrangle or court, as of a college. [Colloq.]

The *quad*, as it was familiarly called, was a small quadrangle. *Trollope*, Warden, v.

2. The quadrangle of a prison where prisoners take exercise; hence, a prison; a jail. More commonly spelled *quod*. [Slang.]

Fancy a nob like you being sent to *quod*! Fiddlededee! You see, sir, you weren't used to it.
Disraeli, Henrietta Temple, vi. 21.

My dear Arminius, . . . do you really mean to maintain that a man can't put old Diggs in *quod* for snaring a hare without all this elaborate apparatus of Roman law?
M. Arnold, Friendship's Garland, vii.

quad² (kwod), *v. t.* [< *quad*², *n.*] To put in prison.

He was *quodded* for two months.
Hewlett, College Life, xxix. (*Hoppe.*)

quad³ (kwod), *n.* [Abbr. of *quadrat*.] In *printing*, a quadrat.

quad³ (kwod), *v. t.*; pret. and pp. *quadded*, ppr. *quadding*. [< *quad*³, *n.*] In *printing*, to fill with quadrats: as, to *quad* out a line.

quad⁴ (kwod), *n.* An abbreviation of *quadruplex* in telegraphy.

quad⁵ (kwod), *n.* A bicycle for four riders. [Colloq.]

quaddy (kwod'i), *a.* [Prob. for **quatty*, < *quat*¹ + *-y*¹.] Short and thick. *Halliwell.* [Prov. Eng.]

quade†, *v. t.* [< ME. *quaden*, < *quad*, bad: see *qued*.] To spoil or destroy. *Halliwell.*

Thine errores will thy worke confounde,
And all thine honoure *quade*.
Halle's Historiall Expostulation (1565). (*Nares.*)

quader¹† (kwā'dėr), *v. i.* [< OF. *quadrer*, F. *cadrer* = Sp. *cuadrar* = Pg. *quadrar* = It. *quadrare*, < L. *quadrare*, make square or four-cornered: see *quadrate*.] To quadrate; match.

The x doth not *quader* well with him, because it sounds harshly. *Hist. Don Quixote* (1675), p. 83.

quader² (kwä'dėr), *n.* [G., square, < MHG. *quâder*, < L. *quadrus* (sc. *lapis*), square: see *quadra*¹.] The German name of a division of the Cretaceous: an abbreviation of *quadersandstein*, paving-sandstone. It is divided into Unter-, Mittel-, and Oberquader. The last is the equivalent of the Upper Chalk of England and France, and is familiar as being the rock which, by its peculiar erosion, has given rise to the picturesque scenery of Saxon Switzerland.

quader³ (kwā'dėr), *n.* [< L. *quadratus*, pp. of *quadrare*, make square: see *quadrate*.] In *anat.*, the quadrate lobule, or præcuneus.

quadness†, *n.* See *quedness*.

quadra¹ (kwod'rạ̈), *n.*; pl. *quadræ* (-rē). [< L. *quadra*, a square, a plinth, a fillet; fem. of (LL.) *quadrus*, square: see *quadrate* and *square*¹.] In *arch.*, etc.: (*a*) A square frame or border inclosing a bas-relief; also, any frame or border.

Quadra.—"Annunciation," by Luca della Robbia, in the Borgo San Jacopo, Florence.

(*b*) The plinth of a podium. (*c*) Any small molding of plain or square section, as one of the fillets above and below the scotia of the Ionic base.

quadra², *n.* See *cuadra*.

quadrable (kwod'rạ-bl), *a.* [< L. as if **quadrabilis*, < *quadrare*, square: see *quadrate*, *v.*] In *geom.*, capable of being squared; having an area exactly equal to that of an assignable square; also, capable of being integrated in finite terms; capable of having its definite integral expressed in exact numerical terms.

quadrad (kwod'rad), *n.* [< L. *quattuor* (*quadr-*), = E. *four*, + *-ad*¹.] Same as *tetrad*.

quadragenarious (kwod"rạ-jẹ̄-nā'ri-us), *a.* [= F. *quadragénaire* = Sp. *cuadragenario* = Pg. It. *quadragenario*, < L. *quadragenarius*, pertaining to the number forty, consisting of forty, < *quadrageni*, forty each: see *quadragene*.] Consisting of forty; forty years old. *Imp. Dict.*

quadragene (kwod'rạ-jēn), *n.* [< L. *quadrageni*, forty each, distributive of *quadraginta*, forty, = E. *forty*.] A papal indulgence for forty days; a remission of the temporal punishment due to sin corresponding to the forty days of the ancient canonical penance. *Imp. Dict.*

You have with much labour and some charge purchased to yourself so many *quadragenes*, or lents of pardon: that is, you have bought off the penances of so many times forty days! *Jer. Taylor*, Dissuasive from Popery, I. ii. § 4.

Quadragesima (kwod-rạ-jes'i-mạ̈), *n.* [= F. *quadragésime* = Sp. *cuadragesima* = Pg. It. *quadragesima*, < ML. *quadragesima*, Lent, < L. *quadragesima*, fem. of *quadragesimus*, *quadragensumus*, fortieth, < *quadraginta*, forty, = F *forty*.] Lent: so called because it continues forty days. See *Lent*¹.—**Quadragesima Sunday**, the first Sunday in Lent.

quadragesimal (kwod-rạ-jes'i-mạl), *a.* and *n.* [= F. *quadragésimal* = Sp. *cuadragesimal* = Pg. *quadragesimal* = It. *quadragesimale*, < ML. *quadragesimalis*, pertaining to Lent, < L. *quadragesima*, Lent: see *Quadragesima*.] **I.** *a.* Pertaining to the forty days of Lent; belonging to Lent; used in Lent; Lenten.

Quadragesimal wits, and fancies lean
As ember weeks. *W. Cartwright*, Ordinary, iii. 5.

This *quadragesimal* solemnity, in which, for the space of some weeks, the church has, in some select days, enjoined a total abstinence from flesh. *South*, Sermons, IX. 134.

II. *n.* An offering formerly made to a mother church by a daughter church on Mid-Lent Sunday.

quadragesms†, *n.* [< L. *quadragesimus*, fortieth: see *Quadragesima*.] A name for a section of the fourth volume of the English Law Reports of the time of Edward III., covering the last twelve years of his reign.

quadrangle (kwod'rang-gl), *n.* [< F. *quadrangle* = Sp. *cuadrángulo* = Pg. *quadrangulo* = It. *quadrangolo*, < LL. *quadrangulum*, a four-cornered figure, a quadrangle, neut. of L. *quadrangulus*, *quadriangulus*, four-cornered, < *quattuor* (combining form *quadr-*, *quadri-*, *quadru-*, the adj. *quadrus*, square, being later), + *angulus*, an angle, a corner: see *angle*³.] **1.** A plane figure having four angles; a foursquare figure; a quadrilateral; in *mod. geom.*, a plane figure formed by six lines intersecting at four points. —**2.** A square or oblong court nearly or quite surrounded by buildings: an arrangement common with public buildings, as palaces, city halls, colleges, etc.

My choler being over-blown
With walking once about the *quadrangle*.
Shak., 2 Hen. VI., i. 3. 156.

At the Palais Royale Henry IV. built a faire *quadrangle* of stately palaces, arched underneath.
Evelyn, Diary, Feb. 4, 1644.

Julian hardly stopped to admire the smooth green *quadrangle* and lofty turrets of King Henry's College.
Farrar, Julian Home, v.

3. In *palmistry*, the space between the line of the heart and that of the head.—**Axis of a quadrangle**, one of the three lines passing each through two centers of the quadrangle.—**Center of a quadrangle**, one of the three points in which opposite sides of a quadrangle meet.—**In quadrangle**, in *her.*, arranged, as charges or groups of charges, so that four will occupy the four quarters of the escutcheon, with no lines of division between the quarters: as, or, four lions *in quadrangle* gules.

quadrangular (kwod-rang'gū-lạ̈r), *a.* [= F. *quadrangulaire* = Sp. *cuadrangular* = Pg. *quadrangular* = It. *quadrangolare*, < L. *quadrangulus*, four-cornered: see *quadrangle*.] Four-cornered; four-angled; having four angles.

That the college consist of three fair *quadrangular* courts and three large grounds, enclosed with good walls behind them. *Cowley*, The College.

As I returned, I diverted to see one of the Prince's Palaces, . . . a very magnificent cloyster'd and *quadrangular* building. *Evelyn*, Diary, Sept. 1, 1641.

Quadrangular lobe, the quadrate lobe of the cerebellum.

quadrangularly (kwod-rang'gū-lạ̈r-li), *adv.* In the form of a quadrangle.

quadrans (kwod'ranz), *n.*; pl. *quadrantes* (kwod-ran'tēz). [L., a fourth part, a quarter, a coin, weight, and measure so called: see *quadrant*.] In *Rom. antiq.*, a copper (or, strictly, bronze) coin, the fourth part of the as. It bore on the obverse the head of Hercules, and on the reverse (like the other coins of the libral series) a prow. It also bore three pellets, to indicate that it was (nominally) of the weight of three unciæ (ounces).—**Quadrans Muralis**, 'the Mural Quadrant,' an obsolete constellation, introduced by Lalande (1795).

quadrant (kwod'rant), *n.* and *a.* [< ME. *quadrant*, < AF. *quadrant*, a farthing, OF. *quadrant*, a Roman coin (*quadrans*), also *quadran*, *cadran*, a sun-dial, F. *cadran*, a sun-dial, dial, = Sp. *cuadrante* = Pg. It. *quadrante* = D. *kwadrant* = G. *quadrant* = Sw. *quadrant* = Dan. *kvadrant*, a quadrant, < L. *quadran(t-)s*, a fourth part, a quarter, applied to a coin (see *quadrans*), a weight (a fourth of a pound), a measure (a fourth of a foot, of an acre, of a sextarius), < *quattuor* (*quadr-*) = E. *four*: see *four*.] **I.** *n.* **1**†. The fourth part; the quarter.

> The sunne, who in his annuall circle takes
> A daye's full *quadrant* from the ensuing yeere,
> Repayes it in foure yeeres, and equall makes
> The number of the dayes within his spheare.
> *Sir J. Beaumont*, End of his Majesty's First Year.

> In sixty-three years there may be lost almost eighteen days, omitting the intercalation of one day every fourth year allowed for this *quadrant*, or six hours supernumerary. *Sir T. Browne*, Vulg. Err., iv. 12.

2. The quarter of a circle; the arc of a circle containing 90°; also, the figure included between this arc and two radii drawn from the center to each extremity; the division of angular magnitude from zero to a right angle, or 90°.—**3.** An astronomical instrument for measuring altitudes, of ancient origin, and consisting of a graduated arc of 90°, with a movable radius carrying sights, or the quadrant, carrying sights, might turn about a fixed radius. Picard in 1669 substituted a telescope for the sights, and Flamsteed (1689) introduced spider-lines in the focal plane of the object-glass. The quadrant was superseded by the mural circle, and this by the meridian circle.

> Howe it commeth to passe that, at the beginnynge of the euenyng twilight, it [the pole-star] is eleuate in that Region only tyue degrees in the moneth of Iune, and in the morninge twylight to bee eleuate xv. degrees by the same *quaadrante*, I doo not vnderstande.
> *R. Eden*, tr. of Peter Martyr (First Books on America, (ed. Arber, p. 90).

> Those curious *Quadrants*, Chimes, and Dials, those kind of Waggons which are used up and down Christendom, were first used by them. *Howell*, Letters, I. ii. 15.

> The astrolabe and *quadrant* are almost the only astronomical instruments used in Egypt.
> *E. W. Lane*, Modern Egyptians, I. 277.

4. An instrument of navigation, for measuring the altitude of the sun, distinctively called the *reflecting quadrant*. It was invented by Thomas Godfrey of Philadelphia in 1730, whence called *Godfrey's bow*, and perhaps independently by Hadley, an instrument-maker of London, about the same time. Among Hadley's papers after his death was found a description of a similar instrument by Newton, of earlier date. The quadrant is now nearly superseded by the sextant.
5. An instrument used in giving a cannon or mortar the angle of elevation necessary to the desired range. In the older forms it has a graduated arc, and a plumb-line which indicates the angle of elevation upon the arc. In a more finished and accurate form a spirit-level is substituted for the plumb, and one of the branches of the instrument is pivoted and slides over the face of the arc so as to show the elevation. Also called *gunners' quadrant* and *gunners' square*.
6. In *elect.*, a name suggested for the practical unit of self-induction. Its value is 10^9 centimeters.—**Adams's quadrant, Coles's quadrant,** varieties of the back-staff, or Davis's quadrant.—**Collins's quadrant,** an instrument for finding the time of day at a fixed latitude, from the date and the altitude or azimuth of the sun, by means of a stereographic projection of a quarter of the celestial zone between the tropics.—**Davis's quadrant,** the back-staff, originally described by John Davis, the discoverer of Davis's Straits, in 1594, and still called by his name, though modified by Hooke, Bouguer, and others. The observer stood with his back to the sun, and, looking through sights, brought the shadow of a pin into coincidence with the horizon.—**Godfrey's quadrant, Hadley's quadrant.** See def. 4.—**Gunter's quadrant,** a quadrant made of wood, brass, or other material—a kind of stereographic projection on the plane of the equator, the eye being supposed to be in one of the poles. It is used to find the hour of the day, the sun's azimuth, etc., as also to take the altitude of an object in degrees.—**Horodictical quadrant,** a sort of movable sun-dial. Upon the plane of the dial are described, first, seven concentric quadrantal arcs marked with the signs of the zodiac, or days of the year, and, secondly, a number of curves the intersections of each of which with the circles are at the same angular distances from one radius that the sun is above the horizon at a given hour of the day in each of the declinations represented by the circles. The radius 90° from that first mentioned carries sights, and from the center hangs a plumb-line whose intersection with the proper circle marks the time of day.—**Mural quadrant.** See *mural*.—**Quadrant electrometer.** See *electrometer*.—**Quadrant electroscope.** See *electroscope*.—**Quadrant of altitude,** an appendage of the artificial globe, consisting of a slip of brass of the length of a quadrant of one of the great circles of the globe, and graduated. It is fitted to the meridian, and can be moved round to all points of the horizon. It serves as a scale in measuring altitudes and other great circles.—**Sinical quadrant,** a diagram, with or without a movable arm, for solving plane triangles. An octant is sufficient.—**Spirit-level quadrant,** an instrument for determining altitudes by the use of a spirit-level.—**Sutton's quadrant.** Same as *Collins's quadrant*.

II.† *a.* Four-sided; square. [Rare.]

> The bishop with Gilbert Bourne his chaplaine, Robert Warnington his commissarie, and Robert Johnson his register, were tarying in a *quadrant* void place before the doore of the same chamber.
> *Foxe*, Martyrs, p. 1206, an. 1550.

Cross nowy quadrant. See *cross*[1].

quadrantal (kwod'ran-tal), *a.* [= Sp. *cuadrantal* = Pg. *quadrantal*, < L. *quadrantalis*, containing the fourth part of, < *quadran(t-)s*, a fourth part, a quarter: see *quadrant*.] **1.** Pertaining to a quadrant; included in the fourth part of a circle: as, a *quadrantal* space.

> Problems in Dialling, both Universal and Particular, and performed by the Lines inscribed on the *Quadrantal* Part of the Instrument.
> Quoted in *N. and Q.*, 7th ser., VIII. 244.

2. Pertaining to the quadrans; of the value of a quadrans.—**Quadrantal dial.** See *dial*.—**Quadrantal triangle,** in *trigon.*, a spherical triangle which has one side equal to a quadrant, or 90°.

quadrantal (kwod'ran-tal), *n.* [< L. *quadrantal*, a liquid measure containing eight congii, also a cube, die, < *quadrantalis*, containing a fourth: see *quadrantal*, *a.*] **1.** A liquid measure used by the Romans, equivalent to the amphora.—**2.** A cube. [Rare.]

quadrant-compass (kwod'rant-kum"pas), *n.* A carpenters' compass with a curved arm or arc, and a binding-screw to hold the limbs in any position.

quadrantes, *n.* Plural of *quadrans*.

quadrantid (kwod'ran-tid), *n.* [< NL. *Quadran(t-)s*, sc. *Muralis* (see *quadrans*), + *-id*[2].] One of a shower of shooting-stars appearing January 2d and 3d, and radiating from the old constellation Quadrans Muralis.

quadrat (kwod'rat), *a.* and *n.* [Another form of *quadrate*; as a noun, in def. 1, < F. *quadrat*, *cadrat*, a quadrat, lit. a square: see *quadrate*.] **I.**† *a.* See *quadrate*.

II. *n.* **1.** In *printing*, a blank type for the larger blank spaces in or at the end of printed lines, cast lower in height, so that it shall not be inked or impressed: made in four forms for all text type—en, em, two-em, three-em. Usually abbreviated to *quad*.

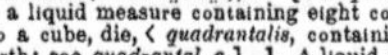

en quad. em quad. 2-em quad. 3-em quad.

> The *low* quadrat, for letterpress work, is about three fourths of an inch high; the *high* quadrat, for stereotype work, is about ten twelfths of an inch high.

> In the lower case, having fifty-four boxes, are disposed the small letters, together with the points, spaces, *quadrats*, etc. *Ure*, Dict., III. 643.

2. An instrument furnished with sights, a plummet, and an index, and used for measuring altitudes, but superseded by more perfect instruments in modern use. Also called *geometrical square*, and *line of shadows*.—**3.** A series or set of four.

quadrata, *n.* Plural of *quadratum*.

quadrate (kwod'rāt), *a.* and *n.* [Formerly also *quadrat*; < OF. *quadrat* (F. *quadrat*, *cadrat*, as a noun: see *quadrat*); OF. vernacularly *quarre* (> E. *quarry*[1]), F. *carré* = Sp. *cuadrato* = Pg. *quadrado* = It. *quadrato* = D. *kwadraat* = G. Sw. *quadrat* = Dan. *kvadrat*, a square; < L. *quadratus*, square (neut. *quadratum*, a square, quadrate), pp. of *quadrare*, make four-cornered, square, put in order, intr. be square, < *quadra*, a square, later *quadrus*, square, < *quattuor* = E. *four*: see *four*. Cf. *quarry*[1], a doublet of *quadrate*; cf. also *square*[1].] **I.** *a.* **1.** Having four equal and parallel sides; square; arranged in a square; four-sided.

> And they followed in a *quadrat* array to the entent to destroy kyng Henry.
> *Hall's Union* (1548), Hen. IV., f. 13. (*Halliwell*.)

> And searching his books, [he] found a book of astronomy . . . with figures, some round, some triangle, some *quadrate*. *Foxe*, Martyrs, an. 1558.

2. Square by being the product of a number multiplied into itself.

> *Quadrate* and cubical numbers.
> *Sir T. Browne*, Vulg. Err., iv. 12.

3†. Square, as typifying justice according to the Pythagoreans; well-balanced.

> The Moralist tells us that a *quadrat* solid wise Man should involve and tackle himself within his own Virtue.
> *Howell*, Letters, I. vi. 58.

4†. Fitted; suited; applicable.

> The word consumption, being applicable . . . to a true and bastard consumption, requires a generical description *quadrate* to both. *Harvey*, Consumptions.

5. In *her.*, of square form, or having square corners: thus, a cross *quadrate* in the center has four rectangular projections in its reëntrant angles. Also *quarter-angled*.—**Quadrate bone,** in *zoöl.*, the special bone by the intervention of which the lower jaw of birds, reptiles, etc., articulates with the skull, thus distinguishing them from mammals, in which the lower jaw articulates directly with the squamosal. See II., 3.—**Quadrate cartilages,** small quadrangular cartilages often found in the nasal alæ.—**Quadrate gyrus** or **lobule.** See *gyrus*, and cut under *cerebral*.—**Quadrate line, lobe, pronator,** etc. See the nouns.—**Quadrate muscle,** in *anat.*: (*a*) The quadratus femoris, or square muscle of the femur, of man, one of the six muscles collectively known in human anatomy as the rotatores femoris, arising from the ischium and passing to the intertrochanteric part of the femur, which bone it rotates outward. (*b*) The quadratus lumborum, or square muscle of the loins, lying on each side of the lumbar region, between the lower ribs and the pelvis. (*c*) The square muscle of the chin, which draws down the lower lip: commonly called *depressor labii inferioris*. (*d*) The quadratus nictitantis, one of the two muscles (the other being the pyramidal) on the back of the eyeball of birds, etc., subserving the movements of the nictitating membrane, or third eyelid. See third cut under *eye*[1].

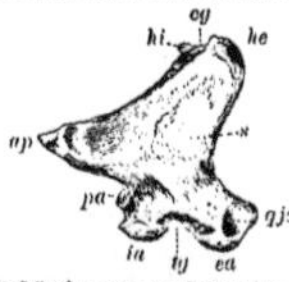

Left Quadrate Bone of an Eagle, outer side, a little enlarged.
s, shaft or body of the bone; *ap*, pterygoid apophysis for muscular attachment; *pa*, articular facet for pterygoid bone; *in*, *ea*, internal and external condyles for articulation with the lower jaw, separated by *tg*, trochlear groove; *qjc*, quadratojugal cup for articulation of quadratojugal bone; *hi*, *he*, internal and external capitulum for articulation with squamosal bone, separated by *cg*, capitular groove.

II. *n.* **1.** A plane figure with four equal sides and four equal angles; a square.

> The one imperfect, mortall, fœminine,
> Th' other immortall, perfect, masculine;
> And twixt them both a *quadrate* was the base,
> Proportiond equally by seven and nine.
> *Spenser*, F. Q., II. ix. 22.

> The powers militant
> . . . in mighty *quadrate* join'd.
> *Milton*, P. L., vi. 62.

2. In *astrol.*, an aspect of two heavenly bodies in which they are distant from each other ninety degrees, or the quarter of a circle; quartile.—**3.** In *zoöl.* and *anat.*: (*a*) The os quadratum, or quadrate bone (see I.); the os pedicellatum, or pedicellate bone; the suspensorium, or suspender bone of the mandible, or that one which is in connection with the lower jaw, in vertebrates below mammals. Also called by Owen and others the *tympanic bone*, and considered to represent that bone of a mammal; by most zoölogists now identified with the malleus or greater part of the malleus of *Mammalia*, formed about the proximal extremity of the Meckelinn cartilage. In birds and reptiles the quadrate is a remarkably distinct bone, generally shaped something like an anvil or a molar tooth, with normally four separate movable articulations—with the squamosal above, the mandible below, the pterygoid internally, and the quadratojugal externally. Such vertebrates are hence called *Quadratifera*. (See cuts under *Gallinæ*, and *quadrate*, *a.*) Below reptiles the quadrate or its equivalent assumes other characters, and its homologies are then disputed; so the bone which has at any rate the same function, that of suspending the lower jaw to the skull, is usually called by another name. See *epitympanic* and *hyoinandibular*, and cuts under *hyoid* and *palatoquadrate*. See also cuts under *Python*, *poison-fang*, *Crotalus*, *Petromyzon*, *teleost*, *palatoquadrate*, and *acrodont*. (*b*) Any quadrate muscle.—**4.** In *musical notation*: (*a*) Same as *natural*, ♮: so called because derived from *B quadratum* (which see, under *B*). (*b*) Same as *breve*, 1.

quadrate (kwod'rāt), *v.*; pret. and pp. *quadrated*, ppr. *quadrating*. [< L. *quadratus*, pp. of *quadrare* (> It. *quadrare* = Pg. *quadrar* = Sp. *cuadrar* = F. *cadrer*, OF. *quadrer*, > E. *quader*[1], q. v.), make four-cornered, square: see *quadrate*, *a.* and *n.*] **I.**† *trans.* **1.** To square; adjust; trim, as a gun on its carriage.—**2.** To divide into four equal parts; quarter. *Moor*, Hindu Pantheon (1810), p. 249.

II. *intrans.* To square; fit; suit; agree: followed by *with*.

> One that . . . has a few general rules, which, like mechanical instruments, he applies to the works of every writer, and as they *quadrate with* them pronounces the author perfect or defective. *Addison*, Sir Timothy Tittle.

> But we should have to make our language over from the beginning, if we would have it *quadrate with* other languages. *F. Hall*, False Philol., p. 85.

quadrated (kwod'rāt-ed), *p. a.* [< *quadrate*, *v.*] In quadrature.

> What time the moon is *quadrated* in Heaven.
> *Poe*, Al Aaraaf, ii.

quadrati, *n.* Plural of *quadratus*.

quadratic (kwod-rat'ik), *a.* and *n.* [< *quadrate* + *-ic*.] **I.** *a.* **1.** In *alg.*, involving the square and no higher power of the unknown quantity or variable of the second degree; of two dimensions.—2. In *crystal.*, tetragonal or dimetric: applied to the system that includes the square prism and related forms. See *crystallography*.—**Quadratic equation, group, logarithm, mean, modulus,** etc. See the nouns.—**Quadratic figure,** a figure of two dimensions; a superficial figure. See *cubical*.—**Quadratic reciprocity,** the relation between any two prime numbers expressed by the law of reciprocity (which see, under *law*[1]).—**Quadratic residue,** a number left as remainder after dividing some square number by a given modulus to which the quadratic residue is said to belong. Thus, 1, 3, 4, 5, and 9 are quadratic residues of 11, for $1 = 1^2 - 0.11$, $3 = 5^2 - 2.11$, $4 = 9^2 - 7.11$, etc.; but 2, 6, 7, 8, and 10 are quadratic non-residues of 11.

II. *n.* 1. In *alg.*, an equation in which the highest power of the unknown quantity is the second, the general form being

$$ax^2 + 2bx + c = 0.$$

Such an equation has two solutions, real, equal, or imaginary, expressed by the formula

$$x = \frac{-b \pm \sqrt{b^2 - ac}}{a}.$$

2. *pl.* That branch of algebra which treats of quadratic equations.—**Affected quadratic,** a quadratic equation having a term containing the unknown to the first degree, and another not containing the unknown.—**Simple quadratic.** See *simple*.

quadratically (kwod-rat'i-kal-i), *adv.* To the second degree.—**To multiply quadratically,** to raise to the second power.

Quadratifera (kwod-rā-tif'e-rä), *n. pl.* [NL., neut. pl. of *quadratifer*: see *quadratiferous*.] Those vertebrates which have a distinct quadrate bone, as birds and reptiles; a series of *Vertebrata* intermediate between the higher *Malleifera* (mammals) and the lower *Lyrifera* (fishes proper and selachians).

quadratiferous (kwod-rā-tif'e-rus), *a.* [< NL. *quadratifer*, < L. *quadratus*, the quadrate muscle, + L. *ferre* = E. *bear*[1].] Having a distinct quadrate bone, as an animal or its skull; of or pertaining to the *Quadratifera*.

quadratiformis (kwod-rā-ti-fôr'mis), *n.*; pl. *quadratiformes* (-mēz). [NL., < L. *quadratus*, the quadrate muscle, + *forma*, form.] The square muscle of the coxal group; the quadratus femoris. *Coues.*

quadratipronator (kwod-rā"ti-prō-nā'tor), *n.* [< L. *quadratus*, square, + NL. *pronator*, q. v.] A square pronator of the forearm: same as *pronator quadratus*. See *pronator*. *Coues.*

quadratocubic (kwod-rā-tō-kū'bik), *a.* Of the fifth degree.—**Quadratocubic root,** the fifth root.

quadratojugal (kwod-rā-tō-jö'gal), *a.* and *n.* I. *a.* Connected with or representing elements of the quadrate and of the jugal or malar bone; common to these two bones: as, the *quadratojugal* arch; the *quadratojugal* articulation.

II. *n.* A bone of the zygomatic arch of birds, etc., interposed between the quadrate bone behind and the jugal or malar bone before: generally a slender rod forming the hinder piece of the zygoma. By some it is identified with the squamosal of mammals—a determination to which few now assent. See cuts under *Gallinæ*, *girdle-bone*, *temporomastoid*, and *Trematosaurus*.

quadratomandibular (kwod-rā"tō-man-dib'ū-lär), *a.* Of or pertaining to the quadrate bone and the lower jaw: as, the *quadratomandibular* articulation. See cut under *Lepidosiren*.

quadratopterygoid (kwod-rā"tō-ter'i-goid), *a.* Of or pertaining to the quadrate and pterygoid bones: as, the *quadratopterygoid* articulation.

quadratoquadratic (kwod-rā"tō-kwod-rat'ik), *a.* Of the fourth degree.—**Quadratoquadratic root,** the fourth root.

quadrator (kwod-rā'tor), *n.* [< LL. *quadrator*, a squarer (used only in sense of 'stone-cutter, quarrier': see *quarrier*[1]), < L. *quadrare*, square: see *quadrate*.] A circle-squarer.

quadratosquamosal (kwod-rā"tō-skwā-mō'sal), *a.* In *anat.*, of or pertaining to the quadrate and the squamosal: as, the *quadratosquamosal* articulation.

quadratrix (kwod-rā'triks), *n.* [NL. (tr. Gr. τετραγωνίζουσα), fem. of LL. *quadrator*, squarer: see *quadrator*.] In *geom.*, a curve by means of which can be found straight lines equal to the circumference of circles or other curves and their several parts; a curve employed for finding the quadrature of other curves.

Quadratrix of Dinostratus.

Deinostratus, to whom is ascribed the invention of the *quadratrix* for solving the two famous problems—the trisection of the angle and the quadrature of the circle.
The Academy, June 1, 1880, p. 381.

Quadratrix of Dinostratus, a curve probably invented by Hippias of Elis about 430 B. C., and named by Dinostratus a century later. Its equation is $r \sin\theta = a\theta$.—**Quadratrix of Tschirnhausen** (named from its inventor, Count E. W. von *Tschirnhausen*, 1651–1708), a curve of sines, having the distance between two successive intersections with the line of abscissas equal to the greatest difference of the ordinates.

quadratum (kwod-rā'tum), *n.*; pl. *quadrata* (-tä). [L., neut. of *quadratus*, square: see *quadrate*, *a.*] 1. In *zoöl.*, the quadrate bone: more fully called *os quadratum*.—2. In *medieval music*, a breve.

quadrature (kwod'rā-tūr), *n.* [= F. *quadrature* = Sp. *cuadratura* = Pg. It. *quadratura*, < LL. *quadratura*, a making square, a squaring, < L. *quadrare*, pp. *quadratus*, square: see *quadrate*.] 1. In *geom.*, the act of squaring an area; the finding of a square or several squares equal in area to a given surface.—2. A quadrate; a square space. [Rare.]

> There let him [God] still victor sway, . . .
> And henceforth monarchy with thee divide
> Of all things, parted by the empyreal bounds,
> His *quadrature*, from thy orbicular world.
> *Milton*, P. L., x. 381.

3. The relative position of two planets, or of a planet and the sun, when the difference of their longitudes is 90°.

But when armillæ were employed to observe the moon in other situations . . . a second inequality was discovered, which was connected, not with the anomalistical, but with the synodical revolution of the moon, disappearing in conjunctions and oppositions, and coming to its greatest amount in *quadratures*. What was most perplexing about this second inequality was that it did not return in every *quadrature*, but, though in some it amounted to 2° 39′, in other *quadratures* it totally disappeared. *Small*, Account of the Astronomical Discoveries [of Kepler (London, 1804), § 11.

Neptune . . . is in *quadrature* with the sun on the 23d.
Sci. Amer., N. S., LVII. 64.

4. A side of a square. [Rare.]

This citie [Cambalu] is foure square, so that euery *quadrature* or syde of the wall hath in it thre principal portes or gates. *R. Eden*, tr. of Sebastian Munster (First Books [on America, ed. Arber, p. 25).

Indefinite quadrature, a rule for the quadrature of the circle, applicable to any sector of it.—**Mechanical quadrature,** an approximate quadrature of a plane surface, effected by the division of it by parallel lines into parts so small that they may be regarded as rectilinear or other quadrable figures; also, the integration of any expression by an analogous method.—**Method of quadratures,** the approximate integration of an expression between given numerical limits by the summation of parts in each of which the difference between the limits is so small that the integral is practically equal to that of some integrable expression.—**The problem of the quadrature, or the quadrature of the circle,** the problem of squaring the circle, of which there are two varieties: first, the *arithmetical quadrature*, exactly to express in square measure the area of a circle whose radius is some exact number in long measure; second, the *geometrical quadrature*, to describe or draw with the rule and compasses alone a square equal in area to a given circle. Both problems have been proved to be insoluble.

quadratus (kwod-rā'tus), *n.*; pl. *quadrati* (-tī). [NL., sc. *musculus*, the square muscle: see *quadrate*.] In *zoöl.* and *anat.*, the musculus quadratus or quadrate muscle of (*a*) the femur; (*b*) the loins; (*c*) the chin; (*d*) the nictitating membrane. See *quadrate muscle*, under *quadrate*.—**Quadratus femoris,** a muscle situated at the back of the hip-joint, arising from the tuberosity of the ischium and inserted into a line running from the posterior intertrochanteric ridge.—**Quadratus labii inferioris.** Same as *depressor labii inferioris* (which see, under *depressor*).—**Quadratus labii superioris,** the combined levator labii superioris alæque nasi, levator labii superioris proprius, and zygomaticus minor muscles, the three different parts being called *caput angulare*, *caput infraorbitale*, and *caput zygomaticum* respectively.—**Quadratus lumborum.** See *lumbus*.—**Quadratus menti.** See *mentum*.

quadrauricular (kwod-râ-rik'ū-lär), *a.* [< L. *quattuor* (*quadr-*), four, + *auricula*, auricle: see *auricle*.] Having four auricles, as the heart of a nautilus.

quadrel (kwod'rel), *n.* [< ML. *quadrellus*, dim. of L. *quadrum*, a square: see *quarrel*[2].] 1. In *arch.*, a square stone, brick, or tile. The term is sometimes restricted in its application to a kind of artificial stone formed of a chalky earth molded to a square form and slowly and thoroughly dried in the shade.
2. A piece of turf or peat cut in a square form. [Prov. Eng.]

quadrelle (kwod-rel'), *n.* [< OF. *quadrelle*, an arrow, shaft, var. of *quarele*, f., *quarel*, m., an arrow, crossbow-bolt, etc.: see *quarrel*[2].] A square-headed or four-edged missile.

quadrennial (kwod-ren'i-al), *a.* and *n.* [For *quadriennial*, q. v.] I. *a.* 1. Comprising four years: as, a *quadrennial* period.—2. Occurring once in four years: as, *quadrennial* elections.

Both States [Montana and Washington] provide for a *quadrennial* election of a governor, lieutenant-governor, secretary of state, state treasurer, state auditor, attorney-general, and superintendent of public instruction.
The Century, XXXIX. 506.

II. *n.* A fourth anniversary, or its celebration.

quadrennially (kwod-ren'i-al-i), *adv.* Once in four years.

quadrenniate (kwod-ren'i-āt), *n.* [< *quadrennium* + *-ate*[3].] A period of four years; a quadrennium.

quadrennium (kwod-ren'i-um), *n.* [For *quadriennium*, q. v.] A period of four years.

Burdening girls, after they leave school, with a *quadrennium* of masculine college regimen.
E. H. Clarke, Sex in Education, p. 125.

quadrequivalent (kwod-rē-kwiv'a-lent), *a.* [< L. *quattuor* (*quadr-*), = E. *four*, + E. *equivalent*.] Same as *quadrivalent*.

quadri-. [L., also *quadru-*, sometimes *quatri-*, combining form of *quattuor*, = E. *four* (the independent adj. *quadrus* or *quadruus*, four-cornered, square, fourfold, < *quattuor*, four, being of later use): see *four*.] An element in many compounds of Latin origin or formation, meaning 'four.' In *quadrangle*, *quadrangular* (as in Latin), and in *quadrennial*, *quadrennium*, it is reduced to *quadr-*.

quadriarticulate (kwod"ri-är-tik'ū-lāt), *a.* [< L. *quattuor* (*quadri-*), = E. *four*, + *articulatus*, pp. of *articulare*, divide into single joints: see *articulate*.] Having four articulations or joints.

quadribasic (kwod-ri-bā'sik), *a.* [< L. *quattuor* (*quadri-*), = E. *four*, + E. *basic*.] In *chem.*, noting an acid which has four hydrogen atoms replaceable by basic atoms or radicals.

quadriblet (kwod'ri-bl), *a.* [Irreg. for the later *quadrable*, q. v.] Capable of being squared. [Rare.]

Sir Isaac Newton had discovered a way of attaining the quantity of all *quadrible* curves analytically, by his method of fluxions, some time before the year 1668.
Derham, Physico-Theol., v. 1, note *y*.

quadric (kwod'rik), *n.* and *a.* [< LL. *quadrus*, square (< L. *quattuor* = E. *four*), + *-ic*.] I. *n.* In *alg.*, a homogeneous expression of the second degree in the variables. *Ternary* and *quaternary quadrics*, equated to zero, represent respectively curves and surfaces which have the property of cutting every line in the plane or in space in two points, real or imaginary, and to such surfaces the name *quadric* is also applied.—**Modular method of generation of quadrics.** See *modular*.

II. *a.* In *alg.* and *geom.*, of the second degree; quadratic. Where there is only one variable, the word *quadratic* is usually employed; in plane geometry, *conic*; and in solid geometry and where the number of non-homogeneous variables exceeds two, *quadric*. Thus, we say *quadric* cone, not *quadratic* or *conic* cone.—**Quadric inversion.** See *inversion*.—**Quadric surface,** a surface of the second order.

quadricapsular (kwod-ri-kap'sū-lär), *a.* [< L. *quattuor* (*quadri-*), = E. *four*, + *capsula*, capsule: see *capsule*, *capsular*.] In *bot.*, having four capsules.

quadricarinate (kwod-ri-kar'i-nāt), *a.* [< L. *quattuor* (*quadri-*), = E. *four*, + *carina*, keel: see *carina*, *carinate*.] In *entom.*, having four carinæ, or longitudinal raised lines: specifically said of the face of an orthopterous insect when the median carina is deeply sulcate, so that it forms two parallel raised lines, which, with the two lateral carinæ, form four raised lines.

quadricellular (kwod-ri-sel'ū-lär), *a.* [< L. *quattuor* (*quadri-*), = E. *four*, + NL. *cellula*, cellule: see *cellular*.] Having or consisting of four cells.

quadricentennial (kwod"ri-sen-ten'i-al), *a.* and *n.* [< L. *quattuor* (*quadri-*), = E. *four*, + ML. *centennis*, a hundred years old: see *centennial*.] I. *a.* Pertaining to or consisting of a period of four hundred years.

II. *n.* The commemoration or celebration of an event which occurred four hundred years before: as, the Luther *quadricentennial*.

quadriceps (kwod'ri-seps), *n.* [NL., < L. *quattuor* (*quadri-*), = E. *four*, + *caput*, head: see *biceps*.] In *anat.*, the quadriceps extensor cruris of the thigh; the great muscle which extends the leg upon the thigh, considered as consisting of the rectus, cruræus, and vastus internus and externus. Called *triceps extensor cruris* when the cruræus is regarded as a part of the vastus internus, or when the rectus is separately enumerated. This great muscle forms nearly all the flesh upon the front of the thigh. See cuts under *muscle*[1].—**Quadriceps suræ,** the combined gastrocnemius externus and internus, soleus, and plantaris, forming the bulk of the muscle of the calf.

quadriciliate (kwod-ri-sil'i-āt), *a.* [< L. *quattuor* (*quadri-*), = E. *four*, + NL. *cilium* + *-ate*[1].] Having four cilia, or flagelliform appendages.

M. Thuret informs us that he has seen the biciliate spores germinate as well as the *quadriciliate*.
M. J. Berkeley, Introd. to Cryptog. Bot., p. 137.

quadricinium (kwod-ri-sin'i-um), *n.*; pl. *quadricinia* (-ä). [NL., < L. *quattuor* (*quadri-*), = E. *four*, + *canere*, sing.] In *music*, a composition for four voices. Also *quatricinium*.

quadricipital (kwod-ri-sip'i-tal), *a.* [< *quadriceps* (*-cipit-*) + *-al*.] Having four heads or origins, as a muscle; of or pertaining to the quadriceps.

quadricone (kwod'ri-kōn), *n.* [< L. *quattuor* (*quadri-*), = E. *four*, + *conus*, cone: see *cone*.] A quadric cone, or surface generated by the motion of a line through a fixed point, one point of which describes a conic section.

quadricorn (kwod'ri-kôrn), *a.* and *n.* [< NL. *quadricornis*, < L. *quattuor* (*quadri-*), = E. *four*, + *cornu* = E. *horn*.] I. *a.* Having four horns or horn-like parts, as antennæ; quadricornous.

II. *n.* A quadricorn animal.

Quadricorn Sheep (*Ovis aries*, var. *quadricornis*).

quadricornous (kwod-ri-kôr'nus), *a.* [< *quadricorn* + *-ous*.] Having four horns; quadricorn.

quadricostate (kwod-ri-kos'tāt), *a.* [< L. *quattuor* (*quadri-*), = E. *four*, + *costa*, rib: see *costa*, *costate*.] Having four ribs or costæ, in any sense.

quadricrescentic (kwod"ri-kre-sen'tik), *a.* [< L. *quattuor* (*quadri-*), = E. *four*, + E. *crescent* + *-ic*.] Having four crescents; quadricrescentoid.

quadricrescentoid (kwod-ri-kres'en-toid), *a.* [< L. *quattuor* (*quadri-*), = E. *four*, + E. *crescent* + *-oid*.] In *odontog.*, having four crescentic folds: noting a pattern of selenodont dentition.

quadricuspidal (kwod-ri-kus'pi-dal), *n.* [< L. *quattuor* (*quadri-*), = E. *four*, + *cuspis* (*cuspid-*), a point: see *cuspidal*.] A ruled surface of the eighth order.—**Limited quadricuspidal**, a ruled surface of the fourth order, generated by the motion of a straight line cutting two given straight lines and touching a given quadric surface.

quadricuspidate (kwod-ri-kus'pi-dāt), *a.* [< L. *quattuor* (*quadri-*), = E. *four*, + *cuspis* (*cuspid-*), a point: see *cusp*, *cuspidate*.] Having four cusps, as a tooth. *W. H. Flower*, Encyc. Brit., XV. 402.

quadricycle (kwod'ri-si-kl), *n.* [< L. *quattuor* (*quadri-*), = E. *four*, + LL. *cyclus*, cycle: see *cycle*[1].] A four-wheeled vehicle intended to be propelled by the feet of the rider.

A *Quadricycle* for pedal propulsion on railways.
The Engineer, LXV. 109.

quadridentate (kwod-ri-den'tāt), *a.* [< L. *quadriden*(*t-*)*s*, having four teeth, < *quattuor* (*quadri-*), = E. *four*, + *den*(*t-*)*s* = E. *tooth*: see *dentate*.] Having four teeth or tooth-like parts, as serrations.

quadriderivative (kwod"ri-dē-riv'a-tiv), *n.* [< L. *quattuor* (*quadri-*), = E. *four*, + E. *derivative*.] A derivative invariant of the second order.

quadridigitate (kwod-ri-dij'i-tāt), *a.* [< L. *quattuor* (*quadri-*), = E. *four*, + L. *digitus*, finger or toe: see *digit*, *digitate*.] Having four digits, whether fingers, toes, or other digitate parts; tetradactyl; quadrisulcate, as a hoofed quadruped.

quadriennial† (kwod-ri-en'i-al), *a.* [= F. *quadriennal*, *quatriennal* = Sp. *cuadrienal* = Pg. *quadriennal*, < LL. *quadriennis*, of four years, < L. *quattuor* (*quadri-*), = E. *four*, + *annus*, a year.] Quadrennial.

quadriennially† (kwod-ri-en'i-al-i), *adv.* Quadrennially.

quadriennium (kwod-ri-en'i-um), *n.* [L. *quadriennium*, a space of four years, < LL. *quadriennis*, of four years: see *quadriennial*.] A quadrennium.—**Quadriennium utile**, in *Scots law*, the four years allowed after majority within which may be instituted an action of reduction of any deed done to the prejudice of a minor.

quadrifarious (kwod-ri-fā'ri-us), *a.* [< LL. *quadrifarius*, fourfold, < L. *quattuor* (*quadri-*), = E. *four*, + *-farius*, as in *bifarius*, etc. (see *bifarious*).] Set, arranged, or disposed in four rows or series: correlated with *unifarious*, *bifarious*, *trifarious*, and *multifarious*.

quadrifariously (kwod-ri-fā'ri-us-li), *adv.* In a quadrifarious manner.

quadrifid (kwod'ri-fid), *a.* [< L. *quadrifidus*, split into four parts, four-cleft, < *quattuor* (*quadri*), = E. *four*, + *findere* (√ *fid*), cleave, split.] Four-cleft; deeply cut, but not entirely divided, into four parts: correlated with *bifid*, *trifid*, and *multifid*.

The mouth of the animal, situated at one of the poles, leads first to a *quadrifid* cavity.
W. B. Carpenter, Micros., § 530.

Quadrifidæ (kwod-rif'i-dē), *n. pl.* [NL., fem. pl. of L. *quadrifidus*, four-cleft: see *quadrifid*.] In *entom.*, a section of noctuid moths; one of the two prime divisions of noctuid moths in Guenée's classification. It includes all those families in which the median vein of the hind wings has four branches. It contains the largest of the noctuids, and the forms are mainly American and East Indian. The character which gives the name is not a stable one, and the term has nearly fallen into disuse.

quadrifocal (kwod-ri-fō'kal), *a.* [< L. *quattuor* (*quadri-*), = E. *four*, + *focus*, focus: see *focus*, *focal*.] Having four foci.

quadrifoliate (kwod-ri-fō'li-āt), *a.* [< L. *quattuor* (*quadri-*), = E. *four*, + *folium*, leaf: see *foliate*.] In *bot.*, four-leaved. (*a*) Having the leaves whorled in fours. (*b*) Same as *quadrifoliolate*: an incorrect use.

Quadrifoliate Stem of *Asclepias quadrifolia*.

quadrifoliolate (kwod-ri-fō'li-ō-lāt), *a.* [< L. *quattuor* (*quadri-*), = E. *four*, + *foliolus*, leaflet.] In *bot.*, having four leaflets: said of a compound leaf.

quadriform (kwod'ri-fôrm), *a.* [< LL. *quadriformis*, four-formed, < L. *quattuor* (*quadri-*), = E. *four*, + *forma*, form.] Having a fourfold aspect, as in shape, arrangement, etc.

We can also apply the principle of group-flashing as easily to a fourfold light as to a single light. According to the number of tiers employed, the arrangement was to be named Biform, Triform, *Quadriform*.
Fortnightly Rev., N. S., XLIII. 815.

quadrifrons (kwod'ri-fronz), *a.* [< L. *quattuor* (*quadri-*), = E. *four*, + *frons* (*front-*), front: see *front*.] Having four faces. See *bifrons*.

quadrifurcate (kwod-ri-fėr'kāt), *a.* [< L. *quattuor* (*quadri-*), = E. *four*, + *furca*, fork: see *furca*, *furcate*.] Having four forks, tines, or branches; twice-forked; doubly dichotomous: correlated with *bifurcate* and *trifurcate*.

quadrifurcated (kwod-ri-fėr'kā-ted), *a.* [< *quadrifurcate* + *-ed*[2].] Same as *quadrifurcate*.

quadriga (kwod-rī'gä), *n.*; pl. *quadrigæ* (-jē). [L., usually in pl. *quadrigæ*, contr. from *quadrijugæ*, a team of four, < *quattuor* (*quadri-*), = E. *four*, + *jugum* (= Gr. ζυγόν), a yoke, pair, team: see *yoke*.] In *classical antiq.*, a two-wheeled chariot drawn by four horses, which were harnessed all abreast. It was used in racing in the Greek Olympian games, and in the circensian games of the Romans. The quadriga is often met with as the reverse type of Greek coins, especially those of Sicily, and is of frequent occurrence in sculpture and vase-painting.

Quadriga.—"The Rape of Proserpine by Pluto," from a Greek red-figured vase.

The *quadriga* for which Praxiteles was said to have made the driver. *A. S. Murray*, Greek Sculpture, I. 182.

quadrigemina (kwod-ri-jem'i-nä), *n. pl.* [NL., neut. pl. of L. *quadrigeminus*, fourfold: see *quadrigeminous*.] The quadrigeminous bodies of the brain, more fully called *corpora quadrigemina*. Below mammals they are represented by the corpora bigemina, or twin bodies. See *corpus*.

quadrigeminal (kwod-ri-jem'i-nal), *a.* [< *quadrigemin-ous* + *-al*.] Fourfold; especially, pertaining to the corpora quadrigemina.

Other fibres, arising in the optic thalamus and *quadrigeminal* body, descend, which preside over the reflex motions. *Frey*, Histol. and Histochem. (trans.), p. 594.

quadrigeminate (kwod-ri-jem'i-nāt), *a.* [< *quadrigemin-ous* + *-ate*[1].] 1. In *bot.*, growing in fours, as the cells of certain algæ.—2. In *anat.*, same as *quadrigeminous*.

quadrigeminous (kwod-ri-jem'i-nus), *a.* [< L. *quadrigeminus*, fourfold, < *quattuor* (*quadri-*), = E. *four*, + *geminus*, twin-born, twin: see *Gemini*, *geminate*.] 1. Consisting of four similar parts; having four parts, as one and the same thing; fourfold; quadrigeminal.—2. In *anat.* and *zoöl.*, specifically, pertaining to the optic lobes or corpora quadrigemina of any mammal, known in human anatomy as the *nates* and *testes*, which appear as two pairs of lobes or tubercles on the morphologically superior surface of the midbrain or mesencephalon, close to the pineal gland, behind the third ventricle, over the aqueduct of Sylvius. See *corpus* and *quadrigemina*.

quadrigenarious (kwod"ri-jē-nā'ri-us), *a.* [< L. *quadrigeni*, *quadringeni*, four hundred each, distributive of *quadringenti*, four hundred, < *quattuor* (*quadri-*), = E. *four*, + *centum* = E. *hund-red*.] Consisting of four hundred.

quadriglandular (kwod-ri-glan'dū-lär), *a.* [< L. *quattuor* (*quadri-*), = E. *four*, + *glan*(*d-*)*s*, gland: see *gland*.] Having four glands or glandular parts.

quadrijugate (kwod-ri-jö'gāt or -rij'ō-gāt), *a.* [< *quadrijug-ous* + *-ate*[1].] In *bot.*, pinnate with four pairs of leaflets: as, a *quadrijugate* leaf.

quadrijugous (kwod-ri-jö'gus or -rij'ō-gus), *a.* [< L. *quadrijugus*, belonging to a team of four, < *quattuor* (*quadri-*), = E. *four*, + *jugum* (= Gr. ζυγόν), a yoke. Cf. *quadriga*.] Same as *quadrijugate*.

quadrilaminar (kwod-ri-lam'i-när), *a.* [< L. *quattuor* (*quadri-*), = E. *four*, + *lamina*, a thin plate: see *lamina*, *laminar*.] Same as *quadrilaminate*.

quadrilaminate (kwod-ri-lam'i-nāt), *a.* [< L. *quattuor* (*quadri-*), = E. *four*, + *lamina*, a thin plate: see *lamina*, *laminate*.] Having four laminæ, layers, or plates; four-layered.

Quadrilatera (kwod-ri-lat'e-rä), *n. pl.* [NL., < L. *quadrilaterus*, four-sided: see *quadrilateral*.] In *Crustacea*, a group of crabs having a quadrate or cordate carapace. *Latreille*.

quadrilateral (kwod-ri-lat'e-ral), *a.* and *n.* [< L. *quadrilaterus*, four-sided, < *quattuor* (*quadri-*), = E. *four*, + *latus* (*later-*), side, flank: see *lateral*.] I. *a.* Having four sides; composed of four lines.—**Quadrilateral map-projection.** See *projection*.

II. *n.* 1. A figure formed of four straight lines. In the old geometry the lines are supposed to terminate at four intersections; in modern geometry the lines are regarded as infinite, and a plane quadrilateral as having six angles. Such a figure has three *diagonals* or *axes*, being straight lines through opposite vertices, and three *centers*, which are the intersections of the axes.

Complete Quadrilateral.

2. *Milit.*, the space inclosed between, and defended by, four fortresses: as, the Bulgarian *quadrilateral*. The most famous quadrilateral was that in northern Italy, inclosed by the fortresses of Peschiera, Mantua, Verona, and Legnago.

Field Marshal Radetsky . . . had collected under his own command all the Austrian forces scattered over the Lombardo-Venetian provinces, and had concentrated them within the well-nigh impregnable stronghold formed in the very heart of these provinces by the fortresses of the *Quadrilateral*. *E. Dicey*, Victor Emmanuel, p. 85.

Inscriptible quadrilateral. See *inscriptible*.—**Plane quadrilateral**, a quadrilateral lying in a plane.—**Skew quadrilateral**, a quadrilateral that does not lie in a plane.

quadrilateralness (kwod-ri-lat'e-ral-nes), *n.* The property of being quadrilateral.

quadriliteral (kwod-ri-lit'e-ral), *a.* and *n.* [< L. *quattuor* (*quadri-*), = E. *four*, + *littera*, *litera*, letter: see *literal*.] I. *a.* Consisting of four letters, or of only four constant letters or consonants.

II. *n.* A word or a root consisting of four letters or containing four consonants.

Arabick roots are as universally [*i. e.*, almost universally] triliteral. . . . If we suppose ten thousand of them (without reckoning *quadriliterals*) to exist, and each of them to admit only five variations, . . . even then a perfect Arabick dictionary ought to contain fifty thousand words.
Sir W. Jones, Asiatic Dissertations, I. 125.

quadrille (kwod-ril' or ka-dril'), *n.* and *a.* [< F. *quadrille*, m., a game at cards, a square dance, music for such a dance, < Sp. *cuadrillo*, m., a small square (cf. F. *quadrille*, f., a troop of horsemen, < Sp. *cuadrilla*, a troop of horsemen, a meeting of four persons, < It. *quadriglia* = Pg. *quadrilha*, a troop of horsemen), dim. of *cuadro*, m., *cuadra*, f., < L. *quadrum*, n., *quadra*, f., a square: see *quadrum*, *quadra*[1]. Cf. *quarrel*[2].] I. *n.* 1. A game played by four persons with forty cards, which are the remainder of the pack after the tens, nines, and eights are discarded.

> They taught him with address and skill
> To shine at ombre and *quadrille*.
> *Cawthorn*, Birth and Education of Genius.

> *Quadrille*, a modern game, bears great analogy to ombre, with the addition of a fourth player, which is certainly a great improvement. *Strutt*, Sports and Pastimes, p. 436.

2. A square dance for four couples, consisting regularly of five parts or movements, each complete in itself—namely, *le pantalon*, *l'été*, *la poule*, *la trénise* (or *la pastourelle*), and *la finale*. These parts are adaptations of popular society dances. They were combined in their present order about 1800, and were soon adopted in France, England, and Germany, giving rise to a quadrille mania similar to the later polka mania.
3. Any single set of dancers or maskers arranged in four sets or groups. [Rare.]

> At length the four *quadrilles* of maskers, ranging their torch-bearers behind them, drew up in their several ranks on the two opposite sides of the hall.
> *Scott*, Kenilworth, xxxvii.

4. Any square dance resembling the quadrille.—5. Music for such square dances. For the movements of the quadrille proper the rhythm is either sextuple or duple, and each section is usually 32 measures long. Quadrille music is usually adapted or arranged, not specially written for the purpose.

II. *a.* Same as *quadrillé*.

quadrille (kwod-ril' or ka-dril'), *v. i.*; pret. and pp. *quadrilled*, ppr. *quadrilling*. [< *quadrille*, *n.*] 1. To play at quadrille. *Imp. Dict.*—2. To dance quadrilles.

> While thus, like motes that dance away
> Existence in a summer ray,
> These gay things, born but to *quadrille*,
> The circle of their doom fulfil.
> *Moore*, Summer Fête.

quadrillé (ka-drē-lyā'), *a.* [F., < **quadrille*, a small square, < Sp. *cuadrillo*, a small square: see *quadrille*.] Divided or marked off into squares; having a pattern composed of small squares: said of textile fabrics, writing-papers ruled with lines crossing at right angles, and the like.

quadrillion (kwod-ril'yon), *n.* [< F. *quadrillion*, < L. *quattuor* (*quadri-*), = E. *four*, + F. (*m*)*illion*, > E. *million*[1].] The fourth power of a million according to the system of numeration called English; but the fifth power of a thousand according to the French system, commonly used in the United States.

quadrilobate (kwod-ri-lō'bāt), *a.* [< L. *quattuor* (*quadri-*), = E. *four*, + NL. *lobus*, lobe.] In *bot.* and *zoöl.*, having four lobes or lobules.

quadrilobed (kwod'ri-lōbd), *a.* [< L. *quattuor* (*quadri-*), = E. *four*, + NL. *lobus*, lobe, + *-ed*[2].] Same as *quadrilobate*.

quadrilocular (kwod-ri-lok'ū-lär), *a.* [< L. *quattuor* (*quadri-*), = E. *four*, + *loculus*, a cell.] 1. In *bot.*, having four cells or compartments; four-celled: as, a *quadrilocular* pericarp.—2. In *anat.* and *zoöl.*, having four cavities or compartments: chiefly an epithet of the heart of mammals and birds.

quadriloculate (kwod-ri-lok'ū-lāt), *a.* [< L. *quattuor* (*quadri-*), = E. *four*, + *loculus*, cell: see *loculus*, *loculate*.] Same as *quadrilocular*.

quadriloge (kwod'ri-lōj), *n.* [= OF. *quadrilogue*, < L. *quattuor* (*quadri-*), = E. *four*, + Gr. λόγος, a saying, speaking, discourse: see *Logos*.] 1. A book written in four parts, as "Childe Harold's Pilgrimage."—2. Any narrative depending on the testimony of four witnesses, as the four Gospels.—3. Any work compiled from four authors, as the "Life of Thomas à Becket." *Brewer*. [Rare in all senses.]

> The very authours of the *quadriloge* itselfe . . . doe all, with one pen and mouth, acknowledge the same.
> *Lambarde*, Perambulation (1596), p. 515. (*Halliwell.*)

Quadrimani (kwod-rim'a-nī), *n. pl.* [NL., pl. of *quadrimanus*: see *quadrimanous*.] In Latreille's system of classification, a group of caraboid beetles, typified by the genus *Harpalus*, having the four anterior tarsi dilated in the males: distinguished from *Simplicimani* and *Patellimani*. See *Harpalinæ*.

quadrimanous (kwod-rim'a-nus), *a.* [< NL. *quadrimanus*, four-handed, < L. *quattuor* (*quadri-*), = E. *four*, + *manus*, hand. Cf. *quadrumanous*.] Same as *quadrumanous*.

> At this malicious game they display the whole of their *quadrimanous* activity.
> *Burke*, Rev. in France, Works, III. 199.

quadrimembral (kwod-ri-mem'bral), *a.* [< LL. *quadrimembris*, four-limbed, four-footed, < L. *quattuor* (*quadri-*), = E. *four*, + *membrum*, a limb, a member.] Having four members (or parts) as limbs: as, most vertebrates are *quadrimembral*.

quadrin†, quadrine† (kwod'rin), *n.* [< ML. *quadrinus* (?); cf. L. *quadran(t-)s*, the fourth part of an as: see *quadrans*, *quadrant*.] A mite; a small piece of money, in value about a farthing.

> One of her paramours sent her a purse full of *quadrines* (which are little pieces of copper money) instead of silver.
> *North*, tr. of Plutarch, p. 722.

quadrinomial (kwod-ri-nō'mi-al), *a.* and *n.* [< L. *quattuor* (*quadri-*), = E. *four*, + *nom(en)*, name (see *nome*[3]), + *-al*. Cf. *binomial*, etc.] I. *a.* In *alg.*, consisting of four terms.

II. *n.* In *alg.*, an expression consisting of four terms.

quadrinomical (kwod-ri-nom'i-kal), *a.* [As *quadrinom(ial)* + *-ic-al*.] Quadrinomial.

quadrinominal (kwod-ri-nom'i-nal), *a.* [< L. *quattuor* (*quadri-*), = E. *four*, + *nomen* (*nomin-*), name: see *nomen*, *nominal*.] Having four terms; quadrinomial.

quadrinucleate (kwod-ri-nū'klē-āt), *a.* [< L. *quattuor* (*quadri-*), = E. *four*, + *nucleus*, a nucleus: see *nucleate*.] In *bot.*, having four nuclei, as the spores of some fungi.

quadrinvariant (kwod-rin-vā'ri-ant), *n.* [< L. *quattuor* (*quadri-*), = E. *four*, + E. *invariant*.] An invariant of the second order in the coefficients.

quadripara (kwod-rip'a-rä), *n.* [NL., < L. *quattuor* (*quadri-*), = E. *four*, + *parere*, bring forth, bear.] A woman who is bearing a child for the fourth time.

Quadriparæ (kwod-rip'a-rē), *n. pl.* [NL., fem. pl. of *quadriparus*: see *quadriparous*.] A group of birds proposed by E. Newman in 1875, being those which lay four eggs, and only four, and place them with the small ends together in the middle of the nest: it includes snipes, sandpipers, plovers, etc., and is practically equivalent to *Limicolæ*, 1.

quadriparous (kwod-rip'a-rus), *a.* [< NL. *quadriparus*, < L. *quattuor* (*quadri-*), = E. *four*, + *parere*, bring forth, bear.] In *ornith.*, laying four eggs, and only four; being of the *Quadriparæ*: as, *quadriparous* birds. *Newman*.

quadripartite (kwod-ri-pär'tīt), *a.* and *n.* [= OF. *quadripartit*, *quadriparty*, < L. *quadripartitus*, *quadripertitus*, divided into four parts, fourfold (LL. also as a finite verb, *quadripartire*, divide into four), < *quattuor* (*quadri-*), = E. *four*, + *partitus*, pp. of *partire*, divide, separate, distribute: see *part*, *v.*, *partite*, etc.] I. *a.* Divided into four parts; specifically, in *bot.* and *zoöl.*, parted into four; divided to the base or entirely into four parts; in *arch.*, divided, as

Quadripartite Vault.—Nave of Amiens Cathedral, France.

a vault, by the system of construction employed, into four compartments. Such a vault is the cardinal type of medieval Pointed vaulting.

> Squire Headlong . . . was *quadripartite* in his locality: that is to say, he was superintending the operations in four scenes of action—namely, the cellar, the library, the picture-gallery, and the dining-room.
> *Peacock*, Headlong Hall, ii.

II. *n.* A book or treatise divided into four parts or treatises; a tetrabiblion: as, the last two books of Ptolemy's *Quadripartite*; the *quadripartite* (four Gospels) of the New Testament.

quadripartitely (kwod-ri-pär'tīt-li), *adv.* In four divisions; in a quadripartite distribution.

quadripartition (kwod″ri-pär-tish'on), *n.* [< L. *quadripartitio(n-)*, a division into four, < *quadripartitus*, divided into four: see *quadripartite*.] A division by four or into four parts.

> Nor would it, perhaps, be possible to entirely deny the position of one who should argue that this convenient *quadri-partition* of the month was first in order of time.
> *Contemporary Rev.*, L. 528.

quadripennate (kwod-ri-pen'āt), *a.* and *n.* [< L. *quattuor* (*quadri-*), = E. *four*, + *penna*, wing: see *penna*, *pennate*.] I. *a.* In *entom.*, having four wings—that is, four functional wings, an anterior pair being not converted into elytra or wing-cases.

II. *n.* A four-winged or quadripennate insect.

quadriphyllous (kwod-ri-fil'us), *a.* [< L. *quattuor* (*quadri-*), = E. *four*, + Gr. φύλλον = L. *folium*, leaf.] In *bot.*, having four leaves; quadrifoliate.

quadriplanar (kwod-ri-plā'när), *a.* [< L. *quattuor* (*quadri-*), = E. *four*, + NL. *planum*, a plane: see *plane*[1], *planar*.] Formed by four planes.—**Quadriplanar coördinates.** See *coördinate*.

quadriplicate (kwod-rip'li-kāt), *a.* and *n.* Same as *quadruplicate*.

quadriplicated (kwod-rip'li-kā-ted), *a.* Same as *quadruplicate*.

quadripulmonary (kwod-ri-pul'mō-nā-ri), *a.* [< L. *quattuor* (*quadri-*), = E. *four*, + L. *pulmo(n-)*, lung: see *pulmonary*.] In *Arachnida*, having two pairs of pulmonary sacs; tetrapneumonous: opposed to *bipulmonary*.

quadriquadric (kwod-ri-kwod'rik), *a.* and *n.* [< *quadri(c)* + *quadric*.] I. *a.* Of the second degree in each of two variables or sets of variables.

II. *n.* A skew quartic curve, the intersection of two quadric surfaces. There are other quartics not of this description.

quadriradiate (kwod-ri-rā'di-āt), *a.* [< L. *quattuor* (*quadri-*), = E. *four*, + *radius*, ray (> *radiatus*, radiate): see *radiate*.] Having four rays, as a fish's fin; tetractinal, as a sponge-spicule; in *bot.*, having four radii or prolongations: as, a *quadriradiate* mass of chlorophyl.

quadrireme (kwod'ri-rēm), *n.* [< L. *quadriremis* (LL. also *quatriremis*), a vessel fitted with four banks of oars, < *quattuor* (*quadri-*), = E. *four*, + *remus*, oar: see *oar*[1].] A galley with four banks of oars or rowers, mentioned as in use occasionally among the ancient Greeks and Romans.

quadrisacramentalist (kwod-ri-sak-ra-men'tal-ist), *n.* [< L. *quattuor* (*quadri-*), = E. *four*, + *sacramentum*, sacrament, + *-al* + *-ist*.] Same as *quadrisacramentarian*.

quadrisacramentarian (kwod-ri-sak″ra-men-tā'ri-an), *n.* [< L. *quattuor* (*quadri-*), = E. *four*, + *sacramentum*, sacrament, + *-arian*.] One of a small body of German Protestants in the middle of the sixteenth century, who held that the four sacraments of baptism, the eucharist, holy orders, and absolution are requisite for salvation.

quadrisection (kwod-ri-sek'shon), *n.* [< L. *quattuor* (*quadri-*), = E. *four*, + *sectio(n-)*, a cutting: see *section*.] A section into four equal parts.

quadriseptate (kwod-ri-sep'tāt), *a.* [< L. *quattuor* (*quadri-*), = E. *four*, + *septum*, a partition: see *septum*, *septate*.] Having four septa or partitions.

quadriserial (kwod-ri-sē'ri-al), *a.* [< L. *quattuor* (*quadri-*), = E. *four*, + *series*, a row: see *serial*.] Set or arranged in four rows or series; four-rowed; quadrifarious; tetrastichous.

> The production of the ambulacral element in some starfishes is much more rapid than general growth, thus producing a crushing together of the plates in the direction of the length, in some cases carried to such an extent that the tube-feet in each furrow become *quadriserial*.
> *Amer. Nat.*, Feb., 1890, p. 161.

quadrisetose (kwod-ri-sē'tōs), *a.* [< L. *quattuor* (*quadri-*), = E. *four*, + *sæta*, *seta*, a bristle: see *seta*, *setose*.] In *entom.*, bearing four setæ or bristles.

quadrispiral (kwod-ri-spī'ral), *a.* [< L. *quattuor* (*quadri-*), = E. *four*, + *spira*, a coil, a spire: see *spire*, *spiral*.] In *bot.*, having four spirals.

> Elaters [of *Fimbriaria*] rather short, uni-*quadrispiral*.
> *Underwood*, Hepaticæ of N. A., p. 39.

Quadrisulcata (kwod″ri-sul-kā'tä), *n. pl.* [NL., neut. pl. of *quadrisulcatus*: see *quadrisulcate*.]

A group of hoofed quadrupeds having four toes; the quadrisulcate ungulate mammals.

quadrisulcate (kwod-ri-sul'kāt), *a.* [< NL. *quadrisulcatus*, < L. *quattuor* (*quadri-*), = E. *four*, + *sulcus*, a furrow: see *sulcus*, *sulcate*.] Having four grooves, furrows, or sulci; specifically, in *mammal.*, having a four-parted hoof; four-toed; quadridigitate.

quadrisyllabic (kwod"ri-si-lab'ik), *a.* [< *quadrisyllab(le)* + *-ic*.] Consisting of four syllables; pertaining to or consisting of quadrisyllables.

quadrisyllabical (kwod"ri-si-lab'i-kal), *a.* [< *quadrisyllabic* + *-al*.] Same as *quadrisyllabic*.

quadrisyllable (kwod-ri-sil'a-bl), *n.* [< L. *quattuor* (*quadri-*), = E. *four*, + *syllaba*, syllable: see *syllable*.] A word consisting of four syllables.

A distinction without a difference could not sustain itself; and both alike disguised their emptiness under this pompous *quadrisyllable*.
De Quincey, Roman Meals. (*Davies*.)

quadritactic (kwod-ri-tak'tik), *a.* [< L. *quattuor* (*quadri-*), = E. *four*, + Gr. τακτικός, pertaining to arrangement: see *tactic*.] Of the nature of a point on a surface or skew curve where four consecutive points are in one plane.—**Quadritactic point.** See *tritactic point*, under *point*[1].

quadritubercular (kwod"ri-tū-bėr'kū-lär), *a.* Same as *quadrituberculate*.

By the suppression of one of the primitive cusps we arrive at the *quadritubercular* tooth. *Nature*, XLI. 467.

quadrituberculate (kwod"ri-tū-bėr'kū-lāt), *a.* [< L. *quattuor* (*quadri-*), = E. *four*, + *tuberculum*, tubercle: see *tubercle*, *tuberculate*.] Having four tubercles: as, a *quadrituberculate* molar.

quadrivalent (kwod-riv'a-lent), *a.* [< L. *quattuor* (*quadri-*), = E. *four*, + *valen(t-)s*, ppr. of *valere*, be strong.] In *chem.*, noting an atom the equivalence of which is four, or an element one atom of which is equivalent, in combining power, to four atoms of hydrogen; tetradic; tetratomic.

quadrivalve (kwod'ri-valv), *a.* and *n.* [< L. *quattuor* (*quadri-*), = E. *four*, + *valva*, a door: see *valve*.] I. *a.* Same as *quadrivalvular*.

II. *n.* One of a set of four folds or leaves forming a door.

quadrivalvular (kwod-ri-val'vū-lär), *a.* [< L. *quattuor* (*quadri-*), = E. *four*, + NL. *valvula*, dim. of L. *valva*, valve: see *valve*.] In *zoöl.* and *bot.*, having four valves or valvular parts.

quadrivia, *n.* Plural of *quadrivium*.

quadrivial (kwod-riv'i-al), *a.* and *n.* [< L. *quadrivius*, having four ways, + *-al*. Cf. *trivial*.] I. *a.* 1. Having four ways meeting in a point; leading in four directions.

A forum, with *quadrivial* streets.
B. *Jonson*, Expostulation with Inigo Jones.

2. Belonging to the quadrivium: thus, *quadrivial astrology* is astrology in the sense in which astrology is a branch of the quadrivium—that is, astronomy.

II. *n.* One of the four arts constituting the quadrivium.

The *quadrivials*—I meane arythmetike, musike, geometrie, and astronomie—& with them all skill in the perspectiues, are now smallie regarded in either of them [the universities]. *Holinshed*, Descrip. of England, ii. 3.

quadrivious (kwod-riv'i-us), *a.* [< L. *quadrivius*, of the cross-roads, lit. having four ways, < *quattuor* (*quadri-*), = E. *four*, + *via* = E. *way*.] Going in four directions.

When the cheese was so rotten with them [vermin] that only the twigs and string kept it from tumbling to pieces and walking off *quadrivious*, it came to table.
C. *Reade*, Cloister and Hearth, xxiv.

quadrivium (kwod-riv'i-um), *n.*; pl. *quadrivia* (-ä). [< LL. *quadrivium*, *quadruvium*, the four branches of mathematics, a particular use of L. *quadrivium*, a place where four ways meet, neut. of *quadrivius*, having four ways: see *quadrivious*. Cf. *trivium*.] The collective name of the four branches of mathematics according to the Pythagoreans—arithmetic (treating of number in itself), music (treating of applied number), geometry (treating of stationary number), and astronomy (treating of number in motion). This Pythagorean quadrivium, preceded by the trivium of grammar, logic, and rhetoric, made up the seven liberal arts taught in the schools of the Roman empire.

quadrivoltine (kwod-ri-vol'tin), *n.* [< L. *quattuor* (*quadri-*), = E. *four*, + It. *volta*, turn, time, + *-ine*[2].] A silkworm which yields four crops of cocoons a year.

quadroon (kwod-rön'), *n.* [An alteration (simulating words in *quadri-*, *quadru-*) of *quarteron*, < Sp. *cuarteron*, a quadroon, one who is one fourth black; also, a fourth part; < *cuarto*, a fourth: see *quart*[1], *quarter*[1].] The offspring of a mulatto and a white person; a person having one fourth African blood.

quadro-quadro-quartic (kwod"rō-kwod"rō-kwâr'tik), *n.* [< *quadric* + *quadric* + *quartic*.] A non-plane curve formed by the intersection of two quadric surfaces.

quadroxid, quadroxide (kwod-rok'sid, -sid or -sīd), *n.* [< L. *quattuor* (*quadri-*, *quadr-*), = E. *four*, + *oxid*, *oxide*.] In *chem.*, a compound of four equivalents of oxygen and one of another element, or a simple oxid containing four atoms of oxygen.

quadrum (kwod'rum), *n.* [L., square, anything square in form, neut. of (LL.) *quadrus*, four-cornered, square: see *quadra*[1], *quadrate*.] In *music*, same as *natural*, 7.

quaduman, quadrumane (kwod'rö-man, -mān), *n.* [< F. *quadrumane*, < NL. *quadrumanus*, four-handed: see *quadrumanous*.] A four-handed quadruped; an animal capable of using all four feet as hands; specifically, a member of the *Quadrumana*.

Quadrumana (kwod-rö'ma-nä), *n. pl.* [NL., neut. pl. of *quadrumanus*, four-handed: see *quadrumanous*.] An order of *Mammalia* named by Blumenbach in 1791, including all kinds of apes, monkeys, and lemurs; the quadrumanous mammals: so called because their hind as well as fore feet can be used as hands. The term is scarcely used now, being superseded by *Primates*; but *Primates* includes both the *Bimana* (man alone) and the *Quadrumana* of the earlier systems. When the name was in vogue the *Quadrumana* were usually divided into *Catarrhini*, Old World apes and monkeys; *Platyrrhini*, New World monkeys; and *Strepsirrhini*, lemurs.

quadrumanous (kwod-rö'ma-nus), *a.* [< NL. *quadrumanus*, four-handed, < L. *quattuor* (*quadru-*), = E. *four*, + *manus*, hand: see *main*[3].] Four-handed; having all four feet fitted for use as hands: said of mammals, as opossums, etc.; specifically, of or pertaining to the *Quadrumana*. Also *quadrimanous*.

The strongly convex upper lip frequently seen among the lower classes of the Irish is a modified *quadrumanous* character. *E. D. Cope*, Origin of the Fittest, p. 291.

quadruped (kwod'rö-ped), *a.* and *n.* [= F. *quadrupède* = Pr. *quadrupedi* = Sp. *cuadrúpede*, *cuadrúpedo* = Pg. *quadrupede* = It. *quadrupede*, *quadrupedo*, < L. *quadrupes*, *quadripes* (*-ped-*), having four feet, a four-footed creature, < *quattuor* (*quadru-*), = E. *four*, + *pes* (*ped-*) = E. *foot*.] I. *a.* Four-footed; having four limbs fitted for sustaining the body and for progression; habitually going on all fours: opposed to *aliped* and *biped*: correlated with *quadrumanous* and *pedimanous*: chiefly said of mammals, but also of four-footed reptiles, as lizards and tortoises. Compare *quadrumanous*.

II. *n.* A four-footed or quadruped animal: especially, a four-footed mammal, as distinguished from a *biped*, as man or a bird.

quadrupedal (kwod'rö-ped-al), *a.* and *n.* [= OF. *quadrupedal* = Sp. *cuadrupedal* = Pg. *quadrupedal*; as *quadruped* + *-al*.] I. *a.* Quadruped or four-footed; especially, going on all fours, or adapted or restricted to that mode of progression: as, the *quadrupedal* shape; *quadrupedal* locomotion.

II.† *n.* A quadruped. [Rare.]

The coldest of any *quadrupedal*.
Howell, Parly of Beasts, p. 11.

quadrupedated (kwod'rö-pe-dā-ted), *a.* [< *quadruped* + *-ate*[1] + *-ed*[2].] Made or become four-footed or like a beast; turned into a quadruped. [Rare.]

Deformed and luxate with the prosecution of vanities; *quadrupedated* with an earthly, stooping, grovelling covetousness. *Rev. T. Adams*, Works, I. 390.

quadrupedism (kwod'rö-ped-izm), *n.* [< *quadruped* + *-ism*.] The state of being a quadruped; the condition of being four-footed, as a beast. [Rare.]

Among the Mahometans . . . *quadrupedism* is not considered an obstacle to a certain kind of canonisation.
Southey, The Doctor, cxcix. (*Davies*.)

quadruplane (kwod'rö-plān), *n.* [< L. *quattuor* (*quadru-*), = E. *four*, + *planum*, a plane: see *plane*[1].] A plane quadrilateral having its opposite or alternate sides equal and one pair of these crossing each other.

Quadruplane or Contraparallelogram.

quadruple (kwod'rö-pl), *a.* and *n.* [< F. *quadruple* = Sp. *cuádruplo* = Pg. It. *quadruplo*, < L. *quadruplus*, fourfold, *quadruplum*, a fourfold quantity, < *quattuor* (*quadru-*), = E. *four*, + *-plus*, -fold: see *-fold*.] I. *a.* Fourfold; four times told.

A law that to bridle theft doth punish thieves with a *quadruple* restitution hath an end which will continue as long as the world itself continueth.
Hooker, Eccles. Polity, iii. 10.

A *quadruple* Jacquard, or four separate Jacquards fixed in one frame. *A. Barlow*, Weaving, p. 275.

Quadruple counterpoint, in *music*, counterpoint in which four melodies are so contrived as to be mutually usable above or below one another by transposition. Twenty-four different dispositions of such melodies are possible. Compare *double* and *triple counterpoint* (which see, under *counterpoint*[2], 3).—**Quadruple crown**, a size of printing-paper, 30 × 40 inches. [Eng.]—**Quadruple demy**, a size of printing-paper, 35 × 45 inches. [Eng.]—**Quadruple foolscap**, a size of printing-paper, 27 × 34 inches. [Eng.]—**Quadruple medium**, a size of printing-paper, 38 × 48 inches. [Eng.]—**Quadruple post**, a size of printing-paper, 32 × 40 inches. [Eng.]—**Quadruple pot**, a size of printing-paper, 26 × 32 inches. [Eng.]—**Quadruple quaver**, in *musical notation*, same as *hemidemisemiquaver*.—**Quadruple ratio.** See *ratio*.—**Quadruple rhythm** or **time**, in *music*, rhythm or time characterized by four beats or pulses to the measure. See *rhythm*.—**Quadruple royal**, a size of printing-paper, 40 × 50 inches. [Eng.]

II. *n.* A number, sum, etc., four times as great as that taken as the standard: as, to receive the *quadruple* of a given sum.

quadruple (kwod'rö-pl), *v.*; pret. and pp. *quadrupled*, ppr. *quadrupling*. [< F. *quadrupler*, < LL. *quadruplare*, make fourfold, < L. *quadruplus*, fourfold: see *quadruple*, *a.*] I. *trans.* To make four times as much or as many; multiply by four; repeat four times; make, do, or cause to happen four times over.

The trade of Scotland has been more than *quadrupled* since the first erection of the two publick banks.
Adam Smith, Wealth of Nations, ii. 2.

II. *intrans.* To become four times as much or as many; repeat itself four times.

quadruplet (kwod'rö-plet), *n.* [< *quadruple* + *-et*.] 1. Any combination of four objects or parts grouped, united, or acting together: as, a *quadruplet* of springs, consisting of four elliptic springs coupled together and acting as one spring. Also called *quartet*.—2. One of four born at a single birth.

quadruplex (kwod'rö-pleks), *a.* and *n.* [< L. *quadruplex*, fourfold, < *quattuor* (*quadru-*), = E. *four*, + *plicare*, fold: see *plicate*.] I. *a.* Fourfold: applied to a system of telegraphy in which four messages may be transmitted simultaneously over one wire.

II. *n.* An instrument by means of which four messages may be transmitted simultaneously over one wire.

Sometimes abbreviated *quad*.

quadruplex (kwod'rö-pleks), *v. t.* [< *quadruplex*, *n.*] To make quadruplex; arrange for fourfold transmission.

If the line is already duplexed, the phonophore will *quadruplex* it. *Elect. Rev.* (Amer.), XIV. 6.

quadruplicate (kwod-rö'pli-kāt), *v. t.*; pret. and pp. *quadruplicated*, ppr. *quadruplicating*. [< L. *quadruplicatus*, pp. of *quadruplicare* (> OF. *quadruplier*, *quadrupliquer*), make fourfold, < *quadruplex*, fourfold: see *quadruplex*.] To make fourfold; double twice.

quadruplicate (kwod-rö'pli-kāt), *a.* and *n.* [Also *quadriplicate*; < L. *quadruplicatus*, make fourfold: see the verb.] I. *a.* Fourfold; four times repeated: as, a *quadruplicate* ratio or proportion. Also *quadriplicated*.

II. *n.* One of four things corresponding in all respects to one another, or to a common original.

quadruplication (kwod-rö-pli-kā'shon), *n.* [= F. *quadruplication* = Sp. *cuadruplicacion* = Pg. *quadruplicação* = It. *quadruplicazione*, < LL. *quadruplicatio(n-)*, a making fourfold, < L. *quadruplicare*, make fourfold: see *quadruplicate*.] The act of making fourfold; a taking of four times the simple sum or amount.

quadruplicature (kwod-rö'pli-kā-tūr), *n.* [< *quadruplicate* + *-ure*.] The act of quadruplicating; also, that which is fourfold—that is, folded twice, so as to make four layers: correlated with *duplicature*: as, the great omentum is a *quadruplicature* of peritoneum.

quadruplicity (kwod-rö-plis'i-ti), *n.* [< ML. *quadruplicita(t-)s*, the character of being fourfold, < L. *quadruplex*, fourfold: see *quadruplex*.] The character of being quadruplex.

This *quadruplicity*, these elements,
From whom each body takes his existence.
Times' Whistle (E. E. T. S.), p. 117.

quadruply (kwod'rö-pli), *adv.* In a quadruple or fourfold degree; to a fourfold extent or amount.

If the person accused makes his innocence plainly to appear upon his trial, the accuser is immediately put to . . . death; and out of his goods or lands the innocent person is *quadruply* recompensed.
Swift, Gulliver's Travels, i. 6.

quære (kwē'rē), *n.* [L., impv. of *quærere*, seek, seek to learn, question; as a noun, in accom. E. spelling, *query*: see *query*.] Same as *query*.

quæsitum (kwę-sī'tum), *n.*; pl. *quæsita* (-tä). [L., neut. of *quæsitus*, pp. of *quærere*, seek, ask: see *quest*[1].] Something sought or required.

A thesis which an argument supposes to be in question is called *quæsitum*; and opposed to that is a thesis from which the argument proceeds — a thesis necessarily connected with the argument, but not in question: such a thesis is called a datum. *Westminster Rev.*, CXXVIII. 747.

quæsta (kwes'tä), *n.*; pl. *quæstæ* (-tē). [ML., fem. of L. *quæsitus*, pp. of *quærere*, seek, obtain: see *quest*[1].] In the middle ages, one of a class of indulgences or remissions of penance which were granted by the Pope to those who contributed certain specified sums of money to the church.

quæstor, quæstorship, *n.* See *questor*, *questorship*.

quæstus, *n.* In *law*. See *questus*.

quaff (kwåf), *v.* [Prob. a reduced form, with change of orig. guttural *gh* to *f* (*ff*) (as in *dwarf*, *trough*, pron. as if *troff*, etc.), of *quaught*, drink, quaff: see *quaught*. There may have been some confusion with the Sc. *quaigh*, *quegh*, *quech*, also *queff*, a cup, < Gael. Ir. *cuach*, a cup, bowl: see *quaigh*.] **I.** *trans.* To drink; swallow in large draughts; drink of copiously or greedily.

He calls for wine, . . . *quaff'd* off the muscadel,
And threw the sops all in the sexton's face.
Shak., T. of the S., iii. 2. 174.

She who, as they voyaged, *quaff'd*
With Tristram that spiced magic draught.
M. Arnold, Tristram and Iseult.

II. *intrans.* To drink largely or luxuriously.

Eate softly, and drinke manerly,
Take heede you doe not *quaffe*.
Babees Book (E. E. T. S.), p. 77.

They *quaffe* and drinke. *Purchas*, Pilgrimage, p. 211.

Near him rode Silenus on his ass,
Pelted with flowers as he on did pass,
Tipsily *quaffing*.
Keats, Endymion, iv. (song).

quaff (kwåf), *n.* [< *quaff*, *v.*] The act of quaffing; also, the quantity of liquor drunk at once; a draught.

Now Alvida begins her *quaff*,
And drinks a full carouse unto her king.
Greene and Lodge, Looking Glass for Lond. and Eng.

quaffer[1] (kwåf'ėr), *n.* [< *quaff* + *-er*[1].] One who quaffs or drinks much.

quaffer[2]†, *v. i.* [Cf. *quaff* (?).] To drink greedily, or to dabble. [The sense is uncertain.]

Ducks, geese, and divers others have such long broad bills to *quaffer* and hunt in waters and mud.
Derham, Physico-Theology, iv. 11, note.

quaffing-pot (kwåf'ing-pot), *n.* A drinking-vessel holding half a gill.

quafftide† (kwåf'tīd), *n.* Drinking-time. [Rare.]

Quaftyde aproacheth,
And showts in nighttyme doo ringe in loftye
Cithærou. *Stanihurst*, Æneid, iv. 314. (*Davies.*)

quag (kwag), *n.* [Abbr. of *quagmire*.] A shaking, marshy soil; a quagmire.

On the left hand there was a very dangerous *quag*, into which if even a good man falls, he can find no bottom for his foot to stand on. Into that *Quag* King David once did fall. *Bunyan*, Pilgrim's Progress, pt. i.

With packhorse constancy we keep the road,
Crooked or straight, through *quags* or thorny dells.
Cowper, Tirocinium, l. 253.

=**Syn.** See *marsh*.

quagga (kwag'ä), *n.* [Also *quacha*; appar. S. African.] 1. An African solidungulate quadruped of the horse family, *Equus* or *Hippotigris quagga*, related to the ass and zebra, but not fully striped like the latter, not being banded on the hind quarters and legs. The ears are short, the head is comparatively small, the tail is tufted, and the color is a dark brown on the head, neck, and shoulders, the back and hind quarters being of a lighter brown, the croup of a russet-gray, and the under parts of the body white. It will breed with the horse, and a mixed race of this kind existed in England some years ago. By the natives the flesh is esteemed palatable.
2. Burchell's zebra, *Equus* or *Hippotigris burchelli*, closely related to the above, but striped throughout like the zebra: more fully called *bonte-quagga*. See cut under *dauw*.

quaggle (kwag'l), *n.* [Dim. of *quake*.] A tremulous motion. *Halliwell.* [Prov. Eng.]

quaggy (kwag'i), *a.* [< *quag* + *-y*[1].] Yielding to the feet or trembling under the foot, as soft wet earth; boggy; spongy.

The watery strath or *quaggy* moss.
Collins, Superstitions of the Highlands.

The *quaggy* soil trembles to a sound like thunder of breakers on a coast. *Harper's Mag.*, LXXVI. 733.

quagmire (kwag'mīr), *n.* [Appar. a var. of the earlier *quakemire*: see *quakemire*.] Soft, wet, boggy land that trembles under the foot; a marsh; a bog; a fen.

Whom the foul fiend hath led through fire and through flame, and through ford and whirlipool, o'er bog and *quagmire*. *Shak.*, Lear, iii. 4. 54.

Faith, I have followed Cupid's Jack-a-lantern, and find myself in a *quagmire* at last. *Sheridan*, The Rivals, iii. 4.

=**Syn.** *Slough*, *Bog*, etc. See *marsh*.

quagmire (kwag'mīr), *v. t.*; pret. and pp. *quagmired*, ppr. *quagmiring*. [< *quagmire*, *n.*] To entangle or sink in or as in a quagmire. [Rare.]

When a reader has been *quagmired* in a dull heavy book, what a refreshing sight it is to see finis!
Laconics (1701), p. 120. (*Latham.*)

A man is never *quagmired* till he stops; and the rider who looks back has never a firm seat.
Landor, Imaginary Conversations, Wellington and Sir [Robert Inglis, p. 376.

quagmiry (kwag'mīr-i), *a.* [< *quagmire* + *-y*[1].] Like a quagmire; boggy; marshy; fenny; quaggy. [Rare.]

They had twenty wigwams, hard by a most hideous swamp, so thick with bushes and so *quagmiry* as men could hardly crowd into it.
Winthrop, Hist. New England, I. 279.

quahog, quahaug (kwą-hog', -hâg'), *n.* [Also *cohog*, *cohaug*, *cohauk*, *quohog*, *quog*, etc.; < Amer. Ind. (Narragansett) *poquauhock*.] The large edible round clam of the Atlantic coast of the United States, *Venus mercenaria*, much used for soups and chowders. See *clam*[3], and cut under *dimyarian*.—**Blood-quahog**, the young or a small specimen of various species of *Arcidæ*, or ark-shells; a bloody clam or hair-clam. [Narragansett Bay.]

Quahog (*Venus mercenaria*).

quaich, *n.* See *quaigh*.

quaid†, *a.* or *pp.* An artificial contracted form of *quailed*, past participle of *quail*[1]. *Spenser.*

quaigh, quaich (kwāċh), *n.* [Also *quegh*, *queigh*, *quech*, *quoich*, *queych*, *queff*; < Gael. Ir. *cuach*, a cup, bowl. Cf. *quaff*.] A shallow drinking-cup, made of small staves hooped together: it is usually of wood, but sometimes of silver. [Scotch.]

She filled a small wooden *quaigh* from an earthen pitcher.
Scott, Pirate, vi.

Nor lacked they, while they sat at dine,
The music, nor the tale,
Nor goblets of the blood-red wine,
Nor mantling *quaighs* of ale.
Scott, Thomas the Rhymer, iii.

The girded *quoich* they brimmed for him.
Prof. Blackie, Lays of Highlands and Islands, p. 171.

quail[1] (kwāl), *v.* [Early mod. E. and dial. also *queal*; < ME. *quelen* (pret. *qual*), < AS. *cwelan* (pret. *cwæl*, pp. *cwolen*), die (also in comp. *ā-cwelan*, die utterly), = OS. *quelan*, die, = MD. *quelen* = MLG. *quelen*, suffer pain, pine, = OHG. *quelan*, *quelen*, *chelen*, MHG. *queln*, die, G. *quälen*, suffer pain; cf. AS. *cwalu*, destruction, ME. *quale*, murrain (see *quale*[1]), and AS. *cwellan*, cause to die, kill, quell: see *quell*, which is the causative form of *quail*, and cf. *qualm*, from the same source.] **I.** *intrans.* 1†. To begin to die; decline; fade; wither.

For as the world wore on, and waxed old,
So virtue *quail'd*, and vice began to grow.
Tancred and Gismunda, ii. 3.

The *quailing* and withering of all things.
Hakewill, Apology, p. 71.

2. To lose heart or courage; shrink before danger or difficulty; flinch; cower; tremble.

And with sharpe threates her often did assayle;
So thinking for to make her stubborne corage *quayle*.
Spenser, F. Q., III. viii. 40.

Plant courage in their *quailing* breasts.
Shak., 3 Hen. VI., ii. 3. 54.

But Pelleas lifted up an eye so fierce
She *quail'd*. *Tennyson*, Pelleas and Ettarre.

3†. To slacken.

And let not search and inquisition *quail*.
Shak., As you Like it, ii. 2. 20.

II. *trans.* To quell; subdue; overpower; intimidate; terrify.

Couetousnesse *quayleth* gentlenesse.
Babees Book (E. E. T. S.), p. 91.

When somer toke in hand the winter to assail,
With force of might, and vertue great, his stormy blasts to
quail. *Surrey*, Complaint of a Lover.

The sword of the spirit Satham *quailes*,
And to attaine the conquest never failes.
Times' Whistle (E. E. T. S.), p. 146.

Am not I here to take thy part?
Then what has *quail'd* thy stubborn heart?
S. Butler, Hudibras, I. iii. 204.

Resist — the thunder *quails* thee! — crouch — rebuff
Shall be thy recompense!
Wordsworth, Eccles. Sonnets, i. 39.

quail[2]† (kwāl), *v. i.* [< ME. *quaylen*, *qualen*, < OF. *coailler*, F. *cailler* = Sp. *cuajar* = Pg. *coalhar* = It. *quagliare*, *cagliare*, < L. *coagulare*, curdle, coagulate: see *coagulate*.] To curdle; coagulate. *Palsgrave.*

The cream is said to be *quailed* when the butter begins to appear in the process of churning.
Batchelor, Orthoep. Anal., p. 140. (*Halliwell.*)

quail[3] (kwāl), *n.* [Early mod. E. also *quayle*, Sc. *quailzie*; < ME. *quaille*, *quayle*, *qwayle*, < OF. *quaille*, F. *caille* = Pr. *calha* = OSp. *coalla* = It. *quaglia*, < ML. *quaquila*, also *quaquara*, *quaquadra*, *quisquila* (also, after OF., etc., *qualia*), < MD. *quakele*, *quackel*, D. *kwakkel* (MD. also *quartel*, D. *kwartel*) = MLG. *quackele*, LG. *quackel*, a quail; so called in reference to its cry, < MD. *quacken*, D. *kwaken* = MLG. *quaken*, quack: see *quack*[1].] 1. A small gallinaceous bird of the Old World, related to the partridge, and belonging to the genus *Coturnix*. The common Messina or migratory quail of Europe and Africa is *C. communis* or *C. dactylisonans*, highly esteemed for the table.

Common Migratory or Messina Quail of Europe (*Coturnix communis*).

The bill is much smaller and weaker than in the partridge, and the nasal fossæ are mostly feathered. The wings are pointed by the first, second, and third quills; the first is emarginate on the inner web; the tail is very short, soft, and slight, not half as long as the wing. The feet are small, with the tarsus shorter than the middle toe and claw, and slightly feathered above. The length of the bird is about 7 inches. The plumage is much variegated, the most conspicuous markings being sharp lance-linear stripes, whitish or buff, over most of the upper parts. This quail has several times been imported into the United States, but has failed thus far to become naturalized. There are many other quails of the same genus in various parts of the Old World, but none are indigenous to the New.
2. One of the various small gallinaceous birds more or less closely resembling the quail proper: loosely applied, with or without a qualifying term, especially in the United States, to all the species of *Ortyx* or *Colinus*, *Lophortyx*, *Oreortyx*, *Callipepla*, *Cyrtonyx*, and other genera of American *Ortyginæ* or *Odontophorinæ*.

Bob-white, or Common Quail of America (*Ortyx virginiana*).

Among such, the species of bob-white, as *Ortyx virginiana*, the common partridge or quail of sportsmen, are the nearest to the Old World species of *Coturnix*. In the United States, wherever the ruffed grouse, *Bonasa umbella*, is called *pheasant*, the bob-white is called *partridge*: where that grouse is called *partridge*, the bob-white is known as *quail*. See also cuts under *Callipepla*, *Cyrtonyx*, *Lophortyx*, and *Oreortyx*.

If we must borrow a name from any Old World birds for our species of Ortyx, Lophortyx, Callipepla, etc., the term "*quail*" is rather more appropriate than "partridge." *Coues*, Key to N. A. Birds, p. 596.

3†. A prostitute. Also called *plover*. [Low.]

Here's Agamemnon — an honest fellow enough, and one that loves *quails*. *Shak.*, T. and C., v. 1. 57.

Painted quail. See *painted*.

quail-call (kwāl'kâl), *n.* A quail-pipe.

quail-dove (kwāl'duv), *n.* An American pigeon of the genus *Starnœnas*. *S. cyanocephalus* is the blue-headed quail-dove, found in the West Indies and Florida.

quail-mutton (kwāl'mut"n), *n.* Diseased mutton. *Halliwell.* [Prov. Eng.]

quail-pigeon (kwāl'pij"on), *n.* A pigeon of the genus *Geophaps*.

quail-pipe (kwāl'pīp), *n.* [< ME. *quail-pipe*; < *quail*[3] + *pipe*[1].] A call or pipe for alluring quail into a net.

> Highe shoos knopped with dagges,
> That frouncen lyke a *quaile-pipe*.
> *Rom. of the Rose*, l. 7259.

Thrush or nightingale, all is one to the fowler; and, Master Varney, you can sound the *quail-pipe* most daintily to wile wantons into his nets. *Scott*, Kenilworth, vii.

Quail-pipe boots†, boots resembling a quail-pipe. *Halliwell.*

A gallant that hides his small-timbered legs with a *quail-pipe boot*. *Middleton*, Blurt, Master-Constable, ii. 1.

quail-snipe (kwāl'snīp), *n.* 1. A South American bird of the family *Thinocoridæ*: same as *lark-plover*.—2. The dowitcher, or red-breasted snipe. *J. P. Giraud*, 1844. [Long Island.]

quaily (kwā'li), *n.*; pl. *quailies* (-liz). [Said to be imitative.] The upland plover, or Bartram's sandpiper, *Tringa bartramia* or *Bartramia longicauda*. See cut under *Bartramia*. [Manitoba.]

quaint (kwānt), *a.* [Early mod. E. also *queint*; dial. (Sc.) *quent*; < ME. *quaint*, *quaynt*, *qwhainte*, *queint*, *queynt*, *quoint*, *coint*, *koint*, < OF. *coint*, *coynt*, *coinct*, *coente*, *cuinte*, *quoint*, *queint*, *quuint*, *quieynt*, well-known, brave, wise, clever, quaint, = Pr. *conte*, *cointe* = It. *conto*, known, noted, also pretty, contr. of *cognito*, known, < L. *cognitus*, known: see *cognizance*, *cognize*, etc. The somewhat remarkable development of senses (which took place in OF.) is partly paralleled by that of *couth*, known, with its negative *uncouth*, and by that of AS. *mǣre*, known, famous, etc. (see *mere*[4]); but some confusion with L. *comptus* (> It. *conto*), neat, and with *computatus* (> It. *conto*, counted, numbered, etc.) is prob. also involved: see *compt*[2]. Cf. *quaint*, *v.*, and *acquaint*, etc.] 1†. Known; familiar.

> The hert & the hinde there thanne hem hed sone,
> As the werwolf hem wissed that ay was here gye,
> Under a *coynte* crag fast bi the quenes chaumber.
> *William of Palerne* (E. E. T. S.), l. 2850.

2†. Artful; clever; cunning; crafty; wily.

> Ovid openly in Eydos tellus
> How Medea the maiden made hym all new,
> By crafte that she kouth of hir *coint* artys.
> *Destruction of Troy* (E. E. T. S.), l. 125.

"Dere brother," quath Peres, "the devell is ful *queynte*
To encombren holy Churche."
Piers Plowman's Crede (E. E. T. S.), l. 482.

> But you, my lord, were glad to be employ'd,
> To show how *quaint* an orator you are.
> *Shak.*, 2 Hen. VI., iii. 2. 274.

3†. Artificial; ingenious; elaborate; curious; pretty; elegant; fine.

> And of Achilles with his *queynte* spere.
> *Chaucer*, Squire's Tale, l. 231.

ȝit schal thou, erthe, for al thi erthe, make thou it neuere so *queynte* & gay.
Hymns to Virgin, etc. (E. E. T. S.), p. 89.

> Our plumes, our spangs, and al our *queint* aray,
> Are pricking spurres, prouoking filthy pride.
> *Gascoigne*, Steele Glas (ed. Arber), p. 60.

> For he was clad in strange accoustrements,
> Fashion'd with *queint* devises, never seene
> In court before. *Spenser*, Mother Hub. Tale, l. 673.

For a fine, *quaint*, graceful, and excellent fashion, yours [your gown] is worth ten on't.
Shak., Much Ado, iii. 4. 22.

> To nurse the saplings tall, and curl the grove
> With ringlets *quaint*. *Milton*, Arcades, l. 47.

4. Fanciful; odd; whimsical: as, a *quaint* phrase; a *quaint* talker.

> We semen wonder wyse,
> Our termes been so clergial and so *queynte*.
> *Chaucer*, Prol. to Canon's Yeoman's Tale, l. 199.

> To move
> His laughter at their *quaint* opinions wide
> Hereafter, when they come to model heaven
> And calculate the stars. *Milton*, P. L., viii. 78.

Some stroke of *quaint* yet simple pleasantry. *Macaulay.*

5. Odd and antique; old-fashioned; curious; odd in any way.

> But sodeinly she saugh a sighte *queynte*.
> *Chaucer*, Knight's Tale, l. 1475.

> A casement high and triple-arched there was,
> . . . diamonded with panes of *quaint* device.
> *Keats*, Eve of St. Agnes, st. 24.

There [in Europe] were to be seen the masterpiece[s] of art, the refinements of highly-cultivated society, the *quaint* peculiarities of ancient and local custom.
Irving, Sketch-Book, p. 14.

Rare fronts of varied mosaic, covered with imagery, wilder and *quainter* than ever filled a Midsummer Night's Dream. *Ruskin.*

> As *quaint* a four-in-hand
> As you shall see — three pyebalds and a roan.
> *Tennyson*, Walking to the Mail.

6†. Affectedly nice; squeamish; prim.

> She, nothing *quaint*,
> Nor sdeignfull of so homely fashion,
> Sith brought she was now to so hard constraint,
> Sat downe upon the dusty ground anon.
> *Spenser*, F. Q., III. vii. 10.

=**Syn. 5.** *Old*, *Antique*, etc. See *ancient*[1].

quaint† (kwānt), *adv.* [ME. *quainte*, *queynte*, etc.; < *quaint*, *a.*] Elegantly.

> What shulde I speke more *queynte*,
> Or peyne me my wordes peynte?
> *Chaucer*, House of Fame, l. 245.

quaint† (kwānt), *v. t.* [< ME. *quainten*, *queinten*, *queynten*, *cointen*; by apheresis from *aquainten*, etc.: see *acquaint*.] To acquaint; inform; cause to know.

> He *coynted* him queyntli with tho two ladies,
> That hade that time thi sone to kepe in warde.
> *William of Palerne* (E. E. T. S.), l. 4644.

> There if he travaile and *quainte* him well,
> The Treasure of Knowledges is his eche deale.
> *Recorde*, Castle of Knowledge (1556). (*Halliwell.*)

> I met a man and bad him stay,
> Requeisting him to mak me *quaint*
> Of the beginning and the event.
> *Battle of Harlaw* (Child's Ballads, VII. 182).

quaintance†, *n.* [ME. *quaintance*, *qweyntance*, *quoyntaunce*; by apheresis from *acquaintance*.] Acquaintance.

> He kysses hir comlyly, & knyȝtly he meleȝ;
> Thay kallen hym of a *quoyntaunce*, & he hit quyk askeȝ,
> To be her seruaunt sothly, if hem-self lyked.
> *Sir Gawayne and the Green Knight* (E. E. T. S.), l. 975.

quaintise†, *n.* [< ME. *quaintise*, *quayntise*, *qwaintis*, *qwantis*, *queyntise*, < OF. *cointise*, *coyntise*, *cointice*, *quointise*, *cuintize*, *coentisce*, *quentis*, etc., cleverness, skilfulness, cunning, artfulness, neatness, < *coint*, known, clever, quaint: see *quaint*.] 1. Cleverness; artfulness; cunning; craft.

> The divill by his dotage dissaueth the chirche,
> And put in the prechours y-paynted withouten:
> And by his *queyntise* they comen in the curates to helpen.
> *Piers Plowman's Crede* (E. E. T. S.), l. 507.

> Into the cuntre of Calaphe cast with a storme,
> There the qwene with hir *qwaintis* qwaitid me to cacche:
> Held me with hir, & my hede knightes.
> *Destruction of Troy* (E. E. T. S.), l. 13245.

> Be waar to whom thou trustis, and spare for no *queyntise*,
> For myche harme hath falle to them that ben not wise.
> *Babees Book* (E. E. T. S.), p. 42.

2. Elegance; beauty; neatness; trimness; daintiness.

They [wives] sholde setten hire entente to pleesen hir housbondes, but nat by hire *queyntise* of array.
Chaucer, Parson's Tale.

quaintise†, *v. t.* [ME. *queintisen*; < *quaintise*, *n.*] To make or adorn cunningly.

> The new guise of Beme was there;
> With sondry thynges well deuised
> I see, wherof thei be *queintised*.
> *Gower*, Conf. Amant., viii.

quaintly (kwānt'li), *adv.* [< ME. *quaintly*, *queintly*, *queyntly*, *cointly*, *coyntly*; < *quaint* + *-ly*[2].] In a quaint manner. (*a*†) Artfully; cunningly; ingeniously; cleverly.

> Bothe that on & that other, myn honoured ladye,
> That thus hor knyȝt wyth hor kest han *koyntly* bigyled.
> *Sir Gawayne and the Green Knight* (E. E. T. S.), l. 2413.

> A ladder *quaintly* made of cords,
> To cast up, with a pair of anchoring hooks.
> *Shak.*, T. G. of V., iii. 1. 117.

> I *queintly* stole a kiss.
> *Gay*, Shepherd's Week, Monday, l. 79.

(*b*†) Prettily; nicely; pleasantly; with neatness or trimness.

> The lorde loutes therto, & the lady als,
> In-to a comly closet *coyntly* ho entre.
> *Sir Gawayne and the Green Knight* (E. E. T. S.), l. 934.

> Yes, yes: the lines are very *quaintly* writ.
> *Shak.*, T. G. of V., ii. 1. 128.

> When was old Sherewood's hair more *quaintly* curl'd,
> Or nature's cradle more enchased and puti'd?
> B. *Jonson.*

(*c*) Fancifully; oddly; whimsically; curiously; especially, in an odd, old-fashioned way: as, *quaintly* dressed; *quaintly* expressed.

> Anon a figure enters, *quaintly* neat,
> All pride and business, bustle and conceit.
> *Crabbe*, Works, I. 14.

quaintness (kwānt'nes), *n.* [< ME. *quaintnes*, *qwhayntnes*; < *quaint* + *-ness*.] The quality of being quaint. (*a*†) Artfulness; cunning; wiliness. (*b*†) Elegance; daintiness; niceness; affectation.

The fancy of some odde *quaintnesses* haue put him cleane beside his Nature.
Bp. Earle, Micro-cosmographie, An Affected Man.

I . . . have therein more solicitously followed the truth of things (many of which I can also assert on my own knowledge) than I have studied *quaintness* in expressions.
N. Morton, New England's Memorial, p. 11.

There is a certain majesty in simplicity which is far above the *quaintness* of wit. *Pope.*

(*c*) Fancifulness; oddity; whimsicality; queerness; especially, odd, old-fashioned appearance or manner.

The great obstacle to Chapman's translations being read is their unconquerable *quaintness*.
Lamb, Eng. Dramatists, Notes.

Healthy seriousness often best expresses itself in playful *quaintness*. *Froude*, Sketches, p. 184.

That peculiar air of *quaintness* which is shared by all places where narrow streets run up a steep hill.
E. A. Freeman, Venice, p. 93.

quair†, *n.* An obsolete form of *quire*[1].

quaisy (kwā'zi), *a.* An obsolete or dialectal form of *queasy*.

quait (kwāt), *n.* A variant of *quoit*. [U. S.]

quake (kwāk), *v.*; pret. and pp. *quaked*, ppr. *quaking*. [< ME. *quaken*, *cwaken* (pret. *quakede*, also *quoke*, *quok*, *quoc*), < AS. *cwacian* (pret. *cwacode*) (whence causative *cweccan*, cause to shake, wag: see *quitch*[1]); perhaps akin to *quick*.] **I.** *intrans.* To shake; tremble; be agitated by tremors or shocks. Specifically—(*a*) To tremble from cold, weakness, or fear; shiver; shudder.

> This Ypermestra caste hire eyen doun,
> And *quok* as doth the leefe of aspe grene.
> *Chaucer*, Good Women, l. 2649.

> We were so ferde we can [began] downe falle,
> And *qwoke* for drede.
> *York Plays*, p. 416.

And so terrible was the sight that Moses said, I exceedingly fear and *quake*. Heb. xii. 21.

> She, . . . while her infant race . . . sit cow'ring o'er the sparks,
> Retires, content to *quake*, so they be warm'd.
> *Cowper*, Task, iv. 386.

(*b*) To tremble from internal convulsions or shocks.

> The erthe *qwoke*, and mounteynes an hight,
> Valeis, & stoonys, bursten a-sundir.
> *Hymns to Virgin*, etc. (E. E. T. S.), p. 48.

The mountains *quake* at him, and the hills melt, and the earth is burned at his presence. Nah. i. 5.

(*c*) To tremble from want of solidity or firmness: as, *quaking* jelly; a *quaking* bog.

> Let custards *quake*, my rage must freely run!
> *Marston*, Scourge of Villanie, ii. 4.

> Next Smedley dived; slow circles dimpled o'er
> The *quaking* mud, that clos'd, and op'd no more.
> *Pope*, Dunciad, ii. 292.

Quaking ash, asp, etc. See the nouns. =**Syn.** (*a*) *Shudder*, etc. See *shiver*.—(*b*) and (*c*) To vibrate, quiver.

II.† *trans.* To cause to shake or tremble; throw into agitation or trembling; cause to shiver or shudder.

> I am not pleas'd at that ill-knotted fire,
> That bushing-staring star. Am I not Duke?
> It should not *quake* me now; had it appear'd
> Before, it I might then haue justly fear'd.
> *Tourneur*, Revenger's Tragedy, v. 3.

> Where ladies shall be frighted,
> And, gladly *quaked*, hear more. *Shak.*, Cor., i. 9. 6.

quake (kwāk), *n.* [< ME. *quake*; < *quake*, *v.*] 1. A shake; a trembling; a tremulous agitation; a shuddering.

> Yet as the earth may sometimes shake,
> For winds shut up will cause a *quake*.
> *Suckling*, Love's World.

2†. Fear; dismay.

> Thou shal bye thi breed ful dere,
> Til thou turne ageyn in *quake*
> To that erthe thou were of-take.
> *Cursor Mundi*, MS. Coll. Trin. Cantab., f. 6. (*Halliwell.*)

quake-breech† (kwāk'brēch), *n.* A coward. [Rare.]

Excors, a hartlesse, a faint-hearted fellow, a *quake-breech*, without boldnes, spirit, wit; a sot. *Withals*, Dict.

quake-grass (kwāk'gràs), *n.* Same as *quaking-grass*.

quakemire† (kwāk'mīr), *n.* [< *quake* + *mire*. Hence *quagmire*, and by abbr. *quag*. Cf. *quavemire*, *quickmire*.] A quagmire. *Stanihurst.*

quaker (kwā'kėr), *n.* [< *quake* + *-er*[1]. Hence (in sense 2) F. *Quacre*, *Quaker* = Sp. *Cudkero* = Pg. *Quacre* = D. *Kwaker* = G. *Quäker* = Dan. *Kvæker* = Sw. *Quäkare*.] 1. One who quakes or trembles.—2. [*cap.*] One of the religious denomination called the *Society of Friends*. The name, originally given in reproach, has never been adopted by the Society. See *Society of Friends*, under *friend*.

> *Quakers* that, like to lanterns, bear
> Their lights within 'em will not swear.
> *S. Butler*, Hudibras, II. ii. 219.

A certain minister in Bremen, . . . reproached with the name of *Quaker*, because of his singular sharpness against the formal lifeless ministers and Christians in the world.
Penn, Travels in Holland, etc.

Get the writings of John Woolman by heart, and love the early *Quakers*. *Lamb*, A Quakers' Meeting.

3. A Quaker gun (which see, under *gun*[1]).

The only other vessel in the port was a Russian government bark, . . . mounting eight guns (four of which we found to be *quakers*).
R. H. Dana, Jr., Before the Mast, p. 271.

4. In *entom.*, one of certain noctuid moths: an English collectors' name. *Agrotis castanea* is the common quaker, and *Mamestra nana* is the small quaker. Also *quaker-moth*.—**Quaker black-drop.** See *black-drop*.—**Quaker buttons.** See *button*.—**Stewed Quaker,** a posset of molasses or honey, stewed with butter and vinegar, and taken hot as a remedy for colds. [Colloq.]

A little saucepan of *stewed Quaker*, prepared by Sarah at the suggestion of the thoughtful Mrs. Hand, was bubbling on the stove. *The Century*, XXXV. 674.

The Quaker City, Philadelphia in Pennsylvania: so called in allusion to its having been founded by Quakers.

quaker-bird (kwā'kėr-bėrd), *n.* The sooty albatross, *Diomedea* or *Phœbetria fuliginosa*: so called from its somber color.

Quaker-color (kwā'kėr-kul'or), *n.* The color of the drab or gray fabrics much worn by Quakers.

The upper parts are a uniform, satiny olive gray or *quaker-color*. *Coues*, Key to N. A. Birds, p. 474.

Quakerdom (kwā'kėr-dum), *n.* [< *Quaker* + *-dom*.] Quakers as a class; the world of Quakers, with their tenets, aims, manners, customs, etc. [Colloq.]

He [Derwent Coleridge] spoke very civilly of modern *Quakerdom*, congratulating them on their preference for the cultivation of the intellect rather than the accomplishments of the person. *Caroline Fox*, Journal, p. 47.

Quakeress (kwā'kėr-es), *n.* [< *Quaker* + *-ess*.] A female Quaker.

Every *Quakeress* is a lily. *Lamb*, A Quakers' Meeting.

quaker-grass (kwā'kėr-grȧs), *n.* Same as *quaking-grass*. [Prov. Eng.]

Quakeric (kwā'kėr-ik), *a.* [< *Quaker* + *-ic*.] Pertaining to a Quaker; Quakerish. [Rare.]

The *Quakeric* dialect. *Macaulay*, in Trevelyan, II. 190.

Quakerish (kwā'kėr-ish), *a.* [< *Quaker* + *-ish*[1].] Pertaining to Quakerism; characteristic of or resembling the Quakers; Quaker-like.

Don't address me as if I were a beauty; I am your plain *Quakerish* governess. *Charlotte Brontë*, Jane Eyre, xxiv.

Quakerism (kwā'kėr-izm), *n.* [< *Quaker* + *-ism*.] The tenets, religious customs, and manners peculiar to the Quakers.—**Wet Quakerism,** the doctrine of those Friends who believe in the propriety and Scriptural sanction of baptism with water: used opprobriously.

Wet Quakerism is largely on the increase, even in the inuermost circle. *H. N. Oxenham*, Short Studies, p. 3.

Quakerly (kwā'kėr-li), *a.* [< *Quaker* + *-ly*[1].] Characteristic of or resembling Quakers; Quaker-like.

You would not have Englishmen, when they are in company, hold a silent *quakerly* meeting.
J. Goodman, Winter Evening Conferences, p. 1.

quaker-moth (kwā'kėr-mȏth), *n.* An English collectors' name for certain modest-colored noctuid moths.

quakers (kwā'kėrz), *n.* [Pl. of *quaker*.] The quaking-grass. [Prov. Eng.]

quakery† (kwā'kėr-i), *n.* [< *Quaker* + *-y*[3] (see *-ery*).] Same as *Quakerism*.

quaketail (kwāk'tāl), *n.* The yellow wagtail; any bird of the genus *Budytes*, as *B. flava*. *Macgillivray; Montagu.* [Local, British.]

quakiness (kwā'ki-nes), *n.* The state of being quaky or shaking: as, the *quakiness* of a bog.

quaking (kwā'king), *n.* [< ME. *quakynge*, < AS. *cwacung*, verbal n. of *cwacian*, quake: see *quake*.] Trembling; fear; agitation.

Son of man, eat thy bread with *quaking*, and drink thy water with trembling. Ezek. xii. 18.

quaking-grass (kwā'king-grȧs), *n.* A grass of the genus *Briza*, especially *B. media*, an Old World plant sparingly introduced into the United States. The spikelets are tremulous on the slender branches of the panicle. Also called *quake-grass*, *quaker-grass*, *dodder-grass*, *cow-quakes*, *dithering grass*, *jockey-grass*, and *maidenhair-grass*.—**Tall quaking-grass.** See *Glyceria*.

quakingly (kwā'king-li), *adv.* In a quaking or trembling manner.

But never pen did more *quakingly* perform his office.
Sir P. Sidney, Arcadia, iii.

quaky (kwā'ki), *a.* [< *quake* + *-y*[1].] Characterized by or prone to quaking; shaky: as, a *quaky* bog.

Poor old Twoshoes is so old and toothless and *quaky* that she can't sing a bit.
Thackeray, Roundabout Papers, Some Carp at Sans Souci.

quale[1]†, *n.* [ME., < AS. *cwalu*, slaughter, destruction (= OS. *quala*, *quale* = MD. *quaele*, D. *kwaal*, sickness, disease, = MLG. *quale*, LG. *quaal*, *kwaal* = OHG. *quala*, *chwala*, *chala*, MHG. *quale*, *kale*, G. *qual* = Icel. *kvöl* = Sw. *qual* = Dan. *kval*, pang, agony), < *cwelan*, die: see *quail*[1].] A plague; murrain. *Layamon.*

quale[2]†, *v. i.* A Middle English form of *quail*[2].

quale[3]†, *n.* A Middle English dialectal form of *whale*[1].

quale[4] (kwā'lē), *n.* [L., neut. of *qualis*, interrog., of what character or quality, of what sort; rel., of such a kind; indef., having some quality or other: see *quality*.] An object named or considered as having a quality.

Moreover, we can directly observe in our own organic sensations, which seem to come nearest to the whole content of infantile and molluscous experience, an almost entire absence of any assignable *quale*.
J. Ward, Encyc. Brit., XX. 40.

qualifiable (kwol'i-fi-a-bl), *a.* [< F. *qualifiable*; as *qualify* + *-able*.] Capable of being qualified, in any sense. *Barrow.*

qualification (kwol'i-fi-kā'shon), *n.* [= F. *qualification* = Sp. *calificacion* = Pg. *qualificação* = It. *qualificazione*, < ML. **qualificatio(n-)*, < *qualificare*, qualify: see *qualify*.] 1. The act of qualifying, or the state of being qualified, by change or modification; specifically, adaptation; fitness.

Neither had the waters of the flood infused such an impurity as thereby the natural and powerful operation of all plants, herbs, and fruits upon the earth received a *qualification* and harmful change. *Raleigh*, Hist. World.

2. A quality adapting a person or thing to particular circumstances, uses, or ends.

The *qualifications* which conduce most to the fixity of a portion of matter seem to be these.
Boyle, Experimental Notes, i.

Strength, agility, and courage would in such a state be the most valuable *qualifications*.
Mandeville, Fable of the Bees, Dialogue vi.

3. That which qualifies a person for or renders him admissible to or acceptable for a place, an office, or an employment; any natural or acquired quality, property, or possession which secures a right to exercise any function, privilege, etc.; specifically, legal power or ability: as, the *qualifications* of an elector.

The true reason of requiring any *qualification* with regard to property in voters is to exclude such persons as are in so mean a situation that they are esteemed to have no will of their own. *Blackstone*, Com., I. ii.

They say a good Maid Servant ought especially to have three *Qualifications*: to be honest, ugly, and high-spirited.
N. Bailey, tr. of Colloquies of Erasmus, I. 304.

Considerable efforts are, however, now being made to have the real gymnasium certificate recognized as a sufficient *qualification* for the study of medicine at least.
Encyc. Brit., XX. 17.

4. In *logic*, the attaching of quality, or the distinction of affirmative and negative, to a term.—5. A qualifying—that is, partially negativing or extenuating—circumstance; modification; restriction; limitation; allowance; abatement: as, to assert something without any *qualification*.

It may be laid down as a general rule, though subject to considerable *qualifications* and exceptions, that history begins in novel and ends in essay. *Macaulay*, History.

But, all *qualifications* being made, it is undeniable that there is a certain specialization of the [nervous] discharge, giving some distinctiveness to the bodily changes by which each feeling is accompanied.
H. *Spencer*, Prin. of Psychol., § 495.

6†. Appeasement; pacification.

Out of that will I cause these of Cyprus to mutiny; whose *qualification* shall come into no true taste again but by the displanting of Cassio. *Shak.*, Othello, ii. 1. 282.

Property qualification, the holding of a certain amount of property as a condition to the right of suffrage or the exercise of some other public function. This condition in the case of suffrage has been common in ancient and modern times, and still prevails to a considerable extent in Europe. In the United States it has disappeared in the different States—the last one, Rhode Island, having abolished it (with a few exceptions) in 1888. In many States a small property qualification is a condition of service as a juror.

qualificative (kwol'i-fi-kā-tiv), *a.* and *n.* [= F. *qualificatif* = Pg. *qualificativo*; < NL. *qualificativus*, < ML. *qualificare*, qualify: see *qualify*.] I. *a.* Serving to qualify or modify, or having the power to do so; qualifying.

II. *n.* That which serves to qualify, modify, or limit; a qualifying term, clause, or statement.

qualificator (kwol'i-fi-kā-tor), *n.* [= F. *qualificateur* = Sp. *calificador* = Pg. *qualificador* = It. *qualificatore*; < ML. *qualificator*, < *qualificare*, qualify: see *qualify*.] In Roman Catholic ecclesiastical courts, an officer whose business it is to examine causes and prepare them for trial.

qualificatory (kwol'i-fi-kā-tō-ri), *a.* [< NL. **qualificatorius*, < ML. *qualificare*, qualify: see *qualify*.] Of or pertaining to qualification. [Rare.]

Some teachers urge that we should have no examinations at all, . . . others that examinations should be solely *qualificatory*. *The Academy*, Oct. 12, 1889, p. 233.

qualified (kwol'i-fid), *p. a.* 1. Having a qualification; fitted by accomplishments or endowments; furnished with legal power or capacity: as, a person *qualified* to hold an appointment; a *qualified* elector.

Well *qualified* and dutiful I know him;
I took him not for beauty.
Beau. and Fl., Philaster, iii. 2.

He only who is able to stand alone is *qualified* for society.
Emerson, Fugitive Slave Law.

2. Affected by some degree of negation, limitation, or modification; modified; limited; restricted: as, a *qualified* statement; *qualified* admiration.

The Quaker's loyalty, said the Earl of Errol at Aberdeen, is a *qualified* loyalty; it smells of rebellion.
Bancroft, Hist. U. S., II. 349.

3. *Eccles.*, noting a person enabled to hold two benefices.—**Estate of inheritance qualified.** See *estate*.—**Qualified acceptance.** See *acceptance*, 1 (c) (2).—**Qualified fee, indorsement, oath, property.** See the nouns. =**Syn.** 1. *Competent, Qualified, Fitted.* To be *competent* is to have the natural abilities or the general training necessary for any given work; to be *qualified* is to have, in addition to competency, a special training, enabling one to begin the work effectively and at once. He who is *competent* may or may not require time to become *qualified*; he who is not *competent* cannot become *qualified*, for it is not in him. *Fitted* is a general word; he who is *fitted* by nature, experience, or general training is *competent*; he who is *fitted* by special preparation is *qualified*.

qualifiedly (kwol'i-fid-li), *adv.* In a qualified manner; with qualification or limitation.

qualifiedness (kwol'i-fid-nes), *n.* The state of being qualified or fitted.

qualifier (kwol'i-fi-ėr), *n.* [< *qualify* + *-er*[1]. Cf. *qualificator*.] One who or that which qualifies; that which modifies, reduces, tempers, or restrains; specifically, in *gram.*, a word that qualifies another, as an adjective a noun, or an adverb a verb, etc.

Your Epitheton or *qualifier*, whereof we spake before, . . . because he serues also to alter and enforce the sence, we will say somewhat more of him.
Puttenham, Arte of Eng. Poesie, p. 152.

Qualifiers of the Holy Office, a body of monks, in the service of the Inquisition, who examined the evidence in regard to accused persons, and made reports to the tribunals. *Encyc. Brit.*

qualify (kwol'i-fi), *v.*; pret. and pp. *qualified*, ppr. *qualifying*. [< OF. *qualifier*, *callifier*, *cualificar*, F. *qualifier* = Sp. *calificar* = Pg. *qualificar* = It. *qualificare*, < ML. *qualificare*, < L. *qualis*, of what kind, + *-ficare*, < *facere*, make: see *quality* and *-fy*.] I. *trans.* 1. To note the quality or kind of; express or mark a quality of.—2. To impart a certain quality or qualification to; fit for any place, office, or occupation; furnish with the knowledge, skill, or other accomplishment necessary for a purpose.

I determined to *qualify* myself for engraving on copper.
Hogarth, in Thackeray's Eng. Humourists, Hogarth, [Smollett, and Fielding, note.

Misanthropy is not the temper which *qualifies* a man to act in great affairs, or to judge of them.
Macaulay, Hallam's Const. Hist.

3. Specifically, to make legally capable; furnish with legal power or capacity: as, to *qualify* a person for exercising the elective franchise.

The first of them, says he, that has a Spaniel by his Side, is a Yeoman of about an hundred Pounds a Year, an honest Man; He is just within the Game Act, and *qualified* to kill an Hare or a Pheasant. *Addison*, Spectator, No. 122.

In 1432 it was ordered that the *qualifying* freehold should be within the county. *Stubbs*, Const. Hist., § 368.

4. In *logic*, to modify by the negative particle or in some similar way.—5. In *gram.*, to express some quality as belonging to; modify; describe: said of an adjective in relation to a noun, of an adverb in relation to a verb, etc.—6. To limit or modify; restrict; limit by exceptions; come near denying: as, to *qualify* a statement or an expression; to *qualify* the sense of words or phrases.

Sometimes wordes suffered to go single do giue greater sence and grace then words *qualified* by attributions do.
Puttenham, Arte of Eng. Poesie, p. 152.

7. To moderate; soothe; abate; soften; diminish; assuage: as, to *qualify* the rigor of a statute.

> I do not seek to quench your love's hot fire,
> But *qualify* the fire's extreme rage.
> *Shak.*, T. G. of V., ii. 7. 22.

Although the seat of the Town be excessive hot, yet it is happily *qualified* by a North-east gale that bloweth from sea. *Sandys*, Travailes, p. 5.

8. To modify the quality or strength of; make stronger, dilute, or otherwise fit for taste: as, to *qualify* liquors.

I have drunk but one cup to-night, and that was craftily *qualified* too. *Shak.*, Othello, ii. 3. 41.

A set of feuars and bonnet lairds who . . . contrived to drink twopenny, *qualified* with brandy or whisky. *Scott*, St. Ronan's Well, i.

9. To temper; regulate; control.

This is the master-piece of a modern politician, how to *qualifie* and mould the sufferance and subjection of the people to the length of that foot that is to tread on their necks. *Milton*, Reformation in Eng., ii.

It [the bittern] hath no fit larynx or throttle to *qualify* the sound. *Sir T. Browne*, Vulg. Err., iii. 27.

10. In *Scotch law*, to prove; authenticate; confirm.

The other [half of the goods forfeited] to be given to him who delates the recepters and *qualifies* the same. *Spalding*, Hist. Troubles in Scotland, I. 273. (*Jamieson.*)

If any individual could *qualify* a wrong, and a damage arising from it. *Thurlow*, quoted in Boswell's Johnson (an. 1776).

=**Syn. 2.** To prepare, capacitate. See *qualified*.—**6** and **7.** To reduce.

II. *intrans.* **1.** To take the necessary steps for rendering one's self capable of holding any office or enjoying any privilege; establish a claim or right to exercise any function.—**2.** To take the oath of office before entering upon its duties.—**3.** To make oath to any fact: as, I am ready to *qualify* to what I have asserted. [U. S.]

qualitative (kwol'i-tā-tiv), *a.* [= F. *qualitative* = Sp. *cualitativo* = Pg. It. *qualitativo*, < LL. *qualitativus*, < L. *qualita(t-)s*, quality: see *quality*.] Originally, depending upon qualities; now, non-quantitative; relating to the possession of qualities without reference to the quantities involved; stating that some phenomenon occurs, but without measurement. The word occurs, according to Dr. Fitzedward Hall, in Gaule's Πῦς-μαντία (1652).

After this quantitative mental distinction [between men and women], which becomes incidentally *qualitative* by telling most upon the most recent and most complex faculties, there come the *qualitative* mental distinctions consequent on the relations of men and women to their children and to one another. *H. Spencer*, Study of Sociol., p. 374.

Qualitative analysis, in *chem.* See *analysis*.—**Qualitative atrophy**, degeneration of tissue combined with atrophy.—**Qualitative definition**, a definition by means of accidental qualities.

qualitatively (kwol'i-tā-tiv-li), *adv.* In a qualitative manner; with reference to quality; in quality.

qualitied (kwol'i-tid), *a.* [< *quality* + *-ed*[2].] Disposed as to qualities or faculties; furnished with qualities; endowed.

Besides all this, he was well *qualitied*. *Chapman*, Iliad, xiv. 104.

> A dainty hand, and small, to have such power
> Of help to dizzy height; and *qualified*
> Divinely. *Harper's Mag.*, LXXVIII. 184.

quality (kwol'i-ti), *n.*; pl. *qualities* (-tiz). [< OF. *qualite*, F. *qualité* = Sp. *cualidad*, *calidad* = Pg. *qualidade* = It. *qualità*, < L. *qualita(t-)s*, property, nature, state, quality (Cicero, tr. Gr. ποιότης), < *qualis*, interrog., of what kind, of what sort; rel., of such a kind, of such sort, such as, as; indef., having some quality or other; < *quis*, fem. abl. *quā*, who, what: see *who*.] **1.** That from which anything can be said to be such or such; a character expressible by an adjective admitting degrees of comparison, but not explicitly relative nor quantitative: thus, blueness, hardness, agility, and mirthfulness are *qualities*. The precise meaning of the word is governed by its prominence in Aristotelian philosophy, which formed part of a liberal education till near the end of the seventeenth century, though the modified doctrine of Ramus was taught at Cambridge. Aristotle makes quality one of his categories, or highest genera, and thereby distinguishes it absolutely from substance, quantity, and relation, as well as from place, time, action, passion, habit, and posture. A quality is further said by Aristotle to be something which has a contrary, which admits of degree, and which is a respect in which things agree and also differ. But no writers, not even Aristotle himself, have strictly observed these distinctions; and Cicero, much followed by the Ramists, uses the word quite loosely. *Quality* has, however, always been opposed to *quantity*; and few writers call the universal attributes of matter or those of mind *qualities*.

There is somewhat contrarie unto *qualitie*, as vertue is contrarie unto vice, wit unto folie, manhode unto cowardise. The thing conteinyng or receivyng any *qualitie* maie be saied to receive either more or less. As one man is thoughte to be wiser then another, not that wisdome it self is either greater or lesse, but that it maie bee in some manne more and in some manne lesse. By *qualitie* things are compted either like or unlike. Those things are like whiche are of like *qualitie* and have proprieties bothe accordingly. *Wilson*, Rule of Reason (1551).

Our good or evil estate after death dependeth most upon the *quality* of our lives. *Hooker*, Eccles. Polity, v. 46.

Every sin, the oftener it is committed, the more it acquireth in the *quality* of evil. *Sir T. Browne*, Religio Medici, i. 42.

Qualities do as well seem to belong to natural bodies generally considered as place, time, motion, and those other things. *Boyle*, Origin of Forms, Pref.

The power to produce any idea in our mind, I call *quality* of the subject wherein that power is. *Locke*, Human Understanding, II. viii. 8.

The three *qualities* which are usually said to distinguish atom from atom are shape, order, and position. *W. Wallace*, Epicureanism, p. 174.

2. One of those characters of a person or thing which make it good or bad; a moral disposition or habit. This use of the word, which comes from Aristotle, was much more common and varied down to the end of the eighteenth century than now. Good characters were called *qualities* more often than bad ones.

> All the *qualities* that man
> Loves woman for. *Shak.*, Cymbeline, v. 5. 166.

> You must now speak Sir John Falstaff fair;
> Which swims against your stream of *quality*.
> *Shak.*, 2 Hen. IV., v. 2. 34.

> To-night we'll wander through the streets, and note
> The *qualities* of people. *Shak.*, A. and C., i. 1. 54.

> You never taught me how to handle cards,
> To cheat and cozen men with oaths and lies;
> Those are the worldly *qualities* to live.
> *Beau. and Fl.*, Honest Man's Fortune, iv. 1.

You must observe all the rare *qualities*, humours, and compliments of a gentleman. *B. Jonson*, Every Man out of his Humour, i. 1.

Thou hast that pretty *Quality* of the familiar Fops of the Town, who, in an Eating-House, always keep Company with all People in 't but those they came with. *Wycherley*, Plain Dealer, v. 1.

He is very great, and a very delightful man, and, with a few bad *qualities* added to his character, would have acted a most conspicuous part in life. *Sydney Smith*, To Lady Holland.

3. A distinguished and characteristic excellence or superiority: as, this wine has *quality*.

We find spontaneity, also, in the rhymes of Allingham, whose "Mary Donnelly" and "The Fairies" have that intuitive grace called *quality* — a grace which no amount of artifice can ever hope to produce. *Stedman*, Vict. Poets, p. 258.

In character the setter should display a great amount of *quality*, a term which is difficult of explanation, though fully appreciated by all experienced sportsmen. It means a combination of symmetry, as understood by the artist, with the peculiar attributes of the breed under examination, as interpreted by the sportsman. *Dogs of Great Britain and America*, p. 102.

4. Degree of excellence or fineness; grade: as, the food was of inferior *quality*; the finest *quality* of cloth.—**5.** A title, or designation of rank, profession, or the like.

When ye will speake giuing euery person or thing besides his proper name a *qualitie* by way of addition, whether it be of good or of bad, it is a figuratiue speach of audible alteration. *Puttenham*, Arte of Eng. Poesie, p. 147.

6. Rank; profession; occupation; function; character sustained.

> A man of such perfection
> As we do in our *quality* much want.
> *Shak.*, T. G. of V., iv. 1. 58.

I am weary of this trade of fortune-telling, and mean to give all over when I come into England; for it is a very ticklish *quality*. *Fletcher (and another)*, Fair Maid of the Inn, v. 2.

Kneeling is the sinner's posture: if thou come hither in the *quality* of a sinner, . . . put thyself into the posture of a sinner, kneel. *Donne*, Sermons, vii.

> The saints would often leave their cells,
> And stroll about, but hide their *quality*,
> To try good people's hospitality.
> *Swift*, Baucis and Philemon.

A marriage, at the Halifax parish church, between John Bateman, of Hipperholme, in that parish, and a Margaret Aldersleye (no address or *quality* given). *N. and Q.*, 6th ser., X. 189.

7. Persons of the same calling or fraternity. [Rare.]

> To thy strong bidding task
> Ariel and all his *quality*. *Shak.*, Tempest, i. 2. 193.

8. Nobility or gentry, either abstractly (as, persons of *quality*) or concretely (as, the *quality*). But the former is obsolescent, the latter obsolete or now vulgar.

Gentlemen of blood and *quality*. *Shak.*, Hen. V., iv. 8. 95.

Two or three great silver flagons, made with inscriptions as gifts of the King to such and such persons of *quality* as did stay in town the late great plague, for the keeping things in order in the town. *Pepys*, Diary, III. 120.

> A nymph of *quality* admires our knight;
> He marries, bows at Court, and grows polite.
> *Pope*, Moral Essays, iii. 385.

9†. Character in respect to dryness or moisture, heat or cold, these being the elemental qualities from which it was supposed other properties, especially those of drugs and the temperaments, were compounded.

> The burning *quality*
> Of that fell poison. *Shak.*, K. John, v. 7. 8.

10†. Cause; occasion: an incorrect use.

> My brother Troilus lodges there to-night:
> Rouse him and give him note of our approach,
> With the whole *quality* wherefore.
> *Shak.*, T. and C., iv. 1. 44.

11. In *logic*: (*a*) The character of a proposition as affirmative or negative. [This use comes from Appuleius, a Latin writer of the second century.]

How is a simple proposition divided according to *qualitie?* Into an affirmative and negative proposition. *Blundeville*, Arte of Logicke, III. i.

(*b*) The character of apprehension as clear and distinct or obscure and confused. [This use is due to Kant.]

In relation to their subject, that is, to the mind itself, they [concepts] are considered as standing in a higher or a lower degree of consciousness—they are more or less clear, more or less distinct; this . . . is called their *quality*. *Sir W. Hamilton*, Logic, viii.

Accidental quality, a quality not distinguishing one species from another, but such that its subject might lose it without ceasing to be the same kind of substance.—**Active, alterative**, or **alterant quality**, a quality by force of which a body acts: thus, heat is an *active quality* of fire.—**Affective quality.** Same as *affection*, 6.—**Categories of quality.** See *category*.—**Contingent quality**, a derivative quality not necessarily involved in any primitive quality.—**Contrariety of quality.** See *contrariety*.—**Corporeal quality**, a natural quality of a kind of substance.—**Cosmical quality**, a quality of a body dependent upon the presence of some unperceived thing, as its color upon the presence of the luminiferous ether.—**Elemental** or **first quality** (tr. Gr. πρώτη διαφορή), one of the four qualities, hot and cold, moist and dry, which, according to Aristotle, distinguish the four elements, earth being dry and somewhat cold, water cold and somewhat moist, air moist and somewhat hot, fire hot and somewhat dry. Of these qualities, hot and cold are active, moist and dry passive. The hot segregates different kinds of substance, the cold brings them together; the moist has no definite boundary of its own, but readily receives one; the dry has its own boundary, and does not easily receive another. The effort of the Aristotelians constantly was to account for the properties of compound bodies by these first qualities, and this was especially done by physicians in regard to drugs.—**Essential quality**, a quality the essential difference of some species.—**Imputed quality†.** See *impute*.—**Intentional quality**, a character the predication of which states a fact, but not the true mode of existence of that fact: thus, it is a fact that the celestial bodies are accelerated toward one another; but, if action at a distance be not admitted, attraction is an *intentional quality*.—**Logical quality.** See def. 10, above.—**Manifest, occult, original qualities.** See the adjectives.—**Mechanical quality**, a quality explicable upon the principles of mechanics.—**Patible quality†** (tr. Gr. ποιότης παθητική), one that directly affects one of the senses.—**Predicamental quality**, quality in the strict sense, in which it is one of the ten predicaments or categories of Aristotle.—**Primary quality**, one of the mathematical characters of bodies, not strictly a quality, and not the object of any single sense exclusively. Locke enumerates these as solidity, extension, figure, motion or rest, and number.—**Primitive quality**, a quality which cannot be conceived to be a result of other qualities.—**Quality of a sound.** See *timbre*.—**Quality of estate**, in *law*, the manner in which the enjoyment of an estate is to be exercised while the right of enjoyment continues.—**Real quality.** (*a*) A quality really existing in a body, and not intentional. (*b*) A quality really existing in a body, and not imputed.—**Secondary quality.** (*a*) A patible quality. (*b*) A derivative quality.—**Secundo-primary quality**, a character which in being known as it affects us is ipso facto known as it exists, as hardness.—**Sensible** or **sensile quality.** Same as *patible quality*.—**Tactile quality.** (*a*) A quality known by the touch. (*b*) A patible quality.—**The quality**, persons of high rank, collectively. [Now vulgar.]

I shall appear at the next masquerade dressed up in my feathers and plumage like an Indian prince, that *the quality* may see how pretty they will look in their travelling habits. *Addison*, Guardian, No. 112.

The quality, as the upper classes in rural districts are designated by the lower. *Trollope*, Barchester Towers, xxxv.

=**Syn. 1** and **2.** *Quality, Property, Attribute, Accident, Characteristic, Character, Affection, Predicate, Mark, Difference, Diathesis, Determination.* *Quality* is that which makes or helps to make a person or thing such as he or it is. It is not universal, and in one popular sense it implies an excellence or a defect. In popular speech a *quality* is intellectual or moral; in metaphysics it may be also physical. A *property* is that which is viewed as peculiarly one's own, a peculiar quality. An *attribute* is a high and lofty character: the *attributes* of God are natural, as omniscience, omnipotence, etc., and moral, as holiness, justice, mercy, etc. "*Accident* is an abbreviated expression for accidental or contingent quality." (*Sir W. Hamilton*, Metaph., vi.) *Characteristic* is not a term of logic or philosophy: it stands for a personal, peculiar, or distinguishing quality: as, yellow in skin, horn, milk, etc., is a *characteristic* of Guernsey cattle. *Characteristics* may be mental, moral, or physical. *Character* is the most general of these words; a *character* is anything which is true of a subject. In another sense *character* (as a collective term) is the sum of the characteristics of a person or thing, especially the moral characteristics. The word always views them as making a unit or whole, and has lower and higher uses. The other words are somewhat technical. *Affection* is used in various senses. *Predicate* and *mark* are very general words in logic. *Difference* is a character distinguishing one class of objects from others. *Diathesis*, the corresponding Greek form, is applied in medicine to peculiarities of constitution. *Determination* is a more recent philosophical term denoting a character in general.

It would be felt as indecorous to speak of the *qualities* of God, and as ridiculous to speak of the *attributes* of matter. *Sir W. Hamilton*, Metaph., vi.

Property is correctly a synonym for peculiar *quality*; but it is frequently used as co-extensive with *quality* in general. *Sir W. Hamilton*, Metaph., vi.

We have no direct cognizance of what may be called the substantive existence of the body, only of its *accidents*. *J. H. Newman*, Parochial Sermons, I. 273.

Affability is a general *characteristic* of the Egyptians of all classes. *E. W. Lane*, Modern Egyptians, I. 261.

To judge human *character*, a man may sometimes have very small experience, provided he has a very large heart. *Bulwer*, What will he Do with it? v. 4.

quality-binding (kwol'i-ti-bīn"ding), *n.* A kind of worsted tape used for binding the borders of carpets and similar work. *Simmonds.*

quallet†, *n.* A Middle English form of *whale*[1].

qualm (kwäm), *n.* [Also dial. *calm*; < ME. *qualm*, *quelm*, pestilence, death, < AS. *cwealm*, death, slaughter, murder, destruction, plague, pestilence (= OS. *qualm*, death, destruction, = D. *kwalm*, suffocating vapor, smoke, = OHG. *qualm*, *chwalm*, MHG. *qualm*, *twalm*, slaughter, destruction, G. *qualm*, suffocating vapor, vapor, steam, damp, smoke, nausea, = Sw. *qvalm*, suffocating air, sultriness, = Dan. *kvalm*, suffocating air, *kvalme*, nausea), < *cwelan*, die, whence *cwellan*, cause to die, kill: see *quail*[1], and cf. *quale*[1] and *quell*.] 1†. Illness; disease; pestilence; plague.

A thousand slain, and not of *qualme* ystorve. *Chaucer*, Knight's Tale, l. 1156.

2. A sudden attack of illness; a turn of faintness or suffering; a throe or throb of pain.

Some sudden *qualm* hath struck me at the heart,
And dimm'd mine eyes. *Shak.*, 2 Hen. VI., i. 1. 54.

3. Especially, a sudden fit or seizure of sickness at the stomach; a sensation of nausea.

Falstaff. How now, Mistress Doll!
Hostess. Sick of a *calm*. *Shak.*, 2 Hen. IV., ii. 4. 40.

For who without a *qualm* hath ever look'd
On holy garbage, though by Homer cook'd?
Roscommon, Translated Verse.

4. A scruple or twinge of conscience; compunction; uneasiness.

Some seek, when queasy conscience has its *qualms*,
To lull the painful malady with alms.
Cowper, Charity, l. 447.

5†. The boding cry of a raven.

As ravenes *qualm*, or schrychynge of thise owlis. *Chaucer*, Troilus, v. 382.

qualm (kwäm), *v. i.* [< *qualm*, *n.*] 1. To be sick; suffer from qualms. [Rare.]

Above the rest,
Let Jesse's sov'reign flow'r perfume my *qualming* breast.
Quarles, Emblems, v. 2.

2. To cause pain or qualms.

Solicitude discomposes the head, jealousy the heart; envy *qualms* on his bowels, prodigality on his purse. *Gentleman Instructed*, p. 560. (*Davies.*)

qualmire† (kwal'mīr), *n.* [A var. of *quavemire*, appar. simulating *quail*[1], *qualm*.] Same as *quagmire*.

Whosoeuer seketh it in ani other place, and goeth about to set it out of men's puddels and *qualmires*, and not out of the most pure and cleare fountaine itselfe. *Bp. Gardiner*, True Obedience, fol. 9.

qualmish (kwä'mish), *a.* [< *qualm* + *-ish*[1].] 1. Sick at the stomach; inclined to vomit; affected with nausea or sickly languor.

I am *qualmish* at the smell of leek. *Shak.*, Hen. V., v. 1. 22.

2. Uneasy.

Elizabeth was not desirous of peace. She was *qualmish* at the very suggestion. *Motley*, Hist. Netherlands, I. 521.

qualmishly (kwä'mish-li), *adv.* In a qualmish manner.

qualmishness (kwä'mish-nes), *n.* The state of being qualmish; nausea.

quamash (kwa-mash'), *n.* Same as *camass*.

quamash-rat (kwa-mash'rat), *n.* Same as *camass-rat*.

quamoclit (kwam'ō-klit), *n.* [Mex.] 1. The cypress-vine, *Ipomæa Quamoclit*.—2. [*cap.*] [NL.] A section of the genus *Ipomæa*, including the cypress-vine, formerly regarded as a genus.

quam proxime (kwam prok'si-mē). [L.: *quam*, as; *proxime*, most nearly, < *proximus*, nearest: see *proxime*.] As near as may be; nearly.

quandang (kwan'dang), *n.* [Australian.] A small Australian tree, *Fusanus acuminatus*, or its fruit. The latter, called *native peach*, is said to be almost the only Australian fruit relished by Europeans. The kernel of the seed (quandang-nut) as well as the pulp is edible. Also *quandong* and *quantong*.

quandary (kwon'da-ri or kwon-dā'ri), *n.*; pl. *quandaries* (-riz). [Origin unknown; perhaps a dial. corruption (simulating a word of L. origin with suffix *-ary*) of dial. *wandreth*, evil, plight, peril, adversity, difficulty: see *wandreth*. The change of initial *w-* to *wh-* (hw-) occurs in some dialectal forms, e. g. in *whant*, a frequently heard pron. of *want* (as, I don't *whant* it). Medial *w* often suffers dialectal change to *qu* (as in *squete* for *sweet*), and instances of the change of *wh-* to *qu-* are numerous (Sc. *qua*, *quha*, for *who*, *quhar* for *where*, etc.). The notion that *quandary* comes from F. *qu'en dirai-je*, 'what shall I say of it,' is absurd.] A state of difficulty or perplexity; a state of uncertainty, hesitation, or puzzlement; a pickle; a predicament.

I leaue you to iudge . . . in what a *quandarie* . . . Pharicles was brought. *Greene*, Mamillia.

That much I fear forsaking of my diet
Will bring me presently to that *quandary*
I shall bid all adieu.
Beau. and Fl., Knight of Burning Pestle, i. 1.

We are in a great *quandary* what to do. *Pepys*, Diary, I. 245.

quandary (kwon'da-ri or kwon-dā'ri), *v.*; pret. and pp. *quandaried*, ppr. *quandarying*. [< *quandary*, *n.*] I. *trans.* To put into a quandary; bring into a state of uncertainty or difficulty.

Methinks I am *quandary'd*, like one going with a party to discover the enemy's camp, but had lost his guide upon the mountains. *Otway*, Soldier's Fortune, iii.

II. *intrans.* To be in a difficulty or uncertainty; hesitate.

He *quandaries* whether to go forward to God, or, with Demas, to turn back to the world. *Rev. T. Adams*, Works, I. 505. (*Davies.*)

quandy (kwan'di), *n.*; pl. *quandies* (-diz). [Origin obscure.] A duck, the oldwife or south-southerly, *Harelda glacialis*. See cut under *Harelda*. [Massachusetts.]

quannet (kwan'et), *n.* [Origin obscure.] 1. A kind of file, used especially for scraping zinc plates for the process denominated anastatic printing. *Ure.*—2. A flat file set in a frame like a plane, used in the manufacture of combs.

Tortoise-shell handles . . . are smoothed with a float or single cut file, technically known as a *quannet*. *O. Byrne*, Artisan's Handbook, p. 410.

quanon, *n.* Same as *kanun*.

quant (kwant), *n.* [Also *quont*; < ME. *quante*, *whante*, a pole, stick, rod; cf. *kent*[1].] 1. A walking-stick. [Prov. Eng.]—2. A pushing-pole with a flat board or cap at one end to prevent it from sinking into the mud, used by bargemen; also, a jumping-pole, similarly fitted, used in marshes. The name is also given to the cap. [Prov. Eng.]

quanta, *n.* Plural of *quantum*.

quantative† (kwon'ta-tiv), *a.* Same as *quantitative*.

The notions of quantity, and of the two most simple differences of *quantative* things, rarity and density. *Sir K. Digby*, Treatise of Bodies (1644), iv.

quantic (kwon'tik), *n.* [< L. *quantus*, how great, how much (see *quantity*), + *-ic*.] In *math.*, a rational integral homogeneous function of two or more variables. Quantics are classified according to their dimensions, as *quadric*, *cubic*, *quartic*, *quintic*, etc., denoting quantics of the second, third, fourth, fifth, etc., degrees. They are further distinguished as *binary*, *ternary*, *quaternary*, etc., according as they contain two, three, four, etc., variables. The word was introduced by Cayley in 1854.—**Order of a quantic**, the degree of a quantic.—**The equation of a quantic.** See *equation*.

quantical (kwon'ti-kal), *a.* Relating to quantics.

quantification (kwon"ti-fi-kā'shon), *n.* [< NL. as if **quantificatio(n-)*, < **quantificare*, quantify: see *quantify*.] 1. The act of attaching quantity to anything: as, the *quantification* of the predicate.—2. The act of determining the quantity.—**Quantification of the predicate**, the attaching of the signs of logical quantity, *every* and *some*, to the predicates of propositions. The resulting propositional forms, according to Hamilton, the protagonist of the opinion that this should be done in formal logic, are: All A is all B; any A is not any B; all A is some B; any A is not some B; some A is all B; some A is not any B; some A is some B; some A is not some B. But these forms include but one decidedly useful addition to the usual scheme (all A is all B), and are systematic only in appearance, as De Morgan has abundantly shown. The doctrine essentially implies that the copula should be considered as a sign of identity; the usual doctrine makes it a sign of inclusion. According to the most modern school of formal logicians, the question is not of great importance, but should be decided against the quantification of the predicate. Aristotle examined and rejected the quantification of the predicate, on the ground that Every A is every B can be true only if A and B are one individual.

The doctrine of the *quantification of the predicate*, set forth in 1827 by Mr. George Bentham, and again set forth under a numerical form by Professor De Morgan, is a doctrine supplementary to that of Aristotle. H. *Spencer*, Study of Sociol., p. 223.

quantify (kwon'ti-fī), *v. t.*; pret. and pp. *quantified*, ppr. *quantifying*. [< NL. **quantificare*, < L. *quantus*, how much, how many, + *-ficare*, < *facere*, make: see *quantity* and *-fy*.] To determine the quantity of; modify or determine with regard to quantity; mark with the sign of quantity: as, to *quantify* a syllable or a verse: more especially a term in logic.—**Quantified proposition.** See *proposition*.

quantitative (kwon'ti-tā-tiv), *a.* [= F. *quantitatif* = Pr. *quantitatiu* = Sp. *cuantitativo* = Pg. It. *quantitativo*, < ML. *quantitativus* (Abelard), < L. *quantita(t-)s*, quantity: see *quantity*.] Relating or having regard to quantity or measurement.

If the thing may be greater or less, . . . then *quantitative* notions enter, and the science must be Mathematical in nature. *Jevons*, Pol. Econ., Int., p. 8.

Perhaps the best *quantitative* verses in our language . . . are to be found in Mother Goose, composed by nurses wholly by ear and beating time as they danced the baby on their knee. *Lowell*, Study Windows, p. 266.

The logic of probability is related to ordinary syllogistic as the *quantitative* to the qualitative branch of the same science. *C. S. Peirce*, Theory of Probable Inference.

Quantitative analysis, in *chem.* See *analysis*.—**Quantitative atrophy.** Same as *simple atrophy*.—**Quantitative feet, meters.** See *accentual feet*, under *accentual*.—**Quantitative geometry.** Same as *metric geometry* (which see, under *geometry*).—**Quantitative logic**, the doctrine of probability.

quantitatively (kwon'ti-tā-tiv-li), *adv.* In a quantitative manner; with regard to quantity.

quantitativeness (kwon'ti-tā-tiv-nes), *n.* The state or condition of being quantitative.

In Geology, in Biology, in Psychology, most of the previsions are qualitative only; and where they are quantitative their *quantitativeness*, never quite definite, is mostly very indefinite. *H. Spencer*, Study of Sociol., p. 45.

quantitive† (kwon'ti-tiv), *a.* Same as *quantitative*. [Rare.]

Compounding and dividing bodies according to *quantitive* parts. *Sir K. Digby*, Man's Soul, iii.

quantitively (kwon'ti-tiv-li), *adv.* So as to be measured by quantity; quantitatively.

quantity (kwon'ti-ti), *n.*; pl. *quantities* (-tiz). [< ME. *quantitee*, *quantite*, < OF. *quantite*, F. *quantité* = Sp. *cantidad* = Pg. *quantidade* = It. *quantità*, < L. *quantita(t-)s*, relative greatness or extent (tr. Gr. ποσότης), < *quantus*, how much, how many, < *quam*, how, in what manner, < *qui*, who, = E. *who*: see *who*, *what*, *how*[1].] 1. The being so much in measure or extent; technically, the intrinsic mode by virtue of which a thing is more or less than another; a system of relationship by virtue of which one thing is said to be more or less than another; magnitude.

Thy zodiak of thin Astralabie is shapen as a compass wich that contienith a large brede, as aftur the *quantite* of thin astralabie. *Chaucer*, Astrolabe, i. 21.

Quantity and number differ only in thought (ratione) from that which has quantity and is numbered. *Descartes*, Prin. of Philos. (tr. by Veitch), ii. § 8.

The science of number is founded on the hypothesis of the distinctness of things; the science of *quantity* is founded on the totally different hypothesis of continuity. *W. K. Clifford*, Lectures, I. 337.

2. In the concrete, an object regarded as more or less; a quantum; any amount, magnitude, or aggregate, in a concrete sense: as, a *quantity* of water: sometimes erroneously used to denote that which should be enumerated rather than measured: as, a *quantity* of people. Any perfectly regular system of objects whose relations are definable in advance, and capable of construction in the imagination, forms a system of quantity capable of being dealt with by mathematical reasoning. The quantities of the mathematician, being constructed according to a definition laid down in advance, are imaginary, and in that sense abstract; but as being objects of the imagination, and not merely of the discursive reason, they are concrete. Mathematical quantities are either discrete (as whole numbers) or continuous. They may also be multiple, as vectors.

Thei don rightfulle Iuggementes in every cause, bothe of riche and pore, smale and grete, aftre the *quantytee* of the trespas that is mys don. *Mandeville*, Travels, p. 287.

Forty thousand brothers
Could not, with all their *quantity* of love,
Make up my sum. *Shak.*, Hamlet, v. 1. 293.

There is a farre greater *quantity* of buildings in this [Exchange] then in ours. *Coryat*, Crudities, I. 212.

Where the ground is seen burning continually about the *quantity* of an acre. *Purchas*, Pilgrimage, p. 19.

Heat, considered with respect to its power of warming things and changing their state, is a *quantity* strictly capable of measurement, and not subject to any variations in quality or in kind. *Clerk Maxwell*, Heat, p. 57.

3. A large or considerable amount.

Warm antiscorbutical plants taken in *quantities* will occasion stinking breath. *Arbuthnot*, Aliments, vi. 7, § 2.

4†. A piece or part, especially a small portion; anything very little or diminutive.

Away, thou rag, thou *quantity*, thou remnant.
Shak., T. of the S., iv. 3. 112.

5†. Proportion; correspondent degree.

Things base and vile, holding no *quantity*,
Love can transpose to form and dignity.
Shak., M. N. D., i. 1. 232.

6. In *anc. orthoëpy*, *pros.*, and *metrics*, the relative time occupied in uttering a vowel or a syllable; that characteristic of a vowel or a syllable by which it is distinguished as long or short; syllabic measure or time; prosodic length. In ancient Greek and Latin pronunciation a long vowel or syllable occupied nearly, or in deliberate enunciation fully, twice the time of a short vowel or syllable, and the grammarians accordingly assumed the average short vowel or syllable as the prosodic unit (mora), and taught that a long vowel or syllable was equal to two short ones. Some vowels or syllables varied in time between these two limits and were called *common*, admitting of metrical use as either longs or shorts. In certain situations (elision, ecthlipsis) vowels were much shorter in pronunciation than the average short, and, although audible, were disregarded in metrical measurement. A syllable was long either by nature or by position (see *long*[1], *a.*, 5 (*a*)). In the English pronunciation of Latin and Greek, quantity in the proper sense is entirely disregarded, except in so far as the length of the penult affects the accent according to the Latin rule; and English writers use the phrase *false quantity* for a false accentuation. Thus, to pronounce *vec-tī′gal vec′ti-gal* is called a "false quantity," but to pronounce the *a* alike in *pāter* and *măter* is not so designated.

All composed in a metre for Catullus,
All in *quantity*, careful of my motion.
Tennyson, Experiments, Hendecasyllabics.

7. In *logic*, that respect in which universal and particular propositions differ. See *proposition*, and *logical quantity*, below.—8. In *elect.*, the amount of electricity which passes through any section of a circuit in a unit of time: more exactly termed the *strength of the current*. A battery is arranged for quantity when the positive poles of all the cells are connected and all the negative poles are connected, so that the current is the maximum when the external resistance is small. —**Absolute quantity**, quantity considered as belonging to an object in itself, without reference to any other.—**Auxiliary quantity.** See *auxiliary*.—**Broken quantity**, discrete quantity.—**Categorical quantity**†, that accident which has parts outside of one another; the quantity of which Aristotle treats in his book of the Categories.—**Categories of quantity.** See *category*, 1.—**Commensurable quantities**, quantities having a common measure.—**Complex quantity**, a multiple quantity, or one which requires two or more numbers to state it; especially, an imaginary quantity of the form A + B*i*, where $i^2 = -1$.—**Compound quantity.** See *compound*[1].—**Constant quantities**, in *math.*, a quantity which remains invariably the same while others increase or decrease; a quantity which, though it may be indeterminate, is not studied in reference to its progressive variation.—**Continuous** or **continued quantity**, a system of concatenated quantity which includes the limit of every convergent series of quantities it contains. See *continuity*, 2.—**Corporeal quantity**, quantity of space or spatial extension, as length, area, volume, etc.—**Definite quantity**, in *logic*, the quantification of a proposition in a more definite way than by the distinction of "some" and "all." There are various systems of definite quantity.—**Dimensive quantity.** Same as *corporeal quantity*.—**Discrete quantity**, quantity proceeding by discrete steps, belonging to a system such that its quantities are susceptible of being connected, one to one, with the whole or a part of the series of whole numbers. The system of ordinal numbers is the most familiar example of discrete quantity; another example is the system of ordinary vulgar fractions.—**Dissimilar quantities**, quantities such that no one is a real multiple of another.—**Dual quantity**, a system of quantity having only two values in any one direction, as in the Boolian algebra.—**Elliptic quantity**, a system of quantity (as the quantity of angles) in which there are no real infinite distances, but in which any quantity on being sufficiently increased returns into itself: so called because the ellipse has no real point at infinity.—**Extensive quantity.** See *extensive*.—**External** or **extrinsic quantity.** See *external*.—**Flowing quantity.** See *flowing*. —**Heterogeneous quantities.** See *heterogeneous*.—**Hyperbolic quantity**, a system of quantity containing such quantities that there are, in some directions at least, two different absolute limits, generally +∞ and −∞. Thus, if it were the property of a yardstick to shorten on receding from a fixed center, this might happen according to such a law that no finite number of layings down of the yardstick could carry the measurement beyond two limits in every, or in some, directions. Points lying beyond these, if such there were, would be at imaginary distances. Such measurement would make a system of hyperbolic quantity.—**Imaginary quantity.** See *imaginary*.—**Impossible quantity.** Same as *imaginary quantity*.—**Improper quantity.** Same as *intensive quantity*. Reid defines *improper quantity* as that which cannot be measured by its own kind—that is, everything not extension, duration, number, nor proportion.—**Incommensurable quantities.** See *incommensurable*.—**Indeterminate quantity.** See *indeterminate*.—**Inference of transposed quantity.** See *inference*.—**Infinite quantity**, a quantity infinitely greater than every measurable quantity. See *infinite*.—**Infinitesimal quantity**, a quantity infinitely less than every measurable quantity. See *infinitesimal*, *n.*—**Intensive quantity.** See *intensive*.—**Internal quantity.** See *internal*.—**Intrinsic quantity**, the older name of *intensive quantity*.—**Irrational quantity**, a quantity not expressible by any whole number or fraction, but usually by means of a square or higher root of a rational quantity; in Euclid, however, by an irrational quantity is meant one incommensurable with the unit of the same kind. In this phrase, *irrational* [tr. Gr. ἄλογος] means 'inexpressible'; it does not mean 'absurd,' though these quantities are called *surds*.—**Like quantities**, quantities one of which multiplied by a scalar quantity gives the other.—**Limited quantity**, a system of quantities all finite, and having an absolute maximum and minimum in every direction.—**Logical quantity**, that character by virtue of which one term contains or is contained by another, and that in three senses: (*a*) *Quantity of extension*, or logical breadth, a relative character of a term such that when it is in excess the term is predicable of all the subjects of which another is predicable, and of more besides; or a relative character of a concept such that when it is in excess the concept is applicable in all the cases in which another is applicable. (*b*) *Quantity of comprehension* or *intension*, or logical depth, a relative character of a term such that when it is in excess the term has all the predicates of another term, and more besides; or a relative character of a proposition such that when it is in excess the proposition is followed by all the consequents of another proposition, and more besides. (*c*) *Quantity of science* (Aquinas) or *of information*, a relative character of a concept such that when it is in excess it has all the subjects and predicates of another concept, and more besides, owing to its being in a mind which has more knowledge. *Logical quantity* is to be distinguished from the *quantity of a proposition*.—**Mathematical quantities.** See *mathematical*.—**Measurable quantity**, a system of quantities every one of which can be stated to any desired degree of approximation by the sums of numerical multiples and submultiples of a finite number of units; a system of quantities embracing only finite quantities together with certain isolated infinities.—**Measure of a quantity.** See *measure*.—**Multiple quantity**, a quantity which can be exactly expressed only by means of two or more numbers, as a geographical position. —**Natural quantity**, quantity in a sense more concrete than the mathematical; quantity as joined to sensible matter, as when we speak of two different but equal quantities of water or lead.—**Negative quantity**, a fictitious quantity in mathematics, in most cases inconceivable, but never involving any logical contradiction in itself, supposed to belong to a line of quantity continuing the line of ordinary or positive quantity below zero for an infinite distance. In many cases a negative quantity has an interpretation: thus, the negative of a dollar owned is a dollar owed, the negative of a temperature above zero is the same degree of temperature below zero, etc.—**Numeral quantity**, number.—**Parabolic quantity**, a quantity belonging to such a system of quantity that on increasing through infinity it immediately reappears on the negative side of zero. Such are Cartesian coördinates in ordinary geometry.—**Permanent quantity.** See *permanent*.—**Physical quantity**, any character in nature susceptible of more or less, such as velocity, atomic weight, elasticity, heat, electric strength of current, etc.—**Positive quantity.** See *positive*.—**Predicamental quantity.** See *predicamental*.—**Proper quantity.** Same as *extensive quantity*. —**Propositional quantity**, the quantity of a proposition in logic. See *logical quantity*, above.—**Protensive quantity**, duration in time.—**Quantity of action**, the line-integral of the momentum.—**Quantity of an eclipse.** See *eclipse*.—**Quantity of curvature**, the reciprocal of the radius of curvature.—**Quantity of electricity**, in *electrostatics*, the amount of electricity upon a charged body. It depends upon the capacity of the body, which, in the case of a sphere, is proportional to the radius (see *capacity*), and upon the potential of the electricity. It is numerically equal to the product of these two factors. In electrodynamics it is measured (in coulombs) by the amount of electricity furnished by a current in one second. —**Quantity of estate**, in *law*, the time during which the right of enjoyment of the property in question is to continue.—**Quantity of heat.** See *heat*, 2.—**Quantity of magnetism**, the strength of a magnetic pole; the force it exerts upon an equal pole at the unit distance.—**Quantity of matter**, the mass, as measured by weighing in a balance.—**Quantity of motion.** See *motion*.—**Quesitive quantity**, quantity expressed by an interrogative numeral. —**Radical quantities.** See *radical*.—**Rational quantity**, a quantity expressible by a whole number or fraction multiplied by the unit of the same kind; in Euclid, a commensurable quantity.—**Real quantity**, that kind of quantity which extends from zero to infinity, and from infinity through the whole series of negative values to zero again. —**Reciprocal of a quantity.** See *reciprocal*.—**Reciprocal quantities.** See *reciprocal*.—**Scalar quantity**, the ratio between two quantities of the same kind; a real number. This is the definition of Hamilton, but subsequent writers sometimes include imaginaries among scalars.—**Semi-infinite quantity**, a system of quantity which is limited at one end and extends to infinity in the other.—**Similar quantities**, quantities of the same kind whose ratios are numbers.—**Sophistic quantity**, an imaginary quantity.—**Superinfinite quantity**, a system of quantity which extends through infinity into a new region. Hyperbolic quantity is a special kind of superinfinite quantity in which there are only two regions.—**Syncategorematic quantity**, quantity as expressed by a syncategorematic word, or generally by any word not a noun.—**Terminal quantity**, in *logic*, the quantity of a term, as opposed to the quantity of a proposition.—**Transcendental quantity**, intensive quantity as opposed to predicamental quantity: so called because different from the quantity treated by Aristotle under the category of quantity.—**Transposed quantity**, logical quantity transposed from one subject in the premise to another in the conclusion.—**Unidimensional quantity**, a system of quantities all of the same kind, otherwise called *simple quantity*.—**Unlike quantities**, quantities which have not a numerical ratio between them.—**Unlimited quantity**, a system of quantities such that, any two A and B being given, a third C exists such that B lies between A and C; a system of quantity which has no absolute maximum nor minimum in any direction.—**Unreal quantity**, an imaginary quantity.—**Variable quantity**, a quantity whose progressive changes are under consideration.—**Vector quantity**, the quantity which belongs to a right line considered as having direction as well as length, but which is equal for all parallel lines of equal length; any quantity capable of representation by a directed right line, without considering its position in space; a quantity whose square is a negative scalar.—**Virtual quantity.** Same as *intensive quantity*.

quantity-culture (kwon′ti-ti-kul″tūr), *n.* See the quotation.

Quantity-culture . . . means a culture, whether pure or not, where a great quantity or bulk of bacteria are growing. *Hueppe*, Bacteriological Investigations (trans.), p. 5.

quantity-fuse (kwon′ti-ti-fūz), *n.* See *fuse*[2].

quantivalence (kwon-tiv′a-lens), *n.* [< *quantivalen(t)* + *-ce*.] In *chem.*, the combining power or value of an atom as compared with that of the hydrogen atom, which is taken as the unit of measure: same as *valence*. Also called *atomicity*.

quantivalency (kwon-tiv′a-len-si), *n.* [As *quantivalence* (see *-cy*).] Same as *quantivalence*.

quantivalent (kwon-tiv′a-lent), *a.* [< L. *quantus*, how much, how many (see *quantity*), + *valen(t-)s*, ppr. of *valere*, be strong: see *valiant*.] Chemically equivalent; having the same saturating or combining power.—**Quantivalent ratio.** Same as *oxygen ratio* (which see, under *ratio*).

quantoid (kwon′toid), *n.* [As *quant(ic)* + *-oid*.] The left-hand side of a linear differential equation whereof the right-hand side is zero.

quantong, *n.* Same as *quandang*.

quantum (kwon′tum), *n.*; pl. *quanta* (-tä). [L., neut. sing. of *quantus*, how much, how many: see *quantity*.] 1. That which has quantity; a concrete quantity.

The objects of outer sense are all *quanta*, in so far as they occupy space, and so also are the objects of inner sense, in so far as they occupy time.
E. Caird, Philos. of Kant, p. 411.

2. A prescribed, proper, or sufficient amount.

In judging the *quantum* of the church's portion, the world thinks every thing too much.
Jer. Taylor, Works (ed. 1835), I. 78.

Quantum meruit, as much as one has merited or deserved; the measure of recovery in law for services the price of which was not fixed by contract.—**Quantum sufficit**, as much as is sufficient. Abbreviated *q. s.*, or *quant. suf.*—**Quantum valebat**, as much as it was worth; the measure of recovery in law for goods sold when no price was fixed by the contract.

quantuplicity† (kwon-tū-plis′i-ti), *n.* [Irreg. (after *duplicity*, *triplicity*, etc.) < **quantuplex*, < L. *quantus*, how much, + *plicare*, fold.] Same as *quotity*. *Wallis.*

quap[1], **quop**[1] (kwop), *v. i.* [< ME. *quappen* = Norw. *kveppa* (pret. *kvapp*, *kropp*), shake, quake, rock; akin to *quave*, *quaver*. Hence later *quab*, *quob*[1], q. v.] Same as *quab*[1]. [Prov. Eng.]

quap[2]†, *n.* Same as *quab*[2], 2.

Gò, *goi* [It.], a fish called a *quap* [a *quap*-fish, ed. 1611], which is poison to man, and man to him. *Florio*, 1598.

quaquaversal (kwā-kwā-vėr′sal), *a.* [< NL. *quaquaversus*, < L. *quaqua*, wheresoever, abl. fem. sing. of *quisquis*, whoever, whatever (< *quis*, who, + *quis*, who), + *versus*, pp. of *vertere*, turn, incline (see *verse*), + *-al*.] Inclined outward in all directions from a central point or area: used chiefly in geology, as in the phrase *quaquaversal dip*, a dipping in all directions from a central area.

quaquaversally (kwā-kwā-vėr′sal-i), *adv.* In a quaquaversal manner; in all directions from a central point or area.

The outer walls are stony ridges rising from 470 to 610 feet above sea-level, and declining *quaquaversally* to the fertile plateau which, averaging 400 feet high, forms the body of the island. *Encyc. Brit.*, XIV. 695.

quaquaversus (kwā-kwā-vėr′sus), *a.* Same as *quaquaversal*. *Brewster*, Phil. Trans., 1852, p. 472.

quaquiner†, *n.* A form of *quaviver*.

There is a little fish in the form of a scorpion, and of the size of the fish *quaquiner* [tr. L. *aranei piscis*].
N. Bailey, tr. of Erasmus's Colloq., p. 393. (*Davies.*)

quar[1]†, *n.* [< ME. *quar*, *quarre*, etc.: see *quarry*[1].] An obsolete form of *quarry*[2].

When temples lye like batter'd *quarrs*,
Rich in their ruin'd sepulchers.
P. Fletcher, Poems, p. 136. (*Halliwell.*)

A chrysolite, a gem, the very agate
Of state and policy, cut from the *quar*
Of Machiavel. *B. Jonson*, Magnetick Lady, i. 1.

The whole citie [Paris], together with the suburbes, is situate upon a *quarre* of free stone.
Coryat, Crudities, I. 27.

quar[1]†, *v. t.* [< *quar*[1], *n.*] To block up.

But as a miller, having ground his grist,
Lets down the flood-gates with a speedy fall,
And *quarring* up the passage therewithal.
W. Browne, Britannia's Pastorals.

quar[2]†, *n.* An obsolete form of *quarry*[3].

When the Falcon (stooping thunder-like)
With sudden souse her [a duck] to the ground shall strike,
And, with the stronk, make on the sense-less ground
The gut-less Quar once, twice, or thrice rebound.
Sylvester, tr. of Du Bartas's Weeks, ii., The Lawe.

quar[3] (kwär), *v. i.* [Origin uncertain.] To coagulate: said of milk in the female breast. *Halliwell.* [Prov. Eng.]

(Garden mint) is very good to be applied to the breastes that are stretched forth and swollen and full of milke, for it slaketh and softeneth the same, and keepeth the mylke from *quarring* and crudding in the brest.
Lyte, Dodoens, p. 246 (quoted in Cath. Ang., p. 84).

quarantinable (kwor′an-tēn-a-bl), *a.* [< *quarantine* + *-able.*] Admitting of quarantine; amenable to or controlled by quarantine.

quarantine (kwor′an-tēn), *n.* [Formerly also *quarantain, quarantaine*, also *carentane* (Lent); = D. *quarantaine, karanteine* = G. *quarantäne* = Sw. *karantän* = Dan. *karantäne* (< F.) = Sp. *cuarentena* = Pg. *quarentena* = Pr. *quarantena, carantena*, < OF. *quarantaine, quarentaine, quarantine*, F. *quarantaine* = Turk. *karantina*, < It. *quarantina, quarentina, quarantana, quarentana*, a number of forty, a period of forty days, esp. such a period of forty days, more or less, for the detention and observation of goods and persons suspected of infection, < ML. *quarantena, quarentena* (after Rom.), a period of forty days, Lent, quarantine, also a measure of forty rods (see *quarentene*), < L. *quadraginta* (> It. *quaranta* = F. *quarante*), forty, = E. *forty*: see *forty*.] 1. A period of forty days. Specifically — (*a*) The season of Lent. (*b*) In *law*, a period of forty days during which the widow of a man dying seized of land at common law may remain in her husband's chief mansion-house, and during which time her dower is to be assigned. (*c*) See def. 2.

2. A term, originally of forty days, but now of varying length according to the exigencies of the case, during which a ship arriving in port and known or suspected to be infected with a malignant contagious disease is obliged to forbear all intercourse with the place where she arrives. The United States first adopted a quarantine law in February, 1799. This law required federal officers to assist in executing State or municipal quarantine regulations. On April 29th, 1878, a national quarantine law was enacted, authorizing the establishment in certain contingencies of national quarantines.

To perform their *quarantine* (for thirty days, as Sir Rd. Browne expressed it in the order of the Council, contrary to the import of the word, though in the general acceptation it signifies now the thing, not the time spent in doing it).
Pepys, Diary, Nov. 26, 1663.

We came into the port of Argostoli on the twenty-second, and went to the town; I desired to be ashoar as one performing *quarantain*.
Pococke, Description of the East, II. ii. 179.

3. The enforced isolation of individuals and certain objects coming, whether by sea or by land, from a place where dangerous communicable disease is presumably or actually present, with a view to limiting the spread of the malady. *Quain.*—4. Hence, by extension: (*a*) The isolation of any person suffering or convalescing from acute contagious disease. [Colloq.] (*b*) The isolation of a dwelling or of a town or district in which a contagious disease exists.

It was . . . a relief when neighbours no longer considered the house in *quarantine* [after typhus].
George Eliot, Middlemarch, xxvii.

5. A place or station where quarantine is enforced.

He happened to mention that he had been three years in *Quarantine*, keeping watch over infected travellers.
B. *Taylor*, Lands of the Saracen, p. 26.

6. The restriction within limits awarded to naval cadets as a punishment. [U. S.]—**Quarantine flag**, a yellow flag displayed by a ship, to indicate that she has been placed in quarantine or that there is contagious disease on board.—**Quarantine of observation.** See the quotation.

A *quarantine of observation*, which is usually for six or three days, and is imposed on vessels with clean bills, may be performed at any port.
Encyc. Brit., XX. 154.

Shot-gun quarantine, forcible quarantine not duly authorized by law. [U. S.]

quarantine (kwor′an-tēn), *v. t.*; pret. and pp. *quarantined*, ppr. *quarantining*. [< *quarantine*, *n.*] 1. To put under quarantine, in any sense of that word.—2. Figuratively, to isolate, as by authority.

The business of these [ministers] is with human nature, and from exactly that are they *quarantined* for years.
W. M. Baker, New Timothy, p. 13.

quare†, *n.* An obsolete form of *quire*[1].

quare impedit (kwā′rē im′pe-dit). [So called from the L. words *quare impedit*, contained in the writ: L. *quare*, why (orig. two words, *quā rē*, for what cause: *quā*, abl. fem. of *quis*, who, what; *rē*, abl. of *res*, thing, cause); *impedit*, 3d pers. sing. pres. ind. of *impedire*, hinder, impede: see *impede*.] In *Eng. law*, the writ (requiring defendant to show why he hindered plaintiff) used to try a right of presentation to a benefice.

quarel†, *n.* See *quarrel*[1], *quarrel*[2], *quarrel*[3].

quarelet†, *n.* An obsolete form of *quarrelet.*

quarellet†, *n.* An obsolete form of *quarrel*[1].

quarentene†, *n.* [< ML. *quarentena* (sc. *terræ*), a furlong, an area of forty rods: see *quarantine.*] A square furlong. *Pearson*, Historical Maps of Eng., p. 51.

quarer†, *n.* Same as *quarry*[2].

quarier†, *n.* See *quarrier*[2].

quark (kwärk), *n.* [Imitative; cf. *quawk.*] Same as *quawk.*

quarl[1] (kwärl), *v.* A dialectal form of *quarrel*[1].

quarl[2] (kwärl), *n.* [Prob. a contr. form of *quarrel*[2] (applied, as *square* is often applied, to an object of different shape).] In *brickmaking*, a piece of fire-clay in the shape of a segment of a circle or similar form: it is used in constructing arches for melting-pots, covers for retorts, and the like.

The erection of nine six-ton pots requires 15,000 common bricks, 10,000 fire-bricks, 160 feet of *quarles*, 80 fire-clay blocks, and 5 tons of fire-clay. *Ure*, Dict., III. 67.

The cover [of a retort] is usually formed of segments of stoneware, or fireclay *quarls*, bound together with iron.
Spons' Encyc. Manuf., I. 156.

quarl[3] (kwärl), *n.* [Origin obscure.] A medusa or jellyfish.

Some on the stony star-fish ride, . . .
And some on the jellied *quarl*, that flings
At once a thousand streamy stings.
J. R. Drake, Culprit Fay, st. 13.

quar-man†, *n.* A quarryman.

The sturdy *Quar-man* with steel-headed Cones
And massie Sledges slenteth out the stones.
Sylvester, tr. of Du Bartas's Weeks, ii., The Magnificence.

quaroft†, *adv.* An obsolete dialectal form of *whereof. Halliwell.*

quar-pit†, *n.* A stone-pit; a quarry. *Whalley.* [West of Eng.]

quarr†, *n.* and *v.* See *quar*[1].

quarre†, *a.* A Middle English form of *quarry*[1].

quarrel[1] (kwor′el), *n.* [Early mod. E. also *quarel, querel*; < ME. *quarel, quarell, quarelle, querel, querele*, < OF. *querele*, F. *querelle* = Pr. *querela, querella* = Sp. *querella* = Pg. *querela* = It. *querela*, < L. *querela*, a complaining, a complaint, < *queri*, pp. *questus*, complain, lament. Cf. *querent*[1], *querimony, querulous*, etc., from the same source.] 1†. A complaint; a lament; lamentation.

Whennes comyn elles alle thyse foreyne Complayntes or *quereles* of pletynges? *Chaucer*, Boëthius, iii. prose 3.

Thou lyf, thou luste, thou mannis hele,
Biholde my cause and my *querele*!
Gower, MS. Soc. Antiq. 134, f. 39. (*Halliwell.*)

As his frendes wepte for hym lyenge on the byere they sayd with swete and deevoute *querelles*, which suffred her devoute seruant to deye without confession and penaunce.
Golden Legend, quoted in Prompt. Parv., p. 419.

If I shulde here answere to all these *querels* particularly and as the woorthynesse of the thynge requireth, I myght fynde matter sufficient to make a volume of iuste quantitie, and perhappes be tedious to summe.
R. Eden (First Books on America, ed. Arber, p. 53).

2. An accusation; in *law*, a complaint; an action, real or personal.

The wars were scarce begun but he, in fear
Of *quarrels* 'gainst his life, fled from his country.
Beau. and Fl., Laws of Candy, i. 1.

3. Cause, occasion, or motive of complaint, objection, dispute, contention, or debate; the basis or ground of being at variance with another; hence, the cause or side of a certain party at variance with another.

My *quarell* is growndid vppon right,
Which gevith me corage for to fight.
Generydes (E. E. T. S.), l. 3210.

Methinks I could not die anywhere so contented as in the King's company; his cause being just and his *quarrel* honourable. *Shak.*, Hen. V., iv. 1. 133.

Herodias had a *quarrel* against him. Mark vi. 19.

He thought he had a good *quarrel* to attack him.
Holinshed.

Rejoice and be merry in the Lord; be stout in his cause and *quarrel*.
J. Bradford, Letters (Parker Soc., 1853), II. 249.

What is your *quarrel* to "shallops"?
Gray, Letters, I. 301.

4†. Cause in general; reason; plea; ground.

I undyrstand that Mastre Fytzwater hathe a syster, a mayd, to mary . . . ye may telle hym, synse he wyll have my servyse, . . . syche a bargayn myght be mad; . . . for then he shold be swer that I shold not be flyttyng, and I had syche a *quarell* to kepe me at home.
Paston Letters, III. 164.

Wives are young men's mistresses, companions for middle age, and old men's nurses, so as a man may have a *quarrel* to marry when he will.
Bacon, Marriage and Single Life (ed. 1887).

5. Altercation; an altercation; an angry dispute; a wrangle; a brawl.

If I can fasten but one cup upon him,
With that which he hath drunk to-night already,
He'll be as full of *quarrel* and offence
As my young mistress' dog. *Shak.*, Othello, ii. 3. 52.

If upon a sudden *quarrel* two persons fight, and one of them kills the other, this is manslaughter.
Blackstone, Com., IV. xiv.

6. A breach of friendship or concord; open variance between parties; a feud.

England was, from the force of mere dynastic causes, dragged into the *quarrel*. *Freeman*, Norman Conq., V. 63.

The Persian Ambassador has had a *quarrel* with the court. *Greville*, Memoirs, June 25, 1819.

7†. A quarreler. [Rare.]

Though 't [pomp] be temporal,
Yet if that *quarrel*, fortune, do divorce
It from the bearer, 'tis a sufferance panging.
Shak., Hen. VIII., ii. 3. 14.

Double quarrel, *eccles.*, a complaint of a clerk to the archbishop against an inferior ordinary, for delay of justice.

No *double quarrel* shall hereafter be granted out of any of the archbishop's courts at the suit of any minister whosoever, except he shall first take his personal oath that the said eight-and-twenty days at the least are expired, etc. *95th Canon of the Church of England* (1603).

To pick a quarrel. See *pick*[1].—**To take up a quarrel**†, to compose or adjust a quarrel; settle a dispute.

I knew when seven justices could not *take up a quarrel*, but when the parties were met themselves, one of them thought but of an If, . . . and they shook hands.
Shak., As you Like it, v. 4. 104.

=**Syn. 5 and 6.** *Quarrel, Altercation, Affray, Fray, Mêlée, Brawl, Broil, Scuffle, Wrangle, Squabble, Feud.* A *quarrel* is a matter of ill feeling and hard words in view of supposed wrong: it stops just short of blows; any use beyond this is now figurative. *Altercation* is the spoken part of a quarrel, the parties speaking alternately. An *altercation* is thus a quarrelsome dispute between two persons or two sides. *Affray* and *fray* express a quarrel that has come to blows in a public place: they are often used of the struggles of war, implying personal activity. *Mêlée* emphasizes the confusion in which those engaged in an affray or struggle are mingled. *Brawl* emphasizes the unbecoming character and noisiness of the quarrel; while *broil* adds the idea of entanglement, perhaps with several: two are enough for a *brawl*; at least three are needed for a *broil*: as, a *brawl* with a neighbor; a neighborhood *broil*. A *scuffle* is, in this connection, a confused or undignified struggle, at close quarters, between two, to throw each other down, or a similar struggle of many. A *wrangle* is a severe, unreasoning, and noisy, perhaps confused, altercation. A *squabble* is a petty wrangle, but is even less dignified or irrational. A *feud* is a deeply rooted animosity between two sets of kindred, two parties, or possibly two persons. See *animosity*.

quarrel[1] (kwor′el), *v.*; pret. and pp. *quarreled* or *quarrelled*, ppr. *quarreling* or *quarrelling*. [Early mod. E. also *quarel, querel*; < OF. *quereler, quereller*, complain, complain of, accuse, sue, claim, F. *quereller*, quarrel with, scold, refl. have a quarrel, quarrel, = Pr. *querelhar* = Sp. *querellar*, complain, lament, bewail, complain of, = Pg. *querelar*, complain, = It. *querelare*, complain of, accuse, indict, refl. complain, lament, < L. *querelari*, make a complaint, ML. *querelare*, complain, complain of, accuse, < L. *querela*, complaint, quarrel: see *quarrel*[1], *n.*] I. *intrans.* 1. To find cause of complaint; find fault; cavil.

There are many which affirme that they haue sayled rownd abowt Cuba. But whether it bee so or not, or whether, enuyinge the good fortune of this man, they seeke occasions of *querelinge* ageynste hym, I can not iudge.
R. Eden, tr. of Peter Martyr (First Books on America, [ed. Arber, p. 90).

I would not *quarrel* with a slight mistake.
Roscommon, tr. of Horace's Art of Poetry.

Viator. I hope we have no more of these Alps to pass over.
Piscator. No, no, Sir, only this ascent before you, which you see is not very uneasy, and then you will no more *quarrel* with your way. *Cotton*, in Walton's Angler, ii. 232.

All are prone to *quarrel*
With fate, when worms destroy their gourd,
Or mildew spoils their laurel.
F. Locker, The Jester's Moral.

2. To dispute angrily or violently; contend; squabble.

Not only, sir, this your all-licensed fool,
But other of your insolent retinue
Do hourly carp and *quarrel*. *Shak.*, Lear, i. 4. 222.

And Jealousy, and Fear, and Wrath, and War
Quarrel'd, although in heaven, about their place.
J. Beaumont, Psyche, i. 105.

If we grumbled a little now and then, it was soon over, for we were never fond enough to *quarrel*.
Sheridan, The Duenna, i. 3.

3†. To disagree; be incongruous or incompatible; fail to be in accordance, in form or essence

Some defect in her
Did *quarrel* with the noblest grace she owed,
And put it to the foil. *Shak.*, Tempest, iii. 1. 45.

Some things arise of strange and *quarrelling* kind,
The forepart lion, and a snake behind.
Cowley, Davideis, ii.

To **quarrel with one's bread and butter**, to fall out with, or pursue a course prejudicial to, one's own material interests or means of subsistence. =**Syn.** 2. To jangle, bicker, spar.

II. *trans.* **1.** To find fault with; challenge; reprove, as a fault, error, and the like. [Scotch.]

Say on, my bonny boy,
Ye'se nae be *quarrell'd* by me.
Young Akin (Child's Ballads, I. 181).

2†. To disagree or contend with.

They [Pharisees] envied the work in the substance, but they *quarrel* the circumstance. *Donne*, Sermons, xviii.

Fitz. You will not slight me, madam?
Wit. Nor you'll not *quarrel* me?
B. *Jonson*, Devil is an Ass, iv. 3.

3. To affect, by quarreling, in a manner indicated by a word or words connected: as, to *quarrel* a man out of his estate or rights.

quarrel[2] (kwor'el), *n.* [< ME. *quarel*, < OF. *quarrel, quarel, carrel*, later *quarreau*, F. *carreau* = Pr. *cairel* = Sp. *cuadrillo*, a small square, = It. *quadrello*, a square tile, a diamond, a crossbow-bolt, < ML. *quadrellus*, a square tile, a crossbow-bolt, dim. of L. *quadrum*, a square: see *quadrum*.] **1.** A small square, or lozenge, or diamond; a tile or pane of a square or lozenge form. Specifically—(*a*) A small tile or paving-stone of square or lozenge form. (*b*) A small lozenge-shaped pane of glass, or a square pane set diagonally, used in glazing a window, especially in the latticed window-frames formerly used in England and elsewhere.

And let your skynner cut both ye sortes of the skynnes in smale peces triangle wyse, lyke halfe a *quarell* of a glasse wyndowe.
Babees Book (E. E. T. S.), p. 247.

We are right Cornish diamonds.
Trim. Yes, we cut
Out *quarrels* and break glasses where we go.
Middleton and Rowley, Fair [Quarrel, ii. 2.

Quarrels of Window.—The form illustrated is the "short quarrel," the acute angle of the pane measuring 77° 29'.

2. A bolt or arrow having a square or four-edged head, especially a cross-bow-bolt of such form.

I sigh [saw] yet arwis reyne,
And grounde *quarels* sharpe of steele.
Rom. of the Rose, l. 1823.

Schot sore alle y-vere;
Quarels, arwes, they fly smerte;
The fyched Men thruȝ heed & herte.
Arthur (ed. Furnivall), l. 461.

A seruaunt . . . was found shooting a *quarrell* of a crossebow with a letter.
Hakluyt's Voyages, II. 87.

Here be two arblasts, comrades, with windlaces and *quarrels*—to the barbican with you, and see you drive each bolt through a Saxon brain!
Scott, Ivanhoe, xxviii.

3. An instrument with a head shaped like that of the crossbow-bolt. (*a*) A glaziers' diamond. (*b*) A kind of graver. (*c*) A stone-masons' chisel.

Quarrel[2], 2.

quarrel[3]† (kwor'el), *n.* [Early mod. E. also *quarrell, quarel*; < ME. *quarelle, querelle*, a quarry, a var. of *quarrer*, < OF. *quarrere*, a quarry: see *quarry*[2].] A quarry where stone is cut. *Cath. Ang.*, p. 296.

quarreler, quarreller (kwor'el-ėr), *n.* [< ME. *querelour*, < OF. *querelour, quereleur*, F. *querelleur*, < *quereler*, quarrel: see *quarrel*[1], *v.*] One who quarrels, wrangles, or fights.

Quenche, fals *querelour*, the quene of heven the will quite!
Booke of Precedence (E. E. T. S., extra ser.), i. 66.

Besides that he's a fool, he's a great *quarreller*.
Shak., T. N., i. 3. 31.

quarrelet (kwor'el-et), *n.* [< *quarrel*[2] + *-et*.] A small square or diamond-shaped piece; a small lozenge.

Some ask'd how pearls did grow and where?
Then spoke I to my girle
To part her lips, and shew'd them there
The *quarelets* of pearl.
Herrick, The Rock of Rubies and Quarrie of Pearls.

quarreller, *n.* See *quarreler*.

quarrelous†, quarrellous† (kwor'el-us), *a.* [Also *quarellous*; < ME. **querelous*, < OF. *querelos, quereleux*, F. *querelleux*, < *querele*, quarrel: see *quarrel*[1].] Apt or disposed to quarrel; petulant; easily provoked to enmity or contention; of things, causing or proceeding from quarreling.

Neither angry without cause, neither *quarellous* without colour. *Lyly*, Euphues, Anat. of Wit, p. 145.

As *quarrelous* as the weasel.
Shak., Cymbeline, iii. 4. 162.

And who can tell what huge outrages might amount of such *quarrelous* and tumultuous causes?
G. Harvey, Foure Letters, ii.

quarrel-pane (kwor'el-pān), *n.* Same as *quarrel*[2], 1 (*b*).

Roland Græme hath . . . broke a *quarrel-pane* of glass in the turret window. *Scott*, Abbot, xxxiv.

quarrel-picker (kwor'el-pik″ėr), *n.* **1.** One who picks quarrels; one who is quarrelsome. [Rare.]—**2.** A glazier: with punning allusion to *quarrel*[2], *n.*, 3 (*a*).

quarrelsome (kwor'el-sum), *a.* [< *quarrel* + *-some*.] Apt to quarrel; given to brawls and contention; inclined to petty fighting; easily irritated or provoked to contest; irascible; choleric; petulant; also, proceeding from or characteristic of such a disposition.

He would say I lied: this is called the Countercheck *Quarrelsome*. *Shak.*, As you Like it, v. 4. 85.

quarrelsomely (kwor'el-sum-li), *adv.* In a quarrelsome manner; with a quarrelsome temper; petulantly.

quarrelsomeness (kwor'el-sum-nes), *n.* The state of being quarrelsome; disposition to engage in contention and brawls; petulance.

Although a man by his *quarrelsomeness* should for once have been engaged in a bad action . . .
Bentham, Introd. to Morals and Legislation, xii. 33, note.

quarrender (kwor'en-dėr), *n.* A kind of apple. *Davies.* [Prov. Eng.]

He . . . had no ambition whatsoever beyond pleasing his father and mother, getting by honest means the maximum of red *quarrenders* and mazard cherries, and going to sea when he was big enough.
Kingsley, Westward Ho, i.

quarrer†, *n.* A Middle English form of *quarry*[2].

quarriable (kwor'i-a̤-bl), *a.* [< *quarry*[1] + *-able*.] Capable of being quarried.

The arable soil, the *quarriable* rock. *Emerson.*

quarried (kwor'id), *a.* [< *quarry*[1] + *-ed*[2].] Paved with quarries. See *quarry*[1], *n.*, 1 (*a*).

In those days the *quarried* parlour was innocent of a carpet. *George Eliot*, Essays, p. 148.

quarrier[1] (kwor'i-ėr), *n.* [< ME. *quaryour, querrour*, < OF. *quarrier*, < LL. *quadratarius*, a stone-cutter, < *quadratus*, squared (*saxum quadratum*, a squared stone): see *quarry*[2]. Cf. LL. *quadrator*, a stone-cutter, lit. 'squarer,' < *quadrare*, make square: see *quadrator, quadrate*.] One who works in a quarry; a quarryman.

Aboute hym lefte he no masoun
That stoon coude leye, ne *querrour*.
Rom. of the Rose, l. 4149.

The men of Rome, which were the conquerors of all nations about them, were now of warriors become *quarriers*, hewers of stone and day laborers.
Holland, tr. of Livy, p. 35. (*Davies.*)

When in wet weather the *quarrier* can sit chipping his stone into portable shape. *Harper's Mag.*, LXX. 243.

quarrier[2]**†, quarier†,** *n.* [Also *currier* (see *currier*[2]); < OF. **quarier*, ult. < L. *quadratus*, square: see *quarry*[1], *quart*[1], *square*.] A wax candle, consisting of a square lump of wax with a wick in the center. Also called *quarion*.

All the endes of *quarriers* and prickets.
Ord. and Reg., p. 295. (*Halliwell.*)

To light the waxen *quariers*
The auncient nurce is prest.
Romeus and Juliet. (*Nares.*)

quarry[1] (kwor'i), *a.* and *n.* [Early mod. E. also *quarrey, quary*; < ME. *quarry, quarrey, quarre*, square, thick, < OF. *quarre*, F. *carré*, square, < L. *quadratus*, squared, square; as a noun, L. *quadratum*, neut., a square, a quadrate, LL. *quadratus*, m., a square: see *quadrate*, of which *quarry*[1] is a doublet.] **I.†** *a.* **1.** Square; quadrate.

Quarré scheld, gode swerd of steil,
And launce stef, biteand wel.
Arthour and Merlin, p. 111. (*Halliwell.*)

The simplest form of mould is that employed for stamping flat diamond-shaped pieces of glass for *quarry* glazing.
Glass-making, p. 88.

The windows were of small *quarry* panes.
Quarterly Rev., CXLVI. 47.

2. Stout; fat; corpulent.

Thycke man he was yron, bot he nas noȝt wel long;
Quarry he was, and wel ymade vorto be strong.
Rob. of Gloucester, p. 412.

A *quarry*, fat man, obesus. *Coles*, Lat. Dict. (*Halliwell.*)

II. *n.*; pl. *quarries* (-iz). **1.** A square or lozenge. Specifically—(*a*) A small square tile or paving-stone: same as *quarrel*[2], 1 (*a*).

To be sure a stone floor was not the pleasantest to dance on, but then, most of the dancers had known what it was to enjoy a Christmas dance on kitchen *quarries*.
George Eliot.

(*b*) A small square or lozenge-shaped pane of glass: same as *quarrel*[2], 1 (*b*).

The Thieves, . . . taking out some *Quaries* of the Glass, put their Hands in and rob the Houses of their Window Curtains.
Quoted in *Ashton's* Social Life in Reign of Queen Anne, [I. 74.

Hartley's rolled coloured-plate, and *quarries* stamped by mechanical pressure, are also largely used where translucency is required without transparency.
Glass-making, p. 92.

2†. A bolt or arrow with a square head: same as *quarrel*[2], 2.

quarry[2] (kwor'i), *n.*; pl. *quarries* (-iz). [< ME. *quarrye*, also *quar*, altered, by confusion with *quarry*[1], from earlier *quarrer, quarrere, quarer, quarere*, < OF. *quarriere*, F. *carrière*, < ML. *quadraria*, a quarry, a place where stones are cut or squared (suggested by LL. *quadratarius*, a stone-cutter, lit. 'a squarer': see *quarrier*[1]), < L. *quadratus*, square, pp. of *quadrare*, make square, square: see *quarry*[1], *quadrate*.] A place, cavern, or pit where stones are dug from the earth, or separated, as by blasting with gunpowder, from a large mass of rock. The word *mine* is generally applied to the excavations from which metals, metalliferous ores, and coal are taken; from *quarries* are taken all the various materials used for building, as marble, freestone, slate, lime, cement, rock, etc. A *quarry* is usually open to the day; a *mine* is generally covered, communicating with the surface by one or more shafts. See *mine*[2].

Thei sale, a litel hem bi-side, a semliche *quarrere*,
Vnder an heiȝ hel, al holwe nowe diked.
William of Palerne (E. E. T. S.), l. 2232.

That Stone rough in the *Quarry* grew
Which now a perfect Venus shews to View.
Congreve, tr. of Ovid's Art of Love.

A *quarry* is an open excavation where the works are visible at the surface. *Bainbridge*, On Mines, p. 2.

quarry[2] (kwor'i), *v. t.*; pret. and pp. *quarried*, ppr. *quarrying*. [< *quarry*[2], *n.*] To dig or take from a quarry: as, to *quarry* marble.

Part of the valley, if not the whole of it, has been formed by *quarrying* away the crags of marble and conglomerate limestone. *B. Taylor*, Lands of the Saracen, p. 89.

Scarped cliff and *quarried* stone.
Tennyson, In Memoriam, lv.

quarry[3] (kwor'i), *n.* [< ME. *querre, kyrre*, < OF. *cuiree, curee*, F. *curée*, quarry, orig. the refuse parts of an animal slain, given to the hounds in its skin, < *cuir*, skin, hide, < L. *corium*, hide: see *corium*.] **1†.** The refuse parts of an animal slain in the chase, given in the skin to the hounds: as, to make the *quarry* (to open and skin the animal slain, and give the refuse to the hounds).

And after, whenne the hert is splayed and ded, he undoeth hym, and maketh his *kyrre*, and enquyrreth or rewardeth his houndes, and so he hath gret likynge.
MS. Bodl. 546. (*Halliwell.*)

Then fersly thay flokked in folk at the laste,
& quykly of the quelled dere a *querré* thay maked.
Sir Gawayne and the Green Knight (E. E. T. S.), l. 1324.

2. A beast of the chase when pursued or slain; any creature hunted by men or by beasts or birds of prey, especially after it has been killed.

I watch'd his eye,
And saw how falcon-like it tower'd, and flew
Upon the wealthy *quarry*.
Fletcher (*and another*), False One, iv. 1.

As a falcon from the rocky height,
Her *quarry* seen, impetuous at the sight,
Forth-springing instant, darts herself from high,
Shoots on the wing, and skims along the sky.
Pope, Iliad, xiii. 92.

3. Hunted or slaughtered game, or any object of eager pursuit.

And let me use my sword, I'ld make a *quarry*
With thousands of these quarter'd slaves.
Shak., Cor., i. 1. 202.

quarry[3]**†** (kwor'i), *v.* [< *quarry*[3], *n.*] **I.** *intrans.* To prey, as a vulture or harpy.

Like the vulture that is day and night *quarrying* upon Prometheus's liver. *Sir R. L'Estrange.*

II. *trans.* To provide with prey.

Now I am bravely *quarried*. *Beau. and Fl.*

A soldier of renown, and the first provost
That ever let our Roman eagles fly
On swarthy Ægypt, *quarried* with her spoils.
B. Jonson, Poetaster, v. 1.

quarry-faced (kwor'i-fāst), *a.* Rough-faced, as taken from the quarry: noting a type of building-stone and masonry built of such stone.

Quarry-faced or Rock-faced Masonry.

quarry-hawk (kwor'i-hâk),

n. An old entered and reclaimed hawk. *Halliwell.*

quarrying-machine (kwor'i-ing-ma-shēn″), *n.* A form of gang-drill for cutting channels in native rock; a rock-drill. Such machines are usually combined in construction with the motor which operates them, and are placed on a railway-track for convenience in moving them along the surface of the stone to be cut.

quarryman (kwor'i-man), *n.*; pl. *quarrymen* (-men). [< *quarry*[2] + *man*.] A man who is occupied in quarrying stones.

quarry-slave (kwor'i-slāv), *n.* A slave compelled to work in a quarry.

> Thou go not, like the *quarry-slave* at night,
> Scourged to his dungeon. *Bryant*, Thanatopsis.

quarry-water (kwor'i-wâ″tėr), *n.* The water which is mechanically held between the particles of a newly quarried rock, and which gradually disappears by evaporation when this is kept from exposure to the weather. A part of this water only disappears after the rock has been heated to the boiling-point, and this is usually called *hygroscopic moisture*. The quantity of quarry-water held by rocks varies greatly in amount, according to their composition and texture. Some rocks which are so soft that they can be cut with a saw or chisel when freshly quarried become much harder after exposure to the air for a few weeks.

> The longer the stone [limestone] has been exposed to the air, the less fuel will be consumed in driving off its inherent moisture, or *quarry-water*. *Spons' Encyc. Manuf.*, I. 619.

quart[1] (kwârt), *n.* [< ME. *quarte*, < OF. *quarte*, F. *quarte*, f., < L. *quarta* (sc. *pars*), a fourth part; cf. OF. *quart*, F. *quart*, m., = Sp. *cuarto* = Pg. *quarto* = It. *quarto*, fourth, a fourth part, quarter; < L. *quartus*, fourth (= E. *fourth*), appar. for **quaturtus*, with ordinal (superl.) formative *-tus* (E. *-th*), < *quattuor* = E. *four*: see *four*, and compare *quadrate*, *quarter*[1], etc.] **1†.** A fourth part or division; a quarter.

> And Camber did possesse the Western *quart*. *Spenser*, F. Q., II. x. 14.

2. A unit of measure, the fourth part of a gallon; also, a vessel of that capacity. Every gallon of liquid measure has a quart, and in the United States there is a quart of dry measure, although the use of the gallon of that measure is confined to Great Britain. In England the peck, or fourth part of a bushel, is sometimes called a *quart*.

1 United States liquid quart	= 0.9468	liter.
1 United States dry quart	= 1.1017	liters.
1 imperial quart	= 1.1359	liters.
1 Scotch quart	= 3.398	liters.

Before the adoption of the metric system, there were measures of capacity corresponding to the quart in almost every part of Europe.

> Go fetch me a *quart* of sack; put a toast in 't. *Shak.*, M. W. of W., iii. 5. 3.

> Yet would you . . . rail upon the hostess, . . .
> Because she brought stone jugs and no seal'd *quarts*. *Shak.*, T. of the S., Ind., ii. 89.

> Glass bottles of all qualities I buys at three for a halfpenny, . . . but very seldom indeed 2*d*., unless it 's something very prime and big like the old *quarts*. *Mayhew*, London Labour and London Poor, II. 122.

3. In *music*, the interval of a fourth: prefixed to the name of an instrument, it denotes one pitched a fourth lower or a fourth higher than the ordinary instrument.

> A succession of parallel *quarts*, quints, and octaves, which would be intolerable to modern ears. *The Academy*, Jan. 18, 1890, p. 51.

4. In Gloucestershire and Leicestershire, England, three pounds of butter; in the Isle of Man, seven pounds—that is, the fourth part of a quarter.—**5.** A Welsh measure of length or surface; a pole of $3\frac{1}{2}$ to $4\frac{1}{2}$ yards.

quart[2] (kärt), *n.* [< F. *quarte*, a sequence of four cards at piquet, also a position in fencing; particular uses of *quarte*, a fourth: see *quart*[1].] **1.** In *card-playing*, a sequence of four cards. A *quart major* is a sequence of the highest four cards in any suit.

> If the elder hand has *quart major* and two other Aces, the odds are only 5 to 4 against his taking in either the Ten to his *quart*, or another Ace. *The American Hoyle*, p. 136.

2. One of the eight thrusts and parries in fencing. A thrust in quart is a thrust, with the nails up, ward, at the upper breast, which is given direct from the ordinary position taken by two fencers when they engage, the left of their foils touching. A parry in quart guards this blow. It is produced by carrying the hand a few inches to the left without lowering hand or point.—**Quart and tierce**, practice between fencers, one thrusting in quart and tierce (see *tierce*) alternately, and the other parrying in the same positions. It is confounded with *tirer au mur* (fencing at the wall), which is simply practice for the legs, hand, and eyes against a stationary mark, usually a plastron hung on the wall.

> The assassin stab of time was parried by the *quart and tierce* of art. *Smollett*, tr. of Gil Blas, iv. 7.

> How subtle at *tierce and quart* of mind with mind! *Tennyson*, In Memoriam, W. G. Ward.

quart[3]†, *a.* [ME. *quart*, *quarte*, *qwarte*, *quert*, *qwert*, *whert*; origin obscure.] Safe; sound; in good health. *Prompt. Parv.*, p. 420.

quart[3]†, *n.* [ME. *quart*, *gwart*, *querte*; < *quart*[3], *a.*] Safety; health.

> Againe alle our care hit is our *quert*. *Holy Rood* (E. E. T. S.), p. 108.

> A! worthy lorde, wolde thou take heede,
> I am full olde and oute of *qwarte*,
> That me liste do no daies dede,
> Bot yf gret mystir me garte. *York Plays*, p. 41.

> With beaute and with bodyly *quarte*
> To serve the I toke noone heede.
> *Political Poems*, etc. (ed. Furnivall), p. 174.

> Loue us helith, & makith in *qwart*,
> And liftith us up in-to heuene-riche.
> *Hymns to Virgin*, etc. (E. E. T. S.), p. 23.

quartan (kwâr'tan), *a.* and *n.* [Early mod. E. also *quartain*; < ME. *quarteyne*, < OF. *quartaine*, F. *quartaine* = Pr. *quartana*, *cartana* = Sp. *cuartana* = Pg. *quartão* = It. *quartana*, < L. *quartana* (sc. *febris*), quartan fever, fem. of *quartanus*, of or pertaining to the fourth, < *quartus*, fourth: see *quart*[1].] **I.** *a.* Having to do with the fourth; especially, occurring every fourth day: as, a *quartan* ague or fever (one which recurs on the fourth day—that is, after three days).

> The *quartan*-fever, shrinking every limb,
> Sets me a-capering straight.
> *Ford*, Perkin Warbeck, iii. 2.

> The sins shall return periodically, like the revolutions of a *quartan* ague. *Jer. Taylor*, Works (ed. 1835), I. 104.

II. *n.* **1.** An intermitting ague that occurs every fourth day, both days of consecutive occurrence being counted, as on Sunday, Wednesday, Saturday, Tuesday, etc.

> After you felt your selfe deliuered of your *quartaine*. *Guevara*, Letters (tr. by Hellowes, 1577), p. 13.

> The *quarteyn* is gendrid of myche haboundaunce of malencolye that is corrumpid withinne the body. *Booke of Quinte Essence* (ed. Furnivall), p. 20.

2. A measure containing the fourth part of some other measure.

quartaner†, *n.* [ME. *quartenare*, < ML. *quartenarius*, < *quartana*, the quartan: see *quartan*.] One who has the quartan.

quartation (kwâr-tā'shon), *n.* [< L. *quartus*, fourth (see *quart*[1]), + *-ation*.] The parting of gold and silver by the use of nitric acid. It is so called because an alloy consisting of more than one part of gold to three parts of silver is very little affected by the acid; hence it is necessary, in the case of alloys very rich in gold, to fuse them with so much additional silver that the gold shall form not more than a fourth of the whole.

> In that operation that refiners call *quartation*, which they employ to purify gold, three parts of silver are so exquisitely mingled by fusion with a fourth part of gold (whence the operation is denominated) that the resulting mass acquires several new qualities by virtue of the composition. *Boyle*, Works, I. 504.

quart d'écu† (kär dā-kü'). [F.] An old French coin: same as *cardecu*.

> Sir, for a *quart-d'écu* he will sell the fee-simple of his salvation. *Shak.*, All's Well, iv. 3. 311.

quarte (kärt), *n.* [F., lit. a fourth part: see *quart*[1], *quart*[2].] Same as *quart*[2].

quarter[1] (kwâr'tėr), *n.* [< ME. *quarter*, *quartere*, dial. *wharter*, quarter (= D. *kwartier* = G. *quartier* = Sw. *quarter* = Dan. *kvarteer*, quarter), < OF. *quartier*, *quarter*, *cartier*, a fourth part, quarter, as of mutton, etc., = Sp. *cuartel* = Pg. *quartel* = It. *quartiero*, *quartiere*, quarter, < L. *quartarius*, a fourth part of any measure, esp. of a sextarius, a quarter, quartern, ML. *quartarius*, also neut. *quartarium*, also (after Rom.) *quarterius*, *quarterium*, a quarter, etc., < L. *quartus*, fourth: see *quart*[1]. Cf. *quarter*[2].] **1.** One of four equal or equivalent parts into which anything is or may be divided; a fourth part or portion; one of four equal or corresponding divisions.

> I have a kinsman not past three *quarters* of a mile hence. *Shak.*, W. T., iv. 3. 85.

Specifically—(*a*) The fourth part of a yard or of an ell.

> The stuarde in honde schalle haue a stafe,
> A fyngur gret, two *wharters* long,
> To reule the men of court ymong.
> *Babees Book* (E. E. T. S.), p. 310.

> His arrowes were fiue *quarters* long, headed with the splinters of a white christall-like stone. *Capt. John Smith*, Works, I. 120.

(*b*) The fourth part of a hundredweight—that is, 28 pounds, the hundredweight being equal to 112 pounds. Abbreviated *qr*. (*c*) In England, as a legal measure of capacity, eight bushels. Locally, 16, 12, or 9 bushels, 8 bushels and 3 pecks, or 8 bushels, 2 pecks, and $2\frac{1}{2}$ quarts are variously called a *quarter*.

> Holding land on which he could sow three-quarters of an imperial *quarter* of corn and three imperial *quarters* of potatoes. *Quarterly Rev.*, CLXII. 387.

(*d*) The fourth part of an hour.

> Sin' your true love was at your yates,
> It 's but twa *quarters* past.
> *The Drowned Lovers* (Child's Ballads, II. 179).

> He always is here as the clock 's going five—
> Where is he? . . . Ah, it is chiming the *quarter*!
> *F. Locker*, The Old Government Clerk.

(*e*) In *astron.*, the fourth part of the moon's period or monthly revolution: as, the first *quarter* after the change or full. (*f*) One of the four parts into which the horizon is supposed to be divided; one of the four cardinal points: as, the four *quarters* of the globe; but, more widely, any region or point of the compass: as, from what *quarter* does the wind blow? people thronged in from all *quarters*; hence, indefinitely, any direction or source: as, my information comes from a high *quarter*.

> Upon Elam will I bring the four winds from the four *quarters* of heaven. *Jer.* xlix. 36.

> I own I was hurt to hear it, as I indeed was to learn, from the same *quarter*, that your guardian, Sir Peter, and Lady Teazle have not agreed lately as well as could be wished. *Sheridan*, School for Scandal, i. 1.

(*g*) In *nav.*, the fourth part of the distance from one point on the compass-card to another, being the fourth of 11° 15′—that is, about 2° 49′. Also called *quarter-point*. (*h*) The fourth part of the year; specifically, in schools, the fourth part of the teaching period of the year, generally ten or eleven weeks.

> I have served your worship truly, sir, this eight years; and if I cannot once or twice in a *quarter* bear out a knave . . . I have but a very little credit. *Shak.*, 2 Hen. IV., v. 1. 53.

> There was a fiction that Mr. Wopsle examined the scholars once a *quarter*. *Dickens*, Great Expectations, vii.

(*i*) A silver coin, equal to one fourth part of a dollar, or twenty-five cents; also, the sum of twenty-five cents. [U. S.] (*j*) One fourth part of the body or carcass of an animal, in the case of butcher's meat including a leg: as, a fore or hind *quarter* of mutton; especially, one of the hind quarters; a haunch: generally in the plural: as, the *quarters* of a horse. See cut under *horse*. (*k*) In *her.*: (1) One of the four parts into which a shield is divided by quartering. The four quarters are numbered as follows: 1, dexter chief; 2, sinister chief; 3, dexter base; 4, sinister base. (2) An ordinary occupying one fourth of the field, and placed (unless otherwise directed) in the dexter chief, as shown in the cut; also, sometimes, same as *canton*[1], 4.

Quarter.

(*l*) In *shoemaking*, the part of the shoe or boot, on either side, between the back of the heel and a line drawn downward from the ankle-bone or thereabout; hence, that part of the leather which occupies the same place, whether the actual upper-leather of the shoe or a stiff lining. See cut under *boot*.

> Lace shoe upper, consisting of vamp, *quarter*, and facing for eyelet holes. *Ure*, Dict., IV. 110.

(*m*) *Naut.*: (1) The part of a ship's side between the after part of the main chains and the stern. (2) The part of a yard between the slings and the yard-arm. (*n*) In *farriery*, the part of a horse's foot between the toe and the heel, being the side of the coffin. A *false quarter* is a cleft in the hoof extending from the coronet to the shoe, or from top to bottom. When for any disorder one of the quarters is cut, the horse is said to be *quarter-cast*. (*o*) In *arch.*, a square panel inclosing a quatrefoil or other ornament; also, an upright post in partitions to which the laths are nailed. (*p*) In a cask, the part of the side between the bulge and the chime. (*q*) In the dress of a millstone, a section of the dress containing one leader and branches. (*r*) In *carp.*, one of the sections of a winding stair. (*s*) In *cork-cutting*, a parallelepiped of cork ready to be rounded into shape. (*t*) In *printing*, any one of the four corners of a cross-barred chase. (*u*) In *music*, same as *quarter-note*.

2. A distinct division of a surface or region; a particular region of a town, city, or country; a district; a locality: as, the Latin *quarter* of Paris; the Jews' *quarter* in Rome.

> Some part of the town was on fire every night; nobody knew for what reason, nor what was the *quarter* that was next to be burnt. *Bruce*, Source of the Nile, II. 624.

> To the right and left of the great thoroughfares are by-streets and *quarters*. *E. W. Lane*, Modern Egyptians, I. 6.

Hence—**3.** A position assigned or allotted; specific place; special location; proper position or station.

> The Lord high-Marshall vnto each his *quarter*
> Had not assigned.
> *Sylvester*, tr. of Du Bartas's Weeks, i. 1.

> Swift to their several *quarters* hasted then
> The cumbrous elements. *Milton*, P. L., iii. 714.

More specifically—(*a*) The proper stations of officers and men on a man-of-war in battle, in exercise, or on inspection: in the plural. The exercise of the guns, as in battle, is distinguished as *general quarters*. (*b*) Place of lodging; temporary residence; shelter; entertainment: usually in the plural.

> The Duke acquaints his Friends, who hereupon fall every one to his Quarter. The Earl of Warwick fell upon the Lord Clifford's Quarter, where the Duke of Somerset hasting to the Rescue was slain. *Baker*, Chronicles, p. 193.

> I shall have time enough to lodge you in your *quarters*, and afterwards to perform my own journey.
> *Cotton*, in Walton's Angler, ii. 223.

(*c*) A station or an encampment occupied by troops; a place of lodgment for officers and men: usually in the plural: as, they went into winter *quarters*. Compare *headquarters*.

> Had all your *quarters* been as safely kept
> As that whereof I had the government,
> We had not been thus shamefully surprised.
> *Shak.*, 1 Hen. VI., ii. 1. 63.

When the service has been read, and the last volley has been fired over the buried soldier, the troops march to *quarters* with a quick step, and to a lively tune.
Thackeray, Philip, xxx.

(*d*) *pl.* The cabins inhabited by the negroes on a plantation, in the period of slavery. [Southern U. S.]

Let us go out to the *quarters*, grandpa; they will be dancing by now. *Harper's Mag.*, LXXVIII. 258.

4†. [Appar. due to the phrase *to keep quarter* (*b*).] Peace; concord; amity. [Rare.]

Friends all but now, even now,
In *quarter*, and in terms like bride and groom.
Shak., Othello, ii. 3. 180.

5†. Friendly intercourse.

If your more serious business do not call you,
Let me hold *quarter* with you; we will talk
An hour out quickly. *Beau. and Fl.*, Philaster, ii. 2.

Alternate quarters, in *her.* See *alternate*.—**Close-quarters.** Same as *close-fights*.—**Grand quarter**, in *her.*, one of the four primary divisions in quartering.—**Great Quarter Court.** Same as Court *of Assistants* (which see, under *court*).—**On the quarter** (*naut.*), strictly, 45° abaft the beam: generally used to designate a position between abeam and astern.—**Quarter binding.** See *binding*.—**Quarter gasket.** See *gasket*.—**To beat to quarters.** See *beat*[1].—**To come to close quarters.** See *close*[2].—**To keep quarter†.** (*a*) To keep the proper place or station.

They do best who, if they cannot but admit love, yet make it *keep quarter*, and sever it wholly from their serious affairs. *Bacon*, Love (ed. 1887).

(*b*) To keep peace. Compare *quarter*[2].

I knew two that were competitors for the secretary's place in Queen Elizabeth's time, and yet *kept* good *quarter* between themselves. *Bacon*, Cunning (ed. 1887).

For the Venetians endeavour, as much as in them lies, to *keep* good *quarters* with the Turk.
Sandys, Travailes, p. 6.

(*c*†) To make noise or disturbance: apparently an ironical use.

Sing, hi ho, Sir Arthur, no more in the house you shall prate;
For all you *kept* such a *quarter*, you are out of the councell of state. *Wright's Political Ballads*, p. 150. (*Halliwell.*)

This evening come Betty Turner and the two Mercers, and W. Batelier, and they had fiddlers, and danced, and *kept a quarter*. *Pepys*, Diary, III. 360.

Weather quarter, the quarter of a ship which is on the windward side.—**Winter quarters**, the quarters of an army during the winter; a winter residence or station.

quarter[1] (kwâr'tėr), *v.* [< *quarter*[1], *n.* In def. II., 5, cf. F. *cartayer*, drive so that one of the two chief ruts shall be between the wheels (thus dividing the road into four sections), < *quart*, fourth: see *quart*[1].] **I.** *trans.* **1.** To divide into four equal parts.

In his silver shield
He bore a bloodie Crosse that *quartred* all the field.
Spenser, F. Q., II. i. 18.

A thought which, *quarter'd*, hath but one part wisdom
And ever three parts coward. *Shak.*, Hamlet, iv. 4. 42.

2. To divide; separate into parts; cut to pieces.

If you frown upon this proffer'd peace,
You tempt the fury of my three attendants,
Lean famine, *quartering* steel, and climbing fire.
Shak., 1 Hen. VI., iv. 2. 11.

Here is a sword baith sharp and broad,
Will *quarter* you in three.
King Malcolm and Sir Colvin (Child's Ballads, III. 380).

The lawyer and the blacksmith shall be hang'd,
Quarter'd. *Ford*, Perkin Warbeck, iii. 1.

3. To divide into distinct regions or compartments.

Then sailors *quartered* heaven, and found a name
For every fixed and every wandering star.
Dryden, tr. of Virgil's Georgics, i. 208.

4. To furnish with lodgings, shelter, or entertainment; supply with temporary means of living; especially, to find lodgings and food for: as, to *quarter* soldiers on the inhabitants.

Divers souldiers were *quarter'd* at my house, but I thank God went away the next day towards Flanders.
Evelyn, Diary, May 1, 1657.

They would not adventure to bring them to us, but *quartered* them in another house, though in the same town. *R. Knox* (Arber's Eng. Garner, I. 344).

5†. To diet; feed.

Scrimansky was his cousin-german,
With whom he served, and fed on vermin;
And when these fail'd, he'd suck his claws,
And *quarter* himself upon his paws.
S. Butler, Hudibras, I. ii. 268.

6. To furnish as portion; deal out; allot; share.

But this isle,
The greatest and the best of all the main,
He *quarters* to his blue-hair'd deities.
Milton, Comus, l. 29.

When the queen frown'd, or smil'd, he knows . . .
Whose place is *quarter'd* out, three parts in four.
Pope, Satires of Donne, iv. 136.

7. In *her.*, to bear quarterly upon one's escutcheon: thus, a man *quarters* the arms of his father with those of his mother, if she has been an heiress. The verb *to quarter* is used even when more than two coats of arms are united upon one escutcheon, and when, therefore, more than four compartments appear. See *quartering*, 4.

Slen. They [the Shallow family] may give the dozen white luces in their coat; . . . I may *quarter*, coz.
Shal. You may, by marrying.
Shak., M. W. of W., i. 1. 23.

"Look at the banner," said the Abbot; "tell me what are the blazonries." "The arms of Scotland," said Edward; "the lion and its tressure, *quartered* . . . with three cushions." *Scott*, Monastery, xxxvii.

8. In *mach.*, to make wrist-pin holes in, 90° apart: said of locomotive driving-wheels.—**9.** In *sporting*, to range or beat (the ground) for game: with indefinite *it*: said of hunting-dogs.

In order to complete the education of the pointer in ranging or beating his ground, it is not only necessary that he should *quarter* it, as it is called, but that he should do it with every advantage of the wind, and also without losing time by dwelling on a false scent.
Dogs of Great Britain and America, p. 229.

To hang, draw, and quarter. See *hang*.—**To quarter the sea**, to bring the sea first on one quarter and then on the other: frequently done with a small boat running before a heavy sea with plenty of sea-room.

II. *intrans.* **1.** To be stationed; remain in quarters; lodge; have a temporary residence.

Some fortunate captains
That *quarter* with him, and are truly valiant,
Have flung the name of Happy Cæsar on him.
Fletcher (and another), False One, iv. 2.

That night they *quartered* in the woods.
Quoted in *Capt. John Smith's* Works, I. 163.

2. *Naut.*, to sail with the wind on the quarter.

We were now assured they were Spaniards; and therefore we put away, *Quartering*, and steering N. W.
Dampier, Voyages, II. ii. 20.

3. To shift; beat about; change position, so as to get advantage of an adversary.

They *quarter* over the ground again and again, Tom always on the defensive.
T. Hughes, Tom Brown at Rugby, ii. 5.

4. In *sporting*, to run back and forth in search of game, as if going about all quarters, as a dog in the field.—**5.** To drive a carriage diagonally from side to side, so as to keep the wheels from entering the ruts.

The postilion . . . was employed, not by fits and starts, but always and eternally, in *quartering*—i. e. in crossing from side to side—according to the casualties of the ground. *De Quincey*, Autob. Sketches, I. 298.

quarter[2] (kwâr'tėr), *n.* [= G. *quartier* = Sw. *quarter* = Dan. *kvarteer*, quarter; < F. *quartier*, "quarter, or fair war, where souldiers are taken prisoners and ransomed at a certain rate" (Cotgrave) (= Sp. *cuartel* = Pg. *quartel* = It. *quartiere*, quarter), in the phrases *donner quartier*, or *faire quartier*, give quarter, *demander quartier*, beg quarter, supposed to have referred orig. to the sending of the vanquished to an assigned 'quarter' or place, there to be detained until his liberation, ransom, or slavery should be decided: see *quarter*[1]. The explanation from an alleged "custom of the Dutch and Spaniards, who accepted as the ransom of an officer or soldier a quarter of his pay for a certain period" (Imp. Dict.) presents obvious difficulties.] Indulgence or mercy shown to a vanquished enemy, in sparing his life and accepting his surrender; hence, in general, indulgence; clemency; mercy.

The three that remain'd call'd to Robin for *quarter*.
Robin Hood's Birth (Child's Ballads, V. 350).

Death a more gen'rous Rage does use;
Quarter to all he conquers does refuse.
Cowley, The Mistress, Thraldom.

He magnified his own clemency, now that they were at his mercy, to offer them *quarter* for their lives, if they gave up the castle. *Clarendon.*

Most people dislike vanity in others, whatever share they have of it themselves; but I give it fair *quarter* wherever I meet with it. *Franklin*, Autobiog., I. 83.

quarterage (kwâr'tėr-āj), *n.* [Early mod. E. also *quarteridge*, *quartridge*; < ME. *quarterage*, < OF. *quarterage*, quarterage, < *quartier*, a quarter: see *quarter*[1].] **1.** A quarterly allowance or payment, as for tuition or rent.

Upon every one of the said quarter days, every one that is a Freeman of the said Company shall pay to the Master for the time being, for his *quarteridge*, one penny.
English Gilds (E. E. T. S.), p. 289.

[A virtuous writer] might have expended more by the year by the revenue of his verse than any riotous elder brother upon the wealthy *quartridges* of three time three hundred acres. *Middleton*, Father Hubbard's Tales.

In 1711 the *quarterage* [of Cartmel Grammar School] was raised to 1*s.* 6*d.* for Latin and 1*s.* for English, the poor children still to be taught free.
Baines, Hist. Lancashire, II. 681.

2. Quarters; lodgment; keeping.

The warre thus being begun and followed, the Scots kept their *quarterage*. *Holinshed*, Scotland, an. 1557.

Any noble residence at which they [great stewards] intended to claim the free *quarterage* due to their official dignity, while engaged in the examination of the state of the district and the administration of the laws by the king's command. *O'Curry*, Ancient Irish, I. xvi.

For *quarterage* of a soldier, 5*s.* per week.
Connecticut Records, II. 386. (*Bartlett.*)

3. A certain special tax. See the quotation.

They [the Roman Catholics] could not obtain the freedom of any town corporate, and were only suffered to carry on their trades in their native cities on condition of paying special and vexatious impositions known by the name of *quarterage*. *Lecky*, Eng. in 18th Cent., ii.

quarter-angled (kwâr'tėr-ang″gld), *a.* In *her.*, same as *quadrate*, 5.

quarter-aspect (kwâr'tėr-as″pekt), *n.* In *astrol.*, the aspect of two planets whose positions are 90° apart on the zodiac.

quarter-back (kwâr'tėr-bak), *n.* A certain player or position in foot-ball. See *back*[1], *n.*, 12.

quarter-badge (kwâr'tėr-baj), *n.* *Naut.*, ornamentation on the quarters of a ship.

quarter-bend (kwâr'tėr-bend), *n.* In a pipe, a bend the arc of which subtends an angle of 90°.

quarter-bill (kwâr'tėr-bil), *n.* *Naut.*, a list of the stations on board a man-of-war for men to take in time of action.

quarter-bitts (kwâr'tėr-bits), *n. pl.* Vertical posts or timbers projecting above the deck on a vessel's quarter, to which hawsers, tow-lines, etc., may be secured.

quarter-blanket (kwâr'tėr-blang″ket), *n.* A horse-blanket intended to cover only the back and a part of the hips. It is usually put on under the harness.

quarter-blocks (kwâr'tėr-bloks), *n. pl.* *Naut.*, blocks underneath a yard close in amidships, for the clew-lines and the sheets of the sail set above them to reeve through.

quarter-board (kwâr'tėr-bōrd), *n.* One of a set of thin boards forming an additional height to the bulwarks of the after part of a vessel. They are also called *topgallant-bulwarks*.

quarter-boat (kwâr'tėr-bōt), *n.* *Naut.*, any boat hung to davits over a ship's quarter.—**Larboard quarter-boat.** See *larboard*.

quarter-boot (kwâr'tėr-böt), *n.* A leather boot to protect the fore feet of horses which overreach with the hind feet.

quarter-bound (kwâr'tėr-bound), *a.* In *bookbinding*, bound with pasteboard covers and leather or cloth on the back only.

quarter-boys (kwâr'tėr-boiz), *n. pl.* Automata which strike the quarter-hours in certain belfries. Compare *jack of the clock*, under *jack*[1].

Their *quarter-boys* and their chimes were designed for this moral purpose as much as the memento which is so commonly seen upon an old clock face, and so seldom upon a new one. *Southey*, Doctor, xxix. (*Davies.*)

quarter-bred (kwâr'tėr-bred), *a.* Having only one fourth pure blood, as horses, cattle, etc.

quarter-cask (kwâr'tėr-kȧsk), *n.* A small cask holding 28 gallons or thereabouts.

quarter-cast (kwâr'tėr-kȧst), *a.* Cut in the quarter of the hoof: said of horses operated upon for some disease of the hoof.

quarter-cleft (kwâr'tėr-kleft), *a.* Same as *quartered*, 4.

quarter-cloth (kwâr'tėr-klôth), *n.* *Naut.*, one of a series of long pieces of painted canvas formerly extended on the outside of the quarter-netting from the upper part of the gallery to the gangway.

quarter-day (kwâr'tėr-dā), *n.* In England, the day that begins each quarter of the year. They are Lady day (March 25th), Midsummer day (June 24th), Michaelmas day (September 29th), and Christmas day (December 25th). These are the usual landlords' and tenants' terms for entering or quitting lands or houses and for paying rent. In Scotland the legal terms are *Whitsunday* (May 15th) and *Martinmas* (November 11th); the conventional terms *Candlemas* (February 2d) and *Lammas* (August 1st) make up the quarter-days.

quarter-deck (kwâr'tėr-dek), *n.* *Naut.*, the part of the spar-deck of a man-of-war between the poop and the main-mast. It is used as a promenade by the officers only.

The officer was walking the *quarter-deck*, where I had no right to go. *R. H. Dana, Jr.*, Before the Mast, p. 5.

quarter-decker (kwâr'tėr-dek″ėr), *n.* *Naut.*, an officer who is more looked upon as a stickler for small points of etiquette than as a thorough seaman. [Colloq.]

quartered (kwâr'tėrd), *p. a.* **1.** Divided into or grouped in four equal parts or quarters; separated into distinct parts.

Nations besides from all the *quarter'd* winds.
Milton, P. R., iv. 202.

2. Lodged; stationed for lodging; of or pertaining to lodging or quarters.

When they hear the Roman horses neigh,
Behold their *quarter'd* fires. *Shak.*, Cymbeline, iv. 4. 18.

3. Having hind quarters (of a specified kind): as, a short-*quartered* horse.—4. Sawed into quarters (said of a tree-trunk), and then cut into planks in such a manner as to show the grain of the wood (especially the silver grain of oak) to advantage. This is done in various ways—that most approved being to cut the quarter into two equal parts from the pith to the bark, and then to saw off boards by cuts parallel to the bisecting section.
5. In *her.*, having a square piece cut out of the center: noting a form of cross. The perforation is usually as wide as the band that forms the cross, so that the arms of the cross do not unite in the middle except at their corners.

A Cross Quartered.

6. In *shoemaking*, made with quarters (of a particular kind): as, low-*quartered* shoes.—**Drawn and quartered.** See *drawn*.—**Quartered oak.** See def. 4.—**Quartered partition**, a partition formed with quarters.—**Quarterly quartered.** See *quarterly*.

quarterer (kwâr'tėr-ėr), *n.* A lodger. *Halliwell.* [Prov. Eng.]

quarter-evil (kwâr'tėr-ē"vl), *n.* Same as *symptomatic anthrax* (which see, under *anthrax*).

quarter-face (kwâr'tėr-fās), *n.* A countenance three parts averted.

> But let this dross carry what price it will
> With noble ignorants, and let them still
> Turn upon scorned verse their *quarter-face*.
> *B. Jonson*, Forest, xii. To Countess of Rutland.

quarter-fast (kwâr'tėr-fâst), *n.* *Naut.* See *fast*1, 1.

quarter-fishes (kwâr'tėr-fish"ez), *n. pl.* Stout pieces of wood hooped on to a mast to strengthen it.

quarterfoil (kwâr'tėr-foil), *n.* See *quatrefoil*.

quarter-franc (kwâr'tėr-frangk), *n.* In *her.*, a quarter used separately as a bearing.

quarter-gallery (kwâr'tėr-gal"ẹ-ri), *n.* *Naut.*, a projecting balcony on each of the quarters, and sometimes on the stern, of a large ship; also, a small structure on the quarters of a ship, containing the water-closet and bath-tub.

quarter-grain (kwâr'tėr-grān), *n.* The grain of wood shown when a log is quartered. See *quartered*, 4. Compare *felt-grain*.

quarter-guard (kwâr'tėr-gärd), *n.* *Milit.*, a small guard posted in front of each battalion in camp.

quarter-gunner (kwâr'tėr-gun"ėr), *n.* In the United States navy, a petty officer whose duty it is, under the direction of the gunner, to care for the guns, gun-gear, small-arms, and ammunition.

quarter-hollow (kwâr'tėr-hol"ō), *n.* and *a.* I. *n.* In *arch.*, etc., a concave molding the arc of which is, or approaches, 90°, or a quadrant: the converse of a *quarter-round*.
II. *a.* Having the form of a quarter-hollow.—**Quarter-hollow tool**, a chisel or gouge used in wood-working to make convex or concave moldings.

quarter-horse (kwâr'tėr-hôrs), *n.* A horse that is good for a dash of a quarter of a mile in a race. [Southern U. S.]

quarter-hung (kwâr'tėr-hung), *a.* Having, as a gun, trunnions with their axis below the line of bore. *Farrow*, Mil. Encyc.

quarteridge†, *n.* An obsolete form of *quarterage*.

quarter-ill (kwâr'tėr-il), *n.* Same as *symptomatic anthrax* (which see, under *anthrax*).

quartering (kwâr'tėr-ing), *n.* [Verbal n. of *quarter*1, *v.*] 1. The act of dividing into fourths.—2. The act of assigning quarters, as for soldiers.—3. Quarters; lodging; a station.

> Divers designations, regions, habitations, mansions, or *quarterings* there. *Bp. Mountagu*, Appeal to Cæsar, xviii.

4. In *her.*, the marshaling or disposal of various escutcheons in one, in order to denote the several alliances of one family with the heiresses of others. When more than three other escutcheons are quartered with that of the family, the arms are still said to be *quartered*, however many compartments the shield may be divided into. The name is also given to the several different coats marshaled and placed together in one escutcheon. See *quarterly*.

Quartering.
First and fourth quarters are of one ancestor, A; second of another, B; third of another, C.

5. In *carp.*, a series of small vertical timber posts, rarely exceeding 4 by 3 inches, used to form a partition for the separation or boundary of apartments. They are usually placed about twelve inches apart, and are lathed and plastered in interiors, but if used for exteriors they are generally boarded. *Gwilt.*
6. In *gun.*, the position or placing of a piece of ordnance when it is so traversed that it will shoot on the same line, or on the same point of the compass, as that on which the ship's quarter has its bearing.—7. In *mech.*, the adjustment of cranks on a single shaft at an angle of 90° with each other; also, the boring of holes for wrist-pins in locomotive driving-wheels at right angles with each other. *E. H. Knight.*

quartering (kwâr'tėr-ing), *p. a.* [Ppr. of *quarter*1, *v.*] 1. *Naut.*: (*a*) Sailing large but not before the wind. *Totten.* (*b*) Being on the quarter, or between the line of the keel and the beam, abaft the latter: as, a *quartering* wind. *Dana.*—2. In *archery*, making an acute angle with the range: said of the wind.

quartering-belt (kwâr'tėr-ing-belt), *n.* Same as *quarter-turn belt* (which see, under *belt*).

quartering-block (kwâr'tėr-ing-blok), *n.* A block on which the body of a person condemned to be quartered was cut in pieces. *Macaulay.*

quartering-hammer (kwâr'tėr-ing-ham"ėr), *n.* A steel hammer used to block out masses of flint for flaking.

quartering-machine (kwâr'tėr-ing-mạ-shēn"), *n.* A machine for boring the wrist-pin holes of driving-wheels accurately at a distance apart of 90°.

quarter-iron (kwâr'tėr-ī"ėrn), *n.* *Naut.*, a boom-iron on the quarter of a lower yard.

quarterland (kwâr'tėr-land), *n.* A small territorial division or estate in the Isle of Man, forming a division of a treen.

quarter-light (kwâr'tėr-līt), *n.* In a carriage, a window in the side of the body, as distinguished from the windows in the doors. *Car-Builder's Dict.*

quarter-line (kwâr'tėr-līn), *n.* 1. The position of ships of a column ranged in a line when one is four points forward or abaft another's beam. Also called *bow-and-quarter line*.—2. An additional line extending to the under side of the bag of a seine. As the bag approaches the shore, this line is from time to time drawn upon to relieve the strain upon the wings.

quarter-look† (kwâr'tėr-lůk), *n.* A side look. *B. Jonson.*

quarterly (kwâr'tėr-li), *a.* and *n.* [< *quarter*1 + *-ly*1.] I. *a.* 1. Containing or consisting of a fourth part.

> The moon makes four *quarterly* seasons within her little year or month of consecution. *Holder*, On Time.

2. Recurring at the end of every quarter of the year: as, *quarterly* payments of rent; a *quarterly* visitation or examination.—**Quarterly conference.** See *conference*, 2 (c) (2).
II. *n.*; pl. *quarterlies* (-liz). A publication or literary periodical issued once every three months.

> So much of our reviewing is done in newspapers and critical notes in magazines and *quarterlies* that this sort of criticism nearly engrosses the name. *Stubbs*, Medieval and Modern Hist., p. 54.

quarterly (kwâr'tėr-li), *adv.* [< *quarterly*, *a.*] 1. In quarters; by quarters.

> They tore in peces *quarterly*
> The corps which they had slaine.
> *Gascoigne*, Philomene (Steele Glas, etc., ed. Arber, p. 107).

2. Once in a quarter of a year: as, the returns are made *quarterly*.—3. In *her.*: (*a*) Arranged according to the four quarters of the shield. (*b*) Arranged according to quartering, even when more than four divisions exist: as, he bears *quarterly* of twelve. Compare *quartering*, 4.—**Quarterly in equerre**, in *her.*, divided into four parts by broken lines, producing an effect similar to gironny.—**Quarterly in saltier**, in *her.*, same as *per saltier*: said of the field. See *saltier*.—**Quarterly pierced**, in *her.*, quartered.—**Quarterly quartered**, in *her.*, divided along the lines which separate the field quarterly: said of any bearing in the field.

Quarterly in Equerre.

quarterman (kwâr'tėr-man), *n.*; pl. *quartermen* (-men). An officer of a subdivision of a navy-yard working force. [U. S.]

quartermaster (kwâr'tėr-màs"tėr), *n.* [= D. *kwartiermeester* = G. *quartiermeister* = Sw. *qvartermästare* = Dan. *kvarteermester*; as *quarter*2 + *master*1.] 1. *Milit.*, a regimental staff-officer, of the relative rank of lieutenant, whose duties are to superintend the assignment of quarters and the distribution of clothing, fuel, and other supplies, to have charge of the barracks, tents, etc., of a regiment, and to keep the regimental stores on the march: he directs the marking out of camp. In the United States army the quartermaster is appointed by the colonel of the regiment, subject to the approval of the Secretary of War. In the British service the quartermaster is generally taken from the ranks, and after thirty years' service, including ten as an officer, he may retire with the honorary rank of captain. *Farrow*, Mil. Encyc.
2. *Naut.*, a petty officer who has charge of the steering of the ship, the signals and soundings, and the running lights, leads, colors, log, compasses, etc., as an assistant to the navigator. Quartermasters keep regular watch during the whole time a ship is in commission, and are selected from the steadiest and most trustworthy seamen. On mail steamers the quartermasters steer and keep the flags and running-lights in order.—**Quartermaster's department**, the staff department of the United States army which provides the quarters and transportation of the army, purchases stores, transports army supplies, and furnishes clothing, camp and garrison equipage, horses for the artillery and cavalry, straw, fuel, forage, and stationery. It disburses the appropriations for the incidental expenses of the army, such as the pursuit and capture of deserters, the burial of officers and soldiers, the extra-duty pay of soldiers, the purchase of veterinary medicines and stores, the hiring of escorts, couriers, guides, spies, and interpreters; and it has charge of the support and maintenance of the national cemeteries.—**Signal** or **chief quartermaster**, in the United States navy, a petty officer who has charge of all the apparatus of navigation, as well as the flags, signals, and lights.

quartermaster-general (kwâr'tėr-màs"tėr-jen'ẹ-ral), *n.* *Milit.*, in the British service, a staff-officer whose department is charged with all orders relating to the marching, embarking, disembarking, billeting, quartering, and cantoning of troops, and to encampments and camp equipage; in the United States army, a staff-officer of the rank of brigadier-general, who is at the head of the quartermaster's department.

quartermaster-sergeant (kwâr'tėr-màs"tėr-sär'jẹnt), *n.* *Milit.*, a non-commissioned officer whose duty it is to assist the quartermaster.

quartern (kwâr'tėrn), *n.* [< ME. *quarteroun*, < OF. *quarteron*, F. *quarteron* = Pr. *cartayron*, *cartairo* = Sp. *cuarteron* = It. *quarterone*, a fourth part, < ML. *quartero(n-)*, a fourth part, < L. *quartus*, fourth: see *quart*1, *quarter*1. Cf. *quarteroon*, *quadroon*.] 1. A fourth part; a quarter.

> And there is not the mone seyn in alle the lunacioun, saf only the seconde *quarteroun*.
> *Mandeville*, Travels, p. 301. (*Halliwell.*)

Specifically—2. The fourth part of certain British measures. (*a*) In *liquid measure*, the fourth of a pint; an imperial gill.

> The waiter . . . returned with a *quartern* of brandy.
> *Smollett*, Launcelot Greaves, xvii.

(*b*) The fourth of a peck, or of a stone. (*c*) A quarter of a pound.

> Applicants for *quarterns* of sugar.
> *Dickens*, Sketches, Tales, iv.

quarter-netting (kwâr'tėr-net"ing), *n.* *Naut.*, netting on the quarter for the stowage of hammocks, which formerly in action served to arrest bullets from small-arms.

quarternion (kwâr-tėr'ni-ọn), *n.* An erroneous form of *quaternion*.

quartern-loaf (kwâr'tėrn-lōf), *n.* A loaf weighing, generally, four pounds.

> Who makes the *quartern-loaf* and Luddites rise?
> H. *Smith*, Rejected Addresses, i.

> In proof of their poverty they [the sweepers] refer you to the workhouse authorities, who allow them certain *quartern-loaves* weekly.
> *Mayhew*, London Labour and London Poor, II. 528.

quarter-noble (kwâr'tėr-nō"bl), *n.* An old English coin, equal in value to the fourth part of a noble. Also *ferling-noble*. See *noble*, 2.

quarter-note (kwâr'tėr-nōt), *n.* In *musical notation*, a note equivalent in time-value to one half of a half-note; a crotchet: marked by the sign ♩ or ♪. Also *quarter*.—**Quarter-note rest.** Same as *quarter-rest*.

quarteroon (kwâr-tẹ-rōn'), *n.* [< Sp. *cuarteron*: see *quartern* and *quadroon*.] Same as *quadroon*.

> Your pale-white Creoles have their grievances: and your yellow *Quarteroons*? . . . Quarteroon Ogé . . . felt for his share too that insurrection was the most sacred of duties.
> *Carlyle*, French Rev., II. v. 4. (*Davies.*)

quarterount†, *n.* A Middle English form of *quartern*.

quarter-pace (kwâr'tėr-pās), *n.* The footpace of a staircase when it occurs at the angle-turns of the stairs.

quarter-partition (kwâr'tėr-pạr-tish"ọn), *n.* In *carp.*, a partition consisting of quarters. See *quartering*, 5.

quarter-pieces (kwâr'tėr-pē"sez), *n. pl.* *Naut.*, projections beyond the quarters of a ship for additional cabin accommodation.

quarter-pierced (kwâr'tėr-pērst), *a.* In *her.*, pierced with a square hole not so large as in *quartered* or *quarterly pierced*. See *quartered*, 5. —**Cross quarter-pierced.** See *cross*[1].

quarter-plate (kwâr'tėr-plāt), *n.* In *photog.*: (*a*) A size of plate measuring 3¼ × 4¼ inches. The *half-plate* measures 4¼ × 5½ inches in the United States (4¾ × 6½ in England), and the *whole-plate* 6½ × 8½ inches. (*b*) A plate of this size, or a picture made from such a plate.

quarter-point (kwâr'tėr-point), *n.* *Naut.*, the fourth part of a point, or 2° 48′ 45″.

quarter-pointed (kwâr'tėr-poin"ted), *a.* In *her.*, representing one quarter of the field cut off saltierwise, usually that quarter which is appended to either side of the field.

quarter-rail (kwâr'tėr-rāl), *n.* *Naut.*, that part of the rail which runs above the quarter of the ship; the rail that serves as a guard to the quarter-deck where there are no ports or bulwarks.

quarter-rest (kwâr'tėr-rest), *n.* A rest or sign for silence, equivalent in time-value to a quarter-note; a crotchet-rest: marked 𝄽 or 𝄾. Also called *quarter-note rest.*

quarter-round (kwâr'tėr-round), *n.* **1.** In *arch.*, a molding whose contour is exactly or approximately a quadrant: same as *ovolo*.

> In the *quarter round* of the cornish without there are spouts carved with a lip and flowers that do not project.
> *Pococke*, Description of the East, II. i. 109.

2. Any tool adapted for forming quarter-rounds, as an ovolo-plane.—**Quarter-round tool,** a chisel adapted for cutting concave or convex moldings.

quarter-saver (kwâr'tėr-sā"vėr), *n.* A device attached to a knitting-machine to prevent the work from running off if the yarn breaks or runs out.

quarter-sawed (kwâr'tėr-sâd), *a.* Same as *quartered*, 4.

quarter-seal (kwâr'tėr-sēl), *n.* The seal kept by the director of the Chancery of Scotland. It is in the shape and impression of the fourth part of the great seal, and is in the Scotch statutes called the *testimonial of the great seal.* Gifts of lands from the crown pass this seal in certain cases. *Bell.*

quarter-section (kwâr'tėr-sek"shon), *n.* In the United States Government Land Survey, a square tract of land containing 160 acres, and constituting one fourth of a section.

quarter-sessions (kwâr'tėr-sesh"onz), *n. pl.* **1.** A criminal court held quarterly in England by justices of the peace in counties (in Ireland by county-court judges), and by the recorder in boroughs, and having jurisdiction of minor offenses and administration of highway laws, poor-laws, etc. In several of the United States a somewhat similar court is known by this name.

> A great broad-shoulder'd genial Englishman, . . .
> A *quarter-sessions* chairman, abler none.
> *Tennyson*, Princess, Conclusion.

2. In Scotland, a court held by the justices of the peace four times a year at the county towns, and having power to review sentences pronounced at the special and petty sessions. Abbreviated *Q. S.*

quarter-sling (kwâr'tėr-sling), *n.* One of the supports for a yard on either side of its center.

quarter-square (kwâr'tėr-skwãr), *n.* The fourth part of the square of a number. Tables of quarter-squares are sometimes used to replace logarithms, on account of the property that $\frac{1}{4}(x+y)^2 + \frac{1}{4}(x-y)^2 = xy$.

quarter-staff (kwâr'tėr-stâf), *n.*; pl. *quarter-staves* (-stävz). An old English weapon formed of a stout pole about 6½ feet long. It was grasped by one hand in the middle, and by the other between the middle and the end. In the attack the latter hand shifted from one quarter of the staff to the other, giving the weapon a rapid circular motion, which brought the ends on the adversary at unexpected points.

> A stout frere I met,
> And a *quarter-staffe* in his hande.
> *Playe of Robyn Hode* (Child's Ballads, V. 420).

> *Quarter-staff* Dr. Johnson explains to be "A staff of defence, so called, I believe, from the manner of using it; one hand being placed at the middle, and the other equally between the end and the middle."
> *Strutt*, Sports and Pastimes, p. 357.

> The two champions, being alike armed with *quarter-staves*, stepped forward. . . . The miller, . . . holding his *quarter-staff* by the middle, and making it flourish round his head, . . . exclaimed boastfully, "Come on, churl, an thou darest!"
> *Scott*, Ivanhoe, xi.

quarter-stanchion (kwâr'tėr-stan"shon), *n.* *Naut.*, a strong stanchion in the quarters of a square-sterned vessel, one such stanchion forming the extreme boundary of the stern on each side.

quarter-stuff (kwâr'tėr-stuf), *n.* Plank one fourth of an inch in thickness. *E. H. Knight.*

quarter-tackle (kwâr'tėr-tak"l), *n.* A purchase sometimes used on the quarter of a lower yard to hoist boats, etc.

quarter-timber (kwâr'tėr-tim"bėr), *n.* **1.** *Naut.*, one of the framing-timbers in a ship's quarters. See cut under *counter*.—**2.** In *carp.*, scantling from two to six inches deep. *E. H. Knight.*

quarter-tone (kwâr'tėr-tōn), *n.* In *musical acoustics*, an interval equivalent to one half of a semitone or half-step. The term is loosely applied to a variety of small intervals, especially to enharmonic ones.

quarter-trap (kwâr'tėr-trap), *n.* In theaters, a small trap on each side of the stage, on a line with the first entrance.

quarter-turn (kwâr'tėr-tėrn), *n.* The arc subtending an angle of 90°; a bend or change of direction at right angles.—**Quarter-turn belt, gooseneck,** etc. See *belt*, etc.

quarter-undulation (kwâr"tėr-un-dū-lā'shon), *n.* In *optics*, a quarter of a wave-length.—**Quarter-undulation plate,** a plate (as of mica) so thin as to cause in a refracted ray a retardation equal to one fourth of a wave-length. Such a plate is used in determining in the polariscope the positive or negative character of a uniaxial crystal.

quarter-vine (kwâr'tėr-vin), *n.* An American vine, *Bignonia capreolata.* It is so called because, owing to the projection of medullary tissue in four winglike layers from the middle to near the surface, a short section of the stem, when gently twisted in the hand, will divide into quarters. See *cross-vine.*

quarter-waiter (kwâr'tėr-wā"tėr), *n.* An officer or gentleman usher of the English court who is one of a number in attendance by turns for a quarter of a year at a time. Also called *quarterly waiter.*

> *Gentleman Usher.* "No, do as I bid thee; I should know something that have beene a *quarter-wayter* [in the queen's service] these fifteen yeares."
> *Sir J. Davies*, Dialogue, Tanner MS. 79.

quarter-watch (kwâr'tėr-woch), *n.* *Naut.*, one half of the watch on deck.

> On the whaling ground in the southern fishery, when a ship is hove to in mid-ocean, they stand *quarter-watches*, one-fourth of the working hands, or half of each watch, being on duty, headed by the boat-steerers.
> *Fisheries of U. S.*, V. ii. 229.

quarter-wind (kwâr'tėr-wind), *n.* *Naut.*, a wind blowing on a vessel's quarter.

quarter-yard (kwâr'tėr-yärd), *n.* An old ale-measure. See *ale-yard* and *half-yard*.

quartet, quartette (kwâr-tet'), *n.* [< It. *quartetto*, a quartet, < L. *quartus*, fourth: see *quart*[1].] **1.** In *music*: (*a*) A composition or movement for four solo parts, either vocal or instrumental, usually without accompaniment. Specifically, an instrumental work, usually for four stringed instruments, written in sonata form, and planned like a small symphony; a string-quartet. The quartet is the highest variety of chamber-music. It first reached its full development at the end of the eighteenth century. (*b*) A company of four singers or players who perform quartets. A mixed vocal quartet properly consists of a soprano (treble), an alto, a tenor, and a bass. A string-quartet consists of two violins, a viola, and a violoncello. (*c*) In an orchestra the stringed instruments collectively, and in oratorio music the principal vocal soloists, are sometimes loosely called the quartet.—**2.** A stanza of four lines.—**3.** Same as *quadruplet.* *Car-Builder's Dict.*—**Double quartet.** (*a*) A composition for eight voices or instruments, especially for four violins, two violas, and two violoncellos. *Grove.* (*b*) The performers of such a composition, whether vocal or instrumental.—**Quartet choir,** a church choir consisting only of a mixed quartet, especially when made up of expert singers.

quartetto (kwâr-tet'ō), *n.* [It.] Same as *quartet.*

quartful†, quartiful†, *a.* [ME. *quartyfulle, quarful*; < *quart*[3] + *-ful.*] In good health; prosperous. *Cath. Ang.*

quartfulness†, *n.* [ME. *quarfulnesse*; < *quartful* + *-ness.*] Prosperity. *Cath. Ang.*

quartic (kwâr'tik), *a.* and *n.* [< L. *quartus*, fourth (see *quart*[1]), + *-ic.*] **I.** *a.* In *math.*, of the fourth degree; especially, of the fourth order.—**Quartic symmetry,** symmetry like that of a regular octagon; in general, symmetry arising from the vanishing of the cubinvariant of a quartic.

II. *n.* An algebraic function of the fourth degree; a quantic of the fourth degree.—**Bicircular quartic.** See *bicircular.*—**Ex-cubo-quartic,** a non-plane curve formed by the intersection of a quadric and a cubic surface which have, besides, two non-intersecting straight lines in common.

quartiful†, *a.* See *quartful.*

quartile (kwâr'til), *n.* [< L. *quartus*, fourth (see *quart*[1]), + *-ile.*] In *astrol.*, an aspect of planets when their longitudes differ by 90°. See *aspect*, 7.

> The heavens threaten us with their comets, stars, planets, with their great conjunctions, eclipses, oppositions, *quartiles*, and such unfriendly aspects.
> *Burton*, Anat. of Mel., p. 87.

> Or Mars and Venus, in a *quartil*, move
> My pangs of jealousy for Arcite's love.
> *Dryden*, Pal. and Arc., i. 500.

quartilunar (kwâr-ti-lū'nãr), *a.* [< L. *quartus*, fourth (see *quart*[1]), + *luna*, moon: see *lunar.*] Pertaining to or consisting of one fourth of a lunar month. [Rare.]

> Such [tidal] waves as these may follow their causes, in periodic times, not diurnally alone, as influenced by sun and moon, but in semilunar or *quartilunar* intervals.
> *Fitz Roy*, Weather Book, p. 96.

quartine (kwâr'tin), *n.* [< L. *quartus*, fourth (see *quart*[1]), + *-ine*[1].] In *bot.*, a supposed fourth integument of some ovules, counting from the outermost. It is really only a layer of the secundine or of the nucleus.

quartinvariant (kwâr-tin-vā'ri-ant), *n.* [< L. *quartus*, fourth, + E. *invariant.*] An invariant of the fourth degree in the coefficients.

quartisection (kwâr-ti-sek'shon), *n.* [< L. *quartus*, fourth, + E. *section.*] Separation into four equal parts; quadrisection.

quartisternal (kwâr-ti-stėr'nal), *n.* [< L. *quartus*, fourth, + *sternum*, breast-bone.] In *anat.*, the fourth sterneber, counting from the manubrium backward; that bone of the sternum which is opposite the fourth intercostal space. [Rare.]

quartle (kwâr'tl), *n.* [A var. of *quarter*[1].] Same as *quarter*[1]. *Halliwell.*

quartlet (kwârt'let), *n.* [ME. *quartelette*, < OF. **quartelet*, < *quart*, fourth: see *quart*[1].] A tankard or goblet holding a quart.

> Item, ij. *quartelettes*, of dyvers sortes, weiyng xlviij. unces.
> *Paston Letters*, I. 472.

quarto (kwâr'tō), *n.* and *a.* [Short for L. (NL.) *in quarto*: L. *in*, in; *quarto*, abl. of *quartus*, fourth: see *quart*[1].] **I.** *n.* A size of book in which the leaf is one fourth of a described or implied size of paper. The sheet folded twice in cross directions makes the square quarto, or regular quarto; folded twice in the same direction makes the long quarto. A cap quarto is 7 × 8½ inches; demy quarto, 8 × 10½ inches; folio-post quarto, 8½ × 11 inches; medium quarto, 9 × 12 inches; royal quarto, 10 × 13 inches. The leaf of a quarto is understood to have a broad and short shape. Abbreviated 4to.

> In my library there is a large copy of the Apocrypha, in what may be called elephant *quarto*, printed for T. Cadell and W. Davies, by Thomas Bensley, 1816.
> *N. and Q.*, 7th ser., IX. 356.

Broad quarto. See *broad folio*, under *broad.*—**Small quarto,** a square octavo; a book having eight leaves to a sheet but the shape of a quarto.

II. *a.* Noting the size of a book in which a sheet makes four leaves: as, a *quarto* volume; being of the size or shape of the leaves of a quarto: as, *quarto* paper; a *quarto* edition.

Quartodeciman (kwâr-tō-des'i-man), *n.* and *a.* [< ML. *quartadecimani*, pl., < L. *quarta decima* (sc. *dies lunæ*), the fourteenth (day of the moon), fem. of *quartus decimus*, fourteenth, < *quartus*, fourth, + *decimus*, tenth: see *quart*[1] and *decimal.*] **I.** *n.* A member of one of those early Christian communities which celebrated the Paschal festival on the fourteenth day of the month Nisan (the same day as that on which the Jews celebrated their Passover), without regard to the day of the week. This practice led to great confusion and to a wide-spread controversy (the *Quartodeciman controversy*). In modern times this question has been much misunderstood, from a failure to distinguish the "Pascha" which was the anniversary of Christ's crucifixion from that which was the anniversary of his resurrection. The Quartodeciman usage was finally condemned by the Council of Nice, A. D. 325.

II. *a.* Relating to the Quartodecimans or to their practice of celebrating the Paschal feast.

> As to the origin and precise nature of the *Quartodeciman* observance, there is not yet an entire agreement.
> *G. P. Fisher*, Begin. of Christianity, p. 331.

Quartodecimani (kwâr-tō-des-i-mā'nī), *n. pl.* [See *Quartodeciman.*] The Quartodecimans.

Quartodecimanian (kwâr-tō-des-i-mā'ni-an), *n.* and *a.* [< *Quartodeciman* + *-ian.*] Same as *Quartodeciman.* Also *Quartadecimanian.*

quartole (kwâr'tōl), *n.* [< L. *quartus*, fourth: see *quart*[1].] In *music*, a group of four notes to be performed in the time of three or six. Compare *decimole, quintole*, etc.

quartrain† (kwâr'trān), *n.* An improper form of *quatrain.*

quartridge† (kwâr'trij), *n.* An obsolete form of *quarterage.*

quartz (kwârts), *n.* [= F. *quartz* = Sp. *cuarzo* = Pg. It. *quarzo* = D. *kwarts* = Sw. *qvarts* = Dan. *kvarts* = Russ. *kvartsŭ*, < MHG. *quarz* (pl. *querze*), G. *quarz*, rock-crystal, quartz.] The common form of native silica, or the oxid of silicon (SiO_2). Silica is also found in nature in the minerals opal and tridymite (which see). Quartz occurs crystallized and massive, and in both states is most abundantly diffused, being one of the constituents of granite, gneiss, and many other crystalline rocks, forming quartzite and sandstone, and making up the mass of the sand of the sea-shore. When crystallized it commonly occurs in hexagonal prisms, terminated by hexagonal pyramids. It belongs, however, to the rhombohedral division of the hexagonal system, and its forms are sometimes very complex. Optically it is remarkable as exhibiting the phenomenon of circular polarization, the right- and left-handed character of the crystals optically corresponding to the arrangement of the modifying trapezohedral planes present. It scratches glass readily (hardness 7), gives fire with steel, becomes electrified by friction, and also by heating and pressure. It is infusible in the flame of the blowpipe, and insoluble in ordinary reagents except hydrofluoric acid. Its specific gravity is 2.66 when pure, and the luster vitreous or in some cases greasy to dull. The colors are various, as white or milky, gray, reddish, yellowish, or brownish, purple, blue, green. When colorless, or nearly so, and crystallized, it is known as rock-crystal (which see): here belong the "Lake George diamonds," etc. Other distinctly crystalline varieties are the pink, called rose-quartz; the milk-white, milk-quartz; the purple or bluish-violet, amethyst; the smoky-yellow or brown, smoky quartz or Cairngorm stone, called *morion* when black or nearly so; the yellow, false topaz or citrine; the aventurin, spangled with scales of mica or hematite; sagenitic, containing acicular crystals of rutile; the cat's-eye, opalescent through the presence of asbestos fibers. The cryptocrystalline varieties are named according either to color or to structure: here belong chalcedony, agate in many forms, onyx, sardonyx, carnelian, heliotrope, prase, chrysoprase, flint, hornstone, jasper, basanite, agatized wood, etc. (see these words). The transparent varieties of quartz (amethyst, smoky quartz, etc.) are used for cheap jewelry, also when colorless for spectacles (then called *pebble*), and for optical instruments. Quartz prisms are useful in spectrum analysis, since quartz is highly transparent to the ultra-violet rays. (See *spectrum*.) Beautiful spheres of rock-crystal, sometimes several inches in diameter, occur in Japan. The massive colored kinds of quartz are much used as ornamental stones, especially the agates and agatized or fossil wood, onyx, etc. In these cases the colors are often produced or at least heightened by artificial means. Pulverized quartz is employed in making sandpaper; also when pure for glass-making, and in the manufacture of porcelain. Quartz-veins are often found in metamorphic rocks, and frequently contain rich deposits of gold; hence, in California and other gold-mining regions mining in the solid rock is commonly called *quartz-mining*, in contradistinction to *placer* and *hydraulic mining*. See cut under *geode*.—**Babel quartz**, a curious form of quartz crystals found at Beer Alston in Devonshire, England, the under surface of which shows the impression of the crystals of fluor-spar upon which the quartz was deposited. Also called *Babylonian quartz*.—**Capped quartz**, a variety of crystallized quartz occurring in Cornwall, England, embedded in compact quartz. When the matrix is broken the crystals are revealed, and a cast of their pyramidal terminations in intaglio is obtained. Another kind consists of separable layers or caps, due to successive interruptions in the growth of the crystal, with perhaps a deposition of a little clay between the layers.—**Milky quartz.** Same as *milk-quartz*.

quartz-crusher (kwârts'krush"ėr), *n.* A machine for pulverizing quartz.

quartziferous (kwârt-sif'ẹ-rus), *a.* [< *quartz* + *-i-ferous*.] Consisting of quartz, or chiefly of quartz; containing quartz.

quartzite (kwârt'sīt), *n.* [< *quartz* + *-ite*[2].] A rock composed essentially of the mineral quartz. It is a rock of frequent occurrence, and often forms deposits of great thickness. Quartzite is rarely without a granular structure, either perceptible to the naked eye or visible with the aid of the microscope. Sometimes, however, this structure is with great difficulty perceptible. It is generally held by geologists that quartzite has resulted from the alteration of quartzose sand, pressure and the presence of siliciferous solutions having thoroughly united the grains of which the rock was originally composed. The quartzose material of which many veins are made up (material which must have been deposited from a solution) is not generally designated as quartzite, this sense being reserved for such quartz as is recognized by its stratigraphic position to have been formed from sedimentary material.

quartzitic (kwârt-sit'ik), *a.* [< *quartzite* + *-ic*.] Of or pertaining to quartzite or quartz; consisting of quartzite or quartz.

quartz-liquefier (kwârts'lik"wẹ-fī-ėr), *n.* An apparatus in which comminuted auriferous quartz is dissolved to liberate the gold.

quartz-mill (kwârts'mil), *n.* 1. A machine for pulverizing quartz, differing in character from the ordinary mill in which the ore is pulverized by stamping, but intended to serve the same purpose. See *stamp-mill*.—2. An establishment where auriferous quartz is stamped or in some other way reduced to a powder, and the gold separated from it by amalgamation; a stamp-mill.

quartzoid (kwârt'soid), *a.* [< *quartz* + *-oid*.] In *crystal.*, a double six-sided pyramid, represented by uniting two six-sided single pyramids base to base.

quartzose (kwârt'sōs), *a.* [< *quartz* + *-ose*.] Composed of quartz. Quartzose rocks are such as are essentially made up of the mineral quartz. Also *quartzous*.

quartz-porphyry (kwârts'pôr"fi-ri), *n.* See *porphyry*.

quartz-reef (kwârts'rēf), *n.* Same as *quartz-vein*. [Australian.]

quartz-rock (kwârts'rok), *n.* Quartzite.

quartz-sinter (kwârts'sin"tėr), *n.* Silicious sinter.

quartz-trachyte, *n.* See *trachyte*.

quartz-vein (kwârts'vān), *n.* A deposit of quartz in the form of a vein. Most of the gold obtained from mining in the solid rock, and not by washing of detrital material, comes from veins of which the gangue is entirely or chiefly quartz; hence auriferous veins are often called *quartz-veins*, and mining for gold in the rock is called *quartz-mining*.

quartzy (kwârt'si), *a.* [< *quartz* + *-y*[1].] Containing or abounding in quartz; pertaining to quartz; partaking of the nature or qualities of quartz; resembling quartz.

The iron ore is still further separated from its granitic or *quartzy* matrix by washing.
Sir George C. M. Birdwood, Indian Arts, II. 4.

quas (kwas), *n.* Same as *kvass*.

quash[1] (kwosh), *v.* [< ME. *quashen*, *quaschen*, *quassen*, *quessen*, < OF. *quasser*, *casser*, *quassier*, *quesser*, *kaisser*, break in pieces, bruise, shatter, maltreat, destroy, F. *casser*, break, shatter, < L. *quassare*, shake or toss violently, shatter, fig. shatter, impair, weaken, freq. of *quatere*, pp. *quassus*, shake, shatter, break in pieces; whence also ult. E. *concuss*, *discuss*, *percuss*, *rescue*. In the fig. sense this verb (L. *quassare*) merges with F. *casser*, annul: see *quash*[2].] **I.** *trans.* 1. To beat down or beat in pieces; crush.

Abowte scho whirles the whele, and whirles me undire,
Tille alle my qwarters that whilie whare *qwaste* al to peces!
Morte Arthure (E. E. T. S.), l. 3390.

The whales
Against sharp rocks, like reeling vessels *quash'd*,
Though huge as mountains, are in pieces dash'd.
Waller, Battle of the Summer Islands, ii.

2. To crush; subdue; put down summarily; quell; extinguish; put an end to.

The word Puritan seemes to be *quasht*, and all that heretofore were counted such are now Brownists.
Milton, Church-Government, i. 6.

The Commotions in Sicily are *quashed*, but those of Naples increase. *Howell*, Letters, iii. 1.

To doubts so put, and so *quashed*, there seemed to be an end for ever. *Lamb*, Witches.

II. *intrans.* To be shaken with a noise; make the noise of water when shaken.

The erthe quook and *quashte* as hit quyke were.
Piers Plowman (C), xxi. 64.

A thin and fine membrane strait and closely adhering to keep it [the brain] from *quashing* and shaking.
Ray, Works of Creation, ii.

quash[2] (kwosh), *v. t.* [< ME. **quashen*, < OF. *quasser*, prop. *casser*, annihilate, annul, F. *casser*, annul, < LL. *cassare*, annihilate, destroy, annul, < L. *cassus*, empty, hollow, fig. empty, vain, useless, futile, null: see *cass*[1], *cash*[1], *cassation*[1], *cashier*[1], etc.] To make void; annul; in *law*, to annul, abate, overthrow, or set aside for insufficiency or other cause: as, to *quash* an indictment.

Pleas in abatement (when the suit is by original) conclude to the writ or declaration by praying "judgment of the writ, or declaration, and that the same may be *quashed*," cassetur, made void, or abated.
Blackstone, Com., III. xx.

quash[3] (kwosh), *n.* [Perhaps so called with ref. to its being easily broken; < *quash*[1], *v.* *Squash*[2] is of Amer. Ind. origin.] 1†. A pompion. *Halliwell*.—2. Same as *squash*[2] (?).

The Indian kale, ochro, *quash*, peppers, ackys, and a variety of pulse being natural to the climate [of Jamaica].
T. *Roughley*, Jamaica Planter's Guide (1823), p. 74.

quashey (kwosh'i), *n.* [Cf. *quash*[3].] A pumpkin.

With regard to these said *quasheys*, . . . the best way of dressing them is to stew them in cream.
Southey, Letters (1823), iii. 391. (*Davies*.)

quashy-quasher (kwosh'i-kwosh"ėr), *n.* A small tree, *Thevetia neriifolia*, of the West Indies and tropical America. It has saffron-colored funnel-shaped flowers, its wood is hard and even-grained, and its seeds yield a fixed oil called *exile-oil*.

quasi (kwā'sī), *conj.* or *adv.* [L., as if, just as, as it were, about, nearly, < *quam*, as, how, + *si*, if.] As if; as it were; in a manner: used in introducing a proposed or possible explanation.

quasi-. [< L. *quasi*, as if, as it were: see *quasi*.] A prefix or apparent adjective or adverb (and hence often written without the hyphen) meaning 'seeming,' 'apparent' (equivalent to 'as it were,' 'in appearance,' in predicate use), expressing some resemblance, but generally implying that what it qualifies is in some degree fictitious or unreal, or has not all the features of what it professes to be: as, a *quasi*-argument; a *quasi*-historical account. In construction and partly in sense it is like *pseudo-*.

The popular poets always represent Macon, Apolin, Tervagant, and the rest as *quasi*-deities, unable to resist the superior strength of the Christian God.
Lowell, Among my Books, 2d ser., p. 110.

A *quasi* hereditary priesthood is in each.
J. F. Clarke, Ten Great Religions, vi. 7.

Henry . . . allowed the Archbishop of Canterbury to exercise a *quasi*-legatine authority under himself, and with a check in Chancery on his proceedings.
Stubbs, Medieval and Modern Hist., p. 259.

Quasi contract, a legal relation existing between parties to which the law attaches some of the characteristics of a contractual relation. See *natural obligation*, under *natural*.—**Quasi corporation, délit, entail.** See the nouns.—**Quasi delict** [LL. *quasi delictum*], in *Rom. law*, the contravention of certain police regulations which imposed a penalty upon a person for certain acts committed by any one belonging to his family—for example, throwing of water out of the windows. The distinction between *delicta* and *quasi delicta* has been followed by some authors whose writings are based on the common law; and *quasi delicta* are defined as those acts by which damage is done to the obligee, though without the negligence or intention of the obligor, and for which damage the obligor is bound to make satisfaction. As, however, intention is not necessary to constitute a delict (tort), the distinction seems to be unnecessary in modern systems.

quasi-evolute (kwā'sī-ev"ọ-lūt), *n.* In *math.*, the envelop of the quasi-normal of a curve.

quasi-fee (kwā'sī-fē), *n.* In *law*, an estate gained by wrong. *Wharton*.

quasi-geometrical (kwā-sī-jē-ọ-met'ri-kạl), *a.* Relating to hyperspace.

quasi-heirloom (kwā'sī-ãr"löm), *n.* See *heirloom*, 1.

Quasimodo (kwas-i-mō'dō). [= F. *quasimodo*; so called because the introit for this day begins with the words "*Quasi modo* geniti infantes," As new-born babes (1 Pet. ii. 2): L. *quasi*, as if; *modo*, just now, lately.] Same as *Low Sunday*. Also called *Quasimodo Sunday* and *Quasimodo-geniti Sunday*. See *low*[2].

quasi-normal (kwā-sī-nôr'mạl), *n.* The harmonic conjugate of the tangent to a curve with respect to the lines joining its point of contact to two fixed points.

quasi-period (kwā-sī-pē'ri-ọd), *n.* That constant which, added to the variable of a quasi-periodic function, multiplies the constant by a fixed function.

quasi-periodic (kwā-sī-pē-ri-od'ik), *a.* Noting a function such that, when the variable is increased by a certain fixed amount, it has its value multiplied by a fixed function: thus, l^x is *quasi-periodic*, because $l^{x+1} = l.\,l^x$.

quasi-radiate (kwā-sī-rā'di-āt), *a.* In *bot.*, slightly radiate: noting the heads of some composites whose ray-florets are small and inconspicuous.

quasi-realty (kwā-sī-rē'ạl-ti), *n.* In *law*, things which are fixed in contemplation of law to realty, but are movable in themselves, as heirlooms, title-deeds, court-rolls, etc. *Wharton*.

quasi-tenant (kwā-sī-ten'ạnt), *n.* In *law*, an undertenant who is in possession at the determination of an original lease, and is permitted by the reversioner to hold over. *Wharton*.

quasi-trustee (kwā"sī-trus-tē'), *n.* In *law*, a person who reaps a benefit from a breach of trust, and so becomes answerable as a trustee. *Wharton*.

quasje, *n.* See *coati*.

quass[1]†, *v.* A Middle English form of *quash*[1].

quass[2]† (kwas), *n.* Same as *kvass*.

With spiced Meades (wholsome but deer),
As Meade Obarne and Mead Cherunk,
And the base *Quasse* by Pesants drunk.
Pimlyco or Runne Red Cap (1609), quoted in Gifford's Jonson, VII. 241.

quassation (kwa-sā'shọn), *n.* [< L. *quassatio(n-)*, a shaking or beating, < *quassare*, shake, shatter: see *quash*[1].] The act of shaking; concussion; the state of being shaken.

Continual contusions, threshing, and *quassations*.
Gayton, Notes on Don Quixote, p. 68.

quassative (kwas'ạ-tiv), *a.* [< L. *quassatus*, pp. of *quassare*, shake: see *quash*[1].] Tremulous; easily shaken.

A Frenchman's heart is more *quassative* and subject to tremor than an Englishman's.
Middleton, Anything for a Quiet Life, iii. 2.

Quassia (kwash'iạ), *n.* [NL. (Linnæus, 1763), named after *Quassi* or *Coissi*, a negro slave in Surinam, who used its bark as a remedy for fever. *Quassi*, *Quassy*, or *Quashy* was a common name of negroes.] 1. A genus of plants, of the order *Simarubaceæ* and tribe *Simarubeæ*.

It is characterized by a large columnar receptacle bearing a small five-lobed calyx, five long erect petals, ten thread-like stamens, and a five-lobed ovary ripening into five fleshy drupes. There are 2 species: one, little known, is from

Branch of *Quassia amara*, with inflorescence. *a*, a flower; *b*, the fruit.

tropical Africa; the other, *Q. amara*, is a tall and smooth tree of tropical America, with intensely bitter wood, bearing alternate pinnate leaves with a winged petiole, and having terminal racemes of large scarlet tubular flowers.
2. [*l. c.*] A drug, also called *bitter-wood*, consisting of the wood of *Picræna* (*Quassia*) *excelsa*, and of two or three related trees; also, a medicinal preparation from these woods. The original tree was *Quassia amara*, the Surinam quassia. Its wood is still in use in France and Germany, but is largely superseded by that of the more abundant *Picræna excelsa*, a tall tree, the bitter-ash of Jamaica and some smaller islands. A substitute for these is *Simaruba amara*, the mountain-damson or bitter damson or stavewood of the West Indies and northern South America. Quassia-wood is imported in billets, and appears in the shops in the form of chips, raspings, etc. As a remedy it possesses in the highest degree the properties of the simple bitters. Its virtues are due to the principle quassin. Cups turned from the wood impart a bitter taste to their contents, and were once popular. A sweetened infusion of quassia is useful to destroy flies. *Picræna excelsa* has sometimes been substituted for hops in brewing, but this use is considered deleterious. See *bitter ash* (under *ash*1), *bitter-wood*, and *mountain-damson*.

quassia-tree (kwash'iạ-trē), *n.* Any of the trees producing the drug quassia; a bitterwood-tree.

Quassilabia (kwas-i-lā'bi-ạ), *n.* [NL. (Jordan and Brayton, 1878), < L. *quassus*, pp. of *quatere*, shake, + *labium*, lip.] A genus of catostomoid fishes of the United States; the hare-lip suckers.

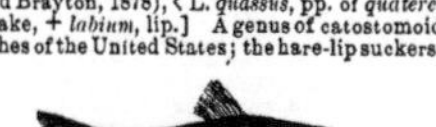
Quassilabia lacera.

Q. lacera is the cutlips, or May, splitmouth, or rabbit-mouth sucker, a singular fish of the Ohio valley and southward, of an olivaceous or brownish color above, the sides and belly silvery, the lower fins tinged with orange, and a peculiar formation of the mouth which has suggested both the technical and the vernacular names.

quassin (kwas'in), *n.* [< *quassia* + *-in*2.] The neutral bitter principle of quassia (*Picræna excelsa*). This substance crystallizes from aqueous solutions in very small white prisms. Its taste is intensely bitter, but it is destitute of odor. It is scarcely soluble in common ether, slightly soluble in water, and more soluble in alcohol. Also called *quassiin*.

quassite (kwas'īt), *n.* [< *quassia* + *-ite*2.] Same as *quassin*.

quasum†, *pron.* [ME., < *qua*, dial. form of *who*, + *sum*, mod. E. *some*.] Whoso.

> *Qua-sum* this tale can beter tende,
> For Cristis loue he hit amende.
> *Holy Rood* (E. E. T. S.), p. 120.

quat1 (kwot), *v.* [< OF. *quatir*, *quattir*, *catir*, press down, strike down, plunge, sink, hide, refl. crouch, squat, hide, = It. *quattare*, dial. *cattare*, crouch, lie close, squat, < L. *coactare*, press together, constrain, force, < *cogere*, pp. *coactus*, press together, urge: see *cogent*. Cf. *squat*, *v.*, the same as *quat*, with a prefix; and cf. also the related *cache*1 and *squash*1.] I. *trans.* 1†. To press down; subdue.

> The renowne of her chastitie was such that it almost *quatted* those sparkes that heated him on to such lawlesse affection.
> *Greene*, Never too Late (Works, ed. Dyce, Int., p. xxi.).

2†. To oppress; satiate.

> Had Philotimus been served in at the first course, when your stomach was not *quatted* with other daintier fare, his relish had perhaps been something loathsome.
> *Philotimus*, 1583. (*Nares.*)

> To the stomack *quatted* with dainties al delicates seeme queasie.
> *Lyly*, Euphues, Anat. of Wit, p. 44.

3. To flatter. *Halliwell.* [Prov. Eng.]
II.† *intrans.* To squat.

quat2† (kwot), *n.* [Origin obscure.] 1. A pustule or pimple.—2. Figuratively, a small, shabby, or insignificant person.

> I have rubb'd this young *quat* almost to the sense,
> And he grows angry.
> *Shak.*, Othello, v. 1. 11.

quat3† (kwot), *v. t.* [A strong pret. and pp. of *quit*, used also as inf.] To quit.

quat3 (kwot), *p. a.* [See *quat*3, *v.*] Quit; free; released. [Scotch.]

quat4, *pron.* A dialectal form of *what*.

quata (kwä'tạ̈), *n.* Same as *coaita*.

quatch1 (kwoch), *v. i.* [Origin obscure.] To tell; be a telltale; peach. *Halliwell.* [Prov. Eng.]

quatch1 (kwoch), *n.* [< *quatch*1, *v.*] A word. *Halliwell.* [Prov. Eng.]

> Noe; not a *quatch*, sad poets; doubt you
> There is not greife enough without you?
> *Bp. Corbet*, Elegy on Death of Queen Anne. (*Davies.*)

quatch2† (kwoch), *a.* [Cf. *quat*1, *squat* (?).] Squat; flat.

> It is like a barber's chair, that fits all buttocks; the pin-buttock, the *quatch*-buttock, the brawn buttock, or any buttock.
> *Shak.*, All's Well, ii. 2. 18.

quater-cousin, *n.* Same as *cater-cousin*.

quaterfoil, *n.* See *quatrefoil*.

quatern (kwā'tėrn), *a.* [< L. *quaterni*, four each, by fours, distributive, < *quattuor*, four: see *quart*1. Cf. *quire*2.] Consisting of four; fourfold; growing by fours: as, *quatern* leaves.

quaternary (kwạ̄-tėr'nạ-ri), *a.* and *n.* [< L. *quaternarius*, consisting of four each, containing four, < *quaterni*, four each, by fours: see *quatern*.] I. *a.* 1. Consisting of four; arranged or grouped in fours.

> Reproductive organs . . . solitary or *quaternary* in the same sporangium.
> *Le Maout and Decaisne*, Botany (trans.), p. 966.

2. [*cap.*] In *geol.*, noting that part of the geological series which is more recent than the Tertiary; Post-tertiary. (See *Tertiary*.) The oldest and most general division of the Quaternary is into *diluvial* and *alluvial*, by which terms are meant respectively coarse detrital material and fine detrital material—the one the result of rapid, the other of slower currents of water. The former presence of ice, both fixed and floating, over a part of the northern hemisphere, and especially in the regions where geology was earliest cultivated, has greatly complicated the question of this division of the Quaternary into subgroups or epochs. Thus *diluvial* has come to be replaced for the most part by *glacial*; and some English geologists divide the Quaternary into *glacial* and *recent*, using the term *Pleistocene* also as the equivalent of *glacial*. The term *recent* has also as its synonym both *alluvial* and *human*. While the essential difference between Tertiary and Quaternary is theoretically supposed to be that in the former a portion of the fossil species are extinct, while in the latter all are living, this does not apply in the case of land-animals, especially the mammals. In fact, there is, over extensive areas, great difficulty in deciding the question whether certain formations shall be called Tertiary or Quaternary, as, for instance, in the case of the Pampean deposits, which, although containing great numbers of species of mammals all or nearly all extinct, are generally considered by geologists as being of Quaternary age.
3. In *old chem.*, noting those compounds which contained four elements, as fibrin, gelatin, etc. —4. In *math.*, containing, as a quantic, or homogeneous integral function, four variables. A surface may be called a *quaternary locus*, because defined by a quaternary equation, or one equating a quaternary quantic to zero.—**Quaternary cubic.** See *cubic*.—**Quaternary number**, ten: so called by the Pythagoreans because equal to $1 + 2 + 3 + 4$. Pythagoras, in the oath of the brotherhood, was called the revealer of the quaternary number, on account of some secret of arithmetic, possibly an abacus.—**Quaternary quadrics.** See *quadric*.
II. *n.* A group of four things.

> The objections I made against the *quaternary* of elements and ternary of principles needed not to be opposed so much against the doctrines themselves.
> *Boyle*, Works, I. 586.

quaternate (kwạ̄-tėr'nāt), *a.* [< NL. *quaternatus*, < L. *quaterni*, four each: see *quatern*.] Consisting of four.—**Quaternate leaf**, a leaf that consists of four leaflets.

quaternion (kwạ̄-tėr'ni-ọn), *n.* [Also *quarternion*; < L. *quaternio(n-)*, the number four, a body or group of four, < *quaterni*, four each, by fours: see *quatern*.] 1. A set, group, or body of four: applied to persons or things.

> He put him in prison, and delivered him to four *quarternions* of soldiers.
> Acts xii. 4.

> Myself . . . am called Anteros, or Love's enemy; the more welcome therefore to thy court, and the fitter to conduct this *quarternion*.
> B. *Jonson*, Cynthia's Revels, v. 3.

> When and where this *quarternion* rhyme, as it is used by Berceo, was first introduced, cannot be determined.
> *Ticknor*, Span. Lit., I. 27.

2. A word of four syllables; a quadrisyllable.

> The triads and *quarternions* with which he loaded his speech.
> *Scott.*

3. A fourfold quantity capable of being expressed in the form $xi + yj + zk + w$, where x, y, z, w are scalars, or real numbers, while i, j, k are vectors, or quantities whose squares are negative scalars. The calculus of such quantities is termed *quaternions*.

> A *Quaternion* is the quotient of two vectors, or of two directed right lines in space, considered as depending on a system of Four Geometrical Elements, and as expressible by an algebraical symbol of Quadrinomial Form. The science, or Calculus, of *Quaternions* is a new mathematical method wherein the foregoing conception of a *quaternion* is unfolded and symbolically expressed, and is applied to various classes of algebraical, geometrical, and physical questions, so as to discover many new theorems, and to arrive at the solution of many difficult problems.
> *Sir W. Rowan Hamilton.*

Conjugate of a quaternion. See *conjugate*.—**Conjugate quaternions.** See *conjugate*.—**Quaternion group.** See *group*1.

quaternion (kwạ̄-tėr'ni-ọn), *v. t.* [< *quaternion*, *n.*] To divide into quaternions, files, or companies.

> The Angels themselves . . . are distinguisht and *quaterniond* into their celestiall Princedomes.
> *Milton*, Church-Government, i. 1.

quaternionist (kwạ̄-tėr'ni-ọn-ist), *n.* [< *quaternion* + *-ist*.] A student of quaternions.

> Do we depart wider from the primary traditions of arithmetic than the *Quaternionist* does?
> *J. Venn*, Symbolic Logic, p. 91.

quaternity (kwạ̄-tėr'ni-ti), *n.* [= F. *quaternité*; as *quatern* + *-ity*.] 1. The state of being four; the condition of making up the number four.

> The number of four stands much admired, not only in the *quaternity* of the elements, which are the principles of bodies, but in the letters of the name of God.
> *Sir T. Browne*, Vulg. Err., iv. 12.

2. A group of four.

> So that their whole scale, of all that is above body, was indeed not a trinity, but a *quarternity*, or four ranks and degrees of beings one below another.
> *Cudworth*, Intellectual System, p. 557.

quateron, *n.* Same as *quadroon*.

quatorzain (ka-tôr'zān), *n.* [Formerly also *quaterzayn*; < OF. *quatorzaine*, *quatorsaine*, the number fourteen, < *quatorze*, fourteen: see *quatorze*.] A stanza or poem of fourteen lines; a sonnet.

> Put out your rush candles, you poets & rimers, and bequeath your crazed *quarterzayne* to the chandlers; for loe! here he commeth that hath broken your legs.
> *Nashe*, quoted in Pierce Penilesse, Int., p. xxiv.

> His [Drayton's] next publication is Idea's mirror; Amours in *Quatorzains*, 1594. It contains fifty-one sonnets.
> *N. and Q.*, 6th ser., X. 61.

quatorze (ka-tôrz'), *n.* [< F. *quatorze*, < L. *quattuordecim*, fourteen, < *quattuor*, four, + *decem*, ten: see *fourteen*.] In the game of piquet, the four aces, kings, queens, knaves, or tens: so called because such a group of four, in the hand that holds the highest, counts fourteen points.

quatrain (kwot'rān), *n.* [Formerly also, improp., *quartrain*; < F. *quatrain*, a stanza of four lines, < *quatre*, four, < L. *quattuor* = E. *four*: see *four*.] A stanza of four lines riming alternately.

> I have chosen to write my poem in *quatrains*, or stanzas of four in alternate rhyme, because I have ever judged them more noble, and of greater dignity both for the sound and number, than any other verse in use amongst us.
> *Dryden*, Account of Annus Mirabilis.

> Who but Landor could have written the faultless and pathetic *quatrain*?—
> I strove with none, for none was worth my strife;
> Nature I loved, and, next to Nature, Art;
> I warmed both hands before the fire of life;
> It sinks, and I am ready to depart.
> *Stedman*, Vict. Poets, p. 69.

quatraylet†, *n.* [< OF. *quatre-ayle*, etc., < *quatre*, four, + *ayle*, grandfather: see *ayle*.] A male ancestor three generations earlier than one's grandfather.

> Thomas Gould, . . . who died in 1520. He was the *quatrayle* of Zaccheus Gould[6], the New England immigrant.
> *New England Bibliopolist*, I. 71.

quatre-cousin†, *n.* Same as *cater-cousin*.

quatrefoil (kat'ėr-foil), *n.* [Also *quaterfoil*, *quarterfoil*; < ME. *katrefoil*, < OF. (and F.) *quatrefeuille*, < *quatre*, four (< L. *quattuor* = E. *four*), + *feuille*, leaf (< L. *folium*, leaf): see *four* and *foil*1.] 1. A leaf with four leaflets, as sometimes that of clover.

> And *katrefoil*, whenne thai beth up ysponge,
> Transplaunte hem into lande ydight with dounge.
> *Palladius*, Husbondrie (E. E. T. S.), p. 191.

2. In *arch.*, an opening or a panel divided by cusps or foliations into four foils, or, more correctly, the figure formed by the cusps. This

Quatrefoils.

ornament resembles the four petals of a cruciform flower, but is certainly not derived from imitation of such a flower. Bands of small quatrefoils are much used as orna-

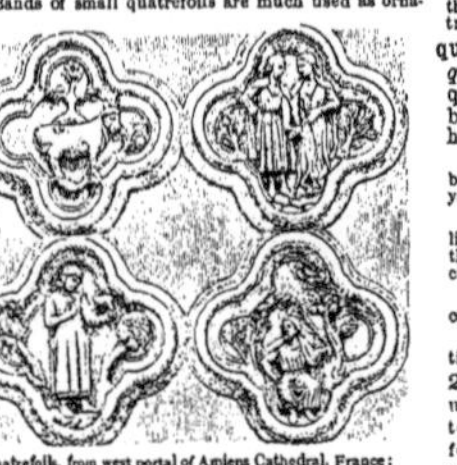

Quatrefoils, from west portal of Amiens Cathedral, France; 13th century.

ments in the English Perpendicular style, and sometimes in the Decorated. The same name is given also to flowers and leaves of similar form carved in relief as ornaments on moldings, etc. See also cut under *gallery*.
3. In *her.*, a four-leaved grass, or leaf divided into four leaflets, used as a bearing.—**Cross quatrefoil.** See *cross*¹.—**Double quatrefoil.** Same as *eight-foil* or *octofoil*.

quatrible (kat'ri-bl), *n.* [< OF. *quadruble*, *quadrouble*, *quadruple*, a piece of music for four voices or four instruments, < *quadruple*, fourfold: see *quadruple*.] In *medieval music*, a descant in parallel fourths to the cantus firmus.

quatrible (kat'ri-bl), *v. i.*; pret. and pp. *quatribled*, ppr. *quatribling*. [< *quatrible*, *n.*] In *medieval music*, to sing a descant at the interval of a fourth from the cantus firmus. See *diaphony*, 2. Compare *quinible*.

quatron†, *a.* An obsolete variant of *quatern*. *Halliwell.*

quatto, *n.* Same as *coaita*.

quattrino (kwä-trē'nō), *n.* [It. (ML. *quatrinus*), < *quattro*, four: see *four*.] An Italian coin of about the value of a half a United States cent.

The *quattrino*, a square coin which was struck during his [Loredano's] reign.
C. C. *Perkins*, Italian Sculpture, p. 356, note.

quattrocentist (kwät-rō-chen'tist), *n.* [= F. *quattrocentiste*, < It. *quattrocentista*, quattrocentist, < *quattrocento* (see *quattrocento*) + *-ist*.] An Italian of the fifteenth century; specifically, an Italian artist of the style of art called quattrocento.

It was a revelation to me, and I began to trace the purity of work in the *quattrocentists* to this drilling of undeviating manipulation which fresco-painting had furnished to them. *Contemporary Rev.*, XLIX. 476.

quattrocento (kwät-rō-chen'tō), *n.* and *a.* [It., lit. 400 (< *quattro*, < L. *quattuor*, four, + *cento*, < L. *centum*, hundred), but used as an abbreviation of *mille quattrocento*, 1400, with ref. to the century (1401–1500) in question. Cf. *cinque-cento*.] I. *n.* The fifteenth century considered as an epoch of art or literature, and especially in connection with Italy: as, the sculpture of the *quattrocento*. The painters of the early part of the period had not yet attained the power to render their conceptions with entire freedom; but their coloring is very beautiful, and their sentiment in general nobler than that of the artists who followed them.

II. *a.* Belonging to, or living or produced in, the fifteenth century; of the style of the fifteenth century: as, *quattrocento* sculpture.

quatuor (kwat'ū-ôr), *n.* [< L. *quatuor*, prop. *quattuor*, = E. *four*: see *four*.] In *music*, a quartet.

quaught (kwâcht), *v. t.* and *i.* [Early mod. E. also *quaght*; Sc. *waught*, *waucht*; origin uncertain. Cf. *quaff*.] To drink; quaff.

I *quaught*, I drinke all out.
Wyll you *quaght* with me? *Palsgrave.*

quave† (kwāv), *v. i.* [Early mod. E. also *queave*; < ME. *quaven*, earlier *cwavien*; akin to *quab*¹, *quap*¹. Hence freq. *quaver*, q. v.] To quiver; shake.

The daye for drede with-drowe, and derke bicam the sonne,
The wal [veil] wagged and clef [was rent], and al the worlde *quaued*. *Piers Plowman* (B), xviii. 61.

While thy mighte
Can keepe my harte *queavinge* or quicke.
Puttenham, Partheniades, vi.

quave† (kwāv), *n.* [< ME. *quave*; < *quave*, *v.*] A shaking; trembling. *Prompt. Parv.*, p. 419.

quavemire† (kwāv'mīr), *n.* [Also contr. *quamire*; < *quave* + *mire*. Cf. *quagmire*, *quakemire*.] Same as *quagmire*. *Palsgrave.*

A muddie *quavemire*. *Mir. for Mags.*, p. 653.

Howbeit, Aratus would not suffer the Achaians to follow them, because of bogs and *quavemires*, but sounded the retreat. *North*, tr. of Plutarch, p. 670.

quaver (kwā'vėr), *v.* [< ME. *quaveren*, freq. of *quave*; cf. LG. *quabbeln* = G. *quabbeln*, *quappeln*, quiver, tremble, freq. of the form represented by E. *quab*¹. Cf. *quiver*¹.] I. *intrans.* 1. To have a tremulous motion; tremble; vibrate.

It semythe that the worlde is alle *qwaveryng*; it will reboyle somwher, so that I deme yonge men shall be cheryshed. *Paston Letters*, III. 174.

At the end of this Hole is a Membrane, . . . stretched like the Head of a Drum, . . . to receive the Impulse of the Sound, and to vibrate or *quaver* according to its reciprocal Motions. *Ray*, Works of Creation, p. 263.

If the finger be moved with a *quavering* motion, they [the colors] appear again. *Newton*, Opticks.

Her hand trembled, her voice *quavered* with that emotion which is not strength. *Stedman*, Vict. Poets, p. 143.

2. To sing or sound with the wavy tones of an untrained voice, or with a distinctly tremulous tone; hence, to sing, in general; also, to perform a shake or similar melodic embellishment with the voice or an instrument.

You'd swear that Randal, in his rustic strains,
Again was *quavering* to the country swains.
Dryden and Soames, tr. of Boileau's Art of Poetry, ii.

Now sportive youth
Carol incondite rhythms with suiting notes,
And *quaver* unharmonious. *J. Philips*, Cider, ii.

II. *trans.* To sing in an artless manner or with tremulous tone.

And for Musick an old hoarse singing man riding ten miles from his Cathedral to *Quaver* out the Glories of our Birth and State. *Shadwell*, The Scowrers.

We will *quaver* out Peccavimus together.
Thackeray, Philip, xxvii.

quaver (kwā'vėr), *n.* [< *quaver*, *v.*] 1. A quivering; a trembling.

The worth of such actions is not a thing to be decided in a *quaver* of sensibility or a flush of righteous common sense. *R. L. Stevenson*, The English Admirals.

2. A tremulous or quivering sound or tone.

And the choristers' song, that late was so strong,
Grew a *quaver* of consternation.
Southey, Old Woman of Berkeley.

3. A shake or similar embellishment, particularly in vocal music.

I hearde a certaine French man who sung very melodiously with curious *quauers*.
Coryat, Crudities, I. 36, sig. D.

It has at least received great improvements among us, whether we consider the instrument itself, or those several *quavers* and graces which are thrown into the playing of it. *Addison*, The Cat-Call.

4. An eighth-note (which see).—**Quaver-rest**, in *musical notation*, same as *eighth-rest*.

quaverer (kwā'vėr-ėr), *n.* One who or that which quavers; a warbler.

quaveringly (kwā'vėr-ing-li), *adv.* In a quavering or tremulous manner.

quavery (kwā'vėr-i), *a.* [< *quaver* + *-y*¹.] Shaky; unstable.

A *quauery* or a maris and unstable foundacion must be holpe with great pylys of alder rammed downe, and with a frame of tymbre called a crossaundre.
Horman, quoted in Prompt. Parv., p. 419.

quaving† (kwā'ving), *n.* [< ME. *quavyng*; verbal n. of *quave*, *v.*] A shaking or trembling, as of the earth. *Sir T. Elyot*, Castle of Health, i. 2.

quaviver†, *n.* [Origin uncertain. Cf. *viver*.] A fish, the sea-dragon or dragonet; a kind of gurnard. See *gurnard* and *Trigla*.

Tumle, the great sea-dragon, or *quaviver*; also the gurnard, called so at Roan. *Cotgrave.*

Vive, the *quaviver*, or sea-dragon. *Cotgrave.*

Traigne, the sea-dragon, viver, *quaviver*. *Cotgrave.*

quawk (kwâk), *v. i.* [Imitative; cf. *squawk*.] To croak; caw. [Prov. Eng.]

quawk (kwâk), *n.* [Imitative; cf. *quawk*, *v.*] The qua-bird or night-heron, *Nyctiardea grisea nævia*. Also *quark*, *squawk*. [Local, U. S.]

quay¹, *n.* An obsolete or dialectal form of *whey*.

quay² (kē), *n.* [A more recent spelling, after the F. *quay*, now *quai*, of the earlier E. *kay*, *key* (the mod. pron. kē prop. belongs to *key* only): see *key*², *kay*².] A landing-place; a place where vessels are loaded and unloaded; a wharf: usually constructed of stone, but sometimes of wood, iron, etc., along a line of coast or a river-bank or round a harbor or dock.

Make *quays*, build bridges, or repair Whitehall.
Pope, Imit. of Horace, II. ii. 120.

To ascertain the limits of all ports, and to assign proper wharfs and *quays* in each port for the exclusive landing and loading of merchandise. *Blackstone*, Com., I. vii.

quay² (kē), *v. t.* [< *quay*², *n.*] To furnish with a quay or quays.

quayage (kē'āj), *n.* [Formerly *keyage*; < F. *quayage*, < *quay*, a key, quay: see *quay*².] Duty paid for repairing a quay, or for the use of a quay; quay-dues; wharfage.

quay-berth (kē'bėrth), *n.* A berth for a ship next to a quay.

quayed†, *a.* A manufactured form of *quailed*, past participle of *quail*¹. *Spenser.*

que¹, *n.* Same as *cue*².

que², *n.* A dialectal form of *cow*¹. *Halliwell.*

queach¹† (kwēch), *v. i.* A variant of *quitch*¹.

queach² (kwēch), *n.* [Also *quitch*; < ME. *queche*, a thicket.] 1. A thick bushy plot; a thorny thicket.

Thei rode so longe till thei com in to a thikke *queche* in a depe valey. *Merlin* (E. E. T. S.), iii. 540.

2. A plat of ground left unplowed on account of queaches or thickets. *Halliwell.* [Prov. Eng.]

queachy¹ (kwē'chi), *a.* [Also *queechy*; < *queach*¹ + *-y*¹.] Shaking; moving, yielding, or trembling under the feet, as wet or swampy ground.

'Twixt Penwith's furthest point and Goodwin's *queachy* sand. *Drayton*, Polyolbion, ii. 396.

I'n got no daughter o' my own—ne'er had one—an' I warna sorry, for they're poor *queechy* things, gells is.
George Eliot, Adam Bede, x. (*Davies.*)

queachy²† (kwē'chi), *a.* [Early mod. E. also *quechy*; < *queach*² + *-y*¹.] Bushy; thick.

The owle, that hates the day and loues to flee by night,
Hath *queachie* bushes to defende him from Apollo's sight.
Turberville, That All Things Have Release.

Our bloud is changed to Inke, our haires to Quils,
Our eyes halfe buried in our *quechy* plots.
Heywood, Golden Age, v. 1.

queal¹ (kwēl), *v. i.* [An earlier and more original form of *quail*¹.] To faint away. *Halliwell.* [Prov. Eng.]

queal², *n.* An obsolete or dialectal form of *wheal*.

quean (kwēn), *n.* [(*a*) Also dial. (Sc.) *quine*; early mod. E. *queane*, *quene*; < ME. *quene*, *quen*, *cwene*, < AS. *cwēne*, *cwȳne* (gen. *cwēnan*), prop. *cwēne*, orig. **cwine*, a woman (L. *femina*, *mulier*), wife (L. *uxor*) (cf. **cwēnfugol*, a hen-bird—a doubtful word in Somner), = OS. *quena*, wife, queen (L. *regina*), harlot (L. *meretrix*), = OD. *quene*, wife, MD. *quene*, a vain or worthless woman, a barren woman, also a barren cow, D. *kween*, a barren woman, a barren cow, = MLG. *quene*, an old woman, LG. *quene*, a barren cow, a heifer, = OHG. *quena* (*quëna*), *chwena*, *chena*, MHG. *chone*, *kone*, *kon*, G. (obs.) *kone*, a woman, G. dial. *kan*, *chan*, a woman, wife, = Icel. *kvenna* = Sw. *qvinna* = Dan. *kvinde*, a woman (cf. contr. Icel. *kona*, woman, = Sw. *kona*, a harlot, = Dan. *kone*, a woman, esp. a married woman, wife), = Goth. *qinō*, a woman, wife (Gr. γυνή); the above forms being distinct from, though partly confused with (*b*) E. *queen* (L. *regina*), < ME. *queen*, *quen*, *quene*, *kuen*, *cwene*, *cwen*, < AS. *cwēn*, rarely *cwǣn* (gen. *cwēne*), a woman (L. *femina*), wife (L. *uxor*), queen (L. *regina*, *imperatrix*, *augusta*), = OS. *quān*, wife, = OHG. *quēna*, *chuuēna* = Icel. *kvān*, *kvæn*, wife, = Goth. *kwēns*, rarely *kweins*, wife (not recorded in sense of 'queen'); both forms ult. akin to Ir. Gael. *coinne*, a woman; Gr. γυνή, a woman, female (see *gynæceum*, *gynarchy*, etc., *gynecocracy*, etc.); Skt. *jāni*, a wife, appar. < √ *jan* = Gr. √ γεν = L. √ *gen* = Teut. √ *ken*, bring forth: see *ken*², *kin*¹, *genus*, *generate*, etc.] A woman; a female person, considered without regard to qualities or position: hence generally in a slighting use. It may be merely neutral or familiar, like *wench* (as, a sturdy *quean*, a thriving *quean*), or be used in various degrees of depreciation (= *jade*, *slut*, *harlot*, *strumpet*). [Eng. and Scotch.]

Bastow with som *quene* al nyght yswonke?
Chaucer, Prol. to Manciple's Tale, l. 18.

At churche in the charnel cheorles aren yuel to knowe,
Other a knyght fro a knaue other a *queyne* fro a queene.
Piers Plowman (C), ix. 46.

Flavia, because her meanes are somewhat scant,
Doth sell her body to relieve her want,
Yet scornes to be reputed as a *quean*.
Times' Whistle (E. E. T. S.), p. 45.

I never was ambitious
Of using congees to my daughter-queen—
A queen! perhaps a *quean*!
Ford, Perkin Warbeck, ii. 3.

I see her yet, the sonsie *quean*
That lighted up my jingle.
Burns, To the Guidwife of Wauchope House.

My young master will . . . call you slut and *quean*, if there be but a speck of soot upon his bandbox.
Scott, Abbot, iv.

queasily (kwē'zi-li), *adv.* In a queasy manner; with squeamishness.

queasiness (kwē'zi-nes), *n.* The state of being queasy; nausea; qualmishness; inclination to vomit; disgust.

They did fight with *queasiness*, constrain'd,
As men drink potions. *Shak.*, 2 Hen. IV., i. 1. 196.

Let them live and die in servile condition and thir scrupulous *queasiness*, if no instruction will confirme them. *Milton*, Eikonoklastes, xxviii.

queasy (kwē'zi), *a.* [Early mod. E. and dial. also *quaisy*; < ME. *quaysy*, *queysy*, causing a feeling of nausea; prob. < Norw. *kveis*, sickness after a debauch, = Icel. *kveisa*, in comp. *idhra-kveisa*, colic, = Sw. dial. *kvesa*, soreness, blister, pimple; perhaps akin to Sw. *qväsa*, bruise, wound, squash, Dan. *kvase*, squash, crush. Cf. AS. *tōcwisan*, crush: see *squeeze*.] 1. Affected with nausea; inclined to vomit.

The Reverend Doctor Gaster found himself rather *queasy* in the morning, therefore preferred breakfasting in bed. *Peacock*, Headlong Hall, vii.

2. Fastidious; squeamish; delicate.

And even so in a manner these instruments make a man's wit so soft and smooth, so tender and *quaisy*, that they be less able to brook strong and tough study. *Ascham*, Toxophilus (ed. 1864), p. 27.

I am so *queasy*-stomached
I cannot taste such gross meat.
Massinger, Bondman, ii. 2.

Is there cause why these men should overween, and be so *queasie* of the rude multitude, lest their deepe worth should be undervalu'd for want of fit umpires? *Milton*, Apology for Smectymnuus.

Deprecation which is unusual even for the *queasy* modesty of sixteenth-century dedications. *S. Lanier*, Sci. of Eng. Verse, p. vi.

3. Apt to cause nausea; occasioning uncomfortable feelings; hence, requiring to be delicately handled; ticklish; nice.

Those times are somewhat *queasy* to be touched. *B. Jonson*, Sejanus, i. 1.

I have one thing, of a *queasy* question,
Which I must act. *Shak.*, Lear, ii. 1. 19.

I was not my own man again for the rest of the voyage. I had a *queasy* sense that I wore my last dry clothes upon my body. *R. L. Stevenson*, Inland Voyage, p. 132.

4. Short; brief. *Halliwell.* [Prov. Eng.]

queazen† (kwē'zn), *v. t.* [For **queasen*, < *queas(y)* + *-en*[1].] To make queasy; sicken.

The spirable odor and pestilent steame . . . would have *queazened* him. *Nashe*, Lenten Stuffe (Harl. Misc., VI. 173).

quebast, *n.* An old game.

Every afternoon at my Lady Briefs and my Lady Meanwell's at ombre and *quebas*. *Etheredge*, She Would if she Could, iii. 3.

Quebec group. In *geol.*, a division of the Lower Silurian established by the Canada Geological Survey, of very uncertain value.

According to recent researches by Mr. Selwyn, the *Quebec group* as defined by Logan embraces three totally distinct groups of rocks, belonging respectively to Archæan, Cambrian, and Lower Silurian horizons. *Geikie*, Text-Book of Geol., p. 691.

Quebec oak. See *oak*.

quebracho (ke-brä'chō), *n.* [Pg., contr. from *quebra-hacho*, 'ax-breaker'; so called in allusion to the hardness of the wood; < *quebrar*, break, + *hacha*, *facha*, ax: see *hatchet*.] The name of several hard-wooded South American trees of economic value. The white quebracho (*quebracho blanco*) is *Aspidosperma Quebracho*, best known for its medicinal bark. (See *quebracho bark*, under *bark*[2].) The red quebracho (*quebracho colorado*) is *Schinopsis* (*Loxopterygium*) *Lorentzii*, of the La Plata region. Its wood and bark form an important tanning-material, very rapid in action, exported to Europe in bulk and in extract. Its timber is extremely hard and strong. Another quebracho is *Iodina rhombifolia* of the *Santalaceæ* (*quebracho flojo*), its wood and bark being mixed with the last.—**Quebracho gum**, the dried juice or watery extract of *Schinopsis Lorentzii*. It is used for the relief of dyspnœa.

quebrada (ke-brä'dạ̈), *n.* [Sp., broken, uneven ground, prop. fem. of *quebrado*, pp. of *quebrar*, break.] A gorge; a ravine; a defile: a word occasionally used by writers in English on Mexican and South American physical geography, and by the Spanish Americans themselves, with about the same meaning as *barranca*.

quecchet, *v. i.* A Middle English form of *quitch*[1].

quech (kwech), *n.* Same as *quaigh*. [Scotch.]

queck†, *n.* [Origin uncertain; cf. *querken*.] A blow (?).

But what and the ladder slyppe, . . .
And yf I fall I catche a *quecke*,
I may fortune to breke my necke, . . .
Nay, nay, not so!
Enterlude of Youth. (*Halliwell.*)

queckshoes†, *n.* See *quelquechose*.

qued†, *a.* and *n.* [ME., also *quede*, *queed*, *quead*, *quad*, *quaad*, *queth*, < AS. **cwǣd* = OFries. *quad* = MD. *quaed*, D. *kwaad* = MLG. *quat*, LG. *quaad*, bad; otherwise found in the neuter, as a noun, AS. **cwǣd*, *cwedd*, filth, dung, = MD. *quaed*, *quaet*, *quat*, *kat* = OHG. *quat*, MHG. *quāt*, *kāt*, *quōt*, *kōt*, G. *kot*, *koth*, filth, dirt, mud.] I. *a.* Bad; evil.

II. *n.* 1. Evil; harm.

For to deme quike and dede
He scal come to gode and *quede*.
King Horn (E. E. T. S.), p. 121.

2. An evil person; especially, the evil one; the devil.

A shrew; an evil person.
Namly an eyre [heir] that ys a *qued*,
That desyreth hys fadrys ded.
MS. Harl. 1701, f. 42. (*Halliwell.*)

And lete me neuere falle in boondis of the *queed!*
Hymns to Virgin, etc. (E. E. T. S.), p. 6.

Quedius (kwē'di-us), *n.* [NL. (Stephens, 1832).] A notable genus of rove-beetles or *Staphylinidæ*, having the prothoracic stigmata each covered by a triangular lamella. About 120 species have been described, the majority from Europe, but many from Asia and America; 18 are found in America north of Mexico. Most of them have the ordinary rove-beetle habits, but *Q. dilatatus* breeds in hornets' nests in Europe, and will also eat honey.

quedship†, *n.* [ME. *quedschipe*, *quedschipe*; < *qued* + *-ship*.] Badness; evilness. *Ancren Riwle*, p. 310.

queed[1], *n.* A dialectal variant of *quid*[1]. *Halliwell.*

queed[2]†, *n.* See *qued*.

queen[1] (kwēn), *n.* [< ME. *queen*, *quen*, *quene*, *qwhene*, *whene*, *kuen*, *cwene*, *cwen*, < AS. *cwēn*, rarely *cwǣn* (gen. *cwēne*), a woman (L. *femina*), wife (L. *uxor*), queen (L. *regina*, *imperatrix*, *augusta*), = OS. *quān*, wife, = OHG. *quēna*, *chuuēna*, wife, = Icel. *kvān*, *kvæn*, wife, = Goth. *kwēns*, rarely *kweins*, wife (not recorded in the sense of 'queen'). See *quean*.] 1. The consort of a king.

Thursdaye, the laste daye of Apryll, to Lasheles, where lyethe *quene* Elyanour of Englonde, and in an abbey of her awne foundacyon. *Sir R. Guylforde*, Pylgrymage, p. 4.

I'll undertake to make thee Henry's *queen*.
Shak., 1 Hen. VI., v. 3. 117.

2. A woman who is the sovereign of a realm; a female sovereign. In countries under monarchical rule females are sometimes excluded from the throne, and seldom if ever succeed in direct lineal descent. In the line of succession to the British throne the eldest son of the sovereign is the heir, to the exclusion of older sisters; but a daughter who has no brothers succeeds, to the exclusion of younger brothers of her father or their male descendants. The exceptionally long reign of Queen Victoria (who succeeded in right of her deceased father, the Duke of Kent, to the exclusion of his younger brothers) has familiarized English-speaking communities of the present day with the form *queen's* instead of *king's* in such phrases as *queen's counsel*, *the queen's English*, etc.

Of lower Syria, Cyprus, Lydia,
Absolute *queen*. *Shak.*, A. and C. iii. 6. 11.

Now what I am ye know right well—your *Queen*,
To whom . . . ye did promise full
Allegiance and obedience to the death.
Tennyson, Queen Mary, ii. 2.

3. Figuratively, a woman who is chief or preeminent among others; one who presides: as, *queen* of beauty; *queen* of the May (see *May-queen*).

Venus, the *queen* of Love, was but thy figure,
And all her graces prophecies of thine.
Shirley, Traitor, iii. 3.

Isabel, thro' all her placid life,
The *queen* of marriage, a most perfect wife.
Tennyson, Isabel.

4. Hence, anything personified as chief or greatest, when considered as possessing female attributes.

The Cathedrall Church of this Citie [Amiens] is dedicated to our Lady, being the very *Queene* of al the Churches in France. *Coryat*, Crudities, I. 15.

Show this *queen* of cities that so fair
May yet be foul. *Cowper*, Task, i. 727.

Seven hundred years and fifty-three
Had Rome been growing up to might,
And now was *queen* of land and sea.
Domett, Christmas Hymn.

5. In *entom.*, a queen bee or queen ant.—6. A playing-card on which a queen is depicted.

The knave of Diamonds tries his wily arts,
And wins (oh shameful chance!) the *Queen* of Hearts.
Pope, R. of the L., iii. 88.

7. In *chess*, the piece which is by far the most powerful of all for attack. See *chess*[1]. Abbreviated *Q.*—8. A variety of roofing-slate, measuring 3 feet long and 2 feet wide. Compare *duchess*, 2.—**Court of Queen's Bench.** See *Court of King's Bench*, under *court*.—**Dollar queen**, in *apiculture*, an untested queen bee, bred from a purely bred mother that has mated with one of her own race: so called because the standard price was supposed to be one dollar. The price of dollar queens, however, varies from 75 cents to $2. *Phin*, Dict. of Apiculture, p. 57.—**Keeper of the Queen's prison.** See *Marshal of the King's* (*or Queen's*) *Bench*, under *marshal*.—**Marshal of the queen's household.** See *marshal*.—**Problem of the queens.** See *problem*.—**Queen Anne's bounty.** See *bounty*.—**Queen Anne style**, in *arch.*, the style which obtained in England in the early part of the eighteenth century, and produced many commodious and dignified buildings, particularly in domestic architecture; also, specifically, a nondescript style purporting to follow the above, and reproducing some of the exterior forms and ornaments of the original, much in vogue in the United States, especially for suburban cottages, from about 1880.—**Queen bee.** See *bee*.—**Queen closer.** See *closer*[1] (*b*).—**Queen consort.** See *consort*[1].—**Queen dowager**, the widow of a deceased king.—**Queen mother**, a queen dowager who is also mother of the reigning sovereign.—**Queen of heaven.** (*a*) A title often given to the goddess Astarte or Ashtoreth.

The women knead their dough to make cakes to the *queen of heaven*, . . . that they may provoke me to anger. Jer. vii. 18.

With these in troop
Came Astoreth, whom the Phœnicians call'd
Astarte, *queen of heaven*, with crescent horns.
Milton, P. L., i. 439.

(*b*) Among Roman Catholics, a title given to the Virgin Mary.—**Queen of the May**, a young girl crowned with flowers and enthroned as the central figure of the May-day sports.—**Queen regent, queen regnant**, a queen who holds the crown in her own right, or a queen who reigns as regent.—**Queen's advocate.** Same as lord *advocate* (which see, under *advocate*).—**Queen's color**, in the British army, one of the pair of colors belonging to every regiment. In the line it is a union jack charged with some regimental devices; in the Guards it is a crimson flag, sometimes having the jack in the dexter chief, but always having the royal cipher and regimental devices. See color, and *a pair of colors*, under *pair*[1]. Boutell, English Heraldry.—**Queen's counsel, enemy, gambit.** See *counsel*, etc.—**Queen's evidence.** See *king's evidence*, under *evidence*.—**Queen's gap**, a gap in a dam, a style of fishway used in British waters. It has been occasionally used in America for alewives. In low dams it answers well for salmon.—**Queen's herb**†, snuff: so called (in the latter part of the sixteenth century) because Catharine de' Medici acquired a taste for it soon after the introduction of tobacco into France.—**Queen's keys.** See *key*[1].—**Queen's messenger.** See *messenger*.—**The queen's English.** See *English*.—**The queen's peace.** See *peace*.

queen[1] (kwēn), *v.* [< *queen*[1], *n.*] I. *intrans.* To play the queen; act the part or character of a queen; domineer: with an indefinite *it*.

A three-pence bow'd would hire me,
Old as I am, to *queen it*.
Shak., Hen. VIII., ii. 3. 37.

Xerxes went out of his way with his army to do homage to the great plane-tree that *queened it* in the desert alone. *P. Robinson*, Under the Sun, p. 85.

II. *trans.* 1. In *chess*, to make a queen of: said of a pawn on its reaching the eighth square.—2. In *apiculture*, to supply with a queen; introduce a queen to: said of a colony of bees. *Phin*, Dict. of Apiculture, p. 57.

queen[2] (kwēn), *n.* Same as *quin*.

In England one hears such names for scallops as "fanshells," "frills," or "*queens*" in South Devon, according to Montagu; and on the Dorset coast the fishermen call them "squinns." *Fisheries of U. S.*, V. ii. 565.

queen-apple (kwēn'ap"l), *n.* A variety of apple.

The *queen-apple* is of the summer kind, and a good cider apple mixed with others. *Mortimer*, Husbandry.

queen-cell (kwēn'sel), *n.* The cell of a honeycomb destined for a queen or female larva. It is larger than the other cells, and generally placed on the edge of the comb, and is said to be provisioned with richer food, the so-called royal jelly.

queen-conch (kwēn'kongk), *n.* The giant stromb or conch, *Strombus gigas*; the fountain-shell, used to make conch-coral, porcelain, etc.

queencraft (kwēn'kráft), *n.* Craft or skill in policy on the part of a queen; kingcraft as practised by a female sovereign.

Elizabeth showed much *queencraft* in procuring the votes of the nobility. *Fuller.*

Queen-day (kwēn'dā), *n.* The Feast of the Annunciation of the Virgin Mary; Lady-day.

queendom (kwēn'dum), *n.* [< *queen*[1] + *-dom*.] 1. The condition or character of a queen; queenly rule, power, or dignity.

Will thy *queendom* all lie hid
Meekly under either lid?
Mrs. Browning, The Dead Pan.

2. The realm or the subjects of a queen.

The mother sat at the head of the table, and regarded her *queendom* with a smile. *George MacDonald*, What's Mine's Mine, p. 9.

[Rare in both uses.]

queenfish (kwēn'fish), *n.* A sciænoid fish, *Seriphus politus*, found on the Pacific coast of the United States. It is a food-fish of good quality, but too small to be of much economic importance, reaching

Queenfish (*Seriphus politus*).

a length of only eight inches and a weight of half a pound. The body is compressed, and covered with rather large deciduous scales. The two dorsal fins are separate; the color is bluish above, silvery below, yellow on the belly, with yellowish vertical fins, and blackish at the base of the pectorals. Also called *kingfish*.

queen-gold (kwēn'gōld), *n.* A royal duty or revenue once enjoyed by every queen of England during her marriage with the king.

queenhood (kwēn'hůd), *n.* [‹ *queen* + *-hood.*] The state or rank of a queen; the dignity of character becoming a queen.

> With all grace
> Of womanhood and *queenhood*.
> *Tennyson*, Geraint.

queening (kwē'ning), *n.* [Appar. ‹ *queen* + *-ing*³; but perhaps connected with *quine*, *quince.*] A name of several varieties of apple: one is distinguished as the *winter queening*.

> The *winter queening* is good for the table.
> *Mortimer*, Husbandry.

queenite (kwē'nīt), *n.* [‹ *queen* + *-ite*².] A partizan of Queen Caroline in her differences with her husband, George IV.

> He thought small beer at that time of some very great patriots and *Queenites*.
> *Southey*, The Doctor, interchapter xvi. (*Davies.*)

queenlet (kwēn'let), *n.* [‹ *queen* + *-let.*] A petty or insignificant queen.

> In Prussia there is a Philosophe King, in Russia a Philosophe Empress; the whole North swarms with kinglets and *queenlets* of the like temper.
> *Carlyle*, Misc., III. 216. (*Davies.*)

queen-lily (kwēn'lil″i), *n.* A plant of the genus *Phædranassa*. *P. chloracea* is a handsome cultivated species from Peru, with flowers 2 inches long, the short tube greenish, the segments of the limb purplish rose-color tipped with green.

queenliness (kwēn'li-nes), *n.* The state or condition of being queenly; the characteristics of a queen; queenly nature or quality; dignity; stateliness.

queenly (kwēn'li), *a.* [‹ *queen* + *-ly*¹.] Like a queen; befitting a queen; suitable to a queen.

> An anthem for the *queenliest* dead that ever died so young.
> *Pope*, Lenore.

queenly (kwēn'li), *adv.* [‹ *queenly*, *a.*] Like a queen; in the manner of a queen.

> *Queenly* responsive when the loyal hand
> Rose from the clay it work'd in as she past.
> *Tennyson*, Aylmer's Field.

queen-mother (kwēn'muᴛʜ″ėr), *n.* See *queen*. —**Queen-mother herb**, tobacco.

queen-of-the-meadows (kwēn'ọv-thẹ̄-med'ōz), *n.* The English meadow-sweet, *Spiræa Ulmaria*, an herb a yard high, with pinnate leaves, and a compound cyme of very numerous small yellowish-white sweet-scented flowers; also, rarely, the American meadow-sweet, *Spiræa salicifolia*.

queen-of-the-prairie (kwēn'ọv-thẹ̄-prā'ri), *n.* A tall American herb, *Spiræa lobata*, of meadows and prairies in the interior. Its pinnate leaves, which are fragrant when bruised, are chiefly near the ground. It bears an ample panicled compound cyme of handsome crowded peach-pink flowers.

queen-pine†, *n.* The pineapple. Also called *king-pine*.

queen-post (kwēn'pōst), *n.* In *carp.*, one of the suspending posts in the framed principal of a

Queen-post Roof.
A A, queen-posts; *B*, tie-beam; *C C*, struts or braces.

roof, or in a trussed partition or other truss, when there are two such posts. When there is only a single post it is called a *king-post* or *crown-post*. Also called *prick-post*.—**Queen-post stay**, in a railroad-car, a rod or bar fastened to a queen-post to secure it against any lateral movement.—**Secondary queen-posts**, a kind of truss-posts set in pairs, each at the same distance from the middle of the truss, for the purpose of hanging the tie-beam below. Also called *side-posts*.

queen's-arm (kwēnz'ärm), *n.* A musket.

> Agin the chimbley crook-necks hung;
> An' in amongst 'em rusted
> The ole *queen's-arm* thet gran'ther Young
> Fetched back frum Concord busted.
> *Lowell*, The Courtin'.

queen's-delight (kwēnz'dẹ̄-līt″), *n.* A berbaceous plant, *Stillingia sylvatica*, order *Euphorbiaceæ*, native of the southern United States. It has clustered stems from 1 to 3 feet high, springing from a thick woody root. The latter is an officinal alterative. Also *queen's-root*.

queen's-flower (kwēnz'flou″ėr), *n.* The blood-wood or jarool, *Lagerstrœmia Flos-Reginæ*, a medium-sized tree of the East Indies, etc., in those regions often planted. The panicled flowers are each 2 or 3 inches in diameter, rose-colored in the morning, becoming purple by evening.

queenship (kwēn'ship), *n.* [‹ *queen* + *-ship.*] The position or dignity of a queen.

> Neither did I at any time so far forget myself in my exaltation or received *queenship* but that I always looked for such an alteration as I now find.
> *Queen Ann Boleyn's last Letter to King Henry* (quoted by [Addison in Spectator, No. 397).

Queensland ebony, see *Maba*; **hemp**, see *Sida*; **laurel**, see *Pittosporum*; **nut, nut-tree**, see *Macadamia*; **olive, poplar**, etc., see *olive*, etc.; **plum**, see *Owenia*, 1.

queen's-lily (kwēnz'lil″i), *n.* 1. See *Kniphofia*.—2. The Mexican lily. See *lily*.

queen's-metal (kwēnz'met″al), *n.* An alloy of which the chief ingredient is tin, answering the purposes of Britannia metal, and somewhat finer and harder than pewter. The proportions of the ingredients vary.

queen's-pigeon (kwēnz'pij″ọn), *n.* A large and handsome ground-pigeon, *Goura victoriæ*: so named from the Queen of England. See *Goura*. Also called *Victoria crown-pigeon*.

queen's-root (kwēnz'röt), *n.* Same as *queen's-delight*.

queen-stitch (kwēn'stich), *n.* A simple pattern in embroidery, made by a square of four stitches drawn within another larger one made in the same way. A checker pattern is produced by a series of these.

queen's-ware (kwēnz'wãr), *n.* A variety of Wedgwood ware, otherwise known as *cream-colored ware*. See *Wedgwood ware*, under *ware*².

queen's-yellow (kwēnz'yel″ō), *n.* The yellow subsulphate of mercury; turpeth-mineral.

queen-truss (kwēn'trus), *n.* A truss framed with queen-posts.

queequehatch, *n.* Same as *quickhatch*.

queer¹ (kwēr), *a.* and *n.* [Formerly also *quire*; ‹ LG. *queer*, *quer*, cross, transverse (› *quere*, obliquity), ≐ MHG. G. *quer*, cross, transverse (› *quere*, obliquity), OHG. MHG. *twer*, cross, transverse (› *twer*, obliquity); a variant, without the final guttural, of OHG. *dwerah*, *dwerih*, *dwerch*, *dwerh*, *thwerah*, *thwereh*, *twerh*, MHG. *dwerch*, *twerch*, G. *zwerch-* = AS. *thweorh*, cross, transverse, = Sw. *tvär* = Dan. *tvær*, cross, obtuse, = Goth. *thwairhs*, angry, = Icel. *thverr*, neut. *thvert*, › ME. *thwert*, *thwart*, E. *thwart*, transverse, transversely: see *thwart*, which is thus a doublet of *queer*.] **I.** *a.* 1. Appearing, behaving, or feeling otherwise than is usual or normal; odd; singular; droll; whimsical; quaint.

> The presence seems, with things so richly odd,
> The mosque of Mahound, or some *queer* pagod.
> *Pope*, Satires of Donne, iv. 239.

> The *queerest* shape that e'er I saw,
> For fient a wame it had ava'.
> *Burns*, Death and Dr. Hornbook.

2. Open to suspicion; doubtful in point of honesty. [Colloq.]

> You drive a *queer* bargain with your friends, and are found out, and imagine the world will punish you.
> *Thackeray.*

> "We've seen his name—the old man's—on some very *queer* paper," says B. with a wink to J.
> *Thackeray*, Philip, iv.

3. Counterfeit; worthless. [Slang.]

> Put it about in the right quarter that you'll buy *queer* bills by the lump. *Dickens*, Our Mutual Friend, ii. 5.

4. Having a sensation of sudden or impending illness; sick or languid. [Colloq.]

> Little of all we value here
> Wakes on the morn of its hundredth year
> Without both feeling and looking *queer*.
> *O. W. Holmes*, The Deacon's Masterpiece.

A queer fish. See *fish*¹.—**Queer Street**, an imaginary place, where persons in financial or other difficulties, and flighty, uncertain, and "shady" characters generally, are feigned to live. [Slang.]

> A fair friend of ours has removed to *Queer-street*; . . . you'll soon be an orphan-in-law.
> *Dickens*, Dombey and Son, xl.

> I am very high in *Queer Street* just now, ma'am, having paid your bills before I left town.
> *Kingsley*, Two Years Ago, xiv. (*Davies.*)

=**Syn.** 1. *Strange*, *Odd*, etc. (see *eccentric*), curious, extraordinary, unique, fantastic.

II. *n.* Counterfeit money; "green goods." [Slang.]—**To shove the queer**, to pass counterfeit money. [Slang.]

queer¹ (kwēr), *v. t.* [‹ *queer*¹, *a.*] 1. To banter; ridicule; deride. [Slang.]

> Who in a row like Tom could lead the van,
> Booze in the ken, or at the spellken hustle?
> Who *queer* a flat? *Byron*, Don Juan, xi. 19.

> A shoulder-knotted puppy, with a grin,
> *Queering* the threadbare curate, let him in.
> *Colman the Younger.*

2. To puzzle. *Halliwell.* [Prov. Eng.]

queer²†, *n.* An obsolete form of *quire*¹. *Cotgrave.*

queer³ (kwēr), *n.* [Formerly also *quare*; prob. ult. ‹ L. *quadrus*, square: see *quarry*¹, *square.*] One of the joints or division-planes of queery rock. [Cornwall, Eng.]

queerer (kwēr'ėr), *n.* One who banters or ridicules. [Slang.]

> 'Twould be most tedious to describe
> The common-place of this facetious tribe,
> These wooden wits, these Quizzers, *Queerers*, Smokers,
> These practical nothing-so-easy Jokers.
> *Colman the Younger.*

queerity (kwēr'i̤-ti), *n.* [Formerly also *quearity*; ‹ *queer*¹ + *-ity.*] Queerness. [Rare.]

> No Person whatsoever shall be admitted [to the "Ugly Club"] without a visible *Queerity* in his Aspect, or peculiar Cast of Countenance. *Steele*, Spectator, No. 17.

queerly (kwēr'li), *adv.* In a queer, odd, or singular manner.

queerness (kwēr'nes), *n.* The state or character of being queer.

queery (kwēr'i), *a.* [Formerly also *quarey*; ‹ *queer*³ + *-y*¹.] Breaking up in cuboidal masses, as rocks in various quarries. [Cornwall, Eng.]

queest (kwēst), *n.* [Also *queast*, *quest*, *quist*, formerly *quoist*, also corruptly *quease*, *queeze*, *quice*; ‹ ME. *quysht*, prob. a contr. form of *cushat.*] The cushat or ring-dove, *Columba palumbus*. [Obsolete or prov. Eng.]

> Askes beth goode, and so hoot is noo dounge
> Of foule as of the douve, a *quysht* outake [excepted].
> *Palladius*, Husbondrie (E. E. T. S.), p. 28.

queet¹ (kwēt), *n.* [A dial. var. of *coot.*] The coot, *Fulica atra*. [Prov. Eng.]

queet² (kwēt), *n.* [Also *quit*, *cuit*, *cute*, *coot*; origin obscure.] An ankle. [Scotch.]

> The first an' step that she stepp'd in,
> She stepped to the *queet*.
> *The Drowned Lovers* (Child's Ballads, II. 179).

> The second brother he stepped in,
> He stepped to the *quit*;
> Then out he jump'd upo' the bank,
> Says, "This water's wond'rous deep."
> *Bondsey and Maisry* (Child's Ballads, II. 379).

queez-madam (kwēz'mad″am), *n.* [F. *cuisse-madame.*] The cuisse-madam, a French jargonelle pear. [Scotch.]

> He'll glowr at an auld-warld barkit aik-snag as if it were a *queez-maddam* in full bearing. *Scott*, Rob Roy, xxi.

queff, quegh, queigh, *n.* Same as *quaigh*.

queint¹†, *a.* A Middle English form of *quaint*.

queint²†. An obsolete preterit and past participle of *quench*. *Chaucer.*

queintise†, *n.* A variant of *quaintise*.

quekeborde†, *n.* [ME., appar. as if **quickboard*, ‹ *quick* + *board.*] An old game, prohibited under Edward IV. *Strutt*, Sports and Pastimes, p. 512.

Quekett's indicator. See *indicator*, 1 (c).

quelch (kwelch), *n.* [Cf. *squelch.*] A blow; a bang. *Halliwell.* [Prov. Eng.]

quele¹†, *v.* An obsolete form of *quail*¹, *queal*.

quele²†, *n.* An obsolete form of *wheel*.

quelea (kwē'lẹ̄-ä), *n.* [African (?).] 1. The crimson-beaked weaver-bird of Africa.—2. [*cap.*]

Quelea sanguinirostris.

[NL. (Reichenbach, 1850).] A genus of African weaver-birds or *Ploceidæ*, containing such species as the above, *Q. sanguinirostris*.

quell (kwel), *v.* [‹ ME. *quellen*, ‹ AS. *cwellan* (= OS. *quellian* = OHG. *quellan*, *cwellan*, *quellen*, *chellen*, *chelen*, MHG. *chwellen*, *chollen*, *quellen*, *queln*, *koln*, G. *quälen* = Icel. *kvelja* = Sw. *qvälja*), kill, lit. cause to die, causal of *cwelan*, etc., die, E. *queal*, now usually *quail*:

see *quail*[1]. The common identification of *quell* with *kill*[1], of which it is said to be the earlier form, is erroneous.] **I.** *trans.* **1†.** To cause to die; put to death; kill; slay.

Take heed that thou reveal it ere thou be *quelled* to death. *Holy Rood* (E. E. T. S.), p. 8.

The dokes criden as men wolde hem *quelle*. *Chaucer*, Nun's Priest's Tale, l. 570.

Hee lete catch the King & kyllen hym soone,
And his Princes of price prestlich hee *quelde*.
Alisaunder of Macedoine (E. E. T. S.), l. 925.

Treading one vpon another, they *quelled* to death . . . a multitude of the common souldiours. *Hakluyt's Voyages*, II. 20.

And *quell'd* the Snakes which round his [William's] Cradle ran. *Prior*, Carmen Seculare (1700), st. 9.

2. To cause to cease; subdue; crush: as, to *quell* an insurrection.

Appointed . . . to *quell* seditions and tumults. *Atterbury.*

The mutiny was *quelled* with much less difficulty than had been feared. *Lecky*, Eng. in 18th Cent., xiv.

3. To reduce to peace or inaction; quiet; allay.

But Consideration is of greater Use, as it suggests Arguments from Reason to *quell* and allay the sudden heat of Passions. *Stillingfleet*, Sermons, III. vii.

Me Agamemnon urg'd to deadly hate;
'Tis past — I *quell* it; I resign to fate.
Pope, Iliad, xviii. 144.

Caroline refused tamely to succumb. . . . Bent on victory over a mortal pain, she did her best to *quell* it. *Charlotte Brontë*, Shirley, xi.

4†. To dash out; destroy.

They fighten, and bryngen hors and man to grounde,
And with hire axes oute the braynes *quelle*.
Chaucer, Troilus, iv. 46.

=**Syn. 2.** To overpower, put down, lay, smother.—**3.** To calm, compose.

II.† *intrans.* **1.** To die; perish.

Yet did he quake and quiver, like to *quell*. *Spenser*, F. Q., VII. vii. 42.

2. To abate.

Winter's wrath beginnes to *quell*. *Spenser*, Shep. Cal., March.

quell (kwel), *n.* [‹ *quell*, *v.*] **1†.** Murder. [Rare.]

What cannot you and I . . . put upon
His spongy officers, who shall bear the guilt
Of our great *quell*? *Shak.*, Macbeth, i. 7. 72.

2. Power or means of quelling or subduing. [Rare and poetical.]

Awfully he [Love] stands,
A sovereign *quell* is in his waving hands;
No sight can bear the lightning of his bow.
Keats, Endymion, ii.

queller (kwel'ėr), *n.* [‹ ME. *queller*, ‹ AS. *cwellere*, a killer, ‹ *cwellan*, kill: see *quell*.] **1†.** One who quells or kills; a slayer.

And our posterite shalbe reproued as children of homecides, ye of regicides, and prince *quellers*. *Hall*, Hen. IV., an. 1.

Mrs. Quickly. Murder! . . . thou art a honey-seed [homicide], a man-*queller*, and a woman-*queller*. *Shak.*, 2 Hen. IV., ii. 1. 59.

2. One who subdues or crushes.

Hail, Son of the Most High, heir of both worlds,
Queller of Satan! *Milton*, P. R., iv. 634.

quellio†, *n.* [‹ Sp. *cuello*, a ruff.] A kind of ruff.

Our rich mockado doublet, with our cut cloth-of-gold sleeves, and our *quellio*. *Ford*, Lady's Trial, ii. 1.

Your Hungerland bands, and Spanish *quellio* ruffs. *Massinger*, City Madam, iv. 4.

quelm, *v. t.* An obsolete or dialectal form of *whelm*. *Babees Book* (E. E. T. S.), p. 323.

quelquechose (kelk'shōz), *n.* [Also *quelkchose* (also *queckshoes*, *keckshose*, *kickshose*, *kickshaws*, etc.: see *kickshaw*), ‹ F. *quelquechose*, something, ‹ *quelque*, some, + *chose*, thing: see *chose*[2]. Cf. *kickshaw*.] A trifle; a kickshaw.

Only let me love none, no, not the sport,
From country grass to comfitures of court,
Or city's *quelque-choses*, let not report
My mind transport. *Donne*, Love's Usury.

queme†, *a.* [ME., also *quem*, *cweme*, earlier *i-queme*, *i-cweme*, ‹ AS. *gecwēme*, pleasing, agreeable, acceptable, fit (cf., with diff. prefix, OHG. *biquāmi*, MHG. *bequæme*, G. *bequem*, fit), ‹ *ge-*, a generalizing prefix, + *cuman* (pret. *cwam*, *com*), come: see *come*, and cf. *become* and *comely*.] Pleasing; agreeable.

Wherfore I beqwethe me to your *queme* spouse,
To lyue with in lykyng to my lyfes ende.
Destruction of Troy (E. E. T. S.), l. 633.

queme†, *v.* [ME. *quemen*, ‹ AS. *cwēman*, also *gecwēman*, please, satisfy, propitiate, ‹ *gecwēme*, pleasing, becoming: see *queme*, *a.*] **I.** *trans.* To become; suit; fit; satisfy; please.

That [virtue] is approperid into noo degree,
But the firste Fadir in magestee,
Which may his heires deeme hem that him *queme*,
Al were he mytre, corone, or diademe.
Chaucer, Gentleness, l. 20.

God geue us grace in oure lyuynge
To serue oure God, & Marie to *queeme*.
Hymns to Virgin, etc. (E. E. T. S.), p. 55.

Parys full pristly with preciouse araye
Worshippit that worthy in wedys full riche,
As *quemet* for a qweno & qwaintly atyret,
That Priam hade purueit & to the place sent.
Destruction of Troy (E. E. T. S.), l. 3404.

Such merimake holy Saints doth *queme*.
Spenser, Shep. Cal., May.

II. *intrans.* To become; come to be.

To *queme* qwyt of all other,
To skape out of skathe and sklaunder to falle.
Destruction of Troy (E. E. T. S.), l. 1809.

quemful†, *a.* [ME., ‹ *queme* + *-ful*.] Becoming; fit.

Now, sothely, na thyng bot a lathyngé of all this werldis blysse, of all flescheley lykynges in thi herte, and a *quemfull* langynge with a thristy zernyng to heuenly joye.
Hampole, Prose Treatises (E. E. T. S.), p. 33.

Haile! *quemfull* Queene, quaintly shape!
Moste of all Macedoine menskfull Ladie!
Alisaunder of Macedoine (E. E. T. S.), l. 582.

quemly†, *adv.* [ME., ‹ *queme* + *-ly*[2].] In a pleasing or fitting manner.

The golde was all gotyn, & the grete sommes
Of qwhete, & of qwhite syluer, *quemly* to-gedur.
Destruction of Troy (E. E. T. S.), l. 11783.

quench (kwench), *v.*; pret. and pp. *quenched*, formerly also *queint*. [‹ ME. *quenchen* (pret. *quencte*, *queynte*), ‹ AS. *cwencan* (also, in comp., *ā-cwencan*), quench, put out, causal of **cwincan* (pret. **cwanc*), in comp. *ā-cwincan* (= OFries. *kwinka*), go out, be extinguished; cf. **cwīnan* (pret. **cwān*), in comp. *ā-cwīnan*, go out, be extinguished.] **I.** *trans.* **1.** To extinguish or put out, as fire.

Thy rage shall burn thee up, and thou shalt turn
To ashes, ere our blood shall *quench* that fire.
Shak., K. John, iii. 1. 345.

The taper, *quenched* so soon,
Had ended merely in a snuff, not stink.
Browning, Ring and Book, I. 112.

2. To extinguish or allay; stop; put an end to, as thirst.

The gentle deare returnd the selfe-same way,
Thinking to *quench* her thirst at the next brooke.
Spenser, Sonnets, lxvii.

In lavish streams to *quench* a country's thirst.
Pope, Moral Essays, iii. 175.

3†. To relieve the thirst of.

A bottle of ale, to *quench* me, rascal.
B. Jonson, Bartholomew Fair, ii. 1.

4. To suppress; stifle; check; repress; destroy: as, to *quench* a passion or emotion.

The supposition of the lady's death
Will *quench* the wonder of her infamy.
Shak., Much Ado, iv. 1. 241.

Parthians should, the next year, tame
The proud Lucanians, and nigh *quench* their Name.
Sylvester, tr. of Du Bartas's Weeks, i. 2.

As I have much *quenched* my senses, and disused my body from pleasure, and so tried how I can endure to be my own grave, so I try now how I can suffer a prison.
Donne, Letters, xxviii.

5. To lay or place in water, as a heated iron. See *temper*.

In *quenching* a tool of which one portion is thick and another thin, the thickest part should generally be the first to enter the water.
C. P. B. Shelley, Workshop Appliances, p. 323.

II. *intrans.* **1.** To be extinguished; go out.

Right anon oon of the fyres *queynte*,
And quykede agayn, and after that anon
That other fyr was queynt, and al agon.
Chaucer, Knight's Tale, l. 1476.

Zif he be chosen to ben Prelate, and is not worthi, his Lampe *quenchethe* anon. *Mandeville*, Travels, p. 60.

That hand shall burn in never-*quenching* fire.
Shak., Rich. II., v. 5. 109.

2. To lose zeal; cool; become cool.

Dost thou think in time
She will not *quench*? *Shak.*, Cymbeline, i. 5. 47.

quench† (kwench), *n.* [‹ *quench*, *v.*] The act of quenching or extinguishing; also, the state of being extinguished.

The same *quench* he hath cast
Upon my life shall quite put out his fame.
Chapman, Byron's Tragedy, v. 1.

quenchable (kwen'cha-bl), *a.* [‹ *quench* + *-able*.] Capable of being quenched or extinguished.

quench-coal† (kwench'kōl), *n.* [‹ *quench*, *v.*, + obj. *coal*.] Anything which quenches or extinguishes fire: applied figuratively to a cold, heartless professor of religion.

Zeal hath in this our earthly mould little fuel, much *quench-coal*; is hardly fired, soon cooled.
Rev. S. Ward, Sermons, p. 71.

You are *quench-coal*; no sparkle of grace can kindle upon your cold hearth. *D. Rogers.*

quencher (kwen'chėr), *n.* **1.** One who or that which quenches or extinguishes.

A griever and *quencher* of the Spirit.
Hammond, Works, IV. 514.

You would-be *quenchers* of the light to be!
Tennyson, Princess, iv.

2. That which quenches thirst; a draught or drink. [Slang.]

The modest *quencher*, . . . coming close upon the heels of the temperate beverage he had discussed at dinner, awakened a slight degree of fever.
Dickens, Old Curiosity Shop, xxxv.

At the bottom [of the hill], however, there is a pleasant public, whereat we must really take a modest *quencher*, for the down air is provocative of thirst.
T. Hughes, Tom Brown at Rugby, i. 1.

quench-fire† (kwench'fīr), *n.* [‹ *quench*, *v.*, + obj. *fire*.] A machine for extinguishing fire; a fire-extinguisher.

I went to see Sir Sam. Morland's inventions and machines, arithmetical wheeles, *quench-fires*, and new harp.
Evelyn, Diary, July 10, 1667.

quenching (kwen'ching), *n.* [Verbal n. of *quench*, *v.*] **1.** The act of extinguishing; also, the state of being extinguished.

Some outward cause fate hath perhaps design'd,
Which to the soul may utter *quenching* bring.
Sir J. Davies, Immortal. of Soul, xxxi.

2. In *metal.*, a method of producing a hard crust on molten metal for convenience in removing it in small plates or disks, called sometimes *rosettes*, instead of allowing it to solidify in one mass. See *rosette*.—**Quenching-tub**, a vessel of water placed beside a blacksmith's forge for cooling or tempering the irons.

quenchless (kwench'les), *a.* [‹ *quench* + *-less*.] That cannot be quenched or repressed; inextinguishable: as, *quenchless* fire or fury.

Come, bloody Clifford, rough Northumberland,
I dare your *quenchless* fury to more rage.
Shak., 3 Hen. VI., i. 4. 28.

His hate
Is *quenchless* as his wrongs.
Shelley, Queen Mab, v.

quenchlessly (kwench'les-li), *adv.* In a quenchless manner.

quenchlessness (kwench'les-nes), *n.* The state of being quenchless or unquenchable.

quenchure†, *n.* [ME., also *quenchour*; irreg. ‹ *quench* + *-ure*.] The act of quenching.

Whanne ȝe haue do ȝoure *quenchour*, putte alle the watris togidere. *Book of Quinte Essence* (ed. Furnivall), p. 6.

quenelle (kẹ-nel'), *n.* [F.] In *cookery*, a forcemeat ball made of a rich and delicately seasoned paste of chicken, veal, or the like. Quenelles are usually served as entrées.

quenouille-training (kẹ-nö'lyė-trā'ning), *n.* [F. *quenouille* = It. *connochia*, ‹ ML. *conucula*, *colucula*, a distaff, dim. of L. *colus*, a distaff.] In *hort.*, a mode of training trees or shrubs in a conical form, with their branches bent downward, so that they resemble a distaff in shape.

quenstedtite (kwen'stet-īt), *n.* [Named after F. A. *Quenstedt* (1809–89), a German geologist and mineralogist.] A hydrous sulphate of iron, occurring in tabular monoclinic crystals of a reddish-violet color: it is found in Chili.

quentise†, *n.* Same as *quaintise*.

quequer†, *n.* A Middle English form of *quiver*[2].

quercetic (kwėr-set'ik), *a.* [‹ *quercet(in)* + *-ic*.] Produced from quercetin: as, *quercetic* acid.

quercetine, *n.* Same as *quercitin*.

quercetum (kwėr-sē'tum), *n.* [L., an oak-wood, ‹ *quercus*, an oak: see *Quercus*.] A collection of living oaks, as in a botanical garden. The word is so applied in the Kew Gardens, London.

quercine (kwėr'sin), *a.* [‹ LL. *quercinus*, of the oak, of oak-leaves, ‹ L. *quercus*, oak: see *Quercus*.] Of or pertaining to the oak or oak-trees.

Quercineæ (kwėr-sin'ẹ̄-ē), *n. pl.* [NL. (Dumortier, 1829), ‹ L. *quercinus*, of the oak, + *-eæ*.] A tribe of dicotyledonous trees and shrubs of the apetalous order *Cupuliferæ*, characterized by the usually three-celled ovary, lobed perianth, numerous stamens, and fruit a nut partly or wholly surrounded by an involucre or cupule. It contains 4 genera, including the oak, beech, and chestnut, for which see Quercus (the type), *Fagus*, *Castanea*, and *Castanopsis*. The range of the whole tribe is included in that of the oak (see *Quercus*), except in the case of the beech, which extends into South America, Australia, and New Zealand.

quercitannic (kwėr-si-tan'ik), *a.* [‹ L. *quercus*, oak, + E. *tannic*.] Same as *tannic*.

The tannin of the quercitron, or *quercitannic* acid.
C. T. Davis, Leather, p. 101.

quercite (kwėr'sīt), *n.* [< L. *quercus*, an oak, + *-ite*[2].] A crystalline substance, $C_6H_7(OH)_5$, derived from acorns, which resembles the sugars in that it is sweet and optically active, but does not ferment with yeast or reduce metallic salts.

quercitin (kwėr'si-tin), *n.* [Accom. from *quercitron*, as if < L. *quercetum*, an oak-wood (< *quercus*, an oak), + *-in*[2].] A substance derived from quercitrin by the action of mineral acids.

quercitrin (kwėr'sit-rin), *n.* [< *quercitr(on)* + *-in*[2].] A glucoside, $C_{36}H_{38}O_{20}$, which forms yellow crystalline needles or tablets. It is the coloring principle of quercitron-bark. Also called *quercitrone*.

quercitron (kwėr'sit-ron), *n.* [Irreg. < L. *quercus*, an oak, + *citrus*, a tree of the lemon kind: see *citron*.] 1. The black or dyers' oak, *Quercus tinctoria*, a tree from 70 to 100 feet high, common through the eastern half of the United States and in southern Canada. Its wood is of some value, and its bark is of considerable importance. The latter, though outwardly dark, is inwardly yellow, whence the tree is also called *yellow* or *yellow-bark oak*.
2. The bark of this tree. It contains, in the principle quercitrin, a yellow dye, which is now used in the form of a preparation called *flavin*. It is also used for tanning, and occasionally in medicine, but the coloring matter hinders these applications.

quercitron-bark (kwėr'sit-ron-bärk), *n.* Same as *quercitron*, 2.

quercitron-oak (kwėr'sit-ron-ōk), *n.* Same as *quercitron*, 1.

quercivorous (kwėr-siv'ō-rus), *a.* [< L. *quercus*, an oak, + *vorare*, devour.] In *zoöl.*, feeding on the oak, as an insect.

Quercus (kwėr'kus), *n.* [NL. (Malpighi, 1675), < L. *quercus*, an oak, = E. *fir*, q. v.] A genus of dicotyledonous trees, the oaks, type of the apetalous order *Cupuliferæ* and of the tribe *Quercineæ*. It is characterized by usually slender and pendulous or erect staminate catkins, the stamens and calyx-lobes of each flower being six in number, and by the scattered or clustered fertile flowers, composed of an ovary commonly with three cells, six ovules, and a three-lobed stigma, surrounded by an involucre of more or less consolidated scales, which becomes a hardened cupule or cup around the flat or rounded base of the nut or acorn. There are about 300 species, natives of all north temperate regions, extending through Mexican mountains and the Andes into the United States of Colombia, and in the mountains of Asia to the Moluccas. They are entirely absent in South America beyond the equator, in Australasia and the Pacific islands, and in Africa outside of the Mediterranean region. They are mainly trees of large size, hard and durable wood, and slow growth, sprouting repeatedly from the root; a few only are never more than shrubs. The characteristic oak-leaf is alternate, thin, and veiny, deeply and pinnately lobed, with the lobes either rounded, as in the white oak, or ending in bristle-points, as in the black and red oaks; but the genus includes great diversity of form, ranging to thick and entire evergreen leaves in the live-oak and others. (See cut under *oak*.) The fruit or acorn matures in one year in the white oak, bur-oak, post-oak, live-oak, and the chestnut-oaks; in other Atlantic species, the biennial-fruited oaks, in two. The yellowish catkins precede or accompany the leaves. The numerous American and European species all belong (with the exception of *Q. densiflora*, the peach-oak of California) to the subgenus *Lepidobalanus* (Endlicher, 1844), with slender and loose-flowered proper aments, and broad cupules with imbricated scales. Of these over 50 are found in Mexico and Central America, and about 40 within the United States, 25 of which occur only east of the Rocky Mountains, and about 15 in California. They extend in North America as far north as 45°, in Europe to 58°. The oaks of central and eastern Asia constitute five other sections, mostly with erect staminate spikes, and include about 106 species. See *oak*, *acorn*, *black-jack*, *blue-jack*, *encino*, *holm-oak*, *kermes-oak*, *live-oak*, *pin-oak*, *post-oak*, *red-oak*, *roble*, *scrub-oak*, *shingle-oak*, *valonia-oak*, *wainscot-oak*, *water-oak*, *willow-oak*.

queret†, *n.* An obsolete form of *quire*[1], *quire*[2].

querela† (kwę-rē'lä), *n.* [L., a complaint, lament: see *quarrel*[1].] A complaint to a court. See *audita querela*.—**Duplex querela.** See *double quarrel*, under *quarrel*.—**Querela inofficiosi testamenti**, in *civil law*, an action by which an inofficious or undutiful will was attacked.—**Querela nullitatis**, in systems of procedure based on the Roman law, an action to get a judicial decree that an act was void.

querelet, **querellet**, *n.* Obsolete (Middle English) forms of *quarrel*[1].

querent[1] (kwē'rent), *n.* [< L. *queren(t-)s*, ppr. of *queri*, complain, lament. Cf. *quarrel*[1], *querela*, *querimony*, etc.] A complainant; a plaintiff.

querent[2] (kwē'rent), *n.* [< L. *quæren(t-)s*, ppr. of *quærere*, ask, inquire: see *quest*[1].] An inquirer. [Rare.]

When a patient or *querent* came to him [Dr. Napier], he presently went to his closet to pray. *Aubrey*, Misc., p. 132.

querimonious (kwer-i-mō'ni-us), *a.* [< L. as if **querimoniosus*, < *querimonia*, a complaint: see *querimony*.] Complaining; querulous; apt to complain.

querimoniously (kwer-i-mō'ni-us-li), *adv.* [< *querimonious* + *-ly*[2].] In a querimonious manner; with complaint; querulously.

To thee, dear Tom, myself addressing,
Most *querimoniously* confessing
That I of late have been compressing.
Sir J. Denham, A Dialogue.

querimoniousness (kwer-i-mō'ni-us-nes), *n.* [< *querimonious* + *-ness*.] The character of being querimonious; disposition to complain; a complaining temper.

querimony† (kwer'i-mō-ni), *n.* [< F. *querimonie* = It. *querimonia*, *querimonio*, < L. *querimonia*, a complaint, < *queri*, complain, lament: see *querent*[1].] A complaint; a complaining.

Hys brother's dayly *querimonye*.
Hall, Edward IV., an. 17.

Here cometh over many *quirimonies*, and complaints against me, of lording it over my brethern.
Cushman, quoted in Bradford's Plymouth Plantation, p. 51.

querist (kwē'rist), *n.* [< *quer-y* + *-ist*.] One who inquires or asks questions.

And yet a late hot *Querist* for Tithes, whom ye may know, by his Wits lying ever beside him in the Margin, to be ever beside his Wits in the Text. *Milton*, Considerations.

I shall propose some considerations to my gentle *querist*.
Spectator.

querister†, *n.* A variant of *quirister*, for *chorister*.

querk[1] (kwėrk), *v.* [< ME. *querken* = OFries. *querka*, *querdza*, North Fries. *querke*, *quirke* = Icel. *kyrkja*, *kvirkja*, throttle, = OSw. *quarka* = Dan. *kværke*, throttle, strangle, suffocate; from the noun, North Fries. *querk* = Icel. *kverk* = Dan. *kværk*, throat. Cf. *querken*.] **I.** *trans.* To throttle; choke; stifle; suffocate.

II. *intrans.* To grunt; moan. *Halliwell.* [Prov. Eng.]

querk[2] (kwėrk), *n.* An obsolete or dialectal form of *quirk*[1].

querken† (kwėr'ken), *v. t.* [Also *quirken*; < ME. *querkenen*; < *querk*[1] + *-en*[1].] Same as *querk*[1].

Chekenyd or *querkenyd*. *Prompt. Parv.* (Halliwell.)

querl (kwėrl), *v. t.* [Also *quirl*; a dial. var. of *twirl*, perhaps due to confusion with *curl*. Cf. G. *querlen*, twirl.] To twirl; turn or wind round; coil: as, to *querl* a cord, thread, or rope. [U. S.]

querl (kwėrl), *n.* [< *querl*, *v.*] A twist; a curl. [U. S.]

And the crooks and *querls* of the branches on the floor.
Harper's Mag., LXX. 21.

quern (kwėrn), *n.* [Also dial. *kern*, and formerly *curn*; < ME. *quern*, *cwerne*, < AS. *cweorn*, *cwyrn* = OS. *quern*, *querna* = OFries. *quern* = D. *kweern* = MLG. *quern*, *querne* = OHG. *chwirna*, *quirn*, *churn*, MHG. *churne*, *kurn*, *kürne* = Icel. *kvern*, mod. *kvörn* = Sw. *qvarn* = Dan. *kværn* = Goth. *kwairnus*, a millstone, a quern.] 1. A stone hand-mill for grinding grain. The most usual form consists of two circular flat stones, the upper one pierced in the center, and revolving on a wooden or metal pin inserted in the lower. In using the quern the grain is dropped with one hand into the central opening, while with the other the upper stone is revolved by means of a stick inserted in a small hole near the edge.

Stone Querns for Grinding.— Dublin Museum.

Men wende that bele Isaude
Ne coude hem noght of love werne;
And yet she that grynt at a *querne*
Is al to good to ese hir harte.
Chaucer, House of Fame, l. 1798.

Some apple-colour'd corn
Ground in faire *quernes*; and some did spindles turn.
Chapman, Odyssey, vii. 139.

We stopped at a little hut, where we saw an old woman grinding with the *quern*. *Boswell*, Johnson, IV. x.

The old hand-mill, or *quern*, such as Pennant sketched the Hebrides women grinding with in the last century, has not yet gone out; Dr. Mitchell says there are thousands of them at work in Scotland, where still
"The music for a hungry wame
Is grinding o' the *quernie*."
E. B. Tylor (Academy, Sept. 18, 1880).

2. A hand-mill used for grinding pepper, mustard, and the like. Such querns were used even on the table, and as early as the sixteenth century.

quern (kwėrn), *v. t.* and *i.* [Formerly also *kern*, *curn*; < *quern*, *n.*] To grind.

Fly where men feel
The *curning* [var. *cunning*] axel-tree; and those that suffer
Beneath the chariot of the snowy beare.
Chapman, Bussy D'Ambois, v.

quern-stone (kwėrn'stōn), *n.* A millstone.

Theyre corne in *quernstoans* they do grind.
Stanihurst, tr. of Virgil, i. (*Nares*.)

querpo, *n.* See *cuerpo*.

Querquedula (kwėr-kwed'ū-lä), *n.* [NL. (Stephens, 1824), < L. *querquedula*, a kind of teal; by some doubtfully connected with Gr. κερκοῦρος, < κέρκουρος, a kind of light boat. Hence ult. E. *kestrel*, q. v.] A genus of *Anatidæ* and subfamily *Anatinæ*, containing a number of species of all countries, notable for their small size, beauty, and excellence of flesh; the teal. The common teal of Europe is *Q. crecca*; the garganey or summer teal is *Q. circia*; the green-winged teal of North America is *Q. carolinensis*; the blue-winged, *Q. discors*; the cinnamon, *Q. cyanoptera*. See *Nettion*, and cut under *teal*.

querquedule (kwėr'kwę-dūl), *n.* [< *Querquedula*, q. v.] A book-name of ducks of the genus *Querquedula*; a teal.

querret, *n.* A Middle English form of *quarry*[2].

querrour†, *n.* A Middle English form of *quarrier*[1].

querry†, *n.* See *equery*.

quert†, *n.* An obsolete form of *quart*[2].

Querula (kwer'ō-lä), *n.* [NL., fem. of L. *querulus*, complaining: see *querulous*.] A genus of

Piahau (*Querula purpurata*).

fruit-crows, giving name to the subfamily *Querulinæ*; the type is *Q. purpurata*, the piahau. *Vieillot*, 1816.

querulation (kwer-ō-lā'shon), *n.* [< ML. **querulatio(n-)*, < *querulari*, complain, < L. *querulus*, complaining: see *querulous*.] A complaint; murmuring.

Will not these mournings, menaces, *querulations*, stir your hearts, because they are derived from God through us, his organ-pipes, as if they had lost their vigour by the way? *Rev. T. Adams*, Works, I. 349.

querulential† (kwer-ō-len'shal), *a.* [< *querul(ous)* + *-ent* + *-ial*.] Having a tendency to querulousness; querulous. [Rare.]

Walpole had by nature a propensity, and by constitution a plea, for being captious and *querulential*, for he was a martyr to the gout. *Cumberland*, Memoirs, I. 23.

Querulinæ (kwer-ō-lī'nē), *n. pl.* [NL., < *Querula* + *-inæ*.] A subfamily of *Cotingidæ*, taking name from the genus *Querula*: same as *Gymnoderinæ*. *Swainson*, 1837.

querulous (kwer'ō-lus), *a.* [< L. *querulus*, full of complaints, complaining, < *queri*, complain, lament: see *querent*[1].] 1. Complaining; habitually complaining; disposed to murmur or express dissatisfaction: as, a *querulous* man.

O *querulous* and weak!— whose useless brain
Once thought of nothing, and now thinks in vain;
Whose eye reverted weeps o'er all the past.
Cowper, Hope, l. 29.

2. Expressing complaint; proceeding from a complaining habit: as, a *querulous* tone of voice.

Quickened the fire and laid the board,
Mid the crone's angry, *querulous* word
Of surly wonder.
William Morris, Earthly Paradise, III. 69.

3†. Quarrelsome.

Warlike, ready to fight, *querulous*, and mischievous. *Holland.*

The cock his crested helmet bent,
And down his *querulous* challenge sent.
Whittier, Snow-Bound.

=**Syn. 1** and **2.** See *plaintive* and *petulant*.

querulously (kwer'ọ̈-lus-li), *adv.* In a querulous or complaining manner.

querulousness (kwer'ọ̈-lus-nes), *n.* The state of being querulous; disposition to complain, or the habit or practice of murmuring.

query (kwē'ri), *n.*; pl. *queries* (-riz). [Formerly, as L., *quære*, being the L. *quære*, ask, inquire (i. e. 'inquire further into this,' 'look this up'), 2d pers. sing. impv. of *quærere*, seek, search for, ask, inquire: much used as a marginal note or memorandum to indicate a question or doubt, and hence taken as a noun: see *quest*.] A question; an inquiry to be answered or resolved; specifically, a doubt or challenge, as of a written or printed statement, represented by the interrogation-point (?), or by an abbreviation, *q.*, *qy.*, or *qu.*, or by both.

This name of Sion, Silon, or Siam may worthily moue a *quære* to Geographers. *Purchas*, Pilgrimage, p. 459.

Answer'd all *queries* touching those at home
With a heaved shoulder and a saucy smile.
Tennyson, Aylmer's Field.

=**Syn.** *Inquiry, Interrogation*, etc. See *question*.

query (kwē'ri), *v.*; pret. and pp. *queried*, ppr. *querying*. [< *query*, *n.*] **I.** *intrans.* To put a query; ask a question or questions; express doubt.

Three college sophs, . . .
Each prompt to *query*, answer, and debate.
Pope, Dunciad, ii. 381.

He *queried*, and reasoned thus within himself.
S. Parker, Bibliotheca Biblica, I. 394.

II. *trans.* **1.** To mark with a query; express a desire to examine as to the truth of.

This refined observation delighted Sir John, who dignifies it as an axiom, yet afterwards came to doubt it with a "sed de hoc quære"—*query* this!
I. D'Israeli, Curios. of Lit., II. 384.

It [Chelsea College] was afterwards repurchased by that monarch (but *query* if purchase money was ever paid).
N. and Q., 7th ser., V. 185.

2. To seek by questioning; inquire or ask: as, to *query* the sum or amount; to *query* the motive or the fact.

We shall not proceed to *query* what truth there is in palmistry. *Sir T. Browne*, Vulg. Err., v. 24.

3. To examine by questions; address queries to: as, to *query* a person. *Gayton.*

quesal, *n.* Same as *quetzal*.

queset (kwēz), *v. t.* [< L. *quæsere*, seek, beg, ask, var. of *quærere*, seek, ask: see *quest*[1].] To search after; look for. *Milton.* [Rare.]

quesitive (kwes'i-tiv), *a.* [< ML. *quæsitivus*, seeking, desirous, < L. *quærere*, pp. *quæsitus*, seek, inquire: see *quest*[1]. Cf. *inquisitive*.] Interrogatory.—**Quesitive quantity.** See *quantity*.

quest[1] (kwest), *n.* [< ME. *queste*, < OF. *queste*, F. *quête* = Pr. *questa*, *quista* = It. *chiesta*, < ML. *quæsta*, < L. *quæsita* (sc. *res*), a thing sought, *quæsitum*, a question, fem. or neut. of *quæsitus*, pp. of *quærere*, also *quæsere*, OL. *quairere*, seek, search for, seek to get, desire, get, acquire, obtain, seek to learn, ask, inquire, etc. From the same L. verb are ult. E. *querent*[2], *query*, *question*, *acquire*, *conquer*, *exquire*, *inquire*, *perquire*, *require*, *acquest*, *conquest*, *inquest*, *request*, etc., *exquisite*, *perquisite*, *inquisition*, *perquisition*, *requisition*, etc. In def. 6 *quest* is in part an aphetic form of *inquest*.] **1.** The act of seeking; search; pursuit; suit.

The Bassa of Sidon's servants, who were abroad in *quest* of Mules for the service of their Master.
Maundrell, Aleppo to Jerusalem, p. 32.

Her sunny locks
Hang on her temples like a golden fleece; . . .
And many Jasons come in *quest* of her.
Shak., M. of V., i. 1. 172.

Greek pirates, roving, like the corsairs of Barbary, in *quest* of men, laid the foundations of Greek commerce.
Bancroft, Hist. U. S., I. 127.

2. An act of searching or seeking, as for a particular object: as, the *quest* of the holy grail.

Thei entred in to many *questes* for to knowe whiche was the beste knyght. *Merlin* (E. E. T. S.), iii. 503.

A long and wearisome *quest* of spiritual joys, which, for all he knows, he may never arrive to.
Bp. Atterbury, Sermons, I. xi., Pref.

And those that had gone out upon the *Quest*,
Wasted and worn, and but a tithe of them,
And those that had not, stood before the King.
Tennyson, Holy Grail.

3. A body of searchers collectively; a searching party.

The senate hath sent about three several *quests*
To search you out. *Shak.*, Othello, i. 2. 46.

4. Inquiry; examination.

Volumes of report
Run with these false and most contrarious *quests*
Upon thy doings. *Shak.*, M. for M., iv. 1. 62.

5. Request; desire; solicitation; prayer; demand.

Gad not abroad at every *quest* and call
Of an untrain'd hope or passion.
G. Herbert, The Temple, Content.

6. A jury of inquest; a sworn body of examiners; also, an inquest.

By God, my maister lost c. marc by a seute of Margyt Bryg upon a defence of atteynt, because a *quest* passed ayenst hyr of xij. penyworth lond by yeer.
Paston Letters, I. 404.

The judge at the empanelling of the *quest* had his grave looks. *Latimer*, 5th Sermon bef. Edw. VI., 1549.

The *quest* of jury-men was call'd.
Sir Hugh of the Grime (Child's Ballads, VI. 249).

What lawful *quest* have given their verdict up
Unto the frowning judge? *Shak.*, Rich. III., i. 4. 189.

xii. they must be to make an enquest or, as some call it, a *quest*. An enquest or *quest* is called a lawfull kind of triall by xii. men. *Smith*, Commonwealth, ii. 18. (*Richardson.*)

Crowner's quest. See *crowner*[2].—**Kirby's quest**, an ancient record remaining with the remembrancer of the Exchequer: so called from its being the inquest of John de Kirby, treasurer of King Edward I. *Rapalje and Lawrence.*

quest[1] (kwest), *v.* [< ME. *questen*, < OF. *quester*, F. *quêter*, seek, < *queste*, a seeking: see *quest*, *n.*] **I.** *intrans.* **1.** To go in search; make search or inquiry; pursue.

And that the Prelates have no sure foundation in the Gospell, their own guiltinesse doth manifest; they would not else run *questing* up as high as Adam, to fetch their originall, as tis said one of them lately did in publick.
Milton, Church-Government, i. 3.

How soon they were recognized by grammarians ought to be ascertainable at the expense of a few hours' *questing* in such a library as that of the British Museum.
F. Hall, Mod. Eng., p. 326.

2. To go begging.

He [Samuel Johnson] dined on venison and champagne whenever he had been so fortunate as to borrow a guinea. If his *questing* had been unsuccessful, he appeased the rage of hunger with some scraps of broken meat.
Macaulay, in Encyc. Brit., XIII. 722.

There was another old beggar-woman down in the town, *questing* from shop to shop, who always amused me.
Fraser's Mag.

3. To give tongue, as a dog on the scent of game.

To bay or *quest* as a dog. *Florio*, p. 1. (*Halliwell.*)

Pup. They are a covey soon scattered, methink; who sprung them, I marle?
Town. Marry, yourself, Puppy, for aught I know; you *quested* last. *B. Jonson*, Gipsies Metamorphosed.

As some are playing young Spaniels, *quest* at every bird that rises: so others, held very good men, are at a dead stand, not knowing what to doe or say.
N. Ward, Simple Cobler, p. 19.

While Redmond every thicket round
Tracked earnest as a *questing* hound.
Scott, Rokeby, iv. 31.

II. *trans.* **1.** To search or seek for; inquire into or examine. [Rare.]

They *quest* annihilation's monstrous theme.
Byrom, Enthusiasm.

2. To announce by giving tongue, as a dog.

Not only to give notice that the dog is on game, but also the particular kind which he is *questing*.
Dogs of Great Britain and America, p. 111.

quest[2] (kwest), *n.* Same as *quest*.

questantt (kwes'tant), *n.* [< OF. *questant*, F. *quêtant*, ppr. of *quester*, F. *quêter*, seek: see *quest*[1], *v.*] A candidate; a seeker of any object; a competitor.

When
The bravest *questant* shrinks, find what you seek,
That fame may cry you loud.
Shak., All's Well, ii. 1. 16.

quest-dovet (kwest'duv), *n.* Same as *quecst*.

Panurge halved and fixed upon a great stake the horns of a roe-buck, together with the skin and the right forefoot thereof, . . . the wings of two bustards, the feet of four *quest-doves*, . . . and a goblet of Beauvois.
Urquhart, tr. of Rabelais, ii. 27. (*Davies.*)

quester (kwes'tėr), *n.* [< OF. *questeur*, F. *quêteur*, < L. *quæsitor*, a seeker, < *quærere*, pp. *quæsitus*, seek: see *quest*[1], *v.* Cf. *questor*.] **1.** A seeker; a searcher.—**2.** A dog employed to find game.

The *quester* only to the wood they loose,
Who silently the tainted track pursues.
Rowe, tr. of Lucan's Pharsalia, iv.

questful (kwest'fůl), *a.* [< *quest*[1] + *-ful*.] Full of quest; searching; investigating.

The summer day he spent in *questful* round.
Lowell, Invita Minerva.

quest-houset (kwest'hous), *n.* The chief watch-house of a parish, generally adjoining a church, where sometimes quests concerning misdemeanors and annoyances were held. *Halliwell.*

A hag, repair'd with vice-complexion'd paint,
A *quest-house* of complaint.
Quarles, Emblems, ii. 10.

questing-stonet, *n.* [Appar. < **questing*, verbal n. of **quest*, rub (< MD. *quisten*, rub, rub away, spend, lavish, D. *kuisten*, spend, lavish). + *stone*.] A stone used for rubbing or polishing (?).

Laden with diuerse goods and marchandises, . . . namely with the hides of oxen and of sheepe, with butter, masts, sparres, boordes, *questing-stones*, and wilde werke.
Hakluyt's Voyages, I. 168.

question (kwes'chọn), *n.* [< ME. *question*, *questioun*, < OF. *question*, F. *question* = Pr. *questio*, *question* = Sp. *cuestion* = Pg. *questão* = It. *questione*, *quistione*, < L. *quæstio*(*n*-), a seeking, investigation, inquiry, question, < *quærere*, pp. *quæsitus*, ML. *quæstus*, seek, ask, inquire: see *quest*[1].] **1.** The act of interrogation; the putting of inquiries: as, to examine by *question* and answer.

Ross. What sights, my lord?
Lady M. I pray you, speak not; he grows worse and worse;
Question enrages him. *Shak.*, Macbeth, iii. 4. 118.

Leodogran . . . ask'd,
Fixing full eyes of *question* on her face, . . .
"But thou art closer to this noble prince?"
Tennyson, Coming of Arthur.

2. That which is asked; an inquiry; a query; the expression of a desire to know something indicated more or less definitely. In grammar, questions are classed as (1) *direct* (*independent*): as, John is here? is John here? who is that? (2) *indirect* (*dependent*), taking the form of an object-clause: as, he asks if John is here; he asks who that is; (3) *simple*: as, is that man a soldier? (4) *double* (*alternative, compound, disjunctive*): as, is that man a soldier or a civilian? (5) *indirect double*: as, he asks whether that man is a soldier or not; (6) *deliberative* or *doubting*: as, shall I do it? shall we remain? (7) *positive*: as, is that right?—with emphasis on the verb this expects the answer "No"; (8) *negative*: as, is not that right?—this expects the answer "Yes."

Answer me
Directly unto this *question* that I ask.
Shak., 1 Hen. IV., ii. 3. 89.

None but they doubtless who were reputed wise had the *Question* propounded to them.
Milton, Eikonoklastes, xxviii.

3. Inquiry; disquisition; discussion.

It is . . . to be put to *question* . . . whether it be lawful for Christian princes or states to make an invasive war only and simply for the propagation of the faith.
Bacon, An Advt. Touching an Holy War.

4. The subject or matter of examination or investigation; the theme of inquiry; a matter discussed or made the subject of disquisition.

Now in things, although not commanded of God, yet lawful because they are permitted, the *question* is what light shall shew us the conveniency which one hath above another. *Hooker*, Eccles. Polity, ii. 4.

The *question* of his [Cæsar's] death is enrolled in the Capitol; his glory not extenuated, . . . nor his offences enforced. *Shak.*, J. C., iii. 2. 41.

The press and the public at large are generally so occupied with the *questions* of the day that . . . the more general aspects of political *questions* are seldom . . . considered. *Nineteenth Century*, XXVI. 733.

5. Dispute or subject of debate; a point of doubt or difficulty.

There arose a *question* between some of John's disciples and the Jews about purifying. John iii. 25.

To be, or not to be: that is the *question*.
Shak., Hamlet, iii. 1. 56.

6. Doubt; controversy; dispute: as, the story is true beyond all *question*.

Our own earth would be barren and desolate without the benign influence of the solar rays, which without *question* is true of all other planets. *Bentley.*

Had they found a linguist half so good,
I make no *question* but the tower had stood.
Pope, Satires of Donne, iv. 85.

In a work which he was, no *question*, acquainted with, we read . . . *F. Hall*, Mod. Eng., p. 178.

7. Judicial trial or inquiry; trial; examination.

He that was in *question* for the robbery.
Shak., 2 Hen. IV., i. 2. 68.

Mr. Endecott was also left out, and called into *question* about the defacing the cross in the ensign.
Winthrop, Hist. New England, I. 188.

8. Examination by torture, or the application of torture to prisoners under criminal accusation in order to extort confession.

Such a presumption is only sufficient to put the person to the rack or *question*, . . . and not bring him to condemnation. *Ayliffe*, Parergon.

A master, when accused, could offer his slaves for the *question*, or demand for the same purpose the slaves of another; and, if in the latter case they were injured or killed in the process, their owner was indemnified.
Encyc. Brit., XXII. 132.

9†. Conversation; speech; talk.

I met the duke yesterday, and had much *question* with him. *Shak.*, As you Like it, iii. 4. 39.

10. In *logic*, a proposition, or that which is to be established as a conclusion, stated by way of interrogation.—11. In *parliamentary usage:* (*a*) The point under discussion by the house; the measure to be voted on: as, to speak to the *question*. (*b*) The putting of the matter discussed to a vote: as, are you ready for the *question?*—**Comparative, complex, double, Eastern question.** See the adjectives.—**Division of the question.** See *division*.—**Horary question,** in *astrol.*, a question the decision of which depends upon the figure of the heavens at the moment it is propounded.—**Hypothetical question.** See *hypothetical*.—**In question,** under consideration or discussion: indicating something just mentioned or referred to.

He is likewise a rival of mine—that is, of my other self's, for he does not think his friend Captain Absolute ever saw the lady *in question*. *Sheridan*, The Rivals, ii. 1.

Mr. Wall and his ally exert themselves to make up for the painful absence *in question* to their utmost power. *W. M. Baker*, New Timothy, p. 213.

Leading question, a question so put as to suggest the answer which is desired, and thus to lead to and prepare the way for such an answer. A party is not allowed to put a leading question to his own witness, except in matters purely introductory, and not touching a point in controversy; and except that if his witness is obviously hostile or defective in memory the court may in its discretion allow a leading question. A party may put leading questions in cross-examining his adversary's witness.—**Mixed questions.** See *mixed*.—**Out of question,** doubtless; beyond question.

Out of question, you were born in a merry hour. *Shak.*, Much Ado, ii. 1. 346.

Out of the question, not worthy of or requiring consideration; not to be thought of.

It is *out of the question* to ask the Diet for money to clear off the enormous debts; so that it is difficult to guess how the matter will end. *Contemporary Rev.*, XLIX. 287.

Previous question, in *parliamentary practice*, the question whether a vote shall be come to on the main issue or not, brought forward before the main or real question is put by the Speaker, and for the purpose of avoiding, if the vote is in the negative, the putting of this question. The motion is in the form, "that the question be now put," and the mover and seconder vote against it. In the House of Representatives of the United States (it is not used in the Senate), and in many State legislatures, the object of moving the previous question is to cut off debate and secure immediately a vote on the question under consideration; here, therefore, the mover and seconder vote in the affirmative.

The great remedy against prolix or obstructive debate is the so-called *previous question*, which is moved in the form "Shall the main question be now put?" and when ordered closes forthwith all debate, and brings the House to a direct vote on that main question. *J. Bryce*, American Commonwealth, I. 130.

Question of fact, question of law. See *fact*, 3.—**Question of order.** See *order*.—**Question of privilege.** See *privilege*.—**Real question.** See *real*[1].—**The Questions,** the Shorter Catechism of the Westminster Assembly of Divines. [Scotch.]—**To beg the question.** See *beg*[1].—**To call in question.** (*a*) To doubt; challenge.

You call *in question* the continuance of his love. *Shak.*, T. N., i. 4. 6.

(*b*) To subject to judicial interrogation.

Touching the resurrection of the dead I am *called in question* by you this day. Acts xxiv. 21.

The governour wrote to some of the assistants about it, and, upon advice with the ministers, it was agreed to *call* . . . them [the offenders] *in question*. *Winthrop*, Hist. New England, I. 172.

To pop the question. See *pop*[1]. =**Syn. 2.** *Question, Query, Inquiry, Interrogation*, and *Interrogatory* agree in expressing a form of words used in calling for information or an answer from another. *Question* is the most general in its meaning, and *inquiry* stands next. *Query* stands for a question asked without force, a point about which one would like to be informed: the word is used with all degrees of weakness down to the mere expression of a doubt: as, I raised a *query* as to the strength of the bridge. A *question* may be put in order to test another's knowledge; the other words express an asking for real information. *Interrogatory* is a strong word, expressing an authoritative or searching question that must be explicitly answered, sometimes in law a written question. *Inquiry* is somewhat milder and less direct than *question*, the order of strength being *query, inquiry, question, interrogation*. There is no perceptible difference between *interrogation* and *interrogatory*, except that the former may express also the act. See *ask*[1] and *examination*.—4 and 5. Proposition, motion, topic, point.

question (kwes'chon), *v.* [‹ OF. *questionner*, ‹ ML. *quæstionare*, question, ‹ L. *quæstio(n-)*, question: see *question*, *n.*] **I.** *intrans.* **1.** To ask a question or questions; inquire or seek to know; examine.

He that *questioneth* much shall learn much. *Bacon*, Discourse.

And mute, yet seem'd to *question* with their Eyes. *Congreve*, Iliad.

2. To debate; reason; consider.

Nor dare I *question* with my jealous thought
Where you may be. *Shak.*, Sonnets, lvii.

3. To dispute; doubt.—**4†.** To talk; converse.

For, after supper, long he *questioned*
With modest Lucrece. *Shak.*, Lucrece, l. 122.

I haue heard him oft *question* with Captaine Martin and tell him, except he could shew him a more substantiall triall, he was not inamoured with their durty skill. Quoted in *Capt. John Smith's* Works, I. 169.

II. *trans.* **1.** To inquire of by asking questions; examine by interrogatories: as, to *question* a witness.

Her father loved me; oft invited me;
Still *question'd* me the story of my life.
Shak., Othello, i. 3. 129.

They *questioned* him apart, as the custom is,
When first the matter made a noise at Rome.
Browning, Ring and Book, I. 127.

2. To doubt of; be uncertain of; mention or treat as doubtful or not to be trusted.

It is much to be *questioned* whether they could ever spin it [asbestos] to a thread. *Pococke*, Description of the East, II. i. 229.

There is no possibility to disprove a matter of fact that was never *questioned* or doubted of before. *Jer. Taylor*, Works (ed. 1835), II. 167.

Nor *question*
The wisdom that hath made us what we are.
Lowell, Under the Willows.

3. To call in question; challenge; take exception to: as, to *question* an exercise of prerogative.

What uproar 's this? must my name here be *question'd*
In tavern-brawls, and by affected ruffians?
Beau. and Fl., Honest Man's Fortune, ii. 2.

Power and right
To *question* thy bold entrance on this place.
Milton, P. L., iv. 882.

Whatever may be *questioned*, it is certain that we are in the presence of an Infinite and Eternal Being. *J. R. Seeley*, Nat. Religion, p. 44.

=**Syn. 1.** *Ask, Inquire of, Interrogate*, etc. (see *ask*[1]), catechize.—3. To controvert, dispute.

questionable (kwes'chon-a-bl), *a.* [= Sp. *cuestionable* = Pg. *questionavel* = It. *questionabile;* as *question* + *-able*.] **1.** Capable of being questioned or inquired of; inviting or seeming to invite inquiry or conversation. [Now rare.]

Thou comest in such a *questionable* shape
That I will speak to thee. *Shak.*, Hamlet, i. 4. 43.

2. Liable to question; suspicious; doubtful; uncertain; disputable: as, the deed is of *questionable* authority; his veracity is *questionable*.

It being *questionable* whether he [Galen] ever saw the dissection of a human body. *Baker*, Reflections upon Learning, xv.

The facts respecting him [Governor Van Twiller] were so scattered and vague, and divers of them so *questionable* in point of authenticity, that I have had to give up the search. *Irving*, Knickerbocker, p. 151.

questionableness (kwes'chon-a-bl-nes), *n.* The character or state of being questionable, doubtful, or suspicious.

questionably (kwes'chon-a-bli), *adv.* In a questionable manner; doubtfully.

questionary (kwes'chon-ā-ri), *a.* and *n.* [= F. *questionnaire* = Sp. *cuestionario* = Pg. *questionario*, ‹ LL. *quæstionarius*, prop. adj., of or pertaining to question, but used only as a noun, LL. a torturer, executioner, ML. also an examiner, a judge, also a solicitor of alms, a beggar, ‹ L. *quæstio(n-)*, question, inquiry: see *question*.] **I.** *a.* Inquiring; asking questions.

I grow laconick even beyond laconicisme; for sometimes I return only Yes or No to *questionary* or petitionary epistles of half a yard long. *Pope*, To Swift, Aug. 17, 1736.

II. *n.*; pl. *questionaries* (-riz). A pardoner; an itinerant seller of indulgences or relics.

One of the principal personages in the comic part of the drama was . . . a *quæstionary* or pardoner, one of those itinerants who hawked about from place to place reliques, real or pretended, with which he excited the devotion at once and the charity of the populace, and generally deceived both the one and the other. *Scott*, Abbot, xxvii.

questioner (kwes'chon-ėr), *n.* [‹ *question* + *-er*[1].] One who asks questions; an inquirer.

He that labours for the sparrow-hawk
Has little time for idle *questioners*.
Tennyson, Geraint.

questioning (kwes'chon-ing), *n.* [Verbal n. of *question*, *v.*] **1.** The act of interrogating; a query.—**2.** Doubt; suspicion.

Those obstinate *questionings*
Of sense and outward things.
Wordsworth, Ode, Immortality, st. 9.

questioningly (kwes'chon-ing-li), *adv.* Interrogatively; as one who questions.

questionist (kwes'chon-ist), *n.* [‹ *question* + *-ist*.] **1.** One who asks questions; a questioner; an inquirer; an investigator; a doubter.

He was not so much a *questionist*, but wrought upon the other's questions, and, like a counsellor, wished him to discharge his conscience, and to satisfy the world. *Bacon*, Charge against Wentworth, Works, XII. 221.

2. In old universities, the respondent in the determinations; hence still at Cambridge, a student of three years, who is consequently qualified to be a candidate for a degree.

Yea, I know that heades were cast together, and counsell deuised, that Duns, with all the rable of barbarous *questionistes*, should haue dispossessed of their place and rowmes Aristotle, Plato, Tullie, and Demosthenes. *Ascham*, The Scholemaster (Arber's reprint, p. 136).

The papers set on the Monday and Tuesday of the week following contain only about one low question a-piece, to amuse the mass of the *Questionists* during the half-hour before the expiration of which they are not allowed to leave the Senate-House. *C. A. Bristed*, English University, p. 291.

questionless (kwes'chon-les), *a.* and *adv.* [‹ *question* + *-less*.] **I.** *a.* Unquestioning.

With the same clear mind and *questionless* faith. *L. Wallace*, Ben-Hur, p. 498.

II. *adv.* Without question; beyond doubt; doubtless; certainly. [An elliptical use of the adjective, standing for the phrase "it is questionless that."]

I have a mind presages me such thrift
That I should *questionless* be fortunate!
Shak., M. of V., i. 1. 176.

She 's abus'd, *questionless*.
Middleton and Rowley, Changeling, iv. 2.

What it [Episcopacy] was in the Apostles time, that *questionlesse* it must be still. *Milton*, Reformation in Eng., ii.

questman† (kwest'man), *n.* [‹ *quest*[1] + *man*.] **1.** One having power to make legal inquiry. Specifically, in *old law:* (*a*) A person chosen to inquire into abuses and misdemeanors, especially such as relate to weights and measures. (*b*) A collector of parish rates. (*c*) An assistant to a churchwarden. Also called *sidesman* and *synod-man*. (*d*) A juryman; a person impaneled to try a cause. Also *questryman*. **2.** One who laid informations and made a trade of petty lawsuits; a common informer.

questmonger† (kwest'mung"gėr), *n.* [‹ *quest*[1] + *monger*.] A juryman.

questor, quæstor (kwes'tor), *n.* [= F. *questeur* = Sp. *cuestor* = Pg. *questor* = It. *questore*, ‹ L. *quæstor*, a magistrate having special jurisdiction in financial matters (see def.), ‹ *quærere*, pp. *quæsitus*, seek, procure: see *quest*[1].] **1.** In ancient Rome, a member of one of two distinct classes of magistrates: (*a*) One of two public accusers (*quæstores parricidii*) whose duty it was to lay accusations against those guilty of murder or other capital offense, and to see to the execution of the sentence. This magistracy was in existence at the earliest historic time, but became obsolete about 366 B. C., its functions being transferred to other officers. (*b*) One of the officers (*quæstores classici*) having the care and administration of the public funds; a public treasurer. It was their duty to receive, pay out, and record the public finances, including the collection of taxes, tribute, etc. Questors accompanied the provincial governors, proconsuls, or pretors, and received everywhere the public dues and imports, paid the troops, etc. After Julius Cæsar, some of their functions were given to the pretors and some to the ediles. The number of questors was originally two, but was gradually increased to twenty. Under Constantine the *quæstor sacri palatii* was an imperial minister of much power and importance. **2.** In the middle ages, one appointed by the Pope or by a Roman Catholic bishop to announce the granting of indulgences, of which the special condition was the giving of alms to the church.—**3.** A treasurer; one charged with the collection and care of dues.

questorship, quæstorship (kwes'tor-ship), *n.* [‹ *questor* + *-ship*.] The office of a questor, or the term of a questor's office.

He whom an honest *quæstorship* has indear'd to the Sicilians. *Milton*, Areopagitica.

questrist† (kwes'trist), *n.* [Irreg. ‹ *quester* + *-ist*.] A person who goes in quest of another. [Rare.]

Some five or six and thirty of his knights,
Hot *questrists* after him, met him at gate.
Shak., Lear, iii. 7. 17.

questryman†, *n.* Same as *questman*.

Then other *questry-men* was call'd; . . .
Twelve of them spoke all in a breast,
Sir Hugh in the Grime, thou'st now guilty.
Sir Hugh of the Grime (Child's Ballads, VI. 249).

questuary† (kwes'tū-ā-ri), *a.* and *n.* [= OF. *questuaire*, ‹ L. *quæstuarius*, pertaining to gain or money-getting, ‹ *quæstus*, gain, acquisition, ‹ *quærere*, pp. *quæstus*, seek, get, obtain: see *quest*[1].] **I.** *a.* Studious of gain; seeking gain; also, producing gain.

Although lapidaries and *questuary* enquirers affirm it, yet the writers of minerals . . . are of another belief, conceiving the stones which bear this name [toad stone] to be a mineral concretion, not to be found in animals. *Sir T. Browne*, Vulg. Err., iii. 13.

Some study *questuary* and gainful arts, and every one would thrive in 's calling. *Middleton*, Family of Love, v. 1.

II. *n.* A pardoner; a questionary. *Jer. Taylor*, Dissuasive from Popery, i. 3.

questus (kwes'tus), *n.* [‹ L. *quæstus*, gain, profit, ‹ *quærere*, seek, obtain: see *quest*[1].] In *law*, land which does not descend by hereditary right, but is acquired by one's own labor and industry. Also *quæstus*.

questword† (kwest'wėrd), *n.* A bequeathment.

The legacies or *questword* of the deceased supplied the rest. *Archæologia* (1792), X. 197. (*Davies.*)

quetch†, *v.* See *quitch*[1].

quethe[1], *v. t.*; pret. *quoth*, ppr. *quething*. [< ME. *quethen* (pret. *quoth*, *quod*, *koth*, *ko*, earlier *quath*, *queth*), < AS. *cwethan* (pret. *cwæth*, pl. *cwædon*, pp. *ge-cwethen*), speak, say. Cf. *bequeath*.] 1. To say; declare; speak. [Obsolete except in the archaic preterit *quoth*.]

I *quethe* hym quyte, and hym relese
Of Egypt alle the wildirnesse.
Rom. of the Rose, l. 6999.

Being alive and seinge I peryshe, i. beinge quycke and *quethyng* I am undone.
Palsgrave, Acolastus (1540). (*Halliwell.*)

"Lordynges," *quoth* he, "now herkneth for the beste."
Chaucer, Prol. to C. T., l. 788.

"I hold by him."
"And I," *quoth* Everard, "by the wassail-bowl."
Tennyson, The Epic.

2†. To bequeath.

Hous and rente and outher thyng
Mow they *quethe* at here endyng.
MS. Harl. 1701, f. 42. (*Halliwell.*)

quethe[2]†, *n.* See *qued*.

quetzal (kwet'sal), *n.* [Native name.] The paradise-trogon, *Pharomacrus mocinno* (or *Calurus elegans*), the most magnificent of the trogons, of a golden-green and carmine color, with long airy upper tail-coverts projecting like sprays a foot or two beyond the tail. It inhabits Central America, especially Costa Rica. See cut under *trogon*. Also *quesal*, *quijal*.

queue (kū), *n.* [< F. *queue*, a tail, < L. *cauda*, tail: see *cue*[1].] 1. A tail; in *her.*, the tail of a beast.—2. A tail or pendent braid of hair; a pigtail: originally part of the wig, but afterward, and toward the close of the eighteenth century, when it was in common use, formed of the hair of the head. See *cue*[1], 1.—3. Same as *cue*[1], 2.

Several dozen [men] standing in a *queue* as at the ticket office of a railway station.
H. *James, Jr.*, International Episode, p. 13.

4. The tail-piece of a violin or similar instrument.—5. In *musical notation*, the stem or tail of a note.

queue (kū), *v. t.*; pret. and pp. *queued*, ppr. *queuing*. [< *queue*, *n.*] To tie, braid, or fasten in a queue or pigtail.

Among his officers was a sturdy veteran named Keldermeester, who had cherished through a long life a mop of hair . . . *queued* so tightly to his head that his eyes and mouth generally stood ajar, and his eyebrows were drawn up to the top of his forehead.
Irving, Knickerbocker, p. 316.

queued (kūd), *a.* [< *queue* + *-ed*[2].] In *her.*, same as *tailed*: used in the phrases *double queued*, *triple queued*, etc.

quever†, *a.* See *quiver*[1].

quew†, *n.* An obsolete spelling of *cue*[1], 3 (*a*).

At the third time the great door openeth, for he shut in one before of purpose to open it when his *quew* came.
Calfhill, Answer to Martiall, p. 209. (*Davies.*)

quey (kwā), *n.* [Also *quee*; ME. *quye*, *qwye*; < Icel. *kviga* = Sw. *qviga* = Dan. *kvie*, a quey.] A young cow or heifer; a cow that has not yet had a calf. [Scotch.]

Nought left me o' four-and-twenty gude ousen and ky,
My weel-ridden gelding, and a white *quey*.
Fray of Suport (Child's Ballads, VI. 116).

queych†, *n.* An obsolete variant of *quaigh*.

queynt†, *a.* An obsolete variant of *quaint*.

quhilk, *pron.* A Scotch form of *which*.

quhilles†, *adv.* An obsolete Scotch form of *whilst*.

quib† (kwib), *n.* [A var. of *quip*; cf. *quibble*.] A sarcasm; a taunt; a gibe; a quip.

After he was gone, Mr. Weston, in lue of thanks to ye Govr and his freinds hear, gave them . . . [a] *quib* (behind their baks) for all their pains.
Bradford, Plymouth Plantation, p. 151.

quibble (kwib'l), *v. i.*; pret. and pp. *quibbled*, ppr. *quibbling*. [Freq. of *quip*; cf. *quib*.] 1. To trifle in argument or discourse; evade the point in question, or the plain truth, by artifice, play upon words, or any conceit; prevaricate.

Quibbling about self-interest and motives, and objects of desire, and the greatest happiness of the greatest number is but a poor employment for a grown man.
Macaulay, Mill on Government.

2. To pun.

His part has all the wit,
For none speakes, carps, and *quibbles* besides him;
I'd rather see him leap, or laugh, or cry,
Than hear the gravest speech in all the play.
Goffe, Careless Shepherdess, Prel. (*Strutt.*)

quibble (kwib'l), *n.* [< *quibble*, *v.*] 1. A start or turn from the point in question, or from plain truth; an evasion; a prevarication.

Quirks and *quibbles* . . . have no place in the search after truth. *Watts*, Improvement of Mind, i. 9, § 27.

His still refuted quirks he still repeats;
New rais'd objections with new *quibbles* meets.
Cowper, Progress of Error, l. 551.

2. A pun; a trivial conceit.

Puns and *quibbles*. *Addison.*

It was very natural, therefore, that the common people, by a *quibble*, which is the same in Flemish as in English, should call the proposed "Moderation" the "Murderation." *Motley*, Dutch Republic, I. 529.

quibbler (kwib'lėr), *n.* 1. One who quibbles; one who evades plain truth by trifling artifices, play upon words, or the like.—2. A punster.

quibblet (kwib'let), *n.* Same as *quibble*, 2. *Nares.*

quibbling (kwib'ling), *n.* A pun; a witticism.

I have made a *quibbling* in praise of her myself.
Shirley, Witty Fair One, iii. 2.

quibblingly (kwib'ling-li), *adv.* In a quibbling manner; evasively; punningly.

quibib†, *n.* [ME., also *quibyb*, *quybibe*, *quybybe*, usually in pl. *quibibes*, < OF. *quibibes*, *cubebes*, cubebs: see *cubeb*.] An obsolete form of *cubeb*.

quiblin†, *n.* [Appar. for *quibbling*.] A quibble.

To o'erreach that head that outreacheth all heads,
'Tis a trick rampant! 'tis a very *quiblyn*!
Marston, Jonson, and Chapman, Eastward Ho, iii. 2.

quice†, *n.* Same as *queest*.

quich†, *v. i.* Same as *quitch*[1].

quick (kwik), *a.* and *n.* [< ME. *quik*, *qwik*, *quyk*, *quek*, *cwic*, *cwuc*, < AS. *cwic*, *cwyc*, *cwicu*, *cucu*, living, alive, = OS. OFries. *quik* = D. *kwik* = LG. *quik* = OHG. *quec*, *queh*, *quek*, *chec*, MHG. *quec* (*queck-*), *kec* (*keck-*), G. *queck* (in *quecksilber* = E. *quicksilver*), living, *keck*, living, lively, quick (> Sw. *käck* = Dan. *kjæk*, lively), = Icel. *kvikr*, *kykr* = Sw. *qvick* = Dan. *kvik* (all these forms having an unorig. *k* developed before the orig. *w*) = Goth. *kwius* (**kwiwa-*), living, quick, = L. *vivus*, living (cf. *vivere*, live, > *vita*, life), for orig. **gvivus*, = Gr. *βίος*, life (> *βιοῦν*, live, *βίοτος*, life, way of life) (the same relation of E. *c* (*k*), L. *v*, Gr. *β* appearing in E. *come* = L. *venire* = Gr. *βαίνειν*), = OBulg. *zhivŭ* = Bohem. *zhiwy* = Russ. *zhivu* = Lith. *givas*, living; Skt. √ *jīv*, live. To the same root in Teut. belongs Icel. *kveikja*, *kveykja*, kindle (a fire).] I. *a.* 1. Living; alive; live. [Archaic.]

Men may see there the Erthe of the Tombe apertly many tymes steren and meven, as there weren *quykke* thinges undre. *Mandeville*, Travels, p. 22.

Seven of their Porters were taken, whom Ieremie commanded to be flayed *quicke*.
Capt. John Smith, True Travels, I. 24.

He shall come to judge the *quick* and the dead.
Apostles' Creed.

Still this great solitude is *quick* with life.
Bryant, The Prairies.

2. Lively; characterized by physical or mental liveliness or sprightliness; prompt; ready; sprightly; nimble; brisk.

The next lesson wolde be some *quicke* and mery dialoges, elect out of Luciane. *Sir T. Elyot*, The Governour, i. 10.

To have an open ear, a *quick* eye, and a nimble hand is necessary for a cutpurse. *Shak.*, W. T., iv. 4. 685.

Where is the boy ye brought me?
A pretty lad, and of a *quick* capacity,
And bred up neatly. *Fletcher*, Pilgrim, ii. 2.

Good intellectual powers, when aided by a comparatively small power of prolonged attention, may render their possessor *quick* and intelligent.
J. Sully, Outlines of Psychol., p. 100.

3. Prompt to perceive or to respond to impressions; perceptive in a high degree; sensitive; hence, excitable; restless; passionate.

Quick is mine ear to hear of good towards him.
Shak., Rich. II., ii. 1. 234.

Quiet to *quick* bosoms is a hell,
And there hath been thy bane.
Byron, Childe Harold, iii. 42.

No more the widow's deafened ear
Grows *quick* that lady's step to hear.
Scott, Marmion, ii., Int.

She was *quick* to discern objects of real utility.
Prescott, Ferd. and Isa., ii. 16.

4. Speedy; hasty; swift; rapid; done or occurring in a short time; prompt; immediate: as, a *quick* return of profits.

Give thee *quick* conduct. *Shak.*, Lear, iii. 6. 104.

Slow to resolve, but in performance *quick*.
Dryden, Hind and Panther, iii. 921.

It may calm the apprehension of calamity in the most susceptible heart to see how *quick* a bound nature has set to the utmost infliction of malice.
Emerson, Essays, 1st ser., p. 239.

So *quick* the run,
We felt the good ship shake and reel.
Tennyson, The Voyage.

5. Hasty; precipitate; irritable; sharp; unceremonious.

In England, if God's preacher, God's minister, be any thing *quick*, or do speak sharply, then he is a foolish fellow, he is rash, he lacketh discretion.
Latimer, Sermon bef. Edw. VI., 1550.

He had rather haue a virgin that could giue a *quicke* aunswere that might cut him then a milde speache that might claw him. *Lyly*, Euphues and his England, p. 280.

6. Pregnant; with child: specifically noting a woman when the motion of the fetus is felt.

Jaquenetta that is *quick* by him.
Shak., L. L. L., v. 2. 687.

His vncles wife surviues, purchance
Left *quick* with child; & then he may goe dance
For a new living. *Times' Whistle* (E. E. T. S.), p. 39.

Puritanism, believing itself *quick* with the seed of religious liberty, laid, without knowing it, the egg of democracy. *Lowell*, Among my Books, 1st ser., p. 238.

7. Active in operation; piercing; sharp; hence, bracing; fresh.

For the word of God is *quick* and powerful, and sharper than any two edged sword. Heb. iv. 12.

The air is *quick* there,
And it pierces and sharpens the stomach.
Shak., Pericles, iv. 1. 28.

Why stay I after? but I deserve to stay,
To feel the *quick* remembrance of my follies.
Steele, Lying Lover, v. 1.

Quick anatomy†, vivisection.—**Quick goods**, cattle or domestic animals. *Norris*, Pamphlet (Charleston, 1712).—**Quick-return gearing.** See *gearing*.—**Quick time.** See *quickstep*, 1.—**Quick water**, a dilute solution of nitrate of mercury and gold, used in the process of water-gilding. *E. H. Knight.*=**Syn.** 2 and 4. Expeditious, rapid, active, alert, agile, hurrying, hurried, fleet, dexterous, adroit. See *quickness*.—3. Acute, keen.

II. *n.* 1†. A living being. [Rare.]

Tho, peeping close into the thicke,
Might see the moving of some *quicke*.
Spenser, Shep. Cal., March.

2. That which is quick, or living and sensitive: with the definite article: as, cut to *the quick*.

This test nippeth, this pincheth, this touches *the quick*.
Latimer.

I know the man,
And know he has been nettled to *the quick* too.
Fletcher, Double Marriage, ii. 3.

How feebly and unlike themselves they reason when they come to *the quick* of the difference. *Fuller.*

You fret, and are gall'd at *the quick*.
Milton, On Def. of Humb. Remonst.

3. A live fence or hedge formed of some growing plant, usually hawthorn; quickset.

The workes and especially the countercamp are curiously hedg'd with *quick*. *Evelyn*, Diary, Sept. 22, 1641.

Wild bird, whose warble, liquid sweet,
Rings Eden thro' the budded *quicks*.
Tennyson, In Memoriam, lxxxviii.

4. The quitch-grass. Also *quicks*, *quitch*. [Prov. Eng.]

quick (kwik), *adv.* [< *quick*, *a.*] 1. In a quick manner; nimbly; with celerity; rapidly; with haste; speedily: as, run *quick*.

But *quick* as thought the change is wrought.
Lady Anne Bothwell's Lament (Child's Ballads, IV. 126).

2. Soon; in a short time; without delay: as, go and return *quick*.

Then rise the tender germs, upstarting *quick*.
Cowper, Task, iii. 521.

quick (kwik), *v.* [< ME. *quikken*, *quiken*, *quyken*; < *quick*, *a.*] I. *trans.* 1†. To make alive; quicken; animate.

"The whiles I *quykke* the corps," quod he, "called am I Anima;
And whan I wilne and wolde Animus ich hatte."
Piers Plowman (B), xv. 23.

Thow seyst thy princes han thee yeven myght
Bothe for to sleen and for to *quike* a wyght.
Chaucer, Second Nun's Tale, l. 481.

2†. To revive; kindle; quicken.

Pandarus to *quyke* alwey the fire
Was ever yholde prest and diligent.
Chaucer, Troilus, iii. 484.

3. In *electroplating*, to prepare for the firmer adhesion of the deposited metal by the use of a solution of nitrate of mercury.

With a brush dipped therein [in a solution of quicksilver and aquafortis] they stroke over the surface of the metal to be gilt, which immediately becomes *quicked*.
Workshop Receipts, 1st ser., p. 308.

II.† *intrans.* To become alive; revive.

Right anon on of the tyres queynte,
And *quykede* agayn.
Chaucer, Knight's Tale, l. 1477.

quick-answered† (kwik'an'sėrd), *a.* [< *quick* + *answer*, *n.*, + *-ed*[2].] Quick in reply; ready at repartee. [Rare.]

Ready in gibes, *quick-answer'd*, saucy.
Shak., Cymbeline, iii. 4. 161.

quick-beam (kwik'bēm), *n.* The Old World mountain-ash or rowan. See *mountain-ash.* Also called *quicken* or *quicken-tree.*

quicken[1] (kwik'n), *v.* [< late ME. *quykenen*; < *quick* + *-en*[1].] **I.** *intrans.* **1.** To become quick or alive; receive life.

Summer flies, . . . that *quicken* even with blowing.
Shak., Othello, iv. 2. 67.

2. To become quick or lively; become more active or sensitive.

Sees by degrees a purer blush arise,
And keener lightnings *quicken* in her eyes.
Pope, R. of the L., i. 144.

3. To enter that state of pregnancy in which the child gives indications of life; begin to manifest signs of life in the womb: said of the mother or the child. The motion of the fetus is first felt by the mother usually about the eighteenth week of pregnancy.

II. *trans.* **1.** To make quick or alive; vivify; revive or resuscitate, as from death or an inanimate state.

You hath he *quickened*, who were dead in trespasses and sins.
Eph. ii. 1.

How a sound shall *quicken* content to bliss.
Browning, By the Fireside.

The idea of universal free labor was only a dormant bud, not to be *quickened* for many centuries.
Bancroft, Hist. U. S., I. 127.

2. To revive; cheer; reinvigorate; refresh.

Music and poesy use to *quicken* you.
Shak., T. of the S., i. 1. 36.

Wake! our mirth begins to die;
Quicken it with tunes and wine.
B. Jonson, Poetaster, iv. 3.

3. To make quick or speedy; hasten; accelerate: as, to *quicken* motion, speed, or flight.

Who got his pension rug,
Or *quickened* a reversion by a drug.
Pope, Satires of Donne, iv. 135.

And we must *quicken*
Our tardy pace in journeying Heavenward,
As Israel did in journeying Canaan-ward.
Longfellow, New Eng. Tragedies, p. 160.

4. To sharpen; give keener perception to; stimulate; incite: as, to *quicken* the appetite or taste; to *quicken* desires.

To *quicken* minds in the pursuit of honour.
B. Jonson, Cynthia's Revels, v. 3.

The desire of fame hath been no inconsiderable motive to *quicken* you.
Swift.

When I speak of civilization, I mean those things that tend to develop the moral forces of Man, and not merely to *quicken* his æsthetic sensibility.
Lowell, Oration, Harvard, Nov. 8, 1886.

5. To work with yeast. *Halliwell.* [Prov. Eng.] =**Syn.** 3. To expedite, hurry, speed.—**4.** To excite, animate.

quicken[2] (kwik'n), *n.* [< *quick* + *-en*, used indefinitely. Cf. *quick-grass* and *quitch*[2].] **1.** The couch- or quitch-grass, *Agropyrum* (*Triticum*) *repens.* Also *quickens.* [Prov. Eng.]—**2.** Same as *quick-beam.*

quickener (kwik'nėr), *n.* [< *quicken*[1] + *-er*[1].] One who or that which quickens, revives, vivifies, or communicates life; that which reinvigorates; something that accelerates motion or increases activity.

Love and enmity, aversation, fear, and the like are notable whetters and *quickners* of the spirit of life.
Dr. H. More, Antidote against Atheism, II. xii. 12.

quickening (kwik'ning), *n.* [< ME. *quykening*; verbal n. of *quicken*[1], *v.*] **1.** The act of reviving or animating. *Wyclif*, Select Works (ed. Arnold), II. 99.—**2.** The time of pregnancy when the fetus is first felt to be quick.

quicker (kwik'ėr), *n.* [< *quick* + *-er*[1].] A quickset hedge. *Halliwell.* [Prov. Eng.]

quick-eyed (kwik'īd), *a.* Having acute sight; of keen and ready perception.

Quick-eyed experience. *Fletcher*, Bonduca, iv. 3.

quick-grass (kwik'gràs), *n.* [= Dan. *kvikgræs*; as *quick* + *grass.* Cf. *quicken*[2], *quitch*[2].] Same as *quitch-grass.*

quickhatch (kwik'hach), *n.* [Amer. Ind.] The American glutton, carcajou, or wolverene, *Gulo luscus.* Also *quecquchatch.*

quick-hedge (kwik'hej), *n.* A live fence or hedge; a quick.

quick-in-hand, quick-in-the-hand (kwik'in-hand', kwik'in-thē̤-hand'), *n.* The yellow balsam or touch-me-not, *Impatiens Noli-tangere*: so called from the sudden bursting of its capsule when handled. [Eng.]

quicklime (kwik'līm), *n.* [< *quick* + *lime*[1].] Calcium oxid, CaO; burned lime; lime not yet slaked with water. Quicklime is prepared by subjecting chalk, limestone, or other natural calcium carbonate to intense heat, when carbonic acid, water, and any organic matter contained in the carbonate are driven off. It is a white amorphous infusible solid, which readily absorbs carbonic acid and water when exposed to the air. In contact with water, quicklime slakes, each molecule of the oxid combining with a molecule of water and forming calcium hydrate, $Ca(OH)_2$, or slaked lime. It is most largely used in making mortar and cement, but has numberless other uses in the arts.

quickling (kwik'ling), *n.* [< *quick* + *-ling*[1].] A young insect. *Halliwell.* [Prov. Eng.]

quickly (kwik'li), *adv.* [< ME. *quykly*, *quicliche*, *cwicliche*; < *quick* + *-ly*[2].] **1.** Speedily; with haste or celerity.

Quickly he walked with pale face downward bent.
William Morris, Earthly Paradise, II. 169.

2. Soon; without delay.

John Earl of Heynault had *quickly* enough of the King of France, and was soon after reconciled to his Brother King Edward.
Baker, Chronicles, p. 118.

quick-march (kwik'märch), *n.* Same as *quick-step.*

quick-match (kwik'mach), *n.* See *match*[2].

quickmire (kwik'mīr), *n.* [ME. *quick mire*; < *quick* + *mire*[1]. Cf. *quakemire*, *quagmire.*] A quagmire. *Halliwell.* [Prov. Eng.]

That al wagged his fleish,
As a *quick mire.*
Piers Plowman's Creed, l. 449.

quickness (kwik'nes), *n.* [< ME. *quyknesse*, *cwicnesse*; < *quick* + *-ness.*] **1.** The state of being quick or alive; vital power or principle.

Touch it with thy celestial *quickness.* *Herbert.*

All the energies seen in nature are . . . but manifestations of the essential life or *quickness* of matter.
Pop. Sci. Mo., XXII. 168.

2. Speed; velocity; celerity; rapidity: as, the *quickness* of motion.

Hamlet, this deed . . . must send thee hence
With fiery *quickness.* *Shak.*, Hamlet, iv. 3. 45.

3. Activity; briskness; promptness; readiness: as, the *quickness* of the imagination or wit.

Iohn Heywood the Epigrammatist, who, for the myrth and *quicknesse* of his conceits more then for any good learning was in him, came to be well benefited by the king.
Puttenham, Arte of Eng. Poesie, p. 49.

With too much *quickness* ever to be taught;
With too much thinking to have common thought.
Pope, Moral Essays, ii. 97.

4. Acuteness; keenness; alertness.

Would not *quickness* of sensation be an inconvenience to an animal that must lie still?
Locke.

In early days the conscience has in most
A *quickness* which in later life is lost.
Cowper, Tirocinium, l. 110.

5. Sharpness; pungency; keenness.

Then would he wish to see my sword, and feel
The *quickness* of the edge.
Beau. and Fl., Maid's Tragedy, i. 1.

A few drops tinge, and add a pleasant *quickness.*
Mortimer.

=**Syn. 2.** *Quickness, Fastness, Speed, Celerity, Swiftness, Fleetness, Rapidity, Velocity*, haste, expedition, despatch, alertness, liveliness. *Quickness* is the generic term. *Quickness, fastness, speed*, and *rapidity* may have relation to time only, or to space passed through or over; the others apply only to space. "*Swift* to hear," in Jas. i. 19, is a bold figure. *Celerity* is swift voluntary movement; but we do not ordinarily speak of the movements of an animal as having *celerity*. *Fleetness* also is voluntary, and is applied to animals; we may speak by figure of the *fleetness* of a yacht. The word suggests quickness in getting over the ground by the use of the feet: we speak of the *swiftness* or *rapidity* of the swallow's or the pigeon's flight; the *fleetness* of Atalanta, a hound, a deer. *Swiftness* is presumably not too great for carefulness or thoroughness; *rapidity* may be too great for either. *Velocity* is the attribute of matter in motion; the word is especially a technical term for the rate of movement of matter, whether fast or slow. We speak also of the *velocity* of sound or light. *Rapidity* has less suggestion of personality than any of the others, except *velocity*. See *nimble.*—**3.** Dexterity, adroitness, expertness, facility, knack.—**4.** Penetration.

quicksand (kwik'sand), *n.* [< ME. *quyksande* (= D. *kwikzand* = G. *quicksand* = Icel. *kviksandr* = Sw. *qvicksand* = Dan. *kviksand*); < *quick* + *sand.*] A movable sand-bank in a sea, lake, or river; a large mass of loose or moving sand mixed with water formed on many sea-coasts, at the mouths and in the channels of rivers, etc., sometimes dangerous to vessels, and especially to travelers.

And fearing lest they should fall into the *quicksands* [should be cast upon the Syrtis, R. V.], [they] strake sail and so were driven.
Acts xxvii. 17.

And what is Edward but a ruthless sea?
What Clarence, but a *quicksand* of deceit?
Shak., 3 Hen. VI., v. 4. 26.

quicksandy (kwik'san-di), *a.* [< *quicksand* + *-y.*] Containing or abounding in quicksands; consisting of or resembling quicksands.

The rotten, moorish, *quicksandy* grounds.
Rev. T. Adams, Works, I. 358.

Unfortunately for this *quicksandy* world, nobody can be sure of his position, however comfortable.
New York Semi-weekly Tribune, April 2, 1867.

quick-scented (kwik'sen″ted), *a.* Having an acute sense of smell; of an acute smell.

I especially commend unto you to be *quick-scented*, easily to trace the footing of sin.
Hales, Golden Remains, p. 168. (*Latham.*)

quickset (kwik'set), *a.* and *n.* [< *quick* + *set*[1].] **I.** *a.* Made of quickset.

He immediately concluded that this huge thicket of thorns and brakes was designed as a kind of fence or *quickset* hedge to the ghosts it enclosed.
Addison, Tale of Marraton.

II. *n.* A living plant set to grow, particularly for a hedge; hawthorn planted for a hedge.

The hairs of the eye-lids are for a *quickset* and fence about the sight. *Bacon*, Advancement of Learning, ii. 167.

quickset (kwik'set), *v. t.*; pret. and pp. *quickset*, ppr. *quicksetting.* [< *quickset*, *n.*] To plant with living shrubs or trees for a hedge or fence: as, to *quickset* a ditch.

quick-sighted (kwik'sī″ted), *a.* Having quick sight or acute discernment; quick to see or discern.

The Judgment, umpire in the strife, . . .
Quick-sighted arbiter of good and ill.
Cowper, Tirocinium, l. 31.

quick-sightedness (kwik'sī″ted-nes), *n.* The quality of being quick-sighted; quickness of sight or discernment; readiness to see or discern.

quicksilver (kwik'sil″vėr), *n.* [< ME. *quyksilver*, < AS. *cwicseolfor* (= D. *kwikzilver* = MLG. *quiksulver* = OHG. *quecsilabar*, *quechsilpar*, MHG. *quecsilber*, G. *quecksilber* = Icel. *kviksilfr*, mod. *kvikasilfr* = Sw. *qvicksilfver* = Norw. *kviksylv* = Dan. *kviksölv*, *kvægsolv*), lit. 'living silver,' so called from its mobility, < *cwic*, living, + *seolfor*, silver: see *quick* and *silver*. So in L., *argentum vivum*, 'living silver'; also *argentum liquidum*, 'liquid silver,' Gr. ἄργυρος χυτός, 'fused silver,' ὑδράργυρος, 'water-silver' (see *hydrargyrum*).] The common popular designation of the metal mercury. See *mercury*, 6, and *mercurial.*

The rogue fled from me like *quicksilver.*
Shak., 2 Hen. IV., ii. 4. 248.

Thou hast *quicksilver* in the veins of thee to a certainty.
Scott, Abbot, xix.

Quicksilver plaster†, a mercury soap, prepared from chlorid of mercury and soap. Also called *quicksilver soap.*—**Quicksilver water**, nitrate of mercury.

quicksilver (kwik'sil″vėr), *v. t.* [< *quicksilver*, *n.*] To overlay with quicksilver; treat with quicksilver: chiefly used in the past and present participles.

quicksilvered (kwik'sil″vėrd), *p. a.* **1.** Overlaid with quicksilver, or with an amalgam, as a plate of glass with quicksilver and tin-foil, to make a mirror.—**2**†. Partaking of the nature of quicksilver; showing resemblance to some characteristic of quicksilver.

Those nimble and *quicksilvered* brains.
Sir E. Sandys, State of Religion, H. 2. b. 1605. (*Latham.*)

This may serve to shew the Difference betwixt the two Nations, the leaden-heel'd Pace of the one, and the *quicksilver'd* Motions of the other. *Howell*, Letters, I. iv. 21.

quicksilvering (kwik'sil″vėr-ing), *n.* [Verbal n. of *quicksilver*, *v.*] **1.** The process of coating with quicksilver or with an amalgam.—**2.** A coating with quicksilver or an amalgam, as in a looking-glass.

quickstep (kwik'step), *n.* **1.** *Milit.*, a march in quick time—that is, at the rate of 110 steps per minute.—**2.** Music adapted to such a rapid march, or in a brisk march rhythm.

quick-tempered (kwik'tem″pėrd), *a.* Passionate; irascible.

quick-witted (kwik'wit″ed), *a.* Having ready wit; sharp; ready of perception.

Bap. How likes Gremio these *quick-witted* folks?
Gre. Believe me, sir, they butt together well.
Shak., T. of the S., v. 2. 38.

quick-wittedness (kwik'wit″ed-nes), *n.* The character of being quick-witted; readiness of wit.

quickwood (kwik'wůd), *n.* The hawthorn. Compare *quickset.* [Prov. Eng.]

He . . . in a pond in the said close, adjoining to a *quickwood* hedge, did drown his wife.
Aubrey, Misc., Apparitions.

quick-work (kwik'wėrk), *n.* In *ship-building*, short planks between the ports; all that part of a ship's side which lies between the chain-wales and the decks: so called because of its being the work most quickly completed in building the ship.

Quicunque (kwi-kung'kwē), *n.* [So called from the opening words of the Latin version, *Quicunque vult*, whosoever will: L. *quicunque*, *quicumque*, whoever, whosoever, < *qui*, who, + *-cumque*, a generalizing suffix.] The Athanasian creed. Also called *Symbolum Quicunque* and the *Psalm Quicunque vult.*

Hilary, . . . Vincentius, . . . and Vigilius, . . . to whom severally the authorship of the *Quicunque* has been ascribed. *Encyc. Brit.*, VI. 562.

quid[1] (kwid), *n.* [Also *queed*; var. of *cud*, q. v.] 1. A cud. [Prov. Eng.]—2. A portion suitable to be chewed; specifically, a piece of tobacco chewed and rolled about in the mouth.

The beggar who chews his *quid* as he sweeps his crossing. *Disraeli.*

quid[1] (kwid), *v. t.* and *i.*; pret. and pp. *quidded*, ppr. *quidding*. [< *quid*[1], *n.*] To drop partly masticated food from the mouth: said of horses.

quid[2] (kwid), *n.* [< L. *quid*, interrog. what, indef. somewhat, something, neut. (= E. *what*) of *quis*, who, = E. *who*: see *who*.] 1. What; nature; substance.

You must know my age
Hath seene the beings and the *quid* of things;
I know the dimensions and the termini
Of all existence. *Marston*, The Fawne, i. 2.

2. Something: used chiefly in the phrase *tertium quid* (see below). See *predication*.—**Tertium quid**, something different from both mind and matter, a representative object in perception, itself immediately known, mediating between the mind and the reality.—**The Quids**, in *U. S. hist.* from 1805 to 1811, a section of the Democratic-Republican party which was attached to extreme State-rights and democratic views, and separated itself from the administration, under the leadership of John Randolph, favoring Monroe as successor to Jefferson: supposed to have been so named as being *tertium quid* to the Federalists and administration Republicans. Also called *Quiddists*.

In his next speech he avowed himself to be no longer a republican; he belonged to the third party, *the quiddists* or *quids*, being that tertium quid, that third something, which had no name, but was really an anti-Madison movement. *H. Adams*, John Randolph, II. 181.

quid[3] (kwid), *n.* [Origin obscure.] A sovereign (£1). [Slang, Eng.]

quidam (kwī'dam), *n.* [L., some, a certain, < *qui*, who, + *-dam*, var. *-dem*, an indef. suffix.] Somebody; one unknown. [Rare.]

So many unworthy *Quidams*, which catch at the garlond which to you alone is dewe. *Spenser*, Shep. Cal., Ded.

quiddany (kwid'a-ni), *n.* [< L. *cydonium*, *cydoneum*, quince-juice, quince-wine, < *cydonia* (*cydonium malum*), a quince: see *Cydonia*. Cf. *quine*[2], *quince*[1].] A confection of quinces prepared with sugar.

quiddative (kwid'a-tiv), *a.* [Contr. of *quidditative*.] Same as *quidditative*.

Quiddist (kwid'ist), *n.* [< *quid*[2] + *-ist*.] See *the Quids*, under *quid*[2].

quiddit (kwid'it), *n.* [A contr. of *quiddity*.] A subtlety; an equivocation; a quibble.

No quirk left, no *quiddit*,
That may defeat him? *Fletcher*, Spanish Curate, i. 3.

By some strange *quiddit*, or some wrested clause,
To find him guiltie of the breach of laws. *Drayton*, The Owl.

quidditative (kwid'i-tā-tiv), *a.* [< F. *quidditatif*, < ML. *quidditativus*, < *quiddita(t-)s*, 'whatness': see *quiddity*.] Constituting the essence of a thing.—**Quidditative being, entity.** See the nouns.—**Quidditative predication**, the predication of the genus or species.

quiddity (kwid'i-ti), *n.*; pl. *quiddities* (-tiz). [= F. *quiddité*, < ML. *quiddita(t-)s*, 'whatness,' < L. *quid*, what (= E. *what*): see *quid*[2].] 1. In *scholastic philos.*, that which distinguishes a thing from other things, and makes it what it is, and not another; substantial form; nature.

I dare vndertake Orlando Furioso, or honest King Arthur, will neuer displease a Souldier: but the *quiddity* of Ens, and Prima materia, will hardely agree with a Corslet. *Sir P. Sidney*, Apol. for Poetrie.

Neither shal I stand to trifle with one that will tell me of *quiddities* and formalities. *Milton*, Church-Government, ii. 1.

The *Quiddity* and Essence of the incomprehensible Creator cannot imprint any formal Conception upon the finite Intellect of the Creature. *Howell*, Letters, ii. 11.

Reason is a common name, and agrees both to the understanding and essence of things as explained in definition. *Quiddity* they commonly call it. The intellect they call reason reasoning, *quiddity* reason reasoned. *Burgersdicius*, tr. by a Gentleman, I. xxi. 4.

2. A trifling nicety; a cavil; a quirk or quibble.

But she, in quirks and *quiddities* of love,
Sets me to school, she is so overwise.
Greene, George-a-Greene.

Evasion was his armature, *quiddity* his defence. *J. T. Fields*, Underbrush, p. 80.

quiddle[1] (kwid'l), *v. i.*; pret. and pp. *quiddled*, ppr. *quiddling*. [A dim. or freq. form, appar. based on L. *quid*, what, as in *quiddit*, *quiddity*, etc.: see *quid*[2], *quiddity*.] 1. To spend or waste time in trifling employments, or to attend to useful subjects in a trifling or superficial manner; be of a trifling, time-wasting character.

You are not sitting as nisi prius lawyers, bound by *quiddling* technicalities. *W. Phillips*, Speeches, etc., p. 181.

2. To criticize. *Davies.*

Set up your buffing base, and we will *quiddell* upon it. *R. Edwards*, Damon and Pythias. (*Davies.*)

quiddle[1] (kwid'l), *n.* [< *quiddle*[1], *v.*] One who quiddles, or busies himself about trifles. Also *quiddler*.

The Englishman is very petulant and precise about his accommodation at inns and on the road, a *quiddle* about his toast and his chop and every species of convenience. *Emerson*, English Traits, vi.

quiddle[2] (kwid'l), *v. i.*; pret. and pp. *quiddled*, ppr. *quiddling*. [Origin obscure.] To quiver; shiver; tremble; creep, as live flesh: as, the fish were still *quiddling*. [New Eng.]

quiddler (kwid'lėr), *n.* [< *quiddle*[1] + *-er*[1].] Same as *quiddle*[1].

quidifical†, *a.* [< L. *quid*, what, + *-fic* + *-al*. Cf. *quiddity*.] Equivocal; subtle.

Diogenes, mocking soch *quidificall* trifles, that were al in the cherubins, said, Sir Plato, your table and your cuppe I see very well, but as for your tabletee and your cupitee, I see none soche. *Udall*, tr. of Apophthegms of Erasmus, p. 139.

quidlibet, *n.* Same as *quodlibet*.

quidnunc (kwid'nungk), *n.* [< L. *quid nunc*, what now: *quid*, what (see *quid*[2]); *nunc*, now (see *now*).] One who is curious to know everything that passes, and is continually asking "What now?" or "What news?" hence, one who knows or pretends to know all that is going on in politics, society, etc.; a newsmonger.

Are not you called a theatrical *quidnunc*, and a mock Mæcenas to second-hand authors? *Sheridan*, The Critic, i. 1.

What a treasure-trove to these venerable *quidnuncs*, could they have guessed the secret which Hepzibah and Clifford were carrying along with them! *Hawthorne*, Seven Gables, xvii.

quid pro quo (kwid prō kwō). [L., something for something: *quid*, interrog. what, indef. something; *pro*, for; *quo*, abl. sing. of *quid*, something.] Something given for something else; a tit for tat; in *law*, an equivalent; a thing given or offered in exchange for or in consideration of another; the mutual consideration and performance of either party as toward the other in a contract.

quien, *n.* [F. *chien*, dial. *quien*, < L. *canis*, a dog: see *hound*.] A dog. [Thieves' cant.]

"Curse the *quiens*," said he. And not a word all dinner-time but "Curse the *quiens!*" I said I must know who they were before I would curse them. "*Quiens!* why, that was dogs. And I knew not even that much?" *C. Reade*, Cloister and Hearth, lv.

quien sabe (kien sä'be). [Sp.: *quien*, who, < L. *quem*, acc. of *quis*, who; *sabe*, 3d pers. sing. pres. ind. of *saber*, know, < L. *sapere*, have taste or sense: see *sapient*.] Who knows? a form of response equivalent to 'how should I know?' or 'I do not know,' occasionally used by Americans on the Pacific coast.

quiert†, *n.* An obsolete variant of *quire*[1].

quiesce (kwi-es'), *v. i.*; pret. and pp. *quiesced*, ppr. *quiescing*. [< L. *quiescere*, rest, keep quiet, < *quies*, rest, quiet: see *quiet*, *n.* Cf. *acquiesce*.] 1. To become quiet or calm; become silent.

The village, after a season of acute conjecture, *quiesced* into that sarcastic sufferance of the anomaly into which it may have been noticed that small communities are apt to subside from such occasions. *Howells*, Annie Kilburn, xxx.

2. In *philol.*, to become silent, as a letter; come to have no sound. *Amer. Jour. Philol.*, VIII. 282.

quiescence (kwi-es'ens), *n.* [< LL. *quiescentia*, rest, quiet, < L. *quiescen(t-)s*, ppr. of *quiescere*, repose, keep quiet: see *quiescent*.] 1. The state or quality of being quiescent or inactive; rest; repose; inactivity; the state of a thing without motion or agitation: as, the *quiescence* of a volcano.

'Tis not unlikely that he [Adam] had as clear a perception of the earth's motion as we think we have of its *quiescence*. *Glanville*, Vanity of Dogmatizing, i.

It is not enough that we are stimulated to pleasure or to pain, we must lapse into muscular *quiescence* to realize either. *A. Bain*, Emotions and Will, p. 149.

2. In *philol.*, silence; the condition of not being heard in pronunciation: as, the *quiescence* of a letter.—3. In *biol.*, quietude or inactivity; a state of animal life approaching torpidity, but in which the animal is capable of some motion, and may receive food: it is observed among insects during either hibernation or pupation, and in many other animals both higher and lower in the scale than these.

quiescency (kwi-es'en-si), *n.* [As *quiescence* (see *-cy*).] Same as *quiescence*.

quiescent (kwi-es'ent), *a.* and *n.* [< L. *quiescen(t-)s*, ppr. of *quiescere*, keep quiet, rest: see *quiesce*.] I. *a.* 1. Resting; being in a state of repose; still; not moving: as, a *quiescent* body or fluid.

Aristotle endeavoureth to prove that in all motion there is some point *quiescent*. *Bacon*, Advancement of Learning, ii. 222.

Quiescent as he now sat, there was something about his nostril, his mouth, his brow, which, to my perceptions, indicated elements within either restless, or hard, or eager. *Charlotte Brontë*, Jane Eyre, xxix.

The overpowering heat inclines me to be perfectly *quiescent* in the daytime. *George Eliot*, Mill on the Floss, vii. 3.

2. In *philol.*, silent; not sounded; having no sound: as, a *quiescent* letter.—3. In *biol.*, physiologically inactive or motionless; resting, as an insect in the chrysalis state, or an encysted amœba.

II. *n.* In *philol.*, a silent letter.

quiescently (kwi-es'ent-li), *adv.* In a quiescent manner; calmly; quietly.

quiet (kwī'et), *a.* [< ME. *quiet*, *quyet* = OF. *quiet*, *quiete*, *quite*, vernacularly *quoi*, *coi* (> E. *coy*), F. *coi* = Pr. *quetz* = Sp. Pg. *quieto*, vernacularly *chedo* = It. *quieto*, vernacularly *queto*, < L. *quietus*, pp. of *quiescere*, keep quiet, rest; cf. *quies* (*quiet-*), quiet, rest: see *quiesce*, *quiet*, *n.* Cf. *coy*[1], a doublet of *quiet*, and *quit*[1], *quite*[1], *acquit*, *requite*, etc.] 1. Being in a state of rest; not being in action or motion; not moving or agitated; still: as, remain *quiet;* the sea was *quiet*.

And they . . . laid wait for him all night in the gate of the city, and were *quiet* all the night, saying, In the morning, when it is day, we shall kill him. Judges xvi. 2.

The holy time is *quiet* as a Nun
Breathless with adoration.
Wordsworth, Misc. Sonnets, i. 30.

2. Left at rest; free from alarm or disturbance; unmolested; tranquil.

In his days the land was *quiet* ten years. 2 Chron. xiv. 1.

A peace above all earthly dignities,
A still and *quiet* conscience.
Shak., Hen. VIII., iii. 2. 380.

3. Peaceable; not turbulent; not giving offense; not exciting controversy, disorder, or trouble.

As long as the Cairiotes are poor and weaken'd by former divisions they are *quiet*, but when they grow rich and great they envy one another, and so fall into divisions. *Pococke*, Description of the East, I. 169.

Be plain in dress, and sober in your diet;
In short, my deary, kiss me! and be *quiet*.
Lady M. W. Montagu, Summary of Lord Lyttelton's Advice [to a Lady.

4. Undisturbed by emotion; calm; patient; contented.

The ornament of a meek and *quiet* spirit. 1 Pet. iii. 4.

Grant . . . to thy faithful people pardon and peace, that they may be cleansed from all their sins, and serve thee with a *quiet* mind. *Book of Common Prayer*, Collect for [21st Sunday after Trinity.

Margaret Duchess of Burgundy, a Woman that could never be *quiet* in her Mind as long as King Henry was quiet in his Kingdom. *Baker*, Chronicles, p. 241.

5. Free from noise or sound; silent; still: as, a *quiet* neighborhood.

Much of mirthe watz that ho made,
Among her ferez that watz so *quyt!*
Alliterative Poems (ed. Morris), i. 1149.

Her days
Henceforth were given to *quiet* tasks of good.
Bryant, Sella.

Till he find
The *quiet* chamber far apart.
Tennyson, Day-Dream, The Arrival.

All was *quiet*, but for faint sounds made
By the wood creatures wild and unafraid.
William Morris, Earthly Paradise, II. 221.

6. Free from fuss or bustle; without stiffness or formality.

A couple of Mrs. Bardell's most particular acquaintance, who had just stepped in to have a *quiet* cup of tea. *Dickens*, Pickwick, xxvi.

7. Not glaring or showy; not such as to attract notice; in good taste: as, *quiet* colors; a *quiet* dress.

A large frame, . . . which I afterwards found to contain a rather highly colored seventeenth-century master, was covered with a *quiet* drapery. *The Century*, XXXVIII. 91.

=**Syn.** 1-5. *Placid, Serene*, etc. (see *calm*[1]), peaceful, unruffled, undisturbed.—4. *Meek*, mild.

quiet (kwī'et), *n.* [< ME. *quiete, quyete* = Sp. *quiete* = It. *quiete*, < L. *quies* (*quiet-*), rest; cf. *quiet, a.*] 1. Rest; repose; stillness.

For now the noonday *quiet* holds the hill. *Tennyson*, Œnone.

That cloistered *quiet* which characterizes all university towns. *Lowell*, Cambridge Thirty Years Ago.

Long be it ere the tide of trade
Shall break with harsh resounding din
The *quiet* of thy banks of shade.
Whittier, Kenoza Lake.

2. An undisturbed condition; tranquillity; peace; repose.

And take hede hou Makamede, thorwe a mylde doue,
He hald al Surrye as hym-self wolde and Sarasyns in *quyete*;
Nouht thorw manslauht and mannes strengthe Makamede hadde the mastrie.
Piers Plowman (C), xviii. 240.

Enjoys his garden and his book in *quiet*.
Pope, Imit. of Horace, II. i. 199.

And, like an infant troublesome awake,
Is left to sleep for peace and *quiet's* sake.
Cowper, Truth, l. 428.

3. An undisturbed state of mind; peace of soul; patience; calmness.

Thy greatest help is *quiet*, gentle Nell.
Shak., 2 Hen. VI., ii. 4. 67.

A certain *quiet* on his soul did fall,
As though he saw the end and waited it.
William Morris, Earthly Paradise, II. 314.

At quiett, still; peaceful.

And they . . . came unto Laish, unto a people that were *at quiet* and secure. Judges xviii. 27.

Death did the only Cure apply;
She was *at quiet*, so was I.
Prior, Turtle and Sparrow.

In quiet, quietly.

York. I shall not sleep *in quiet* at the Tower.
Glou. Why, what should you fear?
Shak., Rich. III., iii. 1. 142.

On the quiet, clandestinely; so as to avoid observation. [Slang.]

I'd just like to have a bit of chinwag with you *on the quiet*.
Punch, Jan. 8, 1881, p. 4.

Out of quiet†, disturbed; restless.

Since the youth of the count's was to-day with my lady, she is much *out of quiet*. *Shak.*, T. N., ii. 3. 144.

=**Syn.** *Repose, Tranquillity*, etc. See *rest*.

quiet (kwī'et), *v.* [< LL. *quietare, quietari*, make quiet, < L. *quietus*, quiet: see *quiet, a.* Cf. *quit*[1], *v.*] I. *trans.* 1. To bring to a state of rest; stop.

Quiet thy cudgel. *Shak.*, Hen. V., v. 1. 54.

The ideas of moving or *quieting* corporeal motion. *Locke.*

2. To make or cause to be quiet; calm; appease; pacify; lull; allay; tranquillize: as, to *quiet* the soul when it is agitated; to *quiet* the clamors of a nation; to *quiet* the disorders of a city.

After that Gallia was thus *quieted*, Cæsar (as he was determined before) went into Italy to hold a parlament.
Golding, tr. of Cæsar, fol. 175.

Surely I have behaved and *quieted* myself, as a child that is weaned of his mother. Ps. cxxxi. 2.

The growth of our dissention was either prevented or soon *quieted*. *Milton*, Eikonoklastes, xxvi.

=**Syn. 2.** To compose, soothe, sober; to still, silence, hush.

II. *intrans.* To become quiet or still; abate: as, the sea *quieted*.

While astonishment
With deep-drawn sighs was *quieting*. *Keats.*

quietage† (kwī'et-āj), *n.* [< *quiet* + *-age.*] Peace; quiet. [Rare.]

Sweet peace and *quiet-age*
It doth establish in the troubled mynd.
Spenser, F. Q., IV. iii. 43.

quieten (kwī'et-n), *v.* [< *quiet, a.*, + *-en*[1].] I. *intrans.* To become quiet or still.

II. *trans.* To make quiet; calm; pacify.

I will stay, . . . partly to *quieten* the fears of this poor faithful fellow. *Mrs. Gaskell*, Ruth, xxxiv. (*Davies.*)

quieter (kwī'et-ėr), *n.* [< *quiet* + *-er*[1].] One who or that which quiets.

quieting-chamber (kwī'et-ing-chām"bėr), *n.* In a steam-engine, an exhaust-pipe fitted with a number of small branch tubes the sections of which, taken together, equal that of the main pipe. It is intended to prevent the usual noise of blowing off steam.

quietism (kwī'et-izm), *n.* [= F. *quiétisme* = Sp. Pg. It. *quietismo* = G. *quietismus*, < NL. *quietismus*; as *quiet* + *-ism.*] 1. That form of mysticism which consists in the entire abnegation of all active exercise of the will and a purely passive meditation on God and divine things as the highest spiritual exercise and the means of bringing the soul into immediate union with the Godhead. Conspicuous exponents of quietism were Molinos and Mme. Guyon, in the seventeenth century. See *Molinist*[2].

If the temper and constitution were cold and phlegmatic, their religion has sunk into *quietism*; if bilious or sanguine, it has flamed out into all the frenzy of enthusiasm.
Warburton, Alliance, i.

The Monks of the Holy Mountain [Mount Athos], from the eleventh century, appeared to have yielded to a kind of *quietism*, and to have held that he who, in silence and solitude, turned his thoughts with intense introspection on himself, would find his soul enveloped in a mystic and ethereal light, the essence of God, and be filled with pure and perfect happiness.
J. M. Neale, Eastern Church, i. 870, note.

2. The state or quality of being quiet; quietness. [Rare.]

He . . . feared that the thoughtlessness of my years might sometimes make me overstep the limits of *quietism* which he found necessary.
Godwin, Mandeville, I. 110. (*Davies.*)

quietist (kwī'et-ist), *n.* [= F. *quiétiste* = Sp. Pg. It. *quietista* = G. *quietist*, < NL. *quietista*; as *quiet* + *-ist.*] 1. One who believes in or practises quietism: applied especially [*cap.*] to a body of mystics (followers of Molinos, a Spanish priest) in the latter part of the seventeenth century. Somewhat similar views were held by the Euchites, Beghards, Beguines, Hesychasts, Brethren of the Free Spirit, and others of less note.

The best persons have always held it to be the essence of religion that the paramount duty of man upon earth is to amend himself; but all except monkish *quietists* have annexed to this the additional duty of amending the world, and not solely the human part of it, but the material, the order of physical nature. *J. S. Mill.*

2. One who seeks or enjoys quietness; one who advocates a policy of quietness or inactivity.

Too apt, perhaps, to stay where I am put. I am a *quietist* by constitution. *The Century*, XXVI. 280.

quietistic (kwī-e-tis'tik), *a.* [< *quietist* + *-ic.*] Of or pertaining to quietists or quietism.

Jeanne Marie . . . Guyon, . . . a leading exponent of the *quietistic* mysticism of the 17th century.
Encyc. Brit., XI. 341.

quietive (kwī'et-iv), *n.* [< *quiet* + *-ive.*] That which has the property of inducing quiet or calm, as a sedative medicine.

Every one knows of a few plants that are good as laxatives, emetics, sudorifics, or *quietives*.
Pop. Sci. Mo., XXVIII. 529.

quietize (kwī'et-īz), *v. t.* [< *quiet, a.*, + *-ize.*] To make quiet; calm.

Solitude, and patience, and religion have now *quietized* both father and daughter into tolerable contentment.
Mme. D'Arblay, Diary, V. 271. (*Davies.*)

quietly (kwī'et-li), *adv.* In a quiet state or manner. Especially—(*a*) Without motion or agitation; in a state of rest.

Lie *quietly*, and hear a little more;
Nay, do not struggle.
Shak., Venus and Adonis, l. 709.

(*b*) Without tumult, alarm, dispute, or disturbance; peaceably: as, to live *quietly*.

After all these Outrages, the King proclaimed Pardon to all such as would lay down Arms and go *quietly* home.
Baker, Chronicles, p. 138.

(*c*) Calmly; tranquilly; without agitation or violent emotion; patiently.

Quietly, modestly, and patiently recommend his estate to God. *Jer. Taylor.*

Then came her father, saying in low tones
"Have comfort," whom she greeted *quietly*.
Tennyson, Lancelot and Elaine.

(*d*) In a manner to attract little or no observation; without noise: as, he *quietly* left the room.

Sometimes . . . [Walpole] found that measures which he had hoped to carry through *quietly* had caused great agitation. *Macaulay*, Horace Walpole.

He shut the gate *quietly*, not to make a noise, but never looked back. *Mrs. Oliphant*, Poor Gentleman, xxxvi.

quietness (kwī'et-nes), *n.* [< ME. *quietness*; < *quiet* + *-ness.*] The state of being quiet, still, or free from action or motion; freedom from agitation, disturbance, or excitement; tranquillity; stillness; calmness.

It is great *quyetnesse* to haue people of good behaviour in a house. *Babees Book* (E. E. T. S.), p. 64.

Peace and *quietness*. *Milton.*

In *quietness* and in confidence shall be your strength.
Isa. xxx. 15.

quietous† (kwī'et-us), *a.* [< *quiet* + *-ous.*] Quiet; peaceable.

Bryngynge men to a *quyetouse* holde and sure step in the Lorde. *Bp. Bale*, Image, i.

quietously† (kwī'et-us-li), *adv.* [< *quietous* + *-ly*[2].] In a quietous manner; quietly. *Bp. Bale.*

quietsome† (kwī'et-sum), *a.* [< *quiet* + *-some.*] Calm; still; undisturbed.

But let the night be calme and *quietsome*.
Spenser, Epithalamion, l. 326.

quietude (kwī'e-tūd), *n.* [< F. *quiétude* = Sp. *quietud* = It. *quietudine*, < L. *quietudo*, quietness, rest, calmness, for **quietitudo*, < *quietus*, quiet: see *quiet, a.*] Rest; repose; quiet; tranquillity.

A future *quietude* and serenitude in the affections.
Sir H. Wotton, Reliquiæ, p. 79.

Never was there a more venerable *quietude* than that which slept among their sheltering boughs.
Hawthorne, Marble Faun, viii.

There broods upon this charming hamlet an old-time *quietude* and privacy. *H. James, Jr.*, Pass. Pilgrim, p. 42.

quietus (kwī-ē'tus), *n.* [< ML. *quietus*, or *quietus est*, (he is) 'free' or 'quitted,' i. e. he is discharged from the debt: a formula in noting the settlement of accounts: see *quiet, a.*] 1. A final discharge of an account; a final settlement; a quittance.

Till I had signed your *quietus*. *Webster.*

I hoped to put her off with half the sum;
That 's truth; some younger brother would have thank'd me,
And given [me] my *quietus*. *Shirley*, The Gamester, v. 1.

Hence—2. A finishing or ending in general; stoppage.

When he himself might his *quietus* make
With a bare bodkin. *Shak.*, Hamlet, iii. 1. 75.

Why, you may think there's no being shot at without a little risk; and if an unlucky bullet should carry a *quietus* with it—I say it will be no time then to be bothering you about family matters. *Sheridan*, The Rivals, v. 3.

3. A severe blow; a "settler." *Halliwell.* [Slang.]

quight†, *adv.* An erroneous spelling of *quite*[1].

qui-hi, qui-hye (kwī'hī'), *n.* [Hind. *koī hai*, 'who is there?'] 1. In Bengal, the Anglo-Indian call for a servant, one being always in attendance, though not in the room.

The seal motto [of a letter] *qui hi* ("who waits") denoting that the bearer is to bring an answer.
J. W. Palmer, The New and the Old, p. 298.

2. Hence, the popular nickname for an Anglo-Indian in Bengal.

The old boys, the old generals, the old colonels, the old *qui-his* from the club came and paid her their homage.
Thackeray, Newcomes, lxii. (*Davies.*)

Quiina (kwi-ī'nä̤), *n.* [NL. (Aublet, 1775), from the native name in Guiana.] A genus of polypetalous plants of the order *Guttiferæ*, type of the tribe *Quiineæ*. It is characterized by ovary-cells with two ovules, the numerous stamens and several styles all filiform, and the fruit a berry with fibrous interior and from one to four woolly seeds, each filled by the two thick and distinct seed-leaves. The 17 species are natives of tropical America. They are trees or shrubs or sometimes climbers, bearing opposite or whorled stipulate leaves, elegantly marked with transverse veinlets. The small flowers are arranged in short axillary panicles or terminal racemed clusters. *Q. Jamaicensis* is an entire-leafed species, known in Jamaica as *old-woman's tree*.

Quiineæ (kwi-in'ẹ̄-ē), *n. pl.* [NL. (Bentham and Hooker, 1862), < *Quiina* + *-eæ.*] A tribe of dicotyledonous polypetalous plants of the order *Guttiferæ*, consisting of the genus *Quiina*, the embryo having large cotyledons and minute radicle, while in the rest of the order, except the *Calophylleæ*, the radicle is large and the seed-leaves are minute.

quilisma (kwi-lis'mä̤), *n.* [ML., < Gr. κύλισμα, a roll, < κυλίειν, roll: see *cylinder.*] In *medieval musical notation*, a sign or neume denoting a shake or trill.

quill[1] (kwil), *n.* [< ME. **quille, quylle*, a stalk (L. *calamus*); cf. LG. *quiele, kiele* = MHG. *kil*, G. *kiel*, dial. *keil*, a quill; connections uncertain. Cf. OF. *quille*, a peg or pin of wood, a ninepin, < OHG. *kegil*, MHG. G. *kegel*, a ninepin, skittle, cone, bobbin: see *kail*[2]. The Ir. *cuille*, a quill, is appar. < E.] 1. The stalk of a cane or reed. [Prov. Eng.]—2. A cane or reed pipe, such as those used in Pan's pipes.

For they bene daughters of the hyghest Jove,
And holden scorne of homely shepheards *quill*.
Spenser, Shep. Cal., June.

On a country *quill* each plays
Madrigals and pretty lays.
Shirley, Love Tricks, iv. 2.

He touch'd the tender stops of various *quills*,
With eager thought warbling his Dorick lay.
Milton, Lycidas, l. 188.

3. One of the large, strong feathers of geese, swans, turkeys, crows, etc., used for writing-pens and the like.

Snatch thee a *quill* from the spread eagle's wing.
Quarles, Emblems, i., Invoc.

And reeds of sundry kinds, . . . more used than *quills* by the people of these countreys.
Sandys, Travailes, p. 110.

4. A quill pen; hence, by extension, any pen, especially considered as the characteristic instrument of a writer.

Thy Pencil triumphs o'er the poet's *Quill*.
Congreve, To Sir Godfrey Kneller.

Mr. Jones has a *quill* of blue ink behind one ear, a *quill* of red ink behind the other, another of black ink in his mouth. *W. M. Baker*, New Timothy, p. 151.

5. One of the comparatively large flight-feathers or remiges of any bird, without reference to the use of such feathers for making quill pens; a quill-feather: as, the *quills* and coverts of the wing; sometimes extended to include the similar feathers of the tail.

Who now so long hath praised the chough's white bill
That he hath left her ne'er a flying *quill*.
Marston, Satires, i. 68.

6. The hard, hollow, horny part of the scape of any feather, which does not bear barbs, and by which the feather is inserted in the skin; the calamus, as distinguished from the rachis.

The whole scape is divided into two parts: one, nearest the body of the bird, the tube or barrel, or *quill* proper, which is a hard, horny, hollow, and semi-transparent cylinder, containing a little pith in the interior; it bears no webs. *Coues*, Key to N. A. Birds, p. 84.

7. One of the much enlarged and peculiarly modified hairs with which some animals, as porcupines, are provided; a large hollow spine.

Like *quills* upon the fretful porpentine.
Shak., Hamlet, i. 5. 20.

Thou 'lt shoote thy *quilles* at mee, when my terrible backe 's turn'd, for all this; wilt not, Porcupine?
Dekker, Humorous Poet, I. 235.

8. A piece of small reed or other light slender tube, used by weavers to wind thread upon, and by manufacturers to hold the wound silk and other thread prepared for sale.

Of works with loom, with needle, and with *quill*.
Spenser.

9. (*a*) A plectrum of quill, as of a goose, for playing on musical instruments of the lute and zither families. (*b*) In the harpsichord, spinet, and virginal, a small piece of quill projecting from the jack of each key (digital), and so set that when the key was depressed the corresponding string was twitched or twanged by it. Various other materials were used instead of quills.—10. In *seal-engraving*, the hollow shaft or mandril of the seal-engravers' lathe, in which the cutting-tools are secured to be revolved while the stones are held against them.—11. In *mining*, a train for igniting a blast, consisting of a quill filled with slow-burning powder: it is now superseded by the safety-fuse.—12. The faucet of a barrel. *Halliwell.* [Prov. Eng.] —13. In *phar.*, bark in a roll, such as is often formed in drying, as of cinnamon or cinchona.—**In the quill**†, a phrase used in the following passage, and interpreted to mean 'penned' (*Steevens*); 'in form and order like a quilled ruff' (*Nares*); 'in the coil' (*Singer*).

My lord protector will come this way by and by, and then we may deliver our supplications *in the quill*.
Shak., 2 Hen. VI., i. 3. 4.

Primary, secondary, tertiary quills. See the adjectives.—**To be under the quill**, to be written about.

The subject which is now *under the quill* is the Bishop of Lincoln. *Bp. Hacket*, Abp. Williams, ii. 28. (*Davies.*)

To carry a good quill, to write well.

quill¹ (kwil), *v.* [‹ *quill*¹, *n.*] **I.** *trans.* **1.** To pluck out quills from.

His wings have been *quilled* thrice, and are now up again. *Swift*, To Stella, xvii.

2. To tap, as a barrel of liquor. *Halliwell.* [Prov. Eng.]

II. *intrans.* To wind thread or yarn on quills for the loom. [New Eng.]

The child Margaret sits in the door of her house, on a low stool, with a small wheel, winding spools—in our vernacular, *quilling*—for her mother. *S. Judd*, Margaret, i. 2.

quill² (kwil), *n.* [Also, as mere F., *quille*; ‹ F. *quille*, a keel: see *keel*¹.] A fold of a plaited or fluted ruff or ruffle.

quill² (kwil), *v. t.* [‹ *quill*², *n.*] To flute; form with small rounded ridges.

What they called his cravat was a little piece of white linen *quilled* with great exactness, and hanging below his chin about two inches.
Addison and Steele, Tatler, No. 257.

quillai (kē-lī'), *n.* [Also *quillay*, *cullay*; ‹ Chilian *quillai*, so called from its soap-like qualities, ‹ *quillcan*, wash.] A middle-sized Chilian tree, *Quillaia Saponaria*.—**Quillai-bark**, the bark of the quillai-tree, the inner layers of which abound in saponin, whence it is commonly used in Chili as soap. It has also come into use elsewhere for washing silks, printed goods, etc.; and an oil for promoting the growth of the hair has been extracted from it. Also *quillia-bark*, *quillaja-bark*, and *soap-bark*.

Quillaia (kwi-lā'yạ), *n.* [NL. (Molina, 1782), ‹ Chilian *quillai.*] A genus of rosaceous trees, type of the tribe *Quillaieæ*. It is characterized by an inferior radicle, five valvate calyx-lobes to which adhere the five dilated and fleshy stamen-bearing lobes of the disk, and five woolly carpels, becoming a stellate crown of five many-seeded follicles. The 3 or 4 species are natives of southern Brazil, Chili, and Peru. They are very smooth evergreen trees, bearing scattered and undivided leaves which are thick, rigid, and veiny. The large and woolly flowers are in small clusters, of which the lateral are staminate and the central are fertile. *Q. Saponaria* is the quillai, cullay, or soap-bark tree of Chili. See *quillai-bark*, under *quillai*. Also spelled *Quillaja*.

Quillaieæ (kwi-lā'yẹ-ē), *n. pl.* [NL. (Endlicher, 1840), ‹ *Quillaia* + *-eæ.*] A tribe of rosaceous plants somewhat resembling the *Spiræeæ*, differing in the usually broadly winged seeds, and characterized by commonly persistent bractless sepals, five, ten, or many stamens, one or many usually ascending ovules, and fruit of five follicles or a capsule. It includes 8 genera, mainly American, of which *Quillaia* is the type. See *Kageneckia*. Also spelled *Quillajeæ*.

quillback (kwil'bak), *n.* The sailfish, spearfish, or skimback, *Carpiodes cyprinus*, a kind of carp-sucker. The name is also given to other fishes of that genus, as C. *difformis*. [Local, U. S.]

quill-bit (kwil'bit), *n.* A small shell-bit: same as *gouge-bit*.

quill-coverts (kwil'kuv"ėrts), *n. pl.* Feathers immediately covering the bases of the large feathers of the wings or tail of a bird; wing-coverts or tail-coverts; tectrices. See *covert*, 6.

quill-driver (kwil'drī"vėr), *n.* One who works with a quill or pen; a scrivener; a clerk. [Slang.]

quill-driving (kwil'drī"ving), *n.* The act of working with a pen; writing. [Slang.]

Some sort of slave's *quill-driving*. *Kingsley*, Hypatia, xii.

quille, *n.* See *quill*².

quilled¹ (kwild), *a.* [‹ *quill*¹ + *-ed*².] **1.** Furnished with quills.

His thighs with darts
Were almost like a sharp-*quill'd* porpentine.
Shak., 2 Hen. VI., iii. 1. 363.

2. Formed into a quill: said of bark: as, *quilled* calisaya, contrasted with *flat* calisaya.

In drying it [cinchona-bark] rolls up or becomes *quilled*. *U. S. Dispensatory* (15th ed.), p. 433.

3. In *her.*, having a quill: said of a feather employed as a bearing, and used only when the quill of a feather is of a different tincture from the rest.

quilled² (kwild), *a.* [‹ *quill*² + *-ed*².] Crimped; fluted.

In the Dahlia the florets are rendered *quilled* [by cultivation], and are made to assume many glowing colours.
Encyc. Brit., IV. 129.

Quilled suture. See *suture*.

quiller (kwil'ėr), *n.* [‹ *quill*¹ + *-er*¹.] An unfledged bird. *Halliwell.* [Prov. Eng.]

quillet¹ (kwil'et), *n.* [Origin obscure. Cf. *quill*².] **1.** A furrow. *Halliwell.* [Prov. Eng.]—**2.** A croft, or small separate piece of ground. [Obsolete or prov. Eng.]

All the account to make of every bag of money, and of every *quillet* of land, whose it is. *Donne*, Sermons, ix.

In the "Cheshire Sheaf," June, 1880, it was stated that there were close to the border town of Holt a number of *quillets* cultivated by the poorer freemen. These were strips of land marked only by mear or boundary stones at a distance of twenty-nine to thirty-two yards.
N. and Q., 6th ser., X. 336.

quillet²† (kwil'et), *n.* [Contr. from L. *quidlibet*, anything you please: *quid*, anything; *libet*, *lubet*, it pleases.] A nicety or subtlety; a quibble.

O, some authority how to proceed;
Some tricks, some *quillets*, how to cheat the devil.
Shak., L. L. L., iv. 3. 288.

He is . . . swallowed in the quicksands of law-*quillets*.
Middleton, Trick to Catch the Old One, i. 1.

quill-feather (kwil'feтн"ėr), *n.* Same as *quill*¹, 5. See *feather*.

quilling (kwil'ing), *n.* [‹ *quill*² + *-ing*¹.] A narrow bordering of net, lace, or ribbon plaited so as to resemble a row of quills.

A plain *quilling* in your bonnet—and if ever any body looked like an angel, it's you in a net *quilling*.
George Eliot, Middlemarch, lxxx.

quill-nib (kwil'nib), *n.* A quill pen from which the feather and a large part of the tube have been cut away, leaving only enough of the substance to give the point of the pen sufficient consistence. This is done for ease of transportation, and the nib requires a holder like the steel pen.

quillon (kē-lyôṅ'), *n.* One of the arms or branches of the cross-guard of a sword. See *cross-guard*, *cross-hilt*, cut in next column, and cut under *hilt*.

quilltail (kwil'tāl), *n.* The ruddy duck, *Erismatura rubida*. Also called *quilltail coot*. [New Jersey.]

quill-turn (kwil'tėrn), *n.* A machine or instrument in which a weavers' quill is turned. *Halliwell.*

quill-work (kwil'wėrk), *n.* Embroidery with porcupine-quills, such as that made by the North American Indians. See *Canadian embroidery*, under *Canadian*.

Sword-hilt. *a*, *a*, quillons.

quillwort (kwil'wėrt), *n.* A plant, *Isoëtes lacustris*: so called from the quill-like leaves; also, any plant of the genus *Isoëtes*. See *Isoëtes* and *Merlin's-grass*.

quilly (kwil'i), *a.* [‹ *quill*¹ + *-y*¹.] Abounding in quills; showing the quills, as a bird's plumage when frayed or worn away.

His wings became *quilly* and draggled and frayed.
J. Owen, Wings of Hope.

quilt (kwilt), *n.* [‹ ME. *quilte*, *quylte*, ‹ OF. *cuilte*, also *cotre*, *coutre*, also *coite*, *coitte*, *coistre*, a tick, mattress, = Sp. Pg. *colcha* = It. *coltre* = W. *cylched*, a quilt, ‹ L. *culcita*, *culcitra*, a cushion, pillow, mattress, quilt: see *cushion*. Cf. *counterpane*¹. The Ir. *cuilte*, a bed, bed-tick, is appar. from the E.] **1**†. A mattress or flock-bed.

Cause to be made a good thycke *quylte* of cotton, or els of pure flockes or of cleane wolle, and let the coueryngeof it be of whyte fustyan, and laye it on the fetherbed that you do lye on. *Babees Book* (E. E. T. S.), p. 245.

After that thei lay down to slepe vpon the grasse, for other *quylles* ne pilowes hadde thei noon.
Merlin (E. E. T. S.), iii. 539.

And you have fastened on a thick *quilt*, or flock-bed, on the outside of the door. *B. Jonson*, Epicœne, ii. 1.

2. A cover or coverlet made by stitching together two thicknesses of a fabric with some soft substance between them; any thick or warm coverlet: as, a patchwork *quilt*.

In both sorts of tables the beds were covered with magnificent *quilts*. *Arbuthnot*, Ancient Coins, p. 134.

There Affectation, with a sickly mien, . . .
On the rich *quilt* sinks with becoming woe.
Pope, R. of the L., iv. 35.

3. A quilted petticoat. [Rural.]—**Log-cabin quilt.** See *log*¹.—**Marseilles quilt**, a double cotton-cloth coverlet woven in patterns which are raised in relief in parts, from having a third thickness there interposed.

quilt (kwilt), *v.* [‹ *quilt*, *n.*] **I.** *trans.* **1.** To stuff or interline in the manner of a quilt; supply with stuffing.

A bag *quilted* with bran is very good, but it drieth too much. *Bacon*, Nat. Hist.

With these [verminous and polluted rags] deformedly to *quilt* and interlace the intire, the spotlesse, and undecaying robe of Truth. *Milton*, Prelatical Episcopacy.

To Charing Cross, and there into the great new Ordinary, . . . being led thither by Mr. Beale, . . . and he sat with me while I had two *quilted* pigeons, very handsome and good meat. *Pepys*, Diary, Sept. 26, 1668.

Dressed
In his steel jack, a swarthy vest,
With iron *quilted* well. *Scott*, Marmion, v. 3.

2. To stitch together, as two pieces of cloth, usually with some soft substance between: as, to *quilt* a petticoat; in general, to stitch together: said of anything of which there are at least three layers or thicknesses, the stitching often taking an ornamental character, the lines crossing one another or arranged in curves, volutes, etc.—3. To pass through a fabric backward and forward at minute intervals, as a needle and thread in the process of making a quilt.

He . . . stoops down to pick up a pin, which he *quilts* into the flap of his coat-pocket with great assiduity.
Goldsmith, The Bee, No. 1.

Quilted armor, stuffed and wadded garments of defense held in place and strengthened by quilting.—**Quilted calves**, sham calves for the legs, made of quilted cloth. *Halliwell.*—**Quilted grape-shot.** See *grape-shot*.

quilter (kwil'tėr), *n.* [‹ *quilt* + *-er*¹.] **1.** One who quilts; one who makes quilting.—**2.** An attachment to sewing-machines for executing quilting upon fabrics.

quilting (kwil'ting), *n.* [Verbal n. of *quilt*, *v.*] **1.** The act or operation of forming a quilt.—**2.** The material used for making quilts; padding or lining.—**3.** Quilted work.

Thick *quiltings* covered with elaborate broidery.
Bulwer, Last Days of Pompeii, i. 3.

4. A kind of cloth resembling diaper, having a pattern slightly marked by the direction of the threads or raised in low relief. It is made of cotton and of linen, and is used, like piqué, for waistcoats.—5. A quilting-bee. [New Eng.]—**French quilting.** Same as *piqué*, 2 (*a*).

quilting-bee (kwil'ting-bē), *n.* A meeting of women for the purpose of assisting one of their number in quilting a counterpane: usually followed by a supper or other entertainment to which men are invited. [New Eng.]

Now [in the days of Peter Stuyvesant] were instituted *quilting bees* . . . and other rural assemblages, where, under the inspiring influence of the fiddle, toil was enlivened by gayety and followed up by the dance.
Irving, Knickerbocker, p. 405.

quilting-cotton (kwil'ting-kot"n), *n.* Same as *cotton wadding* (which see, under *cotton*[1]).

quilting-frame (kwil'ting-frām), *n.* A frame with adjustable bars, wires, etc., used for stretching flat a fabric for quilting or for convenience in embroidering upon it.

Quimper pottery. See *pottery*.

quin (kwin), *n.* [Possibly < Ir. *cuine*, *cun*, coin, money; with ref. to the shape.] A kind of scallop or pecten. Also *queen*, *squin*. [Local, Eng.]

quina (kwī'nä or kē'nä), *n.* [= F. *quina*, < Sp. Pg. *quina* (NL. *quina*), < S. Amer. (Peruv.) *quina*, *kina*, bark.] The bark of various species of *Cinchona*: also applied in Brazil to some other febrifugal barks.

quinamia (kwi-nā'mi-ä), *n.* [NL., < *quina* + *am*(*ide*) + *-ia*.] Same as *quinamine*.

quinamicine (kwi-nam'i-sin), *n.* [< *quinamine*: an arbitrary form.] An artificial alkaloid obtained from quinamine. Its formula is $C_{19}H_{24}N_2O_2$.

quinamidine (kwi-nam'i-din), *n.* [< *quina* + *amide* + *-ine*[2].] An artificial alkaloid obtained from quinamine. It is isomeric with quinamicine.

quinamine (kwi-nam'in), *n.* [< *quina* + *amine*.] A natural crystalline alkaloid, with the formula $C_{19}H_{24}N_2O_2$, obtained from various cinchona barks. Also called *quinamia*.

quinancy†, *n.* An obsolete form of *quinsy*.

quinancy-wort†, *n.* An obsolete form of *quinsy-wort*. *Miller*, English Plant Names.

quinaquina (kē-na-kē'nä), *n.* [Also *quinquina* = F. *quinquina* = Sp. *quinaquina*, < Peruv. *quinaquina*, the tree which yields the bark called *quina*: see *quina*.] The bark of various species of *Cinchona*. See *kin-kina*.

quinarian (kwi-nā'ri-an), *a.* and *n.* [< *quinary* + *-an*.] **I.** *a.* Quinary, as a system of classification; classified in sets of five. In zoölogy the word notes specifically the circular or so-called natural system of classification, originally propounded by Macleay in 1819, and further elaborated especially by Vigors and Swainson. As subsequently modified and formulated by Swainson in 1835, it rests substantially upon the following five propositions: (1) Every natural series of beings, in its progress from a given point, returns or tends to return to that point, thus forming a circle. (2) The primary circular divisions of every group are actually three, or apparently five. (3) The contents of such a circular group are symbolically or analogically represented by the contents of all other circles in the animal kingdom. (4) These primary divisions of every group are characterized by definite peculiarities of form, structure, and economy, which, under diversified modifications, are uniform throughout the animal kingdom, and are therefore to be regarded as the primary types of nature. (5) The different ranks or degrees of the circular groups are nine in number, each being involved within the other. None of these propositions being intelligible, the system soon fell into disuse, and is now regarded as entirely groundless and fanciful.

II. *n.* In *zoöl.*, one who proposed, practised, or taught the quinary system of classification; an adherent of the quinary system.

There were not wanting other men in these islands whose common sense refused to accept the metaphorical doctrine and the mystical jargon of the *Quinarians*; but so strenuously and persistently had the latter asserted their infallibility, and so vigorously had they assailed any who ventured to doubt it, that most peaceable ornithologists found it best to bend to the furious blast, and in some sort to acquiesce at least in the phraseology of the self-styled interpreters of Creative Will.
A. Newton, Encyc. Brit., XVIII. 16.

quinarius (kwī-nā'ri-us), *n.* [L.: see *quinary*.] An ancient Roman republican and imperial silver coin, in value half the denarius, or about 8 cents United States money. It was originally equivalent to five asses, but after the depreciation of the as, to eight. It was also called *victoriatus*, from the figure of Victory stamped upon it. It appears to have been first coined at Rome 177 B. C., after the victories of Clodius in Istria.

quinary (kwī'na-ri), *a.* and *n.* [= F. *quinaire* = Sp. Pg. It. *quinario*, < L. *quinarius*, containing five, < *quini*, five each, < *quinque*, five, = E. *five*.] **I.** *a.* 1. Divided in a set of five, as parts or organs of most radiates.

A *quinary* division of segments.
Adams, Manual of Nat. Hist., p. 328.

2. In *zoöl.*, same as *quinarian*.

Swainson's system of classification was peculiar. He endeavored to establish "circular" or *quinary* analogies throughout the animal kingdom. *Amer. Nat.*, XXI. 889.

The mischief caused by this theory of a *Quinary* System [in zoölogy] was very great, but was chiefly confined to Britain. *A. Newton*, Encyc. Brit., XVIII. 15.

Quinary system, or quinary classification. See *quinarian*.

II. *n.*; pl. *quinaries* (-riz). A whole composed of five parts or elements.

Quaternaries or compounds formed of four elements, *quinaries*, sextaries, etc., according as the number of the constituent elements increases.
Pop. Sci. Mo., XXXIV. 740.

quinate[1] (kwī'nāt), *a.* [< L. *quini*, five each, + *-ate*[1].] In *bot.*, having an arrangement of five similar parts together, as five leaflets on a petiole.

quinate[2] (kwī'nāt), *n.* [< *quin*(*ic*) + *-ate*[1].] In *chem.*, a salt of quinic acid.

quince[1] (kwins), *n.* [Formerly also *quence*; < ME. *quence*, an extension of *quine*, appar. orig. plural taken as singular: see *quine*[2]. Cf. L. *cydonia*, pl., quince. Less prob. a reduction of OF. *coignasse*, the largest kind of quince; < *coin*, quince: see *quine*[2].] 1. The fruit of the tree *Pyrus Cydonia*. (See def. 2.) It is pear-shaped, or in one variety apple-shaped, large, sometimes weighing a pound, of a golden-yellow color when ripe, and

Branch with Fruit of Quince (*Pyrus Cydonia*).

very fragrant. The quince was known to the ancients, and it has been argued that the golden apples of the Hesperides were quinces. While raw it is hard and austere, but it becomes edible by boiling or baking, and is largely used for jelly, preserves, and marmalade (see etymology of *marmalade*), and for flavoring sauces of other fruits. The seeds of the common quince are used in medicine and the arts, on account of their highly mucilaginous coat. In decoction they afford a demulcent application, and they are sometimes used in eye-lotions. Their mucilage is employed in making bandoline and in marbling books. See *bandoline*.

Of ripen'd *Quinces* such the yellow Hue.
Congreve, tr. of Ovid's Art of Love, iii.

2. The fruit-tree *Pyrus Cydonia*, sometimes classed as *Cydonia vulgaris*, the latter genus being based (insufficiently) on the many-seeded cells of the fruit. The quince is a small hardy tree, usually dwarfed, but sometimes reaching 15 or 20 feet in height, having crooked spreading branches which produce the flowers singly at their ends. Besides bearing fruit, the quince often serves as a stock for dwarfing the pear. The local origin of the quince is not clearly known, but it occurs spontaneously from northwestern India westward through the Mediterranean basin. The name *quince* applies also to any of the plants formerly referred to *Cydonia*. See the phrases below.—**Bengal quince,** *Ægle Marmelos*. See *Ægle*.—**Chinese quince,** a species, *Pyrus Cathayensis* (*Cydonia Sinensis*), resembling the Japanese quince, but less ornamental. Its large green egg-shaped fruit can be used to make jelly.—**Japanese quince,** a garden shrub, *Pyrus* (*Cydonia*) *Japonica*, a great favorite, on account chiefly of its abundant early large scarlet or crimson flowers, varying to white. It is well suited for ornamental hedges. The fruit, which resembles a small apple, is inedible, but is sometimes used for making jelly. Also called *japonica* and, locally, *burning-bush*. *P.* (*C.*) *Maulei*, more lately from Japan, bears abundant smaller orange-scarlet flowers on every twig.—**Portugal quince,** a variety of the common quince, having superior finely colored fruit, but less productive than other sorts.—**Quince-essence.** See *œnanthic ether*, under *œnanthic*.

quince[2]† (kwins), *n.* [ME. *quynce*; appar. an abbr. form of *quinsy*, *quinancy*.] Scrofula.

For the *quynce*. Take horehownde and columbyne, and sethe it in wyne or ale, and so thereof let hym dryncke fyrste and laste. *MS. Rec. Med.* (*Halliwell*.)

quince[3] (kwins), *n.* Same as *quinze*.

quincentenary (kwin-sen'te-nā-ri), *a.* and *n.* [Irreg. < L. *quin*(*que*), five, + *centenarius*, consisting of a hundred: see *centenary*.] **I.** *a.* Relating to or consisting of five hundred, especially five hundred years.

II. *n.* 1. That which consists of or comprehends five hundred.—2. A five-hundredth anniversary.

It saves us from the reproach of having allowed the *quincentenary* of the Canterbury Pilgrimage to pass by utterly unnoticed. *The Academy*, Nov. 24, 1888, p. 331.

quince-tree (kwins'trē), *n.* The tree that bears the quince, *Pyrus Cydonia*. See *quince*[1].

quince-wine (kwins'wīn), *n.* A drink made of the fermented juice of the quince.

quinch (kwinch), *v. i.* [A var. of *quitch*[1], appar. simulating *winch* for *wince*.] 1†. To move; stir; wince; flounce.

But Cato did abid it a long time, and never *quinched* for it, nor shewed countenance of fear.
North, tr. of Plutarch, p. 638.

Noe parte of all that realme shall be able or dare soe much as to *quinche*. *Spenser*, State of Ireland.

2. To make a noise. *Halliwell*. [Prov. Eng.]

quincuncial (kwin-kun'shal), *a.* [= F. *quinconcial* = It. *quinconciale*, < L. *quincuncialis*, containing five twelfths, < *quincunx*, five twelfths: see *quincunx*.] Disposed so as to form a quincunx; arranged in a set of five; also, arranged in two sets of oblique rows, at right angles to one another, so that five together form a quincunx; in *bot.*, sometimes noting a pentastichous arrangement of leaves; more often noting an estivation.

Quincuncial arrangement.

Now for the order of setting trees either in groves, hop-yards, or vineyards, we ought to follow the usuall manner of chequer row called *quincuntiall*.
Holland, tr. of Pliny, vii. 11.

Quincuncial estivation, the imbricated arrangement of five petals in a bud, in which the first and second are external, the fourth and fifth internal, and the third has one margin external, overlying the fifth, the other internal, overlapped by the first.—**Quincuncial map-projection.** See *projection*.

quincuncially (kwin-kun'shal-i), *adv.* In a quincuncial manner or order.

It is no wonder that this quincunciall order was first and still affected as gratefull unto the eye: for all things are seen *quincuncially*. *Sir T. Browne*, Urn-burial, iv.

quincunx (kwin'kungks), *n.* [= F. *quinconce* = Pg. *quincunce*, a quincunx; < L. *quincunx* (*quincunc-*), five twelfths (of anything), < *quinque*, = E. *five*, + *uncia*, a twelfth part: see *five* and *ounce*[1].] 1. An arrangement of five objects in a square, one at each corner and one in the middle (thus, ⁙); especially, an arrangement, as of trees, in such squares continuously. A collection of trees in such squares forms a regular grove or wood, presenting parallel rows or alleys in different directions, according to the spectator's position. See diagram under *quincuncial*.

Before them obliquely, in order of *quincunx*, were pits dug three foot deep. *Bladen*, tr. of Cæsar's Com., vii. 31.

The single *quincunx* of the Hyades upon the neck of Taurus. *Sir T. Browne*, Urn-burial, iii.

2. In *bot.*, same as *quincuncial estivation* (which see, under *quincuncial*).—3. In *astrol.*, the position of planets when distant from each other five signs or 150°.

quincunxial (kwin-kungk'shal), *a.* An erroneous form of *quincuncial*.

In *quincunxial* æstivation . . . two of the five pieces are exterior. *Le Maout and Decaisne*, Botany (trans.), p. 86.

quindecagon (kwin-dek'a-gon), *n.* [< L. *quinque*, = E. *five*, + E. *decagon*.] In *geom.*, a plane figure with fifteen sides and fifteen angles.

quindecemvir (kwin-dē-sem'vėr), *n.* [Altered in the second vowel to suit *decemvir*; < L. *quindecimvir*, < *quindecim*, = E. *fifteen* (see *quindecim*), + *vir*, a man.] In *Rom. antiq.*, one of a body of fifteen magistrates who, at the close of the republic, had charge of the Sibylline books. They succeeded the board of the decemvirs (*decemviri sacris faciundis*, or *decemviri sacrorum*), who were keepers of the Sibylline books from 367 B. C., and who continued the functions of the duumvirs, or two patricians of high rank who kept the books under the kings. It was the duty of the quindecemvirs to celebrate the festival of Apollo and the secular games, and they were all regarded as priests of Apollo.

quindecemvirate (kwin-dē-sem'vi-rāt), *n.* [< L. *quindecimviratus*, the dignity of a quindecemvir, < *quindecimviri*, the quindecemvirs: see *quindecemvir*.] The body or office of the quindecemvirs.

quindecim† (kwin'dē-sim), *n.* [< LL. *quindecimus* (L. *quintus decimus*), fifteenth, < L. *quindecim*, fifteen, < *quinque*, = E. *five*, + *decem* = E. *ten*.] A fifteenth part of anything.

Ouer and beside hath also beene declared what vnreasonable collections of monie from time to time, as *quindecims*, subsidies, tenths, &c. *Foxe*, Martyrs, p. 298, an. 1257.

quindecima (kwin-des'i-mä), *n.* [ML., fem. of *quindecimus*, fifteenth: see *quindecim*.] 1. In *music*, the interval of a fifteenth, or double octave.—2. An organ-stop two octaves above the foundation-stops.

quindene†, *n.* [ME. *quyndene*, < OF. *quindesme* (?), < ML. *quindecimus*, fifteenth: see *quindecim*. Cf. ML. *quindena*, a period of fifteen days.] The fifteenth day, counting inclusively from a certain date.

And that done, he toke his leue of seynt Denys about ye *quyndene* of Pasche. *Fabyan*, Chron., II., an. 1347.

quindismet, *v.* Same as *quindecim*.

In the parliament of 6 R. 2. pars 2 num. 11. the bishop of Norwich offered before the king and lords that, if the king would grant him the *quindisme* and disme of the laity and clergy . . . *Prynne*, Treachery and Disloyalty, iv. 7.

quine[1], *n.* A dialectal (Scotch) form of *quean*.

quine[2]†, *n.* [< ME. *quyne*, *coine*, *coin*, < OF. *coin*, F. *coing* = Pr. *codoing*, m., = It. *cotogna*, f., a quince, < L. *Cydonium*, *Cydoneum* (sc. *malum*), < Gr. Κυδώνιον (sc. μῆλον), a quince, lit. 'apple of Cydonia,' < Κυδωνία, Κυδωνίς, Cydonia, an ancient Greek city of Crete: see *Cydonia*. Cf. *quince*[1], *quiddany*.] A quince.

quine[3]†, *adv.* An obsolete dialectal form of *whence*.

quinet (kwī'net), *n.* [< OF. *quignet*, *quoignet*, *coignet*, *cuignet*, a little wedge, dim. of *quoin*, *coin*, a wedge: see *coin*[1], *coign*.] A wedge. *Halliwell*. [Prov. Eng.]

quinia (kwin'i-ä), *n.* [NL., < *quina*, q. v.] An older name for *quinine*.

quinible (kwin'i-bl), *n.* [ME. *quynible*, ult. < L. *quinque* = E. *five*. Cf. *quatrible*.] In *music*, an interval of a fifth; a descant sung at the fifth.

Therto he song som tyme a loud *quynyble*. *Chaucer*, Miller's Tale, l. 146.

To sing a *quinible* means to descant by singing fifths on a plain-song. *Chappell*, Popular Music of the Olden Time, p. 34.

quinible (kwin'i-bl), *v. i.* [< *quinible*, *n.*] In *music*, to sing a descant at the interval of a fifth. See *diaphony*, 2.

quinic (kwin'ik), *a.* [< *quina* + *-ic*.] Same as *kinic*.

quinicia (kwi-nish'iä), *n.* [NL., < *quinic*, q. v.] Same as *quinicine*.

quinicine (kwin'i-sin), *n.* [< *quinic* + *-ine*[2].] The isomeric alkaloid into which quinine or quinidine is converted by heat, differing from them in being dextrogyrate and amorphous.

quinidamine (kwin-i-dam'in), *n.* [< *quina* + *-id-* + *amine*.] An alkaloid of cinchona barks, with the formula $C_{19}H_{24}N_2O_2$. Also called *conchinamine*.

quinidine (kwin'id-in), *n.* [< *quina* + *-id-* + *-ine*[2].] A base ($C_{20}H_{24}N_2O_2$) isomeric with quinine, and occurring associated with it in some cinchona barks. It crystallizes in large transparent prisms, almost insoluble in water, but tolerably soluble in alcohol. It neutralizes acids, and forms salts with them which much resemble the corresponding quinine salts, but crystallize more easily. Their action on the system is similar to that of quinine, but less powerful. Also called *conchinine*.

quinine (kwin'ēn or ki-nēn' or kwī'nīn), *n.* [= F. *quinine* = Sp. Pg. *quinina* = It. *chinina*, *chinino*, < NL. *quinina*, quinine, < *quina*, Peruvian bark: see *quina* and *-ine*[2].] A very important vegetable alkali ($C_{20}H_{24}N_2O_2$), obtained from the bark of several trees of the genus *Cinchona*. It is colorless, inodorous, and extremely bitter. With acids it forms crystallizable salts, the most important of which is the sulphate, extensively used in medicine. It is antiperiodic, antipyretic, antineuralgic, and tonic.

quininism (ki-nēn'izm), *n.* [< *quinine* + *-ism*.] Same as *cinchonism*.

quiniretin (kwin-i-ret'in), *n.* [< *quinine*; second element obscure.] The flocculent precipitate deposited in solutions of quinine by the action of sunlight. It has the same chemical composition as quinine, but no alkaloidal properties.

quinisext (kwin'i-sekst), *a.* [< L. *quini*, five each, five, + *sextus*, sixth.] Bearing some relation to five and six or to the fifth and sixth.—**Quinisext Council.** See *Constantinopolitan Council*, under *Constantinopolitan*.

quinism (kwī'nizm), *n.* [< *quina* + *-ism*.] Same as *cinchonism*.

quink-goose (kwingk'gös), *n.* [< *quink* (imitative) + *goose*.] The brent-goose, *Bernicla brenta*. See cut under *brent-goose*.

quinnat (kwin'at), *n.* [The native name.] The king-salmon, *Oncorhynchus quinnat*. Also called *chavicha* and *equinna*. See *Oncorhynchus* and *salmon*.

quinoa (kē'nọ-ä), *n.* [Also *quinua*; Peruv.] An annual herb, *Chenopodium Quinoa*, native in Peru, Chili, etc., and there much cultivated for its farinaceous seeds. These afford a meal which can be made into cakes, but not into leavened bread. A favorite preparation is a kind of broth or gruel called *carapulque*, prepared from these seeds and seasoned with red pepper, etc. The quinoa is somewhat grown in England, the seed being eaten by fowls, and the leaves used like spinach. The plant resembles some common species of goosefoot or pigweed. A variety having white seeds is the one yielding food; the red seeds of another variety are used in decoction as an application for sores and bruises, and their husk has emetic and antiperiodic properties. Also called *petty-rice*.

They [the Incas of Peru] had also Maiz, *Quinua*, Pulse, Fruit-trees, with Fruit on them all, of Gold and Silver resembling the natural. *S. Clarke*, Geog. Descr. (1671), p. 281.

quinoline (kwin'ō-lin), *n.* [< *quina* + *-ol-* + *-ine*[2].] Same as *chinoline*.—**Quinoline blue**, a coal-tar color formerly used in dyeing: it is very fugitive to light.

quinologist (kwi-nol'ọ-jist), *n.* [< *quinology* + *-ist*.] One who is versed in quinology.

quinology (kwi-nol'ọ-ji), *n.* [< NL. *quina* + Gr. -λογία, < λέγειν, speak, say.] The sum of scientific knowledge concerning quinine and other cinchona alkaloids.

quinone (kwin'ōn), *n.* [< *quina* + *-one*.] 1. The general name applied to all benzene derivatives in which two hydrogen atoms are replaced by two oxygen atoms.—2. Specifically, a compound obtained by distilling kinic acid with diluted sulphuric acid and peroxid of manganese, or by the oxidation of aniline with chromic acid. It is in the form of a sublimate of fine golden-yellow crystals, slightly soluble in cold water and very volatile, and has a piercing irritating odor in the state of vapor. Also written *kinone*.

quinquagenarian (kwin'kwạ-je-nā'ri-ạn), *a.* and *n.* [= F. *quinquagénaire* = Sp. *quincuagenario* = It. *quinquagenario*, < L. *quinquagenarius*, consisting of fifty, < *quinquageni*, fifty each, < *quinquaginta*, fifty, < *quinque* = E. *five*.] **I.** *a.* Being fifty years of age.

II. *n.* A person aged fifty or between fifty and sixty.

Dancers of fifty are a very different sort of *quinquagenarians* from sitters of fifty. *The New Mirror* (1843), II. 34.

quinquagesima (kwin-kwạ-jes'i-mạ), *n.* [L., fem. of *quinquagesimus*, fiftieth, < *quinquaginta*, fifty: see *fifty*.] A period of fifty days.—**Quinquagesima Sunday**, the Sunday immediately preceding Ash Wednesday, being the fiftieth day before Easter (both inclusive), and the last Sunday before Lent; Shrove Sunday.

quinquangular (kwin-kwang'gū-lạr), *a.* [< LL. *quinquangulus*, five-cornered, < L. *quinque*, = E. *five*, + *angulus*, corner, angle: see *angle*[3].] Having five angles.

quinquarticular (kwin-kwär-tik'ū-lạr), *a.* [< L. *quinque*, = E. *five*, + *articulus*, joint, article.] Consisting of or relating to five articles.—**Quinquarticular controversy**, the controversy between the Arminians and the Calvinists on the "five points." See *the Five Articles and the Five Points*, under *article*.

You may perhaps be able to grapple with the difficulties of the *quinquarticular controversy* without discredit to yourselves. *Bp. Horsley*, Charge, Aug., 1806.

quinque-angled (kwin-kwẹ-ang'gld), *a.* [< L. *quinque*, = E. *five*, + E. *angled*.] Quinquangular.

quinquecapsular (kwin-kwẹ-kap'sụ-lạr), *a.* [< L. *quinque*, = E. *five*, + *capsula*, capsule.] In *bot.* and *zoöl.*, having five capsules.

quinquecostate (kwin-kwẹ-kos'tāt), *a.* [< L. *quinque*, = E. *five*, + *costa*, a rib.] In *zoöl.* and *bot.*, having five ribs or costæ, in any sense.

quinquedentate (kwin-kwẹ-den'tāt), *a.* [< L. *quinque*, = E. *five*, + *den(t-)s* = E. *tooth*: see *dentate*.] In *bot.* and *zoöl.*, having five teeth or serrations of any kind.

quinquedentated (kwin-kwẹ-den'tā-ted), *a.* [< *quinquedentate* + *-ed*[2].] Same as *quinquedentate*.

quinquedigitate (kwin-kwẹ-dij'i-tāt), *a.* [< L. *quinque*, = E. *five*, + *digitus*, finger: see *digitate*.] Having five fingers or toes; pentadactyl.

quinquefarious (kwin-kwẹ-fā'ri-us), *a.* [< L. *quinque*, = E. *five*, + *-farius*, as in *bifarious*, etc.] 1. In *bot.*, disposed in five vertical ranks. *Gray*.—2. In *zoöl.*, disposed or arranged in five sets, rows, or series; quinqueserial; pentastichous.

quinquefid (kwin'kwẹ-fid), *a.* [< L. *quinque*, = E. *five*, + *findere* (√ *fid*), cleave, split.] In *bot.*, cleft into five segments. See *cleft*[2], 2.

quinquefoliate (kwin-kwẹ-fō'li-ạt), *a.* [< L. *quinquefolius*, five-leaved (< *quinque*, = E. *five*, + *folium* = Gr. φύλλον, leaf), + *-ate*[1].] In *bot.*, having five leaves, or, more commonly but less properly, five leaflets.

quinquefoliated (kwin-kwẹ-fō'li-ā-ted), *a.* [< *quinquefoliate* + *-ed*[2].] Same as *quinquefoliate*.

quinquefoliolate (kwin-kwẹ-fō'li-ọ-lāt), *a.* [< L. *quinque*, = E. *five*, + NL. *foliolum*, a leaflet: see *foliolate*.] In *bot.*, having five leaflets: said of compound leaves.

quinquegrade (kwin'kwẹ-grād), *a.* [< L. *quinque*, = E. *five*, + *gradus*, degree: see *grade*[1].] In *music*, consisting of five tones.—**Quinquegrade scale.** Same as *pentatonic scale* (which see, under *scale*).

quinqueliteral (kwin-kwẹ-lit'e-rạl), *a.* [< L. *quinque*, = E. *five*, + *littera*, *litera*, letter: see *literal*.] Consisting of five letters.

quinquelobate (kwin-kwẹ-lō'bāt), *a.* [< L. *quinque*, = E. *five*, + NL. *lobus*, lobe: see *lobate*.] In *bot.* and *zoöl.*, having five lobes.

quinquelobed (kwin'kwẹ-lōbd), *a.* [< L. *quinque*, = E. *five*, + E. *lobe* + *-ed*[2].] Same as *quinquelobate*.

quinquelocular (kwin-kwẹ-lok'ū-lạr), *a.* [< L. *quinque*, = E. *five*, + *loculus*, a cell: see *locular*.] In *zoöl.* and *bot.*, having five loculi, cavities, or cells.

quinquenerved (kwin'kwẹ-nėrvd), *a.* [< L. *quinque*, = E. *five*, + *nervus*, nerve, + *-ed*[2].] Same as *quintuplinerved*.

quinquennalia (kwin-kwe-nā'li-ạ), *n. pl.* [L., neut. pl. of *quinquennalis*, that takes place every fifth year: see *quinquennial*.] In *Rom. antiq.*, public games celebrated every fifth year. See *quinquennial*, *n.*, 2.

quinquenniad (kwin-kwen'i-ad), *n.* [< L. *quinquennium*, a period of five years (see *quinquennium*), + *-ad*[1].] A period of five years.

So sleeping, so aroused from sleep
Thro' sunny decads new and strange,
Or gay *quinquenniads*, would we reap
The flower and quintessence of change.
Tennyson, The Day-Dream, L'Envoi.

quinquennial (kwin-kwen'i-ạl), *a.* and *n.* [For *quinquennal, < L. *quinquennalis*, occurring once in five years, < *quinquennis*, of five years, < *quinque*, = E. *five*, + *annus*, year.] **I.** *a.* 1. Occurring once in five years.—2. Recurring in the fifth year, reckoning both years of occurrence; occurring every fourth year. See II., 2.

With joyous banquets had he crown'd
The great *quinquennial* festival of Jove.
West, tr. of Pindar's Nemean Odes, xi.

3. Lasting five years.

II. *n.* 1. A period of five years; a quinquenniad; hence, something characterized by such a period or interval, as an anniversary, or a college catalogue.—2. A festival or celebration occurring once in four years; an anniversary in the fifth year. In this sense both the first and last years of the cycle of occurrence were reckoned, as was the invariable system in antiquity. Thus, the Olympian, Pythian, and Isthmian games, all celebrated once in four years, were all quinquennials.

quinquennially (kwin-kwen'i-ạl-i), *adv.* Once in five years; during a period of five years.

quinquennium (kwin-kwen'i-um), *n.* [L., < *quinquennis*, of five years: see *quinquennial*.] A period of five years.

The lapse of a *quinquennium*. *Lowell*, Among my Books, 2d ser., p. 254.

quinquepartite (kwin-kwẹ-pär'tīt), *a.* [< L. *quinquepartitus*, divided into five parts, fivefold, < *quinque*, = E. *five*, + *partitus*, pp. of *partire*, divide, distribute: see *part*, *v.*] Five-parted; divided into or consisting of five parts.

quinquepetaloid (kwin-kwẹ-pet'ạ-loid), *a.* [< L. *quinque*, = E. *five*, + E. *petaloid*.] Formed of five petaloid ambulacra: as, the *quinquepetaloid* rosette of a spatangoid sea-urchin.

quinqueradiate (kwin-kwẹ-rā'di-āt), *a.* [< L. *quinque*, = E. *five*, + *radius*, ray.] Having five rays; pentactinal, as a fish's fin, a starfish, or a sponge-spicule.

quinquereme (kwin'kwẹ-rēm), *n.* [< L. *quinqueremis*, < *quinque*, = E. *five*, + *remus*, oar.] An ancient galley having five banks of oars.

The great triremes and *quinqueremes* rushed onward. *Kingsley*, Hypatia, xviii.

quinquesect (kwin'kwẹ-sekt), *v. t.* [< L. *quinque*, = E. *five*, + *secare*, pp. *sectus*, cut.] To cut into five equal parts.

quinquesection (kwin-kwẹ-sek'shọn), *n.* [< L. *quinque*, = E. *five*, + *sectio(n-)*, a cutting: see *section*.] Section into five equal parts.

quinqueseptate (kwin-kwẹ-sep'tāt), *a.* [< L. *quinque*, = E. *five*, + *septum*, a partition: see *septum*, *septate*.] Having five septa or partitions.

quinqueserial (kwin-kwẹ-sē'ri-ạl), *a.* [< L. *quinque*, = E. *five*, + *series*, row, series: see *series*, *serial*.] Arranged in five series or rows.

quinquesyllabic (kwin'kwẹ-si-lab'ik), *a.* [< L. *quinque*, = E. *five*, + *syllaba*, syllable: see *syllabic*.] Having five syllables, as a word.

quinquesyllable (kwin-kwē-sil'a-bl), *n.* [< L. *quinque*, = E. *five*, + *syllaba*, syllable: see *syllable*.] A word of five syllables.

Anything beyond a *quinquesyllable* is difficult to pronounce. *Buck's Handbook of Med. Sciences*, VIII. 516.

quinquetactic (kwin-kwē-tak'tik), *a.* [< L. *quinque*, = E. *five*, + Gr. τακτικός, tactic: see *tactic*.] Having five consecutive points in common.—**Quinquetactic point.** See *tritactic point*, under *point*1.

quinquetubercular (kwin"kwē-tū-bėr'kū-lär), *a.* Same as *quinquetuberculate*.

The crowns of the lower molars are *quinquetubercular*. *Amer. Naturalist*, XXII. 663.

quinquetuberculate (kwin"kwē-tū-bėr'kū-lāt), *a.* [< L. *quinque*, = E. *five*, + *tuberculum*, tubercle: see *tubercle*, *tuberculate*.] Having five tubercles: as, a *quinquetuberculate* molar.

quinquevalent (kwin-kwev'a-lent), *a.* [< L. *quinque*, = E. *five*, + E. *valent*.] In *chem.*, capable of being combined with or exchanged for five hydrogen atoms; having an equivalence of five.

quinquevalve (kwin'kwē-valv), *a.* [< L. *quinque*, = E. *five*, + NL. *valva*, door (valve).] In *bot.*, having five valves, as a pericarp.

quinquevalvular (kwin-kwē-val'vū-lär), *a.* [< L. *quinque*, = E. *five*, + NL. *valvula*, dim. of *valva*, valve: see *valve*.] Same as *quinquevalve*.

quinquevir (kwin'kwē-vėr), *n.*; pl. *quinqueviri* (kwin-kwev'i-ri). [L., < *quinque*, = E. *five*, + *vir*, a man.] In *Rom. antiq.*, one of five commissioners who were appointed from time to time under the republic as extraordinary magistrates to carry any measure into effect, as to provide relief in time of public distress, to direct the establishment of a colony, or to provide for the repair of fortifications.

quinqui-. For words so erroneously spelled, see *quinque-*.

quinquina (kin'ki-nä), *n.* Same as *quinaquina*.

quinquino (kin'ki-nō), *n.* [S. Amer.] A tree, *Myroxylon Pereiræ*, the source of the balsam of Peru. It is found on a strip along the coast of San Salvador called the Balsam Coast. It has a height of 50 feet, branching at 8 or 10 feet from the ground; the leaves are pinnate, 6 or 8 inches long, the flowers numerous in erect racemes, the pods 3 or 4 inches long, narrow at the base, broadening and winged above, containing one seed. The balsam is obtained by the natives from the trunk by a process of beating and incision. It was first exported by the way of Peru, whence its name. The fruit also yields to cold pressure a valuable white balsam, and digested in rum furnishes a medicine, balsamito, but neither of these is an article of commerce. See *Myroxylon*, and *balsam of Peru* (under *balsam*).

quinsy (kwin'zi), *n.* [Formerly also *quinsey*, *quinzy*, *quincy* (also *quinancy*); reduced from early *squincy*, **squinsy*, *squinzie*, a contracted form of *squinancy*, < OF. *squinancie*, *squinance*, *esquinance*, F. *esquinancie* (cf. also OF. *quinatique*, *quinatike*) = Sp. *esquinancia* = Pg. *esquinencia* = It. *schinanzia*, quinsy, with prosthetic *s*, < LL. *cynanche*, < Gr. κυνάγχη, a kind of sore throat, also a dog-collar, lit. 'dog-throttling,' < κύων (κυν-), dog, + ἄγχειν, choke, throttle. Cf. *cynanche*.] Tonsillitis; specifically, a deep suppurative tonsillitis.

In steps that insolent insulter,
The cruell *Quincy*, leaping like a Vulture
At Adams throat.
Sylvester, tr. of Du Bartas's Weeks, ii., The Furies.

Why don't you speak out?—not stand croaking like a frog in a *quinsy*! *Sheridan*, The Rivals, iv. 2.

quinsy-berry (kwin'zi-ber"i), *n.* The black currant, *Ribes nigrum*, of the northern Old World, often planted. Its berries are eaten, and a jelly of them is a long-known popular remedy for quinsy and sore throat.

quinsywort (kwin'zi-wėrt), *n.* [Formerly also *quinancy-wort*, *squinancy-wort*; < *quinsy* + *wort*1.] A small trailing European herb, *Asperula cynanchica*, of the *Rubiaceæ*, having narrow leaves whorled in fours, and small, clustered, nearly white flowers. It was once reputed efficacious as a gargle in quinsy and sore throat, whence the common and the specific names. Also *quinsy-woodruff*.

quint (kwint), *n.* [< F. *quinte* (= Sp. Pg. It. *quinta*), f., a fifth part, a fifth (in music, etc.), also *quint*, m., a fifth, < *quint* (= Sp. Pg. It. *quinto*), fifth, < L. *quintus*, fifth, < *quinque*, five: see *five*.] **1.** A set or sequence of five, as in piquet.

For since the State has made a *quint*
Of generals, he's listed in 't.
S. Butler, Hudibras (1541), III. ii.

2. In *music*, same as *fifth*, 2.

As the melody proceeded there resulted a succession of parallel quarts, *quints*, and octaves, which would be intolerable to modern ears.
The Academy, Jan. 18, 1890, p. 51.

3. In *organ-building*, a stop giving tones a fifth above the normal pitch of the digitals used.—**4.** The smallest of the three varieties of viola da bracchio. See *viol*.—**5.** The E string or chanterelle of a violin: probably so called from the highest string of the lute.—**6.** In *fencing*, the fifth of the eight parries in sword-play. It is taught in the schools, but rarely used in practice.

quint-. [L. *quintus*, fifth: see *quint*.] A prefix of the names of musical instruments and of organ-stops, denoting a variety whose pitch is a fifth above or below that of the usual variety.

quinta (kwin'tä), *n.* [Sp. Pg. *quinta*, a country house.] A country house in Madeira.

A Pasco del Molino is the best part of the town, where all the rich merchants reside in *quintas* surrounded by pretty gardens. *Lady Brassey*, Voyage of Sunbeam, I. v.

quintad (kwin'tad), *n.* [< L. *quintus*, fifth (see *quint*), + *-ad*1.] Same as *pentad*.

quintadena (kwin-tä-dē'nä), *n.* [< L. *quintus*, fifth, + *-ad-ena*, an arbitrary termination.] In *organ-building*, a stop having small stopped pipes of metal in the tones of which the second harmonic or twelfth is decidedly prominent.

quintain (kwin'tān), *n.* [Formerly also *quinten*, *quintin*; < ME. *quyntayne*, *qwaintan*, < OF. *quintaine*, *cuintaine*, etc., f., a quintain, F. *quintaine* = Pr. It. *quintana*, < ML. *quintana*, a quintain, also a part of a street where carriages could pass, < L. *quintana*, a street in a camp, between the fifth and sixth maniples, where were the market and forum of the camp, and, it is supposed, the place of martial exercises, etc., whence the ML. use; fem. (sc. *via*) of *quintanus*, fifth: see *quintan*.] **1.** A figure or other object to be tilted at. It was constructed in various ways. A common form in England consisted of an upright post, on the top of which

Movable Quintain, 14th century.
(From Strutt's "Sports and Pastimes of the People of England.")

was a horizontal bar turning on a pivot; to one end of this a sandbag was attached, to the other a broad board; and it was a trial of skill to strike or tilt at the broad end with a lance, and pass on before the bag of sand could whirl round and strike the tilter on the back.

My better parts
Are all thrown down, and that which here stands up
Is but a *quintain*, a mere lifeless block.
Shak., As you Like it, i. 2. 263.

The *quintain* in its original state was not confined to the exercise of young warriors on horseback; it was an object of practice for them on foot, in order to acquire strength and skill in assaulting an enemy with their swords, spears, and battle-axes.
Strutt, Sports and Pastimes, p. 183.

2. The game or exercise of tilting at the quintain.

Somur qwenes, and *qwaintans*, & other qwaint gaumes
There foundyn was first, & yet ben forthe haunted.
Destruction of Troy (E. E. T. S.), l. 1627.

quintal (kwin'tal), *n.* [Also *kintal*, and formerly *kental*, *kintle*, early mod. E. *kyntayl*; < F. *quintal* = It. *quintale*, < Sp. Pg. *quintal*, < Ar. *qintār*, a weight of one hundred pounds, < L. *centum*, a hundred: see *cent* and *cantar*, *cantara*.] A weight of 100 pounds. The old French quintal was equal to 100 livres, or nearly 108 pounds avoirdupois. The *quintal métrique*, or modern quintal, is 100 kilograms, or about 220 pounds avoirdupois.

I give this jewel to thee, richly worth
A *quintal* or an hundred-weight of gold.
Chapman, Blind Beggar of Alexandria.

quintan (kwin'tan), *a.* and *n.* [< L. *quintanus*, pertaining to the fifth, < *quintus*, fifth, < *quinque* = E. *five*: see *five*. Cf. *quintain*.] **I.** *a.* Occurring or recurring every fifth day, both days being counted, as on Sunday and Thursday: as, a *quintan* fever.

II. *n.* An intermittent fever the paroxysms of which recur every fifth day.

quintet†, *a.* A Middle English form of *quaint*.

quintefoil (kwint'foil), *n.* [A corrupt form of *cinquefoil*, as if < OF. *quint*, fifth, + *foil*, leaf.] In *her.*, same as *cinquefoil*.

quintell† (kwin'tel), *n.* An erroneous form of *quintain*.

None crowns the cup
Of wassaile now, or sets the *quintell* up.
Herrick, A Pastorall sung to the King.

quintent, *n.* An obsolete form of *quintain*.

quinternet, *n.* [OF. *quinterne*, a corrupt form of *guinterne*, *guiterne*, a gittern, guitar: see *gittern*, *guitar*.] A musical instrument of the lute family, which was one of the early forms of the modern guitar.

quinteron (kwin'te-ron), *n.* Same as *quintroon*.

quintessence (kwin-tes'ens, formerly kwin'te-sens), *n.* [< ME. *quintessence*, < OF. (and F.) *quintessence* = It. *quintessenza* = ML. *quinta essentia*, fifth essence: L. *quinta*, fem. of *quintus*, fifth; *essentia*, being or essence: see *quint* and *essence*.] **1.** The fifth essence, or fifth body, not composed of earth, water, fire, or air; the substance of the heavenly bodies, according to Aristotle, who seems in this matter to follow Pythagorean doctrine. The quintessence was situated above the four terrestrial elements, and was naturally bright and incorruptible, and endowed with a circular motion.

Forsothe philosophoris clepen the purest substaunce of manye corruptible thingis elementid *quinta essencia*.
Book of Quinte Essence (ed. Furnivall), p. 2.

Paracelsus . . . tells us . . . the lungs consume part of the air, and proscribe the rest. So that . . . it seems we may suppose that there is in the air a little vital *quintessence* (if I may so call it), which serves to the refreshment and restauration of our vital spirits, for which use the grosser and incomparably greater part of the air being unserviceable, it need not seem strange that an animal stands in need of almost incessantly drawing in fresh air.
Boyle, New Experiments touching the Spring of the Air, [Exp. xli. 1.

Hence—**2.** An extract from anything, containing its virtues or most essential part in a small quantity; pure and concentrated essence; the best and purest part of a thing; in *old chem.*, an alcoholic tincture or essence often made by digestion at common temperatures or in the sun's heat, and always at a gentle heat.

To comforte the herte, putte yu oure *5 essense*, the *5 essence* of gold and of peerl, and he schal be delyuerid thereof [of venom] and be hool.
Book of Quinte Essence (ed. Furnivall), p. 23.

More precious I do holde
Maltes pure *quintessence* then king Harries golde.
Times' Whistle (E. E. T. S.), p. 61.

The *quintessence* of every sprite
Heaven would in little show.
Shak., As you Like it, iii. 2. 147.

The large scarlet anemone outshone even the poppy, whose color here is the *quintessence* of flame.
B. Taylor, Lands of the Saracen, p. 116.

Pure *quintessences* of precious oils
In hollow'd moons of gems.
Tennyson, Palace of Art.

quintessence (kwin-tes'ens, formerly kwin'te-sens), *v. t.*; pret. and pp. *quintessenced*, ppr. *quintessencing*. [< *quintessence*, *n.*] To extract as a quintessence; reduce to a quintessence. [Rare.]

If the whole world were *quintessenced* into one perfume, it could not yield so fragrant a smell.
Rev. T. Adams, Works, II. 434.

It is truth *quintessenced* and raised to the highest power.
Quoted in *Littell's Living Age*, CLXXV. 113.

quintessential (kwin-te-sen'shal), *a.* [< *quintessence* (ML. *quinta essentia*) + *-al*.] Consisting of quintessence; of the nature of quintessence.

Here first are born the spirits animal,
Whose matter, almost immaterial,
Resembles heaven's matter *quintessential*.
P. Fletcher, Purple Island, v.

Our states, I have always contended, our various phases, have to be passed through, and there is no disgrace in it so long as they do not levy toll on the *quintessential*, the spiritual element. *G. Meredith*, The Egoist, xiv.

quintessentialize (kwin-te-sen'shal-īz), *v. t.*; pret. and pp. *quintessentialized*, ppr. *quintessentializing*. [< *quintessential* + *-ize*.] To reduce to a quintessence; exhibit in the highest or quintessential form. [Rare.]

Their [the Jews'] national egotism, *quintessentialized* in the prophets, was especially sympathetic with the personal egotism of Milton.
Lowell, Among my Books, 2d ser., p. 273.

quintet, quintette (kwin-tet'), *n.* [= F. *quintette*, < It. *quintetto*, a quintet, < *quinto*, < L. *quintus*, fifth: see *quint*.] In *music*: (*a*) A movement for five solo parts, either vocal or instrumental. Instrumental quintets are essentially similar to quartets. (*b*) A company of five singers or players who perform quintets.

quintetto (kwin-tet'ō), *n.* [It.] Same as *quintet*.

quintfoil (kwint'foil), *n.* See *quintefoil*.

quintic (kwin'tik), *a.* and *n.* [< L. *quintus*, fifth (see *quint*), + *-ic*.] **I.** *a.* Of the fifth degree.—**Quintic equation.** See *equation*.—**Quintic symmetry**, symmetry arising from the possibility of reducing a quintic to the form $ax^5 + by^5$.

II. *n.* An algebraic function of the fifth degree.

quintile (kwin'til), *n.* [< L. *quintus*, fifth, < *quinque*, five, + *-ile.*] The aspect of planets when they are distant from each other the fifth part of the zodiac, or 72°.

Quintillian (kwin-til'ian), *n.* [< *Quintilla*, a Roman female name (see def.), fem. of *Quintillus*, dim. of *quintus*, fifth: see *quintan.*] One of a body of Montanists, said to have been so called from a prophetess Quintilla.

quintillion (kwin-til'yon), *n.* [< L. *quintus*, fifth, + E. (*m*)*illion.*] In the English notation, the fifth power of a million, a unit followed by thirty ciphers; in the French notation, used generally in the United States, the sixth power of one thousand, a unit followed by eighteen ciphers.

quintin†, *n.* An obsolete form of *quintain.*

quintine (kwin'tin), *n.* [< L. *quintus*, fifth, + *-ine*².] In *bot.*, an alleged fifth coat of an ovule, counting from the outermost. Compare *quartine.*

quintisternal (kwin-ti-stėr'nal), *n.* [< L. *quintus*, fifth, + NL. *sternum*, sternum.] In *anat.*, the fifth sterneber, succeeding the quadristernal, and corresponding to the fifth intercostal space. [Rare.]

quintole (kwin'tōl), *n.* [< It. *quinto*, < L. *quintus*, fifth, + *-ole.*] 1. Same as *quintuplet*, 3. Compare *decimole*, *quartole*, etc.—2. A five-stringed variety of viol much used in France in the eighteenth century. See *viol.*

quintroon (kwin-trön'), *n.* [Also *quinteron*; < Sp. *quinteron*, a quintroon, < L. *quintus*, fifth: see *quint.* Cf. *quarteroon*, *quadroon.*] In the West Indies, the child of a white person by one who has one sixteenth part of negro blood.

quintuple (kwin'tụ̈-pl), *a.* [= F. *quintuple* = Sp. *quintuplo* = Pg. It. *quintuplo*, < ML. **quintuplus*, fivefold, < L. *quintus*, fifth (< *quinque*, five), + *-plus*, -fold. Cf. L. *quintuplex*, fivefold, < *quintus*, fifth, + *plicare*, fold.] 1. Fivefold; containing five times the number or amount.

> Owing this name not only unto the *quintuple* number of trees, but the figure declaring that number.
> *Sir T. Browne*, Garden of Cyrus, i.

2. In *bot.*, divided or arranged by a rule of five; fivefold.—**Quintuple rhythm** or **time**, in *music*, rhythm or time characterized by five beats or pulses to the measure. See *rhythm.*

quintuple (kwin'tụ̈-pl), *v.*; pret. and pp. *quintupled*, ppr. *quintupling.* [< *quintuple*, *a.*] I. *trans.* To make fivefold.

II. *intrans.* To increase fivefold.

> The value of land in that district has *quintupled* within the last thirty or forty years.
> *Fortnightly Rev.*, N. S., XLII. 226.

quintuple-nerved (kwin'tụ̈-pl-nėrvd), *a.* Same as *quintuplinerved.*

quintuple-ribbed (kwin'tụ̈-pl-ribd), *a.* Same as *quintuplinerved.*

quintuplet (kwin'tụ̈-plet), *n.* [< *quintuple* + *-et.*] 1. A set of five, as of car-springs, etc. —2. *pl.* Five children born at a birth.

> Five years subsequently she gave birth to *quintuplets.*
> *Lancet*, No. 3417, p. 392.

3. In *music*, a group of five notes to be performed in the time of three, four, or six. Also *quintole.* Compare *nonuplet*, *triplet*, etc.

quintuplicate (kwin-tū'pli-kāt), *v. t.*; pret. and pp. *quintuplicated*, ppr. *quintuplicating.* [< L. *quintuplicatus*, pp. of *quintuplicare*, < *quintus*, fifth, + *plicare*, fold: see *plicate.*] To make fivefold; increase or repeat to the number of five.

quintuplicate (kwin-tū'pli-kạ̄t), *a.* and *n.* [< L. *quintuplicatus*, pp. of *quintuplicare*: see *quintuplicate*, *v.*] I. *a.* Consisting of or relating to a set of five, or to five corresponding parts.

II. *n.* One of five things corresponding in every respect to one another.

> A great many duplicates, not to speak of triplicates, or even such a *quintuplicate* as that which I adduced.
> *Trench*, Study of Words, p. 181

quintuplication (kwin-tū-pli-kā'shọn), *n.* [< *quintuplicate* + *-ion.*] The act or process of repeating five times, or increasing to the number of five.

> The perceptible are evolved out of the imperceptible elements by the process of *quintuplication.*
> *Encyc. Brit.*, XXIV. 119.

quintuplinerved (kwin'tụ̈-pli-nėrvd), *a.* [< ML. **quintuplus*, fivefold, + L. *nervus*, nerve, + *-ed*².] In *bot.*, having a midrib with two lateral ribs or primary nerves on each side: said of palmately nerved leaves, or those approaching the palmate nervation. See *nervation.* Also *quinquenerved.*

quintus (kwin'tus), *n.* [ML., < L. *quintus*, fifth: see *quint.*] In *medieval music*, the fifth voice or part. It either corresponded in compass to one of the other four, though independent, or strengthened the different parts in turn: hence sometimes called *vagans.*

quinzain, quinzaine (kwin'zān; F. pron. kaṅ-zān'), *n.* [< ME. **quinzaine*, *quynsynne*, < OF. (and F.) *quinzaine*, the number of fifteen, a fortnight, < *quinze*, fifteen: see *quinze.*] 1. In *chron.*, the fourteenth day after a feast-day, or the fifteenth if the day of the feast is included.

> And the *quynsynne* after that Merlyn come to courte, and grete was the ioye the kynge made to hym.
> *Merlin* (E. E. T. S.), i. 57.

2. A stanza consisting of fifteen lines.

quinze (kwinz; F. pron. kaṅz), *n.* [Also *quince*; < F. *quinze*, fifteen, < L. *quindecim*, fifteen: see *quindecim.*] A game of cards somewhat similar to vingt-un, in which the object is to count fifteen, or as near as possible to that number without exceeding it.

> Gambling the whole morning in the Alley, and sitting down at night to *quinze* and hazard at St. James's.
> *Colman*, Man of Business, iv.

quinzy†, *n.* See *quinsy.*

quip (kwip), *n.* [< W. *chwip*, a quick turn or flirt, < *chwipio*, whip, move briskly. Cf. *whip.* Hence *quib*, *quibble.*] A smart sarcastic turn; a sharp or cutting jest; a severe retort; a gibe.

> *Psyl.* Why, what's a *quip?*
> *Manes.* Wee great girders call it a short saying of a sharpe wit, with a bitter sense in a sweet word.
> *Lyly*, Alexander and Campaspe, iii. 2.

> If I sent him word again it was not well cut, he would send me word he cut it to please himself. This is called the Quip Modest.
> *Shak.*, As you Like it, v. 4. 79.

> Haste thee, nymph, and bring with thee
> Jest, and youthful jollity,
> *Quips*, and cranks, and wanton wiles.
> *Milton*, L'Allegro, l. 72.

quip (kwip), *v.*; pret. and pp. *quipped*, ppr. *quipping.* [< *quip*, *n.*] I. *intrans.* To use quips or sarcasms; gibe; scoff.

> Are you pleasant or peevish, that you *quip* with suche briefe girdes?
> *Greene*, Theeves Falling Out (Harl. Misc., VIII. 383).

> Ye malitious haue more minde to *quip* then might to cut.
> *Lyly*, Euphues, Anat. of Wit, p. 206.

II. *trans.* To utter quips or sarcasms on; taunt; treat with a sarcastic retort; sneer at.

> The more he laughes, and does her closely *quip*,
> To see her sore lament and bite her tender lip.
> *Spenser*, F. Q., VI. vii. 44.

quipo, *n.* See *quipu.*

quipper† (kwip'ėr), *n.* One who jests or quips.

> And here, peraduenture, some desperate *quipper* will canuaze my proposed comparison.
> *Nashe*, Introd. to Greene's Menaphon, p. 14. (*Davies.*)

quippian (kwip'i-ạn), *n.* [So called because denoted by *Q.*] A curve of the third class, the left-hand member of whose equation is the quintic contravariant of a cubic.

quippish (kwip'ish), *a.* [< *quip* + *-ish*¹.] Abounding in quips; epigrammatic. [Rare.]

> I prefer Fuller's [version], as more *quippish* and adagy.
> *N. and Q.*, 7th ser., VI. 501.

quipu (kē'pö or kwip'ö), *n.* [Also *quippu*, *quipo*, *quippo*; < Peruv. *quipu*, a knot.] A cord about 2 feet in length, tightly spun from variously colored threads, and having a number of smaller threads attached to it in the form of a fringe: used among the ancient Peruvians and elsewhere for recording events, etc. The fringe-like threads were also of different colors and were knotted. The colors denoted sensible objects, as white for silver and yellow for gold, and sometimes also abstract ideas, as white for peace and red for war. They constituted a rude register of certain important facts or events, as of births, deaths, and marriages, the number of the population fit to bear arms, the quantity of stores in the government magazines, etc.

> The mysterious science of the *quipus* . . . supplied the Peruvians with the means of communicating their ideas to one another, and of transmitting them to future generations.
> *Prescott*, Conquest of Peru, i. 4.

> Wampum and *quippus* are mnemonic records of the most elementary kind.
> *Isaac Taylor*, The Alphabet, I. 18.

quiquihatch (kwē'kwẹ̄-hach), *n.* [Amer. Ind.] The quickhatch or wolverene, *Gulo luscus.*

quirace†, *n.* An obsolete form of *cuirass.*

> For all their bucklers, Morions, and *Quiraces*
> Were of no proofe against their poisant maces.
> *Hudson*, tr. of Du Bartas's Judith, v.

quirboille†, quirboilly†, *n.* Obsolete forms of *cuir-bouilli.*

quircal (kwėr'kal), *n.* A kind of marmoset. *Sci. Amer.*, LV. 176.

quire¹ (kwir), *n.* [Early mod. E. also *quier*, *queer*; < ME. *queer*, *quere*, *quer*, *queor*, < OF. *cuer*, F. *chœur* = Pr. *cor* = Sp. Pg. It. *coro* = D. *koor* = G. *chor* = Sw. *kör* = Dan. *kor* = AS. *chor* (rare), < L. *chorus*, < Gr. χορός, a dance, chorus: see *chorus.* Cf. *choir*, a mod. spelling simulating, like the mod. F. *chœur*, the L. spelling, but with pron. of *quire.*] 1. A body of singers; a chorus.

> They rise at mid-night to pray vnto their Idols, which they doe in *Quires*, as the Friers doe.
> *Purchas*, Pilgrimage, p. 459.

> Angelick *quires*
> Sung heavenly anthems of . . . victory.
> *Milton*, P. R., iv. 593.

> When the first low matin-chirp hath grown
> Full *quire.*
> *Tennyson*, Love and Duty.

2. The part of a church allotted to the choristers; the choir.

> Besyde the Queer of the Chirche, at the right syde, as men comen dounward 16 Greces, is the place where oure Lord was born.
> *Mandeville*, Travels, p. 70.

> The fox obscene to gaping tombs retires,
> And savage howlings fill the sacred *quires.*
> *Pope*, Windsor Forest, l. 72.

3†. A company or assembly.

> And then the whole *quire* hold their hips and laugh.
> *Shak.*, M. N. D., ii. 1. 55.

quire¹ (kwīr), *v. i.*; pret. and pp. *quired*, ppr. *quiring.* [< *quire*¹, *n.*] 1. To sing in concert or chorus; chant or sing harmoniously.

> There's not the smallest orb which thou behold'st,
> But in his motion like an angel sings,
> Still *quiring* to the young-eyed cherubims.
> *Shak.*, M. of V., v. 1. 62.

2. To harmonize.

> My throat of war be turn'd,
> Which *quired* with my drum, into a pipe
> Small as . . . the virgin voice
> That babies lulls asleep! *Shak.*, Cor., iii. 2. 113.

quire² (kwir), *n.* [Early mod. E. also *quier*, *queer*, *quere*; < ME. *quayer*, *quaier*, *quair*, *quayre*, *quaer*, *cwaer* (= Icel. *kver*, a quire, a book), < OF. *quaier*, *quayer*, *caier*, *cayer*, *coyer*, a quire (also a square lamp), F. *cahier*, a quire (six sheets), a copy-book, writing-book, written lectures, a memorial, = Pr. *cazern* = It. *quaderno*, a quire, a copy-book, writing-book, cash-book, two fours at dice, < ML. *quaternum*, a set of four sheets of parchment or paper, neut. of *quaternus* (> OF. *quaier*, *caier*, etc., = OIt. *quaderno*, four-square), pl. *quaterni*, four at a time: see *quatern.* For OF. *quaer*, *quaier*, < L. *quaternum*, cf. *enfer*, < L. *infernum.*] 1†. A set of four sheets of parchment or paper folded so as to make eight leaves: the ordinary unit of construction for early manuscripts and books.

> The *quires* or gatherings of which the book was formed generally consisted, in the earliest examples, of four sheets folded to make eight leaves.
> *Encyc. Brit.*, XVIII. 144.

2. A set of one of each of the sheets of a book laid in consecutive order, ready for folding. *E. H. Knight.*—3†. A book.

> Go, litel *quayre*, go unto my lyves quene.
> *Lydgate*, Black Knight, l. 674.

4. Twenty-four sheets of paper; the twentieth part of a ream.—**In quires**, in sheets, not folded or bound: said of printed books.

> The Imprinter to sell this Booke *in Queres* for two shillinges and sixe pence, and not above.
> *Notice in Edward VI.'s Prayer-Book*, 1549.

Inside quires, the eighteen perfect quires of a ream of paper, which were protected by outer quires of imperfect paper, one on each side of the package. This distinction between outside and inside quires is noticeable now only in hand-made papers. Machine-made papers are of uniform quality.

quire² (kwīr), *v. t.*; pret. and pp. *quired*, ppr. *quiring.* [< *quire*², *n.*] To fold in quires, or with marks between quires.

quire³†, *a.* An obsolete form of *queer*¹.

quirewise (kwīr'wīz), *adv.* In *printing*, in single forms on double leaves of paper, so that the leaves can be quired and sewed in sections: in distinction from on single leaves, which have to be side-stitched.

Quirinalia (kwir-i-nā'li-ạ̈), *n. pl.* [L., neut. pl. of *quirinalis*, pertaining to Quirinus or Romulus, or to the Quirinal Hill at Rome, < *Quirinus*, a name of Romulus deified: see *Quirinus.*] In ancient Rome, a festival in honor of Quirinus, celebrated on February 17th, on which day Romulus was said to have been translated to heaven.

quirinca-pods (kwi-ring'kạ̈-podz), *n. pl.* [< S. Amer. *quirinca* + E. *pod.*] The fruit-husks of *Acacia Cavenia*, the espanillo of the Argentine Republic. They contain about 33 per cent. of tannin.

Quirinus (kwi-rī'nus), *n.* [L., < *Cures*, a Sabine town. Cf. *Quirites.*] An Italic warlike divinity, identified with Romulus and assimilated to Mars.

quirister† (kwir'is-tèr), *n.* [Also *quirrister, querister, querester*; < *quire*1, *n.*, + *-ister*. Cf. *chorister*.] Same as *chorister*.

The clear *quiristers* of the woods, the birds.
Ford, Lover's Melancholy, i. 1.

The coy *quiristers* that lodge within
Are prodigal of harmony. Thomson, Spring.

quiritarian (kwir-i-tā'ri-an), *a.* [< *quiritary* + *-an*.] In *Rom. law*, legal: noting a certain class or form of rights, as distinguished from *bonitarian*. The use is equivalent to that of *legal* in modern law, in contradistinction to *equitable*.

They [the Roman lawyers] could conceive land as held (so to speak) under different legal dispensations, as belonging to one person in Quiritarian and to another in Bonitarian ownership, a splitting of ownership which, after feudalism had fallen into decay, revived in our country in the distinction between the legal and the equitable estate.
Maine, Early Law and Custom, p. 343.

quiritary (kwir'i-tā-ri), *a.* [< ML. *quiritarius*, < L. *Quirites*, the Roman citizens: see *Quirites*.] Same as *quiritarian*. *Encyc. Brit.*, XX. 682.

quiritation (kwir-i-tā'shon), *n.* [< L. *quiritatio(n-)*, a cry, a shriek, < *quiritare*, wail, shriek; commonly explained (first by Varro) as orig. 'call upon the Quirites or Roman citizens for aid,' < *Quirites*, Quirites; prob. freq. of *queri*, complain: see *querent*1, and cf. *cry*, ult. < *quiritare*.] A crying for help.

How is it then with thee, O Saviour, that thou thus astonishest men and angels with so wofull a *quiritation*: (My God, my God, why hast thou forsaken me?)?
Bp. Hall, The Crucifixion.

Quirite (kwir'īt), *n.* [< L. *Quiris* (*Quirit-*): see *Quirites*.] One of the Quirites.

Quirites (kwi-rī'tēz), *n. pl.* [L., pl. of *Quiris* (*Quirit-*), orig. an inhabitant of the Sabine town Cures, later a Roman citizen (see def.); < *Cures*, a Sabine town.] The citizens of ancient Rome considered in their civil capacity. The name *Quirites* pertained to them in addition to that of *Romani*, the latter designation having application in their political and military capacity.

quirk1 (kwèrk), *n.* [Formerly also *querk*; perhaps a var. of **quirt* (cf. *jerk*1, *jert*), < W. *chwired*, craft, quirk (< *chwiori*, turn briskly), = Gael. *cuireid*, a turn, wile, trick (cf. *car*, turn).] 1. A sharp turn or angle; a sudden twist.

Then have they neyther-stockes to these gay hosen, . . . curiously knit, with open seame down the legge, with *quirkes* and clockes about the anckles, and sometime (haplie) interlaced with golde or silver threds.
Stubbes, Anat. of Abuses, p. 31. (*Nares*, under *nether-stocks*.)

Hence—2. An artful turn for evasion or subterfuge; a shift; a quibble: as, the *quirks* of a pettifogger.

As one said of a lawyer that, resolving not to be forgotten, he made his will so full of intricate *quirks* that his executors, if for nothing else, yet for very vexation of law, might have cause to remember him.
Rev. T. Adams, Works, I. 76.

3†. A fit or turn; a short paroxysm.

I have felt so many *quirks* of joy and grief.
Shak., All's Well, iii. 2. 51.

4. A smart taunt or retort; a slight conceit or quibble; a quip; a flight of fancy.

I may chance have some odd *quirks* and remnants of wit broken on me. *Shak.*, Much Ado, ii. 3. 245.

Twisted *quirks* and happy hits,
From misty men of letters;
The tavern-hours of mighty wits.
Tennyson, Will Waterproof.

5. Inclination; turn; peculiarity; humor; caprice.

I have heard of some kind of men that put quarrels purposely on others, to taste their valour: belike this is a man of that *quirk*. *Shak.*, T. N., iii. 4. 268.

6. A sudden turn or flourish in a musical air; a fantastic phrase.

Light *quirks* of musick, broken and uneven,
Make the soul dance upon a jig to heaven.
Pope, Moral Essays, iv. 143.

The *quirks* of the melody are not unlike those of very old English ballads. *Lathrop*, Spanish Vistas, p. 126.

7. In *building*, a piece taken out of any regular ground-plot or floor, as to make a court or yard, etc.: thus, if the ground-plan were square or oblong, and a piece were taken out of the corner, such piece is called a *quirk*.—8. In *arch.*, an acute angle or recess; a deep indentation; the incision under the abacus.—9. A pane of glass cut at the sides and top in the form of a rhomb. *Halliwell.* [Prov. Eng.]—10. In a grooving-plane, a projecting fillet on the sole or side, arranged to serve as a fence or gage for depth or distance.—**Bead and quirk, bead and double quirk.** See *bead*, 9.—**Quirk bead,** a molding the round part of which forms more than a semicircle, and which has a sinking on the face termed the *quirk*.—**Quirk molding.** Same as *quirked molding*.

quirk1 (kwèrk), *v.* [< *quirk*1, *n.*] **I.** *intrans.* To turn sharply.

II. *trans.* 1. To twist or turn; form into quirks.—2. To form or furnish with a quirk or channel.

In Grecian architecture, ovolos and ogees are usually *quirked* at the top. *Weale.*

Quirked molding, a molding characterized by a sharp

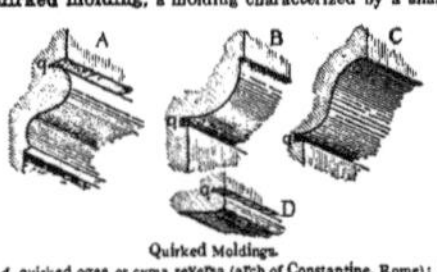

Quirked Moldings.

A, quirked ogee or cyma reversa (arch of Constantine, Rome); *B*, quirked ovolo; *C*, quirked cyma recta; *D*, quirked bead (*B*, *C*, *D*, modern colonial American woodwork). *q q q q*, quirks.

and sudden return from its extreme projection to a reëntrant angle. Also called *quirk molding*. *Gwilt.*

quirk2 (kwèrk), *v. i.* [Cf. *querk*1.] 1. To emit the breath forcibly after retaining it in violent exertion. *Halliwell.* [Prov. Eng.]—2. To grunt; complain. *Halliwell.* [Prov. Eng.]

quirk-float (kwèrk'flōt), *n.* See *float*, 9 (c).

quirking-plane (kwèr'king-plān), *n.* A molding-plane for working on convex surfaces. *E. H. Knight.*

quirkish (kwèr'kish), *a.* [< *quirk*1 + *-ish*1.] Having the character of a quirk; consisting of quirks, quibbles, or artful evasions. [Rare.]

Sometimes it [facetiousness] is lodged in a sly question, in a smart answer, in a *quirkish* reason.
Barrow, Works, I. xiv.

quirky (kwèr'ki), *a.* [< *quirk*1 + *-y*1.] 1. Abounding in quirks or twists; irregular; zigzag; quirkish. [Rare.]

Bordered by *quirky* lines.
Philadelphia Times, June 1, 1885.

2. Full of quirks or subterfuges; shifty; quibbling; characterized by petty tricks: as, a *quirky* attorney; a *quirky* question.—3. Merry; sportive. *Halliwell.* [Prov. Eng.]

quirl (kwèrl), *v.* and *n.* See *querl*.

quirlewind†, *n.* An obsolete dialectal form of *whirlwind*.

quirpele, *n.* [Tamil.] A name for the mongoos: used in India. *Yule and Burnell.*

quirt (kwèrt), *n.* [Perhaps < Sp. *cuerda*, a cord, rope: see *cord*1.] A kind of riding-whip much used in the western parts of the United States and in Spanish-American countries. It usually consists of a short stout stock, a few inches long, of wood, or of leather braided so tightly as to be rigid, and of a braided leather lash, about two feet long, flexible and very loosely attached to the stock. The quirt thus resembles a bull-whip in miniature. It is sometimes entirely braided of leather, like a small black-snake, but so as then to make a short rigid handle and long flexible lash. The quirt is often ornamented fancifully, and generally hung on the right wrist by a leather loop.

quirt (kwèrt), *v. t.* [< *quirt*, *n.*] To strike or flog with a quirt. [Western U. S.]

A first-class rider will sit throughout it all without moving from the saddle, *quirting* his horse all the time, though his hat may be jarred off his head and his revolver out of its sheath. *T. Roosevelt*, The Century, XXXV. 864.

Quiscalinæ (kwis-ka-lī'nē), *n. pl.* [NL., < *Quiscalus* + *-inæ*.] A subfamily of *Icteridæ*, typified by the genus *Quiscalus*, usually having a lengthened and more or less boat-shaped tail, somewhat crow-like or thrush-like bill, stout feet, and in the male the color entirely iridescent-black; the American grackles or crow-blackbirds. The species are mostly terrestrial and gregarious. See *Quiscalus* and *Scolecophagus*.

Quiscalus (kwis'ka-lus), *n.* [NL. (Vieillot, 1816); appar. < ML. *quiscula*, *quisquila*, *quisquilla*, etc., a quail: see *quail*3.] The typical genus of *Quiscalinæ*, having the bill elongated and crow-like, the tail long, graduated or rounded, and more or less keeled or boat-shaped. Several species inhabit the United States and warmer parts of America. The common crow-blackbird, or purple grackle, is *Q. purpureus* (see cut under *crow-blackbird*); the boat-tailed grackle or jackdaw of the Southern States is *Q. major* (see cut under *boat-shaped*); the fan-tailed blackbird is *Q. macrurus*, inhabiting Texas and Mexico.

quish†, *n.* An obsolete form of *cuisse*.

quishin†, *n.* An obsolete form of *cushion*.

Quisqualis (kwis-kwā'lis), *n.* [NL. (Rumphius, 1747), named in allusion to its polymorphous leaves and changing colors of flowers, or from an uncertainty at first as to its classification; < L. *quis*, who, + *qualis*, of what kind.] A genus of polypetalous plants of the order *Combretaceæ* and suborder *Combreteæ*. It is characterized by a calyx with a small deciduous border and a slender tube below, far prolonged beyond the one-celled ovary; by its five petals and ten straight stamens; and by the large, hard, dry fruit with five wings, containing a single five-furrowed oblong seed and sometimes three cotyledons instead of the usual two. The 3 or 4 species are natives of tropical Asia and Africa. They are shrubby climbers with slender branchlets, opposite leaves, and handsome spiked or racemed flowers of changeable colors, passing from white or orange to red. Several species are in cultivation under glass, especially the Rangoon creeper, *Q. Indica*, used by the Chinese as a vermifuge.

quist (kwist), *n.* Same as *queest*. [Prov. Eng.]

quistle, *n.* An obsolete or dialectal form of *whistle*.

quistron†, *n.* [ME. *quystron*, *questeroun*, < OF. *coistron*, *coestron*, *quistron*, *questron*, *coisteron*, a scullion; cf. F. *cuistre*, a college servant, a vulgar pedant.] A scullion.

This god of love of his fasoun
Was lyke no knave ne *quystron*.
Rom. of the Rose, l. 886.

quit1 (kwit), *a.* [< ME. *quit*, *quyt*, *quite*, *quyte*, *cwite* = OFries. *quit* = D. *kwijt* = MLG. *quit*, LG. *quit*, *quiet* = MHG. *quit*, *queit*, G. *quitt* = Icel. *kvittr* = Sw. *quitt* = Dan. *kvit*, < OF. *quite*, *cuite*, F. *quitte* = Pr. *quiti* = Sp. *quito* = Pg. *quite*, discharged, released, freed, < ML. *quietus*, discharged, released, freed, a particular use of L. *quietus*, at rest, quiet: see *quiet*, *a.*, of which *quit* is a doublet. Cf. *quietus*.] Discharged or released from a debt, penalty, or obligation; on even terms; absolved; free; clear.

Yef ye will, leve me, and yef ye ne will, leve me nought; for I ne leve yow nought, and so be we *quyte*.
Merlin (E. E. T. S.), ii. 168.

Tho that ben shryuen & verry contryte,
Of alle here synnes he maketh hem *quyte*.
Political Poems, etc. (ed. Furnivall), p. 118.

I promise you that when I am *quit* of these (public affairs) I will engage in no other.
B. Franklin, Autobiography, p. 317.

Double or quits, in *gambling*, said when the stake due from one person to another is either to become double or to be reduced to nothing, according to the favorable or unfavorable issue of a certain chance.—**To be quit** or **quits** (with one), to have made mutual satisfaction of claims or demands (with him); be on even terms (with him); hence, as an exclamation, *quits!* 'we are even.' [In these phrases the adjective is used as a quasi-noun in a plural form.]

I hope *to be* shortly *quit* with you for all Courtesies.
Howell, Letters, I. iv. 28.

I'll *be quit* with him for discovering me.
Sheridan, School for Scandal, iv. 3.

To get quit of. See *get*1.

quit1 (kwit), *v. t.*; pret. and pp. *quit* or *quitted*, ppr. *quitting*. [Early mod. E. also *quite* (a form still used in *requite*), and erroneously *quight*; < ME. *quiten*, *quyten* (= D. *kwijten* = MLG. *quiten*, LG. *quitten* = MHG. *quiten*, *quiten*, *quitten*, G. *quitten* = Icel. *kvitta* = Sw. *quitta* = Dan. *kvitte*), < OF. *quiter*, *cuiter*, *quitter*, F. *quitter* = Pr. Sp. Pg. *quitar* = It. *quitare*, *chitare* (ML. reflex *quitare*, *quittare*), < ML. *quietare*, pay, discharge, quit, leave, abandon, particular uses of L. *quietare*, make quiet: see *quiet*, *v.*, and cf. *quit*1, *a.* Cf. *acquit*, *requite*.] **I.** To satisfy, as a claim or debt; discharge, as an obligation or duty; make payment for or of; pay; repay; requite.

ȝut more, to make pees and *quyte* menne dettes, . . .
As Crist himself comaundeth to alle Cristene peuple.
Piers Plowman (C), xiv. 76.

I am endetted so therby,
Of gold that I have borwed trewely,
That whyl I lyve, I shal it *quyte* never.
Chaucer, Prol. to Canon's Yeoman's Tale, l. 183.

I'll *quite* his cost or else myself will die.
Greene, Alphonsus, i.

A litle mony from the law will *quite* thee,
Fee but the Sumner, & he shall not cite thee.
Times' Whistle (E. E. T. S.), p. 81.

Like doth *quit* like, and measure still for measure.
Shak., M. for M., v. 1. 416.

First, all our debts are paid; dangers of law,
Actions, decrees, judgments against us, *quitted*.
B. *Jonson*, Catiline, i. 1.

Each looks as if he came to beg,
And not to *quit* a score.
Cowper, The Yearly Distress.

2. To set free; release; absolve; acquit; exonerate.

God *quit* you in his mercy! *Shak.*, Hen. V., ii. 2. 166.

Until they that were accused to be the murtherers were *quitted* or condemned. *Sir P. Sidney*, Arcadia, v.

I must *quit*
Young Florio; Lorenzo and myself
Are only guilty of the prince's death.
Shirley, Traitor, v. 3.

3. To free, as from something harmful or oppressing; relieve; clear; liberate: with *of*.

If I *quit* you not presently, and for ever, *of* this cumber, you shall have power instantly . . . to revoke your act.
B. *Jonson*, Epicœne, v. 1.

Their judicious king
Begins at home; *quits* first his royal palace
Of flattering sycophants.
Webster, Duchess of Malfi, i. 1.

4. To meet the claims upon, or expectations entertained of; conduct; acquit: used reflexively.

Be strong, and *quit yourselves* like men. 1 Sam. iv. 9.

Samson hath *quit himself*
Like Samson. *Milton*, S. A., l. 1709.

5†. To complete; spend: said of time.

Never a worthy prince a day did *quit*
With greater hazard, and with more renown.
Daniel.

6. To depart from; go away from; leave.

Avaunt! and *quit* my sight! *Shak.*, Macbeth, iii. 4. 93.

She ought to play her part in haste, when she considers that she is suddenly to *quit* the stage, and make room for others. *Addison*, Spectator, No. 89.

7. To resign; give up; let go.

The other he held in his sight
A drawen dirk to his breast,
And said, "False carl, *quit* thy staff."
Robin Hood *and the* Beggar (Child's Ballads, V. 197).

I had never *quitted* the lady's hand all this time.
Sterne, Sentimental Journey, p. 23.

8. To forsake; abandon.

Quit thy fear;
All danger is blown over.
Fletcher (and another), Love's Cure, i. 3.

Episcopacy he bids the Queen be confident he will never *quitt*. *Milton*, Eikonoklastes, xviii.

9. In *archery*, to discharge; shoot.

Quit or discharge the arrow by allowing the string to pass smoothly over the finger-points without jerking.
Encyc. Brit., II. 377.

10. To extract; get rid of. *Sportsman's Gazetteer.*—**11.** To remove by force. *Halliwell.* [Obsolete or prov. Eng.]

He strove his combred clubbe to *quight*
Out of the earth. *Spenser*, F. Q., I. viii. 10.

12. To cease; stop; give over. [Now chiefly colloq.]

Quit! quit for shame! this will not move,
This cannot take her.
Suckling (Arber's Eng. Garner, I. 24).

Notice to quit, in *law*, notice to a tenant of real property that he must surrender possession. Where notice to quit is required, as in the case of a tenant at will or by sufferance, it should be in writing, and should state accurately the time for leaving, which, however, varies according to the nature of the tenancy and the relation of the parties.—**To quit cost**, to pay expenses; be remunerative.

Who say I care not, those I give for lost;
And to instruct them, 'twill not *quit* the *cost*.
G. *Herbert*, The Temple, the Church-Porch.

To quit scores, to make even; balance accounts.

Are you sure you do nothing to *quit scores* with them?
Sheridan, St. Patrick's Day, i. 1.

=**Syn.** 6 and 8. *Desert, Abandon*, etc. See *forsake*.

quit[2], *n.* Same as *queet*[2].

quit[3] (kwit), *n.* [Prob. imitative.] The popular name of numerous small birds of Jamaica, belonging to different genera and families. Banana-quits are species of *Certhiola*, as *C. flaveola*; grass-quits are various small sparrow-like birds, as *Spermophila olivacea*; the blue quit is a tanager, *Euphonia jamaica*; the orange quit is another tanager, *Tanagrella ruficollis*.

qui tam (kwī tam). [L.: *qui*, who; *tam*, as well, as much as, equally.] In *law*, an action on a penal statute, brought partly at the suit of the people or state and partly at that of an informer: so called from the words of the old common-law writ, "*Qui tam* pro domino rege quam pro se ipso," etc.

quitasol† (kē'tạ-sol), *n.* [Sp., < *quitar*, quit, + *sol*, sun. Cf. *parasol*.] A parasol.

Then did he incask his pate in his hat, which was so broad as it might serve him excellently for a *quitasol*.
Shelton, tr. of Don Quixote, I. i. 13. (*Richardson*, under [*incask*.)

quitch[1]† (kwich), *v.* [Also *quich, queach, queatch* (also *quinch*, simulating *winch*), more prop. *quetch*; < ME. *quicchen, quycchen, quytchen, quecchen*, < AS. *cweccan* (pret. *cweahte, cwehte*), shake, causative of *cwacian*, shake, quake: see *quake*.] **I.** *trans.* To shake; stir; move. *Layamon.*

II. *intrans.* **1.** To stir; move. *Prompt. Parv.*, p. 421; *Palsgrave.*

An huge great Lyon lay, . . . like captived thrall
With a strong yron chaine and coller bound,
That once he could not move, nor *quich* at all.
Spenser, F. Q., V. ix. 33.

2. To flinch; shrink.

He laid him down upon the wood-stack, covered his face, nor never stirred hand nor foote nor *quitched* when the fire took him. *North*, tr. of Plutarch, p. 587.

quitch[2] (kwich), *n.* [Also *quickens*; an assibilated form of *quick* (= Norw. *kvika, kviku, kvikve, kuku*, quitch-grass), < *quick*, *a*. Cf. *quitch-grass*.] Same as *quitch-grass*.

Full seldom does a man repent, or use
Both grace and will to pick the vicious *quitch*
Of blood and custom wholly out of him,
And make all clean, and plant himself afresh.
Tennyson, Geraint.

Black quitch, mostly the slender foxtail-grass, *Alopecurus agrestis*, a weedy grass with dark-purple flowers. Also *black bent, black couch-grass, black squitch*.

quitch-grass (kwich'gràs), *n.* [Also *couch-grass, cooch-grass*; assibilated form of *quick-grass*: see *quick-grass, quitch*[3].] A weed-grass somewhat resembling wheat, though smaller, formerly regarded as belonging to the wheat genus, *Triticum*, but now known as *Agropyrum repens*. Also *quick-, quack-, cutch-*, and *couch-grass*. See especially *couch-grass*.

The thoroughfares were overrun
with weed
—Docks, *quitchgrass*, loathy mallows no man plants.
Browning, Sordello, iv.

1, Flowering Plant of Quitch-grass (*Agropyrum* (*Triticum*) *repens*); 2, the spike on a larger scale; *a*, a spikelet; *b*, the flowering glume; *c*, the palet.

quitclaim (kwit'klām), *n.* [< ME. *quiteclayme*, < OF. *quiteclame*, a giving up, abandonment, release, < *quiter*, quit, + *clame*, claim: see *claim*[1].] In *law*: (*a*) A deed of release; an instrument by which some claim, right, or title to an estate is relinquished to another. (*b*) A conveyance without any covenant or warranty, expressed or implied.

Sin ye wyll do so,
Of vs shal he haue a *quite-clayme* fully.
Rom. of Partenay (E. E. T. S.), l. 1885.

quitclaim (kwit'klām), *v. t.* [Early mod. E. also *quiteclaim*; < ME. *quitclaymen, quiteclaymen, quytecleymen*, < OF. *quiteclamer, quiteclaimer*, give up, release, < *quiteclame*, a quitclaim: see *quitclaim, n.*] **1.** To quit or give up claim to; relinquish; release; acquit, as of an obligation.

The quene *quyte cleymed* the x knyghtes that were prisoners that hir knyghtes hadde her sent.
Merlin (E. E. T. S.), iii. 502.

Fram henne to Ynde that cité
Quiteclaym thai schul go fre.
Gy of Warwike, p. 310. (*Halliwell.*)

Wee haue *quite claimed*, and for vs and our heires released, our welbeloued the Citizens of Colen and their marchandise from the payment of those two shillings which they were wont to pay. *Hakluyt's Voyages*, I. 131.

2. In *law*, to quit or abandon a claim or title to by deed; convey without covenants of warranty against adverse titles or claims: as, to *quitclaim* a certain parcel of ground.

If any freke be so telle to fonde that I telle,
Lepe lyztly me to, & lach this weppen,
I *quit clayme* hit for euer, kepe hit as his auen.
Sir Gawayne and the Green Knight (E. E. T. S.), l. 293.

quitclaimance (kwit'klā"mạns), *n.* [< ME. *quite-clamance*, < OF. *quiteclamance* (ML. *quieta clamantia*), < *quiteclamer*, quitclaim: see *quitclaim*.] Same as *quitclaim*.

Of that Philip, for he suld haf grantise,
Mad Richard a *quite clamance* fro him & alle hise,
& neuer thorgh no distresse suld Clayme ther of no right.
Rob. of Brunne, tr. of Langtoft's Chron. (ed. Hearne), p. 186.

quite[1]†, *a.* An obsolete form of *quit*[1].

quite[1] (kwit), *adv.* [Early mod. E. also, erroneously, *quight*; < ME. *quite, quyte*, adv., < *quite*[1], *a*.] **1.** Completely; wholly; entirely; totally; fully; perfectly.

Generydes hym sette so vppon the hede
That his helme flew *quyte* in to the feld.
Generydes (E. E. T. S.), l. 2636.

No gate so strong, no locke so firme and fast,
But with that percing noise flew open *quite*, or brast.
Spenser, F. Q., I. viii. 4.

Shut me nightly in a charnel-house,
O'er-covered *quite* with dead men's rattling bones.
Shak., R. and J., iv. 1. 82.

Something much more to our concern,
And *quite* a scandal not to learn.
Pope, Imit. of Horace, II. vi. 146.

Books *quite* worthless are *quite* harmless.
Macaulay, Machiavelli.

2. To a considerable extent or degree; noticeably: as, *quite* warm; *quite* pretty; *quite* clever; *quite* an artist: in this sense now chiefly colloquial and American.

Billings . . . was but three months old, but, as the Americans say, was *quite* a town.
W. Shepherd, Prairie Experiences, p. 76.

The lithographer has done his work *quite*, though hardly very, well. *Science*, VII. 403.

Quite a few. See *few*.—**Quite a little**, considerable: as, *quite a little* business; *quite a little* curiosity. [Colloq.]—**Quite so**, a form of assent in conversation.

quite[1]†, *v. t.* An obsolete form of *quit*[1].

quite[2]†, *a.* An obsolete dialectal form of *white*.

Ther cam on in a *qwyte* surplisse,
And pryvely toke him be the slefe.
MS. Cantab. Ff. v. 48, f. 67. (*Halliwell.*)

quitely†, *adv.* [ME., also *quitly*; < *quite*[1], *quit*[1], *a.*, + *-ly*[2].] **1.** Completely; entirely; quite.

ȝour ancestres conquered all France *quitely*.
Rob. of Brunne, p. 115.

2. Freely; unconditionally.

Ther-fore, ȝif godes wille were i wold haue al the payne,
To mode ȝe were fro this quarrere *quitly* a-schaped.
William of Palerne (E. E. T. S.), l. 2341.

Qui tollis (kwī tol'is). [So called from the first words: L. *qui*, who; *tollis*, 2d pers. sing. pres. ind. act. of *tollere*, raise, take away.] In the *Rom. Cath.* and *Anglican liturgy*: (*a*) A part of the Gloria in Excelsis. (*b*) A musical setting of the words of the above.

Quito orange. See *orange*[1].

Qui transtulit sustinet (kwī trȧns'tụ̄-lit sus'-ti-net). [L.: *qui*, who; *transtulit*, 3d pers. sing. perf. ind. of *transferre*, transfer; *sustinet*, 3d pers. sing. pres. ind. of *sustinere*, sustain.] He who transplanted still sustains: the motto of the State of Connecticut.

quit-rent (kwit'rent), *n.* [< ME. *quiterent*; < *quit*[1] + *rent*[2].] Rent paid by the freeholders and copyholders of a manor in discharge or acquittance of other services. Also called *chief-rent*.

Consydre what seruyce longyth ther-to,
And the *quyterent* that there-of owte shalle goo.
Political Poems, etc. (ed. Furnivall), p. 24.

There was nothing before him but contests for *quitrents* with settlers resolved on governing themselves.
Bancroft, Hist. U. S., II. 355.

quits (kwits). See *quit*, *a*.

quit-shilling† (kwit'shil"ing), *n.* A gratuity given by a prisoner on his acquittal.

Were any one lucky enough to be acquitted, he had to spend a *Quit Shilling* for their delight.
J. Ashton, Social Life in Reign of Queen Anne, II. 245.

quittable (kwit'ạ-bl), *a.* [< *quit*[1] + *-able*.] Capable of being quitted or vacated.

quittal† (kwit'ạl), *n.* [< *quit*[1] + *-al*. Cf. *acquittal, requital*.] Requital; return; repayment.

As in revenge or *quittal* of such strife.
Shak., Lucrece, l. 236.

Let him unbind thee that is bound to death,
To make a *quital* for thy discontent.
Kyd, Spanish Tragedy, iii.

quittance (kwit'ans), *n.* [< ME. *quytance*, < F. *quittance* (= Sp. *quitanza* = Pg. *quitança* = It. *quitanza*), a release, receipt, < *quitter*, quit, release: see *quit*[1], *v*.] **1.** Acquittance; discharge from a debt or obligation; a receipt.

Hauing paid the custome, it behoueth to haue a *quittance* or cocket sealed and firmed.
Hakluyt's Voyages, II. 272.

Who writes himself "Armigero" in any bill, warrant, *quittance*, or obligation. *Shak.*, M. W. of W., i. 1. 10.

Gurth . . . folded the *quittance*, and put it under his cap. *Scott*, Ivanhoe, x.

2. Recompense; requital; return; repayment.

But those mine eyes saw him in bloody state,
Rendering faint *quittance*; wearied and outbreathed,
To Harry Monmouth. *Shak.*, 2 Hen. IV., i. 1. 108.

In *quittance* of your loving, honest counsel
I would not have you build an airy castle.
Shirley, Hyde Park, i. 1.

To cry quittance, to get even.

Cry quittance, madam, then, and love not him.
Marlowe, Edward II., i. 4.

Against whom [certain ladies of the bed-chamber], at their first being appointed, the French shut the doors, . . . whereas now ours have *cried quittance* with them.
Court and Times of Charles I., I. 122.

quittance† (kwit'ạns), *v. t.* [< *quittance*, *n*.] To repay; make requital or return for.

Hate calls on me to *quittance* all my ills.
Greene, Orlando Furioso.

We dread not death to *quittance* injuries.
Tourneur, Revenger's Tragedy, iii. 5.

quitter[1] (kwit'ėr), *n.* [< *quit*[1] + *-er*[1].] **1.** One who quits.—**2†.** A deliverer.

quitter[2] (kwit'ėr), *n.* [Also *quittor*, and formerly *quitture*; < ME. *quiter, quitere, quitoure, quiture, quytur, whitour*; cf. LG. *kwater, kwader*, rottenness.] **1†.** Matter flowing from a sore or wound.

Qwytur or rotunnes, putredo.
Nominale MS. (*Halliwell.*)

Still drink thou wine, and eat,
Till fair-hair'd Hecamed hath giv'n a little water-heat
To cleanse the *quitture* from thy wound.
Chapman, Iliad, xiv. 7. (*Davies.*)

2. In *farriery*, a fistulous wound upon the quarters or the heel of the coronet, caused by treads, pricks in shoeing, corns, or other injuries which produce suppuration at the coronet or within the foot.—3†. Scoria of tin.

quitter[2] (kwit'ėr), *v. i.* [< ME. *quiteren, whitouren;* from the noun.] To suppurate.

quittor, *n.* See *quitter*[2].

quitture†, *n.* An obsolete variant of *quitter*[2].

quiver[1]† (kwiv'ėr), *a.* [Also dial. *quever;* < ME. **quiver, quever, cwiver*, < AS. **cwifer*, in comp. *cwiferlice*, eagerly; cf. *quiver*[1], *v.*] Nimble; active; spry.

> There was a little *quiver* fellow, and a' would manage you his piece thus; and a' would about and about.
> *Shak.*, 2 Hen. IV., iii. 2. 301.

quiver[1] (kwiv'ėr), *v. i.* [Cf. MD. *kuyveren*, tremble, quiver, freq. form, associated with *kuyven*, tremble, quiver, and with the E. adj. *quiver*[1]: see *quiver*[1], *a.* Cf. *quaver*.] **1.** To quake; tremble; shake tremulously; shudder; shiver.

> In glaunces bright she glittered from the ground,
> Holding in hand her targe and *quiuering* spere.
> *Surrey*, Æneid, ii.

> That jewel 's mine that *quivers* in his ear,
> Mocking his master's chilness and vain fear.
> *Tourneur*, Revenger's Tragedy, i.

> Her pale lip *quivered*, and the light
> Gleamed in her moistening eyes.
> *O. W. Holmes*, Illustration of a Picture.

2. To flutter or be agitated with a tremulous motion.

> *Quivering* beams, which daz'd the wondering eye.
> *Fairfax*, tr. of Tasso.

> Willows whiten, aspens *quiver*.
> *Tennyson*, Lady of Shalott.

=**Syn.** *Quake*, etc. See *shiver*[2].

quiver[1] (kwiv'ėr), *n.* [< *quiver*[1], *v.*] The act or state of quivering; a tremulous motion; a tremor; a flutter; a shudder; a shiver.

> But Figs, all whose limbs were in a *quiver*, and whose nostrils were breathing rage, put his little bottle-holder aside.
> *Thackeray*, Vanity Fair, v.

quiver[2] (kwiv'ėr), *n.* [< ME. *quiver, quyver, quywere, quequer*, < OF. *quivre, cuivre, querre, cuerre, coivre, couvre* (ML. *cucurum* = MGr. κούκουρον), < OHG. *chohhar, chochar, chohhāri*, MHG. *kocher, kochære*, also *koger, keger*, G. *köcher*, also MHG. *koger, keger* = LG. *koker, kaker* = D. *koker* = OS. *cocar* = OFries. *koker* = AS. *cocur, cocer*, ME. *koker* = Sw. *kogger* = Dan. *kogger*, a quiver.] A case for holding arrows or crossbow-bolts. Quivers were formerly nearly as long as the arrows, so that only the feathers projected, these being covered by a piece of leather or cloth when not likely to be required. Medieval archers in war generally used the quiver on the march only, and in battle carried their arrows secured by a strap, usually with the addition of a small socket in which the points only were covered.

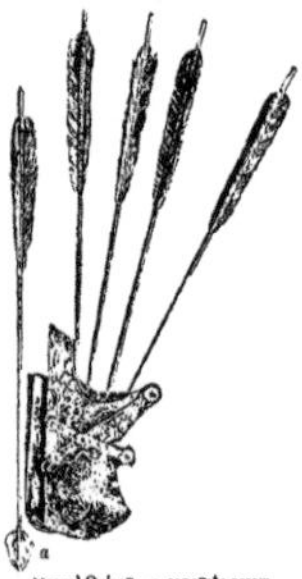

Mongol Quiver. *a*, separate arrow.

> But Mosco did vs more service then we expected, for, having shot away his *quiver* of Arrowes, he ran to the Boat for more. Quoted in *Capt. John Smith's* Works, I. 186.

> Now in her hand a slender spear she bore,
> Now a light *quiver* on her shoulders wore.
> *Addison*, tr. of Ovid's Metamorph., ii.

quivered (kwiv'ėrd), *a.* [< *quiver*[2], *n.*, + *-ed*[2].] **1.** Furnished with a quiver; wearing a quiver.

> The *quiver'd* Arabs' vagrant clan, that waits
> Insidious some rich caravan. *J. Philips*, Cercalia.

> Him, thus retreating, Artemis upbraids,
> The *quiver'd* huntress of the sylvan shades.
> *Pope*, Iliad, xxi. 546.

2. Held or covered in or as if in a quiver: said of a feathered arrow, or, as in the quotation, of a quill.

> From him whose quills stand *quiver'd* at his ear
> To him who notches sticks at Westminster.
> *Pope*, Imit. of Horace, I. i. 83.

quivering (kwiv'ėr-ing), *n.* [Verbal n. of *quiver*[1], *v.*] The act of trembling, wavering, or vibrating; a tremulous shaking.

> The *quivering* of objects seen through air rising over a heated surface is due to irregular retraction, which incessantly shifts the directions of the rays of light.
> *Tyndall*, Light and Elect., p. 43.

quiveringly (kwiv'ėr-ing-li), *adv.* In a quivering manner; with quivering.

quiverish (kwiv'ėr-ish), *a.* [< *quiver*[1] + *-ish*[1].] Tremulous; trembling.

> Then furth with a *quiverish* horror.
> *Stanihurst*, Æneid, iii. 30. (*Davies.*)

quiver-tree (kwiv'ėr-trē), *n.* A species of aloe, *Aloë dichotoma*.

qui vive (kē vēv). [F., lit. who lives? i. e. who goes there? as a noun in the phrase *être sur le qui vive*, be on the alert: *qui* (< L. *qui*), who; *vive*, 3d pers. sing. pres. subj. of *vivre*, < L. *vivere*, live: see *vivid*.] Who goes there?—the challenge of French sentries addressed to those who approach their posts.—**To be on the qui vive**, to be on the alert; be watchful, as a sentinel.

> Our new King Log we cannot complain of as too young, or too much *on the qui-vive*.
> *Miss Edgeworth*, Patronage, viii. (*Davies.*)

quixote (kwik'sọt), *v. i.* [< *Quixote* (see def. of *quixotic*) (Sp. *Quixote*, now spelled *Quijote*, pronounced kē-hō'te).] To act like Don Quixote; play the Quixote: with indefinite *it*.

> When you have got the devil in your body, and are upon your rantipole adventures, you shall *Quixote it* by yourself for Lopez. *Vanbrugh*, False Friend, v. 1.

quixotic (kwik-sot'ik), *a.* [< *Quixote* (see def.) + *-ic*.] Pertaining to or resembling Don Quixote, the hero of Cervantes's celebrated romance of that name; hence, extravagantly or absurdly romantic; striving for an unattainable or impracticable ideal; characterized by futile self-devotion; visionary.

> The project seemed rash and *quixotic*, and one that he could not countenance. *Everett*, Orations, I. 464.

> This family training, too, combined with their turn for combativeness, makes them eminently *quixotic*. They can't let anything alone which they think going wrong.
> *T. Hughes*, Tom Brown at Rugby, i. 1.

quixotically (kwik-sot'i-kạl-i), *adv.* [< *quixotic* + *-al* + *-ly*[2].] After the manner of Don Quixote; in an absurdly romantic manner.

quixotism (kwik'sọt-izm), *n.* [< *Quixote* (see *quixotic*) + *-ism*.] Quixotic extravagance in notions, actions, or undertakings; pursuit of absurdly romantic enterprises; uncalled-for or useless chivalry or magnanimity.

> Since his [Cervantes's] time, the purest impulses and the noblest purposes have perhaps been oftener stayed by the devil under the name of *Quixotism* than any other base name or false allegation.
> *Ruskin*, Lectures on Architecture and Painting, ii.

quixotry (kwik'sọt-ri), *n.* [< *Quixote* (see *quixotic*) + *-ry*.] Quixotism; visionary notions or undertakings.

> Many persons will . . . consider it as a piece of *Quixotry* in M'Intyre to give you a meeting [in a duel] while your character and circumstances are involved in such obscurity. *Scott*, Antiquary, xx.

quiz[1] (kwiz), *n.*; pl. *quizzes* (kwiz'ez). [Orig. slang; perhaps a made word, based on *question* (with which it is vaguely associated), or (as a school term) on the L. *quæso*, I ask: see *quese, quest*[1]. No reliance is to be placed on the various anecdotes which purport to give the origin of the word.] **1.** A puzzling question; something designed to puzzle one or make one ridiculous; banter; raillery.—**2.** One who quizzes.—**3.** One who or that which is obnoxious to ridicule or quizzing; a queer or ridiculous person or thing.

> Where did you get that *quiz* of a hat? it makes you look like an old witch. *Jane Austen*, Northanger Abbey, p. 33.

> 'Twas the Queen dressed her; you know what a figure she used to make of herself with her odd manner of dressing herself; but mamma said, "Now really, Princess Royal, this one time is the last, and I cannot suffer you to make such a *quiz* of yourself." . . . The word *quiz*, you may depend, was never the Queen's.
> *Mme. D'Arblay*, Diary (1797), VI. 138. (*Davies.*)

4. An oral questioning of a student or class by a teacher, conducted with the object of communicating instruction and preparing for some examination: as, the surgery *quiz;* the practice *quiz*. [Colloq.]—**5.** A collection of notes made by a student from a professor's lectures, especially when printed for the use of other students. [Colloq.]—**6.** A monocular eye-glass, with or without a handle; a quizzing-glass.

quiz[1] (kwiz), *v.*; pret. and pp. *quizzed*, ppr. *quizzing*. [< *quiz*[1], *n.*] **I.** *trans.* **1.** To puzzle; banter; make sport of by means of puzzling questions, hints, and the like; chaff.

> The zeal for *quizzing* him grew less and less
> As he grew richer. *Halleck*, Fanny.

> His [Sydney Smith's] constant *quizzing* of the national foibles and peculiarities. *Encyc. Brit.*, XXII. 177.

> I hate to be *quizzed*, and I think most people do, particularly those who indulge in the habit of *quizzing* others.
> *J. Jefferson*, Autobiog., iii.

2. To look at through or as through a quizzing-glass; peer at; scrutinize suspiciously.

> To inquire the name of an individual who was using an eye-glass, in order that he might complain . . . that the person in question was *quizzing* him.
> *Dickens*, Sketches.

3. In *med.*, to examine (a student) orally or informally, as in a quiz- or question-class. [Colloq.]

II. *intrans.* **1.** To practise bantering or chaffing; be addicted to teasing.—**2.** In *med.*, to attend oral or informal examinations, as in a quiz-class. [Colloq.]

quiz[2] (kwiz), *n.* [Perhaps a var. of *whiz*.] A toy, formerly popular, consisting of a small cylinder or wheel grooved to receive a string, by which the wheel is made to wind and unwind itself. Also called *bandalore*.

> Moore says that his earliest verses were composed on the use of the toy "called in French a bandalore, and in English a *quiz*." *N. and Q.*, 7th ser., III. 67.

quiz-class (kwiz'klȧs), *n.* In *med.*, a number of medical students enrolled in a class for the purpose of being orally questioned, either by their teacher or by one another. [Colloq.]

quiz-master (kwiz'mȧs"tėr), *n.* The teacher or leader of a quiz-class. Compare *quiz*[1], *n.*, 4.

quizzer (kwiz'ėr), *n.* One who quizzes others, or makes them the object of banter or raillery.

quizzery (kwiz'ėr-i), *n.*; pl. *quizzeries* (-iz). [< *quiz*[1] + *-ery*.] The act or practice of quizzing; a quizzical observation or comment.

> Of Mrs. Carlyle's *quizzeries*, he [Sterling] thinks she puts them forth as such evident fictions that they cannot mislead with reference to the character of others.
> *Caroline Fox*, Journal, p. 133.

quizzical (kwiz'i-kạl), *a.* [< *quiz*[1] + *-ic-al*.] Characteristic of a quiz; bantering; teasing; shy; queer: as, a *quizzical* look or remark.

> I believe you have taken such a fancy to the old *quizzical* fellow that you can't live without him.
> *Miss Edgeworth*, Belinda, ix. (*Davies.*)

quizzicality (kwiz-i-kal'i-ti), *n.* [< *quizzical* + *-ity*.] The quality of being quizzical; a quizzical look or remark.

> The poor Duke, . . . with the old *quizzicality* in his little face, declared . . . *Carlyle*, in Froude, II.

quizzically (kwiz'i-kạl-i), *adv.* In a quizzical or bantering manner; with playful slyness.

> "Look here," said one of them, *quizzically*, "Ogden, have you lived all your life in every house in Crofield and in Mertonville and everywhere?". *St. Nicholas*, XVII. 611.

quizzification (kwiz"i-fi-kā'shọn), *n.* [< *quizzify* + *-ation*.] A joke; a quiz.

> After all, my dear, the whole may be a *quizzification* of Sir Philip's—and yet he gave me such a minute description of her person! *Miss Edgeworth*, Belinda, xi. (*Davies.*)

quizzify (kwiz'i-fī), *v. t.*; pret. and pp. *quizzified*, ppr. *quizzifying*. [< *quiz*[1] + *-i-fy*.] To turn into a quiz; make odd or ridiculous.

> The caxon *quizzifies* the figure, and thereby mars the effect of what would otherwise have been a pleasing as well as appropriate design.
> *Southey*, The Doctor, cxii. (*Davies.*)

quizziness (kwiz'i-nes), *n.* Oddness; eccentricity.

> His singularities and affectation of affectation always struck me; but both these and his spirit of satire are mere *quizziness*. *Mme. D'Arblay*, Diary, VI. 187. (*Davies.*)

quizzing (kwiz'ing), *n.* [Verbal n. of *quiz*[1], *v.*] Banter; raillery; teasing.

quizzing-glass (kwiz'ing-glȧs), *n.* A single eye-glass, or monocle; especially, one that is held to the eye by the muscles of the face.

quo†, *pron.* An obsolete form of *who*.

quo'. A clipped form of *quoth*.

quoad hoc (kwō'ad hok). [L.: *quoad*, so far as (< *quod*, what, as, + *ad*, to); *hoc*, neut. of *hic*, this: see *he*[1].] To this extent; as far as this.

quoad omnia (kwō'ad om'ni-ạ). [L.: *quoad*, so far as; *omnia*, neut. pl. of *omnis*, all.] As regards or in respect of all things: as, a *quoad omnia* parish. See *parish*.

quoad sacra (kwō'ad sā'krạ). [L.: *quoad*, so far as; *sacra*, neut. pl. of *sacer*, sacred, consecrated.] In respect of or as far as concerns sacred matters: as, a *quoad sacra* parish. See *parish*.

quob, *v.* and *n.* See *quab*[1].

quod[1]†. An obsolete form of *quoth*.

quod[2] (kwod), *n.* and *v.* See *quad*[2], 2.

quoddle[1], *v. t.* An obsolete or dialectal form of *coddle*[1].

It seemes it is the fashion with you to sugar your papers with Carnation phrases, and spangle your speeches with new *quodled* words. *N. Ward*, Simple Cobler, p. 89.

quoddle[2] (kwod'l), *v. i.*; pret. and pp. *quoddled*, ppr. *quoddling*. [Cf. *waddle* (?).] To paddle.

You will presently see the young eagle mounting into the air, the duck *quoddling* in a pool. *Bp. Stillingfleet*, Origines Sacræ, iii. 1, § 16.

quoddy (kwod'i), *n.*; pl. *quoddies* (-iz). [Abbr. of *Passamaquoddy*.] A kind of large herring found in Passamaquoddy Bay.

quodlibet (kwod'li-bet), *n.* [= F. *quolibet*, a joke, pun; < ML. *quodlibetum*, a quodlibet, < L. *quodlibet* (*quidlibet*), what you please, anything you please, anything at all (neut. of *quilibet*, any one you please, any one at all), < *quod*, what, neut. of *qui*, who, which, + *libet*, impers., it pleases. Cf. *quillet*[2].] 1. A scholastic argumentation upon a subject chosen at will, but almost always theological. These are generally the most elaborate and subtle of the works of the scholastic doctors. There are about a dozen printed books of quodlibets, all written between 1250 and 1350.

These are your *quodlibets*, but no learning, brother. *Fletcher (and another)*, Elder Brother, ii. 1.

He who, reading on the Heart
(When all his *Quodlibets* of Art
Could not expound its Pulse and Heat),
Swore he had never felt it beat.
Prior, Alma, iii.

2. In *music*: (*a*) A fantasia or potpourri. (*b*) A fanciful or humorous harmonic combination of two or more well-known melodies: sometimes equivalent to a *Dutch concert*.

quodlibetal (kwod'li-bet-al), *a.* [< ML. *quodlibetalis*; as *quodlibet* + *-al*.] Consisting of quodlibets.—**Quodlibetal question.** Same as *quodlibet*.

quodlibetarian (kwod″li-be-tā'ri-an), *n.* [< ML. *quodlibetarius* (< *quodlibetum*, a quodlibet: see *quodlibet*) + *-an*.] One given to quodlibets or argumentative subtleties.

quodlibetic (kwod-li-bet'ik), *a.* [< ML. *quodlibeticus*, < *quodlibetum*, a quodlibet: see *quodlibet*.] 1. Not restrained to a particular subject; moved or discussed at pleasure for curiosity or entertainment; pertaining to quodlibets.

To speak with the schools, it is of *quodlibetic* application, ranging from least to greatest. *Sir W. Hamilton.*

2. Given to niceties and subtle points.

quodlibetical (kwod-li-bet'i-kal), *a.* [< *quodlibetic* + *-al*.] Same as *quodlibetal*. *W. Watson*, A Decachordon of Ten *Quodlibetical* Questions.

quodlibetically (kwod-li-bet'i-kal-i), *adv.* In a quodlibetical manner; at pleasure; for curiosity; so as to be debated for entertainment.

Many positions seem *quodlibetically* constituted, and, like a Delphian blade, will cut on both sides. *Sir T. Browne*, Christ. Mor., ii. § 3.

quodling†, **quodlin**†, *n.* See *codling*[1], 2.

Dol. A fine young *quodling*.
Face. O,
My lawyer's clerk, I lighted on last night.
B. Jonson, Alchemist, i. 1.

quod permittat (kwod pėr-mit'at). [So called from these words in the writ: L. *quod*, which, neut. of *qui*, who; *permittat*, 3d pers. sing. pres. subj. of *permittere*, permit: see *permit*[1].] In *Eng. law*, a writ (requiring defendant to permit plaintiff to, etc.) used to prevent interference with the exercise of a right, such as the enjoyment of common of pasture, or the abatement of a nuisance.

quod vide (kwod vī'dē). [L.: *quod*, which, neut. of *qui*, who; *vide*, impv. sing. of *videre*, see.] Which see: common, in the abbreviated form *q. v.*, after a dictionary-word, book-title and page, or the like, to which the reader is thus referred for further information.

quog (kwog), *n.* Same as *quahog*.

quohog, *n.* Same as *quahog*.

quoich, *n.* Same as *quaigh*.

quoif†, *n.* An obsolete spelling of *coif*.

quoiffure†, *n.* An obsolete spelling of *coiffure*.

quoil†, *n.* An obsolete spelling of *coil*[1].

quoin (koin), *n.* [< F. *coin*, an angle, a corner, a wedge: see *coin*[1].] 1. An external solid angle; specifically, in *arch.* and *masonry*, the external angle of a building. The word is generally applied to the separate stones or blocks of which the angle is formed; when these project beyond the general surface of the walls, and have their corners chamfered off, they are called *rustic quoins* or *bossage*.

2. A wedge-like piece of stone, wood, metal, or other material, used for various purposes. (*a*) In *masonry*, a wedge to support and steady a stone. (*b*) In *printing*, a short blunt wedge used by printers to secure the types in a chase or on a galley. Mechanical quoins are made of iron in many forms, pressure being applied by means of the screw or by combined wedges.

Small wedges, called *quoins*, are inserted and driven forward by a mallet and a shooting-stick, so that they gradually exert increasing pressure upon the type. *Encyc. Brit.*, XXIII. 700.

(*c*) In *gem-cutting*, any one of the four facets on the crown of a brilliant; also, any one of the four facets on the pavilion or base. These facets divide each portion of the brilliant into four parts. Also called *lozenge*. See cut under *brilliant*. (*d*) *Naut.*, a wedge placed beneath a cask when stowed on shipboard, to prevent it from rolling. (*e*) In *gun.*, a wooden wedge used to hold a gun at a desired elevation.—**Cantick-quoin.** Same as *canting-coin*.

quoin (koin), *v. t.* [< *quoin*, *n.*] To wedge, steady, or raise with quoins, as a stone in building a wall, the types in a chase, etc.: generally with *up*. See *quoin*, *n.*, 2.

"They [flat stones] are exactly what I want for my wall—just the thing for *quoining up*." What Mr. Grey meant by *quoining up* was filling in the spaces under the large stones when they did not fit exactly to those below them, and thus wedging them up to their proper level. *Jacob Abbott*, Wallace, vii.

quoin-post (koin'pōst), *n.* In *hydraul. engin.*, the heel-post of a lock-gate. *E. H. Knight.*

quoit (kwoit), *v.* [Also *coit*; < ME. *coiten*, *coyten*, < OF. *coiter*, *coitier*, *quoitier*, *cuiter*, press, push, hasten, incite, prob. < L. *coactare*, force, freq. of *cogere*, compel: see *cogent*. Cf. *quat*[1]; cf. also *quail*[2], ult. < L. *coagulare*.] **I.** *trans.* To throw as a quoit; throw.

Quoit him down, Bardolph. *Shak.*, 2 Hen. IV., ii. 4. 206.

Hundreds of tarred and burning hoops were skilfully *quoited* around the necks of the soldiers, who struggled in vain to extricate themselves from these fiery ruffs. *Motley*, Dutch Republic, II. 468.

II. *intrans.* To throw quoits; play at quoits.

For Python slain, he Pythian games decreed,
Where noble youths for mastership should strive,
To *quoit*, to run, and steeds and chariots drive.
Dryden, tr. of Ovid's Metamorph., i. 600.

quoit (kwoit), *n.* [Also *coit*, also dial. *quait*; < ME. *coite*, *coyte*; cf. *quoit*, *v.*] 1. A flattish ring of iron, used in playing a kind of game. It is generally from 8½ to 9½ inches in external diameter, and between 1 and 2 inches in breadth, convex on the upper side and slightly concave on the under side, so that the outer edge curves downward, and is sharp enough to cut into soft ground.

Quoit.
a, central opening; *b*, marginal edge, which, when the quoit is skilfully pitched, cuts into the earth; *c*, thumb-notch, by which the thrower is enabled to give the quoit a spinning motion on an axis at right angles with the marginal edge.

He willed vs also himselfe to sit downe before him the distance of a *quoit's* cast from his tent. *Hakluyt's Voyages*, I. 355.

'Tis not thine to hurl the distant dart,
The *quoit* to toss, the pond'rous mace to wield,
Or urge the race, or wrestle on the field.
Pope, Iliad, xxiii. 713.

Formerly in the country the rustics, not having the round perforated *quoits* to play with, used horse-shoes, and in many places the *quoit* itself, to this day, is called a shoe. *Strutt*, Sports and Pastimes, p. 142.

2. *pl.* The game played with such rings. Two pins, called *hobs*, are driven part of their length into the ground some distance apart; and the players, who are divided into two sides, stand beside one hob, and in regular succession throw their quoits (of which each player has two) as near the other hob as they can. The side which has the quoit nearest the hob counts a point toward game, or, if the quoit is thrown so as to surround the hob, it counts two. The game only slightly resembles the ancient exercise of throwing the discus, which has, however, been often translated by this English word.

A' plays at *quoits* well. *Shak.*, 2 Hen. IV., ii. 4. 266.

The game of *quoits*, or coits, . . . is more moderate, because this exercise does not depend so much upon superior strength as upon superior skill. *Strutt*, Sports and Pastimes, p. 141.

3. A quoit-shaped implement used as a weapon of war; a discus. Those used by the Sikhs are of polished steel with sharp edges, and are sometimes richly ornamented with damascening or the like.

quoivest, *n.* Plural of *quoif*, an old form of *coif*.

quo jure (kwō jö'rē). [So called from these words in the writ: L. *quo*, by what, abl. sing. neut. of *quis*, who, which, what; *jure*, abl. sing. of *jus*, law, right.] In *law*, a writ which formerly lay for him who had land wherein another challenged common of pasture time out of mind: it was to compel him to show by what title he challenged it. *Wharton.*

quok†, **quoket**†. Obsolete strong preterits of *quake*.

quoll (kwol), *n.* [Australian.] An Australian marsupial mammal, *Dasyurus macrurus*.

quo minus (kwō mī'nus). [So called from these words in the writ: L. *quo*, by which, abl. sing. of *quod*, which, neut. of *qui*, who; *minus*, less: see *minus*.] An old English writ, used in a suit complaining of a grievance which consisted in diminishing plaintiff's resources, as for instance, waste committed by defendant on land from which plaintiff had a right to take wood or hay. The Court of Exchequer, whose original jurisdiction related to the Treasury, acquired its jurisdiction between private suitors by allowing a plaintiff by the use of this writ to allege that, by reason of the defendant's not paying the debt sued for, the plaintiff was less able (quo minus) to discharge his obligations to the crown.

quondam (kwon'dam), *a.* and *n.* [L., formerly, < *quom*, *cum*, when, + *-dam*, a demonstr. particle.] **I.** *a.* Having been formerly; former: as, one's *quondam* friend; a *quondam* schoolmaster.

This is the *quondam* king. *Shak.*, 3 Hen. VI., iii. 1. 23.

Farewell, my hopes! my anchor now is broken:
Farewell, my *quondam* joys, of which no token
Is now remaining.
Beau. and Fl., Woman-Hater, iii. 2.

II. *n.* A person formerly in an office; a person ejected from an office or a position.

Make them *quondams*, out with them, cast them out of their office. *Latimer*, 4th Sermon bef. Edw. VI., 1549.

As yet there was never learned man, or any scholar or other, that visited us since we came into Bocardo, which now in Oxford may be called a college of *quondams*. *Bp. Ridley*, in Bradford's Letters (Parker Soc., 1853), II. 84.

quondamship† (kwon'dam-ship), *n.* [< *quondam* + *-ship*.] The state of being a quondam.

As for my *quondamship*, I thank God that he gave me the grace to come by it by so honest a means. *Latimer*, 4th Sermon bef. Edw. VI., 1549.

Quoniam (kwō'ni-am), *n.* [So called from the initial word in the L. version: L. *quoniam*, since now, although, < *quom*, *cum*, when, since, + *jam*, now.] 1. In the *Rom. Cath. liturgy*: (*a*) A part of the Gloria. (*b*) A musical setting of the words of the above.—2†. [*l. c.*] A sort of drinking-cup.

Out of can, *quoniam*, or jourdan. *Healy*, Disc. of New World, p. 69. (*Nares.*)

quont, *n.* See *quant*.

quook†, **quooke**†. Obsolete preterits and past participles of *quake*.

quorl†, *v.* A Middle English form of *whirl*.

quorum (kwō'rum), *n.* [Formerly also *corum*; < L. *quorum*, 'of whom,' gen. pl. of *qui*, who: see *who*. In commissions, etc., written in Latin, it was common, after mentioning certain persons generally, to specify one or more as always to be included, in such phrases as *quorum unum A. B. esse volumus* (of whom we will that A. B. be one); such persons as were to be in all cases necessary therefore constituted a quorum.] 1. In England, those justices of the peace whose presence is necessary to constitute a bench. Among the justices of the peace it was formerly customary to name some eminent for knowledge and prudence to be of the quorum; but the distinction is now practically obsolete, and all justices are generally "of the quorum."

He that will not cry "amen" to this, let him live sober, seem wise, and die o' the *corum*. *Beau. and Fl.*, Scornful Lady, i. 2.

I must not omit that Sir Roger is a justice of the *quorum*. *Addison*, Spectator, No. 2.

2. The number of members of any constituted body of persons whose presence at or participation in a meeting is required to render its proceedings valid, or to enable it to transact business legally. If no special rule exists, a majority of the members is a quorum; but in a body of considerable size the quorum may by rule be much less than a majority, or in a smaller one much more. Forty members constitute a quorum or "house" in the British House of Commons.

In such cases, two thirds of the whole number of Senators are necessary to form a *quorum*. *Calhoun*, Works, I. 175.

Others [regulations] prescribe rules for the removal of unworthy members, and guard against the usurpation of individuals by fixing a *quorum*. *Stubbs*, Const. Hist., § 367.

3†. Requisite materials.

Here the Dutchmen found fullers' earth, a precious treasure, whereof England hath, if not more, better than all Christendom besides; a great commodity of the *quorum* to the making of good cloath. *Fuller*, Ch. Hist., III. ix. 12. (*Davies.*)

Quorum of Twelve, or **Quorum**, a name given collectively to the twelve apostles in the Mormon Church. See *Mormon*[2].

quost†, *n.* An obsolete spelling of *coast*.

quota (kwō'tạ̈), *n.* [< It. *quota*, a share, < L. *quota* (sc. *pars*), fem. of *quotus*, of what number, how many, < *quot*, how many, as many as, akin to *qui*.] A proportional part or share; share or proportion assigned to each; any required or proportionate single contribution to a total sum, number, or quantity.

They never once furnished their *quota* either of ships or men. *Swift*, Conduct of the Allies.

The power of raising armies, by the most obvious construction of the articles of the confederation, is merely a power of making requisitions upon the states for *quotas* of men. *A. Hamilton*, Federalist, No. 22.

quotability (kwō-tạ-bil'į-ti), *n.* [< *quotable* + *-ity* (see *-bility*).] Capability of or fitness for being quoted; quotable quality.

It is the prosaicism of these two writers [Cowper and Moore] to which is owing their especial *quotability*.
Poe, Marginalia, xxviii. (*Davies.*)

quotable (kwō'tạ-bl), *a.* [< *quote* + *-able.*] Capable of or suitable for being quoted or cited.

Mere vividness of expression, such as makes *quotable* passages, comes of the complete surrender of self to the impression, whether spiritual or sensual, of the moment.
Lowell, Among my Books, 1st ser., p. 176.

quotableness (kwō'tạ-bl-nes), *n.* Quotability. *Athenæum*, Nov. 24, 1888, p. 693.

quotably (kwō'tạ-bli), *adv.* So as to be quoted; in a quotable manner.

All qualities of round coal prices are weak, though not *quotably* lower. *The Engineer*, LXV. 513.

quotation (kwọ-tā'shọn), *n.* [< *quote* + *-ation.*] 1. The act of quoting or citing.

Classical *quotation* is the parole of literary men all over the world. *Johnson*, in Boswell, an. 1781.

Emerson . . . believed in *quotation*, and borrowed from everybody, . . . not in any stealthy or shame-faced way, but proudly. *O. W. Holmes*, Emerson, xii.

2. That which is quoted; an expression, a statement, or a passage cited or repeated as the utterance of some other speaker or writer; a citation.

When the *quotation* is not only apt, but has in it a term of wit or satire, it is still the better qualified for a medal, as it has a double capacity of pleasing.
Addison, Ancient Medals, iii.

3. In *com.*, the current price of commodities or stocks, published in prices-current, etc.

A *quotation* of price such as appears in a daily price list is, if there has been much fluctuation, only a very rough guide to the actual rates of exchange that have been the basis of the successive bargains making up the day's business. *Encyc. Brit.*, XXII. 465.

4. [Abbr. of *quotation-quadrat.*] In *printing*, a large hollow quadrat, usually of the size 3 × 4 picas, made for the larger blanks in printed matter. [U. S.] = **Syn. 2.** Extract. See *quote*.

quotational (kwọ-tā'shọn-ạl), *a.* [< *quotation* + *-al.*] Of or pertaining to quotations; as a quotation.

quotationist (kwọ-tā'shọn-ist), *n.* [< *quotation* + *-ist.*] One who makes quotations.

Considered not altogether by the narrow intellectuals of *quotationists* and common places.
Milton, Divorce, To the Parlament.

quotation-mark (kwọ-tā'shọn-märk), *n.* One of the marks used to note the beginning and the end of a quotation. In English, quotation-marks generally consist of two inverted commas at the beginning and two apostrophes at the end of a quotation; but a single comma and a single apostrophe are also used, especially in Great Britain. In the former case the marking of a quotation within a quotation is single; in the latter, properly double. Single quotation-marks are often used, as in this work, to mark a translation. Quotation-marks for printing in French, German, etc., are types specially cut and cast for this use; and in some fonts for printing in English characters have been made for the beginning of quotations corresponding in reverse to the apostrophes at the end.

quote (kwōt), *v.*; pret. and pp. *quoted*, ppr. *quoting*. [Formerly also *cote*; < OF. *quoter*, *coter*, F. *coter*, letter, number, quote (in commercial use), < ML. *quotare*, mark off into chapters and verses, give a reference, < L. *quotus*, of what number, how many, < *quot*, as many as.] **I.** *trans.* **1†.** To note down; set down in writing; hence, in general, to note; mark; observe.

A fellow by the hand of nature mark'd,
Quoted and sign'd to do a deed of shame.
Shak., K. John, iv. 2. 222.

I am sorry that with better heed and judgement
I had not *quoted* him. *Shak.*, Hamlet, ii. 1. 112.

Wherfore I was desirous to see it again, and to read it with more deliberation, and, being sent to me a second time, it was thus *quoted* in the margent as ye see.
Foxe, Martyrs, p. 1110, an. 1543.

2. To adduce from some author or speaker; cite, as a passage from some author or a saying of some speaker; name, repeat, or adduce as the utterance of some other person, or by way of authority or illustration; also, to cite the words of: as, to *quote* a passage from Homer; to *quote* Shakspere or one of his plays; to *quote* chapter and verse.

He *quoted* texts right upon our Saviour, though he expounded them wrong. *Atterbury.*

As long as our people *quote* English standards they dwarf their own proportions. *Emerson*, Conduct of Life.

3. In *writing* or *printing*, to inclose within quotation-marks; distinguish as a quotation or as quoted matter by marking: as, the dialogue in old books is not *quoted*.—4. In *com.*, to name, as the price of stocks, produce, etc.; name the current price of.—**Quoted matter**, in *printing*, composed types that are inclosed by quotation-marks: thus, " ". = **Syn. 2.** *Quote, Cite, Adduce, Recite*. When we *quote* or *recite*, we repeat the exact words; when we *cite* or *adduce*, we may only refer to the passage without quoting it, or we may give the substance of the passage. We may *quote* a thing for the pleasure that we take in it or for any other reason: as, to *quote* a saying of Izaak Walton's. We *cite* or *adduce* a thing in proof of some assertion or doctrine: as, to *cite* an authority in court; to *adduce* confirmatory examples. *Adduce*, besides being broader in its use, is stronger than *cite*, as to urge in proof. *Recite*, in this connection, applies to the quoting of a passage of some length: as, to *recite* a law; to *recite* the conversation of Lorenzo and Jessica at Belmont. It generally implies that the passage is given orally from memory, but not necessarily, as a petition *recites*, etc.; the others may be freely used of that which is read aloud or only written.

II. *intrans.* To cite the words of another; make a quotation.

quote (kwōt), *n.* [In def. 1, < OF. *quote*; in other senses < *quote*, *v.*] **1†.** A note upon an author.

O were thy margents cliffes of itching lust,
Or *quotes* to chalke out men the way to sin,
Then were there hope that multitudes wold thrust
To buy thee. *C. Tourneur*, Transformed Metamorphosis, Author to his Booke.

2. A quotation, or the marking of a quotation.

This column of "Local Notes and Queries" . . . has been succeeded by a column entitled "Notes and *Quotes*."
N. and Q., 7th ser., VII. 505.

3. A quotation-mark: usually in the plural. [Colloq.]—**4†.** A quotient. [Rare.]

quoteless (kwōt'les), *a.* [< *quote* + *-less.*] Not capable or worthy of being quoted; unquotable. *Wright.*

quoter (kwō'tėr), *n.* One who quotes or cites the words of an author or a speaker.

Next to the originator of a good sentence is the first *quoter* of it. *Emerson*, Quotation and Originality.

quoteworthy (kwōt'wėr"ᴛʜi), *a.* Deserving of quotation. [Rare.]

In Horne's "Spirit of the Age" are some *quoteworthy* remarks. *The New Mirror* (N. Y., 1843), III.

quoth (kwōth). Preterit of *quethe*. [Obsolete or archaic.]

"Good morrow, fool," *quoth* I. "No, sir," *quoth* he,
"Call me not fool till heaven hath sent me fortune."
Shak., As you Like it, ii. 7. 18.

Quoth the raven, "Nevermore." *Poe*, The Raven.

quotha (kwō'thạ̈), *interj.* [For *quoth a*, and that for *quoth he*, *a* being a corruption of *he*: see *a*6.] Forsooth! indeed! originally a parenthetical phrase used in repeating the words of another with more or less contempt or disdain.

Here are ye clavering about the Duke of Argyle, and this man Martingale gaun to break on our hands, and lose us gude sixty pounds—I wonder what duke will pay that, *quotha*. *Scott*, Heart of Mid-Lothian, xxiv.

quotidian (kwọ-tid'i-ạn), *a.* and *n.* [< ME. *cotidien*, < OF. *quotidien*, *cotidien*, F. *quotidien* = Pr. *cotidian*, *cotedian* = Sp. *cotidiano* = Pg. It. *quotidiano*, < L. *quotidianus*, *cottidianus*, daily, < *quotidie*, *cottidie*, *cotidie*, daily, < *quot*, as many as, + *dies*, day: see *dial.*] **I.** *a.* Daily; occurring or returning daily: as, a *quotidian* fever.

Common and *quotidian* infirmities that so necessarily attend me. *Sir T. Browne*, Religio Medici, ii. 7.

Like the human body, with a *quotidian* life, a periodical recurrence of ebbing and flowing tides.
Gladstone, Might of Right, p. 173.

Double quotidian fever. See *fever*1.

II. *n.* **1.** Something that returns or is expected every day; specifically, in *med.*, a fever whose paroxysms return every day.

He seems to have the *quotidian* of love upon him.
Shak., As you Like it, iii. 2. 383.

A disposition which to his he finds will never cement, a *quotidian* of sorrow and discontent in his house.
Milton, Divorce, ii. 16.

2†. A cleric or church officer who does daily duty.—**3†.** Payment given for such duty.

quotient (kwō'shẹnt), *n.* [= F. *quotient*; with accom. term. *-ent*, < L. *quoties*, *quotiens*, how often, how many times, < *quot*, how many, as many as.] In *math.*, the result of the process of division; the number of times one quantity or number is contained in another. See *division*, 2.—**Differential quotient.** Same as *differential coefficient* (which see, under *coefficient*).

quotiety (kwọ-ti'e-ti), *n.* [< L. *quoties*, how often (see *quotient*) + *-e-ty.*] The proportionate frequency of an event.

quotity (kwot'ị-ti), *n.* [< L. *quot*, how many, + *-i-ty.*] **1.** The number of individuals in a collection.—**2.** A collection considered as containing a number of individuals. *Carlyle*, French Rev., I. ii.

quotquean†, *n.* A corruption of *cotquean*.

Don *Quot-quean*, Don Spinster! wear a petticoat still, and put on your smock a' Monday.
Fletcher (*and another*), Love's Cure, ii. 2.

quotum (kwō'tum), *n.* [L., neut. of *quotus*, of what number, how many, < *quot*, how many, as many as.] A quota; a share; a proportion. [Rare.]

The number of names which are really formed by an imitation of sound dwindles down to a very small *quotum* if cross-examined by the comparative philologist.
Max Müller.

quo warranto (kwō wo-ran'tō). [So called from these words in the writ: L. *quo*, by what (abl. sing. neut. of *quis*, who, which, what); ML. *warranto*, abl. of *warrantum*, warrant: see *warrant.*] In *law*, a writ calling upon a person or body of persons to show by what warrant they exercise a public office, privilege, franchise, or liberty. It is the remedy for usurpation of office or of corporate franchises, etc.—**Information or action in the nature of a quo warranto**, a statement of complaint by a public prosecutor or complainant to the court: now used in many jurisdictions in lieu of the ancient writ of *quo warranto*.

Quran, *n.* Same as *Koran*.

quy†, *n.* Same as *quey*. *Halliwell.*

quyrboille†, **quyrboilly†**. Obsolete forms of *cuir-bouilli*.

The Gentyles han schorte Speres and large, and fulle trenchant on that o syde: and thei han Plates and Helmes made of *Quyrboylle*, and hire Hors covertoures of the same. *Mandeville*, Travels, p. 251.

His jambeux were of *quyrboilly*.
Chaucer, Sir Thopas, l. 164.

quyssewes†, *n.* A Middle English form of *cuishes*.

quysshen†, *n.* An obsolete form of *cushion*.

And doun she sette hire by hym on a stone
Of jasper, on a *quysshen* [var. (16th century) *quishin*] gold ybette. *Chaucer*, Troilus, ii. 1229.

q. v. An abbreviation (*a*) of the Latin phrase *quantum vis*, 'as much as you will'; (*b*) of *quod vide*, 'which see.'

qw. See *qu*.

qwelet†, *n.* An obsolete form of *wheel*.

qweseyn†, *n.* An obsolete form of *cushion*.

qwether†, *adv.* An obsolete dialectal variant of *whether*.

qwh-. See *wh-*.

qwhat†, *pron.* A Middle English dialectal form of *what*.

qwiche†, *pron.* An obsolete dialectal form of *which*.

qy. An abbreviation of *query*.

1. The eighteenth letter and fourteenth consonant in the English alphabet, representing a character having a like position and value in the alphabets from which the English is derived—the Latin, Greek, and Phenician. Specimens of its early forms (as in the case of the other letters: see especially *A*) are given below:

Egyptian. Hieroglyphic. Hieratic. Phenician. Early Greek and Latin.

The tag below the curve by which the English (and the Latin) R differs from the later Greek form P was added to the latter in order to distinguish it from the *p*-sign after this had assumed its present form; the addition was first made on Greek ground, but was abandoned there when the distinction of the *p*- and *r*-signs had become established in another way. The value of the character has always been essentially the same; it represents a continuous sonant utterance made between the tip of the tongue and the roof of the mouth, at a point more or less removed backward from the upper front teeth. The sound is so resonant and continuable as to be nearly akin with the vowels; and it is, in fact, used as a vowel in certain languages, as Sanskrit and some of the Slavic dialects: in normal English pronunciation, however, it never has that value. By its mode of production it is nearly akin with *l*, and r and *l* are to a large extent interchangeable with one another in linguistic history. It is often classed as a "liquid," along with *l*, *m*, *n*; less often, but more accurately, as a semivowel, with *l*, *y*, *w*. It also, on no small scale, answers as corresponding sonant (in languages that have no *z*) to *s* as surd, and comes from *s* under sonantizing influences: so in Sanskrit, in Latin (as *ara* from *asa*), and in Germanic (as in our *were*, plural of *was*). In Anglo-Saxon the initial r of many words was aspirated (that is, pronounced with an *h* before it), as *hring* (our *ring*); but the aspiration was long ago abandoned, both in pronunciation and in spelling. In Greek initial *r* was always thus aspirated, and the combination was transliterated in Latin by *rh* instead of *hr*: hence the frequency of *rh* in our words of Greek derivation. Moreover, such an r, when by inflection or composition made medial, became *rrh*, and double r was in general viewed as *rrh*: whence that spelling in many of our words (for example, *diarrhea*, *hemorrhage*, *catarrh*, etc.): in recent scientific words and names taken from Greek, the Greek rule and Latin practice as regards the doubling and aspiration of the r are often neglected. The mode of production of the *r*-sound itself varies greatly in different languages and dialects. Normally its utterance is combined with a distinct trilling or vibration of the tip of the tongue, in various degrees (the sound is thence often called the "dog's letter," *littera canina*). But in ordinary English pronunciation this vibration is either extremely slight, or, more commonly, altogether wanting; in fact, the tip of the tongue is drawn too far back into the dome of the palate to admit of vibration; the English *r* is a smooth r. But further, in many localities, even among the most cultivated speakers, no r is ever really pronounced at all unless followed (in the same word, or, if final, in the word following) by a vowel (for example, in *are*, *farther*, pronounced *ah*, *father*): it either simply disappears, or, as after most long vowels, is replaced by a bit of neutral-vowel sound, of ă or ė; and after such a long vowel, if it comes to be pronounced by the addition of a vowel, it retains the same neutral-vowel sound as transition-sound (for example, in *faring*, *fearing*, *pouring*, *during*, *firing*, *souring*: the pronunciation is indicated in this work by retaining the r in the same syllable with the long vowel: thus, fãr'ing, fēr'ing, etc.). An *r* has a stronger and more frequent influence upon the character of the preceding vowel than any other consonant; hence the reduction to similarity of the vowel-sounds in such words as *pert*, *dirt*, *curt*, *earn*, *myrrh*. If all our *r*'s that are written are pronounced, the sound is more common than any other in English utterance (over seven per cent.); the instances of occurrence before a vowel, and so of universal pronunciation, are only half as frequent. There are localities where the normal vibration of the tip of the tongue is replaced by one of the uvula, making a guttural trill, which is still more entitled to the name of "dog's letter" than is the ordinary r: such are considerable parts of France and Germany; the sound appears to occur only sporadically in English pronunciation.

2. As a medieval Roman numeral, 80, and with a line over it (R̄), 80,000.—3. As an abbreviation: (*a*) Of *Rex* or *Regina*, as in George *R.*, Victoria *R.* (*b*) Of *Royal*, as in *R. N.* for *Royal Navy*, *R. A.* for *Royal Academy* or *Academician*, or for *Royal Arch* (in freemasonry). (*c*) Prefixed to a medical prescription (℞), of *recipe*, take. (*d*) [*l. c.*] *Naut.*: (1) In a ship's log-book, of *rain*. (2) When placed against a man's name in the paymaster's book, of *run away*. (*e*) Of *right* (right-hand), as in *R. A.* for *right ascension*, *R. II. E.* for *right second entrance* (on the stage of a theater). (*f*) In *math.*, r is generally a radius vector of coördinates, R the radius of a circle, ρ a radius of curvature.—**The three R's**, reading, writing, and arithmetic: a humorous term. It originated with Sir William Curtis (1752–1829), an eminent but illiterate alderman and lord mayor of London, who, on being asked to give a toast, said, "I will give you the three R's, Riting, Reading, and Rithmetic."

> Parochial education in Scotland had never been confined to *the three R's*. *Times* (London).

ra†, *n.* An obsolete form of roe[1]. *Chaucer.*

Ra (rä), *n.* [Egypt.] In *Egypt. mythol.*, the sovereign sun-god of the Memphite system, the chief Egyptian personification of the Supreme Being. He was often confounded to some extent with the Theban Amen. In art he was typically represented as a hawk-headed man bearing on his head the solar disk and the royal uræus.

R. A. An abbreviation of (*a*) *Royal Academy*; (*b*) *Royal Academician*; (c) *Royal Arch*; (*d*) *right ascension*.

ra-. [See *re-*.] A prefix in some words of French origin, ultimately from *re-* and *ad-*. See *rabate*, *rabbet*, *rapport*, etc.

raad, *n.* [< Ar. *ra'd*, thunder.] A nematognathous fish, *Malapterurus electricus*, inhabiting the Nile; the electric catfish. It reaches a length of 3 to 4 feet, and gives a sharp galvanic shock on being touched.

rab[1] (rab), *n.* [Origin obscure.] A kind of loam; a coarse hard substance for mending roads. *Halliwell.* [Cornwall, Eng.]

rab[2]† (rab), *n.* [An abbr. of *rabbit*[2].] Same as *rabbit*[2], 1.

rab[3] (rab), *n.* [Heb.: see *rabbi*.] A title of respect given to Jewish doctors or expounders of the law. See *rabbi*.

rabanna (ra-ban'ạ̈), *n.* [Native name.] Cloth or matting made from the raffia and perhaps other fibers: an article of export from Madagascar to Mauritius. See *raffia*.

rabat (ra-bat'; F. pron. ra-bä'), *n.* [F., < *rabat*, a turned-down collar, a band or ruff, OF. also a plasterers' beater, a penthouse, eaves, also a beating down, suppression, < *rabattre*, beat down, bring down: see *rabate*. Cf. *rabato*.] 1. A kind of linen collar worn by some ecclesiastics, falling down upon the chest and leaving the neck exposed.—2. A polishing-material made from unglazed pottery which has failed in baking, used by marble-workers, etc.

rabate (ra-bāt'), *v. t.*; pret. and pp. *rabated*, ppr. *rabating*. [Early mod. E. also *rabbate*; < F. *rabattre*, OF. *rabatre*, beat down, bring down, < *re-*, back, + *abattre*, beat down: see *abate*. Cf. *rebate*.] 1†. To beat down; rebate.

> This alteration is sometimes by adding, sometimes by *rabatting*, of a sillable or letter to or from a worde either in the beginning, middle, or ending. *Puttenham*, Arte of Eng. Poesie, p. 134.

2. In *falconry*, to bring down or recover (the hawk) to the fist.

rabate† (ra-bāt'), *n.* [< *rabate*, *v.*] Abatement.

> And your figures of *rabbate* be as many. *Puttenham*, Arte of Eng. Poesie, p. 135.

rabatine† (rab'ạ-tin), *n.* [< F. **rabatine* (?), dim. of *rabat*, a neck-band: see *rabat*, *rabato*.] Same as *rabato*.

> Reform me, Janet, that precise ruff of thine for an open *rabatine* of lace and cut work, that will let men see thou hast a fair neck. *Scott*, Kenilworth, xxiii.

rabato† (ra-bä'tō), *n.* [Also *rebato*; with altered termination (as if of Sp. or It. origin), < OF. (and F.) *rabat*, a turned-down collar, a band or ruff: see *rabat*.] 1. A falling band; a collar turned over upon the shoulders, or supported in a horizontal position like a ruff.

> Where is your gowne of silke, your periwigs,
> Your fine *rebatoes*, and your costly iewels?
> *Heywood*, 2 Edw. IV. (Works, ed. Pearson, 1874, I. 168).
>
> Your stiffnecked *rabatos*, that have more arches for pride to row under than can stand under five London bridges. *Dekker*, Gull's Hornbook.

2. A wire or other stiffener used to hold this band in place.

> I pray you, sir, what say you to these great ruffes, which are borne up with supporters and *rebatoes*, as it were with poste and raile? *Dent'd Pathway*, p. 42. (*Halliwell.*)

rabattement (ra-bat'mẹnt), *n.* [< F. *rabattement*, < *rabattre*, beat down: see *rabate*.] An operation of descriptive geometry consisting in representing a plane as rotated about one of its traces until it is brought into a plane of projection, with a view of performing other operations more easily performed in such a situation, after which the plane is to be rotated back to its proper position.

rabban (rab'ạn), *n.* [Heb. *rabban*, lord; cf. Ar. *rabbani* (> Pers. *rabboni*), belonging to a lord or the Lord, divine; as a noun, a rabbi; *rabbana* (Pers.), O our Lord! etc.: see *rabbi*, and cf. *rabboni*.] A title of honor (of greater dignity than *rabbi*) given by the Jews to the patriarchs or presidents of the Sanhedrim—Gamaliel I., who was patriarch in Palestine about A. D. 30–50, being the first to whom it was applied.

rabbanist (rab'ạn-ist), *n.* Same as *rabbinist*.

rabbate†, *v. t.* An obsolete form of *rabate*.

rabbet (rab'et), *v. t.* [Early mod. E. also *rabbot*, *rabot*; < ME. *rabeten*, rabbet, < OF. (and F.) *raboter*, plane, level, lay even; cf. F. *robot*, a joiners' plane (also a plasterers' beater, cf. OF. *rabat*, a plasterers' beater: see *robot*); cf. F. *raboteux*, rugged, knotty, rough; < OF. *robouter*, thrust back (= Pr. *rebotar* = It. *ributtare*, push back), < *re-*, again, + *aboter*, *abouter*, thrust against: see *re-* and *abut*. Cf. *rebut*.] To cut the edge of (a board) so that it will overlap that of the next piece, which is similarly cut out, and will form a close joint with this adjoining board; cut or form a rabbet in (a board or piece of timber). See *rabbet*, *n.*—**Rabbeted lock**, a lock of which the face-plate is sunk in a rabbet in the edge of a door. *E. H. Knight.*

rabbet (rab'et), *n.* [< ME. *robet*, < OF. (and F.) *rabot*, a joiners' plane, < *raboter*, plane: see *rabbet*, *v.*] 1. A cut made on the edge of a board so that it may join by lapping with another board similarly cut; also, a rectangular recess, channel, or groove cut along the edge of a board or the like to receive a corresponding projection cut on the edge of another board, etc., required to fit into it. Rabbets are common in paneling. See also cut under *match-joint*.—2. Same as *rabbet-plane*.

Rabbets.

rabbeting-machine (rab'et-ing-mạ-shēn'), *n.* A machine for cutting rabbets: a form of matching-, molding-, or planing-machine. *E. H. Knight.*

rabbet-joint (rab'et-joint), *n.* A joint formed by rabbeting, as the edges of two boards or pieces of timber.

rabbet-plane (rab'et-plān), *n.* A plane for plowing a groove along the edge of a board. Rabbet-planes are so shaped as to adapt them to peculiar kinds of work. In a *square-rabbet plane* the cutting edge is square across the sole; in a *skew-rabbet plane* the bit is set obliquely

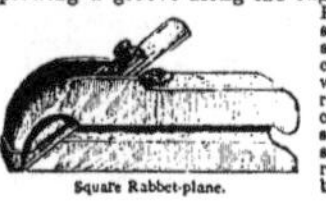

Square Rabbet-plane.

across the sole; in a *side-rabbet plane* the cutter is on the side, not on the sole.

rabbet-saw (rab'et-sâ), *n.* A saw used for making rabbets. Such saws commonly have an adjustable fence or gage to insure the proper placing of the groove.

rabbi (rab'i or rab'ī), *n.*; pl. *rabbis* (rab'iz or rab'īz). [Early mod. E. also *rabbie, rabby*; < ME. *rabi, raby* = OF. *rabbi, rabi, raby*, < LL. *rabbi*, < Gr. ῥαββί, < Heb. (Aramaic) *rabbī*, master, lord (much used in the Targums for all degrees of authority, from king and high priest down to chief shepherd), lit. 'my master' or 'my lord' (= Ar. *rabbi*, 'my master' or 'my lord'); with pronominal suffix *-i*, < *rab*, master, lord (= Ar. *rabb*, master, lord, the Lord, God, cf. *rabba*, mistress), < *rābab*, be great. Cf. *rab*[2], *rabbin, rabban, rabboni*.] Literally, 'my master': a title of respect or of office (of higher dignity than *rab*) given to Jewish doctors or expounders of the law. In modern Jewish usage the term is strictly applied only to those who are authorized by ordination to decide legal and ritualistic questions, and to perform certain designated functions, as to receive proselytes, etc.; but it is given by courtesy to other distinguished Jewish scholars. By persons not Hebrews it is often applied to any one ministering to a Jewish congregation, to distinguish him from a Christian clergyman.

God liketh nat that *Raby* men us calle.
Chaucer, Summoner's Tale, l. 470.

They said unto him, *Rabbi* (which is to say, being interpreted, Master [*i. e.*, Teacher]). John i. 38.

Those whose heads with age are hoary growen,
And those great *Rabbies* that do grauely sit,
Revolving volumes of the highest Writ.
Sylvester, tr. of Du Bartas's Weeks, ii., The Captaines.

rabbin (rab'in), *n.* [< F. *rabbin*, < LL. *rabbi*, < Gr. ῥαββί, rabbi: see *rabbi*.] Same as *rabbi*.

It is expressly against the laws of our own government when a minister doth serve as a stipendiary curate, which kind of service nevertheless the greatest *rabbins* of that part do altogether follow. *Hooker*, Eccles. Polity, v. 80.

Now he [Salmasius] betakes himself to the fabulous *rabbins* again. *Milton*, Ans. to Salmasius, iii. 85.

rabbinate (rab'in-āt), *n.* [< *rabbin* + *-ate*[3].] The dignity or office of a rabbi.

Gradually the Talmud, which had been once the common pabulum of all education, passed out of the knowledge of the laity, and was abandoned almost entirely to candidates for the *rabbinate*. *Encyc. Brit.*, XIII. 681.

rabbinic (ra-bin'ik), *a.* and *n.* [= F. *rabbinique*; as *rabbin* + *-ic*.] **I.** *a.* Same as *rabbinical*.

II. *n.* [*cap.*] The language or dialect of the rabbis; the later Hebrew.

rabbinical (ra-bin'i-kal), *a.* [< *rabbinic* + *-al*.] Pertaining to the rabbis, or to their opinions, learning, and language. The term *rabbinical* has been applied to all the Jewish exegetical writings composed after the Christian era.

We will not buy your *rabbinical* fumes; we have One that calls us to buy of him pure gold tried in the fire.
Milton, On Def. of Humb. Remonst.

It is but a legend, I know,
A fable, a phantom, a show,
Of the ancient *rabbinical* lore.
Longfellow, Sandalphon.

Rabbinical Hebrew. See *Hebrew*.

rabbinically (ra-bin'i-kal-i), *adv.* In a rabbinical manner; like a rabbi.

rabbinism (rab'in-izm), *n.* [< F. *rabbinisme* = Sp. *rabinismo*; as *rabbin* + *-ism*.] **1.** A rabbinic expression or phrase; a peculiarity of the language of the rabbis.—**2.** A system of religious belief prevailing among the Jews from the return from the Jewish captivity to the latter part of the eighteenth century, the distinguishing feature of which was that it declared the oral law to be of equal authority with the written law of God.

rabbinist (rab'in-ist), *n.* [Also *rabbanist*; < F. *rabbiniste* = Sp. *rabinista*; as *rabbin* + *-ist*.] Among the Jews, one who adhered to the Talmud and the traditions of the rabbins, in opposition to the Karaites, who rejected the traditions. See *rabbinism*.

Those who stood up for the Talmud and its traditions were chiefly the rabbins and their followers; from whence the party had the name of *rabbinists*.
Stackhouse, Hist. Bible, II. vii. 4.

rabbinite (rab'in-īt), *n.* [< *rabbin* + *-ite*[2].] Same as *rabbinist*.

rabbit[1] (rab'it), *n.* [Early mod. E. also *rabbale, rabet*; < ME. *rabet*, rabbit, appar. < OF. **rabot*, indicated in F. dial. *rabotte*, a rabbit; cf. OD. *robbe*, D. *rob*, a rabbit; LG. G. *robbe*, a sea-dog, seal; Gael. *rabaid, rabait*, a rabbit. Cf. F. *râble*, the back of a rabbit, Sp. Pg. *rabo*, tail, hind quarters, Sp. *rabel*, hind quarters. An older E. name is *cony*. The native name for the rabbit is *hare* (including hares and rabbits).] **1.** A rodent mammal, *Lepus cuniculus*, of the hare family, *Leporidæ*; a kind of hare notable for burrowing in the ground. This animal is indigenous to Europe, but has been naturalized in many other countries, and is the original of all the domestic breeds. It is smaller than the common hare of Europe, L. *timidus* or *variabilis*, with shorter ears

Rabbit (white lop-eared variety).

and limbs. The natural color is brownish, but in domestication black, gray, white, and pied individuals are found. The ears are naturally erect, but in some breeds they fall; such rabbits are called *lopped* or *lop-eared*, and degrees of lopping of the ears are named *half-lops* and *full-lops*. Rabbits breed in their burrows or warrens, and also freely in hutches: they are very prolific, bringing forth several times a year, usually six or eight at a litter, and in some countries where they have been naturalized they multiply so rapidly as to become a pest, as in Australia for example. The fur is used in the manufacture of hats and for other purposes, and the flesh is esteemed for food.

Hence—**2.** Any hare; a leporid, or any member of the *Leporidæ*. The common gray rabbit or wood-rabbit of the United States is L. *sylvaticus*, also called *cottontail* and *molly cottontail*, a variety of which (or a closely related species) is the sage-rabbit of western North America, L. *artemisia*. The marsh-rabbit is L. *palustris*; the swamp-rabbit of the Southern States is L. *aquaticus*. Various large long-eared and long-limbed hares of western North America are called *jack-rabbits* or *jackass-rabbits*. The South American rabbit or hare is the tapeti, L. *brasiliensis*. See cuts under *cottontail, jack-rabbit*, and *hare*.—**Native rabbit**, in Australia, a long-eared kind of bandicoot, *Macrotis lagotis*.—**Snow-shoe rabbit**, that variety of the American varying hare which is found in the Rocky Mountains. It turns white in winter, and at that season the fur of the feet is very heavy. It has been described as a distinct species, *Lepus bairdi*, but is better treated as a local race of *L. americanus*.—**Welsh rabbit.** [A term of jocular origin, formed after the fashion of *Norfolk capon*, a red herring, etc. (see quotation). Owing to an absurd notion that *rabbit* in this phrase is a corruption of *rarebit* (as if 'a rare bit'), the word is often so written.] Cheese melted with a little ale, and poured over slices of hot toast. Cream, mustard, or Worcestershire sauce are occasionally added. The name has been given to cheese toasted but not entirely melted, and laid on toast.

Welsh rabbit is a genuine slang term, belonging to a large group which describe in the same humorous way the special dish or product or peculiarity of a particular district. For examples: . . . an Essex lion is a calf; a Field-lane duck is a baked sheep's head; Glasgow magistrates or Norfolk capons are red herrings; Irish apricots or Munster plums are potatoes; Gravesend sweetmeats are shrimps. *Macmillan's Mag.*

rabbit[1] (rab'it), *v. i.* [< *rabbit*[1], *n.*] To hunt or trap rabbits.

She liked keeping the score at cricket, and coming to look at them fishing or *rabbiting* in her walks.
T. Hughes, Tom Brown at Oxford, II. vii.

"I suppose," pursued Mr. Morley presently, "that you have been indulging in the Englishman's usual recreation of slaughter." "I've been *rabbiting*, if that's what you mean," answered Sir Christopher shortly.
W. E. Norris, Miss Shafto, xix.

rabbit[2]† (rab'it), *n.* [< OF. (and F.) *rabot*, a plasterers' beater: see *rabbet*.] **1.** A wooden implement used in mixing mortar. *Cotgrave.*—**2.** A wooden can used as a drinking-vessel.

Strong beer in *rabits* and cheating penny cans,
Three pipes for two-pence, and such like trepans.
Praise of Yorkshire Ale (1697), p. 1. (*Halliwell.*)

rabbit[3] (rab'it), *v. t.* [Appar. a corruption of *rabate* (cf. *rabbet*), used as a vague imprecation.] An interjectional imperative, equivalent to *confound*.

"*Rabbit* the fellow," cries he; "I thought, by his talking so much about riches, that he had a hundred pounds at least in his pocket."
Fielding, Joseph Andrews. (*Latham.*)

Rabbit me, I am no soldier. *Scott.*

rabbit-berry (rab'it-ber″i), *n.* The buffalo-berry, *Shepherdia argentea*.

Flowering Plant of Rabbit-brush (*Bigelovia graveolens*). *a*, a head; *b*, a flower.

rabbit-brush (rab'it-brush), *n.* A tall shrubby composite plant, *Bigelovia graveolens*, growing abundantly in alkaline soils of western North America, often, like the sage-brush (but at lower elevations), monopolizing the ground over large tracts. It furnishes a safe retreat for the large jack-rabbits of the plains. It is a disagreeably scented plant, with numerous bushy branches which are more or less whitened by a close tomentum, narrow leaves, and yellow flowers. There are 4 or 5 well-marked varieties, differing chiefly in the width of the leaves, in the degree of whiteness, and in size.

rabbitear (rab'it-ēr), *n.* A long slender oyster; a razorblade.

rabbit-eared (rab'it-ērd), *a.* Having long or large ears, like those of a rabbit; lagotic: as, the *rabbit-eared* bandicoot or native rabbit of Australia, *Macrotis lagotis*.

rabbiter (rab'i-tėr), *n.* One who hunts or traps rabbits.

The majority of the men engaged as *rabbiters* [in Australia] were making a very high rate of wages.
Sci. Amer., N. S., LVI. 294.

rabbit-fish (rab'it-fish), *n.* **1.** A holocephalous fish, *Chimæra monstrosa*. Also called *king of the herrings*. [Local, British.]—**2.** A plectognathous fish of the family *Tetrodontidæ* and genus *Lagocephalus*. The name refers to the peculiarity of the front teeth, which resemble the incisors of a rabbit. The rabbit-fish of the eastern United States is *L. lævigatus*, also called *smooth puffer* and *tambor*. It is mostly olive-green, but silver-white below, and attains a length of 2 feet or more. The name is also extended to kindred plectognaths.
3. The streaked gurnard, *Trigla lineata*. [Local, Eng.]

rabbit-foot clover. See *clover*, 1, and *hare's-foot*, 1.

rabbit-hutch (rab'it-huch), *n.* A box or cage for the confinement and rearing of tame rabbits.

rabbit-moth (rab'it-môth), *n.* The bombycid moth *Lagoa opercularis*: so called from its soft furry appearance and rabbit-like coloration. See cut under *stinging-caterpillar*. [U. S.]

rabbit-mouth (rab'it-mouth), *n.* A mouth like that of a hare; used attributively, having a formation of the jaws which suggests harelip: as, the *rabbit-mouth* sucker, a catostomoid fish, otherwise called *splitmouth, harelip, harelipped sucker, cutlips*, and *Lagochila* or *Quassilabia lacera*. This fish has the form of an ordinary sucker, but the lower lip is split into two separate lobes, and the upper lip is greatly enlarged and not protractile. It is most common in the streams flowing from the Ozark mountains. See cut under *Quassilabia*.

rabbit-rat (rab'it-rat), *n.* An Australian rodent of the genus *Hapalotis*, as *H. albipes*.

rabbit-root (rab'it-röt), *n.* The wild sarsaparilla, *Aralia nudicaulis*.

rabbitry (rab'it-ri), *n.*; pl. *rabbitries* (-riz). [< *rabbit*[1] + *-ry*.] A collection of rabbits, or the place where they are kept; a rabbit-warren.

rabbit-spout (rab'it-spout), *n.* The burrow of a rabbit. [Prov. Eng.]

Here they turn left-handed, and run him into a *rabbit-spout* in the gorse.
Field (London), Feb. 27, 1886. (*Encyc. Dict.*)

rabbit-squirrel (rab'it-skwur″el), *n.* A South

South American Chincha or Rabbit-squirrel (*Lagidium cuvieri*).

American rodent of the family *Chinchillidæ* and genus *Lagidium*, as *L. cuvieri*. *Coues.*

rabbit-sucker† (rab'it-suk″ėr), *n.* **1.** A sucking rabbit; a young rabbit.

I preferre an olde cony before a *rabbet-sucker*, and an ancient henne before a young chicken peeper.
Lyly, Endymion, v. 2.

If thou dost it half so gravely, so majestically, both in word and matter, hang me up by the heels for a *rabbit-sucker*. *Shak.*, 1 Hen. IV., ii. 4. 480.

2. A gull; a dupe; a cony. See *cony*, 7.

rabbit-warren (rab'it-wor″en), *n.* A piece of ground appropriated to the perservation and breeding of rabbits.

rabble[1] (rab'l), *v.*; pret. and pp. *rabbled*, ppr. *rabbling*. [Also *ravel*; < ME. *rablen*, speak confusedly; cf. OD. *rabbelen*, chatter, trifle, toy, = G. dial. *rabbeln, robbeln*, chatter, prattle; cf. ML. *rabulare*, scold, < L. *rabula*, a brawling advocate, a pettifogger. Cf. Gr. ῥαβάσσειν, make a noise, Ir. *rapal*, noise, *rapach*, noisy, Gael. *rapair*, a noisy fellow. The word may have been in part confused or associated with *ramble*; cf. dial. *rabbling*, winding, rambling.] I. *intrans.* To speak confusedly; talk incoherently; utter nonsense.

II. *trans.* To utter confusedly or incoherently; gabble or chatter out.

Let thy tunge serve thyn hert in skylle,
And *rable* not wordes recheles owt of reson.
MS. Cantab. Ff. ii. 38, f. 24. (*Halliwell.*)

Thus, father Traves, you may see my rashness to *rabble* out the Scriptures without purpose, time [in other editions *rime*], or reason.
J. Bradford, Letters (Parker Soc., 1853), II. 23.

[Obsolete or prov. Eng. and Scotch in both uses.]

rabble[2] (rab'l), *n.* and *a.* [Early mod. E. *rable*; ‹ ME. *rabel*; cf. *rabble*[1], *v.*] I. *n.* 1. A tumultuous crowd of vulgar, noisy people; a confused, disorderly assemblage; a mob.

I saw, I say, come out of London, even unto the presence of the prince, a great *rable* of mean and light persones.
Ascham, The Scholemaster, i.

Then the Nabob Vizier and his *rabble* made their appearance, and hastened to plunder the camp of the valiant enemies.
Macaulay, Warren Hastings.

2. Specifically, the mass of common people; the ignorant populace; the mob: with the definite article.

The rabble now such freedom did enjoy
As winds at sea that use it to destroy.
Dryden, Astræa Redux, l. 43.

3. Any confused crowd or assemblage; a haphazard conglomeration or aggregate, especially of things trivial or ignoble.

This miscreant [Mahomet] . . . instituted and published a sect, or rather a *rabble*, of abhominable preceptes and detestable counselles, thereby to chaunge the vertuous, and therewith to delight the vicious and wicked.
Guevara, Letters (tr. by Hellowes, 1577), p. 327.

For the solace they may geue the readers, after such a *rable* of scholastical precepts which be tedious, these reports being of the nature of matters historicall, they are to be embraced.
Puttenham, Arte of Eng. Poesie, p. 221.

Flies, Butterflies, Gnats, Bees, and all the *rabbles*
Of other Insects.
Sylvester, tr. of Du Bartas's Weeks, i. 5.

=Syn. 1. *Mob*, etc. See *populace*.

II. *a.* Pertaining to or consisting of a rabble; riotous; tumultuous; disorderly; vulgar; low.

To gratify the barbarous party of my audience, I gave them a short *rabble*-scene, because the mob (as they call them) are represented by Plutarch and Polybius with the same character of baseness and cowardice.
Dryden, Cleomenes, Pref.

How could any one of English education and prattique swallow such a low, *rabble* suggestion?
Roger North, Examen, p. 306. (*Davies.*)

The victory of Beaumont proved to MacMahon that his only resource left was to abandon the attempt to reach Bazaine, and to concentrate his *rabble* army around the frontier fortress of Sedan.
Lowe, Bismarck, I. 548.

rabble[2] (rab'l), *v. t.*; pret. and pp. *rabbled*, ppr. *rabbling*. [‹ *rabble*[2], *n.*] To assault in a violent and disorderly manner; mob. [Scotch.]

Unhappily, throughout a large part of Scotland, the clergy of the established church were, to use the phrase then common, *rabbled*.
Macaulay, Hist. Eng., xiii.

The desolation of Ireland, the massacre of Glencoe, the abandonment of the Darien colonists, the *rabbling* of about 300 Episcopal clergymen in Scotland . . .
Lecky, Eng. in 18th Cent., i.

It seems but as yesterday since in the streets of Edinburgh ladies were insulted and *rabbled* on their way to a medical lecture-room.
Fortnightly Rev., N. S., XXXIX. 19.

rabble[3] (rab'l), *n.* [‹ OF. *roable*, F. *râble*, an implement for stirring or mixing, a poker, etc., dial. *redable*, ‹ L. *rutabulum*, ML. also *rotabulum*, a poker or shovel.] An iron bar bent at right angles at one end, used in the operation of puddling for stirring the melted iron, so as to allow it to be more fully exposed to the action of the air and the lining of the furnace.

rabble[3] (rab'l), *v. t.*; pret. and pp. *rabbled*, ppr. *rabbling*. [‹ *rabble*[3], *n.*] To stir and skim with a rabble or puddling-tool, as melted iron in a furnace.

rabble-fish (rab'l-fish), *n.* Fish generally rejected for market, as the dogfishes, rays, gurnards, scad, and wrasses. [West of Eng.]

rabblement[1] (rab'l-ment), *n.* [‹ *rabble*[1] + *-ment*.] Idle, silly talk; babblement. *Halliwell.* [Prov. Eng.]

rabblement[2]† (rab'l-ment), *n.* [Formerly also *rablement*; ‹ *rabble*[2] + *-ment*.] 1. A tumultuous crowd or assemblage; a disorderly rout; a rabble.

The first troupe was a monstrous *rablement*
Of fowle misshapen wightes.
Spenser, F. Q., II. xi. 8.

The *rabblement* hooted, and clapped their chopped hands.
Shak., J. C., i. 2. 245.

I saw . . . giants and dwarfs,
Clowns, conjurors, posture-masters, harlequins,
Amid the uproar of the *rabblement*,
Perform their feats.
Wordsworth, Prelude, vii.

2. Refuse; dregs. *Halliwell.* [Prov. Eng.]

rabbler (rab'lėr), *n.* One who works with or uses a rabble, especially in the operation of puddling.

rabbling (rab'ling), *a.* Same as *rambling*. See *ramble*. [Prov. Eng.]

rabboni (ra-bō'ni), *n.* [Heb.: see *rabbi*.] Literally, 'my great master': a title of honor among the Jews; specifically, the highest title given to doctors or expounders of the law. It was publicly given to only seven persons of great eminence, all of the school of Hillel.

She turned herself, and saith unto him, *Rabboni*; which is to say, Master [i. e., Teacher].
John xx. 16.

rabd, rabdoid, etc. See *rhabd*, etc.

rabel, *n.* Same as *rebec*.

Rabelaisian (rab-e-lā'zi-an), *a.* [‹ F. *rabelaisien*, ‹ *Rabelais* (see def.).] Of or pertaining to François Rabelais (about 1490–1553), a French priest, author of "Gargantua and Pantagruel"; resembling or suggestive of Rabelais and the characteristics of his thought and style. Compare *Pantagruelism*.

Gleams of the truest poetical sensibility alternate in him [John Skelton] with an almost brutal coarseness. He was truly *Rabelaisian* before Rabelais.
Lowell, N. A. Rev., CXX. 340.

rabet[1]†, *n.* An obsolete spelling of *rabbit*[1].

rabet[2]†, *n.* An obsolete spelling of *rabbet*.

rabi[1]†, *n.* An obsolete spelling of *rabbi*.

rabi[2] (rab'i), *n.* [Also written *rubbee*; ‹ Hind. *rabi*, the spring, the crop then gathered.] The great grain-crop of Hindustan, consisting of wheat, barley, oats, and millet. It is the last of the three crops, being laid down in August and September, partly on land which has lain fallow and partly on land which has been cleared of the bhadoee or earliest crop. It furnishes about five sixteenths of the food-supply in a normal year.

rabiate (rā'bi-āt), *a.* [‹ ML. *rabiatus*, pp. of *rabiare*, go mad, rave, rage, ‹ L. *rabies*, madness: see *rabies*. Cf. *rage*, *rave*[1].] Rabid; maddened.

Ah! ye Jewes, worse than dogges *rabiate*.
Lamentation of Mary Magdalen.

rabiator (rā'bi-ā-tor), *n.* [‹ ML. *rabiator*, a furious man, ‹ *rabiare*, rave, go mad: see *rabiate*. The Sc. *rubiature*, a robber, bully, It. *rubatore*, a robber, ‹ ML. **rubator*, does not seem to be connected.] A furious animal or person; a violent, greedy person. [Scotch.]

rabic (rab'ik), *a.* [‹ *rabi(es)* + *-ic*.] Of or pertaining to rabies; affected or caused by rabies.

Of eight unvacciuated dogs, six succumbed to the intravenous inoculation of *rabic* matter.
Tyndall, Int. to Lady C. Hamilton's tr. of Life of Pasteur, [p. 40.

In the interval it [a dog] manifests *rabic* symptoms.
Medical News, XLVIII. 223.

rabid (rab'id), *a.* [= OF. *rabi*, *rabit* = Sp. *rábido* = Pg. It. *rabido*, ‹ L. *rabidus*, mad, furious, ‹ *rabere*, be mad, rage: see *rabies*, and cf. *rage*, *n.*] 1. Furious; raging; mad.

With *rabid* hunger feed upon your kind.
Dryden, tr. of Ovid's Metamorph., xv. 258.

Like *rabid* snakes that sting some gentle child
Who brings them food. *Shelley*, Revolt of Islam, v. 7.

Sleep is the sure antidote of insanity, the cure of idiocy, . . . without whose potent anodynes every creature would run *rabid*.
A. B. Alcott, Table-Talk, p. 71.

2. Specifically—(*a*) Affected with rabies or hydrophobia, as a dog, wolf, horse, or man; hydrophobic; mad. (*b*) Pertaining to rabies: as, *rabid* virus.—3. Excessively or foolishly intense; rampant: as, a *rabid* Tory; a *rabid* teetotaler.

In the *rabid* desire to say something easily, I scarcely knew what I uttered at all.
Poe, Tales, I. 289.

rabidity (rā-bid'i-ti), *n.* [‹ ML. *rabidita(t-)s*, rabidness, ‹ L. *rabidus*, rabid: see *rabid*.] The state of being rabid; rabidness; specifically, rabies. [Rare.]

Although the term hydrophobia has been generally applied to this terrible disease, I have preferred that of rabies, or *rabidity*, as being more characteristic of the chief phenomena manifested by it both in man and the lower animals.
Copland, Dict. Pract. Med., Rabies, § 2.

I fear that he [Macaulay] is one of those who, like the individual whom he has most studied, will "give up to party what was meant for mankind." At any rate, he must get rid of his *rabidity*. He writes now on all subjects as if he certainly intended to be a renegade.
Disraeli, Young Duke, v. 6.

rabidly (rab'id-li), *adv.* [‹ *rabid* + *-ly*[2].] In a rabid manner; madly; furiously.

rabidness (rab'id-nes), *n.* [‹ *rabid* + *-ness*.] The state of being rabid; furiousness; madness.

rabies (rā'bi-ēz), *n.* [‹ L. *rabies*, rage, madness, fury: see *rage*, *n.*] An extremely fatal infectious disease of man and many other animals, with predominant nervous symptoms. In man (where it is called *hydrophobia*) the period of incubation lasts in a majority of cases from three to six months or more. Cases where it is said to have lasted several years are ill sustained. The outbreak begins with malaise, anorexia, headache, and slight difficulty in swallowing. After one or two days of these prodromal symptoms the stage of tonic spasms begins, most marked at first in the pharyngeal muscles and in the attempt to swallow, especially liquids, but proceeding to involve the respiratory muscles and others of the trunk and those of the extremities. These convulsions are accompanied by extreme anxiety and oppression, and may be elicited by any stimulus, but especially by attempts to drink or by the sound or sight of liquids. They may last from a few minutes to half an hour. The pulse-rate increases, the temperature is more or less raised, and there may be decided delirium. After from one to three days the period of paralysis succeeds, followed shortly by death. The mortality after the development of the malady is nearly 100 per cent. The disease is communicated to man by inoculation from a rabid animal, usually by a dog-bite. The maximum number of inoculations occur in the early spring or winter, the minimum in late summer or fall. The saliva of rabid dogs seems to be somewhat rabigenic two or three days before the animal shows any evident signs of ill-health. Of persons bitten by rabid animals only a fraction develop rabies, estimated at from 16 per cent. for light wounds through the clothing up to 80 per cent. for wounds of exposed parts. The records of Pasteur's laboratories show a reduction to less than 1 per cent. when such persons are treated by his method. See *Pasteurism*.

rabietic (rā-bi-et'ik), *a.* [Irreg. ‹ *rabies* + *-et* + *-ic*.] Pertaining or relating to rabies; of the nature of or resembling rabies.

To M. Grancher was most justly accorded the very agreeable task of expounding in a few simple and unadorned sentences the results of the anti-*rabietic* treatment of M. Pasteur.
Nature, XXXIX. 73.

rabific (rā-bif'ik), *a.* [‹ L. *rabies*, madness, + *facere*, make (see *-fic*).] Communicating rabies or canine madness; capable of causing hydrophobia.

Rabific virus is obtained from a rabbit which has died after inoculation by trepanning.
Encyc. Brit., XX. 202.

rabigenic (rab-i-jen'ik), *a.* [‹ L. *rabies*, madness, + *gignere*, *genere*, produce, √ **gen*, bear, produce: see *-gen*.] Same as *rabific*.

rabinet† (rab'i-net), *n.* [Origin obscure.] A small piece of ordnance formerly in use, weighing about 300 pounds, and carrying a ball about 1½ inches in diameter.

rabious† (rā'bi-us), *a.* [‹ OF. *rabieux* = Sp. *rabioso* = Pg. *raivoso* = It. *rabbioso*, ‹ L. *rabiosus*, full of rage, raging, ‹ *rabies*, rage, fury: see *rabies* and *rage*.] Wild; raging; fierce.

Ethelred languishing in minde and body, Edmond his sonne, surnamed Ironside (to oppose youth to youth), was imployed against this *rabious* inuador.
Daniel, Hist. Eng., p. 15. (*Davies.*)

rabite†, *n.* [ME., also *rabett*, *rabyghte*, war-horse, ‹ Icel. *rābītr*, an Arabian steed (cf. Icel. *rābitar*, Arabs), = MHG. *rāvit*, *ravit*, a war-horse, ‹ OF. *arabit*, *arrabi*, an Arabian horse, ‹ *Arabe*, Arab: see *Arab*.] A war-horse.

Syr Gye bestrode a *rabyghte*,
That was moche and lyghte.
MS. Cantab. Ff. ii. 38, f. 121. (*Halliwell.*)

rabone†, *n.* [= Sp. *rábano* = Pg. *rabano*, *rabão*, ‹ L. *raphanus*, a radish: see *Raphanus*.] A radish. *Gerarde*, Herball.

rabot (rab'ot), *n.* [‹ F. *rabot*: see *rabbet*.] A hard-wood rubber used in rubbing marble to prepare it for polishing. *E. H. Knight.*

raca (rä'kä), *a.* [Formerly also *racha*; LL. *raca*, ‹ Gr. ῥακά, ‹ Chal. *rēkā*, an insulting epithet of doubtful meaning, connected perhaps with *raq*, spit, spit upon (Ar. *riq*), or with *riqā*, empty, valueless (Ar. *raiq*, vain, futile).] Worthless; naught: a transliterated word occurring in Mat. v. 22, common among the Jews in Christ's time as an expression of contempt.

raccahout (rak'a-höt), *n.* [‹ F. *racahout*, a corruption of Ar. *rāqaut*, *rāqoūt*, or *rāqaout*, a nourishing starch with analeptic properties. But this Ar. word may be the F. *ragoût*, OF. *ragoust*, imported into the East during the Crusades: see *ragout*.] A starch or meal prepared from the edible acorns of the belote oak, *Quercus Ballota*, sometimes recommended as a food for invalids. Mixed with sugar and aromatics, it is used by the Arabs as a substitute for chocolate. (*Encyc. Dict.*) The so-called *racahout des Arabes*, sold in France, is a mixture made from edible acorns, salep, chocolate, potato-starch, rice-flour, vanilla, and sugar. *Larousse.*

raccoon, *n.* See *racoon*.

raccourcy (ra-kör'si), *a.* [‹ OF. *raccourcé*, pp. of *raccourcir*, shorten, cut off, ‹ *re-*, again, + *ac-*

courcir, shorten, < *a-* + *court*, short: see *curt*.] In *her.*, same as *couped*.

race[1] (rās), *n.* [Early mod. E. also *rase*; < ME. *rase*, *ras*, commonly *rees*, *res*, a rush, running, swift course, swift current, a trial of speed, etc., < AS. *rǣs*, a rush, swift course, onset (cf. *gār-rǣs*, 'spear-rush,' fight with spears), = Icel. *rās*, a race, running, course, channel: see *race*[1], *v.*, and cf. *race*[2]. The AS. form *rǣs*, ME. *rees*, *res*, would produce a mod. E. **reese*; the form in noun and verb, *race*, prop. *rase*, is due to the Scand. cognates, and perhaps also in part, in the verb, to confusion with *race*[5], *v.*] **1.** A rush; running; swift course.

Whenne thei were war of Moises,
Thei fleyȝe away al in a *res*.
Cursor Mundi. (*Halliwell.*)

That I ful ofte, in suche a *res*,
Am werye of myn owen lyf.
Gower, Conf. Amant.

The flight of many birds is swifter than the *race* of any beasts. *Bacon*, Nat. Hist., § 681.

2. A course which has to be run, passed over, or gone through; onward movement or progression; career.

How soon hath thy prediction, Seer blest,
Measured this transient world, the *race* of time,
Till time stand fix'd! *Milton*, P. L., xii. 554.

Eternity! that boundless *Race*
Which Time himself can never run.
Congreve, Imit. of Horace, II. xiv. 1.

Succeeding Years their happy *Race* shall run,
And Age unheeded by Delight come on.
Prior, Henry and Emma.

My Arthur, whom I shall not see
Till all my widow'd *race* be run.
Tennyson, In Memoriam, ix.

3. A contest of speed; a competitive trial of speed, especially in running, but also in riding, driving, sailing, rowing, walking, or any mode of progression. The plural, used absolutely, commonly means a series of horse-races run at a set time over a regular course: as, to go to the *races*; the Epsom *races*.

To the bischope in a *ras* he ran.
Old Eng. Metr. Homilies, l. 141.

Part on the plain, or in the air sublime,
Upon the wing or in swift *race* contend,
As at the Olympian games. *Milton*, P. L., ii. 529.

The *races* were then called bell courses, because . . . the prize was a silver bell. *Strutt*, Sports and Pastimes, p. 107.

4†. Course, as of events; progress.

The prosecution and *race* of the war carrieth the defendant to assail and invade the ancient and indubitate patrimony of the first aggressor. *Bacon*, War with Spain.

5†. Struggle; conflict; tumult; trouble.

Others hue him sworen in stude ther he wes,
To bueu him hold ant trewe for alles cunnes *res*.
Execution of Sir Simon Fraser (Child's Ballads, VI. 276).

Hem rued the *res* that thei ne rest had.
Alisaunder of Macedoine (E. E. T. S.), l. 389.

Redeliche in that *res* the recuuerere that me falles,
As whan I haue ani hap to here of that barne.
William of Palerne (E. E. T. S.), l. 439.

6†. Course; line of onward movement; way; route.

The souldier victourer is not woonte to spare any that commethe in his *rase*. *R. Eden*, tr. of Peter Martyr (First Books on America, [ed. Arber, p. 122).

Consolation race. See *consolation*.—**Flat race**, a horse-race over level or clear ground, as opposed to a hurdle-race or steeplechase.—**Obstacle-race.** See *obstacle*.

race[1] (rās), *v.*; pret. and pp. *raced*, ppr. *racing*. [< ME. *rasen*, *resen*, rush, run, hasten, < AS. *rǣsan*, rush, move violently, also rush on, attack, rush into; = OD. *rāsen*, rage, = MLG. *rasen*, MHG. G. *rasen*, rage, = Icel. *rāsa* = Sw. *rasa* = Dan. *rase*, race, rush, hurry: see *race*[1], *n.*, 1. The form *race*, prop. *rase*, is due to the Scand. cognates: see the noun.] **I.** *intrans.* **1.** To run swiftly; run in, or as if engaged in, a contest of speed.

Saladin began to *rase* for ire.
Richard Coer de Lion, l. 3633.

The *racing* place, call'd the Hippodromus, without the gate of Canopus, was probably in the plain towards the canal. *Pococke*, Description of the East, I. 10.

But I began
To thrid the musky-circled mazes, wind
And double in and out the holes, and *race*
By all the fountains: fleet I was of foot.
Tennyson, Princess, iv.

2. To run with uncontrolled speed; go or revolve wildly or with improper acceleration: said of a steam-engine, a wheel, a ship's screw, or the like, when resistance is diminished without corresponding diminution of power.

No centrifugal governor could have so instantaneously cut off the steam: it would not have acted till the engine began to *race*. *S. P. Thompson*, Dynamo-Elect. Mach., p. 98.

A big steamer in a heavy seaway often rests upon two waves, one under her bows and the other under her stern, while the 'midship section has practically no support from the water; and, again, her bows will be almost out of water and her screw *racing*. *Sci. Amer.*, N. S., LVII. 144.

3. To practise horse-racing as an occupation; be engaged in the business of running horses.

II. *trans.* **1.** To cause to run or move swiftly; push or drive onward in, or as if in, a trial of speed: as, to *race* a horse; to *race* steamers.—**2.** To run, or cause horses, etc., to run, in competition with; contend against in a race.

Swore, boxed, fought cocks, and *raced* their neighbor's horses. *Irving*, Knickerbocker, p. 176.

[Colloquial in both uses.]

race[2] (rās), *n.* [A particular use of *race*[1], as 'a swiftly running stream'; but perhaps in part due to OF. *rase*, *raise*, a ditch, channel, = Pr. *rasa*, a channel; origin uncertain.] A strong or rapid current of water, or the channel or passage for such a current; a powerful current or heavy sea sometimes produced by the meeting of two tides: as, the *Race* of Alderney; Portland *Race*.

This evening the Talbot weighed and went back to the Cowes, because her anchor would not hold here, the tide set with so strong a *race*.
Winthrop, Hist. New England, I. 4.

Near the sides of channels and near the mouths of bays the changes of the currents are very complex; and near the headlands separating two bays there is usually at certain times a very swift current, termed a *race*.
Encyc. Brit., XXIII. 353.

(*a*) A canal or watercourse from a dam to a water-wheel: specifically called the *head-race*. (*b*) The watercourse which leads away the water after it leaves the wheel: specifically called the *tail-race*.

race[3] (rās), *n.* and *a.* [< F. *race* (> G. *rasse*, *race* = Sw. *ras* = Dan. *race*, breed of horses, etc.), dial. *raice* = Pr. Sp. *raza* = Pg. *raça* = It. *razza*, race, breed, lineage, < OHG. *reiz*, *reiza*, MHG. *reiz* (G. *riss*), line, scratch, stroke, mark, = Icel. *reitr*, scratch, < *rita*, scratch, = AS. *writan* = E. *write*: see *write*. No connection with *race*[4], root, < L. *radix*, though *race*[3] may have been influenced by this word in some of its uses: see *race*[4].] **I.** *n.* **1.** A genealogical line or stock; a class of persons allied by descent from a common ancestry; lineage; family; kindred: as, the Levites were a *race* of priests; to be of royal or of ignoble *race*.

She is a gentlewoman of very absolute behaviour, and of a good *race*. *B. Jonson*, Epicœne, iii. 2.

He lives to build, not boast, a generous *race*;
No tenth transmitter of a foolish face.
Savage, The Bastard.

2. An ethnical stock; a great division of mankind having in common certain distinguishing physical peculiarities, and thus a comprehensive class appearing to be derived from a distinct primitive source: as, the Caucasian *race*; the Mongolian *race*; the Negro *race*. See *man*, 1.

I cannot with any accuracy speak of the English *race*; that would be claiming for ourselves too great a place among the nations of the earth.
E. A. Freeman, Amer. Lects., p. 14.

3. A tribal or national stock; a division or subdivision of one of the great racial stocks of mankind, distinguished by minor peculiarities: as, the Celtic *race*; the Finnic *race* is a branch of the Mongolian; the English, French, and Spaniards are mixed *races*.—**4.** The human family; human beings as a class; mankind: a shortened form of *human race*: as, the future prospects of the *race*; the elevation of the *race*.

She had no companions of mortal *race*.
Shelley, Sensitive Plant, ii. 4.

5. A breed, stock, or strain of domesticated animals or cultivated plants; an artificially propagated and perpetuated variety. Such races differ from natural species or varieties in their tendency to revert to their original characters, and lose those artificially acquired, when they are left to themselves. Many thousands of races have been produced and named.

There is a *race* of sheep in this country with four horns, two of them turning upwards, and two downwards.
Pococke, Description of the East, II. i. 196.

The truth of the principle of prepotency comes out more clearly when distinct *races* are crossed.
Darwin, Var. of Animals and Plants, xiv.

Specifically—(*a*) In *zoöl.*, a geographical variety; a subspecies, characteristic of a given faunal area, intergrading with another form of the same species. (*b*) In *bot.*: (1) A variety so fixed as to reproduce itself with considerable certainty by seed. Races may be of spontaneous origin or the result of artificial selection. (2) In a broader use, any variety, subspecies, species, or group of very similar species whose characters are continued through successive generations. *Bentham*, Address to Linn. Soc., 1869.

6. Any fixed class of beings more or less broadly differentiated from all others; any general aggregate of mankind or of animals considered as a class apart; a perpetuated or continuing line of like existences: as, the human *race*; the *race* of statesmen; the equine or the feline *race*.

That provident care for the welfare of the offspring which is so strongly evinced by many of the insect *race*.
Say.

7†. A line or series; a course or succession: used of things.

A *race* of wicked acts
Shall flow out of my anger, and o'erspread
The world's wide face. *B. Jonson*, Sejanus, ii. 2.

8†. A strong peculiarity by which the origin or species of anything may be recognized, as, especially, the flavor of wine.

Order. There came not six days since from Hull a pipe of rich canary. . . .
Greedy. Is it of the right *race*?
Massinger, New Way to Pay Old Debts, i. 3.

9†. Intrinsic character; natural quality or disposition; hence, spirit; vigor; pith; raciness.

Now I give my sensual *race* the rein.
Shak., M. for M., ii. 4. 160.

I think the Epistles of Phalaris to have more *race*, more spirit, more force of wit and genius than any others I have ever seen. *Sir W. Temple*, Anc. and Mod. Learning.

=**Syn.** *Tribe*, *Clan*, etc. See *people*.

II. *a.* Of or pertaining to a race. [Rare.]

The pyramids are *race* monuments.
New Princeton Rev., V. 285.

race[4] (rās), *n.* [Formerly also *raze*; < OF. *raïs*, *raïz* = Sp. *raiz* = Pg. *raiz* = It. *radice*, a root, < L. *radix*, a root: see *radix*, *radish*.] A root. See *race-ginger*, and *hand*, 13 (*a*).

I have a gammon of bacon, and two *razes* of ginger, to be delivered as far as Charing Cross.
Shak., 1 Hen. IV., ii. 1. 27.

By my troth, I spent eleven pence, beside three *races* of ginger.
Greene and Lodge, Looking Glass for Lond. and Eng.

race[5]† (rās), *v. t.* [< ME. *racen*, *rasen*, by apheresis from *aracen*, root up: see *arace*[1], and cf. *rash*[3].] To tear up; snatch away hastily.

After he be-heilde towarde the fier, and saugh the flesshe that the knaue hadde rosted that was tho I-nough, and *raced* it off with his hondes madly, and rente it a-sonder in peces. *Merlin* (E. E. T. S.), iii. 424.

And *raas* it frome his riche mene and ryste it in sondyre.
Morte Arthure (E. E. T. S.), l. 362.

race[6]†, *v. t.* An obsolete form of *rase*[1], *raze*[1].

race[7] (rās), *n.* [Origin obscure.] A calcareous concretion in brick-earth. [Prov. Eng.]

What were at first supposed to be pebbles in one of the samples from Tantah prove on examination to be calcareous concretions (*race* or kunkur).
Proc. Roy. Soc., XXXIX. 213.

racé (ra-sā'), *a.* In *her.*, same as *indented*.

race-card (rās'kärd), *n.* A printed card containing information about the races to be run at a meeting on a race-course.

I remember it because I went to Epsom races that year to sell *race cards*.
Mayhew, London Labour and London Poor, I. 431.

race-cloth (rās'klôth), *n.* A saddle-cloth used in horse-racing, having pockets for the weights that may be prescribed.

race-course (rās'kōrs), *n.* **1.** A plot of ground laid out for horse-racing, having a track for the horses, usually elliptical, and accommodations for the participants and spectators.—**2.** The canal along which water is conveyed to or from a water-wheel.

race-cup (rās'kup), *n.* A piece of plate forming a prize at a horse-race. Originally such a piece of plate had the form of a goblet or drinking-cup, whence the name.

race-ginger (rās'jin"jėr), *n.* Ginger in the root, or not pulverized.

race-ground (rās'ground), *n.* Ground appropriated to races.

race-horse (rās'hôrs), *n.* **1.** A horse bred or kept for racing or running in contests; a horse that runs in competition. The modern race-horse, though far inferior to the Arab in point of endurance, is perhaps the finest horse in the world for moderate heats, such as those on common race-tracks. It is generally longer-bodied than the hunter, and the same power of leaping is not required. This animal is of Arabian, Berber, or Turkish extraction, improved and perfected by careful crossing and training. See *racer*, 2.
2. The steamer-duck.—**3.** A rear-horse; any mantis.

race-knife (rās'nīf), *n.* A tool with a bent-over lip for scribing, marking, numbering, and other purposes. *E. H. Knight.*

Race-knife.

racemation (ras-ē-mā'shon), *n.* [< LL. *racematio(n-)*, the gleaning of grapes, < L. *racemus*, a cluster of grapes: see *raceme*.] **1.** The gathering or trimming of clusters of grapes. [Rare.]

Having brought over some curious instruments out of Italy for *racemation*, engrafting, and inoculating, he was a great master in the use of them. *Bp. Burnet*, Bp. Bedell, p. 120. (*Latham.*)

2. A cluster, as of grapes; the state of being racemose, or having clustered follicles, as a gland. [Rare.]

The whole *racemation* or cluster of eggs. *Sir T. Browne*, Vulg. Err., iii. 28.

raceme (ra-sēm'), *n.* [= F. *racème*, a cluster, = Sp. Pg. *racimo* = It. *racemo*, < L. *racemus*, a cluster of grapes; allied to Gr. ῥάξ (gen. ῥαγός), a berry, esp. a grape. Cf. *raisin*1, from the same source.] A cluster; specifically, in *bot.*, a simple inflorescence of the centripetal or indeterminate type, in which the several or many flowers are borne on somewhat equal axillary pedicels along a relatively lengthened axis or rachis. Examples are furnished by the currant, the lily-of-the-valley, the locust, etc. A raceme becomes compound when the single flowers are replaced by racemes. See *inflorescence*, compare *spike*, and see cuts under *Actæa*, *inflorescence*, and *Ornithogalum*.

racemed (ra-sēmd'), *a.* [< *raceme* + *-ed*2.] In *bot.*, disposed in racemes: said of flowers or fruits, or of the branches of a racemosely compound inflorescence.

race-meeting (rās'mē"ting), *n.* A meeting for the purpose of horse-racing.

How many more *race-meetings* are there now than there were in 1850? *Quarterly Rev.*, CXLV. 70.

racemic (ra-sem'ik), *a.* [< *raceme* + *-ic.*] Pertaining or relating to grapes in clusters, or to racemes.—**Racemic acid**, $C_4H_6O_6$, an acid isomeric with tartaric acid, found along with the latter in the tartar obtained from certain vineyards on the Rhine. It is a modification of the ordinary tartaric acid, differing from it in its physical but not in its chemical properties. Also called *paratartaric acid*.

racemiferous (ras-ē-mif'e-rus), *a.* [< L. *racemus*, a cluster (see *raceme*), + *ferre* = E. *bear*1.] Bearing racemes.

racemiform (ra-sē'mi-fôrm), *a.* [< L. *racemus*, a cluster, + *forma*, form.] In *bot.*, having the form of a raceme.

racemocarbonic (ra-sē"mō-kär-bon'ik), *a.* [< *racemic* + *carbonic.*] Formed from or consisting of racemic and carbonic acids.—**Racemocarbonic acid.** Same as *desoxalic acid* (which see, under *desoxalic*).

racemose (ras'ē-mōs), *a.* [Also *racemous*; = F. *racemeux* = Sp. Pg. *racimoso* = It. *racemoso*, < L. *racemosus*, full of grapes, < *racemus*, bunch of grapes: see *raceme*, *raisin.*] 1. In *bot.*: (*a*) Having the character or appearance of a raceme: said of a flower-cluster. (*b*) Arranged in racemes: said of the flowers.—2. In *anat.*, clustered or aggregate, as a gland; having ducts which divide and subdivide and end in bunches of follicles. It is a common type of glandular structure, well exemplified in the salivary glands and the pancreas. See cut under *parotid*.—**Racemose adenoma**, a tumor originating from glandular tissue, and resembling closely the appearance and structure of a racemose gland: found in the breast and in salivary and sebaceous glands.

racemosely (ras'ē-mōs-li), *adv.* So as to form or resemble a raceme or racemes.

racemous (ras'ē-mus or ra-sē'mus), *a.* Same as *racemose*.

racemule (ras'ē-mūl), *n.* [< NL. **racemulus*, dim. of L. *racemus*, a cluster: see *raceme.*] In *bot.*, a small raceme.

racemulose (ra-sem'ū-lōs), *a.* [< NL. *racemulosus*, full of small racemes, < **racemulus*, a small raceme: see *racemule.*] In *bot.*, resembling a racemule, or arranged in racemules.

race-plate (rās'plāt), *n.* A wrought-iron or steel traversing-platform for heavy guns, upon which the gun is moved in a horizontal arc and moves backward in recoil.

racer (rā'sėr), *n.* [= Icel. *rāsari*, a racer, race-horse; as *race*1 + *-er*1.] 1. One who races; a runner or contestant in a race or in races of any kind.

Besmear'd with filth, and blotted o'er with clay,
Obscene to sight, the rueful *racer* lay.
Pope, Iliad, xxiii. 912.

2. A race-horse.

The *racer* is generally distinguished by his beautiful Arabian head; his fine and finely-set-on neck; his oblique lengthened shoulders; well-bent hinder legs; his ample muscular quarters; his flat legs, rather short from the knee downwards; and his long and elastic pastern. Quoted in *T. Bell's British Quadrupeds*, p. 382.

3. Hence, anything having great speed.

Coal will be transferred across the Atlantic in cargo boats for the use of the ocean *racers*. *Engineer*, LXVI. 77.

4. In a braiding-machine, a traversing support for tension and spool-holding apparatus.—5. A snake of the genus *Scotophis* (or *Coluber*), *S. obsoletus*, also called *pilot black-snake* or *pilot-snake*. It is black, with a mottled black and yellow belly, and has the median dorsal scales carinated.—6. A snake, *Bascanion constrictor*, the common black-snake of the eastern United States. It is blue or blue-black, with greenish-blue belly, and has smooth scales.—7. A poor, thin, or spent fish; a slink: applied to mackerel, shad, salmon, etc.—8. A sand-crab. See *Ocypoda*.—**Blue racer.** See *blue-racer*.

race-track (rās'trak), *n.* The track or path over which a race is run; a race-course.

raceway (rās'wā), *n.* 1. An artificial passage for water flowing from a fall or dam; a mill-race. Compare *mill-race*. See *race*2.—2. In *fish-culture*, a fishway.

racht, *n.* See *ratch*2.

rachamah, *n.* In *ornith.* See *Neophron*.

rache1†, *n.* See *ratch*1.

rache2†, *v.* An obsolete form of *reach*1.

rache3†, *v. t.* An obsolete assibilated form of *rack*1.

rachial (rā'ki-al), *a.* [< *rachis* + *-al.*] Pertaining to a rachis; rachidial. Also *rhachial*.

rachialgia (rā-ki-al'ji-ä), *n.* [NL., prop. *rhachialgia*, < Gr. ῥάχις, spine, + ἄλγος, pain.] Pain in the spine, especially neuralgic pain. Also *rhachialgia*.

rachialgic (rā-ki-al'jik), *a.* [< *rachialgia* + *-ic.*] Affected with rachialgia. Also *rhachialgic*.

Rachianectes (rā"ki-a-nek'tēz), *n.* [NL. (Cope), also *Rhachianectes*, < Gr. ῥαχία, a rocky shore, + νήκτης, a swimmer, < νήχειν, swim.] A genus of whalebone whales of the family *Balænopteridæ* and subfamily *Agaphelinæ*, containing the gray whale of the North Pacific, *R. glaucus*, combining the small head, slender form, and narrow flippers of a finner-whale with the lack of a dorsal fin and absence of folds of skin on the throat of a right whale. This whale attains great size, and its pursuit is an important branch of the fisheries in the waters it is found in, sometimes attended with special dangers. The parasites chiefly affecting *R. glaucus* are a whale-louse, *Cyamus scammoni*, and a barnacle, *Cryptolepas rachianecti*.

Rachicallis (rā-ki-kal'is), *n.* [NL. (A. P. de Candolle, 1830), < Gr. ῥαχία, a rocky shore, + κάλλος, beauty.] A genus of rubiaceous shrubs belonging to the tribe *Rondeletieæ*, differing from *Rondeletia* chiefly in its half-superior septicidal capsule. There is only one species, *R. rupestris*, called *earwort*, growing on the rocky coasts of the West Indies. It is a low shrub bearing narrow decussate leaves with sheathing stipules, and small solitary yellow flowers sessile in the axils.

rachides, *n.* Plural of *rachis*.

rachidial (rą-kid'i-ąl), *a.* [Also *rhachidial*; < Gr. ῥάχις (assumed stem *ῥαχιδ-), the spine, + *-al.*] Of or pertaining to a rachis, in any sense; rachial.

rachidian (rą-kid'i-ąn), *a.* [Also *rhachidian*; < F. *rachidien*, < Gr. ῥάχις (assumed stem *ῥαχιδ-), the spine, + *-ian.*] Same as *rachidial*.

The teeth of the radula are divided by nearly all students of that organ into *rhachidian* or median, lateral, and uncinal. *W. H. Dall*, Science, iv. No. 81, Aug. 22, 1884.

Rachidian bulb. Same as *medulla oblongata*.—**Rachidian canal**, the spinal or neural canal.

Rachiglossa (rā-ki-glos'ä), *n. pl.* [Also *Rhachiglossa*; NL., < Gr. ῥάχις, the spine, + γλῶσσα, tongue.] Those mollusks which are rachiglossate; specifically, a division of gastropods so characterized, including the *Buccinidæ*, *Muricidæ*, *Volutidæ*, etc. See cut under *ribbon*.

rachiglossate (rā-ki-glos'āt), *a.* [Also *rhachiglossate*; < Gr. ῥάχις, the spine, + γλῶσσα, tongue.] In *Mollusca*, having upon the lingual ribbon or radula only a single median tooth, or a median tooth with only an admedian one on each side of it, in any one of the many transverse series or cross-rows of radular teeth. The formula is 0-I-0 or I-I-I, where the 0 is a cipher and I means one.

rachilla (rą-kil'ä), *n.* [Also *rhachilla*; NL., < Gr. ῥάχις, the spine, + dim. *-illa.*] In *bot.*, a little rachis; a secondary rachis in a compound inflorescence, as of a spikelet in a grass.

Rachiodon (rā-kī'ō-don), *n.* [NL.: see *rachiodont.*] The typical genus of *Rachiodontidæ*, having a series of enamel-tipped vertebral processes projecting into the esophagus and serving as teeth: synonymous with *Dasypeltis* (which see). The type is *R. scaber*, of Africa, a snake which lives much on eggs, and has this contrivance for not smashing them till they get down its throat, when the sagacious serpent swallows the contents and spits out the shell. Also *Rhachiodon*.

rachiodont (rā'ki-ō-dont), *a.* [Also *rhachiodont*; < Gr. ῥάχις, the spine, + ὀδούς (ὀδοντ-) = E. *tooth.*] Having processes of the spinal column which function as teeth; belonging to the *Rachiodontidæ*.

Rachiodontidæ (rā"ki-ō-don'ti-dē), *n. pl.* [NL., < *Rachiodon* (*-odont-*) + *-idæ.*] A family of colubriform ophidians, named from the genus *Rachiodon*: same as the subfamily *Dasypeltinæ*. Also *Rhachiodontidæ*.

Rachiopteris (rā-ki-op'te-ris), *n.* [NL., < Gr. ῥάχις, the spine, + πτερίς, fern: see *Pteris.*] A name under which Schimper has grouped various fragments of the rachides or stems of fossil ferns. Specimens of this nature have been described by Lesquereux as occurring in the coal-measures of Illinois, and by Dawson as having been found in the Devonian of New York.

rachipagus (rą-kip'ä-gus), *n.*; pl. *rachipagi* (-jī). [NL., < Gr. ῥάχις, the spine, + πάγος, that which is fixed or firmly set, < πηγνύναι, make fast.] In *teratol.*, a double monster united at the spine.

rachis (rā'kis), *n.*; pl. *rachides* (-ki-dēz). [Also *rhachis*; NL., < Gr. ῥάχις, the spine, a ridge (of a mountain-chain), a rib (of a leaf).] 1. In *bot.*: (*a*) The axis of an inflorescence when somewhat elongated; the continuation of the peduncle along which the flowers are ranged, as in a spike or a raceme. (*b*) In a pinnately compound leaf or frond, the prolongation of the petiole along which the leaflets or pinnæ are disposed, corresponding to the midrib of a pinnately veined simple leaf. See cut under *compound*.—2. In *zoöl.* and *anat.*: (*a*) The vertebral column. (*b*) The stem, shaft, or scape of a feather, as distinguished from the web, vane, or vexillum; especially, that part of the stem which bears the vexillum, as distinguished from the calamus or quill. See *quill*, 4.

Rye-grass (*Lolium perenne*). *a*, Rachis.

The differentiation of the feather into *rachis* and vexillum. *Gegenbaur*, Comp. Anat. (trans.), p. 419.

(*c*) The median part of the radula of a mollusk, usually bearing teeth which differ from those on each side of it.—3. The axial skeleton of various polyp-colonies, as of *Gorgonia*; some axial part, or formation like a midrib, as in crinoids.—**Generative rachis**, in crinoids, a cellular rod or cord which lies in the genital canal in connection with the visceral generative tissue, and the enlargements of which in the pinnules form the genital glands.

rachitic (rā-kit'ik), *a.* [Also *rhachitic*; < F. *rachitique*; as *rachitis* + *-ic.*] 1. In *anat.*, of or pertaining to the spinal column; spinal; vertebral. [Rare.]—2. Pertaining to or affected with rachitis; rickety.

rachitis (rā-kī'tis), *n.* [NL. (Dr. Glisson, 1650, in his work "De *Rachitide*"), as if lit. 'inflammation of the spine' (prop. *rhachitis*, < Gr. ῥάχις, the spine, + *-itis*), but adopted as a Latinized form for E. *rickets*: see *rickets.*] 1. A disease of very early life, characterized by a perversion of nutrition of the bones, by which uncalcified osteoid tissue is formed in place of bone, and the resorption of bone is quickened. Hence the bones are flexible, and distortions occur, such as crooked legs, heart-shaped pelvis, or curvature of spine. See *rickets*. 2. In *bot.*, a disease producing abortion of the fruit or seed.—**Rachitis fœtalis annularis**, intra-uterine formation of annular thickenings on the diaphyses of the long bones. Also called *rachitis intra-uterina annularis*.—**Rachitis fœtalis micromelica**, intra-uterine stunting of the bones in their longitudinal growth. Also called *rachitis uterina micromelica*.

rachitome (rak'i-tōm), *n.* [Also *rhachitome*; < F. *rachitome*, < Gr. ῥάχις, the spine, + -τομος, < τέμνειν, ταμεῖν, cut.] An anatomical instrument for opening the spinal canal, without injuring the medulla.

rachitomous (rā-kit'ō-mus), *a.* [Also *rhachitomous*; < Gr. ῥάχις, the spine, + -τομος, < τέμνειν, ταμεῖν, cut.] Segmented, as a vertebra of many of the lower vertebrates which consists of a neural arch resting on a separate piece on each side, the pleurocentrum, which in turn rests on a single median piece below, the intercentrum; having or characterized by such vertebræ, as a fish or batrachian, or the backbone of such animals. See *embolomerous*. *E. D. Cope.*

Both kinds of vertebræ (*rachitomous* and embolomerous) can be found in the same animal. *Science*, VI. 98.

racial (rā'sią l), *a.* [< *race*3 + *-ial.* Cf. *facial.*] Relating or pertaining to race or lineage, or to a race or races of living beings; characteristic of race or of a race.

Man, as he lived on the earth during the time when the most striking *racial* characteristics were being developed. *W. H. Flower*, Encyc. Brit., XV. 445.

racially (rā'sią l-i), *adv.* In a racial manner; in relation to or as influenced by race or lineage.

The unification of the *racially* most potent people of whom we have record. *The Academy*, Aug. 3, 1889, p. 66.

Raciborskia (ras-i-bôr'ski-ä), *n.* [NL. (Berlese), < *Racyborski*, a Polish botanist.] A genus of myxomycetous fungi, giving name to the family *Raciborskiaceæ*.

Raciborskiaceæ (ras-i-bôr-ski-ā'sē-ē), *n. pl.* [NL., < *Raciborskia* + *-aceæ*.] A small family of myxomycetous fungi, taking its name from the genus *Raciborskia*, and having the peridium naked and distinctly stipitate, and the capillitium violaceous.

racily (rā'si-li), *adv.* [< *racy* + *-ly*².] In a racy manner; piquantly; spicily.

racinet, *n.* [ME.; < OF. *racine, rachine*, F. *racine* = Pr. *racina, razina*, root, < ML. as if **radicina*, dim. of L. *radix* (*radic-*), root: see *radix*. Cf. *race*⁴.] A root.

> Unlefulle lust, though it be sote,
> And of alle yvelle the *racyne*.
> *Rom. of the Rose*, l. 4881.

raciness (rā'si-nes), *n.* [< *racy* + *-ness*.] The quality of being racy; peculiarly characteristic and piquant flavor or style; spiciness; pungency.

racing (rā'sing), *n.* [Verbal n. of *race*¹, *v.*] The running of races; the occupation or business of arranging for or carrying on races, especially between horses.

> The Queen [Anne] was fond of *racing*, and gave her 100*l.* gold cups to be run for, as now: nay more, she not only kept race horses, but ran them in her own name.
> *Ashton*, Social Life in Reign of Queen Anne, I. 302.

racing-bell (rā'sing-bel), *n.* A grelot or small bell given as a prize for a horse-race: such a prize was frequent in the sixteenth century. Bells of this form exist of silver, from an inch to two inches and a half in diameter, with inscriptions and dates.

racing-bit (rā'sing-bit), *n.* A light jointed-ring bit, the loose rings of which range in size from 3 to 6 inches.

racing-calendar (rā'sing-kal'en-dạ̈r), *n.* A detailed list of races run or to be run.

rack¹ (rak), *v. t.* [Early mod. E. also *wrack* (by confusion with *wrack*¹); not found as a verb in ME. or AS., except the secondary forms AS. *reccan*, as below, and ME. *raxen*, < AS. *raxan*, **racsan*, stretch oneself (see *rax*); prob. < MD. *racken*, stretch, reach out, torture, rack, = G. *racken*, stretch, torture; a collateral form of AS. *reccan* (pret. *reahte*), stretch out, also correct, direct, rule, guide, tell, etc. (> ME. *rechen*, stretch, also tell: see *retch*¹ and *rack*⁷, *reckon*), = OS. *rekkian*, stretch, = MD. *recken*, D. *rekken* = MLG. *reken*, stretch, = OHG. *recchan*, MHG. *recken*, stretch, extend, = Icel. *rekja*, stretch, trace (cf. *rekkja*, strain), = Dan. *række* = Sw. *räcka*, reach, hand, stretch, = Goth. **rakjan*, in comp. *uf-rakjan*, stretch out; prob. = L. *regere*, rule, lit. 'stretch out,' 'make straight' (in *por-rigere*, stretch forth, *e-rigere*, straighten out, erect, etc.) (pp. *rectus*, straight, = E. *right*), = Gr. ὀρέγειν, stretch, = Lith. *rasau*, *razyti*, stretch, = Skt. √ *arj*, stretch. Akin to *rake*², reach, extend, but prob. not to *rake*¹, nor to *reach*¹, with which, however, *rack*¹ has been partly confused. The verb and esp. the noun *rack* show great confusion and mixture of senses, and complete separation is difficult. In some senses the verb is from the noun.] 1. To stretch; stretch out; strain by force or violence; extend by stretching or straining.

> Which yet they *rack* higher to foure hundred threescore and ten thousand yeares.
> *Purchas*, Pilgrimage, p. 54.

> I know your hearts are like two lutes *rack'd* up
> To the same pitch. *The Slighted Maid*, p. 53. (*Nares.*)

> Suits in love should not,
> Like suits in law, be *rack'd* from term to term.
> *Shirley*, Hyde Park, i. 2.

2. To strain so as to rend; wrench by strain or jar; rend; disintegrate; disjoint: as, a *racking* cough; to *rack* a ship to pieces by slanting shot.

> The duke
> Dare no more stretch this finger of mine than he
> Dare *rack* his own. *Shak.*, M. for M., v. 1. 317.

3. To torture by violent stretching; stretch on a frame by means of a windlass; subject to the punishment of the rack. See *rack*¹, *n.*, 2 (*b*).

> He was *racked* and miserably tormented, to the intent he should either change his opinion or confesse other of his profession. *Foxe*, A Table of French Martyrs, an. 1551.

> An answer was returned by Lord Killultagh to the effect that "you ought to *rack* him if you saw cause, and hang him if you found reason." *Encyc. Brit.*, XXIII. 466.

> Noblemen were exempt, the vulgar thought,
> From *racking*; but, since law thinks otherwise,
> I have been put to the rack.
> *Browning*, Ring and Book, I. 202.

Hence—4. To put in torment; affect with great pain or distress; torture in any way; disturb violently.

> My soul is *rack'd* till you dissolve my fears.
> *Beau. and Fl.* (?), Faithful Friends, i. 1.

> Lord, how my soul is *rack'd* betwixt the world and thee!
> *Quarles*, Emblems, v. 9.

> I will not *rack* myself with the Thought.
> *Steele*, Grief A-la-Mode, v. 1.

> Kinraid was *racked* with agony from his dangling broken leg, and his very life seemed leaving him.
> *Mrs. Gaskell*, Sylvia's Lovers, xxxviii.

5. To strain with anxiety, eagerness, curiosity, or the like; subject to strenuous effort or intense feeling; worry; agitate: as, to *rack* one's invention or memory.

> A barbarous phrase has often made me out of love with a good sense; and doubtful writing hath *wracked* me beyond my patience. *B. Jonson*, Discoveries.

> It doth *rack* my brain why they should stay thus.
> *Shirley*, Love in a Maze, v. 5.

6. To stretch or draw out of normal condition or relation; strain beyond measure or propriety; wrest; warp; distort; exaggerate; overstrain: chiefly in figurative uses.

> Albeit this is one of the places that hath been *racked*, as I told you of *racking* Scriptures.
> *Latimer*, Sermon of the Plough.

> For it so falls out
> That what we have we prize not to the worth
> While we enjoy it, but, being lack'd and lost,
> Why, then we *rack* the value.
> *Shak.*, Much Ado, iv. 1. 222.

> Pray, *rack* not honesty. *Fletcher*, Loyal Subject, ii. 6.

> Hyperbole is *racked* to find terms of adoring admiration for the queen. *Whipple*, Ess. and Rev., II. 28.

7. To exact or obtain by rapacity; get or gain in excess or wrongfully. See *rack-rent*. [Obsolete or archaic.]

> Each place abounding with fowle injuries,
> And fild with treasure *rackt* with robberies.
> *Spenser*, Mother Hub. Tale, l. 1306.

> Why, honest master, here lies all my money,
> The money I ha' *rack'd* by usury.
> *Fletcher* (*and another*), Sea Voyage, i. 1.

> Good for nought but to persuade their lords
> To *rack* their rents and give o'er housekeeping.
> *Middleton*, Anything for a Quiet Life, i. 1.

8†. To subject to extortion; practise rapacity upon; oppress by exaction.

> The commons hast thou *rack'd*; the clergy's bags
> Are lank and lean with thy extortions.
> *Shak.*, 2 Hen. VI., i. 3. 131.

> Here are no hard Landlords to *racke* vs with high rents, or extorting fines. *Capt. John Smith*, Works, II. 186.

9. In *mining*, to wash on the rack. See *rack*¹, *n.*, 5 (*i*).—10. To place on or in a rack or frame made for the purpose, either for storage or for temporary need, as for draining, drying, or the like.—11. To form into or as if into a rack or grating; give the appearance of a rack to.—12. *Naut.*, to seize together with cross-turns, as two ropes.—**Racking turns**, turns taken alternately over and under ropes, to bind them together.—**To rack a tackle**, to seize two parts of a tackle together with rope-yarn or spun-yarn, so that, if the fall is let go, the strain will not be loosened.

rack¹ (rak), *n.* [< ME. *racke*, a rack (for torture), *rakke*, a straight bar, a rack for hay, a framework, *rekke*, a bar, a framework above a manger, a bar, a rack (for torture), later *rak*, rack (as a roost, a frame for dishes, weapons, etc.); < MD. *racke*, D. *rak*, a rack, = LG. *rakk*, a shelf, = G. *rack*, a bar, rail, *recke*, a frame, trestle, rack for supporting things, dial. *reck*, scaffold, wooden horse; the lit. sense being either (*a*) active, 'that which stretches,' as an appliance for bending a bow, a frame for stretching the limbs in torture (*rack* in this sense also involving the sense of 'framework' merely), or (*b*) passive, 'that which is stretched,' hence a straight bar (cf. Icel. *rakkr*, *rakr*, straight, = Sw. *rak*, straight), a frame of bars (such as the grating above a manger), a framework used in torture (involving also the orig. active notion of 'stretching'), a bar with teeth, a thing extorted, etc.; from the verb. Cf. G. *reckbank*, a rack (means of torture), < *recken*, stretch, + *bank*, bench.] 1†. A bar.

> Hevie *rekkes* binde to hire fet.
> *Early Eng. Poems and Lives of Saints* (ed. Furnivall), xv. [192.

2. A frame or apparatus for stretching or straining. Specifically—(*a*) A windlass or winch for bending a bow; the part of the crossbow in which the gaffle moved. *Halliwell.*

> These bows . . . were bent only by a man's immediate strength, without the help of any bender or *rack*.
> *Bp. Wilkins*, Math. Magick. (*Latham.*)

(*b*) An instrument of torture by means of which the limbs were pulled in different directions, so that the whole body was subjected to a great tension, sufficient sometimes to cause the bones to leave their sockets. The form of application of the torture differed at different times. The rack consisted essentially of a platform on which the body was laid, having at one end a fixed bar to which one pair of limbs was fastened, and at the other end a movable bar

Rack.

to which the other limbs were fastened, and which could be forcibly pulled away from the fixed bar or rolled on its own axis by means of a windlass. See *judicial torture*, under *torture*.

> Galows and *racke*.
> *Caxton*, tr. of Reynard the Fox (ed. Arber), p. 24.

> Take him hence; to the *rack* with him! We'll touse you Joint by joint, but we will know his purpose.
> *Shak.*, M. for M., v. 1. 313.

3. Punishment by the rack, or by some similar means of torture.

> You have found a Person who would suffer *Racks* in Honour's Cause. *Congreve*, Way of the World, iv. 13.

Hence—4. A state of torture or extreme suffering, physical or mental; great pain; rending anxiety; anguish. See *on the rack*, below.

> A fit of the stone puts a king to the *rack*, and makes him as miserable as it does the meanest subject.
> *Sir W. Temple.*

5. A grating or open framework of bars, wires, or pegs on or in which articles are arranged or deposited: much used in composition, as in bottle-*rack*, card-*rack*, hat-*rack*, letter-*rack*, etc. Specifically—(*a*) A grating on which bacon is laid. (*b*) An open wooden framework placed above a manger or the like, in which fodder for horses or cattle is laid.

> From their full *racks* the generous steeds retire.
> *Addison.*

(*c*) An openwork siding, high and flaring outward, placed on a wagon for the conveyance of hay or straw, grain in the sheaf, or other light and bulky material. (*d*) In *printing*, an upright framework, with side-cleats or other supports, for the storing of cases, of boards or galleys of type, etc.: distinguished as *case-rack*, *galley-rack*, etc. (*e*) *Naut.*, a fair-leader for a running rigging. (*f*) The cob-iron of a grate. *Halliwell.* (*g*) A framework for a table aboard ship to hold dishes, etc., so as to keep them from sliding or falling off: same as *fiddle*, 2. (*h*) A frame for holding round shot in holes; a shot-rack. (*i*) In *metal.*, an inclined wooden table on which fine ore is washed on a small scale. It is one of the various simpler forms of the buddle. (*j*) In *woolen-cloth manuf.*, a frame in a stove or room heated by steam-pipes on which the cloth is stretched tightly after washing with fullers' earth. (*k*) In *organ-building*, one of the thin boards, with perforations, which support the upper part of the feet of the pipes.

6. In *mach.*, a straight or very slightly curved metallic bar, with teeth on one of its edges, adapted to work into the teeth of a wheel, pinion, or endless screw, for converting a circular

a c b

Rack and Worm. Rack and Pinion.

into a rectilinear motion, or vice versa. If the rack is curved, it is called a *segment-rack*. If the teeth are placed on the rack obliquely and it is used with a worm instead of a wheel, it forms a *rack-and-worm gear*; in the cut, *a* is the worm, *b* the rack, and *c* a friction-wheel on which the back of *b* rolls, and which holds *b* intermeshed with *a*. See also cut under *mutilated*.

7. An anglers' creel or fish-basket.—8. A fish-weir.—9. A measure of lacework counting 240 meshes perpendicularly.—10. Reach: as, to work by *rack* of eye (that is, to be guided by the eye in working).—11†. That which is extorted; exaction.

> The great rents and *racks* would be insupportable.
> *Sir E. Sandys*, State of Religion.

In a high rack, in a high position. *Halliwell.* [Prov. Eng.]—**On the rack**, on the stretch by or as if by means of a rack; hence, in a state of tension or of torturing pain or anxiety.

> I wou'd have him ever to continue *upon the Rack* of Fear and Jealousie. *Congreve*, Way of the World, ii. 1.

> My Head and Heart are *on the Rack* about my Son.
> *Steele*, Conscious Lovers, iv. 1.

Rack and pinion. See def. 6, above.—**Rack-and-pinion jack**, a lifting-jack in which power is applied by means of a rack and pinion.—**Rack-and-pinion press**, a press in which force is transmitted through a pinion to a rack connected with the follower. *E. H. Knight.*—**Rack-cutting machine**, a milling-machine for cutting the teeth of racks.—**To live at rack and manger**, to live sumptuously and recklessly without regard to pecuniary means; live on the best without reck of payment.

> But while the Palatine was thus busily employ'd, and lay with all his sea-horses, unbridl'd, unsaddl'd, *at rack*

and manger, secure and careless of any thing else but of carrying on the great work which he had begun . . .
The Pagan Prince (1690). (*Nares.*)

A blustering, dissipated human figure . . . tearing out the bowels of St. Edmundsbury Convent (its larders namely and cellars) in the most ruinous way, by *living at rack and manger* there. *Carlyle*, Past and Present, ii. 1.

To **put to the rack**, to subject to the torture of the rack; cause to be racked; hence, to torment with or about anything; subject to a state of keen suffering.

rack[2] (rak), *n.* [< ME. *rakke, < AS. *hracca, hreccea, hreca*, the back of the head (L. *occiput*: Sweet, Old Eng. Texts, p. 549).] The neck and spine of a fore quarter of veal or mutton, or the neck of mutton or pork. *Halliwell.*

A rack of mutton, sir,
And half a lamb. *Middleton*, Chaste Maid, ii. 2.

rack[3]† (rak), *v. i.* [Altered, to conform to *rack*[3], *n.*, from ME. *reken* (pret. *rac*), drive, move, tend, < Icel. *reka*, drive, drift, toss, = Sw. *vräka* = Dan. *vrage*, reject, drift, = AS. *wrecan*, drive, wreak, E. *wreak*: see *wreak*. Cf. *rack*[3], *n.*] 1. To drive; move; go forward rapidly; stir.

His spere to his hoorte *rac*. *Layamon*, l. 9320.

To her sone sche gan to *reke*. *Octovian*, l. 182.

Ichwule forthur *reke*. *Owl and Nightingale*, l. 1666.

2. To drive, as flying clouds.

Three glorious suns, each one a perfect sun;
Not separated with the *racking* clouds,
But sever'd in a pale clear-shining sky.
Shak., 3 Hen. VI., ii. 1. 27.

The clouds *rack* clear before the sun. *B. Jonson.*

rack[3] (rak), *n.* [< ME. *rac, rak, rakke*, < Icel. *rek*, drift, a thing drifted ashore, jetsam; cf. *reki*, drift, jetsam; < *reka*, drive, drift: see *rack*[3], *v.* Cf. *rack*[4] = *wrack*[1], *wreck*.] Thin flying broken clouds; especially, detached fragments of raggy cloud, commonly occurring with rain-clouds.

There a tempest hom toke on the torres hogh:
A *rak* and a royde wynde rose in hor saile.
Destruction of Troy (E. E. T. S.), l. 1984.

The great globe itself,
Yea, all which it inherit, shall dissolve
And, like this insubstantial pageant faded,
Leave not a *rack* behind.
Shak., Tempest, iv. 1. 156.

The cloudy *rack* slow journeying in the west.
Keats, Endymion, ii.

As when across the sky the driving *rack* of the rain-cloud
Grows for a moment thin, and betrays the sun by its brightness. *Longfellow*, Miles Standish, ix.

rack[4] (rak), *n.* [Another spelling of *wrack*: see *wrack*[1], *n.*, and cf. *rack*[3], from the same ult. source.] Same as *wrack*[1]: now used in the phrases *to go to rack, to go to rack and ruin*.

We fell to talk largely of the want of some persons understanding to look after the business, but all *goes to rack*.
Pepys.

rack[5] (rak), *n.* [A var. of *rake*[2], a path, track: see *rake*[2].] 1. A rude narrow path, like the track of a small animal. *Halliwell.* [Prov. Eng.]—2. A rut in a road. *Halliwell.* [Prov. Eng.]

rack[6] (rak), *v.* A dialectal form of *reck*.

rack[7]† (rak), *v. t.* [A dial. form for what would be reg. *retch, < ME. *recchen, racchen, rechen* (pret. *rahte, rehte, raugte*), rule, < AS. *reccan*, direct, extend, reach forth, explain, say: see *rack*[1], and cf. *retch*[1] and *reckon*.] To relate; tell. *Halliwell.*

rack[8] (rak), *v. i.* [Perhaps a particular use of *rack*[3], *v.* By some supposed to be a var. of *rock*[2].] To move with the gait called a rack.

His Rain-deer, *racking* with proud and stately pace,
Giveth to his flock a right beautiful grace.
Peele, An Eclogue.

Berratto [It.], a boulting cloth, a sieue; a *racking* of a horse. *Borattare*, to sift or boult mealo. Also a *racking* between an amble and a trot. *Florio.*

rack[8] (rak), *n.* [< *rack*[8], *v.*] A gait of the horse between a trot and a gallop (or canter), in which the fore feet move as in a slow gallop, while the hind feet move as in a trot (or pace). It is usually an artificial gait, but is sometimes hereditary or natural. There is much confusion of terms in respect to this gait, due to the fact that the gait itself is somewhat varied, according as the racker carries the one or the other fore foot foremost in the galloping motion of the fore feet; that many confound the rack with the pace, the two words often being used as synonymous; and that many have mistaken the use of the words *pace* and *amble*. There is abundant evidence that the American "pace" of to-day is the "amble" of Europeans of the last century and earlier. The motion of the hind feet is the same in the trot, the pace, and the rack. In the trot the diagonal hind and fore feet move nearly simultaneously. In the pace or amble the hind and fore feet of the same side move nearly simultaneously. See cut in next column.

rack[9] (rak), *n.* [A var. of *rock*[3], by confusion with *rack*[1]. Cf. *rack*[8], a supposed var. of *rock*[2].] A distaff; a rock.

Successive Positions of a Horse in one Stride of the Rack. (After instantaneous photographs by Eadweard Muybridge.)

The sisters turn the wheel,
Empty the woolly *rack*, and fill the reel.
Dryden, tr. of Virgil's Georgics, iv. 423.

rack[10] (rak), *v. t.* [Appar. first in pp. *racked, rackt*; < OF. *raquer*, pp. *raqué*, in *vin raqué*, "small or corse wine, squeezed from the dregs of the grapes, already drained of all their best moisture" (Cotgrave); origin uncertain; according to Wedgwood, < Languedoc *arrou*, rack, < *raco*, husks or dregs of grapes; according to Skeat, for orig. *rasquer = Sp. Pg. Pr. *rascar*, scratch; cf. Sp. Pg. *rasgar*, tear apart: see *rash*[5].] To draw off from the lees; draw off, as pure liquor from its sediment: as, to *rack* cider or wine; to *rack* off liquor.

Rockt wines—that is, wines cleansed and so purged that it may be sud is drawne from the loose. *Minsheu*, 1617.

rack[11] (rak), *n.* [Partly by apheresis from *arrack*; cf. Sp. *raque*, arrack, Turk. *raqi*, a spirituous drink, from the same ult. source: see *arrack*.] 1. Same as *arrack*.

Their ordinary drink is Tea: but they make themselves merry with hot *Rack*, which sometimes also they mix with their Tea. *Dampier*, Voyages, II. i. 53.

2. A liquor made chiefly of brandy, sugar, lemons (or other fruit), and spices. *Halliwell.*—**Rack punch**, a punch made with arrack.

I don't love *rack punch*. *Swift*, To Stella, xxxv.

If slices of ripe pineapple be put into good arrack, and the spirit kept for a considerable time, it mellows down and acquires a very delicious flavour. This quality is much valued for making *rack-punch*.
Spons' Encyc. Manuf., I. 220.

rack[12] (rak), *n.* [Origin obscure.] A young rabbit. See the quotation.

Racks, or young rabbits about two months old, which have not lost their first coat. *Ure*, Dict., IV. 380.

rackabones (rak'a-bōnz), *n.* [< *rack*[1], *v.*, + *a* (insignificant) + *bones*.] A very lean person or animal. [Colloq., U. S.]

He is a little afraid that this mettlesome charger cannot be trusted going down hill; otherwise he would let go of the old *rackabones* that hobbles behind [the vehicle].
New York Tribune, June 13, 1862.

rackapelt (rak'a-pelt), *n.* [Cf. *rackabones*.] An idle rascal. *Halliwell.* [Prov. Eng.]

rackarock (rak'a-rok), *n.* [< *rack*[1], *v.*, + *a*[2] + *rock*[1]. Cf. *rendrock*.] An explosive consisting of about three parts of potassium chlorate to one part of nitrobenzol.

rack-bar (rak'bär), *n.* *Naut.*, a billet of wood used to twist the bight of a rope called a swifter, in order to bind a raft firmly together.

rack-block (rak'blok), *n.* *Naut.*, a range of sheaves cut in one piece of wood for running-ropes to lead through.

rack-calipers (rak'kal″i-pėrz), *n. pl.* Calipers of which the legs are actuated by a rack-and-pinion motion. *E. H. Knight.*

rack-car (rak'kär), *n.* A freight-car roofed over and with sides formed of slats with open spaces between.

rack-compass (rak'kum″pas), *n.* A joiners' compass with a rack adjustment. *E. H. Knight.*

racker[1] (rak'ėr), *n.* [= D. *rakker* = MLG. *racker, racher*, LG. *rakker* = G. *racker* = Sw. *rackare* = Dan. *rakker*; as *rack*[1], *v.*, + *-er*[1].] 1. One who puts to the rack; a torturer or tormentor.—2. One who wrests, twists, or distorts.

Such *rackers* of orthography. *Shak.*, L. L. L., v. 1. 21.

3. One who harasses by exactions: as, a *racker* of tenants. *Swift.*

racker[2] (rak'ėr), *n.* [< *rack*[8] + *-er*[1].] A horse that moves with a racking gait.

racker[3] (rak'ėr), *n.* [< *rock*[10] + *-er*[1].] A device for racking liquor, or drawing it off from the lees; also, a person who racks liquors.

The filling of casks is effected by Smith's *rackers*.
Engineer, LXVI. 151.

racket[1] (rak'et), *n.* [< Gael. *racaid*, a noise, disturbance, < *rac*, make a noise like geese or ducks; Ir. *racan*, noise, riot. Cf. *rackle*.] 1. A disorderly, confusing noise, as of commingled play or strife and loud talk; any prolonged clatter; din; clamor; hurly-burly.

Pray, what's all that *racket* over our heads? . . . My brother and I can scarce hear ourselves speak.
Sterne, Tristram Shandy, ii. 6.

2. A disturbance; a row; also, a noisy gathering; a scene of clamorous or eager merriment. [Colloq.]

Chav. Adzflesh, forsooth, yonder haz been a most heavy *racket*; by the zide of the wood there is a curious hansom gentlewoman lies as dead as a herring, and bleeds like any stuck pig. *Unnatural Mother* (1698). (*Nares.*)

3. A clamorous outburst, as of indignation or other emotion; a noisy manifestation of feeling: as, to make a *racket* about a trifle; to raise a *racket* about one's ears. [Colloq.]—4. Something going on, whether noisily and openly or quietly; a special proceeding, scheme, project, or the like: a slang use of very wide application: as, what's the *racket*? (what is going on?); to go on a *racket* (to engage in a lark or go on a spree); to be on to a person's *racket* (to detect his secret aim or purpose); to work the *racket* (to carry on a particular scheme or undertaking, especially one of a "shady" character); to stand the *racket* (to take the consequences, or abide the result).

He is ready as myself to stand the *racket* of subsequent proceedings.
Daily Telegraph (London), Sept. 8, 1882. (*Encyc. Dict.*)

He had been off on the *racket*, perhaps for a week at a time.
Daily Telegraph (London), Nov. 16, 1885. (*Encyc. Dict.*)

"Lucky I learned that signal *racket*," said Jack, as, still at a furious pace, he made cuts in different directions with his extemporized flag. *The Century*, XXXIX. 527.

To give the name of legislation to the proceedings at Albany over the Fair Bill yesterday would be an abuse of language. The proper name for them was "tumbling to the *racket*." The Assembly passed the bill without debate and almost unanimously, much as they might pass a bill authorizing a man to change his name.
New York Evening Post, Jan. 29, 1890.

5. A smart stroke; a rap. [Prov. Eng. and Scotch.]

racket[1] (rak'et), *v.* [< *racket*[1], *n.*] **I.** *intrans.* 1. To make a rattling or clattering noise; raise a tumult; move noisily.

The wind blazed and *racketed* through the narrow space between the house and the hill. *S. Judd*, Margaret, i. 17.

2. To engage or take part in a racket of any kind; frequent noisy or tumultuous scenes; carry on eager or energetic action of some special kind. [Colloq.]

Old Gineral Pierpont, his gret-gret-grandfather, was a gineral in the British army in Injy, an' he *racketed* round 'mong them nabobs out there, an' got no end o' gold an' precious stones. *H. B. Stowe*, Oldtown, p. 571.

3. To be dissipated; indulge to excess in social pleasures. [Colloq.]

I have been *racketing* lately, having dined twice with Rogers and once with Grant.
Macaulay, in Trevelyan, I. 302.

II. *trans.* To utter noisily or tumultuously; clamor out. [Rare.]

Then think, then speak, then drink their sound again,
And *racket* round about this body's court
These two sweet words, 'Tis safe.
B. Jonson, Case is Altered, iv. 4.

racket[2] (rak'et), *n.* [Also *racquet, raquet*; < ME. *raket* = D. *raket* = MLG. *ragget* = G. *racket, raket, rakett* = Dan. Sw. *raket*, < OF. assibilated *rachete, rachette, rasquete, rasquette*, a racket, battledore, also the palm of the hand, F. *raquette*, a racket, battledore, < Sp. *raqueta* = It. *racchetta*, also *lacchetta*, a racket, battledore (cf. ML. *racha*), < Ar. *rāhat*, palm of the hand, pl. *rāh*, the palms; cf. *palm*[1], 7, the game so called, tennis.] 1. The instrument with which players at tennis and like games strike the ball; a bat consisting usually of a thin strip of wood bent into a somewhat elliptical hoop,

Rackets.
a, b, racket and ball used in Italy in the 17th century; *c, d*, racket and ball in present use.

across which a network of cord or catgut is stretched, and to which a handle is attached.

> But kanstow pleyen *raket* to and fro?
> *Chaucer*, Troilus, iv. 460.

> Th' Hail, which the Winde full in his face doth yerk,
> Smarter than *Racquets* in a Court re-ierk
> Balls 'gainst the Walls of the black-hoorded house.
> *Sylvester*, tr. of Du Bartas's Weeks, ii., The Captaines.

> 'Tis but a ball bandied to and fro, and every man carries a *racket* about him, to strike it from himself among the rest of the company.
> *Swift*, Tale of a Tub, Author's Pref.

2. *pl.* A modern variety of the old game of tennis.

> He could shoot, play *rackets*, whist, and cricket better than most people. and was a consummate horseman on any animal under any circumstances.
> *Whyte Melville*, White Rose, I. xiii.

> Some British officers, playing *rackets*, had struck a ball to where he was sitting. *Nineteenth Century*, XXVI. 801.

3. A kind of net. *Halliwell*.—4. A snow-shoe: an Anglicized form of the French *raquette*. [Rare.]

> Their [the Canadian Indians'] Dogges are like Foxes, which spend not, neuer giue ouer, and haue *rackets* tyed vnder their feet, the better to runne on the snow.
> *Purchas*, Pilgrimage, p. 753.

5. A broad wooden shoe or patten for a horse or other draft-animal, to enable him to step on marshy or soft ground.—6. A bird's tail-feather shaped like a racket; a spatule. The racket may result from a spatulate enlargement of the webs at or near the end of the feather; or from the lack, natural or artificial, of webbing along a part of the feather, beyond which the feather is webbed; or from coiling of the end of the feather. These formations are exhibited in the motmots, in some humming-birds and birds of paradise, and in various others, and are illustrated in the figures under *Momotus*, *Prioniturus*, and *Cincinnurus*. Some feathers springing from the head acquire a similar shape. See cut under *Parotia*.

7†. A musical instrument of the seventeenth century, consisting of a mouthpiece with a double reed, and a wooden tube repeatedly bent upon itself, and pierced with several finger-holes. Its compass was limited, and the tone weak and difficult to produce. Several varieties or sizes were made, as of the bombard, which it resembled. Early in the eighteenth century it was replaced by the modern bassoon. 8. An organ-stop giving tones similar to those of the above instrument.

racket[2]† (rak'et), *v. t.* [< *racket*[2], *n.*] To strike with or as if with a racket; toss.

> Thus, like a tennis-ball, is poor man *racketed* from one temptation to another, till at last he hazard eternal ruin.
> *Hewyt*, Nine Sermons, p. 60.

racket-court (rak'et-kōrt), *n.* A court or area in which the game of rackets is played; a tennis-court.

racketer (rak'et-ėr), *n.* [< *racket*[1] + *-er*[1].] A person given to racketing or noisy frolicking; one who leads a gay or dissipated life.

> At a private concert last night with my cousins and Miss Clements: and again to be at a play this night; I shall be a *racketer*, I doubt.
> *Richardson*, Sir Charles Grandison, I. letter xvi.

racket-ground (rak'et-ground), *n.* Same as *racket-court*.

> The area, it appeared from Mr. Roker's statement, was the *racket-ground*. *Dickens*, Pickwick, xli.

rackettail (rak'et-tāl), *n.* A humming-bird of the genus *Discurus* and related forms, having two feathers of the tail shaped like rackets.

racket-tailed (rak'et-tāld), *a.* Having the tail formed in part like a racket; having a racket on the tail, as the motmots (*Momotidæ*), certain humming-birds (*Discurus*, etc.), or a parrakeet of the genus *Prioniturus*.

rackety (rak'et-i), *a.* [< *racket*[1] + *-y*[1].] Making or characterized by a racket or noise; noisy: as, a *rackety* company or place. [Colloq.]

> This strange metamorphosis in the *racketty* little Irishman. *Kingsley*, Two Years Ago, vii. (*Davies.*)

> In the *rackety* bowling-alley.
> *C. F. Woolson*, Anne, p. 193.

rack-fish† (rak'fish), *n.* [Origin unknown; prob. either for **wrackfish* or for *rockfish*, q. v.] A fish, of what kind is not determined. *S. Clarke*, Four Plantations in America (1670), p. 5.

rack-hook (rak'hůk), *n.* In a repeating clock, a part of the striking-mechanism which engages the teeth of the rack in succession when the hours are struck; the gathering-piece or pallet. *E. H. Knight.*

racking[1] (rak'ing), *n.* [Verbal n. of *rack*[1], *v.*] 1. The act of torturing on the rack.—2. *Naut.*, a piece of small stuff used to rack a tackle.—3. In *metallurgical operations*, same as *ragging*, 2.

racking[2] (rak'ing), *n.* [Verbal n. of *rack*[8], *v.*] In the *manège*, same as *rack*[8].

racking-can (rak'ing-kan), *n.* A vessel from which wine can be drawn without disturbing the lees, which remain at the bottom.

racking-cock (rak'ing-kok), *n.* A form of faucet used in racking off wine or ale from the cask or from the lees in the fermenting-vat.

racking-crook (rak'ing-krůk), *n.* A hook hung in an open chimney to support a pot or kettle. See *trammel*. Also called *ratten-crook*.

racking-faucet (rak'ing-fâ"set), *n.* Same as *racking-cock*.

racking-pump (rak'ing-pump), *n.* A pump for the transfer of liquors from vats to casks, etc., when the difference of level is such as to prevent the use of a siphon or faucet.

racking-table (rak'ing-tā"bl), *n.* A wooden table or frame used in Cornwall for washing tin ore, which is distributed over the surface of the table with a solid rake or hard brush, whence the name: sometimes corrupted into *ragging-table*. See *framing-table*.

rackle (rak'l), *v. t.* and *i.*; pret. and pp. *rackled*, ppr. *rackling*. [Perhaps a var. of *rattle*[1]; but cf. *racket*[1].] To rattle. [Prov. Eng.]

rackle (rak'l), *n.* [Cf. *rackle*, *v.*, *racket*[1].] Noisy talk. [Prov. Eng.]

rackoon†, *n.* An obsolete spelling of *racoon*.

rack-pin (rak'pin), *n.* A small rack-stick.

rack-rail (rak'rāl), *n.* A rail laid alongside the bearing-rails of a railway, having cogs into which works a cog-wheel on the locomotive: now used only in some forms of inclined-plane railway.

rack-railway (rak'rāl"wā), *n.* A railway operated with the aid of rack-rails.

> The first *rack-railway* in France was opened lately at Langres. *Nature*, XXXVII. 328.

rack-rent (rak'rent), *n.* [< *rack*[1], *v.*, + *rent*[2], *n.*] A rent raised to the highest possible limit; a rent greater than any tenant can reasonably be expected to pay: used especially of land-rents in Ireland.

> Some thousand families are . . . preparing to go from hence and settle themselves in America, . . . the farmers, whose beneficial bargains are now become a *rackrent* too hard to be borne, and those who have any ready money, or can purchase any by the sale of their goods or leases, because they find their fortunes hourly decaying.
> *Swift*, Intelligencer, No. 19.

> *Rack-rent* . . . is the highest annual rent that can be obtained by the competition of those who desire to become tenants. It is not a strictly legal term, though sometimes used in Acts of Parliament; in legal documents it is represented by "the best rent that can be obtained without a fine." *F. Pollock*, Land Laws, p. 152.

rack-rent (rak'rent), *v.* [< *rack-rent*, *n.*] I. *trans.* To subject to the payment of rack-rent.

> The land-lord *rack-renting* and evicting him [the tenant] with the help of the civil and military resources of the law. *W. S. Gregg*, Irish Hist. for Eng. Readers, p. 160.

II. *intrans.* To impose rack-rents.

> Hence the chief gradually acquired the characteristics of what naturalists have called "synthetic" and "prophetic" types, combining the features of the modern gombeen-man with those of the modern *rack-renting* landlord.
> *Huxley*, Pop. Sci. Mo., XXXVI. 783.

rack-renter (rak'ren"tėr), *n.* [< *rack-rent* + *-er*[1].] 1. One who is subjected to the payment of rack-rent.

> The yearly rent of the land, which the *rack-renter* or under tenant pays. *Locke.*

2. One who rack-rents his tenants.

> The entire Tory and Unionist alliance went on its knees, so to speak, during the Autumn to implore the *rack-renters* to moderation. *Contemporary Rev.*, LI. 124.

rack-saw (rak'sâ), *n.* A wide-toothed saw.

rack-stick (rak'stik), *n.* A stick suitably prepared for stretching or straining a rope or the like, as in fastening a load on a wagon.—**Rack-stick and lashing**, a piece of two-inch rope, about 6 feet long, fastened to a picket about 15 inches long, having a hole in its head to receive the rope. *Farrow*, Mil. Encyc.

rack-tail (rak'tāl), *n.* In a repeating clock, a bent arm connected with the striking-mechanism, having a pin at its end which drops upon the notched wheel that determines the number of strokes.

rackwork (rak'wėrk), *n.* A piece of mechanism in which a rack is used; a rack and pinion or the like. See cut under *rack*[1].

raconteur (ra-kôṅ-tėr'), *n.* [F., < *raconter*, relate: see *recount*[1].] A story-teller; a person given to or skilled in relating anecdotes, recounting adventures, or the like.

> There never was, in my opinion, a *raconteur*, from Charles Lamb or Theodore Hook down to Gilbert à Beckett or H. J. Byron, . . . who spoke and told anecdotes at a dinner-table, . . . that was not conscious that he was going to be funny.
> *Lester Wallack*, in Scribner's Mag., IV. 721.

racoon, raccoon (ra-kön'), *n.* [Formerly also *rackoon*, *rackcoon*, by apheresis from earlier *arocoun*, *aroughcun*, *aroughcond*, < Amer. Ind. *arathcone*, *arrathkune*, a racoon. Hence, by further apheresis, *coon*. The F. *raton*, racoon, is an accom. form, simulating F. *raton*, a rat: see *ratten*.] A small plantigrade carnivorous quadruped of the arctoid series of the order *Feræ*, belonging to the family *Procyonidæ* and genus *Procyon*. The common racoon is *P. lotor*, so called from its habit of dipping its food in water, as if

Common Racoon (*Procyon lotor*).

washing it, before eating. This animal is about 2 feet long, with a stout body, a bushy ringed tail, short limbs, pointed ears, broad face, and very sharp snout, of a general grayish coloration, with light and dark markings on the face. It is common in southerly parts of the United States, and feeds on fruits and other vegetable as well as animal substances. Its flesh is eatable, and the fur, much used for making caps, is called *coonskin*. The racoon is readily tamed, and makes an amusing pet. Other members of the genus are *P. psora* of California (perhaps only a nominal species) and the quite distinct *P. cancrivorus*, the crab-eating racoon, of the warmer parts of America, known as the *agouara*.

> A beast they call *Aroughcun*, much like a badger, but vseth to liue on trees as squirrels doe.
> *Capt. John Smith*, Virginia, I. 124.

> Quil-darting Porcupines and *Rackcoones* be
> Castled in the hollow of an aged Tree.
> *S. Clarke*, Four Plantations in America (1670), p. 32.

racoon-berry (ra-kön'ber"i), *n.* The May-apple, *Podophyllum peltatum*. [U. S.]

racoon-dog (ra-kön'dog), *n.* An Asiatic and Japanese animal of the family *Canidæ*, *Nyctereutes procyonoides*, a kind of dog having an aspect suggesting a racoon. See cut under *Nyctereutes*.

racoon-oyster (ra-kön'ois"tėr), *n.* An uncultivated oyster growing on muddy banks exposed at low tide. [Southern coast, U. S.]

racoon-perch (ra-kön'pėrch), *n.* The common yellow perch, *Perca americana*, of the Mississippi valley: so called from bands around the body something like those of a racoon's tail. See cut under *perch*[1].

Racovian (ra-kō'vi-an), *a.* and *n.* [< *Racow* (in Poland) (NL. *Racovia*) + *-ian*.] I. *a.* Pertaining or relating to Rakow, a town of Poland, or to the Socinians, who made it their chief seat in the first part of the seventeenth century: as, the *Racovian* Catechism (a popular exposition of Socinianism: see *catechism*, 2).

II. *n.* An inhabitant of Rakow, or an adherent of the Unitarian doctrines formerly taught there; specifically, a Polish Socinian.

racquet, *n.* See *racket*[2].

racy (rā'si), *a.* [< *race*[3] + *-y*[1].] 1. Having an agreeably peculiar flavor, of a kind that may be supposed to be imparted by the soil, as wine; peculiarly palatable.

The hospitable sage, in sign
Of social welcome, mix'd the *racy* wine.
Pope, Odyssey, iii. 503.

2. Having a strong distinctive and agreeable quality of any kind; spirited; pungent; piquant; spicy: as, a *racy* style; a *racy* anecdote.

Brisk *racy* verses, in which we
The soil from whence they came taste, smell, and see.
Cowley, Ans. to Verses.

His ballads are *raciest* when brimmed with the element that most attracts the author.
E. C. Stedman, Poets of America, p. 282.

Book English has gone round the world, but at home we still preserve the *racy* idioms of our fathers.
R. L. Stevenson, The Foreigner at Home.

3. Pertaining to race or kind; racially distinctive or peculiar; of native origin or quality.

Yorkshire has such families here and there, . . . peculiar, *racy*, vigorous; of good blood and strong brain.
Charlotte Brontë, Shirley, ix.

The eyes [of a Gordon setter] must be full of animation, of a rich color, between brown and gold; the neck must be clean and *racy*.
The Century, XXXI. 118.

=**Syn.** 1 and **2.** *Racy, Spicy.* These words agree in expressing a quality that is relished, physically or mentally. Literally, *racy* applies to the peculiar flavor which wines derive from the soil, and *spicy* to the flavor given to food, breezes, etc., by spice. Figuratively, that is *racy* which is agreeably fresh and distinctive in thought and expression; that is *spicy* which is agreeably pungent to the mind, producing a sensation comparable to that which spice produces in taste. Pointedness is essential to *spiciness*, and likely to be found in *raciness*.

rad[1] (rad), *a.* [< ME. *rad*, < Icel. *hræddr* = Sw. *rädd* = Dan. *ræd*, afraid.] Afraid; frightened. [Old Eng. and Scotch.]

We were so *rad* euerilkon,
When that he put besyde the stone,
We qwoke for ferd, and durst styr none,
And sore we were abast.
York Plays, p. 416.

She seyd, "Without consent of me,
That an Outlaw suld come befor a King;
I am right *rad* of treasonrie."
Sang of the Outlaw Murray (Child's Ballads, VI. 27).

rad[2]†, *a.* A Middle English form of *rath*[1].

rad[3]†. A Middle English preterit of *ride*.

rad[4]†. An obsolete preterit of *read*[1].

rad[5] (rad), *n.* [Abbr. of *radical*.] A radical. [Low.]

He's got what will buy him bread and cheese when the *Rads* shut up the Church. *Trollope*, Dr. Thorne, xxxv.

radde†. An obsolete preterit of *read*[1].

raddle[1] (rad'l), *n.* [Early mod. E. *radel*, *redle*; also (in verb) *ruddle*; perhaps a transposed form of *hurdle*; or formed from *wreathe* or *writhe* (cf. *writhle*, *v.*) and confused with *hurdle*, or with *riddle*[3] (ME. *redel*, etc.), a curtain.] **1.** A hurdle. [Prov. Eng.]—**2.** *pl.* Small wood or sticks split like laths to bind a wall for the plastering it over with loam or mortar. *Kennett.* (*Halliwell.*)

In old time the houses of the Britons were slightlie set vp with a few posts and many *radels*, with stable and all offices under one roofe.
Harrison, Descrip. of Britain, ii. 12. (*Holinshed's Chron.*)

3. A piece of wood interwoven with others between stakes to form a fence. [Prov. Eng.]—**4.** A hedge formed by interweaving the shoots and branches of trees or shrubs. [Prov. Eng.]—**5.** A wooden bar with a row of upright pegs, employed by domestic weavers in some places to keep the warp of a proper width, and to prevent it from becoming entangled when it is wound upon the beam.—**6.** In *metal-working*, a rabble.

raddle[1] (rad'l), *v. t.*; pret. and pp. *raddled*, ppr. *raddling*. [Formerly also *redle*, *ruddle*; < *raddle*[1], *n.*] **1.** To weave; interweave; wind together; wattle.

Raddling or working it up like basket work.
Defoe, Robinson Crusoe, xxv.

2†. To "baste"; beat.

Robin Hood drew his sword so good,
The peddler drew his brand,
And he hath *raddled* him, bold Robin Hood,
So that he scarce can stand.
Ballad of Robin Hood.

raddle[2] (rad'l), *n.* [Var. of *reddle*, *ruddle*[1].] **1.** Same as *reddle*.—**2.** A layer of red pigment.

Some of us have more serious things to hide than a yellow cheek behind a *raddle* of rouge.
Thackeray, Roundabout Papers, A Medal of George the [Fourth.

raddle[2] (rad'l), *v. t.*; pret. and pp. *raddled*, ppr. *raddling*. [< *raddle*[2], *n.*] **1.** To paint with or as if with raddle; color coarsely, as with rouge.

Can there be any more dreary object than those whitened and *raddled* old women who shudder at the slips?
Thackeray, Newcomes, xx.

2. To get over (work) in a careless, slovenly manner. [Prov. Eng.] *Imp. Dict.*

raddle-hedge (rad'l-hej), *n.* Same as *raddle*[1], 4.

raddleman†, *n.* Same as *reddleman*. *Fuller*, Worthies, III. 38.

raddock (rad'ọk), *n.* A dialectal form of *ruddock*.

raddour†, *n.* See *redour*.

rade[1]† (rād). A dialectal (Old English and Scotch) preterit of *ride*.

rade[2] (rād), *n.* A dialectal (Scotch) or obsolete form of *road*.

radeau (ra-dō'), *n.*; pl. *radeaux* (-dōz'). [< F. *radeau* = Pr. *radelh*, < ML. **ratellus* (also, after OF., *rodellus*, *rasellus*), dim. of L. *ratis*, raft, vessel.] A raft.

Three vessels under sail, and one at anchor, above Split Rock, and behind it the *radeau* Thunderer.
Irving. (*Webster.*)

Rademacher's plaster. See *plaster*.

radevore†, *n.* [ME., prob. of OF. origin; perhaps orig. OF. **ras de Vore*: *ras* (Sp. It. *raso*), a sort of smooth cloth (see *rash*[4]); *de*, of; **Vore*, perhaps the town of *Lavaur* in Languedoc. Cf. F. *ras de Châlons*, *ras de Gennes*, similar cloth from the places named.] A sort of cloth or textile fabric usually explained as 'tapestry' or 'striped stuff tapestry.'

This woful lady ylerned had in youthe
So that she werken and embrowden kouthe,
And weven in stole the *radevore*,
As hyt of wymmen hath be woved yore.
Chaucer, Good Women, l. 2352.

radge† (raj), *n.* Same as *rodge*.

radial (rā'di-ạl), *a.* and *n.* [< F. *radial* = It. *radiale*, < NL. *radialis*, < L. *radius*, ray, radius: see *radius*, *ray*[1].] **I.** *a.* Of or pertaining to a ray or a radius (or radii); having the character or appearance of a ray or a radius; grouped or appearing like radii or rays; shooting out as from a center; being or moving in the direction of the radius.

At a little distance from the center the wind is probably nearly *radial*. *Science*, III. 94.

Specifically—(*a*) In *anat.*, of or pertaining in any way to the radius (see *radius*, 2): as, the *radial* artery, nerve, vein; *radial* articulations or movements; the *radial* side or aspect of the arm, wrist, or hand; the *radial* group of muscles; the *radial* pronator or supinator. (*b*) In *zoöl.*, rayed, radiate, or radiating; of or pertaining to the rays, arms, or radiating processes of an animal; relating to the radially disposed or actinomeric parts of the *Radiata* and similar animals. See cut under *medusiform*. (*c*) In *ichth.*, of or pertaining to the radialia. See *radiale* (*c*).

The cartilaginous, or ossified, basal and *radial* supports of the fins. *Huxley*, Anat. Vert., p. 38.

(*d*) In *bot.*: (1) Belonging to a ray, as of an umbel or of a flower-head in the *Compositæ*. (2) Developing uniformly on all sides of the axis: opposed to *bifacial* or *dorsiventral*. *Goebel.*—**Radial ambulacral vessels.** See *ambulacral*.—**Radial artery**, the smaller of the branches resulting from the bifurcation of the brachial artery at the elbow, extending in a straight line on the outer side of the front of the forearm to the wrist, where it turns around the radial side of the carpus and descends to the upper part of the first interosseous space, where it penetrates the palm of the hand to help form the deep palmar arch. Just above the wrist it lies subcutaneously on the ulnar side of the tendon of the long supinator, and is here commonly felt in ascertaining the pulse. Its chief branches, besides the muscular and cutaneous ones, are the radial recurrent and the anterior and posterior carpals.—**Radial axle-box.** See *axle-box*.—**Radial bundle**, in *bot.*, a fibrovascular bundle in which the phloëm and xylem are arranged in alternating radii. Compare *closed*, *collateral*, and *concentric bundle*, under *bundle*.

The last form is the *radial*, where the *bundles* of phloem and xylem are arranged alternately in the central fibro-vascular axis. *Encyc. Brit.*, XII. 18.

Radial cells, in *entom.*, same as *postcostal cellules* (which see, under *postcostal*).—**Radial curve**, in *geom.*, a curve most conveniently expressed by means of the radius vector as one coördinate: spirals and the quadratrix of Dinostratus are *radial curves*.—**Radial drilling-machine.** See *drilling-machine*.—**Radial fibers of the retina.** See *sustentacular fibers*, under *sustentacular*.—**Radial formula**, the expression of the number of rays in the fins of a fish by the initial letters of the names of the fins and the numbers of their rays: thus, the *radial formula* for the yellow perch is D. XIII. + I. 14; A. II. + 7; P. 15; V. I. 5—where the Roman numerals are the spines and the Arabic the rays of the dorsal, anal, pectoral, and ventral fins respectively.—**Radial nerve.** See *nerve*.—**Radial-piston water-wheel.** See *water-wheel*.—**Radial plates**, in crinoids, the set or system of plates which includes the joints of the stem, arms and pinnules, the centrodorsal plate, and the radial plate proper: distinguished from *perisomatic plates*.—**Radial recurrent artery**, a branch of the radial artery, given off near its origin, that turns backward to join in the anastomosis about the elbow.—**Radial symmetry.** See *symmetry*.—**Radial vein.** See *marginal vein*, under *marginal*.

II. *n.* A radiating or radial part; a ray. Specifically, in *anat.* and *zoöl.*: (*a*) A radiale. (*b*) In *ichth.*, the radius or hypercoracoid (a bone). (*c*) One of the joints of the branches of a crinoid, between the brachials and the basals; one of the joints of the second order, or of a division of the basals. See cut under *Crinoidea*.

The two *radials* [of a crinoid] on either side of the largest basal . . . are broader than the other two.
Quart. Jour. Geol. Soc., XLV. 150.

(*d*) The fourth joint, counting from the base, of the pedipalp of a spider.

radiale (rā-di-ā'lē), *n.*; pl. *radialia* (-li-ä). [NL., neut. of *radialis*, radial: see *radial*.] In *zoöl.* and *anat.*: (*a*) The radiocarpal bone; that bone of the wrist which is situated on the radial side of the proximal row of carpals, in special relation with the radius. In man this bone is the scaphoid. Compare *ulnare*, and see cuts under *hand* and *carpus*. (*b*) One of the rays of the cup of a crinoid. See *radial*, *n.* (*c*), and cut under *Crinoidea*. (*c*) A cartilage radiating from the base of the fins of elasmobranchiate fishes. See cut under *pterygium*. (*d*) Same as *radial*, *n.* (*b*). See *hypercoracoid*.

radialis (rā-di-ā'lis), *n.*; pl. *radiales* (-lēz). [NL. *radialis* (sc. *musculus*, etc.), radial: see *radial*.] In *anat.*, a radial muscle, artery, vein, or nerve: chiefly used adjectively as a part of certain Latin phrase-names of muscles: as, flexor carpi *radialis*; extensor carpi *radialis* longior or brevior. See *flexor*, *extensor*.

radiality (rā-di-al'i-ti), *n.* [< *radial* + *-ity*.] The character or structure of a radiate organism; formation of rays, or disposition of rayed parts; radial symmetry. Sometimes called *radiateness* and *radiism*.

radialization (rā-di-ạl-i-zā'shọn), *n.* [< *radialize* + *-ation*.] Arrangement in radiating forms; radiation.

Thus the rocks exhibit much evidence of a silicification (and often of a *radialization* possibly connected with it).
Quart. Jour. Geol. Soc., XLV. 267.

radialize (rā'di-ạl-īz), *v. t.*; pret. and pp. *radialized*, ppr. *radializing*. [< *radial* + *-ize*.] To render radiate; make ray-like.

One fragment exhibits part of a large *radialized* structure within a spherulitic matrix.
Quart. Jour. Geol. Soc., XLV. 249.

radially (rā'di-ạl-i), *adv.* **1.** In a radial or radiating manner; in the manner of radii or rays: as, lines diverging *radially*.

As the growth [of the fungus] spreads outward *radially*, the inner hyphæ, having sucked all the organic matter out of the ground, perish.
S. B. Herrick, Wonders of Plant Life, p. 82.

2. In *entom.*, toward or over the radius (a vein of the wing): as, a color-band *radially* dilated.

radian (rā'di-ạn), *n.* [< *radius* + *-an*.] The angle subtended at the center of a circle by an arc equal in length to the radius. Also called the *unit angle* in circular measure. It is equal to 57° 17′ 44″.80625 nearly.

radiance (rā'di-ạns), *n.* [< F. *radiance*, < ML. *radiantia*, radiance, < L. *radian(t-)s*, radiant: see *radiant*.] **1.** Brightness shooting in rays or beams; hence, in general, brilliant or sparkling luster; vivid brightness.

The sacred *radiance* of the sun. *Shak.*, Lear, i. 1. 111.

The Son, . . .
Girt with omnipotence, with *radiance* crown'd
Of majesty divine. *Milton*, P. L., vii. 194.

Life, like a dome of many-coloured glass,
Stains the white *radiance* of eternity.
Shelley, Adonais, lii.

2. Radiation.

Thus we have . . . (3) Theory of *radiance*.
J. Clerk Maxwell, in Encyc. Brit., XIX. 2.

=**Syn. 1.** *Radiance, Brilliance, Brilliancy, Effulgence, Refulgence, Splendor, Luster.* These words agree in representing the shooting out of rays or beams in an impressive way. *Radiance* is the most steady; it is generally a light that is agreeable to the eyes; hence the word is often chosen for corresponding figurative expressions: as, the *radiance* of his cheerfulness; the *radiance* of the gospel. *Brilliance* represents a light that is strong, often too strong to be agreeable, and marked by variation or play and penetration: as, the *brilliance* of a diamond or of fireworks. Hence, figuratively, the *brilliancy* of the scene at a wedding; the *radiance* of humor, the *brilliancy* of wit. *Brilliance* is more often literal, *brilliancy* figurative. *Effulgence* is a splendid light, seeming to fill to overflowing every place where it is—a strong, flooding, but not necessarily intense or painful light: as, the *effulgence* of the noonday sun; the *effulgence* of the attributes of God. Hence a courtier might by figure speak of the *effulgence* of Queen Elizabeth's beauty. *Refulgence* is often the same as *effulgence*, but sometimes weaker. *Splendor*, which is more often used figuratively, is, when used literally, about the same as *refulgence*. *Luster* is the only one of these words which does not imply that the object gives forth light; *luster* may be used where the light is either emitted or reflected, but latterly more often reflected: as, the *luster* of silk. *Luster* is generally like *brilliance*, a varying light, but it may be simply two or three degrees weaker than *splendor*. For comparison with *glisten*, *glitter*, etc., see *glare*, *v. i.*

'Twere all one
That I should love a bright particular star
And think to wed it, he is so above me.
In his bright *radiance* and collateral light
Must I be comforted. *Shak.*, All's Well, i. 1. 90.

There is an appearance of *brilliancy* in the pleasures of high life which naturally dazzles the young. *Craig.*

Effulgence of my glory, Son beloved.
Milton, P. L., vi. 680.

Though they fell, they fell like stars,
Streaming *splendour* through the sky.
Montgomery, Battle of Alexandria.

The smiling infant in his hand shall take
The crested basilisk and speckled snake,
Pleased the green *lustre* of the scales survey,
And with their forky tongues shall innocently play.
Pope, Messiah, l. 82.

radiancy (rā'di-an-si), *n.* [As *radiance* (see *-cy*).] Same as *radiance*.

radiant (rā'di-ant), *a.* and *n.* [Early mod. E. *radiaunt*; < OF. *radiant*, F. *radiant* = Sp. Pg. *radiante* = It. *radiante*, *raggiante*, < L. *radian(t-)s*, ppr. of *radiare*, radiate, shine: see *radiate*.] **I.** *a.* **1.** Darting, shooting, or emitting rays of light or heat; shining; sparkling; beaming with brightness, literally or figuratively: as, the *radiant* sun; a *radiant* countenance.

Mark, what *radiant* state she spreads.
Milton, Arcades, l. 14.

A sudden star, it shot through liquid air,
And drew behind a *radiant* trail of hair.
Pope, R. of the L., v. 128.

His features *radiant* as the soul within.
O. W. Holmes, Vestigia Quinque Retrorsum.

2. Giving out rays; proceeding in the form of rays; resembling rays; radiating; also, radiated; radiate: as, *radiant* heat.

Jonas . . . made him a shadowynge place for his defence agaynst the *radyaunt* heet of the sonne in the syde of an hyll. *Bp. Fisher*, Seven Penitential Psalms, Ps. cxxx.

The passage of *radiant* heat, as such, through any medium does not heat it at all.
W. L. Carpenter, Energy in Nature (1st ed.), p. 45.

When this [radiation of fibers] takes place in an open cavity, producing brush-like forms, they are termed *radiant*.
Encyc. Brit., XVI. 370.

3. In *her.*: (*a*) Edged with rays: said of an ordinary or other bearing such as is usually bounded with straight lines, the rays generally appearing like long indentations. See *ray*¹, 8. (*b*) Giving off rays, which do not form a broken or indented edge to the bearing, but stream from it, its outline being usually perfect and the rays apparently streaming from behind it.—**4.** In *bot.*, radiating; radiate.—**Radiant energy.** See *energy*.—**Radiant heat.** See *heat*, 2.—**Radiant matter**, a phrase used by Crookes to describe a highly rarefied gas, or "ultra-gaseous matter," which is found to produce certain peculiar mechanical and luminous effects when a charge of high-potential electricity is passed through it. For example, in a vacuum-tube exhausted to one millionth of an atmosphere (a Crookes tube) the molecules of the gas present are projected from the negative pole in streams, and if they are made to strike against a delicately poised wheel they set it in motion; if on a piece of calcite, they make it phosphoresce, etc.—**Radiant neuration**, in *entom.*, neuration characterized by a number of veins radiating outward from a small roundish areolet or cell in the disk of the wing, as in certain *Diptera*.—**Radiant point**, in *physics*, the point from which rays of light or heat proceed. Also called *radiating point*.—**Radiant veins or nervures**, in *entom.*, veins or nervures radiating from a single small wing-cell. = **Syn.** 1. Beaming, resplendent. See *radiance*.

Or, a Chief Radiant, Sable.

II. *n.* **1.** In *optics*, a luminous point or object from which light radiates to the eye, or to a mirror or lens; a point considered as the focus of a pencil of rays.—**2.** In *astron.*, the point in the heavens from which the shooting-stars of a meteoric shower seem to proceed: thus, the *radiant* of the shower of November 13th is near the star ζ Leonis, and these meteors are hence called the *Leonides*. Similarly the meteors of November 27th (which are connected with Biela's comet, and are often called the *Bielides*) have their radiant not far from γ Andromedæ, and are also known as the *Andromedes* or *Andromedids*.

radiantly (rā'di-ant-li), *adv.* **1.** With radiant or beaming brightness; with glittering splendor.—**2.** By radiation; in the manner of rays; radiatingly. [Rare.]

Healthy human actions should spring *radiantly* (like rays) from some single heart motive.
Ruskin, Elements of Drawing, iii.

Radiaria† (rā-di-ā'ri-ä), *n. pl.* [NL., neut. pl. of *radiarius*, radiate: see *radiary*.] **1.** In Lamarck's classification (1801–12), a class of animals, divided into the orders *Mollia*, or acalephs, and *Echinoderma* (the latter including the *Actiniæ*).—**2.** In Owen's classification (1855), a subprovince of the province *Radiata*, containing the five classes *Echinodermata*, *Bryozoa*, *Anthozoa*, *Acalephæ*, and *Hydrozoa*.—**3.** In H. Milne-Edwards's classification (1855), the first subbranch of *Zoöphytes* (contrasted with *Sarcodaria*), containing the three classes of echinoderms, acalephs, and corals or polyps.

radiary† (rā'di-ā-ri), *a.* and *n.* [= F. *radiaire*, < NL. *radiarius*, < L. *radius*, a ray, radius: see *radius*.] In *zoöl.*, same as *radiate*.

Radiata (rā-di-ā'tä), *n. pl.* [NL., neut. pl. of L. *radiatus*, radiate: see *radiate*, *a.*] **1.** In Cuvier's system of classification, the fourth grand branch of the animal kingdom, containing "the radiated animals or zoöphytes." It was divided into five classes: (1) *Echinodermata*; (2) *Entozoa*, or intestinal worms; (3) *Acalepha*, or sea-nettles; (4) *Polypi*; (5) *Infusoria*: thus a mere waste-basket for animals not elsewhere located to Cuvier's satisfaction. It was accepted and advocated by L. Agassiz after its restriction to the echinoderms, acalephs, and polyps, in which sense it was very generally adopted for many years. But the group has now been abolished, and its components are widely distributed in other phyla and classes of the animal kingdom, as *Protozoa*, *Cœlentera*, *Echinodermata*, and *Vermes*.

The lower groups of which he [Cuvier] knew least, and which he threw into one great heterogeneous assemblage, the *Radiata*, have been altogether remodelled and rearranged. . . . Whatever form the classification of the Animal Kingdom may eventually take, the Cuvierian *Radiata* is, in my judgment, effectually abolished.
Huxley, Classification (1869), p. 86.

2. In later classifications, with various limitations and restrictions of sense 1. (*a*) The old *Radiata* without the *Infusoria*. (*b*) Same as *Echinodermata* proper; *Ambulacraria* (which see) without the genus *Balanoglossus*. *Metschnikoff*. (*c*) In Owen's system (1855), one of four provinces of the animal kingdom, divided into *Radiaria*, *Entozoa* (cœlelminths and sterelminths), and *Infusoria* (the latter containing *Rotifera* and *Polygastria*).

radiate (rā'di-āt), *v.*; pret. and pp. *radiated*, ppr. *radiating*. [< L. *radiatus*, pp. of *radiare*, furnish with spokes, give out rays, radiate, shine (> It. *radiare*, *raggiare* = Sp. Pg. *radiar* = F. *radier*, radiate, shine), < *radius*, a spoke, ray: see *radius*, *ray*¹.] **I.** *intrans.* **1.** To issue and proceed in rays or straight lines from a point; spread directly outward from a center or nucleus, as the spokes of a wheel, heat and light, etc.

Light . . . *radiates* from luminous bodies directly to our eyes. *Locke*, Elem. of Nat. Phil., xi.

But it [the wood] is traversed by plates of parenchyma, or cellular tissue of the same nature as the pith, which *radiate* from that to the bark.
A. Gray, Structural Botany, p. 74.

When the light diminishes, as in twilight, the circular fibers relax, the previously stretched *radiating* fibers contract by elasticity, and enlarge the pupil.
Le Conte, Sight, p. 39.

2. To emit rays; be radiant: as, a *radiating* body.—**3.** To spread in all directions from a central source or cause; proceed outward as from a focus to all accessible points.

The moral law lies at the center of nature, and *radiates* to the circumference. *Emerson*, Nature, p. 51.

Enjoyment *radiates*. It is of no use to try and take care of all the world; that is being taken care of when you feel delight in art or in anything else.
George Eliot, Middlemarch, xxii.

II. *trans.* **1.** To emit or send out in direct lines, as from a point or focus; hence, to cause to proceed or diverge in all directions, as from a source or cause; communicate by direct emanation: as, the sun *radiates* heat and light.

Donatello . . . seemed to *radiate* jollity out of his whole nimble person. *Hawthorne*, Marble Faun, x.

The Wonder . . . looked full enough of life to *radiate* vitality into a statue of ice.
O. W. Holmes, A Mortal Antipathy, vi.

Mountain tops gather clouds around them for the same reason: they cool themselves by *radiating* their heat, through the dry superincumbent air, into space.
R. J. Mann, in Modern Meteorology, p. 23.

2. To furnish with rays; cause to have or to consist of rays; make radial.

Elsewhere, a brilliant *radiated* formation was conspicuous, spreading, at four opposite points, into four vast luminous expansions, compared to feather-glumes, or aigrettes. *A. M. Clerke*, Astron. in 19th Cent., p. 83.

Radiating keyboard or pedals, in *organ-building*, a pedal keyboard in which the pedals are placed closer together in front than behind, so as to enable the player to reach them with equal ease.—**Radiating point.** Same as *radiant point* (which see, under *radiant*).—**Radiating power.** Same as *radiative power* (which see, under *radiative*).

radiate (rā'di-āt), *a.* and *n.* [< L. *radiatus*, having rays, radiating, pp. of *radiare*, radiate, furnish with spokes: see *radiate*, *v.*] **I.** *a.* **1.** Having a ray, rays, or ray-like parts; having lines or projections proceeding from a common center or surface; rayed: as, a *radiate* animal (a member of the *Radiata*); a *radiate* mineral (one with rayed crystals or fibers); a *radiate* flower-head. Specifically—(*a*) In *zoöl.*: (1) Characterized by or exhibiting radial symmetry, or radiation; having the whole structure, or some parts of it, radiating from a common center; radiatory; rayed; actinomeric. (2) Of or pertaining to the Cuvierian *Radiata*: as, "the *radiate* mob," *Huxley*. (*b*) In *bot.*, bearing ray-flowers: said chiefly of a head among the *Compositæ*, in which a disk of tubular florets is encircled by one or more rows of radially spreading ligulate florets, as in the daisy and sunflower; or in which all the florets are ligulate, as in the dandelion and chicory.

Radiate Structure.—Wavellite.

2. Constituting a ray or rays; proceeding or extending outward from a center or focus; radiating: as, the *radiate* fibers of some minerals and plants; the *radiate* petals of a flower or florets of a head.

A school-house plant on every hill,
Stretching in *radiate* nerve-lines thence
The quick wires of intelligence.
Whittier, Snow-Bound.

3. In numismatic and similar descriptions, represented with rays proceeding from it, as a head or bust: as, the head of the Emperor Caracalla, *radiate*; the head of Helios (the sun-god), *radiate*.

Radiate Head of Gallienus.—From an aureus in the British Museum. (Four times the size of the original.)

The sun-god Helios rising from the sea, showing radiate head. (Metope from New Ilium in the Troad.)

II. *n.* **1.** A ray-like projection; a ray.

The tin salt crystallised out in transparent, shining needles, arranged in clusters of *radiates* about nuclei.
Amer. Chem. Jour., XI. 82.

2. A member of the *Radiata*, in any sense.

radiated (rā'di-ā-ted), *p. a.* [< *radiate* + *-ed*².] Same as *radiate*.—**Radiated animals.** See *Radiata*.—**Radiated falcon.** See *falcon*.—**Radiated wing-cells**, in *entom.*, wing-cells formed principally by diverging nervures, as in the earwig.

radiately (rā'di-āt-li), *adv.* In a radiate manner; with radiation from a common center; radially.—**Radiately veined or nerved**, in *bot.*, same as *palmately veined* or *nerved*. See *nervation*.

radiateness (rā'di-āt-nes), *n.* Same as *radiality*.

radiate-veined (rā'di-āt-vānd), *a.* In *bot.*, palmately veined. See *nervation*.

radiatiform (rā-di-ā'ti-fôrm), *a.* [< L. *radiatus*, radiate, + *forma*, form.] In *bot.*, having the appearance of being radiate: said of heads, as in some species of *Centaurea*, having some of the marginal flowers enlarged, but not truly ligulate.

radiatingly (rā'di-ā-ting-li), *adv.* Same as *radiately*.

radiation (rā-di-ā'shon), *n.* [< F. *radiation* = Sp. *radiacion* = Pg. *radiação* = It. *radiazione*, < L. *radiatio(n-)*, shining, radiation, < *radiare*, shine, radiate: see *radiate*.] **1.** The act of radiating, or the state of being radiated; specifically, emission and diffusion of rays of light and the so-called rays of heat. Physically speaking, radiation is the transformation of the molecular energy of a hot body—that is, any body above the absolute zero (−273° C.)—into the wave-motion of the surrounding ether, and the propagation of these ether waves through space. Hence, every body is the source of radiation, but the character of the radiation varies, depending chiefly upon the temperature of the body; it is called *luminous* or *obscure*, according as it is or is not capable of exciting the sensation of light. See further *radiant energy* (under *energy*), also *heat*, *light*[1], *spectrum*.

> *Radiation* is the communication of vibratory motion to the ether, and when a body is said to be chilled by *radiation*, as for example the grass of a meadow on a starlight night, the meaning is that the molecules of the grass have lost a portion of their motion, by imparting it to the medium in which they vibrate. *Tyndall*, Radiation, § 2.

> Any substance . . . will become heated by *radiation* to the greatest degree when its surface is made rough and completely black, so that it can absorb all the rays falling upon it. *Lommel*, Light (trans.), p. 198.

2. The divergence or shooting forth of rays from a point or focus.—3. In *zoöl.*, the structural character of a radiate; the radiate condition, quality, or type; the radiate arrangement of parts. Also *radiism*.—**Direct radiation** and **indirect radiation**, phrases used in describing the method of heating by steam-radiators, according as the radiator is actually in the room heated or is inclosed in a space beneath, from which the hot air is distributed by tin pipes, as in simple heating by a hot-air furnace. In both cases the heat is communicated by convection, and in the case of indirect radiation not at all by radiation.—**Dynamic radiation**, a phrase introduced by Tyndall to describe the radiation of a gas when the heat is not due to an outside source, but is developed by the molecular motion as the gas passes rapidly into an exhausted vessel.—**Solar radiation**, the radiation of the sun as measured by the heat which the earth receives from it.—**Terrestrial radiation**, the communication of heat by the earth to the surrounding ether, by means of radiation.

radiative (rā'di-ā-tiv), *a.* [< *radiate* + *-ive*.] Having a tendency to radiate; possessing the quality of radiation.—**Radiative** or **radiating power**, the ability of a body to radiate heat—that is, physically, to transform its own heat-energy into the wave-motion of the surrounding ether. It depends, other things being equal, upon the nature of the surface of the body, being a maximum for lampblack and a minimum for polished metallic surfaces: thus, a mass of hot water will cool more rapidly in a vessel with a dull-black surface than in one which is polished and bright, like silver. The radiative and absorbing powers of a substance are identical, and are the opposite of the reflecting power. Also called *emissive power*.

radiator (rā'di-ā-tọr), *n.* [< *radiate* + *-or*[1].] 1. Anything which radiates; a body or substance from which rays of heat emanate or radiate.—2. A part of a heating apparatus designed to communicate heat to a room, chiefly by convection, but partly, in some cases, by radiation.

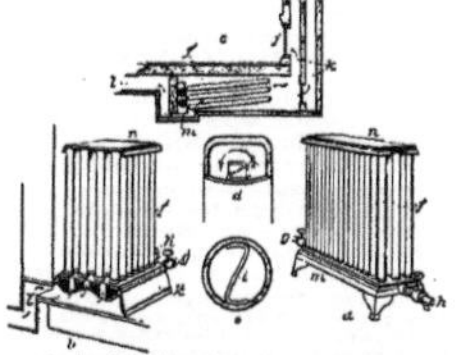

a, a direct radiator with cast-iron base *m* and cap *n*; *f*, vertical tubes of wrought-iron screwed into the base; *g*, inlet; *h*, outlet; *d* and *e*, detail sections of tube; *i*, diaphragm used in one kind of vertical-tube steam-radiators, steam passing through it, as indicated by arrow. *b*, a direct-indirect radiator, air entering at *l*, and circulating upward through passages in base *k*. *c*, an indirect steam-radiator: *m*, base; *f*, tubes; cold air from without is admitted at *l*, and passes over radiator as indicated by arrows; *k*, flues up which warm air passes to register *j*.

A common form of radiator is a sheet-iron drum or cylinder containing deflectors or baffle-plates, placed over a fireplace to cause the volatile products of combustion to give up their heat as they pass: a heating-drum. A steam-radiator consists of a mass of coiled or flexed pipes to which steam for heating is conveyed through a continuous pipe from a boiler, and which is provided with suitable valves for the control of the steam.

radiatory (rā'di-ā-tō-ri), *a.* [< *radiate* + *-ory*.] Radiating; having parts arranged like rays around a center or axis; rayed; actinomeric.

radical (rad'i-kạl), *a.* and *n.* [< F. *radical* = Pr. Sp. Pg. *radical* = It. *radicale* = D. *radikaal* = G. Sw. Dan. *radikal*, < LL. *radicalis*, of or pertaining to the root, having roots, radical, < L. *radix* (*radic-*), root: see *radix*.] **I.** *a.* 1. Pertaining or relating to a root or to roots.

> The cause of a thynne and watery *radycall* moyster to suche thynges as drawe theyr nuryshement therof. *R. Eden*, tr. of Gonzalus Oviedus (First Books on America, (ed. Arber, p. 227).

Specifically—(*a*) In *bot.*, belonging to the root: opposed to *cauline*. See *radical leaves* and *radical peduncle*, below. (*b*) In *philol.*, of the nature of or pertaining to a root, or a primary or underived word or main part of a word: as, a *radical* word: a *radical* letter or syllable: *radical* accentuation. (*c*) In *math.*, consisting of or indicating one of the roots of a number: as, a *radical* expression; the *radical* sign. (*d*) In *chem.*, noting any atom or group of atoms which is, for the moment, regarded as a chief constituent of the molecules of a given compound, and which does not lose its integrity in the ordinary chemical reactions to which the substance is liable. *Cooke*, Chem. Philos., p. 106.

2. Making part of the essential nature of the subject or thing concerned; existing inherently; intrinsic; organic: as, *radical* defects of character; a *radical* fault of construction; the *radical* principles of an art or of religion. The Latin word first occurs, about the beginning of the thirteenth century, in the phrase *humidum radicale*, or radical moisture, that moisture in an animal or a plant which cannot be expelled without killing the organism which was supposed to remain unchanged throughout life, and to be the chief principle of vitality. The word seems to translate the pseudo-Aristotelian ὡς ἂν εἴποι τις ῥίζαι, 'as one may say, roots'—an expression applied to moisture and certain other conditions as being essential to the life of plants.

> *Radicall* moisture, or first or naturall moisture, spred like a dew thorow all the parts of the bodie, wherewith such parts are nourished: which moisture, being once wasted, can neuer be restored. *Minsheu*.

> Whilst thus my sorrow-wasting soul was feeding
> Upon the *radical* humour of her thought.
> *Quarles*, Emblems, iv. 12.

> This *radical* error . . . has contributed more than any other cause to prevent the formation of popular constitutional governments. *Calhoun*, Works, I. 30.

3. Of or pertaining to the root or foundation of the subject; concerned with or based upon fundamental principles; hence, thoroughgoing; extreme: as, a *radical* truth; a *radical* difference of opinion; *radical* views or measures; the *Radical* party in British politics.

> His works . . . are more *radical* in spirit and tendency than any others, for they strike at all cant whatever, whether it be the cant of monarchy or the cant of democracy. *Whipple*, Ess. and Rev., I. 147.

4. [*cap.*] Of or pertaining to a political party or body of persons known as Radicals (see II., 4, below): as, a *Radical* candidate; the *Radical* program.—**Radical axis of two circles.** See *axis*[1].—**Radical bass**, in *music*, same as *fundamental bass* (which see, under *fundamental*).—**Radical cadence**, in *music*, a cadence consisting of chords in their original position.—**Radical center of three circles in a plane**, the intersection of the three radical axes of the three pairs of the three circles.—**Radical curve.** See *curve*.—**Radical expression**, an expression containing radical signs, especially a quantity expressed as a root of another. Sometimes loosely called a *radical quantity*.—**Radical function.** See *function*.—**Radical leaves**, leaves springing from the root, or, properly, from a part of the stem near to and resembling the root. In many herbs (primrose, dandelion, etc.) all or nearly all the leaves are thus clustered at the base of the stem. See cuts under *Hieracium* and *Ornithogalum*.—**Radical moisture**†. See above, def. 2.—**Radical peduncle**, a peduncle that proceeds from the axil of a radical leaf, as in the primrose and cowslip.—**Radical pitch**, the pitch or tone with which the utterance of a syllable begins.—**Radical plane**, the plane of intersection of two spheres other than the plane at infinity, whether the circle of intersection be real or not.—**Radical sign**, the sign $\surd$ (a modified form of the letter *r*, the initial of Latin *radix*, root), placed before any quantity, denoting that its root is to be extracted: thus, $\sqrt{a}$ or $\sqrt{a+b}$. To distinguish the particular root, a number is written over the sign: thus, $\sqrt[3]{\ }$, $\sqrt[4]{\ }$, $\sqrt[5]{\ }$, etc., denote respectively the square root, cube root, fourth root, etc. In the case of the square root, however, the number is usually omitted, and merely the sign written. The same sign is much used to mark a so-called root or radical element of words.—**Radical stress**, in *elocution*, the force of utterance falling on the initial part of a syllable or word. =**Syn.** 3. There may be a distinction between a *radical* reform, change, cure, or the like, and one that is *thorough*, *entire*, *complete*, or *thoroughgoing*, *radical* emphasizing only the fact of going to the root, whether there is thoroughness or entireness or not. Yet that which is *radical* is likely to be *thorough*, etc.

Radical Axes and Radical Center.

II. *n.* 1. In *philol.*: (*a*) A radical word or part of a word; especially, a primitive word or verbal element serving as a root of inflected or derivative words. (*b*) A radical letter; a letter forming an essential part of the primitive form or root of a word. Also *radicle*.—2. In *chem.*, an element or group of combined elements which remains after one or more elements have been removed from a compound. (See the quotation.) The term is chiefly applied to compound radicals, which are assumed to exist in compound bodies and to remain intact in many of the chemical changes which these bodies undergo. Thus the compound radical ethyl, C_2H_5, appears in alcohol ($C_2H_5.OH$), in ether ($(C_2H_5)_2O$), in ethylamine ($C_2H_5.NH_2$), etc., and may be transferred without change, like an element, from one of these compounds to the other. Also *radicle*.

> The word *radical* stands for any atom or group of atoms which is, for the moment, regarded as a chief constituent of the molecules of a given compound, and which does not lose its integrity in the ordinary chemical reactions to which the substance is liable. . . . As a general rule the metallic atoms are basic *radicals*, while the non-metallic atoms are acid *radicals*. . . . Among compound *radicals* those consisting of carbon and hydrogen alone are usually basic, and those containing oxygen also are usually acid. *Cooke*, Chem. Philos., p. 106.

3. In *music*, same as *root*.—4. A person who holds or acts according to radical principles; one who pursues a theory to its furthest apparent limit; an extremist, especially in politics. In the political sense, in which the word has been most used, a Radical is one who aims at thorough reform in government from a liberal or democratic point of view, or desires the establishment of what he regards as abstract principles of right and justice, by the most direct and uncompromising methods. The political Radicals of a country generally constitute the extreme faction or wing of the more liberal of the two leading parties, or act as a separate party when their numbers are sufficient for the exertion of any considerable influence. The name *Radical* is often applied as one of reproach to the members of a party by their opponents. In the United States it has been so applied at times to Democrats, and to Republicans especially in the South about the period of reconstruction. The French Radicals are often called the *Extreme Left*. The British Radicals form an important section of the Liberal party.

> In politics they [the Independents] were, to use the phrase of their own time, "Root-and-Branch men," or, to use the kindred phrase of our own, *Radicals*. *Macaulay*.

> He [President Johnson] did not receive a single Southern vote, and was detested through every Southern State with a cordiality unknown in the case of any Northern *Radical*. *The Nation*, III. 141.

5. In *alg.*, a quantity expressed as a root of another quantity.—**Negative, organic**, etc., **radical.** See the adjectives.

radicalise, *v.* See *radicalize*.

radicalism (rad'i-kạl-izm), *n.* [= F. *radicalisme* = Sp. Pg. It. *radicalismo*; as *radical* + *-ism*.] The state or character of being radical; the holding or carrying out of extreme principles on any subject; specifically, extreme political liberalism; the doctrine or principle of uncompromising reform in government; the system or methods advocated by the political Radicals of a country.

> *Radicalism* endeavours to realize a state more in harmony with the character of the ideal man. H. *Spencer*, Social Statics, p. 511.

> The year 1769 is very memorable in political history, for it witnessed the birth of English *Radicalism*, and the first serious attempts to reform and control Parliament by a pressure from without, making its members habitually subservient to their constituents. *Lecky*, Eng. in 18th Cent., xi.

radicality (rad-i-kal'i-ti), *n.* [< *radical* + *-ity*.] 1. The state or character of being radical, in any sense. [Rare.]—2†. Origination.

> There may be equivocal seeds and hermaphroditical principles which contain the *radicality* and power of different forms. *Sir T. Browne*, Vulg. Err., iii. 17.

radicalize (rad'i-kạl-īz), *v.*; pret. and pp. *radicalized*, ppr. *radicalizing*. [< *radical* + *-ize*.] **I.** *trans.* To make radical; cause to conform to radical ideas, or to political radicalism. [Recent.]

> It is inferred . . . that Lord Salisbury means to *radicalize* his land programme for England. *New York Tribune*, Feb. 18, 1887.

II. *intrans.* To become radical; adopt or carry out radical principles, or the doctrines of political radicalism. [Recent.]

> Indeed, it is hard to say which is the more surprising—the goodwill shown by the Russians, and even by the Russian Government, for a *radicalising* Republic, or the fatuous admiration of certain French Republicans for the most autocratic State in Europe. *Contemporary Rev.*, LIII. 308.

Also spelled *radicalise*.

radically (rad'i-kạl-i), *adv.* 1. By root or origin; primitively; originally; naturally.

> Tho' the Word [*bless*] be *radically* derived from the Dutch Word, yet it would bear good Sense, and be very pertinent to this Purpose, if we would fetch it from the French Word "blesser," which is to hurt. *Howell*, Letters, I. vi. 55.

> These great Orbs thus *radically* bright. *Prior*, Solomon, i.

2. In a radical manner; at the origin or root; fundamentally; essentially: as, a scheme or system *radically* wrong or defective.

> The window tax, long condemned by universal consent as a *radically* bad tax. *S. Dowell*, Taxes in England, II. 313.

radicalness (rad'i-kạl-nes), *n.* The state of being radical, in any sense.

radicand (rad-i-kand'), *n.* [< L. *radicandus*, ger. of *radicari*, take root: see *radicate*.] In *math.*, an expression of which a root is to be extracted.

radicant (rad'i-kạnt), *a.* [< F. *radicant*, < L. *radican(t-)s*, ppr. of *radicari*, take root: see *radicate*.] In *bot.*, rooting; specifically, producing roots from some part other than the descending axis, as for the purpose of climbing. Also *radicating*.

radicarian (rad-i-kā'ri-an), *a.* [‹ L. *radix* (*radic-*), root, + *-arian.*] Of or relating to roots.

The strength of the *radicarian* theory is that it accords with all that we have learned as to the nature of language. *Whitney*, Amer. Jour. Philol., Nov., 1880, p. 338.

Radicata (rad-i-kā'tạ), *n. pl.* [NL., neut. pl. of L. *radicatus*, rooted: see *radicate.*] A division of polyzoans: same as *Articulata* (*d*): opposed to *Incrustata.*

radicate (rad'i-kāt), *v.*; pret. and pp. *radicated*, ppr. *radicating.* [‹ L. *radicatus*, pp. of *radicari* (› It. *radicare* = Sp. Pg. Pr. *radicar*), take or strike root, ‹ *radix* (*radic-*), root: see *radix.*] **I.** *intrans.* To take root.

For evergreens, especially such as are tender, prune them not after planting till they do *radicate.* *Evelyn*, Sylva.

II. *trans.* To cause to take root; root; plant deeply and firmly.

Often remembrance to them [noblemen] of their astate may happen to *radycate* in theyr hartes intollerable pride. *Sir T. Elyot*, The Governour, i. 4.

This medical feature in the Essenes is not only found in the Christians, but is found *radicated* in the very constitution of that body. *De Quincey*, Essenes, iii.

radicate (rad'i-kāt), *a.* [‹ L. *radicatus*, pp. of *radicari*, take root: see *radicate*, *v.*] 1. In *zoöl.*: (*a*) Rooted; fixed at the bottom as if rooted; growing from a fixed root or root-like part. (*b*) Specifically, in *conch.*: (1) Byssiferous; fixed by a byssus. (2) Adherent by the base to some other body, as a limpet to a rock. (*c*) Rooted and of a plant-like habit, as a polyzoan; not incrusting like a lichen; belonging to the *Radicata.*—2. In *bot.*, rooted.

radicated (rad'i-kā-ted), *p. a.* [‹ *radicate*, *v.*, + *-ed*[2].] Rooted, or having taken root: same as *radicate*: as, a *radicated* stem.

If, therefore, you would not cheat yourselves, as multitudes in this age have done, about your love to the brethren, try not by the bare act, but by the *radicated*, prevalent degree of your love. *Baxter*, Saints' Rest, iii. 11.

radicating (rad'i-kā-ting), *p. a.* In *bot.*, same as *radicant.*

radication (rad-i-kā'shọn), *n.* [‹ F. *radication* = Sp. *radicacion* = Pg. *radicação* = It. *radicazione*, ‹ ML. *radicatio*(*n-*), ‹ L. *radicari*, pp. *radicatus*, take root: see *radicate.*] 1. The process of taking root, or the state of being rooted.

Pride is a sin of so deep *radication*, and so powerful in the hearts of carnal men, that it will take advantage of any condition. *Baxter*, Life of Faith, iii. 15.

2. In *bot.*, the manner in which roots grow or are arranged.—3. In *zoöl.*, fixation at the base, as if rooted; the state of being radicate or radicated.

radicet, *n.* An obsolete form of *radish.*

radicel (rad'i-sel), *n.* [‹ F. *radicelle* = It. *radicella*, ‹ NL. **radicella*, little root, dim. of L. *radix* (*radic-*), root.] 1. In *bot.*, a minute root; a rootlet. Also *radicle.* *A. Gray.*—2. In *zoöl.*, a rootlet or radicle.

radices, *n.* Plural of *radix.*

radicicolous (rad-i-sik'ọ-lus), *a.* [‹ L. *radix* (*radic-*), root, + *colere*, inhabit.] Living upon or infesting roots: specifically noting the root-form of the phylloxera or vine-pest: contrasted with *gallicolous.* See *Phylloxera*, 2.

radiciflorous (rạ-dis-i-flō'rus), *a.* [‹ L. *radix* (*radic-*), root, + *flos* (*flor-*), flower, + *-ous.*] Flowering (apparently) from the root. *A. Gray.*

radiciform (rạ-dis'i-fôrm), *a.* [= F. It. *radiciforme*, ‹ L. *radix* (*radic-*), root, + *forma*, form: see *form.*] 1. In *bot.*, of the nature or appearance of a root. *A. Gray.*—2. In *zoöl.*, root-like in aspect or function.

radicle (rad'i-kl), *n.* [= F. *radicule* = Sp. *radícula*, ‹ L. *radicula*, rootlet, small root, also radish, soapwort, dim. of *radix* (*radic-*), root: see *radix.* Cf. *radicel.*] 1. In *bot.*: (*a*) A rootlet: same as *radicel.* (*b*) Specifically, same as *caulicle*: by late writers appropriately restricted to the rudimentary root at the lower extremity of the caulicle.—2. In *anat.* and *zoöl.*, a little root or root-like part; a radix: as, the *radicles* of a vein (the minute vessels which unite to form a vein); the *radicle* of a nerve.—3. In *philol.*, same as *radical*, 1. [Unusual.]

Radicles are elementary relational parts of words. They are generally single sounds—oftenest a consonant sound. *F. A. March*, Anglo-Saxon Grammar (1869), p. 33.

4. In *chem.*, same as *radical*, 2.

A *radicle* may consist of a single elementary atom, and it then forms a simple *radicle*; or it may consist of a group of atoms, in which case it constitutes a compound *radicle.* *W. A. Miller*, Elem. of Chemistry, § 1061.

Adverse, centrifugal, centripetal radicle. See the adjectives.

radicolous (rạ-dik'ọ-lus), *a.* A contracted form of *radicicolous.*

radicose (rad'i-kōs), *a.* [= Sp. Pg. *radicoso*, ‹ L. *radicosus*, full of roots, ‹ *radix* (*radic-*), a root: see *radix.*] In *bot.*, having a large root.

radicula (rạ-dik'ụ-lạ), *n.*; pl. *radiculæ* (-lē). [L.: see *radicle.*] In *entom.*, a radicle.

radicular (rạ-dik'ụ-lạr), *a.* [‹ *radicule* + *-ar*[3].] Characterized by the presence of a radicle or radicles.

As the first leaves produced are the cotyledons, this stem is called the cotyledonary extremity of the embryo, while the other is the *radicular.* *Balfour.*

Radicular odontome, an odontome formed on the neck or root of a tooth.

radicule (rad'i-kūl), *n.* [‹ F. *radicule*, ‹ L. *radicula*, little root: see *radicle.*] In *bot.*, same as *radicle*, 1.

radiculose (rạ-dik'ụ-lōs), *a.* [‹ NL. **radiculosus*, ‹ L. *radicula*, rootlet: see *radicle.*] In *bot.*, covered with radicles or rootlets.

radii, *n.* Plural of *radius.*

radiism (rā'di-izm), *n.* [‹ L. *radius*, ray, + *-ism.*] In *zoöl.*, same as *radiation*, 3. *Forbes*, Brit. Sea Urchins.

radiocarpal (rā"di-ō-kär'pạl), *a.* [‹ L. *radius*, radius, + NL. *carpus*, the wrist: see *carpal.*] 1. Pertaining to the radius and the carpus or wrist: as, the *radiocarpal* articulation; *radiocarpal* ligaments.—2. Situated on the radial side of the wrist: as, the *radiocarpal* bone. See *radiale.*—**Radiocarpal arteries**, the anterior and posterior carpal arteries; small branches given off from the radial at the wrist and passing to the front and back to help form the anterior and posterior carpal arches.—**Radiocarpal articulation**, the wrist-joint proper; the jointing of the manus or third segment of the forelimb of any vertebrate with the second or preceding segment. In animals whose ulna is shorter than the radius this joint is formed wholly by the radius in articulation with some or all of the proximal row of carpal bones, constituting a radiocarpal articulation in literal strictness; but the ulna often enters into this joint without altering its name. In man, whose pronation and supination are perfect, the ulna reaches the wrist, but is cut off from direct articulation with any carpal by a button of cartilage interposed between itself and the cuneiform, and the radius articulates with both the scaphoid and the semilunar, so that the human wrist-joint is properly radiocarpal.—**Radiocarpal ligament**, the external lateral ligament of the radiocarpal articulation. It extends from the summit of the styloid process of the radius to the outer side of the scaphoid.

Radioflagellata (rā"di-ọ-flaj-e-lā'tạ), *n. pl.* [NL.: see *radioflagellate.*] An order of animalcules emitting numerous ray-like pseudopodia, after the manner of the *Radiolaria*, and provided at the same time with one or more flagellate appendages, but having no distinct oral aperture. They are mostly marine. In Kent's system they consist of two families, *Actinomonadidæ* and *Euchitonidæ.*

radioflagellate (rā"di-ọ-flaj'e-lāt), *a.* [‹ L. *radius*, ray, + *flagellum*, a whip: see *flagellate*[1].] Having radiating pseudopodia and flagella; of or pertaining to the *Radioflagellata.*

radiograph (rā'di-ō-gràf), *n.* [‹ L. *radius*, ray, + Gr. γράφειν, write.] 1. An instrument for measuring and recording the intensity of solar radiation.—2. An impression produced on a sensitive photographic plate by the Röntgen rays. See *ray.*

radiohumeral (rā"di-ō-hū'mẹ-rạl), *a.* [‹ L. *radius*, ray, + *humerus*, prop. *umerus*, a shoulder: see *humeral.*] Relating to the radius and the humerus: as, the *radiohumeral* articulation or ligament.

Radiola (rạ-dī'ọ-lạ), *n.* [NL. (J. F. Gmelin, 1791), so named in reference to the many branches; ‹ L. *radiolus*, a little ray, also a plant resembling a fern, dim. of *radius*, a ray: see *radius*, *ray*[1].] A genus of polypetalous plants of the order *Lineæ*, or flax family, and tribe *Eulineæ*, distinguished from the nearly related genus *Linum* (flax) by its complete numerical symmetry in fours (instead of fives), having four toothed sepals, four twisted petals, four distinct stamens, a four-celled ovary, four styles, and an eight-celled, eight-seeded capsule. The only species, *R. Millegrana*, native of the temperate and subtropical parts of the Old World, is a little annual with forking stem, opposite leaves, and minute white corymbose flowers. See *allseed* (d) and *flaxseed*, 2.

Radiolaria (rā"di-ō-lā'ri-ạ), *n. pl.* [NL., neut. pl. of **radiolaris*, ‹ L. *radiolus*, a little ray: see *Radiola.*] A class of filose non-corticate *Protozoa*: a name applied by Haeckel (in 1862) to the protozoans called by Ehrenberg *Polycystina.* The radiolarians are marine gymnomyxine protozoans in which no contractile vacuoles are observed, having an amœbiform body of spherical or conical figure with radiant filose pseudopods, inclosing a similarly shaped perforated test of membranous texture called the central capsule. The intracapsular protoplasm is continuous through the perforations with that which is extracapsular, and has a large specialized nucleus or several such nuclei. There is usually a skeleton of silicious spicules or of the substance called acanthin, and embedded in the protoplasm may be oil-globules, pigment-granules, and crystals. Most radiolarians contain peculiar nucleated yellow corpuscles regarded as parasitic algals. Reproduction both by fission and by sporulation has been observed. The *Radiolaria* have been divided into the subclasses *Silicoskeleta* and *Acanthometridea*, according to the chemical composition of the skeleton, the former subclass into *Peripylæa*, *Monopylæa*, and *Tripylæa* (or *Phæodaria*); into *Monocyttaria*, with one central capsule, and *Polycyttaria*, with several such; and in various other ways. The latest monographer arranges them under four subclasses or "legions": (1) *Peripylea* or *Spumellaria*, with 32 families; (2) *Actipylea* or *Acantharia*, with 12 families; (3) *Monopylea* or *Nassellaria*, with 26 families; and (4) *Cannopylea* or *Phæodaria*, with 15 families. The term *Radiolaria* appears to have been first used by Johannes Müller, in 1858, for the organisms known as *Polycystina*, *Thalassicolla*, and *Acanthometra.* The marine radiolarians all inhabit the superficial stratum of the sea, and fabricate their skeletons of the infinitesimally small proportion of silex which is dissolved in sea-water. When they die these skeletons sink to the bottom, forming geological strata. Extensive masses of Tertiary rock, such as that which is found at Oran in Algeria, and that which occurs at Bissex Hill in Barbados, are very largely made up of exquisitely preserved skeletons of *Radiolaria*, which are erroneously named "fossil *Infusoria.*" But, though there can be little doubt that *Radiolaria* abounded in the Cretaceous sea, none are found in the Chalk, their silicious skeletons having probably been dissolved and redeposited as flint. Recent remains of radiolarians enter largely into the composition of the so-called radiolarian ooze.

A Radiolarian (*Heliosphæra pectinata*), 160 times natural size.

radiolarian (rā"di-ō-lā'ri-ạn), *a.* and *n.* [‹ *Radiolaria* + *-an.*] **I.** *a.* Of or pertaining to the *Radiolaria*; containing or consisting of radiolarians.—**Radiolarian ooze**, the ooze or sediment at the bottom of the sea, composed in part of the shells of radiolarians. See *globigerina-mud.*

Their siliceous skeletons accumulate in some localities . . . to such an extent as to form a *Radiolarian ooze.* *W. B. Carpenter*, Micros., § 507.

II. *n.* Any member of the *Radiolaria.*

radioli, *n.* Plural of *radiolus.*

radiolite (rā'di-ọ-līt), *n.* [‹ NL. *radiolites*, ‹ *radiolus*, dim. of L. *radius*, ray: see *radius.*] 1. A member of the genus *Radiolites.*—2. A variety of natrolite, occurring in radiated forms in the zircon-syenite of southern Norway.

Radiolites (rā"di-ọ-lī'tēz), *n.* [NL.: see *radiolite.*] A genus of *Rudistæ*, typical of the family *Radiolitidæ.* The typical species have at maturity valves elevated in a coniform manner in opposite directions, and sculptured with radiating grooves and ridges.

Radiolitidæ (rā"di-ọ-lit'i-dē), *n. pl.* [NL., ‹ *Radiolites* + *-idæ.*] A family of *Rudistæ*, typified by the genus *Radiolites.* The shell is very inequivalve and fixed by one valve; the hinge has one cardinal tooth and two fossæ in the fixed valve, and two cardinal teeth in the free; the external layer of the shell is thick and the internal thin; the summit of the free valve is nearly central in the adult, but submarginal in the young. The family is characteristic of the Cretaceous period.

radiolus (rạ-dī'ọ-lus), *n.*; pl. *radioli* (-lī). [NL., dim. of L. *radius*, a ray: see *radius.*] In *ornith.*, one of the barbules, or rays of the second order, of the main shaft of a feather.—**Radioli accessorii**, the barbules of the aftershaft or hypoptilum of a feather.

radiometer (rā-di-om'e-tėr), *n.* [= F. *radiomètre* = Sp. *radiómetro*, ‹ L. *radius*, a ray, + Gr. μέτρον, measure.] 1. An old instrument for

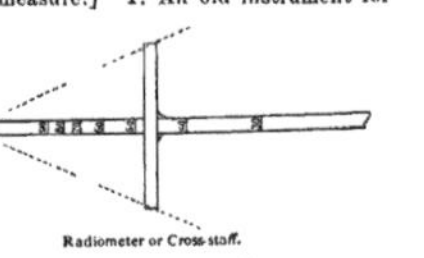

Radiometer or Cross-staff.

measuring angles; the cross-staff. The end of the staff was held to the eye, and the crosspiece was shifted until it just covered the angle to be measured, when the latter was read off on the longitudinal staff.

2. An instrument which serves to transform radiant energy into mechanical work. It consists of four crossed arms of very fine glass, supported in the center by a needle-point, and having at the extreme ends thin vertical disks or squares of pith, blackened on one side. When placed in a glass vessel nearly exhausted of air, and exposed to rays of light or heat, the blackened surfaces absorb the radiant energy and become heated, the molecules of the air remaining in the vessel striking against them gain from them greater velocity, and there results an increased pressure, causing a more or less rapid revolution of the arms. By varying the conditions as to degree of exhaustion, size of bulb, etc., a number of experiments are performed with the radiometer which serve to illustrate the mechanical effects of the rapidly moving molecules of a gas.

Crookes's Radiometer.

radiometric (rā″di-ọ̄-met′rik), *a.* Pertaining to the radiometer, or to the experiments performed by it.

radiomicrometer (rā″di-ọ̄-mī-krom′e-tėr), *n.* [< L. *radius*, ray, + E. *micrometer*.] An instrument serving as a very delicate means of measuring small amounts of heat. It consists essentially of an antimony-bismuth thermo-electric couple of very small dimensions, with the ends joined by a hoop of copper wire, and suspended by a slender thread in a powerful magnetic field. It is claimed for it that it can be made even more sensitive than Langley's bolometer.

radiomuscular (rā″di-ō-mus′kụ̄-lär), *a.* [< L. *radius*, radius, + *musculus*, muscle: see *muscle*¹, *muscular*.] In *anat.*, pertaining to the radius and to muscles: specifically noting muscular branches of the radial artery and of the radial nerve. *Coues.*

radiophone (rā′di-ọ̄-fōn), *n.* [< L. *radius*, ray, + Gr. φωνή, voice, sound: see *phone*¹.] An instrument in which a sound is produced by the successive expansions and contractions of a body under the action of an intermittent beam of radiant heat thrown upon and absorbed by it.

radiophonic (rā″di-ọ̄-fon′ik), *a.* [< *radiophone* + *-ic*.] Pertaining to radiophony, or the production of sound by the action of a beam of light and heat; relating to the radiophone, or produced by it.

radiophonics (rā″di-ọ̄-fon′iks), *n.* [Pl. of *radiophonic* (see *-ics*).] Same as *radiophony*.

radiophony (rā′di-ọ̄-fō-ni), *n.* [< L. *radius*, ray, + Gr. φωνή, voice, sound: see *phone*¹.] The production of sound by the action of an intermittent beam of radiant heat; that branch of acoustics which considers sound so produced. For example, if the beam from a lime-light is thrown upon a rotating disk perforated with a series of holes, and, after thus being rendered intermittent, is made to fall upon a confined mass of a liquid or gas capable of absorbing radiant heat, a musical note is obtained from the latter whose pitch depends upon the rapidity of the rotation. Similar results are obtained with a plate of an appropriate solid, as hard rubber. Radiophony also includes the more complex case where an intermittent beam of light, falling upon a substance like selenium (also in a less degree sulphur), serves to vary its electrical resistance, and hence the strength of current passing through it, so as to produce a corresponding sound in a telephone-receiver placed in the circuit. This is illustrated in the photophone.

radio-ulnar (rā′di-ō-ul′nạ̈r), *a.* [< L. *radius*, radius, + *ulna*, ulna: see *ulna*, *ulnar*.] Of or belonging to the radius and the ulna: as, the *radio-ulnar* articulation.—**Radio-ulnar fibrocartilage.** See *fibrocartilage*.

radious (rā′di-us), *a.* [< ME. *radious*, *radyous*, *radius*, < OF. **radios*, F. *radieux* = Sp. Pg. It. *radioso*, < L. *radiosus*, radiant, beaming, < *radius*, a ray: see *radius*.] 1†. Consisting of rays, as light. *Berkeley.*—2†. Radiating; radiant.

His *radious* head with shameful thorns they tear.
G. Fletcher, Christ's Triumph over Death, st. 35.

3. In *bot.*, same as *radiant*. [Rare.]

radish (rad′ish), *n.* [Formerly also *raddish* (also dial. *redish*, *reddish*, appar. simulating *reddish*, of a red color); early mod. E. *radice*, *radyce*; < ME. *radish* = D. *radijs* = LG. *radys* = G. *radies* = Dan. *radis* = Sw. *rädisa*, *radis*, *radisa*, < OF. *radis*, F. *radis*, a radish, < Pr. *raditz*, a root, a radish, = OF. *rais*, *raiz* (also *radice*), a root, = It. *radice*, a root, radish, = AS. *rǣdic*, *rēdic*, erroneously *hrǣdic*, ME. *radik* = MLG. *redik*, *redek*, *redich* = OHG. *rātih*, *rātich*, MHG. *ratich*, *rätich*, *retich*, G. *rettich*, *rettig* = Dan. *rǣddike* = Sw. *rättika*, a radish, < L. *radix* (*radic-*), a root, in particular an edible root, esp. a radish: see *radix*.] 1. A plant, *Raphanus sativus*, cultivated for its edible root; also other species of the same genus. (See phrases below.) The radish of cultivation is unknown in a wild state, but is thought by many to be derived from the wild radish, *R. Raphanistrum*. It has been highly prized from the days of ancient Egypt for its crisp fleshy root, which is little nutritious, but pleasantly pungent and antiscorbutic, and is mostly eaten raw as a relish or in salads. The radish commonly must be young and fresh, but some varieties are grown for winter use. The root varies greatly in size (but is ordinarily eaten when small), in form (being long and tapering, turnip-shaped, olive-shaped, etc.), and also in color (being white, scarlet, pink, reddish-purple, yellowish, or brown). The leaves were formerly boiled and eaten, and the green pods make a pickle somewhat resembling capers.

2. A root of this plant.

When a' was naked, he was, for all the world, like a forked *radish*, with a head fantastically carved upon it with a knife.
Shak., 2 Hen. IV., iii. 2. 334.

3. Same as *water-radish*.—**Horse radish.** See *horse-radish*.—**Rat-tail radish**, a species (*Raphanus caudatus*) or perhaps a variety of the common radish, a curiosity from the East Indies, with narrow pods a foot or more long, which are boiled or pickled for the table.—**Sea-radish**, or **seaside radish**, a variety of the wild radish, sometimes regarded as a species (*Raphanus maritimus*) found on European coasts.—**Wild radish**, a noxious field-weed, *Raphanus Raphanistrum*, resembling charlock, but having necklace-formed pods, and hence sometimes called *jointed charlock*. It has rough lyrate leaves, and yellowish petals turning whitish or purplish. It is adventive in the eastern United States.

radish-fly (rad′ish-flī), *n.* An American dipterous insect, *Anthomyia raphani*, injurious to the radish.

radius (rā′di-us), *n.*; pl. *radii* (-ī). [< L. *radius*, a staff, rod, spoke of a wheel, a measuring-rod, a semidiameter of a circle (as it were a spoke of the wheel), a shuttle, spur of a bird, sting of a fish, the radius of the arm; by transfer, a beam of light, a ray. Cf. *ray*¹ (a doublet of *radius*) and the derived *radiant*, *radiate*, *irradiate*, etc.] 1. In *math.*, one of a number of lines proceeding from a center; a ray; especially, a line drawn from the center to the periphery of a circle or sphere; also, the measure of the semidiameter.—2. In *anat.* and *zoöl.*, the outer one of the two bones of the forearm, or corresponding part of the fore leg; the bone on the thumb side of the forearm, extending from the humerus to the carpus, and bearing upon its distal end the manus or hand: so called from its revolving, somewhat like a spoke, about the ulna, as in man and other mammals whose fore limb exhibits the motions called *pronation* and *supination*. In most animals, however, the radius is motionless, being fixed in a state of pronation, when it appears as the inner rather than the outer of the two bones, or as by far the larger bone, of the forearm, the ulna being often much reduced. In man the radius is as long as the ulna without the olecranon, and somewhat stouter, especially in its distal parts. It presents a small, circular, cupped and button-like head, for articulation with the capitulum of the humerus and lesser sigmoid cavity of the ulna, following which is a constriction termed the *neck*, and next to this a tubercle for the insertion of the biceps muscle. The shaft enlarges from above downward, and is of somewhat prismatic form, with the sharpest edge of the prism presenting toward the ulna. The lower end has two large articular facets for articulation with the scaphoid and lunar bones (forming the radiocarpal articulation, or wrist-joint), a lateral facet for the radio-ulnar articulation, and a stout projection called the *styloid process*, for the insertion of the supinator longus muscle. The radius is pronated by the pronator radii teres and pronator quadratus, and supinated by the supinator longus and supinator brevis, assisted by the biceps. Quite a similar form and disposition of the radius characterize various mammals which use their fore paws like hands, as monkeys, mice, squirrels, opossums, etc. The radius of others, as the horse and ox, is more different, and associated with a much reduced and ankylosed ulna. In birds the radius is so peculiarly articulated with the humerus that it slides lengthwise back and forth upon the ulna in the opening and closing of the wing, pronation and supination being absent in this class of animals. See *pronation* and *supination*, and cuts under *carpus*, *Catarrhina*, *Equidæ*, *forearm*, *ox*, *pinion*, *Plesiosaurus*, and *solidungulate*.

CA, CD, CB, CE, Radii of Circle.

3. In *ichth.*, a bone of the pectoral arch, wrongly identified by some naturalists with the radius of higher vertebrates. The one so called by Cuvier is the hypercoracoid, and that of Owen is the hypocoracoid.—4. In *entom.*, a vein of the wing of some insects, extending from the pterostigma to the tip of the wing.—5. [*cap.*] In *conch.*, a genus of *Ovulidæ*. *R. volva* is the shuttle-shell or weaver-shell.—6. *pl.* In *ornith.*, the barbs of the main shaft of a feather; the rays of the first order of the rachis.—7. In *arachnology*, one of the radiating lines of a geometrical spider's web, which are connected by a single spiral line.—8. In echinoderms, one of the five radial pieces of the dentary apparatus of a sea-urchin, being an arched rod-like piece articulated at its base with the inner extremity of each rotula, running more or less nearly parallel with the rotula, and ending in a free bifurcated extremity. Also called the *compass of the lantern of Aristotle* (which see, under *lantern*). See also cut B under *lantern*.—9. *pl.* Specifically, in *Cirripedia*, the lateral parts of the shell, as distinguished from the paries, when they overlap: when overlapped by others, they are called *alæ*.—10. In *bot.*, a ray, as of a composite flower, etc.—11. The movable limb or arm of a sextant; also, a similar feature in any other instrument for measuring angles.—12. In *fort.*, a line drawn from the center of the polygon to the end of the outer side.—**Auricular radii.** See *auricular*.—**Geometrical radius** of a cog-wheel, the radius of the pitch-circle of the wheel, in contradistinction to its real radius, which is that of the circle formed by the crests of the teeth.—**Oblique line of the radius.** See *oblique*.—**Pronator radii quadratus.** See *pronator quadratus*, under *pronator*.—**Pronator radii teres.** See *pronator*.—**Proportional radii**, in a system of gears, or in a set of gears of the same pitch, radii proportioned in length to the number of teeth in the respective wheels. The proportional radii of any two geared wheels, when taken together, are equal to the line connecting the centers of the wheels, which line is the basis of computation in determining them. Also called *primitive radii*.—**Radii accessorii**, the barbs of the aftershaft or hyporachis of a feather.—**Radius astronomicus.** Same as *radiometer*, 1.—**Radius of concavity.** Same as *radius of curvature*.—**Radius of curvature**, the radius of the circle of curvature—that is, of the osculating circle at any point of a curve. In the cut, AHBC is the primitive curve (in this case an ellipse); KHJ, the circle of curvature, osculating the primitive curve at H; T, the center of curvature; TH, the radius of curvature; GFTED, the locus of centers of curvature, or the evolute. The radius of curvature wrapping itself upon the evolute gives the primitive curve.—**Radius of dissipation.** See *dissipation*.—**Radius of explosion.** See *mine*², 2 (*b*).—**Radius of gyration**, in *mech.*, the distance from the axis to a point such that, if the whole mass of a body were concentrated into it, the moment of inertia would remain unchanged. If the axis is a principal axis, this radius becomes a *principal radius of gyration*.—**Radius of rupture.** See *mine*², 2 (*b*).—**Radius of the evolute.** Same as *radius of curvature*.—**Radius of torsion**, the element of the arc of a curve divided by the angle of torsion.—**Radius vector** (pl. *radii vectores*), the length of the line joining a variable point to a fixed origin: in astronomy the origin is taken at the sun or other central body. See *vector*.—**Real radius.** See *geometrical radius*.

Radius of Curvature.

radius-bar (rā′di-us-bär), *n.* In a steam-engine, one of a pair of rods pivoted at one end and connected at the other with some concentrically moving part which it is necessary to keep at a definite distance from the pivot or center. Also called *radius-rod* and *bridle-rod*. See cuts under *grasshopper-beam* and *paddle-wheel*.

radius-saw (rā′di-us-sâ), *n.* A circular saw journaled at the end of a swinging frame or radial shaft, used in cross-cutting timber.

radix (rā′diks), *n.*; pl. *radices* (rā-dī′sēz). [< L. *radix* (*radic-*), a root, = Gr. ῥάδιξ, a branch, rod. Hence ult. E. *race*⁴ and *radish* (doublets of *radix*), *radical*, *radicel*, *radicle*, *radicule*, *radicate*, *eradicate*, *arace*¹, etc.] 1. The root of a plant: used chiefly with reference to the roots of medicinal plants or preparations from them. Hence—2. The primary source or origin; that from which anything springs, or in which it originates. [Rare.]

Her wit is all spirit, that spirit fire, that fire flies from her tongue, able to burne the *radix* of the best invention; in this element she is the abstract and briefe of all the eloquence since the incarnation of Tully.
Heywood, Fair Maid of the Exchange (Works, 1874, II. 54).

Judaism is the *radix* of Christianity—Christianity the integration of Judaism.
De Quincey, Essenes, iii.

3. In *etym.*, a primitive word or form from which spring other words; a radical; a root.—4. In *math.*, a root. (*a*) Any number which is arbitrarily made the fundamental number or base of any system of numbers, to be raised to different powers. Thus, 10 is the radix of the decimal system of numeration (Briggs's). In the common system of logarithms, the radix is also 10; in the Napierian it is 2.7182818284; every other number is considered as some power of the radix, the exponent of which power constitutes the logarithm of that number. (*b*) The root of a finite expression from which a series is derived.

5. In *zoöl.* and *anat.*, a root; a rooted or root-like part: a radicle: as, the *radix* or root of a tooth; the *radix* of a nerve.—**Radix cerebelli**, the posterior peduncle of the cerebellum.—**Radix motoria**, the smaller motor root of the trigeminal nerve.—**Radix sensoria**, the larger sensory root of the trigeminal nerve.

radly†, *adv.* See *rathly*.

radness† (rad'nes), *n.* [ME., < *rad*[1] + *-ness*.] Fear; fright; terror.

> The Romaynes for *radnesse* ruschte to the erthe,
> Fforde ferdnesse of hys face, as they fey were.
> *Morte Arthure* (E. E. T. S.), l. 120.

radoub (ra-döb'), *n.* [F., repairs made on a vessel, < *radouber*, formerly also *redouber*, mend, repair: see *redub*.] In *mercantile law*, the repairing and refitting of a ship for a voyage. *Wharton.*

radula (rad'ū-lä), *n.*; pl. *radulæ* (-lē). [NL., < L. *radula*, a scraper, scraping-iron, < *radere*, scrape: see *rase*[1], *raze*[1].] In *conch.*, the tongue or lingual ribbon of a mollusk, specifically called *odontophore*, and more particularly, the rasping surface or set of teeth of the odontophore, which bites like a file. This structure is highly characteristic of the cephalophorous classes, among which it presents great diversity in detail. It bears the numerous small chitinous processes or teeth of these mollusks, which serve to triturate food with a kind of filing or rasping action. According to the disposition of the teeth in any one of the many cross-rows which beset the length of the radula, mollusks are called *rachiglossate*, *tænioglossate*, *rhipidoglossate*, *toxoglossate*, *ptenoglossate*, and *docoglossate*. See these words, and *odontophore*.

A, median tooth and teeth of one row of right half of radula of *Trochus cinerarius*. *B*, one row of radular teeth of *Cypræa europæa*: *A* is rhipidoglossate, and *B* is tænioglossate.

radular (rad'ū-lär), *a.* [< *radula* + *-ar*[3].] Pertaining to the radula: as, *radular* teeth.

radulate (rad'ū-lāt), *a.* [< *radula* + *-ate*[1].] Provided with a radula, as a cephalophorous mollusk; raduliferous.

raduliferous (rad-ū-lif'e-rus), *a.* [< NL. *radula* + L. *ferre* = E. *bear*[1].] Bearing a radula; radulate.

raduliform (rad'ū-li-fôrm), *a.* [< L. *radula*, a scraper, + *forma*, form.] Rasp-like; having the character or appearance of the teeth of a file; cardiform: specifically noting, in ichthyology, the conical, sharp-pointed, and close-set teeth of some fishes, resembling villiform teeth, but larger and stronger.

rae (rā), *n.* A Scotch form of *roe*.

rafe†. A Middle English preterit of *reave*.

raff† (råf), *v. t.* [< OF. *raffer*, *rafer*, catch, snatch, slip away, = It. **raffare*, in comp. *arraffare*, snatch, seize, = MHG. *raffen*, *reffen*, G. *raffen*, snatch, sweep away, carry off suddenly, = MLG. LG. *rapen*, snatch, = Sw. *rappa*, snatch, seize, = Dan. *rappe*, hasten: see *rap*[2], from the Scand. form cognate with the G. Hence ult. *raffle*[1].] To sweep; snatch, draw, or huddle together; take by a promiscuous sweep.

> Their causes and effects . . . I thus *raffe* vp together.
> *R. Carew*, Survey of Cornwall, fol. 69.

raff (råf), *n.* and *a.* [< ME. *raffe*, *raf*, esp. in the phrase *rif and raf* (now *riffraff*), < OF. *rif et raf*, every bit, in which *raf* is due to the verb *raffer*, snatch: see *raff*, *v.* Cf. *riffraff*. Cf. It. *raffola*, a crowd, press.] **I.** *n.* **1.** A promiscuous heap or collection; a jumble; a medley. [Obsolete or archaic.]

> The synod of Trent was convened to settle a *raff* of errors and superstitions. *Barrow*, Unity of the Church.

2. Trashy material; lumber; rubbish; refuse. [Old and prov. Eng.]

> And maken of the rym and *raf*
> Suche gylours for pompe and pride.
> *Appendix to W. Mapes*, p. 340. (*Halliwell.*)

> Let *raffs* be rife in prose and rhyme,
> We lack not rhymes and reasons,
> As on this whirligig of Time
> We circle with the seasons.
> *Tennyson*, Will Waterproof.

3. Abundance; affluence. *Halliwell.* [Prov. Eng. and Scotch.]—4. A worthless or disorderly person; a rowdy; a scapegrace: now applied to students of Oxford by the townspeople. *Halliwell.*

> Myself and this great peer
> Of these rude *raffs* became the jeer.
> *W. Combe*, Dr. Syntax, i. 20. (*Davies.*)

> One of the *raffs* we shrink from in the street,
> Wore an old hat, and went with naked feet.
> *Leigh Hunt*, High and Low. (*Davies.*)

5. Collectively, worthless persons; the scum or sweepings of society; the rabble. Compare *riffraff*.

> "People, you see," he said, "won't buy their 'accounts' of *raff*; they won't have them of any but respectable."
> *Mayhew*, London Labour and London Poor, I. 325.

II. *a.* Idle; dissolute. *Halliwell.* [Prov. Eng.]

Raffaelesque, *a.* See *Raphaelesque*.

raffe, raffie (raf, raf'i), *n.* [Origin obscure.] *Naut.*, a three-cornered sail set on schooners when before the wind or nearly so. The head hoists up to the foretopmast-head and the clues haul out to the square-sail yard-arms. It is rarely used except on the Great Lakes of North America. Sometimes it is in two pieces, one for each side of the mast.

Raffe.

raffia, roffia (raf'i-ä, rof'i-ä), *n.* [Malagasy.] **1.** A palm, *Raphia Ruffia*, growing in Madagascar. It bears pinnate leaves 20 or 30 feet long upon a moderate trunk. The cuticle is peeled from both sides of the leaf-stalk, for use as a fiber, being largely made into matting, and also applied by the natives to finer textile purposes. (See *rabanna*.) It is now somewhat largely used for agricultural tie-bands, as is also a similar product of the jupati-palm, *R. tædigera*, included under the same name. Also spelled *raphia*.

2. The fiber of this plant.

raffish (råf'ish), *a.* [< *raff* + *-ish*[1].] Resembling or having the character of the raff or rabble; scampish; worthless; rowdy. Compare *raff*, *n.*, 5.

> Five or six *raffish*-looking men had surrounded a fair, delicate girl, and were preparing to besiege her in form.
> *Lawrence*, Guy Livingstone, xxiii.

> The *raffish* young gentleman in gloves must measure his scholarship with the plain, clownish laddie from the parish school. *R. L. Stevenson*, The Foreigner at Home.

raffle[1] (raf'l), *n.* [< ME. *rafle*, a game at dice (= Sw. *raffel*, a raffle); < OF. *rafle*, *raffle*, F. *rafle*, a pair royal at dice (*faire rafle*, sweep the stakes), also a grape-stalk, < *rafler*, snatch, seize, carry off, < G. *raffeln*, snatch up, freq. of *raffen*, snatch, snatch away, carry off hastily: see *raff*, *v.* Cf. *raffle*[2].] **1**†. A game with dice.

> Now comth hasardrie with hise apurtenaunces, as tables and *rafles*, of which comth deceite, false othes, chidynges, and alle ravynes, blasphemynge and reneyinge of God.
> *Chaucer*, Parson's Tale.

2. A method of sale by chance or lottery, in which the price of the thing to be disposed of is divided into equal shares, and the persons taking the shares cast lots for its possession by throwing dice or otherwise.

raffle[1] (raf'l), *v.*; pret. and pp. *raffled*, ppr. *raffling*. [= Sw. *raffla* = Dan. *rafle*, raffle; from the noun.] **I.** *intrans.* To try the chance of a raffle; engage in a raffle: as, to *raffle* for a watch.

> They were *raffling* for his coat.
> *S. Butler*, Satire upon Gaming.

> The great Rendezvous is at night, after the Play and Opera are done; and *Raffling* for all Things Vendible is the great Diversion. *Lister*, Journey to Paris, p. 176.

II. *trans.* To dispose of by means of a raffle: often with *off*: as, to *raffle* or *raffle off* a watch.

raffle[2] (raf'l), *v.*; pret. and pp. *raffled*, ppr. *raffling*. [Perhaps < Icel. *hrafla*, scrape together (a slang term); cf. *hrapa*, hurry, hasten: see *raff*, *v.* Cf. *raffle*[1].] **I.** *intrans.* **1.** To move or fidget about. *Halliwell.* [Prov. Eng.]—**2.** To live in a disorderly way. *Halliwell.* [Prov. Eng.]

II. *trans.* **1.** To stir (a fire).—**2.** To brush off (walnuts). *Halliwell.* [Prov. Eng.]

raffle[2] (raf'l), *n.* [< *raffle*[2], *v.* Cf. *raff*, *n.*] *Naut.*, raff; lumber; rubbish.

> Her decks were heavily encumbered with what sailors call *raffle*—that is, the muddle of ropes, torn canvas, staves of boats and casks, . . . with which the ocean illustrates her violence. *W. C. Russell*, Death Ship, xxx.

raffle[3] (raf'l), *n.* [Origin obscure.] Same as *raffle-net*.

raffled (raf'ld), *a.* [Origin obscure.] Having the edge finely divided or serrated.

> A peculiar small cut or *raffled* leaf resembling an ivy, or more nearly a vine leaf.
> *Soulages Catalogue*, p. 116, note to No. 365.

raffle-net (raf'l-net), *n.* A kind of fishing-net.

raffler (raf'lėr), *n.* [< *raffle*[2] + *-er*[1].] One who raffles.

Rafflesia (raf-lē'zi-ä), *n.* [NL. (R. Brown, 1821), named after Sir Stamford *Raffles*, British governor in Sumatra, and companion to the botanist Dr. Joseph Arnold, who discovered there the first known species, *R. Arnoldi*, in 1818.] A genus of apetalous parasitic plants of the order *Cytinaceæ* and type of the tribe *Rafflesieæ*, characterized by a perianth of five large entire and fleshy imbricated lobes, numerous stigmas, and globose many-chambered anthers, each opening by a single pore, which form a ring at the revolute top of a column rising in the center of the flower. The flowers are diœcious, and the pistillate ones contain an ovary with a labyrinth of small cells and numerous ovules. The 4 species are natives of hot and damp jungles in the Malay archipelago. The whole plant consists of a single flower, without leaves or proper stem, growing out from the porous root or stem of species of *Vitis* (*Cissus*), at a time when the leaves and flowers of the foster-plant have withered. The flower of the parasite protrudes as a knob from the bark at first, and enlarges for some months, resembling before opening a close cabbage, and remaining fully expanded only a few days. It exhales an odor of tainted meat, securing cross-fertilization by aid of the flies thus attracted to it. The flower reaches 3 inches or more in diameter in *R. Rochusseni* (valued by the Javanese for astringent and styptic properties), 6 inches in others, and 2 feet in *R. Patma*. *R. Arnoldi* has long been famed for its size, greatly exceeding the Victoria lily (23 inches), and even exceeding the *Aristolochia Goldieana* (a specimen of which at Kew, March, 1890, was 28 inches long and 16 broad). The first flower

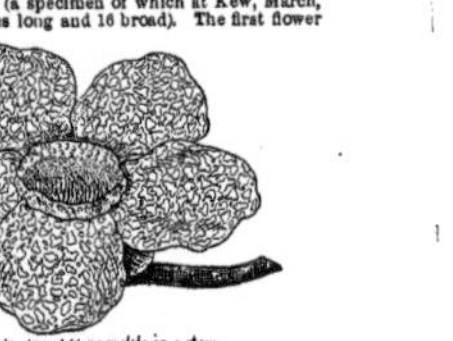

Rafflesia Arnoldi, parasitic on a stem.

of *R. Arnoldi* found measured 3 feet across its flat circular top, and weighed about 15 pounds; the roundish calyx-lobes were each a foot long, and in places an inch thick; and the globular central cup was a foot across and held about 6 quarts. The fruit ripens into a chestnut-brown and truncated nut, about 5 inches thick, with irregularly furrowed and broken surface, and containing thousands of hard, curiously appendaged and lacunose seeds. The flower is flesh-colored and mottled pink and yellow within, and with brown or bluish scales beneath. It is called *ambun-ambun* or *wonder-wonder* by the Malays, and *krubut*, a name which they also give to another gigantic plant which grows with it, the ovoid *Amorphophallus Titanum*.

Rafflesiaceæ (raf-lē-zi-ā'sē-ē), *n. pl.* [NL. (Schott and Endlicher, 1832), < *Rafflesia* + *-aceæ*.] Same as *Rafflesieæ*, but formerly regarded as a separate order.

Rafflesieæ (raf-lē-zī'ē-ē), *n. pl.* [NL. (Robert Brown, 1844), < *Rafflesia* + *-eæ*.] A tribe of apetalous parasitic plants, constituting with the smaller tribe *Hydnoreæ* the order *Cytinaceæ*. It is characterized by the presence of scattered or imbricated scales in place of leaves, and flowers with from four to ten usually imbricated calyx-lobes, the anthers forming one, two, or three circles about a column in the center of the staminate flower, and the one or many stigmas terminating a similar column in the pistillate flower. It includes about 21 species in 5 genera, scattered through warm climates, and extending into the Mediterranean region, South Africa, and Mexico. All are indwelling parasites, issuing out of the roots or branches of various trees and shrubs. They vary in habit, having in *Cytinus* a colored fleshy and distinct stem and many-flowered spike, while in the other genera the whole plant consists of a single flower sessile on its embedded rhizome. They range from a minute size in *Apodanthes* and large in other genera to the monster flower of *Rafflesia*, the type. The plants are called *palma-worts* by some botanists.

raffling-net (raf'ling-net), *n.* Same as *raffle-net*.

raffman† (råf'man), *n.* [< *raff* + *man*.] A dealer in miscellaneous stuff; a chandler.

> Grocers and *raffemen*. *Norwich Records.* (*Nares.*)

raff-merchant (råf'mėr"chant), *n.* A dealer in lumber or old articles. Also *raft-merchant*. [Prov. Eng.]

raft[1] (råft), *n.* [< ME. *raft*, *ræft*, *rafte*, a rafter, spar, beam, < Icel. *raptr* (*raftr*), a rafter, beam (*r* final being sign of nom. case); = Sw. Dan. *raft*, rafter; with formative *-t*, perhaps < Icel. *râf*, *ræfr*, a roof, = OHG. *râfo*, MHG. *râvo*, G. dial. *raff*, a spar, rafter; cf. Gr. ὀροφος, a roof, ἐρέφειν, cover. Cf. *rafter*[1].] **1**†. A beam; spar; rafter.

> Aythir gripus a schafte
> Was als rude as a *rafte*.
> *Avowynge of King Arthur*, xxv.

2. A sort of float or framework formed of logs, planks, or other pieces of timber fastened or lashed together side by side, for the convenience of transporting the constituent materials down rivers, across harbors, etc. Rafts of logs

tobe floated to a distant point are often very large, strongly constructed, and carry huts for the numerous men required to manage them. Those of the Rhine are sometimes 400 or 500 feet long, with 200 or more hands. A cigar-shaped raft of large logs, 560 feet long, 50 feet wide, and 35 feet deep, was lost in December, 1887, under towage by sea from Nova Scotia to New York; but other large rafts have been successfully transported.
3. A structure similarly formed of any materials for the floating or transportation of persons or things. In cases of shipwreck, planks, spars,

Life-raft.
a, b, tanks or air-chambers; *c, c',* decks; *e,* fender; *f, f',* life-lines; *g,* rowlocks; *g',* steering and sculling rowlock; *h,* lashings.

barrels, etc., are often hastily lashed together to form a raft for escape. In passenger-vessels life-rafts frequently form part of the permanent equipment. See *life-raft*.

> Where is that son
> That floated with thee on the fatal *raft*?
> *Shak.*, C. of E., v. 1. 348.

4. An accumulation of driftwood from fallen trees in a river, lodged and compacted so as to form a permanent obstruction. Rafts of this kind exist or have existed in the Mississippi and other rivers of the western United States, the largest ever formed being that of the Red River, which during many years completely blocked the channel for 45 miles.
5. A conglomeration of eggs of some animals, as certain insects and mollusks, fastened together and forming a mass; a float. See cut under *Ianthina*.

A great many eggs [of the common cockroach] are laid at one time, the whole number being surrounded by a stiff chitinous coat, forming the so-called *raft*. *Amer. Nat.*, XXII. 857.

raft[1] (råft), *v. t.* [< *raft*[1], *n.*] **I.** *trans.* **1.** To transport or float on a raft.

Guns taken out of a ship to lighten her when aground should be hoisted out and *rafted* clear, if there is any danger of bilging on them. *Luce*, Seamanship, p. 182, note.

The idea of *rafting* timber by the ocean. *Sci. Amer.*, N. S., LVIII. 17.

2. To make a raft of; form into a raft.

As soon as the blubber is taken off, it is *rafted*—tied together with ropes in a sort of raft—and lies in the water until taken on board ship. *C. M. Scammon*, Marine Mammals, p. 63.

I could see him securing these planks to one another by lashings. By the time he had *rafted* them, nearly an hour had passed since he had left the sandbank. *W. C. Russell*, A Strange Voyage, xlvi.

II. *intrans.* To manage a raft; work upon a raft or rafts; travel by raft.

They canoed, and *rafted*, and steam-boated, and travelled with packhorses. *Academy*, Nov. 10, 1888, p. 301.

raft[2] (råft), *n.* [A var. of *raff*, appar. by confusion with *raft*[1].] A miscellaneous collection or heap; a promiscuous lot: used slightingly: as, a *raft* of papers; a whole *raft* of things to be attended to. [Colloq., U. S.]

This last spring a *raft* of them [Irish maids] was out of employment. *Philadelphia Times*, Oct. 24, 1886.

raft[3] (råft), *n.* [Origin uncertain: cf. *raff*.] A damp fusty smell. *Halliwell.* [Prov. Eng.]
raft[4]†. An obsolete preterit and past participle of *reave*.
raft-breasted (råft'bres"ted), *a.* In *ornith.*, ratite. *W. K. Parker.*
raft-dog (råft'dog), *n.* An iron bar with ends bent over and pointed, for securing logs together in a raft. The points are driven respectively into adjacent or juxtaposed logs, which are thus bonded to each other.

Raft-dog.

raft-duck (råft'duk), *n.* The scaup or blackhead duck, *Aithyia* or *Fuligula* or *Fulix marila*: so called in the United States from its flocking closely on the water, as if forming a raft of ducks. Also called *bluebill*, *shuffler*, and *flocking-fowl*. See cut under *scaup*.—**Red-headed raft-duck.** Same as *redhead*, 2.
rafte†. An obsolete preterit and past participle of *reave*. *Chaucer.*
rafter[1] (råf'tėr), *n.* [< ME. *rafter*, *refter*, < AS. *ræfter*, pl. *ræftras*, *reftres* (= MD. *rafter* = MLG. *rafter*, *raffert*), a beam, rafter; with formative *-er*, from **ræft* = Icel. *raptr* (*raftr*) = Sw. Dan. *raft*, a rafter, beam: see *raft*.] **1.** In *building*, one of the beams which give the slope of a roof, and to which is secured the lath or other framework upon which the slate or other outer covering is nailed. The rafters extend from the eaves to the ridge of the roof, abutting at their upper ends on corresponding rafters rising from the opposite side of the roof, or resting against a crown-plate or ridge-plate as the case may be. For the different kinds of rafters in a structure, see *roof*, and cuts under *curb-roof*, *jack-rafter*, and *pontoon*.

> Shepherd, I take thy word,
> And trust thy honest offer'd courtesy,
> Which oft is sooner found in lowly sheds
> With smoky *rafters* than in tap'stry halls.
> *Milton*, Comus, l. 324.

2. Same as *carline*[4], 2.—**3.** In *anat.*, a trabecula or trabeculum: as, the *rafters* of the embryonic skull.—**Binding-rafter.** See *binding*.—**Intermediate rafter,** a rafter placed between the ordinary rafters, or between principal rafters, to strengthen a roof.—**Principal rafter,** a main timber in an assemblage of carpentry; especially, one of those rafters which are larger than the common rafters, and are framed at their lower ends into the tie-beam, and either abut at their upper ends against the king-post or receive the ends of the straining-beams when queen-posts are used. The principal rafters support the purlins, which again carry the common rafters: thus the whole weight of the roof is sustained by the principal rafters.
rafter[1] (råf'tėr), *v. t.* [< *rafter*[1], *n.*] **1.** To form into or like rafters: as, to *rafter* timber.—**2.** To furnish or build with rafters: as, to *rafter* a house.

Buildyng an hous euen from the foundacion vnto the vttermoste *raftreyng* and reiring of the roofe. *Udall*, tr. of Apophthegms of Erasmus, p. 260. (*Davies.*)

3. In *agri.*, to plow, as a piece of land, by turning the grass side of the plowed furrow on a strip of ground left unplowed.
rafter[2] (råf'tėr), *n.* [< *raft*[1] + *-er*[1].] One who is employed in rafting timber, or transporting it in rafts, as from a ship to the shore.

How the 900 casual deal-porters and *rafters* live during . . . six months of the year . . . I cannot conceive. *Mayhew*, London Labour and London Poor, III. 293.

rafter-bird (råf'tėr-bėrd), *n.* The beam-bird or wall-bird, *Muscicapa grisola*; the spotted flycatcher: from the site of its nest. [Eng.]
rafting-dog (råf'ting-dog), *n.* Same as *raft-dog*.
raft-like (råft'lik), *a.* Flat-bottomed or keelless, as the breast-bone of a bird; ratite.
raft-merchant (råft'mėr"chạnt), *n.* Same as *raff-merchant*.
raft-port (råft'pōrt), *n.* In some ships, a large square hole framed and cut immediately under the counter, or forward between the breast-hooks of the bow, for loading or unloading timber. See cut under *lumber-port*.
raft-rope (råft'rōp), *n.* A rope about three fathoms long, with an eye-splice, used for stringing seal-blubber to be towed to a whaling-vessel. A raft-rope is also sometimes used by a blubber-logged vessel for rafting or towing whale-blubber.

The horse-pieces [blubber of the sea-elephant] are strung on a *raft-rope* . . . and taken to the edge of the surf. *C. M. Scammon*, Marine Mammals, p. 119.

raftsman (råfts'mạn), *n.*; pl. *raftsmen* (-men). [< *raft's*, poss. of *raft*[1], + *man*.] A man employed in the management of a raft.
rafty (råf'ti), *a.* [< *raft*[3] + *-y*[1].] **1.** Musty; stale.—**2.** Damp; muggy.—**3.** High-tempered; violent. [Prov. Eng. in all senses.]
rag[1] (rag), *n.* and *a.* [< ME. *ragge*, pl. *ragges*, shred of cloth, rag; cf. AS. **raggig*, in neut. pl. *raggie*, shaggy, bristly, ragged, as applied to the rough coat of a horse (as if from an AS. noun, but prob. from the Scand. adj.); < Icel. *rögg*, shagginess (*raggathr*, shaggy), = Sw. *ragg*, rough hair (Sw. *raggig*, shaggy, Sw. dial. *raggi*, having rough hair, slovenly), = Norw. *ragg*, rough hair (*raggad*, shaggy); root unknown. The orig. sense 'shagginess' or 'roughness' is now more obvious in uses of *ragged*.] **I.** *n.* **1.** A sharp or jagged fragment rising from a surface or edge: as, a *rag* on a metal plate; hence, a jagged face of rock; a rocky headland; a cliff; a crag.

And taking up their standing upon the craggie rockes and *ragges* round about, with all their might and maine defended their goods. *Holland*, tr. of Ammianus Marcellinus (1609). (*Nares.*)

2. A rock having or weathering with a rough irregular surface. [Eng.]

The material is Kentish *rag*, laid in regular courses, with flue joints. Quoted in *N. and Q.*, 7th ser., V. 466.

> We wound
> About the cliffs, the copses, out and in,
> Hammering and clinking, chattering stony names
> Of shale and hornblende, *rag* and trap and tuff.
> *Tennyson*, Princess, iii.

3. In *bot.*: (*a*) A lichen, *Sticta pulmonaria* (see *hazel-crottles*). (*b*) Another lichen, *Parmelia saxatilis* (stone-rag). (*c*) A catkin of the hazel, or of the willow, *Salix caprea*. Also *raw*. [Prov. Eng.]—**4.** A torn, worn, or formless fragment or shred of cloth; a comparatively worthless piece of any textile fabric, either wholly or partly detached from its connection by violence or abrasion: as, his coat was in *rags*; cotton and linen *rags* are used to make paper, and woolen *rags* to make shoddy.

> Hir *ragges* thei anone of drawe, . . .
> She had bathe, she had reste,
> And was arraied to the beste.
> *Gower*, Conf. Amant., i.

> Cowls, hoods, and habits with their wearers toss'd,
> And flutter'd into *rags*. *Milton*, P. L., iii. 491.

5. A worn, torn, or mean garment; in the plural, shabby or worn-out clothes, showing rents and patches.

If you will embrace Christ in his robes, you must not think scorn of him in his *rags*. *J. Bradford*, Letters (Parker Soc., 1853), II. 111.

Drowsiness shall clothe a man with *rags*. Prov. xxiii. 21.

> Trust me, I prize poor virtue with a *rag*
> Better than vice with both the Indies.
> *Beau. and Fl.* (?), Faithful Friends, iv. 4.

The poore inhabitants were dispers'd, . . . some under tents, some under miserable hutts and hovells, many without a *rag* or any necessary utensills. *Evelyn*, Diary, Sept. 5, 1666.

> The man forget not, though in *rags* he lies,
> And know the mortal through a crown's disguise.
> *Akenside*, Epistle to Curio.

6. Any separate fragment or shred of cloth, or of something like or likened to it: often applied disparagingly or playfully to a handkerchief, a flag or banner, a sail, the curtain of a theater, a newspaper, etc.

It cost three men's lives to get back that four-by-three flag—to tear it from the breast of a dead rebel—for the name of getting their little *rag* back again. *Walt Whitman*, The Century, XXXVI. 827.

7. Figuratively, a severed fragment; a remnant; a scrap; a bit.

> So he up with his rusty sword,
> And chopped the old saddle to *rags*.
> *Saddle to Rags* (Child's Ballads, VIII. 267).

They [fathers] were not hearkened to, when they were heard, but heard perfunctorily, fragmentarily, here and there a *rag*, a piece of a sentence. *Donne*, Sermons, v.

Not having otherwise any *rag* of legality to cover the shame of their cruelty. *Fuller.*

8. A base, beggarly person; a ragamuffin; a tatterdemalion. [Colloq.]

> Lash hence these overweening *rags* of France,
> These famish'd beggars, weary of their lives.
> *Shak.*, Rich. III., v. 3. 328.

Out of my doore, you Witch, you *Ragge*, you Baggage! *Shak.*, M. W. of W. (folio 1623), iv. 2. 194.

9. A farthing. *Halliwell.* [Eng. cant.]

> *Jac.* 'Twere good she had a little foolish money
> To rub the time away with.
> *Host.* Not a *rag*,
> Not a denier. *Beau. and Fl.*, Captain, iv. 2.

10†. A herd of colts. *Strutt.* [Prov. Eng.]—**11.** In *type-founding*, the bur or rough edge left on imperfectly finished type.—**Coral rag,** one of the limestones of the Middle Oölite, consisting in part of continuous beds of petrified corals.—**Rag, tag, and rag†.** See *hag*[3].—**Kentish rag.** See *Kentish*.—**Litmus on rags.** See *litmus*.—**Rag, tag, and bobtail,** a rabble; everybody indiscriminately. See *rag-tag*. [Colloq.]—**Rowley rag,** a basaltic rock occurring in the South Staffordshire coal-field, much quarried for road-mending. See *ragstone*.

II. *a.* Made of or with rags; formed from or consisting of refuse pieces or fragments of cloth: as, *rag* pulp for paper-making; a *rag* carpet.—**Rag baby.** (*a*) A doll made entirely of rags or scraps of cloth, usually in a very artless manner. (*b*) In *U. S. political slang*, the paper currency of the government; greenback money: so called with reference to the contention of the Greenback party, before and after the resumption of specie payments in 1879, in favor of making such money a full legal tender for the national debt and all other purposes.

Fortunately, the "specie basis" of the national banks is now chiefly paper—the *rag-baby*—three hundred and forty-six millions of greenbacks! *N. A. Rev.*, CXLI. 207.

Rag carpet, a cheap kind of carpeting woven with strips or shreds of woolen and other cloth, usually from worn-out garments, for the weft. A better kind is made with strips of list from new cloth, when it is also called *list carpet*.—**Rag money, rag currency,** paper money; circulating notes issued by United States banks or by the government: so called in depreciation or contempt, in allusion to the origin of the material, to the ragged appearance of paper money when much handled, and to its intrinsic worthlessness. [Slang.]

All true Democrats were clamorous for "hard-money" and against *rag-money*. *The Nation*, July 29, 1875, p. 66.

Rag paper. See *paper*.
rag[1] (rag), *v.*; pret. and pp. *ragged*, ppr. *ragging*. [< *rag*[1], *n.*] **I.** *intrans.* **1.** To become ragged; fray: with *out*.

Leather thus leisurely tanned and turned many times in the fat will prove serviceable, which otherwise will quickly fleet and *rag out*.
Fuller, Worthies, Middlesex, II. 312.

2. To dress; deck one's self: in the phrase *to rag out*, to dress in one's best. [Slang, U. S.]

A finely dressed woman *rags out*.
S. Bowles, Our New West, p. 506.

II. *trans.* 1. To make ragged; abrade; give a ragged appearance to, as in the rough-dressing of the face of a grindstone.

In straggling or *ragging* [a grindstone] the stone is kept running as usual. *O. Byrne*, Artisan's Handbook, p. 422.

2. In *mining*, to separate by ragging or with the aid of the ragging-hammer. See *ragging*, 2.

rag[2] (rag), *v. t.*; pret. and pp. *ragged*, ppr. *ragging*. [Prob. < *rag*[1], *n.*, 5. In another view, < Icel. *rægja*, calumniate, = AS. *wrēgan*, accuse: see *wray*.] To banter; badger; rail at; irritate; torment. Compare *bullyrag*. [Local.]

To *rag* a man is good Lincolnshire for chaff or tease. At school, to get a boy into a rage was called getting his rag out. *N. and Q.*, 7th ser., VI. 38.

rag[3] (rag), *n.* [< Icel. *hragg*, storm and rain.] A drizzling rain. [Prov. Eng.]

rag[4] (rag), *n.* An abbreviation of *raginee*.

ragabash (rag′a̤-bash), *n.* [Also *raggabash*, *ragabrash*, Sc. *rag-a-buss*, *ragabush*; appar. a made word, vaguely associated with *rag*[1] or *ragamuffin*.] 1. A shiftless, disreputable fellow; a ragamuffin. [Prov. Eng. and Scotch.]

The most unalphabetical *raggabashes* that ever bred louse. *Discov. of a New World*, p. 81. (*Nares.*)

2. Collectively, idle, worthless people. *Halliwell.* [Prov. Eng.]

ragamuffin (rag′a̤-muf-in), *n.* and *a.* [Early mod. E. also *raggemuffin*, *ragamofin*, *rayomofin*; erroneously analyzed *rag-a-muffin*, *rag of Muffins*; < ME. *Ragamoffyn*, the name of a demon, prob., like many other names of demons, merely fanciful. The present sense has been partly determined by association with *rag*[1]. For the sense 'demon,' cf. *ragman*[2].] I. 1†. [*cap.*] The name of a demon.

Ac rys vp, *Ragamoffyn*, and reche me alle the barres
The Belial thy bel-syre beot with thy danme.
Piers Plowman (C), xxi. 283.

2. An idle, worthless fellow; a vagabond; now, especially, a disreputably ragged or slovenly person: formerly used as a general term of reprehension.

I have led my *ragamuffins* where they are peppered.
Shak., 1 Hen. IV., v. 3. 36.

Did that same tiranicall-tongu'd *rag-a-muffin*
Horace turne bald-pates out so naked?
Dekker, Humorous Poet.

Once, attended with a crew of *raggamuffins*, she broke into his house, turned all things topsy-turvy, and then set it on fire. *Swift*, Story of an Injured Lady.

3. A titmouse: same as *muffin*.

II. *a.* Base; beggarly; ragged or disorderly.

Here be the emperor's captains, you *ragamuffin* rascal, and not your comrades. *B. Jonson*, Poetaster, i. 1.

Mr. Aldworth . . . turned over the rest of this *ragamuffin* assembly to the care of his butler.
Graves, Spiritual Quixote, viii. 23. (*Davies.*)

ragamuffinly (rag′a̤-muf-in-li), *a.* [< *ragamuffin* + *-ly*[1].] Like a ragamuffin; marked by raggedness or slovenliness. [Rare.]

His attire was . . . shabby, not to say *ragamuffinly* in the extreme, . . . as to inherent disreputableness of appearance. *J. Fothergill*, March in the Ranks, x.

rag-bolt (rag′bōlt), *n.* An iron pin with a barbed shank, chiefly used where a common bolt cannot be clinched. Also called *barb-bolt* and *sprig-bolt*.

Rag-bolts.

rag-bush (rag′bush), *n.* In some heathen countries, a bush in some special locality, as near a sacred well, on which pieces of cloth are hung to propitiate the spirits supposed to dwell there. The rags are generally pieces torn from the garments of pilgrims or wayfarers.

There is usually a *rag-bush* by the well, on which bits of linen or worsted are tied as a gift to the spirits of the watch. *C. Elton*, Origins of Eng. Hist., p. 286.

rag-dust (rag′dust), *n.* The refuse of woolen or worsted rags pulverized and dyed in various colors to form the flock used by paper-stainers for their flock-papers.

rage (rāj), *n.* [< ME. *rage*, < OF. *rage*, *raige*, F. *rage*, F. dial. *raige* = Pr. *rabia*, *rotje* = Sp. *rabia* = Pg. *raiva*, *rabia* = It. *rabbia*, dial. *raggia*, madness, rage, fury, < ML. (and prob. LL.) *rabia*, a later form of L. *rabies*, madness, rage, fury, < *rabere*, be mad, rave, = Skt. √ *rabh*, seize. Cf. *rage*, *v.*, *enrage*, *rave*[1], *rabies*, *rabid*, etc.] 1†. Madness; insanity; an access of maniacal violence.

Now, out of doubt Antipholus is mad. . . .
The reason that I gather he is mad,
Besides this present instance of his *rage*,
Is a mad tale he told to-day.
Shak., C. of E., iv. 3. 88.

2. Violent anger manifested in language or action; indignation or resentment excited to fury and expressed in furious words and gestures, with agitation.

Words well dispost
Have secrete powre t' appease inflamed *rage*.
Spenser, F. Q., II. viii. 26.

So he [Naaman] turned and went away in a *rage*.
2 Ki. v. 12.

Heaven has no *rage* like love to hatred turned,
Nor hell a fury like a woman scorned.
Congreve, Mourning Bride, iii. 8.

3. Extreme violence of operation or effect; intensity of degree, force, or urgency: used of things or conditions: as, the *rage* of a storm or of the sea; the *rage* of fever or of thirst.

And in wynter, and especially in lente, it ys mervelows flowyng with *rage* of watir that comyth with grett violence thorow the vale of Josophat.
Torkington, Diarie of Eng. Travell, p. 27.

Fear no more the heat o' the sun,
Nor the furious winter's *rages*.
Shak., Cymbeline, iv. 2 (song).

Ere yet from rest or food we seek relief,
Some rites remain, to glut our *rage* of grief.
Pope, Iliad, xxii. 14.

4. Vehement emotion; generous ardor or enthusiasm; passionate utterance or eloquence.

Thurgh which her grete sorwe gan aswage;
She may not alwey duren in swich *rage*.
Chaucer, Franklin's Tale, l. 108.

And your true rights be term'd a poet's *rage*,
And stretched metre of an antique song.
Shak., Sonnets, xvii.

The soldiers shout around with generous *rage*,
And in that victory their own presage.
Dryden, Pal. and Arc., i. 117.

Chill penury repressed their noble *rage*,
And froze the genial current of the soul.
Gray, Elegy.

5. Vehement desire or pursuit; ardent eagerness, as for the attainment or accomplishment of something; engrossing tendency or propensity: as, the *rage* for speculation, for social distinction, etc.

So o'er this sleeping soul doth Tarquin stay,
His *rage* of lust by gazing qualified.
Shak., Lucrece, l. 424.

What *rage* for fame attends both great and small!
Better be d—d than mentioned not at all.
Wolcot (*P. Pindar*), To the Royal Academicians.

In our day the *rage* for accumulation has apotheosized work. *H. Spencer*, Social Statics, p. 178.

Croquet, which is now so far lost in the mists of antiquity that men of thirty are too young to remember the *rage* for it, was actually not yet [1837] invented.
W. Besant, Fifty Years Ago, p. 88.

6. An object of general and eager desire or pursuit; fashion; vogue; fad: as, music is now all the *rage*. [Colloq.]—7†. A violent wind.

Therout cam a *rage* and such a vese
That it made al the gates for to rese.
Chaucer, Knight's Tale, l. 1127.

=**Syn.** 2. *Vexation*, *Indignation*, etc. (see *anger*[1]); frenzy, madness, raving.

rage (rāj), *v.*; pret. and pp. *raged*, ppr. *raging*. [< ME. *ragen*, < OF. *ragier*, *rager*, be furious, rage, romp, play, F. *rager*, Picard dial. *rabier*, be furious, rage, = Pr. *raviar*, *ratjar* = Sp. *rabiar* = Pg. *raivar* = OIt. *rabbiare*, be furious, < ML. *rabiare*, be furious, rage, < *rabia*, L. *rabies*, madness, fury, rage: see *rage*, *n.* Cf. *enrage*, *rave*[1], *rabiate*.] I. *intrans.* 1. To be furious with anger; be excited to fury; be violently agitated with passion of any kind.

He inly *raged*, and, as they talk'd,
Smote him into the midriff with a stone.
Milton, P. L., xi. 444.

2. To speak with passionate utterance, or act with furious vehemence; storm; rave.

The fool *rageth*, and is confident. Prov. xiv. 16.

Poets, when they *rage*,
Turn gods to men, and make an hour an age.
Beau. and Fl., Maid's Tragedy, i. 2.

As hee was thus madde and *raging* against the true Religion. *Purchas*, Pilgrimage, p. 84.

I expect Mr. Tickler this evening, and he will *rage* if he miss his free-and-easy. *Noctes Ambrosianæ*, Feb., 1832.

3. To act violently; move impetuously; be violently driven or agitated; have furious course or effect: said of things: as, a *raging* fever; the storm *rages*; war is *raging*.

The chariots shall *rage* in the streets, they shall justle one against another in the broad ways. Nahum ii. 4.

Like the hectic in my blood he *rages*.
Shak., Hamlet, iv. 3. 68.

If the Sickness *rage* in such Extremity at London, the Term will be held at Reading. *Howell*, Letters, I. iv. 23.

The storm of cheers and counter-cheers *rages* around him [Mr. Gladstone], as it can *rage* nowhere except in the House of Commons. *T. W. Reid*, Cabinet Portraits, p. 24.

4†. To frolic wantonly; play; frisk; romp.

When sche seyth galantys revell yn hall,
Yn here hert she thynkys owtrage,
Desyrynge with them to pley and *rage*,
And stelyth fro yow full prevely.
Reliq. Antiq., i. 29. (*Halliwell.*)

On a day this hende Nicholas
Fil with this yonge wyf to *rage* and pleye.
Chaucer, Miller's Tale, l. 87.

She bygan to plaie and *rage*,
As who saith, I am well enough.
Gower, Conf. Amant., i.

5. To be very eager or anxious. [Rare.]

II. *trans.* To enrage; chafe; fret.

Deal mildly with his youth;
For young hot colts being *raged* do rage the more.
Shak., Rich. II., ii. 1. 70.

ragee, *n.* See *raggee*.

rageful (rāj′fu̇l), *a.* [< *rage* + *-ful*.] Full of rage; furious.

With *rageful* eyes she bad him defend himself.
Sir P. Sidney, Arcadia, ii.

Nor thou be *rageful*, like a handled bee.
Tennyson, Ancient Sage.

rageman†, *n.* See *ragman*[3].

rag-engine (rag′en″jin), *n.* In *paper-manuf.*, a tank fitted with rotating cylindrical cutters or other devices for the rapid disintegration of rags to form paper-pulp.

rageous† (rā′jus), *a.* [Also *ragious*; < *rage* + *-ous*, perhaps by association with the unrelated *outrageous*.] Full of rage; furious.

Our Sauyour whiche redeemed vs with so great a price may not thincke that it longeth to hym to se vs peryshe, neyther to suffer the shippe of his churche to bee so shaken with many great and *ragious* flodes.
Bp. Fisher, Seven Penitential Psalms.

rageousness† (rā′jus-nes), *n.* The quality of being rageous; fury. Also *ragiousness*.

What a *ragiousnes* is it, to set thy chastity common like an harlot, that thou maiest gather riches!
Vives, Instruction of a Christian Woman, iii. 7.

ragery† (rā′jėr-i), *n.* [< ME. *ragerie*, < OF. *ragerie*, rage, anger, < *rager*, rage: see *rage*, *v.*] 1. Rage; an ebullition of fury.

Plucked off . . . in a *ragery*.
W. Browne, Shepherd's Pipe, i.

2. Wantonness; frolic.

He was al coltissh, ful of *ragerye*.
Chaucer, Merchant's Tale, l. 603.

rag-fair (rag′fãr), *n.* A market for vending old clothes and cast-off garments.

ragg†, *n.* See *rag*[1].

raggabash, *n.* See *ragabash*.

ragged (rag′ed), *a.* [< ME. *ragged*, *raggyd*, shaggy, tattered, torn; < Icel. *raggathr* (= Norw. *raggad*), shaggy, < Icel. *rögg*, shagginess, = Norw. *ragg*, rough, uneven hair: see *rag*[1].] 1. Having a rough shaggy coat, as a horse or sheep; shaggy.

A *ragged* colt. *King Alisaunder*, l. 684.

What shepherd owns those *ragged* sheep?
Dryden, tr. of Virgil's Eclogues, iii. 1.

2. Rough, uneven, or rocky, as a sea-bottom.—3. Roughly broken, divided, or disordered; having disjointed parts, or a confusedly irregular surface or outline; jagged; craggy; ruggedly uneven or distorted: often used figuratively.

My voice is *ragged*; I know I cannot please you.
Shak., As you Like it, ii. 5. 15.

I am so bold as to call so piercing and so glorious an Eye as your Grace to view those poore *ragged* lines.
Capt. John Smith, Works, I. 57.

Then, foraging this Isle, long-promis'd them before,
Amongst the *ragged* cleeves those monstrous Giants sought.
Drayton, Polyolbion, i. 471.

We went somewhat out of ye way to see the towne of Bourbon l'Archambaut, from whose antient and *ragged* castle is deriv'd the name of the present Royal Family of France. *Evelyn*, Diary, Sept. 24, 1644.

Ragged clouds still streamed the pale sky o'er.
William Morris, Earthly Paradise, III. 162.

4. Rent or worn into rags or tatters; tattered; frayed: as, a *ragged* coat; *ragged* sails.

He [the sheik] came out to us in a *ragged* habit of green silk, lined with fur.
Pococke, Description of the East, II. i. 266.

5. Wearing torn or frayed clothes; dressed in rags or tatters.

Since noble arts in Rome have no support,
And *ragged* virtue not a friend at court.
Dryden, tr. of Juvenal's Satires, iii.

He . . . perhaps thinks that after all gipsies do not look so very different from other *ragged* people.
E. A. Freeman, Venice, p. 58.

6. Shabby; ill-furnished.

In a small, low, *ragged* room . . . Margaret saw an old woman with a dish of coals and two tallow candles burning before her on a table. *S. Judd*, Margaret, i. 15.

7. In *her.*, same as *raguly*, especially of anything which is raguly on both sides. See *ragged staff*, below.—**Ragged staff**, in *her.*, a pale couped at each end and raguly on each side: more commonly represented as an actual knotted stick, or stout staff with short stumps of branches on each side.

The Earl of Warwick's *ragged staff* is yet to be seen pourtrayed in their church steeple. *R. Carew*, Survey of Cornwall.

ragged-lady (rag'ed-lā'di), *n.* A garden flower, *Nigella Damascena.*

raggedly (rag'ed-li), *adv.* In a ragged condition or manner; roughly; brokenly.

Raggedly and meanly apparelled. *Bp. Hacket*, Abp. Williams (1693), p. 219. (*Latham.*)

Sometimes I heard the foxes as they ranged over the snow crust in moonlight nights, . . . barking *raggedly* and demoniacally like forest dogs. *Thoreau*, Walden, p. 293.

raggedness (rag'ed-nes), *n.* The state or character of being ragged, in any sense.

Poor naked wretches, . . . How shall
Your loop'd and window'd *raggedness* defend you
From seasons such as these? *Shak.*, Lear, iii. 4. 31.

ragged-robin (rag'ed-rob'in), *n.* The cuckoo-flower, *Lychnis Flos-cuculi.*

Ragged-robin (*Lychnis Flos-cuculi*). 1, upper part of stem with inflorescence; 2, lower part of stem with rhizome; *a*, a fruit.

ragged-sailor (rag'ed-sā'lor), *n.* A plant of the genus *Polygonum*: same as *prince's-feather*, 2.

ragged-school (rag'ed-sköl), *n.* See *school*[1].

ragged-staff (rag'ed-ståf), *n.* A kind of polyzoan, *Alcyonidium glutinosum.* Also called *mermaid's-glove.*

raggee (rag'ē), *n.* [Also *raggy*, *ragee*; < Hind. Canarese *rāgi.*] A grass, *Eleusine coracana*, a prolific grain-plant cultivated in Japan and parts of India.

raggery (rag'ėr-i), *n.* [< *rag*[1] + *-ery.*] Rags collectively; raggedness. [Rare.]

Grim, portentous old hags, such as Michael Angelo painted, draped in majestic *raggery.* *Thackeray*, Newcomes, xxxv.

ragging (rag'ing), *n.* [Verbal n. of *rag*[1], *v.*] 1. A method of fishing for the striped-bass, etc., in which a red rag is used as a fly. [U. S.] —2. In *mining*, the first and roughest separation of the ore (mixed with more or less veinstone), by which the entirely worthless portion is selected and rejected. Nearly the same as *spalling*; but sometimes the latter term is used to designate a second and more thorough ragging, while *cobbing* may mean a still more thorough separation; but all are done with the hammer, without special machinery.

ragging-frame (rag'ing-frām), *n.* Same as *racking-table.*

raggle (rag'l), *v. t.*; pret. and pp. *raggled*, ppr. *raggling.* [Freq. of *rag*[1].] To notch or groove irregularly.

raggle (rag'l), *n.* [< *raggle*, *v.*] A ragged piece; a torn strip.

Striding swiftly over the heavy snow, he examines each trap in turn, to find perhaps in one a toe, in another a nail, and in a third a splendid ermine torn to *raggles* by "that internal carcajou." *Cosmopolitan*, Feb., 1888.

raggy† (rag'i), *a.* [< ME. **raggy*, < AS. *raggig* (pl. *raggie*), rough, shaggy, < Sw. *raggig*, shaggy, Sw. dial. *raggi*, rough-haired, slovenly, < *ragg*, rough hair, = Icel. *rögg*, shagginess: see *rag*[1].] Rough; rugged; rocky.

A stony and *raggy* hill. *Holland.*

raght†. Same as *raught*[1] for *reached.*

ragi (rag'ē), *n.* See *ragee.*

raginee (rag'i-nē), *n.* [Hind. *rāginī*, a mode in music (= Skt. *rāginī*, possessing color or passion), cf. *rāg*, a mode in music, < Skt. *rāga*, coloring, color, feeling, passion; < √*raj*, be colored.] One of a class of Hindu melodies founded on fixed scales. Often contracted to *rag.*

ragingly (rā'jing-li), *adv.* In a raging manner; with fury; with violent impetuosity.

ragious†, **ragiousness**†. See *rageous*, *rageousness.*

rag-knife (rag'nīf), *n.* In a rag-engine, one of the knives in the cylindrical cutter, working against those in the bed or bottom-plate.

raglan (rag'lan), *n.* [So called after Lord *Raglan*, commander-in-chief of the British forces in the Crimea.] A kind of loose overcoat, having very full sleeves, or a sort of cape covering the arms, worn about 1855 and later.

As it was quite dark in the tent, I picked up what was supposed to be my *raglan*, a water-proof light overcoat, without sleeves. *The Century*, XXXIX. 506.

rag-looper (rag'lö"pėr), *n.* An apparatus for knotting together strips and pieces of fabrics in making a rag carpet.

ragman[1] (rag'man), *n.*; pl. *ragmen* (-men). [< ME. *ragmann*; < *rag*[1] + *man.*] 1†. A ragged person.

Ragmann, or he that goythe wythe iaggyd [var. *raggyd*] clothys, pannicius vel pannicia. *Prompt. Parv.*, p. 421.

2. A man who collects or deals in rags.

ragman[2]†, *n.* [ME. **ragman*, *rageman*, *raggeman*, prob. < Icel. *ragmenni*, a craven (cf. *regimadhr*, a craven), < *ragr*, craven, cowardly (appar. a transposed form of *argr*, craven, cowardly, = AS. *earg*, cowardly: see *arch*[3]), + *madhr* (**mannr*), man, = E. *man.* Cf. *ragman-roll.*] 1. A craven. [Not found in this sense, except as in *ragman-roll* and the particular application in definition 2 following.]—2. The devil.

Filius by the faders wil degh with Spiritus Sanctus,
To ransake that *rageman* and reue hym hus apples,
That fyrst man deceyuede thorgh frut and false by-heste.
Piers Plowman (C), xix. 122.

ragman[3]† (rag'man), *n.* [ME. *ragman*, *ragmon*, *rageman*, *ragemon*, *ragment*, a deed sealed, a papal bull, a list, a tedious story, a game so called: an abbr. of *ragman-roll*, q. v.] 1. Same as *ragman-roll*, 1.

He blessed hem with his breuet, and blered hure eyen,
And raghte with hus *ragman* rynges and broches.
Piers Plowman (C), i. 72.

Rede on this *ragmon*, and rewle yow theraftur.
MS. Cantab. Ff. v. 48, f. 7. (*Halliwell.*)

The records in connexion with the financial operations of Richard II. and Richard III. make it clear that a *ragman* or *rageman*—I believe the word is spelled both ways—meant simply a bond or personal obligation. *The Academy*, Jan. 18, 1890, p. 47.

2. Same as *ragman-roll*, 2.

Mr. Wright . . . has printed two collections of ancient Verses used in the game of *ragman.* *Halliwell.*

ragman-roll† (rag'man-rōl), *n.* [ME. **ragman-rolle*, *ragmane-roelle*; < *ragman*[2] + *roll*, *n.* Also *ragman's roll*, *ragman's rewe* (i. e. *row*). Hence by abbr. *ragman*[3], by corruption *rig-my-roll*, *rigmarole*: see *rigmarole.*] 1. A parchment roll with pendent seals, as an official catalogue or register, a deed, or a papal bull; hence, any important document, catalogue, or list. The name was applied specifically, and perhaps originally (in the supposed invidious sense 'the Cravens' Roll'), to the collection of those instruments by which the nobility and gentry of Scotland were tyrannically constrained to subscribe allegiance to Edward I. of England in 1296, and which were more particularly recorded in four large rolls of parchment, consisting of thirty-five pieces bound together, and kept in the Tower of London. (*Jamieson.*)

What one man emong many thousandes . . . hath so moche vacaunte tyme, that he maie bee at leasure to tourne ouer and ouer in the bookes of Plato the *ragmannes rolles* . . . whiche Socrates doeth there vse? *Erasmus*, Pref. to Apophthegms, tr. by Udall.

The list of names in Fame's book is called *ragman roll* in Skelton, i. 420. *Halliwell.*

2. A game played with a roll of parchment containing verses descriptive of character, to each of which was attached a string with a pendant. The parchment being rolled up, each player selected one of the projecting strings, and the verse to which it led was taken as his description.

3. A written fabrication; a vague or rambling story; a rigmarole.

Mayster parson, I marvayll ye wyll gyve lycenc
To this false knave in this audience
To publish his *ragman rolles* with lyes.
The Pardoner and the Frere (1533). (*Halliwell.*)

ragman's rewe†. Same as *ragman-roll*, 2.

These songes or rimes (because their originall beginnyng issued out of Fescenium) wer called in Latine Fescennina Carmina or Fescennini rythmi or versus: whiche I doe here translate (according to our English prouerbe) a *ragman's rewe* or a bible. For so doe we call a long jeste that railleth on any persone by name, or toucheth a bodie's honestee somewhat nere. *Udall's Erasmus's Apophth.*, p. 274.

ragman's roll† (rag'manz rōl), *n.* See *ragman-roll.*

rag-money (rag'mun"i), *n.* See *rag money*, under *rag*[1].

Ragnarök (räg'nä-rėk'), *n.* [< Icel. *ragna rökr*, 'twilight of the gods' (G. *götterdämmerung*): *ragna*, gen. of *rögn*, *regin*, neut. pl., the gods (= Goth. *ragin*, counsel, will, determination, > *ragineis*, counselor); *rökr*, twilight, dimness, vapor (see *reek*[1]); but orig. *ragna rök*, the history of the gods and the world, esp. with ref. to the last judgment, doomsday: *rök*, reason, judgment.] In *Scand. myth.*, the general destruction of the gods in a great battle with the evil powers, in which the latter and the earth also perish, followed by regeneration of all things through the power of the supreme God, and the reappearance of those gods who represent the regenerative forces of nature.

ragoa (ra-gō'ä), *n.* Same as *goa*, 1.

ragondin, *n.* The pelt or fur of the La Plata beaver or coypou, *Myopotamus coypus*; nutria.

ragoo†, *n.* An obsolete English spelling of *ragout.*

ragout (ra-gö'), *n.* [Formerly spelled *ragoo* or *ragou*, in imitation of the F. pron., also *ragoust*, < OF. *ragoust*, F. *ragoût*, a stew, a seasoned dish, < *ragouster*, *ragoûter*, bring back to one's appetite; < *re-* (< L. *re-*), again, + *a-* (< L. *ad*), to, + *gouster*, F. *goûter*, < L. *gustare*, taste: see *gust*[2].] 1. A dish of meat (usually mutton or veal) and vegetables cut small, stewed brown, and highly seasoned.

Spongy Morells in strong *Ragousts* are found,
And in the Soupe the slimy Snail is drown'd.
Gay, Trivia.

And thus they bid farewell to carnal dishes,
And solid meats, and highly-spiced *ragoûts*,
To live for forty days on ill-dress'd fishes.
Byron, Beppo, st. 7.

When he found her prefer a plain dish to a *ragout*, had nothing to say to her. *Jane Austen*, Pride and Prejudice, p. 29.

2. Figuratively, a spicy mixture; any piquant combination of persons or things.

I assure you she has an odd *Ragoût* of Guardians, as you will find when you hear the Characters. *Mrs. Centlivre*, Bold Stroke, ii.

rag-picker (rag'pik"ėr), *n.* 1. One who goes about to collect rags, bones, and other waste articles of some little value, from streets, ash-pits, dunghills, etc.—2. A machine for tearing and pulling to shreds rags, yarns, hosiery, old carpet, and other waste, to reduce them to cotton or wool staple; a shoddy-machine.—**Rag-pickers' disease**, malignant anthrax.

ragshag (rag'shag), *n.* [A riming variation of *rag*, as if < *rag*[1] + *shag.*] A very ragged person; especially, one who purposely dresses in grotesque rags for exhibition. [Colloq.]

While the *Ragshags* were marching, . . . [he] caught his foot in his ragged garment and fell. *Conn. Courant*, July 7, 1887.

rag-shop (rag'shop), *n.* A shop in which rags and other refuse collected by rag-pickers are bought, sorted, and prepared for use.

rag-sorter (rag'sôr"tėr), *n.* A person employed in sorting rags for paper-making or other use.

The subjects were grouped as follows: six *ragsorters*, four female cooks, etc. *Medical News*, LIII. 600.

ragstone (rag'stōn), *n.* [< *rag*[1] + *stone.*] 1. In *Eng. geol.*, a rock forming a part of a series of rough, shelly, sandy limestones, with layers of marl and sandstone, occurring in the Lower or Bath Oölite. The shale series is sometimes called the *Ragstone* or *Ragstone series.*—2. In *masonry*, stone quarried in thin blocks or slabs.

rag-tag (rag'tag), *n.* [Also *tag-rag*, short for *tag and rag*: see *rag*[1], *tag*, *n.*, *tag-rag.*] Ragged people collectively; the scum of the populace; the rabble: sometimes used attributively. [Colloq.]—**Rag-tag and bobtail**, all kinds of shabby or shiftless people; persons of every degree of worthlessness; a disorderly rabble. [Colloq.]

Rag-tag and bobtail, disguised and got up with make-shift arms, hovering in the distance, have before now decided battles. *Gladstone*, Gleanings of Past Years, I. 169.

rag-turnsol (rag'tėrn"sol), *n.* Linen impregnated with the blue dye obtained from the juice of the plant *Chrozophora tinctoria*, used as a test for acids. See *turnsol*, 2.

ragulated (rag'ū-lā-ted), *a.* In *her.*, same as *raguly.*

ragulé (rag-ū-lā'), *a.* Same as *raguly.*

raguled (rag'ūld), *a.* [< *ragul-y* + *-ed*[2].] Same as *raguly.*

raguly (rag'ū-li), *a.* [< Heraldic F. *ragulé*; < E. *rag*[1] + *-ul-* + *-é.*] In *her.*, broken into regular projections and depressions like battlements, except that the lines make oblique angles with one another: said of one of the lines in heraldry, which is used to separate the divisions of the field or to form the boundary of any ordinary.

A Cross Raguly.

Ragusan (ra-gö'san), *a.* and *n.* [< *Ragusa* (see def.) + *-an*. Cf. *argosy*.] **I.** *a.* Of or pertaining to Ragusa in Dalmatia, on the Adriatic, a city belonging to Austria, but for many centuries prior to the time of Napoleon I. an independent republic.

II. *n.* A native or an inhabitant of Ragusa.

ragweed (rag'wēd), *n.* **1.** Any plant of the composite genus *Ambrosia*; especially, the common North American species *A. trifida*, the great ragweed or horse-cane, and *A. artemisiæfolia*, the Roman wormwood or hogweed. Both are sometimes called *bitterweed*. The former is commonly found on river-banks, has three-lobed leaves, and is sometimes 12 feet high. The latter, a much-branching plant from 1 to 3 feet high, with dissected leaves, grows everywhere in waste places, along roads, etc., and is troublesome in fields. Its pollen is regarded as a cause of hay-fever. The plants of this genus are monœcious, the flowers of the two sexes borne in separate heads, the female heads producing a single flower with the ovoid involucre closed over it. The flowers are greenish and inconspicuous. See *Ambrosia*, 2.

2. The ragwort or St.-James-wort, *Senecio Jacobæa*. [Prov. Eng.]

rag-wheel (rag'hwēl), *n.* **1.** In *mach.*, a wheel having a notched or serrated margin.—**2.** A cutlers' polishing-wheel or soft disk made by clamping together a number of disks cut from some fabric.—**Rag-wheel and chain**, a contrivance for use instead of a band or belt when great resistance is to be overcome, consisting of a wheel with pins or cogs on the rim, and a chain in the links of which the pins catch. See cut under *chain-wheel*.

rag-wool (rag'wůl), *n.* Wool from rags; shoddy.

rag-work (rag'wėrk), *n.* **1.** Masonry built with undressed flat stones of about the thickness of a brick, and having a rough exterior, whence the name.—**2.** A manufacture of carpeting or similar heavy fabric from strips of rag, which are either knitted or woven together. Compare *rag carpet*, under *rag*[1].

ragworm (rag'wėrm), *n.* Same as *mud-worm*.

ragwort (rag'wėrt), *n.* The name of several plants of the genus *Senecio*; primarily, *S. Jacobæa* of Europe and northern Asia. This is an erect herb from 2 to 4 feet high, with bright-yellow radiate heads in a compact terminal corymb; the leaves are irregularly lobed and toothed, whence the name. Also called *benweed*, *cankerweed*, *St.-James-wort*, *kadle-dock*, *jacobæa*, etc.: in Ireland *fairies'-horse*. Sometimes *ragweed*.—**African ragwort.** See *Othonna*.—**Golden ragwort**, a North American plant, *Senecio aureus*, from 1 to 3 feet high, sometimes lower, bearing corymbs of golden-yellow heads in spring: very common and extremely variable. It is said to have been a favorite vulnerary with the Indians, and is by some regarded as an emmenagogue and diuretic. Also called *squaw-weed* and *liferoot*.—**Purple ragwort**, the purple jacobæa, *Senecio elegans*, a handsome garden species from the Cape of Good Hope: a smooth herb with pinnatifid leaves and corymbed heads, the rays purple, the disk yellow or purple.—**Sea-ragwort.** Same as *dusty-miller*, 2.—**Woolly ragwort**, *Senecio tomentosus* of the southern United States, a plant covered with scarcely deciduous hoary wool.

1, the upper part of the stem with the heads of golden ragwort (*Senecio aureus*); 2, the rhizome with the lower part of the stem and the leaves; *a*, the achene.

rahate†, *n. t.* An erroneous form of *rate*[1].

> He neuer linned *rahatyng* of those persones that offred sacrifice for to haue good health of bodie.
> *Udall*, tr. of Apophthegms of Erasmus, p. 86. (*Davies.*)

Rahu (rä'hö), *n.* [Skt. *Rāhu*; derivation obscure.] In *Hindu myth.*, the demon that is supposed to be the cause of the eclipses of the sun and moon.

Raia (rā'ä), *n.* [NL., also *Raja*, < L. *raia*, a ray: see *ray*[2].] A genus of batoid selachians: used with various limits. (*a*) By the old authors it was extended to all the species of the order or suborder *Raiæ*. (*b*) By modern authors it is restricted to those *Raiidæ* (in the narrowest sense) which have the pectorals separated by the snout, the caudal rudimentary, and the ventrals distinct and notched. It comprises nearly 40 species, generally called *skates* or *rays*. See cuts under *skate* and *ray*[1].

Raiæ (rā'ē), *n. pl.* [NL., pl. of L. *raia*, a ray: see *Raia*.] An order or suborder of selachians, comprising the rays or skates, and distinguished by the position of the branchial apertures on the lower surface of the body, and the depressed and disk-like trunk in combination with the outspread pectorals. Also called *Batoidei*.

raian (rā'an), *a.* and *n.* [< NL. *Rai(a)* + *-an*.] Same as *raioid*.

raible (rā'bl), *v.* A Scotch form of *rabble*[1].

> Wee Miller neist the guard relieves,
> And orthodoxy *raibles*. *Burns*, Holy Fair.

raid (rād), *n.* [Also *rade*; < ME. *rade*, Northern form of *rode*, < AS. *rād*, a riding, = Icel. *reidh*, a riding, a raid: see *road*, of which *raid* is a variant, prob. in part from the cognate Icel. form.] **1.** A hostile or predatory incursion; especially, an inroad or incursion of mounted men; a swooping assault for injury or plunder; a foray.

> Then he a proclamation maid,
> All men to meet at Inverness,
> Throw Murray land to mak a *raid*.
> *Battle of Harlaw* (Child's Ballads, VII. 184).

> So the ruffians growl'd,
> Fearing to lose, and all for a dead man,
> Their chance of booty from the morning's *raid*.
> *Tennyson*, Geraint.

Hence—**2.** A sudden onset in general; an irruption for or as if for assault or seizure; a descent made in an unexpected or undesired manner: as, a police *raid* upon a gambling-house. [Chiefly colloq.]

raid (rād), *v.* [< *raid*, *n.*] **I.** *intrans.* To go upon a raid; engage in a sudden hostile or disturbing incursion, foray, or descent.

> The Saxons were perpetually *raiding* along the confines of Gaul. *The Atlantic*, LXV. 153.

II. *trans.* **1.** To make a raid or hostile attack upon; encroach upon by foray or incursion. Hence—**2.** To attack in any way; affect injuriously by sudden or covert assault or invasion of any kind: as, to *raid* a gambling-house. [Colloq.]—**To raid the market**, to derange prices or the course of trade, as on the stock-exchange, by exciting distrust or uncertainty with regard to values; disturb or depress prices by creating a temporary panic. [Colloq.]

raider (rā'dėr), *n.* [< *raid* + *-er*[1].] One who makes a raid; one engaged in a hostile or predatory incursion.

raign[1]†, *v. t.* [ME. *reynen*; by apheresis for *arraign*[1] (ME. *araynen*, etc.).] To arraign.

> And many other extorcioners and promoters in dyuers contreys within the reame was broght to London, and put in to prysons, and *reyned* at the Gyld Halle with Empson and Dudley. *Arnold's Chronicle*, p. xliv.

raign[2]†, *n.* and *v.* An obsolete spelling of *reign*.

Raiidæ (rā'i-dē), *n. pl.* [NL., < *Raia* + *-idæ*.] A family of hypotreme selachians, or *Raiæ*, typified by the genus *Raia*; the skates and rays proper. The species have a moderately broad rhombic disk, a more or less acute snout, the tail slender but not whip-like, and surmounted by two small dorsals without spines, and no electrical apparatus. The females are oviparous, eggs inclosed in quadrate corneous capsules being cast. In this respect the *Raiidæ* differ from all the other ray-like selachians. The species are quite numerous, and every sea has representatives. Formerly the family was taken in a much more extended sense, embracing all the representatives of the suborder except the saw-fishes. Also *Rajidæ*.

Raiinæ (rā-ī'nē), *n. pl.* [NL., < *Raia* + *-inæ*.] A subfamily of rays, coextensive with the family *Raiidæ* in its most restricted sense.

raik†, *v. i.* See *rake*[2].

rail[1] (rāl), *n.* [< ME. *rail*, *raile*, *rayl*, **regel*, **regol* (in comp. *regolsticke*, a ruler), partly < AS. *regol* (not found in sense of 'bar' or 'rail' except as in *regolsticca* (> ME. *regolsticke*), a ruler, a straight bar, but common in the derived sense 'a rule of action,' = MD. *reghel*, *rijghel*, *rijchel*, *richel*, a bar, rail, bolt, later *richgel*, a bar, shelf, D. *rigchel*, a bar, = MLG. *regel*, LG. *regel*, a rail, cross-bar, = OHG. *rigil*, MHG. *rigel*, G. *riegel*, a bar, bolt, rail, = Sw. *regel* = Dan. *rigel*, a bar, bolt; partly < OF. *reille*, *raille*, *roille*, *roile*, *reilhe*, *relle*, *rele*, a bar, rail, bolt, board, plank, ladder, plow-handle, furrow, row, etc., F. dial. *reille*, ladder, *reille*, *raille*, plowshare (< LG.); < L. *regula*, a straight piece of wood, a stick, bar, staff, rod, rule, ruler, hence a rule, pattern, model: see *rule*[1]. *Rail*[1] is thus a doublet of *rule*[1], derived through AS., while *rule*[1] is derived through OF., from the same L. word. Cf. *rail*[2].] **1.** A bar of wood or other material passing from one post or other support to another. Rails, variously secured, as by being mortised to or passing through slots in their supports, etc., are used to form fences and barriers and for many other purposes. In many parts of the United States rail fences are commonly made of rails roughly split from logs and laid zigzag with their ends resting upon one another, every intersection so formed being often supported by a pair of cross-stakes driven into the ground, upon which the top rails rest.

2. A structure consisting of rails and their sustaining posts, balusters, or pillars, and constituting an inclosure or line of division: often used in the plural, and also called a *railing*. The rails of massive stone, elaborately sculptured, which form the ceremonial inclosures of ancient Buddhist topes, temples, sacred trees, etc., in India, are among the most characteristic and important features of Buddhist architecture, and are the most remarkable works of this class known.

> The Grownd within the *Rayles* must bee coveryd with blake Cloth.
> *Books of Precedence* (E. E. T. S., extra ser.), i. 33.

> There lyeth a white marble in form of a graves-stone, environed with a *rale* of brasse. *Sandys*, Travailes, p. 127.

> The Bharhut *rail*, according to the inscription on it, was erected by a Prince Vādha Pala. . . . The Buddh Gaya *rail* is a rectangle, measuring 131 ft. by 98 ft.
> *J. Fergusson*, Hist. Indian Arch., p. 85.

3. In *joinery*, a horizontal timber in a piece of framing or paneling. Specifically—(*a*) In a door, sash, or any paneled work, one of the horizontal pieces between which the panels lie, the vertical pieces being called *stiles*. See cut under *door*. (*b*) The course of pieces into which the upper ends of the balusters of a stair are mortised. (*c*) In furniture-making and fine joinery, any piece of the construction passing between two posts or other members of the frame: as, the head-*rail* or foot-*rail* in a bedstead. Hence—(*d*) A corresponding member in construction in other materials than wood, as a tie in brass or iron furniture.

4. *Naut.*, one of several bars or timbers in a ship, serving for inclosure or support. The *rail*, specifically so called, is the fence or upper part of the bulwarks, consisting of a course of molded planks or small timbers mortised to the stanchions, or sometimes to the timber-heads. The part passing round the stern is the *taffrail*. The *forecastle-rail*, *poop-rail*, and *top-rail* are bars extended on stanchions across the after part of the forecastle-deck, the fore part of the poop, and the after part of each of the tops, respectively. A *pin-rail* is part of a rail with holes in it for belaying-pins; and a *fife-rail* is a rail around the lower part of a mast, above the deck, with similar holes. The *rails of the head* are curved pieces of timber extending from the bows on each side to the hull of the head, for its support.

5. One of the iron or (now generally) steel bars or beams used on the permanent way of a railway to support and guide the wheels of cars and motors. The general form now most in use for steam-railways is that known as the *T-rail*. But, though these rails all have a section vaguely resembling the letter T, the proportions of the different parts and the weights of the rails are nearly as various as the railways themselves. In the accompanying diagram is shown a section of a rail weighing 75 pounds per yard in length, the weight of the length of one yard being the common mode of stating the weights of rails. These weights are in modern rails sometimes as great as 100 or more pounds per yard, the more recent tendency having been toward heavier locomotives and heavier rails. The cut shows the comparative dimensions of the various parts. (Compare *fish-joint*, *fish-plate*, and *fish*[1], *v. t.*, 8.) The curved junctions of the web with the head and the base are called the *fillets*.

Section of Rail.
a, head; *b*, web; *c*, base; the part *d* is at the inner side of the head, and made to correspond with the throat of the car-wheel.

6. The railway or railroad as a means of transport: as, to travel or send goods by *rail*. [Colloq.]

> French and English made rapid way among the dragomanish officials of the *rail*.
> *W. H. Russell*, Diary in India, I. 24.

> On the question of *rail* charges a good deal might be written. *Quarterly Rev.*, CXLV. 319.

> The tourists find the steamer waiting for them at the end of the *rail*. *C. D. Warner*, Their Pilgrimage, p. 270.

7. In *cotton-spinning*, a bar having an up-and-down motion, by which yarn passing through is guided upon the bar and is distributed upon the bobbins.—**Adhesion of wheels to rails.** See *adhesion*.—**Capped rail.** See *cap*[1].—**Compound rail**, a railway-rail made in two longitudinal counterparts bolted together in such manner that opposite ends of each project beyond the other part to produce a lapping joint when the rails are spiked to the ties or sleepers. Also called *continuous rail*.—**Double-headed rail**, a railway-rail without flanges, with two opposite heads united by a web. It is always used with chairs, and by turning it upside down it can be used after the upper head has become so worn as to be useless.—**False rail**, in *ship-carp.*, a thin piece of timber attached inside of a curved head-rail in order to strengthen it.—**Fish-bellied rail**, a cast-iron railway-rail having a convex or downwardly arching under surface to strengthen its middle part, after the manner of some cast-iron beams and girders. It was introduced in 1805.—**Flat rail**, a railway-rail of cast-iron or wrought-iron fastened by spikes to longitudinal sleepers. The cast-iron flat rail was first used in 1776.—**Middle rail**, in *carp.*, that rail of a door which is on a level with the hand, and on which the lock is usually fixed, whence it is sometimes called the *lock-rail*. See cut under *door*.—**Pipe rail**, a rail of iron pipe joined by fittings as in pipe-fitting. Such rails, of iron or brass, are now much used in engine-rooms of ships, at the sides of locomotives, on iron bridges, elevated railways, etc.—**Pipe-rail fittings**, the screw-threaded fittings, including couplings, elbows, crosses, tees, flanges, etc., used in putting together pipe-railings, and usually of an ornamental pattern.—**Point-rail**, a pointed rail used in the construction of a railway-switch.—**Rail-drilling machine**, a machine for drilling holes in the web of steel rails for the insertion of fish-plate bolts.—**Rail-**

straightening machine, a portable screw-press for straightening bent or crooked rails or iron bars.—**Rail under** (*naut.*), with the lee rail submerged: as, the vessel sailed *rail under*.—**Rolled rail**, a rail made of wrought-iron or steel by rolling.—**Steel-headed rail**, a railway-rail having a wrought-iron base and web and a steel head. Such rails were too expensive for general use, and have given place to the Bessemer-steel rails. Also called *steel-topped rail*.—**Steel rail**, a rolled-steel railway-rail. The first steel rails were manufactured in England by Mushet in 1857. The development of the use of steel rails, stimulated by the invention of the celebrated Bessemer process for making cheap mild steel from which rails of far greater durability than those of wrought-iron can be manufactured, has been rapid, and has resulted in the substitution of steel rails for wrought-iron rails on nearly all important railways in the world.—**To ride on a rail.** See *ride*.—**Virginia rail fence.** Same as *snake fence* (which see, under *fence*).

rail[1] (rāl), *v.* [< ME. *railen*, *raylen* (= OHG. *rigilōn*, MHG. *rigelen*, G. *riegeln*), rail; cf. OF. *reillier*, *roillier*, *ruillier*, inclose with rails, bar; from the noun. Cf. *rail*[2], *v.*] **I.** *trans.* **1.** To inclose with rails: often with *in* or *off*.

The sayd herse must bee *raylyd* about, and hangyd with blake Cloth. *Booke of Precedence* (E. E. T. S., extra ser.), i. 33.

It is a spot *railed in*, and a piece of ground is laid out like a garden bed. *Pococke*, Description of the East, II. ii. 101.

Mr. Langdon . . . has now reached the *railed* space. *W. M. Baker*, New Timothy, p. 150.

2. To furnish with rails; lay the rails of, as a railway; construct a railway upon or along, as a street. [Recent.]

Fifty miles of new road graded last year, which was to receive its rails this spring, will not be *railed*, because it is not safe for the company to make further investments in that State. *Harper's Mag.*, LXXVII. 125.

II. *intrans.* To fish with a hand-line over the rail of a ship or boat. [Colloq.]

In England, the summer fishing for mackerel is carried on by means of hand lines, and small boats may be seen *railing* or "whiffing" amongst the schools of mackerel. *Nature*, XLI. 180.

rail[2]† (rāl), *v. t.* [< ME. *railen*, *raylen*, < AS. as if **regolian* (= D. *regelen* = G. *regeln*), set in order, rule, < *regol* = D. G. Sw. Dan. *regel*, < L. *regula*, a rule: see *rail*[1], and cf. *rule*[1]. Cf. OF. *reillier*, *roillier*, rail, bar, also stripe, from the noun.] To range in a line; set in order.

Al watz *rayled* on red ryche golde nayles,
That al glytered & glent as glem of the sunne.
Sir Gawayne and the Green Knight (E. E. T. S.), l. 603.

They were brought to London all *railed* in ropes, like a team of horses in a cart, and were executed, some at London, and the rest at divers places. *Bacon*, Hist. Hen. VII.

Audley, Flammock, Joseph,
The ringleaders of this commotion,
Railed in ropes, fit ornaments for traitors,
Wait your determinations.
Ford, Perkin Warbeck, iii. 1.

rail[3]† (rāl), *n.* [Early mod. E., also *rayle*; < ME. *rail*, *reil*, *regel*, < AS. *hrægel*, *hrægl*, a garment, dress, robe, pl. clothes, = OS. *hregil* = OFries. *hreil*, *reyl*, *reil* = OHG. *hregil*, clothing, garment, dress; root unknown.] **1.** A garment; dress; robe: now only in the compound *night-rail*.—**2.** A kerchief.

Rayle for a womans neck, crevechief, en quarttre doubles. *Palsgrave*.

And then a good grey frocke,
A kercheffe, and a *raile*.
Friar Bacon's Prophesie (1604). (*Halliwell*.)

rail[3]† (rāl), *v. t.* [ME. *railen*; < *rail*[3], *n.*] To dress; clothe.

Reali *railled* with wel riche clothes.
William of Palerne (E. E. T. S.), l. 1618.

rail[4] (rāl), *n.* [Early mod. E. *rayle*; < OF. *raale*, *rasle*, F. *râle* (> G. *ralle*, ML. *rallus*), F. dial. *reille*, a rail; so called from its cry; cf. OF. *rasle*, F. *râle*, a rattling in the throat; < OF. *raller*, F. *râler*, rattle in the throat, < MD. *ratelen*, rattle, make a noise: see *rattle*. Cf. also D. *rallen*, *rellen*, make a noise, Sw. *ralla*, chatter (*rallfågel*, a rail), Dan. *ralle*, rattle.] A bird of the subfamily *Rallinæ*, and especially of the genus *Rallus*; a water-rail, land-rail, marsh-hen, or crake. Rails are small marsh-loving wading birds, related to coots and gallinules. They abound in the marshes and swamps of most parts of the world, where they thread their way in the mazes of the reeds with great ease and celerity, the body being thin and compressed, and the legs stout and strong with long toes. They nest on the ground, and lay numerous spotted eggs; the young run about as soon as hatched. The common rail of Europe is *Rallus aquaticus*; the clapper-rail or salt-water marsh-hen of the United States is *R. crepitans*; the king-rail or fresh-water marsh-hen is *R. elegans*; the Virginia rail is *R. virginianus*, also called *red rail*, *little red-breasted rail*, *lesser clapper-rail*, *small mud-hen*, etc. Very generally, in the United States, the word *rail* used absolutely means the sora or soree, *Porzana carolina*, more fully called *rail bird*, *chicken-billed rail*, *English rail*, *Carolina rail*, *American rail*, *common rail*, *sora-rail*, *ortolan*, *Carolina crake*, *crake-gallinule*, etc. See *Crex*, *Porzana*, and cut under *Rallus*.—**Golden rail**, a snipe of the genus *Rhynchæa*; a painted-snipe or rail-snipe.—**Spotted rail**, the spotted crake, *Porzana maruetta*, also called *spotted skitty* and *spotted water-hen*.—**Weka rail.** See *Ocydromus*.

rail[5] (rāl), *v.* [Early mod. E. *rayle*; < OF. *roiller*, F. *railler*, jest, deride, mock, = Sp. *rallar*, grate, scrape, vex, molest, = Pg. *ralar*, scrape, rub, vex, < L. as if **radulare*, dim. or freq. of *radere*, scrape, scratch: see *rase*[1], *raze*[1]. Cf. L. *rallum* (contr. of **radlum*), a scraper, *radula*, a scraping-iron: see *radula*. Hence *rally*[2], *raillery*.] **I.** *intrans.* To speak bitterly, opprobriously, or reproachfully; use acrimonious expressions; scoff; inveigh.

Thou *rayled* on, right withouten reason,
And blamest hem much for small encheason.
Spenser, Shep. Cal., May.

Angels . . . bring not *railing* accusation against them. 2 Pet. ii. 11.

A certain Spaniard . . . *railed* . . . extremely at me. *Coryat*, Crudities, I. 126.

With God and Fate to *rail* at suffering easily.
M. Arnold, Empedocles on Etna.

=**Syn.** of *rail at*. To upbraid, scold or scold at or scold about, inveigh against, abuse, objurgate. *Railing* and scold*ing* are always undignified, if not improper; literally, *abusing* is improper; all three words may by hyperbole be used for talk which is proper.

II.† *trans.* To scoff at; taunt; scold; banter; affect by railing or raillery.

Till thou canst *rail* the seals from off my bond,
Thou but offend'st thy lungs to speak so loud.
Shak., M. of V., iv. 1. 139.

Such as are capable of goodness are *railed* into vice, that might as easily be admonished into virtue. *Sir T. Browne*, Religio Medici, ii. 4.

rail[6]† (rāl), *v. i.* [Early mod. E. *rayle*; < ME. *railen*, *reilen*, *roilen*, flow, prob. a var. of *roilen*, roll, wander: see *roil*[1].] To run; flow.

Whan the Geaunte felt hym wounded and saugh the blode *raile* down by the lifte iye, he was nygh wode oute of witte. *Merlin* (E. E. T. S.), ii. 342.

I saw a spring out of a rocke forth *rayle*,
As clear as Christall gainst the Sunnie beames.
Spenser, Visions of Bellay, l. 155.

rail-bender (rāl'ben″dėr), *n.* A screw-press or hydraulic press for straightening rails, or for bending them in the construction of railway-curves and -switches. The rail is supported upon two bearers, between which the pressure is applied. Also called *rail-bending machine*.

rail-bird (rāl'bėrd), *n.* The Carolina rail or sora, *Porzana carolina*. [U. S.]

rail-bittern (rāl'bit″ėrn), *n.* One of the small bitterns of the genus *Ardetta*, as *A. neoxena*, which in some respects resemble rails. *Coues*.

rail-board (rāl'bōrd), *n.* A board nailed to the rail of a vessel engaged in fishing for mackerel with hand-lines.

rail-borer (rāl'bōr″ėr), *n.* A hand-drill for making holes in the web of rails for the fish-plate bolts.

rail-brace (rāl'brās), *n.* A brace used to prevent the turning over of rails or the spreading of tracks at curves, switches, etc., on railways.

rail-chair (rāl'chãr), *n.* An iron block, used especially in Great Britain, by means of which railway-rails are secured to the sleepers. With the flat-bottomed rail common in the United States, chairs are not required, the rails being attached to the sleepers by spikes.

Double-headed Rail and Rail-chair, as used on the London and North-Western Railway, England.

a, upper head of rail; *a′*, lower head of rail; *b*, chair; *c*, sleeper; *c′*, wedge of wood; *d*, wood-screws; *e*, spikes.

rail-clamp (rāl'klamp), *n.* A wedge or tightening-key for clamping a rail firmly in a rail-chair, so as to prevent lateral play.

rail-coupling (rāl'kup″ling), *n.* A bar or rod connecting the opposite rails of a railway together at critical points, as curves or switches, where a firmer connection than is afforded by the sleepers is needed.

railer[1] (rā'lėr), *n.* [< *rail*[1] + *-er*[1].] One who makes or furnishes rails.

railer[2] (rā'lėr), *n.* [Early mod. E. *rayler*, < F. *railleur*, railer, jester, < *railler*, rail, jest, mock: see *rail*[5].] One who rails, scoffs, insults, censures, or reproaches with opprobrious language.

I am so far off from deserving you,
My beauty so unfit for your affection,
That I am grown the scorn of common *railers*.
Fletcher, Wildgoose Chase, iii. 1.

Junius is never more than a *railer*, and very often he is third-rate even as a *railer*. *John Morley*, Burke, p. 47.

rail-guard (rāl'gärd), *n.* **1.** In English locomotives, one of two stout rods, reaching down to about two inches from the track, before a front wheel. In America the cow-catcher or pilot serves the same purpose.—**2.** A guard-rail.

railing (rā'ling), *n.* [< ME. *raylynge*; verbal n. of *rail*[1], *v.*] **1.** Rails collectively; a combination of rails; a construction in which rails form an important part. Hence—**2.** Any openwork construction used as a barrier, parapet, or the like, primarily of wood, but also of iron bars, wire, etc.—**Post and railing.** See *post*[1].

railingly (rā'ling-li), *adv.* In a railing manner; with scoffing or opprobrious language.

railing-post (rā'ling-pōst), *n.* Same as *rail-post*.

railipotent (rā-lip'ǫ-tent), *a.* [Irreg. < *rail*[5] + *potent*, as in *omnipotent*.] Powerful in railing or vituperation, or as incentive to railing; extremely abusive. [Rare.]

The most preposterous principles have, in requital, shown themselves, as an old author phrases it, valiantly *railipotent*. *F. Hall*, Mod. Eng., Pref.

rail-key (rāl'kē), *n.* A wedge-piece used to clamp a rail to a chair by driving it in between the rail and the chair. Compare *rail-clamp*.

raillery (rāl'- or ral'ėr-i), *n.* [Early mod. E. *raillerie*, *ralliery*, *rallery*; < F. *raillerie*, jesting, mockery, < *railler*, jest: see *rail*[5] and *rally*[2].] **1.** Good-humored pleasantry or ridicule; satirical merriment; jesting language; banter.

Let *raillery* be without malice or heat. *B. Jonson*.

When you have been Abroad, Nephew, you'll understand *Rallery* better. *Congreve*, Way of the World, iii. 16.

That conversation where the spirit of *raillery* is suppressed will ever appear tedious and insipid.
Sheridan, School for Scandal, i. 1.

2†. A jest. [Rare.]

They take a pleasing *raillery* for a serious truth.
Gentleman Instructed, p. 13. (*Davies*.)

railleur (ra-lyėr'), *n.* [F. *railleur*, railer, jester, mocker: see *railer*[2].] One who turns what is serious into ridicule; a jester; a banterer; a mocker.

The family of the *railleurs* is derived from the same original with the philosophers. The founder of philosophy is confessed by all to be Socrates; and he was also the famous author of all irony.
Bp. Sprat, Hist. Royal Soc.

railly (rā'li), *n.*; pl. *raillies* (-liz). [Dim. of *rail*[3].] Same as *rail*[3]. [Scotch.]

rail-post (rāl'pōst), *n.* In *carp.*: (*a*) A baluster for a stair-rail, hand-rail, or a balustrade. (*b*) A newel. Also called *railing-post*.

rail-punch (rāl'punch), *n.* A machine for punching holes in the webs of rails, and for analogous uses.

railroad (rāl'rōd), *n.* [< *rail*[1] + *road*.] A road upon which are laid one or more lines of rails to guide and facilitate the movement of vehicles designed to transport passengers or freight, or both. [In this sense the words *railroad* and *railway* (which are of about equal age) are synonymous; but the former is more commonly (and preferably) used in the United States, the latter now universally in England. In both countries steam-railroads are called *roads*, seldom *ways*. For convenience, the subject of railroads, and the various compound words, are treated in this dictionary under *railway*.]

The London "Courier," in detailing the advantages of *rail-roads* upon the locomotive steam engine principle, contains a remark relative to Mr. Rush, our present minister in London . . . : "Whatever parliament may do, they cannot stop the course of knowledge and improvement! The American government has possessed itself, through its minister, of the improved mode of constructing and making *rail-roads*, and there can be no doubt of their immediate adoption throughout that country."
Niles's Register, April 2, 1825.

Alas! even the giddiness attendant on a journey on this Manchester *rail-road* is not so perilous to the nerves as that too frequent exercise in the merry-go-round of the ideal world.
Scott, Count Robert of Paris, Int., p. xi. (Oct. 15, 1831).

On Monday I shall set off for Liverpool by the *railroad*, which will then be opened the whole way.
Macaulay, in Trevelyan, II. 20.

Lady Buchan of Athlone writes thus in 1833: "I have a letter from Sir John, who strongly recommends my going by the *railroad*." *N. and Q.*, 7th ser., VIII. 379.

Commissioner of Railroads. See *commissioner*.—**Elevated railroad.** See *railway*.—**Railroad euchre.** See *euchre*.—**Underground railroad.** (*a*) See *underground railway*, under *railway*. (*b*) In the United States before the abolition of slavery, a secret arrangement for enabling slaves to escape into free territory, by passing them along from one point of concealment to another till they reached Canada or some other place of safety.

railroad (rāl'rōd), *v. t.* [< *railroad*, *n.*] To hasten or push forward with railroad speed; expedite rushingly; rush: as, to *railroad* a bill through a legislature. [Slang, U. S.]

A New York daily some time ago reported that a common thief . . . was *railroaded* through court in a few days. *Pop. Sci. Mo.*, XXXII. 758.

The Alien act, that was *railroaded* through at the close of the last session. *Sci. Amer.*, N. S., LVII. 37.

railroader (rāl'rō-dėr), *n.* A person engaged in the management or operation of a railroad or railroads; one employed in or about the running of railroad-trains or the general business of a railroad. [U. S.]

The Inter-State Commerce Commission is endeavoring to harmonize the interests of shippers and *railroaders*.
The Engineer, LXVI. 18.

railroading (rāl'rō-ding), *n.* [< *railroad* + *-ing*[1].] The management of or work upon a railroad or railroads; the business of constructing or operating railroads. [U. S.]

Wonders in the science of *railroading* that the tourist will go far to see.
Harper's Weekly, XXXIII., Supp., p. 60.

railroad-worm (rāl'rōd-wėrm), *n.* The apple-maggot (larva of *Trypeta pomonella*): so called because it has spread along the lines of the railroads. [New Eng.]

rail-saw (rāl'sâ), *n.* A portable machine for sawing off railway-rails in track-laying and -repairing. The most approved form clamps to the rail to be sawn, its frame carrying a reciprocating segmental saw working on a rock-shaft, which is operated by laterally extending detachable rock-levers. It has mechanism which slowly moves the saw toward the rail. A rail can be cut off by it in fifteen minutes.

rail-snipe (rāl'snīp), *n.* A bird of the genus *Rhynchæa* (or *Rostratula*), as *R. capensis*, the Cape rail-snipe, also called *painted Cape snipe* and *golden rail*.

rail-splitter (rāl'split"ėr), *n.* One who splits logs into rails for making a rail fence. Abraham Lincoln, President of the United States from 1861 to 1865, who in his youth had occasionally split rails, was sometimes popularly called *the rail-splitter*, and clubs of his partizans assumed the name *Rail-splitters*. [U. S.]

Yes: he had lived to shame me from my sneer,
To lame my pencil, and confute my pen;
To make me own this hind of princes peer,
This *rail-splitter* a true-born king of men.
Tom Taylor, Abraham Lincoln.

railway (rāl'wā), *n.* [< *rail*[1] + *way*.] 1. In *mech. engin.*, broadly, a way composed of one or more rails, or lines of rails, for the support, and commonly also for the direction of the motion, of a body carried on wheels adapted to roll on the rail or rails, or lines of rails. The wheels of railway-cars are now more usually flanged; but in railways forming parts of machines they are sometimes grooved, or they may run in grooves formed in the rails.
2. A way for the transportation of freight or passengers, or both, in which vehicles with flanged or grooved wheels are drawn or propelled on one or more lines of rails that support the wheels of the vehicles, and guide their course by the lateral pressure of the rails against the wheels; a railroad. (See *railroad*.) The parts of an ordinary passenger- and freight-railway proper are the road-bed, ballast, sleepers, rails, rail-chairs, splices, spikes, switches and switch mechanism, collectively called *permanent way*, and the signals; but in common and accepted usage the meaning of the terms *railway* and *railroad* has been extended to include not only the permanent way, but everything necessary to its operation, as the rolling-stock and buildings, including stations, warehouses, round-houses, locomotive-shops, car-shops, and repair-shops, and also all other property of the operating company, as stocks, bonds, and other securities. Most existing railways employ steam-locomotives; but systems of propulsion by endless wire ropes or cables, by electric locomotives, and by electromotors placed on individual cars to which electricity generated by dynamos at suitable stations is supplied from electrical conductors extending along the line, or from storage-batteries carried by the cars, have recently made notable progress. Horse-railways or tramways, in which the cars are drawn by horses or mules, are also extensively used for local passenger and freight traffic; but in many places such railways are now being supplanted by electric or cable systems.

Railway.—A new iron *railway* has been invented in Bavaria. On an exactly horizontal surface, on this improvement, a woman, or even a child, may, with apparent ease, draw a cart loaded with more than six quintals. . . . It is proved that those iron railings are two-thirds better than the English, and only cost half as much.
Niles's Register, Jan. 26, 1822.

Abandonment of railway. See *abandonment*.—**Aërial, Archimedean, atmospheric, centripetal, electric railway.** See the adjectives.—**Elevated railway,** or *elevated railroad*, in contradistinction to *surface railway*, an elevated structure, in form analogous to a bridge, used in New York and elsewhere for railway purposes, to avoid obstruction of surface roadways. The elevated structures are usually made of a good quality of steel and iron, and cars are moved on them either by steam-locomotives or by cable-traction, more commonly the former. Electricity has also been applied to the propulsion of cars on elevated railways.—**Inclined railway,** a railway having such a steep grade that special means other than ordinary locomotive driving-wheels are necessary for drawing or propelling cars on it. The use of locomotives with gripping-wheels engaging a rail extending midway between the ordinary rails, or having a pinion engaging the teeth of a rack-rail similarly placed, is a feature of many such railways. Cables operated by a stationary engine are also used.—**Marine railway.** See *marine*.—**Military railway,** a railway equipped for military service. Armored locomotives, and armor-plated cars having port-holes for rifles and some of them carrying swivel-guns, are prominent features of a military railway outfit.—**Pneumatic railway.** (*a*) A railway in which cars are propelled by air-pressure behind them. In one form of pneumatic railway the cars were pushed like pistons through a tunnel by pressure of air on the rear. The system failed of practical success from the difficulties met with in the attempt to carry it out on a large scale. Also called *atmospheric railway* (which see, under *atmospheric*). (*b*) A railway in which cars are drawn by pneumatic locomotives. Scarcely more success has been reached in this method than in that described above.—**Portable railway,** or *portable railroad*, a light railway-track made in detachable sections, or otherwise constructed so that it may be easily taken up, carried about, and transported to a distance, for use in military operations, in constructing roads, in building operations, in making excavations, etc. The rails are frequently of wood, or of wood plated with iron.—**Prismoidal railway,** a railway consisting of a single continuous beam or truss supported on posts or columns. The engine and cars run astride of the beam, the former being provided with grip-wheels to obtain the hold on the track requisite for draft.—**Railway brain,** a term applied to certain cases developed by railway accident, in which a traumatic neurosis is believed to be of cerebral origin.—**Railway Clauses Consolidation Act,** an English statute of 1845 (8 and 9 Vict., c. 20) consolidating the usual statutory provisions applicable to railway corporations, enabling them to take private property, and giving them special rights or special duties.—**Railway cut-off saw.** See *saw*[1].—**Railway post-office.** See *post-office*.—**Railway scrip.** See *scrip*.—**Railway spine,** an affection of the spine resulting from concussion produced by a railway accident. See under *spine*.

The *railway spine* has taken its place in medical nomenclature.
Sci. Amer., N. S., LX. 22.

Underground railway, a railway running through a continuous tunnel, as under the streets or other parts of a city; a subterranean railway.

railway-car (rāl'wā-kär), *n.* Any vehicle in general (the locomotive or other motor and its tender excepted) that runs on a railway, whether for the transportation of freight or of passengers.

railway-carriage (rāl'wā-kar"āj), *n.* A railway-car for passenger-traffic. [Eng.]

railway-chair (rāl'wā-chãr), *n.* Same as *rail-chair*.

railway-company (rāl'wā-kum"pa-ni), *n.* A stock company, usually organized under a charter granted by special legislative enactment, for the purpose of constructing and operating a railway, and invested with certain special powers, as well as subject to special restrictions, by the terms of its charter.

railway-crossing (rāl'wā-krôs"ing), *n.* 1. An intersection of railway-tracks.—2. The intersection of a common roadway or highway with the track of a railway.

railway-frog (rāl'wā-frog), *n.* See *frog*[2], 2.

railway-slide (rāl'wā-slīd), *n.* A turn-table. [Eng.]

railway-stitch (rāl'wā-stich), *n.* 1. In *crochet*, same as *tricot-stitch*.—2. In *embroidery*, a simple stitch usually employed in white embroidery, or with floss or filoselle.—3. In worsted-work or Berlin-wool work, a kind of stitch used on leviathan canvas, large and loose, and covering the surface quickly.

railway-switch (rāl'wā-swich), *n.* See *switch*.

railway-tie (rāl'wā-tī), *n.* See *tie*.

railway-train (rāl'wā-trān), *n.* See *train*.

raim (rām), *v. t.* Same as *ream*[2].

raiment (rā'ment), *n.* [Early mod. E. *rayment*; < ME. *raiment*, *rayment*, short for *arayment*, later *arraiment*, mod. *arrayment*: see *arrayment*. Cf. *ray*, by apheresis for *array*.] That in which one is arrayed or clad; clothing; vesture; formerly sometimes, in the plural, garments. [Now only poetical or archaic.]

On my knees I beg
That you'll vouchsafe me *raiment*, bed, and food.
Shak., Lear, ii. 4. 158.

Truth's Angel on horseback, his *raiment* of white silk powdered with stars of gold.
Middleton, Triumphs of Truth.

=**Syn.** Clothes, dress, attire, habiliments, garb, costume, array. These words are all in current use, while *raiment* and *vesture* have a poetic or antique sound.

raimondite (rā'mon-dīt), *n.* [Named after A. *Raimondi*, an Italian scientist who spent many years in exploring Peru.] A basic sulphate of iron, occurring in hexagonal tabular crystals of a yellow color.

rain[1] (rān), *n.* [Early mod. E. *rayne*, < ME. *rein*, *reyn*, *reyne*, *reane*, *regn*, *rien*, *ren*, *ran*, < AS. *regn* (often contr. *rēn*) = OS. *regan*, *regin* = OFries. *rein* = D. *regen* = MLG. *regen* = OHG. *regan*, MHG. *regen*, G. *regen* = Icel. Sw. Dan. *regn* = Goth. *rign*, rain; cf. L. *rigare*, moisten (see *irrigation*), Gr. βρέχειν, wet (see *embrocation*).] 1. The descent of water in drops through the atmosphere, or the water thus falling. In general, clouds constitute the reservoir from which rain descends, but the fall of rain in very small quantities from a cloudless sky is occasionally observed. The aqueous vapor of the atmosphere, which condenses into cloud, and falls as rain, is derived from the evaporation of water, partly from land, but chiefly from the vast expanse of the ocean. At a given temperature, only a certain amount of aqueous vapor can be contained in a given volume, and when this amount is present the air is said to be saturated. If the air is then cooled below this temperature, a part of the vapor will be condensed into small drops, which, when suspended in the atmosphere, constitute clouds. Under continued cooling and condensation, the number and size of the drops increase until they begin to descend by their own weight. The largest of these, falling fastest, unite with smaller ones that they overtake, and thus drops of rain are formed whose size depends on the thickness and density of the cloud and on the distribution of electrical stress therein. Sometimes the rate of condensation is so great that the water appears to fall in sheets rather than in drops, and then the storm is popularly called *a cloud-burst*. It is now generally held that dynamic cooling (that is, the cooling of air by expansion, when raised in altitude, and thereby brought under diminished pressure), if not the sole cause of rain, is the only cause of any importance, and that other causes popularly appealed to—such as the intermingling of warm and cold air, contact with cold mountain-slopes, etc.—are either inoperative or relatively insignificant. The requisite ascent of air may be occasioned either by convection currents, a cyclonic circulation, or the upward deflection of horizontal currents by hills or mountains; and rain may be classified as *convective*, *cyclonic*, or *orographic*, according as the first, second, or third of these methods is brought into operation to produce it. The productiveness of the soil and the maintenance of life in most parts of the earth depend largely upon an adequate fall of rain. In some regions it is more or less evenly distributed throughout the year, in others it is confined to a part of the year (the rainy season), and in others still it is entirely absent, or too slight for need, according to variation of local atmospheric conditions. In a ship's log-book abbreviated r.

A muchel wind alith mid a lutel *rein*.
Ancren Riwle, p. 246.

Also a man that was born in thys yle told vs that they had no *Rayne* by the space of x months; they sow ther whete with owt *Rayne*.
Torkington, Diarie of Eng. Travell, p. 61.

2. Figuratively—(*a*) A fall of any substance through the atmosphere in the manner of rain, as of blossoms or of the pyrotechnic stars from rockets and other fireworks. *Blood-rain* is a fall of fragments of red algæ or the like, raised in large quantities by the wind and afterward precipitated. *Sulphur-rain* or *yellow rain* is a similar precipitation of the pollen of fir-trees, etc. (*b*) A shower, downpour, or abundant outpouring of anything.

Whilst Wealth it self doth roll
In to her bosom in a golden *Rain*.
J. Beaumont, Psyche, i. 38.

The former and the latter rain, in Palestine, the rains of autumn and of spring; hence, rain in its due season.—**The Rains**†, a tract of the Atlantic ocean formerly so called. See the quotation.

Crossing toward the west, from Africa, it is now known that between about five and fifteen north latitude is a space of ocean, nearly triangular, the other limit being about twenty (long.) and ten (lat.), which used to be called by the earlier navigators *the Rains*, on account of the calms and almost incessant rain always found there.
Fitz Roy, Weather Book, p. 115.

=**Syn. 1.** *Rain, Haze, Fog, Mist, Cloud.* A *cloud* resting upon the earth is called *mist* or *fog*. In *mist* the globules are very fine, but are separately distinguishable, and have a visible motion. In *fog* the particles are separately indistinguishable, and there is no perceptible motion. A *dry fog* is composed largely of dust-particles on which the condensed vapor is too slight to occasion any sense of moisture. *Haze* differs from *fog* and *cloud* in the greater microscopic minuteness of its particles. It is visible only as a want of transparency of the atmosphere, and in general exhibits neither form, boundary, nor locus. Thus, among *haze*, *fog*, *mist*, and *rain*, the size of the constituent particles or globules is a discriminating characteristic, though frequently cloud merges into fog or mist, and mist into rain, by insensible gradations.

rain[1] (rān), *v.* [< ME. *raynen*, *reinen*, *reynen*, *regnen*, *rinen*, *rynen* (pret. *rainde*, *reinede*, *rinde*; sometimes strong, *ron*, *roon*), < AS. *rignan*, rarely *regnan*, usually contracted *rīnan*, *rȳnan* (pret. *rīnde*; rarely strong, *rān*), = D. *regenen* = MLG. *regenen* = OHG. *reganōn*, *regonōn*, MHG. *regenen*, G. *regnen* = Icel. *regna*, *rigna* = Sw. *regna* = Dan. *regne* = Goth. *rignjan*, rain; from the noun: see *rain*[1], *n.*] **I.** *intrans.* 1. To fall in drops through the air, as water: generally used impersonally.

There *it reyneth* not but litylle in that Contree; and for that Cause they have no Watre, but zif it be of that Flood of that Ryvere.
Mandeville, Travels, p. 45.

Evermore so sternliche *it ron*,
And blew therwith so wonderliche loude,
That wel neighe no man heren other koude.
Chaucer, Troilus, iii. 677.

And in Elyes tyme heuene was yclosed,
That no reyne ne *rone*.
Piers Plowman (B), xiv. 66.

The rain *it raineth* every day. *Shak.*, T. N., v. 1. 401.

2. To fall or drop like rain: as, tears *rained* from their eyes.

The Spaniards presented a fatal mark to the Moorish missiles, which *rained* on them with pitiless fury.
Prescott, Ferd. and Isa., ii. 7.

Down *rained* the blows upon the unyielding oak.
William Morris, Earthly Paradise, III. 252.

II. *trans.* To pour or shower down, like rain from the clouds; pour or send down abundantly.

Behold, I will *rain* bread from heaven for you. Ex. xvi. 4.

Does he *rain* gold, and precious promises, Into thy lap? *Fletcher*, Wife for a Month, i. 1.

Why, it *rains* princes: though some people are disappointed of the arrival of the Pretender. *Walpole*, Letters, II. 24.

To rain cats and dogs. See *cat*.

rain[2] (rān), *n.* [Origin obscure.] 1. A ridge. *Halliwell*.—2. A furrow. [Prov. Eng. in both senses.]

They reaped the corne that grew in the *raine* to serve that turne, as the corne in the ridge was not readie. *Wynne*, History of the Gwedir Family, p. 87. (*Encyc. Dict.*)

rain[3]†, *n.* An obsolete spelling of *rein*[1].

rainball (rān'bâl), *n.* One of the festoons of the mammato-cumulus, or pocky cloud: so called because considered to be a sign of rain. [Prov. Eng.]

rainband (rān'band), *n.* A dark band in the solar spectrum, situated on the red side of the D line, and caused by the absorption of that part of the spectrum by the aqueous vapor of the atmosphere. The intensity of the rainband varies with the amount of vapor in the air, and is thus of some importance as an indication of rain. Direct-vision spectroscopes of moderate dispersion are best adapted for observing it. Pocket instruments of this kind, designed for the purpose, are called *rainband-spectroscopes*.

At every hour, when there is sufficient light, the intensity of the *rainband* is observed and recorded. *Nature*, XXXV. 589.

rain-bird (rān'bėrd), *n.* [< ME. *reyne-bryde*; < *rain*[1] + *bird*[1].] A bird supposed to foretell rain by its cries or actions, as the rain-crow. Many birds become noisy or uneasy before rain, the popular belief having thus considerable foundation in fact. (*a*) The green woodpecker, *Gecinus viridis*. Also *rain-fowl*, *rain-pie*. [Eng.] (*b*) The large ground-cuckoo of Jamaica, *Saurothera vetula*; also, a related cuckoo, *Piaya pluvialis*.

rainbow (rān'bō), *n.* [< ME. *reinbowe*, *reinboge*, *renboge*, < AS. *regn-boga*, *rēnboga* (= OFries. *reinboga* = D. *regenboog* = MLG. *regenboge*, *regensboge* (cf. LG. *water-boog*) = OHG. *reganbogo*, MHG. *regenboge*, G. *regenbogen* = Icel. *regnbogi* = Sw. *regnbåge* = Dan. *regnbue*), < *regn*, rain, + *boga*, bow: see *rain*[1] and *bow*[3], *n.*] 1. A bow, or an arc of a circle, consisting of the prismatic colors, formed by the refraction and reflection of rays of light from drops of rain or vapor, appearing in the part of the heavens opposite to the sun. When large and strongly illuminated, the rainbow presents the appearance of two concentric arches, the inner being called the *primary* and the outer the *secondary* rainbow. Each is formed of the colors of the solar spectrum, but the colors are arranged in reversed order, the red forming the exterior ring of the primary bow and the interior of the secondary. The primary bow is formed by rays of the sun that enter the upper part of falling drops of rain, and undergo two refractions and one reflection; the secondary, by rays that enter the under part of rain-drops, and undergo two refractions and two reflections. Hence, the colors of the secondary bow are fainter than those of the primary. The rainbow is regarded as a symbol of divine beneficence toward man, from its being made the token of the covenant that the earth should never again be destroyed by a flood (Gen. ix. 13–17). Smaller bows, sometimes circular and very brilliant, are often seen through masses of mist or spray, as from a waterfall or from waves about a ship. (See *fog-bow*.) The moon sometimes forms a bow or arch of light, more faint than that formed by the sun, and called a *lunar rainbow*.

Thanne ic ofe[r]-téo hefenes mid wicne. thanne bith atéwed min *rén boge*. betwuxe than folce [vel wicne]. thanne beo ic gemenéged mines weddes. that ic nelle henon forth mancyn. mid watere adrenche. *Old Eng. Homilies* (ed. Morris), 1st ser., xxiv. 225. (*Rich.*)

Tannede [showed] him in the wa[l]kene a-buuen *Rein-bowe*. *Genesis and Exodus*, l. 637.

When in Heav'n I see the *Rain-bowe* bent, I hold it for a Pledge and Argument. *Sylvester*, tr. of Du Bartas's Weeks, i. 2.

Intersecting *rainbows* are not uncommon. They require, of course, for their production, two sources of parallel rays; and they are seen when, behind the spectator, there is a large sheet of calm water. *Tait*, Light, § 165.

2. In *her.*, the representation of a half-ring divided into seven concentric narrow rings and arched upward, each end resting on a clump of clouds. To avoid the difficulty of finding seven different tinctures, the number of concentric rings is sometimes diminished to three, usually *azure*, *or*, and *gules*—that is, blue, gold, and red.

3. In *ornith.*, a humming-bird of the genus *Diphlogena*, containing two most brilliantly plumaged species, *D. iris* of Bolivia, and *D. hesperus* of Ecuador.—4. The rainbow-fish.—**Rainbow style**, a method of calico-printing in which the colors are blended with one another at the edges.—**Spurious** or **supernumerary rainbow**, a bow always seen in connection with a fine rainbow, lying close inside the violet of the primary bow, or outside that of the secondary one. Its colors are fainter and less pure, as they proceed from the principal bow, and finally merge in the diffused white light of the primary bow, and outside the secondary.

rainbow-agate (rān'bō-ag"āt), *n.* An iridescent variety of agate.

rainbow-darter (rān'bō-där"tėr), *n.* The soldier-fish or blue darter, *Pœcilichthys cæruleus*, of gorgeous and varied colors, about 2½ inches long, found in the waters of the Mississippi basin; as a book-name, any species of this genus.

rainbowed (rān'bōd), *a.* [< *rainbow* + *-ed*[2].] 1. Formed by or like a rainbow.—2. Encircled with a rainbow or halo. *Davies.*

See him stand Before the altar, like a *rainbowed* saint. *Kingsley*, Saint's Tragedy, i. 3.

rainbow-fish (rān'bō-fish), *n.* One of several different fishes of bright or varied coloration. (*a*) The blue darter, *Pœcilichthys cæruleus*. [U. S.] (*b*) A sparoid fish, *Scarus* or *Pseudoscarus quadrispinosus*. [Bermuda.]

rainbow-hued, rainbow-tinted (rān'bō-hūd, -tin"ted), *a.* Having hues or tints like those of a rainbow.

rainbow-quartz (rān'bō-kwârts), *n.* An iridescent variety of quartz.

rainbow-trout (rān'bō-trout), *n.* A variety or subspecies of the Californian *Salmo gairdneri*, specifically called *S. irideus*. It is closely related to the brook-trout of Europe, but not to that of the United States. It has been quite widely distributed by pisciculturists. In the breeding season its colors are resplendent, giving rise to the popular name.

Rainbow-trout (*Salmo irideus*).

rainbow-worm (rān'bō-wėrm), *n.* A species of tetter, the *herpes iris* of Bateman.

rainbow-wrasse (rān'bō-ras), *n.* A labroid fish, *Coris julis*, the only British species of that genus: so called from its bright and varied colors.

rain-box (rān'boks), *n.* A device in a theater for producing an imitation of the sound of falling rain.

rain-chamber (rān'chām"bėr), *n.* An attachment to a furnace, hearth, or smelting-works in which the fumes of any metal, as lead, are partly or entirely condensed by the aid of water.

rain-chart (rān'chärt), *n.* A chart or map giving information in regard to the fall and distribution of rain in any part or all parts of the world. Also called *rain-map*.

rain-cloud (rān'kloud), *n.* Any cloud from which rain falls: in meteorology called *nimbus*. Two general classes may be distinguished—(*a*) cumulo-nimbus, where rain falls from cumulus clouds, generally in squalls or showers, and (*b*) strato-nimbus, where rain falls from stratus clouds. The name is sometimes especially given, in a more restricted sense, to the ragged, detached masses of cumulus (called by Poey *fracto-cumulus*), or to the low, torn fragments of cloud called *scud*, which are characteristic associates of rain-storms. See cut under *cloud*.

rain-crow (rān'krō), *n.* A tree-cuckoo of the genus *Coccygus*, either *C. americanus* or *C. erythrophthalmus*: so named from its cries, often heard in lowering weather, and supposed to predict rain. [Local, U. S.]

raindeer†, *n.* See *reindeer*.

rain-doctor (rān'dok"tor), *n.* Same as *rain-maker*.

rain-door (rān'dōr), *n.* In Japanese houses, one of the external sliding doors or panels in a veranda which are closed in stormy weather and at night.

raindrop (rān'drop), *n.* [< ME. *raindrope* (also *reines drope*), < AS. *regndropa* (= D. dim. *regendroppel*, *regendruppel* = OHG. *regentropho*, MHG. G. *regentropfen* = Sw. *regndroppe* = Dan. *regndraabe*, raindrop), < *regn*, rain, + *dropa*, drop: see *rain*[1] and *drop*, *n.*] A drop of rain.—**Raindrop glaze**, in *ceram.*, a glaze with very slight drop-like bosses, used for porcelain.

raine†, *n.* An obsolete spelling of *reign*.

raines[1]†, *n. pl.* An obsolete spelling of *reins*.

raines[2]†, *n.* [Also *raynes*, *reins*; < *Rennes* (see def.).] A kind of linen or lawn, manufactured at Rennes in France.

She should be apparelled beautifully with pure white silk, or with most fine *raines*. *Bale*, Select Works, p. 542. (*Davies.*)

rainfall (rān'fâl), *n.* 1. A falling of rain; a shower.—2. The precipitation of water from clouds; the water, or the amount of water, coming down as rain. The rainfall is measured by means of the pluviometer or rain-gage. The average rainfall of a district includes the snow, if any, reduced to its equivalent in water.—**Rainfall chart**, an isohyetal chart. See *isohyetal*.

rain-fowl (rān'foul), *n.* [< ME. *reyn fowle*; < *rain*[1] + *fowl*[1].] 1. Same as *rain-bird* (*a*). [Eng.]—2. The Australian *Scythrops novæ-hollandiæ*.

rain-gage (rān'gāj), *n.* An instrument for collecting and measuring the amount of rainfall at a given place. Many forms have been used; their size has been a few square inches or square feet in area, and their material has been sheet-metal, porcelain, wood, or glass. The form adopted by the United States Signal Service consists of three parts—(*a*) a funnel-shaped receiver, having a turned brass rim 8 inches in diameter; (*b*) a collecting tube, made of seamless brass tubing of 2.53 inches inside diameter, making its area one tenth that of the receiving surface; and (*c*) a galvanized iron overflow-cylinder, which in time of snow is used alone as a snow-gage. A cedar measuring-stick is used to measure the depth of water collected in the gage. By reason of the ratio between the area of the collecting tube and that of the receiving surface, the depth of rain is one tenth that measured on the stick. See cut under *pluviometer*.

rain-goose (rān'gös), *n.* The red-throated diver or loon, *Urinator* or *Colymbus septentrionalis*, supposed to foretell rain by its cry. [Local, British.]

rain-hound† (rān'hound), *n.* A variety of the hound. See the quotation.

Mastiffs are often mentioned in the proceedings at the Forest Courts [in England], in company with other breeds which it is not easy now to identify, such as the *rain-hound*, which keeps watch by itself in rainy weather. *The Academy*, Feb. 4, 1888, p. 71.

raininess (rā'ni-nes), *n.* [< *rainy* + *-ness*.] The state of being rainy.

rainless (rān'les), *a.* [< *rain*[1] + *-less*.] Without rain: as, a *rainless* region; a *rainless* zone.

rain-maker (rān'mā"kėr), *n.* Among superstitious races, as those of Africa, a sorcerer who pretends to have the power of producing a fall of rain by incantation or supernatural means. Also called *rain-doctor*.

The African chief, with his *rain-makers* and magicians. *The Century*, XL. 303.

rain-map (rān'map), *n.* Same as *rain-chart*.

rainment† (rān'ment), *n.* An aphetic form of *arraignment*.

rain-paddock (rān'pad"ok), *n.* The batrachian *Breviceps gibbosus*, of South Africa, which lives in holes in the ground and comes out in wet weather.

rain-pie (rān'pī), *n.* Same as *rain-bird* (*a*). [Eng.]

rainpour (rān'pōr), *n.* A downpour of rain; a heavy rainfall. [Colloq.]

The red light of flitting lanterns blotched the steady *rainpour*. *Harper's Mag.*, LXXVI. 572.

rain-print (rān'print), *n.* In *geol.*, the print of raindrops in some aqueous rocks, formed when they were in a soft state, such as may be seen on a muddy or sandy sea-beach after a heavy shower. It is possible for the geologist to tell by inspection of the prints from what direction the wind was blowing at the time of their formation.

rain-proof (rān'pröf), *n.* Proof against rain; not admitting the entrance of rain or penetration by it; rain-tight; water-proof in a shower.

Their old temples, . . . which for long have not been *rain-proof*, crumble down. *Carlyle*, Sartor Resartus, ii. 7.

rain-quail (rān'kwāl), *n.* The quail *Coturnix coromandelicus*, of Africa and India, whose migrations are related in some way to rainy seasons.

rain-storm (rān'stôrm), *n.* A storm of rain; a rain.

The fells sweep skyward with a fine breadth, freshened by strong breezes; clouds and sunshine, ragged *rainstorms*, thunder and lightning, chase across them forever. *The Atlantic*, LXV. 824.

rain-tight (rān'tīt), *a.* So tight as to exclude rain.

rain-tree (rān'trē), *n.* The genisaro or guango, *Pithecolobium Saman*. It is said to be so called because occasionally in South America, through the agency of cicadas which suck its juices, it sheds moisture to such an extent as to wet the ground. Another explanation is that its foliage shuts up at night, so that the rain and dew are not retained by it. See *genisaro*.

rain-wash (rān'wosh), *n.* See *wash*.

rain-water (rān'wâ"tėr), *n.* [< ME. *reyne water*, *reinwater*, < AS. **regnwæter*, *rēnwæter* (= OHG. *reganwazar*), < *regn*, *rēn*, rain, + *wæter*, water: see *rain*[1] and *water*.] Water that has fallen from the clouds in rain, and has not sunk into the earth.

No one has a right to build his house so as to cause the *rain water* to fall over his neighbour's land, . . . unless he has acquired a right by a grant or prescription. *Bouvier*, Law Dict., II. 419.

rainy (rā'ni), *a.* [< late ME. *rayne*, < AS. **regnig*, *rēnig*, rainy, < *regn*, *rēn*, rain: see *rain*[1].] Abounding with or giving out rain; dropping with or as if with rain; showery: as, *rainy* weather; a *rainy* day or season; a *rainy* sky.

A continual dropping in a very *rainy* day. Prov. xxvii. 15.

Both mine eyes were *rainy* like to his. *Shak.*, Tit. And., v. 1. 117.

A rainy day, figuratively, a time of greater need or of clouded fortunes; a possible time of want or misfortune in the future: as, to lay by something for *a rainy day*.

The man whose honest industry just gives him a competence exerts himself that he may have something against *a rainy day*. *Everett*, Orations, I. 285.

raioid (rā'oid), *a.* and *n.* [< L. *raia*, ray, + Gr. εἶδος, form.] **I.** *a.* Resembling or related to the ray or skate.

II. *n.* A selachian of the family *Raiidæ* or suborder *Raiæ*.

Raioidea (rā-oi'dē-ä), *n. pl.* [NL.: see *raioid*.] A superfamily of rays represented by the family *Raiidæ*.

raip (rāp), *n.* A dialectal form of *rope*.

rair (rãr), *v.* and *n.* A dialectal form of *roar*.

rais (rā'is), *n.* Same as *reis*[1].

raisable (rā'za-bl), *a.* [< *rais(e)*[1] + *-able*.] Capable of being raised or produced; that may be lifted up. [Rare.]

They take their sip of coffee at our expense, and celebrate us in song; a chorus is *raisable* at the shortest possible notice, and a chorus is not easily cut off in the middle. *C. W. Stoddard*, Mashallah, xviii.

raise[1] (rāz), *v.*; pret. and pp. *raised*, ppr. *raising*. [Early mod. E. also *rayse*; < ME. *raisen*, *raysen*, *reisen*, *reysen*, < Icel. *reisa* (= Sw. *resa* = Dan. *reise* = Goth. *raisjan* = AS. *rǣran*, E. *rear*[1]), raise, cause to rise, causal of *rísa*, rise, = AS. *rīsan*, E. *rise*: see *rise*[1]. Cf. *rear*[1], the native (AS.) form of *raise*.] **I.** *trans.* **1.** To lift or bring up bodily in space; move to a higher place; carry or cause to be carried upward or aloft; hoist: as, to *raise* one's hand or head; to *raise* ore from a mine; to *raise* a flag to the masthead.

When the morning sun shall *raise* his car
Above the border of this horizon,
We'll forward towards Warwick.
Shak., 3 Hen. VI., iv. 7. 80.

The oxen *raise* the water by a bucket and rope, without a wheel, and so by driving them from the well the bucket is drawn up. *Pococke*, Description of the East, II. i. 61.

The high octagon summer house you see yonder is *raised* on the mast of a ship, given me by an East-India captain. *Colman and Garrick*, Clandestine Marriage, ii.

2. To make upright or erect; cause to stand by lifting; elevate on a base or support; stand or set up: as, to *raise* a mast or pole; to *raise* the frame of a building; to *raise* a fallen man.

He wept tendirly, and *reised* the kynge be the hande. *Merlin* (E. E. T. S.), ii. 354.

The elders of his house arose and went to him, to *raise* him up from the earth. 2 Sam. xii. 17.

3. To elevate in position or upward reach; increase the height of; build up, fill, or embank; make higher: as, to *raise* a building by adding a garret or loft; to *raise* the bed of a road; the flood *raised* the river above its banks. —**4.** To make higher or more elevated in state, condition, estimation, amount, or degree; cause to rise in grade, rank, or value; heighten, exalt, advance, enhance, increase, or intensify: as, to *raise* a man to higher office; to *raise* one's reputation; to *raise* the temperature; to *raise* prices; to *raise* the tariff.

Merrick said only this: The Earl of Essex *raised* me, and he hath overturned me. *Baker*, Chronicles, p. 392.

Those who have carnal Minds may have some *raised* and spiritual Thoughts, but they are too cold and speculative. *Stillingfleet*, Sermons, III. viii.

I was both weary and hungry, and I think my appetite was *raised* by seeing so much food. *Dampier*, Voyages, II. i. 93.

The duty [on salt] was *raised* by North, in the war of American Independence, to 5s. the bushel. *S. Dowell*, Taxes in England, IV. 4.

Steam-greens after printing are frequently brightened, or *raised* as it is technically called, by passing through a weak bath of bichrome. *W. Crookes*, Dyeing and Calico-printing, p. 607.

5. To estimate as of importance; cry up; hence, to applaud; extol.

Like Cato, give his little Senate laws,
And sit attentive to his own applause;
While wits and templars every sentence *raise*,
And wonder with a foolish face of praise.
Pope, Epistle to Dr. Arbuthnot, l. 211.

6. To form as a piled-up mass, or by upward accretion; erect above a base or foundation; build or heap up: as, to *raise* a cathedral, a monument, or a mound; an island in the sea *raised* by volcanic action.

I will *raise* forts against thee. Isa. xxix. 3.

All these great structures were doubtless *raised* under the bishops of Damascus, when Christianity was the established religion here. *Pococke*, Description of the East, II. i. 121.

7. To lift off or away; remove by or as if by lifting; take off, as something put on or imposed: as, to *raise* a blockade.

Once already have you prisoned me,
To my great charge, almost my overthrow,
And somewhat *raisde* the debt by that advantage.
Heywood, Fair Maid of the Exchange (Works, ed. Pearson, [1874, II. 28).

The Sorbonne *raised* the prohibition it had so long laid upon the works of the Grecian philosopher [Aristotle]. *Mind*, XII. 257.

8. To cause to rise in sound; lift up the voice in; especially, to utter in high or loud tones.

When I *raised* the psalm, how did my voice quaver for fear! *Swift*, Mem. of P. P.

In sounds now lowly, and now strong,
To *raise* the desultory song.
Scott, Marmion, Int., iii.

They both, as with one accord, *raised* a dismal cry. *Dickens*, Haunted Man.

9. To cause to rise in air or water; cause to move in an upward direction: as, to *raise* a kite; to *raise* a wreck.

The dust
Should have ascended to the roof of heaven,
Raised by your populous troops.
Shak., A. and C., iii. 6. 50.

10. To cause to rise from an inert or lifeless condition; specifically, to cause to rise from death or the grave; reanimate: as, to *raise* the dead.

Also in ye myddes of that chapell is a rounde marble stone, where the very hooly crosse was prouyd by *reysinge* of a deed woman, whanne they were in doubte whiche it was of the thre. *Sir R. Guylforde*, Pylgrymage, p. 25.

We have testified of God that he *raised* up Christ: whom he *raised* not up, if so be that the dead rise not. 1 Cor. xv. 15.

Thou must restore him flesh again and life,
And *raise* his dry bones to revenge this scandal.
Beau. and Fl., Maid's Tragedy, iv. 1.

11. To cause to rise above the visible horizon, or to the level of observation; bring into view; sight, as by approach: chiefly a nautical use: as, to *raise* the land by sailing toward it.

When first seeing a whale from the mast-head or other place, it is termed *raising* a whale. *C. M. Scammon*, Marine Mammals (Glossary), p. 311.

In October, 1832, the ship Hector of New Bedford *raised* a whale and lowered for it. *The Century*, XL. 562.

12. To cause to rise by expansion or swelling; expand the mass of; puff up; inflate: as, to *raise* bread with yeast.

I learned to make wax work, japan, paint upon glass, to *raise* paste, make sweetmeats, sauces, and everything that was genteel and fashionable. Quoted in *J. Ashton*, Social Life in Reign of Queen Anne, [I. 23.

The action of the saltpetre on the hides or skins, it is claimed, is to plump or *raise* them, as it is called. *C. T. Davis*, Leather, p. 240.

13. To cause to rise into being or manifestation; cause to be or to appear; call forth; evoke: as, to *raise* a riot; to *raise* a ghost.

I will *raise* up thy seed after thee, which shall be of thy sons. 1 Chron. xvii. 11.

He commandeth and *raiseth* the stormy wind. Ps. cvii. 25.

I'll learn to conjure and *raise* devils. *Shak.*, T. and C., ii. 3. 6.

Come, come, leave conjuring;
The spirit you would *raise* is here already.
Beau. and Fl., Custom of the Country, iii. 2.

14. To promote with care the growth and development of; bring up; rear; grow; breed: as, to *raise* a family of children (a colloquial use); to *raise* crops, plants, or cattle.

A bloody tyrant and a homicide;
One *raised* in blood. *Shak.*, Rich. III., v. 3. 247.

Most can *raise* the flowers now,
For all have got the seed.
Tennyson, The Flower.

"Where is Tina?" . . .
"Asphyxia 's took her to *raise*."
"To what?" said the boy, timidly.
"Why, to fetch her up—teach her to work," said the little old woman. *H. B. Stowe*, Oldtown, p. 112.

15. To cause a rising of, as into movement or activity; incite to agitation or commotion; rouse; stir up: as, the wind *raised* the sea; to *raise* the populace in insurrection; to *raise* a covey of partridges.

We are betray'd. Fly to the town, cry "Treason!"
And *raise* our faithful friends!
Fletcher, Double Marriage, v. 1.

Raise up the city; we shall be murder'd all!
Ford, 'Tis Pity, v. 6.

He sow'd a slander in the common ear, . . .
Raised my own town against me in the night.
Tennyson, Geraint.

16. To cause to arise or come forth as a mass or multitude; draw or bring together; gather; collect; muster: as, to *raise* a company or an army; to *raise* an expedition.

The Lord Mayor Walworth had gone into the City, and *raised* a Thousand armed Men. *Baker*, Chronicles, p. 139.

He had by his . . . needless *raising* of two Armies, intended for a civil Warr, begger'd both himself and the Public. *Milton*, Eikonoklastes, v.

Send off to the Baron of Meigallot; he can *raise* threescore horse and better. *Scott*, Monastery, xxxiv.

17. To take up by aggregation or collection; procure an amount or a supply of; bring together for use or possession: as, to *raise* funds for an enterprise; to *raise* money on a note; to *raise* revenue.

At lenght they came to *raise* a competente & comforteable living, but with hard and continuall labor. *Bradford*, Plymouth Plantation, p. 17.

He was commissioned to *raise* money for the Hussite crusade. *Stubbs*, Const. Hist., § 334.

These young men find that they have to *raise* money by mortgaging their land, and are often obliged to part with the land because they cannot meet the interest on the mortgages. *W. F. Rae*, Newfoundland to Manitoba, vi.

18. To give rise to, or cause or occasion for; bring into force or operation; originate; start: as, to *raise* a laugh; to *raise* an expectation or a hope; to *raise* an outcry.

The plot I had, to *raise* in him doubts of her,
Thou hast effected.
Beau. and Fl., Knight of Malta, iii. 2.

This will certainly give me Occasion to *raise* Difficulties. *Steele*, Conscious Lovers, ii. 1.

There, where she once had dwelt 'mid hate and praise,
No smile, no shudder now her name could *raise*.
William Morris, Earthly Paradise, III. 161.

19. To hold up to view or observation; bring forward for consideration or discussion; exhibit; set forth: as, to *raise* a question or a point of order.

Moses' third excuse, *raised* out of a natural defect. *Donne*, Sermons, v.

They excepted against him for these 2. doctrins *raised* from 2 Sam. xii. 7. *Bradford*, Plymouth Plantation, p. 177.

What a beautiful Description has our Author *raised* upon that Hint in one of the Prophets! *Addison*, Spectator, No. 339.

20. To rouse; excite; inflame. [Scotch.]

The herds that came set a' things here asteer,
And she ran aff as *rais'd* as ony deer.
Ross, Helenore, p. 45. (*Jamieson.*)

Nahum was *raised*, and could give no satisfaction in his answers. *Galt*, Ringan Gilhaize, II. 138. (*Jamieson.*)

He should been tight that daur' to *raise* thee
Ance in a day.
Burns, Auld Farmer's Salutation to his Auld Mare.

21. To incite in thought; cause to come or proceed; bring, lead, or drive, as to a conclusion, a point of view, or an extremity.

I cannot but be *raised* to this persuasion, that this third period of time will far surpass that of the Græcian and Roman learning. *Bacon*, Advancement of Learning, ii. 358.

22. In the arts, to shape in relief, as metal which is hammered, punched, or spun from a thin plate in raised forms. See *spin*, *repoussé*. —**Raised bands, battery, beach.** See *band*[1], etc.—**Raised canvas-work.** See *canvas-work*, 2.—**Raised couching.** See *couching*[1], 5.—**Raised crewel-work**, ornamental needlework done with crewel-wool in raised loops.—**Raised embroidery.** (*a*) Embroidery in which the pattern is raised in relief from the ground, usually by applying the main parts of the pattern to the ground in locks of cotton or wool or pieces of stuff, and covering these with the embroidery-silk. (*b*) Embroidery by means of which a nap or pile like that of velvet is produced, the pattern being worked in looped stitches and thus raised in relief from the background.—**Raised loop-stitch**, a stitch in crochet-work by which a soft surface of projecting loops of worsted is produced.—**Raised mosaic.** (*a*) Mosaic in which the inlaid figures are left in relief above the background, instead of being polished down to a uniform surface, as in some examples of Florentine mosaic. (*b*) Mosaic of small tesseræ, in which the principal surface is modeled in relief, as in stucco or plaster, the tesseræ being afterward applied to this surface and following its curves: a variety of the art practised under the Roman empire, but not common since.—**Raised panel.** See *panel*.—**Raised patchwork**, patchwork in which some or all of the pieces are stuffed with wadding, so that they present a rounded surface.—**Raised plan** of a house. Same as *elevation*, 6.—**Raised point**, in *lace-making*, a point or stitch by means of which a part of the pattern is raised in relief. Compare *rose-point*, and *Venice point*, under *point*[1].—**Raised roof.** See *roof*.—**Raised stitch**, in worsted-work or Berlin work, a stitch by means of which a surface like velvet is produced, the wool being first raised in loops, which are then cut or shaved and combed until the pile is soft and uniform.—**Raised velvet.** See *velvet*.—**Raised work**, in *lace-making*, work done in the point or stitch used in some kinds of bobbin-lace, by means of which the edge or some other part of the pattern is raised in relief, as in Honiton lace.—**To have one's dander raised.** See *dander*[2].—**To raise a bead**, to cause a bead or mass of bubbles to rise, as on a glass of liquor, by agitation in pouring or drawing. See *bead*, *n.*, 6.—**To raise a blockade.** See *blockade*.—**To raise a bobbery, Cain, the devil, hell, the mischief, a racket, a row, a rumpus,** etc., to make mischief or trouble; create confusion, disturbance, conflict, or riot. [Slang.]

Sir, give me an Account of my Necklace, or I'll make such a Noise in your House I'll *raise the Devil* in it.
Vanbrugh, Confederacy, v.

The head-editor has been in here *raising the mischief* and tearing his hair.
Mark Twain, Sketches, i. (Mr. Bloke's Item).

I expect Susy's boys 'll be *raising Cain* round the house; they would if it wasn't for me.
H. B. Stowe, Oldtown, p. 242.

To raise a check or a note, to make a check or a note larger by dishonestly altering the amount for which it was drawn.—**To raise a dust.** See *dust*1.—**To raise a house,** to raise and join together the parts of the frame of a house built of wood. See *house-raising* and *raising-bee*. [Rural, U. S.]—**To raise a purchase** (*naut.*), to dispose or arrange appliances or apparatus in such a way as to exert the required mechanical power.—**To raise a siege,** to relinquish the attempt to capture a place by besieging it, or to cause the attempt to be relinquished.—**To raise bread, cake,** etc., to render bread, etc., light, porous, and spongy by the development of carbonic-acid gas in the substance of the dough, as by the use of yeast or leaven.—**To raise money on** (something), to procure money by pledging or pawning (something).—**To raise one's bristles or one's dander,** to excite one to anger or resentment; make one angry. [Vulgar, U. S.]

They began to *raise my dander* by belittling the Yankees.
Haliburton, Sam Slick, The Clockmaker, 1st ser., xxii.

To raise the curtain. See *curtain*.—**To raise the dust.** Same as *to raise the wind* (*b*). [Slang.]—**To raise the land.** See *land*1.—**To raise the market upon,** to charge more than the current or regular price. [Colloq.]

Sweyn Erickson had gone too far in *raising the market upon* Mr. Mertoun.
Scott, Pirate, ii.

To raise the wind. (*a*) To make a disturbance. [Colloq.] (*b*) To obtain ready money by some shift or other. [Colloq.]—**To raise up**†, to collect.

To *reysen up* a rente
That longeth to my lordes duetee.
Chaucer, Friar's Tale, l. 90.

=**Syn.** 1 and 2. *Raise, Lift, Erect, Elevate, Exalt, Heighten, Heave, Hoist.* *Raise* is the most general and the most freely figurative of these words, and in its various uses represents all the rest, and also many others, as shown in the definitions. *Lift* is peculiar in implying the exercise of physical or mechanical force, moving the object generally a comparatively short distance upward, but breaking completely its physical contact with the place where it was. To *lift* a ladder is to take it wholly off the ground, if only an inch; to *raise* a ladder, we may *lift* one end and carry it up till it is supported in some way. To *lift* one's head or arm is a more definite and energetic act than to *raise* it. We *lift* a child over a place; we *raise* one that has fallen. To *erect* is to set up perpendicularly: as, to *erect* a flagstaff. To *elevate* is to raise relatively, generally by an amount not large; the word is often no more than a dignified synonym for *raise*. To *exalt* is to raise to dignity; the word is thus used in a physical sense in Isa. xl. 4, "Every valley shall be *exalted*," and elsewhere in the Bible; but the figurative or moral sense has now become the principal one, so that the other seems antique. To *heighten* is to increase in height, either physically or morally: he whom we esteem already is *heightened* in our esteem by an especially honorable act. To *heave* is to raise slowly and with effort, and sometimes to throw in like fashion. To *hoist* is to raise a thing of some weight with some degree of slowness or effort, generally with mechanical help, to a place: as, to *hoist* a rock, or a flag.—14. *Rear, Bring up, Raise.* To *rear* offspring through their tenderer years till they can take care of themselves; to *bring up* a child in the way he should go; to *raise* oats and other products of the soil; to *raise* horses and cattle. Where were you *brought up?* not, where were you *raised?* The use of *raise* in application to persons is a vulgarism. *Rear* applies only to physical care; *bring up* applies more to training or education in mind and manners.

II. *intrans.* To bring up phlegm, bile, or blood from the throat, lungs, or stomach. [Colloq.]

raise1 (rāz), *n.* [< *raise*1, *v.*] 1. Something raised, elevated, or built up; an ascent; a rise; a pile; a cairn. [Prov. Eng.]

There are yet some considerable remains of stones which still go by the name of *raises*.
Hutchinson, Hist. Cumberland. (*Halliwell.*)

That exquisite drive through Ambleside, and . . . up Dunmail *Raise* by the little Wythburn church.
Congregationalist, July 14, 1887.

2. A raising or lifting; removal by lifting or taking away, as of obstructions. [Colloq.]

No further difficulty is anticipated in making permanent the *raise* of the freight blockade in this city [St. Louis].
Philadelphia Times, April 6, 1886.

3. A raising or enlarging in amount; an increase or advance: as, a *raise* of wages; a *raise* of the stakes in gaming. [Colloq.]—4. An acquisition; a getting or procuring by special effort, as of money or chattels: as, to make a *raise* of a hundred dollars. [Colloq.]

raise2 (rāz). A dialectal (Scotch) preterit of *rise*.

raiser (rā'zėr), *n.* [< *raise*1 + *-er*1.] 1. A person who raises or is occupied in raising anything, as buildings, plants, animals, etc.

A *raiser* of huge melons and of pine.
Tennyson, Princess, Conclusion.

The head of the Victor Verdier type [of roses] originated with the greatest of all the *raisers*, Lacharme, of Lyons.
The Century, XXVI. 351.

2. That which raises; a device of any kind used for raising, lifting, or elevating anything: as, a water-*raiser*. Specifically—(*a*) In *carp.*, same as *riser*. (*b*) In a vehicle, a support or stay of wood or metal under the front seat, or some material placed under the trimmings to give them greater thickness. (*c*) In *whale-fishing*, a contrivance for raising or buoying up a dead whale.

raisin (rā'zn), *n.* [< ME. *raisin, reisin, reysyn, reysone, reysynge*, a cluster of grapes, also a dried grape, raisin, = D. *razijn, rozijn* = MLG. *rosin* = MHG. *rasin, rosine*, G. *rosine* = Dan. *rosin* = Sw. *russin* (ML. *rosina*), raisin; < OF. *raisin, reisin*, a cluster of grapes, a grape, a dried grape (*raisins de cabas*, dried grapes, raisins), F. *raisin*, dial. *rasin, roisin, rosin*, grapes (*un grain de raisin*, a grape; *raisins de caisse*, raisins), = Pr. *razim, rozim, razain* = Cat. *rahim* = Sp. *racimo* = Pg. *racimo* = It. *racemo* (dim. *racimolo*), a cluster of grapes, < L. *racemus*, a cluster of grapes: see *raceme*, a doublet of *raisin*.] 1†. A cluster of grapes; also, a grape.

Nether in the vyneyerd thou schalt gadere *reysyns* and greynes fallynge doun, but thou schalt leeve to be gaderid of pore men and pilgryms.
Wyclif, Lev. xix. 10. (*Trench.*)

2. A dried grape of the common Old World species, *Vitis vinifera*. Only certain saccharine varieties of the grape, however, thriving in special localities, are available for raisins. The larger part of ordinary large raisins are produced on a narrow tract in Mediterranean Spain. These are all sometimes classed as *Malaga raisins*, but this name belongs more properly to the "dessert-raisins" grown about Malaga: they are also called *muscatels* from the variety of grape, *blooms* from retaining a glaucous surface, and, in part at least, *raisins of the sun* or *sun-raisins* because dried on the vine, the leaves being removed, and sometimes the cluster-stem half-severed. When packed between sheets of paper, these are known as *layer raisins*. Raisins suitable for cookery, or "pudding-raisins," sometimes called *lexias*, are produced especially at Valencia. These are cured, after cutting from the vine, in the sun, or in bad weather in heated chambers, the quality in the latter case being inferior. The clusters are often dipped in potash lye to soften the skin, favor drying, and impart a gloss. Excluding the "Corinthian raisin" (see below), the next most important source of raisins is the vicinity of Smyrna, including Chesme, near Chios. Here are produced nearly all the sultanas, small seedless raisins with a golden-yellow delicate skin and sweet aromatic flavor. Raisins are also a product of Persia, of Greece, Italy, and southern France, of the Cape of Good Hope, Australia, and California. No variety of native American grape has yet been developed suitable for the preparation of raisins. See *raisin-wine*.

Then Abigail made haste, and took . . . an hundred clusters of *raisins*.
1 Sam. xxv. 18.

I must have saffron to colour the warden pies; . . . four pounds of prunes, and as many of *raisins* o' the sun.
Shak., W. T., iv. 3. 51.

Black Smyrna raisin, a small black variety of raisin with large seeds.—**Corinthian raisin,** the currant, or Zante currant, the dried fruit of the variety *Corinthiaca* of the grape. The cluster is about three inches long, and the berry is not larger than a pea. It is produced in very large quantities in the Morea and the neighboring islands, and is consumed in baking and cookery.—**Eleme raisin,** a Smyrna raisin of good size and quality, hand-picked from the s em, used chiefly for ships' stores or sent to distant markets.

raising (rā'zing), *n.* [< ME. *reysynge*; verbal n. of *raise*1, *v.*] 1. The act of lifting, elevating, etc. (in any sense of the verb). Specifically —(*a*) An occasion on which the frame of a new building, the pieces of which have been previously prepared, but require many hands to put into place, is raised with the help of neighbors. See *house-raising* and *raising-bee*. [Rural, U. S.] (*b*) In *metal-work*, the embossing or ornamentation of sheet-metal by hammering, spinning, or stamping. (*c*) A method of treating hides with acids to cause them to swell and to open the pores in order to hasten the process of tanning. (*d*) In *dyeing*, the process or method of intensifying colors.

2. Same as *raising-piece*.

Franke-posts, *raisins*, beames . . . and such principals.
W. Harrison, Descrip. of England, ii. 12.

3. That with which bread is raised; yeast or yeast-cake; leaven. *Gayton*, Festivous Notes on Don Quixote (cited by Lowell, Biglow Papers, 2d ser., Int.). [Old or prov. Eng. and U. S.]—4. In *printing*, the overlays in a press for woodcut-printing.

raising-bee (rā'zing-bē), *n.* A gathering of neighbors to help in putting together and raising the framework of a new building. Such gatherings are nearly obsolete. Compare *husking-bee, quilting-bee*. [U. S.]

Raising-bees . . . were frequent, where houses sprung up at the wagging of the fiddle-sticks, as the walls of Thebes sprang up of yore to the sound of the lyre of Amphion.
Irving, Knickerbocker, p. 405.

raising-board (rā'zing-bōrd), *n.* In *leather-manuf.*, a corrugated board used to rub the surface of tanned leather to raise the grain; a crippler. *E. H. Knight.*

raising-gig (rā'zing-gig), *n.* In *cloth-manuf.*, a machine for raising a nap on cloth; a gig-machine. *E. H. Knight.*

raising-hammer (rā'zing-ham″ėr), *n.* A hammer with a long head and a rounded face, used by silversmiths and coppersmiths to form a sheet of metal into a cup or bowl shape.

raising-knife (rā'zing-nīf), *n.* A coopers' knife used to set up staves in form for a cask.

raising-piece (rā'zing-pēs), *n.* In *carp.*, a piece of timber laid on a brick wall, or on the top of the posts or puncheons of a timber-framed house, to carry a beam or beams; a templet.

raising-plate (rā'zing-plāt), *n.* In *carp.*, a horizontal timber resting on a wall, or upon vertical timbers of a frame, and supporting the heels of rafters or other framework; a wall-plate.

raisin-tree (rā'zn-trē), *n.* The common currant-shrub, *Ribes rubrum*, the fruit of which is often confounded with the Corinthian raisin, or currant. [Prov. Eng.]—**Japanese raisin-tree,** a small rhamnaceous tree, *Hovenia dulcis*. The peduncle of its fruit is edible.

raisin-wine (rā'zn-wīn), *n.* Wine manufactured from dried grapes. Malaga wine is mostly of this kind, and the Tokay of Hungary is made from partly dried fruit. Raisin-wine was known to the ancients.

raison d'être (rā-zōṅ' dā'tr). [F.: *raison*, reason; *d'* for *de*, of, for; *être*, being, < *être*, be.] Reason or excuse for being; rational cause or ground for existence.

raisonné (rā-zo-nā'), *a.* [< F. *raisonné*, pp. of *raisonner*, reason, prove or support by reasoning, arguments, etc.: see *reason*1, *v.*] Reasoned out; systematic; logical: occurring in English use chiefly in the phrase *catalogue raisonné* (which see, under *catalogue*).

raivel (rāvl), *n.* A Scotch form of *ravel*1, 3.

raj (räj), *n.* [Hind. *rāj*, rule, < Skt. √ *rāj*, rule. Cf. *raja*2.] Rule; dominion. [India.]

But Delhi had fallen when these gentlemen threw their strength into the tide of revolt, and they were too late for a decisive superiority over the British *raj*.
Capt. M. Thomson, Story of Cawnpore, xvi.

Raja1, *n.* Same as *Raia*.

raja2, **rajah** (rä'jä), *n.* [Hind. *rāja*, < Skt. *rāja*, the form in comp. of *rājan*, a king, as in *mahārāja*, great king; akin to L. *rex*, king (see *rex*); < √ *rāj*, rule: see *regent*.] In India, a prince of Hindu race ruling a territory, either independently or as a feudatory; a king; a chief: used also as a title of distinction for Hindus in some cases, without reference to sovereignty, as *nabob* is for Mohammedans. The power of nearly all the rajas is now subordinate to that of British officials resident at their courts. Those who retain some degree of actual sovereignty are commonly distinguished by the title *maharaja* (great raja).

Rajania (rā-jā'ni-ä), *n.* [NL. (Linnæus, 1737), an adapted form of *Jan-Raja* (Plumier, 1703), so called after John *Ray* (Latinized *Raius*), 1628–1705, a celebrated English naturalist, founder of a natural system of classification.] A genus of monocotyledonous plants of the order *Dioscoreaceæ*, the yam family. It is characterized by diœcious bell-shaped or flattened six-lobed flowers, with six stamens and a three-celled ovary, ripening into a flattened broad-winged and one-celled samara. The 6 species are all natives of the West Indies. They are twining vines resembling the yam, and bear alternate leaves, either halberd- or heart-shaped or linear, and small flowers in racemes. Several species are occasionally cultivated under glass. *R. pleioneura*, common in woods of the larger West Indies, is there called *wild yam* and *waw-waw*.

rajaship, rajahship (rä'jä-ship), *n.* [< *raja*2 + *-ship*.] The dignity or principality of a raja.

Rajidæ, *n. pl.* Same as *Raiidæ*.

Rajput, Rajpoot (raj-pöt'), *n.* [< Hind. *rajpût*, a prince, son of a raja, < Skt. *rājaputra*, a king's son, a prince, < *rājan*, a king, + *putra*, son.] A member of a Hindu race, divided into numerous clans, who regard themselves as descendants of the ancient Kshatriya or warrior caste. They are the ruling (though not the most numerous) race of the great region named from them Rajputana, consisting of several different states. Their hereditary profession is that of arms, and no race in India has furnished so large a number of princely families. The Rajputs are not strict adherents of Brahmanism.

rake1 (rāk), *n.* [< ME. *rake*, < AS. *raca, racu, ræce* = MD. *rake, raecke*, D. *rake*, dim. *rakel* = MLG. *rake*, LG. *rake*, a rake, = Sw. *raka*, an oven-rake, = Dan. *rage*, a poker; in another form, MD. *reke*, D. *reek* = LG. *reek* = OHG. *recho, rehho*, MHG. *reche*, G. *rechen*, a rake, = Icel. *reka*, a shovel; from the verb represented by MD. *reken*, OHG. *rechan, rehhan*, MHG. *rechen*, scrape together, = Goth. *rikan* (pret. *rak*), collect, heap up (cf. *rake*1, *v.*, which depends on the noun).] 1. An implement of wood or iron, or partly of both, with teeth or tines for drawing or scraping things together, evening a surface of loose materials, etc. In its simplest form, for use by hand, it consists of a bar in which the teeth are set, and which is fixed firmly at right angles to a handle. Rakes are made in many ways for a great variety of purposes, and the

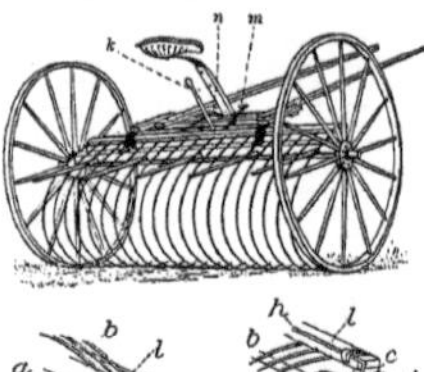

Horse-rake. *A* and *B* show details of dumping-apparatus.

a, backpiece for holding cleaner-sticks; *b*, steel teeth; *c*, pawl engaged with ratchet; *c*, pawl disengaged from ratchet; *d*, trip for pawl; *e*, pawl acting by its gravity to disengage ratchet; *f*, clearer-sticks, which clear the rake when dumping; *g*, ratchet; *h*, wood axle and cap for axle and tooth-holder; *i*, counter-balance for pawl; *j*, axle; *k*, "hand-up," by which the driver can raise the teeth and keep them from the ground; *l*, trip-rod for self-dump; *m*, foot-lever for holding down teeth; *n*, trip-lever attached to trip-rod *l* for dumping the rake. Pressure of the foot on *n* locks the pawls into the ratchet *g*, then axle and cap trim with the wheels until the pawls automatically disengage from the ratchet by striking *d*, when the teeth fall back again into original position.

teeth are inserted either perpendicularly or at a greater or less inclination, according to requirement. Their most prominent uses are in agriculture and gardening, for drawing together hay or grain in the field, leveling beds, etc. For farm-work on a large scale horse-rakes of many forms are used; the above figures represent the so-called *sulky-rake*.

2. An instrument of similar form and use with a blade instead of teeth, either entire, as a gamblers' or a maltsters' rake, or notched so as to form teeth, as a furriers' rake. See the quotations.

The *rake* (for malt) . . . is an iron blade, about 30 inches long and perhaps 2 inches broad, fixed at each end by holders to a massive wood head, to which is attached a strong wood shaft, with a cross-head handle.
Ure, Dict., III. 188.

The skin is first carded with a *rake*, which is the blade of an old shear or piece of a scythe with large teeth notched into its edge.
Ure, Dict., IV. 380.

Clam-rake, an instrument used for collecting the sea-clam, *Mactra solidissima*.—**Under-rake**, a kind of oyster-rake, used mostly through holes in the ice, with handle 15 to 20 feet long, head 1 to 2 feet wide, and iron teeth 6 to 10 inches long. [Rhode Island.]

rake[1] (rāk), *v.*; pret. and pp. *raked*, ppr. *raking*. [< ME. *raken*, scrape, < AS. **racian* = MD. *raken* = MLG. *raken* = Icel. Sw. *raka* = Dan. *rage*, rake; from the noun: see *rake*[1], *n.* Cf. MD. *reken*, OHG. *rechan*, *rehhan*, MHG. *rechen*, scrape together, G. *rechen*, rake, Goth. *rikan* (pret. *rak*), collect, heap up: see *rake*[1], *n.*] **I.** *trans.* **1.** To gather, clear, smooth, or stir with or as if with a rake; treat with a rake, or something that serves the same purpose: as, to *rake* up hay; to *rake* a bed in a garden; to *rake* the fire with a poker or raker.

They *rake* these coales round in the forme of a cockpit, and in the midst they cast the offenders to broyle to death.
Capt. John Smith, Works, I. 144.

Rake well the cinders, sweep the floor,
And sift the dust behind the door.
Cowper, Epistle to Robert Lloyd.

2. To collect as if by the use of a rake; gather assiduously or laboriously; draw or scrape together, up, or in.

All was *rak'd* up for me, your thankful brother,
That will dance merrily upon your grave.
Fletcher, Spanish Curate, I. 1.

Who had hence *raked* some objections against the Christians, for these things which had not authoritie of Scripture.
Purchas, Pilgrimage, p. 68.

Times when chimney-corners had benches in them, where old people sat poking into the ashes of the past, and *raking* out traditions like live coals.
Hawthorne, Seven Gables, xviii.

3. To make minute search in, as if with a rake; look over or through carefully; ransack: as, to *rake* all history for examples.

The statesman *rakes* the town to find a plot.
Swift, On Dreams.

4. To pass along with or as if with a scraping motion; impinge lightly upon in moving; hence, to pass over swiftly; scour.

Thy thunders roaring *rake* the skies,
Thy fatal lightning swiftly flies.
Sandys, Paraphrase of Ps. lxxvii.

Every mast, as it passed,
Seemed to *rake* the passing clouds.
Longfellow, Sir Humphrey Gilbert.

5. *Milit.*, to fire upon, as a ship, so that the shot will pass lengthwise along the deck; fire in the direction of the length of, as a file of soldiers or a parapet; enfilade.

They made divers shot through her (being but inch board), and so *raked* her fore and aft as they must needs kill or hurt some of the Indians.
Winthrop, Hist. New England, I. 226.

Raking a ship is the act of cannonading a ship on the stern or head, so as that the balls shall scour the whole length of her decks; which is one of the most dangerous incidents that can happen in a naval action.
Falconer, Marine Dict. (ed. 1778).

6†. To cover with earth raked together; bury. See *to rake up*, below.

Whanne thi soule is went out, & thi bodi in erthe *rakid*,
Than thi bodi that was rank & Vndeuout, Of alle men is bihatid.
Hymns to Virgin, etc. (E. E. T. S.), p. 89.

To rake hell, to search, as it were, among the damned, implying that the person or thing referred to in the context is so bad or so extreme that an equal could scarcely be found even in hell.

This man I brought to the general, assuring his excellency that if I had *raked hell* I could not find his match for his skill in mimicking the covenanters.
Swift, Mem. of Capt. Creichton.

To rake up. (*a*) To cover with material raked or scraped together; bury by overlaying with loose matter: as, to *rake up* a fire (to cover it with ashes, as in a fireplace).

Here, in the sands,
Thee [a corpse] I'll *rake up*, the post unsanctified
Of murderous lechers.
Shak., Lear, iv. 6. 281.

The Bellowes whence they blowe the fire
Of raging Lust (before) whose wanton flashes
A tender brest *rak't-up* in shamefac't ashes.
Sylvester, tr. of Du Bartas's Weeks, i. 2.

(*b*) To draw from oblivion or obscurity, as something forgotten or abandoned; bring to renewed attention; resuscitate; revive: used in a more or less opprobrious sense: as, to *rake up* a forgotten quarrel.

Nobody thinks any more of the late King than if he had been dead fifty years, unless it be to abuse him and to *rake up* all his vices and misdeeds.
Greville, Memoirs, July 16, 1830.

To *rake up* old claims based on a forgotten state of things, after treaty or long use had buried them, is profligate.
Woolsey, Introd. to Inter. Law, App. iii., p. 438.

II. *intrans.* **1.** To use a rake; work with a rake, especially in drawing together hay or grain.—**2.** To make search with or as if with a rake; seek diligently for something; pry; peer here and there.

Those who take pleasure to be all thir life time *rakeing* in the Foundations of Old Abbies and Cathedrals.
Milton, Hist. Eng., iv.

But what pleasure is it to *rake* into the sores or to reprove the Vices of a degenerate age?
Stillingfleet, Sermons, II. iii.

rake[2]† (rāk), *n.* [< ME. *rake* (also *raike*), < AS. *racu*, a path (*eá-racu*, a river-path), from the root of *rack*[1]: see *rack*[5]. Cf. *rake*[2], *v.*] A course, way, road, or path.

Rydes one a rawndoune, and his *rayke* holdes.
Morte Arthure (E. E. T. S.), l. 2986.

Out of the *rake* of rigtwysnes renne sald he nevire.
King Alisaunder, p. 115.

rake[2] (rāk), *v. i.*; pret. and pp. *raked*, ppr. *raking*. [Early mod. E. (Sc.) also *raik*; < ME. *raken*, < AS. *racian*, run, take a course, = Sw. *raka*, run hastily; mixed with ME. *raiken*, *rayken*, *reyken*, < Icel. *reika*, wander: see *rake*[2], *n.*] **1.** To take a course; move; go; proceed. [Obsolete or prov. Eng. and Scotch.]

Then Paris aprochyt, the Percians hym with:
Radli on the right syde *rakit* he furth,
And bounet into batell with a brym will.
Destruction of Troy (E. E. T. S.), l. 6904.

Now pass we to the bold beggar
That *raked* o'er the hill.
Robin Hood and the Beggar (Child's Ballads, V. 196).

2. In *hunting*: (*a*) Of a hawk, to range wildly; fly wide of the game.

Their talk was all of training, terms of art,
Diet and seeling, jesses, leash and lure.
"She is too noble," he said, "to check at pies,
Nor will she *rake*; there is no baseness in her."
Tennyson, Merlin and Vivien.

(*b*) Of a dog, to follow a wrong course. See the quotation.

All young dogs are apt to *rake*: that is, to hunt with their noses close to the ground, following their birds by the track rather than by the wind.
Sportsman's Gazetteer, p. 466.

To rake about, to gad or wander about. [Scotch.]

rake[3] (rāk), *v.*; pret. and pp. *raked*, ppr. *raking*. [< OSw. *raka*, project, reach (*raka fram*, reach over, project), = Dan. *rage*, project, protrude, jut out; allied to AS. *reccan*, stretch: see *rack*[1], *retch*[1].] **I.** *intrans.* To incline from the perpendicular or the horizontal, as the mast, stem, or stern of a ship, the rafters of a roof, the end of a tool, etc. See the noun.

The stern, when viewed in the sheer plan, *rakes* aft, the bounding line being straight, and making an obtuse angle with the line forming the boundary of the buttock.
Thearle, Naval Arch., § 107.

II. *trans.* To give a rake to; cause to incline or slope. [Rare.]

Every face in it [the theater] commanding the stage, and the whole so admirably *raked* and turned to that centre that a hand can scarcely move in the great assemblage without the movement being seen from thence.
Dickens, Uncommercial Traveller, Journey iii.

rake[3] (rāk), *n.* [< *rake*[3], *v.*] **1.** Inclination or slope away from a perpendicular or a horizontal line. The rake of a ship's mast is its inclination backward, or rarely (in some peculiar rigs) forward; that of its stem or its stern (the fore rake and the rake aft of the ship) is the slope inward from the upper works to the keel: also called *hang*. (See cut under *patamar*.) The rake of a roof is its pitch or slope from the ridge to the eaves. The rake of a saw-tooth is the angle of inclination which a straight line drawn through the middle of the base of the tooth and its point forms with a radius also drawn through the middle of the base of the tooth; of a cutting-tool, the slope backward and downward from the edge on either side or both sides. Rake in a grinding-mill is a sloping or want of balance of the runner, producing undue pressure at one edge.

2. In *coal-mining*, a series of thin layers of ironstone lying so near each other that they can all be worked together. [Derbyshire, Eng.]

rake[4] (rāk), *n.* [Abbr. of *rakehell*, ult. of *rakel*.] An idle, dissolute person; one who goes about in search of vicious pleasure; a libertine; an idle person of fashion.

We have now and then *rakes* in the habit of Roman senators, and grave politicians in the dress of *rakes*.
Steele, Spectator, No. 14.

I am in a fair Way to be easy, were it not for a Club of Female *Rakes* who, under p e en e of taking their innocent rambles, forsooth, and diverting the Spleen, seldom fail to plague me twice or thrice a day to Cheapen Tea, or buy a Skreen. . . . These *Rakes* are your idle Ladies of Fashion, who, having nothing to do, employ themselves in tumbling over my Ware.
Steele, Spectator, No. 336.

rake[4] (rāk), *v. i.*; pret. and pp. *raked*, ppr. *raking*. [< *rake*[4], *n.*] To play the part of a rake; lead a dissolute, debauched life; practise lewdness.

'Tis his own fault, that will *rake* and drink when he is but just crawled out of his grave.
Swift, Journal to Stella, xx.

Women hid their necks, and veil'd their faces,
Nor romp'd, nor *rak'd*, nor star'd at public places.
Shenstone, Epil. to Dodsley's Cleone.

rake-dredge (rāk'drej), *n.* A combined rake and dredge used for collecting specimens in natural history. It is a heavy A-shaped iron frame, to the arms of which bars of iron armed with long, thin, sharp teeth, arranged like those of a rake, are bolted back to back. A rectangular frame of round iron, supporting a deep and fine dredge-net, is placed behind the rake, to receive and retain the animals raked from the mud or sand.

rakee, *n.* See *raki*.

rake-head (rāk'hed), *n.* In *her.*, a bearing representing the head of a rake, or, more usually, four or five hooks or curved teeth inserted in a short rod.

rakehell (rāk'hel), *a.* and *n.* [A corruption of *rakel*, simulating *rake*[1], *v.*, + obj. *hell*, as if one so bad as to be found only by raking hell, or one so reckless as to rake hell (in double allusion to the "*harrowing* of hell": see *harrow*[2] and *harrow*[1]): see *rakel*, and cf. *to rake hell*, under *rake*[1], *v.*] **I.** *a.* Dissolute; base; profligate.

And farre away, amid their *rakehell* bands,
They spide a Lady left all succourlesse.
Spenser, F. Q., V. xi. 44.

II. *n.* An abandoned fellow; a wicked wretch; especially, a dissolute fellow; a rake.

I thought it good, necessary, and my bounden duty to acquaint your goodness with the abominable, wicked, and detestable behaviour of all these rowsey, ragged rabblement of *rake-hells*, that under the pretence of great misery, diseases, and other innumerable calamities, which they feign through great hypocrisy, do win and gain great alms in all places where they wily wander, to the utter deluding of the good givers.
Harman, Caveat for Cursetors, p. ii.

A sort of lewd *rake-hells*, that care neither for God nor the devil.
B. Jonson, Every Man in his Humour, iv. 1.

A *rakehell* of the town, whose character is set off with no other accomplishment but excessive prodigality, profaneness, intemperance, and lust, is rewarded with a lady of great fortune to repair his own, which his vices had almost ruined.
Swift, Against Abolishing Christianity.

rakehellonian† (rāk-he-lō'ni-an), *n.* [< *rakehell* + *-onian*, as in *Babylonian*, etc.] A wild, dissolute fellow; a rakehell. [Rare.]

I have been a man of the town, or rather a man of wit, and have been confess'd a beau, and admitted into the family of the *rakehellonians*.
Tom Brown, Works, II. 313. (*Davies*.)

rakehelly (rāk'hel-i), *a.* [< *rakehell* + *-y*1. Cf. *rakely.*] Like or characteristic of a rakehell.

I scorne and spue out the *rakehellye* route of our ragged rymers. *Spenser*, Shep. Cal., Ded.

Dissipated, not to say *rakehelly*, countenances. *J. Payn*, Mystery of Mirbridge, p. 32.

rakel†, *a.* and *n.* [Early mod. E. also *rakyl*, Sc. *rackel*; < ME. *rakel, rakle, racle, rakyl, rakil*, hasty, rash, wild, < Icel. *reikull, reikall*, wandering, unsettled (< Icel. *reika*, wander, roam: see *rake*2); cf. Sw. dial. *rakkel*, a vagabond, < *rakkla*, wander, rove, freq. of *raka*, run hastily: see *rake*2. Cf. Icel. *rækall*, Sw. *räkel*, Dan. *rækel*, a hound, lout, used as a term of abuse.] I. *a.* Rash; hasty.

O *rakel* hand, to doon so foule amys. *Chaucer*, Manciple's Tale, l. 174.

II. *n.* A dissolute man. See *rakehell.*

rakel†, *v. i.* [ME. *rakelen*; < *rakel*, *a.*] To act rashly or hastily.

Ne I nyl not *rakle* as for to greven here. *Chaucer*, Troilus, iii. 1642.

rakelnesse†, *n.* [< ME. *rakelnesse*, haste, rashness; < *rakel* + *-ness.*] Hastiness; rashness.

O every man, be war of *rakelness*,
Ne trowe no thyng withouten strong witnesse.
Chaucer, Manciple's Tale, l. 179.

rakely†, *a.* [< *rake*4 + *-ly*1. Cf. *rakehelly.*] Rakish; rakehelly.

Our *rakely* young Fellows live as much by their Wits as ever. *C. Shadwell*, Humours of the Army (1713).

raker (rā'kėr), *n.* [< ME. *rakere, rakyer*; < *rake*1 + *-er*1.] 1. One who or that which rakes. Specifically—(*a*) A person who uses a rake; formerly, a scavenger or street-cleaner.

Their business was declared to be that they should hire persons called *rakers*, with carts, to clean the streets and carry away the dirt and filth thereof, under a penalty of 40*s*. *Mayhew*, London Labour and London Poor, II. 232.

(*b*) A machine for raking hay, straw, etc., by horse or other power. (*c*) An instrument for raking out the ashes from a fire or grate; in locomotives, a self-acting contrivance for cleaning the grate. (*d*) A gun so placed as to rake an enemy's vessel.

Down! she 's welcome to us:
Every man to his charge! man her i' the bow well,
And place your *rakers* right.
Fletcher, Double Marriage, ii. 1.

(*e*) A piece of iron having pointed ends bent at right angles in opposite directions, used for raking out decayed mortar from the joints of old walls, in order to replace it with new mortar.

2. A rake-like row of internal branchial arch appendages of some fishes. See *gill-raker.*

rakery (rā'kėr-i), *n.* [< *rake*4 + *-ery.*] The conduct or practices of a rake; dissoluteness. [Rare.]

He . . . instructed his lordship in all the *rakery* and intrigues of the lewd town. *Roger North*, Lord Guilford, II. 300.

rakeshame† (rāk'shām), *n.* [< *rake*1, *v.*, + obj. *shame*, *n.*, as if 'one who gathers shame to himself'; formed in moral amendment of *rakehell.*] A vile, dissolute wretch.

Tormentors, rooks, and *rakeshames*, sold to lucre. *Milton*, Reformation in Eng., ii.

rakestale† (rāk'stāl), *n.* [Also dial. *rakestele*; < *rake*1 + *stale*1, *steal*2.] A rake-handle.

That tale is not worth a *rakestele.* *Chaucer*, Wife of Bath's Tale, l. 93.

rake-vein (rāk'vān), *n.* In *lead-mining*, in England, a vertical or highly inclined fissure-vein, as distinguished from the flat-vein, or flat, and the pipe-vein (a mass of ore filling an irregularly elongated cavern-like opening). [Derbyshire, Eng.]

raki, rakee (rak'ē), *n.* [< Turk. *raki*, spirits, brandy. Cf. *arrack, rack*11.] A colorless aromatic spirituous liquor, prepared from grain-spirit, as in Greece, or from distilled grape-juice, as in the Levant.

The hill-men on such occasions consume a coarse sort of *rakee* made from corn. *W. H. Russell*, Diary in India, II. 181.

Raw grain spirit, which is used in the country for making *raki*. *U. S. Cons. Rep.*, No. lxviii. (1886), p. 640.

raking1 (rā'king), *n.* [< ME. *rakynge*; verbal n. of *rake*1, *v.*] 1. The art of using a rake; a gathering or clearance with or as if with a rake; also, that which is raked or raked up.

But such a *raking* was never seen
As the *raking* o' the Rullien Green.
Battle of Pentland Hills (Child's Ballads, VII. 242).

2. The act of raking into or exploring something; hence, a rigid scrutiny or examination; a depreciatory overhauling; censorious criticism.

The average common school received a *raking* which would even gratify the sharp-set critical appetite. *Jour. of Education*, XVIII. 136.

raking1 (rā'king), *p. a.* [Ppr. of *rake*1, *v.*] Such as to rake: as, a *raking* fire.

raking2 (rā'king), *p. a.* [Ppr. of *rake*3, *v.*] Inclining; having a rake or inclination.—**Raking bond, molding**, etc. See the nouns.

raking-piece (rā'king-pēs), *n.* 1. In a bridge-centering, a piece laid upon the sill supported by the footing or impost of a pier. Upon the raking-pieces rest the striking-plates, which support the ribs of the centering, and are driven in to allow the centering to drop clear when the arch is completed.

2. In a theater, a low and pointed bit of scenery used to mask an incline.

rakish1 (rā'kish), *a.* [< *rake*3 + *-ish*1.] *Naut.*, having an unusual amount of rake or inclination of the masts, as a vessel. The piratical craft of former times were distinguished for their rakish build.

But when they found, as they soon did, that the beautiful, *rakish*-looking schooner was averse to piracy, and careless of plunder, . . . they declared first neutrality, then adhesion. *Whyte Melville*, White Rose, II. i.

rakish2 (rā'kish), *a.* [< *rake*4 + *-ish*1.] 1. Resembling or given to the practices of a rake; given to a dissolute life; lewd; debauched.

The arduous task of converting a *rakish* lover. *Macaulay.*

2. Jaunty.

rakishly (rā'kish-li), *adv.* [< *rakish*2 + *-ly*2.] 1. In a rakish or dissolute manner.—2. Jauntily.

rakishness1 (rā'kish-nes), *n.* [< *rakish*1 + *-ness.*] The aspect of a rakish vessel.

rakishness2 (rā'kish-nes), *n.* [< *rakish*2 + *-ness.*] 1. The character of being rakish or dissolute; dissoluteness.

If the lawyer had been presuming on Mrs. Transome's ignorance as a woman, or on the stupid *rakishness* of the original heir, the new heir would prove to him that he had calculated rashly. *George Eliot*, Felix Holt, ii.

2. Jauntiness.

rakke†, *n.* A Middle English form of *rack*1.

rakle†, *v. i.* A variant of *rakel.*

rakshas, rakshasa (rak'shas, rak'sha-sä), *n.* [Skt.] In *Hind. myth.*, one of a class of evil spirits or genii. They are cruel monsters, frequenting cemeteries, devouring human beings, and assuming any shape at pleasure. They are generally hideous, but some, especially the females, allure by their beauty.

Rakusian (ra-kū'si-an), *n.* [Ar.] A member of a Christian sect mentioned by Mohammedan writers as having formerly existed in Arabia. Little is known of it, but its tenets appear to be a further corruption of those of the Mendæans or Sabians. *Blunt.*

râle (räl), *n.* [< F. *râle*, OF. *raale, rasle*, rattling in the throat, < F. *râler*, OF. *raller*, rattle, < LG. *ratelen, rateln*, rattle: see *rattle.* Cf. *rail*4.] In *pathol.*, an abnormal sound heard on auscultation of the lungs, additional to and not merely a modification of the normal respiratory murmur.—**Cavernous râle.** See *cavernous.*—**Crepitant râle**, a very fine crackling râle heard during inspiration in the first stage of pneumonia. Also called *vesicular râle.*—**Dry râle**, a non-bubbling respiratory râle, caused by constriction of a bronchial tube or larger air-passage. The high-pitched whistling dry râle is called a *sibilant râle*, and the low-pitched snoring dry râle is called a *sonorous râle.*—**Moist râles**, bubbling râles, fine or coarse, produced by liquid or semiliquid in the bronchial tubes, bronchi, trachea, or larynx.—**Pleural râle**, an abnormal sound produced within the pleura, as a friction sound, or metallic tinkling, or a succussion sound.—**Subcrepitant râle**, a very fine bronchial bubbling râle.—**Vesicular râle.** Same as *crepitant râle.*

Ralfsia (ralf'si-ä), *n.* [NL. (Berkeley), named in honor of John *Ralfs*, an English botanist.] A small genus of olive-brown seaweeds of the class *Phæosporeæ*, type of the order *Ralfsiaceæ.* They are rather small homely plants, growing on stones, rocks, or the shells of mollusks and crustaceans. Three species are found on the New England coast.

Ralfsiaceæ (ralf-si-ā'sẹ-ē), *n. pl.* [NL., < *Ralfsia* + *-aceæ.*] An order of olive-brown seaweeds, typified by the genus *Ralfsia.* The fronds are horizontally expanded, sometimes crustaceous; and fructification is in raised spots, composed of a few club-shaped paraphyses and spheroidal sporangia.

rall. An abbreviation of *rallentando.*

rallentando (räl-len-tän'dọ̄), *a.* [It., ppr. of *rallentare* = F. *ralentir*, slacken, relent, abate, retard: see *relent.*] In *music*, becoming slower; with decreasing rapidity. Also *rallentato.* Abbreviated *rall.* Compare *ritardando* and *ritenuto.*

ralliance† (ral'i-ans), *n.* [< *rally*1 + *-ance.*] The act of rallying. [Rare.] *Imp. Dict.*

Rallidæ (ral'i-dē), *n. pl.* [NL., < *Rallus* + *-idæ.*] A family of paludicole grallatorial precocial birds, typified by the genus *Rallus*, and divided into *Rallinæ, Gallinulinæ*, and *Fulicinæ*, or rails, gallinules, and coots, to which some add *Ocydrominæ* and *Himantornithinæ*; the rails and their allies. There are upward of 150 species, found in nearly all parts of the world, in swamps and marshes. See cuts under *coot, gallinule, Porzana*, and *Rallus.*

rallier1 (ral'i-ėr), *n.* [< *rally*1 + *-er*1.] One who rallies or reassembles; one who reunites, as disordered or scattered forces.

rallier2 (ral'i-ėr), *n.* [< *rally*2 + *-er*1.] One who rallies or banters. [Rare.] *Imp. Dict.*

ralliform (ral'i-fôrm), *a.* [< NL. *ralliformis*, < *Rallus*, a rail, + L. *forma*, form.] Having the structure of or an affinity with the rails; ralline in a broad sense; of or pertaining to the *Ralliformes.*

Ralliformes (ral-i-fôr'mēz), *n. pl.* [NL., pl. of *ralliformis*: see *ralliform.*] A superfamily of paludicole precocial grallatorial birds, represented by the family *Rallidæ* in a broad sense, containing the rails and their allies, as distinguished from the *Gruiformes*, or related birds of the crane type.

Rallinæ (ra-lī'nē), *n. pl.* [NL., < *Rallus* + *-inæ.*] The leading subfamily of *Rallidæ*, including the genus *Rallus* and related genera; the rails. The species are strictly paludicole; the body is greatly compressed; the form tapers in front, and is thick-set behind, with a short tipped-up tail; the wings are short and rounded; the tail has twelve feathers; the thighs are very muscular, and the flank-feathers are notably colored; the tibiæ are naked below; the tarsi are scutellate in front; and the toes are long, cleft to the base, and not lobed or obviously margined. Besides *Rallus*, the leading genera are *Porzana* and *Crex.* There are about 60 species, found in most countries.

ralline (ral'in), *a.* [NL., < *Rallus* + *-ine*1.] Pertaining or related to the genus *Rallus* or family *Rallidæ*; resembling a rail; ralliform in a narrow sense.

rallum (ral'um), *n.*; pl. *ralla* (-ä). [L., < *radere*, scrape, scratch: see *rase*1, *raze*1.] An implement used as a scraper by husbandmen among the Romans, consisting of a straight handle and a triangular blade.—**Rallum-shaped**, growing wider toward the end and terminating squarely, as the blade of a stylus.

Rallus (ral'us), *n.* [NL., < F. *râle*, OF. *rasle*, a rail: see *rail*4.] The leading genus of *Rallinæ*, containing the true rails, water-rails, or marsh-hens, having the bill longer than the head, slender, compressed, and decurved, with long nasal groove and linear subbasal nostrils, and the coloration plain below, but with conspicuously banded flanks. See *rail*4.

Virginia Rail (*Rallus virginianus*).

rally1 (ral'i), *v.*; pret. and pp. *rallied*, ppr. *rallying.* [Early mod. E. *rallie*, < OF. *rallier, ralier*, F. *rallier*, rally, < *re-*, again, + *alier, allier*, bind, ally: see *ally*1, and cf. *rely*1 and *rely*2.] I. *trans.* 1. To bring together or into order again by urgent effort; urge or bring to reunion for joint action; hence, to draw or call together in general for a common purpose: as, to *rally* a disorganized army; to *rally* voters to the polls.

There 's no help now;
The army 's scatter'd all, through discontent,
Not to be *rallied* up in haste to help this.
Fletcher, Loyal Subject, iii. 1.

2. To call up or together, unite, draw, gather up, concentrate, etc., energetically.

Prompts them to *rally* all their sophistry. *Decay of Christian Piety.*

Grasping his foe in mortal agony, he *rallied* his strength for a final blow. *Prescott*, Ferd. and Isa., ii. 7.

Philip *rallied* himself, and tried to speak up to the old standard of respectability. *Mrs. Gaskell*, Sylvia's Lovers, xxxiv.

II. *intrans.* 1. To come together or into order again with haste or ardor; reunite energetically; hence, to gather or become conjoined for a common end; cohere for aid or support.

And then we *rally'd* on the hills.
Up and War Them A', Willie (Child's Ballads, VII. 266).

They *rallied* round their flags, and renewed the assault.
The Century, XXIX. 297.

2. To come into renewed energy or action; acquire new or renewed strength or vigor; undergo restoration or recovery, either partial or complete: as, the market *rallied* from its depression; the patient *rallied* about midnight.

Innumerable parts of matter chanced then to *rally* together and to form themselves into this new world.
Tillotson.

Catholicism had *rallied*, and had driven back Protestantism even to the German Ocean.
Macaulay, Von Ranke's Hist. Popes.

rally[1] (ral'i), *n.*; pl. *rallies* (-iz). [‹ *rally*[1], *v.*] 1. A rapid or ardent reunion for effort of any kind; a renewal of energy in joint action; a quick recovery from disorder or dispersion, as of a body of troops or other persons.—2. *Theat.*, specifically, the general scramble or chase of all the players in a pantomime; a mêlée of pantomimists, as at the end of a transformation scene.

The last scene of all, which in modern pantomime follows upon the shadowy chase of the characters called the *rally*.
Encyc. Brit., XVIII. 216.

3. In *lawn-tennis*, the return of the ball over the net from one side to the other for a number of times consecutively.—4. A quick recovery from a state of depression or exhaustion; renewal of energy or of vigorous action; return to or toward the prior or normal condition, as in disease, trade, active exertion of any kind, etc.: as, a *rally* in the course of a disease; a *rally* in prices.

The two stand to one another like men; *rally* follows *rally* in quick succession, each fighting as if he thought to finish the whole thing out of hand.
T. Hughes, Tom Brown at Rugby, ii. 5.

rally[2] (ral'i), *v.*; pret. and pp. *rallied*, ppr. *rallying*. [‹ F. *railler*, rail: see *rail*[5].] I. *trans.* To attack with raillery; treat with jocose, satirical, or sarcastic pleasantry; make merry with in regard to something; poke fun at; quiz.

Strephon had long confess'd his amorous pain,
Which gay Corinna *rallied* with disdain.
Gay, The Fan, i. 40.

Snake has just been *rallying* me on our mutual attachment.
Sheridan, School for Scandal, i. 1.

=**Syn.** *Banter*, etc. (see *banter*), joke, quiz, tease.

II. *intrans.* To use pleasantry or satirical merriment.

Juvenal has railed more wittily than Horace has *rallied*.
Dryden, Orig. and Prog. of Satire.

This gentleman *rallies* the best of any man I know; for he forms his ridicule upon a circumstance which you are in your heart not unwilling to grant him: to wit, that you are guilty of an excess in something which is in itself laudable.
Steele, Spectator, No. 422.

rally[2] (ral'i), *n.* [‹ *rally*[2], *v.*] An exercise of good humor or satirical merriment. [Rare.]

rallyingly (ral'i-ing-li), *adv.* In a rallying, bantering, or quizzical manner. [Rare.]

"What! tired already, Jacob's would-be successor?" asks she *rallyingly*.
R. Broughton, Doctor Cupid, ix.

rallying-point (ral'i-ing-point), *n.* A place, person, or thing at or about which persons rally, or come together for action.

ralph (ralf), *n.* [Appar. from the personal name *Ralph*.] 1. An alleged or imagined evil spirit who does mischief in a printing-house. [Printers' slang, Eng.]—2. A familiar name of the raven, *Corvus corax*.

ralstonite (râl'ston-īt), *n.* [After J. Grier *Ralston*, of Norristown, Pennsylvania.] A fluoride of aluminium and calcium, occurring in transparent isometric octahedrons with cryolite in Greenland.

ram[1] (ram), *n.* [‹ ME. *ram*, *ramme*, *rom*, ‹ AS. *ram*, *ramm*, *rom*; = D. *ram* = MLG. LG. *ram* = OHG. *ram*, *rammo*, MHG. *ram*, G. *ramm*, a ram, male sheep. Hence *ram*[2]. Cf. *ram*[3].] The male of the sheep, *Ovis aries*, and other ovine quadrupeds; a tup. See cuts under *Ovis* and *quadricornous*.—**The Ram**, Aries, one of the signs and constellations of the zodiac. See *Aries*.

ram[2] (ram), *n.* [‹ ME. *ram*, *ramme*, ‹ AS. *ram*, *ramm* = D. *ram*, m., = MHG. G. *ramme*, f., a battering-ram; orig. a particular use of *ram*[1], in allusion to the way a ram uses his head in fighting.] 1. An instrument for battering, crushing, butting, or driving by impact. Specifically—(*a*) Same as *battering-ram*.

Bring up your *rams*,
And with their armed heads make the fort totter.
Fletcher, Bonduca, iv. 4.

(*b*) A solid pointed projection or beak jutting from the bow of a war-vessel, used both in ancient and in recent times for crushing in an enemy's vessel by being driven against it. See def. 2, and cut under *embolon*. (*c*) The heavy weight of a pile-driving machine, which falls upon the head of the pile: same as *monkey*, 3. (*d*) The piston in the large cylinder of a hydraulic press. (*e*) A hooped spar used in ship-building for moving timbers by a jolting blow on the end. (*f*) In *metal-working*, a steam-hammer used in forming a bloom.

2. A steam ship of war armed at the prow below the water-line with a heavy metallic beak

Ram. *a*, bow-rudder.

or spur, intended to destroy an enemy's ship by the force of collision. The beak is often so far independent of the vital structure of the ship that, in the event of a serious collision, it may be carried away without essential injury to the ship to which it belongs. See also cuts under *beak*.—**Hydraulic ram.** See *hydraulic*.

ram[2] (ram), *v.*; pret. and pp. *rammed*, ppr. *ramming*. [‹ ME. *rammen*, *ram*, ram; cf. D. *rammen* = MLG. *rammen*, ram, batter, = G. *rammen*, ram, bore or drive in (› Dan. *ramme*, hit, strike, ram, drive); from the noun: see *ram*[1], *n.*] I. *trans.* 1. To strike with a ram; drive a ram or similar object against; batter: as, the two vessels tried to *ram* each other.—2. To force in; drive down or together: as, to *ram* down a cartridge; to *ram* a charge; to *ram* piles into the earth.

Somewhat of trepidation might be observed in his manner as he *rammed* down the balls.
Barham, Ingoldsby Legends, I. 143.

3. To fill or compact by pounding or driving.

Lady Len. No man shall ever come within my gates.
Men. Fos. Wilt thou *ram* up thy porch-hold?
Marston and Barksted, Insatiate Countess, i.

A Ditch . . . was filled with some sound materials, and *ramm'd* to make the foundation solid.
Arbuthnot, Ancient Coins, p. 76.

4. To stuff as if with a ram; cram.

By the Lord, a buck-basket! *rammed* me in with foul shirts and smocks, socks, foul stockings, greasy napkins.
Shak., M. W. of W., iii. 5. 90.

They *ramme* in great piles of woode, which they lay very deep.
Coryat, Crudities, I. 206.

Do not bring your Æsop, your politician, unless you can *ram* up his mouth with cloves.
B. Jonson, Poetaster, iii. 1.

II. *intrans.* To beat or pound anything, in any of the transitive senses of *ram*.

So was it impossible that the wals of Iericho should fall downe, being neither vndermined nor yet *rammed* at with engines.
Hakluyt's Voyages, II. 134.

Finding that he could do no good by *ramming* with logs of timber, he set one of the gates on fire.
Bacon, Hist. Hen. VII.

With all the watchfulness and all the skill in the world, it would be futile to attempt to pass through the real ice-pack without a ship built for *ramming*.
Schley and Soley, Rescue of Greely, p. 160.

ram[3] (ram), *a.* [‹ Icel. *ramr*, strong (*ramliga*, strongly), = Sw. *ram*, strong, perfect, mere (*en ram bonde*, 'a perfect boor'), = Dan. *ram*, sharp, acrid, rank, mere (*ram jydsk*, 'pure Jutish').] 1. Strong; as a prefix, very: used as a prefix in *ramshackle*, *rambustious*, etc.—2. Strong-scented; stinking: as, *ram* as a fox. *Latham.*

Ramadan, Ramadhan (ram-a-dan'), *n.* [Also *Ramazan*, *Ramadzan*, and *Rhamazan*; = F. *ramazan*, *ramadan* = Sp. *ramadan* = Pg. *ramadan*, *remedão* = Turk. Pers. *ramazān*, ‹ Ar. *ramadān*, the name of the 9th month of the Moslem year, ‹ *ramed* (*ramad*), be heated or hot.] The ninth month of the Mohammedan year, and the period of the annual thirty days' fast or Mohammedan Lent, rigidly observed daily from dawn until sunset, when all restrictions are removed. The lunar reckoning of the Mohammedan calendar brings its recurrence about eleven days earlier each year, so that it passes through all the seasons successively in a cycle of about thirty-three years; but it is supposed that when it was named it was regularly one of the hot months, through lunisolar reckoning. The close of the fast is followed by the three days' feast called the *Lesser Bairam*.

ramage[1]† (ram'āj), *a.* and *n.* [I. *a.* ‹ ME. *ramage*, ‹ OF. *ramage*, of or belonging to branches, wild, rude, ‹ LL. **ramaticus*, of branches, ‹ L. *ramus*, a branch: see *ramus*. II. *n.* ‹ OF. *ramage*, branches, branching, song of birds on the branches, etc., ‹ LL. **ramaticum*, neut. of **ramaticus*, of branches: see I.] I. *a.* 1. Having left the nest and begun to sit upon the branches: said of birds.

A brancher, a *ramage* hawke.
Cotgrave.

Nor must you expect from high antiquity the distinctions of eyes and *ramage* hawks.
Sir T. Browne, Misc. Tracts, v.

Hence—2. Wild or savage; untamed.

Longe ye gan after hym abyde,
Cerching, enquering in wodes *ramage*,
A wilde swine chasing at that houred tyde.
Rom. of Partenay (E. E. T. S.), l. 527.

Ellis he is not wise ne sage,
No more than is a gote *ramage*.
Rom. of the Rose, l. 5384.

Yet if she were so tickle as ye would take no stand, so *ramage* as she would be reclaimed with no leave.
Greene, Gwydonius (1593). (*Halliwell.*)

Also *ramish*, *rammish*.

II. *n.* 1. The branching of trees or plants; branches collectively.—2. The warbling of birds among branches; bird-song.

When immelodious winds but made thee [a lute] move,
And birds their *ramage* did on thee bestow.
Drummond, Sonnets, ii. 10.

3. A branch of a pedigree; lineage; kindred. *Cotgrave.*—4. Courage. *Prompt. Parv.*, p. 422.

ramage[2]†, *n.* Same as *rummage*.

ramagious† (ra-mā'jus), *a.* [‹ ME. *ramagous*, *ramagious*, ‹ *ramage*, wild: see *ramage*[1].] Untamed; wild. *Coles*, 1717.

ramal (rā'mal), *a.* [‹ NL. **ramalis*, ‹ L. *ramus*, a branch: see *ramus*.] 1. In *bot.*, of or belonging to a branch; growing or originating on a branch; rameal.—2. In *anat.* and *zoöl.*, pertaining to a ramus; of the character of a ramus: as, the *ramal* part of the jaw-bone.

Ramalina (ram-a-lī'nä), *n.* [NL. (Acharius), ‹ L. *ramale*, twigs, shoots, ‹ *ramus*, a branch: see *ramus*.] A genus of crustaceous lichens of the tribe *Parmeliacei* and family *Usneei*. The thallus is fruticulose or finally pendulous, mostly compressed or at length subfoliaceous; the apothecia are scutelliform; the spores are ellipsoid or oblong, bilocular, and colorless. *R. scopulorum* furnishes a dye comparable with archil.

ramass† (ra-mas'), *v. t.* [‹ F. *ramasser*, bring together, gather, ‹ *re-*, again, + *amasser*, heap up: see *amass*.] To bring together; gather up; unite.

And when they have *ramast* many of several kindes and tastes, according to the appetite of those they treat, they open one vessel, and then another.
Comical Hist. of the World in the Moon (1659). (*Halliwell.*)

ramastrum† (ra-mas'trum), *n.*; pl. *ramastra* (-trä). [NL., ‹ L. *ramus*, a branch, + dim. *-aster*.] In *bot.*, one of the secondary petioles, or petiolules, of compound leaves. *Lindley.*

Ramayana (rä-mä'ya-nä), *n.* [Skt. *Rāmāyana*, ‹ *Rama* (see def.) + *ayana*, a going, course, progress, expedition, ‹ *i*, go: see *go*.] The name of one of the two great epic poems of ancient India, the other being the Mahabharata. It gives the history of Rama, especially of his expedition through the Deccan to Ceylon, to recover, by the aid of the monkey-god Hanuman, his wife Sita, carried away thither by Ravana.

rambade (ram'bād), *n.* [‹ F. *rambade*, "the bend or wale of a gally" (Cotgrave), also *rambate*; cf. Pg. *ar-rombada*, a platform of a galley.] *Naut.*, the elevated platform built across the prow of a galley for boarding, etc.

rambeh (ram'be), *n.* [Said to be connected with Malay *rambūtan*, ‹ *rambut*, hair: see *rambutan*.] The fruit of a middle-sized tree, *Baccaurea sapida*, of the *Euphorbiaceæ*, found in Malacca, Burma, etc. The fruit is globose, half an inch long, yellowish in color, several-celled, with a pleasant subacid pulp.

ramberge† (ram'bėrj), *n.* [Also *remberge*; ‹ OF. *ramberge*; origin obscure.] A long, narrow war-ship, swift and easily managed, formerly used on the Mediterranean.

By virtue thereof, through the retention of some aerial gusts, are the huge *ramberges*, mighty gallions, &c., launched from their stations.
Ozell, tr. of Rabelais, iii. 51. (*Nares.*)

ramble (ram'bl), *v. i.*; pret. and pp. *rambled*, ppr. *rambling*. [An altered form (with dissimilation of *mm* to *mb*) of dial. *rammle*, ‹ ME. **ramelen*, freq. of *ramen*, E. dial. *rame*, roam, ramble: see *roam*.] 1. To roam or wander about in a leisurely manner; go from point to point carelessly or irregularly; rove: as, to *ramble* about the city or over the country.

Bold Robin Hood he would *ramble* away.
Robin Hood and the Ranger (Child's Ballads, V. 207).

My first Entrance upon this *Rambling* kind of Life.
Dampier, Voyages, II., Pref.

2. To take a wavering or wandering course; proceed with irregular turns, windings, or transitions; show a lack of definite direction or arrangement: as, a *rambling* path or house;

a *rambling* discourse; the vine *rambles* every way; he *rambled* on in his incoherent speech.

> But wisdom does not lie in the *rambling* imaginations of men's minds. *Stillingfleet*, Sermons, I. ii.

> O'er his ample sides the *rambling* sprays
> Luxuriant shoot. *Thomson*, Spring, l. 794.

> Our home is a *rambling* old place, on the outskirts of a country town. *The Century*, XL. 278.

3. To reel; stagger. *Halliwell*. [Prov. Eng.] =**Syn.** 1. *Ramble, Stroll, Saunter, Rove, Roam, Wander, Range, Stray*. *Ramble*, by derivation, also *stroll* and *saunter*, and *stray* when used in this sense, express a less extended course than the others. To *ramble* or *stroll* is to go about, as fancy leads, for the pleasure of being abroad. To *saunter* is to go along idly, and therefore slowly. One may *saunter* or *stroll*, *stray* or *wander*, along one street as far as it goes. To *ramble*, *rove*, or *roam* is to pursue a course that is not very straight. One may *rove*, *roam*, or *wander* with some briskness or for some object, as in search of a lost child. One may *wander* about or *stray* about because he has lost his way. The wild beast *ranges*, *roves*, or *roams* in search of prey. *Roam* expresses most of definite purpose: as, to *roam* over Europe.

ramble (ram'bl), *n.* [< *ramble*, *v.*] 1. A roving or wandering movement; a going or turning about irregularly or indefinitely; especially, a leisurely or sauntering walk in varying directions.

> Coming home after a short Christmas *ramble*, I found a letter upon my table. *Swift*.

> In the middle of a brook, whose silver *ramble*
> Down twenty little falls, through reeds and bramble,
> Tracing along, it brought me to a cave.
> *Keats*, Endymion, i.

> On returning from our *ramble*, we passed the house of the Governor. *B. Taylor*, Lands of the Saracen, p. 57.

2. A place to ramble in; a mazy walk or tract. —3. In *coal-mining*, thin shaly beds of stone, taken down with the coal, above which a good roof may be met with. *Gresley*.

rambler (ram'blėr), *n.* [< *ramble*, *v.*, + *-er*1.] One who rambles; a rover; a wanderer.

> There is a pair of Stocks by every Watch house, to secure night *ramblers* in. *Dampier*, Voyages, II. i. 77.

rambling (ram'bling), *n.* [Verbal n. of *ramble*, *v.*] 1. The act of wandering about, or from place to place.

> *Rambling* makes little alteration in the mind, unless proper care be taken to improve it by the observations that are made. *Pococke*, Description of the East, II. ii. 277.

2. A roving excursion or course; an indefinite or whimsical turning back and forth.

> Thy money she will waste
> In the vain *ramblings* of a vulgar taste.
> *Crabbe*, Works, I. 73.

> And oft in *ramblings* on the wold . . .
> I saw the village lights below.
> *Tennyson*, Miller's Daughter.

ramblingly (ram'bling-li), *adv.* In a rambling manner.

ramboose†, ramboozet, *n.* See *rumbooze*.

ram-bow (ram'bou), *n.* A ship's bow of such construction that it may be efficiently used in ramming.

rambunctious (ram-bungk'shus), *a.* Same as *rambustious*. [Colloq., U. S.]

rambustious (ram-bus'tyus), *a.* [Also *rambunctious*; a slang term of no definite formation, as if < *ram*3 + *bust*2 + *-ious*. Cf. E. dial. *rumbustical*, *rumgumptious*, *rumbumptious*, etc., boisterous, slang forms of the same general type.] Boisterous; careless of the comfort of others; violent; arrogant. [Low.]

> And as for that black-whiskered alligator, . . . let me first get out of those *rambustious* unchristian filbert-shaped claws of his. *Bulwer*, My Novel, xi. 19.

rambutan, rambootan (ram-bö'tąn), *n.* [Also *rambostan*; < Malay *rambûtan*, so called in allusion to the villose covering of the fruit, < *rambut*, hair.] The fruit of *Nephelium lappaceum*, a lofty tree of the Malay archipelago. It is of an oval form, somewhat flattened, 2 inches long, of a reddish color, and covered with soft spines or hairs. The edible part is an aril, and is of a pleasant subacid taste. The tree is related to the lichi and longan, and is cultivated in numerous varieties.

ramby†, *a.* [ME.; cf. *ramp*.] Spirited; prancing; ramping (?).

> I salle be at journee with gentille knyghtes,
> On a *ramby* stede fulle jolyly graythide.
> *Morte Arthure* (E. E. T. S.), l. 373.

ram-cat (ram'kat), *n.* A tom-cat.

> Egad! old maids will presently be found
> Clapping their dead *ram-cats* in holy ground,
> And writing verses on each mousing devil.
> *Wolcot* (P. Pindar), Peter's Pension.

> *Ram-cat* is older than Peter. Smollett uses the word in his translation of Gil Blas: "They brought me a ragout made of *ram-cat*" (vol. i. ch. vii.).
> *N. and Q.*, 7th ser., V. 351.

ramé (ra-mā'), *a.* [OF. *rame*, branched, < L. **ramatus*, branched, < *ramus*, a branch: see *ramus*.] In *her.*, same as *attired*.

rameal (rā'mē-al), *a.* [< *rameous* + *-al*.] Growing upon or otherwise pertaining to a branch. Also *rameous*.

Ramean (rā'mę-an), *n.* [< *Ramée* or *Ramus* (see *Ramist*) + *-an*.] A Ramist.

ramed (rāmd), *a.* [Appar., with E. suffix *-ed*2, < F. *ramé*, pp. of *ramer*, prop, support (creeping plants), < *rame*, f., OF. *raim*, m., a branch, stake, F. dial. *rain*, *raime* = Pr. *ram*, *ramp* = It. *ramo*, < L. *ramus*, a branch: see *ramus*.] Noting a vessel on the stocks when all the frames are set upon the keel, the stem and stern-post put up, and the whole adjusted by the ram-line.

ramee, *n.* See *ramie*.

ramekin (ram'e-kin), *n.* [Also *rammekin*, *ramequin*; < F. *ramequin*, a sort of pastry made with cheese, < OFlem. *rammeken*, toasted bread.] Toasted cheese and bread, or toast and cheese; Welsh rabbit; also, bread-crumb baked in a pie-pan with a farce of cheese, eggs, and other ingredients. *E. Phillips*, 1706.

ramel†, *n.* See *rammel*.

ramellose (ram'el-ōs), *a.* [< *ramellus* + *-ose*.] In *algology*, bearing or characterized by ramelli. See *ramellus*.

> Fasciculi of extreme branches densely *ramellose*.
> *H. C. Wood*, Fresh-Water Algæ, p. 207.

ramellus (rą-mel'us), *n.*; pl. *ramelli* (-ī). [NL., dim. of L. *ramus*, a branch: see *ramus*, *ramulus*.] In *algology*, a ramulus, or, more specifically, a branch smaller and simpler than a ramulus, occurring at the growing tip.

rament (rą-ment'), *n.* [< L. *ramentum*, usually in pl. *ramenta*, scrapings, shavings, chips, scales, bits, < *radere*, scrape, shave: see *rase*1, *raze*1.] 1. A scraping; shaving.—2. In *bot.*, same as *ramentum*. [Rare.]

ramentaceous (ram-en-tā'shius), *a.* [< *rament* + *-aceous*.] In *bot.*, covered with ramenta.

ramentum (rą-men'tum), *n.*; pl. *ramenta* (-tą). [NL.: see *rament*.] 1. Same as *rament*, 1.—2. In *bot.*, a thin, chaffy scale or outgrowth from the epidermis, sometimes appearing in great abundance on young shoots, and particularly well developed on the stalks of many ferns: same as *palea* (which see for cut).

rameous (rā'mę-us), *a.* [< L. *rameus*, of or belonging to boughs or branches, < *ramus*, a branch: see *ramus*. Cf. *ramous*, *ramose*.] Same as *rameal*.

ramequin†, *n.* See *ramekin*.

Rameside (ram'e-sid), *a.* and *n.* [< *Rameses* + *-ide*2.] I. *a.* Pertaining or relating to any of the ancient Egyptian kings named Rameses or Ramses, or to their families or government. The principal kings of the name were Rameses II. of the nineteenth dynasty and Rameses III. of the twentieth.

II. *n.* A member of the line or the family of Rameside kings.

ramfeezle (ram-fē'zl), *v. t.*; pret. and pp. *ramfeezled*, ppr. *ramfeezling*. [Appar. < *ram*3 + *feeze*.] To fatigue; exhaust. [Scotch.]

> My awkward muse sair pleads and begs
> I would na write.
> The tapetless *ramfeezl'd* hizzie,
> She's saft at best, and something lazy.
> *Burns*, Second Epistle to John Lapraik.

ram-goat (ram'gōt), *n.* A low, tortuous, leafy shrub, *Xanthoxylum spinifex* (*Fagara microphyllum*), found on arid shores in the West Indies and South America.

ramgunshock (ram-gun'shok), *a.* [Also *ramgunshoch*, *rangunshock*, rugged; origin obscure.] Rough; rugged. [Scotch.]

> Our *ramgunshock*, glum gudeman
> Is out and owre the water.
> *Burns*, Had I the Wyte.

ram-head (ram'hed), *n.* 1. An iron lever for raising up great stones.—2†. *Naut.*, a halyard-block.—3†. A cuckold.

> To be called *ram-head* is a title of honour, and a name proper to all men. *John Taylor*.

ram-headed (ram'hed″ed), *a.* Represented with the head of a ram, as a sphinx; furnished with ram's horns, as a sphinx's head; criocephalous (which see).

rami, *n.* Plural of *ramus*.

ramicorn (rā'mi-kôrn), *n.* and *a.* [< NL. *ramicornis*, < L. *ramus*, a branch, + *cornu*, horn.] I. *n.* In *ornith.*, the horny sheath of the side of the lower mandible, in any way distinguished from that covering the rest of the bill.

> The *ramicorn*, which covers the sides of the rami of the lower mandible. *Coues*, Proc. Phila. Acad. (1866), p. 276.

II. *a.* In *entom.*, having ramified antennæ, as a hemipterous insect; pertaining to the *Ramicornes*.

ramicorneous (rā-mi-kôr'nę-us), *a.* [< *ramicorn* + *-eous*.] Of or pertaining to the ramicorn.

Ramicornes (rā-mi-kôr'nēz), *n. pl.* [NL., pl. of *ramicornis*: see *ramicorn*.] In *entom.*, a group of hemipterous insects, having ramified antennæ. See *ramose*.

ramie (ram'ē), *n.* [Also *ramee*; Malay.] A plant, the so-called China grass, *Bœhmeria nivea*, or its fiber. The plant is a perennial shrub with herbaceous shoots, native in the Malay islands, China, and Japan. It has long been cultivated in parts of the East Indies to supply fiber for fish-nets and cloths, and in China and Japan textiles of great beauty are made from this material. (See *grass-cloth*.) In length, thickness, and woodiness the stems most nearly resemble hemp. The fiber is unsurpassed in strength, is in an exceptional degree unaffected by moisture, in fineness rivals flax, and has a silky luster shared only by jute. The plant can be grown in any moderate climate—in the southern United States and as far north as New Jersey, as demonstrated by experiment. Also called *cambric-grass*, *silk-grass*, and *ramie-hemp*; in India, *rhea*. See cut under *Bœhmeria*.

ramie-fiber (ram'ē-fī″bėr), *n.* See *ramie*.

ramie-plant (ram'ē-plant), *n.* See *ramie*.

ramification (ram″i-fi-kā'shǫn), *n.* [= F. *ramification* = Sp. *ramificacion* = Pg. *ramificação* = It. *ramificazione*, < ML. **ramificatio(n-)*, < *ramificare*, ramify: see *ramify*.] 1. The act or process of ramifying, or the state of being ramified; a branching out; division into branches, or into divergent lines, courses, or parts, as of trees or plants, blood-vessels, a mountain-chain, a topic or subject, etc.—2. The manner or result of ramifying or branching; that which is ramified or divided into branches; a set of branches: as, the *ramification* of a coral; the *ramifications* of an artery or a nerve; the *ramifications* of the capillaries, or of nerves in an insect's wing. See cuts under *Dendrocœla* and *embryo*.

> Infinite vascular *ramifications*, . . . revealed only by the aid of the highest powers of the microscope.
> *Is. Taylor*.

3. In *bot.*, the branching, or the manner of branching, of stems and roots.—4. One of the branches or divergent lines or parts into which anything is divided; a division or subdivision springing or derived from a main stem or source: as, the *ramifications* of a conspiracy; to pursue a subject in all its *ramifications*.

> When the radical idea branches out into parallel *ramifications*, how can a consecutive series be formed of senses in their nature collateral? *Johnson*, Eng. Dict., Pref.

5. The production of figures resembling branches.—**Point of ramification**, in the *integral calculus*, a point on the plane of imaginary quantity where two or more values of the function become equal. Also called *critical point*.

ramified (ram'i-fid), *a.* In *zoöl.* and *anat.*, branched; having branches; dividing and redividing: as, *ramified* nervures of the wings.—**Ramified corpuscle**, a lacuna of bone, having long slender processes which ramify and inosculate with those of other lacunæ; an ordinary bone-cell.

ramiflorous (rā-mi-flō'rus), *a.* [< L. *ramus*, branch, + *flos* (*flor-*), flower.] Flowering on the branches. *Gray*.

ramiform (rā'mi-fôrm), *a.* [= F. *ramiforme*, < L. *ramus*, a branch, + *forma*, form.] In *bot.* and *zoöl.*, resembling a branch. *Henslow*.

ramify (ram'i-fī), *v.*; pret. and pp. *ramified*, ppr. *ramifying*. [< F. *ramifier* = Pr. Sp. Pg. *ramificar* = It. *ramificare*, < ML. **ramificare* (in pp. *ramificatus*), branch, ramify, < L. *ramus*, a branch (see *ramus*), + *-ficare*, < *facere*, make.] I. *intrans.* 1. To form branches; shoot into branches, as the stem of a plant, or anything analogous to it; branch out.

> When they [asparagus-plants] are older, and begin to *ramify*, they lose this quality. *Arbuthnot*, Aliments, p. 61.

> The "test" has a single round orifice, from which, when the animal is in a state of activity, the sarcodic substance streams forth, speedily giving off *ramifying* extensions.
> *W. B. Carpenter*, Micros., § 397.

2. To diverge in various ways or to different points; stretch out in different lines or courses; radiate.

> The establishments of our large carriers *ramify* throughout the whole kingdom. *H. Spencer*, Social Statics, p. 441.

II. *trans.* To divide into branches or parts; extend in different lines or directions.

> Whoever considers the few radical positions which the Scriptures afforded him will wonder by what energetic operations he expanded them to such an extent, and *ramified* them to so much variety. *Johnson*, Milton.

> It is also infinitely *ramified*, diversified, extending everywhere, and touching everything.
> *D. Webster*, Speech, March 18, 1834.

Ramilie (ram'i-lē), *n.* [< *Ramillies*: see def.] A name given to various articles or modes of dress, in commemoration of Marlborough's victory at Ramillies in Belgium over the French under Villeroi, in 1706: chiefly used attributively. The Ramilie hat was a form of cocked hat worn in the time of George I. Its peculiarity consisted in the adjustment of the hat-brim—apparently the one in which the three cocks are nearly equal in length and similar in arrangement. The Ramilie wig, worn as late as the time of George III., had a long, gradually diminishing plait, called the Ramilie plait or tail, with a very large bow at the top and a smaller one at the bottom.

A peculiar-shaped hat was known as the "*Ramilie* cock."
N. and Q., 6th ser., XII. 35.

While in this country, the natural hair tied in a pig-tail and powdered passed for as good as the *Ramilie* wig and *Ramilie* tail. *S. Dowell*, Taxes in England, III. 290.

ramiparous (rā-mip'a-rus), *a.* [< L. *ramus*, a branch, + *parere*, produce.] Producing branches.

ramish†, *a.* [A corruption of *ramage*[1].] Same as *ramage*[1].

The plaintiff had declared for a *ramish* hawk, which is a hawk living inter ramos (amongst the boughs), and by consequence feræ naturæ.
Nelson, Laws Conc. Game, p. 151. (*Encyc. Dict.*)

Ramism (rā'mizm), *n.* [< *Ramus* (see def.) + *-ism.*] The logical doctrine of Petrus Ramus, or Pierre de la Ramée (born in Picardy, 1515; massacred on St. Bartholomew's day, 1572). The doctrine was that of Aristotle, with the omission of the more difficult and metaphysical parts, and with a few additions drawn from rhetoric and from Platonic sources (such as the doctrine of dichotomy). It was characterized by simplicity and good sense, and was set forth with some literary skill. It attracted considerable attention, owing to the unbounded hostility to Aristotle professed by Ramus, and was taught for many years in the Scottish universities and at Cambridge. John Milton wrote a Ramist logic.

In England, Cambridge alone, always disposed to reject the authority of Aristotle, and generally more open to new ideas than the sister university, was a stronghold of *Ramism*. *R. Adamson*, Encyc. Brit., XIV. 803.

Ramist (rā'mist), *n.* and *a.* [< F. *ramiste*, a Ramist, pertaining to Ramus, < *Ramus* (see *Ramism*).] **I.** *n.* A follower of Peter Ramus. See *Ramism*. The main position of Ramus was that "everything that Aristotle taught was false," but there was nothing original in his writings. He introduced into logic the dilemma, which had always been taught as a part of rhetoric, to which he greatly inclined.

II. *a.* Pertaining to Ramus or Ramism; characterized by or characteristic of Ramism.—**Ramist consonants** (French *consonnes ramistes*), the letters *j* and *v*: so called by French writers, because Ramus was the first, in his grammatical writings, to distinguish them as consonants from the vowels *i* and *u*.

ram-line (ram'līn), *n.* [< *ram* (?) (see *ramed*) + *line*[2].] 1. In *ship-building*, a small rope or line used for setting the frames fair, assisting in forming the sheer of the ship, or for other similar purposes.—2. In *spar-making*, a line used to make a straight middle line on a spar.

rammed (ramd), *a.* [Pp. of *ram*[2], *v.*] Excessive. *Halliwell.* [Prov. Eng.]

rammekin†, *n.* See *ramekin*.

rammel (ram'el), *n.* [Also *ramell*, *ramel*; < late ME. *ramel*, rubbish, < OF. *ramaille*, *ramille*, usually in pl. *ramailles*, *ramilles*, F. *ramilles*, branches, twigs, < LL. *ramale*, usually in pl. *ramalia*, branches, twigs, sticks, < L. *ramus*, a branch: see *ramus*.] 1. Refuse wood, as of twigs or small branches, or decayed woody matter.

Rubbish, *rammel*, and broken stones. *Holland.*

2. Rubbish, especially bricklayers' rubbish.

The Pictes ridding away the earth and *ramell* wherewith it was closed up.
Holinshed, Hist. Scot., M. b, col. 1, c. (*Nares.*)

[Obsolete or prov. Eng. in both senses.]

rammel† (ram'el), *v. i.* [< *rammel*, *n.*] To turn to rubbish; molder.

Franare [It.], . . . to *rammell* or moulder in pieces, as sometimes mud walles or great masses of stone will doe of themselves.
Florio (1611), p. 195.

rammelsbergite (ram'elz-bėrg-īt), *n.* [After K. F. *Rammelsberg* (born 1813), a German chemist.] An arsenide of nickel, like chloanthite in composition, but crystallizing in the orthorhombic system.

rammel-wood† (ram'el-wůd), *n.* Natural copsewood.

There growyth many allers and other *ramell-wood*, which servethe muche for the buyldinge of suche small houses.
MS. Cotton. Calig. B. viii. (*Halliwell.*)

Rammers.
a, wooden rammer, with iron band or hoop; *b*, *c*, paving-rammers—*b* being used to compact sand, and *c* for cobblestones, etc.

rammer (ram'ėr), *n.* [= G. *rammer*; as *ram*[2], *v.*, + *-er*[1].] An instrument for ramming, or driving by impact. The pavers' rammer, used in settling stones or compacting earth, is a heavy mass of iron-bound wood, of tapering form, with handles at the top and on one or both sides. (See *beetle*[1], 1.) Founders' rammers are made in different ways, for various purposes, as forcing the sand into the pattern, solidifying it in the flask, etc. A gunners' rammer is a staff with a cylindrical head, for driving home the charge in a cannon, usually having for field-artillery a swab (called a *sponge*) at the other end for cleaning out the gun after firing. Ramrods, and some kinds of ram, as that of a ship of war, are also sometimes called *rammers*. See *ram*[2], 2, and *ramrod*; see also cut in preceding column, and cut under *gun-carriage*.

The earth is to bee wel driven and beaten downe close with a *rammer*, that it may be fast about the roots.
Holland, tr. of Pliny, xvii. 11.

rammish[1] (ram'ish), *a.* [< ME. *rammish*; < *ram*[1] + *-ish*[1].] Resembling or characteristic of a ram; rammy; strong-scented; hence, coarse; lewd; lascivious: used like *goatish* in the same sense. Compare *hircine*.

For al the world, they stinken as a goot:
Her savour is so *rammish* and so hoot,
That though a man from hem a myle be,
The savour wol infecte him, trusteth me.
Chaucer, Prol. to Canon's Yeoman's Tale, l. 334.

Whose father being a *rammish* ploughman, himself a perfumed gentleman. *Middleton*, Phœnix, i. 2.

rammish[2]**†** (ram'ish), *a.* Same as *ramage*[1].

rammishness (ram'ish-nes), *n.* [< *rammish*[1] + *-ness.*] The state or character of being rammish.

rammy (ram'i), *a.* [< *ram*[1] + *-y*[1].] Like a ram; rammish.

Galen takes exception at mutton, but without question he means that *rammy* mutton which is in Turkie and Asia Minor. *Burton*, Anat. of Mel., ii. § 2.

ramollescence (ram-o-les'ens), *n.* [< F. *ramollir*, soften, refl. become soft (< *re-*, again, + *amollir*, soften: see *amollish*), + *-escence*. Cf. L. *remollescere*, become soft again, become soft.] A softening or mollifying; mollification. *Imp. Dict.* [Rare.]

ramollissement (ra-mo-lēs'moṅ), *n.* [< F. *ramollissement*, < *ramollir*, soften, become soft: see *ramollescence*.] In *pathol.*, a morbid condition of some part of the body, as the brain or the liver, in which it becomes softened.

ramoon (ra-mön'), *n.* [< Sp. *ramon*, the top of branches cut as food for sheep in snowy weather (= F. *ramon*, a broom of twigs or branches), < *ramo*, < L. *ramus*, a branch: see *ramus*.] A low West Indian tree, *Trophis Americana*, belonging to the mulberry tribe, with milky juice and drupe-like fruit. Its leaves and twigs are sometimes fed to cattle.

ramose (rā'mōs), *a.* [< L. *ramosus*, full of branches: see *ramous*.] 1. Same as *ramous*.—2. In *zoöl.*: (*a*) Branching; much-branched; ramifying frequently, as corals and other zoöphytes; ramous. (*b*) Resembling a branch or branches; shooting out like a branch: as, the *ramose* spines of some shells.—**Ramose antennæ**, antennæ in which the joints are rather long, a few of them emitting from the base or apex—generally on the outer side, rarely on both sides—long cylindrical processes or branches.

ramosely (rā'mōs-li), *adv.* In a ramose or branching manner. *H. C. Wood*, Fresh-Water Algæ, p. 21.

ramous (rā'mus), *a.* [< F. *rameux* = Pr. *ramos* = Sp. Pg. It. *ramoso*, < L. *ramosus*, full of branches, < *ramus*, a branch: see *ramus*.] Branched or branchy, or full of branches; having branches, or divisions of the character of branches; ramifying; ramose.

Which vast contraction and expansion seems unintelligible, by feigning the particles of air to be springy and *ramous*. *Newton*, Opticks, iii. query 31.

A *ramous* efflorescence of a fine white spar found hanging from a crust of like spar, at the top of an old wrought cavern. *Woodward*, Fossils.

ramp (ramp), *v.* [Also *romp* (now partly differenced in use: see *romp*); < ME. *rampen*, < OF. *ramper*, *raumper*, creep, crawl, also climb, F. *ramper*, creep, crawl, cringe (cf. *rampe*, a flight of stairs (> G. *rampe*), = It. *rampare*, clutch (*rampa*, a claw, a grip, *rampo*, a grappling-iron), a nasalized form of **rappare*, in comp. *ar-rappare*, = Pr. Sp. Pg. *rapar*, snatch up, carry off, seize upon; of Teut. origin: LG. *rappen*, *rapen*, snatch up hastily; Bavar. dial. *rampfen*, G. *raffen*, snatch, etc.: see *rap*[2], *rape*[2], *raff*.] **I.** *intrans.* 1. To rise by climbing or shooting up, as a plant; run or grow up rapidly; spring up in growth.

Some Sorts of Plants . . . are either endued with a Faculty of twining about others that are near, or else furnish'd with Claspers and Tendrils, whereby . . . they catch Hold of them, and so *ramping* upon Trees, Shrubs, Hedges or Poles, they mount up to a great Height.
Ray, Works of Creation, p. 111.

Trees of every sort
On three sides, slender, spreading, long and short;
Each grew as it contrived, the poplar *ramped*,
The fig-tree reared itself. *Browning*, Sordello.

2. To rise for a leap or in leaping, as a wild beast; rear or spring up; prepare for or make a spring; jump violently. See *rampant*.

Tho, rearing up his former feete on hight,
He *rampt* upon him with his ravenous pawes.
Spenser, F. Q., VI. xii. 29.

Surely the Prelates would have Saint Paul's words *rampe* one over another, as they use to clime into their Livings and Bishopricks. *Milton*, On Def. of Humb. Remonst.

Thither I climb'd at dawn
And stood by her garden-gate;
A lion *ramps* at the top,
He is claspt by a passion-flower.
Tennyson, Maud, xiv. 1.

3. To move with violent leaps or starts; jump or dash about; hence, to act passionately or violently; rage; storm; behave with insolence.

Whan she comth hoom, she *rampeth* in my face,
And cryeth, "False coward, wreck thy wyf."
Chaucer, Prol. to Monk's Tale, l. 16.

The Gov[r], hearing y[e] tumulte, sent to quiet it, but he *ramped* more like a furious beast then a man.
Bradford, Plymouth Plantation, p. 174.

For the East Lynn (which is our river) was *ramping* and roaring frightfully.
R. D. Blackmore, Lorna Doone, xlviii.

4. To spring about or along gaily; frolic; gambol; flirt; romp. See *romp*.

Good wenches would not so *rampe* abrode ydelly.
Udall, Roister Doister, ii. 4.

Then the wild boar, being so stout and strong, . . .
Thrashed down the trees as he *ramped* him along.
Jovial Hunter of Bromsgrove (Child's Ballads, VIII. 146).

Peace, you foul *ramping* jade!
B. Jonson, Bartholomew Fair, iv. 3.

[This verb, although still employed in literature, is not common in colloquial use.]

II. *trans.* 1. To hustle; rob with violence. [Thieves' slang.]—2. To bend upward, as a piece of iron, to adapt it to the woodwork of a gate or the like. *Halliwell.*

Mr. R. Phipps is introducing at Campbell Road, Bow, Messrs. Parkin and Webb's patent *ramped* wheel tire.
The Engineer, LXVIII. 535.

To ramp and reavel, to get (anything) by fair means or foul. *Halliwell.*

ramp (ramp), *n.* [< ME. *rampe*; < *ramp*, *v.* Cf. *romp*, *n.*] 1. A leap; a spring; a bound. [Obsolete or archaic.]

The bold Ascalonite
Fled from his lion *ramp*. *Milton*, S. A., l. 139.

2. A rising passage or road; specifically (*milit.*), a gradual slope or ascent from the interior level of a fortification to the general level behind the parapet.

The ascent is by easy *ramps*.
B. Taylor, Lands of the Saracen, p. 400.

We crossed literally a *ramp* of dead bodies loosely covered with earth. *W. H. Russell*, Diary in India, I. 312.

3. In *masonry* and *carp.*, a concave bend or slope in the cap or upper member of any piece of ascending or descending workmanship, as in the coping of a wall; the concave sweep that connects the higher and lower parts of a railing at a half- or quarter-pace.—4. In *arch.*, etc., any slope or inclined plane, particularly an inclined plane affording communication between a higher and a lower level.

In some parts [of the temple at Khorsabad] even the parapet of the *ramp* still remains in situ.
J. Fergusson, Hist. Arch., I. 154.

5†. A coarse, frolicsome woman; a jade; a romp.

Nay, fy on thee, thou *rampe*, thou ryg, with al that take thy part. *Bp. Still*, Gammer Gurton's Needle, iii. 3.

Although that she were a lusty bouncing *rampe*, somewhat like Gallimetta, or Maid Marian. *G. Harvey.*

The bouncing *ramp*, that roaring girl my mistress.
Middleton and Dekker, Roaring Girl, iii. 3.

6. The garden rampion, or its root.—7†. A highwayman; a robber. *Halliwell.*—8. In the game of pin-pool, a stroke by which all the pins but the center one are knocked down. A player making a ramp at any stage of the game wins the pool.—**Ramp and twist**, in *carp.*, any line that rises and winds simultaneously.

ramp† (ramp), *a.* [< *ramp*, *v.*] Ramping; leaping; furiously swift or rushing.

Ride out, ride out, ye *ramp* rider!
Your steed 's baith stout and strang.
The Broom of Cowdenknows (Child's Ballads, IV. 46).

rampacious (ram-pā'shus), *a.* [A var. of *rampageous*, prob. confused with *rapacious*.] Same as *rampageous*. [Colloq.]

A stone statue of some *rampacious* animal with flowing mane and tail, distantly resembling an insane cart-horse.
Dickens, Pickwick, xxii.

rampadgeon (ram-pā'jọn), *n.* [< *rampage-ous* + *-on*.] A furious, boisterous, or quarrelsome fellow. *Halliwell.* [Prov. Eng.]

rampage (ram'pāj or ram-pāj'), *n.* [< *ramp* + *-age*.] A leaping or jumping about, as from anger or excitement; violent or furious movement; excited action of any kind: as, to be on the *rampage;* to go on a *rampage.* [Colloq.]

She's been on the *ram-page* this last spell about five minutes. *Dickens*, Great Expectations, ii.

A diplomatist like Prince Bismarck, possessed of that faculty of plain speech, and out for the time on the *rampage*, seems to Continental Courts a terror.
Spectator (London), June 28, 1890.

rampage (ram'pāj or ram-pāj'), *v. i.*; pret. and pp. *rampaged*, ppr. *rampaging.* [Also (Sc.) *rampauge;* < *rampage, n.*] 1. To act or move in a ramping manner; spring or rush violently; rage or storm about. [Colloq.]

Were I best go to finish the revel at the Griffin? But then Maudie will *rampauge* on my return.
Scott, Fair Maid of Perth, xvi.

Now we will see how these *rampaging* Hurons lived when outlying in ambushments.
J. F. Cooper, Last of Mohicans, xii.

2. To run or prance about; move springily or friskily; romp; riot. [Colloq.]

An' they *rampaged* about [on horseback] wi' their grooms, and was 'untin' arter the men.
Tennyson, Village Wife, vii.

How do you propose to go *rampaging* all over Scotland, and still be at Oban on the fifteenth?
W. Black, Princess of Thule, xxvii.

rampageous (ram-pā'jus), *a.* [Also *rampagious* (and *rampacious*, q. v.); < *rampage* + *-ous*.] 1. Of a ramping character; behaving rampantly; unruly; raging; boisterous; stormy. [Colloq.]

The farmers and country folk [had] no cause to drive in their herds and flocks as in the primitive ages of a *rampageous* antiquity. *Galt*, Provost, xv. (*Davies.*)

A lion—a mighty, conquering, generous, *rampageous* Leo Belgicus.
Thackeray, Roundabout Papers, A Week's Holiday.

There's that Will Maskery, sir, as is the *rampageousest* Methodis as can be. *George Eliot*, Adam Bede, v.

Hence—2. Glaring or "loud" in style or taste; "stunning." [Colloq.]

There comes along a missionary, . . . with a *rampagious* gingham.
Daily Telegraph, Oct. 6, 1885. (*Encyc. Dict.*)

The ornamentation is for the most part in *rampageous* rocaille style, bright burnished gold on whitewash or white imitation marble. *Harper's Mag.*, LXXIX. 200.

rampageousness (ram-pā'jus-nes), *n.* The character of being rampageous. [Colloq.]

One there is, a lover-cousin, who out-Herods every one else in *rampagiousness* and lack of manners.
Athenæum, No. 3249, p. 145.

rampair†, *v. t.* [< F. *remparer*, fortify, inclose with a rampart: see *rampire, rampart.*] To make secure; intrench; shield; cover.

Theyr frame is rayned of excedynge hyghe trees, sette close together and fast *rampaired* in the grounde, so standyng a slope and bending inward that the toppes of the trees ioyne together.
Peter Martyr (tr. in Eden's First Books on America, [ed. Arber, p. 68).

rampallian†, rampallion† (ram-pal'yan, -yọn), *n.* [< *ramp* + *-allian, -allion*, a vague termination of contempt, as in *rapscallion, rumgallion.*] Rapscallion; villain; rascal: a vituperative word.

Away, you scullion! you *rampallian*, you fustilarian!
Shak., 2 Hen. IV., ii. 1. 65.

Out upon them, *rampallions!* I'll keep myself safe enough out of their fingers.
Beau. and Fl., Honest Man's Fortune, ii. 2.

I was almost strangled with my own band by twa *rampallians*, wha wanted yestreen . . . to harle me into a change-house. *Scott*, Fortunes of Nigel, xxvi.

rampancy (ram'pạn-si), *n.* [< *rampan(t)* + *-cy*.] The state or quality of being rampant; excessive activity; exuberance; extravagance.

The pope had over mastered all, the temporall power being quite in a manner evacuated by the *rampancy* of the spiritual. *Dr. H. More*, Epistles to the Seven Churches, Pref.

This height and *rampancy* of vice. *South.*

rampant (ram'pạnt), *a.* [< ME. **rampant*, also *rampand, rampend*, < OF. *rampant*, ppr. of *ramper*, creep, climb: see *ramp.*] 1. Climbing or springing unchecked; rank in growth; exuberant: as, *rampant* weeds.

The cactus is here very abundant and *rampant*.
C. D. Warner, Roundabout Journey, p. 95.

2. Overleaping restraint or usual limits; unbridled; unrestricted.

He is tragicall on the Stage, but *rampant* in the Tyring-house, and sweares oathes there which he neuer con'd.
Bp. Earle, Micro-cosmographie, A Player.

The custom of street-hawking is *rampant* in Spain.
Lathrop, Spanish Vistas, p. 10.

Happily the love of red rags which is so *rampant* on either side of Parenzo, at Trieste and at Zara, seems not to have spread to Parenzo itself.
E. A. Freeman, Venice, p. 104.

The style of the pulpit in respect of imagery, I conceive, should be grave, severe, intense, not luxuriant, not *rampant*. *A. Phelps*, English Style, p. 144.

They were going together to the Doncaster spring meeting, where Bohemianism would be *rampant*.
Miss Braddon, Only a Clod, xxvi.

3. Ramping; rearing.

The tawny lion . . . springs, as broke from bonds,
And *rampant* shakes his brinded mane.
Milton, P. L., vii. 466.

When he chaseth and followeth after other beasts, hee goeth alwaies saltant or *rampant;* which he neuer useth to doe when he is chased in sight, but is onely passant.
Holland, tr. of Pliny, viii. 16.

4. In *her.*, rising with both fore legs elevated, the dexter uppermost, and the head seen sidewise, the dexter hind leg also higher than the sinister, as if the weight of the creature were borne upon the latter: noting a lion or other beast of prey. Also *ramping, effrayé.* See also cut under *affronté.*

Lion Rampant.

Old Nevil's crest,
The *rampant* bear chain'd to the ragged staff.
Shak., 2 Hen. VI., v. 1. 203.

Rampant affronté, rampant combatant. See *counter-rampant.*—**Rampant arch**, in *arch.*, an arch whose imposts or abutments are not on the same level.—**Rampant bandage**, a bandage applied in such a manner that the turns of the spiral do not touch each other, but leave uncovered spaces between.—**Rampant displayed**, in *her.*, facing directly out from the shield and seated on the haunches or raised erect on the hind legs, the fore paws extended: noting a lion or other beast of prey.—**Rampant gardant**, in *her.*, having the same attitude as in rampant, but with the head turned so as to look directly out from the shield—that is, affronté.—**Rampant indorsed.** See *counter-rampant.*—**Rampant in full aspect.** Same as *rampant displayed.*—**Rampant passant**, said of an animal when walking with the dexter fore paw raised somewhat higher than the mere passant position.—**Rampant regardant**, in *her.*, rampant, but with the head turned round, so that the creature looks in the direction of its tail.—**Rampant sejant**, in *her.*, seated on the hind quarters, but with the fore paws raised, the dexter above.—**Rampant vault.** See *vault.*

Rampant Arches.
a, grand staircase of the Nouvel Opéra, Paris; *b*, crowning arcade in façade of Sta. Maria del Orto, Venice.

rampantly (ram'pạnt-li), *adv.* In a rampant manner.

rampart (ram'pärt), *n.* [Early mod. E. also *rampar, ramper, rampare, rampire, rampier;* < OF. *rempart* (with excrescent *t*), *rempar* (F. *rempart*), a rampart of a fort, < *remparer*, defend, fortify, inclose with a rampart (F. *remparer*, refl., fortify oneself), < *re-*, again, + *emparer*, defend, fortify, surround, seize, take possession of (F. *emparer*, seize, take possession of), < *en-* + *parer*, defend: see *pare*[1], *parry*. Cf. It. *riparo* (= Pg. *reparo*), a defense, < *riparare*, defend, = Pg. *reparar*, repair, shelter: see *repair*[1]. Cf. *parapet*, which contains the same ult. verb.] 1. In *fort.*, an elevation or mound of earth round a place, capable of resisting cannon-shot, and having the parapet raised upon it; a protecting enceinte; also, this elevation together with the parapet. The rampart is built of the earth taken out of the ditch, but the lower part of the outer slope is usually constructed of masonry. The top of the rampart behind the parapet should have sufficient width for the free passage of troops, guns, etc. See cut under *parapet.*

Thrice . . . did he set up his banner upon the *rampier* of the enemy. *Sir P. Sidney*, Arcadia, iii.

When bands
Of pioneers, with spade and pickaxe arm'd,
Forerun the royal camp, to trench a field,
Or cast a *rampart*. *Milton*, P. L., i. 678.

The term *rampart*, though strictly meaning the mound on which the parapet stands, generally includes the parapet itself.
Brande and Cox, Dict. of Sci., Lit., and Art, III. 205.

Hence—2. Something that serves as a bulwark or defense; an obstruction against approach or intrusion; a protecting inclosure.

What *rampire* can my human frailty raise
Against the assault of fate?
Fletcher (and Massinger ?), Lovers' Progress, iv. 2.

At length they reached an open level, encompassed on all sides by a natural *rampart* of rocks.
Prescott, Ferd. and Isa., ii. 7.

Rampart gun. See *gun*[1].=**Syn.** See *fortification.*

rampart (ram'pärt), *v. t.* [Formerly also *rampire, ramper;* < *rampart, rampire, n.*] To fortify with ramparts; protect by or as if by a rampart; bolster; strengthen.

Set but thy foot
Against our *rampired* gates, and they shall ope.
Shak., T. of A., v. 4. 47.

Those grassy hills, those glittering dells,
Proudly *ramparted* with rocks.
Coleridge, Ode to the Departing Year, vii.

'Neath *rampired* Solidor pleasant riding on the Rance!
Browning, Hervé Riel.

rampart-grenade (ram'pärt-grẹ-nād'), *n.* See *grenade.*

rampart-slope (ram'pärt-slōp), *n.* In *fort.*, the slope which terminates the rampart on the interior, connecting the terre-plein with the parade; the ramp or talus.

rampet, *v.* and *n.* An obsolete form of *ramp.*

ramper[1] (ram'pėr), *n.* 1. An obsolete or dialectal form of *rampart.*—2. A turnpike road. *Halliwell.* [Prov. Eng.]

ramper[2] (ram'pėr), *n.* [< *ramp* + *-er*[1].] A ruffian who infests race-courses. [Slang.] *Encyc. Dict.*

ramph-. For words beginning thus, see *rhamph-.*

rampick, rampike (ram'pik, ram'pīk), *n.* [Formerly also *ranpick, ranpike;* appar. < *ran-* (identified by some with *ran-* in *ran-tree, roan-tree*, mountain-ash (cf. *rantle-tree*)) + *pick*[1] or *pike*[1].] A tree having dead boughs standing out of its top; any dead tree: also used attributively (in this use also *rampicked*). [Old and prov. Eng.; U. S. and New Brunswick, in the form *rampike.*]

When their fleeces gin to waxen rough,
He combes and trims them with a *rampicke* bough.
The Affectionate Shepheard (1594). (*Halliwell.*)

The aged *ranpick* trunk where plow-men cast their seed.
Drayton, Polyolbion, ii. 205.

The march of the fire was marked next morning by . . . hundreds of blackened trees which would never bud again. The sight of these bare and lifeless poles is a common one here; the poles are termed *ram-pikes.*
W. F. Rae, Newfoundland to Manitoba, iii.

rampicked (ram'pikt), *a.* [< *rampick* + *-ed*[2].] See *rampick.*

According to Wilbraham, a *rampicked* tree is a stag-headed tree, i. e. like an overgrown oak, having the stumps of boughs standing out of its top. *Halliwell.*

rampier†, *n.* An obsolete form of *rampart.*

rampike, *n.* See *rampick.*

ramping (ram'ping), *p. a.* In *her.*, same as *rampant*, 4.

rampion (ram'pi-ọn), *n.* [Appar. corrupted from It. *ramponzolo, raperonzolo, raperonzo* = Sp. *reponche, ruiponce* = Pg. *raponto, ruiponto* = OF. *raiponce, reponce, raiponse* = LG. *rapunsje* = G. *rapunzel* = Sw. Dan. *rapunzel* (ML. *rapuncium*), a plant, the *Campanula Rapunculus*, also the *Phyteuma spicatum*, < ML. *rapunculus*, dim. of L. *rapa, rapum*, a turnip: see *rape*[3]. For the form, cf. Sp. *rampion*, a species of lobelia.] 1. One of the bellflowers, *Campanula Rapunculus*, a native of central and southern Europe, formerly much cultivated in gardens for its white tuberous roots, which were used as a salad. More fully *garden rampion.*—2. A name of several plants of other genera.—**Horned rampion**, a general name of the species of *Phyteuma*, plants related to the bellflowers, and called *horned* because the slender corolla-lobes in some species remain long coherent in a conical beak.—**Large rampion**, said to be a name of the evening primrose, *Œnothera biennis.*

rampire, *n.* and *v.* An obsolete or archaic variant of *rampart* (which see).

rampired (ram'pīrd), *a.* [< *rampire* + *-ed*[2].] Furnished with ramparts. See quotations under *rampart, v.*

rampish† (ram'pish), *a.* [< *ramp* + *-ish*[1].] Rampant. *Palsgrave.* (*Halliwell.*)

rampler (ramp'lėr), *n.* and *a.* [Also *ramplor;* appar. equiv. to *ramper*[2], lit. one who ramps, or to *rambler*, one who rambles or roves: see *ramper*[2], *rambler.*] I. *n.* A gay, roving, or unsettled fellow. [Scotch.]

He's ——, a mischievous clever *ramplor*, and never devals with cracking his jokes on me.
Galt, Sir Andrew Wylie, I. 226.

II. *a.* Roving; unsettled. *Galt.* [Scotch.]

Rampoor chudder. A soft shawl of fine wool of the kind made at Rampoor in the Northwest Provinces, India. Such shawls are called in England and America simply *chudder.* See *chudder.*

rampostan, *n.* Same as *rambutan.*

ramps[1] (ramps), *n. pl.* Same as *ramsons.* [Prov. Eng.]

ramps[2] (ramps), *n.* Same as *rampion.*

rampse (ramps), *v. i.*; pret. and pp. *rampsed,* ppr. *rampsing.* [Variant of *ramp.*] To climb. *Halliwell.* [Prov. Eng.]

rampsman (ramps'man), *n.*; pl. *rampsmen* (-men). [Appar. ‹ *ramp* + poss. gen. *-s* + *man.* Cf. *cracksman.*] A highway robber who uses violence when necessary. *The Slang Dictionary,* p. 211.

ram-riding (ram'rī"ding), *n.* See the quotation.

> One summer evening, when the scandalised townsmen and their wedded wives assembled, and marched down to the cottage with intent to lead the woman in a *Ram-riding,* i. e. in a shameful penitential procession through the streets, the sight of Kit playing in the garden, and his look of innocent delight as he ran in to call his mother out, took the courage out of them.
> *The Speaker,* April 19, 1890, I. 427.

ramrod (ram'rod), *n.* [‹ *ram*[2] + *rod.*] A rod for ramming down the charge of a gun, pistol, or other firearm, especially for small hand-firearms. (Compare *rammer.*) Now that most small-arms load at the breech, ramrods are much less used than formerly. The ordinary ramrod for shot-guns, rifles, and the like was an unjointed wooden or iron rod, enlarged at the head or there fitted with a metal cap, and furnished at the other end with a screw or wormer for extracting a charge; when not in use it was carried in thimbles on the under side of the barrel.

ramrod-bayonet (ram'rod-bā"ọ-net), *n.* A steel rod one end of which is fitted for cleaning the bore of a rifle, while the other is pointed to serve as a bayonet: when intended for use as a weapon, the bayonet end is drawn a certain distance beyond the muzzle, and is held by a catch.

ramroddy (ram'rod-i), *a.* [‹ *ramrod* + *-y*[1].] Like a ramrod; stiff or unbending as a ramrod; prim; formal; obstinate. [Colloq.]

> The inevitable English nice middle-class tourist with his wife, the latter *ramroddy* and uncompromising.
> *C. D. Warner,* Their Pilgrimage, p. 60.

Ramsden's eyepiece. See *eyepiece.*

ramshackle[1] (ram'shak-l), *a.* and *n.* [Also, as adj., *ramshackled,* Sc. *ramshackled;* ‹ Icel. *ramskakkr,* quite wrong, absurd (Cleasby and Vigfusson); otherwise defined as "ramshackle, crazy"; ‹ *ramr,* strong, very, as intensive prefix, very, + *skakkr,* wry, distorted, unequal, › Sc. *shach,* distort: see *shach.* The second element in the E. word is appar. conformed to *shackle;* cf. Icel. *skökull,* Sw. *skakel,* Dan. *skagle,* the pole of a carriage that shakes about: see *shackle.*] I. *a.* Loose-jointed; ill-made; out of gear or repair; crazy; tumble-down; unregulated; chaotic.

> There came . . . my lord the cardinal, in his *ramshackle* couch, and his two, nay three, footmen behind him.
> *Thackeray,* Newcomes, xxxv.

> To get things where you wanted them, until they shook loose again by the *ram-shackle* movements of the machine.
> *Bramwell,* Wool-Carding, p. 136.

> In the present complex, artificial, and generally *ramshackle* condition of municipal organization in America.
> *The American,* IX. 229.

II. *n.* A thoughtless fellow. [Scotch.]

> Gin yon chield had shaved twa niches nearer you, your head, my man, would have lookit very like a bluidy pancake. This will learn ye again, ye young *ramshackle.*
> *Lockhart,* Reginald Dalton, I. 199.

ramshackle[2] (ram'shak-l), *v.* A corrupt form of *ransack,* confused with *ramshackle*[1].

ramshackled (ram'shak-ld), *a.* [Sc. *ramshackled,* ‹ *ramshackle*[1] + *-ed*[2].] Same as *ramshackle*[1].

ramshackly (ram'shak-li), *a.* [‹ *ramshackle*[1] + *-y*[1].] Same as *ramshackle*[1].

> This old lady was immeasurably fond of the old *ramshackly* house she lived in.
> *C. Reade,* Clouds and Sunshine, p. 15.

ram's-head (ramz'hed), *n.* 1. A species of lady's-slipper or moccasin-flower, *Cypripedium arietinum,* a rare plant of northern swamps in North America. The solitary flower has the three sepals distinct, is smaller than that of the common lady's-slipper, is colored brownish and reddish, and is drooping and of an odd form suggesting the name.—2. A seed of the chick-pea, *Cicer arietinum.*

ram's-horn (ramz'hôrn), *n.* 1. A semicircular work in the ditch of a fortified place, sweeping the ditch, and itself commanded by the main work.—2. An ammonite: a general name of fossil cephalopods whose shells are spiral, twisted, or bent.—3. A winding net supported by stakes, to inclose fish that come in with the tide. *Halliwell.* [Prov. Eng.]

ramskin (ram'skin), *n.* [Prob. a corruption of *ramekin.*] A species of cake made of dough and grated cheese. Also called *Sefton cake,* as said to have been invented at Croxteth Hall, England, the seat of Lord Sefton. *Imp. Dict.*

ramsons (ram'zọnz), *n. pl.* [Formerly also *ramsens, ramsins,* sometimes corruptly *ramshorns;* irreg., with additional plural suffix *-s,* for **ramson, *ramsen,* itself a plural in ME., ‹ ME. **ramsen* (‹ AS. *hramsan*), pl. (for which are found *ramsis, ramzys, ramseys,* with pl. *-s*) of singular **ramse* (› E. dial. **ramse, ramps, ramsh,* also *ramsy, ramsey*), ‹ AS. *hramsa* (pl. *hramsan*), broad-leafed garlic, = Bav. dial. *ramsen, ramsel* = Sw. **rams* (in comp. *rams-lök* (*lök* = E. *leek*), bear-garlic) = Dan. *rams,* also in comp. *rams-lög* (*lög* = E. *leek*), garlic; cf. Lith. *kremusze, kremuszis,* wild garlic, Ir. *creamh,* garlic, Gr. κρόμυον, an onion.] A species of garlic, *Allium ursinum,* of the northern parts of the Old World.

> Eate leekes in Lide and *ramsins* in May,
> And all the yeare after physicians may play.
> *Aubrey's Wilts,* MS. Royal Soc., p. 124. (*Halliwell.*)

ram-stag (ram'stag), *n.* A gelded ram. *Halliwell.* [Prov. Eng.]

ram-stam (ram'stam), *a.* and *n.* [A riming compound, ‹ *ram*[3] + *stam,* var. of *stamp.*] I. *a.* Forward; thoughtless; headstrong. *Halliwell.* [Scotch and North. Eng.]

> The hairum-scairum, *ram-stam* boys.
> *Burns,* To James Smith.

II. *n.* A giddy, forward person. [Scotch.]

> Watty is a lad of a methodical nature, and no a hurly-burly *ram-stam,* like you flea-luggit thing, Jamie.
> *Galt,* The Entail, III. 70.

ram-stam (ram'stam), *adv.* [‹ *ram-stam, a.*] Precipitately; headlong. [Scotch.]

> The least we'll get, if we gang *ram-stam* in on them, will be a broken head, to learn us better havings.
> *Scott,* Rob Roy, xxviii.

ramstead, ramsted (ram'sted), *n.* Same as *ranstead.*

ramstead-weed (ram'sted-wēd), *n.* Same as *ranstead.*

ramtil (ram'til), *n.* [E. Ind.] A plant, *Guizotia Abyssinica,* with oleiferous seeds.

ramule (ram'ūl), *n.* [‹ F. *ramule,* ‹ L. *ramulus,* a little branch: see *ramulus.*] In *bot.,* same as *ramulus.*

ramuli, *n.* Plural of *ramulus.*

ramuliferous (ram-ū-lif'ẹ-rus), *a.* [‹ L. *ramulus,* a little branch, + *ferre* = E. *bear*[1].] In *bot.,* bearing ramuli or branchlets.

ramulose (ram'ū-lōs), *a.* [‹ L. *ramulosus:* see *ramulous.*] Same as *ramulous.*—**Ramulose cell** or **areolet** of the wing, in *entom.,* a cell or areolet emitting a short nervure from the outer or posterior side.

ramulous (ram'ū-lus), *a.* [= F. *ramuleux,* ‹ L. *ramulosus,* full of little branches (applied by Pliny to veined leaves), ‹ *ramulus,* a little branch: see *ramulus.*] 1. In *bot.,* having many small branches.—2. In *entom.,* having one or more small branches; ramulose.

ramulus (ram'ū-lus), *n.*; pl. *ramuli* (-lī). [L., a little branch, dim. of *ramus,* a branch: see *ramus.* Cf. *ramule.*] 1. In *bot., anat.,* and *zoöl.,* a branchlet or twig; a small ramus or branch, as of an artery.—2. [*cap.*] [NL.] A genus of orthopterous insects. *Saussure,* 1861.—**Ramulus carotico-tympanicus,** one of the small branches of the internal carotid artery given off in the carotid canal to the mucous membrane of the tympanic cavity.

ramus (rā'mus), *n.*; pl. *rami* (-mī). [= F. *rame,* f., OF. *raim,* m., = Sp. Pg. It. *ramo,* m., ‹ L. *rāmus,* a branch, bough, twig, club, orig. **radmus* = Gr. ῥάδαμος, a young branch; cf. Gr. ῥάδιξ, a branch, = L. *radix,* a root: see *radix.*] In *biol.,* a branch or branching part, as of a plant, vein, artery, or forked bone. The rami of the ischium and pubis are their narrowed projecting parts. The rami of the lower jaw, as in man, are the ascending branches at each end, as distinguished from the intermediate horizontal part, called the *body;* but in any case where such distinction is not marked, as in birds and reptiles, a ramus is either half of the mandible, or one of the gnathidia, usually composed of several distinct bones. See diagram under *bill,* and cuts under *Felidæ* and *pleurodont.*—**Mandibular, pubic,** etc., **ramus.** See the adjectives.

ramuscule (rạ-mus'kūl), *n.* [= F. *ramuscule,* ‹ LL. *ramusculus,* dim. of L. *ramus,* a branch: see *ramus.*] 1. A branchlet; a small spray.—2. In *anat.,* a ramulus, branchlet, or twig, as of the arteries of the pia mater, which penetrate the substance of the brain.

ran[1] (ran). Preterit of *run.*

ran[2]† (ran), *n.* [‹ ME. **ran,* ‹ AS. *rān,* robbery, open rapine, ‹ Icel. *rān* = Dan. *ran,* robbery, depredation.] Open robbery and rapine; force; violence.

ran[3] (ran), *n.* [Also *rann;* ‹ ME. *ran, ron,* ‹ W. *rhan,* a part, division, share, portion, section, = Ir. Gael. *rann,* part, division, verse, poem.] A song.

ran[4] (ran), *n.* [Perhaps a confused form of *rand*[1], strip of leather.] 1. The hank of a string. *Halliwell.* [Prov. Eng.]—2. In *rope-making,* twenty cords of twine wound on a reel, every cord being so parted by a knot as to be easily separated from the others.—3. *Naut.,* yarns coiled on a spun-yarn winch. *Encyc. Dict.*

ran[5] (ran), *n.* Same as *runn.*

Rana[1] (rā'nạ̈), *n.* [NL., ‹ L. *rāna,* frog, prob. orig. **racna,* a croaker; cf. *raccare,* cry as a tiger.] 1. An extensive Linnean genus of aquatic salient anurous batrachians, typical of the family *Ranidæ;* the frogs proper. It was formerly more than conterminous with the present family *Ranidæ.* See *frog*[1], and also cuts under *bullfrog, girdle-bone, Anura*[2], and *temporomastoid.*—2. A genus of mollusks. *Humphreys,* 1797.

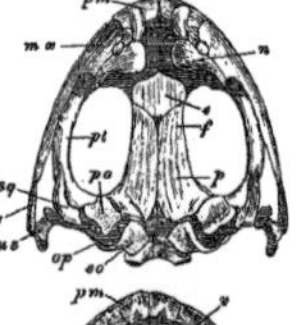

Rana.—Skull of the Frog: upper figure from above, lower from below.

e, girdle-bone, or os-en-ceinture; *eo,* exoccipital; *f,* frontal part of frontoparietal bone; *mx,* maxillary; *n,* nasal; *op,* opisthotic; *p,* parietal part of frontoparietal; *par,* parasphenoid; *pm,* premaxilla; *po,* proötic; *pt,* pterygoid; *q,* quadratojugal; *sq,* squamosal; *sus,* suspensorium of lower jaw; *v,* vomer; 1, optic foramen; 2, foramen ovale; 3, condyloid foramen.

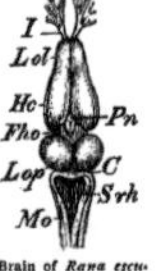

Brain of *Rana esculenta,* from above, ×4.

Lol, olfactory lobe, or rhinencephalon, with *I,* olfactory nerves; *Hc,* cerebral hemisphere, or prosencephalon; *Fho,* thalamencephalon; *Pn,* pineal body; *Lop,* optic lobe; *C,* cerebellum; *Srh,* fourth ventricle; *Mo,* medulla oblongata.

Rana[2] (rä'nạ̈), *n.* [Hind. *rānā,* a prince, ‹ Skt. *rājanya,* princely, royal, ‹ *rājan,* a king, prince: see *raja*[2]. Cf. *rani.*] Prince: the title of some sovereign princes or ruling chiefs in Rajputana and other parts of India.

> *Ránd* Bhim Sink [of Dholpur], the tenth in descent from *Ránd* Singan Deo, seized upon the fortress of Gwalior.
> *Encyc. Brit.,* VII. 147.

Ranæ (rā'nē), *n. pl.* [NL., pl. of L. *rana,* frog: see *Rana*[1].] The salient batrachians as an order of reptiles. *Wagler,* 1830.

Ranales (rạ-nā'lēz), *n. pl.* [NL. (Lindley, 1833), ‹ *Ran(unculus),* the type of the cohort.] A cohort of dicotyledonous plants of the polypetalous series *Thalamifloræ.* It is characterized by the commonly numerous stamens and pistils, all distinct and inserted on the receptacle or within it, and by the fleshy and usually copious albumen, surrounding a small or minute embryo. It includes about 1,800 species, grouped in 8 orders, of which the *Ranunculaceæ,* the leading family, and the *Dilleniaceæ* have generally one row of petals and one of five sepals. The other orders are remarkable among plants in having their petals commonly in two or more rows, and include the calycanthus and barberry families, the leaves in the first opposite, in the second usually compound; the magnolia and custard-apple families, trees with alternate leaves, in the first mainly stipulate; the moonseed family, consisting of vines; and the water-lilies, a family of aquatics.

ranarium (rạ-nā'ri-um), *n.*; pl. *ranaria* (-ạ̈). [NL., ‹ L. *rana,* frog (see *Rana*[1]), + *-arium.*] A collection of live frogs; a place where frogs are kept alive, to study their transformations, for vivisection in physiological experiments, etc.

> The institute also contains a large room full of rabbits and guinea-pigs, for which a little lawn is provided in summer. It also possesses a *ranarium,* in which are 700 frogs, divided into thirty-one departments, to prevent the spread of the frog disease.
> *Lancet,* No. 3426, p. 862.

Ranatra (ran'a̤-trạ̈), *n.* [NL.] **1.** A Fabrician (1794) genus of hemipterous insects of the family *Nepidæ*. In these curious water-bugs the body is extremely long and cylindric, the short acute rostrum is directed forward, there is a long anal respiratory tube, and the fore legs are raptorial. The species are aquatic and carnivorous. They are found in fresh-water ponds, and feed on fish-eggs, fry, and other water-bugs. *R. linearis* of Europe is an example; *R. fusca* is common in North America, where it is called *needle-bug*. **2.** [*l. c.*] A bug of this genus; a needle-bug.

Needle-bug (*Ranatra fusca*), two thirds natural size.

rance[1] (rans), *n.* [< OF. *ranche*, a stick, wooden pin, F. *ranche*, a round (of a ladder), rack, prop, or brace; cf. OF. *ranchier*, *rancher*, F. *rancher*, a rack, ladder, a crosspiece of wood placed in front of or behind a cart; < L. *ramex* (*ramic-*), a staff, < *ramus*, a branch, bough, twig, club: see *ramus*.] **1.** A shore or prop acting as a strut for the support of something, as of a Congreve rocket.—**2.** One of the cross-bars between the legs of a chair.

rance[1] (rans), *v. t.*; pret. and pp. *ranced*, ppr. *rancing*. [< OF. *rancer*, prop, < *rance*, a prop: see *rance*[1].] To shore or prop. [Scotch.]

Rance[2]† (rans), *a.* An obsolete form of *Rhenish*.

Ane great peis of *Rance* wyne.
Aberdeen Reg., 16th cent. (*Jamieson.*)

rance[3]†, **rauncet**, *n.* [Early mod. E. *rance*, *raunce* (?), a kind of fine stone; < F. *rance*, *rance marbre*, defined by Larousse as a white and red-brown marble veined with ashen-white and blue; prob. lit. 'Rhenish' (< *Rance*[2]), belonging to the Rhine, as it were a sort of 'Rhine-stone.'] An unknown hard mineral or fine stone, supposed to be some sort of marble.

What liuing *Rance*, what rapting Ivory,
Swims in these streams?
Sylvester, tr. of Du Bartas's Weeks, ii., The Trophies.

She's empty; hark! she sounds; there's nothing in't;
The spark-engendering flint
Shall sooner melt, and hardest *raunce* shall first
Dissolve and quench thy thirst.
Quarles, Emblems, ii. 10.

rancescent (ran-ses'e̤nt), *a.* [< LL. *rancescen(t-)s*, ppr. of *rancescere*, inceptive of L. (ML.) *rancere*, stink: see *rancid* and *rancor*.] Becoming rancid or sour. *Imp. Dict.*

ranch[1] (ranch), *v. t.* [Also *raunch*; prob. a var. form of **rench* for *wrench*.] To wrench; tear; wound. [Obsolete or prov. Eng.]

Hasting to *raunch* the arrow out.
Spenser, Shep. Cal., August.

Against a stump his tusk the monster grinds, . . .
And *ranched* his hips with one continued wound.
Dryden, tr. of Ovid's Metamorph., i.

ranch[1] (ranch), *n.* [< *ranch*[1], *v.*] A deep scratch or wound. [Obsolete or prov. Eng.]

Griffade [F.], a *ranche* or clinch with a beast's claw.
Cotgrave.

ranch[2] (rȧnch), *n.* [Also *ranche*; < Sp. *rancho*: see *rancho*.] **1.** In the western part of the United States, especially in the parts formerly Mexican, on the great plains, etc., a herding establishment and estate; a stock-farm; by extension, in the same regions, any farm or farming establishment. The tract of land over which the animals of a ranch or of several ranches roam for pasturage is called a *range*. See *range*, 7 (*a*).
2. In a restricted sense, a company of ranchers or rancheros; the body of persons employed on a ranch.

The Spanish rancho means a mess, and so the American herder speaks of his companions collectively as the *ranch* or the "outfit." *L. Swinburne*, Scribner's Mag., II. 509.

ranch[2] (rȧnch), *v. i.* [< *ranch*[2], *n.*] To conduct or work upon a ranch; engage in herding. [Western U. S.]

Ranching is an occupation like those of vigorous, primitive pastoral peoples, having little in common with the humdrum, workaday business world of the nineteenth century. *T. Roosevelt*, The Century, XXXV. 500.

Patients who have exchanged the invalid's room at home for cattle *ranching* in Colorado.
Lancet, No. 3481, p. 1079.

rancher (rȧn'chėr), *n.* [< *ranch*[2] + *-er*[1]. Cf. *ranchero*.] A person engaged in ranching; one who carries on or works upon a ranch; a ranchman. [Western U. S.]

To misdirect persons was a common enough trick among *ranchers*. *W. Shepherd*, Prairie Experiences, p. 97.

rancheria (rȧn-che-rē'ạ̈), *n.* [Mex. Sp., < *rancho*, a ranch: see *ranch*[2].] In Mexico, the dwelling-place of a ranchero or of rancheros; a herdsman's hut, or a village of herders; hence, a settlement, more or less permanent, of Indians.

Prior to the occupation of California by the Europeans the Indians dwelt, more or less, in temporary villages, later called *rancherias*, where they had an imperfect government, controlled by chiefs, councils, and priests.
Johns Hopkins Univ. Studies, 8th ser., IV. 35.

By evening all the Indians had betaken themselves to their own *rancherias*, and the agency was comparatively deserted for another week. *The Century*, XXXVIII. 398.

ranchero (rȧn-chā'rō), *n.* [< Mex. Sp. *ranchero*, steward of a rancho or mess, ranchman, herdsman, also owner of a rancho or small farm, < *rancho*, a ranch: see *rancho*.] In Mexico, a herdsman; a person employed on a rancho; specifically, one who has the oversight of a rancho, or the care of providing for its people; by extension, same as *ranchman*.

Ranchero.

A fancy serape hanging on a hook, with a *ranchero's* bit and lariat. *J. W. Palmer*, The New and the Old, p. 85.

ranch-house (rȧnch'hous), *n.* The principal dwelling-house on a ranch; the abode of a ranchman. [Western U. S.]

Meanwhile the primitive *ranch-house*, outbuildings, and corrals are built. *T. Roosevelt*, The Century, XXXV. 499.

ranching (ran'ching), *n.* [Native name.] A slender dagger used in the Malay Islands.

ranchman (rȧnch'man), *n.*; pl. *ranchmen* (-men). A man who is employed on a ranch; one of the herdsmen of a ranch; specifically, one who owns or who has the charge or control of a ranch; a rancher.

At the main ranch there will be a cluster of log buildings, including a separate cabin for the foreman or *ranchman*. *T. Roosevelt*, The Century, XXXV. 499.

rancho (rȧn'chō), *n.* [< Sp. *rancho*, a mess, small farm, clan, hamlet, a clear passage, = Pg. *rancho*, mess on a ship, soldiers' quarters; cf. *ranchar*, divide seamen into messes, Sp. *arrancharse*, dwell together; origin doubtful.] In Spanish America, a rude hut or cluster of huts where herdsmen or stockmen live or only lodge; hence, an establishment for breeding cattle and horses; a stock-farm. It is thus distinguished from a *hacienda*, which is a cultivated farm or plantation. See *ranch*[2], *n.*

rancid (ran'sid), *a.* [= OF. *rancide*, F. *rance*, *rance* (> MD. *ranst*, *ranstigh*, D. *rans*, *ransig* = G. *ranzig*) = Pr. *ranc* = Sp. *rancio* = Pg. It. *rancido*, < L. *rancidus*, stinking, rank, rancid, offensive, < *rancere* (ML.), stink, in L. used only in ppr. *rancen(t-)s*, stinking; cf. *rancor*, from the same verb. The adj. *rank*[1] is not related.] **1.** Rankly offensive to the senses; having a tainted smell or taste; fetid or soured from chemical change.

The oil with which fishes abound often turns *rancid*, and lies heavy on the stomach, and affects the very sweat with a *rancid* smell. *Arbuthnot*, Aliments, p. 79.

2. Repulsive to the moral sense; disgusting; loathsome. [Rare.]

One of the most *rancid* and obnoxious pieces that have ever disgraced the stage.
New York Tribune, May 16, 1890.

rancidify (ran-sid'i-fī), *v. i.* and *t.*; pret. and pp. *rancidified*, ppr. *rancidifying*. [< *rancid* + *-i-fy*.] To become or make rancid. [Rare.]

The oxidation or *rancidifying* of the cacao butter.
Therapeutic Gazette, XI. 314.

rancidity (ran-sid'i-ti), *n.* [= F. *rancidité* (cf. Sp. *rancidez*, It. *rancidezza*), < L. as if **rancidita(t-)s*, < *rancidus*, rancid: see *rancid*.] The quality of being rancid; a rankly sour or tainted smell and taste, as of old oil.

rancidly (ran'sid-li), *adv.* With a rancid odor; mustily.

rancidness (ran'sid-nes), *n.* The quality of being rancid; rancidity.

rānck†, *a.* and *v.* An obsolete spelling of *rank*[1].

rancor, rancour (rang'kọr), *n.* [Formerly also *rankor*; < ME. *rancor*, *rancour*, *rankoure*, < OF. *rancor*, *rancuer*, *rancoeur*, dial. *rancœur*, disgust, rancor, hatred, = Pr. *rancor* = OSp. *rancor*, Sp. *rencor* = Pg. *rancor* = It. *rancore*, < LL. *rancor*, a stinking smell or flavor, rancidness, also bitterness, grudge, < L. (ML.) *rancere*, stink, be rancid: see *rancid*. Cf. the var. form OF. **rancure*, *rancune*, F. *rancune* = OPg. *rancura* = It. *rancura*, < ML. *rancura*, *rancuna*, rancor.] **1†.** Sourness; bitterness.

For Banquo's issue . . . Duncan have I murder'd;
Put *rancours* in the vessel of my peace
Only for them. *Shak.*, Macbeth, iii. 1. 67.

2. Rankling malice or spitefulness: bitter animosity; in general, a soured or cankered disposition, inciting to vindictive action or speech; a nourished hatred or grudge.

In her corage no *rancour* dooth abide.
Babees Book (E. E. T. S.), p. 33.

Some whom emulation did enrage
To spit the venom of their *rancour's* gall.
Ford, Fame's Memorial.

The *rancor* of an evil tongue.
Milton, Apology for Smectymnuus.

=**Syn. 2.** *Asperity*, *Harshness*, etc. (see *acrimony*), *Ill-will*, *Enmity*, etc. (see *animosity*), gall, spleen, spite, spitefulness, rankling, hate, hatred, malevolence, bad blood.

rancorous, rancourous (rang'kọr-us), *a.* [< OF. *rancuros*, *rancorus*, *rancurus* = Sp. *rencoroso*, < ML. *rancorosus*, rancorous, full of hate or spite, < L. *rancor*, rancor: see *rancor*.] Full of rancor; implacably spiteful or malicious; intensely virulent.

Can you in words make show of amity,
And in your shields display such *rancorous* minds?
Marlowe, Edward II., ii. 2.

He [Warren Hastings] was beset by *rancorous* and unprincipled enemies. *Macaulay*, Warren Hastings.

=**Syn.** See *rancor*.

rancorously, rancourously (rang'kọr-us-li), *adv.* In a rancorous manner; with spiteful malice or vindictiveness.

rand[1] (rand), *n.* [< ME. *rand*, border, margin, edge, strip, slice, < AS. *rand*, *rond*, border, edge, brink, margin, shore, the rim or boss of a shield, a shield, buckler, = D. *rand* = MLG. *rant*, edge, border, etc., = OHG. *rant*, MHG. *rant*, border, rim or boss of a shield, a shield, G. *rand*, border, brim, rim, edge, etc., = Icel. *rönd*, a stripe, a shield, = Sw. Dan. *rand*, a stripe, = Goth. **randa* (prob. found in the derived Sp. *randa*, lace or edging on garments); cf. Lith. *rumbas*, OBulg. *rebŭ*, border, edge, rind, seam; akin to *rim*[1], q. v. Hence ult., through OF., E. *random*.] **1†.** A margin, border, or edge, as the bank of a stream.—**2†.** A strip or slice of flesh cut from the margin of a part or from between two parts.

A great bolle-full of benen were betere in his wombe,
And with the *randes* of bakun his baly for to fillen,
Than pertriches or plouers or pekokes y-rosted.
Piers Plowman's Crede (E. E. T. S.), l. 763.

Giste de bœuf [F.], a rand of beef: a long and fleshie piece cut out from between the flank and buttock. *Cotgrave.*

They came with chopping knives
To cut me into *rands*, and sirloins, and so powder me.
Fletcher, Wildgoose Chase, v. 2.

3. A hank of line or twine; a strip of leather. *Halliwell.* [Local, Eng.]—**4.** Rushes on the borders and edges of land near a river. *Halliwell.* [Prov. Eng.]—**5.** In *shoemaking*: (*a*†) The edge of the upper-leather; a seam of a shoe. *Bailey.* (*b*†) A thin inner shoe-sole, as of cork. *Simmonds.* (*c*) One of the slips beneath the heel of a sole to bring the rounding surface to a level ready to receive the lifts of the heel: distinctively called *heel-rand*. See cut under *boot*.

rand[2]† (rand), *v. i.* [A var. of *rant*.] To storm; rant.

He was born to fill thy mouth, . . . he will teach thee to tear and *rand*. *B. Jonson*, Poetaster, iii. 1.

randall-grass (ran'dạl-grȧs), *n.* The meadow-fescue. See *Festuca*. [Virginia.]

Randallite (ran'dal-īt), *n.* [After Benjamin *Randall* (1749–1808), founder of the body of Freewill Baptists at New Durham, New Hampshire, in 1780.] A Freewill Baptist. [Rare.]

randan (ran′dan), *n.* [Cf. *rand*[2]; perhaps in part due to *randon*, random: see *random*. In the 3d and 4th senses uncertain; perhaps with ref. to quick movement; but in def. 3 possibly a corrupt form, connected with *range*, *v.*, 6.] 1. A noise or uproar. *Halliwell.* [Prov. Eng.]—2. A spree: used only in the phrase *on the randan* (also *on the randy*), on a spree. [Prov. Eng.]—3. The finest part of the bran of wheat; the product of the second sifting of meal. [Prov. Eng.]—4. A boat impelled by three rowers, the one amidships using a pair of sculls, and the bowman and strokesman one oar each. Also called *randan-gig*. [Eng.]

randan-gig (ran′dan-gig), *n.* Same as *randan*, 4.

A sort of boat, . . . a *randan-gig* built for us by Searle of Putney, where . . . we used to keep her.
Yates, Fifty Years of London Life.

randanite (ran′dan-it), *n.* [< *Randan*, Puy de Dôme, Auvergne, France, where it is found, + *-ite*[2].] The name given in France to infusorial silica, or kieselguhr, found under the soil in peat-bogs in the department of Puy de Dôme, at Randan and in other localities in the neighborhood of Clermont.

Randia (ran′di-ä), *n.* [NL. (A. A. Houston, 1737, in Linnæus's "Genera Plantarum"), named after Isaac *Rand*, a London botanist of the 18th century.] A genus of gamopetalous plants of the order *Rubiaceæ* and tribe *Gardenieæ*. It is characterized by hermaphrodite and axillary flowers, united style-branches bearing a club-shaped or fusiform stigma, a two-celled ovary with many ovules, seeds with membranaceous coats, and short intrapetiolar stipules which are almost connate. There are about 100 species, natives of tropical regions, especially in Asia and Africa. They are trees and shrubs, erect or climbing, with or without thorns, and bearing opposite leaves which are obovate or narrower, and either small or large flowers, which are solitary or in clusters, and white or yellow, rarely red. The fruit is a many-seeded, two-celled roundish berry, yielding a blue dye in the West Indian species, as *R. aculeata*, known as *indigo-berry* and *inkberry*. These species also furnish a valuable wood, used for cask-staves, ladders, etc. *R. dumetorum*, a small thorny tree, widely distributed from Africa to Java, is used as a hedge-plant in India, while its fruit, called *emetic nut*, is there a current drug, said also, like *Cocculus Indicus*, to have the property of stupefying fish.

randie, *a.* and *n.* See *randy*.

randing-machine (ran′ding-ma-shēn″), *n.* In *shoe-manuf.*, a machine for fitting rands to heel-blanks for shoes, after the rands have been formed from rand-strips in a rand-forming machine.

randing-tool (ran′ding-töl), *n.* In *shoe-manuf.*, a hand-tool for cutting out strips of leather for rands.

randle-balk (ran′dl-bâk), *n.* Same as *randle-bar*.

randle-bar (ran′dl-bär), *n.* The horizontal bar built into the walls of an open chimney, from which to hang hooks for supporting cooking-vessels. See *back-bar*.

randle-tree, *n.* See *rantle-tree*.

random (ran′dum), *n.*[1] [An altered form (assimilated to *whilom*, *seldom*, *ransom*, the latter also with orig. *n*) of the early mod. E. *randon*, < ME. *randon*, *randun*, *randoun*, force, impetuosity, < OF. *randon*, force, impetuosity, impetuous course, as of a torrent (*grands randons de pluie*, great torrents of rain); esp. in the phrases *à randon*, *à grand randon*, with force or fury, very fast, with great force (*courir du grant randon*, run with great fury); cf. It. dim. *randello*, *a randello*, at random; *a randa*, near, with difficulty, exactly; cf. Sp. *de rendon*, *de rondon*, rashly, intrepidly, abruptly (nearly like E. *at random*); perhaps < OHG. MHG. *rant*, G. *rand*, edge, brim, rim, margin: see *rand*[1].] 1†. A rushing, as of a torrent; an impetuous course; impetuosity; violence; force: especially with *great*, as in the phrase *a great randon*, with great speed or force.

And thei rennen to gidre *a gret randoun*.
Mandeville, Travels, p. 238.

The two kynges were fierce and hardy, and mette with so *grete raundon* with speres that were grete and shorte.
Merlin (E. E. T. S.), iii. 628.

But of hym thought he to faill in no wise,
With *gret raundon* cam to hym in his gise.
Rom. of Partenay (E. E. T. S.), l. 5866.

Corragiously the two kynges newely fought with *great randon* and force.
Hall, Hen. VIII., an. 12.

2†. A rush; spurt; gush.

When thei saugh come the dragon that Merlin bar, that caste oute of his throte so grete *raundon* of fiere in to the aire, that was full of duste and powder, so that it semed all reade . . .
Merlin (E. E. T. S.), ii. 219.

3†. A continuous flow of words; a harangue.

Randone, or longe renge of wurdys, or other thyngys, haringga, etc.
Prompt. Parv., p. 423.

4. An indeterminate course or proceeding; hence, lack of direction, rule, or method; haphazard; chance: used only in the phrase *at random*—that is, in a haphazard, aimless, and purely fortuitous manner.

You flee with winges of often change *at random* where you please.
Turberville, The Lover to a Gentlewoman.

Sith late mischaunce had her compeld to chaunge
The land for sea, *at randon* there to raunge.
Spenser, F. Q., III. viii. 20.

Come not too neere me, I *at random* strike,
For gods and men I now hate both alike.
Heywood, Dialogues (Works, ed. Pearson, 1874, VI. 178).

Like orient pearls *at random* strung.
Sir W. Jones, Song of Hafiz.

5. The distance traversed by a missile; range; reach.

The angle which the missive is to mount by, if we will have it go to its furthest *random*, must be the half of a right one.
Sir K. Digby.

random (ran′dum), *a.* and *n.*[2] [By ellipsis from *at random*.] I. *a.* Proceeding, taken, done, or existing at random; aimless; fortuitous; haphazard; casual.

In common things that round us lie
Some *random* truths he can impart.
Wordsworth, A Poet's Epitaph.

I would shoot, howe'er in vain,
A *random* arrow from the brain.
Tennyson, Two Voices.

You feel that the whole of him [Dryden] was better than any *random* specimen, though of his best, seems to prove.
Lowell, Among my Books, 1st ser., p. 8.

Random choice, the selection of objects, subject to the condition that they shall belong to a given class or collection, but not voluntarily subject to any other condition. The assumption is that objects so selected will in the long run occur as objects of the same kind occur in general experience. This assumption is natural, it leads to no difficulty, and no serious doubt has ever been thrown upon it. It is the fundamental postulate of the theory of probability. See *probability*.—**Random courses**, in *masonry* and *paving*, courses of stones in horizontal beds, the stones being of unequal thickness, but exactly fitted together.—**Random line.** (*a*) In local probability, an infinite straight line supposed to be chosen in such a manner that the infinitesimal probability of its cutting any limited straight line is proportional to the length of the latter. (*b*) In United States public land-surveying, a trial line on which temporary mile and half-mile stakes are set, for the purpose of getting the data for rerunning the same line and setting permanent stakes at the corners.—**Random point**, in local probability, a point supposed to be so chosen that the infinitesimal probability of its lying within any closed surface is proportional to the solid contents of that surface.—**Random-range ashler, random-tooled ashler.** See *ashler*, 3.—**Random shot**, a shot not intentionally directed to any point; also, a shot with the muzzle of the gun elevated above the horizontal line.—**Random stonework**, in *masonry*, a construction formed of squared stones varying in thickness and not laid in courses. See cut under *ashler*.—**Random tooling**, the act of bringing the face of a stone to a nearly smooth surface by hewing it over with a broad-pointed chisel, which produces a series of minute waves at right angles to its path. It is called *droving* in Scotland.—**Random work**, random stonework.—**Random yarn**, in *dyeing*, yarn dipped into a bath of water with a layer of color at the top, so as to produce a clouded effect; clouded yarn.

On the large scale the *random yarns* are coloured in machines.
W. Crookes, Dyeing and Calico-Printing, p. 102.

II. *n.* Something done or produced without definite method, or with irregular or haphazard effect. (*a*) In *masonry*, one of a number of dressed stones of irregular or unmatched sizes. See *random stonework*, under I.

50 tons squares, 250 tons dressed *randoms*, and 1000 tons 2 in. ringsmall.
Engineer, LXVII. 117.

(*b*) In *dyeing*, clouded yarn. See *random yarn*, under I.

randomly (ran′dum-li), *adv.* [< *random* + *-ly*[2].] In a random manner; at random, or without aim, purpose, or guidance.

An infusorium swims *randomly* about.
H. *Spencer*, Data of Ethics, § 4.

randon†, *n.* An obsolete form of *random*.

randon† (ran′don), *v. i.* [< OF. *randonner*, run swiftly, < *randon*, a swift course: see *random*.] To stray in a wild manner or at random.

Shall leave them free to *randon* of their will.
Norton and Sackville, Ferrex and Porrex, i. 2.

randy (ran′di), *a.* and *n.* [Also *randie*, *ranty*; < *rand*[2], *rant*, + *-y*[1]. Cf. *randan*.] I. *a.* Disorderly; boisterous; obstreperous; riotous; also, noisily wanton. [Scotch and North. Eng.]

A merry core
O' *randie*, gangrel bodies.
Burns, Jolly Beggars.

II. *n.*; pl. *randies* (-diz). 1. A sturdy beggar or vagrant; one who exacts alms by threatenings and abusive language. Also called *randy-beggar*. [Scotch.]—2. A romping girl; a noisy hoyden; a scold; a violent and vulgar quarrelsome woman. *Jamieson.* [Scotch and North. Eng.]

That scandalous *randy* of a girl.
Carlyle, in Froude (Life in London, xviii.).

3. A spree: as, to be on the *randy*. *Halliwell.* [Prov. Eng.]

ranedeer†, *n.* An obsolete form of *reindeer*.

ranee, *n.* See *rani*.

Ranelagh mob†, Ranelagh cap†. A cap worn by women in the eighteenth century, apparently a form of the mob-cap: the name is taken from Ranelagh, a place of fashionable resort near Dublin.

ranforce†, *v. t.* Same as *reinforce*. *Bailey.*

rang[1] (rang). Preterit of *ring*[2].

rang[2]†, *n.* and *v.* An old form of *rank*[2].

range (rānj), *v.*; pret. and pp. *ranged*, ppr. *ranging*. [Early mod. E. also *raunge*; < ME. *rengen*, < OF. *renger*, F. *ranger* (= Pr. *rengar*), range, rank, order, array, < *rang*, a rank, row: see *rank*[2]. Cf. *arrange*, *derange*.] I. *trans.* 1. To make a row or rows of; place in a line or lines; hence, to fix or set in any definite order; dispose with regularity; array; arrange.

Than two of hem *renged* hem, and priked after the messagers as faste as the horse myght hem bere.
Merlin (E. E. T. S.), i. 127.

They had *raunged* their ships broad in a front ranke.
Holland, tr. of Livy, p. 957.

For all the Etruscan armies
Were *ranged* beneath his eye.
Macaulay, Horatius.

2. To rank or class; place or reckon as being of or belonging to some class, category, party, etc.; fix the relative place or standing of; classify; collocate.

The late Emperour Augustus all the world *raungeth* in this ranke of men fortunate.
Holland, tr. of Pliny, vii. 45.

So they *ranged* all their youth under some family, and set upon such a course, which had good success, for it made all hands very industrious.
N. Morton, New England's Memorial, p. 93.

The great majority of the Indians, if they took part in the war, *ranged* themselves on the side of the Crown.
Lecky, Eng. in 18th Cent., xiv.

Among those inhabitants of the Roman dominion who were personally free, there were four classes, *ranged* in an ascending scale—provincials, Italians, Latins, Romans.
E. A. Freeman, Amer. Lects., p. 320.

3†. To rank or reckon; consider; count.

The Æthiops were as fair
As other dames; now black with black despair:
And in respect of their complexious changed,
Are eachwhere since for luckless creatures *ranged*.
B. Jonson, Masque of Blackness.

4†. To engage; occupy.

That, of all other, was the most fatal and dangerous exploit that ever I was *ranged* in.
B. Jonson, Every Man in his Humour, iii. 1.

5. To pass over or through the line, course, or extent of; go along or about, especially for some definite purpose; rove over or along: as, to *range* the forest for game or for poachers; to *range* a river or the coast in a boat.

I found this credit,
That he did *range* the town to seek me out.
Shak., T. N., iv. 3. 7.

As they *ranged* the coast at a place they named Whitson Bay, they were kindly vsed by the Natiues.
Quoted in Capt. *John Smith's* Works, I. 108.

To *range* the woods, to roam the park.
Tennyson, In Memoriam, Conclusion.

6. To sift; pass through a range or bolting-sieve. [Obsolete or local.]

They made a decree, and tooke order that no corne maisters that bought and sold grain should beat this mule away from their *raunging* sives.
Holland, tr. of Pliny, viii. 44.

II. *intrans.* 1. To constitute or be parallel to a line or row; have linear course or direction; be in or form a line: as, a boundary *ranging* east and west; houses *ranging* evenly with the street.

Than thei rode forth and *renged* close that wey where as the childeren foughten full sore, ffor the Saisnes were mo than vij[m] in a flote.
Merlin (E. E. T. S.), ii. 198.

Direct my course so right as with thy hand to show
Which way thy forests *range*.
Drayton, Polyolbion, i. 14.

The stones are of the same thickness as the walls, and the pilasters have no capitals; there is a cornish below that *ranges* round, which might belong to a basement.
Pococke, Description of the East, II. i. 135.

2. To be on a level; agree in class or position; have equal rank or place; rank correspondingly.

'Tis better to be lowly born,
And *range* with humble livers in content,
Than to be perk'd up in a glistering grief,
And wear a golden sorrow.
Shak., Hen. VIII., ii. 3. 20.

This was cast upon the board,
When all the full-faced presence of the Gods
Ranged in the halls of Peleus.
Tennyson, Œnone.

3. To go in a line or course; hence, to rove freely; pass from point to point; make a course or tour; roam; wander.

Let reason *range* beyonde his creede.
Puttenham, Parthenlades, xiii.

The Gaules from the Albane Glinnes . . . *raunged* all over the champion and the sea coaste, and wasted the countrie. *Holland*, tr. of Livy, p. 265.

How wild his [man's] thoughts! how apt to *range!*
How apt to vary! apt to change!
Quarles, Emblems, iv. 5.

Watch him, for he *ranges* swift and far.
M. Arnold, Empedocles on Etna.

4. To move in a definite manner, as for starting game; beat about; of dogs, to run within the proper range.

All shrank — like boys who, unaware,
Ranging the woods to start a hare,
Come to the mouth of the dark lair
Where, growling low, a fierce old bear
Lies amidst bones and blood.
Macaulay, Horatius.

Next comes the teaching to *range*, which is about the most difficult part of breaking.
Dogs of Great Britain and America, p. 226.

Down goes old Sport, *ranging* a bit wildly.
The Field (London), March 27, 1886. (*Encyc. Dict.*)

5. To have course or direction; extend in movement or location; pass; vary; stretch; spread: as, prices *range* between wide limits; the plant *ranges* from Canada to Mexico.

Man *ranges* over the whole earth, and exists under the most varied conditions.
A. R. Wallace, Nat. Select., p. 226.

In temperate climates, toward the higher latitudes, the quicksilver *ranges*, or rises and falls, nearly three inches.
Fitz Roy, Weather Book, p. 13.

The Cyprinoids also afford an instance of an Indian species *ranging* into Africa. *Encyc. Brit.*, XII. 673.

6. In *gun.*, to have range: said of a missile, and denoting length of range and also direction: as, that shot *ranged* too far, or too much to the right: rarely, of the gun itself.—**To range by**, to sail by; pass ahead of, as a vessel. =**Syn. 3.** *Roam, Rove*, etc. See *ramble*, v.

range (rānj), *n.* [Early mod. E. also *raunge;* < late ME. *range, reenge*, order, range, row (cf. OF. *rangie*, F. *rangée*, range, row, etc.); < *range*, v. The noun prob. in part involves ME. *reng*, pl. *renges, ringes*, rank, series, row: see *rank*[2]. Cf. also (in def. 10) *rung*[2].] **1.** A line or row (usually straight or nearly straight); a linear series; a regular sequence; a rank; a chain: used especially of large objects permanently fixed or lying in direct succession to one another, as mountains, trees, buildings, columns, etc.

Ther be iiij rowes or *Ranges* of pylers thorow the Chirche.
Torkington, Diarie of Eng. Travell, p. 47.

There is a long row or *range* of buildings.
Coryat, Crudities, I. 192.

Altogether this arcade only makes us wish for more, for a longer *range* from the same hand.
E. A. Freeman, Venice, p. 247.

A row of Corinthian columns, standing on brackets, once supported the archivolts of a *range* of niches.
J. Fergusson, Hist. Arch., I. 367.

Specifically—(*a*) A line or chain of mountains; a cordillera: as, to skirt the *range;* to cross the *ranges*. [In mountainous regions, as parts of Australia and America, this specific use is common.] (*b*) In United States surveys of public land, one of a series of divisions numbered east or west from the prime meridian of the survey, consisting of townships which are numbered north or south in every division from a base-line. See *township*. (*c*) In *geom.*, a series of points lying in one straight line.

2. A rank, class, or order; a series of beings or things belonging to the same grade or having like characteristics. [Rare.]

The next *range* of beings above him are the immaterial intelligences. *Sir M. Hale.*

3. The extent of any aggregate, congeries, or complex, material or immaterial; array of things or sequences of a specific kind; scope; compass: as, the *range* of industries in a country; the whole *range* of events or of history; the *range* of prices or of operations; the *range* of one's thoughts or learning.

The *range* and compass of his [Hammond's] knowledge filled the whole circle of the arts.
Bp. Fell, Hammond, p. 99.

A man has not enough *range* of thought to look out for any good which does not relate to his own interest.
Addison.

When I briefly speak of the Greek school of art with reference to questions of delineation, I mean the entire *range* of the schools from Homer's days to our own.
Ruskin, Aratra Pentelici, p. 157.

In the *range* of historical geography, the most curious feature is the way in which certain political names have kept on an abiding life in this region, though with singular changes of meaning. *E. A. Freeman*, Venice, p. 4.

4. Extent of operating force or activity; scope or compass of efficient action; space or distance over or through which energy can be exerted; limit of effect or of capability; extent of reach: as, the *range* of a gun or a shot; the *range* of a thermometer or a barometer (the extent of its variation in any period, or of its capacity for marking degrees of change); the *range* of a singer or of a musical instrument. Range in shooting is the horizontal distance to which a projectile is or may be thrown by a gun or other arm under existing conditions: distinguished from *trajectory*, or the curvilinear distance traversed by the projectile when the arm is elevated out of a horizontal line. The effective range depends upon the amount or the absence of elevation and the consequent trajectory. (Compare *point-blank*.) To get the range of a point to be fired at is to ascertain, either by calculation or by experiment, or by both, the degree of elevation for the muzzle of the piece necessary to bring the shot to bear upon it.

Far as creation's ample *range* extends,
The scale of sensual, mental powers ascends.
Pope, Essay on Man, i. 207.

Her warbling voice, a lyre of widest *range*,
Struck by all passion, did fall down and glance
From tone to tone. *Tennyson*, Fair Women.

No obstacle was encountered until the gunboats and transports were within *range* of the fort.
U. S. Grant, Personal Memoirs, I. 489.

The proposal [advocating cremation] was not to be regarded as coming within the *range* of a practical policy.
Nineteenth Century, XXIII. 2.

5. Unobstructed distance or interval from one point or object to another; length of course for free direct ranging through the air, as of a missile or of sight; a right line of aim or of observation, absolute or relative: as, the *range* is too great for effective firing; the *range* of vision.—**6.** The act of ranging; a wandering or roving; movement from point to point in space.

He may take a *range* all the world over. *South.*

7. An area or course of ranging, either in space or in time; an expanse for movement or existence; the region, sphere, or space over which any being or thing ranges or is distributed: as, the *range* of an animal or a plant within geographical limits or during geological time, or of a marine animal in depth; the *range* of Gothic architecture; the *range* of a man's influence.

The free bison's amplitude of *range*.
Whittier, The Panorama.

Specifically—(*a*) A tract or district of land within which domestic animals in large numbers range for subsistence; an extensive grazing-ground: used on the great plains of the United States for a tract commonly of many square miles, occupied by one or by different proprietors, and distinctively called a *cattle-, stock-*, or *sheep-range*. The animals on a range are usually left to take care of themselves during the whole year without shelter, excepting when periodically gathered in a "round-up" for counting and selection, and for branding when the herds of several proprietors run together. In severe winters many are lost by such exposure.

Cowboys from neighboring ranches will ride over, looking for lost horses, or seeing if their cattle have strayed off the *range*. *T. Roosevelt*, The Century, XXXV. 500.

(*b*) A course for shooting at marks or targets; a space of ground appropriated or laid out for practice in the use of firearms: distinctively called a *rifle-range* or *shooting-range*.

8. A fire-grate.

He was bid at his first coming to take off the *range*, and let down the cinders. *Sir R. L'Estrange.* (*Latham.*)

9. A cooking-stove built into a fireplace, or sometimes portable but of a similar shape, having a row or rows of openings on the top for carrying on several operations at once. Fixed ranges usually have two ovens, either on each side of the fire-chamber or above it at the back, and in houses supplied with running water a hot-water reservoir or permanent boiler. The origin of the modern cooking-range may be sought in the furnaces of masonry of the ancient Romans, arranged to receive cooking-utensils on the top. Throughout the middle ages only open-chimney fires were used, until in France, in the course of the fourteenth century, built furnaces with openings above for pots began to be added in great kitchens, for convenience in preparing the soups and sauces then in greater favor than before. The range in the modern sense, involving the application of heat conducted by and reflected from iron plates, was first advanced and practically improved by Count Rumford.

It [the kitchen] was a vaut ybuilt for great dispence,
With many *raunges* reard along the wall,
And one great chimney, whose long tonnell thence
The smoke forth threw. *Spenser*, F. Q., II. ix. 29.

Every thing whereupon any part of their carcase falleth shall be unclean; whether it be oven, or *ranges* for pots, they shall be broken down. Lev. xi. 35.

And so home, where I found all clean, and the hearth and *range*, as it is now enlarged, both up.
Pepys, Diary, May 25, 1661.

10. A step of a ladder; a round; a rung. [Obsolete or local.]

The first *range* of that ladder which should serve to mount over all their customs. *Clarendon*, Great Rebellion.

11. *Naut.*: (*a*†) A large cleat with two arms or branches, bolted in the waist of ships to belay the tacks and sheets to. (*b*) A certain quantity of cable hauled up on deck from the chain-locker, of a length slightly greater than the depth of water, in order that the anchor, when let go, may reach the bottom without being checked. —**12.** In *shoemaking*, a strip cut from a butt or side of sole-leather.

The butt is first cut into long strips known as *ranges*, of varying width according to the purposes for which required. *Ure*, Dict., IV. 110.

13. A bolting-sieve for meal. *Cotgrave; Halliwell.* [Old and prov. Eng.]—**Battle-range.** See *battle*[1].—**Broken-range stonework**, range stonework in which thicker or thinner stones are occasionally inserted, thus breaking the uniformity. Compare *random stonework*, under *random*.—**Constituent of a range.** See *constituent*.—**Double-oven range**, a range which has two ovens, one on each side of the fire-pot.—**Point-blank range.** See *point-blank*.—**Random-range ashler.** See *ashler*[3]. —**Range curve.** See *curve*.—**Range stonework**, masonry laid in courses. The courses may vary in height, but in each a level joint is preserved.—**Single-oven range**, a range having but one oven, usually at one side of the fire-pot: in contradistinction to *double-oven range*. —**To get the range** of anything, to find by experiment and calculation the exact angle of elevation of the gun, the amount of charge, etc., necessary to throw projectiles so as to strike the object aimed at. =**Syn. 1.** Line, tier, file.—**4.** Sweep, reach.

rangé (roṅ-zhā'), *n.* [F., pp. of *ranger*, range, order: see *range*, v.] In *her.*, arranged in order: said of small bearings set in a row fessewise, or the like. The epithet is not often needed: thus, "six mullets in bend or bendwise" is sufficient without the use of the expression "*rangé* in bend."

range-finder (rānj'fīn"dėr), *n.* An instrument for measuring the range or distance of an object. The range-finder used in the United States navy is the invention of Lieutenant Fiske, U. S. N. Two telescopes, at the ends of the ship, are fitted with contacts, which move along arcs of resistance wire as the telescopes are directed at any object. The wires are connected as a Wheatstone bridge, the galvanometer of which is placed in a secure place below the water-line of the ship. The act of directing the telescopes toward any object disturbs the "balance of the bridge," and makes the galvanometer needle deflect by an amount proportional to the conveyance of the telescopes and inversely proportional to the distance. The scale of the galvanometer is divided into yards; so that the needle automatically points to the graduation representing the distance of the object.

range-heads (rānj'hedz), *n. pl.* *Naut.*, the windlass-bitts.

range-lights (rānj'līts), *n. pl.* **1.** Two or more lights, generally in lighthouses, so placed that when kept in line a fair course can be made through a channel: where two channels meet, the bringing of two range-lights into line serves to mark the turning-point into the new channel. —**2.** Lights placed aboard ship at a considerable horizontal distance from each other, and in the same vertical plane with the keel. They are used to give a better indication of changes of course to approaching vessels than is afforded by the ordinary side and steaming lights.

rangement† (rānj'ment), *n.* [< OF. *rangement*, < *renger, ranger*, range: see *range*, v.] The act of ranging; arrangement.

Lodgement, *rangement*, and adjustment of our other ideas. *Waterland*, Works, IV. 468.

ranger (rān'jėr), *n.* [Early mod. E. also *raunger;* < *range* + *-er*[1]. Cf. F. *rangeur*, one who arranges.] **1.** One who ranges, or roams, or roves about; especially, one engaged in ranging or going about for some specific purpose, as search or ward.

O where are all my *rangers* bold,
That I pay meat and fee
To search the forest far an' wide?
Young Akin (Child's Ballads, I. 186).

Specifically—**2.** In England, formerly, a sworn officer of a forest, appointed by the king's letters patent, whose business it was to walk through the forest, watch the deer, prevent trespasses, etc.; now, merely a government official connected with a royal forest or park.

They [wolves] walke not widely as they were wont,
For feare of *raungers* and the great hunt.
Spenser, Shep. Cal., September.

3. One of a body of regular or irregular troops, or other armed men, employed in ranging over a region, either for its protection or as marauders: as, the Texan *rangers*. Military rangers are generally mounted, but may fight on foot if occasion requires. The name is sometimes used in the plural for a permanent body of troops, as the Connaught *Rangers* in the British army.

"Do you know, friend," said the scout gravely, . . . "that this is a band of *rangers* chosen for the most desperate service?" *J. F. Cooper*, Last of Mohicans, xxxii.

4. One who roves for plunder; a robber. [Rare.] —**5.** A dog that beats the ground.—**6**†. A sieve. *Holland.*—**7.** A kind of fish. See the quotation.

[At Gibraltar] the Sp. besugo, a kind of sunbream, is called in English *ranger*. *N. and Q.*, 7th ser., IV. 278.

8. A kind of seal, probably the young bay-seal. [Newfoundland.]—**Partizan ranger.** See *partizan*[1].

rangerine (ran'jėr-in), *a.* Same as *rangiferine*.

Rangifer tarandus (Gray), the name usually given to the Old World species of *rangerine* deer, of which the American woodland and barren ground caribou are believed to be mere varieties. *Amer. Cyc.*, XIV. 265.

rangership (rān'jėr-ship), *n.* [< *ranger* + *-ship.*] The office of ranger or keeper of a forest or park. *Todd.*

range-stove (rānj'stōv), *n.* A cooking-stove made like a range; a portable range.

range-table (rānj'tā"bl), *n.* A table for a particular firearm containing the range and the time of flight for every elevation, charge of powder, and kind of projectile.

Rangia (ran'ji-ạ̈), *n.* [NL., named after *Rang*, a French conchologist.] 1. In *conch.*, the typical genus of *Rangiidæ*. The *R. cyrenoides* is common in the States bordering on the Gulf of Mexico. Also called *Gnathodon*. *Des Moulins*, 1832.
2. In *Actinozoa*, a genus of ctenophorous acalephs, ranking as the type of a family. *Agassiz*, 1860.

Rangifer (ran'ji-fėr), *n.* [NL. (Hamilton Smith), perhaps accom. < OF. *rangier, ranger, rancher, ranglier*, a reindeer (appar. < Icel. *hreinn* = OSw. *ren*, reindeer), + L. *fera*, a wild beast.] A genus of *Cervidæ*, containing arctic and subarctic species with large irregularly branching horns in both sexes, the brow-antler of which is highly developed, usually unsymmetrical, and more or less palmate, and very broad spreading hoofs; the reindeer. See cuts under *reindeer* and *caribou*.

rangiferine (ran-jif'e-rin), *a.* [< *Rangifer* + *-ine*[1].] Belonging or relating to the genus *Rangifer*; resembling a reindeer. Also *rangerine*.

Rangiidæ (ran-ji'i-dē), *n. pl.* [NL., < *Rangia* + *-idæ.*] 1. A family of bivalves, typified by the genus *Rangia*. The animal has short siphons connected at the base, a large linguiform foot, long palpi, and two pairs of gills, of which the outer is narrow and appendiculate. The shell is equivalve with salient umbones, and the hinge has two cardinal teeth and anterior and posterior lateral teeth in each valve, as well as an internal median fossa and cartilage.
2. A family of eurystomatous ctenophorans, represented by the genus *Rangia*. It was based on an African species, and characterized by the deep indentation between the rows of locomotive flappers and a tentacle projecting from the angle of each indentation.

ranging-rod (rān'jing-rod), *n.* A surveyors' rod or pole.

Rangoon creeper. See *Quisqualis*.

Rangoon tar. See *tar*.

rangy (rān'ji), *a.* [< *range* + *-y*[1].] 1. In *stock-breeding*, adapted for ranging or running about, or indicating such adaptation; quick or easy in movement; of roving character or capability: as, a *rangy* yoke of oxen (that is, good travelers, capable of making good speed, as in plowing): *rangy* steers (that is, steers disposed to wander away to a distance, as on a stock-range). The word is also sometimes applied to a roving person, as a lad who wanders from home, or who has a predilection for a roving life, as that of a sailor. [U. S.]

> The ponies . . . used for the circle-riding in the morning have need rather to be strong and *rangey*.
> *T. Roosevelt*, Hunting Trips, i.

2. Having or permitting range or scope; roomy; commodious. [U. S.]

> A large *rangy* shed for the horses.
> *Sportsman's Gazetteer*, p. 452.

rani, ranee (ran'ē), *n.* [Also *rany, rannee, ranny*; < Hind. *rānī*, < Skt. *rājñī*, queen, fem. of *rājan*: see *raja*.] In India, the wife of a raja, or a reigning princess; a queen.

Raniceps (ran'i-seps), *n.* [NL., < L. *rana*, a frog, + *caput*, head.] 1. In *ichth.*, a Cuvierian genus of gadoid fishes, typical of the family *Ranicipitidæ*. *R. raninus* is known as the *tadpole-hake*.—2. In *herpet.*, a genus of fossil labyrinthodont amphibians of the Carboniferous.

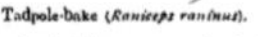

Tadpole-hake (*Raniceps raninus*).

Ranicipitidæ (ran"i-si-pit'i-dē), *n. pl.* [NL., < *Raniceps* (*Ranicipit-*) + *-idæ.*] A family of gadoid fishes, represented by the genus *Raniceps*. Their characters are mostly shared with the *Gadidæ*, but the suborbital chain is enlarged and continued backward over the operculum, the suspensorium of the lower jaw is very oblique, and the pyloric cæca are rudimentary or reduced to two.

Ranidæ (ran'i-dē), *n. pl.* [NL., < *Rana*[1] + *-idæ.*] A family of firmisternal salient amphibians, typified by the genus *Rana*, with premaxillary and maxillary teeth, subcylindrical sacral diapophyses and precoracoids, and with omosternum: the frog family. It is the most extensive family of batrachians, about 250 species, of several genera, being known. See *frog*[1], and cuts under *omosternum* and *Rana*[1].

raniform (ran'i-fôrm), *a.* [< NL. *raniformis*, < L. *rana*, a frog, + *forma*, form.] Frog-like; resembling or related to a frog; belonging to the *Raniformes*; ranine: distinguished from *bufoniform*.

Raniformes (ran-i-fôr'mēz), *n. pl.* [NL., pl. of *raniformis*: see *raniform*.] A division of batrachians, including the true frogs: distinguished from *Bufoniformes*.

Ranina[1] (rạ̈-nī'nạ̈), *n.* [NL. (Lamarck, 1801), fem. sing. of *raninus*: see *ranine*.] In *Crustacea*, the typical genus of *Raninidæ*, containing such frog-crabs as *R. dorsipeda*.

Frog-crab (*Ranina dorsipeda*), natural size.

Ranina[2] (rạ̈-nī'nä), *n. pl.* [NL., < *Rana*[1] + *-ina*[2].] In Günther's classification, a division of oxydactyl opisthoglossate batrachians, containing 6 families of frogs.

Raninæ (rạ̈-nī'nē), *n. pl.* [NL., < *Rana*[1] + *-inæ.*] The true frogs as a subfamily of batrachians, corresponding to the family *Ranidæ*.

ranine (rā'nin), *a.* [< F. *ranin*, < NL. *raninus*, < L. *rana*, a frog: see *Rana*[1].] 1. In *herpet.*, pertaining to frogs; related or belonging to the *Ranidæ*; raniform.—2. In *anat.*, pertaining to the under side of the tip of the tongue, where a tumor called a *ranula* is sometimes formed. The ranine artery is the termination of the lingual artery, running to the tip of the tongue; it is accompanied by the ranine vein.

raninian (rạ̈-nin'i-ạn), *a.* and *n.* [< *ranine* + *-ian.*] I. *a.* Pertaining to the *Raninidæ*.
II. *n.* A crab of the family *Raninidæ*.

Raninidæ (rạ̈-nin'i-dē), *n. pl.* [NL., < *Ranina*[1] + *-idæ.*] A family of anomurous crustaceans, typified by the genus *Ranina*. They have a smooth ovate-oblong carapace, the last pair of legs reduced and subdorsal, and the abdomen short, partially extended, and not folded under the thorax. The species are almost entirely confined to the tropics. See cut under *Ranina*[1].

raninoid (ran'i-noid), *a.* Pertaining to the *Raninoidea*; raninian.

Raninoidea (ran-i-noi'dẹ̄-ạ̈), *n. pl.* [NL., < *Ranina*[1] + *-oidea.*] A superfamily of anomurous crustaceans, represented by the raninians.

ranite (ran'īt), *n.* [< Icel. *Rān*, a giant goddess, queen of the sea, + *-ite*[2].] A hydrated silicate of aluminium and sodium, derived from the alteration of elæolite: it occurs in southern Norway, and is essentially the same as hydronephelite.

ranivorous (rạ̈-niv'ọ̄-rus), *a.* [< L. *rana*, a frog, + *vorare*, devour.] Frog-eating; subsisting habitually or chiefly upon frogs: as, the marsh-hawk is *ranivorous*.

rank[1] (rangk), *a.* [< ME. *rank, ranc, ronk, raunk, renk*, strong, proud, also rancid (influenced by OF. *rance, ranci*, rancid: see *rancid*); < AS. *ranc*, proud, forward, arrogant, showy, bold, valiant, = D. MLG. LG. G. *rank*, slender, projecting, lank, = Icel. *rakkr* (for **rankr*), straight, slender, bold, valiant, = Sw. *rank*, long and thin, = Dan. *rank*, straight, erect, slender.] 1†. Strong; powerful; capable of acting or of being used with great effect; energetic; vigorous; headstrong.

> There arof all the rowte with there *Ranke* shippes,
> Cast ancres with cables that kene were of byt.
> *Destruction of Troy* (E. E. T. S.), l. 4701.

> Soch a *rancke* and full writer must vse, if he will do wiselie, the exercise of a verie good kinde of Epitome.
> *Ascham*, The Scholemaster, p. 112.

> When folke bene fat, and riches *rancke*,
> It is a signe of helth. *Spenser*, Shep. Cal., July.

> Her *rank* teeth the glittering poisons chaw.
> *Middleton*, Entertainment to King James.

2. Strong of its kind or in character; unmitigated; virulent; thorough; utter: as, *rank* poison; *rank* treason; *rank* nonsense.

> The *renke* rebelle has been un-to my rounde table,
> Redy aye with Romaynes!
> *Morte Arthure* (E. E. T. S.), l. 2402.

> Whose sacred filletes all besprinkled were
> With filth of gory blod, and venim *rank*.
> *Surrey*, Æneid, ii.

> Willie mourns o'er her in vain,
> And to his mother he has gane,
> That vile *rank* witch, o' vilest kind!
> *Willie's Ladye* (Child's Ballads, I. 163).

> *Rank* corruption, mining all within,
> Infects unseen. *Shak.*, Hamlet, iii. 4. 148.

> Run, run, ye rogues, ye precious rogues, ye *rank* rogues!
> *Fletcher*, Bonduca, iv. 2.

> What are these but *rank* pedants?
> *Addison*, The Man of the Town.

3. Strong in growth; growing with vigor or rapidity; hence, coarse or gross: said of plants.

> Seven ears of corn came up upon one stalk, *rank* and good. Gen. xli. 5.

> *Rank* weeds, that every art and care defy,
> Reign o'er the land, and rob the blighted rye.
> *Crabbe*, Works, I. 5.

> As o'er the verdant waste I guide my steed,
> Among the high *rank* grass that sweeps his sides.
> *Bryant*, The Prairies.

4. Suffering from overgrowth or hypertrophy; plethoric. [Rare.]

> I know not, gentlemen, what you intend,
> Who else must be let blood, who else is *rank*.
> *Shak.*, J. C., iii. 1. 152.

5. Causing strong growth; producing luxuriantly; rich and fertile.

> Where land is *rank*, 'tis not good to sow wheat after a fallow. *Mortimer*, Husbandry.

6. Strong to the senses; offensive; noisome; rancid: as, a *rank* taste or odor.

> To thy fair flower add the *rank* smell of weeds.
> *Shak.*, Sonnets, lxix.

> And because they [the Caphrarians] alwayes annoint themselues with grease and fat, they yeeld a *ranke* smell.
> *Purchas*, Pilgrimage, p. 693.

> Whence arise
> But weeds of dark luxuriance, tares of haste,
> *Rank* at the core, though tempting to the eyes.
> *Byron*, Childe Harold, iv. 120.

> A number held pipes between their teeth, filling the room with the *rank* smoke of the strongest and blackest tobacco. *C. J. Bellamy*, Breton Mills, ii.

Hence—7. Coarse or gross morally; offensive to the mind; obscene; indecent; foul.

> My wife 's a hobby-horse, deserves a name
> As *rank* as any flax-wench. *Shak.*, W. T., i. 2. 277.

> The London Cuckolds, the most *rank* play that ever succeeded, was then [in the time of King Charles II.] in the highest court favour. *Life of Quin* (reprint 1887), p. 14.

> The euphemisms suggested by the American Revisers were certainly desirable, instead of the *rank* words which offend American sensibilities.
> *Bibliotheca Sacra*, XLIII. 557.

8†. Ruttish; in heat.

> The ewes, being *rank*,
> In the end of autumn turned to the rams.
> *Shak.*, M. of V., i. 3. 81.

9. In *law*, excessive; exceeding the actual value: as, a *rank* modus.—10. In *mech.*, cutting strongly or deeply, as the iron of a plane set so as to project more than usual.

> A roughing tool with *rank* feed or a finish tool with fine feed. *Sci. Amer.*, N. S., LI. 32.

11. Eager; anxious; impatient: as, he was *rank* to do it. [Slang, U. S.]—12. Very angry; in a passion. [Prov. Eng.]

rank[1]† (rangk), *adv.* [< *rank*[1], *a.*] Rankly; strongly; furiously.

> The seely man, seeing him ryde so *ranck*,
> And ayme at him, fell flatt to ground for feare.
> *Spenser*, F. Q., II. iii. 6.

> He 's irrecoverable; mad, *ranke* mad.
> *Marston*, What you Will, i. 1.

rank[1]† (rangk), *v. i.* [ME. **ranken, ronken*; < *rank*[1], *a.*] To become rank.

> Er hit *ronke* on rote. *Anglia*, iv. 19.

rank[2] (rangk), *n.* [Early mod. E. also *ranck, ranke*; < ME. *renk*, usually *reng*, pl. *renges, ringes*, a row or line of soldiers, class, order, grade, station, < OF. *renc, reng*, later *rang*, F. *rang* (> D. G. Dan. Sw. *rang*), F. dial. *ringue, raing* = Pr. *renc* = OCat. *renc*, a rank, row, range; < OHG. *hring, hrinc*, MHG. *rinc*, G. *ring*, a ring, = E. *ring*: see *ring*[1], *n.* Cf. *harangue*, from the same ult. (OHG.) source. The Bret. *renk* is < F.; Ir. *ranc* < E.] 1. A line, row, or range. [Obsolete or archaic except in specific uses. See *range*, 1.]

> And all the fruitfull spawne of fishes hew
> In endlesse *rancks* along enranged were.
> *Spenser*, F. Q., III. vi. 35.

> If therefore we look upon the *rank* or chain of things voluntarily derived from the positive will of God, we behold the riches of his glory proposed as the end of all.
> *Hooker*, Eccles. Polity, v., App. 1.

> The *rank* of osiers by the murmuring stream.
> *Shak.*, As you Like it, iv. 3. 80.

> Two equall *ranks* of Orient Pearls impale
> The open throat.
> *Sylvester*, tr. of Du Bartas's Weeks, i. 6.

In my juvenile days, and even long since, there was, hereabouts, a hackney-coach *rank* that had endured time out of mind, but was in latter years called a cab-stand.
N. and Q., 6th ser., X. 398.

Specifically—(*a*) One of the rows of a body of troops, or of any persons similarly ranged in a right-and-left line; a line of soldiers or other persons standing abreast in a formation: distinguished from *file*3, 5. See *rank and file*, under *file*3.

And Merlin that rode fro oo *renge* to a-nother ascride hem often "ore auaunt." *Merlin* (E. E. T. S.), iii. 588.

Olotocara, which had not learned to keepe his *ranke*, or rather moued with rage, lept on the platforme, and thrust him through the bodie with his pike and slew him.
Hakluyt's Voyages, III. 358.

Meanwhile the Tuscan army,
Right glorious to behold,
Came flashing back the noonday light,
Rank behind *rank*, like surges bright
Of a broad sea of gold. *Macaulay*, Horatius.

Hence—(*b*) *pl.* The lines or divisions of an army or any armed force; organized soldiery; the body or class of common soldiers: as, the *ranks* are full; to rise from the *ranks*; to reduce an officer to the *ranks*.

The Knight of Rokeby led his *ranks*
To aid the valiant northern Earls
Who drew the sword for royal Charles.
Scott, Rokeby, i. 28.

In 1887 the number was fifty-one; and in 1888, up to the 1st September, forty-five commissions were given to men from the *ranks*. *Harper's Mag.*, LXXX. 340.

(*c*) In *organ-building*, a row or set of pipes, one for each digital of the keyboard. A mixture-stop is said to be of two, three, four, or five ranks, according to the numbers of pipes sounded at once by a single digital. (*d*) One of the lines of squares on a chess-board running from side to side, in distinction from the files, which run from player to player. (*e*) A row, as of leaves on a stem.

2†. A continuous line or course; a stretch.

Presently after he was baptized, hee went to fast in the desert, xl. dayes & xl. nights on a *rancke*.
Guevara, Letters (tr. by Hellowes, 1577), p. 360.

3. A class, order, or grade of persons; any aggregate of individuals classed together for some common reason, as social station, occupation, character, or creed: as, the Prohibition *ranks*; the *ranks* of the Anarchists.

Thou wert honest,
Ever among the *rank* of good men counted.
Fletcher, Wife for a Month, v. 1.

All *ranks* and orders of men, being equally concerned in public blessings, equally join in spreading the infection. *Bp. Atterbury*.

Then from his Lordship I shall learn
Henceforth to meet with unconcern
One *rank* as weel 's another.
Burns, On Meeting Basil, Lord Daer.

The nearest practical approach to the theological estimate of a sin may be found in the *ranks* of the ascetics.
Lecky, Europ. Morals, I. 117.

4. Grade in a scale of comparison; class or classification; natural or acquired status; relative position; standing.

Not i' the worst *rank* of manhood.
Shak., Macbeth, iii. 1. 103.

These are all virtues of a meaner *rank*. *Addison*.

Specifically, of persons—(*a*) Titular distinction or dignity; gradation by hereditary, official, or other title: as, civil, judicial, or military *rank*; the *rank* of baron or marquis; the *rank* of general or admiral; the *rank* of ambassador or governor. The relative rank of officers of the United States army and navy is as follows: General ranks with admiral; lieutenant-general with vice-admiral; major-general with rear-admiral; brigadier-general with commodore; colonel with captain; lieutenant-colonel with commander; major with lieutenant-commander; captain with lieutenant (senior grade); first lieutenant with lieutenant (junior grade); second lieutenant with ensign.

The *rank* of an ambassador has nothing to do with the transaction of affairs.
Woolsey, Introd. to Inter. Law, § 94.

(*b*) Eminent standing or dignity; especially, aristocratic station or hereditary distinction, as in European monarchies; inherited or conferred social eminence.

Respect for *Rank*, fifty years ago universal and profound, is rapidly decaying. There are still many left who believe in some kind of superiority by Divine Right and the Sovereign's gift of *Rank*, even though that *Rank* be but ten years old, and the grandfather's shop is still remembered.
W. Besant, Fifty Years Ago, p. 118.

5†. A ranging or roving; hence, discursive wandering; divagation; aberration.

Instead of a manly and sober form of devotion, all the extravagant *ranks* and silly freaks of enthusiasm!
Bp. Atterbury, Sermons, I. ii.

6. In *geom.*, the degree of a locus of lines. (*a*) The number of lines of a singly infinite system which cut any given line in tridimensional space. (*b*) The number of lines of a triply infinite system which lie in one plane and pass through one point in that plane.—**A split in the ranks**, dissension and division in a party, sect, society, or the like. [Colloq.]

They must submit to the humiliation of acknowledging a *split in* their own *ranks*.
Nineteenth Century, XXVI. 749.

Rank and file. See *file*3.—**Rank of a complex**, the number of its rays lying in an arbitrary plane and passing through an arbitrary point in that plane.—**Rank of a curve**, the rank of the system of its tangents, or the number of tangents which cut any arbitrarily taken line in space.—**Rank of a surface**, the number of tangent lines to the surface which lie in a given plane and pass through a given point in that plane.—**To break ranks.** See *break*.—**To fill the ranks**, to make up the whole number, or a competent number.—**To keep rank†**, to be in keeping; be consistent.

Some strange effect which will not well *keep ranck*
With the rare temperance which is admired
In his life hitherto.
Beau. and Fl., Knight of Malta, iii. 3.

To take rank, to have rank or consideration; be classed or esteemed, with reference to position or merit: as, he *takes rank* as a very original poet.—**To take rank of**, to have the right of taking a higher place than; outrank: as, in Great Britain the sovereign's sons *take rank of* all other nobles. Compare *rank*2, *v. t.*, 3.—**To take rank with**, to have the same or coördinate rank with; be entitled to like official or social consideration: as, a captain in the navy *takes rank with* a colonel in the army.

rank2 (rangk), *v.* [Early mod. E. also *ranck*; < *rank*2, *n.*, q. v.] **I.** *trans.* **1.** To arrange in a rank or ranks; place in a rank or line.

And every sort is in a sondry bed
Sett by it selfe, and *ranckt* in comely rew.
Spenser, F. Q., III. vi. 35.

A many thousand warlike French
That were embattailed and *rank'd* in Kent.
Shak., K. John, iv. 2. 200.

These as enemies tooke their stands a musket shot one from another; *ranked* themselues 15 a breast, and each ranke from another 4 or 5 yards.
Capt. John Smith, Works, I. 135.

Horse and chariots *rank'd* in loose array.
Milton, P. L., ii. 887.

2. To assign to a particular class, order, or division; fix the rank of; class.

Thou bor'st the face once of a noble gentleman,
Rank'd in the first file of the virtuous.
Fletcher, Double Marriage, ii. 2.

I will not *rank* myself in the number of the first.
I. Walton, Complete Angler, p. 40.

How shall we *rank* thee upon glory's page?
Thou more than soldier and just less than sage!
Moore, To Thomas Hume.

3. To take rank of or over; outrank: as, in the United States army, an officer commissioned simply as general *ranks* all other generals. [U. S.]—**4.** To dispose in suitable order; arrange; classify.

Antiently the people [of Magnesia] were *ranked* according to their different tribes.
Pococke, Description of the East, II. ii. 55.

By *ranking* all things under general and special heads, it [Logic] renders the nature or any of the properties, powers, and uses of a thing more easy to be found out when we seek in what rank of beings it lies.
Watts, Logic, I. vi. § 13.

5†. To fix as to state or estimation; settle; establish.

We cannot *rank* you in a nobler friendship
Than your great service to the state deserves.
Beau. and Fl., Laws of Candy, i. 2.

I, that before was *ranked* in such content.
B. *Jonson*, Every Man in his Humour, iii. 3.

6†. To range; give the range to, as a gun in firing.

Their shot replies, but they were *rank'd* too high
To touch the pinnace.
Legend of Captain Jones (1659). (*Halliwell*, under *range*.)

II. *intrans.* **1.** To move in ranks or rows. [Rare.]

Your cattle, too; Allah made them; serviceable dumb creatures; . . . they come *ranking* home at evening time.
Carlyle.

2. To be ranged or disposed, as in a particular order, class, or division; hold rank or station; occupy a certain position as compared with others: as, to *rank* above, below, or with some other man.

There is reason to believe that he [William of Orange] was by no means equal as a general in the field to some who *ranked* far below him in intellectual powers.
Macaulay, Hist. Eng., vii.

Gorizia *ranks* as an ecclesiastical metropolis.
E. A. Freeman, Venice, p. 50.

3†. To range; go or move about; hence, to bear one's self; behave.

His men were a' clad in the grene;
The knight was armed capapie,
With a bended bow, on a milk-white steed;
And I wot they *rank'd* right bonnilie.
Sang of the Outlaw Murray (Child's Ballads, VI. 25).

Harke! they are at hande; *ranke* handsomly.
Marston, Dutch Courtezan, iv. 1.

4. In *British law*: (*a*) To have rank or standing as a claim in bankruptcy or probate proceedings.

£19,534 is expected to *rank* against assets estimated at £18,120 15*s.* 2*d.*
Daily Telegraph, April 8, 1886. (*Encyc. Dict.*)

(*b*) To put in a claim against the property of a bankrupt person or a deceased debtor: as, he *ranked* upon the estate.

rank-axis (rangk'ak"sis), *n.* A line considered as the envelop of planes.

rank-brained† (rangk'brānd), *a.* Wrong-headed; crack-brained.

rank-curve (rangk'kėrv), *n.* A curve considered as the envelop of its tangents.

ranker (rang'kėr), *n.* [< *rank*2 + *-er*1.] **1.** One who ranks or arranges; one who disposes in ranks.—**2.** A military officer who has risen or been promoted from the ranks. [Colloq., Eng.]

The new coast battalion, most of whose officers are *rankers*.
St. James's Gazette, June 2, 1886, p. 12. (*Encyc. Dict.*)

ranking (rang'king), *n.* [Verbal n. of *rank*2, *v.*] The act of one who ranks.—**Ranking and sale**, or **ranking of creditors**, in *Scots law*, the process whereby the heritable property of an insolvent person is judicially sold and the price divided among his creditors according to their several rights and preferences. This is the most complex and comprehensive process known in the law of Scotland, but is now practically obsolete. It corresponds to the English process of marshaling securities in an action for redemption or foreclosure.

rankle (rang'kl), *v.*; pret. and pp. *rankled*, ppr. *rankling*. [Early mod. E. also *rankill*, *rankyll*; < ME. *ranclen*, freq. of *rank*1, *v.*] **I.** *intrans.* **1.** To operate rankly or with painful effect; cause inflammation or irritation; produce a festering wound: used of either physical or mental influences.

Look, when he fawns, he bites; and when he bites,
His venom tooth will *rankle* to the death.
Shak., Rich. III., i. 3. 291.

[He] looked the rage that *rankled* in his heart.
Crabbe, Works, I. 76.

Or jealousy, with *rankling* tooth,
That inly gnaws the secret heart.
Gray, On a Distant Prospect of Eton College.

Say, shall I wound with satire's *rankling* spear
The pure warm hearts that bid me welcome here?
O. W. Holmes, A Rhymed Lesson.

Resentment long *rankled* in the minds of some whom Endicott had perhaps too passionately punished.
Bancroft, Hist. U. S., I. 322.

2. To continue or grow rank or strong; continue to be painful or irritating; remain in an inflamed or ulcerous condition; fester, as a physical or mental wound or sore.

My words might cast rank poison to his pores,
And make his swoln and *rankling* sinews crack.
Peele, David and Bethsabe.

A leper shut up in a pesthouse *rankleth* to himself, infects not others. *Rev. T. Adams*, Works, III. 19.

A wound i' the flesh, no doubt, wants prompt redress; . . .
But a wound to the soul? That *rankles* worse and worse.
Browning, Ring and Book, I. 197.

II. *trans.* **1.** To irritate; inflame; cause to fester.

Then shall the Britons, late dismayd and weake,
From their long vassalage gin to respire,
And on their Paynim foes avenge their *rankled* ire.
Spenser, F. Q., III. iii. 36.

2†. To corrode.

Here, because his mouth waters at the money, his [Judas's] teeth *rankle* the woman's credit, for so I find malignant reprovers styled: corrodunt, non corrigunt; correptores, immo corruptores—they do not mend, but make worse; they bite, they gnaw.
Rev. T. Adams, Works (Sermon on John xii. 6), II. 224.

rankly (rangk'li), *adv.* [< ME. *rankly*, *ronkly*; < *rank*1 + *-ly*2.] **1†.** With great strength or force; fiercely; rampantly.

Herk renk! is this ryȝt, so *ronkly* to wrath
For any dede that I haf don other demed the ȝet?
Alliterative Poems (ed. Morris), iii. 431.

2. In an excessive manner or degree; inordinately; intensely; profusely; exuberantly: as, *rankly* poisonous; *rankly* treasonable; weeds that grow *rankly*.—**3.** Offensively; noisomely; fetidly.

The smoking of incense or perfumes, and the like, smells *rankly* enough, in all conscience, of idolatry.
Dr. H. More, Antidote against Idolatry, viii. (*Latham*.)

4. Grossly; foully.

The whole ear of Denmark
Is by a forged process of my death
Rankly abused. *Shak.*, Hamlet, i. 5. 38.

rankness (rangk'nes), *n.* [< ME. *ranknesse*; < *rank*1 + *-ness*.] **1†.** Physical strength; effective force; potency.

The crane's pride is in the *rankness* of her wing.
Sir R. L'Estrange, Fables.

2. Strength of kind, quality, or degree, in a disparaging sense; hence, extravagance; excess; grossness; repulsiveness: as, *rankness* of growth; the *rankness* of a poison, or of one's pride or pretensions.—**3†.** Insolence; presumption.

I will physic your *rankness*, and yet give no thousand crowns neither. *Shak.*, As you Like it, i. 1. 91.

4. Strength of growth; rapid or excessive increase; exuberance; extravagance; excess, as of plants, or of the wood of trees. Rankness is a condition often incident to fruit-trees in gardens and orchards, in consequence of which great shoots or feeders are given out with little or no bearing wood. Excessive richness of soil and a too copious supply of manure are generally the inducing causes.

I am stifled
With the mere rankness of their joy.
Shak., Hen. VIII., iv. 1. 59.

5. Excessive fertility; exuberant productiveness, as of soil.

By reason of the *rankenesse* and frutefulnesse of the grounde, kyne, swyne, and horses doo maruelously increase in these regions.
Peter Martyr (tr. of Eden's First Books on America, ed. [Arber, p. 164).

Bred by the *rankness* of the plenteous land.
Drayton, Legend of Thomas Cromwell.

6. Offensive or noisome smell or taste; repulsiveness to the senses.

The native *rankness* or offensiveness which some persons are subject to, both in their breath and constitution.
Jer. Taylor (?), Artificial Handsomeness, p. 46.

rank-plane (rangk'plān), *n.* The plane of a plane pencil.

rank-point (rangk'point), *n.* The focus of a plane pencil.

rank-radiant (rangk'rā″di-ant), *n.* A point considered as the envelop of lines lying in a plane.

rank-riding† (rangk'rī″ding), *a.* Riding furiously; hard-riding.

And on his match as much the Western horseman lays
As the *rank-riding* Scots upon their Galloways.
Drayton, Polyolbion, iii. 28.

rank-scented (rangk'sen″ted), *a.* Strong-scented; having a coarse or offensive odor.

The mutable, *rank-scented* many. *Shak.*, Cor., iii. 1. 66.

rank-surface (rangk'sėr″fās), *n.* A surface considered as the envelop of its tangents.

rann, *n.* See *ran*[3].

rannee, *n.* See *rani*.

rannel† (ran'el), *n.* [< F. *ranelle*, toad, dim. of L. *rana*, frog.] A strumpet; a prostitute.

Such a roinish *rannel*, such a dissolute Gillian-flirt.
G. *Harvey*, Pierce's Supererogation (1600).

rannel-balk (ran'el-bâk), *n.* Same as *randle-bar*.

rannen†. A Middle English preterit plural of *run*. *Chaucer*.

ranny† (ran'i), *n.* [Also *ranney*; supposed to be ult. a corroption (through OF.) of L. *araneus*, sc. *mus*, a kind of mouse: see *shrew* and *araneous*.] The shrew or shrew-mouse, *Sorex araneus*.

Sammonicus and Nicander do call the mus araneus, the shrew or *ranney*, blind. *Sir T. Browne*, Vulg. Err., iii. 18.

ranoid (rā'noid), *a.* [< L. *rana*, a frog, + Gr. εἶδος, form.] In *herpet.*, same as *ranine*: distinguished from *bufonoid*.

ranpick†, ranpike†, *n.* Same as *rampick*.

ransack (ran'sak), *v.* [Prop. *ransake*, the form *ransack* being due in part to association with *sack*[2], pillage (see def. 2); < ME. *ransaken*, *ransakyn*, *raunsaken*, < Icel. *rannsaka* (= Sw. Norw. *ransaka* = Dan. *ransage*), search a house, ransack, < *rann* (for **rasn*), a house, abode (= AS. *ræsn*, a plank, ceiling, = Goth. *razn*, a house), + *saka*, fight, hurt, harm, appar. taken in this compound with the sense of the related *sækja*, seek, = AS. *sēcan*, seek: see *seek* and *sake*.] I. *trans.* 1. To search thoroughly; seek carefully in all parts of; explore, point by point, for what is desired; overhaul in detail.

In a morwenyng
When Phebus, with his firy torches rede,
Ransaked hath every lover in hys drede.
Chaucer, Complaint of Mars, l. 28.

All the articlis there in conteynid they shall *ransakyn* besyly, and discussyn soo discretly in here remembraunce that both in will . . . shal not onyttyn for to complishe the seyd articles. *Paston* Letters, I. 458.

In the third Year of his Reign, he *ransacked* all Monasteries, and all the Gold and Silver of either Chalices or Shrines he took to his own use. *Baker*, Chronicles, p. 26.

Cicero . . . *ransacks* all nature, and pours forth a redundancy of figures even with a lavish hand.
Goldsmith, Metaphors.

2†. To sack; pillage completely; strip by plundering.

Their vow is made
To *ransack* Troy.
Shak., T. and C., Prol., l. 8.

I observed only these two things, a village exceedingly *ransacked* and ruinated by meanes of the civil warres.
Coryat, Crudities, I. 23.

3†. To obtain by ransacking or pillage; seize upon; carry off; ravish.—4†. To violate; deflower: as, "*ransackt* chastity," *Spenser*.

II. *intrans.* To make penetrating search or inquisition; pry; rummage. [Obsolete or rare.]

With sacrilegious Tools we rudely rend her,
And *ransack* deeply in her bosom tender.
Sylvester, tr. of Du Bartas's Weeks, i. 5.

Such words he gaue, but deepe with dynt the sword enforced furst
Had *ransakt* through his ribs and sweete white brest at once had burst. *Phaer*, Æneid, ix.

ransack (ran'sak), *n.* [Cf. Icel. *rannsak*, *rannsókn*, a ransacking; from the verb.] 1. Detailed search or inquisition; careful investigation. [Rare.]

What secret corner, what unwonted way,
Has scap'd the *ransack* of my rambling thought?
Quarles, Emblems, iv. 12.

To compile, however, a real account of her [Madame Récamier] would necessitate the *ransack* of all the memoirs, correspondence, and anecdotage concerning French political and literary life for the first half of this century. *Encyc. Brit.*, XX. 309.

2†. A ransacking; search for plunder; pillage; sack.

Your Highness undertook the Protection of the English Vessels putting into the Port of Leghorn for shelter, against the Dutch Men of War threatning 'em with nothing but *Ransack* and Destruction.
Milton, Letters of State, Sept., 1652.

Even your father's house
Shall not be free from *ransack*. *J. Webster*.

ransacker† (ran'sak-ėr), *n.* [< ME. *raunsaker*; < *ransack* + *-er*[1].] One who ransacks; a careful searcher; a pillager.

That es to say, *Raunsaker* of the myghte of Godd and of His Maieste with-owttene gret clennes and meknes sall be ouerlayde and oppresside of Hym-selfe.
Hampole, Prose Treatises (E. E. T. S.), p. 42.

ransake†, *v.* An obsolete form of *ransack*.

ranshackle† (ran'shak-l), *v. t.* A variant of *ransack*, simulating *ramshackle*[1].

They loosed the kye out, ane and a',
And *ranshackled* the house right wel.
Jamie Telfer (Child's Ballads, VI. 106).

ransom (ran'sum), *n.* [Early mod. E. also *ransome*, *raunsom*; < ME. *ransome*, *raunsom*, *rawnsome*, *ranson*, *ransoun*, *raunson*, *raunsun*, *rawnison* (for the change of *n* to *m*, cf. *random*) = D. *rantsoen* = MLG. LG. *ransūn*, *ransūn* = G. *ranzion* = Dan. *ranson* = Sw. *ranson*, < OF. *rançon*, *renҫon*, *raenson*, *raenchon*, F. *rançon* = Pr. *reemsos*, *rezempto*, mod. *rançoun*, < L. *redemptio(n-)*, ransom, redemption: see *redemption*, of which *ransom* is a much shrunken form.] 1. Redemption for a price; a holding for redemption; also, release from captivity, bondage, or the possession of an enemy for a consideration; liberation on payment or satisfaction of the price demanded.

And Galashin seide than sholde he dye with-oute *raunsom*. *Merlin* (E. E. T. S.), iii. 571.

You beseche and pray,
Fair sir, saue my life, lete me on-lif go,
Taking this peple to *ranson* also!
Rom. of Partenay (E. E. T. S.), l. 4205.

Then he shall give for the *ransom* of his life whatsoever is laid upon him. Ex. xxi. 30.

The Money raised for his *Ransom* was not so properly a Taxation as a Contribution. *Baker*, Chronicles, p. 66.

2. The money or price awarded or paid for the redemption of a prisoner, captive, or slave, or for goods captured by an enemy; payment for liberation from restraint, penalty, or punishment.

Vpon a crosse naylyd I was for the,
Soffred deth to pay the *rawnson*.
Political Poems, etc. (ed. Furnivall), p. 111.

Even the Son of man came not to be ministered unto, but to minister, and to give his life a *ransom* for many.
Mark x. 45.

3†. Atonement; expiation.

If hearty sorrow
Be a sufficient *ransom* for offence,
I tender't here. *Shak.*, T. G. of V., v. 4. 75.

ransom (ran'sum), *v. t.* [Early mod. E. also *raunsome*; < ME. **raunsonen*, *raunceounen*, < OF. *rançonner*, ransom; from the noun.] 1. To redeem from captivity, bondage, forfeit, or punishment by paying or giving in return that which is demanded; buy out of servitude; buy off from penalty.

A robbere was *yraunceouned* rather than thei alle,
With-outen any penaunce of purgatorie, to perpetuel blisse. *Piers Plowman* (B), x. 420.

This was hard fortune; but, if alive and taken,
They shall be *ransom'd*, let it be at millions.
Fletcher, Humorous Lieutenant, ii. 4.

Walk your dim cloister, and distribute dole
To poor sick people, richer in His eyes
Who *ransom'd* us, and haler too, than I.
Tennyson, Guinevere.

2†. To redeem; rescue; deliver.

I will *ransom* them from the power of the grave; I will redeem them from death. Hos. xiii. 14.

3†. To hold at ransom; demand or accept a ransom for; exact payment on.

And he and hys company . . . dyde great domage to the countre, as well by *raunsomynge* of the townes as by pillage ouer all the countrey.
Berners, tr. of Froissart's Chron., II. (*Richardson.*)

4†. To set free for a price; give up the custody of on receipt of a consideration.

I would . . . *ransom* him to any French courtier for a new-devised courtesy. *Shak.*, L. L. L., i. 2. 65.

5†. To atone for; expiate.

Those tears are pearl which thy love sheds,
And they are rich and *ransom* all ill deeds.
Shak., Sonnets, xxxiv.

ransomable (ran'sum-a̤-bl), *a.* [< *ransom* + *-able*.] Capable of being ransomed or redeemed for a price.

I passed my life in that bath with many other gentlemen and persons of condition, distinguished and accounted as *ransomable*.
Jarvis, tr. of Don Quixote, I. iv. 13. (*Davies.*)

ransom-bill (ran'sum-bil), *n.* A war contract by which it is agreed to pay money for the ransom of property captured at sea and for its safe-conduct into port.

ransomer (ran'sum-ėr), *n.* [Early mod. E. *raunsomer*, < OF. *rançonneur*, < *rançonner*, ransom: see *ransom*, *v.*] One who ransoms or redeems.

The onlie sauior, redeemer, and *raunsomer* of them which were lost in Adam our forefather.
Foxe, Martyrs, an. 1555.

ransom-free (ran'sum-frē), *a.* Free from ransom; ransomless.

Till the fair slave be render'd to her sire,
And *ransom-free* restor'd to his abode.
Dryden, Iliad, i. 147.

ransomless (ran'sum-les), *a.* [< *ransom* + *-less*.] Free from ransom; without the payment of ransom.

Cosroe, Cassana, and the rest, be free,
And *ransomless* return!
Fletcher (*and another?*), Prophetess, iv. 5.

For this brave stranger, so indear'd to thee,
Passe to thy country, *ransomlesse* and free.
Heywood, Fair Maid of the West (Works, ed. Pearson, [1874, II. 423).

ranstead (ran'sted), *n.* [Also *ransted*; frequently also *ramstead*, *ramsted*; said to have been introduced at Philadelphia as a garden flower by a Welsh gentleman named *Ranstead*.] The common toad-flax, *Linaria vulgaris*, a weed with herbage of rank odor, erect stem, narrow leaves, and a raceme of spurred flowers, colored light-yellow, part of the lower lip bright-orange.

rant (rant), *v. i.* [< OD. *ranten*, also *randen*, dote, be enraged, = LG. *randen*, attack any one, call out to any one, = G. *ranzen*, toss about, make a noise; cf. G. dial. *rant*, noise, uproar; root uncertain.] 1. To speak or declaim violently and with little sense; rave: used of both the matter and the manner of utterance, or of either alone: as, a *ranting* preacher or actor.

Nay, an thou'lt mouth,
I'll *rant* as well as thou.
Shak., Hamlet, v. 1. 307.

They say you're angry, and *rant* mightily,
Because I love the same as you.
Cowley, The Mistress, Rich Rival.

Make not your Hecuba with fury rage,
And show a *ranting* grief upon the stage.
Dryden and Soames, tr. of Boileau's Art of Poetry, iii. 563.

2. To be jovial or jolly in a noisy way; make noisy mirth. [North. Eng. and Scotch.]

Wi' quaffing and laughing,
They *ranted* and they sang.
Burns, Jolly Beggars.

rant (rant), *n.* [< *rant*, *v.*] 1. Boisterous, empty declamation; fierce or high-sounding language without much meaning or dignity of thought; bombast.

This is stoical *rant*, without any foundation in the nature of man or reason of things. *Atterbury*.

2. A ranting speech; a bombastic or boisterous utterance.

After all their *rants* about their wise man being happy in the bull of Phalaris, &c., they yet allow'd him to dispatch himself if he saw cause. *Stillingfleet*, Sermons, I. v.

He sometimes, indeed, in his *rants*, talked with Norman haughtiness of the Celtic barbarians; but all his sympathies were really with the natives.
Macaulay, Hist. Eng., vi.

3. The act of frolicking; a frolic; a boisterous merrymaking, generally accompanied with dancing. [Scotch.]

Thou art the life o' public haunts;
But [without] thee, what were our fairs and *rants*!
Burns, Scotch Drink.

I hae a good conscience, . . . unless it be about a *rant* amang the lasses, or a splore at a fair.
Scott, Black Dwarf, ii.

4. A kind of dance, or the music to which it was danced. = **Syn. 1.** *Fustian, Turgidness*, etc. See *bombast*.

ran-tan (ran'tan), *n.* [Prob. an imitative var. of *randon*.] Same as *randan*.

ranter[1] (ran'tėr), *n.* [< *rant* + *-er*[1].] 1. One who rants; a noisy talker; a boisterous preacher, actor, or the like.—2. [*cap.*] A name applied—(*a*) By way of reproach, to the members of an English Antinomian sect of the Commonwealth period, variously associated with the Familists, etc. (*b*) Also, opprobriously, to the Primitive Methodists, who formed themselves into a society in 1810, although the founders had separated from the old Methodist society some years before, the ground of disagreement being that the new body favored street preaching, camp-meetings, etc.—3. A merry, roving fellow; a jolly drinker. [North. Eng. and Scotch.]

Mistake me not, custom, I mean not tho,
Of excessive drinking, as great *ranters* do.
Praise of Yorkshire Ale (1697), p. 5. (*Halliwell*.)

Yours, saint or sinner, Rob the *Ranter*.
Burns, To James Tennant.

ranter[2] (ran'tėr), *n.* [Origin obscure.] A large beer-jug.

ranter[2] (ran'tėr), *v. i.* [Cf. *ranter*[2], *n.*] To pour liquor from a large into a smaller vessel. [Prov. Eng.]

ranter[3] (ran'tėr), *v. t.* Same as *renter*[2].

ranterism (ran'tėr-izm), *n.* [< *ranter*[1] + *-ism*.] The practice or tenets of the Ranters; rantism.

ranters† (ran'tėrz), *n. pl.* A woolen stuff made in England in the eighteenth century. *Drapers' Dict.*

rantingly (ran'ting-li), *adv.* In a ranting manner. (*a*) With sounding empty speech; bombastically. (*b*) With boisterous jollity; frolicsomely.

Sae *rantingly*, sae wantonly,
Sae dauntingly gaed he;
He play'd a spring, and danc'd it round,
Below the gallows-tree.
Burns, Macpherson's Farewell.

rantipole (ran'ti-pōl), *a.* and *n.* [Appar. < *ranty* + *pole* = *poll*[1], head: see *poll*[1]. Cf. *dodipoll*.] **I.** *a.* Wild; roving; rakish.

Out upon't, at years of discretion, and comport yourself at this *rantipole* rate!
Congreve, Way of the World, iv. 10.

This *rantipole* hero had for some time singled out the blooming Katrina for the object of his uncouth gallantries.
Irving, Sketch-Book, p. 431.

II. *n.* A rude, romping boy or girl; a wild, reckless fellow.

What strange, awkward *rantipole* was that I saw thee speaking to? *J. Baillie.*

I was always considered as a *rantipole*, for whom anything was good enough.
Marryat, Frank Mildmay, xv. (*Davies.*)

rantipole (ran'ti-pōl), *v. i.*; pret. and pp. *rantipoled*, ppr. *rantipoling*. [< *rantipole*, *n.*] To run about wildly.

The elder was a termagant, imperious wench; she used to *rantipole* about the house, pinch the children, kick the servants, and torture the cats and dogs. *Arbuthnot.*

rantism[1]† (ran'tizm), *n.* [< Gr. ῥαντισμός, a sprinkling, < ῥαντίζειν, sprinkle, besprinkle.] A sprinkling; hence, a small number; a handful. [Rare.]

We, but a handful to their heap, a *rantism* to their baptism. *Bp. Andrews.*

rantism[2] (ran'tizm), *n.* [< *rant* + *-ism*.] The practice or tenets of the Ranters; ranterism. *Johnson.*

rantle-tree, randle-tree (ran'tl-trē, -dl-trē), *n.* [Cf. *ran-tree*, a dial. form of *roan-tree*; cf. also *ranpick*, *rampick*.] 1. A tree chosen with two branches, which are cut short, and left somewhat in the form of the letter Y, set close to or built into the gable of a cottage to support one end of the rooftree.—2. A beam which runs from back to front of a chimney, and from which the crook is suspended.—3. Figuratively, a tall, raw-boned person.

If ever I see that auld *randle-tree* of a wife again, I'll gie her something to buy tobacco.
Scott, Guy Mannering, xxvi.

[Scotch in all uses.]

rantock (ran'tok), *n.* The goosander, *Mergus merganser*. [Orkneys.]

ran-tree (ran'trē), *n.* A dialectal variant of *roan-tree*. Also *rantry*.

ranty (ran'ti), *a.* and *n.* [< *rant* + *-y*[1].] Same as *randy*. [Prov. Eng.]

ranula (ran'ū-lạ̈), *n.*; pl. *ranulæ* (-lē). [= F. *ranule*, < L. *ranula*, a little frog, also a small swelling on the tongue of cattle, dim. of *rana*, a frog: see *Rana*[1].] A cystic tumor caused by the obstruction of the duct of a small mucous gland on the under surface of the tongue, the so-called Blandin-Nuhn gland. The term has been applied, however, with considerable looseness, to other tumors in or near this place presenting some resemblance to true ranulæ.

ranular (ran'ū-lär), *a.* [= F. *ranulaire*; as *ranula* + *-ar*[3].] Of or pertaining to a ranula; of the character of a ranula.

Ranunculaceæ (rạ̈-nung-kū-lā'sẹ̄-ē), *n. pl.* [NL. (A. L. de Jussieu, 1789), < *Ranunculus* + *-aceæ*.] An order of polypetalous plants of the cohort *Ranales*, characterized by the numerous stamens inserted on the receptacle, five deciduous and commonly colored sepals, not more than one complete circle of petals, and seeds with a minute embryo in fleshy albumen, and without an aril. They have usually many separate pistils which mature into distinct dry fruits, either achenes or follicles, or coalesce into berries. The species, estimated by some at 1,200, by Durand at 680, are included in 5 tribes and 30 genera. They occur throughout the world, but in the tropics more rarely and chiefly on mountains, elsewhere forming a conspicuous part of the flora of almost every region, especially in Europe, which contains one fifth, and in North America, which has one seventeenth, of all the species. Their wide distribution is aided by the long-continued vitality of the seeds, many of which are also remarkably slow to germinate after planting, those of several species requiring two years. They are annual or perennial herbs—rarely undershrubs, as *Xanthorhiza*. Many have dissected alternate or radical leaves, the petiole with an expanded sheathing base, but without stipules; *Clematis* is exceptional in its opposite leaves and climbing stem. The order is often known as the buttercup or crowfoot family, from the type, and contains an unusually large proportion of other characteristic plants, as the hepatica of America, the Christmas rose of Germany, and the lesser celandine of England. It includes also many of the most beautiful flowers of garden cultivation. Most of the species contain in their colorless juice an acrid and caustic principle, which sometimes becomes a dangerous narcotic poison, is often of great medicinal value (see *hellebore*, *aconite*, *Hydrastis*, *Actæa*, *Cimicifuga*), is usually most concentrated in the roots, but very volatile in the foliage and stems, and is dissipated by drying or in water, but intensified by the action of acids, alcohol, etc. The order was one of the earliest to be defined by botanists with substantially its present limits (as *Multisiliquæ* by Linnæus, 1751), and has long been placed at the head of the polypetalous families of dicotyledons, standing as the first order of plants in the most widely accepted classifications, from De Candolle in 1819 to Durand in 1888.

ranunculaceous (rạ̈-nung-kū-lā'shius), *a.* [< NL. *ranunculaceus*, < *Ranunculus*, q. v. Cf. *Ranunculaceæ*.] Of or pertaining to the *Ranunculaceæ*; resembling the ranunculus.

Ranunculeæ (rā-nung-kū'lẹ̄-ē), *n. pl.* [NL. (A. P. de Candolle, 1818), < *Ranunculus* + *-eæ*.] A tribe of plants of the order *Ranunculaceæ*. It is characterized by carpels with one ascending ovule, becoming achenes in fruit, by numerous radical leaves, and (excepting in the two species of *Oxygraphis*) by the additional presence of alternate stem-leaves. It includes the type genus *Ranunculus*, and 3 other genera embracing 8 species.

Ranunculus (rā-nung'kū-lus), *n.* [NL. (Kaspard Bauhin, 1623), < L. *ranunculus*, a medicinal plant, also called *batrachion*, perhaps crowfoot (> It. *ranuncolo*, Sp. *ranúnculo*, Pg. *ranunculo*, D. *ranonkel*, G. Dan. Sw. *ranunkel*, crowfoot), dim. of *rana*, a frog: see *Rana*[1].] 1. A large genus of polypetalous plants, type of the order *Ranunculaceæ* and of the tribe *Ranunculeæ*. It is characterized by the perfect flowers with from three to five caducous sepals, three to five or even fifteen conspicuous petals, each marked at the base by a nectar-bearing scale or pit, and by the many achenes in a head or spike, each beaked with a short persistent style. There are about 200 species, scattered throughout the world, abundant in temperate and cold regions, with a few on mountain-tops in the tropics; 15 species are British, and about 47 occur in the United States, besides at least 9 others in Alaska; 28 are found in the Atlantic States. The genus is remarkable for its development northward, extending to the Aleutian Islands and Point Barrow, and even to Fort Conger, 81° 44′ north. Others extend well to the south, as the Fuegian *R. biternatus*. The species have usually a perennial base or rootstock, and bear deeply divided leaves, entire in a few species, and yellow or white terminal flowers (pink in *R. Andersoni* of Nevada), which are generally bright and showy, and have numerous and conspicuous short yellow stamens and a smaller central mass of yellow or greenish pistils. The more common species, with bright-yellow flowers and palmately divided leaves, are known as *buttercup* and *crowfoot*, especially *R. acris* and *R. bulbosus*, which have also the old local names of *butter-flower*, *butter-daisy*, *blister-plant*, *crow-flower*, and in Scotland *yellow gowan*. (See also *goldcup*, and cut under *ovary*[1].) A number of yellow species are cultivated under the name *garden ranunculus*, as *R. speciosus*, a favorite source of cut flowers, and especially the Persian *R. Asiaticus*, with three-parted leaves, parent of a hundred varieties, mostly double, and including scarlet and other colors. *R. aconitifolius*, a tall European species with five-parted leaves, is cultivated in white double-flowered varieties under the names *bachelor's-buttons* and *fair-maids-of-France* or *-of-Kent*. The bright-yellow flowers of *R. insignis*, a densely woolly New Zealand species, are nearly 2 inches across. Several white-flowered species are remarkable for their growth in rock-crevices amid perpetual snow, especially *R. glacialis* of the Alps, and also the yellow-flowered *R. Thora*, the mountain wolf's-bane. A few weedy species have prickly fruit, as *R. arvensis* of England (for which see *hungerweed*, *hedgehog*, 3, and *joy*, 4). Many species are so acrid as to raise blisters when freshly gathered, but are sometimes eaten, when dried, by cattle. *R. sceleratus*, said to be the most acrid species, is eaten boiled as a salad in Wallachia, as are also the roots of *R. bulbosus*, the acridity disappearing on boiling. *R. auricomus* (see *goldilocks*) is exceptional in the absence of this acrid principle, as also *R. aquatilis*, which sometimes forms almost the entire food of cattle. This and several other species, the water-crowfoots, are immersed aquatics with finely dissected foliage, forming deep-green feathery masses which bear white emersed flowers; among them is *R. Lyallii* of New Zealand, one of the most ornamental species, there known as *water-lily*. The yellow water-crowfoot, *R. multifidus*, found from North Carolina to Point Barrow, has kidney-shaped and cut floating leaves. Several species with long and mainly undivided leaves are known as *spearwort*. For *R. Ficaria*, celebrated as one of the earliest English flowers, and as *Wordsworth's flower*, see *celandine*, 2, *pilewort*, and *figwort*, 2. See also cut under *achenium*.

Flowering Plant of *Ranunculus bulbosus* (buttercup).

2. [*l. c.*; pl. *ranunculi* (-lī).] A plant of the genus *Ranunculus*.

ranverse†, *v. t.* See *renverse*.

Ranvier's nodes. See *nodes of Ranvier*, under *node*.

Ranzania (ran-zā'ni-ạ̈), *n.* [NL., named (in def. 1 by Nardo, 1840) after C. *Ranzani*, an Italian naturalist.] 1. In *ichth.*, a genus of gymnodont fishes of the family *Molidæ*.—2. In *entom.*, a genus of coleopterous insects.

ranz des vaches (roṅs dā vash). [Swiss F. (see def.), explained as lit. (*a*) 'the lowing of the cows': Swiss dial. *ranz*, connected, in this view, with G. *ranzen*, make a noise, drum with the fingers (cf. *ranken*, bray as an ass); *des*, comp. of *de*, of, and *les*, pl. of def. art.; *vaches*, pl. of *vache*, < L. *vacca*, a cow (see *vaccine*); (*b*) in another view, 'the line of cows,' *ranz* being taken as a var. of *rangs*, pl. of *rang*, row, line (because the cows fall into line when they hear the alpenhorn): see *rank*[2].] One of the melodies or signals of the Swiss herdsmen, commonly played on the alpenhorn. It consists of irregular phrases made up of the harmonic tones of the horn, which are singularly effective in the open air and combined with mountain echoes. The melodies vary in the different cantons. They are sometimes sung.

Raoulia (rạ̈-ö'li-ạ̈), *n.* [NL. (Sir J. D. Hooker, 1867), named after E. *Raoul*, a French naval surgeon, who wrote on New Zealand plants in 1846.] A genus of composite plants of the tribe *Inuloideæ* and subtribe *Gnaphalieæ*. It is characterized by the solitary, sessile, and terminal heads of many flowers, which are mostly perfect and fertile, the outer circles of pistillate flowers being only one or two, or less than in the related genus *Gnaphalium* (the everlasting), but more than in the other next-allied genus, *Helichrysum*. All the flowers bear a bifid style and a pappus which is not plumose. The 14 species are mostly natives of New Zealand, and are small densely tufted plants of rocky mountainous places, resembling mosses, with numerous branches thickly clothed with minute leaves. They bear white starry flower-heads, one at the end of each short twig, closely surrounded with leaves, and in *R. grandiflora* and others ornamented by an involucre with white bracts. *R. eximia* and *R. mammillaris* are known in New Zealand as *sheep-plants*, from their growth in sheep-pastures in large white woolly tufts, readily mistaken for sheep even at a short distance.

rap[1] (rap), *v.*; pret. and pp. *rapped* or *rapt*, ppr. *rapping*. [< ME. *rappen*, < Sw. *rappa*, strike, beat, rap; cf. *rap*[1], *n.* Cf. MHG. freq. *raffeln*, G. *rappeln*, intr., rattle. Perhaps connected with *rap*[2].] **I.** *trans.* 1. To beat upon; strike heavily or smartly; give a quick, sharp blow to, as with the fist, a door-knocker, a stick, or the like; knock upon.

His hote newe chosen love he chaunged into hate,
And sodainly with mighty mace gan *rap* hir on the pate.
Gascoigne, In Praise of Lady Sandes.

With one great Peal they *rap* the Door,
Like Footmen on a Visiting Day.
Prior, The Dove, st. 9.

2. To use in striking; make a blow or blows with. [Rare.]

Dunstan, as he went along through the gathering mist, was always *rapping* his whip somewhere.
George Eliot, Silas Marner, iv.

3. To utter sharply; speak out: usually with *out* (see phrase below).

> One *raps* an oath, another deals a curse;
> He never better bowl'd; this never worse.
> *Quarles*, Emblems, i. 10.

To rap out. (*a*) To throw out violently or suddenly in speech; utter in a forcible or striking manner: as, to *rap out* an oath or a lie.

> He could roundlie *rap out* so manie vgle othes.
> *Ascham*, The Scholemaster, p. 57.

> The first was a judge, who *rapped out* a great oath at his footman. *Addison*, Freeholder, No. 44.

(*b*) To produce or indicate by rapping sounds; impart by a series of significant raps: as, to *rap out* a communication or a signal: used specifically of the supposed transmission of spiritual intelligence in this way through the instrumentality of mediums. =Syn. 1. To thump, whack.

II. *intrans.* 1†. To deal a heavy blow or heavy blows; beat.

> The elementes gonne to rusche & *rappe*,
> And smet downe chirches & templis with crak.
> *Political Poems*, etc. (ed. Furnivall), p. 206.

2†. To fall with a stroke or blow; drop so as to strike.

> Now, by this time the tears were *rapping* down
> Upon her milk-white breast, aneth her gown.
> *Ross*, Helenore, p. 70. (*Jamieson.*)

3. To strike a quick, sharp blow; make a sound by knocking, as on a door: as, to *rap* for admittance.

> Villain, I say, knock me at this gate,
> And *rap* me well. *Shak.*, T. of the S., i. 2. 12.

> Whan she cam to the king's court,
> She *rappit* wi' a ring.
> *Earl Richard* (Child's Ballads, III. 397).

> Comes a dun in the morning and *raps* at my door.
> *Shenstone*, Poet and Dun.

4. To take an oath; swear; especially, to swear falsely: compare *to rap out* (*a*), above. [Thieves' cant.]

> It was his constant maxim that he was a pitiful fellow who would stick at a little *rapping* for his friend.
> *Fielding*, Jonathan Wild, i. 13. (*Davies.*)

rap[1] (rap), *n.* [< ME. *rap*, *rappe* = Sw. Norw. *rapp* = Dan. *rap*, a rap, tap, smart blow; cf. *rap*[1], *v.*] 1. A heavy or quick, smart blow; a sharp or resounding knock; concussion from striking.

> The right arme with a *rappe* reft fro the shuldurs.
> *Destruction of Troy* (E. E. T. S.), l. 7680.

> And therewith (as in great anger) he clapped his tyste on the borde a great *rappe*. *Hall*, Edw. V.

> Bolus arriv'd, and gave a doubtful tap,
> Between a single and a double *rap*.
> *Colman the Younger*, Broad Grins, The Newcastle Apothecary.

2. A sound produced by knocking, as at a door, or by any sharp concussion; specifically, in modern spiritualism, a ticking or knocking noise produced by no apparent physical means, and ascribed to the agency of disembodied spirits.

> We may first take the *raps* and the "astral bells," which Mr. Sinnett seems to regard as constituting important test phenomena.
> *R. Hodgson*, Proc. Soc. Psych. Research, III. 261.

rap[2] (rap), *v. t.*; pret. and pp. *rapped* or *rapt*, ppr. *rapping*. [< ME. *rappen*, < Sw. *rappa*, snatch, seize, carry off, = MHG. G. *raffen*, snatch; dial. (LG.) *rappen*, snatch up, take up (> ult. E. *raff*). Cf. *rope*[1] and *rape*[2]. The pp. *rapped*, *rapt*, became confused with *rapt*, < L. *raptus*, pp. of *rapere*, snatch, which is not connected with the Teut. word: see *rapt*[1], *rapt*[2].] 1†. To snatch or hurry away; seize by violence; carry off; transport; ravish.

> Some shall be *rapt* and taken alive, as St. Paul saith.
> *Latimer*, 2d Sermon bef. Edw. VI., 1550.

> Think ye that . . . they will not pluck from you whatsoever they can *rap* or reave?
> *Apostolic Benediction of Adrian VI.*, Nov. 25, 1522 [(Foxe's Martyrs, II. 59).

> He ever hastens to the end, and so
> (As if he knew it) *raps* his hearer to
> The middle of his matter.
> *B. Jonson*, tr. of Horace's Art of Poetry.

> But when these people grew niggardly in their offerings, it [the room] was *rapt* from thence.
> *Sandys*, Travailes, p. 160.

> *Rapt* in a chariot drawn by fiery steeds.
> *Milton*, P. L., iii. 522.

2. To transport out of one's self; affect with ecstasy or rapture; carry away; absorb; engross.

> What, dear sir,
> Thus *raps* you? Are you well?
> *Shak.*, Cymbeline, i. 6. 51.

> I found thee weeping, and . . .
> Am *rapt* with joy to see my Marcia's tears.
> *Addison*, Cato, iv. 3.

> *Rapt* into future times, the bard begun.
> *Pope*, Messiah, l. 7.

To rap and rend (originally *to rape and ren*: see *rape*[2]), to seize and strip: fall on and plunder; snatch by violence.

> All they could *rap and rend*, and pilfer,
> To scraps and ends of gold and silver.
> *S. Butler*, Hudibras, II. ii. 789.

> From foe and from friend
> He'd *rap and he'd rend*, . . .
> That Holy Church might have more to spend.
> *Barham*, Ingoldsby Legends, II. 206.

rap[3] (rap), *v. t.*; pret. and pp. *rapped*, ppr. *rapping*. [Also *rape*; prob. due in part to *rap*[1], but in part representing ME. *repen*, < AS. *hrepian*, touch, treat, = OFries. *reppa*, touch, move, = MD. *reppen*, move, = LG. *reppen*, touch, move, > G. *rappen*, scrape, = Icel. *hreppa*, catch, obtain, = Sw. *repa*, scratch. Cf. *rape*[6].] To scratch. *Halliwell.* [Prov. Eng.]

rap[4] (rap), *n.* [Perhaps a particular use of *rap*[1]. There is nothing to connect the word with MHG. G. *rappe*, a coin so called: see *rappe*[2].] A counterfeit coin of bad metal which passed current in Ireland for a halfpenny in the reign of George I., before the issue of Wood's halfpence. Its intrinsic value was half a farthing. Hence the phrases *not worth a rap*, *to care not a rap*, implying something of no value.

> It having been many years since copper halfpence or farthings were last coined in this Kingdom, they have been for some time very scarce, and many counterfeits passed about under the name of *raps*.
> *Swift*, Drapier's Letters, letter i.

> They [his pockets] was turned out afore, and the devil a *rap*'s left. *Barham*, Ingoldsby Legends, I. 76.

> I don't care a *rap* where I go.
> *C. D. Warner*, Their Pilgrimage, p. 201.

Rap halfpenny, a rap.

> It is not of very great moment to me that I am now and then imposed on by a *rap halfpenny*.
> *Blackwood's Mag.*, XCVI. 392.

rap[5]†, *n.* A Middle English form of *rope*.

rap[6]†. A Middle English preterit of *reap*. *Wyclif.*

rap[7] (rap), *n.* [Origin obscure.] A lay or skein of yarn containing 120 yards. *E. H. Knight.*

Rapaces (rā-pā'sēz), *n. pl.* [NL., pl. of L. *rapax*, rapacious: see *rapacious*.] 1. In *mammal.*, the beasts of prey; carnivorous quadrupeds; the *Carnivora*, now called *Feræ*. Also *Rapacia*.—2. In *ornith.*, the birds of prey; rapacious birds; the *Accipitres* or *Raptores*.

Rapacia (rā-pā'shi-ä), *n. pl.* [NL., neut. pl. of L. *rapax*: see *Rapaces*.] Rapacious mammals; beasts of prey: synonymous with *Rapaces*, 1.

rapacious (rā-pā'shus), *a.* [= F. *rapace* = Pr. *rapatz* = Sp. *rapaz* = It. *rapace*, < L. *rapax* (*rapac-*), rapacious, < *rapere*, seize: see *rape*[2].] 1. Of a grasping habit or disposition; given to seizing for plunder or the satisfaction of greed, or obtaining wrongfully or by extortion; predatory; extortionate: as, a *rapacious* usurer; specifically, of animals, subsisting by capture of living prey; raptorial; predaceous: as, *rapacious* birds or fishes.

> What trench can intercept, what fort withstand
> The brutal soldier's rude *rapacious* hand.
> *Rowe*, tr. of Lucan's Pharsalia, vii.

> A *rapacious* man he [Warren Hastings] certainly was not. Had he been so, he would infallibly have returned to his country the richest subject in Europe.
> *Macaulay*, Warren Hastings.

2. Of a grasping nature or character; characterized by rapacity; immoderately exacting; extortionate: as, a *rapacious* disposition; *rapacious* demands.

> Well may then thy Lord, appeased,
> Redeem thee quite from Death's *rapacious* claim.
> *Milton*, P. L., xi. 258.

> There are two sorts of avarice; the one is but of a bastard kind, and that is the *rapacious* appetite of gain.
> *Cowley*, Avarice.

=Syn. 1. *Rapacious, Ravenous, Voracious.* *Rapacious*, literally disposed to seize, may note, as the others do not, a distinctive characteristic of certain classes of animals; the tiger is a *rapacious* animal, but often not *ravenous* or *voracious*. *Ravenous* implies hunger of an extreme sort, shown in eagerness to eat. *Voracious* means that one eats or is disposed to eat a great deal, without reference to the degree of hunger: a glutton is *voracious*. Samuel Johnson tended to be a *voracious* eater, because in his early life he had often gone hungry till he was *ravenous*.

rapaciously (rā-pā'shus-li), *adv.* In a rapacious manner; by rapine; by violent seizure.

rapaciousness (rā-pā'shus-nes), *n.* The character of being rapacious; inclination to seize violently or unjustly.

rapacity (rā-pas'i-ti), *n.* [< F. *rapacité* = Pr. *rapacitat* = Sp. *rapacidad* = Pg. *rapacidade* = It. *rapacità*, < L. *rapacita(t-)s*, rapacity, < *rapax* (*rapac-*), rapacious: see *rapacious*.] The character of being rapacious; the exercise of a rapacious or predaceous disposition; the act or practice of seizing by force, as plunder or prey, or of obtaining by extortion or chicanery, as unjust gains: as, the *rapacity* of pirates, of usurers, or of wild beasts.

> Our wild profusion, the source of insatiable *rapacity*.
> *Bolingbroke*, To Pope.

> In the East the *rapacity* of monarchs has sometimes gone to the extent of taking from cultivators so much of their produce as to have afterwards to return part for seed.
> *H. Spencer*, Prin. of Sociol., § 443.

rapadura (rap-a-dö'rä), *n.* [Also *rappadura*; < Sp. Pg. *rapadura*, shavings or scrapings, < *rapar*, shave, scrape, = F. *râper*, OF. *rasper*, scrape: see *rasp*[1], *v.*] A coarse unclarified sugar, made in Mexico and some parts of South America, and cast in molds.

raparee, *n.* See *rapparee*.

Rapatea (rä-pā'tē-ä), *n.* [NL. (Aublet, 1775), from a native name in Guiana.] A genus of monocotyledonous plants, the type of the order *Rapateaceæ*. It is characterized by an ovary with three cells and three ovules, six anthers each with a spiral appendage, and numerous flowers in a globose head with an involucre of two long leaf-like bracts dilated at the base, and each flower provided with many closely imbricated obtuse appressed bractlets. There are 5 or 6 species, natives of Guiana and northern Brazil. They bear long and narrow radical leaves from a low or robust rootstock, and flowers on a leafless scape, each with three rigid and chaff-like erect sepals, and three broad and spreading petals united below into a hyaline tube.

Rapateaceæ (rä-pā-tē-ā'sē-ē), *n. pl.* [NL. (Koernicke, 1871), < *Rapatea* + *-aceæ*.] An order of monocotyledonous plants of the series *Coronarieæ*, typified by the genus *Rapatea*. It is characterized by regular flowers with three greenish sepals and three petals, six stamens with long anthers opening by a pore, a three-celled ovary with few or solitary anatropous ovules, and a lenticular embryo in farinaceous albumen. It includes about 22 species, of 6 genera, once classed among the rushes, and now placed between them and the spiderworts. They are perennial herbs, natives of Brazil, Guiana, and Venezuela, and are mostly robust marsh-plants, with long radical tapering leaves, sessile or petioled, and flowers on a naked scape, commonly in dense involucrate heads resembling those of the *Compositæ*.

rape[1]† (rāp), *v. i.* [< ME. *rapen*, < Icel. *hrapa*, fall, rush headlong, hurry, hasten, = Norw. *rapa*, slip, fall, = Dan. *rappe*, make haste; cf. MLG. *reppen*, hasten, hurry, G. refl. *rappeln*, hasten, hurry. Cf. *rape*[1], *a.* and *n.*, also *rape*[2], *rap*[2], of which *rape*[1] is in part a doublet.] To make haste; hasten; hurry: often used reflexively.

> Pas fro my presens on payne of thi lyffe,
> And *rape* of [from] my rewme in a rad haste,
> Or thou shall lelly be lost and thou leng oghter.
> *Destruction of Troy* (E. E. T. S.), l. 1898.

> "For I may nougt lette," quod that leode, and lyarde he bistrydeth,
> And *raped hym* to-Iherusalem-ward the rigte waye to ryde.
> *Piers Plowman* (B), xvii. 79.

rape[1]† (rāp), *n.* [ME., < *rape*[1], *v.*] Haste; precipitancy; a precipitate course.

> Row forthe in a *rape* right to the banke,
> Tit vnto Troy, tary no lengur.
> *Destruction of Troy* (E. E. T. S.), l. 5633.

> So oft a day I mote thy werke renewe,
> It to correct and eke to rubbe and scrape;
> And al is thorgh thy necligence and *rape*.
> *Chaucer*, Scrivener, l. 7.

rape[1]† (rāp), *a.* [< ME. *rape* = D. *rap*, < Sw. Norw. *rapp* = Dan. *rap*, quick, brisk: see *rape*[1], *v.*] Quick; hasty.

> Than byspak his brother, that *rape* was of rees.
> *Tale of Gamelyn*, l. 101.

rape[1]† (rāp), *adv.* [ME., < *rape*[1], *a.*] Quickly; hastily.

> I sey and swere hym ful *rape*.
> *Rom. of the Rose*, l. 6516.

rape[2] (rāp), *v.*; pret. and pp. *raped*, ppr. *raping*. [< ME. *rapen* (= MD. *rapen*, *raepen*, D. *rapen*, gather, = MLG. LG. *rapen*, snatch, seize, = Norw. *rapa*, tear off), a var. of *rappen*, seize: see *rap*[2]. This verb has been partly confused with L. *rapere*, seize, whence ult. E. *rapid*, *rapine*, *rapacious*, *rapt*[2], etc.: see *rap*[2], *rapt*[1], *rapt*[2], etc.] I. *intrans.* 1†. To seize and carry off; snatch up; seize; steal.

> Ravenows fiches han sum mesure; whanne thei hungren thei *rapyn*; whanne thei ben ful they sparyn.
> *Wimbelton's Sermon*, 1388, MS. Hatton 57, p. 16. (*Halliwell.*)

2. To commit the crime of rape.

> There's nothing new, Menippus; as before,
> They *rape*, extort, forswear.
> *Heywood*, Hierarchy of Angels (1635), p. 349. (*Latham.*)

II. *trans.* 1. To carry off violently; hence, figuratively, to enrapture; ravish.

> To *rape* the fields with touches of her string.
> *Drayton*, Eclogues, v.

> My son, I hope, hath met within my threshold
> None of these household precedents, which are strong,
> And swift to *rape* youth to their precipice.
> *B. Jonson*, Every Man in his Humour, ii. 3.

2. To commit rape upon; ravish.—**To rape and rent**, to seize and plunder. Compare *to rap and rend*, under *rap*[2].

For, though ye loke never so brode and stare,
Ye shul nat winne a myte in that chaffare,
But wasten al that ye may rape and renne.
Chaucer, Canon's Yeoman's Tale, l. 411.

rape[2] (rāp), *n.* [< *rape*[2], *v.*] 1. The act of snatching by force; a seizing and carrying away by force or violence, whether of persons or things; violent seizure and carrying away: as, the *rape* of Proserpine; the *rape* of the Sabine women; Pope's "*Rape* of the Lock."

Death is cruell, suffering none escape;
Olde, young, rich, poore, of all he makes his *rape*.
Times' Whistle (E. E. T. S.), p. 128.

Pear grew after pear,
Fig after fig came; time made never *rape*
Of any dainty there. *Chapman*, Odyssey.

2. In *law*, the violation or carnal knowledge of a woman forcibly and against her will. *Forcibly* is usually understood not necessarily to mean violence, but to include negative consent. Statutes in various jurisdictions modify the definition, some by extending it to include carnal knowledge of a girl under 10 either with or without her consent. Rape is regarded as one of the worst felonies. The penalty for it was formerly death, as it is still in some jurisdictions, but is now generally imprisonment for life or for a long term of years. It is now often called *criminal assault*.
3. Something taken or seized and carried away; a captured person or thing. [Rare.]

Where now are all my hopes? oh, never more
Shall they revive, nor Death her *rapes* restore!
Sandys.

Rape of the forest, in *Eng. law*, trespass committed in the forest by violence.

rape[3] (rāp), *n.* [< Icel. *hreppr*, a district, prob. orig. 'share' or 'allotment,' < Icel. *hreppa*, catch, obtain, = AS. *hrepian*, *hreppan*, touch: see *rap*[3].] A division of the county of Sussex, in England, intermediate between a hundred and the shire. The county is divided into six rapes.

The *Rape* . . . is . . . a mere geographical expression, the judicial organisation remaining in the hundred.
Stubbs, Const. Hist., § 45.

rape[4] (rāp), *n.* [< ME. *rape*, also *rave*, < OF. **rape*, also *rabe*, later *rave*, F. dial. *reuve*, *reve*, *rabe*, *rova* = Pr. Sp. *raba*, rape, turnip (cf. Pg. *rabão*, horse-radish), = D. *raap* = OHG. *raba*, MHG. *rabe*, *rape*, *rappe*, rape, turnip, G. *rapps*, rape-seed, = LG. *raap*, rape; akin to OHG. *ruoba*, *ruoppa*, MHG. *ruobe*, *rüebe*, G. *rübe*, rape, turnip, etc., = LG. *rove*, *rowe* = Dan. *roe* = Sw. *rofva*, turnip; cf. OBulg. *riepa* = Serv. *repa* = Bohem. *rzhepa* = Pol. *rzepa* = Russ. *riepa* = Lith. *rope*, *rape* = Albanian *repe*, a turnip. < L. *rapa*, also *rapum*, a turnip, rape, = Gr. ῥάπυς, ῥάφυς, turnip; cf. Gr. ῥαφανίς, ῥαφάνη, a radish; ῥάφανος, a cabbage; root unknown.] 1†. A turnip. *Halliwell*.—2. The colza, cole-seed, or rape-seed, a cruciferous plant including the *Brassica campestris* and *B. Napus* of Linnæus, the latter form now considered to be a variety, together with the common turnip, of *B. campestris*, which occurs in a wild state as a weed throughout Europe and Asiatic Russia. Of the two forms named, the former, sometimes called *summer rape*, has rough leaves, and the latter, called *winter rape*, smooth leaves. Rape is extensively grown in Europe and in India for its oleaginous seeds, the source of rape-oil. It is also sown for its leaves, which are used as food for sheep, and are produced in gardens for use as a salad.

rape[5] (rāp), *n.* [< ME. *rape* = MHG. *rappe*, *rape*, G. *rapp*, a stalk of grapes, < OF. *rape*, F. *râpe* = Pr. *raspa* = It. *raspo*, a stem or stalk of grapes.] 1. The stem or stalk of grapes.

Til grapes to the presse beo set
Ther renneth no red wyn in *rape*.
Holy Rood (E. E. T. S.), p. 135.

2. *pl.* The stalks and skins of grapes from which the must has been expressed. *E. H. Knight*.—3. Loose or refuse grapes used in wine-making.

The juice of grapes is drawn as well from the *rape*, or whole grapes plucked from the cluster, and wine poured upon them in a vessel, as from a vat, where they are bruised. *Ray*.

4. A filter used in a vinegar-manufactory to separate the mucilaginous matter from the vinegar. It derives its name from being charged with rapes. *E. H. Knight*.

rape[6] (rāp), *v. t.*; pret. and pp. *raped*, ppr. *raping*. [Prob. a var. of *rasp*, perhaps affected by F. *râper* (= Sp. Pg. *rapar*), rasp: see *rasp*[1].] To scratch; abrade; scarify. [Prov. Eng.]

Interesting reading; wasn't it? I wish they'd *rape* the character of some other innocent—ha!
The Money-makers, p. 78.

rape[7] (rāp), *n.* An obsolete or dialectal form of *rope*.

rape-butterfly (rāp'but″ėr-flī), *n.* A pierian, *Pieris rapæ*, known in the United States as the *imported cabbage-butterfly*, to distinguish it from several similar native species. See cut under *cabbage-butterfly*, and compare figures under *Pieris*. [Eng.]

rape-cake (rāp'kāk), *n.* A hard cake formed of the residue of the seed and husks of rape (see *rape*[4]) after the oil has been expressed. It is used for feeding oxen and sheep, but is inferior to linseed-cake and some other kinds of oil-cakes; it is also used in considerable quantity as a rich manure.

rapeful† (rāp'fụl), *a.* [< *rape*[2] + *-ful*.] Given to rape or violence. [Rare.]

To teach the *rapeful* Hyenus marriage.
Chapman, Byron's Tragedy, iv. 1. (*Nares*.)

rapely† (rāp'li), *adv.* [ME., also *raply*, *rappliche*, etc.; < *rape*[1], *a.*, + *-ly*[2].] Hastily; hurriedly; quickly; rapidly.

Then seih we a Samaritan cam syttynge on a mule,
Rydynge full *raply* the way that we wente.
Piers Plowman (C), xx. 48.

Upsterte the champioun *rapely* anon.
Tale of Gamelyn, l. 219.

rape-oil (rāp'oil), *n.* A thick brownish-yellow oil expressed from rape-seed. It was formerly, as in India still, applied chiefly to illumination, but is now largely consumed for lubricating and in india-rubber manufacturing. Also called *cabbage-oil*, *colza-oil*, *rape-seed oil*.

rape-seed (rāp'sēd), *n.* The seed of the rape, or the plant itself; cole-seed.—**Rape-seed oil.** Same as *rape-oil*.

rape-wine (rāp'wīn), *n.* A poor thin wine prepared from the murk or stalks, skins, and other refuse of grapes which have been pressed.

rap-full (rap'fụl), *a.* and *n.* [< *rap*[1] + *full*[1].] I. *a.* Full of wind: applied to sails when on a wind every sail stands full without lifting.
II. *n.* A sail full of wind: also called a *smooth full*.

rapfully† (rap'fụl-i), *adv.* With beating or striking; with resounding blows; batteringly. [Rare.]

Then far of vplandish we doe view theo fird Sicil Ætna,
And a seabelch grounting on rough rocks *rapfulye* trapping. *Stanihurst*, Æneid, iii.

Raphaelesque (raf″ā-el-esk'), *a.* [Also *Raffaelesque*; < *Raphael* (It. *Raffaello*), a chief painter of the Italian Renaissance (see *Raphaelism*), + *-esque*.] Of or resembling the style, color, or art of the great Renaissance painter Raphael (Raffaello Sanzio da Urbino).

A strange opulence of splendour, characterisable as half-legitimate half-meretricious—a splendour hovering between the *raffaelesque* and the japannish.
Carlyle, Sterling, i. 6.

Raphaelism (raf'ā-el-izm), *n.* [< *Raphael* (see def.) + *-ism*.] The principles of art introduced by Raphael, the famous Italian painter (1483–1520); the style or method of Raphael.

Raphaelite (raf'ā-el-īt), *n.* [< *Raphael* + *-ite*[2]: see *Raphaelism*.] One who adopts the principles or follows the style of the painter Raphael.

Raphaelitism (raf'ā-el-ī-tizm), *n.* [< *Raphaelite* + *-ism*.] The principles or methods of the Raphaelites; pursuit of or adherence to the style of the painter Raphael.

Raphaneæ (rā-fā'nē-ē), *n. pl.* [NL. (A. P. de Candolle, 1821), < *Raphanus* + *-eæ*.] A tribe of polypetalous plants of the order *Cruciferæ*. It is characterized by an elongated unjointed indehiscent pod, which is a cylindrical or moniliform one-celled and many-seeded silique, or is divided into many small one-seeded cells (in one or two rows), which at length fall apart. It includes 9 genera, of which *Raphanus* is the type, all of them plants of the Old World, and chiefly Asiatic.

Raphanus (raf'a-nus), *n.* [NL. (Tournefort, 1700), < L. *raphanus*, < Gr. ῥάφανος, cabbage, radish, ῥαφανίς, radish, akin to ῥάπυς, ῥάφυς, turnip, L. *rapa*, *rapum*, turnip: see *rape*[4].] A genus of cruciferous plants, including the radish, type of the tribe *Raphaneæ*. It is characterized by globose seeds, solitary in the single row of cells formed by constrictions of the pods, which are closed by a pithy substance or sometimes remain continuous throughout. The 6 species are natives of Europe and temperate parts of Asia, and are branching annuals or biennials, with fleshy roots, lyrate lower leaves, and elongated bractless racemes of slender-pedicelled white or yellow purplish-veined flowers, followed by erect spreading, thick, and corky or spongy pods. Some species (genus *Raphanistrum*, Tournefort, 1700) have a short seedless joint below, forming a stalk to the long inflated necklace-like cell which composes the rest of the pod, as *R. Landra*, a yellow-flowered Italian weed with large radical leaves, eaten as a salad, and *R. Raphanistrum*, a coarse weed, the wild or field radish. See *radish*.

raphe (rā'fē), *n.* [NL., prop. *rhaphe*; < Gr. ῥαφή, a seam, suture, < ῥάπτειν, sew: see *rhapsode*.] 1. In *bot.*: (*a*) In an anatropous or amphitropous (hemitropous) ovule or seed, the adnate cord which connects the hilum with the chalaza, commonly appearing as a more or less salient ridge, sometimes completely embedded in a fleshy testa of the seed. See cuts under *anatropous* and *hemitropous*. (*b*) A longitudinal line or rib on the valves of many diatoms, connecting the three nodules when present. (See *nodule*.) The usual primary classification of genera depends upon its presence or absence.—2. In *anat.*, a seam-like union of two lateral halves, usually in the mesial plane, and constituting either a median septum of connective tissue or a longitudinal ridge or furrow; specifically, in the brain, the median lamina of decussating fibers which extends in the tegmental region from the oblongata up to the third ventricle.—**Raphe of the corpus callosum**, a longitudinal furrow on the median line of its dorsal surface, bounded by the mesial longitudinal striæ.—**Raphe of the medulla oblongata**, the median septum, composed of fibers which run in part dorsoventrally, in part longitudinally, and in part across the septum more or less obliquely, together with nerve-cells.—**Raphe of the palate**, a linear median ridge extending from a small papilla in front, corresponding with the inferior opening of the anterior palatine foramen, back to the uvula.—**Raphe of the penis**, the extension of the raphe of the scrotum forward on the under side of the penis.—**Raphe of the perineum**, the extension of the raphe of the scrotum backward on the perineum.—**Raphe of the pharynx**, the median seam on the posterior wall of the pharynx.—**Raphe of the scrotum**, a slight median ridge extending forward to the under side of the penis, and backward along the perineum to the margin of the anus.—**Raphe of the tongue**, a slight furrow along the middle of the dorsal surface, terminating posteriorly in the foramen cæcum.

Raphia (rā'fi-ä), *n.* [NL. (Palisot de Beauvois, 1804), < *raffia*, the native name of the Madagascar species.] A genus of palms of the tribe *Lepidocaryeæ*, type of the subtribe *Raphieæ* (which is distinguished from the true ratan-palms, *Calameæ*, by a completely three-celled ovary). It is characterized by pinnately divided leaves crowning an erect and robust trunk, and by a fruit which becomes one-celled, is beaked with the three terminal stigmas, and has a thick pericarp tessellated with overlapping scales, spongy within and containing a single oblong furrowed seed with very hard osseous albumen. There are 5 species, natives of tropical Africa and Madagascar, with one, *R. tædigera*, the jupati-palm (which see), native in America from the mouths of the Amazon to Nicaragua. All inhabit low swampy lands and banks near tide-water. Their trunks are unarmed and of little height, but their leaves are spiny and often over 50 feet in length, the entire tree becoming thus 60 or 70 feet in height to their erect tips. The large pendulous flower-spikes reach 6 feet in length, contain flowers of both sexes, and have their numerous branches set in two opposite rows, their flower-bearing branchlets resembling flattened catkins. In fruit the spike sometimes becomes 15 feet long, and weighs 200 or even 300 pounds, bearing numerous egg-like brown and hard fruits often used as ornaments. *R. Ruffia*, which produces the largest spadices, is known as the *raffia-palm*. (See *raffia*.) *R. vinifera* supplies the toddy of western tropical Africa, and its leafstalks are used in various ways.

Raphia vinifera.

raphides, *n.* Plural of *raphis*.

Raphidia (rā-fid'i-ạ̈), *n.* [NL. (Linnæus, 1748), < Gr. ῥαφίς (ῥαφιδ-), a needle, a pin: see *raphis*.] A notable genus of neuropterous insects, of the family *Sialidæ* or giving name to the family *Raphidiidæ*. The prothorax is cylindrical, and the wings are furnished with a pterostigma. The larvæ differ from all other *Sialidæ* in not being aquatic; they live under bark. The genus is represented in North America only on the Pacific coast, although common in Europe.

raphidian (rā-fid'i-ạn), *a.* 1. In *bot.*, of the nature of or containing raphides: as, *raphidian* cells in a plant.—2. In *zoöl.*, of or pertaining to the genus *Raphidia*.

raphidiferous (raf-i-dif'e̤-rus), *a.* [< Gr. ῥαφίς (ῥαφιδ-), a needle, pin, + L. *ferre*, bear, carry.] In *bot.*, containing raphides.

Raphidiidæ (raf-i-dī'i-dē), *n. pl.* [NL. (Leach, 1824), < *Raphidia* + *-idæ*.] A family of neuropterous insects: now merged in the *Sialidæ*.

raphigraph (raf'i-gråf), *n.* [< Gr. ῥαφίς, a needle, pin, + γράφειν, write.] A machine intended to provide a means of communication with the blind, by the use of characters made by pricking paper with ten needle-pointed pegs, actuated by a keyboard, and operating in conjunction with mechanism for shifting the paper. The machine has proved practically valueless from its complication and its extreme slowness of operation, resulting from the requisite number of motions.

raphis (rā'fis), *n.*; pl. *raphides* (raf'i-dēz). [NL., < Gr. ῥαφίς, ῥαπίς, a needle, pin, < ῥάπτειν, sew, stitch. Cf. *raphe*.] In *bot.*, one of the acicular crystals, most often composed of oxalate of lime, which occur in bundles in the cells of many plants. The term has less properly been used to include crystals of other forms found in the same situations. Also *rhaphis*.

rapid (rap'id), *a.* and *n.* [I. *a.* F. *rapide* (OF. vernacularly *rade*, *ra*) = Sp. *rápido* = Pg. It. *rapido*, swift, < L. *rapidus*, snatching, tearing, usually hasty, swift, lit. 'quick,' < *rapere*, snatch, akin to Gr. ἁρπάζειν, seize (see *harpy*): see *rap*[2], *rape*[2]. II. *n.* F. *rapide*, a swift current in a stream, pl. *rapides*, rapids; from the adj.] I. *a.* 1. Moving or doing swiftly or with celerity; acting or performing with speed; quick in motion or execution: as, a *rapid* horse; a *rapid* worker or speaker.

> Part curb their fiery steeds, or shun the goal
> With *rapid* wheels. *Milton*, P. L., ii. 532.

> Be fix'd, you *rapid* orbs, that bear
> The changing seasons of the year.
> *Carew*, Cœlum Britannicum, iv.

> Against his Will, you chain your frighted King
> On *rapid* Rhine's divided Bed.
> *Prior*, Imit. of Horace, iii. 2.

2. Swiftly advancing; going on or forward at a fast rate; making quick progress: as, *rapid* growth; *rapid* improvement; a *rapid* conflagration.

> The *rapid* decline which is now wasting my powers.
> *Farrar*, Julian Home, xiv.

3. Marked by swiftness of motion or action; proceeding or performed with velocity; executed speedily.

> My father's eloquence was too *rapid* to stay for any man; — away it went. *Sterne*, Tristram Shandy, v. 3.

> Thus inconsiderately, but not the less maliciously, Oldmixon filled his *rapid* page.
> *I. D'Israeli*, Amen. of Lit., II. 416.

> It pleased me to watch the curious effect of the *rapid* movement of near objects contrasted with the slow motion of distant ones. *O. W. Holmes*, Old Vol. of Life, p. 20.

4. Gay. *Halliwell*. [Prov. Eng.] = **Syn.** 1-3. Fast, fleet, expeditious, hasty, hurried.

II. *n.* A swift current in a river, where the channel is descending; a part of a river where the current runs with more than its ordinary celerity; a sudden descent of the surface of a stream, more or less broken by obstructions, but without actual cataract or cascade: usually in the plural.

> No truer Time himself
> Can prove you, tho' he make you evermore
> Dearer and nearer, as the *rapid* of life
> Shoots to the fall. *Tennyson*, A Dedication.

> The *rapids* above are a series of shelves, bristling with jutting rocks and lodged trunks of trees.
> *C. D. Warner*, Their Pilgrimage, p. 310.

rapidamente (rà-pē-dä-men'te), *adv.* [It., < *rapido*, rapid: see *rapid*.] In *music*, rapidly; in a rapid manner.

rapidity (ra-pid'i-ti), *n.* [< F. *rapidité* (cf. Sp. Pg. *rapidez*) = It. *rapidità*, < L. *rapidita(t-)s*, rapidity, swiftness, < *rapidus*, rapid: see *rapid*.] The state or property of being rapid; celerity of motion or action; quickness of performance or execution; fast rate of progress or advance.

> Where the words are not monosyllables, we make them so by our *rapidity* of pronunciation. *Addison*.

> The undulations are present beyond the red and violet ends of the spectrum, for we have made them sensible through their actions on other reagents, and have measured their *rapidities*.
> *G. H. Lewes*, Probs. of Life and Mind, II. 208.

= **Syn.** *Speed, Swiftness*, etc. (see *quickness*), haste, expedition, despatch.

rapidly (rap'id-li), *adv.* In a rapid manner; swiftly; quickly; at a fast rate.

rapidness (rap'id-nes), *n.* The condition of being rapid, or of acting or proceeding rapidly; rapidity.

rapido (rà'pi-dō), *adv.* [It.: see *rapid*.] In *music*, with rapidity or agility: commonly applied to a running passage.

rapier (rā'piėr), *n.* [= D. *rapier*, *rappier* = LG. *rapier* = G. *rappier* = Sw. Dan. *rapier*, < OF. *rapiere*, *raspiere*, F. *rapière*, F. dial. *raipeire* (ML. *rapperia*), a rapier; prob., as the form *raspiere* and various allusions indicate, of Spanish origin, a name given orig. in contempt, as if 'a poker,' < Sp. *raspadera*, a raker, < *raspar*, *rapar* = Pg. *rapar* = OF. *rasper*, F. *râper*, scrape, scratch, rasp, < OHG. *raspôn*, rasp, etc.: see *rasp*[1].] 1. A long, narrow, pointed, two-edged sword, used, especially in the sixteenth and seventeenth centuries, with a guard for the hand, adapted for both cutting and thrusting, but used chiefly for thrusting. Rapier practice was usually with a dagger or hand-buckler held in the left hand to parry the thrust. See cut under *sword*.

> And I will turn thy falsehood to thy heart,
> Where it was forged, with my *rapier's* point.
> *Shak.*, Rich. II., iv. 1. 40.

> Who had girt vnto them a *Rapyer* and Dagger, gilt, point pendante. *Greene*, Quip for an Upstart Courtier.

> Some . . . will not sticke to call Hercules himselfe a dastard, because forsooth he fought with a club and not at the *rapier* and dagger.
> *Sir J. Harington*, tr. of Ariosto's Orlando Furioso.

> The offense . . . caused her Majesty [Queen Elizabeth] to . . . place selected grave citizens at every gate to cut the ruffes and break the *rapiers'* points of all passengers that exceeded a yard in length of their *rapiers*.
> *Stowe*, quoted in Encyc. Brit., IX. 70.

2. In later English usage, a fencing-sword used only for thrusting.

> By a *rapier* is now always meant a sword for the thrust, in contradistinction to one adapted for cutting.
> *Encyc. Brit.*, IX. 70.

rapier-dance† (rā'piėr-dàns), *n.* A dance formerly practised in Yorkshire, England, by men in costume who represented ancient heroes and flourished rapiers, ending with a mock execution of one of their number by uniting their rapiers round his neck. See *sword-dance*. *Halliwell*.

rapier-fish (rā'piėr-fish), *n.* A sword-fish.

rapillo (ra-pil'ō), *n.* [< F. *rapille* (Cotgrave) = It. *rapillo*, dross and ashes from a volcano, a kind of sand used in making mortar.] Pulverized volcanic substances.

rapine (rap'in), *n.* [Early mod. E. also *rapin*; < OF. *rapine*, F. *rapine* = Pr. *rapina* = Sp. *rapiña* = Pg. It. *rapina*, < L. *rapina*, rapine, plunder, robbery, < *rapere*, seize: see *rapid*, *rape*[2]. Cf. *ravine*[2], *raven*[2], from the same source.] 1. The violent seizure and carrying off of property; open plunder by armed or superior force, as in war or by invasion or raid.

> They lived therefore mostly by *rapin*, pillaging their Neighbours, who were more addicted to traffick than fighting. *Dampier*, Voyages, II. i. 107.

> Plunder and *rapine* completed the devastations which war had begun. *Bp. Atterbury*, Sermons, II. xiii.

2†. Violence; force; ravishment.

> Her graceful innocence, her every air
> Of gesture, or least action, overawed
> His malice, and with *rapine* sweet bereaved
> His fierceness of the fierce intent it brought.
> *Milton*, P. L., ix. 461.

= **Syn.** 1. Plunder, spoliation, robbery, depredation. See *pillage*.

rapine† (rap'in), *v. t.* [< F. *rapiner*, rapine, plunder; from the noun. Cf. *raven*[2], *v.*, from the same source.] To plunder violently or by superior force.

> A Tyrant doth not only *rapine* his Subjects, but spoils and robs Churches. *Sir G. Buck*, Hist. Richard III., v.

raping (rā'ping), *p. a.* [Ppr. of *rape*[2], *v.*] 1. In *her.*, devouring or tearing its prey: said of any carnivorous beast used as a bearing. It is necessary to mention the position of the creature, as rampant, etc., and also the nature of the prey.

2. Ravishing.

> Or had the Syrens, on a neighbour shore,
> Heard in what *raping* notes she did deplore
> Her buried glory. *W. Browne*, Pastorals, i. 5.

rapinous† (rap'i-nus), *a.* [= It. *rapinoso*, < ML. **rapinosus*, < L. *rapina*, rapine: see *rapine*. Cf. *ravenous*, a doublet of *rapinous*.] Committing or characterized by rapine; rapacious.

> All the close shrouds too, for his *rapinous* deedes
> In all the caue, he knew.
> *Chapman*, Homeric Hymn to Hermes.

raplach (rap'lach), *n.* Same as *raploch*.

raploch, raplock (rap'loch, -lok), *n.* and *a.* [Also *raplach*, *raplack*; origin obscure.] I. *n.* Coarse woolen cloth, made from the worst kind of wool, homespun, and not dyed. [Scotch and North. Eng.]

II. *a.* Unkempt; rough; coarse. [Scotch.]

> My Muse, poor hizzie !
> Tho' rough an' *raploch* be her measure,
> She's seldom lazy.
> *Burns*, Second Epistle to Davie.

raply† (rap'li), *adv.* See *rapely*.

rappt, *v. t.* An obsolete form of *rap*[2].

rappadura, *n.* See *rapadura*.

rapparee, raparee (rap-a-rē'), *n.* [< Ir. *rapaire*, a noisy fellow, sloven, robber, thief, = Gael. *rapair*, noisy fellow; cf. Ir. *rapal*, noise; *rapach*, noisy: see *rabble*[1].] An armed Irish plunderer; in general, a vagabond.

> The frequent robberies, murders, and other notorious felonies committed by robbers, *rapparees*, and tories, upon their keeping, hath greatly discouraged the replanting of this kingdom.
> *Laws of Will. III.* (1695), quoted in Ribton-Turner's Vagrants and Vagrancy, p. 396.

> The Irish formed themselves into many bodies . . . called *rapparees*. *Bp. Burnet*, Hist. Own Times, an. 1690.

> The confiscations left behind them many "wood kerns," or, as they were afterwards called, *rapparees*, who were active in agrarian outrage, and a vagrant, homeless, half-savage population of beggars.
> *Lecky*, Eng. in 18th Cent., vi.

rappe†, *v.* A Middle English form of *rap*[1], *rap*[2], etc.

rappee (ra-pē'), *n.* [= G. *rapee*, *rappeh* = Dan. *rapee*, < F. *râpé*, a kind of snuff, < *râpé*, pp. of *râper*, rasp, scrape, grate: see *rasp*[1].] A strong kind of snuff, coarser than maccouba, of either a black or a brown color, made from the darker and ranker kinds of tobacco-leaves.

> In early times the duly sauced and fermented leaves were made up into "carottes"—tightly tied up spindle-formed bundles, from the end of which the snuffer, by means of a "snuff rasp," rasped off his own supply, and hence the name "râpé," which we have still as *rappee*, to indicate a particular class of snuff. *Encyc. Brit.*, XXIII. 427.

rappel (ra-pel'), *n.* [< F. *rappel*, OF. *rapiel* (ML. *rapellum*), verbal n. of *rapeler*, F. *rappeler*, repeal, revoke: see *repeal*.] 1. The roll or beat of the drum to call soldiers to arms.— 2. An ancient musical instrument, still used in Egypt, consisting of a ring to which are attached small bells or metal plates, forming a sort of rattle.

rappen (rap'en), *n.*; pl. *rappen*. [Swiss G. *rappen*, a coin of Basel, of small value, bearing the impress of a raven, < MHG. *rappe*, a coin first struck at Freiburg in Baden, with the head of a bird on it representing the Freiburg coat of arms, < *rappe*, a collateral form of *rabe* = E. *raven*: see *raven*[1].] A Swiss coin and denomination of money. At the present day the rappen is equivalent to a centime: thus, 100 *rappen* (equal to 100 centimes) make 1 franc.

Obverse. Reverse.
Rappen of Billon, 1802; British Museum. (Size of original.)

rapper (rap'ėr), *n.* [< *rap*[1] + *-er*[1].] 1. One who raps or knocks; specifically, a spirit-rapper.— 2. The knocker of a door. [Rare.]— 3. In *coal-mining*, a lever with a hammer attached at one end, placed at the mouth of a shaft or incline for giving signals to the banksman, by rapping on an iron plate.— 4. An extravagant oath or lie; a "whopper." See *to rap out* (*a*), under *rap*[1], *v. t.* [Prov. Eng.]

> Bravely sworn ! though this is no flower of the sun, yet I am sure it is something that deserves to be called a *rapper*.
> *Bp. Parker*, Reproof of Rehearsal Transposed, p. 200.

rapping (rap'ing), *n.* [Verbal n. of *rap*[1], *v.*] The production of sound by a rap; specifically, the sound of significant raps or knocks supposed to be produced by spirits through the instrumentality of mediums or spirit-rappers; spirit-rapping.

rapping (rap'ing), *a.* [Ppr. of *rap*[1], *v.*] Remarkably large; of striking or astonishing size; "whopping." [Prov. Eng.]

Rappist (rap'ist), *n.* [< *Rapp*, name of the founder (see *Harmonist*, 4), + *-ist*.] Same as *Harmonist*, 4.

Rappite (rap'īt), *n.* [< *Rapp* (see *Rappist*) + *-ite*[2].] Same as *Harmonist*, 4.

rapport (ra-pōrt'), *v. i.* [< F. *rapporter*, relate, refer: see *report*, *v.*] To have relation or reference; relate; refer. [Rare.]

> When God hath imprinted an authority upon a person, . . . others are to pay the duty which that impression demands; which duty, because it *rapports* to God, and touches not the man, . . . extinguishes all pretences of opinion and pride. *Jer. Taylor*, Works (ed. 1835), I. 142.

rapport (ra-pōr'), *n.* [F. *rapport*, OF. *raport*, account, also resemblance, correspondence, accord, agreement, = Pg. *raporte* = It. *rapporto*, report, relation: see *report*, *n.*] 1. Harmonious relation; correspondence; accord or agreement; affinity; analogy: used as a French word, often in the phrase *en rapport*, in or into close relation, accord, or harmony.

> It is obvious enough what *rapport* there is, and must ever be, between the thoughts and words, the conceptions and languages of every country.
> *Sir W. Temple*, Anc. and Mod. Learning.

2. In *French law*, a report on a case, or on a subject submitted; a return.

rapprochement (ra-prōsh'moṅ), *n.* [F., reunion, reconciliation, < *rapprocher*, approach again, <

re-, back, + *approcher*, approach: see *approach*.] A coming or bringing together or into accord; establishment of harmonious relations; reconciliation.

The present *rapprochement* between the Turk and the Muscovite. *The Academy*, Dec. 15, 1888, p. 379.

He [Lewes] here seeks to effect a *rapprochement* between metaphysic and science. *Encyc. Brit.*, XIV. 491.

rapscallion (rap-skal'yon), *n.* [A modified form of *rascallion*.] A rascally, disorderly, or despicable person; a wretch or vagabond; a rascallion.

Well, *rapscallions!* and what now!
Barham, Ingoldsby Legends, I. 87.

There isn't any low, friendless *rapscallion* in this town that hasn't got me for his friend.
Howells, Annie Kilburn, xi.

rapscallionry (rap-skal'yon-ri), *n.* [< *rapscallion* + *-ry*.] Rascals collectively. [Rare.]

rapt[1] (rapt). A preterit and past participle of *rap*[1].

rapt[2] (rapt), *p. a.* [Early mod. E. spelling of *rapped*, pp. of *rap*[2], confused with L. *raptus*, pp. of *rapere*, seize: see *rap*[2], and cf. *rapt*[3].] Seized with ecstasy; transported; exalted; ecstatic; in a state of rapture.

More dances my *rapt* heart
Than when I first my wedded mistress saw
Bestride my threshold. *Shak.*, Cor., iv. 5. 122.

Looks commercing with the skies,
Thy *rapt* soul sitting in thine eyes.
Milton, Il Penseroso, l. 40.

Their faces wore a *rapt* expression, as if sweet music were in the air around them.
Hawthorne, Hall of Fantasy.

rapt[3]† (rapt), *v. t.* [< L. *raptare*, seize and carry off, freq. of *rapere*, pp. *raptus*, seize: see *rapt*[2], and cf. *rap*[2], *rape*[2].] **1.** To seize or grasp; seize and carry off; ravish.

The Lybian lion, . . .
Out-rushing from his den, *rapts* all away.
Daniel, Civil Wars, vii. 97.

We are a man distinct . . .
From those whom custom *rapteth* in her press.
B. Jonson, Poetaster, v. 1.

2. To transport as with ecstasy; enrapture.

So those that dwell in me, and live by frugal toil,
When they in my defence are reasoning of my soil,
As *rapted* with my wealth and beauties, learned grow.
Drayton, Polyolbion, xiii. 411.

rapt[3]† (rapt), *n.* [< F. *rapt*, OF. *rat*, *rap* = Pr. *rap* = Sp. Pg. *rapto* = It. *ratto*, < L. *raptus*, a seizure, plundering, abduction, rape, ML. also forcible violation, < *rapere*, pp. *raptus*, seize, snatch: see *rapt*[2], *a.*, and cf. *rapture*.] **1.** Transporting force or energy; resistless movement.

And therefore in this Encyclopedic and round of knowledge, like the great and exemplary wheels of heaven, we must observe two circles: that while we are daily carried about, and whirled on by the swing and *rapt* of the one, we may maintain a natural proper course in the slow and sober wheel of the other. *Sir T. Browne*, Vulg. Err., Pref.

2. An ecstasy; a trance.

Dissimulyng traunces and *raptes*.
Hall, Hen. VIII., an. 25.

He seemeth to lye as thoughe he were in great payne or in a *rapte*, wonderfully tormentynge hym selfe.
R. Eden, tr. of Gonzalus Oviedus (First Books on America, [ed. Arber, p. 215).

An extraordinary *rapt* and act of prophesying.
Bp. Morton, Discharge of Imput. (1633), p. 174.

Raptatores (rap-ta-tō'rēz), *n. pl.* [NL., pl. of *raptator*, < L. *raptare*, seize and carry off, waste, ravage, plunder: see *rapt*[2], *rapt*[3].] In *ornith.*, same as *Raptores*. *Illiger*, 1811.

Raptatoria (rap-ta-tō'ri-ä), *n. pl.* [NL.: see *Raptatores*.] In *entom.*, same as *Raptoria*.

raptatorial (rap-ta-tō'ri-al), *a.* [< *raptatory* + *-al*.] Same as *raptorial*.

raptatory (rap'ta-tō-ri), *a.* [< NL. **raptatorius*, < *raptator*, a robber, plunderer: see *Raptatores*.] In *entom.*, formed for seizing prey; raptorial.

rapter† (rap'tėr), *n.* Same as *raptor*, 1.

raptor (rap'tor), *n.* [= Sp. Pg. *raptor* = It. *rattore*, < L. *raptor*, robber, plunderer, abductor, < *rapere*, pp. *raptus*, seize, carry off: see *rapt*[2], *rapt*[3].] **1**†. A ravisher; a plunderer.

To have her harmless life by the lewd *rapter* spilt.
Drayton, Polyolbion, x. 149.

2. [*cap.*] [NL.] A genus of coleopterous insects.

Raptores (rap-tō'rēz), *n. pl.* [NL., pl. of L. *raptor*, robber, plunderer: see *raptor*.] An order of *Aves*, the *Accipitres* of Linnæus, the *Raptatores*, *Rapaces*, or *Aëtomorphæ* of some authors; the raptorial or rapacious birds; the birds of prey. They have an epignathous cered beak, and talons generally fitted for grasping live prey. The bill is hooked and often also toothed. The toes are four, three in front and one behind, with large crooked claws; the outer toe is sometimes versatile. The plumage is aftershafted or not; the oil-gland is present and usually tufted. The carotids are two; the syrinx has not more than one pair of intrinsic muscles. Cæca are present (except in *Cathartidæ*). The maxillopalatines are united to an ossified septum; the angle of the mandible is not recurved. The *Raptores* are found in every part of the world. There are upward of 500 species, mostly belonging to the two families *Falconidæ* and *Strigidæ*. The *Raptores* are divided into 4 suborders or superfamilies: (1) the African *Gypogeranidæ*; (2) the American *Cathartidæ*; (3) the cosmopolitan diurnal birds of prey, *Accipitres*; and (4) the cosmopolitan nocturnal birds of prey, the owls, *Striges*.

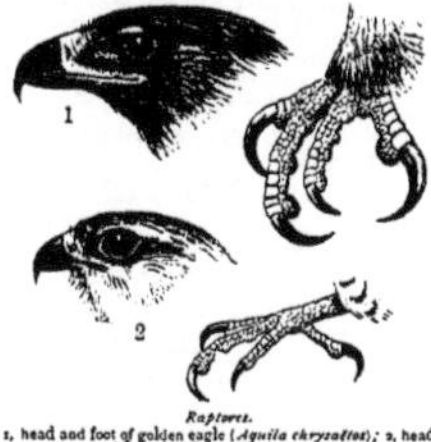

Raptores.
1, head and foot of golden eagle (*Aquila chrysaëtos*); 2, head and foot of gerfalcon (*Falco gyrfalco*).

Raptoria (rap-tō'ri-ä), *n. pl.* [NL., < L. *raptor*, robber: see *Raptores*.] In *entom.*, in Westwood's system (1839), a division of orthopterous insects; the *Mantidæ* (which see). Westwood's *Raptoria* were a part of Latreille's *Cursoria*, the rest of which Westwood called *Ambulatoria* and *Cursoria*. Also *Raptatoria*.

raptorial (rap-tō'ri-al), *a.* and *n.* [< *raptori-ous* + *-al*.] **I.** *a.* **1.** Rapacious; predatory; preying upon animals; of or pertaining to the *Raptores* or *Raptoria*.—**2.** Fitted for seizing and holding; prehensile: as, the *raptorial* beak or claws of birds; the *raptorial* palps of insects.—**Raptorial legs**, in *entom.*, legs in which the tibiæ and tarsi turn back on the femur, often fitting into it like the blade of a pocket-knife into a handle; the tibiæ may also be armed with teeth or spines, thus forming very powerful seizing-organs. This type is found only in the front legs, and it is most fully developed in the *Mantidæ*. See cut under *Mantis*.

II. *n.* A bird of prey; a member of the *Raptores*.

raptorious (rap-tō'ri-us), *a.* [< NL. **raptorius*, < L. *raptor*, a robber, plunderer: see *raptor*.] In *entom.*, same as *raptorial*. *Kirby*. [Rare.]

rapture (rap'tūr), *n.* [< *rapt*[1] + *-ure*.] **1**†. A violent taking and carrying away; seizure; forcible removal.

Spite of all the *rapture* of the sea,
This jewel holds his building on my arm.
Shak., Pericles, ii. 1. 161.

When St. Paul had his *rapture* into heaven, he saw fine things. *Jer. Taylor*, Works (ed. 1835), II. 131.

2. Violent transporting movement; a rapid carrying or going along; moving energy.

Wave rolling after wave, where way they found;
If steep, with torrent *rapture*; if through plain,
Soft ebbing. *Milton*, P. L., vii. 299.

With the *rapture* of great winds to blow
About earth's shaken coignes.
Lowell, Agassiz, vi. 1.

3. A state of mental transport or exaltation; ecstasy. (*a*) Ecstatic pleasure; rapt delight or enjoyment; extreme joy over or gladness on account of something.

I have never heard
Praise of love or wine
That panted forth a flood of *rapture* so divine.
Shelley, To a Skylark.

To exercise a devilish ingenuity in inventions of mutual torture became not only a duty but a *rapture*.
Motley, Dutch Republic, II. 426.

(*b*) Ecstatic elevation of thought or feeling; lofty or soaring enthusiasm; exalted or absorbing earnestness.

This man, beyond a Stoick apathy, sees truth as in a *rapture*, and cleaves to it. *Milton*, Apology for Smectymnuus.

You grow correct that once with *rapture* writ.
Pope, Epil. to the Satires, i. 3.

There is a *rapture* on the lonely shore . . .
By the deep sea, and music in its roar.
Byron, Childe Harold, iv. 178.

4. A manifestation of mental transport; an ecstatic utterance or action; an expression of exalted or passionate feeling of any kind; a rhapsody.

Her [Cassandra's] brain-sick *raptures*
Cannot distaste the goodness of a quarrel
Which hath our several honours all engaged
To make it gracious. *Shak.*, T. and C., ii. 2. 122.

Are not groans and tears
Harmonious *raptures* in th' Almighty's ears?
Quarles, Emblems, iv. 15.

5†. An ecstasy of passionate excitement; a paroxysm or fit from excessive emotion. [Rare.]

Your prattling nurse
Into a *rapture* lets her baby cry.
Shak., Cor., ii. 1. 223.

=**Syn.** 3. Transport, bliss, exaltation.

raptured (rap'tūrd), *a.* [< *rapture* + *-ed*[2].] In a state of rapture; characterized by rapture or ecstasy; enraptured.

Raptur'd I stood, and as this hour amaz'd,
With rev'rence at the lofty wonder gaz'd.
Pope, Odyssey, vi. 199.

The intent Damon drew
Such maddening draughts of beauty to his soul,
As for a while o'erwhelm'd his *raptured* thought
With luxury too-daring. *Thomson*, Summer, l. 1333.

That favored strain was Surrey's *raptured* line.
Scott, L. of L. M., vi. 19.

rapturist (rap'tūr-ist), *n.* [< *rapture* + *-ist*.] One who habitually manifests rapture; an enthusiast. [Rare.]

Such swarms of prophets and *rapturists* have flown out of those hives in some ages.
J. Spencer, Vanity of Vulgar Prophecies (1665), p. 43.

rapturous (rap'tūr-us), *a.* [< *rapture* + *-ous*.] Of the character of rapture; marked by rapture; exciting or manifesting rapture; ecstatically joyous or exalted: as, *rapturous* exultation; a *rapturous* look; a *rapturous* scene.

His welcome, before enthusiastic, was now *rapturous*.
Everett, Orations, I. 480.

rapturously (rap'tūr-us-li), *adv.* In a rapturous manner; with rapture; ecstatically.

raptus melancholicus (rap'tus mel-an-kol'i-kus). [NL.: L. *raptus*, a seizure; *melancholicus*, melancholic: see *rapt*[2], *n.*, and *melancholic*.] A motor crisis or outbreak of uncontrollable violence developed in a melancholic person from the intensity of his mental anguish.

raquet, *n.* See *racket*[2].

raquette (ra-ket'), *n.* [F.] A racket.—**Raquette head-dress**, a kind of head-dress in use toward the close of the sixteenth century, in which the hair is drawn back from the forehead and temples, and raised in a sort of crest; a kind of chignon was arranged at the back of the head and covered by a cap of fine linen, darned net embroidery, or some similar material.

rara (rä'rä), *n.* [S. Amer.; imitative of its cry.] A bird, the South American plant-cutter, *Phytotoma rara*. Also called *rarita*. See cut under *Phytotoma*.

rara avis (rā'rä ā'vis); pl. *raræ aves* (rā'rē ā'-vēz). [L., in full *rara avis in terris*, 'a rare bird on earth'—a phrase applied by Horace (Sat. ii. 2, 26) to the peacock: *rara*, fem. of *rarus*, rare, uncommon; *avis*, bird: see *rare*[1] and *Aves*.] A rare bird; hence, a person or an object of a rare kind or character; a prodigy.

rare[1] (rãr), *a.* [< ME. *rare* = D. *raar* = MLG. *rār*, LG. *raar* = G. Dan. Sw. *rar*, < OF. *rare*, *rere*, F. *rare*, dial. *raire*, *rale*, *rase* = Sp. Pg. It. *raro*, < L. *rarus*, thin, not dense, thinly scattered, few, rare, uncommon; root unknown.] **1.** Thin; porous; not dense; of slight consistence; rarefied; having relatively little matter in a given volume: as, a *rare* substance; the *rare* atmosphere of high mountains.

The fiend
O'er bog or steep, through strait, rough, dense, or *rare*,
With head, hands, wings, or feet pursues his way.
Milton, P. L., ii. 948.

Water is nineteen times lighter, and by consequence nineteen times *rarer* than gold. *Newton*, Opticks, II. iii. 8.

2. Thinly scattered; coming or occurring at wide intervals; sparse; dispersed.

Cucumber in this moone is sowen *rare*.
Palladius, Husbondrie (E. E. T. S.), p. 110.

The cattle in the fields and meadows green:
Those *rare* and solitary, these in flocks
Pasturing at once, and in broad herds upsprung.
Milton, P. L., vii. 461.

He left the barren-beaten thoroughfare,
Chose the green path that show'd the *rarer* foot.
Tennyson, Lancelot and Elaine.

3. Very uncommon or infrequent; seldom occurring or to be found; hardly ever met with.

She calls me proud, and that she could not love me
Were man as *rare* as phœnix.
Shak., As you Like it, iv. 3. 17.

It is the *rarest* thing that ever I saw in any place, neyther do I thinke that any citie of Christendome hath the like. *Coryat*, Crudities, I. 192.

When so many have written too much, we shall the more readily pardon the *rare* man who has written too little or just enough. *Lowell*, New Princeton Rev., I. 161.

Hence—**4.** Remarkable from uncommonness; especially, uncommonly good, excellent, valuable, fine, or the like; of an excellence seldom met with.

Good discent, rare features, vertuous partes.
Times' Whistle (E. E. T. S.), p. 43.

I think my love as rare
As any she belied with false compare.
Shak., Sonnets, cxxx.

They write to me from England of rare News in France.
Howell, Letters, I. vi. 37.

Ha! ha! ha! yes, yes, I think it a *rare* joke.
Sheridan, School for Scandal, iii. 3.

She's a rare hand at sausages; there's noane like her in a' the three Ridings. *Mrs. Gaskell*, Sylvia's Lovers, viii.

=**Syn.** 3. *Rare, Scarce*, infrequent, unusual. *Rare* implies that only few of the kind exist: as, perfect diamonds are rare. *Scarce* properly implies a previous or usual condition of greater abundance. *Rare* means that there are much fewer of a kind to be found than may be found where *scarce* would apply.

A perfect union of wit and judgment is one of the *rarest* things in the world. *Burke.*

Where words are *scarce*, they are seldom spent in vain.
Shak., Rich. II., ii. 1. 7.

Then touch'd upon the game, how *scarce* it was
This season. *Tennyson*, Audley Court.

4. Singular, extraordinary, incomparable, choice.

rare[2] (rãr), *a.* [A dial. form of *rear*[2], q. v.] Not thoroughly cooked; partly cooked; underdone: applied to meat: as, *rare* beef; a *rare* chop. [In common use in the United States, but now only dialectal in Great Britain.]

New-laid eggs, which Baucis' busy care
Turned by a gentle fire, and roasted *rare*.
Dryden, tr. of Ovid's Metamorph., viii. 98.

Scanty mutton scrags on Fridays, and rather more savoury, but grudging, portions of the same flesh, rotten-roasted or *rare*, on the Tuesdays. *Lamb*, Christ's Hospital.

The word *rare*, applied to meat not cooked enough, did sound really strange to me; but an eminent citizen of yours presently showed me that it had for it the authority of Dryden. *E. A. Freeman*, Amer. Lects., p. 69.

rare[3] (rãr), *adv.* [Also *rear*; prob. a reduction of *rather* (with sense of the positive *rath*): see *rather*, *rath*[1], *adv.* Cf. *rareripe* for *rathripe*.] Early. [Prov. Eng.]

rare[4] (rãr), *v.* A dialectal form of *rear*[1]. [U. S.]

rare[5]†, *v.* An obsolete form of *roar*.

rarebit (rãr'bit), *n.* [An altered form of *rabbit*[1] in the phrase *Welsh rabbit*, simulating an absurd derivation from *rare*[1] + *bit*, as if 'a rare delicacy.'] See *Welsh rabbit*, under *rabbit*[1].

raree-show (rar'ē-shō), *n.* [Appar. contracted from **rarity-show*, < *rarity* + *show*, *n.* (cf. G. *raritäten-kabinet*, a 'cabinet of curiosities or rarities,' *raritätenkasten*, peep-show, D. *rarekykkas*, a 'rare show,' show-box).] A peep-show; a show carried about in a box.

Thou didst look into it with as much innocency of heart as ever child look'd into a *raree-show* box.
Sterne, Tristram Shandy, viii. 24.

rarefaction (rar-ẹ̄-fak'shon), *n.* [< F. *raréfaction* = Pr. *rarefaccio* = Sp. *rarefaccion* = Pg. *rarefacção* = It. *rarefazione*, < L. as if **rarefactio(n-)*, < *rarefacere*, pp. *rarefactus*, rarefy: see *rarefy*.] The act or process of rarefying or making rare, or of expanding or distending a body or mass of matter, whereby the bulk is increased, or a smaller number of its particles occupy the same space; also, the state or condition so produced: opposed to *condensation*. The term is used chiefly in speaking of gases, the terms *dilatation* and *expansion* being applied in speaking of solids and liquids. There was formerly a dispute as to whether rarefaction consisted merely of an increase in the mean distance of the particles (as it is now held to do), or in an enlargement of the particles themselves, or finally in an intrusion of foreign particles. In the strictest sense, the word was understood to signify the second action.

Either we must say . . . that the selfsame body does not only obtain a greater space in *rarefaction*, . . . but adequately and exactly filled it, and so when rarefied acquires larger dimensions without either leaving any vacuities betwixt its component corpuscles or admitting between them any new or extraneous substance whatsoever. Now it is to this last (and, as some call it, rigorous) way of *rarefaction* that our adversary has recourse.
Boyle, Spring of the Air, I. iii.

When the *rarefaction* of a gas is extreme (one-millionth) its matter becomes radiant.
A. Daniell, Prin. of Physics, p. 584.

rarefactive (rar-ẹ̄-fak'tiv), *a.* [= F. *raréfactif* = Pr. *rarefactiu* = Sp. Pg. *rarefactivo*; as *rarefact(ion)* + *-ive*.] Causing rarefaction; making rarer or less dense. [Rare.]

The condition of the bone was not a tumour, but a *rarefactive* disease of the whole bone accompanied by new growth. *Lancet*, No. 3423, p. 684.

rarefiable (rar'ẹ̄-fī-ạ-bl), *a.* [< *rarefy* + *-able*.] Capable of being rarefied.

rarefy (rar'ẹ̄-fī), *v.*; pret. and pp. *rarefied*, ppr. *rarefying*. [Also, incorrectly, *rarify*; < F. *raréfier* = Pr. *rareficar* = Sp. *rarificar* = It. *rarificare*, < ML. as if **rareficare*, < L. *rarefacere* (> Pg. *rarefazer*), make thin or rare, < *rarus*, thin, rare, + *facere*, make.] **I.** *trans.* To make rare, thin, porous, or less dense; expand or enlarge without adding any new matter; figuratively, to spread or stretch out; distend: opposed to *condense*.

Presently the water, very much *rarified* like a mist, began to rise. *Court and Times of Charles I.*, I. 113.

For plain truths lose much of their weight when they are *rarify'd* into subtilities. *Stillingfleet*, Sermons, I. iv.

A body is commonly said to be *rarefied* or dilated (for I take the word in a larger sense than I know many others do) . . . when it acquires greater dimensions than the same body had before. *Boyle*, Works, I. 144.

Rarefying osteitis, an osteitis in which the Haversian canals become enlarged and the bone rarefied. Also called *osteoporosis*.

II. *intrans.* To become rare; pass into a thinner or less dense condition.

Earth *rarefies* to dew; expanded more,
The subtil dew in air begins to soar. *Dryden.*

rarely[1] (rãr'li), *adv.* [< *rare*[1], *a.*, + *-ly*[2].] 1. Seldom; not often: as, things *rarely* seen.

His friend alwayes shall doe best, and you shall *rarely* heare good of his enemy.
Bp. Earle, Micro-cosmographie, A Partiall Man.

The good we never miss we *rarely* prize.
Cowper, Retirement, l. 406.

2. Finely; excellently; remarkably well; with a rare excellence.

I could play Ercles *rarely*, or a part to tear a cat in, to make all split. *Shak.*, M. N. D., i. 2. 31.

Argyll has raised an hunder men,
An hunder harness'd *rarely*.
Bonnie House of Airly (Child's Ballads, VI. 186).

You can write *rarely* now, after all your schooling, I should think. *George Eliot*, Mill on the Floss, iii. 3.

3. In excellent health: in quasi-adjective use. Compare *purely* in like use. [Prov. Eng. and U. S.]

rarely[2] (rãr'li), *adv.* [< *rare*[2], *a.*, + *-ly*[2].] So as to be underdone or only partially cooked: said of meats: as, a roast of beef *rarely* cooked.

rareness[1] (rãr'nes), *n.* [< *rare*[1], *a.*, + *-ness*.] 1. Thinness; tenuity; rarity: as, the *rareness* of air or vapor.—2. The state of being scarce, or of happening seldom; uncommonness; infrequency.

If that the follye of men hadde not sette it [gold] in higher estimation for the *rarenesse* sake.
Sir T. More, Utopia (tr. by Robinson), ii. 6.

Rareness and difficulty give estimation
To all things are i' th' world.
Webster, Devil's Law-Case, v. 6.

3. Uncommon character or quality; especially, unusual excellence, fineness, or the like. [Rare.]

Roses set in the midst of a pool, being supported by some stay; which is matter of *rareness* and pleasure, though of small use. *Bacon*, Nat. Hist., § 407.

His providences toward us are to be admired for the *rareness* and graciousness of them. *Sharp*, Sermons, II. i.

rareness[2] (rãr'nes), *n.* [< *rare*[2], *a.*, + *-ness*.] The state of being rare or underdone in cooking.

rareripe (rãr'rīp), *a.* and *n.* [A reduction of *rathripe*, q. v.] **I.** *a.* Early ripe; ripe before others, or before the usual season: as, *rareripe* peaches.

II. *n.* An early fruit, particularly a kind of peach which ripens early.

rarify (rar'i-fī), *v.*; pret. and pp. *rarified*, ppr. *rarifying*. A common but incorrect spelling of *rarefy*.

rarita (rä-rē'tạ̈), *n.* [S. Amer.] Same as *rara*.

rarity (rar'i-ti), *n.*; pl. *rarities* (-tiz). [= OF. *rarite, rarete*, F. *rareté* = Pr. *raritat, raretat* = Sp. *raridad* = Pg. *raridade* = It. *rarità* = D. *rariteit* = G. *rarität* = Dan. Sw. *raritet*, < L. *rarita(t-)s*, the state of being thin or not dense, looseness of texture, tenuity, also fewness, rarity, a rare or curious thing, esp. in pl., < *rarus*, thin, rare: see *rare*[1].] 1. The condition of being rare, or not dense, or of occupying, as a corporeal substance, much space with little matter; thinness; tenuity: opposed to *density*: as, the *rarity* of a gas.

This I do . . . only that I may better demonstrate the great *rarity* and tenuity of their imaginary chaos.
Bentley, Sermons.

A few birds . . . seemed to swim in an atmosphere of more than usual *rarity*.
R. L. Stevenson, Treasure of Franchard.

2. The state of being uncommon or of infrequent occurrence; uncommonness; infrequency.

Alas, for the *rarity*
Of Christian charity
Under the sun!
Hood, Bridge of Sighs.

3. Something that is rare or uncommon; a thing valued for its scarcity or for its unusual excellence.

Gon. But the rarity of it is—which is indeed almost beyond credit.
Seb. As many vouched *rarities* are.
Shak., Tempest, ii. 1. 60.

How ignorant had we been of the beauty of Florence, of the monuments, urns, and *rarities* that yet remain.
I. Walton, Complete Angler, p. 34.

In climates where wine is a *rarity* intemperance abounds. *Macaulay*, Milton.

ras[1] (ras), *n.* [< Ar. *ras*, head; cf. *rais*, *reis*, head, chief: see *reis*[2].] 1. A promontory; cape; peak: a term prefixed to the names of promontories or capes on the Arabian and African coasts, etc. —2. In Abyssinia, the title of the vizir or chief minister, and also of generals and governors. The ras of the empire was for a long period—down to the accession of the usurping King Theodore in 1855—the actual ruler, the nominal Negus being merely a puppet. The ras commonly owed his position to superior military strength as governor of some province.

ras[2] (rä), *n.* [F.: see *rash*[4].] A smooth material of wool, and also of silk: a French term used in English, especially in certain combinations.

rasamala (ras-ạ-mä'lạ̈), *n.* [Native name.] A tree of Java and parts of India, *Altingia excelsa*, of the *Hamamelideæ*, closely related to the liquidambars. It has a tall straight trunk, ascending 90 or 100 feet before branching.

rasant (rā'zạnt), *a.* [< F. *rasant*, m., *rasante*, f., ppr. of *raser*, touch, graze, raze: see *rase*[1], *raze*[1].] In *fort.*, sweeping or grazing. A *rasant fire* is a flanking fire that impinges on or grazes the face which it defends, or a low fire that sweeps along near the ground. A *rasant line* is a direct line of fire of this kind. A *rasant flank* is the flank of a bastion the fire from which passes along the face of an adjoining bastion.

rasberry†, *n.* An obsolete form of *raspberry*.

Rasbora (ras-bō'rạ̈), *n.* [NL. (Hamilton); from a native name.] The typical genus of *Rasborina*, containing numerous small cyprinoids of the Oriental and African waters. The lateral line runs along the lower half of the caudal part.

Rasborina (ras-bọ̄-rī'nạ̈), *n. pl.* [NL., < *Rasbora* + *-ina*[2].] A division of *Cyprinidæ*, represented by *Rasbora* and four other genera.

rascabilian† (ras-kạ-bil'yạn), *n.* [A perverted form of *rascallion*.] A rascal.

Their names are often recorded in a court of correction, where the register of rogues makes no little gaine of *rascabilians*. *Breton*, Strange News, p. 6. (*Davies.*)

rascaille†, *n.* A Middle English form of *rascal*.

rascal (ràs'kạl), *n.* and *a.* [Early mod. E. *rascall*; < ME. *rascall*, *raskalle*, *rascaile*, *rascaille*, *rascayle*, *raskaille*, *rasskayle*, *rascalie*, *rascalye*, < OF. (AF.) *rascaille*, *raskaylle*, *raskayle*, a rabble, mob, F. *racaille*, "the rascality or base and rascall sort, the scumme, dregs, offals, outcasts, of any company" (Cotgrave), lit. 'scrapings,' < OF. **rasquer*, scrape, = Sp. Pg. *rascar*, scratch, *rasgar*, tear, rend, scrape, = OIt. *rascare*, burnish, rub, furbish (see *rash*[5]), < LL. **rasicare*, freq. of L. *radere*, pp. *rasus*, scrape: see *rase*[1], *raze*[1].] **I.** *n.* 1†. The commonalty of people; the vulgar herd; the general mass.

So rathely they rusche with roselde speris
That the *raskaille* was rade, and rane to the grefes.
Morte Arthure (E. E. T. S.), l. 2882.

Lo! here the fyn and guerdon for travaille,
Of Jove, Apollo, of Mars and swich *rescaille*.
Chaucer, Troilus, v. 1853.

The church is sometime taken for the common *rascal* of all that believe, whether with the mouth only, and carnally without spirit, neither loving the law in their hearts.
Tyndale, Ans. to Sir T. More, etc. (Parker Soc., 1850), [p. 114.

2. In *hunting*, a refuse or despicable beast or class of beasts; an animal, or animals collectively, unfit to chase or to kill, on account of ignoble quality or lean condition; especially, a lean deer.

I wondir not byly thouȝ heed-dere thou ffallid;
ffor litill on ȝoure lyf the list ffor to rewe
On *rascaile* that rorid with ribbis so lene,
ffor ffaute of her ffode that fflatereris stelen.
Richard the Redeless, ii. 119.

Other bestys all,
Where so ye theym fynde, *rascall* ye shall them call.
Quoted in *Walton's* Complete Angler, p. 31.

Horns? Even so. Poor men alone? No, no; the noblest deer hath them as huge as the *rascal*.
Shak., As you Like it, iii. 3. 58.

3†. A low or vulgar person; one of the rabble; a boor or churl.

'Tis true, I have been a *rascal*, as you are,
A fellow of no mention, nor no mark,
Just such another piece of dirt, so fashion'd.
Fletcher (and another?), Prophetess, v. 2.

4. A low or mean fellow; a tricky, dishonest person; a rogue; a knave; a scamp: used in

objurgation with much latitude, and often, like *rogue*, with slight meaning. Compare *rascally*.

> I have matter in my head . . . against your cony-catching *rascals*, Bardolph, Nym, and Pistol. — *Shak.*, M. W. of W., i. 1. 128.

> Shall a *rascal*, because he has read books, talk pertly to me? — *Cibber.*

> There were many men who wore green turbans, he said, that were very great *rascals*; but he was a Saint, which was better than a Sherriffe. — *Bruce*, Source of the Nile, I. 76.

II. *a.* **1.** Paltry; worthless; unworthy of consideration; in a special use, unfit for the chase, as a lean deer: used of things or animals. [Obsolescent.]

> When Marcus Brutus grows so covetous,
> To lock such *rascal* counters from his friends,
> Be ready, gods, with all your thunderbolts!
> — *Shak.*, J. C., iv. 3. 80.

2. Low; mean; base; common; ignoble; vulgar; knavish: used of persons, formerly with reference to class or occupation, but now only with an implication of moral baseness or dishonesty. [Not now common as an adjective.]

> Paul, being in prison in Rome, did write divers epistles, in which he expresseth the names of many which were in comparison of Peter but *rascal* personages; but of Peter he speaketh never a word. — *J. Bradford*, Letters (Parker Soc., 1853), II. 145.

> Metaphore . . . as one should in reproch say to a poore man, thou *raskall* knaue, where *raskall* is properly the hunter's terme giuen to young deere, leane and out of season, and not to people. — *Puttenham*, Arte of Eng. Poesie (ed. Arber), p. 191.

> Clodius shrieked for help. His *rascal* followers rushed in with lighted torches. — *Froude*, Cæsar, xv.

rascaldom (räs'kal-dum), *n.* [< *rascal* + *-dom.*] **1.** The sphere or domain of rascals; a class or body of rascally persons.

> How has this turbulent Alexandrian *rascaldom* been behaving itself in my absence? — *Kingsley*, Hypatia, ii.

> View of the *rascaldom* of Paris, tragical at this time (for where is now that reiving and stealing, that squeaking and jabbering—of lies?), otherwise unprofitable. — *Carlyle*, in Froude (First Forty Years, II. xvii.).

2. Rascally character or action; the spirit or practice of rascals; rascalism. [Rare.]

> The "three R's," if no industrial training has gone along with them, are apt, as Miss Nightingale observes, to produce a fourth R—of *rascaldom*. — *Froude*, at St. Andrews, March, 1869.

> Falstaff . . . is a character of the broadest comedy, . . . enjoying the confusion betwixt reason and the negation of reason—in other words, the rank *rascaldom* he is calling by its name. — *Emerson*, Letters and Social Aims, The Comic.

rascaldry† (räs'kal-dri), *n.* [For **rascalry*, < *rascal* + *-ry.*] A body or the class of rascals; the common herd; the rabble. [Rare.]

> So base a *rascaldry*
> As is too farre from thought of chyualry.
> — *Breton*, Pasquil's Fooles-cappe, p. 21. (*Davies.*)

rascalism (räs'kal-izm), *n.* [< *rascal* + *-ism.*] The spirit or practice of a rascal or of rascals; rascally character or quality.

> A tall handsome man with ex-military whiskers, with a look of troubled gaiety and *rascalism*. — *Carlyle*, Diamond Necklace, xiv. (*Davies.*)

rascality (räs-kal'i-ti), *n.* [< *rascal* + *-ity.*] **1.** Low or mean people collectively; rascals in general; rascaldom: now used chiefly in the moral sense. See *rascal*, *a.*, 2.

> Your baboons, and your jackanapes, being the scum and *rascality* of all hedge-creepers, they go in jerkins and mandilions. — *Dekker*, Gull's Hornbook, p. 69.

> Pretended philosophers judge as ignorantly in their way as the *rascality* in theirs. — *Glanville.*

> A favorite remedy [expulsion] with the Scotch for the purpose of disembarrassing themselves of their superfluous *rascality*. — *Ribton-Turner*, Vagrants and Vagrancy, p. 129.

2. The character or an action of a rascal; the quality of being a rascal; low or mean trickery; base or dishonest procedure; villainy; fraud.

> Why, goodman Hobby-horse, if we out of our gentility offer'd you to begin, must you out of your *rascality* needs take it? — *R. Taylor*, Hog hath Lost its Pearl, iii.

> This letter (full of *rascalities* against King Ch. II. and his Court). — *Wood*, Athenæ Oxon., II. 629.

rascal-like (räs'kal-lik), *a.* Like a rascal, in any sense; in the quotation, like a lean deer.

> If we be English deer, be then in blood;
> Not *rascal-like*, to fall down with a pinch.
> — *Shak.*, 1 Hen. VI., iv. 2. 49.

rascallion (räs-kal'yon), *n.* [< *rascal* + *-ion.* Hence var. *rapscallion.*] A low, mean wretch; a rapscallion.

> Used him so like a base *rascallion*. — *S. Butler*, Hudibras, I. iii. 327.

rascally (räs'kal-i), *a.* [< *rascal* + *-ly*[1].] Like or characteristic of a rascal; base; mean; trickish; scampish: used of persons or things with much latitude, often with slight meaning.

> These same abominable, vile, . . . *rascally* verses. — *B. Jonson*, Every Man in his Humour, i. 3.

> Well, Mr. Sharper, would you think it? In all this time—as I hope for a Truncheon—this *rascally* Gazette-writer never so much as once mention'd me. — *Congreve*, Old Batchelor, ii. 2.

> None of your *rascally* "dips"—but sound,
> Round, ten-penny moulds of four to the pound.
> — *Barham*, Ingoldsby Legends, II. 94.

rasclet, *v. i.* See *raxle.*

rase[1], **raze**[1] (rāz), *v. t.*; pret. and pp. *rased*, ppr. *rasing.* [Early mod. E. also *race* (confused with *race*[6]); < ME. *rasen*, *racen* (= D. *rasen* = G. *rasiren* = Sw. *rasera*), < OF. *raser*, F. *raser* = Sp. Pg. *rasar* = It. *rasare*, < ML. *rasare*, freq. of L. *radere*, pp. *rasus*, scrape, scratch, shave, rub, smooth, level, graze, touch, strip; akin to *rodere*, gnaw (see *rodent*). Hence ult. *erase*, *razor*, *razee*, *rascal*, *rash*[6], *abrade*, etc.] **1.** To scrape or glance along the surface of; scratch; graze; shave.

> A friendly checke killeth thee, when a rasor cannot *rase* thee. — *Lyly*, Euphues and his England, p. 381.

> Have you been stung by wasps, or angry bees,
> Or *rased* with some rude bramble or rough briar?
> — *B. Jonson*, Sad Shepherd, ii. 2.

> His breast 's of such well tempered proofe
> It may be *rac'd*, not pearc't, by savage tooth
> Of foaming malice.
> — *Marston*, Antonio and Mellida, II., ii. 2.

> Nor miss'd its aim, but where the plumage danc'd
> *Raz'd* the smooth cone, and thence obliquely glanc'd.
> — *Pope*, Iliad, xi. 464.

> This inside line is *rased* or scratched in. — *Thearle*, Naval Arch., § 39.

2. To obliterate by scraping; erase; cancel; hence, to strike out of existence; annul; destroy: often with *out.* [Obsolete or archaic.]

> I have a licence and all; it is but *razing out* one name and putting in another. — *B. Jonson*, Bartholomew Fair, v. 2.

> I write, indite, I point, I *rase*, I quote,
> I interline, I blot, correct, I note.
> — *Drayton*, Matilda to K. John.

> And in derision sets
> Upon their tongues a various spirit, to *rase*
> Quite *out* their native language.
> — *Milton*, P. L., xii. 53.

> He *razeth* all his foes with fire and sword. — *Marlowe*, Tamburlaine the Great, I., iv. 1.

3. To level with the ground or the supporting surface; tear down or demolish; reduce to ruins: in this sense now always spelled *raze.*

> Bellona storms,
> With all her battering engines bent to *rase*
> Some capital city.
> — *Milton*, P. L., ii. 923.

> We touch'd with joy
> The royal hand that *razed* unhappy Troy.
> — *Dryden*, Æneid, xi. 378.

> Sacrilegious and rebellious hands had *razed* the church, even to the foundation thereof, and laid the honour of the crown low in the dust. — *Bp. Atterbury*, Sermons, I. xvii.

> The strangers . . . who found a fiendish pleasure in *razing* magnificent cities. — *Macaulay*, Machiavelli.

=**Syn.** 3. *Raze, Demolish.* See *demolish.*

rase[1], **raze**[1] (rāz), *n.* [< *rase*[1], *v.*] A scratch; an abrasion; a slight wound.

> They whose tenderness shrinketh at the least *rase* of a needle point. — *Hooker*, Eccles. Polity. (*Latham.*)

rase[2]†, *n.* A Middle English form of *race*[1].

rase[3]†, *v. t.* Same as *race*[5].

rased (rāzd), *a.* [< *rase*[1] + *-ed*[2].] In *her.*, same as *raguly.*

rasée (ra-zā'), *a.* [< F. *rasé*, pp. of *raser*, rase: see *rase*[1].] In *her.*, same as *raguly.*

rasgado (räs-gä'dō), *n.* [Sp., a rent, break, laceration, < *rasgar*, rend, break: see *rascal.*] In guitar-playing, an effect produced by sweeping the strings with the thumb; a kind of arpeggio.

rash[1] (rash), *a.* [< ME. *rash*, *rasch*, hasty, headstrong; not found in AS. except in the rare verb *ræscan*, move quickly (of light), quiver, glitter, *ræscettan*, crackle, sparkle (= OHG. *raskezzan*, sparkle); = D. *rasch*, quick, swift, = MLG. *rasch* = OHG. *rasc*, also *rosch*, MHG. *rasch*, also *resch*, *risch*, G. *rasch*, quick, swift, = Dan. Sw. *rask*, brisk, quick, rash, = Icel. *röskr*, strong, vigorous (> *röskir*, quick); with adj. formative *-sk* (*-sh*), from the root of AS. *ræde*, quick (> *rædnes*, quickness), = MD. *rade*, *raede*, D. *rad* = MLG. *rat* (*rad-*), quick (see *rath*[1]), and of OFries. *reth*, *rad* = MD. D. *rad* = MLG. *rat*, LG. *rad* = OHG. *rad*, MHG. *rat*, G. *rad*, wheel, = Ir. *roth* = L. *rota* = Lith. *ratas*, wheel, = Skt. *ratha*, a wagon, chariot, war-chariot. Cf. *rash*[2].] **1**†. Quick; sudden; hasty.

> Ouer meruelous meres so mad arayed,
> Of raas [race, way, course] thaz I were *rasch* & ronk,
> Set rapely ther-inne I watz restayed.
> — *Alliterative Poems* (ed. Morris), i. 1166.

> As strong
> As aconitum or *rash* gunpowder.
> — *Shak.*, 2 Hen. IV., iv. 4. 48.

2. Hasty in council or action; precipitate; headstrong; impetuous; venturesome: as, a *rash* statesman or minister; a *rash* commander.

> In her faire eyes two living lamps did flame, . . .
> That quite bereav'd the *rash* beholders sight.
> — *Spenser*, F. Q., II. iii. 23.

> Be not *rash* with thy mouth. — Eccl. v. 2.

> For, though I am not splenitive and *rash*,
> Yet have I something in me dangerous.
> — *Shak.*, Hamlet, v. 1. 284.

> Her *rash* hand in evil hour
> Forth reaching to the fruit, she pluck'd, she eat!
> — *Milton*, P. L., ix. 780.

> Of the dead what hast thou heard
> That maketh thee so *rash* and unafeared?
> — *William Morris*, Earthly Paradise, III. 240.

3. Marked by or manifesting inconsiderate haste in speech or action; resulting from temerity or recklessness: as, *rash* words; *rash* measures.

> Of all my *rash* adventures past
> This frantic feat must prove the last!
> — *Scott*, L. of the L., iv. 28.

> The plan is *rash*; the project desperate. — *Browning*, Ring and Book, II. 52.

4†. Requiring haste; urgent.

> My lord, I scarce have leisure to salute you,
> My matter is so *rash*.
> — *Shak.*, T. and C., iv. 2. 62.

=**Syn. 2** and **3.** *Enterprising, Foolhardy*, etc. (see *adventurous*), precipitate, hasty, headlong, inconsiderate, careless, heedless. See list under *reckless.*

rash[1] (rash), *v. t.* [< *rash*[1], *a.* Cf. AS. *ræscan* = G. *raschen* = Sw. *raska*, move quickly, = Dan. *raske*, refl., rise; from the adj.] **1**†. To put together hurriedly; prepare with haste.

> In my former edition of Acts and Monuments, so hastily *rashed* [var. *raked*] vp at that present, in such shortnesse of time. — *Foxe*, Martyrs, p. 645, an. 1439. (*Richardson.*)

2. To publish imprudently; blab. *Jamieson.* [Scotch.]—**3.** To cook too rapidly; burn from haste: as, the beef has been *rashed* in the roasting. *Halliwell.* [Prov. Eng.]

rash[2] (rash), *a.* and *n.* [Prob. < Sw. Dan. *rask*, quick, = Icel. *röskr*, strong, vigorous; cf. Icel. *röskvask*, refl., ripen (said of persons): see *rash*[1].] **I.** *a.* So ripe or dry as to break or fall readily, as corn from dry straw in handling. [Local, Eng.]

II. *n.* Corn in the straw, so dry as to fall out with handling. [Local, Eng.]

rash[3]† (rash), *v. t.* [By apheresis from **arash*, var. of *arace*, < ME. *aracen*, *arasen*, also *arachen*, < AF. *aracer*, OF. *aracier*, *arachier*, mixed with *crachier*, *esrachier*, F. *arracher*, uproot, tear up, eradicate: see *arace*[1] and *eradicate*, and cf. *race*[5]. But the form and sense seem to be due in part to the verb *rash*[1]. Hence perhaps *rasher*[1].] To tear or slash violently; lacerate; rend; hack; hew; slice.

> Like two mad mastiffes, each on other flew,
> And shields did share, and mailes did *rash*, and helmes did hew.
> — *Spenser*, F. Q., IV. ii. 17.

> He dreamt the boar had *rashed* off his helm. — *Shak.*, Rich. III., iii. 2. 11. (*Nares.*)

> He strikes Clarindo, and *rashes* off his garland. — *Daniel*, Hymen's Triumph, iv. 3. (*Nares.*)

> I mist my purpose in his arm, *rashed* his doublet-sleeve, ran him close by the left cheek, and through his hair. — *B. Jonson*, Every Man out of his Humour, iv. 4.

rash[4] (rash), *n.* [(*a*) = D. LG. *ras* = G. *rasch*, woolen cloth, = Dan. *rask*, serge, = Sw. *rask*, a kind of cloth; prob. < OF. *ras*, a woolen stuff, F. *ras*, short-nap cloth, = Sp. It. *raso*, a smooth cloth material; cf. Sp. dim. *rasilla*, serge; perhaps < L. *rasus*, pp. of *radere*, scrape, rub: see *rase*[1]. (*b*) Cf. It. *rascia*, serge, 'rash,' said by Muratori to be < *Rascia*, a region in Bosnia where this stuff is said to have originated. (*c*) Cf. also *arras*, tapestry, = It. *arazzo* = MHG. *arraz*, *arras* (ML. *arrasium*, *arracium*), also, by apheresis, It. *razzo* = Pg. *raz*, arras, < F. *Arras*, also *Aras*, a town in northern France where arras was first made. Some confusion of these forms seems to have occurred.] A kind of inferior manufacture of silk or of silk and stuff.

> Be it therefore enacted, for the maintenance of the same trade in velvets, satins, sylkes, *rashe*, and other stuffs, as fitt for tearing as fine for wearing . . . — *Sixth Decree of Christmas Prince*, p. 21. (*Nares.*)

> Sleeveless his jerkin was, and it had been
> Velvet, but 'twas now (so much ground was seen)
> Become tufftaffaty; and our children shall
> See it plain *rash* awhile, then nought at all.
> — *Donne*, Satires, iv. 34.

> I see it, mistress; 'tis good stuff indeed;
> It is a silk *rash*; I can pattern it.
> — *Middleton*, Anything for a Quiet Life, iv. 3.

rash[5] (rash), *n.* [< OF. *rasche*, also *rasque*, rash, scurf, F. *rache*, an eruption on the head, scurf, = Pr. *rasca*, itch; < Pr. *rascar* = Sp. Pg. *rascar*, scratch, *rasgar*, tear, rend, scrape, etc., < LL. **rasicare*, scratch (cf. L. *rasitare*, shave often), freq. of L. *radere*, pp. *rasus*, scrape, shave: see *rase*[1], *raze*[1], and cf. *rascal*.] A more or less extensive eruption on the skin.

rash[6] (rash), *n.* An obsolete or dialectal form of *rush*[1].

They biggit a bower on yon burn brae,
And theekit it o'er wi' *rashes*.
Bessy Bell and Mary Gray, in Aitken's Scottish Song, p. 20.

rasher[1] (rash'ėr), *n.* [(*a*) < *rash*[1] + *-er*[1] (cf. "*rasher* on the coals, quasi *rashly* or hastily roasted"—Minsheu) (see *rash*[1], *v.*); or (*b*) < *rash*[3], slice, + *-er*[1]; the suffix *-er* being taken passively in either case.] In *cookery*, a slice of bacon, and formerly of any meat, for frying or broiling.

Carbonata, a carbonada, meat broiled vpon the coles, a *rasher*. *Florio*, 1598.

This making of Christians will raise the price of hogs; if we grow all to be pork-eaters, we shall not shortly have a *rasher* on the coals for money. *Shak.*, M. of V., iii. 5. 28.

He that eats nothing but a red herring a-day shall ne'er be broiled for the devil's *rasher*. *Beau. and Fl.*, Love's Cure, ii. 1.

He had done justice to a copious breakfast of fried eggs and broiled *rashers*. *Thackeray*, Pendennis, I. 313.

rasher[2] (rash'ėr), *n.* [Perhaps < Sp. *rascacio* = Pg. *rascacio*, also *rascas*, names of the European *Scorpæna scrofa* and related fishes.] A scorpænoid fish of California, *Sebastichthys* or *Sebastodes miniatus*, of a red color variously marked. It is one of a large group of rock-fish or rock-cod, others of which no doubt have the same name.

rashful† (rash'fůl), *a.* [< *rash*[1] + *-ful*.] Rash; hasty; precipitate. [Rare.]

Then you with hastie doome and *rashfull* sentence straight Will vaunt that women in that age were all with vertue fraught.
Turberville, Dispraise of Women that allure and love not.

rashling† (rash'ling), *n.* [< *rash*[1] + *-ling*[1].] A rash person. [Rare.]

What *rashlings* doth delight, that sober men despise.
Sylvester, tr. of Du Bartas.

rashly (rash'li), *adv.* In a rash manner; hastily; with precipitation; inconsiderately; presumptuously; at a venture.

rashness (rash'nes), *n.* 1. The character of being rash; inconsiderate or presumptuous haste; headstrong precipitation in decision or action; temerity; unwarranted boldness.

Such bold asseverations as in him [the apostle Paul] were admirable should in your mouths but argue *rashness*.
Hooker, Eccles. Polity, Pref., vi.

And though he stumbles in a full career,
Yet *rashness* is a better fault than fear.
Dryden, Tyrannic Love, Prol., l. 21.

2. A rash act; a reckless or foolhardy deed.

Why not set forth, if I should do
This *rashness*, that which might ensue
With this old soul in organs new?
Tennyson, Two Voices.

=Syn. 1. *Rashness*, *Temerity*. *Rashness* has the vigor of the Anglo-Saxon, *temerity* the selectness and dignity of the Latin. *Temerity* implies personal danger, physical or other: as, the *temerity* of undertaking to contradict Samuel Johnson; *temerity* in going upon thin ice. *Rashness* is broader in this respect. *Rashness* goes by the feelings without the judgment; *temerity* rather disregards the judgment. *Temerity* refers rather to the disposition, *rashness* to the conduct. See *adventurous*.

For *rashness* is not courage. *Rashness* flings itself into danger without consideration or foresight. But courage counts the cost, and does not make any display of itself.
J. F. Clarke, Self-Culture, p. 336.

As the note of warlike preparation reached them [the Moors] in their fastnesses, they felt their *temerity* in thus bringing the whole weight of the Castilian monarchy on their heads. *Prescott*, Ferd. and Isa., ii. 7.

rasin†, *n.* An obsolete form of *resin*.

rasing (rā'zing), *n.* [Verbal n. of *rase*[1], *v.*] In *ship-building*, the act of marking by the edges of molds any figure upon timber, etc., with a rasing-knife, or with the points of compasses.

rasing-iron (rā'zing-ī″ėrn), *n.* A kind of calking-iron for clearing the pitch and oakum out of a vessel's seams, preparatory to recalking.

rasing-knife (rā'zing-nīf), *n.* A small edged tool fixed in a handle, and hooked at its point, used for making particular marks on timber, lead, tin, etc.

rasion (rā'zhon), *n.* [< L. *rasio*(*n-*), a scraping, shaving, < *radere*, pp. *rasus*, scrape, shave: see *rase*[1].] 1†. A scraping or shaving; rasure. *Bailey*, 1731.—2. In *phar.*, the division of substances by the rasp or file. *Dunglison*.

raskaile†, *n.* An obsolete form of *rascal*.

Raskolnik (ras-kol'nik), *n.* [Russ.] In Russia, a schismatic; a dissenter. There are many sects of Raskolniks, most of them differing from the Orthodox Church by even greater conservatism in ritual, etc. Some sects retain the office of priest, while others are Presbyterian or Independent in polity; others, again, are of wildly fanatical and antinomian character.

rasoo (ra-sö'), *n.* [E. Ind.] A flying-squirrel of India, a species of *Pteromys*.

Rasores (rā-sō'rēz), *n. pl.* [NL., pl. of L. *rasor*, a scraper (applied to a fiddler), < *radere*, pp. *rasus*, scrape, scratch: see *rase*[1], *raze*[1].] 1†. In Illiger's system (1811), the rasorial birds, or scratchers, an order of *Aves*, including the gallinaceous and columbaceous birds.—2. The same excluding the pigeons: now usually called *Gallinæ* (which see).

Rasores.
1, 1, head and foot of dunghill-cock; 2, 2, head and foot of moor-fowl (*Lagopus scoticus*).

rasorial (rā-sō'ri-al), *a.* [NL., < *Rasores* + *-ial*.] Given to scratching the ground for food, as poultry; belonging to the *Rasores*, especially in the second sense of that word; gallinaceous.

rasp[1] (rasp), *v.* [< ME. *raspen*, *rospen*, < OF. *rasper*, F. *râper*, scrape, grate, rasp, = Sp. Pg. *raspar* = It. *raspare*, scrape, rasp, < ML. *raspare*, scrape, rake, < OHG. *raspôn*, MHG. *raspen*, scrape together (cf. D. MLG. *raspen* = MHG. freq. *raspelen*, G. *raspeln*, rasp, = Dan. *raspe* = Sw. *raspa*, rasp, in part from the noun); cf. OHG. *hrespan*, MHG. *respen*, rake together, pluck; Icel. *rispa*, scratch (> Sc. *risp*); prob. from the root of OHG. **raffon*, MHG. G. *raffen*, etc., seize: see *rap*[2]. Cf. *rasp*[1], *n.* Hence ult. (prob.) *rapier*.] I. *trans.* 1. To abrade by rubbing or grating with a coarsely rough instrument; grate, or grate away, with a rasp or something comparable to it.

Al that thise first vii [years of plenty] maken,
Sulen this othere vii [years of famine] *rospen* & raken.
Genesis and Exodus (E. E. T. S.), l. 2132.

That fellow . . . who insists that the shoe must fit him because it fitted his father and grandfather, and that, if his foot will not enter, he will pare and *rasp* it.
Landor, Imaginary Conversations, Solon and Pisistratus.

When the cane [in sugar-making] has been *rasped* to shreds [by a rasper], it is reduced to pulp by disintegrating apparatus. *Spons' Encyc. Manuf.*, II. 1879.

2. Figuratively, to affect or perform harshly, as if by the use of a rasp; grate upon; utter with a rough and jarring effect: as, to *rasp* one's feelings; to *rasp* out a refusal.

Through all the weird September-eves
I heard the harsh, reiterant katydids
Rasp the mysterious silence.
J. G. Holland, Kathrina, i.

Grating songs a listening crowd endures,
Rasped from the throats of bellowing amateurs.
O. W. Holmes, An After-Dinner Poem.

II. *intrans.* To rub against something gratingly; produce a rasping effect: as, the vessel *rasped* against the quay: literally or figuratively.

Rasped harshly against his dainty nature.
Lowell, Vision of Sir Launfal, i. 5.

rasp[1] (rasp), *n.* [= D. Dan. Sw. *rasp* = G. *raspe*, < OF. *raspe*, F. *râpe* (> G. *rappe*) (= It. *raspa*), a rasp, grater, < *rasper*, F. *râper*, grate, rasp, file: see *rasp*[1], *v.*] 1. A coarse form of file, having its surface dotted with separate protruding teeth, formed by the indentations of a pointed punch. In cabinet-rasps, wood-rasps, and farriers' rasps the teeth are cut in lines sloping down from the left- to the right-hand side; in rasps for use in making boot- and shoe-lasts the teeth slope in the opposite way; and rasps for makers of gun-stocks and saddletrees are cut with teeth arrayed in circular lines or in crescent form: sometimes used figuratively.

The horses from the country were a goodly sight to see, with the *rasp* of winter bristles rising through and among the soft summer-coat.
R. D. Blackmore, Lorna Doone, lxix.

2. A machine or large instrument for use in rasping; a rasper.

The juice [of beet-roots] from the *rasp* and the press is brought into a boiler and heated by steam.
Spons' Encyc. Manuf., I. 210.

3. The radula or odontophore of a mollusk; the lingual ribbon. See cut under *radula*.—4. A rasping surface. (*a*†) The steel of a tinder-box. [Prov. Eng.] (*b*) The rough surface of the tongue of some animals.

He dismounted when he came to the cattle, and walked among them, stroking their soft flanks, and feeling in the palm of his hand the *rasp* of their tongues.
The Century, XXXV. 947.

rasp[2] (rasp), *n.* [Formerly also *respe*, also *raspis*, *raspise*, *raspice*, *respass* (with occasional pl. *raspisses*), appar. orig. pl., prop. *raspes* (the berries), used as sing. (the bush, and later transferred to a single berry ?), prob. < *rasp*[1], *n.*, or abbr. of *raspberry*, < *rasp*[1] + *berry*[1], with ref. to its rough outside; cf. It. *raspo*, a raspberry (Florio): see *rasp*[1].] The fruit of the common (European) raspberry. See *raspberry*. [Obsolete or prov. Eng.]

The soyle of this playne bryngeth foorth ferne and bramble busshes bearynge blacke berries or wylde *raspes*, which two are tokens of coulde regions.
Peter Martyr (tr. in Eden's First Books on America, ed. [Arber, p. 172).

For kindes of fruites, they haue . . . *rasps*, strawberies, and hurtilberies. *Hakluyt's Voyages*, I. 477.

Rosey had done eating up her pine-apple, artlessly confessing . . . that she preferred it to the *rasps* and hinny-blobs in her grandmamma's garden.
Thackeray, Newcomes, xxiii.

rasp[3] (rasp), *v. i.* [Cf. G. *räuspern*, hawk or clear the throat; prob. imitative.] To belch; eject wind from the stomach. [Old and prov. Eng.]

Let them bind gold to their aching head, drink Cleopatra's draught (precious stones dissolved), to ease their *rasping* stomach. *Rev. T. Adams*, Works, I. 424.

This man of nice education hath a feeble stomacke, and (*rasping* since his last meale) doubts whether he should eat of his laste meale or nothing.
Bp. Hall, Heaven upon Earth, § 26.

raspatory (ras'pa-tō-ri), *n.*; pl. *raspatories* (-riz). [< ML. *raspatorium* (cf. Sp. Pg. *raspador*, a scraper), < *raspare*, rasp, scrape: see *rasp*[1], *v.*] A surgeons' rasp; an instrument for scraping or abrading bones in surgical or anatomical operations.

raspberry (raz'ber″i), *n.*; pl. *raspberries* (-iz). [Formerly also *rasberry* and *raspis-berry*; < *rasp*[1], or *rasp*[2] (see *rasp*[2]), + *berry*[1].] 1. The fruit of several plants of the genus *Rubus*, consisting of many small juicy grains or drupes, which, unlike those of the blackberry, separate from the convex receptacle together when ripe, thus giving the fruit the shape of a thimble. Besides its extensive use as a dessert fruit, the raspberry is used for jellies and jam, and its juice for flavoring, for cooling drinks, and in wines and brandies.

Herewith (at hand) taking her horne of plentie,
Fill'd with the choyse of every orchard's daintie,
As peares, plums, apples, the sweet *raspis-berry*.
W. Browne, Britannia's Pastorals, i. 5.

2. The plant that produces this berry. The common garden raspberry, the first of the name, is *Rubus Idæus*, a native of Europe and Asiatic Russia—a shrub with perennial creeping rootstock, nearly erect, prickly, biennial stems, and a red pleasant fruit. It was cultivated by the Romans in the fourth century, and is the source of the best raspberries, affording many varieties, some of them yellow-fruited. The wild red raspberry, *R. strigosus*, of North America, is a very similar plant, but not quite so tall, the leaves being thinner, and the fruit not so firm, large, or well-flavored. It is common northward, especially on newly cleared grounds, and its fruit is much gathered; while under cultivation it has yielded several good varieties. The black raspberry, thimbleberry, or blackcap is the American *R. occidentalis*, a shrub with long recurved biennial stems, rooting at the tips, and a black fruit. It is very productive with little care, and affords good garden varieties.—**Dwarf raspberry**, an unimportant American species, *Rubus triflorus*, with herbaceous trailing or ascending stems, resembling a blackberry.—**Flowering raspberry**, a name of two American species, *Rubus odoratus*, the purple, and *R. Nutkanus*, the white flowering raspberry. The former is a rather ornamental shrub of the eastern United States, with ample three- to five-lobed leaves, and showy purple or pink flowers blooming all summer, the fruit of little worth. In England it is sometimes called *Virginian raspberry*. *R. Nutkanus* is a similar western species with white flowers; also, and better, called *salmon-berry*.—**Himalayan raspberry**, *Rubus rosæfolius*, an East Indian species widely naturalized and cultivated in warm countries, and often grown as a greenhouse shrub, on account of its profusion of white, often double, flowers. The large fruit consists of many minute orange-red grains.—**Raspberry vinegar**, a drink made with sugar, vinegar, and the juice of raspberries.—**Virginian raspberry**. See *flowering raspberry*.

raspberry-borer (räz'ber-i-bōr'ėr), *n.* The larva of one of the clear-winged sphinxes or hornet-moths, *Bembecia marginata*, common in the United States. It bores the roots of raspberries and blackberries. The larva of a beetle, *Oberea bimaculata*, which also bores into the same plants, is often called by this name.

Raspberry-borer (*Bembecia marginata*).
a, male; *b*, female. (Natural size.)

raspberry-bush (räz'ber-i-bush), *n.* The shrub, bush, or bramble producing any of the kinds of raspberry.

raspberry-jam tree (räz'ber-i-jam trē). One of the Australian wattle-trees, *Acacia acuminata*. Its wood is used in cabinet-work, and has the odor of jam made from raspberries.

rasped (rąspt), *a.* [Pp. of *rasp*¹, *v.*] **1.** Affected as if by rasping; hoarse or raucous, as the voice; raspy; nervous or irritable, as from continued slight provocations.—**2.** In *bookbinding*, said of book-covers which have the sharp angles taken off, but are not beveled.

rasper (rąs'pėr), *n.* [< *rasp*¹ + *-er*¹.] **1.** One who or that which rasps; a cutting scraper. Specifically—(*a*) A coarse file for removing the burnt crust from over-baked bread. (*b*) A rasping-machine; an instrument for rasping sugar-cane, beet-root, or the like to shreds; a large grater.

The typical representative of the internal system of grating is Champonnois' *rasper*.
Spons' Encyc. Manuf., II. 1838.

2. In *hunting*, a difficult fence. [Colloq.]

Three fourths of our fences . . . average somewhat better than four feet in height, with an occasional *rasper* that will come well up to five. *The Century*, XXXII. 336.

3. A contrivance for taking fish, consisting of several bare hooks fastened back to back, to be jerked through the water with a line; a pull-devil. [Canada.]

rasp-house (rąsp'hous), *n.* A place where wood is dressed or reduced to powder by rasping, for use in dyeing, etc.

We went to see the *Rasp-house*, where the lusty knaves are compell'd to worke, and the rasping of Brasill and Logwood is very hard labour.
Evelyn, Diary, Aug. 19, 1641.

raspice†, *n.* Same as *rasp*².

rasping (rąs'ping), *n.* [Verbal n. of *rasp*¹, *v.*] A particle rasped off from a body or mass of matter. Compare *filing*¹, 2.

The wood itself, either reduced to shavings, *raspings*, or powder. *W. Crookes*, Dyeing and Calico-printing, p. 337.

rasping (rąs'ping), *p. a.* [Ppr. of *rasp*¹, *v.*] **1.** Characterized by grating or scraping: as, a *rasping* sound; hence, irritating; exasperating. —**2.** In *hunting*, said of a fence difficult to take.

You cannot . . . make him keep his seat over a *rasping* fence. *Dr. J. Brown*, Spare Hours, 3d ser., p. 60.

raspingly (rąs'ping-li), *adv.* With a harsh, rasping sound or effect; in a coarse, harsh manner; gratingly; irritatingly; exasperatingly.

I told him to stay at home, quite *raspingly*, and he was very ready to admit that I had done him a good turn in doing so. *F. H. Burnett*, Pretty Polly Pemberton, vii.

rasping-machine (rąs'ping-ma-shēn"), *n.* **1.** A machine for rasping wood and bark for making dyes, tinctures, etc.; a bark-cutting machine. —**2.** A machine for grating beet-root, for making sugar. *E. H. Knight.*

rasping-mill (rąs'ping-mil), *n.* A saw-like machine for reducing a substance to shreds or fine particles, as a bark-cutter or a grinding-mill for beet-roots; a rasping-machine; a rasper.

raspist, *n.* Same as *rasp*².

The *raspis* is planted in gardens. *Gerard.*

Raspis are of the same vertue that common brier or bramble is of. It were good to keepe some of the juyce of *raspis*-berries in some wooden vessel, and to make it, as it were, *raspis* wine. *Langham*, Garden of Health, p. 522.

rasp-palm (rąsp'päm), *n.* A common palm of the Amazon region, *Iriartea exorhiza*, notable in that its stem is supported by a cone of aërial roots, of sufficient height for a man to pass beneath. These roots are covered with hard tubercles, and are used by the natives as graters, whence the name.

rasp-pod (rąsp'pod), *n.* An Australian tree, *Flindersia australis*: so named from its woody capsules, covered with tubercles and used as graters.

rasp-punch (rąsp'punch), *n.* A tool, rather more like a cold-chisel than a punch, used for forming the teeth of rasps by cutting into, and turning upward above the surface, parts of the metal before it has been hardened and tempered.

raspy (rąs'pi), *a.* [< *rasp*¹ + *-y*¹.] Grating; harsh; rough.

Such a *raspy*, untamed Voice as that of his I have hardly heard. *Carlyle*, Misc., IV. 197. (*Davies.*)

rasse¹ (ras), *n.* [< Javanese *rosa*, smell, taste, < Skt. *rasa*, sap, taste, savor.] A kind of civet-cat; the lesser civet, a viverrine quadruped of the genus *Viverricula*, *V. malaccensis*, widely distributed in China, India, the Malay peninsula, Java, etc. It is about 20 inches long without the tail, and is sometimes called the *Malacca weasel*. Its perfume, called by the natives *dedes*, is secreted in a double pouch like that of the civet; it is much valued by the Javanese. For its sake the animal is often kept in captivity. It is savage and irritable, and can inflict a very severe bite.

rasse²†, *n.* [ME.] An eminence; a mound; a summit.

On a *rasse* of a rok hit reste at the laste,
On the mounte of Mararach of Armene hilles.
Alliterative Poems (ed. Morris), ii. 446.

rastral (ras'tral), *n.* [< *rastrum* + *-al.*] Same as *rostrum*.

rastrite (ras'trīt), *n.* A zoöphyte of the genus *Rastrites*; a graptolite.

Rastrites (ras-trī'tēz), *n.* [NL., < L. *rastrum*, a rake, + *-ites.*] A genus of fossil Silurian zoöphytes: same as *Graptolithus*.

rastrum (ras'trum), *n.*; pl. *rastra* (-trä). [NL., < L. *rastrum*, a rake, hoe, mattock, < *radere*, scrape: see *rase*¹.] **1.** A five-pointed pen for ruling staffs for music; a music-pen.—**2.** A herse.

rasure (rā'zūr), *n.* [Early mod. E. also *razure*; < F. *rasure* = Sp. Pg. It. *rasura*, a shaving, a blotting off, also the priest's tonsure, < L. *rasura*, a shaving, scraping, < *radere*, pp. *rasus*, scrape: see *rase*¹. Cf. *erasure.*] **1.** The act of scraping or shaving; a rasing or erasing; a scratch. [Rare.]

With the tooth of a small beast like a rat they race some their faces, some their bodies, after diuers formes, as if it were with the scratch of a pin, the print of which *rasure* can neuer be done away againe during life.
Hakluyt's Voyages, III. 674.

A forted residence 'gainst the tooth of time
And *razure* of oblivion. *Shak.*, M. for M., v. 1. 13.

2†. Same as *erasure*.

There were many *razures* in the book of the treasury.
Bp. Burnet.

rat¹ (rat), *n.* [Formerly also *ratt*; < ME. *ratte*, *rotte*, pl. *rattes*, < AS. *ræt* (*rætt-*) = MD. *ratte*, D. *rat* = OLG. *ratta*, MLG. *ratte*, LG. *ratte*, also *rat*, *rot* = OHG. *rato*, m., *ratta*, f., MHG. *rat*, *rate*, m., *ratte*, *rate*, f., MHG. also *ratz*, *ratze*, G. *ratze*, m., = Icel. *rotta* = Sw. *råtta* = Dan. *rotte*, a rat; cf. F. Pr. *rat* = Sp. Pg. *rato* = It. *ratto* = ML. *ratus*, *rattus*; cf. also Ir. Gael. *radan*, Bret. *raz*, a rat. The relations of the Teut., Rom., and Celtic groups to one another, and the ult. source of the word, are unknown. Some refer the word to the root seen in L. *radere*, scratch, scrape (see *rase*¹, *raze*¹), *rodere*, gnaw (see *rodent*). The forms of the word *cat* are equally wide-spread.] **1.** A rodent of some of the larger species of the genus *Mus*, as *M. rattus*, the black rat, and *M. decumanus*, the gray, brown, or Norway rat: distinguished from *mouse*. The distinction between *rat* and *mouse*, in the application of the names to animals everywhere parasitic with man, is obvious and familiar. But these are simply larger and smaller species of the same genus, very closely related zoölogically, and in the application of the two names to the many other species of the same genus all distinction between them is lost.

2. Any rodent of the family *Muridæ*; a murine; in the plural, the *Muridæ*. In this sense, *rat* includes *mouse*. American rats or mice are a particular section of the subfamily *Murinæ*, called *Sigmodontes*, confined to America, where no other *Murinæ* are indigenous. Field-rats, water-rats, meadow-mice, or voles are *Muridæ* of the subfamily *Arvicolinæ*. See cuts under *Arvicola*, *Muridæ*, *muskrat*, *Neotoma*, *Nesokia*, and *Nesomys*.

3. Any rodent of the suborder *Myomorpha*. Different animals of several families, as *Dipodidæ*, *Zapodidæ*, *Saccomyidæ*, *Geomyidæ*, *Spalacidæ*, are often known as *rats* of some kind distinguished by qualifying words or compound names. See cut under *mole-rat*.

4. Some other rodent, or some insectivore, marsupial, or other animal like or likened to a rat. Thus, among hystricomorphic rodents, many species of *Octodontidæ* are called *rats*: as, the *spiny rats* of the subfamily *Echinomyinæ*. Some large aquatic shrews are known as *muskrats*. (See *Myogale*.) Some rat-like marsupials are known as *kangaroo-rats*. (See *bettong*, and cuts under *kangaroo-rat* and *Echimys*.)

5. A person who is considered to act in some respect in a manner characteristic of rats: so called in opprobrium. Specifically—(*a*) A man who deserts a party or an association of any kind for one opposed to it in order to gain some personal advantage or benefit; a self-seeking turncoat; a renegade. [Colloq.]

He [Wentworth] was the first of the *Rats*, the first of those statesmen whose patriotism had been only the coquetry of a political prostitution, and whose profligacy has taught governments to adopt the old maxim of the slave-market, that it is cheaper to buy than to breed, to import defenders from an Opposition than to rear them in a Ministry. *Macaulay*, Hallam's Const. Hist.

(*b*) A workman who accepts lower wages than those current at the time and place or required by an authorized scale, or one who takes a position vacated by a striker, or one who refuses to strike when others do. [Colloq.]

The men who agree to go into the strike are always the more united and determined class. The *rats* who refuse suffer accordingly. *The American*, III. 181.

(*c*†) A clergyman: so called in contempt. *Halliwell.*

6. Something suggesting the idea of a rat, as a curving roll of stuffed cloth or of crimped hair-work, with tapering ends, formerly (about 1860–70) and still occasionally used by women to puff out the hair, which was turned over it.

At one time even a small amount of natural hair easily served the purpose of covering the crescent-shaped pillows on which it was put up, the startling names of which were *rats* and mice. *The Century*, XXXVI. 709.

Alexandrian rat, a gray or rufous-backed and white-bellied variety of *Mus rattus*, to which the name *M. alexandrinus* has been applied, owing to its having been first discovered at Alexandria in Egypt, but which is not specifically distinct from the black rat.—**Bamboo-rat**, an Indian murine rodent mammal of the genus *Rhizomys*, as *R. sumatranus*. The bay bamboo-rat is *R. badius*. The species are also called *canets*. See cut under *Rhizomys*.—**Bandicoot rat.** (*a*) The Anglo-Indian name of the large murine rodents of India, of the family *Muridæ*, subfamily *Phlœomyinæ*, and genus *Nesokia*, of which there are several species, all Indian. *N. griffithi* is an example. See cut under *Nesokia*. (*b*) Same as *bandicoot*, 2.—**Black rat**, *Mus rattus*, one of the most anciently known rats, now almost cosmopolitan, and typically of a blackish color, but very variable in this respect. It is rather smaller than the Norway gray rat. In one of its varieties it is known as *roof-rat* (*Mus tectorum*) and *white-bellied rat*. See cut under *Muridæ*.—**Hare-tailed rat.** See *lemming*.—**Maori rat**, the black rat, *Mus rattus*, introduced and naturalized in New Zealand.—**Mountain rat**, the large bushy-tailed wood-rat of the Rocky Mountain region, *Neotoma cinerea*; the pack-rat. [U. S.]—**Norway rat**, the common rat, *Mus decumanus*.—**Pack-rat**, the mountain rat, *Neotoma cinerea*: so called on account of its curious and inveterate habit of dragging off to its hole any object it can move. [Western U. S.]—**Pharaonic rat, Pharaoh's rat**, the ichneumon: a phrase traceable back at least to Belon (about 1555). See *Herpestes*. Also called *Pharaoh's mouse*.—**Pouched rat.** See *pouched*.—**To have a rat in the garret**, to be slightly crack-brained: same as *to have a bee in one's bonnet* (which see, under *bee*).—**To smell a rat**, to be suspicious that all is not right; have an inkling of some mischief, plot, or underhand proceeding.

Quoth Hudibras, "I *smell a rat*:
Ralpho, thou dost prevaricate."
S. Butler, Hudibras, I. i. 821.

rat¹ (rat), *v.*; pret. and pp. *ratted*, ppr. *ratting*. [< *rat*¹, *n.*] **I.** *intrans.* **1.** To catch or kill rats; follow the business of a ratter or rat-catcher. —**2.** To go over from one party or cause to another, especially from a party or cause that is losing or likely to lose, as rats run from a falling house; desert one's party or associates for advantage or gain; become a renegade. [Colloq.]

His ci-devant friends curse the hour that he *ratted*.
Barham, Ingoldsby Legends, II. 385.

I am fully resolved to oppose several of the clauses. But to declare my intention publicly, at a moment when the Government is in danger, would have the appearance of *ratting*. *Macaulay*, in Trevelyan, I. 275.

3. To work for less than current wages, to refuse to strike with fellow-workmen, or to take the place of one who has struck: often with indefinite *it*. See *rat*¹, *n.*, 5 (*b*). [Colloq.]

II. *trans.* **1.** To puff out (the hair) by means of a rat. See *rat*¹, *n.*, 6. [Rare.]

Next morning, at breakfast, Sin Saxon was as beautifully ruffled, *ratted*, and crimped—as gay, as bewitching, and defiant—as ever. *Mrs. Whitney*, Leslie Goldthwaite, x.

2. To displace or supplant union workers in: as, to *rat* an office or a shop. [Colloq.]

rat²† (rat), *n.* [Usually in pl. *rats*, < ME. *rattes*, rags; either from the verb, ME. *ratten*, tear (see *rat*², *v.*), or < Icel. *hrat*, *hrati*, rubbish, trash, = Norw. *rat*, rubbish; cf. Sw. Norw. *rata*, reject, refuse (see *rate*¹).] A rag; tatter. [Prov. Eng.]

I *ratles* and i clutes. *Old Eng. Homilies*, I. 227.

rat²† (rat), *v. t.* [< ME. *ratten* = MHG. *ratzen*, tear; cf. *rat*², *n.*] To tear.

How watȝ thou hardy this hous for thyn vnhap [to] neȝe,
In on so *ratted* a robe & rent at the sydes?
Alliterative Poems (ed. Morris), ii. 144.

rat³ (rat), *v. t.* [Prob. a var. of *rot*; cf. *drat*², in similar use.] A term of objurgation, used in the imperative.

rat[4]†. A Middle English contracted form of *redeth*, the third person singular present indicative of *read*[1]. *Piers Plowman.*

rata (rä'tạ̈), *n.* [New Zealand.] A tree of New Zealand, *Metrosideros robusta*, growing from 60 to 80 feet high, the wood of which is used in cabinet-work, and in civil and naval architecture. The name belongs also to *M. florida*, a stout-trunked climber ascending the highest trees; it is also more or less extended by settlers to other species of the genus. Besides in several cases yielding valuable wood, these trees are notable for their profusion of brilliant flowers, which are generally, as in *M. robusta*, scarlet. See *fire-tree* and *Metrosideros*.

ratability (rā-tạ-bil'ị-ti), *n.* [< *ratable* + *-ity* (see *-bility*).] The quality of being ratable. *Athenæum*, No. 3261, p. 535.

ratable (rā'ta-bl), *a.* [Also *rateable*; < *rate*[2] + *-able*.] 1. Capable of being rated, or set at a certain value.

I collect out of the abbay booke of Burton, that 20 Ores were *ratable* to two markes of siluer.
Camden, Remains, Money.

2. Reckoned according to a certain rate; proportional.

In conscience and credit [poets were] bound, next after the diuine praises of the immortall gods, to yeeld a like *ratable* honour to all such amongst men as most resembled the gods by excellencie of function.
Puttenham, Arte of Eng. Poesie, p. 28.

A *ratable* payment of all the debts of the deceased, in equal degree, is clearly the most equitable method.
Blackstone, Com., III. ii.

3. Liable or subjected by law to be rated or assessed for taxation.

ratableness (rā'tạ-bl-nes), *n.* Ratability.

ratably (rā'tạ-bli), *adv.* According to rating or valuation; at a proportionate rate; proportionally.

I will thus charge them all *ratablye*, according to theyr abilityes, towardes theyr maintenaunce.
Spenser, State of Ireland.

The shareholders of every national banking association shall be held individually responsible, equally and *ratably*.
National Bank Act, U. S. (ed. 1882), p. 14.

ratafia (rat-ạ-fē'ạ̈), *n.* [Formerly also *ratifia*, *ratifie*, *ratifee*, also *ratafiaz*; = D., etc., *ratafia*, < F. *ratafia*, formerly also *ratafiat* (cf. F. *tafia*, rum, arrack), = Sp. *ratafia* = Pg. *ratafia*, < Malay *araq*, a distilled spirit, arrack (< Ar. *'araq*, juice, distilled spirit: see *arrack*), + *tafia*, *taffia*, a spirit distilled from molasses.] 1. A sweet cordial flavored with fruits: sometimes limited to those the flavor of which is obtained from black currants, bitter almonds, or peach- and cherry-kernels.

It would make a Man smile to behold her Figure in a front Box, where her twinkling Eyes, by her Afternoon's Drams of *Ratifee* and cold Tea, sparkle more than her Pendants. Quoted in *Ashton's* Social Life in Reign of [Queen Anne, I. 201.

2. A kind of fancy cake or biscuit.

Give him three *ratafias*, soaked in a dessert-spoonful of cream. *George Eliot*, Mill on the Floss, vi. 1.

ratan, rattan[2] (ra-tan'), *n.* [Formerly also *rattoon*, *rotan*, rot*ang*, *rottang*; = D. Sw. Dan. *rotting* (NL. *Rotang*), < F. *rotin*, *rotang* = Sp. rota, < Malay ro*tan*, ratan. The E. accent, on the last syllable, is appar. in imitation of the F.; the Malay word is accented on the first syllable.] 1. A palm of one among numerous species, mostly of the genus *Calamus*, a few of the genus *Rhapis*; a ratan-palm. The species of *Calamus* are prevailingly climbing palms, attaining a length sometimes of 500 feet, with a thickness not exceeding an inch—ascending the tallest trees, falling in festoons, and again ascending. A few species are found in Africa and Australia, but they abound chiefly in the East Indies, on the mainland and islands. The species of *Rhapis* are erect slender canes growing in dense tufts, and are natives of China and Japan. Ratans of this habit are commercially distinguished from the climbing ones as *ground-ratans*.
2. The stems of the ratan collectively as an economic material. Among its chief commercial sources are *Calamus Rotang*, C. *rudentum*, C. *verus*, C. *erectus*, and C. *Royleanus*. The most valuable ratan is produced in Borneo. On account of its length and light, tough, flexible, and fissile character, ratan is applied to very numerous uses. In native regions the product of C. *rudentum* and other species is split and twisted in vast quantities into all sizes of cordage from cables to fishing-lines. Basket-making is another common use. In some places the stems of climbing ratans are used for the suspension of foot-bridges of great length. In China whole houses are made of ratan, there afforded chiefly by *Rhapis flabelliformis*. Matting made of split ratan is exported thence to all parts of the world. The same fiber serves also to make hats, the bottoms of rice-sieves, thread for sewing palm-leaves, etc. In recent times ratan has become an important article in western commerce. It is now not only used for walking-sticks, but extensively made into chairs and chair-bottoms, bodies for fancy carriages, fine and coarse basket-work, etc. It has almost superseded willow in making the large baskets required in manufacturing and other industries.
3. A switch or stick of ratan, especially a walking-stick.

Mr. Hunley did give me a little black *rattoon*, painted and gilt. *Pepys*, Diary, an. 1660.

ratan, rattan[2] (ra-tan'), *v. t.* [< *ratan*, *rattan*[2], *n.*] 1. To use ratan in making; cover or form with interlaced lengths of ratan.

The second class coach is finished in native ash with Moorish designed ceilings, *rattaned* sofa seats, and closet and toilet rooms. *Sci. Amer.*, N. S., LIX. 3.

2. To use a ratan upon; beat with or as with a ratan-cane. [Colloq.]

ratan-cane (ra-tan'kān), *n.* Same as *ratan*, 3.

ratanhine (rat'an-in), *n.* [< Braz. Pg. *ratanhia* (see *ratany*) + *-ine*[2].] An alkaloid ($C_{10}H_{13}NO_3$) occurring in small quantity in the extract of ratany-root.

ratany (rat'a-ni), *n.* [Also *rattany*, *ratanhy*, and *rhatany*; = F. *ratanhia*, < Braz. Pg. *ratanhia*, < Peruv. *ratana*, native name.] 1. A procumbent South American shrub, *Krameria triandra*, yielding a medicinal root. Its foliage is silver-gray with silky hairs, and it bears star-like lake-colored flowers singly in the upper axils. See *Krameria* and *ratany-root*.
2. A medicinal substance procured from this plant: same as *ratany*-root. — **Pará, Brazilian**, or **Ceara ratany**, a substitute for the true ratany, obtained from *Krameria argentea* of northeastern Brazil.

Ratany (*Krameria triandra*).

ratany-root (rat'ạ-ni-röt), *n.* The root-substance of the ratany, used in medicine for its astringent, diuretic, and detergent properties, and in the adulteration of port-wine.

rataplan (rat-a-ploṅ'), *n.* [F.; imitative. Cf. *rattan*[3], *rat-a-tat*.] The sound or music of the military drum; a tattoo or "rub-a-dub."

rat-a-tat (rat'ạ-tat'), *n.* [Imitative. Cf. *rat-tat*, *rat-tat-too*.] A rattling sound or effect, as from the beating of a drum.

rat-catcher (rat'kach″ėr), *n.* One whose business is the catching of rats; a ratter.

rat-catching (rat'kach″ing), *n.* The catching of rats, now pursued as a business by rat-catchers, and formerly to a large extent in Great Britain, with dogs or ferrets, as a popular amusement.

ratch[1] (rach), *v.* [An assibilated form of *rack*[1], or in part a var. of *retch*[1] or *reach*[1]: see *rack*[1], *v.*] I. *trans.* 1. To stretch or pull asunder.—2. To spot or streak. *Halliwell.*
[Prov. Eng. in both uses.]
II. *intrans. Naut.*, to make a stretch or varying stretches in sailing; sail by the wind or by tacks; stand off and on.

There was a fleet of smacks *ratching* to the eastward on our port bow. *W. C. Russell*, Jack's Courtship, xxiii.

ratch[1] (rach), *n.* [An assibilated form of *rack*[1]: see *rack*[1], *n.* In defs. 3 and 4, directly from the verb. Cf. dim. *ratchet*.] 1. In a machine, a bar having angular teeth, into which a pawl drops, to prevent the machine from being reversed in motion. A circular ratch is a *ratchet-wheel*.—2. In *clockwork*, a sort of wheel having fangs, which serve to lift the detents and thereby cause the clock to strike.—3. A straight line. [Prov. Eng.]—4. A white mark on the face of a horse. [Eng.]

ratch[2]† (rach), *n.* [Early mod. E. also *rach*, *rache*; < ME. *racche*, *rache*, < AS. *ræcc*, a dog, = Icel. *rakki*, a dog.] A dog that hunts by scent.

As they ryde talkynge,
A *rach* ther come flyngynge
Overtwert the way.
Thanne seyde old and yonge,
From her first gynnynge,
They ne sawe bonde never so gay.
Lybeaus Disconus (Ritson's Metr. Rom., II.).

There are in England and Scotland two kinds of hunting dogs: the first is called a *rache*; and this is a foot-scenting creature, both of wild beasts, birds, and fishes also which lie hid among the rocks; the female hereof is called in England a brache. *Gentleman's Recreation*, p. 28.

ratch[3] (rach), *v. t.* Same as *rash*[3]. [Scotch.]

ratch[4] (rach), *n.* [Origin obscure. Cf. *ratchel*.] A subsoil of stone and gravel mixed with clay. *Halliwell.* [Prov. Eng.]

ratched (racht), *p. a.* [Pp. of *ratch*[3], *v.*] Ragged: in a ruinous state. *Jamieson.* [Scotch.]

ratchel (rach'el), *n.* [Also *ratchell*, *ratchil*; cf. *ratch*[4], *ratcher*. Perhaps < G. *rutschel*, the fragments from two masses of rock sliding one on the other, < *rutschen*, slide, slip.] Fragments of stone; gravelly stone; also, a hard, rocky crust below the soil. *Jamieson.* [Prov. Eng. and Scotch.]

ratcher (rach'ėr), *n.* [Cf. *ratch*[4], *ratchel*.] A rock. *Halliwell.* [Prov. Eng.]

ratchet (rach'et), *n.* [< *ratch*[1] + *-et*.] A detent or pivoted piece designed to fit into the teeth of a ratchet-wheel, permitting the wheel to rotate in one direction, but not in the other. A similar device so arranged as to move the wheel is termed a *pallet*. (See *ratchet-wheel*, *click*[1], 3, *pawl*, and *detent*.) Combined with the ratchet-wheel as a means of converting a reciprocating into a rotary motion, the ratchet appears in a number of tools and gives its name to each: as, the *ratchet* bed-key, etc.

ratchet-brace (rach'et-brās), *n.* See *brace*[1].

ratchet-burner (rach'et-bėr″nėr), *n.* A burner for a lamp in which the wick is moved up and down by means of a wheel with notched points.

ratchet-coupling (rach'et-kup″ling), *n.* A device for uncoupling machinery in the event of a sudden stoppage of the motion of a driving-wheel, as by an obstruction. It consists of a ratchet-wheel inserted in a sleeve on the exterior shaft of a driving-wheel. The ratchet is efficient as long as it transmits the initial motion; but if the revolution of the driver is checked, the sleeve slips over the ratchet until the machinery loses its momentum, thus avoiding a shock.

ratchet-drill (rach'et-dril), *n.* A tool for drilling holes by means of a ratchet in a narrow plane where there is no room for the common brace.

ratchet-jack (rach'et-jak), *n.* A form of screw-jack in which the lever-socket is fitted with a pallet engaging a ratchet-wheel, so that the jack may be operated by oscillation of the lever.

ratchet-lever (rach'et-lev″ėr), *n.* A lever with a collar fitted around a ratchet-wheel which engages a pallet on the lever, used for operating a drill or screw by oscillation of the lever.

ratchet-pedal (rach'et-ped″ạl), *n.* See *pedal*.

ratchet-post (rach'et-pōst), *n.* *Milit.*, a metallic post fastened to the rear transom of the top-carriage of a heavy gun, to serve as a support or fulcrum for the elevating-bar.

ratchet-punch (rach'et-punch), *n.* A punch worked by a screw which is revolved by means of a ratchet-lever.

ratchet-wheel (rach'et-hwēl), *n.* A wheel with pointed and angular teeth, against which a ratchet abuts, used either for converting a reciprocating into a rotatory motion on the shaft to which it is fixed, or for admitting of its motion in one direction only. For both purposes an arrangement similar to that shown in the cut is employed. *a* is the ratchet-wheel, and *b* the reciprocating lever, to the end of which is jointed a small ratchet or pawl c, furnished with a catch of the same form as the teeth of the wheel, which, when the lever is moved in one direction, slides over the teeth, but in returning draws the wheel with it. The pawl c is forced into engagement with the teeth of the ratchet-wheel by the spring *f*. The other ratchet, d, which may be used either separately or in combination with the first, permits of the motion of the wheel in the direction of the arrow, but opposes its return in the opposite direction. Also called *click-wheel*. See also cut under *pawl*.

Ratchet-wheel.

ratchet-wrench (rach'et-rench), *n.* A ratchet bed-key wrench.

ratchety (rach'e-ti), *a.* [< *ratchet* + *-y*[1].] Like the movement of a ratchet; jerky; clicking.

Raikes . . . poured out a *ratchety* but vehement panegyric. *The Money-Makers*, p. 128.

ratchil, *n.* See *ratchel*.

ratchment (rach'mẹnt), *n.* [< *ratch*[1] + *-ment*.] In *arch.*, a flying-buttress which springs from the principals of a herse and abuts against the central or chief principal. *Oxford Glossary.*

rate[1] (rāt), *v.*; pret. and pp. *rated*, ppr. *rating*. [< ME. *raten*, chide, scold, in comp., < Sw. *rata*, reject, refuse, slight, find fault with (cf. *rat-gods*, refuse goods), = Norw. *rata*, reject, cast aside as rubbish; akin to Norw. *rat*, refuse, rubbish, trash, = Icel. *hrat*, *hrati*, rubbish, trash, skins, stones, etc., of berries; Norw. *rata*, bad, worthless: see *rat*[2].] I. *trans.* 1. To chide with vehemence; reprove; scold; censure violently.

He shal be *rated* of his studying.
Chaucer, Miller's Tale, l. 277.

Go, *rate* thy minions, proud insulting boy!
Shak., 3 Hen. VI., ii. 2. 84.

His mother is angry, *rates* him.
B. *Jonson*, Sad Shepherd, Arg.

2†. To affect by chiding or reproving; restrain by vehement censure.

No words may *rate*, nor rigour him remove
From greedy hold of that his blouddy feast.
Spenser, F. Q., IV. ix. 31.

II. *intrans.* To utter vehement censure or reproof; inveigh scoldingly: with *at*.

Yea, the Moores, meeting with this beast, doe *rate* and braule *at* him. *Purchas*, Pilgrimage, p. 42.

Such a one
As all day long hath *rated at* her child,
And vext his day.
Tennyson, Gareth and Lynette.

rate[2] (rāt), *n.* [< OF. *rate*, price, value, = Pr. Sp. Pg. It. *rata* = G. *rate*, < ML. *rata*, rate, proportion (L. *pro rata parte*, or *pro rata portione*, or simply *pro rata*, according to a certain part or portion (see *pro rata*, *pro-rate*)); fem. of L. *ratus*, determined, fixed, settled, pp. of *reri* (ind. *reor*), think, deem, judge, orig. reckon, calculate. From the same L. verb are ult. derived E. *rate*[3], *ratio*, *ration*, *reason*, *areason*, *arraign*[1], etc., *ratify*, etc.] **1.** A reckoning by comparative values or relations; proportional estimation according to some standard; relative amount, quantity, range, or degree: as, the *rate* of interest is 6 per cent. (that is, $6 for every $100 for every year); the *rate* per mile of railroad charges, expenses, or speed; a rapid *rate* of growth or of progress.

He lends out money gratis, and brings down
The *rate* of usance here with us in Venice.
Shak., M. of V., i. 3. 46.

One of the necessary properties of pure Motion is Velocity. It is not possible to think of Motion without thinking of a corresponding *Rate* of motion.
A. Daniell, Prin. of Physics, p. 52.

As regards travelling, the fastest *rate* along the high roads was ten miles an hour.
W. Besant, Fifty Years Ago, p. 5.

It was no longer practicable to levy the duties on the old plan of one *rate* for unrefined and another *rate* for refined sugars. *S. Dowell*, Taxes in England, IV. 31.

2. Charge or valuation according to a scale or standard; comparative price or amount of demand; a fixed measure of estimation.

A jewel that I have purchased at an infinite *rate*.
Shak., M. W. of W., ii. 2. 213.

I am not . . . content to part with my commodities at a cheaper *rate* than I accustomed; look not for it.
B. *Jonson*, Volpone, ii. 1.

They have no Goods but what are brought from Manilo at an extraordinary dear *rate*. *Dampier*, Voyages, I. 308.

Servants could be hired of their nominal owners at a barley-corn *rate*. *The Century*, XXXIX. 130.

3. A fixed public tax or imposition assessed on property for some local purpose, usually according to income or value: as, poor-*rates* or church-*rates* in Great Britain.

They paid the Church and Parish *Rate*,
And took, but read not the Receit.
Prior, An Epitaph.

The empowering of certain boards to borrow money repayable from the local *rates*, to employ and pay those out of work. H. *Spencer*, Man vs. State, p. 9.

A sewers *rate*, however, was known as early as the sixth year of Henry VI. (1427).
Mayhew, London Labour and London Poor, II. 477.

4†. A proportion allotted or permitted; an allotment or provision; a regulated amount or supply.

The one right feeble through the evill *rate*
Of food which in her duresse she had found.
Spenser, F. Q., IV. viii. 19.

The people shall go out and gather a certain *rate* every day. Ex. xvi. 4.

5. A relative scale of being, action, or conduct; comparative degree or extent of any mode of existence or procedure; proportion in manner or method: as, an extravagant *rate* of living or of expenditure. See *at any rate*, *at no rate*, below.

With wyse men there is rest & peace, after a blessed *rate*.
Babees Book (E. E. T. S.), p. 92.

With might and delight they spent all the night,
And liv'd at a plentiful *rate*.
Robin Hood and the Ranger (Child's Ballads, V. 210).

Tom hinting his dislike of some trifle his mistress had said, she asked him how he would talk to her after marriage, if he talked at this *rate* before. *Addison.*

Hence—**6†.** Mode or manner of arrangement; order; state.

Thus sate they all around in seemely *rate*.
Spenser, F. Q., IV. x. 52.

7†. Degree, rank, or estimation; rating; appraisement: used of persons and their qualities.

I am a spirit of no common *rate*.
Shak., M. N. D., iii. 1. 157.

With the common *rate* of men there is nothing commendable but what they themselves may hope to be partakers of. *Steele*, Spectator, No. 188.

8. The order or class of a vessel, formerly regulated in the United States navy by the number of guns carried, but now by the tonnage displacement. Vessels of 5,000 tons displacement and over are of the first rate, of 3,000 and above but below 5,000 tons of the second rate, of 1,000 and above but below 3,000 tons of the third rate, of less than 1,000 tons of the fourth rate. In classifying the navies of England, France, and the other principal European powers the term *class* is used instead of *rate*, and relates not so much to the actual weight or power of the ships as to arbitrary divisions of types of vessels, and to their relative importance as battle-ships, cruisers, etc.

9. In the United States navy, the grade or position of any one of the crew: same as *rating*[2], 2.—**10.** In *horology*, the daily gain or loss of a chronometer or other timepiece. A losing rate is called by astronomers a positive rate, because it entails a positive correction to the difference of readings of the clock-face.—**At any rate**, in any manner, or by any means; in any case; at all events; positively; assuredly: as, I shall stay *at any rate*; *at any rate* the claim is a valid one.

I have no friend,
Project, design, or country but your favour,
Which I'll preserve *at any rate*.
Fletcher (*and another*), False One, i. 1.

At no rate†, in no manner; by no means; not at all. [Rare.]

This day *at no rate*
Shalt thou performe thy worke, least thou doe draw
My heavy wrath vpon thee.
Times' Whistle (E. E. T. S.), p. 16.

County rates, landing-rates, police rate, etc. See *county*[1], *landing*, etc.—**Rate of change**, in *math.*, the ratio of an infinitesimal increment of any function to that of the independent variable. Thus, the *rate of change* of x^2 relatively to x is $2x$.—**Rate of exchange.** Same as *course of exchange* (which see, under *exchange*).—**Rate of profit.** See *profit*. (See also *church-rate*, *poor-rate*.)=**Syn.** 3. *Assessment*, *Impost*, etc. See *tax*.

rate[2] (rāt), *v.*; pret. and pp. *rated*, ppr. *rating*. [< *rate*[2], *n.*] **I.** *trans.* **1.** To reckon by comparative estimation; regard as of such a value, rank, or degree; hold at a certain valuation or estimate; appraise; fix the value or price of.

If thou be'st *rated* by thy estimation.
Shak., M. of V., ii. 7. 26.

The frigid productions of a later age are *rated* at no more than their proper value. *Macaulay*, Dryden.

2. To assess as to payment or contribution; fix the comparative liability of, for taxation or the like; reckon at so much in obligation or capability; set a rate upon.

Tell us (I pray you) how ye would have the sayd landes *rated*, that both a rente may rise thereout unto the Queene, and also the souldiours paye.
Spenser, State of Ireland.

Look on my George; I am a gentleman;
Rate me at what thou wilt, thou shalt be paid.
Shak., 2 Hen. VI., iv. 1. 30.

Charles S. What do you *rate* him at, Moses?
Moses. Four guineas. *Sheridan*, School for Scandal, iv. 1.

3. To fix the relative scale, rank, or position of: as, to *rate* a ship; to *rate* a seaman.—**4.** To determine the rate of, or rate-error of, as a chronometer or other timepiece. See *rate*[1], *n.*, 10.

Our chronometers, *rated* but two weeks ago at Upernavik. *Kane*, Sec. Grinn. Exp., I. 68.

Rating-instrument, a rude transit-instrument for determining time accurately to half a second, in order to rate watches.

II. *intrans.* To have value, rank, standing, or estimation: as, the vessel *rates* as a ship of the line.

When he began milling in a small way at the Falls of St. Anthony, Minneapolis flour *rated* very low.
The Century, XXXII. 46.

rate[3]† (rāt), *n.* [< ML. *rata*, f., a stipulation, contract, *ratum*, neut., a decision, fem. or neut. of L. *ratus*, pp. of *reri*, think, deem, judge: see *rate*[2].] A ratification.

Neuer without the *rates*
Of all powers else. *Chapman*, Iliad, i. 508.

rate[3]†, *v. t.* [< *rate*[3], *n.* Cf. *ratify*.] To ratify.

To *rate* the truce they swore. *Chapman.*

rateable, *a.* See *ratable*.

rate-book (rāt'bůk), *n.* A book in which a record of rates is kept; a book of valuations.

Horses by papists are not to be ridden;
But sure the Muses' horse was ne'er forbidden;
For in no *rate-book* was it ever found
That Pegasus was valued at five pound.
Dryden, Don Sebastian, Prol., i. 43.

rateen, *n.* See *ratteen*.

ratel (rā'tel), *n.* [< F. *ratel*, dim. of *rat*, a rat: see *rat*[1].] A carnivorous quadruped of the family *Mustelidæ* and subfamily *Mellivorinæ*, as *Mellivora capensis* or *M. ratellus*, the honey-ratel of the Cape of Good Hope, and *M. indica*, that of India; a honey-badger. See *Mellivora*, and cut in next column.

ratepayer (rāt'pā"ėr), *n.* One who is assessed and pays a rate or local tax. [Great Britain.]

In the vestry-meeting the freemen of the township, the *ratepayers*, still assemble for purposes of local interest, not involved in the manorial jurisdiction.
Stubbs, Const. Hist., § 43.

Ratel (*Mellivora capensis*).

They have already in many towns supplied us, at the expense of the *ratepayers*, with hospitals, museums, free libraries, art galleries, baths, and parks.
Westminster Rev., CXXV. 17.

ratepaying (rāt'pā"ing), *a.* Paying a local tax; relating to taxation by assessment.

In addition to the . . . eccentricity from an Australian point of view of a *ratepaying* or property basis for the parliamentary franchise, Tasmania has another legislative peculiarity which she copied from Victoria, and shares only with that colony and with New Zealand.
Sir C. W. Dilke, Probs. of Greater Britain, ii. 4.

rater (rā'tėr), *n.* [< *rate*[2] + *-er*[1].] One who rates or sets a value; one who makes an estimate.

rate-tithe (rāt'tīth), *n.* In *old Eng. law*, a tithe paid for sheep or cattle which are kept in a parish for less than a year, in which case the owner must pay tithe for them pro rata, according to the custom of the place. *Sir A. Fitzherbert*, Natura Brevium (1534 and later).

rat-fish (rat'fish), *n.* A selachian fish, the *Chimæra colliæi*. [Pacific coast, U. S.]

rat-goose (rat'gös), *n.* [< *rat-*, said to be imitative, + *goose*. Cf. *clack-goose*, another name of the same bird.] The brent- or brant-goose, *Bernicla brenta*: so called from its cry.

rath[1] (rāth), *a.* [Also improp. *rathe*; < ME. *rath*, *rad*, *ræd*, quick, early, < AS. *hræth*, *hreth*, also *hræd* (pl. *hrade*), quick, swift, fleet, sudden, active, = D. *rad* = MLG. *rat* (*rad-*) = OHG. *hrad*, *hrat*, *rat*, MHG. *rad*, *rat* = Icel. *hradhr*, quick, swift, fleet; root uncertain; the forms without the aspirate merge with similar forms mentioned under *rash*[1], q. v. Hence *rath*[1], *adv.*, and *rather*.] **1†.** Quick; swift; speedy.—**2.** Early; coming before others, or before the usual time; youthful. [Obsolete or archaic.]

Last of all, vnto quhose actionis, in speciall, suld Kyngis geue *rathest* actendence.
Lauder, Dewtie of Kyngis (E. E. T. S.), To the Redar.

The *rather* lambes bene starved with cold.
Spenser, Shep. Cal., Februarie.

Bring the *rathe* primrose that forsaken dies.
Milton, Lycidas, l. 142.

Thy converse drew us with delight,
The men of *rathe* and riper years.
Tennyson, In Memoriam, cx.

3†. Near; proximate.

rath[1] (rāth), *adv.* [Also *rathe*; < ME. *rathe*, < AS. *hrathe*, quickly, < *hræth*, quick: see *rath*[1], *a.*] **1†.** Quickly; swiftly; speedily.

With hise salte teris gan he bathe
The ruby in his signet, and it sette
Upon the wex deliverliche and *rathe*.
Chaucer, Troilus, ii. 1088.

Thane this rychc mane *rathe* arayes his byernez,
Rowlede his Romaynez, and realle knyghtez.
Morte Arthure (E. E. T. S.), l. 2022.

2. Early; soon. [Obsolete or archaic.]

Dobet is hir damoisele sire Doweles dougter,
To serue this lady lelly bothe late and *rathe*.
Piers Plowman (B), ix. 13.

What eyleth yow so *rathe* for to ryse?
Chaucer, Shipman's Tale, l. 90.

But lesynges with her false flaterye . . .
Accepte ben now *rathest* unto grace.
Lydgate, Complaint of the Black Knight, l. 427.

Rathe she rose, half-cheated in the thought
She needs must bid farewell to sweet Lavaine.
Tennyson, Lancelot and Elaine.

Rath ripe, early ripe. See *rathripe*.

rath[2] (rath), *n.* [Early mod. E. also *rathe*; < Ir. *rath*, an earthen fort or fortified dwelling.] A fortified dwelling of an ancient Irish chief. The word occurs as the initial element in many Irish place-names, as *Rathkeale*, *Rathlin*, etc.

There is a great use amongst the Irish to make great assemblies togither upon a *rath* or hill, there to parley (they say) about matters of wronge betwene township and township, or one private person and another.
Spenser, State of Ireland, p. 642.

The *Rath* was a simple circular wall or enclosure of mixed earth, enclosing a space of more or less extent, in which stood the residence of the chief and sometimes the dwellings of one or more of the officers or chief men of

the tribe or court. Sometimes also the *Rath* consisted of two or three concentric walls or circumvallations; but it does not appear that the erection so called was ever intended to be surrounded with water.
O'Curry, Anc. Irish, II. xix.

rath[3] (rät), *n.* [E. Ind.] A name given to certain rock-cut Buddhist temples in India.

The oldest and most interesting group of monuments at Mahavellipore are the so-called five *raths* or monolithic temples standing on the sea-shore.
J. Fergusson, Hist. Indian Arch., p. 328.

rath[4] (rät), *n.* [Hind. *rath*, a carriage, < Skt. *ratha*, chariot.] A Burmese state carriage.

Every day the State *rath*, or chariot, of the Bhavnagar Dunbar is drawn by two oxen about the Upper Gardens.
Colonial and Indian Exhibition, 1886, p. 30.

rat-hare (rat'hãr), *n.* Same as *pika*.

rathe, *a.* and *adv.* See *rath*[1].

rathelt, *v. t.* [ME. *rathelen*; origin obscure.] To fix; root.

Gawayn graythely hit bydez & glent with no membré, Bot stode stylle as the ston, other a stubbe auther, That *ratheled* is in roche grounde, with rotez a hundreth.
Sir Gawayne and the Green Knight (E. E. T. S.), l. 2292.

rathely†, *adv.* See *rathly*.

rather (raтн'ėr), *adv.* [< ME. *rather*, *rether*, < AS. *hrathor*, more quickly, sooner, earlier, compar. of *hrathe*, quick, soon, early: see *rath*[1], *adv.* Cf. superl. *rathest* (obs.), < ME. *rathest*, *rathestc*, soonest, earliest, < AS. *hrathost*: see *rath*[1].] 1†. More quickly; quicker. See *rath*[1], *adv.*, 1.—2†. Earlier; sooner.

Thilke sterres that ben cleped sterres of the north arisen *rather* than the degree of hire longitude, and alle the sterres of the south arisen after the degree of hire longitude.
Chaucer, Astrolabe, i. 21.

And ȝit schal erthe vn-to erthe *rather* than he wolde.
Hymns to Virgin, etc. (E. E. T. S.), p. 88.

3. More readily or willingly; with better liking; with preference or choice; in preference, as compared with something else.

Men loved darkness *rather* than light, because their deeds were evil.
John iii. 19.

4. In preference; preferably; with better reason; better.

Give us of your oil. . . . Not so: . . . but go ye *rather* to them that sell, and buy for yourselves.
Mat. xxv. 9.

Dye *rather*, dye, then ever from her service swerve.
Spenser, F. Q., III. v. 46.

Had he who drew such gladness ever wept?
Ask *rather* could he else have seen at all,
Or grown in Nature's mysteries an adept?
Lowell, To a Friend.

5. More properly; more correctly speaking; more.

The Doctor by this oversight (or cunningness, *rather*) got a supply of money.
Howell, Letters, IV. 2.

A certain woman . . . had spent all that she had, and was nothing bettered, but *rather* grew worse.
Mark v. 26.

This is an art
Which does mend nature, change it *rather*, but
The art itself is nature.
Shak., W. T., iv. 4. 96.

Covered with dust and blood and wounds, and haggard with fatigue and horror, they looked like victims *rather* than like warriors.
Irving, Granada, p. 92.

6. On the contrary; to the contrary of what has been just stated.—7. In a greater degree; much; considerably; also, in colloquial use, in some degree; somewhat: qualifying a verb.

He sought her through the world, but sought in vain,
And, no-where finding, *rather* fear'd her slain.
Dryden, tr. of Ovid's Metamorph., l. 709.

Wal, of course he made his court to Ruth; and the General, he *rather* backed him up in it.
H. B. Stowe, Oldtown, p. 37.

8. In some degree or measure; somewhat; moderately: usually qualifying an adverb or an adjective: as, she is *rather* pretty. [Chiefly colloq.]

An Indian camp is a *rather* interesting, though very dirty, place to visit.
The Century, XXXVI. 39.

[In this sense often used ironically, in answering a question, as an emphatic affirmative.

"Do you know the mayor's house?" "*Rather*," replied the boots significantly, as if he had some good reason to remember it.
Dickens.]

Had rather. See *to have rather*, under *have*.—**Leet rather.** See *leet*[4].—**Rather better than**, somewhat in excess of; rather more than.

Five hundred and fifty musketeers, *rather better than* three to one.
G. P. R. James, Arrah Neil, p. 60.

Rather . . . than otherwise. See *otherwise*.—**The rather**, by so much the more; especially; for better reason; for particular cause.

You are come to me in happy time;
The rather for I have some sport in hand.
Shak., T. of the S., Ind., l. 91.

This I *the rather* write, that we may know there are other Parts of the World than those which to us are known.
Baker, Chronicles, p. 50.

ratherish (raтн'ėr-ish), *adv.* [< *rather* + *-ish*[1].] Slightly; to a small extent; in some degree. [Colloq.]

Lavalette is *ratherish* against Popish temporality; Gen. Guyon is rather favorable to it.
New York Tribune, April 22, 1862.

Rathke's duct. The Müllerian duct when it is persistent in the male.

Rathke's trabeculæ. See *trabecula*.

rathly†, *adv.* [ME., also *rathely*, *radly*, *radliche*, < AS. *hrædlice*, quickly, hastily, speedily, < *hræth*, quick: see *rath*[1].] In a rath manner; quickly; suddenly.

Thomas *rathely* vpe he rase.
Thomas of Erseldoune (Child's Ballads, I. 100).

Ryse we now full *radly*, rest here no longer,
And I shall tell you full tyte, and tary no thing.
Destruction of Troy (E. E. T. S.), l. 772.

rat-hole (rat'hōl), *n.* 1. A hole gnawed in woodwork, etc., by a rat or rats.—2. In *printing*, same as *pigeonhole*, 6.

ratholite (rath'ō-līt), *n.* Same as *pectolite*.

rathripe (räтн'rīp), *a.* and *n.* [< ME. **rathripe*, < AS. *rædrīpe*, *hrædrīpe*, early ripe, < *hræth*, quick, + *ripe*, ripe: see *rath*[1] and *ripe*. Cf. *rareripe*.] I. *a.* Early ripe; ripe before the season; rareripe. [Obsolete or prov. Eng.]

Such as delight in *rathripe* fruits.
Fuller.

Rathripe barley, barley derived from a long succession of crops on warm gravelly soil, so that it ripens earlier than common barley under different circumstances.

II. *n.* A rareripe. [Obsolete or prov. Eng.]

ratifiat, **ratifiet**, *n.* Obsolete forms of *ratafia*.

ratification (rat″i-fi-kā'shǫn), *n.* [Early mod. E. *ratificacion*, < OF. *ratification*, *ratificacion*, F. *ratification* = Pr. *ratiffication* = Sp. *ratificacion* = Pg. *ratificação* = It. *ratificazione*, < ML. *ratificatio(n-)*, < *ratificare*, ratify: see *ratify*.] 1. The act of ratifying; the act by which a competent authority gives sanction and validity to something done by another; also, the state of being ratified; confirmation: as, the *ratification* of a treaty, or of a contract or promise.

The kyng of England sent Sir Nicholas Carew, knight, master of his horses, and Doctor Sampson, to Bononie, for the *ratificacion* of the league concluded at Cambray.
Hall, Hen. VIII., an. 21.

It was argued by Monroe, Gerry, Howel, Ellery, and myself that by the modern usage of Europe the *ratification* was considered as the act which gave validity to a treaty, until which it was not obligatory.
Jefferson, Autobiography, p. 46.

2. In *law*, the adoption by a person, as binding upon himself, of an act previously done in his name or on his behalf, or in such relation that he may claim it as done for his benefit, although done under such circumstances as would not bind him except by his subsequent consent, as in the case of an act done by a stranger having at the same time no authority to act as his agent, or by an agent not having adequate authority to do the act. Intention to ratify is not necessary in order to constitute a ratification, for an acceptance of the results of the act may itself be conclusive upon the party. But a knowledge of all the material circumstances is usually necessary in order to make a ratification binding.—**Ratification by a wife**, in *Scots law*, a declaration on oath made by a wife in presence of a justice of the peace (her husband being absent) that a deed she has executed has been made freely, and that she has not been induced to make it by her husband through force or fear.—**Ratification meeting**, in the United States, a political meeting called for the purpose of expressing approval of the nominations made by a political party, and of creating enthusiasm for their support.

ratifier (rat'i-fī-ėr), *n.* One who or that which ratifies or sanctions.

Antiquity forgot, custom not known,
The *ratifiers* and props of every word.
Shak., Hamlet, iv. 5. 105.

ratify (rat'i-fī), *v. t.*; pret. and pp. *ratified*, ppr. *ratifying*. [< OF. *ratefier*, F. *ratifier* = Pr. Sp. Pg. *ratificar* = It. *ratificare*, < ML. *ratificare*, confirm, ratify, < L. *ratus*, fixed, settled, + *-ficare*, < *facere*, make: see *rate*[2] and *-fy*.] 1. To confirm; establish; settle conclusively or authoritatively; make certain or lasting.

We have *ratified* to them the borders of Judea.
1 Mac. xi. 34.

Covenants will be *ratified* and confirmed, as it were by the Stygian oath.
Bacon, Political Fables, ii., Expl.

Shaking hands with emphasis, . . . as if they were *ratifying* some solemn league and covenant.
Charlotte Brontë, Shirley, xvii.

2. To validate by some formal act of approval; accept and sanction, as something done by an agent or a representative; confirm as a valid act or procedure.

This Accord and final Peace signed by both Kings was *ratified* by their two eldest Sons.
Baker, Chronicles, p. 125.

A solemn compact let us *ratify*,
And witness ev'ry power that rules the sky.
Pope, Odyssey, xiv.

The unfortunate king, unable to make even a protest for the rights of his son, was prevailed on to *ratify* the agreement.
Stubbs, Const. Hist., § 677.

Ratifying convention, a convention held for the purpose of ratifying certain measures, acts, etc.: specifically used in United States politics of the conventions held by the several States of the American Union for the purpose of ratifying the Federal Constitution of 1787.

ratihabition† (rat″i-hạ-bish'ǫn), *n.* [= Sp. *ratihabicion* = Pg. *ratihabição* = It. *ratiabizione*, < LL. *ratihabitio(n-)*, ratification at law, < L. *ratus*, fixed, settled (see *rate*[2]), + *habere*, have: see *habit*.] Approval, as of something done or to be done; precedent or subsequent consent; sanction; confirmation of authority or of action.

In matters criminal *ratihabition*, or approving of the act, does always make the approver guilty.
Jer. Taylor.

To assure their full powers, they had letters of commission or of *ratihabition*, or powers of attorney, such as were usually furnished to proctors or representative officers.
Stubbs, Const. Hist., § 747.

rating[1] (rā'ting), *n.* [Verbal n. of *rate*[1], *v.*] A scolding.

rating[2] (rā'ting), *n.* [Verbal n. of *rate*[2], *v.*] 1. A fixing of rates; proportionate distribution as to charge or compensation; determination of relative values or rights.

The loss by any railway company of its whole share of this traffic, in consequence of being crippled in competition by regulations as to *rating*.
Contemporary Rev., LI. 78.

The following table of *ratings* and of the number pensioned at each rate shows how the allowance is distributed among invalid survivors.
The Century, XXXVIII. 636.

2. Classification according to grade or rank; determination of relative standing; hence, rank or grade. The rating of men in the navy signifies the grade in which they are rated or entered in the ship's books. The rating of ships is the division into grades (see *rate*[2], *n.*, 8) by which the complement of officers and certain allowances are determined.

ratio (rā'shiō), *n.* [< L. *ratio*, a reckoning, account, calculation, relation, reference, reason, etc., < *reri*, pp. *ratus*, think, deem, estimate: see *rate*[2], and cf. *ration* and *reason*, from the same L. noun.] 1. The relation between two similar magnitudes in respect to quantity; the relation between two similar quantities in respect to how many times one makes so many times the other. There is no intelligible difference between a ratio and a quotient of similar quantities; they are simply two modes of expression connected with different associations. But it was contrary to the old usage to speak of a ratio as a quantity—a usage leading to intolerable complications. Thus, instead of saying that the momentum of a moving particle is the product of its mass into its velocity—a mode of expression both convenient and philosophical—the older writers say that the momenta of two particles are in the compound ratio of their masses and velocities. This language, which betrays several errors of logic, is now disused; although some writers still persist in making numbers the only subjects of addition and multiplication. By mathematicians *ratio* is now conceived and spoken of as synonymous with *quotient*.

The numbers which specify a strain are mere *ratios*, and are therefore independent of units.
J. D. Everett, Units and Physical Constants, p. 45.

2. Proportion of relations or conditions; coincident agreement or variation; correspondence in rate; equivalence of relative movement or change.

There has been a constant *ratio* kept between the stringency of mercantile restraints and the stringency of other restraints.
H. *Spencer*, Social Statics, p. 327.

3. Reason; cause: often used as a Latin word in current Latin phrases.

In this consists the *ratio* and essential ground of the gospel doctrine.
Waterland.

4. In *musical acoustics*, the relation between the vibration-numbers of two tones. It is the physical or mathematical representation of the interval between them.—5. In *civil law*, an account; a cause, or the giving of judgment therein.—**Alternate ratio**, the ratio of the first to the third or the second to the fourth term of a proportion.—**Anharmonic ratio.** See *anharmonic*.—**Arithmetical ratio.** See *arithmetical*.—**Change-ratio.** See *change*.—**Composition of ratios**, the uniting of two or more simple ratios into one, by taking the product of the antecedents and the product of the consequents.—**Compound ratio.** See *compound*[1].—**Consequent of a ratio.** See *consequent*.—**Direct ratio.** (*a*) A ratio not inverse. (*b*) Loosely, a direct and simple ratio: as, the weights of bodies are in the *direct ratio* of their masses—that is, the weight of one is to that of another as the mass of the former is to that of the latter. Also *direct proportion*.—**Direction ratio, duple ratio.** See the qualifying words.—**Dissimilar ratios**, unequal quotients.—**Division of a ratio.** See *division*.—**Duplicate ratio**, a ratio of squares. The old writers, instead of saying that the distance passed over by a falling body is proportional to the square of the time, say that the spaces are in the *duplicate ratios* of the times.—**Inverse or reciprocal ratio**, in *math.*, the ratio of the reciprocals of two quantities.—**Irrational ratio**, a ratio of surds.—**Measure of a ratio.** See *measure*.—**Mixed ratio.** See *mixed*[1].—**Modular ratio.** See *modular*.—**Multiplicate ratio**, a ratio of powers.—**Oxygen ratio**, in *mineral.*, the ratio between the number of oxygen

atoms belonging to the different groups of acidic or basic compounds in the composition of a mineral. The oxygen ratio of silica, sesquioxid, and protoxid in garnet is 2 : 1 : 1. —**Pedal ratio**, in *anc. pros.*, the proportion of the number of times in the arsis to that in the thesis, or vice versa. The pedal ratio (λόγος ποδικός) is usually either *equal* or *isorrhythmic ratio* (1 : 1), *diplasic* or *double ratio* (1 : 2), or *hemiolic ratio* (2 : 3 = 1 : 1½). Besides these three, the ordinary pedal ratios, two others were anciently recognized—the *triplasic* or *triple* ratio (1 : 3), and the *epitritic ratio* (3 : 4 = 1 : 1⅓). The dochmius, regarded as a single foot, had a pedal ratio different from all these (3 : 5; ⏑ – | ⏑ ⏑ –). Isorrhythmic, diplasic, hemiolic, triplasic, epitritic, and dochmiac feet are feet having the pedal ratios just named. See *foot*, 11, *irrational*, *rhythm*.—**Prime and ultimate ratios**, phrases first introduced, at least in a system, by Newton, who preferred them to the terms suggested by his own method of fluxions. The method of prime and ultimate ratios is a method of calculation which may be considered as an extension of the ancient method of exhaustions. It may be thus explained: let there be two variable quantities constantly approaching each other in value, so that their ratio or quotient continually approaches to unity, and at last differs from unity by less than any assignable quantity; the ultimate ratio of these two quantities is said to be a ratio of equality. In general, when different variable quantities respectively and simultaneously approach other quantities, considered as invariable, so that the differences between the variable and the invariable quantities become at the same time less than any assignable quantity, the ultimate ratios of the variables are the ratios of the invariable quantities or limits to which they continually and simultaneously approach. They are called *prime ratios* or *ultimate ratios* according as the ratios of the variables are considered as receding from or approaching to the ratios of the limits. The first section of Newton's "Principia" contains the development of prime and ultimate ratios, with various propositions.—**Progression with *n* ratios**. See *progression*.—**Quadruple ratio**, the ratio of 4 to 1.—**Quadruplicate ratio**, a ratio of fourth powers.—**Quintuple ratio**, the ratio of 5 to 1.—**Ratio cognoscendi** (L.), a reason.—**Ratio decidendi** (L.), in *law*, the ground or reason on which a judicial decision is conceived as proceeding. The effect of such a decision as a precedent or evidence of the law is largely dependent on the ratio decidendi, which is usually indicated in the opinions of the court, but often obscurely or with conflict; hence what was the ratio decidendi is often a question for commentators and text-writers.—**Ratio essendi** (L.), a cause.—**Rational ratio**, a ratio between rational quantities.—**Ratio of equality**. See *equality*.—**Ratio of exchange**, in *polit. econ.*, the proportion in which a given quantity of one commodity may be exchanged for a given quantity of another, especially when the commodities correspond in form and mode of measurement: as, the *ratio of exchange* between gold and silver, or between wheat and barley.

When I proposed in the first edition of this book to use *Ratio of Exchange* instead of the word value, the expression had been so little if at all employed by English Economists that it amounted to an innovation. . . . Yet *ratio* is unquestionably the correct scientific term, and the only term which is strictly and entirely correct.
W. S. Jevons, Theory of Polit. Econ., p. 89.

Ratio of greater (or lesser) inequality, the ratio of a greater quantity to a lesser one (or of a lesser to a greater).—**Ratio of similitude**, in *geom.*, the ratio between corresponding dimensions of similar figures. See *homothetic*.—**Ratio sufficiens** (L.). Same as *sufficient reason* (which see, under *reason*).—**Reciprocal ratio**. Same as *inverse ratio*.—**Simple ratio**. (a) A ratio between first powers. (b) A ratio not compound.—**Subduple ratio**. See *duple*.—**Subduplicate ratio**, an inverse ratio of squares (*sub* in all names of ratio indicating the inversion of the ratio): as, the gravity of two equal masses is in the *subduplicate ratio* of their distances from the gravitating center.—**Submultiple ratio**, the ratio which exists between an aliquot part of any number or quantity and the number or quantity itself: thus, the ratio of 3 to 21 is submultiple, 21 being a multiple of 3.—**To cut a line in extreme and mean ratio**. See *extreme*.—**Triple ratio**, the ratio of 3 to 1.

ratiocinant (rash-i-os'i-nant), *a.* [< L. *ratiocinan(t-)s*, ppr. of *ratiocinari*, reason: see *ratiocinate*.] Reasoning.—**Ratiocinant reason**. See *reason*.

ratiocinate (rash-i-os'i-nāt), *v. i.*; pret. and pp. *ratiocinated*, ppr. *ratiocinating*. [< L. *ratiocinatus*, pp. of *ratiocinari* (> It. *raziocinare* = Sp. Pg. *raciocinar* = F. *ratiociner*), reckon, compute, calculate, consider, deliberate, meditate, reason, argue (cf. *ratiocinium*, a reckoning, a computation, > It. *raziocinio* = Sp. Pg. *raciocinio*, reasoning), < *ratio(n-)*, reckoning, reason: see *ratio*, *reason*.] To reason; from two judgments to infer a third. The word usually implies an elaborate deductive operation.

ratiocinate (rash-i-os'i-nāt), *a.* [< L. *ratiocinatus*, pp. of *ratiocinari*, reason: see the verb.] Reasoned about.—**Ratiocinate reason**. See *reason*.

ratiocination (rash-i-os-i-nā'shọn), *n.* [< F. *ratiocination* = Pr. *raciocinacio* = Sp. *raciocinacion* = Pg. *raciocinação* (cf. It. *raziocinamento*, *raziocinio*, reasoning), < L. *ratiocinatio(n-)*, reasoning, argumentation, a syllogism, < *ratiocinari*, pp. *ratiocinatus*, reason: see *ratiocinate*.] 1. The mental process of passing from the cognition of premises to the cognition of the conclusion; reasoning. Most writers make *ratiocination* synonymous with *reasoning*. J. S. Mill and others hold that the word is usually limited to necessary reasoning. The Latin word is especially applied by Cicero to probable reasoning.

The great instrument that this work [spiritual meditation] is done by is *ratiocination*, reasoning the case with yourselves, discourse of mind, cogitation, or thinking; or, if you will, call it consideration.
Baxter, Saints' Rest, iv. 8.

The schoolmen make a third act of the mind, which they call *ratiocination*, and we may stile it the generation of a judgement from others actually in our understanding.
A. Tucker, Light of Nature, I. i. 11.

Ratiocination is the great principle of order in thinking; it reduces a chaos into harmony; it catalogues the accumulations of knowledge; it maps out for us the relations of its separate departments; it puts us in the way to correct its own mistakes.
J. H. Newman, Gram. of Assent, p. 273.

2. A mental product and object consisting of premises and a conclusion drawn from them; inference; an argumentation.

Can any kind of *ratiocination* allow Christ all the marks of the Messiah, and yet deny him to be the Messiah?
South.

Ratiocination denotes properly the process, but, improperly, also the product of reasoning.
Sir W. Hamilton, Logic, xv.

=**Syn.** *Reasoning*, etc. See *inference*.

ratiocinative (rash-i-os'i-nā-tiv), *a.* [< F. *ratiocinatif*, < L. *ratiocinativus*, of or belonging to reasoning, syllogistic, argumentative, < *ratiocinari*, reason: see *ratiocinate*.] Of the nature of reasoning; pertaining to or connected with the act of reasoning. The word is misused by some modern writers. See *ratiocination*, 2.

The conclusion is attained quasi per saltum, and without any thing of *ratiocinative* process.
Sir M. Hale, Orig. of Mankind, p. 51.

The *ratiocinative* meditativeness of his character.
Coleridge.

Again, it not unfrequently happens that, while the keenness of the *ratiocinative* faculty enables a man to see the ultimate result of a complicated problem in a moment, it takes years for him to embrace it as a truth, and to recognize it as an item in the circle of his knowledge.
J. H. Newman, Gram. of Assent, p. 150.

ratiocinatory (rash-i-os'i-nā-tọ-ri), *a.* [< *ratiocinate* + *-ory*.] Same as *ratiocinative*. [Rare.]

ration (rā'shọn or rash'ọn), *n.* [< F. *ration* = Sp. *racion* = Pg. *ração*, *reção* = It. *razione*, a ration, a rate or allowance, < L. *ratio(n-)*, a calculation, reckoning, hence in ML. a computed share or allowance of food: see *ratio*, *reason* (which are doublets of *ration*), and cf. *rate*[2].] 1. An allowance of means of subsistence for a fixed period of time; specifically, in the army and navy, an allotment or apportionment of provisions for daily consumption to each officer and man, or of forage for each horse. Officers' rations are generally commuted for a money payment at a prescribed rate; and soldiers' and sailors' rations may be partly or wholly commuted under some circumstances.

2. Any stated or fixed amount or quantity dealt out; an allowance or allotment.

At this rate [two years and a half for three vowels], to master the whole alphabet, consonants and all, would be a task fitter for the centurial adolescence of Methuselah than for our less liberal *ration* of years.
Lowell, Harvard Anniversary.

ration (rā'shọn or rash'ọn), *v. t.* [< *ration*, *n.*] 1. To supply with rations; provision.

It had now become evident that the army could not be *rationed* by a wagon train over the single narrow and almost impassable road between Milliken's Bend and Perkins' plantation.
U. S. Grant, Personal Memoirs, I. 471.

2. To divide into rations; distribute or apportion in rations. [Rare.]

The presence of hunger began; they began to *ration* out the bread.
The Nation, March 9, 1871, p. 160.

rationability (rash'ọn-ạ-bil'i-ti), *n.* [= Sp. *racionabilidad* = Pg. *racionabilidade* = It. *razionabilità*, < LL. *rationabilita(t-)s*, < *rationabilis*, reasonable: see *rationable*.] The possession of reason, as the distinctive attribute of man.

Rationability, being but a faculty or specifical quality, is a substantial part of a man, because it is a part of his definition, or his essential difference.
Bramhall, ii. 24. (*Davies.*)

rationable (rash'ọn-ạ-bl), *a.* [= OF. *rationable* = Sp. *racionable* = Pg. *racionavel* = It. *razionabile*, < LL. *rationabilis*, reasonable, rational, < L. *ratio(n-)*, reason: see *reason*.] Reasonable, as an agent or an act.

She was, I take it, on this matter not quite *rationable*.
Miss Edgeworth, Belinda, xxvi.

rational (rash'ọn-ạl), *a.* and *n.* [I. *a.* < OF. *rationel*, *rational*, F. *rationnel* = Pr. Sp. Pg. *racional* = It. *razionale*, < L. *rationalis*, of or belonging to reason, rational, reasonable, < *ratio(n-)*, reason: see *ratio*, *ration*, *reason*. II. *n.* < OF. *rational*, < ML. *rationale*, a pontifical stole, a pallium, an ornament worn over the chasuble, neut. of L. *rationalis*, rational: see I.] I. *a.* 1. Of, pertaining to, or springing from the reason, in the sense of the highest faculty of cognition.

He confesses a *rational* sovrantie of soule, and freedom of will in every man.
Milton, Eikonoklastes, vi.

Devout from constitution rather than from *rational* conviction.
Macaulay, Essays, History, p. 304.

Contradiction . . . must be absurd when it is regarded as fixed, and *rational* when it is regarded as superable.
Veitch, Introd. to Descartes's Method, p. clxxviii.

2. Endowed with reason, in the sense of that faculty which distinguishes man from the brutes: as, man is a *rational* animal.

It is our glory and happiness to have a *rational* nature.
Law.

Are these men *rational*, or are not the apes of Borneo more wise?
Goldsmith, Citizen of the World, let. x.

He [man] is *rational* and moral according to the organic internal conformation of his mind.
Swedenborg, Christian Psychol. (tr. by Gorman), p. 72.

There has been an idea of good, suggested by the consciousness of unfulfilled possibilities of the *rational* nature common to all men.
T. H. Green, Prolegomena to Ethics, § 207.

3. Conformable to the precepts of reason, especially of the practical reason; reasonable; wise.

You are one
Of the deepest politics I ever met,
And the most subtly *rational*.
B. Jonson, Magnetick Lady, iii. 4.

He had his Humour as other Men, but certainly he was a solid *rational* Man.
Howell, Letters, I. vi. 17.

His bounties are more *rational* and moderate than before.
Goldsmith, Vicar, iii.

4. In *arith.* and *alg.*: (*a*) Expressible in finite terms: applied to expressions in which no extraction of a root is left, or, at least, none such indicated which cannot be actually performed by known processes. The contraries of these are called *surd* or *irrational* quantities. Thus 2, 12¼, ⅔, are rational quantities, and $\sqrt{2}$, $\sqrt[3]{4}$, etc., are irrational or surd quantities, because their values can only be approximately and not accurately assigned. (*b*) In Euclid's "Elements" and commentaries, etc., on that work, commensurable with a given line. In senses (*a*) and (*b*) *rational* (Latin *rationalis*) translates Greek ῥητός, expressible. It may be remarked that some inconvenience arises from the fact that words derived from Latin *ratio*, originally signifying an account, are used to translate words connected with Greek λόγος, whose original meaning (a word) is entirely different.

5. In *anc. pros.*, capable of measurement in terms of the metrical unit (semeion or mora). A *rational time* (χρόνος ῥητός) is a time divisible by this unit without remainder. Thus, disemic times (times of two semeia) are rational, while irrational times (χρόνοι ἄλογοι) can be expressed only by fractions (as ½, 1½, 2½, 2⅔) of a semeion.—**Geometrically rational**, algebraic.—**Rational and integral function**. See *function*.—**Rational certainty, cognition, cosmology**. See the nouns.—**Rational class of functions**, a class which is relative to a group of operations produced by combinations of additions, subtractions, multiplications, and divisions.—**Rational composition**, in *logic*: (*a*) The composition of elements which only differ as viewed by the mind, and not as they exist, as the composition of essence and existence, of being and relation, etc. (*b*) The union of several objects so far as they are brought together into or under one concept.—**Rational derivative**. See *derivative*.—**Rational formula**. See *chemical formula*, under *chemical*.—**Rational fraction, function**. See the nouns.—**Rational horizon**. (*a*) The astronomical horizon. (*b*) The limits of rational knowledge.—**Rational inference**, a ratiocinative inference or syllogism.—**Rational instinct**, an innate idea, or natural belief.—**Rational knowledge**. (*a*) Knowledge of an object through its cause or causes.

The knowledge why or how a thing is is termed the knowledge of the cause; philosophical, scientific, *rational knowledge*.
Sir W. Hamilton, Metaph., iii.

(*b*) Knowledge springing directly or indirectly from reason, and not from experience.—**Rational mechanics**, the science which establishes and puts into shape the laws of motion.—**Rational number**, a number expressible as an ordinary fraction, in contradistinction to a continued fraction.—**Rational power, proposition, ratio**, etc. See the nouns.—**Rational psychology**. See *psychology*.—**Rational theology**, theology so far as drawn from a priori ideas.—**Rational transformation**, the transformation of a geometrical continuum into another, so as to make a one-to-one correspondence between the points of the two, except for a finite number of exceptional points. =**Syn.** *Rational*, *Reasonable*, sensible, enlightened, discreet, intelligent, sane, sound. The first two words are somewhat different, according as they refer to persons or things. As to persons, *rational* is the more speculative, *reasonable* the more practical term; *rational* means possessing the faculty of reason, while *reasonable* means exercising reason in its broader sense, in opposition to *unreasonable*—that is, guided by prejudice, fancy, etc. In fever the patient may become *irrational* and give *irrational* answers; when he is *rational* he may through weakness and fretfulness make *unreasonable* demands of his physician. As to things, the distinction continues between the narrower and the broader senses: a *rational* proposition is one that might proceed from a *rational* mind; a *reasonable* proposition is one that is marked by common sense and fairness. It is *irrational* to look for a coal-mine in a granite-ledge; it is *unreasonable* to expect good work for poor pay. See *absurd*.

II. *n.* 1. A quiddity; a universal; a nature. Thus, in the first quotation "the world of *rationals*" is the rational world, the system of general or possible entities. The conception is Platonic.

He, the great Father, kindled at one flame
The world of *rationals*. *Young*, Night Thoughts, iv.

This absolute end, prescribed by Reason necessarily and a priori, which is for all rational beings as such, can be nothing but Reason itself, or the Universe of *Rationals*.
H. *Sidgwick*, Methods of Ethics, p. 362.

2. *Eccles.*: (*a*) The breastplate of the Jewish high-priest. The name *rational* for the Jewish high-priest's breastplate (Hebrew *chōshen*, an 'ornament,' according to others a 'pouch' or 'receptacle') comes from the Latin *rationale*, a mistaken translation in the Vulgate of the word λόγιον or λογεῖον in the Septuagint, etc., meaning an 'oracle' or 'oracular instrument,' with allusion to the consultation of the Urim and Thummim. Hence—(*b*) A square plate of gold, silver, or embroidery, either jeweled or enameled, formerly worn on the breast over the chasuble by bishops during the celebration of mass. Also *pectoral* and *rationale* in both senses.

But upon the English chasuble there was to be seen, more or less often, up to the fourteenth century, an appendage, the *rational*, as beautiful as becoming, which is never found adorning the same Anglo-Saxon vesture.
Rock, Church of our Fathers, I. 363.

rationale (rash-o-nā'lē), *n.* [L., neut. sing. of *rationalis*, of or belonging to reason, rational: see *rational*.] 1. The rational basis or motive of something; that which accounts for or explains the existence of something; reason for being.

The *rationale* of your scheme is just:
"Pay toll here, there pursue your pleasure free."
Browning, Ring and Book, II. 292.

Thoroughly to realize the truth that with the mind as with the body the ornamental precedes the useful, it is needful to glance at its *rationale*.
H. Spencer, Education, p. 25.

2. A rational explanation or statement of reasons; an argumentative or theoretical account; a reasoned exposition.

I admire that there is not a *rationale* to regulate such trifling accidents, which consume much time, and is a reproch to the gravity of so greate an assembly of sober men.
Evelyn, Diary, Nov. 23, 1666.

Since the religion of one seems madness unto another, to afford an account or *rationale* of old rites requires no rigid reader.
Sir T. Browne, Urn-burial, iv.

Theological dogma is nothing in the world but a *rationale* of the relations in which God places Himself towards us in the very act of revealing Himself.
Contemporary Rev., XLIX. 345.

3. Same as *rational*, 2.

rationalisation, rationalise, etc. See *rationalization*, etc.

rationalism (rash'on-al-izm), *n.* [= F. *rationalisme* = Sp. Pg. *racionalismo* = It. *razionalismo* = G. *rationalismus*; as *rational* + *-ism*.] 1. In general, adherence to the supremacy of reason in matters of belief or conduct, in contradistinction to the submission of reason to authority; thinking for one's self.

From the infinite variability of opinion our great writers deduced the necessity of toleration in the place of persecution and of *rationalism* in place of obedience to authority.
Leslie Stephen, Eng. Thought, ii. ¶ 4.

2. In *theol.*: (*a*) In general, the subjection of religious doctrine and Scriptural interpretation to the test of human reason or understanding; the rejection of dogmatic authority as against reason or conscience; rational latitude of religious thought or belief.

What seemed most to protect the dogma of the Church from depravation really left it without defence against the scholastic *rationalism*.
Caird, Philos. of Kant, p. 25.

(*b*) More specifically, as used with reference to the modern school or party of rationalists, that system of doctrine which, in its extreme form, denies the existence of any authoritative and supernatural revelation, and maintains that the human reason is of itself, and unaided by special divine inspiration, adequate to ascertain all attainable religious truth. As a theological system rationalism regards the reason as the sole, final, and adequate arbiter of all religious questions, and is thus opposed to *mysticism*, which maintains the existence in man of a spiritual power transcending observation and the reasoning faculty. As a doctrinal system, it includes the doctrines founded upon rationalistic philosophy as a postulate, and embraces a denial of the authority of the Scripture and the supernatural origin of Christianity, but maintains as at least probable opinions the existence of a God and the immortality of the soul, and as indisputable facts the great principles of the moral law. As an interpretation of Scripture, it holds that the Scriptures themselves, rightly interpreted, corroborate rationalism, and thus it eliminates from them all supernatural elements. The term is, however, one of somewhat vague import, and is used with various modified meanings in modern polemical theology.

3. In *metaph.*, the doctrine of a priori cognitions; the doctrine that knowledge is not all produced by the action of outward things upon the senses, but partly arises from the natural adaptation of the mind to think things that are true.

The form of *Rationalism* which is now in the ascendant resembles the theory of natural evolution in this, that as the latter finds the race more real than the individual, and the individual to exist only in the race, so the former looks upon the individual reason as but a finite manifestation of the universal reason.
W. R. Sorley, Ethics of Naturalism, p. 18.

rationalist (rash'on-al-ist), *n.* [= F. *rationaliste* = Sp. Pg. *racionalista* = It. *razionalista* = D. G. Dan. Sw. *rationalist*; as *rational* + *-ist*.] 1. One who follows reason and not authority in thought or speculation; a believer in the supremacy of reason over prescription or precedent.

There is a new sect sprung up among them, and these are the *rationalists*; and what their reason dictates them in church or state stands for good, until they be convinced with better.
Clarendon, State Papers, II. xl., Introd.

2. In *theol.*, one who applies rational criticism to the claims of supernatural authority or revelation; specifically, one of a school or party, originating in Germany in the eighteenth century, who maintain as an ultimate conclusion that the human reason is of itself, and unaided by special divine inspiration, adequate to ascertain all attainable truth, and who accordingly, in interpretation of the Scripture, regards it as only an illustration and affirmation, not as a divine revelation, of truth. See *rationalism*, 2 (*b*).—3. A believer in metaphysical rationalism.

rationalistic (rash"on-a-lis'tik), *a.* [< *rationalist* + *-ic*.] Of or pertaining to rationalists or rationalism; conformable to or characterized by rationalism: as, *rationalistic* opinions; a *rationalistic* interpretation.

From the publication of the essays of Montaigne we may date the influence of that gifted and ever enlarging *rationalistic* school who gradually effected the destruction of the belief in witchcraft.
Lecky, Rationalism, I. 114.

Rationalistic Monarchians. See *Monarchian*.

rationalistical (rash"on-a-lis'ti-kal), *a.* [< *rationalistic* + *-al*.] Same as *rationalistic*.

rationalistically (rash"on-a-lis'ti-kal-i), *adv.* In a rationalistic manner.

rationality (rash-o-nal'i-ti), *n.* [< F. *rationalité* = Sp. *racionalidad* = Pg. *racionalidade* = It. *razionalità*, < LL. *rationalita(t-)s*, reasonableness, rationality, < L. *rationalis*, reasonable: see *rational*.] 1. The rational faculty; the power of reasoning; possession of reason; intelligence.

God has made *rationality* the common portion of mankind.
Dr. H. More.

Yes, the highest and most improved parts of *rationality* are frequently caught in the entanglements of a tenacious imagination, and submit to its obstinate but delusory dictamens.
Glanville, Vanity of Dogmatizing, xi.

2. The character of being rational; accordance with reason; reasonableness; congruity; fitness.

Well directed intentions, whose *rationalities* will not bear a rigid examination.
Sir T. Browne.

"It may do good, and it can do no harm," is the plea for many actions which have scarcely more *rationality* than worship of a painted stone.
H. *Spencer*, Prin. of Sociol., App. A.

3. The exercise, result, or manifestation of reason; rational principle, motive, or causation; basis in reason.

An essay on the "*Rationality* of History," . . . in which history is represented as a "struggle towards rational freedom."
H. *Sidgwick*, Mind, XIII. 406.

The solid black vote, cast, we said, without *rationality* at the behest of a few scoundrels.
The Century, XXX. 676.

rationalization (rash"on-al-i-zā'shon), *n.* [< *rationalize* + *-ation*.] 1. The act of rationalizing; a making rational or intelligible; subjection to rational tests or principles.

Lysons argues very strongly in favour of the famous story of "Whittington and his Cat," and rejects the *rationalization* which explains the legend by supposing Whittington's fortunes to have been made in the voyages of a mediæval cat or merchant-vessel.
Encyc. Brit., XXIV. 556.

2. In *alg.*, the process of clearing an equation from radical signs.

Also spelled *rationalisation*.

rationalize (rash'on-al-iz), *v.*; pret. and pp. *rationalized*, ppr. *rationalizing*. [< F. *rationaliser*; as *rational* + *-ize*.] I. *trans.* 1. To make conformable to reason; give rationality to; cause to be or to appear reasonable or intelligible.

Eusebius tells us that religion was divided by the Romans into three parts: the mythology, or legends that had descended from the poets; the interpretations or theories by which the philosophers endeavoured to *rationalise*, filter, or explain away these legends; and the ritual or official religious observances.
Lecky, European Morals, I. 429.

When life has been duly *rationalized* by science, it will be seen that among a man's duties care of the body is imperative.
H. Spencer, in Pop. Sci. Mo., XXII. 357.

The faculties of the mind have been *rationalised* into functions of the mind; so many sorts of operations, classified as observation demands.
Hodgson, Phil. of Reflection, II. 247.

2. To subject to the test of reason; explain or interpret by rational principles; treat in the manner of a rationalist: as, to *rationalize* religion or the Scriptures.—3. In *alg.*, to free from radical signs.

II. *intrans.* To think for one's self; employ the reason as a supreme test; argue or speculate upon the basis of rationality or rationalism; act as a rationalist.

If they [certain theologians] *rationalise* as the remarkable school of Cambridge Platonists *rationalised*, it is with a sincere belief that they are only bringing out the full meaning of the doctrine which they expound.
Leslie Stephen, Eng. Thought, ii. ¶ 60.

To *rationalise* meant to apply the canons of our limited enlightenment to the unlimited ranges of actuality.
W. Wallace, Logic of Hegel, Prolegomena, vi.

In order to know, in any wide and large sense, we must *rationalize*.
Henry Calderwood, New Princeton Rev., III. 23.

Also spelled *rationalise*.

rationalizer (rash'on-al-ī-zėr), *n.* One who rationalizes, or practises the methods of the rationalists; one who tests doctrines, principles, etc., by the light of abstract reason, or who employs reason alone in interpretation or explanation. Also spelled *rationaliser*.

Like many other *rationalisers*, he [Thomas Burnet] fancied himself to be confirming instead of weakening Scriptural authority.
Leslie Stephen, Eng. Thought, i. ¶ 8.

rationally (rash'on-al-i), *adv.* In a rational manner; in consistency with reason; reasonably: as, to speak *rationally*; to behave *rationally*.

rationalness (rash'on-al-nes), *n.* The state of being rational, or consistent with reason.

rationary (rash'on-ā-ri), *a.* [= F. *rationnaire*, one who receives rations, one who receives a salary, < ML. *rationarius*, relating to accounts, an accountant, < L. *ratio(n-)*, a reckoning, an account, ML. allowance: see *ration*.] Of or pertaining to accounts. [Rare.]

ration-money (rā'shon-mun"i), *n.* Money paid as commutation for rations.

Ratitæ (rā-tī'tē), *n. pl.* [NL., fem. pl. (sc. *Aves*, birds) of *ratitus*: see *ratite*.] One of the prime divisions of birds, including the ostriches, cassowaries, emus, and kiwis; the group of struthious birds, as contrasted with *Carinatæ*, to which all other existing birds belong. The *Ratitæ* are flightless, with more or less rudimentary wings; the sternum is a flattened or concavo-convex buckler-like bone, without a keel, developing from paired lateral centers of ossification. Associated with this condition of the sternum is a special configuration of the scapular arch, the scapula and coracoid meeting at a very obtuse angle, or with nearly coincident axes, and clavicles being absent or defective. The bones of the palate are peculiarly arranged, the pterygoids articulating with the basisphenoid in a manner only paralleled in *Carinatæ* in the tinamous. The Cretaceous genus *Hesperornis* was ratite in sternal characters, but is excluded from *Ratitæ* by the possession of teeth. The families of living *Ratitæ* usually recognized are the *Struthionidæ*, *Rheidæ*, *Casuariidæ*, and *Apterygidæ*; the genera are *Struthio*, *Rhea*, *Casuarius* and *Dromæus*, and *Apteryx*; the species are few. The extinct New Zealand moas (*Dinornithidæ* and *Palapterygidæ*) and the Madagascar *Æpyornithidæ* are also *Ratitæ*. The name was introduced by B. Merrem in 1813; it passed almost unnoticed for some years, but has lately come into almost universal use.

ratitate (rat'i-tāt), *a.* [< *ratite* + *-ate*[1].] Same as *ratite*. [Rare.]

ratite (rā'tīt), *a.* [< NL. *ratitus*, < L. *ratitus*, marked with the figure of a raft, < *ratis*, a raft.] Raft-breasted, as a bird; having a flat breastbone or sternum with no keel; having no keel, as a breast-bone; ecarinate; of or pertaining to the *Ratitæ*.

ratiuncule (rā-shi-ung'kūl), *n.* [< NL. *ratiunculus, dim. of L. *ratio(n-)*, a ratio: see *ratio*.] A ratio very near unity.

rati-weight, *n.* Same as *retti-weight*.

rat-kangaroo (rat'kang-ga-rö"), *n.* A kangaroo-rat; any species of *Hypsiprymnus*. See cut under *kangaroo-rat*.

ratline, ratlin (rat'lin), *n.* [Also corruptly *ratling*, *rattling*; formerly also *rare-line*; appar. < *rat*[1] + *line*[2] (corrupted to *rare-line*, as if 'thin line'?); a seamen's jocular name, as if forming ladders for the rats to climb by. Cf. D. *weeflijn*, ratline, lit. 'web-line.'] *Naut.*,

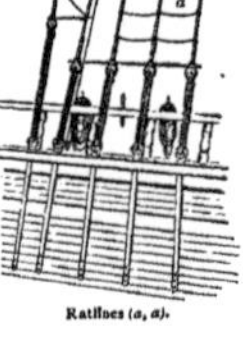

Ratlines (*a*, *a*).

one of a series of small ropes or lines which traverse the shrouds horizontally, thus forming the steps of ladders for going aloft.—**Sheer ratline**, every fifth ratline, which is extended to the swifter and after shroud.

ratline-stuff (rat'lin-stuf), *n.* *Naut.*, small tarred rope, of from 12 to 24 threads, from which ratlines are made.

ratling (rat'ling), *n.* A corruption of *ratline*.

ratmara (rat'ma-rä), *n.* [Native name.] An East Indian lichen, used in dyeing.

rat-mole (rat'mōl), *n.* Same as *mole-rat*.

ratont, *n.* An obsolete form of *ratten*.

ratonert, *n.* See *rattener*.

Ratonia (rā-tō'ni-ä), *n.* [NL.] A former genus of *Sapindaceæ*, now referred to *Matayba*. See *bastard mahogany*, under *mahogany*.

ratoon (ra-tön'), *n.* [Also *rattoon*; = Sp. *retoño*, a new sprout or shoot (> *retoñar*, sprout anew, put forth shoots again), < Hind. *ratun*, a second crop of sugar-cane from the same roots.] **1.** A sprout or shoot springing up from the root of a plant after it has been cropped; especially, a new shoot from the root of a sugar-cane that has been cut down. Compare *plant-cane*.

Plant canes generally take more lime than *ratoons* to cause the juices to granulate.
T. Roughley, Jamaica Planter's Guide (1823), p. 344.

Next year [second crop] the cane sprouts from the stubble, and is called first *ratoons*. . . . The second year it sprouts again, and is called second *ratoons*.
The Century, XXXV. 111.

2. The heart-leaves in a tobacco-plant. *Imp. Dict.*

ratoon (ra-tön'), *v. i.* [= Sp. *retoñar*, sprout or spring up anew; from the noun: see *ratoon*, *n.*] To sprout or send up new shoots from the root after being cropped or cut down: said of the sugar-cane and some other plants.

The cocoa, cassavas, and sweet potatoes will *ratoon* in two or three years; the negro yams are a yearly crop, but the white yams will last in the ground for several years.
T. Roughley, Jamaica Planter's Guide, p. 317.

On the Upper Coast, above New Orleans, it is customary to let the stubble *ratoon* but once. In Cuba it often *ratoons* six successive years, but the cane becomes constantly more woody and poorer in saccharine matter.
The Century, XXXV. 111.

ratount, *n.* An obsolete form of *ratten*.

rat-pit (rat'pit), *n.* An inclosure in which rats are baited or killed. The object is to ascertain how many rats a dog can kill in a given time, or which of two or more dogs can kill them most rapidly.

rat-poison (rat'poi"zn), *n.* **1.** Something used to poison rats with, as a preparation of arsenic. —**2.** A West African shrub, *Chailletia toxicaria*, whose seeds are used to destroy rats. The genus belongs to the *Chailletiaceæ*, a small order allied to the *Celastrineæ* and *Rhamnaceæ*. In the West Indies *Hamelia patens* is called *rat-poison*.

ratsbane (rats'bān), *n.* [< *rat's*, poss. of *rat*[1], + *bane*[1], as in *henbane*, etc.: see *bane*[1].] **1.** Rat-poison. Arsenious acid is often so called.

Wherefore . . . you see by the example of the Romans that playes are *ratsbane* to government of common-weales.
Prynne, Histrio-Mastix, I., iv. 1.

We live like vermin here, and eat up your cheese—
Your mouldy cheese that none but rats would bite at;
Therefore 'tis just that *ratsbane* should reward us.
Fletcher, Sea Voyage, iv. 3.

2. A plant, *Chailletia toxicaria*. See *rat-poison*, 2.

ratsbane (rats'bān), *v. t.*; pret. and pp. *ratsbaned*, ppr. *ratsbaning*. [< *ratsbane*, *n.*] To poison with ratsbane.

rat-snake (rat'snāk), *n.* A colubrine serpent of the genus *Ptyas*, *P. mucosus*, a native of India, Ceylon, etc., attaining a length of 7 feet, frequently entering houses. Some similar snakes are also called by the same name.

rat's-tail (rats'tāl), *n.* **1.** Same as *rat-tail*.—**2.** A slender rib or tongue tapering to a point, used to reinforce or stiffen a bar, plate, or the like, as on the back of a silver spoon.

rattt, *n.* An obsolete form of *rat*[1].

rat-tail (rat'tāl), *n.* and *a.* **I.** *n.* In *farriery*: (*a*) An excrescence on a horse's leg, growing from the pastern to the shank. (*b*) A disease which causes the hair of a horse's tail to fall off; also, a horse's tail thus denuded of hair. Also *rat's-tail*.

II. *a.* Same as *rat-tailed*.—**Rat-tail file, radish,** etc. See the nouns.—**Rat-tail maggot.** See under *rat-tailed*.

rattail (rat'tāl), *n.* **1.** A fish of the genus *Macrurus*, as *M. fabricii* or *M. rupestris*; the onion-fish or grenadier. See cut under *Macrurus*.—**2.** A horse which has a tail bare or nearly bared of hair.—**3.** One of various plants having tail-like flower-spikes, as the common plantain and the ribwort plantain, and various grasses, including species of *Rottbœllia* in the United States and *Ischæmum laxum* (*Andropogon nervosus*) in Australia.

rat-tailed (rat'tāld), *a.* **1.** Having a tail like a rat's; having a rat-tail, as a horse.

Here comes the wonderful one-hoss shay,
Drawn by a *rat-tailed*, ewe-necked bay.
O. W. Holmes, The Deacon's Masterpiece.

2. Like a rat's tail in shape.—**Rat-tailed kangaroo-rat**, *Hypsiprymnus murinus*, an Australian marsupial.—**Rat-tailed larva** or **maggot**, the larva of certain syrphid flies, ending in a long slender stigmatophorous

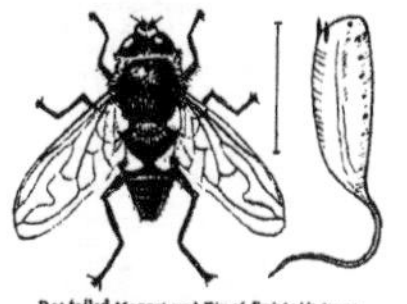

Rat-tailed Maggot and Fly of *Eristalis tenax*. (Line shows natural size of fly.)

tail of two telescopic joints, forming an organ which enables the larva to breathe from the surface while lying hidden in mud, etc. The larva of *Eristalis tenax* is an example.—**Rat-tailed serpent**, *Bothrops lanceolatus*, a very venomous American pit-viper.—**Rat-tailed shrew.** See *shrew*.

rattan[1], *n.* See *ratten*.

rattan[2], *n.* and *v.* See *ratan*.

rattan[3] (ra-tan'), *n.* [Imitative; cf. F. *rataplan*, imitation of the sound of a drum; cf. also *rat-tat*.] The continuous beat or reverberation of a drum; rataplan; rat-a-tat. [Rare.]

They had not proceeded far, when their ears were saluted with the loud *rattan* of a drum. *W. H. Ainsworth.*

rattanas (rat'a-nas), *n.* [Native name.] A kind of coarse sacking made in Madagascar and Mauritius.

rattany, *n.* See *ratany*.

rat-tat (rat-tat'), *n.* Same as *rat-a-tat*.

A breeze always blowing and playing *rat-tat*
With the bow of the ribbon round your hat.
Lowell, Appledore.

rat-tat-too (rat'tat-tö'), *n.* An intensified form of *rat-a-tat*.

The *rat-tat-too* of a drum was heard in the distance.
Philadelphia Times, Oct. 24, 1886.

ratteen (ra-tēn'), *n.* [Also *rateen*; = D. *ratijn* = G. Sw. Dan. *ratin*, < F. *ratine*, a kind of cloth, = Sp. Pg. *ratina* = It. *rattina*; origin uncertain; prob. (like F. *rate*, milt, spleen) so called from its loose cellular texture and likeness to a honeycomb, < LG. *rate*, honeycomb.] A kind of stuff, usually thick and resembling drugget or frieze: it is chiefly employed for linings.

ratten (rat'n), *n.* [Also *rattan*, *ratton*, *rattin*, *rotten*, *rotton*; < ME. *raton*, *ratoun*, *ratone*, < OF. (and F.) *raton*, a rat, = Sp. *raton*, a mouse, < ML. *rato(n-)*, a rat: see *rat*[1]. Cf. *kitten* as related to *cat*.] A rat. [Obsolete or prov. Eng. and Scotch.]

Thanoe ran ther a route of *ratones*, as it were,
And smale mys with hem mo than a thousand.
Piers Plowman (C), i. 165.

I comawnde alle the *ratons* that are here abowte,
That non dwelle in this place with-inne ne with-owte.
Political Poems, etc. (ed. Furnivall), p. 23.

The bald *rattons*
Had eaten his yellow hair.
Young Bekie (Child's Ballads, IV. 11).

"A Yorkshire burr," he affirmed, "was as much better than a Cockney's lisp as a bull's bellow than a *rattan's* squeak." *Charlotte Brontë*, Shirley, p. 64.

ratten (rat'n), *v. t.* [< *ratten*, *n.* Cf. *rat*[1], *v.*] To play mischievous tricks upon, as an obnoxious person, for the purpose of coercion or intimidation. The members of a trades-union ratten a fellow-workman who refuses to join the union, to obey its behests, or to pay his dues, by secretly removing or breaking his tools or machinery, spoiling his materials, or the like, and ironically ascribing the mischief to rats. The practice was at one time prevalent in some of the manufacturing districts of Great Britain.

For enforcing payment of entrance-fees, contributions towards paying the fermes (dues), as well as of fines, the Craft-Gilds made use of the very means so much talked of in the case of the Sheffield Trade-Unions, namely *rattening*: that is, they took away the tools of their debtors.
English Gilds (E. E. T. S.), Int., p. cxxvii.

A piece of sulphate of copper put into an indigo-vat throws it out of order, by oxidising the white indigo and sending it—in an insoluble state—to the bottom. This is a method of *rattening* not unknown in dye-works.
W. Crookes, Dyeing and Calico-printing, p. 548.

Rattening, as defined by the Report of the Royal Commission, is "the abstraction of the workman's tools, so as to prevent him from earning his livelihood until he has obeyed the arbitrary orders of the union." It is satisfactory to know that this system . . . was chiefly confined to Sheffield and Manchester.
George Howell, Conflicts of Capital and Labor, vii. § 13.

rattenert, rattonert, *n.* [< ME. *ratoner*, *ratonere*, rat-catcher, < OF. *raton*, a rat: see *ratten*.] A ratter or rat-catcher.

A rybidour and a *ratoner*, a rakere and hus knaue.
Piers Plowman (C), vii. 371.

ratter[1] (rat'ėr), *n.* [< *rat*[1], *v.*, + *-er*[1].] **1.** One who catches rats; a rat-catcher.—**2.** An animal which catches rats, as a terrier.

ratter[2] (rat'ėr), *n.* [< *rat*[1], *v.*, 2, + *-er*[1].] One who rats, or becomes a renegade; also, a workman who renders himself obnoxious to a trades-union. See *ratting*, 2. [Colloq.]

The Essay on Faction is no less frank in its recognition of self-interest as a natural and prevailing motive, and almost cynical in its suppression of resentment against *ratters* and traitors. *E. A. Abbott*, Bacon, p. 84.

rat-terrier (rat'ter"i-ėr), *n.* A small active dog used to kill rats.

rattery (rat'ėr-i), *n.* [< *ratter*[2] + *-y* (see *-ery*).] The qualities or practices of a ratter; apostasy; tergiversation. [Rare.]

Such a spectacle refreshes me in the *rattery* and scoundrelism of public life.
Sydney Smith, Letters, 1822. (*Davies.*)

rattinet (rat-i-net'), *n.* [< F. *ratine*, a kind of cloth (see *ratteen*), + dim. *-et*.] A woolen stuff thinner than ratteen.

ratting (rat'ing), *n.* [Verbal n. of *rat*[1], *v.*, 2.] **1.** The act of deserting one's principles, and going over to the opposite party.—**2.** In the trades, the act of working for less than established or demanded prices, or of refusing to strike, or of taking the place of a striker.—**3.** A low sport consisting in setting a dog upon a number of rats confined in a tub, cage, or pit, to see how many he will kill in a given time.

rattish (rat'ish), *a.* [< *rat*[1] + *-ish*[1].] Characteristic of rats; having a rat-like character; like a rat.

rattle[1] (rat'l), *v.*; pret. and pp. *rattled*, ppr. *rattling*. [< ME. *ratelen*, rattle, clatter, etc., < AS. **hrætelan* (cf. *hrætelwyrt*, 'rattlewort') = D. *ratelen*, rattle, = LG. *rateln*, *räteln* = MHG. *razzeln*, rage, roar, G. *rasseln* (> Dan. *rasle* = Sw. *rasla*), rattle; freq. of a simple verb seen in MHG. *razzen*, *ratzen*, rattle; perhaps akin to Gr. κραδαίνειν, swing, wave, brandish, shake; perhaps in part imitative (cf. *rat-a-tat*, *rat-tat*, in imitation of a knock at a door, *rattan*[3], F. *rataplan*, in imitation of a drum, etc.), and in so far comparable with Gr. κρότος, a rattling noise, κροτεῖν, knock, rattle, κρόταλον, a rattle, κροταλίζειν, rattle (see *Crotalus*, rattlesnake). Cf. dial. *rackle*, a var. of *rattle*. Hence ult. *rail*[4], *Rallus*, *râle*.] **I.** *intrans.* **1.** To give out a rapid succession of short, sharp, jarring or clattering sounds; clatter, as by continuous concussions.

The quiver *rattleth* against him. Job xxxix. 23.

To the dread *rattling* thunder
Have I given fire, and rifted Jove's stout oak
With his own bolt. *Shak.*, Tempest, v. 1. 44.

"Farewell!" she said, and vanished from the place;
The sheaf of arrows shook, and *rattled* in the case.
Dryden, Pal. and Arc., iii. 282.

Swift Astolpho to the *rattling* horn
His lips applies.
Hoole, tr. of Orlando Furioso, xxxiii.

One or two [rattlesnakes] coiled and *rattled* menacingly as I stepped near. T. *Roosevelt*, The Century, XXXVI. 201.

2. To move or be carried along with a continuous rapid clatter; go or proceed or bear one's self noisily: often used with reference to speed rather than to the accompanying noise.

And off my mourning-robes; grief, to the grave;
For I haue gold, and therefore will be brave;
In silks I'll *rattle* it of every colour.
J. Cook, Green's Tu Quoque.

I'll take a good *rattling* gallop.
Sterne, Tristram Shandy, iv. 20.

Wagons . . . *rattling* along the hollow roads, and over the distant hills. *Irving*, Sketch-Book, p. 445.

We *rattled* away at a merry pace out of the town.
R. D. Blackmore, Lorna Doone, xiv.

3. To speak with noisy and rapid utterance; talk rapidly or in a chattering manner: as, to *rattle* on about trifles.

The *rattling* tongue
Of saucy and audacious eloquence.
Shak., M. N. D., v. 1. 102.

The girls are handsome, dashing women, without much information, but *rattling* talkers.
C. D. Warner, Their Pilgrimage, p. 183.

II. *trans.* **1.** To cause to make a rattling sound or a rapid succession of hard, sharp, or jarring sounds.

Her chain she *rattles*, and her whip she shakes.
Dryden.

Rattle his bones over the stones!
He's only a pauper whom nobody owns!
T. *Noel*, The Pauper's Drive.

2. To utter in sharp, rapid tones; deliver in a smart, rapid manner: as, to *rattle* off a string of names.

He *rattles* it out against Popery and arbitrary power.
Swift, Against Abolishing Christianity.

The rolls were *rattled* off; the short, crisp commands went forth. *The Century*, XXXVII. 466.

3. To act upon or affect by rattling sounds; startle or stir up by any noisy means.

Sound but another, and another shall
As loud as thine *rattle* the welkin's ear.
Shak., K. John, v. 2. 172.

These places [woodlands] are generally strongholds for foxes, and should be regularly *rattled* throughout the season. *Encyc. Brit.*, XII. 395.

4. To scold, chide, or rail at noisily; berate clamorously.

If my time were not more precious
Than thus to lose it, I would *rattle* thee,
It may be beat thee.
Beau. and Fl., Honest Man's Fortune, v. 3.

I to Mrs. Ann, and, Mrs. Jem being gone out of the chamber, she and I had a very high bout. I *rattled* her up, she being in bed; but, she becoming more cool, we parted pretty good friends. *Pepys*, Diary, Feb. 6, 1660.

5. To shake up, unsettle, or disturb by censure, annoyance, or irritation; bring into an agitated or confused condition. [Colloq. or slang.]

The king hath so *rattled* my lord-keeper that he is now the most pliable man in England.
Cottington, To Strafford (1633), quoted in Hallam's Const. [Hist., II. 89.

Unpleasant stories came into my head, and I remember repeating to myself more than once (candor is better than felicity of phrase), "Be careful, now; don't get *rattled!*"
Atlantic Monthly, LXIV. 110.

rattle[1] (rat'l), *n.* [< ME. *ratele*, a rattle, < AS. **hrætele*, in comp. *hrætelwyrt*, 'rattlewort,' a plant in whose pods the seeds rattle; = MD. *ratele*, D. *ratel* = G. *rassel*, a rattle; from the verb: see *rattle*[1], *v.* Cf. G. *ratsche*, a rattle, clapper; Sw. *rassel*, clank, clash, clatter, etc.] 1. A rapid succession of short, sharp, clattering sounds, as of intermitting collision or concussion.

"I'll hold ten Pound my Dream is out;
I'd tell it to you but for the *Rattle*
Of those confounded Drums.
Prior, English Ballad on tr. of Boileau's Taking of Namur, [st. 10.

I aren't like a bird-clapper, forced to make a *rattle* when the wind blows on me. *George Eliot*, Adam Bede, lii.

2. A rattling clamor of words; sharp, rapid talk of any kind; hence, sharp scolding or railing.

This *rattle* in the crystal hall
Would be enough to deaf them all.
Cotton (Arber's Eng. Garner, I. 218).

Receiving such a *rattle* for his former contempt by the Bishop of London that he came out blubbering.
Heylin, Life of Laud, p. 257. (*Davies.*)

I chid the servants and made a *rattle*.
Swift, Journal to Stella, lx.

3. An instrument or toy contrived to make a rattling sound. The watchman's rattle, formerly used for giving an alarm, and the child's toy resembling it, consist of a vibrating tongue slipping over the teeth of a rotating ratchet-wheel, and producing much noise when rapidly twirled by the handle. Other toy rattles for children, and those used by some primitive races for various purposes, commonly consist of a box or casing, or even a hollow gourd or shell, with or without a handle, containing loose pebbles or other hard objects.

The *rattles* of Isis and the cymbals of Brasilea nearly enough resemble each other. *Raleigh.*

They vse *Rattles* of the shell of a certaine fruite, in which they put stones or Graines, and call them Maraca, of which they haue some superstitious conceit.
Purchas, Pilgrimage, p. 837.

Behold the child, by Nature's kindly law,
Pleased with a *rattle*, tickled with a straw.
Pope, Essay on Man, ii. 276.

4. One who talks rapidly and without moderation or consideration; a noisy, impertinent talker; a jabberer.

She had not been brought up to understand the propensities of a *rattle*, nor to know to how many idle assertions and impudent falsehoods the excess of vanity will lead.
Jane Austen, Northanger Abbey, ix.

They call me their agreeable *Rattle*.
Goldsmith, She Stoops to Conquer.

It may seem strange that a man who wrote with so much perspicuity, vivacity, and grace should have been, whenever he took a part in conversation, an empty, noisy, blundering *rattle*. *Macaulay*, Goldsmith.

5. The crepitaculum of the true rattlesnake, consisting of a series of horny epidermic cells of an undulated pyramidal shape, articulated one within the other at the extremity of the tail. See *rattlesnake*.—6. (*a*) An annual herb, *Rhinanthus Crista-galli*, of meadows and pastures in Europe and northern Asia. It attaches itself by its fibrous roots to the roots of living grasses, etc., thus doing much damage. Its calyx in fruit is orbicular, inflated but flattened, containing a capsule of similar form with a few large flat, generally winged seeds. This is the common or yellow rattle, also called locally *penny-grass*, *penny-rattle*, *rattlebags*, *rattlebox*, and *rattle-penny*. (*b*) One of the Old World lousewort, *Pedicularis palustris*, the red rattle.—**The rattles.** (*a*) Croup. (*b*) The death-rattle.

rattle[2] (rat'l), *v. t.*; pret. and pp. *rattled*, ppr. *rattling*. [A back formation from *rattling*, a corruption of *ratline* but taken as a verbal noun in *-ing*, whence the assumed verb *rattle*.] *Naut.*, to furnish with ratlines.—**To rattle down,** to seize or fasten ratlines on (the shrouds of a vessel).

rattlebags (rat'l-bagz), *n.* See *rattle*[1], 6 (*a*).

rattle-barrel (rat'l-bar"el), *n.* In *founding*, a tumbling-box for castings, used to free them from sand, and sometimes to remove the cores.

rattlebox (rat'l-boks), *n.* 1. A toy that makes a rattling noise; a rattle.—2. (*a*) A plant, the yellow rattle. See *rattle*[1], 6 (*a*). (*b*) Any of the North American species of *Crotalaria*; chiefly, *C. sagittalis*, a low herb of sandy soil in the eastern half of the United States. The seeds rattle in the inflated leathery pod. (*c*) The calico-wood, snowdrop-, or silverbell-tree, *Halesia tetraptera*: so named from its large dry fruit, which is bony within and contains a single seed in each of its 1 to 4 cells. See *Halesia* and *calico-wood*.

Plant, with Flowers and Pods, of Rattlebox (*Crotalaria sagittalis*).

rattlebrain (rat'l-brān), *n.* A giddy, chattering person; a rattlepate.

rattle-brained (rat'l-brānd), *a.* Giddy; chattering; whimsical; rattle-headed.

rattlebush (rat'l-bush), *n.* The wild indigo, *Baptisia tinctoria*, a bushy herb with inflated pods.

rattlecap (rat'l-kap), *n.* A giddy, volatile person; a madcap: generally said of a girl. [Colloq.]

rattled (rat'ld), *a.* 1. Confused; flurried. [Colloq. or slang.]—2. Affected by eating the loco or rattleweed; locoed. [Western U. S.]

rattlehead (rat'l-hed), *n.* A giddy, chattering person; a rattlepate.

rattle-headed (rat'l-hed"ed), *a.* Noisy; giddy; trifling.

rattle-mouse† (rat'l-mous), *n.* [< *rattle*[1] + *mouse*. Cf. *flittermouse*, *reremouse*.] A bat.

Not vnlike the tale of the *rattle mouse*.
Puttenham, Arte of Eng. Poesie, ii. 13 [18].

rattlepate (rat'l-pāt), *n.* A noisy, empty fellow; a trifling or impertinent chatterer.

rattle-pated (rat'l-pā"ted), *a.* Same as *rattle-headed*.

rattler (rat'lėr), *n.* [< *rattle*[1] + *-er*[1].] 1. One who rattles, or talks away without reflection or consideration; a giddy, noisy person.—2. Anything which causes a person to become rattled, as a smart or stunning blow. [Slang or colloq.]

And once, when he did this in a manner that amounted to personal, I should have given him a *rattler* for himself if Mrs. Boffin had not thrown herself betwixt us.
Dickens, Our Mutual Friend.

3. A rattlesnake. [U. S.]

We have had *rattlers* killed every year; copperheads less frequently. *Sci. Amer.*, N. S., LVI. 85.

4. A big or bold lie. [Colloq.]—5. Among cutlers, a special form of razor with a very thin blade, the faces of which are ground to an angle of fifteen degrees.—**Diamond rattler**, the diamond rattlesnake.

rattleran (rat'l-ran), *n.* The lower half of a fore quarter of beef; a plate-piece. [U. S.]

rattleskull (rat'l-skul), *n.* Same as *rattlepate*.

rattlesnake (rat'l-snāk), *n.* [< *rattle*[1] + *snake*.] A venomous serpent of the family *Crotalidæ*, whose tail ends in a rattle or crepitaculum; a crotaliform or solenoglyphic serpent, or pit-viper, of either of the genera *Crotalus* and *Crotalophorus*. These poisonous reptiles are confined to America, where there are many species. Those whose head is covered on top with scales like those of the back belong to the genus *Crotalus*; others, with the top of the head plated, belong to *Crotalophorus*, *Caudisona*, or *Sistrurus*. The former are the larger species; both are equally venomous, in proportion to their size, and both have the pit between the eyes and nose characteristic of all the pit-vipers. (See cut under *pit-viper*.) The rattle is an epidermal or cuticular

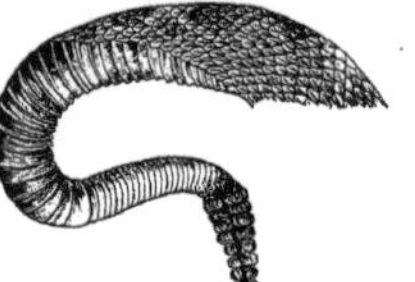

Hinder Part of a Rattlesnake, showing the rattle, with seven "rings" and a "button."

structure, representing the extreme of development of the horn or spine in which the tail of many other serpents ends. It consists of several hard horny pieces loosely articulated together, so that when rapidly vibrated they make a peculiar whirring or rattling noise. Rattlesnakes are sluggish and naturally inoffensive reptiles, only seeking to destroy their prey, like other animals. When alarmed or irritated they prepare to defend themselves by coiling in the attitude best adapted for striking with the fangs, at the same time sounding the warning rattle, during which process both the head and the tail are held erect. The

Rattlesnake (*Crotalus durissus*) coiled to strike.

snake can strike to a distance of about two thirds of its own length. The mechanism of the jaws is such that, when the mouth is wide open, the fangs are erected in position for piercing; and, when the mouth closes upon the wound the fangs have made in the flesh, a tiny stream of venom is spirted through each fang into the bitten part. (See cuts under *Crotalus* and *poison-fang*.) The poison, which is specially modified saliva, is secreted in a venom-gland near the angle of the jaw, and is conveyed by a venom-duct to the tooth. It is extremely dangerous, readily killing the small animals upon which the snake feeds, and is often fatal to man and other large animals. It has an acid reaction, neutralizable by an alkali, and is harmless when swallowed, if there is no lesion of the mucous membrane, though exceedingly poisonous when introduced into the circulation. The flesh of the rattlesnake is edible, and some animals, as hogs and peccaries, habitually feed upon these snakes. Among the best-known species are the banded and the diamond rattlesnakes, which inhabit eastern as well as other regions of the United States, and sometimes attain a length of 5 or 6 feet; many similarly large ones are found in the west, among them *Crotalus pyrrhus*, of a reddish color. The commonest species of the west is the Missouri rattlesnake, *C. confluentus*, very widely distributed from the British to the Mexican boundary. Among the smaller species are the massasauga, *Crotalophorus tergeminus* (*Sistrurus catenatus*), also known as the *sidewiper*, from its habit of wriggling obliquely. One species, *C. cerastes*, has a small horn over each eye.

rattlesnake-fern (rat'l-snāk-fėrn), *n.* One of the moonworts or grape-ferns, *Botrychium Virginianum*, found through a large part of North America and in the Old World. The sterile segment of the frond is broadly triangular, thin and finely divided, and of ample size or often reduced. The name is apparently from the resemblance of the fruit to the rattles of a rattlesnake.

rattlesnake-grass (rat'l-snāk-grås), *n.* An American grass, *Glyceria Canadensis*, a handsome stout species with a large panicle of drooping spikelets, which are ovate, and flattish but turgid, like those of *Briza*, the quaking-grass. It is a useful forage-grass in wet places. Sometimes called *tall quaking-grass.*

rattlesnake-herb (rat'l-snāk-ėrb), *n.* The baneberry or cohosh. See *Actæa.*

rattlesnake-master (rat'l-snāk-mås"tėr), *n.* One of several American plants at some time reputed to cure the bite of the rattlesnake. (*a*) The false aloe, *Agave Virginica*, said to be so called in South Carolina. A tincture of this plant is sometimes used for flatulent colic. (*b*) According to Pursh, *Liatris scariosa* and *L. squarrosa*, in Virginia, Kentucky, and the Carolinas. (*c*) A species of eringo, *Eryngium yuccæfolium*, also called, like *Liatris, button-snakeroot*; but the plants are quite unlike. See the generic names.

Rattlesnake-master (*Eryngium yuccæfolium*).
1, upper part of the stem with the heads; 2, a leaf; *a*, a flower, with the bract.

rattlesnake-plantain (rat'l-snāk-plan"tān), *n.* Any one of the three American species of *Goodyera.*

rattlesnake-root (rat'l-snāk-röt), *n.* A plant, *Prenanthes serpentaria*, also *P. alba* and *P. altissima*, the first at least

Rattlesnake-root (*Prenanthes alba*).
1, the inflorescence; 2, lower part of stem with root; *a*, a head, after anthesis; *b*, the achenium with the pappus.

having some repute in North Carolina, etc., as a remedy for snake-bites. See *Prenanthes* and *cancer-weed.*

rattlesnake-weed (rat'l-snāk-wēd), *n.* A hawkweed, *Hieracium venosum*, of the eastern half of the United States. It has a slender stem a foot or two high, forking above into a loose corymb of a few yellow heads. The leaves, which are marked with purple veins, are situated mostly at the base. These and the root are thought to possess an astringent virtue.

rattletrap (rat'l-trap), *n.* A shaky, rattling object; especially, a rattling, rickety vehicle; in the plural, objects clattering or rattling against each other. [Colloq.]

> Hang me if I'd ha' been at the trouble of conveying her and her *rattle-traps* last year across the channel.
> *Mrs. Gore*, Castles in the Air, xxxiv.

> "He'd destroy himself, and me too, if I attempted to ride him at such a *rattletrap* as that." A *rattletrap!* The quintain that she had put up with so much anxious care.
> *Trollope*, Barchester Towers, viii.

rattleweed (rat'l-wēd), *n.* A plant of the genus *Astragalus*, in numerous species. It includes various loco-weeds, and is presumably extended to *Oxytropis* in the Rocky Mountain region.

rattlewing (rat'l-wing), *n.* The golden-eyed duck, or whistlewing, *Clangula glaucion.* Also called *whistler.* [Eng.]

rattlewort (rat'l-wėrt), *n.* [Not found in ME.; < AS. *hrætelwyrt*, rattlewort, < **hrætele*, a rattle, + *wyrt*, wort: see *rattle*[1], *wort*[1].] A plant of the genus *Crotalaria.* Compare *rattlebox*, 2 (*b*).

rattling[1] (rat'ling), *n.* [Verbal n. of *rattle*[1], *v.*] 1. The act of making a rattle, clatter, or continuous jarring noise.

> The noise of a whip, and the noise of the *rattling* of the wheels, and of the prancing horses, and of the jumping chariots.
> Nahum iii. 2.

2. The act of berating or railing at or otherwise assailing or attacking: as, to give one a *rattling.*

rattling[1] (rat'ling), *p. a.* [Ppr. of *rattle*[1], *v.*] 1. Making or adapted for making a rattle; hence, smart; sharp; lively in action, movement, or manners: as, a *rattling* rider; a *rattling* pace; a *rattling* game; a *rattling* girl.

> He ance tell'd me . . . that the Psalms of David were excellent poetry! as if the holy Psalmist thought o' *rattling* rhymes in a blether, like his ain silly clinkum-clankum things that he ca's verse.
> *Scott*, Rob Roy, xxi.

2. Bewilderingly large or conspicuous: as, *rattling* stakes or bets. [Colloq. or slang.]

rattling[2] (rat'ling), *n.* A corruption of *ratline.*

ratton, *n.* See *ratten.*

rattoner†, *n.* See *rattener.*

rattoon[1], *n.* See *ratoon.*

rattoon[2]†, *n.* Same as *ratan.*

rat-trap (rat'trap), *n.* A trap for catching rats; also, something resembling or suggesting such a trap.—**Rat-trap pedal.** See *pedal.*

rauchwacke (råk'wak; G. pron. rouċh'vä"ke), *n.* [G., < *rauch*, smoke (= E. *reek*), + *wacke*, a sort of stone consisting of quartz, sand, and mica: see *wacke.* Cf. *graywacke.*] Dolomite or dolomitic limestone, containing many small irregular cavities, frequently lined with crystals of brown-spar: a characteristic mode of occurrence of the Zechstein division of the Permian in various parts of Germany.

raucid (râ'sid), *a.* [< L. **raucidus*, LL. dim. *raucidulus*, hoarse, < *raucus*, hoarse: see *raucous.*] Same as *raucous.*

> Methinks I hear the old boatman (Charon) paddling by the weedy wharf, with *raucid* voice, bawling "sculls."
> *Lamb*, To the Shade of Elliston.

raucity (râ'si-ti), *n.* [< F. *raucité*, hoarseness, < L. *raucita(t-)s*, hoarseness, also snoring, < *raucus*, hoarse: see *raucous.*] Roughness or harshness of utterance; hoarseness.

> The purling of a wreathed string, and the *raucity* of a trumpet.
> *Bacon*, Nat. Hist., § 700.

raucle (râ'kl), *a.* [A var. of *rackel*, *rackle*, rash, fearless, also stout, firm, strong: see *rackle*, *rakel.*] Coarse; harsh; strong; firm; bold. [Scotch.]

> Auld Scotland has a *raucle* tongue.
> *Burns*, Prayer to the Scotch Representatives.

raucous (râ'kus), *a.* [= F. *rauque* = Pr. *rauc*, *rauch* = Cat. *ronc* = Sp. *ronco*, *rauco* = Pg. *rouco* = It. *rauco*, < L. *raucus*, hoarse; cf. Skt. √ *ru*, cry out.] Hoarse; harsh; croaking in sound: as, a *raucous* voice or cry.

raucously (râ'kus-li), *adv.* In a raucous manner; with a croaking sound; hoarsely.

raught[1]†. An obsolete preterit and past participle of *reach*[1].

raught[2]†. An obsolete preterit and past participle of *reck.*

raun (rân), *n.* A dialectal form of *roe*[2].

raunce†, *n.* See *rance*[3].

raunceoun†, *v. t.* A Middle English form of *ransom.*

raunch (räuch), *v. t.* Same as *ranch*[1].

raunson†, **raunsoun**†, *n.* and *v.* Middle English forms of *ransom.*

rauracienne (rō-ras-ien'), *n.* In *dyeing*, same as *orseillin.*

Rausan (F. pron. rē-zoṅ'), *n.* [F.: see def.] A wine of Bordeaux, of the commune of Margaux: its best variety is the wine of Château Rausan, often exported under the name of *Rausan-Margaux.*

Rauwolfia (rau-wol'fi-ä), *n.* [NL. (Plumier, 1703), named after Leonhard *Rauwolf*, a German botanist and traveler of the sixteenth century.] A genus of gamopetalous plants of the order *Apocynaceæ*, the dogbane family, tribe *Plumerieæ*, and type of the subtribe *Rauwolficæ.* It is characterized by a salver-shaped corolla with included stamens, an annular or cup-shaped disk, and an ovary with two carpels, each with two ovules, in fruit becoming drupaceous and united, often beyond the middle. There are about 42 species, natives of the tropics in America, Asia, and Africa, also in South Africa. They are trees or shrubs, commonly with smooth whorled leaves which are three or four in a circle, and finely and closely feather-veined. The small flowers and fruit are in cymose clusters which become lateral and commonly resemble umbels. Most species are actively poisonous; some, as *R. nitida*, are in repute as cathartics and emetics. Several medicinal species, with remarkably twisted roots and stems, were formerly separated as a genus *Ophioxylon* (Linnæus, 1767), on account of their producing both sterile flowers with two stamens and fertile flowers with five: as *R. serpentina*, the East Indian serpentwood, a climber with handsome leaves, the root of which is used in India and China as a febrifuge. *R. Sandwicensis*, the hao of the Hawaiians, a small milky tree with white scarred branches, is unlike all other species in its leafy sepals.

ravage (rav'āj), *n.* [< F. *ravage*, ravage, havoc, spoil, < *ravir*, bear away suddenly: see *ravish.*] Desolation or destruction wrought by the violent action of men or beasts, or by physical or moral causes; devastation; havoc; waste; ruin: as, the *ravage* of a lion; the *ravages* of fire or tempest; the *ravages* of an invading army; the *ravages* of passion or grief.

> Would one think 'twere possible for love
> To make such *ravage* in a noble soul? *Addison.*

> And many another suppliant crying came
> With noise of *ravage* wrought by beast and man.
> *Tennyson*, Gareth and Lynette.

=**Syn.** Pillage, plunder, spoliation, despoilment. These words all apply not to the treatment of people directly, but to the destruction or appropriation of property.

ravage (rav'āj), *v. t.*; pret. and pp. *ravaged*, ppr. *ravaging.* [< F. *ravager*, ravage; from the noun.] To desolate violently; lay waste, as by force, storm, etc.; commit havoc on; devastate; pillage; despoil.

> Cæsar
> Has *ravaged* more than half the globe, and sees
> Mankind grown thin by his destructive sword.
> *Addison*, Cato i. 1.

> While oft in whirls the mad tornado flies,
> Mingling the *ravaged* landscape with the skies.
> *Goldsmith*, Des. Vil., l. 358.

=**Syn.** To plunder, waste. See the noun.

ravager (rav'āj-ėr), *n.* [< F. *ravageur*, < *ravager*, ravage: see *ravage.*] One who ravages; a plunderer; a spoiler; one who or that which lays waste.

Ravaton's operation. See *operation.*

rave[1] (rāv), *v.*; pret. and pp. *raved*, ppr. *raving.* [< ME. *raven*, rave, talk like a madman (cf. MD. freq. *ravelen*, D. *revelen*, dote, etc.), < OF. *raver*, *resver*, rave, dote, speak idly, F. *rêver*, dream (cf. OF. *ravasser*, rave, talk idly, *reve*, madness), = Sp. *rabiar*, rave, = Pg. *raivar*, rage (cf. It. *ar-rabbiare*, rage, go mad), < LL. **rabiare*, rave, rage, < L. *rabies*, ML. *rabia*, rage, < L. *rabere*, rave, rage: see *rage*, *n.*, and cf. *rage*, *v.*, practically a doublet of *rave*[1]. Cf. also *reverie.*] I. *intrans.* 1. To talk like a madman; speak with delirious or passionate extravagance; declaim madly or irrationally; rage in speech.

> Peter was angry and rebuked Christ, and thought earnestly that he had *raued*, and not wist what he sayde.
> *Tyndale*, Works, p. 25.

> Have I not cause to *rave* and beat my breast?
> *Addison*, Cato, iv. 3.

> Three days he lay and *raved*
> And cried for death.
> *William Morris*, Earthly Paradise, I. 336.

2. To talk about something with exaggerated earnestness, and usually with little judgment or coherence; declaim enthusiastically, immoderately, or ignorantly.

> He must fight singly to-morrow with Hector: and is so prophetically proud of an heroical cudgelling that he *raves* in saying nothing.
> *Shak.*, T. and C., iii. 3. 249.

> Fire in each eye, and papers in each hand,
> They *rave*, recite, and madden round the land.
> *Pope*, Prol. to Satires, l. 6.

3. To produce a brawling or turbulent sound; move or act boisterously: used of the action of the elements.

> His bowre is in the bottom of the maine,
> Under a mightie rocke, gainst which doe *rave*
> The roring billowes in their proud disdaine.
> *Spenser*, F. Q., III. viii. 37.

> On one side of the church extends a wide woody dell, along which *raves* a large brook among broken rocks and trunks of fallen trees.
> *Irving*, Sketch-Book, p. 444.

II. *trans.* To utter in frenzy; say in a wild and excited manner.

> Pride, like the Delphic priestess, with a swell
> *Rav'd* nonsense, destin'd to be future sense.
> *Young*, Night Thoughts, vii. 506.

rave[2]† (rāv). An obsolete preterit of *rive.*

rave[3]† (rāv), *v. t.* [< ME. *raven*; a secondary form of *riven*, after the pret. *rave*: see *rive*[1].] To rive.

> And he worowede him, and slowhe him; ande thanne he ranne to the false emperes, ande *ravide* hir evino to the bone, but more harme dide he not to no mane.
> *Gesta Romanorum*, p. 202. (*Halliwell.*)

rave[4] (rāv), *v. t.* [A dial. form of *reave.*] 1. Same as *reave*, 3.

> Thairfoir I hald the subject vaine,
> Wold *rave* us of our right.
> *Battle of Balrinnes* (Child's Ballads, VII. 220).

2. To tear up; pull or tear the thatch or covering from (a house): same as *reave*, 4. *Halliwell.* [Prov. Eng.]—**To rave up**, to pull up; gather together. [Prov. Eng.]

rave[4] (rāv), *n.* [< *rave*[4], *v.*] A tearing; a hole or opening made by tearing out or away: as, a *rave* in an old building. *Halliwell.* [Prov. Eng.]

rave[5] (rāv), *n.* [Origin obscure.] One of the side pieces of the body of a wagon or other vehicle.

The *rave* bolts [in a bob-sleigh] extend upward from the runners in front and rear of the knees, and the *raves* rest between their ends on the bottom of the recess.
Sci. Amer., N. S., LIV. 130.

Floating raves, a light open frame of horizontal bars, attached along the top of the sides of wagons, and sloping upward and outward from them. They are convenient for supporting and securing light bulky loads. *Farrow*, Mil. Encyc., I. 679.

rave[6]† (rāv), *n.* [ME., < OF. *rave*, < L. *rapa*, *rapum*, a turnip: see *rape*[4].] A turnip.

Rave, as brassik for vyne as ille is fonde.
Palladius, Husbondrie (E. E. T. S.), p. 173.

rave-hook (rāv'hůk), *n.* In *ship-carp.*, a hooked iron tool used when enlarging the butts for receiving a sufficient quantity of oakum; a ripping-iron.

ravel[1] (rav'el or rav'l), *v.*; pret. and pp. *raveled* or *ravelled*, ppr. *raveling* or *ravelling*. [Formerly also *reavel* and (as a var. of the noun) *revel*; early mod. E. also **rivel*, *ryvell* (< OF. *riuler*, unravel, < LG.); < MD. *ravelen*, entangle (L. *intricare*, Kilian), ravel (Hexam, Sewel) (*uit ravelen*, ravel out, unravel), D. *rafelen*, unravel, unweave, = LG. *reffeln*, *rebeln*, *rebbeln*, unravel, unweave; origin unknown. There is no obvious connection with G. *raffeln*, snatch up, rake, *raffel*, a rake, grate for flax, < *raffen*, snatch: see *raff*, *raffle*[1].] **I.** *trans.* **1.** To tangle; entangle; entwine confusedly; involve in a tangled or knotted mass, as thread or hair mingled together loosely.

Sleepe that knits vp the *rauel'd* Sleeue [that is, floss-silk] of Care. *Shak.*, Macbeth (folio 1623), ii. 2. 37.

I've *reavell'd* a' my yellow hair
Coming against the wind.
Glenkindie (Child's Ballads, II. 12).

Minute glands, which resemble *ravelled* tubes, formed of basement membrane and epithelial scales.
J. R. Nichols, Fireside Science, p. 186.

Hence—**2.** To involve; perplex; confuse.

What glory 's due to him that could divide
Such *ravel'd* int'rests, has the knot untied? *Waller.*

3†. To treat confusedly; jumble; muddle.

They but *ravel* it over loosely, and pitch upon disputing against particular conclusions. *Sir K. Digby.*

4. To disentangle; disengage the threads or fibers of (a woven or knitted fabric, a rope, a mass of tangled hair, etc.); draw apart thread by thread; unravel: commonly with *out*: in this sense (the exact contrary of the first sense), originally with *out*, *ravel out* being equivalent to *unravel.*

Must I *ravel out*
My weaved-up folly?
Shak., Rich. II., iv. 1. 228.

The fiction pleas'd; their loves I long elude;
The night still *ravell'd* what the day renew'd.
Fenton, in Pope's Odyssey, xix.

A favorite gown had been woven by her maids, of cotton, striped with silk procured by *raveling* the general's discarded stockings. *The Century*, XXXVII. 841.

II. *intrans.* **1.** To become entangled or snarled, as the ends of loose and dangling threads, or a mass of loose hair. Hence—**2.** To become involved or confused; fall into perplexity.

As you unwind her love from him,
Lest it should *ravel* and be good to none,
You must provide to bottom it on me.
Shak., T. G. of V., iii. 2. 52.

Till, by their own perplexities involved,
They *ravel* more, still less resolved.
Milton, S. A., l. 305.

3. To curl up, as a hard-twisted thread. *Jamieson.* [Scotch.]—**4.** To become untwisted or disjoined, as the outer threads of a loosely made fabric or the strands of a rope; become disjoined thread by thread; fray, as a garment at the edges: commonly with *out.*

I *ryvell out*, as sylke doth, je rivle. *Palsgrave.*

Hence—**5.** To suffer gradual disintegration or decay.

Do's my lord *ravell out*? do's he fret?
Marston, The Fawne, ii. 1.

And this vast Work all *ravel out* again
To its first Nothing. *Cowley*, Davideis, i.

6†. To make a minute and careful examination in order to straighten what is confused, unfold what is hidden, or clear up what is obscure; investigate; search; explore.

It can be little pleasure to us to *rave* [*sic* ed. 1660, 1671; *rake*, ed. 1681, 1686: read *ravel*] into the infirmities of God's servants, and bring them upon the stage.
Bp. Sanderson, Works, I. 100.

It will be needless to *ravel* far into the records of elder times. *Decay of Christian Piety.*

The humour of *ravelling* into all these mystical or entangled matters . . . produced infinite disputes.
Sir W. Temple.

ravel[1] (rav'el or rav'l), *n.* [Formerly or dial. also *revel*; < *ravel*[1], *v.*] **1.** A raveled thread; a raveling. [Rare.]

Life goes all to *ravels* and tatters. *Carlyle*, in Froude.

2. *pl.* The broken threads cast away by women at their needlework. *Halliwell* (spelled *revels*).—**3.** In *weaving*, a serrated instrument for guiding the separate yarns when being distributed and wound upon the yarn-beam of a loom, or for guiding the yarns wound on a balloon; an evener; a separator.

Also, in Scotch spelling, *raivel.*

ravel[2] (rav'el), *v.* Same as *rabble*[1]. [Prov. Eng.]

ravel-bread (rav'el-bred), *n.* Same as *raveled bread.* See *raveled.* *Halliwell.* [Prov. Eng.]

raveled†, **ravelled**†, *a.* [< OF. *ravalé*, *ravallé*, brought low, abated, lessened in price, pp. of *ravaler*, *ravaller*, *ravailler*, bring down, bring low, abate, diminish, lessen in price, < *re-*, back, + *avaler*, let down, come down: see *avale.*] Lower-priced: distinctively noting wheaten bread made from flour and bran together.

The *raveled* is a kind of cheat bread, but it reteineth more of the grosse and lesse of the pure substance of the wheat. *Harrison*, p. 168. (*Halliwell.*)

They had four different kinds of wheaten bread: the finest called manchet, the second cheat or trencher bread, the third *ravelled*, and the fourth in England called mescelin [see *maslin*[2]], in Scotland mashloch. The *ravelled* was baken up just as it came from the mill, flour, bran, and all. *Arnot*, Hist. of Edin. (*Jamieson.*)

ravelin (rav'lin), *n.* [Formerly also *rav'lin*, corruptly *raveling*; < OF. *ravelin*, F. *ravelin*, m., OF. also *raveline*, f., = Sp. *revellin* = Pg. *revelim*, < OIt. *ravellino*, *revellino*, It. *rivellino*, a ravelin; origin unknown; hardly, as supposed, < L. *re-*, back, + *vallum*, a wall, rampart: see *wall*[1]. Cf. F. dial. *ravelin*, dim. of *ravin*, a ravine, hollow: see *ravine*[2].] A detached triangular work in fortification, with two embankments which form a projecting angle. In the figure BB is the ravelin, with *A* its redout, and *CC* its ditch. *DD* is the main ditch of the fortress, and *E* the passage giving access from the fortress to the ravelin.

Ravelin.

We will erect
Wals and a *raveling* that may safe our fleet and us protect. *Chapman*, Iliad, vii.

This book will live, it hath a genius; . . .
. . . here needs no words' expence
In bulwarks, *rav'lins*, ramparts for defence.
B. Jonson, On the Poems of Sir John Beaumont.

raveling[1], **ravelling** (rav'el-ing), *n.* [Verbal n. of *ravel*[1], *v.*] A raveled thread or fiber; a thread drawn out from a woven, knitted, or twisted fabric: as, to use *ravelings* for basting.

raveling[2]†, *n.* An obsolete form of *ravelin.*

raveling-engine (rav'el-ing-en"jin), *n.* In *paper-manuf.*, a machine for tearing rags for making into pulp; a rag-engine or tearing-cylinder.

ravelled†, **ravelling.** See *raveled*, *raveling*[1].

ravelly (rav'el-i), *a.* [< *ravel*[1] + *-y*[1].] Showing loose or disjoined threads; partly raveled out. [Colloq.]

Dressed in a dark suit of clothes that looked seamed and *ravelly*, as if from rough contact with thorny undergrowth.
The Century, XXXIX. 444.

ravelment (rav'el-ment), *n.* [< *ravel*[1] + *-ment.*] A pulling or drawing apart, as in raveling a fabric; hence, disunion of feeling; disagreement; embroilment.

raven[1] (rā'vn), *n.* and *a.* [< ME. *raven*, *reven*, *revin*; pl. *ravenes*, *refnes*, *remes*; < AS. *hræfn*, *hrefn*, *hræmn*, *hremn* = D. *raven*, *rave*, *raaf* = MLG. *raven*, *rave*, LG. *rave* = OHG. *rabo*, also *hraban*, *raban*, *hram*, *ram*, MHG. *rabe*, also *rappe*, *raben*, *ram*, *ramm* (forms remaining in the proper names *Rapp* and *Wolf-ram*) = Icel. *hrafn* = OSw. *rafn*, *ramn* = Dan. *ravn* (not recorded in Goth.), a raven; perhaps, like the crow and owl, named from its cry, namely from the root seen in L. *crepare*, rattle: see *crepitation*, *discrepant*. The alleged etymological connection with L. *corvus*, Gr. *κόραξ*, raven, L. *cornix*, Gr. *κορώνη*, crow, Pol. *kruk*, a raven, Skt. *kārava*, a raven, is not made out.] **I.** *n.* **1.** A bird of the larger species of the genus *Corvus*, having the feathers of the throat lanceolate and distinct from one another. The plumage is entirely black, with more or less lustrous or metallic sheen; the bill and feet are ebony-black; the wings are pointed, the tail is rounded, and the nostrils are concealed beneath large tufts of antrorse plumules. The voice is raucous. The common raven is *C. corax*, about

Raven (*Corvus corax*).

2 feet long and 50 inches in extent of wings. It inhabits Europe, Asia, and some other regions, and the American bird, though distinguished as *C. carnivorus*, is scarcely different. There are several similar though distinct species of various countries, among them *C. cryptoleucus* of western North America, which has the concealed bases of the feathers of the neck snowy-white. Ravens are easily tamed, and make very intelligent pets, but are thievish and troublesome. They may be taught to imitate speech to some extent. In the wild state the raven is omnivorous, like the crow; it nests on trees, rocks, and cliffs, preferring the most inaccessible places, and lays four or five greenish eggs heavily speckled with brown and blackish shades. The American raven is now almost unknown in the eastern parts of the United States, but is still abundant in the west. Ravens have from time immemorial been viewed with superstitious dread, being supposed to bring bad luck and forebode death.

The *raven* himself is hoarse
That croaks the fatal entrance of Duncan
Under my battlements. *Shak.*, Macbeth, i. 5. 40.

2. A kind of fish. See *sea-raven* and *Hemitripteridæ.*

II. *a.* Black as a raven; evenly and glossily or lustrously black: as, *raven* locks.

Smoothing the *raven* down
Of darkness till it smiled.
Milton, Comus, l. 251.

raven[2] (rav'n), *n.* [Also *ravine*; early mod. E. also *ravin*; < ME. *ravin*, *ravine*, *ravyne*, *raveyne*, < OF. *ravine*, *raveine*, *rabine*, prey, plunder, rapine, also rapidity, impetuosity, prob. = Pr. *rabina*, < L. *rapina*, plunder, pillage: see *rapine*, a doublet of *raven*[2].] **1.** Plunder; rapine; robbery; rapacity; furious violence. [Archaic.]

And whan thei herde the horne a-noon thei slaked theire reynes and spored theire horse and smote in to the hoste with grete *ravyne*. *Merlin* (E. E. T. S.), ii. 324.

Oh gods!
Why do we like to feed the greedy *raven*
Of these blown men? *Fletcher*, Valentinian, v. 4.

2. Plunder; prey; food obtained with rapacity.

That is to seyn, the foulis of *ravyne*
Were heyest set.
Chaucer, Parliament of Fowls, l. 323.

Egles, Gledes, Ravenes, and othere Foules of *raveyne*, that eten Flesche. *Mandeville*, Travels, p. 309.

The lion . . . filled his holes with prey, and his dens with *ravin*. Nah. ii. 12.

raven[2] (rav'n), *v.* [Also *ravin*; < OF. *raviner*, seize by force, ravage, < L. **rapinare* (in deriv.), plunder, < *rapina*, plunder, impetuosity: see *raven*[2], *n.*] **I.** *trans.* **1**†. To seize with rapacity, especially food; prey upon; ravage. See *ravined.*—**2.** To subject to rapine or ravage; obtain or take possession of by violence.

Master Carew of Antony, in his Survay of Cornewall, witnesseth that the Sea hath *ravened* from that Shire that whole Country of Lionesse. *Hakewill*, Apology, i. 3, § 2.

Woe to the wolves who seek the flock to *raven* and devour! *Whittier*, Cassandra Southwick.

3. To devour with great eagerness; eat with voracity; swallow greedily.

Our natures do pursue,
Like rats that *ravin* down their proper bane,
A thirsty evil. *Shak.*, M. for M., i. 2. 133.

They rather may be said to *raven* then to eate it; and, holding the flesh with their teeth, cut it with rasors of stone. *Purchas*, Pilgrimage, p. 778.

II. *intrans.* To prey with rapacity; show rapacity.

Benjamin shall *ravin* as a wolf. Gen. xlix. 27.

Ravenala (rav-e-nā'lạ̈), *n.* [NL. (Adanson, 1763), from a native name in Madagascar.] A genus of monocotyledonous plants, of the order

Musaceæ, the banana family. It is characterized by a loculicidally three-valved and three-celled capsule with numerous seeds in six rows, and by separate long and narrow sepals and petals, three of each, all similar and unappendaged. There are but 2 species, natives one of Madagascar, the other of northern Brazil and Guiana. In both the stem is sometimes short, with the leaves almost all radical, at other times forming a tall woody trunk reaching 30 feet high, ringed by leaf-scars. The handsome oblong and two-ranked leaves resemble those of the banana, and are of immense size, being considered the largest undivided leaves known, with the exception perhaps of the Victoria lily. The long concave leafstalks are divided within into small cubical chambers, about a half-inch square, filled with a clear watery sap which forms a refreshing drink, whence the name *traveler's-tree*, used in botanic gardens for *R. Madagascariensis*. The leaves are also used as a thatch for the native huts. The large flowers form a short many-flowered raceme within the spathe, and are followed by woody capsules and edible seeds with a lacerate and pulpy blue aril which yields an essential oil. See *traveler's-tree*.

raven-cockatoo (rā'vn-kok-a-tö'), *n.* A black cockatoo. See *cockatoo*.

ravener† (rav'n-ėr), *n.* [< ME. *raviner*, *ravinere*, *ravyner*, *ravinour*, *ravynour*, *raveynour*, < OF. *ravineor*, *ravinour*, < L. *rapinator*, a plunderer, robber, < **rapinare*, plunder, rob: see *raven*[2].] 1. One who ravens or plunders; a greedy plunderer; a devourer or pursuer.

We scorne swich *raviners* and honters of fouleste thinges. *Chaucer*, Boëthius, i. prose 3.

And then he is such a *ravener* after fruit. B. *Jonson*, Bartholomew Fair, i. 1.

2. A bird of prey. *Holland.*

ravening (rav'n-ing), *n.* [Verbal n. of *raven*[2], *v.*] Eagerness for plunder; rapacity.

Your inward part is full of *ravening* [*extortion*, R. V.] and wickedness. Luke xi. 39.

raveningly (rav'n-ing-li), *adv.* In a ravening or ravenous manner; voraciously; greedily.

Liguirire somtymes is auidè and helluosè, that is griedily and *raueninglye* or gluttonously to devour very much. *Udall*, Flowers, fol. 98.

ravenous (rav'n-us), *a.* [< OF. *ravinos*, *ravinous*, *ravineus*, F. *ravineux*, violent, impetuous, = It. *rapinoso*, ravenous, etc., < ML. **rapinosus*, < L. *rapina*, rapine: see *raven*[2]. Cf. *rapinous*.] 1. Furiously voracious; hungry even to rage; devouring with rapacious eagerness: as, a *ravenous* wolf, lion, or vulture; to be *ravenous* with hunger.

I will give thee unto the *ravenous* birds of every sort, and to the beasts of the field, to be devoured. Ezek. xxxix. 4.

I wish some *ravenous* wolf had eaten thee! *Shak.*, 1 Hen. VI., v. 4. 31.

2. Greedily eager for gratification; tending to rapacity or voracity: as, *ravenous* appetite or desire.

Thy desires
Are wolvish, bloody, starved, and *ravenous*.
Shak., M. of V., iv. 1. 138.

=**Syn.** *Voracious*, etc. See *rapacious*.

ravenously (rav'n-us-li), *adv.* In a ravenous manner; with raging voracity.

ravenousness (rav'n-us-nes), *n.* The state or character of being ravenous; furious avidity; rage for prey.

The *ravenousness* of a lion or bear are natural to them. *Sir M. Hale.*

ravenry (rā'vn-ri), *n.*; pl. *ravenries* (-riz). [< *raven*[1] + *-ry*.] A place where ravens nest and breed or are kept.

Nothing short of a reward given on the hatching-off of a *ravenry* . . . would insure protection. *Nature*, XXXVII. 602.

Ravensara (rav-en-sä'rä), *n.* [NL. (Sonnerat, 1782), < Malagasy *ravin-dzara*, said to mean 'good leaf.'] A genus of trees of the order *Laurineæ* and tribe *Perseaceæ*. It is distinguished by having the parts of the flower in threes, two-celled anthers, an enlarged perianth-tube closed over the ovary in fruit, and a seed with six lobes descending into as many false cells of the pericarp. The 3 or 4 species are smooth aromatic trees of Madagascar. *R. aromatica* has a clove-like fragrance throughout, and its fruit, called *clove-nutmeg* or *ravensara-nut*, is used in Madagascar as a spice.

raven's-duck (rā'vnz-duk), *n.* A fine kind of hempen sail-cloth.

ravenstone (rā'vn-stōn), *n.* [Tr. G. *rabenstein*, a gallows (also a black stone), < *rabe*, = E. *raven*, + *stein* = E. *stone*: so called as a place where ravens (birds of ill omen) and vultures congregate. Cf. D. *raven-kop*, hangman, lit. 'raven-head': see *raven*[1] and *stone*[1].] A gallows. [Rare.]

To and fro, as the night-winds blow,
The carcass of the assassin swings;
And then alone, on the *raven-stone*,
The raven flaps his dusky wings.
Byron, Manfred (first MS.), iii.

raver (rā'vėr), *n.* [< ME. *ravare*; < *rave*[1] + *-er*[1]. Cf. F. *rêveur*, dreamer.] One who raves or is furious; a maniac.

As old decrepite persons, yong Infantes, tooles, Madmen, and *Ravers*. *Touchstone of Complexions*, p. 94. (*Davies.*)

ravery† (rā'vėr-i), *n.* [< OF. *reverie*, raving, dreaming: see *rave*[1], and cf. *reverie*.] The act or practice of raving; extravagance of speech or expression; a raving.

Reject them not as the *raveries* of a child. *Sir J. Sempill*, Sacrilege Sacredly Handled, Int. (*Davies.*)

ravin† (rav'in), *n.* and *v.* See *raven*[2].

ravine[1], *n.* Same as *raven*[2].

ravine[2] (ra-vēn'), *n.* [< ME. *ravine*, *ravyne*, < OF. *ravine*, *rabine*, a raging flood, a torrent, an inundation, a hollow worn by a torrent, a ravine, F. *ravine*, *ravin*, a ravine; a particular use of *ravine*, violence, impetuosity, plunder, < L. *rapina*, rapine, violence, plunder: see *rapine*, and cf. *raven*[2].] 1†. A raging flood.

A *ravine*, or inundation of waters, which overcometh all things that come in its way. *Cotgrave.*

2. A long deep hollow worn by a stream or torrent of water; hence, any deep narrow gorge, as in a mountain; a gully. =**Syn.** 2. *Glen*, *Gorge*, etc. See *valley*.

ravined† (rav'ind), *a.* [Irreg. < *ravin*, *raven*[2], + *-ed*[2].] Ravenous.

Witches' mummy, maw and gulf
Of the *ravin'd* salt-sea shark.
Shak., Macbeth, iv. 1. 24.

ravine-deer (ra-vēn'dēr), *n.* The goat-antelope of the Deccan, which inhabits rocky places.

Ravine-deer (*Tetraceros quadricornis*).

It has many names, vernacular and technical, as *blacktail*, *chikara*, *chousingha*, *kalsiepie*, *Antilope chikara* or *quadricornis*, *Tetraceros quadricornis*, and *Tragops bennetti*.

raving (rā'ving), *n.* [< ME. *ravynge*; verbal n. of *rave*[1], *v.*] Furious exclamation; irrational incoherent talk.

They are considered as lunatics, and therefore tolerated in their *ravings*. *Steele*, Tatler, No. 178.

raving (rā'ving), *p. a.* 1. Furious with delirium; mad; distracted.—2. Fit to excite admiration or enthusiasm; hence, amazing, intense, superlative, or the like. [Colloq. or slang.]

A letter of *raving* gallantry, which Orlando Furioso himself might have penned, potent with the condensed essence of old romance. *I. D'Israeli*, Amen. of Lit., II. 262.

The veterans liked to recall over the old Madeira the wit and charms of the *raving* beauties who had long gone the way of the famous vintages of the cellar. *New Princeton Rev.*, I. 6.

ravingly (rā'ving-li), *adv.* In a raving manner; with furious wildness or frenzy; distractedly.

The swearer is *ravingly* mad; his own lips so pronounce him. *Rev. T. Adams*, Works, I. 288.

ravisable†, *a.* [ME., < OF. *ravissable*, < *ravir*, ravish: see *ravish*.] Ravenous.

And inward we, withouten fable,
Ben gredy wolves *ravisable*.
Rom. of the Rose, l. 7016.

ravisant†, *a.* [ME., also *ravisaunt*; < OF. *ravisant*, *ravissant*, ppr. of *ravir*, ravish: see *ravish*. Cf. *ravissant*.] Ravishing; ravening; predatory.

The wolf, wilde and *ravisaunt*,
With the schep ȝeode so milde so lomb.
MS. Laud. 108, f. 11. (*Halliwell.*)

ravish (rav'ish), *v. t.* [< ME. *ravisshen*, *ravischen*, *ravisen*, *ravichen*, < OF. (and F.) *raviss-*, stem of certain parts of *ravir*, ravish, snatch away hastily, = It. *rapire*, < L. *rapere*, snatch, seize: see *rape*[2] and *rapid*. Cf. *ravage*.] 1. To seize and carry off; transport or take away forcibly; snatch away. [Obsolete or archaic.]

Thanne thei seyn that he is *ravissht* in to another world, where he is a grettre Lord than he was here. *Mandeville*, Travels, p. 254.

And the gret fray that the [they] mad in the tyme of masse it *ravyched* my witts and mad me ful hevyly dysposyd. *Paston Letters*, II. 81.

These hairs, which thou dost *ravish* from my chin,
Will quicken, and accuse thee. *Shak.*, Lear, iii. 7. 38.

2. To transport mentally; enrapture; bring into a state of ecstasy, as of delight or fear.

Sore were all their mindes *ravished* wyth feare, that in maner half beside themselves they said . . . *Golding*, tr. of Cæsar, fol. 173.

Thou hast *ravished* my heart. Cant. iv. 9.

The view of this most sweet Paradise [Mantua] . . . did even *ravish* my senses. *Coryat*, Crudities, I. 145.

My friend was *ravished* with the beauty, innocence, and sweetness that appeared in all their faces. *Addison*, Freeholder, No. 47.

3. To deprive by seizure; dispossess violently: with *of*.

They may *ravish* me o' my life,
But they canna banish me fro' Heaven hie.
Hughie the Graeme (Child's Ballads, VI. 57).

And am I blasted in my bud with treason?
Boldly and basely *of* my fair name *ravish'd*?
Beau. and Fl., Knight of Malta, ii. 5.

4. To violate the chastity of; commit rape upon; deflower.

Their houses shall be spoiled, and their wives *ravished*. Isa. xiii. 16.

My heroes slain, my bridal bed o'erturn'd,
My daughters *ravish'd*, and my city burn'd,
My bleeding infants dash'd against the floor.
Pope, Iliad, xxii. 89.

ravish† (rav'ish), *n.* [< *ravish*, *v.*] Ravishment; ecstasy; a transport or rapture.

Most of them . . . had builded their comfort of salvation upon unsound grounds, viz. some upon dreams and *ravishes* of spirit by fits; others upon the reformation of their lives. *Winthrop*, Hist. New England, I. 219, an. 1636.

ravisher (rav'ish-ėr), *n.* [< ME. *ravischour*, *ravissour*, < OF. *raviseor*, *raviseur*, F. *ravisseur*, ravisher, < *ravir*, ravish: see *ravish*.] 1. One who ravishes or takes by violence.

Gods! shall the *ravisher* display your hair,
While the fops envy and the ladies stare?
Pope, R. of the L., iv. 103.

2. One who violates the chastity of a woman.

Thou *ravisher*, thou traitor, thou false thief!
Shak., Lucrece, l. 888.

3. One who or that which transports with delight.

ravishing (rav'ish-ing), *n.* [< ME. *ravisshing*, *ravyschynge*; verbal n. of *ravish*, *v.*] Ecstatic delight; mental transport. [Rare.]

The *ravishings* that sometimes from aboue do shoot abroad in the inward man. *Feltham*, Resolves, ii. 66.

ravishing (rav'ish-ing), *p. a.* 1. Snatching; taking by violence; of or pertaining to ravishment.

Tarquin's *ravishing* strides. *Shak.*, Macbeth, ii. 1. 55.

2. Exciting rapture or ecstasy; adapted to enchant; exquisitely lovely; enrapturing.

Those delicious villas of St. Pietro d'Arena, which present another Genoa to you, the *ravishing* retirements of the Genoese nobility. *Evelyn*, Diary, Oct. 17, 1644.

He [Emerson] . . . gave us *ravishing* glimpses of an ideal under the dry husk of our New England. *Lowell*, Study Windows, p. 380.

3†. Moving furiously along; hurrying. *Chaucer*, Boëthius, i. meter 5.

ravishingly (rav'ish-ing-li), *adv.* In a ravishing manner; so as to delight or enchant.

ravishment (rav'ish-ment), *n.* [< OF. (and F.) *ravissement*, a ravishing, ravishment, < *ravir*, ravish: see *ravish*.] 1. The act of seizing and carrying off, or the act or state of forcible abduction; violent transport or removal.—2. Mental transport; a carrying or being carried away with delight; ecstasy; rapture.

All things joy, with *ravishment*
Attracted by thy beauty still to gaze.
Milton, P. L., v. 46.

The music and the bloom
And all the mighty *ravishment* of Spring.
Wordsworth, Sonnets, ii. 18.

3. Violation of female chastity; rape.

In bloody death and *ravishment* delighting.
Shak., Lucrece, l. 430.

ravissant (rav'i-sant), *a.* [See *ravisant*.] In *her.*, leaping in a position similar to rampant: usually noting the wolf.

ravisse†, *v. t.* A Middle English form of *ravish*. *Chaucer.*

raw[1] (rà), *a.* and *n.* [< ME. *raw*, *raw*, *ra*, < AS. *hreáw*, *hrǣw*, raw, uncooked, unprepared, sore, = OS. *hrā* = D. *rauw* = MLG. *rauw*, *rô*, LG. *rau* = OHG. *rāo*, *rō*, *rou* (*raw-*), MHG. *rō* (*raw-*), G. *roh* = Icel. *hrār* = Sw. *rå* = Dan. *raa*, raw, crude; akin to L. *crudus*, raw, *cruentus*, bloody, *cruor*, gore, blood (see *crude*), Gr. *κρέας*, flesh, Skt. *kravis*, raw meat, *krūra*, cruel, hard, OSlav.

krūvì, Lith. *kraujas*, blood.] **I.** *a.* **1.** Existing in the state of natural growth or formation; unchanged in constitution by subjection to heat or other alterative agency; uncooked, or chemically unaltered: as, *raw* meat, fish, oysters, etc.; most fruits are eaten *raw*; *raw* medicinal substances; *raw* (that is, unburnt) umber.

Distilled waters will last longer than *raw* waters.
Bacon, Nat. Hist., § 347.

On this brown, greasy napkin . . . lie the *raw* vegetables she is preparing for domestic consumption.
H. *James, Jr.*, Little Tour, p. 165.

2. In an unchanged condition as regards some process of fabrication; unwrought or unmanufactured. In this sense *raw* is used either of substances in their primitive state, or of partly or wholly finished products fitted for working into other forms, according to the nature of the case: as, the *raw* materials of a manufacture; *raw* silk or cotton (the prepared fiber); *raw* marble; *raw* clay.

Eight thousand bailes of *raw* silke are yearly made in the Island. *Sandys*, Travailes, p. 192.

Like a cautious man of business, he was not going to speak rashly of a *raw* material in which he had had no experience. *George Eliot*, Mill on the Floss, iii. 5.

It [the German mind] has supplied the *raw* material in almost every branch of science for the defter wits of other nations to work on.
Lowell, Among my Books, 1st ser., p. 293.

3. In a rudimental condition; crude in quality or state; primitively or coarsely constituted; unfinished; untempered; coarse; rough; harsh.

Her lips were, like *raw* lether, pale and blew.
Spenser, F. Q., V. xii. 29.

The coast scene of Hoguet . . . copied in water-color, . . . and blind-haltered with a blazing space of *raw*-white all around it. *The Nation*, Feb., 1875, p. 84.

The *raw* vessels fresh from the wheel, which only require a moderate heat to prepare them for being glazed, are piled in the highest chamber. *Encyc. Brit.*, XIX. 638.

The glycerine is of a brownish colour and known as *raw*, in which state it is sold for many purposes.
Workshop Receipts, 2d ser., p. 310.

4. Harshly sharp or chilly, as the weather; bleak, especially from cold moisture; characterized by chilly dampness.

Once, upon a *raw* and gusty day. *Shak.*, J. C., i. 2. 100.

Dreadful to me was the coming home in the *raw* twilight, with nipped fingers and toes.
Charlotte Brontë, Jane Eyre, i.

A *raw* mist rolled down upon the sea.
B. *Taylor*, Northern Travel, p. 15.

5. Crude or rude from want of experience, skill, or reflection; of immature character or quality; awkward; untrained; unfledged; ill-instructed or ill-considered: said of persons and their actions or ideas.

No newelle practised worshippinges alloweth he for hys, but vtterlye abhorreth them all as thinges *rawe* and unsauerye. *Bp. Bale*, Image, ii.

An opinion hath spread itself very far in the world, as if the way to be ripe in faith were to be *raw* in wit and judgment. *Hooker*, Eccles. Polity, iii. 8.

I have within my mind
A thousand *raw* tricks of these bragging Jacks,
Which I will practise. *Shak.*, M. of V., iii. 4. 77.

He had also a few other *raw* Seamen, but such as would have made better Landmen, they having served the King of Siam as Soldiers. *Dampier*, Voyages, II. i. 112.

His [Sherman's] division was at that time wholly *raw*, no part of it ever having been in an engagement.
U. S. Grant, Personal Memoirs, I. 338.

6. Looking like raw meat, as from lividness or removal of the skin; deprived or appearing destitute of the natural integument: as, a *raw* sore; a *raw* spot on a horse.

His cheeke-bones *raw*, and eie-pits hollow grew,
And brawney armes had lost their knowen might.
Spenser, F. Q., IV. xii. 20.

When *raw* flesh appeareth in him [a leper], he shall be unclean. Lev. xiii. 14.

Since yet thy cicatrice looks *raw* and red
After the Danish sword. *Shak.*, Hamlet, iv. 3. 62.

7. Feeling sore, as from abrasion of the skin; harshly painful; galled.

And all his sinews waxen weak and *raw*
Through long imprisonment.
Spenser, F. Q., I. x. 2.

Sec. Gent. Have you no fearful dreams?
Steph. Sometimes, as all have
That go to bed with *raw* and windy stomachs.
Fletcher, Pilgrim, iii. 7.

8. In *ceram.*, unbaked—that is, either fresh from the potters' wheel or the mold, or merely dried without the use of artificial heat.—**Raw edge**, that edge of any textile fabric which is not finished with a selvage, nor hemmed or bound or otherwise secured, and which is therefore liable to ravel out.—**Raw hide.** See *hide*[2] and *rawhide*.—**Raw material oil, sienna, silk**, etc. See the nouns.=**Syn.** *Raw, Crude.* These words, the same in ultimate origin and in earlier meaning, have drawn somewhat apart. *Raw* continues to apply to food which is not yet cooked, as *raw* potatoes; but *crude* has lost that meaning. *Raw* is applied to material not yet manufactured, as cotton, silk; *crude* rather to that which is not refined, as petroleum, or matured, as a theory or an idea.

II. *n.* **1.** A raw article, material, or product. Specifically—(*a*) An uncooked oyster, or an oyster of a kind preferred for eating raw: as, a plate of *raws*. [Colloq.] (*b*) Raw sugar. [Colloq. or trade use.]

The stock of *raws* on hand on the 31st of December, 1884, amounted to 1,000,000 kilograms.
U. S. Cons. Rep., No. lx. (1886), p. 96.

2. A raw, galled, or sore place; an established sore, as on a horse; hence, soreness or sensitiveness of feeling or temper. [Colloq.]

Like savage hackney coachmen, they know where there is a *raw*. *De Quincey*. (*Webster*.)

It's a tender subject, and every one has a *raw* on it.
Lever, Davenport Dunn.

Here is Baynes, . . . in a dreadfully wicked, murderous, and dissatisfied state of mind. His chafing, bleeding temper is one *raw*; his whole soul one rage and wrath.
Thackeray, Philip, xxvii.

3. In *bot.*, same as *rag*[1], 3 (*b*). [Prov. Eng.]—**To touch one on the raw**, to irritate one by alluding to or joking him about any matter in respect to which he is especially sensitive.

raw[2] (râ), *n.* An obsolete or dialectal form of *row*[2].

Clavers and his Highlandmen
Came down upo' the *raw*.
Battle of Killiecrankie (Child's Ballads, VII. 153).

rawbone† (râ'bōn), *a.* [< *raw*[1] + *bone*, *n.*] Same as *raw-boned*. *Spenser*, F. Q., IV. v. 34.

raw-boned (râ'bōnd), *a.* Having little flesh on the bones; lean and large-boned; gaunt.

Lean *raw-boned* rascals! who would e'er suppose
They had such courage and audacity?
Shak., 1 Hen. VI., i. 2. 35.

rawhead (râ'hed), *n.* **1.** A specter; a nursery bugbear of frightful aspect: usually coupled with *bloody-bones*.

I was told before
My face was bad enough; but now I look
Like Bloody-Bone and Raw-Head, to fright children.
Fletcher (*and another?*), Prophetess, iv. 4.

The indiscretion of servants, whose usual method is to awe children, and keep them in subjection, by telling them of *raw-head* and *bloody-bones*.
Locke, Education, § 138.

2. The cream which rises on the surface of raw milk, or milk that has not been heated. *Halliwell.* [Prov. Eng.]

rawhide (râ'hīd), *n.* and *a.* [< *raw*[1] + *hide*[1], *n.*] **I.** *n.* **1.** The material of untanned skins of cattle, very hard and tough when twisted in strips for ropes or the like, and dried.—**2.** A riding-whip made of twisted rawhide.

II. *a.* Made of rawhide: as, a *rawhide* whip.

rawish (râ'ish), *a.* [< *raw*[1] + *-ish*[1].] Somewhat raw; rather raw, in any sense of that word.

The *rawish* dank of clumsy winter.
Marston, Prol. to Antonio's Revenge.

rawly (râ'li), *adv.* **1.** In a raw, crude, unfinished, immature, or untempered manner; crudely; roughly.

Nothing is so prosaic as the *rawly* new.
W. W. Story, Roba di Roma, i.

2†. In an unprepared or unprovided state.

Some crying for a surgeon, some upon their wives left poor behind them, some upon the debts they owe, some upon their children *rawly* left. *Shak.*, Hen. V., iv. 1. 147.

rawness (râ'nes), *n.* [< ME. *rawenes*, *rawnesse*, *rownes*; < *raw*[1] + *-ness*.] **1.** The state or quality of being raw, in any sense.

Of what Comodity such vse of arte wilbe in our tounge may partely be seene by the scholasticall *rawnesse* of some newly Commen from the vniuersities.
Booke of Precedence (E. E. T. S., extra ser.), i. 2.

Much if not most of this *rawness* in the use of English must come, not merely from defective training in schools, but from defective training at home.'
The Nation, XLVIII. 392.

2†. Unprepared or precipitate manner; want of provision or foresight.

Why in that *rawness* left you wife and child, . . .
Without leave-taking? *Shak.*, Macbeth, iv. 3. 26.

rawnsake†, *v. t.* An old form of *ransack*.

raw-port (râ'pōrt), *n.* A port-hole in a small sailing vessel through which in a calm an oar can be worked.

raw-pot (râ'pot), *n.* A young crow. [Local, Irish.]

The crows . . . feeding the young *rawpots* that kicked up such a bobbery in their nests wid hunger.
Mrs. S. C. Hall, Sketches of Irish Char., p. 36.

rax (raks), *v.* [< ME. *raxen*, *roxen*, *rasken*, *rosken*, stretch oneself, < AS. **racsan*, *raxan*, stretch oneself after sleep; with formative *-s* (as in *cleanse*, *rinse*, etc.), from the root of *rack*[1], stretch: see *rack*[1].] **I.** *trans.* To stretch, or stretch out; reach out; reach or attain to; extend the hand to; hand: as, *rax* me ower the pitcher. [North. Eng. and Scotch.]

He raise, and *raxed* him where he stood,
And bade him match him with his marrows.
Raid of the Reidswire (Child's Ballads, VI. 134).

When ye gang to see a man that never did ye nae ill *raxing* a halter [that is, hanging].
Scott, Heart of Mid-Lothian, v.

So he *raxes* his hand across t' table, an' mutters summat as he grips mine. *Mrs. Gaskell*, Sylvia's Lovers, xliii.

II. *intrans.* To perform the act of reaching or stretching; stretch one's self; reach for or try to obtain something. [North. Eng. and Scotch.]

raxle†, *v. i.* [ME. *raxlen*, *roxlen*, *rasclen*, a var. or freq. of *raxen*, stretch: see *rax*.] To stretch one's self; rouse up from sleep. Compare *rax*.

I *raxled* & fel in gret affray [after a dream].
Alliterative Poems (ed. Morris), i. 1173.

Benedicite he by-gan with a bolke and hus brest knokede, *Rascled* and remed and routte at the laste.
Piers Plowman (C), viii. 7.

ray[1] (rā), *n.* [< ME. *raye*, < OF. *ray*, *rai*, *raid*, F. *rais*, a spoke, ray, = Pr. *rai*, *raig*, *rait*, spoke, ray, = Sp. *rayo*, a spoke, ray, thunderbolt, right line, radius, *radio*, radius, = Pg. *raio*, a spoke, ray, thunderbolt, *radio*, radius, = It. *razzo*, a spoke, ray, beam, *raggio*, a ray, beam, radius, *radio*, ray; also in fem., OF. *raie*, F. *raie*, a line, stroke, = Pr. Sp. *raya*, a line, streak, stroke, limit, boundary (see *ray*[2]); < L. *radius*, a staff, rod, a beam or ray, etc.: see *radius*.] **1.** Light emitted in a given direction from a luminous body; a line of light, or, more generally, of radiant energy; technically, the straight line perpendicular to the wave-front in the propagation of a light- or heat-wave. For different waves the rays may have different wave-lengths. Thus, in a pencil or beam of light, which is conceived to be made up of an indefinite number of rays, the rays all have the same wave-length if the beam is monochromatic; but if it is of white light, the wave-lengths of the rays vary by insensible degrees from that of red to that of violet light. (See *radiant energy* (under *energy*), *spectrum*.) A collection of parallel rays constitutes a *beam*; a collection of diverging or converging rays a *pencil*.

Full many a gem of purest *ray* serene
The dark, unfathomed caves of ocean bear.
Gray, Elegy.

2. A beam of intellectual light.

A *ray* of reason stole
Half through the solid darkness of his soul.
Pope, Dunciad, iii. 225.

3. A stripe; streak; line.

Wrought with little *raies*, streames, or streaks.
Baret, Alvearie, 1580.

4. In *geom.*, an unlimited straight line. As it is desirable to give the line different names according as it is conceived (1) as a locus of points, (2) as an intersection of planes, or (3) as an element of a plane, in 1865 the practice was begun of calling the unlimited straight line considered as a locus of points a *ray*. But as it was found that the word did not readily suggest that idea, owing to other associations, the practice was changed, and the line so considered is now called a *range*, while the word *ray* is taken to mean an unlimited straight line as an element of a plane. In older geometrical writings *ray* is synonymous with *radius*, while a line considered as a radial emanation is called a *beam*.

5. In *bot.*: (*a*) One of the branches or pedicels in an umbel. (*b*) The marginal part as opposed to the central part or disk in a head, umbel, or other flower-cluster, when there is a difference of structure, as in many *Compositæ* and in wild hydrangeas. (*c*) A ray-flower. (*d*) A radius. See *medullary rays*, under *medullary*.—**6.** One of the ray-like processes or arms of the *Radiata*, as of a starfish; a radiated or radiating part or organ; an actinomere. See cuts under *Asterias* and *Asteriidæ*.—**7.** One of the hard spinous or soft jointed processes which support and serve to extend the fin of a fish; a part of the skeleton of the fin; specifically, one which is articulated, thus contradistinguished from a hard or inarticulated one called specifically a *spine*; a fin-ray.—**8.** In *entom.*, one of the longitudinal nervures or veins of an insect's wing.—**9.** *pl.* In *her.*: (*a*) Long indentations or dents by which a heraldic line is broken, whether dividing two parts of the escutcheon or bounding any ordinary. Compare *radiant*, 3 (*a*). (*b*) A representation of rays, whether issuing from the sun or from a corner of the escutcheon, a cloud, or an ordinary. They are sometimes straight, sometimes waving, and sometimes alternately straight and waving; it is in the last form that they are usually represented when surrounding the sun.—**Branchial ray, branchiostegal rays.** See the adjectives.—**Calorific rays**, heat-rays. See *heat* and *spectrum*.—**Cone of rays.** See *cone*.—**Deviation of a ray of light.** See *deviation*.—**Direct rays.** See *direct illumination*, under *direct*.—**Divergent rays.** See *divergent*.

— **Extraordinary ray.** See *refraction.*— **Herschelian rays of the spectrum.** See *Herschelian.*— **Medullary rays.** (*a*) See *medullary.* (*b*) Bundles of straight or collecting tubules of the kidney contained in the cortex; the pyramids of Ferrein. See *tubule.*— **Obscure rays.** See *obscure* and *spectrum.*— **Ordinary ray.** See *refraction.*— **Principal ray.** See *principal.*— **Ritteric rays.** See *Ritteric.*— **Visual rays.** See *visual.*— **Cathode rays,** a form of radiation generated in a vacuum-tube, in connection with the cathode, or negative pole, when an electric discharge is passed through it.— **X-rays,** or **Röntgen rays,** a form of radiation having characteristic and distinctive properties, discovered by Professor Wilhelm Konrad Röntgen, of Würzburg (announced by him in December, 1895). He showed that the discharge of a large Ruhmkorff coil through a vacuum-tube produces a form of radiation external to the latter, which has the property of causing various substances to fluoresce; of affecting the ordinary photographic plate like light (though itself invisible); and of penetrating opaque bodies in various degrees, according to their density and relative thickness, platinum, lead, and silver being quite opaque, while aluminium, wood, and paper are quite transparent. He also found that these rays are not refracted by prisms of carbon disulphid, and that uncertain refraction occurs with vulcanized rubber prisms and those made of aluminium; that powdered substances, opaque to white light, are quite as transparent to these rays as solid bodies of equal mass; and that bodies having rough surfaces act like those whose surfaces are polished. These facts forced him to conclude that refraction and regular reflection do not exist, but that such bodies behave to X-rays as muddy media to light. Other conclusions were that these rays pass through all substances at the same speed; that air absorbs a very much smaller part of them than of cathode rays; that they are not deflected by a magnet; that the spot on the wall of the tube which fluoresces most decidedly is to be regarded as the principal point of their radiation; that when the cathode rays are deflected within the tube, the spot is changed, thus producing a new source of radiation; that, therefore, cathode rays and X-rays are not identical: that X-rays are rectilinearly propagated; that no interference phenomena of X-rays were found to exist; that the above facts tend to show that they have properties not hitherto known in connection with ultra-violet, visible, and infra-red light; and that, therefore, they do not consist of transverse vibrations of the ether, but of longitudinal vibrations. The source of X-rays has been shown to be the surface upon which the cathode rays first strike, whether that surface be the wall of the tube or an object placed within the tube: when this object within the tube is the anode itself, the emanations are most powerful. It has also been found that X-rays have the property, in common with ultra-violet light, of dispersing negative charges on insulated surfaces and the power of positively electrifying such surfaces; and that regular reflection, though weak, may be demonstrated by the use of the photographic plate and long exposure. Hertz had previously shown that cathode rays penetrate opaque bodies, and Lenard that such rays may pass through aluminium forming a part of the wall of the tube and affect the photographic plate, but that their absorption is excessive beyond a few millimeters from the aluminium window.

X-ray photograph of a foot in a shoe.

ray[1] (rā), *v.* [< OF. *raier,* F. *rayer,* mark with lines, streak, stripe, mark out, scratch, = Pr. *raiar* = Sp. *rayar,* form lines or strokes, streak, = Pg. *raiar,* radiate, sparkle, = It. *raggiare, razzare,* radiate, also Sp. Pg. *radiar* = It. *radiare,* radiate, sparkle; < L. *radiare,* furnish with spokes or beams, radiate, shine forth, < *radius,* a staff, rod, spoke of a wheel, ray, etc.: see *ray*[1], *n.,* and cf. *radiate.*] **I.** *trans.* **1.** To mark with long lines; form rays of or in.

> Unloved, the sun-flower, shining fair,
> *Ray* round with flames her disk of seed.
> *Tennyson,* In Memoriam, ci.

2. To shoot forth or emit; cause to shine out.

> Shines o'er the rest, the pastoral queen, and *rays*
> Her smiles, sweet-beaming, on her shepherd-king.
> *Thomson,* Summer, l. 401.

3†. To stripe.

> I wil yif him a feder bedde
> *Rayed* with golde.
> *Chaucer,* Death of Blanche, l. 252.

II. *intrans.* To shine forth or out as in rays.

> In a molten glory shrined
> That rays off into gloom. *Mrs. Browning.*

ray[2] (rā), *n.* [< ME. *raye,* < OF. *raie, raye,* F. *raie* = OCat. *raja* = Sp. *raya* = It. *raja, razza* (cf. ML. *ragadia*), < L. *rāia,* a ray; prob. orig. **ragia,* akin to D. *roch, rog* = LG. *ruche* (> LG. *roche*), a roach, a ray, = Dan. *rokke,* a ray, = AS. *reohhe, reohche* (glossed by ML. *fannus*), ME. *rehʒe, rohʒe,* a roach: see *roach*[1].] **1.** One of the elasmobranchiate fishes constituting the genus *Raia,* recognized by the flattened body, which becomes a broad disk from its union with the extremely broad and fleshy pectorals, which are joined to each other before or at the snout, and extend behind the two sides of the abdomen as far as the base of the ventrals, resembling the rays of a fan.— **2.** Any member of the order *Hypotremi, Batoidei,* or *Raiæ,* such as the sting-ray, eagle-ray, skate, torpedo, etc. See cuts under *Elasmobranchii, skate, sting-ray,* and *torpedo.*— **Beaked rays,** *Rhinobatidæ.*— **Clear-nosed ray,** *Raia eglanteria.*— **Cow-nosed ray,** *Rhinoptera quadriloba.* Also called *clam-cracker, corn-cracker, whipperee,* etc.— **Fuller or fuller's ray,** *Raia fullonica.*— **Horned ray,** a ray or batoid fish of the family *Cephalopteridæ* or *Mantidæ*: so called from the horn-like projections on the head. See cut under *devil-fish.*— **Painted ray.** See *painted.*— **Sandy ray,** *Raia circularis.*— **Starry ray** or **skate,** *Raia radiata.*— **Stingless rays,** *Anacanthidæ.*— **Torpedo rays,** *Torpedinidæ.* See *torpedo.* (See the generic and family names; also *bishop-ray, butterfly-ray, eagle-ray, sting-ray.*)

ray[3]† (rā), *n.* [< ME. *raye, ray,* < OF. *rei, rai, roi,* array: see *array,* of which *ray*[3] is in part an aphetic form.] Array; order; arrangement; rank; dress. *Mir. for Mags.,* I. 237.

ray[3]† (rā), *v. t.* [< ME. *rayen*; < *ray*[3], *n.* Cf. *array, v.,* of which *ray*[3] is in part an aphetic form. In def. 2, the same verb used (as *array* also was used) in an ironical application; hence, in comp., *beray.*] **1.** To array.— **2.** To beray with dirt or filth; daub; defile.

> Fie on . . . all foul ways! Was ever man so beaten? was ever man so *rayed*? *Shak.,* T. of the S., iv. 1. 3.

ray[4]† (rā), *n.* [Early mod. E. also *rey*; < ME. *raye*; prob. a particular application of *ray*[1], a stripe, line, etc.] A kind of striped cloth.

> Ich drow me among drapers, . . .
> Among the riche *rayes* ich rendered a lesson.
> *Piers Plowman* (C), vii. 217.

> Foure yards of broad Cloth, rowed or striped thwart with a different colour, to make him a Goune, and these were called *Rey* Gounes. *Stow,* Survey of London, p. 652.

ray[5] (rā), *n.* [Cf. MHG. *reige, reie, rei,* G. *reihen, reigen,* a kind of dance.] A kind of dance. *Halliwell.* [Prov. Eng.]

ray[6] (rā), *n.* [Origin obscure.] A certain disease of sheep, also called *scab, shab,* or *rubbers.*

ray[7]†, *n.* Same as *roy.*

Raya[1], **Rayah** (rä'yä), *n.* [= F. *rayah, raïa,* < Ar. *raiya,* pl. *ra'āyā,* people, peasants, subjects, cattle, < *ra'a,* pasture, feed; cf. *rānya,* flocks, herds. Cf. *ryot,* ult. the same word.] Any subject of the Sultan of Turkey who is not a Mohammedan.

raya[2] (rä'yä), *n.* [E. Ind.] An Indian broadthroat of the family *Eurylæmidæ, Psarisomus dalhousiæ,* inhabiting the Himalayas. The term is also one of the several generic designations which this species has received.

Rayah, *n.* See *Raya*[1].

rayat, rayatwari. See *ryot, ryotwar.*

rayed (rād), *a.* [< ME. *rayed, rayyd, rayid*; < *ray*[1] + *-ed*[2].] **1.** Having rays or ray-like processes, as a flower-head or an animal; specifically, in *zoöl.,* radiate.— **2.** Having rays (of this or that kind): as, a many-*rayed* fin; a soft-*rayed* fish.— **3**†. Striped.

> The sheriffs of London should give yearly *rayed* gowns to the recorder, chamberlain, etc.
> *Archæologia,* XXXIX. 367.

Rayed animals. See *Radiata.*

rayer† (rā'ėr), *n.* [< ME. *rayere,* < *raye,* striped cloth: see *ray*[4].] A seller of ray-cloth. *Piers Plowman.*

rayey (rā'i), *a.* [< *ray*[1] + *-ey* = *-y*[1].] Having or consisting of rays.

> The *rayey* fringe of her faire eyes. *Cotton,* Song.

ray-floret (rā'flō"ret), *n.* A ray-flower: used chiefly of *Compositæ.*

ray-flower (rā'flou"ėr), *n.* One of the flowers which collectively form the ray (see *ray*[1], 5 (*b*)); most often, one from the circle of ligulate flowers surrounding a disk of tubular flowers in the heads of many *Compositæ.*

ray-grass (rā'gràs), *n.* A good forage-grass, *Lolium perenne.* Also *rye-grass.*

rayket, raylet. See *rake*[2], *rail.*

rayless (rā'les), *a.* [< *ray*[1] + *-less.*] **1.** Without rays or radiance; unilluminated; lightless; dark; somber; gloomy. *Young,* Night Thoughts, i. 19.— **2.** In *bot.* and *zoöl.,* having no rays or ray-like parts.

raymet, *v. i.* A Middle English form of *roam.*

Raymond's blue. See *blue.*

Raynaud's disease. See *disease.*

Raynaud's gangrene. Same as *Raynaud's disease.*

rayne[1]†, **rayne**[2]†. See *rain*[1], *reign.*

ray-oil (rā'oil), *n.* Oil prepared from the livers of batoid fishes or rays.

rayon† (rā'on), *n.* [< F. *rayon,* a ray, beam, < *rais,* a ray: see *ray*[1].] A beam or ray. *Spenser,* Visions of Bellay (ed. 1591), ll.

rayonnant (rā'o-nant), *a.* [< F. *rayonnant,* ppr. of *rayonner,* radiate, shine, < *rayon,* a ray: see *rayon.*] Radiating; arranged in the direction of rays issuing from a center. Decoration is often said to be *rayonnant* when, as in the case of a round dish or other circular object, the surface is divided into panels growing larger as they approach the circumference, and bounded by the radii and by arcs of larger and smaller circles.

rayonned (rā'ond), *a.* [< *rayon* + *-ed*[2].] Same as *rayonnant.*

raze[1] (rāz), *v. t.* See *rase*[1].

raze[2]†, *n.* An obsolete form of *race*[4].

raze[3] (rāz), *n.* [Origin obscure.] A swinging fence set up in a watercourse to prevent the passage of cattle. *Halliwell.* [Prov. Eng.]

razed (rāzd), *p. a.* [Pp. of *raze*[1], *v.*] In *her.,* same as *ragged,* 7.

razee (ra-zē'), *n.* [< F. *rasé,* cut down (*vaisseau rasé,* a vessel cut down), pp. of *raser,* shave, rase: see *rase*[1], *raze*[1].] A ship of war cut down to a smaller size by reducing the number of decks.

razee (ra-zē'), *v. t.* [< *razee, n.*] To cut down or reduce to a lower class, as a ship; hence, to lessen or abridge by cutting out parts: as, to *razee* a book or an article.

razor (rā'zor), *n.* [Early mod. E. also *rasour, raser*; < ME. *rasour, rasoure, rasowre, rasure,* a razor, < OF. (and F.) *rasoir* = Pr. *razor* = OCat. *rasó* = It. *rasoio,* < ML. *rasorium,* a razor (cf. *rasorius,* razor-fish), < L. *radere,* pp. *rasus,* scrape, shave: see *rase*[1], *raze*[1].] **1.** A sharp-edged instrument used for shaving the face or head. The blade is usually made with a thick rounded back, sides hollowed or sloping to a very thin edge, and a tang by which it is pivoted to and swings freely in a two-leafed handle. The tang has a prolongation by the aid of which the razor is firmly grasped and controlled. There are also razors formed on the principle of the carpenters' plane, by the use of which the risk of cutting the skin is avoided. In Eastern countries razors are made with an immovable handle continuous with the blade. Compare *rattler,* 5.

Cross-sections of Razors.

a and *b,* ordinary forms; *c,* section known as "half-rattler"; *d,* backed razor.

2. A tusk: as, the *razors* of a boar. *Johnson.*— **Occam's razor,** the principle that the unnecessary supposition that things of a peculiar kind exist, when the observed facts may be equally well explained on the supposition that no such things exist, is unwarranted (*Entia non sunt multiplicanda præter necessitatem*). So called after William of Occam (died about 1349); but, as a historical fact, Occam does not make much use of this principle, which belongs rather to the contemporary nominalist William Durand de St. Pourçain (died 1332).

razorable† (rā'zor-a-bl), *a.* [< *razor* + *-able.*] Fit to be shaved.

> Till new-born chins
> Be rough and *razorable.*
> *Shak.,* Tempest, ii. 1. 250.

razorback (rā'zor-bak), *n.* **1.** A rorqual, finfish, or finner-whale, of the family *Balænopteridæ.*— **2.** A hog whose back has somewhat the form of a sharp ridge. This formation, accompanied by long legs, is characteristic of breeds of hogs that have long been allowed to run wild in woods and waste places and feed upon mast, wild fruits, etc. The flesh of such swine, particularly that of the hams, is usually of superior quality for the table.

razor-backed (rā'zor-bakt), *a.* **1.** Having a sharp back; hog-backed: as, the *razor-backed* buffalo, a fish, *Ictiobus urus,* of the Mississippi valley.— **2.** Having a long sharp dorsal fin which cuts the water like a razor, as the rorqual.

razorbill (rā'zor-bil), *n.* **1.** The razor-billed auk, or tinker, *Alca* or *Utamania torda,* so called from the deep, compressed, and trenchant bill. The bill is feathered for about one half its length, in the rest of its extent being vertically furrowed, and hooked at the

Razorbill (*Alca torda*), in winter plumage.

tip; one of the furrows is white, the bill being otherwise black, like the feet; the mouth is yellow. The plumage is black on the upper parts, the lower parts from the neck in summer, and from the bill in winter, being white; there is a narrow white line from the bill to the eye, and the tips of the secondaries are white. The bird is about 18 inches long, and 27 in extent of wings. It inhabits arctic and northerly regions of both hemispheres, subsists chiefly on fish, and nests on rocky sea-coasts, laying a single egg about 3 by 2 inches, white or whitish, spotted and blotched with different shades of brown. The flesh is eatable.

2. The skimmer or cutwater, *Rhynchops nigra*. See *skimmer* and *Rhynchops*.

razor-billed (rā'zor-bild), *a.* Having a bill likened to a razor in any way: specifically noting certain birds.—**Razor-billed auk.** See *razorbill*, 1.—**Razor-billed curassow**, a bird of the genus *Mitua*, as *M. tuberosa* of Guiana.

razorblade (rā'zor-blād), *n.* A long, slim oyster. [Connecticut.]

razor-clam (rā'zor-klam), *n.* A bivalve mollusk of the family *Solenidæ*, especially of the genera *Ensis*, *Solen*, or *Siliqua*; a razor-fish or razor-shell: so called from its shape. See cut under *Ensis*.

razor-fish (rā'zor-fish), *n.* 1. A fish of the family *Labridæ*, *Xyrichthys lineatus*, of the West Indies, occasional on the southern coast of the United States.—2. A related fish, *Xyrichthys novacula*, of the Mediterranean.—3. A razor-clam: so called from the shape of the shell, which resembles a razor. The common razor-fish of Great Britain is *Ensis siliqua*, also called *spout-fish* and *razor-shell*. *Siliqua patula* is a Californian species, used for food.

razor-grass (rā'zor-gràs), *n.* A West Indian nut-rush, *Scleria scindens*, with formidable cutting leaves.

razor-grinder (rā'zor-grīn"dėr), *n.* The nightjar: same as *grinder*, 3.

razor-hone (rā'zor-hōn), *n.* A fine hone used for sharpening or setting razors. See *hone*[1].

razor-paper (rā'zor-pā"pėr), *n.* Smooth unsized paper coated on one side with a composition of powdered crocus and emery, designed as a substitute for a strop.

razor-paste (rā'zor-pāst), *n.* A paste of emery-powder or the like, for spreading on the surface of a razor-strop to give it its sharpening property.

razor-shell (rā'zor-shel), *n.* The shell of a razor-fish; a bivalve mollusk of the genera *Ensis*, *Solen*, or *Siliqua*: so called from the shape of the shell, which resembles a razor. Compare *razor-fish*, 3.

razor-stone (rā'zor-stōn), *n.* Same as *novaculite*.

razor-strop (rā'zor-strop), *n.* An implement for sharpening razors. See *strop*. Also called *razor-strap*.

razure† (rā'zhūr), *n.* [= F. *rasure*, < L. *rasura*, < *radere*, pp. *rasus*, scrape: see *rase*[1], *raze*[1].] See *rasure*.

razzia (rat'si-ä), *n.* [< F. *razzia* = Pg. *gazia*, *gazira*, a raid, < Algerian Ar. *ghazia* (Turk. *ghazya*) (pron. nearly *razia* in Algiers, the initial letter *gh* being represented by the F. r *grasséyé*), a military expedition against infidels, a crusade, a military incursion.] Properly, a military raid intended for the subjection or punishment of hostile or rebellious people by the carrying off of cattle, destruction of crops, etc.; by extension, any plundering or destructive incursion in force. Razzias were formerly common in Arabian countries. They were practised by the Turkish authorities in Algeria and other provinces against tribes or districts which refused to pay taxes; and the word was adopted, and the practice continued for a time, by the French in Algeria after its conquest.

> It was probable he should hand the troops over to John Jones for the *razzia* against the Moulvie.
>
> *W. H. Russell*, Diary in India, II. 27.

Rb. The chemical symbol of *rubidium*.

R. C. An abbreviation of *Roman Catholic*.

R. D. An abbreviation (*a*) of *Royal Dragoons*; (*b*) of *Rural Dean*.

R. E. An abbreviation (*a*) of *Royal Engineers*; (*b*) of *Royal Exchange*.

re[1] (rā), *n.* [See *gamut*.] In *solmization*, the syllable used for the second tone of the scale. In the scale of C this tone is D—a tone which is therefore sometimes called *re* in France and Italy.

re[2] (rē), *n.* [L., abl. of *res*, thing, case, matter, affair: see *res*[2].] A word used in legal language in the phrase *in re*: as, '*in re* Bardell vs. Pickwick,' in the case of Bardell against Pickwick: often elliptically *re*: as, *re* Bardell vs. Pickwick; *re* Brown.

re-. [ME. *re-* = OF. *re-*, F. *re-*, *ré-* = Sp. Pg. *re-* = It. *re-*, *ri-*, < L. *re-*; before a vowel or *h* generally *red-*, but later also *re-* (the form *red-* also occurring in *red-dere*, render, and, assimilated, in *rel-ligio*, religion, *rel-liquiæ*, relics, *rec-cidere*, fall back, and with a connecting vowel in *redi-vivus*, living again), an inseparable prefix, back, again, against: see def. The OF. and It. form *re-* often appears as *ra-* by confusion with the true *ra-* (< L. *re-* + *ad-*), and the following consonant is often doubled, as in OF. *reppeller*, < L. *repellere*, repel; It. *rappresentare*, < L. *repræsentare*, represent; etc. Words with the prefix *ra-* in OF. usually appear with *re-* in E., except when the accent has receded, as in *rally*[1].] An inseparable prefix of Latin origin (before a vowel usually in the form *red-*), meaning 'back,' 'again.' It occurs in a great number of verbs and derived adjectives and nouns taken from the Latin, and is also common as an English formative. It denotes (*a*) a turning back ('back'), as in *recede*, *recur*, *remit*, *repel*, etc.; (*b*) opposition ('against'), as in *reluctant*, *repugnant*, etc.; (*c*) restoration to a former state ('back,' 'again,' English *un-*[2]), as in *restitution*, *relegate*, *redintegrate* or *reintegrate*, and with some words of non-Latin origin, as in *recall*, *remind*, *renew*, etc.; (*d*) transition to an opposite state, as in *reprobate*, *retract*, *reveal*, etc.; (*e*) repetition of an action ('again'), as in *revise*, *resume*, etc., becoming in this use an extremely common English formative, applicable to any English verb whatever, whether of Latin origin, as in *react*, *reënter*, *recreate*, *readdress*, *reappear*, *reproduce*, *reunite*, etc., or of Anglo-Saxon or other origin, as in *rebind*, *rebuild*, *redye*, *refill*, *refit*, *reheat*, *relight*, *reline*, *reload*, *reset*, *rewrite*, etc. In many words taken from the Latin, either directly or through the Old French, the force of *re-* (*red-*) has been lost, or is not distinctly felt, in English, as in *receive*, *reception*, *recommend*, *recover*[2], *reduce*, *redeem*, *recuperate*, *recreate*[1], *refer*, *rejoice*, *relate*, *religion*, *remain*, *renown*, *repair*[1], *repair*[2], *report*, *request*, *require*, and other words containing a radical element not used in the particular sense concerned, or not used at all, in English. Some of these words, as *recover*[2], *recreate*[1], are distinguished from English formations with the clear prefix *re-*, again, often written distinctively with a hyphen, as in *re-cover*, *re-create*, etc. In many instances the prefix, by shifting of accent and change of sound, or loss of adjacent elements, loses the character of a prefix, as in *rebel*, *a.*, *relic*, *relict*, *remnant*, *rest*[2], *restive*, etc., and in words from Old French in which the prefix *re-* combines with the prefix *a-* in the form *ra-*, not recognized as an English prefix, as in *rally*[1], *rabate*, etc. In some other words also *re-* is reduced to *r-*, as in *ransom* (doublet of *redemption*), *rampart*, *rencounter*, etc. The prefix *re-* is found in many words formed in Old French from non-Latin elements, as in *regret*, *regard*, *reward*, etc. As an English formative *re-* may be prefixed to a primitive verb, adjective, or noun, or to derivatives, indifferently, and such secondary forms as *reëstablishment*, *reaction*, etc., may be analyzed either as *re-* + *establishment*, *re-* + *action*, etc., or as *reëstablish* + *-ment*, *react* + *-ion*, etc. Prefixed to a word beginning with *e*, *re-* is separated by a hyphen, as *re-establish*, *re-estate*, *re-edify*, etc.; or else the second *e* has a dieresis over it: as, *reëstablish*, *reëmbark*, etc. The hyphen is also sometimes used to bring out emphatically the sense of repetition or iteration: as, *sung* and *re-sung*. The dieresis is not used over other vowels than *e* when *re-* is prefixed: thus, *reinforce*, *reunite*, *reabolish*.

reabsorb (rē-ab-sôrb'), *v. t.* [= F. *réabsorber*; as *re-* + *absorb*.] To draw or take in anew by absorption, imbibition, or swallowing, as something previously ejected, emitted, or put forth.

> During the embryo stage of the higher vertebrata temporary organs appear, serve their purpose awhile, and are subsequently *reabsorbed*.
>
> *H. Spencer*, Social Statics, p. 458.

reabsorption (rē-ab-sôrp'shon), *n.* [= F. *réabsorption*; as *re-* + *absorption*.] The act of reabsorbing, or the state of being reabsorbed.

reaccommodate† (rē-a-kom'ō-dāt), *v. t.* [< *re-* + *accommodate*.] To readjust; resettle; bring into renewed order.

> King Edward, . . . discovering the Disturbance made by the Change of Place, instantly sends to charge that Part, without giving them Time to *re-accommodate* themselves.
>
> *Baker*, Chronicles, p. 121.

reaccuse (rē-a-kūz'), *v. t.* [< *re-* + *accuse*.] To accuse again or afresh; make a renewed accusation against.

> Her'ford, . . . who *re-accus'd*
> Norfolk for words of treason he had us'd.
>
> *Daniel*, Civil Wars, i. 60.

reach[1] (rēch), *v.*; pret. and pp. *reached* (formerly *raught*), ppr. *reaching*. [Also dial., with shortened vowel, *retch*, and unassibilated *reek*; < ME. *rechen* (pret. *raughte*, *raghte*, *raght*, *rehte*, *reahte*, pp. *raught*, *raugt*), < AS. *rǣcan*, *rǣcean* (pret. *rǣhte*), reach, get into one's power, = OFries. *reka*, *retsia*, *resza* = MD. *reijcken*, D. *reiken* = MLG. *reken*, LG. *reiken* = OHG. *reihhen*, *reichen*, MHG. G. *reichen*, reach, extend, stretch out. The word has been more or less associated with the group to which belong *rack*[1], *rake*[1], *rax*, *retch*[1], etc., Goth. *rakjan*, etc., stretch, and L. *reg-ere*, *por-rigere*, Gr. ὀρέγειν, stretch, but an orig. connection is on phonetic grounds improbable.] **I.** *trans.* 1. To hold or stretch forth; extend outward.

> *Reach* hither thy finger, and behold my hands; and *reach* hither thy hand, and thrust it into my side.
>
> John xx. 27.

> He shall flourish,
> And, like a mountain cedar, *reach* his branches
> To all the plains about him.
>
> *Shak.*, Hen. VIII., v. 5. 53.

> To his
> She *reached* her hands, and in one bitter kiss
> Tasted his tears.
>
> *William Morris*, Earthly Paradise, II. 307.

2. To deliver by or as if by the outstretched hand; hand out or over; extend out to.

> First, Christ took the bread in his hands; secondarily, he gave thanks; thirdly, he broke it; fourthly, he *raught* it them, saying, Take it.
>
> *Tyndale*, Ans. to Sir T. More, etc. (Parker Soc., 1850), [p. 241.

> The prince he *reacht* Robin Hood a blow.
>
> *Robin Hood and the Stranger* (Child's Ballads, v. 415).

> *Reach* a chair;
> So; now, methinks, I feel a little ease.
>
> *Shak.*, Hen. VIII., iv. 2. 3.

> I stand at one end of the room, and *reach* things to her woman.
>
> *Steele*, Spectator, No. 137.

3. To make a stretch to; bring into contact by or as if by stretching out the hand; attain to by something held or stretched out: as, to *reach* a book on a shelf; to *reach* an object with a cane.

> He slough man and horse whom that he *raught* with his axe that he heilde with bothe hondes.
>
> *Merlin* (E. E. T. S.), ii. 288.

> Wilt thou *reach* stars, because they shine on thee?
>
> *Shak.*, T. G. of V., iii. 1. 156.

4. To take, seize, or move by stretching out the hand, or by other effort.

> Than Troiell with tene the tourfer beheld, . . .
> *Reiches* his reynis & his roile [rowel] strykes,
> Caires to the kyng with a kant wille.
>
> *Destruction of Troy* (E. E. T. S.), l. 10215.

> The damesell hym thanked, and *raught* hym vp be the honde.
>
> *Merlin* (E. E. T. S.), iii. 697.

> Lest therefore his now bolder hand
> *Reach* also of the tree of life, and eat,
> And live for ever.
>
> *Milton*, P. L., xi. 94.

5. To attain to by movement or progress; arrive at, physically or mentally; come or get to: as, to *reach* a port or destination; to *reach* high office or distinction; to *reach* a conclusion by study or by reasoning.

> And through the Tyrrhene Sea, by strength of toiling oars,
> *Raught* Italy at last.
>
> *Drayton*, Polyolbion, i. 325.

> He must have *reached* a very advanced age.
>
> *Barham*, Ingoldsby Legends, I. 98.

> He [Dante] has shown us the way by which that country far beyond the stars may be *reached*.
>
> *Lowell*, Among my Books, 2d ser., p. 124.

6. To extend to in continuity or scope; stretch or be prolonged so as to extend to, literally or figuratively; attain to contact with or action upon; penetrate to.

> There is no mercy in mankind can *reach* me.
>
> *Fletcher*, Bonduca, iv. 3.

> Thy desire . . . leads to no excess
> That *reaches* blame, but rather merits praise.
>
> *Milton*, P. L., iii. 697.

> The loss might be repaired again; or, if not, could not however destroy us by *reaching* us in our greatest and highest concern.
>
> *South*, Sermons, II. i.

> When he addresses himself to battle against the guardian angels, he stands like Teneriffe or Atlas; his stature *reaches* the sky.
>
> *Carlyle.*

7. To come or get at; penetrate or obtain access to; extend cognizance, agency, or influence to: as, to *reach* a person through his vanity.

> The fewness and fulness of his [George Fox's] words have often struck even strangers with admiration, as they used to *reach* others with consolation.
>
> *Penn*, Rise and Progress of Quakers, v.

> It is difficult indeed in some places to *reach* the sense of the inspired writers.
>
> *Bp. Atterbury*, Sermons, II. ix.

> He [Atterbury] could be *reached* only by a bill of pains and penalties.
>
> *Macaulay*, Francis Atterbury.

8†. To attain to an understanding of; succeed in comprehending.

> But how her fawning partner fell I *reach* not,
> Unless caught by some springe of his own setting.
>
> *Middleton*, Women Beware Women, v. 1.

> *Sir P.* I *reach* you not.
> *Lady P.* Right, sir, your policy
> May bear it through thus.
>
> *B. Jonson*, Volpone, iv. 1.

II. *intrans.* 1. To stretch; have extent in course or direction; continue to or toward a term, limit, or conclusion.

> By hym that *rauhte* on rode [the cross].
>
> *Piers Plowman* (C), v. 179.

> And he dreamed, and behold a ladder set up on the earth, and the top of it *reached* to heaven.
>
> Gen. xxviii. 12.

> Thus far the fable *reaches* of Proteus, and his flock, at liberty and unrestrained.
>
> *Bacon*, Physical Fables, vii., Expl.

They [consequences] *reach* only to those of their posterity who abet their forefathers' crime, and continue in their infidelity. *Bp. Atterbury*, Sermons, II. v.

There are the wide-*reaching* views of fruitful valleys and of empurpled hill-sides.
D. G. Mitchell, Wet Days at Edgewood, Pliny's Country [Places.

In the distance . . . the mountains *reach* away in faint and fainter shades of purple and brown.
Harper's Weekly, Jan. 19, 1889.

2. To extend in amount or capacity; rise in quantity or number; amount; suffice: with *to* or *unto*.

What may the king's whole battle [army] *reach unto*?
Shak., 1 Hen. IV., iv. 1. 129.

Every one was to pay his part according to his proportion towards ye purchass, & all other debts, what ye profite of ye trade would not *reach* too.
Bradford, Plymouth Plantation, p. 215.

A very exceptional grant was made, two fifteenths and tenths first, and then another sum of the same amount, *reaching*, according to Lord Bacon, *to* £120,000.
Stubbs, Medieval and Modern Hist., p. 300.

3. To make a stretch to or toward something, as with the hand or by exertion; stretch forward or onward; make a straining effort: as, to *reach* out for an apple; to *reach* at or after gain.

Ful semely after hire mete she *raughte*.
Chaucer, Gen. Prol. to C. T., l. 136.

He slytte the sheilde as fer as that he *raught*, and the kynge Ban seute hym a stroke with Corsheuse, his goode swerde. *Merlin* (E. E. T. S.), ii. 344.

One may *reach* deep enough, and yet
Find little. *Shak.*, T. of A., iii. 4. 15.

Oft the first that (without right or reason)
Attempt Rebellion and do practice Treason,
And so at length are iustly tumbled down
Beneath the foot, that *raught* aboue the Crown.
Sylvester, tr. of Du Bartas's Weeks, i. 1.

Why was I not contented? Wherefore *reach*
At things which, but for thee, O Latmian!
Had been my dreary death? *Keats*, Endymion, iii.

4. To attain; arrive; get, as to a point, destination, or aim.

Festus, . . . whose ears were unacquainted with such matter, heard him [the apostle Paul], but could not *reach* unto that whereof he spake. *Hooker*, Eccles. Polity, iii. 8.

The wind being very great at S. W., he could *reach* no farther than Cape Ann harbour that night.
Winthrop, Hist. New England, I. 115.

5†. To turn; start forth.

Up he sterte, and on his weye he *raughte*,
Til she agayn hym by the lappe caughte.
Chaucer, Troilus, ii. 447.

6. *Naut.*, to sail with the wind free.

reach[1] (rēch), *n.* [‹ *reach*[1], *v.*] 1. A continuous stretch or course; an uninterrupted line of extension or continuity: as, a *reach* of level ground; an inland *reach* of the sea; a *reach* of a river (a straight course between bends); a *reach* of a canal (the part between locks, having a uniform level).

And, on the left hand, hell
With long *reach* interposed. *Milton*, P. L., x. 322.

The silver Phea's glittering rills they lost,
And skimm'd along by Elis' sacred coast,
Then cautious through the rocky *reaches* wind,
And, turning sudden, shun the death designed.
Pope, Odyssey, xv.

We walk'd
Beside the river's wooded *reach*.
Tennyson, In Memoriam, lxxi.

2. Limit or scope of stretch or extension; power of reaching by the outstretched hand or any other agency; the act of or capacity for reaching: as, the *reach* of the arm; to be within one's *reach*, or within the *reach* of the law.

All others have a dependent being, and within the *reach* of destruction. *Sir T. Browne*, Urn-burial, v.

Out of the *reach* of danger, he [Junius] has been bold; out of the *reach* of shame, he has been confident.
Johnson, Thoughts on late Trans. in the Falkland Islands.

Poor the *reach*,
The undisguised extent, of mortal sway!
Wordsworth, Canute and Alfred, on the Sea-Shore.

The study of spectra has opened a new world of research, and added some such *reach* to our physics and chemistry as the telescope brought to vision.
C. A. Young, The Sun, p. 67.

Most of the villages of Egypt are situated upon eminences of rubbish, which rise a few feet above the *reach* of the inundation. *E. W. Lane*, Modern Egyptians, I. 24.

3. Effective extent or scope; range of capacity or ability; power of accomplishment; grasp; penetration; comprehension.

Men more audacious and precipitant then of solid and deep *reach*. *Milton*, Reformation in Eng., ii.

Be sure yourself and your own *reach* to know,
How far your genius, taste, and learning go.
Pope, Essay on Criticism, l. 153.

Groves that inspire the Nightingale to trill
And modulate, with subtle *reach* of skill
Elsewhere unmatched, her ever-varying lay.
Wordsworth, Sonnets, iii. 6.

His [Wordsworth's] mind had not that *reach* and elemental movement of Milton's.
Lowell, Among my Books, 2d ser., p. 241.

4. A reaching out for something; forecast in aim or purpose; a scheme of effort for some end.

I have brains
That beat above your *reaches*.
Fletcher, Mad Lover, i. 1.

The Duke of Parma had particular *reaches* and ends of his own underhand to cross the design. *Bacon*.

Others
Think heaven a world too high for our low *reaches*.
Chapman, Cæsar and Pompey, iv. 3.

5. The pole connecting the rear axle to the bolster of a wagon or other vehicle; a coupling-pole. See cut under *hound*, 7.—6. *Naut.*, the distance sailed between tacks: same as *board*, 13 (*c*).—7. An extended point of land; a promontory. [Local, U. S.]—**Head reach**, the distance to windward traversed by a vessel while tacking.

reach[2] (rēch), *v.* A variant of *retch*[2]. [Prov. Eng.]

reachable (rē'cha-bl), *a.* [‹ *reach*[1] + *-able*.] Capable of being reached; within reach.

reacher (rē'chėr), *n.* 1. One who or that which reaches, or is capable of or serves for reaching.

Hold in your rapier; for, though I have not a long *reacher*, I have a short hitter.
Greene and Lodge, Looking Glass for Lond. and Eng.

He . . . spoke to *Jennings*, the *reacher* of the records, that he should let him have any record.
Life of A. Wood, p. 205.

2†. An exaggeration; a "stretcher." [Slang.]

I can hardly believe that *reacher*, which another writeth of him, that "with the palms of his hands he could touch his knees, though he stood upright."
Fuller, Worthies, Monmouthshire, II. 435.

reaching-post (rē'ching-pōst), *n.* In *rope-making*, a post fixed in the ground at the lower end of a rope-walk.

reachless (rēch'les), *a.* [‹ *reach*[1] + *-less*.] Beyond reach; unattainable; lofty.

To raise her silent and inglorious name
Unto a *reachlesse* pitch of praises hight.
Bp. Hall, A Defiance to Envy.

reach-me-down (rēch'mē-doun'), *a.* [‹ *reach*[1], *v.*, + *me*, indirect object, + *down*[1], *adv.* Cf. *pick-me-up*.] Ready-made. [Colloq., Eng.]

You know in the Palais Royal they hang out the most splendid *reach-me-down* dressing-gowns, waistcoats, and so forth. *Thackeray*, Philip, xxiv.

reacquite† (rē-a-kwīt'), *v. t.* [‹ *re-* + *acquite*.] To pay back; give a return to or for; requite.

You shall assuredly find the gentleman very honest and thankful, and me ready to *re-acquite* your courtesy and favour to him so shewn, in that I possibly may.
G. *Harvey*, Four Letters, i.

react (rē-akt'), *v.* [‹ *re-* + *act*, *v.* Cf. F. *réagir*, react.] I. *trans.* To act or perform anew; reenact: as, to *react* a play.

II. *intrans.* 1. To exert, as a thing acted upon, an opposite action upon the agent.

If fire doth heate water, the water *reacteth* againe . . . upon the fire and cooleth it.
Sir K. Digby, Treatise of Bodies (1644), xvi.

Great minds do indeed *re-act* on the society which has made them what they are; but they only pay with interest what they have received. *Macaulay*, Dryden.

Every opinion *reacts* on him who utters it. It is a thread-ball thrown at a mark, but the other end remains in the thrower's bag. *Emerson*, Compensation.

2. To act, after being acted upon, in a manner directly opposed to the first action, and in increased measure. Thus, when the body has been chilled by a bath, it is said to *react* in becoming warmer than before; and, in like manner, when misfortune stimulates the mind to greater efforts, the mind is said to *react*. 3. To act mutually or reciprocally upon each other, as two or more chemical agents.

reaction (rē-ak'shon), *n.* [= F. *réaction* = Sp. *reaccion* = Pg. *reacção* = It. *reazione*; as *re-* + *action*.] 1. Any action in resistance or response to the influence of another action or power; reflexive action or operation; an opposed impulse or impression.

Of *reaction* in locall motion, that each agent must suffer in acting and act in suffering.
Sir K. Digby, Treatise of Bodies (1644), xvi.

Sense being nothing else, as some conceit, but motion, or rather *re-action* of a body pressed upon by another body. *Dr. H. More*, Immortal. of Soul (1662), i. 12.

Attack is the *re-action*; I never think I have hit hard, unless it re-bounds. *Johnson*, in Boswell, an. 1775.

Every trespass produces a *reaction*, partly general and partly special—a *reaction* which is extreme in proportion as the trespass is great. *H. Spencer*, Social Statics, p. 484.

2. In *dynamics*, a force called into being along with another force, being equal and opposite to it. All forces exist in pairs: and it is a fundamental law (Newton's third law of motion) in mechanics that "action and reaction are always equal and contrary," or that the mutual actions of two bodies are always equal and exerted in opposite directions. This law was announced, in the form that the quantity of motion is preserved in all percussion, simultaneously in 1660 by Christian Huygens, John Wallis, and Sir Christopher Wren, but was experimentally proved by Wallis only.

3. Action contrary to a previous influence, generally greater than the first effect; in *politics*, a tendency to revert from a more to a less advanced policy, or the contrary.

The violent *reaction* which had laid the Whig party prostrate was followed by a still more violent *reaction* in the opposite direction. *Macaulay*, Hist. Eng., ii.

4. In *chem.*, the mutual or reciprocal action of chemical agents upon each other.—**Achilles tendon reaction**, the contraction of the calf-muscles evoked by tapping the Achilles tendon.—**Amphigenous, amphoteric, etc., reaction.** See the adjectives.—**Color-reaction**, in *chem.*, a reaction which causes a characteristic development or change of color: used in testing.—**Diazo-reaction.** Same as *Ehrlich's reaction*.—**Ehrlich's reaction**, a reaction in the urine of typhoid and other patients in which it strikes a deep dark red on being treated with a mixture containing sodium nitrite, sulphanilic acid, and hydrochloric acid, and alkalinized with ammonia. Also called *Ehrlich's test*, and *diazo-reaction*.—**Law of action and reaction.** See *action*.—**Paradoxical reaction.** See *paradoxical*.—**Reaction of degeneration**, a modification of the normal reaction of nerve and muscle to electric stimuli, observable in cases where the lesion lies in the motor nerve or its immediate central or peripheral terminations. The complete form presents (*a*) total loss of irritability of the nerve below the lesion; (*b*) on direct stimulation of the muscle, (1) loss of irritability for very brief currents, such as induction-shocks; (2) retention and even increase of irritability for making and breaking of currents of longer duration (this galvanic irritability also becomes lost in the terminal stages of the severest forms); (3) increase of irritability for making currents at the anode as compared with the cathode, so that the anode closing contraction may exceed the cathode closing contraction; (4) a sluggishness of contraction and relaxation.

reactionary (rē-ak'shon-ā-ri), *a.* and *n.* [= F. *réactionnaire*; as *reaction* + *-ary*.] I. *a.* 1. Of or pertaining to reaction in general; consisting of or characterized by reflex or reciprocal action; reactive.

The *reactionary* excitement that gave her a proud self-mastery had not subsided.
George Eliot, Mill on the Floss, vi. 10.

Specifically—2. Of or pertaining to political reaction; favoring reaction: as, *reactionary* principles or movements.

The poverty and suffering of millions of the working classes came in aid of the *reactionary* party and the more egotistical line of policy.
W. R. Greg, Misc. Essays, 1st ser., p. 33.

II. *n.*; pl. *reactionaries* (-riz). A promoter of reaction; specifically, one who attempts to check, undo, or reverse political action.

The *reactionaries* and conservatives of Sweden—and there are many of them in this old country—are afraid that free Norway will lead Sweden into the path of reforms.
Harper's Mag., LXXVIII. 804.

reactionist (rē-ak'shon-ist), *n.* [‹ *reaction* + *-ist*.] A favorer of reaction; an advocate of old methods or principles; a reactionary.

Those who are not afraid of the nickname of *reactionists* will be slow to condemn her [Austria] for the maintenance of a principle on which she has grown into power.
Stubbs, Medieval and Modern Hist., p. 239.

reaction-period (rē-ak'shon-pē"ri-od), *n.* Same as *reaction-time*.

reaction-time (rē-ak'shon-tīm), *n.* The time between the application of a stimulus and some reaction, as when a signal is rendered on the perception of some sensation. The *reduced reaction-time* is the part of this which is consumed in perception and willing, as distinct from what is consumed in transmission and in the period of muscular latency.

reaction-wheel (rē-ak'shon-hwēl), *n.* See *turbine*.

reactive (rē-ak'tiv), *a.* [= F. *réactif*; as *react* + *-ive*.] Pertaining to or causing reaction; acting reflexively or reciprocally; resulting from reflex action.

Ye fish, assume a voice, with praises fill
The hollow rock and loud *reactive* hill.
Sir R. Blackmore, Creation, vii.

Knowledge of Sanscrit . . . will be kept alive by the *reactive* influence of Germany and England.
Maine, Village Communities, p. 25.

This equilibration between new outer forces and *reactive* inner forces, which is thus directly produced in individuals. *H. Spencer*, Prin. of Biol., § 296.

reactively (rē-ak'tiv-li), *adv.* By reaction.

reactiveness (rē-ak'tiv-nes), *n.* The quality of being reactive.

reactivity (rē-ak-tiv'i-ti), *n.* [‹ *reactive* + *-ity*.] The state of being reactive; the process or course of reaction, as from a diseased condition.

The occurrence of colour, therefore, is more frequently than not concomitant with a high degree of *reactivity*.
Nature, XXXVII. 503.

read[1] (rēd), *v.*; pret. and pp. *read* (red), ppr. *reading*. [Early mod. E. also *reed*, *reede*, *rede*; ‹

ME. *reden*, earlier *ræden*, *rathen*, *rothen* (a weak verb, pret. *redde*, *radde*, pp. *red*, *rad*, *i-rad*), < AS. (*a*) *rǣdan* (a weak verb, pret. *rǣdde*, pl. *rǣddon*, pp. *rǣded*, *rǣdd*, *gerǣd*), mixed with (*b*) *rǣdan*, Anglian also *rēdan*, *rēthan* (a strong redupl. verb, pret. *reórd*, pp. *rǣden*; found only in poet. or Anglian use), counsel, advise, consult, etc., read (a writing, whether aloud or to oneself), = OS. *rādan* (pret. *rēd*, pp. *girādan*), counsel, take counsel upon, provide, = OFries. *rēda* (pret. *rēd*), counsel, = MD. D. *raden*, counsel, advise, interpret, guess, = MLG. *rāten*, LG. *raten*, counsel, advise, = OHG. *rātan*, MHG. *rāten*, G. *raten*, *rathen* (pret. *riet*, *rieth*, pp. *geraten*, *gerathen*), counsel, advise, interpret, guess, = Icel. *rādha* (pret. *rēdh*, pp. *rādhinn*), counsel, advise, etc., = Sw. *råda*, counsel, advise, prevail, *rå*, can, may, = Dan. *raade*, counsel, rule, control, also interpret, = Goth. **rēdan*, in comp. *ga-rēdan* (pret. *ga-rairōth*), provide for; perhaps akin (having then an orig. present formative *-d*) to L. *reri* (pp. *ratus*), think, deem, consider: see *rate*[2], *ratio*, *reason*. Some compare Skt. √ *rādh*, be successful, Russ. *radŭ*, glad, happy, ready, Lith. *rodas*, willing, etc. Hence *read*[1], *n.*, *riddle*[1], *aread*, etc. The verb *read* in the already obsolete sense 'counsel, advise,' was much affected by Spenser, and in the early modern and ME. spelling *rede* which he used has likewise been much affected by his archaizing imitators; but there is no historical ground for a difference in spelling. The pret. *read* (red) should be written *red*, as it was formerly; it is exactly parallel with *led*, pret. of *lead*[1], and with *let*, pret. of *let*[1] (inf. formerly *lete*, with long vowel).] **I.** *trans.* **1**†. To counsel; advise; recommend.

> And she thus breuneth bothe in love and drede,
> So that she nyste what was best to *rede*.
> *Chaucer*, Troilus, iv. 679.

> And seththe he *radde* religioun the rule for to holde —
> "Leste the kyng and his counseil ȝor comunes apeire,
> And beo stiward in oure stude til ȝe be stouwet betere."
> *Piers Plowman* (A), v. 38.

> We may *read* constancy and fortitude
> To other souls. *B. Jonson*, Poetaster, i. 1.

> If there 's a hole in a' your coats,
> I *rede* you tent it.
> *Burns*, Captain Grose's Peregrinations.

> My Ladye *reads* you swith return.
> *Scott*, L. of L. M., iv. 22.

2. To teach; instil, as a lesson.

> Are these the arts,
> Robin, you *read* your rude ones of the wood,
> To countenance your quarrels and mistakings?
> *B. Jonson*, Sad Shepherd, ii. 2.

3. To explain the meaning of; explain; interpret; make out; solve: as, to *read* a riddle; to *read* a dream.

> Joseph, . . . he that *redde* so
> The kynges metynge, Pharao.
> *Chaucer*, Death of Blanche, l. 281.

> Did you draw bonds to forfeit, sign to break?
> Or must we *read* you quite from what you speak?
> *Donne*, Expostulation (ed. 1819).

> "I'll *read* your dream, sister," he says,
> "I'll *read* it into sorrow."
> *The Braes o' Yarrow* (Child's Ballads, III. 71).

> I can *read* my uncle's riddle. *Scott*, Waverley, lxii.

4†. To declare; tell; rehearse.

> That hast my name and nation *redd* aright.
> *Spenser*, F. Q., I. x. 67.

5†. To suppose; guess; imagine; fancy.

> Right hard it was for wight which did it heare
> To *read* what manner musicke that mote bee.
> *Spenser*, F. Q., II. xii. 70. (*Nares.*)

6. To understand by observation or scrutiny; acquire a knowledge of (something not otherwise obvious) by interpreting signs or indications; study out; interpret: as, to *read* the signs of the times: to *read* the sky or a person's countenance.

> Who is 't can *read* a woman?
> *Shak.*, Cymbeline, v. 5. 48.

> Let thy ambitious eye
> *Read* noble objects. *Quarles*, Emblems, v. 8.

7. To discover by observation or scrutiny; perceive from signs or indications.

> Those about her
> From her shall *read* the perfect ways of honour.
> *Shak.*, Hen. VIII., v. 5. 38.

> Let vs looke backe to Adam, who in this wicked fruit of his bodie might *reade* continuall lectures of repentance for the sinne of his soule. *Purchas*, Pilgrimage, p. 34.

> All the gazers on the skies
> *Read* not in fair heaven's story
> Expresser truth, or truer glory,
> Than they might in her bright eyes.
> *B. Jonson*, Epigrams, xl.

> If once the reality of the phenomena were established, we should all be able to *read* each other's secrets.
> *Proc. Soc. Psych. Research*, II. 10.

8. (*a*) To observe and apprehend the meaning of (something written, printed, inscribed, or stamped in letters or other significant characters); go over with the eyes (or, in the case of the blind, with the fingers) and take in the meaning of (significant characters forming or representing words or sentences); peruse: as, to *read* a book, newspaper, poem, inscription, or piece of music.

> He . . . *radde* it over, and gan the letre fold.
> *Chaucer*, Troilus, ii. 1085.

> A man of Ethiopia . . . sitting in his chariot *read* Esaias the prophet. Acts viii. 27, 28.

> I heard of a late Secretary of State that could not *read* the next Morning his own Hand-writing.
> *Howell*, Letters, I. v. 37.

> In his short life, and without ostentation, he [Shelley] had in truth *read* more Greek than many an aged pedant who, with pompous parade, prides himself upon this study alone. *Hogg*, in Dowden's Shelley, I. 73.

(*b*) To note the indication of (a graduated instrument): as, to *read* a thermometer or a circle.—**9.** To utter aloud: said of words or sounds represented by letters or other significant characters.

> The king . . . *read* in their ears all the words of the book of the covenant. 2 Ki. xxiii. 2.

> In their Synagogues they make one of the best sort to *read* a Chapter of Moses. *Howell*, Letters, I. vi. 14.

10. To peruse or study (a subject in the books written about it): learn through reading: as, to *read* law or philosophy; to *read* science for a degree; to *read* the news; we *read* that the meek shall inherit the earth.

> Chyffe of folis, men yn bokys *redythe*,
> Able yn his toly to holde residence,
> Ys he that nowther God louethe nor dredethe,
> Nor to his chyrche bathe none aduertence.
> *Books of Precedence* (E. E. T. S., extra ser.), i. 79.

> At Iberico, as it is *red*, our Lord dyde many grete myracles. *Sir R. Guylforde*, Pylgrymage, p. 41.

11. To perceive or assume in the reading or study of a book or writing (something not expressed or directly indicated); impute or import by inference: as, to *read* a meaning in a book which the author did not intend; to *read* one's own notions into a book; to *read* something between the lines.

> Nascent philosophy and dawning science are *read* into the sacred literature. *Maine*, Early Law and Custom, i.

> After their usual manner of speculating about primitive practices, men *read* back developed ideas into undeveloped minds. *H. Spencer*, Prin. of Sociol., § 346.

12. To affect by reading so as to bring into a specified condition: as, to *read* a child asleep; to *read* one's self blind.

> No, no; give him a Young Clark's Guide. What, we shall have you *read* yourself into a Humour of rambling and fighting, and studying military Discipline, and wearing red Breeches. *Wycherley*, Plain Dealer, iii. 1.

13†. To read about.

> Of the fynest stones faire
> That men *rede* in the Lapidaire.
> *Chaucer*, House of Fame, l. 1352.

To read (one) **a chapter.** See *chapter*.—**To read one's self in**, in the *Church of England*, to read the Thirty-nine Articles of Religion, and repeat the Declaration of Assent (to the Articles, Prayer-book, and Ordinary) prescribed by law, which is required of every incumbent on the first Sunday on which he officiates in the church of his benefice, or on some other Sunday appointed and allowed by the ordinary.

> On the following Sunday Mr. Arabin was to *read himself in* at his new church.
> *Trollope*, Barchester Towers, xxii.

To read out of, to expel from, or declare no longer to belong to (some organization), by proclamation of any kind: as, to *read* a person *out of* a political party.

II. *intrans.* **1**†. To counsel; advise; give advice or warning.

> "Syr," he seyd, "now haue I *redd*;
> Ete we now, and make vs glad,
> And euery man fle care."
> *The Horn of King Arthur* (Child's Ballads, I. 22).

> A monster vile whom God and man does hate:
> Therefore I *read* beware. *Spenser*, F. Q., I. i. 13.

> As for this carping girl, Iphigena,
> Take her with thee to bear thee company,
> And in my land I *rede* be seen no more.
> *Greene*, Alphonsus, iii.

2†. To speak; discourse; declare; tell.

> Sojourned hath this Mars, of which I *rede*,
> In chambre amyd the paleys prively.
> *Chaucer*, Complaint of Mars, l. 78.

3. To peruse something written or printed; acquire information from a record of any kind.

> I have *read* of Caligula's Horse, that was made Consul.
> *Howell*, Letters, I. v. 37.

> To *read* well—that is, to read true books in a true spirit—is a noble exercise. *Thoreau*, Walden, p. 110.

4. To utter aloud the words of something written or printed; enunciate the words of a book or writing.

> So they *read* in the book of the law of God distinctly, and gave the sense. Neh. viii. 8.

5. In *music*: (*a*) To perform or render music at first sight of the notes: applied to either vocal or instrumental performance: as, he plays well, but *reads* very slowly. (*b*) To perform or render music in a particular way; put a certain expression upon it; interpret it: used of a performer or conductor.—**6.** To give a recital or lecture; rehearse something written or learned: as, to *read* before a public audience.

> For, if I take ye in hand, I shall dissect you,
> And *read* upon your phlegmatic dull carcases.
> *Fletcher* (*and another*), Elder Brother, iv. 3.

7. To study systematically from books or writings: sometimes with *up*.

> The Bachelors, most of them Scholars, *reading* for Fellowships, and nearly all of them private tutors.
> *C. A. Bristed*, English University, p. 36.

> Men should . . . be compelled to *read up* on questions of the time, and give in public a reason for the faith which is in them. *Harper's Mag.*, LXXVIII. 209.

8. To appear on reading; have a (specified) meaning.—**9.** To have a certain quality or effect in perusal; used absolutely, to be suitable or desirable for perusal.

> Then again, his [Sheridan's] works, unlike those of Burke, do not *read*, possess no attractions, are not indispensable to the library. *Jon Bee*, Samuel Foote.

> The following passage, however, with some historical basis, *reads* rather curiously. *Mind*, XII. 624.

To read between the lines, to detect a meaning or purpose not specifically expressed in a book or other writing; discover some recondite motive or implication in what is read.—**To read by sound**, in *teleg.*, to make out the words or terms of a message from the sounds made by the instrument in transmitting it.

read[1] (red), *p. a.* [Pp. of *read*[1], *v.*] Having knowledge gained from reading; instructed by reading; in general, versed: now usually with *well*: as, *well read* in the classics.

> You are all *read* in mysteries of state.
> *Ford*, Perkin Warbeck, ii. 3.

> An Oxford-Man, extremely *read* in Greek,
> Who from Euripides makes Phædra speak.
> *Prior*, Epilogue to Phædra.

> One cannot be *well read* unless well seasoned in thought and experience. *A. B. Alcott*, Tablets, p. 134.

read[1] (rēd), *n.* [Early mod. E. also *rede*; < ME. *rede*, < AS. *rǣd* = OS. *rād* = OFries. *rēd* = D. *raad* = MLG. *rād*, LG. *rad* = OHG. MHG. *rāt*, G. *rat*, *rath* = Icel. *rādh* = Sw. *råd* = Dan. *raad*, counsel, advice; from the orig. verb: see *read*[1], *v.* In the sense 'counsel, advice,' the noun is used archaically, in the spelling *rede*, like the verb.] **1**†. Counsel; advice.

> But who so wol nat trowen *rede* ne lore,
> I kan not sen in hym no remedie,
> But lat hym worchen with his fantasie.
> *Chaucer*, Troilus, v. 327.

> And whan the kynge was come to Cardoel, he sente after the men of hys counseile, and asked what was theire *rede* in this thinge. *Merlin* (E. E. T. S.), i. 81.

> To whose wise *read* she hearkning sent me streight
> Into this land. *Spenser*, F. Q., VI. ii. 30.

> May you better reck the *rede*
> Than ever did th' adviser!
> *Burns*, Epistle to a Young Friend.

2†. Interpretation.

> I repeated
> The *read* thereof for guerdon of my paine,
> And taking downe the shield with me did it retaine.
> *Spenser*, F. Q., IV. x. 10.

3†. Speech; tale; narrative.

> Why then a final note prolong,
> Or lengthen out a closing song,
> Unless to bid the gentles speed,
> Who long have listened to my *rede*?
> *Scott*, Marmion, L'Envoy.

4†. A saying; a proverb.

> This *reede* is ryfe, that oftentime
> Great clymbers fall unsoft.
> *Spenser*, Shep. Cal., July.

5. Reading; perusal. [Colloq.]

> My first *read* of the newspaper.
> *Thackeray*, Great Hoggarty Diamond, x.

> I got the other day a hasty *read* of your "Scenes of Clerical Life." *E. Hall*, in Cross's George Eliot, II. ix.

read[2]†, *a.* An obsolete form of *red*[1].

read[3] (rēd), *v. t.* A dialectal form of *red*[3].

readability (rē-da-bil'i-ti), *n.* [< *readable* + *-ity* (see *-bility*).] Readableness.

readable (rē'da-bl), *a.* [< *read*[1] + *-able*.] **1.** Capable of being read; legible.—**2.** Of sufficient interest to be read; worth reading; easy or interesting to read: as, a *readable* story.

> Nobody except editors and school-teachers and here and there a literary man knows how common is the capacity of rhyming and prattling in *readable* prose.
> *O. W. Holmes*, Poet at the Breakfast-Table.

3. Enabling to read; capable of being read by. [Rare.]

Those who have been labouring to introduce into our railway carriages not only a good *readable* light, but a light generally acceptable to everyone. *Elect. Rev.* (Eng.), XXV. 601.

readableness (rē'da-bl-nes), *n.* The state or character of being readable.

A book remarkable for its succinctness, its vividness, and its eminent *readableness*. *Harper's Mag.*, LXXVI. 805.

readably (rē'da-bli), *adv.* In a readable manner; legibly.

readdress (rē-a-dres'), *v. t.* [< *re-* + *address*.] To address or direct again.

He . . . *re-addressed* himself to her. *Boyle*, Works, VI. 290.

readept† (rē-a-dept'), *v. t.* [< *re-* + *adept*.] To regain; recover.

The which Duoble if he might by their meanes *readept* and recover, he would never let passe out of hys memorie so great a benifite. Hall, Edward IV., f. 25. (*Halliwell*.)

readeption (rē-a-dep'shon), *n.* [< *re-* + *adeption*.] A regaining; recovery of something lost.

In whose begynnyng of *raedepcion* [*rea-*], the erle of Worcester, whiche for his crueltesse was called the bochier of Englo[n]de, was taken and put in streyght pryson. *Fabyan*, Chron., II. 659, an. 1570.

Will any say that the *readeption* of Trevigi was matter of scruple? *Bacon.*

reader (rē'dėr), *n.* [< ME. *reder*, *redere*, *redare*, *redar*, reader, counselor, adviser, < AS. *rǣdere*, *rēdere*, a reader, scholar, church reader (lector), reader of riddles, diviner (= D. *rader*, adviser, = OHG. *rātari*, *rātiri*, MHG. *rātære*, counselor, adviser, guesser, diviner), < *rǣdan*, advise, read: see *read*[1].] 1†. One who counsels; a counselor; an adviser.

Loke . . . uram [from] kueade [evil] *rederes*, and ne akse no red at foles. *Ayenbite of Inwyt* (E. E. T. S.), p. 184.

2. One who interprets; one who acquires knowledge from observation or impression; an interpreter: as, a *reader* of weather-signs or of probabilities. See *mind-reader*.—3. One who reads; a person who peruses, studies, or utters aloud that which is written or printed.

And the *reader* droned from the pulpit,
Like the murmur of many bees,
The legend of good Saint Guthlac.
Longfellow, King Witlaf's Drinking-Horn.

Readers are multiplying daily; but they want guidance, help, plan. *Nineteenth Century*, XXIV. 499.

Specifically—(*a*) One who reads for examination or criticism; an examiner of that which is offered or proposed for publication: as, an editorial or a publisher's *reader*. (*b*) One who is employed to read for correction for the press; a proof-reader. (*c*) One who recites before an audience anything written: as, an elocutionary *reader*. Particularly—(*d*) One whose office it is to read before an audience; an officer appointed to read for a particular purpose; a lector; a lecturer. (1) In the early church, the Greek Church, the Roman Catholic Church, and some other churches, a member of one of the minor clerical orders, appointed to read Scripture lections in the church. The order of reader existed as early as the second century. At an early date it was not unusual to admit young boys, even of five or six, to the office of reader, but by the sixth century the age of eighteen was required by law. In the Roman Catholic Church this order is little more than one of the steps to the priesthood. The reader (lector) ranks above a door-keeper and below an exorcist, and the form of ordination is the delivery to him of the book from which he is to read. In the Greek Church the reader (anagnost) ranks below a subdeacon, and it is his office, as it was in the early church, to read the Epistle, the deacon reading the Gospel. In the Church of England the order fell into abeyance after the Reformation, but lay readers were frequently licensed, especially in churches or chapels without a clergyman. They could not minister the sacraments and other rites of the church, except the burial of the dead and the churching of women, nor pronounce the absolution and benediction. Of late years, however, bishops have regularly admitted candidates to the office of reader by delivery of a copy of the New Testament. In the American Episcopal Church lay readers conduct services in vacant churches or under a rector by his request with license from the bishop for a definite period (a year or less). They cannot give absolution or benediction, administer sacraments, nor use the occasional offices of the church except those for the burial of the dead and visitation of the sick and prisoners, nor deliver sermons of their own composition. (2) One who reads the law in a Jewish synagogue. (3) In the Universities of Oxford and Cambridge, the English Inns of Court, etc., a lecturer, or, where there are two grades of lecturers, a lecturer of the higher grade, the others being called *sub-lectors* or *lecturers*.

4. A reading-book for schools; a book containing exercises in reading.—**Gentle reader, lay reader**, etc. See the adjectives.

readership (rē'dėr-ship), *n.* [< *reader* + *-ship*.] The office of reader. See *reader*, 3 (*d*) (3).

Oxford has decided to establish a *Readership* in Geography. *Nature*, XXXV. 475.

readily (red'i-li), *adv.* [< ME. *redely*, *reddely*, *redili*, *rediliche*; < *ready* + *-ly*[2].] 1. In a ready manner; with facility; quickly; speedily; promptly; easily.

On hir fete wexen saugh I
Partriches winges *redely*.
Chaucer, House of Fame, l. 1392.

Mr. Carlyle is for calling down fire from Heaven whenever he cannot *readily* lay his hand on the match-box. *Lowell*, Study Windows, p. 128.

2. With readiness or alacrity; without delay or objection; willingly.

She answered that she could *readily* obey what her father and mother had done. *Pepys*, Diary, July 17, 1665.

I *readily* grant that one truth cannot contradict another. *Locke.*

3†. Just now; at once.

A tydynge for to here . . .
That shal nat now be told for me,
For it no nede is *redely*.
Chaucer, House of Fame, l. 2137.

=**Syn.** See *ready*.

readiness (red'i-nes), *n.* [Early mod. E. *readines*, *redynes*; < ME. *redinesse*, *redynesse*; < *ready* + *-ness*.] 1. The condition of being ready; the state of being adapted or in condition for immediate use or action; present preparedness or fitness; ready availability or qualification.

At the Archynale there be closed within, alwaye in a *redynesse* to set forth whan they woll.
Sir R. Guylforde, Pylgrymage, p. 7.

If it [death] be not now, yet it will come; the *readiness* is all. *Shak.*, Hamlet, v. 2. 234.

Probed many hearts, beginning with his own,
And now was far in *readiness* for God.
Browning, Ring and Book, I. 16.

2. Ready action or movement; instant facility or aptitude; promptness; quickness: as, *readiness* of thought or of speech; *readiness* in off-hand drawing.

I thought, by your *readiness* in the office, you had continued in it some time. *Shak.*, M. for M., ii. 1. 275.

Good abstractive power shows itself in a superior *readiness* to frame any kind of concept.
J. Sully, Outlines of Psychol., p. 385.

3. Ready disposition; present willingness; mental preparedness.

They received the word with all *readiness* of mind.
Acts xvii. 11.

Digby made his peace with Cromwell, and professes his *readiness* to spend his blood for him.
Lowell, Among my Books, 1st ser., p. 274.

=**Syn. 2.** *Readiness*, *Facility*, *Expertness*, *Knack*, promptitude, aptness, preparation, preparedness, inclination. The first four words agree in meaning that the person can do a thing with ease and quickness. *Readiness* emphasizes promptitude: as, *readiness* in repartee. *Facility* by derivation emphasizes ease, whether partly natural or wholly acquired. (See *ease*, *n.*) *Expertness* is facility acquired: as, *expertness* with the pen, at figures, in working a sewing-machine; it is primarily physical, and especially manual, but also mental. *Knack* is a familiar word, applying to facility or expertness viewed as a happy and rather surprising possession of skill or faculty.

reading (rē'ding), *n.* [< ME. *redynge*, *ræding*, reading, < AS. *rǣding*, reading, a reading, a passage or lesson, also rule, government; verbal n. of *rǣdan*, counsel, rule, read: see *read*[1].] 1. The act of interpreting; interpretation; exposition, as of a riddle or dream; interpretation of signs, marks, or the like; a rendering or discovery of what is signified by the state or marking of an instrument, by arbitrary signs of any kind, or by the existing condition or action of anything: as, the *readings* of a steam-indicator; a correct *reading* of the sky (as to weather), or of a person's countenance or proceedings.

For instance, if the freezing-point is lowered, we must subtract the amount of fall from each *reading*.
J. Trowbridge, New Physics, p. 187.

Take the *readings* of the two pegs [in adjusting a field level], which will give their true difference of level.
Sci. Amer. Supp., p. 8905.

2. The particular interpretation given to a composition of any kind, an event or a series of events, etc.; also, a rendering in speech, act, or performance; delineation; representation.

You charm me, Mortimer, with your *reading* of my weaknesses. By-the-by, that very word *Reading*, in its critical use, always charms me. An actress's *reading* of a chamber-maid, a dancer's *reading* of a hornpipe, a singer's *reading* of a song, a marine-painter's *reading* of the sea, the kettle-drum's *reading* of an instrumental passage, are phrases ever youthful and delightful.
Dickens, Our Mutual Friend, iii. 10.

For Englishmen in their own tongue to have from such a man [Von Ranke] a *reading* of the most critical period of English history would be a boon of incalculable value.
Stubbs, Medieval and Modern Hist., p. 68.

His *reading* of Bach's Italian Concerto was a scramble, so far as the first and last movements were concerned.
The Academy, June 29, 1889, p. 456.

3. The act of perusing that which is written or printed; perusal.

You write with ease to show your breeding,
But easy writing 's curst hard *reading*.
Sheridan, Clio's Protest.

4. The utterance or recital of recorded words, either from the record (as a printed page) or from memory; specifically, a public lection or lecture: as, to give *readings* from the poets, or upon law or philosophy. See *read*[1], *v. i.*, 6.

The Jews had their weekly *readings* of the law.
Hooker.

The *readings* [in the Inns of Court] were from the very first deemed of vital importance, and were delivered in the halls with much ceremony. *Encyc. Brit.*, XIII. 88.

5. That which is read or to be read; any written or printed medium of thought or intelligence; recorded matter or material.

It is in newspapers that we must look for the main *reading* of this generation. *De Quincey*, Style, i.

Remembering his early love of poetry and fiction, she unlocked a bookcase, and took down several books that had been excellent *reading* in their day.
Hawthorne, Seven Gables, ix.

6. The indication of a graduated instrument: as, the *reading* of a barometer.—7. Textual structure or construction; a form, expression, or collocation in a writing, or in a particular copy or impression of it; a version: as, the various *readings* of a passage in Shakspere; the *reading* seems to be corrupt.

When you meet with several *Readings* of the Text, take heed you admit nothing against the Tenets of your Church.
Selden, Table-Talk, p. 22.

Disjunctor reading. See *disjunctor*.—**Penny reading**, an amateur entertainment consisting of readings, recitations, music, etc., admission to which is only one penny: common in the British Islands, where such entertainments seem to have been introduced about 1860.—**Reading ægrotat.** See *ægrotat*.—**Reading notice.** See *notice*.

reading (rē'ding), *p. a.* Inclined to read; having a taste for reading; of a studious disposition: as, a *reading* community.—**Reading man.** See *man*.

William himself was not a *reading man*.
Macaulay, Hist. Eng., vii.

reading-book (rē'ding-bůk), *n.* [< ME. **reding-bok*, < AS. *rǣding-bōc*, reading-book, lectionary, < *rǣding*, reading, + *bōc*, book.] 1. A lectionary.—2. A book containing selections to be used as exercises in reading.

reading-boy (rē'ding-boi), *n.* In *printing*, a boy employed to read copy to a proof-reader; a reader's assistant: in the United States called *copy-holder*.

reading-desk (rē'ding-desk), *n.* A desk adapted for use in reading; specifically, a high desk for holding a book or manuscript to be read by a person while standing; in a church, same as *lectern*, 1.

He feared he should acquit himself badly in St. Ewold's *reading-desk*. *Trollope*, Barchester Towers, xxiii.

reading-glass (rē'ding-glàs), *n.* A magnifying lens set in a frame with a handle, for use in reading fine print, or for persons with defective vision.

reading-lamp (rē'ding-lamp), *n.* A lamp especially adapted for use in reading; specifically, a form of lamp for use in public reading or speaking, arranged so that its light is concentrated upon the reading-desk.

reading-pew (rē'ding-pū), *n.* In English churches, a pew from which to read part of the service; especially, after the Reformation, an inclosure in the body of a church, with a door, seat, and desk or desks, used instead of the older and later form of reading-desk or stalls.

reading-room (rē'ding-röm), *n.* 1. An apartment appropriated to reading; a room furnished with newspapers, periodicals, etc., to which persons resort for reading.—2. A room or closet set apart for the use of professional proof-readers.

reading-stand (rē'ding-stand), *n.* A stand to support a book. (*a*) Same as *reading-table*. (*b*) Same as *reading-desk*.

reading-table (rē'ding-tā''bl), *n.* A table providing support for a heavy book or books, when in use, and frequently space for other books needed for consultation, and the like. There are many patterns, some having a revolving top.

readjourn (rē-a-jėrn'), *v. t.* and *i.* [< F. *réajourner*, readjourn; as *re-* + *adjourn*. Cf. *rejourn*.] To adjourn again.

Parliament assembling again . . . was then *re-adjourned* by the king's special command till Tuesday next.
Sir H. Wotton, Reliquiæ, p. 443.

readjournment (rē-a-jėrn'ment), *n.* [< F. *réajournement*, readjournment; as *readjourn* + *-ment*.] A succeeding adjournment; adjournment anew.

readjust (rē-a-just'), *v. t.* [< *re-* + *adjust*.] 1. To settle again; put in order again, as what had been discomposed.

The beau sheathed his hanger, and *readjusted* his hair. *Fielding.*

2. To adjust in a new way; make a different adjustment, arrangement, or settlement of.

The problem these gentlemen had to solve was to *readjust* the proportion between their wants and their income. *George Eliot*, Mill on the Floss, ii. 4.

My scheme, your better knowledge broke,
Presently *readjusts* itself, the small
Proportioned largelier, parts and whole named new.
Browning, Ring and Book, II. 221.

readjuster (rē-ạ-jus'tėr), *n.* [< *readjust* + *-er*¹.] 1. One who readjusts, or takes part in a readjustment of something.—2. [*cap.*] Specifically, a member of a party in Virginia, formed about 1878, under the leadership of General William Mahone, and originally composed principally of Democrats, for the forcible readjustment of the debt on terms dictated by the State without the consent of the bondholders. The exceptional losses of the State in the civil war made the large debt previously contracted very burdensome; and the amount of its liability was in dispute with the State of West Virginia, which had been set off from Virginia without a decision of this question. The Readjusters elected the State government in 1879, and also United States senators for the terms 1881–7 and 1883–9, in opposition to the Conservative Democrats, or Funders; but the party failed to effect a permanent settlement of the debt, and was merged in the Republican party about 1882.

Further news from Virginia indicates that the Repudiators, or *Readjusters*, as they call themselves, have elected a majority of the General Assembly. *The Nation*, Nov. 13, 1879, p. 317.

readjustment (rē-ạ-just'mẹnt), *n.* [< *readjust* + *-ment.*] 1. The act of readjusting, or the state of being readjusted.—2. Specifically, in *U. S. politics*, the political schemes of the Readjusters.

readmission (rē-ad-mish'ọn), *n.* [< F. *réadmission* = Sp. *readmision* = Pg. *readmissão*; as *re-* + *admission.*] The act of admitting again; the state of being readmitted; renewed admission.

In an exhausted receiver, animals that seem as they were dead revive upon the *readmission* of fresh air. *Arbuthnot.*

readmit (rē-ad-mit'), *v. t.* [= F. *réadmettre* = Sp. *readmitir* = Pg. *readmittir* = It. *riammettere*, readmit; as *re-* + *admit.*] To admit again.

Whose ear is ever open, and his eye
Gracious to *re-admit* the suppliant.
Milton, S. A., l. 1173.

readmittance (rē-ad-mit'ạns), *n.* [< *re-* + *admittance.*] Permission to enter again; readmission.

Humbly petitioning a *readmittance* into his college. *T. Warton*, Sir T. Pope, p. 84. (*Latham.*)

readvance (rē-ạd-vȧns'), *v. i.* [< *re-* + *advance*, *v.*] To advance again or afresh.

Which if they miss, they yet should *readvance*
To former height.
B. Jonson, Epigrams, xxxv., To Sir H. Goodyere.

readvertency (rē-ad-vėr'tẹn-si), *n.* [< *re-* + *advertency.*] The act of adverting to or reviewing again. [Rare.]

Memory he does not make to be a recovery of ideas that were lost, but a *re-advertency* or reapplication of mind to ideas that were actually there, though not attended to. *Norris*, Reflections on Locke, p. 9.

ready (red'i), *a.* and *n.* [< ME. *redy*, *redi*, *rædi*, *rædig*, *i-redi*, ready, prepared, prompt, near, < AS. *rǣde* (rare and uncertain), usually *gerǣde*, ready, swift, prompt, easy, plain (suffix *-e* becoming *-i* by confusion with the common adj. suffix ME. *-i*, *-y*, > E. *-y*¹); = OFries. *rede*, *red* = D. *ree* = MLG. *rēde*, *reide*, *rēt*, *reit*, LG. *rede*, *reed* = OHG. *bi-reiti*, MHG. *bereite*, *be-reit*, G. *be-reit*, ready, prepared, = Icel. *g-reithr* (**ga reithr*), ready (whence ult. E. *graith*, *grade*²), = OSw. *reda*, Sw. *be-red* = Dan. *rede*, *be-redt*, ready; perhaps = Goth. *garaids*, set, appointed; cf. *raidjan*, appoint, *ga-raidjan*, enjoin, command, *ga-raideins*, an ordinance, rule, authority. Otherwise akin to Icel. *reithi*, harness, outfit, gear, implements; or to AS., etc., *rīdan* (pret. *rād*), ride, *rād*, a riding, expedition: see *ride*, *road*, *raid*. Hence, in comp., *already*, and ult. *array*, *curry*¹, *ray*³, *raiment*, etc.] I. *a.* 1. Completely prepared, as for immediate action or use, or for present requirement; suitably equipped, ordered, or arranged; in proper trim or condition.

Comaund, sir kyng, that a clene nauy
Be redy to rode on the rugh see,
All well for the werre, with wight men ynogh.
Destruction of Troy (E. E. T. S.), l. 2549.

My oxen and my fatlings are killed, and all things are *ready*. Mat. xxii. 4.

Be *ready*, Claudio, for your death to-morrow. *Shak.*, M. for M., iii. 1. 107.

2†. Dressed.

Up ryseth fresshe Canacee hir-selue, . . .
Noon hyer was he [the sun] whan she *redy* was.
Chaucer, Squire's Tale, l. 379.

The French leap over the walls in their shirts. Enter, several ways, . . . Alençon and Reignier, half *ready*, and half unready. *Shak.*, 1 Hen. VI., ii. 1 (stage direction).

Bid my wife make herself *ready* handsomely,
And put on her best apron.
Fletcher (*and another*), Queen of Corinth, ii. 4.

3. Suitably disposed in mind; mentally prepared; willing; inclined; not reluctant.

The spirit truly is *ready*, but the flesh is weak. Mark xiv. 38.

A persecutor who inflicts nothing which he is not *ready* to endure deserves some respect. *Macaulay*, Hallam's Const. Hist.

4. Prepared by what has gone before; brought to a fit state or condition; not unlikely; immediately liable: with an infinitive.

The blessing of him that was *ready* to perish came upon me. Job xxix. 13.

Our king, being *ready* to leap out of himself for joy of his found daughter, . . . cries, "O, thy mother!" *Shak.*, W. T., v. 2. 54.

The miserable prisoner is *ready* to famish. *Dekker*, Seven Deadly Sins, p. 45.

5. Already prepared or provided; available for present use or requirement; immediately at hand or within reach; opportune: as, a *ready* means of escape; a *ready* way.

And the olde knyght seide that he sholde do sette ther a cheyer, that euer more sholde be *redy* for the knyght in to sitte that sholde be so trewe in lovynge whan he were come. *Merlin* (E. E. T. S.), ii. 362.

It sometimes cometh to pass that the *readiest* way which a wise man hath to conquer is to fly. *Hooker*, Eccles. Polity, Pref.

Nine-score and seventeen pounds; of which he made five marks, *ready* money. *Shak.*, M. for M., iv. 3. 7.

He pays in *ready* guineas very liberally. *Swift*, Letter, May 13, 1727.

6. Prompt in action or movement; expert; dexterous; facile.

Ready in gibes, quick-answer'd, saucy, and
As quarrelous as the weasel.
Shak., Cymbeline, iii. 4. 161.

Reading maketh a full man, conference a *ready* man, . . . and therefore, if a man . . . confer little, he had need have a present wit. *Bacon*, Studies.

There's a sudden turn now! You have a *ready* wit for intrigue, I find. *Colman*, Jealous Wife, i.

7. Prompt; quick; offhand: as, a *ready* reply or retort; a *ready* admission; a *ready* welcome.

My tongue is the pen of a *ready* writer. Ps. xlv. 1.

Unless he had done this with great dexterity and *ready* address, he would frequently have been involved in imminent danger. *Bacon*, Physical Fables, x., Expl.

8†. Present; at hand; here: used in answering a call.

Duke. What, is Antonio here?
Ant. Ready. *Shak.*, M. of V., iv. 1. 2.

[*Ready* is much used in compounds, with participles and sometimes nouns, or in combinations that are properly compounds: as, *ready*-made; *ready*-cooked, etc.]—**Making ready**, in *printing*, the process of preparation for taking regular impressions from a form on the press. It includes the adjustment of the form on the press, the proper distribution of the pressure on type and cuts by means of underlays and overlays, and the adaptation of ink to paper.—**Ready about.** See *about.*—**Ready money.** See *money.*—To **make ready.** (*a*) To prepare; set in order.

Whiche the ffryers kepte and ther thei *made* the *redy* in ornaments and began ther a very solempne procession. *Torkington*, Diarie of Eng. Travell, p. 41.

They sit downe at tables, and then must the Bridegrome make triall of his breast in singing a long prayer: others in the meane time call to *make readie* the hens. *Purchas*, Pilgrimage, p. 214.

(*b*†) To dress.

While Master Mathew reads, Bobadill *makes* himself *ready*. *B. Jonson*, Every Man in his Humour, i. 4.

Go, and *make* thee *ready* straight
In all thy best attire. *B. Jonson*, Volpone, ii. 3.

A man may *make* him *ready* in such clothes
Without a candle.
Middleton (*and others*), The Widow, iii. 3.

=**Syn.** *Ready*, *Easy*; disposed, apt, expert, handy, skilful, clever, smart; expeditious, unhesitating. So many of the meanings of *ready* convey the idea of a movement of mind, and especially a consent of the will, that there is a tendency to use other words where disposition is not included. Hence it is better to say this may *easily* be seen, than this may *readily* be seen. See quotation from Locke under *readily*. *Easy* of approach; *easy* to be done; *ready* to hear. All the senses of *ready*, active or passive, grow out of that of being prepared.

II. *n.* 1. Ready money; cash: usually with the definite article. [Slang.]

Lord Strutt was not flush in *ready*, either to go to law, or clear old debts. *Arbuthnot*, Hist. John Bull. (*Latham.*)

2. The condition of being ready. [Colloq.]—3. The position of a soldier's weapon following the command "Make ready!" or "Ready!" [Colloq.]

[The hunter] beats patiently and noiselessly from the leeward . . . with his rifle at the *ready*. *T. Roosevelt*, Hunting Trips, p. 119.

A good **ready**, a state of being fully ready or prepared; a good condition of readiness. [Colloq.]

ready (red'i), *v. t.*; pret. and pp. *readied*, ppr. *readying*. [< ME. *redien*, *redyen* (= D. *reeden*, prepare, dress, = MLG. *rēden*, *reiden* = MHG. *reiten*, *reiden*; cf. ME. *beredien* = G. *be-reiten* = Sw. *be-reda* = Dan. *be-rede*, prepare, get ready, etc.); < *ready*, *a.*] 1. To make ready; put into proper condition or order; dispose; arrange; prepare. [Obsolete or archaic.]

Thare-fore what-so-euer thou bee that *redies* the for to lufe Gode, . . . haue in mynde besely for to halde the name of Ihesu in thi mynde. *Hampole*, Prose Treatises (E. E. T. S.), p. 3.

And, having *readied* all these costly things,
In a poore pedlers trusse he packs his wares.
Heywood, Troia Britannica (1609). (*Nares.*)

2†. To direct.

For, for the gretnesse of the Erthe and of the See, men may go be a 1000 and a 1000 other weyes, that no man cowde *redye* him perfitely toward the parties that he cam fro, but zif it were be aventure and happ, or be the grace of God. *Mandeville*, Travels, p. 185.

ready-made (red'i-mād), *a.* 1. Previously made and now ready for use; furnished or obtained in a formed state; specifically, in trade, made ready for chance sale, and not made to order for a particular person: as, *ready-made* clothing; *ready-made* opinions or excuses.

When he hears
The tale of horror, to some *ready-made* face
Of hypocritical assent he turns.
Shelley, Queen Mab, iii.

The provision-man had honestly the effect of having got for the day only into the black coat which he had bought *ready-made* for his first wife's funeral. *Howells*, Annie Kilburn, xxii.

2. Pertaining to articles prepared beforehand: as, the *ready-made* department of a tailor's or shoemaker's business. [Trade use.]

ready-man (red'i-mạn), *n.* One of the men sent aloft in a man-of-war to prepare for evolutions with spars or sails.

ready-pole (red'i-pōl), *n.* A bar fixed across a chimney to support the pot-hook. It is now commonly of iron, but was formerly made of wood. *Halliwell.* [Prov. Eng.]

ready-reckoner (red″i-rek'nėr), *n.* A book of tabulated calculations, giving the value of any number of things from the lowest monetary unit upward, as also the interest on any sum of money for any period from a day upward, etc.; a book of tables to facilitate calculations.

I could almost think from the preface (but such deductions are very deceptive) that the earliest of the books which are now called *ready reckoners*, meaning those which have totals at given prices ready cast up, was the following: London 1693. Wm. Leyborn. Panarithmologia; being a mirror for merchants, a brieviate for bankers, a treasure for tradesmen, a mate for mechanics, and a sure guide for purchasers, sellers, or mortgagers of land, leases, annuities, rents, pensions, etc., in present possession or reversion, and a constant concomitant fitted for all men's occasions. *De Morgan.*

The Clerk in Eastcheap cannot spend the day in verifying his *Ready-Reckoner*; he must take it as verified, true and indisputable. *Carlyle.*

reaf†, *n.* [Usually in Sc. spelling *reif*, *rief*; < ME. *ref*, *ræf*, *reaf*, *reve*, < AS. *réaf*, spoil, plunder: see *reave.*] Spoil; plunder; robbery.

Meaning to live by *reif* of other mennes goodes, wherein they have no maner of propertie. *Holinshed*, Chron. (*Nares.*)

The man that wons yon foreste intill,
He lives by *reif* and felonie!
Sang of the Outlaw Murray (Child's Ballads, VI. 32).

reaffirm (rē-ạ-fėrm'), *v. t.* [= F. *réaffirmer*; as *re-* + *affirm.*] To affirm again.

I close with *re-affirming* the truth that I have aimed to impress. *Channing*, Perfect Life, p. 25.

reaffirmance (rē-ạ-fėr'mạns), *n.* [< *reaffirm* + *-ance.*] Renewed affirmation; reaffirmation.

A *reaffirmance* after such revocation. *Aylife*, Parergon.

reaffirmation (rẹ-af-ėr-mā'shọn), *n.* [< *reaffirm* + *-ation.*] Renewed affirmation; a repeated affirmation.

The great movement of thought which characterises the nineteenth century is a movement through negation to *reaffirmation*, through destruction to reconstruction. *E. Caird*, Hegel, p. 1.

reafforest (rē-a-for'est), *v. t.* [< *re-* + *afforest.*] To convert anew into a forest; renew the forest-growth of; reforest.

The Legislature was obliged to take steps to *reafforest* considerable tracts. *The American*, VII. 229.

reafforestation (rē-a-for-es-tā'shọn), *n.* [< *re-* + *afforest* + *-ation.*] A second afforestation; promotion of renewed forest-growth.

Even partial *reafforestation* in Brescia. *The Century*, XXXI. 536.

reagency (rē-ā'jen-si), *n.* [< *re-* + *agency.*] Action of or as of a reagent; reflex agency or activity; counter-agency; reaction.

Still, the mind, when acted on, is only excited to self-agency, to manifest what it is in itself, in the way of *re-agency.* — *H. B. Smith*, Christian Theology, p. 173.

reagent (rē-ā'jent), *n.* [< *re-* + *agent.* Cf. *react.*] 1. One who or that which exerts reflex action or influence; an agency that produces reciprocal effects; a cause or source of counter-results.

These tools have some questionable properties. They are *reagents.* Machinery is aggressive. The weaver becomes a web, the machinist a machine. — *Emerson*, Works and Days.

2. In *chem.*, a substance used to effect chemical change in another substance for the purpose of identifying its component parts or of ascertaining its percentage composition. Thus, the infusion of galls is a reagent which indicates iron in solution by a dark-purple precipitate. Barium chlorid is a reagent which separates sulphuric acid from a solution in the insoluble form of barium sulphate which can be weighed, and from the weight of which the actual amount of sulphuric acid can readily be deduced. 3. Anything used for the treatment of a substance under investigation to render its nature or condition more evident. Ordinarily the object is to see what changes are thus produced, but the word is used more loosely, as in *hardening reagents.*—**Nessler's reagent**, a reagent used to detect and determine minute quantities of ammonia, particularly in water. It consists of a strongly alkaline solution of potassium iodide and mercuric chlorid. A few drops added to a few fluidounces of water will cause a slight reddish-yellow tinge if one part of ammonia is present in twenty million parts of water.

reaggravation (rē-ag-ra-vā'shon), *n.* [< *reaggravate* + *-ion.*] In *Rom. Cath. eccles. law*, the last monitory, published after three admonitions and before the excommunication.

reagree (rē-a-grē'), *v.* [< *re-* + *agree.*] I. *intrans.* To agree again; become reconciled.

II.† *trans.* To cause to agree again; reconcile.

And fain to see that glorious holiday
Of union which this discord *reagreed.*
Daniel, Civil Wars, vii. 111.

reak†, *v. i.* An obsolete spelling of *reck*[1].

reake†, *n.* [Perhaps an erroneous form for *wrack* or *wreck*, or an error for *reate*, q. v.: see *wrack*, *wreck.*] A kind of plant. [The word occurs only in the passage quoted, where it is used as a translation of Latin *ulva*, seaweed.]

The bore is yll in Laurente soyle,
That teedes on *reakes* and reedes;
Somtymes frome goodly pleasant vine
A sower tendrell speedes.
Drant, tr. of Horace's Satires, ii. 4.

reaks†. See *to play rex*, under *rex.*

reaks-player†, *n.* One who plays reaks (rex). *Cotgrave.*

real[1] (rē'al), *a.* and *n.* [< ME. *real*, *reall*, < OF. *real*, *reel*, F. *réel* = Pr. Sp. Pg. *real* = It. *reale*, < ML. *realis*, belonging to the thing itself (in the disputes of the Nominalists and Realists), < L. *res*, a thing; perhaps allied to Skt. √ *rā*, give. Hence *realize*, *realization*, *realism*, *realist*, *reality*, etc.; also, from L. *res*, E. *rebus*, *republic*, *republican*, etc.] I. *a.* 1. Actual; genuine; true; authentic; not imaginary, artificial, counterfeit, or factitious: as, *real* lace.

I waked, and found
Before mine eyes all *real*, as the dream
Had lively shadow'd. *Milton*, P. L., viii. 310.

Homer tells us that the blood of the gods is not real blood, but only something like it. *Addison*, Spectator, No. 275.

The hatred of unreality was uppermost with Carlyle; the love of what is real with Emerson. *O. W. Holmes*, Emerson, iv.

It is probable that the American inventor of the first anæsthetic has done more for the real happiness of mankind than all the moral philosophers from Socrates to Mill. *Lecky*, Europ. Morals, I. 91.

The Teutonic words are all of them real words, words which we are always wanting. *E. A. Freeman*, Amer. Lects., p. 163.

2. Of genuine character; not pretended or pretending; unassumed or unassuming.

Phœbe's presence made a home about her. . . . She was *real!* *Hawthorne*, Seven Gables, ix.

Real kings hide away their crowns in their wardrobes, and affect a plain and poor exterior. *Emerson*, Works and Days.

3. Specifically, in *philos.*, existing in or pertaining to things, and not words or thought merely; being independent of any person's thought about the subject; possessing characters independently of the attribution of them by any individual mind or any number of minds; not resulting from the mind's action: opposed to *imaginary* or *intentional.* *Real* differs from *actual*, inasmuch as what is only in germ or in posse, in so far as it has a power of developing into a definite actuality, is real, and independent of what we may think about it. Real objects are either external to the mind, when they are independent altogether of our thought, or they are internal, when they depend upon thought, but not upon thought about them.

The term *real* (*realis*), though always importing the existent, is used in various significations and oppositions. . . . 1. As denoting existence, in contrast to the nomenclature of existence—the thing as contradistinguished from its name. Thus we have definitions and divisions *real*, and definitions and divisions nominal or verbal. 2. As expressing the existent as opposed to the non-existent—a something in contrast to a nothing. In this sense the diminutions of existence, to which reality in the following significations is counterposed, are all *real.* 3. As denoting material or external, in contrast to mental, spiritual, or internal, existence. This meaning is improper. . . . 4. As synonymous with *actual*; and this (*a*) as opposed to potential, (*b*) as opposed to possible existence. 5. As denoting absolute or irrespective, in opposition to phænomenal or relative, existence; in other words, as denoting things in themselves and out of relation to all else, in contrast to things in relation to, and as known by, intelligences, like men, who know only under the conditions of plurality and difference. In this sense, which is rarely employed and may be neglected, the *real* is only another term for the unconditioned or absolute—τὸ ὄντως ὄν. 6. As indicating existence considered as a subsistence in nature (ens extra animam, ens naturæ), it stands counter to an existence considered as a representation in thought. In this sense, *reale*, in the language of the older philosophy (Scholastic, Cartesian, Gassendian), as applied to *esse* or *ens*, is opposed to *intentionale*, *notionale*, *conceptibile*, *imaginarium*, *rationis*, *cognitionis*, *in anima*, *in intellectu*, *prout cognitum*, *ideale*, etc.; and corresponds with *a parte rei* as opposed to *a parte intellectus*, with *subjectivum* as opposed to *objectivum*, with *proprium*, *principale*, and *fundamentale* as opposed to *vicarium*, with *materiale* as opposed to *formale*, and with *formale in seipso* and *entitativum* as opposed to *representativum*, etc. Under this head, in the vacillating language of our more recent philosophy, *real* approximates to, but is hardly convertible with, objective, in contrast to subjective in the signification there prevalent. 7. In close connection with the sixth meaning, *real*, in the last place, denotes an identity or difference founded on the conditions of the existence of a thing in itself, in contrast to an identity or difference founded only on the relation or point of view in which the thing may be regarded by the thinking subject. In this sense it is opposed to logical or rational, the terms being here employed in a peculiar meaning. Thus a thing which really (*re*) or in itself is one and indivisible may logically (*ratione*) by the mind be considered as diverse or plural. *Sir W. Hamilton*, Reid's Works, Note B, § 1, 5, foot-note.

Ideas of substances are *real* when they agree with the existence of things. *Locke*, Human Understanding, II. xxx. 5.

We substitute a *real* for a dramatic person, and judge him accordingly. *Lamb*, Artificial Comedy.

For the first time the ideal social compact was *real.* *Emerson*, Hist. Discourse at Concord.

4†. Sincere; faithful; loyal.

Then the governor told them, if they were *real*, as they professed, he should expect their ready and free concurrence with him in all affairs tending to the public service. *Memoirs of Colonel Hutchinson* (1643). (*Nares.*)

5†. Relating to things, not to persons; not personal.

Many are perfect in men's humours that are not greatly capable of the *real* part of business. *Bacon.*

6. In *law*, pertaining to or having the quality of things fixed or immovable. See *real estate*, etc., below.—**Chattel real.** See *chattel.*—**Covenant real.** See *covenant.*—**Real abstraction.** See *abstraction.*—**Real action**, in *law.* See *action*, 8.—**Real assets.** See *assets*, 1.—**Real attribute**, an attribute known by ordinary observation, generalization, and abstraction, and signified by a term of first intention: opposed to a *notional attribute*, which is signified by a term of second intention.—**Real burden**, in *Scots law*, a burden in money imposed on the subject of a right, as on an estate, in the deed by which the right is constituted, and thus distinguished from a *personal burden*, which is imposed merely on the receiver of the right.—**Real character.** See *character.*—**Real component of a force.** See *component.*—**Real composition.** (*a*) The union of objects having existences distinct from one another. (*b*) In *Eng. eccles. law*, an agreement made between the owner of lands and the parson or vicar, with consent of the ordinary, that such lands shall be discharged from payment of tithes, in consequence of other land or recompense given to the parson in lieu and satisfaction thereof. Also called *composition of tithes.*—**Real concordance.** See *concordance*, 3.—**Real contract.** See *contract.*—**Real convenience**†, the agreement of a thing with itself.—**Real definition**, the definition of a thing—that is to say, of a species—by stating the components of its essence, or its place in natural classification. For the nominalists there could be no real definition, in the proper sense; hence, finding the definitions so called useful, they invented new definitions of the phrase. The real definition, for Leibnitz and Wolf, is the definition from which the possibility of the thing defined follows; for Kant, the definition which sets forth the possibility of the thing from its essential marks; for Mill, the definition of a name with an implied assumption of the existence of the thing.—**Real degradation.** See *degradation*, 1 (*a*).—**Real distinction.** (*a*) A distinction independent of any person's thought. (*b*) A distinction between real objects. The Scotists made subtle and elaborate definitions of this phrase.—**Real diversity, division, ens, essence.** See the nouns.—**Real estate**, in *law*: (*a*) Land, including with it whatever by nature or artificial annexation inheres with it as a part of it or as the means of its enjoyment, as minerals on or in the earth, standing or running water, growing trees, permanent buildings, and fences. In this sense the term refers to those physical objects of ownership which are immovable. (*b*) The ownership of or property in lands, etc.; any legal or equitable interest in lands, etc., except some minor, temporary, or inchoate rights which by the laws of most jurisdictions are deemed to be personal estate. "At common law, any estate in lands, etc., the date of the termination of which is not determined by or ascertainable from or at the date of the act which creates it, is *real estate.*" (*Robinson.*) The line between the two classes of property is differently drawn in detail, according as the object of the law is to define what shall be taxed, or what shall go to the heir in case of intestacy as distinguished from what shall go through the administrator to the next of kin, or what shall come within the rules as to recording titles, or other purposes.—**Real evidence, exchange, focus, fugue.** See the nouns.—**Real horse-power.** Same as *indicated horse-power* (which see, under *horse-power*).—**Real identity**, the non-difference in reality of the extremes of a relation.—**Real immunity** (*eccles.*). See *immunity*, 3.—**Real induction.** See *induction*, 5.—**Real laws**, laws which directly and indirectly regulate property, and the rights of property, without changing the state of the person.—**Real noon.** Same as *apparent noon* (which see, under *apparent*).—**Real partition**, the mental separation of an object into parts which might be physically separated.—**Real poinding, possibility, power, precision, presence, privilege.** See the nouns.—**Real property.** Same as *real estate.*—**Real quality, quantity, relation, representative, restriction, right.** See the nouns.—**Real question**, a question where the attribute in regard to whose presence or absence inquiry is made is a real one.—**Real science** or **philosophy.** (*a*) A science or philosophy that is caused in the mind by a real thing, as physics, mathematics, metaphysics; a speculative science: opposed to *practical science*, which is caused in the mind by an idea of a thing to be brought about. (*b*) A science which has a determinate reality for its object, and is conversant about existences other than forms of thought: in this sense, mathematics is not a real science.—**Real services.** Same as *predial services* (which see, under *predial*).—**Real things**, in *law*, things substantial and immovable, and the rights and profits annexed to or issuing out of them.—**Real truth**, the agreement of a judgment with its object: opposed to *formal truth*, which consists in the agreement of a reasoning with the principles of logic.—**The real stuff**, the genuine thing; that which is really what is represented or supposed: used especially of liquors. [Colloq.]

In this exhibition there are, of course, a certain number of persons who make believe that they are handing you round tokay—giving you the *real* imperial *stuff*, with the seal of genuine stamped on the cork. *Thackeray*, Men and Pictures.

Real warrandice. See *warrandice.* = **Syn. 1** and **2.** *Real, Actual, Positive*, veritable, substantial, essential. *Real* applies to that which certainly exists, as opposed to that which is imaginary or feigned: as, *real* cause for alarm; a *real* occurrence; a *real* person, and not a ghost or a shadow; *real* sorrow. *Actual* applies to that which is brought to be or to pass, as opposed to that which is possible, probable, conceivable, approximate, estimated, or guessed at. *Actual* has a rather new but natural secondary sense of present. *Positive*, from the idea of a thing's being placed, fixed, or established, is opposed to *uncertain* or *doubtful.*

II. *n.* 1. That which is real; a real existence or object; a reality.

While it is true that correlatives imply each other, it is not true that all correlatives imply *Reals.* . . . The only meaning we can attach to Reality is that every *Real* has a corresponding feeling or group of feelings. *G. H. Lewes*, Probs. of Life and Mind, II. 19.

2†. A realist.

Scotists, Thomists, *Reals*, Nominals. *Burton*, Anat. of Mel., p. 677.

The real. (*a*) Reality. (*b*) The real thing; the genuine article. [Colloq.]

A cynic might suggest as the motto of modern life this simple legend,—"Just as good as *the real.*" *C. D. Warner*, Backlog Studies, p. 4.

real[1] (rē'al), *adv.* [< *real*[1], *a.*] Really; truly; very; quite. [Colloq., Eng. and U. S.]

real[2]† (rē'al), *a.* [< ME. *real*, *riall*, *rial*, *ryall*, *ryell*, *roial*, royal, regal, < AF. *reial*, *roial*, OF. *real*, F. *réal* (used only in certain antique locutions), = Sp. Pg. *real* = It. *reale*, *regale*, < L. *regalis*, regal, kingly, royal: see *royal* and *regal*[1], doublets of *real*[2]. Cf. *leal*, *loyal*, *legal*, similarly related.] Royal; regal; royally excellent or splendid.

Thus, *real* as a prince is in his hallé,
Leve I this chauntecleer in his pasture.
Chaucer, Nun's Priest's Tale, l. 364.

Sir, I could wish that for the time of your vouchsafed abiding here, and more *real* entertainment, this my house stood on the Muses' hill. *B. Jonson*, Every Man out of his Humour, ii. 1.

Reall, magnanimous, bountious. *Marston*, Antonio and Mellida, I., ii. 1.

real[3] (rā-äl'), *n.*; pl. *reales* (rā-ä'les). [Also *rial*; < Sp. *real*, a coin so called, lit. 'royal,' < L. *regalis*, regal, royal: see *real*[2], *royal*, *regal*[1].] A subsidiary silver coin and money of account in Spain and Spanish-American countries. The current real of Spain (*real de vellon*) is one quarter of the peseta or franc, and worth about 5 United States cents. The Mexican real, corresponding to the old Spanish *real de plata*, is one eighth of a dollar (Mexican *peso*), and reckoned at 12½ cents. The latter coin, both Spanish and Mexican, circulated largely in the United States down to about 1850,

Obverse. Reverse.
Silver Real of Isabella II.—British Museum. (Size of original.)

being called a Spanish or Mexican shilling in New York, a levy (see *levy*[3], 1) in the South, etc.

real[4] (rē´al), *n.* [Cuban, perhaps < Sp. *real*, royal: see *real*[2], *real*[3]. Cf. OF. *real*, a kind of sturgeon.] The big-eyed herring, or saury, *Elops saurus*. [Cuba.]

reales, *n.* Plural of *real*[3].

realgar (rē-al´gär), *n.* [Also *resalgar*, < ME. *resalgar*, *rysalgar*, *rosalgar*; = OF. *realgal*, *reagal*, *riagal*, *realgal*, *risigal*, F. *réalgar* = Sp. *rejalgar* = Pg. *rosalgar* = It. *risigallo* (ML. *risigallum*), < Ar. *rahj al-ghar*, realgar, lit. 'powder of the mine,' mineral powder (so called because derived orig. from silver-mines): *rahj*, *rehj*, dust, powder; *al*, the; *ghār* (*gār*), cavern, mine. Cf. Ar. *rahj asfar*, orpiment.] Arsenic disulphid (As_2S_2), a combination of an equal number of sulphur and arsenic atoms; red sulphuret of arsenic, which is found native in transparent crystals, and also massive. Realgar differs from orpiment in that orpiment is composed of two equivalents of arsenic and three of sulphur, and has a yellow color. Realgar, also called *red arsenic* or *ruby sulphur*, is prepared artificially for use as a pigment and for making white fire, which is a mixture of 2 parts of ruby sulphur and 10 parts of niter.

realisation, realise. See *realization*, *realize*.

realism (rē´al-izm), *n.* [= F. *réalisme* = Sp. Pg. It. *realismo* = G. *realismus*, < NL. *realismus*; as *real*[1] + *-ism*.] 1. The doctrine of the realist, in any of the senses of that word. See especially *realist*, *n.*, 1.

(1) Extreme *realism* taught that universals were substances or things, existing independently of and separately from particulars. This was the essence of Plato's theory of ideas. . . . (2) Moderate *realism* also taught that universals were substances, but only as dependent upon and inseparable from individuals, in which each inhered: that is, each universal inhered in each of the particulars ranged under it. This was the theory of Aristotle, who held that the τόδε τι or individual thing was the first essence, while universals were only second essences, real in a less complete sense than first essences. He thus reversed the Platonic doctrine, which attributed the fullest reality to universals only, and a merely participative reality to individuals. . . . (3) Extreme nominalism taught that universals had no substantive or objective existence at all, but were merely empty names or words. [See *nominalism*.] (4) Moderate nominalism or conceptualism taught that universals have no substantive existence at all, but yet are more than mere names signifying nothing; and that they exist really, though only subjectively, as concepts in the mind, of which names are the vocal symbols. . . . (5) [The medieval schoolmen] Albertus Magnus, Thomas Aquinas, Duns Scotus, and others fused all these views into one, and taught that universals exist in a threefold manner: universalia ante rem, as thoughts in the mind of God; universalia in re, as the essence [quiddity] of things, according to Aristotle; and universalia post rem, as concepts in the sense of moderate nominalism. This is to-day the orthodox philosophy of the Catholic Church, as opposed to the prevailingly exclusive conceptualism of the Protestant world. . . . In contrast with all the views above presented, another and sixth view will now be stated. . . . (6) Relationism or scientific *realism* teaches that universals, or genera and species, are, first, objective relations of existence among objectively existing things; secondly, subjective concepts of these relations, determined in the mind by the relations themselves; and thirdly, names representative both of the relations and of the concepts, and applicable alike to both. This is the View logically implied in all scientific classifications of natural objects, regarded as objects of real scientific knowledge.
F. E. Abbot, Scientific Theism, Int.

2. In *literature* and *art*, the representation of what is real in fact; the effort to exhibit the literal reality and unvarnished truth of things; treatment of characters, objects, scenes, events, circumstances, etc., according to actual truth or appearance, or to intrinsic probability, without selection or preference over the ugly of what is beautiful or admirable: opposed to *idealism* and *romanticism*. Compare *naturalism*.

I wish the reader particularly to observe, throughout all these works of Tintoret, the distinction of the imaginative Verity from falsehood on the one hand, and from *realism* on the other. *Ruskin*, Modern Painters, III. ii. 3.

A far fuller measure of the ease and grace and life of the *realism* which Giotto had taught.
D. G. Mitchell, Bound Together, ii.

By *realism* I mean simply the observation of things as they are, the familiarity with their aspect, physical and intellectual, and the consequent faculty of reproducing them with approximate fidelity.
Contemporary Rev., L. 241.

Exact realism. See *Herbartian*.—**Hypothetic realism.** See *hypothetic*.—**Natural realism**, the doctrine that in sensation (if not also in volition) we have a direct consciousness of a real object other than ourselves, so that we are as sure of the existence of the outer world as we are of our own, or even of the presence of ideas.

In the act of sensible perception, I am conscious of two things;—of myself as the perceiving subject, and of an external reality . . . as the object perceived. . . . I am conscious of knowing each of them, not mediately, in something else, as represented, but immediately in itself, as existing. . . . Each is apprehended equally, and at once, in the same indivisible energy . . . ; and . . . each is apprehended out of, and in direct contrast to, the other. . . . The contents of the fact of perception, as given in consciousness, being thus established, what are the consequences to philosophy, according as the truth of its testimony is, or is not, admitted? On the former alternative, the veracity of consciousness, in the fact of perception, being unconditionally acknowledged, we have established at once, without hypothesis or demonstration, the reality of mind and the reality of matter; while no concession is yielded to the sceptic, through which he may subvert philosophy in manifesting its self-contradiction. The one legitimate doctrine, thus possible, may be called *natural realism* or natural dualism. . . . If the testimony of consciousness to our knowledge of an external world existing be rejected with the idealist, but with the realist the existence of that world be affirmed, we have a scheme which—as it by many various hypotheses endeavours on the one hand not to give up the reality of an unknown material universe, and on the other to explain the ideal illusion of its cognition—may be called the doctrine of cosmothetic idealism, hypothetical realism, or hypothetical dualism. This last [system] . . . is the one which . . . has found favour with the immense majority of philosophers.
Sir W. Hamilton, Reid's Works, Note A, § 1, 10.

realist (rē´al-ist), *n.* and *a.* [= F. *réaliste* = Sp. Pg. It. *realista* = G. *realist*, < NL. *realista*; as *real*[1] + *-ist*.] **I.** *n.* 1. A logician who holds that the essences of natural classes have some mode of being in the real things: in this sense distinguished as a *scholastic realist*: opposed to *nominalist*. As soon as intellectual development had reached the point at which men were capable of conceiving of an essence, they naturally found themselves realists. But reflection about words inclined them to be nominalists. Thus, a controversy sprang up between these sects in the eleventh century (first in the Irish monasteries, and then spread through the more civilized countries of northern Europe), and was practically settled in favor of the realists toward the end of the twelfth century. During the fourteenth century a reaction from the subtleties of Scotus produced a revival of nominalistic views, which were brought into a thorough-going doctrine by Occam, his followers being distinguished as *terminists* from other schools of nominalists. At the time when scholasticism came to a rather violent end, owing to the revival of learning, the terminists were in the ascendant, though some of the universities were Scotist. The Cartesians did not profess to be realists; and Leibnitz was a decided nominalist; while the whole weight of the English school (Occam, Hobbes, Locke, Berkeley, Hume, Hartley, Reid, Brown, the Mills, and others) went in the same direction. At the present day philosophy seems to be, and science certainly is, prevailingly realistic. See quotation under *realism*, 1.

2. A philosopher who believes in the real existence of the external world as independent of all thought about it, or, at least, of the thought of any individual or any number of individuals.—3. In *literature* and *art*, a believer in or a practiser of realism; one who represents persons or things as he conceives them to be in real life or in nature; an opponent of idealism or romanticism.

How hard and meagre they seem, the professed and finished *realists* of our own day, ungraced by that spiritual candor which makes half the richness of Ghirlandaio!
H. *James, Jr.*, Trans. Sketches, p. 298.

4. One who advocates technical as opposed to classical education; one who upholds the method of the real-schools. [A German use.]

II. *a.* Of or pertaining to realism; realistic; naturalistic.

realistic (rē-a-lis´tik), *a.* [< *realist* + *-ic*.] 1. Of or pertaining to the realists in philosophy; characteristic of speculative realism.

The *realistic* tendency—the disposition to mistake words for things—is a vice inherent in all ordinary thinking.
J. Fiske, Cosmic Philos., I. 122.

2. Exhibiting or characterized by realism in description or representation; objectively real or literal; lifelike, usually in a bad or depreciatory sense: as, a *realistic* novel or painting; a *realistic* account of a murder.

A bit of *realistic* painting, in the midst of a piece of decorative painting, would offend us, and yet the *realistic* bit would add a certain amount of veracity.
P. G. Hamerton, Graphic Arts, v.

Realistic they are in the nobler sense: that is, they are true to nature without being slavish copies of nature.
C. C. *Perkins*, Italian Sculpture, p. 91

Realistic dualism. See *dualism*.

realistically (rē-a-lis´ti-kal-i), *adv.* In a realistic manner; in a manner that has regard to the actual appearance of objects or circumstances, or the real facts of existence.

reality[1] (rē-al´i-ti), *n.*; pl. *realities* (-tiz). [= F. *réalité* = Sp. *realidad* = Pg. *realidade* = It. *realità*, < ML. *realita(t-)s*, < *realis*, real: see *real*[1]. Cf. *realty*[1].] 1. The being real; truth as it is in the thing; objective validity; independence of the attributions of individual thought; positively determinate being.

Hee exhorted him to beleeve the *reality* of the sacrament after the consecration.
Foxe, Martyrs, p. 1159, an. 1543.

Reality shall rule, and all shall be as they shall be for ever. *Sir T. Browne*, Christ. Mor., iii. 24.

For this, in *reality*, is the port of Acre, where ships lie at anchor. *Pococke*, Description of the East, II. i. 56.

In the English plays alone is to be found the warmth, the mellowness, and the *reality* of painting.
Macaulay, Dryden.

Nothing can have *reality* for us until it enters within the circle of Feeling, either directly through perception, or indirectly through Intuition. Conception is the symbolical representation of such real presentation.
G. *H. Lewes*, Probs. of Life and Mind, II. 11.

2. That which is real or genuine; something that really is or exists, as opposed to what is imagined or pretended; an essential verity or entity, either in fact or in representation.

Of that skill the more thou know'st,
The more she will acknowledge thee her head,
And to *realities* yield all her shows.
Milton, P. L., viii. 575.

Only shadows are dispensed below,
And Earth has no *reality* but woe.
Cowper, Hope, l. 68.

They who live only for wealth, and the things of this world, follow shadows, neglecting the great *realities* which are eternal on earth and in heaven.
Sumner, Orations, I. 194.

3. In *law*, same as *realty*[1]. [Now rare.]—**Absolute reality.** See *absolute*.—**Empirical reality**, the reality of an object of actual or conditionate experience.

What we insist on is the *empirical reality* of time, that is, its objective validity, with reference to all objects which can ever come before our senses. What we deny is that time has any claim to absolute reality, so that, without taking into account the form of our sensuous condition, it should by itself be a condition or quality inherent in things; for such qualities as belong to things by themselves can never be given to us through the senses.
Kant, Critique of Pure Reason, tr. by Müller.

Objective reality, truth; reference to a real object. This is the sense in which this phrase is used by Kant. At an earlier date it would have meant existence in the mind. With later writers it means nearly the same as *absolute reality*.—**Practical reality**, in the *Kantian philos.*, that force in a postulate of the practical reason by which it becomes the source of the possibility of realizing the summum bonum.

I have, indeed, no intuition which should determine its objective theoretic reality of the moral law, but not the less it has a real application, which is exhibited in concreto in intentions or maxims: that is, it has a *practical reality* which can be specified, and this is sufficient to justify it even with a view to noumena.
Kant, Critique of Practical Reason, tr. by T. K. Abbott, [p. 146.

Reality of laws, a legal phrase for all laws concerning property and things.—**Subjective reality**, real existence in the mind.

Time has *subjective reality* with regard to internal experience; that is, I really have the representation of time, and of my determinations in it.
Kant, Critique of Pure Reason, tr. by Müller, p. 37.

Theoretical reality, in the *Kantian philos.*, validity as a hypothesis.—**Transcendental reality.** Same as *absolute reality*. = **Syn.** 1 and 2. Verity (see *real*1). *Reality* means that a thing certainly is; *truth* applies to the correctness of what is said or believed about the thing, the conformity of such report or belief to reality. The *reality* of a danger; the *actuality* of the arrival of help; the *truth* about the matter.

reality[2]†, *n.* Same as *realty*[2].

Our *reality* to the emperor. *Fuller*.

realizability (rē-a-li-za-bil´i-ti), *n.* [< *realizable* + *-ity* (see *-bility*).] Capability of being realized. [Rare.]

realizable (rē´a-li-za-bl), *a.* [< F. *réalisable*; as *realize* + *-able*.] Capable of being realized.

realization (rē´al-i-zā´shon), *n.* [< OF. *realisation*, F. *réalisation*; as *realize* + *-ation*.] 1. A bringing or coming into real existence or manifestation, as of something conceived or imagined: as, the *realization* of a project.

The *realization* of the rights of humanity in the nation is the fulfillment of righteousness.
E. Mulford, The Nation, vi.

The desire is the direction of a self-conscious subject to the *realisation* of an idea.
T. *H. Green*, Prolegomena to Ethics, § 151.

2. Perception of the reality or real existence of something; a realizing sense or feeling: as, the *realization* of one's danger.

An intrinsic and awful *realization* of eternal truths.
Islay Burns, Memoir of W. C. Burns, p. 98.

3. The act of realizing upon something; conversion into money or its equivalent; exchange of property for its money value. [Trade use.]—4. The act of converting money into land or real estate. *Imp. Dict.*

Also spelled *realisation*.

realize (rē´al-īz), *v.*; pret. and pp. *realized*, ppr. *realizing*. [< OF. *realiser*, F. *réaliser* = Sp. Pg. *realizar*; as *real*[1] + *-ize*.] **I.** *trans.* 1. To make or cause to become real; bring into existence or fact: as, to *realize* a project, or a dream of empire.

His [Clive's] dexterity and resolution *realised*, in the course of a few months, more than all the gorgeous visions which had floated before the imagination of Dupleix.
Macaulay, Lord Clive.

All art is the endeavour to *realise* in material forms and colours an idea of beauty latent in the human spirit from the beginning. *Faiths of the World*, p. 5.

Children are, as it were, fresh blocks of marble, in which, if we have any ideal, we have a new chance of *realizing* it after we have failed in ourselves. *J. R. Seeley*, Nat. Religion, p. 128.

2. To perceive or comprehend the reality of; make real or distinct to one's self; recognize the real nature or the actual existence of: as, to *realize* the horrors of war; to *realize* one's danger or one's deficiencies.

Intrenched within these many walls, the people of this gay capital cannot *realize* war. *W. Ware*, Zenobia, II. xi.

In order to pity suffering we must *realise* it. *Lecky*, Europ. Morals, I. 138.

He [Samuel Adams] wanted the whole world to *realize* that the rule of a republic is a rule of law and order. *J. Fiske*, Critical Period of Amer. Hist., iv.

3. To manifest as real or as a reality; exhibit the actual existence or character of; cause to appear real or distinct.

To put these materials to poetical use is required an imagination capable of painting nature, and *realizing* fiction. *Johnson*, Milton.

The child *realizes* to every man his own earliest remembrance, and so supplies a defect in our education, or enables us to live over the unconscious history with a sympathy so tender as to be almost personal experience. *Emerson*, Domestic Life.

Correggio appears to have been satisfied with *realising* the tumult of heaven rushing to meet earth, and earth straining upwards to ascend to heaven in violent commotion. *J. A. Symonds*, Italy and Greece, p. 274.

4. To bring or get into actual possession; make one's own; clear as a profit or gain; obtain a return of: as, to *realize* a fortune from speculation.

Send me an account of the number of crowns you *realize*. *Shelley*, To H. Reveley, Oct. 18, 1819.

Pope was the first Englishman who, by the mere sale of his writings, *realised* a sum which enabled him to live in comfort and in perfect independence. *Macaulay*, Montgomery's Poems.

Man begins with nothing *realized* (to use the word), and he has to make capital for himself by the exercise of those faculties which are his natural inheritance. *J. H. Newman*, Gram. of Assent, ix.

The question of imposing upon what has been termed *realised* income a higher poundage than that for what has been termed precarious income has been frequently raised. *S. Dowell*, Taxes in England, III. 136.

5. To bring into form for actual or ready use; exchange for cash or ready means: as, to *realize* one's stock or securities. [Trade use.]—6. To fetch as a price or return; bring in exchange or as compensation; make a return of: as, how much did the cargo *realize*? his labor *realizes* but little.

A farm he sold *realised* less than was anticipated. *Whyte Melville*, White Rose, II. xxvi.

7. To convert into real estate; make real property of. *Imp. Dict.*

II. *intrans.* To obtain ready money or profits by sale of property.

Also spelled *realise*.

realizedness (rē'al-ī-zed-nes), *n.* The state of being realized. [Rare.]

But taking pleasure to be the feeling of the *realizedness* of the will or self, we should doubt if apart from some present function or activity pleasure could exist. *F. H. Bradley*, Ethical Studies, p. 119.

realizer (rē'al-ī-zėr), *n.* One who realizes. *Coleridge.*

realizingly (rē'al-ī-zing-li), *adv.* So as to realize. [Rare.]

reallege (rē-a-lej'), *v. t.* [= OF. *realleguer*, F. *réalléguer*; as *re-* + *allege*[1].] To allege again. *Cotgrave.*

realliance (rē-a-lī'ans), *n.* [< *re-* + *alliance.*] A renewed alliance.

reallich†, *adv.* See *really*[2].

really[1] (rē'al-i), *adv.* [< *real*[1] + *-ly*[2].] 1. In a real manner; with or in reality; in fact, and not in appearance only; in truth; actually; truly.

The bread therefore changeth not to his essence, but is bread *realie*, and is the bodie of Christ sacramentallie. *Foxe*, Martyrs, p. 456.

James . . . hoped to obtain a law, nominally for the removal of all religious disabilities, but *really* for the excluding of all Protestants from all offices. *Macaulay*, Sir J. Mackintosh.

2. Indeed; to tell the truth; as a fact: often used as a slight corroboration of an opinion or declaration, or interrogatively or exclamatorily to express slight surprise. [Colloq.]

Why, *really*, sixty-five is somewhat old. *Young.*

Really, no; a dyspeptic demigod it makes one dyspeptic to think of! *De Quincey*, Homer, ii.

=**Syn.** 1. Truly, absolutely, certainly, verily, positively.

really[2]† (rē'al-i), *adv.* [< ME. *realyche*, *realy*, *rially*, *realliche*; < *real*[2] + *-ly*[2]. Cf. *royally*.] Royally; in a royal or regal manner; like a king.

It is ful fair to ben yclept madame,
And gon to vigilies al byfore,
And han a mantel *riallyche* ibore.
Chaucer, Gen. Prol. to C. T., l. 378.

really[3] (rē-a-lī'), *v. t.* [< *re-* + *ally.* Cf. *rally*[1].] To form or arrange again; recompose.

That whil'st the Gods . . .
Were troubled, and amongst themselves at ods,
Before they could new counsels *re-allie*,
To set upon them in that extasie.
Spenser, F. Q., VII. vi. 23.

realm (relm), *n.* [< ME. *realme*, *ryalme*, *roialme*, *royalme*, *reaume*, *reume*, *rewme*, *reame*, *reme*, *rem*, < OF. *realme*, *reaume*, *roialme*, *royaume*, F. *royaume* = Pr. *realme*, *reyalme*, *reialme* = OSp. *reame*, *realme* = It. *reame*, < ML. as if **regalimen*, a kingdom, < L. *regalis*, of a king: see *real*[2], *royal*, *regal*.] 1. A royal jurisdiction or extent of government; a king's dominions; a kingdom.

Pes among the puple he put to the *reaume*.
William of Palerne (E. E. T. S.), l. 5240.

Sydrak, Misak, and Abdenago: that is to seye, God glorious, and God victorious, and God over alle Thinges and *Remes*. *Mandeville*, Travels, p. 35.

Whoso wol seken actes of sondry *remes*
May rede of dremes many a wonder thing.
Chaucer, Nun's Priest's Tale, l. 310.

Which Salique land the French unjustly glose
To be the *realm* of France. *Shak.*, Hen. V., i. 2. 41.

Thou, great Anna! whom three *realms* obey.
Pope, R. of the L., iii. 7.

These are our *realms*, no limit to their sway—
Our flag the sceptre all who meet obey.
Byron, Corsair, i. 1.

2. Figuratively, a jurisdiction or domain in general; a sphere of power, influence, or operation; province; arena.

The Goddess goes exulting from his sight,
And seeks the seas profound, and leaves the *realms* of light.
Dryden, Iliad, i.

3. In *zoögeog.*, a prime division of the earth's surface; a faunal area of the largest extent; a zoölogical region of the first order.—**To abjure the realm.** See *abjure*.

realness (rē'al-nes), *n.* The state or condition of being or appearing real; manifest genuineness; freedom from artifice or any deception.

There is such a *realness* to his narration that one is willing to overlook his many deficiencies in the art of expression. *Science*, VI. 472.

real-school (rē'al-sköl), *n.* [Tr. G. *realschule*, < *real*, real, practical, = E. *real*[1], + *schule*, school, = E. *school*[1].] One of a class of preparatory scientific or technical schools in Germany, corresponding in grade to the gymnasia or classical schools.

realty[1] (rē'al-ti), *n.* [< OF. **realte* = It. *realtà*, < ML. *realita(t-)s*, reality: see *reality*[1]. Cf. *lealty* and *legality*, *specialty* and *speciality*, *personalty* and *personality*, etc.] 1†. Reality.—2. In *law*: (*a*) Immobility, or the fixed, permanent nature of that kind of property termed *real*. (*b*) Landed property; real estate. See *real*[1] and *personalty*.

realty[2]† (rē'al-ti), *n.* [< ME. *realte*, *rielte*, *reaute*, *roialtee*, < OF. *realte*, *reaute*, *royaulte*, F. *royauté*, royalty, = It. *realtà*, < ML. *regalita(t-)s*, < L. *regalis*, regal: see *regal*, *real*[2]. Cf. *reality*[2], *royalty*.] 1. Royalty.

Whi sholdys thou my *realte* oppress?
Chaucer, Fortune, l. 60.

Kings do . . . hazard infinitely
In their free *realties* of rights and honours,
Where they leave much for favourites' powers to order.
Chapman and Shirley, Admiral of France, i.

2. Loyalty; fealty.

O heaven! that such resemblance of the Highest
Should yet remain, where faith and *realty*
Remain not. *Milton*, P. L., vi. 115.

ream[1] (rēm), *n.* [Also *reem*, *raim*; < ME. *rem*, *reme*, < AS. *reám* = D. *room* = MLG. *rôm*, LG. *rom* = MHG. *roum*, G. *raum*, *rahm* = Icel. *rjómi*, cream; origin unknown.] Cream; also, the cream-like froth on ale or other liquor; froth or foam in general. [Prov. Eng. and Scotch.]

Soone aftir ȝe schal se as it were a liqour of oyle ascende vp fletynge aboue in maner of a skyn or of a *reme*.
Book of Quinte Essence (ed. Furnivall), p. 9.

Cristened we weore in red *rem*
Whon his bodi bledde on the Beem
Of Cipresse and Olyue.
Holy Rood (E. E. T. S.), p. 146.

ream[1] (rēm), *v. i.* [< *ream*[1], *n.*] 1. To cream; mantle; foam; froth. [Prov. Eng. and Scotch.]

Wi' *reaming* swats [ale] that drank divinely.
Burns, Tam o' Shanter.

A huge pewter measuring pot, . . . which, in the language of the hostess, *reamed* . . . with excellent claret.
Scott, Waverley, xi.

2. To appear like foam; be fleecy. [Rare.]

Farewell the flax and *reaming* wooll
With which thy house was plentifull.
Herrick, The Widdowes Teares.

ream[2] (rēm), *v. t.* [Also *reem*, dial. *rim*, *rime*; < ME. *remen*, *rimen*, *rumen*, < AS. *rȳman*, widen, extend, spread, enlarge, etc. (= OS. *rûmian* = OFries. *rêma* = MD. D. *ruimen* = MLG. *rûmen* = OHG. *rûmian*, *rûman*, MHG. *rûmen*, yield, give way, make room, retire, relax, G. *räumen*, make room, etc., = Icel. *rȳma*, make room, clear, quit, = Sw. *rymma* = Dan. *römme*, quit), < *rûm*, wide, roomy: see *room*[1].] 1†. To make wide; widen; extend; extend by stretching; stretch or draw out.

His full growne stature, high his head, lockes higher rise;
His pearching hornes are *ream'd* a yard beyond assise.
A Herrings Tayle (1598). (*Nares.*)

Specifically—2. To widen or enlarge by the use of a rotatory cutter: often with *out*: used especially of a hole or an opening in metal, and most commonly in connection with splayed or funnel-shaped holes.—3. *Naut.*, to open (seams) for calking.—4†. To leave; quit.

Thu makedest me fleme (flee),
And thi lond to *reme*.
King Horn (E. E. T. S.), p. 36.

ream[3] (rēm), *n.* [Early mod. E. *reme*; < late ME. *reeme* = D. *riem*, < OF. *rayme*, *raime*, *rame*, F. *rame* (ML. reflex *rama*) = It. *risma*, formerly also *risima*, < Sp. Pg. *resma* (ML. *risma*) (cf. late MHG. *ris*, *riz*, *rist*, G. *ries*, *riess* = Dan. Sw. *ris*, with loss of final syllable), < Ar. *rizma* (pl. *rizam*), a bundle, esp. of clothes, also of paper. The word was brought into Europe by the Moors, who introduced the manufacture of cotton paper into Spain.] A quantity of paper, consisting, for ordinary writing-paper, of 20 quires of 24 sheets each, or 480 sheets; for some kinds of drawing-paper, of 472 or 500 sheets; for printing-paper, of 21½ quires, or 516 sheets. Writing-paper is usually put up in half- or quarter-ream packages, printing-paper in bundles of two reams.—**A ream of insides**, 480 sheets of perfect paper.—**Perfect ream**, an improper use for *printers' ream*.—**Printers' ream**, or **printing ream**. See *printer*.

ream†, *n.* A Middle English form of *realm*.

reamer (rē'mėr), *n.* [Also *rimer* (= G. *räumer*, a person who or an instrument that makes clean); < *ream*[2] + *-er*[1].] One who or that which reams; specifically, a tool used for reaming out holes. Reamers have a variety of forms, of which triangular, square, or pentagonal shafts or bodies with sharp angles, fluted bodies with sharp edges, and bodies formed with intersecting right and left spiral grooves with sharp edges are prominent types. The bodies are of uniform thickness for reaming straight holes, and tapered for reaming tapered holes or for enlarging holes. Compare *ream*[2], *v. t.*, 2.—**Expanding reamer**, a reamer having a device which can be extended after the insertion of the reamer into a hole, so as to make an undercut.

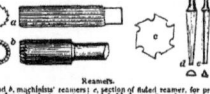

Reamers.
a and *b*, machinists' reamers; *c*, section of fluted reamer, for producing salient edges; *d* and *e*, flat-sided reamers, or broaches.

reamer-bit (rē'mėr-bit), *n.* Same as *reaming-bit*.

reaminess (rē'mi-nes), *n.* [< *reamy* + *-ness*.] A creaming or foaming condition; an appearance as of foaming or frothing. [Rare.]

Reaminess, or wavy marks, of uneven thickness in the film . . . are most likely to occur in thick viscous samples of collodion. *Silver Sunbeam*, p. 457.

reaming-bit (rē'ming-bit), *n.* A bit used for enlarging or splaying holes in metal.

reaming-iron (rē'ming-ī"ėrn), *n.* *Naut.*, an iron instrument used for opening the seams of planks so that they may be more readily calked.

ream-kit (rēm'kit), *n.* A cream-pot. *Halliwell.* [Yorkshire, Eng.]

reamy (rē'mi), *a.* [< *ream*[1] + *-y*[1].] Creamy; creaming; in a foaming condition; appearing frothy. [Rare.]

rean[1] (rēn), *n.* [< ME. *rene*, a watercourse: see *rine*, *run*[1].] A watercourse; a gutter; specifically, the furrow between ridges of plowed land to take off the water. *Halliwell.* [Prov. Eng.]

rean[2]†, *n.* and *v.* An old spelling of *rein*[1].

reanimate (rē-an'i-māt), *v.* [< *re-* + *animate*. Cf. F. *réanimer* = Sp. Pg. *reanimar* = It. *rianimare*.] I. *trans.* 1. To revive; resuscitate;

restore to life, as a person dead or apparently dead: as, to *reanimate* a person apparently drowned.

We are our *re-animated* ancestours, and antedate their resurrection. *Glanville*, Vanity of Dogmatizing, xv.

We may suppose that the creative power returns and *reanimates* some among the dead. *Isaac Taylor*, Nat. Hist. Enthusiasm, p. 66.

2. To revive when dull or languid; invigorate; infuse new life or courage into: as, to *reanimate* disheartened troops; to *reanimate* drowsy senses or languid spirits.

Variety *reanimates* the attention, which is apt to languish under a continual sameness. *Sir J. Reynolds*, Discourses, viii.

II. *intrans.* To revive; become lively again. [Rare.]

"There spoke Miss Beverley!" cried Delvile, *reanimating* at this little apology. *Miss Burney*, Cecilia, ix. 5.

reanimation (rē-an-i-mā'shọn), *n.* [< *reanimate* + *-ion.*] The act or operation of reanimating, or reviving from apparent death; the act or operation of giving fresh spirits, courage, or vigor; the state of being reanimated.

Having opened his father's casque, he was rejoiced to see him give symptoms of *reanimation*. *Scott*, Anne of Geierstein, xxxvi.

reannex (rē-a-neks'), *v. t.* [< *re-* + *annex.*] To annex again; annex what has been separated; reunite.

King Charles was not a little inflamed with an ambition to repurchace and *re-annex* that duchie. *Bacon*, Hist. Hen. VII., p. 40.

reannexation (rē-an-ek-sā'shọn), *n.* [< *reannex* + *-ation.*] The act of annexing again.

reanoint (rē-a-noint'), *v. t.* [< *re-* + *anoint.*] To anoint again or anew.

And Edward, . . .
Proud in his spoils, to London doth repair,
And, *reanointed*, mounts th' imperial chair.
Drayton, Miseries of Queen Margaret.

reanswer (rē-ån'sėr), *v. t.* [< *re-* + *answer.*] 1. To answer again; make a renewed reply to.— 2†. To answer or satisfy as a return; correspond to; equal; balance.

Bid him therefore consider of his ransome; which must proportion the losses we have borne, . . . which in weight to *re-answer*, his pettiness would bow under. *Shak.*, Hen. V., iii. 6. 136.

reap (rēp), *v.* [< ME. *repen*, *reopen*, *ripen* (pret. *rap*, *rep*, pl. *ropen*, *ropen*, pp. *repen*, *ropen*, later *reaped*), < AS. *rīpan*, a variable verb, being in part strong (pret. pl. *ripon*), also *geripan* (pret. pl. *geripon*), also with short vowel *ripan*, Anglian *riopan*, *rioppan*, *hrioppan*, *hrippan* (pret. **ræp*, pl. *rǣpon*), and in part (and appar. orig.) weak, *rȳpan* (pret. **rȳpte*, not found), reap (cf. *rip*, *rȳp*, a reaping, harvest): appar. a particular use of *rīpan*, prop. *rȳpan* (pret. pl. *rȳpton*, *rǣpton*), plunder, spoil, = OHG. *roufen*, MHG. *roufen*, *reufen*, *röufen*, G. *raufen*, pluck, pull, etc., = Goth. *raupjan*, pluck. Cf. D. *rapen*, reap, gather.] I. *trans.* 1. To cut with a sickle or other implement or machine; cut down and gather: used specifically of cutting grain: as, to *reap* wheat or rye.

When ye *reap* the harvest of your land, thou shalt not wholly reap the corners of thy field. Lev. xix. 9.

That which they *reapt* on the land was put into storehouses built for that purpose. *Purchas*, Pilgrimage, p. 876.

And no Man ever *reapt* his Corn,
Or from the Oven drew his Bread,
Ere Hinds and Bakers yet were born,
That taught them both to sow and knead.
Prior, Alma, i.

2. To cut a crop of grain, or something likened to such a crop, from; clear by or as if by reaping.

His chin new *reap'd*
Show'd like a stubble-land at harvest-home.
Shak., 1 Hen. IV., i. 3. 34.

3. Figuratively, to gather in by effort of any kind; obtain as a return or recompense; garner as the fruit of what has been done by one's self or others.

They have sown the wind, and they shall *reap* the whirlwind. Hos. viii. 7.

Of our labours thou shalt *reap* the gain.
Shak., 3 Hen. VI., v. 7. 20.

He cannot justly expect to *reape* aught but dishonour and dispraise. *Milton*, Eikonoklastes, v.

Do thou the deeds I die too young to do,
And *reap* a second glory in thine age!
M. Arnold, Sohrab and Rustum.

II. *intrans.* 1. To perform the act or operation of reaping; cut and gather a harvest.

Yf y *repe*, [I] ouere-reche, other gaf hem red that *repen*
To sese to me with here sykel; that ich sew neuere.
Piers Plowman (C), vii. 270.

Thou shalt sow, but thou shalt not *reap*. Micah vi. 15.

I would the globe from end to end
Might sow and *reap* in peace.
Tennyson, Epilogue.

2. Figuratively, to gather the fruit of labor or works; receive a return for what has been done.

For wel I wot that ye han herbeforne
Of makynge [poetry] *ropen*, and lad awey the corne.
Chaucer, Good Women, l. 74.

They that sow in tears shall *reap* in joy. Ps. cxxvi. 5.

reap† (rēp), *n.* [Early mod. E. also *repe*; < ME. *reepe*, *rep*, *rip*, < AS. *rīp*, *rȳp*, a reaping, a crop, harvest (also in comp., as *rīp-man*, harvester, *rīp-tīma*, harvest), also a sheaf of grain, etc., < *rīpan*, *rȳpan*, reap: see *reap*, *v.*] A sheaf of grain. [Prov. Eng.]

As mych as oone *reepe*.
Towneley Mysteries, p. 13. (*Halliwell.*)

reaper (rē'pėr), *n.* [< ME. *repare*, *ripere*, < AS. *rīpere*, a reaper, < *rīpan*, reap: see *reap*, *v.*] 1. One who reaps; one who cuts grain with a sickle or other implement or machine; hence, one who gathers in the fruits of his own or others' labor or work.

When brown August o'er the land
Call'd forth the *reapers'* busy band.
Scott, Rokeby, vi. 35.

In the vast field of criticism on which we are entering, innumerable *reapers* have already put their sickles. *Macaulay.*

Only *reapers*, reaping early
In among the bearded barley,
Hear a song that echoes cheerly.
Tennyson, Lady of Shalott, i.

2. A machine for cutting grain; a reaping-machine.—**The reaper**, an ancient sophism, to the following effect: If you are to reap, it is not true that perhaps you will reap and perhaps not, but you will certainly reap. On the other hand, if you are not to reap, it is not true that perhaps you will reap and perhaps not, but you will certainly not. Thus you will either necessarily reap, or necessarily not reap, and the statement that there is a "perhaps" is false.

reap-hook (rēp'hůk), *n.* Same as *reaping-hook*. *Halliwell.* [Prov. Eng.]

reaping-hook (rē'ping-hůk), *n.* A curved blade with a short handle for reaping; a sickle; specifically, a sickle without the notched edge which formerly distinguished that implement.

The reapers in Palestine and Syria still make use of the *reaping-hook* in cutting down their crops: and "fill their hand" with the corn, and those who bind up the sheaves their "bosom."—Ps. cxxix. 7; Ruth ii. 5. *Kitto.*

reaping-machine (rē'ping-ma-shēn"), *n.* A harvesting-machine for grain-crops; a mechanical reaper drawn over a field of standing grain by horses. The reaping-machine is a modified mowing-machine or mower, both mower and reaper being harvesters; the two machines are identical in their mechanism for cutting down the standing grain, of which mechanism the essential feature is the reciprocating knife moving within the fingers of a finger-bar. The reaper is distinguished from the mower by the addition of a reel for bending the grain down upon the knives, and by a platform, a raking mechanism, a discharging mechanism or dropper (by which the gavels or sheaves are thrown out of the machine), and a binding mechanism; of these devices any or all may be present in one machine. Reaping-machines are often distinguished according to their attachments: thus, a *dropper* is a reaping-machine that automatically throws out the cut grain at intervals; a *self-raker* or a *self-binder*, sometimes called a *harvester and binder*, is one with a raking or a binding attachment. The discharging mechanism or dropper is a device for causing the platform upon which the grain falls when cut to throw off its load. The raking attachment consists of a series of rakes moving over the platform to gather the grain into gavels and sweep it off upon the ground. The binding attachment consists essentially of an endless-belt elevator for lifting the cut grain, and a pair of curved arms for gathering and compressing it into a bundle and holding it while the binding mechanism proper draws wire or twine around it, twists the wire or loops and knots the twine, cuts the bundle from the wire or twine, and discharges the bound sheaf.

Reaping-machine.

a, driving-wheel; *b*, pole; *c*, whiffletrees; *d*, driver's seat; *e*, cutter-bar, arranged at front edge of platform *f* and carried by the latter; *g*, supporting wheel for outside extremity of the platform; *h*, tilting-lever, by which the front edge of the platform may be depressed for cutting grain that is lodged; *i*, *i'*, *i''*, *i'''*, rakes; *j*, cam-mechanism for operating rakes; *k*, outside divider, which separates the standing grain; *k'*, inside divider, which separates the cut grain on the ground from that on the platform. The grain as cut falls on the platform, and is formed into gavels by the rakes *i*, *i'*, etc., which move from the front to the rear of the platform after reaching the position shown at *i*.

reapman† (rēp'man), *n.* [< ME. *repman*, < AS. **rīpman* (Anglian *hripeman*), a harvestman, < *rīp*, harvest, + *man*, man.] A reaper; a harvestman.

Oon daywerk of a goode *repman* may gete
V strik, a febbler for III may swete.
Palladius, Husbondrie (E. E. T. S.), p. 158.

reapparel (rē-a-par'el), *v. t.* [< *re-* + *apparel*, *v.* Cf. *reparel.*] To apparel or clothe again or anew.

Then [at the resurrection] we shall all be invested, *reapparelled*, in our own bodies. *Donne*, Devotions, Expostulation, xiv.

reapparition (rē-ap-a-rish'ọn), *n.* [< *re-* + *apparition.*] A renewed apparition; a coming again; reappearance. [Rare.]

There would be presented the phenomena of colonies, *reapparitions*, and other faunal dislocations in the vertical and horizontal distribution of fossil remains. *Winchell*, World-Life, p. 281.

reappear (rē-a-pēr'), *v. i.* [= It. *riapparire*; as *re-* + *appear*. Cf. OF. *rapparoitre*, F. *réapparaître*, reappear.] To appear again or anew; return to sight or apprehension; be seen again, in either the same or a different example.

The law of harmonic sounds *reappears* in the harmonic colors. *Emerson*, Nature, v.

Energy . . . only vanishes to *reappear* under some other form. *W. L. Carpenter*, Energy in Nature, p. 12.

The river that *reappears* at Ombla is an old friend. *E. A. Freeman*, Venice, p. 238.

reappearance (rē-a-pēr'ans), *n.* [< *reappear* + *-ance.*] A new appearance; another coming into view or apprehension: as, the *reappearance* of Encke's comet.

reapplication (rē-ap-li-kā'shọn), *n.* [< *re-* + *application.*] The act of applying again, or the state of being reapplied.

A readvertency or *reapplication* of mind to ideas that are actually there. *Norris*, Reflections on Locke, p. 9. (*Latham.*)

reapply (rē-a-plī'), *v. t.* and *i.* [< *re-* + *apply.*] To apply again.

reappoint (rē-a-point'), *v. t.* [< *re-* + *appoint.*] To appoint again.

reappointment (rē-a-point'mẹnt), *n.* [< *reappoint* + *-ment.*] A renewed appointment.

reapportion (rē-a-pōr'shọn), *v. t.* [< *re-* + *apportion.*] To apportion again; make a new apportionment.

reapportionment (rē-a-pōr'shọn-mẹnt), *n.* [< *reapportion* + *-ment.*] A renewed apportionment; a new proportional distribution or arrangement: as (in the United States), the *reapportionment* of members of Congress or of Congressional districts under a new census.

reapproach (rē-a-prōch'), *v.* [< *re-* + *approach.*] I. *intrans.* To come near again.

II. *trans.* To bring near together again.

We were able to produce a lovely purple, which we can destroy or recompose at pleasure, by severing and *re-approaching* the edges of the two irises. *Boyle*, Works, I. 738.

reap-silver† (rēp'sil"vėr), *n.* [ME. *repsilver*; < *reap*, *n.*, + *silver.*] Money paid by feudal serfs or tenants to their lord as a commutation for their services in reaping his crops.

rear[1] (rēr), *v.* [Early mod. E. also *reer*, *rere*, also dial. *rare*; < ME. *reren*, < AS. *rǣran* (= Icel. *reisa* = Goth. *raisjan*), cause to rise, lift up, establish, rouse, elevate, etc.; causative of *rīsan* (pret. *rās*), rise: see *rise*[1], and cf. *raise*[1], which is from the Icel. form (*reisa*) of the same verb. The change of the orig. medial *s* to *r* occurs also in *were* (pl. of *was*), *ear*[1], *iron*, *lorn*, etc.] I. *trans.* 1. To raise, lift, or hoist by or as if by main strength; bring to or place in an elevated position; set or hold up; elevate; bear aloft.

Off with the traitor's head,
And *rear* it in the place your father's stands.
Shak., 3 Hen. VI., ii. 6. 86.

And higher yet the glorious temple *rear'd*
Her pile. *Milton*, P. R., iv. 546.

2. To form by raising or setting up the parts of; lift up and fix in place the materials of; erect; construct; build.

Seint dauid aboute this holi ȝerde a strong wal let *rere*. *Holy Rood* (E. E. T. S.), p. 28.

O'er his Grave a Monument they *rear'd*. *Congreve*, Iliad.

3†. To raise from a prostrate state or position; uplift; exalt.

The Ladie, hearing his so courteous speach,
Gan *reare* her eyes as to the chearefull light.
Spenser, F. Q., VI. ii. 42.

In adoration at his feet I fell
Submiss; he *rear'd* me.
Milton, P. L., viii. 316.

Charity, decent, modest, easy, kind,
Softens the high, and *rears* the abject mind.
Prior, Charity.

4†. To lift or carry upward; give an upward bent or turn to.

Up to a hill anon his steps he *rear'd*,
From whose high top to ken the prospect round.
Milton, P. R., ii. 285.

5†. To cause to rise into view; approach (an object) so that it appears above the visible horizon. See *raise*[1], 10.

And in .xv. degrees, we dyde *reere* the crossiers; and we myght haue *rered* them sooner if we had loked for theym.
R. Eden, First three Eng. Books on America (ed. Arber), [p. 380.

6†. To carry off, as by conquest; take away by or as if by lifting; wrest. See *raise*[1], 6.

He, in an open Turney lately held,
Fro me the honour of that game did *reare*.
Spenser, F. Q., IV. vi. 6.

It *rereth* our hearts from vain thoughts.
Barrow. (*Webster.*)

7†. To cause to rise to action; stir up; rouse.

Item, the Kyng cometh to London ward, and, as it is seyd, *rereth* the pepyll as he come. *Paston Letters*, I. 506.

Into the naked woods he goes,
And seeks the tusky boar to *rear*,
With well-mouthed hounds and pointed spear.
Dryden, tr. of Horace's Epode ii.

They were not in any hope that the citye wold hastelye consent to *rere* war. *Golding*, tr. of Cæsar, fol. 201.

The waves come rolling, and the billowes rore,
For not one puffe of winde there did appeare,
That all the three thereat woxe much afrayd,
Unweeting what such horrour straunge did *reare*.
Spenser, F. Q., II. xii. 22.

8†. To raise in amount; make a rise in; increase.

He stirs men up to outrageous *rearing* of rents.
Latimer, 6th Sermon bef. Edw. VI.

9. To develop or train physically or mentally or both, as young; care for while growing up; foster; nurture; educate: used of human beings, and less frequently of animals and plants. See *raise*[1].

The pokok men may *rere* up esily
Yf bestes wilde or theves hem ne greve.
Palladius, Husbondrie (E. E. T. S.), p. 23.

She [Pharaoh's daughter] takes him vp, and *rears* him royal-like;
And his quick Spirit, train'd in good Arts, is like
A wel breath'd Body, nimble, sound, and strong.
Sylvester, tr. of Du Bartas's Weeks, ii., The Lawe.

Delightful task! to *rear* the tender Thought,
To teach the young Idea how to shoot.
Thomson, Spring, l. 1150.

10. To mock; gibe. *Halliwell.* [Prov. Eng.] =**Syn.** 9. *Bring up*, etc. See *raise*[1].

II. *intrans.* **1.** To rise up; assume an elevated posture, as a horse or other animal in standing on its hind legs alone.

Ofte hit [the ark] roled on-rounde, and *rered* on ende.
Alliterative Poems (ed. Morris), ii. 423.

Anon he *rears* upright, curvets, and leaps.
Shak., Venus and Adonis, l. 279.

2. To rise up before the plow, as a furrow. *Halliwell.* [Prov. Eng.]—**Rearing vein**, in *coal-mining*, a vein that seems to rear like a horse or mule. See *rearer*, 3.

rear[2] (rēr), *a.* [Early mod. E. also *reer*, *rere*, also dial. (now in common use in the U. S.) *rare*; < ME. *rere*, < AS. *hrēr*, underdone (said only of eggs): *hrēr henne æg*, 'a rear hen's egg,' *hrērenbrǣden æg*, *hrērebrǣd æg*, 'a rear roasted egg,' *gebrǣddan hrēro ægeran*, 'roasted rear eggs'; appar. not an independent adj., but the stem of a verb, in comp. **hrēr-æg* (= G. *rühr-ei*, a scrambled egg, buttered egg; cf. *eier rühren*, beat eggs), < *hrēran*, move, shake, stir, + *æg*, egg: see *rear*[4].] Underdone; nearly raw; rare: formerly said of eggs, now (in the United States, in the form *rare*) of meats. Compare *rear-boiled*, *rear-roasted*. [Obsolete or provincial.]

Rere, or nesche, as eggys. Mollis, sorbilis.
Prompt. Parv., p. 430.

If they [eggs] be *rere*, they do clense the throte and brest.
Sir T. Elyot, Castle of Health, ii. 13.

Maces and ginger, *rere egges*, and poched eggs not hard, theyr yolkes be a cordiall. *Borde*, Breviary of Health.

Can a soft, *rear*, poor poach'd iniquity
So ride upon thy conscience?
Middleton, Game at Chess, iv. 2.

rear[3] (rēr), *n.* and *a.* [Early mod. E. also *reer*, *rere*; < ME. *rere*, in comp. *rereward*, rearward and *arere*, arrear (see *arrear*[2], *adv.*), < OF. *rere*, *riere*, back, < L. *retro*, back, backward, < *re*, back, + compar. suffix (in abl.) *-tro*. But in ME. and mod. E. *rear* as a prefix is rather an aphetic form of *arear*, *arrear*: see *arrear*[2], *adv.*] **I.** *n.* **1.** The space behind or at the back; a tract or a position lying backward; the background of a situation or a point of view.

Tom Pipes, knowing his distance, with great modesty took his station in the *rear*. *Smollett*, Peregrine Pickle, ii.

Crook . . . conducted his command south in two parallel columns until he gained the *rear* of the enemy's works.
P. H. Sheridan, Personal Memoirs, II. 37.

2. The back or hinder part; that part of anything which is placed or comes last in order or in position.

His yeomen all, both comly and tall,
Did quickly bring up the *rear*.
Robin Hood and Maid Marian (Child's Ballads, V. 375).

Like a gallant horse fall'n in first rank,
Lie there for pavement to the abject *rear*,
O'er-run and trampled on.
Shak., T. and C., iii. 3. 162.

While the cock, with lively din,
Scatters the *rear* of darkness thin.
Milton, L'Allegro, l. 50.

Were they in the front or in the *rear* of their generation?
Macaulay, Sir J. Mackintosh.

3. In specific military use, the hindmost body of an army or a fleet; the corps, regiment, squadron, or other division which moves or is placed last in order: opposed to *van*: as, the *rear* was widely separated from the main body.

The Vanguard he commits to his Brother the Count de Alanson, the *Reer* to the Earl of Savoy.
Baker, Chronicles, p. 121.

To bring up the rear. See *bring*. [In comp. *rear* is practically a prefix. In older words it is always *rere*; for such words, see entries in *rere-*.]

II. *a.* Pertaining to or situated in the rear; hindermost; last: as, the *rear* rank.—**Rear front**, the rear rank of a company or body of men when faced about and standing in that position.—**Rear supper†**. See *rere-supper*.—**Rear vault**, in *arch.*, a small vault over the space between the tracery or glass of a window and the inner face of the wall.

rear[3]† (rēr), *v. t.* [< *rear*[3], *v.*] To send to or place in the rear.

rear[4]†, *v. t.* [< ME. *reren*, < AS. *hrēran*, move, shake, stir, = OS. *hrōrian*, *hrōrien*, *hruorian*, shake, = OHG. *hruorjan*, *hrōrjan*, *ruoran*, MHG. *rüeren*, G. *rühren*, shake, touch, = Icel. *hræra* = Sw. *röra* = Dan. *röre*, move, stir; perhaps = Goth. **hrōzjan* (not recorded), akin to *hrisjan*, shake. Hence, in comp., *rearmouse*, *reremouse*, and *uproar*. Cf. *rear*[2].] **1.** To move; stir.—**2.** To carve: applied to the carving of geese. *Halliwell.*

Rere that goose. *Babees Book* (E. E. T. S.), p. 265.

rear[5]†, *adv.* Same as *rare*[3].

O'er yonder hill does scant the dawn appear,
Then why does Cuddy leave his cot so *rear?*
Gay, Shepherd's Week, Monday, l. 6.

rear-admiral (rēr'ad'mi-ral), *n.* See *admiral*, 2.

rearage† (rēr'āj), *n.* [ME., by apheresis for *arerage*: see *arrearage*.] Arrearage.

Such dedes I did wryte, ʒif he his day breke.
I haue mo maneres [manors] thorw *rerages* than thorw misseretur et comodat. *Piers Plowman* (B), v. 246.

ffor he wylle gyfe a rekonyng that rewe salle aftyre, . . .
Or the *rereage* be requit of rentez that he claymez!
Morte Arthure (E. E. T. S.), l. 1680.

rear-boiled† (rēr'boild), *a.* [Formerly *rere-boiled*; < *rear*[2] + *boiled*.] Partly boiled.

A *rere-boiled* egg, Een half gaar gekookt ey.
Sewel, Eng.-Dutch Dict.

reard†, *n.* [< ME. *rerd*, *rerid*, *reorde*, *rorde*, *rurd*, < AS. *reord* (for **reard*), voice, speech, language, = OHG. *rarta* = Icel. *rödd* (gen. *raddar*) = Goth. *razda*, a voice, sound.] A voice; sound.

Ecko . . . is the *rearde* thet ine the heʒe helles [high hills] comth ayen. *Ayenbite of Inwit* (E. E. T. S.), p. 60.

reardorse†, *n.* [< ME. *reredors*: see *reredos*.] **1.** An open fireplace against the rear wall of a room, without a chimney, the smoke rising and escaping through the louver.

In their [the old men's] yoong daies there were not aboue two or three [chimneys], if so manie, in most vplaudish townes of the realme (the religious houses, manour places of their lords, alwaies excepted, and peraduenture some great personages), but ech one made his fire against a *reredosse* in the hall, where he dined and dressed his meat.
Harrison, Descrip. of Eng., ii. 12. (*Holinshed.*)

Also, you shall inquire of all armorers and other artificers using to work in mettal, which have or use any *reardorses*, or any other places dangerous or perillous for fire.
Calthrop's Reports (1670). (*Nares.*)

2. A piece of armor for the back.

Ane hole brest-plate, with a *rere-dors*
Behynde shet, or elles on the syde.
Clariodes, MS. (*Halliwell.*)

rear-egg†, *n.* An underdone egg. See *rear*[2], *a.*

rearer (rēr'ėr), *n.* **1.** One who rears or raises; one who brings up.

Pholoë, . . . the *rearer* of the steed.
Lewis, tr. of Statius's Thebaid, x.

2. A rearing horse, ass, or mule; an animal that has a habit of rearing.—**3.** In *coal-mining*, a seam of coal having an inclination of more than thirty degrees.

rear-guard (rēr'gärd), *n.* [Early mod. E. *rere-garde*, for **areregarde*, < OF. **ariere-garde*, *ariere-garde*, F. *arrièregarde*, rear-guard; as *rear*[3] + *guard*, *n.* Cf. *rearward*.] Part of an army detached during a march for the protection of the rear, especially in retreating when the attacks of a pursuing enemy are feared.

We can nat se aboute vs, nor haue knoledge of your *reregarde* nor vowarde.
Berners, tr. of Froissart's Chron., II. cxlii.

reargue (rē-är'gū), *v. t.* [< *re-* + *argue*.] To argue over again.

reargument (rē-är'gū-ment), *n.* [< *re-* + *argument*.] A renewed argumentation, as of a case in court; a new arguing or pleading upon the same matter.

rearhorse (rēr'hôrs), *n.* A gressorial and raptorial orthopterous insect of the family *Mantidæ*; a praying-mantis, camel-insect, or devil's coach-horse: so called from the way in which it rears upon its hind legs. The common rearhorse of the United States is *Phasmomantis carolina*. See *Empusa*, and cut under *mantis*.

rearing-bit (rēr'ing-bit), *n.* A bit intended to prevent a horse from lifting his head when rearing. In the accompanying cut, *a*, *a* are rings for check-straps, to which also the chain *b* is attached, in use passing under the horse's lower jaw; *c*, *c* are rings for attachment of curb-reins. The side-pieces, d, d act as levers when the reins are pulled, and force open the horse's jaw, the curved part of the bit pressing forward and downward upon the tongue of the animal, thus causing him pain when he attempts to rear.

a a d b c c

Rearing-bit.

rearing-box (rēr'ing-boks), *n.* In *fish-culture*, a fish-breeder.

rearly (rēr'li), *adv.* [< *rear*[5] + *-ly*[2].] Early. [Prov. Eng.]

Jailer's Brother. I'll bring it to-morrow.
Jailer's Daughter. Do, very *rearly*, I must be abroad else,
To call the maids.
Fletcher (and another), Two Noble Kinsmen, iv. 1.

rearmost (rēr'mōst), *a. superl.* [< *rear*[3] + *-most*.] Furthest in the rear; last of all.

The rest pursue their course before the wind,
These of the *rear-most* only left behind.
Rowe, tr. of Lucan's Pharsalia, iii.

rearmouse, *n.* See *reremouse*.

rearrange (rē-a-rānj'), *v. t.* [< *re-* + *arrange*.] To arrange anew; make a different arrangement of.

rearrangement (rē-a-rānj'ment), *n.* [< *rearrange* + *-ment*.] A new or different arrangement.

rear-roasted† (rēr'rōs'ted), *a.* Partly roasted. Compare *rear*[2].

There we complaine of one *reare-roasted* chick,
Here meat worse cookt nere makes us sick.
Sir J. Harington, Epigrams, iv. 6. (*Nares.*)

reart (rērt), *v. t.* [A corruption of *reet*, a dial. var. of *right*, *v.*] To right or mend. *Halliwell.* [Local, Eng.]

rearward[1]† (rēr'wârd), *n.* [Early mod. E. *rereward*; < ME. *rerewarde*, short for *arere-warde*, < OF. *arere-warde*, < *arere*, back, + *ward*, *garde*, ward, guard: see *arrear*[2] and *ward*. Cf. doublet *rear-guard*.] **1.** A rear-guard; a body or force guarding the rear.

The standard of the camp of the children of Dan set forward, which was the *rereward* [rearward, R. V.] of all the camps. Num. x. 25.

The God of Israel will be your *rereward* [rearward, R. V.].
Isa. lii. 12.

Because . . . it was bootlesse for them [the Turks] to assaile the forefront of our battell, . . . they determined to set vpon our *rereward*. *Hakluyt's Voyages*, II. 20.

Hence—**2.** Any company or body of persons bringing up the rear; the rear.

He . . . speaks to the tune of a country lady, that comes ever in the *rearward* or train of a fashion.
B. Jonson, Cynthia's Revels, iv. 1.

rearward[2] (rēr'wärd), *adv.* [< *rear*[3] + *-ward*.] At or to the rear; toward the hinder part; backward from anything.

Rearward extended the curtain of mountains, back to the Wolkenburg. *Longfellow*, Hyperion, i. 1.

rearward[2] (rēr'wärd), *a.* and *n.* [< *rearward*[2], *adv.*] **I.** *a.* Situated at or toward the rear; being or coming last.

II. *n.* Place or position at the rear; the part that comes last; rear; end; conclusion; wind-up.

'A came ever in the *rearward* of the fashion.
Shak., 2 Hen. IV., iii. 2. 339.

rearwardly (rēr'wärd-li), *adv.* In a rearward direction; toward the rear; rearward. [Objectionable.]

Having a handle . . . extending *rearwardly* beyond the suction tube. *The Engineer*, LXV. 374.

reascend (rē-a-send'), *v. i.* and *t.* [< *re-* + *ascend.*] To ascend, mount, or climb again.

Taught by the heavenly Muse to venture down
The dark descent, and up to *reascend.*
Milton, P. L., iii. 20.

He mounts aloft and *reascends* the skies. *Addison.*

reascension (rē-a-sen'shon), *n.* [< *re-* + *ascension.*] The act of reascending; a remounting.

reascent (rē-a-sent'), *n.* [< *re-* + *ascent.*] A rise of ground following a descent.

Hence the declivity is sharp and short,
And such the *reascent.* *Cowper*, Task, i. 327.

reason[1] (rē'zn), *n.* [< ME. *reson, resun, resoun, raisoun, reisun*, < OF. *reson, resoun, reison, reasoun, reason, raison, raisoun, raisun*, F. *raison*, F. dial. *roison* = Pr. *razo, razio* = Cat. *raho* = Sp. *razon* = Pg. *razão* = It. *ragione*, < L. *ratio(n-)*, reckoning, list, register, sum, affair, relation, regard, course, method, etc., also the faculty of reckoning, or of mental action, reason, etc., < *reri*, pp. *ratus*, think: see *rate*[2]. *Reason*[1] is a doublet of *ratio* and *ration*.] 1. An idea acting as a cause to create or confirm a belief, or to induce a voluntary action; a judgment or belief going to determine a given belief or line of conduct. A premise producing a conclusion is said to be the *reason* of that conclusion; a perceived fact or reflection leading to a certain line of conduct is said to be a *reason* for that conduct; a cognition giving rise to an emotion or other state of mind is said to be a *reason* of or for that state of mind.

And be ready always to give an answer to every man that asketh you a *reason* of the hope that is in you.
1 Pet. iii. 15.

Give you a *reason* on compulsion! If *reasons* were as plentiful as blackberries, I would give no man a *reason* upon compulsion. *Shak.*, 1 Hen. IV., ii. 4. 264.

2. A fact, known or supposed, from which another fact follows logically, as in consequence of some known law of nature or the general course of things; an explanation.

No sooner sighed but they asked one another the *reason*; no sooner knew the *reason* but they sought the remedy.
Shak., As you Like it, v. 2. 39.

Not even the tenderest heart, and next our own,
Knows half the *reasons* why we smile or sigh.
Keble, Christian Year, 24th Sunday after Trinity.

3. An intellectual faculty, or such faculties collectively. (*a*) The intellectual faculties collectively. (*b*) That kind and degree of intelligence which distinguishes man from the brutes.

And at the end of the days I Nebuchadnezzar lifted up mine eyes unto heaven, and mine understanding returned unto me, and I blessed the most High. . . . At the same time my *reason* returned unto me. Dan. iv. 36.

O judgement! thou art fled to brutish beasts,
And men have lost their *reason.*
Shak., J. C., iii. 2. 110.

For smiles from *reason* flow,
To brute denied. *Milton*, P. L., ix. 239.

(*c*) The logical faculties generally, including all that is subservient to distinguishing truth and falsehood, except sense, imagination, and memory on the one hand, and the faculty of intuitively perceiving first principles, and other lofty faculties, on the other.

The knowledge which respecteth the Faculties of the Mind of man is of two kinds: the one respecting his Understanding and *Reason*, and the other his Will, Appetite, and Affection; whereof the former produceth Position or Decree, the later Action or Execution. . . . The end of Logic is to teach a form of argument to secure *reason*, and not to entrap it; the end of Morality is to procure the affections to obey *reason*, and not to invade it; the end of Rhetoric is to fill the imagination to second *reason*, and not to oppress it. *Bacon*, Advancement of Learning, ii.

But God left free the will; for what obeys
Reason is free, and *reason* he made right,
But bid her well be ware, and still erect;
Lest, by some fair-appearing good surprised,
She dictate false, and misinform the will
To do what God expressly hath forbid.
Milton, P. L., ix. 352.

We may in *reason* discover these four degrees; the first and highest is the discovering and finding out of proofs; the second, the regular and methodical disposition of them, and laying them in a clear and fit order, to make their connection and force be plainly and easily perceived; the third is the perceiving of their connection; and the fourth is a making a right conclusion.
Locke, Human Understanding, iv. 17, § 3.

(*d*) The faculty of drawing conclusions or inferences, or of reasoning.

When she rates things, and moves from ground to ground,
The name of *reason* she obtains by this;
But when by *reason* she the truth hath found,
And standeth fix'd, she understanding is.
Sir J. Davies, Immortal. of Soul, § 25.

The Latins called accounts of money rationes, and accounting ratiocinatio; and that which we in books of accounts call items they call nomina, that is, names; and thence it seems to proceed that they extended the word ratio to the faculty of reckoning in all other things. The Greeks have but one word, λόγος, for both speech and *reason*; not that they thought there was no speech without *reason*, but no reasoning without speech. . . . Out of all which we may define, that is to say determine, what that is which is meant by this word *reason*, when we reckon it amongst the faculties of the mind. For *reason*, in this sense, is nothing but reckoning.
Hobbes, Leviathan, i. 4.

(*e*) The faculty by which we attain the knowledge of first principles; a faculty for apprehending the unconditioned.

Some moral and philosophical truths there are so evident in themselves that it would be easier to imagine half mankind run mad, and joined precisely in the same species of folly, than to admit anything as truth which should be advanced against such natural knowledge, fundamental *reason*, and common sense. *Shaftesbury.*

Reason is the faculty which supplies the principles of knowledge a priori.
Kant, Critique of Pure Reason, tr. by Müller, p. 11.

4. Intelligence considered as having universal validity or a catholic character, so that it is not something that belongs to any person, but is something partaken of, a sort of light in which every mind must perceive.—5. That which recommends itself to enlightened intelligence; some inward intimation for which great respect is felt and which is supposed to be common to the mass of mankind; reasonable measure; moderation; right; what mature and cool reflection, taking into account the highest considerations, pronounces for, as opposed to the prompting of passion.

You shall find me reasonable; if it be so, I shall do that that is *reason.* *Shak.*, M. W. of W., i. 1. 218.

Reason is the life of the law; nay, the common law itself is nothing else but *reason.* *Sir E. Coke*, Institutes.

To subdue
By force who *reason* for their law refuse,
Right *reason* for their law, and for their King
Messiah, who by right of merit reigns.
Milton, P. L., vi. 41.

Many are of opinion that the most probable way of bringing France to *reason* would be by the making an attempt upon the Spanish West Indies.
Addison, Present State of the War.

6. A reasonable thing; a rational thing to do; an idea or a statement conformable to common sense.

And telle he moste his tale as was *resoun*,
By forward and by composicioun,
As ye han herd.
Chaucer, Prol. to Knight's Tale (ed. Morris), l. 847.

It is not *reason* that we should leave the word of God and serve tables. Acts vi. 2.

Men cannot retire when they would, neither will they when it were *reason.* *Bacon*, Great Place.

7. The exercise of reason; reasoning; right reasoning; argumentation; discussion.

Your *reasons* at dinner have been sharp and sententious.
Shak., L. L. L., v. 1. 2.

I follow'd her; she what was honour knew,
And with obsequious majesty approved
My pleaded *reason.* *Milton*, P. L., viii. 510.

8. The intelligible essence of a thing or species; the quiddity.

That other opinion, that asserts that the abstract and universal rationes, *reasons*, of things, as distinct from phantasms, are nothing else but mere names without any signification, is so ridiculously false that it deserves no confutation at all.
Cudworth, Eternal and Immutable Morality, iv. 1.

9. In *logic*, the premise or premises of an argument, especially the minor premise.

A premiss placed after its conclusion is called the *Reason* of it, and is introduced by one of those conjunctions which are called causal: viz., "since," "because," &c.
Whately, Logic, i. § 2.

By reason†. (*a*) For the reason that; because.

'Tis not unusual in the Assembly to revoke their Votes, *by reason* they make so much haste.
Selden, Table-Talk, p. 108.

(*b*) By right or justice; properly; justly.

And, as my body and my beste ougte to be my liegis,
So rithfully be *reson* my rede shulde also.
Richard the Redeless, Prol.

By reason of, on account of; for the cause of.

And *by reson of* gentill fader ought come gentill issue.
Merlin (E. E. T. S.), iii. 660.

The days of our years are threescore years and ten; and if *by reason of* strength they be fourscore years, yet is their strength labour and sorrow. Ps. xc. 10.

Mr. Bradford and Mr. Collier of Plimouth came to Boston, having appointed a meeting here the week before, but *by reason of* foul weather were driven back.
Winthrop, Hist. New England, I. 166.

The Parliament is adjourned to Oxford, *by reason of* the Sickness which increaseth exceedingly.
Howell, Letters, I. iv. 20.

I cannot go so fast as I would, *by reason of* this burden that is on my back. *Bunyan*, Pilgrim's Progress, p. 89.

We elected a president, as many of the ancients did their kings, *by reason of* his height.
Addison, Spectator, No. 108.

Discourse of reason, the operation or faculty of reasoning, or the conscious and voluntary use of beliefs already had to determine others.

O God! a beast, that wants *discourse of reason*,
Would have mourn'd longer. *Shak.*, Hamlet, i. 2. 150.

Discursive reason, reason in the sense 3 (d); the dianoetic faculty, or faculty of drawing conclusions and inferences. Compare *intuitive reason*, below.

Whence the soul
Reason receives, and *reason* is her being,
Discursive or *intuitive*; discourse
Is oftest yours, the latter most is ours,
Differing but in degree, of kind the same.
Milton, P. L., v. 487.

Diversity of reason†. See *diversity*.—**Ens of reason.** See *ens*.—**False reason**, an inconclusive reason.—**Feast of reason.** (*a*) Delightful intellectual discourse.

There St. John mingles with my friendly bowl
The *feast of reason* and the flow of soul.
Pope, Imit. of Horace, II. i. 128.

(*b*) [*caps.*] In *French hist.*, an act of worship of human reason, represented by a woman as the goddess of Reason, performed on November 10th, 1793, in the cathedral of Notre Dame, and also in other churches (renamed temples of Reason) in France on that and succeeding days. The worship of Reason was designed to take the place of the suppressed Christian worship; recognition of the Supreme Being was restored through the influence of Robespierre.—**Generative reason.** See *generative*.—**In reason.** (*a*) In the view or estimation of reason; reasonably; justly; properly.

His unjust unkindness, that *in* all *reason* should have quenched her love. *Shak.*, M. for M., iii. 1. 250.

The Oath which binds him to performance of his ought *in reason* to contain the summ of what his chief trust and Office is. *Milton*, Eikonoklastes, vi.

(*b*) Agreeable to reason; reasonable; just; proper: as, I will do anything *in reason*.—**Intuitive reason**, reason in the sense 3 (*e*); the noetic faculty, or sense of primal truth. See quotation under *discursive reason*.—**Logical reason**, discursive reason.—**Objective reason.** See *objective*.—**Out of reason**, without or beyond reason; devoid of cause or warrant.

If we desyre no redresse of dedis before,
We may boldly vs byid with bostis *out of Reason.*
Destruction of Troy (E. E. T. S.), l. 2222.

Practical reason. See *practical*.—**Principle of sufficient reason**, the proposition that nothing happens without a good and sufficient reason why it should be as it is and not otherwise. This doctrine denies, first, that anything happens by chance or spontaneity, and, second, that anything happens by irrational and brute force. It is inextricably bound up with the principle of the identity of indiscernibles. It requires that there should be a general reason why the constants of nature should have the precise values they have. It is in conflict with every form of nominalism, teaching that general reasons are not only real, but that they exclusively govern phenomena; and it appears to lead logically to an idealism of a Platonic type. It is not the mere statement that everything has a cause, but that those causes act according to general and rational principles, without any element of blind compulsion. The principle was first enunciated by Leibnitz in 1710, and has met with extraordinary favor, the more so as it has often been misunderstood.—**Pure reason**, reason strictly a priori; reason quite independent of experience. See *pure*, 8.

Reason is *pure* if in reasoning we admit only definitions and propositions known a priori.
Baumeister, Philosophia Definitiva (trans.), 2d ed., 1738, [§ 823.

Pure reason is that faculty which supplies the principles of knowing anything entirely a priori.
Kant, Critique of Pure Reason, tr. by Müller, p. 11.

Ratiocinant reason. (*a*) A reason or cause as it exists in the mind: opposed to *ratiocinate reason*.

I have not asked this question without cause causing, and *reason* truly very *ratiocinant.*
Urquhart, Rabelais, III. vi. (*Davies.*)

(*b*) The human understanding; the discursive reason.—**Ratiocinate reason**, a reason as an element of the quiddity of things, according to the Aristotelian conception: opposed to *ratiocinant reason*.—**Reason of state**, a political motive for a public act which cannot be accounted for publicly; a concealed ground of action by a government or a public officer in some matter concerning the state's welfare or safety, or the maintenance of a policy.—**Relation of reason.** See *relation*.—**Right reason**, reason in sense 5, above.—**Rime nor reason.** See *rime*[1].—**Speculative reason**, reason employed about supersensuous things.—**Subjective reason**, reason which is determined by the subject or agent.—**Sufficient reason.** See *principle of sufficient reason*, above.—**Theoretical reason**, reason as productive of cognition.—**There is no reason but**, there is no reason why not; it is inevitable; it cannot be helped.

There is no reason but I shall be blind.
Shak., T. G. of V., ii. 4. 212.

To do one reason†. (*a*) To do what is desired, or what one desires; act so as to give satisfaction.

Lord Titus, by your leave, this maid is mine.
. . . [I am] resolved withal
To do myself this *reason* and this right.
Shak., Tit. And., i. 1. 279.

Strike home, and *do me reason* in thy heart. *Dryden.*

(*b*) See *dot*.—**To have reason**, to have reason or right on one's side; be in the right. [A Gallicism.]

Mr. Mechlin *has reason.* *Foote*, Commissary, iii. 1.

To hear reason, to yield to reasoning or argument; accept a reason or reasons adduced; act according to advice.

Con. You should *hear reason.*
D. John. . . . What blessing brings it?
Con. If not a present remedy, at least a patient sufferance. *Shak.*, Much Ado, i. 3. 6.

To stand to reason. See *stand*.=**Syn.** 1. *Inducement*, etc. (see *motive*), account, object, purpose, design.

reason[1] (rē'zn), *v.* [< ME. *resonen*, < OF. *raisoner, raisonner, raisnier*, reason, argue, discourse, speak, F. *raisonner*, reason, argue, reply, = Pr. *razonar*, *rasonar* = Cat. *rahonar* = Sp. *razonar* = Pg. *razoar* = It. *ragionare*, reason, < ML. *rationare*, reason, argue, discourse, speak, calculate, < L. *ratio(n-)*, reason, calculation: see *reason*[1], *n*. Cf. *areason*.] **I.** *intrans*. **1.** To exercise the faculty of reason; make rational deductions; think or choose rationally; use intelligent discrimination.

He [the serpent] hath eaten and lives,
And knows, and speaks, and *reasons*, and discerns,
Irrational till then. *Milton*, P. L., ix. 765.

We only *reason* in so far as we note the resemblances among objects and events. *J. Sully*, Outlines of Psychol., p. 415.

2. To practise reasoning in regard to something; make deductions from premises; engage in discussion; argue, or hold arguments.

Let us dispute again,
And *reason* of divine Astrology.
Marlowe, Doctor Faustus, ii. 2.

Come now, and let us *reason* together, saith the Lord. Isa. i. 18.

3†. To hold account; make a reckoning; reckon.

Since the affairs of men rest still incertain,
Let's *reason* with the worst that may befall.
Shak., J. C., v. 1. 97.

4. To hold discourse; talk; parley.

They *reasoned* among themselves, saying, This is the heir: come, let us kill him. Luke xx. 14.

But *reason* with the fellow,
Before you punish him. *Shak.*, Cor., iv. 6. 51.

II. *trans*. **1.** To reason about; consider or discuss argumentatively; argue; debate.

Why *reason* ye these things in your hearts? Mark ii. 8.

Condescends, even, to *reason* this point. *Brougham*.

2. To give reasons for; support by argument; make a plea for: often with *out*: as, to *reason out* a proposition or a claim.

This boy, that cannot tell what he would have,
But kneels and holds up hands for fellowship,
Does *reason* our petition with more strength
Than thou hast to deny 't. *Shak.*, Cor., v. 3. 176.

3. To persuade by reasoning or argument.

Men that will not be *reasoned* into their senses may yet be laughed or drolled into them. *Sir R. L'Estrange*.

4†. To hold argument with; engage in speech or discussion; talk with; interrogate.

reason[2]†, *n*. An obsolete spelling of *raisin*[1]. In the following passage it is apparently applied to some other fruit than the grape.

A medlar and a hartichoke,
A crab and a small *reason*.
Cotgrave, Wits Interpreter (1671), p. 219. (*Nares*.)

reasonable (rē'zn-a̤-bl), *a*. [< ME. *resonable*, *resunable*, *resnabyl*, *resnable*, *renable*, *runnable*, < OF. *resonable*, *raisonnable*, *regnable*, *resnable*, *rationable*, F. *raisonnable* = Pr. *razonable* = Cat. *rahonable* = Sp. *razonable* = Pg. *razoavel* = It. *razionabile*, < L. *rationabilis*, reasonable, < *ratio(n-)*, reason, calculation: see *reason*[1] and *-able*.] **1.** Having the faculty of reason; endowed with reason; rational, as opposed to *brute*.

If he have wit enough to keep himself warm, let him bear it for a difference between himself and his horse; for it is all the wealth that he hath left, to be known a *reasonable* creature. *Shak.*, Much Ado, i. 1. 71.

2. Characterized by the use of reason; amenable to reason or sound sense; not senseless, foolish, or extravagant in thought or action.

Hir maners might no man amend;
Of tong she was trew and *renable*,
And of hir semblant soft and stabile.
Ywaine and Gawaine (Ritson's Metr. Rom., I. 10), l. 208.
[(*Piers Plowman*, Notes, p. 17.)

The adjective *reasonable* . . . denotes a character in which reason (taking it in its largest acceptation) possesses a decided ascendant over the temper and passions; and implies no particular propensity to a display of the discursive power, if indeed it does not exclude the idea of such a propensity. *D. Stewart*, Human Mind, ii. 10, note.

3. Conformable to or required by reason; due to or resulting from good judgment; rationally sound, sensible, natural, etc.

Ther doth no wyghte nothing so *resonable*
That nys harme in her [jealousy's] ymagynynge.
Chaucer, Complaint of Venus, l. 35.

I beseech you . . . present your bodies a living sacrifice, holy, acceptable unto God, which is your *reasonable* service. Rom. xii. 1.

A law may be *reasonable* in itself, though a man does not allow it. *Swift*.

The terrors of the child are quite *reasonable*, and add to his loveliness. *Emerson*, Courage.

4. Not exceeding the bounds of reason or common sense; moderate; tolerable.

I will marry her upon any *reasonable* demands.
Shak., M. W. of W., i. 1. 233.

5. Moderate in amount or price; not high or dear: as, *reasonable* charges or prices; *reasonable* goods.—**6.** In *law*, befitting a person of reason or sound sense; such as a prudent man would exercise or act upon in his own affairs: as, *reasonable* care; *reasonable* diligence; *reasonable* cause.—**7**†. Calculable; computable; hence, detailed; itemized.

And rekene byfore reson a *resonable* acounte,
What one hath, what another hath, and what hy hadde bothe. *Piers Plowman* (C), xiv. 35.

8†. Talkative; ready in conversation.

Lo! how goodly spak this knight . . .
I . . . gan me aqueynte
With him, and fond him so tretable,
Right wonder skilful and *resonable*.
Chaucer, Death of Blanche, l. 534.

Proof beyond a reasonable doubt, such proof as will produce an abiding conviction to a moral certainty, so that a prudent man would feel safe to act upon that conviction in matters of the highest concern to his personal interests.—**Reasonable aid**, a euphemistic expression for *aid*[1], 3, corresponding to the term *benevolence* as used for forced loans or gifts.—**Reasonable alms.** See *alms*.—**Reasonable doubt**, in *law*, doubt for which a pertinent reason can be assigned; that state of a case which, after the entire comparison and consideration of the evidence, leaves the minds of jurors in that condition that they cannot say they feel an abiding conviction, to a moral certainty, of the truth of the charge. *Shaw, C. J.*—**Reasonable dower.** See *dower*[2], 2.=**Syn.** *Rational*, *Reasonable*. See *rational*.

reasonable† (rē'zn-a̤-bl), *adv*. [< *reasonable*, *a*.] Reasonably.

I have a *reasonable* good ear in music. Let's have the tongs and the bones. *Shak.*, M. N. D., iv. 1. 31.

The Library of the Sorbonne is a very long and large Gallery, *reasonable* well stored with Books.
Lister, Journey to Paris, p. 128.

reasonableness (rē'zn-a̤-bl-nes), *n*. The character of being reasonable; conformity to or compliance with the requirements of reason; agreeableness to rational ideas or principles.

The method of inwardness and the secret of self-renouncement, working in and through this element of mildness, produced the total impression of his [Jesus's] "epieikeia," or sweet *reasonableness*.
M. Arnold, Literature and Dogma, vii. § 5.

reasonably (rē'zn-a̤-bli), *adv*. [ME. *resonably*, *renably*; < *reasonable* + *-ly*[2].] **1.** In a reasonable manner; agreeably to reason; with good sense or judgment.

And speke as *renably* and faire and wel
As to the Phitonissa did Samuel.
Chaucer, Friar's Tale, l. 211.

The abuse of the judicial functions that were properly and *reasonably* assumed by the House was scandalous and notorious. *Lecky*, Eng. in 18th Cent., iii.

2. Within the bounds of reason; with good reason or cause; justly; properly.

Whate'er Lord Harry Percy then had said . . .
May *reasonably* die. *Shak.*, 1 Hen. IV., i. 3. 74.

It might seem that an egg which has succeeded in being fresh has done all that can *reasonably* be expected of it.
H. James, Jr., Little Tour, p. 248.

3. To a reasonable extent; in a moderately good degree; fairly; tolerably.

Verely she was heled, and left her styltes thore,
And on her fete wente home *resonably* well.
Joseph of Arimathie (E. E. T. S.), p. 47.

As a general rule, Providence seldom vouchsafes to mortals any more than just that degree of encouragement which suffices to keep them at a *reasonably* full exertion of their powers. *Hawthorne*, Seven Gables, iii.

reasoned (rē'znd), *p. a*. Characterized by or based upon reasoning; following a logical or rational method; carefully argued or studied.

reasoner (rē'zn-ėr), *n*. [< *reason*[1] + *-er*[1]. Cf. F. *raisonneur* = Pr. *razonador* = Sp. *razonador* = Pg. *raciocinador* = It. *ragionatore*, < ML. *rationator*, a reasoner, < *rationare*, reason: see *reason*[1], *v*.] One who reasons or argues, or exercises his reasoning powers; one who considers a subject argumentatively.

They are very bad *reasoners*, and vehemently given to opposition. *Swift*, Gulliver's Travels, iii. 2.

reasonfully† (rē'zn-fůl-i), *adv*. [ME., < *reason*[1] + *-ful* + *-ly*[2].] With full reason; most reasonably.

So then *reasonfulli* maye we sey that mercy both right and lawe passeth. *Testament of Love*, iii.

reasoning (rē'zn-ing), *n*. [Verbal n. of *reason*[1], *v*.] **1.** The use of the faculty of reason; discriminative thought or discussion in regard to a subject; rational consideration.—**2.** A presentation of reasons or arguments; an argumentative statement or expression; a formal discussion.

Hear now my *reasoning*, and hearken. Job xiii. 6.

3†. Discussion; conversation; discourse.

Then there arose a *reasoning* among them, which of them should be greatest. Luke ix. 46.

Chain of reasoning. See *chain*.—**Deductive, diagrammatic, dilemmatic, Fermatian reasoning.** See the adjectives.=**Syn.** *Reasoning*, *Argumentation*. *Reasoning* is much broader than *argumentation*. The latter is confined to one side of the question, or, in another sense, supposes a proposition, supported by arguments on the affirmative side and attacked by arguments on the negative. *Reasoning* may be upon one side of a proposition, and is then the same as *argumentation*; but it may also be the method by which one reaches a belief, and thus a way of putting together the results of investigation: as, the *reasoning* in Euclid, or in Butler's Analogy; the *reasoning* by which a thief justifies himself in stealing.

A piece of *reasoning* is like a suspended chain, in which link is joined to link by logical dependence.
J. F. Clarke, Self-Culture, p. 158.

A poem does not admit *argumentation*, though it does admit development of thought. *Coleridge*, Table-Talk.

reasonless (rē'zn-les), *a*. [< *reason*[1] + *-less*.] **1.** Lacking the faculty of reason; irrational, as an animal. [Rare.]

The *reasonless* creatures [the two kine] also do the will of their maker.
Bp. Hall, Contemplations (ed. Tegg, 1836), II. 144.

2. Deficient in reason or judgment; lacking in good sense; unreasoning. [Archaic.]

When any of them [animals] dieth, it is . . . buried in a holy place, the *reasonlesse* men howling and knocking their breasts in the exequies of these vnreasonable beasts.
Purchas, Pilgrimage, p. 574

3. Not marked or justified by reason; senseless; causeless; unwarranted.

This proffer is absurd and *reasonless*.
Shak., 1 Hen. VI., v. 4. 137.

reason-piece (rē'zn-pēs), *n*. [A corruption of *raising-piece*.] In *building*, a timber lying under the ends of beams in the side of a house; a wall-plate.

reassemblage (rē-a̤-sem'bla̤j), *n*. [< *re-* + *assemblage*.] A renewed assemblage.

New beings arise from the *re-assemblage* of the scattered parts. *Harris*, Three Treatises, Note 7 on Treatise I.

reassemble (rē-a̤-sem'bl), *v*. [< *re-* + *assemble*. Cf. F. *rassembler*, reassemble.] **I.** *trans*. To assemble or bring together again; gather anew.

Reassembling our afflicted powers,
Consult how we may henceforth most offend.
Milton, P. L., i. 186.

II. *intrans*. To assemble or meet together again.

The forces of Surajah Dowlah were dispersed, never to *reassemble*. *Macaulay*, Lord Clive.

reassert (rē-a̤-sėrt'), *v. t*. [< *re-* + *assert*.] To assert again; proclaim or manifest anew.

With equal fury, and with equal fame,
Shall great Ulysses *reassert* his claim.
Pope, Odyssey, xvii. 147.

reassertion (rē-a̤-sėr'shọn), *n*. [< *reassert* + *-ion*.] A repeated assertion of the same thing; the act of asserting anew.

reassess (rē-a̤-ses'), *v. t*. [< *re-* + *assess*.] To assess again.

reassessment (rē-a̤-ses'mẹnt), *n*. [< *reassess* + *-ment*.] A renewed or repeated assessment.

reassign (rē-a̤-sīn'), *v. t*. [= F. *réassigner*; as *re-* + *assign*.] To assign again; transfer back or to another what has been assigned.

reassignment (rē-a̤-sīn'mẹnt), *n*. [< *reassign* + *-ment*.] A renewed or repeated assignment.

reassume (rē-a̤-sūm'), *v. t*. [= Sp. *reasumir* = Pg. *reassumir* = It. *riassumere*; as *re-* + *assume*.] To assume or take again; resume.

And when the sayd v. dayes were expyred, yᵉ kynge *reassumyd* the crowne of Pandulph.
Fabyan, Chron., II., an. 1212.

reassumption (rē-a̤-sump'shọn), *n*. [< *re-* + *assumption*.] A resuming; a second assumption.

reassurance (rē-a̤-shör'a̤ns), *n*. [= F. *réassurance*; as *reassure* + *-ance*.] **1.** Assurance or confirmation repeated.

A *reassurance* of his tributary subjection.
Prynne, Treachery and Disloyalty, iii. 25.

2. Restoration of courage or confidence; deliverance from apprehension or doubt.

How plainly I perceived hell flash and fade
O' the face of her—the doubt that first paled joy,
Then, final *reassurance*.
Browning, Ring and Book, II. 49.

3. Same as *reinsurance*.

No *re-assurance* shall be lawful, except the former insurer shall be insolvent, a bankrupt, or dead.
Blackstone, Com., II. xxx.

reassure (rē-a̤-shör'), *v. t*. [= F. *réassurer* = Pg. *reassegurar* = It. *riassicurare*; as *re-* + *assure*.] **1.** To assure or establish anew; make sure again; confirm.

Let me fore-warn'd each sign, each system learn,
That I my people's danger may discern,
Ere 'tis too late wish'd health to *reassure*.
Churchill, Gotham, iii.

But let me often to these solitudes
Retire, and in thy presence *reassure*
My feeble virtue. *Bryant*, Forest Hymn.

2. To give renewed assurance to; free from doubt or apprehension; restore to confidence.

They rose with fear, and left the unfinished feast,
Till dauntless Pallas *re-assured* the rest.
Dryden, Æneid, viii. 146.

3. Same as *reinsure*.

reassurer (rē-a-shör'ėr), *n.* One who reassures, or assures or insures anew.

reassuringly (rē-a-shör'ing-li), *adv.* In a reassuring manner; so as to reassure.

reast[1] (rēst), *v.* [Also *reest* (and *reese*, *reeze*, in pp. *reased*, *reezed*), Sc. *reist* (as *v. t.*); prob. < Dan. *riste*, broil, grill; cf. Sw. *rosta*, roast: see *roast*.] **I.** *trans.* To dry (meat) by the heat of the sun or in a chimney; smoke-dry.

Let us cut up bushes and briars, pile them before the door and set fire to them, and smoke that auld devil's dam as if she were to be *reisted* for bacon.
Scott, Black Dwarf, ix.

They bequeath so great sums for masses, and dirges, and trentals, . . . that their souls may at the last be had to heaven, though first for a while they be *reezed* in purgatory.
Rev. T. Adams, Works, I. 65.

II. *intrans.* 1†. To become rusty and rancid, as dried meat. *Cath. Ang.*, p. 304.

The scalding of Hogges keepeth the flesh whitest, plumpest, and fullest, neither is the Bacon so apt to *reast* as the other; besides, it will make it somewhat apter to take salt. *Markham*, Countrey Farme (1616), p. 107.

2. To take offense. *Halliwell.* [Prov. Eng.]

reast[2]†, *v.* An obsolete spelling of *rest*[1].

reasted (rēs'ted), *p. a.* [Also *reested*, *reestit*, **reased*, *reezed*, *rezed*, *reised*; < ME. *rested*, contr. *reste*; pp. of *reast*[1], *v.*] Become rusty and rancid, as dried meat. *Cath. Ang.*, p. 304.

Or once a weeke, perhaps, for novelty,
Reez'd bacon soords shall feaste his family.
Bp. Hall, Satires, IV. ii.

What accademick starved satyrist
Would gnaw *rez'd* bacon?
Marston, Scourge of Villanie, iii. (*Nares.*)

Of beef and *reised* bacon store,
That is most fat and greasy,
We have likewise to feed our chaps,
And make them glib and easy.
King Alfred and the Shepherd. (*Nares.*)

reastiness (rēs'ti-nes), *n.* [< *reasty* + *-ness.*] The state or quality of being reasty; rancidness. [Prov. Eng.]

reasty[1] (rēs'ti), *a.* [Also *resty* and *rusty* (simulating *rust*); < *reast*[1] + *-y*[1]. Cf. the earlier adj. *reasted.*] Same as *reasted.*

Through folly, too beastly,
Much bacon is *reasty*.
Tusser, Husbandry, November Abstract.

And than came haltynge Jone,
And broughte a gambone
Of bakon that was *resty*.
Skelton, Elynour Rummyng, l. 328.

Thy flesh is *restie* or leane, tough & olde,
Or it come to borde unsavory and colde.
Barclay, Cytezen & Uplondyshman (Percy Soc.), p. 39.
[(*Cath. Ang.*, p. 304.)

reasty[2] (rēs'ti), *a.* Same as *resty*[1].

reata (rē-ä'tä), *n.* [Also *riata*; < Sp. *reata*, a rope, also a leader mule (= Pg. *reata*, *ar-riata*, a halter), < Sp. *reatar*, tie one beast to another, retie (= Pg. *reatar*, *ar-riatar*, bind again), < *re-* (< L. *re-*), again, back, + Sp. Pg. Cat. *atar*, bind, < L. *aptare*, fit on, fit together, etc.: see *apt.*] A rope, usually of rawhide, with or without a noose, used in western and Spanish America for catching or picketing animals; a lariat.

Dick jingled his spurs and swung his *riata*. Jovita bounded forward.
Bret Harte, Tales of the Argonauts, p. 17.

reate (rēt), *n.* [Also *reit*; prop. *reat* or *reet*; origin obscure. Cf. *reake.*] The water-crowfoot, *Ranunculus aquatilis*: probably applied also to fresh-water algæ and various floating plants. [Obsolete or prov. Eng.]

This is the onely fish that buildeth upon the *reites* and mosse of the sea, and laieth her egs, or spawneth, in her nest. *Holland*, tr. of Pliny, ix. 26.

Reits, sea weed, of some called *reits*, of others wrack, and of the Thanet men wore. *Bp. Kennett.*

The soft tree-tent
Guards with its face of *reate* and sedge.
Browning, Sordello.

reattach (rē-a-tach'), *v. t.* [< *re-* + *attach.* Cf. F. *rattacher*, attach again.] To attach again, in any sense.

reattachment (rē-a-tach'ment), *n.* [< *reattach* + *-ment.*] A second or repeated attachment.

reattempt (rē-a-tempt'), *v. t.* [< *re-* + *attempt.*] To attempt again.

His voyage then to be *re-attempted.*
Hakluyt's Voyages, III. 158.

reaume†, *n.* An obsolete form of *realm.*

Reaumuria (rē-ǭ-mū'ri-ä), *n.* [NL. (Linnæus, 1762), named after René A. F. de *Réaumur* (1683–1757), a French naturalist.] 1. A genus of polypetalous shrubs of the order *Tamariscineæ* and type of the tribe *Reaumurieæ.* It is characterized by numerous stamens which are free or somewhat united into five clusters, from five to ten bracts close to the calyx, five awl-shaped styles, and densely hairy seeds. There are about 12 species, natives of the Mediterranean region and of central Asia. They are generally very branching and procumbent undershrubs, with small or cylindrical crowded leaves and terminal solitary flowers, which are sometimes showy and red or purple. Several species are occasionally cultivated as ornamental shrubs. *R. vermiculata*, a pink-flowered species, is used as an external remedy for the itch.

2. In *entom.*, a genus of dipterous insects. *Desvoidy*, 1830.

Reaumurieæ (rē″ǭ-mū-rī'ę-ē), *n. pl.* [NL. (Ehrenberg, 1827), < *Reaumuria* + *-eæ.*] A tribe of polypetalous plants of the order *Tamariscineæ*, the tamarisk family, characterized by free petals, long-haired seeds, and solitary axillary or terminal flowers. It includes 2 genera, *Hololachne*, a monotypic undershrub of the salt marshes of central Asia, and *Reaumuria.*

Réaumur's porcelain. See *porcelain*[1].

Réaumur's scale. See *thermometer.*

reave (rēv), *v.*; pret. and pp. *reaved*, *reft* (formerly also *raft*), ppr. *reaving.* [Early mod. E. also *reve*, *reeve* (Sc. *reive*, etc.), dial. *rave*; < ME. *reven* (pret. *revede*, *reved*, *refde*, *rafte*, *refte*, pp. *raft*, *reft*), < AS. *reáfian*, rob, spoil, plunder, = OS. **rōbhōn* (in comp. *bi-rōbhōn*) = OFries. *rāvia*, *rāva* = D. *rooven* = MLG. LG. *roven* = OHG. *roubōn*, MHG. *rouben*, G. *rauben*, rob, deprive, = Icel. *raufa* = Sw. *röfva* = Dan. *röve*, rob, = Goth. **raubōn*, in comp. *bi-raubon*, rob, spoil; a secondary verb associated with the noun, AS. *reáf*, spoil, plunder, esp. clothing or armor taken as spoil, hence clothing in general, = OFries. *rāf* = D. *roof* = MLG. *rōf* = OHG. *roub*, *roup*, *raup*, MHG. *roup*, G. *raub* = Icel. *rauf* = Sw. *rof* = Dan. *rov*, spoil, plunder (see *reaf*); from the primitive verb, AS. **reófan*, in comp. *be-reófan*, *bi-reófan*, deprive, = Icel. *rjúfa* (pp. *rofinn*), break, rip, violate, = L. *rumpere* (√ *rup*), break: see *rupture.* Hence, in comp., *bereave.* From the Teut. are It. *ruba*, spoil, etc., *rubare*, spoil, = OF. *rober*, *robber*, rob, whence E. *rob*, etc.; It. *roba* = OF. (and F.) *robe*, garment, robe, whence E. *robe*, *rubble*, *rubbish*: see *robe* and *rob.* From the D. form are E. *rove*[1], *rover.*] **I.** *trans.* 1. To take away by force or stealth; carry off as booty; take violently; purloin, especially in a foray: with a thing as object. [Now rare.]

Aristotill sais that the bees are feghtande agaynes hym that will drawe thaire hony fra thaym, swa sulde we do agaynes deuells that afforces tham to *reue* fra vs the hony of poure lyfe. *Hampole*, Prose Treatises (E. E. T. S.), p. 8.

Since he himself is *reft* from her by death.
Shak., Venus and Adonis, l. 1174.

A good cow was a good cow, had she been twenty times *reaved.* *G. MacDonald*, What's Mine's Mine, p. 303.

2. To take away; remove; abstract; draw off. [Obsolete or archaic.]

Hir clothes ther scho *rafe* hir fro,
And to the wodd gane scho go.
Perceval, 2157. (*Halliwell.*)

And ffrom ȝoure willffull werkis ȝoure will was chaungid,
And *rafte* was ȝoure riott and rest, ffor ȝoure daiez
Weren wikkid thoru ȝoure cursid councelll.
Richard the Redeless, i. 6.

The derke nyght
That *revith* bestis from here besynesse.
Chaucer, Parliament of Fowls, l. 86.

Sith nothing ever may redeeme nor *reave*
Out of your endlesse debt so sure a gage.
Spenser, F. Q., To Lord Grey of Wilton.

We *reave* thy sword,
And give thee armless to thy enemies.
Beau. and Fl., Knight of Malta, v. 2.

3. To rob; plunder; dispossess; bereave: with a person as object. [Obsolete or archaic.]

And sitthe he is so leel a lorde, ich leyue that he wol nat *Reuen* ous of oure ryght. *Piers Plowman* (C), xxi. 310.

To *reave* the orphan of his patrimony.
Shak., 2 Hen. VI., v. 1. 187.

So *reft* of reason Athamas became.
Longfellow, tr. of Dante's Inferno, xxx. 4.

Then he *reft* us of it
Perforce, and left us neither gold nor field.
Tennyson, Gareth and Lynette.

4. To tear up, as the rafters or roof of a house. [Obsolete or prov. Eng.]

Agaynst them Troians down the towres and tops of houses rold,
And rafters vp they *reaue*. *Phaer*, Æneid, ii.

5. To ravel; pull to pieces, as a textile fabric. — **To ramp and reave.** See *ramp.*

II. *intrans.* To practise plundering or pillaging; carry off stolen property. [Now only Scotch.]

Where we shall robbe, where we shall *reve*,
Where we shall bete and bynde.
Lytell Geste of Robyn Hode (Child's Ballads, V. 46).

To slink thro' slaps, an' *reive* an' steal
At stacks o' pess, or stocks o' kail.
Burns, Death of Poor Mailie.

reavel†, *v.* An obsolete form of *ravel*[1].

reaver (rē'vėr), *n.* [Early mod. E. also *reever* (Sc. *reiver*); < ME. *revere*, < AS. *reáfere* (= OFries. *rāvere*, *rāver* = D. *roover* = MLG. *rover* = OHG. *roubare*, MHG. *roubære*, G. *räuber* = Icel. *raufari*, *reyfari* = Sw. *röfvare* = Dan. *röver*), a robber, < *reáfian*, rob, reave: see *reave.* Cf. *rover*, from the D. cognate of *reaver.*] One who reaves or robs; a plundering forager; a robber. [Obsolete or archaic, or Scotch.]

To robbers and to *reueres.* *Piers Plowman* (B), xiv. 182.

Those were the days when, if two men or three came riding to a town, all the township fled for them and weened that they were *reavers.*
E. A. Freeman, Norman Conquest, V. 189.

reavery (rē'vėr-i), *n.* [= D. *rooverij* = MLG. *roverie* = G. *räuberei* = Sw. *röfveri* = Dan. *röveri*; as *reave* + *-ery.*] A carrying off, as of booty; a plundering or pillaging; robbery. [Rare.]

Wallace was ner, quhen he sic *reueré* saw.
Wallace, iv. 40. (*Jamieson.*)

reballing (rę-bâ'ling), *n.* [< *re-* + *ball*[1] + *-ing*[1].] The catching of eels with earthworms attached to a ball of lead which is suspended by a string from a pole. *Halliwell.* [Prov. Eng.]

rebaptism (rē-bap'tizm), *n.* [< *re-* + *baptism.*] A new or second baptism. It has always been the generally accepted teaching that to perform the ceremony on one known to have been really baptized already is sacrilegious; and what is or may be rebaptism is permissible only because the validity of the previous ceremony has been denied, or because the fact of its administration, or the manner in which it was performed, is disputed or doubtful. *Conditional* or *hypothetical baptism* is administered in the Roman Catholic Church to all candidates coming from Protestant churches, under a form beginning "If thou hast not been baptized," the question of the validity of Protestant baptism being held in abeyance. Such rebaptism is also administered in the Anglican churches in special cases, as where the candidate himself desires it. Baptist churches require rebaptism of all who have not been immersed on profession of faith.

rebaptist (rē-bap'tist), *n.* [< *re-* + *baptist.*] One who baptizes again, or who undergoes baptism a second time; also, a Baptist or Anabaptist.

Some for *rebaptist* him bespatter,
For dipping rider oft in water.
T. *Brown*, Works, IV. 270. (*Davies.*)

rebaptization (rē-bap-ti-zā'shọn), *n.* [= F. *rebaptisation*; as *rebaptize* + *-ation.*] The act of rebaptizing; renewed or repeated baptism.

St. Cyprian . . . persisted in his opinion of *rebaptization* until death. *Jer. Taylor*, Works (ed. 1835), II. 313.

rebaptize (rē-bap-tīz'), *v. t.* [< OF. *rebaptiser*, *rebaptiser*, F. *rebaptiser* = Sp. *rebautizar* = Pg. *rebaptizar* = It. *ribattezzare*, < LL. *rebaptizare*, baptize again, < *re-*, again, + *baptizare*, baptize: see *baptize.*] 1. To baptize again or anew; repeat the baptism of.

Cyprian was no hereticke, though he beleeued *rebaptising* of them which were baptised of hereticks.
Foxe, Martyrs, p. 1468, an. 1555.

2. To give a new name to, as at a second baptism.

Of any Paganism at that time, or long before, in the Land we read not, or that Pelagianism was *rebaptiz'd.*
Milton, Hist. Eng., iii.

rebaptizer (rē-bap-tī'zėr), *n.* One who rebaptizes, or who believes in rebaptism; also, an Anabaptist.

There were Adamites in former Times and *Rebaptizers.*
Howell, Letters, iv. 29.

rebate[1] (rę-bāt'), *v.*; pret. and pp. *rebated*, ppr. *rebating.* [< ME. *rebaten*, < OF. *rebatre*, *rebattre*, beat or drive back again, repel, repulse, F. *rebattre*, beat again, repeat (= It. *ribattere*, beat again, beat down, blunt, reflect, etc.), < *re-*, back, again, + *batre*, *battre*, beat: see *bate*[1], *batter*[1]. Cf. *rabate.*] **I.** *trans.* 1†. To beat back; drive back by beating; fend or ward off; repulse.

This is the city of great Babylon,
Where proud Darius was *rebated* from.
Greene, Orlando Furioso.

This shirt of mail worn near my skin
Rebated their sharp steel.
Beau. and Fl. (?), Faithful Friends, iii. 3.

2†. To beat down; beat to bluntness; make obtuse or dull, literally or figuratively; blunt; bate.

One who . . .
. . . doth *rebate* and blunt his natural edge
With profits of the mind, study and fast.
Shak., M. for M., i. 4. 60.

Thou wilt belie opinion, and *rebate*
The ambition of thy gallantry.
Beau. and Fl., Laws of Candy, i. 2.

But the broad belt, with plates of silver bound,
The point *rebated*, and repelled the wound.
Pope, Iliad, xi. 304.

3. To set or throw off; allow as a discount or abatement; make a drawback of. See the noun. [Rare or obsolete.]

Yet was I verie ill satisfied, and forced to *rebate* part [of a debt], and to take wares as payment for the rest.
Hakluyt's Voyages, I. 332.

II.† *intrans.* To draw back or away; withdraw; recede.

He began a little to *rebate* from certain points of popery.
Foxe, Martyrs, p. 1621, an. 1555.

rebate[1] (rẹ-bāt'), *n.* [< *rebate*[1], *v.* Cf. *rabate*, *n.*] Diminution; retrenchment; specifically, an allowance by way of discount or drawback; a deduction from a gross amount.—**Rebate and discount**, in *arith.*, a rule by which abatements and discounts upon ready-money payments are calculated.

rebate[2] (rẹ-bāt'), *n.* [An altered form of *rabate*: see *rabate* and *rabbet*.] **1.** A longitudinal space or groove cut back or sunk in a piece of joinery, timber, or the like, to receive the edge of some other part.

On the periphery at the socket end [of the brush] a shallow *rebate* is formed, to receive the binding string.
Spons' Encyc. Manuf., I. 544.

2. A kind of hard freestone used in pavements. *Elwes.*—**3.** A piece of wood fastened to a handle, used for beating mortar. *Elwes.*

rebate[2] (rẹ-bāt'), *v. t.*; pret. and pp. *rebated*, ppr. *rebating*. [< *rebate*[2], *n.*] To make a rebate or rabbet in, as a piece of joinery or other work; rabbet.

rebated (rẹ-bā'ted), *p. a.* **1.** In *her.*, cut short: noting any ordinary, especially a cross, characterized by having one or more of its arms too short to reach the edge of the field.—**2.** Blunt.

rebatement (rẹ-bāt'ment), *n.* [< *rebate*[1] + *-ment*.] **1.** The act of rebating, or the state of being rebated; a blunting; abatement; drawback. [Rare.]—**2.** In *her.*: (*a*) A cutting off, or shortening, as of one arm of a cross, or the like. (*b*) Same as *abatement*, in the sense of degradation of or dishonorable addition to a coat-armor.—**3.** A narrowing.

For without in the wall of the house he made narrowed rests [margin: narrowings, or *rebatements*] round about, that the beams should not be fastened in the walls of the house.
1 Ki. vi. 6.

In the description of the side-chambers of the temple, the *rebatement* signifies the narrowing of the walls which left a ledge for the joists of the upper chambers to rest on.
W. A. Wright, Bible Word-Book, p. 497.

rebato†, *n.* Same as *rabato*.

rebaud†, rebawde†, rebaudry†. Obsolete forms of *ribald*, *ribaldry*.

rebec, rebeck (rē'bek), *n.* [(*a*) Early mod. E. also *rebeke*; < ME. *rebecke*, *rebekke*, *rebeke*, < OF. *rebec*, *rebeke*, F. *rebec* = Pg. *rabeca* = It. *ribeca*, *ribecca* (ML. *rebeca*, *rebecca*); also with diff. terminations, (*b*) F. dial. *rebay* = Pr. *rubey*; (*c*) Sp. *rabel* = Pg. *rabil*, *arrabil*; (*d*) ME. *rebibe*, *ribibe*, *rubibe*, *ribible*, < OF. *rebebe*, *rebesbe*, *reberbe*, It. *ribeba*, *ribebla*, < Ar. *rabāba* = Hind. *rabāb*, *rubāb*, Pers. *rabāb*, *rubāb*, a rebec, a fiddle with one or two strings.] **1.** A musical instrument, the earliest known form of the Viol class. It had a pear-shaped body, which was solid above, terminating in a slender neck and a carved head, and hollow below, with sound-holes and a sound-post. The number of strings was usually three, but was sometimes only one or two. They were tuned in fifths, and sounded by a bow. The tone was harsh and loud. The rebec is known to have been in use in Europe as early as the eighth century. Its origin is disputed, but is usually attributed to the Moors of Spain. It was the precursor of the true Viol in all its forms, and continued in vulgar use long after the latter was artistically established.

When the merry bells ring round,
And the jocund *rebecks* sound
To many a youth, and many a maid.
Milton, L'Allegro, l. 94.

2†. An old woman: so called in contempt. Compare *ribibe*, 2.

"Brother," quod he, "heere woneth an old *rebekke*,
That hadde almoost as lief to lese hire nekke
As for to geve a peny of hir good."
Chaucer, Friar's Tale, l. 275.

Rebeccaism (rẹ-bek'a-izm), *n.* [< *Rebecca*(*ite*) + *-ism*.] The principles and practices of the Rebeccaites.

Rebeccaite (rẹ-bek'a-īt), *n.* [< *Rebecca* (see def.) + *-ite*[2].] A member of a secret anti-turnpike society in Wales, about 1843–4. The grievance of the Rebeccaites was the oppressive number of toll-gates, and they turned out at night in large parties, generally mounted, to destroy them. Their leader, dressed in woman's clothes, received the title of Rebecca from a fanciful application of the Scriptural passage Gen. xxiv. 60; and the parties were called "Rebecca and her daughters."

rebel (reb'el), *a.* and *n.* [< ME. *rebel*, *rebele*, < OF. *rebelle*, *rebele*, F. *rebelle* = Sp. Pg. *rebelde* = It. *ribello*, rebellious, a rebel, < L. *rebellis*, adj., making war again, insurgent, rebellious; as noun, a rebel; < *re-*, again, + *bellum*, war: see *belligerent*, *duel*. Cf. *rebel*, *v.*] **I.** *a.* **1.** Resisting authority or law; rebellious.

Qwo-so be *rebele* of his tonge a3ein the aldirman, or dispise the aldirman in time that he holden here mornspeche, scal paien, to amendement of the gilde, vj. d.
English Gilds (E. E. T. S.), p. 95.

His pride
Had cast him out from heaven, with all his host
Of *rebel* angels.
Milton, P. L., i. 38.

2. Of a rebellious nature or character; characteristic of a rebel. [Rare.]

Thow drowe in skorne Cupide eke to recorde
Of thilke *rebel* worde that thow hast spoken,
For which he wol no lenger be thy lorde.
Chaucer, Envoy of Chaucer to Scogan, l. 23.

II. *n.* **1.** A person who makes war upon the government of his country from political motives; one of a body of persons organized for a change of government or of laws by force of arms, or by open defiance.

Know whether I be dextrous to subdue
Thy *rebels*, or be found the worst in heaven.
Milton, P. L., v. 742.

For rebellion being an opposition not to persons, but authority, which is founded only in the constitution and laws of the government, those, whoever they be, who by force break through, and by force justify their violation of them, are truly and properly *rebels*.
Locke, Civil Government, I.

Kings will be tyrants from policy, when subjects are *rebels* from principle.
Burke.

Hence—**2.** One who or that which resists authority or law; one who refuses obedience to a superior, or who revolts against some controlling power or principle.

As reason is a *rebel* unto faith, so passion unto reason.
Sir T. Browne, Religio Medici, i. 19.

She shall die unshrived and unforgiven,
A *rebel* to her father and her God.
Shelley, The Cenci, iv. 1.

=**Syn.** 1. *Traitor*, etc. See *insurgent*, *n.*

rebel (rẹ-bel'), *v. i.*; pret. and pp. *rebelled*, ppr. *rebelling*. [< ME. *rebellen*, < OF. *rebeller*, *rebeler*, *reveler*, F. *rebeller* = Sp. *rebelar* = Pg. *rebellar* = It. *ribellare*, < L. *rebellare*, wage war again (said of the conquered), make an insurrection, revolt, rebel, < *re-*, again, + *bellare*, wage war, < *bellum*, war. Cf. *rebel*, *a.*] To make war against one's government, or against anything deemed oppressive, by arms or other means; revolt by active resistance or repulsion.

In his days Nebuchadnezzar king of Babylon came up, and Jehoiakim became his servant three years: then he turned and *rebelled* against him.
2 Ki. xxiv. 1.

The deep fall
Of those too high aspiring, who *rebell'd*
With Satan.
Milton, P. L., vi. 899.

Our present life, in so far as it is healthy, *rebels* once for all against its own final and complete destruction.
W. K. Clifford, Lectures, I. 231.

rebeldom (reb'el-dum), *n.* [< *rebel* + *-dom*.] **1.** A seat of rebellion; a region or sphere of action controlled by rebels. [Rare.]—**2.** Rebellious conduct. [Rare.]

Never mind his *rebeldom* of the other day; never mind about his being angry that his presents were returned.
Thackeray, Virginians, li.

rebeller† (rẹ-bel'ėr), *n.* [< *rebel*, *v.*, + *-er*[1].] One who rebels; a rebel.

God . . . shal . . . scourge and plague this nacion, beeing nowe many a long daie a continuall *rebeller* agaynste God.
J. Udall, On Luke xxi.

rebellion (rẹ-bel'yon), *n.* [< ME. *rebellion*, < OF. *rebellion*, F. *rébellion* = Sp. *rebelion* = Pg. *rebellião* = It. *ribellione*, < L. *rebellio*(*n-*), a renewal of war, revolt, rebellion, < *rebellis*, making war again: see *rebel*, *a.*] **1.** War waged against a government by some part of its subjects; armed opposition to a government by a party of citizens, for the purpose of changing its composition, constitution, or laws; insurrectionary or revolutionary war.

He told me that *rebellion* had bad luck,
And that young Harry Percy's spur was cold.
Shak., 2 Hen. IV., i. 1. 41.

Then shall you find this name of liberty
(The watch-word of *rebellion* ever us'd . . .)
But new-turn'd servitude.
Daniel, Civil Wars, ii. 15.

2. The act of rebelling or taking part in a rebellious movement; open or armed defiance to one's government; the action of a rebel.

Boling. On what condition stands it [my fault], and wherein?
York. Even in condition of the worst degree,
In gross *rebellion*, and detested treason.
Shak., Rich. II., ii. 3. 109.

From all sedition, privy conspiracy, and *rebellion*, . . . Good Lord, deliver us.
Book of Common Prayer, Litany.

Hence—**3.** Revolt against or defiance of authority in general; resistance to a higher power or to an obligatory mandate; open disobedience or insubordination; determination not to submit.

For he addeth *rebellion* unto his sin; he . . . multiplieth his words against God.
Job xxxiv. 37.

Civil rebellion, in *Scots law*, disobedience to letters of horning. See *horning*.—**Commission of rebellion**, in *law*. See *commission*[1].—**Shays's rebellion**, an insurrection in Massachusetts, under the lead of Daniel Shays, directed against the State authorities, which broke out in 1786 and was suppressed in 1787.—**The Great Rebellion**, in *Eng. hist.*, the war waged by the Parliamentary army against Charles I. from 1642 till his execution in 1649, and the subsequent maintenance by armed force of a government opposed to the excluded sovereign Charles II. till the Restoration (1660).—**The Rebellion**, in *U. S. hist.*, the civil war of 1861–5. See *civil*.—**Whisky Insurrection or Rebellion.** See *insurrection*. =**Syn.** *Sedition*, *Revolt*, etc. See *insurrection*.

rebellious (rẹ-bel'yus), *a.* [< *rebelli*(*on*) + *-ous*.] **1.** Acting as a rebel, or having the disposition of one; defying lawful authority; openly disobedient or insubordinate.

Rebellious subjects, enemies to peace,
Profaners of this neighbour-stained steel.
Shak., R. and J., i. 1. 88.

2. Pertaining to or characteristic of a rebel or rebellion; of rebel character, relation, or use.

These are his substance, sinews, arms, and strength,
With which he yoketh your *rebellious* necks.
Shak., 1 Hen. VI., ii. 3. 64.

3. Hard to treat or deal with; resisting effort or operation; refractory: applied to things.—**Rebellious assembly**, in *old Eng. law*, a gathering of twelve persons or more, intending, going about, or practising unlawfully, and of their own authority, to change any laws of the realm, or to destroy any property, or do any other unlawful act. =**Syn. 1.** Insubordinate, disobedient. See *insurgent*, *n.*, and *insurrection*.

rebelliously (rẹ-bel'yus-li), *adv.* In a rebellious manner; with violent or obstinate disobedience or resistance to lawful authority.

rebelliousness (rẹ-bel'yus-nes), *n.* The state or character of being rebellious.

rebellow (rē-bel'ō), *v. i.* [< *re-* + *bellow*.] To bellow in return; echo back as a bellow; resound loudly.

And all the aire *rebellowed* againe,
So dreadfully his hundred tongues did bray.
Spenser, F. Q., V. xii. 41.

rebelly (reb'el-i), *a.* [< *rebel* + *-y*[1].] Inclined to rebellion; rebellious. [Rare.]

It was called "*Rebelly* Belfast" in those days [of 1798, etc.].
The American, VIII. 198.

rebibe†, rebible†, *n.* Same as *rebec*.

rebind (rē-bīnd'), *v. t.* [< *re-* + *bind*.] To bind anew; furnish with a new binding, as a book or a garment.

rebirth (rē-bėrth'), *n.* [< *re-* + *birth*.] **1.** Renewed birth; a repeated birth into temporal existence, as of a soul, according to the doctrine of metempsychosis; a new entrance into a living form: now oftener called *reincarnation*.

Gautama Buddha's main idea was that liberation from the cycle of *rebirths* (Samsâra) was to be by means of knowledge.
The Academy, Feb. 4, 1888, p. 84.

2. Renewed life or activity; entrance into a new course or phase of existence; reanimation; resuscitation; renascence; regeneration.

This *rebirth* of the spirit of free inquiry.
Guizot, Hist. Civilization (trans.), p. 148.

rebite (rē-bīt'), *v. t.* [< *re-* + *bite*.] In *engraving*, to deepen or restore worn lines in (an engraved plate) by the action of acid.

rebiting (rē-bī'ting), *n.* [Verbal n. of *rebite*, *v.*] In *etching*, a repetition of the process of biting, in order to restore or freshen worn lines, or to deepen lines which have been but imperfectly attacked.

reboant (reb'ọ-ant), *a.* [< L. *reboan*(*t-*)*s*, ppr. of *reboare*, bellow back, resound, reëcho, < *re-*, back, + *boare*, bellow: see *boation*.] Rebellowing; loudly resounding. [Rare.]

The echoing dance
Of *reboant* whirlwinds.
Tennyson, Supposed Confessions.

reboation (reb-ọ-ā'shon), *n.* [< ML. *reboatio*(*n-*), *reboacio*(*n-*), < L. *reboare*, resound, bellow back: see *reboant*.] A resounding; the return of a loud sound.

I imagine that I should hear the *reboation* of an universal groan.
Bp. Patrick, Divine Arithmetick (1650), p. 2. (*Latham.*)

reboil (rē-boil'), *v.* [< ME. *reboylen*, < OF. *rebouillir*, *resbouillir*, F. *rebouillir* = It. *ribollire*, < L. *rebullire*, bubble up, cause to bubble up, < *re-*, again, + *bullire*, bubble, boil: see *boil*[2].] **I.** *intrans.* **1†.** To bubble up; effervesce; ferment.

Also take good hede of your wynes euery nyght with a candell, bothe rede wyne and swete wyne, & loke they *reboyle* nor leke not, & wasshe ye pype hedes euery nyght with colde water. *Babees Book* (E. E. T. S.), p. 267.

Some of his companyons therat *reboyleth*, infamynge hym to be a manne without charytie. *Sir T. Elyot*, Governour, ii. 7.

2. To boil again.

II. *trans.* To cause to boil again; subject again to boiling.

reboise (rē-boiz'), *v. t.* [< F. *reboiser*, reforest, < *re-*, = E. *re-*, + *bois*, a wood, forest: see *bush*[1].] To reëstablish a growth of wood upon, as a tract of land; reforest; reafforest. [A recent Gallicism.]

reboisement (rē-boiz'ment), *n.* [< F. *reboisement*, < *reboiser*, reforest: see *reboise*.] A replanting of trees on land which has been denuded of a former growth of wood, especially with a view to their effect on climate and moisture; reforestation: used chiefly with reference to French practice. [A recent Gallicism.]

reborn (rē-bôrn'), *a.* [< *re-* + *born*.] Born again or anew; reappearing by or as if by a new birth; endowed with new life. See *rebirth*.

reboso, rebosa, *n.* Same as *rebozo*.

Reboulleau's blue. See *blue*.

rebound (rē-bound'), *v.* [< ME. *rebounden*, < OF. *rebundir*, *rebondir*, F. *rebondir*, leap back, rebound, < *re-*, back, + *bondir*, leap, bound, *bundir*, resound: see *re-* and *bound*[2], *v.*] **I.** *intrans.* **1.** To bound or spring back; fly back from force of impact, as an elastic or free-moving body striking against a solid substance.

As cruel waves full oft be found
Against the rockes to rore and cry,
So doth my hart full oft *rebound*
Agaynst my brest full bitterly.
Surrey, The Lover describes, etc.

Bodies which are either absolutely hard, or so soft as to be void of elasticity, will not *rebound* from one another. *Newton*, Opticks, iii. query 31.

2. To bound or bounce again; repeat a bound or spring; make repeated bounds or springs.

Clamours from Earth to Heav'n, from Heav'n to Earth, *rebound*. *Congreve*, On the Taking of Namure.

Along the court the fiery steeds *rebound*. *Pope*, Odyssey, xv. 162.

3. To fall back; recoil, as to a starting-point or a former state; return as with a spring.

Make thereof no laugheng, sporte, ne Iape;
For ofte tymes it doith *rebounde*
Vppon hym that list to crie and gape.
Booke of Precedence (E. E. T. S., extra ser.), i. 110.

When it does Hardness meet and Pride,
My Love does then *rebound* t' another side.
Cowley, The Mistress, Resolved to be Beloved, ii.

4†. To send sounds back and forth; reverberate; resound; reëcho.

Every hall where in they stay'd
Wi' their mirth did *reboun'*.
Sir Patrick Spens (Child's Ballads, III. 340).

Where the long roofs *rebounded* to the din
Of spectre chiefs.
T. Warton, On his Majesty's Birthday, June 4, 1788.

Rebounding lock. See *lock*[1]. =**Syn. 1.** *Rebound, Reverberate, Recoil. Rebound* and *reverberate* apply to that which strikes an unyielding object and bounds back or away; *recoil* applies to that which springs back from a position of rest, as a cannon or rifle when discharged, or a man and a rattlesnake when they discover their proximity to each other. *Reverberate*, by onomatopœia, applies chiefly to heavy sounds, but has other special uses (see the word); it has no figurative extension. *Recoil* is most freely used in figure: as, a man's treachery *recoils* upon himself; in sudden fright the blood *recoils* upon the heart.

II.† *trans.* To throw or drive back, as sound; make an echo or reverberation of; repeat as an echo or echoes.

The dogge tyger . . . rored soo terrybly that it grated the bowels of suche as harde hym, and the wooddes and montaynes neare aboute *rebounded* the noyse of the horryble crye.
Peter Martyr (tr. in Eden's First Books on America, ed. [Arber, p. 144).

Through rocks and caves the name of Delia sounds;
Delia each cave and echoing rock *rebounds*.
Pope, Autumn, l. 50.

rebound (rē-bound'), *n.* [< *rebound*, *v.*] The act of flying back on collision with another body; a bounding back or in reverse; resilience; recoil; reëcho; reverberation.

Ye haue another figure which by his nature we may call the *Rebound*, alluding to the tennis ball which being smitten with the racket reboundes backe againe.
Puttenham, Arte of Eng. Poesie, p. 173.

I do feel,
By the *rebound* of yours, a grief that smites
My very heart at root. *Shak.*, A. and C., v. 2. 104.

Xenophon. The fall of a king is terrible.
Cyrus. The *rebound* is worse. When your Saturn fell from heaven, did any god or mortal lend a hand to raise him up again?
Landor, Imaginary Conversations, Xenophon and Cyrus [the Younger.

Comedy often springs from the deepest melancholy, as if in sudden *rebound*. *G. H. Lewes.*

rebozo (Sp. re-bō'thō; Sp.-Am. -zō), *n.* [Sp., a muffler, short mantle, < *rebozar*, muffle, overlay, < *re-*, back, + *bozo*, a headstall.] A shawl or long scarf worn by Mexican and other Spanish-American women, covering the head and shoulders, and sometimes part of the face, one end being thrown over the left shoulder; a kind of mantilla. Also written *reboso*, *rebosa*, and *ribosa*.

The ladies wear no hats, but wind about their heads and shoulders a graceful scarf called the *rebozo*. This is passed across the face, leaving only one eye of the lady exposed.
J. Jefferson, Autobiog., p. 292.

Rebozo.

rebrace (rē-brās'), *v. t.* [< *re-* + *brace*.] To brace up anew; renew the strength or vigor of.

Oh! 'tis a cause
To arm the hand of childhood, and *rebrace*
The slacken'd sinews of time-wearied age.
Gray, Agrippina, i. 1.

rebucous† (rē-bū'kus), *a.* [< *rebuke* + *-ous*.] Of the nature of rebuke; rebuking; reproving. [Rare.]

She gaue vnto hym many *rebucous* wordys.
Fabyan, Chron. (ed. Ellis), p. 557, an. 1399.

rebuff (rē-buf'), *v. t.* [< OF. *rebuffer* (also *rabuffer*) (= It. *rebuffare*, *ribuffare*, also *rabbuffare*), check, chide, repulse, < *re-* + *buffer* (= It. *buffare*), puff, blow: see *buff*[2] and *buff*[3].] To repel; make inflexible resistance to; check; put off with an abrupt and unexpected denial.

Marvelling that he who had neuer heard such speeches from any knight should be thus *rebuffed* by a woman.
Sir P. Sidney, Arcadia, iii.

=**Syn.** To repel, repulse, throw back. See *refuse*[1].

rebuff (rē-buf'), *n.* [< OF. *rebuffe* = It. *rebuffo*, *ribuffo*; from the verb.] **1.** A repelling; a repercussion.

The strong *rebuff* of some tumultuous cloud,
Instinct with fire and nitre, hurried him
As many miles aloft. *Milton*, P. L., ii. 936.

2. An interposed check; a defeat.

These perplexing *rebuffs* gave my uncle Toby Shandy more perturbations than you would imagine.
Sterne, Tristram Shandy, ii. 1.

The *rebuffs* we received in the progress of that experiment. *Burke*, A Regicide Peace, iii.

3. A holding off or in check; repulsion, as of inquiry or solicitation; peremptory denial or refusal.

Who listens once will listen twice;
Her heart, be sure, is not of ice,
And one refusal no *rebuff*. *Byron*, Mazeppa, vi.

All eyes met her with a glance of eager curiosity, and she met all eyes with one of *rebuff* and coldness.
Charlotte Brontë, Jane Eyre, xviii.

rebuild (rē-bild'), *v. t.*; pret. and pp. *rebuilt*, ppr. *rebuilding*. [< *re-* + *build*.] To build or build up again; build or construct after having been demolished; reconstruct or reconstitute: as, to *rebuild* a house, a wall, a wharf, or a city; to *rebuild* one's credit.

rebuilder (rē-bil'dėr), *n.* One who reconstructs or builds again.

The *rebuilders* of Jerusalem after the captivity.
Bp. Bull, Works, I. 240.

rebukable (rē-bū'ka-bl), *a.* [< *rebuke* + *-able*.] Deserving of rebuke or reprehension.

Rebukeable
And worthy shameful check it were to stand
On more mechanic compliment.
Shak., A. and C., iv. 4. 30.

rebuke (rē-būk'), *v. t.*; pret. and pp. *rebuked*, ppr. *rebuking*. [< ME. *rebuken*, < OF. *rebouquer*, later *reboucher*, dull, blunt (a weapon), < *re-*, back, + *bouquer*, F. *boucher*, stop, obstruct, shut up, also hoodwink, < *bouque*, F. *bouche*, mouth, < L. *bucca*, cheek: see *bouche*, *bucca*.] **1.** To reprove directly and pointedly; utter sharp disapproval of; reprimand; chide.

In grete anger *rebukyng* hym full soore.
Generydes (E. E. T. S.), l. 1443.

Thus the duke was at the same time superseded and publicly *rebuked* before all the army.
Swift, Mem. of Capt. Creichton.

2. To treat or affect reprehendingly; check or restrain by reprimand or condemnation.

He stood over her, and *rebuked* the fever; and it left her. Luke iv. 39.

To spread his colours, boy, in thy behalf,
And to *rebuke* the usurpation
Of thy unnatural uncle. *Shak.*, K. John, ii. 1. 9.

The manna dropping from God's hand
Rebukes my painful care. *Whittier*, My Psalm.

3†. To buffet; beat; bruise.

A head *rebuked* with pots of all size, daggers, stools, and bed-staves. *Beau. and Fl.*

=**Syn. 1.** *Reprove, Reprimand*, etc. See *censure*.

rebuke (rē-būk'), *n.* [< *rebuke*, *v.*] **1.** A direct reprimand; reproof for fault or wrong; reprehension; chiding.

And refuse not the sweete *rebuke*
Of him that is your friend.
Babees Book (E. E. T. S.), p. 102.

But yet my caution was more pertinent
Than the *rebuke* you give it. *Shak.*, Cor., ii. 2. 68.

2. A manifestation of condemnation; a reprehending judgment or infliction; reprobation in act or effect.

They perish at the *rebuke* of thy countenance.
Ps. lxxx. 16.

And who before the King of kings can boast?
At his *rebuke* behold a thousand flee.
Jones Very, Poems, p. 76.

3. A check administered; a counter-blow.

He gave him so terrible a *rebuke* upon the forehead with his heel that he laid him at his length.
Sir R. L'Estrange.

The gods both happy and forlorn
Have set in one world each to each to be
A vain *rebuke*, a bitter memory.
W. Morris, Earthly Paradise, III. 109.

4†. Behavior deserving rebuke; rudeness. [Rare.]

She would not in discourteise wise
Scorne the faire offer of good will profest;
For great *rebuke* it is love to despise.
Spenser, F. Q., III. i. 55.

=**Syn. 1.** *Monition, Reprehension*, etc. See *admonition*.

rebukeful (rē-būk'fůl), *a.* [Early mod. E. also *rebukful*; < *rebuke* + *-ful*.] Of a rebuking character; full of or abounding in rebuke.

Therfore he toke vpon him the *rebukful* miserie of our mortalitee, to make us partakers of his godlye glorie.
J. Udall, On John i.

rebukefully (rē-būk'fůl-i), *adv.* With reproof or repreheusion.

Unto euery man disclose nat thy harte, leest . . . he . . . reporte *rebukefully* of the.
Sir T. Elyot, The Governour, iii. 28.

When I returned to the hotel that night, Smith stood *rebukefully* . . . before the parlor fire.
T. B. Aldrich, Ponkapog to Pesth, p. 187.

rebuker (rē-bū'kėr), *n.* One who rebukes.

These great *Rebukers* of Nonresidence.
Milton, Hist. Eng., iii.

rebukingly (rē-bū'king-li), *adv.* In a rebuking manner; by way of rebuke.

A certain stillness of manner, which, as my friends often *rebukingly* declared, did but ill express the keen ardour of my feelings. *Carlyle*, Sartor Resartus, ii. 4.

rebullition† (rē-bu-lish'on), *n.* [< L. *rebullire*, pp. *rebullitus*, bubble up, also cause to bubble up: see *reboil*.] A renewed ebullition, effervescence, or disturbance.

There may be a *rebullition* in that business.
Sir H. Wotton, Reliquiæ, p. 582.

reburse† (rē-bėrs'), *v. t.* [< *re-* + *burse*. Cf. *reimburse*.] To pay over again; expend anew.

I am in danger to *reburse* as much
As he was robbed on; ay, and pay his hurts.
B. *Jonson*, Tale of a Tub, iii. 1.

rebus (rē'bus), *n.* [< OF. *rebus*, F. *rebus*, a rebus; derived, according to Ménage, from satirical pieces which the clerics of Picardy composed at the annual carnival, and which, as they referred to current topics, follies, etc., were entitled *de rebus quæ geruntur*, 'of things which are going on'; otherwise explained as words represented 'by things'; < L. *rebus*, abl. pl. of *res*, a thing, an object: see *real*[1].] **1.** A puzzle or riddle consisting of words or phrases represented by figures or pictures of objects whose names resemble in sound those words or phrases or the syllables of which they are composed; an enigmatical representation of words by means of figures or pictures suggestive of them.—**2.** In *her.*: (*a*) A bearing or succession of bearings which make up the name or a word expressing the profession or office of the bearer. The origin of many bearings in early heraldry is such an allusion; and on the other hand many proper names have been derived from the bearings, these having been granted originally to persons having a name or territorial designation which a descendant, perhaps of a younger branch, abandoned for the allusive surname suggested by the bearing: thus, in the case of the name *Tremain*, and the bearing of three human hands, either the bearing or the name may have originated the other. Also called *allusive arms*.

Rebus of Bishop Oldham ("owldom"), Exeter Cathedral.

Excellent have been the conceipt[s] of some citizens, who, wanting armes, have coined themselves certaine devices as neere as may be alluding to their names, which we call *rebus*.
H. Peacham, The Gentleman's Exercise (1634), p. 155. [(*Skeat*.)

(*b*) A motto in which a part of the phrase is expressed by representations of objects instead of by words. In a few rare cases the whole motto is thus given. Such mottos are not commonly borne with the escutcheon and crest, but form rather a device or impresa, as the figure of a sun-dial preceded by the words "we must," meaning "we must die all."

You will have your *rebus* still, mine host.
B. Jonson, New Inn, i. 1.

rebus (rē′bus), *v. t.* [< *rebus*, *n.*] To mark with a rebus; indicate by a rebus. *Fuller*, Ch. Hist., IV. iv. 34.

rebut (rẹ̄-but′), *v.*; pret. and pp. *rebutted*, ppr. *rebutting*. [Early mod. E. *rebutte*; < OF. *rebouter*, repulse, drive back, reject, F. *rebouter*, also *rebuter* = Pr. *rebotar* = It. *ributtare*, repulse, reject; as *re-* + *butt*[2].] **I.** *trans.* **1**†. To repel by force; rebuff; drive back.

He . . . rusht upon him with outragious pryde;
Who him rencountring fierce, as hauke in flight,
Perforce *rebutted* backe. *Spenser*, F. Q., I. xi. 53.

Philosophy lets her light descend and enter wherever there is a passage for it; she takes advantage of the smallest crevice, but the rays are *rebutted* by the smallest obstruction.
Landor, Imaginary Conversations (Epicurus, Leontion, and [Ternissa).

2. To thrust back or away, as by denial; refuse assent to; repel; reject.

The compliment my friend *rebutted* as best he could, but the proposition he accepted at once.
Poe, Tales, I. 218.

3. To repel by evidence or argument; bring counter-arguments against; refute, or strive to refute: much used in legal procedure.

Some of them he has objected to; others he has not attempted to *rebut*; and of others he has said nothing.
D. Webster, Speech, Senate, June 27, 1834.

4†. To withdraw: used reflexively.

Themselves . . .
Doe backe *rebutte*, and ech to other yealdeth land.
Spenser, F. Q., I. ii. 15.

II. *intrans.* **1.** In *law*, to make an answer, as to a plaintiff's surrejoinder. Compare *surrebut*.

The plaintiff may answer the rejoinder by a sur-rejoinder; upon which the defendant may *rebut*.
Blackstone, Com., III. xx.

2. In *curling*, to make a random stroke with great force, in the hope of gaining some advantage in the striking and displacement of the stones about the tee.

rebuttable (rẹ̄-but′ạ-bl), *a.* [< *rebut* + *-able*.] That may be rebutted.

rebuttal (rẹ̄-but′ạl), *n.* [< *rebut* + *-al*.] **1.** The act of rebutting; refutation; confutation; contradiction.

There is generally preserved an amazing consistency in the delusion, in spite of the incessant *rebuttals* of sensation. *Warren*, Diary of a Physician, xiv.

2. In *law*, that part of a trial in which the plaintiff endeavors to meet the defendant's evidence by counter-evidence.

rebutter[1] (rẹ̄-but′ėr), *n.* [< *rebut* + *-er*[1].] One who rebuts or refutes. [Rare.]

rebutter[2] (rẹ̄-but′ėr), *n.* [< OF. *rebouter*, inf. used as noun: see *rebut*.] An act of rebutting; specifically, in *law*, an answer, such as a defendant makes to a plaintiff's surrejoinder. Compare *surrebutter*.

recadency (rẹ̄-kā′dẹn-si), *n.* [< *re-* + *cadency*. Cf. L. *recidere*, fall back: see *recidivous*.] The act of falling back or descending again; relapse. [Rare.]

Defection is apt to render many sincere progressions in the first fervor suspected of unsoundness and *recadency*.
W. Montague, Devoute Essays, Address to the Court.

recalcitrance (rẹ̄-kal′si-trạns), *n.* [< *recalcitran(t)* + *-ce*.] Refusal of submission; obstinate noncompliance or nonconformity; refractoriness.

recalcitrant (rẹ̄-kal′si-trạnt), *a.* [= F. *récalcitrant* = It. *ricalcitrante*, < L. *recalcitran(t-)s*, < *recalcitrare*, kick back: see *recalcitrate*.] Refusing to submit; exhibiting repugnance or opposition; not submissive or compliant; refractory.

recalcitrate (rẹ̄-kal′si-trāt), *v.*; pret. and pp. *recalcitrated*, ppr. *recalcitrating*. [< L. *recalcitratus*, pp. of *recalcitrare* (> OF. *recalcitrer*, F. *récalcitrer* = Sp. Pg. *recalcitrar* = It. *ricalcitrare*), kick back, deny access, < *re-*, back, + *calcitrare*, kick.] **I.** *intrans.* To show repugnance or resistance to something; refuse submission or compliance; be refractory.

Wherefore *recalcitrate* against that will
From which the end can never be cut off?
Longfellow, tr. of Dante's Inferno, ix. 94.

II. *trans.* To kick against; show repugnance or opposition to. [Rare.]

The more heartily did one disdain his disdain, and *recalcitrate* his tricks. *De Quincey*.

recalcitration (rẹ̄-kal-si-trā′shọn), *n.* [< *recalcitrate* + *-ion*.] The act of recalcitrating; opposition; repugnance.

Inwardly chuckling that these symptoms of *recalcitration* had not taken place until the fair malecontent was, as he mentally termed it, under his thumb, Archibald coolly replied, "That the hills were none of his making."
Scott, Heart of Mid-Lothian, xii.

recalesce (rē-ka-les′), *v. i.*; pret. and pp. *recalesced*, ppr. *recalescing*. [< L. *re-*, again, + *calescere*, grow hot, inceptive of *calere*, be hot: see *calid*.] To show renewed calescence; resume a state of glowing heat.

recalescence (rē-ka-les′ẹns), *n.* [< *recalesce* + *-ence*.] Renewed calescence; reglow; specifically, in *physics*, a phenomenon exhibited by iron as it cools gradually from a white heat (point of high incandescence): at certain temperatures, as at 1,000°, the cooling seems to be arrested, and the iron glows more brilliantly for a short time. It has also been found that certain other properties of the metal, magnetic and electrical, undergo a sudden change at these points of recalescence.

recall (rẹ̄-kâl′), *v. t.* [< *re-* + *call*[1].] **1.** To call back from a distance; summon or cause to return or to be returned; bring back by a call, summons, or demand: as, to *recall* an ambassador or a ship; we cannot *recall* our lost youth.

If Henry were *recall'd* to life again,
These news would cause him once more yield the ghost.
Shak., 1 Hen. VI., i. 1. 66.

At the expiration of six years he was suddenly *recalled* to his native country by the death of his father.
Prescott, Ferd. and Isa., ii. 5.

2. To call back to mind or perception; renew the memory or experience of; bring again, as something formerly experienced.

How soon
Would highth *recall* high thoughts!
Milton, P. L., iv. 95.

I *recall* it, not see it;
Could vision be clearer?
Lowell, Fountain of Youth.

3. To revoke; take back, as something given or parted with; countermand; abrogate; cancel: as, to *recall* a decree or an order; to *recall* an edition of a book.

Passed sentence may not be *recall'd*.
Shak., C. of E., i. 1. 148.

The doore of grace turnes upon smooth hinges wide opening to send out; but soon shutting to *recall* the precious offers of mercy to a nation.
Milton, Church-Government, i. 7.

The Gods themselves cannot *recall* their gifts.
Tennyson, Tithonus.

=**Syn.** **3.** *Recant*, *Abjure*, etc. (see *renounce*); *Repeal*, *Rescind*, etc. (see *abolish*).

recall (rẹ̄-kâl′), *n.* [< *recall*, *v.*] **1.** A calling back; a summons to return; a demand for reappearance, as of a performer after he has left the stage (usually indicated by long-continued applause): as, the *recall* of an ambassador; the *recall* of an actor.—**2.** A calling back to mind; the act of summoning up the memory of something; a bringing back from the past.

The *recall*, resuscitation, or reproduction of ideas already formed takes place according to fixed laws, and not at random. *Mind*, XII. 161.

3. Revocation; countermand; retraction; abrogation.

Those indulgent laws
Will not be now vouchsafed; other decrees
Against thee are gone forth without *recall*.
Milton, P. L., v. 885.

'Tis done, and, since 'tis done, 'tis past *recall*.
Dryden, Spanish Friar, iii. 3.

4. A musical call played on a drum, bugle, or trumpet to summon back soldiers to the ranks or to camp.—**5.** A signal-flag used to recall a boat to a ship.

recallable (rẹ̄-kâl′ạ-bl), *a.* [< *recall* + *-able*.] Capable of being recalled, in any sense.

Delegates *recallable* at pleasure. *Madison*.

The glow of a gorgeous sunset continues to be *recallable* long after faintly coloured scenes of the same date have been forgotten. *H. Spencer*, Prin. of Psychol., § 90.

recallment, recalment (rẹ̄-kâl′mẹnt), *n.* [< *recall* + *-ment*.] The act of recalling, or the state of being recalled. [Rare.]

I followed after,
And asked, as a grace, what it all meant?
If she wished not the rash deed's *recalment*?
Browning, The Glove.

recant (rẹ̄-kant′), *v.* [< OF. *recanter*, *rechanter*, sing again, = Pr. *rechantar* = Pg. *recantar* = It. *ricantare*, sing again, < L. *recantare*, sing back, reëcho, also sing again, repeat in singing, recant, recall, revoke, charm back or away, < *re-*, back, + *cantare*, sing: see *chant* and *cant*[2].] **I.** *trans.* **1**†. To sing over again; utter repeatedly in song.

They were wont ever after in their wedding songs to *recant* and resound this name—Thalassius.
Holland, tr. of Plutarch, p. 704.

2. To unsay; contradict or withdraw formally (something which one had previously asserted); renounce; disavow; retract: as, to *recant* one's opinion or profession of faith.

Which duke . . . did *recant* his former life.
Fabyan, Chron. (ed. Ellis), II. 712, an. 1553.

We haue another manner of speech much like to the repentant, but doth not as the same *recant* or vnsay a word that hath bene said before.
Puttenham, Arte of Eng. Poesie, p. 180.

He shall do this, or else I do *recant*
The pardon that I late pronounced here.
Shak., M. of V., iv. 1. 391.

=**Syn.** **2.** *Abjure*, *Forswear*, etc. See *renounce*.

II. *intrans.* To revoke a declaration or proposition; unsay what has been said; renounce or disavow an opinion or a dogma formerly maintained; especially, to announce formally one's abandonment of a religious belief.

And many, for offering to maintain these Ceremonies, were either punish'd or forced to *recant*.
Baker, Chronicles, p. 304.

It is against all precedent to burn
One who *recants*; they mean to pardon me.
Tennyson, Queen Mary, iv. 2.

recantation (rē-kan-tā′shọn), *n.* [= Sp. *recantacion* = Pg. *recantação* = It. *ricantazione*; < L. as if **recantatio(n-)*, < *recantare*, recant: see *recant*.] The act of recanting; retraction; especially, solemn renunciation or abjuration of a doctrine or religious system previously maintained, with acknowledgment that it is erroneous.

Your lord and master did well to make his *recantation*.
Shak., All's Well, ii. 3. 195.

Cranmer, it is decided by the Council
That you to-day should read your *recantation*
Before the people in St. Mary's Church.
Tennyson, Queen Mary, iv. 2.

recanter (rẹ̄-kan′tėr), *n.* One who recants.

The public body, which doth seldom
Play the *recanter*. *Shak.*, T. of A., v. 1. 149.

recapacitate (rē-kạ̄-pas′i-tāt), *v. t.* [< *re-* + *capacitate*.] To qualify again; confer capacity on again. *Bp. Atterbury*, To Bp. Trelawney.

recapitulate (rē-ka-pit′ụ̄-lāt), *v.* [< LL. *recapitulatus*, pp. of *recapitulare* (> It. *ricapitolare* = Sp. Pg. Pr. *recapitular* = F. *récapituler*), go over the main points of a thing again, < L. *re-*, again, + *capitulum*, a head, main part, chapter (> ML. *capitulare*, capitulate): see *capitulate*.] **I.** *trans.* To repeat, as the principal things mentioned in a preceding discourse, argument, or essay; give a summary of the principal facts, points, or arguments of; mention or relate in brief.

When they met, Temple began by *recapitulating* what had passed at their last interview.
Macaulay, Sir William Temple.

=**Syn.** *Recapitulate*, *Repeat*, *Recite*, *Rehearse*, *Reiterate*. *Recapitulate* is a precise word, applying to the formal or exact naming of points that have been with some exactness named before: as, it is often well, after an extended argument, to *recapitulate* the heads. In this it differs from *repeat*, *recite*, *rehearse*, which are freer in their use. To *reiterate* is to say a thing a second time or oftener.

II. *intrans.* To repeat in brief what has already been said.

recapitulation (rē-ka-pit-ụ̄-lā′shọn), *n.* [< OF. *recapitulacion*, *recapitulation*, F. *récapitulation* = Sp. *recapitulacion* = Pg. *recapitulação* = It. *ricapitulazione*, < LL. *recapitulatio(n-)* (technical as trans. of Gr. ἀνακεφαλαίωσις), < L. *recapitulare*, recapitulate: see *recapitulate*.] **1.** The act or process of recapitulating.

> *D. Fer.* Were e'er two friends engag'd in an adventure
> So intricate as we, and so capricious?
> *D. Jul.* Sure never in this world; methinks it merits
> A special *recapitulation*. *Digby*, Elvira, iii.

2. In *rhet.*, a summary or concise statement or enumeration of the principal points or facts in a preceding discourse, argument, or essay. Also *anacephalæosis*, *enumeration*. See *epanodos*.

> Such earnest and hastie heaping vp of speaches be made by way of *recapitulation*, which commonly is in the end of euery long tale and Oration, because the speaker seemes to make a collection of all the former materiall points, to binde them as it were in a bundle and lay them forth to enforce the cause. *Puttenham*, Arte of Eng. Poesie, p. 198.

recapitulative (rē-ka-pit̤'ṳ̄-lā̤-tiv), *a.* [< *recapitulate* + *-ive*.] Of or pertaining to recapitulation; resulting from or characterized by recapitulation; giving a summary of the chief parts or points.

> It has been shown that these [rudimentary structures] are the last *recapitulative* remnant of an independent series of structures developed outside the spore in the fern. *Nature*, XLI. 316.

recapitulator (rē-ka-pit̤'ṳ̄-lā-tọr), *n.* [< *recapitulate* + *-or*[1].] One who recapitulates.

recapitulatory (rē-ka-pit̤'ṳ̄-lā̤-tō̤-ri), *a.* [< *recapitulate* + *-ory*.] Of the nature of or containing recapitulation.

> This law is comprehensive and *recapitulatory* (as it were) of the rest concerning our neighbour, prescribing universal justice toward him. *Barrow*, Expos. of the Decalogue.

reception (rẹ̄-kap'shọn), *n.* [< *re-* + *caption*.] The act of retaking; reprisal; in *law*, the retaking, without force or violence, of one's own goods, chattels, wife, or children from one who has taken them and wrongfully detains them. Also called *reprisal*.—**Writ of recaption**, a writ to recover property taken by a second distress pending a replevin for a former distress for the same rent or service.

recaptor (rẹ̄-kap'tọr), n. [< *re-* + *captor*.] One who recaptures; one who takes a prize which had been previously taken.

recapture (rẹ̄-kap'tṳ̄r), *n.* [< *re-* + *capture*, *n.*] **1.** The act of retaking; particularly, the retaking of a prize or goods from a captor.—**2.** That which is recaptured; a prize retaken.

recapture (rẹ̄-kap'tṳ̄r), *v. t.* [< *re-* + *capture*, *v.*] To capture back or again; retake, particularly a prize which had been previously taken.

recarburization (rē-kär"bṳ̄-ri-zā'shọn), *n.* [< *recarburize* + *-ation*.] The adding of carbon to take the place of that removed.

recarburize (rē-kär'bṳ̄-rīz), *v. t.* [< *re-* + *carburize*.] To restore to (a metal) the carbon previously removed, especially in any metallurgical operation connected with the manufacture of iron or steel.

recarnify (rẹ̄-kär'ni-fī), *v. t.* [< *re-* + *carnify*.] To convert again into flesh.

> Looking upon them [a herd of kine] quietly grazing up and down, I fell to consider that the Flesh which is daily dish'd upon our Tables is but concocted Grass, which is *recarnified* in our Stomachs and transmuted to another Flesh. *Howell*, Letters, ii. 50.

recarriage (rē-kar'ā̤j), *n.* [< *re-* + *carriage*.] A carrying back or again; repeated carriage.

> Another thing there is in our markets worthie to be looked vnto, and that is the *recariage* of graine from the same into lofts and sollars.
> *Harrison*, Descrip. of Eng., ii. 18 (Holinshed's Chron., I.).

recarry (rẹ̄-kar'i), *v. t.* [< *re-* + *carry*.] To carry back, as in returning; carry again or in a reversed direction.

> When the Turks besieged Malta or Rhodes, . . . pigeons are then related to carry and *recarry* letters.
> *I. Walton*, Complete Angler, i. 1.

recast (rẹ̄-kȧst'), *v. t.* [< *re-* + *cast*[1].] **1.** To throw again.

> In the midst of their running race they would cast and *recast* themselves from one to another horse.
> *Florio*, tr. of Montaigne, p. 155.

2. To cast or found again: as, to *recast* cannon.—**3.** To cast or form anew; remodel; remold: as, to *recast* a poem.

> Your men of close application, though taking their terms from the common language, find themselves under a necessity of *recasting* them in a mould of their own.
> *A. Tucker*, Light of Nature, I. i. 6.

> Not painlessly doth God *recast*
> And mould anew the nation.
> *Whittier*, "Ein Feste Burg ist unser Gott."

4†. To cover anew with plaster: said of an old wall or building.—**5.** To compute anew; recalculate: as, to *recast* an account.

recast (rē-kȧst'), *n.* [< *recast*, *v.*] A fresh molding, arrangement, or modification, as of a work of art, a writing, etc.

> Popular feeling called for a diaskeué, or thorough *recast*. *De Quincey*, Homer, iii.

recaulescence (rē-kâ-les'ẹns), *n.* [< *re-* + *caulescen(t)* + *-ce*.] In *bot.*, the adnation of a petiole to a peduncle or a leafy branch: a term of Schimper's.

recchet†, *v.* A Middle English form of *reck*.

recchelest†, *a.* A Middle English form of *reckless*.

recede[1] (rẹ̄-sēd'), *v. i.*; pret. and pp. *receded*, ppr. *receding*. [< OF. *receder*, F. *recéder* = It. *recedere*, < L. *recedere*, go back, withdraw, retreat, < *re-*, back, + *cedere*, go: see *cede*.] **1.** To move back; retreat; withdraw; fall away.

> The world *receded* from her rising view,
> When heaven approach'd as earthly things withdrew.
> *Crabbe*, Works, IV. 186.

2. To withdraw an affirmation, a belief, a demand, or the like; turn back or aside.

> It is plain that the more you *recede* from your grounds, the weaker do you conclude.
> *Bacon*, Advancement of Learning, ii. 369.

3. To have a backward inclination, slope, or tendency: as, a *receding* coast-line; a *receding* chin. =**Syn.** 1. To retire, retrograde, give way. See *retreat*[1].

recede[2] (rē-sēd'), *v. t.* [< *re-* + *cede*.] To cede back; grant or yield to a former possessor: as, to *recede* conquered territory.

recedence (rẹ̄-sē'dẹns), *n.* [< *recede*[1] + *-ence*.] Same as *recession*[1]. [Rare.]

> The beaded brown kelp deepens to bronze in . . . the wet, rich, pulpy *recedence* of the ebb.
> *Harper's Mag.*, LXXII. 94.

receipt (rẹ̄-sēt'), *n.* [Formerly also *receit* (the *p* being inserted in imitation of the L. original, and the proper spelling being *receit*, like *conceit*, *deceit*); (*a*) < ME. *receit*, *receyt*, *receite*, receipt, recipe, < AF. *receite*, OF. *recete*, *recepte*, *reçoite*, F. *recette* = Pr. *recepta* = Sp. *receta* = Pg. *receita* = It. *ricetta*, f., receipt, recipe, < ML. *recepta*, f., receipt, recipe, money received, a treasury, a right of pasture, lit. (sc. *res*, a thing) 'a thing received,' fem. of L. *receptus*, pp. of *recipere*, receive; (*b*) in defs. 5 and 6, also *reset* (see *reset*[1]), < ME. *recet*, *reset*, *resset*, *resset*, *resate*, < OF. *recet*, *receit*, *recept*, *reset*, *reçoit*, *rechet*, *rechiet*, etc., = Sp. *recepto* = It. *ricetto*, m., a retreat, refuge, abode, asylum (see *recheat*), < L. *receptus*, m., a receiving, place of retreat, refuge, < *recipere*, pp. *receptus*, receive: see *receive*. Cf. *reset*[1] and *recheat*, doublets of *receipt*; cf. also *recept*.] **1.** A thing received; that which is received by transfer; the amount or quantity of what is received from other hands: as, the *receipts* of cotton at a port.

> Three parts of that *receipt* I had for Calais
> Disbursed I duly to his highness' soldiers.
> *Shak.*, Rich. II., i. 1. 126.

> He wintered for the second time in Dublin; where his own pieces, and Macklin's "Love-a-la-Mode," brought great *receipts* to Crow-Street theatre.
> *W. Cooke*, Memoirs of S. Foote, I. 51.

2. The act or state of receiving by transfer or transmission; a taking of that which is delivered or passed over; a getting or obtaining: as, the *receipt* of money or of a letter; he is in the *receipt* of a good income.

> Christ in us is that *receipt* of the same medicine whereby we are every one particularly cured.
> *Hooker*, Eccles. Polity, v. 55.

> Villain, thou did'st deny the gold's *receipt*.
> *Shak.*, C. of E., ii. 2. 17.

3. A written acknowledgment of having received something specified, with date, source, signature, and such other particulars as the case requires. A receipt may be for something received as a trust or a purchase, or for money or other valuable thing taken either in part or in full payment of a debt. At common law a mere unsealed receipt, though expressed to be in full for a debt, does not by its own force operate to discharge the debt if the payment in fact be of a part only. A receipt is not deemed a contract within the rule that a written contract cannot be varied by oral evidence.

4. A formula or prescription for the making of something, or the production of some effect; a statement of that which is to be taken or done for some purpose: distinguished from *recipe* by the common restriction of that word to medical or related uses: as, a *receipt* for a pudding; a *receipt* for gaining popularity.

> Come, sir, the sight of Golde
> Is the most sweet *recent* for melancholy,
> And will reuiue your spirits.
> *Heywood*, Woman Killed with Kindness (Works, ed. Pearson, 1874, II. 107).

> We have the *receipt* of fern-seed, we walk invisible.
> *Shak.*, 1 Hen. IV., ii. 1. 96.

> No *Receipt* can Human-kind relieve,
> Doom'd to decrepit Age without Reprieve.
> *Congreve*, tr. of Ovid's Art of Love.

5†. Reception; admittance; a granting of entrance or admission.

> He wayted hym aboute, & wylde hit hym thoȝt,
> & seȝe no syngne of *resette*.
> *Sir Gawayne and the Green Knight* (E. E. T. S.), l. 2164.

> Ther [in heaven] entreȝ non to take *reset*,
> That bereȝ any spot.
> *Alliterative Poems* (ed. Morris), i. 1066.

> Come, cave, become my grave; come, death, and lend
> *Receipt* to me within thy bosom dark.
> *Sir P. Sidney*, Arcadia, iii.

6†. A place for the reception of persons or things; a place where anything is received or taken in; a station or a receptacle for lodgment.

> Men han made a lityle *Receyt*, besyde a Pylere of that Chirche, for to resceyve the Offrynges of Pilgrymes.
> *Mandeville*, Travels, p. 112.

> Go forth, tary we not behynd,
> Vnto som *receit* nye the wodes lynde,
> Wher we mow thys tym receyued to be.
> *Rom. of Partenay* (E. E. T. S.), l. 159.

> He saw Levi . . . sitting at the *receipt* of custom [place of toll, R. V.]. Mark ii. 14.

> Memory, the warder of the brain,
> Shall be a fume, and the *receipt* of reason
> A limbeck only. *Shak.*, Macbeth, i. 7. 66.

7†. Power of receiving or taking in; extent of accommodation; fitness for holding or containing.

> The foresaid ships were of an huge and incredible capacitie and *receipt*. *Hakluyt's Voyages*, I. 593.

> In things of great *receipt* with ease we prove
> Among a number one is reckon'd none.
> *Shak.*, Sonnets, cxxxvi.

> Such be the capacity and *receipt* of the mind of man.
> *Bacon*, Advancement of Learning, i. 9.

Accountable receipt. See *accountable*.=**Syn.** *Recipe*, etc. See *reception*.

receipt (rẹ̄-sēt'), *v. t.* [Also in technical legal use *reset* (see *reset*[1]); < ME. *recetten*, *reseten*; from the noun: see *receipt*, *n.*] **1†.** To receive; harbor.

> And ȝe hit make, and that me greves,
> A den to *reset* inne theves.
> *Cursor Mundi*, MS. Coll. Trin. Cantab., f. 91. (*Halliwell*.)

> My lorde hym *recetted* in hys castell
> For the dewkys dethe oton.
> *MS. Cantab.*, Ff. ii. 38, f. 220. (*Halliwell*.)

2. To give a receipt for; acknowledge in writing the payment of: as, to *receipt* a bill (usually by writing upon the bill "Received payment" and the creditor's signature).

receiptable (rẹ̄-sē'ta-bl), *a.* [< *receipt* + *-able*.] Capable of being receipted; for which a receipt may be granted.

receipt-book (rẹ̄-sēt'bu̇k), *n.* A book containing receipts, in either sense 3 or sense 4.

receiptment (rẹ̄-sēt'mẹnt), *n.* [< *receipt* + *-ment*.] In *old Eng. law*, the receiving or harboring of a felon with knowledge on the part of the harborer of the commission of a felony. *Burrill.*

receiptor (rẹ̄-sē'tọr), *n.* [< *receipt* + *-or*[1].] One who gives a receipt; specifically, in *law*, a person to whom property is bailed by an officer, who has attached it upon mesne process, to answer to the exigency of the writ and satisfy the judgment, the obligation of the receiptor being to have it forthcoming on demand. *Wharton.*

receit†, *n.* A former spelling of *receipt* (and of the ultimately identical *recheat*).

receivability (rẹ̄-sē-va-bil'i̤-ti), *n.* [< *receivable* + *-ity* (see *-bility*).] The quality of being receivable. *Imp. Dict.*

receivable (rẹ̄-sē'va̤-bl), *a.* [< F. *recevable* (cf. Pg. *recebivel* = It. *ricevevole*), receivable; as *receive* + *-able*.] **1.** Capable of being received; fit for reception or acceptance.—**2.** Awaiting receipt of payment; that is to be paid: as, bills *receivable*. See *bill payable*, *bill receivable*, under *bill*[3].

receivableness (rẹ̄-sē'va̤-bl-nes), *n.* The character of being receivable; capability of being received.

receive (rẹ̄-sēv'), *v.*; pret. and pp. *received*, ppr. *receiving*. [Early mod. E. also *receve*, *receave*; < ME. *receiven*, *receyven*, *resceyven*, *resseyven*, *resceyven*, *resayven*, *resaven*, < OF. *recever*, *recevoir*, *reçoivre*, F. *recevoir* = Pr. *recobre* = Sp. *recibir* = Pg. *receber* = It. *ricevere*, receive, < L. *recipere*, pp. *receptus*, take back, get back, regain, recover, take to oneself, admit, accept, receive, take in, assume, allow, etc., < *re-*, back, + *capere*, take: see *capacious*. Cf. *conceive*, *deceive*, *perceive*. Hence ult. (from the L. verb) *receipt*, *receptacle*, *recipe*, etc.] **I.** *trans.* **1.** To take from a source or agency of transmission; get by transfer: as, to *receive* money or a letter; to *receive* gifts.

They be like Gray Friars, that will not be seen to *receive* bribes themselves, but have others to *receive* for them.
Latimer, 5th Sermon bef. Edw. VI., 1549.

Son, remember that thou in thy lifetime *receivedst* thy good things, and likewise Lazarus evil things.
Luke xvi. 25.

2. To take or get from a primary source: as, to *receive* favors or a good education; to *receive* an impression, a wound, or a shock.

Receives not thy nose court-odour from me?
Shak., W. T., iv. 4. 757.

The idea of solidity we *receive* by our touch. *Locke.*

No Norman or Breton ever saw a Mussulman, except to give and *receive* blows on some Syrian field of battle.
Macaulay, Von Ranke's Hist. Popes.

3. To take notice of on coming or appearing; greet the advent of; salute or treat upon approach: as, to *receive* an actor with applause; to *receive* news joyfully.

To Westmynstur the kyng be water did glide,
Worshypfully *resayeid* with procession in frett,
Resayeid with reverence, his dewte not denye.
MS. Bibl. Reg. 17 D. xv. (*Halliwell.*)

My father was *received* with open arms by all his old friends. *Lady Holland*, Sydney Smith, vi.

4. To take or consider favorably; admit as credible, worthy, acceptable, etc.; give admission or recognition to: as, to *receive* a person into one's friendship; a *received* authority.

What he hath seen and heard, that he testifieth; and no man *receiveth* his testimony. John iii. 32.

He is a Gentleman so *receiv'd*, so courted, and so trusted.
Steele, Tender Husband, i. 1.

Every person who should now leave *received* opinions . . . might be regarded as a chimerical projector.
Goldsmith, The Bee, No. 4.

5. To admit for intercourse or entertainment; grant audience or welcome to; give a friendly reception to: as, to *receive* an ambassador or guests.

The quen with hire companie com him a-ȝens,
& *reseyued* as reali as swiche rinkes ouȝt.
William of Palerne (E. E. T. S.), l. 3930.

It was so fre that Men *resceyved* there alle manere of Fugityfes of other places for here evyl Dedis.
Mandeville, Travels, p. 66.

They kindled a fire, and *received* us every one, because of the present rain, and because of the cold. Acts xxviii. 2.

6. To take in or on; give entrance to; hold; contain; have capacity for: as, a box to *receive* contributions.

The brasen altar that was before the Lord was too little to *receive* the burnt offerings. 1 Ki. viii. 64.

This cave, fashion'd
By provident Nature in this solid rock
To be a den for beasts, alone *receives* me.
Beau. and Fl., Knight of Malta, iv. 1.

7†. To perceive; comprehend; take into the mind.

To be *received* plain, I'll speak more gross.
Shak., M. for M., ii. 4. 82.

8. In *law*: (*a*) To take by transfer in a criminal manner; accept the custody or possession of from a known thief: as, to *receive* stolen goods.

You must restore all stoln goods you *receiv'd*.
Fletcher (*and another*), Love's Cure, v. 3.

(*b*) To admit as pertinent; take into consideration; permit the reception of: as, the court refused to *receive* the evidence, and ordered it to be stricken out.—**To receive the canvas†.** See *canvas*.—**To receive the coif.** See *coif*.=**Syn. 1** and **2.** *Receive, Take, Accept.* These words are in the order of strength in regard to the willingness with which the thing in question is received, etc., but none of them is warm. One may *receive* a letter, a challenge to a duel, a remittance, detriment, or a wound; the word thus may be wholly neuter. One may *take* cold, but, more often, *take* that which he might refuse, as a present, a bribe, offense, a pinch of snuff, or an orange. One may *accept* one's fate, but even then the word means a mental consent, a movement of mind; more often it means to receive with some willingness, as to *accept* a proposition, an invitation, or an offer. An offer, etc., may be *received* and not *accepted*.

II. *intrans.* 1. To be a receiver or recipient; come into custody or possession of something by transfer.

Every one shall *receive* of thy words. Deut. xxxiii. 3.

Freely ye have *received*, freely give. Mat. x. 8.

2. To give, or take part in holding, a reception; greet and entertain visitors, especially at certain fixed times.

As this name was called the person presented advanced, bowed first to the prince and then separately to the two members of the royal family who were *receiving* with him.
T. C. Crawford, English Life, p. 38.

received (rē-sēvd'), *a.* In *entom.*, projecting between other parts.—**Received scutellum**, a scutellum which lies between the bases of the elytra, as in most beetles.

receivedness (rē-sē'ved-nes), *n.* The state of being received; general allowance or belief.

Others will, upon account of the *receivedness* of this opinion, think it rather worth to be examined, than acquiesced in. *Boyle.*

receiver (rē-sē'vėr), *n.* [Early mod. E. also *receaver*, *receauer*; < ME. *resaver*, *receyvour*, < OF. *recevour*, *receveur*, F. *receveur*, < *recevoir*, receive: see *receive*.] 1. One who or that which receives, in any general sense; a recipient; a receptacle; a taker or container of anything transmitted: as, a *receiver* of taxes; a *receiver* for odds and ends.

We are *receivers* through grace and mercy, authors through merit and desert we are not, of our own salvation.
Hooker, Eccles. Polity, v., App. 1.

But in this thankless World the Givers
Are envy'd ev'n by the *Receivers*.
Cowley, Pindaric Odes, i. 11.

This invention covers a combined grass *receiver* and dumper to catch and carry the grass while the lawn mower is being operated. *Sci. Amer.*, N. S., LXII. 364.

2. An officer appointed to receive public money; a treasurer; specifically, a person appointed by a court of equity or other judicial tribunal to take, pending litigation, the custody and management or disposal of property in controversy, or to receive the rents and profits of land or the produce of other property.—3. One who, for purposes of profit or concealment, takes stolen goods from a thief, knowing them to be stolen, thus making himself a party to the crime.

Were there noe *receavers*, there would be noe theeves.
Spenser, State of Ireland.

4. In *chem.*: (*a*) A vessel for receiving and containing the product of distillation. (*b*) A vessel for receiving and containing gases.—5. The glass vessel placed on the plate of an air-pump, in order to be exhausted of air: so named because it is the recipient of those things on which experiments are made. See *air-pump*.—6. The receiving magnet of an electric telegraph, the receiving apparatus of a telephone, or the like.—**Exhausted receiver.** See *exhaust*.—**Florentine receiver.** See *Florentine*.—**Knitting-needle receiver**, an apparatus consisting of a magnetizing coil with a knitting-needle in its axis, used by Reis as a telephonic receiver. The action of this receiver depends on Page's discovery that an iron bar gives a sharp click when magnetized; the rapid succession of clicks in the receiver, corresponding to the successive make-and-breaks of the Reis transmitter, reproduces the sound.—**Mail-bag receiver and discharger.** See *mail-catcher*.—**Receiver and manager.** See *manager*, 4.—**Receiver of the fines**, formerly, in England, an officer who received the money of all such as compounded with the crown on original writs sued out of Chancery.—**Receiver's certificates**, evidences of debt, issued by a receiver of property in litigation, for the discharge of obligations incurred in the management of it, to be redeemed out of its proceeds when finally disposed of or restored to its owners. Such certificates may be authorized by the proper court, and made a lien upon the property, when the expenses connected with it cannot be otherwise met without detriment.—**Receivers of wreck**, officers appointed by the British Board of Trade for the preservation of wreck, etc., for the benefit of the shipping interests. They were formerly called *receivers of droits of admiralty*.

receiver-general (rē-sē'vėr-jen'e-ral), *n.* In some countries or states, an officer who receives the public revenues in general or in a particular territory: in some of the United States, an additional title of the State treasurer.

receivership (rē-sē'vėr-ship), *n.* [< *receiver* + *-ship*.] The office of a receiver of public money, or of money or other property in litigation; the collection and care of funds awaiting final distribution by legal process.

receiving (rē-sē'ving), *n.* [< ME. *receyving*; verbal n. of *receive*, *v.*] The act of one who receives, in any sense of that verb.—**Receiving apparatus** or **instrument**, in *teleg.*, any appliance used at a telegraph-station, by the action of which the signals transmitted from another station are rendered perceptible to any of the senses of the receiving operator.—**Receiving tubes of the kidney**, the straight tubules of the kidney.

receiving-house (rē-sē'ving-hous), *n.* A house where letters or parcels are received for transmission; a place of deposit for things to be forwarded; a depot. [Great Britain.]

receiving-magnet (rē-sē'ving-mag'net), *n.* See *magnet*.

receiving-office (rē-sē'ving-of'is), *n.* In Great Britain, a branch post-office where letters, parcels, etc., may be posted, but from which no delivery is made to persons addressed.

receiving-ship (rē-sē'ving-ship), *n.* A ship stationed permanently in a harbor to receive recruits for the navy until they can be transferred to a cruising ship.

receiving-tomb (rē-sē'ving-töm), *n.* Same as *receiving-vault*.

receiving-vault (rē-sē'ving-vâlt), *n.* A building or other structure in which the bodies of the dead may be placed temporarily when it is impossible or inconvenient to inter them in the usual manner.

recency (rē'sen-si), *n.* [< ML. *recentia*, < L. *recen(t-)s*, new, fresh: see *recent*.] The state or quality of being recent; recentness; newness; lateness; freshness.

So also a scirrhus in its *recency*, whilst it is in its augment, requireth milder applications than the confirmed or inveterate one. *Wiseman*, Surgery, i. 19.

An impression of *recency* is given which some minds are clearly unable to shake off.
Maine, Early Law and Custom, p. 198.

recense (rē-sens'), *v. t.*; pret. and pp. *recensed*, ppr. *recensing*. [< OF. *recenser*, number, count, peruse, muster, review, F. *recenser*, number, take the census of, = Pr. *recensar* = Pg. *recensear*, examine, survey, < L. *recensere*, recount, examine closely, review, muster, revise, etc., < *re-*, again, + *censere*, think, deem, judge: see *census*.] To review; revise. [Rare.]

Sixtus and Clemens, at a vast exponce, had an assembly of learned divines to *recense* and adjust the Latin Vulgate.
Bentley.

recension (rē-sen'shon), *n.* [< F. *recension*, < L. *recensio(n-)*, an enumeration, reviewing, recension, < *recensere*, review: see *recense*.] 1. Review; examination; enumeration. [Obsolete or rare.]

In this *recension* of monthly flowers, it is to be understood for the whole period that any flower continues, from its first appearing to its final withering.
Evelyn, Calendarium Hortense, January.

2. A critical or methodical revision, as of the text of a book or document; alteration of a text according to some authority, standard, or principle; a reëditing or systematic revisal.

He who . . . spends nine years in the elaboration and *recension* of his book . . . will find that he comes too late.
G. P. Marsh, Lects. on Eng. Lang., xxi.

3. A text established by critical or systematic revision; an edited version.

The genuine ballad-book thus published was so successful that in less than ten years three editions or *recensions* of it appeared. *Ticknor*, Span. Lit., I. 115.

Using the ancient versions in this way, we can recover a *recension* (or *recensions*) differing more or less widely from that represented by the traditional Hebrew text.
Contemporary Rev., L. 595.

4. A critical examination, as of a book; a review; a critique.

He was . . . bitterly convinced that his old acquaintance Carp had been the writer of that depreciatory *recension* which was kept locked in a small drawer of Mr. Casaubon's desk, and also in a small dark closet of his verbal memory. *George Eliot*, Middlemarch, xxix.

recensionist (rē-sen'shon-ist), *n.* [< *recension* + *-ist*.] One who reviews or revises, as the text of an ancient author; an editor.

recent (rē'sent), *a.* [< OF. *recent*, F. *récent* = Pr. *recent* = Sp. *reciente* = Pg. It. *recente*, < L. *recen(t-)s*, fresh, new; (*a*) in one view, < *re-* + *-cen(t-)s*, supposed to be allied to W. *cynt*, first, earliest, Skt. *kanīyāṅs*, smaller, *kanistha*, smallest (cf. Russ. *po-chinati*, begin); (*b*) in another view, orig. ppr. from a root **rec* = Zend √ *raç*, come (cf. *recens a victoria*, 'just coming from a victory'; *Rhodo recentes Romam venerunt*, 'they came to Rome just from Rhodes,' etc.: see def. 5).] 1. Of or pertaining to time just before the present; not long past in occurrence or existence; lately happening or being; newly appearing, done, or made: as, *recent* events; *recent* importations; *recent* memories; *recent* news; a *recent* speech.—2. Of modern date, absolutely or relatively; not of primitive or remote origin; belonging to or occurring in times not far removed.—3. Still fresh in quality or existence; not old or degenerate; unchanged by time: said of things liable to rapid change, as newly gathered plants or specimens in natural history.

The odour [of essential oils] is seldom as pleasant as that of the *recent* plant. *Ure*, Dict., III. 450.

4. In *geol.*, of or pertaining to the epoch regarded as the present from a geological point of view. Strata so called contain few, if any, fossils belonging to extinct species. The alluvial formations in the valleys are generally of recent formation, as well as most of the superficial detrital material. The deposits which belong to the Post-tertiary, or which are more recent than the Tertiary, are with difficulty classified, except for purposes of local geology. In glaciated regions, the traces of the former presence of ice adds variety to the phenomena, and complexity to the classification, of the various forms of detrital material. The existence of very ancient remains and works of man is a further element of interest in the geology of the recent formations.

5. Lately come; not long removed or separated. [Poetical and rare.]

Shall I not think that, with disorder'd charms,
All heav'n beholds me *recent* from thy arms?
Pope, Iliad, xiv. 382.

Amphitryon *recent* from the nether sphere.
Lewis, tr. of Statius's Thebaid, viii.

=**Syn. 1.** *Late, Fresh*, etc. See *new*.

recently (rē'sent-li), *adv.* At a recent time; newly; lately; freshly; not long since: as, advices *recently* received; a town *recently* built or repaired; an isle *recently* discovered.

recentness (rē'sent-nes), *n.* The state or quality of being recent; newness; freshness; recency; lateness of origin or occurrence: as, the *recentness* of alluvial land; the *recentness* of news or of events.

recept (rē'sept), *n.* [< L. *receptum*, neut. of *receptus*, pp. of *recipere*, receive: see *receive*. Cf. *receipt*.] That which is received; especially, something taken into the mind from an external source; an idea derived from observation. [Recent.]

The bridge between *recept* and concept is equally impassable as that between percept and concept.
Athenæum, No. 3193, p. 12.

receptacle (rē-sep'tạ-kl, formerly also res'ep-tạ-kl), *n.* [< OF. *receptacle*, F. *réceptacle* = Pr. *receptacle* = Sp. *receptáculo* = Pg. *receptaculo* = It. *ricettacolo*, *recettaculo*, < L. *receptaculum*, a receptacle, place to receive or store things in, < *recipere*, pp. *receptus*, receive, hold, contain: see *receive*.] **1.** That which receives or holds anything for rest or deposit; a storing-place; a repository; a container; any space, open or closed, that serves for reception and keeping.

As in a vault, an ancient *receptacle*,
Where, for these many hundred years, the bones
Of all my buried ancestors are pack'd.
Shak., R. and J., iv. 3. 39.

Least his neighbor's countrey might be an harborugh or *receptacle* of his toes and aduersaries.
Hall, Edw. III., an. 10.

2. In *bot.*: (*a*) In a single flower, the more or less enlarged and peculiarly developed apex of the peduncle or pedicel, upon which all the organs of the flower are directly or indirectly

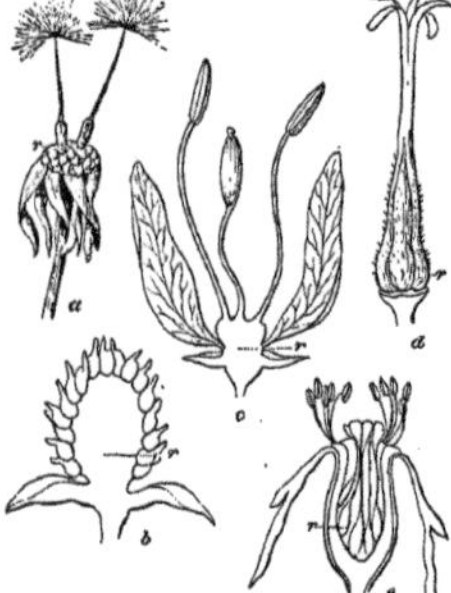

Various Forms of Receptacle (*r*).
a, Dandelion (*Taraxacum officinale*); *b*, *Fragaria elatior* (longitudinal section); *c*, *Cleome integrifolia* (longitudinal section); *d*, *Geranium maculatum*; *e*, *Rosa rubiginosa* (longitudinal section).

borne: the Linnæan and usual name: same as the more specific and proper *torus* of De Candolle and the *thalamus* of Tournefort. The receptacle varies in size and texture. In form it may be convex or conical (as most often), elongated, as in *Magnolia*, or concave, as in the rose; it may develop into a *stipe*, *gynobase*, *disk*, *carpophore*, or *hypanthium* (see these words), or it may greatly enlarge in fruit, as in the strawberry. As belonging to a single flower, sometimes termed *proper receptacle*. (*b*) In an inflorescence, the axis or rachis of a head or other short dense cluster; most often, the expanded disk-like summit of the peduncle in *Compositæ* (dandelion, etc.), on which are borne the florets of the head, surrounded by an involucre of bracts; a clinanthium. In contrast with the above, sometimes called *common receptacle*. (*c*) In an ovary, same as *placenta*, 4. (*d*) Among cryptogams—(1) In the vascular class, the placenta. (2) In *Marchantiaceæ*, one of the umbrella-like branches of the thallus, upon which the reproductive organs are borne. (3) In *Fucaceæ*, a part of the thallus in which conceptacles (see *conceptacle*) are congregated. They are either terminal portions of branches or parts sustained above water by air-bladders. (4) In *Fungi*, sometimes same as *stroma*; in *Ascomycetes*, same as *pycnidium*, 1 (also the stalk of a discocarp); in *Phalloideæ*, the inner part of the sporophore, supporting the gleba. (5) In lichens, the cup containing the soredia. The term has some other analogous applications.—**3.** In *zoöl.* and *anat.*, a part or an organ which receives and contains or detains a secretion; a receptaculum: as, the gall-bladder is the *receptacle* of the bile.

receptacula, *n.* Plural of *receptaculum*.

receptacular (rē-sep-tak'ū-lär), *a.* [= F. *réceptaculaire*, < L. *receptaculum*, a receptacle: see *receptacle*.] **1.** In *bot.*, of or pertaining to a receptacle.—**2.** In *zoöl.* and *anat.*, serving as a receptacle or reservoir; pertaining to a receptaculum.

receptaculite (rē-sep-tak'ū-līt), *n.* [< NL. *Receptaculites*.] A fossil of the genus *Receptaculites*.

Receptaculites (rē-sep-tak-ū-lī'tēz), *n.* [NL. (Defrance, 1827), < L. *receptaculum*, a receptacle (see *receptacle*), + *-ites* (see *-ite*[2]).] The typical genus of *Receptaculitidæ*.

Receptaculitidæ (rē-sep-tak-ū-lit'i-dē), *n. pl.* [NL., < *Receptaculites* + *-idæ*.] A family of fossil organisms, typified by the genus *Receptaculites*, of a very doubtful nature. They have been referred by many to the silicious sponges; but the skeleton was originally calcareous, and the silicious examples are the result of fossilization. They are of a spherical or pyriform shape, with a central closed cavity and an upper and lower pole, and the wall is composed of pillar-like spicules at right angles to the surface and expanded at their outer ends into rhomboidal summit-plates forming a mosaic-like outer layer. The species lived in the seas of the Silurian and Devonian epochs. Also called *Receptaculidæ*.

receptaculum (rē-sep-tak'ū-lum), *n.*; pl. *receptacula* (-lạ̈). [L.: see *receptacle*.] In *zoöl.*, *anat.*, and *bot.*, a receptacle; a reservoir of fluid; a saccular or vesicular organ to receive and retain a fluid.—**Receptaculum chyli**, a dilatation of the thoracic duct, situated upon the body of the first or second lumbar vertebra, into which the lymphatics of the lower extremities and the lacteals of the intestine discharge. Also called *receptaculum Pecqueti*, *cistern* or *reservoir of Pecquet*, *lacteal sac*.—**Receptaculum ganglii petrosi**, a depression in the lower border of the petrous portion of the temporal bone, for the lodgment of the petrous ganglion.—**Receptaculum Pecqueti.** Same as *receptaculum chyli*.—**Receptaculum seminis**, in *zoöl.*, a spermatheca in the female; any kind of seminal vesicle which may receive semen from the male and store it up. See cut under *Nematoidea*.

receptary† (res'ep-tạ̄-ri), *a.* and *n.* [= OF. *receptaire* = Sp. *recetario* = It. *ricettario*, a book of prescriptions or receipts, < ML. **receptarius*, adj. (as a noun *receptarius*, m., a receiver, collector), < *recepta*, a receipt, prescription: see *receipt*.] **I.** *a.* Commonly received or accepted but not proved; uncertain. [Rare.]

Baptista Porta, in whose works, although there be contained many excellent things, and verified upon his own experience, yet are there many also *receptary* and such as will not endure the test. *Sir T. Browne*, Vulg. Err., i. 8.

II. *n.* **1.** A collection of receipts.

Receptaire [F.], a *receptary*: a note of physical receits.
Cotgrave.

2. A thing commonly received but not proved; an assumption; a postulate. [Rare.]

Nor càn they which behold the present state of things, and controversy of points so long received in divinity, condemn our sober enquiries in the doubtful appertinancies of arts and *receptaries* of philosophy.
Sir T. Browne, Vulg. Err., To the Reader.

receptibility (rē-sep-ti-bil'i-ti), *n.* [< F. *réceptibilité* = Pg. *receptibilidade* = It. *recettibilità*; as *receptible* + *-ity* (see *-bility*).] **1.** The quality of being receptible; receivableness.

The peripatetick matter is a pure unactuated power, and this conceited vacuum a mere *receptibility*.
Glanville, Vanity of Dogmatizing, xvi.

2†. Something that may be received or believed in. *Imp. Dict.*

receptible (rē-sep'ti-bl), *a.* [< OF. *receptible* = Pg. *receptivel* = It. *recettibile*, < LL. *receptibilis*, that may be acquired again, recoverable, < L. *recipere*, pp. *receptus*, acquire, recover, receive: see *receive*.] Capable of or suited for being received; receivable. *Imp. Dict.*

reception (rē-sep'shon), *n.* [< ME. *reception* (in astrology), < OF. *reception*, F. *réception* = Pr. *receptio* = Sp. *recepcion* = Pg. *recepção* = It. *ricezione*, *recezione*, < L. *receptio(n-)*, a receiving, reception, < *recipere*, pp. *receptus*, receive: see *receive*.] **1.** The act of receiving by transfer or delivery; a taking into custody or possession of something tendered or presented; an instance of receipt: as, the *reception* of an invitation; a taking into place, position, or association; admission to entrance or insertion; a taking or letting in: as, a groove or socket for the *reception* of a handle; the *reception* of food in the stomach; *reception* of a person into society.—**2.** Admission into the mind; a taking into cognizance or consideration; a granting of credence; acceptance: as, the *reception* of a doctrine.

God never intended to compel, but only to persuade, us into a *reception* of divine truth.
Bp. Atterbury, Sermons, II. vii.

3. A receiving into audience, intercourse, or entertainment; treatment of a person on approach or presentation; greeting or welcome, as of a visitor: as, a cordial *reception*.—**4.** An occasion of ceremonious or complimentary greeting; an assemblage of persons to be individually received or greeted by an entertainer or by a guest selected for special attention: as, to give weekly *receptions*.

He assembled all his train,
Pretending so commanded, to consult
About the great *reception* of their King,
Thither to come. *Milton*, P. L., v. 769.

5†. A retaking; recapture; recovery.

He was right glad of the French King's *reception* of those Townes from Maximilian. *Bacon*, Hist. Hen. VII., p. 44.

6†. Power or capacity of receiving; receptivity; susceptivity.

That were to extend
His sentence beyond dust and nature's law,
By which all causes else, according still
To the *reception* of their matter, act,
Not to the extent of their own sphere.
Milton, P. L., x. 807.

7. In *astrol.*, the interchange of the dignities of two planets, owing to each being in the other's house or exaltation.=**Syn. 1** and **3.** *Reception*, *Receipt*, *Recipe*. *Reception* is used of a person or a thing: as, he got a very gracious *reception*; *receipt* of a thing: as, the *reception* or, better, the *receipt* of news or a letter; *recipe*, in medicine or, latterly, in cooking. We say a *receipt* or *recipe* for making a cake, a *receipt* for money paid.

reception-room (rē-sep'shon-röm), *n.* A room for the reception of visitors.

receptive (rē-sep'tiv), *a.* [< OF. *receptif* = Sp. Pg. *receptivo* = It. *ricettivo*, *recettivo* = G. *receptiv*, < NL. **receptivus*, < L. *recipere*, pp. *receptus*, receive: see *receive*.] Having the quality of or capacity for receiving, admitting, or taking in; able to hold or contain.

The soul being in this sort, as it is active, perfected by love of that infinite good, shall, as it is *receptive*, be also perfected with those supernatural passions of joy, peace, and delight. *Hooker*, Eccles. Polity, i. 11.

To acquire knowledge is to receive an object within the sphere of our consciousness. The acquisitive faculty may therefore, also, be called a *receptive* faculty.
Sir W. Hamilton, Metaph., xxi.

I am somehow *receptive* of the great soul. . . . More and more the surges of everlasting nature enter into me.
Emerson, Essays, 1st ser., p. 260.

The outer layer of rods and cones (bacillary) is undoubtedly the true *receptive* layer. *Le Conte*, Sight, p. 58.

Receptive power. See *power*[1].—**Receptive spot**, in *bot.*, the hyaline spot in an oösphere at which the male gamete enters. *Goebel.*

receptiveness (rē-sep'tiv-nes), *n.* Power or readiness to receive; receptivity.

Many of her opinions . . . seemed too decided under every alteration to have been arrived at otherwise than by a wifely *receptiveness*. *George Eliot*, Daniel Deronda, iii.

receptivity (rē-sep-tiv'i-ti), *n.* [= F. *réceptivité* = G. *receptivität*, < NL. **receptivita(t-)s*, < **receptivus*, receptive: see *receptive*.] The state or property of being receptive; ability to receive or take in; specifically, a natural passive power of the mind.

We call sensibility the *receptivity* of the soul, or its power of receiving representations whenever it is in any wise affected. *Kant*, Critique of Pure Reason, tr. by Müller, p. 51.

Objectivity, with subjectivity, causativity, plasticity, *receptivity*, and several other kindred terms, have come into vogue, during the two last generations, through the influence of German philosophy and æsthetics.
F. Hall, Mod. Eng., p. 308.

In our social system, so marked by the dovetailing of classes, the quality of *receptivity* for these influences . . . is raised to its maximum. *Gladstone*, Gleanings, I. 46.

receptory† (rē-sep'tō-ri), *n.* [< LL. *receptorius*, fit for receiving (neut. *receptorium*, a place of shelter), < L. *recipere*, pp. *receptus*, receive: see *receive*.] A receptacle. *Holland.*

receptrix (rē-sep'triks), *n.* [< LL. *receptrix*, fem. of *receptor*, a receiver, < L. *recipere*, pp. *receptus*, receive: see *receive*.] In *physics*, a dynamo-machine used to transform back into mechanical energy the electrical energy produced by a generatrix; an electric motor. See *generatrix*.

receptual (rẹ̄-sep'tụ̄-al), *a.* [< L. *receptus* (*receptu-*), a receiving (see *receipt*, *recept*), + *-al*.] Relating or pertaining to that which is received or taken in; consisting or of the character of a recept or recepts. [Recent.]

The difference between a mind capable of however limited a degree of conceptual ideation and one having only *receptual* ideation is usually agreed to be the possession of language by the first, and its absence in the other. *Science*, XV. 90.

receptually (rẹ̄-sep'tụ̄-al-i), *adv.* In a receptual manner; by receiving or taking in. [Recent.]

There is then the denotative stage, in which the child uses names *receptually* by more association. *Science*, XV. 90.

recercelé (rẹ̄-ser-se-lā'), *a.* [OF., also *recercellé*, pp. of *recerceler*, *recerceller*, curl up, curve, also hoop, encircle, < *re-*, back, + *cerceler*, hoop, encircle, < *cercel*, *cerceau*, hoop, ring, < L. *circellus*, dim. of *circus*, a ring: see *circus*.] In *her.*: (*a*) Curved at the ends more decidedly than in other forms, such as moline: noting a cross each end of which is divided into two points rolled backward into a spiral. (*b*) Same as *moline*.

recercelled (rẹ̄-sėr'seld), *a.* In *her.*, same as *recercelé*.

recess (rẹ̄-ses'), *n.* [< OF. *reces*, *recez*, a departure, retreat, recess (as of a school), setting (of a star), repose, = Sp. *receso* = Pg. It. *recesso*, recess, retreat, < L. *recessus*, a going back, retreat, departure, also a retired place, corner, retreat, etc., < *recedere*, pp. *recessus*, recede, retreat, etc.: see *recede*[1].] **1.** The act of receding, or going back or away; withdrawal; retirement; recession. [Obsolete or archaic.]

Men . . . have made too untimely a departure and too remote a *recess* from particulars. *Bacon*, Advancement of Learning, ii. 164.

Every day of sin, and every criminal act, is a degree of *recess* from the possibilities of heaven. *Jer. Taylor*, Works (ed. 1835), I. 182.

Pliny hath an odd and remarkable passage concerning the death of men and animals upon the *recess* or ebb of the sea. *Sir T. Browne*, To a Friend.

The access of frost in the autumn, and its *recess* in the spring, do not seem to depend merely on the degree of cold. *Jefferson*, Notes on Virginia (1787), p. 182.

2†. A state of being withdrawn or retired; seclusion; privacy.

In these are faire parks or gardens call'd villas, being onely places of *recess* and pleasure, at some distance from the streetes, yet within the walls. *Evelyn*, Diary, May 6, 1645.

Good verse *recess* and solitude requires. *Dryden.*

3. A time of withdrawal or retirement; an interval of release from occupation; specifically, a period of relief from attendance, as of a school, a jury, a legislative body, or other assembly; a temporary dismissal.

Before the Revolution the sessions of Parliament were short and the *recesses* long. *Macaulay*, Sir William Temple.

It was *recess* as I passed by, and forty or fifty boys were creating such a hubbub in the school-yard. *The Century*, XXVIII. 12.

4. A place of retirement or seclusion; a remote or secret spot or situation; a nook; hence, a hidden or abstruse part of anything: as, the *recesses* of a forest; the *recesses* of philosophy.

Departure from this happy place, our sweet *Recess*. *Milton*, P. L., xi. 304.

I went to Dorking to see Mr. Charles Howard's amphitheatre, garden, or solitary *recess*, environed by a hill. *Evelyn*, Diary, Aug. 1, 1655.

Every man who pretends to be a scholar or a gentleman should . . . acquaint himself with a superficial scheme of all the sciences, . . . yet there is no necessity for every man of learning to enter into their difficulties and deep *recesses*. *Watts*, Improvement of Mind, I. xx. § 10.

The pair
Frequent the still *recesses* of the realm
Of Hela, and hold converse undisturb'd.
M. Arnold, Balder Dead.

5. A receding space or inward indentation or depression in a line of continuity; a niche, alcove, or the like: as, a *recess* in a room for a window or a bed; a *recess* in a wall or the side of a hill. See cut under *ambry*.

A bed which stood in a deep *recess*. *Irving.* (*Webster.*)

Inside the great portal at Koyunjik was a hall, 180 ft. in length by 42 in width, with a *recess* at each end, through which access was obtained to two courtyards, one on the right and one on the left. *J. Fergusson*, Hist. Arch., I. 178.

6. A treaty, law, decree, or contract embodying the results of a negotiation; especially, a decree or law promulgated by the Diet of the old German empire, or by that of the Hanseatic League.—**7.** In *bot.*, a sinus of a lobed leaf.—**8.** In *anat.* and *zoöl.*, a receding or hollowed-out part; a depression or sinus; a recessus.—**Contrariety of access and recess.** Same as *contrariety of motion* (which see, under *contrariety*).—**Lateral recess.** See *recessus lateralis ventriculi quarti*, under *recessus*.—**Peritoneal recesses.** Same as *peritoneal fossæ* (which see, under *peritoneal*).=**Syn. 3.** *Prorogation*, *Dissolution*, etc. (see *adjournment*), intermission, respite.—**4.** Retreat, nook, corner.

recess (rẹ̄-ses'), *v.* [< *recess*, *n.*] **I.** *trans.* **1.** To make a recess in; form with a space sunk beyond the general surface: as, to *recess* a wall.

Cutters for boring bars should be, if intended to be of standard size, *recessed* to fit the bar. *J. Rose*, Pract. Machinist, p. 218.

2. To place in a recess; form as a recess; make a recess of or for; hence, to conceal in or as if in a recess.

Behind the screen of his prodigious elbow you will be comfortably *recessed* from curious impertinents. *Miss Edgeworth*, Manœuvring, xiv.

The inscription is engraved on a *recessed* tablet, cut in the wall of the tunnel a few yards from its lower end. *Isaac Taylor*, The Alphabet, I. 233.

The head of Zeus on these interesting coins is of the leonine type, with deeply *recessed* eye. *B. V. Head*, Historia Numorum, p. 88.

Recessed arch. See *arch*[1].

II. *intrans.* To take a recess; adjourn or separate for a short time: as, the convention *recessed* till the afternoon. [Colloq.]

recession[1] (rẹ̄-sesh'ọn), *n.* [< F. *récession*, going back, withdrawing, < L. *recessio(n-)*, a going back, receding, < *recedere*, recede: see *recede*[1] and *recess*.] **1.** The act of receding or going back; withdrawal; retirement, as from a position reached or from a demand made.

Our wandering thoughts in prayer are but the neglects of meditation, and *recessions* from that duty. *Jer. Taylor*, Works (ed. 1835), I. 73.

2. The state of being put back; a position relatively withdrawn.

But the error is, of course, more fatal when much of the building is also concealed, as in the well-known case of the *recession* of the dome of St. Peter's. *Ruskin.*

recession[2] (rē-sesh'ọn), *n.* [< *re-* + *cession*.] A cession or granting back; retrocession: as, the *recession* of conquered territory to its former sovereign.

We believe a large sentiment in California would support a bill for the *recession* [of the Yosemite Park] to the United States. *The Century*, XXXIX. 475.

recessional (rẹ̄-sesh'ọn-ạl), *a.* and *n.* [< *recession*[1] + *-al*.] **I.** *a.* Pertaining to or connected with recession, or a receding movement, as that of the choir or congregation at the close of a service: as, a *recessional* hymn.

II. *n.* A hymn sung while the clergy and choir are leaving a church at the end of a service of public worship.

recessive (rẹ̄-ses'iv), *a.* [< *recess* + *-ive*.] Tending to recede; receding; going back: used especially of accent regarded as transferred or moved backward from the end toward the beginning of a word. In Greek grammar the accent is said to be *recessive* when it stands as far back from the end of the word as the laws of Greek accentuation permit—that is, on the antepenult if the ultimate is short, or on the penult if the ultimate is long.

recessively (rẹ̄-ses'iv-li), *adv.* In a recessive or retrograde manner; with a backward movement or course.

As she [Greece] passes *recessively* from the grand Attic period to the Spartan, the Theban, the Macedonian, and the Asiatic. *Edinburgh Rev.*, CLXIV. 494.

recessus (rẹ̄-ses'us), *n.*; pl. *recessus*. [L.: see *recess*.] In *anat.* and *zoöl.*, a recess.—**Recessus chiasmatis.** Same as *recessus opticus*.—**Recessus infrapinealis**, a small cleft extending from the third ventricle into the conarium. Also called *ventriculus conarii*.—**Recessus infundibuli**, the funnel-shaped cavity at the bottom of the third ventricle; the cavity of the infundibulum.—**Recessus labyrinthi.** Same as *ductus endolymphaticus* (which see, under *ductus*).—**Recessus lateralis ventriculi quarti**, the lateral recess of the fourth ventricle, containing the lateral choroid plexus.—**Recessus opticus**, a V-shaped recess of the floor of the third ventricle, in front of the infundibulum, bounded anteriorly by the lamina terminalis, posteriorly by the optic chiasm. Also called *recessus chiasmatis*. *Mihalcovics*.—**Recessus præpontilis**, a name given by Wilder in 1881 to the median pit formed by the overhanging of the front border of the pons Varolii.

Rechabite (rek'ạ-bīt), *n.* [= F. *Réchabite*; < *Rechab*, father of Jonadab, who founded the sect, + *-ite*[2].] **1.** A member of a Jewish family and sect descended from Rechab, which, in obedience to the command of Jonadab, refused to drink wine, build or live in houses, sow seed, or plant or own vineyards. Jer. xxxv. 6, 7. Hence—**2.** A total abstainer from strong drink.

A *Rechabite* poor Will must live,
And drink of Adam's Ale.
Prior, Wandering Pilgrim.

3. A member of a society composed of total abstainers from intoxicating drinks, called the Independent Order of Rechabites.

Rechabitism (rek'ạ-bi-tizm), *n.* [< *Rechabite* + *-ism*.] **1.** The practice of the ancient Rechabites in respect to abstinence from strong drink.

The praises of *Rechabitism* afford just as good an opportunity for the exhibition of sportive fancy and a lively humor as lyrical panegyrics on the most exquisite vintage of France or the Rhine. *R. J. Hinton*, Eng. Radical Leaders, p. 220.

2. The principles and practice of the Independent Order of Rechabites.

The advantages which *Rechabitism* offered above other friendly societies. *Rechabite Mag.*, July, 1886, p. 175. (*Encyc. Dict.*)

rechant† (rẹ̄-chànt'), *v. t.* and *i.* [< *re-* + *chant*. Cf. *recant*.] To chant in alternation; sing antiphonally.

Hark, hark the cheerfull and *re-chaunting* cries
Of old and young singing this ioyfull Dittie.
Sylvester, tr. of Du Bartas's Weeks, ii., The Handy-Crafts.

rechase (rẹ̄-chās'), *v. t.* [< ME. *rechasen*, < OF. (and F.) *rechasser*, drive back, < *re-*, back, + *chasser*, drive: see *chase*[1].] **1.** To chase or drive back or away, as to a forest or covert; turn back by driving or chasing: as, to *rechase* sheep by driving them from one pasture to another. *Halliwell.* [Obsolete or prov. Eng.]

Withynne a while the herte y-founde ys,
I-hallowed, and *rechased* faste
Longe time. *Chaucer*, Death of Blanche, l. 379.

Then these assail; then those *re-chase* again;
Till stay'd with new-made hills of bodies slain.
Daniel, Civil Wars, iv. 47.

2. To call back (hounds) from a wrong scent.

rechase†, *n.* [< *rechase*, *v.*] A call (in hunting).

Seven score raches at his *rechase*.
Squyr of Lowe Degré, l. 772. (*Halliwell.*)

rechate†, *n.* and *v.* Same as *recheat*.

réchauffé (rā-shō-fā'), *n.* [F., pp. of *réchauffer*, dial. *récaufer*, *recofer*, warm up, warm over, < *re-*, again, + *échauffer*, warm, < L. *excalfacere*, warm: see *excalfaction*, and cf. *eschaufe*, *chafe*.] A warmed-up dish; hence, a new concoction of old materials; a literary rehash.

We suffer old plots willingly in novels, and endure without murmur *réchauffés* of the most ancient stock of fiction. *Saturday Rev.*

reche†, *v.* An old spelling of *reach*[1].

recheat† (rẹ̄-chēt'), *n.* [Early mod. E. also *rechate*, *recait*; < OF. *recet*, *receit*, etc., also *rechet*, *rechiet*, a retreat, refuge: see *receipt*.] In *hunting*, a melody which the huntsman winds on the horn to call back the dogs from a wrong course, or to call them off at the close of the hunt; a recall on the horn.

In hunting I had as leeve stand at the *receit* as at the loosing. *Lyly*, Euphues. (*Nares.*)

That I will have a *recheat* winded in my forehead, or hang my bugle in an invisible baldrick, all women shall pardon me. *Shak.*, Much Ado, i. 1. 242.

recheat† (rē-chēt'), *v. i.* [Early mod. E. also *rechate*; < ME. *rechaten*, < OF. *receter*, *recheter*, *rechaiter*, receive, give refuge, refl. take refuge, retreat, < *recet*, *rechet*, etc., recheat: see *recheat*, *n.*] In *hunting*, to play the recheat; call back the hounds by the tones of the recheat on the horn.

Huntes hyzed hem theder, with hornez ful mony
Ay *rechatande* aryzt til thay the renk sezen.
Sir Gawayne and the Green Knight (E. E. T. S.), l. 1911.

Rechating with his horn, which then the hunter chears,
Whilst still the lusty stag his high-palm'd head up-bears.
Drayton, Polyolbion, xiii. 127.

recherché (rē-sher'shā), *a.* [F., pp. of *rechercher*, seek again: see *research*.] Much sought after; hence, out of the common; rare; dainty.

We thought it a more savoury meat than any of the *recherché* culinary curiosities of the lamented Soyer. *Capt. M. Thomson*, Story of Cawnpore, v.

rechristen (rē-kris'n), *v. t.* [< *re-* + *christen*.] To christen or name again; fix a new name upon.

Abbeys which have since been . . . *rechristened* with still homelier names. *Trevelyan*, Early Hist. Chas. Jas. Fox, p. 47.

The faculties . . . are in part *rechristened*, and also rearranged. *Nature*, XXXIX. 244.

recidivate† (rẹ̄-sid'i-vāt), *v. i.* [< ML. *recidivatus*, pp. of *recidivare* (> F. *récidiver*), fall back, relapse, < L. *recidivus*, falling back, etc. (cf. *recidivatus*, a restoration): see *recidivous*.] To fall back, relapse, or backslide; return to an abandoned course of conduct.

To *recidivate*, and to go against her own act. *Bp. Andrewes*, Opuscula, Speech, p. 79 (1629). (*Latham.*)

recidivation† (rẹ̄-sid-i-vā'shọn), *n.* [< OF. *recidivation*, F. *récidivation*, < ML. *recidivatio(n-)*, falling back, < *recidivare*, fall back: see *recidivate*.] A falling back; relapse; return to an abandoned course; backsliding.

Recidivation is so much more dangerous than our first sickness, as our natural strength is then the more feebled, and unable to endure means of restoring.
Rev. T. Adams, Works, I. 447.

recidivist (rẹ-sid'i-vist), *n.* [< F. *récidiviste*, < *récidive*, a repetition of a fault or crime, < L. *recidivus*, falling back: see *recidivous*.] In *French law*, a relapsed criminal; one who falls back into the same criminal course for which he has already been condemned.

The French Cabinet offered a pledge that no *recidivists* should be sent to the islands.
Appleton's Ann. Cyc., 1886, p. 60.

recidivous† (rẹ-sid'i-vus), *a.* [= OF. *recidif* = It. *recidivo*, < L. *recidivus*, falling back, returning, recurring, < *recidere*, *reccidere*, fall back, < *re-*, back, + *cadere*, fall: see *cadent*.] Liable to backslide to a former state. *Imp. Dict.*

recipe (res'i-pē), *v. t.* [L., impv. of *recipere*, take: see *receive*.] Take: a Latin imperative used (commonly abbreviated R. or ℞) at the beginning of physicians' prescriptions, as formerly and in part still written in Latin.

recipe (res'i-pē), *n.* [= OF. *recipe*, F. *récipé* = Sp. *récipe* = Pg. It. *recipe*, a recipe, < L. *recipe*, take, used as the first word in a prescription, and hence taken as a name for it: see *recipe*, *v.*] 1. A formula for the compounding of a remedy, with directions for its use, written by a physician; a medical prescription.

He deals all
With spirits, he; he will not hear a word
Of Galen or his tedious *recipes*.
B. Jonson, Alchemist, ii. 1.

2. A prescribed formula in general, but especially one having some relation or resemblance to a medical prescription; a receipt.

There was a greatness of mind in Paracelsus, who, having furnished a *recipe* to make a fairy, had the delicacy to refrain from its formation.
I. D'Israeli, Curios. of Lit., IV. 186.

The one grand *recipe* remains for you — the be-all and the end-all of your strange existence upon earth. Move on!
Dickens, Bleak House, xix.

=**Syn.** *Receipt*, etc. See *reception*.

recipiangle (rẹ-sip'i-ang-gl), *n.* [< F. *récipiangle*, irreg. < L. *recipere*, receive, + *angulus*, angle: see *receive*, and *angle*³, *n.*] In *engin.*, an instrument formerly used for measuring angles, especially in fortification. *Buchanan.*

recipience (rẹ-sip'i-ẹns), *n.* [< *recipien(t)* + *-ce*.] A receiving; the act of or capacity for receiving; receptivity. [Rare.] *Imp. Dict.*

recipiency (rẹ-sip'i-ẹn-si), *n.* [As *recipience* (see *-cy*).] Same as *recipience*.

We struggle — fain to enlarge
Our bounded physical *recipiency*,
Increase our power, supply fresh oil to life.
Browning, Cleon.

recipient (rẹ-sip'i-ẹnt), *a.* and *n.* [= F. *récipient*, a receiver, water-clock, = Sp. Pg. It. *recipiente*, receiving, a receiver, < L. *recipien(t-)s*, ppr. of *recipere*, receive: see *receive*.] I. *a.* Receiving; receptive; acting or serving as a receiver; capable of receiving or taking in.

The step from painting on a ground of stanniferous enamel to a similar surface on a metallic *recipient* body is an easy and obvious one. *Cat. Soulages Coll.*, p. 99.

Recipient cavity, in *entom.*, a cavity in which an organ or part is received at the will of the insect; specifically, a cavity of the mesosternum which corresponds to a spine of the prosternum, the spine and cavity forming in the *Elateridæ* a springing-organ. See *spring*.

II. *n.* 1. A receiver or taker; especially, one who receives or accepts something given or communicated; a taker of that which is offered or bestowed: as, *recipients* of charity or of public education; the *recipients* of the eucharist.

Whatever is received is received according to the capacity of the *recipient*.
Cudworth, Intellectual System, p. 725.

Something should have been inserted to signify that, when the *recipient* is fitly qualified and duly disposed, there is a salutary life-giving virtue annexed to the sacrament. *Waterland*, Works, V. 428.

The first *recipients* of the Revelation.
J. H. Newman, Development of Christian Doctrine, ii. § 1.

2. That which receives; formerly, the receiver in an apparatus or instrument.

The form of sound words, dissolved by chymical preparation, ceases to be nutritive, and, after all the labours of the alembeck, leaves in the *recipient* a fretting corrosive. *Decay of Christian Piety.*

recipiomotor (rẹ-sip'i-ọ-mō'tọr), *a.* [Irreg. < L. *recipere*, receive, + *motor*, mover.] Receiving a motor impulse or stimulus; afferent, as a nerve, in an ordinary sense: correlated with *liberomotor* and *dirigomotor*. See *motor*.

Each afferent nerve is a *recipio-motor* agent.
H. *Spencer*, Prin. of Psychol., § 18.

reciprocal (rẹ-sip'rọ-kạl), *a.* and *n.* [< NL. as if **reciprocalis*, < L. *reciprocus*, returning, alternating, reciprocal (> It. Pg. *reciproco* = Sp. *recíproco* = OF. *reciproque*, > obs. E. *reciprock*); perhaps lit. 'moving backward and forward,' < **recus* (< *re-*, back, + adj. formative *-cus*: see *-ic*) + *procus* (< *pro*, forward, + adj. formative *-cus*). Cf. *reciprocous*, *reciprock*.] I. *a.* 1. Moving backward and forward; alternating; reciprocating.

The stream of Jordan, south of their going over, was not supplied with any *reciprocal* or refluous tide out of the Dead Sea.
Fuller, Pisgah Sight, II. i. 17. (*Davies*, under *refluous*.)

Obedient to the moon, he spent his date
In course *reciprocal*, and had his fate
Link'd to the mutual flowing of the seas.
Milton, Second Epitaph on Hobson the Carrier.

2. Mutually exchanged or exchangeable; concerning or given or owed by each (of two or more) with regard to the other or others: as, *reciprocal* aid; *reciprocal* rights, duties, or obligations; *reciprocal* love or admiration.

Let our *reciprocal* vows be remembered.
Shak., Lear, iv. 6. 267.

The Liturgy or service . . . consisteth of the *reciprocal* acts between God and man.
Bacon, Advancement of Learning, ii. 378.

I take your gentle offer, and withal
Yield love again for love *reciprocal*.
Beau. and Fl., Knight of Burning Pestle, i. 2.

The king assured me of a *reciprocal* affection to the king my master, and of my particular welcome to his court.
Lord Herbert of Cherbury, Life (ed. Howells), p. 129.

The liberty of the enemy's fishermen in war has been protected by many French ordinances, and the English observed a *reciprocal* indulgence.
Woolsey, Introd. to Inter. Law, § 170.

There is much the same relation of *reciprocal* dependence between judgment and reasoning as between conception and judgment.
J. Sully, Outlines of Psychol., p. 414.

3. Having an interchangeable character or relation; mutually equivalent or correspondent; concordant; agreeing.

Knowledge and power are *reciprocal*.
Bacon, Physical Fables, x., Expl., note.

Sometimes a universal affirming may be converted saving the quantity, to wit when consisting of *reciprocal* terms: as, every man is a rational animal, and therefore every rational animal is a man.
Burgersdicius, tr. by a Gentleman, i. 32.

He [the king] must guide the vast and complicated machine of government, to the *reciprocal* advantage of all his dominions. *A. Hamilton*, Works, II. 56.

Thence came her friends of either sex, and all
With whom she lived on terms *reciprocal*.
Crabbe, Works, V. 51.

Reciprocal consecution. See *consecution*.—**Reciprocal cross**, a reciprocal hybrid.

A *reciprocal cross* is a double cross between two species or varieties, one form being used in one case as the father and in the other case as the mother.
W. K. Brooks, Law of Heredity, p. 126.

Reciprocal determinant, diagrams, equation. See *determinant*, *diagram*, etc.—**Reciprocal ellipsoid of expansion.** See *ellipsoid*.—**Reciprocal figures** in *geom.*, two figures of the same kind (triangles, parallelograms, prisms, pyramids, etc.) so related that two sides of the one form the extremes of an analogy of which the means are the two corresponding sides of the other.—**Reciprocal functions, hybrids, matrix.** See *function*, etc. —**Reciprocal polars**, two curves such that the polar of any point on either (with respect to a fixed conic) is a tangent of the other.—**Reciprocal pronoun**, a pronoun expressing mutual or reciprocal relation, such as Greek ἀλλήλοιν (of each other, of one another).—**Reciprocal proportion.** See *proportion*.—**Reciprocal quantities**, in *math.*, those quantities which, multiplied together, produce unity.—**Reciprocal ratio.** See *ratio*.—**Reciprocal screws**, a pair of screws so related that a wrench about one produces no twist about the other. Given any five screws, a screw reciprocal to them all can be found.—**Reciprocal terms**, in *logic*, those terms that have the same signification, and consequently are convertible and may be used for each other. = **Syn.** *Reciprocal*, *Mutual*. There is a theoretical difference between these words, although it often is not important. That is *mutual* which is a common act on the part of both persons at the same time. *Mutual* is not properly applicable to physical acts or material things, as blows or gifts. *Reciprocal* means that one follows another, being caused by it, with emphasis upon that which is viewed as caused: as, *reciprocal* love or hate. See remarks under *mutual* as to the propriety of using *mutual* for *common*.

II. *n.* 1. That which is reciprocal to another thing.

No more
Ye must be made your own *reciprocals*
To your loved city and fair severals
Of wives and houses.
Chapman, tr. of Homer's Hymn to Apollo.

Love is ever rewarded either with the *reciprocal*, or with an inward or secret contempt. *Bacon*, Love (ed. 1887).

2. In *math.*, the quotient resulting from the division of unity by the quantity of which the quotient is said to be the reciprocal. Thus, the reciprocal of 4 is ¼, and conversely the reciprocal of ¼ is 4; the reciprocal of 2 is ½, and that of $a + x$ is $1/(a + x)$. A fraction made by inverting the terms of another fraction is called the reciprocal of that other fraction: thus, 4/3 is the reciprocal of ¾.—**Polar reciprocals.** Same as *reciprocal polars*. See I.

reciprocality (rẹ-sip-rọ-kal'i-ti), *n.* [< *reciprocal* + *-ity*.] The state or character of being reciprocal.

An acknowledged *reciprocality* in love sanctifies every little freedom. *Richardson*, Clarissa Harlowe, II. l.

reciprocally (rẹ-sip'rọ-kạl-i), *adv.* 1. In a reciprocal manner; with reciprocating action or effect; alternatingly; interchangeably; correspondingly.

The Aristotelians . . . believe water and air to be *reciprocally* transmutable. *Boyle*, Works, II. 342.

Virtue and sentiment *reciprocally* assist each other.
Goldsmith, Cultivation of Taste.

Faults in the life breed errors in the brain,
And these *reciprocally* those again.
Cowper, Progress of Error, l. 505.

2. In a reciprocal ratio or proportion; inversely. Thus, in bodies of the same weight the density is reciprocally as the magnitude — that is, the greater the magnitude the less in the same proportion the density, and the less the magnitude the greater in the same proportion the density. In geometry two magnitudes are said to be reciprocally proportional to two others when one of the first pair is to one of the second as the remaining one of the second is to the remaining one of the first.

reciprocalness (rẹ-sip'rọ-kạl-nes), *n.* The state or character of being reciprocal.

reciprocant (rẹ-sip'rọ-kạnt), *n.* [< L. *reciprocan(t-)s*, ppr. of *reciprocare*, move back and forth: see *reciprocate*.] 1. The contravariant expressing the condition of tangency between the primitive quantic and an adjoint linear form.—2. A differential invariant; a function of partial differential coefficients of *n* variables connected by a single relation, this function being such that, if the variables are interchanged in cyclical order, it remains unchanged except for multiplication by some *n*th root of unity into some power of the same root of the continued product of the first differential coefficients of one of the variables relatively to all the others. For an example, see *Schwartzian*, *n.*—**Absolute reciprocant**, one whose extrinsic factor reduces to unity, so that the interchange of variables produces no change except multiplication by a root of unity.—**Binary reciprocant**, one having two variables.—**Characteristic of a reciprocant**, the root of unity with which it becomes multiplied on interchange of the variables.—**Character of a reciprocant**, its kind with respect to its characteristic.—**Circular reciprocant**, a reciprocant which, equated to zero, gives the equation of a locus which is its own inverse with respect to every point.—**Degree of a reciprocant**, the number of factors (differential coefficients) in that term which has the greatest number. Thus, if that term is $(D_xy)^a(D_x^2y)^b(D_x^2y)^c$, the degree is $a + b + c$. —**Even reciprocant**, one whose characteristic is 1.—**Extent of a reciprocant**, the weight of the most advanced letter which it contains.—**Homogeneous reciprocant**, a reciprocant all the terms of which are of the same degree in the differential coefficients.—**Homographic binary reciprocant**, one which remains unaltered when x and y are changed respectively into $(Lx + M)/(x + N)$ and $(Py + Q)/(y + R)$, where the capitals are constants.—**Integrable reciprocant**, a reciprocant which, equated to zero, gives an equation which can be integrated. —**Isobaric reciprocant**, a reciprocant having the sum of the orders of the differential coefficients the same in all the terms.—**Odd reciprocant**, one whose characteristic is not 1.—**Orthogonal reciprocant**, one which remains unchanged by an orthogonal transformation of the variables.—**Type of a reciprocant**, the combination of its character, weight, degree, and extent.—**Weight of a reciprocant**, the sum of the orders, each diminished by two, of the factors (differential coefficients) of the term having the greatest weight. Thus, if that term is $(D_xy)^a(D_x^2y)^b(D_x^3y)^c(D_x^4y)^d$, the weight is $-a + c + 2d$.

reciprocantive (rẹ-sip'rọ-kạn-tiv), *a.* [< *reciprocant* + *-ive*.] Pertaining to a reciprocant.

reciprocate (rẹ-sip'rọ-kāt), *v.*; pret. and pp. *reciprocated*, ppr. *reciprocating*. [< L. *reciprocatus*, pp. of *reciprocare*, move back and forth, reverse (> It. *reciprocare* = Sp. Pg. *reciprocar* = F. *réciproquer*, reciprocate, interchange), < *reciprocus*, reciprocal: see *reciprocal*.] I. *trans.* 1. To cause to move back and forth; give an alternating motion to.

The sleeve is *reciprocated* from a rock shaft journaled in the lower aligning ends of the main frame.
Sci. Amer., N. S., LXII. 75.

2. To give and return mutually; yield or perform each to each; interchange: as, to *reciprocate* favors.

For 'tis a union that bespeaks
Reciprocated duties.
Cowper, Friendship, l. 48.

At night men crowd the close little caffè, where they *reciprocate* smoke, respiration, and animal heat.
Howells, Venetian Life, iii.

3. To give or do in response; yield a return of; requite correspondingly.

It must happen, no doubt, that frank and generous women will excite love they do not *reciprocate*.
Margaret Fuller, Woman in 19th Cent., p. 140.

II. *intrans.* 1. To move backward and forward; have an alternating movement; act interchangeably; alternate.

One brawny smith the puffing bellows plies,
And draws and blows *reciprocating* air.
Dryden, tr. of Virgil's Georgics, iv. 249.

2. To act in return or response; do something equivalent or accordant: as, I did him many favors, but he did not *reciprocate*. [Colloq.]—**Reciprocating engine**, a form of engine in which the piston and piston-rod move back and forth in a straight line, absolutely or relatively to the cylinder, as in oscillating-cylinder engines: in contradistinction to *rotatory engine*. See *rotatory*.—**Reciprocating force.** See *force*1.—**Reciprocating motion**, in *mach.*, a contrivance frequently employed in the transmission of power from one part of a machine to another. A rigid bar is suspended upon a center or axis, and the parts situated on each side of the axis take alternately the positions of those on the other. See cut under *pitman*.—**Reciprocating propeller**, a propeller having a paddle which has a limited stroke and returns in the same path.—**Reciprocating proposition.** See *proposition*.

reciprocation (rẹ̄-sip-rọ̄-kā'shọn), *n.* [< F. *réciprocation* = Sp. *reciprocacion* = Pg. *reciprocação* = It. *reciprocazione*, < L. *reciprocatio(n-)*, a going back upon itself, a returning by the same way, a retrogression, alternation, reflux, ebb, < *reciprocare*, pp. *reciprocatus*, move back and forth: see *reciprocate*.] 1. A going back and forth; alternation of movement.

When the bent spring is freed, when the raised weight falls, a converse series of motions must be effected, and this . . . would lead to a mere *reciprocation* [of force].
W. R. Grove, Corr. of Forces, p. 24.

2. The act of reciprocating; interchange of acts; a mutual giving and returning: as, the *reciprocation* of kindnesses.

We do therefore lie, in respect of each other, under a *reciprocation* of benefits.
Scott, Heart of Mid-Lothian, Prol.

3. In *logic*, the relation of two propositions each the converse of the other.—**Polar reciprocation**, in *geom.*, the process of forming the polar reciprocal of a figure.

reciprocative (rẹ̄-sip'rọ̄-kā̤-tiv), *a.* [< *reciprocate* + *-ive*.] Of a reciprocating character; giving and taking reciprocally.

Our four-handed cousins apparently credit their biped kinsmen with *reciprocative* tendencies.
Pop. Sci. Mo., XXXIV. 111.

reciprocatory (rẹ̄-sip'rọ̄-kā̤-tọ̄-ri), *a.* [< *reciprocate* + *-ory*.] Going backward and forward; alternating in direction or in action; reciprocating: opposed to *rotatory*.

Impart a *reciprocatory* motion to the carriage.
C. T. Davis, Leather, p. 457.

A rotatory movement could be combined with the *reciprocatory* one. *Dredge's Electric Illumination*, I. 388.

reciprocity (res-i-pros'ị-ti), *n.* [< F. *réciprocité* = Sp. *reciprocidad* = Pg. *reciprocidade* = It. *reciprocità*, < ML. **reciprocita(t-)s*, < L. *reciprocus*, reciprocal: see *reciprocal*.] 1. Reciprocal action or relation; free interchange; mutual responsiveness in act or effect: as, *reciprocity* of benefits or of feeling; *reciprocity* of influence.

By the Convention of 1815 a *reciprocity* of intercourse was established between us and Great Britain.
D. Webster, Speech, Jan. 24, 1832.

2. Equality of commercial privileges between the subjects of different governments in each other's ports, with respect to shipping or merchandise, to the extent established by treaty.

On the Continent, after the fourteenth century, a system of *reciprocity* was frequently established between the several towns, as for instance in 1865 at Tournay.
English Gilds (E. E. T. S.), p. cxxix.

The *reciprocity* stipulations in our previous treaties were thought to operate disadvantageously to American navigation in the case of the Hanse towns, especially in regard to tobacco. *E. Schuyler*, Amer. Diplomacy, p. 432.

Another illustration may be found in the history of *reciprocity* with Canada.
G. F. Edmunds, Harper's Mag., LXXVI. 428.

3. In the *Kantian philos.*, mutual action and reaction in the strict mechanical sense.

Reciprocity, which, as a pure conception, is but the relation of parts or species in a generic whole, becomes . . . invariable coexistence, or coexistence according to a universal rule. *E. Caird*, Philos. of Kant, p. 412.

Glance once again at *reciprocity* and causality. The one is a necessary to and fro; the other only a necessary fro.
J. H. Stirling, Mind, X. 65.

4. In *geom.*, the mutual relationship between points and straight lines in a plane, or points and planes in space, etc.; duality.—**Hermite's law of reciprocity** [named from the French mathematician Charles *Hermite*, born 1822], the proposition that the number of invariants of the *n*th order in the coefficients possessed by a binary quantic of the *p*th degree is equal to the number of invariants of the order *p* in the coefficients possessed by a quantic of the *n*th degree.—**Law of reciprocity of prime numbers.** See *law*1.—**Plane birational reciprocity**, a one to one correspondence between the elements of a field of points and those of a field of rays.—**Quadratic reciprocity.** See *quadratic*.—**Reciprocity treaty**, a treaty granting equal privileges of commercial intercourse in certain specified particulars to the people of the countries concerned. The reciprocity treaty between Great Britain and the United States, existing from 1854 to 1866, provided for freedom of trade in certain commodities, chiefly raw or half-manufactured products, between the latter country and the Canadian provinces. It was abrogated on previous notice given under its terms by the United States. The United States government formed a similar treaty with that of Hawaii in 1876. =**Syn.** 1. Exchange, interchange, reciprocation.

reciprock†, *a.* [Also *reciproque*; < OF. *reciproque*, F. *réciproque* = Pr. *reciproc* = Sp. *reciproco* = Pg. It. *reciproco*, < L. *reciprocus*, reciprocal: see *reciprocous* and *reciprocal*.] Reciprocal.

'Twixt whom and them there is this *reciprock* commerce.
B. Jonson, Cynthia's Revels, v. 2.

reciprocornous (rẹ̄-sip-rọ̄-kôr'nus), *a.* [< L. *reciprocicornis*, having horns curved backward, < *reciprocus*, turning back the same way (see *reciprocal*), + *cornu*, a horn: see *corn*2 and *horn*.] Having horns turned backward and then forward, as a ram. This form is characteristic of the sheep tribe, though not peculiar to it. See *arietiform*, and cuts under *bighorn*, *argali*, *aoudad*, and *Ovis*.

reciprocous† (rẹ̄-sip'rọ̄-kus), *a.* [< L. *reciprocus*, turning back the same way: see *reciprocal*.] Reciprocal.

For the removing of which imparity, the cardinal acquainted Taylor "That he had devised to make the band *reciprocous* and egal."
Strype, Memorials, Hen. VIII., I. i. 5.

reciproque†, *a.* See *reciprock*.

recision (rẹ̄-sizh'ọn), *n.* [< OF. *recision*, F. *récision* = Sp. *recision* = Pg. *recisão* = It. *recisione*, < L. *recisio(n-)*, a cutting off, retrenchment, diminution, < *recidere*, pp. *recisus*, cut off, < *re-*, back, again, + *cædere*, cut.] 1. The act of cutting off. *Cotgrave*.—2. Specifically, in *surg.*, same as *resection*.

recital (rẹ̄-sī'tal), *n.* [< *recite* + *-al*.] 1. The reciting or repeating of something previously prepared; especially, an elocutionary recitation; the rhetorical delivery before an audience of a composition committed to memory: as, the *recital* of a poem; a dramatic *recital*.—2. A telling over; a narration; a relation of particulars about anything, either orally or in writing: as, the *recital* of evidence.

Some men . . . give us in *recitals* of disease
A doctor's trouble, but without the fees.
Cowper, Conversation, l. 313.

He poured out a *recital* of the whole misadventure.
Howells, Undiscovered Country, p. 154.

3. That which is recited; a story; a narrative: as, a harrowing *recital*.—4. In *law*: (*a*) That part of a deed which rehearses the circumstances inducing or leading to its execution. (*b*) Any incidental statement of fact in a deed or contract: as, a *recital* is evidence of the fact recited, as against the party making it. —5. A musical performance or concert, vocal or instrumental, especially one given by a single performer, or a concert consisting of selections from the works of some one composer: as, a Wagner *recital*; a piano *recital*.=**Syn.** 2 and 3. *Relation*, *Narrative*, etc. (see *account*), repetition, speech, discourse.

recitation (res-i-tā'shọn), *n.* [< OF. *recitation*, F. *récitation* = Sp. *recitacion* = Pg. *recitação* = It. *recitazione*, < L. *recitatio(n-)*, a reading aloud of judicial decrees or literary works, < *recitare*, pp. *recitatus*, read aloud, recite: see *recite*.] 1. The act of reciting or repeating what has been committed to memory; the oral delivery of a composition without the text, especially as a public exercise or performance. —2. The rehearsal by a pupil or student of a lesson or exercise to a teacher or other person; a meeting of a class for the purpose of being orally examined in a lesson.—3. In *music*: (*a*) Same as *recitative*. (*b*) Same as *reciting-note*. —**Mystic recitation.** See *mystic*.

recitationist (res-i-tā'shọn-ist), *n.* [< *recitation* + *-ist*.] One who practises recitation; a public reciter of his own or others' compositions.

The youth who has heard this last of the *recitationists* deliver one of his poems will recall in future years the fire and spirit of a veteran whose heart was in his work.
Stedman, Poets of America, viii. § 3.

recitation-room (res-i-tā'shọn-röm), *n.* A room for college or school recitations.

recitative (res″i-ta-tēv'), *a.* and *n.* [< F. *récitatif*, n., < It. *recitativo*, n., a recitative in music; as *recite* + *-ative*.] I. *a.* In *music*, in the style of a recitative; as if spoken.

II. *n.* In *music*: (*a*) A form or style of song resembling declamation—that is, in which regularity of rhythmic, melodic, and harmonic structure is reduced to the minimum. It is a union of song and speech, with the emphasis sometimes on one element and sometimes on the other, but with a careful avoidance of technical "form" in the musical sense. The division into phrases is properly governed by rhetorical reasons only. The strictly tonal and metrical qualities of a balanced melody are usually but meagerly represented. The sequence of harmonies and of tonalities is often entirely unrestricted. An unaccompanied recitative (*recitativo secco*) has only a few detached instrumental chords, or a *basso continuo*, to suggest or sketch the harmonic basis of the melody. Accompaniments of this sort have been given at different periods to different instruments, such as the harpsichord, the Violoncello, or the string orchestra alone. An accompanied recitative (*recitativo stromentato*) has a continuous instrumental background, which occasionally becomes highly descriptive or dramatic, and may be assigned to a full orchestra. This Variety of recitative passes over insensibly into the *arioso* and the *aria parlante*. The recitative was invented, in the latter part of the sixteenth century, in the course of an attempt by certain Florentine musicians to recover the dramatic declamation of the ancient Greeks. Its recognition as a legitimate style of composition opened the way for the development of the dramatic forms of the opera and the oratorio, in both of which it has always retained a prominent place. Its value in such extended forms is due to its adaptability to descriptive, explanatory, and epic matter generally, as well as to strictly dramatic utterance of every kind. It has been customary to introduce lyric arias by recitatives; but in the operatic works of the present century the formal distinction between recitative and aria has been more or less abandoned as arbitrary. The *melos* of Wagner is an intermediate form, capable of extension in either direction. Also *recitation*.

What they call *Recitative* in Musick is only a more tuneable Speaking; it is a kind of Prose in Musick.
Congreve, Semele, Arg.

Ballads, in the seventeenth century, had become the delight of the whole Spanish people. . . . The blind beggar gathered alms by chanting them, and the puppet-showman gave them in *recitative* to explain his exhibition.
Ticknor, Span. Lit., III. 77.

(*b*) A section, passage, or movement in the style described above.

recitatively (res″i-ta-tēv'li), *adv.* In the manner of recitative.

recitativo (rā-chē-tā-tē'vọ̄), *n.* [It., a recitativo in music: see *recitative*.] Recitative.

She tripp'd and laugh'd, too pretty much to stand; . . .
Then thus in quaint *recitativo* spoke.
Pope, Dunciad, iv. 52.

recite (rẹ̄-sīt'), *v.*; pret. and pp. *recited*, ppr. *reciting*. [< OF. *reciter*, F. *réciter* = Pr. Sp. Pg. *recitar* = It. *recitare*, < L. *recitare*, read aloud, recite, repeat from memory, < *re-*, again, + *citare*, cite: see *cite*1.] I. *trans.* 1. To repeat or say over, as something previously prepared or committed to memory; rehearse the words of; deliver orally: as, to *recite* the Litany; to *recite* a poem.

All the parties concerned were then called together; and the tedtsh, or prayer of peace, used in long and dangerous journies, was solemnly *recited* and assented to by them all.
Bruce, Source of the Nile, II. 504.

2. In *music*, to deliver in recitative.

The dialogue [in the first operas] was neither sung in measure, nor declaimed without Music, but *recited* in simple musical tones. *Burney*, Hist. Music, IV. 18.

3. To relate the facts or particulars of; give an account or statement of; tell: as, to *recite* one's adventures or one's wrongs.

Till that, as comes by course, I doe *recite*
What fortune to the Briton Prince did lite,
Pursuing that proud Knight.
Spenser, F. Q., VI. vi. 17.

Lest the world should task you to *recite*
What merit lived in me. *Shak.*, Sonnets, lxxii.

"I make," cries Charley, *reciting* the shield, "three merions on a field or, with an earl's coronet."
Thackeray, Virginians, xxxii.

4. To repeat or tell over in writing; set down the words or particulars of; rehearse; cite; quote.

Which booke (de Ratione Studii et de Liberis Educandis) is oft *recited*, and moch praysed, in the fragmentes of Nonius, even for authoritie sake.
Ascham, The Scholemaster, ii.

Lucianus, the merry Greeke, *reciteth* a great number of them [prophecies], devised by a coosening companion, one Alexander. *Puttenham*, Arte of Eng. Poesie, p. 218.

The thoughts of gods let Granville's verse *recite*.
Pope, Windsor Forest, l. 425.

To recite one's beads. See *to bid beads*, under *bead*. =**Syn.** 3. *Cite*, *Adduce*, etc. (see *quote*); *Rehearse*, *Reiterate*, etc. (see *recapitulate*); enumerate, detail.

II. *intrans.* To make a recitation or rehearsal; rehearse or say over what has been learned: as, to *recite* in public or in a class.

They *recite* without book.
E. W. Lane, Modern Egyptians, II. 126.

recite† (rẹ̄-sīt'), *n.* [< *recite*, *v.*] Recital.

All former *recites* or observations of long-liv'd races.
Sir W. Temple, Health.

reciter (rẹ-sī'tėr), *n.* [< OF. *reciteur, recitateur*, F. *récitateur* = It. *recitatore*, < L. *recitator*, a reciter, < *recitare*, recite: see *recite*.] One who recites or rehearses; a narrator or declaimer, especially of what has been previously written or told.

Narrative songs were committed to memory, and delivered down from one *reciter* to another.
Bp. Percy, On Anc. Metrical Romances, § 1. (*Latham*.)

reciting-note (rẹ-sī'ting-nōt), *n.* In *chanting*, a note or tone on which several or many syllables are recited in monotone. In Gregorian music this tone is regularly the dominant of the mode, but in Anglican chants it may be any tone. Usually every chant contains two, or a double chant four, reciting-notes.

reck (rek), *v.*; pret. and pp. *recked* (formerly *raught*). [Formerly also *reak*, sometimes misspelled *wreak*; < ME. *recken, rekken*, assibilated *recchen*, later forms, with shortened vowel, of *reken*, assibilated *rechen* (pret. *roughte, rouhte, rogte, roghte, rohte*), < AS. *rēcan, rēccan* (pret. *rōhte*), care, reck, = OS. *rōkian* = MLG. *rōken, rūken*, LG. *roken, ruken, rochen* = OHG. *ruohhjan, ruochan, ruochen*, MHG. *ruochen* (also, in comp., OHG. *geruochan*, MHG. *geruochen*, G. *geruhen*) = Icel. *rækja*, reck, regard, etc. (cf. Dan. *rögte*, care, tend, etc.); cf. AS. **rōc* (not recorded) = OHG. *ruoh, ruah*, MHG. *ruoch*, care, heed; perhaps akin to Gr. ἀλέγειν (for *ἀρέγειν), have care, heed, reck.] **I.** *intrans.* **1.** To take heed; have a care; mind; heed; care: usually in a negative clause, often followed by *of*.

And whether thei had good ansuere or euell, thei *raught* neuer. *Book of the Knight of La Tour Landry*, p. 2.

Sith that he myghte do her no companye,
He ne *roghte* not a myte for to dye.
Chaucer, Complaint of Mars, l. 126.

He *recketh* not, be so he wynne,
Of that another man shall lese.
Gower, Conf. Amant., ii.

I *reck* not though I end my life to-day.
Shak., T. and C., v. 6. 26.

Of God, or hell, or worse,
He *reck'd* not. *Milton*, P. L., ii. 50.

Light *recking of* his cause, but battling for their own.
Scott, Vision of Don Roderick, The Vision, st. 45.

2†. To think.

Forthe ther ys oon, y *reke*,
That can well Frensche speke.
MS. Cantab. Ff. ii. 38, f. 115. (*Halliwell*.)

II. *trans.* To take heed of; care for; regard; consider; be concerned about. [Obsolete or poetical.]

This son of mine, not *recking* danger, . . . came hither to do this kind office, to my unspeakable grief.
Sir P. Sidney.

An' may you better *reck* the rede
Than ever did th' adviser!
Burns, Epistle to a Young Friend.

It **recks** (impersonal), it concerns.

Of night, or loneliness, *it recks* me not.
Milton, Comus, l. 404.

reckent, *v.* An obsolete (the more correct) form of *reckon*.

reckless (rek'les), *a.* [Formerly also assibilated *rechless, retchless*, and misspelled *wreckless, wretchless*; < ME. *rekles, reckeles, rekkeles*, assibilated *recheles, reccheles, rechlesse*, < AS. *rēceleás, rēcceleás*, careless, reckless, thoughtless, heedless, etc., = D. *roekeloos*, reckless, rash, = MLG. *rokelôs, rocelos* = OHG. *ruahchalôs*, MHG. *ruochelos*, G. *ruchlos*, careless, untroubled, wicked, notorious; < **rōc* or **rēce* (not recorded) = OHG. *ruoh*, MHG. *ruoch*, care (see *reck, v.*), + *-leás* = E. *-less*.] **1†.** Not recking; careless; heedless; inattentive: in a mild sense.

A monk, whan he is *recchelees*,
Is likned to a fissch that is waterles—
This is to seyn, a monk out of his cloystre.
Chaucer, Gen. Prol. to C. T., l. 179.

First when thu spekist be not *rekles*,
Kepe feete and fingeris and handes still in pese.
Babees Book (E. E. T. S.), p. 26.

2. Not recking of consequences; desperately heedless, as from folly, passion, or perversity; impetuously or rashly adventurous.

I am one, my liege,
Whom the vile blows and buffets of the world
Have so incensed that I am *reckless* what
I do to spite the world. *Shak.*, Macbeth, iii. 1. 110.

Unhappily, James, instead of becoming a mediator, became the fiercest and most *reckless* of partisans.
Macaulay, Hist. Eng., vi.

=**Syn. 2.** *Enterprising, Rash*, etc. (see *adventurous*), incautious, unwary, unconcerned, indifferent, thoughtless. See list under *rash*[1].

recklessly (rek'les-li), *adv.* [< ME. *reklesly, rekkelesly*, < AS. **rēceleáslice, rēcceleáslice*, < *rēcceleás*, reckless: see *reckless* and *-ly*[2].] In a reckless manner; with rash or desperate heedlessness.

recklessness (rek'les-nes), *n.* [Formerly also assibilated *rechlessness, retchlessness*; < ME. *reklesnes, rechelesnesse, recchelesnes*, < AS. *rēceleásnes*, < *rēceleás*, reckless: see *reckless* and *-ness*.] The state or quality of being reckless or heedless; perverse or desperate rashness.

reckling (rek'ling), *n.* and *a.* [Also *ruckling*; prob. < Icel. *reklingr*, an outcast, < *reka*, drive, toss, drift, etc. (= *wreak*), + *-lingr* = E. *-ling*[1]. Cf. *wretchcock*, the smallest of a brood of fowls.] **I.** *n.* **1.** The smallest and weakest one in a litter, as of puppies, kittens, or pigs; the runt. Hence—**2.** A helpless babe.

There lay the *reckling*, one
But one hour old! What said the happy sire?
Tennyson, Merlin and Vivien.

II. *a.* Small; puny; stunted.

A mother dotes upon the *reckling* child
More than the strong.
Sir H. Taylor, Ph. van Artevelde, II., v. 3.

reckmaster† (rek'mås″tėr), *n.* [Irreg. < *reck(on)* + *master*.] A professional computer and accountant. [Rare.]

The common logist, *reckmaster*, or arithmetician.
Dr. John Dee, Preface to Euclid (1570).

reckon (rek'n), *v.* [Early mod. E. *recken*; < ME. *reckenen, rekenen, reknen*, count, account, reckon, esteem, etc., < AS. **recenian*, found only in the once-occurring comp. *ge-recenian*, explain, = OFries. *rekenia, reknia* = D. *rekenen* = MLG. LG. *rekenen* = OHG. *rehhanon*, MHG. *rechenen*, G. *rechnen* = Icel. *reikna* (for **rekna*?) = Sw. *räkna* = Dan. *regne*, reckon, = Goth. *rahnjan* (for **raknjan*?), reckon; a secondary verb, with formative *-n* (see *-en*[1]), parallel with another verb (the common one in AS.), AS. *reccan* (pret. *reahte, rehte*), narrate, tell, say, explain, expound, = OS. *rekkian*, narrate, explain, = OHG. *rachjan, recchen*, narrate, explain, reckon; these verbs being derived from a noun, AS. *racu*, f., an account or reckoning, an account or narrative, an exposition, explanation, history, comedy, = OHG. *rahha*, f., a subject, thing, = Icel. *rök*, neut. pl., a reason, ground, origin; prob. akin to Gr. λόγος, an account, saying, word, reason, λέγειν, say: see *Logos, logic, legend*, etc. The AS. verb *reccan*, narrate, is generally confused with *reccan*, direct, rule, also stretch: see *rack*[1], *retch*[1]. The former spelling *recken* is historically the proper one, the termination *-on*, as with *beckon*, being prop. *-en*: see *-en*[1].] **I.** *trans.* **1.** To count, or count up; compute; calculate; tell over by items or one by one: often with *up*.

No man vpon molde schuld now deuise
Men richlier a-raid to *rekene* alle thinges.
William of Palerne (E. E. T. S.), l. 1934.

I have not art to *reckon* my groans.
Shak., Hamlet, ii. 2. 121.

If we *reckon up* only those days which God hath accepted of our lives, a life of good years will hardly be a span long.
Sir T. Browne, To a Friend.

To *reckon* right it is required, (1.) That the mind distinguish carefully two ideas which are different one from another only by the addition or subtraction of one unit. (2.) That it retain in memory the names or marks of the several combinations from an unit to that number.
Locke, Human Understanding, II. xvi. 7.

2. To take into account; include in an account or category; set to one's account; impute; charge or credit.

Faith was *reckoned* to Abraham for righteousness.
Rom. iv. 9.

Also these Yles of Ynde, which beth evene azenst us, beth noght *reckned* in the Climates; for thei ben azenst us that ben in the lowe Contree.
Mandeville, Travels, p. 186.

Was any man's lust or intemperance ever *reckoned* among the Titles of his honour? *Stillingfleet*, Sermons, I. ii.

Among the costs of production have to be *reckoned* taxes, general and local. *H. Spencer*, Man vs. State, p. 23.

3†. To take account of; inquire into; consider.

Thane salle we *rekkene* fulle rathe whatt ryghte that he claymes. *Morte Arthure* (E. E. T. S.), l. 1275.

4. To hold in estimation as; regard; consider as being.

We ought not to *reken* and coumpt the thynge harde
That bryngeth ioye and pleasure afterwarde.
Babees Book (E. E. T. S.), p. 339.

For that they *reckened* this demeanoure attempted, not so specially againste the other Lordes, as agaynste the Kinge hymselfe. *Sir T. More*, Works, p. 43.

Though it be not expressly spoken against in Scripture, yet I *reckon* it plainly enough implied in the Scripture.
Latimer, Sermon bef. Edw. VI., 1550.

This is *reckoned* a very polite and fashionable amusement here. *Goldsmith*, Citizen of the World, lxxxvi.

A friend may well be *reckoned* the masterpiece of nature.
Emerson, Friendship.

=**Syn. 1.** To enumerate, cast, cast up.—**1** and **2.** *Compute, Count*, etc. (see *calculate*).

II. *intrans.* **1.** To make a computation; cast up an account; figure up.

And when he had begune to *recken*, won was browghte vnto hym whiche ought hym ten thousande talenttes.
Tyndale, Mat. xviii. 24.

2. To make an accounting; settle accounts; come to an adjustment or to terms: commonly followed by *with*.

"Parfay," seistow, "som tyme he *rekne* shal, . . .
For he noght helpeth needfulle in her nede."
Chaucer, Man of Law's Tale, l. 12.

The lorde of those servauntes cam, and *reckened with* them. *Tyndale*, Mat. xxv. 19.

Know that ye shall to-morrow be placed before God, and *reckoned with* according to your deeds.
E. W. Lane, Modern Egyptians, I. 104.

3†. To give an account of one's self; make an explanation.

Pandarus, withouten *rekenynge*,
Out wente anon to Eleyne and Deiphebus.
Chaucer, Troilus, ii. 1640.

4†. To take account of the points or details of a subject; reason; discriminate.

Nothing at all, to *rekin* rycht,
Different, in to Goddis sycht,
Than bene the purest Creature
That euir wes formit of nature.
Lauder, Dewtie of Kyngis (E. E. T. S.), l. 63.

5. To base a calculation or expectation; rely; count; depend: with *on* or *upon*.

My Lord Ambassador Aston *reckons upon* you, that you will be one of his Train at his first Audience in Madrid.
Howell, Letters, I. vi. 28.

Thus they [men] adore the goodly scheme by which they brought all these things to pass, and *reckon upon* it as sure and infallible for the future.
Bp. Atterbury, Sermons, I. vii.

In the whole corporation [of Newcastle-on-Tyne], the government could not *reckon on* more than four votes.
Macaulay, Hist. Eng., viii.

6. To hold a supposition or impression; have a notion; think; suppose; guess: as, I *reckon* a storm is coming. [The use of *reckon* in this sense, though regularly developed and found in good literature, like the corresponding sense of the transitive verb (definition 4), has by reason of its frequency in colloquial speech in some parts of the United States, especially in the South (where it occupies a place like that of *guess* in New England), come to be regarded as provincial or vulgar.]

I *reckoned* [*thought*, R. V., margin] till morning that as a lion so will he break all my bones. Isa. xxxviii. 13.

For I *reckon* that the sufferings of this present time are not worthy to be compared with the glory which shall be revealed in us. Rom. viii. 18.

What, you are a courtier, I *reckon*? No wonder you wish the press was demolished. *Foote*, The Bankrupt, iii.

There is one thing I must needs add, though I *reckon* it will appear to many as a very unreasonable paradox.
Swift, Nobles and Commons, v.

I *reckon* you will be selling out the whole—it's needless making twa bites of a cherry. *Scott*, St. Ronan's Well, x.

I *reckon* they will always be "the girls" to us, even if they're eighty. *Harper's Mag.*, LXXVIII. 444.

7. To expect; intend. [Obsolete or colloq.]

Another sweet invention,
The which in brief I *reckon* to name.
Undaunted Londonderry (Child's Ballads, VII. 249).

To reckon for, to give an account for; be answerable for.

If they fail in their bounden duty, they shall *reckon for* it one day. *Bp. Sanderson*.

To reckon without one's host. See *host*[2].

reckoner (rek'n-ėr), *n.* [< ME. *rekenere, rekenare* (= D. *rekenaar* = G. *rechner* = Sw. *beräknare* = Dan. *be-regner*); < *reckon* + *-er*[1].] **1.** One who reckons or computes: as, a rapid *reckoner*.

But retrospects with bad *reckoners* are troublesome things. *Warburton*, On Occasional Reflections.

In Ireland, where the *reckoner* would begin by saying "The two thumbs is one." *Harper's Mag.*, LXXVIII. 489.

2. Something that assists a person to reckon or cast up accounts, as a book containing a series of tables; a ready-reckoner.

reckoning (rek'n-ing), *n.* [Early mod. E. also *recking*; < ME. *rekeninge, rekninge, rekning, recning* (= D. *rekening*, a bill, account, reckoning, = MLG. *rekeninge* = OHG. *rechenunga*, MHG. *rechenunge*, G. *rechnung* = Sw. *räkning* = Dan. *regning*, a reckoning, a computation); verbal n. of *reckon, v.*] **1.** The act of counting or computing; hence, an account or calculation; an adjustment of accounts.

For it pleaseth a Mayster much to haue a true *reckoning*. *Babees Book* (E. E. T. S.), p. 66.

I am ill at *reckoning*. *Shak.*, L. L. L., i. 2. 42.

The way to make *reckonings* even is to make them often.
South.

2. A bill of charges, especially in a hotel, tavern, inn, or other place of entertainment; an itemized statement of what is due; a score.

> Cervicius pales for all, his purse
> Dolraies all *reckninge*.
> *Times' Whistle* (E. E. T. S.), p. 61.

We were treated in the most friendly manner by these good people, and had no reason to complain of our *reckoning* on leaving. *B. Taylor*, Northern Travel, p. 300.

> He paid the goodwife's *reckoning*
> In the coin of song and tale.
> *Whittier*, Cobbler Keezar's Vision.

> Till issuing arm'd he found the host, and cried,
> "Thy *reckoning*, friend?" *Tennyson*, Geraint.

3. An account of time.

> Truth is truth
> To the end of *reckoning*.
> *Shak.*, M. for M., v. 1. 46.

4. The estimated time of a cow's calving. [Now only Scotch.]

> Canst thou their *reck'nings* keep, the time compute?
> *Sandys*, Paraphrase upon Job, xxxix.

5. A summing up in general; a counting of cost or expenditure; a comparison of items or particulars in any matter of accountability.

> Let us care
> To live so that our *reckonings* may fall even
> When we're to make account.
> *Ford*, Broken Heart, ii. 3.

The waste of it [time] will make you dwindle, alike in intellectual and moral stature, beyond your darkest *reckonings*. *Gladstone*, Might of Right, p. 21.

6. An accounting for action or conduct; explanation; inquisition; scrutiny.

> We two to *rekenynge* must be brougt;
> Biwaare! free wille wole make thee woode.
> *Hymns to Virgin*, etc. (E. E. T. S.), p. 60.

7. A holding in estimation; assignment of value; appreciation.

You make no further *reckoning* of it [beauty] than of an outward fading benefit nature bestowed.
Sir P. Sidney.

8. Standing as to rank, quality, or worthiness; rating; consideration; reputation.

Neither ought they [certain men] to be of such *reckoning* that their opinion or conjecture should cause the laws of the Church of England to give place.
Hooker, Eccles. Polity, Pref., iv.

> Of honourable *reckoning* are you both.
> *Shak.*, R. and J., i. 2. 4.

One M. Harvey, a right honest man, of good *reckoning*; and one that above twenty years since bare the chiefest office in Walden with good credit.
G. *Harvey*, Four Letters, i.

9. *Naut.*, the calculation of the position of a ship from the rate as determined by the log, and the course as determined by the compass, the place from which the vessel started being known. See *dead-reckoning*.—**Astronomical reckoning**, a mode of stating dates before Christ, used by astronomers. The year B. C. 1 is called 0; B. C. 2 is called −1, etc.—**Count and reckoning.** See *count*¹.—**The day of reckoning**, the day of judgment; the day when account must be rendered and settlement made.—**To be astern of the reckoning.** See *astern*.—**To run ahead of one's reckoning** (*naut.*), to sail beyond the position erroneously estimated in the dead-reckoning.

reckoning-book (rek'n-ing-bùk), *n.* A book in which money received and expended is set down. *Johnson.*

reckoning-penny (rek'n-ing-pen'i), *n.* [= G. *rechenpfennig*.] A metallic disk or counter, with devices and inscriptions like a coin, formerly used in reckoning or casting up accounts.

reclaim (rē-klām'), *v.* [Early mod. E. also *reclame*; < ME. *reclaimen*, *reclaymen*, *recleimen*, *recleymen*, < OF. *reclaimer*, *recleimer*, *reclamer*, F. *réclamer*, claim, reclaim, cry out against, exclaim upon, sue, claim, = Pr. Sp. Pg. *reclamar* = It. *richiamare*, < L. *reclamare*, cry out against, exclaim against, contradict, call repeatedly, < *re-*, again, + *clamare*, call: see *claim*¹.] **I.** *intrans.* 1†. To cry out; exclaim against something.

Hereunto Polomar *reclaiming* againe, began to aduance and magnifie the honour and dignitie of generall councels.
Foxe, Martyrs, p. 637, an. 1438.

"I do not design it," says Tom, "as a reflection on Virgil: on the contrary, I know that all the manuscripts *reclaim* against such a punctuation." *Addison*, Tom Folio.

2. In *Scots law*, to appeal from a judgment of the lord ordinary to the inner house of the Court of Session.—3†. To draw back; give way.

> Ne from his currish will a whit *reclaim*.
> *Spenser.* (*Webster.*)

4. To effect reformation.

> They, harden'd more by what might most *reclaim*,
> Grieving to see his glory, at the sight
> Took envy. *Milton*, P. L., vi. 791.

II. *trans.* 1†. To cry out against; contradict; gainsay.

Herod, instead of *reclaiming* what they exclaimed, embraced and hugged their praises.
Fuller, Pisgah Sight, ii. 8. (*Trench.*)

2†. To call back; call upon to return; recall; urge backward.

> And willed him for to *reclayme* with speed
> His scattred people, ere they all were slaine.
> *Spenser*, F. Q., V. xii. 9.

3. To claim the return or restoration of; demand renewed possession of; attempt to regain: as, to *reclaim* one's rights or property.

A tract of land [Holland] snatched from an element perpetually *reclaiming* its prior occupancy. *Coxe.*

A truly great historian would *reclaim* those materials which the novelist has appropriated. *Macaulay*, History.

4. To effect the return or restoration of; get back or restore by effort; regain; recover.

> So shall the Briton blood their crowne agayn *reclame*.
> *Spenser*, F. Q., III. iii. 48.

> This arm, that hath *reclaim'd*
> To your obedience fifty fortresses.
> *Shak.*, 1 Hen. VI., iii. 4. 5.

5†. In *falconry*, to draw back; recover.

> Another day he wol, peraventure,
> *Reclayme* thee and bringe thee to lure.
> *Chaucer*, Prol. to Manciple's Tale, l. 72.

To the bewits was added the creance, or long thread, by which the bird in tutoring was drawn back, after she had been permitted to fly; and this was called the *reclaiming* of the hawk. *Strutt*, Sports and Pastimes, p. 91.

6†. To bring under restraint or within close limits; check; restrain; hold back.

By this means also the wood is *reclaimed* and repressed from running out in length beyond all measure.
Holland, tr. of Pliny, xvii. 22.

> Or is her tow'ring Flight *reclaim'd*
> By Seas from Icarus' Downfall nam'd?
> *Prior*, Carmen Seculare (1700), st. 23.

It cannot be intended that he should delay his assistance till corruption is *reclaimed*.
Johnson, Debates in Parliament (ed. 1787), II. 375.

7. To draw back from error or wrong-doing; bring to a proper state of mind; reform.

> If he be wild,
> The *reclaiming* him to good and honest, brother,
> Will make much for my honour.
> *Fletcher*, Wildgoose Chase, i. 1.

'Tis the intention of Providence, in its various expressions of goodness, to *reclaim* mankind. *Rogers*, Sermons.

8. To bring to a subdued or ameliorated state; make amenable to control or use; reduce to obedience, as a wild animal; tame; subdue; also, to fit for cultivation, as wild or marshy land.

> Thou [Jason] madest thy *reclaymynge* and thy lures
> To ladies of thy staately aparaunce,
> And of thy wordes farsed with plesaunce.
> *Chaucer*, Good Women, l. 1371.

> The elephant is never won with anger,
> Nor must that man that would *reclaim* a lion
> Take him by the teeth. *Fletcher*, Valentinian, i. 3.

> Upon his fist he bore, for his delight,
> An eagle well *reclaimed*, and lily white.
> *Dryden*, Pal. and Arc., iii. 80.

> A pathless wilderness remains
> Yet unsubdued by man's *reclaiming* hand.
> *Shelley*, Queen Mab, ix.

9†. To call or cry out again; repeat the utterance of; sound back; reverberate.

Melt to teares, poure out thy plaints, let Eccho *reclame* them. *Greene*, The Mourning Garment.

Reclaimed animals, in *law*, those animals, naturally wild, that are made tame by art, industry, or education, whereby a qualified property is acquired in them.=**Syn.** 4 and 6. To recover, regain, restore, amend, correct.

reclaim (rē-klām'), *n.* [< ME. *reclayme*, *recleyme*, < OF. *reclaim*, F. *réclame* = Sp. Pg. It. *reclamo*, calling back (in falconry); from the verb.] The act of reclaiming, or the state of being reclaimed, in any sense; reclamation; recall; restoration; reformation.

> Non of hem all that him hide myȝh
> But cam with him a *reclayme* ffro costis aboute,
> And ffell with her ffetheris ffiat vppon the erthe.
> *Richard the Redeles*, ii. 182.

> I see you are e'en past hope
> Of all *reclaim*.
> B. *Jonson*, Every Man in his Humour, i. 1.

reclaimable (rē-klā'ma-bl), *a.* [< *reclaim* + *-able*.] Capable of being reclaimed, reformed, or tamed.

He said that he was young, and so *reclaimable*: that this was his first fault. *Dr. Cockburn*, Rem. on Burnet, p. 41.

reclaimably (rē-klā'ma-bli), *adv.* So as to be capable of being reclaimed.

reclaimant† (rē-klā'mant), *n.* [< OF. *reclamant*, F. *réclamant* (= Pg. It. *reclamante*), ppr. of *réclamer*, reclaim: see *reclaim*.] One who reclaims, or opposes, contradicts, or remonstrates.

reclaimer (rē-klā'mėr), *n.* One who reclaims.

reclaiming (rē-klā'ming), *p. a.* [< ME. *recleymynge*; ppr. of *reclaim*, *v.*] 1. Serving or tending to reclaim; recalling to a regular course of life; reforming.—2. In *Scots law*, appealing from a judgment of the lord ordinary to the inner house of the Court of Session.—**Reclaiming days**, in *Scots law*, the days allowed within which to take an appeal.—**Reclaiming note**, in *Scots law*, the petition of appeal in a case of reclaiming.

reclaimless (rē-klām'les), *a.* [< *reclaim* + *-less*.] Incapable of being reclaimed; that cannot be reclaimed; not to be reclaimed; irreclaimable. [Rare.]

> And look on Guise as a *reclaimless* Rebel.
> *Lee*, Duke of Guise, ii. 1.

reclamation (rek-lạ̄-mā'shọn), *n.* [< OF. *reclamation*, F. *réclamation* = Sp. *reclamacion* = Pg. *reclamação* = It. *richiamazione*, a contradiction, gainsaying, < L. *reclamatio(n-)*, a cry of opposition or disapprobation, < *reclamare*, cry out against: see *reclaim*.] 1. A reclaiming of something as a possession; a claim or demand for return or restoration; a requirement of compensation for something wrongly taken or withheld; also, a claim to a discovery as having been previously made.

When Denmark delivered up to Great Britain three prizes, carried into a port of Norway by Paul Jones in the revolutionary war, we complained of it, and continued our *reclamations* through more than sixty years.
Woolsey, Introd. to Inter. Law, App. iii., p. 448.

2. A calling or bringing back, as from aberration or wrong-doing; restoration; reformation.

Not for a partnership in their vice, but for their *reclamation* from evill.
Bp. Hall, Satan's Fiery Darts Quenched, iii. § 6.

3. The act of subduing to fitness for service or use; taming; amelioration: as, the *reclamation* of wild animals or waste land.

A thorough course of *reclamation* was then adopted with this land, which was chiefly bog and cold boulder clay. *Fortnightly Rev.*, N. S., XL. 205.

4. A remonstrance; representation made in opposition; a cry of opposition or disapprobation.

I suspect you must allow there is some homely truth at the bottom of what called out my worthy secretary's admonitory *reclamation*. *Noctes Ambrosianæ*, Sept., 1832.

reclamation-plow (rek-lạ̄-mā'shọn-plou), *n.* A heavy plow used for breaking new land and clearing it of roots and stones. Some forms are drawn by a steam-plow engine, others by oxen or horses.

reclinant (rē-klī'nạnt), *a.* [< F. *réclinant*, ppr. of *récliner*: see *recline*.] In *her.*, bending or bowed.

reclinate (rek'li-nāt), *a.* [= F. *récliné* = Sp. Pg. *reclinado* = It. *reclinato*, < L. *reclinatus*, pp. of *reclinare*, bend back, recline: see *recline*.] Bending downward. (*a*) In *bot.*, said of stems or branches when erect or ascending at the base, then turning toward the ground; of leaves in the bud in which the blade is bent down upon the petiole or the apex of the blade upon its base; of a cotyledon doubled over in the seed. (*b*) In *entom.*, said of parts, processes, hairs, etc., which curve down toward a surface, as if to rest on it.

reclination (rek-li-nā'shọn), *n.* [= F. *réclinaison* = Sp. *reclinacion* = Pg. *reclinação*, < L. *reclinare*, pp. *reclinatus*, bend back: see *recline* and *reclinate*.] 1. The act of leaning or reclining; the state of reclining or being reclined.—2. In *dialing*, the angle which the plane of the dial makes with a vertical plane which it intersects in a horizontal line.—3. In *surg.*, one of the operations once used for the cure of cataract. It consists in applying a specially constructed needle in a certain manner to the anterior surface of the lens, and depressing it downward or backward into the vitreous humor.

reclinatory† (rē-klī'nạ̄-tẹ̄-ri), *n.* [ME. *reclinatorye*; < ML. *reclinatorium*, a place for reclining, a pillow, < L. *reclinare*, recline: see *recline*.] Something to recline on; a rest.

> Therinne sette his *reclynatorye*.
> *Lydgate*, MS. Soc. Antiq. 134, f. 3. (*Halliwell.*)

recline (rē-klīn'), *v.*; pret. and pp. *reclined*, ppr. *reclining*. [< OF. *recliner*, F. *récliner* = Sp. Pg. *reclinar* = It. *reclinare*, lean back, < L. *reclinare*, lean back, recline, < *re-*, back, + **clinare*, lean: see *cline* and *lean*¹, *v.*] **I.** *intrans.* 1. To lean backward or downward upon something; rest in a recumbent posture.—2. To bend downward; lean; have a leaning posture. [Rare.]

> Eastward, in long perspective glittering, shine
> The wood-crowned cliffs that o'er the lake *recline*.
> *Wordsworth*, Descriptive Sketches.

Reclining dial. See *dial*.=**Syn.** *Recline* is always as strong as *lean*, and generally stronger, indicating a more completely recumbent position, and approaching *lie*.

II. *trans.* To place at rest in a leaning or recumbent posture; lean or settle down upon something: as, to *recline* the head on a pillow, or upon one's arm.

> The mother
> *Reclined* her dying head upon his breast. *Dryden.*

In a shadowy saloon,
On silken cushions half *reclined*,
I watch thy grace. *Tennyson*, Eleänore.

recline (rẹ-klīn'), *a.* [< L. *reclinis*, *reclinus*, leaning back, bent back, reclining, < *reclinare*, lean back, recline: see *recline*, *v.*] Leaning; being in a reclining posture. [Rare.]

They sat *recline*
On the soft downy bank damask'd with flowers.
Milton, P. L., iv. 333.

recliner (rẹ-klī'nėr), *n.* One who or that which reclines; specifically, a reclining dial.

reclining-board (rẹ-klī'ning-bōrd), *n.* A board to which young persons are sometimes strapped, to prevent stooping and to give erectness to the figure. *Mrs. S. C. Hall.*

reclining-chair (rẹ-klī'ning-chār), *n.* A chair the back of which can be tilted as desired, to allow the occupant to assume a reclining position; an invalid-chair.

reclivate (rek'li-vāt), *a.* [< LL. *reclivis*, leaning backward, < L. *re-*, back, + *clivus*, sloping: see *clivous*.] In *entom.*, forming a double curve; curving outward and then inward: noting margins, parts of jointed organs, and processes.

reclothe (rē-klōᴛʜ'), *v. t.* [< *re-* + *clothe*.] To clothe again.

The varying year with blade and sheaf
Clothes and *reclothes* the happy plains.
Tennyson, Day Dream, The Sleeping Palace.

reclude† (rẹ-klöd'), *v. t.* [= OF. *reclure*, *reclorre*, F. *reclure* = Pr. *reclaure*, *resclure* = Sp. Pg. *recluir*, shut up, seclude, = It. *richiudere*, unclose, open, < LL. *recludere*, shut up or off, close, < L. *recludere*, unclose, open, also in LL. shut up, < *re-*, back, + *claudere*, shut: see *close*[1], and cf. *conclude*, *exclude*, *include*, *preclude*, *seclude*, *occlude*.] To open; unclose.

Hem softe enclude,
And towarde nyght hir yates thou *reclude*.
Palladius, Husbondrie (E. E. T. S.), p. 39.

recluse (rẹ-klös'), *a.* and *n.* [1. < ME. *recluse*, *n.*, < OF. *reclus*, F. *reclus*, fem. *recluse* = Pr. *reclus* = Sp. Pg. *recluso* = It. *richiuso*, < LL. *reclusus*, shut up (ML. *reclusus*, m., *reclusa*, f., a recluse), pp. of *recludere*, shut up, L. unclose, open, etc.: see *reclude*. 2. < ME. *recluse*, < OF. *recluse*, a convent, monastery, < LL. *reclusa*, fem. of *reclusus*, shut up: see above.] I. *a.* Shut up or apart from the world; retired from public notice; sequestered; solitary; existing or passed in a solitary state: as, a *recluse* monk or hermit; a *recluse* life.

Here, as *recluse* as the Turkish Spy at Paris, I am almost unknown to every body.
Goldsmith, To Rev. Thomas Contarine.

II. *n.* 1. A person who withdraws from the world to spend his days in seclusion and meditation; specifically, a member of a religious community who is voluntarily immured for life in a single cell. The life of a monastic recluse was a privilege accorded only to those of exceptional virtue, and only by express permission of the abbot, chapter, and bishop. In earlier monasticism, the recluse was immured in a cell, sometimes underground, and usually within the precincts of the monastery. He was to have no other apparel than that which he wore at the time of his incarceration. The doorway to the cell was walled up, and only a sufficient aperture was left for the conveyance of provisions, but so contrived as not to allow the recluse to see or be seen. Later monasticism greatly modified this rigor.

2†. A place of seclusion; a retired or quiet situation; a hermitage, convent, or the like.

It is certain that the church of Christ is the pillar of truth, or sacred *recluse* and peculiar asylum of Religion.
J. Wise, The Churches' Quarrel Espoused.

recluse† (rẹ-klöz'), *v. t.* [< ME. *reclusen*; < *recluse*, *a.*] To shut up; seclude; withdraw from intercourse.

Religious out-ryders *reclused* in here cloistres.
Piers Plowman (C), v. 116.

I had a shrewd Disease hung lately upon me, proceeding, as the Physicians told me, from this long *reclused* Life.
Howell, Letters, ii. 29.

reclusely (rẹ-klös'li), *adv.* In a recluse manner; in retirement or seclusion from society; as a recluse. *Lee*, Eccles. Gloss.

recluseness (rẹ-klös'nes), *n.* The state of being recluse; retirement; seclusion from society.

A kind of calm *recluseness* is like rest to the overlabour'd man. *Feltham*, On Eccles. ii. 11. (Resolves, p. 349.)

reclusion (rẹ-klö'zhon), *n.* [< F. *reclusion* = Sp. *reclusion* = Pg. *reclusão* = It. *reclusione*, < ML. *reclusio(n-)*, < LL. *recludere*, pp. *reclusus*, shut up: see *reclude* and *recluse*.] 1. A state of retirement from the world; seclusion. *Johnson.* —2. Specifically, the life or condition of a recluse or immured solitary.

reclusive (rẹ-klö'siv), *a.* [< *recluse* + *-ive*.] Affording retirement from society; recluse.

And if it sort not well, you may conceal her . . .
In some *reclusive* and religious life.
Shak., Much Ado, iv. 1. 244.

reclusory (rẹ-klö'sọ-ri), *n.*; pl. *reclusories* (-riz). [= Sp. It. *reclusorio*, < ML. *reclusorium*, < LL. *recludere*, pp. *reclusus*, shut up, close: see *recluse*.] The abode or cell of a recluse.

recoct† (rẹ-kokt'), *v. t.* [< L. *recoctus*, pp. of *recoquere*, cook again, < *re-*, again, + *coquere*, cook: see *cook*[1], *v.*] To cook over again; hence, to vamp up or renew.

Old women and men, too, . . . seek, as it were, by Medea's charms, to *recoct* their corps, as she did Æson's, from feeble deformities to sprightly handsomeness.
Jer. Taylor (?), Artif. Handsomeness, p. 71.

recoction (rẹ-kok'shọn), *n.* [< *recoct* + *-ion*.] A second coction or preparation. *Imp. Dict.*

recognisable, recognise, etc. See *recognizable*, etc.

recognition[1] (rek-ọg-nish'ọn), *n.* [< OF. *recognition*, F. *récognition* = It. *ricognizione*, *recognizione*, < L. *recognitio(n-)*, < *recognoscere*, pp. *recognitus*, recognize, know again: see *recognize*[1].] 1. The act of recognizing; a knowing again; consciousness that a given object is identical with an object previously cognized.

Every species of fancy hath three modes: *recognition* of a thing as present, memory of it as past, and foresight of it as to come. *N. Grew.*

Sense represents phenomena empirically in perception, imagination in association, apperception in the empirical consciousness of the identity of these reproductive representations with the phenomena by which they were given therefore in *recognition*.
Kant, Critique of Pure Reason, tr. by Müller, p. 115.

A person's *recognition* of a colour is in part an act of inference. *J. Sully*, Sensation and Intuition, p. 67.

2. A formal avowal of knowledge and approval or sanction; acknowledgment: as, the *recognition* of one government by another as an independent sovereignty or as a belligerent.

The lives of such saints had, at the time of their yearly memorials, solemn *recognition* in the church of God.
Hooker.

This Byzantine synod assumed the rank and powers of the seventh general council; yet even this title was a *recognition* of the six preceding assemblies.
Gibbon, Decline and Fall, xlix.

On the 4th he was received in procession at Westminster, seized the crown and sceptre of the Confessor, and was proclaimed king by the name of Edward IV. . . . From the 4th of March the legal *recognition* of Edward's royal character begins, and the years of his reign date.
Stubbs, Const. Hist., § 355.

That a man's right to the produce of his brain is equally valid with his right to the produce of his hands is a fact which has yet obtained but a very imperfect *recognition*.
H. *Spencer*, Social Statics, p. 155.

3. Cognizance; notice taken; acceptance.

The interesting fact about Apollonius is the extensive *recognition* which he obtained, and the ease with which his pretensions found acceptance in the existing condition of the popular mind. *Froude*, Sketches, p. 103.

4. In *Scots law*, the recovery of lands by the proprietor when they fall to him by the fault of the vassal; or, generally, any return of the feu to the superior, by whatever ground of eviction. =**Syn. 1.** See *recognize*[1].

recognition[2] (rē"kog-nish'ọn), *n.* A repeated cognition.

recognitive (rẹ-kog'ni-tiv), *a.* [< L. *recognitus*, pp. of *recognoscere*, recognize, + *-ive*. Cf. *cognitive*.] Recognizing; recognitory.

recognitor† (rẹ-kog'ni-tọr), *n.* [< AF. *recognitor*, < ML. *recognitor*, < L. *recognitus*, pp. of *recognoscere*, recognize: see *recognize*[1].] In *law*, one of a jury impaneled on an assize: so called because they acknowledge a disseizin by their verdict. The recognitor was a witness rather than a juror in the modern sense.

The inquests by *Recognitors* which we hear of from the time of the Conqueror onwards—the sworn men by whose oaths Domesday was drawn up—come much more nearly [than compurgators] to our notion of Jurors, but still they are not the thing itself.
E. A. Freeman, Norman Conquest, V. 303.

recognitory (rẹ-kog'ni-tọ-ri), *a.* [< L. *recognitus*, pp. of *recognoscere*, recognize, + *-ory*[1].] Pertaining to or connected with recognition.

A pun and its *recognitory* laugh must be co-instantaneous. *Lamb*, Distant Correspondents.

recognizability (rek-ọg-ni-zạ-bil'i-ti), *n.* [< *recognizable* + *-ity* (see *-bility*).] The state of being recognizable; capacity for being recognized.

recognizable (rek'ọg-ni-zạ-bl or rẹ-kog'ni-zạ-bl), *a.* [< *recognize*[1] + *-able*. Cf. OF. *reconnoissable*, F. *reconnaissable*.] Capable of being recognized, known, or acknowledged. Also spelled *recognisable*.

recognizably (rek'ọg-nī-zạ-bli or rẹ-kog'ni-zạ-bli), *adv.* So as to be recognized.

recognizance (rẹ-kog'ni-zạns or rẹ-kon'i-zạns), *n.* [< ME. *recognisance*, *reconyssaunce*, < OF. *recognoissance*, *reconnoisance*, *reconoisance*, *recunuissance*, *reconisance*, etc., F. *reconnaissance* (> E. *reconnaissance*) = Pr. *reconaissensa*, *regonoyssensa* = Pg. *reconhecença* = It. *riconoscenza*, < ML. *recognoscentia*, a recognizing, acknowledgment, an obligation binding one over to do some particular act, < L. *recognoscen(t-)s*, ppr. of *recognoscere*, recognize: see *recognize*[1]. Cf. *cognizance*.] 1. The act of recognizing; acknowledgment of a person or thing; avowal; recognition.

The great bell that heaves
With solemn sound—and thousand others more,
That distance of *recognizance* bereaves,
Make pleasing music and not wild uproar.
Keats, Sonnet, "How many Bards."

2. Mark or badge of recognition; token.

She did gratify his amorous works
With that *recognizance* and pledge of love
Which I first gave her [a handkerchief].
Shak., Othello, v. 2. 214.

3. In *law*: (*a*) An obligation of record entered into before some court of record or magistrate duly authorized, conditioned to do some particular act, as to appear at court, to keep the peace, or pay a debt.

He was bounden in a *reconyssaunce*
To paye twenty thousand sheeld anon.
Chaucer, Shipman's Tale, l. 330.

This fellow might be in 's time a great buyer of land, with his statutes, his *recognizances*, his fines, his double vouchers, his recoveries. *Shak.*, Hamlet, v. 1. 113.

(*b*†) The verdict of a jury impaneled upon assize.—**To enter into recognizances.** See *enter*[1].

recognizant (rẹ-kog'ni-zạnt or rẹ-kon'i-zạnt), *a.* [< OF. *recognoissant*, ppr. of *recognoistre*, etc., recognize: see *recognize*[1].] Recognizing; perceiving.

The laird did his best to help him; but he seemed nowise *recognizant*.
George MacDonald, Warlock o' Glenwarlock, xv.

recognization (rẹ-kog-ni-zā'shọn), *n.* [< *recognize*[1] + *-ation*.] The act of recognizing.

recognize[1] (rek'ọg-nīz), *v.*; pret. and pp. *recognized*, ppr. *recognizing*. [With accom. term. *-ize* (as if from *recognizance*), after OF. *recognoistre*, F. *reconnaître* (> E. *reconnoiter*) = Pr. *recognoscer*, *reconoscer* = Sp. *reconocer* = Pg. *reconhecer* = It. *riconoscere*, < L. *recognoscere*, know again, recall to mind, recognize, examine, certify, < *re-*, again, + *cognoscere*, know: see *cognition*. Cf. *cognize*.] I. *trans.* 1. To know (the object) again; recall or recover the knowledge of; perceive the identity of with something formerly known or in the mind.

Then first he *recognis'd* the ætherial guest;
Wonder and joy alternate fire his breast.
Fenton, in Pope's Odyssey, i. 415.

To *recognize* an object is to identify it with some object previously seen. *J. Sully*, Outlines of Psychol., p. 226.

2. To avow or admit a knowledge of, with approval or sanction; acknowledge or accept formally: as, to *recognize* one as ambassador; to *recognize* a government as an independent sovereignty or as a belligerent.

He brought several of them . . . to *recognize* their sense of their undue procedure used by them unto him.
Bp. Fell, Life of Hammond. (*Latham.*)

Only that State can live in which injury to the least member is *recognized* as damage to the whole.
Emerson, Address, Soldiers' Monument, Concord.

Holland, immediately after the surrender of Yorktown, had *recognized* the independence of America, which had as yet only been *recognized* by France.
Lecky, Eng. in 18th Cent., xv.

3. To indicate one's acquaintance with (a person) by a salute: as, to pass one without *recognizing* him.—4. To indicate appreciation of: as, to *recognize* merit.—5. To review; reëxamine; take cognizance of anew.

However their causes speed in your tribunals, Christ will *recognize* them at a greater. *South.*

6. To acknowledge; admit or confess as an obligation or duty.

It is more to the purpose to urge that those who have so powerful an engine [as the press] in their hands should *recognize* their responsibility in the use of it.
H. N. Oxenham, Short Studies, p. 87.

=**Syn. 2-4.** *Recognize*, *Acknowledge*. The essential difference between these words lies in the difference between letting in to one's own knowledge (*recognize*) and letting out to other people's knowledge (*acknowledge*). Hence the opposite of *recognize* is *disown* or some kindred word; that of *acknowledge* is *conceal* or *deny*. To *recognize* an obligation and to *acknowledge* an obligation differ precisely in this way. The preacher may be able to make a man *recognize*, even if he cannot make him *acknowledge*, his need of moral improvement. See *acknowledge*.

II. *intrans.* In *law*, to enter an obligation of record before a proper tribunal: as, A. B. *recognized* in the sum of twenty dollars.

Also spelled *recognise*.

recognize[2] (rē-kog'nīz), *v. t.* To cognize again.

By the aid of Reasoning we are guided in our search, and by it *re-cognize* known relations under somewhat different attendant circumstances.
G. H. Lewes, Probs. of Life and Mind, II. 172.

recognizee (rẹ-kog-ni-zē' or rẹ-kon-i-zē'), *n.* [< *recognize*[1] + *-ee*[1].] In *law*, the person to whom a recognizance is made.

The recognizance is an acknowledgment of a former debt upon record, the form whereof is "that A. B. doth acknowledge to owe to our lord the king, to the plaintiff, to C. D., or the like, the sum of ten pounds" . . . : in which case the king, the plaintiff, C. D., &c., is called the *recognizee*, "is cui cognoscitur"; as he that enters into the recognizance is called the cognizor, "is qui cognoscit."
Blackstone, Com., II. xx.

recognizer (rek'og-nī-zėr), *n.* [< *recognize*[1] + *-er*[1]. Cf. *recognizor*.] One who recognizes.

recognizingly (rek'og-nī-zing-li), *adv.* With recognition; consciously; appreciatively.

I know not if among all his "friends" he [John Wilson] has left one who feels more *recognizingly* what he was . . . than I.
Carlyle, in Froude, Life in London, xxii.

recognizor (rẹ-kog'ni-zor or rẹ-kon'i-zor), *n.* [< OF. **recognoisseur*, F. *reconnaisseur*; as *recognize*[1] + *-or*[1].] In *law*, one who enters into a recognizance.

recognoscet, *v. t.* [< L. *recognoscere*, recognize: see *recognize*[1].] Same as *recognize*[1]. *Boyle.*

The Examiner [Boyle] might have remembered . . . who it was that distinguished his style with "ignore" and "*recognosce*," and other words of that sort, which nobody has yet thought fit to follow him in.
Bentley (quoted in F. Hall's Mod. Eng., p. 118).

recoil[1] (rẹ-koil'), *v.* [Early mod. E. also *recoyle*, *recule*; < ME. *recoilen*, *reculen*, < OF. *reculer*, F. *reculer*, draw back, go back, recoil, retire, defer, drive off (= Pr. Sp. *recular* = Pg. *recuar* = It. *reculare*, *rinculare*), < ML. *reculare*, go backward, < L. *re-*, back, + *culus* (> F. *cul*), the hinder parts, posteriors; cf. Ir. Gael. *cúl*, the back, hinder part, = W. *cil*, back, a retreat.] I. *intrans.* 1. To draw back; go back; retreat; take a sudden backward motion after an advance.

Sodainely he blewe the retraite, and *reculed* almoste a myle backewarde.
Hall, Hen. V., an. 6.

We were with vyolence and rage of the sayde tempest constreyned to *recoyle* and turne backwardes, and to seke some haayn vpon the coste of Turkey.
Sir R. Guylforde, Pylgrymage, p. 59.

Ye both forwearied be; therefore a whyle
I read you rest, and to your bowres *recoyle*.
Spenser, F. Q., I. x. 17.

Looking on the lines
Of my boy's face, methoughts I did *recoil*
Twenty-three years, and saw myself unbreech'd.
Shak., W. T., i. 2. 154.

Their manner is, when any will inuade them, to allure and drawe them on by flying and *reculing* (as if they were afraide).
Hakluyt's Voyages, I. 489.

His men were compelled to *recoil* from the dense array of German pikes.
Prescott, Ferd. and Isa., ii. 12.

2. To start or draw back, as from anything repulsive, distressing, alarming, or the like; shrink.

First Fear his hand, its skill to try,
Amid the chords bewildered laid,
And back *recoiled*, he knew not why,
E'en at the sound himself had made.
Collins, The Passions.

The heart
Recoils from its own choice.
Cowper, Task, i. 467.

3. To fall, rush, start, bound, or roll back, as in consequence of resistance which cannot be overcome by the force impressed; return after a certain strain or impetus: literally or figuratively.

These dread curses, like the sun 'gainst glass,
Or like an overcharged gun, *recoil*.
Shak., 2 Hen. VI., iii. 2. 331.

Revenge, at first though sweet,
Bitter ere long, back on itself *recoils*.
Milton, P. L., ix. 172.

4†. To fall off; degenerate.

Be revenged;
Or she that bore you was no queen, and you
Recoil from your great stock.
Shak., Cymbeline, i. 6. 128.

II.† *trans.* To drive back.

Mariners and merchants with much toyle
Labour'd in vaine to have secur'd their prize, . . .
But neither toyle nor traveill might her backe *recoyle*.
Spenser, F. Q., II. xii. 19.

recoil[1] (rẹ-koil'), *n.* [Early mod. E. also *recule*; < OF. *recul*, recoil, backward movement, retreat, F. *recul*, recoil, rebound, = Pg. *recuo*, a recoil; from the verb.] 1†. A drawing back; retreat.

Where, having knowledge of Omore his *recule*, he pursued him.
Holinshed, Descrip. of Ireland. (*Nares.*)

2. A backward movement; a rebound: literally or figuratively.

On a sudden open fly
With impetuous *recoil* and jarring sound
The infernal doors.
Milton, P. L., ii. 880.

The *recoil* from formalism is scepticism.
F. W. Robertson.

Who knows it not — this dead *recoil*
Of weary fibres stretched with toil?
O. W. Holmes, Midsummer.

3. Specifically, the rebound or resilience of a firearm or a piece of ordnance when discharged.

Like an unskilful gunner, he usually misses his aim, and is hurt by the *recoil* of his own piece.
Sheridan, The Duenna, i. 3.

Energy of recoil. See *energy*.— **Recoil-check.** See *check*[1].

recoil[2] (rē-koil'), *v. t.* [< *re-* + *coil*[1].] To coil again.

He [the driller] then reverses the motion, uncoils it [the cable], and *recoils* it up the other way.
Sci. Amer., N. S., LV. 116.

recoiler (rẹ-koi'lėr), *n.* One who recoils or falls back. *Bp. Hacket*, Abp. Williams, p. 98.

recoil-escapement (rẹ-koil'es-kāp"ment), *n.* In *horol.*, an escapement in which after each beat the escape-wheel recoils, or moves backward slightly: opposed to a *dead-beat escapement*, in which the escape-wheel rests dead, or without motion in the interval between the beats.

recoilment (rẹ-koil'ment), *n.* [Formerly also *recuilment*; < OF. (and F.) *reculement*, < *reculer*, recoil: see *recoil*[1].] The act of recoiling.

The sharp pains of the stone were allay'd by that heaviness of sense which the *recuilment* of serous moisture into the habit of the body and insertions of the nerves occasion'd.
Hammond, in Bp. Fell.

recoil-pallet (rẹ-koil'pal"et), *n.* One of the pallets which form an essential part of the mechanism of a recoil-escapement.

Recoil pallets — and dead ones too — should only just clear the teeth.
Sir E. Beckett, Clocks and Watches, p. 79.

recoil-wave (rẹ-koil'wāv), *n.* A dicrotic wave.

recoin (rē-koin'), *v. t.* [< *re-* + *coin*[1].] To coin again: as, to *recoin* gold or silver. *Locke.*

recoinage (rē-koi'nāj), *n.* [< *recoin* + *-age*.] 1. The act of coining anew.— 2. That which is coined anew.

recoiner (rē-koi'nėr), *n.* One who recoins.

recollect[1] (rē-ko-lekt'), *v.* [< L. *recollectus*, pp. of *recolligere* (> It. *raccogliere*, *raccorre*, *ricogliere*, *ricorre* = Pg. *recolher* = Sp. *recolegir* = F. *recueillir*, also *récolliger*), gather up again, recollect, < *re-*, again, + *colligere*, pp. *collectus*, gather, collect: see *collect*. Cf. *recollect*[2] and *recueil*.] I. *trans.* 1. To collect or gather again; collect what has been scattered: often written distinctively *re-collect*: as, to *re-collect* routed troops.

So oft shalt thou eternal favour gain,
Who *recollectedst* Ireland to them twain.
Ford, Fame's Memorial.

The Lake of Zembre, . . . now dispersed into ample lakes, and againe *recollecting* his extravagant waters.
Sandys, Travailes, p. 73.

He [Gray] asks his friend Stonehewer, in 1760, "Did you never observe (while rocking winds are piping loud) that pause as the gust is *re-collecting* itself?"
Lowell, New Princeton Rev., I. 163.

2†. To summon back, as scattered ideas; reduce to order; gather together.

"Young man" (quoth she), "thy spirites *recollect*;
Be not amazde mine vncouth shape to see."
Times' Whistle (E. E. T. S.), p. 138.

Recollecting of all our scattered thoughts and exterior extravagances . . . is the best circumstance to dispose us to a heavenly visitation.
Jer. Taylor, Works (ed. 1835), I. 29.

3. To recover (one's self); collect (one's self): used reflexively in the past participle.

Thor. You'll be temperate,
And hear me.
Ger. Speak, I am *re-collected*.
Shirley, Love in a Maze, ii. 3.

Now if Joseph would make one of his long speeches, I might *recollect* myself a little.
Sheridan, School for Scandal, v. 3.

4†. To gather; collect.

These fishers . . . from their watery empire *recollect*
All that may men approve or men detect.
Shak., Pericles, ii. 1. 54.

II. *intrans.* To come together again; reunite.

Though diffus'd, and spread in infinite,
Shall *recollect*, and in one all unite.
Donne, To Lady Bedford.

recollect[2] (rek-o-lekt'), *v. t.* [In form and origin same as *recollect*[1], but in pronunciation and sense depending upon the noun *recollection*.] To recover or recall knowledge of; bring back to the mind or memory; remember.

Conscious of age, she *recollects* her youth.
Cowper, Truth, l. 153.

Perchance
We do but *recollect* the dreams that come
Just ere the waking.
Tennyson, Lucretius.

=Syn. To call up, call to mind. See *remember* and *memory*.

Recollect[3] (rek'o-lekt), *n.* Same as *Recollet*.

The *Recollects* were uninfected by Jansenism.
Rom. Cath. Dict., p. 709.

recollectedness (rek-o-lek'ted-nes), *n.* 1. The result of searching the memory, as putting a person into complete possession of what he remembers.

Recollectedness to every good purpose; unpremeditatedness to every bad purpose.
Bentham, Judicial Evidence, II. iv.

2. Self-possession; mastery of what is in one's mind.

I spoke with *recollectedness* and power.
Bp. Wilberforce, Diary, March 3, 1857.

recollection (rek-o-lek'shon), *n.* [< OF. *recollection*, F. *récollection* = Sp. *recoleccion*, recollection, = Pg. *recoleição*, retirement, < L. *recollectio(n-)*, < *recolligere*, pp. *recollectus*, collect again: see *recollect*[1], *recollect*[2].] 1. The act of recollecting, or recalling to the memory; the act by which objects are voluntarily recalled to the memory or ideas are revived in the mind; the searching of the memory; reminiscence; remembrance.

If it [the idea] be sought after by the mind, and with pain and endeavour found, and brought again in view, it is *recollection*.
Locke, Human Understanding, II. xix. 1.

2. The power of recalling ideas to the mind, or the period over which such power extends; remembrance: as, the events mentioned are not within my *recollection*.

When I think of my own native land,
In a moment I seem to be there;
But alas! *recollection* at hand
Soon hurries me back to despair.
Cowper, Alexander Selkirk.

How dear to this heart are the scenes of my childhood,
When fond *recollection* presents them to view!
S. Woodworth, The Bucket.

3. That which is recollected; something recalled to mind.

One of his earliest *recollections*.
Macaulay.

Thinks I, "Aha!
When I can talk, I'll tell Mamma."
— And that's my earliest *recollection*.
F. Locker, A Terrible Infant.

4. The operation or practice of collecting or concentrating the mind; concentration; collectedness.

From such an education Charles contracted habits of gravity and *recollection* which scarcely suited his time of life.
W. Robertson, Charles V.

=Syn. 1-3. *Remembrance*, *Reminiscence*, etc. See *memory*.

recollective (rek-o-lek'tiv), *a.* [< *recollect*[2] + *-ive*.] Having the power of recollecting. *Foster.*

Recollet (rek'o-let), *n.* [Sometimes spelled *Recollect*; < OF. *recollet*, F. *récollet* = Sp. Pg. *recoleto* = It. *recolletto*, m. (F. *récollette* = Sp. Pg. *recoleta* = It. *recolletta*, f.), < L. *recollectus*, pp. of *recolligere*, recollect: see *recollect*[1].] A member of a congregation of a monastic order which follows an especially strict rule. The most noted Recollets belong to the Franciscan order, and form a branch of the Observantines. See *Franciscan*.

recolor, recolour (rē-kul'or), *v.* [< *re-* + *color*, *colour*.] I. *trans.* To color or dye again.

The monuments which were restored . . . may also in part have been *recoloured*.
Athenæum, No. 3237, p. 643.

II. *intrans.* To reassume a color; flush again. [Rare.]

The swarthy blush *recolours* in his cheeks.
Byron, Lara, i. 13.

recomand†, *v.* A Middle English form of *recommend*.

recombine (rē-kom-bīn'), *v. t.* [= F. *récombiner* = Sp. *recombinar*; as *re-* + *combine*.] To combine again.

Which when to-day the priest shall *recombine*,
From the mysterious holy touch such charms
Will flow.
Carew, On the Marriage of P. K. and C. C.

recomfort (rẹ-kum'fėrt), *v. t.* [< ME. *recomforten*, *reconforten*, *recounforten*, < OF. *reconforter*, *recunforter*, F. *réconforter* = It. *riconfortare*, strengthen anew; as *re-* + *comfort*.] 1†. To give new strength to.

The kynge Pyngnores com with viji[m] Salanes, that hem *recounforted* and moche sustened, for thei smyten in among the kynge Ventres meyne.
Merlin (E. E. T. S.), ii. 245.

In strawberries . . . it is usual to help the ground with muck, and likewise to *recomfort* it sometimes with muck put to the roots.
Bacon, Nat. Hist., § 463.

2. To comfort again; console anew.

> And hym with al hire wit to *reconforte*,
> As sche best koude, she gan hym to disport.
> *Chaucer*, Troilus, ii. 1672.

> *Recomfort* thyself, wench, in a better choice.
> *Middleton*, Family of Love, ii. 4.

recomfortless† (rē-kum'fėrt-les), *a.* [< **recomfort*, *n.* (< F. *reconfort*, succor, consolation), + *-less*.] Without comfort.

> There all that night remained Britomart,
> Restlesse, *recomfortlesse*, with heart deepe grieved.
> *Spenser*, F. Q., V. vi. 24.

recomforture† (rē-kum'fėr-tūr), *n.* [< *recomfort* + *-ure*.] Renewal or restoration of comfort.

> They shall breed
> Selves of themselves, to your *recomforture* [orig. *recomfiture*].
> *Shak.*, Rich. III., iv. 4. 425.

recommence (rē-ko-mens'), *v.* [< F. *recommencer* = Pr. *recomensar* = It. *ricominciare*; as *re-* + *commence*.] **I.** *intrans.* To begin again to be; begin again.

> He seemed desirous enough of *recommencing* courtier.
> *Johnson*, Swift.

> The transport of reconciliation was soon over; and the old struggle *recommenced*.
> *Macaulay*, Sir William Temple.

II. *trans.* To cause again to begin to be; begin again.

> I could be well content, allow'd the use
> Of past experience, . . .
> To *recommence* life's trial. *Cowper*, Four Ages.

recommencement (rē-ko-mens'ment), *n.* [< OF. (and F.) *recommencement* = It. *ricominciamento*; as *recommence* + *-ment*.] A commencement anew.

recommend (rek-o-mend'), *v. t.* [Early mod. E. also *recommaund*; < ME. *recommenden*, *recomanden*, *recomaunden*, < OF. *recommander*, *recumander*, F. *recommander* = Pr. *recommandar* = Cat. *recomanar* = Sp. *recomendar* = Pg. *recommendar* = It. *raccomandare*, < ML. *recommendare*, recommend, < L. *re-*, again, + *commendare*, commend: see *commend*.] **1.** To commend to another's notice; put in a favorable light before another; commend or give favorable representations of; bring under one's notice as likely to be of service.

> Custance, your child, hir *recomandeth* ofte
> Un-to your grace.
> *Chaucer*, Man of Law's Tale, l. 180.

> And we praye the kynge of Fraunce that he wyll vs *recommaunde* to the myghty kyng of Englande.
> *R. Eden*, tr. of Amerigo Vespucci (First Books on America, ed. Arber, p. xxxvi).

> In my most hearty wise I *recommend* me to you.
> *Sir T. More* (Arber's Eng. Garner, I. 297).

> He *recommends* a red striped silk to the pale complexion, white to the brown, and dark to the fair.
> *Addison*, Spectator, No. 265.

2. To make acceptable; attract favor to.

> Conversing with the meanest of the people, and choosing such for his Apostles, who brought nothing to *recommend* them but innocency and simplicity.
> *Stillingfleet*, Sermons, I. iii.

> As shades more sweetly *recommend* the light,
> So modest plainness sets off sprightly wit.
> *Pope*, Essay on Criticism, l. 301.

3. To commit or intrust, as in prayer.

> Alle the bretherin and sistrin . . . han *recomoundid* in here mynde the stat of holi Chirche, and for pes and vnite in the lond.
> *English Gilds* (E. E. T. S.), p. 37.

> Paul chose Silas, and departed, being *recommended* by the brethren unto the grace of God. Acts xv. 40.

4. To advise, as to an action, practice, measure, remedy, or the like; advise (that something be done).

> If there be a particular inn . . . where you are well acquainted, . . . *recommend* your master thither.
> *Swift*, Advice to Servants, To the Groom.

> He *recommended* that the whole disposition of the camp should be changed. *Irving*, Granada, p. 67.

> I was . . . strongly *recommended* to sell out by his Royal Highness the Commander-in-Chief.
> *Thackeray*, Fitz-Boodle's Confessions.

5†. To give or commit in kindness.

> Denied me mine own purse,
> Which I had *recommended* to his use
> Not half an hour before. *Shak.*, T. N., v. 1. 94.

To recommend itself, to be agreeable; make itself acceptable.

> This castle hath a pleasant seat; the air
> Nimbly and sweetly *recommends itself*
> Unto our gentle senses. *Shak.*, Macbeth, i. 6. 2.

recommendable (rek-o-men'da-bl), *a.* [< OF. (and F.) *recommandable* = Sp. *recomendable* = Pg. *recommendavel*; as *recommend* + *-able*.] Capable of being or suitable to be recommended; worthy or deserving of recommendation or praise. *Glanville*, Vanity of Dogmatizing, Pref.

recommendableness (rek-o-men'da-bl-nes), *n.* The quality of being recommendable. *Dr. H. More*.

recommendably (rek-o-men'da-bli), *adv.* In a recommendable manner; so as to deserve recommendation.

recommendation (rek"o-men-dā'shon), *n.* [< ME. *recomendacyon*, < OF. (and F.) *recommandation* = Pr. *recomandatio* = Sp. *recomendacion* = Pg. *recommendação* = It. *raccommandazione*, < ML. *recommendatio(n-)*, < *recommendare*, recommend: see *recommend*.] **1.** The act of recommending or of commending; the act of representing in a favorable manner for the purpose of procuring the notice, confidence, or civilities of another.

> My wife . . . referred her to all the neighbors for a character; but this our peeress declined as unnecessary, alleging that her cousin Thornhill's *recommendation* would be sufficient. *Goldsmith*, Vicar, xi.

2. That which procures a kind or favorable reception; any thing, quality, or attribute, which produces or tends to produce a favorable acceptance, reception, or adoption.

> Poplicola's doors were opened on the outside, to save the people even the common civility of asking entrance; where misfortune was a powerful *recommendation*.
> *Dryden*.

3†. Favor; repute.

> Whome I founde a lorde of hyghe *recomendacyon*, noble, lyberall, and curtesse.
> *Berners*, tr. of Froissart's Chron., II. xxvii.

> It [the burying of the dead] hath always been had in an extraordinary *recommendation* amongst the ancients.
> *North*, tr. of Plutarch, ii.

4. A letter of recommendation. [Colloq.]—**Letter of recommendation**, a letter given by one person to another, and addressed to a third or "to whom it may concern," in which the bearer is represented as worthy of consideration and confidence.

recommendative† (rek-o-men'da-tiv), *n.* [= OF. *recommandatif* = It. *raccomandativo*; as *recommend* + *-ative*.] That which recommends; a recommendation. *Imp. Dict.*

recommendatory (rek-o-men'dā-tō-ri), *a.* [= Sp. *recomendatorio* = It. *raccomandatorio*; < *recommend* + *-at-ory*. Cf. *commendatory*.] Serving to recommend; recommending.

> If you . . . send us withal a Copy of your *Recommendatory* Letters, we shall then take care that you may with all speed repair to us upon the Public Faith.
> *Milton*, Letters of State (Works, VIII. 271).

recommender (rek-o-men'dėr), *n.* [< OF. (and F.) *recommandeur* = Pg. *recommendador* = It. *raccomandatore*; from the verb.] One who or that which recommends.

> This letter is in your behalf, fair maid;
> There's no denying such a *recommender*.
> *Digby*, Elvira, i. 1.

recommit (rē-ko-mit'), *v. t.* [= It. *ricommettere*; as *re-* + *commit*. Cf. ML. *recommittere*, commend.] **1.** To commit again: as, to *recommit* persons to prison.

> When they had bailed the twelve bishops who were in the Tower, the House of Commons expostulated with them, and caused them to be *recommitted*. *Clarendon*.

2. To refer again as to a committee.

> I shall propose to you to suppress the Board of Trade and Plantations, and to *recommit* all its business to the council. *Burke*, Economical Reform.

> If a report is *recommitted* before it has been agreed to by the assembly, what has heretofore passed in the committee is of no validity.
> *Cushing*, Manual of Parliamentary Practice, § 291.

recommitment (rē-ko-mit'ment), *n.* [< *recommit* + *-ment*.] **1.** A second or renewed commitment.—**2.** A renewed reference to a committee.

recommittal (rē-ko-mit'al), *n.* [< *recommit* + *-al*.] Same as *recommitment*.

recompact (rē-kom-pakt'), *v. t.* [< *re-* + *compact*[1], *v.*] To compact or join anew.

> Repair
> And *recompact* my scatter'd body.
> *Donne*, A Valediction of my Name.

recompence†, *v.* and *n.* An old spelling of *recompense*.

recompensation (rē-kom-pen-sā'shon), *n.* [< ME. *recompensacion*, *recompensacioun*, < OF. *recompensation* = Sp. *recompensacion* = Pg. *recompensação* = It. *ricompensazione*, < ML. *recompensatio(n-)*, a rewarding, < *recompensare*, reward: see *recompense*.] **1†.** A recompense.

> They ne owhte nat ryht for the *recompensacyon* for to geten hem hounto and prowesse.
> *Chaucer*, Boëthius, iv. prose 4.

> And that done, he shuld geue vnto the duke, in *recompensacion* of his costys, so many wedgys of golde as shulde charge or lade viii. charettis.
> *Fabyan*, Chron., II., an. 1391.

2. In *Scots law*, a case in which the plaintiff pursues for a debt, and the defendant pleads compensation, to which the pursuer replies by pleading compensation also.

recompense (rek'om-pens), *v.*; pret. and pp. *recompensed*, ppr. *recompensing*. [Formerly also *recompence*; < ME. *recompensen*, < OF. *recompenser*, F. *récompenser* = Pr. Sp. Pg. *recompensar* = It. *ricompensare*, < ML. *recompensare*, reward, remunerate, < L. *re-*, again, + *compensare*, compensate: see *compensate*.] **I.** *trans.* **1.** To make a return to; give or render an equivalent to, as for services or loss; compensate: with a person as object.

> For they cannot *recompence* the, butt thou shalt be *recompensed* at the resurreccion of the iuste men.
> *Tyndale*, Luke xiv. 14.

> Yet fortune cannot *recompense* me better
> Than to die well and not my master's debtor.
> *Shak.*, As you Like it, ii. 3. 75.

2. To return an equivalent for; pay for; reward; requite.

> I will *recompense* their iniquity. Jer. xvi. 18.

> He means to *recompense* the pains you take
> By cutting off your heads. *Shak.*, K. John, v. 4. 15.

> He shall *recompense* them their wickedness, and destroy them in their own malice.
> *Book of Common Prayer*, Psalter, xciv. 23.

3. To pay or give as an equivalent; pay back.

> *Recompense* to no man evil for evil. Rom. xii. 17.

4. To make amends for by some equivalent; make compensation for; pay some forfeit for.

> If the man have no kinsman to *recompense* the trespass unto. Num. v. 8.

> So shall his father's wrongs be *recompensed*.
> *Shak.*, 1 Hen. VI., iii. 1. 161.

> The sun, whose presence they are long depriued of in the winter (which is *recompensed* in their nightlesse Summer), is worshipped amongst them.
> *Purchas*, Pilgrimage, p. 434.

> Where thou mightst hope to change
> Torment with ease, and soonest *recompense*
> Dole with delight. *Milton*, P. L., iv. 893.

> He is a very licentious translator, and does not *recompense* his neglect of the author by beauties of his own.
> *Johnson*, Stepney.

5. To serve as an equivalent or recompense for.

> The tenderness of an uncle *recompensed* the neglect of a father. *Goldsmith*, The Bee, No. 2.

=Syn. 1 and 2. *Remunerate*, *Reimburse*, etc. (see *indemnify*), repay.

II.† *intrans.* To make amends or return. *Chaucer*.

recompense (rek'om-pens), *n.* [Formerly also *recompence*; < OF. *recompense*, F. *récompense* = Sp. Pg. *recompensa* = It. *ricompensa*, f., *ricompenso*, m., < ML. *recompensa*, recompense; from the verb.] An equivalent returned for anything given, done, or suffered; compensation; reward; amends; requital.

> To me belongeth vengeance and *recompence*.
> Deut. xxxii. 35.

> Is this a child's love? or a *recompense*
> Fit for a father's care?
> *Beau. and Fl.*, Captain, i. 3.

> Large was his bounty, and his soul sincere;
> Heaven did a *recompense* as largely send.
> *Gray*, Elegy.

recompensement† (rek'om-pens-ment), *n.* [< OF. *recompensement* = It. *ricompensamento*; as *recompense* + *-ment*.] Recompense; requital.

> Edfryde had great summes of money in *recompencement* of his brother's deth. *Fabyan*, Chron., I. cxxxv.

recompenser (rek'om-pen-sėr), *n.* [< OF. *recompenseur*, F. *récompenseur* = Pg. *recompensador*, < ML. *recompensator*, < *recompensare*, recompense: see *recompense*.] One who or that which recompenses.

recompensive (rek'om-pen-siv), *a.* [< *recompense* + *-ive*.] Having the character of a recompense; compensative.

> Reduce those seeming inequalities and respective distributions in this world to an equality and *recompensive* justice in the next. *Sir T. Browne*, Religio Medici, i. § 47.

recompile (rē-kom-pīl'), *v. t.* [< *re-* + *compile*.] To compile anew. *Bacon*.

recompilement (rē-kom-pīl'ment), *n.* [< *recompile* + *-ment*.] A new compilation or digest.

> Although I had a purpose to make a particular digest or *recompilement* of the laws, I laid it aside.
> *Bacon*, A Compiling an Amendment of the Laws.

recomplete (rē-kom-plēt'), *v. t.* [< *re-* + *complete*.] To complete anew; make complete again, as after an injury.

> The ability of an organism to *recomplete* itself when one of its parts has been cut off is of the same order as the ability of an injured crystal to *recomplete* itself.
> *H. Spencer*, Prin. of Biol., § 64.

recompletion (rē-kom-plē'shon), *n.* [< *re-* + *completion*.] Completion again, as after an injury which has caused incompleteness.

In this way, by successive destruction and *re-completion*. *J. D. Dana*, Text-book of Geology (3d ed.), p. 38.

recompose (rē-kom-pōz'), *v. t.* [< OF. (and F.) *recomposer*; as *re-* + *compose*. Cf. Sp. *recomponer* = Pg. *recompôr* = It. *ricomporre*, recompose.] 1. To quiet anew; compose or tranquilize that which is ruffled or disturbed: as, to *recompose* the mind.

By music he was *recomposed* and tamed. *Jer. Taylor*, Holy Living, iv. 8.

2. To compose anew; form or adjust again.

We were able to produce a lovely purple, which we can destroy or *recompose* at pleasure. *Boyle*, Works, I. 788.

recomposer (rē-kom-pō'zėr), *n.* One who or that which recomposes.

No animal figure can offer to move or wagge amisse but it meets with a proper corrector and *re-composer* of its motions. *Dr. H. More*, Moral Cabbala, i.

recomposition (rē-kom-pō-zish'on), *n.* [< F. *recomposition* = Sp. *recomposicion* = Pg. *recomposição*; as *re-* + *composition*.] The act of recomposing; composition renewed.

I have taken great pains with the *recomposition* of this scene. *Lamb*, To Coleridge. (*Latham.*)

recompt†, *v. t.* An obsolete form of *recount*[1].

reconcilable (rek'on-sī-la-bl), *a.* [Also *reconcileable*; < *reconcile* + *-able*. Cf. F. *réconciliable* = Sp. *reconciliable* = Pg. *reconciliavel* = It. *riconciliabile*, < L. as if **reconciliabilis*, < *reconciliare*, reconcile: see *reconcile*.] Capable of being reconciled. Specifically — (*a*) Capable of being brought again to friendly feelings; capable of renewed friendship. (*b*) Capable of being made to agree or be consistent; able to be harmonized or made congruous.

Acts not *reconcileable* to the rules of discretion, decency, and right reason. *Bp. Atterbury*, Sermons, I. ii.

The different accounts of the Numbers of Ships . . . are *reconcileable* by supposing that some spoke of the men of war only and others added the Transports. *Arbuthnot*, Ancient Coins, p. 250.

So *reconcilable* are extremes, when the earliest extreme is laid in the unnatural. *De Quincey*, Plato.

=**Syn.** (*a*) Appeasable, placable. (*b*) Consistent (with).

reconcilableness (rek'on-sī-la-bl-nes), *n.* The quality of being reconcilable. (*a*) Possibility of being restored to friendship and harmony. (*b*) Consistency; harmony. Also spelled *reconcileableness*.

Discerning how the several parts of Scripture are fitted to several times, persons, and occurrences, we shall discover not only a *reconcileableness*, but a friendship and perfect harmony, betwixt texts that here seem most at variance. *Boyle*.

reconcilably (rek'on-sī-la-bli), *adv.* In a reconcilable manner. Also *reconcileably*. *Imp. Dict.*

reconcile (rek'on-sīl), *v.*; pret. and pp. *reconciled*, ppr. *reconciling*. [< ME. *reconcilen*, *reconsylen*, *reconsuelen*, < OF. *reconcilier*, *reconseiller*, F. *réconcilier* = Pr. Sp. Pg. *reconciliar* = It. *riconciliare*, < L. *reconciliare*, bring together again, reunite, reconcile, < *re-*, again, + *conciliare*, bring together, conciliate: see *conciliate*.] **I.** *trans.* 1. To conciliate anew; restore to union and friendship after estrangement or variance; bring again to friendly or favorable feelings.

First be *reconciled* to thy brother, and then come and offer thy gift. Mat. v. 24.

We pray you, in Christ's stead, be ye *reconciled* to God. 2 Cor. v. 20.

To be friends for her sake, to be *reconciled*. *Tennyson*, Maud, xix.

2. To adjust; pacify; settle: as, to *reconcile* differences or quarrels.

You never shall, so help you truth and God!
Embrace each other's love in banishment; . . .
Nor never write, regreet, nor *reconcile*
This louring tempest of your home-bred hate.
Shak., Rich. II., i. 3. 186.

3. To bring to acquiescence, content, or quiet submission: with *to*.

The treasurer's talent in removing prejudice, and *reconciling* himself to wavering affections. *Clarendon*.

I found his voice distinct till I came near Front street. . . . This *reconciled me* to the newspaper accounts of his having preached to twenty-five thousand people in the fields. *B. Franklin*, Autobiog., p. 109.

Men *reconcile* themselves very fast *to* a bold and good measure when once it is taken, though they condemned it in advance. *Emerson*, Amer. Civilization.

4. To make consistent or congruous; bring to agreement or suitableness: often followed by *with* or *to*.

Such welcome and unwelcome things at once
'Tis hard to *reconcile*. *Shak.*, Macbeth, iv. 3. 139.

If it be possible to *reconcile* contradictions, he will praise him by displeasing him, and serve him by disserving him. *Milton*, Eikonoklastes, xxv.

5. To rid of apparent discrepancies; harmonize: as, to *reconcile* the accounts of a fact given by two historians: often with *with* or *to*.

However, it breeds much difficulty to *reconcile* the ancient Historie of the Babylonian and Assyrian great and long continued Empire *with* the kingdomes and Kings in that Chapter by Moses mentioned. *Purchas*, Pilgrimage, p. 71.

6. *Eccles.*, to restore to sacred uses after desecration, or to unity with the church, by a prescribed ceremonial: as, to *reconcile* a church or a cemetery which has been profaned, as by murder; to *reconcile* a penitent (that is, to restore to communion one who has lapsed, as into heresy or schism).

Oure righte Heritage before seyd [Palestine] scholde be *reconsyled* and put in the Hondes of the righte Heires of Jesu Crist. *Mandeville*, Travels, p. 4.

The chirche is entredited til it be *reconciled* by the bysshop. *Chaucer*, Parson's Tale.

Innocent III. ordered that the remains of the excommunicated person . . . should . . . be exhumed; if not, that the cemetery should be *reconciled* by the aspersion of holy water solemnly blessed. *Rom. Cath. Dict.*, p. 134.

7†. To recover; regain.

Othir kynges of the kith, that comyn fro Troy,
That were put fro there prouyns, Repairet agayne,
Recounseled to there cuntre, comyns & other.
And were welcom, I-wis, to wyuis & all.
Destruction of Troy (E. E. T. S.), l. 12931.

8. In *ship-building*, to join (a piece of work) fair with another. The term refers particularly to the reversion of curves. = **Syn. 1.** *Reconcile*, *Conciliate*, pacify, appease. *Reconcile* may apply to one or both parties to a quarrel; *conciliate* to only one. With either word, if only one side is meant, the person or persons seem to be rather in a position of superiority. — **2.** To compose, heal.

II.† *intrans.* To become reconciled.

Your thoughts, though much startled at first, *reconcile* to it. *Abp. Sancroft*, Sermons, p. 104. (*Latham.*)

reconcilement (rek'on-sīl-ment), *n.* [< OF. *reconciliement*, F. *réconciliement* = Pr. *reconciliament* = It. *riconciliamento*; as *reconcile* + *-ment*.] 1. The act of reconciling, in any sense; reconciliation; renewal of interrupted friendship.

Reconcilement is better managed by an amnesty, and passing over that which is past, than by apologies and excusations. *Bacon*, Advancement of Learning, ii. 316.

2. Adjustment.

By *reconcilement* exquisite and rare,
The form, port, motions, of this Cottage-girl
Were such as might have quickened and inspired
A Titian's hand. *Wordsworth*, Excursion, vi.

reconciler (rek'on-sī-lėr), *n.* One who reconciles; especially, one who brings parties at variance into renewed friendship.

reconciliation (rek-on-sil-i-ā'shon), *n.* [< OF. *reconciliation*, F. *réconciliation* = Pr. *reconciliatio* = Sp. *reconciliacion* = Pg. *reconciliação* = It. *riconciliazione*, < L. *reconciliatio(n-)*, a restoration, renewal, reconciliation, < *reconciliare*, reconcile: see *reconcile*.] 1. The act of reconciling parties at variance; renewal of friendship after disagreement or enmity.

A man that languishes in your displeasure,
. . . your lieutenant, Cassio. Good my lord,
If I have any grace or power to move you,
His present *reconciliation* take.
Shak., Othello, iii. 3. 47.

I have found out a Pique she has taken at him, and have fram'd a letter that makes her sue for *Reconciliation* first. *Congreve*, Old Batchelor, iii. 11.

2. The act of harmonizing or making consistent; an agreement of things seemingly opposite, different, or inconsistent.

These distinctions of the fear of God give us a clear and easy *reconciliation* of those seeming inconsistencies of Scripture with respect to this affection. *D. Rogers*.

3. *Eccles.*: (*a*) Removal of the separation made between God and man by sin; expiation; propitiation; atonement. 2 Chron. xxix. 24. (*b*) Restoration to sacred uses after desecration, or to communion with the church. See *reconcile*, 6.

The local interdict is quite peculiar to the Church of Rome. It is removed by what is termed *reconciliation*. *Encyc. Brit.*, XIII. 188.

=**Syn. 1.** *Atonement*, *Expiation*, etc. (see *propitiation*); reconcilement, appeasement, pacification, reunion.

reconciliatory (rek-on-sil'i-a-tō-ri), *a.* [= OF. *reconciliatoire*, F. *réconciliatoire* = Sp. *reconciliatorio*, < L. *reconciliare*, pp. *reconciliatus*, reconcile: see *reconcile*.] Able or tending to reconcile.

Those *reconciliatory* papers fell under the eyes of some grave divines on both parts. *Bp. Hall*, Specialties of the Life of Bp. Bull.

recondensation (rē-kon-den-sā'shon), *n.* [< *recondense* + *-ation*.] The act of recondensing.

recondense (rē-kon-dens'), *v. t.* [= OF. *recondenser* = It. *ricondensare*; as *re-* + *condense*.] To condense again.

recondite (rē-kon'dit or rek'on-dīt), *a.* [< ME. **recondit*, *recondet*, < OF. *recondit* = Sp. *recóndito* = Pg. It. *recondito*, hidden, secret, etc., < L. *reconditus*, put away, hidden, secret, pp. of *recondere*, put back again, put away, hide, < *re-*, back, + *condere*, put together: see *condiment*, *condite*[1].] 1. Hidden from mental view; secret; abstruse: as, *recondite* causes of things.

When the most inward and *recondite* spirits of all things shall be dislodged from their old close residences. *Glanville*, Pre-existence of Souls, xiv. (*Latham.*)

Occasionally, . . . when a question of theological or political interest touches upon the more *recondite* stores of history, we have an industrious examination of ancient sources. *Stubbs*, Medieval and Modern Hist., p. 55.

2. Profound; dealing with things abstruse.

Men of more *recondite* studies and deep learning. *Felton*, On Reading the Classics. (*Latham.*)

It is this mine of *recondite* quotations in their original languages, most accurately translated, which has imparted such an enduring value to this treasure of the ancient theology, philosophy, and literature. *I. D'Israeli*, Amen. of Lit., II. 400.

The most trivial passages he regards as oracles of the highest authority, and of the most *recondite* meaning. *Macaulay*, Dryden.

3. In *bot.*, concealed; not easily seen. — 4. In *entom.*, said of organs which are concealed in repose: opposed to *exserted*. Specifically applied to the aculeus or sting of a hymenopterous insect when it is habitually withdrawn into the body. =**Syn. 1.** Occult, mystical, mysterious, deep.

reconditeness (rē-kon'dit-nes or rek'on-dīt-nes), *n.* The character or state of being recondite; profound or hidden meaning.

reconditory (rē-kon'di-tō-ri), *n.*; pl. *reconditories* (-riz). [= Pg. It. *reconditorio*, a hiding-place, < ML. *reconditorium*, a repository for archives, < L. *recondere*, pp. *reconditus*, put or hide away: see *recondite*.] A repository; a storehouse or magazine. [Rare.] *Imp. Dict.*

reconduct (rē-kon-dukt'), *v. t.* [< L. *reconductus*, pp. of *reconducere*, bring back, hire anew (> It. *ricondurre*, prorogue, continue, = Sp. *reconducir*, renew a lease, = Pg. *reconduzir* = F. *reconduire*, reconduct), < *re-*, back, + *conducere*, lead: see *conduct*.] To conduct back or again.

Amidst this new creation want'st a guide
To *reconduct* thy steps?
Dryden, State of Innocence, ii. 1.

reconduction (rē-kon-duk'shon), *n.* [= F. *réconduction* = Sp. *reconduccion*, renewal of a lease, = Pg. *reconducção*, prorogation, continuance, < NL. **reconductio(n-)*, < L. *reconducere*, pp. *reconductus*, hire anew: see *reconduct*.] In *law*, a renewal of a lease.

reconfirm (rē-kon-fėrm'), *v. t.* [< OF. (and F.) *reconfirmer*, < ML. *reconfirmare*, confirm anew, < L. *re-*, again, + *confirmare*, confirm: see *confirm*.] To confirm anew. *Clarendon*, Life, III. 835.

reconjoin (rē-kon-join'), *v. t.* [= It. *ricongiugnere*, < ML. *reconjungere*, join again, < L. *re-*, again, + *conjungere*, conjoin: see *conjoin*.] To conjoin or join anew. *Boyle*, Works, I. 739.

reconnaissance (rē-kon'ā-sans), *n.* [Also *reconnoissance*; < F. *reconnaissance*, formerly *reconnoissance*, recognition, reconnaissance: see *recognizance*.] The act or operation of reconnoitering; preliminary examination or survey. Specifically — (*a*) An examination of a territory or of an enemy's position, for the purpose of directing military operations. (*b*) An examination or survey of a region in reference to its general geological character. (*c*) An examination of a region as to its general natural features, preparatory to a more particular survey for the purposes of triangulation, or of determining the location of a public work, as a road, a railway, or a canal. — **Reconnaissance in force** (*milit.*), a demonstration or attack by a considerable body of men for the purpose of discovering the position or strength of an enemy.

reconnoissance (rek-o-noi'sans), *n.* Same as *reconnaissance*.

reconnoiter, reconnoitre (rek-o-noi'tėr), *v.*; pret. and pp. *reconnoitered*, *reconnoitred*, ppr. *reconnoitering*, *reconnoitring*. [< OF. *recognoistre*, *reconoistre*, F. *reconnaître*, recognize, take a precise view of: see *recognize*[1].] **I.** *trans.* 1†. To know again; recognize.

So incompetent has the generality of historians been for the province they have undertaken, that it is almost a question whether, if the dead of past ages could revive, they would be able to *reconnoitre* the events of their own times as transmitted to us by ignorance and misrepresentation. *Walpole*, Historic Doubts, Pref.

He would hardly have *reconnoitred* Wildgoose, however, in his short hair and his present uncouth appearance. *Graves*, Spiritual Quixote, iv. 1. (*Davies.*)

2. To examine with the eye; make a preliminary survey of; specifically, to examine or survey, as a tract or region, for military, engineering, or geological purposes. See *reconnaissance*.

These gardens also seem to be those where Titus was in such great danger when he came to *reconnoitre* the city.
Pococke, Description of the East, II. i. 19.

An aged, sour-visaged domestic *reconnoitered* them through a small square hole in the door.
Scott, Kenilworth, iii.

II. *intrans.* To make a survey or inspection preliminary to taking some action; examine a position, person, opinion, etc., as a precaution.

He . . . thrust out his head, and, after *reconnoitering* for a couple of minutes, drew it in again.
Barham, in Mem. prefixed to Ingoldsby Legends, I. 51.

She saw a tardigrade slowly walking round a bladder [of *Utricularia clandestina*], as if *reconnoitring*.
Darwin, Insectiv. Plants, p. 408.

reconnoiter, reconnoitre (rek-o̤-noi'tėr), *n.* [< *reconnoiter, reconnoitre, v.*] A preliminary survey; a reconnaissance.

Satisfied with his *reconnoitre*, Losely quitted the skeleton pile.
Bulwer, What Will He Do with It? x. 1.

reconquer (rē̤-kong'kėr), *v. t.* [< OF. *reconquerir, reconquerre*, F. *reconquérir* (cf. Sp. Pg. *reconquistar* = It. *riconquistare*); as *re-* + *conquer*.] 1. To conquer again; recover by conquest.

Belisarius has *reconquered* Africa from the Vandals.
Brougham.

2. To recover; regain.

Nor has Protestantism in the course of two hundred years been able to *reconquer* any portion of what she then lost.
Macaulay, Von Ranke's Hist. Popes.

reconquest (rē̤-kong'kwest), *n.* [< OF. *reconqueste*, F. *reconquête* = Sp. Pg. *reconquista* = It. *riconquista*; as *re-* + *conquest*.] A second or repeated conquest. *Hall.*

reconsecrate (rē-kon'sē̤-krāt), *v. t.* [< *re-* + *consecrate*.] To consecrate anew.

If a church should be consumed by fire, it shall, in such a case, be *reconsecrated*.
Aylife, Parergon.

reconsecration (rē-kon-sē̤-krā'shon), *n.* [< *re-* + *consecration*.] A renewed consecration.

reconsider (rē-kon-sid'ėr), *v. t.* [< OF. *reconsiderer*, F. *reconsidérer* = It. *riconsiderare*; as *re-* + *consider*.] 1. To consider again; turn over in the mind again; review.

Reconsider from time to time, and retain the friendly advice which I send you.
Chesterfield.

He had set himself . . . to *reconsider* his worn suits of clothes, to leave off meat for breakfast, to do without periodicals.
George Eliot, Daniel Deronda, xxiv.

2. In *parliamentary language*, to take into consideration a second time, generally with the view of rescinding or of amending: as, to *reconsider* a motion in a legislative body; to *reconsider* a vote.

It is believed the motion to *reconsider*, as in use in this country [the United States], is of American origin.
Cushing, Manual of Parliamentary Practice, § 257

reconsideration (rē-kon-sid-e̤-rā'shon), *n.* [< *reconsider* + *-ation*.] The act of reconsidering. (*a*) A renewed consideration or review in the mind.

Unless on *reconsideration* it should appear that some of the stronger inductions have been expressed with greater universality than their evidence warrants, the weaker one must give way.
J. S. Mill, Logic, III. iv. § 3.

(*b*) A second consideration; specifically, in *deliberative assemblies*, the taking up for renewed consideration that which has been passed or acted upon previously, as a motion, vote, etc. Usually a motion to reconsider can be made only by a person who voted with the majority.

The inconvenience of this rule [that a decision by vote cannot be again brought into question] . . . has led to the introduction into the parliamentary practice of this country [the United States] of the motion for *reconsideration*.
Cushing, Manual of Parliamentary Practice, § 254.

reconsolate† (rē-kon'sō̤-lāt), *v. t.* [< *re-* + *consolate*. Cf. OF. (and F.) *reconsoler* = It. *riconsolare*.] To console or comfort again.

That only God who can *reconsolate* us both.
Sir H. Wotton, Reliquiæ, p. 439.

reconsolidate (rē-ko̤n-sol'i-dāt), *v. t.* [< *re-* + *consolidate*. Cf. F. *reconsolider*, reconsolidate.] To consolidate anew.

reconsolidation (rē-kon-sol-i-dā'shon), *n.* [< *reconsolidate* + *-ion*.] The act of reconsolidating, or the state of being reconsolidated; a second or renewed consolidation.

reconstituent (rē-ko̤n-stit'ṳ̄-ent), *a.* Reconstituting; forming anew; giving a new character or constitution to. *Nature*, XL. 636. [Rare.]

reconstitute (rē-kon'sti-tūt), *v. t.* [< *re-* + *constitute*.] To constitute anew; furnish again with a constitution, whether the original or a different one.

reconstitution (rē-kon-sti-tū'shon), *n.* [= F. *reconstitution*; as *reconstitute* + *-ion*.] The act or process of forming anew, or of bringing together again the parts or constituents of anything that has been broken up or destroyed.

No thorough *reconstitution* of the council was, however, made during the reign.
Stubbs, Const. Hist., § 367.

reconstruct (rē-ko̤n-strukt'), *v. t.* [< *re-* + *construct*. Cf. OF. (and F.) *reconstruire* = Pg. *reconstruir*, reconstruct.] To construct again; rebuild.

The aim of the hour was to *reconstruct* the South; but first the North had to be *reconstructed*.
Emerson, Address, Soldiers' Monument, Concord.

Out of an enormous amount of material, Carlyle *reconstructs* for us Frederick William I. of Prussia, a living, moving, tantalising reality.
Stubbs, Medieval and Modern Hist., p. 92.

reconstruction (rē-ko̤n-struk'sho̤n), *n.* [= F. *reconstruction* = Sp. *reconstruccion* = Pg. *reconstrucção*; as *reconstruct* + *-ion*.] 1. The act of constructing again.

Goethe . . . has left an interesting memorial of Euripidean study in his attempted *reconstruction* of the lost Phaethon.
Encyc. Brit., VIII. 679.

2. Specifically, in *U. S. hist.*, the process by which, after the civil war, the States which had seceded were restored to the rights and privileges inherent in the Union. The period of reconstruction extended from 1865 to about 1870. —3. That which is reconstructed. [Rare.]

A fleet of above thirty vessels, all carrying cannon, was in about three months little less than created, though a few of the largest were *reconstructions*, having been first framed and sent over from Great Britain.
Belsham, Hist. Great Britain, an. 1777.

Reconstruction Acts, two acts of Congress, of which the first, entitled "an act to provide for the more efficient government of the rebel States," was passed over the President's veto on March 2d, 1867; and the second, a supplementary act, was passed later in the same month. These acts embodied the congressional plan of reconstruction, providing that every State should remain under military government until certain acts should be performed. The principal conditions were that each State should hold a convention and frame a constitution; that this constitution must be ratified by popular vote and approved by Congress; that the new State legislature must ratify the Fourteenth Amendment to the United States Constitution; and that when the requisite number of States had ratified this amendment, any State which had fulfilled all requirements should be readmitted to the Union, and entitled to congressional representation. By 1870 all the seceding States were readmitted, but they were not all represented in Congress until 1871.

reconstructionary (rē-kon-struk'sho̤n-ā̤-ri), *a.* [< *reconstruction* + *-ary*.] Of or pertaining to reconstruction, especially to reconstruction in the southern United States: as, "*reconstructionary* influence," *Congregationalist*, June 17, 1886. [Rare.]

reconstructionist (rē-ko̤n-struk'sho̤n-ist), *n.* [< *reconstruction* + *-ist*.] An adherent of reconstruction; specifically, in *U. S. politics*, an adherent of the policy of reconstruction in the South.

The Republican *reconstructionists* . . . barred the way.
J. C. Harris, Harper's Mag., LXXVI. 703.

reconstructive (rē-ko̤n-struk'tiv), *a.* and *n.* [< *reconstruct* + *-ive*.] I. *a.* Tending to reconstruct; having the power of reconstructing.

II. *n.* In *med.*, that which is adapted or serviceable for reconstructing.

Oysters, on the other hand, are extremely useful as nerve *reconstructives*.
Science, XV. 219.

recontinuance (rē-ko̤n-tin'ṳ̄-a̤ns), *n.* [< *recontinue* + *-ance*.] The state of recontinuing; renewed continuance. [Rare.]

Of which course some have wished a *recontinuance*.
Selden, Illustrations of Drayton's Polyolbion, iv. 177.

recontinue (rē-ko̤n-tin'ū), *v. t.* and *i.* [< OF. (and F.) *recontinuer*; as *re-* + *continue*.] To continue again or anew. [Rare.]

All at an instant shall together go,
To *recontinue*, not beginning so.
Stirling, Doomesday, The Fourth Hour.

reconvalescence (rē-kon-va̤-les'e̤ns), *n.* [< *re-* + *convalescence*.] Complete restoration of health.

reconvene (rē-ko̤n-vēn'), *v.* [< ML. *reconvenire*, make an additional demand in a suit at law, lit. 'come together again,' < L. *re-*, again, + *convenire*, come together: see *convene*.] I. *intrans.* To come together again.

II. *trans.* To call together again.

reconvent† (rē-ko̤n-vent'), *v. t.* [< ML. *reconventus*, pp. of *reconvenire*, in lit. sense 'come together again': see *reconvene, convent*.] To bring together, assemble, or collect again.

He *reconuenting* armes therefore.
Warner, Albion's England, v. 27.

reconvention (rē-ko̤n-ven'sho̤n), *n.* [< OF. (and F.) *reconvention* = Sp. *reconvencion* = Pg. *reconvenção* = It. *riconvenzione*, < ML. *reconventio(n-)*, a contrary action brought by a defendant, < *reconvenire*: see *reconvene*.] In *law*, an action by a defendant against a plaintiff in a previous or pending action; a cross-bill or counter-claim. Thus, one who could not be made defendant in an original action, by reason of not being subject to the jurisdiction, may in some cases, if he sues as plaintiff, be compelled to respond to a cross-action or counter-claim, by way of *reconvention* in reduction or extinction of his demand.

reconversion (rē-ko̤n-vėr'sho̤n), *n.* [< *re-* + *conversion*.] A second or renewed conversion; also, a conversion back to a previous belief.

reconvert (rē-kon-vėrt'), *v. t.* [< OF. (and F.) *reconvertir* = It. *riconvertire*; as *re-* + *convert, v.*] To convert a second time; also, to convert back to a previously abandoned belief.

About this time the East Saxons, who . . . had expell'd their Bishop Mellitus, and renounc'd the Faith, were by the means of Oswi . . . *reconverted*.
Milton, Hist. Eng., iv.

reconvey (rē-ko̤n-vā'), *v. t.* [< OF. (and F.) *reconvier*, also *reconvoyer*, reconvey, reconvoy; as *re-* + *convey*.] 1. To convey back or to its former place: as, to *reconvey* goods.

As rivers, lost in seas, some secret vein
Thence *reconveys*, there to be lost again.
Sir J. Denham, Cooper's Hill.

2. To transfer back to a former owner: as, to *reconvey* an estate.

reconveyance (rē-ko̤n-vā'a̤ns), *n.* [< *reconvey* + *-ance*.] The act of reconveying; especially, the act of transferring a title back to a former proprietor.

record (rē̤-kôrd'), *v.* [< ME. *recorden*, < OF. *recorder*, repeat, recite, report, F. *recorder* = Pr. Sp. Pg. *recordar* = It. *ricordare*, < L. *recordari*, LL. also *recordare*, call to mind, remember, recollect, think over, meditate upon, ML. also recite, record, revise, < *re-*, again, + *cor(d-)*, heart, = E. *heart*: see *cordial*. Cf. *accord, concord, discord*.] I. *trans.* 1†. To call to mind; recall; remember; bear in mind.

Preyeth to God, lord of misericorde,
Our olde giltes that he nat *recorde*.
Chaucer, Mother of God, l. 119.

In solitary silence, far from wight,
He gan *record* the lamentable stowre
In which his wretched love lay day and night.
Spenser, F. Q., IV. xii. 10.

2†. To recall (to another's mind); remind.

Ye woote youre forward, and I it you *recorde*.
Chaucer, Gen. Prol. to C. T., l. 829.

3†. To bring to mind; suggest.

For every other wey ye kan *recorde*,
Myn herte ywis may therwith noght acorde.
Chaucer, Troilus, iv. 1513.

4†. To see or know by personal presence; bear witness to; attest.

For thei that misseden here mete wold make gret noyse,
& *record* it redeli in Rome al a-boute.
William of Palerne (E. E. T. S.), l. 1828.

And alle ryghtful *recordeden* that Reson treuthe seyde.
Piers Plowman (C), v. 151.

I call heaven and earth to *record* this day against you, that I have set before you life and death.
Deut. xxx. 19.

How proud I am of thee and of thy gifts
Rome shall *record*.
Shak., Tit. And., i. 1. 255.

5. To recite; repeat; sing; play.

Lay al this mene while Troyius
Recordynge his lesson in this manere:
"Ma fey!" thoght he, "thus wol I seye and thus."
Chaucer, Troilus, iii. 51.

And to the nightingale's complaining notes
Tune my distresses and *record* my woes.
Shak., T. G. of V., v. 4. 6.

For you are fellows only know by rote,
As birds *record* their lessons.
Fletcher, Valentinian, ii. 1.

6. To preserve the memory of by written or other characters; take a note of; register; enroll; chronicle; note; write or inscribe in a book or on parchment, paper, or other material, for the purpose of preserving authentic or correct evidence of: as, to *record* the proceedings of a court; to *record* a deed or lease; to *record* historical events.

The Levites were *recorded* . . . chief of the fathers.
Neh. xii. 22.

That he do *record* a gift,
Here in the court, of all he dies possess'd,
Unto his son Lorenzo and his daughter.
Shak., M. of V., iv. 1. 388.

And I *recorded* what I heard,
A lesson for mankind.
Cowper, The Doves.

7. To mark distinctly. [Rare.]

So even and morn *recorded* the third day.
Milton, P. L., vii. 338.

8. Figuratively, to imprint deeply on the mind or memory: as, to *record* the sayings of another in the heart.—**Recording bell, secretary, telegraph**, etc. See the nouns.—**Recording gage**, a gage provided with means for leaving a visible record of its indications. =**Syn.** 6. *Record, Register, Chronicle, Enroll, Enlist.* To *record* events, facts, words; to *register* persons, voters, things; to *enroll* volunteers, scholars; to *chronicle*

events; to *enlist* soldiers, marines. To *record* a mortgage or deed; to *register* a marriage.

II. *intrans.* 1†. To reflect; meditate; ponder.

Praying all the way, and *recording* upon the words which he before had read. *Fuller.*

2. To sing or repeat a tune: now only of birds.

She had no sooner ended with the joining her sweet lips together but that he *recorded* to her music like rural poesy; and with the conclusion of his song he embraced her. *Sir P. Sidney*, Arcadia, iii.

Sweet robin, linnet, thrush,
Record from every bush.
B. Jonson, The Penates.

The young males [birds] continue practising, or, as the bird-catchers say, *recording*, for ten or eleven months. *Darwin*, Descent of Man, I. 53.

record (rek'ọrd, formerly also rē-kôrd'), *n.* [< ME. *record*, *recorde*, < OF. *record*, *recort*, witness, record, mention, = Pr. *recort* = Cat. *record* = Sp. *recuerdo*, remembrance, = It. *ricordo*, remembrance, warning, instruction, < ML. *recordum*, witness, record, judgment; from the verb: see *record*, *v.*] 1. Attestation of a fact or event; testimony; witness.

Purely hir symple *recorde*
Was founde as trewe as any bonde.
Chaucer, Death of Blanche, l. 934.

Though I bear *record* of myself, yet my *record* is true. John viii. 14.

Heaven be the *record* to my speech! *Shak.*, Rich. II., i. 1. 30.

The *record* of a nameless woe
In the dim eye's imploring stare.
Whittier, The Human Sacrifice.

2†. Memory; remembrance.

Vio. My . . . died that day when Viola from her birth
Had number'd thirteen years.
Seb. O, that *record* is lively in my soul!
Shak., T. N., v. 1. 253.

3. That which preserves remembrance or memory; a memorial.

Nor Mars his sword nor war's quick fire shall burn
The living *record* of your memory. *Shak.*, Sonnets, lv.

4. Something set down in writing or delineated for the purpose of preserving memory; specifically, a register; an authentic or official copy of any writing, or an account of any facts and proceedings, whether public or private, usually entered in a book for preservation; also, the book containing such copy or account: as, the *records* of a court of justice; the *records* of a town or parish; the *records* of a family. In law the term is often used, even without qualification, to designate the records of a family, a corporation, a priest or church, etc., but these, except when rendered public by law or legal sanction, are really private records.

He commanded to bring the book of *records* of the chronicles; and they were read before the king. Esther vi. 1.

Burn all the *records* of the realm. *Shak.*, 2 Hen. VI., iv. 7. 16.

Probably the very earliest *record* which we possess of any actual event is the scene depicted on a fragment of an antler, which was found in the rock shelter at Laugerie Basse, in Auvergne. *Isaac Taylor*, The Alphabet, I. 16.

5. The aggregate of known facts in a person's life, especially in that of a public man; personal history: as, a good *record*; a candidate with a *record*.

Because in America party loyalty and party organization have been hitherto so perfect that any one put forward by the party will get the full party vote if his character is good and his record, as they call it, unstained. *J. Bryce*, American Commonwealth, I. 76.

6. In *racing*, *sports*, etc., the best or highest recorded achievement of speed, distance, endurance, or the like: as, to beat the *record* in leaping.—7†. Same as *recorder*, 4. [Rare.]

Melodious instruments, as Lutes, Harpes, Regals, *Records* and such like. *Puttenham*, Arte of Eng. Poesie, p. 53.

Assurances or **conveyances by record**, those made or evidenced by the authority of a court of record, as a conveyance by private act of Parliament or royal grant, or a fine and recovery.—**Closing the record**, in *Scots law*, the judicial declaration that the pleadings in a cause are at issue for trial.—**Contract of record.** See *contract*.—**Court of record.** See *court*, 7.—**Debt of record**, a debt which is shown by public record to exist.—**Estoppel by record.** See *estoppel*.—**In record, on record, upon record**, set down; registered; recorded.

Mine were the very cipher of a function,
To fine the faults whose fine stands *in record*,
And let go by the actor. *Shak.*, M. for M., ii. 2. 40.

Convicted fools they are, madmen *upon record*. *Burton*, Anat. of Mel., To the Reader, p. 75.

Judgment record. See *judgment*.—**Matter of record.** See *matter*.—**Nisi prius record.** See *nisi prius*.—**Public records**, official entries of facts, transactions, or documents, made by public officers pursuant to law, for the purpose of affording public notice or preserving a public memorial or continuing evidence thereof. More specifically—(*a*) In *old Eng. law*, authentic documents in official rolls of parchment, particularly of judicial proceedings, and preserved in a court of record. (*b*) In modern use, the original process and pleadings in an action or suit, with the judgment and such other proceedings as are involved therein and required to be included by the law of the forum, which are filed and registered as containing a permanent memorial of the essential features of the adjudication.—**To beat, break, or cut the record**, in contests of speed, skill, endurance, etc., to surpass any recorded exploit in the line in question: as, *to break the record* for the running jump. [Colloq.]—**To discharge of record.** See *discharge*.—**To falsify a record.** See *falsify*.—**Trial by record**, a common-law mode of trial, had when a matter of record is pleaded and the opposite party pleads that there is no such record. The trial is by inspection of the record itself; no other evidence is admissible.=**Syn. 4.** Note, chronicle, account, minute, memorandum.

recordable (rē-kôr'da-bl), *a.* 1. Capable of recordation or being known as past.—2. Worthy of being recorded; deserving of record.

Of very important, very *recordable* events, it was not more productive than such meetings usually are. *Jane Austen*, Emma, xxxviii.

recordance† (rē-kôr'dans), *n.* [< OF. *recordance*, remembrance, < *recorder*, remember: see *record*.] Remembrance; recollection. *Howell*, Letters.

recordari facias loquelam (rek-ôr-dā'rī fā'shi-as lō-kwē'lam). [So called from these words in the writ, in the L. (ML.) form, lit. 'cause the complaint to be recorded': L. *recordari*, pass. of *recordare*, usually deponent *recordari*, remember, ML. also recite, record; *facias*, 2d pers. sing. pres. subj. (in impv. use) of *facere*, make, cause; *loquelam*, acc. of *loquela*, complaint.] In *law*, an old writ directed to the sheriff to make a record of the proceedings of a cause depending in an inferior court, and remove the same to the King's (Queen's) Bench or Common Pleas.

recordation (rek-ọr-dā'shọn), *n.* [Early mod. E. *recordacion*; < OF. *recordation*, *recordacion*, F. recor*dation* = Pr. *recordacio* = Sp. recor*dacion* = Pg. recor*dação* = It. *ricordazione*, < L. *recordatio(n-)*, recalling to mind, recollection, remembrance, < recor*dari*, remember: see *record*.] 1†. Recollection; remembrance.

For suche as be in sorowe, care, or peyne can not sicape soundely, for the often *recordacion* of theyr cuils. *Udall*, Flowers, fol. 138.

To rain upon remembrance with mine eyes,
That it may grow and sprout as high as heaven,
For *recordation* to my noble husband.
Shak., 2 Hen. IV., ii. 3. 61.

Sinfull man, whose very heart should bleed
With *recordation* of soe straunge a deed.
Times' Whistle (E. E. T. S.), p. 68.

2. The act of recording; also, a record; a register.

I think that the wittes of many readers haue diuerted from the weyght of great affaires, to the *recordation* of such pleasaunt thynges.
Peter Martyr (tr. in Eden's First Books on America, ed. [Arber, p. 200).

Ulyss. Why stay we, then?
Tro. To make a *recordation* to my soul
Of every syllable that here was spoke.
Shak., T. and C., v. 2. 116.

Papers pertaining to the probate and *recordation* of wills. *Code of Virginia*, 1873, clv. § 7.

recorder (rē-kôr'dėr), *n.* [< ME. recor*der*, a pipe, **recordour*, *recordowre*, a witness, < OF. *recordeor*, *recordeour*, *recordeur*, one who records or narrates, a witness, a judge, a minstrel, = Sp. recor*dador*, recorder, = It. ricor*datore*, remembrancer, < ML. *recordator*, a recorder, < L. recor*dari*, remember: see recor*d*.] 1†. One who bears witness; a witness. *Prompt. Parv.*, p. 426.—2. One who records; specifically, a person whose official duty is to register writings or transactions, as the keeper of the rolls of a city, or the like.

Elihoreph and Ahiah, . . . scribes; Jehoshaphat the son of Ahilud, the *recorder*. 1 Ki. iv. 3.

I . . . asked the mayor what meant this wilful silence;
His answer was, the people were not wont
To be spoke to but by the *recorder*.
Shak., Rich. III., iii. 7. 30.

3. A judge having local criminal jurisdiction in a city or borough. [The designation is little used in the United States except in the State of New York.]—4†. A musical instrument of the flageolet family, having a long tube with seven holes and a mouthpiece. In some cases an eighth hole, covered with gold-beaters' skin, appears near the mouthpiece, apparently to influence the quality of the tone. The compass of the instrument was about two octaves. Also *record*.

O, the *recorders*! let me see one. . . . Will you play upon this pipe? *Shak.*, Hamlet, iii. 2. 360.

Anon they move
In perfect phalanx to the Dorian mood
Of flutes and soft *recorders*. *Milton*, P. L., i. 551.

5. A registering apparatus; specifically, in *teleg.*, a receiving instrument in which a permanent record of the signals is made. In the earlier form, as invented by Morse, the record was made by embossing on a ribbon of paper by means of a style fixed to one end of a lever, which carried at the other end the armature of an electromagnet. Several devices for using ink were afterward substituted for the style. In Bain's chemical recorder the dots and dashes were registered by

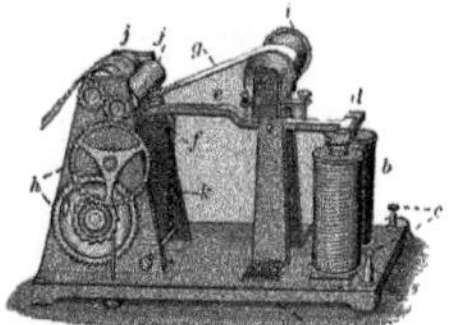

Morse Recorder or Register.

a, base; *b*, electromagnet; *c*, screws for terminals of the wires; *d*, armature; *e*, armature-lever; *f*, stylus, carried by lever *e*; *g*, paper tape; *h*, mechanism for unwinding the tape from the spool *i*, and feeding it between the rolls *j*, *j*; *k*, armature-lever spring.

the chemical decomposition of some substance with which the paper was impregnated, the decomposition being produced on the passage of a current of electricity. In Thomson's siphon recorder, used principally on long cable-lines, a fine glass tube bent into the shape of a siphon is attached to the movable part of the receiving instrument, one arm

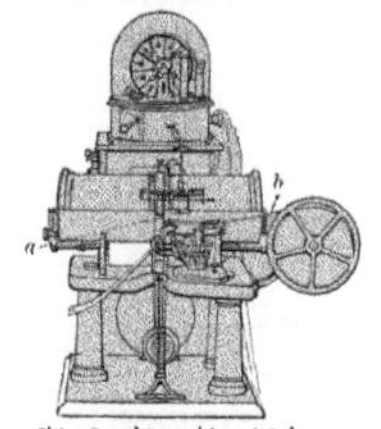

Siphon Recorder. *a*, siphon; *b*, reel.

of which dips into a vessel of ink, and the other moves back and forth at right angles to a strip of paper which is regularly moved by clockwork. The electrification of the ink causes it to be projected from the end of the tube in minute drops, so that the movements of the coil are recorded on the slip of paper in very fine dots very near one another. The principal advantage of this instrument is that only a very feeble current is required to give a permanent record of the signals.

recordership (rę-kôr'dėr-ship), n. [< *recorder* + *-ship*.] The office of recorder; also, the period during which a person holds this office.

record-office (rek'ọrd-of"is), *n.* A place where public records are kept and may be consulted.

recorporification (rē-kôr"pō-ri-fi-kā'shọn), *n.* [< *re-* + *corporification*.] The act of embodying again, or the state of being reëmbodied; the state of being invested anew with a body. *Boyle*, Works, III. 53. [Rare.]

recouch (rē-kouch'), *v. i.* [< OF. (and F.) *recoucher* = It. ri*collocare*, replace; as *re-* + *couch*, *v.*] To lie down again; retire again to a couch. *Sir H. Wotton*, Reliquiæ, p. 386. [Rare.]

recounsel†, *v. t.* A Middle English form of recon*cile*.

recount[1] (rę-kount'), *v. t.* [Early mod. E. also *recompt*; < ME. *recompten*, < OF. *reconter* (cf. F. *raconter*) = Sp. Pg. *recontar* = It. *ricontare*, < ML. *recomputare*, recall to mind, narrate, count, relate, < L. *re-*, again, + *computare*, count, compute: see *count*[1].] 1. To relate in detail; recite; tell or narrate the particulars of; rehearse.

The greatest enimyes to discipline, as Plato *recompteth*, are labours and sleepe.
Lyly, Euphues, Anat. of Wit, p. 143.

I must
Once in a month *recount* what thou hast been.
Shak., Tempest, i. 2. 262.

The lawyer . . .
Went angling down the Saco, and, returning,
Recounted his adventures and mishaps.
Whittier, Bridal of Pennacook.

2†. To account; consider.

Thy wordes as japes ought wel to be *recompted*.
Lydgate, The Bayte.

=**Syn. 1.** To narrate, repeat, detail.

recount[2] (rē-kount'), *v. t.* [< *re-* + *count*[1].] To count again.

recount[2] (rē-kount'), *n.* [< *recount*[2], *v.*] A counting anew; a second or repeated count.

recountal (rę-koun'tạl), *n.* [< *recount*[1] + *-al*.] The act of recounting; a detailed narration. [Rare.]

A mere *recountal* of facts.
A. V. J. Allen, Jonathan Edwards, p. v.

recountment (rẹ̄-kount'ment), *n.* [‹ *recount*[1] + *-ment.*] Relation in detail; recital. [Rare.]

When from the first to last betwixt us two
Tears our *recountments* had most kindly bathed.
Shak., As you Like it, iv. 3. 141.

recoup (rẹ̄-köp'), *v. t.* [‹ OF. *recouper*, *recoupper*, *recolper*, *recoper*, cut again, cut back, cut off, strike, F. *recouper*, cut again, ‹ *re-*, again, + *couper*, cut: see *coupon*, *coupé*.] 1. In *law*, to keep back as a set-off or discount; diminish by keeping back a part: as, to *recoup* from a servant's wages the damages caused by his negligence; to *recoup* from the price of goods sold a claim for breach of warranty as to quality.—2. To reimburse or indemnify for a loss or damage by a corresponding advantage: commonly used reflexively.

Elizabeth had lost her venture; but, if she was bold, she might *recoup herself* at Philip's cost. *Froude.*

It was necessary for parliament to intervene to compel the landlord to *recoup* the tenant for his outlay on the land. *W. S. Gregg*, Irish Hist. for Eng. Readers, p. 161.

3. To return or bring in an amount equal to.

Why should the manager be grudged his ten per cent. . . . when it would be the means of securing to the shareholders dividends that in three or four years would *recoup* their whole capital?
Saturday Rev., Aug. 1, 1868, p. 151. (*Latham.*)

recoup (rẹ̄-köp'), *n.* [‹ OF. *recoupe*, *recouppe*, something cut off, a shred, ‹ *recouper*, cut off: see *recoup*, *v.*] In *law*, the keeping back of something which is due; a deduction; recoupment; discount. *Wharton.*

recoupé (rē-kö-pā'), *a.* [‹ F. *recoupé*, pp. of *recouper*, cut again: see *recoup*, *v.*] In *her.*, cut or divided a second time: especially noting an escutcheon which, being divided per fesse, is divided again barwise, usually in the base.

recouped (rẹ̄-köpt'), *a.* [‹ *recoup* + *-ed*[2], after F. *recoupé*: see *recoup*, *v.*] In *her.*: (*a*) Same as *couped*. (*b*) Same as *recoupé*.

recouper (rẹ̄-kö'pėr), *n.* In *law*, one who recoups or keeps back. *Story.*

recoupment (rẹ̄-köp'mẹnt), *n.* [‹ OF. (and F.) *recoupement*, ‹ *recouper*, recoup: see *recoup*, *v.*] In *law*, the act of recouping or retaining a part of a sum due by reason of a legal or equitable right to abate it because of a cross-claim arising out of the same transaction or relation.

recourt, **recouret**, *v. t.* Obsolete forms of *recover*[2].

recourse (rẹ̄-kōrs'), *n.* [‹ ME. *recours*, ‹ OF. (and F.) *recours* = Pr. *recors* = Sp. Pg. *recurso* = It. *ricorso*, recourse, retreat, ‹ L. *recursus*, a running back, return, retreat, ‹ *recurrere*, pp. *recursus*, run back, retreat: see *recur*. Cf. *course*[1].] 1. Resort for help or protection, as when in difficulty or perplexity.

As I yow saie, so schall it bee,
Ye nedis non othir recours to craue.
York Plays, p. 237.

Hippomenes, therefore, had *recourse* to stratagem.
Bacon, Physical Fables, iv.

Though they [the Italians] might have *recourse* to barbarity as an expedient, they did not require it as a stimulant. *Macaulay*, Machiavelli.

2. Resort; customary visitation or communication.

Vpon their countrye bordered the Nerutans, of whose nature and condicions Cesar founde thus muche by enquirye, that there was no *recourse* of merchants vnto them.
Golding, tr. of Cæsar, fol. 53.

3†. Access; admittance.

I'll give you a pottle of burnt sack to give me *recourse* to him, and tell him my name is Brook.
Shak., M. W. of W., ii. 1. 223.

4†. Return; new attack; recurrence.

Preventive physick . . . preventeth sickness in the healthy, or the *recourse* thereof in the valetudinary.
Sir T. Browne.

5†. Repeated course; frequent flowing.

Priamus and Hecuba on knees,
Their eyes o'ergalled with *recourse* of tears.
Shak., T. and C., v. 3. 55.

6. In *Scots law*, the right of an assignee or disponee under the warrandice of the transaction to recur on the vendor or cedent for relief in case of eviction or of defects inferring warrandice.—**Indorsement without recourse.** See *indorsement.*

recourse† (rẹ̄-kōrs'), *v. i.* [‹ L. *recursare*, run back, freq. of *recurrere*, run back: see *recur*, and cf. *recourse*, *v.*] 1. To return; recur.

The flame departing and *recoursing* thrise ere the wood took strength to be the sharper to consume him.
Foxe, Martyrs, p. 924.

Recoursing to the thinges forepaste, and divining of thinges to come. *Spenser*, F. Q., To the Reader.

2. To have recourse.

The Court *re-courst* to Lakes, to Springs, and Brooks:
Brooks, Springs, and Lakes had the like taste and looks.
Sylvester, tr. of Du Bartas's Weeks, ii., The Lawe.

recourseful† (rẹ̄-kōrs'fụl), *a.* [‹ *recourse* + *-ful.*] Returning; moving alternately.

Thetis' handmaids still in that *recourseful* deep
With those rough Gods of sea continual revels keep.
Drayton, Polyolbion, i. 279.

recover[1] (rē-kuv'ėr), *v. t.* [‹ OF. (and F.) *recouvrir*, cover again, cover up, = Pr. *recobrir* = OCat. *ricobrir* = It. *ricoprire*, cover again, ‹ L. *re-*, again, + *cooperire*, cover, hide: see *cover*[1], *v.*] To cover again or anew. Sometimes written distinctively *re-cover*.

When they [old shoes] are in great danger, I *recover* them. *Shak.*, J. C., i. 1. 28.

recover[2] (rẹ̄-kuv'ėr), *v.* [‹ ME. *recoveren*, *recoevren*, *recocuren*, *recouren*, *recuren*, *rekeveren*, *rekeuren*, ‹ OF. *recovrer*, *recouvrer*, *recuvrer*, *recovrer*, *recoverer*, *recouverer*, regain, recover, get, obtain, etc., F. *recouvrer*, recover, = Pr. Sp. *recobrar* = Pg. *recuperar* = It. *recuperare*, ‹ L. *recuperare*, *reciperare*, get again, regain, recover, revive, restore; in ML. also intr., revive, convalesce, recover; ‹ *re-* + *-cuperare*, *-ciperare*, of uncertain origin; perhaps orig. 'make good again,' ‹ Sabine **cuprus*, *cyprus*, good; or orig. 'desire,' ‹ L. *cupere*, desire: see *Cupid*. Cf. *recuperate*, and *recure*[1], a contracted form, and *cover*[2], a reduced form, of *recover*[2].] **I.** *trans.* 1. To regain; get or obtain again (after it has been lost).

And some to ryde and to *recoeure* that vnrigtfully was wonne. *Piers Plowman* (B), xix. 239.

Than com alle the Bretouns oute of the wode, and haue *recouered* the felde. *Merlin* (E. E. T. S.), iii. 654.

And David *recovered* all that the Amalekites had carried away. 1 Sam. xxx. 18.

I spier'd for my cousin fu' couthy and sweet,
Gin she had *recover'd* her hearin'.
Burns, Last May a Braw Wooer.

2. To restore from sickness, faintness, or the like; cure; heal.

Am I God, . . . that this man doth send unto me to *recover* a man of his leprosy? 2 Ki. v. 7.

He's most desperate ill, sir;
I do not think these ten months will *recover* him.
Fletcher, Rule a Wife, v. 3.

3. To repair the loss or injury of; retrieve; make up for: as, to *recover* lost time.

"For los of catel may *recovered* be,
But los of tyme shendeth us," quod he.
Chaucer, Prol. to Man of Law's Tale, l. 27.

Yet this loss,
Thus far at least *recover'd*, hath much more
Establish'd in a safe unenvied throne.
Milton, P. L., ii. 22.

Diligence . . . gives great advantages to men: it loses no time, it conquers difficulties, *recovers* disappointments, gives dispatch, supplies want of parts.
Penn, Advice to his Children, iii. § 10.

Jamaica society has never *recovered* the mixture of Buccaneer blood.
Dr. Arnold, Life and Correspondence, p. 505.

He had given a shake to her confidence which it never could *recover*. *J. H. Newman*, Loss and Gain, p. 263.

4. To rescue; save from danger.

That they may *recover* themselves out of the snare of the devil. 2 Tim. ii. 26.

If you will not undo what you have done—that is, kill him whom you have *recovered* [saved from drowning]—desire it not. *Shak.*, T. N., ii. 1. 39.

He fell into the water, near the shore, where it was not six feet deep, and could not be *recovered*.
Winthrop, Hist. New England, I. 291.

5†. To reach by some effort; get; gain; find; come to; return to.

With cormerantes make thy nek long,
In pondys depe thy pray to *recouere*.
Political Poems, etc. (ed. Furnivall), p. 25.

If she be lost, we shal *recovere* another.
Chaucer, Troilus, iv. 406.

Sir And. If I cannot *recover* your niece, I am a foul way out. *Shak.*, T. N., ii. 3. 200.

The forest is not three leagues off;
If we *recover* that, we are sure enough.
Shak., T. G. of V., v. 1. 12.

Your son-in-law came to me so near the time of his going away as it had been impossible to have *recovered* him with a letter at so far a distance as he was lodged.
Donne, Letters, lix.

6†. To reconcile; reëstablish friendly relations with.

What, man! there are ways to *recover* the general again: you are but now cast in his mood; . . . sue to him again, and he's yours. *Shak.*, Othello, ii. 3. 273.

7. In *law*, to obtain by judgment in a court of law or by legal proceedings: as, to *recover* lands in ejectment; to *recover* damages for a wrong, or for a breach of contract. It does not necessarily imply the actual gain of satisfaction or possession, but ordinarily only the obtaining of judgment therefor.

There is no Iuge y-sette of suche trespace
By which of right one may *recouered* be.
Political Poems, etc. (ed. Furnivall), p. 74.

8. In *hunting*, to start (a hare) from her cover or form. *Halliwell.*—9†. To fetch; deal.

He [Pounce] . . . smote the kynge vpon the helme, . . . and whan Pounce wolde have *recovered* a-nother stroke, the kynge spored his horse in to the stour.
Merlin (E. E. T. S.), iii. 391.

10†. To restore to a previous state.

To hiden his desire al in mewe
From every wyght yborne, alle outrely,
But he myghte aught *recovered* be therby.
Chaucer, Troilus, i. 383.

Recover arms (*milit.*), a word of command, in firing, requiring the piece to be brought back or recovered from the position of aim to that of ready.—**To recover one's self.** (*a*) To regain one's strength, consciousness, composure, or the like.

He fell down for dead; . . .
But Robin he soon *recovered himself*,
And bravely fell to it again.
Robin Hood and the Ranger (Child's Ballads, V. 209).

(*b*†) To recoup one's self.

I shall pay the Wager in the Place appointed, and try whether I can *recover myself* at Gioco d'amore, which the Italian saith is a Play to cozen the Devil.
Howell, Letters, I. v. 25.

To recover the wind of, to cause (an animal pursued) to run with the wind, that it may not perceive the snare.

Why do you go about to *recover the wind of* me, as if you would drive me into a toil? *Shak.*, Hamlet, iii. 2. 361.

=**Syn. 1 and 2.** To get back, repair, recruit, recuperate, reëstablish.

II. *intrans.* 1. To regain health after sickness; grow well again: often followed by *of* or *from*.

Go, enquire of Baal-zebub, the god of Ekron, whether I shall *recover of* this disease. 2 Ki. i. 2.

With the help of a surgeon he might yet *recover*.
Shak., M. N. D., v. 1. 317.

2. To regain a former state or condition, as after misfortune or disturbance of mind: as, to *recover* from a state of poverty or depression. In this sense formerly and still sometimes used elliptically without *from*.

Twelue of the men in the flyboat were throwne from the Capstern by the breaking of a barre, and most of them so hurt that some never *recovered* it.
Quoted in *Capt. John Smith's* Works, I. 102.

Two of . . . [the men] fell into the ice, yet *recovered* again. *Winthrop*, Hist. New England, I. 302.

As soon as Jones had a little *recovered* his first surprise.
Fielding, Tom Jones, v. 6.

Just as we were *recovering* the effects of breakfast, the sound of firing from Outram's position summoned all idlers to the front. *W. H. Russell*, Diary in India, I. 284.

3†. To come; arrive; make one's way.

With much ado the Christians *recovered* to Antioch.
Fuller.

4. To obtain a judgment at law; succeed in a lawsuit: as, the plaintiff has *recovered* in his suit.

recover[2] (rẹ̄-kuv'ėr), *n.* [‹ ME. *recover*, *recure*; from the verb.] 1†. Recovery.

He was in peril to deye,
And but if he hadde *recourere* the rather that rise shulde he neure. *Piers Plowman* (B), xvii. 67.

I'le witness when I had recovered him,
The prince's head being split against a rocke
Past all *recover*. *Tragedy of Hoffman* (1631).

2. In *boating*, the movement of the body by which a rower reaches forward from one stroke in preparation for the next: as, the bow oar is slow in the *recover*.

recoverability (rẹ̄-kuv"ėr-ạ-bil'ị-ti), *n.* [‹ *recoverable* + *-ity* (see *-bility*).] The state or property of being recoverable.

recoverable (rẹ̄-kuv'ėr-ạ-bl), *a.* [‹ OF. (and F.) *recouvrable*; as *recover*[2] + *-able*. Cf. *recuperable*.] 1. Capable of being regained or recovered.

You have lost nothing by missing yesterday at the trials, but a little additional contempt for the High Steward; and even that is *recoverable*, as his long paltry speech is to be printed. *Walpole*, Letters, II. 43.

2. Restorable from sickness, faintness, danger, or the like.

It is a long time . . . to spend in [mental] darkness; . . . If I am *recoverable*, why am I thus?
Cowper, To Rev. John Newton, Jan. 13, 1784.

3. Capable of being brought back to a former condition.

A prodigal course
Is like the sun's; but not, like his, *recoverable*.
Shak., T. of A., iii. 4. 13.

4. Obtainable from a debtor or possessor: as, the debt is *recoverable*.

Being the only case in which damages were *recoverable* in any possessory actions at the common law.
Blackstone, Com., III. x.

5. That may be recovered from. [Rare.]

Whether the sicknesse or disease be curable and *recoverable*, yea, or no? *J. Gaule*, Πῦς-μαντία, an. 1652, p. 240.

recoverableness (rḗ-kuv'ėr-ạ-bl-nes), *n.* The state of being recoverable; capability of being recovered.

recoverance† (rḗ-kuv'ėr-ạns), *n.* [< OF. *recoverance*, *recovrance*, *recuvrance*, *recourrance*, F. *recouvrant*, pp. of *recouvrer*, recover: see *recover*[2].] Recovery. *York Plays*, p. 223.

recoveree (rḗ-kuv-ėr-ē'), *n.* [< *recover*[2] + *-ee*[1].] In *law*, the tenant or person against whom a judgment is obtained in common recovery. See *common*.

recoverer[1] (rḗ-kuv'ėr-ėr), *n.* [< ME. *recoverer*, < OF. *recovreor*, *recouvreur*, < *recovrer*, recover: see *recover*[2].] One who recovers; a recoveror.

recoverer[2]†, *n.* [ME., < OF. *recovrier*, aid, help, recovery, < *recovrer*, recover: see *recover*[2].] Aid; help; recovery.

And by that Castell where-of I spoke hadde the saisnes all her *recouerer* and all her socour of the contrey.
Merlin (E. E. T. S.), ii. 185.

recoveror (rḗ-kuv'ėr-ọr), *n.* [< OF. *recovreor*, etc.: see *recoverer*[1].] In *law*, the demandant or person who obtains a judgment in his favor in common recovery. See *common*.

recovery (rḗ-kuv'ėr-i), *n.*; pl. *recoveries* (-iz). [Early mod. E. *recovery*, *recoverie*; < AF. *recovery* (Littleton), OF. *recovree*, *recuvree*, *recouvree*, recovery, < *recovrer*, recover: see *recover*[2], *v.* Cf. *recover*[2], *n.*, and *discovery*.] 1. The act or power of recovering, regaining, retaking, conquering again, or obtaining renewed possession: as, to offer a reward for the *recovery* of stolen goods.

What the devil should move me to undertake the *recovery* of this drum? *Shak.*, All's Well, iv. 1. 38.

Mario Sanudo, a Venetian, . . . lived about the 14th Age, a Man full of zeal for the *recovery* of the Holy Land.
Arbuthnot, Ancient Coins, p. 269.

2. Restoration from a bad to a good condition; especially, restoration from sickness, faintness, or the like; also, restoration from low condition or misfortune.

Let us come in, that we may bind him fast,
And bear him home for his *recovery*.
Shak., C. of E., v. 1. 41.

This year much of the wheat is destroyed, . . . but the Lord hath sent much rain for the *recovery* of the remainder.
N. Morton, New England's Memorial, p. 321.

Pray tell me how you are, and if you are making a good *recovery*. *Sydney Smith*, To Countess Grey.

3†. Attainment; reaching.

To thintent that his adversaryes showld not have ready *recovery* of the shore, and coome a land.
Polydore Vergil, Hist. Eng., xxv. (Camden Soc.), p. 213.

4. In *law*, the obtaining of right to something by a verdict or judgment of court from an opposing party in a suit: as, the *recovery* of debt, damages, and costs by a plaintiff; the *recovery* of costs by a defendant; the *recovery* of land in ejectment. Compare *fine*[1], *n.*, 3.—5. In *fencing*, the return of the fencer to his original position "on guard" after extending himself in the hinge (which see). It is done by raising the left hand sharply, withdrawing the right foot from its place in extension, and flexing the right elbow more or less till the foil or sword is in the proper position to await the opponent's riposte (which see).—**Abolition of Fines and Recoveries Act.** See *fine*[1].—**Common or feigned recovery.** See *common*.

recrayed†, *a.* [ME., < OF. *recreü* (= It. *ricreduto*), pp. of *recroire*, be recreant (see *recreant*), + E. *-ed*[2].] Recreant.

Ac reddestow neuere Regum, thow *recrayed* Mede,
Whi the veniaunce fel on Saul and on his children?
Piers Plowman (B), iii. 257.

recreance (rek'rḗ-ạns), *n.* [< ME. *recreance*, < OF *recreance*, weariness, faintness, faint-heartedness, < *recreant*, weary, faint-hearted, cowardly: see *recreant*.] Recreancy. *Chaucer*.

recreancy (rek'rḗ-ạn-si), *n.* [As *recreance* (see *-cy*).] The quality of being recreant; a cowardly yielding; mean-spiritedness.

Amidst the poignancy of her regrets, her shame for her *recreancy* was sharper still.
Howells, Annie Kilburn, xxvii.

recreandise†, *n.* [ME. *recreaundise*, < OF. *recreandise*, *recreantise*, weakness, cowardice, recreancy, < *recreant*, recreant: see *recreant*.] Recreancy; apostasy; desertion of principle.

I seye nought for *recreaundise*,
For I nought doute of youre servise.
Rom. of the Rose, l. 2107.

recreant (rek'rḗ-ạnt), *a.* and *n.* [< ME. *recreant*, *recreaunt*, *recrayhand*, < OF. *recreant*, *recreaunt*, giving up the contest, acknowledging defeat, weary; as a noun, one who acknowledges defeat, a craven, recreant; < ML. *recreden(t-)s*, ppr. (cf. equiv. *recreditus*, a recreant, prop. pp.) of *recredere* (> OF. *recroire*), give in, recant; *se recredere*, own oneself beaten in a duel or judicial combat; lit. 'believe again,' < L. *re-*, again, + *credere*, believe: see *credent*. Cf. *miscreant*.] **I.** *a.* 1. Ready to yield in fight; acknowledging defeat; hence, craven; cowardly. Compare *craven*.

He that despeireth hym is lyke the coward champioun *recreaunt*, that seith "recreaunt" withoute nede.
Chaucer, Parson's Tale.

Thou wear a lion's hide! doff it for shame,
And hang a calf's-skin on those *recreant* limbs.
Shak., K. John, iii. 1. 128.

2. Unfaithful to duty; betraying trust.

And if I eny man it graunte,
Holdeth me for *recreaunte*.
Rom. of the Rose, l. 4090.

Who, for so many benefits received,
Turn'd *recreant* to God, ingrate and false.
Milton, P. R., iii. 138.

Then and there I . . . offered up a vow . . . that I would in no manner prove *recreant* to her dear memory, or to the memory of the devout affection with which she had blessed me. *Poe*, Tales, I. 449.

II. *n.* One who yields in combat and cries craven; one who begs for mercy; hence, a mean-spirited, cowardly, or unfaithful wretch.

With his craftes gaume he calle,
And callede thame *recrayhandes* alle,
Kynge, knyghtes in-with walle.
Perceval, 610. (*Halliwell.*)

You are all *recreants* and dastards.
Shak., 2 Hen. VI., iv. 8. 28.

We find St. Paul
No *recreant* to this faith delivered once.
Browning, Ring and Book, II. 84.

recreantly (rek'rḗ-ạnt-li), *adv.* [< ME. *recreantly*; < *recreant* + *-ly*[2].] In a recreant or cowardly manner; basely; falsely.

That he wold be dede ful *recreantly*,
Or discomfite wold this cruell geant.
Rom. of Partenay (E. E. T. S.), l. 4436.

recreate[1] (rek'rḗ-āt), *v.* [< L. *recreatus*, pp. of *recreare* (> It. *ricreare* = Sp. Pg. Pr. *recrear* = OF. *recreer*, F. *récréer*), create or make again, revive, refresh, recruit, < *re-*, again, + *creare*, create: see *create*.] **I.** *trans.* To revive or refresh after toil or exertion; reanimate, as languid spirits or exhausted strength; amuse; divert; gratify.

Sweete sauers [savors] greatly *recreatynge* and comfortynge nature.
Peter Martyr (tr. in Eden's First Books on America, [ed. Arber, p. 151).

Go, *recreate* yourselves abroad; go, sport.
B. Jonson, Volpone, v. 3.

Painters, when they work on white grounds, place before them colours mixed with blue and green to *recreate* their eyes. *Dryden*.

As every day brought her stimulating emotion, so every night yielded her *recreating* rest.
Charlotte Brontë, Shirley, xx.

=**Syn.** To reanimate, enliven, cheer, entertain.

II. *intrans.* To take recreation.

They suppose the souls in purgatory have liberty to *recreate*. *L. Addison*, State of the Jews, p. 121. (*Latham.*)

recreate[2] (rē-krḗ-āt'), *v. t.* [< L. *recreatus*, pp. of *recreare*, create again: see *recreate*[1].] To create anew: often written distinctively *re-create*.

On opening the campaign of 1776, instead of reinforcing, it was necessary to *recreate* the army.
Marshall. (*Webster.*)

The mass of men, whose very souls even now
Seem to need *re-creating*.
Browning, Ring and Book, II. 225.

recreation[1] (rek-rḗ-ā'shọn), *n.* [< ME. *recreation*, *recreacyon*, *recreacioun*, < OF. *recreation*, F. *récréation* = Pr. *recreacio* = Sp. *recreacion* = Pg. *recreação* = It. *ricreazione*, recreation, diversion, < L. *recreatio(n-)*, recovery from illness, restoration, < *recreare*, pp. *recreatus*, refresh, revive: see *recreate*[1].] 1. The act of recreating, or the state of being recreated; refreshment of the strength and spirits after toil; amusement; diversion; also, some occupation which serves to recreate or amuse.

Vnkyndely thei kidde them ther kyng for to kenne,
With carefull comforth and colde [poor] *recreacioun*.
York Plays, p. 481.

God never did make a more calm, quiet, innocent *recreation* than angling. *I. Walton*, Complete Angler, i. 5.

Soft *Recreations* fit the Female-kind;
Nature for Men has rougher Sports design'd.
Congreve, tr. of Ovid's Art of Love.

2. A short piece of music introduced among technical exercises for variety and practice in style.—3†. Dinner; refreshment; refection.

We will to our *recreation*. *Shak.*, L. L. L., iv. 2. 173.

=**Syn.** 1. *Amusement*, *Entertainment*, etc. (see *pastime*), sport, play.

recreation[2] (rē-krḗ-ā'shọn), *n.* [< L. *recreatio(n-)*, in lit. sense: see *recreation*[1] and *recreate*[2].] The act of creating or forming anew; a new creation; specifically, in *theol.*, regeneration. Also written *re-creation*.

recreational (rek-rḗ-ā'shọn-ạl), *a.* [< *recreation*[1] + *-al*.] Of, pertaining to, or conducing to recreation. *The Century*, XL. 176.

recreation-ground (rek-rḗ-ā'shọn-ground), *n.* A place set apart for sports and other recreations.

recreative (rek'rḗ-ạ̄-tiv), *a.* [< OF. *recreatif*, F. *récréatif*, diverting, amusing, = Sp. Pg. *recreativo* = It. *ricreativo*, < L. *recreare*, pp. *recreatus*, recreate, revive, restore, etc.: see *recreate*[1].] Tending to recreate; refreshing: giving new vigor or animation; giving relief after labor or pain; amusing; diverting.

Another Vision happned to the same Authoure, as comfortable *recreatyce* as the former was dolorous.
Puttenham, Partheniades.

Let not your recreations be lavish spenders of your time; but choose such which are healthful, short, transient, *recreative*. *Jer. Taylor*, Holy Living, i. 1.

In this "Manual of Sins" . . . our *recreative* monk has introduced short tales, some grave and some he deemed facetious, which convey an idea of domestic life and domestic language. *I. D'Israeli*, Amen. of Lit., I. 138.

recreatively (rek'rḗ-ạ̄-tiv-li), *adv.* In a recreative manner; with recreation or diversion. *Imp. Dict.*

recreativeness (rek'rḗ-ạ̄-tiv-nes), *n.* The quality of being recreative, refreshing, or diverting.

recrement (rek'rḗ-mẹnt), *n.* [< OF. *recrement*, F. *récrément* = Sp. Pg. *recremento*, refuse, < L. *recrementum*, dross, slag, < **recernere*, < *re-*, back, + *cernere*, pp. *cretus*, separate: see *concern*, *concrete*, and cf. *excrement*[1].] 1. Superfluous matter separated from that which is useful; dross; scoria; spume.

Of all the visible creatures that God hath made, none is so pure and simple as light; it discovers all the foulness of the most earthly *recrements*, it mixeth with none of them. *Bp. Hall*, Remains, p. 41.

2. In *med.*, a fluid which, after having been separated from the blood, is returned to it, as the saliva, the secretion of serous membranes, etc.

recremental (rek-rḗ-men'tạl), *a.* [< *recrement* + *-al*.] Consisting of or pertaining to recrement; recrementitious. *Armstrong*, Art of Preserving Health, iii. 254.

recrementitial (rek″rḗ-men-tish'ạl), *a.* [< F. *récrémentitiel*; as *recrement* + *-it-ial*.] Same as *recrementitious*.

recrementitious (rek″rḗ-men-tish'us), *a.* [= Sp. Pg. *recrementicio*; as *recrement* + *-it-ious*.] Drossy; consisting of superfluous matter separated from that which is valuable. *Boyle*, Works, I. 645.

recrew† (rḗ-krö'), *v. t.* [< **recrew*, < OF. *recreue*, *recrue*, a supply, spare stores, recruit, F. *recrue*, supply, addition, recruit, levy: see *recruit*.] To recruit.

One intire troop with some other odd troopers, and some stragling foot, that were to *recrew* other companies.
Prince Rupert's beating up of the Rebel Quarters at Post-[comb and Chinner (1643), p. xvi. (*Davies.*)

recriminate (rḗ-krim'i-nāt), *v.* [< ML. *recriminatus*, pp. of *recriminare* (> It. *recriminare* = Sp. Pg. *recriminar* = OF. *recriminer*, F. *récriminer*), accuse in return, < L. *re-*, back, + *criminari*, accuse: see *criminate*.] **I.** *intrans.* To return one accusation with another; retort a charge; charge an accuser with a like crime.

Such are some of the personalities with which Decker *recriminated*. *I. D'Israeli*, Calamities of Authors, II. 339.

II. *trans.* To accuse in return. [Rare.]

Did not Joseph lie under black infamy? he scorned so much as to clear himself, or to *recriminate* the strumpet.
South.

recrimination (rḗ-krim-i-nā'shọn), *n.* [< OF. *recrimination*, F. *récrimination* = Sp. *recriminacion* = Pg. *recriminação* = It. *recriminazione*, < ML. *recriminatio(n-)*, < *recriminare*, recriminate: see *recriminate*.] 1. The act of recriminating; the meeting of an accusation by a counter-accusation: as, to indulge in mutual *recriminations*.

Let us endeavour to remove this objection, not by *recrimination* (which is too easie in such cases), but by living suitably to our holy Religion.
Stillingfleet, Sermons, II. vi.

Short-sighted and injudicious, however, as the conduct of England may be in this system of aspersion, *recrimination* on our part would be equally ill-judged.
Irving, Sketch-Book, p. 76.

2. In *law*, an accusation, brought by an accused person against the accuser, of being in a similar guilt as charged, or derelict in a corresponding duty; a counter-accusation.

recriminative (rē-krim'i-nā-tiv), *a.* [< *recriminate* + *-ive*.] Of the nature of or pertaining to recrimination; indulging in recrimination; recriminatory. *Imp. Dict.*

recriminator (rē-krim'i-nā-tor), *n.* [Cf. F. *récriminateur* = Sp. *recriminador*, one who recriminates, recriminating; as *recriminate* + *-or*[1].] One who recriminates; one who accuses the accuser of a like crime.

recriminatory (rē-krim'i-nā-tō-ri), *a.* [= F. *récriminatoire* = Pg. *recriminatorio*; as *recriminate* + *-ory*.] Retorting accusation; recriminating.

They seem to have been so entirely occupied with the defence of the French directory, so very eager in finding *recriminatory* precedents to justify every act of its intolerable insolence. *Burke*, A Regicide Peace, iii.

recrossed (rē-krôst'), *a.* In *her.*: (*a*) Having the ends crossed. (*b*) Same as *crossed* when noting a crosslet: thus, a cross crosslet *recrossed* is the same as a cross crosslet crossed.

recrucify (rē-krö'si-fī), *v. t.* [< *re-* + *crucify*.] To crucify again.

By it [wilful sin] we do, as the Apostle teaches, *recrucify* the Son of God, and again expose Him to open shame. *Barrow*, Works, VI. 79.

recrudency (rē-krö'den-si), *n.* [As *recrud(esce)* + *-ency*.] Same as *recrudescence*.

recrudesce (rē-krö-des'), *v. i.*; pret. and pp. *recrudesced*, ppr. *recrudescing*. [= Pg. *recrudescer*, < L. *recrudescere*, become raw again, < *re-*, back, again, + *crudescere*, grow harsh, < *crudus*, raw: see *crude*.] 1. To become raw or exacerbated again.—2. To revive; become alive again; be renewed.

Ideas which have made no part of the waking life are apt to *recrudesce* in the sleep-waking state. *Mind*, IX. 118.

recrudescence (rē-krö-des'ens), *n.* [< F. *recrudescence* = Sp. Pg. *recrudescencia*; as *recrudescen(t)* + *-ce*.] 1. The state of being recrudescent, or becoming raw or exacerbated again. Hence—2. A reopening; renewal; a coming into existence anew; a fresh outbreak.

The king required some regulations should be made for obviating the *recrudescence* of those ignoramus abuses for the future that had been so scandalous before. *Roger North*, Examen, p. 632. (*Davies.*)

That *recrudescence* of military organization which followed the Conquest. *H. Spencer*, Prin. of Sociol., § 525.

3. In *med.*, increased activity of a disease or morbid process after partial recovery.

A kind of *recrudescence* [of scarlet fever], but without the reappearance of the rash, would seem possible up to the eighth week. *Quain*, Med. Dict., p. 1392.

4. In *bot.*, the production of a fresh shoot from the top of a ripened spike.

recrudescency (rē-krö-des'en-si), *n.* [As *recrudescence* (see *-cy*).] Same as *recrudescence*. *Browning*, Ring and Book, I. 578.

recrudescent (rē-krö-des'ent), *a.* [= Pg. *recrudescente*, < L. *recrudescen(t-)s*, ppr. of *recrudescere*, break out afresh, become raw again, < *re-*, again, + *crudescere*, become raw.] 1. Growing raw, sore, or painful again.—2. Coming into existence or renewed vigor again.

recruit (rē-kröt'), *v.* [Formerly also *recrute*; = D. *recruteren* = G. *recrutieren* = Dan. *rekrutere* = Sw. *rekrytera*, < OF. *recruter*, levy, prop. *recluter*, mend, = Pg. *recrutar*, *reclutar*, levy, = Sp. *reclutar*, complete, supply, also recruit, = It. *reclutare*, complete, levy, < ML. *reclutare* (after Rom.), recruit, orig. mend, patch, < L. *re-* + Teut. (AS.) *clūt* (> OF. *clut*), clout, lit. 'rag,' 'piece': see *clout*[1]. The orig. sense was forgotten, and confusion ensued with OF. *recreue*, *recrue*, a supply, spare stores, etc., *recrue*, a levy of troops, prop. an addition, supply, fem. of *recreu*, F. *recru*, pp. of *recroître*, *recroistre*, grow again, < L. *re-*, again, + *crescere*, grow, increase: see *crease*[2], *increase*, etc. Cf. *accrew*, *recrew*, *crew*[1].] I. *trans.* 1. To repair by fresh supplies; supply lack or deficiency in.

Her cheeks glow the brighter, *recruiting* their colour. *Granville*, Phyllis Drinking.

2. To restore the wasted vigor of; renew the health, spirits, or strength of; refresh: as, to *recruit* one's health.

And so I began the world anew; and, by the blessing of God, was again pretty well *recruited* before I left this town. *R. Knox* (Arber's Eng. Garner, I. 385).

I sat down and talked with the family while our guide *recruited* himself with a large dish of thick sour milk. B. *Taylor*, Northern Travel, p. 410.

3. To supply with new men; specifically, to supply with new men for any deficiency of troops; make up by enlistment: as, to *recruit* an army.

His [Amurath's] forces, . . . though daily *recruited* by the new supplies which came to them, yet mouldred away. *North*, tr. of Thevet's Lives.

The Frank population of Cyprus . . . was either constantly diminishing or *recruited* by arrivals from the West. *Stubbs*, Medieval and Modern Hist., p. 168.

4. To provision; take supplies on board of, as a vessel: as in the phrase *to recruit ship*. = **Syn.** Reinforce, replenish.

II. *intrans.* 1. To gain new supplies of anything lost or wasted; gain flesh, health, spirits, etc.

My master, said I, honest Thomas . . . is come to Bath to *recruit*. Yes, sir, I said to *recruit*—and whether for men, money, or constitution, you know, sir, is nothing to him, nor any one else. *Sheridan*, The Rivals, ii. 1.

2. To gain new supplies of men for any object; specifically, to raise new soldiers.

When a student in Holland he there met Carstairs, on a mission into that country to *recruit* for persons qualified to fill the chairs in the several universities of Scotland. *Sir W. Hamilton.*

3. To enter port for supplies, as a vessel.

recruit (rē-kröt'), *n.* [= D. *recruut* = G. *recrut* = Dan. *rekrut* = Sw. *rekryt*, < OF. *recreute* = Sp. *recluta* = Pg. *recruta* = It. *recluta*, recruit; from the verb, confused in OF. with *recrene*, a supply, *recrue*, a levy of troops.] 1. A fresh supply of anything wasted or used, as of provisions and supplies on shipboard, etc.

Carrying also plentiful *recruits* of provisions. *Beverley*, Virginia, i. ¶ 9.

A *Recruit* of new People. *Howell*, Letters, I. i. 38.

The state is to have *recruits* to its strength, and remedies to its distempers. *Burke.*

2. A soldier or sailor newly enlisted to supply the deficiency of an army or a navy; one who has newly filled a vacancy in any body or class of persons.

The powers of Troy
With fresh *recruits* their youthful chief sustain. *Dryden.*

3. A substitute for something wanting. [Rare.]

Whatever Nature has in worth deny'd,
She gives in large *recruits* of needful pride. *Pope*, Essay on Criticism, l. 206.

Port of recruit (*naut.*), a recruiting-station.

recruital (rē-krö'tal), *n.* [< *recruit* + *-al*.] A renewed supply of anything lost or exhausted, especially of strength or vigor, bodily or mental. [Rare.]

Shortly after this communion Mr. Chalmers sought relief and *recruital* in an excursion to Fifeshire. *W. Hanna*, Chalmers, II. 65.

recruiter (rē-krö'tėr), *n.* One who recruits.

recruithood (rē-kröt'hud), *n.* [< *recruit* + *-hood*.] The condition of a recruit; the state or the period of being a recruit. [Rare.]

Old soldiers who read this will remember their green *recruithood* and smile assent. *The Century*, XXIX. 108.

recruiting-ground (rē-krö'ting-ground), *n.* A place or region where recruits are or may be obtained.

The murderers of Cæsar had turned the provinces which they governed into one vast *recruiting-ground* for a last decisive struggle. *W. W. Capes*, The Early Empire, Int.

recruiting-party (rē-krö'ting-pär"ti), *n.* A number of soldiers, in charge of an officer or a non-commissioned officer, who are detached from their regiment or post for the purpose of enlisting recruits.

recruiting-sergeant (rē-krö'ting-sär"jent), *n.* A sergeant deputed to enlist recruits.

recruitment (rē-kröt'ment), *n.* [< F. *recrutement* = Sp. *reclutamiento* = Pg. *recrutamento*, the act of recruiting; as *recruit* + *-ment*.] The act or business of recruiting; the act of raising new supplies of men for an army or a navy.

The theoretical *recruitment* is partly voluntary and partly by lot for the militia. *Fortnightly Rev.*, N. S., XLIII. 40.

Rec. Sec. An abbreviation of *Recording Secretary*.

rect†, *a.* [ME., < L. *rectus*, straight, direct, right: see *right*.] Direct; immediate.

Thus ys mede and mercede as two manere relacions,
Rect and indyrect. *Piers Plowman* (C), iv. 336.

rect. An abbreviation of (*a*) in pharmacy, (*rectificatus*) *rectified*; (*b*) rector.

recta, *n.* Plural of *rectum*.

rectal (rek'tal), *a.* [< *rectum* + *-al*.] Pertaining to or connected with the rectum or straight gut: as, *rectal* parts or organs; *rectal* disease, operation, instrument; *rectal* action, evacuation.—**Rectal alimentation**, the administration of enemeta containing food specially prepared for absorption by the mucous membrane of the large intestine.—**Rectal anæsthesia**, the administration of ether or other anesthetics by the rectum.—**Rectal chemise.** See *chemise*.—**Rectal crises**, paroxysms of pain in the rectum, often with tenesmus, and sensations as of a foreign body, met with in cases of locomotor ataxia.—**Rectal diaphragm**, the sheet of muscles closing the rectal outlet of the pelvis, consisting of the sphincter ani externus superficially, and a deeper layer composed of the levator ani and coccygeus.—**Rectal fissure**, a very painful crack-like opening in the mucous membrane of the lower part of the rectum.—**Rectal glands.** See *gland*.

rectalgia (rek-tal'ji-ä), *n.* [NL., < *rectum*, rectum, + Gr. ἄλγος, pain.] Neuralgia of the rectum: same as *proctalgia*.

rectangle (rek'tang-gl), *a.* and *n.* [< OF. (and F.) *rectangle* = Sp. *rectángulo* = Pg. *rectangulo* = It. *rettangolo*, rectangular, a rectangle, < LL. *rectiangulum*, having a right angle, < *rectus*, right, + *angulus*, an angle: see *right* and *angle*[3].] I.† *a.* Rectangular; right-angled.

If all Athens should decree that . . . in *rectangle* triangles the square which is made of the side that subtendeth the right angle is equal to the squares which are made of the sides containing the right angle, . . . geometricians . . . would not receive satisfaction without demonstration thereof. *Sir T. Browne*, Vulg. Err., i. 7.

II. *n.* 1. A quadrilateral plane figure having all its angles right angles and its opposite sides consequently equal. When the adjacent sides are equal, it is a square. The area of a rectangle is equal to the product of two adjacent sides; thus, if its sides measure 6 feet and 4 feet, its area is 24 square feet.

Rectangle.

2. The product of two lengths. Thus, especially in old books, "the *rectangle* under two lines" is spoken of, meaning substantially the product of their lengths.

3†. A right angle.

Th' acute, and the *rect-Angles* too,
Stride not so wide as obtuse Angles doo.
Sylvester, tr. of Du Bartas's Weeks, ii., The Columnes.

rectangled (rek'tang-gld), *a.* [< *rectangle* + *-ed*[2].] 1. Having a right angle or right angles; right-angled.—2. In *her.*, forming a right angle, or broken twice, forming two right angles: said of a heraldic line and also of a division of the field so bounded by it: as, a chief *rectangled*.—**Fesse rectangled.** See *fesse*.

Argent, a Chief Rectangled gules.

rectangular (rek-tang'gū-lär), *a.* [= F. *rectangulaire* = Sp. Pg. *rectangular*, < L. *rectangulus*, rectangled: see *rectangle*.] Right-angled; having an angle or angles of ninety degrees.—**Rectangular coördinates**, in *analytical geom.* See *coördinate*.—**Rectangular hyperbola**, a hyperbola whose asymptotes are at right angles to one another.—**Rectangular map-projection.** See *projection*.—**Rectangular solid**, in *geom.*, a solid whose axis is perpendicular to its base.

Rectangular Hyperbola.

rectangularity (rek-tang-gū-lar'i-ti), *n.* [< F. *rectangularité*; as *rectangular* + *-ity*.] The quality or state of being rectangular or right-angled; rectangularness.

rectangularly (rek-tang'gū-lär-li), *adv.* In a rectangular manner; with or at right angles.—**Rectangularly polarized**, in *optics*, oppositely polarized.

rectangularness (rek-tang'gū-lär-nes), *n.* Rectangularity. *Imp. Dict.*

rectascension (rek-ta-sen'shon), *n.* [< L. *rectus*, right, + *ascensio(n-)*, ascension.] In *astron.*, right ascension.

recti, *n.* Plural of *rectus*.

recticruræus (rek"ti-krö-rē'us), *n.*; pl. *recticruræi* (-ī). [NL., < L. *rectus*, straight, + *crus* (*crur-*), leg: see *cruræus*.] The straight muscle of the front of the thigh; the rectus femoris. *Coues.*

rectifiable (rek'ti-fī-a-bl), *a.* [< F. *rectifiable* = Sp. *rectificable* = Pg. *rectificavel*; as *rectify* + *-able*.] 1. Capable of being rectified, corrected, or set right: as, a *rectifiable* mistake.—2. In *geom.*, said of a curve admitting the construction of a straight line equal in length to any definite part of the curve.

rectification (rek"ti-fi-kā'shon), *n.* [< OF. (and F.) *rectification* = Pr. *rectificatio* = Sp. *rectificacion* = Pg. *rectificação* = It. *rettificazione*, < ML. *rectificatio(n-)*, < *rectificare*, rectify: see *rectify*.] The act or operation of rectifying. (*a*) The act of correcting, amending, or setting right that which is wrong or erroneous: as, the *rectification* of errors, mistakes, or abuses.

The proper *rectification* of the expression would be to insert the adverb as. H. *Blair*, Rhetoric, xxii.

(*b*) The process of refining a substance by repeated or fractional distillation: it is in this way freed from other substances which are either more or less volatile than itself, or from non-volatile matters: as, the *rectification* of spirits. The concentration of sulphuric acid in platinum or glass vessels is sometimes (improperly) called *rectification.*

The process of *rectification* is generally done by redistilling, and filtering through alternate layers of woolen blankets, sand, and granulated bone or maple charcoal. *Pop. Sci. Mo.*, XXIX. 80.

(c) In *geom.*, the determination of a straight line whose length is equal to a given portion of a curve; the finding a formula for the length of the arc of a given curve.—**Rectification of a globe**, in *astron.* and *geog.*, the adjustment of it preparatory to the solution of a proposed problem.

rectified (rek'ti-fīd), *p. a.* [Pp. of *rectify.*] **1.** Made right; corrected.

Be just therefore to thyself all the way, pay thyself, and take acquittances of thyself, all the way, which is only done under the seal and in the testimony of a *rectified* conscience. *Donne*, Sermons, ix.

2. In *hort.*, developed in a desired direction, as when plain tulips are propagated till they sport into variegated forms.

Some of the progeny "break," that is, produce flowers with the variegation which is so much prized. The flower is then said to be "*rectified*." *Encyc. Brit.*, XII. 259.

rectifier (rek'ti-fī-ėr), *n.* [< *rectify* + *-er*[1].] One who or that which rectifies. (a) One who corrects or amends.

Fast friend he was to reformation, . . .
Next *rectifier* of wry law.
S. Butler, Hudibras, I. ii. 432.

(b) One who refines a substance by repeated distillations or by filtering or any other method; specifically, one who rectifies liquors. (c) In the distillation of alcoholic liquors: (1) A vessel or receptacle in which a second distillation is carried on, to condense the liquor and increase its alcoholic strength, or to flavor it by exposing the flavoring substance to the vaporized spirit. (2) A cylindrical vessel continuous with a primary still, in which repeated distillations occur till the alcohol reaches the desired strength. Also called *rectifying column*, and simply *column*. (d) An instrument formerly used for indicating the errors of the compass. *Falconer.*

rectify (rek'ti-fī), *v. t.*; pret. and pp. *rectified*, ppr. *rectifying.* [Early mod. E. *rectifie, rectyfye*; < OF. (and F.) *rectifier* = Pr. Sp. Pg. *rectificar* = It. *rettificare*, < ML. *rectificare*, make right, rectify, < L. *rectus*, straight (= E. *right*), + *-ficare*, < *facere*, make.] **1.** To make right or straight; correct when wrong, erroneous, or false; amend: as, to *rectify* errors, mistakes, or abuses: sometimes applied to persons.

I meant to *rectify* my conscience.
Shak., Hen. VIII., ii. 4. 203.

I onlie strive
To *rectifie* abuses which deprive
The Gospell of his propagation
And plentifull encrease.
Times' Whistle (E. E. T. S.), p. 16.

To *rectifie* a common-wealth with debaushed people is impossible. *Capt. John Smith*, Works, II. 106.

When an authentic watch is shown,
Each man winds up and *rectifies* his own.
Suckling, Aglaura, Epil.

This morning I received from him the following letter, which, after having *rectified* some little orthographical mistakes, I shall make a present of to the public.
Addison, Husbands and Wives.

Specifically—**2.** In *distilling*: (a) To remove impurities from (an alcoholic distillate) and raise to a required proof or strength by repeated distillation. As flavoring materials are often added during rectification in the manufacture of gin, cordials, factitious brandy, etc., the term *rectify* has been extended to the performance of these processes. Hence—(b) To bring (a spirit) by repeated distillation to the strength required, and at the same time to impart to it the desired flavor. See *rectifier.* —**3.** In *chemical manuf.* and in *phar.*: (a) To separate impurities from (a crystalline body) by dissolving and recrystallizing it, sometimes repeatedly, and sometimes also with intermediate washing of the crystals. (b) To raise (a liquid) to a prescribed strength by extraction of some part of its liquid components. Distillation under ordinary atmospheric pressure or in a vacuum, and absorption of water by substances having strong affinity for water, as caustic lime, calcium chlorid, etc., when such substances do not affect the chemical constitution of the substances under treatment, are common processes employed in rectification. (c) To remove impurities from (solutions) by filtering them through substances absorbent of dissolved impurities, but non-absorbent of, and chemically inactive upon, the substance to be purified. Of such materials bone-black is a typical example, especially in sugar-refining. (d) To purify by one or more resublimations.—**4.** In *math.*, to determine the length of (a curve, or a part of a curve) included between two limits.—**5.** In the use of the globes, to place (a globe) in such a position that the solution of a given problem may be effected with it.—**Rectifying developable**, or **rectifying developable surface of a non-plane curve**, a developable surface such that, when it is unrolled into a plane with the curve to which it belongs, the latter is unrolled into a right line: it is perpendicular to the normal and the osculating planes.—**Rectifying edge**, the cuspidal edge of the rectifying developable.—**Rectifying line**, the line common to two consecutive rectifying planes.—**Rectifying plane**, a plane tangent to the rectifying surface.—**To rectify alcoholic liquors.** See def. 2.—**To rectify a sun-dial.** See the quotation.

To rectify the dial (using the old expression, which means to prepare the dial for an observation).
Encyc. Brit., VII. 161.

To rectify the course of a vessel, in *nav.*, to determine its true course from indications of the ship's compass, by correcting the errors of the compass due to magnetic variations and local attractions.—**To rectify the globe**, in *astron.* and *geog.*, to bring the sun's place in the ecliptic on a globe to the brass meridian, or otherwise to adjust it in order to prepare it for the solution of any proposed problem. = **Syn. 1.** *Improve, Better*, etc. (see *amend*), redress, adjust, regulate.

Rectigradæ (rek-tig'rā-dē), *n. pl.* [NL.: see *rectigrade.*] A group of spiders; the rectigrade spiders. Also *Rectigrada, Rectigrades.*

rectigrade (rek'ti-grād), *a.* [< L. *rectus*, straight, + *gradi*, step: see *grade*[1].] Walking straight forward, as a spider; pertaining to the *Rectigradæ*: correlated with *laterigrade*, *saltigrade*, etc.

rectilineal (rek-ti-lin'ē-al), *a.* [Cf. It. *rettilineo* = OF. (and F.) *rectiligne*; < ML. **rectilineus*, having a straight line, < L. *rectus*, straight, right, + *linea*, a line: see *right* and *line*[2], *n.*] Same as *rectilinear.*

rectilineally (rek-ti-lin'ē-al-i), *adv.* Same as *rectilinearly.*

rectilinear (rek-ti-lin'ē-ār), *a.* [< L. *rectilineus*, rectilineal (see *rectilineal*), + *-ar*[3].] Straight-lined; bounded by straight lines; consisting of a straight line or of straight lines; straight: as, a *rectilinear* figure or course. Also *rectilineal.*

Whenever a ray of light is by any obstacle turned out of its *rectilinear* way, it will never return to the same *rectilinear* way, unless perhaps by very great accident.
Newton, Opticks.

Rectilinear lens, motion, etc. See the nouns.—**Rectilinear muscle.** See *muscle*[1], 2.

rectilinearity (rek-ti-lin-ē-ar'i-ti), *n.* [< *rectilinear* + *-ity.*] The state of being rectilinear. *Coleridge.*

rectilinearly (rek-ti-lin'ē-ār-li), *adv.* In a rectilinear manner or direction; in a right line.

rectilinearness (rek-ti-lin'ē-ār-nes), *n.* The quality or condition of being rectilinear. *W. R. Greg*, Misc. Essays, 2d ser., p. 230.

rectilineous† (rek-ti-lin'ē-us), *a.* [= OF. (and F.) *rectiligne* = Sp. *rectilineo* = Pg. *rectilineo* = It. *rettilineo*, < ML. **rectilineus*: see *rectilineal.*] Rectilinear. *Ray*, Works of Creation, i.

rectinerved (rek'ti-nėrvd), *a.* [< L. *rectus*, straight, + *nervus*, nerve, + *-ed*[2].] In *bot.*, having nerves running straight from their origin to the apex or to the margin: said mostly of parallel-nerved leaves.

rection (rek'shon), *n.* [< L. *rectio(n-)*, a leading, guiding, government, direction, < *regere*, pp. *rectus*, rule, govern: see *regent.*] In *gram.*, the influence or power of a word in consequence of which another word in the sentence must have a certain form, in regard to number, case, person, mode, or the like; government.

rectipetality (rek"ti-pe-tal'i-ti), *n.* [< L. *rectus*, straight, + *petere*, seek (see *petition*), + *-al* + *-ity.*] In *bot.*, the inherent tendency of stems to grow in a right line, as indicated by Voechting's experiments with the clinostat. Even parts grown crooked incline to straighten when freed from deflecting influences. This general tendency is modified, however, by an irregularity called *heterauxesis* (which see).

rectirostral (rek-ti-ros'tral), *a.* [Cf. F. *rectirostre*; < L. *rectus*, straight, + *rostrum*, beak, + *-al.*] Having a straight bill or beak, as a bird.

rectischiac (rek-tis'ki-ak), *a.* [< NL. *rectum* + *ischium* + *-ac.*] Same as *ischiorectal.*

rectiserial (rek-ti-sē'ri-al), *a.* [< L. *rectus*, straight, + *series*, a row: see *serial.*] **1.** Disposed in a right line; rectilinear or straight, as a row or series of parts.—**2.** In *bot.*, disposed in one or more straight ranks: specifically used by Bravais, in contrast with *curviserial* (which see), to describe those forms of phyllotaxy in which a second leaf soon stands exactly over any given leaf, and thus all fall into right lines.

rectitic (rek-tit'ik), *a.* [< *rectitis* + *-ic.*] Pertaining to or affected with rectitis.

rectitis (rek-tī'tis), *n.* [NL., < *rectum* + *-itis.*] Inflammation of the rectum.

rectitude (rek'ti-tūd), *n.* [< OF. *rectitude, rectitude*, F. *rectitude* = Pr. *rectetut* = Cat. *rectitut* = Sp. *rectitud* = Pg. *rectitude* = It. *rettitudine*, < L. *rectitudo* (*-in-*), straightness, uprightness, < *rectus*, straight, = E. *right*: see *right.*] **1.** Straightness: as, the *rectitude* of a line. *Johnson.*

Young pines, bent by . . . snowfalls or other accident, in seeking to recover their *rectitude*, describe every graceful form of curve or spiral. *A. B. Alcott*, Tablets, p. 12.

2. Rightness of principle or practice; uprightness of mind; exact conformity to truth, or to the rules prescribed for moral conduct by either divine or human laws; integrity; honesty; justice.

Of the *rectitude* and sincerity of their life and doctrine to judge rightly, wee must judge by that which was to be their rule. *Milton*, Reformation in Eng., i.

Provided they "keep o' the windy side of the law," the great majority are but little restrained by regard for strict *rectitude.* *H. Spencer*, Social Statics, p. 465.

3. Correctness; freedom from error, as of conduct.

Perfectly conscious of the *rectitude* of her own appearance, [she] attributed all this mirth to the oddity of mine.
Goldsmith, The Bee, No. 2.

= **Syn. 2.** *Integrity, Uprightness*, etc. (see *honesty*), principle, equity.

recto (rek'tō), *n.* [1. < L. *recto*, abl. of *rectum*, right: see *right*, n. 2. For recto *folio*, 'the right page,' opposed to *verso folio*, 'the opposite page': L. *recto*, abl. of *rectus*, right; *folio*, abl. of *folium*, a leaf, sheet: see *folio.*] **1.** In *law*, a writ of right, now abolished.—**2.** In *printing*, the right-hand page of an open book: opposed to the left-hand, *reverso* or *verso*. In books as commonly printed, the odd folios, pages 1, 3, 5, 7, etc., are the rectos; the even folios, pages 2, 4, 6, 8, etc., the reverses.

Junius had seen books of this kind printed by Coster (the beginnings of his labours) on the *rectos* of the leaves only, not on both sides. *Encyc. Brit.*, XXIII. 689.

recto-. In composition, rectal; of the rectum.

rectocele (rek'tō-sēl), n. [< NL. *rectum*, rectum, + Gr. κήλη, tumor.] Prolapse of the rectovaginal wall through the vagina. Compare *proctocele.*

rectogenital (rek-tō-jen'i-tal), *a.* [< NL. *rectum*, rectum, + L. *genitalis*, genital.] Of or pertaining at once to the rectum and to the genitalia: as, the *rectogenital* chamber.

rector (rek'tor), *n.* [= OF. *retteur*, *recteur*, F. *recteur* = Pr. Sp. *rector* = Pg. *rector*, *reitor* = It. *rettore*, < L. *rector*, a ruler, director, rector, < *regere*, pp. *rectus*, rule: see *regent.*] **1.** A ruler or governor. [Rare.]

The *rector* of the vniuersitie called to counsell all the doctors regentes that were that tyme at Tholose.
Hall, Hen. VIII., an. 22.

Reason (which in right should be
The special *rector* of all harmony).
B. Jonson, Poetaster, v. 1.

Who shall be the *rectors* of our daily rioting?
Milton, Areopagitica (ed. Hales), p. 24.

2. In the *Ch. of Eng.*, a clergyman who has the charge of a parish and full possession of all the rights and privileges attached thereto. He differs from the *vicar* in that the latter is entitled only to a certain proportion of the ecclesiastical income specially set apart to the vicarage. The latter, again, differs from the *curate* (in the narrower or popular sense of that word), who is subject to the incumbent, whether rector or vicar, and the amount of whose salary is determined not by the law, but by the patron of the benefice, or by the incumbent employing him. Abbreviated *Rect.*

The bishops that are spoken of in the time of the primitive Church, all such as parsons or *rectors* of parishes are with us. *Hooker*, Eccles. Polity, vii. 13.

3. In the United States, a clergyman in charge of a parish in the Protestant Episcopal Church. —**4.** In the *Rom. Cath. Ch.*, an ecclesiastic in charge of a congregation, a college, or a religious house; specifically, the superior of a Jesuit seminary or college.

His wife . . . fled . . . to Saint Jaques le Grand; . . . her death . . . was faithfully confirmed by the *rector* of the place. *Shak.*, All's Well, iv. 3. 69.

5. The chief elective officer of some universities, as in France and Scotland. In Scotland *rector* is also the title of the head master of an academy or important public school: in England, of the heads of Exeter and Lincoln colleges, Oxford. In the United States it is a title assumed by the principals of some private schools: as, the *rectors* of St. John's and St. Paul's. In Germany *rector* is the title of the head of a higher school; the chief officer of a university is styled *rector magnificus* or, when the prince of the country is the titular head, *rector magnificentissimus.*

The *rector* . . . in the first instance was head of the faculty of arts. . . . It was not until the middle of the 14th century that the *rector* became the head of the collective university [of Paris]. *Encyc. Brit.*, XXIII. 835.

6. The presiding officer or chairman of certain gilds and associations.

Many artists . . . as *rectors* represented the greater and lesser art guilds in the city government [of Siena].
C. C. Perkins, Italian Sculpture, p. 51.

Lay rector, in the *Ch. of Eng.*, a layman who receives and possesses the rectorial tithes of a benefice. *Lee*, Glossary. —**Missionary rector**, in the *Rom. Cath. Ch.*, a priest appointed by the bishop to certain parishes in England, in the United States to the charge of any parish.—**Rector of a Board of Trustees**, the presiding officer.

rectorage (rek'tọr-āj), *n.* [OF. *rectorage*, < *rector* + *-age*.] A rector's benefice. Compare *vicarage*.

> Sic pastoris wyll be weill content
> To leif vpon the fer les rent,
> Nor hes sum Vicare for his waige,
> Or Rector for his *Recturaige*.
> Lauder, Dewtie of Kyngis (E. E. T. S.), l. 326.

rectoral (rek'tọr-ạl), *a.* [< F. *rectoral* = Sp. *rectoral*, < ML. **rectoralis*, < L. *rector*, a rector: see *rector*.] Same as *rectorial*. *Blackstone*.

rectorate (rek'tọr-āt), *n.* and *a.* [< F. *rectorat* = Sp. *rectorado* = Pg. *reitorado* = It. *rettorato*, < ML. *rectoratus*, the office of a rector, < L. *rector*, a rector: see *rector*.] **I.** *n.* The office or rank of rector; the period of incumbency of a rector.

> His two *rectorates* in our city, from 1829 to 1845, saw the beginning of a successful revolt against the leadership of Evangelicals. *The American*, X. 297.

II. *a.* Same as *rectorial*.

> His very instructive *rectorate* address on The Backwardness of the Ancients in Natural Science. *Pop. Sci. Mo.*, XIII. 263.

rectoress, rectress (rek'tọr-es, -tres), *n.* [< *rector* + *-ess*.] 1. A female rector or ruler; a governess. [Rare.]

> Be thou alone the *rect'ress* of this isle,
> With all the titles I can thee enstile.
> *Drayton*, Legend of Matilda, st. 39.

> Great mother Fortune, queen of human state,
> *Rectress* of action, arbitress of fate.
> B. *Jonson*, Sejanus, v. 4.

2. A rector's wife. [Humorous.]

> In this way the worthy *Rectoress* consoled herself.
> *Thackeray*, Vanity Fair, xlviii.

Also *rectrix*.

rectorial (rek-tō'ri-ạl), *a.* [< *rector* + *-ial*.] Of or pertaining to a rector or a rectory.—**Rectorial tithes**, tithes payable to the rector, ordinarily those of corn, hay, and wood. Also *great tithes*.

> The tithes of many things, as wood in particular, are in some parishes *rectorial*, and in some vicarial *tithes*.
> Blackstone, Com., I. xi.

rectorship (rek'tọr-ship), *n.* [< *rector* + *-ship*.] 1. The office or rank of a rector.—2†. Rule; direction; guidance.

> Why, had your bodies
> No heart among you? or had you tongues to cry
> Against the *rectorship* of judgement?
> *Shak.*, Cor., ii. 3. 213.

rectory (rek'tọr-i), *n.*; pl. *rectories* (-iz). [< OF. *rectorie* = Sp. *rectoria* = Pg. *reitoria* = It. *rettoria*, < ML. *rectoria*, the office or rank of a rector, < L. *rector*, a rector: see *rector*.] 1. A parish church, parsonage, or spiritual living, with all its rights, tithes, and glebes.—2. A rector's mansion or parsonage-house.

> The *Rectory* was on the other side of the river, close to the church, of which it was the fitting companion.
> *George Eliot*, Felix Holt, xxiii.

rectoscope (rek'tọ-skōp), *n.* [< NL. *rectum*, rectum, + Gr. σκοπεῖν, view.] A speculum used for rectal examination.

rectostenosis (rek″tọ-stẹ-nō'sis), *n.* [NL., < *rectum* (see *rectum*) + Gr. στένωσις, stricture: see *stenosis*.] Stricture of the rectum.

rectotomy (rek-tot'ọ-mi), *n.* [< NL. *rectum*, rectum, + Gr. -τομία, < τέμνειν, ταμεῖν, cut.] The operation for dividing a rectal stricture.

recto-urethral (rek″tō-ụ-rē'thrạl), *a.* Pertaining to the rectum and to the urethra: as, the *recto-urethral* space (a vertical triangular interval between the membranous urethra above and the rectum below, with the apex at the prostate gland).—**Recto-urethral fistula**, a fistula connecting the rectum and the urethra.

recto-uterine (rek-tō-ū'tẹ-rin), *a.* Of or belonging to the rectum and the uterus.—**Recto-uterine folds or ligaments**, semilunar folds of peritoneum passing one on each side from the rectum to the posterior upper surface of the uterus, forming the lateral walls of the rectovaginal pouch.—**Recto-uterine fossa**, the space between the uterus and the rectum above the borders of the recto-uterine folds.—**Recto-uterine pouch.** See *pouch*.

rectovaginal (rek-tō-vaj'i-nạl), *a.* Of or belonging to the rectum and the vagina.—**Rectovaginal fistula**, a fistulous opening between the rectum and the vagina.—**Rectovaginal hernia.** Same as *rectocele*.—**Rectovaginal pouch.** See *pouch*.—**Rectovaginal septum**, the tissues separating the rectum and the vagina.

rectovesical (rek-tō-ves'i-kạl), *a.* [< NL. *rectum* + E. *vesical*.] Of or belonging to the rectum and the bladder.—**Rectovesical fascia.** See *fascia*.—**Rectovesical folds**, the posterior false ligaments of the bladder, lunate folds of peritoneum between the bladder and the rectum in the male. Also called *semilunar folds of Douglas*.—**Rectovesical fossa**, the pouch of peritoneum lying between the bladder and the rectum.—**Rectovesical pouch.** See *pouch*.

rectress, *n.* See *rectoress*.

rectrices, *n.* Plural of *rectrix*.

rectricial (rek-trish'ạl), *a.* [< NL. *rectrix* (*rectric-*), a tail-feather (see *rectrix*), + *-ial*.] Of or pertaining to rectrices.

rectrix (rek'triks), *n.*; pl. *rectrices* (rek-trī'sēz). [< L. *rectrix*, directress, governess, mistress, fem. of *rector*, ruler, governor: see *rector*.] 1. Same as *rectoress*.

> A late queen *rectrix* prudently commanded.
> *Sir T. Herbert*, Travels in Africa. (*Latham.*)

2. In *ornith.*, a tail-feather; one of the long or large quill-feathers of a bird's tail: so called from its use in directing or steering the course of a bird in flight, like a rudder. The rectrices are comparable to the similar large flight-feathers of the wing, called *remiges*. In the *Saururæ*, or Jurassic birds with long lizard-like bony tail, the rectrices are biserially or distichously arranged in a row on each side of the caudal vertebræ. In all modern birds they are set together in a fan-like manner upon the pygostyle. (See *Eurhipidura*.) In a few birds they are rudimentary, as in grebes. The most frequent number by far is twelve, which prevails (with few anomalous exceptions) throughout the great order *Passeres*, and also in very many other birds of different orders. In many picarian birds the number is ten; in a very few eight. In various water-birds the rectrices run up to higher numbers, twenty-four being probably the maximum. There is normally always an even number, these feathers being paired. In size, shape, and texture they are endlessly varied, giving rise to all the different shapes a bird's tail presents.

rectum (rek'tum), *n.*; pl. *recta* (-tạ̈). [= F. *rectum* = Sp. Pg. *recto* = It. *retto*, < NL. *rectum*, abbr. of L. *rectum intestinum*, the straight intestine: *rectum*, neut. of *rectus*, straight: see *right*.] In *anat.* and *zoöl.*, a terminal section of the intestine, ending in the anus: so called from its comparatively straight course in man; the lower bowel: more fully called *intestinum rectum*. In man the rectum is the continuation of the sigmoid flexure of the colon, beginning about opposite the promontory of the sacrum, a little to the left side, and running through the pelvis to the anus. It is supported by a proper duplication of peritoneum, the mesorectum, and other fasciæ. Its structure includes well-developed longitudinal and circular muscular fibers, the latter being aggregated into a stout internal sphincter muscle near the lower end. In animals whose colon has no special sigmoid flexure there is no distinction of a rectum from the rest of the large intestine; and the term applies only to any given or taken terminal section of the bowel, of whatever character. In mammals above monotremes the rectum is entirely shut off from the urogenital organs, ending in a distinct anus; but in most animals it ends in a cloaca common to the digestive and urogenital systems. The rectum receives the refuse of digestion, and retains the feces until voided. See cuts under *intestine*, *peritoneum*, *Pulmonata*, *Pycnogonida*, *Appendicularia*, and *Blattidæ*.—**Columns of the rectum.** See *column*.

rectus (rek'tus), *n.*; pl. *recti* (-tī). [NL., abbr. of L. *rectus musculus*, straight muscle: *rectus*, straight: see *right*.] In *anat.*, one of several muscles so called from the straightness of their course, either in their own axis or in the axis of the body or part where they lie.—**Recti capitis**, five pairs of small muscles, the anticus major and minor, posticus major and minor, and the lateralis, all arising from the lower part of the occipital bone and inserted into the transverse processes of the upper cervical vertebræ.—**Rectus abdominis externus.** Same as *pyramidalis* (*a*).—**Rectus abdominis internus**, the straight muscle of the abdomen, in the middle line in front, mostly inclosed in an aponeurotic sheath formed by the tendons of other abdominal muscles, usually intersected by several transverse tendons, and extending from the pubis to the sternum, in some animals to the top of the sternum.—**Rectus femoris**, the anterior part of the quadriceps extensor. It is a fusiform, bipennate muscle, arising by two heads from the ilium, and inserted into the base of the patella. See cut under *muscle*[1].—**Rectus lateralis**, the lateral straight muscle of the head, arising from the transverse process of the axis, and inserted into the jugular process of the occipital.—**Rectus medialis oculi.** Same as *rectus oculi internus*.—**Rectus oculi externus, inferior, internus, superior**, the external, inferior, internal, superior straight muscle of the eyeball, turning the ball outward, downward, inward, or upward. See cut under *eyeball*.—**Rectus sternalis**, in man, an occasional slip lying lengthwise upon the sternum, representing the prolongation upward of the rectus abdominis externus, as is normal in many animals.—**Rectus thoracis**, in man, an occasional slip, similar to the last, but lying deep-seated, supposed to represent the continuation upward of the rectus abdominis internus.

recubant (rek'ụ-bạnt), *a.* [< L. *recuban(t-)s*, ppr. of *recubare*, lie back: see *recubation*.] Lying down; reclining; recumbent.

recubation (rek-ụ-bā'shọn), *n.* [< L. *recubare*, pp. *recubatus*, lie upon the back, lie back, recline: see *recumbent*.] The act of lying down or reclining. [Rare.]

> The French and Italian translations, expressing neither position of session or *recubation*, do only say that he placed himself at the table. *Sir T. Browne*, Vulg. Err., v. 6.

recueil (rē-kėy'), *n.* [F., a collection: see *recule*[2].] A collection of writings.

recuile†, *v.* and *n.* An obsolete form of *recoil*[1].

recuilement†, *n.* An obsolete form of *recoilment*.

recule[1]†, *v.* and *n.* An obsolete form of *recoil*[1].

recule[2]†, *n.* [ME., also *recuyell*, < OF. *recueil*, F. *recueil*, a collection, < *recueillir*, collect: see *recollect*.] A collection of writings; a book or pamphlet. *Caxton; Halliwell.*

recultivate (rē-kul'ti-vāt), *v. t.* [< *re-* + *cultivate*. Cf. OF. *recultiver*, recultivate.] To cultivate anew.

recultivation (rē-kul-ti-vā'shọn), *n.* [< *recultivate* + *-ion*.] The act of cultivating anew, or the state of being cultivated anew.

recumb† (rẹ-kum'), *v. i.* [< L. *recumbere*, lie back, recline: see *recumbent*.] To recline; lean; repose.

> The king makes an overture of pardon and favour unto you, upon condition that any one of you will *recumbe*, rest, lean upon, or roll himself upon the person of his son.
> *Barrow*, Works, II. iv.

recumbence (rẹ-kum'bẹns), *n.* [< *recumben(t)* + *-ce*.] Same as *recumbency*.

> A *recumbence* or reliance upon Christ for justification and salvation. *Lord North*, Light to Paradise, p. 64.

recumbency (rẹ-kum'bẹn-si), *n.* [As *recumbence* (see *-cy*).] 1. The state of being recumbent; the posture of reclining, leaning, or lying.

> But relaxation of the languid frame,
> By soft *recumbency* of outstretched limbs,
> Was bliss reserved for happier days.
> *Cowper*, Task, i. 82.

2. Rest; repose; idleness.

> When the mind has been once habituated to this lazy *recumbency* and satisfaction, . . . it is in danger to rest satisfied there. *Locke.*

3. The act of reposing or resting in confidence.

> There are yet others [Christians] who hope to be saved by a bare act of *recumbency* on the merits of Christ.
> *Bp. Atterbury*, Sermons, II. xiv.

recumbent (rẹ-kum'bẹnt), *a.* [< L. *recumben(t-)s*, ppr. of *recumbere*, lie back, recline, < *re-*, back, + *cubare*, lie: see *cumbent*.] 1. Leaning; reclining.

> The Roman *recumbent* . . . posture in eating was introduced after the first Punic war.
> *Arbuthnot*, Ancient Coins, p. 134.

2. Reposing; inactive; idle; listless.

> What smooth emollients in theology
> *Recumbent* virtue's downy doctors preach!
> *Young*, Night Thoughts, iv. 644.

3. In *zoöl.* and *bot.*, noting a part that leans or reposes upon anything.—**Recumbent hairs**, in *entom.*, hairs that lie partly against the surface, but are not pressed close to it.

recumbently (rẹ-kum'bẹnt-li), *adv.* In a recumbent manner or posture.

recuperability (rẹ-kū″pẹ-rạ-bil'i-ti), *n.* [< *recuperable* + *-ity* (see *-bility*).] Ability to recuperate; power of recuperation. [Rare.]

> A state of almost physiological *recuperability*.
> *Alien. and Neurol.*, VII. 463.

recuperable (rẹ-kū'pẹ-rạ-bl), *a.* [< ME. *recuperable*, < OF. *recuperable* = Sp. *recuperable* = Pg. *recuperavel*, < ML. **recuperabilis*, < L. *recuperare*, recover, recuperate: see *recuperate*, *recover*[2]. Cf. *recoverable*.] Recoverable; that may be regained.

> And hard it is to ravysshe a treasour
> Which of nature is not *recuperable*.
> *Lydgate*, The Tragedies.

> Therfore, if thou yet by counsaile arte *recuperable*,
> Flee thou from idlenesse and alway be stable.
> *Sir T. Elyot*, The Governour, i. 13.

recuperate (rẹ-kū'pẹ-rāt), *v.*; pret. and pp. *recuperated*, ppr. *recuperating*. [< L. *recuperatus*, pp. of *recuperare*, *reciperare* (> It. *recuperare* = Sp. Pg. *recuperar* = F. *récupérer*), get again, regain, recover, revive, restore, ML. also intr., revive, convalesce, recover: see *recover*[2], the older form in E.] **I.** *trans.* 1. To recover; regain: as, to *recuperate* one's health or spirits.—2. To recoup. [Rare.]

> More commonly he [the agent] paid a fixed sum to the clergyman, and *recuperated* himself by a grinding tyranny of the tenants. *Lecky*, Eng. in 18th Cent., xvi.

II. *intrans.* To recover; regain strength or health. [U. S.]

recuperation (rẹ-kū-pẹ-rā'shọn), *n.* [< OF. *recuperation*, F. *récupération* = Sp. *recuperacion* = Pg. *recuperação* = It. *recuperazione*, < L. *recuperatio(n-)*, a getting back, regaining, recovery, < *recuperare*, pp. *recuperatus*, regain, recover: see *recuperate* and *recover*[2].] 1. Recovery, as of something lost.

> The reproduction or *recuperation* of the same thing that was before. *Dr. H. More*, Mystery of Godliness, p. 225.

2. Specifically, recovery of strength or health.

recuperative (rẹ-kū'pẹ-rā-tiv), *a.* [= Sp. Pg. *recuperativo*, < L. *recuperativus*, recoverable, < *recuperare*, pp. *recuperatus*, recover: see *recover*[2] and *recuperate*.] Tending to recovery;

pertaining to recovery, especially of strength or health.

The seasons being in turn *recuperative*, . . . even the frosts of winter impart virtues that pass into summer, preserving the mind's vigor and fertility during the reign of the dog-star. *A. B. Alcott*, Table-Talk, p. 68.

recuperator (rē-kū'pe-rā-tor), *n.* [= Sp. Pg. *recuperador*, < L. *recuperator*, a recoverer, < *recuperare*, pp. *recuperatus*, recover: see *recuperate*.] 1. One who or that which recuperates or recovers.—2. That part of the Ponsard furnace which answers the same purpose as the regenerator of the Siemens regeneration furnace. See *regenerator*.

recuperatory (rē-kū'pe-rā-tō-ri), *a.* [= Sp. Pg. *recuperatorio*, < L. *recuperatorius*, < *recuperator*, a recoverer, < *recuperare*, pp. *recuperatus*, recover: see *recuperate*.] Same as *recuperative*. *Bailey*.

recur (rē-kėr'), *v. i.*; pret. and pp. *recurred*, ppr. *recurring*. [< OF. *recourer*, *recorir*, *recourre*, *recourir*, F. *recourir* = Pr. *recorre* = Cat. *recorrer* = Sp. *recurrir* = Pg. *recorrer* = It. *ricorrere*, < L. *recurrere*, run back, return, recur, < *re-*, back, + *currere*, run: see *current*[1].] 1. To go or come back; return: literally or figuratively.

When the fear of Popery was over, the Tories *recurred* to their old principles. *Brougham.*

And Fancy came and at her pillow sat, . . .
And chased away the still-*recurring* gnat.
Tennyson, Three Sonnets to a Coquette, i.

2. To return in thought or recollection.

He . . . had received a liberal education at a charity school, and was apt to *recur* to the days of his muffin-cap and leathers. *Barham*, Ingoldsby Legends, I. 25.

3. To return to the thought or mind.

When any word has been used to signify an idea, that old idea will *recur* in the mind when the word is heard. *Watts*, Logic, I. vi. § 3.

Acted crime,
Or seeming-genial venial fault,
Recurring and suggesting still.
Tennyson, Will.

4. To resort; have recourse; turn for aid.

For if his grace were minded, or would intend to do a thing inique or unjust, there were no need to *recur* unto the pope's holiness for doing thereof. *Bp. Burnet*, Records, I. ii., No. 22.

5. To occur again or be repeated at stated intervals, or according to some rule.

Food, sleep, amusement *recur* in uniform succession. *Bacon*, Advancement of Learning, ii. 272.

In volcanic archipelagos . . . the greater eruptions usually *recur* only after long intervals. *Darwin*, Geol. Observations, i. 144.

recure[1]† (rē-kūr'), *v.* [< ME. *recuren*, < OF. *recurer*, < L. *recurare*, restore by taking care of, make whole again, cure, also take care of, prepare carefully, < *re-*, again, + *curare*, care, cure: see *cure*, *v.* The verb was partly confused with *recure*[2], ME. *recouren*, a form of *recoveren*, recover: see *recure*[2], *recover*[2].] I. *trans.* To cure again; cure; heal.

Which [ills] to *recure*, we heartily solicit
Your gracious self to take on you the charge
And kingly government of this your land.
Shak., Rich. III., iii. 7. 130.

Jarumannus, a Faithfull Bishop, who with other his fellow Labourers, by sound Doctrin and gentle dealing, soon *recur'd* them [the East-Saxons] of thir second relaps. *Milton*, Hist. Eng., iv.

II. *intrans.* To recover; get well.

Rabert Lauerawns is wele amendyd, and I hope xall *recure*. *Paston Letters*, I. 112.

recure[1]† (rē-kūr'), *n.* [< ME. *recure*; < *recure*[2], partly < *recure*[1], *v.*] Recovery.

Recure to fynde of myn adversite.
Lydgate, Complaint of a Lover's Life, l. 681.

Had she been my daughter,
My care could not be greater than it shall be
For her *recure*. *Middleton*, Spanish Gypsy, iii. 2.

recure[2]† (rē-kūr'), *v. t.* [Early mod. E. also *recoure*; < ME. *recuren*, *recouren*, var. of *recoveren*, recover: see *recover*[2].] To recover; get again.

Fredom of kynde so lost hath he
That never may *recured* be.
Rom. of the Rose, l. 4920.

But Hector fyrst, of strength most assured,
His stede agayne hath anone *recured*.
Lydgate, Troye (1555), sig. P, v. (*Halliwell.*)

For sometimes Paridell and Blandamour
The better had, and bet the others backe:
Eftsoones the others did the field *recoure*.
Spenser, F. Q., IV. ix. 25.

recureful† (rē-kūr'fůl), *a.* [< *recure*[1] + *-ful*.] Curative; healing.

Let me forever hide this staine of beauty
With this *recureful* maske.
Chapman, Gentleman Usher, v. 1.

recureless† (rē-kūr'les), *a.* [< ME. *rekeurles*; < *recure*[1] + *-less*.] Incapable of recovery or remedy; incurable.

Ye are to blame to sette yowre hert so sore,
Sethyn that ye wote that hyt [ys] *rekeurles*.
MS. Cantab. Ff. i. 6, f. 14. (*Halliwell.*)

My *recureless* sore. *G. Ferrars.*

'Tis foolish to bewail *recureless* things.
Greene, James the Fourth, ii.

recurelessly† (rē-kūr'les-li), *adv.* So as not to be cured.

Recurelessly wounded with his own weapons.
Greene, Groats-worth of Wit (Works, ed. Dyce, Int., p. xxvi.).

recurrence (rē-kur'ens), *n.* [= F. *récurrence*; as *recurren(t)* + *-ce*.] 1. The act of recurring, or the state of being recurrent; return.

Atavism, which is the name given to the *recurrence* of ancestral traits, is proved by many and varied facts. *H. Spencer*, Prin. of Biol., § 83.

2. Resort; the having recourse.

In the use of this, as of every kind of alleviation, I shall insensibly go on from a rare to a frequent *recurrence* to the dangerous preparations. *Jer. Taylor.*

recurrency (rē-kur'en-si), *n.* [As *recurrence* (see *-cy*).] Same as *recurrence*. *Bailey*.

recurrent (rē-kur'ent), *a.* and *n.* [< OF. *recurrent*, F. *récurrent* = Pg. *recurrente* = It. *ricorrente*, < L. *recurren(t-)s*, ppr. of *recurrere*, run back, return, recur: see *recur*.] I. *a.* 1. Recurring; returning from time to time; reappearing; repeated: as, *recurrent* pains of a disease. *Prof. Blackie*.

The music would swell out again, like chimes borne onward by a *recurrent* breeze. *George Eliot*, Mill on the Floss, v. 1.

Nature, with all her changes, is secure in certain noble *recurrent* types. *Stedman*, Vict. Poets, p. 150.

2. In *crystal.*, noting a crystal which exhibits an oscillatory combination of two sets of planes. See *oscillatory*.—3. In *anat.*, turned back in its course, and running in a direction the opposite of its former one: specifically noting the inferior laryngeal branch of the pneumogastric. See the following phrases.—4. In *entom.*, turning back toward the base: as, a *recurrent* process.—**Posterior interosseous recurrent artery**, a branch of the posterior interosseous artery which gives off branches in the region of the olecranon which anastomose with the superior profunda, posterior ulnar recurrent, and radial recurrent arteries.—**Radial recurrent artery.** See *radial*.—**Recurrent arteries of the deep palmar arch**, branches which pass from the upper side of the palmar arch and anastomose with branches of the anterior carpal arch.—**Recurrent branch of the ophthalmic nerve**, a small branch arising near the Gasserian ganglion, and running backward across the fourth nerve to be distributed in the tentorium.—**Recurrent fever.** See *fever*[1].—**Recurrent fibroid tumor.** Same as *small spindle-cell sarcoma*. See *sarcoma*.—**Recurrent laryngeal.** See *laryngeal*.—**Recurrent mania.** Same as *periodical mania*.—**Recurrent nerve.** Same as *meningeal nerve* (which see, under *nerve*).—**Recurrent nerve of the inferior maxillary**, a branch from the inferior maxillary as it passes through the foramen ovale, which passes back into the skull through the foramen spinosum, giving rise to two branches, one going to the great wing of the sphenoid, the other to the mastoid cells.—**Recurrent nerve of the superior maxillary**, a branch given off from the superior maxillary near its origin, which passes to the dura mater and middle meningeal artery.—**Recurrent nervure** of an insect's wing. (*a*) A branch which is more or less turned toward the base of the wing, in a direction contrary to the nervure from which it arises. Many of these recurrent nervures are distinguished. (*b*) A vein of the wing which, after running toward the apex, is bent or curved back toward the base, as in many *Coleoptera*.—**Recurrent pulse.** See *pulse*[1].—**Recurrent radial artery**, an artery which arises from the radial artery near its origin, and anastomoses with the anterior terminal branch of the superior profunda.—**Recurrent sensibility**, the sensibility manifested by the anterior root of a spinal nerve. This is due to fibers derived from the posterior root.—**Recurrent tibial arteries.** (*a*) The *posterior*, arising near the perforation of the interosseous membrane, and anastomosing with the lower articular popliteal arteries. (*b*) The *anterior*, a larger branch, arising just behind the perforation of the interosseous membrane, and anastomosing with the lower articular popliteal arteries.—**Recurrent ulnar arteries.** (*a*) The *anterior*, arising from the upper part of the ulnar, and joining the anastomotic branch of the brachial. (*b*) The *posterior*, arising a little lower than the anterior (though they often have a common origin), and communicating with the inferior profunda, the anastomotic, and posterior interosseous recurrent.

II. *n.* Any recurrent nerve or artery.

recurrently (rē-kur'ent-li), *adv.* In a recurrent manner; with recurrence.

For a long time I had under observation a middle-aged man who, throughout his life, has *recurrently* been tormented by this parasite. *B. W. Richardson*, Preventive Medicine, p. 568.

recurring (rē-kėr'ing), *p. a.* Returning again.—**Recurring continued fraction.** See *continued fraction*, under *continued*.—**Recurring decimal.** See *decimal*.—**Recurring series**, in *alg.*, a series in which the coefficients of the successive powers of x are formed from a certain number of the preceding coefficients according to some invariable law. Thus, $a + bx + (a + b)x^2 + (a + 2b)x^3 + (2a + 3b)x^4 + (3a + 5b)x^5 + \ldots$ is a recurring series.—**Recurring utterances**, a form of aphasia in which the patient can repeat only the word last uttered when taken ill.

recursant (rē-kėr'sant), *a.* [< L. *recursan(t-)s*, ppr. of *recursare*, run or hasten back, come back, return, recur, freq. of *recurrere*, run back, recur: see *recur*.] In *her.*, turned in a way contrary to the usual position, or with the back displayed instead of the front. Thus, an eagle *recursant* shows the back of the bird with the wings crossed.—**Displayed recursant.** See *displayed*.

recursion (rē-kėr'shon), *n.* [< L. *recursio(n-)*, a running back, return, < *recurrere*, pp. *recursus*, run back, return: see *recur*.] Return. [Rare.]

When the receiver was full of air, the included pendulum continued its *recursions* about fifteen minutes. *Boyle*, Works, I. 61.

recurvant (rē-kėr'vant), *a.* [< L. *recurvan(t-)s*, ppr. of *recurvare*, bend or curve backward, turn back: see *recurve*.] In *her.*, of a serpent, coiled up, with the head projecting from the folds; bowed-embowed.

recurvate (rē-kėr'vāt), *v. t.* [< L. *recurvatus*, pp. of *recurvare*, bend backward, curve back: see *recurve*.] Same as *recurve*. *Imp. Dict.*

recurvate (rē-kėr'vāt), *a.* [< L. *recurvatus*, pp.: see *recurvate*, *v.*] In *bot.* and *zoöl.*, recurved.

recurvation (rē-kėr-vā'shon), *n.* [< *recurvate* + *-ion*.] The act or process of recurving; the state of being curved up or back: opposed to *decurvation*: as, the *recurvation* of a bird's bill. Also *recurvature*, *recurvity*.

By a serpentine and trumpet *recurvation*, it [the windpipe] ascendeth again into the neck. *Sir T. Browne*, Vulg. Err., iii. 27.

recurvature (rē-kėr'vā-tūr), *n.* [< *recurvate* + *-ure*.] Same as *recurvation*.

recurve (rē-kėrv'), *v.* [= OF. *recorber*, *recurber*, *recourber*, F. *recourber* = Pr. Pg. *recurvar*, < L. *recurvare*, bend or curve backward, turn up or back, < *re-*, back, + *curvare*, curve: see *curve*, *v.*] I. *trans.* To curve back; turn backward. Also *recurvate*.

II. *intrans.* To be recurved.

recurved (rē-kėrvd'), *p. a.* 1. In *bot.*, curved back or downward: as, a *recurved* leaf, petal, etc.—2. In *zoöl.*, bent upward: the opposite of *decurved*: as, the *recurved* beak of the avoset.

recurviroster (rē-kėr-vi-ros'tėr), *n.* [< NL. *recurvirostrus*, < L. *recurvus*, bent or curved back, crooked (see *recurvous*), + *rostrum*, beak, bill: see *rostrum*.] A bird of the genus *Recurvirostra*; an avoset.

Recurvirostra (rē-kėr-vi-ros'trä), *n.* [NL., fem. of *recurvirostrus*: see *recurviroster*.] A genus of precocial limicoline grallatorial birds, type of the family *Recurvirostridæ*, having a long and very slender depressed and recurved bill, extremely long slender legs, and four toes, the three front ones of which are webbed; the avosets. The body is depressed, and the under parts are clothed with thick plumage like a duck's, so that the birds swim with ease by means of their webbed feet. See *avoset*. Also called *Avocetta*.

recurvirostral (rē-kėr-vi-ros'tral), *a.* [As *recurviroster* + *-al*.] Having a recurved bill, as an avoset; belonging to the genus *Recurvirostra*; pertaining to a recurviroster.

Recurvirostridæ (rē-kėr-vi-ros'tri-dē), *n. pl.* [NL., < *Recurvirostra* + *-idæ*.] A family of wading birds with long and slender bill and legs, typified by the genus *Recurvirostra*, and divided into the *Recurvirostrinæ* and *Himantopodinæ*; the avosets and stilts.

Recurvirostrinæ (rē-kėr"vi-ros-trī'nē), *n. pl.* [NL., < *Recurvirostra* + *-inæ*.] A subfamily of *Recurvirostridæ*, having the characters of the genus *Recurvirostra*, as distinguished from those of *Himantopus*, and including only the avosets.

recurvity (rē-kėr'vi-ti), *n.* [< L. *recurvus*, bent back (see *recurvous*), + *-ity*.] Same as *recurvation*. *Bailey*.

recurvo-patent (rē-kėr'vō-pat"ent), *a.* [< L. *recurvus*, bent back, + *paten(t-)s*, open, spreading: see *patent*[1].] In *bot.*, bent back and spreading.

recurvous (rē-kėr'vus), *a.* [= Pg. *recurvo* = It. *ricurvo*, < L. *recurvus*, bent or curved back, < *re-*, back, + *curvus*, curve: see *curve*.] Bent backward.

recusance (rek'ū-zans), *n.* [< *recusan(t)* + *-ce*.] Same as *recusancy*.

The parliament now passed laws prohibiting Catholic worship, and imposing a line of one shilling, payable each Sunday, for *recusance*. *W. S. Gregg*, Irish Hist. for Eng. Readers, p. 54.

recusancy (rek'ū-zan-si), *n.* [As *recusance* (see *-cy*).] 1. Obstinate refusal or opposition.

> It is not a *recusancy*, for I would come; but it is an excommunication, I must not.
> *Donne*, Devotions, III., Expostulation.

> If any one, or two, or ten, or twenty members of congress should manifest symptoms of *recusancy*, . . . the weird sisters of ambitious hearts shall play before their eyes images of foreign missions, and departments, and benches of justice. *R. Choate*, Addresses, p. 339.

2. The state of being a recusant.

> The papists made no scruple of coming to our churches; *recusancy* was not then so much as a chrisom, not an embryo. *Jer. Taylor*, Works (ed. 1835), II. 98.

> There is also an inferior species of *recusancy* (refusing to make the declaration against popery enjoined by statute 30 Car. II. st. 2, when tendered by the proper magistrate). *Blackstone*, Com., IV. iv.

> We shall see that mere *recusancy* was first made punishable, later on in the reign, by the Second Act for Uniformity of Edward.
> *R. W. Dixon*, Hist. Church of Eng., xv., note.

3. The tenets of the recusants, or adherence to those tenets.

> The penalties of *recusancy* were particularly hard upon women, who . . . adhered longer to the old religion than the other sex. Hallam, Const. Hist., vii., note.

recusant (rek'ū-zant or rē-kū'zant), *a.* and *n.* [< OF. *recusant*, F. *récusant* = Sp. Pg. *recusante* = It. *ricusante*, < L. *recusan(t-)s*, ppr. of *recusare*, reject, object: see *recuse*.] I. *a.* Obstinate in refusal; specifically, in *Eng. hist.*, refusing to attend divine service in Anglican churches, or to acknowledge the ecclesiastical supremacy of the crown.

> No *recusant* lord might have a vote in passing that act.
> *Clarendon.*

II. *n.* 1. One obstinate in refusing; one who will not conform to general opinion or practice.

> The last rebellious *recusants* among the family of nations. *De Quincey.*

> He that would not take the oath should be executed, though unarmed; and the *recusants* were shot on the roads, . . . or as they stood in prayer.
> *Bancroft*, Hist. U. S., II. 411.

2. Specifically, in *Eng. hist.*, one who refused to attend divine worship in Anglican churches, or to acknowledge the ecclesiastical supremacy of the crown. Heavy penalties were inflicted on such persons, but they pressed far more lightly on the simple recusant or nonconformist than on the Roman Catholic recusant, the chief object being to secure national unity and loyalty to the crown, in opposition to papal excommunications, which declared British subjects absolved from their allegiance (as in 1570), and to plots against the government. The name *recusant*, though legally applied to both Protestants and Roman Catholics, was in general given especially to the latter.

> As well those restrained . . . as generally all the papists in this kingdom, not any of them did refuse to come to our church, and yield their formal obedience to the laws established. And thus they all continued, not any one refusing to come to our churches, during the first ten years of her Majesty's [Queen Elizabeth's] government. And in the beginning of the eleventh year of her reign, Cornwallis, Bedingfield, and Silyarde were the first *recusants*, they absolutely refusing to come to our churches. And until they in that sort began, the name of *recusant* was never heard of amongst us.
> *Sir Edward Coke* [in 1607], in Blunt, Annotated Book of [Common Prayer, p. 24.

recusation (rek-ū-zā'shon), *n.* [< OF. *recusation*, F. *récusation* = Pr. *recusatio* = Sp. *recusacion* = Pg. *recusação* = It. *ricusazione*, < L. *recusatio(n-)*, a declining, refusal, objection, protest, also nausea, rejection, < *recusare*, pp. *recusatus*, object, decline, reject: see *recuse*.] In *law*, the interposition of an objection or challenge for cause to a judge or arbitrator, or to an expert appointed by a court; also, the objection or challenge so presented.

> He [Bonner], to deface his Authority (as he thought), did also then exhibit in writing a *Recusation* of the Secretaries Judgment against him.
> *Foxe*, Martyrs, II. 35, an. 1549.

recusative (rē-kū'zā-tiv), *a.* [< *recuse* + *-ative*.] Tending or prone to recuse or refuse; refusing; denying; negative. [Rare.]

> The act of the will produces material and permanent events; it is acquisitive and effective, or *recusative* and destructive, otherwise than it is in any other faculties.
> *Jer. Taylor*, Rule of Conscience, IV. i. 1.

recuse (rē-kūz'), *v. t.*; pret. and pp. *recused*, ppr. *recusing*. [< OF. *recuser*, F. *récuser* = Pr. Sp. Pg. *recusar* = It. *ricusare*, < L. *recusare*, object, decline, reject, refuse, protest against, plead in defense, < *re-*, back, + *causa*, a cause: see *cause*. Cf. *accuse*.] To refuse; reject; specifically, in *law*, to reject or challenge (a judge or juror) as disqualified to act.

> Yet she [the queen] nevertheless persisting in her former wilfulness and in her Appeal, which also by the said Judges was likewise *recused*, incontinently departed out of the Court. *Bp. Burnet*, Records, I. ii., No. 28.

> A judge may proceed notwithstanding my appeal, unless I *recuse* him as a suspected judge. *Ayliffe*, Parergon.

recussion (rē-kush'on), *n.* [< L. *recutere*, pp. *recussus*, strike back, beat back, etc., < *re-*, back, + *quatere*, strike, shake: see *quash*[1]. Cf. *concussion*, *discussion*, *percussion*.] The act of beating back. *Bailey.*

red[1] (red), *a.* and *n.* [< ME. *red*, *reed*, *rede*, earlier *read*, *reod*, < AS. *reád* = OS. *rōd* = OFries. *rād* = D. *rood* = MLG. *rōt*, LG. *rod* = OHG. MHG. *rōt*, G. *rot*, *roth* = Icel. *rauthr* = Sw. Dan. *röd* = Goth. *rauths* (*raud-*), red; cf. AS. *reód* (= Icel. *rjódhr*), red, *rud*, *rudu*, redness (see *rud*); < AS. *reódan*, make red, kill, = Icel. *rjódha* (pret. *raudh*), redden (see *red*[1], *v.*); akin to L. *ruber* (*rubr-*, for *ruthr-*, = Gr. ἐρυθρός), red, *rufus*, red, *rubidus*, dark-red, *rubere*, turn red, blush, *rubicundus*, red, reddish, *russus*, reddish, *rutilus*, reddish, *robigo*, rust, etc.; Gr. ἐρυθρός, red, ἔρευθος, redness, ἐρευθεῖν, redden; Ir. Gael. *ruadh* = W. *rhudd*, red; OBulg. *rŭdrŭ*, red, *rŭdieti*, blush, etc., *ruda*, metal, etc., = Bohem. Pol. *ruda*, ore, rust, mildew, etc., = Russ. *ruda*, ore, mineral, a mine, blood, etc.; Lith. *rudas*, *rusvas*, red-brown, *raūdas*, *raudónas*, red, *raudà*, red color; Skt. *rudhira*, red, blood, *rohita* (for **rodhita*), red. From the E. root, besides *redden*, *reddish*, etc., are derived *rud*, *ruddle*, *ruddock*, *ruddy*, *rust*, etc.; from the L. are derived E. *ruby*, *rubescent*, *rubric*, *rubicund*, *rufous*, *russet*, *rutilate*, *rutilant*; from the Gr. are *Erythræa*, *erythric*, etc. *Red*, like *lead*[2] (led), with which it is phonetically parallel, had in ME. a long vowel, which has become shortened. The long vowel remains, however, in the surnames *Read*, *Reade*, *Reed*, *Reid*, which represent old forms of the adj., and the existence of which as surnames explains the almost total absence of the expected surname *Red*, parallel to *Black*, *Brown*, *White*, etc. As a noun, cf. ME. *rede*, redness, = OHG. *rōtī*, G. *röthe*, redness, red; from the adj.] I. *a.* 1. Of a bright, warm color resembling that of blood or of the highest part of the primary rainbow. See II.

> Dropes *rede* as ripe cherrees,
> That fro his flesshe gan lave.
> *Holy Rood* (E. E. T. S.), p. 217.

> The ladye blushed scarlette *redde*,
> And fette a gentill sighe.
> *Sir Cauline* (Child's Ballads, III. 181).

> Your colour, I warrant you, is as *red* as any rose.
> *Shak.*, 2 Hen. IV., ii. 4. 28.

2. Ultra-radical; revolutionary; violent: from the use of a red flag as a revolutionary emblem: as, a *red* republican.

> Ev'n tho' thrice again
> The *red* fool-fury of the Seine
> Should pile her barricades with dead.
> *Tennyson*, In Memoriam, cxxvii.

> The Social Democratic Federation has degenerated into a *red* Anarchist organization. *The Nation*, XLVII. 450.

Black-breasted red game. See *game*[1].—**Neither flesh, fowl, nor good red herring**, nondescript; lacking distinctive character; neither one thing nor another: same as *neither hay nor grass*.—**Order of the Red Eagle.** See *eagle*.—**Red adder.** Same as *copperhead*, 1. *Bartlett*.—**Red admiral.** See *admiral*, 5.—**Red algæ**, red or purplish seaweeds constituting the class *Florideæ*. Also known as the *Rhodosporeæ* and *Rhodospermeæ*. See *Rhodospermeæ* and *Algæ*.—**Red ant**, a small ant of a red color, as Pharaoh's ant and some similar species. See cut under *Monomorium*.—**Red antimony.** Same as *kermesite*.—**Red arsenic.** Same as *realgar*.—**Red ash, band-fish, bark, bay.** See the nouns.—**Red bat**, the common New York bat, *Lasiurus* or *Atalapha noveboracensis*, a small reddish bat of wide distribution in North America, and one of the most abundant in eastern parts of the United States. It is rather larger than the brown bat, *Vespertilio subulatus*, and easily recognized by its coloration and the densely furry interfemoral membrane.—**Red bead-vine.** See *Rhynchosia*.—**Red bear-cat**, the panda or wah. See cut under *panda*.—**Red beds**, a conspicuous formation in the Rocky Mountains; a series of deep-red, sandy, gypsiferous strata lying upon the Carboniferous, and generally considered to be of Triassic age. They are often eroded into fantastic and picturesque forms.—**Red beech, beefwood, birch, bird's-eye.** See the nouns.—**Red body**, in *ichth.*, an aggregation of capillaries forming a gland-like body.

> These tufts of radiating capillaries are much localized at various places, as in Esocidæ; or the tufts are so aggregated as to form gland-like *red bodies*, the capillaries reuniting into larger vessels, which again ramify freely round the border of the *red body*.
> *Günther*, Study of Fishes, p. 147.

Red Book. (*a*) A book containing the names of all the persons in the service of the state. (*b*) The Peerage. See *peerage*, 3. [Colloq.]

> I hadn't a word to say against a woman who was intimate with every duchess in the *Red Book*.
> *Thackeray*, Book of Snobs, xxv.

Red Book of the Exchequer, an ancient record in which are registered the names of all the holders of lands per baroniam in the time of Henry II.—**Red buckeye**, a shrub or low tree, *Æsculus Pavia*, of the southern United States. Its flowers are red, and showy in cultivation.—**Red button.** Same as *red rosette*.—**Red cabbage**, a strongly marked variety of the common cabbage, with purple or reddish-brown heads, used chiefly for pickling.—**Red cedar.** See *cedar*, 2.—**Red cent**, a copper cent. The copper cent is no longer current, but the phrase *red cent* remains in use as a mere emphatic form of *cent*: as, it is not worth a *red cent*. [Colloq., U. S.]

> Every thing in New Orleans sells by dimes, bits, and picayunes; and as for copper money, I have not seen the first *red cent*. *B. Taylor*, in N. Y. Tribune. (*Bartlett*.)

Red chalk, chickweed, copper, coral. See the nouns.—**Red cock**, an incendiary fire. [Scottish Gipsies' slang.]

> We'll see if the *red cock* craw not in his bonnie barn yard ae morning before day dawning. *Scott*, Guy Mannering.

Red crab. See *crab*[1], 1.—**Red Crag**, the local name of a division of the Pliocene in England. It is a dull-red iron-stained shelly sandstone of inconsiderable thickness, containing a large number of fossils—molluscan, coralline, and mammalian remains—among which last are the elephant, mastodon, rhinoceros, tapir, hog, horse, hyena, and stag.—**Red cross.** See *cross*[1], and *union jack* (under *union*).—**Red crossbill, currant, deal.** See the nouns.—**Red cusk.** See *red-cusk*.—**Red cypress.** See *Taxodium*.—**Red dace.** See *red-dace*.—**Red deer, ear, elder.** See the nouns.—**Red ensign**, in England, the usual British flag—that is, a plain red flag with the canton filled by the union jack. It is used at sea for all British vessels not belonging to the navy, but previous to 1864 was also the special flag of the so-called Red Squadron of the navy.—**Red fever**, dengue.—**Red fir**, a name of the Oregon pine, and of *Abies nobilis* and *A. magnifica* of the western United States: the last two are trees sometimes 200 feet high, but of moderate economic worth.—**Red flag.** See *flag*[2].—**Red flamingo, fog, fox, game, gilthead, goose, grouper.** See the nouns.—**Red grouse.** Same as *red game*.—**Red gum.** See *red-gum*.—**Red gurnard, hand, hat, hawk.** See the nouns.—**Red hay**, mowburnt hay, in distinction from green hay, or hay which has taken a moderate heat, and from vinny or moldy hay. *Halliwell*. [Prov. Eng.]—**Red heat, hematite, hepatization, herring, Indian.** See the nouns.—**Red iodide of mercury ointment.** See *ointment*.—**Red iron ore.** See *iron*.—**Red ironwood.** See *Darling plum*, under *plum*[1].—**Red jasmine, land.** See the nouns.—**Red lane**, the throat. See *lane*[1], 3. [Slang.]—**Red lattice, lead, linnet.** See the nouns.—**Red lead ore.** Same as *crocoite*.—**Red liquor, lump-fish, magnetism, mahogany.** See the nouns.—**Red man.** Same as *Red Indian*.—**Red manganese, mangrove, maple, marlin, meat.** See the nouns.—**Red Marl Series.** See *marl*[1].—**Red Men's Act**, an act of West Virginia (L. 1882, c. 135) prohibiting the carrying of dangerous weapons, and providing for the punishment of unlawful combinations and conspiracies to injure persons and property, designated in the act as "Red Men," "Regulators," "Vigilance Committees," etc.—**Red milk, minnow, mulberry, mullet.** See the nouns.—**Red murrain on.** Same as *plague on*.

> A *red murrain* o' thy jade's tricks!
> *Shak.*, T. and C., ii. 1. 20.

Red nucleus, ocher, oil, osier. See the nouns.—**Red orpiment.** Same as *realgar*.—**Red owl**, the reddish phase of the common gray screech-owl of the United States, *Scops* (*Megascops*) *asio*, formerly considered a distinct species, now known to be an erythrism.—**Red oxid of manganese.** See *manganese*.—**Red oxid of mercury ointment.** See *ointment*.—**Red pepper.** See *Capsicum*.—**Red perch.** See *perch*[1].—**Red pestilence.** Same as *red plague*.

> Now the *red pestilence* strike all trades in Rome!
> *Shak.*, Cor., iv. 1. 13.

Red phalarope. See *phalarope*.—**Red pheasant**, a tragopan; a pheasant of the genus *Ceriornis*.—**Red phosphorus.** See *phosphorus*, 2.—**Red pimpernel.** See *pimpernel*, 4.—**Red pine.** See *pine*[1].—**Red plague**, a form of the plague characterized, according to the physicians of the middle ages, by a red spot, boil, or bubo. Compare *black death*, under *death*.

> You taught me language, and my profit on 't
> Is, I know how to curse. The *red plague* rid you!
> *Shak.*, Tempest, i. 2. 364.

Red pole, poppy, precipitate. See the nouns.—**Red porphyry.** See *pebbleware*.—**Red puccoon.** See *puccoon*, 1.—**Red rail.** Same as *Virginia rail* (which see, under *rail*[4]).—**Red republican, Ribbon, rosette.** See the nouns.—**Red rock-cod.** See *cod*[2].—**Red roncador.** See *roncador*.—**Red ruffed grouse.** See *ruffed grouse*, under *grouse*.—**Red rust.** See *rust*[1].—**Red sandalwood, red sanderswood.** See the nouns.—**Red sandstone.** See *sandstone*.—**Red saunders**, the sliced or rasped heartwood of *Pterocarpus santalinus*. It imparts a red color to alcohol, ether, and alkaline solutions. It is used for coloring alcoholic liquors, and in pharmacy for coloring tinctures.—**Red seaweeds.** Same as *red algæ*.—**Red silver.** See *proustite* and *pyrargyrite*.—**Red snapper.** See *snapper*.—**Red snow.** See *Protococcus*.—**Red softening**, a form of acute softening of the cerebral substance characterized by a red punctiform appearance due to the presence of blood. See *softening*.—**Red sword-grass moth**, *Calocampa vetusta*: a British collectors' name.—**Red tape.** See *tape*.—**Red tiger.** Same as *cougar*.—**Red tincture.** Same as *great elixir* (which see, under *elixir*, 1).—**Red twin-spot carpet-moth**, a British geometrid moth, *Coremia ferrugata*.—**Red venison.** See *venison*.—**Red viper.** Same as *copperhead*, 1.—**Red vitriol.** Same as *colcothar*.—**Red wind.** See *wind*[2].—**The red chop.** See *the grand chop*, under *chop*[4].—**To fly the red flag.** See *fly*[1].—**To paint the town red.** See *paint*. =**Syn.** Flashing, flaming, fiery, bloody.

II. *n.* 1. A color more or less resembling that of blood or the lower end of the spectrum. *Red* is one of the most general color-names, and embraces colors ranging in hue from rose aniline to scarlet iodide of mercury and red lead. A red yellower than vermilion is called *scarlet*; one much more purple is called *crimson*. A very dark red, if pure or crimson, is called *maroon*; if brownish, *chestnut* or *chocolate*. A pale red—that is, one of low chroma and high luminosity—is called a pink, ranging from rose-pink, or pale crimson, to salmon-pink, or pale scarlet.

2. A red pigment. The most useful reds for painting are carmine, obtained from the cochineal-insect; the lakes and madders, of vegetable origin; vermilion, chrome-red, Indian red, and burnt sienna.

3. An object of a red color, as wine, gold, etc.

> Now kepe yow fro the whyte and fro the *rede*,
> And namely fro the whyte wyn of Lepe,
> That is to selle in Fish strete or in Chepe.
> *Chaucer*, Pardoner's Tale, l. 100.

> No pint of white or *red*
> Had ever half the power to turn
> This wheel within my head.
> *Tennyson*, Will Waterproof.

4. Specifically, a red cent. See under I. [Slang, U. S.]—**5.** A red republican (which see, under *republican*).—**6.** *pl.* The catamenial discharges; menses.—**Adrianople red.** Same as *Turkey red*.—**Alizarin red**, in *leather-manuf.*, a pale flesh-color produced by rubbing the cleansed and trodden skins with a solution of alizarin or extract of madder in weak soda-lye, and rinsing in water. C. T. *Davis*, Leather, p. 735.—**Aniline red.** Same as *fuchsin*.—**Anisol red**, a coal-tar color of the oxy-azo group, formerly used in dyeing silk and wool, but not now a commercial product.—**Antimony red**, a sulphid of antimony suggested as a pigment, but not permanent: used for coloring rubber and the heads of friction-matches.—**Aurora red**, a light red, like that of the spinel ruby.—**Barwood red.** See *barwood*.—**Bengal red**, a coal-tar color used in dyeing. It produces brilliant reds similar to those of eosin, but more blue in tone. It is the alkali salt of tetraiododichloro-fluorescein. Also called *rose bengale*.—**Bristol red**, a dye for stuffs, in favor in the sixteenth century.

> Her kyrtel *Brystow red*.
> *Skelton*, Elynour Rummyng, l. 70.

Brown red. Same as *red ocher* (which see, under *ocher*).—**Cadmium red**, an artists' pigment composed of the cadmium sulphid. It is more orange in hue than vermilion, but is very brilliant and permanent.—**Chica** or **chico red.** See *chico*, 1.—**Cobalt red**, a phosphate of cobalt sometimes used as an artists' color. It is durable, but poor in hue.—**Congo red**, a coal-tar color used in dyeing. It may be applied to cotton and wool, producing a bright scarlet fast to soap, but not to light or acids. It is a sodium salt of a tetrazo dye from benzidine.—**Corallin red**, a coal-tar color used in dyeing, produced by treating aurin with ammonia at a high temperature. It is used by calico- and woolen-printers, but is quite fugitive. See *coralline*, 3.—**English red.** Same as *Venetian red*.—**Fast red**, a coal-tar color used in dyeing a garnet-red on woolen. It is of complex composition, and belongs to the azo-group. Also known in commerce as *rocellin*, *orseillin*, *rubidin*, and *rauracienne*.—**French red**, a coal-tar color used in dyeing, being a mixture of claret-red and naphthol orange.—**Indian red**, an important pigment used by artists and house-painters. Originally it was a natural earth rich in oxid of iron, brought from India. It is now prepared artificially by heating iron sulphate in a reverberatory furnace. The sulphuric acid is driven off, and the iron is immediately oxidized to the red oxid. The color varies from a purple to a light-yellowish red, according to the temperature at which the process is conducted. It is a color of much body, and is very permanent. Also called *Indian ocher*.—**Jewelers' red.** See *jeweler*.—**Light red**, a light yellowish-red oxid of iron prepared similarly to Indian red. It is also sometimes made by calcining Oxford ocher. It is used as an artists' pigment.—**Madder-red.** See *madder*[1].—**Magdala red**, a coal-tar color used to produce bright pinks on silk. It is the hydrochlorid of the base rosa-naphthylamine.—**Mars red**, a pigment used by artists. It is somewhat similar in composition and color to Indian red.—**Mock Turkey red.** See *barwood*.—**Naphthalene red.** See *naphthalene*.—**New red.** See *fuchsin*.—**Paris red.** Same as *minium*.—**Peony red.** Same as *corallin red*.—**Persian red.** Same as the normal form of *Indian red*.—**Phenetol red.** Same as *coccinin*.—**Piccolpasso red**, a name given to the deep red of the Italian majolica, obtained by the use of silicate of alumina, in which there is much oxid of iron, and applied upon the yellow enamel already fired: so called from *Piccolpasso*, a sixteenth-century writer on Italian potteries.—**Pompadour red.** See *rose pompadour*, under *rose*[2].—**Pompeian red.** See *Pompeian*.—**Prussian red.** Same as *Venetian red*.—**Saturnine red.** Same as *red lead* (which see, under *lead*[2]).—**Spanish red.** Same as *Venetian red*.—**Turkey red**, an intense scarlet red produced on fabrics by dyeing with the color-giving principles of the madder-root. This has been almost entirely superseded by exactly the same color produced on fabrics by means of artificial alizarin. See *alizarin*. Also called *Adrianople red*.—**Turkey-red oil**, an oil with which cloth is treated in dyeing the color called Turkey red. It is p epa ed by mixing castor-oil with dilute sulphuric acid; the acid is then washed away with a solution of common salt, and the fatty acids saponified with ammonia. The oil consists chiefly of ammonium sulpho-ricinoleate. Compare *Gallipoli oil*, under *oil*.—**Venetian red**, an important pigment used by artists and house-painters. Formerly it was a natural earth simulating Indian red. It is now made by calcining a mixture of lime and iron sulphate, the resulting product being a mixture of calcium sulphate and oxid of iron in nearly equal proportions. It is somewhat darker than brick-red in color, and is very permanent. (See also *chrome-red*, *claret-red*.)

red[1] (red), *v. t.*; pret. and pp. *redded*, ppr. *redding*. [< ME. *reden*, *readen*, redden, < AS. *reódan*, a strong verb (pret. *reád*, pl. *rudon*), redden, stain with blood, also wound, kill, = Icel. *rjódha* (pret. *raudh*, *rautt*, pp. *rodhinn*), redden with blood (see *red*[1], *a.*); also (and in other languages only) weak, AS. *reádian*, also *reódian*, = G. *röten*, *röthen*, become red; from the adj. Cf. *redden*.] To make red; redden.

> For he did *red* and die them with their own blood.
> *Foxe*, Martyrs, I. 664.

red[2] (red), *v. t.* A dialectal form of *rid*[1].

red[3] (red), *v. t.*; pret. and pp. *red*, ppr. *redding*. [Also *redd*, dial. *rid*; < ME. *reden*, put in order; in part same as *reden*, *redien*, make ready, but prob. from the related Sw. *redo*, prepare, put in order (*reda ut sit hår*, comb out one's hair), = Dan. *rede*, prepare: see *ready*, *v.* This verb has become confused with *red*[2], var. of *rid*[1]: see *rid*[1].] **1.** To put in order; tidy: often with *up*: as, to *red up* a house or one's self.

> When the derke was done, and the day sprange,
> All the renkes to row *redyn* hor shippes,
> Halit out of hauyn to the hegh see,
> There plainly thaire purpos put to an end.
> *Destruction of Troy* (E. E. T. S.), l. 5648.

> When you *rid up* the parlour-hearth in a morning, throw the last night's ashes into a sieve.
> *Swift*, Advice to Servants (House-Maid).

> Jeanie, my woman, gang into the parlour—but stay, that winna be *redd up* yet.
> *Scott*, Heart of Mid-Lothian, xxvi.

> The fire . . . was *redd up* for the afternoon—covered with a black mass of coal, over which the equally black kettle hung on the crook.
> *Mrs. Gaskell*, Sylvia's Lovers, xvi.

2. To disentangle; clear; put a stop to, as a quarrel, by interference; adjust.

> Up rose the laird to *red* the camber.
> *Raid of the Reidswire* (Child's Ballads, VI. 135).

> He maun take part wi' hand and heart; and weel his part it is, for *redding* his quarrel might have cost you dear.
> *Scott*, Guy Mannering, liii.

3. To separate, as two combatants.—**To red one's feet**, to free one's self from entanglement: used chiefly in reference to moral complications.—**To red the hair**, specifically, to comb the hair.

[Now chiefly colloquial in all uses.]

red[4] (red), *n.* [Perhaps < *red*[3].] In *coal-mining*, rubbish; attle; waste. [Prov. Eng.]

red[5] (red), *n.* [Also *redd*; perhaps < *red*[2], *v.*] The nest of a fish; a trench dug by a fish in which to spawn. [Prov. Eng.]

> A trout's *redd* or nest is a mound of gravel which would fill one or even two wheelbarrows.
> *Day*, Fishes of Great Britain and Ireland, II. 105.

red[6], *v.* and *n.* An obsolete or dialectal form of *read*[1].

red-. A form of *re-* used before vowels.

-red. [< ME. *-rede*, *-reden*, *-ræden*, < AS. *ræden*, condition, rule, reckoning, estimation, occurring as second part of about 25 compounds, being a form, with suffix *-en*, of *ræd*, counsel, advice, etc. (= OHG. MHG. *rāt*, advice, counsel, etc., frequent in comp., as *haus-rat*, household things, *hei-rath*, marriage, = AS. *hiw-ræden*, household, = ME. *hired*): see *read*[1], *n.*] A suffix of Anglo-Saxon origin, meaning 'condition,' 'state,' occurring in *hatred*, *kindred* (for **kin-red*), *gossipred*, etc. It is analogous to *-hood*, which has taken its place in a few instances, as in *brotherhood*, *neighborhood*.

redact (rẹ-dakt'), *v. t.* [< OF. *redacter* = Sp. *redactar*, redact, edit, < L. *redactus*, pp. of *redigere* (> F. *rédiger* = D. *redigeren* = G. *redigiren* = Sw. *redigera* = Dan. *redigere*), drive, lead, or bring back, call in, collect, raise, receive, reduce to a certain state, < *red-*, back, + *agere*, drive, do: see *act*.] **1†.** To bring to a specified form or condition; force or compel to assume a certain form; reduce.

> Then was the teste or potsherd [the brasse, golde, and syluer] *redacte* into dust. *Joye*, Expos. of Daniel ii.

> They were now become miserable, wretched, sinful, *redact* to extreme calamity.
> *Bacon*, Works, p. 46. (*Halliwell.*)

> Plants they had, but metals whereby they might make use of those plants, and *redact* them to any form or instruments of work, were yet (till Tubal Cain) to seek.
> *Bp. Hall*, Character of Man.

2. To bring into a presentable literary form; edit.

> I saw the reporters' room, in which they *redact* their hasty stenographs. *Emerson*, Eng. Traits, p. 265.

redacteur (re-dak-tėr'), *n.* Same as *redactor*.

redaction (rẹ-dak'shọn), *n.* [= D. *redaktie* = G. Sw. Dan. *redaktion* = F. *rédaction*, a compiling, also a working over, editing, the editorial staff, = Sp. *redaccion* = Pg. *redacção* = It. *redazione*, < NL. *redactio(n-)*, redaction, < L. *redigere*, pp. *redactus*, lead back, collect, prepare, reduce to a certain state: see *redact*.] **1.** The act of reducing to order; the act of preparing for publication: said of literary or historical matter.

> To work up literary matter and give it a presentable form is neither compiling, nor editing, nor resetting; and the operation performed on it is exactly expressed by *redaction*. *F. Hall*, Mod. Eng., p. 310.

2. A work thus prepared; a special form, edition, or version of a work as digested, revised, or rewritten.

> In an early *redaction* of the well-known ballad of Lord Ronald . . . the name of the unfortunate victim to "eels boil'd in brue" is Laird Rowland.
> *N. and Q.*, 6th ser., XII. 134.

> This fresh discovery does not furnish us with the date of the story, but it gives us the date of one of its *redactions*, and shows it must have existed in the middle of the fourteenth century. *Edinburgh Rev.*, CLXIV. 192.

> Ionic *redaction* of Cynaithos of Chios about the middle of the sixth century. *Amer. Jour. Philol.*, VII. 233.

3. The staff of writers on a newspaper or other periodical; an editorial staff or department. *Imp. Dict.*—**4†.** The act of drawing back; a withdrawal.

> It . . . takes away all reluctation and *redaction*, infuseth a pliable willingness; of wolfish and dogged, makes the will lamb-like and dove-like.
> *Rev. S. Ward*, Sermons, p. 31.

redactor (rẹ-dak'tọr), *n.* [Also, as F., *redacteur*; < F. *rédacteur* = Sp. Pg. *redactor* = It. *redattore*, < NL. *redactor*, an editor, < L. *redigere*, pp. *redactus*, lead back, collect, reduce to a certain state: see *redact*.] One who redacts; one who prepares matter for publication; an editor.

> Each successive singer and *redactor* furnishes it (the primeval mythus) with new personages, new scenery, to please a new audience. *Carlyle*, Nibelungen Lied.

> Distrust of Dorothea's competence to arrange what he had prepared was subdued only by distrust of any other *redactor*. *George Eliot*, Middlemarch, I.

redactorial (rē-dak-tō'ri-ạl), *a.* [< *redactor* + *-ial*.] Of or pertaining to a redactor or redaction; having the character of a redaction.

> Three chief documents, viz. the Yahwistic, the Elohistic, and the Editorial or *Redactorial*.
> *The Academy*, Feb. 11, 1888, p. 92.

redan (rẹ-dan'), *n.* [More prop. *redent*; < OF. *redan*, *redent*, F. *redan* = Pg. *redente*, a double notching or jagging, as in a saw, < L. *re-*, back, + *den(t-)s* = E. *tooth*.] **1.** In *field fort.*, the simplest kind of work employed, consisting of two parapets of earth raised so as to form a salient angle, with the apex toward the enemy and unprotected on the rear. Two redans connected form a *queue d'aronde*, and three connected form a *bonnet à* (or *de*) *prêtre*. Several redans connected by curtains form lines of intrenchment.

Redans.

2. A downward projection in a wall on uneven ground to render it level.—**Redan battery, redan line.** See *battery*, *line*[2].=**Syn. 1.** See *fortification*.

redargue (re-där'gū), *v. t.*; pret. and pp. *redargued*, ppr. *redarguing*. [< OF. *redarguer*, F. *rédarguer*, blame, reprehend, = Pr. *redarguire* = Sp. Pg. *redarguir* = It. *redarguire*, < L. *redarguere*, disprove, confute, refute, contradict, < *red-*, back, against, + *arguere*, argue: see *argue*.] **1.** To put down by argument; disprove; contradict; refute.

> Sir, I'll *redargue* you
> By disputation.
> B. *Jonson*, Magnetick Lady, iii. 4.

> Wherefore, says he, the libel maun be *redargued* by the panel proving her defences.
> *Scott*, Heart of Mid-Lothian, xii.

> Consciousness cannot be explained nor *redargued* from without. *Sir W. Hamilton*.

2†. To accuse; blame.

> When he had *redargued* himself for his slothfulness, he began to advise how he should eschew all danger.
> *Pitscottie*, Chron. of Scotland, p. 19. (*Jamieson.*)

> How shall I be able to suffer that God should *redargue* me at doomsday, and the angels reproach my lukewarmness? *Jer. Taylor*. (*Allibone.*)

redargution† (red-är-gū'shọn), *n.* [ME. *redarguacion*, < OF. *redarguacion*, *redargation* (prop. *redargucion*, *redargution*) = Sp. *redargucion* = It. *redarguizione*, < L. *redargutio(n-)*, a refutation, < *redarguere*, disprove, refute: see *redargue*.] Refutation; conviction.

> To pursue all tho that do reprobacion
> Agayns our lawes by ony *redarguacion*.
> *Digby Mysteries*, p. 33. (*Halliwell.*)

> The more subtile forms of sophisms and illaqueations with their *redargutions*, which is that which is termed elenches. *Bacon*, Advancement of Learning, ii. 224.

redargutory† (re-där'gụ-tọ-ri), *a.* [< *redargut(ion)* + *-ory*.] Tending to redargue or refute; pertaining to refutation; refutatory.

> My privileges are an ubiquitary, circumambulatory, speculatory, interrogatory, *redargutory* immunity over all the privy lodgings. *Carew*, Cœlum Britannicum.

redback (red'bak), *n.* **1.** The red-backed sandpiper, or American dunlin. *A. Wilson*. See cut under *dunlin*. [New Jersey.]—**2.** The pectoral sandpiper, *Tringa maculata*. [Local, U. S.]

red-backed (red'bakt), *a.* Having a red back: as, the *red-backed* sandpiper, *Tringa alpina*; the *red-backed* shrike, *Lanius rufus*; the *red-backed* humming-bird, *Selasphorus rufus*.

red-bass (red'bås), *n.* The redfish, *Sciænops ocellatus*.

red-beaked (red'bēkt), *a.* Same as *red-billed*: as, the *red-beaked* hornbill, *Buceros erythrorhynchus*, of Africa.

redbeard (red'bērd), *n.* The red sponge, *Microciona prolifera*, which commonly grows on oysters, forming a beard on the shell. [Local, U. S.]

red-bellied (red'bel'id), *a.* Having a red belly, or the under parts red: as, the *red-bellied* nuthatch, *Sitta canadensis*; the *red-bellied* snipe, *Macrorhamphus scolopaceus*; the *red-bellied* woodpecker, *Centurus carolinus*; the *red-bellied* monkey of Africa, *Cercopithecus erythrogaster*; the *red-bellied* terrapin, *Chrysemys* or *Pseudemys rubriventris*.—**Red-bellied perch.** See *perch*[1].

redbelly (red'bel"i), *n.* 1. The slider, potter, or red-fender, *Chrysemys rubriventris*, an edible terrapin of the United States. See *red-fender*.—2. The torgoch, a Welsh variety of the char, *Salvelinus umbla*.—3. The red-bellied minnow, *Chrosomus erythrogaster*. [Southern U. S.]—4. The red-bellied perch or sunfish, a centrarchoid, *Lepomis auritus*. [South Carolina.]—5. The red grouper, *Epinephelus morio*. [U. S.]

red-belted (red'bel"ted), *a.* Belted or banded with red: as, the *red-belted* clearwing, a moth, *Trochilium myopæforme*.

redberry (red'ber"i), *n.*; pl. *redberries* (-iz). A plant of the genus *Rhagodia*. [Australia.]

red-billed (red'bild), *a.* Having a red bill or beak, as a bird: as, the *red-billed* curlew, *Ibidorhynchus struthersi*, of Asia; the *red-billed* wood-hoopoe, *Irrisor erythrorhynchus*. See cut under *Irrisor*.

redbird (red'bėrd), *n.* A name of sundry red or partly red birds. Specifically—(*a*) The common bullfinch of Europe, *Pyrrhula vulgaris*. (*b*) The cardinal grosbeak of the United States, *Cardinalis virginianus*. See *cardinal-bird*, and cut under *Cardinalis*. (*c*) The summer tanager, *Piranga æstiva*, or scarlet tanager, *P. rubra*, both of the United States. (*d*) *Pericrocotus speciosus*.

> All day the *red-bird* warbles
> Upon the mulberry near.
> *Bryant*, Hunter's Serenade.

red-blooded (red'blud"ed), *a.* Having red or reddish blood: specifically noting the higher worms, or annelids, in which, however, the blood is often greenish.

redbreast (red'brest), *a.* and *n.* [< ME. *redbreste*; < *red* + *breast*.] I. *a.* Red-breasted.

II. *n.* 1. A small sylviine bird of Europe, *Erithacus rubecula*; the robin, or robin redbreast. See *robin*. [Eng.]

> To relish a love-song like a robin-*redbreast*.
> *Shak.*, T. G. of V., ii. 1. 21.

> The *redbreast* warbles still, but is content
> With slender notes. *Cowper*, Task, vi. 77.

2. The American robin or migratory thrush, *Merula migratoria* or *Turdus migratorius*. See *robin*. [U. S.]—3. The red-breasted sandpiper, or knot, *Tringa canutus*. See *robin-snipe*.—4. The red-bellied sunfish, *Lepomis auritus*.

red-breasted (red'bres"ted), *a.* Having a red or reddish breast.—**Little red-breasted rail.** Same as *Virginia rail* (which see, under *rail*[4]).—**Red-breasted finch**[1]. See *finch*[1].—**Red-breasted goose**, *Anser ruficollis*.—**Red-breasted merganser**, *Mergus serrator*.—**Red-breasted plover.** Same as *redbreast*, 3.—**Red-breasted sandpiper**, *Tringa canutus*.—**Red-breasted snipe.** (*a*) *Macrorhamphus griseus*, the dowitcher: also called *gray snipe*, *brown snipe*, *quail-snipe*, *German snipe* (compare *dowitcher*), *robin-snipe*, *grayback*, *brownback*, *driver*, *sea-pigeon*, and *New York godwit*. (*b*) A misnomer of the American woodcock, *Philohela minor*. [Local, U. S.] (*c*) Same as *redbreast*, 3.

redbuck (red'buk), *n.* The roodebok, *Cephalophus natalensis*. See *roodebok*.

redbud (red'bud), *n.* Any tree of the American species of *Cercis*; the Judas-tree. The best-known, common in the interior and southern United States, is *C. Canadensis*, a small tree, the branches clothed in early spring with fascicles of small flowers of nearly peach-blossom color, followed by rather large heart-shaped pointed leaves. In southwestern woods it is very conspicuous when in blossom, and it is often cultivated for ornament. The flowers have an acid taste, and are said to be used, like those of the Old World Judas-tree, in salads, etc. The name is from the color of the flowers, and doubtless from their bud-like aspect even when open. *C. reniformis*, a Texan and Mexican species, is a smaller tree or a shrub often forming dense thickets, and *C. occidentalis* is a Californian shrubby species.

red-bug (red'bug), *n.* A heteropterous insect, *Dysdercus suturellus*, which damages cotton in the southern United States and in the West Indies. Also called *cotton-stainer*.

redcap (red'kap), *n.* 1. The goldfinch, *Carduelis elegans*, more fully called *King Harry redcap*. [Local, British.]

> The *redcap* whistled; and the nightingale
> Sang loud. *Tennyson*, Gardener's Daughter.

2. A variety of the domestic hen, of English origin. The plumage resembles that of the golden-spangled Hamburg, but is duller; the fowl is larger than the Hamburg; and the flat rose-comb is very large.

3. A specter having long teeth, popularly supposed to haunt old castles in Scotland.

red-capped (red'kapt), *a.* Having red on the head: as, the *red-capped* snake, a venomous Australian species, *Brachysoma diadema*.

red-carpet (red'kär"pet), *n.* A British geometrid moth, *Coremia munitata*.

red-cheeked (red'chēkt), *a.* In *ornith.*, having red lores: as, the *red-cheeked* coly, *Colius erythromelas*.

red-chestnut (red'ches"nut), *n.* A British moth, *Tæniocampa rubricosa*.

redcoat (red'kōt), *n.* A British soldier. [Colloq.]

> King Shames' *red-coats* should be hung up.
> *Battle of Killiecrankie* (Child's Ballads, VII. 155).

> You know the *redcoats* are abroad; . . . these English must be looked to. *Cooper*, Spy, xii.

red-cockaded (red'ko-kā"ded), *a.* Having a tuft of red feathers on each side of the back of the head: only in the phrase *red-cockaded woodpecker*, a bird of the southern United States, *Picus borealis* or *querulus*.

red-cod (red'kod), *n.* A fish of the family *Gadidæ*, *Pseudophycis bacchus*, having two dorsal fins and one anal, of a reddish-silvery color. [New Zealand.]

red-corpuscled (red'kôr"pus-ld), *a.* Having red blood-disks.

red-crested (red'kres"ted), *a.* Having a red crest: as, the *red-crested* duck or pochard, *Fuligula rufina*.

red-cross (red'krôs), *a.* Wearing or bearing a red cross, such as the badge of the Order of the Temple, the cross of St. George, or one with a religious, social, or national meaning: as, a *red-cross* knight (which see, below); the *red-cross* banner, the national flag of Great Britain.

> And their own sea hath whelm'd yon *red-cross* Powers!
> *Scott*, Vision of Don Roderick, Conclusion, st. 2.

Red-cross knight, a knight bearing on his shield or crest a red cross as his principal cognizance, whether as being a Templar or with religious significance, as in Spenser's "Faerie Queene," I. i. 2.

> A *red-cross knight* for ever kneel'd
> To a lady in his shield.
> *Tennyson*, Lady of Shalott.

Red-Cross Society, a philanthropic society founded to carry out the views of the Geneva Convention of 1864. Its objects are to care for the wounded in war, and secure the neutrality of nurses, hospitals, etc., and to relieve suffering occasioned by pestilence, floods, fire, and other calamities.

red-cusk (red'kusk), *n.* A brotuloid fish, *Dinematichthys* or *Brosmophycis marginatus*, of the coast of California, of a pale-reddish color.

redd[1], *v. t.* See *red*[3].

redd[2], *n.* See *red*[5].

red-dace (red'dās), *n.* A common fish of the eastern United States, *Notropis megalops*, formerly named *Leuciscus cornutus*. Also called *redfin* and *rough-head*.

reddet. A Middle English preterit of *read*[1].

redden (red'n), *v.* [< *red*[1] + *-en*[1]. Cf. Icel. *rodhna* = Dan. *rödme*, redden.] I. *intrans.* 1. To become red; grow red.

> For me the balm shall bleed, and amber flow,
> The coral *redden*, and the ruby glow.
> *Pope*, Windsor Forest, l. 394.

Hence—2. To blush; become flushed.

> Sir Roderick, who to meet them came,
> *Redden'd* at sight of Malcolm Græme.
> *Scott*, L. of the L., ii. 27.

II. *trans.* 1. To make red.

> And this was what had *redden'd* her cheek
> When I bow'd to her on the moor.
> *Tennyson*, Maud, xix. 6.

2. To cure (herrings). *Halliwell.* [Prov. Eng.]

reddendo (re-den'dō), *n.* [So called from the first word of the clause in the Latin form, *reddendo inde annuatim*, etc.: L. *reddendo*, abl. of *reddendum*, neut. gerundive of *reddere*, render, return, give up or back: see *render*[2].] In *Scots law*, a clause indispensable to an original charter, and usually inserted in charters by progress. It specifies the feu-duty and other services which have been stipulated to be paid or performed by the vassal to his superior.

reddendum (re-den'dum), *n.* [So called from the first word in the Latin form of the deed or clause (see def.): L. *reddendum*, neut. gerundive of *reddere*, return, render, give up or back: see *render*[2].] In *law*, a reservation in a deed whereby the grantor creates or reserves some new thing to himself, out of what he had granted before. (*Broom and Hadley.*) Thus, the clause in a lease which specifies the rent or other service to be rendered to the lessor is termed the *reddendum*, or *reddendum clause*.

redder (red'ėr), *n.* [< *red*[3] + *-er*[1].] One who settles or puts in order; especially, one who endeavors to settle a quarrel. [Scotch.]

> "But, father," said Jenny, "if they come to lounder ilk ither as they did last time, suldna I cry on you?" "At no hand, Jenny; the *redder* gets aye the warst lick in the fray." *Scott*, Old Mortality, iv.

reddidit (red'i-dit). [L. *reddidit*, 3d pers. sing. pret. ind. of *reddere*, give up, render: see *render*[2].] In *law*, a term used in cases where a man delivers himself in discharge of his bail.

redding[1] (red'ing), *n.* [< ME. *redynge*; verbal n. of *red*[1], *v.*] 1. Reddle. [Prov. Eng.]

> *Redynge* colowre. Rubiculum, rubiatura.
> *Prompt. Parv.*, p. 427.

> The traveller with the cart was a reddleman—a person whose vocation it was to supply farmers with *redding* for their sheep. *T. Hardy*, Return of the Native, i. 1.

2. A compound used to redden the jambs and hearth of an open wood-fireplace. *Bartlett.* [U. S.]

> The brick hearth and jambs aglow with fresh *redding*.
> *Mrs. Whitney*, Leslie Goldthwaite, vii.

redding[2] (red'ing), *n.* [Verbal n. of *red*[3], *v.*] The act or process of clearing up or putting in order.

redding-comb (red'ing-kōm), *n.* A large-toothed comb for combing the hair. (See *red*[3].) *Trans. Amer. Philol. Ass.*, XVII. 42.

reddingite (red'ing-īt), *n.* [< *Redding* (see def.) + *-ite*[2].] A hydrous phosphate of iron and manganese, resembling scorodite in form, found at Branchville, in the town of Redding, Connecticut.

redding-straik (red'ing-strāk), *n.* A stroke received in attempting to separate combatants in a fray; a blow in return for officious interference. Compare *red*[3], 2, 3, and *redder*. [Scotch.]

> Said I not to ye, Make not, meddle not?—Beware of the *redding straik!* You are come to no house o' fair-strae death. *Scott*, Guy Mannering, xxvii.

reddish (red'ish), *a.* and *n.* [< *red*[1] + *-ish*[1].] I. *a.* Of a color approaching red.

> A bright spot, white, and somewhat *reddish*.
> Lev. xiii. 19.

Reddish egrets. See *egret*.—**Reddish light-arches**, a British noctuid moth, *Xylophasia sublustris*.

II. *n.* A reddish color.

reddishness (red'ish-nes), *n.* The state or quality of being reddish; redness in a moderate degree.

> The *reddishness* of copper. *Boyle*, Works, I. 721.

reddition (re-dish'on), *n.* [< F. *reddition* = It. *reddizione*, < L. *redditio(n-)*, a giving back, returning, rendering, also (in gram.) the apodosis, < *reddere*, pp. *redditus*, give back, return, render: see *render*[2]. Cf. *rendition*.] 1. A returning of something; restitution; surrender.

> She [Ireland] is . . . reduc'd . . . to a perfect obedience, . . . partly by voluntary *reddition* and desire of protection, and partly by conquest.
> *Howell*, Vocall Forrest, p. 32.

2. Explanation; rendering.

> When they used [to carry branches] in procession about their altars, they used to pray "Lord, save us; Lord, prosper us"; which hath occasioned the *reddition* of "Hoschiannah" to be, amongst some, that prayer which they repeated at the carrying of the "Hoschiannah," as if itself did signify "Lord, save us."
> *Jer. Taylor*, Works (ed. 1835), I. 288.

3. In *law*, a judicial acknowledgment that the thing in demand belongs to the demandant, and not to the adversary. [Rare.]

redditive (red'i-tiv), *a.* [< L. *redditivus*, of or belonging to the apodosis (in gram.), consequential (cf. *redditio*, the apodosis of a clause), < *reddere*, pp. *redditus*, give back: see *reddition*.] Conveying a reply; answering: as, *redditive* words.

> For this sad sequel is, if not a relative, yet a *redditive* demonstration of their misery; for after the infection of sin follows that infliction of punishment.
> *Rev. T. Adams*, Works, I. 261.

reddle (red'l), *n.* [Also *raddle*; var. of *ruddle*[1], q. v.] An earthy variety of hematite iron ore. It is fine-grained, and sufficiently compact to be cut into strips, which are used for various purposes, as for marking sheep and drawing on board. This material is found in several localities in England, and much more rarely in the United States, where it is generally called *red chalk*.

> *Reddle* spreads its lively hues over everything it lights on, and stamps unmistakably, as with the mark of Cain, any person who has handled it for half an hour.
> *T. Hardy*, Return of the Native, i. 9.

reddleman (red'l-man), *n.*; pl. *reddlemen* (-men). [< *reddle* + *-man*.] A dealer in reddle or red chalk, usually a sort of peddler. Also *raddleman*, *ruddleman*.

Raddleman then is a *Reddleman*, a trade (and that a poor one) only in this county [Rutland], whence men bring on their backs a pack of red stones, or ochre, which they sell to the neighbouring countries for the marking of sheep. *Fuller*, Worthies, Rutlandshire, III. 38.

Reddlemen of the old school are now but seldom seen. Since the introduction of railways Wessex farmers have managed to do without these somewhat spectral visitants, and the bright pigment so largely used by shepherds in preparing sheep for the fair is obtained by other routes. *T. Hardy*, Return of the Native, i. 9.

reddock (red'ok), *n.* Same as *ruddock*. [Prov. Eng.]

red-dog (red'dog), *n.* The lowest grade of flour produced in the roller-milling processes. Originally the term was applied to a poor flour made from middlings; now it is applied to the lowest grade produced by the new-process milling.

reddour†, *n.* See *redour*.

red-drum (red'drum), *n.* The southern redfish, or red-bass, *Sciænops ocellatus*, an important food-fish of the Atlantic coast of the United States from Chesapeake Bay southward. See cut under *redfish*.

rede[1]†, *v.* and *n.* See *read*[1].

rede[2]†, *a.*, *n.*, and *v.* An obsolete form of *red*[1].

rede[3]†, *v. t.* An obsolete form of *red*[3].

rede[4]†, *a.* An obsolete variant of *ready*.

redecraft (rēd'kräft), *n.* [A pseudo-archaism, purporting to represent a ME. **rede-craft* or AS. **ræd-cræft*, which was not in use.] The art or power of reasoning; logic. *Barnes.*

red-edge (red'ej), *n.* A bivalve mollusk of the family *Lucinidæ*, *Codakia tigerina*. [Florida.]

redeem (rē-dēm'), *v. t.* [Early mod. E. *redeme*; < OF. *redimer*, vernacularly *raembre*, *reembre*, *raimbre*, *raiembre*, etc., F. *rédimer* = Sp. *redimir* = Pg. *remir* = It. *redimere*, < L. *redimere*, buy back, redeem, < *red-*, back, + *emere*, buy, orig. take: see *emption*, *exempt*, etc. Hence ult. *redemption*, *ransom*, etc.] **1.** To buy back; recover by purchase; repurchase.

If a man sell a dwelling house in a walled city, then he may *redeem* it within a whole year after it is sold. Lev. xxv. 29.

2. Specifically—(*a*) In *law*, to recover or disencumber, as mortgaged property, by payment of what is due upon the mortgage. Commonly applied to the property, as in the phrase "to *redeem* from the mortgage"; but sometimes applied, with the same meaning, to the encumbrance: as, "to *redeem* the mortgage." (*b*) In *com.*, to receive back by paying the obligation, as a promissory note, bond, or any other evidence of debt given by a corporation, company, or individual.—**3.** To ransom, release, or liberate from captivity or bondage, or from any obligation or liability to suffer or be forfeited, by paying an equivalent: as, to *redeem* prisoners, captured goods, or pledges.

Alas, sweet wife, my honour is at pawn;
And, but my going, nothing can *redeem* it.
Shak., 2 Hen. IV., ii. 3. 8.

Prepare to die to-morrow; for the world
Cannot *redeem* ye.
Fletcher (and another), Sea Voyage, v. 2.

Thrice was I made a slave, and thrice *redeem'd*
At price of all I had. *Beau. and Fl.*, Captain, ii. 1.

One Abraham, found a Delinquent, *redeems* himself for seven hundred Marks. *Baker*, Chronicles, p. 82.

If a pawnbroker receives plate or jewels as a pledge or security for the repayment of money lent thereon on a day certain, he has them upon an express contract or condition to restore them if the pledger performs his part by *redeeming* them in due time. *Blackstone*, Com., II. xxx.

4. To rescue; deliver; save, in general.

Redeem Israel, O God, out of all his troubles. Ps. xxv. 22.

How if . . .
I wake before the time that Romeo
Come to *redeem* me? *Shak.*, R. and J., iv. 3. 32.

That valiant gentleman you *redeem'd* from prison.
Fletcher, Beggars' Bush, iv. 3.

Six thousand years of fear have made you that
From which I would *redeem* you.
Tennyson, Princess, iv.

5. In *theol.*, to deliver from sin and spiritual death by means of a sacrifice offered for the sinner. See *redemption* (*c*).

I learn to believe in . . . God the Son, who hath *redeemed* me, and all mankind. *Book of Common Prayer*, Catechism.

Christ hath *redeemed* us from the curse of the law, being made a curse for us. Gal. iii. 13.

6. To perform or fulfil, as a promise; make good by performance: as, to *redeem* an obligation.

Had he lived, I doubt not that he would have *redeemed* the rare promise of his earlier years.
O. W. Holmes, Old Vol. of Life, p. 69.

7. To make amends for; atone for; compensate for.

This feather stirs; she lives; if it be so,
It is a chance which does *redeem* all sorrows
That ever I have felt. *Shak.*, Lear, v. 3. 266.

You have shewn much worth this day, *redeem'd* much error. *Fletcher*, Bonduca, v. 5.

Passages of considerable beauty, especially in the last two acts, frequently occur; but there is nothing to *redeem* the absurdity of the plot.
Gifford, Int. to Ford's Plays, p. xxii.

To *redeem* defeat by new thought, by firm action, that is not easy. *Emerson*, Success.

Detect at least
A touch of wolf in what showed whitest sheep,
A cross of sheep *redeeming* the whole wolf.
Browning, Ring and Book, I. 27.

8. To improve, or employ to the best advantage.

Redeeming the time, because the days are evil.
Eph. v. 16.

He [Voltaire] worked, not by faith, but by sight, in the present moment, but with indefatigable energy, *redeeming* the time. *J. F. Clarke*, Self-Culture, p. 78.

9†. To restore; revive.

Hee wyll *redeme* our deadly drowping state.
Gascoigne, De Profundis, The Auctor.

redeemability (rē-dē-ma-bil'i-ti), *n.* [< *redeemable* + *-ity* (see *-bility*).] Redeemableness. *Imp. Dict.*

redeemable (rē-dē'ma-bl), *a.* [< *redeem* + *-able*.] **1.** Capable of being redeemed; admitting of redemption.—**2.** Capable of being paid off; subject to a right on the part of the debtor to discharge, satisfy, recover, or take back by payment: as, a *redeemable* annuity.

Every note issued is receivable by any bank for debt due, and is *redeemable* by the national government in coin if the local bank should fail. *Harper's Mag.*, LXXX. 458.

Redeemable rights, in *law*, those conveyances in property or in security which contain a clause whereby the grantor, or any other person therein named, may, on payment of a certain sum, redeem the lands or subjects conveyed.

redeemableness (rē-dē'ma-bl-nes), *n.* The state of being redeemable. *Johnson.*

redeemer (rē-dē'mėr), *n.* [< *redeem* + *-er*[1].] **1.** One who redeems, ransoms, or atones for another. See *redemption*.

And his *redeemer* challeng'd for his foe,
Because he had not well mainteind his right.
Spenser, F. Q., II. v. 20.

Specifically—**2.** [*cap.*] The Saviour of the world, Jesus Christ.

The precious image of our dear *Redeemer*.
Shak., Rich. III., ii. 1. 123.

Christian libertie purchas'd with the death of our *Redeemer*. *Milton*, Eikonoklastes, xiii.

My *Redeemer* and my Lord,
I beseech thee, I entreat thee,
Guide me in each act and word.
Longfellow, Golden Legend, ii.

Congregation of the Redeemer, one of several Roman Catholic fraternities, the most famous of which is entitled the *Congregation of the Most Holy Redeemer*. See *Redemptorist*.—**Order of the Redeemer**, an order of the kingdom of Greece, founded in 1834.

redeeming (rē-dē'ming), *p. a.* [Ppr. of *redeem*.] Saving; making amends; noting what is good as exceptional to what is generally bad: as, there is not a single *redeeming* feature in the scheme.

redeemless (rē-dēm'les), *a.* [< *redeem* + *-less*.] Incapable of being redeemed; without redemption; irrecoverable; incurable.

The duke, the hermit, Lodowick, and myselfe
Will change his pleasures into wretched
And *redeemelesse* misery.
Tragedy of Hoffman (1631). (*Nares.*)

redel†, **redelest**, *n.* and *v.* Obsolete forms of *riddle*[1].

redelet, *n.* An obsolete form of *riddle*[2].

redeless†, *a.* [ME. *redeles*, *redles*, < AS. *rǣdleás* (= OHG. *rātilos*, MHG. G. *ratlos* = Icel. *rādhlauss*), without counsel, unwise, confused, < *rǣd*, counsel (see *read*[1], *n.*), + *-leás*, E. *-less*.] Without counsel or wisdom; wild.

For drede of hire drem [she] deulfulli quaked, . . .
& romed than redli al *redles* to hure chapel,
& godly be-sougt God to gode turne hire sweuen.
William of Palerne (E. E. T. S.), l. 2915.

Now, Richard the *redeles*, reweth [have pity] on zou-self,
That lawelesse leddyn zoure lyf, and zoure peple bothe.
Richard the Redeless (ed. Skeat), i. 1.

The opponents of Eadward . . . dreaded that he would "govern by his own unbridled will," that he would be, in a word, what they afterwards called Æthelred—a king *redeless*, or uncounselled.
J. R. Green, Conq. of England, p. 339.

redeliver (rē-dē-liv'ėr), *v. t.* [< OF. *redelivrer*; as *re-* + *deliver*[1].] **1.** To deliver back; return to the sender; restore.

But at the coming of Cesar, when thinges were altered, the Heduanes had theyr hostages *redelivered*, theyr old alyes and confederaces restored, new brought in by Cesar.
Golding, tr. of Cæsar, fol. 154.

My lord, I have remembrances of yours
That I have longed long to *redeliver*.
Shak., Hamlet, iii. 1. 94.

Having assembled their forces, [they] boldly threatned at our Ports to force Smith to *redeliver* seven Salvages, which for their villanies he detained prisoners.
Quoted in *Capt. John Smith's* Works, I. 171.

2. To deliver again; liberate a second time.—**3.** To report; repeat.

Osr. Shall I *re-deliver* you e'en so?
Ham. To this effect, sir. *Shak.*, Hamlet, v. 2. 186.

redeliverance (rē-dē-liv'ėr-ans), *n.* [< *re-* + *deliverance*.] A second deliverance; redelivery. *Imp. Dict.*

redelivery (rē-dē-liv'ėr-i), *n.* [< *re-* + *delivery*.] The act of delivering back; also, a second deliverance or liberation.

They did at last procure a sentence for the *redelivery* of what had been taken from them.
Clarendon, Life, an. 1665.

redemand (rē-dē-månd'), *v. t.* [< OF. (and F.) *redemander* = Pr. *redemandar* = It. *ridomandare*; as *re-* + *demand*, *v.*] To demand the return of; also, to demand a second time.

They would say, God hath appointed us captains of these our bodily forts, which, without treason to that majesty, were never to be delivered over till they were *redemanded*. *Sir P. Sidney*, Arcadia, iv.

Our Long-boats, sent to take in fresh Water, were assail'd in the Port, and one taken and detain'd: which being *redemanded*, answer was made, That neither the Skiff nor the Seamen should be restor'd.
Milton, Letters of State, May, 1658.

She sang the Bell Song with brilliant effect, and it was *redemanded*. *New York Tribune*, March 8, 1887.

redemand (rē-dē-månd'), *n.* [< *redemand*, *v.*] The repetition of a demand; also, a demand for the return of anything.

redemise (rē-dē-mīz'), *v. t.* [< *re-* + *demise*.] To demise back; convey or transfer back, as an estate in fee simple, fee tail, for life, or for a term of years.

redemise (rē-dē-mīz'), *n.* [< *redemise*, *v.*] Reconveyance; the transfer of an estate back to the person who has demised it: as, the demise and *redemise* of an estate in fee simple, fee tail, or for life or years, by mutual leases.

redemptible (rē-demp'ti-bl), *a.* [< L. *redemptus*, pp. of *redimere*, redeem: see *redeem* and *-ible*.] Capable of being redeemed; redeemable.

redemption (rē-demp'shon), *n.* [< ME. *redempcion*, < OF. *redemption*, *redemptiun*, F. *rédemption* = Pr. *redempcio* = Sp. *redencion* = Pg. *redempção* = It. *redenzione*, < L. *redemptio(n-)*, a buying back or off, a releasing, ransoming, redemption, < *redimere*, buy back, redeem: see *redeem*. Cf. *ransom*, a reduced form of the same word.] The act of redeeming, or the state of being redeemed; ransom; repurchase; deliverance; release: as, the *redemption* of prisoners of war, of captured goods, etc.

But peaceful measures were also employed to procure the *redemption* of slaves; and money sometimes accomplished what was vainly attempted by the sword.
Sumner, Orations, I. 232.

Such a sacrifice
Alone the fates can deem a fitting price
For thy *redemption*.
William Morris, Earthly Paradise, I. 318.

Specifically—(*a*) In *law*, the recovering or disencumbering of property by one who had a right to it subject to the encumbrance or defeasible conveyance, as where a debtor by paying his debt gets back a pledge or a mortgaged estate; also, the right of redeeming and reëntering. (*b*) In *com.*, payment to the holders by the issuer of notes, bills, or other evidences of debt. (*c*) In *theol.*, deliverance from sin and its consequences by the obedience and sacrifice of Christ the Redeemer. The word *redemption* presupposes that man is in a state of bondage to the powers of evil—either spiritual powers external to himself, or evil passions and p[illegible] within himself, or both—and that he can be delivered from them only by the sacrifice and suffering of another. This suffering is regarded as the price or ransom paid to redeem the captive. Thus, redemption is substantially equivalent to salvation, but involves the idea of a new and additional right over man acquired by God; and the doctrine of redemption includes the doctrines of atonement, justification, regeneration, and sanctification.

The Mounte of Caluery, where our Sauyour Criste was crucyfyed and suffred dethe for our *redempcion*.
Sir R. Guylforde, Pylgrymage, p. 26.

Plantagenet,
Which held thee dearly as his soul's *redemption*.
Shak., 3 Hen. VI., ii. 1. 102.

By sin man was principally bound to God, as relates to punishment, because he had principally sinned against God; but he was bound to the devil as a tormentor, to whom he was justly delivered by God's permission; but the price of *redemption* ought to be paid to the principal, not to the intervening agent, and therefore Christ exhibited His death as the price of our *redemption* to God the Father for our reconciliation, and not to the devil.
Durandus, in Owen's Dogmatic Theology, p. 279.

Brethren of the Redemption of Captives. See *brother*.—**Covenant of redemption,** in *New Eng. theol.* See *covenant*.—**Equity of redemption.** See *equity*.

redemptionary (rẹ̄-demp'shọn-ā̤-ri), *n.*; pl. *redemptionaries* (-riz). [< *redemption* + *-ary*.] One who is or may be redeemed or set at liberty by paying a compensation; one who is or may be released from a bond or obligation by fulfilling the stipulated terms or conditions.

None other then such as haue aduentured in the first voyage, or shall become aduenturers in this supply at any time hereafter, are to be admitted in the seid society, but as *redemptionaries*, which will be very chargeable.
Hakluyt's Voyages, III. 176.

redemptioner† (rẹ̄-demp'shọn-ėr), *n.* [< *redemption* + *-er*[1].] One who redeemed himself or purchased his release from debt or obligation to the master of a ship by his services, or one whose services were sold to pay the expenses of his passage to America.

Sometimes they [indented servants] were called *redemptioners*, because, by their agreement with the master of the vessel, they could redeem themselves from his power by paying their passage. *Jefferson*, Correspondence, I. 405.

Poor wretch! . . . he had to find out what the life of a *Redemptioner* really was, by bitter experience.
J. Ashton, Social Life in Reign of Queen Anne, II. 247.

redemptionist (rẹ̄-demp'shọn-ist), *n.* [< *redemption* + *-ist*.] See *Trinitarian*.

redemptive (rẹ̄-demp'tiv), *a.* [< L. *redemptus*, pp. of *redimere*, redeem: see *redeem*.] Redeeming; serving to redeem.

The *redemptive* and the completive work of Messiah.
Schaff, Hist. Christ. Church, I. § 83.

redemptor†, redemptour†, *n.* [< ME. *redemptour*, < OF. *redempteur*, vernacularly *raembeor*, *raiembeor*, F. *rédempteur* = Pr. *redemptor* = Sp. *redentor* = It. *redentore*, < L. *redemptor*, redeemer, < *redimere*, pp. *redemptus*, redeem, etc.: see *redeem*.] A redeemer.

Record of prophets thou shalt be *redemptour*,
And singuler repast of everlastyng lyf.
Candlemas Day, ap. *Hawkins*, i. 23. (*Nares.*)

redemptoric†, *a.* [< *redemptor* + *-ic*.] Redemptory; redemptive. [Rare.]

Till to her loved sire
The black-ey'd damsell he resign'd; no *redemtoric* hire
Tooke for her freedome; not a gift; but all the ransome quit.
Chapman, Iliad, i.

Redemptorist (rẹ̄-demp'tọr-ist), *n.* [< F. *rédemptoriste*; as *redemptor* + *-ist*.] A member of a Roman Catholic order founded by Alfonso Maria da Liguori of Naples in 1732. The especial object of the order (which is called the Congregation of the Most Holy Redeemer) is missionary work among the poor. The Redemptorists exist in the United States, in several European countries, etc. On account of their coöperation with the Jesuits, they have been excluded in some countries, as in Germany at the time of the Kulturkampf. Also *Liguorian*, *Liguorist*.

Redemptoristine (rẹ̄-demp-tọ-ris'tin), *n.* [< *Redemptorist* + *-ine*[2].] A member of the Order of the Most Holy Redeemer, a Roman Catholic order of cloistered and contemplative nuns, founded in connection with the congregation of the Redemptorists.

redemptory (rẹ̄-demp'tọ̄-ri), *a.* [< L. *redemptus*, pp. of *redimere*, redeem, etc.: see *redeem*.] 1. Serving to redeem; paid for ransom.

Omega sings the exequies,
And Hector's *redemptorie* prise.
Chapman, Iliad, xxiv., Arg.

2. Of or pertaining to redemption.

Clinging to a great, vivifying, *redemptory* idea.
The Century, XXXI. 211.

redemptour†, *n.* See *redemptor*.

redempture† (rẹ̄-demp'tụ̄r), *n.* [< L. *redemptura*, an undertaking by contract, a contracting, < *redimere*, contract, hire, redeem: see *redeem*.] Redemption.

Thou moost mylde mother and vyrgyn moost pure,
That barest swete Jhesu, the worldys *redempture*.
Fabyan, Chron., II., an. 1326.

redent†, *n.* Same as *redan*.

redented (rẹ̄-den'ted), *a.* [As *redent* + *-ed*[2].] Formed like the teeth of a saw; indented.

redescend (rē-dẹ̄-send'), *v. i.* [= F. *redescendre*; as *re-* + *descend*.] To descend again. *Howell.*

redescent (rē-dẹ̄-sent'), *n.* [< *re-* + *descent*.] A descending or falling again. *Sir W. Hamilton.*

redescribe (rē-dẹs-krīb'), *v. t.* [< *re-* + *describe*.] To describe a second time; describe again: as, *Nasua narica* was *redescribed* by Von Tschudi as *N. leucorhynchus*.

redetermine (rē-dẹ̄-tėr'min), *v. t.* [< *re-* + *determine*.] To determine again.

The titanium was then . . . *redetermined* in the solution by the calorimetric method.
Amer. Chem. Jour., X. 38.

redevable†, *a.* [< F. *redevable*, < *redevoir*, remain in one's debt, < *re-*, back, again, + *devoir*, owe, be in debt: see *due*[1], *devoir*.] Beholden; under obligation.

I must acknowledge my self exceedingly *redevable* to Fortunes kindnesse (continued he) for addressing me into the company of a man whose acquaintance I shall be proud to purchase. *Comical History of Francion* (1655). (*Nares.*)

redevelop (rē-dẹ̄-vel'up), *v.* [< *re-* + *develop*.] I. *intrans.* To develop again.

II. *trans.* To develop again or a second time; specifically, in *photog.*, to intensify by a second developing process.

redevelopment (rē-dẹ̄-vel'up-mẹnt), *n.* [< *re-* + *development*.] Specifically, in *photog.*, the act or process of redeveloping: a form of intensification in which the negative is bleached with cupric or mercuric chlorid and then subjected anew to the action of the developer.

redeye (red'ī), *n.* 1. A cyprinoid fish, *Leuciscus erythrophthalmus*, having a red iris; the rudd.—2. The blue-spotted sunfish, *Lepomis cyanellus*.—3. The rock-bass, *Ambloplites rupestris*. See cut under *rock-bass*. [Ohio.]—4. The red-eyed vireo or greenlet, *Vireo olivaceus*, having the iris red. See cut under *greenlet*.—5. A strong and fiery whisky: so called from its effect upon the eyes of drinkers. [Low, U. S.]

red-eyed (red'īd), *a.* [= Icel. *raudheygdhr*; as *red* + *eye* + *-ed*[2].] 1. Having red eyes, the iris being of that color: as, the *red-eyed* vireo or greenlet or flycatcher, *Vireo olivaceus*. See cut under *greenlet*.—2. Having a bare red space about the eyes, as some birds.—3. Having congested eyelids, as after shedding tears.—**Red-eyed pochard.** See *pochard*.

red-faced (red'fāst), *a.* 1. Having a red face.—2. In *ornith.*, having the front of the head red: as, the *red-faced* or Pallas's cormorant, *Phalacrocorax perspicillatus*.

red-fender (red'fen"dėr), *n.* The red-bellied salt-water terrapin of the United States, *Chrysemys* or *Pseudemys rubriventris*, also called *potter*, *redbelly*, and *slider*. It grows much larger than the true diamond-back, often attaining a length of eighteen or twenty inches, but the meat is coarse and fishy. The market value is much less than that of the diamond-back, and this terrapin is much used to adulterate dishes of the latter.

red-fighter (red'fī"tėr), *n.* The common bullfinch, *Pyrrhula vulgaris*. See cut under *bullfinch*.

red-figured (red'fig"ụ̈rd), *a.* Bearing or marked with red figures: specifically noting the class of Greek pottery bearing red figures or ornament on a solid black ground, which succeeded the archaic black-figured pottery about the second quarter of the fifth century B. C., and includes the vases of the highest artistic type. See *vase*, and cuts under *Poseidon*, *psykter*, and *pyxis*.

Chaclurylion painted none but *red-figured* Vases, but he is one of the earliest masters of the style, and must be placed early in the fifth century.
Harrison and Verrall, Ancient Athens, p. cxi.

redfin (red'fin), *n.* 1. The red-dace, *Notropis megalops*. [U. S.]—2. The common yellow perch of the United States, *Perca flavescens*. Also *yellowfin*. [Southern U. S.]—3. The red-cusk, *Dinematichthys* or *Brosmophycis marginatus*. [California.]—4. The cyprinoid fish *Notropis* or *Lythrurus ardens*.

redfish (red'fish), *n.* 1. The blue-backed salmon, *Oncorhynchus nerka*. [Idaho.]—2. The red perch or rose-fish, *Sebastes marinus* or *viviparus*.—3. The labroid fish *Trochocopus* or *Pimelometopon pulcher*; the fathead. See cut under *fathead*. [Pacific coast, U. S.]—4. The red-drum, *Sciæna ocellata* or *Sciænops ocellatus*;

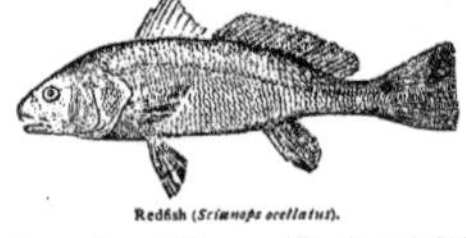

Redfish (*Sciænops ocellatus*).

the southern red-horse. [Florida and Gulf Coast.]—5. A preparation of fish, very popular among the Malays. After the heads have been removed, the fish are cleaned, salted in the proportion of one part salt to eight parts of fish, and deposited in flat, glazed earthen vessels, in which they are for three days submitted to the pressure of stones placed on thin boards or dried plantain-leaves. The fish are next freed from salt and saturated with vinegar of cocoa-palm toddy, after which powdered ginger, black pepper, brandy, and powdered red rice are added. The anchovy (*Stolephorus* or *Engraulis*) is the most esteemed constituent, but other fishes are used in the same way. The preparation is also called *Malacca fish*. *Cantor.*

red-footed (red'fu̇t"ed), *a.* Having red feet: as, the *red-footed* douroucouli, *Nyctipithecus rufipes*.—**Red-footed falcon.** See *falcon*.

redgound†, *n.* [Also *redgown* (and, by further corruption. *red-gum*, q. v.), early mod. E. *reed gounde*; < ME. *redgownd*, *radegounde*, < *rede*, red, + *gownde*, < AS. *gund* (= OHG. *gund*, *gunt*), matter, pus, virus: see *red*[1] and *gound*[1].] A corruption of *red-gum*[2]. [Prov. Eng.]

Reed gounde, sicknesse of chyldren. *Palsgrave.*

red-green (red'grēn), *a.* Of a reddish-green color: as, the *red-green* carpet (a British moth).—**Red-green blindness,** a form of color-blindness in which there is inability to recognize either the red of the spectrum or the complementary color bluish-green—the former appearing blackish-gray and the latter whitish-gray. Also called *anerythroblepsia*, *anerythropsia*.

redgullet (red'gul"et), *n.* Same as *redmouth*.

red-gum[1] (red'gum), *n.* [< *red*[1] + *gum*[2].] 1. A disease of grain: same as *rust*. [Prov. Eng.]—2. The resinous product of several eucalypts; Australian kino.—3. A red-gum tree.—4. See *Liquidambar*, 1.—**Red-gum tree,** one of several species of *Eucalyptus*—*E. resinifera*, *E. calophylla*, *E. tereticornis*, *E. rostrata*, and others: so named from the red gum which they exude. *E. resinifera*, next to the blue-gum, is most frequently planted in Europe for sanitary purposes. *E. rostrata* is exceptionally 200 feet high, and its timber is one of the best of eucalyptus woods, being heavy, hard, and strong, and very durable in all situations. It is employed for railway-ties, piles, many ship-building purposes, etc.

red-gum[2] (red'gum), *n.* [A corruption of *redgound*, q. v.] An unimportant red papular eruption of infants. Also called *gum-rash* and *strophulus*.

Their heads are hid with skalls,
Their Limbs with *Red-gums*.
Sylvester, tr. of Du Bartas's Weeks, ii., The Furies.

I found Charlotte quite in a fuss about the child: she was sure it was very ill; it cried and fretted, and was all over pimples. So I looked at it directly, and "Lord! my dear," says I, "it is nothing in the world but the *red-gum*."
Jane Austen, Sense and Sensibility, xxxvii.

red-haired (red'hãrd), *a.* [= Icel. *raudhhærdhr*; as *red*[1] + *hair* + *-ed*[2].] Having red or reddish hair.

red-hand (red'hand), *a.* Same as *red-handed*.

red-handed (red'han"ded), *a.* With red or bloody hands; hence, in the very act, as if with red or bloody hands: said originally of a person taken in the act of homicide, but extended figuratively to one caught in the perpetration of any crime: generally in the phrase *to be taken red-handed*.

I was pushed over by Pumblechook, exactly as if I had that moment picked a pocket, or fired a rick; indeed it was the general impression in court that I *had been taken red-handed*; for as Pumblechook shoved me before him through the crowd I heard some people say, "What 's he done?" and others, "He 's a young 'un too."
Dickens, Great Expectations, xiii.

redhead (red'hed), *n.* [< *red*[1] + *head*, *n.*] 1. A person having red hair.—2. A red-headed duck, the pochard, *Fuligula* or *Æthyia ferina*, a common bird of Europe, a variety of which bears the same name in America and is called more fully *red-headed duck*, *red-headed raft-duck*, *red-headed broadbill*, also *grayback*, *Washington canvasback*, and *American pochard*. In the male the head is of a bright chestnut-red with coppery or bronzy reflection. It is a near relative of the canvasback, for which it is sometimes sold, and is much esteemed for the table. See *pochard*. 3. The red-headed woodpecker, *Melanerpes erythrocephalus*. See cut under *Melanerpes*.—4. A tropical milkweed, *Asclepias Curassavica*, with umbels of bright-red flowers. The root and the expressed juice are emetic, or in smaller doses cathartic. Also called *blood-flower* and *bastard ipecacuanha*. [West Indies.]

red-headed (red'hed"ed), *a.* 1. Having red hair, as a person.—2. Having a red head, as a bird: as, the *red-headed* woodpecker, *Melanerpes erythrocephalus*. See cut under *Melanerpes*.—**Red-headed curre, duck, pochard, poker, raft-duck, or widgeon.** Same as *redhead*, 2.—**Red-headed finch or linnet,** the redpoll.—**Red-headed smew,** the female smew or white nun, *Mergellus albellus*.—**Red-headed teal.** Same as *greenwing*.

redhibition (red-hi-bish'ọn), *n.* [= F. *rédhibition* = Sp. *redhibicion* = Pg. *redhibição* = It. *redibizione*, < L. *redhibitio(n-)*, a taking back, the giving or receiving back of a damaged article sold, < *redhibere*, give back, return, < *red-*, back, + *habere*, have: see *habit*.] In *law*, an action by a buyer to annul the sale of a movable and oblige the seller to take it back because of a defect or of some deceit. Also *rehibition*.

redhibitory (red-hib'i-tọ-ri), *a.* [= OF. *redhibitoire*, F. *rédhibitoire* = Sp. Pg. *redhibitorio* = It. *redibitorio*, < LL. *redhibitorius*, < L. *redhibere*, give back, return: see *redhibition*.] In *law*, pertaining to redhibition. Also *rehibitory*.

redhorn (red'hôrn), *n.* An insect of the family *Rhodoceridæ*.

red-horse (red'hôrs), *n.* 1. The common white or lake sucker, a catostomoid fish, *Moxostoma macrolepidotum*, or any other of the same genus; a stone-roller or white mullet. The golden red-horse is *M. aureolum*. The long-tailed red-horse is *M. anisurum*.—2. The red-drum, *Sciænops occllatus*. See cut under *redfish*. [Florida and Gulf States.]

red-hot (red'hot), *a.* 1. Red with heat; heated to redness: as, *red-hot* iron; *red-hot* balls. Hence—2. Extreme; violent; ardent: as, a *red-hot* political speech. [Slang.]—**Red-hot poker.** Same as *flame-flower*.—**Red-hot shot**, cannon-balls heated to redness and fired at shipping, magazines, wooden buildings, etc., to combine destruction by fire with battering by concussion.

red-humped (red'humpt), *a.* Having a red hump: noting a bombycid moth of the genus *Notodonta*: as, the *red-humped* prominent, *N. concinna*. See cut under *Notodonta*.

redit, *a.* A Middle English form of *ready*.

redia (rē'di-ạ), *n.*; pl. *rediæ* (-ē). [NL., so called after *Redi*, an Italian naturalist.] The second larval stage of some fluke-worms or *Trematoda*, as *Distoma*, intervening between the condition of the ciliated embryo and the more advanced form known as *cercaria*. A redia is a sporocyst, containing the germs of other rediæ, which eventually develop into cercariæ. The redia of *Distoma* is also known as *king's yellow worm*. See *cercaria* (with cut) and *Distoma*.

From each ovum [of *Distoma*] issues a ciliated larva, showing the rudiments of . . . a *Redia*. The perfect *Redia* . . . bursts, and these new zoöids [cercariæ] are set free. . . . Several generations of *Rediæ* may intervene between the third and fourth stages; or the mature animal may appear at the close of this stage, having undergone no Cercarian metamorphosis.
Huxley, Anat. Invert., p. 180.

redient (rō'di-ent), *a.* [< L. *redien(t-)s*, ppr. of *redire*, go back, return, < *red-*, back, + *ire*, go: see *iter*[1].] Returning. *E. H. Smith.* [Rare.]

redifferentiate (rē-dif-ẹ-ren'shi-āt), *v. i.* [< *re-* + *differentiate*.] To differentiate a differential or differential coefficient.

redifferentiation (rē-dif-ẹ-ren-shi-ā'shon), *n.* [< *re-* + *differentiation*.] The differentiation of a result of differentiation.

redigest (rē-di-jest'), *v. t.* [< *re-* + *digest*, *v.*] To digest or reduce to form a second time.

redingking†, *n.* [ME. *redyngkynge*, prob. erroneously for **redyngynge*, lit. 'riding-man,' < **redyng*, for *ridyng*, *riding*, + *-ynge*, E. *-ing*[3], indicating a dependent. Cf. AS. *rādcniht*, E. as if **roadknight*, one of "certain seruitours who held their lands by seruing their lord on horseback" (Minsheu, under *rodknights*, *radknights*).] One of a class of feudal retainers; a lackey.

Reynald the reue, and *redyngkynges* menye,
Munde the mylnere, and meny mo othere.
Piers Plowman (C), iii. 112.

redingote (red'ing-gōt), *n.* [= Sp. *redingote*, < F. *rédingote*, a corruption of E. *riding-coat*.] 1. A double-breasted outside coat with long plain skirts not cut away at the front.—2. A similar garment for women, worn either as a wrap or as part of the house dress, frequently cut away at the front.

The existing *redingote*, which has been fashionable for the last few years, and is highly popular just now, is a garment of silk, plush, or cloth, cut somewhat after the manner of a gentleman's tail-coat, richly trimmed, and adorned with very large buttons.
Fortnightly Rev., N. S., XLIII. 287.

redingtonite (red'ing-tọn-īt), *n.* [< *Redington* + *-ite*[2].] A hydrous chromium sulphate, occurring in fibrous masses having a pale-purple color. It is found at the Redington mine, Knoxville district, California.

red-ink plant. See *Phytolacca*.

redintegrate (re-din'tẹ-grāt), *v. t.*; pret. and pp. *redintegrated*, ppr. *redintegrating*. [< L. *redintegratus*, pp. of *redintegrare* (> It. *redintegrare* = Pg. *redintegrar*), restore, make whole again, < *red-*, again, + *integrare*, make whole: see *integrate*. Cf. *reintegrate*.] To bring back to an integral condition; recombine or reconstruct; renew; restore to a perfect state.

Redintegrate the fame first of your house,
Restore your ladyship's quiet.
B. Jonson, Magnetick Lady, iv. 2.

Christendom should be no longer rent in pieces, but would be *redintegrated* in a new pentecost.
Jer. Taylor, Works (ed. 1835), II. 304.

Cut off the legs, the tail, the jaws [of the newt], separately or all together, and . . . these parts not only grow again, but the *redintegrated* limb is formed on the same type as those which were lost.
Huxley, Lay Sermons, p. 261.

redintegrate (re-din'tẹ-grāt), *a.* [< *redintegrate*, *v.*] Renewed; restored to wholeness or a perfect state.

The ignorances and prevarications and partial abolitions of the natural law might be cured and restored, and by the dispersion of prejudices the state of natural reason be *redintegrate*. *Jer. Taylor*, Great Exemplar, Pref., p. 11.

redintegration (re-din-tẹ-grā'shon), *n.* [< F. *rédintégration* = Pg. *redintegração* = It. *redintegrazione*, < L. *redintegratio(n-)*, restoration, renewal, < *redintegrare*, pp. *redintegratus*, restore, renew: see *redintegrate*. Cf. *reintegration*.] 1. The act or process of redintegrating; recombination, restoration, or reconstruction; restoration to a whole or sound state.

Let us all study first the *redintegration* of that body of which Christ Jesus hath declared himself to be the head.
Donne, Sermons, xxii.

This *redintegration*, or renewing of us into the first condition, is . . . called repentance.
Jer. Taylor, Works (ed. 1835), I. 181.

They . . . absurdly commemorated the *redintegration* of his natural body by mutilating and dividing his mystical. *Decay of Christian Piety.*

2. In *chem.*, the restoration of any mixed body or matter to its former nature and constitution.—3. In *psychol.*, the law that those elements which have previously been combined as parts of a single mental state tend to recall or suggest one another—a term adopted by many psychologists to express phenomena of mental association.

redirect (rē-di-rekt'), *v. t.* [< *re-* + *direct*.] To direct again or anew: as, the parcel was sent to Boston and there *redirected* to Cambridge.

redirect (rē-di-rekt'), *a.* [< *re-* + *direct*.] Direct a second time: used only in the legal phrase *redirect examination* (which see, under *examination*, 2).

redisburse (rē-dis-bėrs'), *v. t.* [Early mod. E. also *redisbourse*; < *re-* + *disburse*.] To repay or refund.

But when the flond is spent, then backe againe,
His borrowed waters forst to *redisbourse*,
He sends the sea his owne with double gaine,
And tribute eke withall, as to his Soveraine.
Spenser, F. Q., IV. iii. 27.

rediscover (rē-dis-kuv'ėr), *v. t.* [< *re-* + *discover*.] To discover again or afresh.

rediscovery (rē-dis-kuv'ėr-i), *n.* [< *re-* + *discovery*.] A discovering again or afresh: as, the *rediscovery* of Encke's comet.

redispose (rē-dis-pōz'), *v. t.* [< *re-* + *dispose*.] To dispose or adjust again.

redisposition (rē-dis-pọ-zish'ọn), *n.* [< *redispose* + *-ition*.] The act or process of redisposing; a disposing afresh or anew; a rearrangement.

redisseize (rē-dis-sēz'), *v. t.* [< *re-* + *disseize*.] In *law*, to disseize anew or a second time.

redisseizin (rē-dis-sē'zin), *n.* [< *re-* + *disseizin*.] In *law*, a writ to recover seizin of lands or tenements against a redisseizor.

redisseizor (rē-dis-sē'zọr), *n.* [< *re-* + *disseizor*.] A person who disseizes lands or tenements a second time, or after a recovery of the same from him in an action of novel disseizin.

redissolution (rē-dis-ọ-lū'shọn), *n.* [< *re-* + *dissolution*.] A dissolving again or anew; a second dissolution.

After the protoplasm in a tentacle has been aggregated, its *redissolution* always begins in the lower part.
Darwin, Insectiv. Plants, p. 243.

redissolve (rē-di-zolv'), *v. t.* [= F. *redissoudre*; as *re-* + *dissolve*.] To dissolve again.

The protoplasm last aggregated is first *redissolved*.
Darwin, Insectiv. Plants, p. 243.

redistribute (rē-dis-trib'ụt), *v. t.* [< *re-* + *distribute*. Cf. F. *redistribuer*, redistribute.] To distribute again; deal back; apportion afresh.

redistribution (rē-dis-tri-bū'shọn), *n.* [= F. *redistribution*; as *re-* + *distribution*.] A dealing back; a second or new distribution.

A state of raised molecular vibration is favourable to those *re-distributions* of matter and motion which constitute Evolution. *H. Spencer*, Prin. of Biol., § 18.

We have said that in our opinion the *redistribution* of seats [see the phrase below] formed an essential part of reform. *Gladstone.*

Redistribution of Seats Act, an English statute of 1885 (48 and 49 Vict., c. 23) making extensive changes in the subdivision of the country into districts entitled to elect members of Parliament, mostly with the object of equalizing them as regards the number of electors.

redistrict (rē-dis'trikt), *v. t.* [< *re-* + *district*.] To divide or apportion again, as a State, into districts or other electoral units. [U. S.]

redistricting (rē-dis'trik-ting), *n.* [Verbal n. of *redistrict*, *v.*] The act or practice of rearranging (a State or other territory) into new electoral districts. [U. S.]

redition (rẹ-dish'ọn), *n.* [< L. *reditio(n-)*, a returning, going or coming back, < *redire*, pp. *reditus*, go or come back, return: see *redient*.] The act of going back; return. [Rare.]

Address suite to my mother, that her meane
May make the day of your *redition* scene.
Chapman, Odyssey, vi.

redivide (rē-di-vīd'), *v. t.* [< *re-* + *divide*.] To divide again.

redivived† (red-i-vīvd'), *a.* [< L. *redivivus*, living again (see *redivivus*), + *-ed*[2].] Made to live again; revived.

New-devised or *redivived* errours of opinion.
Bp. Hall, Revelation Unrevealed, § 11.

redivivus (red-i-vī'vus), *a.* [L., living again, < *red-(i-)*, again, + *vivus*, living: see *vivid*. Cf. *revive*.] Alive again; renewed; restored.

The Napoleonic empire *redivivus*.
G. W. Curtis, Potiphar Papers.

redknees (red'nēz), *n.* The water-pepper, *Polygonum Hydropiper*. [Prov. Eng.]

red-lac (red'lak), *n.* The Japan wax-tree, *Rhus succedanea*. See *wax-tree*.

red-legged (red'leg"ed or -legd), *a.* Having red legs or feet, as a bird: specifically noting several birds.—**Red-legged crow.** See *crow*[2].—**Red-legged gull**, the black-headed gull, *Chroïcocephalus ridibundus*. [Local, British.]—**Red-legged ham-beetle.** See *ham-beetle*.—**Red-legged kittiwake**, *Rissa brevirostris*, a three-toed gull of the North Pacific, having coral-red legs.—**Red-legged mew.** Same as *redshank*, 3.—**Red-legged partridge**, *Caccabis rufa*.—**Red-legged plover.** See *plover*.

redlegs (red'legz), *n.* 1. In *ornith.*: (*a*) The red-legged partridge. (*b*) The red-legged plover or turnstone, *Strepsilas interpres*. [Massachusetts.] (*c*) The purple sandpiper, *Tringa maritima*. [Caermarthen.] (*d*) The redshank.—2. In *bot.*, the bistort, *Polygonum Bistorta*, so named from the redness of its stems. The name is applied also to some other species of *Polygonum*. [Prov. Eng.]

redlest, *a.* See *redeless*.

red-letter (red'let"ėr), *a.* Having red letters; marked by red letters.—**Red-letter day.** (*a*) *Eccles.*, one of the more important church festivals: so called because formerly marked in the calendar of the Book of Common Prayer (as still in some copies, and in Roman Catholic missals and breviaries) by red-letter characters. Only the red-letter days have special services provided for them in the Prayer-book. Opposed to *black-letter day*.

The Calendar was crowded with *Red-Letter Days*, nominally indeed consecrated to Saints; but which, by the encouragement of Idleness and Dissipation of Manners, gave every kind of countenance to Sinners.
Bourne's Pop. Antiq. (1777), p. viii.

The *red-letter days* now become, to all intents and purposes, dead-letter days. *Lamb*, Oxford in the Vacation.

Hence—(*b*) A fortunate or auspicious day.

It is the old girl's birthday; and that is the greatest holiday and *reddest-letter day* in Mr. Bagnet's calendar.
Dickens, Bleak House, xlix.

redlichet, *adv.* A Middle English form of *rathly*.

red-litten (red'lit"n), *a.* [< *red*[1] + *lit*, pp. of *light*[1], **litten*, an extended form with suffix *-en*[1], after the analogy of *hidden*.] Exhibiting a red light or illumination. [Rare.]

And travellers, now, within that valley,
Through the *red-litten* windows see
Vast forms, that move fantastically
To a discordant melody.
Poe, Haunted Palace.

red-looked (red'lůkt), *a.* Having a red look; causing or indicated by a red face. [Rare.]

Let my tongue blister,
And never to my *red-look'd* anger be
The trumpet any more. *Shak.*, W. T., ii. 2. 34.

red-louse (red'lous), *n.* See *louse*[1] (*i*).

redly (red'li), *adv.* [< *red*[1] + *-ly*[2].] With redness; with a red color or glow.

red-mad (red'mad), *a.* [< *red*[1] + *mad*[1]. Cf. *redwood*[2].] Quite mad. *Halliwell.* [Prov. Eng.]

redman (red'man), *n.*; pl. *redmen* (-men). A holocentroid fish, *Holocentrus ascensionis*, of a brilliant reddish color. [St. Thomas, W. I.]

red-metal (red'met"ạl), *n.* A name given to several metallic compounds, mostly alloys of copper, used in modern silverware; also, a Japanese alloy much used in decorative metal-work.

red-morocco (red'mọ-rok'ō), *n.* The plant pheasant's-eye, *Adonis autumnalis*: so called from its red petals.

It is one of those plants which are annually cried about our streets under the name *Red Morocco*. *Curtis*, Flora Londinensis.

redmouth (red'mouth), *n.* and *a.* **I.** *n.* A fish of the genus *Hæmulon* (or *Diabasis*); a grunt. Also called *redgullet*. See *Hæmulon*, and cut under *grunt*.

II. *a.* Having a red mouth or lips; redmouthed: as, the *redmouth* buffalo-fish, *Ictiobus bubalus*. *D. S. Jordan.*

red-necked (red'nekt), *a.* Having a red neck. — **Red-necked footman**, *Lithosia rubricollis*, a British moth. — **Red-necked grebe**, *Podiceps griseigena* or *P. rubricollis*, one of the largest species of the family. — **Red-necked phalarope**, *Lobipes hyperboreus*, the northern phalarope.

redness (red'nes), *n.* [< ME. *rednesse*, *rednes*, < AS. *reádness*, *reádnyss*, *reádnes*, redness, < *reád*, red: see *red*[1].] The quality of being red; a red color.

There was a pretty *redness* in his lip. *Shak.*, As you Like it, iii. 5. 120.

red-nose (red'nōz), *a.* Same as *red-nosed*.

The *red-nose* innkeeper of Daventry. *Shak.*, 1 Hen. IV., iv. 2. 51.

red-nosed (red'nōzd), *a.* **1.** Having a red nose, as a toper. — **2.** Having a red beak: as, the *red-nosed* auklet, *Simorhynchus pygmæus*, also called *whiskered auklet*.

redo (rē-dö'), *v. t.* [< *re-* + *do*[1].] To do over again.

Prodigality and luxury are no new crimes, and . . . we doe but *re-doe* old vices. *Sandys*, Travailes, p. 204.

red-oak (red'ōk), *n.* **1.** An oak-tree, *Quercus rubra*, common in eastern North America, there extending further north than any other species. Its height is from 70 to 90 feet. Its wood is of a light-brown or red color, heavy, hard, strong, and coarse-grained, now much employed for clapboards and cooperage, and to some extent for inside finish. A Texan variety is smaller, with the wood much closer-grained. Also *black-oak*.

2. Another American species, *Q. falcata*, the Spanish oak. See *Spanish*.

redolence (red'ō-lens), *n.* [OF. *redolence*, < *redolent*, redolent: see *redolent*.] The state of being redolent; sweetness of scent; fragrance; perfume.

We have all the *redolence* of the perfumes we burn upon his altars. *Boyle.*

=**Syn.** See *smell*.

redolency (red'ō-len-si), *n.* [As *redolence* (see *-cy*).] Same as *redolence*.

Their flowers attract spiders with their *redolency*. *Mortimer.*

redolent (red'ō-lent), *a.* [< ME. *redolent*, < OF. *redolent* = It. *redolente*, < L. *redolen(t-)s*, ppr. of *redolere* (> It. *redolere*, OF. *redoler*), emit odor, be redolent, < *red-*, again, + *olere*, be odorous: see *olid*.] Having or diffusing a sweet scent; giving out an odor; odorous; smelling; fragrant: often with *of*.

In this graue full derke nowe is her bowre,
That by her lyte was sweete and *redolent*.
Fabyan, Chron., I. ccxxxviii.

Thy love excells the joy of wine;
Thy odours, O how *redolent*!
Sandys, Paraphrase of Song of Solomon, i.

Gales . . . *redolent* of joy and youth.
Gray, Prospect of Eton College.

redolently (red'ō-lent-li), *adv.* In a redolent manner; fragrantly.

redondilla (red-on-dē'lyä), *n.* [< Sp. *redondilla* (= Pg. *redondilha*), a roundel or roundelay, dim. of *redondo*, round, < L. *rotundus*, round: see *rotund*, and cf. *round*, *roundel*, *roundelay*, *rondeau*.] A form of versification formerly used in the south of Europe, consisting of a union of verses of four, six, and eight syllables, of which generally the first rimed with the fourth and the second with the third. At a later period verses of six and eight syllables in general, in Spanish and Portuguese poetry, were called *redondillas*, whether they made perfect rimes or assonances only. These became common in the dramatic poetry of Spain.

redorse (rē-dôrs'), *n.* [A reduction of *reredorse*, as if < *re-* + *dorse*[1].] The back or reverse side of a dorsal or dorse. See quotation under *dorse*[1], 2.

redoss (rē-dos'), *n.* Same as *redorse*.

redouble (rē-dub'l), *v.* [< OF. (and F.) *redoubler* = Sp. *redoblar* = Pg. *redobrar* = It. *raddoppiare*, < ML. *reduplicare*, redouble, double, < L. *re-*, again, + *duplicare*, double: see *double*, *v.* Cf. *reduplicate*.] **I.** *trans.* **1.** To double again or repeatedly; multiply; repeat often.

So they
Doubly *redoubled* strokes upon the foe.
Shak., Macbeth, i. 2. 38.

Often tymes the omittynge of correction *redoubleth* a trespace. *Sir T. Elyot*, The Governour, iii. 21.

2. To increase by repeated or continued additions.

And Ætna rages with *redoubled* heat.
Addison, tr. of Ovid's Metamorph.

Each new loss *redoubles* all the old.
Lowell, Nightwatches.

3†. To repeat in return.

So ended she; and all the rest around
To her *redoubled* that her undersong. *Spenser.*

Redoubled interval, in *music*, same as *compound interval*. See *interval*, 5.

II. *intrans.* To become twice as much; be repeated; become greatly or repeatedly increased.

Envy ever *redoubleth* from speech and fame.
Bacon, Envy (ed. 1887), p. 92.

Peal upon peal *redoubling* all around.
Cowper, Truth, l. 240.

redoubt[1] (rē-dout'), *v. t.* [< ME. *redouten*, *redowten*, < OF. *redouter*, *redoter*, *reduter*, later *redoubter*, F. *redouter* (= Pr. *redoptar* = It. *ridottare*), fear, < *re-* + *douter*, fear: see *doubt*, *v.*] **1.** To fear; dread. [Obsolete or archaic.]

Sholde I thanne *redowte* my blame?
Chaucer, Boëthius, i. prose 3.

The more superstitious crossed themselves on my approach; . . . it began at length to dawn upon me that if I was thus *redoubted* it was because I had stayed at the residencia. *R. L. Stevenson*, Olalla.

2†. To venerate; honor.

Sholde thilke honour maken hym worshipful and *redouted* of straunge folk? *Chaucer*, Boëthius, iii. prose 4.

redoubt[2], *n.* See *redout*[2].

redoubtable (rē-dou'ta-bl), *a.* [Also *redoutable*; < ME. *redoutable*, *redowtable*, < OF. *redoutable*, *redotable*, later *redoubtable*, F. *redoutable* (= Pr. *redoptable*), feared, redoubtable, < *redouter*, *redoubter*, fear: see *redoubt*[1].] **1.** That is to be dreaded; formidable; terrible: as, a *redoubtable* hero; hence, valiant: often used in irony or burlesque.

The Queen growing more *redoubtable* and famous by the Overthrow of the Fleet of Eighty eight.
Howell, Letters, I. vi. 3.

The enterprising Mr. Lintot, the *redoubtable* rival of Mr. Tonson, overtook me. *Pope*, To Earl of Burlington, 1716.

This is a tough point, shrewd, *redoubtable*;
Because we have to supplicate the judge
Shall overlook wrong done the judgment-seat.
Browning, Ring and Book, II. 104.

2†. Worthy of reverence.

Redowtable by honour and strong of power.
Chaucer, Boëthius, iv. prose 5.

redoubted (rē-dou'ted), *p. a.* [ME. *redouted*; < *redoubt*[1] + *-ed*[2].] Dreaded; formidable; honored or respected on account of prowess; valiant; redoubtable.

Lord regent and *redoubted* Burgundy.
Shak., 1 Hen. VI., ii. 1. 8.

redoubting† (rē-dou'ting), *n.* [ME. *redoutyng*; verbal n. of *redoubt*[1], *v.*] Honor; reverence; celebration.

With sotyl pencil depeynted was this storie
In *redoutyng* of Mars and of his glorie.
Chaucer, Knight's Tale, l. 1192.

redound (rē-dound'), *v. i.* [< OF. *redonder*, *rendonder*, F. *redonder*, *rédonder* = Pr. *redondar* = Sp. Pg. *redundar* = It. *ridondare*, < L. *redundare*, overflow, abound, < *red-*, again, back, + *undare*, surge, flow, abound, < *unda*, a wave: see *red-* and *ound*, and cf. *abound*, *surround*. Cf. *redundant*.] **1†.** To overflow; be redundant; be in excess; remain over and above.

For every dram of hony therein found
A pound of gall doth over it *redound*.
Spenser, F. Q., IV. x. 1.

The gates wide open stood, . . . and, like a furnace mouth,
Cast forth *redounding* smoke and ruddy flame.
Milton, P. L., ii. 889.

2. To be sent, rolled, or driven back; roll or flow back, as a wave; rebound.

Indeed, I never yet took box o' th' ear,
But it *redounded*, I must needs say so.
Fletcher (and another?), Nice Valour, iv. 1.

The evil, soon
Driven back, *redounded* as a flood on those
From whom it sprung. *Milton*, P. L., vii. 57.

3. To conduce; result; turn out; have effect.

I will, my lord; and doubt not so to deal
As all things shall *redound* unto your good.
Shak., 2 Hen. VI., iv. 9. 47.

Whenever he imagines the smallest advantage will *redound* to one of his foot-boys by any new oppression of me and my whole family and estate, he never disputeth it a moment. *Swift*, Story of the Injured Lady.

He thinks it will *redound* to his reputation.
Goldsmith, Criticisms.

redound (rē-dound'), *n.* [< *redound*, *v.*] **1.** The coming back, as of consequence or effect; result; reflection; return.

Not without *redound*
Of use and glory to yourselves ye come,
The first-fruits of the stranger.
Tennyson, Princess, ii.

2. Reverberation; echo. [Rare.] *Imp. Dict.*

redounding† (rē-doun'ding), *n.* [Verbal n. of *redound*, *v.*] Reverberation; resounding.

Such as were next to the abby herde clerely the *redoundynge* of the Naueroyse, for, as they went, their harneys clatteredde and made some noyse.
Berners, tr. of Froissart's Chron., I. clxxxv.

redour†, **reddour†**, *n.* [< ME. *redour*, *redur*, also *raddour*, *reddour*, *reddur*, < OF. *rador*, *radour*, *radeur*, violence, rapidity, < *rade*, < L. *rapidus*, rapid (see *rapid*); prob. confused also with *raidour*, *raideur*, *roideur*, stiffness, < L. *rigidus*, stiff, rigid: see *rigid*.] Violence; roughness.

His londes, his legemen, out of lyue broght;
His suster into seruage & to syn put;
And other *redurs* full ryfe in his rewme dyd.
Destruction of Troy (E. E. T. S.), l. 1805.

But trewely no fors of thi *reddour*
To hym that over hymself hath the maystrye.
Chaucer, Fortune, l. 14.

redout[1]†, *v.* See *redoubt*[1].

redout[2], **redoubt**[2] (rē-dout'), *n.* [The form *redoubt* is erroneous, due to confusion with *redoubt*[1] and *redoubtable*; prop. *redout* (= D. G. *redoute* = Sw. *redutt* = Dan. *redute*), formerly also *reduit* (and, after L., *reduct*); < OF. *reduit*, m., *reduite*, f., F. *réduit*, also (fem. It.) *redoute* = Sp. *reducto* = Pg. *reducto*, *reduto* = It. *ridotto*, a retreat, refuge, redout, < ML. *reductus* (> E. *reduct*), a retreat, refuge, redout, < L. *reducere*, bring back: see *reduce*.] In *fort.*, a general name for nearly every class of works wholly inclosed and undefended by reëntering or flanking angles. The word is, however, most generally used for a small inclosed work of various form — polygonal, square, triangular, or even circular — serving mainly as a temporary field-work. The name is also given to a central or retired work constructed within another, to serve as a place of retreat for the defenders: in this sense generally *reduit*. Redouts are usually provided with parapet, ditch, scarps, banquette, etc., as in regular fortification. They are especially useful in fortifying the tops of hills, in commanding passes, or in feeling the way through a hostile or wooded country. — **Demilune redout**, a redout placed within the demilune. =**Syn.** See *fortification*.

redout[3] (rē-dout'), *a.* [< OF. *reduit*, < L. *reductus*, brought back, pp. of *reducere*, bring back: see *reduce*. Cf. *redout*[2], *n.*] In *her.*, bent in many angles: noting a cross with hooked extremities, in the form of the fylfot or swastika.

redoutable, *a.* See *redoubtable*.

redowa (red'ō-ä), *n.* [< F. *redowa*, < Bohem. *rejdowák*, *rejdowačka*, the dance so called, < *rejdowati*, turn, turn around, bustle about.] **1.** A Bohemian dance, which has two forms — the *rejdowák*, resembling the waltz or the mazurka, and the *rejdowačka*, resembling the polka. — **2.** Music for such a dance or in its rhythm, which is properly triple and quick, but in another form is duple, and readily assimilated to that of the polka.

red-paidle, *n.* The lumpsucker. [Scotch.]

redpoll (red'pōl), *n.* [Also *redpole*: so called from the red color on the head; < *red*[1] + *poll*[1].] **1.** A small fringilline bird of the genus *Ægiothus* (or *Acanthis*), the male of which has a crimson poll, a rosy-red breast, and the plumage streaked with flaxen and dusky brown and white. The bill is small, conic-acute, with a nasal ruff; the wings are pointed; the tail is emarginate. Several species inhabit the arctic and north temperate regions of Europe, Asia, and America. The common redpoll is *Æ. linaria*; the mealy redpoll is *Æ. canescens*; the American mealy redpoll is *Æ. exilipes*.

Redpoll (*Ægiothus linaria*).

2. The red-polled warbler, or palm-warbler, of North America, *Dendrœca palmarum*, having a chestnut-red poll: more fully called *yellow red-poll*. See *palm-warbler*.

red-polled (red'pōld), *a.* Having a red poll, or the top of the head red.

redraft (rē-dràft'), *v. t.* [< *re-* + *draft.*] To draft or draw anew.

redraft (rē-dràft'), *n.* [< *redraft*, *v.*] 1. A second draft or copy.—2. A new bill of exchange which the holder of a protested bill draws on the drawer or indorsers, by which he reimburses to himself the amount of the protested bill with costs and charges.

redraw (rē-drâ'), *v.* [< *re-* + *draw.*] I. *trans.* To draw again; make a second draft or copy of.

II. *intrans.* In *com.*, to draw a new bill of exchange to meet another bill of the same amount, or, as the holder of a protested bill, on the drawer or indorser.

redress[1] (rẹ̄-dres'), *v.* [< ME. *redressen*, < OF. *redrescer*, *redrecer*, *redrecier*, *redresser*, F. *redresser*, set up again, straighten, < *re-*, again, + *dresser*, direct, dress: see *dress.*] I. *trans.* 1†. To set up or upright; make erect; reërect.

> Right as floures, thorgh the cold of nyghte
> Yclosed, stoupen on her stalkes lowe,
> *Redressen* hem agein the soune brighte.
> *Chaucer*, Troilus, ii. 960.

2. To set right again; restore; amend; mend.

> *Redresse* me, mooder, and me chastise;
> For certeynly my Faderes chastisinge,
> That dar I nought abiden in no wise.
> *Chaucer*, A. B. C., l. 129.

> As broken glass no cement can *redress*,
> So beauty blemish'd once 's for ever lost.
> *Shak.*, Pass. Pilgrim, l. 178.

> In yonder spring of roses intermix'd
> With myrtle, find what to *redress* till noon.
> *Milton*, P. L., ix. 219.

3. To put right, as a wrong; remedy; repair, relieve against, as an injury: as, to *redress* injuries; to *redress* grievances. See *redress*[1], *n.*, 2.

> And *redresse* vs the domage that he don has,
> By Paris his proude son, in our prise londis.
> *Destruction of Troy* (E. E. T. S.), l. 4917.

> Orisouns or preyers is for to seyn a pitous wyl of herte that *redresseth* it in God and expresseth it by word outward to remoeven harmes. *Chaucer*, Parson's Tale.

> The state of this unconstant world . . . bringeth forth daily such new evils as must of necessity by new remedies be *redrest*. *Hooker*, Eccles. Polity, vi. 2.

> Their duty
> And ready service shall *redress* their needs,
> Not prating what they would be.
> *Fletcher*, Valentinian, ii. 3.

> He who best knows how to keep his necessities private is the most likely person to have them *redressed*.
> *Goldsmith*, The Bee, No. 3.

4. To relieve of anything unjust or oppressive; bestow relief upon; compensate; make amends to.

> *Redres* mans sowle from alle mysery,
> That he may enter the eternal glorye.
> *Political Poems*, etc. (ed. Furnivall), p. 82.

> Will Gaul or Muscovite *redress* ye?
> *Byron*, Childe Harold, ii. 76.

II.† *intrans.* To rise again; reërect one's self.

> Yet like the valiant Palme they did sustaine
> Their peisant weight, *redressing* vp againe.
> *Hudson*, tr. of Du Bartas's Judith, ii.

redress[1] (rẹ̄-dres'), *n.* [< OF. *redresse*, *redresce*, *redrece*, redress; from the verb: see *redress*[1], *v.*] 1†. A setting right again; a putting into proper order; amendment; reformation.

> The *redresse* of boistrous & sturdie courages by perswasion. *Puttenham*, Arte of Eng. Poesie, p. 19.

> The father, with sharpe rebukes sesoned with louing lookes, causeth a *redresse* and amendment in his childe.
> *Lyly*, Euphues, Anat. of Wit, p. 150.

> For us the more necessary is a speedy *redress* of ourselves. *Hooker*.

2. Deliverance from wrong, injury, or oppression; removal of grievances or oppressive burdens; undoing of wrong; reparation; indemnification. In its most general sense *redress* includes whatever relief can be afforded against injustice, whether by putting an end to it, by compensation in damages, by punishing the wrong-doer, or otherwise.

> Is not the swoord the most violent *redress* that may be used for any evill? *Spenser*, State of Ireland.

> Be factious for *redress* of all these griefs.
> *Shak.*, J. C., i. 3. 118.

> Fair majesty, the refuge and *redress*
> Of those whom fate pursues and wants oppress.
> *Dryden*, Æneid, i. 838.

> Think not
> But that there is *redress* where there is wrong,
> So we are bold enough to seize it.
> *Shelley*, The Cenci, iii. 1.

> Ring in *redress* to all mankind.
> *Tennyson*, In Memoriam, cvi.

> To every one o' my grievances law gave
> *Redress*. *Browning*, Ring and Book, I. 237.

=**Syn.** 2. Relief, amends, compensation.

redress[2] (rē-dres'), *v. t.* [< *re-* + *dress.*] To dress again, in any sense: as, to *redress* furniture or leather; to *redress* a wound.

redressal (rẹ̄-dres'al), *n.* [< *redress*[1] + *-al.*] The act of redressing. *Imp. Dict.*

redresser (rẹ̄-dres'ėr), *n.* One who gives redress.

> Don Quixote of the Mancha, the righter of wrongs, the *redresser* of injuries.
> *Shelton*, Don Quixote, iv. 25. (*Latham.*)

redressible (rẹ̄-dres'i-bl), *a.* [< *redress*[1] + *-ible.*] Capable of being redressed. *Imp. Dict.*

redressive (rẹ̄-dres'iv), *a.* [< *redress*[1] + *-ive.*] Affording redress; giving relief. [Rare.]

> Can I forget the generous band
> Who, touch'd with human woe, *redressive* search'd
> Into the horrors of the gloomy jail?
> *Thomson*, Winter, l. 360.

redressless (rẹ̄-dres'les), *a.* [< *redress*[1] + *-less.*] Without redress or amendment; without relief.

redressment (rẹ̄-dres'mẹnt), *n.* [< OF. *redrecement*, *redressement*, F. *redressement*; as *redress* + *-ment.*] Redress; the act of redressing.

red-ribbon (red'rib"ọn), *n.* The band-fish.

redrive (rē-drīv'), *v. t.* [< *re-* + *drive.*] To drive back; drive again. *Southey.*

red-roan (red'rōn), *a.* See *roan*[1].

red-robin (red'rob"in), *n.* The red-rust, *Puccinia graminis*. [Eng.]

redroot (red'röt), *n.* 1. An American shrub, *Ceanothus Americanus*, the New Jersey tea. The stems are from 1 to 3 feet high from a dark-red root, the leaves ovate or oblong-ovate, the small white flowers gathered in rather pretty dense clusters at the ends of leafy shoots. The name is more or less extended to other members of the genus.

2. A herbaceous plant, *Lachnanthes tinctoria*, of the *Hæmodoraceæ*, or bloodwort family. It grows in wet sandy places in the eastern United States near the coast. It has a simple stem with sword-shaped leaves mostly from near the base, and woolly flowers, yellow within, crowded in a dense compound cyme. The root is red, and has been used in dyeing. Upon authority adduced by Darwin ("Origin of Species," ch. i.), the root of this plant is fatally poisonous to white pigs which eat it, but not to black; the statement, however, requires confirmation. Also *paintroot*.

3. The alkanet, *Alkanna tinctoria*.—4. One of the pigweeds, *Amarantus retroflexus*. [U. S.]

redruthite (red'röth-īt), *n.* [< *Redruth*, in Cornwall, England, + *-ite*[2].] Copper-glance: same as *chalcocite*.

redsear (red'sēr), *v. i.* [< *red* + *sear* (?).] To break or crack when too hot, as iron under the hammer: a word used by workmen. Also *redshare*.

red-seed (red'sēd), *n.* Small crustaceans, as ostracodes, copepods, etc., which float on the surface of the sea, and upon which mackerel, menhaden, etc., feed. Some red-seed is said to injure the fish.

red-shafted (red'shȧf"ted), *a.* Having red shafts of the wing- and tail-feathers: specifically applied to *Colaptes mexicanus*, the red-shafted woodpecker or Mexican flicker, related to the common flicker or yellow-shafted woodpecker. It abounds in western North America.

redshank (red'shangk), *n.* [< *red*[1] + *shank.*] 1. The fieldfare, *Turdus pilaris*. [Local, Eng.] —2. A wading bird of the family *Scolopacidæ* and genus *Totanus*, having red shanks. The common redshank is *T. calidris*, about 11 inches long, common in many parts of Europe, Asia, and Africa. The spotted redshank, T. *fuscus*, is a related species of similar distribution. Compare *greenshank*, *yellowshank*.

Redshank (*Totanus calidris*).

3. The hooded or black-headed gull, *Chrœcocephalus ridibundus*: so called from its red legs: more fully called *redshank gull* and *red-legged gull* or *mew*.—4. *pl.* A name given in contempt to Scottish Highlanders, and formerly to native Irish, in allusion to their dress leaving the legs exposed.

> Mamertinus . . . dooth note the *Redshanks* and the Irish (which are properlie the Scots) to be the onlie enimies of our nation.
> *Harrison*, Descrip. of Britain, p. 6 (Holinshed's Chron., I.).

> And when the *Redshanks* on the borders by
> Incursions made, and rang'd in battell stood
> To beare his charge, from field he made them flie,
> Where fishie Moine [in Galway] did blush with crimson blood. *Mir. for Mags.* (England's Eliza, st. 105).

> They lay upon the ground covered with skins, as the *red-shanks* do on heather. *Burton*, Anat. of Mel., p. 527.

> Though all the Scottish hinds would not bear to be compared with those of the rich counties of South Britain, they would stand very well in competition with the peasants of France, Italy, and Savoy, not to mention the mountaineers of Wales, and the *red-shanks* of Ireland.
> *Smollett*, Humphrey Clinker, ii. 41. (*Davies.*)

redshanks (red'shangks), *n.* 1. Same as *herb-robert*.—2. See *Polygonum*.

redshare (red'shãr), *v. i.* A variant of *redsear*.

red-short (red'shôrt), *a.* Noting iron or steel when it is of such a character that it is brittle at a red heat.

> The former substance [sulphur] rendering the steel more or less brittle when hot (*red-short* or hot-short).
> *Encyc. Brit.*, XIII. 283.

red-shortness (red'shôrt"nes), *n.* In *metal.*, the quality or state of being red-short.

> *Red-shortness* is often the result of the presence of an undue proportion of sulphur in the metal.
> *W. H. Greenwood*, Steel and Iron, p. 10.

> The cold-shortness or *red-shortness* of iron or steel is due principally to an admixture of oxide of iron.
> *Sci. Amer.*, N. S., LX. 408.

red-shouldered (red'shōl"dėrd), *a.* Having the "shoulder"—that is, the carpal angle or bend of the wing—red, as a bird. The red-shouldered blackbird is *Agelæus gubernator*, common in western North America, where it replaces to some extent the common red-winged blackbird, from which it differs in having the scarlet patch on the wing not bordered with buff. The red-shouldered buzzard is *Buteo lineatus*, one of the commonest of the large hawks of the United States, having the lesser wing-coverts reddish when adult.—**Red-shouldered falcon**†, the adult red-shouldered buzzard.

red-sided (red'sī"ded), *a.* Having red on the sides: specifically noting the red-winged thrush, *Turdus iliacus*.

redsides (red'sīdz), *n.* A small cyprinoid fish, *Notropis* or *Lythrurus ardens*, common in the streams of the southern United States. Also called *redfin*.

redskin (red'skin), *n.* A Red Indian; a North American Indian.

> The Virginia frontiersmen were angry with the Pennsylvania traders for selling rifles and powder to the *redskins*. *The Atlantic*, LXIV. 819.

red-spider (red'spī"dėr), *n.* A small red mite or acarine, *Tetranychus telarius*, formerly called *Acarus telarius*, now placed in the family *Tetranychidæ*: found in conservatories.

red-staff (red'stȧf), *n.* A millers' straight-edge, used in dressing millstones. The true edge, reddened by ocher, is gently rubbed on the stone, and the projecting points are thus detected, even when the irregularity of surface is very minute.

redstart (red'stärt), *n.* [< *red*[1] + *start*[2].] One of several entirely different birds which have the tail more or less red. (*a*) A small sylviine bird, *Ruticilla phœnicura*, of Europe, Asia, and Africa, related to the redbreast and bluethroat. Also *firetail*, *redtail*, etc. A similar species, *R. titys* or *tithys*, is known as the *black redstart*. (*b*) In the United States, a fly-catching warbler, *Setophaga ruticilla*, of the family *Sylvicolidæ* or *Mniotiltidæ*. The male is lustrous blue-black, with white belly and vent, the sides of the breast, the lining of the wings, and much of the extent of the wing- and tail-feathers fiery orange or flame-color, the bill and feet black. The female is mostly plain olivaceous, with the parts which are orange in the male clear pale yellow. The length is 5¼ inches, the extent 7¾. This beautiful bird abounds in woodland in eastern North America; it is migratory and insectivorous, has a singular song, builds

European Redstart (*Ruticilla phœnicura*).

American Redstart (*Setophaga ruticilla*).

a neat nest in the fork of a branch, and lays four or five eggs, which are white, speckled with shades of reddish brown.—**Blue-throated redstart.** Same as *bluethroat.*

redstreak (red'strēk), *n.* **1.** A sort of apple, so called from the color of the skin.

The *redstreak*, of all cyder fruit, hath obtained the preference. *Mortimer*, Husbandry.

2. Cider pressed from redstreak apples.

Herefordshire *redstreak* made of rotten apples at the Three Cranes, true Brunswick Mum brew'd at S. Katherines. *Character of a Coffee-house* (1673), p. 3. (*Halliwell.*)

redtail (red'tāl), *n.* and *a.* **I.** *n.* **1.** Same as *redstart* (*a*).—**2.** The red-tailed buzzard, *Buteo borealis*, one of the commonest and largest hawks of North America, when adult having the upper side of the tail bright chestnut-red. The plumage otherwise is very variable, not only with age, but also according to geographical distribution, there being several varieties or local races in western parts of the continent. It is commonly known as *hen-hawk* or *chicken-hawk*, and the young, without the red tail, is the *white-breasted hawk*. The male is from 19 to 22 inches long, and 48 inches or more in spread of wing; the female is 21 to 24 inches long, and spreads 56 inches. See cut under *Buteo.*

II. *a.* Having a red tail.

red-tape (red'tāp'), *a.* [< *red tape*: see *tape.*] Pertaining to or characterized by official routine or formality. See *red tape*, under *tape.*

Exposures by the press and criticisms in Parliament leave no one in ignorance of the vices of *red-tape* routine. H. *Spencer*, Man vs. State, p. 55.

We working men, when we do come out of the furnace, come out not tinsel and papier maché, like those fops of *red-tape* statesmen, but steel and granite. *Kingsley*, Alton Locke, iv. (*Davies.*)

red-taped (red'tāpt'), *a.* [< *red tape* + *-ed*[2].] Same as *red-tape. Nature*, XLII. 106.

red-tapery (red'tā'pe̤-ri), *n.* [< *red tape* + *-ery.*] Same as *red-tapism.*

red-tapism (red'tā'pizm), *n.* [< *red tape* + *-ism.*] Strict observance of official formalities; a system of vexatious or tedious official routine.

He at once showed . . . how little he had of the official element which is best described as *red-tapeism.* T. *W. Reid*, Cabinet Portraits, p. 52.

He loudly denounces the Tchinovnik spirit—or, as we should say, *red-tapeism* in all its forms. *D. M. Wallace*, Russia, p. 201.

red-tapist (red'tā'pist), *n.* [< *red tape* + *-ist.*] **1.** A clerk in a public office. *Quarterly Rev.*—**2.** One who adheres strictly to forms and routine in official or other business.

You seem a smart young fellow, but you must throw over that stiff *red-tapist* of yours, and go with Public Opinion and Myself. *Bulwer*, My Novel, x. 20. (*Davies.*)

In no country is the *red-tapist* so out of place as here. Every calling is filled with bold, keen, subtle-witted men, fertile in expedients and devices, who are perpetually inventing new ways of buying cheaply, underselling, or attracting custom. *W. Mathews*, Getting on in the World, p. 90.

red-thighed (red'thīd), *a.* Having or characterized by red thighs.—**Red-thighed locust.** See *locust*[1].

red-throated (red'thrō'ted), *a.* Having a patch of red on the throat: as, the *red-throated* diver, *Colymbus* or *Urinator septentrionalis.*

red-thrush (red'thrush), *n.* The redwing, *Turdus iliacus.*

red-tipped (red'tipt), *a.* Having the wings tipped with red: as, the *red-tipped* clearwing, a British moth, *Sesia formicæformis.*

redtop (red'top), *n.* A kind of bent-grass, *Agrostis vulgaris* (*A. alba*, var. *vulgaris*). The species is common throughout the northern parts of the Old World, and is thoroughly naturalized in America. It is marked to the eye by its large light panicle of minute spikelets on delicate branches, which is of a reddish hue. Other varieties, called *fiorin*, *white bent*, etc., have a whitish top and a longer ligule. Redtop, at least in the United States, is a highly valued pasture-grass, and is also sown for hay. It forms a fine turf, and is suitable for lawns. Also called *fine bent*, *finetop-grass*, and *herd's-grass.* (U. S.)—**False redtop**, the fowl meadow-grass, *Poa serotina*, which has somewhat the aspect of redtop.—**Northern** or **mountain redtop**, *Agrostis exarata*, a species found from Wisconsin to the Pacific, allied to the common redtop, and giving promise of similar service in its own range.—**Tall redtop**, a tall reddish wiry grass, *Triodia cuprea*, found in the United States.

red-tubs (red'tubz), *n.* The sapphirine gurnard, *Trigla hirundo.* [Local, Eng.]

redub† (rē̤-dub'), *v. t.* [Early mod. E. also *redoub*; < OF. *redouber*, *redauber* (also *radauber*, *radouber*, F. *radouber*), repair, mend, fit, < *re-*, again, + *douber* (*adouber*), mend, repair, etc.: see *dub*[1].] To repair or make reparation for; make amends for; requite.

Whiche domage . . . neither with treasure ne with powar can be *redoubed.* *Sir T. Elyot*, The Governour, ii. 14.

I doubte not by Coddes grace so honestly to *redubbe* all thynges that have been amys. *Ellis*, Literary Letters, p. 4.

O Gods, *redubbe* them vengeaunce iust. *Phaer*, Æneid, vi.

Whether they [monks] will conform themselves gladly, for the *redubbing* of their former trespasses, to go to other houses of their coat, where they shall be well received. *State Papers*, I. 540, in R. W. Dixon's Hist. Church of [Eng., vii., note.

redubber† (rē̤-dub'ėr), *n.* [Also *redubbor*; < OF. **redoubeur*, *radoubeur*, one who mends or repairs a ship, < *redouber*, *radouber*, mend: see *redub.*] One who bought stolen cloth and so altered it in color or fashion that it could not be recognized.

reduce (rē̤-dūs'), *v. t.*; pret. and pp. *reduced*, ppr. *reducing.* [< ME. *reducen*, < OF. *reducier*, vernacularly *reduire*, F. *réduire* = Pr. *reduzir*, *reduire* = Cat. *reduir* = Sp. *reducir* = Pg. *reduzir* = It. *ridurre*, < L. *reducere*, lead or bring back, draw back, restore, replace, bring to a certain condition, reduce, < *re-*, back, + *ducere*, lead, bring: see *duct.* Cf. *reduct*, *reduit*, *redout*[2].] **1**†. To lead or bring back; restore; resolve to a former state.

Therupon he *reduced* to their memorie the battailes they had fought. *J. Brende*, tr. of Quintus Curtius, iv.

Abate the edge of traitors, gracious Lord,
That would *reduce* these bloody days again.
Shak., Rich. III., v. 5. 36.

A good man will go a little out of his road to *reduce* the wandring traveller; but if he will not return, it will be an unreasonable compliance to go along with him to the end of his wandring. *Jer. Taylor*, Rule of Conscience, II. iii. 19.

Mr. Cotton . . . did spend most of his time, both publicly and privately, to discover . . . errors, and to *reduce* such as were gone astray. *Winthrop*, Hist. New England, I. 304.

And 'cause I see the truth of his affliction,
Which may be your's, or mine, or any body's,
Whose passions are neglected, I will try
My best skill to *reduce* him.
Shirley, Hyde Park, v. 1.

It were but right
And equal to *reduce* me to my dust.
Milton, P. L., x. 748.

2. In *surg.*, to restore to its proper place, or so that the parts concerned are brought back to their normal topographical relations: as, to *reduce* a dislocation, fracture, or hernia.—**3.** To bring to any specified state, condition, or form: as, to *reduce* civil affairs to order; to *reduce* a man to poverty or despair; to *reduce* glass to powder; to *reduce* a theory to practice; to *reduce* a Latin phrase to English.

Being inspired with the holy spirite of God, they [the 72 Interpreters chosen by Eleazar out of each tribe] *reduced* out of Hebrue into Greeke all the partes of the olde Testament. *Guevara*, Letters (tr. by Hellowes, 1577), p. 380.

Doe you then blame and finde faulte with soe good an Acte in that good pope as the *reducing* of such a greate people to Christianitye? *Spenser*, State of Ireland.

He had beene a peace-maker to *reduce* such and such, which were at oddes, to amitie. *Purchas*, Pilgrimage, p. 453.

Reduc'd to practice, his beloved rule
Would only prove him a consummate fool.
Cowper, Conversation, l. 139.

Holland was *reduced* to such a condition that peace was her first necessity. *Lecky*, Eng. in 18th Cent., p. 463.

4. In *metal.* and *chem.*, to bring into the metallic form; separate, as a metal, from the oxygen or other mineralizer with which it may be combined, or change from a higher to a lower degree of oxidation: as, to *reduce* the ores of silver or copper.—**5**†. To atone for; repair; redress.

Till they *reduce* the wrongs done to my father.
Marlowe.

6. To bring down; diminish in length, breadth, thickness, size, quantity, value, or the like: as, to *reduce* expenses; to *reduce* the quantity of meat in diet; to *reduce* the price of goods; to *reduce* the strength of spirit; to *reduce* a figure or design (to make a smaller copy of it without changing the form or proportion).

He likes your house, your housemaid, and your pay;
Reduce his wages, or get rid of her,
Tom quits you. *Cowper*, Truth, l. 211.

7. To bring to an inferior condition; weaken; impoverish; lower; degrade; impair in fortune, dignity, or strength: as, the family were in *reduced* circumstances; the patient was much *reduced* by hemorrhage.

Yet lo! in me what authors have to brag on!
Reduced at last to hiss in my own dragon.
Pope, Dunciad, iii. 286.

The Chamber encroached upon the sovereign, thwarted him, *reduced* him to a cypher, imprisoned him, and slew him. *W. R. Greg*, Misc. Essays, 2d ser., p. 93.

I dare say he was some poor musicianer, or singer, or a *reduced* gentleman, perhaps, for he always came after dusk, or else on bad, dark days. *Mayhew*, London Labour and London Poor, I. 331.

8. To subdue, as by force of arms; bring into subjection; render submissive: as, to *reduce* mutineers to submission; Spain, Gaul, and Britain were *reduced* by the Roman arms.

Charles marched northward at the head of a force sufficient, as it seemed, to *reduce* the Covenanters to submission. *Macaulay*, Nugent's Hampden.

Montpensier was now closely besieged, till at length, *reduced* by famine, he was compelled to capitulate. *Prescott*, Ferd. and Isa., ii. 2.

The fortresses garrisoned by the French in Spain were *reduced*; but at what a prodigious expenditure of life was this effected! *Encyc. Brit.*, IX. 457.

9. To bring into a class, order, genus, or species; bring within certain limits of definition or description.

I think it [analogy between words and reason] very worthy to be *reduced* into a science by itself. *Bacon*, Advancement of Learning, ii. 236.

Zanchius *reduceth* such infidels to four chief sects. *Burton*, Anat. of Mel., p. 598.

I shall . . . *reduce* these authors under their respective classes. *Addison*, Of the Christian Religion, § i. 1.

The variations of languages are *reduced* to rules. *Johnson*, Dict.

10. To show (a problem) to be merely a special case of one already solved.—**11.** To change the denomination of (numbers): as, to *reduce* a number of shillings to farthings, or conversely (see *reduction* (*i*)); change the form of (an algebraic expression) to one simpler or more convenient.—**12.** To prove the conclusion of (an indirect syllogism) from its premises by means of direct syllogism and immediate inference alone.—**13.** To adjust (an observed quantity) by subtracting from it effects due to the special time and place of observation, especially, in astronomy, by removing the effects of refraction, parallax, aberration, precession, and nutation, changing a circummeridian to a meridian altitude, and the like.—**14.** In *Scots law*, to set aside by an action at law; rescind or annul by legal means: as, to *reduce* a deed, writing, etc.—**15.** *Milit.*, to take off the establishment and strike off the pay-roll, as a regiment. When a regiment is reduced, the officers are generally put upon half-pay.—**Reduced eye**, an ideal eye in which the two nodal points of the refractive system are considered as united into one, and also the two principal points: this simplifies the mathematical treatment of certain problems.—**Reduced form of an imaginary**, the form $r(\cos\phi + i\sin\phi)$, first used in 1828 by Cauchy.—**Reduced hub.** See *hub*, 7.—**Reduced inertia of a machine.** See *inertia* and *machine.*—**Reduced iron**, metallic iron in a fine powder, obtained by reducing ferric oxid by hydrogen at a dull-red heat. Also called *powder of iron*, *iron-powder*, *iron by hydrogen.*—**Reduced latitude.** Same as *geocentric latitude* (which see, under *latitude*).—**Reduced reaction-time.** See *reaction-time.*—**Reducing flame**, in blowpipe analysis. See *flame*, 1.—**Reducing square.** See *square.*—**To reduce the square** (*milit.*), to bring back a battalion which has been formed in a square to its former position in line or column. *Farrow.*—**To reduce to the ranks** (*milit.*), to degrade, for misconduct, to the condition of a private soldier.=**Syn. 6.** To lessen, decrease, abate, curtail, shorten, abridge, contract, retrench.

reduceable† (rē̤-dū'sa-bl), *a.* [= OF. *reduisable*; as *reduce* + *-able.* Cf. *reducible.*] Same as *reducible.*

They [young students] should be habituated to consider every excellence as *reduceable* to principles. *Sir J. Reynolds*, Discourses, I. viii.

reducement (rē̤-dūs'mẹnt), *n.* [= Sp. *reducimiento* = It. *riducimento*; as *reduce* + *-ment.*] **1.** The act of reducing; a bringing back; restoration.

This once select Nation of God . . . being ever since incapable of any Coalition or *Reducement* into one Body politic. *Howell*, Letters, ii. 8.

By this we shall know whether yours be that ancient Prelaty which you say was first constituted for the *reducement* of quiet and unanimity into the Church.
Milton, Church-Government, i. 6.

2. Reduction; abatement.

After a little *reducement* of his passion, and that time and further meditation had disposed his senses to their perfect estate.
History of Patient Grisel, p. 40. (*Halliwell.*)

reducent (rē̤-dū'sent), *a.* and *n.* [< L. *reducen(t-)s*, ppr. of *reducere*: see *reduce*.] **I.** *a.* Tending to reduce.

II. *n.* That which reduces. *Imp. Dict.*

reducer (rē̤-dū'sėr), *n.* **1.** One who or that which reduces, in any sense.

The last substances enumerated are those in general use as *reducers* or developers in photography.
Silver Sunbeam, p. 95.

An accumulator is indeed merely a chemical converter which is unequalled as a pressure-*reducer*.
Electric Rev. (Eng.), XXV. 583.

2. A joint-piece for connecting pipes of varying diameter. It may be of any form, straight, bent, etc. Also called *reducing-coupling*.

a, reducer, connecting the pipe of larger diameter *b* with the pipe of smaller diameter *c*.

reducibility (rē̤-dū-si-bil'i̤-ti), *n.* [< *reducible* + *-ity* (see *-bility*).] Reducibleness; reductibility.

The theorem of the *reducibility* of the general problem of transformation to the rational is, however, stated without proof in this paper. *Encyc. Brit.*, XIII. 70.

It was, however, quite evident, from . . . the history and the complete *reducibility* of the tumour, that it must be a pulmonary hernia. *Lancet*, No. 3429, p. 1002.

reducible (rē̤-dū'si-bl), *a.* [< OF. *redusible* = Sp. *reducible* = Pg. *reduzivel* = It. *riducibile*; as *reduce* + *-ible*. Cf. *reduceable*.] Capable of being reduced; convertible.

In the new World they have a World of Drinks; for there is no Root, Flower, Fruit, or Pulse but is *reducible* to a notable Liquor. *Howell*, Letters, ii. 54.

The line of its motion was neither straight nor yet *reducible* to any curve or mixed line that I had met with among mathematicians. *Boyle*, Works, III. 683.

I have never been the less satisfied that no cause *reducible* to the known laws of nature occasioned my sufferings.
Barham, Ingoldsby Legends, I. 198.

Reducible circuit. See *circuit*.—**Reducible hernia**, a hernia whose contents can be returned by pressure or posture.

reducibleness (rē̤-dū'si-bl-nes), *n.* The quality of being reducible.

The *reducibleness* of ice back again into water.
Boyle, Works, III. 50.

reducibly (rē̤-dū'si-bli), *adv.* In a reducible manner.

reducine (rē̤-dū'sin), *n.* [< *reduce* + *-ine*[2].] A decomposition product of urochrome.

reducing-coupling (rē̤-dū'sing-kup'ling), *n.* Same as *reducer*, 2.

reducing-press (rē̤-dū'sing-pres), *n.* An auxiliary press used in sheet-metal work to complete shapes that have been partially struck up.

reducing-scale (rē̤-dū'sing-skāl), *n.* A form of scale used by surveyors to reduce chains and links to acres and roods by inspection, and also in mapping and drawing to different scales; a surveying-scale.

reducing-T (rē̤-dū'sing-tē), *n.* A T-shaped pipe-coupling, having arms different from the stem in diameter of opening. It is used to unite pipes of different sections. Also written *reducing-tee*.

reducing-valve (rē̤-dū'sing-valv), *n.* In *steam-engin.*, a peculiar valve controlled by forces acting in opposite directions. The parts are so arranged that the valve opens to its extreme limit only when the pressure on the delivery side is at a prescribed minimum, closing the part in the valve-seat more or less when this minimum is exceeded. The pressure on the delivery side of the valve is thus kept from varying (except between very narrow limits) from its predetermined pressure, although the pressure on the opposite side may be variable, and always higher than on the delivery side. Such valves are much used for maintaining lower pressures in steam-heating and -drying apparatus than is carried in the boiler. They are also used in automatic air-brakes for railways and in other pneumatic machines, and, in some forms, as gas-regulators for equalizing the pressure of gas delivered to gas-burners, etc. Also called *pressure-reducing valve*.

reduct† (rē̤-dukt'), *v. t.* [< L. *reductus*, pp. of *reducere*, lead or bring back: see *reduce*.] To reduce.

All the kynges host there heying assembled and *reducte* into one companye. Hall, Edw. IV., an. 10.

Pray let me *reduct* some two or three shillings for points and ribands.
B. *Jonson*, Every Man out of his Humour, iv. 5.

reduct (rē̤-dukt'), *n.* [< ML. *reductus*, a withdrawing-place: see *redout*[2].] In *building*, a little piece or cut taken out of a part, member, etc., to make it more uniform, or for any other purpose; a quirk. *Gwilt.*

reductibility (rē̤-duk-ti-bil'i̤-ti), *n.* [= F. *réductibilité*; as *reduct* + *-ibility*.] The quality of being reducible; reducibleness. *Imp. Dict.*

reductio ad absurdum (rē̤-duk'shi-ō ad ab-sėr'dum). [L.: *reductio*, a leading, reduction; *ad*, to; *absurdum*, neut. of *absurdus*, absurd: see *absurd*.] A reduction to an absurdity; the proof of a proposition by proving the falsity of its contradictory opposite: an indirect demonstration. In geometry the reductio ad absurdum consists in drawing a figure whose parts are supposed to have certain relations, and then showing that this leads to a conclusion contrary to a known proposition, whence it follows that the parts of the figure cannot have those relations. Thus, in Euclid's "Elements" the proposition that if a triangle has two angles equal the sides opposite those angles will be equal is proved as follows. In the triangle ABC, let the angles ABC and ACB be equal. Then, suppose AB to be greater than AC. Lay off DB = AC and join DC. Then, comparing the two triangles ACB and DBC, we have in the former the sides AC and BC and their included angle ACB equal in the latter to the sides DB and CB and their included angle DBC. Hence, these two triangles would be equal, or the part would be equal to the whole. This proof is a *reductio ad absurdum*. This kind of reasoning is considered somewhat objectionable as not showing the principle from which the proposition flows; but it is a perfectly conclusive mode of proof, and, in fact, is in all cases readily converted into a direct proof. Thus, in the above example, we have only to compare the triangle ABC with itself, considering it as two triangles according as the angle B is named before C or vice versa. In the triangle ABC the angles B and C with the included side BC are respectively equal in the triangle ACB to the angles C and B with the included side CB; hence the other parts of the triangles are equal, and the side AC opposite the first angle B in the first triangle is equal to the side AB opposite the first angle C in the second triangle.

reduction (rē̤-duk'shon), *n.* [< OF. *reduction*, F. *réduction* = Pr. *reductio* = Sp. *reduccion* = Pg. *reducção* = It. *riduzione*, < L. *reductio(n-)*, a leading or bringing back, a restoring, restoration, < *reducere*, lead or bring back: see *reduce*, *reduct*.] The act of reducing, or the state of being reduced. (*a*†) The act of bringing back or restoring.

For *reduction* of your majesty's realm of Ireland to the unity of the Church. *Bp. Burnet*, Records, II. ii.

(*b*) Conversion into another state or form: as, the *reduction* of a body to powder; the *reduction* of things to order. (*c*) Diminution: as, the *reduction* of the expenses of government; the *reduction* of the national debt; a *reduction* of 25 per cent. made to wholesale buyers.

Let him therefore first make the proper *reduction* in the account, and then see what it amounts to.
Waterland, Works, VI. 186.

(*d*) Conquest; subjugation: as, the *reduction* of a province under the power of a foreign nation; the *reduction* of a fortress. (*e*) A settlement or parish of South American Indians converted and trained by the Jesuits.

Governing and civilizing the natives of Brazil and Paraguay in the missions and *reductions*, or ministering, at the hourly risk of his life, to his coreligionists in England under Elizabeth and James I., the Jesuit appears alike devoted, indefatigable, cheerful, and worthy of hearty admiration and respect. *Encyc. Brit.*, XIII. 649.

The Indians [under the Jesuits in Paraguay] were gathered into towns or communal villages called bourgaden or *reductions*, where they were taught the common arts, agriculture, and the practice of rearing cattle.
Johns Hopkins Univ. Studies, 8th ser., IV. 32.

(*f*) The bringing of a problem to depend on a problem already solved. (*g*) The transformation of an algebraic expression into another of a simpler kind. (*h*) The lowering of the values of the numerator and denominator of a fraction, or of the antecedent and consequent of a ratio, by dividing both by the same quantity. (*i*) The conversion of a quantity expressed in terms of one denomination so as to express it in terms of another denomination. *Ascending reduction* is conversion to terms of larger units; *descending reduction*, conversion to terms of smaller units. (*j*) The proof of the conclusion of an indirect syllogism from its premises by means of a direct syllogism and immediate inferences. This is said to be a *reduction* to the mode of direct syllogism employed. (*k*) A direct syllogism proving, by means of conversions and other immediate inferences, that the conclusion of an indirect syllogism follows from its premises. (*l*) The act or process of making a copy of a figure, map, design, draft, etc., on a smaller scale, preserving the original proportions; also, the result of this process. (*m*) In *surg.*, the operation of restoring a dislocated or fractured bone to its former place. (*n*) Separation of a metal from substances combined with it: used especially with reference to lead, zinc, and copper, and also applied to the treatment of iron ore, as when steel is made from it by a direct process. (*o*) In *astron.*, the correction of observed quantities for instrumental errors, as well as for refraction, parallax, aberration, precession, and nutation, so as to bring out their cosmical significance. A similar process is applied to observations in other physical sciences. (*p*) In *Scots law*, an action for setting aside a deed, writing, etc.—**Apagogical reduction**, in *logic*, a reduction in which the contradictory of the conclusion becomes one of the premises, and the contradictory of one of the premises the conclusion. Apagogical reduction is an application of the *reductio ad absurdum*, and is also called *reductio per impossibile*. Example:

Baroco.	*Reductio per impossibile.*
All M is P.	All M is P.
Some S is not P.	All S is M.
Ergo, Some S is not M.	Ergo, All S is P.

Chasles-Zeuthen reduction, a method of finding how many figures fulfil certain conditions, by the consideration of degenerate figures composed of simpler figures with lower constants. Thus, in this way we readily find that the number of conics touching five given conics in a plane is 3,264.—**Iron-reduction process.** See *process*.—**Long reduction**, in *logic*, a reduction in which the major premise of the original syllogism becomes the minor premise, and vice versa, and in which one of the premises and the conclusion are converted. Example:

Camestres.	*Long Reduction.*
All M is P.	No P is S.
No S is P.	All M is P.
Ergo, No S is M.	Ergo, No M is S.

Ostensive reduction, that reduction which has for its premises the original premises or their conversions, and for its conclusion the original conclusion or its converse.—**Reduction and reduction-improbation**, in *Scots law*, the designations given to the two varieties of rescissory actions. See *improbation*, 2.—**Reduction reductive**, an action in which a decree of reduction which has been erroneously or improperly obtained is sought to be reduced.—**Reduction to the ecliptic**, the difference between the anomaly of a planet reckoned from its node and the longitude reckoned from the same point.—**Short reduction**, in *logic*, a reduction which differs from the original syllogism only in having one of its premises converted. The following is an example:

Cesare.	*Short Reduction.*
No M is P.	No P is M.
All S is P.	All S is P.
Ergo, No S is M.	Ergo, No S is M.

=**Syn.** (*c*) Lessening, decrease, abatement, curtailment, abridgment, contraction, retrenchment.

reduction-compasses (rē̤-duk'shon-kum'pas-ez), *n. pl.* Proportional dividers, or whole-and-half dividers.

reduction-formula (rē̤-duk'shon-fôr'mṳ̄-lä̤), *n.* In the *integral calculus*, a formula depending on integration by parts, reducing an integral to another nearer to one of the standard forms.

reduction-works (rē̤-duk'shon-wėrks), *n. sing.* and *pl.* A metallurgical establishment; smelting-works.

reductive (rē̤-duk'tiv), *a.* and *n.* [= F. *réductif* = Sp. Pg. *reductivo* = It. *riduttivo*, < L. *reductus*, pp. of *reducere*, lead or bring back: see *reduct*, *reduce*.] **I.** *a.* Having the property, power, or effect of reducing; tending to reduce.

Inquire into the repentance of thy former life particularly; whether it were of a great and perfect grief, and productive of fixed resolutions of holy living, and *reductive* of these to act. *Jer. Taylor*, Holy Dying, iv. 6.

Reduction reductive. See *reduction*.—**Reductive conversion**, in *logic*, a conversion of a proposition in which there is some modification of the subject or predicate: as, no man is a mother, therefore no mother is some man. See *conversion*, 2.—**Reductive principle**, a principle by which an indirect syllogism is reduced to a direct mood. The reductive principles were said to be conversion, transposition, and reductio per impossibile.

II. *n.* That which has the power of reducing.

So that it should seem there needed no other *reductive* of the numbers of men to an equability than the wars that have happened in the world.
Sir M. Hale, Orig. of Mankind, p. 215.

reductively (rē̤-duk'tiv-li), *adv.* By reduction; by consequence.

Love, and simplicity, and humility, and usefulness: . . . I think these do *reductively* contain all that is excellent in the whole conjugation of Christian graces.
Jer. Taylor, Works (ed. 1835), II. 44.

reduit†, *n.* See *redout*[2].

redundance (rē̤-dun'dans), *n.* [< OF. *redondance*, F. *redondance*, *rédondance* = Sp. Pg. *redundancia* = It. *ridondanza*, < L. *redundantia*, an overflow, superfluity, excess, < *redundan(t-)s*, redundant: see *redundant*.] **1.** The character of being redundant; superfluity; superabundance.

He is a poor unwieldy wretch that commits faults out of the *redundance* of his good qualities.
Steele, Tatler, No. 27.

2. That which is redundant or in excess; anything superfluous.

redundancy (rē̤-dun'dan-si), *n.* [As *redundance* (see *-cy*).] Same as *redundance*.

The mere
Redundancy of youth's contentedness.
Wordsworth, Prelude, vi.

=**Syn.** *Verbosity*, *Tautology*, etc. (see *pleonasm*); surplusage.

redundant (rē̤-dun'dant), *a.* [< OF. *redondant*, F. *redondant*, *rédondant* = Sp. Pg. *redundante* = It. *ridondante*, < L. *redundan(t-)s*, ppr. of *redundare*, overflow, redound: see *redound*.] **1**†. Rolling or flowing back, as a wave or surge.

On his rear,
Circular base of rising folds, that tower'd
Fold above fold, a surging maze! his head . . .
Amidst his circling spires, that on the grass
Floated *redundant*. *Milton*, P. L., ix. 503.

2. Superfluous; exceeding what is natural or necessary; superabundant; exuberant.

Notwithstanding the *redundant* oil in fishes, they do not increase fat so much as flesh. *Arbuthnot*, Aliments, iv. 1.

With foliage of such dark *redundant* growth.
Cowper, Task, i. 226.

A farmer's daughter, with *redundant* health.
Crabbe, Works, VIII. 216.

3. Using or containing more words or images than are necessary or useful: as, a *redundant* style.

Where the author is *redundant*, mark those paragraphs to be retrenched. *Watts.*

Redundant chord or **interval**, in *music*, same as *augmented chord* or *interval* — that is, one greater by a half-step than the corresponding major chord or interval. Also *pluperfect*, *extreme*, *superfluous chord* or *interval*. So *redundant fourth*, *fifth*, *sixth*, etc.—**Redundant hyperbola**, a curve having three or more asymptotes.—**Redundant number**, a number the sum of whose divisors exceeds the number itself.

redundantly (rẹ̄-dun′dant-li), *adv.* In a redundant manner; with superfluity or excess; superfluously; superabundantly.

red-underwing (red′un″dėr-wing), *n.* A large British moth, *Catocala nupta*, expanding three inches, having the under wings red bordered with black. See *underwing*.

reduplicate (rẹ̄-dū′pli-kāt), *v.* [< ML. (LL. in derived noun) *reduplicatus*, pp. of *reduplicare* (> It. *reduplicare* = Sp. Pg. *reduplicar*), redouble, < L. *re-*, again, + *duplicare*, double, duplicate: see *duplicate*. Cf. *redouble*.] **I.** *trans.* 1. To double again; multiply; repeat.

That *reduplicated* advice of our Saviour.
Bp. Pearson, Expos. of Creed, xii.

Then followed that ringing and *reduplicated* laugh of his, so like the joyous bark of a dog when he starts for a ramble with his master.
Lowell, The Century, XXXV. 514.

2. In *philol.*, to repeat, as a syllable or the initial part of a syllable (usually a root-syllable). See *reduplication*.

II. *intrans.* In *philol.*, to be doubled or repeated; undergo reduplication: as, *reduplicating* verbs.

reduplicate (rẹ̄-dū′pli-kāt), *a.* [= F. *rédupliqué* = Sp. Pg. *reduplicado* = It. *reduplicato*, < ML. *reduplicatus*, pp.: see the verb.] 1. Redoubled; repeated; reduplicative.

Reduplicate words are formed of repetitions of sound, as in murmur, singsong. *S. S. Haldeman*, Etymology, p. 23.

2. In *bot.*: (*a*) Valvate, with the edges folded back so as to project outward: said of petals and sepals in one form of estivation. (*b*) Describing an estivation so characterized. Also *reduplicative*.

reduplication (rẹ̄-dū-pli-kā′shọn), *n.* [= F. *réduplication* = Sp. *reduplicacion* = Pg. *reduplicação* = It. *reduplicazione*, < L. *reduplicatio(n-)*, < (ML.) *reduplicare*, redouble, reduplicate: see *reduplicate*.] 1. The act of reduplicating, redoubling, or repeating, or the state of being reduplicated.

Jesus, by *reduplication* of his desire, fortifying it with a command, made it in the Baptist to become a duty.
Jer. Taylor, Works (ed. 1835), I. 97.

The memory-train is liable to change in two respects, which considerably modify its structure: viz., (1) through the evanescence of some parts, and (2) through the partial recurrence of like impressions, which produces *reduplications* of varying amount and extent in other parts.
J. Ward, Encyc. Brit., XX. 61.

2. In *rhet.*, a figure in which a verse ends with the same word with which the following begins. —3. In *philol.*: (*a*) The repetition of a syllable (usually a root-syllable), or of the initial part, often with more or less modification, in various processes of word-formation and inflection. In our languages, it is especially the perfect tense that exhibits reduplication: thus, Gothic *haihald*, Latin *cecini*, Greek πέφευγα, Sanskrit *babhāra*; but also the present tense: thus, Latin *sisto*, Greek δίδωμι, Sanskrit *dadāmi*, etc.; and elsewhere. (*b*) The new syllable formed by reduplication.—4. In *logic*, an expression affixed to the subject of a proposition, showing the formal cause of its possession of the predicate: as, "man, as an animal, has a stomach," where the expression "as an animal" is the reduplication.—5. In *anat.* and *zoöl.*, a folding of a part; a folded part; a fold or duplication, as of a membrane, of the skin, etc. Also *reduplicature*.—**Attic reduplication**, in Gr. *gram.*, reduplication in the perfect of some verbs beginning with α, ε, ο, by prefixing the first two letters of the stem to the same letters with temporal augment: as ἀλήλιφα from ἀλείφω, ἀκήκοα from ἀκούω. A similar reduplication is found in the second aorist (ἤγαγον from ἄγω) and in the present (ἀραρίσκω). This reduplication did not especially characterize the Attic as distinguished from contemporary dialects, but was called *Attic* by late grammarians as opposed to the less classic form used in their own days.

reduplicative (rẹ̄-dū′pli-kā-tiv), *a.* [< F. *réduplicatif* = Sp. Pg. *reduplicativo* = It. *reduplicativo*, < NL. *reduplicativus*, < ML. *reduplicare*, reduplicate: see *reduplicate*.] 1. Containing or effecting reduplication, in any sense.

Some logicians refer *reduplicative* propositions to this place, as "Men, considered as men, are rational creatures" —that is, because they are men. *Watts*, Logic, ii. 2.

2. In *bot.*, same as *reduplicate*, 2.

reduplicature (rẹ̄-dū′pli-kā-tūr), *n.* [< *reduplicate* + *-ure*.] Same as *reduplication*, 5. [Rare.]

The body (in *Phyllopoda*) is either cylindrically elongated and clearly segmented, without free *reduplicature* of the skin, e. g. Branchipus, or it may be covered by a broad and flattened shield. *Claus*, Zoölogy (trans.), p. 416.

Reduviidæ (red-ū-vī′i-dē), *n. pl.* [NL. (Stephens, 1829), < *Reduvius* + *-idæ*.] An important family of predaceous bugs, named from the genus *Reduvius*. They have the thoracic segments concentrated, the coxæ short, two ocelli, four-jointed antennæ, a three-jointed rostrum, three-jointed tarsi, and long strong legs, of which the anterior are sometimes prehensile. It is a large and wide-spread family, containing a great variety of forms grouped into nine subfamilies and many genera. Throughout their life they are predaceous and feed on other insects. A very few species, like *Conorhinus sanguisugus*, suck the blood of warm-blooded animals. See also cuts under *Conorhinus*, *Harpactor*, *Pirates*, and *Reduvius*.

Sinea diadema, one of the *Reduviidæ*. (Line shows natural size.)

reduvioid (rẹ̄-dū′vi-oid), *a.* and *n.* [< *Reduvius* + *-oid*.] **I.** *a.* Of or pertaining to the *Reduviidæ*; resembling a reduviid.

II. *n.* A member of the family *Reduviidæ*.

Reduvius (rẹ̄-dū′vi-us), *n.* [NL. (Fabricius, 1776), < L. *reduvia*, a hangnail.] A genus of heteropterous insects, typical of the family *Reduviidæ*, formerly of very large extent, but now restricted to species which have the postocular section of the head longer than the anteocular section, and the first joint of the head scarcely shorter than the second. About 50 species are now included, most of them African. A few are European, and one only is found in America. *R. personatus* is a European species, an inch long, known as the *fly-bug*, of a dark-brown color with reddish legs.

Reduvius personatus.
b, fly (parts of right side removed); *c*, larva.

redux (rē′duks), *a.* [L., that leads or brings back, also led or brought back, < *reducere*, lead or bring back: see *reduce*.] 1. Led or brought back, as from a distance, from captivity, etc.: as, "Astræa *Redux*" (the title of a poem by Dryden on the restoration and return of Charles II.).

Lady Laura Standish is the best character in "Phineas Finn" and its sequel "Phineas *Redux*."
Trollope, Autobiog., xvii.

2. In *med.*, noting the return of certain physical signs, after their disappearance in consequence of disease.

redware (red′wãr), *n.* A seaweed, *Laminaria digitata*, the common tangle.

red-wat (red′wot′), *a.* [< *red*[1] + *wat*, a Sc. form of *wet*: see *wet*.] Wetted by something red, as blood. [Scotch.]

The hand of her kindred has been *red-wat* in the heart's blude o' my name; but my heart says, Let byganes be byganes. *Blackwood's Mag.*, VII. 334.

redwater (red′wâ″tėr), *n.* A disease of cattle, also called *hemoglobinuria*, or *hemoglobinemia*, because the coloring matter (hemoglobin) of the red blood-corpuscles which have been broken up in the system appears in the urine, and imparts to it a pale-red or a dark-red, port-wine color. The disease prevails in various countries in undrained, unimproved meadows and in woods, whence it is also called *wood-evil*. According to some, it is caused by the ingestion of food growing in such localities; others attribute it to rheumatic attacks, resulting from exposure. Redwater is also a prominent symptom of Texas cattle-fever, and occasionally accompanies anthrax in cattle. It is rarely observed among sheep and swine.

red-water tree (red′wâ″tėr trē). The sassy-bark tree. See *Erythrophlæum*.

redweed (red′wēd), *n.* 1. The corn-poppy, *Papaver Rhœas*, whose red petals have been used as a dye. Also applied locally to various reddish-stemmed plants. [Eng.]—2. A species of *Phytolacca*, or pokeweed. [West Indies.]

red-whelk (red′hwelk), *n.* A whelk, *Chrysodomus antiquus*. See cut under *reversed*. [Local, Eng.]

red-whiskered (red′hwis″kėrd), *a.* Having red whiskers: applied in ornithology to several birds: as, the *red-whiskered* bulbul, *Otocompsa jocosa* of India.

redwing (red′wing), *n.* 1. The red-winged thrush of Europe, *Turdus iliacus*.—2. The red-winged marsh-blackbird of America, *Agelæus phœniceus*. See *Agelæus* and *blackbird*.

red-winged (red′wingd), *a.* Having red wings, or red on the wings.

red-withe (red′with), *n.* A high-climbing vine of tropical America, *Combretum Jacquini*. [West Indies.]

redwood (red′wụ̂d), *n.* 1. The most valuable of Californian timber-trees, *Sequoia sempervirens*, or its wood. It occupies the Coast ranges, where exposed to ocean fogs, from the northern limit of the State to the southern borders of Monterey county, but is most abundant north of San Francisco. It is the only congener of the famous big-or mammoth tree, which it almost rivals in size. It grows commonly from 200 to 300 feet high, with a straight cylindrical trunk, naked to the height of 70 or

Branch with Cones of Redwood (*Sequoia sempervirens*).
a, a cone; *b*, a seed.

100 feet; the diameter is from 8 to 12 feet. The bark is from 6 to 12 inches thick, of a bright cinnamon color; the wood is of a rich brownish red, light, straight-grained, easily worked and taking a fine finish, and very durable in contact with the soil. It is the prevailing and most valuable building-timber of the Pacific coast; in California it is used almost exclusively for shingles, fence-posts, railway-ties, telegraph-poles, wine-butts, etc.

2. The name is also applied to various other trees. Thus, the East Indian redwoods are *Soymida febrifuga*, also called *East Indian mahogany*; *Pterocarpus santalinus*, the red sandalwood (see *sandalwood*); and *P. Indicus* (including *P. dalbergioides*), the Andaman redwood, or padouk. The last is a lofty tree of India, Burma, the Andaman Islands, etc., with the heart-wood dark-red, close-grained, and moderately hard, used to make furniture, gun-carriages, carts, and for many other purposes. Other trees called *redwood* are *Cornus mas*, of Turkey; *Rhamnus Erythroxylon*, the Siberian buckthorn; *Melhania Erythroxylon* of the *Sterculiaceæ*, an almost extinct tree of St. Helena; the Jamaican *Laplacea* (Gordonia) *Hæmatoxylon* of the *Ternstrœmiaceæ*; *Colubrina ferruginosa*, a rhamnaceous tree of the Bahamas; *Ochna arborea* of the Cape of Good Hope; *Ceanothus spinosus*, a shrub or small tree of southern California; and any tree of the genus *Erythroxylon*. *Redwood* is also a local name of the Scotch pine. See *pine*[1].

red-wood (red′wụ̂d), *a.* [Also *red-wud*; < *red*[1] intensive (cf. *red-mad*, etc.) + *wood*[2], mad: see *wood*[2].] Stark mad. [Scotch.]

An' now she's like to rin *red-wud*
About her Whisky.
Burns, Prayer to the Scotch Representatives.

ree[1] (rē), *v. t.* [Also *rie*; supposed to be a dial. reduction of *riddle*[2].] To riddle; sift; separate or throw off. [Prov. Eng.]

After malt is well rubbed and winnowed, you must then *ree* it over in a sieve. *Mortimer*, Husbandry.

ree[2] (rē), *a.* [< ME. **ree*, *reh*, < AS. *hreóh*, *hrióh*, contr. *hreó*, fierce, wild, stormy, troubled, = OS. *hrē*, wild.] 1. Wild; outrageous; crazy. [Prov. Eng.]—2. Half-drunk; tipsy. [Prov. Eng.]

ree[2] (rē), *n.* [Cf. *ree*[2], *a.*] A state of temporary delirium. [Prov. Eng.]

ree[3] (rē), *n.* [Origin obscure.] A river; a flood. [Prov. Eng.]

ree[4] (rē), *interj.* A reduction (as an exclamation) of *reet*, dialectal form of *right*: used in driving horses.

reebok (rā′bok), *n.* [< D. *reebok* = E. *roebuck*: see *roebuck*.] A South African antelope, *Pelea capreola*: so called by the Dutch colonists. The horns are smooth, long, straight, and slender, and so sharp at the point that the Hottentots and Bushmen use them for needles and bodkins. The reebok is nearly 5 feet in length, 2½ feet high at the shoulder, of a slighter and more graceful form than most other antelopes, and extremely swift. Also *reh-bok* and *rheebok*.

reecht, *n.* [< ME. *reche*, *rech*, an assibilated form of *reek*, smoke: see *reek*[1].] Smoke.

Such a rothun of a *reche* ros.
Alliterative Poems (E. E. T. S.), ii. 1009.

reechily†, *adv.* [< *reechy* + *-ly*[2].] Smokily; squalidly.

And wash his face, he lookt so *reechilie*,
Like bacon hanging on the chimnie roofe.
D. Belchier, See me and See me not, sig. C. 2 b. (*Nares.*)

reëcho (rẹ-ek'ō), *v.* [Early mod. E. *re-eccho*; < *re-* + *echo*.] **I.** *intrans.* To echo back; sound back or reverberate again.

A charge of snuff the wily virgin threw; . . .
And the high dome *re-echoes* to his nose.
Pope, R. of the L., v. 86.

II. *trans.* To echo back; return; send back; repeat; reverberate again: as, the hills *reëcho* the roar of cannon.

The consecrated root
Re-echoing pious anthems! *Cowper*, Task, i. 343.

reëcho (rẹ-ek'ō), *n.* [< *reëcho*, *v.*] The echo of an echo; a second or repeated echo.

The hills and vallies here and there resound
With the *re-echoes* of the deepe-mouth'd hound.
W. Browne, Britannia's Pastorals, i. 4.

reechy† (rē'chi), *a.* [An assibilated form of *reeky*.] Tarnished with smoke; sooty; foul; squalid; filthy.

The kitchen malkin pins
Her richest lockram 'bout her *reechy* neck.
Shak., Cor., ii. 1. 225.

reed[1] (rēd), *n.* [< ME. *reed*, *red*, *reod*, irreg. *rehed*, *reheed*, < AS. *hreód* = OD. *ried*, D. *riet* = MLG. *rēt*, LG. *ried* = OHG. *hriot*, *riot*, MHG. *riet*, G. *ried*, *riet*, a reed; root unknown.] **1.** Any tall broad-leafed grass growing on the margins of streams or in other wet places; especially, any grass of one of the genera *Phragmites*, *Arundo*, or *Ammophila*. The common reed is *Phragmites communis*, a stately grass from 5 to 12 feet high, found in nearly all parts of the world. It serves by its creeping rootstocks to fix alluvial banks; its stems form perhaps the most durable thatch, and are otherwise useful; and it is planted for ornament. See the generic names, and phrases below. Compare *reed-grass*.

Common Reed (*Phragmites communis*). 1, flowering plant; 2, the panicle; *a*, a spikelet.

He lieth under the shady trees, in the covert of the *reed*, and fens. Job xl. 21.

We glided winding under ranks
Of iris, and the golden *reed*.
Tennyson, In Memoriam, ciii.

2. Some one of other more or less similar plants. See phrases below.—**3.** A musical pipe of reed or cane, having a mouthpiece made by slitting the tube near a joint, and usually several finger-holes; a rustic or pastoral pipe; hence, figuratively, pastoral poetry. See cut under *pipe*[1].

I'll . . . speak between the change of man and boy
With a *reed* voice. *Shak.*, M. of V., iii. 4. 67.

Sound of pastoral *reed* with oaten stops.
Milton, Comus, l. 345.

Now she tries the *Reed*, anon attempts the Lyre.
Congreve, Epistle to Lord Halifax.

4. In *music*: (*a*) In musical instruments of the oboe and clarinet classes, and in all kinds of organs, a thin elastic plate or tongue of reed, wood, or metal, so fitted to an opening into a pipe as nearly to close it, and so arranged that, when a current of air is directed through the opening, the reed is drawn into or driven against it so as to close it, but immediately springs back by its own elasticity, only to be pressed forward again by the air, thus producing a tone, either directly by its own vibrations or indirectly by the sympathetic vibrations of the column of air in the pipe. When the reed is of metal, the pitch of the tone depends chiefly on its size; but when of reed or cane, it may be so combined with a tube that the pitch shall depend chiefly on the size of the air-column. A *free reed* is one that vibrates in the opening without touching its edges; a *beating* or *striking reed* is one that extends slightly beyond the opening. In orchestral instruments, the wood wind group includes several reed-instruments, which have either double reeds (two wooden reeds which strike against each other, as in the oboe, the bassoon, the English horn, etc.), or a single reed (a wooden reed striking against an opening in a wooden mouthpiece or beak, as in the clarinet, the basset-horn, etc.). A pipe-organ usually contains one or more sets of reed-pipes, the tongues of which are nearly always striking reeds of brass. (See *reed-pipe*.) A reed-organ is properly a collection of several sets of reeds, the tongues of which are free reeds of brass. (See *reed-organ*.) In the brass wind group of instruments, with but few exceptions, the tone is produced by the player's lips acting as free membranous reeds within the cup of the mouthpiece. The mechanism of the human voice, also, is essentially a reed-instrument, the vocal cords being simply free membranous reeds which may be stretched within the tube of the larynx. The quality of the tone produced by a reed varies indefinitely, according to the material and character of the reed itself, the method in which it is set in vibration, and especially the arrangement of the tube or cavity with which it is connected. The accompanying fig. 1 shows the construction of an organ-reed: *a* is the reed-block, which in use is inserted in its proper slot in the reed-board; *b*, the metal tongue, which is set in sonorous vibration when air is forced through the opening *c*. Fig. 2 shows the mouthpiece of a clarinet, in which *a* is the reed, held to the body of the mouthpiece by the split-bands *b*, which are drawn tight by the screws *c*. Air entering between the reed and the margin of an opening which it covers causes it to produce a musical tone, the pitch of which is varied partly by the position of the mouthpiece in the mouth and partly by the action of the keys. Fig. 3 shows the mouthpiece of an oboe, and similar reeds are used for bassoons and bagpipes. The reed is made of two counterparts of the same shape bound together by the thread *a*. The lower and middle parts of the mouthpiece are circular in cross-section, but the upper part *c*, the reed proper, is flattened. Air forced through this opening causes the reed to emit a harsh tone, which is softened in quality by the tube of the instrument.

Reeds.

(*b*) In reed-instruments of the oboe class, and in both pipe- and reed-organs, the entire mechanism immediately surrounding the reed proper, consisting of the tube or box the opening or eschallot of which the reed itself covers or fills, together with any other attachments, like the tuning-wire of reed-pipes. (See *reed-organ* and *reed-pipe*.) In the clarinet the analogous part is called the *beak* or *mouthpiece*. (*c*) Any reed-instrument as a whole, like an oboe or a clarinet: as, the *reeds* of an orchestra. (*d*) In *organ-building*, same as *reed-stop*.—**5.** A missile weapon; an arrow or a javelin: used poetically.

With cruel Skill the backward *Reed*
He sent, and, as he lied, he slew.
Prior, To a Lady, st. 8.

The viewless arrows of his thoughts were headed
And wing'd with flame,
Like Indian *reeds* blown from his silver tongue.
Tennyson, The Poet.

6. Reeds or straw prepared for thatching; thatch: a general term: as, a bundle of *reed*.—**7.** A long slender elastic rod of whalebone, ratan, or steel, of which several are inserted in a woman's skirt to expand or stiffen it.—**8.** In *mining*, any hollow plant-stem which can be filled with powder and put into the cavity left by the withdrawal of the needle, to set off the charge at the bottom. Such devices are nearly or entirely superseded by the safety-fuse. Also called *spire*.—**9.** An instrument used for pressing down the threads of the woof in tapestry, so as to keep the surface well together.—**10.** A weavers' instrument for separating the threads of the warp, and for beating the weft up to the web. It is made of parallel slips of metal or reed, called *dents*, which resemble the teeth of a comb. The dents are fixed at their ends into two parallel pieces of wood set a few inches apart.

The *reed* for weaving the same is measured in an equally complex manner, for the unit of length is 37 inches, and according to the number of hundreds of dents or splits it contains, so is the *reed* called. For instance, a "fourteen-hundred *reed*" means that 37 inches of a *reed* of that number, no matter what length, contains 1400 dents, or about 38 per inch. *A. Barlow*, Weaving, p. 329.

11. In *her.*, a bearing representing a weavers' reed. See *slay*[2].—**12.** A Hebrew and Assyrian unit of length, equal to 6 cubits, generally taken as being from 124 to 130 inches.

A measuring *reed* of six cubits long, of a cubit and a handbreadth each. Ezek. xl. 5.

13. Same as *rennet-bag*. *W. B. Carpenter*.—**14.** In *arch.*, *carp.*, etc., a small convex molding; in the plural, same as *reeding*, 2.

The three pillars [of the temple] which stand together are fluted; and the lower part, filled with cablins of *reeds*, is of one stone, and the upper part of another.
Pococke, Description of the East, II. ii. 169.

Canary reed, the reed canary-grass. See *Phalaris*.—**Dutch reeds**, in the *arts*, the stems of several kinds of horsetail or scouring-rush (*Equisetum*) used, on account of their silicious crust, to polish wood and even metals.—**Egyptian reed**, the papyrus.—**Fly-reed**, in *weaving*, a reed of a fly-shuttle loom, provided with springs which limit the force with which the reed strikes the weft-thread to a constant or very nearly a constant quantity, and thus produce a greater uniformity of texture.—**Great reed**, a reed of the genus *Arundo*, especially *Arundo Donax*.—**Harmonic reed**. See *harmonic*.—**Indian reed**, the canna or Indian-shot.—**New Zealand reed**, a fine ornamental grass, *Arundo conspicua*, blooming earlier than pampas-grass.—**Number of the reed, set of the reed**, in *weaving*. See *number*.—**Paper reed**. See *paper-reed*.—**Reed bent**. See *bent*[2].—**Reed bent-grass**. Same as *small reed* (which see, below).—**Reed meadow-grass**. See *meadow-grass*.—**Reed of hemp**. Same as *boon*.—**Sea-reed**, or **sea-sand reed**, the marram or mat-grass, *Ammophila arundinacea*.—**Small reed**, any species of *Calamagrostis* or of *Deyeuxia*, including the useful blue-joint grass.—**Trumpet-reed**, *Arundo occidentalis*, of tropical America (West Indies).—**Wood-reed, writing-reed**, *Calamagrostis Epigeios*, of the northern parts of the Old World.

reed[1] (rēd), *v. t.* [< ME. *reden*; < *reed*[1], *n.*] **1.** To thatch. Compare *reed*[1], *n.*, 6.

Where houses be *reeded*,
Now pare of the moss, and go beat in the reed.
Tusser, Husbandry.

2. In *carp.*, *arch.*, etc., to fashion into, or decorate with, reeds or reeding.

reed[2]†, *a.* An obsolete form of *red*[1] (still extant in the surname *Reed*).

reed[3]†, *v.* and *n.* An obsolete form of *read*[1].

reedbeere†, *n.* [< *reed*[1] + *beer* as in *pillow-beer*, etc.] A bed of reeds.

A place where reedes grow: a *reedebeere*.
Nomenclator. (*Nares.*)

reed-bird (rēd'bėrd), *n.* **1.** The bobolink, *Dolichonyx oryzivorus*: so called in the late summer and early fall months, when the male has exchanged his black-and-buff dress for a plain yellowish streaked plumage like that of the female, and when it throngs the marshes in great flocks, becomes very fat, and is highly esteemed for the table. The name *reed-bird* obtains chiefly in the Middle States, where the birds haunt the fields of water-oats or wild rice (*Zizania aquatica*); further south, where it similarly throngs the rice-fields, it is called *rice-bird*. It is known as *butter-bird* in the West Indies, and is also called *ortolan*. See *bobolink*, *Dolichonyx*, *ortolan*.

2. A reed-warbler.

reedbuck (rēd'buk), *n.* [Tr. D. *rietbok*.] A name of several kinds of aquatic African antelopes; specifically, *Eleotragus arundinaceus*. Also *rietbok*.

reed-bunting (rēd'bun″ting), *n.* The black-headed bunting, *Emberiza schœniclus*. It is a common bird of Europe, frequenting the reeds of marshes and fens, and is about six inches long. Also called *reed-sparrow*.

reeden† (rē'dn), *a.* [< *reed*[1] + *-en*[2].] Consisting of a reed or reeds; made of reeds.

Through *reeden* pipes convey the golden flood,
T' invite the people [bees] to their wonted food.
Dryden, tr. of Virgil's Georgics, iv. 385.

reeder (rē'dėr), *n.* [< ME. **redere*, *redare*; < *reed*[1] + *-er*[1].] **1.** One who thatches with reeds; a thatcher. *Prompt. Parv.*, p. 426.—**2.** A thatched frame covering blocks or tiles of dried china-clay, to protect them from the rain while permitting free ventilation.

A number of thatched gates or *reeders*.
Spons' Encyc. Manuf., I. 687.

reed-gound†, *n.* See *redgound*.

reed-grass (rēd'gràs), *n.* [= D. *rietgras* = G. *riet-* (*ried-*) *gras*; as *reed*[1] + *grass*.] **1**†. The bur-reed, *Sparganium ramosum*.—**2.** Any one of the grasses called reeds, and of some others, commonly smaller, of similar habit. See phrases.—**Salt reed-grass**, *Spartina polystachya*, a tall stout salt-marsh grass with a dense oblong purplish raceme, found along the Atlantic coast of the United States.—**Small reed-grass**. Same as *small reed* (which see, under *reed*[1]).—**Wood reed-grass**, either of the two species of *Cinna*, *C. arundinacea* and *C. pendula*, northern grasses in America, the latter also in Europe. They are graceful sweet-scented woodland grasses, apparently of no great value.

reëdification† (rẹ-ed″i-fi-kā'shọn), *n.* [= OF. *reedification*, F. *réédification* = Sp. *reedificacion* = Pg. *reedificação* = It. *riedificazione*; as *re-* + *edification*.] The act or operation of rebuilding, or the state of being rebuilt.

The toun was compellid to help to the *Reedification* of it.
Leland, Itinerary (1769), III. 11.

reëdify† (rẹ-ed'i-fī), *v. t.* [Early mod. E. also *reædify*; ME. *redifyen*; < OF. *reedifier*, F. *réédifier* = Sp. Pg. *reedificar* = It. *riedificare*, < LL. *reædificare*, build again, rebuild, < L. *re-*, again, + *ædificare*, build: see *edify*.] To rebuild; build again after destruction.

The ruin'd wals he did *reædifye*.
Spenser, F. Q., II. x. 46.

Return'd from Babylon by leave of kings
Their lords, whom God disposed, the house of God
They first *re-edify*. *Milton*, P. L., xii. 350.

reediness (rē'di-nes), *n.* The state or property of being reedy, in any sense.

It [the Liszt organ] possesses great freedom from *reediness* in sound. *Sci. Amer.*, N. S., LVIII. 402.

The greater number of these tests are to detect *reediness*, lamination, or looseness in the fibrous structure of the iron, these defects occurring more frequently in angle, T, and beam irons than in plates.
Thearle, Naval Arch., § 332.

reeding (rē'ding), *n.* [< ME. *redynge*; verbal n. of *reed*[1], *v.*] 1. Thatching. [Obsolete or prov. Eng.]

Redynge of howses. Arundinacio.
Prompt. Parv., p. 427.

2. In *arch.*, a series of small convex or beaded moldings designed for ornament; also, the convex fluting or cabling characterizing some types of column.

These [external walls of Wuswus at Wurka] were plastered and covered by an elaborate series of *reedings* and square sinkings, forming a beautiful and very appropriate mode of adorning the wall of a building that had no external openings. *J. Fergusson*, Hist. Arch., I. 162.

3. The milling on the edge of a coin.—4. In *silk-weaving*. See the quotation.

Reeding and harnessing are subsidiary processes in putting the warp in proper shape on the loom. These consist in putting each warp-thread through its proper slit in the reed and eyelet in the harness.
Harper's Mag., LXXI. 256.

reed-instrument (rēd'in"strö-ment), *n.* A musical instrument the tone of which is produced by the vibration of a reed; especially, an orchestral instrument of the oboe or of the clarinet family.

reed-knife (rēd'nīf), *n.* A long knife-shaped implement of metal for reaching and adjusting the tuning-wires of reed-pipes in a pipe-organ. Also called *tuning-knife*.

reedless (rēd'les), *a.* [< *reed*[1] + *-less*.] Destitute of reeds.

Youths tombed before their parents were,
Whom foul Cocytus' *reedless* banks enclose. *May.*

reedling (rēd'ling), *n.* [< *reed*[1] + *-ling*[1].] The bearded tit, *Panurus* or *Calamophilus biarmicus*, a common bird of Europe and Asia: so called from frequenting reeds. Also called *reed-pheasant*.

reed-mace (rēd'mās), *n.* The cattail; any plant of the genus *Typha*, chiefly *T. latifolia* and *T. angustifolia*, the great and the lesser reed-mace, the two species known in England and North America. *T. latifolia* is the common plant. It is a tall, straight, erect aquatic with long flag-like leaves and long dense spikes of small flowers, brown when mature. The abundant down of the ripened spikes makes a poor material for stuffing pillows, etc.; the leaves were formerly much used by coopers to prevent the joints of casks from leaking, and have been made into mats, chair-bottoms, etc. It is so named either directly from its reed-like character and the resemblance of its head to a mace (club), or (*Prior*, "Popular Names of British Plants") from its being placed in the hands of Christ as a mace or scepter in pictures and in statues. Less properly called *bulrush*. In the United States known almost exclusively as *cattail* or *cattail flag*.

reed-mote (rēd'mōt), *n.* Same as *fescue*, 1. *Halliwell.* [Prov. Eng.]

reed-moth (rēd'mōth), *n.* A British moth, *Macrogaster arundinis*.

reed-motion (rēd'mō"shon), *n.* In *weaving*, the mechanism which, in power-looms, moves the batten, carrying the reed for beating up the weft between the threads of the warp. The term has also been inappropriately applied to a "stop-motion" whereby, when the shuttle is trapped in its passage through the warp, the movement of the batten is stopped, to prevent breaking warp-threads by the impact of the reed against the shuttle. See *stop-motion*.

reed-organ (rēd'ôr"gan), *n.* A musical instrument consisting essentially of one or more graduated sets of small free reeds of metal, which are sounded by streams of air set in motion by a bellows, and controlled from a keyboard like that of the pianoforte. The two principal varieties are the *harmonium*, which is common in Europe, and the so-called *American organ*, the chief essential difference between which is that the former is sounded by a compression-bellows driving the air outward through the reeds, and the latter by a suction-bellows drawing it inward through them. The tone of the harmonium is usually keener and more nasal than that of the American organ. The apparatus for compressing or exhausting the air, and for distributing the current among the various sets of reeds and among the channels belonging to the various digitals of the keyboard, is not essentially different from that of a pipe-organ, though on a much smaller scale. (See *organ*[1].) The bellows, however, is usually operated by means of alternating treadles. The keyboard is exactly similar to that of the pipe-organ or the pianoforte, and has a compass of about four or five octaves. The tone-producing apparatus consists of one or more sets of small brass *vibrators* or *reeds* (see illustration); the pitch of the tone depends on the size of their vibratile tongues, and its quality on their proportions and on the character of the resonating cavities with which they are connected. Each set of vibrators constitutes a *stop*, the use of which is controlled by a stop-knob. The possible variety of qualities is rather limited. The treadles operate feeders, which are connected with a general bellows, so that the current of air may be maintained at a constant tension; but in the harmonium the waste-valve of the bellows may be closed by drawing a stop-knob called the *expression-stop*, so that the force of the tones may be directly varied by the rapidity of the treadling. In the American organ the force of the tones is varied by a lever, operated by the player's knee, which opens or closes a shutter in the box inclosing the vibrators. The harmonium sometimes has a mechanism called the *percussion*, providing a little hammer to strike the tongue of each reed as its digital is depressed, thus setting it into Vibration very promptly.

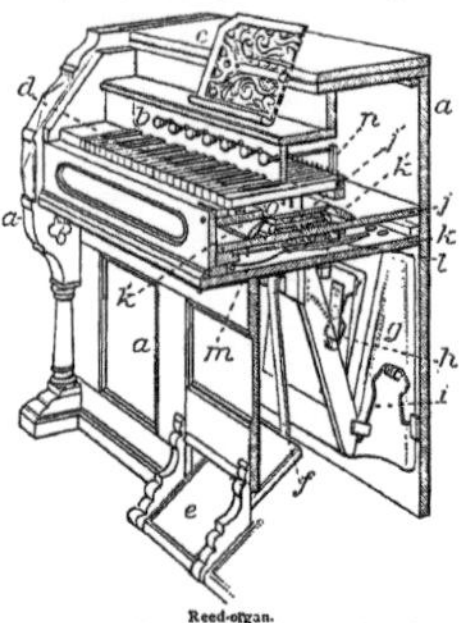

Reed-organ.

a, Case; *b*, stop-rail and stops; *c*, music-rack; *d*, keyboard; *e*, one of the pedals or treadles; *f*, one of the pedal- or treadle-straps which operate the bellows *g*; *h*, pedal-spring which lifts the pedal after the latter has been relieved from the pressure of the foot; *i*, bellows-spring which opens the bellows after compression; *j* and *k*, upper and lower boards of wind-chest, inclosing space into which air is delivered from the bellows; *j'*, reed-board, which supports the reeds in slots formed therein (see cut under *reed*[1]); *k'*, *k'*, swells (see cut below); *l*, reed-valve; *m*, valve-spring which closes the valve after the latter is opened by push-pin shown in the cut below. There is one of these valves for each key, admitting wind to one or more reeds of a set or such sets of reeds as are allowed to act by the stops pulled out, and of a particular tone corresponding with the key; *n*, stop-arm; *o*, key-frame.

A *tremulant* is often introduced, consisting of a revolving fan, by which the current of air is made to oscillate slightly. More than one manual keyboard and a pedal keyboard, with separate stops for each, as in the pipe-organ, occur in large instruments. Occasionally a set of pipes is also added. Various devices for sustaining tones in the bass after the fingers have left the digitals, or for emphasizing the treble, are sometimes introduced. Pianofortes are made with a harmonium attached (sometimes called an *æolian attachment*). The reed-organ has become one of the commonest of musical instruments. Its popularity rests upon its capacity for concerted music, like the pianoforte and pipe-organ, combined with simplicity, portability, cheapness, and stability of intonation. Artistically regarded, its tone is apt to be either weak and negative or harsh and unsympathetic. A variety of recent invention, the *vocalion*, has a remarkably powerful and mellow tone.

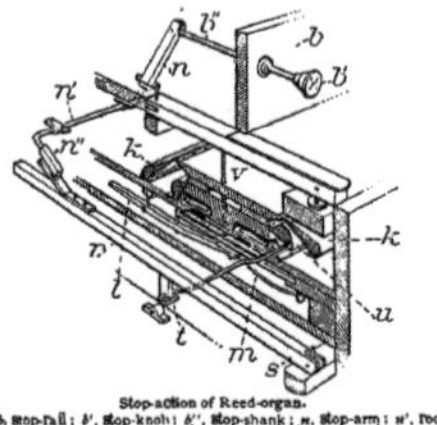

Stop-action of Reed-organ.

b, stop-rail; *b'*, stop-knob; *b''*, stop-shank; *n*, stop-arm; *n'*, rock-lever, connected at *n''* to the lever *r*, the latter being pivoted to a rail at *s*. A downwardly projecting arm engages the crank of another rock-lever *t*, connecting with and actuating the stop-valve *u*; *k*, *k*, swells; *l*, reed-valve opened by the push-pin *v*, and closed by the spring *m*.

reed-palm (rēd'päm), *n.* A ratan-palm; a palm of the genus *Calamus*.

reed-pheasant (rēd'fez"ant), *n.* The bearded titmouse or reedling, *Panurus biarmicus*: so called in allusion to the long tail. Also called simply *pheasant*. [Norfolk, Eng.]

reed-pipe (rēd'pīp), *n.* In *organ-building*, a pipe whose tone is produced by the vibration of a reed or tongue: opposed to *flue-pipe*. Such pipes consist of a *foot* or *mouthpiece* containing the reed, and a tubular *body* furnishing a column of air for sympathetic vibration. The term *reed* is applied to both the vibratile tongue and the mechanism immediately surrounding it. In the latter sense, a reed consists of a metal tube connecting the foot and the body of the pipe; at its lower end is an oblong opening or eschallot, over or in which is fixed the brass tongue or reed proper. The effective length of the tongue is controlled by a movable spring or *tuning-wire*, the head of which projects outside the pipe-foot. The pitch of the tone depends primarily upon the vibrating length of the tongue, but is modified by the length of the air-column in the body of the pipe. A reed-pipe, therefore, is tuned both on the reed and on the top of the pipe. The quality of the tone depends somewhat on the form of the tongue, but chiefly on that of the body as a whole. The force of the tone depends on the pressure of the air-current, on the size of the inlet to the foot, and on the exact adjustment of the tongue to the eschallot. Most reed-pipes have striking reeds, but free reeds are occasionally used. A set of reed-pipes is called a *reed-stop*.

reed-pit (rēd'pit), *n.* [ME. *reede pytte*; < *reed*[1] + *pit*[1].] A fen. *Prompt. Parv.* (*Halliwell.*)

reed-plane (rēd'plān), *n.* In *joinery*, a concave-soled plane used in making beads.

reed-sparrow (rēd'spar"ō), *n.* Same as *reed-bunting*. [Local, Eng.]

reed-stop (rēd'stop), *n.* In *organ-building*, a set or register of reed-pipes the use of which is controlled by a single stop-knob: opposed to *flue-stop*. Each partial organ usually has one or more such stops, though they are less invariable in the pedal organ than in the others. They are generally intended to imitate some orchestral instrument, as the *trumpet* (usually placed in the great organ), the *oboe* (usually in the swell organ), the *clarinet* (usually in the choir organ), the *trombone* (usually in the pedal organ), the *cornopean*, the *clarion*, the *contrafagotto*, etc. They may be of eight-feet, four-feet, or sixteen-feet tone. (See *organ*[1].) Reed-stops are specially valuable because of their powerful, incisive, and individual quality, which is suited both for solo effects and for the enrichment of all kinds of combinations. The most peculiar reed-stop is the *vox humana*. A reed-stop is often called simply a *reed*.

reed-thrush (rēd'thrush), *n.* The greater reed-warbler, *Acrocephalus turdoides*.

Specimens of the . . . *reed-thrush*, to use its oldest English name.
Yarrell, Brit. Birds (4th ed.), I. 365. (*Encyc. Dict.*)

reed-tussock (rēd'tus"ok), *n.* A British moth, *Orgyia cænosa*. See *tussock*.

reed-wainscot (rēd'wān"skot), *n.* A British moth, *Nonagria cannæ*.

reed-warbler (rēd'wâr"blėr), *n.* One of a group of Old World sylviine birds, constituting the genus *Acrocephalus*. The species to which the name specially applies is *A. streperus* or *A. arundinaceus*, also called *Calamoherpe* or *Salicaria arundinacea*. Another species, *A. turdoides*, is known as the *greater reed-warbler*, *reed-thrush*, and *reed-wren*.

reed-work (rēd'wėrk), *n.* In *organ-building*, the reed-stops of an organ, or of a partial organ, taken collectively: opposed to *flue-work*.

reed-wren (rēd'ren), *n.* 1. The greater reed-warbler.—2. An American wren of the family *Troglodytidæ* and genus *Thryothorus*, as the great Carolina wren, *T. carolinensis*, or Bewick's wren, *T. bewicki*. There are many species, chiefly of the subtropical parts of America, the two named being the only ones which inhabit much of the United States.

reedy (rē'di), *a.* [< *reed*[1] + *-y*[1]. Cf. AS. *hreódiht*, reedy.] 1. Abounding with reeds.

Ye heathy wastes, immix'd with *reedy* fens.
Burns, Elegy on Miss Burnet.

2. Consisting of or resembling a reed.

With the tip of her *reedy* wand
Making the sign of the cross.
Longfellow, Blind Girl of Castèl Cuillè, i.

3. Noting a tone like that produced from a reed-instrument. Such tones are usually somewhat nasal, and are often thin and cutting.

The blessed little creature answered me in a voice of such heavenly sweetness, with that *reedy* thrill in it which you have heard in the thrush's even-song, that I hear it at this moment. *O. W. Holmes*, Autocrat, ix.

4. Noting a quality of iron in which bars or plates of it have the nature of masses of rods imperfectly welded together.

reef[1] (rēf), *n.* [Formerly *riff*; < D. *rif* = MLG. *rif*, *ref*, LG. *riff*, *reff* (> G. *riff*), a reef, = Icel. *rif* = Dan. *rev*, a reef, sand-bank; akin to Icel. *rifa*, a fissure, rift, rent, = Sw. *refva*, a strip, cleft, gap; Sw. *refvel*, a sand-bank, = Dan. *revle*, a sand-bank, bar, shoal, a strip of land, a lath; prob. from the verb, Icel. *rífa*, etc., rive, split: see *rive*[1]. Cf. *rift*[1].] 1. A low, narrow ridge of rocks, rising ordinarily but a few feet above the water. A reef passes by increase of size into an island. The word is especially used with reference to those low islands which are formed of coralline debris. See *atoll*, and *coral reef*, below.

Atolls have been formed during the sinking of the land by the upward growth of the *reefs* which primarily fringed the shores of ordinary islands.
Darwin, Coral Reefs, p. 105.

The league-long roller thundering on the *reef*.
Tennyson, Enoch Arden.

2. Any extensive elevation of the bottom of the sea; a shoal; a bank: so called by fishermen.

The *riff*, or bank of rocks, on which the French fleet was lost, runs along from the east and to the northward about three miles. *Dampier*, Voyages, I., an. 1681, note.

3. In Australia, the same as *lode*, *rein*, or *ledge* of the Cordilleran miner: as, a quartz-*reef* (that is, a quartz-vein).

Many a promising gold field has been ruined by having bad machinery put up on it. *Reefs* that would have paid handsomely with good machinery are abandoned as unpayable, and the field is deserted. *H. Finch-Hatton*, Advance Australia, p. 218.

4. A kind of commercial sponge which grows on reefs. [A trade-name.]

British Consul Little of Havana says, according to the "Journal of the Society of Arts," that the classes [of sponges] included are sheep wool, velvet, hard-head, yellow, grass, and glova. Very little *reef*, if any, is found in Cuba. *Science*, XIV. 861.

Coral reef, an accumulation of calcareous material which has been secreted from the water of the tropical ocean, and especially of the Pacific to the south of the equator, by the reef-building corals. Such accumulations, which are often of great dimensions, offer curious peculiarities of form and distribution. They have been classified under the names of *fringing* and *barrier reefs* and *atolls*. *Fringing reefs* border the land; *barrier reefs* extend parallel with but at some distance from the shore; *atolls* are approximately circular or elliptical in form, and typical atolls inclose a lagoon, which usually communicates with the ocean by one or more passages through the reef. Barrier reefs may be hundreds of miles in length; that off the shore of Australia is 1,250 miles long, and from 10 to 90 broad. Atolls vary from 1 to 50 miles and over in diameter. The principal mass of a coral reef consists essentially of dead coral, together with more or less of the skeletons and shells of other marine organisms; this dead material is mingled with debris resulting from the action of breakers and currents on the coralline formation. The exterior of such a reef, where conditions are favorable to the development of the coral animals, especially on its seaward face, is covered with a layer or mantle of living and growing coral, and the rapidity and vigor of this growth depend on the supply of food brought by the oceanic currents. Where the conditions for this supply have not been favorable, there the reefs are not found; where the conditions have been such as to encourage growth, but have ceased to have this character, there the formation of the reef has slackened or been stopped altogether. Investigations have shown that the reef-building corals cannot flourish where the temperature of the surface-water sinks below 70°; in the typical coral regions the temperature is decidedly higher than that, and its range very small. Neither can the reef-builders work at a considerable depth, or above the level of low tide; their entire vertical range is not more than 15 or 20 fathoms at the utmost. These conditions of coral-reef formation, coupled with the fact that the carbonate of lime in the form in which it has been left by the death of the organisms by which it was secreted is decidedly soluble in sea-water, are sufficient to account for all the peculiarities in the distribution and mode of occurrence of these remarkable structures. It is because the currents sweeping toward the eastern shores of the continents are warm and constant that, while the western sides of Africa and South America exhibit only isolated patches of coral, the eastern borders are abundantly supplied with it. It is not now considered necessary to call in the assistance of a general subsidence of the Pacific Ocean bottom in order to account for the form of the atolls; for it is the opinion of most of the recent investigators that all the characteristic features of the coral formations—whether these occur as fringing or barrier reefs, or as atolls—can be produced in regions of subsidence or of elevation, as well as in those where no change of level is taking place.

reef[2] (rēf), *n.* [Formerly *riff*; < ME. *riff*, < MD. *rif* (also *rift*), D. *reef* = LG. *reff*, *riff* (> G. *reef*, *reff*) = Icel. *rif* = Sw. *ref* = Dan. *rev*, a reef of a sail; of uncertain origin; perhaps of like origin with *reef*[1]. Hence *reef*[2], *v.*, and *reeve*[3].] *Naut.*, a part of a sail rolled or folded up, in order to diminish the extent of canvas exposed to the wind. In topsails and courses, and sometimes in topgallantsails, the reef is the part of the sail between the head and the first reef-band, or between any two reef-bands; in fore-and-aft sails reefs are taken on the foot. There are generally three or four reefs in topsails, and one or two in courses.

Calms are our dread; when tempests plough the deep,
We take a *reef*, and to the rocking sleep.
Crabbe, Works, I. 48.

Close reef. See *close*[2].—**French reef**, reefing of sails when they are fitted with rope jackstays instead of points.

reef[2] (rēf), *v.* [< *reef*[2], *n.* Cf. the doublet *reeve*[3].] **I.** *trans.* **1.** *Naut.*, to take a reef or reefs in; reduce the size of (a sail) by rolling or folding up a part and securing it by tying reef-points about it. In square sails the reef-points are tied round the yard as well as the sail; in fore-and-aft sails they may or may not be tied round the boom which extends the foot of the sail. In very large ships, where the yards are so large as to make it inconvenient to tie the reef-points around them, the sails are sometimes reefed to jackstays on the yards.

Up, aloft, lads! Come, *reef* both topsails!
Davenant and Dryden, Tempest, i. 1.

2. To gather up stuff of any kind in a way similar to that described in def. 1. Compare *reefing*.—**Close reefed**, the condition of a sail when all its reefs have been taken in.—**To reef paddles**, in steamships, to disconnect the float-boards from the paddle-arms and bolt them again nearer the center of the wheel, in order to diminish the dip when the vessel is deep.—**To reef the bowsprit**, to rig in the bowsprit. The phrase usually has application to yachts; men-of-war are said to *rig in* their bowsprits.

The *bowsprits* on cutters can be *reefed* by being drawn closer in and fidded. *Yachtsman's Guide.*

II. *intrans.* See the quotation. [Colloq.]

In some subtle way, however, when the driver moves the bit to and fro in his mouth, the effect is to enliven and stimulate the horse, as if something of the jockey's spirit were thus conveyed to his mind. If this motion be performed with an exaggerated movement of the arm, it is called *reefing*. *The Atlantic*, LXIV. 115.

reef[3] (rēf), *a.* and *n.* [Also (Sc.) *reif*, *rief*; < ME. *ref*, < AS. *hreóf*, scabby, leprous, rough (> *hreófol*, *hreófl*, scabbiness, leprosy, *hreóflig*, leprous, *hreófla*, a leper), = OHG. *riob*, leprous, = Icel. *hrjúfr*, scabby, rough. Cf. Icel. *ruf*, scurf, eruption of the skin; perhaps connected with *rifa*, break: see *rive*.] **I.** *a.* Scabby; scurvy.

Kings and nations, swith awa!
Reif randies, I disown ye!
Burns, Louis, What Reck I by Thee?

II. *n.* **1.** The itch; also, any eruptive disorder. [Prov. Eng.]—**2.** Dandruff. [Prov. Eng.]

reef-band (rēf'band), *n.* A strong strip of canvas extending across a sail, in a direction parallel to its head or foot, to strengthen it. The reef-band has eyelet-holes at regular intervals for the reef-points which secure it when reefed.—**Balance reef-band**, a reef-band extending diagonally across a fore-and-aft sail. See *reef*[2], *n.*

reef-builder (rēf'bil"dėr), *n.* Any coral which builds a reef.

reef-building (rēf'bil"ding), *a.* Constructing or building up a coral reef, as a reef-builder.

reef-cringle (rēf'kring"gl), *n.* See *cringle* (*a*).

reef-earing (rēf'ēr"ing), *n.* See *earing*[1].

reefer[1] (rē'fėr), *n.* [< *reef*[1] + *-er*[1].] An oyster that grows on reefs in the wild or untransplanted state; a reef-oyster.

reefer[2] (rē'fėr), *n.* [< *reef*[2] + *-er*[1].] **1.** One who reefs: a name familiarly applied to midshipmen, because they attended in the tops during the operation of reefing. *Admiral Smyth.*

The steerage or gun-room was ever heaven, the scene of happiness unalloyed, the home of darling *reefers* who own the hearts they won long years ago, the abode of briny mirth, of tarry jollity. *Harper's Mag.*, LXXVII. 166.

2. A short coat or jacket worn by sailors and fishermen, and copied for general use by the fashions of 1888–90.

reef-goose (rēf'gös), *n.* The common wild goose of North America, *Bernicla canadensis*. See cut under *Bernicla*. [North Carolina.]

reefing (rē'fing), *n.* [Verbal n. of *reef*[2], *v.*] In *upholstery*, the gathering up of the material of a curtain, valance, or the like, as in short festoons.

reefing-beckets (rē'fing-bek"ets), *n. pl.* Sennet straps fitted with an eye and toggle, used in reefing when sails are fitted with French reefs. The toggle part is generally seized to the iron jackstay on the yard, and the tail of the strap is taken around the rope jackstay on the sail, the eye being then placed over the toggle.

reefing-jacket (rē'fing-jak"et), *n.* A close-fitting jacket or short coat made of strong heavy cloth.

reefing-point (rē'fing-point), *n.* *Naut.*, a reef-point.

reef-jig, reef-jigger (rēf'jig, -jig"ėr), *n.* *Naut.*, a small tackle sometimes used in reefing to stretch the reef-band taut before knotting the points.

reef-knot (rēf'not), *n.* Same as *square knot* (which see, under *knot*[1]).

reef-line (rēf'lin), *n.* *Naut.*, a temporary means of spilling a sail, arranged so that it can serve when the wind is blowing fresh.

reef-oyster (rēf'ois"tėr), *n.* A reefer. See *reefer*[1] and *oyster*.

reef-pendant (rēf'pen"dant), *n.* *Naut.*, in fore-and-aft sails, a rope through a sheave-hole in the boom, with a tackle attached, to haul the after-leech down to the boom while reefing; in square sails, a rope fastened to the leech of the sail and rove up through the yard-arm, having a purchase hooked to the upper end, to serve as a reef-tackle.

reef-point (rēf'point), *n.* *Naut.*, a short piece of rope fastened by the middle in each eyelet-hole of a reef-band, to secure the sail in reefing.

reef-squid (rēf'skwid), *n.* A lashing or earing used aboard the luggers on the south coast of England to lash the outer cringle of the sail when reefing.

reef-tackle (rēf'tak"l), *n.* *Naut.*, a tackle fastened to the leeches of a sail below the close-reef band, used to haul the leeches of the sail up to the yard to facilitate reefing.

reek[1] (rēk), *v.* [< ME. *reken*, *reoken*; (*a*) < AS. *reócan* (strong verb, pret. *reác*, pl. *rucon*), smoke, steam, = OFries. *riaka* = D. *rieken*, *ruiken* = MLG. *ruken*, LG. *ruiken*, *rieken* = OHG. *riuhhan*, *riohhan*, MHG. *riechen*, G. *riechen* (pret. *roch*), smell, *rauchen*, smoke, = Icel. *rjúka* (pret. *rauk*, pl. *ruku*) = Sw. *röka*, *ryka* = Dan. *röge*, *ryge* = Goth. **riukan* (not recorded), smoke; (*b*) < AS. *rēcan* (pret. *rēhte*) (= OFries. *rēka* = D. *rooken* = MLG. *röken* = OHG. *rouhan* = Icel. *reykja*), tr., smoke, steam. Hence *reek*[1], *n.* No connection with Skt. *raja*, *rajas*, dimness, sky, dust, pollen, *rajani*, night, √ *ranj*, dye.] **I.** *intrans.* To smoke; steam; exhale.

The encence out of the fyr *reketh* sote [sweet].
Chaucer, Good Women, l. 2612.

Frae many a spout came running out
His *reeking*-het red gore.
Battle of Tranent-Muir (Child's Ballads, VII. 170).

I found me laid
In balmy sweat, which with his beams the sun
Soon dried, and on the *reeking* moisture fed.
Milton, P. L., viii. 256.

The *reeking* entrails on the fire they threw,
And to the gods the grateful odour flew.
Dryden, tr. of Ovid's Metamorph., xii. 211.

The floor *reeked* with the recent scrubbing, and the goddess did not like the smell of brown soap.
Thackeray, Pendennis, lxvi.

II. *trans.* To smoke; expose to smoke.

After the halves [of the moulds] are so coated or *reeked*, they are fitted together.
W. H. Greenwood, Steel and Iron, p. 423.

reek[1] (rēk), *n.* [< ME. *reek*, *rek*, *rike*, *reik* (also assibilated *reche*, > E. *reech*), < AS. *rēc*, smoke, vapor, = OS. *rōk* = OFries. *rēk* = D. *rook* = MLG. *roke*, LG. *rook* = OHG. *rouh*, MHG. *rouch*, G. *rauch*, smoke, vapor, = Icel. *reykr*, smoke, steam (cf. *rökr*, twilight: see *Ragnarök*), = Sw. *rök* = Dan. *rög*, smoke; from the verb. Cf. Goth. *rikwis*, darkness, smoke.] **1.** Smoke; vapor; steam; exhalation; fume. [Obsolete, archaic, or Scotch.]

You common cry of curs! whose breath I hate
As *reek* o' the rotten fens. *Shak.*, Cor., iii. 3. 121.

As hateful to me as the *reek* of a lime-kiln.
Shak., M. W. of W., iii. 3. 86.

The *reek* it rose, and the flame it flew,
And oh the fire augmented high.
Quoted in *Child's Ballads*, VI. 178.

The *reek* o' the cot hung over the plain
Like a little wee cloud in the world its lane.
Hogg, Kilmeny.

2†. Incense.

Reke, that is a gretyngful prayer of men that do penance. *MS. Coll. Eton.* 10, f. 25. (*Halliwell.*)

Kale through the reek. See *kale*.

reek[2]† (rēk), *n.* [< ME. *reek*, < AS. *hreác* = Icel. *hraukr*, a heap, rick. Cf. the related *rick* and *ruck*.] A rick; also, a small bundle of hay. *Halliwell.* [Prov. Eng.]

I'll instantly set all my hinds to thrashing
Of a whole *reek* of corn.
B. Jonson, Every Man out of his Humour, ii. 1. (*Nares.*)

reeky (rē'ki), *a.* [Also in Sc. spelling *reekie*, and assibilated *reechy*; < *reek*[1] + *-y*[1].] **1.** Smoky; soiled with smoke.

Now he [the devil] 's taen her hame to his ain *reeky* den.
Burns (1st ed.), There lived a Carle on Kellyburn Braes.

2. Giving out reek or vapor; giving out fumes or odors, especially offensive odors. See *reek*[1].

Shut me nightly in a charnel-house, . . .
With *reeky* shanks, and yellow chapless skulls.
Shak., R. and J., iv. 1. 83.

Seeing the *reeky*
Repast placed before him, scarce able to speak, he
In ecstasy mutter'd, "By Jove, Cocky-leeky!"
Barham, Ingoldsby Legends, I. 310.

reel[1] (rēl), *n.* [< ME. *reel*, *reele*, *rele*, *reyle*, a reel, < AS. *reól*, also *hreól* (glossing ML. *alibrum*), a reel; cf. Icel. *hræll*, *ræll*, a weavers' rod or sley; Gael. *ruidhil*, a reel for winding yarn on. Root unknown. Cf. *reel*[2].] A cylinder or frame turning on an axis, on which thread, yarn, string, rope, etc., are wound. Specifically —(*a*) A roller or bobbin for thread used in sewing; a spool.

Down went the blue-frilled work-basket, . . . dispersing on the floor *reels*, thimble, muslin-work.
George Eliot, Felix Holt, v.

(*b*) A machine on which yarn is wound to form it into hanks, skeins, etc.

Oh leeze me on my spinning-wheel,
Oh leeze me on my rock an' *reel*.
Burns, Bess and her Spinning-Wheel.

(*c*) In *rope-making*, the frame on which the spun-yarns are wound as each length is twisted, previous to tarring or laying up into strands. (*d*) The revolving frame upon which silk-fiber is wound from the cocoon. (*e*) Anything prepared for winding thread upon, as an open framework turning on a pivot at each end, upon which thread is wound as it is spun, or when a skein is opened for use. (*f*) In *teleg.*, a barrel on which the strip of paper for receiving the message is wound in a recording telegraph. *Encyc. Dict.* (*g*) A winch used by English and Scotch whalemen for regaining the tow-line. It is not employed by Americans. (*h*) *Naut.*, a revolving frame varying in size, used for winding up hawsers, hose, lead-line, log-lines, etc. (*i*) A windlass for hoisting oyster-dredges. (*j*) In *milling*, the drum on which the bolting-cloth is placed. (*k*) In *agri.*, a cylinder formed of light slats and radial arms, used with a reaper to gather the grain into convenient position for the knives to operate on it, and to direct its fall on the platform. (*l*) In *baking*, a cylindrical frame carrying bread-pans suspended from the horizontal arms of the frame. It is used in a form of oven called a *reel oven.* (*m*) A device used in angling, attached to the rod, for winding the line, consisting of a cylinder revolving on an axis moved by a small crank or spring. The salmon-reel is about four inches, and the trout-reel about two inches in diameter; the length is about two inches. In angling the reel plays an important part, its use and action requiring to be in perfect accord or correspondence with the play of the rod and line. To meet these requirements, clicks and multipliers are employed. The click checks the line from running out too freely, and the multiplier gathers in the slack with increased speed. (*n*) A hose-carriage.—**Off the reel**, one after another without a break; in uninterrupted succession: as, to win three games *off the reel.* [Colloq.]—**Reel-and-bead molding**, in *arch.*, etc., a simple molding consisting of elongated or spindle-shaped bodies alternating with beads either spherical or flattened in the direction of the molding.—**Reel of paper**, a continuous roll of paper as made for use on web printing-machines. [Eng.]—**Reel oven.** See *oven.*

Click-reel.

a, spool journaled in sides of the frame or case *b*; *c*, pinion on the axis of the spool; *d*, small gear meshing with *c* (in use these wheels are covered by the cover *e*); *f*, axis of the wheel *d* (this axis is squared on the outer end and fits into the crank-socket *g*, when the cover *e* is attached to the frame by small screws *i*); *h*, crank fitted to crank-socket *g*; *j*, reel-seat; *k*, *k*, reel-bands which fasten the reel-seat to the rod *r*; *s*, click which, when not pressed out of engagement with a small serrated wheel on the end of the spool-shaft opposite the pinion *c*, emits a sound when the line is running out and warns the sportsman that his bait is taken; *t*, click-button, which presses out the click from its engagement with the serrated wheel, as when winding in the line.

Reel-and-bead Molding.
1. Greek (Erechtheum). 2. Renaissance (Venice).

reel[1] (rēl), *v. t.* [< ME. *relen*, *reolen*, *relien*, reel; from the noun: see *reel*[1], *n.* Cf. *reel*[2], *v.*] To wind upon a reel, as yarn or thread from the spindle, or a fishing-line.

> To karde and to kembe, to clouten and to wasche,
> To rubbe and *rely.* *Piers Plowman* (C), x. 81.

> I say nothing of his lips; for they are so thin and slender that, were it the fashion to *reel* lips as they do yarn, one might make a skein of them.
> *Jarvis*, tr. of Don Quixote, II. iii. 15. (*Davies.*)

> Silk *reeling* is one of the industries.
> *Harper's Mag.*, LXXVII. 47.

To reel in, in *angling*, to recover by winding on the reel (the line that has been paid out).—**To reel off**, to give out or produce with ease and fluency, or in a rapid and continuous manner. [Colloq.]

> Mr. Wark and Mr. Paulhamus [telegraphers], who sent in the order named, *reeled off* exactly the same number of words. *Electric Rev.* (Amer.), XVI. viii. 7.

To reel up, to wind up or take in on a reel (all the line).

reel[2] (rēl), *v.* [Early mod. E. also *rele*; < ME. *relen*, turn round and round; appar. a particular use of *reel*[1], *v.*, but cf. Icel. *ridhlask*, rock, waver, move to and fro (as ranks in battle), < *ritha*, tremble. Not connected with *roll.*] **I.** *intrans.* **1.** To turn round and round; whirl.

> Hit [the boat] *reled* on roun[d] vpon the roȝe ythes [rough waves]. *Alliterative Poems* (ed. Morris), iii. 147.

2. To sway from side to side in standing or walking; stagger, especially as one drunk.

> To knyȝtez he kest his yȝe,
> & *reled* hym vp & doun.
> *Sir Gawayne and the Green Knight* (E. E. T. S.), l. 229.

> But when they saw the Almayne *rele* and staggar, then they let fall the rayle betwene them.
> *Hall*, Hen. VIII., an. 6.

> The tinker he laid on so fast,
> That he made Robin *reel.*
> *Robin Hood and the Tinker* (Child's Ballads, V. 235).

> Nathelesse so sore a buff to him it lent
> That made him *reele*, and to his brest his bever bent.
> *Spenser*, F. Q., II. v. 6.

> Flecked darkness like a drunkard *reels*
> From forth day's path. *Shak.*, R. and J., ii. 3. 3.

> She [France] staggered and *reeled* under the burden of the war. *Bolingbroke*, State of Europe, viii.

3. To be affected with a whirling or dizzy sensation: as, his brain *reeled.*

> Your fine Tom Jones and Grandisons,
> They make your youthful fancies *reel.*
> *Burns*, Oh leave Novels.

> When all my spirit *reels*
> At the shouts, the leagues of lights,
> And the roaring of the wheels.
> *Tennyson*, Maud, xxvi.

=**Syn.** 2. *Reel, Stagger*, and *Totter* have in common the idea of an involuntary unsteadiness, a movement toward falling. Only animate beings *reel* or *stagger*; a tower or other erect object may *totter. Reel* suggests dizziness or other loss of balance; *stagger* suggests a burden too great to be carried steadily, or a walk such as one would have in carrying such a burden; *totter* suggests weakness: one *reels* upon being struck on the head; a drunken man, a wounded man, *staggers*; the infant and the very aged *totter.*

> Pale he turn'd, and *reel'd*, and would have fall'n,
> But that they stay'd him up. *Tennyson*, Guinevere.

> His breast heaved, and he *staggered* in his place,
> And stretched his strong arms forth with a low moan.
> *William Morris*, Earthly Paradise, II. 279.

> He [Newcastle] thought it better to construct a weak and rotten government, which *tottered* at the smallest breath, . . . than to pay the necessary price for sound and durable materials. *Macaulay*, William Pitt.

II.† *trans.* **1.** To turn about; roll about.

> Runischly his rede yȝen [eyes] he *reled* aboute.
> *Sir Gawayne and the Green Knight* (E. E. T. S.), l. 304.

2. To roll.

> And Sisyphus an huge round stone did *reele*
> Against an hill. *Spenser*, F. Q., I. v. 35.

3. To reel or stagger through.

> You are too indulgent. Let us grant, it is not
> Amiss to . . . keep the turn of tippling with a slave;
> To *reel* the streets at noon. *Shak.*, A. and C., i. 4. 20.

4. To cause to reel, stagger, totter, or shake.

reel[2] (rēl), *n.* [< *reel*[2], *v.*] A staggering motion, as that of a drunken man; giddiness.

> (The attendant . . . carries off Lepidus [drunk].) . . .
> *Eno.* Drink thou; increase the *reels.*
> *Shak.*, A. and C., ii. 7. 100.

> Instinctively she paused before the arched window, and looked out upon the street, in order to seize its permanent objects with her mental grasp, and thus to steady herself from the *reel* and vibration which affected her more immediate sphere. *Hawthorne*, Seven Gables, xvi.

reel[3] (rēl), *n.* [Formerly also *reill*; < Gael. *righil*, a reel (dance).] **1.** A lively dance, danced by two or three couples, and consisting of various circling or intertwining figures. It is very popular in Scotland. The *strathspey* (which see) is slower, and full of sudden jerks and turns.

> There's threesome *reels*, there's foursome *reels*,
> There's hornpipes and strathspeys, man.
> *Burns*, The Deil cam Fiddlin' thro' the Town.

> Blythe an' merry we's be a', . . .
> And dance, till we be like to fa',
> The *reel* of Tullochgorum.
> *Rev. J. Skinner*, Tullochgorum.

2. Music for such a dance or in its rhythm, which is duple (or rarely sextuple), and characterized by notes of equal length.

> Ceilles Duncane did goe before them, playing this *reill* or daunce upon a small trump.
> *Newes from Scotland* (1591), sig. B. iii.

Virginia reel, a country-dance supposed to be derived from the English "Sir Roger de Coverley." [U. S.]

reel[3] (rēl), *v. i.* [< *reel*[3], *n.*] To dance the reel; especially, to describe the figure 8 as in a reel.

> The dancers quick and quicker flew;
> They *reel'd*, they set, they cross'd, they cleekit.
> *Burns*, Tam o' Shanter.

reelable (rē'la-bl), *a.* [< *reel*[1] + *-able.*] Capable of being reeled, or wound on a reel.

> At least six species of Bombyx . . . form *reelable* cocoons. *Encyc. Brit.*, XXII. 60.

reel-band (rēl'band), *n.* A band of metal used to confine a reel in the reel-bed of a fly-rod.

reel-bed (rēl'bed), *n.* The place on an anglers' rod where the reel is fitted; a reel-seat.

reel-check (rēl'chek), *n.* Any device for checking the run of a fishing-line from the reel.

reel-click (rēl'klik), *n.* An attachment to an anglers' reel, by a light pressure of which the movement of the line is directed. It checks the line from running out too freely. Some clicks graduate the strain upon the line, checking it almost entirely, or permitting it to run without any check at all. The click also indicates to the ear what the fish is doing.

reel-cotton (rēl'kot"n), *n.* Sewing-cotton which is sold on reels instead of being made up into balls, including generally the finer grades. Compare *spool-cotton.*

reëlect (rē-ē-lekt'), *v. t.* [< *re-* + *elect.* Cf. F. *réélire*, reëlect, = Sp. *reelegir* = Pg. *reeleger* = It. *rieleggere.*] To elect again.

> The chief of these was the strategos or commander-in-chief, who held his office for a year, and could only be *re-elected* after a year's interval. *Brougham.*

reëlection (rē-ē-lek'shon), *n.* [= F. *réélection* = Sp. *reeleccion* = Pg. *reeleição* = It. *rielezione*; as *re-* + *election.*] Election a second time for the same office: as, the *reëlection* of a former representative.

> Several acts have been made, and rendered ineffectual by leaving the power of *reelection* open. *Swift.*

> Several Presidents have held office for two consecutive terms. . . . Might it not be on the whole a better system to forbid immediate *re-election*, but to allow *re-election* at any later vacancy? *E. A. Freeman*, Amer. Lects., p. 381.

reeler (rē'lėr), *n.* **1.** One who reels, in any sense; specifically, a silk-winder.

> The syndicate were able to advance somewhat the price of cocoons, and to induce the *reelers* to provide themselves liberally for fear of a further rise.
> *U. S. Cons. Report*, No. 73 (1887), p. lxxxiv.

2. The grasshopper-warbler, *Acrocephalus nævius*: so called from its note. [Local, Eng.]

> In the more marshy parts of England . . . this bird has long been known as the *Reeler*, from the resemblance of its song to the noise of the reel used, even at the beginning of the present century, by the hand-spinners of wool. But, this kind of reel being now dumb, in such districts the country-folks of the present day connect the name with the reel used by the fishermen.
> *Yarrell*, Brit. Birds (4th ed.), I. 385. (*Encyc. Dict.*)

reel-holder (rēl'hōl"dėr), *n.* **1.** A frame or box with pins upon which reels of silk, cotton, etc., for use in sewing can be put, free to revolve, and kept from being scattered. See *spool-holder.* [Eng.]—**2.** *Naut.*, on a man-of-war, one of the watch on deck who is stationed to hold the reel and haul in the line whenever the log is heaved to ascertain the ship's speed.

reëligibility (rē-el"i-ji-bil'i-ti), *n.* [= F. *rééligibilité*; as *reëligible* + *-ity* (see *-bility*).] Eligibility for being reëlected to the same office.

> With a positive duration [of the presidency] of considerable extent I connect the circumstance of *re-eligibility.*
> *A. Hamilton*, The Federalist, No. 72.

> There is another strong feature in the new constitution which I as strongly dislike. That is, the perpetual *re-eligibility* of the President.
> *Jefferson*, Correspondence, II. 291.

reëligible (rē-el'i-ji-bl), *a.* [= F. *rééligible* = It. *rieleggibile*; as *re-* + *eligible.*] Capable of being elected again to the same office.

> One of his friends introduced a bill to make the tribunes legally *reeligible.* *Froude*, Cæsar, p. 29.

reeling (rē'ling), *n.* [Verbal n. of *reel*[1], *v.*] **1.** The act or process of winding silk, as from the cocoons.—**2.** The use of the reel of an anglers' rod. *Forest and Stream.*

reeling-machine (rē'ling-ma-shēn"), *n.* **1.** A machine for winding thread on reels or spools; a spooling-machine or silk-reel. *E. H. Knight.*—**2.** In *cotton-manuf.*, a machine which takes the yarn from the bobbins of the spinning- or twisting-frames, and winds it into hanks or skeins.

reel-keeper (rēl'kē"pėr), *n.* In *angling*, any device, as a clamping ring, etc., for holding a reel firmly on the butt section of a rod.

reel-line (rēl'lin), *n.* A fishing-line used upon a reel by anglers; that part of the whole line which may be reeled, as distinguished from the casting-line or leader.

reel-oven (rēl'uv"n), *n.* See *oven.*

reel-pot† (rēl'pot), *n.* A drunkard. *Middleton.* (*Encyc. Dict.*)

reel-rall (rēl'ral), *adv.* [Appar. a repetition of *reel*; cf. *whim-wham*, *rip-rap*, etc.] Upside down; topsy-turvy. [Scotch.]

> The warld's a' *reel-rall* but wi' me and Kate. There's nothing but broken heads and broken hearts to be seen.
> *Donald and Flora*, p. 17. (*Jamieson.*)

reel-seat (rēl'sēt), *n.* **1.** The plate, groove, or bed on an anglers' rod which receives the reel.—**2.** A device used by anglers to fasten the reel to the butt of the rod. It is a simple bed-plate of sheet-brass, or of silver, screwed down upon the butt of the rod, with a pair of clamps into which the plate of the reel slides.

> Adjusting a light . . . reel . . . to the *reel-seat* at the extreme butt of the [fishing-]rod.
> *The Century*, XXVI. 378.

reel-stand (rēl'stand), *n.* A form of reel-holder.

reem[1]†, *n.* and *v.* An obsolete form of *ream*[1].

reem[2], *v. t.* Same as *ream*[2].

reem[3] (rēm), *v. i.* [< ME. *remen*, < AS. *hrȳman*, *hrēman*, cry, call out, boast, exult, also murmur, complain, < *hrēm*, cry, shout.] To cry or moan. *Halliwell.* [North. Eng.]

reem[4] (rēm), *n.* A dialectal variant of *rime*[2].

reem[5] (rēm), *n.* [< Heb.] The Hebrew name of an animal mentioned in the Old Testament (Job xxxix. 9, etc.), variously translated 'unicorn,' 'wild ox,' and 'ox-antelope,' now identified as *Bos primigenius.*

> Will the tall *reem*, which knows no Lord but me,
> Low at the crib, and ask an alms of thee?
> *Young*, Paraphrase on Job, l. 241.

reëmbark (rē-em-bärk'), *v.* [= F. *rembarquer* = Sp. Pg. *reembarcar;* as *re-* + *embark.*] **I.** *trans.* To embark or put on board again.

> On the 22d of August, 1776, the whole army being *re-embarked* was safely landed, under protection of the shipping, on the south-western extremity of Long Island.
> *Belsham*, Hist. Great Britain, George III.

II. *intrans.* To embark or go on board again.

> Having performed this ceremony [the firing of three volleys] upon the island, . . . we *re-embarked* in our boat.
> *Cook*, First Voyage, II. v.

reëmbarkation (rē-em-bär-kā'shon), *n.* [< *re-* + *embarkation.*] A putting on board or a going on board again.

> Reviews, *re-embarkations*, and councils of war.
> *Smollett*, Hist. Eng., iii. 2. (*Latham.*)

reeming†, *n.* [Verbal n. of *reem*[3], *v.*] Lamenting; groaning.

> On this wise, all the weke, woke thai within,
> With *Remyng* & rauthe, Renkes to be-hold.
> *Destruction of Troy* (E. E. T. S.), l. 8606.

reënact (rē-e-nakt'), *v. t.* [< *re-* + *enact.*] To enact again, as a law.

> The Construction of Ships was forbidden to Senators, by a Law made by Claudius, the Tribune, . . . and *re-enacted* by the Julian Law of Concessions.
> *Arbuthnot*, Ancient Coins, p. 259.

> The Southern Confederacy, in its short-lived constitution, *re-enacted* all the essential features of the constitution of the United States.
> *E. A. Freeman*, Amer. Lects., p. 397.

reënactment (rē-e-nakt'ment), *n.* [< *reënact* + *-ment.*] The enacting of a law a second time; the renewal of a law. *Clarke.*

reënforce, reënforcement, etc. See *reinforce*, etc.

reëngender (rē-en-jen'dėr), *v. t.* [< *re-* + *engender.*] To regenerate.

> The renovating and *reingendering* spirit of God.
> *Milton*, On Def. of Humb. Remonst., § 4.

reënslave (rē-en-slāv'), *v. t.* [< *re-* + *enslave.*] To enslave again; cast again into bondage.

reënslavement (rē-en-slāv'ment), *n.* [< *reënslave* + *-ment.*] The act of reënslaving, or subjecting anew to slavery.

> Consenting to their *reënslavement*, we shall pass . . . under the grasp of a military despotism.
> *The Independent*, April 24, 1862.

reënstamp (rē-en-stamp'), *v. t.* [< *re-* + *enstamp.*] To enstamp again. *Bedell.*

reënter (rē-en'tėr), *v.* [< *re-* + *enter.* Cf. F. *rentrer*, reënter, = It. *rientrare*, shrink.] **I.** *intrans.* **1.** To enter again or anew.

> That glory . . . into which He *re-entered* after His passion and ascension. *Waterland*, Works, IV. 66.

2. In *law*, to resume or retake possession of lands previously parted with. See *reëntry*, 2.

> As in case of Disseisin, the law hath been, that the disseisor could not *re-enter* without action, unless he had as it were made a present and continual claim.
> *Selden*, Illustrations of Drayton's Polyolbion, xvii. 128.

II. *trans.* **1.** To enter anew: as, (*a*) to *reënter* a house; (*b*) to *reënter* an item in an account or record.—**2.** In *engraving*, to cut deeper, as lines of an etched plate which the aqua fortis has not bitten sufficiently, or which have become worn by repeated printing.

reëntering (rē-en'tėr-ing), *n.* In *hand-block calico-printing*, the secondary and subsequent colors, which are adapted to their proper place in the pattern on the cloth by means of pin-points. Also called *grounding-in. E. H. Knight.*

reëntering (rē-en'tėr-ing), *p. a.* Entering again or anew.—**Reëntering angle**, an angle pointing inward (see *angle*[3]); specifically, in *fort.*, the angle of a work whose point turns inward toward the defended place.

Reëntering Angle.

> All that can be seen of the fortress from the river, upon which it fronts, is a long, low wall of gray stone broken sharply into salient and *reëntering angles* with a few cannon en barbette. *The Century*, XXXV. 521.

Reëntering polygon. See *polygon.*

reënthrone (rē-en-thrōn'), *v. t.* [< *re-* + *enthrone.*] To enthrone again; restore to the throne.

> He disposes in my hands the scheme
> To *reenthrone* the king. *Southerne.*

reënthronement (rē-en-thrōn'ment), *n.* [< *reënthrone* + *-ment.*] The act of enthroning again; restoration to the throne.

reënthronize (rē-en-thrō'nīz), *v. t.* [< *re-* + *enthronize.*] To reënthrone. [Rare.]

> This Mustapha they did *re-inthronize*, and place in the Ottoman Empire. *Howell*, Letters, I. iii. 22.

reëntrance (rē-en'trans), *n.* [< *re-* + *entrance*[1].] The act of entering again.

> Their repentance, although not their first entrance, is notwithstanding the first step of their *re-entrance* into life. *Hooker.*

> It is not reasonable to think but that so many of their orders as were outed from their fat possessions would endeavour a *re-entrance* against those whom they account heretics. *Dryden*, Religio Laici, Pref.

reëntrant (rē-en'trant), *a.* [= F. *rentrant* = Pg. *reintrante* = It. *rientrante;* as *re-* + *entrant.*] Same as *reëntering.*

> A *reëntrant* fashion. *Amer. Jour. Sci.*, XXX. 210.

Reëntrant angle. See *angle*[3].—**Reëntrant branch**, in *geom.* See *branch*, 2 (d).

reëntry (rē-en'tri), *n.* [< *re-* + *entry.*] **1.** The act of reëntering; a new or fresh entry.

> A right of *re-entry* was allowed to the person selling any office on repayment of the price and costs at any time before his successor, the purchaser, had actually been admitted. *Brougham.*

2. In *law*, the resuming or retaking possession of lands previously parted with by the person so doing or his predecessors: as, a landlord's *reëntry* for non-payment of rent.—**Proviso for reëntry**, a clause usually inserted in leases, providing that upon non-payment of rent, public dues, or the like, the term shall cease.

reënverse†, *v. t.* [For *renverse*, < OF. *renverser*, reverse: see *renverse.*] To reverse.

> *Reenversing* his name.
> *Donne*, Pseudo-Martyr, p. 274. (*Encyc. Dict.*)

reeper (rē'pėr), *n.* A longitudinal section of the Palmyra-palm, used in the East as a building-material.

reermouse, *n.* See *rearmouse.*

rees[1]†, *n.* See *race*[1].

rees[2] (rēs), *n.* A unit of tale for herrings (=375).

reescate†, *v. t.* Same as *rescat.*

reesk (rēsk), *n.* [Also *reysk*, *reyss;* < Gael. *riasg*, coarse mountain-grass, a marsh, fen. Cf. *rish*[1], *rush*[1].] **1.** A kind of coarse or rank grass.—**2.** Waste land which yields such grass. [Scotch in both senses.]

reest[1]†, *v.* See *reast*[1].

reest[2] (rēst), *v.* [Also *reist*, a dial. form of *rest*[2]: see *rest*[2].] **I.** *intrans.* To stand stubbornly still, as a horse; balk. [Scotch.]

> In cart or car thou never *reestit*,
> The steyest brae thou wad ha'e fac'd it.
> *Burns*, Auld Farmer's Salutation to his Auld Mare.

II. *trans.* To arrest; stop suddenly; halt. [Scotch.]

reëstablish (rē-es-tab'lish), *v. t.* [< *re-* + *establish.* Cf. OF. *restablir*, *retablir*, F. *rétablir*, Pr. *restablir*, Sp. *restablecer*, Pg. *restabelecer*, It. *ristabilire*, reëstablish.] To establish anew; set up again: as, to *reëstablish* one's health.

> And thus was the precious tree of the crosse *reestablyshid* in his place, and thauncyent myracles renewid.
> *Holy Rood* (E. E. T. S.), p. 164.

> The French were *re-established* in America, with equal power and greater spirit, having lost nothing by the war which they had before gained.
> *Johnson*, State of Affairs in 1756.

reëstablisher (rē-es-tab'lish-ėr), *n.* One who reëstablishes.

> Restorers of virtue, and *re-establishers* of a happy world.
> *Sir E. Sandys*, State of Religion.

reëstablishment (rē-es-tab'lish-ment), *n.* [< *reëstablish* + *-ment.* Cf. OF. *restablissement*, *retablissement*, F. *rétablissement*, Sp. *restablecimiento*, Pg. *restabelecimento*, It. *ristabilimento.*] The act of establishing again, or the state of being reëstablished; restoration.

> The Jews . . . made such a powerful effort for their *re-establishment* under Barchocab, in the reign of Adrian, as shook the whole Roman empire.
> *Addison*, Of the Christian Religion, viii. 6.

> The *re-establishment* of the old system, by which the dean and chapter (jointly) may have the general conduct of the worship of the church, and the care of the fabric.
> *Edinburgh Rev.*, CLXIII. 183.

reëstate† (rē-es-tāt'), *v. t.* [< *re-* + *estate.*] To reëstablish; reinstate.

> Had there not been a degeneration from what God made us at first, there had been no need of a regeneration to *re-estate* us in it. *Wallis*, Two Sermons, p. 20.

reested, reestit (rēs'ted, -tit), *p. a.* See *reasted.*

reet[1] (rēt), *n.* A dialectal variant of *root*[1].

> The highest tree in Elmond's-wood,
> He's pu'd it by the *reet.*
> *Young Akin* (Child's Ballads, I. 180).

reet[2] (rēt), *a.* and *n.* A dialectal variant of *right.*

reet[2] (rēt), *v. t.* [A dialectal variant of *right.*] To smooth, or put in order; comb, as the hair. *Halliwell.* [Prov. Eng.]

reetle, *v. t.* [A freq. of *reet*[2].] To put to rights; repair. *Halliwell.* [Prov. Eng.]

reeve[1] (rēv), *n.* [< ME. *reeve*, *reve*, < AS. *gerēfa* (rarely *gerēafa*, with loss of prefix *rēfa*, with syncope in Anglian *grǣfa*), a prefect, steward, fiscal officer of a shire or county, reeve, sheriff, judge, count; origin uncertain. The form *gerēfa* suggests a derivation (as orig. an honorary title), < *ge-*, a generalizing prefix, + *rōf* (= OS. *rōf*, *ruof*), famous, well-known or valiant, stout, a poetical epithet of unprecise meaning and unknown origin. But *gerēfa* may perhaps stand for orig. **grēfa* (Anglian *grǣfa*) = OFries. *grēva* = D. *graaf* = OHG. *grāvo*, MHG. *grāve*, *grǣve*, G. *graf*, a count, prefect, overseer, etc.: see *graf*, *grave*[6], *greeve*[1].] **1.** A steward; a prefect; a bailiff; a business agent. The word enters into the composition of some titles, as *borough-reeve*, *hog-reeve*, *portreeve*, *sheriff* (*shire-reeve*), *town-reeve*, etc., and is itself in use in Canada and in some parts of the United States.

> Selde falleth the seruant so deepe in arerages
> As doth the *reyue* other the conterroller that rekene mot and a-counte
> Of al that thei hauen had of hym that is here maister.
> *Piers Plowman* (C), xii. 298.

> His lordes scheep, his neet, his dayerie,
> His swyn, his hors, his stoor, and his pultrie,
> Was holly in this *reeves* governynge.
> *Chaucer*, Gen. Prol. to C. T. (ed. Morris), l. 599.

> In auncient time, almost every manor had his *reve*, whose authoritie was not only to levie the lords rents, to set to worke his servaunts, and to husband his demesnes to his best profit and commoditie, but also to governe his tenants in peace, and to leade them foorth to war, when necessitie so required.
> *Lambarde*, Perambulation (1596), p. 484. (*Halliwell.*)

> A lord "who has so many men that he cannot personally have all in his own keeping" was bound to set over each dependent township a *reeve*, not only to exact his lord's dues, but to enforce his justice within its bounds.
> *J. R. Green*, Conq. of Eng., p. 217.

> The council of every village or township [in Canada] consists of one *reeve* and four councillors, and the county council consists of the *reeves* and deputy-*reeves* of the townships and villages within the county.
> *Sir C. W. Dilke*, Probs. of Greater Britain, i. 2.

2. A foreman in a coal-mine. *Edinburgh Rev.* [Local.]—**Fen reeve**, in some old English municipal corporations, an officer having supervision of the fens or marshes.

> The *Fen Reeve* [at Dunwich] superintends the stocking of the marshes, and his emoluments are from 5*l.* to 6*l.* a year.
> *Municip. Corp. Report* (1835), p. 2222.

reeve[2]† (rēv), *v. i.* An obsolete variant of *reave.*

reeve[3] (rēv), *v. t.*; pret. and pp. *reeved* or *rove*, ppr. *reeving.* [< D. *reven* = Dan. *rebe*, reef or reeve, < *reef*, a reef: see *reef*[2], *n.* Cf. *reef*[2], *v.*, a doublet of *reeve*[3]. The pp. *rove* is irreg., appar. in imitation of *hove*, pret. and pp. of *heave.*] *Naut.*, to pass or run through any hole in a block, thimble, cleat, ring-bolt, cringle, etc., as the end of a rope.

> When first leaving port, studding-sail gear is to be *rove*, all the running rigging to be examined, that which is unfit for use to be got down, and new rigging *rove* in its place. *R. H. Dana, Jr.*, Before the Mast, p. 15.

reeve[4] (rēv), *n.* [Appar. formed by irreg. vowel-change from the original of *ruff*[2]: see *ruff*[2].] A bird, the female of the ruff, *Machetes pugnax.* See *Pavoncella*, and cut under *ruff*[2].

> The *reeves* lay four eggs in a tuft of grass, the first week in May. *Pennant*, Brit. Zoöl. (ed. 1776), p. 458. (*Jodrell.*)

Reeves's pheasant. See *Phasianus.*

reëxamination (rē-eg-zam-i-nā'shon), *n.* [= Sp. *reexaminacion* = Pg. *reexaminação;* as *re-* + *examination.*] A renewed or repeated examination; specifically, in *law*, the examination of a witness after a cross-examination.

reëxamine (rē-eg-zam'in), *v. t.* [= Sp. Pg. *reexaminar;* as *re-* + *examine.*] To examine anew; subject to another examination.

> Spend the time in *re-examining* more duly your cause.
> *Hooker.*

reëxchange (rē-eks-chānj'), *n.* [< *re-* + *exchange*, *n.*] **1.** A renewed exchange.—**2.** In *com.*, the difference in the value of a bill of exchange occasioned by its being dishonored in a foreign country in which it was payable. The existence and amount of it depend on the rate of exchange between the two countries. *Wharton.*

reëxchange (rē-eks-chānj'), *v. t.* [< *re-* + *exchange*, *v.*] To exchange again or anew.

reëxhibit (rē-eg-zib'it), *v. t.* [< *re-* + *exhibit.*] To exhibit again or anew.

reëxhibit (rē-eg-zib'it), *n.* [< *reëxhibit*, *v.*] A second or renewed exhibit.

reëxperience (rē-eks-pē′ri-ens), *n.* [< *re-* + *experience, n.*] A renewed or repeated experience.

reëxperience (rē-eks-pē′ri-ens), *v. t.* [< *re-* + *experience, v.*] To experience again.

reëxport (rē-eks-pōrt′), *v. t.* [= F. *réexporter*; as *re-* + *export.*] To export again; export after having imported.

The goods, for example, which are annually purchased with the great surplus of eighty-two thousand hogsheads of tobacco annually *re-exported* from Great Britain, are not all consumed in Great Britain.
Adam Smith, Wealth of Nations, iv. 7.

reëxport (rē-eks′pōrt), *n.* [< *reëxport, v.*] 1. A commodity that is reëxported.—2. Reëxportation.

Foreign sugars have not been taken to Hawaii for *re-export* to the Pacific Coast. *The American*, VI. 387.

reëxportation (rē-eks-pōr-tā′shon), *n.* [= F. *réexportation*; as *reëxport* + *-ation.*] The act of exporting what has been imported.

In allowing the same drawbacks upon the *re-exportation* of the greater part of European and East India goods to the colonies as upon their *re-exportation* to any independent country, the interest of the mother country was sacrificed to it, even according to the mercantile ideas of that interest. *Adam Smith*, Wealth of Nations, iv. 7.

reëxtent (rē-eks-tent′), *n.* [< *re-* + *extent.*] In *law*, a second extent on lands or tenements, on complaint that the former was partially made, or the like. See *extent*, 3.

reezet, *v. t.* See *reast*[1].

reezedt, *a.* See *reasted.*

ref. An abbreviation of (*a*) *reformed*; (*b*) *reference.*

refaction† (rē-fak′shon), *n.* [= F. *réfaction* = Sp. *refaccion*, < L. as if **refactio(n-)*, for *refectio(n-)*, a restoring (cf. *refactor*, a restorer): see *refection.*] Retribution.

The Soveraigne Minister, who was then employed in Elaiana, was commanded to require *refaction* and satisfaction against the informers or rather inventours and forgers of the aforesaid mis-information.
Howell, Vocall Forrest, p. 113.

refait (F. pron. rė-fā′), *n.* [F., a drawn game, < *refait*, pp. of *refaire*, do again, < *re-*, again, + *faire*, do: see *feat*[1].] A drawn game; specifically, in *rouge-et-noir*, a state of the game in which the cards dealt for the players who bet on the red equal in value those dealt for the players who bet on the black.

refashion (rē-fash′on), *v. t.* [= OF. *refaçoner*, *refaçonner*, F. *refaçonner*, fashion over, refashion; as *re-* + *fashion, v.*] To fashion, form, or mold into shape a second time or anew.

refashionment (rē-fash′on-ment), *n.* [< *refashion* + *-ment.*] The act of fashioning or forming again or anew. *L. Hunt.*

refasten (rē-fås′n), *v. t.* [< *re-* + *fasten.*] To fasten again.

refect† (rē-fekt′), *v. t.* [< L. *refectus*, pp. of *reficere*, restore, refresh, remake, < *re-*, again, + *facere*, make: see *fact.* Cf. *refete*, *refit.*] To refresh; restore after hunger or fatigue; repair.

A man in the morning is lighter in the scale, because in sleep some pounds have perspired; and is also lighter unto himself, because he is *refected.*
Sir T. Browne, Vulg. Err., iv. 7.

refect† (rē-fekt′), *p. a.* [ME., < L. *refectus*, refreshed, restored, pp. of *reficere*, restore, refresh: see *refect, v.*] Recovered; restored; refreshed.

Tak thanne this drawht, and, whan thou art wel refresshed and *refect*, thow shal be moore stydefast to stye [rise] into heyere questiouns.
Chaucer, Boëthius, iv. prose 6.

refection (rē-fek′shon), *n.* [< ME. *refeccion*, *refeccyon*, < OF. *refection*, F. *réfection* = Pr. *refectio* = Sp. *refeccion* = Pg. *refeição*, *refecção* = It. *refezione*, < L. *refectio(n-)*, a restoring, refreshment, remaking, < *reficere*, pp. *refectus*, restore, remake: see *refect.*] 1. Refreshment after hunger or fatigue; a repast: applied especially to meals in religious houses.

And whan we were retourned ayen into ye sayde chapell of oure Lady, after a lytel *refeccyon* with mete and drynke . . . *Sir R. Guylforde*, Pylgrymage, p. 27.

But now the peaceful hours of sacred night
Demand *refection*, and to rest invite.
Pope, Iliad, xxiv. 754.

Beside the rent in kind and the feudal services, the chief who had given stock was entitled to come with a company . . . and feast at the Daer-stock tenant's house at particular periods. . . . This "right of *refection*" and liability to it are among the most distinctive features of ancient Irish custom.
Maine, Early Hist. of Institutions, p. 161.

2. In *civil law* and *old Eng. law*, repair; restoration to good condition.

refectioner (rē-fek′shon-ėr), *n.* [< *refection* + *-er*[2].] One who has charge of the refectory and the supplies of food in a monastery.

Two most important officers of the Convent, the Kitchener and *Refectioner*, were just arrived with a sumpter-mule loaded with provisions. *Scott*, Monastery.

refective (rē-fek′tiv), *a.* and *n.* [< *refect* + *-ive.*] I. *a.* Refreshing; restoring.

II. *n.* That which refreshes.

refectorer (rē-fek′tō-rėr), *n.* [< F. *refectorier* = Sp. *refitolero* = Pg. *refeitoreiro* = It. *refettoriere*, < ML. *refectorarius*, one who has charge of the refectory, < *refectorium*, refectory: see *refectory.*] Same as *refectioner.*

refectory (rē-fek′tō-ri), *n.*; pl. *refectories* (-riz). [= OF. *refectoir*, *refeitoir*, also (with intrusive r) *refrectoir*, *refreitoir*, *refrictur*, *refretor*, etc., F. *réfectoire* and *réfectoir* = Pr. *refector*, *refeitor* = Sp. *refectorio*, *refitorio* = Pg. *refeitorio* = It. *refettorio*, < ML. *refectorium*, a place of refreshment, < L. *reficere*, pp. *refectus*, refresh, restore, refect: see *refect.*] A room of refreshment;

Refectory of the Monastery of Mont St. Michel, Normandy; 13th century.

an eating-room; specifically, a hall or apartment in a convent, monastery, or seminary where the meals are eaten. Compare *fraiter.*

Scenes
Sacred to neatness and repose, th' alcove,
The chamber, or *refectory*. *Cowper*, Task, vi. 572.

To whom the monk: . . . "a guest of ours
Told us of this in our *refectory*."
Tennyson, Holy Grail.

refel† (rē-fel′), *v. t.* [< OF. *refeller*, < L. *refellere*, show to be false, refute, < *re-*, again, back, + *fallere*, deceive (> *falsus*, false): see *fail*[1].] To refute; disprove; overthrow by arguments; set aside.

How I persuaded, how I pray'd and kneel'd,
How he *refell'd* me, and how I replied.
Shak., M. for M., v. 1. 94.

I shall confute, refute, repel, *refel*,
Explode, exterminate, expunge, extinguish
Like a rush-candle this same heresy.
Chapman, Revenge for Honour, i. 2.

refeoff (rē-fef′), *v. t.* [< ME. *refeffen*; as *re-* + *feoff.*] To feoff again; reinvest; reëndow.

Kynge Arthur *refeffed* hym a-gein in his londe that he hadde be-fore. *Merlin* (E. E. T. S.), iii. 479.

refer (rē-fėr′), *v.*; pret. and pp. *referred*, ppr. *referring.* [< ME. *referren*, < OF. *referer*, F. *référer* = Pr. *referre* = Sp. *referir* = Pg. *referir-se*, *referir* = It. *riferire*, < L. *referre*, bear back, relate, refer, < *re-*, back, + *ferre*, bear, = E. *bear*[1]. Cf. *confer*, *defer*, *differ*, *infer*, *prefer*, *transfer*, etc. Cf. *relate.*] I. *trans.* 1†. To bear or carry back; bring back.

Alle thinges ben *referred* and browht to nowht.
Chaucer, Boëthius, iii. prose 11.

He lives in heav'n, among the saints *referred.*
P. Fletcher, Eliza.

Cut from a crab his crooked claws, and hide
The rest in earth, a scorpion thence will glide,
And shoot his sting; his tail, in circles tossed,
Refers the limbs his backward father lost.
Dryden, tr. of Ovid's Metamorph., xv.

2. To trace back; assign to as origin, source, etc.; impute; assign; attribute.

Wo be to the land, to the realm, whose king is a child: which some interpret and *refer* to childish conditions.
Latimer, 2d Sermon bef. Edw. VI., 1550.

Mahomet *referred* his new laws to the angel Gabriel, by whose direction he gave out they were made.
Burton, Anat. of Mel., p. 603.

In the political as in the natural body, a sensation is often *referred* to a part widely different from that in which it really resides. *Macaulay*, Hallam's Const. Hist.

3. To hand over or intrust for consideration and decision; deliver over, as to another person or tribunal for treatment, information, decision, and the like: as, to *refer* a matter to a third person; parties to a suit *refer* their cause to arbitration; the court *refers* a cause to individuals for examination and report, or for trial and decision.

Now, touching the situation of measures, there are as manie or more proportions of them which I *referre* to the makers phantasie and choise.
Puttenham, Arte of Eng. Poesie, p. 74.

I *refer* it to your own judgment.
B. Jonson, Every Man in his Humour, ii. 2.

4. Reflexively, to betake one's self to; appeal.

I do *refer me* to the oracle. *Shak.*, W. T., iii. 2. 116.

My father's tongue was loosed of a suddenty, and he said aloud, "I *refer myself* to God's pleasure, and not to yours." *Scott*, Redgauntlet, letter xi.

5. To reduce or bring in relation, as to some standard.

You profess and practise to *refer* all things to yourself.
Bacon.

6. To assign, as to a class, rank, historical position, or the like.

A science of historical palmistry . . . that attempts to *refer*, by distinctions of penmanship, parchment, paper, ink, illumination, and abbreviation, every manuscript to its own country, district, age, school, and even individual writer. *Stubbs*, Medieval and Modern Hist., p. 76.

7. To defer; put off; postpone. [Rare.]

Marry, all but the first [challenge] I put off with engagement; and, by good fortune, the first is no madder of fighting than I; so that that's *referred*: the place where it must be ended is four days' journey off.
Beau. and Fl., King and no King, iii. 2.

My account of this voyage must be *referred* to the second part of my travels. *Swift*, Gulliver's Travels, i. 8.

8. To direct for information; instruct to apply for any purpose.

My wife . . . *referred* her to all the neighbors for a character. *Goldsmith*, Vicar, xi.

I would *refer* the reader . . . to the admirable exposition in the August issue of the "Westminster Review."
Contemporary Rev., LIV. 329.

=Syn. 2. *Ascribe*, *Charge*, etc. See *attribute.*

II. *intrans.* 1. To have relation; relate.

Breaking of Bread: a Phrase which . . . manifestly *refers* to the Eucharist. *Bp. Atterbury*, Sermons, I. vii.

2. To have recourse; apply; appeal: as, to *refer* to an encyclopedia; to *refer* to one's notes.

Of man, what see we but his station here,
From which to reason, or to which *refer?*
Pope, Essay on Man, i. 20.

3. To allude; make allusion.

I proceed to another affection of our nature which bears strong testimony to our being born for religion. I *refer* to the emotion which leads us to revere what is higher than ourselves. *Channing*, Perfect Life, p. 11.

4. To direct the attention; serve as a mark or sign of reference.

Some suspected passages . . . are degraded to the bottom of the page, with an asterisk *referring* to the places of their insertion. *Pope*, Pref. to Shakspere.

5. To give a reference: as, to *refer* to a former employer for a recommendation. =Syn. 1. To belong to, pertain to, concern.—1 and 3. *Allude*, *Hint*, etc. See *advert.*

referable (ref′ėr-a-bl), *a.* [< OF. *referable*, < *referer*, refer: see *refer* and *-able.* Cf. *referrible.*] Capable of being referred; that may be assigned; admitting of being considered as belonging or related to.

As for those names of Ἀφροδίτη, Ζύγια, &c., they are all *referable* to Γάμος, which we have already taken notice of in our defence of the Cabbala.
Dr. H. More, The Cabbala, iv. 4.

Other classes of information there were—partly obtained from books, partly from observation, to some extent *referable* to his two main employments of politics and law. *R. Choate*, Addresses and Orations, p. 304.

France is the second commercial country of the world; and her command of foreign markets seems clearly *referable*, in a great degree, to the real elegance of her productions. *Gladstone*, Might of Right, p. 47.

Isaac Barrow, Sir Thomas Browne, Henry More, Dr. Johnson, and many other writers, down to our own time, have *referrible* [instead of *referable*]. . . . Possibly it was pronunciation, in part, that debarred *preferrible*, and discouraged *referrible*. *F. Hall*, Adjectives in -able, p. 47.

referee (ref-ė-rē′), *n.* [< F. *référé*, pp. of *référer*, refer: see *refer.*] 1. One to whom something is referred; especially, a person to whom a matter in dispute has been referred for settlement or decision; an arbitrator; an umpire.

He was the universal *referee*; a quarrel about a bet or a mistress was solved by him in a moment, and in a manner which satisfied both parties. *Disraeli*, Coningsby, i. 5.

2. Specifically, in *law*, a person selected by the court or parties under authority of law to try a cause in place of the court, or to exam-

ine and report on a question in aid of the court, or to perform some function involving judicial or quasi-judicial powers.=**Syn.** *Umpire*, *Arbitrator*, etc. See *judge*, *n*.

referee (ref-e-rē′), *v. t.* [‹ *referee*, *n*.] To preside over as referee or umpire. [Colloq.]

The boys usually asked him to keep the score, or to *referee* the matches they played. *St. Nicholas*, XIV. 50.

reference (ref′ėr-ens), *n*. [‹ F. *référence* = Sp. Pg. *referencia* = It. *riferenza*, ‹ ML. **referentia*, ‹ L. *referen(t-)s*, ppr. of *referre*, refer: see *refer*.] 1. The act of referring. (*a*) The act of assigning: as, the *reference* of a work to its author, or of an animal to its proper class. (*b*) The act of having recourse to a work or person for information; consultation: as, a work of *reference*: also used attributively. (*c*) The act of mentioning or speaking of (a person or thing) incidentally.

But distance only cannot change the heart;
And, were I call'd to prove th' assertion true,
One proof should serve—a *reference* to you.
Cowper, Epistle to Joseph Hill.

(*d*) In *law*: (1) The process of assigning a cause pending in court, or some particular point in a cause, to one or more persons appointed by the court under authority of law to act in place of or in aid of the court. (2) The hearing or proceeding before such person. Abbreviated *ref*.
2. Relation; respect; regard: generally in the phrase *in* or *with reference to*.

Ros. But what will you be call'd?
Cel. Something that hath a *reference to* my state;
No longer Celia, but Aliena.
Shak., As you Like it, i. 3. 129.

I have dwelt so long on this subject that I must contract what I have to say *in reference to* my translation.
Dryden, tr. of Juvenal, Ded.

If we take this definition of happiness, and examine it *with reference to* the senses, it will be acknowledged wonderfully adapt. *Swift*, Tale of a Tub, ix.

3. That which is or may be referred to. (*a*) A written testimonial to character or ability. Hence—(*b*) One of whom inquiries may be made in regard to a person's character, abilities, or the like.
4. A direction in a book or writing to refer to some other place or passage: often a mere citation, as of book, chapter, page, or text.—
5†. Assignment; apportionment.

I crave fit disposition for my wife,
Due *reference* of place and exhibition [maintenance].
Shak., Othello, i. 3. 238.

6†. An appeal.

Make your full *reference* freely to my lord,
Who is so full of grace that it flows over
On all that need. *Shak.*, A. and C., v. 2. 23.

Book or **work of reference**, a book, such as a dictionary or an encyclopedia, intended to be consulted as occasion requires.—**Reference Bible**, a Bible having references to parallel passages, with or without brief explanations, printed on the margin.—**Reference book**, a book or work of reference.—**Reference library**, a library containing books which can be consulted only on the spot: in contradistinction to a *lending* or *circulating library*.—**Reference-marks**, in *printing*, the characters * † ‡ ‖ § ¶, or figures, or letters, used in a printed page to refer the reader from the text to notes, or vice versa.

referendar (ref′ėr-en-där′), *n*. [G.: see *referendary*.] In Germany, a jurist, or one not yet a full member of a judicial college, whose functions vary in different states. In Prussia, since 1869, two examinations are required in the judicial service; after passing the first the candidate becomes a referendar, and serves generally without pay and without a vote.

referendary (ref-e-ren′da-ri), *n*. [‹ OF. *referendaire*, *referendaire*, F. *référendaire* = Sp. Pg. *referendario* = It. *riferendario*, *referendario* = G. *referendar*, ‹ ML. *referendarius*, an officer through whom petitions were presented to and answered by the sovereign, and by whom the sovereign's mandates were communicated to the courts, commissions signed, etc., ‹ L. *referendus*, to be referred to, gerundive of *referre*, refer: see *refer*.] 1. One to whom or to whose decision anything is referred; a referee.

In suits which a man doth not well understand, it is good to refer them to some friend of trust and judgment; . . . but let him chuse well his *referendaries*, for else he may be led by the nose. *Bacon*, Suitors (ed. 1887).

If I were by your appointment your *referendary* for news, I should write but short letters, because the times are barren. *Donne*, Letters, xxiv.

2. An officer acting as the medium of communication with a sovereign.—3. [Tr. Gr. ῥεφερενδάριος.] An official who is the medium of communication between the patriarch of Constantinople and the civil authorities. This office has existed since the sixth century.

referendum (ref-e-ren′dum), *n*. [= G. *referendum*, etc., ‹ NL. *referendum*, neut. of L. *referendus*, gerundive of *referre*, refer: see *referendary*.] 1. A note from a diplomatic agent addressed to his government, asking for instructions on particular matters.—2. In Switzerland, the right of the people to decide on certain laws or measures which have been passed by the legislative body. In one of its two forms, *facultative referendum* (contingent on certain conditions) or *obligatory referendum*, it exists in nearly all the cantons. Since 1874 the facultative referendum forms part of the federal constitution: if 8 cantons or 30,000 voters so demand, a federal measure must be submitted to popular vote.

referential (ref-e-ren′shal), *a*. [‹ *reference* (ML. **referentia*) + *-al*.] Relating to or having reference; relating to or containing a reference or references.

Any one might take down a lecture, word for word, for his own *referential* use. *Athenæum*, No. 2944, p. 411.

referentially (ref-e-ren′shal-i), *adv*. By way of reference.

referment[1]† (rē-fėr′ment), *n*. [= It. *riferimento*; as *refer* + *-ment*.] A reference for decision.

There was a *referment* made from his Majesty to my Lord's Grace of Cant., my Lords of Durham and Rochester, and myself, to hear and order a matter of difference in the church of Hereford. *Abp. Laud*, Diary, Dec. 6, 1624.

referment[2] (rē-fėr-ment′), *v*. [= Pg. *refermentar*; as *re-* + *ferment*.] **I.** *intrans.* To ferment again. *Maunder*.
II. *trans.* To cause to ferment again.

Th' admitted nitre agitates the flood,
Revives its fire, and *referments* the blood.
Sir R. Blackmore, Creation, vi.

referrer (rē-fėr′ėr), *n*. One who refers.

referrible (rē-fėr′i-bl), *a*. [= Sp. *referible* = Pg. *referivel*; as *refer* + *-ible*. Cf. *referable*.] Same as *referable*.

Acknowledging . . . the secondary [substance] to be *referrible* also to the primary or centrall substance by way of causall relation. *Dr. H. More*, Immortal. of Soul, i. 4.

I shall only take notice of those effects of lightning which seem *referrible* . . . partly to the distinct shapes and sizes of the corpuscles that compose the destructive matter. *Boyle*, Works, III. 682.

Some of which may be *referrible* to this period.
Hallam.

refete†, *v. t.* [‹ ME. *refeten*, ‹ OF. *refeter*, *refaiiter*, ‹ *refait*, ‹ L. *refectus*, pp. of *reficere*, refect: see *refect*. Cf. *refit*.] To refect; refresh.

Thay ar happen also that hungeres after ryȝt,
For thay schal frely be *refete* ful of alle gode.
Alliterative Poems (ed. Morris), iii. 20.

refigure (rē-fig′ūr), *v. t.* [‹ ME. *refiguren*; ‹ *re-* + *figure*.] 1. To go over again; figure anew; represent anew.

Refigurynge hire shap, hire wommanhede,
Withinne his herte, and every word or dede
That passed was. *Chaucer*, Troilus, v. 472.

The child doth not more expresly *refigure* the visage of his Father then that book resembles the stile of the Remonstrant. *Milton*, Apology for Smectymnuus.

When the fog is vanishing away,
Little by little doth the sight *refigure*
Whate'er the mist that crowds the air conceals.
Longfellow, tr. of Dante's Inferno, xxxi. 35.

Specifically—2. In *astron.*, to correct or restore the parabolic figure of: said of a parabolic mirror.

refill (rē-fil′), *v. t.* and *i*. [‹ *re-* + *fill*[1].] To fill again.

See! round the verge a vine-branch twines.
See! how the mimic clusters roll,
As ready to *refill* the bowl!
Broome, tr. of Anacreon's Odes, l.

refine (rē-fīn′), *v*. [= Sp. Pg. *refinar*; as *re-* + *fine*[2]. Cf. F. *raffiner* (= It. *raffinare*), refine, ‹ *re-* + *affiner*, refine, fine (metal): see *affine*[2].] **I.** *trans.* 1. To bring or reduce to a pure state; free from impurities; free from sediment; defecate; clarify; fine: as, to *refine* liquor, sugar, or petroleum.

Wines on the lees well *refined*. Isa. xxv. 6.

The temper of my love, whose flame I find
Fin'd and *refin'd* too oft, but faintles flashes,
And must within short time fall down in ashes.
Stirling, Aurora, Sonnet xxii.

Now the table was furnished with fat things, and wine that was well *refined*. *Bunyan*, Pilgrim's Progress, p. 122.

2. In *metal.*, to bring into a condition of purity as complete as the nature of the ore treated will allow. Used chiefly with reference to gold and silver, especially with reference to the separation (parting) of these two metals from each other and from the baser metals with which they are combined in what are known as bullion-bars or bricks of mixed metals, as they come from the mills located at or near the mines. Refining is, in general, the last stage or stages in the metallurgical treatment of an ore. As the term *refining* is commonly used with reference to the manufacture of iron, it means the partial decarburization and purification of pig in the open-hearth furnace, for the purpose of rendering it more suitable for use in the puddling-furnace in which the process of converting it into malleable iron is completed. This method of puddling is called *dry puddling*. The operation of converting pig- into wrought-iron in the open-hearth furnace, when begun and completed without puddling, is generally called *fining*, and in this process charcoal or coke is used. There are many modifications of the fining process, but the principle is the same in all. In puddling, raw coal is used, and the fuel does not come in contact with the metal; in fining, the ore and fuel (either charcoal or coke) are together upon the same hearth. The various fining processes for converting pig- into wrought-iron, with charcoal as fuel, were of great importance before the invention of puddling, by which method much the larger part of the wrought-iron now used in the world is prepared, and this is done, for the most part, without previous partial decarburization of the pig in the refinery, by the process known as *wet puddling*, or *pig-boiling*. See *puddle*[1] and *finery*[2].

I will bring the third part through the fire, and will *refine* them as silver is *refined*. Zech. xiii. 9.

To gild *refined* gold, to paint the lily.
Shak., K. John, iv. 2. 11.

3. To purify from what is gross, coarse, debasing, low, vulgar, inelegant, rude, clownish, and the like; make elegant; raise or educate, as the taste; give culture to; polish: as, to *refine* the manners, taste, language, style, intellect, or moral feelings.

So it more faire accordingly it [beauty] makes,
And the grosse matter of this earthly myne
Which clotheth it thereafter doth *refyne*.
Spenser, In Honour of Beautie, l. 47.

Love *refines*
The thoughts, and heart enlarges.
Milton, P. L., viii. 590.

Refined madder. See *madder*[1].
II. *intrans.* 1. To become pure; be cleared of feculent matter.

So the pure limpid stream, when foul with stains,
Works itself clear, and, as it runs, *refines*. *Addison*.

2. To improve in accuracy, delicacy, or in anything that constitutes excellence.

Chaucer has *refined* on Boccace, and has mended the stories which he has borrowed. *Dryden*, Pref. to Fables.

But let a lord once own the happy lines,
How the wit brightens! how the style *refines*!
Pope, Essay on Criticism, l. 421.

A new generation, *refining* upon the lessons given by himself [Shelley] and Keats, has carried the art of rhythm to extreme variety and finish. *Stedman*, Vict. Poets, p. 380.

3. To exhibit nicety or subtlety in thought or language, especially excessive nicety.

You speak like good blunt soldiers; and 'tis well enough;
But did you live at court, as I do, gallants,
You would *refine*, and learn an apter language.
Fletcher (*and another*), False One, iii. 2.

Who, too deep for his hearers, still went on *refining*,
And thought of convincing, while they thought of dining.
Goldsmith, Retaliation, l. 35.

refined (rē-fīnd′), *p. a.* Purified; elevated; cultivated; subtle: as, a *refined* taste; a *refined* discrimination; *refined* society.

There be men that be so sharp, and so over-sharpe or *refined*, that it seemeth little unto them to interprete words, but also they holde it for an office to diuine thoughts.
Guevara, Letters (tr. by Hellowes, 1577), p. 133.

Modern taste
Is so *refin'd*, and delicate, and chaste.
Cowper, Table-Talk, l. 511.

refinedly (rē-fī′ned-li), *adv*. With refinement; with nicety or elegance, especially excessive nicety.

Will any dog . . .
Refinedly leave his bitches and his bones,
To turn a wheel? *Dryden*, Essay upon Satire, l. 135.

Some have *refinedly* expounded that passage in Matt. xii.
Calvin, On Jonah (Calv. Trans. Soc., 1847), p. 20.

refinedness (rē-fī′ned-nes), *n*. The state of being refined; purity; refinement; also, affected purity.

Great semblances of peculiar sanctimony, integrity, scrupulosity, spirituality, *refinedness*. *Barrow*, Works, III. xv.

refinement (rē-fīn′ment), *n*. [= Pg. *refinamento*; as *refine* + *-ment*. Cf. F. *raffinement* = It. *raffinamento*.] 1. The act of refining or purifying; the act of separating from a substance all extraneous matter; purification; clarification: as, the *refinement* of metals or liquors.

The soul of man is capable of very high *refinements*, even to a condition purely angelical.
Dr. H. More, Immortal. of Soul, iii. 1.

2. The state of being pure or purified.

The more bodies are of a kin to spirit in subtilty and *refinement*, the more diffusive are they. *Norris*.

3. The state of being free from what is coarse, rude, inelegant, debasing, or the like; purity of taste, mind, etc.; elegance of manners or language; culture.

I am apt to doubt whether the corruptions in our language have not at least equalled the *refinements* of it.
Swift, Improving the English Tongue.

This refined taste is the consequence of education and habit: we are born only with a capacity of entertaining this *refinement*, as we are born with a disposition to receive and obey all the rules and regulations of society.
Sir J. Reynolds, Discourses, xiii.

Refinement as opposed to simplicity of taste is not necessarily a mark of a good æsthetic faculty.
J. Sully, Outlines of Psychol., p. 544.

4. That which proceeds from refining or a desire to refine; a result of elaboration, polish, or nicety: often used to denote an over-nicety, or

affected subtlety: as, the *refinements* of logic or philosophy; the *refinements* of cunning.

It is the Poet's *Refinement* upon this Thought which I most admire. *Addison*, Spectator, No. 303.

From the small experience I have of courts, I have ever found *refinements* to be the worst sort of all conjectures; . . . of some hundreds of facts, for the real truth of which I can account, I never yet knew any refiner to be once in the right. *Swift*, Change in Queen's Ministry.

As used in Greece, its [the Doric column's] beauty was very much enhanced by a number of *refinements* whose existence was not suspected till lately, and even now cannot be detected but by the most practised eye. *J. Fergusson*, Hist. Arch., I. 249.

5†. Excessive or extravagant compliment; a form of expression intended to impose on the hearer.

I must tell you a great piece of *refinement* of Harley. He charged me to come to him often; I told him I was loth to trouble him in so much business as he had, and desired I might have leave to come at his levee; which he immediately refused, and said that was not a place for friends to come to. *Swift*, Journal to Stella, v.

=Syn. 3. *Cultivation*, etc. See *culture*.

refiner (rȩ̄-fī'nėr), *n.* 1. One who refines liquors, sugar, metals, etc.

And he shall sit as a *refiner* and purifier of silver. Mal. iii. 3.

2. An improver in purity and elegance.

As they have been the great *refiners* of our language, so it hath been my chief ambition to imitate them. *Swift*.

3. An inventor of superfluous subtleties; one who is overnice in discrimination, or in argument, reasoning, philosophy, etc.

Whether (as some phantasticall *refyners* of phylosophy will needes perswade vs) hell is nothing but error, and that none but tooles and idiots and mechanicall men, that haue no learning, shall be damnd. *Nashe*, Pierce Penilesse, p. 66.

No men see less of the truth of things than these great *refiners* upon incidents, who are so wonderfully subtle and over wise in their conceptions. *Addison*.

4†. One who indulges in excessive compliment; one who is over-civil; a flatterer.

The worst was, our guilded *refiners* with their golden promises made all men their slaues in hope of recompences. Quoted in *Capt. John Smith's* Works, I. 169.

For these people have fallen into a needless and endless way of multiplying ceremonies, which have been extremely troublesome to those who practise them, and insupportable to every body else; insomuch that wise men are often more uneasy at the over civility of these *refiners* than they could possibly be in the conversation of peasants or mechanics. *Swift*, Good Manners.

5. An apparatus for refining; specifically, in England, a gas-purifier.

refinery (rȩ̄-fī'nėr-i), *n.*; pl. *refineries* (-iz). [< *refine* + *-ery*. Cf. F. *raffinerie*, a refinery, < *raffiner*, refine: see *refine*.] A place or establishment where some substance, as petroleum, is refined; specifically, in *metal.*, a place where metals are refined. See *refine* and *finery*[2].

refit (rȩ̄-fit'), *v.* [< *re-* + *fit*[1], *v.* Partly due to ME. *refeten*, repair: see *refete*.] I. *trans.* 1. To fit or prepare again; restore after damage or decay; repair: as, to *refit* ships of war.

Permit our ships a shelter on your shores,
Refitted from your woods with planks and oars.
Dryden, Æneid, i. 777.

We landed, in order to *refit* our vessels and store ourselves with provisions. *Addison*, Frozen Words.

2. To fit out or provide anew.

II. *intrans.* To repair damages, especially damages of ships.

Having received some Damage by a Storm, we . . . put in here to *refit* before we could adventure to go farther. *Dampier*, Voyages, I. 413.

At each place [Tampa Bay and Pensacola Bay] we have a railroad terminus, while at the latter harbor are ample means for *refitting*. *Jour. of Mil. Service Inst.*, X. 586.

refit (rȩ̄-fit'), *n.* [< *refit*, *v.*] The repairing or renovating of what is damaged or worn out; specifically, the repair of a ship: as, the vessel came in for *refit*.

refitment (rȩ̄-fit'mẹnt), *n.* [< *refit* + *-ment*.] The act of refitting.

refl. An abbreviation of *reflexive*.

reflair†, *n.* [< ME.; as *re-* + *flair*.] An odor.

Alf hit watz semly on to sene,
A fayre *reflayr* ȝet fro hit flot,
Ther wonys that worthyly I wot & wene.
Alliterative Poems (ed. Morris), i. 46.

reflair†, *v. i.* [ME. *reflaren*; < *reflair*, *n.*] To arise, as an odor.

Haill! floscampy, and flower vyrgynall,
The odour of thy goodnes *reflars* to vs all.
York Plays, p. 444.

reflame (rȩ̄-flām'), *v. i.* [< *re-* + *flame*.] To blaze again; burst again into flame.

Stamp out the fire, or this
Will smoulder and *re-flame*, and burn the throne
Where you should sit with Philip.
Tennyson, Queen Mary, i. 5.

reflect (rȩ̄-flekt'), *v.* [< OF. *reflecter*, F. *refléter* (= Sp. *reflectar*, *reflejar*), reflect; vernacularly, OF. *reflechir*, bend back, F. *réfléchir*, reflect, etc., = Pr. Sp. Pg. *reflectir* = It. *riflettere*, *reflettere*, reflect; < L. *reflectere*, bend backward, < *re-*, back, + *flectere*, bend: see *flection*.] I. *trans.* 1. To bend back; turn back; cast back; throw back again.

Reflect I not on thy baseness court-contempt?
Shak., W. T., iv. 4. 758.

And dazled with this greater light, I would *reflect* mine eyes to that reflexion of this light. *Purchas*, Pilgrimage, p. 13.

Let me mind the reader to *reflect* his eye upon other quotations. *Fuller*.

Do you *reflect* that Guilt upon me?
Congreve, Way of the World, ii. 3.

2. Hence, figuratively, to bend the will of; persuade. [Rare.]

Such rites beseem ambassadors, and Nestor urgèd these,
That their most honours might *reflect* enraged Æacides.
Chapman, Iliad, ix. 180. (*Davies.*)

3. To cause to return or to throw off after striking or falling on any surface, and in accordance with certain physical laws: as, to *reflect* light, heat, or sound; incident and *reflected* rays. See *reflection*, 2.

Then, grim in arms, with hasty vengeance flies,
Arms that *reflect* a radiance through the skies.
Pope, Iliad, xv. 137.

Like a wave of water which is sent up against a sea-wall, and which *reflects* itself back along the sea. *W. K. Clifford*, Lectures, II. 40.

4. To give back an image or likeness of; mirror.

Nature is the glass *reflecting* God,
As by the sea *reflected* is the sun.
Young, Night Thoughts, ix. 1007.

Heav'n *reflected* in her face. *Cowper*, A Comparison.

The vast bosom of the Hudson was like an unruffled mirror, *reflecting* the golden splendor of the heavens. *Irving*, Knickerbocker, p. 344.

Among the lower forms of life there is but little variation among the units; the one *reflects* the other, and species are founded upon differences that are only determined by using the micrometer. *Amer. Nat.*, June, 1890, p. 578.

II. *intrans.* 1. To bend or turn back; be reflected.

Let thine eyes
Reflect upon thy soul, and there behold
How loathed black it is.
Beau. and Fl., Captain, iv. 5.

Not any thing that shall
Reflect injurious to yourself.
Shirley, Love's Cruelty, i. 1.

2. To throw back light, heat, sound, etc.; give reflections; return rays or beams: as, a *reflecting* mirror or gem.

She lifts the coffer-lids that close his eyes,
Where, lo, two lamps, burnt out, in darkness lies;
Two glasses, where herself herself beheld
A thousand times, and now no more *reflect*.
Shak., Venus and Adonis, l. 1130.

3. To throw or turn back the thoughts upon something; think or consider seriously; revolve matters in the mind, especially in relation to conduct; ponder or meditate.

Who saith, Who could such ill events expect?
With shame on his own counsels doth *reflect*.
Sir J. Denham, Prudence.

Content if hence the unlearn'd their wants may view,
The learn'd *reflect* on what before they knew.
Pope, Essay on Criticism, l. 740.

We cannot be said to *reflect* upon any external object except in so far as that object has been previously perceived, and its image become part and parcel of our intellectual furniture. *Sir W. Hamilton*, Metaph., x.

Let boys and girls in our schools be taught to think; let them not be drilled so much in remembering as in *reflecting*. *J. F. Clarke*, Self-Culture, p. 137.

4. To bring reproach; cast censure or blame: followed by *on* or *upon*.

This kind of language *reflects* with the same ignominy *upon* all the Protestant Reformations that have bin since Luther. *Milton*, Eikonoklastes, xiiii.

She could not hear to hear Charles *reflected on*, notwithstanding their difference.
Sheridan, School for Scandal, i. 1.

5†. To shine.

Lord Saturnine; whose virtues will, I hope,
Reflect on Rome as Titan's rays on earth,
And ripen justice. *Shak.*, Tit. And., i. 1. 226.

=Syn. 3. To consider, meditate upon, etc. (see list under *contemplate*), cogitate, ruminate, study.

reflect†, *n.* [< *reflect*, *v.*] A reflection. [Rare.]

Would you in blindnesse live? these raies of myne
Give that *reflect* by which your Beauties shine.
Heywood, Apollo and Daphne (Works, ed. Pearson, 1874, [VI. 280).

reflected (rȩ̄-flek'ted), *p. a.* 1. Cast or thrown back: as, *reflected* light.—2. In *anat.*, turned back upon itself. See *reflection*, 10.—3. In *entom.*, turned upward or back: as, a *reflected* margin.—4. In *her.*, same as *reflexed*, 3.—**Flected and reflected.** See *flected*.—**Reflected light**, in *painting*, the subdued light which falls on objects that are in shadow, and serves to bring out their forms. It is treated as reflected from some object on which the light falls directly, whether seen in the picture or supposed to influence it from without.

reflectent† (rȩ̄-flek'tẹnt), *a.* [< L. *reflecten(t-)s*, ppr. of *reflectere*, reflect: see *reflect*.] 1. Bending or flying back; reflected.

The ray descendent, and the ray *reflectent*.
Sir K. Digby, Nature of Man's Soul. (*Latham.*)

2. Capable of reflecting.

When light passes through such bodies, it finds at the very entrance of them such resistences, where it passes, as serve it for a reflecting body, and yet such a *reflectent* body as hinders not the passage through, but only from being a straight line with the line incident.
Sir K. Digby, Of Bodies, xiii.

reflectible (rȩ̄-flek'ti-bl), *a.* [< *reflect* + *-ible*. Cf. *reflexible*.] Capable of being reflected or thrown back.

reflecting (rȩ̄-flek'ting), *p. a.* 1. Throwing back light, heat, etc., as a mirror or other polished surface.

A perfectly *reflecting* body is one which cannot absorb any ray. Polished silver suggests such a body.
Tait, Light, § 307.

2. Given to reflection; thoughtful; meditative; provident: as, a *reflecting* mind.

No *reflecting* man can ever wish to adulterate manly piety (the parent of all that is good in the world) with mummery and parade.
Sydney Smith, in Lady Holland, iii.

Reflecting circle, an instrument for measuring altitudes and angular distances, constructed on the principle of the sextant, the graduations, however, being continued completely round the limb of the circle.—**Reflecting dial.** See *dial*.—**Reflecting galvanometer.** See *Thomson's mirror galvanometer*, under *galvanometer*.—**Reflecting goniometer.** See *goniometer*.—**Reflecting lamp**, a lamp with an upper reflector so arranged as to throw downward those rays of light which tend upward.—**Reflecting level.** (*a*) An instrument for determining a horizontal direction by looking at the reflection of an object at a distance. Thus, in Mariotte's level, the level is determined by bisecting the distance between the direct image of an object and its reflection in a sort of artificial horizon. In Cassini's level, a telescope hangs vertically, carrying before its object-glass a plane mirror inclined 45° to the line of sight. (*b*) An instrument in which a slow-moving bubble is viewed by reflection, so that the image of the middle of it can be seen by the side of the direct image of a distant object. Such are Abney's and Locke's levels, used by topographers. See *Locke level*, under *level*[1].—**Reflecting microscope.** See *microscope*.—**Reflecting power**, the power possessed by any surface of throwing off a greater or less proportion of incident heat. This power is a maximum for the polished metals and a minimum for a surface of lampblack; it is the reciprocal of the absorptive (and radiating) power.—**Reflecting quadrant.** See *quadrant*, 4.—**Reflecting sight**, in firearms, a reflecting surface placed at such an angle as to reflect to the eye light from one direction only. *E. H. Knight.*—**Reflecting telescope.** See *telescope*.

reflectingly (rȩ̄-flek'ting-li), *adv.* 1. With reflection.—2. With censure; reproachfully; censoriously. [Rare.]

A great indiscretion in the archbishop of Dublin, who applied a story out of Tacitus very *reflectingly* on Mr. Harley. *Swift*, Journal to Stella, xx.

reflection, reflexion (rȩ̄-flek'shọn), *n.* [< ME. *reflexion*, *reflexioun*, < OF. *reflexion*, F. *réflexion*, *réflection* = Pr. *reflexio* = Sp. *reflexion* = Pg. *reflexão* = It. *riflessione*, < LL. *reflexio(n-)*, a bending or turning back, < L. *reflectere*, pp. *reflexus*, bend back, reflect: see *reflect*.] 1. A bending back; a turning.

Crooked Erimanthus wyth hys manye turnynges and *reflexions* is consumed by the inhabytours with wateryng their ground. *J. Brende*, tr. of Quintus Curtius, fol. 232.

2. The act of reflecting, or the state of being reflected; specifically, in *physics*, the change of direction which a ray of light, radiant heat, or sound experiences when it strikes upon a surface and is thrown back into the same medium from which it approached. Reflection follows two laws, viz.—(1) the angle of reflection is equal to the angle of incidence; and (2) the reflected and incident rays are in the same plane with a normal to the surface. If DE represents the surface of a mirror and CB the incident ray, then HBC is the *angle of incidence*, and HBA, equal to it, is the *angle of reflection*. This applies alike to sound, to radiant energy (heat and light), and also to a perfectly elastic body bounding from a perfectly elastic rigid surface. The plane passing through the perpendicular to the reflecting surface at the point of incidence and the path of the reflected ray of light or heat is called the *plane of reflection*. (See *mirror*, *echo*.) For the total reflection of rays when the critical angle is passed, see *refraction*.

Lights, by clear *reflection* multiplied
From many a mirror. *Cowper*, Task, iv. 268.

Reflection always accompanies refraction; and if one of these disappear, the other will disappear also.
Tyndall, Light and Elect., p. 39.

3. That which is produced by being reflected; an image given back from a reflecting surface.

As the sun in water we can bear,
Yet not the sun, but his *reflection*, there.
Dryden, Eleonora, l. 137.

Mountain peak and village spire
Retain *reflection* of his fire.
Scott, Rokeby, v. 1.

The mind is like a double mirror, in which *reflexions* of self within self multiply themselves till they are undistinguishable. *J. H. Newman*, Gram. of Assent, p. 185.

4. The act of shining. [Rare.]

As whence the sun 'gins his *reflection*
Shipwrecking storms and direful thunders break.
Shak., Macbeth, i. 2. 25.

5. The turning of thought back upon past experiences or ideas; attentive or continued consideration; meditation; contemplation; deliberation: as, a man much given to *reflection*.

Education begins the gentleman; but reading, good company, and *reflection* must finish him.
Locke. (*Allibone*.)

Where under heav'n is pleasure more pursued,
Or where does cold *reflection* less intrude?
Cowper, Expostulation, l. 8.

6. A mental process resulting from attentive or continued consideration; thought or opinion after deliberation.

A gentleman whose conversation and friendship furnish me still with some of the most agreeable *reflections* that result from my travels.
Bruce, Source of the Nile, Int., p. xxii.

He made very wise *reflections* and observations upon all I said. *Swift*, Gulliver's Travels, ii. 3.

"I am sorry, but I must do it; I am driven to it; every body has to do it; we must look at things as they are;" these are the *reflections* which lead men into violations of morality. *J. R. Seeley*, Nat. Religion, p. 57.

7. A kind of self-consciousness resulting from an outward perception, whether directly or indirectly; the exercise of the internal sense; the perception of a modification of consciousness; the faculty of distinguishing between a datum of sense and a product of reason; the consideration of the limitations of knowledge, ignorance, and error, and of other unsatisfactory states as leading to knowledge of self; the discrimination between the subjective and objective aspects of feelings. The Latin word *reflexio* was first used as a term of psychology by Thomas Aquinas, who seems to intend no optical metaphor, but to conceive that consciousness is turned back upon itself by the reaction of the object of outward perception. According to Aquinas, pure thought in itself can know nothing of singulars, or particular things; but in perception there is a peculiar sense of reaction or reciprocation which he calls *reflection*, and this first makes us aware of the existence of actual singulars and also of thought as being an action; and this, according to him, is the first self-consciousness. Scotus accepted reflection, not as affording the first knowledge of singulars, but as a perception of what passes in the mind, and thus the original meaning of the term was modified. Walter Burleigh, who died in 1337, affords an illustration of this when he says that the thing without is apprehended before the passion which is in the soul, because the thing without is apprehended directly, and the passion of the soul only indirectly, by reflection. Ramus, in his dissertation on reflection, defines it as "the successive direction of the attention to several partial perceptions." A still further change of meaning had come about when Goclenius, in 1613, defined reflection as "the inward action of the soul, by which it recognizes both itself and its acts and ideas." The importance of the word in the English school of philosophy (Berkeley, Hume, etc.) may be said to be due entirely to its use by Locke, who explains it as follows:

The other fountain from which experience furnisheth the understanding with ideas is the perception of the operations of our own mind within us, as it is employed about the ideas it has got; which operations, when the soul comes to reflect on and consider, do furnish the understanding with another set of ideas, which could not be had from things without; and such are perception, thinking, doubting, believing, reasoning, knowing, willing, and all the different actings of our own minds; which we being conscious of, and observing in ourselves, do from these receive into our understandings as distinct ideas as we do from bodies affecting our senses. This source of ideas every man has wholly in himself; and though it be not sense, as having nothing to do with external objects, yet it is very like it, and might properly enough be called internal sense. But as I call the other sensation, so I call this *reflection*, the ideas it affords being such only as the mind gets by reflecting on its own operations within itself. By *reflection*, then, in the following part of this discourse, I would be understood to mean that notice which the mind takes of its own operations, and the manner of them; by reason whereof there come to be ideas of these operations in the understanding.
Locke, Human Understanding, II. i. 4.

Reid endeavored to revive the Ramist use of the word, for which he is condemned by Hamilton. Kant, in his use of the term, returns to something like the Thomist view, for he makes it a mode of consciousness by which we are made aware whether knowledge is sensuous or not. Kant makes use of the term *reflection* to denote a mode of consciousness in which we distinguish between the relations of concepts and the corresponding relations of the objects of the concepts. Thus, two concepts may be different, and yet it may be conceived that their objects are identical; or two concepts may be identical, and yet it may be conceived that their objects (say, two drops of water) are different. Mr. Shadworth Hodgson, in his "Philosophy of Reflection," 1878, uses the term to denote one of three fundamental modes of consciousness, namely that in which the objective and subjective aspects of what is present are discriminated without being separated as person and thing.

The faculty by which I place the comparison of representations in general by the side of the faculty to which they belong, and by which I determine whether they are compared with each other as belonging to the pure understanding or to sensuous intuition, I call transcendental *reflection*.
Kant, Critique of Pure Reason, tr. by Müller, p. 261.

The particular *reflection* that states of consciousness are things, or that the Subject is its Objects, constitutes . . . the reflective mode of consciousness. . . . Perception . . . is the rudimentary function in *reflection* as well as in primary consciousness; and reflective conception is a derivative from it. *S. Hodgson*, Philosophy of Reflection, i. 2, § 3.

8†. That which corresponds to and reflects something in the mind or in the nature of any one.

As if folkes complexiouns [constitutions, temperaments]
Make hem dreme of *reflexiouns*.
Chaucer, House of Fame, l. 22.

9. Reproach cast; censure; criticism.

To suppose any Books of Scripture to be lost which contained any necessary Points of Faith is a great *Reflexion* on Divine Providence. *Stillingfleet*, Sermons, III. ii.

He bore all their weakness and prejudice, and returned not *reflection* for *reflection*.
Penn, Rise and Progress of Quakers, v.

10. In *anat.*: (*a*) Duplication; the folding of a part, as a membrane, upon itself; a bending back or complete deflection. (*b*) That which is reflected; a fold: as, a *reflection* of the peritoneum forming a mesentery.—11. In *zoöl.*, a play of color which changes in different lights: as, the *reflections* of the iridescent plumage of a humming-bird. *Coues*.—**Axis of reflection.** See *axis*[1].—**Logical reflection.** See *logical*.—**Point of reflection.** See *point*[1].—**Total reflection.** See *refraction*[1]. =**Syn.** 5. Rumination, cogitation.—6. See *remark*[1], *n.*

reflection† (rē̤-flek'shon), *v. t.* [< *reflection*, *n.*] To reflect. [Rare.]

But, *reflectioning* apart, thou seest, Jack, that her plot is beginning to work.
Richardson, Clarissa Harlowe, IV. xxi.

reflectionist (rē̤-flek'shon-ist), *n.* [< *reflection* + *-ist*.] An adherent of Shadworth Hodgson's philosophy of reflection. The doctrine is that a power of perceiving the relations of subjective and objective aspects and elements is the highest mode of consciousness.

reflective (rē̤-flek'tiv), *a.* [= F. *réflectif*; as *reflect* + *-ive*. Cf. *reflexive*.] 1. Throwing back rays or images; giving reflections; reflecting.

In the *reflective* stream the sighing bride
Viewing her charms impair'd. *Prior*.

A mirror . . . of the dimensions of a muffin, and about as *reflective*. *L. M. Alcott*, Hospital Sketches, p. 62.

2. Taking cognizance of the operations of the mind; exercising thought or reflection; capable of exercising thought or judgment.

Forc'd by *reflective* Reason, I confess
That human Science is uncertain Guess.
Prior, Solomon, i.

His perceptive and *reflective* faculties . . . thus acquired a precocious and extraordinary development.
Motley. (*Webster*.)

3. Having a tendency to or characterized by reflection.

The Greeks are not *reflective*, but perfect in their senses and in their health, with the finest physical organization in the world. *Emerson*, Essays, 1st ser., p. 23.

Several persons having the true dramatic feeling . . . were overborne by the *reflective*, idyllic fashion which then began to prevail in English verse.
Stedman, Vict. Poets, p. 2.

4. Devoted to reflection; containing reflections. [Rare.]—5. In *gram.*, reflexive.—**Reflective faculties**, in *phren.*, a division of the intellectual faculties, comprising the two so-called organs of comparison and causality.—**Reflective judgment**, in the *Kantian terminology*, that kind of judgment that mounts from the particular to the general.

reflectively (rē̤-flek'tiv-li), *adv.* In a reflective manner; by reflection, in any sense of that word.

reflectiveness (rē̤-flek'tiv-nes), *n.* The state or quality of being reflective.

The meditative lyric appeals to a profounder *reflectiveness*, which is feelingly alive to the full pathos of life, and to all the mystery of sorrow.
J. C. Shairp, Aspects of Poetry, p. 118.

reflectoire (ref-lek-twor'), *n.* [< F. *réflectoire*; as *reflect* + *-ory*.] A geometrical surface whose form is that of the appearance of a horizontal plane seen through a layer of water with air above it.—**Reflectoire curve**, a curve which is a central vertical section of the surface called a reflectoire. It is a curve of the fourth order and sixth class, having a tacnode on the surface of the water at infinity, and a double point at the eye.

Reflectoire.

Reflectoire.

reflector (rē̤-flek'tor), *n.* [= F. *réflecteur*; as *reflect* + *-or*[1].] 1. One who reflects or considers.

There is scarce anything that nature has made, or that men do suffer, whence the devout *reflector* cannot take an occasion of an aspiring meditation. *Boyle*, On Colours.

2. One who casts reflections; a censurer.

This answerer has been pleased to find fault with about a dozen passages; . . . the *reflector* is entirely mistaken, and forces interpretations which never once entered into the writer's head. *Swift*, Tale of a Tub, Apol.

3. That which reflects. Specifically—(*a*) A polished surface of metal or any other suitable material, used for the purpose of reflecting rays of light, heat, or sound in any required direction. Reflectors may be either plane or curvilinear; of the former the common mirror is a familiar example. Curvilinear reflectors admit of a great variety of forms, according to the purposes for which they are employed; they may be either convex or concave, spherical, elliptical, parabolic, or hyperbolic, etc. The parabolic form is perhaps the most generally serviceable, being used for many purposes of illumination as well as for various highly important philosophical instruments. Its property is to reflect, in parallel lines, all rays diverging from the focus of the parabola, and conversely. A series of parabolic mirrors, by which the rays from one or more lamps were reflected in a parallel beam, so as to render the light visible at a great distance, was the arrangement generally employed in lighthouses previous to the invention of the Fresnel lamp, or dioptric light. The annexed cut is a section of a ship's lantern fitted with an Argand lamp and parabolic reflector. *a a* is the reflector, *b* the lamp, situated in the focus of the polished concave paraboloid, c the oil-cistern, d the outer frame of the lantern, and *e* the chimney for the escape of the products of combustion. (*b*) A reflecting telescope, the speculum of which is an example of the converse application of the parabolic reflector, the parallel rays proceeding from a distant body being in this case concentrated into the focus of the reflector. See *telescope*, and cut under *catoptric*.

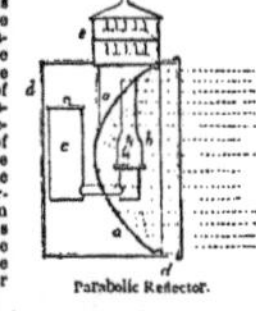

Parabolic Reflector.

Reflectors have been made as large as six feet in aperture, the greatest being that of Lord Rosse.
Newcomb and Holden, Astron., p. 68.

Double-cone reflector, a form of ventilating-reflector, connected with a chandelier or a similar device for supplying artificial light: used in the ceiling of a hall or other place of public assembly.—**Parabolic reflector**, a reflector of paraboloidal shape: used either for concentrating rays upon an object at the focus, as in the microscope, or, with a light at the focus, for reflecting the rays in parallel lines to form a beam of light, as in lighthouse and some other lanterns. See def. 3, and cut above.

reflectory (rē̤-flek'tō̤-ri), *a.* [< *reflect* + *-ory*.] Capable of being reflected.

reflet (F. pron. rė-flā'), *n.* [F., reflection, < L. *reflectere*, reflect: see *reflect*.] 1. Brilliancy of surface, as in metallic luster or glaze on pottery, especially when having an iridescent or many-colored flash.

A full crimson tint with a brilliant metallic *reflet* or iridescence. *J. C. Robinson*, S. K. Spec. Ex., p. 421.

2. A piece of pottery having such a glaze, especially a tile: sometimes used attributively.

There is in this place an enormous *reflet* tile. . . . The *reflet* tiles in which a copper tint is prominent.
S. G. W. Benjamin, Persia and the Persians, pp. 285, 287.

Reflet métallique. See *metallic luster*, under *luster*[2], 2. —**Reflet nacré**, a luster having an iridescent appearance like that of mother-of-pearl.

reflex (rē̤-fleks'), *v. t.* [< L. *reflexus*, pp. of *reflectere*, reflect: see *reflect*.] 1. To bend back; turn back.

A dog lay, . . . his head *reflext* upon his tail.
J. Gregory, Posthuma, p. 118.

2†. To reflect; cast or throw, as light; let shine.

May never glorious sun *reflex* his beams
Upon the country where you make abode.
Shak., 1 Hen. VI., v. 4. 87.

reflex (rē'fleks or rē̤-fleks'), *a.* [< L. *reflexus*, pp. of *reflectere*, reflect: see *reflect*.] 1. Thrown or turned backward; having a backward direction; reflective; reactive.

A *reflex* act of the soul, or the turning of the intellectual eye inward upon its own actions. *Sir M. Hale*.

The order and beauty of the inanimate parts of the world, the discernible ends of them, do evince by a *reflex* argument that it is the workmanship, not of blind mechanism or blinder chance, but of an intelligent and benign agent.
Bentley.

2. In *painting*, illuminated by light reflected from another part of the same picture. See *reflected light*, under *reflected*.—3. In *biol.*, bent back; reflexed.—**Reflex action, motion,** or **movement**, in *physiol.*, those comparatively simple actions of the nervous system in which a stimulus is transmitted along sensory nerves to a nerve-center, from which again it is reflected along efferent nerves to call into play some muscular, glandular, or other activity. These actions are performed involuntarily, and often unconsciously, as the contraction of the pupil of the eye when exposed to strong light.

There is another *action*, namely, that of aggregation, which in certain cases may be called *reflex*, and it is the only known instance in the vegetable kingdom.
Darwin, Insectiv. Plants, p. 242.

Reflex movements have slightly more of the appearance of a purposive character than automatic movements, though this is in many cases very vague and ill-defined.
J. Sully, Outlines of Psychol., p. 504.

Reflex angle. See *angle*³, 1.—**Reflex epilepsy**, epilepsy dependent on some peripheral irritation, as a nasal polypus.—**Reflex excitation**, muscular movement produced by the irritation of an efferent nerve.—**Reflex neuralgia**, neuralgia dependent on a source of irritation in some more or less distant part.—**Reflex paralysis.** See *paralysis*.—**Reflex perception.** (*a*) Consciousness of our states of mind; reflection; internal sense; self-consciousness. (*b*) A sensation supposed to be produced by the irritation of an efferent or motor nerve: but the existence of the phenomenon is denied.—**Reflex science**, the science of science; logic.—**Reflex sense**, the power of perceiving relations among objects of imagination. This term, in the form *reflected sense*, was introduced by Shaftesbury, with whom, however, it merely means secondary sensation, or a sensation produced by ideas. Hutcheson modified the meaning and form of the expression.—**Reflex theory**, any one of the theories proposed to account for or explain the phenomena of reflex action in physiology.—**Reflex vision**, vision by means of reflected light, as from mirrors.—**Reflex zenith-tube**, an instrument used at Greenwich to observe the transit of γ Draconis in an artificial horizon, that star coming nearly to the zenith at that observatory.

reflex (rē'fleks, formerly also rẹ-fleks'), *n.* [< F. *réflexe* = Sp. *reflejo* = Pg. *reflexo* = It. *riflesso*, a reflex, reflection, < L. *reflexus*, a bending back, a recess, < *reflectere*, pp. *reflexus*, bend back: see *reflect*, *reflex*, *v.*] 1. Reflection; an image produced by reflection.

Yon grey is not the morning's eye,
'Tis but the pale *reflex* of Cynthia's brow.
Shak., R. and J., iii. 5. 20.

To cut across the *reflex* of a star.
Wordsworth, Influence of Natural Objects (ed. of 1842; [in ed. of 1820, *reflection*).

Like the *reflex* of the moon
Seen in a wave under green leaves.
Shelley, Prometheus Unbound, iii. 4.

2. A mere copy; an adapted form: as, a Middle Latin *reflex* of an Old French word.—3. Light reflected from an illuminated surface to one in shade; hence, in *painting*, the illumination of one body or a part of it by light reflected from another body represented in the same piece. See *reflected light*, under *reflected*.

Yet, since your light hath once enlumind me,
With my *reflex* yours shall encreased be.
Spenser, Sonnets, lxvi.

4. Same as *reflex action* (which see, under *reflex*, *a.*).

These *reflexes* are caused by mechanical irritation of the pleural surface. *Medical News*, LII. 496.

Abdominal reflex. See *abdominal*.—**Cornea-reflex**, winking on irritation of the cornea.—**Cremasteric reflex**, contraction of the cremaster muscle on stimulation of the skin on the inside of the thigh.—**Deep reflexes**, reflexes developed by percussion of tendons or bones, as the knee-jerk.—**Epigastric reflex**, irritation of the skin in the fifth or sixth intercostal space on the side of the chest, causing a contraction of the highest fibers of the rectus abdominis muscle.—**Gluteal reflex**, contraction of the gluteal muscles, due to irritation of the skin of the nates. The center is in the spinal cord in the region of the fourth or fifth lumbar nerve.—**Knee-reflex.** Same as *knee-jerk*.—**Paradoxical pupillary reflex**, the dilatation of the pupil on stimulation of the retina by light. Also called *paradoxical pupillary reaction*.—**Patellar-tendon reflex.** Same as *knee-jerk*.—**Plantar reflex**, the reflex action producing movements in toes and foot evoked by tickling the sole of the foot. Also called *sole-reflex*.—**Pupillary light-reflex**, the contraction of the pupil when light falls on the retina. The action is bilateral, both pupils contracting though only one retina is stimulated. The paradoxical pupillary reflex or reaction is the dilatation of the pupil when light falls on the retina: it occurs in rare abnormal states.—**Pupillary skin-reflex**, the dilatation of the pupil on more or less intense stimulation of the skin. The motor path is through the cervical sympathetic.—**Reflex-center**, the collection of nerve-cells or nucleus in the brain in which the afferent sensory impulse becomes changed to the efferent motor impulse.—**Scapular reflex**, contraction of the posterior axillary fold, due to irritation of the skin in the interscapular region.—**Sole-reflex.** Same as *plantar reflex*.—**Spinal reflexes**, such reflex actions as have their centers in the spinal cord.—**Superficial reflexes**, such reflexes as are developed from skin-stimulation, as the plantar, cremasteric, abdominal, or other reflexes.—**Tendon-reflex.** Same as *myotatic contraction* (which see, under *myotatic*).

reflexed (rẹ-flekst'), *a.* [< *reflex*, *v.*, + *-ed*².] 1. In *bot.*, bent abruptly backward: said of petals, sepals, leaf-veins, etc.—2. In *zoöl.*, bent back or up; reflex.—3. In *her.*, curved twice: same as *bowed*, but applied especially to the chain secured to the collar of a beast, which often takes an S-curve. Also *reflected*.—**Reflexed antennæ**, antennæ carried constantly bent back over the head and body.—**Reflexed ovipositor**, an ovipositor which is turned back so as to lie on the upper surface of the abdomen, as in certain *Chalcididæ*.

reflexibility (rẹ-flek-si-bil'i̤-ti), *n.* [= F. *réflexibilité* = Sp. *reflexibilidad* = Pg. *reflexibilidade* = It. *reflessibilità*; as *reflexible* + *-ity* (see *-bility*).] The quality of being reflexible, or capable of being reflected: as, the *reflexibility* of light-rays.

Reflexibility of Rays is their disposition to be reflected or turned back into the same Medium from any other Medium upon whose surface they fall.
Newton, Opticks, I. i. 3.

reflexible (rẹ-flek'si-bl), *a.* [= F. *réflexible* = Sp. *reflexible* = Pg. *reflexivel* = It. *reflessibile*; as *reflex*, *v.*, + *-ible* (cf. *flexible*).] Capable of being reflected or thrown back.

Rays are more or less *reflexible* which are turned back more or less easily. *Newton*, Opticks, I. i. 3.

reflexion, *n.* See *reflection*.

reflexity (rẹ-flek'si̤-ti), *n.* [< *reflex*, *a.*, + *-ity*.] The capacity of being reflected. [Rare.]

reflexive (rẹ-flek'siv), *a.* and *n.* [< OF. *reflexif*, F. *réflexif* = Pr. *reflexiu* = Sp. Pg. *reflexivo* = It. *reflessivo*, *riflessivo*, < L. *reflexus*, pp. of *reflectere*, bend backward: see *reflect*.] **I.** *a.* 1. Reflective; bending or turning backward; having respect to something past.

Assurance *reflexive* . . . cannot be a divine faith.
Hammond, Pract. Catechism, i. § 3.

The *reflexive* power of flame is nearly the same as that of tracing-paper. *A. Daniell*, Prin. of Physics, p. 413.

2. Capable of reflection; reflective.

In general, brute animals are of such a nature as is devoid of that free and *reflexive* reason which is requisite to acquired art and consultation.
Dr. H. More, Immortal. of Soul, iii. 13.

3†. Casting or containing a reflection or censure.

I would fain know what man almost there is that does not resent an ugly *reflexive* word. *South*, Sermons, X. vi.

Reflexive verb, in *gram.*, a verb of which the action turns back upon the subject, or which has for its direct object a pronoun representing its agent or subject: as, I *bethought myself*; the witness *forswore himself*. Pronouns of this class are called *reflexive pronouns*, and in English are generally compounds with *self*; though such examples as he *bethought him* how he should act also occur.

I do *repent me*, as it is an evil,
And take the shame with joy.
Shak., M. for M., ii. 3. 35.

II. *n.* A reflexive verb or pronoun.

What I wish to say is, that the *reflexive* which serves to express the passive is a causal *reflexive*.
J. Hadley, Essays, p. 209.

reflexively (rẹ-flek'siv-li), *adv.* 1. In a reflexive manner; in a direction backward: as, to meditate *reflexively* upon one's course.—2. In *gram.*, after the manner of a reflexive verb.—3†. Reflectingly; slightingly; with censure.

Ay, but he spoke slightly and *reflexively* of such a lady.
South, Sermons, VI. iii.

reflexiveness (rẹ-flek'siv-nes), *n.* The state or quality of being reflexive.

reflexly (rē'fleks-li or rẹ-fleks'li), *adv.* In a reflex manner.

reflexogenic (rẹ-flek-sọ̄-jen'ik), *a.* [< L. *reflexus*, reflex (see *reflex*, *a.*), + *-genus*, producing: see *-genic*.] Producing an increased tendency to reflex motions.

refloat† (rē-flōt'), *n.* [< *re-* + *float*, after F. *reflot*, reflux, ebb: see *float*.] A flowing back; reflux; ebb.

Of which kind we conceive the main float and *refloat* of the sea is, which is by consent of the universe as part of the diurnal motion. *Bacon*, Nat. Hist., § 907.

reflorescence (rē-flọ̄-res'ẹns), *n.* [< L. *reflorescen(t-)s*, ppr. of *reflorescere*, begin to bloom again, < *re-*, again, + *florescere*, begin to bloom: see *flourish*. Cf. *reflourish*.] A blossoming anew; reflowering.

Nor can we, it is apprehended, peruse the account of the flowering rod of Aaron . . . without being led to reflect on the ascertainment of the Melchisedekian priesthood to the person of Christ, by the *reflorescence* of that mortal part which he drew from the stem of Jesse.
Horne, Works, IV. xvi.

reflourish (rē-flur'ish), *v. i.* [< OF. *refleuriss-*, stem of certain parts of *reflurir*, *reflorir*, *refleurir*, F. *refleurir* = It. *rifiorire*, < L. **reflorere*, bloom again (cf. Sp. Pg. *reflorecer*, < L. *reflorescere*, begin to bloom again), < *re-*, again, + *florere*, bloom: see *flourish*.] To revive, flourish, or bloom anew.

For Israel to *reflourish*, and take new life by the influxes of the Holy Spirit. *Waterland*, Works, III. 421.

reflow (rē-flō'), *v. i.* [< *re-* + *flow*, *v.*] To flow back; ebb.

When any one blessed spirit rejoices, his joy goes round the whole society; and then all their rejoicings in his joy *reflow* upon and swell and multiply it.
J. Scott, Christian Life, I. iii. § 3.

reflow (rē-flō'), *n.* [< *reflow*, *v.*] A reflux; a flowing back; refluence; ebb.

reflower (rē-flou'ėr), *v.* [< *re-* + *flower*, *v.* Cf. *reflorescence*, *reflourish*.] **I.** *intrans.* To flower again.

II. *trans.* To cause to flower or bloom again.

Her footing makes the ground all fragrant-fresh;
Her sight *re-flowres* th' Arabian Wildernes.
Sylvester, tr. of Du Bartas's Weeks, ii., The Magnificence.

reflowing (rē-flō'ing), *n.* A flowing back; reflux.

By . . . working upon our spirits they can moderate as they please the violence of our passions, which are nothing but the flowings and *reflowings* of our spirits to and fro from our hearts.
J. Scott, Christian Life, II. vii. § 10.

refluence (ref'lọ̈-ẹns), *n.* [< *refluen(t)* + *-ce*.] 1. A flowing back; reflux; ebb.—2. A backward movement.

Nay but, my friends, one hornpipe further, a *refluence* back, and two doubles forward.
Greene, James the Fourth, iv.

refluency (ref'lọ̈-ẹn-si), *n.* [As *refluence* (see *-cy*).] Same as *refluence*.

All things sublunary move continually in an interchangeable flowing and *refluencie*.
W. Montague, Devoute Essays, I. vi. 2.

refluent (ref'lọ̈-ẹnt), *a.* [= F. *refluant* = Sp. Pg. *refluente* = It. *rifluente*, < L. *refluen(t-)s*, ppr. of *refluere* (> It. *rifluire* = Sp. Pg. *refluir* = F. *refluer*), flow back, < L. *re-*, back, + *fluere*, flow: see *fluent*.] Flowing or surging back; ebbing: as, the *refluent* tide.

And *refluent* through the pass of fear
The battle's tide was poured.
Scott, L. of the L., vi. 18.

And in haste the *refluent* ocean
Fled away from the shore, and left the line of the sand-beach
Covered with waifs of the tide.
Longfellow, Evangeline, i. 5.

refluous† (ref'lọ̈-us), *a.* [= It. *refluo*, < L. *refluus*, flowing back, < *refluere*, flow back: see *refluent*.] Flowing back; refluent; ebbing.

The stream of Jordan, south of their going over, was not supplied with any reciprocall or *refluous* tide out of the Dead Sea. *Fuller*, Pisgah Sight, II. i. 17. (*Davies.*)

reflux (rē'fluks), *n.* [< *reflux* = Sp. *reflujo* = F. Pg. *refluxo* = It. *riflusso*, < ML. **refluxus*, a flowing back, ebb, < L. *refluere*, pp. *refluxus*, flow back: see *refluent*.] A flowing back: as, the flux and *reflux* of the tides.

If man were out of the world, who were then to search out the causes of the flux and *reflux* of the sea, and the hidden virtue of the magnet?
Dr. H. More, Antidote against Atheism, ii. 12.

There will be disputes among its neighbours, and some of these will prevail at one time and some at another, in the perpetual flux and *reflux* of human affairs.
Bolingbroke, The Occasional Writer, No. 2.

The old miracle of the Greek proverb, . . . which adopted the *reflux* of rivers towards their fountains as the liveliest type of the impossible. *De Quincey*, Homer, iii.

reflux-valve (rē'fluks-valv), *n.* An automatic valve designed to prevent reflux; a back-pressure valve. *E. H. Knight.*

refocillate† (rẹ-fos'i-lāt), *v. t.* [< LL. *refocillatus*, pp. of *refocillare* (> It. *rifocillare*, *refocillare* = Sp. *refocilar* = Pg. *refocillar*), warm into life again, revive, revivify, < L. *re-*, again, + *focillare*, *focillari*, revive by warmth, cherish, < *focus*, a hearth, fireplace: see *focus*.] To warm into life again; revive; refresh; reinvigorate.

The first view thereof did even *refocillate* my spirits.
Coryat, Crudities, I. 110.

refocillation† (rẹ-fos-i-lā'shọn), *n.* [= Sp. *refocilacion* = Pg. *refocillação*, < LL. as if **refocillatio(n-)*, < *refocillare*, refocillate: see *refocillate*.] The act of refocillating or imparting new vigor; restoration of strength by refreshment; also, that which causes such restoration.

Marry, sir, some precious cordial, some costly *refocillation*, a composure comfortable and restorative.
Middleton, Mad World, iii. 2.

refold (rē-fōld'), *v. t.* [< *re-* + *fold*¹.] To fold again.

refolded (rẹ-fōl'ded), *a.* In *entom.*, replicate: noting the wings when fluted or folded longitudinally, like a fan, and then turned back on themselves, as in the earwigs.

refoot (rē-fût'), *v. t.* [< *re-* + *foot*.] To repair by supplying with a new foot, as a boot or a stocking.

reforest (rē-for'est), *v. t.* [< *re-* + *forest.*] To replant with forest-trees; restore to the condition of forest or woodland; reafforest.

Within the last twenty years, France has *reforested* about two hundred and fifty thousand acres of mountain-lands. *Pop. Sci. Mo.*, XXXII. 228.

The *reforesting* of the denuded areas in the lower hills. *Nature*, XXXVII. 467.

reforestation (rē-for-es-tā'shon), *n.* [< *reforest* + *-ation.*] The act or process of reforesting; replanting with forest-trees.

Quite recently districts have been enclosed for *reforestation*, and the eucalyptus and other trees have been planted. *Encyc. Brit.*, XXII. 93.

reforge (rē-fōrj'), *v. t.* [= F. *reforger*; as *re-* + *forge.*] To forge or form again; hence, to fabricate or fashion anew; make over.

The kyngdome of God receiueth none but suche as be *reforged* and chaunged according to this paterne. *J. Udall*, On Luke xviii.

reforger (rē-fōr'jėr), *n.* One who reforges; one who makes over.

But Christe, beyng a newe *reforger* of the olde lawe, in stede of burnte offreyng did substitute charitee. *J. Udall*, On Luke xxiv.

reform (rē-fôrm'), *v.* [Early mod. E. also *reforme*; < ME. *reformen*, *refourmen* (= D. *reformeren* = G. *reformiren* = Sw. *reformera* = Dan. *reformere*), < OF. *reformer*, *refurmer*, *reffourmer*, *refourmer*, form anew, reform, rectify, etc., F. *reformer*, form anew, *réformer*, reform, rectify, correct, reduce, put on half-pay, = Pr. Sp. Pg. *reformar* = It. *riformare*, reform, < L. *reformare*, form anew, remodel, remold, transform, metamorphose, change, alter, amend, reform (as manners or discipline), < *re-*, again, + *formare*, form: see *form.*] **I.** *trans.* **1.** To form again or anew; remake; reconstruct; renew. [In this, the original sense, and in the following sense, usually with a full pronunciation of the prefix, and sometimes written distinctively *re-form.*]

Then carppez to syr Gawan the knyȝt in the grene,
"*Refourme* we oure forwardes [covenants], er we fyrre passe."
Sir Gawayne and the Green Knight (E. E. T. S.), l. 377.

And right so in the same forme,
In flesshe and bloud he shall *reforme*,
Whan time cometh, the quicke and dede.
Gower, Conf. Amant., ii.

Beholde the buyldynge of the towre; yf it be well I am contente, and yf ony thynge be amysse yt shall be *refourmed* after your deuyse.
Berners, tr. of Froissart's Chron., II. lxxxiii.

She saw the bees lying dead in heaps. . . . She could render back no life; she could set not a muscle in motion; she could *re-form* not a filament of a wing.
S. Judd, Margaret, i. 5.

Napoleon was humbled; the map of Europe was *re-formed* on a plan which showed a respect for territorial rights, and a just recognition both of the earnings of force and of the growth of ideas.
Stubbs, Medieval and Modern Hist., p. 237.

2. To restore to the natural or regular order or arrangement: as, to *reform* broken or scattered troops.

In accustoming officers to seek all opportunities for *re-forming* dispersed men at the earliest possible moment. *Encyc. Brit.*, XXIV. 354.

Then came the command to *re-form* the battalion.
The Century, XXXVII. 409.

3. To restore to a former and better state, or to bring from a bad to a good state; change from worse to better; improve by alteration, rearrangement, reconstruction, or abolition of defective parts or imperfect conditions, or by substitution of something better; amend; correct: as, to *reform* a profligate man; to *reform* corrupt manners or morals; to *reform* the corrupt orthography of English or French.

And now, forsooth, takes on him to *reform*
Some certain edicts, and some strait decrees
That lie too heavy on the commonwealth.
Shak., 1 Hen. IV., iv. 3. 78.

In the Beginning of his Reign, he refined and *reformed* the Laws of the Realm. *Baker*, Chronicles, p. 56.

When Men have no mind to be *reformed*, they must have some Terms of Reproach to fasten upon those who go about to do it. *Stillingfleet*, Sermons, III. v.

Reforming men's conduct without *reforming* their natures is impossible. *H. Spencer*, Social Statics, p. 384.

4. To abandon, remove, or abolish for something better. [Rare.]

1 Play. I hope we have reformed that [bombastic acting] indifferently with us, sir.
Hamlet. O, *reform* it altogether.
Shak., Hamlet, iii. 2. 40.

5†. To mend, in a physical sense; repair.

He gave towardes the *reforming* of that church [St. Helen's] five hundred markes. *Stowe*, Survey of London, p. 181.

6. To correct. [Rare.]

The prophet Esay also saith, "Who hath *reformed* the Spirit of the Lord, or who is of His council to teach Him?"
Becon, Works, ii. 39. (*Davies.*)

To reform an instrument, in *law*, to adjudge that it be read and taken differently from what it is expressed, as when it was drawn without correctly expressing the intent of the parties. =**Syn. 3.** *Improve*, *Better*, etc. (see *amend*), repair, reclaim, remodel.

II. *intrans.* **1.** To form again; get into order or line again; resume order, as troops or a procession. [In this use treated as in I., 1, above.] —**2.** To abandon that which is evil or corrupt and return to that which is good; change from worse to better; be amended or redeemed.

Experience shows that the Turk never has *reformed*, and reason, arguing from experience, will tell us that the Turk never can *reform*. *E. A. Freeman*, Amer. Lects., p. 422.

reform (rē-fôrm'), *n.* [= D. *reforme* = G. Sw. Dan. *reform*; < F. *réforme* = Sp. Pg. *reforma* = It. *riforma*, reform; from the verb.] Any proceeding which either brings back a better order of things or reconstructs the present order to advantage; amendment of what is defective, vicious, depraved, or corrupt; a change from worse to better; reformation: as, to introduce *reforms* in sanitary matters; to be an advocate of *reform*.

A variety of schemes, founded in visionary and impracticable ideas of *reform*, were suddenly produced.
Pitt, Speech on Parliamentary Reform, May 7, 1783.

Great changes and new manners have occur'd,
And blest *reforms*. *Cowper*, Conversation, l. 804.

Our fervent wish, and we will add our sanguine hope, is that we may see such a *reform* of the House of Commons as may render its votes the express image of the opinion of the middle orders of Britain.
Macaulay, Utilitarian Theory of Government.

Revolution means merely transformation, and is accomplished when an entirely new principle is—either with force or without it—put in the place of an existing state of things. *Reform*, on the other hand, is when the principle of the existing state of things is continued, and only developed to more logical or just consequences. The means do not signify. A reform may be carried out by bloodshed, and a revolution in the profoundest tranquillity.
Lassalle, quoted in Rae's Contemporary Socialism, p. 66.

Ballot reform, reform in the manner of voting in popular elections. Since about 1887 several of the United States have passed laws designed to promote secrecy in voting, to discourage corruption at elections, and to provide for an exclusively official ballot; these laws are modeled more or less on the so-called Australian system in elections.—**Civil-service reform**, in *U. S. politics*, reform in the administration of the civil service of the United States; more generally, reform in the administration of the entire public service, federal, State, and local. The main objects of this reform are the abolition of abuses of patronage and the spoils system, discouragement of the interference of office-holders in active politics, abolition of arbitrary appointments to and removals from office, qualification by competitive examination for appointment to all offices of a clerical nature, and promotion for merit. Since the passage of the Civil-service Act in 1871 this reform has been one of the leading questions for public discussion. See *Civil-service Act* (under *civil*) and *spoils system* (under *spoil*).—**Reform Act.** See *Reform Bill*.—**Reform Bill**, specifically, in *Eng. hist.*, a bill for the purpose of enlarging the number of voters in elections for members of the House of Commons, and of removing inequalities in representation. The first of these bills, passed in 1832 by the Liberals after a violent struggle, and often called specifically The Reform Bill, disfranchised many rotten boroughs, gave increased representation to the large towns, and enlarged the number of the holders of county and borough franchise. The effect of the second Reform Bill, passed by the Conservatives in 1867, was in the direction of a more democratic representation, and the same tendency was further shown in the Franchise Bill (see *franchise*) passed by the Liberals in 1884.—**Reform school**, a reformatory. [U. S.]—**Spelling reform.** See *spelling*.—**Tariff reform.** See *tariff*. =**Syn.** *Amendment*, etc. See *reformation*.

reformable (rē-fôr'ma-bl), *a.* [< ME. *reformable*, < OF. *reformable*, F. *réformable* = Sp. *reformable* = Pg. *reformavel* = It. *riformabile*, < ML. **reformabilis*, < L. *reformare*, reform: see *reform*, *v.*] Capable of being reformed; inclined to reform.

Yf ony of the said articlis be contrary to the liberte of the said cite, or old custumes of the same, thanh hit be *reformabyll* and corrigabill by the Mayre, Baliffs, and the comen counsayle of the citee.
English Gilds (E. E. T. S.), p. 337.

A seruaunt not *reformable*, that
Takes to his charge no heede,
Ofte tymes falleth to pouertye;
In wealth he may not byde.
Babees Book (E. E. T. S.), p. 83.

Woman [Eliz. Young], I have sued for thee indeed, and I promise thee, if thou wilt be *reformable*, my Lord will be good unto thee. *Foxe*, Martyrs, III. 769, an. 1558.

reformade† (ref-ọr-mād'), *n.* [Appar. an Anglicization of *reformado.*] A reduced or dismissed officer; a disbanded or non-effective soldier.

They also that rode *Reformades*, and that came down to see the Battle, they shouted . . . and sung. [Marginal note by author, "The *Reformades* joy."]
Bunyan, Holy War, p. 128.

reformado† (ref-ọr-mā'dō), *n.* and *a.* [< Sp. *reformado* = Pg. *reformado* = It. *riformato* = F. *réformé*, reformed, reduced, < L. *reformatus*, pp. of *reformare*, reform, refashion, amend: see *reform*, *v.*] **I.** *n.* **1.** A monk who demands or favors the reform of his order.

Amongst others, this was one of Celestin the pope's caveats for his new *reformadoes*. *Weever.* (*Latham.*)

2. A military officer who, for some disgrace, is deprived of his command, but retains his rank and perhaps his pay; also, generally, an officer without a command.

He had . . . writhen himself into the habit of one of your poor infantry, your decayed, ruinous, worm-eaten gentlemen of the round. . . . Into the likeness of one of these *reformados* had he moulded himself.
B. Jonson, Every Man in his Humour, iii. 2.

II. *a.* **1.** Penitent; reformed; devoted to reformation.

Venus, and all her naked Loves,
The *reformado* nymph removes.
Fenton, The Fair Nun.

2. Pertaining to or in the condition of a reformado; hence, inferior, degraded.

Although your church be opposite
To ours, as Black-friars are to White,
In rule and order, yet I grant
You are a *reformado* saint.
S. Butler, Hudibras, II. ii. 116.

reformalize† (rē-fôr'mạl-īz), *v. i.* [Irreg. < *reform* + *-al* + *-ize*; or < *re-* + *formalize.*] To make pretension to improvement or to formal correctness.

Christ's doctrine [is] pure, correcting all the unpure glosses of the *reformalizing* Pharisees.
Loe, Blisse of Brightest Beauty (1614), p. 25. (*Latham.*)

reformation (ref-ọr-mā'shon), *n.* [< OF. *reformacion*, *reformation*, F. *réformation* = Pr. *reformacio* = Sp. *reformacion* = Pg. *reformação* = It. *riformazione*, < L. *reformatio(n-)*, a reforming, amending, reformation, transformation, < *reformare*, pp. *reformatus*, reform: see *reform*, *v.*] **1.** The act of forming anew; a second forming in order: as, the *reformation* of a column of troops into a hollow square. [In this literal sense usually pronounced rē-fôr-mā'shon, and sometimes written distinctively with a hyphen.] **2.** The act of reforming what is defective or evil, or the state of being reformed; correction or amendment, as of life or manners, or of a government.

I would rather thinke (sauing *reformacion* of other better learned) that this Tharsis . . . were rather some other countrey in the south partes of the world then this Tharsis of Cilicia.
R. Eden, First Books on America (ed. Arber), p. 8.

Never was such a sudden scholar made;
Never came *reformation* in a flood
With such a heady currance, scouring faults.
Shak., Hen. V., i. 1. 33.

God has set before me two great objects, the suppression of the slave trade and the *reformation* of manners.
Wilberforce, Journal, Oct. 28, 1787 (Life, v.).

Specifically, with the definite article—**3.** [*cap.*] The great religious revolution in the sixteenth century, which led to the establishment of the Protestant churches. The Reformation assumed different aspects and resulted in alterations of discipline or doctrine more or less fundamental in different countries and in different stages of its progress. Various reformers of great influence, as Wyclif and Huss, had appeared before the sixteenth century, but the Reformation proper began nearly simultaneously in Germany under the lead of Luther and in Switzerland under the lead of Zwingli. The chief points urged by the Reformers were the need of justification by faith, the use and authority of the Scriptures and the right of private judgment in their interpretation, and the abandonment of the doctrine of transubstantiation, the adoration of the Virgin Mary and saints, the supremacy of the Pope, and various other doctrines and rites regarded by the Reformers as unscriptural. In the German Reformation the leading features were the publication at Wittenberg of Luther's ninety-five theses against indulgences in 1517, the excommunication of Luther in 1520, his testimony before the Diet of Worms in 1521, the spread of the principles in many of the German states, as Hesse, Saxony, and Brandenburg, and the opposition to them by the emperor, the Diet and Confession of Augsburg in 1530, and the prolonged struggle between the Protestants and the Catholics, ending with comparative religious equality in the Peace of Passau in 1552. The Reformation spread in Switzerland under Zwingli and Calvin, in France, Hungary, Bohemia, the Scandinavian countries, Low Countries, etc. In Scotland it was introduced by Knox about 1560. In England it led in the reign of Henry VIII. to the abolition of the papal supremacy and the liberation from papal control of the Church of England, which, after a short Roman Catholic reaction under Mary, was firmly established under Elizabeth. In many countries the Reformation occasioned an increased strength and zeal in the Roman Catholic Church sometimes called the *Counter-Reformation*. The term *Reformation* as applied to this movement is not of course accepted by Roman Catholics, who use it only with some word of qualification.

Prophesies and Forewarnings . . . sent before of God, by divers and sundry good men, long before the time of Luther, which foretold and prophesied of this *Reformation* of the Church to come.
Foxe, Martyrs (ed. 1684), II. 43.

Festival of the Reformation, an annual commemoration in Germany, and among Lutherans generally, of the nailing of the ninety-five theses on the doors of the Castle church at Wittenberg on October 31st, 1517.—**Reformation of the calendar**, the institution of the Gregorian calendar. See *calendar*. =**Syn.** 2. *Amendment*, *Reform*, *Reformation*. *Amendment* may be of any degree, however small; *reform* applies to something more thorough, and *reformation* to that which is most important, thorough, and lasting of all. Hence, when we speak of temperance *reform*, we dignify it less than when we call it temperance *reformation*. Moral *reform*, religious *reformation*; temporary *amendment* or *reform*, permanent *reformation*. *Reform* represents the state more often than *reformation*.

reformative (rē̦-fôr'mạ-tiv), *a.* [= Sp. Pg. *reformativo*; as *reform* + *-ative*.] Forming again; having the property of renewing form.

reformatory (rē̦-fôr'mạ-tō-ri), *a.* and *n.* [= F. *réformatoire* = Sp. Pg. *reformatorio*; as *reform* + *-atory*.] **I.** *a.* Having a tendency to reform or renovate; reformative.—**Reformatory school**, a reformatory. See II.

II. *n.*; pl. *reformatories* (-riz). An institution for the reception and reformation of youths who have already begun a career of vice or crime. Reformatories, or reformatory schools, are, in Great Britain, identical in character with certified industrial schools, admission to either being determined by differences of age and criminality, and they differ from ragged schools in so far as they are supported by the state, and receive only such children or youths as are under judicial sentence.

reformed (rē̦-fôrmd'), *p. a.* [Early mod. E. also *refourmed*; < *reform* + *-ed*[2].] 1. Corrected; amended; restored to a better or to a good state: as, a *reformed* profligate; *reformed* spelling.

> Very noble and *refourmed* knight, by the words of your letter I understood howe quickly ye medicine of my writing came to your heart.
> *Guevara*, Letters (tr. by Hellowes, 1577), p. 181.

2†. Deprived of rank or position, or reduced in pay. See *reformado*, 2.—**Captain reformed†**. See *captain*.—**Reformed Bernardines.** See *Feuillant*, 1.—**Reformed Church.** (*a*) A general name for the Protestant bodies on the continent of Europe which trace their origin to the Swiss reformation under Zwingli and Calvin, as distinguished from the Lutheran Church. In France the Reformed were known as Huguenots. In the Netherlands the Arminians afterward separated from the Calvinists (Gomarists). In Germany, after 1817, the greater part of the Reformed and Lutherans combined to form the United Evangelical Church. Specifically—(*b*) In the United States: (1) The Reformed (Dutch) Church in America, growing out of a union among the Dutch churches in America in 1770 and finally perfected in 1812. The territory of the denomination was at first limited to the States of New York and New Jersey and a small part of Pennsylvania, but was gradually extended to the West. The affairs of each congregation are managed by a consistory, consisting of elders and deacons chosen for two years. The elders, with the pastor, receive and dismiss members and exercise discipline; the deacons have charge of the alms. Both together are ex officio trustees of the church, hold its property, and call its minister. Ex-elders and ex-deacons constitute what is called the Great Consistory, which may be summoned to give advice in important matters. The minister and one elder from each congregation in a certain district constitute a classis, which supervises spiritual concerns in that district. Four ministers and four elders from each classis in a larger district make a Particular Synod, with similar powers. Representatives, clerical and lay, from each classis, proportioned in number to the size of the classis, constitute the General Synod, which has supervision of the whole, and is a court of last resort in judicial cases. The church is Calvinistic in its theological belief, and possesses a liturgy the greater part of which is optional except the offices for the sacraments, for ordination, and for church discipline. (2) The Reformed (German) Church in the United States. This church was constituted by colonies from Germany in New York, Maryland, Virginia, and North and South Carolina. The first synod was organized September 27th, 1747, under the care of the Reformed Classis of Amsterdam. The church holds to the parity of the ministry, maintains a presbyterian form of government, is moderately Calvinistic in its theology, and provides liturgical forms of service, which are, however, chiefly optional. (3) The True Reformed Dutch Church, the result of a secession from the Reformed Dutch Church in America in 1822. (4) The Reformed Episcopal Church, an Episcopal church organized in the United States in 1873, by eight clergymen and twenty laymen previously members of the Protestant Episcopal Church. It maintains the episcopacy as a desirable form of church polity, but not as of divine obligation, continues to use the Book of Common Prayer, but in a revised form, and rejects the doctrines of apostolic succession, the priesthood of the clergy, the sacrifice or oblation in the Lord's Supper, the real presence, and baptismal regeneration.—**Reformed officer**, in the British army, one who is continued on full pay or half-pay after his troops are broken up. *Farrow*, Mil. Encyc.—**Reformed Presbyterian Church**, a Presbyterian denomination originating in Scotland. See *Cameronian*, *n.*, 1, and *Covenanter*, 2.—**Reformed procedure.** See *equity*, 2 (*b*).—**The Reformed**, on the continent of Europe, Calvinistic Protestants as distinguished from Lutherans.

reformedly† (rē̦-fôr'med-li), *adv.* In or after the manner of a reform. [Rare.]

> A fierce Reformer once, now rankl'd with a contrary heat, would send us back, very *reformedly* indeed, to learn Reformation from Tyndarus and Rebuffus, two canonical Promoters.
> *Milton*, Touching Hirelings.

reformer (rē̦-fôr'mėr), *n.* [< *reform* + *-er*[1].] 1. One who effects a reformation or amendment: as, a *reformer* of manners or of abuses; specifically [*cap.*], one of those who instituted or assisted in the religious reformatory movements of the sixteenth century and earlier.

> God's passionless *reformers*, influences
> That purify and heal and are not seen.
> *Lowell*, Under the Willows.

2. One who promotes or urges reform: as, a tariff *reformer*; a spelling *reformer*.

> They could not call him a revenue *reformer*, and still less could they call him a civil-service *reformer*, for there were few abuses of the civil service of which he had not, during the whole of his life, been an active promoter.
> *The Nation*, XV. 68.

reformist (rē̦-fôr'mist), *n.* [= F. *réformiste*; as *reform* + *-ist*.] 1†. [*cap.*] One who is of the reformed religion; a Protestant.

> This comely Subordination of Degrees we once had, and we had a visible conspicuous Church, to whom all other *Reformists* gave the upper Hand. *Howell*, Letters, iv. 36.

2. One who proposes or favors a political reform. [Rare.]

> Such is the language of reform, and the spirit of a *reformist!* *I. D'Israeli*, Calam. of Authors, p. 204.

refortify (rē-fôr'ti-fī), *v. t.* [= OF. (and F.) *refortifier* = It. *rifortificare*, < ML. *refortificare*, < L. *re-*, again, + ML. *fortificare*, fortify: see *fortify*.] To fortify anew.

refossion† (rē̦-fosh'o̤n), *n.* [< L. *refossus*, pp. of *refodere*, dig up or out again, < *re-*, again, + *fodere*, dig: see *fossil*.] The act of digging up again.

> Hence are . . . *refossion* of graues, torturing of the surviving, worse than many deaths.
> *Bp. Hall*, St. Paul's Combat.

refound[1] (rē-found'), *v. t.* [< OF. (and F.) *refonder*, found or build again, < *re-*, again, + *fonder*, found: see *found*[2].] To found again or anew; establish on a different basis.

> George II. *refounded* and reformed the Chair which I have the honour to fill.
> *Stubbs*, Medieval and Modern Hist., p. 4.

refound[2] (rē-found'), *v. t.* [< OF. (and F.) *refondre* = Pr. *refondre* = Sp. Pg. *refundir* = It. *rifondere*, cast over again, recast, < L. *refundere*, pour back or out, < *re-*, back, + *fundere*, pour: see *found*[3].] To found or cast anew.

> Perhaps they are all antient bells *refounded*.
> *T. Warton*, Hist. Kiddington, p. 8.

refounder (rē-foun'dėr), *n.* [< *refound*[1] + *-er*[1].] One who refounds, rebuilds, or reëstablishes.

> Charlemagne, . . . the *refounder* of that empire which is the ideal of despotism in the Western world.
> *Lowell*, Study Windows, p. 142.

refract (rē̦-frakt'), *v. t.* [= F. *réfracter*, < L. *refractus*, pp. of *refringere*, break back, break up, break open, hence turn aside, < *re-*, back, + *frangere*, break: see *fraction*. Cf. *refrain*[2].] To bend back sharply or abruptly; especially, in *optics*, to break the natural course of, as of a ray of light; deflect at a certain angle on passing from one medium into another of a different density. See *refraction*.

> Visual beams *refracted* through another's eye.
> *Selden*, Pref. to Drayton's Polyolbion.

refractable (rē̦-frak'tạ-bl), *a.* [< *refract* + *-able*.] Capable of being refracted; refrangible, as a ray of light or heat. *Dr. H. More.*

refractary† (rē̦-frak'tạ-ri), *a.* [= OF. *refractaire*, F. *réfractaire* = Sp. Pg. *refractario* = It. *refrattario*, < L. *refractarius*, stubborn, obstinate, refractory, < *refringere*, pp. *refractus*, break in pieces: see *refract* and *-ary*[1]. Cf. *refractory*.] The earlier and more correct form of *refractory*. *Cotgrave.*

refracted (rē̦-frak'ted), *a.* In *bot.*, same as *reflexed*, but abruptly bent from the base. *Gray.*

refracting (rē̦-frak'ting), *p. a.* Serving or tending to refract; turning from a direct course.—**Doubly refracting spar**, Iceland spar. See *calcite* and *spar*[3].—**Refracting angle of a prism**, the angle formed by the two faces of the triangular prism used to decompose white or solar light.—**Refracting dial.** See *dial*.—**Refracting surface**, a surface bounding two transparent media, at which a ray of light, in passing from one into the other, undergoes refraction.—**Refracting system**, in lighthouses, same as *dioptric system* (which see, under *dioptric*).—**Refracting telescope.** See *telescope*.

refraction (rē̦-frak'sho̤n), *n.* [< OF. *refraction*, F. *réfraction* = Sp. *refraccion* = Pg. *refracção* = It. *rifrazione*, *refrazione*, < ML. *refractio(n-)*, lit. a breaking up (in logic tr. Gr. ἀνάκλασις), NL. refraction, < L. *refringere*, pp. *refractus*, break up, break open, break to pieces: see *refract*.] 1. The act of refracting, or the state of being refracted: almost exclusively restricted to physics, and applied to a deflection or change of direction of rays, as of light, heat, or sound, which are obliquely incident upon and pass through a smooth surface bounding two media not homogeneous, as air and water, or of rays which traverse a medium the density of which is not uniform, as the atmosphere. It is found (1) that, when passing into a denser isotropic medium, the ray is refracted toward the perpendicular to the surface, and bent away from it when passing into one less dense; (2) that the sines of the angles of incidence and refraction bear a constant ratio to each other for any two given media; and (3) that the incident ray and the refracted ray are in the same plane. Thus, if (fig. 1) SP represents a ray incident upon the surface of water at P, it will be bent away from its original direction SPL toward the perpendicular Qq in passing into the denser medium, and make an angle qPR, such that the $\frac{\sin SPQ}{\sin RPq}$ is a constant quantity—that is, the perpendicular distance of a point q (such that the line from it to P, the point of incidence, is normal to the surface) from the refracted path bears a constant ratio to its distance from the path as it would be without refraction, however the angle of incidence varies; but this constant depends on the nature of the two media. If the first medium is air, this constant ratio is called the *index of refraction* or *refractive index* of the given substance (or *n*). Again, if the ray proceeded from R to P, it would be bent away from the perpendicular in the direction PS. The latter case is peculiar, however, in that for a certain angle of incidence called the critical angle (whose sine = $1/n$) the angle of refraction of QPS is a right angle and a ray incident at P at any greater angle cannot pass out into the rarer medium at all, but suffers total reflection at P. In fig. 2, AHC is the angle of incidence, and EHK the angle of refraction, CD being the normal to the surface; if, further, the second surface is parallel to the first, the ray emerging into the original medium at E has a direction EF parallel with its first direction, AH. If (fig. 3) the refracting medium has the form of a prism (ABC), the incident ray LF suffers a double change of direction, first (FE) in passing into the prism, and second (EG) in emerging from it; the total angle of deviation IDL varies in value with a change in the direction of LF, but has a definite minimum value when the angles of incidence and emergence are equal. If *d* represents the angle of the prism BAC, and *r* the angle of minimum deviation, LDI, then the refractive index *n* of the material of which the prism is made is given by the relation $n = \frac{\sin \frac{1}{2}(d + r)}{\sin \frac{1}{2} d}$. The angle of deviation or refraction also increases as the wave-length of the ray diminishes, and hence a beam of white light in passing through a prism is both refracted and dispersed, thus yielding a spectrum. The phenomena of the refraction of light explain the properties of lenses (see *lens*) and of prisms (see *prism* and *spectrum*). Sound-waves may also be refracted when passing from one medium to another of different density, obeying the same laws as light. *Double refraction* is the separation of a ray of light into two rays, which are unequally refracted upon passing through an anisotropic medium. This property belongs to all transparent crystalline substances except those of the isometric system. A striking example is calcite, hence called *doubly refracting spar*. In uniaxial crystals (those belonging to the tetragonal and hexagonal systems) one of the rays follows the ordinary law of refraction (see law (2), above), and is called the *ordinary ray*; the other, which does not, is called the *extraordinary ray*; both rays are polarized (see *polarization*), the ordinary ray having vibrations perpendicular to and the extraordinary ray vibrations parallel to the vertical axis. If the index of refraction is greater for the ordinary ray than for the extraordinary ray, the crystal is said to be *negative*, and in the opposite case *positive*: otherwise expressed, a crystal is negative or positive according as the crystallographic axis (optical axis) is the axis of greatest or of least elasticity. In the direction of the vertical axis a ray suffers no double refraction, and this direction is called the *optic axis*. In biaxial crystals (those belonging to the orthorhombic, monoclinic, and triclinic systems) neither ray follows the ordinary law of refraction, and there are two directions, called *optic axes*, lying in the plane of the axes of greatest and least elasticity, in which a ray suffers no double refraction. There are also three indices of refraction, corresponding to the rays propagated by vibrations parallel to the three axes of elasticity. A biaxial crystal is called *negative* or *positive* according as the acute bisectrix coincides with the axis of greatest or of least elasticity. According to the degree of difference between the two indices of refraction of a uniaxial crystal and between the greatest and least of the three indices of a biaxial crystal, the double refraction is said to be *strong* or *weak*; upon this difference depends the brilliancy of color of thin sections of a crystal as seen in polarized light. Amorphous substances like glass do not show double refraction, except under abnormal conditions, as when subjected to unequal strains, as in glass suddenly cooled. This is also true of crystals belonging to the isometric system, which, however, sometimes show secondary or abnormal double refraction (as garnet), due to internal molecular strain or other cause. For the refraction of the eye, see *eye*[1], and *crystalline humor* (under *crystalline*). Errors of refraction in the eye are tested by trial with lenses, test types, etc., by the ophthalmoscope, or by skiascopy or the shadow-test, and are corrected by appropriate glasses.

Fig. 1.

Fig. 2.

Fig. 3.
Section of a Prism, showing the refraction of a transmitted light-ray along the path LF, FE, EG.

2. In *logic*, the relation of the Theophrastian moods to the direct moods of the first figure.—**Astronomical** or **atmospheric refraction**, the apparent angular elevation of the heavenly bodies above their true places, caused by the refraction of the rays of light in their passage through the earth's atmosphere, so that in consequence of this retraction those bodies appear higher than they really are. It is greatest when the body is on the horizon, and diminishes all the way to the zenith, where it is zero.—**Axis of double refraction.** See *optic axis* (b), under *optic*.—**Axis of refraction.** See *axis*.—**Caustic by refraction.** See *diacaustic*.—**Conical refraction**, the refraction of a single ray of light, under certain conditions, into an infinite number of rays in the form of a hollow luminous cone, consisting of two kinds, *external conical refraction* and *internal conical refraction*, the ray in the former case issuing from the refracting crystal as a cone with its vertex at the point of emergence, and in the latter being converted into a cone on entering the crystal, and issuing as a hollow cylinder.—**Double refraction.** See def. 1.—**Dynamic refraction**, refraction of the eye as increased in accommodation.—**Electrical double refraction**, the double refraction produced in an isotropic dielectric medium, as glass, under the action of an electrical strain.—**Index of refraction.** See *index*, and def. 1.—**Plane of refraction**, the plane passing through the normal or perpendicular to the refracting surface at the point of incidence and the refracted ray.—**Point of refraction.** See *point*1.—**Refraction equivalent**, a phrase used by Landolt to express in the case of a liquid the quantity obtained by multiplying the molecular weight of the liquid by the so-called specific refractive energy, as defined by Gladstone and Dale (namely, the refractive index less unity divided by its density referred to water). The refraction equivalent of a compound is said to be equal to the sum of the equivalents of its component parts.—**Refraction of altitude and declination, of ascension and descension, of latitude and longitude**, the change in the altitude, declination, etc., of a heavenly body due to the effect of atmospheric refraction.—**Refraction of sound**, the bending of a beam of sound from its rectilinear course whenever it undergoes an unequal acceleration or retardation, necessarily turning toward the side of least velocity and from the side of greatest velocity.—**Static refraction**, refraction of the eye when the accommodation is entirely relaxed.—**Terrestrial refraction**, that refraction which makes terrestrial objects appear to be raised higher than they are in reality. This arises from the air being denser near the surface of the earth than it is at higher elevations, its refractive power increasing as the density increases. The mirage is a phenomenon of terrestrial refraction.

refractive (rē-frak'tiv), *a.* [< F. *réfractif* = Pg. *refractivo*; as *refract* + *-ive*.] Of or pertaining to refraction; serving or having power to refract or turn from a direct course.—**Refractive index.** Same as *index of refraction*. See *index* and *refraction*.—**Refractive power**, in *optics*, the degree of influence which a transparent body exercises on the light which passes through it: used also in the same sense as *refractive index*.

refractiveness (rē-frak'tiv-nes), *n.* The state or quality of being refractive.

refractivity (rē-frak-tiv'i-ti), *n.* [< *refractive* + *-ity*.] See the quotation.

The *refractivity* of a substance is the difference between the index of refraction of the substance and unity.
Philosophical Mag., 5th ser., XXVIII. 400.

refractometer (rē-frak-tom'e-tėr), *n.* [Irreg. < L. *refractus*, pp. of *refringere*, break up (see *refract*), + Gr. μέτρον, measure.] An instrument used for measuring the refractive indices of different substances. Many forms of this have been devised; and the term is specifically applied to an instrument which employs interference fringes and which allows of the measurement of the difference of path of two interfering rays—the immediate object of observation being the displacement produced by the passage of the ray through a known thickness of the given medium, from which its refractive power can be found. Such refractometers (*interferential refractometers*) may also be employed for other purposes, for example, in certain cases of linear measurement.

refractor (rē-frak'tor), *n.* [= F. *réfracteur*; as *refract* + *-or*1.] A refracting telescope. See *telescope*.

refractorily (rē-frak'tō-ri-li), *adv.* In a refractory manner; perversely; obstinately. *Imp. Dict.*

refractoriness (rē-frak'tō-ri-nes), *n.* The state or character of being refractory, in any sense.

refractory (rē-frak'tō-ri), *a.* and *n.* [Erroneously for the earlier *refractary*, < L. *refractarius*, stubborn, obstinate, refractory: see *refractary*.] I. *a.* 1. Resisting; unyielding; sullen or perverse in opposition or disobedience; obstinate in non-compliance; stubborn and unmanageable.

There is a law in each well-order'd nation
To curb those raging appetites that are
Most disobedient and *refractory*.
Shak., T. and C., ii. 2. 182.

Our care and caution should be more carefully employed in mortification of our natures and acquist of such virtues to which we are more *refractory*.
Jer. Taylor, Works (ed. 1835), II. 8.

He then dissolved Parliament, and sent its most *refractory* members to the Tower.
D. Webster, Speech, Senate, May 7, 1834.

2. Resisting ordinary treatment or strains, etc.; difficult of fusion, reduction, or the like: said especially of metals and the like that require an extraordinary degree of heat to fuse them, or that do not yield readily to the hammer. In metallurgy an ore is said to be *refractory* when it is with difficulty treated by metallurgical processes, or when it is not easily reduced. Stone, brick, etc., are refractory when they resist the action of fire without melting, cracking, or crumbling. Refractory materials are such as can be used for the lining of furnaces and crucibles, and for similar purposes.

3. Not susceptible; not subject; resisting (some influence, as of disease). [Rare.]

Pasteur claimed to so completely tame the virus that a dog would, in being rendered *refractory* to rabies by hypodermic inoculation or trepanning, show no sign of illness.
Science, III. 744.

Refractory period of a muscle, the time after a first stimulus when the muscle is not irritable by a second stimulus. This has been found for striated frog's muscle, after a maximal first stimulation, to be about $\frac{1}{250}$ second. = **Syn.** 1. *Stubborn, Intractable*, etc. (see *obstinate*), unruly, ungovernable, unmanageable, headstrong, mulish.

II. *n.*; pl. *refractories* (-riz). 1†. One who is obstinate in opposition or disobedience.

Render not yourself a *refractory* on the sudden.
B. Jonson, Cynthia's Revels, v. 2.

2†. Obstinate opposition.

Glorying in their scandalous *refractories* to public order and constitutions.
Jer. Taylor (?), Artif. Handsomeness, p. 138.

3. In *pottery*, a piece of ware covered with a vaporable flux and placed in a kiln to communicate a glaze to other articles. *E. H. Knight.*

refracture (rē-frak'tūr), *n.* [< *re-* + *fracture*. In def. 2 with ref. to *refractory*.] 1. A breaking again, as of a badly set bone.—2†. Refractoriness; antagonism. [Rare.]

More veniall and excusable may those verball reluctancies, reserves, and *refractures* (rather than anything of open force and hostile rebellions) seem.
Bp. Gauden, Tears of the Church, p. 562. (*Davies.*)

refragability (ref"ra-ga-bil'i-ti), *n.* [< ML. *refragabilita(t-)s*, < *refragabilis*, refragable: see *refragable*.] The state or quality of being refragable; refragableness. *Bailey.*

refragable (ref'ra-ga-bl), *a.* [= Pg. *refragavel*, < ML. *refragabilis*, resistible, < L. *refragari*, oppose, resist, gainsay, contest: see *refragate*.] Capable of being opposed or resisted; refutable. *Bailey.*

refragableness (ref'ra-ga-bl-nes), *n.* The character of being refragable. [Rare.]

refragate† (ref'ra-gāt), *v. i.* [< L. *refragatus*, pp. of *refragari*, oppose, resist, contest, gainsay, < *re-*, back, again, + *fragari*, perhaps < *frangere* (√ *frag*), break: see *fragile*.] To oppose; be opposite in effect; break down under examination, as theories or proofs.

And 'tis the observation of the noble St. Alban that that philosophy is built on a few vulgar experiments; and if, upon further inquiry, any were found to *refragate*, they were to be discharg'd by a distinction.
Glanville, Vanity of Dogmatizing, xix.

refrain1 (rē-frān'), *v.* [Early mod. E. *refrayne*, *refreyne*, < ME. *refreinen*, *refreynen*, *refraynen*, < OF. *refraindre*, *refreindre*, also *refrener*, F. *réfréner*, bridle, restrain, repress, = Pr. Sp. *refrenar* = Pg. *refrear* = It. *raffrenare*, < LL. *refrenare*, bridle, hold in with a bit, < L. *re-*, back, + *frenum*, *frænum*, a bit, curb, pl. *frena*, curb and reins, a bridle: see *frenum*.] I. *trans.* 1. To hold back; restrain; curb; keep from action.

My son, . . . *refrain* thy foot from their path.
Prov. i. 15.

In this plight, therefore, he went home, and *refrained* himself as long as he could, that his wife and children should not perceive his distress.
Bunyan, Pilgrim's Progress, p. 84.

The fierceness of them shalt thou *refrain*.
Ps. lxxvi. 10 (Psalter).

2†. To forbear; abstain from; quit.

Men may also *refreyne* venial sinne by receyvynge worthily of the precious body of Jhesu Crist.
Chaucer, Parson's Tale.

At length, when the sun waxed low,
Then all the whole train the grove did *refrain*,
And unto their caves they did go.
Robin Hood and Little John (Child's Ballads, V. 222).

I cannot *refrain* lamenting, however, in the most poignant terms, the fatal policy too prevalent in most of the states.
Washington, quoted in Bancroft's Hist. Const., I. 282.

II. *intrans.* To forbear; abstain; keep one's self from action or interference.

Dreadfull of daunger that mote him betyde,
She oft and oft adviz'd him to *refraine*
From chase of greater beastes.
Spenser, F. Q., III. i. 37.

Refrain from these men, and let them alone.
Acts v. 38.

The chat, the nuthatch, and the jay are still;
The robin too *refrains*.
Harper's Mag., LXXVII. 718.

refrain2 (rē-frān'), *n.* [< ME. *refraine*, *refreyne*, < OF. (and F.) *refrain*, a refrain (= Pr. *refranh*, *refrim*, a refrain, = Sp. *refran* = Pg. *refrão*, a proverb, an oft-repeated saying), < *refraindre*, repeat, sing a song, = Pr. *refranher*, *refrenher*, repeat, = It. *refrangere*, refract, reverberate, < L. *refringere*, break back, break off: see *refract*.] 1. A burden or chorus recurring at regular intervals in the course of a song or ballad, usually at the end of each stanza.

Everemo "allas?" was his *refreyne*.
Chaucer, Troilus, ii. 1571.

They sang the *refrain*:—
"The roads should blossom, the roads should bloom,
So fair a bride shall leave her home!"
Longfellow, Blind Girl of Castèl-Cuillè.

2. The musical phrase or figure to which the burden of a song is set. It has the same relation to the main part of the tune that the burden has to the main text of the song.

3. An after-taste or -odor; that impression which lingers on the sense: as, the *refrain* of a Cologne water, of a perfume, of a wine.

refrainer (rē-frā'nėr), *n.* [Early mod. E. *refreinor*; < *refrain*1 + *-er*1.] One who refrains.

So these ii. persons were euer cohibetors and *refreinors* of the kinges wilfull skope and vnbrideled libertie.
Hall, Hen. VII., an. 18.

refraining† (rē-frā'ning), *n.* [< ME. *refraining*, the singing of the burden of a song; verbal n. of **refrain*2, v., < OF. *refrener*, sing a refrain, *refraindre*, repeat, sing a song: see *refrain*2.] The singing of the burden of a song.

She . . . couthe make in song sich *refreynynge*,
It sat [became] hir wonder wel to synge.
Rom. of the Rose, l. 749.

refrainment (rē-frān'ment), *n.* [= F. *refrènement* = Sp. *refrenamiento* = Pg. *refreamento* = It. *raffrenamento*; as *refrain*1 + *-ment*.] The act of refraining; abstinence; forbearance.

Forbearance and Indurance . . . we may otherwise call *Refrainment* and Support.
Shaftesbury, Judgment of Hercules, vi. § 4.

refrait†, *n.* [Also *refret*; < ME. *refraite*, *refraide*, *refrayde*, *refret*, < OF. *refrait*, a refrain, < *refraindre*, repeat: see *refrain*2.] Same as *refrain*2.

The *refraite* of his laye salewed the Kynge Arthur and the Quene Gonnore, and alle the other atter.
Merlin (E. E. T. S.), iii. 615.

reframe (rē-frām'), *v. t.* [< *re-* + *frame*.] To frame or put together again.

refranation (ref-ra-nā'shon), *n.* [Irreg. < L. *refrænatio(n-)*, refrenation: see *refrenation*.] In *astrol.*, the failure of a planetary aspect to occur, owing to a retrograde motion of one of the planets.

refrangibility (rē-fran-ji-bil'i-ti), *n.* [= F. *réfrangibilité* = Sp. *refrangibilidad* = Pg. *refrangibilidade* = It. *rifrangibilità*; as *refrangible* + *-ity* (see *-bility*).] The property of being refrangible; susceptibility of refraction; the disposition of rays of light, etc., to be refracted or turned out of a direct course in passing out of one medium into another.

refrangible (rē-fran'ji-bl), *a.* [= F. *réfrangible* = Sp. *refrangible* = Pg. *refrangivel* = It. *rifrangibile*, refrangible, < L. *refringere*, refract (see *refract*), + *-ible*.] Capable of being refracted in passing from one medium to another, as rays of light. The violet rays in the spectrum are more refrangible than those of greater wave-length, as the red rays.

Some of them [rays of light] are more *refrangible* than others.
Locke, Elem. of Nat. Philos., xi.

refrangibleness (rē-fran'ji-bl-nes), *n.* The character or property of being refrangible; refrangibility. *Bailey.*

refreeze (rē-frēz'), *v. t.* [< *re-* + *freeze*.] To freeze a second time.

Partially *refrozen* under continual agitation.
Proc. Physical Soc., London, ii. 62. (*Encyc. Dict.*)

refreid†, **refroid**†, *v.* [ME. *refreiden*, *refreyden*, *refroiden*, < OF. *refreider*, *refreidier*, *refroidir*, *reffroidir*, F. *refroidir*, render cold or cool, chill, etc., = Pr. *refreidar*, *refreydir* = Sp. Pg. *resfriar* = It. *raffreddare*, < ML. *refrigidare*, make cold or cool, < L. *re-*, again, + *frigidus*, cold: see *frigid*. Cf. *refrigerate*.] I. *trans.* To make cool; chill.

He . . . shal som tyme be moeved in hymself, but if he were al *refreyded* by siknesse, or by malefice of sorcerie, or colde drynkes.
Chaucer, Parson's Tale.

Nevew, be not so roth, *refroide* youre maltalente, ffor wrath hath many a worthi man and wise made to be holde for foles while the rage endureth.
Merlin (E. E. T. S.), iii. 500.

II. *intrans.* To grow cool.

God wot, *refreyden* may this boote fare,
Er Calkas sende Troylus Cryseyde.
Chaucer, Troilus, v. 507.

refrenation† (ref-rē-nā'shon), *n.* [< OF. *refrenation*, F. *réfrénation* = Sp. *refrenacion*, < L. *refrenatio(n-)*, a bridling, curbing, restraining, < *refrenare*, bridle, curb, check: see *refrain*[1].] The act of restraining. *Cotgrave.*

refresh (rē-fresh'), *v.* [< ME. *refreshen*, *refreschen*, *refrisschen*, < OF. *refreschir*, *refraischir*, also *refreschier*, *refraissier* (= Sp. Pg. *refrescar* = It. *rinfrescare*, < ML. *refrescare*, *refriscare*), refresh, cool, < L. *re-*, again, + *friscus*, *frescus*, new, recent, fresh: see *fresh*.] **I.** *trans.* **1.** To make fresh or as if new again; freshen; improve; restore; repair; renovate.

I have desirid hym to move the Counsell for *refreshing* of the toun of Yermowth with stuff of ordnance and gonnes and gonne powdre, and he seid he wolde.
Paston Letters, I. 427.

Before I entered on my voyage, I took care to *refresh* my memory among the classic authors.
Addison, Remarks on Italy, Pref.

I remember, old gentleman, how often you went home in a day to *refresh* your countenance and dress when Teraminta reigned in your heart.
Steele, Tatler, No. 95.

As in some solitude the summer rill
Refreshes, where it winds, the faded green.
Cowper, In Memory of John Thornton.

2. To make fresh or vigorous again; restore vigor or energy to; give new strength to; reinvigorate; recreate or revive after fatigue, privation, pain, or the like; reanimate.

I am glad of the coming of Stephanas and Fortunatus, . . . for they have *refreshed* my spirit and yours.
1 Cor. xvi. 17, 18.

And labour shall *refresh* itself with hope,
To do your grace incessant services.
Shak., Hen. V., ii. 2. 37.

There are two causes by the influence of which memory may be *refreshed*, and by that means rendered, at the time of deposition, more vivid than, by reason of the joint influence of the importance of the fact and the ancientness of it, it would otherwise be. One is intermediate statements. . . . Another is fresh incidents.
Bentham, Judicial Evidence, i. 10.

3. To steep and soak, particularly vegetables, in pure water with a view to restore their fresh appearance. =**Syn. 1** and **2.** To revive, renew, recruit, recreate, enliven, cheer.

II. *intrans.* **1.** To become fresh or vigorous again; revive; become reanimated or reinvigorated.

I went to visite Dr. Tenison at Kensington, whither he was retired to *refresh* after he had ben sick of the small-pox.
Evelyn, Diary, March 7, 1684.

2. To take refreshment, as food or drink. [Colloq.]

Tumblers *refreshing* during the cessation of their performances.
Thackeray, Vanity Fair, lxvi.

3. To lay in a fresh stock of provisions. [Colloq.]

We met an American whaler going in to *refresh*.
Simmond's Colonial Mag. (*Imp. Dict.*)

refresh† (rē-fresh'), *n.* [< *refresh*, *v.*] The act of refreshing; refreshment.

Beauty, sweete love, is like the morning dew,
Whose short *refresh* upon the tender green
Cheers for a time.
Daniel, Sonnets, xlvii.

refreshen (rē-fresh'n), *v. t.* [< *re-* + *freshen*.] To make fresh again; refresh; renovate. [Rare.]

In order to keep the mind in repair, it is necessary to replace and *refreshen* those impressions of nature which are continually wearing away.
Sir J. Reynolds, On Du Fresnoy's Art of Painting, Note 28.

It had begun to rain, the clouds emptying themselves in bulk . . . to animate and *refreshen* the people.
S. Judd, Margaret, i. 13.

refresher (rē-fresh'ėr), *n.* **1.** One who or that which refreshes, revives, or invigorates; that which refreshes the memory.

This [swimming] is the purest exercise of health,
The kind *refresher* of the summer heats.
Thomson, Summer, l. 1258.

Every fortnight or so I took care that he should receive a *refresher*, as lawyers call it — a new and revised brief memorialising my pretensions.
De Quincey, Sketches, I. 72. (*Davies.*)

Miss Peccher [a schoolmistress] went into her little official residence, and took a *refresher* of the principal rivers and mountains of the world.
Dickens, Our Mutual Friend, ii. 1.

2. A fee paid to counsel for continuing attention or readiness, for the purpose of refreshing his memory as to the facts of a case before him, in the intervals of business, especially when the case is adjourned. [Colloq., Eng.]

Had he gone to the bar, he might have attained to the dignity of the Bench, after feathering his nest comfortably with retainers and *refreshers*.
Fortnightly Rev., N. S., XL. 28.

refreshful (rē-fresh'fůl), *a.* [< *refresh* + *-ful.*] Full of refreshment; refreshing.

They spread the breathing harvest to the sun,
That throws *refreshful* round a rural smell.
Thomson, Summer, l. 364.

refreshfully (rē-fresh'fůl-i), *adv.* In a refreshing manner; so as to refresh.

Refreshfully
There came upon my face . . .
Dew-drops.
Keats, Endymion, i.

refreshing (rē-fresh'ing), *n.* [Verbal n. of *refresh*, *v.*] Refreshment; that which refreshes; relief after fatigue or suffering.

And late vs rest us for a daye or twayne,
That your pepill may haue *refreshing*;
Thanne we wolle geve them batell new ageyn.
Generydes (E. E. T. S.), l. 2091.

Secret *refreshings* that repair his strength.
Milton, S. A., l. 665.

refreshing (rē-fresh'ing), *p. a.* [Ppr. of *refresh*, *v.*] Tending or serving to refresh; invigorating; reviving; reanimating: sometimes used with a humorous or sarcastic implication.

Who [Ceres] with thy saffron wings upon my flowers
Diffusest honey-drops, *refreshing* showers.
Shak., Tempest, iv. 1. 79.

And one good action in the midst of crimes
Is "quite *refreshing*," in the affected phrase
Of these ambrosial Pharisaic times.
Byron, Don Juan, viii. 90.

refreshingly (rē-fresh'ing-li), *adv.* In a refreshing manner; so as to refresh or give new life.

refreshingness (rē-fresh'ing-nes), *n.* The character of being refreshing. *Imp. Dict.*

refreshment (rē-fresh'ment), *n.* [< OF. *refreschement*, *refraischement*, etc. (also *rafrechissement*, *rafraischissement*, *rafraichissement*, F. *rafraîchissement*), refreshment; as *refresh* + *-ment.*] **1.** The act of refreshing, or the state of being refreshed; relief after exhaustion, etc.

Although the worship of God is the chief end of the institution [the Sabbath], yet the *refreshment* of the lower ranks of mankind by an intermission of their labours is indispensably a secondary object.
Bp. Horsley, Works, II. xxiii.

2. That which refreshes; a recreation; that which gives fresh strength or vigor, as food, drink, or rest: in the plural it is now almost exclusively applied to food and drink.

When we need
Refreshment, whether food or talk between,
Food of the mind.
Milton, P. L., ix. 237.

Having taken a little *refreshment*, we went to the Latin Convent, at which all Frank Pilgrims are wont to be entertained.
Maundrell, Aleppo to Jerusalem, p. 67.

Such honest *refreshments* and comforts of life our Christian liberty has made it lawful for us to use. *Bp. Sprat.*

"May I offer you any *refreshment*, Mr. ——? I haven't the advantage of your name." *Thackeray*, Pendennis, xv.

Refreshment Sunday, the fourth Sunday in Lent; Mid-lent Sunday. The name of *Refreshment* or *Refection Sunday* (*Dominica Refectionis*) is generally explained as referring to the feeding of the multitude mentioned in the Gospel for the day (John vi. 1–14). Also called *Bragget Sunday*, *Jerusalem Sunday*, *Lætare*, *Mothering Sunday*, *Rose Sunday*, *Simnel Sunday*.

refret†, refrete†, *n.* See *refrait*.

refrication† (ref-ri-kā'shon), *n.* [< L. *refricare*, rub or scratch open again, < *re-*, again, + *fricare*, rub: see *friction*.] A rubbing up afresh.

In these legal sacrifices there is a continual *refrication* of the memory of those sins every year which we have committed.
Bp. Hall, Hard Texts, Heb. x. 3.

refrigerant (rē-frij'e-rant), *a.* and *n.* [< OF. *refrigerant*, F. *réfrigérant* = Sp. Pg. *refrigerante* = It. *refrigerante*, *rifrigerante*, < L. *refrigeran(t-)s*, ppr. of *refrigerare*, make cool, grow cool again: see *refrigerate*.] **I.** *a.* Abating heat; cooling.

Unctuous liniments or salves . . . devised as lenitive and *refrigerant*.
Holland, tr. of Pliny, xxxiv. 18.

II. *n.* **1.** Anything which abates the sensation of heat, or cools.—**2.** Figuratively, anything which allays or extinguishes.

This almost never fails to prove a *refrigerant* to passion.
Blair.

refrigerate (rē-frij'e-rāt), *v. t.*; pret. and pp. *refrigerated*, ppr. *refrigerating*. [< L. *refrigeratus*, pp. of *refrigerare* (> It. *refrigerare*, *rifrigerare* = Sp. Pg. *refrigerar* = F. *réfrigérer*), make cool again, < *re-*, again, + *frigerare*, make cool: see *frigerate*.] To cool; make cold; allay the heat of.

The great brizes which the motion of the air in great circles (such as are under the girdle of the world) produceth, which do *refrigerate*.
Bacon, Nat. Hist., § 398.

The air is intolerably cold, either continually *refrigerated* with frosts or disturbed with tempests.
Goldsmith, Animated Nature, I. 142.

refrigerate† (rē-frij'e-rāt), *a.* [< ME. *refrigerate*, < L. *refrigeratus*, pp.: see the verb.] Cooled; made or kept cool; allayed.

Nowe benes, . . .
. . . upplucked soone,
Made clene, and sette up wel *refrigerate*,
From grobbes saue wol kepe up theire estate.
Palladius, Husbondrie (E. E. T. S.), p. 100.

refrigerating-chamber (rē-frij'e-rā-ting-chām"bėr), *n.* A chamber in which the air is artificially cooled, used especially for the storage of perishable provisions during warm weather.

refrigerating-machine (rē-frij'e-rā-ting-ma-shēn"), *n.* A machine for the artificial production of cold. In such machines mechanical power is employed for the conversion of heat into work by operating upon a gas at a temperature far removed from that at which such gas becomes a liquid. They perform the following cycle of operations: first, the gas is compressed into a smaller volume, in which compression its contained heat is increased by the heat-equivalent of the work performed in the compression; secondly, the compressed gas is cooled under constant pressure, and thus brought near to the temperature of the cooling medium (usually water), and the increase of heat due to compression is removed; thirdly, the compressed and cooled gas is permitted to expand, expending a portion of its expansive force in the performance of work. This work having been performed at the expense of the store of heat originally contained in the gas, the latter has now lost the heat-equivalent of the work, and its temperature is greatly lowered. The now cold gas can be used for the refrigeration of any other substance which has a higher temperature by methods described under *ice-machine* and *refrigeration*. In other machines a gas or vapor the ordinary temperature of which is near to that at which it liquefies is compressed and cooled, and subsequently permitted to assume the gaseous form. By the compression the temperature of liquefaction is raised till it becomes the same as or a little higher than that of a conveniently available cooling medium, such as ordinary atmospheric air, or, most commonly, water at ordinary temperature, the application of which to cooling the gas still under constant pressure reduces it to the liquid state, or to a state of intermixed liquid and gas. The subsequent expansion of the liquid into gas is performed at the expense of its inner heat. It therefore suffers a reduction of temperature, to restore which it absorbs its latent heat of vaporization from a surrounding or contiguous substance (usually a saline solution), which, thus made cold, is used for cooling air-spaces, or refrigerators or substances therein contained, or for making ice. Machines of either of the above classes are very commonly called *ice-machines*, and are so styled in the classifications of inventions in both the United States and British patent-offices, whether designed for the manufacture of ice, for merely cooling substances in insulated spaces or refrigerators, or for both these purposes.

refrigeration (rē-frij-e-rā'shon), *n.* [< OF. *refrigeration*, F. *réfrigération* = Sp. *refrigeracion* = Pg. *refrigeração* = It. *refrigerazione*, < L. *refrigeratio(n-)*, a cooling, coolness, mitigation (of diseases), < *refrigerare*, pp. *refrigeratus*, make cool again: see *refrigerate*.] **1.** The act of refrigerating or cooling; the abatement of heat; the state of being cooled.

Suche thynges as are fyned by continuall heate, mouynge, and circulation are hyndered by *refrigeration* or coulde.
R. Eden, tr. of Jacobus Gastaldus (First Books on America, ed. Arber, p. 294).

The testimony of geological evidence . . . indicates a general *refrigeration* of climate.
Croll, Climate and Time, p. 530.

Specifically—**2.** The operation of cooling various substances by artificial processes. This is effected by the use of inclosures in which the articles to be cooled are placed on or in proximity to ice or other refrigerating substances or freezing-mixtures, or in air cooled by a refrigerating-machine or -apparatus; or, as in beer-cooling, by floating metallic pans or vessels containing ice upon the surface of the liquid to be cooled, or by circulating the latter over an extended surface of some good conductor of heat cooled by continuous contact of cold water, cold air, or cold brine with the opposite surface. See *ice-machine* and *refrigerating-machine*.—**Chemical refrigeration**, refrigeration by the use of mixtures of substances which, during their admixture, by mutual solution of each in the other, or the solution of one or more in another or others, become lowered in temperature by absorption of the latent heat of liquefaction from the sensible heat. Remarkable changes of temperature are thus produced by a variety of refrigerating mixtures or freezing-mixtures. See *freezing-mixture*.—**Mechanical refrigeration.** (*a*) In its strictest sense, the conversion of heat into work by the expansion of a volume of gas or vapor which performs work during the act of expansion, as in moving a piston against some resistance, usually that of a pump or compressor for compressing another volume of such gas or vapor. The gas during the expansion, if it expands adiabatically, is reduced in temperature by the conversion of its inner heat into work, the reduction being found in degrees by dividing the work due to the expansion by the product of the specific heat of the gas, the weight of the volume expanded, and the mechanical equivalent of heat. Air mechanically refrigerated is frequently discharged directly into refrigerators or rooms it is desired to cool, but in apparatus for cooling by the use of other gases and vapors a strong solution of some salt which resists freezing at low temperatures — as sodium, calcium, or magnesium chlorid — is used as a medium for extracting heat from the substances and spaces to be cooled, and as a vehicle for conveying the heat so abstracted to the mechanically cooled gas. See *ice-machine*. (*b*) In a broader sense, a process of refrigeration in which the cycle of heat-changes is only partly produced by mechanical action, as in compression ice-machines using anhydrous ammonia, wherein the cooling of the vapor takes place entirely during the formation from the liquid, and is caused by absorption of the latent heat of vaporization from the sensible heat of the substance, the mechanical part of the process being wholly confined to compressing the ammonia-vapor while liquefying it under the action of cold and pressure. Such machines are the most effective and the most extensively used.

refrigerative (rẹ̄-frij'e-rā-tiv), *a.* and *n.* [= OF. *refrigeratif*, F. *réfrigératif* = Sp. Pg. *refrigerativo* = It. *refrigerativo*, *rifrigerativo*; as *refrigerate* + *-ive*.] **I.** *a.* Cooling; refrigerant: as, a *refrigerative* treatment.

All lectuces are by nature *refrigerative*, and doe coole the bodie. *Holland*, tr. of Pliny, xix. 8.

II. *n.* A medicine that allays the sensation of heat; a refrigerant.

refrigerator (rẹ̄-frij'e-rā-tor), *n.* [< *refrigerate* + *-or*1.] That which refrigerates, cools, or keeps cool; specifically, any vessel, chamber, or apparatus designed to keep its contents at a temperature little if at all above the freezing-point. In a restricted sense, a refrigerator is an inclosed chamber or compartment where meats, fish, fruit, or liquors, etc., are kept cool by the presence of ice or freezing-mixtures, or by the circulation of currents of cold air or liquid supplied by an ice-machine or a refrigerating-machine. Domestic refrigerators are made in a great variety of shapes, and may be either portable or built into the walls of a house. They range from the common ice-box (which in its simplest form is merely a metal-lined wooden box with facilities for drainage, kept partly filled with ice on which fish or meat may be kept) to large and elaborate ice-chests and ice-rooms. Small refrigerators are sometimes called *ice-safes*.—**Anesthetic refrigerator.** See *anesthetic*.

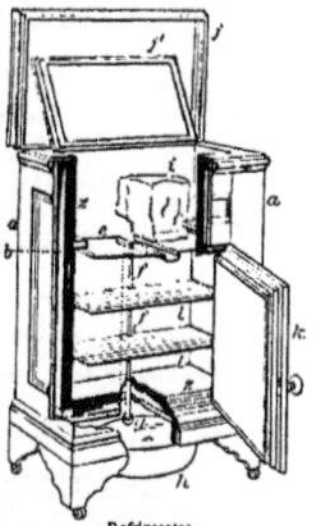

Refrigerator.
a, body of the refrigerator; *b*, paper sheathing; *c*, a shelf for supporting ice; *d*, drip-pipe; *e*, air-trap; *h*, drip-pan; *f*, *f*, lids covering ice-chamber; *k*, door of compartment containing shelves *l*, of corrugated galvanized iron, on which are supported the articles to be preserved by refrigeration; *s*, zinc lining.

refrigerator-car (rẹ̄-frij'e-rā-tor-kär), *n.* A freight-car fitted up for the preservation by means of cold of perishable merchandise. Such cars are supplied with an ice-chamber, and sometimes with a blower, which is driven by a belt from one axle of the car, and causes a constant circulation of air over the ice and through the car. [U. S.]

refrigeratory (rẹ̄-frij'e-rā-tō-ri), *a.* and *n.* [= Sp. Pg. It. *refrigeratorio*, < L. *refrigeratorius*, cooling, refrigeratory, < *refrigerare*, pp. *refrigeratus*, cool: see *refrigerate*.] **I.** *a.* Cooling; mitigating heat.

This grateful acid spirit that first comes over is . . . highly *refrigeratory*, diuretic, sudorific. *Bp. Berkeley*, tr. of Siris, § 120.

II. *n.*; pl. *refrigeratories* (-riz). Anything which refrigerates; a refrigerant; a refrigerator; any vessel, chamber, or pipe in which cooling is effected.

A delicate wine, and a durable *refrigeratory*. *Mortimer.*

refrigerium† (ref-ri-jē'ri-um), *n.* [= It. Sp. Pg. *refrigerio*, a cooling, mitigation, consolation, < LL. *refrigerium*, < L. *refrigerare*, make cool: see *refrigerate*.] Cooling refreshment; refrigeration.

It must be acknowledged, the ancients have talked much of annual *refrigeriums*. *South.*

refringe†, *v. t.* [< L. *refringere*, break up, break open, < *re-*, back, + *frangere*, break: see *fraction*. Cf. *refract*, *refrain*2, and *infringe*.] To infringe upon. *Palsgrave.* (*Halliwell.*)

refringency (rẹ̄-frin'jen-si), *n.* [< *refringen(t)* + *-cy*.] The power of a substance to refract a ray; refringent or refractive power.

refringent (rẹ̄-frin'jent), *a.* [< F. *réfringent* = Sp. *refringente*, < L. *refringen(t-)s*, ppr. of *refringere*, break up, break off: see *refract*.] Possessing the quality of refractiveness; refractive; refracting: as, a *refringent* prism. [Rare.]

Refraction is the deflection or bending which luminous rays experience in passing obliquely from one medium to another. . . . According as the refracted ray approaches or deviates from the normal, the second medium is said to be more or less *refringent* or refracting than the first. *Atkinson*, tr. of Ganot's Physics (10th ed.), § 536.

refroide†, *v.* Same as *refreid*.

reft1 (reft). Preterit and past participle of *reave*.

reft2†, **refte**†, *n.* Obsolete forms of *rift*1.

refuge1 (ref'ūj), *n.* [< ME. *refuge*, < OF. (and F.) *refuge* = Pr. *refug*, *refuch* = Sp. Pg. It. *refugio*, < L. *refugium*, a taking refuge, refuge, a place of refuge, < *refugere*, flee back, retreat, < *re-*, back, + *fugere*, flee: see *fugitive*. Cf. *refuit*, *refute*2.] **1.** Shelter or protection from danger or distress.

And as thou art a rightful lord and juge,
Ne yeve us neither mercy ne *refuge*.
Chaucer, Knight's Tale, l. 862.

Rocks, dens, and caves! But I in none of these
Find place or *refuge*. *Milton*, P. L., ix. 119.

2. That which shelters or protects from danger, distress, or calamity; a stronghold which protects by its strength, or a sanctuary which secures safety by its sacredness; any place where one is out of the way of a threatened danger or evil; specifically, an institution where the destitute or homeless find temporary shelter; an asylum.

God is our *refuge* and strength, a very present help in trouble. Ps. xlvi. 1.

The high hills are a *refuge* for the wild goats, and the rocks for the conies. Ps. civ. 18.

Drawn from his *refuge* in some lonely elm,
. . . ventures forth . . .
The squirrel. *Cowper*, Task, vi. 310.

3. An expedient to secure protection, defense, or excuse; a device; a contrivance; a shift; a resource.

Their latest *refuge*
Was to send him. *Shak.*, Cor., v. 3. 11.

O, teach me how to make mine own excuse!
Or at the least this *refuge* let me find;
Though my gross blood be stain'd with this abuse,
Immaculate and spotless is my mind.
Shak., Lucrece, l. 1654.

A youth unknown to Phœbus, in despair,
Puts his last *refuge* all in heaven and prayer.
Pope, Dunciad, ii. 214.

Patriotism is the last *refuge* of a scoundrel.
Johnson, in Boswell, an. 1775.

City of Refuge. See *city*.—**Harbor of refuge.** See *harbor*1.—**House of refuge,** an institution for the shelter of the homeless or destitute.—**School of refuge,** a charity, ragged, or industrial school. Also called *boys'* or *girls' house of refuge*. =**Syn. 1.** Safety, security.—**2.** Asylum, retreat, sanctuary, harbor, covert.

refuge1 (ref'ūj), *v.*; pret. and pp. *refuged*, ppr. *refuging*. [< OF. *refugier*, F. *réfugier* = Sp. Pg. *refugiar* = It. *refugiare*, take refuge; from the noun.] **I.** *trans.* To shelter; protect; find refuge or excuse for.

Silly beggars,
Who, sitting in the stocks, *refuge* their shame,
That many have and others must sit there.
Shak., Rich. II., v. 5. 26.

Even by those gods who *refuged* her abhorred.
Dryden, Æneid, ii. 782.

II. *intrans.* To take shelter. [Rare.]

The Duke de Soubise *refuged* hether from France upon miscarriage of some undertakings of his there.
Sir J. Finett, Foreign Ambassadors, p. 111.

Upon the crags
Which verge the northern shore, upon the heights
Eastward, how few have *refuged*! *Southey.*

refuge2 (ref'ūj), *n.* A dialectal form of *refuse*2. *Halliwell.*

refugee (ref-ū-jē'), *n.* [< F. *réfugié* (= Sp. Pg. *refugiado* = It. *refugiato*), pp. of *réfugier*, take refuge: see *refuge*1, *v.*] **1.** One who flees to a refuge or shelter or place of safety.

Under whatever name, the city on the rocks, small at first, strengthened by *refugees* from Salona, grew and prospered. *E. A. Freeman*, Venice, p. 229.

2. One who in times of persecution or political commotion flees to a foreign country for safety.

Poor *refugees* at first, they purchase here;
And soon as denizen'd they domineer.
Dryden, tr. of Satires of Juvenal, iii.

3. One of a band of marauders during the American Revolution: so called because they placed themselves under the refuge or protection of the British crown: same as *cow-boy*, 3.

refugeeism (ref-ū-jē'izm), *n.* [< *refugee* + *-ism*.] The state or condition of a refugee.

A Pole, or Czech, or something of that fermenting sort, in a state of political *refugeeism*.
George Eliot, Daniel Deronda, xxii.

refuit†, *n.* [ME., also *refuyt*, *refute*, *refut*, *refutt*, < OF. *refuit*, *refuyt*, *refui*, m., *refuite*, *refute*, F. *refuite*, f., flight, escape, < *refuir*, flee, < L. *refugere*, flee: see *refuge*1.] Refuge; protection.

Thou art largesse of pleyn felicitee,
Havene of *refute*, of quiete, and of reste.
Chaucer, A. B. C., l. 14.

How myght ye youre-self guyde that may nought se to bore a baner in bateile of a kynge that ought to be *refute* and counfort to alle the hoste.
Merlin (E. E. T. S.), iii. 622.

refulgence (rẹ̄-ful'jens), *n.* [< OF. *refulgence* = Sp. Pg. *refulgencia* = It. *refulgenza*, < L. *refulgentia*, reflected luster, refulgence, < *refulgen(t-)s*, refulgent: see *refulgent*.] The state or character of being refulgent; a flood of light; splendor; brilliancy.

A bar of ore, the heat and *refulgence* of which were almost insupportable to me at ten feet distance.
Wraxall, Tour through Northern Parts of Europe, p. 169.

=**Syn.** *Effulgence*, *Splendor*, etc. (see *radiance*), brightness.

refulgency (rẹ̄-ful'jen-si), *n.* [As *refulgence* (see *-cy*).] Same as *refulgence*.

refulgent (rẹ̄-ful'jent), *a.* [< OF. *refulgent*, F. *refulgent* = Sp. Pg. *refulgente* = It. *rifulgente*, < L. *refulgen(t-)s*, ppr. of *refulgere*, flash back, shine brilliantly, < *re-*, back, + *fulgere*, flash, shine: see *fulgent*.] Emitting or reflecting a bright light; shining; splendid.

If those *refulgent* beams of Heav'n's great light
Gild not the day, what is the day but night?
Quarles, Emblems, v. 12.

Where some *refulgent* sunset of India
Streams o'er a rich ambrosial ocean isle.
Tennyson, Experiments, Milton.

refulgently (rẹ̄-ful'jent-li), *adv.* With refulgence; with great brightness.

refund1 (rẹ̄-fund'), *v. t.* [< OF. *refondre*, remelt, recast, *refondre*, *refonder*, restore, pay back, F. *refondre*, remelt, recast, remodel, reform, = Pr. *refondre* = Sp. Pg. *refundir*, pour out again, = It. *rifondere*, pour out, remelt, recast, < L. *refundere*, pour back, restore, < *re-*, back, + *fundere*, pour: see *refound*2. The OF. *refondre*, in the form *refonder*, in the sense 'restore,' seems to be confused with *refonder*, *refunder*, reëstablish, rebuild, restore: see *refound*1. In def. 2 the E. verb appar. associated with *fund*1, *n.* Cf. *refund*2.] **1**†. To pour back.

Were the humours of the eye tinctured with any color, they would *refund* that colour upon the object.
Ray, Works of Creation, ii.

2. To return in payment or compensation for what has been taken; repay; restore.

With this you have repaid me two thousand Pound, and if you did not *refund* thus honestly, I could not have supply'd her. *Steele*, Tender Husband, i. 1.

3. To resupply with funds; reimburse; indemnify. [Rare.]

The painter has a demand . . . to be fully *refunded*, both for his disgraces, his losses, and the apparent danger of his life. *Swift*, to Bp. Horte, May 12, 1736.

Refunding Act, a United States statute of July 14th, 1870, providing for the issue of 5, 4½, and 4 per cent. bonds, and for devoting the proceeds to the redemption of outstanding bonds.

refund1 (rẹ̄-fund'), *n.* [< *refund*1, *v.*] Repayment; return of money. [Colloq.]

Their lots were confiscated; no *refund* was made of the purchase money or compensation allowed for improvements. *Pop. Sci. Mo.*, XXVIII. 784.

No *refund* of duty shall be allowed after the lapse of fourteen days from the time of entry.
U. S. Cons. Reports (1886), No. 72, p. 532.

refund2 (rẹ̄-fund'), *v. t.* [< *re-* + *fund*1.] To fund again or anew, as a public debt.

refunder1 (rẹ̄-fun'dėr), *n.* [< *refund*1 + *-er*1.] One who refunds or repays.

refunder2 (rẹ̄-fun'dėr), *n.* [< *refund*2 + *-er*1.] One who refunds or favors refunding or funding anew.

refundment (rẹ̄-fund'ment), *n.* [< *refund*1 + *-ment*.] The act of refunding or returning in payment or compensation that which has been borrowed or taken; also, that which is refunded.

Church land, alienated to lay uses, was formerly denounced to have this slippery quality (like thawing snow). But some portions of it somehow always stuck so fast that the denunciators have been fain to postpone the prophecy of *refundment* to a late posterity.
Lamb, Popular Fallacies, ii.

refurbish (rē-fėr'bish), *v. t.* [< *re-* + *furbish*. Cf. OF. *reforbir*, *refourbir*, F. *refourbir* = It. *riforbire*, refurbish.] To furbish anew; polish up.

It requires a better poet to *refurbish* a trite thought than to exhibit an original.
Landor, Imaginary Conversations, Abbe Delille and Walter Landor.

refurnish (rē-fėr'nish), *v. t.* [< *re-* + *furnish*. Cf. OF. *refournir*, F. *refournir* = It. *rifornire*, refurnish.] To furnish or supply anew; refit with furniture.

By his moste excellent witte, he (Henry VII.) . . . reulued the lawes, . . . *refurnisshed* his dominions, and repayred his manours. *Sir T. Elyot*, The Governour, i. 24.

refusable (rẹ̄-fū'za-bl), *a.* [< OF. (and F.) *refusable*; as *refuse*1 + *-able*.] Capable of being refused; admitting refusal.

A *refusable* or little thing in one's eye.
Young, Sermons, ii.

refusal (rẹ̄-fū'zal), *n.* [< AF. *refusal*; as *refuse*1 + *-al*.] **1.** The act of refusing; denial or rejection of anything demanded, solicited, or offered for acceptance.

For upon theyr *refusall* and forsakinge of the gospell, the same was to you by so muche yͤ rather offered. *J. Udall*, On Rom. xi.

I beseech you
That my *refusal* of so great an offer
May make no ill construction.
Fletcher, Spanish Curate, i. 1.

2. The choice of refusing or taking; the right of taking in preference to others; option of buying; preëmption.

I mean to be a suitor to your worship
For the small tenement. . . .
Why, if your worship give me but your hand,
That I may have the *refusal*, I have done.
B. Jonson, Volpone, v. 4.

Neighbour Steel's wife asked to have the *refusal* of it, but I guess I won't sell it. *Haliburton.*

Barnard's Act [passed in 1735], which avoided and prohibited all speculative dealings in the British public funds, "puts" and *refusals*, and even such ordinary transactions as selling stocks which the vendor has not in his possession at the time. *Nineteenth Century*, XXVI. 852.

3. In *hydraul. engin.*, the resistance of a pile at any point to further driving.—**To buy the refusal of.** See *buy*.

refuse[1] (rē-fūz'), *v.*; pret. and pp. *refused*, ppr. *refusing*. [< ME. *refusen*, *reffusen*, < OF. *refuser*, *reufuser*, *ranfuser*, F. *refuser* = Sp. *rehusar* = Pg. *refusar* = It. *rifusare*, refuse, deny, reject; origin uncertain; perhaps (1) < LL. **refusare*, freq. of L. *refundere*, pp. *refusus*, pour back, give back, restore (see *refund*[1], and cf. *refuse*[2]); or (2) irreg. < L. *refutare*, refuse (see *refute*[1]), perhaps by confusion with *recusare*, refuse (see *recuse*); or (3) < OF. *refus*, refuse, leavings (see *refuse*[2]).] **I.** *trans.* **1.** To deny, as a request, demand, or invitation; decline to do or grant: as, to *refuse* admittance; she *refused* herself to callers.

Accepteth than of us the trewe entente,
That never yet *refuseden* your heste.
Chaucer, Clerk's Tale, l. 72.

If you *refuse* your aid
In this so never-needed help, yet do not
Upbraid 's with our distress. *Shak.*, Cor., v. 1. 33.

He then went to the town-hall; on their *refusing* him entrance, he burst open the door with his foot, and seated himself abruptly. *Walpole*, Letters, II. 2.

2. To decline to accept; reject: as, to *refuse* an office; to *refuse* an offer.

And quhome ʒe aucht for to *refuse*
Frome that gret office, chairge, and cure.
Lauder, Dewtie of Kyngis (E. E. T. S.), l. 508.

The stone which the builders *refused* is become the head stone of the corner. Ps. cxviii. 22.

I, Anthony Lumpkin, Esquire, of Blank place, *refuse* you, Constantia Neville, spinster, of no place at all.
Goldsmith, She Stoops to Conquer, v.

3†. To disown; disavow; forsake. *Nares.* ["God *refuse* me!" was formerly a fashionable imprecation.]

Reffuse me nat oute of your Reme[m]braunce.
Political Poems, etc. (ed. Furnivall), p. 41.

He that yn yowthͤ no vertue wyll vse,
In Age all honour wyll hym *Refuse*.
Booke of Precedence (E. E. T. S., extra ser.), i. 68.

Deny thy father, and *refuse* thy name.
Shak., R. and J., ii. 2. 34.

4. *Milit.*, to hold (troops) back, or move (them) back from the regular alinement, when about to engage the enemy in battle. In the oblique order of battle, if either flank attack, the other flank is *refused*.—5. Fail to receive; resist; repel.

The acid, by destroying the alkali on the lithographic chalk, causes the stone to *refuse* the printing ink except where touched by the chalk.
Workshop Receipts, 1st ser., p. 152.

=**Syn. 1** and **2.** *Decline, Refuse, Reject, Repel*, and *Rebuff* are in the order of strength.

II. *intrans.* To decline to accept or consent; fail to comply.

Our [women's] hearts are form'd, as you yourselves would choose,
Too proud to ask, too humble to *refuse*.
Garth, Epil. to Addison's Cato.

Free in his will to choose or to *refuse*,
Man may improve the crisis, or abuse.
Cowper, Progress of Error, l. 25.

refuse[1]† (rē-fūz'), *n.* [< ME. *refuse*, < OF. *refus*, m., *refuse*, f., = It. *refuso*, m., a refusal; from the verb: see *refuse*[1], *v.* Cf. *refuse*[2].] A refusal.

He hathe hurte ful fele that list to make
A yifte lightly, that put is in *refuse*.
Political Poems, etc. (ed. Furnivall), p. 70.

Thy face tempts my soul to leave the heavens for thee,
And thy words of *refuse* do pour even hell on me.
Sir P. Sidney (Arber's Eng. Garner, I. 567).

refuse[2] (ref'ūs), *n.* and *a.* [< ME. *refus*, *refuce*, < OF. *refus*, *reffus*, repulse, refusal, rejection (*faire refus de* . . . , object to, refuse, *à refus*, so as to cause rejection, *etre de refus*, be refused, *cerf de refus*, a refuse stag, etc.), associated with the verb *refuser*, refuse, and prob. < L. *refusus*, pp. of *refundere*, pour back, give back, restore: see *refuse*[1], *refund*[1]. Some confusion may have existed with OF. *refus*, refugee, *refus*, *refuit*, refuge: see *refuit*, *refute*[2].] **I.** *n.* That which is refused or rejected; waste or useless matter; the worst or meanest part; rubbish.

Thou hast made us as *refuse*. Lam. iii. 45.

Yet man, laborious man, by slow degrees . . .
Gleans up the *refuse* of the general spoil.
Cowper, Heroism, l. 70.

Shards and scurf of salt, and scum of dross,
Old plash of rains, and *refuse* patch'd with moss.
Tennyson, Vision of Sin, v.

= **Syn.** Dregs, scum, dross, trash, rubbish.

II. *a.* Refused; rejected; hence, worthless; of no value: as, the *refuse* parts of stone or timber.

To sen me languyshinge,
That am *refus* of every creature.
Chaucer, Troilus, i. 570.

They fought not against them, but with the *refuse* and scattered people of the overthrown army his father had lost before. *North*, tr. of Plutarch, p. 207.

Everything that was vile and *refuse*, that they destroyed utterly. 1 Sam. xv. 9.

refuse[3] (rē-fūz'), *v. t.* [< *re-* + *fuse*[1], *v.*] To fuse or melt again.

refuser (rẹ-fū'zėr), *n.* One who refuses or rejects.

The only *refusers* and condemners of this catholic practice. *Jer. Taylor.*

refusion (rē-fū'zhọn), *n.* [< OF. *refusion*, F. *réfusion* = It. *rifusione*, < L. *refusio(n-)*, an overflowing, < *refundere*, pp. *refusus*, pour back: see *refuse*[1], *refund*.] **1.** A renewed or repeated melting or fusion.—**2.** The act of pouring back; a reflowing.

It hath been objected to me that this doctrine of the *refusion* of the soul was very consistent with the belief of a future state of rewards and punishments, in the intermediate space between death and the resolution of the soul into the τὸ ἕν. *Warburton*, Legation, iii., note cc.

refutability (rẹ-fū-tạ-bil'ị-ti), *n.* [< *refutable* + *-ity* (see *-bility*).] Capability of being refuted.

refutable (rẹ-fū'tạ-bl), *a.* [= OF. **refutable* = Sp. *refutable* = Pg. *refutavel*; as *refute*[1] + *-able*.] Capable of being refuted or disproved; that may be proved false or erroneous.

He alters the text, and creates a *refutable* doctrine of his own. *Junius*, Letters, liv.

refutably (rẹ-fū'tạ-bli), *adv.* In a refutable manner; so as to be refuted or disproved.

refutal (rẹ-fū'tạl), *n.* [< *refute*[1] + *-al*.] Refutation. [Rare.]

A living *refutal* of the lie that a good soldier must needs be depraved. *National Baptist*, XXI. xiii. 1.

refutation (ref-ụ-tā'shọn), *n.* [< OF. *refutation*, F. *réfutation* = Sp. *refutacion* = Pg. *refutação* = It. *rifutazione*, < L. *refutatio(n-)*, a refutation, < *refutare*, pp. *refutatus*, refute: see *refute*[1].] The act of refuting or disproving; the overthrowing of an argument, opinion, testimony, doctrine, or theory by argument or countervailing proof; confutation; disproof. *Refutation* is distinguished as direct or ostensive, indirect or apagogical, a priori or a posteriori, according to the kind of reasoning employed.

It was answered by another boke called the *Refutacion* or Ouercommyng of the appollogie, of the conuencion of Madrill. *Hall*, Hen. VIII., an. 18.

As for the first interpretation, because it is altogether wasted, it nedeth no *refutation*.
Caluine, Declaration on the Eighty-seventh Psalm.

The error referred to . . . is too obvious to require a particular *refutation*.
Bushnell, Nature and the Supernat., xi.

refutatory (rẹ-fū'tạ-tọ-ri), *a.* [< F. *réfutatoire* = Sp. Pg. *refutatorio*, < LL. *refutatorius*, of or belonging to refutation, refutatory, < L. *refutare*, pp. *refutatus*, refute: see *refute*[1].] Tending to refute; containing refutation.

refute[1] (rẹ-fūt'), *v. t.*; pret. and pp. *refuted*, ppr. *refuting*. [< OF. *refuter*, refute, confute, F. *réfuter* = Sp. Pg. *refutar* = It. *rifutare*, *refutare*, < L. *refutare*, check, drive back, repress, repel, rebut, etc., < *re-* + **futare* as in *confutare*, confute: see *confute*.] **1.** To disprove and overthrow by argument or countervailing proof; prove to be false or erroneous: as, to *refute* a doctrine or an accusation.

And then the Law of Nations gainst her rose,
And reasons brought that no man could *refute*.
Spenser, F. Q., V. ix. 44.

Then I began to *refute* that foule error, howbeit my speach did nothing at all preuaile with him.
Hakluyt's Voyages, II. 60.

How wilt thou reason with them, how *refute*
Their idolisms, traditions, paradoxes?
Milton, P. R., iv. 233.

And he says much that many may dispute,
And cavil at with ease, but none *refute*.
Cowper, Truth, l. 360.

2. To overcome in argument; prove to be in error: as, to *refute* a disputant.

There were so many witnesses to these two miracles that it is impossible to *refute* such multitudes. *Addison.*

=**Syn. 1.** *Confute* and *Refute* agree in representing a quick and thorough answer to assertions made by another. *Confute* applies to arguments, *refute* to both arguments and charges.

refute[2]†, *n.* See *refuit*.

refuter (rẹ-fū'tėr), *n.* One who or that which refutes.

My *refuter's* forehead is stronger, with a weaker wit.
Bp. Hall, Honour of Married Clergy, i. § 3.

reg. An abbreviation of (*a*) *regent*; (*b*) *register*; (*c*) *registrar*; (*d*) *regular*; (*e*) *regularly*.

regain (rẹ-gān'), *v. t.* [< OF. *regaignier*, *regaagner*, *rewaignier*, F. *regagner* (= Sp. *reganar* = Pg. *reganhar* = It. *riguadagnare*), < *re-*, again, + *gaagnier*, *gaigner*, gain: see *gain*[1].] **1.** To gain anew; recover, as what has escaped or been lost; retrieve.

But by degrees, first this, then that *regain'd*,
The turning tide bears back with flowing chance
Unto the Dauphin all we had attain'd.
Daniel, Civil Wars, v. 44.

If our Fathers have lost their Liberty, why may not we labour to *regain* it? *Selden*, Table-Talk, p. 40.

Hopeful to *regain*
Thy love, the sole contentment of my heart.
Milton, P. L., x. 972.

Ah, love! although the morn shall come again,
And on new rose-buds the new sun shall smile,
Can we *regain* what we have lost meanwhile?
William Morris, Earthly Paradise, I. 338.

2. To arrive at again; return to; succeed in reaching once more: as, they *regained* the shore in safety.

The leap was quick, return was quick, he has *regain'd* the place. *Leigh Hunt*, The Glove and the Lions.

= **Syn. 1.** To repossess.

regal[1] (rē'gạl), *a.* and *n.* [< ME. *regal*, *regall*, < OF. *regal*, regal, royal (as a noun, a royal vestment), in vernacular form *real*, F. *réal* (> E. *real*[2]) and *royal* (> E. royal); = Pr. *reial*, *rial* = Sp. Pg. *real* (> E. *real*[3], a coin) = It. *regale*, *reale*, < L. *regalis*, royal, kingly, < *rex* (*reg-*), a king: see *rex*. Cf. *real*[2], *real*[3], *royal*, *regale*[2].] **I.** *a.* Pertaining to a king; kingly; royal: as, a *regal* title; *regal* authority; *regal* pomp.

Most manifest it is that these [the pyramids], as the rest, were the *regall* sepulchres of the Ægyptians.
Sandys, Travailes, p. 99.

With them [Ithuriel and Zephon] comes a third of *regal* port,
But faded splendour wan. *Milton*, P. L., iv. 869.

Among the gems will be found some portraits of kings in the Macedonian period, which may be best studied in connexion with the *regal* coins of the same period.
C. T. Newton, Art and Archæol., p. 374.

Regal or **royal fishes**, whales and sturgeons: so called from an enactment of Edward II. that when thrown ashore or caught on the British coasts they can be claimed as the property of the sovereign.=**Syn.** *Kingly*, etc. See *royal*.

II.† *n. pl.* Royalty; royal authority.

Now be we duchesses, both I and ye,
And sikered to the *regals* of Athenes.
Chaucer, Good Women, l. 2128.

regal[2] (rē'gạl), *n.* [Early mod. E. *regall*, *regalle*, also *rigole*, *regole*; < OF. *regale*, F. *régale*, < OIt. *regale*, a regal, It. *regale*, a hand-organ (Sp. *regalia*, an organ-pipe), < *regale*, regal, royal, < L. *regalis*, regal, royal: see *regal*[1].] **1.** A small portable organ, much used in the sixteenth and seventeenth centuries, consisting of one or sometimes two sets of reed-pipes played with keys for the player's right hand, with a small bellows for the left hand. Its compass included only a few tones. In many cases the instrument was made to shut up within covers, like a large book: hence the name *Bible-organ*. If there was but one pipe to each note, the instrument was called a *single regal*, if two pipes to each note, a *double regal*. The invention of the regal is often erroneously ascribed to Roll, an organ-builder of Nuremberg, in 1575; the instrument was common in England in the reign of Henry VIII. It is now obsolete, but the name is still applied in Germany to certain reed-stops

Regal.
(From an old painting.)

of the organ. In England a single instrument was usually called a *pair of regals*.

With dulsemers and the *regalls*,
Sweet sittrons melody.
Leighton, Teares or Lamentations (1613). (*Halliwell.*)

And in *regals* (where they have a pipe they call the nightingale pipe, which containeth water) the sound hath a continuall trembling. *Bacon*, Nat. Hist., § 172.

Representations of *regals* shew as if they were fastened to the shoulder, while the right hand touches the keys, and the left is employed in blowing a small pair of bellows. *Gentleman's Mag.*, LXXIV. 328.

2. An old instrument of percussion, composed of sonorous slabs or slips of wood. It was a sort of harmonica, and was played by striking the slips of wood with a stick armed with a ball or knob.

regale[1] (rē-gāl'), *v.*; pret. and pp. *regaled*, ppr. *regaling*. [< OF. *regaler*, *regalier*, F. *régaler*, entertain, regale (= Sp. *regalar*, entertain, caress, fondle, pet, = Pg. *regalar*, entertain, charm, please, = It. *regalare*, entertain, treat); of doubtful origin: (*a*) in one view orig. 'treat like a king,' 'treat royally,' < *regal*, royal (cf. OF. *regaler*, *regaller*, take by royal authority) (see *regal*[1]); (*b*) in another view, lit. 'rejoice oneself,' < *re-* + *galer*, rejoice: see *gala*[1]; (c) the Sp. is identified by Diez with *regalar*, melt, < L. *regelare*, melt, thaw, warm, lit. 'unfreeze,' < *re-*, back, + *gelare*, freeze: see *congeal*, and cf. *regelation*; (*d*) cf. OF. *regaler*, *regaller*, divide or share equally, distribute, equalize, < *re-* + *egal*, equal: see *egal*, *equal*.] I. *trans.* To entertain sumptuously or delightfully; feast or divert with that which is highly pleasing; gratify, as the senses: as, to *regale* the taste, the eye, or the ear.

The Portuguese general then invited the monks on board his vessel, where he *regaled* them, and gave to each presents that were most suitable to their austere life.
Bruce, Source of the Nile, II. 144.

Every old burgher had a budget of miraculous stories to tell about the exploits of Hardkoppig Piet, wherewith he *regaled* his children of a long winter night.
Irving, Knickerbocker, p. 361.

Heliogabalus and Galerius are reported, when dining, to have *regaled* themselves with the sight of criminals torn by wild beasts. *Lecky*, Europ. Morals, I. 298.

II. *intrans.* To feast; have pleasure or diversion.

See the rich churl, amid the social sons
Of wine and wit, *regaling!*
Shenstone, Economy, i. 14.

On twigs of hawthorn he *regal'd*,
On pippins' russet peel.
Cowper, Epitaph on a Hare.

The little girl . . . was met by Mrs. Norris, who thus *regaled* in the credit of being foremost to welcome her.
Jane Austen, Mansfield Park, ii.

regale[1] (rē-gāl'), *n.* [< F. *régal*, also *régale*, a banquet, amusement, pleasure-party (= Sp. Pg. It. *regalo*, a present, gift: see *regalia*[2], *regalio*), < *régaler*, regale, entertain: see *regale*[1], *v.*] A choice repast; a regalement, entertainment, or treat; a carouse.

The damned . . . would take it for a great *regale* to have a dunghill for their bed, instead of the burning coals of that eternal fire. *Jer. Taylor*, Works (ed. 1835), I. 386.

Our new acquaintance asked us if ever we had drank egg-flip? To which we answering in the negative, he assured us of a *regale*, and ordered a quart to be prepared.
Smollett, Roderick Random, xiv.

That ye may garnish your profuse *regales*
With summer fruits brought forth by wintry suns.
Cowper, Task, iii. 551.

regale[2] (rē-gā'lē), *n.*; pl. *regalia* (-liạ). [= OF. *regale*, F. *régale* = Sp. *regale* = It. *regalia*, a royal privilege, prerogative, < ML. *regale*, royal power or prerogative, *regalia*, pl. (also as fem. sing.), royal powers, royal prerogatives, the ensigns of royalty, etc., neut. of L. *regalis*, regal, royal: see *regal*[1].] 1. A privilege, prerogative, or right of property pertaining to the sovereign of a state by virtue of his office. The regalia are usually reckoned to be six—namely, the power of judicature; of life and death; of war and peace; of masterless goods, as estrays, etc.; of assessments; and of minting of money.

The prerogative is sometimes called jura regalia or *regalia*, the *regalia* being either majora, the regal dignity and power, or minora, the revenue of the crown.
Encyc. Brit., XIX. 672.

2. In *eccles. hist.*, the power of the sovereign in ecclesiastical affairs. In monarchical countries where the papal authority is recognized by the state, the regale is usually defined by a concordat with the papal see; in other monarchical countries it takes the form of the royal supremacy (see *supremacy*). In medieval times especially the regale involved the right of enjoyment of the revenues of vacant bishoprics, and of presentation to all ecclesiastical benefices or positions above the ordinary parochial cures during the vacancy of a see. These rights were exercised by the Norman and Plantagenet kings of England and by the French kings from the eleventh century onward with constantly widening application and increased insistence till the time of Louis XIV. Opposed to *pontificale*. See *investiture*.

Those privileges and liberties of the Church which were not derogatory to the *regale* and the kingdom.
R. W. Dixon, Hist. Church of Eng., i.

3. *pl.* Ensigns of royalty; the apparatus of a coronation, as the crown, scepter, etc. The regalia of England consist of the crown, the scepter with the cross, the verge or rod with the dove, the so-called staff of Edward the Confessor, several swords, the ampulla for the sacred oil, the spurs of chivalry, and several other pieces. These are preserved in the jewel-room in the Tower of London. The regalia of Scotland consist of the crown, the scepter, and the sword of state. They, with several other regal decorations, are exhibited in the crown-room in the castle of Edinburgh.

4. *pl.* The insignia, decorations, or "jewels" of an order, as of the Freemasons.—**Regalia of the church**, in England, the privileges which have been conceded to the church by kings; sometimes, the patrimony of the church.

Regalecidæ (reg-a-les'i-dē), *n. pl.* [NL., < *Regalecus* + *-idæ*.] A family of tæniosomous fishes, typified by the genus *Regalecus*. They have the body much compressed and elongated or ribbon-like, the head oblong and with the opercular apparatus produced backward, several of the anterior dorsal rays elongated and constituting a kind of crest, and long, single, oar-like rays in the position of the ventral fins. The species are pelagic and rarely seen. Some attain a length of more than 20 feet.

Regalecus (re-gal'e-kus), *n.* [NL. (Brünnich), lit. 'king of the herrings,' < L. *rex* (*reg-*), king, + NL. *alec*, herring: see *alec*.] A genus of ribbon-fishes, typical of the family *Regalecidæ*.

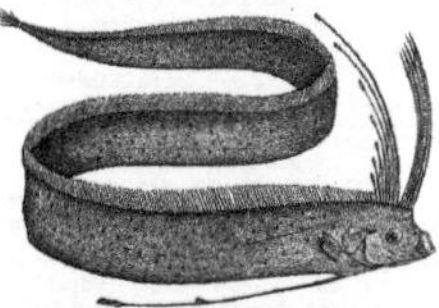

King of the Herrings, or Oar-fish (*Regalecus glesne*).

The northern *R. glesne* is popularly known as the *king of the herrings*. Also called *Gymnetrus*.

regalement (rē-gāl'ment), *n.* [= F. *régalement* = Sp. *regalamiento*; as *regale*[1] + *-ment*.] Refreshment; entertainment; gratification.

The Muses still require
Humid *regalement*, nor will aught avail
Imploring Phœbus with unmoisten'd lips.
J. Philips, Cider, ii.

regaler (rē-gā'lėr), *n.* One who or that which regales. *Imp. Dict.*

regalia[1], *n.* Plural of *regale*[2].

regalia[2]†, *n.* [Confused in E. with *regalia*[1]; < Sp. Pg. It. *regalo*, < F. *régale*, a banquet: see *regale*[1].] Same as *regale*[1].

The Town shall have its *regalia*; the Coffee-house gapers, I'm resolv'd, shan't want their Diversion.
D'Urfey, Two Queens of Brentford, i. (*Davies.*)

regalia[3] (rē-gā'liạ), *n.* [< Cuban Sp. *regalia*, a fine grade of cigar (*regalia imperial*, imperial regalia, *media regalia*, medium regalia), lit. 'royal privilege': see *regale*[2].] A superior kind of cigar. See the quotation.

The highest class of Cuban-made cigars [are] called "vegueras." . . . Next come the *regalias*, similarly made of the best Vuelta Abajo tobacco; and it is only the lower qualities, "ordinary *regalias*," which are commonly found in commerce, the finer . . . being exceedingly high-priced. *Encyc. Brit.*, XXIII. 426.

regalian (rē-gā'lian), *a.* [< F. *régalien*, appertaining to royalty, < *régal*, regal: see *regal*[1], *regale*[2].] Pertaining to a king or suzerain; regal; sovereign; belonging to the regalia.

Chester was first called a county palatine under Henry II., but it previously possessed all *regalian* rights of jurisdiction. *Hallam*, Middle Ages.

He had a right to the *regalian* rights of coining.
Brougham.

regalio†, *n.* Same as *regale*[1].

Do you think . . . that the fatal end of their journey being continually before their eyes would not alter and deprave their palate from tasting these *regalios?*
Cotton, tr. of Montaigne's Essays, xvi. (*Davies.*)

Fools, which each man meets in his dish each day,
Are yet the great *regalios* of a play.
Dryden, Sir Martin Mar-All, Prol., l. 3.

regalism (rē'gal-izm), *n.* [< *regal*[1] + *-ism*.] The control or interference of the sovereign in ecclesiastical matters.

Nevertheless in them [the Catholic kingdoms of Europe] *regalism*, which is royal supremacy pushed to the very verge of schism, has always prevailed. *Card. Manning.*

regality (rē-gal'i-ti), *n.* [Early mod. E. *regalitie*, < OF. *regalite* = It. *regalità*, < ML. *regalita(t-)s*, kingly office or character, royalty, < L. *regalis*, kingly, regal: see *regal*[1]. Cf. *regalty*, *realty*[2], *royalty*, doublets of *regality*.] 1. Royalty; sovereignty; kingship.

The nobles and commons were wel pleased that Kyng Richard should frankely and frely of his owne mere mocion resigne his croune and departe from his *regalite*.
Hall, Hen. IV., Int.

Is it possible that one so grave and judicious should . . . be persuaded that ecclesiastical regiment degenerateth into civil *regality*, when one is allowed to do that which hath been at any time the deed of more?
Hooker, Eccles. Polity, vii. 14.

He came partly in by the sword, and had high courage in all points of *regality*. *Bacon*, Hist. Hen. VII.

2. In Scotland, a territorial jurisdiction formerly conferred by the king. The lands over which this jurisdiction extended were said to be given *in liberam regalitatem*, and the persons receiving the right were termed lords *of regality*, and exercised the highest prerogatives of the crown.

There be civill Courts also in everie *regalitie*, holden by their Bailiffes, to whom the kings have gratiously granted royalties. *Holland*, tr. of Camden, ii. 8. (*Davies.*)

3†. *pl.* Things pertaining to sovereignty; insignia of kingship; regalia.

For what purpose was it ordayned that christen kynges . . . shulde in an open and stately place before all their subiectes receyue their crowne and other *Regalities?*
Sir T. Elyot, The Governour, iii. 2.

Such which God . . . hath reserved as his own appropriate *regalities*. *Jer. Taylor*, Works (ed. 1835), I. 201.

Burgh of regality. See *burgh*.

regally (rē'gal-i), *adv.* In a regal or royal manner.

regalo† (rē-gā'lō), *n.* [< It. Sp. Pg. *regalo*: see *regale*[1].] Same as *regale*[1].

I thank you for the last *regalo* you gave me at your Musæum, and for the good Company.
Howell, Letters, I. vi. 20.

I congratulate you on your *regalo* from the Northumberlands. *Walpole*, To Mann, July 8, 1758.

regals† (rē'galz), *n. pl.* Same as *regalia*[1]. See *regale*[2], 3.

regalty† (rē'gal-ti), *n.* [< ME. *regalty*, < OF. **regalte*, *regalite*, royalty: see *regality*, *realty*[2].] Same as *regality*.

For all Thebes with the *regalty*
Put his body in such jeopardy.
Lydgate, Story of Thebes, ii.

This was dangerous to the peace of the kingdom, and entrenched too much upon the *regalty*.
Jer. Taylor, Works (ed. 1835), II. 99.

regaly†, *n.* [< ME. *regalie*, *regalye*, < OF. *regalie*, f., < ML. *regalia*, royalty, royal prerogative, prop. neut. pl. of L. *regalis*, royal: see *regal*[1], *regale*[2].] 1. Royalty; sovereignty; prerogative.

Hit stondeth thus, that youre contraire, crueltee,
Allyed is agenst your *regalye*
Under colour of womanly beaute. *Chaucer*, Pity, l. 65.

To the entente to make John, sone of the same Duke, King of this your seid realme, and to depose you of your heigh *regalie* therof. *Paston Letters*, I. 100.

2. *pl.* Same as *regalia*[1]. See *regale*[2], 3.

The *regalies* of Scotland, that is to meane the crowne, with the septer and cloth of estate.
Fabyan, Chron. (ed. 1559), II. 140.

regar, *n.* See *regur*.

regard (rē-gärd'), *v.* [Formerly also *reguard* (like *guard*); < OF. *regarder*, *reguarder*, *rewarder*, F. *regarder* (= Pr. *regardar*, *reguardar* = Pg. *regardar* = It. *riguardare*, ML. *regardare*), look at, observe, regard, < *re-* + *garder*, keep, heed, mark: see *guard*. Cf. *reward*.] I. *trans.* 1. To look upon; observe; notice with some particularity; pay attention to.

If much you note him,
You shall offend him; . . .
Feed, and *regard* him not.
Shak., Macbeth, iii. 4. 58.

Him Sir Bedivere
Remorsefully *regarded* thro' his tears.
Tennyson, Passing of Arthur.

The horse sees the spectacle; it is only you who *regard* and admire it. *H. James*, Subs. and Shad., p. 295.

2†. To look toward; have an aspect or prospect toward.

Calais is an extraordinary well fortified place, in the old Castle and new Citadell, *reguarding* the Sea.
Evelyn, Diary, Nov. 11, 1643.

3. To attend to with respect; observe a certain respect toward; respect; reverence; honor; esteem.

He that *regardeth* the day *regardeth* it unto the Lord.
Rom. xiv. 6.

This aspect of mine . . .
The best-*regarded* virgins of our clime
Have loved. *Shak.*, M. of V., ii. 1. 10.

4. To consider of importance, value, moment, or interest; mind; care for: as, to *regard* the feelings of others; not to *regard* pain.

His bookes of Husbandrie are moch to be *regarded*.
Ascham, The Scholemaster, p. 152.

Facts from various places and times prove that in militant communities the claims to life, liberty, and property are little *regarded*. *H. Spencer*, Prin. of Sociol., § 560.

5. To have or to show certain feelings toward; show a certain disposition toward; treat; use.

His associates seem to have *regarded* him with kindness.
Macaulay.

6. To view; look on; consider: usually followed by *as*.

They are not only *regarded as* authors, but *as* partisans.
Addison.

A face perfectly quiescent we *regard as* signifying absence of feeling. *H. Spencer*, Prin. of Psychol., § 497.

I *regard* the judicial faculty, "judgment," . . . *as* that on which historical study produces the most valuable results. *Stubbs*, Medieval and Modern Hist., p. 94.

7. To have relation or respect to; concern: as, this argument does not *regard* the question.

This fable seems to *regard* natural philosophy.
Bacon, Physical Fables, xi., Expl.

The deed is done,
And what may follow now *regards* not me.
Shelley, The Cenci, iv. 4.

8†. To show attention to; care for; guard.

But ere we go, *regard* this dying prince,
The valiant Duke of Bedford. Come, my lord,
We will bestow you in some better place.
Shak., 1 Hen. VI., iii. 2. 86.

As regards, with regard to; as respects; as concerns: as, *as regards* that matter, I am quite of your opinion. =**Syn.** To remark, heed, estimate, value.

II. *intrans.* To have concern; care.

The Knight nothing *regarded*
To see the Lady scoffed.
Constance of Cleveland (Child's Ballads, IV. 229).

regard (rē̦-gärd′), *n.* [Formerly also *reguard* (like *guard*); < ME. *regard*, < OF. *regard*, *regort*, *reguard*, F. *regard* = Pr. *regart*, *reguart* = OSp. *reguardo* = Pg. *regardo* = It. *riguardo* (ML. *regardum*), regard, respect; from the verb: see *regard*, *v.*] 1. Look or gaze; aspect.

I extend my hand to him thus, quenching my familiar smile with an austere *regard* of control.
Shak., T. N., ii. 5. 731.

You are now within *regard* of the presence.
B. Jonson, Cynthia's Revels, ii. 1.

2. Attention, as to a matter of importance or interest; heed; consideration.

Beleue me (Lord), a souldiour cannot haue
Too great *regarde* whereon his knife should cut.
Gascoigne, Steele Glas (ed. Arber), p. 65.

Things without all remedy
Should be without *regard*; what's done is done.
Shak., Macbeth, iii. 2. 12.

We have sufficient proof that hero-worship is strongest where there is least *regard* for human freedom.
H. Spencer, Social Statics, p. 481.

3. That feeling or view of the mind which springs especially from estimable qualities in the object; esteem; affection; respect; reverence: as, to have a great *regard* for a person.

Will ye do aught for *regard* o' me?
Jamie Telfer (Child's Ballads, VI. 111).

To him they had *regard*, because that of long time he had bewitched them with sorceries. Acts viii. 11.

I have heard enough to convince me that he is unworthy my *regard*. *Sheridan*, School for Scandal, iii. 1.

4. Repute, good or bad, but especially good; note; account.

Mac Tirrelaghe was a man of meanest *regarde* amongest them. *Spenser*, State of Ireland.

I am a bard of no *regard*,
Wi' gentle folks and a' that.
Burns, Jolly Beggars.

5. Relation; respect; reference; view: often in the phrases *in regard to*, *with regard to*.

Thus conscience does make cowards of us all; . . .
And enterprises of great pitch [folios have *pith*] and moment
With this *regard* their currents turn awry.
Shak., Hamlet, iii. 1. 87.

To . . . persuade them to pursue and persevere in virtue *with regard to* themselves, in justice and goodness *with regard to* their neighbours, and piety toward God.
Watts.

6. Matter; point; particular; consideration; condition; respect.

Love 's not love
When it is mingled with *regards* that stand
Aloof from the entire point. *Shak.*, Lear, i. 1. 242.

I never beheld so delicate a creature [a horse]; . . . in all *reguards* beautifull, and proportioned to admiration.
Evelyn, Diary, Nov. 17, 1684.

Nature . . . in the first sentiment of kindness anticipates already a benevolence which shall lose all particular *regards* in its general light. *Emerson*, Love.

7†. Prospect; object of sight; view.

Throw out our eyes for brave Othello,
Even till we make the main and the aerial blue
An indistinct *regard*. *Shak.*, Othello, ii. 1. 40.

8. In *old English forest law*: (*a*) Official view or inspection. (*b*) The area within the jurisdiction of the regarders.—9. *pl.* Respects; good wishes; compliments: as, give my best *regards* to the family. [Colloq.]—**At regard of†**, in comparison with.

Thanne shewede he hym the litel erthe that here is, *At regard of* the hevenes quantite.
Chaucer, Parliament of Fowls, l. 57.

Court of regard (or survey) of dogs, an old forest court in England which was held every third year for the lawing or expeditation of mastiffs.—**Field of regard**, a surface conceived as plane or spherical, fixed with regard to the head, in which the fixation-point wanders with the movements of the eyeball. Also called *field of fixation*.—**In regard†**, (*a*) In view (of the fact that): usually with ellipsis of *that* following.

England . . . hath been . . . an overmatch [of France], *in regard* the middle people of England make good soldiers, which the peasants of France do not.
Bacon, True Greatness of Kingdoms and Estates.

I fear it [my last letter] miscarried, *in regard* you make no mention of it in yours. *Howell*, Letters, I. i. 15.

(*b*) Comparatively; relatively. Compare *in respect*.

How wonderfully dyd a fewe Romayns, *in regarde*, defend this litel territory.
Sir T. Elyot, Image of Governaunce, fol. 62, b. (*Encyc. Dict.*)

In regard of. (*a*) In view of; on account of.

Change was thought necessary *in regard of* the great hurt which the church did receive by a number of things then in use. *Hooker*.

In regard of his hurt, Smith was glad to be so rid of him.
Capt. John Smith, True Travels, I. 5.

(*b*) In regard to; in respect to. [Objectionable.]

In regard of its security, it [the chest of drawers] had a great advantage over the bandboxes.
Dickens, Martin Chuzzlewit, xlix.

In this (that) regard, in this (that) respect. [Objectionable.]—**Point of regard.** See *point*[1].—**With regard of†**, with regard to; considering.

How in safety best we may
Compose our present evils, *with regard*
Of what we are, and where. *Milton*, P. L., ii. 281.

=**Syn. 2.** Notice, observance (of), care, concern.—**3.** *Estimate*, *Estimation*, etc. See *esteem*, *love*[1].

regardable (rē̦-gär′da-bl), *a.* [< OF. (and F.) *regardable*; as *regard* + *-able*.] Capable of being regarded; observable; worthy of notice; noticeable.

Herein is not only *regardable* a mere history, but a mystery also. *Rev. T. Adams*, Works, I. 1.

regardant (rē̦-gär′dant), *a.* [Formerly also *reguardant*; < OF. *regardant*, ppr. of *regarder*, look at, regard: see *regard*, *v.*] 1. Regarding; looking to; looking behind or backward; watching.

You might have known that by my looks and language,
Had you been *regardant* or observant.
B. Jonson, New Inn, iv. 3.

With lockes *regardiant* [read *reguardant*] did the Thracian gaze. *Marston and Barksted*, Insatiate Countess, ii.

2. In *her.*, looking backward: applied to any animal whose face is turned toward its tail.—3. Looking at one another; turned so as to face one another.

Two *regardant* portraits of a lady and gentleman (in a marble relief).
Soulages Catalogue, No. 440.

Lion Passant Regardant.

Passant regardant. See *passant*.—**Rampant regardant.** See *rampant*.—**Regardant reversed**, having the head turned backward and downward: especially said of a serpent bent into a figure of eight, with the head below.—**Villein regardant, regardant villein**, in *feudal law*, a villein or retainer annexed to the land or manor, charged with the doing of all base services within the same.

regarder (rē̦-gär′dėr), *n.* 1. One who or that which regards.

Modern science is of itself . . . a slight *regarder* of time and space. *J. N. Lockyer*, Spect. Anal., p. 35.

2. In *Eng. law*, an officer whose business it was to view the forest, inspect the officers, and inquire concerning all offenses and defaults.

A Forest . . . hath also her peculiar Officers, as Foresters, Verderers, *Regarders*, Agisters, &c.
Howell, Letters, iv. 16.

regardful (rē̦-gärd′fu̇l), *a.* [< *regard* + *-ful.*] Having or paying regard. Especially—(*a*) Full of regard or respect; respectful.

To use all things and persons upon whom his name is called, or any ways imprinted, with a *regardful* and separate manner of usage, different from common, and far from contempt and scorn. *Jer. Taylor*, Holy Dying, iv. 8.

(*b*) Taking notice; heedful; observing with care; attentive.

When with *regardfull* sight
She, looking backe, espies that griesly wight.
Spenser, F. Q., IV. vii. 22.

Let a man be very tender and *regardful* of every pious motion made by the Spirit of God to his heart. *South.*

=**Syn.** (*b*) Observant, mindful, watchful, careful.

regardfully (rē̦-gärd′fu̇l-i), *adv.* In a regardful manner, in any sense.

regarding (rē̦-gär′ding), *prep.* [Ppr. of *regard*, *v.*] Respecting; concerning; in reference to: as, to be at a loss *regarding* one's position.

"*Regarding* personalities," he added, "I have not the same clear showing." *George Eliot*, Felix Holt, xxiv.

regardless (rē̦-gärd′les), *a.* [< *regard* + *-less.*] 1. Not having regard or heed; not looking or attending; heedless; negligent; indifferent; careless.

My eyes
Set here unmov'd, *regardless* of the world,
Though thousand miseries encompass me!
Beau. and Fl., King and No King, i. 1.

Blindeth the beauty everywhere revealed,
Treading the May-flowers with *regardless* feet.
Whittier, Among the Hills, Prel.

2. Not regarded; slighted. [Rare.]

Yes, Traitor; Zara, lost, abandon'd Zara,
Is a *regardless* Suppliant, now, to Osmyn.
Congreve, Mourning Bride, ii. 9.

=**Syn. 1.** Unmindful, inattentive, unobservant, neglectful, unconcerned.

regardlessly (rē̦-gärd′les-li), *adv.* In a regardless manner; heedlessly; carelessly; negligently.

regardlessness (rē̦-gärd′les-nes), *n.* Heedlessness; inattention; negligence.

regard-ring (rē̦-gärd′ring), *n.* A ring set with stones the initial letters of whose names make up the word *regard*, as ruby, emerald, garnet, amethyst, ruby, and diamond.

regather (rē-gaᴛʜ′ėr), *v. t.* [< *re-* + *gather*.] To gather or collect again.

When he had renewed his provisions and *regathered* more force. *Hakluyt's Voyages*, III. 640.

regatta (rē̦-gat′ä), *n.* [= F. *régate*, < It. *regatta*, *rigatta*, *regata*, a boat-race, yacht-race, a rowing-match, a particular use (orig. Venetian) of OIt. *regatta*, *rigatta*, a strife or contention for the mastery, < OIt. *regattare*, *rigattare*, sell by retail, haggle as a huckster, wrangle, contend, cope or fight for the mastery (cf. Sp. *regatear*, retail provisions, haggle, rival in sailing; *regateo*, a haggling, a regatta), prob. a dial. form of *recatare*, **recattare*, buy and sell again by retail, retail, regrate, forestall (cf. Sp. *recatear*, retail; *recatar*, take care, be cautious), < *re-*, again, + *cattare*, get, acquire, purchase (cf. Sp. *catear*, taste, try, view), < L. *captare*, catch, capture, procure: see *catch*[1], and cf. *acate*. Cf. *regrate*[1].] Originally, a gondola-race in Venice; now, any regularly appointed boat-race in which two or more row-boats, yachts, or other boats contend for prizes.

A *regatta* of wherries raced past us.
Hawthorne, Our Old Home.

They penetrated to Cowes for the race-balls and *regatta* gayeties. *Thackeray*, Vanity Fair, xxxix.

regelate (rē′jē̦-lāt), *v. i.*; pret. and pp. *regelated*, ppr. *regelating*. [< L. *regelatus*, pp. of *regelare* (> It. *regalare* = Pg. *regelar* = F. *regeler*), air, cool off, < *re-*, back, + *gelare*, congeal: see *geal*[1].] To freeze or become congealed again; specifically, to freeze together.

Everything yields. The very glaciers are viscous, or *regelate* into conformity, and the stiffest patriots palter and compromise. *Emerson*, Fortune of the Republic.

regelation (rē-jē̦-lā′sho̤n), *n.* [= F. *regélation*, a freezing over, < LL. *regelatio*(*n*-), a thawing, < L. *regelare*, thaw, warm, < *re-*, back, again, also = *un-*, + *gelare*, freeze: see *regelate*.] The phenomenon of congelation and cohesion exemplified by two pieces of melting ice when brought into contact at a temperature above the freezing-point. Not only does this occur in air, but also in water. The phenomenon, first observed by Faraday, is obscure.

Two pieces of ice at 32° Fahr., with moist surfaces, when placed in contact, freeze together to a rigid mass. This is called *regelation*. *Faraday.* (*Webster.*)

An attempt . . . has been made of late years to reconcile the brittleness of ice with its motion in glaciers. It is founded on the observation, made by Mr. Faraday in 1850, that when two pieces of thawing ice are placed together they freeze together at the place of contact. . . . The word *Regelation* was proposed by Dr. Hooker to express the freezing together of two pieces of thawing ice observed by Faraday; and the memoir in which the term was first used was published by Mr. Huxley and Mr. Tyndall in the Philosophical Transactions for 1857.
Tyndall, Forms of Water, p. 164.

regence† (rē′jens), *n.* [= OF. *regence*, F. *régence* = Sp. Pg. *regencia* = It. *reggenza*, < ML. *regentia*, rule, < L. *regen*(*t*-)*s*, ruling: see *regent*.] Government; rule.

Some for the gospel, and massacres
Of spiritual affidavit-makers,
That swore to any human *regence*
Oaths of suprem'cy and allegiance.
S. Butler, Hudibras, III. ii. 275.

regency (rē′jen-si), *n.*; pl. *regencies* (-siz). [As *regence* (see *-cy*).] 1. Rule; authority; government.

The sceptre of Christ's *regency*. *Hooker.*

2. More specifically, the office, government, or jurisdiction of a regent; deputed or vicarious government. See *regent*, 2.

The king's illness placed the queen and the duke of York in direct rivalry for the *regency*. *Stubbs*, Const. Hist., § 349.

3. The district under the jurisdiction of a regent or vicegerent.

Regions they pass'd, the mighty *regencies*
Of seraphim. *Milton*, P. L., v. 748.

4. The body of men intrusted with vicarious government: as, a *regency* constituted during a king's minority, insanity, or absence from the kingdom.

By the written law of the land, the sovereign was empowered to nominate a *regency* in case of the minority or incapacity of the heir apparent. *Prescott*, Ferd. and Isa., ii. 17.

5. The existence of a regent's rule; also, the period during which a regent administers the government.

I can just recall the decline of the grand era. . . . The ancient habitués, . . . contemporaries of Brummell in his zenith—boon companions of George IV. in his *regency*—still haunted the spot. *Bulwer*, My Novel, xi. 2.

To the forced and gloomy bigotry which marked the declining years of Louis Quatorze succeeded the terrible reaction of the *regency* and the following reigns. *W. R. Greg*, Misc. Essays, 2d ser., p. 17.

6. The office of a university regent, or master regent.—7. The municipal administration of certain towns in northern Europe.—**Albany regency**, in *U. S. hist.*, a group of politicians who, by the skilful use of patronage, controlled the nominating conventions and other machinery of the Democratic party in the State of New York, from about 1820 to about 1850. The most noted members were Wright, Martin Van Buren, Marcy, and Dix.—**Regency Act**, a name given to special statutes regulating regency, as, for instance, an English statute of 1840 (3 and 4 Vict., c. 52), which authorized the Prince Consort to act as regent, in case of the demise of Queen Victoria, during the minority of her successor.—**The Regency**, in *French hist.*, the period of the minority of Louis XV., 1715–23, when Philip of Orleans was regent.

regender† (rē-jen′dėr), *v. t.* [‹ *re-* + *gender*. Cf. *regenerate*.] To gender again; renew.

Furth spirts fyre freshlye *regendred*. *Stanihurst*, Æneid, ii. 496.

regeneracy (rẹ-jen′ẹ-rā-si), *n.* [‹ *regenera(te)* + *-cy*.] The state of being regenerated.

Though Saul were, yet every blasphemous sinner could not expect to be, called from the depth of sin to *regeneracy* and salvation. *Hammond*, Works, IV. 686.

regenerate (rẹ-jen′ẹ-rāt), *v. t.* [‹ L. *regeneratus*, pp. of *regenerare* (› It. *regenerare*, *rigenerare* = Sp. Pg. *regenerar* = F. *régénérer*), generate again, ‹ *re-*, again, + *generare*, generate: see *generate*.] 1. To generate or produce anew; reproduce.

In a divided worm, he [Bülow] says, the tail is *regenerated* from cell-layers developed in the same way and exactly equivalent to the three layers of the embryo. *Mind*, IX. 417.

2. In *theol.*, to cause to be born again; cause to become a Christian; give by direct divine influence a new spiritual life to. See *regeneration*, 2.

No sooner was a convert initiated . . . but by an easy figure he became a new man, and both acted and looked upon himself as one *regenerated* and born a second time. *Addison*, Def. of Christ. Relig., ix. 2.

regenerate (rẹ-jen′ẹ-rāt), *a.* [= F. *régénéré* = Sp. Pg. *regenerado* = It. *regenerato*, *rigenerato*, ‹ L. *regeneratus*, pp.: see the verb.] 1. Reproduced; restored; renewed.

O thou, the earthly author of my blood,
Whose youthful spirit, in me *regenerate*,
Doth with a twofold vigour lift me up.
Shak., Rich. II., i. 3. 70.

Who brought a race *regenerate* to the field, . . .
And raised fair Lusitania's fallen shield.
Scott, Vision of Don Roderick, Conclusion, st. 14.

2. In *theol.*, begotten or born anew; changed from a natural to a spiritual state.

Seeing now . . . that this child is *regenerate*, and grafted into the body of Christ's Church, let us give thanks unto Almighty God for these benefits. *Book of Common Prayer*, Office of Public Baptism of [Infants.

regenerateness (rẹ-jen′ẹ-rāt-nes), *n.* The state of being regenerated. *Bailey.*

regeneration (rẹ-jen-ẹ-rā′shọn), *n.* [‹ ME. *regeneracioun*, ‹ OF. *regeneration*, F. *régénération* = Sp. *regeneracion* = Pg. *regeneração* = It. *regenerazione*, *rigenerazione*, ‹ LL. *regeneratio(n-)*, a being born again, regeneration: see *regenerate*.] 1. The act of regenerating or producing anew.—2. In *theol.*: (*a*) A radical change in the spirit of an individual, accomplished by the direct action of the Spirit of God. Evangelical theologians agree that there is a necessity for such a radical spiritual change in man in order to the divine life; but they differ widely in their psychological explanations of the change. They are, however, generally agreed that it consists of or at least necessarily involves a change in the affections and desires of the soul. Regeneration is also understood, as by the Roman Catholic Church, to be the gift of the germ of a spiritual life conferred regularly by God's ordinance in baptism, which is accordingly called the *sacrament of regeneration*, or simply *regeneration*. The word *regeneration* occurs only once in the New Testament in its ordinary theological meaning; but equivalent expressions are found, such as "begotten again," "born again," "born of God," "born of water and of the Spirit."

According to his mercy he saved us, by the washing of *regeneration*, and renewing of the Holy Ghost. Tit. iii. 5.

Baptism is . . . a sign of *Regeneration* or New-Birth, whereby, as by an instrument, they that receive Baptism rightly are grafted into the Church. *Thirty-nine Articles of Religion*, xxvii.

(*b*) The renovation of the world to be accomplished at the second coming of the Messiah.

Ye which have followed me, in the *regeneration*, when the Son of Man shall sit in the throne of his glory, ye also shall sit upon twelve thrones, judging the twelve tribes of Israel. Mat. xix. 28.

3 (rē-jen-ẹ-rā′shọn). In *biol.*, the genesis or origination of new tissue to repair the waste of the body, or to replace worn-out tissue; also, the reproduction of lost or destroyed parts or organs. Regeneration of tissue constantly goes on in all animals in the ordinary repair of waste products of vital action; but the replacing of lost parts, as a limb, is nearly confined to animals below vertebrates, in many of which it is an easy or usual process.—**Baptismal regeneration.** See *baptismal*.=**Syn.** 2. See *conversion*.—3. See *reproduction*.

regenerative (rẹ-jen′ẹ-rā-tiv), *a.* [= OF. *regeneratif*, F. *regénératif* = Sp. Pg. *regenerativo*; as *regenerate* + *-ive*.] 1. Producing regeneration; renewing.

She identified him with the struggling *regenerative* process in her which had begun with his action. *George Eliot*, Daniel Deronda, lxv.

In Mahommedanism there is no *regenerative* power; it is "of the letter, which killeth"—unelastic, sterile, barren. *Faiths of the World*, p. 331.

2. In *metal.*, on the principle of the Siemens regenerator, or so constructed as to utilize that method of economizing fuel, as in the term *regenerative gas-furnace*. See *regenerator*.—**Regenerative burner.** See *burner*.—**Regenerative chamber**, in a furnace, a regenerator.—**Regenerative furnace.** See *furnace*.

regeneratively (rẹ-jen′ẹ-rā-tiv-li), *adv.* In a regenerative manner; so as to regenerate.

regenerator (rẹ-jen′ẹ-rā-tọr), *n.* [= F. *régénérateur*, n.; as *regenerate* + *-or*[1].] 1. One who regenerates.

He is not his own *regenerator*, or parent at all, in his new birth. *Waterland*, Works, VI. 352.

All these social *regenerators* panted to be free. *The American*, XIV. 23.

2. In *metal.*, a chamber filled with a checker-work of fire-bricks; that part of a regenerative furnace in which the waste heat of the gases escaping from the hearth is, by reversal of the draft at suitable intervals, alternately stored up and given out to the gas and air entering the furnace. The idea of employing what is now generally called the "regenerative system" of heating was first conceived by Robert Stirling, in 1816, but his arrangement for carrying it out was not a practical one. The present form of the furnace, and in general the successful application of the principle, constituting a highly important improvement in the consumption of fuel, are due to the brothers Siemens. The regenerative system has already been extensively applied in various metallurgical and manufacturing processes, and is likely to receive still further development. According to the Siemens regenerative method, there must be at least one pair of regenerative chambers, in order that the heat may be in process of being stored up in one while being utilized in the other. In the Siemens regenerative reheating- or mill-furnace there are two pairs of chambers, each pair consisting of one larger and one smaller chamber, through one of which the air passes, and through the other the gas on its way to the furnace. The so-called "Ponsard recuperator" is a form of regenerator in which, by an ingenious arrangement of solid and hollow fire-bricks, the current is made continuous in one direction, instead of requiring reversal as in the Siemens regenerative furnace. This form of furnace has been employed for reheating in rolling-mills.

regenerator-furnace (rẹ-jen′ẹ-rā-tọr-fėr″nās), *n.* Any form of furnace with which a regenerator is connected.

regeneratory (rẹ-jen′ẹ-rā-tō-ri), *a.* [‹ *regenerate* + *-ory*.] Regenerative; having the power to renew; tending to reproduce or renovate.

regenesis (rẹ-jen′e-sis), *n.* [‹ *re-* + *genesis*.] The state of being renewed or reproduced.

There tended to be thereafter a continual *regenesis* of dissenting sects. *H. Spencer*, Pop. Sci. Mo., XXVIII. 368.

regent (rē′jent), *a.* and *n.* [‹ OF. *regent*, F. *régent* = Sp. Pg. *regente* = It. *reggente*, ruling, as a noun a regent, vicegerent, ‹ L. *regen(t-)s*, ruling; as a noun, a ruler, governor, prince; ppr. of *regere*, pp. *rectus*, direct, rule, correct, lit. 'make straight,' 'stretch,' = Gr. ὀρέγειν, stretch, = Skt. √ *raj*, stretch out, = Goth. *uf-rakjan*, stretch out, etc. (see *rack*[1]); cf. Skt. √ *rāj*, direct, rule, *rājan*, king, L. *rex* (*rēg-*), king (see *rex*). The two roots in Skt. may be orig. identical, as they have become in L. From the L. *regere* are also ult. *regimen*, *regiment*, *régime*, *region*, *rector*, *rectum*, *rectangle*, *rectilineal*, etc., *correct*, *direct*, *erect*, etc., *dress*, *address*, *redress*, etc. Related E. words of Teut. origin are *right*, *rack*[1], etc.] I. *a.* 1. Ruling; governing.

To follow nature's too affected fashion,
Or travel in the *regent* walk of passion.
Quarles, Emblems, ii. 4.

He together calls,
Or several, one by one, the *regent* powers,
Under him *regent*. *Milton*, P. L., v. 697.

Some other active *regent* principle that resides in the body. *Sir M. Hale.*

2. Exercising vicarious authority: as, a prince *regent*.—3. Taking part in the government of a university.—**Queen regent.** See *queen*.

II. *n.* 1. A ruler; a governor: in a general sense.

Uriel, . . . *regent* of the sun, and held
The sharpest-sighted spirit of all in Heaven.
Milton, P. L., iii. 690.

The moon (sweet *regent* of the sky)
Silver'd the walls of Cumnor Hall.
Mickle, Cumnor Hall.

2. One who is invested with vicarious authority; one who governs a kingdom in the minority, absence, or disability of the king. In most hereditary governments this office is regarded as belonging to the nearest relative of the sovereign capable of undertaking it; but this rule is subject to many modifications.

I say, my sovereign, York is meetest man
To be your *regent* in the land of France.
Shak., 2 Hen. VI., i. 3. 164.

3. In the old universities, a master or doctor who takes part in the regular duties of instruction or government. At Cambridge all resident masters of arts of less than four years' standing, and all doctors of less than two, are regents. At Oxford the period of regency is shorter. At both universities those of a more advanced standing, who keep their names on the college books, are called *non-regents*. At Cambridge the regents compose the upper house and the non-regents the lower house of the senate, or governing body. At Oxford the regents compose the congregation, which confers degrees and does the ordinary business of the university. The regents and non-regents collectively compose the convocation, which is the governing body in the last resort.

Only *regents*—that is, masters actually engaged in teaching—had any right to be present or to vote in congregations [at Bologna]. *Encyc. Brit.*, XXIII. 835.

4. In the State of New York, a member of the corporate body known as the University of the State of New York. The university is officially described as consisting "of all incorporated institutions of academic and higher education, with the State Library, State Museum, and such other libraries, museums, or other institutions for higher education in the state as may be admitted by the regents. . . . The regents have power to incorporate, and to alter or repeal the charters of colleges, academies, libraries, museums, or other educational institutions belonging to the University; to distribute to them all funds granted by the state for their use; to inspect their workings and require annual reports under oath of their presiding officers; to establish examinations as to attainments in learning, and confer on successful candidates suitable certificates, diplomas, and degrees, and to confer honorary degrees."—**House of regents.** See *house*[1].—**Necessary regent**, one who is obliged to serve as regent: opposed to a *regent ad placitum*, who has served the necessary term and is at liberty to retire.

regent-bird (rē′jent-bėrd), *n.* An Australian bird of the genus *Sericulus*, *S. chrysocephalus* or *melinus*, the plumage of which is velvety-black and golden-yellow in the male: so called

Regent-bird (*Sericulus chrysocephalus*).

during the regency of the Prince of Wales, afterward George IV., in compliment to him. It is related to the bower-birds, but has been variously classified. See *Sericulus*. Also *regent-oriole*.

regentess (rē′jen-tes), *n.* [‹ *regent* + *-ess*.] A female regent; a protectress of a kingdom.

regent-oriole (rē′jent-ō″ri-ōl), *n.* Same as *regent-bird*.

regentship (rē'jent-ship), *n.* [< *regent* + *-ship.*] The office or dignity of a regent, especially of a vicegerent, or one who governs for a king; regency.

If York have ill demean'd himself in France,
Then let him be denay'd the *regentship.*
Shak., 2 Hen. VI., i. 3. 107.

regerminate (rē-jėr'mi-nāt), *v. i.* [< L. *regerminatus*, pp. of *regerminare*, sprout again, < *re-*, again, + *germinare*, sprout, germinate: see *germinate.*] To germinate again.

regermination (rē-jėr-mi-nā'shon), *n.* [< L. *regerminatio(n-)*, < *regerminare*, pp. *regerminatus*, sprout again: see *regerminate.*] A sprouting or germination anew.

The Jews commonly express resurrection by *regermination*, or growing up again like a plant.
Gregory, Notes on Scripture, p. 125.

regest† (rē-jest'), *v. t.* [< L. *regestus*, pp. of *regerere*, throw or cast back, retort, also record, chronicle, < *re-*, back, + *gerere*, carry: see *gest*[2].] To throw back; retort.

Who can say, it is other than righteous, that thou shouldest *regest* one day upon us, Depart from me, ye wicked?
Bp. Hall, Contemplations, iii. 5.

regest† (rē-jest'), *n.* [< F. (obs.) *regeste*, pl. *regestes* (= Pg. *registo*, *resisto*), a register, < L. *regestum* (pl. *regesta*), neut. of *regestus*, pp. of *regerere*, record: see *regest*, *v.* Cf. *register*[1].] A register.

Old legends and Cathedrall *regests.*
Milton, Hist. Eng., iii.

reget (rē-get'), *v. t.* [< *re-* + *get*[1].] **1.** To get or obtain again.

And then desire in Gascoign to *reget*
The glory lost.
Daniel, Civil Wars, vi. 71.

2†. To generate or bear again.

Tovy, although the mother of vs all,
Regets [read *regests*?] thee in her wombe.
Davies, Scourge of Folly, p. 52. (*Davies.*)

reghte†, *adv.* A Middle English form of *right.*

regiam majestatem (rē'ji-am maj-es-tā'tem). [So called from these words at the beginning of the collection; L.: *regiam*, acc. fem. of *regius*, pertaining to a king, royal (< *rex* (*reg-*), king); *majestatem*, acc. of *majestas*, majesty: see *majesty.*] A collection of early laws, said to have been compiled by the order of David I., king of Scotland. It resembles so closely the *Tractatus de Legibus*, supposed to have been written by Glanvil in the reign of Henry II., that no doubt one was copied from the other.

regian (rē'ji-an), *n.* [< L. *regius*, of a king (see *regious*), + *-an.*] **1.** An adherent or upholder of regalism.

This is alleged and urged by our *regians* to prove the king's paramount power in ecclesiasticis.
Fuller, Ch. Hist., II. iii. 38.

2. A royalist.

Arthur Wilson . . . favours all Republicans, and never speaks well of *regians* (it is his own distinctions) if he can possibly avoid it.
Bp. Hacket, Abp. Williams, i. 39. (*Davies.*)

regible† (rej'i-bl), *a.* [= It. *reggibile* = Sp. *regible*, < LL. *regibilis*, that may be ruled, governable, tractable, < L. *regere*, rule: see *regent.*] Governable.

regicidal (rej'i-si-dal), *a.* [< *regicide*[2] + *-al.*] Consisting in, relating to, or having the nature of regicide; tending to regicide.

regicide[1] (rej'i-sīd), *n.* [= F. *régicide* = Sp. Pg. It. *regicida*, < L. *rex* (*reg-*), a king, + *-cida*, < *cædere*, kill.] A king-killer; one who puts a king to death; specifically, in *Eng. hist.*, a member of the high court of justice constituted by Parliament for the trial of Charles I., by which he was found guilty of treason and sentenced to death in 1649.

The *regicides* who sat on the life of our late King were brought to tryal in the Old Bailey.
Evelyn, Diary, Oct. 11, 1660.

regicide[2] (rej'i-sīd), *n.* [= F. *régicide* = Sp. Pg. It. *regicidio*, the slaying of a king, < L. *rex* (*reg-*), king, + *-cidium*, a killing, < *cædere*, kill.] The killing of a king.

Did Fate, or we, when great Atrides dy'd,
Urge the bold traitor to the *Regicide?*
Fenton, in Pope's Odyssey, i. 48.

regifugium (rē-ji-fū'ji-um), *n.*; pl. *regifugia* (-ä). [= Pg. *regifugio*, < LL. *regifugium*, 'the king's flight,' < L. *rex* (*reg-*), king, + *fuga*, flight, < *fugere*, flee: see *fugitive.*] An ancient Roman annual festival, held, according to some ancient writers, in celebration of the flight of Tarquin the Proud.

regild (rē-gild'), *v. t.* [< *re-* + *gild*[1].] To gild anew.

régime (rā-zhēm'), *n.* [< F. *régime*, < L. *regimen*, direction, government: see *regimen.*] **1.** Mode, system, or style of rule or management; government, especially as connected with certain social features; administration; rule.

The industrial *régime* is distinguished from the predatory *régime* in this, that mutual dependence becomes great and direct, while mutual antagonism becomes small and indirect.
H. Spencer, Prin. of Psychol., § 525.

2. In *French law*, specifically, the system of property rights under the marriage relation, fixed upon by the parties by an ante-nuptial contract. The principal systems are *régime de communauté* (see *community property*, under *community*), *régime de separation de biens*, and *régime dotal* (see *dotal*).—**Ancient régime** [F. *ancien régime*], a former style or system of government; an ancient social system; specifically, the political and social system which prevailed in France before the revolution of 1789.

regimen (rej'i-men), *n.*; pl. *regimens*, *regimina* (rej'i-menz, rē-jim'i-nā). [= OF. *regime*, F. *régime* = Sp. *regimen* = Pg. *regimen*, *regime* = It. *regimine*, < L. *regimen*, guidance, direction, government, rule, < *regere*, rule: see *regent.* Cf. *régime.*] **1.** Orderly government or system; system of order; government; control.

It concerneth the *regimen* and government of every man over himself, and not over others.
Bacon, Advancement of Learning, ii. 278.

Time . . . restored the giddy revellers to the *regimen* of sober thought.
O. W. Holmes, Emerson, xvi.

2. Any regulation or remedy which is intended to produce beneficial effects by gradual operation; specifically, in *med.*, the regulation of diet, exercise, etc., with a view to the preservation or restoration of health, or for the attainment of a determinate result; a course of living according to certain rules: sometimes used as equivalent to *hygiene*, but most commonly used as a synonym for *diet*[1], 2.

My Father's disorder appeared to be a dropsy, an indisposition the most unsuspected, being a person so exemplaryly temperate, and of admirable *regimen.*
Evelyn, Diary, Oct. 30, 1640.

Yet I have heard you were ill yourself, and kept your bed: . . . this was (I imagine) only by way of *regimen*, and not from necessity.
Gray, Letters, I. 340.

3. In *zoöl.*, habit or mode of life with regard to eating; choice of food; dietetics: as, an animal or a vegetable *regimen;* carnivorous *regimen.*—**4.** In *gram.*: (*a*) Government; the control which one word exercises over the form of another in connection with it.

The grammarians posit the absence of *regimen* as one of the differential features of a conjunction.
F. Hall, False Philol., p. 84.

(*b*) The word or words so governed.

regiment (rej'i-ment), *n.* [< ME. *regiment*, *regement*, < OF. *regiment*, *regement*, government, sway, later a regiment of soldiers, = Pr. *regiment* = Sp. *regimiento*, government, a regiment, = Pg. *regimento* = It. *reggimento*, < LL. *regimentum*, rule, government, < L. *regere*, rule: see *regent.* Cf. *regimen*, *régime.*] **1**†. Rule; government; authority.

That for hens forth y[t] he be under the *regement* and gouernance of the Mayr and Aldermen of the same cite.
Charter of London, in Arnold's Chronicle, p. 43.

The first Blast of the Trumpet against the monstrous *Regiment* of Women.
Knox, title of work.

The *regiment* of Debora, who ruled twentie yeares with religion.
Lyly, Euphues and his England, p. 455.

2†. A district ruled; a kingdom.

The triple-parted *regiment*
That froward Saturn gave unto his sons.
Greene, Orlando Furioso.

3†. Rule of diet; regimen.

This may bring her to eat, to sleep, and reduce what's now out of square with her into their former law and *regiment.*
Fletcher (*and another*), Two Noble Kinsmen, iv. 3.

4. *Milit.*, a body of soldiers, consisting of one or more battalions of infantry, or of several squadrons of cavalry, commanded by a colonel, or of a certain division of artillery. It is the largest permanent association of soldiers, and the third subdivision of an army-corps, several regiments constituting a brigade, and several brigades a division. These combinations are, however, temporary, while in the regiment the same officers serve continuously, and in command of the same bodies of men. The strength of a regiment may vary greatly, as any regiment may comprise any number of battalions. The organization of the British Royal Artillery is anomalous, the whole body forming one regiment. In 1880 it comprised nearly 35,000 officers and men, distributed in 30 brigades, each of which is as large as an ordinary regiment. In the United States service the full strength of cavalry regiments is about 1,200 each; of artillery, about 600; of infantry, 500; but these numbers are subject to inevitable variations. Abbreviated *regt.*

We'll set forth
In best appointment all our *regiments.*
Shak., K. John, ii. 1. 296.

Marching regiment. See *march*[2].—**Royal regiment of artillery.** See *artillery.*

regiment (rej'i-ment), *v. t.* [= Sp. *regimentar*, form into regiments; from the noun.] To form into a regiment or into regiments with proper officers; hence, to organize; bring under a definite system of command, authority, or interdependence.

If women were to be *regimented*, he would carry an army into the field without beat of drum.
Richardson, Sir Charles Grandison, III. 314. (*Davies.*)

regimental (rej-i-men'tal), *a.* and *n.* [= Pg. *regimental;* as *regiment* + *-al.*] **I.** *a.* Of or pertaining to a regiment: as, *regimental* officers; *regimental* clothing.

The band led the column, playing the *regimental* march.
Thackeray, Vanity Fair, xxx.

Regimental adjutant, fund, etc. See the nouns.

II. *n. pl.* (rarely used in the singular). Military clothing: so named from the former practice of discriminating the uniforms of different regiments very decidedly one from another—a fashion nearly abandoned at the present time.

If they had been ruled by me, they would have put you into the guards. You would have made a sweet figure in a *regimental.*
Colman, Man of Business, ii. (*Davies.*)

You a soldier!—you're a walking block, fit only to dust the company's *regimentals* on.
Sheridan, The Rivals, iii. 1.

In their ragged *regimentals*
Stood the old Continentals,
Yielding not.
G. H. McMaster, Carmen Bellicosum.

regimentation (rej"i-men-tā'shon), *n.* [< *regiment*, *v.*, + *-ation.*] The act of forming into regiments, or the state of being formed into regiments or classified systems; organization.

The process of militant organization is a process of *regimentation*, which, primarily taking place in the army, secondarily affects the whole community.
H. Spencer, Prin. of Sociol., § 553.

regimina, *n.* Latin plural of *regimen.*

regiminal (rē-jim'i-nal), *a.* [< L. *regimen* (*regimin-*), rule, + *-al.*] Of or pertaining to regimen: as, strict *regiminal* rules.

Regina (rē-ji'nä), *n.* [NL. (Baird and Girard, 1853), < L. *regina*, a queen, fem. of *rex* (*reg-*), a king: see *rex.*] In *herpet.*, a genus of water-snakes or aquatic harmless serpents of the family *Colubridæ.* The type is the striped water-snake of the United States, *R. leberis.*

Regina purple. See *purple.*

region (rē'jon), *n.* [< ME. *region*, *regioun*, < OF. *region*, F. *région* = Pr. *regio*, *reio* = Sp. *region* = Pg. *região* = It. *regione*, a region, < L. *regio(n-)*, a direction, line, boundary-line, boundary, territory, quarter, province, region, < *regere*, direct, rule: see *regent.*] **1.** Any considerable and connected part of a space or surface; specifically, a tract of land or sea of considerable but indefinite extent; a country; a district; in a broad sense, place without special reference to location or extent: as, the equatorial *regions;* the temperate *regions;* the polar *regions;* the upper *regions* of the atmosphere.

Zit there is, toward the parties meridionales, many Contrees and many *Regyouns.*
Mandeville, Travels, p. 262.

The *regions* of Artois,
Wallon, and Picardy.
Shak., 1 Hen. VI., ii. 1. 9.

Gawain the while thro' all the *region* round
Rode with his diamond, wearied of the quest.
Tennyson, Lancelot and Elaine.

2. An administrative division of a city or territory; specifically, such a division of the city of Rome and of the territory about Rome, of which the number varied at different times; a district, quarter, or ward (modern *rione*). Under Servius Tullius there were four regions in the city and twenty-six in the Roman territory.

The series of Roman Macedonia begins with coins of the *regions* issued by permission of the senate and bearing the name of the Macedonians, from 158 to 146 B. C.
Encyc. Brit., XVII. 640.

His [Alberic's] chief attention was given to the militia, which was still arranged in scholæ, and it is highly probable that he was the author of the new divison of the city [Rome] into twelve *regions.*
Encyc. Brit., XX. 788.

Rome has seven ecclesiastical *regions*, each with its proper deacons, subdeacons, and acolytes. Each *region* has its own day of the week for high ecclesiastical functions, which are celebrated by each in rotation.
Encyc. Brit., XVI. 509.

3. Figuratively, the inhabitants of a region or district of country.

All the *regions*
Do smilingly revolt.
Shak., Cor., iv. 6. 102.

4. In *anat.*, a place in or a part of the body in any way indicated: as, the abdominal *regions.*

Let it fall rather, though the fork invade
The *region* of my heart.
Shak., Lear, i. 1. 147.

The mouth, and the *region* of the mouth, . . . were about the strongest feature in Wordsworth's face.
De Quincey (Personal Traits of Brit. Authors, Wordsworth).

5†. Place; rank; station; dignity.

He is of too high a *region*; he knows too much. *Shak.*, M. W. of W., iii. 2. 75.

6†. Specifically, the space from the earth's surface out to the orbit of the moon: properly called the *elemental region*.

The orb below
As hush as death, anon the dreadful thunder
Doth rend the *region*. *Shak.*, Hamlet, ii. 2. 509.

I should have fatted all the *region* kites
With this slave's offal. *Shak.*, Hamlet, ii. 2. 607.

7. In *zoögeog.*, a large faunal area variously limited by different authors. Especially—(*a*) A realm: one of several primary divisions of the earth's surface, characterized by its fauna: as, the Palearctic or the Nearctic *region*. The term acquired specific application to certain large principal areas from its use in this sense by P. L. Sclater in 1857. Sclater's regions, adopted with little modification by Günther and Wallace, were six in number: the Palearctic, Ethiopian, Oriental or Indian, Australian, Nearctic, and Neotropical. (See these words.) Baird added a seventh, the West Indian, now considered a division of the Neotropical. In 1874 Sclater, following Huxley, recognized as primary divisions (1) *Arctogæa*, comprising the Palearctic, Ethiopian, Indian, and Nearctic regions; (2) *Dendrogæa*, represented by the Neotropical region; (3) *Antarctogæa*, with an Australasian region; and (4) *Ornithogæa*, with a New Zealand region. (*b*) A secondary faunal area, the primary being called a *realm*: as, the Antillean, Central American, and Brazilian *regions* of the American Tropical realm. In this sense it has been used by most American zoölogists. Various other divisions have been proposed, as by A. Murray in 1866, Huxley in 1868, W. T. Blanford in 1869, E. Blyth in 1871, A. Newton in 1875, T. Gill in 1878, and J. A. Allen in 1878. Each of the main divisions, however defined by different naturalists, is subdivided into several subregions or provinces, more or less minutely in different systems. Thus, for example, the Ethiopian region is divided by Newton into the Libyan, Guinean, Caffrarian, Mozambican, and Madagascarian subregions, and the Libyan subregion itself into the Arabian, Egyptian, Abyssinian, and Gambian provinces. The waters of the globe have been either included in the prime divisions based on the land faunas, or segregated in peculiar ones.—**Abdominal regions.** See *abdominal*.—**Agrarian region, anal region.** See the adjectives.—**Axillary region**, a region on the side of the thorax, extending from the axilla to a line drawn from the lower border of the mammary to that of the scapular region.—**Basilar region**, the region of the base of the skull.—**Blue-grass region.** See *grass*.—**Broca's region.** Same as *Broca's convolution*. See *convolution*.—**Ciliary region**, that part of the eyeball just back from the cornea which corresponds to the ciliary muscle and processes.—**Clavicular region**, the region on the front of the chest immediately over the clavicle.—**Clypeal region.** See *clypeal*.—**Cordilleran region.** See *cordillera*.—**Cyclic, dorsolumbar, epigastric, gluteal, hypogastric region.** See the adjectives.—**Hyomental region**, the space between the lower jaw and the hyoid bone.—**Hypochondriac region.** (*a*) Of the abdomen. See *abdominal regions*. (*b*) Of the thorax, same as *inframammary region*.—**Iliac region.** See *abdominal regions*.—**Indo-Pacific region.** See *Indo-Pacific*.—**Infra-axillary region**, the region on the side of the chest extending from the axillary region to the free border of the ribs. Also called *subaxillary region*.—**Infraclavicular region.** See *infraclavicular*.—**Infrahyoid region**, the space between the hyoid bone and the sternum.—**Inframammary region.** See *inframammary*.—**Infrascapular region**, the region on the back of the thorax on either side of the median line below a horizontal line through the inferior angle of each scapula. Also called *subscapular region*.—**Interscapular region**, the region on the back of the thorax between the shoulder-blades.—**Ischiorectal region**, the space corresponding to the posterior part of the pelvic outlet.—**Lenticulostriate region**, the anterior parts of the lenticular and caudate nuclei and the intervening part of the internal capsule.—**Lenticulothalamic region**, the posterior part of the lenticular nucleus, the optic thalamus, and the intervening part of the internal capsule.—**Lumbar region.** See *lumbar*[1].—**Mammary region**, the region on the front of the chest extending from the upper border of the third to the upper border of the sixth rib.—**Mesogastric region**, the umbilical and right and left lumbar regions taken together.—**Multiply-connected region**, in *math.*, a region such that between any two points of it several paths can be drawn which cannot be changed one into the other by gradual changes or variations without going out of the region in question.—**Parasternal, pelvic, Polynesian, popliteal, precordial, etc., region.** See the adjectives.—**Region of calms.** See *calm*[1].—**Sternal region**, *superior* and *inferior*. See *sternal*.—**Subaxillary region.** Same as *infra-axillary region*.—**Subclavicular region.** Same as *infraclavicular region*.—**Submammary region.** Same as *inframammary region*.—**Subscapular region.** Same as *infrascapular region*.—**Suprahyoid region**, the region of the front of the neck above the hyoid bone; the hyomental region.—**Supramammary region.** Same as *infraclavicular region*.—**Suprascapular region**, the region on the back above the spine of the scapula.—**Suprasternal region.** See *suprasternal*. =**Syn.** 1. Quarter, locality, clime, territory.

regional (rē'jon-al), *a.* [< F. *régional* = Sp. Pg. *regional* = It. *regionale*, < LL. *regionalis*, of or belonging to a region or province, < L. *regio(n-)*, a region, province: see *region*.] 1. Of or pertaining to a particular region or place; sectional; topical; local.

The peculiar seasonal and *regional* distribution of hurricanes. *The Atlantic*, XLIX. 334.

2. Of or pertaining to division into regions, as in anatomy and zoögeography; topographical.

It is curious that the Japanese should have anticipated Europe in a kind of rude *regional* anatomy. *O. W. Holmes*, Med. Essays, p. 224.

Regional anatomy. Same as *topographical anatomy*. See *anatomy*.

regionally (rē'jon-al-i), *adv.* With reference to a region or particular place; topically; locally; in *zoögeog.*, with reference to faunal regions or areas.

He thought it was the duty of the surgeon to treat it *regionally*. *Medical News*, LII. 273.

The preservation of rock-oils in every formation, of every geological age, all over the world—subject, however, locally or *regionally*, to subsequent change or destruction. *Science*, VIII. 233.

regionarius (rē"ji-ō-nā'ri-us), *n.*; pl. *regionarii* (-ī). [NL., < L. *regio(n-)*, a region: see *region*.] A title given to various Roman Catholic ecclesiastics who are assigned to duty in or jurisdiction over certain regions or districts in the city of Rome.

regionary (rē'jon-ā-ri), *a.* [< *region* + *-ary*.] 1. Of or pertaining to a region or regions.

But to this they attributed their successes, namely, to the tropical and *regionary* deities, and their entertaining so numerous a train of gods and goddesses. *Evelyn*, True Religion, I. 104.

2. Of or pertaining to a region or administrative district, especially of the city of Rome.—**Regionary deacon.** See *deacon*.

From the time of Honorius II., Rome had twelve *regionary deacons*. *Rom. Cath. Dict.*, p. 714.

regionic (rē-ji-on'ik), *a.* [< *region* + *-ic*.] Same as *regional*. [Rare.]

A *regionic* association. *Buck's Handbook of Med. Sciences*, IV. 758.

regious† (rē'ji-us), *a.* [= Sp. Pg. It. *regio*, < L. *regius*, kingly, royal, regal, < *rex* (*reg-*), a king: see *rex*.] Pertaining to a king; royal. *J. Harington.*

register[1] (rej'is-tėr), *n.* [< ME. *regester* (= D. G. Sw. Dan. *register*), < OF. *registre*, F. *registre*, a record, register, = Pr. *registre* = Sp. *registro* = Pg. *registro*, *registo*, *resisto* = It. *registro*, a register, record, < ML. *registrum*, also *registra*, *register*, a register, an altered form of *regestum*, a book in which things are recorded, a register, orig. pl., L. *regesta*, things recorded, records, neut. pl. of *regestus*, pp. of *regerere*, record: see *regest*, *n.* and *v.* In the later senses 6–10, from the verb, and in part practically identical, as 'that which registers,' with *register*[2], 'one who registers': see *register*[2].] 1. An official written account or entry, usually in a book regularly kept, as of acts, proceedings, or names, for preservation or for reference; a record; a list; a roll; also, the book in which such a record is kept: as, a parish *register*; a hotel *register*.

Of soules fynde I nat in this *registre*. *Chaucer*, Knight's Tale, l. 1954.

Each time of sorrow is naturally evermore a *register* of all such grievous events as have happened either in or near about the same time. *Hooker*, Eccles. Polity, v. 72.

2. In *old Eng. law*, a compilation of the forms of writs in use, both original and judicial, which seems to have grown up gradually in the hands of clerks and of copyists, and therefore to vary much in different copies. *Harvard Law Review*, Oct., 1889.—3. In *com.*, a document issued by the customs authorities as evidence of a ship's nationality. See *registration of British ships*, under *registration*.—4. The printed list of signatures at the end of early printed books. —5. In *music*: (*a*) The compass or range of a voice or an instrument. (*b*) A particular series of tones, within the compass of a voice or of certain instruments, which is produced in the same way and with the same quality: as, the chest-*register* of the voice, or the chalumeau *register* of the clarinet. The vocal registers are distinguished by quality more than by pitch, since the same tone can often be produced in more than one register. The difference lies in the way in which the larynx is used, but the exact nature of the process is disputed. The so-called *head-register* and *chest-register* include tones that call the cavities of the head and chest respectively into decided sympathetic vibration. The different vocal qualities are also called the *low*, *middle*, and *high registers*, or the *thick*, *middle*, and *thin registers*, depending in the first case upon the pitch of the tones for which they are best suited, and in the second upon the supposed condition of the vocal cords in producing them, or the quality of the tones produced.

It is true that alto boys cannot be made effective when choir-masters prohibit the use of the chest *register*. *Harper's Mag.*, LXXVII. 73.

6. In *organ-building*: (*a*) Same as *stop* or *stop-knob*. (*b*) A perforated frame or board for holding a set of trackers in place.—7. A device for registering automatically the number of revolutions made or the amount of work done by machinery, or for recording the pressure of steam, air, or water, or other data, by means of apparatus deriving motion from the object or objects whose force, velocity, etc., it is desired to ascertain.—8. A contrivance for regulating the passage of heat or air, as the draft-regulating plate of a furnace, or the damper-plate of a locomotive engine; a perforated plate with valves governing the opening into a duct which admits warm air into a room for heat, or fresh air for ventilation, or which allows foul air to escape.

Look well to the *register*;
And let your heat still lessen by degrees.
B. Jonson, Alchemist, ii. 1.

I should like to know if an artist could ever represent on canvas a happy family gathered round a hole in the floor called a *register*. *C. D. Warner*, Backlog Studies, p. 13.

9. In *printing*, exact adjustment of position in the presswork of books or papers printed on both sides of the leaf. When pages, columns, and lines are truly square, and back one another precisely on the leaf, or when two or more adjacent colors meet without impinging, they are said to be *in register*; otherwise, *out of register*.

10. The inner part of the mold in which types are cast.—11. In *bookbinding*, a ribbon attached to a full-bound book to serve as a marker of place for the reader.—**Anemometrographic register.** See *anemometer*.—**Army Register.** See *army-list*, 1.—**Lloyd's Register of British and Foreign Shipping.** See *Lloyd's*.—**Meteorological register.** See *meteorological table* (*a*), under *meteorological*.—**Morse register.** Same as *indicator*, 1 (*b*).—**Out of register.** See def. 9.—**Parish register**, a book in which the births, deaths, and marriages that occur in a given parish are registered.—**Register counties**, in *Eng. law*, certain counties or parts of counties, including Middlesex except London, the North, East, and West Ridings of Yorkshire, and Kingston-upon-Hull, in which peculiar laws for registration of matters affecting land-titles are in force.—**Register ship**, a ship which once obtained permission by treaty to trade to the Spanish West Indies, and whose capacity, per registry, was attested before sailing.—**Register thermometer.** See *thermometer*.—**Seamen's register**, a record containing the number and date of registration of each foreign-going ship and her registered tonnage, the length and general nature of her voyage or employment, the names, ages, etc., of the master and crew, etc. [Eng.]—**Ship's register**, a document showing the ownership of a vessel and giving a general description of her. It is used as a permit issued by the United States government to give protection and identification to an American vessel in a foreign trade, being practically for the vessel what a deed is for a house.—**To make register**, in *printing*, to arrange on the press pages, plates, or woodcuts in colors exactly in their proper positions. =**Syn.** 1. *Catalogue*, etc. (see *list*[5]), chronicle, archives.

register[1] (rej'is-tėr), *v.* [< F. *registrer* = Pr. Sp. Pg. *registrar* = It. *registrare*, < ML. *registrare*, register; from the noun: see *register*[1], *n.*] I. *trans.* 1. To enter in a register; indicate by registering; record in any way.

Here are thy virtues shew'd, here *register'd*,
And here shall live forever.
Fletcher, Double Marriage, v. 2.

Many just and holy men, whose names
Are *register'd* and calendar'd for saints.
Tennyson, St. Simeon Stylites.

The gray matter of the nervous system is the part in which sensory impulses are received and *registered*. *Science*, V. 258.

2. To mark or indicate on a register or scale. —3. In *rope-making*, to twist, as yarns, into a strand.—**Light-registering apparatus.** See *light*[1]. =**Syn.** 1. See *record*.

II. *intrans.* 1. To enter one's name, or cause it to be entered, in a register, as at a hotel, or in the registry of qualified voters.—2. In *printing*, etc.: (*a*) To correspond exactly in symmetry, as columns or lines of printed matter on opposite sides of a leaf, so that line shall fall upon line and column upon column. (*b*) To correspond exactly in position, as in color-printing, so that every different color-impression shall fall exactly in its proper place, forming no double lines, and neither leaving blank spaces nor passing the limits proper to any other color.—3. In *organ-playing*, same as *registrate*.

register[2] (rej'is-tėr), *n.* [An altered form, due to confusion with *register*[1], of *registrer*, now usually written *registrar*: see *registrar*.] 1. One who registers: same as *registrar*.

O comfort-killing Night! . . .
Dim *register* and notary of shame!
Shak., Lucrece, l. 765.

And hauing subscribed their names, certaine *Registers* copie the said Orations. *Purchas*, Pilgrimage, p. 439.

Specifically—2. In *law*: (*a*) An officer of a United States district court, formerly appointed under the United States bankruptcy act, for the purpose of assisting the judge in the performance of his duties under that act, by attending to matters of detail and routine, or purely administrative in their character. *Bump.* (*b*) In some parts of the United States, an officer who receives and records deeds so as to give public notice thereof.—**Lord register, or lord clerk register**, a Scottish officer of state who has the custody of the archives.—**Register in bankruptcy.** Same as *bankruptcy commissioner* (which see, under *bankruptcy*).—**Register of deeds**, in the United States, a public officer who records at length deeds, conveyances, and mortgages of real estate situated within a given district.—**Register of probate or of wills**, in some of the United States, a public officer who records all wills admitted to probate.—**Register of the Treasury**, an officer of the Treasury Department of the United States government, who has charge of the account-books of the United States, registers all warrants drawn by the Secretary of the Treasury upon the treasurer, signs and issues all government securities, and has charge of the registry of vessels.

registerable (rej'is-tėr-a-bl), *a.* [< *register*1 + *-able.*] Admitting of registration, or of being registered or recorded. *Fortnightly Rev.*, N. S., XXXIX. 26.

registered (rej'is-tėrd), *p. a.* Recorded, as in a register or book; enrolled: as, a *registered* voter (one whose name is duly entered in the official list of persons qualified to vote in an election).—**Registered bond, invention, letter**, etc. See the nouns.—**Registered company**, a company entered in an official register, but not incorporated by act or charter.

registerer† (rej'is-tėr-ėr), *n.* [< *register*1, *v.*, + *-er*1. Cf. *registrar.*] One who registers; a registrar; a recorder.

The Greekes, the chiefe *registerers* of worthy actes.
Golding, tr. of Cæsar, To the Reader.

register-grate (rej'is-tėr-grāt), *n.* A grate furnished with an apparatus for regulating the admission of air and the heat of the fire.

registering (rej'is-tėr-ing), *n.* [Verbal n. of *register*, *v.*] Same as *registration.*

register-office (rej'is-tėr-of"is), *n.* 1. An office where a register is kept, or where registers or records are kept; a registry; a record-office.—2. An agency for the employment of domestic servants. [U. S.]

register-plate (rej'is-tėr-plāt), *n.* In rope-making machines, a concave metallic disk having holes so arranged concentrically as to give the yarns passed through them the proper positions for entering into the general twist.

register-point (rej'is-tėr-point), *n.* The adjustable point or spur attached to a printing-press and used to aid in getting register. See *point*1, 2 (*c*).

registership (rej'is-tėr-ship), *n.* [< *register*2 + *-ship.*] The office of a register or registrar.

registrable (rej'is-tra-bl), *a.* [< *register*1 + *-able.*] Admitting of registration; that may or can be registered. *Lancet*, No. 3474, p. 733.

registrar (rej'is-trär), *n.* [Formerly *registrer*; < ME. *registrere*, < ML. *registrarius*, one who keeps a register or record, a registrar, notary, < *registrum*, a register, record: see *register*1. Cf. *registrary* and *register*2. Cf. also OF. *registreur*, *registrateur*, < ML. *registrator*, < *registrare*, register.] 1. One whose business it is to write or keep a register or record; a keeper of records.

I make Pieres the Plowman my procuratour and my reve,
And *registrere* to receyue. *Piers Plowman* (B), xix. 254.

The patent was sealed and delivered, and the person admitted sworne before the *registrar*.
T. Warton, Bathurst, p. 136.

2. An official who acts as secretary to the congregation of a university.—**Registrar's license.** See *license.*

registrar-general (rej'is-trär-jen'e-ral), *n.* An officer who superintends a system of registration; specifically, in Great Britain, an officer appointed by the crown, under the great seal, to whom is intrusted, subject to such regulations as shall be made by a principal secretary of state, the general superintendence of the system of registration of births, deaths, and marriages.

registrarship (rej'is-trär-ship), *n.* [< *registrar* + *-ship.*] The office of registrar.

registrary (rej'is-trā-ri), *n.*; pl. *registraries* (-riz). [< ML. *registrarius*, one who registers: see *registrar.*] A registrar. The registrar of the University of Cambridge is so called.

Lo, hither commyth a goodly maystres,
Occupacyon, Famys *regestary*.
Skelton, Garland of Laurel, l. 521.

registrate (rej'is-trāt), *v.*; pret. and pp. *registrated*, ppr. *registrating*. [< ML. *registratus*, pp. of *registrare*, register: see *register*1, *v.*] I.† *trans.* To register; enroll.

Why do ye toil to *registrate* your names
On icy pillars, which soon melt away?
Drummond, Flowers of Sion.

II. *intrans.* In *organ-playing*, to arrange or draw stops for playing; make or set a combination. See *registration*, 3. Also *register*.

registrate†, *a.* Registered; recorded.

Those madrigals we sung amidst our flocks . . .
Are *registrate* by echoes in the rocks.
Drummond, To Sir W. Alexander.

registration (rej-is-trā'shon), *n.* [< OF. *registration*, < ML. *registratio(n-)*, a registering, < *registrare*, register: see *registrate* and *register*1, *v.*] 1. The act of inserting or recording in a register; the act of recording in general: as, the *registration* of deeds; the *registration* of births, deaths, and marriages; the *registration* of voters.

Man's senses were thus indefinitely enlarged as his means of *registration* were perfected.
J. Fiske, Idea of God, p. 48.

2. Specifically, in the *law of conveyancing*, a system for the recording of conveyances, mortgages, and other instruments affecting the title to real property, in a public office, for the information of all concerned. The general policy of registry laws is to make a duly registered instrument notice to all the world, so that no one can claim any advantage over the registered owner by dealing with an unregistered owner or claimant in ignorance of the registered title. Under some systems a specified time is allowed for registering; and in some neglect to register an instrument within the time limited marks it with infirmity. The more generally accepted principle is to give effect to each instrument in the order of its registration, as against all unregistered instruments of which the purchaser, etc., had no actual notice. Another important element in registry laws is a provision that the record or certified copy shall be evidence in all courts equally as the original; but in some systems the non-production of the original must be accounted for before the record can be received in lieu of it. 3. In *organ-playing*, the act, process, art, or result of selecting or combining stops for playing given pieces of music. It includes every effect of light and shade, of quality or power, that is needed for a complete rendering, including the choice of manuals, the drawing and retiring of stops, and the use of all mechanical accessories, like couplers, the swell pedal, etc. In most recent organ-music the registration is somewhat carefully indicated by the composer or editor, but organs are so diverse that every player must interpret such marks for himself. Older music is usually unmarked, and the registration requires special study as well as special talent.—**Decree of registration.** See *decree.*—**Parliamentary Registration Act**, an English statute of 1843 (6 and 7 Vict., c. 18), which requires the registration of voters and defines certain rights of voting. It has been amended by later statutes.—**Registration Act.** (*a*) An English statute of 1885 (48 Vict., c. 15), which extends the borough system of registration of voters to county voters. (*b*) One of numerous American statutes in various States, providing for registration, and often requiring it as a condition of the right to vote.—**Registration of births, marriages, and deaths**, the system of collecting vital statistics by requiring attending physicians, etc., in case of births and deaths, and clergymen and magistrates solemnizing marriages, to report at once each case, with appropriate particulars, to the public authorities, for the purpose of preserving permanent and systematic records.—**Registration of British ships**, a duty imposed on ship-owners in order to secure to their vessels the privileges of British ships. Registration is to be made by the principal officer of customs at any port or place in the United Kingdom, and by certain specified officers in the colonies. The registration comprises the name of the ship, the names and descriptions of the owners, the tonnage, build, and description of the vessel, the particulars of her origin, and the name of the master, who is entitled to the custody of the certificate of registry. The vessel is considered to belong to the port at which she is registered.—**Registration of copyright**, the name given in England to the recording of the title of a book for the purpose of securing the copyright: corresponding to *entry of copyright* in the United States.—**Registration of trade-marks**, the system by which one claiming the exclusive right to a trade-mark may register it for the purpose of giving public notice of his claim, and preserving record evidence thereof from the time of entry.—**Registration of voters or electors.** (*a*) In the United States, a system for the prevention of frauds in the exercise of the suffrage, by requiring voters to cause their names to be registered in books provided for the purpose in each election district, with appropriate particulars of residence, age, etc., to enable investigation to be made, and the right of the voter to cast the ballot to be challenged, if there be occasion. (*b*) In Great Britain and Ireland, the making up of a list of voters which, after judicial revision, is the accredited record of an elector's title to vote.

registrational (rej-is-trā'shon-al), *a.* [< *registration* + *-al.*] Of or pertaining to registration. *Lancet*, No. 3457, p. 1135.

registry (rej'is-tri), *n.*; pl. *registries* (-triz). [Early mod. E. also *regestery*, *regestary*; < ME. *regestery*, < ML. **regestarium*, < *regestum*, a register: see *register*1.] 1. The act of recording or writing in a register, or depositing in the place of public record: as, the *registry* of a deed; the *registry* of a will, etc.—2. The place where a register is kept.—3. A series of facts recorded; a record.

I have sometimes wondered why a *registry* has not been kept in the colleges of physicians of all such [specific remedies] as have been invented by any professors of every age. *Sir W. Temple*, Health and Long Life.

Our conceptions are but the *registry* of our experience, and can therefore be altered only by being temporarily annihilated. *J. Fiske*, Cosmic Philos., I. 59.

Certificate of registry. See *certificate*, 2.—**District registry**, in *Eng. law*, an office in a provincial town for the transaction or record of steps incidental to litigation by attorneys within the district, in order to avoid the necessity of taking every step in the central offices in London.

regitive† (rej'i-tiv), *a.* [Irreg. < L. *regere*, rule (see *regent*), + *-itive.*] Ruling; governing.

Their *regitive* power over the world.
Gentleman's Calling, vii. § 5. (*Latham.*)

regium donum (rē'ji-um dō'num). [L.: *regium*, neut. of *regius*, royal (see *regious*); *donum*, a gift, grant: see *donate.*] A royal grant; specifically, an annual grant of public money formerly given in aid of the maintenance of the Presbyterian and other dissenting clergy in Ireland, commuted in 1869 for £791,372.

He had had something to do with both the *regium donum* and the Maynooth grant.
Trollope, Barchester Towers, iii.

regius professor (rē'ji-us prọ-fes'ọr). [L.: *regius*, royal; *professor*, professor.] A royal professor; specifically, one of those professors in the English universities whose chairs were founded by Henry VIII. In the Scotch universities the same name is given to all professors whose professorships have been founded by the crown. Abbreviated *reg. prof.*

regive (rē-giv'), *v. t.* [< *re-* + *give.*] To give back; restore.

Bid day stand still,
Bid him drive back his car, and reimport
The period past, *regive* the present hour.
Young, Night Thoughts, ii. 309.

regle†, *n.* [Also *reigle*; < OF. *regle*, *reigle*, *riegle*, *rigle*, *reule*, *rieule*, F. *règle*, a rule, etc.: see *rule*1. Cf. *reglet*, *reglement*. In def. 2, cf. *reglet*, and also *rule*1 and the doublet *rail*1, a straight bar, etc.] 1. A rule; a regulation. *Halliwell.*—2. A hollow cut or channel for guiding anything; a groove in which something runs: as, the *regle* of a side-post for a flood-gate.

In one of the corners next the sea standeth a flood-gate, to bee drawne vp and let downe through *reigles* in the side postes, whose mouth is encompassed with a double frith.
R. Carew, Survey of Cornwall, fol. 105.

regle†, *v. t.* [Also *reigle*; < OF. *regler*, *reigler*, < LL. *regulare*, rule: see *rule*1, *regulate.*] To rule; govern; regulate.

All ought to *regle* their lives, not by the Pope's Decrees, but Word of God. *Fuller*, Worthies, Wales, III. 49.

reglement† (reg'l-mẹnt), *n.* [Also *reiglement*; < OF. *reglement*, F. *réglement* = Sp. *reglamento* = Pg. *regulamento* = It. *regolamento*, < ML. *regulamentum*, ruling, regulation, < LL. *regulare*, rule, regulate: see *regle*, *rule*1.] Regulation.

To speak now of the reformation and *reglement* of usury, how the discommodities of it may be best avoided.
Bacon, Usury.

reglementary (reg-lẹ-men'tạ-ri), *a.* [< OF. *reglementaire*, conformable to rule, < *reglement*, a rule, regulation: see *reglement.*] Of, pertaining to, or embodying regulations; regulative: as, a *reglementary* charter. *Encyc. Dict.* [Rare.]

reglet (reg'let), *n.* [Also *riglet*; < OF. *reglet*, F. *réglet* (= Sp. *regleta* = Pg. *regreta*), a reglet, < *regle*, a rule: see *regle.*] 1. In *printing*, a thin strip of wood, less than type-high, used in composition to make blanks about a page, or between the lines of large types in open display. Reglets are made of the width of ordinary text-types, from pearl to great primer. Broader strips of wood are known as *furniture*.
2. In *arch.*, a narrow flat molding, employed to separate panels or other members, or to form knots, frets, and other ornaments.

reglet-plane (reg'let-plān), *n.* A plane used for making printers' reglets. Reglets are not made in America with planes, but with fine circular saws. [Eng.]

reglow (rē-glō'), *v. i.* [< *re-* + *glow.*] Same as *recalesce.*

reglow (rē-glō'), *n.* [< *reglow*, *v.*] Same as *recalescence.*

regma (reg'mạ), *n.*; pl. *regmata* (-mạ-tạ). [< Gr. ῥῆγμα, a fracture, breakage, < ῥηγνύναι, break: see *break.*] In *bot.*, a capsule with two or more lobes and as many one-seeded, two-valved cells, which separate at maturity, splitting elastically from the persistent axis (carpophore), as in *Euphorbia* and *Geranium*. It is one form of schizocarp.

regmacarp (reg'mạ-kärp), *n.* [< Gr. ῥῆγμα, a fracture (see *regma*), + καρπός, fruit.] In *bot.*, any dehiscent fruit. *Masters.*

regna, *n.* Plural of *regnum*.

regnal (reg'nal), *a.* [< ML. *regnalis*, < L. *regnum*, kingdom, reign: see *reign.*] Pertaining to the reign of a monarch.—**Regnal years**, the number of years a sovereign has reigned. It has been the practice in various countries to date public documents and other deeds from the year of accession of the sovereign. The practice still prevails in Great Britain in the enumeration of acts of Parliament.

regnancy (reg'nan-si), *n.* [< *regnan(t)* + *-cy.*] The act of reigning; rule; predominance. *Coleridge.*

regnant (reg'nant), *a.* [= F. *régnant* = Sp. *reinante* = Pg. *reguante, reinante* = It. *regnante*, < L. *regnan(t-)s*, ppr. of *regnare*, reign: see *reign.*] 1. Reigning; exercising regal authority by hereditary right.

The church of martyrs, and the church of saints, and doctors, and confessors, now *regnant* in heaven.
Jer. Taylor, Works (ed. 1835), II. 214.

2. Ruling; predominant; prevalent; having the chief power.

His guilt is clear, his proofs are pregnant,
A traitor to the vices *regnant*. *Swift.*

This intense and *regnant* personality of Carlyle.
The Century, XXVI. 532.

Queen regnant. See *queen.*

regnative† (reg'na-tiv), *a.* [< L. *regnatus*, pp. of *regnare*, reign, + *-ive.*] Ruling; governing. [Rare.]

regnet, *n.* and *v.* An obsolete spelling of *reign.*

regnicide (reg'ni-sid), *n.* [< L. *regnum*, a kingdom, + *-cida*, < *cædere*, kill.] The destroyer of a kingdom. [Rare.]

Regicides are no less than *regnicides*, Lam. iv. 20; for the life of a king contains a thousand thousand lives, and traitors make the land sick which they live in.
Rev. T. Adams, Works, I. 418.

Regnoli's operation. See *operation.*

regnum (reg'num), *n.*; pl. *regna* (-nä). [ML., a particular use of L. *regnum*, kingly government, royalty: see *reign.*] 1. A badge or mark of royalty or supremacy, generally a crown of some unusual character. The word is especially applied to early forms of the papal tiara, a crown similar to a royal crown with a high conical cap rising from within it.

St. Peter (in the seal of the mayor of Exeter) has a lofty *regnum* on his head.
Jour. Brit. Archæol. Ass., XVIII. 257.

2. [*cap.*] [NL.] One of three main divisions of natural objects (collectively called *Imperium Naturæ*), technically classed as the *Regnum Animale, R. Vegetabile*, and *R. Minerale*: used by the older naturalists before and for some time after Linnæus, and later represented by the familiar English phrases *animal, vegetable*, and *mineral kingdom.* (See *kingdom*, 6.) A fourth, *R. Primigenium*, was formally named by Hogg. See *Primalia, Protista.*

regorge† (rē-gôrj'), *v. t.* [< OF. (and F.) *regorger* = Pr. *regorgar* = It. *ringorgare*, vomit up; as *re-* + *gorge, v.*] 1. To vomit up; eject from the stomach; throw back or out again.

It was scoffingly said, he had eaten the king's goose, and did then *regorge* the feathers. *Sir J. Hayward.*

2. To swallow again or back.

And tides at highest mark *regorge* the flood.
Dryden, Sig. and Guis., l. 186.

3. To devour to repletion. [Rare.]

Drunk with idolatry, drunk with wine,
And fat *regorged* of bulls and goats.
Milton, S. A., l. 1671.

regraces†, *n. pl.* [ME., < OF. *regraces*, thanks, < *regracier*, < ML. *regratiare, regratiari*, thank again, thank, < L. *re-*, again, + ML. *gratiare*, thank: see *grace.*] Thanks.

With dew *regraces.*
Plumpton Correspondence, p. 5. (*Halliwell.*)

regrade† (rē-grād'), *v. i.* [Altered to suit the orig. *grade*, and *degrade, retrograde*, etc.; < L. *regredi*, go or come back, turn back, retire, retreat, < *re-*, back, + *gradi*, go: see *grade*[1]. Cf. *regrede.* Cf. LL. *regradare*, restore to one's rank or to a former condition, also degrade from one's rank.] To retire; go back; retrograde.

They saw the darkness commence at the eastern limb of the sun, and proceed to the western, till the whole was eclipsed; and then *regrade* backwards, from the western to the eastern, till his light was fully restored.
Hales, New Analysis of Chronology, III. 230.

regrant (rē-grȧnt'), *v. t.* [< AF. *regranter, regraunter*, grant again; as *re-* + *grant.*] To grant again.

This their grace is long, containing a commemoration of the benefits vouchsafed their fore-fathers, & a prayer for *regranting* the same. *Purchas*, Pilgrimage, p. 200.

regrant (rē-grȧnt'), *n.* [< *regrant, v.*] The act of granting again; a new or fresh grant.

As there had been no forfeiture, no *regrant* was needed.
E. A. Freeman, Norman Conquest, V. 9.

regrate[1] (rē-grāt'), *v. t.* [< ME. *regraten*, < OF. *regrater*, sell by retail, regrate, F. *regratter*, haggle, higgle; with intrusive r (appar. due to confusion with OF. *regrater*, dress, mend, scour, furbish up for sale: see *regrate*[2]) for **regater* = Sp. *regatear*, rival in sailing, prob. formerly sell by retail, haggle (cf. deriv. *regateur*, retail, haggle, wriggle, avoid), = Pg. *regatar*, buy, sell, traffic (cf. deriv. *regatear*, haggle, bargain hard), = OIt. *regattare, rigattare*, sell by retail, haggle, strive for mastery, also **recattare, recatare*, buy and sell again by retail, retail, regrate, forestall the market (ML. refl. *regatare*, buy back, redeem), < *re-*, again, + *cattare*, get, obtain, acquire, purchase, < L. *captare*, strive to seize, lay hold of, snatch at, chase, etc.: see *chase*[1], *catch*[1], and cf. *acate* and *purchase.* Cf. also *regatta*, from the same source.] To retail; specifically, to buy, as corn or provisions, and sell again in or near the same market or fair—a practice which, from its effect in raising the price, was formerly made a criminal offense, often classed with *engrossing* and *forestalling.*

And that they *regrate* no corne commynge to the market, in peyne of lesynge xx. s. for euery of the seid offences.
English Gilds (E. E. T. S.), p. 381.

Neither should they likewise buye any corne to sell the same agayne, unless it were to make malte therof: for by such engrossing and *regrating* we see the dearthe that nowe comonly raigneth heere in England to have bene caused.
Spenser, Present State of Ireland.

regrate[2] (rē-grāt'), *v. t.* [< OF. *regrater*, dress, mend, scour, furbish up for sale, lit. 'scrape again,' F. *regratter*, scrape or scratch again, regrate (masonry), < *re-*, again, + *grater*, F. *gratter*, scrape, scratch, grate: see *grate*[1]. The word has hitherto been confused with *regrate*[1]: see *regrate*[1].] 1. In *masonry*, to remove the outer surface of (an old hewn stone), so as to give it a fresh appearance.—2†. To grate or rasp; in a figurative sense, to offend; shock. [Rare.]

The most sordid animal, those that are the least beautified with colours, or rather whose clothing may *regrate* the eye. *Derham*, Physico-Theology, iv. 12.

regrate[3]†, *n.* A Middle English form of *regret.*

regrater, regrator (rē-grā'tėr, -tor), *n.* [(*a*) E. *regrater*, < ME. *regratere*, < OF. *regratier*, F. *regrattier*, a huckster, = Pr. *regratier* = Sp. *regatero* = Pg. *regateiro* = It. *rigattiere* (ML. *regratarius*, later also *regraterius*), huckster; (*b*) E. *regrator*, < ME. *regratour*, < OF. *regrateor, regratour, regratteur* (= Pg. *regateador*; ML. as if **regratator*), a huckster, regrater, < *regrater*, regrate: see *regrate*[1].] A retailer; a huckster; specifically, one who buys provisions and sells them, especially in the same market or fair.

At Mede the mayde the maire hath bisougte,
Of alle suche sellers syluer to take,
Or presentz with-oute pens as peces of siluer,
Ringes or other richesse the *regrateres* to maynetene.
Piers Plowman (B), iii. 90.

No *regratour* ne go owt of towne for to engrosy the chaffare, vpon payne for to be fourty-dayes in the kynges prysone. *English Gilds* (E. E. T. S.), p. 353.

Regrater or *Regrator*, a Law-word formerly us'd for one that bought by the Great, and sold by Retail: but it now signifies one that buys and sells again any Wares or Victuals in the same Market or Fair or within five Miles of it. Also one that trims up old Wares for Sale; a Broker, or Huckster. *E. Phillips*, 1706.

Regraters of bread corn. *Tatler*, No. 118.

Forestallers and *regrators* haunted the privy councils of the king. *I. D'Israeli*, Amen. of Lit., I. 379.

regratery†, *n.* [ME., < OF. **regraterie* (ML. *regrataria*), < *regrater*, regrate: see *regrate*[1].] The practice of regrating.

For thise aren men on this molde that moste harm worcheth
To the pore peple that parcel-mele buggen [buy at retail]; . . .
Thei rychen thorw *regraterye.* *Piers Plowman* (B), iii. 83.

regratiatory† (rē-grā'shi-ạ̄-tọ̄-ri), *n.* [< ML. *regratiator*, one who gives thanks, < *regratiari*, give thanks (cf. AF. *regraces*, thanks): see *regraces.* Cf. *ingratiate.*] A returning or giving of thanks; an expression of thankfulness.

That welnere nothynge there doth remayne
Wherewith to gyue you my *regraciatory.*
Skelton, Garland of Laurel.

regrator, *n.* See *regrater.*

regratorie†, *n.* A variant of *regratery.*

regratress† (rē-grā'tres), *n.* [< *regrater* + *-ess.*] A woman who sells at retail; a female huckster.

No baker shall give unto the *regratresses* the six-pence . . . by way of hansel-money.
Riley, tr. of Liber Albus, p. 232, quoted in Piers Plowman [(ed. Skeat), Notes, p. 43.

regrede (rē-grēd'), *v. i.* [< L. *regredi*, go or come back, return, retire, retreat, regrade, < *re-*, back, + *gradi*, go: see *grade*[1], and cf. *regress, regrade.*] To go back: retrograde, as the apse of a planet's orbit. *Todhunter.* [Rare.]

regredience† (rē-grē'di-ens), *n.* [< L. *regredien(t-)s*, ppr. of *regredi*, go back: see *regrede.*] A returning; a retrograding; a going back.

No man comes late unto that place from whence
Never man yet had a *regredience.*
Herrick, Never too Late to Dye.

regreet (rē-grēt'), *v. t.* [< *re-* + *greet*[1].] 1. To greet again; resalute.

You, cousin Hereford, upon pain of life,
Till twice five summers have enrich'd our fields,
Shall not *regreet* our fair dominions.
Shak., Rich. II., i. 3. 142.

2. To salute; greet. [Rare.]

Lo, as at English feasts, so I *regreet*
The daintiest last, to make the end more sweet.
Shak., Rich. II., i. 3. 67.

regreet (rē-grēt'), *n.* [< *regreet, v.*] A return or exchange of salutation; a greeting.

One that comes before
To signify the approaching of his lord;
From whom he bringeth sensible *regreets.*
Shak., M. of V., ii. 9. 89.

Thus low in humblest heart
Regreets unto thy truce do we impart.
Ford, Honour Triumphant, Monarch's Meeting.

regress (rē-gres'), *v. i.* [= Sp. *regresar* = Pg. *regressar*, < L. *regressus*, pp. of *regredi*, go back, < *re-*, back, + *gradi*, go: see *regrede.* Cf. *digress, progress, v.*] 1. To go back; return to a former place or state.

All . . . being forced into fluent consistences, do naturally *regress* into their former solidities.
Sir T. Browne, Vulg. Err., ii. 1.

2. In *astron.*, to move from east toward west.

regress (rē'gres), *n.* [= OF. *regres, regrez*, F. *regrès* = Sp. *regreso* = Pg. It. *regresso*, < L. *regressus*, a returning, return, < *regredi*, pp. *regressus*, go back: see *regress, v.*] 1. Passage back; return.

The standing is slippery, and the *regress* is either a downfall, or at least an eclipse.
Bacon, Great Place (ed. 1887).

'Tis their natural place which they always tend to, and from which there is no progress nor *regress.* *Burnet.*

2. The power or liberty of returning or passing back.

My hand, bully; thou shalt have egress and *regress.*
Shak., M. W. of W., ii. 1. 226.

3. In *Scots law*, reëntry. Under the feudal law, *letters of regress* were granted by the superior of a wadset, under which he became bound to readmit the wadsetter, at any time when he should demand an entry to the wadset.

4. In *canon law.* See *access*, 7.—5. In *logic*, the passage in thought from effect to cause.—**Demonstrative regress**, demonstrative reasoning from effect to cause.

regression (rē-gresh'on), *n.* [= OF. *regression*, F. *régression* = Sp. *regresion* = Pg. *regressão* = It. *rigressione*, < L. *regressio(n-)*, a going back, return, etc., < *regredi*, pp. *regressus*, go back: see *regress.*] 1. The act of passing back or returning; retrogression.

I will leave you whilst I go in and present myself to the honourable count; till my *regression*, so please you, your noble feet may measure this private, pleasant, and most princely walk. *B. Jonson*, Case is Altered, iii. 3.

2. In *astron.*, motion from east toward west.—3. In *geom.*, contrary flexure; also, the course of a curve at a cusp.—**Edge of regression**, the cuspidal edge of a developable surface. See *cuspidal.*—**Regression of nodes**, a gyratory motion of the orbit of a planet, causing the nodes to move from east to west on the ecliptic.

regressive (rē-gres'iv), *a.* [= F. *régressif*; as *regress* + *-ive.*] Passing back; returning: opposed to *progressive.*—**Regressive assimilation**, assimilation of a sound to one preceding it.—**Regressive method**, the analytic method, which, departing from particulars, ascends to principles. *Sir W. Hamilton*, Logic, xxiv.—**Regressive paralysis.** See *paralysis.*

regressively (rē-gres'iv-li), *adv.* In a regressive manner; in a backward way; by return. *De Quincey.*

regressus (rē-gres'us), *n.* [NL.: see *regress.*] In *bot.*, that reversion of organs now known as retrogressive and retrograde metamorphosis. See *metamorphosis.*

regret (rē-gret'), *v. t.*; pret. and pp. *regretted*, ppr. *regretting.* [< F. *regretter*, regret, OF. *regretter, regreter, regrater*, desire, wish for, long after, bewail, lament, = Pr. *regretar* (after F.); not found in other Rom. languages, and variously explained: (*a*) Orig. 'bewail,' < OF. *re-* + **greter*, from the OLG. form cognate with AS. *grǣtan*, ME. *greten*, E. *greet* = Icel. *grāta*, weep, wail, mourn, = Sw. *gråta* = Dan. *græde* = Goth. *grētan*, weep: see *greet*[2]. (*b*) < L. *re-*, taken as privative, + *gratus*, pleasing, as if orig. adj., 'unpleasing,' then a noun, 'displeasure, grief, sorrow': see *grate*[3], *gree*[2], *agree, maugre.* (c) < ML. as if **regradus*, a return (of a disease), as in Walloon *li r'gret d'on man*, 'the return of a disease,' < *regredi*, go back: see *regrede*, *regress*. (*d*) < L. as if **requiritari*, < *re-* + *quiritare*, bewail: see *cry*. (*e*) < L. *requiritare*, ask after, inquire for, freq. of *requirere*, ask after, require: see *require*. Of these explanations only the first is in any degree plausible.] 1. To look back at with sorrow; feel grief or sorrowful longing for on looking back.

Sure, if they catch, to spoil the toy at most,
To covet flying, and regret when lost.
Pope, Moral Essays, ii. 234.

Beauty which you shall feel perfectly but once, and *regret* forever. *Howells*, Venetian Life, ii.

2. To grieve at; be mentally distressed on account of: as, to *regret* one's rashness; to *regret* a choice made.

Ah, cruel fate, thou never struck'st a blow
By all mankind *regretted* so.
Cotton, Death of the Earl of Ossory.

Those the impiety of whose lives makes them *regret* a Deity, and secretly wish there were none, will greedily listen to atheistical notions. *Glanville.*

Poets, of all men, ever least *regret*
Increasing taxes and the nation's debt.
Cowper, Table-Talk, l. 176.

Alone among the Spaniards the Catalans had real reason to *regret* the peace. *Lecky*, Eng. in 18th Cent., i.

=**Syn.** To rue, lament. See *repentance*.

regret (rē-gret'), *n.* [Early mod. E. also *regrate*; < OF. *regret*, desire, will, grief, sorrow, regret, F. *regret*, regret; from the verb (which, however, is later in E.): see *regret*, *v.*] 1. Grief or trouble caused by the want or loss of something formerly possessed; a painful sense of loss; desire for what is gone; sorrowful longing.

When her eyes she on the Dwarf had set,
And saw the signes that deadly tydinges spake,
She fell to ground for sorrowfull *regret*.
Spenser, F. Q., I. vii. 20.

Anguish and *regret*
For loss of life and pleasure overloved.
Milton, P. L., x. 1018.

A pain of privation takes the name of a pain of *regret* in two cases: (1) where it is grounded on the memory of a pleasure which, having been once enjoyed, appears not likely to be enjoyed again; (2) where it is grounded on the idea of a pleasure which was never actually enjoyed, nor perhaps so much as expected, but which might have been enjoyed (it is supposed) had such or such a contingency happened, which, in fact, did not happen.
Bentham, Introd. to Morals and Legislation, v. 20.

2. Pain or distress of mind, as at something done or left undone; the earnest wish that something had not been done or did not exist; bitterness of reflection.

A passionate *regret* at sin, a grief and sadness at its memory, enters us into God's roll of mourners.
Decay of Christian Piety.

Many and sharp the num'rous ills
Inwoven with our frame!
More pointed still we make ourselves
Regret, remorse, and shame.
Burns, Man was Made to Mourn.

3†. Dislike; aversion.

Is it a virtue to have some ineffective *regrets* to damnation? *Decay of Christian Piety.*

4. An expression of regret: commonly in the plural. [Colloq.]—5. A written communication expressing sorrow for inability to accept an invitation. [Colloq.] =**Syn.** 1. Concern, sorrow, lamentation.—2. *Penitence*, *Compunction*, etc. See *repentance*.

regretful (rē-gret'fu̇l), *a.* [< *regret* + *-ful.*] Full of regret; sorrowful.

regretfully (rē-gret'fu̇l-i), *adv.* With regret.

regrettable (rē-gret'a-bl), *a.* [< *regret* + *-able.*] Admitting of or calling for regret.

Of *regrettable* good English examples can be quoted from 1632 onwards.
J. A. H. Murray, N. and Q., 7th ser., VIII. 134.

regrettably (rē-gret'a-bli), *adv.* With regret; regretfully.

My mother and sisters, who have so long been *regrettably* prevented from making your acquaintance.
H. James, Jr., International Episode, p. 126.

regrowth (rē-grōth'), *n.* [< *re-* + *growth.*] A growing again; a new or second growth. *Darwin.*

regt. An abbreviation of (*a*) *regent*; (*b*) *regiment*.

reguardant†, *a.* See *regardant*.

reguerdon† (rē-gėr'don), *n.* [< ME. *reguerdoun*, < OF. *reguerdon*; as *re-* + *guerdon*, *n.*] A reward; a recompense.

And in *reguerdon* of that duty done,
I gird thee with the valiant sword of York.
Shak., 1 Hen. VI., iii. 1. 170.

reguerdon† (rē-gėr'don), *v. t.* [< OF. *reguerdonner*, reward; as *re-* + *guerdon*, *v.*] To reward; recompense.

Yet never have you tasted our reward,
Or been *reguerdon'd* with so much as thanks.
Shak., 1 Hen. VI., iii. 4. 23.

reguerdonment (rē-gėr'don-ment), *n.* [< *reguerdon* + *-ment.*] Reward; return; requital.

In generous *reguerdonment* whereof he sacramentally obliged himselfe.
Nashe, Lenten Stuffe (Harl. Misc., VI. 163).

regula (reg'ū-lä), *n.*; pl. *regulæ* (-lē). [< L. *regula*, a rule: see *rule*¹, and cf. *regle.*] 1. A book of rules or orders governing a religious house; the rule. *Rev. F. G. Lee.*—2. In *arch.*, a short band or fillet, bearing guttæ or drops on the lower side, corresponding, below the crowning tænia of the Doric architrave, to the triglyphs of the frieze. See cut under *ditriglyph*.—**Regula cæci**, a rule of arithmetic for solving two linear equations between three unknown quantities in whole numbers.—**Regula falsi**, the rule of false. See *position*, 7.

regulable (reg'ū-la-bl), *a.* [< *regula(te)* + *-ble.*] Admitting of regulation; capable of being regulated.

regulæ, *n.* Plural of *regula*.

regular (reg'ū-lär), *a.* and *n.* [< ME. *reguler*, < OF. *regulier*, F. *régulier* = Pr. *reglar* = Sp. *reglar*, *regular* = Pg. *regular* = It. *regolare*, < L. *regularis*, regular, < *regula*, a rule, < *regere*, rule, govern: see *regula* and *rule*¹.] **I.** *a.* 1. Conformed to or made in accordance with a rule; agreeable to an established rule, law, type, or principle, to a prescribed mode, or to established customary forms; normal: as, a *regular* epic poem; a *regular* verse in poetry; a *regular* plan; *regular* features; a *regular* building.

The English Speech, though it be rich, copious, and significant, and that there be divers Dictionaries of it, yet, under Favour, I cannot call it a *regular* Language.
Howell, Letters, ii. 55.

But soft—by *regular* approach—not yet—
First through the length of yon hot terrace sweat.
Pope, Moral Essays, iv. 129.

Philip was of the middle height; he had a fair, florid complexion, *regular* features, long flowing locks, and a well-made, symmetrical figure.
Prescott, Ferd. and Isa., ii. 19.

2. Acting, proceeding, or going on by rule; governed by rule or rules; steady or uniform in a course or practice; orderly; methodical; unvarying: as, *regular* in diet; *regular* in attendance on divine worship; the *regular* return of the seasons.

Not a man
Shall . . . offend the stream
Of *regular* justice in your city's bounds,
But shall be rendered to your public laws.
Shak., T. of A., v. 4. 61.

True Courage must be a *Regular* thing; it must have not only a good End, but a wise Choice of Means.
Stillingfleet, Sermons, III. v.

This gentleman is a person of good sense, and some learning, of a very *regular* life, and obliging conversation.
Addison, Spectator, No. 106.

3. Specifically, in *law*, conformable to law and the rules and practice of the court.—4. In *math.*, governed by one law throughout. Thus, a *regular* polygon is one which has all its sides and all its angles equal; a *regular* body is one which has all its faces regular polygons, and all its summits formed by the junction of equal numbers of edges, those of each summit being equally inclined to one line.
5. In *gram.*, adhering to the more common form in respect to inflectional terminations, as, in English, verbs forming their preterits and past participles by the addition of *-d* or *-ed* to the infinitive; as nouns forming their plurals with *-s* or *-es*; as the three conjugations of French verbs known as *regular*; and so on.—6. Belonging to and subject to the rule of a monastic order; pertaining to a monastic order: as, *regular* clergy, in distinction from *secular* clergy.

As these chanouns *regulers*,
Or white monkes, or these blake.
Rom. of the Rose, l. 6694.

7. Specifically, in *bot.*, having the members of each circle of floral organs (sepals, petals, stamens, and pistils) normally alike in form and size: properly restricted to symmetry of form, as distinguished from symmetry of number.—8. In *zoöl.*, noting parts or organs which are symmetrically disposed. See *Regularia*.—9. In *music*: (*a*) Same as *strict*: as, *regular* form; a *regular* fugue, etc. (*b*) Same as *similar*: as, *regular* motion.—10. *Milit.*, permanent; standing: opposed to *volunteer*: said of an army or of troops.—11. In *U. S. politics*, of, pertaining to, or originating from the recognized agents or "machinery" of a party: as, a *regular* ticket.—12. Thorough; out-and-out; perfect; complete: as, a *regular* humbug; a *regular* deception; a *regular* brick. [Colloq.]—**Regular abbot, body, canon.** See the nouns.—**Regular benefice**, a benefice which could be conferred only on a regular priest.—**Regular curve.** (*a*) A curve without contrary flexure. (*b*) A curve defined by the same equation or equations throughout.—**Regular decagon, dodecagon, dodecahedron.** See the nouns.—**Regular function**, a function connected with the variable by the same general law for all values of the latter.—**Regular physician**, a practitioner of medicine who has acquired an accepted grade of knowledge of such things as pertain to the art of healing, and who does not announce himself as employing any single and peculiar rule or method of treatment, in contrast with the allopath (if such there be), homeopath, botanic physician, hydropath, electrician, or mind-cure practitioner. But nothing in his character of regular physician prevents his using drugs which may be made to produce in a healthy person effects opposite to or similar to those of the disease in hand, or using drugs of vegetable origin, or water in its various applications, or electricity, or recognizing the tonic effects of faith.—**Regular place**, a place within the precincts of a religious house.—**Regular polygon, polyhedron.** See the nouns.—**Regular proof**, a proof drawn up in strict form, with all the steps accurately stated in their proper order.—**Regular relation.** See *relation*.—**Regular sales**, in *stock-broking* and similar transactions, sales for delivery on the following day.—**Regular syllogism**, a syllogism set forth in the form usual in the books of logic, the major premise first, then the minor premise, and last the conclusion, each proposition being formally stated, with the same expressions used for the terms in the different propositions, and the construction of the proposition being that which logic contemplates.—**The regular system**, in *crystal.*, the isometric system. =**Syn.** 1. *Ordinary*, etc. See *normal*.—2. Systematic, uniform, periodic, settled, established, stated.

II. *n.* 1. A member of any duly constituted religious order which is bound by the three monastic vows.

They declared positively that he [Archbishop Abbot] was not to fall from his Dignity or Function, but should still remain a *Regular*, and in statu quo prius.
Howell, Letters, I. iii. 7.

As in early days the *regulars* sustained Becket and the seculars supported Henry II. *Stubbs*, Const. Hist., § 405.

2. A soldier who belongs to a standing army, as opposed to a militiaman or volunteer; a professional soldier.

He was a *regular* in our ranks; in other services only a volunteer. *Sumner*, John Pickering.

3. In *chron.*: (*a*) A number attached to each year such that added to the concurrents it gives the number of the day of the week on which the paschal full moon falls. (*b*) A fixed number attached to each month, which assists in ascertaining on what day of the week the first day of any month fell, or the age of the moon on the first day of any month.—**College of regulars.** See *college*.—**Congregation of Bishops and Regulars.** See *congregation*, 5 (*a*) (8).

Regularia (reg-ū-lā'ri-ä), *n. pl.* [NL., neut. pl. of L. *regularis*, regular: see *regular*.] Regular sea-urchins, with biserial ambulacral plates, centric mouth, and aboral anus interior. Also called *Endocyclica*.

regularise, *v. t.* See *regularize*.

regularity (reg-ū-lar'i-ti), *n.* [< OF. *regularite*, *regulairete*, F. *régularité* = Sp. *regularidad* = Pg. *regularidade* = It. *regolarità*, < ML. **regularita(t-)s*, < L. *regularis*, regular: see *regular*.] The state or character of being regular, in any sense: as, *regularity* of a plan or of a building; *regularity* of features; the *regularity* of one's attendance at church; the watch goes with great *regularity*.

He was a mighty lover of *regularity* and order.
Bp. Atterbury.

There was no *regularity* in their dancing.
E. W. Lane, Modern Egyptians, II. 212.

Regularity and proportion appeal to a primary sensibility of the mind. *A. Bain*, Emotions and Will, p. 236.

regularization (reg″ū-lär-i-zā'shon), *n.* [< *regularize* + *-ation.*] The act or process of regularizing, or making regular; the state of being made regular. [Rare.]

At present (1885), a scheme combining the two systems of *regularization* and canalization is being carried out, for the purpose of securing everywhere at low water a depth of 5 feet 3 inches. *Encyc. Brit.*, XX. 528.

An ancient Chinese law, moreover, prescribed the *regularization* of weights and measures at the spring equinox.
Encyc. Brit., XXIV. 792.

regularize (reg'ū-lär-īz), *v. t.* [< F. *régulariser*; as *regular* + *-ize.*] To make regular.

The labor bestowed in *regularizing* and modulating our language had operated not only to impoverish it, but to check its growth. *F. Hall*, Mod. Eng., p. 282.

Their [the alkaline metals'] mode of action is greatly *regularised* by being made into amalgam with mercury.
W. Crookes, Dyeing and Calico-printing, p. 440.

Also spelled *regularise*.

regularly (reg'ū-lär-li), *adv.* In a regular manner, in any sense of the word *regular*.

regularness (reg'ū-lär-nes), *n.* Regularity.

Long crystals . . . that did emulate native crystal as well in the *regularness* of shape as in the transparency of the substance. *Boyle*, Works, III. 530.

regulatable (reg'ū-lā-ta-bl), *a.* [< *regulate* + *-able.*] Capable of being regulated. *E. H. Knight.*

regulate (reg'ū-lāt), *v. t.*; pret. and pp. *regulated*, ppr. *regulating*. [< L. *regulatus*, pp. of *regulare* (> It. *regolare* = Sp. *reglar*, *regular* = Pg. *regular*, *regrar* = F. *régler*), direct, rule, regulate, < *regula*, rule: see *rule*[1]. Cf. *regle*, *rail*[2], *v.*] 1. To adjust by rule, method, or established mode; govern by or subject to certain rules or restrictions; direct.

If we think to *regulat* Printing, thereby to rectifie manners, we must *regulat* all recreations and pastimes, all that is delightfull to man. *Milton*, Areopagitica, p. 23.

When I travel, I always choose to *regulate* my own supper. *Goldsmith*, She Stoops to Conquer, ii. 1.

One of the settled conclusions of political economy is that wages and prices cannot be artificially *regulated*. *H. Spencer*, Social Statics, p. 501.

2. To put or keep in good order: as, to *regulate* the disordered state of a nation or its finances; to *regulate* the digestion.

You must learn by trial how much half a turn of the screw accelerates or retards the watch per day, and after that you can *regulate* it to the utmost nicety. *Sir E. Beckett*, Clocks, Watches, and Bells, p. 300.

3. Specifically, in musical instruments with a keyboard, so to adjust the action that it shall be noiseless, prompt, and sensitive to the touch. =**Syn.** 1. *Rule, Manage*, etc. See *govern*.

regulating (reg'ū-lā-ting), *n.* 1. The act indicated by the verb *regulate*. Specifically—2. In *rail.*, the work in the yard of making up trains, storing cars, etc.; drilling or switching.

regulating-screw (reg'ū-lā-ting-skrö), *n.* In *organ-building*, a screw by which the dip of the digitals of the keyboard may be adjusted.

regulation (reg-ū-lā'shon), *n.* and *a.* [= F. *régulation* = Sp. *regulacion* = Pg. *regulação* = It. *regolazione*, < ML. **regulatio(n-)*, < *regulare*, regulate: see *regulate*.] I. *n.* 1. The act of regulating, or the state of being regulated or reduced to order.

No form of co-operation, small or great, can be carried on without *regulation*, and an implied submission to the regulating agencies. *H. Spencer*, Man vs. State, p. 39.

2. A rule or order prescribed by a superior or competent authority as to the actions of those under its control; a governing direction; precept; law: as, police *regulations*; more specifically, a rule prescribed by a municipality, corporation, or society for the conduct of third persons dealing with it, as distinguished from (*a*) *by-law*, a term which is generally used rather with reference to the standing rules governing its own internal organization and the conduct of its officers and members, and (*b*) *ordinance*, which is generally used in the United States for the local legislation of municipalities.—3. In musical instruments with a keyboard, the act or process of adjusting the action so that it shall be noiseless, prompt, and sensitive to every variation of touch.—**Army regulations.** See *army*[2].—**General regulations**, a system of ordinances for the administration of the affairs of the army, and for better prescribing the respective duties and powers of officers and men in the military service, and embracing all forms of a general character. *Ives.* =**Syn.** 1. Disposition, ordering, adjustment.—2. *Ordinance, Statute*, etc. See *law*[1].

II. *a.* Having a fixed or regulated pattern or style; in accord with a rule or standard. [Colloq.]

The *regulation* mode of cutting the hair. *Dickens*, Oliver Twist, xviii.

My *regulation* saddle-holsters and housings. *Thackeray*, Vanity Fair, xxx.

regulation (reg-ū-lā'shon), *v. t.* [< *regulate* + *-ion.*] To bring under regulations; cause to conform to rules. [Rare.]

The Javanese knows no freedom. His whole existence is *regulationed*. Quoted in *Encyc. Brit.*, XIII. 604.

regulative (reg'ū-lā-tiv), *a.* [< *regulate* + *-ive.*] Regulating; tending to regulate.

Ends and uses are the *regulative* reasons of all existing things. *Bushnell*, Sermons for New Life, p. 12.

It is the aim of the Dialectic to show . . . that there are certain ideas of reason which are *regulative* of all our empirical knowledge, and which also limit it. *E. Caird*, Philos. of Kant, p. 197.

Regulative faculty, Sir W. Hamilton's name for the faculty of principles; the noetic faculty.—**Regulative idea**, a conception resulting from or carrying with it a regulative principle.—**Regulative principle.** (*a*) In *logic*, the leading principle of an argumentation or inference: that general proposition whose truth is required to justify the habit of inference which has given rise in any case to the particular inference of which this proposition is said to be the regulative principle: opposed to *constitutive principle*, or pre-major premise. [This use of the term originated in the fifteenth century.]

Which be the principles irregulatiue? The *Principles regulatiue* of a syllogisme be these two phrases of speech: to be spoken of all, and to be spoken of none. *Blundeville*, Arte of Logicke (ed. 1619), v. 1.

(*b*) Since Kant, a rule showing what we ought to assume, without giving any assurance that the fact to be assumed is true; or a proposition which will lead to the truth if it be true, while if it be false the truth cannot be attained: such, for example, is the rule that we must not despair of answering any question by sufficient investigation. (*c*) A rule of conduct which, if it be pursued, may lead us to our desired end, while, if it be not pursued, that end cannot be attained in any way.—**Regulative use of a conception.** See *constitutive use of a conception*, under *constitutive*.

regulator (reg'ū-lā-tor), *n.* [= F. *régulateur* = Sp. Pg. *regulador* = It. *regolatore*, < ML. *regulator*, a regulator, ruler, < *regulare*, regulate: see *regulate*.] 1. One who or that which regulates. Members of the unauthorized associations which have at various times been formed in parts of the United States for the carrying out of a rough substitute for justice in the case of heinous or notorious crimes have been called *regulators*.

2. A mechanical contrivance intended to produce uniformity of motion, temperature, power, etc. (*a*) In *engin.* and *mach.*: (1) A governor in the sense described and illustrated under *governor*, 6. (2) A governor employed to control the closing of the port-opening for admission of steam to the cylinder of an automatically variable cut-off steam-engine. This is a numerous class of regulators, in which the ball-governor described under *governor*, 6, is used to control the motion of the induction-valve instead of that of the throttle-valve. By leaving the throttle-valve fully open and closing the induction-valve earlier or later in the stroke, the steam arrives in the cylinder nearly at full pressure, and with its full store of available heat for conversion into work by expansion. (3) An arrangement of weights, springs, and an eccentric or eccentrics, carried on the fly-wheel shaft or on the fly-wheel of a steam-engine, connected with the stem of the induction-valve by an eccentric-rod, and automatically varying

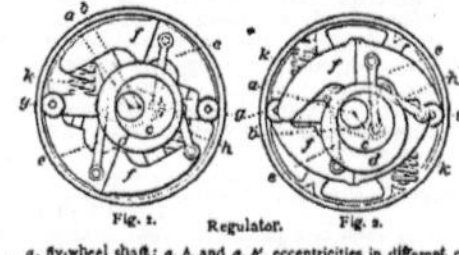

Fig. 1. Regulator. Fig. 2.

a, fly-wheel shaft; *a*, *b*, and *a*, *b'*, eccentricities in different positions of the eccentrics *c* and *d*. The eccentric *c* turns freely on the shaft *a*, and is actuated by links *e*, that are pivoted to ears formed on the eccentric, and are also pivoted to weights *f*. The weights have the form of curved bars, and are pivoted at one end to spokes of the wheel, as shown at *g*. The eccentric *d* is fitted to and turns freely upon the perimeter of the eccentric *c*. It is also connected by a link *h* to the toe of one of the weights, and is rotated on *c* by the motion of the weight toward or away from the center of the shaft *a*. The eccentric *c* is also rotated on the shaft *a* by the motion of the weights to or from the center of the shaft, but it is turned in a direction opposite to that in which *d* is turned. These two eccentricities, therefore, constitute a compound eccentric, the eccentricity or "throw" of which varies with the position of the weights, while the "lead" remains practically the same. Coiled springs *k* constantly press the weights *f* toward the center, and the action of these springs is more or less overcome by centrifugal force as the shaft *a* rotates with greater or less velocity. The higher the velocity the less will be the throw of the valve and the shorter the cut-off, and vice versa. Fig. 1 shows the weights in their extreme outward position, in which the throw *ab* is the least possible. Fig. 2 shows the extreme inward position of the weights, in which the throw *ab'* is the greatest possible. The range of variable cut-off is thus carried from simple lead to 0.7 of the stroke, and a very small percentage of change in the velocity is sufficient to change the cut-off from its least to its greatest limit.

the cut-off, maintaining a uniform speed of rotation under conditions of widely varying work. One of the most ingenious and scientific of this class is illustrated in the cut with an accompanying explanation. (4) A throttle-valve. (5) The induction-valve of a steam-engine. (6) The brake-hand of a crab or crane which regulates the descent of a body raised by or suspended on a machine. (*b*) In heating apparatus: (1) A register. (2) A thermostat. (3) An automatic draft-damper for the furnace or fire-box of a steam-boiler. Also called *damper-regulator*. (*c*) In *horol.*: (1) A clock of superior order, by comparison with which other time-pieces are regulated. (2) A clock which, being electrically connected with other clocks at a distance, causes them to keep time in unison with it. (3) A device (commonly a screw and small nut) by which the bob of a pendulum is raised or lowered, causing the clock to go faster or slower. (4) The fly of the striking mechanism of a clock. (See *fly*[1], 3 (*a*) (1).) (5) A small lever which shortens or lengthens the hair-spring of a watch, thus causing the watch to go faster or slower according as the regulator is moved toward a part marked F. or *S.* (*d*) In the electric light, the contrivance, usually an electromagnet, by which the carbon-points are kept at a constant distance, so that the light is steady (see *electric light*, under *electric*); or, in general, a contrivance for making the current produced by the dynamo-machines of constant strength.—**Many-light regulator**, a regulator for voltaic arc-lights, controlling numerous lights on one circuit.—**Regulator-box.** (*a*) A valve-chest or -box. (*b*) The original valve-motion of Watt's double-action condensing pumping-engine. It was a valve-box having a spindle through one of its sides, on which was a toothed sector working on a central bearing, and meshing with a rack attached to a valve. A tripping-lever attached to the sector and operated by the plug-tree caused the oscillations of the latter to open and close the valve.—**Regulator-cock**, one of the oil-cocks which admit oil to the steam-chest or valve-chest of a locomotive engine.—**Regulator-cover**, the cover or bonnet of a valve-chest or steam-chest of a steam-engine cylinder.—**Regulator-shaft and -levers**, in locomotive engines, the shaft and levers placed in front of the smoke-box when each cylinder has a separate regulator: now collectively called *valve-gear* or *valve-motion*.—**Regulator-valve**, a throttle-valve.

regulatory (reg'ū-lā-tō-ri), *a.* [< *regulate* + *-ory.*] Tending to regulate; regulative. *N. Y. Med. Jour.*, XL. 476.

regulatress (reg'ū-lā-tres), *n.* [< *regulator* + *-ess.*] A female regulator; a directrix. *Knight*, Anc. Art and Myth. (1876), p. 99.

Regulinæ (reg-ū-lī'nē), *n. pl.* [NL., < *Regulus* + *-inæ.*] The kinglets as a subfamily of *Sylviidæ* (or of *Turdidæ*), typified by the genus *Regulus*. They are only 4 or 5 inches long, generally with a conspicuous colored crest. The tarsi are booted, and the first primary is strictly spurious. The species are numerous, and inhabit chiefly the Old World. Sometimes *Regulidæ*, as a separate family.

reguline[1] (reg'ū-lin), *a.* [< F. *régulin*, having the character of regulus, the condition of perfect purity; as *regulus* + *-ine*[1].] Of or pertaining to a regulus.

The *reguline* condition is that of the greater number of deposits made in electrometallurgy. *Jour. Franklin Inst.*, CXIX. 90.

reguline[2] (reg'ū-lin), *a.* In *ornith.*, of or pertaining to the *Regulinæ*.

regulize (reg'ū-līz), *v. t.*; pret. and pp. *regulized*, ppr. *regulizing*. [< *regulus* + *-ize.*] To reduce to regulus.

regulus (reg'ū-lus), *n.*; pl. *reguli* (-lī). [< L. *regulus*, a little king, a king's son, a king bee, a small bird so called, LL. a kind of serpent, ML. *regulus*, metallic antimony, later also applied to various alloys and metallic products; dim. of *rex* (*reg-*), a king: see *rex*.] 1. In *ornith.*: (*a*) An old name of the goldcrest or crested wren of Europe; a kinglet. (*b*) [*cap.*] [NL.] The typical genus of *Regulinæ*; the kinglets. The common goldcrest of Europe is *R. cristatus* (see cut under *goldcrest*); the fire-crested wren of the same country is *R. ignicapillus*. The corresponding species of America is the golden-crowned kinglet, *R. satrapa*. The ruby-crowned kinglet is *R. calendula*. See *kinglet*.

2. In *alchemy* and *early chemistry*, the reduced or metallic mass obtained in the treatment of various ores, particularly those of the semi-metals (see *metal*); especially, metallic antimony (*regulus antimonii*): but various alloys of antimony, other brittle metals, and even the more perfect metals were also occasionally so called, to indicate that they were in the metallic condition.—3. [*cap.*] [NL. (Copernicus), tr. Gr. βασιλίσκος, the name of the star in Ptolemy.] A very white star, of magnitude 1.4, on the heart of the Lion; α Leonis.—4. In *geom.*, a ruled surface or singly infinite system of straight lines, where consecutive lines do not intersect.—**Dalmatian regulus.** See *Dalmatian*.

regur, regar (rē'gėr, rē'gär), *n.* [Hind. *rēgur*, prop. *rēgada*, *rēgadi*, black loam (see def.), < *reg*, sand.] The name given in India to a dark-colored, loamy, superficial deposit or soil rich in organic matter, and often of very considerable thickness. It is distinguished by its fineness and the absence of forest vegetation, thus resembling in character the black soil of southern Russia (tschernozem) and of the prairies of the Mississippi valley.

regurgitant (rē-gėr'ji-tant), *a.* [< ML. *regurgitan(t-)s*, ppr. of *regurgitare*, regurgitate: see *regurgitate*.] Characterized by or pertaining to regurgitation.

The diseases of the valves and orifices of the heart which produce mechanical disorders of the circulation . . . are of two kinds, obstructive and *regurgitant*. *Quain*, Med. Dict., p. 623.

Regurgitant cardiac murmurs. See *murmur*.

regurgitate (rē-gėr'ji-tāt), *v.*; pret. and pp. *regurgitated*, ppr. *regurgitating*. [< ML. *regurgitatus*, pp. of *regurgitare* (> It. *regurgitare* = Sp. Pg. *regurgitar* = OF. *regurgiter*, F. *régurgiter*), regurgitate, < LL. *re-*, back, + *gurgitare*, engulf, flood: see *gurgitation*.] I. *trans.* To pour or cause to rush or surge back; pour or throw back in great quantity.

For a mammal, having its grinding apparatus in its mouth, to gain by the habit of hurriedly swallowing unmasticated food, it must also have the habit of *regurgitating* the food for subsequent mastication. *H. Spencer*, Prin. of Biol., § 297.

II. *intrans.* To be poured back; surge or rush back.

Many valves, all so situate as to give a free passage to the blood and other humours in their due channels, but not permit them to *regurgitate* and disturb the great circulation. *Bentley.*

Nature was wont to evacuate its vicious blood out of these veins, which passage being stopt, it *regurgitates* upwards to the lungs. *Harvey.*

regurgitation (rē-gėr-ji-tā'shon), *n.* [= F. *régurgitation* = Sp. *regurgitacion* = Pg. *regurgitação*, < ML. *regurgitatio(n-)*, < *regurgitare*, regurgitate: see *regurgitate*.] 1. The act of regurgitating or pouring back.—2. The act of swallowing again; reabsorption.

In the lowest creatures, the distribution of crude nutriment is by slow gurgitations and *regurgitations*.
H. Spencer, Universal Progress, p. 417.

3. In *med.*: (*a*) The puking or posseting of infants. (*b*) The rising of solids or fluids into the mouth in the adult. (*c*) Specifically, the reflux through incompetent heart-valves: as, aortic *regurgitation* (reflux through leaking aortic valves).

reh (rā), *n.* [Hind.] A saline efflorescence rising to the surface and covering various extensive tracts of land in the Indo-Gangetic alluvial plain, rendering the soil worthless for cultivation. It consists chiefly of sodium sulphate mixed with more or less common salt (sodium chlorid) and sodium carbonate. It is known in the Northwest Provinces of India as *reh*, and further west, in the Upper Punjab, as *kalar* or *kullar*.

Those who have travelled through Northern India cannot fail to have noticed whole districts of land as white as if covered with snow, and entirely destitute of vegetation. . . . This desolation is caused by *reh*, which is a white flocculent efflorescence, formed of highly soluble sodium salts, which are found in almost every soil. Where the subsoil water-level is sufficiently near the surface, the strong evaporating force of the sun's heat, aided by capillary attraction, draws to the surface of the ground the water holding these salts in solution, and these compel the water, which passes off in the form of vapour, to leave behind the salts it held as a white efflorescence.
A. G. F. Eliot James, Indian Industries, p. 195.

rehabilitate (rē-hā̦-bil'i-tāt), *v. t.* [< ML. *rehabilitatus*, pp. of *rehabilitare* (> It. *riabilitare* = Sp. Pg. *rehabilitar* = OF. *rehabiliter*, F. *réhabiliter*), restore, < *re-*, again, + *habilitare*, habilitate: see *habilitate*.] 1. To restore to a former capacity or standing; reinstate; qualify again; restore, as a delinquent, to a former right, rank, or privilege lost or forfeited: a term drawn from the civil and canon law.

He is *rehabilitated*, his honour is restored, all his attainders are purged! *Burke*, A Regicide Peace, iv.

Assured
The justice of the court would presently
Confirm her in her rights and exculpate,
Re-integrate, and *rehabilitate*.
Browning, Ring and Book, II. 327.

2. To reëstablish in the esteem of others or in social position lost by disgrace; restore to public respect: as, there is now a tendency to *rehabilitate* notorious historical personages; Lady Blank was *rehabilitated* by the influence of her family at court.

rehabilitation (rē-hā̦-bil-i-tā'shon), *n.* [= OF. *rehabilitation*, F. *réhabilitation* = Sp. *rehabilitacion* = Pg. *rehabilitação* = It. *riabilitazione*, < ML. *rehabilitatio(n-)*, < *rehabilitare*, pp. *rehabilitatus*, rehabilitate: see *rehabilitate*.] The act of rehabilitating, or reinstating in a former rank, standing, or capacity; restoration to former rights; restoration to or reëstablishment in the esteem of others.

This old law-term [rehabilitate] has been gaining ground ever since it was introduced into popular discourse by Burke, to whom it may have been suggested by the French réhabiliter. Equally with its substantive, *rehabilitation*, it enables us to dispense with a tedious circumlocution.
F. Hall, Mod. Eng., p. 299, note.

rehait†, rehete†, *v. t.* [ME. *rehaiten*, *rehayten*, *reheten*, < OF. *rehaitier*, make joyful, < *re-*, again, + *haitier*, make joyful.] To revive; cheer; encourage; comfort.

Thane the conquerour kyndly carpede to those lordes,
Rehetede the Romaynes with realle speche.
Morte Arthure (E. E. T. S.), l. 221.

Hym wol I comforte and *rehete*,
For I hope of his gold to gete.
Rom. of the Rose, l. 6509.

rehandle (rē-han'dl), *v. t.* [< *re-* + *handle*.] To handle or have to do with again; remodel; revise. *The Academy*, March 29, 1890, p. 218.

rehash (rē-hash'), *v. t.* [< OF. *rehacher*, hack or chop again, < *re-*, again, + *hacher*, chop, hash: see *hash*[1].] To hash anew; work up, as old material, in a new form.

rehash (rē-hash'), *n.* [< *rehash*, *v.*] Something hashed afresh; something concocted from materials formerly used: as, a literary *rehash*. [Colloq.]

I understand that Dr. O——'s speech here, the other evening, was principally a *rehash* of his Yreka effort.
Senator Broderick, Speech in California, Aug., 1859. (*Bartlett*.)

Your finest method in her hands is only a *rehash* of the old mechanism. *Jour. of Education*, XVIII. 377.

rehead (rē-hed'), *v. t.* [< *re-* + *head*.] To fit or furnish with a head again, as a cask or a nail.

rehear (rē-hēr'), *v. t.* [< *re-* + *hear*.] To hear again; try a second time: as, to *rehear* a cause in a law-court. *Bp. Horne*, Com. on Ps. lxxxii.

rehearing (rē-hēr'ing), *n.* [Verbal n. of *rehear*, *v.*] A second hearing; reconsideration; especially, in *law*, a second hearing or trial; more specifically, a new trial in chancery, or a second argument of a motion or an appeal.

If by this decree either party thinks himself aggrieved, he may petition the chancellor for a *rehearing*.
Blackstone, Com., III. xxvii.

rehearsal (rē̦-hėr'sa̤l), *n.* [Early mod. E. *rehersall*; < ME. *rehersaille*, < OF. *rehearsal*, *rehersall*, repeating, < *reherser*, rehearse: see *rehearse*.] The act of rehearsing. (*a*) Repetition of the words of another.

Twice we appoint that the words which the minister pronounceth the whole congregation shall repeat after him: as first in the publick confession of sins, and again in *rehearsal* of our Lord's prayer after the blessed sacrament. *Hooker*, Eccles. Polity.

(*b*) Narration: a telling or recounting, as of particulars: as, the *rehearsal* of one's wrongs or adventures.

Be not Autour also of tales newe,
For callyng to *rehersaill*, lest thou it rewe.
Booke of Precedence (E. E. T. S., extra ser.), i. 110.

You haue made mine cares glow at the *rehearsall* of your loue. *Lyly*, Euphues, Anat. of Wit, p. 75.

(*c*) In *music* and the *drama*: (1) The process of studying by practice or preparatory exercise: as, to put a work in *rehearsal*. (2) A meeting of musical or dramatic performers for practice and study together, preliminary to a public performance.

Here's a marvellous convenient place for our *rehearsal*. This green plot shall be our stage.
Shak., M. N. D., iii. 1. 3.

Full rehearsal, a rehearsal in which all the performers take part.—**Public rehearsal**, a rehearsal to which a limited number of persons are admitted by way of compliment or for their criticism, or even as to a regular performance.

rehearse (rē̦-hėrs'), *v.*; pret. and pp. *rehearsed*, ppr. *rehearsing*. [Early mod. E. also *reherse*; < ME. *rehercen*, *rehersen*, *rehearsen*, < AF. *reherser*; *rehercer*, repeat, rehearse, a particular use of OF. *reherser*, harrow over again, < *re-*, again, + *hercer*, harrow, < *herce*, F. *herse*, a harrow: see *hearse*[1].] **I.** *trans.* 1. To repeat, as what has already been said or written; recite; say or deliver again.

Her faire locks up stared stiffe on end,
Hearing him those same bloody lynes *reherse*.
Spenser, F. Q., III. xii. 36.

When the words were heard which David spake, they *rehearsed* them before Saul. 1 Sam. xvii. 31.

We *rehearsed* our rhymes
To their fair auditor.
Whittier, Bridal of Pennacook.

2. To mention; narrate; relate; recount; recapitulate; enumerate.

With many moe good deedes, not *rehearsed* heere.
Rob. of Gloucester, p. 582.

Of swiche unkynde abhomynacions
Ne I wol noon *reherce*, if that I may.
Chaucer, Man of Law's Tale, l. 89.

There shall they *rehearse* the righteous acts of the Lord.
Judges v. 11.

3. To repeat, act, or perform in private for experiment and practice, preparatory to a public performance: as, to *rehearse* a tragedy; to *rehearse* a symphony.

A mere boy, with but little physical or dramatic strength, coming upon the stage to *rehearse* so important a character, must have been rather a shock . . . to the great actor whom he was to support. *J. Jefferson*, Autobiog., p. 129.

4. To cause to recite or narrate; put through a rehearsal; prompt. [Rare.]

A wood-sawyer, living by the prison wall, is under the control of the Defarges, and has been *rehearsed* by Madame Defarge as to his having seen her [Lucie] . . . making signs and signals to the prisoners.
Dickens, Two Cities, iii. 12.

=**Syn.** 2. To detail, describe. See *recapitulate*.

II. *intrans.* To repeat what has already been said, written, or performed; go through some performance in private, preparatory to public representation.

Meet me in the palace wood . . . there will we *rehearse*.
Shak., M. N. D., i. 2. 105.

rehearser (rē̦-hėr'sėr), *n.* One who rehearses, recites, or narrates.

Such *rehearsers* [of genealogies] who might obtrude fictitious pedigrees. *Johnson*, Jour. to Western Isles.

rehearsing (rē̦-hėr'sing), *n.* [< ME. *rehersyng*, *rehersynge*; verbal n. of *rehearse*, *v.*] Rehearsal; recital; discourse.

Of love, of hate, and other sondry thynges,
Of whiche I may not maken *rehersynges*.
Chaucer, Good Women, l. 24.

reheat (rē-hēt'), *v. t.* [< *re-* + *heat*.] To heat again or anew.—**Reheating-furnace.** See *furnace*.

reheater (rē-hē'tėr), *n.* An apparatus for restoring heat to a previously heated body which has entirely or partially cooled during some stage of a manufacture or process. In a diffusion apparatus for extraction of sugar from beet-roots or from sugar-canes, reheaters are arranged in alternation with diffusers, commonly twelve in number, containing the sliced roots. The hot water for diffusion is directed through pipes connecting the diffusers with the reheaters by means of cocks or valves, and is reheated by passing through a reheater after passing through a diffuser. Thus, through the aid of heat and pressure, the water becomes charged with sugar. See *diffusion apparatus* (under *diffusion*), and *diffuse*.

rehed†, *n.* A corrupt Middle English form of *reed*[1].

reheel (rē-hēl'), *v. t.* [< *re-* + *heel*[1].] To supply a heel to, especially in knitting, as in mending a stocking.

rehelm (rē-helm'), *v. t.* [< *re-* + *helm*[2].] To cover again, as the head, with a helm or helmet.

With the crossynge of their speares the erle was vnhelmed; than he retourned to his men, and incontynent he was *rehelmed*, and toke his speare.
Berners, tr. of Froissart's Chron., II. cxlviii.

rehersaille†, *n.* A Middle English form of *rehearsal*.

reherse†, *v.* An obsolete spelling of *rehearse*.

rehete†, *v. t.* See *rehait*.

rehibition (rē-hi-bish'on), *n.* Same as *redhibition*.

rehibitory (rē̦-hib'i-tō̦-ri), *a.* Same as *redhibitory*.

rehybridize (rē-hī'bri-dīz), *v. t.* [< *re-* + *hybridize*.] To cause to hybridize or interbreed a second time and with a different species.

Hybrid plants may be again crossed or even *re-hybridized*. *Encyc. Brit.*, XII. 216.

rehypothecate (rē-hī-poth'ē̦-kāt), *v. t.* [< *re-* + *hypothecate*.] To hypothecate again, as by lending as security bonds already pledged. See *hypothecate*.

rehypothecation (rē-hī-poth-ē̦-kā'shon), *n.* [< *re-* + *hypothecation*.] The pledging of property of any kind as security for a loan by one with whom it has already been pledged as security for money be has loaned.

rei, *n.* Plural of *reus*.

reichardtite (rī'chär-tīt), *n.* [< *Reichardt* + *-ite*.] A massive variety of epsomite from Stassfurt, Prussia.

Reichertian (rī-chėr'ti-an), *a.* [< *Reichert* (see def.) + *-ian*.] Pertaining to the German anatomist K. B. Reichert (1811–83).

Reichsrath (G. pron. rīchs'rät), *n.* [G., < *reichs*, gen. of *reich*, kingdom, empire (= AS. *rīce*, kingdom: see *riche*), + *rath*, council, parliament: see *read*[1], *rede*[1].] The chief deliberative body in the Cisleithan division of Austria-Hungary. It is composed of an upper house (*Herrenhaus*) of princes, certain nobles and prelates, and life-members nominated by the emperor, and of a lower house of 353 deputies elected by landed proprietors and other persons having a certain property or particular individual qualification.

Reichsstadt (G. pron. rīch'stät), *n.* [G., < *reichs*, gen. of *reich*, kingdom, empire, + *stadt*, a town. Cf. *stadtholder*.] In the old Roman-German empire, a city which held immediately of the empire and was represented in the Reichstag.

Reichstag (G. pron. rīchs'tāch), *n.* [G., < *reichs*, gen. of *reich*, kingdom, empire, + *tag*, parliament: see *day*[1]. Cf. *Landtag*.] The chief deliberative body in certain countries of Europe. For the Reichstag of the old Roman-German empire, see *diet*[2]. In the present empire of Germany, the Reichstag, in combination with the Bundesrath (which see), exercises the legislative power in imperial matters; it is composed of 397 deputies, elected by universal suffrage. In the Transleithan division of Austria-Hungary it is composed of a House of Magnates and a lower House of Representatives. *Reichstag* in all these senses is often rendered in English by *diet* or *parliament*.

reichsthaler (G. pron. rīchs'tä"lėr), *n.* [G., < *reichs*, gen. of *reich*, kingdom, empire, + *thaler*, dollar: see *dollar*.] Same as *rix-dollar*.

reif†, *n.* See *reef*[3].

reification (rē"i-fi-kā'shon), *n.* [< *reify* + *-ation* (see *-fication*).] Materialization; objectivization; externalization; conversion of the abstract into the concrete; the regarding or treating of an idea as a thing, or as if a thing. [Rare.]

reify (rē'i-fī), *v. t.*; pret. and pp. *reified*, ppr. *reifying*. [< L. *res*, a thing, + *-ficare*, < *facere*, make (see *-fy*).] To make into a thing; make real or material; consider as a thing.

The earliest objects of thought and the earliest concepts must naturally be those of the things that live and move about us; hence, then—to seek no deeper reason for the present—this natural tendency, which language by providing distinct names powerfully seconds, to *reify* or personify not only things, but every element and relation of things which we can single out, or, in other words, to concrete our abstracts. *J. Ward*, Encyc. Brit., XX. 78.

reighte†. A Middle English variant of *raughte* for *reached*.

reiglet†, *n.* and *v.* See *regle*.

reiglement†, *n.* See *reglement*.

reign (rān), *n.* [Early mod. E. also *raign*, *raine*; < ME. *regne*, *rengne*, < OF. *reigne*, *regne*, F. *règne* = Pr. *regne* = Sp. Pg. *reino* = It. *regno*, < L. *regnum*, kingly government, royalty, dominion, sovereignty, authority, rule, a kingdom, realm, estate, possession, < *regere*, rule: see *regent*.] 1. Royal or imperial authority; sovereignty; supreme power; control; sway.

Why, what is pomp, rule, *reign*, but earth and dust?
Shak., 3 Hen. VI., v. 2. 27.

That fix'd mind . . .
That with the Mightiest raised me to contend,
And to the fierce contention brought along
Innumerable force of spirits arm'd,
That durst dislike his *reign*. *Milton*, P. L., i. 102.

In Britain's isle, beneath a George's *reign*.
Cowper, Heroism, l. 90.

2. The time during which a monarch occupies the throne: as, an act passed in the present *reign*.

In the fifteenth year of the *reign* of Tiberius Cæsar . . . the word of God came unto John. Luke iii. 1.

3†. The territory over which a sovereign holds sway; empire; kingdom; dominions; realm.

He conquerede al the *regne* of Femenye.
Chaucer, Knight's Tale, l. 8.

Then stretch thy sight o'er all her rising *reign*, . . .
Ascend this hill, whose cloudy point commands
Her boundless empire over sea and lands.
Pope, Dunciad, iii. 65.

4. Power; influence; sway; dominion.

She gan to stoupe, and her proud mind convert
To meeke obeysance of loves mightie *raine*.
Spenser, F. Q., V. v. 28.

In her the painter had anatomized
Time's ruin, beauty's wreck, and grim care's *reign*.
Shak., Lucrece, l. 1451.

That characteristic principle of the Constitution, which has been well called "The *Reign* of Law," was established.
J. Bryce, American Commonwealth, I. 215.

Reign of Terror. See *terror*.

reign (rān), *v. i.* [Early mod. E. also *raign*, *raine*; < ME. *reinen*, *reignen*, *regnen*, < OF. *regner*, F. *régner* = Pr. *regnar*, *renhar* = Sp. Pg. *reinar* = It. *regnare*, < L. *regnare*, reign, rule, < *regnum*, authority, rule: see *reign*, *n.* Cf. *regnant*.] 1. To possess or exercise sovereign power or authority; govern, as a king or emperor; hold the supreme power; rule.

In the Cytee of Tyre *regned* Agenore the Fadre of Dydo.
Mandeville, Travels, p. 30.

Alleluia: for the Lord God omnipotent *reigneth*.
Rev. xix. 6.

Better to *reign* in hell than serve in heaven.
Milton, P. L., i. 263.

2. To prevail; be in force.

The spavin
Or springhalt *reigned* among 'em.
Shak., Hen. VIII., i. 3. 13.

The sultry Sirius burns the thirsty plains,
While in thy heart eternal winter *reigns*.
Pope, Summer, l. 22.

Fear and trembling *reigned*, for a time, along the frontier. *Irving*, Granada, p. 101.

Silence *reigned* in the streets; from the church no Angelus sounded. *Longfellow*, Evangeline, i. 5.

3. To have dominion or ascendancy; predominate.

Let not sin therefore *reign* in your mortal body, that ye should obey it in the lusts thereof. Rom. vi. 12.

Our Jovial star *reign'd* at his birth.
Shak., Cymbeline, v. 4. 105.

Insatiate Avarice then first began
To *raigne* in the depraved minde of man
After his fall. *Times' Whistle* (E. E. T. S.), p. 41.

Two principles in human nature *reign*;
Self-love to urge, and Reason to restrain.
Pope, Essay on Man, ii. 53.

reigner (rā'nėr), *n.* [< *reign* + *-er*[1]. Cf. It. *regnatore*, ruler, < L. *regnator*, ruler.] One who reigns; a ruler. [Rare.]

reik†, *n.* A variant of *reck*[1].

reil†, *n.* A Middle English form of *rail*[3].

Reil's band. A fibrous or muscular band extending across the right ventricle of the heart, from the base of the anterior papillary muscle to the septum. It is frequent in man, and represents the moderator band found in the heart of some lower animals.

reim (rēm), *n.* Same as *riem*.

reimbark, *v.* See *reëmbark*.

reimbursable (rē-im-bėr'sa-bl), *a.* [= F. *remboursable* = Sp. *reembolsable*; as *reimburse* + *-able*.] Capable of being or expected to be reimbursed or repaid.

Let the sum of 550,000 dollars be borrowed, . . . *reimbursable* within five years.
A. Hamilton, To House of Rep., Dec. 3, 1792.

reimburse (rē-im-bėrs'), *v. t.* [Accom. < OF. (and F.) *rembourser* = Sp. Pg. *reembolsar* = It. *rimborsare*, reimburse; as *re-* + *imburse*.] 1. To replace in a purse, treasury, or fund, as an equivalent for what has been taken, expended, or lost; pay back; restore; refund: as, to *reimburse* the expenses of a war.

It was but reasonable that I should strain myself as far as I was able to *reimburse* him some of his charges.
Swift, Story of the Injured Lady.

If any of the Members shall give in a Bill of the Charges of any Experiments which he shall have made, . . . the Money is forthwith *reimbursed* by the King.
Lister, Journey to Paris, p. 79.

2. To pay back to; repay to; indemnify.

As if one who had been robbed . . . should allege that he had a right to *reimburse* himself out of the pocket of the first traveller he met. *Paley*, Moral Philos., iii. 7.

=**Syn.** 2. *Remunerate*, *Recompense*, etc. See *indemnify*.

reimbursement (rē-im-bėrs'ment), *n.* [Accom. < OF. (and F.) *remboursement* = It. *rimborsamento*; as *reimburse* + *-ment*.] The act of reimbursing or refunding; repayment.

She helped them powerfully, but she exacted cautionary towns from them, as a security for her *reimbursement* whenever they should be in a condition to pay.
Bolingbroke, The Occasional Writer, No. 2.

reimburser (rē-im-bėr'sėr), *n.* One who reimburses; one who repays or refunds what has been lost or expended.

reimplace† (rē-im-plās'), *v. t.* [Accom. < OF. *remplacer*, replace; as *re-* + *emplace*.] To replace.

For this resurrection of the soul, for the *reimplacing* the Divine image, . . . God did a greater work than the creation. *Jer. Taylor*, Works (ed. 1835), I. 865.

reimplant (rē-im-plant'), *v. t.* [< *re-* + *implant*.] To implant again.

How many grave and godly matrons usually graffe or *reimplant* on their now more aged heads and brows the reliques, combings, or cuttings of their own or others' more youthful hair!
Jer. Taylor (?), Artit. Handsomeness, p. 45.

reimplantation (rē-im-plan-tā'shon), *n.* [< *reimplant* + *-ation*.] The act or process of reimplanting.

Successful *Reimplantation* of a Trephined Button of Bone. *Medical News*, LII. p. 1. of Adv'ts.

reimport (rē-im-pōrt'), *v. t.* [< F. *réimporter*, reimport; as *re-* + *import*.] 1. To bring back.

Bid him [day] drive back his car, and *reimport*
The period past. *Young*, Night Thoughts, ii. 308.

2. To import again; carry back to the country of exportation.

Goods . . . clandestinely *reimported* into our own [country]. *Adam Smith*, Wealth of Nations, iv. 4.

reimport (rē-im'pōrt), *n.* [< *reimport*, *v.*] Same as *reimportation*.

The amount available for *reimport* probably has been returned to us. *The American*, VI. 244.

reimportation (rē-im-pōr-tā'shon), *n.* [< F. *réimportation*; as *reimport* + *-ation*.] The act of reimporting; that which is reimported.

By making their *reimportation* illegal.
The American, VI. 244.

reimpose (rē-im-pōz'), *v. t.* [< OF. *reimposer*, F. *réimposer*; as *re-* + *impose*.] 1. To impose or levy anew: as, to *reimpose* a tax.—2. To tax or charge anew; retax. [Rare.]

The parish is afterwards *reimposed*, to reimburse those five or six. *Adam Smith*, Wealth of Nations, v. 2.

3. To place or lay again: as, to *reimpose* burdens upon the poor.

reimposition (rē-im-pō-zish'on), *n.* [< F. *réimposition*; as *re-* + *imposition*.] 1. The act of reimposing: as, the *reimposition* of a tax.

The attempt of the distinguished leaders of the party opposite to form a government, based as it was at that period on an intention to propose the *reimposition* of a fixed duty on corn, entirely failed. *Gladstone.*

2. A tax levied anew.

Such *reimpositions* are always over and above the taille of the particular year in which they are laid on.
Adam Smith, Wealth of Nations, v. 2.

reimpress (rē-im-pres'), *v. t.* [< *re-* + *impress*.] To impress anew.

Religion . . . will glide by degrees out of the mind unless it be reinvigorated and *reimpressed* by external ordinances, by stated calls to worship, and the salutary influence of example. *Johnson*, Milton.

reimpression (rē-im-presh'on), *n.* [< F. *réimpression* = Sp. *reimpresion* = Pg. *reimpressão*; as *re-* + *impression*.] 1. A second or repeated impression; that which is reimpressed.

In an Appendix I have entered into particulars as to my *reimpression* of the present poem.
F. Hall, Pref. of Lauder's Dewtie of Kyngis (E. E. T. S.), p. v.

2. The reprint or reprinting of a work.

reimprison (rē-im-priz'n), *v. t.* [< *re-* + *imprison*.] To imprison again.

reimprisonment (rē-im-priz'n-ment), *n.* [< *reimprison* + *-ment*.] The act of confining in prison a second time for the same cause, or after a release from prison.

rein[1] (rān), *n.* [Early mod. E. also *rain*, *reigne*; < ME. *reine*, *reyne*, *reene*, < OF. *reine*, *resne*, *resgne*, F. *rêne* = Pr. *regna* = Sp. *rienda* (transposed for **redina*) = Pg. *rédea* = It. *redine*, < LL. **retina*, a rein (cf. L. *retinaculum*, a tether, halter, rein), < L. *retinere*, hold back, restrain: see *retain*.] 1. The strap of a bridle, fastened to the curb or snaffle on each side, by which the rider or driver restrains and guides the animal driven; any thong or cord used for the same purpose. See cut under *harness*.

Ther sholde ye haue sein speres and sheldes flote down the river, and the horse all quyk withoute maister, her *reynes* traillinge with the strem.
Merlin (E. E. T. S.), iii. 403.

How like a jade he stood, tied to the tree,
Servilely master'd with a leathern *rein*!
Shak., Venus and Adonis, l. 392.

She look'd so lovely as she sway'd
The *rein* with dainty finger-tips.
Tennyson, Sir Launcelot and Queen Guinevere.

2. A rope of twisted and greased rawhide. *E. H. Knight*.—3. *pl.* The handles of blacksmiths' tongs, on which the ring or coupler slides. *E. H. Knight*.—4. Figuratively, any means of curbing, restraining, or governing; government; restraint.

Dr. Davenant held the *reins* of the disputation; he kept him within the even boundals of the cause.
Bp. Hacket, Abp. Williams, i. 26. (*Davies*, under *boundal*.)

No more *rein* upon thine anger
Than any child. *Tennyson*, Queen Mary, iii. 4.

Overhead rein, a guiding-rein that passes over the head of a horse between the ears, and thus to the bit. It is used with an overcheck bridle. Also called *overcheck rein*. —**To draw rein.** See *draw*.—**To give the rein** or **the reins**, to give license; leave without restraint.

Do not *give* dalliance
Too much *the rein*: the strongest oaths are straw
To the fire i' the blood. *Shak.*, Tempest, iv. 1. 52.

To take the reins, to take the guidance or government.

rein[1] (rān), *v.* [< OF. **reiner*, *resner*, F. *réner*, bridle a horse, < *rêne*, a rein; from the noun.] I. *trans.* 1. To govern, guide, or restrain by reins or a bridle.

As skilful Riders *rein* with diff'rent force
A new-back'd Courser and a well-train'd Horse.
Congreve, tr. of Ovid's Art of Love.

She [Queen Elizabeth] was mounted on a milk-white horse, which she *reined* with peculiar grace and dignity.
Scott, Kenilworth, xxx.

2. To restrain; control.

Being once chafed, he cannot
Be *rein'd* again to temperance; then he speaks
What 's in his heart. *Shak.*, Cor., iii. 3. 28.

3. To carry stiffly, as a horse does its head or neck under a bearing-rein.—**To rein in**, to curb; keep under restraint, as by reins.

The cause why the Apostles did thus conform the Christians as much as might be according to the pattern of the Jews was to *rein* them *in* by this mean the more, and to make them cleave the better.
Hooker, Eccles. Polity, iv. 11.

II. *intrans.* To obey the reins.

He will bear you easily, and *reins* well.
Shak., T. N., iii. 4. 358.

To rein up, to halt; bring a horse to a stand.

But, when they won a rising hill,
He bade his followers hold them still: . . .
"*Rein up*; our presence would impair
The fame we come too late to share."
Scott, Lord of the Isles, vi. 18.

rein[2]†, *n.* An obsolete singular of *reins*.

reina, *n.* See *rena*.

reincarnate (rē-in-kär'nāt), *v. t.* [< *re-* + *incarnate*.] To incarnate anew.

reincarnation (rē-in-kär-nā'shon), *n.* [< *reincarnate* + *-ion*.] The act or state of being incarnated anew; a repeated incarnation; a new embodiment.

reincense† (rē-in-sens'), *v. t.* [< *re-* + *incense*[1].] To incense again; rekindle.

She, whose beams do *re-incense*
This sacred fire. *Daniel*, Civil Wars, viii. 1.

Indeed, Sir James Croft (whom I never touched with the least tittle of detractions) was cunningly incensed and *reincensed* against me. *G. Harvey*, Four Letters, iii.

reincite (rē-in-sīt'), *v. t.* [= OF. *reinciter*, F. *réinciter*; as *re-* + *incite*.] To incite again; reanimate; reëncourage.

To dare the attack, he *reincites* his band,
And makes the last effort.
W. L. Lewis, tr. of Statius's Thebaid, xii.

reincrease (rē-in-krēs'), *v. t.* [< *re-* + *increase*.] To increase again; augment; reinforce.

When they did perceaue
Their wounds recur'd, and forces *reincreast*,
Of that good Hermite both they tooke their leave.
Spenser, F. Q., VI. vi. 15.

reincrudation (rē-in-krö-dā'shon), *n.* [< *re-* + **incrudation* (< *in-*2 + *crude* + *-ation*), equiv. to *incrudescence.*] Recrudescence. [Rare.]

This writer [Artephius, an adept] proceeds wholly by *reincrudation*, or in the via humida.
Swift, Tale of a Tub, i.

reindeer (rān'dēr), *n.* [Formerly also *rain-deer, ranedeer;* < ME. *raynedere* (= D. *rendier* = G. *rennthier* = Dan. *rensdyr*), < **rein* (< Icel.) or *ron*, < AS. *hrān*, a reindeer (cf. F. *renne* = Sp. *reno* = Pg. *renna*, *renno* = It. *renna*, a reindeer), < Icel. *hreinn* = Sw. *ren*, a reindeer (cf. Sw. *ren-ko*, a female reindeer (*ko* = E. *cow*1), > Lapp and Finn. *raingo*, a reindeer); < Lapp *reino*, pasturage or herding of cattle, a word much associated with the use and care of the reindeer (for which the Lapp word is *patso*), and mistaken by the Scandinavians for the reindeer itself.] 1. A deer of the genus *Rangifer* or *Tarandus*, having horns in both sexes, and inhabiting arctic and cold temperate regions; the *Cervus tarandus*, *Rangifer tarandus*, or *Tarandus rangifer*.

Reindeer (*Rangifer tarandus*).

It has branched, recurved, round antlers, the crowns of which are more or less palmated; the antlers of the male are much larger than those of the female, and are remarkable for the size and asymmetry of the brow-antler. The body is of a thick and square form, and the legs are shorter in proportion than those of the red-deer. The size varies much according to climate: about 4 feet 6 inches may be given as the average height of a full-grown specimen. The reindeer is keen of sight and swift of foot, being capable of maintaining a speed of 9 or 10 miles an hour for a long time, and can easily draw a weight of 200 pounds, besides the sledge to which it is usually attached when used as a beast of draft. Among the Laplanders the reindeer is a substitute for the horse, the cow, and the sheep, as it furnishes food, clothing, and the means of conveyance. The caribou of North America, if not absolutely identical with the reindeer, would seem to be at least a well-marked variety, usually called *R. caribou*. The American barren-ground reindeer has been described as a different species, *R. grœnlandicus*. See also cut under *caribou*.

2. In *her.*, a stag having two sets of antlers, the one pair bending downward, and the other standing erect.—**Reindeer period**, the time when the reindeer flourished and was prominent in the fauna of any region, as it is now in Lapland: used chiefly with reference to Belgium and France.

M. Dupont recognizes two stages in the Palæolithic Period, one of which is called the Mammoth period, and the other, which is the more recent, the *Reindeer period*. These names . . . have never met with much acceptance in England, . . . for it is quite certain that the reindeer occupied Belgium and France in the so-called Mammoth period. *J. Geikie*, Prehistoric Europe, p. 101.

Reindeer tribe, a tribe using the reindeer, as do the Laplanders at the present time, and as the dwellers in central Europe have done in prehistoric times: used chiefly with regard to the prehistoric tribes of central France and Belgium.

reindeer-lichen (rān'dēr-lī″ken), *n.* Same as *reindeer-moss*.

reindeer-moss (rān'dēr-môs), *n.* A lichen, *Cladonia rangiferina*, which constitutes almost the sole winter food for the reindeer in high northern latitudes, where it is said to attain sometimes the height of one foot. Its nutritive properties depend chiefly on the gelatinous or starchy matter of which it is largely composed. Its taste is slightly pungent and acrid, and when boiled it forms a jelly possessing nutritive and tonic properties, and is sometimes eaten by man during scarcity of food, being powdered and mixed with flour. See *Cladonia* and *lichen*.

reinfect (rē-in-fekt'), *v. t.* [< OF. *reinfecter;* as *re-* + *infect.*] To infect again. *Cotgrave.*

reinfection (rē-in-fek'shon), *n.* [< *reinfect* + *-ion.*] Infection a second time or subsequently.

reinflame (rē-in-flām'), *v. t.* [< *re-* + *inflame.*] To inflame anew; rekindle; warm again.

To *re-inflame* my Daphnis with desires.
Dryden, tr. of Virgil's Pastorals, viii. 92.

reinforce, reënforce (rē-in-fōrs', rē-en-fōrs'), *v. t.* [Formerly also *renforce, ranforce;* accom. < OF. *renforcer*, *renforchier*, F. *renforcer* = It. *rinforzare*, strengthen, reinforce; as *re-* + *in-force.*] 1. To add new force, strength, or weight to; strengthen: as, to *reinforce* an argument.

A meane to supply her wants, by *renforcing* the causes wherein shee is impotent and defectiue.
Puttenham, Arte of Eng. Poesie, p. 253.

To insure the existence of the race, she [Nature] *reinforces* the sexual instinct, at the risk of disorder, grief, and pain. *Emerson*, Old Age.

Specifically—2. (*a*) *Milit.*, to strengthen with additional military or naval forces, as troops, ships, etc.

But hark! what new alarum is this same?
The French have *reinforced* their scatter'd men;
Then every soldier kill his prisoners.
Shak., Hen. V., iv. 6. 36.

(*b*) To strengthen any part of an object by an additional thickness, support, or other means.

Another mode of *reinforcing* the lower pier is that which occurs in the nave of Laon. . . . In this case five detached monolithic shafts are grouped with the great cylinder, four of them being placed so as to support the angles of the abacus, and the fifth containing the central member of the group of vaulting shafts.
C. H. Moore, Gothic Architecture, p. 66.

3†. To enforce; compel. [Rare.]

Yet twise they were repulsed backe againe,
And twise *renforst* backe to their ships to fly.
Spenser, F. Q., II. x. 48.

reinforce (rē-in-fōrs'), *n.* [< *reinforce, v.*] An additional thickness or support imparted to any part of an object in order to strengthen it. (*a*) A strengthening patch or additional thickness sewed round a cringle or eyelet-hole in a sail or tent-cover. (*b*) A second outer thickness of cloth, applied to those parts of trousers or breeches which come next the saddle. (*c*) The part of a cannon nearest to the breech, which is made stronger to resist the explosive force of the powder. The *first reinforce* is that which extends from the base-ring of the gun to the seat of the projectile. The *second reinforce* is that which is forward of the first reinforce and connects it with the chase of the gun, and from which the trunnions project laterally.—**Reinforce-band**, in *ordnance*, a flat ring or molding formed at the junction of the first and second reinforces of a gun.—**Reinforce-rings**, flat hoop-like moldings on the reinforces of a cannon, on the end nearest to the breech. See *hooping* and *frettage*.

reinforcement, reënforcement (rē-in-fōrs'-, rē-en-fōrs'ment), *n.* [Accom. < OF. (and F.) *renforcement* = It. *rinforzamento;* as *reinforce*, *v.*, + *-ment.*] 1. The act of reinforcing.

The dreadful Sagittary
Appals our numbers; haste we, Diomed,
To *reinforcement*, or we perish all.
Shak., T. and C., v. 5. 16.

2. Additional force; fresh assistance; specifically, additional troops or forces to augment the strength of a military or naval force.

Alone he [Coriolanus] enter'd, . . .
And with a sudden *re-inforcement* struck
Corioli like a planet. *Shak.*, Cor., ii. 2. 117.

3. Any augmentation of strength or force by something added.

Their faith may be both strengthened and brightened by this additional *reinforcement*.
Waterland, Works, V. 287.

reinforcer, reënforcer (rē-in-, rē-en-fōr'sėr), *n.* One who reinforces or strengthens.

Writers who are more properly feeders and *re-enforcers* of life itself. *The Century*, XXVII. 929.

reinforcible, reënforcible (rē-in-, rē-en-fōr'si-bl), *a.* [< *reinforce, v.*, + *-ible.*] Capable or susceptible of reinforcement; that may be strengthened anew.

Both are *reinforcible* by distant motion and by sensation.
Medical News, LII. 680.

reinform (rē-in-fôrm'), *v. t.* [< *re-* + *inform*1.] To inform again.

Redintegrated into humane bodies, and *reinformed* with their primitive souls. *J. Scott*, Christian Life, ii. 7.

reinfund (rē-in-fund'), *v. i.* [< *re-* + *infund.*] To flow in again, as a stream. *Swift*, Works (ed. 1768), I. 109. [Rare.]

reinfuse (rē-in-fūz'), *v. t.* [< *re-* + *infuse.*] To infuse again.

reingratiate (rē-in-grā'shi-āt), *v. t.* [< *re-* + *ingratiate.*] To ingratiate again; recommend again to favor.

Joining now with Canute, as it were to *reingratiate* himself after his revolt, whether real or complotted.
Milton, Hist. Eng., vi.

reinhabit (rē-in-hab'it), *v. t.* [< *re-* + *inhabit.*] To inhabit again.

Towns and Citties were not *reinhabited*, but lay ruin'd and wast. *Milton*, Hist. Eng., iii.

rein-holder (rān'hōl″dėr), *n.* A clip or clasp on the dashboard of a carriage, to hold the reins when the driver has alighted. *E. H. Knight.*

rein-hook (rān'hůk), *n.* A hook on a gig-saddle to hold the bearing-rein. *E. H. Knight.*

reinite (rī'nīt), *n.* [Named after Prof. *Rein* of Marburg.] A tungstate of iron, occurring in blackish-brown tetragonal crystals. It is found in Japan.

reinless (rān'les), *a.* [< *rein*1 + *-less.*] Without rein; without restraint; unchecked.

A wilfull prince, a *rainelesse* raging horse.
Mir. for Mags., p. 388.

Lyfe corrupt, and *rainlesse* youth.
Drant, tr. of Horace's Satires, i. 6.

reinoculation (rē-in-ok-ū-lā'shon), *n.* [< *re-* + *inoculation.*] Inoculation a second time or subsequently.

rein-orchis (rān'ôr″kis), *n.* See *orchis*2.

reins (rānz), *n. pl.* [Early mod. E. also *raines;* < ME. *reines, reynes, reenus*, < OF. *reins*, pl. of *rein*, F. *rein* (cf. Sp. *reñon*, *riñon*) = Pg. *rim* = It. *rene*, < L. *ren*, kidney, pl. *renes*, the kidneys, reins, loins; perhaps akin to Gr. *φρήν*, the midriff, pl. *φρένες*, the parts about the heart and liver: see *phren.*] 1. The kidneys or renes.

What man soever . . . is a leper, or hath a running of the *reins*. Lev. xxii. 4 (margin).

Hence—2. The region of the kidneys; the loins, or lower parts of the back on each side.

All living creatures are fattest about the *raines* of the backe. *Holland*, tr. of Pliny, xi. 25.

3. The seat of the affections and passions, formerly supposed to be situated in that part of the body; hence, also, the emotions and affections themselves.

I will bless the Lord, who hath given me counsel: my *reins* also instruct me in the night seasons. Ps. xvi. 7.

Reins of a vault, in *arch.*, the sides or walls that sustain the vault or arch.

reinscribe (rē-in-skrīb'), *v. t.* [< *re-* + *inscribe.*] In *French law*, to record or register a second time, as a mortgage, required by the law of Louisiana to be periodically reinscribed in order to preserve its priority.

reinsert (rē-in-sėrt'), *v. t.* [< *re-* + *insert.*] To insert a second time.

reinsertion (rē-in-sėr'shon), *n.* [< *reinsert* + *-ion.*] The act of reinserting, or what is reinserted; a second insertion.

rein-slide (rān'slīd), *n.* A slipping loop on an extensible rein, holding the two parts together near the buckle, which is adjustable on the standing part. *E. H. Knight.*

reinsman (rānz'man), *n.*; pl. *reinsmen* (-men). A person skilled in managing reins or driving. [Recent.]

Stage-drivers, who, proud of their skill as *reinsmen*, . . . look down on and sneer at the plodding teamsters.
T. Roosevelt, The Century, XXXV. 501.

rein-snap (rān'snap), *n.* In a harness, a spring-hook for holding the reins; a harness-snap or snap-hook. *E. H. Knight.*

reinspect (rē-in-spekt'), *v. t.* [< *re-* + *inspect.*] To inspect again.

reinspection (rē-in-spek'shon), *n.* [< *reinspect* + *-ion.*] The act of inspecting a second time.

reinspire (rē-in-spīr'), *v. t.* [< *re-* + *inspire.*] To inspire anew.

While Phœbus hastes, great Hector to prepare . . .
His lab'ring Bosom *re-inspires* with Breath,
And calls his Senses from the Verge of Death.
Pope, Homer's Iliad, xv. 65.

With youthful fancy *re-inspired*.
Tennyson, Ode to Memory, v.

reinstall, reinstal (rē-in-stâl'), *v. t.* [= F. *réinstaller;* as *re-* + *install.*] To install again; seat anew.

That which alone can truly *re-install* thee
In David's royal seat. *Milton*, P. R., iii. 372.

reinstalment, reinstallment (rē-in-stâl'ment), *n.* [< *reinstall* + *-ment;* or < *re-* + *instalment.*] The act of reinstalling; a renewed or additional instalment.

reinstate (rē-in-stāt'), *v. t.* [< *re-* + *instate.*] 1. To instate again; place again in possession or in a former state; restore to a state from which one had been removed.

David, after that signal victory which had preserved his life [and] *reinstated* him in his throne . . .
Government of the Tongue.

Theodore, who reigned but twenty days,
Therein convoked a synod, whose decree
Did *reinstate*, repope the late unpoped.
Browning, Ring and Book, II. 171.

2. In *fire insurance*, to replace or repair (property destroyed or damaged).

The condition that it is in the power of the company to *reinstate* property rather than to pay the value of it.
Encyc. Brit., XIII. 165.

reinstatement (rē-in-stāt'ment), *n.* [< *reinstate* + *-ment.*] 1. The act of reinstating; restoration to a former position, office, or rank; reëstablishment.

The *re-instatement* and restoration of corruptible things is the noblest work of natural philosophy.
Bacon, Physical Fables, iii., Expl.

2. In *fire-insurance*, the replacement or repairing of damaged property.

The insured has not the option of requiring *reinstatement.*
Encyc. Brit., XIII. 165.

reinstation (rē-in-stā'shon), *n.* [< *reinstate* + *-ion.*] The act of reinstating; reinstatement. *Gentleman's Mag.*

reinsurance (rē-in-shör'ans), *n.* [< *reinsure* + *-ance.*] 1. A renewed or second insurance.—2. A contract by which the first insurer relieves himself from the risks he had undertaken, and devolves them upon other insurers, called *reinsurers.* Also called *reassurance.*

reinsure (rē-in-shör'), *v. t.* [< *re-* + *insure.*] To insure again; insure a second time and take the risks, so as to relieve another or other insurers. Also *reassure.*

reinsurer (rē-in-shör'ėr), *n.* One who reinsures. See *reinsurance.*

reintegrate (rē-in'tē-grāt), *v. t.* [< ML. *reintegratus*, pp. of *reintegrare* (> It. *reintegrare* = Pg. Sp. Pr. *reintegrar* = F. *réintégrer*, OF. *reintegrer*) for earlier (L.) *redintegrare*, make whole again, restore, renew: see *redintegrate.*] 1†. To make whole again; bring into harmony or concord.

For that heauenly city shall be restored and *reintegrate* with good Christian people.
Bp. Fisher, Seven Penitential Psalms.

Desiring the King nevertheless, as being now freed from her who had been the occasion of all this, to take hold of the present time, and to *reintegrate* himself with the Pope.
Wood, Athenæ Oxon., I. 117.

2. To renew with regard to any state or quality; restore; renew the integrity of.

The league drove out all the Spaniards out of Germany, and *reintegrated* that nation in their ancient liberty.
Bacon.

To *reintegrate* the separate jurisdictions into one.
J. Fiske, Amer. Pol. Ideas, p. 49.

reintegration (rē-in-tē-grā'shon), *n.* [= OF. *reintegration*, F. *réintégration* = Sp. *reintegracion* = Pg. *reintegração* = It. *reintegrazione*, < ML. *reintegratio(n-)*, making whole, restoring, renewing, < *reintegrare*, pp. *reintegratus*, make whole again: see *reintegrate.* Cf. *redintegration.*] The act of reintegrating; a renewing or making whole again.

During activity the *reintegration* falls in arrear of the disintegration.
H. Spencer, Prin. of Biol., § 62.

reinter (rē-in-tėr'), *v. t.* [< *re-* + *inter*[1].] To inter again.

They convey the Bones of their dead Friends from all Places to be *re-interred.*
Howell, Letters, ii. 8.

reinterrogate (rē-in-ter'ō-gāt), *v. t.* [< *re-* + *interrogate*; cf. OF. *reinterroger*, F. *réinterroger.*] To interrogate again; question repeatedly. *Cotgrave.*

reinthrone (rē-in-thrōn'), *v. t.* [< *re-* + *inthrone.*] Same as *reënthrone.*

A pretence to *reinthrone* the king.
Sir T. Herbert, Memoirs of King Charles I. (*Latham.*)

reinthronize† (rē-in-thrō'nīz), *v. t.* [< *re-* + *inthronize.*] An obsolete form of *reënthronize.*

reintroduce (rē-in-trō-dūs'), *v. t.* [< *re-* + *introduce.*] To introduce again.

reintroduction (rē-in-trō-duk'shon), *n.* [< *re-* + *introduction.*] A repeated introduction.

reinundate (rē-in-un'dāt or rē-in'un-dāt), *v. t.* [< *re-* + *inundate.*] To inundate again.

reinvent (rē-in-vent'), *v. t.* [< *re-* + *invent.*] To devise or create anew, independently and without knowledge of a previous invention.

It is immensely more probable that an alphabet of the very peculiar Semitic style should have been borrowed than that it should have been *reinvented* from independent germs.
Isaac Taylor, The Alphabet, II. 311.

reinvest (rē-in-vest'), *v. t.* [< ML. *reinvestire*, invest again; as *re-* + *invest.*] 1. To invest anew, with or as with a garment.

They that thought best amongst them believed that the souls departed should be *reinvested* with other bodies.
Jer. Taylor, Works (ed. 1835), II. 131.

2. To invest anew, as money or other property.

reinvestment (rē-in-vest'ment), *n.* [< *reinvest* + *-ment*; or < *re-* + *investment.*] The act of investing anew; a second or repeated investment.

The question of *re-investment* in securities bearing a higher rate of interest has been discussed at both Oxford and Cambridge.
The Academy, March 8, 1880, p. 168.

reinvigorate (rē-in-vig'or-āt), *v. t.* [< *re-* + *invigorate.*] To revive vigor in; reanimate.

reinvigoration (rē-in-vig-o-rā'shon), *n.* [< *reinvigorate* + *-ion.*] A strengthening anew; reinforcement.

reinvite (rē-in-vīt'), *v. t.* [< OF. *reinviter*, invite again; as *re-* + *invite.*] To invite again.

reinvolve (rē-in-volv'), *v. t.* [< *re-* + *involve.*] To involve anew.

To *reinvolve* us in the pitchy cloud of infernal darkness.
Milton, Reformation in Eng.

reird†, *n.* A variant of *reard.*

reis[1] (rās), *n.* [Pg. *reis*, pl. of *real*: see *real*[3].] A Portuguese money of account: 1,000 reis make a milreis, which is of the value of 4*s.* 5*d.* sterling, or about $1.08. Large sums are calculated in contos of reis, or amounts of 1,000,000 reis ($1,080). In Brazil the milreis is reckoned at about 55 cents. Also *rais.*

reis[2], *n.* Same as *ras*[1], 2.

reise†, *v.* An obsolete form of *raise*[1].

reissuable (rē-ish'ö-a-bl), *a.* [< *reissue* + *-able.*] Capable of being reissued: as, *reissuable* bank-notes.

reissue (rē-ish'ö), *v.* [< *re-* + *issue*, *v.*] I. *intrans.* To issue or go forth again.

But even then she gain'd
Her bower; whence *reissuing*, robed and crown'd,
To meet her lord, she took the tax away.
Tennyson, Godiva.

II. *trans.* To issue, send out, or put forth a second time: as, to *reissue* an edict; to *reissue* bank-notes.

reissue (rē-ish'ö), *n.* [< *reissue*, *v.*] A second or renewed issue: as, the *reissue* of old notes or coinage.

reist[1], *v. t.* See *reast*[1].

reist[2], *v.* A dialectal form of *rest*[2].

reister†, *n.* See *reiter.*

reit† (rēt), *n.* An obsolete form of *reate.*

reiter (rī'tėr), *n.* [Early mod. E. also *reister*, < OF. *reistre*, "a reistor or swartrutter, a German horseman" (Cotgrave), < G. *reiter*, a rider, trooper, cavalryman, = E. *rider*: see *rider.* Cf. *ritter.*] Formerly, especially in the sixteenth and seventeenth centuries, a German cavalry-soldier; in particular, a soldier of those bodies of troops which were known to the nations of western Europe during the religious wars, etc.

Offer my services to Butrech, the best doctor among *reisters*, and the best *reister* among Doctors.
Sir P. Sidney, To Hubert Languet, Oct., 1577 (Zurich Letters, ii. 293). (*Davies.*)

reiterant (rē-it'e-rant), *a.* [= OF. *reiterant*, F. *réitérant*, < L. *reiteran(t-)s*, ppr. of *reiterare*, repeat: see *reiterate.*] Reiterating. [Rare.]

In Heaven they said so, and at Eden's gate,
And here, *re-iterant*, in the wilderness.
Mrs. Browning, Drama of Exile.

reiterate (rē-it'e-rāt), *v. t.*; pret. and pp. *reiterated*, ppr. *reiterating.* [< L. *reiteratus*, pp. of *reiterare* (> It. *reiterare* = Sp. Pg. *reiterar* = F. *réitérer*), repeat again, repeat, < *re-*, again, + *iterare*, say again, repeat: see *iterate.*] 1. To repeat again and again; do or say (especially say) repeatedly: as, to *reiterate* an explanation.

You never spoke what did become you less
Than this; which to *reiterate* were sin.
Shak., W. T., i. 2. 283.

Th' employs of rural life,
Reiterated as the wheel of time
Runs round.
Cowper, Task, iii. 626.

He *reiterated* his visits to the flagon so often that at length his senses were overpowered.
Irving, Sketch-Book, p. 55.

Simple assertion, however *reiterated*, can never make proof.
Stubbs, Medieval and Modern Hist., p. 18.

2†. To walk over again; go along repeatedly.

No more shall I *reiterate* thy Strand,
Whereon so many stately Structures stand.
Herrick, Hesperides, Teares to Thamasis.

=**Syn.** 1. See *recapitulate.*

reiterate (rē-it'e-rāt), *a.* [= F. *réitéré* = Sp. Pg. *reiterado* = It. *reiterato*, < L. *reiteratus*, pp. of *reiterare*, repeat: see the verb.] Reiterated. *Southey.* [Rare.]

reiteratedly (rē-it'e-rā-ted-li), *adv.* By reiteration; repeatedly. *Burke*, Regicide Peace, iv.

reiteration (rē-it-e-rā'shon), *n.* [= OF. *reiteration*, F. *réitération* = Sp. *reiteracion* = Pg. *reiteração* = It. *reiterazione*, < L. *reiteratio(n-)*, a repeating, reiteration, < *reiterare*, pp. *reiteratus*, repeat: see *reiterate.*] 1. The act of reiterating; repetition.

The *reiteration* again and again in fixed course in the public service of the words of inspired teachers . . . has in matter of fact been to our people a vast benefit.
J. H. Newman, Gram. of Assent, p. 54.

2. In *printing*, printing on the back of a sheet by reversing it, and making a second impression on the same form.

reiterative (rē-it'e-rā-tiv), *n.* [< *reiterate* + *-ive.*] 1. A word or part of a word repeated so as to form a reduplicated word: as, prittle-prattle is a *reiterative* of prattle.—2. In *gram.*, a word, as a verb, signifying repeated action.

Reithrodon (rī'thrō-don), *n.* [NL. (Waterhouse, 1837), < Gr. ῥεῖθρον, a channel, + ὀδούς (ὀδοντ-) = E. *tooth.*] A genus of South American sigmodont rodents of the family *Muridæ*, having grooved upper incisors. It includes several species of peculiar appearance, named *R. cuniculoides*, *R. typicus*, and *R. chinchilloides.* The name has been erroneously extended to include the small North American mice of the genus *Ochetodon.*

reive, reiver. Scotch spellings of *reave*, *reaver.*

reject (rē-jekt'), *v. t.* [< OF. *rejecter*, *regeter*, F. *rejeter* = Pr. *regetar* = Sp. *rejitar* = Pg. *regeitar*, *rejeitar* = It. *rigettare*, reject, < L. *rejectare*, throw away, cast away, vomit, etc., freq. of *reicere*, *rejicere*, pp. *rejectus*, throw back, reject, < *re-*, back, + *jacere*, throw: see *jet*[1]. Cf. *adject*, *conject*, *deject*, *eject*, *inject*, *project*, etc.] 1†. To throw or cast back.

By torse whereof [the wind] we were put ayen bak and *rejecte* unto the coste of a desert yle.
Sir R. Guylforde, Pylgrymage, p. 62.

2. To throw away, as anything undesirable or useless; cast off; discard: as, to pick out the good and *reject* the bad; to *reject* a lover.

At last, *rejecting* her barbarous condition, [she] was maried to an English Gentleman.
Quoted in *Capt. John Smith's* Works, II. 31.

Favours to none, to all she smiles extends;
Oft she *rejects*, but never once offends.
Pope, R. of the L., ii. 12.

3. To refuse to receive; decline haughtily or harshly; slight; despise.

Because thou hast *rejected* knowledge, I will also *reject* thee.
Hos. iv. 6.

Then woo thyself, be of thyself *rejected.*
Shak., Venus and Adonis, l. 159.

Good counsel *rejected* returns to enrich the giver's bosom.
Goldsmith, Vicar, xxvii.

=**Syn.** 2. To throw aside, cast off. See *refuse*[1].

rejectable (rē-jek'ta-bl), *a.* [= OF. *rejettable*, *rejetable*, F. *rejetable*; as *reject* + *-able.*] Capable of being rejected; worthy or suitable to be rejected. Also *rejectible.*

rejectamenta (rē-jek-ta-men'tä), *n. pl.* [NL., pl. of ML. **rejectamentum*, < L. *rejectare*, throw away: see *reject.* Cf. *rejectment.*] Things rejected; ejecta; excrement.

Discharge the *rejectamenta* again by the mouth.
Owen, Anat., ix. (*Latham.*)

rejectaneous† (rē-jek-tā'nē-us), *a.* [< L. *rejectaneus*, that is to be rejected, rejectable, < *reicere*, pp. *rejectus*, reject: see *reject.*] Not chosen or received; rejected.

Profane, *rejectaneous*, and reprobate people.
Barrow, Works, III. xxix.

rejected (rē-jek'ted), *p. a.* Thrown back: in *entom.*, noting the scutellum when it is exteriorly visible, but lies between the pronotum and the elytra, instead of between the bases of the latter, as in the coleopterous genus *Passalus.*

rejecter (rē-jek'tėr), *n.* One who rejects or refuses.

rejectible (rē-jek'ti-bl), *a.* [< *reject* + *-ible.*] Same as *rejectable.*

Will you tell me, my dear, what you have thought of Lovelace's best and of his worst?—How far eligible for the first, how far *rejectible* for the last?
Richardson, Clarissa Harlowe, I. 237.

rejection (rē-jek'shon), *n.* [< OF. *rejection*, F. *réjection*, < L. *rejectio(n-)*, < *reicere*, pp. *rejectus*, throw away: see *reject.*] The act of rejecting, of throwing off or away, or of casting off or forsaking; refusal to accept or grant: as, the *rejection* of what is worthless; the *rejection* of a request.

The *rejection* I use of experiments is infinite; but if an experiment be probable and of great use, I receive it.
Bacon.

rejectitious† (rē-jek-tish'us), *a.* [< *reject* + *-itious.*] Worthy of being rejected; implying or requiring rejection.

Persons spurious and *rejectitious*, whom their families and allies have disowned.
Waterhouse, Apology, p. 151. (*Latham.*)

rejective (rē-jek'tiv), *a.* [< *reject* + *-ive.*] Rejecting or tending to reject or cast off. *Imp. Dict.*

rejectment (rē-jekt'ment), *n.* [< OF. *rejectement*, F. *rejettement* = It. *rigettamento*, < ML. **rejectamentum*, what is thrown away, the act of throwing away, < L. *rejectare*, throw away: see *reject*.] Matter thrown away.

rejector (rē-jek'tor), *n.* One who rejects.

The *rejectors* of it [revelation], therefore, would do well to consider the grounds on which they stand. *Warburton*, Works, IX. xiii.

rejoice (rē-jois'), *v.*; pret. and pp. *rejoiced*, ppr. *rejoicing*. [< ME. *rejoicen*, *rejoisen*, *rejoischen*, < OF. *resjois-*, stem of certain parts of *resjoir*, F. *réjouir*, gladden, rejoice: see *rejoy*, and cf. *joice*.] **I.** *trans.* **1.** To make joyful; gladden; animate with lively and pleasurable sensations; exhilarate.

Whoso loveth wisdom *rejoiceth* his father. Prov. xxix. 3.

I love to *rejoice* their poor hearts at this season [Christmas], and to see the whole village merry in my great hall. *Addison*, Spectator, No. 269.

2†. To enjoy; have the fruition of.

To do so that here sone after mi dessece,
Mizte *reioische* that reaume as rizt eir bi kinde.
William of Palerne (E. E. T. S.), l. 4102.

For lenger that ye keep it thus in veyne,
The lesse ye gette, as of your hertis reste,
And to *rejoise* it shal ye neuere atteyne.
Political Poems, etc. (ed. Furnivall), p. 66.

3†. To feel joy on account of.

Ne'er mother
Rejoiced deliverance more.
Shak., Cymbeline, v. 5. 370.

II. *intrans.* To experience joy and gladness in a high degree; be exhilarated with lively and pleasurable sensations; be joyful; feel joy; exult: followed by *at* or *in*, formerly by *of*, or by a subordinate clause.

When the righteous are in authority, the people *rejoice*. Prov. xxix. 2.

Rejoice, O young man, *in* thy youth. Eccl. xi. 9.

He *rejoiceth* more *of* that sheep, than *of* the ninety and nine which went not astray. Mat. xviii. 13.

To *rejoice in* the boy's correction. *Shak.*, T. G. of V., iii. 1. 394.

May they *rejoice*, no wanderer lost,
A family in Heaven!
Burns, Verses Left at a Friend's House.

rejoice† (rē-jois'), *n.* [< *rejoice*, *v.*] The act of rejoicing. [Rare.]

There will be signal examples of God's mercy, and the angels must not want their charitable *rejoices* for the conversion of lost sinners. *Sir T. Browne*, Christian Morals, ii. 6.

rejoicement† (rē-jois'ment), *n.* [< *rejoice* + *-ment*.] Rejoicing.

It is the most decent and comely demeanour of all exultations and *rejoycements* of the hart, which is no lesse naturall to man then to be wise or well learned or sober. *Puttenham*, Arte of Eng. Poesie, p. 244.

rejoicer (rē-joi'sėr), *n.* **1.** One who causes to rejoice: as, a *rejoicer* of the comfortless and widow. *Pope*.—**2.** One who rejoices.

rejoicing (rē-joi'sing), *n.* [< ME. *rejoisyng*, etc.; verbal n. of *rejoice*, *v.*] **1.** The feeling and expression of joy and gladness; procedure expressive of joy; festivity.

The voice of *rejoicing* and salvation is in the tabernacles of the righteous. Ps. cxviii. 15.

A day of thanksgiving was proclaimed by the King, and was celebrated with pride and delight by his people. The *rejoicings* in England were not less enthusiastic or less sincere. *Macaulay*, Frederic the Great.

2. The experience of joy.

Iff he [a child] be vicius, and no thing will lerne, . . . no man off hym *reioysynge* will haue. *Booke of Precedence* (E. E. T. S., extra ser.), i. 57.

But let every man prove his own work, and then shall he have *rejoicing* in himself alone, and not in another. Gal. vi. 4.

3. A subject of joy.

Thy testimonies have I taken as an heritage for ever: for they are the *rejoicing* of my heart. Ps. cxix. 111.

rejoicingly (rē-joi'sing-li), *adv.* With joy or exultation.

She hath despised me *rejoicingly*, and
I'll be merry in my revenge.
Shak., Cymbeline, iii. 5. 150.

rejoie†, *v. t.* Same as *rejoy*.

rejoin (rē-join'), *v.* [Early mod. E. *rejoyne*; < OF. *rejoindre*, F. *rejoindre* = It. *riggiugnere*, rejoin, overtake, < L. *re-*, again, + *jungere*, join: see *join*.] **I.** *trans.* **1.** To join again; unite after separation.

A short space severs ye,
Compared unto that long eternity
That shall *rejoine* ye.
B. Jonson, Elegy on my Muse.

The Grand Signior . . . conveyeth his galleys . . . down to Grand Cairo, where they are taken in pieces, carried upon camels' backs, and *rejoined* together at Suez. *Sir T. Browne*, Vulg. Err., vi. 8.

The letters were written not for publication . . . and to *rejoin* heads, tails, and betweenities which Hayley had severed. *Southey*, Letters, III. 448

2. To join the company of again; bestow one's company on again.

Thoughts which at Hyde-park corner I forgot
Meet and *rejoin* me in the pensive Grot.
Pope, Imit. of Horace, II. ii. 209.

3. To say in answer to a reply or a second or later remark; reply or answer further: with a clause as object.

It will be replied that he receives advantage by this lopping of his superfluous branches; but I *rejoin* that a translator has no such right. *Dryden*, tr. of Ovid's Epistles, Pref.

"Are you that Lady Psyche?" I *rejoin'd*.
Tennyson, Princess, ii.

II. *intrans.* **1.** To answer to a reply; in general, to answer.

Your silence argues it, in not *rejoining*
To this or that late libel.
B. *Jonson*, Apol. to Poetaster.

2. In *law*, to answer the plaintiff's replication.

I *rejoyne*, as men do that answere to the lawe, and make answere to the byll that is put up agaynst them. *Palsgrave*.

rejoinder (rē-join'dėr), *n.* [< F. *rejoindre*, rejoin, inf. used as noun: see *rejoin*. Cf. *attainder*, *remainder*.] **1.** An answer to a reply; in general, an answer.

The quality of the person makes me judge myself obliged to a *rejoinder*. *Glanville*, To Albius.

Rejoinder to the churl the King disdain'd;
But shook his head, and rising wrath restrain'd.
Fenton, in Pope's Odyssey, xx. 231.

2. In *law*, the fourth stage in the pleadings in an action at common law, being the defendant's answer to the plaintiff's replication. The next allegation of the plaintiff is called *surrejoinder*. =**Syn.** **1.** Reply, retort.

rejoinder† (rē-join'dėr), *v. i.* [< *rejoinder*, *n.*] To make a reply.

When Nathan shall *rejoinder* with a "Thou art the man." *Hammond*, Works, IV. 604.

rejoindure† (rē-join'dūr), *n.* [< *rejoin* (*rejoinder*) + *-ure*.] A joining again; reunion. [Rare.]

Rudely beguiles our lips
Of all *rejoindure*, forcibly prevents
Our lock'd embrasures.
Shak., T. and C., iv. 4. 38.

rejoint (rē-joint'), *v. t.* [< *re-* + *joint*. Cf. F. *rejointoyer*, rejoint, < *rejoint*, pp. of *rejoindre*, rejoin.] **1.** To reunite the joints of; joint anew.

Ezekiel saw dry bones *rejoynted* and reinspired with life. *Barrow*, Resurrection of the Body or Flesh.

2. To fill up the joints of, as of stone in buildings when the mortar has been displaced by age or the action of the weather.

rejolt (rē-jōlt'), *v. t.* [< *re-* + *jolt*.] To jolt again; shake or shock anew; cause to rebound. *Locke*.

rejolt (rē-jōlt'), *n.* [< *rejolt*, *v.*] A reacting jolt or shock.

These inward *rejolts* and recoilings of the mind. *South*, Sermons, II. v.

rejourn† (rē-jėrn'), *v. t.* [For ***readjourn*, < F. *réajourner*, adjourn again; as *re-* + *adjourn*.] **1.** To adjourn to another hearing; defer.

You wear out a good wholesome forenoon in hearing a cause between an orange wife and a fosset-seller, and then *rejourn* the controversy of threepence to a second day of audience. *Shak.*, Cor., ii. 1. 79.

Concerning mine own estate, I am right sorry that my coming to Venice is *rejourned* a month or two longer. *Sir H. Wotton*, Reliquiæ, p. 702.

2. To refer; send for information, proof, or the like.

To the Scriptures themselves I *rejourne* all such Atheistical spirits. *Burton*, Anat. of Mel., p. 27.

rejournment† (rē-jėrn'ment), *n.* [< *rejourn* + *-ment*.] Adjournment.

So many *rejournments* and delays. *North*, tr. of Plutarch, p. 713.

rejoy† (rē-joi'), *v. t.* [< ME. *rejoyen*, *rejoien*, < OF. *resjoir*, F. *réjouir*, gladden, rejoice, < *re-*, again, + *esjoir*, F. *éjouir*, joy, rejoice, < *es-* (< L. *ex-*, out) + *joir*, F. *jouir*, joy, rejoice: see *joy*, *v.*, and cf. *enjoy* and *rejoice*.] To rejoice; enjoy.

Ris, lat us speke of lusty lif in Troye,
That we have led, and forth the tyme dryve,
And ek of tyme comynge us *rejoye*.
Chaucer, Troilus, v. 395.

And that I and my assignez may peasseble *rejoie* theym [certain lands]. *Paston Letters*, II. 332.

rejudge (rē-juj'), *v. t.* [< OF. (and F.) *rejuger*; as *re-* + *judge*.] To judge again; reëxamine; review; call to a new trial and decision.

'Tis hers the brave man's latest steps to trace,
Rejudge his acts, and dignify disgrace.
Pope, Epistle to Harley, l. 30.

It appears now too late to *rejudge* the virtues or the vices of those men. *Goldsmith*, Pref. to Roman History.

rejuvenate (rē-jö've-nāt), *v. t.* [< *re-* + *juvenate*. Cf. OF. *rejovenir*, *rejovener*, *rejoennir*, *rejeunir*, *renjovenir*, *rajeunir*, F. *rajeunir* = Pr. *rejovenir* = OSp. *rejuvenir* = It. *ringiovanire*, *ringiovenire*, rejuvenate.] To restore the appearance, powers, or feelings of youth to; make as if young again; renew; refresh.

Such as used the bath in moderation, refreshed and restored by the grateful ceremony, conversed with all the zest and freshness of *rejuvenated* life. *Bulwer*, Last Days of Pompeii, i. 7.

No man was so competent as he to *rejuvenate* those dead old skulls and relics, lifting a thousand years from the forgotten past into the middle of the nineteenth century. *Harper's Mag.*, LXXX. 398.

rejuvenation (rē-jö-ve-nā'shon), *n.* [< *rejuvenate* + *-ion*.] The act of rejuvenating, or the state or process of being rejuvenated; rejuvenescence.

Instances of fecundity at advanced ages are not rare. Contemporaneous writers mention examples of *rejuvenation* which must be regarded as probably legendary. *Pop. Sci. Mo.*, XX. 99.

rejuvenator (rē-jö've-nā-tor), *n.* [< *rejuvenate* + *-or*[1].] One who or that which rejuvenates.

A great beautifier and *rejuvenator* of the complexion. *Lancet*, No. 3433, p. 1193.

rejuvenesce (rē-jö-ve-nes'), *v. i.*; pret. and pp. *rejuvenesced*, ppr. *rejuvenescing*. [< ML. *rejuvenescere*, grow young again, < L. *re-*, again, + *juvenescere*, grow young: see *rejuvenescent*.] To grow young again; renew one's youthfulness by reacquiring vitality; specifically, in *biol.*, to accomplish rejuvenescence, or repair vitality by conjugation and subsequent fission, as an infusorian.

The dark, double-bordered cells are those which were sown but did not *rejuvenesce*. *Pasteur*, On Fermentation (trans.), p. 177.

rejuvenescence (rē-jö-ve-nes'ens), *n.* [< *rejuvenescen(t)* + *-ce*.] **1.** A renewal of the appearance, powers, or feelings of youth.

That degree of health I give up entirely; I might as well expect *rejuvenescence*. *Chesterfield*, Misc. Works, IV. 275. (*Latham*.)

2. In *biol.*, a transformation whereby the entire protoplasm of a vegetative cell changes into a cell of a different character—that is, into a primordial cell which subsequently invests itself with a new cell-wall and forms the starting-point of the life of a new individual. It occurs in numerous algæ, as *Œdogonium*, and also in some diatoms.

rejuvenescency (rē-jö-ve-nes'en-si), *n.* [As *rejuvenescence* (see *-cy*).] Same as *rejuvenescence*.

The whole creation, now grown old, expecteth and waiteth for a certain *rejuvenescency*. *J. Smith*, Portrait of Old Age, p. 264.

rejuvenescent (rē-jö-ve-nes'ent), *a.* [< ML. *rejuvenescen(t-)s*, ppr. of *rejuvenescere*, become young again: see *rejuvenesce*. Cf. *juvenescent*.] Becoming or become young again.

Rising
Rejuvenescent, he stood in a glorified body.
Southey.

rejuvenize (rē-jö've-nīz), *v. t.*; pret. and pp. *rejuvenized*, ppr. *rejuvenizing*. [< *rejuven(esce)* + *-ize*.] To render young again; rejuvenate.

reke[1]†, *v.* A Middle English form of *reek*[1].

reke[2]†, *n.* A variant of *reek*[2].

reke[3], *v.* An obsolete or dialectal form of *rake*[1].

rekels†, *n.* [ME., also *rekils*, *rekyls*, *rekles*, assibilated *rychellys*, *rechles*, *recheles*, < AS. *rēcels*, incense, < *rēcan*, smoke, reek: see *reek*[1].] Incense. *Prompt. Parv.*, p. 433. (*Stratmann*.)

reken[1]†, *v.* A Middle English form of *reckon*.

reken[2]†, *a.* [ME., < AS. *recen*, ready, prompt, swift.] Ready; prompt; noble; beautiful.

Thou so ryche a *reken* rose.
Alliterative Poems (ed. Morris), i. 905.

The *rekeneste* redy mene of the rownde table.
Morte Arthure (E. E. T. S.), l. 4082.

rekindle (rē-kin'dl), *v.* [< *re-* + *kindle*[1].] **I.** *trans.* **1.** To kindle again; set on fire anew.

On the pillar raised by martyr hands
Burns the *rekindled* beacon of the right.
O. W. Holmes, Commemoration Services, Cambridge, [July 21, 1865.

2. To inflame again; rouse anew.

Rekindled at the royal charms,
Tumultuous love each beating bosom warms.
Fenton, in Pope's Odyssey, i. 465.

II. *intrans.* To take fire or be animated anew.

Straight her *rekindling* eyes resume their fire.
Thomson, To th[illegible]

reking† (rē-king'), *v. t.* [< r[illegible] make king again; raise to th[illegible] [Rare.]

[illegible] of the company to [illegible] he value of it. [illegible] *yc. Brit.*, XIII. 165.

You hassard lesse, re-kinging him,
Then I vn-king'd to bee.
Warner, Albion's England, iii. 104.

rekket, *r.* A Middle English form of *reck*.

reknet, *v.* A Middle English form of *reckon*.

reknowledge† (rē̤-nol'ej), *v. t.* [< *re-* + *knowledge*.] To confess a knowledge of; acknowledge.

But in that you have *reknowledged* Jesus Criste the autor of saluacion. *J. Udall*, On John ii.

Although I goe bescattered and wandering in this Courte, I doe not leaue to *reknowledge* the good. *Guevara*, Letters (tr. by Hellowes, 1577), p. 192.

relais (re-lā'), *n.* [< F. *relais*, a space left: see *relay*[1].] In *fort.*, a walk, four or five feet wide, left without the rampart, to receive the earth which may be washed down and prevent it from falling into the ditch.

relapsable (rē̤-lap'sa-bl), *a.* [< *relapse* + *-able*.] Capable of relapsing, or liable to relapse. *Imp. Dict.*

relapse (rē̤-laps'), *v. i.* [< L. *relapsus*, pp. of *relabi*, slide back, fall back, < *re-*, back, + *labi*, slip, slide, fall: see *lapse*, *v.*] **1.** To slip or slide back; return.

Agreeably to the opinion of Democritus, the world might *relapse* into its old confusion. *Bacon*, Physical Fables, i., Expl.

It then remains that Church can only be
The guide which owns unfailing certainty;
Or else you slip your hold and change your side,
Relapsing from a necessary guide.
Dryden, Hind and Panther, ii. 480.

2. To fall back; return to a former bad state or practice; backslide: as, to *relapse* into vice or error after amendment.

The oftener he hath *relapsed*, the more significations he ought to give of the truth of his repentance. *Jer. Taylor.*

But grant I may *relapse*, for want of grace,
Again to rhyme. *Pope*, Imit. of Horace, II. ii. 88.

3. To fall back from recovery or a convalescent state.

He was not well cured, and would have *relapsed*. *Wiseman.*

And now — alas for unforeseen mishaps!
They put on a damp nightcap, and *relapse*.
Cowper, Conversation, l. 322.

relapse (rē̤-laps'), *n.* [< *relapse*, *v.*] **1.** A sliding or falling back, particularly into a former evil state.

Ease would recant
Vows made in pain, as violent and void, . . .
Which would but lead me to a worse *relapse*
And heavier fall. *Milton*, P. L., iv. 100.

2†. One who has refallen into vice or error; specifically, one who returns into error after having recanted it.

As, when a man is falne into the state of an outlaw, the lawe dispenseth with them that kils him, & the prince excludes him from the protection of a subiect, so, when a man is a *relaps* from God and his lawes, God withdrawes his prouidence from watching ouer him, & authorizeth the deuill, as his instrument, to assault him and torment him, so that whatsoeuer he dooth is limitata potestate, as one saith. *Nashe*, Pierce Penilesse, p. 84.

3. In *med.*, the return of a disease or symptom during or directly after convalescence. See *recrudescence*.

Sir, I dare sit no longer in my waistcoat, nor have anything worth the danger of a *relapse* to write. *Donne*, Letters, vi.

A true *relapse* [in typhoid] is not merely a recurrence of pyrexia, but a return of all the phenomena of the fever. *Quain*, Med. Dict., p. 1683.

relapser (rē̤-lap'sėr), *n.* One who relapses, as into vice or error.

Of indignation, lastly, at those speculative *relapsers* that have out of policy or guiltinesse abandoned a knowne and received truth. *Bp. Hall*, St. Paul's Combat.

relapsing (rē̤-lap'sing), *p. a.* Sliding or falling back; marked by a relapse or return to a former worse state.—**Relapsing fever.** See *fever*[1].

relata, *n.* Plural of *relatum*.

relate (rē̤-lāt'), *v.*; pret. and pp. *related*, ppr. *relating*. [< OF. *relater*, F. *relater* = Sp. Pg. *relatar* = It. *relatare*, < ML. *relatare*, refer, report, relate, freq. of *referre*, pp. *relatus*, bring back, refer, relate: see *refer*.] **I.** *trans.* **1**†. To bring back; restore.

Mote not mislike you also to abate
Your zealous hast, till morrow next againe
Both light of heven and strength of men *relate*.
Spenser, F. Q., III. viii. 51.

2†. To bring into relation; refer.

[illegible] ...t have thought this holy religious father ment. [illegible] ...onised and related into the number of *Becon*, Works, p. 137. (*Halliwell.*)

The question o[illegible] higher rate of inte[illegible] and Cambridge. [illegible] ...cribe as to a source or origin; [illegible] ...ert a relation with.

There has been anguish enough in the prisons of the Ducal Palace, but we know little of it by name, and cannot confidently *relate* it to any great historic presence. *Howells*, Venetian Life, i.

4. To tell; recite; narrate: as, to *relate* the story of Priam.

When you shall these unlucky deeds *relate*,
Speak of me as I am. *Shak.*, Othello, v. 2. 341.

Misses! the tale that I *relate*
This lesson seems to carry.
Cowper, Pairing Time Anticipated.

5. To ally by connection or blood.

How lov'd, how honour'd once, avails thee not,
To whom *related*, or by whom begot.
Pope, Elegy on an Unfortunate Lady.

To relate one's self, to vent one's thoughts in words. [Rare.]

A man were better *relate himself* to a statue or picture than suffer his thoughts to pass in smother. *Bacon*, Friendship.

=**Syn. 4.** To recount, rehearse, report, detail, describe. See *account*, *n.*

II. *intrans.* **1.** To have reference or respect; have regard; stand in some relation; have some understood position when considered in connection with something else.

This challenge that the gallant Hector sends . . .
Relates in purpose only to Achilles.
Shak., T. and C., i. 3. 323.

Pride *relates* more to our opinion of ourselves; vanity to what we would have others think of us. *Jane Austen*, Pride and Prejudice, v.

It was by considerations *relating* to India that his [Clive's] conduct as a public man in England was regulated. *Macaulay*, Lord Clive.

2†. To make reference; take account.

Reckoning by the years of their own consecration, without *relating* to any imperial account. *Fuller.*

3. To have relation or connection.

There are also in divers rivers, especially that *relate* to, or be near to the sea, as Winchester, or the Thames about Windsor, a little Trout called a Samlet. *I. Walton*, Complete Angler, i. 4.

relate (rē̤-lāt'), *n.* [< ML. *relatum*, a relate, an order, report, neut. of L. *relatus*, pp.: see *relate*, *v.*] Anything considered as being in a relation to another thing; something considered as being the first term of a relation to another thing. Also *relatum*.

If the relation which agrees to heteronyms has a name, one of the two relateds is called the *relate:* to wit, that from which the relation has its name; the other the correlate. *Burgersdicius.*

Heteronymous, predicamental, etc., **relates.** See the adjectives.—**Synonymous relates.** See *heteronymous relates*.—**Transcendental relates.** See *predicamental relates*.

related (rē̤-lā'ted), *p. a.* and *n.* [Pp. of *relate*, *v.*] **I.** *p. a.* **1.** Recited; narrated.—**2.** Allied by kindred; connected by blood or alliance, particularly by consanguinity: as, a person *related* in the first or second degree.

Because ye're surnam'd like his grace;
Perhaps *related* to the race.
Burns, Dedication to Gavin Hamilton.

3. Standing in some relation or connection: as, the arts of painting and sculpture are closely *related*.

No one and no number of a series of *related* events can be the consciousness of the series as related. *T. H. Green*, Prolegomena to Ethics, § 16.

4. In *music*: (*a*) Of tones, belonging to a melodic or harmonic series, so as to be susceptible of close connection. Thus, the tones of a scale when taken in succession are *melodically related*, and when taken in certain sets are *harmonically related*. See *relation*, 8. (*b*) Of chords and tonalities, same as *relative*.

II.† *n.* Same as *relate*. [Rare.]

Relateds are reciprocated. That is, every *related* is referred to a reciprocal correlate. *Burgersdicius*, tr. by a Gentleman, i. 7.

relatedness (rē̤-lā'ted-nes), *n.* The state or condition of being related; affinity.

We are not strong by our power to penetrate, but by our *relatedness*. The world is enlarged for us, not by new objects, but by finding more affinities and potencies in those we have. *Emerson*, Success.

relater (rē̤-lā'tėr), *n.* [< *relate* + *-er*[1].] One who relates, recites, or narrates; a historian. Also *relator*.

Her husband the *relater* she preferr'd
Before the angel, and of him to ask
Chose rather. *Milton*, P. L., viii. 52.

relation (rē̤-lā'shon), *n.* [< ME. *relation*, *relacion*, < OF. *relation*, F. *relation* = Pr. *relation* = Sp. *relacion* = Pg. *relação* = It. *relazione*, < L. *relatio(n-)*, a carrying back, bringing back, restoring, repaying, a report, proposition, motion, hence a narration, relation, also reference, regard, respect, < *referre*, pp. *relatus*, refer, relate: see *refer*, *relate*.] **1.** The act of relating or telling; recital; narration.

He schalle telle it anon to his Conseille, or discovere it to sum men that wille make *relacioun* to the Emperour. *Mandeville*, Travels, p. 235.

I shall never forget a story of our host Zachary, who on the *relation* of our perill told us another of his owne. *Evelyn*, Diary, Oct. 16, 1644.

I remember to have heard an old gentleman talk of the civil wars, and in his *relation* give an account of a general officer. *Steele*, Spectator, No. 497.

2. That which is related or told; an account; narrative: formerly applied to historical narrations or geographical descriptions: as, the Jesuit *Relations*.

Sometime the Countrie of Strabo, to whom these our *Relations* are so much indebted. *Purchas*, Pilgrimage, p. 320.

Oftimes *relations* heertofore accounted fabulous have bin after found to contain in them many foot-steps and reliques of somthing true. *Milton*, Hist. Eng., i.

Political and military *relations* are for the greater part accounts of the ambition and violence of mankind. *Burke*, Abridg. of Eng. Hist.

3. A character of a plurality of things; a fact concerning two or more things, especially and more properly when it is regarded as a predicate of one of the things connecting it with the others; the condition of being such and such with regard to something else: as, the *relation* of a citizen to the state; the *relation* of demand and supply. Thus, suppose a locomotive blows off steam; this fact constitutes a relation between the locomotive and the steam so far as the "blowing" is conceived to be a character of the locomotive, and another relation so far as the "being blown" is conceived as a character of the steam, and both these relations together are embraced in the same relationship, or plural fact. This latter, also often called a *relation*, is by logicians called the *foundation* of the relation. The two or more subjects or things to which the plural fact relates are termed the *relates* or *correlates;* the one which is conceived as subject is specifically termed the *subject* of the relation, or the *relate;* the others the *correlates*. Words naming things in their character as relates are called *relatives*, as father, cousin. A set of relatives referring to the same relationship according as one or another object is taken as the relate are called *correlatives:* such are buyer, seller, commodity, price. The logical nomenclature of relations depends on the consideration of *individual relations*, or relations subsisting between the individuals of a single set of correlates, as opposed to *general relations*, which, really or in conception, subsist between many such sets. Relations are either *dual* — that is, connecting couples of objects, as in the examples above — or *plural* — that is, connecting more than two correlates, as the relation of a buyer to the seller, the thing bought, and the price. Every individual dual relation is either a relation of a thing to itself or a relation of a thing to something else. *Logical relations* are those which are known from logical reflection: opposed to *real relations*, which are known by generalization and abstraction from ordinary observations. The chief logical relations are those of *incompossibility*, *coexistence*, *identity*, and *otherness*. Real dual relations are of five classes: (1) *differences* or *alio-relations*, being relations which nothing can bear to itself, as being greater than; (2) *sibi-relations* or *concurrencies*, being relations which nothing can bear to anything else, as self-consciousness; (3) *agreements*, or relations which everything bears to itself, as similarity; (4) relations which everything bears to everything else, which may be called *distances;* and (5) *variform relations*, which some things only bear to themselves, and which subsist between some pairs of things only. Other divisions of relations are important in logic, as the following. An *iterative* or *repeating relation* is such that a thing may at once be in that relation and its converse to the same or different things, as the relation of father to son, or spouse to spouse: opposed to a *finial* or *non-repeating relation*, as that of husband to wife. An *equiparance* or *convertible relation*, opposed to a *disquiparance* or *inconvertible relation*, is such that, if anything is in that relation to another, the latter is in the same relation to the former, as that of cousins. A relation which cannot subsist between two things reciprocally, as that of greater and less, may be called an *irreciprocable relation*, opposed to a *reciprocable relation*, which admits reciprocation as possible merely. A relation such that if A is so related to B, and B so related to C, then A is so related to C, is called a *transitive*, in opposition to an *intransitive relation*. A relation such that if A is so related to something else, C, there is a third thing, B, which is so related to C, and to which A is so related, is called a *concatenated*, in opposition to an *inconcatenated relation*. A relation subsisting between objects in an endless or self-returning series is called an *inexhaustible*, in opposition to an *exhaustible relation*. If there is a self-returning series, the relation is termed *cyclic*, in opposition to *acyclic*. A translative relation such that of any two objects of a certain category one has this relation to the other may be called a *linear relation;* and the series of objects so formed may be called the *line* of the relation. According as this is continuous or discontinuous, finite or infinite, and in the latter case discretely or absolutely, these designations may be applied to the relation. According to the nominalistic (including the conceptualistic) view, a relation is a mere product of the mind. Adding to this doctrine that of the relativity of knowledge, that we know only relations, Kant reached his conclusion that things in themselves are absolutely incognizable. But most Kantian students come to deny the existence of things in themselves, and so reach an idealistic realism which holds relations to be as real as any facts. The realistic view is expressed in the dictum of Scotus that every relation without which, or a term of which, its foundation cannot be is, in the thing (*realiter*), identical with that foundation — that is, what really is is a fact relating to two or more things, and that fact viewed as a predicate of one of those things is the relation.

> Thus is *relacion* rect, ryht as adiectif and substantif
> A-cordeth in alle kyndes with his antecedent.
> *Piers Plowman* (C), iv. 363.

> The last sort of complex ideas is that we call *relation*, which consists in the consideration and comparing one idea with another. *Locke*, Human Understanding, ii. 12.

> The only difference between relative names and any others consists in their being given in pairs; and the reason of their being given in pairs is not the existence between two things of a mystical bond called a *relation* and supposed to have a kind of shadowy and abstract reality, but a very simple peculiarity in the concrete fact which the two names are intended to mark.
> *J. S. Mill*, Note to James Mill's Human Mind, xiv. 2.

> In natural science, I have understood, there is nothing petty to the mind that has a large vision of *relations*.
> *George Eliot*, Mill on the Floss, iv. 1.

> Most *relations* are feelings of an entirely different order from the terms they relate. The *relation* of similarity, e. g., may equally obtain between jasmine and tuberose, or between Mr. Browning's verses and Mr. Story's: it is itself neither odorous nor poetical, and those may well be pardoned who have denied to it all sensational content whatever. *W. James*, Mind, XII. 13.

4. Intimate connection between facts; significant bearing of one fact upon another.

> For the intent and purpose of the law
> Hath full *relation* to the penalty,
> Which here appeareth due upon the bond.
> *Shak.*, M. of V., iv. 1. 248.

> The word *relation* is commonly used in two senses considerably different from each other. Either for that quality by which two ideas are connected together in the imagination, and the one naturally introduces the other . . . ; or for that particular circumstance in which . . . we may think proper to compare them. . . . In a common way we say that "nothing can be more distant than such or such things from each other, nothing can have less *relation*," as if distance and *relation* were incompatible.
> *Hume*, Human Nature, part i. § 5.

5. Connection by consanguinity or affinity; kinship; tie of birth or marriage; relationship.

> *Relations* dear, and all the charities
> Of father, son, and brother, first were known.
> *Milton*, P. L., iv. 756.

6. Kindred; connection; a group of persons related by kinship. [Rare.]

> He hath need of a great stock of piety who is first to provide for his own necessities, and then to give portions to a numerous *relation*. *Jer. Taylor*, Works (ed. 1835), I. 644.

7. A person connected by consanguinity or affinity; a kinsman or kinswoman; a relative.

> Sir, you may spare your application,
> I'm no such beast, nor his *relation*.
> *Pope*, Imit. of Horace, I. vii. 60.

> I am almost the nearest *relation* he has in the world, and am entitled to know all his dearest concerns.
> *Jane Austen*, Pride and Prejudice, lvi.

8. In *math.*: (*a*) A ratio; proportion. (*b*) A connection between a number of quantities by which certain systems of values are excluded; especially, such a connection as may be expressed by a plexus of general equations.—9. In *music*, that connection or kinship between two tones, chords, or keys (tonalities) which makes their association with each other easy and natural. The relation of tones is perceived by the ear without analysis. Physically it probably depends upon how far the two series of upper partial tones or harmonics coincide. Thus, a given tone is closely related to its perfect fifth, because the 2d, 5th, 8th, 11th, etc., harmonics of the one are respectively identical with the 1st, 3d, 5th, 7th, etc., of the other; while for converse reasons it is hardly at all related to its minor second. Tones that have but a distant relation to each other, however, are often both closely related to a third tone, and then, particularly if they are associated together in some melodic series, like a scale, may acquire a close relation. Thus, the seventh and eighth tones of a major scale have a close relation which is indirectly harmonic, but apparently due to their habitual melodic proximity. The relation of chords depends primarily on the identity of one or more of their respective tones. Thus, a major triad is closely related to a minor triad on the same root, or to a minor triad on the minor third below itself, because in each case there are two tones in common. Thus, the tonic triad of a key is related to the dominant and subdominant triads through the identity of one of its tones with one of theirs. As with tones, chords having but a distant relation to each other may acquire a relation through their respective close relations to a third chord, especially if habitually brought together in harmonic progressions. Thus, the dominant and subdominant triads of a key have a substantial but indirect relation; and, indeed, a relation is evident between all the triads of a key. The relation of keys (tonalities) depends properly on the number of tones which they have in common; though it is often held that a key is closely connected with every key whose tonic triad is made up of its tones. Thus, a major key is most intimately related to the major keys of its dominant and subdominant and to the minor key of its submediant, because each of them differs from it by but one tone, and also to the minor keys of its mediant and supertonic, because their tonic triads are also composed of its tones. Hence a major key and the minor key of its submediant are called mutually relative (*relative major* and *relative minor*), in distinction from the tonic major and tonic minor, which are more distantly related. When carefully analyzed, the fact of relation is found to be profoundly concerned in the entire structure and development of music. It has caused the establishment of the major diatonic scale as the norm of all modern music. It is the kernel of tonality, of harmonic and melodic progression, of form in general, and of many extended forms in particular.

10. In *law*: (*a*) A fiction of law whereby, to prevent injustice, effect is given to an act done at one time as if it had been done at a previous time, it being said to have *relation* back to that time: as, where a deed is executed and acted on, but its delivery neglected, the law may give effect to its subsequent delivery by *relation* back to its date or to its execution, as may be equitable. (*b*) Suggestion by a relator; the statement or complaint of his grievance by one at whose instance an action or special proceeding is brought by the state to determine a question involving both public and private right.—11. In *arch.*, the direct dependence upon one another, and upon the whole, of the different parts of a building, or members of a design.—**Abelian relation**, a relation expressed by certain identical linear equations given by Abel connecting roots of unity with the roots of the equation which gives the values of the elliptic functions for rational fractions of the periods.—**Accidental relation**, an indirect relation of A to C, constituted by A being in some relation to B, and B being in an independent relation to C. Thus, if a man throws away a date-stone, and that date-stone strikes an invisible genie, the relation of the man to the genie is an accidental one.—**Actual relation.** See *actual*.—**Aggregate relation.** (*a*) A relation resulting from a disjunctive conjunction of several relations, such that, if any of the latter are satisfied, the aggregate relation is satisfied. (*b*) Same as *composite relation* (*a*). [This is the signification attached to the word by Cayley, contrary to the established terminology of logic.]—**Alio relation**, a relation of such a nature that a thing cannot be in that relation to itself: as, being previous to.—**Aptitudinal relation.** See *aptitudinal*.—**Categories of relation.** See *category*, 1.—**Composite relation.** (*a*) A relation consisting in the simultaneous existence of several relations. (*b*) Same as *aggregate relation* (*a*). [This is the signification attached to the phrase by Cayley, in opposition to the usage of logicians.]—**Confidential, cyclical, discriminant relation.** See the adjectives.—**Definite relation**, a relation unlike any relation of the same relate to other correlates. [This is Kempe's nomenclature, but is objectionable. *Peculiar relation* would better express the idea.]—**Distributively satisfied composite relation.** See *distributively*.—**Double relation, dual relation**, relation between a pair of things, or between a relate and a single correlate.—**Dynamic relations.** See *dynamic*.—**Enharmonic relation.** See *enharmonic*.—**Exterior relations.** See *exterior*.—**Extrinsic relation**, a relation which is established between terms already existing.—**False or inharmonic relation**, in *music*. See *false*.—**In relation to**, in the characters that connect the subject with the correlate which is the object of the preposition *to*: as, music *in relation* to poetry (music in those characters that connect it with poetry).—**Intrinsic relation.** See *intrinsic*.—**Involutorial relation.** See *involutorial*.—**Irregular relation**, a relation not regular.—**Jacobian relation**, the relation expressed by equating the Jacobian to zero.—**K-fold relation**, a relation which reduces by *k* the number of independent ways in which a system of quantities may vary.—**Legal relation**, the aggregate of legal rights and duties characterizing one person or thing in respect to another.—**Omal relation**, a relation expressed by a system of linear equations. [With Legendre, *omal* means having the differential coefficient constantly of one sign; but Cayley uses the word as a synonym of *homaloidal* or *linear*.]—**Order of a relation**, in *math.* See *order*, 12.—**Parametric relation**, a relation involving parameters, or variables over and above the coördinates.—**Plural relation**, a relation between a relate and two or more correlates, as when A aims a shot, B, at C.—**Predicamental relation**, a relation which comes under Aristotle's category of relation.—**Prime relation**, a relation not resulting from the conjunction of relations alternatively satisfied.—**Real relation**, a relation the statement of which cannot be separated into two facts, one relating to the relate and the other to the correlate, such as the relation of Cain to Abel as his killer. For the facts that Cain killed somebody and that Abel was killed do not together make up the fact that Cain killed Abel: opposed to *relation of reason*.—**Regular relation**, a relation of definite manifoldness. [So defined by Cayley; but it would have been better to denominate this a *homoplasial relation*, reserving the term *regular relation* for one which follows one law, expressible by general equations, for all values of the coördinates—this meaning according better with that usually given to *regular*.]—**Relation of disquiparance**, a relation which confers unlike names upon relate and correlate.—**Relation of equiparance**, a relation which confers the same relative name upon relate and correlate: thus, the being a cousin of somebody is such a relation, for if A is cousin to B, B is cousin to A.—**Relation of reason**, a relation which depends upon a fact which can be stated as an aggregate of two facts (one concerning the relate, the other concerning the correlate), such that the annihilation of the relate or the correlate would destroy only one of these facts, but leave the other intact: thus, the fact that Franklin and Rumford were both scientific Americans constitutes a relationship between them with two correlative relations; but these are *relations of reason*, because the two facts are that Franklin was a scientific American and that Rumford was a scientific American, the first of which facts would remain true even if Rumford had never existed, and the second even if Franklin had never existed.—**Resultant relation**, a relation between parameters involved in a superdeterminate relation.—**Self-relation.** (*a*) A relation of such a sort that a thing can be in that relation to itself: as, being the killer of; but better (*b*) a relation of such a sort that nothing can be so related to anything else, as the relations of self-consciousness, self-depreciation, self-help, etc.—**Superdeterminate relation**, a relation whose manifoldness is as great as or greater than the number of coördinates.—**Transcendental relation**, a relation which does not come under Aristotle's category of relation, as cause and effect, habit and object. = **Syn.** 1. *Narration, Recital*, etc. See *account*.—3. Attitude, connection.—5. Affiliation.—5 and 7. *Relation, Relative, Connection.* When applying to family affiliations, *relation* is used of a state or of a person, but in the latter sense *relative* is much better; *relative* is used of a person, but not of a state; *connection* is used with equal propriety of either person or state. *Relation* and *relative* refer to kinship by blood; *connection* is increasingly restricted to ties resulting from marriage.—6. Kindred, kin.

relational (rẹ-lā'shọn-al), *a.* [< *relation* + *-al.*] 1. Having relation or kindred.

> We might be tempted to take these two nations for *relational* stems. *Tooke.*

2. Indicating or specifying some relation: used in contradistinction to *notional*: as, a *relational* part of speech. Pronouns, prepositions, and conjunctions are *relational* parts of speech.

relationality (rẹ-lā-shọ-nal'i-ti), *n.* [< *relational* + *-ity.*] The state or property of having a relational force.

> But if the remarks already made on what might be called the *relationality* of terms have any force, it is obvious that mental tension and conscious intensity cannot be equated to each other. *J. Ward*, Mind, XII. 56.

relationism (rẹ-lā'shọn-izm), *n.* [< *relation* + *-ism.*] 1. The doctrine that relations have a real existence.

> *Relationism* teaches . . . that things and relations constitute two great, distinct orders of objective reality, inseparable in existence, yet distinguishable in thought.
> *F. E. Abbot*, Scientific Theism, Introd., ii.

2. The doctrine of the relativity of knowledge.

relationist (rẹ-lā'shọn-ist), *n.* [< *relation* + *-ist.*] 1†. A relative; a relation. *Sir T. Browne.*—2. An adherent of the doctrine of relationism.

relationship (rẹ-lā'shọn-ship), *n.* [< *relation* + *-ship.*] 1. The state of being related by kindred, affinity, or other alliance.

> Faith is the great tie of *relationship* betwixt you [and Christ]. *Chalmers*, On Romans viii. 1 (ed. R. Carter).

> Mrs. Mugford's conversation was incessant regarding the Ringwood family and Firmin's *relationship* to that noble house. *Thackeray*, Philip, xxi.

2. In *music*, same as *relation*, 8. Also called *tone-relationship*.

relatival (rel-a-tī'val or rel'a-tiv-al), *a.* [< *relative* + *-al.*] Pertaining to relative words or forms.

> Conjunctions, prepositions (personal, relative, and interrogative), *relatival* contractions.
> *E. A. Abbott*, Shakespearian Grammar (cited in The [Nation, Feb. 16, 1871, p. 110).

relative (rel'a-tiv), *a.* and *n.* [< ME. *relatif*, < OF. (and F.) *relatif* = Pr. *relatiu* = Sp. Pg. It. *relativo*, < LL. *relativus*, having reference or relation, < L. *relatus*, pp. of *referre*, refer, relate: see *refer*, *relate*.] I. *a.* 1. Having relation to or bearing on something; close in connection; pertinent; relevant; to the purpose.

> The devil hath power
> To assume a pleasing shape; yea, and perhaps . . .
> Abuses me to damn me. I'll have grounds
> More *relative* than this. *Shak.*, Hamlet, ii. 2. 633.

2. Not absolute or existing by itself; considered as belonging to or respecting something else; depending on or incident to relation.

> Everything sustains both an absolute and a *relative* capacity: an absolute, as it is such a thing, endued with such a nature; and a *relative*, as it is a part of the universe, and so stands in such a relation to the whole.
> *South.*

> Not only simple ideas and substances, but modes also, are positive beings: though the parts of which they consist are very often *relative* one to another.
> *Locke*, Human Understanding, II. xxvi. § 6.

> Religion, it has been well observed, is something *relative* to us; a system of commands and promises from God towards us. *J. H. Newman*, Parochial Sermons, i. 317.

3. In *gram.*, referring to an antecedent; introducing a dependent clause that defines or describes or modifies something else in the sentence that is called the antecedent (because it usually, though by no means always, precedes the relative): thus, he *who* runs may read; he lay on the spot *where* he fell. Pronouns and pronominal adverbs are relative, such adverbs having also the value of conjunctions. A relative word used without an antecedent, as implying in itself its antecedent, is often called a *compound relative*: thus, *who* breaks pays; I saw *where* he fell. Relative words are always either demonstratives or interrogatives which have acquired secondarily the relative value and use.

4. Not intelligible except in connection with something else; signifying a relation, without stating what the correlate is: thus, *father*, *better*, *west*, etc., are *relative* terms.

> Profundity, in its secondary as in its primary sense, is a *relative* term. *Macaulay*, Sadler's Ref. Refuted.

5. In *music*, having a close melodic or harmonic relation. Thus, *relative chords*, in a narrow sense, the triads of a given key (tonality) having as roots the successive tones of its scale; *relative keys*, keys (tonalities) having several tones in common, thus affording opportunity for easy modulation back and forth, or, more narrowly, keys whose tonic triads are relative chords of each other; *relative major*, *relative minor*, a major key and the minor key of its submediant regarded with respect to each other. Also *related*, *parallel*. See cut under *chord*, 4.—**Relative beauty**, beauty consisting in the adaptation of the object to its end.—**Relative chronology**, in *geol.*, the geological method of computing time, as opposed to the *absolute* or *historical* method.—**Relative end, ens, equilibrium.** See the nouns.—**Relative enunciation**, an enunciation whose clauses are connected by a relative: as, "Wheresoever the carcase is, there will the eagles be gathered together."—**Relative gravity.** (*a*) The acceleration of gravity at a station referred to that at another station, and not expressed in terms of space and time. (*b*) Same as *specific gravity* (which see, under *gravity*).—**Relative ground of proof**, a premise which itself requires proof.—**Relative humidity, hypermetropia, locality.** See the nouns.—**Relative motion.** See *motion*.—**Relative opposites**, the two terms of any dual relation.—**Relative place**, the place of one object as defined by the situations of other objects.—**Relative pleasure or pain**, a state of feeling which is pleasurable or painful by force of contrast with the state which preceded it.—**Relative pronoun, proposition**, etc. See the nouns.—**Relative syllogism**, a syllogism whose major premise is a relative enunciation: as, Where Christ is, there will also the faithful be; but Christ is in heaven; therefore there also will the faithful be.—**Relative term**, a term which, to become the complete name of any class, requires to be completed by the annexation of another name, generally of another class: such terms are, for example, father of, the qualities of, tangent to, identical with, man that is, etc. Strictly speaking, all adjectives are of this nature.—**Relative time**, the sensible measure of any part of duration by means of motion.

II. *n.* 1. Something considered in its relation to something else; one of two things having a certain relation.—2. A person connected by blood or affinity; especially, one allied by blood; a kinsman or kinswoman; a relation.

> Our friends and *relatives* stand weeping by,
> Dissolv'd in tears to see us die.
> *Pomfret*, Prospect of Death.

> There is no greater bugbear than a strong-willed *relative* in the circle of his own connections. *Hawthorne*, Seven Gables, xi.

3. In *gram.*, a relative word; a relative pronoun or adverb. See I., 3.—4. In *logic*, a relative term.—**Logic of relatives**, that branch of formal logic which treats of relations, and reasonings concerning them. =**Syn. 2.** *Connection*, etc. See *relation*.

relatively (rel'a̤-tiv-li), *adv.* In a relative manner; in relation or respect to something else; with relation to each other and to other things; not absolutely; comparatively: often followed by *to*: as, his expenditure in charity was large *relatively to* his income.—**Relatively identical**, the same in certain respects.—**Relatively prime.** See *prime*, 7.

relativeness (rel'a̤-tiv-nes), *n.* The state of being relative or having relation.

> Therefore, while for a later period of the dialect-life of Hellas the expression "dialect" is one of peculiar *relativeness*, it is a justifiable term for certain aggregations of morphological and syntactical phenomena in the earlier periods of language, when dialect-relations were more sharply defined. *Amer. Jour. Philol.*, VII. 444.

relativity (rel-a-tiv'i̤-ti), *n.* [= F. *relativité*, < NL. **relativita(t-)s*, < LL. *relativus*, relative: see *relative*.] 1. The character of being relative; relativeness; the being of an object as it is by force of something to which it is relative. Specifically—2. Phenomenality; existence as an immediate object of the understanding or of experience; existence only in relation to a thinking mind.—**The doctrine of the relativity of existence**, the doctrine that the real existence of the subject, and also of the object, depends on the real relation between them.—**The doctrine of the relativity of knowledge.** The phrase *relativity of knowledge* has received divergent significations. (*a*) The doctrine that it is impossible to have knowledge of anything except by means of its relations to the mind, direct and indirect, cognized as relations. (*b*) The doctrine of phen mena sm, that only appearances can be known, and that the relations of these appearances to external substrata, if such there be, are completely incognizable. This doctrine is sometimes associated with a denial of the possibility of any knowledge of relations as such, or at least of any whose terms are not independently present together in consciousness. It would therefore better be denominated *the doctrine of the impossibility of relativity of cognition*. (*c*) The doctrine that we can only become conscious of objects in their relations to one another. This doctrine is almost universally held by psychologists.

> Relative and correlative are each thought through the other, so that in enouncing *relativity* as a condition of the thinkable—in other words, that thought is only of the relative—this is tantamount to saying that we think one thing only as we think two things mutually and at once; which again is equivalent to the doctrine that the absolute (the non-relative) is for us incogitable, and even inconceivable. *Sir W. Hamilton*, Metaph., App. V. (*c*).

> When a philosopher lays great stress upon the *relativity of our knowledge*, it is necessary to cross-examine his writings, and compel them to disclose in which of its many degrees of meaning he understands the phrase. . . . To most of those who hold it, the difference between the Ego and the Non-ego is not one of language only, nor a formal distinction between two aspects of the same reality, but denotes two realities, each having a separate existence, and neither dependent on the other. . . . They believe that there is a real universe of "things in themselves," and that whenever there is an impression on our senses, there is a "thing in itself," which is behind the phænomenon, and is the cause of it. But as to what this thing is "in itself," we, having no organs except our senses for communicating with it, can only know what our senses tell us; and as they tell us nothing but the impression which the thing makes upon us, we do not know what it is in itself at all. . . . Of the ultimate realities, as such, we know the existence, and nothing more. . . . It is in this form that *the doctrine of the relativity of knowledge* is held by the greater number of those who profess to hold it, attaching any definite idea to the term. *J. S. Mill*, Examination of Hamilton, ii.

relator (rē̤-lā'to̤r), *n.* [< F. *relateur* = Sp. Pg. *relator* = It. *relatore*, < L. *relator*, a relater, narrator, < *referre*, pp. *relatus*, relate, etc.: see *relate*.] 1. Same as *relater*.

> When this place affords anything worth your hearing, I will be your *relator*. *Donne*, Letters, xxxi.

2. In *law*, a person on whose suggestion or complaint an action or special proceeding in the name of the state (his name being usually joined therewith) is brought, to try a question involving both public and private right.

relatrix (rē̤-lā'triks), *n.* [ML., fem. of *relator*.] In *law*, a female relator or petitioner. *Story*.

relatum (rē̤-lā'tum), *n.*; pl. *relata* (-tä̤). [ML.: see *relate*, *n.*] Same as *relate*.

> The *Relatum* and its Correlate seem to be simul naturâ. *Grote*, Aristotle, I. iii.

relax (rē̤-laks'), *v.* [< OF. (and F.) *relaxer* = Pr. *relaxar*, *relachar* = Sp. *relajar* = Pg. *relaxar* = It. *rilassare*, *rilasciare*, release, < L. *relaxare*, relax, < *re-*, back, + *laxare*, loosen, < *laxus*, loose: see *lax*[1]. Doublet of *release*[1].] I. *trans.* 1. To slacken; make more lax or less tense or rigid; loosen; make less close or firm: as, to *relax* a rope or cord; to *relax* the muscles or sinews.

> Nor served it to *relax* their serried files.
> *Milton*, P. L., vi. 599.

> The self-complacent actor, when he views . . .
> The slope of faces from the floor to th' roof . . .
> *Relax'd* into a universal grin. *Cowper*, Task, iv. 204.

2. To make less severe or rigorous; remit or abate in strictness: as, to *relax* a law or rule.

> The statute of mortmain was at several times *relaxed* by the legislature. *Swift*.

> His principles, though not inflexible, were not more *relaxed* than those of his associates and competitors. *Macaulay*, Burleigh and his Times.

3. To remit or abate in respect to attention, assiduity, effort, or labor: as, to *relax* study; to *relax* exertions or efforts.—4. To relieve from attention or effort; afford a relaxation to; unbend: as, conversation *relaxes* the mind of the student.—5. To abate; take away.—6. To relieve from constipation; loosen; open: as, medicines *relax* the bowels.—7. To set loose or free; give up or over.

> The whole number of convicts amounted to thirty, of whom sixteen were reconciled, and the remainder *relaxed* to the secular arm: in other words, turned over to the civil magistrate for execution. *Prescott*.

=**Syn. 1.** To loose, unbrace, weaken, enervate, debilitate.—**2.** To mitigate, ease.—**4.** To divert, recreate.

II. *intrans.* 1. To become loose, feeble, or languid.

> His knees *relax* with toil. *Pope*, Iliad, xxi. 309.

2. To abate in severity; become more mild or less rigorous.

> The bill has ever been petitioned against, and the mutinous were likely to go great lengths, if the Admiralty had not bought off some by money, and others by *relaxing* in the material points. *Walpole*, Letters, II. 147.

> She would not *relax* in her demand.
> *Lamb*, Imperfect Sympathies.

3. To remit in close attention; unbend.

> No man can fix so perfect an idea of that virtue [justice] as that he may not afterwards find reason to add or *relax* therefrom. *A. Tucker*, Light of Nature, II. iii. 24.

> The mind, *relaxing* into needful sport,
> Should turn to writers of an abler sort.
> *Cowper*, Retirement, l. 715.

relax† (rē̤-laks'), *n.* [< *relax*, *v.*] Relaxation.

> Labours and cares may have their *relaxes* and recreations. *Feltham*, Resolves, ii. 58.

relax† (rē̤-laks'), *a.* [= It. *relasso*, weary, < ML. *relaxus*, relaxed: see *relax*, *v.*] Relaxed; loose.

> The sinews, . . . when the southern wind bloweth, are more relax. *Bacon*, Nat. Hist., § 381.

relaxable (rē̤-lak'sa̤-bl), *a.* [< *relax* + *-able*.] Capable of being relaxed or remitted.

> How, saith Ambrose, can any one dare to reckon the Holy Ghost among creatures? or who doth so render himself obnoxious that, if he derogate from a creature, he may not suppose it to be *relaxable* to him by some pardon? *Barrow*, Works, II. xxxiv.

relaxant (rē̤-lak'sa̤nt), *n.* [= F. *relaxant* = Sp. *relajante* = Pg. *relaxante* = It. *rilassante*, < L. *relaxan(t-)s*, ppr. of *relaxare*, relax: see *relax*.] A medicine that relaxes or opens. *Thomas*, Med. Dict.

relaxate (rē̤-lak'sāt), *v. t.* [< L. *relaxatus*, pp. of *relaxare*, relax: see *relax*.] To relax. [Rare.]

> Man's body being *relaxated* . . . by reason of the heat of . . . Summer.
> *T. Venner*, Via Recta ad Vitam Longam, p. 265.

relaxation (rē-lak-sā'sho̤n), *n.* [< OF. (and F.) *relaxation* = Pr. *relaxatio* = Sp. *relajacion* = Pg. *relaxação* = It. *rilassazione*, < L. *relaxatio(n-)*, a relaxing, < *relaxare*, relax, etc.: see *relax*.] 1. The act of relaxing, or the state of being relaxed. (*a*) A diminution of tone, tension, or firmness; specifically, in *pathol.*, a looseness; a diminution of the natural and healthy tone of parts: as, *relaxation* of the soft palate.

> All lassitude is a kind of contusion and compression of the parts; and bathing and anointing give a *relaxation* or emollition. *Bacon*, Nat. Hist., § 730.

> But *relaxation* of the languid frame
> By soft recumbency of outstretch'd limbs
> Was bliss reserv'd for happier days.
> *Cowper*, Task, i. 81.

(*b*) Remission or abatement of rigor.

> Abatements and *relaxations* of the laws of Christ.
> *Waterland*, Works, VI. 25.

> The late ill-fortune had dispirited the troops, and caused an indifference about duty, a want of obedience, and a *relaxation* in discipline in the whole army.
> *Bruce*, Source of the Nile, II. 373.

(*c*) Remission of attention or application: as, *relaxation* of efforts.

> A *relaxation* of religion's hold
> Upon the roving and untutor'd heart
> Soon follows. *Cowper*, Task, ii. 569.

> There is no better known fact in the history of the world than that a deadly epidemic brings with it a *relaxation* of moral instincts. *E. Sartorius*, In the Soudan, p. 76.

2. Unbending; recreation; a state or occupation intended to give mental or bodily relief after effort.

> There would be no business in solitude, nor proper *relaxations* in business. *Addison*, Freeholder.

> For what kings deem a toil, as well they may,
> To him is *relaxation* and mere play.
> *Cowper*, Table-Talk, l. 156.

> Hours of careless *relaxation*. *Macaulay*.

> It is better to conceal ignorance, but it is hard to do so in *relaxation* and over wine.
> *Heraclitus* (trans.), Amer. Jour. Psychol., I. 668.

Letters of relaxation, in *Scots law*, letters passing the signet, whereby a debtor is relieved from personal diligence, or whereby an outlaw is reponed against sentence of outlawry: now employed only in the latter sense.

relaxative (rē̤-lak'sa̤-tiv), *a.* and *n.* [< *relax* + *-at-ive*.] I. *a.* Having the quality of relaxing; laxative.

II. *n.* 1. That which has power to relax; a laxative medicine.

> And therefore you must use *relaxatives*.
> *B. Jonson*, Magnetick Lady, iii. 4.

2. That which gives relaxation; a relaxation.

> The Moresco festivals seem . . . *relaxatives* of corporeal labours. *L. Addison*, West Barbary, xvii.

relay[1] (rē̤-lā'), *n.* [< ME. *relaye*, < OF. *relais*, rest, stop, remission, delay, a relay, F. *relais*, relay, = It. *rilasso*, relay; cf. *rilasso*, *relasso*, same as *rilascio*, a release, etc.; < OF. *relaisser*, release, let go, relinquish, intr. stop, cease, rest, = It. *rilassare*, *relasciare*, relax, release, < L. *relaxare*, loosen, let loose, allow to rest: see *relax* and *release*[1].] 1. A fresh supply, especially of animals to be substituted for others; specifically, a fresh set of dogs or horses, in hunting, held in readiness to be cast off or to remount the hunters should occasion require, or a relief supply of horses held in readiness for the convenience of travelers.

> Ther overtok I a gret route
> Of huntes and eke of foresteres,
> With many *relayes* and lymeres.
> *Chaucer*, Death of Blanche, l. 362.

> *Rob.* What *relays* set you?
> *John.* None at all; we laid not
> In one fresh dog. *B. Jonson*, Sad Shepherd, i. 2.

> Through the night goes the diligence, passing *relay* after relay. *Thackeray*, Philip, xxix.

2. A squad of men to take a spell or turn of work at stated intervals; a shift.—3. Generally, a supply of anything laid up or kept in store for relief or fresh supply from time to time.

> Who call aloud . . .
> For change of follies, and *relays* of joy.
> *Young*, Night Thoughts, ii. 250.

4. An instrument, consisting principally of an electromagnet with the armature delicately adjusted for a slight motion about an axis, and with contact-points so arranged that the movement of the armature in obedience to the signals transmitted over the line puts a battery, known as the *local battery*, into or out of a short local circuit in which is the recording or receiving apparatus. Also called *relay-magnet*.—**Microphone relay.** See *microphone*.—**Polarized relay**, a relay in which the armature is permanently magnetized. The movements of the armature are accomplished without the use of a retractile spring, and the instrument is thus more sensitive than one of the ordinary form.—**Relay of ground**, ground laid up in fallow. *Richardson.*

relay[2] (rē-lā'), *v. t.* [< *re-* + *lay*[1].] To lay again; lay a second time: as, to *relay* a pavement.

relbun (rel'bun), *n.* See *Calceolaria*.

releasable (rẹ-lē'sạ-bl), *a.* [< *release* + *-able*.] Capable of being released.

He [Ethelbald, king of Mercland] discharged all monasteries and churches of all kind of taxes, works, and imposts, excepting such as were for building of forts and bridges, being (as it seems the law was then) not *releasable*. *Selden*, Illustrations of Brayton's Polyolbion, xi.

release[1] (rẹ-lēs'), *v. t.*; pret. and pp. *released*, ppr. *releasing*. [< ME. *relesen*, *relessen*, *releschen*, < OF. *relaissier*, *relessier*, *relesser*, release, let go, relinquish, quit, intr. stop, cease, rest, F. *relaisser* (also OF. *relacher*, *relascher*, F. *relâcher*), relax, release, = Pr. *relaxar*, *relachar* = Sp. *relajar* = Pg. *relaxar* = It. *relassare*, *rilassare*, *rilasciare*, relax, release, < L. *relaxare*, relax: see *relax*, of which *release* is a doublet. Cf. *relay*[1].] 1. To let loose; set free from restraint or confinement; liberate, as from prison, confinement, or servitude.

But Pilate answered them, saying, Will ye that I *release* unto you the King of the Jews? Mark xv. 9.

The Earls Marchar and Syward, with Wolnoth, the Brother of Harold, a little before his Death, he [King William] *released* out of Prison. *Baker*, Chronicles, p. 26.

And I arose, and I *released*
The casement, and the light increased.
Tennyson, Two Voices.

2. To free from pain, care, trouble, grief, or any other evil.

They would be so weary of their liues as either fly all their Countries, or giue all they had to be *released* of such an hourely misery.
Quoted in *Capt. John Smith's* Works, II. 91.

Leisure, silence, and a mind *releas'd*
From anxious thoughts how wealth may be increas'd.
Cowper, Retirement, l. 139.

3. To free from obligation or penalty: as, to *release* one from debt, or from a promise or covenant.

About this time William Cecil, Lord Burleigh, and High Treasurer of England, finding himself to droop with Age, . . . sent Letters to the Queen, entreating her to *release* him of his publick Charge. *Baker*, Chronicles, p. 387.

The people begged to be *released* from a part of their rates. *Emerson*, Hist. Discourse at Concord.

"Good friends," he said, "since both have fled, the ruler and the priest,
Judge ye if from their further work I be not well *released*." *Whittier*, Cassandra Southwick.

4†. To forgive.—5. To quit; let go, as a legal claim; remit; surrender or relinquish: as, to *release* a debt, or to *release* a right to lands or tenements by conveying to another already having some right or estate in possession. Thus, a remainder-man *releases* his right to the tenant in possession; one coparcener *releases* his right to the other; or the mortgagee *releases* to the mortgager or owner of the equity of redemption.

I *releshe* the my ryght with a rank will,
And graunt the the gouernanse of this grete yle.
Destruction of Troy (E. E. T. S.), l. 13626.

Item, that the duchy of Anjou and the county of Maine shall be *released* and delivered to the king her father.
Shak., 2 Hen. VI., i. 1. 51.

We here *release* unto our faithful people
One entire subsidy, due unto the crown
In our dead brother's days.
Webster and Dekker, Sir Thomas Wyatt, p. 31.

Tithes therfore, though claim'd, and Holy under the Law, yet are now *releas'd* and quitted, both by that command to Peter and by this to all Ministers above cited.
Milton, Touching Hirelings.

6†. To relax.

It may not seem hard if in cases of necessity certain profitable ordinances sometimes be *released*, rather than all men always strictly bound to the general rigor thereof. *Hooker*.

7†. To let slip; let go; give up.

Bidding them fight for honour of their love,
And rather die then Ladies cause *release*.
Spenser, F. Q., IV. ii. 19.

8. To take out of pawn. *Nabbes*, The Bride (4to, 1640), sig. F. iv. (*Halliwell*.) =**Syn.** 1. To loose, deliver.—1-3. *Liberate*, etc. See *disengage*.—3. To acquit.

release[1] (rē-lēs'), *n.* [< ME. *relees*, *reles*, *relece*, < OF. *reles*, *relez*, *relais*, *rellais*, F. *relais* = It. *rilascio*, a release, relay; from the verb: see *release*[1], *v.*, and cf. *relay*[1].] 1. Liberation or discharge from restraint of any kind, as from confinement or bondage.

Confined together,
. . . all prisoners, sir, . . .
They cannot budge till your *release*.
Shak., Tempest, v. 1. 11.

Thou . . .
Who boast'st *release* from hell, and leave to come
Into the heaven of heavens. *Milton*, P. R., i. 409.

2. Liberation from care, pain, or any burden.

It seem'd so hard at first, mother, to leave the blessed sun,
And now it seems as hard to stay, and yet His will be done!
But still I think it can't be long before I find *release*.
Tennyson, May Queen, Conclusion.

When the Sabbath brings its kind *release*,
And care lies slumbering on the lap of Peace.
O. W. Holmes, A Rhymed Lesson.

3. Discharge from obligation or responsibility, as from debt, tax, penalty, or claim of any kind; acquittance.

The king made a great feast, . . . and he made a *release* to the provinces, and gave gifts. Esther ii. 18.

Henry III. himself . . . sought in a papal sentence of absolution a *release* from the solemn obligations by which he had bound himself to his people.
Stubbs, Const. Hist., § 403.

4. In *law*, a surrender of a right; a remission of a claim in such form as to estop the grantor from asserting it again. More specifically—(*a*) An instrument by which a creditor or lienor discharges the debt or lien, or frees a particular person or property therefrom, irrespective of whether payment or satisfaction has actually been made. Hence usually it implies a sealed instrument. See *receipt*. (*b*) An instrument by which a person having or claiming an ulterior estate in land, or a present estate without possession, surrenders his claim to one having an inferior estate, or having an alleged wrongful possession; a quitclaim. See *lease and release*, under *lease*[2].

5. In a steam-engine, the opening of the exhaust-port before the stroke is finished, to lessen the back-pressure.—6. In *archery*, the act of letting go the bowstring in shooting; the mode of performing this act, which differs among different peoples.—**Out of release**†, without cessation.

Whom erthe and se and heven, *out of relees*,
Ay herien. *Chaucer*, Second Nun's Tale, l. 46.

Release of dower. See *dower*[2]. =**Syn.** 1-3. Deliverance, excuse, exemption, exoneration, absolution, clearance. See the verb.

release[2] (rē-lēs'), *v. t.* [< *re-* + *lease*[2].] To lease again or anew. *Imp. Dict.*

releasee (rē-lē-sē'), *n.* [< *release*[1] + *-ee*[1]. Cf. *lessee*, *relessee*.] In *law*, a person to whom a release is given; a relessee.

releasement (rẹ-lēs'mẹnt), *n.* [< *release*[1] + *-ment*. Cf. OF. *relaschement*, F. *relâchement* = Pr. *relaxamen* = Sp. *relajamiento* = Pg. *relaxamento* = It. *relassamento*, releasement.] The act of releasing, in any sense; a release.

'Tis I am Hercules, sent to free you all.—
. . . In this club behold
All your *releasements*. *Shirley*, Love Tricks, iii. 5.

The Queen interposeth for the *Releasement* of my Lord of Newport and others, who are Prisoners of War.
Howell, Letters, I. v. 8.

releaser (rẹ-lē'sėr), *n.* 1. One who releases.—2. In *mech.*, any device in the nature of a tripping mechanism whereby one part is released from engagement with another. [Rare.]

release-spring (rẹ-lēs'spring), *n.* A spring attached to the end-piece of a truck for the purpose of throwing the brakes out of contact with the wheels. *Car-Builder's Dict.*

releasor (rẹ-lē'sọr), *n.* [< *release*[1] + *-or*[1].] In *law*, one who grants a release; one who quits or renounces that which he has; a relessor.

releest†, *n.* A Middle English form of *release*[1].

releet (rẹ-lēt'), *n.* [< *re-* + *leet*.] A crossing of roads. *Halliwell.* [Prov. Eng.]

relefe†, *n.* An obsolete spelling of *relief*.

relegate (rel'ē-gāt), *v. t.*; pret. and pp. *relegated*, ppr. *relegating*. [< L. *relegatus*, pp. of *relegare* (> It. *relegare* = Sp. *relegar* = Pr. *relegar*, *releguar* = F. *reléguer*), send away, despatch, remove, < *re-*, away, back, + *legare*, send: see *legate*.] 1. To send away or out of the way; consign, as to some obscure or remote destination; banish; dismiss.

We have not *relegated* religion (like something we were ashamed to shew) to obscure municipalities or rustic villages. *Burke*, Rev. in France.

Relegate to worlds yet distant our repose.
M. Arnold, Empedocles on Etna.

Relegated by their own political sympathies and Whig liberality . . . to the comparative uselessness of literary retirement. *Stubbs*, Medieval and Modern Hist., p. 6.

2. In *Rom. law*, to send into exile; cause to remove a certain distance from Rome for a certain period.—3. In *law*, to remit or put off to an inferior remedy.

relegation (rel-ē-gā'shon), *n.* [< OF. *relegacion*, *relegation*, F. *relégation* = Sp. *relegacion* = It. *relegazione*, < L. *relegatio(n-)*, a sending away, exiling, banishing, < *relegare*, send away: see *relegate*.] The act of relegating; banishment: specifically a term in ancient Roman law, and also in ecclesiastical law, and in that of universities, especially in Germany. See *relegate*, 2.

The exiles are not allowed the liberty of other banished persons, who, within the isle or region of *relegation*, may go or move whither they please.
Jer. Taylor, Works (ed. 1835), I. 388.

Arius behaved himself so seditiously and tumultuarily that the Nicene fathers procured a temporary decree for his *relegation*. *Jer. Taylor*, Liberty of Prophesying, Ep. Ded.

relent (rē-lent'), *v.* [< ME. *relenten*, < OF. *ralentir*, *rallentir*, slacken, relent, F. *ralentir* = Pg. *relentar* (cf. Sp. *relentecer*, soften, relent, < L. *relentescere*, slacken) = It. *rallentare*, < L. *re-*, back, + *lentus*, slow, slack, tenacious, pliant; akin to *lenis*, gentle, and E. *lithe*[1]: see *lenient*.] I. *intrans.* 1†. To slacken; stay.

Yet scarcely once to breath would they *relent*.
Spenser, F. Q., IV. ii. 18.

2†. To soften in substance; lose compactness; become less rigid or hard.

He stired the coles til *relente* gan
The wex agayn the fyr.
Chaucer, Canon's Yeoman's Tale, l. 267.

There be some houses wherein sweet-meats will *relent* . . . more than in others. *Bacon*, Nat. Hist., § 809.

When op'ning buds salute the welcome day,
And earth *relenting* feels the genial ray.
Pope, Temple of Fame, l. 4.

3†. To deliquesce; dissolve; melt; fade away.

The colours, beynge nat suerly wrought, . . . by moystnesse of wether *relenteth* or fadeth.
Sir T. Elyot, The Governour, iii. 19.

All nature mourns, the skies *relent* in showers.
Pope, Spring, l. 69.

4. To become less severe or intense; relax. [Rare.]

The workmen let glass cool by degrees, and in such *relentings* of fire as they call their nealing heats, lest it should shiver in pieces by a violent succeeding of air.
Sir K. Digby, On Bodies.

The slave-trade had never *relented* among the Mahometans. *Bancroft*, Hist. U. S., I. 129.

5. To become less harsh, cruel, or obdurate; soften in temper; become more mild and tender; give way; yield; comply; feel compassion.

Relent and yield to mercy. *Shak.*, 2 Hen. VI., iv. 8. 11.

Stern Proserpine *relented*,
And gave him back the fair.
Pope, Ode on St. Cecilia's Day, l. 85.

No light had we: for that we do repent;
And, learning this, the bridegroom will *relent*.
Too late, too late! ye cannot enter now.
Tennyson, Guinevere.

II.† *trans.* 1. To slacken; remit; stay; abate.

But nothing might *relent* her hasty flight.
Spenser, F. Q., III. iv. 49.

2. To soften; mollify; dissolve.

In water first this opium *relent*,
Of sape until it have similitude.
Palladius, Husbondrie (E. E. T. S.), p. 102.

All his body shulde be dyssolued and *relented* into salte dropes. *Sir T. Elyot*, The Governour, ii. 12.

relent† (rē-lent'), *n.* [< *relent*, *v.*] 1. Remission; stay.

Ne rested till she came without *relent*
Unto the land of Amazons.
Spenser, F. Q., V. vii. 24.

2. Relenting.

Fear of death enforceth still
In greater minds submission and *relent*.
Greene, Orlando Furioso.

relenting (rē-len'ting), *p. a.* Inclining to relent or yield; soft; too easily moved; soft-hearted; weakly complaisant.

Relenting tool, and shallow, changing woman!
Shak., Rich. III., iv. 4. 431.

relentless (rē-lent'les), *a.* [< *relent* + *-less*.] Incapable of relenting; unmoved by pity; unpitying; insensible to the distress of others; destitute of tenderness.

Only in destroying I find ease
To my *relentless* thoughts. *Milton*, P. L., ix. 130.

=**Syn.** *Implacable*, etc. See *inexorable*, and list under *unrelenting*.

relentlessly (rē-lent'les-li), *adv.* In a relentless manner; without pity.

relentlessness (rē-lent'les-nes), *n.* The quality of being relentless, or unmoved by pity. *Imp. Dict.*

relentment (rē-lent'mẹnt), *n.* [= It. *rallentamento;* as *relent* + *-ment.*] The act or state of relenting; compassion. *Imp. Dict.*

reles[1]†, *n.* A Middle English form of *release*[1].

reles[2]†, *n.* A Middle English form of *relish.*

relesse†, *v.* A Middle English form of *release*[1].

relessee (rẹ̄-le-sē'), *n.* [Var. of *releasee*, imitating the simple *lessee.*] In *law*, the person to whom a release is executed.

relessor (rẹ̄-les'ọr), *n.* [Var. of *releasor.* Cf. *relessee.*] In *law*, the person who executes a release.

There must be a privity of estate between the *relessor* and relessee. *Blackstone*, Com., II. xx.

relet (rē-let'), *v. t.* [< *re-* + *let*[1], *v.*] To let anew, as a house.

relevance (rel'ẹ̄-vạns), *n.* [= Pg. *relevancia;* as *relevan(t)* + *-ce.*] Same as *relevancy.*

relevancy (rel'ẹ̄-vạn-si), *n.* [As *relevance* (see *-cy*).] 1†. The state of affording relief or aid.— 2. The state or character of being relevant or pertinent; pertinence; applicableness; definite or obvious relation; recognizable connection.

Much I marvelled this ungainly fowl to hear discourse so plainly,
Though its answer little meaning—little *relevancy* bore.
Poe, The Raven.

3. In *Scots law*, fitness or sufficiency to bring about a decision. The *relevancy* of the libel, in Scots law, is the sufficiency of the matters therein stated to warrant a decree in the terms asked.

The presiding Judge next directed the counsel to plead to the *relevancy:* that is, to state on either part the arguments in point of law, and evidence in point of fact, against and in favour of the criminal.
Scott, Heart of Mid-Lothian, xxii.

relevant (rel'ẹ̄-vạnt), *a.* [< OF. *relevant*, assisting, = Sp. Pg. *relevante*, raising, important, < L. *relevan(t-)s*, ppr. of *relevare*, lift up again, lighten, relieve, hence in Rom. help, assist: see *relieve*, and cf. *levant*[1].] 1. To the purpose; pertinent; applicable: as, the testimony is not *relevant* to the case.

Close and *relevant* arguments have very little hold on the passions. *Sydney Smith.*

2. In *law*, being in subject-matter germane to the controversy; conducive to the proof or disproof of a fact in issue or a pertinent hypothesis. See *irrelevant.*

The word *relevant* means that any two facts to which it is applied are so related to each other that, according to the common course of events, one, either taken by itself or in connection with other facts, proves or renders probable the past, present, or future existence of the other.
Stephen.

3. In *Scots law*, sufficient legally: as, a *relevant* plea.

The Judges . . . recorded their judgment, which bore that the indictment, if proved, was *relevant* to infer the pains of law: and that the defence, that the panel had communicated her situation to her sister, was a *relevant* defence. *Scott*, Heart of Mid-Lothian, xxii.

=**Syn.** 1 and 2. Apposite, appropriate, suitable, fit.

relevantly (rel'ẹ̄-vạnt-li), *adv.* In a relevant manner; with relevancy.

relevation† (rel-ẹ̄-vā'shọn), *n.* [= Sp. *relevacion*, < L. *relevatio(n-)*, a lightening, relief, < *relevare*, lighten, relieve: see *relevant*, *relieve.*] A raising or lifting up. *Bailey.*

releve†, *v.* A Middle English form of *relieve.*

reliability (rẹ̄-lī-a-bil'ị-ti), *n.* [< *reliable* + *-ity* (see *-bility*).] The state or quality of being reliable; reliableness.

He bestows all the pleasures, and inspires all that ease of mind on those around him or connected with him, which perfect consistency, and (if such a word might be framed) absolute *reliability*, equally in small as in great concerns, cannot but inspire and bestow.
Coleridge, Biog. Lit., iii.

reliable (rẹ̄-lī'ạ-bl), *a.* [< *rely*[1] + *-able.*] That may be relied on; fit or worthy to be relied on; worthy of reliance; to be depended on; trustworthy. [This word, which involves a use of the suffix *-able* superficially different from its more familiar use in *provable*, 'that may be proved,' *eatable*, 'that may be eaten,' etc., has been much objected to by purists on philological grounds. The objection, however, really has no philological justification, being based on an imperfect knowledge of the history and uses of the suffix *-able*, or on a too narrow view of its office. Compare *available*, *conversable*, *dispensable*, *laughable*, and many other examples collected by Fitzedward Hall in his work cited below, and see *-able.* As a matter of usage, however, the word is shunned by many fastidious writers.]

The Emperor of Russia may have announced the restoration of monarchy as exclusively his object. This is not considered as the ultimate object, by this country, but as the best means, and most *reliable* pledge, of a higher object, viz. our own security, and that of Europe.
Coleridge, Essays on His Own Times, p. 296 (on a speech by [Mr. Pitt (Nov. 17, 1800), as manipulated by Coleridge): [quoted in F. Hall's Adjectives in *-able*, p. 29.

According to General Livingston's humorous account, his own village of Elizabethtown was not much more *reliable*, being peopled in those agitated times by "unknown, unrecommended strangers, guilty-looking tories, and very knavish whigs." *Irving.* (*Webster.*)

He [Mr. Grote] seems to think that the *reliable* chronology of Greece begins before its *reliable* history.
Gladstone, Oxford Essays (1857), p. 49.

She [the Church] has now a direct command, and a *reliable* influence, over her own institutions, which was wanting in the middle ages.
J. H. Newman, Lectures and Essays on University Subjects (ed. 1859), p. 302.

Above all, the grand and only *reliable* security, in the last resort, against the despotism of the government, is in that case wanting—the sympathy of the army with the people. *J. S. Mill*, Representative Government, xvi.

The sturdy peasant . . . has become very well accustomed to that spectacle, and regards the said lord as his most *reliable* source of trinkgelds and other pecuniary advantages.
Leslie Stephen, Playground of Europe (1871), p. 47.

=**Syn.** Trustworthy, trusty.

reliableness (rẹ̄-lī'ạ-bl-nes), *n.* The state or quality of being reliable; reliability.

The number of steps in an argument does not subtract from its *reliableness*, if no new premises of an uncertain character are taken up by the way.
J. S. Mill, Logic (ed. 1865), I. 303.

reliably (rẹ̄-lī'ạ-bli), *adv.* In a reliable manner; so as to be relied on.

reliance (rẹ̄-lī'ạns), *n.* [< *rely*[1] + *-ance.*] 1. The act of relying, or the state or character of being reliant; confident rest for support; confidence; dependence: as, we may have perfect *reliance* on the promises of God; to have *reliance* on the testimony of witnesses.

His days and times are past,
And my *reliances* on his fracted dates
Have smit my credit. *Shak.*, T. of A., ii. 1. 22.

Who would lend to a government that prefaced its overtures for borrowing by an act which demonstrated that no *reliance* could be placed on the steadiness of its measures for paying? *A. Hamilton*, The Federalist, No. xxx.

2. Anything on which to rely; sure dependence; ground of trust.

reliant (rẹ̄-lī'ạnt), *a.* [< *rely*[2] + *-ant.*] Having or indicating reliance or confidence; confident; self-trustful: as, a *reliant* spirit; a *reliant* bearing.

Dinah was too *reliant* on the Divine will to attempt to achieve any end by a deceptive concealment.
George Eliot, Adam Bede, lii.

relic (rel'ik), *n.* [Formerly also *relick*, *relique;* < ME. *relyke*, *relike*, chiefly pl., < OF. *reliques*, pl., F. *relique*, pl. *reliques* = Pr. *reliquias* = Sp. Pg. It. *reliquia* = AS. *reliquias*, relics (also in comp. *relic-gong*, a going to visit relics), < L. *reliquiæ*, remains, relics, < *relinquere* (pret. *reliqui*, pp. *relictus*), leave behind: see *relinquish.* Cf. *relict.*] 1. That which remains; that which is left after the consumption, loss, or decay of the rest.

The Mouse and the Catte fell to their victualles, beeing such *reliques* as the olde manne had left.
Lyly, Euphues and his England, p. 234.

They shew monstrous bones, the *Reliques* of the Whale from which Perseus freed Andromeda.
Purchas, Pilgrimage, p. 95.

Fair Greece! sad *relic* of departed worth!
Byron, Childe Harold, ii. 73.

2. The body of a deceased person; a corpse, as deserted by the soul. [Usually in the plural.]

What needs my Shakspeare, for his honour'd bones,
The labour of an age in piled stones?
Or that his hallow'd *reliques* should be hid
Under a star-ypointing pyramid?
Milton, Epitaph on Shakspeare.

3. That which is preserved in remembrance; a memento; a souvenir; a keepsake.

His [Peter Stuyvesant's] silver-mounted wooden leg is still treasured up in the store-room as an invaluable *relique.* *Irving*, Knickerbocker, p. 466.

4. An object held in reverence or affection because connected with some sacred or beloved person deceased; specifically, in the *Rom. Cath. Ch.*, the *Gr. Ch.*, and some other churches, a saint's body or part of it, or an object supposed to have been connected with the life or body of Christ, of the Virgin Mary, or of some saint or martyr, and regarded therefore as a personal memorial worthy of religious veneration. Relics are of three classes: (*a*) the entire bodies or parts of the bodies of venerated persons, (*b*) objects used by them or connected with their martyrdom, and (*c*) objects connected with their tombs or sanctified by contact with their bodies. Relics are preserved in churches, convents, etc., to which pilgrimages are on their account frequently made. The miraculous virtues which are attributed to them are defended by such instances from Scripture as that of the miracles which were wrought by the bones of Elisha (2 Ki. xiii. 21).

The in a Chirche of Seynt Silvester ys many grett *reliquis*, a pece of the vesture of our blyssyd lady.
Torkington, Diarie of Eng. Travell, p. 4.

What make ye this way? we keep no *relics* here,
Nor holy shrines. *Fletcher*, Pilgrim, i. 2.

Lists of *relics* belonging to certain churches in this country are often to be met with in Anglo-Saxon manuscripts.
Rock, Church of our Fathers, III. i. 357, note.

5†. Something dear or precious.

It is a fulle noble thing
Whanne thyne eyen have metyng
With that *relike* precious,
Wherof they be so desirous.
Rom. of the Rose, l. 2907.

6†. A monument.

Shall we go see the *reliques* of this town?
Shak., T. N., iii. 3. 19.

=**Syn.** 4. *Remains*, *Relics.* The *remains* of a dead person are his corpse or his literary works; in the latter case they are, for the sake of distinction, generally called *literary remains.* We speak also of the *remains* of a feast, of a city, building, monument, etc. *Relics* always suggests antiquity: as, the *relics* of ancient sovereigns, heroes, and especially saints. The singular of *relics* is used; that of *remains* is not.

relic-knife (rel'ik-nīf), *n.* A knife made so as to contain the relic or supposed relic of a saint, either in a small cavity provided for the purpose in the handle, or by incorporating the relic, if a piece of bone or the like, in the decoration of the handle itself. *Jour. Brit. Archæol. Ass.*, X. 89.

relicly† (rel'ik-li), *adv.* [< *relic* + *-ly*[2].] As a relic; with care such as is given to a relic. [Rare.]

As a thrifty wench scrapes kitchen-stuff,
And barrelling the droppings, and the snuff
Of wasting candles, which in thirty year,
Relicly kept, perchance buys wedding cheer.
Donne, Satires, ii.

relic-monger (rel'ik-mung″gėr), *n.* One who traffics in relics; hence, one who has a passion for collecting objects to serve as relics or souvenirs.

The beauty and historic interest of the heads must have tempted the senseless and unscrupulous greed of mere *relic-mongers.* *Harper's Mag.*, LXXVI. 302.

relict (rel'ikt), *n.* and *a.* [< OF. *relict*, m., *relicte*, f., a person or thing left behind, esp. *relicte*, f., a widow, < L. *relictus*, fem. *relicta*, neut. *relictum*, left behind, pp. of *relinquere*, leave behind: see *relic*, *relinquish.*] I. *n.* 1†. One who is left or who remains; a survivor.

The eldest daughter, Frances, . . . is the sole *relict* of the family. *B. Jonson*, New Inn, Arg.

2. Specifically, a widower or widow, especially a widow.

He took to Wife the virtuous Lady Emma, the *Relict* of K. Ethelred. *Baker*, Chronicles, p. 16.

Though the *relict* of a man or woman hath liberty to contract new relations, yet I do not find they have liberty to cast off the old. *Jer. Taylor*, Works (ed. 1835), II. 84.

Who cou'd love such an unhappy *Relict* as I am?
Steele, Grief A-la-Mode, iii. 1.

3†. A thing left behind; a relic.

To breake the eggeshell after the meat is out, wee are taught in our childhood, and practice it all our lives, which neverthelesse is but a superstitious *relict.*
Sir T. Browne, Pseud. Epid. (1646), v. 21.

II. *a.* Left; remaining; surviving.

His *Relict* Lady . . . lived long in Westminster.
Fuller, Worthies, Lincoln, II. 13. (*Davies.*)

relict†, *v. t.* [< L. *relictus*, pp. of *relinquere*, leave: see *relinquish.*] To leave.

A vyne whoos fruite humoure wol potrifie
Pampyned [pruned] is to be by every side,
Relicte on hit oonly the croppes hie.
Palladius, Husbondrie (E. E. T. S.), p. 186.

relicted (rẹ̄-lik'ted), *a.* [< L. *relictus*, pp. of *relinquere*, relinquish, leave behind (see *relinquish*, *relict*), + *-ed*[2].] In *law*, left dry, as land by the recession of the sea or other body of water.

reliction (rẹ̄-lik'shọn), *n.* [< L. *relictio(n-)*, a leaving behind, forsaking, < *relinquere*, pp. *relictus*, forsake, abandon: see *relict*, *relinquish.*] In *law*, the recession of the sea or other body of water from land; also, land thus left uncovered.

relief (rẹ̄-lēf'), *n.* [< ME. *releef*, *relefe*, *relef*, also *relif*, *relyf*, *relyee*, relief, also remnants left over, relics, a basket of fragments, < OF. *relef*, *relief*, a raising, relieving, a relief, a thing raised, scraps, fragments, also raised or embossed work, relief, F. *relief*, relief, embossed work, = Pr. *releu* = Cat. *relleu* = Sp. *relieve*, a relief, *relievo*, embossed work, *relevo*, relief (milit.), = Pg. *relevo*, embossed work, = It. *rilevo*, remnants, fragments, *rilievo*, embossed work (see *bas-relief*, *basso-rilievo*); from the verb: see *relieve.*] 1. The act of relieving, or the state of being relieved; the removal, in whole or in part, of any pain, oppression, or burden, so that some ease is obtained; alleviation; succor; comfort.

Bycause it was a deserte yle, there was no thynge to be founde that myght be to our *releſe*, nother in vytaylles nor otherwyse, whiche discomforted vs right moche.
Sir R. Guylforde, Pylgrymage, p. 62.

Wherever sorrow is, *relief* would be.
Shak., As you Like it, iii. 5. 86.

To the catalogue of pleasures may accordingly be added the pleasures of *relief*, or the pleasures which a man experiences when, after he has been enduring a pain of any kind for a certain time, it comes to cease, or to abate.
Bentham, Introd. to Morals and Legislation, v. 16.

2. That which mitigates or removes pain, grief, want, or other evil.

What *releefe* I should haue from your Colony I would satisfie and spare them (when I could) the like courtesie.
Capt. *John Smith*, Works, II. 80.

Pity the sorrows of a poor old man. . . .
Oh! give *relief*, and Heaven will bless your store.
T. Moss, Beggar's Petition.

He [James II.] . . . granted to the exiles some *relief* from his privy purse, and, by letters under his great seal, invited his subjects to imitate his liberality.
Macaulay, Hist. Eng., vi.

3. In Great Britain, assistance given under the poor-laws to a pauper: as, to administer outdoor *relief*.—4. Release from a post of duty by a substitute or substitutes, who may act either permanently or temporarily; especially, the going off duty of a sentinel or guard whose place is supplied by another soldier.

For this *relief*, much thanks; 'tis bitter cold,
And I am sick at heart. *Shak.*, Hamlet, i. 1. 8.

5. One who relieves another, as from a post of duty; a soldier who relieves another who is on guard; collectively, a company of soldiers who relieve others who are on guard.

Even in front of the National Palace the sentries on duty march up and down their beats in a slipshod fashion, while the *relief* loll about on the stone benches, smoking cigarettes and otherwise making themselves comfortable.
Harper's Mag., LXXIX. 820.

6. In *sculp.*, *arch.*, etc., the projection (in *painting*, the apparent projection) of a figure or feature from the ground or plane on which it is formed. Relief is, in general, of three kinds: high relief (*allo-rilievo*), low relief (*basso-rilievo*, *bas-relief*), and middle or half relief (*mezzo-rilievo*). The distinction lies in the degree of projection. *High relief* is that in which

High Relief.—The Rondanini mask of Medusa in the Glyptothek, Munich—illustrating the late beautified type of the Gorgon.

the figures project at least one half of their natural circumference from the background. In *low relief* the figures project but slightly from the ground, in such a manner that no part of them is entirely detached from it, as in medals, the chief effect being produced by the treatment of light and shadow. *Middle* or *half relief* is intermediate between the other two. The varieties of relief are still further distinguished as *stiacciato rilievo*, or very flat relief, the lowest possible relief, of which the projection in parts hardly exceeds the thickness of a sheet of paper; and *cavo-rilievo*, hollow relief, also called *intaglio rilevato*, or cœlanaglyphic sculpture, an Egyptian form of relief obtained by cutting a furrow with sloping sides around a figure previously outlined on a stone surface, leaving the highest parts of the finished work on a level with the original surface-plane. See also cut in next column, and cuts under *orant*, *Proserpine*, *allo-rilievo*, and *bas-relief*.

You find the figures of many ancient coins rising up in a much more beautiful *relief* than those on the modern.
Addison, Ancient Medals, iii.

7. A work of art or decoration in relief of any of the varieties described above.

On each side of the door-place [of several grottos] there are rough unfinished pillars cut in the rock, which support a pediment, and over the door there is a *relief* of a spread eagle. *Pococke*, Description of the East, II. i. 135.

Hollow-relief or Cavo-rilievo Sculpture.—Court of Edfu, Egypt; Ptolemaic age, 2d century B. C.

8. In *her.*, the supposed projection of a charge from the surface of the field, represented by shading with a heavier bounding-line on the sinister side and toward the base than on the dexter side and toward the chief. Thus, if an escutcheon is divided into seven vertical stripes, alternately red and white, it would not be blazoned paly of seven gules and argent, as the rule is that paly is always of an even number, but the sinister side of three alternate stripes would be shaded to indicate relief, and the blazoning would be gules, three pallets argent, the assumption being that the pallets are in relief upon the field.
9. In *phys. geog.*, the form of the surface of any part of the earth, considered in the most general way, and with special regard to differences of elevation: little used except in the name *relief-map*, by which is meant a geographical or geological map in which the form of the surface is expressed by elevations and depressions of the material used. Unless the scale of such relief-maps is very large, there must be considerable exaggeration, because differences of vertical elevations in nature are small as compared with superficial extent. Relief-maps are occasionally made by preparing a model of the region it is desired to exhibit, and then photographing this model under an oblique illumination. The relief of the surface is also frequently indicated on maps by various colors or by a number of tints of one color. Both hachure and contour-line maps also indicate the relief of the surface, to a greater or less extent, according to their scale and artistic perfection. Thus, the Dufour map of Switzerland, especially when photographed down to a small size, has in a very striking degree the effect of a photograph from an actual model, although in reality a hachure-map.
10. In *fort.*, the perpendicular height of the interior crest of the parapet above the bottom of the ditch.—11. Prominence or distinctness given to anything by something presenting a contrast to it, or brought into close relation with or proximity to it; a contrast.

Here also grateful mixture of well-match'd
And sorted hues (each giving each *relief*,
And by contrasted beauty shining more).
Cowper, Task, iii. 634.

Miss Brooke had that kind of beauty which seems to be thrown into *relief* by poor dress.
George Eliot, Middlemarch, i.

12. In *hunting*, a note sounded on the horn on reaching home after the chase.

Now, Sir, when you come to your stately gate, as you sounded the recheat before, so now you must sound the *releefe* three times. *Return from Parnassus* (1606), ii. 5.

13†. What is picked up; fragments left; broken meat given in alms.

After dener, ther shall come all ffre sowerys, and take the *relef* of the mete and drynke that the fforsayde M. and shopholderis levyth. *English Gilds* (E. E. T. S.), p. 315.

14. In *law*, that which a court of justice awards to a suitor as redress for the grievance of which he complains.—15. In *feudal law*, a fine or composition which the heir of a tenant holding by knight's service or other tenure paid to the lord at the death of the ancestor, for the privilege of succeeding to the estate, which, on strict feudal principles, had lapsed or fallen to the lord on the death of the tenant. This relief consisted of horses, arms, money, etc., the amount of which was originally arbitrary, but afterward fixed by law. The term is still used in this sense in Scots law, being a sum exigible by a feudal superior from the heir who enters on a feu. Also called *casualty of relief*.

On taking up the inheritance of lands, a *relief* [was paid to the king]. The *relief* originally consisted of arms, armour and horses, and was arbitrary in amount, but was subsequently "ascertained," that is, rendered certain, by the Conqueror, and fixed at a certain quantity of arms and habiliments of war. After the assize of arms of Henry II., it was commuted for a money payment of 100*s.* for every knight's fee, and as thus fixed continued to be payable ever afterwards. *S. Dowell*, Taxes in England, I. 25.

Absolute relief, in *fort.*, the height of any point of a work above the bottom of the ditch.—**Alternative relief**, in *law*, different modes of redress asked in the alternative, usually because of uncertainty as to some of the facts, or because of a discretionary power in the court to award either.—**Bond of relief.** See *bond*[1].—**Constructive relief**, in *fort.*, the height of any point of a work above the plane of construction.—**Conversion of relief.** See *conversion*.—**Indoor relief**, accommodation in the poorhouse, as distinguished from *outdoor relief*, the assistance given to those paupers who live outside. [Great Britain.]—**Infeftment of relief.** See *infeftment*.—**Outdoor relief.** See *indoor relief*.—**Parochial relief.** See *parochial*.—**Relief Church**, a body of Presbyterian dissenters in Scotland, who separated from the Established Church on account of the oppressive exercise of patronage. Thomas Gillespie, its founder, was deposed by the General Assembly of the Church of Scotland in 1752, and organized the "Presbytery of Relief" on October 22d, 1761. In 1847 the Relief and United Secession churches amalgamated, forming the United Presbyterian Church.—**Relief law.** See *law*[1].—**Relief processes**, those processes in mechanical or "process" engraving by which are produced plates or blocks with raised lines, capable of being printed from like type, or together with type, in an ordinary press.—**Relief satiné, or satiné relief.** Same as *raised satin-stitch* (which see, under *satin-stitch*).—**Roman Catholic Relief Acts.** See *Catholic*.—**Specific relief**, in *law*, action of the court directly on the person or property, as distinguished from that in which an award of damages only is made, to be collected by execution. =**Syn. 1.** Mitigation.—2. Help, aid, support.

relief-ful (rẹ-lēf'fůl), *a.* [< *relief* + *-ful.*] Full of relief; giving relief or ease.

Never was there a more joyous heart, . . . ready to burst its bars for *relief-ful* expression.
Richardson, Clarissa Harlowe, III. lix.

reliefless (rẹ-lēf'les), *a.* [< *relief* + *-less.*] Destitute of relief, in any sense.

relief-map (rẹ-lēf'map), *n.* See *relief*, 9.

relief-perspective (rẹ-lēf'pėr-spek"tiv), *n.* The art of constructing homological figures in space, and of determining the relations of the parts of bas-reliefs, theatrical settings, etc., to make them look like nature. Every such representation refers to a fixed center of perspective and to a fixed plane of homology. The latter in a theater setting is the plane in which the actors generally stand; in a bas-relief it is the plane of life-size figures. Every natural plane is represented by a plane cutting it in a line lying in the plane of homology. Every natural point is represented by a point in the same ray from the center of perspective. The plane of homology represents itself, and the center of perspective represents itself. One other point can be taken arbitrarily to represent a given point. There is a vanishing plane, parallel to the plane of homology, which represents the portions of space at an infinite distance.

relief-valve (rẹ-lēf'valv), *n.* 1. In a steam-engine, a valve through which the water escapes into the hot-well when shut off from the boiler.—2. A valve set to open at a given pressure of steam, air, or water; a safety-valve.—3. A valve for automatically admitting air to a cask when the liquid in it is withdrawn.

relief-work (rẹ-lēf'wėrk), *n.* Work in road-making, the construction of public buildings, or the like, put in hand for the purpose of affording employment to the poor in times of public distress. [Eng.]

Those . . . who believe that any employment given by the guardians on *relief-works* would be wasteful and injurious may find that the entire question is one of administration, and that such work proved a success in Manchester during the cotton famine. *Contemporary Rev.*, LIII. 51.

relier (rẹ-lī'ėr), *n.* [< *rely*[1] + *-er*[1].] One who relies or places confidence.

My friends [are] no *reliers* on my fortunes.
Fletcher, Tamer Tamed, i. 3.

relievable (rẹ-lē'vạ-bl), *a.* [< *relieve* + *-able.*] Capable of being relieved; fitted to receive relief.

Neither can they, as to reparation, hold plea of things wherein the party is *relievable* by common law.
Sir M. Hale.

relieve (rẹ-lēv'), *v.*; pret. and pp. *relieved*, ppr. *relieving*. [Early mod. E. also *releeve*; < ME. *releven*, < OF. *relever*, F. *relever* = Pr. Sp. Pg. *relevar* = It. *rilevare*, lift up, relieve, < L. *relevare*, lift up, raise, make light, lighten, relieve, alleviate, lessen, ease, comfort, < *re-*, again, + *levare*, lift: see *levant*[1], *levity*, etc., and cf. *relief*, *relevant*, etc.] **I.** *trans.* 1†. To lift up; set up a second time; hence, to collect; assemble.

Supposing ever, though we sore smerte,
To be *releved* by him afterward.
Chaucer, Prol. to Canon's Yeoman's Tale, l. 319.

That that deth doun brouhte deth shal *releue*.
Piers Plowman (C), xxi. 145.

2. To remove, wholly or partially, as anything that depresses, weighs down, pains, oppresses, etc.; mitigate; alleviate; lessen.

Misery . . . never *relieved* by any.
Shak., Venus and Adonis, l. 708.

I cannot behold a beggar without *relieving* his necessities with my purse, or his soul with my prayers.
Sir T. Browne, Religio Medici, ii. 13.

Accident in some measure *relieved* our embarrassment.
Goldsmith, Vicar, vii.

3. To free, wholly or partly, from pain, grief, want, anxiety, trouble, encumbrance, or anything that is considered to be an evil; give ease, comfort, or consolation to; help; aid; support; succor: as, to *relieve* the poor and needy.

He *relieveth* the fatherless and widow. Ps. cxlvi. 9.

And to remember the lady's love
That last *reliev'd* you out of pine.
Young Beichan and Susie Pye (Child's Ballads, IV. 8).

The pain we feel prompts us to *relieve* ourselves in *relieving* those who suffer. *Burke*, Sublime and Beautiful.

4. Specifically, to bring efficient help to (a besieged place); raise the siege of.

The King of Scots, with the Duke of Gloucester, about the 8th of July besieged Dreux; which agreed, if it were not *relieved* by the twentieth of that Month, then to surrender it. *Baker*, Chronicles, p. 176.

5. To release from a post, station, task, or duty by substituting another person or party; put another in the place of, or take the place of, in the performance of any duty, the bearing of any burden, or the like: as, to *relieve* a sentinel or guard.

Mar. Farewell, honest soldier.
Who hath *relieved* you?
Fran. Bernardo has my place.
Shak., Hamlet, i. 1. 17.

6. To ease of any burden, wrong, or oppression by judicial or legislative interposition, by indemnification for losses, or the like; right.—7. To give assistance to; support.

Parallels or like relations alternately *relieve* each other, when neither will pass asunder, yet they are plausible together. *Sir T. Browne.*

8. To mitigate; lessen; soften.

Not a lichen *relieves* the scintillating whiteness of those skeleton cliffs. *Harper's Mag.*, LXV. 197.

9. To give relief or prominence to, literally or figuratively; hence, to give contrast to; heighten the effect or interest of, by contrast or variety.

The poet must take care not to encumber his poem with too much business; but sometimes to *relieve* the subject with a moral reflection.
Addison, Essay on Virgil's Georgics.

The vegetation against which the ruined colonnades are *relieved* consists almost wholly of almond and olive trees, . . . both enhancing the warm tints of the stone.
J. A. Symonds, Italy and Greece, p. 189.

Relieving arch. Same as *arch of discharge* (which see, under *arch*[1]).—**Relieving officer**, in England, a salaried official appointed by the board of guardians of a poor-law union to superintend the relief of the poor in the parish or district. He receives applications for relief, inquires into facts, and ascertains whether the case is or is not within the conditions required by the law. He visits the houses of the applicants in order to pursue his inquiries, and gives immediate relief in urgent cases.—**Relieving tackles.** See *tackle*.—**To relieve nature.** See *nature*.—**To relieve of**, to take from; free from: said of that which is burdensome.

He shook hands with none until he had helped Miss Brown to unfurl her umbrella, [and] had *relieved* her *of* her prayer-book. *Mrs. Gaskell*, Cranford i.

=**Syn. 2.** *Mitigate*, *Assuage*, etc. (see *alleviate*); diminish, lighten.

II.† *intrans.* To rise; arise.

As soon as I might I *releved* up again.
Lamentation of Mary Magdalene, st. 29.

Thane *relevis* the renkes of the rounde table
Be the riche revare, that rynnys so faire.
Morte Arthure (E. E. T. S.), l. 2278.

At eche tyme that he [Frolle] didde *releve*, he [Galashin] smote hym with his swerde to grounde, that his men wende wele that he hadde be deed. *Merlin* (E. E. T. S.), iii. 397.

relievement† (rē̤-lēv'ment), *n.* [= F. *relèvement* = Pr. *relevament* = It. *rilevamento*, < ML. *relevamentum*, relieving, relief, < *relevare*, relieve: see *relieve*.] The act of relieving, or the state of being relieved, in any sense; that which mitigates or lightens; relief.

His [Robert's] delay yields the King time to confirm him Friends, under-work his Enemies, and make himself strong with the English, which he did by granting relaxation of tribute, with other *relievements* of their doleances.
Daniel, Hist. Eng., p. 53.

reliever (rē̤-lē'vėr), *n.* [< *relieve* + *-er*[1].] 1. One who or that which relieves or gives relief.

O welcome, my *reliever*;
Aristius, as thou lov'st me, ransom me.
B. Jonson, Poetaster, iii. 1.

It acts in three ways . . . (2) as a *reliever* of congestion.
Lancet, No. 3449, p. 3 of Adv'ts.

2. In *gun.*, an iron ring fixed to a handle by means of a socket, which serves to disengage the searcher of a gun when one of its points is retained in a hole.—3. A garment kept for being lent out. [Slang.]

In some sweating places there is an old coat kept called the *reliever*, and this is borrowed by such men as have none of their own to go out in.
Kingsley, Cheap Clothes and Nasty. (*Davies.*)

relievo, *n.* See *rilievo*.

relight (rē-līt'), *v.* [< *re-* + *light*[1].] I. *trans.* 1. To light anew; illuminate again.

His power can heal me and *relight* my eye. *Pope.*

2. To rekindle; set on fire again.

II. *intrans.* To burn again; rekindle; take fire again.

The desire . . . *relit* suddenly, and glowed warm in her heart. *Charlotte Brontë*, Shirley, xviii.

religieuse (rē-lē-zhi-ėz'), *n.* [< F. *religieuse* (fem. of *religieux*), a religious woman, a nun, = Sp. Pg. It. fem. *religiosa*, < L. *re-(rel-)ligiosa*, fem. of *religiosus*, religious: see *religious*.] A nun.

religieux (rē-lē-zhi-ė'), *n.*; pl. *religieux*. [< F. *religieux*, n. and a., religious, a religious person, esp. a monk: see *religious*.] One who is engaged by vows to follow a certain rule of life authorized by the church; a member of a monastic order; a monk.

religion (rē̤-lij'on), *n.* [< ME. *religiun*, *religioun*, < OF. *religium*, *religion*, F. *religion* = Pr. *religio*, *religion* = Sp. *religion* = Pg. *religião* = It. *religione* = D. *religie* = G. Sw. Dan. *religion*, < L. *religio(n-)*, *relligio(n-)*, reverence toward the gods, fear of God, piety, conscientious scrupulousness, religious awe, conscientiousness, exactness; origin uncertain, being disputed by ancient writers themselves: (*a*) according to Cicero, < *relegere*, go through or over again in reading, speech, or thought ("qui omnia quæ ad cultum deorum pertinerent diligenter retractarent et tamquam *relegerent* sunt dicti *religiosi* ex *relegendo*, ut *elegantes* ex *eligendo*," etc.—Cicero, Nat. Deor., ii. 28, 72), whence ppr. *religen(t-)s* (rare), revering the gods, pious (cf. the opposite *neglegen(t-)s*, negligent); cf. Gr. ἀλέγειν, reverence. (*b*) According to Servius, Lactantius, Augustine, and others, and to the common modern view, < *religare*, bind back, bind fast, as if 'obligation' (cf. *obligation*, of same radical origin), < *re-*, back, + *ligare*, bind: see *ligament*. (*c*) < *relegere*, the same verb as in (*a*) above, in the lit. sense 'gather again, collect,' as if orig. 'a collection of religious formulas.' Words of religious use are especially liable to lose their literal meanings, and to take on the aspect of sacred primitives, making it difficult to trace or impossible to prove their orig. meaning or formation.] 1. Recognition of and allegiance in manner of life to a superhuman power or superhuman powers, to whom allegiance and service are regarded as justly due.

. . . One rising, eminent
In wise deport, spake much of right and wrong,
Of justice, of *religion*, truth, and peace,
And judgment from above. *Milton*, P. L., xi. 667.

By *Religion* I understand the belief and worship of Supreme Mind and Will, directing the universe and holding moral relations with human life.
J. Martineau, A Study of Religion, I. 15.

By *Religion* I mean the knowledge of God, of His Will, and of our duties towards Him.
J. H. Newman, Gram. of Assent, p. 378.

Religion is the communion between a worshipping subject and a worshipped object—the communion of a man with what he believes to be a god.
Faiths of the World, p. 345.

2. The healthful development and right life of the spiritual nature, as contrasted with that of the mere intellectual and social powers.

For *religion*, pure *religion*, I say, standeth not in wearing of a monk's cowl, but in righteousness, justice, and well doing. *Latimer*, Sermons, p. 392.

Religion is Christianity, which, being too spiritual to be seen by us, doth therefore take an apparent body of good life and works, so salvation requires an honest Christian.
Donne, Letters, xxx.

Religion, if we follow the intention of human thought and human language in the use of the word, is ethics heightened, enkindled, lit up by feeling; the passage from morality to religion is made when to morality is applied emotion. *M. Arnold*, Literature and Dogma, i.

3. Any system of faith in and worship of a divine Being or beings: as, the Christian *religion*; the *religion* of the Jews, Greeks, Hindus, or Mohammedans.

The church of Rome, they say, . . . did almost out of all *religions* take whatsoever had any fair and gorgeous show. *Hooker*, Eccles. Polity, iv. 11.

After the most straitest sect of our *religion* I lived a Pharisee. Acts xxvi. 5.

No *religion* binds men to be traitors.
B. Jonson, Catiline, iii. 2.

4†. The rites or services of religion; the practice of sacred rites and ceremonies.

What she was pleased to believe apt to minister to her devotions, and the *religions* of her pious and discerning soul. *Jer. Taylor*, Works (ed. 1835), I. 756.

The invisible
Glory of him that made them to transform
Oft to the image of a brute adorn'd
With gay *religions* full of pomp and gold.
Milton, P. L., i. 372.

5. The state of life of a professed member of a regular monastic order: as, to enter *religion*; her name in *religion* is Mary Aloysia: now especially in Roman Catholic use.

He [Dobet] is lowe as a lombe, and loueliche of speche, . . .
And is ronne in-to *religion*, and rendreth hus byble,
And precheth to the puple seynt Poules wordes.
Piers Plowman (C), xi. 88.

And thus when that thei were counselled,
In black clothes thei them clothe,
The doughter and the lady both,
And yolde hem to *religion*.
Gower, Conf. Amant., viii.

He buryed Bedewere
Hys frend and hys Botyler,
And so he dude other Echon
In Abbeys of *Relygyoun*
That were cristien of name.
Arthur (ed. Furnivall), l. 488.

6. A conscientious scruple; scrupulosity. [Obsolete or provincial.]

Out of a *religion* to my charge,
And debt professed, I have made a self-decree
Ne'er to express my person.
B. Jonson, New Inn, i. 1.

Its [a jelly's] acidity sharpens Mr. Wall's teeth as for battle, yet, under the circumstances, he makes a *religion* of eating it. *W. M. Baker*, New Timothy, p. 109.

7. Sense of obligation; conscientiousness; sense of duty.

Ros. Keep your promise.
Orl. With no less *religion* than if thou wert indeed my Rosalind. *Shak.*, As you Like it, iv. 1. 201.

Established religion, that form of religion in a country which is recognized and sanctioned by the state. See *establishment*, 6.—**Evidences of revealed religion.** See *evidences of Christianity*, under *Christianity*.—**Experimental religion.** See *experimental*.—**Natural religion**, that knowledge of and reverent feeling toward God, and that knowledge and practice of our duties toward our fellow-men, which is based on and derived from nature, apart from revelation.—**Religion of Humanity.** See *positive philosophy*, under *positive*.—**Revealed religion**, that knowledge of God and right feeling toward him, and that recognition and practice of duty toward our fellow-men, which is derived from and based upon positive revelation.—**To experience religion.** See *experience*.—**To get religion.** See *get*[1]. =**Syn. 1.** *Religion*, *Devotion*, *Piety*, *Sanctity*, *Saintliness*, *Godliness*, *Holiness*, *Religiosity*. In the subjective aspect of these words *religion* is the most general, as it may be also the most formal or external; in this sense it is the place of the will and character of God in the heart, so that they are the principal object of regard and the controlling influence. *Devotion* and *piety* have most of fervor. *Devotion* is a religion that consecrates itself, being both a close attention to God with complete inward subjection and an equal attention to the duties of religion. *Piety* is religion under the aspect of filial feeling and conduct, the former being the primary idea. *Sanctity* is generally used objectively; subjectively it is the same as *holiness*. *Saintliness* is more concrete than *sanctity*, more distinctly a quality of a person, likeness to a saint, ripeness for heaven. *Godliness* is higher than *saintliness*; it is likeness to God, or the endeavor to attain such likeness, fixed attention given immediately to God, especially obedience to his will and endeavor to copy his character. *Holiness* is the most absolute of these words; it is moral and religious wholeness, completeness, or something approaching so near to absolute freedom from sin as to make the word appropriate; it includes not only being free from sin, but refusing it and hating it for its own sake. *Religiosity* is not a very common nor a very euphonious word, but seems to meet a felt want by expressing a susceptibility to the sentiments of religion, awe, reverence, admiration for the teachings of religion, etc., without much disposition to obey its commands.

religionary (rē̤-lij'on-ā-ri), *a.* and *n.* [< F. *religionnaire* = Sp. Pg. It. *religionario*; as *religion* + *-ary*.] I. *a.* 1. Relating to religion.—2†. Pious.

His [Bishop Saunderson's] *religionary* professions in his last will and testament contain something like prophetical matter. *Bp. Barlow*, Remains, p. 638.

II. *n.*; pl. *religionaries* (-riz). Same as *religionist*. [Rare.]

religioner (rē̤-lij'on-ėr), *n.* [< F. *religionnaire* = Sp. *religionario*, a religionist, < NL. **religionarius*, < L. *religio(n-)*, religion: see *religion*.] A religionist. [Rare.]

These new-fashioned *religioners* have fast-days.
Scott, Monastery, xxv.

religionise, *v.* See *religionize*.

religionism (rē̤-lij'on-izm), *n.* [< *religion* + *-ism*.] 1. Outward practice or profession of religion.

This subject of "Political *Religionism*" is indeed as nice as it is curious; politics have been so cunningly worked into the cause of religion that the parties themselves will never be able to separate them.
I. D'Israeli, Curios. of Lit., IV. 138.

2. Affected religious zeal.

religionist (rē-lij'ọn-ist), *n.* [= Sp. *religionista;* as *religion* + *-ist.*] A religious bigot, partizan, or formalist; a sectarian: sometimes used in other than a condemnatory sense.

From the same source from whence, among the *religionists*, the attachment to the principle of asceticism took its rise, flowed other doctrines and practices, from which misery in abundance was produced in one man by the instrumentality of another: witness the holy wars, and the persecutions for religion.
Bentham, Introd. to Morals and Legislation, ii. 8.

There is a verse . . . in the second of the two detached cantos of "Mutability," "Like that ungracious crew which feigns demurest grace," which is supposed to glance at the straiter *religionists*.
Lowell, Among my Books, 2d ser., p. 167.

religionize (rē-lij'ọn-īz), *v.*; pret. and pp. *religionized*, ppr. *religionizing*. [< *religion* + *-ize.*] I. *trans.* To imbue with religion; make religious. [Recent.]

I have quoted Othello and Mrs. Craven's heroine as types of love when *religionised*.
Mallock, Is Life Worth Living? p. 122.

II. *intrans.* To make professions of religion; play the religionist. [Recent.]

How much *religionizing* stupidity it requires in one to imagine that God can be propitiated or pleased with them [human inventions].
S. H. Cox, Interviews Memorable and Useful, p. 138.

Also spelled *religionise*.

religionless (rē-lij'ọn-les), *a.* [< *religion* + *-less.*] Without religion; not professing or believing in religion; irreligious.

Picture to yourself, O fair young reader, a worldly, selfish, graceless, thankless, *religionless* old woman, writhing in pain and fear, . . . and ere you be old, learn to love and pray!
Thackeray, Vanity Fair, xiv.

religiosity (rē-lij-i-os'i-ti), *n.* [< ME. *religiosite*, < OF. *religiosete*, *religieusete*, F. *religiosité* = Sp. *religiosidad* = Pg. *religiosidade* = It. *religiosità*, < LL. *religiosita(t-)s*, religiousness, ML. religious or monastic life, < L. *religiosus*, religious: see *religious.*] 1. Religiousness; the sentiment of religion; specifically, in recent use, an excessive susceptibility to the religious sentiments, especially wonder, awe, and reverence, unaccompanied by any corresponding loyalty to divine law in daily life; religious sentimentality.

One Jewish quality these Arabs manifest, the outcome of many or of all high qualities: what we may call *religiosity*.
Carlyle, Heroes and Hero-Worship, ii.

Away . . . from that *religiosity* which is one of the curses of our time, he studied his New Testament, and in this, as in every other matter, made up his mind for himself.
Dr. J. Brown, Spare Hours, 3d ser., p. 174.

Is there a more patent and a more stubborn fact in history than that intense and unchangeable Semitic nationality with its equally intense *religiosity?*
Schaff, Hist. Christ. Church, I. § 17.

2. Religious exercise or service. [Rare.]

Soporific sermons . . . closed the domestic *religiosities* of those melancholy days.
Southey, The Doctor, ix.

3†. Members of the religious orders.

Hir [Diana's] law [the law of chastity] is for *religiosite*.
Court of Love, l. 686.

=**Syn.** 1. *Piety*, *Holiness*, etc. See *religion*.

religioso (re-lē-ji-ō'sō), *adv.* [It.: see *religious.*] In *music*, in a devotional manner; expressing religious sentiment.

religious (rẹ-lij'us), *a.* and *n.* [< ME. *religious*, *religius*, < OF. *religios*, *religius*, *religieus*, *religiouz*, F. *religieux* = Pr. *religios*, *relegios* = Sp. Pg. It. *religioso*, < L. *religiosus*, *relligiosus*, religious, < *religio(n-)*, *relligio(n-)*, religion: see *religion.*] I. *a.* 1. Imbued with, exhibiting, or arising from religion; pious; godly; devout: as, a *religious* man; *religious* behavior: used in the authorized version of the Bible of outward observance (Jas. i. 26; Acts xiii. 43).

Such a prince,
Not only good and wise, but most *religious*.
Shak., Hen. VIII., v. 3. 116.

That sober race of men whose lives
Religious titled them the sons of God.
Milton, P. L., xi. 622.

It [dogma] is discerned, rested in, and appropriated as a reality by the *religious* Imagination; it is held as a truth by the theological intellect.
J. H. Newman, Gram. of Assent, p. 94.

2. Pertaining or devoted to a monastic life; belonging to a religious order; in the *Rom. Cath. Ch.*, bound by the vows of a monastic order; regular.

Shal I nat love in cas if that me liste?
What, pardieux, I am nought *religiouse?*
Chaucer, Troilus, ii. 759.

Hie thee to France,
And cloister thee in some *religious* house.
Shak., Rich. II., v. 1. 23.

The fourth, which was a painter called Iohn Story, became *religious* in the College of S. Paul in Goa.
Hakluyt's Voyages, II. 270.

3. Bound by or abiding by some solemn obligation; scrupulously faithful; conscientious.

Whom I most hated living, thou hast made me,
With thy *religious* truth and modesty,
Now in his ashes honour: peace be with him.
Shak., Hen. VIII., iv. 2. 74.

4. Of or pertaining to religion; concerned with religion; teaching or setting forth religion; set apart for purposes connected with religion: as, a *religious* society; a *religious* sect; a *religious* place; *religious* subjects; *religious* books or teachers; *religious* liberty.

And storied windows richly dight,
Casting a dim *religious* light.
Milton, Il Penseroso, l. 160.

Fanes which admiring gods with pride survey, . . .
Some felt the silent stroke of mould'ring age,
Some hostile fury, some *religious* rage.
Pope, To Addison, l. 12.

Religious corporation. See *corporation.*—**Religious house**, a monastery or a nunnery.—**Religious liberty.** See *liberty.*—**Religious marks**, in *printing*, signs such as ✠, ℞, ℣, indicating respectively 'sign of the cross,' 'response,' and 'versicle.'—**Religious uses.** See *use.* =**Syn.** 1. Devotional.—3. Scrupulous, exact, strict, rigid. See *religion*.

II. *n.* One who is bound by monastic vows, as a monk, a friar, or a nun.

Ac there shal come a kyng and confesse gow *religiouses*,
And bete gow, as the bible telleth, for brekynge of goure reule.
Piers Plowman (B), x. 317.

It is very lucky for a *religious*, who has so much time on his hands, to be able to amuse himself with works of this nature [inlaying a pulpit].
Addison, Remarks on Italy (ed. Bohn), I. 370.

A *religious* in any other order can pass into that of the Carthusians, on account of its great austerity.
Rom. Cath. Dict., p. 699.

religiously (rẹ-lij'us-li), *adv.* In a religious manner. (*a*) Piously; with love and reverence to the Supreme Being; in obedience to the divine commands; according to the rites of religion; reverently; with veneration.

For their brethren slain
Religiously they ask a sacrifice.
Shak., Tit. And., i. 1. 124.

We most *religiously* kiss'd the sacred Rust of this Weapon, out of Love to the Martyr.
N. Bailey, tr. of Colloquies of Erasmus, II. 27.

(*b*) Exactly; strictly; conscientiously: as, a vow or promise *religiously* observed.

The privileges justly due to the members of the two Houses and their attendants are *religiously* to be maintained.
Bacon.

My old-fashioned friend *religiously* adhered to the example of his forefathers.
Steele, Tatler, No. 263.

religiousness (rẹ-lij'us-nes), *n.* The character or state of being religious, in any sense of that word. *Baxter.*

relike†, *n.* A Middle English form of *relic*.

relinquent (rẹ-ling'kwent), *a.* and *n.* [< L. *relinquen(t-)s*, ppr. of *relinquere*, relinquish: see *relinquish.*] I. *a.* Relinquishing. [Rare.] *Imp. Dict.*

II. *n.* One who relinquishes. [Rare.] *Imp. Dict.*

relinquish (rẹ-ling'kwish), *v. t.* [< OF. *relinquiss-*, stem of certain parts of *relinquir*, *relenquir*, < L. *relinquere*, pp. *relictus*, leave, < *re-* + *linquere*, leave: see *license*, and cf. *relic*, *relict*, and *delinquent.*] 1. To give up the possession or occupancy of; withdraw from; leave; abandon; quit.

To be *relinquished* of the artists, . . . both of Galen and Paracelsus, . . . of all the learned and authentic fellows . . . that gave him out incurable.
Shak., All's Well, ii. 3. 10.

Having formed an attachment to this young lady, . . . I have found that I must *relinquish* all other objects not connected with her.
Monroe, To Jefferson (Bancroft's Hist. Const., I. 503).

2. To cease from; give up the pursuit or practice of; desist from: as, to *relinquish* bad habits.

With commandement to *relinquish* (for his owne part) the intended attempt.
Hakluyt's Voyages, II. ii. 194.

Sir C. Cornwallis, in a Letter to the Lord Cranburne, asserts that England never lost such an Opportunity of winning Honour and Wealth unto it, as by *relinquishing* War against an exhausted Kingdom.
Bolingbroke, Remarks on Hist. Eng., let. 22.

3. To renounce a claim to; resign: as, to *relinquish* a debt. =**Syn.** 1. *Abandon*, *Desert*, etc. (see *forsake*), let go, yield, cede, surrender, give up, lay down. See list under *desert*.

relinquisher (rẹ-ling'kwish-ėr), *n.* One who relinquishes, leaves, or quits; one who renounces or gives up.

relinquishment (rẹ-ling'kwish-ment), *n.* [< *relinquish* + *-ment.*] The act of relinquishing, leaving, or quitting; a forsaking; the renouncing of a claim.

This is the thing they require in us, the utter *relinquishment* of all things popish.
Hooker, Eccles. Polity, iv. § 3.

reliqua (rel'i-kwạ̈), *n. pl.* [ML. (OF., etc.), neut. pl. of L. *reliquus*, *relicuus*, that which is left or remains over (> Pg. *reliquo*, remaining), < *relinquere*, leave behind: see *relic*, *relinquish.*] In *law*, the remainder or debt which a person finds himself debtor in, upon the balancing or liquidating of an account. *Wharton.*

reliquaire (rel-i-kwãr'), *n.* [< F. *réliquaire:* see *reliquary*[1].] Same as *reliquary*[1]. *Scott*, Rokeby, vi. 6.

reliquary[1] (rel'i-kwạ̄-ri), *n.*; pl. *reliquaries* (-riz). [< OF. *reliquaire*, F. *réliquaire* = Pr. *reliquiari* = Sp. Pg. *relicario* = It. *reliquiario*, < ML. *reliquiare* or *reliquiarium*, a reliquary, < L. *reliquiæ*, relics: see *relic.*] A repository for relics, often, though not necessarily, small enough to be carried on the person. See *shrine*, and cut under *phylacterium*.

Under these cupolas is yᵉ high altar, on which is a *reliquarie* of severall sorts of jewells.
Evelyn, Diary, June, 1645.

Sometimes, too, the hollow of our Saviour's image, wrought in high relief upon the cross, was contrived for a *reliquary*, and filled full of relics.
Rock, Church of our Fathers, III. i. 357.

reliquary[2] (rel'i-kwạ̄-ri), *n.*; pl. *reliquaries* (-riz). [< ML. **reliquarius*, < *reliqua*, what is left over: see *reliqua.*] In *law*, one who owes a balance; also, a person who pays only piecemeal. *Wharton.*

relique, *n.* An obsolete or archaic spelling of *relic*.

reliquiæ (rẹ-lik'wi-ē), *n. pl.* [L., leavings, remains, relics, remnants: see *relic.*] 1. Relics; remains, as those of fossil organisms.—2. In *bot.*, same as *induviæ*.—3. In *archæol.*, artifacts. See *artifact*.

Without the slightest admixture of either British or Saxon *reliquiæ*.
Jour. Brit. Archæol. Ass., XIII. 291.

reliquian (rē-lik'wi-ạn), *a.* [< L. *reliquiæ*, relics (see *relic*), + *-an.*] Of, pertaining to, or being a relic or relics.

A great ship would not hold the *reliquian* pieces which the Papists have of Christ's cross.
R. Hill, Pathway to Piety (1629), p. 149. (*Encyc. Dict.*)

reliquidate (rē-lik'wi-dāt), *v. t.* [< *re-* + *liquidate.*] To liquidate anew; adjust a second time. *Wright.*

reliquidation (rē-lik-wi-dā'shọn), *n.* [< *reliquidate* + *-ion;* or < *re-* + *liquidation.*] A second or renewed liquidation; a renewed adjustment. *Clarke.*

relish[1] (rel'ish), *v.* [Not found in ME. (where, however, the noun exists); according to the usual view, < OF. *relecher*, lick over again, < *re-*, again, + *lecher*, *lescher*, F. *lécher*, lick: see *lick*, and cf. *lecher*, etc. But the word may have been due in part to OF. *relescier*, *releichier*, *resleechier*, *reslcecier*, *relesser*, please, cause or inspire joy in, gratify, < *re-* + *leecier*, *leechier*, *leesser*, etc., rejoice, live in pleasure.] I. *trans.* 1. To like the taste or flavor of; partake of with pleasure or gratification.

No marvel if the blind man cannot judge of colours, nor the deaf distinguish sounds, nor the sick *relish* meats.
Rev. T. Adams, Works, I. 364.

2. To be pleased with or gratified by, in general; have a liking for; enjoy; experience or cause to experience pleasure from.

There's not a soldier of us all that, in the thanksgiving before meat, do *relish* the petition well that prays for peace.
Shak., M. for M., i. 2. 16.

No one will ever *relish* an author thoroughly well who would not have been fit company for that author had they lived at the same time.
Steele, Tatler, No. 173.

He's no bad fellow, Blougram—he had seen
Something of mine he *relished*.
Browning, Bishop Blougram's Apology.

3. To give an agreeable taste to; impart a pleasing flavor to; cause to taste agreeably.

A sav'ry bit that serv'd to *relish* wine.
Dryden, tr. of Ovid's Metamorph., viii. 109.

4†. To savor of; have a smack or taste of; have the cast or manner of.

'Tis ordered well, and *relisheth* the soldier.
Fletcher, Beggar's Bush, v. 1.

Inc. Sir, he's found, he's found.
Phil. Ha! where? but reach that happy note again,
And let it *relish* truth, thou art an angel.
Fletcher (and another), Love's Pilgrimage, iv. 2.

II. *intrans.* 1. To have a pleasing taste; in general, to give pleasure.

Had I been the finder out of this secret, it would not have *relished* among my other discredits.
Shak., W. T., v. 2. 132.

Without which their greatest dainties would not *relish* to their palates. *Hakewill*, On Providence.

He intimated . . . how ill it would *relish*, if they should advance Capt. Underhill, whom we had thrust out for abusing the court. *Winthrop*, Hist. New England, I. 353.

2. To have a flavor, literally or figuratively.

Nothing of friend or foe can be unwelcome unto me that savoureth of wit, or *relisheth* of humanity, or tasteth of any good. *G. Harvey*, Four Letters.

This act of Propertius *relisheth* very strange with me.
B. Jonson, Poetaster, iv. 1.

A theory which, how much soever it may *relish* of wit and invention, hath no foundation in nature. *Woodward.*

relish[1] (rel'ish), *n.* [< ME. *reles, relees, relece,* odor, taste; from the verb: see *relish*[1], *v.*] 1. A sensation of taste; savor; flavor; especially, a pleasing taste; hence, pleasing quality in general.

Veins which, through the tongue and palate spread,
Distinguish ev'ry *relish*, sweet and sour.
Sir J. Davies, Immortal. of Soul, xvi.

Her hunger gave a *relish* to her meat.
Dryden, Cock and Fox, l. 22.

I would not anticipate the *relish* of any happiness, nor feel the weight of any misery, before it actually arrives.
Addison, Omens.

What Professor Bain describes as sense of *relish*, quite apart from taste proper, and felt perhaps most keenly just as food is leaving or just after it has left the region of the voluntary and entered that of the involuntary muscles of deglutition. *G. S. Hall*, German Culture, p. 253.

2. Perception or appreciation of peculiar, especially of pleasing, quality in anything; taste, in general; liking; appetite: generally used with *for* before the thing, sometimes with *of*.

Who the *relish* of these guests will fit
Needs set them but the alms-basket of wit.
B. Jonson, Ode to himself.

They have a *relish for* everything that is news, let the matter of it be what it will. *Addison*, The Newspaper.

This love of praise dwells most in great and heroic spirits; and those who best deserve it have generally the most exquisite *relish of* it. *Steele*, Tatler, No. 92.

Boswell had a genuine *relish for* what was superior in any way, from genius to claret.
Lowell, Among my Books, 1st ser., p. 351.

3. A peculiar or characteristic, and especially a pleasing, quality in an object; the power of pleasing; hence, delight given by anything.

His fears . . . of the same *relish* as ours are.
Shak., Hen. V., iv. 1. 114.

In the time of Youth, when the Vanities and Pleasures and Temptations of the World have the greatest *relish* with us, and when the things of Religion are most apt to be despised. *Stillingfleet*, Sermons, III. xiii.

When liberty is gone,
Life grows insipid, and has lost its *relish*.
Addison, Cato, ii. 3.

It preserves some *relish* of old writing. *Pope.*

4. A small quantity just perceptible; tincture; smack.

Some act
That has no *relish* of salvation in 't.
Shak., Hamlet, iii. 3. 92.

5. That which is used to impart a flavor; especially, something taken with food to increase the pleasure of eating, as sauce; also, a small highly seasoned dish to stimulate the appetite, as caviare, olives, etc. See *hors-d'œuvre*.

This is not such a supper as a major of the Royal Americans has a right to expect; but I've known stout detachments of the corps glad to eat their venison raw, and without a relish too. *J. F. Cooper*, Last of Mohicans, v.

Happiness was not happy enough, but must be drugged with the *relish* of pain and fear.
Emerson, Essays, 1st ser., p. 150.

"Knowing as you was partial to a little *relish* with your wittles, . . . we took the liberty" [of bringing a present of shrimps]. *Dickens*, David Copperfield, vii.

For our own part, we prefer a full, old-fashioned meal, with its side-dishes of spicy gossip, and its last *relish*, the Stilton of scandal, so it be not too high.
Lowell, Study Windows, p. 91.

6. In *harpsichord music*, an embellishment or grace consisting of a repetition of a principal note with a trill and a turn after it: usually *double relish*, but see also *single relish*, under *single*. =**Syn.** 2. Zest, gusto, predilection, partiality.—4. Tinge, touch.—5. Appetizer.

relish[2] (rel'ish), *v. t.* [Origin obscure.] In *joinery*, to shape (the shoulders of a tenon which bear against a rail). See *relishing-machine*.

relish[2] (rel'ish), *n.* [See *relish*[2], *v.*] In *joinery*, projection of the shoulder of a tenoned piece beyond the part which enters the mortise. *E. H. Knight.*

relishable (rel'ish-a-bl), *a.* [< *relish*[1] + *-able*.] Capable of being relished; having an agreeable taste.

By leaven soured we made *relishable* bread for the use of man. *Rev. T. Adams*, Works, II. 340.

relishing-machine (rel'ish-ing-ma-shēn"), *n.* In *joinery*, a machine for shaping the shoulders of tenons. It combines several circular saws cutting simultaneously in different planes so as to form the piece at one operation.

relisten (rē-lis'n), *v. i.* [< *re-* + *listen*.] To listen again or anew.

The brook . . . seems, as I *re-listen* to it,
Prattling the primrose fancies of the boy.
Tennyson, The Brook.

relive (rē-liv'), *v.* [< *re-* + *live*[1].] I. *intrans.* To live again; revive.

For I wil *relive* as I sayd on the third day, &, being *relived*, will goe before you into Galile.
J. Udall, Paraphrase of Mark xiii.

Will you deliver
How this dead queen *re-lives?*
Shak., Pericles, v. 3. 64.

II.† *trans.* To recall to life; reanimate; revive.

Had she not beene devoide of mortall slime,
Shee should not then have bene *relyv'd* againe.
Spenser, F. Q., III. iv. 35.

By Faith, Saint Paul did Eutichus *re-lyve:*
By Faith, Elias rais'd the Sareptite.
Sylvester, tr. of Du Bartas's Triumph of Faith, iii. 12.

Rellyanist (rel'i-an-ist), *n.* [< *Relly* (see def.) + *-an* + *-ist*.] A member of a small Universalist body, followers of James Relly (1720–80).

reload (rē-lōd'), *v. t.* [< *re-* + *load*[1], *v.*] To load again, as a gun, a ship, etc. *Imp. Dict.*

relocate (rē-lō'kāt), *v. t.* [< LL. *relocare*, let out again, < L. *re-*, again, + *locare*, place, let: see *locate*. In the def. taken in lit. sense, as < *re-* + *locate*.] To locate again. *Imp. Dict.*

relocation (rē-lō-kā'shon), *n.* [< F. *relocation*, < ML. *relocatio(n-)* (?), < LL. *relocare*, let out again: see *relocate*. In def. 1 taken in lit. sense, as < *relocate* + *-ion*.] 1. The act of relocating.—2. In *Scots law*, a reletting; renewal of a lease.—**Tacit relocation**, the tacit or implied renewal of a lease: inferred where the landlord, instead of warning the tenant to remove at the stipulated expiration of the lease, has allowed him to continue without making any new agreement.

relong† (rē-lông'), *v. t.* [Accom. < OF. *ralonger*, prolong, lengthen (cf. *reloignement*, delay), < *re-* + *alonger*, lengthen: see *allonge* and *long*[1].] 1. To prolong; extend.

I thynke it were good that the trewce were *relonged*.
Berners, tr. of Froissart's Chron., I. ccxii.

2. To postpone.

Then the kyng sent to Parys, commaundynge that the iourney and batayle betwene the squyer and yᵉ knyght sholde be *relonged* tyl his comynge to Parys.
Berners, tr. of Froissart's Chron., II. lxi.

relove† (rē-luv'), *v. t.* [< *re-* + *love*[1].] To love in return.

To own for him so familiar and levelling an affection as love, much more to expect to be *reloved* by him, were not the least saucy presumption man could be guilty of, did not his own commandments make it a duty. *Boyle.*

relucent† (rē-lū'sent), *a.* [ME. *relusaunt*, < OF. *reluisant*, F. *reluisant* = Sp. *reluciente* = Pg. *reluzente* = It. *rilucente*, < L. *relucen(t-)s*, ppr. of *relucere*, shine back or out, < *re-*, back, + *lucere*, shine: see *lucent*.] Throwing back light; shining; luminous; glittering; bright; eminent.

I seg by-zonde that myry mere
A crystal clyffe ful *relusaunt;*
Mony ryal ray con fro hit rere.
Alliterative Poems (ed. Morris), i. 159.

That college wherein piety and beneficence were *relucent* in despite of jealousies.
Bp. Hacket, Abp. Williams, p. 46.

In brighter mazes, the *relucent* Stream
Plays o'er the mead. *Thomson*, Summer, l. 162.

reluct (rē-lukt'), *v. i.* [= OF. *relucter, reluicter, relutier*, F. *relutter* = Sp. *reluchar* = Pg. *reluctar* = It. *reluttare*, < L. *reluctare, reluctari*, struggle against, oppose, resist, < *re-*, back, + *luctari*, struggle: see *luctation*.] To strive or struggle against something; make resistance; exhibit reluctance. [Obsolete or archaic.]

We with studied mixtures force our *relucting* appetites, and with all the spells of epicurism conjure them up, that we may lay them again. *Decay of Christian Piety.*

I care not to be carried with the tide that smoothly bears human life to eternity, and *reluct* at the inevitable course of destiny. *Lamb*, New Year's Eve.

Such despotic talk had never been heard before in that Directors' Room. They relucted a moment.
T. Winthrop, Love and Skates.

reluctance (rē-luk'tans), *n.* [= Pg. *reluctancia* = It. *reluttanza*, < ML. **reluctantia*, < L. *reluctan(t-)s*, reluctant: see *reluctant*.] The state of being reluctant; aversion; repugnance; unwillingness: often followed by *to*, sometimes by *against*.

That . . . savours only . . .
Reluctance against God and his just yoke.
Milton, P. L., x. 1045.

When he [Æneas] is forced, in his own defence, to kill Lausus, the poet shows him compassionate, and tempering the severity of his looks with a *reluctance to* the action.
Dryden, Parallel of Poetry and Painting.

Lay we aside all inveterate prejudices and stubborn *reluctances*. *Waterland*, Works, VIII. 383.

There is in most people a *reluctance* and unwillingness to be forgotten. *Swift*, Thoughts on Various Subjects.

Magnetic reluctance. See *magnetic resistance*, under *resistance*. =**Syn.** Hatred, *Dislike* (see *antipathy*), backwardness, disinclination. See list under *aversion*.

reluctancy (rē-luk'tan-si), *n.* [As *reluctance* (see *-cy*).] Same as *reluctance*.

reluctant (rē-luk'tant), *a.* [= OF. *reluttant* = Sp. *reluchante* = Pg. *reluctante* = It. *riluttante*, < L. *reluctan(t-)s*, ppr. of *reluctare, reluctari*, struggle against: see *reluct*.] 1. Striving against some opposing force; struggling or resisting.

Down he fell,
A monstrous serpent on his belly prone,
Reluctant, but in vain; a greater Power
Now ruled him. *Milton*, P. L., x. 515.

And bent or broke
The lithe *reluctant* boughs to tear away
Their tawny clusters. *Tennyson*, Enoch Arden.

2. Struggling against some requirement, demand, or duty; unwilling; acting with repugnance; loath: as, he was very *reluctant* to go.

From better habitation spurn'd,
Reluctant dost thou rove?
Goldsmith, The Hermit.

The great body of the people grew every day more *reluctant* to undergo the inconveniences of military service, and better able to pay others for undergoing them.
Macaulay, Hallam's Const. Hist.

3. Proceeding from an unwilling mind; granted with unwillingness: as, *reluctant* obedience.

My friend . . . at length yielded a *reluctant* consent.
Barham, Ingoldsby Legends, I. 180.

4. Not readily brought to any specified behavior or action.

In Italy, Spain, and those hot countries, or else nature and experience too lies, a temporal man cannot swallow a morsel or bit of spiritual preferment but it is *reluctant* in his stomach, up it comes again.
Rev. T. Adams, Works, II. 228.

The liquorice renders it [ink] easily dissolvable on the rubbing up with water, to which the isinglass alone would be somewhat *reluctant*. *Workshop Receipts*, 2d ser., p. 337.

=**Syn.** 2. *Averse, Reluctant* (see *averse*), disinclined, opposed, backward, slow.

reluctantly (rē-luk'tant-li), *adv.* In a reluctant manner; with opposition; unwillingly.

reluctate (rē-luk'tāt), *v.*; pret. and pp. *reluctated*, ppr. *reluctating*. [< L. *reluctatus*, pp. of *reluctari*, struggle against: see *reluct*.] I. *intrans.* To struggle against something; be reluctant. [Obsolete or provincial.]

Men devise colours to delude their *reluctating* consciences; but when they have once made the breach, their scrupulosity soon retires. *Decay of Christian Piety.*

I have heard it within the past year from one of the Southern Methodist bishops: "You *reluctate* at giving up the good opinion men have of you." He told me that he got it from his old Scotch-Irish professor, who died a few years ago at the age of ninety or more.
Trans. Amer. Philol. Ass., XVII. 42.

II. *trans.* To struggle against; encounter with reluctance or unwillingness. [Rare.]

The mind that *reluctates* any emotion directly evades all occasion for bringing that object into consciousness.
Hickok, Mental Science, p. 101.

reluctation† (rē-luk-tā'shon), *n.* [< *reluctate* + *-ion*.] Reluctance; repugnance; resistance.

I have done as many villanies as another,
And with as little *reluctation*.
Fletcher, Pilgrim, ii. 2.

Relapse and *reluctation* of the breath.
A. C. Swinburne, Anactoria.

relume (rē-lūm'), *v. t.*; pret. and pp. *relumed*, ppr. *reluming*. [< OF. *relumer*, < L. *reluminare*, light up again: see *relumine*.] To rekindle; light again.

Poet or patriot, rose but to restore
The faith and moral Nature gave before;
Relumed her ancient light, not kindled new.
Pope, Essay on Man, iii. 287.

relumine (rē-lū'min), *v. t.*; pret. and pp. *relumined*, ppr. *relumining*. [< L. *reluminare*, light up again, < *re-*, again, + *luminare*, light, < *lumen*, a light: see *luminate*. Cf. *relume*.] 1. To light anew; rekindle.

When the light of the Gospel was *relumined* by the Reformation. *Bp. Lowth*, Sermons and Other Remains, p. 168.

2. To illuminate again.

Time's *relumined* river. *Hood.*

rely (rē-lī'), *v.*; pret. and pp. *relied*, ppr. *relying*. [Early mod. E. *relye, relie;* < ME. *relyen, relien*, < OF. *relier*, fasten again, attach, bind together, bind up, bandage, tie up, shut up, fix, repair, join, unite, assemble, rally, fig. bind, oblige, F. *relier*, bind, tie up, = Pr. *religuar*, reliar = Sp. Pg. religar = It. rilegare, fasten again, bind again, < L. *religare*, bind back, bind fast, fasten, moor (a ship), etc., < *re-*, back, again, + *ligare*, bind: see *ligament*. Cf. *ally*¹ and *rally*¹. The verb *rely*, in the orig. sense 'fasten, fix, attach,' came to be used with a special reference to attaching one's faith or oneself to a person or thing (cf. 'to *pin* one's faith to a thing,' 'a man to *tie* to,' colloquial phrases containing the same figure); in this use it became, by omission of the object, intransitive, and, losing thus its etymological associations (the other use, 'bring together again, rally,' having also become obsolete), was sometimes regarded, and has been by some etymologists actually explained, as a barbarous compound of *re-* + E. *lie*¹, rest, whence appar. the occasional physical use (def. II., 3). But the pret. would then have been *relay, pp. *relain.] **I.** *trans.* **1†.** To fasten; fix; attach.

> Therefore [they] must needs *relye* their faithe upon the sillie Ministers faithlesse fidelitie.
> H. T., in Anthony Wotton's Answer to a Popish Pamphlet, (etc. (1605), p. 19, quoted in F. Hall's Adjectives in *-able*, [p. 159.

> Let us now consider whether, by our former description of the first age, it may appeare whereon these great admirers and contemners of antiquitie rest and *rely* themselves. *A World of Wonders* (1607), p. 21, quoted in F. [Hall's Adjectives in *-able*, p. 160.

> No faith her husband doth in her *relie*.
> Breton (?), Cornucopiæ (1612), p. 96, quoted in F. Hall's [Adjectives in *-able*, p. 160.

2†. To bring together again; assemble again; rally.

> Petrius, that was a noble knyght, and bolde and hardy, *relied* his peple a-boute hym. *Merlin* (E. E. T. S.), iii. 654.

3. To polish. *Coles; Halliwell.* [Prov. Eng.]

II. *intrans.* **1.** To attach one's faith to a person or thing; fix one's confidence; rest with confidence, as upon the veracity, integrity, or ability of another, or upon the certainty of facts or of evidence; have confidence; trust; depend: used with *on* or *upon*, formerly also with *in* and *to*. Compare *reliable*.

> Because thou hast *relied on* the king of Syria, and not *relied on* the Lord thy God, therefore is the host of the king of Syria escaped out of thine hand. 2 Chron. xvi. 7.

> Bade me *rely on* him as on my father.
> *Shak.*, Rich. III., ii. 2. 25.

> It is a like error to *rely upon* advocates or lawyers, which are only men of practice, and not grounded in their books.
> *Bacon*, Advancement of Learning, i. 17.

> Instead of apologies and captation of good will, he [Paul] *relies to* this fort (a good conscience).
> *Rev. S. Ward*, Sermons, p. 107.

> We also reverence the Martyrs, but *relye* only *upon* the Scriptures. *Milton*, Apology for Smectymnuus.

2†. To assemble again; rally.

> Thus *relyed* Lyf for a litel [good] fortune,
> And pryked forth with Pryde.
> *Piers Plowman* (B), xx. 147.

> Whan these saugh hem comynge thei *relien* and closed hem to-geder, and lete renne at the meyne of Pounce Antonye. *Merlin* (E. E. T. S.), iii. 393.

3†. To rest, in a physical sense; recline; lean.

> Ah se how His most holy Hand *relies*
> Vpon His knees to vnder-prop His charge.
> *Davies*, Holy Roode, p. 13. (*Davies.*)

> It [the elephant] sleepeth against a tree, which the Hunters observing doe saw almost asunder; whereon the beast *relying*, by the fall of the tree falls also down itselfe and is able to rise no more.
> *Sir T. Browne*, Pseud. Epid., iii. 1.

rely¹†, *v.* See *rely*.

rely²†, *v. t.* [ME. *relyen*, a reduced form of *releven*, E. *relieve*; cf. *reprie*, similarly related to *reprieve*.] To raise; elevate.

> To life ayin lykynge that lorde the *relyede*.
> *Religious Pieces*, etc., edited by the Rev. G. H. Perry (1867), [p. 87, quoted in F. Hall's Adjectives in *-able*, p. 159.

remain (rẹ̄-mān′), *v. i.* [Early mod. E. *remayne*; < OF. *remaindre* (ind. pres. impers. *il remaint*, it remains) = Pr. *remandre*, *remaner*, *remaner* = OSp. *remaner* = It. *rimanere* (cf. mod. Pg. Sp. *remanecer*, remain), < L. *remanere*, remain, < *re-*, behind, back, + *manere*, remain, = Gr. μένειν, remain, stay. From the same L. verb (*manere*) are also ult. E. *mansel*, *mansion*, *manor*, etc., *menage*¹, *menial*, *immanent*, *permanent*, *remanent*, *remnant*.] **1.** To continue in a place; stay; abide; dwell.

> He should have *remained* in the city of his refuge.
> Num. xxxv. 28.

> You dined at home:
> Where would you had *remain'd* until this time!
> *Shak.*, C. of E., iv. 4. 60.

> And fools, who came to scoff, *remained* to pray.
> *Goldsmith*, Des. Vil., l. 180.

2. To continue without change as to some form, state, or quality specified: as, to *remain* active in business; to *remain* a widow.

> If she depart, let her *remain* unmarried. 1 Cor. vii. 11.

> Great and active minds cannot *remain* at rest.
> *Macaulay*, Dante.

3. To endure; continue; last.

> They shall perish; but thou *remainest*; . . . thy years shall not fail. Heb. i. 11, 12.

4. To stay behind after others have gone; be left after a part, quantity, or number has been taken away or destroyed.

> And all his fugitives with all his bands shall fall by the sword, and they that *remain* shall be scattered.
> Ezek. xvii. 21.

> Hitherto
> I have liv'd a servant to ambitious thoughts
> And fading glories: what *remains* of life
> I dedicate to Virtue.
> *Fletcher and another* (?), Prophetess, iv. 5.

> Shrine of the mighty! can it be
> That this is all *remains* of thee?
> *Byron*, The Giaour, l. 107.

5. To be left as not included or comprised; be held in reserve; be still to be dealt with: formerly followed in some instances by a dative.

> And such end, perdie, does all *hem remayne*
> That of such falsers freendship bene fayne.
> *Spenser*, Shep. Cal., May.

> Norfolk, for thee *remains* a heavier doom.
> *Shak.*, Rich. II., i. 3. 148.

> The easier conquest now
> *Remains thee.* *Milton*, P. L., vi. 38.

> That a father may have some power over his children is easily granted; but that an elder brother has so over his brethren *remains* to be proved. *Locke.*

Remaining velocity. See *velocity*. =**Syn. 1.** To wait, tarry, rest, sojourn.—**2.** To keep.

remain (rẹ̄-mān′), *n.* [< *remain*, *v.*] **1†.** The state of remaining; stay; abode.

> A most miraculous work in this good king,
> Which often, since my here-*remain* in England,
> I have seen him do. *Shak.*, Macbeth, iv. 3. 148.

2†. That which is left to be done.

> I know your master's pleasure and he mine;
> All the *remain* is "Welcome!"
> *Shak.*, Cymbeline, iii. 1. 87.

3. That which is left; remainder; relic: used chiefly in the plural.

> Come, poor *remains* of friends, rest on this rock.
> *Shak.*, J. C., v. 5. 1.

> Among the *remains* of old Rome the grandeur of the commonwealth shows itself chiefly in works that were either necessary or convenient.
> *Addison*, Remarks on Italy, Rome.

> Their small *remain* of life. *Pope.*

> Of labour on the large scale, I think there is no *remain* as respectable as would be a common ditch for the draining of lands: unless indeed it be the Barrows, of which many are to be found all over the country.
> *Jefferson*, Notes on Virginia (1787), p. 156.

Specifically—**4.** *pl.* That which is left of a human being after life is gone; a dead body; a corpse.

> Be kind to my *remains*; and oh, defend,
> Against your judgment, your departed friend!
> *Dryden*, To Congreve, l. 72.

> A woman or two, and three or four undertaker's men, . . . had charge of the *remains*, which they watched turn about. *Thackeray*, Vanity Fair, xli.

5. *pl.* The productions, especially the literary works, of one who is dead; posthumous works: as, "Coleridge's Literary *Remains*."—**Fossil remains**, fossils. See *fossil*.—**Organic remains.** See *organic*. =**Syn. 3.** Scraps, fragments.—**3-5.** See *relic*.

remainder (rẹ̄-mān′dėr), *n.* and *a.* [< OF. *remaindre*, inf. used as a noun: see *remain*.] **I.** *n.* **1.** That which remains; anything left after the separation, removal, destruction, or passing of a part.

> As much as one sound cudgel of four foot—
> You see the poor *remainder*—could distribute,
> I made no spare, sir. *Shak.*, Hen. VIII., v. 4. 20.

> What madness moves you, matrons, to destroy
> The last *remainders* of unhappy Troy?
> *Dryden*, Æneid, v.

2. In *math.*, the sum or quantity left after subtraction or after any deduction; also, the part remaining over after division: thus, if 19 be divided by 4, the *remainder* is 3, because 19 is three more than an exact multiple of 4. In the old arithmetics called the *remainer*.—**3.** In *law*, a future estate so created as to take effect in possession and enjoyment after another estate (as a life-interest) is determined; a remnant of an estate in land, depending upon a particular prior estate, created at the same time, and by the same instrument, and limited to arise immediately on the determination of that estate. (*Kent.*) It is thus distinguished from a *reversion*, which is the estate which by operation of law arises in the grantor or his heirs when a limited estate created without creating also a remainder comes to an end; and distinguished also from an *executory interest*, which may take effect although there be no prior estate upon the termination of which it is to commence in possession. At the time when by the common law no grant could be made but by livery of seizin, a person who wished to give to another a future estate was obliged to create at the same time an intermediate estate commencing immediately, and he could limit this temporary estate by the event which he wished to fix for the commencement of the ultimate estate, which was hence called the *remainder*—that is, what remained after the precedent or particular estate—and was said to be supported by the precedent or particular estate. (See *particular estate* and *executory estate*, both under *estate*.) A remainder is *vested* when the event which will terminate the precedent estate is certain to happen, and the person designated to take in remainder is in existence. The fact that the person may not survive to enjoy the estate, or that others may come into existence who will also answer the designation and therefore be entitled to share it with him, does not prevent the *remainder* from being deemed vested meanwhile.

> With Julius Caesar, Decimus Brutus had obtained that interest, as he set him down in his testament for heir in *remainder* after his nephew. *Bacon*, Friendship (ed. 1887).

4. In the *publishing trade*, that which remains of an edition the sale of which has practically ceased, and which is sold out at a reduced price.

> In 1843 he felt strong enough to start as a publisher in Soho Square, his main dealings before this having been in *remainders*, and his one solitary publication a failure.
> *Athenæum*, No. 3191, p. 850.

Contingent remainder, in *law*, a remainder which is not vested. The epithets *contingent* and *vested* are, however, often loosely used to indicate the distinction between remainders of which the enjoyment is in any way contingent and others.—**Cross remainder**, in *law*, that state of affairs in which each of two grantees or devisees has reciprocally a remainder in the property in which a particular estate is given to the other. Thus, if land be devised, one half to A for life with remainder to B in fee simple, and the other half to B for life with remainder to A in fee simple, these remainders are called *cross remainders*. Cross remainders arise on a grant to two or more as tenants in common, a particular estate being limited to each of the grantees in his share, with remainders to the other or others of them. =**Syn. 1.** *Rest, Remainder, Remnant, Residue, Balance.* *Rest* is the most general term; it may represent a large or a small part. *Remainder* and *residue* generally represent a comparatively small part, and *remnant* a part not only very small, but of little or no account. *Rest* may be applied to persons as freely as to things; *remainder* and *residue* only to things; but we may speak of the *remainder* of a party. *Remnant* and *residue* are favorite words in the Bible for *rest* or *remainder*, as in Mat. xxii. 6 and Isa. xxi. 17, but such use of them in application to persons is now antique. *Balance* cannot, literally or by legitimate figure, be used for *rest* or *remainder*: we say the *balance* of the time, week, space, party, money. It is a cant word of trade.

II.† *a.* Remaining; refuse; left.

> As dry as the *remainder* biscuit
> After a voyage. *Shak.*, As you Like it, ii. 7. 39.

remainder-man (rẹ̄-mān′dėr-man), *n.* In *law*, one who has an estate after a particular estate is determined.

remainer (rẹ̄-mā′nėr), *n.* **1.** One who remains. —**2†.** Same as *remainder*, 2.

remake (rē-māk′), *v. t.* [< *re-* + *make*¹.] To make anew; reconstruct.

> My business is not to *remake* myself,
> But make the absolute best of what God made.
> *Browning*, Bishop Blougram's Apology.

Remak's fibers. See *nerve-fiber*.

remanation (rē-mạ̄-nā′shọn), *n.* [< L. *remanatus*, pp. of *remanare*, flow back, < *re-*, back, + *manare*, flow: see *emanation*.] The act of returning, as to its source; the state of being reabsorbed; reabsorption. [Rare.]

> [Buddhism's] pantheistic doctrine of emanation and *remanation*. *Macmillan's Mag.*

remand (rẹ̄-månd′), *v. t.* [< late ME. *remanden*, < OF. *remander*, send for again, F. *remander* = Sp. *remandar*, order several times, = It. *rimandare*, < L. *remandare*, send back word, < *re-*, back, + *mandare*, enjoin, send word: see *mandate*.] **1.** To send, call, or order back: as, to *remand* an officer from a distant place.

> When a prisoner first leaves his cell he cannot bear the light of day. . . . But the remedy is, not to *remand* him into his dungeon, but to accustom him to the rays of the sun. *Macaulay*, Milton.

> The ethical writer is not likely to *remand* to Psychology proper the analysis of Conscience.
> *A. Bain*, Mind, XIII. 536.

2. In *law*, to send back, as a prisoner, on refusing his application to be discharged, or a cause from an appellate court to the court of original jurisdiction.

> Morgan is sent back into Custody, whither also I am *remanded*. *Smollett*, Roderick Random, xxx., Contents.

remand (rẹ̄-månd′), *n.* [< *remand*, *v.*] The state of being remanded, recommitted, or held over; the act of remanding.

> He will probably apply for a series of *remands* from time to time, until the case is more complete.
> *Dickens*, Bleak House, lii.

remandment (rẹ̄-månd′mẹnt), *n.* [< *remand* + *-ment*.] The act of remanding.

remanence (rem′ạ-nẹns), *n.* [< *remanen(t)* + *-ce*.] **1.** The state or quality of being remanent; continuance; permanence.

Neither St. Augustin nor Calvin denied the *remanence* of the will in the fallen spirit. *Coleridge.*

2†. That which remains; a residuum.

This salt is a volatile one, and requires no strong heat to make it sublime into finely figured crystals without a *remanence* at the bottom. *Boyle*, Works, III. 81.

remanency† (rem'a-nen-si), *n.* [As *remanence* (see *-cy*).] Same as *remanence*. *Jer. Taylor*, Works (ed. 1835), II. 392.

remanent (rem'a-nent), *a.* and *n.* [I. *a.* < L. *remanen(t-)s*, ppr. of *remanere*, remain: see *remain*. II. *n.* < ME. *remanent*, *remanaunt*, *remenant*, *remenaunt*, *remelant*, also syncopated *remnant*, *remlant*, < OF. *remenant*, *remanent* = Sp. *remanente* = It. *rimanente*, a remnant, residue, < L. *remanen(t-)s*, remaining: see I. Cf. *remnant*, a syncopated form of *remanent*.] I. *a.* 1. Remaining.

There is a *remanent* felicity in the very memory of those spiritual delights. *Jer. Taylor*, Works (ed. 1835), II. 251.

The residual or *remanent* magnetism of the electro-magnets is neutralised by the use of a second and independent coil wound in the opposite direction to the primary helix. *Dredge's Electric Illumination*, I., App., p. cxvii.

2. Additional; other: as, the moderator and *remanent* members of a church court. [Scotch.]

II.† *n.* The part remaining; remnant.

Her majesty bought of his executrix the *remanent* of the last term of three years. *Bacon.*

Breke as myche as thou wylle ete,
The *remelant* to pore thou shalle lete.
Babees Book (E. E. T. S.), p. 300.

remanet (rem'a-net), *n.* [< L. *remanere*, remain: see *remain*.] In *Eng. law*, a suit standing over, or a proceeding connected with one which is delayed or deferred.

remanié (rē-man-i-ā'), *a.* [F., pp. of *remanier*, handle again, change, < *re-* + *manier*, handle: see *manage*.] Derived from an older bed: said of fossils. *Sir C. Lyell.*

remark¹ (rē-märk'), *v.* [< OF. *remarquer*, *remerquier*, F. *remarquer*, mark, note, heed, < *re-*, again, + *marquer*, mark: see *mark¹*, *v.* Cf. *remark²*.] I. *trans.* 1. To observe; note in the mind; take notice of without audible expression.

Then with another humourous ruth *remark'd*
The lusty mowers laboring dinnerless,
And watch'd the sun blaze on the turning scythe.
Tennyson, Geraint.

He does not look as if he hated them, so far as I have *remarked* his expression. *O. W. Holmes*, A Mortal Antipathy, xiv.

2. To express, as a thought that has occurred to the speaker or writer; utter or write by way of comment or observation.

The writer well *remarks*, a heart that knows
To take with gratitude what Heav'n bestows
. . . is all in all. *Cowper*, Hope, l. 420.

Bastian *remarks* that the Arabic language has the same word for epilepsy and possession by devils. *H. Spencer*, Prin. of Sociol., § 122.

3†. To mark; point out; distinguish.

They are moved by shame, and punished by disgrace, and *remarked* by punishments, . . . and separated from sober persons by laws. *Jer. Taylor*, Works (ed. 1835), I. 683.

Offic. Hebrews, the prisoner Samson here I seek.
Chor. His manacles *remark* him; there he sits.
Milton, S. A., l. 1309.

II. *intrans.* To make observations; observe.

remark¹ (rē-märk'), *n.* [< OF. *remarque*, *remerque*, F. *remarque* (= It. *rimarco*, importance), < *remarquer*, remark: see *remark¹*, *v.*] 1. The act of remarking or taking notice; notice or observation.

The cause, tho' worth the search, may yet elude
Conjecture, and *remark*, however shrewd.
Cowper, Table-Talk, l. 205.

2. A notice, note, or comment; an observation: as, the *remarks* of an advocate; the *remarks* made in conversation; the *remarks* of a critic.

Then hire a slave . . . to make *remarks*,
Who rules in Cornwall, or who rules in Berks: . . .
"That makes three members, this can choose a mayor."
Pope, Imit. of Horace, I. vi. 103.

3. Noticeable appearance; note.

There was a man of special grave *remark*.
Thomson, Castle of Indolence, i. 57.

4. In *line-engraving* and *etching*: (*a*) A distinguishing mark or peculiarity of any kind, indicating any particular state of the plate prior to its completion. The remark may be a slight sketch made by the engraver on the margin of his plate, or it may consist merely in the absence of certain detail or features of the finished work. Thus, in a first proof of an etching the absence of retouching with the dry point, or of a final rebiting, constitutes a remark; or in a line-engraving it may consist in the presence or absence of some minor object, or of certain lines representing texture or shading, which in a later state of the plate are removed or added.

The old legend still lingers that the *remarque* began when some unknown etcher tried his point upon the edge of his plate just before taking his first impressions. The belief yet obtains that the *remarque* testifies to the etcher's supreme satisfaction with a supreme effort. But as a matter of fact the *remarque* has become any kind of a fanciful supplementary sketch, not necessarily appropriate, not always done by the etcher, and appearing upon a number of impressions which seem to be limited only at the will of artist or dealer. Sometimes we see 50 *remarque* proofs announced, and again 300. *New York Tribune*, Feb. 6, 1887.

(*b*) A print or proof bearing or characterized by a remark; a remarked proof, or remark proof. Also written *remarque*. =**Syn.** 2. *Remark, Observation, Comment, Commentary, Reflection, Note, Annotation, Gloss.* A *remark* is brief and cursory, suggested by present circumstances and presumably without previous thought. An *observation* is made with some thought and care. A *comment* is a remark or observation bearing closely upon some situation of facts, some previous utterance, or some published work. *Remark* may be substituted by modesty for *observation*. When printed, *remarks, observations*, or *comments* may be called *reflections*: as, Burke's "*Reflections* on the Revolution in France"; when they are systematic in explanation of a work, they may be called a *commentary*: as, Lange's "*Commentary* on Matthew." A *note* is primarily a brief writing to help the memory; then a marginal comment: *notes* is sometimes used modestly for *commentary*: as, Barnes's "*Notes* on the Psalms"; Trench's "*Notes* on the Parables." A marginal comment is more definitely expressed by *annotation*. A *gloss* is a comment made for the purpose of explanation, especially upon a word or passage in a foreign language or a peculiar dialect.

remark² (rē-märk'), *v. t.* [< *re-* + *mark¹*; cf. F. *remarquer* = Sp. *remarcar*, mark again.] To mark anew or a second time.

remarkable (rē-mär'ka-bl), *a.* and *n.* [< OF. (and F.) *remarquable* = It. *rimarcabile*; as *remark¹* + *-able*.] I. *a.* 1. Observable; worthy of notice.

This day will be *remarkable* in my life
By some great act. *Milton*, S. A., l. 1388.

'Tis *remarkable* that they
Talk most who have the least to say.
Prior, Alma, ii.

2. Extraordinary; unusual; deserving of particular notice; such as may excite admiration or wonder; conspicuous; distinguished.

There is nothing left *remarkable*
Beneath the visiting moon.
Shak., A. and C., iv. 15. 67.

I have breakfasted again with Rogers. The party was a *remarkable* one—Lord John Russell, Tom Moore, Tom Campbell, and Luttrell. *Macaulay*, Life and Letters, I. 207.

=**Syn.** Noticeable, notable, rare, strange, wonderful, uncommon, singular, striking.

II.† *n.* Something noticeable, extraordinary, or exceptional; a noteworthy thing or circumstance.

Jerusalem won by the Turk, with wofull *remarkables* thereat. *Fuller*, Holy War, ii. 46 (title). (*Davies.*)

Some few *remarkables* are not only still remembered, but also well attested. *C. Mather*, Mag. Chris., iv. 1.

remarkableness (rē-mär'ka-bl-nes), *n.* The character of being remarkable; observableness; worthiness of remark; the quality of deserving particular notice.

remarkably (rē-mär'ka-bli), *adv.* In a remarkable manner; in a manner or degree worthy of notice; in an extraordinary manner or degree; singularly; surprisingly.

remarked (rē-märkt'), *p. a.* 1. Conspicuous; noted; remarkable.

You speak of two
The most *remark'd* i' the kingdom.
Shak., Hen. VIII., v. 1. 33.

2. In *plate-engraving* and *etching*, bearing or characterized by a remark. See *remark¹*, *n.*, 4.

remarker (rē-mär'kėr), *n.* One who remarks; one who makes remarks; a critic.

She pretends to be a *remarker*, and looks at every body. *Steele*, Lying Lover, iii. 1.

remarque, *n.* See *remark¹*, 4.

remarriage (rē-mar'āj), *n.* [< OF. (and F.) *remarriage*; as *re-* + *marriage*.] Any marriage after the first; a repeated marriage.

With whom [the Jews] polygamy and *remarriages*, after unjust divorces, were in ordinary use. *Bp. Hall*, Honour of Married Clergy, i. § 18.

remarry (rē-mar'i), *v. t.* and *i.* [< F. *remarier* = Pr. *remaridar*; as *re-* + *marry¹*.] To marry again or a second time.

remasticate (rē-mas'ti-kāt), *v. t.* [< *re-* + *masticate*. Cf. F. *remastiquer*.] To chew again, as the cud; ruminate. *Imp. Dict.*

remastication (rē-mas-ti-kā'shon), *n.* [< *remasticate* + *-ion*.] The act or process of remasticating; rumination. *Imp. Dict.*

remberge†, *n.* Same as *ramberge*.

remblai (roṅ-blā'), *n.* [< F. *remblai*, < *remblayer*, OF. *remblayer*, *rembler*, embank, < *re-* + *emblayer*, *emblaer*, embarrass, hinder, lit. 'sow with grain': see *emblement*.] 1. In *fort.*, the earth or materials used to form the whole mass of rampart and parapet. It may contain more than the déblai from the ditch.—2. In *engin.*, the mass of earth brought to form an embankment in the case of a railway or canal traversing a natural depression of surface.

remble (rem'bl), *v. t.*; pret. and pp. *rembled*, ppr. *rembling*. [Perhaps a var. of *ramble*: see *ramble*.] To move; remove. [Prov. Eng.]

Theer wur a boggle in it [the waste], . . .
But I stubb'd 'um oop wi' the lot, and raäved an' *rembled* 'um oot. *Tennyson*, Northern Farmer (Old Style).

Remboth, *n.* See *Remoboth*.

Rembrandtesque (rem-bran-tesk'), *a.* [< *Rembrandt* (see def.) + *-esque*.] Resembling the manner or style of the great Dutch painter and etcher Rembrandt (died 1669); specifically, in *art*, characterized by the studied contrast of high lights and deep shadows, with suitable treatment of chiaroscuro.

Rembrandtish (rem'brant-ish), *a.* [< *Rembrandt* + *-ish¹*.] Same as *Rembrandtesque*. *Athenæum*, No. 3201, p. 287.

reme¹†, *v. i.* A Middle English form of *ream¹*.

reme²†, *n.* A Middle English form of *realm*.

remead, *n.* See *remede*.

remean† (rē-mēn'), *v. t.* [ME. *remenen*; < *re-* + *mean¹*.] To give meaning to; interpret. *Wyclif.*

Of love y schalle hem so *remene*
That thou schalt knowe what they mene.
Gower, MS. Soc. Antiq. 134, f. 40. (*Halliwell.*)

remeant (rē'mē-ant), *a.* [< L. *remean(t-)s*, ppr. of *remeare*, go or come back, < *re-*, back, + *meare*, go: see *meatus*.] Coming back; returning. [Rare.]

Most exalted Prince,
Whose peerless knighthood, like the *remeant* sun
After too long a night, regilds our clay.
Kingsley, Saint's Tragedy, ii. 8.

remede (rē-mēd'), *n.* [Also *remeud*, *remeed*, Sc. *remeid*; < OF. *remede*, F. *remède*, a remedy: see *remedy*.] Remedy; redress; help. [Old Eng. or Scotch.]

But what is thanne a *remede* unto this,
But that we shape us soone for to mete?
Chaucer, Troilus, iv. 1272.

If it is for ony heinous crime,
There 's nae *remeid* for thee.
Lang Johnny Moir (Child's Ballads, IV. 276).

The town's people were passing sorry for bereaving them of their arms by such an uncouth slight—but no *remead*. *Spalding*, Hist. Troubles in Scotland, I. 230. (*Jamieson.*)

An' strive, wi' al' your wit an' lear,
To get *remead*.
Burns, Prayer to the Scotch Representatives.

remediable (rē-mē'di-a-bl), *a.* [< OF. *remediable*, F. *remédiable* = Sp. *remediable* = Pg. *remediavel* = It. *rimediabile*, < ML. **remediabilis*, capable of being remedied, < *remediare*, remedy: see *remedy*, *v.*] Capable of being remedied or cured.

Not *remediable* by courts of equity.
Bacon, Advice to the King.

remediableness (rē-mē'di-a-bl-nes), *n.* The state or character of being remediable. *Imp. Dict.*

remediably (rē-mē'di-a-bli), *adv.* In a remediable manner or condition; so as to be susceptible of remedy or cure. *Imp. Dict.*

remedial (rē-mē'di-al), *a.* [< L. *remedialis*, healing, remedial, < *remediare*, *remediari*, heal, cure: see *remedy*, *v.*] Affording a remedy; intended for a remedy or for the removal of an evil: as, to adopt *remedial* measures.

They shall have redress by audita querela, which is a writ of a most *remedial* nature. *Blackstone*, Com., III. xxv.

But who can set limits to the *remedial* force of spirit? *Emerson*, Nature, p. 85.

Remedial statutes. See *statute*.

remedially (rē-mē'di-al-i), *adv.* In a remedial manner. *Imp. Dict.*

remediate† (rē-mē'di-āt), *a.* [< L. *remediatus*, pp. of *remediari*, heal, cure: see *remedy*, *v.*] Remedial.

All you unpublish'd virtues of the earth,
Spring with my tears! be aidant and *remediate*
In the good man's distress! *Shak.*, Lear, iv. 4. 17.

remediless (rem'e-di-les), *a.* [< ME. *remedylesse*; < *remedy* + *-less*.] 1†. Without a remedy; not possessing a remedy.

Thus welle y wote y am *remedylesse*,
For me no thyng may comforte nor amend.
MS. Cantab. Ff. i. 6, f. 131. (*Halliwell.*)

2. Not admitting a remedy; incurable; desperate: as, a *remediless* disease.

The other sought to stanch his *remediless* wounds.
Sir P. Sidney, Arcadia, iii.

As if some divine commission from heav'n were descended to take into hearing and commiseration the long *remedilesse* afflictions of this kingdome.
Milton, Apology for Smectymnuus.

3. Irreparable, as a loss or damage.

She hath time enough to bewail her own folly and *remediless* infelicity. *Jer. Taylor*, Works (ed. 1835), II. 139.

This is the affliction of hell, unto whom it affordeth despair and *remediless* calamity. *Sir T. Browne*, Vulg. Err.

4†. Not answering as a remedy; ineffectual; powerless. *Spenser*. =**Syn.** 2 and 3. Irremediable, irrecoverable, irretrievable, hopeless.

remedilessly (rem'ẹ-di-les-li), *adv.* In a manner or degree that precludes a remedy.

He going away *remedilessly* chafing at his rebuke.
Sir P. Sidney, Arcadia, i.

remedilessness (rem'ẹ-di-les-nes), *n.* The state of being remediless, or of not admitting of a remedy; incurableness.

The *remedilessness* of this disease may be justly questioned. *Boyle*, Works, II. ii. 3.

remedy (rem'ẹ-di), *n.*; pl. *remedies* (-diz). [< ME. *remedie*, < OF. **remedie*, *remede*, F. *remède* = Pr. *remedi*, *remoyi* = Sp. Pg. It. *remedio*, < L. *remedium*, a remedy, cure, < *re-*, again, + *mederi*, heal: see *medicine*. Cf. *remede*.] 1. That which cures a disease; any medicine or application or process which promotes restoration to health or alleviates the effects of disease: with *for* before the name of a disease.

A cool well by, . . .
Growing a bath and healthful *remedy*
For men diseased. *Shak.*, Sonnets, cliv.

When he [a scorpion] is hurt with one Poison, he seeks his *Remedy* with another.
N. Bailey, tr. of Colloquies of Erasmus, I. 165.

Colchicum with alkalis and other *remedies for* gout, such as a course of Friedrichshall or Carlsbad waters, will prove of great service. *Quain*, Med. Dict., p. 188.

2. That which corrects or counteracts an evil of any kind; relief; redress; reparation.

For in holi writt thou made rede,
"In helle is no *remedie*."
Hymns to Virgin, etc. (E. E. T. S.), p. 50.

Things without all *remedy*
Should be without regard.
Shak., Macbeth, iii. 2. 11.

3. In *law*, the means given for obtaining through a court of justice any right or compensation or redress for a wrong.—4. In *coining*, a certain allowance at the mint for deviation from the standard weight and fineness of coins: same as *allowance*[1], 7.—5†. A course of action to bring about a certain result.

Ye! nere it [were it not] that I wiste a *remedye*
To come ageyn, right here I wolde dye.
Chaucer, Troilus, iv. 1623.

Provisional remedy. See *provisional*.—**The divine remedy.** See *divine*. =**Syn.** 1 and 2. Cure, restorative, specific, antidote, corrective.

remedy (rem'ẹ-di), *v. t.*; pret. and pp. *remedied*, ppr. *remedying*. [< late ME. *remedyen*, < OF. *remedier*, F. *remédier* = Pr. Sp. Pg. *remediar* = It. *rimediare*, < L. *remediare*, *remediari*, heal, cure, < *remedium*, a remedy: see *remedy*, *n.*] 1. To cure; heal: as, to *remedy* a disease.—2. To repair or remove something evil from; restore to a natural or proper condition.

I desire your majesty to *remedy* the matter.
Latimer, 5th Sermon bef. Edw. VI., 1549.

3. To remove or counteract, as something evil; redress.

If you cannot even as you would *remedy* vices which use and custom have confirmed, yet for this cause you must not leave and forsake the common-wealth.
Sir T. More, Utopia (tr. by Robinson), i.

Whoso believes that spiritual destitution is to be *remedied* only by a national church may with some show of reason propose to deal with physical destitution by an analogous instrumentality.
H. Spencer, Social Statics, p. 348.

remeed, remeid, *n.* See *remede*.

remelant†, *n.* A Middle English form of *remanent*, *remnant*.

remember (rẹ-mem'bėr), *v.* [< ME. *remembren*, < OF. *remembrer* (refl.), F. *remembrer* = Pr. *remembrar* = OSp. *remembrar* = Pg. *lembrar* = It. *rimembrare* (also in mod. form directly after L., F. *rémemorer* = Pr. Sp. Pg. *rememorar* = It. *rimemorare*), < LL. *rememorari*, ML. also *rememorare*, recall to mind, remember, < L. *re-*, again, + *memorare*, bring to remembrance, mention, recount, < *memor*, remembering, mindful: see *memorate*, *memory*.] I. *trans.* 1. To bring again to the memory; recall to mind; recollect.

Now calleth us to *remember* our sins past.
J. Bradford, Letters (Parker Soc., 1853), II. 36.

To *remember* is to perceive any thing with memory, or with a consciousness that it was known or perceived before.
Locke, Human Understanding, I. iv. 20.

2. To bear or keep in mind; have in memory; be capable of recalling when required; preserve unforgotten: as, to *remember* one's lessons; to *remember* all the circumstances.

Remember thee!
Ay, thou poor ghost, while memory holds a seat
In this distracted globe. *Shak.*, Hamlet, i. 5. 95.

Remembering no more of that other day
Than the hot noon *remembereth* of the night,
Than summer thinketh of the winter white.
William Morris, Earthly Paradise, I. 427.

3. To be continually thoughtful of; have present to the attention; attend to; bear in mind: opposed to *forget*.

Remember whom thou hast aboard.
Shak., Tempest, i. 1. 20.

Remember what I warn thee, shun to taste.
Milton, P. L., viii. 327.

But still *remember*, if you mean to please,
To press your point with modesty and ease.
Cowper, Conversation, l. 103.

4†. To mention.

The selfe same sillable to be sometime long and sometime short for the cares better satisfaction, as hath bene before *remembred*. *Puttenham*, Arte of Eng. Poesie, p. 89.

Now call we our high court of parliament. . . .
Our coronation done, we will accite,
As I before *remember'd*, all our state.
Shak., 2 Hen. IV., v. 2. 142.

Pliny, Solinus, Ptolemy, and of late Leo the African, *remember* unto us a river in Æthiopia, famous by the name of Niger. *B. Jonson*, Masque of Blackness.

5†. To put in mind; remind; reflexively, to remind one's self (to be reminded).

This Eneas is comen to Paradys
Out of the swolowe of helle: and thus in joye
Remembreth him of his estaat in Troye.
Chaucer, Good Women, l. 1105.

I may not ease me hert as in this case,
That doth me harme whanne I *remembre me*.
Generydes (E. E. T. S.), l. 588.

One only thing, as it comes into my mind, let me *remember* you of.
Sir P. Sidney (Arber's Eng. Garner, I. 308).

I'll not *remember* you of my own lord.
Shak., W. T., iii. 2. 231.

She then *remembered* to his thought the place
Where he was going. *B. Jonson*, A Panegyre.

Ile tell ye, or at least *remember* ye, for most of ye know it already. *Milton*, Church-Government, ii., Conc.

6. To keep in mind with gratitude, favor, confidence, affection, respect, or any other feeling or emotion.

Remember the sabbath day, to keep it holy. Ex. xx. 8.

If thou wilt indeed look on the affliction of thine handmaid and *remember* me. 1 Sam. i. 11.

That they may have their wages duly paid 'em,
And something over to *remember* me by.
Shak., Hen. VIII., iv. 2. 151.

Old as I am, for ladies' love unfit,
The power of beauty I *remember* yet.
Dryden, Cym. and Iph., l. 2.

7. To take notice of and give money or other present to: said of one who has done some actual or nominal service and expects a fee for it.

[Knocking within.] *Porter*. Anon, anon! I pray you *remember* the porter. [Opens the gate.]
Shak., Macbeth, ii. 3. 23.

Remember your courtesy†, be covered; put on your hat: addressed to one who remained bareheaded after saluting, and intended to remind him that he had already made his salute.

I do beseech thee, *remember thy courtesy*; I beseech thee, apparel thy head. *Shak.*, L. L. L., v. 1. 103.

Pray you *remember your court'sy*. . . . Nay, pray you be cover'd.
B. Jonson, Every Man in his Humour (ed. Gifford), i. 1.

To be remembered†, to recall; recollect; have in remembrance. Compare def. 5.

To your extent I canne right wele agree;
Ther is a land I *am remembryd* wele,
Men call it Perse, a plenteuous contre.
Generydes (E. E. T. S.), l. 619.

Now by my troth, if I *had been remember'd*,
I could have given my uncle's grace a flout.
Shak., Rich. III., ii. 4. 23.

She always wears a muff, if you *be remembered*.
B. Jonson, Cynthia's Revels, ii. 1.

To remember one to or **unto**, to recall one to the remembrance of; commend one to: used in complimentary messages: as, *remember me to* your family.

Remember me
In all humility unto his highness.
Shak., Hen. VIII., iv. 2. 160.

Remember me to my old Companions. *Remember me to* my Friends. *N. Bailey*, tr. of Colloquies of Erasmus, I. 27.

=**Syn.** 1. *Remember*, *Recollect*. *Remember* implies that a thing exists in the memory, not that it is actually present in the thoughts at the moment, but that it recurs without effort. *Recollect* means that a fact, forgotten or partially lost to memory, is after some effort recalled and present to the mind. *Remembrance* is the store-house, *recollection* the act of culling out this article and that from the repository. He *remembers* everything he hears, and can *recollect* any statement when called on. The words, however, are often confounded, and we say we cannot *remember* a thing when we mean we cannot *recollect* it. See *memory*.

II. *intrans.* 1. To hold something in remembrance; exercise the faculty of memory.

I *remember*
Of such a time: being my sworn servant,
The duke retain'd him his.
Shak., Hen. VIII., i. 2. 190.

As I *remember*, there were certain low chairs, that looked like ebony, at Esher, and were old and pretty.
Gray, Letters, I. 217.

2†. To return to the memory; come to mind: used impersonally.

But, Lord Crist! whan that it *remembreth* me
Upon my yowthe and on my jolitee,
It tikleth me aboute myn herte roote.
Chaucer, Prol. to Wife of Bath's Tale, l. 469.

rememberable (rẹ-mem'bėr-a̤-bl), *a.* [< *remember* + *-able*.] Capable or worthy of being remembered.

The earth
And common face of Nature spake to me
Rememberable things. *Wordsworth*, Prelude, i.

rememberably (rẹ-mem'bėr-a̤-bli), *adv.* In a rememberable manner; so as to be remembered.

My golden rule is to relate everything as briefly, as perspicuously, and as *rememberably* as possible.
Southey, 1805 (Mem. of Taylor of Norwich, II. 77). (*Davies*.)

rememberer (rẹ-mem'bėr-ėr), *n.* One who remembers.

A brave master to servants, and a *rememberer* of the least good office; for his flock, he transplanted most of them into plentiful soils. *Sir H. Wotton*. (*Latham*.)

remembrance (rẹ-mem'brans), *n.* [Early mod. E. also *remembraunce*; < ME. *remembrance*, *remembraunce*, < OF. *remembrance*, *remembraunce*, F. *remembrance* = Pr. *remembransa* = Sp. *remembranza* = Pg. *remembrança*, *lembrança* = It. *rimembranza*, < ML. as if **rememorantia*, < *rememorare*, remember: see *remember*.] 1. The act of remembering; the keeping of a thing in mind or recalling it to mind; a revival in the mind or memory.

All knowledge is but *remembrance*.
Bacon, Advancement of Learning, i. 2.

Remembrance is but the reviving of some past knowledge. *Locke*, Human Understanding, IV. i. 9.

Remembrance and reflection, how allied;
What thin partitions sense from thought divide!
Pope, Essay on Man, i. 225.

2. The power or faculty of remembering; memory; also, the limit of time over which the memory extends.

Thee I have heard relating what was done
Ere my *remembrance*. *Milton*, P. L., viii. 204.

When the word perception is used properly and without any figure, it is never applied to things past. And thus it is distinguished from *remembrance*.
Reid, Intellectual Powers, i. 1.

3. The state of being remembered; the state of being held honorably in memory.

The righteous shall be in everlasting *remembrance*.
Ps. cxii. 6.

Grace and *remembrance* be to you both.
Shak., W. T., iv. 4. 76.

Oh! scenes in strong *remembrance* set!
Scenes never, never to return!
Burns, The Lament.

4. That which is remembered; a recollection.

How sharp the point of this *remembrance* is!
Shak., Tempest, v. 1. 138.

The sweet *remembrance* of the just
Shall flourish when he sleeps in dust.
Tate and Brady, Ps. cxii. 6.

5. That which serves to bring to or keep in mind.

I pray, Sir, be my continual *remembrance* to the Throne of grace.
W. Bradford, in Appendix to New England's Memorial, [p. 435.

(*a*) An account preserved; a memorandum or note to preserve or assist the memory; a record; mention.

Auferius, the welebelouyd kyng
That was of Ynd, and ther had his dwellyng
Till he was putte [from] his enheritaunce,
Wherof be fore was made *remembraunce*.
Generydes (E. E. T. S.), l. 2177.

Let the understanding reader take with him three or four short *remembrances*. . . . The memorandums I would commend to him are these.
Chillingworth, Relig. of Protestants, Ans. to Fifth Chapter, [§ 29.

(*b*) A monument; a memorial.

And it is of trouthe, as they saye there, and as it is asygned by token of a fayre stone layde for *remembraunce*, yt our blessyd Lady and seynt John Euangelyste stode not aboue vpon the hyghest pte of the Mounte of Caluery at the passyon of our Lord.
Sir R. Guylforde, Pylgrymage, p. 27.

If I neuer deserue anye better *remembraunce*, let mee . . . be epitaphed the Inuentor of the English Hexameter.
G. Harvey, Four Letters.

(c) A token by which one is kept in the memory; a keepsake.

> I am glad I have found this napkin;
> This was her first *remembrance* from the Moor.
> *Shak.*, Othello, iii. 3. 291.

> I pray you accept
> This small *remembrance* of a father's thanks
> For so assur'd a benefit.
> *Fletcher* (*and another*), Love's Pilgrimage, v. 2.

6. The state of being mindful; thought; regard; consideration; notice of something absent.

> In what place that euer I be in, the moste *remembraunce* that I shall haue shall be vpon yow, and on yowre nedes.
> *Merlin* (E. E. T. S.), i. 49.

> We with wisest sorrow think on him,
> Together with *remembrance* of ourselves.
> *Shak.*, Hamlet, i. 2. 7.

> The Puritans, to keep the *remembrance* of their unity one with another, and of their peaceful compact with the Indians, named their forest settlement Concord.
> *Emerson*, Hist. Discourse at Concord.

7†. Admonition; reminder.

> I do commit into your hand
> The unstained sword that you have used to bear;
> With this *remembrance*, that you use the same
> With the like bold, just, and impartial spirit
> As you have done 'gainst me.
> *Shak.*, 2 Hen. IV., v. 2. 115.

Clerks of the remembrance. See *remembrancer*, 2.— **To make remembrance†**, to bring to remembrance; recount: relate.=**Syn.** 1, 2, and 4. *Recollection, Reminiscence*, etc. See *memory*.

remembrancer (rē-mem'brạn-sėr), *n.* [< *remembrance* + *-er*[1].] 1. One who or that which reminds or revives the memory of anything.

> Astronomy in all likelihood was knowne to Abraham, to whom the heauenly stars might be *Remembrancers* of that promise, so shall thy seed be. *Purchas*, Pilgrimage, p. 66.

> Premature consolation is but the *remembrancer* of sorrow. *Goldsmith*, Vicar, iii.

> All the young fellows crowd up to ask her to dance, and, taking from her waist a little mother-of-pearl *remembrancer*, she notes them down.
> *Thackeray*, Fitz-Boodle Papers, Dorothea.

2. An officer in the Exchequer of England, employed to record documents, make out processes, etc.; a recorder. These officers were formerly called *clerks of the remembrance*, and were three in number — the *king's remembrancer*, the *lord treasurer's remembrancer*, and the *remembrancer of first-fruits*. The *queen's remembrancer's department* now has a place in the central office of the Supreme Court. The name is also given to an officer of certain corporations: as, the *remembrancer* of the city of London.

> These rents [ceremonial rents, as a horseshoe, etc.] are now received by the Queen's *Remembrancer* a few days before the beginning of Michaelmas term.
> *F. Pollock*, Land Laws, p. 8.

rememorance†, *n.* [ME. *rememoraunce*, a var., after ML. **rememorantia*, of *remembraunce*: see *remembrance*.] Remembrance.

> Nowe menne it call, by all *rememoraunce*,
> Constantyne noble, wher to dwell he did enclyne.
> *Hardyng's Chronicle*, f. 50. (*Halliwell.*)

rememorate† (rẹ-mem'ọ-rāt), *v. t.* [< LL. *rememoratus*, pp. of *rememorari*, remember: see *remember*.] To remember; revive in the memory.

> We shall ever find the like difficulties, whether we *rememorate* or learne anew.
> *L. Bryskett*, Civil Life (1606), p. 128.

rememoration† (rẹ-mem-ọ-rā'shọn), *n.* [Early mod. E. *rememoracioun*; < OF. *rememoration*, F. *remémoration*, < ML. *rememoratio(n-)*, < LL. *rememorari*, remember: see *remember*, *rememorate*.] Remembrance.

> The story requires a particular *rememoration*.
> *Jer. Taylor*, Works (ed. 1835), II. 256.

rememorative† (rẹ-mem'ọ-rạ-tiv), *a.* [< F. *remémoratif* = Sp. Pg. *rememorativo*; as *rememorate* + *-ive*.] Recalling to mind; reminding.

> For whi, withoute *rememoratif* signes of a thing, or of thingis, the rememoracioun, or the remembraunce, of thilk thing or thingis muste needis be the febler.
> *Pocock*, quoted in Waterland's Works, X. 254.

remenant†, *n.* An obsolete form of *remnant*.

remene[1]**†**, *v. t.* See *remean*.

remene[2]**†**, *v. t.* [< OF. (and F.) *remener* (= Pr. *ramenar* = It. *rimenare*), < *re-*, again, + *mener*, < ML. *minare*, conduct, lead, bring: see *mien*.] To bring back. *Vernon MS.* (*Halliwell.*)

remercie†, remercy† (rẹ-mėr'si), *v. t.* [< OF. F. *remercier* (= Pr. *remarciar*), thank, < *re-*, again, + *mercier*, thank, < *merci*, thanks: see *mercy*.] To thank.

> She him *remercied* as the Patrone of her life.
> *Spenser*, F. Q., II. xi. 16.

remerciest, *n. pl.* [< *remercie*, *v.*] Thanks.

> So mildely did he, beying the conquerour, take the vnthankefulnesse of persones by hym conquered & subdued who did . . . not render thaunkes ne sale *remercies* for that thei had been let bothe safe and sounde.
> *Udall*, tr. of Apophthegms of Erasmus, ii. Philippos, § 7.

remercy†, *v. t.* See *remercie*.

remerge (rē-mėrj'), *v. i.* [< L. *remergere*, dip in or immerse again, < *re-*, again, + *mergere*, dip: see *merge*.] To merge again.

> That each, who seems a separate whole,
> Should move his rounds, and, fusing all
> The skirts of self again, should fall
> *Remerging* in the general Soul,
> Is faith as vague as all unsweet.
> *Tennyson*, In Memoriam, xlvii.

remeve†, *v.* A Middle English variant of *remove*.

remew†, remue†, *v. t.* [ME. *remewen*, *remuen*, < OF. *remuer*, F. *remuer*, move, stir, = Pr. Sp. Pg. *remudar* = It. *rimutare*, change, alter, transform, < ML. *remutare*, change, < L. *re-*, again, + *mutare*, change: see *mew*[3] and *mue*. The sense in ME. and OF. is appar. due in part to confusion with *remove* (ME. *remeven*, etc.).] To remove.

> The hors of bras, that may nat be *remewed*,
> It stant as it were to the ground yglewed.
> *Chaucer*, Squire's Tale, l. 173.

> Sette eke noon almondes but greet and newe,
> And hem is best in Feveryere *remewe*.
> *Palladius*, Husbondrie (E. E. T. S.), p. 54.

remex (rē'meks), *n.*; pl. *remiges* (rem'i-jēz). [NL., < L. *remex* (*remig-*), a rower, oarsman, < *remus*, an oar, + *agere*, move.] In *ornith.*, one of the flight-feathers; one of the large stiff quill-feathers of a bird's wing which form most of its spread and correspond to the rectrices or rudder-feathers of the tail. They are distinguished from ordinary contour-feathers by never having aftershafts, and by being almost entirely of pennaceous structure. They are divided into three series, the primaries, the secondaries, and the tertiaries or tertials, according to their seat upon the pinion, the forearm, or the upper arm. See diagram under *bird*[1].

remiform (rem'i-fôrm), *a.* [< L. *remus*, an oar, + *forma*, form.] Shaped like an oar.

remigable (rem'i-gạ-bl), *a.* [< L. *remigare*, row (< *remus*, an oar, + *agere*, move), + *-able*.] Capable of being rowed upon; fit to float an oared boat.

> Where steril *remigable* marshes now
> Feed neighb'ring cities, and admit the plough.
> *Cotton*, tr. of Montaigne, xxiv. (*Davies.*)

remiges, *n.* Plural of *remex*.

Remigia (rẹ-mij'i-ạ̈), *n.* [NL. (Guenée, 1852), < L. *remigium*, a rowing: see *remex*.] A genus of noctuid moths, typical of the family *Remigiidæ*, distinguished by the vertical, moderately long palpi with the third joint lanceolate. The genus is wide-spread, and comprises about 20 species, more common in tropical America than elsewhere.

remigial (rẹ-mij'i-ạl), *a.* [< NL. *remex* (*remig-*) + *-al*.] Of or pertaining to a remex or remiges.

> In this the *remigial* streamers do not lose their barbs.
> *A. Newton*, Encyc. Brit., X. 712.

Remigiidæ (rem-i-jī'i-dē), *n. pl.* [NL. (Guenée, 1852), < *Remigia* + *-idæ*.] A family of noctuid moths, typified by the genus *Remigia*, with stout bodies, and in the male sex with very hairy legs, the hind pair woolly and the tarsi densely tufted. It is a widely distributed family, comprising 7 genera. Usually written *Remigidæ*, and, as a subfamily, *Remiginæ*.

remigrate (rem'i-grāt or rē-mī'grāt), *v. i.* [< L. *remigratus*, pp. of *remigrare*, go back, return, < *re-*, back, + *migrare*, migrate: see *migrate*.] To migrate again; remove to a former place or state; return.

> When the salt of tartar from which it is distilled hath retained or deprived it of the sulphurous parts of the spirit of wine, the rest, which is incomparably the greater part of the liquor, will *remigrate* into phlegm.
> *Boyle*, Works, I. 499.

remigration (rem-i-grā'shọn or rē-mī-grā'shọn), *n.* [< *remigrate* + *-ion*.] Repeated migration; removal back; a migration to a place formerly occupied.

> The Scots, transplanted hither, became acquainted with our customs, which, by occasional *remigrations*, became diffused in Scotland. *Hale.*

Remijia (rẹ-mij'i-ạ̈), *n.* [NL. (A. P. de Candolle, 1829), named from a surgeon, *Remijo*, who used its bark instead of cinchona.] A genus of gamopetalous shrubs of the order *Rubiaceæ*, tribe *Cinchoneæ*, and subtribe *Eucinchoneæ*. It is characterized by a woolly and salver-shaped corolla with five valvate lobes and a smooth and enlarged throat, and by a septicidal two-celled and somewhat ovoid capsule, with numerous peltate seeds and subcordate seed-leaves. The 13 species are all natives of tropical America. They are shrubs or small and slender trees, with weak and almost unbranched stem, bearing opposite or whorled revolute leaves, sometimes large, thick, and coriaceous, often with very large lanceolate stipules. The flowers are rather small, white or rose-colored, and fragrant, clustered in axillary and prolonged racemes. Several species are still in medicinal use. See *cuprea-bark*, *cupreine*, and *cinchonamine*.

remind (rẹ-mīnd'), *v. t.* [< *re-* + *mind*[1]; appar. suggested by *remember*.] To put in mind; bring to the remembrance of; recall or bring to the notice of: as, to *remind* a person of his promise.

> Where mountain, river, forest, field, and grove
> *Remind* him of his Maker's pow'r and love.
> *Cowper*, Retirement, l. 30.

> I have often to go through a distinct process of thought to *remind* myself that I am in New England, and not in Middle England still.
> *E. A. Freeman*, Amer. Lects., p. 170.

reminder (rẹ-mīn'dėr), *n.* [< *remind* + *-er*[1].] One who or that which reminds; anything which serves to awaken remembrance.

remindful (rẹ-mīnd'fůl), *a.* [< *remind* + *-ful*.] 1. Tending or adapted to remind; careful to remind. *Southey.*

> The slanting light touched the crests of the clods in a newly ploughed field to her left with a vivid effect, *remindful* of the light-capped wavelets on an eventful bay.
> *Harper's Mag.*, LXXVI. 212.

2. Remembering.

> Meanwhile, *remindful* of the convent bars,
> Bianca did not watch these signs in vain.
> *Hood*, Bianca's Dream, st. 32.

remingtonite (rem'ing-tọn-īt), *n.* [Named after Mr. Edward *Remington*, at one time superintendent of the mine where it was found.] A little-known mineral occurring as a thin rose-colored coating in serpentine in Maryland. It is essentially a hydrated carbonate of cobalt.

Remington rifle. See *rifle*[2].

reminiscence (rem-i-nis'ẹns), *n.* [< OF. *reminiscence*, F. *réminiscence* = Pr. Sp. Pg. *reminiscencia* = It. *reminiscenza*, *reminiscenzia*, < LL. *reminiscentiæ*, pl., remembrances, < L. *reminiscen(t-)s*, ppr. of *reminisci*, remember: see *reminiscent*.] 1. The act or power of recollecting; recollection; the voluntary exertion of the reproductive faculty of the understanding; the recalling of the past to mind.

> I cast about for all circumstances that may revive my memory or *reminiscence*.
> *Sir M. Hale*, Orig. of Mankind. (*Latham.*)

> The reproductive faculty is governed by the laws which regulate the succession of our thoughts — the laws, as they are called, of mental association. If these laws are allowed to operate without the intervention of the will, this faculty may be called suggestion or spontaneous suggestion. Whereas, if applied under the influence of the will, it will properly obtain the name of *reminiscence* or recollection. *Sir W. Hamilton*, Metaph., xx.

2. That which is recollected or recalled to mind; a relation of what is recollected; a narration of past incidents, events, and characteristics within one's personal knowledge: as, the *reminiscences* of a quinquagenarian.

> I will here mention what is the most important of all my *reminiscences*, viz. that in my childhood my mother was to me everything.
> H. C. *Robinson*, Diary, Reminiscences and Correspondence, i.

3. In *music*, a composition which is not intended to be original in its fundamental idea, but only in its manner of treatment.=**Syn.** 1. *Recollection, Remembrance*, etc. See *memory*.

reminiscency† (rem-i-nis'ẹn-si), *n.* [As *reminiscence* (see *-cy*).] Reminiscence.

> *Reminiscency*, when she [the soul] searches out something that she has let slip out of her memory.
> *Dr. H. More*, Immortal. of Soul, ii. 5.

reminiscent (rem-i-nis'ẹnt), *a.* and *n.* [< L. *reminiscen(t-)s*, ppr. of *reminisci*, remember, < *re-*, again, + *min-*, base of *me-min-isse*, remember, think over, akin to *men(t-)s*, mind: see *mental*[1], *mind*[1], etc. *Reminiscent* is not connected with *remember*.] I. *a.* Having the faculty of memory; calling to mind; remembering; also, inclined to recall the past; habitually dwelling on the past.

> Some other state of which we have been previously conscious, and are now *reminiscent*. *Sir W. Hamilton.*

> During the earlier stages of human evolution, then, imagination, being almost exclusively *reminiscent*, is almost incapable of evolving new ideas.
> *H. Spencer*, Prin. of Psychol., § 492.

II. *n.* One who calls to mind and records past events.

reminiscential (rem'i-ni-sen'shạl), *a.* [< *reminiscent* + *-ial*.] Of or pertaining to reminiscence or recollection.

> Would truth dispense, we could be content, with Plato, that knowledge were but remembrance, that intellectual acquisition were but *reminiscential* evocation, and new impressions but the colouring of old stamps which stood pale in the soul before.
> *Sir T. Browne*, Vulg. Err., Pref., p. i.

> At the sound of the name, no *reminiscential* atoms . . . stirred and marshalled themselves in my brain.
> *Lowell*, Fireside Travels, p. 90.

reminiscentially (rem″i-ni-sen′shal-i), *adv.* In a reminiscential manner; by way of calling to mind.

Reminiscere Sunday. [So called because the Sarum introit, taken from Ps. xxv. 6, begins with the word *reminiscere* (L. *reminiscere*, impv. of *reminisci*, remember: see *reminiscent*).] The second Sunday in Lent. Also *Reminiscere*.

reminiscion†, *n.* [Irreg. < *reminisc(ent)* + *-ion*.] Remembrance; reminiscence.

> Stir my thoughts
> With *reminiscion* of the spirit's promise.
> *Chapman*, Bussy D'Ambois, v. 1.

reminiscitory (rem-i-nis′i-tō-ri), *a.* [< *reminisc(ent)* + *-it-ory*.] Remembering, or having to do with the memory; reminiscential. [Rare.]

> I still bore a *reminiscitory* spite against Mr. Job Jonson, which I was fully resolved to wreak. *Bulwer*, Pelham, lxxiii.

remiped (rem′i-ped), *a.* and *n.* [< LL. *remipes*, oar-footed, < L. *remus*, an oar, + *pes* (*ped-*) = E. *foot*.] **I.** *a.* Having oar-shaped feet, or feet that are used as oars; oar-footed.

II. *n.* A remiped animal, as a crustacean or an insect.

Remipes (rem′i-pēz), *n.* [NL.: see *remiped*.] 1. In *Crustacea*, a genus of crabs of the family *Hippidæ*. *R. testudinarius* is an Australian species.—2. In *entom.*: (*a*) A genus of coleopterous insects. (*b*) A genus of hemipterous insects.

remise (rē-mīz′), *n.* [< OF. *remise*, delivery, release, restoration, reference, remitting, etc., F. *remise*, a delivery, release, allowance, delay, livery (*voiture de remise*, a livery-carriage); cf. LL. *remissa*, pardon, remission; < L. *remissa*, fem. of *remissus* (> F. *remis*), pp. of *remittere* (> F. *remettre*), remit, release: see *remit*.] 1. In *law*, a granting back; a surrender; release, as of a claim.—2. A livery-carriage: so called (for French *voiture de remise*) as kept in a carriage-house, and distinguished from a fiacre or hackney-coach, which is found on a stand in the public street.

> This has made Glass for Coaches very cheap and common, so that even many of the Fiacres or Hackneys, and all the *Remises*, have one large Glass before. *Lister*, Journey to Paris, p. 142.

3. In *fencing*, a second thrust which hits the mark after the first thrust has missed, made while the fencer is extended in the lunge. In modern fencing for points the remise is discouraged, being often ignored by judges as a count, because greater elegance and fairness are obtained if the fencer returns to his guard when his first thrust has not reached, and parries the return blow of his opponent.

remise (rē-mīz′), *v. t.*; pret. and pp. *remised*, ppr. *remising*. [< *remise*, *n.*] 1†. To send back; remit.

> Yet think not that this Too-too-Much *remises*
> Ought into nought; it but the Form disguises.
> *Sylvester*, tr. of Du Bartas's Weeks, i. 2.

2. To give or grant back; release a claim to; resign or surrender by deed.

> The words generally used therein [that is, in releases] are *remised*, released, and for ever quit-claimed. *Blackstone*, Com., II. xx.

remiss (rē-mis′), *a.* and *n.* [= OF. *remis*, F. *remis* = Sp. *remiso* = Pg. *remisso* = It. *rimesso*, < L. *remissus*, slack, remiss, pp. of *remittere*, remit, slacken, etc.: see *remit*.] **I.** *a.* **1.** Not energetic or diligent in performance; careless in performing duty or business; not complying with engagements at all, or not in due time; negligent; dilatory; slack.

> The prince must think me tardy and *remiss*. *Shak.*, T. and C., iv. 4. 143.

> It often happens that they who are most secure of truth on their side are most apt to be *remiss* and careless, and to comfort themselves with some good old sayings, as God will provide, and Truth will prevail. *Stillingfleet*, Sermons, II. i.

> Bashfulness, melancholy, timorousness, cause many of us to be too backward and *remiss*. *Burton*, Anat. of Mel., p. 107.

2. Wanting earnestness or activity; slow; relaxed; languid.

> The water deserts the corpuscles, unless it flow with a precipitate motion; for then it hurries them out along with it, till its motion becomes more languid and *remiss*. *Woodward*.

=**Syn.** 1. *Neglectful*, etc. (see *negligent*), careless, thoughtless, inattentive, slothful, backward, behindhand.

II.† *n.* An act of negligence.

> Such manner of men as, by negligence of Magistrates and *remisses* of lawes, euery countrie breedeth great store of. *Puttenham*, Arte of Eng. Poesie (ed. Arber), p. 55.

remissailes†, *n. pl.* [ME. *remyssailes*, < OF. **remissailles*, < *remis*, pp. of *remettre*, cast aside: see *remiss*, *remit*.] Leavings; scraps; pieces of refuse.

> Laade not thy trenchour with many *remyssailes*. *Babees Book* (E. E. T. S.), p. 28.

remissful (rē-mis′fůl), *a.* [< *remiss* + *-ful*.] Ready to grant remission or pardon; forgiving; gracious. [Rare.]

> As though the Heavens, in their *remissful* doom,
> Took those best-lov'd from worser days to come.
> *Drayton*, Barons' Wars, i. 11.

remissibility (rē-mis-i-bil′i-ti), *n.* [< *remissible* + *-ity* (see *-bility*).] Capability of being remitted or abated; the character of being remissible.

> This is a greater testimony of the certainty of the *remissibility* of our greatest sins. *Jer. Taylor*, Holy Dying, v. 5.

> The eleventh and last of all the properties that seem to be requisite in a lot of punishment is that of *remissibility*. *Bentham*, Introd. to Morals and Legislation, xv. 25.

remissible (rē-mis′i-bl), *a.* [< OF. *remissible*, F. *rémissible* = Sp. *remisible* = Pg. *remissivel* = It. *remissibile*, < LL. *remissibilis*, pardonable, easy, light, < L. *remittere*, pp. *remissus*, remit, pardon: see *remit*, *remiss*.] Capable of being remitted or forgiven.

> They [papists] allow them [certain sins] to be such as deserve punishment, although such as are easily pardonable: *remissible*, of course, or expiable by an easy penitence. *Feltham*, Resolves, ii. 9.

remissio injuriæ (rē-mis′i-ō in-jö′ri-ē). [L.: *remissio*, remission; *injuriæ*, gen. of *injuria*, injury: see *injury*.] In *Scots law*, in an action of divorce for adultery, a plea implying that the pursuer has already forgiven the offense; condonation.

remission (rē-mish′on), *n.* [< ME. *remission*, *remissioun*, < OF. *remission*, F. *rémission* = Pr. *remissio* = Sp. *remision* = Pg. *remissão* = It. *remissione*, *rimissione*, < L. *remissio(n-)*, a sending back, relaxation, < *remittere*, pp. *remissus*, send back, remit: see *remit*.] The act of remitting. (*a*†) The act of sending back.

> The fate of her [Lot's wife] . . . gave rise to the poets' fiction of the loss of Eurydice and her *remission* into hell, for her husband's turning to look upon her. *Stackhouse*, Hist. Bible, iii. 1. (*Latham.*)

(*b*) The act of sending to a distant place, as money; remittance.

> The *remission* of a million every year to England. *Swift*, To the Abp. of Dublin, Concerning the Weavers.

(*c*) Abatement; a temporary subsidence, as of the force or violence of a disease or of pain, as distinguished from *intermission*, in which the disease leaves the patient entirely for a time.

> Remittent [fever] has a morning *remission*; yellow fever has not. *Quain*, Med. Dict., p. 1335.

(*d*) Diminution or cessation of intensity; abatement; relaxation; moderation: as, the *remission* of extreme rigor; the *remission* of close study or of labor.

> As too much bending breaketh the bowe, so too much *remission* spoyleth the minde. *Lyly*, Euphues, Anat. of Wit, p. 112.

> Darkness fell
> Without *remission* of the blast or shower.
> *Wordsworth*.

(*e*) Discharge or relinquishment, as of a debt, claim, or right; a giving up: as, the *remission* of a tax or duty.

> Another ground of the bishop's fears is the *remission* of the first fruits and tenths. *Swift*.

(*f*) The act of forgiving; forgiveness; pardon; the giving up of the punishment due to a crime.

> Neuerthelesse, to them that with deuocion beholde it afer is graunted clene *remyssyon*. *Sir R. Guylforde*, Pylgrymage, p. 30.

> My penance is to call Lucetta back,
> And ask *remission* for my folly past.
> *Shak.*, T. G. of V., i. 2. 65.

> All wickedness is weakness; that plea therefore
> With God or man will gain thee no *remission*.
> *Milton*, S. A., l. 835.

Intension and remission of forms†. See *intension*.—**Remission of sins**, in *Scrip.*, deliverance from the guilt and penalty of sin. The same word (ἄφεσις) is in the authorized version translated *remission* (Mat. xxvi. 28, etc.), *forgiveness* (Col. i. 14), and *deliverance* (Luke iv. 18).—**Remission Thursday.** Same as *Maundy Thursday* (which see, under *maundy*). =**Syn.** (*f*) *Absolution*, etc. See *pardon*.

remissive (rē-mis′iv), *a.* [= Sp. *remisivo*, < L. *remissivus*, relaxing, laxative: see *remiss*.] 1. Slackening; relaxing; causing abatement.

> Who bore by turns great Ajax' seven-fold shield;
> Whene'er he breathed *remissive* of his might,
> Tired with the incessant slaughters of the fight.
> *Pope*, Iliad, xiii. 887.

2. Remitting; forgiving; pardoning.

> O Lord, of thy abounding love
> To my offence *remissive* be.
> *Wither*, tr. of the Psalms, p. 96. (*Latham.*)

remissly (rē-mis′li), *adv.* In a remiss or negligent manner; carelessly; without close attention; slowly; slackly; not vigorously; languidly; without ardor.

remissness (rē-mis′nes), *n.* The state or character of being remiss; slackness; carelessness; negligence; lack of ardor or vigor; lack of attention to any business, duty, or engagement in the proper time or with the requisite industry.

> The extraordinary *remissenesse* of discipline had (til his coming) much detracted from the reputation of that Colledg. *Evelyn*, Diary, May 10, 1687.

=**Syn.** *Oversight*, etc. See *negligence*.

remissory (rē-mis′ō-ri), *a.* [= Sp. *remisorio*, < ML. **remissorius*, remissory, < L. *remittere*, pp. *remissus*, remit: see *remiss*, *remit*.] Pertaining to remission; serving or tending to remit; obtaining remission.

> They would have us saved by a daily oblation propitiatory, by a sacrifice expiatory or *remissory*. *Latimer*, Sermon of the Plough.

remit (rē-mit′), *v.*; pret. and pp. *remitted*, ppr. *remitting*. [Early mod. E. also *remytte*; < ME. *remitten*, < OF. *remettre*, *remetre*, also *remitter*, F. *remettre* = Pr. *remetre* = Sp. *remitir* = Pg. *remittir* = It. *rimettere*, < L. *remittere*, send back, abate, remit (LL. pardon), < *re-*, back, + *mittere*, send: see *missile*, *mission*. Cf. *admit*, *commit*, *emit*, *permit*[1], etc.] **I.** *trans.* **1**†. To send back.

> And, reverent maister, *remitte* me summe letter by the bringer her of. *Paston Letters*, II. 67.

> Whether earth 's an animal, and air
> Imbibes, her lungs with coolness to repair,
> And what she sucks, *remits*, she still requires
> Inlets for air, and outlets for her fires.
> *Dryden*, tr. of Ovid's Metamorph., xv.

2. To transmit or send, as money, bills, or other things in payment for goods received.

> I have received that money which was *remitted* here in order to release me from captivity. *Goldsmith*, Citizen of the World, lxxvi.

> He promised to *remit* me what he owed me out of the first money he should receive, but I never heard of him after. *Franklin*, Autobiog., p. 58.

3. To restore; replace.

> In this case the law *remits* him to his ancient and more certain right. *Blackstone*. (*Imp. Dict.*)

4. To transfer. [Rare.]

> He that vsed to teache did not commonlie vse to beate, but *remitted* that ouer to an other mans charge. *Ascham*, The Scholemaster, p. 48.

5. In *law*, to transfer (a cause) from one tribunal or judge to another, particularly from an appellate court to the court of original jurisdiction. See *remit*, *n.*—6. To refer.

> Wheche mater I *remytte* ondly to youre ryght wyse discrecion. *Paston Letters*, I. 321.

> In the sixth Year of his Reign, a Controversy arising between the two Archbishops of Canterbury and York, they appealed to Rome, and the Pope *remitted* it to the King and Bishops of England. *Baker*, Chronicles, p. 28.

> How I have
> Studied your fair opinion, I *remit*
> To time. *Shirley*, Hyde Park, ii. 4.

> The arbiter, an officer to whom the prætor is supposed to have *remitted* questions of fact as to a jury. *Encyc. Brit.*, II. 312.

7. To give or deliver up; surrender; resign.

> *Prin.* Will you have me, or your pearl again?
> *Biron.* Neither of either; I *remit* both twain.
> *Shak.*, L. L. L., v. 2. 459.

> The Egyptian crown I to your hands *remit*.
> *Dryden*, Tyrannic Love, iii. 1.

8. To slacken; relax the tension of; hence, figuratively, to diminish in intensity; make less intense or violent; abate.

> Those other motives which gave the animadversions no leave to *remit* a continuall vehemence throughout the book. *Milton*, Apology for Smectymnuus.

> As when a bow is successively intended and *remitted*. *Cudworth*, Intellectual System, p. 222.

> In a short time we *remit* our fervour, and endeavour to find some mitigation of our duty, and some more easy means of obtaining the same end. *Johnson*, Rambler, No. 65.

9. To refrain from exacting; give up, in whole or in part: as, to *remit* punishment.

> Thy slanders I forgive; and therewithal
> *Remit* thy other forfeits. *Shak.*, M. for M., v. 1. 526.

> *Remit* awhile the harsh command,
> And hear me, or my heart will break.
> *Crabbe*, Works, I. 248.

10. To pardon; forgive.

> Whose soever sins ye *remit*, they are *remitted* unto them. John xx. 23.

> 'Tis the law
> That, if the party who complains *remit*
> The offender, he is freed: is 't not so, lords?
> *Beau. and Fl.*, Laws of Candy, v. 1.

> *Remit*
> What 's past, and I will meet your best affection.
> *Shirley*, Hyde Park, v. 1.

11†. To omit; cease doing. [Rare.]

> I have *remitted* my verses all this while; I think I have forgot them. *B. Jonson*, Poetaster, iii. 1.

=**Syn.** 2. To forward.—9. To release, relinquish.

II. *intrans.* 1. To slacken; become less intense or rigorous.

> When our passions *remit*, the vehemence of our speech *remits* too. W. Broome, Notes on the Odyssey. (Johnson.)

> How often have I blest the coming day,
> When toil *remitting* lent its turn to play.
> Goldsmith, Des. Vil., l. 16.

> She [Sorrow] takes, when harsher moods *remit*,
> What slender shade of doubt may flit,
> And makes it vassal unto love.
> Tennyson, In Memoriam, xlviii.

2. To abate by growing less earnest, eager, or active.

> By degrees they *remitted* of their industry, loathed their business, and gave way to their pleasures. South.

3. In *med.*, to abate in violence for a time without intermission: as, a fever *remits* at a certain hour every day.—4. In *com.*, to transmit money, etc.

> They obliged themselves to *remit* after the rate of twelve hundred thousand pounds sterling per annum. Addison.

Remitting bilious fever, remitting icteric fever. See *fever*1.

remit (rē̦-mit′), *n.* [< *remit*, *v.*] 1. In *Scots law*, a remission; a sending back. In judicial procedure, applied to an interlocutor or judgment transferring a cause either totally or partially, or for some specific purpose, from one tribunal or judge to another, or to a judicial nominee, for the execution of the purposes of the remit.
2. A formal communication from a body having higher jurisdiction, to one subordinate to it.

remitment (rē̦-mit′me̤nt), *n.* [< *remit* + *-ment*. Cf. It. *rimettimento*.] The act of remitting, or the state of being remitted; remission; remittance; forgiveness; pardon.

> Yet all law, and God's law especially, grants every where to error easy *remitments*, even where the utmost penalty exacted were no undoing. Milton, Tetrachordon.

remittable (rē̦-mit′a̤-bl), *a.* [< *remit* + *-able*.] Same as *remissible*. Cotgrave.

remittal (rē̦-mit′al), *n.* [< *remit* + *-al*.] 1. A remitting; a giving up; surrender.—2. The act of sending, as money; remittance.

> I received letters from some bishops of Ireland, to solicit the Earl of Wharton about the *remittal* of the first-fruits and tenths to the clergy there. Swift, Change in the Ministry.

remittance (rē̦-mit′a̤ns), *n.* [< *remit* + *-ance*.] 1. The act of transmitting money, bills, or the like, to another place.—2. A sum, bills, etc., remitted in payment.

remittancer (rē̦-mit′a̤n-sėr), *n.* [< *remittance* + *-er*1.] One who sends a remittance.

> Your memorialist was stopped and arrested at Bayonne, by order from his *remittancers* at Madrid. Cumberland, Memoirs, II. 170. (Latham.)

remittee (rē̦-mit-ē′), *n.* [< *remit* + *-ee*1.] A person to whom a remittance is sent.

remittent (rē̦-mit′e̤nt), *a.* and *n.* [= F. *rémettant* = Sp. *remitente* = Pg. *remittente* = It. *rimettente*, < L. *remitten(t-)s*, ppr. of *remittere*, remit, abate: see *remit*.] I. *a.* Temporarily abating; having remissions from time to time: noting diseases the symptoms of which diminish very considerably, but never entirely disappear as in intermittent diseases.—**Bilious, epidemic, infantile, marsh remittent fever.** See *fever*1.—**Remittent bilious fever.** See *fever*1.—**Remittent fever.** See *fever*1.—**Yellow remittent fever.** See *fever*1.
II. *n.* Same as *remittent fever* (which see, under *fever*1).

remitter1 (rē̦-mit′ėr), *n.* [< *remit* + *-er*1.] One who remits. (*a*) One who makes remittance for payment. (*b*) One who pardons.

> Not properly pardoners, forgivers, or *remitters* of sin, as though the sentence in heaven depended upon the sentence in earth. Fulke, Against Allen, p. 143. (Latham.)

remitter2 (rē̦-mit′ėr), *n.* [< OF. *remitter*, *remettre*, inf. used as a noun: see *remit*, *v.*] In *law*, the sending or setting back of a person to a title or right he had before; the restitution of a more ancient and certain right to a person who has right to lands, but is out of possession, and has afterward the freehold cast upon him by some subsequent defective title, by operation of law, by virtue of which he enters, the law in such case reinstating him as if possessing under his original title, free of encumbrances suffered by the possessor meanwhile.

> In Hillary term I went.
> You said, if I returned next 'size in Lent,
> I should be in *remitter* of your grace.
> Donne, Satires, ii.

remittor (rē̦-mit′o̤r), *n.* [< *remit* + *-or*1.] In *law*, same as *remitter*2.

remnant (rem′na̤nt), *a.* and *n.* [Contr. from *remenant*, *remanent*, < ME. *remenant*, *remenaunt*, < OF. *remenant*, *remenaunt*, remainder: see *remanent*.] I.† *a.* Remaining; yet left.

> But when he once had entred Paradise,
> The *remnant* world he lustly did despise.
> Sylvester, tr. of Du Bartas's Weeks, ii., Eden.

> And quiet dedicate her *remnant* Life
> To the just Duties of a humble Wife.
> Prior, Solomon, ii.

II. *n.* 1. That which is left or remains; the remainder; the rest.

> The *remenant* were anhanged, moore and lesse,
> That were consentant of this cursednesse.
> Chaucer, Physician's Tale, l. 275.

> The *remnant* that are left of the captivity there in the province are in great affliction and reproach. Neh. i. 3.

> Westward the wanton Zephyr wings his flight,
> Pleas'd with the *remnants* of departing light.
> Dryden, tr. of Ovid's Metamorph., i. 78.

2. Specifically, that which remains after the last cutting of a web of cloth, bolt of ribbon, or the like.

> Away, thou rag, thou quantity, thou *remnant!*
> Shak., T. of the S., iv. 3. 112.

> It is a garment made of *remnants*, a lite ravelled out into ends, a line discontinued. Donne, Letters, iv.

> I am old and good for nothing; but, as the store-keepers say of their *remnants* of cloth, I am but a fag end, and you may have me for what you please to give. The Century, XXXV. 742.

=**Syn.** *Residue*, etc. See *remainder*.

Remoboth, Remboth (rem′ō-both, rem′both), *n.* [Appar. Egypt.] In the *early church*, a class of monks who lived chiefly in cities in companies of two or three, without an abbot, and were accused of leading worldly and disorderly lives. Also called *Sarabaitæ*.

remodel (rē-mod′el), *v. t.* [< F. *remodeler*, remodel; as *re-* + *model*, *v.*] To model, shape, or fashion anew; reconstruct.

remodification (rē-mod″i-fi-kā′sho̤n), *n.* [< *remodify* + *-ation*, after *modification*.] The act of modifying again; a repeated modification or change. *Imp. Dict.*

remodify (rē-mod′i-fī), *v. t.* [< *re-* + *modify*.] To modify again; shape anew; reform. *Imp. Dict.*

remold, remould (rē-mōld′), *v. t.* [< *re-* + *mold*4.] To mold or shape anew. *H. Spencer*, Prin. of Sociol., § 578.

remoleculization (rē-mol-e-kū-li-zā′sho̤n), *n.* [< *re-* + *molecule* + *-ize* + *-ation*.] A rearrangement among the molecules of a body, leading to the formation of new compounds.

> The purpose of this [book] . . . is to suggest a theory of the manner in which the germs act in producing disease. It is that, through the power which the bacteria possess in the *remoleculization* of matter, they cause the formation and diffusion through the system of organic alkalies having poisonous qualities comparable with those of strychnine. Pop. Sci. Mo., XXVI. 134.

remollient (rē̦-mol′i-e̤nt), *a.* [< L. *remollien(t-)s*, ppr. of *remollire*, make soft again, soften: see *re-* and *mollify*.] Mollifying; softening. [Rare.]

remolten (rē-mōl′tn), *p. a.* [Pp. of *remelt*.] Melted again.

> It were good, therefore, to try whether glass *remoulten* do leese any weight. Bacon, Nat. Hist., § 799.

remonetization (rē-mon″e-ti-zā′sho̤n), *n.* [< F. *rémonétisation*; as *remonetize* + *-ation*.] The act of remonetizing.

remonetize (rē-mon′e-tīz), *v. t.*; pret. and pp. *remonetized*, ppr. *remonetizing*. [< F. *rémonétiser*; as *re-* + *monetize*.] To restore to circulation in the shape of money; make again a legal or standard money of account, as gold or silver coin. Also spelled *remonetise*.

remonstrable† (rē̦-mon′stra̤-bl), *a.* [< *remonstra(te)* + *-able*.] Capable of demonstration.

> Was it such a sin for Adam to eat a forbidden apple? Yes; the greatness is *remonstrable* in the event. Rev. T. Adams, Works, II. 356.

remonstrance (rē̦-mon′stra̤ns), *n.* [< OF. *remonstrance*, F. *remontrance* = It. *rimostranza*, < ML. *remonstrantia*, < *remonstran(t-)s*, ppr. of *remonstrare*, remonstrate: see *remonstrant*.] 1†. The act of remonstrating; demonstration; manifestation; show; exhibit; statement; representation.

> Make rash *remonstrance* of my hidden power.
> Shak., M. for M., v. 1. 397.

> The committee . . . concluded upon "a new general *remonstrance* to be made of the state of the kingdom." Clarendon, Civil Wars, I. 157.

> 'Tis strange,
> Having seven years expected, and so much
> *Remonstrance* of her husband's loss at sea,
> She should continue thus. Shirley, Hyde Park, i. 1.

2. The act of remonstrating; expostulation; strong representation of reasons, or statement of facts and reasons, against something complained of or opposed; hence, a paper containing such a representation or statement.

> A large family of daughters have drawn up a *remonstrance*, in which they set forth that, their father having refused to take in the Spectator . . . Addison.

> The English clergy, . . . when they have discharged the formal and exacted duties of religion, are not very forward, by gratuitous inspection and *remonstrance*, to keep alive and diffuse a due sense of religion in their parishioners. Sydney Smith, in Lady Holland, iii.

3. In the *Rom. Cath. Ch.*, same as *monstrance*.—4. [*cap.*] In *eccles. hist.*, a document consisting of five articles expressing the points of divergence of the Dutch Arminians (Remonstrants) from strict Calvinism, presented to the states of Holland and West Friesland in 1610.—**The Grand Remonstrance**, in *Eng. hist.*, a remonstrance presented to King Charles I., after adoption by the House of Commons, in 1641. It recited the recent abuses in the government, and outlined various reforms. =**Syn. 2.** Protest. See *censure*, *v.*

remonstrant (rē̦-mon′stra̤nt), *a.* and *n.* [= F. *remontrant* = It. *rimostrante*, < ML. *remonstran(t-)s*, ppr. of *remonstrare*, exhibit, remonstrate: see *remonstrate*.] I. *a.* 1. Expostulatory; urging strong reasons against an act; inclined or tending to remonstrate.

> "There are very valuable books about antiquities. . . . Why should Mr. Casaubon's not be valuable? . . ." said Dorothea, with more *remonstrant* energy. George Eliot, Middlemarch, xxii.

2. Belonging or pertaining to the Arminian party called Remonstrants.
II. *n.* 1. One who remonstrates.

> The defence of the *remonstrant*, as far as we are informed of it, is that he ought not to be removed because he has violated no law of Massachusetts. W. Phillips, Speeches, etc., p. 159.

Specifically—2. [*cap.*] One of the Arminians, who formulated their creed (A. D. 1610) in five articles entitled the *Remonstrance*.

> They have projected to reconcile the papists and the Lutherans and the Calvinists, the *remonstrants* and contra-remonstrants. Jer. Taylor, Works (ed. 1835), II. 54.

remonstrantly (rē̦-mon′strant-li), *adv.* In a remonstrant manner; remonstratively; as or by remonstrance.

> "Mother," said Deronda, *remonstrantly*, "don't let us think of it in that way." George Eliot, Daniel Deronda, liii.

remonstrate (rē̦-mon′strāt), *v.*; pret. and pp. *remonstrated*, ppr. *remonstrating*. [< ML. *remonstratus*, pp. of *remonstrare* (> It. *rimostrare* = F. *remontrer*), exhibit, represent, demonstrate, < L. *re-*, again, + *monstrare*, show, exhibit: see *monstration*, *monster*, *v.*, and cf. *demonstrate*.] I. *intrans.* 1†. To exhibit; demonstrate; prove.

> It [the death of Lady Carbery] was not . . . of so much trouble as two fits of a common ague; so careful was God to *remonstrate* to all that stood in that sad attendance that this soul was dear to him. Jer. Taylor, Funeral Sermon on Lady Carbery.

2. To exhibit or present strong reasons against an act, measure, or any course of proceedings; expostulate: as, to *remonstrate* with a person on his conduct; conscience *remonstrates* against a profligate life.

> Corporal Trim by being in the service had learned to obey, and not to *remonstrate*. Sterne, Tristram Shandy, ii. 16.

=**Syn. 2.** *Reprove*, *Rebuke*, etc. (see *censure*), object, protest, reason, complain.

II.† *trans.* 1. To show by a strong representation of reasons; set forth forcibly; show clearly.

> I consider that in two very great instances it was *remonstrated* that Christianity was the greatest prosecution of natural justice and equality in the whole world. Jer. Taylor, Great Exemplar, Pref., p. 15.

> De L'Isle, alarmed at the cruel purport of this unexpected visit, *remonstrated* to his brother officer the undesigning and good-natured warmth of his friend. Hist. Duelling (1770), p. 145.

2. To show or point out again.

> I will *remonstrate* to you the third door. B. Jonson.

remonstration (rē-mo̤n-strā′sho̤n), *n.* [< ML. *remonstratio(n-)*, < *remonstrare*, exhibit: see *remonstrate*.] The act of remonstrating; a remonstrance.

> He went many times over the case of his wife, the judgment of the doctor, his own repeated *remonstration*. Harper's Mag., LXIV. 243.

remonstrative (rē̦-mon′stra̤-tiv), *a.* [< *remonstrate* + *-ive*.] Of, belonging to, or characterized by remonstrance; expostulatory; remonstrant. *Imp. Dict.*

remonstratively (rē̦-mon′stra̤-tiv-li), *adv.* In a remonstrative manner; remonstrantly. *Imp. Dict.*

remonstrator (rē̦-mon′strā-to̤r), *n.* [< *remonstrate* + *-or*1.] One who remonstrates; a remonstrant.

> And orders were sent down for clapping up three of the chief *remonstrators*. Bp. Burnet, Hist. Own Times, an. 1660.

remonstratory (rẹ̄-mon'strạ̄-tọ̄-ri), *a.* [< *remonstrate* + *-ory.*] Expostulatory; remonstrative. [Rare.]

"Come, come, Sikes," said the Jew, appealing to him in a *remonstratory* tone. *Dickens*, Oliver Twist, xvi.

remontant (rẹ̄-mon'tạnt), *a.* and *n.* [< F. *remontant*, ppr. of *remonter*, remount: see *remount.*] I. *a.* In *hort.*, blooming a second time late in the season: noting a class of roses.

The Baronne Prévost, which is now the oldest type among hybrid *remontant* roses. *The Century*, XXVI. 350.

II. *n.* In *hort.*, a hybrid perpetual rose which blooms twice in a season.

Beautiful white roses, whose places have not been filled by any of the usurping *remontants*. *The Century*, XXVI. 350.

remontoir (re-mon-twor'), *n.* [< F. *remontoir*, < *remonter*, wind up: see *remount.*] In *horol.*, a kind of escapement in which a uniform impulse is given to the pendulum or balance by a special contrivance upon which the train of wheel-work acts, instead of communicating directly with the pendulum or balance.

remora (rem'ọ̄-rạ̈), *n.* [= F. *rémora*, *rémore* = Sp. *rémora* = Pg. It. *remora*, < L. *remora*, a delay, hindrance, also the fish *echeneis*, the sucking-fish (cf. *remorari*, stay, delay), < *re-*, back, + *mora*, delay, the fish *echeneis* (see *Echeneis*).] 1†. Delay; obstacle; hindrance.

A gentle answer is an excellent *remora* to the progresses of anger, whether in thyself or others. *Jer. Taylor*, Works (ed. 1835), I. 214.

We had his promise to stay for us, but the *remora's* and disappointments we met with in the Road had put us backward in our Journey. *Maundrell*, Aleppo to Jerusalem, p. 46.

2. (*a*) The sucking-fish, *Echeneis remora*, or any fish of the family *Echeneididæ*, having on the top of the head a flattened oval adhesive surface by means of which it can attach itself firmly to various objects, as another fish, a ship's bottom, etc., but whether for protection or convoyance, or both, has not been satisfactorily ascertained. It was formerly believed to have the power of delaying or stopping ships. See cuts under *Echeneis* and *Rhombochirus*. (*b*) [*cap.*] [NL. (Gill, 1862).] A genus of such fishes, based on the species above-named.

All sodainely there clove unto her keele
A little fish, that men call *Remora*,
Which stopt her course.
Spenser, Worlds Vanitie, l. 108.

I am seized on here
By a land *remora;* I cannot stir,
Nor move, but as he pleases.
B. Jonson, Poetaster, iii. 1.

3. In *med.*, a stoppage or stagnation, as of the blood.—4. In *surg.*, an instrument to retain parts in place: not now in use.—5. In *her.*, a serpent: rare, confined to certain modern blazons.

remorate† (rem'ọ̄-rāt), *v. t.* [< L. *remoratus*, pp. of *remorari*, stay, linger, delay, hinder, defer, < *re-*, back, + *morari*, delay. Cf. *remora.*] To hinder; delay. *Imp. Dict.*

remorce†, *n.* An obsolete spelling of *remorse*.

remord† (rē-môrd'), *v.* [< ME. *remorden*, < OF. *remordre*, F. *remordre* = Pr. *remordre* = Cat. *remordir* = Sp. Pg. *remorder* = It. *rimordere*, < L. *remordere*, vex, disturb, lit. 'bite again,' < *re-*, again, + *mordere*, bite: see *mordant*. Cf. *remorse.*] I. *trans.* 1. To strike with remorse; touch with compassion.

Ye shul dullen of the rudenesse
Of us sely Trojans, but if routhe
Remorde yow, or vertu of youre trouthe.
Chaucer, Troilus, iv. 1491.

2. To afflict.

God . . . *remordith* som folk by adversite. *Chaucer*, Boëthius, iv. 6.

3. To rebuke.

Noght euere-like man that cales the lorde,
Or mercy askes, sal hafe thi blisc,
His consciencȝ bot he *remorde*,
And wirke thi wil, & mende his lyte.
Political Poems, etc. (ed. Furnivall), p. 108.

Rebukynge and *remordyng*,
And nothynge accordynge.
Skelton, Against the Scots.

II. *intrans.* To feel remorse.

His conscience *remording* agayne the destruction of so noble a prince. *Sir T. Elyot*, The Governour, ii. 5.

remordency† (rẹ̄-môr'dẹn-si), *n.* [< **remorden(t)* (< L. *remorden(t-)s*, ppr. of *remordere*, vex: see *remord*) + *-cy.*] Compunction; remorse.

That *remordency* of conscience, that extremity of grief, they feel within themselves. *Killingbeck*, Sermons, p. 175.

remore†, *v. t.* [< L. *remorari*, stay, hinder: see *remorate.*] To check; hinder.

No bargains or accounts to make:
Nor Land nor Lease to let or take:
Or if we had, should that *remore* us,
When all the world 's our own before us?
Brome, Jovial Crew, i.

remorse (rē-môrs'), *n.* [Formerly also *remorce;* < ME. *remors*, < OF. *remors*, F. *remords* = Pg. *remorso* = It. *rimorso*, < LL. *remorsus*, remorse, < L. *remordere*, pp. *remorsus*, vex: see *remord.*] 1. Intense and painful regret due to a consciousness of guilt; the pain of a guilty conscience; deep regret with self-condemnation.

The *Remorse* for his [King Richard's] Undutifulness towards his Father was living in him till he died. *Baker*, Chronicles, p. 67.

It is natural for a man to feel especial *remorse* at his sins when he first begins to think of religion; he ought to feel bitter sorrow and keen repentance. *J. H. Newman*, Parochial Sermons, i. 182.

We have her own confession at full length,
Made in the first *remorse*.
Browning, Ring and Book, I. 104.

2†. Sympathetic sorrow; pity; compassion.

"Pity," she cries, "some favour, some *remorse!*" *Shak.*, Venus and Adonis, l. 257.

I am too merciful, I find it, friends,
Of too soft a nature, to be an officer;
I bear too much *remorse*.
Fletcher (and another ?), Prophetess, iii. 2.

=**Syn.** 1. *Compunction, Regret*, etc. (see *repentance*), self-reproach, self-condemnation, anguish, stings of conscience.

remorsed† (rẹ̄-môrst'), *a.* [< *remorse* + *-ed*[2].] Feeling remorse or compunction.

The *remorsed* sinner begins first with the tender of burnt offerings. *Bp. Hall*, Contemplations (ed. Tegg), V. 169.

remorseful (rẹ̄-môrs'fụ̇l), *a.* [Formerly also *remorceful;* < *remorse* + *-ful.*] 1. Full of remorse; impressed with a sense of guilt.—2†. Compassionate; feeling tenderly.

He was none of these *remorseful* men,
Gentle and affable; but fierce at all times, and mad then.
Chapman, Iliad, xx.

3†. Causing compassion; pitiable.

Eurylochus straight hasted the report
Of this his fellowes most *remorceful* fate.
Chapman, Odyssey, x.

=**Syn.** 1. See *repentance*.

remorsefully (rẹ̄-môrs'fụ̇l-i), *adv.* In a remorseful manner.

remorsefulness (rẹ̄-môrs'fụ̇l-nes), *n.* The state of being remorseful.

remorseless (rẹ̄-môrs'les), *a.* [Formerly also *remorceless;* < *remorse* + *-less.*] Without remorse; unpitying; cruel; insensible to distress.

Women are soft, mild, pitiful, and flexible;
Thou stern, obdurate, flinty, rough, *remorseless*.
Shak., 3 Hen. VI., i. 4. 142.

Atropos for Lucina came,
And with *remorseless* cruelty
Spoil'd at once both fruit and tree.
Milton, Epitaph on M. of Win., l. 29.

=**Syn.** Pitiless, merciless, ruthless, relentless, unrelenting, savage.

remorselessly (rẹ̄-môrs'les-li), *adv.* In a remorseless manner; without remorse.

remorselessness (rẹ̄-môrs'les-nes), *n.* The state or quality of being remorseless; insensibility to distress.

remote (rẹ̄-mōt'), *a.* [< ME. *remote*, < OF. *remot*, m., *remote*, f., = Sp. Pg. *remoto* = It. *remoto*, *rimoto*, < L. *remotus*, pp. of *removere*, remove: see *remove.*] 1. Distant in place; not near; far removed: as, a *remote* country; a *remote* people.

Here oon [tree], there oon to leve a fér *remote*
I holde is goode.
Palladius, Husbondrie (E. E. T. S.), p. 150.

Remote, unfriended, melancholy, slow,
Or by the lazy Scheldt, or wandering Po.
Goldsmith, Traveller, l. 1.

2. Distant or far away, in any sense. (*a*) Distant in time, past or future: as, *remote* antiquity.

It is not all *remote* and even apparent good that affects us. *Locke*.

The hour conceal'd, and so *remote* the fear,
Death still draws nearer, never seeming near.
Pope, Essay on Man, iii. 75.

When *remote* futurity is brought
Before the keen inquiry of her thought.
Cowper, Table-Talk, l. 492.

Some say that gleams of a *remoter* world
Visit the soul in sleep. *Shelley*, Mont Blanc, iii.

Do we not know that what is *remote* and indefinite affects men far less than what is near and certain? *Macaulay*, Disabilities of Jews.

(*b*) Mediate; by intervention of something else; not proximate.

From the effect to the *remotest* cause. *Granville*.

Their nimble nonsense takes a shorter course, . . .
And gains *remote* conclusions at a Jump.
Cowper, Conversation, l. 154.

The animal has sympathy, and is moved by sympathetic impulses, but these are never altruistic; the ends are never *remote*. *G. H. Lewes*, Probs. of Life and Mind, I. ii. § 61.

(*c*) Alien; foreign; not agreeing: as, a proposition *remote* from reason. (*d*) Separated; abstracted.

As nothing ought to be more in our wishes, so nothing seems more *remote* from our hopes, than the Universal Peace of the Christian World. *Stillingfleet*, Sermons, II. vi.

These small waves raised by the evening wind are as *remote* from storm as the smooth reflecting surface. *Thoreau*, Walden, p. 140.

Wherever the mind places itself by any thought, either amongst or *remote* from all bodies, it can in this uniform idea of space nowhere find any bounds. *Locke*, Human Understanding, II. xvii. 4.

(*e*) Distant in consanguinity or affinity: as, a *remote* kinsman. (*f*) Slight; inconsiderable; not closely connected; having slight relation: as, a *remote* analogy between cases; a *remote* resemblance in form or color; specifically, in the *law of evidence*, having too slight a bearing upon the question in controversy to afford any ground for inference. (*g*) In *music*, having but slight relation. See *relation*, 8. (*h*) In *zoöl.* and *bot.*, distant from one another; few or sparse, as spots on a surface, etc.—**Remote cause**, the cause of a cause; a cause which contributes to the production of the effect by the concurrence of another cause of the same kind.—**Remote key.** See *key*[1].—**Remote matter.** (*a*†) In *metaph.*, matter unprepared for the reception of any particular form. (*b*) In *logic:* (1) The terms of a syllogism, as contradistinguished from the propositions, which latter are the immediate matter. (2) Terms of a proposition which are of such a nature that it is impossible that one should be true of the other.

When is a proposition said to consist of *matter remote* or unnatural? When the predicat agreeth no manner of way with the subject: as, a man is a horse. *Blundeville*, Arte of Logicke (1599), iii. 3.

Remote mediate mark. See *mark*[1].—**Remote possibility**, in *law*. See *possibility*, 3.

remoted†, *a.* [< *remote* + *-ed*[2].] Removed; distant.

I must now go wander like a Caine
In forraigne Countries and *remoted* climes.
Heywood, Woman Killed with Kindness.

remotely (rẹ̄-mōt'li), *adv.* In a remote manner. (*a*) At a distance in space or time; not nearly. (*b*) Not proximately; not directly: as, *remotely* connected. (*c*) Slightly; in a small degree: as, to be *remotely* affected by an event.

remoteness (rẹ̄-mōt'nes), *n.* 1. The state of being remote, in any sense.—2. In the *law of conveyancing*, a ground of objection to the validity of an estate in real property, attempted to be created, but not created in such manner as to take effect within the time prescribed by law (computed with reference to a life or lives in being), so that, if carried into effect, it would protract the inalienability of land against the policy of the law. See *perpetuity*.

remotion (rẹ̄-mō'shọn), *n.* [< OF. **remotion* = Sp. *remocion* = Pg. *remoção* = It. *rimozione*, < L. *remotio(n-)*, a removing, removal, < *removere*, pp. *remotus*, remove: see *remove*, *remote.*] 1†. The act of removing; removal.

This act persuades me
That this *remotion* of the duke and her
Is practice only. *Shak.*, Lear, ii. 4. 115.

2. The state of being remote; remoteness. [Rare.]

The sort of idealized life—life in a state of *remotion*, unrealized, and translated into a neutral world of high cloudy antiquity—which the tragedy of Athens demanded for its atmosphere. *De Quincey*, Theory of Greek Tragedy.

remotive† (rẹ̄-mō'tiv), *a.* [< *remote* + *-ive.*] Removing, in the sense of declaring impossible.—**Remotive proposition**, in *logic*, a proposition which declares a relation to be impossible: thus, to say that a man is blind is only privative, but to say that a statue is incapable of seeing is *remotive*.

remould, *v. t.* See *remold*.

remount (rē-mount'), *v.* [< ME. *remounten*, < OF. (and F.) *remonter*, mount again, reascend, F. *remonter*, mount again, furnish again, wind again, etc., = Sp. Pg. *remontar* = It. *rimontare*, < ML. *remontare*, mount again, < *re-*, again, + *montare*, mount: see *mount*[2], *v.*] I. *trans.* To mount again or anew, in any sense.

So peyned thei that were with kynge Arthur that thei haue hym *remounted* on his horse. *Merlin* (E. E. T. S.), i. 119.

One man takes to pieces the syringes which have just been used, burns the leathers, disinfects the metal parts, and sends them to the instrument-maker to be *remounted*. *Nineteenth Century*, XXIV. 853.

II. *intrans.* 1. To mount again; reascend; specifically, to mount a horse again.

He, backe returning by the Yvorie dore,
Remounted up as light as chearefull Larke.
Spenser, F. Q., I. i. 44.

Stout Cymon soon *remounts*, and cleft in two
His rival's head. *Dryden*, Cym. and Iph., l. 600.

2. To go back, as in order of time or of reasoning.

The shortest and the surest way of arriving at real knowledge is to unlearn the lessons we have been taught, to *remount* to first principles, and take nobody's word about them. *Bolingbroke*, Idea of a Patriot King.

remount (rē-mount'), *n.* [< *remount, v.*] The opportunity or means of remounting; specifically, a fresh horse with its furniture; also, a supply of fresh horses for cavalry.

removability (rē-mö-vạ-bil'i̤-ti), *n.* [< *removable* + *-ity* (see *-bility*).] The capacity of being removable, as from an office or a station; liability to removal.

removable (rē̤-mö'vạ-bl), *a.* [< *remove* + *-able.* Cf. Pg. *removivel* = It. *rimovibile.*] Capable of being removed; admitting of or subject to removal, as from one place to another, or from an office or station.

Such curate is *removable* at the pleasure of the rector of the mother church. *Ayliffe*, Parergon.

The wharves at the water level are provided with a railroad and with *removable* freight sheds. *Harper's Mag.*, LXXIX. 92.

removably (rē̤-mö'vạ-bli), *adv.* So as to admit of removal: as, a box fitted *removably*.

removal (rē̤-mö'vạl), *n.* [< *remove* + *-al.*] The act of removing, in any sense of that word. = **Syn.** Displacement, dislodgment, transference, withdrawal, dismissal, ejection, elimination, suppression, abatement.

remove (rē̤-möv'), *v.*; pret. and pp. *removed*, ppr. *removing*. [Early mod. E. also *remeve*; < ME. *removen, remeven*, < OF. **remover*, **remouver*, later *removoir, remouvoir* = Sp. Pg. *remover* = It. *rimuovere, remuovere*, < L. *removere*, move back, draw back, set aside, remove, < *re-*, back, + *movere*, move: see *move.*] **I.** *trans.* **1.** To move from a position occupied; cause to change place; transfer from one point to another; put from its place in any manner.

To trusten som wyght is a preve
Of trouthe, and forthy wolde I fayne *remeve*
Thy wrong conceyte. *Chaucer*, Troilus, i. 691.

Remeve thi rewle up and down til that the stremes of the sonne shyne thorgh bothe holes of thi rewle.
Chaucer, Astrolabe, ii. 2.

Whan thei saugh Claudas men assembled thei smote on hem so harde that thei made hem *remeve* place.
Merlin (E. E. T. S.), iii. 410.

Thou shalt not *remove* thy neighbour's landmark.
Deut. xix. 14.

Moved! in good time; let him that moved you hither
Remove you hence. *Shak.*, T. of the S., ii. 1. 197.

Does he not see that he is only *removing* the difficulty one step farther? *Macaulay*, Sadler's Refutation Refuted.

2. To displace from an office, post, or situation.

He *removed* the Bishop of Hereford from being Treasurer, and put another in his Place.
Baker, Chronicles, p. 146.

But does the Court a worthy man *remove*,
That instant, I declare, he has my love.
Pope, Epil. to Satires, ii. 74.

3. To take or put away in any manner; take away by causing to cease; cause to leave or depart; put an end to; do away with; banish.

Remove sorrow from thy heart. Eccl. xi. 10.

Good God, betimes *remove*
The means that makes us strangers!
Shak., Macbeth, iv. 3. 162.

What drop or nostrum can this plague *remove*?
Pope, Prol. to Satires, l. 29.

If the witch could produce disease by her incantations, there was no difficulty in believing that she could also *remove* it. *Lecky*, Rationalism, I. 92.

4. To make away with; cut off; take away by death: as, to *remove* a person by poison.

When he's *removed*, your highness
Will take again your queen as yours at first.
Shak., W. T., i. 2. 335.

Forgive my grief for one *removed*,
Thy creature, whom I found so fair.
I trust he lives in thee.
Tennyson, In Memoriam, Int.

5. In *law*, to transfer from one court to another.

Wee *remove* our cause into our adversaries owne Court.
Milton, Prelatical Episcopacy.

= **Syn. 1.** To dislodge, transfer.—**2.** To dismiss, eject, oust.—**3.** To abate, suppress.

II. *intrans.* To change place in any manner; move from one place to another; change the place of residence: as, to *remove* from Edinburgh to London.

Merlin seide he neded not nothinge ther-of hym to prayen, and bad make hem redy, "for to-morowe moste we *remove*." *Merlin* (E. E. T. S.), ii. 380.

Till Birnam wood *remove* to Dunsinane
I cannot taint with fear. *Shak.*, Macbeth, v. 3. 2.

They [the Carmelite nuns] *remove* shortly from that wherein they now live to that which is now building.
Coryat, Crudities, I. 18.

remove (rē̤-möv'), *n.* [< *remove, v.*] **1.** The act of removing, or the state of being removed; removal; change of place.

I do not know how he [the King] will possibly avoid . . . the giving way to the *remove* of divers persons, as . . . will be demanded by the parliament.
Lord Northumberland (1640), quoted in Hallam's Const. [Hist., II. 105.

Not to feed your ambition with a dukedom,
By the *remove* of Alexander, but
To serve your country. *Shirley*, The Traitor, ii. 1.

Three *removes* is as bad as a fire.
Franklin, Way to Wealth.

2. The distance or space through which anything is removed; interval; stage; step; especially, a step in any scale of gradation or descent.

That which we boast of is not anything, or at the most but a *remove* from nothing.
Sir T. Browne, Religio Medici, i. 60.

Our cousins too, even to the fortieth *remove*, all remembered their affinity. *Goldsmith*, Vicar, i.

3. In English public schools: (*a*) Promotion from one class or division to another.

Keeping a good enough place to get their regular yearly *remove*. *T. Hughes*, Tom Brown at Rugby, i. 9.

The desire of getting his *remove* with Julian.
F. W. Farrar, Julian Home, iii.

Hence—(*b*) A class or division.

When a boy comes to Eton, he is "placed" by the head master in some class, division, or *remove*.
Westminster Rev., N. S., XIX. 496.

4†. A posting-stage; the distance between two resting-places on a road.

Here's a petition from a Florentine,
Who hath for four or five *removes* come short
To tender it herself. *Shak.*, All's Well, v. 3. 131.

5†. The raising of a siege.

If they set down before 's, for the *remove*
Bring up your army. *Shak.*, Cor., i. 2. 28.

6†. The act of changing a horse's shoe from one foot to another, or for a new one.

His horse wanted two *removes*, your horse wanted nails.
Swift, Advice to Servants (Groom).

7. A dish removed from table to make room for something else; also, a course.

removed (rē̤-mövd'), *p. a.* [< ME. *removed*; pp. of *remove, v.*] Remote; separate from others; specifically, noting a grade of distance in relationship and the like: as, "a lie seven times *removed*," *Shak.*, As you Like it, v. 4. 71.

Look, with what courteous action
It waves you to a more *removed* ground.
Shak., Hamlet, i. 4. 61.

The nephew is two-degrees *removed* from the common ancestor: viz., his own grandfather, the father of Titius.
Blackstone, Com., II. xiv.

removedness (rē̤-mö'ved-nes), *n.* The state of being removed; remoteness; retirement.

I have eyes under my service, which look upon his *removedness*. *Shak.*, W. T., iv. 2. 41.

remover[1] (rē̤-mö'vėr), *n.* [< *remove* + *-er*[1].] **1.** One who or that which removes: as, a *remover* of landmarks.

Love is not love
Which alters when it alteration finds,
Or bends with the *remover* to remove.
Shak., Sonnets, cxvi.

2†. An agitator.

A hasty fortune maketh an enterpriser and *remover*.
Bacon, Fortune (ed. 1887).

remover[2] (rē̤-mö'vėr), *n.* [< OF. **remover*, inf. used as a noun: see *remove, v.*] In *law*, the removal of a suit from one court to another. *Bouvier.*

Remphan (rem'fan), *n.* [LL. *Rempham*, Gr. Ῥεμφάν (N. T.), Ῥαιφάν (LXX.).] **1.** A name of a god mentioned in Acts vii. 43.—**2.** [NL.] In *entom.*, a genus of coleopterous insects. *Waterhouse*, 1836.

rempli (roṅ-plē'), *a.* [< F. *rempli*, pp. of *remplir*, fill up, < *re-* + *emplir*, fill, < L. *implere*, fill up: see *implement.*] In *her.*, having another tincture than its own laid over or covering the greater part: thus, a chief azure *rempli* or has a broad band of gold occupying nearly the whole space of the chief, so that only a blue fimbriation shows around it. Also *coupu*.

Argent, a chief azure rempli or.

remplissage (roṅ-plē-säzh'), *n.* [< F. *remplissage*, < *rempliss-*, stem of certain parts of *remplir*, fill up: see *rempli.*] That which serves only to fill up space; filling; padding: used specifically in literary and musical criticism.

remuable†, *a.* [< OF. (and F.) *remuable*, changeable, < *remuer*, change: see *remew.*] Changeable; fickle; inconstant.

And this may length of yeres nought fordo,
Ne *remuable* fortune deface.
Chaucer, Troilus, iv. 1682.

remuet, *v. t.* See *remew*.

remugient† (rē̤-mū'ji-ẹnt), *a.* [< L. *remugien(t-)s*, ppr. of *remugire*, bellow again, reëcho, resound, < *re-*, back, + *mugire*, bellow, low: see *mugient.*] Rebellowing.

Earthquakes accompanied with *remugient* echoes, and ghastly murmurs from below.
Dr. H. More, Mystery of Godliness, p. 63.

remuner† (rē̤-mū'nėr), *v. t.* [< OF. *remunerer*, F. *rémunérer* = Sp. Pg. *remunerar* = It. *rimunerare*, < L. *remunerari, remunerare*, reward, remunerate: see *remunerate.*] To remunerate.

Eschewe the evyll, or ellys thou shalt be deceyved atte last; and ever do wele, and atte last thou shal be *remunered* therfor.
Lord Rivers, Dictes and Sayings of the Philosophers, sig. [E. iii. b. (*Latham.*)

remunerability (rē̤-mū'ne-rạ-bil'i̤-ti), *n.* [< *remunerable* + *-ity* (see *-bility*).] The capacity of being remunerated or rewarded.

The liberty and *remunerability* of human actions.
Bp. Pearson, Expos. of Creed, ii.

remunerable (rē̤-mū'ne-rạ-bl), *a.* [= Sp. *remunerable*; as *remuner* + *-able.*] Capable of being remunerated or rewarded; fit or proper to be recompensed. *Bailey.*

remunerate (rē̤-mū'ne-rāt), *v. t.*; pret. and pp. *remunerated*, ppr. *remunerating*. [< L. *remuneratus*, pp. of *remunerari, remunerare*, reward, remunerate, < *re-*, again, + *munerari, munerare*, give: see *munerate*. Cf. *remuner.*] To reward; recompense; requite, in a good sense; pay an equivalent to for any service, loss, expense, or other sacrifice.

She no doubt with royal favour will *remunerate*
The least of your deserts.
Webster and Dekker, Sir Thomas Wyatt, p. 13.

The better hour is near
That shall *remunerate* thy toils severe.
Cowper, To Wm. Wilberforce, 1792.

= **Syn.** *Recompense, Compensate*, etc. (see *indemnify*), repay.

remuneration (rē̤-mū-ne-rā'shọn), *n.* [< OF. *remuneracion, remuneration*, F. *rémunération* = Pr. *remuneration* = Sp. *remuneracion* = Pg. *remuneração* = It. *remunerazione*, < L. *remuneratio(n-)*, a repaying, recompense, reward, < *remunerari*, remunerate: see *remunerate.*] **1.** The act of remunerating, or paying for services, loss, or sacrifices.—**2.** What is given to remunerate; the equivalent given for services, loss, or sufferings.

O, let not virtue seek
Remuneration for the thing it was.
Shak., T. and C., iii. 3. 170.

We have still in vails and Christmas-boxes to servants, &c., the remnants of a system under which fixed *remuneration* was eked out by gratuities.
H. Spencer, Prin. of Sociol., § 375.

= **Syn. 1.** Repayment, indemnification.—**2.** Reward, recompense, compensation, payment. See *indemnify*.

remunerative (rē̤-mū'ne-rā-tiv), *a.* [= F. *rémunératif* = Pg. *remunerativo* = It. *rimunerativo*; as *remunerate* + *-ive.*] **1.** Affording remuneration; yielding a sufficient return: as, a *remunerative* occupation.—**2.** Exercised in rewarding; remuneratory.

Fit objects for *remunerative* justice to display itself upon. *Cudworth*, Intellectual System, p. 690.

= **Syn. 1.** Profitable, paying.

remuneratively (rē̤-mū'ne-rā-tiv-li), *adv.* So as to remunerate; in a remunerative manner; so as to afford an equivalent for what has been expended.

remunerativeness (rē̤-mū'ne-rā-tiv-nes), *n.* The character of being remunerative.

The question of *remunerativeness* seems to me quite of a secondary character. *Elect. Rev.* (Amer.), XV. ix. 6.

remuneratory (rē̤-mū'ne-rā-tọ-ri), *a.* [= F. *rémunératoire* = Sp. Pg. It. *remuneratorio*; as *remunerate* + *-ory.*] Affording recompense; rewarding; requiting.

Remuneratory honours are proportioned at once to the usefulness and difficulty of performances.
Johnson, Rambler, No. 145.

remurmur (rē-mėr'mėr), *v.* [< L. *remurmurare*, murmur back, < *re-*, back, + *murmurare*, murmur: see *murmur, v.*] **I.** *intrans.* To repeat or echo a murmuring or low rumbling sound. [Rare.]

Swans *remurmuring* to the floods,
Or birds of different kinds in hollow woods.
Dryden, Æneid, xi.

II. *trans.* To utter back in murmurs; return in murmurs; repeat in low hoarse sounds. [Rare.]

The trembling trees, in every plain and wood,
Her fate *remurmur* to the silver flood.
Pope, Winter, l. 64.

remutation (rē-mṳ̄-tā'shọn), *n.* [< *re-* + *mutation*. Cf. *remue, remew.*] The act or process of changing back; alteration to a previous form or quality. [Rare.]

The mutation or rarefaction of water into air takes place by day, the *remutation* or condensation of air into water by night. *Southey*, The Doctor, cxxvii.

ren[1]†, *v. i.*; pret. *ran*, *ron*, pp. *ronnen*. A Middle English form of *run*[1].

Pitee *renneth* soone in gentil herte. *Chaucer*, Merchant's Tale, l. 742.

ren[2]†, *v. t.* [ME. *rennen*, < Icel. *ræna*, rob, plunder, < *rān*, plunder: see *ran*[2].] To plunder: only in the phrase *to rape and ren* (which see, under *rape*[2]).

ren[3] (ren), *n.*; pl. *renes* (rē'nēz). [NL., < L. *rien* (rare), sing. form of *renes*, pl., the kidneys: see *reins*, *renal*.] The kidney: little used, though the derivatives, as *renal*, *adrenal*, are in constant employ.—**Renes succenturiati**, the adrenals, or suprarenal capsules.—**Renes succenturiati accessorii**, accessory adrenals.—**Ren mobilis**, movable kidney; floating kidney.

rena, reina (rā'nä), *n.* [NL., < Sp. *reina*, < L. *regina*, queen, fem. of *rex* (*reg-*), king: see *rex*.] A small rockfish of the family *Scorpænidæ*, *Sebastichthys elongatus*. [California.]

renable (ren'a-bl), *a.* [Also *renible*; < ME. *renable*, also *resnable*, *resonable*: see *reasonable*.] 1†. A Middle English form of *reasonable*.

Thyse thri thinges byeth nyeduolle to alle the thinges thet in the erthe wexeth. Guod molde, wocnesse norissynde, and *renable* hete. *Ayenbite of Inwit* (E. E. T. S.), p. 95.

2. Talkative; loquacious. [Obsolete or prov. Eng.]

A raton of renon, most *renable* of tonge. *Piers Plowman* (B), Prol., l. 158.

renably†, *adv.* [ME., < *renable* + *-ly*[2]. See *reasonably*.] Reasonably.

Sometime we . . . speke as *renably* and faire and wel As to the Phitonesse dide Samuel. *Chaucer*, Friar's Tale, l. 211.

renaissance (rē-nā-sons' or re-nā'sans), *n.* and *a.* [F. *renaissance*, OF. *renaissance*, *renaiscence*, < ML. *renascentia*, new birth: see *renascence*.] **I.** *n.* A new birth; hence, the revival of anything which has long been in decay or desuetude. Specifically [*cap.*], the movement of transition in Europe from the medieval to the modern world, and especially the time, spirit, and activity of the revival of classical arts and letters. The earliest traces and most characteristic development of this revival were in Italy, where Petrarch and the early humanists and artists of the fourteenth century may be regarded as its precursors. The movement was greatly stimulated by the influx of Byzantine scholars, who brought the literature of ancient Greece into Italy in the fifteenth century, especially after the taking of Constantinople by the Turks in 1453. The Italian Renaissance was at its height at the end of the fifteenth and in the early sixteenth century, as seen in the lives and works of such men as Lorenzo dei Medici, Michelangelo, Leonardo da Vinci, Raphael, Machiavelli, Politian, Ariosto, Correggio, Titian, and Aldus Manutius. The Renaissance was aided everywhere by the spirit of discovery and exploration of the fifteenth century—the age which saw the invention of printing, the discovery of America, and the rounding of Africa. In Germany the Renaissance advanced about the same time with the Reformation (which commenced in 1517). In England the revival of learning was fostered by Erasmus, Colet, Grocyn, More, and their fellows, about 1500, and in France there was a brilliant artistic and literary development under Louis XII. (1498–1515) and Francis I. (1515–47). Also, in English form, *renascence*.

I have ventured to give to the foreign word *Renaissance*—destined to become of more common use amongst us as the movement which it denotes comes, as it will come, increasingly to interest us—an English form [*Renascence*]. *M. Arnold*, Culture and Anarchy, iv., note.

The *Renaissance* and the Reformation mark the return to experience. They showed that the doctrine of reconciliation was at last passing from the abstract to the concrete. *E. Caird*, Philos. of Kant, p. 28.

II. *a.* [*cap.*] Of or pertaining to the Renaissance; in the style of the Renaissance.—**Renaissance architecture**, the style of building and decoration which succeeded the medieval, and was based upon study and emulation of the outward forms and ornaments of Roman art, though with imperfect understanding of their principles. This style had its origin in Italy in the first half of the fifteenth century, and afterward spread over Europe. Its main characteristic is an attempted return to the classical forms which had been the forerunners of the Byzantine and the medieval. The Florentine Brunelleschi (died about 1446) was one of the first masters of the style, having prepared himself by earnest study of the remains of the monuments of ancient Rome. From Florence the style was introduced into Rome, where the works of Bramante (died 1514) are among its finest examples, the chief of these being the palace of the Chancellery, the foundations of St. Peter's, part of the Vatican, and the small church of San Pietro in Montorio. One of the greatest achievements of the Renaissance is the dome of St. Peter's, the work of Michelangelo; but this must yield in grandeur of conception to the earlier Florentine dome of Brunelleschi. After Michelangelo the style declined rapidly. Another chief Renaissance school arose in Venice, where in the majority of the buildings of the sixteenth and seventeenth centuries predominance is given to external decoration. From this school sprung Palladio (1518–1580), whose distinctive style of architecture received the name of *Palladian*. Renaissance architecture was introduced into France by Lombardic and Florentine architects at the beginning of the sixteenth century, and flourished there during that century, but especially in the first half, under Louis XII. and Francis I. During the seventeenth century the style degenerated in France, as it had in Italy, and gave rise to the inorganic and insipid productions of the so-called *rococo* or Louis XV. style of the first half of the eighteenth century.

Renaissance Architecture.—French Renaissance tomb of Loys de Brézé (died 1531), Grand Seneschal of Normandy, etc., in the cathedral of Rouen; erected by his wife, Diane de Poitiers, and attributed to Jean Goujon and Jean Cousin.

In England the Renaissance style was introduced later than in France, and it is represented there by the works of Inigo Jones, Sir Christopher Wren, and their contemporaries—St. Paul's, London, being a grand example by Wren. While all Renaissance architecture is far inferior to medieval building of the best time, it represents a distinct advance over the debased and over-elaborated forms of the medieval decadence. For an Italian example, see cut under *Italian*; see also cuts under *loggia* and *Palladian*.—**Renaissance braid-work**, a kind of needlework similar in its make to needle-point lace, but of much stouter material, as fine braid.—**Renaissance lace**. Same as *Renaissance braid-work*.—**Renaissance painting**, next to architecture the chief art of the Renaissance, had by far its most important and characteristic development in Italy, where, based upon the art of the Byzantine painters of the middle ages, a number of important art-centers or -schools arose, differing from one another in their ideals and methods, but all distinctively Italian. The central one of these schools was that of Florence, which took the lead under the impulse and example of the great artist Giotto in the early part of the fourteenth century. Among the greatest of those after Giotto, whose genius influenced the development of the art, were Fra Angelico (Fra Giovanni da Fiesole), Masolino, Masaccio, Filippo Lippi, Sandro Botticelli, Filippino Lippi, and Leonardo da Vinci. The chief glory of Renaissance painting is that it advanced that art beyond any point that it had attained before, or has since reached. For other schools of Renaissance painting, see *Bolognese*, *Roman*, *Sienese*, *Umbrian*, *Venetian*; and see *Italian painting*, under *Italian*.—**Renaissance sculpture**, the sculpture of the Renaissance, characterized primarily by seeking its models and inspiration in the works of Roman antiquity, instead of in contemporary life, like medieval sculpture. As an adjunct to architecture, this sculpture reached its highest excellence in Italy and in France. Eminent names are those of Niccolà Pisano, Donatello, Ghiberti, Luca della Robbia, Sansovino, Sangallo, and Michelangelo (1475–1564), one of the half-dozen names that rank as greatest in the world's art-history. See cut of Benvenuto Cellini's "Perseus and Medusa," under *Perseus*, and see, under *quadra*, another example by Luca della Robbia.—**Renaissance style**, properly the style of art and decoration (see *Renaissance architecture*) which prevailed in Italy during the fifteenth century and later, and the styles founded upon these which were in vogue in northern Europe at a date somewhat later—as in France from about 1520 to 1560. By extension the phrase is made to cover all the revived classic styles of the last four centuries, including the above, and to embrace everything which shows a strong classic influence. This use is generally avoided by French writers, who speak of the styles following the religious wars in France as the styles of Henry IV., Louis XIII., etc., excluding these from the Renaissance style proper; but English writers commonly include the whole period from 1400 to the French Revolution or the end of the eighteenth century, and divide it into various epochs or subordinate styles, according to the writer's fancy.

Renaissance Sculpture.—The "David" of Michelangelo, in the Accademia, Florence, Italy.

Renaissance Sculpture.—Cherub by Donatello, in the Basilica of San Antonio, Padua.

renal (rē'nal), *a.* [< OF. *renal*, F. *rénal* = Sp. Pg. *renal* = It. *renale*, < L. *renalis*, pertaining to the kidneys, < *renes*, kidneys, reins: see *reins*.] Of or pertaining to the kidneys: as, a *renal* artery or vein; *renal* structure or function; *renal* disease.—**Renal alterative**. Same as *diuretic*.—**Renal apoplexy**, a hemorrhage into the kidney-substance. [Obsolescent.]—**Renal artery**, one of the arteries arising from the sides of the aorta about one half-inch below the superior mesenteric artery, the right being a trifle lower than the left. They are directed outward at nearly right angles to the aorta. As they approach the kidney, each artery divides into four or five branches which pass deeply into the substance of the kidney. Small branches are given off to the suprarenal capsule.—**Renal asthma**, paroxysmal dyspnœa occurring in Bright's disease.—**Renal calculus**, a calculus in the kidney or its pelvis.—**Renal canal**, a ureter, especially in a rudimentary state.

The kidneys of the Mammalia vary in several points, and especially as to the characters of the orifice of the ureters, after the differentiation of the rudiment which is known as the *renal canal*. *Gegenbaur*, Comp. Anat. (trans.), p. 607.

Renal capsule. Same as *adrenal*.—**Renal cast**, **colic**, **ganglion**. See the nouns.—**Renal cyst**, a thin-walled cyst in the substance and on the surface of the kidney, with serous, rarely sanguinolent or gelatinous contents.—**Renal dropsy**, dropsy resulting from disease of the kidney.—**Renal gland**. Same as *adrenal*.—**Renal impression**. See *impression*.—**Renal ischuria**, retention of urine from some kidney trouble.—**Renal nerves**, small nerves, about fifteen in number, arising from the renal plexus and renal splanchnic nerve. They contain fibers from both central and sympathetic nervous systems, and are distributed in the kidney along with the renal artery.—**Renal plexus**. See *plexus*.—**Renal portal system**. See *reniportal*.—**Renal splanchnic nerve**, the smallest splanchnic nerve. See *splanchnic*.—**Renal veins**, short wide vessels which begin at the hilum of the kidney and pass inward to join the vena cava. Also called *emulgent veins*.

renald†, *n.* An obsolete form of *reynard*.

renaldry†, *n.* [< *renald* + *-ry*.] Intrigue; cunning, as of a fox.

First, she used all malitious *renaldrie* to the end I might stay there this night. *Benvenuto*, Passengers' Dialogues. (*Nares.*)

rename (rē-nām'), *v. t.* [< *re-* + *name*[1].] To give a new name to.

renard, *n.* See *reynard*.

renardine (ren'är-din), *a.* [< *renard* + *-ine*[1].] Of, pertaining to, or characteristic of the legend of "Reynard the Fox."

There has been much learning expended by Grimm and others on the question of why the lion was king in the *Renardine* tales. *Athenæum*, Aug. 7, 1886, p. 165.

renascence (rę̄-nas'ens), *n.* [= F. *renaissance* = Pg. *renascença* = It. *rinascenza*, < ML. **renascentia*, new birth, < L. *renascen(t-)s*, new-born: see *renascent*. Cf. *renaissance*.] 1. The state of being renascent.

Read the Phœnix, and see how the single image of *renascence* is varied. *Coleridge*. (*Webster.*)

2. A new birth; specifically [*cap.*], same as *Renaissance*.

"For the first time," to use the picturesque phrase of M. Taine, "men opened their eyes and saw." The human mind seemed to gather new energies at the sight of the vast field which opened before it. It attacked every province of knowledge, and in a few years it transformed all. Experimental science, the science of philology, the science of politics, the critical investigation of religious truth, all took their origin from this *Renascence* — this "New Birth" of the world. *J. R. Green*, Short Hist. Eng., vi. 4.

renascency (rę̄-nas'ęn-si), *n.* [As *renascence* (see *-cy*).] Same as *renascence*.

Job would not only curse the day of his nativity, but also of his *renascency*, if he were to act over his disasters and the miseries of the dunghill. *Sir T. Browne*, Christ. Mor., iii. 25.

Leave the stools as close to the ground as possible, especially if you design a *renascency* from the roots. *Evelyn*, Sylva, iii. 3.

renascent (rę̄-nas'ęnt), *a.* [= F. *renaissant* = Sp. *renaciente* = Pg. *renascente* = It. *rinascente*, < L. *renascen(t-)s*, ppr. of *renasci*, be born again, grow, rise or spring up again, revive, < *re-* + *nasci*, be born: see *nascent*.] Springing or rising into being again; reproduced; reappearing; rejuvenated.

renascible (rę̄-nas'i-bl), *a.* [< L. *renasci*, be born again (see *renascent*), + *-ible*.] Capable of being reproduced; able to spring again into being. *Imp. Dict.*

renat†, *n.* An obsolete form of *rennet*[2].

renate[1]† (rę̄-nāt'), *a.* [= F. *rené* = It. *rinato*, < L. *renatus*, pp. of *renasci*, be born again: see *renascent*.] Born again; regenerate.

Father, you shall know that I put my portion to use that you have given me to live by;
And, to confirm yourself in me *renate*,
I hope you'll find my wit's legitimate.
Beau. and Fl., Wit at Several Weapons, i. 2.

renate[2]†, *n.* An obsolete form of *rennet*[2].

renated† (rę̄-nā'ted), *a.* [< *renate*[1] + *-ed*[2].] Same as *renate*[1].

Suche a pernycious fable and ficcion, being not onely straunge and marveylous, but also prodigious and unnaturall, to feyne a dead man to be *renated* and newely borne agayne. *Hall*, Hen. VII., f. 32. (*Halliwell.*)

renay†, *v.* See *reny*.

rench (rench), *v. t.* A dialectal form of *rinse*. [Prov. Eng. and U. S.]

rencounter (ren-koun'tėr), *v.* [Also *rencontre*; < OF. (and F.) *rencontrer* (= It. *rincontrare*), encounter, meet, < *re-*, again, + *encontrer*, meet: see *encounter*.] I. *trans.* 1. To meet unexpectedly; fall in with. [Rare.] — 2†. To attack hand to hand; encounter.

And him *rencountring* fierce, reskewd the noble pray. *Spenser*, F. Q., I. iv. 39.

As yet they sayd, blessed be God they kepte the feldes, and none to *rencontre* them. *Berners*, tr. of Froissart's Chron., II. lxxxviii.

II. *intrans.* To meet an enemy unexpectedly; clash; come in collision; fight hand to hand.

rencounter (ren-koun'tėr), *n.* [Also *rencontre*, and early mod. E. also *re-encounter*; < OF. (and F.) *rencontre* = It. *rincontro*, a meeting, encounter; from the verb: see *rencounter*, *v.*] 1. An antagonistic or hostile meeting; a sudden coming in contact; collision; combat.

The Vice-Admiral of Portugal . . . was engaged in close Fight with the Vice-Admiral of Holland, and after many tough *Rencounters* they were both blown up, and burnt together. *Howell*, Letters, I. vi. 40.

The justling chiefs in rude *rencounter* join. *Granville*, Progress of Beauty.

2. A casual combat or action; a sudden contest or fight; a slight engagement between armies or fleets.

Will reckons every misfortune that he has met with among the women, and every *rencounter* among the men, as parts of his education. *Addison*, The Man of the Town.

= **Syn.** 2. *Skirmish*, *Brush*, etc. See *encounter*.

renculus (reng'kū̦-lus), *n.*; pl. *renculi* (-lī). [NL., < L. *reniculus*, a little kidney, dim. of *ren*, pl. *renes*, the kidneys: see *ren*[3], *reins*.] A lobe of a kidney.

rend[1] (rend), *v.*; pret. and pp. *rent* (formerly also *rended*), ppr. *rending*. [< ME. *renden*, *reenden* (pret. *rende*, *rente*, *rent*, pl. *rendden*, pp. *rended*, *irend*, *rent*), < AS. (ONorth.) *rendan* (pret. pl. *rendun*, *rindon*), also *hrendan* (and in comp. *tō-rendan*: see *torend*), cut down, tear down, = OFries. *renda*, *randa*, North Fries. *renne*, tear, break; perhaps akin to *hrindan* (pret. *hrand*), push, thrust, = Icel. *hrinda* (pret. *hratt*), push, kick, throw; Skt. √ *krit*, cut, cut down, Lith. *kirsti*, cut, hew; cf. L. *crēna*, a notch: see *crenate*[1], *cranny*[1]. Cf. *rent*[1].] I. *trans.* 1. To separate into parts with force or sudden violence; tear asunder; split.

He *rent* the sayle with hokes lyke a sithe,
He bringeth the cappe and biddeth hem be blithe.
Chaucer, Good Women, l. 646.

An evil beast hath devoured him; Joseph is without doubt *rent* in pieces. Gen. xxxvii. 33.

With this, the grave venerable bishop, giving me his benediction, fetcht such a sigh that would have *rended* a rock asunder. *Howell*, Twelve Several Treatises, etc., p. 331.

Aloud they beat their Breasts, and tore their Hair,
Rending around with Shrieks the suff'ring Air.
Congreve, Iliad.

2. To remove or pluck away with violence; tear away.

I will surely *rend* the kingdom from thee. 1 Ki. xi. 11.

If I thought that, I tell thee, homicide,
These nails should *rend* that beauty from my cheeks.
Shak., Rich. III., i. 2. 126.

They from their mothers' breasts poor orphans *rend*,
Nor without gages to the needy lend.
Sandys, Paraphrase upon Job, xxiv.

To rap and rend. See *rap*[2]. = **Syn.** I. *Rip*, *Tear*, *Rend*, *Split*, *Cleave*, *Fracture*, *Chop*. In garments we *rip* along the line at which they were sewed; we *tear* the texture of the cloth; we say, "It is not *torn*; it is only *ripped*." More broadly, *rip*, especially with *up*, stands for a cutting open or apart with a quick, deep stroke: as, to *rip up* a body or a sack of meal. *Rend* implies great force or violence. To *split* is primarily to divide lengthwise or by the grain: as, to *split* wood. *Cleave* may be a more dignified word for *split*, or it may express a cutting apart by a straight, heavy stroke. *Fracture* may represent the next degree beyond cracking, the lightest kind of breaking, leaving the parts in place: as, a *fractured* bone or plate of glass; or it may be a more formal word for *break*. To *chop* is to cut apart with a heavy stroke, which is generally across the grain or natural cleavage, or through the narrow dimension of the material: *chopping* wood is thus distinguished from *splitting* wood.

II. *intrans.* 1. To be or to become rent or torn; become disunited; split; part asunder.

The very principals did seem to *rend*,
And all-to topple. *Shak.*, Pericles, iii. 2. 16.

She from the *rending* earth and bursting skies
Saw gods descend, and fiends infernal rise.
Pope, Essay on Man, iii. 253.

2. To cause separation, division, or strife.

But ye, keep ye on earth
Your lips from over-speech, . . .
For words divide and *rend*,
But silence is most noble to the end.
Swinburne, Atalanta in Calydon.

rend[2]†, *v.* An obsolete variant of *ren*[1].

render[1] (ren'dėr), *n.* [< *rend*[1] + *-er*[1].] One who rends or tears by violence.

Our *renders* will need be our reformers and repairers. *Bp. Gauden*, Bp. Brownrigg, p. 242. (*Latham.*)

render[2] (ren'dėr), *v.* [< ME. *renderen*, *rendren*, < OF. (and F.) *rendre* = Pr. *rendre*, *reddre*, *redre*, *retre* = Cat. Sp. *rendir* = Pg. *render* = It. *rendere*, < ML. *rendere*, nasalized form of L. *reddere*, restore, give back, < *red-*, back, + *dare*, give: see *date*[1]. Cf. *reddition*, *rendition*, etc., and *surrender*, *rendezvous*. Besides the intrusion of *n* by dissimilation of the orig. *dd*, this word in E. is further irregular in the retention of the inf. termination *-er*. It would be reg. **rend*; cf. *defend*, *offend*, from OF. *defendre*, *offendre*. The form of the verb *render*, however, may be due to conformity with the noun, which is in part the OF. inf. used as a noun (like *remainder*, *trover*, etc.).] I. *trans.* 1. To give or pay back; give in return, or in retribution; return: sometimes with *back*.

I will *render* vengeance to mine enemies. Deut. xxxii. 41.

See that none *render* evil for evil unto any man. 1 Thes. v. 15.

And *render back* their cargo to the main. *Addison*, Remarks on Italy, Pesaro, etc., to Rome.

What shall I *render* to my God
For all his kindness shown?
Watts, What shall I Render?

2. To give up; yield; surrender.

Orestes be right shuld *render* his londes,
And be exilede for euermore, as orible of dede.
Destruction of Troy (E. E. T. S.), l. 13069.

To Cæsar will I *render*
My legions and my horse.
Shak., A. and C., iii. 10. 33.

My sword lost, but not forc'd; for discreetly
I *render'd* it, to save that imputation.
Beau. and Fl., King and No King, iv. 3.

3. To give; furnish; present; afford for use or benefit; often, to give officially, or in compliance with a request or duty: as, to *render* assistance or service; the court *rendered* judgment.

The sluggard is wiser in his own conceit than seven men that can *render* a reason. Prov. xxvi. 16.

Cres. In kissing, do you *render* or receive?
Patr. Both take and give. *Shak.*, T. and C., iv. 5. 36.

You buy much that is not *rendered* in the bill. *Emerson*, Conduct of Life.

4. To make or cause to be; cause to become; invest with certain qualities: as, to *render* a fortress more secure or impregnable.

Oh ye gods,
Render me worthy of this noble wife!
Shak., J. C., ii. 1. 303.

What best may ease
The present misery, and *render* hell
More tolerable. *Milton*, P. L., ii. 459.

5. To translate, as from one language into another.

Thus with Mammonaes moneie he hath made hym frendes,
And is ronne in-to Religioun, and hath *rendred* the bible,
And precheth to the peple seynt Poules wordes.
Piers Plowman (B), viii. 90.

The Hebrew Sheōl, which signifies the abode of departed spirits, and corresponds to the Greek Hades, or the under world, is variously *rendered* in the Authorised Version by "grave," "pit," and "hell." *Pref. to Revised Version of Holy Bible* (1884).

6. To interpret, or express for others, the meaning, spirit, and effect of; reproduce; represent: as, to *render* a part in a drama, a piece of music, a scene in painting, etc.

I observe that in our Bible, and other books of lofty moral tone, it seems easy and inevitable to *render* the rhythm and music of the original into phrases of equal melody. *Emerson*, Books.

Under the strange-statued gate,
Where Arthur's wars were *render'd* mystically.
Tennyson, Lancelot and Elaine.

7†. To report; exhibit; describe.

I have heard him speak of that same brother;
And he did *render* him the most unnatural
That lives amongst men.
Shak., As you Like it, iv. 3. 123.

8. To reduce; try out; clarify by boiling or steaming: said of fats: as, kettle-*rendered* lard.

Tallow is chiefly obtained from the fat of sheep and oxen, the tallow being first *rendered*, as it is technically called — that is, separated from the membranous matter with which it is associated in the form of suet. *Watt*, Soap-making, p. 26.

9. In *building*, to plaster directly on the brickwork and without the intervention of laths. — 10. To pass or pull through a pulley or the like, as a rope. — **Account rendered.** See *account*. — **To render up**, to surrender; yield up.

You have our son; touch not a hair of his head;
Render him *up* unscathed. *Tennyson*, Princess, iv.

= **Syn.** 1. To restore. — 3. To contribute, supply. — 5 and 6. *Interpret*, etc. See *translate*.

II. *intrans.* 1†. To give an account; make explanation or confession.

My boon is, that this gentleman may *render*
Of whom he had this ring.
Shak., Cymbeline, v. 5. 135.

2. To be put or passed through a pulley or the like.

render[2] (ren'dėr), *n.* [< *render*[2], *v.*; in part < OF. *rendre*, used as a noun: see *render*[2], *v.*] 1. A return; a payment, especially a payment of rent.

In those early times the king's household (as well as those of inferior lords) were supported by specific *renders* of corn and other victuals from the tenants of the respective demesnes. *Blackstone*, Com., I. viii.

Each person of eighteen years old on a fief paid a certain head-money and certain *renders* in kind to the lord, as a personal payment. *Brougham.*

The rent or *render* was 2*s.* yearly. *Baines*, Hist. Lancashire, II. 49.

2†. A giving up; surrender.

Take thou my oblation, poor but free,
Which is not mix'd with seconds, knows no art
But mutual *render*, only me for thee.
Shak., Sonnets, cxxv.

Three Years after this the disinherited Barons held out, till at length Conditions of *Render* are propounded. *Baker*, Chronicles, p. 88.

3. An account given; a statement; a confession. [Obsolete or prov. Eng.]

Newness
Of Cloten's death . . . may drive us to a *render*
Where we have lived, and so extort from 's that
Which we have done. *Shak.*, Cymbeline, iv. 4. 11.

4. Plaster put directly on a wall. — **Render and set**, in *plastering*, two-coat work applied directly on stone or brick walls. — **Render, float, and set**, three-coat plastering executed directly on stone or brick. — **To lie in render**, in *old Eng. law*, to be subject to an obligation of offering to deliver the thing, as rent, release, heriots, etc., which it was for the obligor to perform: distinguished from *to lie in prender*, which is said of things that might be taken by the lord without any offer by the tenant, such as an escheat.

renderable (ren'dėr-a̤-bl), *a.* [< *render*[2] + *-able*.] Capable of being rendered. *Cotgrave.*

renderer (ren'dėr-ėr), *n.* [< *render*[2] + *-er*[1].] One who renders.

The heathen astrologers and *renderers* of oracles wisely forbore to venture on such predictions. *Boyle*, Works, VI. 679.

The *renderer's* name shall be distinctly marked on each tierce at the time of packing, with metallic brand, marking-iron, or stencil. *New York Produce Exchange Report* (1888-9), p. 172.

rendering (ren'dėr-ing), *n.* [< ME. *renderynge*; verbal n. of *render*[2], *v.*] 1. The act of translating; also, a version; translation.

In case of doubt the alternative *rendering* has been given in the margin. *Pref. to Revised Version of Holy Bible* (1884).

2. In the *fine arts* and the *drama*, interpretation; delineation; reproduction; representation; exhibition.

When all is to be reduced to outline, the forms of flowers and lower animals are always more intelligible, and are felt to approach much more to a satisfactory *rendering* of the objects intended, than the outlines of the human body. *Ruskin.*

An adequate *rendering* of his [Liszt's] pieces requires not only great physical power, but a mental energy . . . which few persons possess. *Grove*, Dict. Music, II. 741.

3. In *plastering*: (*a*) The laying on of a first coat of plaster on brickwork or stonework. (*b*) The coat thus laid on.

The mere . . . *rendering* is the most economical sort of plastering, and does for inferior rooms or cottages. *Workshop Receipts*, 1st ser., p. 121.

4. The process of trying out or clarifying.

rendering-pan (ren'dėr-ing-pan), *n.* Same as *rendering-tank*.

rendering-tank (ren'dėr-ing-tangk), *n.* A tank or boiler, usually steam-jacketed, for rendering lard or oil from fat. It is sometimes provided with mechanical devices for stirring and breaking up the fat

Rendering-tank and Condenser.

A, tank or kettle jacketed over the part exposed to direct action of furnace; *L*, condenser through which gases and vapors are carried and condensed, and subsequently either purified for illumination or utilized as fuel in the furnace; *H*, pressure-gage. For regulating flow and discharging the rendered lard, various cocks are provided. There are also a safety-valve (shown at the right of the figure), and a manhole at the top for charging and cleansing.

while under treatment in the tank by steam- or fire-heat, and a condensing apparatus for cooling and condensing the vapors that arise from the tank, in order that they may be burned and destroyed.

rendezvous (ren'de-vö or ron'dā̤-vö), *n.*; pl. *rendezvous* (formerly *rendezvouses*). [Formerly also *rendesvous*, *randevous*, *rendevous*; < F. *rendez-vous*, betake or assemble yourselves (at the place appointed), < *rendez*, 2d pers. pl. impv. of *rendre*, render, betake (see *render*[2]), + *vous*, you, yourself, yourselves, < L. *vos*, you, pl. of *tu*, thou.] 1. A place of meeting; a place at which persons (or things) commonly meet; specifically, a place appointed for the assembling of troops, or the place where they assemble; the port or place where ships are ordered to join company.

Go, captain. . . . You know the *rendezvous*. *Shak.*, Hamlet, iv. 4. 4.

The Greyhound, the Greyhound in Blackfriars, an excellent *rendezvous*. *Dekker and Webster*, Westward Ho, ii. 3.

The air is so vast and rich a *rendezvous* of innumerable seminal corpuscles. *Boyle*, Hidden Qualities of Air.

To be sure it is extremely pleasant to have one's house made the motley *rendezvous* of all the lackeys of literature — the very high 'change of trading authors and jobbing critics! *Sheridan*, The Critic, i. 1.

An inn, the free *rendezvous* of all travellers. *Scott*, Kenilworth, i.

2. A meeting; a coming together; an associating. [Rare.]

There Time is every Wednesday, . . . perhaps, in memory of the first occasions of their *Rendezvouses*. *Bp. Sprat*, Hist. Royal Soc., p. 93.

The general place of *rendezvous* for all the servants, both in winter and summer, is the kitchen. *Swift*, Advice to Servants (General Directions).

3. An appointment made between two or more persons for a meeting at a fixed place and time.—4†. A sign or occasion that draws men together.

The philosopher's stone and a holy war are but the *rendezvous* of cracked brains. *Bacon.*

5†. A refuge; an asylum; a retreat.

A *rendezvous*, a home to fly unto. *Shak.*, 1 Hen. IV., iv. 1. 57.

Within a taverne; whilst his coine did last
Ther was his *randevous*. *Times' Whistle* (E. E. T. S.), p. 65.

If I happen, by some Accident, to be disappointed of that Allowance I am to subsist by, I must make my Address to you, for I have no other *Rendezvous* to flee unto. *Howell*, Letters, I. i. 2.

rendezvous (ren'de-vö or ron'dā̤-vö), *v.*; pret. and pp. *rendezvoused*, ppr. *rendezvousing*. [< *rendezvous*, *n.*] I. *intrans.* To assemble at a particular place, as troops.

The rest that escaped marched towards the Thames, and with others *rendezvoused* upon Blackheath. *Sir T. Herbert*, Memoirs of King Charles I.

Our new recruits are *rendezvousing* very generally. *Jefferson*, Correspondence, I. 183.

II. *trans.* To assemble or bring together at a certain place.

All men are to be *rendezvoused* in a general assembly. *J. T. Phillips*, Conferences of the Danish Missionaries [(trans.), 1719, p. 310.

rendezvouser (ren'de-vö-ėr), *n.* One who makes a rendezvous; an associate. [Rare.]

His Lordship retained such a veneration for the memory of his noble friend and patron Sir Jeofry Palmer that all the old *rendezvousers* with him were so with his lordship. *Roger North*, Lord Guilford, I. 291. (*Davies.*)

rendible[1]† (ren'di-bl), *a.* [< *rend*[1] + *-ible*; more prop. *rendable*.] Capable of being rent or torn asunder. *Imp. Dict.*

rendible[2]† (ren'di-bl), *a.* [Prop. **rendable*, < OF. *rendable*, < *rendre*, render: see *render*[2].] 1. Capable of being yielded or surrendered; renderable.—2. Capable of being translated.

Every Language hath certain Idioms, Proverbs, peculiar Expressions of it's own, which are not *rendible* in any other, but paraphrastically. *Howell*, Letters, iii. 21.

rendition (ren-dish'on), *n.* [< F. *rendition* = Sp. *rendicion* = Pg. (obs.) *rendição* = It. *redditione*, < L. *redditio(n-)*, a giving back, < *reddere*, ML. *rendere*, give back: see *render*[2]. Cf. *reddition*.] 1. The act of rendering or translating; a rendering or giving the meaning of a word or passage; translation.

"Let us therefore lay aside every weight, and the sin that doth so easily beset us:" so we read the words of the apostle; but St. Chrysostom's *rendition* of them is better. *Jer. Taylor*, Works, III. ii.

2. The act of rendering up or yielding possession; surrender.

These two lords . . . were carried with him [the king] to Oxford, where they remained till the *rendition* of the place. *Hutchinson*, Memoirs, II. 133.

3. The act of rendering or reproducing artistically. [An objectionable use.]

He [a painter] is contented to set himself delightful and not insoluble problems of *rendition*, and draws infinite pleasure from their resolution. *Harper's Mag.*, LXXVIII. 554.

rendle-balk (ren'dl-bâk), *n.* Same as *randle-bar*.

rend-rock (rend'rok), *n.* [< *rend*[1], *v.*, + obj. *rock*[1].] Same as *lithofracteur*.

rene[1]†, *n.* A Middle English form of *reign*.

rene[2]†, *n.* and *v.* An obsolete form of *rein*[1].

reneague†, *v.* See *renege*. *Shak.*

reneg, *v.* An obsolete or dialectal form of *renege*.

renegade (ren'ẹ-gād), *n.* [Also *renegado*; < Sp. Pg. *renegado*, a renegade: see *renegate*.] 1. An apostate from a religious faith.

In the most flourishing days of Ottoman power the great mass of the holders of high office were *renegades* or sons of *renegades*; the native Turk lay almost under a ban. *E. A. Freeman*, Amer. Lects., p. 427.

2. One who deserts to an enemy; one who deserts his party and joins another; a deserter.

He [Wentworth] abandoned his associates, and hated them ever after with the deadly hatred of a *renegade*. *Macaulay*, Nugent's Hampden.

=**Syn.** 1. *Neophyte*, *Proselyte*, etc. (see *convert*), backslider, turncoat.—2. Traitor, runaway.

renegado (ren-ẹ-gā'dō), *n.* [< Sp. Pg. *renegado*: see *renegade*.] Same as *renegade*.

He was a *Renegado*, which is one that first was a Christian, and afterwards becommeth a Turke. *Hakluyt's Voyages*, II. 186.

You are first (I warrant) some *Renegado* from the Inns of Court and the Law; and thou'lt come to suffer for't by the Law — that is, be hang'd. *Wycherley*, Plain Dealer, ii. 1.

renegate (ren'ẹ-gāt), *n.* and *a.* [< ME. *renegat* (= D. *renegaat* = G. Sw. Dan. *renegat*), < OF. *renegat*, F. *renégat* (OF. vernacularly *renié*, *renoié*) = Pr. *renegat* = Sp. Pg. *renegado* = It. *rinegato*, *rinnegato*, < ML. *renegatus*, one who denies his religion, pp. of *renegare*, deny again, < L. *re-*, again, + *negare*, deny: see *negate* and *renay*, *reny*. Hence, by corruption, *runagate*.] I. *n.* A renegade; an apostate. [Now only prov. Eng.]

How may this wayke womman han this strengthe
Hire to defende agayn this *renegat*? *Chaucer*, Man of Law's Tale, l. 835.

II. *a.* Apostate; false; traitorous.

Here may all true Christian hearts see the wonderfull workes of God shewed vpon such infidels, blasphemers, . . . and *renegate* Christians. *Hakluyt's Voyages*, II. 187.

renegation (ren-ẹ-gā'shon), *n.* [< ML. **renegatio(n-)*, < *renegare*, pp. *renegatus*, deny: see *renegate*.] Denial. [Rare.]

The inexorable leader of the monkish party asserted that it was worse than the worst heresy, being absolute *renegation* of Christ. *Milman.*

renege (rẹ-nēg'), *v.* [Formerly also *reneague*, *reneg*, *renig*; = F. *renier* = Pr. *renegar*, *renejar* = Sp. Pg. *renegar* = It. *rinegare*, *rinnegare*, deny, renounce: see *reny*, *renay*, *renegate*.] I.† *trans.* To deny; disown; renounce.

Shall I *renege* I made them then?
Shall I denye my cunning tounde? *Mir. for Mags.*, I. 113.

His captain's heart,
Which in the scuffles of great fights hath burst
The buckles on his breast, *reneges* all temper. *Shak.*, A. and C., i. 1. 8.

II. *intrans.* 1†. To deny.

Such smiling rogues as these . . .
Renege, affirm, and turn their halcyon beaks
With every gale and vary of their masters. *Shak.*, Lear, ii. 2. 84.

2. In *card-playing*, to play a card that is not of the suit led (as is allowable in some games); also, by extension, to revoke. Also *renig*. [U. S.]

reneger† (rẹ-nē'gėr), *n.* One who denies; a renegade.

Their forefathers . . . were sometimes esteemed blest Reformers by most of these modern *Renegers*, Separates, and Apostates. *Bp. Gauden*, Tears of the Church, p. 57. (*Davies.*)

reneie†, *v.* See *reny*.

renerve (rē-nėrv'), *v. t.* [< *re-* + *nerve*, *v.*] To nerve again; give new vigor to.

The sight *re-nerved* my courser's feet. *Byron*, Mazeppa, xvii.

renes, *n.* Plural of *ren*[3].

renew (rẹ-nū'), *v.* [< ME. *renewen*, *renuen*; < *re-* + *new*, *v.* Cf. *renovate*.] I. *trans.* 1. To make new again; restore to former freshness, completeness, or perfection; revive; make fresh or vigorous again; restore to a former state, or to a good state after decay or impairment.

Let us go to Gilgal and *renew* the kingdom there. 1 Sam. xi. 14.

Thou *renewest* the face of the earth. Ps. civ. 30.

Restore his years, *renew* him, like an eagle. *B. Jonson*, Alchemist, ii. 1.

Thou wilt *renew* thy beauty morn by morn;
I earth in earth forget these empty courts. *Tennyson*, Tithonus.

2. To make again: as, to *renew* a treaty or covenant; to *renew* a promise; to *renew* an attempt.

They turne afresh, and oft *renew* their former threat. *Spenser*, F. Q., V. xi. 45.

And [I have] endeavoured to *renew* a faint image of her several virtues and perfections upon your minds. *Bp. Atterbury*, Sermons, I. vi.

3. To supply, equip, furnish, or fill again.

Loke the cup of Wyne or ale be not empty, but ofte *renued*. *Babees Book* (E. E. T. S.), p. 67.

Come, bumpers high, express your joy,
The bowl we maun *renew* it. *Burns*, Impromptu on Willie Stewart.

4. To begin again; recommence.

Either *renew* the fight,
Or tear the lions out of England's coat. *Shak.*, 1 Hen. VI., i. 5. 27.

Day light returning *renu'd* the conflict. *Milton*, Hist. Eng., vi.

5. To go over again; repeat; iterate.

Then gan he all this storie to *renew*. *Spenser*, F. Q., IV. viii. 64.

The birds their notes *renew*, and bleating herds
Attest their joy. *Milton*, P. L., ii. 494.

The lady *renewed* her excuses. *Steele*, Tatler, No. 266.

6. To grant or furnish again, as a new loan on a new note for the amount of a former one.—7. In *theol.*, to make new spiritually. See *renovation*, 2.

Be *renewed* in the spirit of your mind. Eph. iv. 23.

=**Syn.** 1. To reëstablish, reconstitute, recreate, rebuild.

II. *intrans.* 1. To become new; grow afresh.

Renew I could not, like the moon. *Shak.*, T. of A., iv. 3. 68.

Their temples wreathed with leaves that still *renew*. *Dryden.*

2. To begin again; cease to desist.

Renew, *renew*! The fierce Polydamas
Hath beat down Menon. *Shak.*, T. and C., v. 5. 6.

renewability (rẹ-nū-a̤-bil'i̤-ti), *n.* [< *renewable* + *-ity* (see *-bility*).] The quality of being renewable.

renewable (rẹ̄-nū'a-bl), *a.* [< *renew* + *-able.*] Capable of being renewed: as, a lease *renewable* at pleasure.

renewal (rẹ̄-nū'al), *n.* [< *renew* + *-al.*] The act of renewing, or of forming anew.

One of those *renewals* of our constitution. *Bolingbroke*, On Parties, xviii.

Such originality as we all share with the morning and the spring-time and other endless *renewals*. *George Eliot*, Middlemarch, xxii.

Renewal Sunday, a popular name for the second Sunday after Easter: so called because of the post-communion of the mass, according to the Sarum rite, formerly used on that day.

renewedly (rẹ̄-nū'ed-li), *adv.* Again; anew; once more. [Rare.] *Imp. Dict.*

renewedness (rẹ̄-nū'ed-nes), *n.* The state of being renewed.

The Apostle here [Gal. vi.] shewethe unprofitableness of all these [ceremonies], and sets up an inward sanctity and *renewedness* of heart against them all. *Hammond*, Works, IV. 663.

renewer (rẹ̄-nū'ėr), *n.* One who renews. See *bounder*, 3.

The restfull place, *renuer* of my smart. *Wyatt*, Complaint vpon Loue.

renewing (rẹ̄-nū'ing), *n.* [< ME. *renewyng*; verbal n. of *renew*, *v.*] The act or process of making new again, in any sense.

Be ye transformed by the *renewing* of your mind. Rom. xii. 2.

renewl†, *v.* Same as *renovel*.

reneye†, *v.* Same as *reny*.

renfierse†, *v. t.* [Appar. a var., but simulating *fierce*, of *renforce*, *reinforce*.] To reinforce.

Whereat *renfierst* with wrath and sharp regret,
He stroke so hugely with his borrowd blade
That it empierst the Pagans burganet.
Spenser, F. Q., II. viii. 45.

renforce†, *v. t.* An obsolete form of *reinforce*.

reng†, *n.* An obsolete form of *rung*2.

renge1†, *n.* A Middle English form of *rank*2.

renge2†, *v.* An obsolete form of *range*.

reniant†, *n.* [< OF. *reniant*, ppr. of *renier*, deny: see *reny* and *renegate*.] A renegade. *Testament of Love.*

renicapsular (ren-i-kap'sū-lär), *a.* [< *renicapsule* + *-ar*3.] Pertaining to the suprarenal capsules; adrenal. Also *reniglandular*.

renicapsule (ren-i-kap'sūl), *n.* [< L. *ren*, kidney, + NL. *capsula*, capsule: see *capsule*.] The adrenal or suprarenal capsule.

renicardiac (ren-i-kär'di-ak), *a.* [< L. *ren*, kidney, + *cardiacus*, cardiac: see *cardiac*.] Pertaining to the renal and cardiac organs of a mollusk; renipericardial: as, the *renicardiac* orifice.

reniculus (rẹ̄-nik'ū-lus), *n.*; pl. *reniculi* (-lī). [LL., dim. of *ren*, kidney: see *ren*3, *reins*.] In *entom.*, a small reniform or kidney-shaped spot.

renidification (rē-nid″i-fi-kā'shon), *n.* [< *renidify* + *-ation* (see *-fication*).] Renewed nidification; the act of nidifying again, or building another nest.

renidify (rē-nid'i-fī), *v. i.* [< *re-* + *nidify*.] To make another nest.

reniform (ren'i-fôrm), *a.* [< L. *ren*, kidney, + *forma*, form.] Having the form or shape of the human kidney; kidney-form; bean-shaped; in *bot.* (when said of flat organs), having the outline of a longitudinal section through a kidney (see cut under *kidney-shaped*).

Reniform Structure.—Hematite.

—**Reniform spot**, a large kidney-shaped spot on the wing of a noctuid moth, near the center. It is rarely absent in this family.

renig (rẹ̄-nig'), *v. t.* A form of *renege* (II., 2). [U. S.]

reniglandular (ren-i-glan'dū-lär), *a.* [< L. *ren*, kidney, + NL. *glandula*, glandule, + *-ar*3.] Same as *renicapsular*.

renipericardial (ren-i-per-i-kär'di-al), *a.* [< L. *ren*, kidney, + NL. *pericardium*: see *pericardial*.] Pertaining to the nephridium and the pericardium of a mollusk: as, a *renipericardial* communication. Also, less properly, *renopericardial*. *E. R. Lankester.*

reniportal (ren-i-pōr'tal), *a.* [< L. *ren*, kidney, + *porta*, gate: see *portal*1.] In *zoöl.* and *anat.*, noting the portal venous system of the kidneys, an arrangement by which venous blood circulates in the capillaries of the kidneys before reaching the heart, as it does in those of the liver by means of the hepatic portal system. See *portal vein*, under *portal*1.

renisexual (ren-i-sek'sū-al), *a.* [< L. *ren*, kidney, + LL. *sexualis*, sexual.] Combining the functions of a renal and a sexual organ, as the nephridium of mollusks.

renitence (ren'i-tens or rẹ̄-nī'tens), *n.* [< OF. *renitence*, F. *rénitence*, resistance, = Sp. Pg. *renitencia* = It. *renitenza*, < ML. **renitentia*, < L. *reniten(t-)s*, resistant: see *renitent*.] Same as *renitency*.

Out of indignation, and an excessive *renitence*, not separating that which is true from that which is false. *Wollaston*, Religion of Nature. (*Latham.*)

renitency (ren'i- or rẹ̄-nī'ten-si), *n.* [As *renitence* (see *-cy*).] 1. The resistance of a body to pressure; the effect of elasticity.—2. Moral resistance; reluctance; disinclination.

Nature has form'd the mind of man with the same happy backwardness and *renitency* against conviction which is observed in old dogs—"of not learning new tricks." *Sterne*, Tristram Shandy, iii. 34.

renitent (ren'i-tent or rẹ̄-nī'tent), *a.* [< OF. *renitent*, F. *rénitent* = Sp. Pg. It. *renitente*, < L. *reniten(t-)s*, ppr. of *reniti*, strive or struggle against, resist, < *re-*, back, + *niti*, struggle: see *nisus*1.] 1. Resisting pressure or the effect of it; acting against impulse by elastic force.

To me it seems most probable that it is done by an inflation of the muscles, whereby they become both soft and yet *renitent*, like so many pillows. *Ray*, Works of Creation, ii.

2. Persistently opposing.

renk1†, *n.* See *rink*1.

renk2†, *n.* An obsolete form of *rank*2. *Nominale MS.*

renne†, **renner**†. Middle English forms of *run*1, *runner*.

rennelesse†, *n.* [ME.: see *rennet*1.] Same as *rennet*1.

rennet1 (ren'et), *n.* [Early mod. E. *renet*; also dial. *runnet*, < ME. *rennet*, var. of **renel*, **rennels*, *rennelesse*, *renels*, *renlys*, *rendlys* (= MD. *rinsel*, *runsel*), rennet, < *rennen*, run: see *run*1.] 1. The fourth stomach of a calf prepared for curdling milk; the rennet-bag.—2. Anything used to curdle milk.

It is likely enough that Galium, or, as it is popularly called, lady's bedstraw, is still used as *rennet* in some neighbourhoods, its use having formerly been common all over England, especially in Cheshire. *N. and Q.*, 7th ser., VIII. 231.

rennet1 (ren'et), *v. t.* [< *rennet*1, *n.*] To mix or treat with rennet.

Come thou not neere those men who are like bread
O're-leven'd, or like cheese o're-*renetted*.
Herrick, To His Booke.

rennet2 (ren'et), *n.* [Formerly also *renat*, *renate* (simulating *renate*1, as if in allusion to grafting) (= D. *renet* = G. *renette* = Sw. *renett* = Dan. *reinette*), < F. *reinette*, *rainette*, a pippin, rennet; either (*a*) < OF. *reinette*, *roynette*, a little queen (a name given to meadow-sweet), dim. of *reine*, < L. *regina*, queen, fem. of *rex* (*reg-*), king (see *rex*); or (*b*) < OF. *rainette*, a little frog (because, it is supposed, the apple was speckled like the skin of a frog), dim. of *raine*, a frog, < L. *rana*, a frog: see *Rana*1.] A kind of apple, said to have been introduced into England in the reign of Henry VIII. Also called *renneting*.

Pippins grafted on a pippin stock are called *renates*, bettered in their generous nature by such double extraction. *Fuller*, Worthies, Lincolnshire, II. 264.

There is one sort of Pippin peculiar to this Shire [Lincolnshire], growing at Kirton and thereabouts, and from thence called Kirton-Pippin, which is a most wholesome and delicious Apple, both which being grafted on their own Stock are much bettered, and then called *Renates*. T. Cox, Magna Britannia (Lincolnshire), p. 1457 (an. 1720).

rennet-bag (ren'et-bag), *n.* The abomasum, or fourth stomach of a ruminant. Also called *reed*.

rennet-ferment (ren'et-fėr″ment), *n.* The ferment of the gastric juice of young ruminants, which coagulates casein.

renneting (ren'et-ing), *n.* [< *rennet*2 + *-ing*2.] Same as *rennet*2.

rennet-whey (ren'et-hwā), *n.* The serous part of milk, separated from the caseous by means of rennet. It is used in pharmacy.

rennet-wine (ren'et-win), *n.* A vinous extract of dried rennet.

renniblet, *a.* Same as *renable*.

renning (ren'ing), *n.* [< ME. *rennynge*, a stream (not found in sense 'rennet'), < AS. **rinning*, *rynning* (= D. *renninge*), rennet, lit. 'a running,' verbal n. of *rinnan*, run: see *run*1, *running*, and cf. *rennet*1, *runnet*.] 1†. Same as *running*.—2. Rennet. *Baret.* [Obsolete or prov. Eng.]

rennish (ren'ish), *a.* [< ME. *renysche*, fierce; prob. of OF. origin.] Furious; passionate. *Halliwell.* [Prov. Eng.]

Than has sire Dary dedeyne and derfely he lokes;
Kysys him up *renyshe* and rest in his sete.
King Alexander, p. 100.

rennishly (ren'ish-li), *adv.* [< ME. *renyschly*; < *rennish* + *-ly*2.] Fiercely; furiously. [Prov. Eng.]

The tyste with the fyngeres that flayed thi hert,
That rusped *renyschly* the woze with the roz penne.
Alliterative Poems (ed. Morris), ii. 1724.

renome†, **renomed**†. Middle English forms of *renown*, *renowned*.

renomee†, *n.* [ME., < OF. *renommee*, F. *renommée*, renown: see *renown*.] Renown.

For gentilesse nys but *renomee*
Of thyne auncestres for hire heigh bountee,
Which is a strange thyng to thy persone.
Chaucer, Wife of Bath's Tale, l. 303.

renominate (rē-nom'i-nāt), *v. t.* [< *re-* + *nominate*.] To nominate again or anew.

renomination (rē-nom-i-nā'shon), *n.* [< *renominate* + *-ion*.] The act of nominating again or anew; a repeated nomination.

renon†, *n.* A Middle English variant of *renown*.

renopericardial (ren-ō-per-i-kär'di-al), *a.* Same as *renipericardial*. *Huxley and Martin*, Elementary Biology, p. 284.

renoum†, **renoumed**†. Obsolete forms of *renown*, *renowned*.

renoun†, *n.* An obsolete form of *renown*.

renounce (rẹ̄-nouns'), *v.*; pret. and pp. *renounced*, ppr. *renouncing*. [< ME. *renouncen*, *renonsen*, < OF. *renoncier*, *renuncer*, *renoncer*, F. *renoncer* = Pr. Sp. Pg. *renunciar* = It. *rinunziare*, *renunziare*, renounce, < L. *renuntiare*, *renunciare*, bring back a report, also disclaim, renounce, < *re-*, back, + *nuntiare*, *nunciare*, bring a message, < *nuntius*, a messenger: see *nuncio*. Cf. *announce*, *denounce*, *enounce*, *pronounce*.] I. *trans.* 1. To declare against; disown; disclaim; abjure; forswear; refuse to own, acknowledge, or practise.

My ryght I *renonse* to that rynk sone. *Destruction of Troy* (E. E. T. S.), l. 13620.

Minister. Dost thou *renounce* the devil and all his works, the vain pomp and glory of the world, . . . and the sinful desires of the flesh . . . ?

Answer. I *renounce* them all; and, by God's help, will endeavour not to follow nor be led by them.
Book of Common Prayer, Baptism of those of Riper Years.

It is impossible to conceive that a whole nation of men should all publicly reject and *renounce* what every one of them, certainly and infallibly, knew to be a law. *Locke*, Human Understanding, I. iii. § 11.

2. To cast off or reject, as a connection or possession; forsake.

She that had *renounc'd*
Her sex's honour was *renounc'd* herself
By all that priz'd it. *Cowper*, Task, iii. 76.

The conditions of earthly existence were *renounced*, rather than sanctified, in the religious ideal [of the medieval church]. *Gladstone*, Might of Right, p. 208.

He only lives with the world's life
Who hath *renounced* his own.
M. Arnold, Stanzas in memory of the Author of Obermann.

3. In *card-playing*, to play (a suit) different from what is led: as, he *renounced* spades. =**Syn.** *Renounce*, *Recant*, *Abjure*, *Forswear*, *Retract*, *Revoke*, *Recall*, abandon, forsake, quit, forego, resign, relinquish, give up, abdicate, decline, cast off, lay down. *Renounce*, to declare strongly, with more or less of formality, that we give up some opinion, profession, or pursuit forever. Thus, a pretender to a throne may *renounce* his claim. *Recant*, to make publicly known that we give up a principle or belief formerly maintained, from conviction of its erroneousness; the word therefore implies the adoption of the opposite belief. *Abjure*, *forswear*, literally to renounce upon oath, and, metaphorically, with protestations and utterly. They do not necessarily imply any change of opinion. *Retract*, to take back what has been once given or made, as a pledge, an accusation. *Revoke*, to take back that which has been pronounced by an act of authority, as a decree, a command, a grant. *Recall*, the most general word for literal or figurative calling back: as, to *recall* an expression. *Forswear* is somewhat out of use. A man may *renounce* his birthright, *forswear* a habit, *recant* his professions, *abjure* his faith, *retract* his assertions, *revoke* his pledges, *recall* his promises.

II. *intrans.* 1†. To declare a renunciation.

He of my sons who fails to make it good
By one rebellious act *renounces* to my blood.
Dryden, Hind and Panther, iii. 143.

2. In *card-games* in which the rule is to follow suit, to play a card of a different suit from that led; in a restricted sense, to have to play a card of another suit when the player has no card of the suit led. Compare *revoke*.

renounce (rẹ̄-nouns'), *n.* [< F. *renonce* = Sp. Pg. *renuncia* = It. *rinunzia*, a renounce; from the verb: see *renounce, v.*] In *card-games* in which the rule is to follow suit, the playing of a card of a different suit from that led.

renouncement (rẹ̄-nouns'mẹnt), *n.* [< OF. F. *renoncement* = Pr. *renunciamen* = Sp. *renunciamiento* = It. *rinunziamento*; as *renounce, v.,* + *-ment.*] The act of renouncing, or of disclaiming or rejecting; renunciation.

> I hold you as a thing ensky'd and sainted,
> By your *renouncement* an immortal spirit.
> *Shak.*, M. for M., i. 4. 35.

renouncer (rẹ̄-noun'sėr), *n.* One who renounces; one who disowns or disclaims.

renovant (ren'ọ̄-vạnt), *a.* [< OF. *renovant*, < L. *renovan(t-)s*, ppr. of *renovare*, renew, renovate: see *renovate.*] Renovating; renewing. *Cowel.*

renovate (ren'ọ̄-vāt), *v. t.*; pret. and pp. *renovated*, ppr. *renovating*. [< L. *renovatus*, pp. of *renovare*, renew (> It. *rinovare, rinnovare* = Sp. Pg. *renovar*), < *re-*, again, + *novus*, new, = E. *new*: see *new*. Cf. *renew.*] **1.** To renew; render as good as new; restore to freshness or to a good condition: as, to *renovate* a building.

> Then prince Edward, *renouating* his purpose, tooke shipping againe. *Hakluyt's Voyages*, II. 37.

> In hopes that by their poisonous weeds and wild incantations they may regenerate the paternal constitution, and *renovate* their father's life. *Burke*, Rev. in France.

> Till food and wine again should *renovate* his powers.
> *Crabbe*, Works, V. 93.

2. To give force or effect to anew; renew in effect.

> He *renouateth* by so doing all those sinnes which before times were forgiven him.
> *Latimer*, Sermon on the Lord's Prayer.

renovater (ren'ọ̄-vā-tėr), *n.* [< *renovate* + *-er*[1].] Same as *renovator*.

renovation (ren-ọ̄-vā'shọn), *n.* [< OF. *renovacion*, F. *rénovation* = Pr. *renovacio* = Sp. *renovacion* = Pg. *renovação* = It. *rinovazione, rinnovazione*, < L. *renovatio(n-)*, a renewing, renewal, < *renovare*, renew, renovate: see *renovate.*] **1.** The act of renovating, or the state of being renovated or renewed; a making new after decay, destruction, or impairment; renewal.

> This ambassade was sent . . . for the *renouation* of the old league and amitie. *Grafton*, Hen. VII., an. 19.

> Death becomes
> His final remedy; and, . . . to second life,
> Waked in the *renovation* of the just,
> Resigns him up with heaven and earth renew'd.
> *Milton*, P. L., xi. 65.

> The regular return of genial months,
> And *renovation* of a faded world.
> *Cowper*, Task, vi. 124.

> Mr. Garrick, in conjunction with Mr. Lacey, purchased the property of that theatre [Drury Lane], together with the *renovation* of the patent.
> *Life of Quin* (reprint, 1887), p. 42.

2. In *theol.*, the renewal wrought by the Holy Spirit in one who has been regenerated. Renovation differs from regeneration inasmuch as, while regeneration is a single act, and confers a divine life, which can never be wholly lost in this life, or, according to Calvinistic theology, continues forever, renovation is a continuous process or a repetition of acts whereby the divine life is preserved and matured.

renovationist (ren-ọ̄-vā'shọn-ist), *n.* [< *renovation* + *-ist.*] One who believes in the improvement of society by the spiritual renovation of the individual, supernaturally wrought through divine influence rather than by the development of human nature through purely natural and human influences.

renovator (ren'ọ̄-vā-tọr), *n.* [= OF. *renovateur*, F. *rénovateur* = Sp. Pg. *renovador* = It. *rinnovatore*, < L. *renovator*, a renewer, < *renovare*, renew: see *renovate.*] One who or that which renovates or renews.

> Just as sleep is the *renovator* of corporeal vigor, so, with their [the Epicureans'] permission, I would believe death to be of the mind's.
> *Landor*, Imaginary Conversations (Marcus Tullius and Quinctus Cicero).

renovel†, *v. t.* and *i.* [ME. *renovelen, renovellen* (also contr. *renuelen, renulen*, simulating *new*), < OF. *renoveler, renuveler, renouveler, renouveller*, F. *renouveler* = Pr. *renovellar* = It. *rinovellare, rinnovellare*, renew, < L. *re-*, again, + *novellus*, new: see *novel.*] To renew.

> Yet sang this foule, I rede yow alle awake, . . .
> And ye that han ful chosen, as I devise,
> Yet at the leste *renovelcth* your servyse.
> *Chaucer*, Complaint of Mars, l. 17.

renovelance†, *n.* [ME. *renoveilaunce*, < OF. *renovelaunce*, < *renoveler*, renew: see *renovel.*] A renewal.

> *Renoveilaunces*
> Of olde forleten aqueyntaunces.
> *Chaucer*, House of Fame, l. 693.

renowm†, **renowmed**†. Obsolete forms of *renown, renowned*.

renown (rẹ̄-noun'), *v.* [< ME. *renownen, renoumen, renomen* (in pp. *renowned, renomed*), < OF. *renomer, renumer, renommer*, make famous (pp. *renommé*, renowned, famous), F. *renommer*, name over, repeat, rename, = Pr. *renomnar, renompnar, renomenar* = Sp. *renombrar* = It. *rinomare* (> G. *renommiren*, boast), < ML. *renominare*, make famous, < L. *re-*, again, + *nominare*, name: see *nominate.*] **I.** *trans.* To make famous.

> Nor yron bands abord
> The Pontick sea by their huge Navy cast
> My volume shall *renowne*, so long since past.
> *Spenser*, Virgil's Gnat, l. 48.

> The memorials and the things of fame
> That do *renown* this city. *Shak.*, T. N., iii. 3. 24.

> Soft elocution does thy style *renown*.
> *Dryden*, tr. of Persius's Satires, v. 19.

II. *intrans.* To behave or pose as a renowner; swagger; boast: with indefinite *it*. [Slang, imitating German.]

> To *renown it* . . . is equivalent to the American phrase "spreads himself."
> *C. G. Leland*, tr. of Heine's Pictures of Travel, The [Hartz Journey, note.

> A general tumult ensued, and the student with the sword leaped to the floor. . . . He was *renowning it*.
> *Longfellow*, Hyperion, ii. 4.

renown (rẹ̄-noun'), *n.* [Early mod. E. also *renowm, renoum*; < ME. *renoun, renowne, renon, renowme*, < OF. *renoun, renun, renon, renom*, F. *renom* = Pr. Cat. *renom* = Sp. *renombre* = Pg. *renome* = It. *rinomo*, fame, renown; from the verb: see *renown, v.*] **1.** The state of having a great or exalted name; fame; celebrity; exalted reputation derived from the widely spread praise of great achievements or accomplishments.

> "O perle," quoth I, "of rych *renoun*,
> So watz hit me dere that thou con deme,
> In thys veray avysyoun."
> *Alliterative Poems* (ed. Morris), i. 1183.

> Better it is to haue *Renowme* among the good sorte then to be lorde over the whole world.
> *Booke of Precedence* (E. E. T. S., extra ser.), i. 12.

> I loved her old *renown*, her stainless fame—
> What better proof than that I loathed her shame?
> *Lowell*, To G. W. Curtis.

2†. Report; rumor; éclat.

> And [they] diden so well that the worde and the *renon* com to Agrausin and to Gaheret that the childeren foughten be-nethe fer from hem. *Merlin* (E. E. T. S.), ii. 285.

> Socrates, . . . by the . . . uniuersall *renoume* of all people, was approued to be the wisest man of all Grecia.
> *Sir T. Elyot*, The Governour, iii. 22.

> The Rutherfoords, with grit *renown*,
> Convoy'd the town of Jedbrugh out.
> *Raid of the Reidswire* (Child's Ballads, VI. 132).

3†. A token of fame or reputation; an honor; a dignity.

> For I ride on the milk-white steed,
> And aye nearest the town:
> Because I was a christen'd knight,
> They gave me that *renown*.
> *The Young Tamlane* (Child's Ballads, I. 121).

4†. Haughtiness.

> Then out spake her father, he spake wi' *renown*,
> "Some of you that are maidens, ye'll loose aff her gown."
> *Lord Salton and Auchanachie* (Child's Ballads, II. 169).

=**Syn. 1.** *Fame, Honor*, etc. (see *glory*[1], *n.*), repute, note, distinction, name.

renowned (rẹ̄-nound'), *p. a.* [< ME. *renowned, renomed* (Sc. *renownit, renommit*); pp. of *renown, v.*] Having renown; famous; celebrated.

> To ben riht cleer and *renomed*.
> *Chaucer*, Boëthius, iii. prose 2.

> And made his compere a godsone of hys, that he hadden houe fro the fontstone, and was cleped after the kynge ban Bawdewyn, whiche was after full *renomede*.
> *Merlin* (E. E. T. S.), i. 124.

> They that durst to strike
> At so exampless and unblamed a life
> As that of the *renowned* Germanicus.
> *B. Jonson*, Sejanus, ii. 4.

=**Syn.** *Celebrated, Illustrious*, etc. (see *famous*), famed, far-famed.

renownedly (rẹ̄-nou'ned-li), *adv.* With, or so as to win, renown; with fame or celebrity. *Imp. Dict.*

renowner (rẹ̄-nou'nėr), *n.* **1.** One who gives renown or spreads fame.

> Through his great *renowner* I have wrought,
> And my safe saile to sacred anchor brought.
> *Chapman*, Odyssey, xxiii.

> Above them all I preferr'd the two famous *renowners* of Beatrice and Laura, who never write but honour of them to whom they devote their verse.
> *Milton*, Apology for Smectymnuus.

2. [= G. *renommist*, in university slang, a boaster.] A boaster; a bully; a swaggerer.

> Von Kleist was a student, and universally acknowledged among his young acquaintance as a devilish handsome fellow, notwithstanding a tremendous scar on his cheek, and a cream-colored mustache as soft as the silk of Indian corn. In short, he was a *renowner*, and a duellist.
> *Longfellow*, Hyperion, ii. 4.

renownful† (rẹ̄-noun'fụl), *a.* [< *renown* + *-ful.*] Renowned; illustrious.

> Man of large fame, great and abounding glory,
> *Renownfull* Scipio. *Marston*, Sophonisba, i. 1.

rense (rens), *v. t.* A dialectal form of *rinse*.

rensselaerite (ren-se-lār'īt), *n.* [After Stephen Van *Rensselaer*.] A variety of massive talc or steatite. It has a fine compact texture, and is worked in the lathe into inkstands and other articles.

rent[1] (rent). Preterit and past participle of *rend*[1].

rent[1]†, *v.* An obsolete variant of *rend*[1].

> Maligne interpretours whiche fayle not to *rente* and deface the renoume of wryters.
> *Sir T. Elyot*, The Governour, The Proheme.

> Though thou *rentest* thy face with painting [enlargest (margin, Heb. *rendest*) thine eyes with paint, R. V.], in vain shalt thou make thyself fair. Jer. iv. 30.

> In an extreame rage, *renting* his clothes and tearing his haire. *Lyly*, Euphues and his England, p. 230.

> Repentance must begin with a just sorrow, a sorrow of heart, and such a sorrow as *renteth* the heart.
> *Hooker*, Eccles. Polity, vi. 3.

> They assaulted me on all sides, buffeting me and *renting* my Cloaths. *Dampier*, Voyages, II. i. 92.

rent[1] (rent), *n.* [< *rent*[1], *v.*, ult. *rend*[1], *v.*] **1.** An opening made by rending or tearing; a tear; a fissure; a break or breach; a crevice or crack.

> You all do know this mantle. . . .
> Look, in this place ran Cassius' dagger through;
> See what a *rent* the envious Casca made.
> *Shak.*, J. C., iii. 2. 179.

2. A schism; a separation: as, a *rent* in the church.

> Heer sing I Isaac's civill Brauls and Broils;
> Jacobs Revolt; their Cities sack, their Spoils:
> Their cursed Wrack, their Godded Calues; the *rent*
> Of th' Hebrew Tribes from th' Isbeans Regiment.
> *Sylvester*, tr. of Du Bartas's Weeks, ii., The Schisme.

> We care not to keep truth separated from truth, which is the fiercest *rent* and disunion of all.
> *Milton*, Areopagitica, p. 53.

=**Syn.** Tear, rupture, rift.

rent[2] (rent), *n.* [< ME. *rent, rente* = D. G. Dan. *rente* = Sw. *ränta*, < OF. *rente*, F. *rente*, income, revenue, rent, annuity, pension, funds, = Pr. *renta, renda* = Sp. *renta* = Pg. *renda* = It. *rendita*, income, revenue, rent, < L. *reddita* (sc. *pecunia*), 'money paid,' fem. of *redditus*, pp. of *reddere*, give back, pay, yield: see *render*[2].] **1**†. Income; revenue; receipts from any regular source.

> Litel was hire catel and hire *rente*.
> *Chaucer*, Nun's Priest's Tale, l. 7.

> She seyde, "O Love, to whom I have and shal
> Ben humble suget, trewe in myn entente,
> As I best can, to you, Lord, geve Ich al
> For everemo myn hertes lust to *rente*."
> *Chaucer*, Troilus, ii. 830.

2. In *law*: (*a*) A compensation or return made periodically, or fixed with reference to a period of time, for the possession and use of property of any kind.

> Of all the tulkes of Troy, to telle them by name,
> Was non so riche of *renttes*, ne of renke godes,
> Of castels full close, & mony clene tounes.
> *Destruction of Troy* (E. E. T. S.), l. 3945.

> Thus the poete preiseth the pocok for hus federes,
> And the riche for hus *rentes*, othere rychesse in hus schoppe. *Piers Plowman* (C), xv. 186.

> Money, if kept by us, yields no *rent*, and is liable to loss.
> *Emerson*, Essays, 1st ser., p. 213.

(*b*) Technically, a definite compensation or return reserved by a lease, to be made periodically, or fixed with reference to a period of tenure, and payable in money, produce, or other chattels or labor, for the possession and use of land or buildings. Compensation of any other nature is not termed *rent*, because not enforceable in the same manner. The time of paying rents is either by the particular appointment of the parties in the deed, or by appointment of law, but the law does not control the express appointment of the parties, when such appointment will answer their intention. In England Michaelmas and Lady-day are the usual days appointed for payment of rents; and in Scotland Martinmas and Whitsunday.

> Take (deer Son) to thee
> This Farm's demains, . . .
> And th' only *Rent* that of it I reserue is
> One Trees fair fruit, to shew thy sute and service.
> *Sylvester*, tr. of Du Bartas's Weeks, ii., Eden.

> *Rent* is said to be due at the first moment of the day appointed for payment, and in arrear at the first moment of the day following. *Encyc. Brit.*, XIV. 275.

(*c*) The right to such compensation, particularly in respect of lands. Rents, at common law, are of three kinds: *rent-service, rent-charge* or *fee-farm rent*, and *rent-seck*. *Rent-service* is when some corporal service is incident to it, as by fealty and a sum of money: *rent-charge*, or *fee-farm rent*, is when the owner of the rent has no future interest or reversion expectant in the land, but the rent is reserved in the deed by a clause of distress for rent in arrear (in other words, it is a charge on lands, etc., in the form of rent, in favor of one who is not the landlord): *rent-seck* is a like rent, but without any clause of distress. There are also *rents of assize*, certain established rents of freeholders and copyholders of manors, which cannot be varied: also called *quit-rents*. These, when payable in silver, are called *white rents*, in contradistinction to rents reserved in work or the baser metals, called *black rents* or *black mail*.

3. In *polit. econ.*, that part of the produce of the soil which is left after deducting what is necessary to the support of the producers (including the wages of the laborers), the interest on the necessary capital, and a supply of seed for the next year; that part of the produce of a given piece of cultivated land which it yields over and above that y e ded by the poorest land in cultivation undor equal circumstances in respect to transportation, etc. The rent theoretically goes to the owner of the soil, whether cultivator or landlord. Also called *economic rent*.

Rent is that portion of the produce of the earth which is paid to the landlord for the use of the original and indestructible powers of the soil. It is often, however, confounded with the interest and profit of capital, and, in popular language, the term is applied to whatever is annually paid by a farmer to his landlord. *Ricardo*, Pol. Econ., ii.

The *rent*, therefore, which any land will yield, is the excess of its produce beyond what would be returned to the same capital if employed on the worst land in cultivation. *J. S. Mill*, Pol. Econ., II. xvi. § 3.

Rent is that portion of the regular net product of a piece of land which remains after deducting the wages of labor and the interest on the capital usual in the country incorporated into it. *W. Roscher*, Pol. Econ. (trans.), II. § 149.

No part of Ricardo's theory is more elementary or more unchallenged than this, that the *rent* of land constitutes no part of the price of bread, and that high *rent* is not the cause of dear bread, but dear bread the cause of high *rent*. *Rae*, Contemporary Socialism, p. 428.

4. An endowment; revenue.

The kynge hym graunted, and yaf hym *rentes*, and lefte with hym of his auoir grete plente for to make the hospitall, and ther lefte the clerke in this manere, that was after a goode man and holy of lif. *Merlin* (E. E. T. S.), ii. 369.

Alwyn Childe, a Citizen of London, founded the Monastery of S. Saviour's at Bermondsey in Southwark, and gave the Monks there divers *Rents* in London. *Baker*, Chronicles, p. 29.

Annual rent. See *annual*.—**Black rent.** (*a*) See *black*. (*b*) See def. 2 (*c*).—**Double rent**, rent payable by a tenant who continues in possession after the time for which he has received notice to quit until the time of his quitting possession.—**Forehand rent.** (*a*) A fine or premium given by the lessee at the time of taking his lease: otherwise called a *fore-gift* or *income*. (*b*) Rent paid in advance.—**Paschal rents.** See *paschal*.—**Peppercorn rents.** See *peppercorn*.—**Rents of assize.** See def. 2 (*c*).—**Tithe Rent-charge Redemption Act**, an English statute of 1885 (48 and 49 Vict., c. 32), which extends the Commutation of Tithes Act (which see, under *commutation*) to all rents or payments charged on lands, by virtue of any act, in lieu of tithes.

rent[2] (rent), *v.* [< ME. *renten*, < OF. *renter*, give rent or revenue to, = Sp. *rentar*, produce, yield; from the noun.] **I.** *trans.* **1**†. To endow; secure an income to.

And sette scoleres to scole or to somme other craftes;
Releue religioun [religious orders] and *renten* hem bettere. *Piers Plowman* (B), vii. 32.

Here is a stately Hospitall built by Cassachi, or Rosa, the Wife of great Soliman, richly *rented*, and nourishing many poore people. *Purchas*, Pilgrimage, p. 271.

2. To grant the possession and enjoyment of for a consideration in the nature of rent; let on lease.

There is no reason why an honourable society should *rent* their estate for a trifle. *Swift*, To Mr. Alderman Barber, March 30, 1737.

3. To take and hold for a consideration in the nature of rent: as, the tenant *rents* his farm for a year.

Not happier . . .
In forest planted by a father's hand
Than in five acres now of *rented* land.
Pope, Imit. of Horace, II. ii. 136.

Who was dead,
Who married, who was like to be, and how
The races went, and who would *rent* the hall.
Tennyson, Audley Court.

4. To hire; obtain the use or benefit of for a consideration, without lease or other formality, but for a more or less extended time: as, to *rent* a row-boat; to *rent* a piano.=**Syn.** 3 and 4. *Lease*, etc. See *hire*[1].

II. *intrans.* To be leased or let for rent: as, an estate *rents* for five thousand dollars a year.

rent[3]†, *v. i.* An obsolete variant of *rant*.

rent[4]† (rent). A Middle English contracted form of *rendeth*, 3d person singular present indicative of *rend*[1]. *Chaucer*.

rentable (ren'ta-bl), *a.* [< *rent*[2] + *-able*.] Capable of being rented.

rentage† (ren'tāj), *n.* [< OF. *rentage*, rentage, < *renter*, give rent to: see *rent*[2] and *-age*.] Rent.

Nor can we pay the fine and *rentage* due.
P. Fletcher, Purple Island, vii.

rental (ren'tal), *n.* [< ME. *rental*, < *rent*[2] + *-al*. Cf. OF. *rental*, charged with rent.] 1. A schedule or an account of rents, or a roll wherein the rents of a manor or an estate are set down; a rent-roll.

I have heard of a thing they call Doomsday-book—I am clear it has been a *rental* of back-ganging tenants. *Scott*, Redgauntlet, letter xi.

The nations were admonished to cease their factions; the heads of houses were ordered to surrender all their charters, donations, statutes, bulls, and papistical muniments, and to transmit a complete *rental* and inventory of all their effects to their Chancellor. *R. W. Dixon*, Hist. Church of Eng., iv.

2. The gross amount of rents drawn from an estate or other property: as, the *rental* of the estate is five thousand a year.—**Minister's rental.** See *minister*.—**Rental right**, a species of lease at low rent, usually for life. The holders of such leases were called *rentallers* or *kindly tenants*.

rentaller (ren'tal-ėr), *n.* [< *rental* + *-er*[1].] One who holds a rental right. See *rental*.

Many of the more respectable farmers were probably descended of the *rentallers* or kindly tenants described in our law books, who formed in the Middle Ages a very numerous and powerful body. *Edinburgh Rev.*, CXLV. 194.

rent-arrear (rent'a-rēr'), *n.* Unpaid rent.

rent-charge (rent'chärj), *n.* See *rent*[2], 2 (*c*).

rent-day (rent'dā), *n.* The day for paying rent.

rente (ront), *n.* [< F. *rente*: see *rent*[2].] Annual income; revenue; rent; interest; specifically, in the plural, *rentes* (or *rentes sur l'état*), sums paid annually by a government as interest on public loans; hence, the bonds or stocks on which such interest is paid.

renter[1] (ren'tėr), *n.* [< OF. *rentier*, F. *rentier* (= Pr. *rendier* = OCat. *render* = Sp. *rentero* = Pg. *rendeiro*), a tenant, renter, < *rente*, rent: see *rent*[2].] 1. One who leases an estate; more commonly, the lessee or tenant who takes an estate or a tenement on rent.

The estate will not be let for one penny more or less to the *renter*, amongst whomsoever the rent he pays be divided. *Locke*.

2. One who rents or hires anything.

renter[2] (ren'tėr), *v. t.* [Also *ranter*; < F. *rentraire*, sew together, < *re-*, again, + *en-*, in, + *traire*, draw: see *trace*, *tract*, etc.] 1. In *tapestry*, to work new warp into in order to restore the original pattern or design. Hence—2. To finedraw; sew together, as the edges of two pieces of cloth, without doubling them, so that the seam is scarcely visible.

renterer (ren'tėr-ėr), *n.* [< *renter*[2] + *-er*[1].] One who renters, especially in tapestry-work. See *renter*[2], *v. t.*, 1.

renter-warden (ren'tėr-wâr'dn), *n.* The warden of a company who receives rents.

rent-free (rent'frē), *adv.* Without payment of rent.

All such inmates which fell to decay, and so to be kept by the parish, they were to be continued in their houses *rent-free*, and to be kept at the only charge of the landlord which admitted them. *Court and Times of Charles I.*, II. 282.

rent-gatherer†, *n.* [ME. *rente-gaderer*; < *rent*[2] + *gatherer*.] A collector of rents. *Prompt. Parv.*, p. 430.

rentier (roṅ-tiā'), *n.* [F. *rentier*: see *renter*[1].] One who has a fixed income, as from lands, stocks, etc.; a fund-holder.

rent-roll (rent'rōl), *n.* A rental; a list or account of rents or income. See *rental*.

Godfrey Bertram . . . succeeded to a long pedigree and a short *rent-roll*, like many lairds of that period. *Scott*, Guy Mannering, ii.

rent-seck (rent'sek), *n.* See *rent*[2], 2 (*c*).

rent-service (rent'sėr'vis), *n.* See *rent*[2], 2 (*c*).

renuent (ren'ū-ent), *a.* [< L. *renuen(t-)s*, ppr. of *renuere*, nod back the head, deny by a motion of the head, disapprove (> Pg. *renuir*, refuse; cf. Sp. *renuencia*, reluctance), < *re-*, back, + **nuere* (in comp. *abnuere*, etc.), nod: see *nutation*.] Throwing back the head: specifically applied in anatomy to muscles which have this effect.

renule[1]†, *v.* An obsolete form of *renovel*.

renule[2] (ren'ūl), *n.* [< NL. **renulus*, dim. of L. *ren*, kidney: see *ren*[3], and cf. *renculus*.] A small kidney; a renal lobe or lobule, several of which may compose a kidney. *Encyc. Brit.*, XV. 366.

renumber (rē-num'bėr), *v. t.* [< *re-* + *number*.] To count or number again; affix a new number to, as a house.

renumerate (rē-nū'me-rāt), *v. t.* [< L. *renumeratus*, pp. of *renumerare*, count over (> It. *rinumerare*), < *re-*, again, + *numerare*, number: see *numerate*, and cf. *renumber*.] To count or number again. *Imp. Dict.*

renunciance (rē-nun'sians), *n.* [< L. *renuntian(t-)s*, ppr. of *renuntiare*, renounce: see *renounce*.] Renunciation. [Rare.]

Yet if they two . . . each, in silence, in tragical *renunciance*, did find that the other was all too-lovely? *Carlyle*, French Rev., II. v. 3.

renunciation (rē-nun-si-ā'shon), *n.* [< OF. *renunciation*, *renonciation*, F. *renonciation* = Pr. *renunciatio* = Sp. *renunciacion* = Pg. *renunciação* = It. *rinunziazione*, *renunziazione*, < L. *renuntiatio(n-)*, *renunciatio(n-)*, a renouncing, < *renuntiare*, pp. *renuntiatus*, renounce: see *renounce*.] The act of renouncing. (*a*) A disowning or disclaiming; rejection.

He that loves riches can hardly believe the doctrine of poverty and *renunciation* of the world. *Jer. Taylor*.

Renunciation remains sorrow, though a sorrow borne willingly. *George Eliot*, Mill on the Floss, iv. 3.

(*b*) In *law*, the legal act by which a person abandons a right acquired, but without transferring it to another: applied particularly in reference to an executor or trustee who has been nominated in a will, or other instrument creating a trust, but who, having an option to accept it, declines to do so, and in order to avoid any liability expressly renounces the office. In Scots law the term is also used in reference to an heir who is entitled, if he chooses, to succeed to heritable property, but, from the extent of the encumbrances, prefers to refuse it. (*c*) In *liturgics*, that part of the baptismal service in which the candidate, either in person or by his sureties, renounces the world, the flesh, and the devil.—**Renunciation of a lease**, in Scotland, the surrender of a lease.=**Syn.** (*a*) Abandonment, relinquishment, surrender. See *renounce*.

renunciatory (rē-nun'si-ā-tō-ri), *a.* [< ML. *renuntiatorius*, < L. *renuntiare*, renounce: see *renounce*.] Of or pertaining to renunciation.

renverse† (ren-vėrs'), *v. t.* [Also *ranverse*; < OF. *renverser*, overthrow, overturn, < *re-*, back, + *enverser*, overturn, invert, < *envers*, against, toward, with, < L. *inversus*, turned upside down, inverted: see *inverse*.] 1. To overthrow; overturn; upset; destroy.

God forbid that a Business of so high a Consequence as this . . . should be *ranversed* by Differences 'twixt a few private Subjects, tho' now public Ministers. *Howell*, Letters, I. iii. 20.

2. To turn upside down; overthrow.

First he his beard did shave, and fowly shent,
Then from him reft his shield, and it *renverst*.
Spenser, F. Q., V. iii. 37.

Whiles all my hopes were to the winds disperst,
Erected whiles, and whiles againe *renverst*.
Stirling, Aurora, st. 77.

renverse (ren-vėrs'), *a.* [< *renverse*, *v.*; cf. F. adv. *à la renverse*, on one's back, upside down.] In *her.*, same as *reversed*.

renversement† (ren-vėrs'ment), *n.* [< OF. *renversement*, < *renverser*, reverse: see *renverse* and *-ment*.] The act of renversing.

A total *renversement* of the order of nature. *Stukeley*, Palæographia Sacra, p. 60.

renvoy† (ren-voi'), *v. t.* [< OF. *renveier*, *renvoyer*, F. *renvoyer* (= It. *rinviare*), send back, < *re-*, back, + *envoyer*, send: see *envoy*[1].] To send back. *Bacon*, Hist. Hen. VIII.

renvoy† (ren-voi'), *n.* [< OF. *renvoy*, *renvoi*, F. *renvoi*, a sending back: see *renvoy*, *v.*] The act of sending back or dismissing home.

The *renvoy* of the Ampelonians was ill taken by the royal vine. *Howell*, Vocall Forrest. (*Latham.*)

reny†, *v. i.* and *t.* [Also *renay*; < ME. *renyen*, *reneyen*, *reneien*, *renayen*, < OF. *renier*, *reneier*, *renoier*, F. *renier*, < ML. *renegare*, deny: see *renegate*, and cf. *renege*, a doublet of *reny*. Cf. *deny*, *denay*.] To renounce; abjure; disown; abandon; deny.

That Ydole is the God of false Cristene, that han *reneyed* hire Feythe. *Mandeville*, Travels, p. 173.

For though that thou *reneyed* hast my lay,
As other wrecches han doon many a day, . . .
If that thou live, thou shalt repenten this.
Chaucer, Good Women, l. 336.

renye†, *n.* [ME., < OF. *renié*, < ML. *renegatus*, one who has denied his faith, a renegade: see *renegate*.] A renegade.

Raynalde of the rodes, and rebelle to Criste,
Pervertede with Paynyms that Cristene persewes; . . .
The *renye* relys abowte and ruschez to the erthe.
Morte Arthure (E. E. T. S.), l. 2795.

reobtain (rē-ob-tān'), *v. t.* [< *re-* + *obtain*.] To obtain again.

I came to *re-obtaine* my dignitie,
And in the throne to seate my sire againe.
Mir. for Mags., p. 758.

reobtainable (rē-ọb-tā'nạ-bl), *a.* [< *reobtain* + *-able.*] That may be obtained again.

reoccupy (rẹ̄-ok'ū-pī), *v. t.* [< F. *réoccuper;* as *re-* + *occupy.*] To occupy anew.

reometer, *n.* See *rheometer.*

reopen (rẹ̄-ō'pn), *v.* [< *re-* + *open, v.*] **I.** *trans.* To open again: as, to *reopen* a theater.

II. *intrans.* To be opened again; open anew: as, the schools *reopen* to-day.

reophore, *n.* See *rheophore.*

reoppose (rē-ọ-pōz'), *v. t.* [< *re-* + *oppose.*] To oppose again.

> We shall so far encourage contradiction as to promise no disturbance, or *re-oppose* any pen that shall fallaciously or captiously refute us.
> *Sir T. Browne,* Vulg. Err., Pref., p. 6.

reordain (rē-ôr-dān'), *v. t.* [= OF. *reordonner,* F. *réordonner* = Sp. *reordenar* = Pg. *reordenar,* *reordinar* = It. *riordinare,* reordain (cf. ML. *reordinare,* restore to one's former name or place); as *re-* + *ordain.*] To ordain again, as when the first ordination is defective or otherwise invalid.

> They did not pretend to *reordain* those that had been ordained by the new book in King Edward's time.
> *Bp. Burnet,* Hist. Reformation, ii. 2.

> A person, if he has been validly ordained by bishops of the apostolic succession, cannot be *reordained.* . . . It is not a reordination to confer orders upon one not episcopally set apart for the ministry. But it is reordination to do this to one previously so ordained. If it is done at all, it is a mockery, and the parties to it are guilty of a profanity. *Church Cyc.*

reorder (rē-ôr'dėr), *v. t.* [< *re-* + *order.*] **1.** To order a second time; repeat a command to or for.—**2.** To put in order again; arrange anew.

> At that instant appeared, as it were, another Armie comming out of a valley, . . . which gave time to Assan to *reorder* his disordered squadrons.
> *Capt. John Smith,* True Travels, I. 13.

reordination (rē-ôr-di-nā'shọn), *n.* [= F. *réordination* = Pg. *reordenação;* as *re-* + *ordination.*] A second or repeated ordination.

reorganization (rẹ̄-ôr"gạn-i-zā'shọn), *n.* [= F. *réorganisation;* < *reorganize* + *-ation.*] The act or process of organizing anew. Also spelled *reorganisation.*

reorganize (rẹ̄-ôr'gạn-īz), *v. t.* [= F. *réorganiser;* as *re-* + *organize.*] To organize anew; bring again into an organized state: as, to *reorganize* a society or an army. Also spelled *reorganise.*

re-orient (rē-ō'ri-ẹnt), *a.* [< *re-* + *orient.*] Arising again or anew, as the life of nature in spring. [Rare.]

> The life *re-orient* out of dust.
> *Tennyson,* In Memoriam, cxvi.

reossify (rē-os'i-fī), *v. i.* [< *re-* + *ossify.*] To ossify again. *Lancet,* No. 3487, p. 1424.

reotrope, *n.* See *rheotrope.*

rep[1] (rep), *n.* [Also *repp, reps;* origin unknown; supposed to be a corruption of *rib.*] A corded fabric the cords of which run across the width of the stuff. Silk rep is used for women's dresses, ecclesiastical vestments, etc., and is narrow; woolen rep is used for upholstery and curtains, and is about a yard and a half wide. It is sometimes figured, but more often dyed in plain colors.

> The reception-room of these ladies was respectable in threadbare brussels and green *reps.*
> *Howells,* A Woman's Reason, viii.

Cotton rep. See *cotton*[1].

rep[2] (rep), *n.* An abbreviation of *reputation,* formerly much used (as slang), especially in the asseveration *upon* or *'pon rep.*

> In familiar writings and conversations they [some of our words] often lose all but their first syllables, as in mob. *rep.* pos. incog. and the like.
> *Addison,* Spectator, No. 135.

> *Nev.* Madam, have you heard that Lady Queasy was lately at the play-house incog?
> *Lady Smart.* What! Lady Queasy of all women in the world! Do you say it upon *rep?*
> *Nev.* Pozz; I saw her with my own eyes.
> *Swift,* Polite Conversation, i.

rep. Same as *repet.*

repace (rē-pās'), *v. t.* [< *re-* + *pace*[1]. Doublet of *re-pass.*] To pace again; go over again in a contrary direction. *Imp. Dict.*

repacify (rē-pas'i-fī), *v. t.* [< *re-* + *pacify.*] To pacify again.

> Which, on th intelligence was notify'd
> Of Richard's death, were wrought to mutiny;
> And hardly came to be *repacify'd,*
> And kept to hold in their fidelity.
> *Daniel,* Civil Wars, iv. 9.

repack (rē-pak'), *v. t.* [< *re-* + *pack*[1], *v.*] To pack a second time: as, to *repack* beef or pork. *Imp. Dict.*

repacker (rē-pak'ėr), *n.* One who repacks. *Imp. Dict.*

repair[1] (rẹ̄-pãr'), *v. t.* [< ME. *reparen, repayren,* < OF. *reparer,* F. *réparer,* repair, mend, = Pr. Sp. Pg. *reparar* = It. *riparare,* repair, mend, remedy, shelter, restore, defend, parry, oppose, hinder, < L. *reparare,* get again, recover, regain, retrieve, repair, < *re-,* again, + *parare,* get, prepare: see *pare*[1].] **1.** To restore to a sound, good, or complete state after decay, injury, dilapidation, or partial destruction; restore; renovate.

> Thenne themperour dyde doo *repayre* the chirches.
> *Holy Rood* (E. E. T. S.), p. 164.

> Seeking that beauteous roof to ruinate
> Which to *repair* should be thy chief desire.
> *Shak.,* Sonnets, x.

> To *repair* his numbers thus impair'd.
> *Milton,* P. L., ix. 144.

2. To make amends for, as for an injury, by an equivalent; give indemnity for; make good: as, to *repair* a loss or damage.

> I'll *repair* the misery thou dost bear
> With something rich about me.
> *Shak.,* Lear, iv. 1. 79.

> King Henry, to *repair* the Loss of the Regent, caused a great Ship to be built, such a one as had never been seen in England. *Baker,* Chronicles, p. 257.

> She [Elizabeth] gained more . . . by the manner in which she *repaired* her errors than she would have gained by never committing errors. *Macaulay,* Burleigh.

3†. To fortify; defend.

> When the Soudan vnderstode his malice, he caused the Holy Lande to be better *repared* and more suerly kept, for yᵉ more displesur of the Turke. *Arnold's Chron.,* p. 162.

4†. To recover, or get into position for offense again, as a weapon.

> He, ere he could his weapon backe *repaire,*
> His side all bare and naked overtooke,
> And with his mortal steel quite through the body strooke.
> *Spenser,* F. Q., V. xi. 13.

=**Syn. 1.** To mend, refit, retouch, vamp (up), patch, tinker (up).

repair[1] (rẹ̄-pãr'), *n.* [Early mod. E. also *repayer;* < ME. *repaire, repeire* = Sp. Pg. *reparo,* repair, recovery, = It. *riparo,* remedy, resource, defense (cf. *rampart*); from the verb.] **1.** Restoration to a sound or good state after decay, waste, injury, or partial destruction; supply of loss; reparation.

> Even in the instant of *repair* and health,
> The fit is strongest. *Shak.,* K. John, iii. 4. 113.

> We have suffer'd beyond all *repair* of honour.
> *Fletcher,* Loyal Subject, v. 4.

> It is not that during the period of activity [of the nerve-centers] waste goes on without *repair,* while during the period of inactivity *repair* goes on without waste; for the two always go on together.
> H. *Spencer,* Prin. of Psychol., § 37.

2. Good or sound condition kept up by repairing as required; with a qualifying term, condition as regards repairing: as, a building in good or bad *repair.*

> Her sparkling Eyes she still retains,
> And Teeth in good *Repair.* *Congreve,* Doris.

> All highways, causeways, and bridges . . . within the bounds of any town shall be kept in *repair* and amended . . . at the proper charge and expense of such town.
> *R. I. Pub. Stats.,* ch. 65, § 1.

3†. Reparation for wrong; amends.

> In the quier make his *repayer* openly, and crave forgiveness of the other vicars choral and clerks.
> Quoted in *Contemporary Rev.,* LIII. 60.

4†. Attire; apparel.

> Rial *repeire,* riche roobis, and rent,
> What mowe thei helpe me at myn eende?
> *Political Poems,* etc. (ed. Furnivall), p. 201.

repair[2] (rẹ̄-pãr'), *v. i.* [< ME. *repairen, repeiren, reparen,* < OF. *repairer, repairier, repeirer, reparer, reperer,* return, come back, retire, tr. get back to, regain, lodge in, haunt, frequent; prob. the same, in a restricted use, as Sp. *repatriar* = It. *ripatriare,* return to one's country, < LL. *repatriare,* return to one's country, < L. *re-,* back, + *patria,* native land: see *patria,* and cf. *repatriate.* The It. *ripararsi,* frequent, repair to, is a reflexive use of *reparar,* shelter, defend, repair: see *repair*[1].] **1.** To go to a (specified) place; betake one's self; resort: as, to *repair* to a sanctuary for safety.

> "Lete be these wordes," quod sir Ewein, "and take youre horse, and lete vs *repeire* hom to the Court."
> *Merlin* (E. E. T. S.), iii. 572.

> Bid them *repair* to the market-place.
> *Shak.,* Cor., v. 6. 3.

2†. To return.

> Natheles, I thoughte he was so trewe,
> And eek that he *repaire* shulde ageyn
> Withinne a litel whyle.
> *Chaucer,* Squire's Tale, l. 581.

repair[2] (rẹ̄-pãr'), *n.* [< ME. *repair, repayre,* < OF. *repaire,* F. *repaire,* haunt, den, lair, = Pr. *repaire* = Sp. Pg. *reparo,* haunt; from the verb: see *repair*[2], *v.*] **1.** The act of betaking one's self to a (specified) place; a resorting.

> This noble marchaunt heeld a worthy hous,
> For which he hadde alday so greet *repair*
> For his largesse, and for his wyf was fair,
> That wonder is. *Chaucer,* Shipman's Tale, l. 21.

> Lastly, the king is sending letters for me
> To Athens, for my quick *repair* to court.
> *Ford,* Broken Heart, iii. 1.

2. A place to which one repairs; haunt; resort.

> I will it be cleped the mountain of the catte, ffor the catte hadde ther his *repeire,* and was ther slain.
> *Merlin* (E. E. T. S.), iii. 669.

> Where the fierce winds his tender force assail,
> And beat him downward to his first *repair.*
> *Dryden,* Annus Mirabilis, st. 220.

3†. Probably, an invitation or a return.

> As in an evening when the gentle ayre
> Breathes to the sullen night a soft *repaire.*
> *W. Browne,* Britannia's Pastorals, ii. 4. (*Nares.*)

repairable (rẹ̄-pãr'ạ-bl), *a.* [< *repair*[1] + *-able.* Cf. *reparable.*] Capable of being repaired; reparable.

> It seems scarce pardonable, because 'tis scarce a repentable sin or *repairable* malice.
> *Bp. Gauden,* Tears of the Church, p. 65. (*Davies.*)

repairer (rẹ̄-pãr'ėr), *n.* One who or that which repairs, restores, or makes amends.

> Sleep, which the Epicureans and others have represented as the image of death, is, we know, the *repairer* of activity and strength.
> *Landor,* Imaginary Conversations (Marcus Tullius and Quinctus Cicero).

repairment (rẹ̄-pãr'mẹnt), *n.* [< OF. *reparement* = Sp. *reparamiento* = It. *riparamento,* < ML. *reparamentum,* a repairing, restoration, < L. *reparare,* repair, restore: see *repair*[1].] The act of repairing.

repair-shop (rẹ̄-pãr'shop), *n.* A building devoted to the making of repairs, as in the rolling-stock of a railway.

repand (rẹ̄-pand'), *a.* [< L. *repandus,* bent back, turned up, < *re-,* back, + *pandus,* bent, crooked, curved.] In *bot.,* wavy or wavy-margined; tending to be sinuate, but less uneven; undulate: said chiefly of leaves and leaf-margins.

Repand Leaf of *Solanum nigrum.*

repandodentate (rẹ̄-pan"dō-den'tāt), *a.* In *bot.,* repand and toothed.

repandous (rẹ̄-pan'dus), *a.* [< L. *repandus,* bent back: see *repand.*] Bent upward; convexly crooked.

> Though they [pictures] be drawn *repandous,* or convexedly crooked in one piece, yet the dolphin that carrieth Arion is concavously inverted.
> *Sir T. Browne,* Vulg. Err., v. 2.

reparability (rep"ạ-rạ-bil'i-ti), *n.* [< *reparable* + *-ity* (see *-bility*).] The state or property of being reparable.

reparable (rep'ạ-rạ-bl), *a.* [< OF. *reparable,* F. *réparable* = Pr. Sp. *reparable* = Pg. *reparavel* = It. *riparabile,* < L. *reparabilis,* that may be repaired, restored, or regained, < *reparare,* repair, restore, regain: see *repair*[1].] Capable of being repaired; admitting of repair.

> An adulterous person is tied to restitution of the injury so far as it is *reparable* and can be made to the wronged person. *Jer. Taylor,* Holy Living, iii. § 4, 9.

=**Syn.** Restorable, retrievable, recoverable.

reparably (rep'ạ-rạ-bli), *adv.* So as to be reparable.

reparail†, *v.* See *reparel.*

reparation (rep-ạ-rā'shọn), *n.* [< ME. *reparacioun, reparacyoun,* < OF. *reparacion, reparation,* F. *réparation* = Pr. Sp. *reparacion* = Pg. *reparação* = It. *riparazione,* < LL. *reparatio(n-),* a restoration, < L. *reparare,* restore, repair: see *repair*[1].] **1.** The act of repairing; repair; restoration; upbuilding. [Now rare.]

> Whan the Mynystres of that Chirche neden to maken ony *reparacyoun* of the Chirche or of ony of the Ydoles, thei taken Gold and Silver . . . to quyten the Costages.
> *Mandeville,* Travels, p. 174.

> No German clock nor mathematical engine whatsoever requires so much *reparation* as a woman's face.
> *Dekker and Webster,* Westward Ho, i. 1.

2. What is done to repair a wrong; indemnification for loss or damage; satisfaction for any injury; amends.

> I am sensible of the scandal I have given by my loose writings, and make what *reparation* I am able. *Dryden.*

3†. A renewal of friendship; reconciliation.

> Mo dissymulaciouns
> And feyned *reparaciouns* . . .
> Ymade than greynes be of sondes.
> *Chaucer,* House of Fame, l. 688.

=**Syn. 1.** Restoration.—**2.** Compensation.

reparative (rē-par'ạ-tiv), *a.* and *n.* [= Sp. *reparativo*, < ML. ***reparativus*, < L. *reparare*, repair: see *repair*[1].] **I.** *a.* **1.** Capable of effecting or tending to effect repair; restoring to a sound or good state; tending to amend defect or make good: as, a *reparative* process.

Reparative inventions by which art and ingenuity studies to help and repair defects or deformities.
Jer. Taylor, Artif. Handsomeness (?), p. 60. (*Latham.*)

2. Pertaining to reparation or the making of amends.

Between the principle of *Reparative* and that of Retributive Justice there is no danger of confusion or collision, as one is concerned with the injured party, and the other with the wrongdoer.
H. *Sidgwick*, Methods of Ethics, p. 256.

II. *n.* That which restores to a good state; that which makes amends.

repare[1]†, *v. t.* A Middle English form of *repair*[1].

repare[2]†, *v. i.* A Middle English form of *repair*[2].

repareil† (rē-par'el), *v. t.* [< ME. *reparelen*, *reparellen*, *reparailen*, < OF. *repareiller*, *repareiller*, etc., repair, renew, reunite, < *re-*, again, + *apareiller*, prepare, apparel: see *apparel*. The word seems to have been confused with *repair*[1].] To repair.

He salle . . . come and *reparelle* this citee, and bigge it agayne also wele als ever it was.
MS. Lincoln A. i. 17, f. 11. (*Halliwell.*)

repareil† (rē-par'el), *n.* [Also *reparrel*; < *reparel*, *v.*] Apparel.

Mayest thou not know me to be a lord by my *reparrel?*
Greene, Friar Bacon and Friar Bungay.

Let them but lend him a suit of *reparel* and necessaries.
Beau. and Fl., Knight of Burning Pestle, Ind.

repart (rē-pärt'), *v. t.* [< OF. *repartir*, divide again, subdivide, reply, answer a thrust, < ML. **repartiri*, divide again, < L. *re-*, again, + *partire*, part, divide, share: see *part*, *v.*, and *party*[1].] To divide; share; distribute.

To glue the whole heart to one [friend] is not much, but howe much lesse when amongst many it is *reparted*.
Guevara, Letters (tr. by Hellowes, 1577), p. 77.

First, these Judges, in al cities and townes of their jurisdiction, do number the housholds, and do *repart* them in ten and tenne housholds; and upon the tenth house they do hang a table or signe, whereon is writen the names of those ten housholders, &c.
R. Parke, Hist. China, etc. (1588), p. 83. (*F. Hall*, Adjectives in *-able*, p. 205.)

repartee (rep-är-tē'), *n.* [Formerly also *reparty* (the spelling *repartee* being intended at the time (the 17th century) to exhibit the F. sound of the last syllable); < OF. *repartie*, an answering thrust, a reply, fem. of *reparti*, pp. of *repartir*, answer a thrust with a thrust, reply, divide again: see *repart*.] **1.** A ready, pertinent, and witty reply.

They [wicked men] know there is no drolling with so sour a piece as that [conscience] within them is, for that makes the smartest and most cutting *repartees*, which are uneasie to bear, but impossible to answer.
Stillingfleet, Sermons, I. xi.

There were the members of that brilliant society which quoted, criticised, and exchanged *repartees* under the rich peacock-hangings of Mrs. Montague.
Macaulay, Warren Hastings.

2. Such replies in general or collectively; the kind of wit involved in making sharp and ready retorts.

As for *repartee* in particular, as it is the very soul of conversation, so it is the greatest grace of comedy, where it is proper to the characters.
Dryden, Mock Astrologer, Pref.

You may allow him to win of you at Play, for you are sure to be too hard for him at *Repartee*. Since you monopolize the Wit that is between you, the Fortune must be his of Course.
Congreve, Way of the World, i. 6.

=**Syn.** 1. *Repartee*, *Retort*. A *repartee* is a witty and good-humored answer to a remark of similar character, and is meant to surpass the latter in wittiness. A *retort* is a keen, prompt answer. A *repartee* may be called a *retort* where the wit is keen. *Retort*, however, is quite as commonly used for a serious turning back of censure, derision, or the like, in a short and sharp expression.

Repartee is the witty retort in conversation.
J. De Mille, Rhetoric, § 453.

repartee (rep-är-tē'), *v. i.* [< *repartee*, *n.*] To make ready and witty replies.

High Flights she had, and Wit at Will,
And so her Tongue lay seldom still;
For in all Visits who but she
To argue, or to *repartee?*
Prior, Hans Carvel.

reparter† (rē-pär'tėr), *n.* [< *repart* + *-er*[1].] A distributor.

Of the temporall goods that God giues us, we be not lords but *reparters*.
Guevara, Letters (tr. by Hellowes, 1577), p. 152.

repartimiento (re-pär-ti-mien'tō), *n.* [< Sp. *repartimiento*, partition, division, distribution: see *repartment*.] **1.** A partition or division; also, an assessment or allotment.

In preparing for the siege of this formidable place, Ferdinand called upon all the cities and towns of Andalusia and Estremadura . . . to furnish, according to their *repartimientos* or allotments, a certain quantity of bread, wine, and cattle, to be delivered at the royal camp before Loxa.
Irving, Granada, p. 64.

2. In Spanish America, the distribution of certain sections of the country, including the native inhabitants (as peons), made by the early conquerors among their comrades and followers.

There was assigned to him [Las Casas] and his friend Renteria a large village in the neighbourhood of Xagua, with a number of Indians attached to it, in what was known as *repartimiento* (allotment).
Encyc. Brit., XIV. 320.

repartition (rē-pär-tish'ọn), *n.* [= F. *répartition* = Sp. *reparticion* = Pg. *repartição* = It. *ripartigione*, < ML. **repartitio(n-)*, < **repartiri*, divide again: see *repart*, and cf. *partition*.] A repeated or fresh partition; redistribution. *Bailey.*

repartment†, *n.* [< OF. *repartement*, division, F. *répartement*, assessment, = Sp. *repartimiento* = Pg. *repartimento* = It. *ripartimento*, assessment, < ML. **repartimentum*, < **repartiri*, divide again: see *repart*.] A division; distribution; classification.

In these *repartments* of Epaminondas it apperteyneth not unto your honour and mee that we come in a good houre, nor that we stande in a good houre; for wee are now come to be of the number that goe in a good houre.
Guevara, Letters (tr. by Hellowes, 1577), p. 135.

repass (rē-pȧs'), *v.* [< OF. *repasser*, pass again, F. *repasser*, pass again, iron, set, hone, grind, = Sp. *repasar* = Pg. *repassar* = It. *ripassare*, < ML. *repassare*, pass back, return, < L. *re-*, back, + ML. *passare*, pass, go: see *pass*.] **I.** *intrans.* To pass or go back; move back: used specifically by conjurers or jugglers.

Nothing but hey-pass, *repass!*
Fletcher, Humorous Lieutenant, iv. 4.

Five girdles bind the skies: the torrid zone
Glows with the passing and *repassing* sun.
Dryden, tr. of Virgil's Georgics, i. 322.

II. *trans.* To pass again, in any sense.

Well have we pass'd and now *repass'd* the seas,
And brought desired help. *Shak.*, 3 Hen. VI., iv. 7. 5.

The bill was thoroughly revised, discussed, and *repassed* a little more than one year afterwards.
The Century, XXXVII. 559.

repassage (rē-pas'ạj), *n.* [< OF. *repassage*, F. *repassage* (ML. reflex *repassagium*), a returning, ironing, setting, honing, whetting, raking, etc., < *repasser*, return: see *repass*.] **1.** The act of repassing; a passing again; passage back.—**2.** In *gilding*, the process of passing a second coat of deadening glue as a finish over dead or unburnished surfaces. *Gilder's Manual*, p. 24.

repassant (rē-pas'ạnt), *a.* [< F. *repassant*, ppr. of *repasser*, repass: see *repass*.] In *her.*, same as *counter-passant*.

repassion (rē-pash'ọn), *n.* The reception of an effect by one body from another which is more manifestly affected by the action than the former.

repast (rē-pȧst'), *n.* [< ME. *repast*, < OF. *repast*, *repas*, F. *repas*, a repast, meal (= Sp. *repasto*, increase of food), < ML. *repastus*, a meal, < L. *re-*, again, + *pastus*, food: see *pasture*.] **1.** A meal; the act of taking food.

What neat *repast* shall feast us, light and choice,
Of Attick taste, with wine? *Milton*, To Mr. Lawrence.

And hie him home, at evening's close,
To sweet *repast*, and calm repose.
Gray, Ode, Pleasure arising from Vicissitude, l. 88.

2. Food; victuals.

Go, and get me some *repast*,
I care not what, so it be wholesome food.
Shak., T. of the S., iv. 3. 15.

A buck was then a week's *repast*,
And 'twas their point, I ween, to make it last.
Pope, Imit. of Horace, II. ii. 93.

3†. Refreshment through sleep; repose.

Forthwith he runnes with feigned faithfull hast
Unto his guest, who, after troublous sights
And dreames, gan now to take more sound *repast*;
Whom suddenly he wakes. *Spenser*, F. Q., I. ii. 4.

repast† (rē-pȧst'), *v.* [= Sp. Pg. *repastar*, feed again: from the noun.] **I.** *trans.* To feed; feast.

To his good friends thus wide I'll ope my arms,
And, like the kind life-rendering pelican,
Repast them with my blood. *Shak.*, Hamlet, iv. 5. 147.

He then also, as before, left arbitrary the dyeting and *repasting* of our minds. *Milton*, Areopagitica, p. 10.

II. *intrans.* To take food; feast. *Pope.*

repaster† (rē-pȧs'tėr), *n.* One who takes a repast.

They doe plye theire commons, lyke quick and greedye *repasturs*,
Thee stagg vpbreaking they slit to the dulcet or inchepyn.
Stanihurst, Æneid, i.

repastination† (rē-pas-ti-nā'shọn), *n.* [< L. *repastinatio(n-)*, a digging up again, < *repastinare*, dig up again, < *re-*, again, + *pastinare*, dig: see *pastinate*.] A second or repeated digging up, as of a garden or field.

Chap. vi.—Of composts, and stercoration, *repastination*, dressing and stirring the earth or mould of a garden.
Evelyn, Misc. Writings, p. 730.

repasture† (rē-pȧs'tūr), *n.* [< *repast* + *-ure*.] Food; entertainment.

Food for his rage, *repasture* for his den.
Shak., L. L. L., iv. 1. 95.

repatriate (rē-pā'tri-āt), *v. t.* [< LL. *repatriatus*, pp. of *repatriare* (> It. *ripatriare* = Sp. Pg. *repatriar* = F. *repatrier*, *rapatrier*), return to one's country again, return home, < L. *re-*, back, + *patria*, native land: see *patria*. Cf. *repair*[2].] To restore to one's own country. *Cotgrave.*

He lived in a certain Villa Garibaldi, which had belonged to an Italian refugee, now long *repatriated*, and which stood at the foot of the nearest mountain.
Harper's Mag., LXXVI. 578.

repatriation (rē-pā-tri-ā'shọn), *n.* [< ML. *repatriatio(n-)*, < LL. *repatriare*, pp. *repatriatus*, return to one's country: see *repatriate*.] Return or restoration to one's own country.

I wish your Honour (in our Tuscan Phrase) a most happy *Repatriation*.
Sir H. Wotton, To Lord Zouch, Florence, June 13, 1592.

repay (rē-pā'), *v.* [< OF. *repayer* = Sp. Pg. *repagar* = It. *ripagare*, pay back; as *re-* + *pay*[1].] **I.** *trans.* **1.** To pay back; refund.

In common worldly things, 'tis call'd ungrateful
With dull unwillingness to *repay* a debt.
Shak., Rich. III., ii. 2. 92.

He will repay you; money can be *repaid*;
Not kindness such as yours.
Tennyson, Enoch Arden.

2. To make return, retribution, or requital for, in a good or bad sense: as, to *repay* kindness; to *repay* an injury.

And give God thanks, if forty stripes
Repay thy deadly sin. *Whittier*, The Exiles.

Repaying incredulity with faith.
Browning, Ring and Book, II. 150.

3. To make return or repayment to.

When I come again, I will *repay* thee. Luke x. 35.

Now hae ye play'd me this, fause love,
In simmer, mid the flowers?
I sall *repay* ye back again
In winter, 'mid the showers.
The Fause Lover (Child's Ballads, IV. 90).

II. *intrans.* To requite either good or evil; make return.

Vengeance is mine; I will *repay*, saith the Lord.
Rom. xii. 19.

'Tis not the grapes of Canaan that *repay*,
But the high faith that failed not by the way.
Lowell, Comm. Ode.

repayable (rē-pā'ạ-bl), *a.* [< *repay* + *-able*.] That may or must be repaid; subject to repayment or refunding: as, money lent, *repayable* at the end of sixty days.

repayment (rē-pā'mẹnt), *n.* [< *repay* + *-ment*.] **1.** The act of repaying or paying back.

To run into debt knowingly . . . without hopes or purposes of *repayment*. *Jer. Taylor*, Holy Dying, iv. § 8.

2. The money or other thing repaid.

What was paid over it was reckoned as a *Repayment* of part of the Principal. *Arbuthnot*, Ancient Coins, p. 200.

repe†, *v.* and *n.* A Middle English form of *reap*.

repeal (rē-pēl'), *v. t.* [< ME. *repelen*, < OF. *rapeler*, call back, recall, revoke, repeal, F. *rappeler*, call again, call back, call after, call in, recall, retract, call up, call to order, recover, regain, < *re-*, back, + *apeler*, later *appeler*, call, appeal: see *appeal*.] **1**†. To call back; recall, as from banishment, exile, or disgrace.

For syn my fader in so heigh a place
As parlement hath hire eschaunge enseled,
He nyl for me his lettre be *repeled*.
Chaucer, Troilus, iv. 560.

I here forget all former griefs,
Cancel all grudge, *repeal* thee home again.
Shak., T. G. of V., v. 4. 143.

2†. To give up; dismiss.

Yet may ye weel *repele* this busynesse,
And to reson sumwhat haue attendance.
Political Poems, etc. (ed. Furnivall), p. 72.

Which my liege Lady seeing thought it best
With that his wife in friendly wise to deale, . . .
And all forepast displeasures to *repeale*.
Spenser, F. Q., V. viii. 21.

Adam soon *repeal'd*
The doubts that in his heart arose.
Milton, P. L., vii. 59.

3. To revoke; abrogate, as a law or statute: it usually implies a recalling of the act by the power that made or enacted it.

Divers laws had been made, which, upon experience, were *repealed*, as being neither safe nor equal.
Winthrop, Hist. New England, I. 380.

The land, once lean, . . .
Exults to see its thistly curse *repeal'd*.
Cowper, Task, vi. 768.

A law for paying debts in lands or chattels was *repealed* within eight months of its enactment.
Bancroft, Hist. Const., I. 234.

=**Syn.** 3. *Annul, Rescind*, etc. See *abolish*, and list under *abrogate*.

repeal (rẹ̄-pēl'), *n.* [Early mod. E. *repel, repell*; < OF. *rapel*, F. *rappel*, a recall, appeal, < *rappeler*, call back: see *repeal, v.*] 1†. Recall, as from exile.

Her intercession chafed him so,
When she for thy *repeal* was suppliant,
That to close prison he commanded her.
Shak., T. G. of V., iii. 1. 234.

Begge not thy fathers free *repeale* to Court,
And to those offices we have bestow'd.
Heywood, Royal King (Works, ed. Pearson, 1874, VI. 52).

2. The act of repealing; revocation; abrogation: as, the *repeal* of a statute.—**Freedom of repeal†.** See *freedom*.—**Repeal agitation**, in *British hist.*, a movement for the repeal of the legislative union between Great Britain and Ireland. Its leader was Daniel O'Connell, and its climax was reached in the monster meetings in its favor in 1843. After the trial of O'Connell in 1844, the agitation subsided.=**Syn.** 2. See *abolish*.

repealability (rẹ̄-pē-la-bil'i-ti), *n.* [< *repealable* + *-ity* (see *-bility*).] The character of being repealable.

repealable (rẹ̄-pē'la-bl), *a.* [< OF. *rapelable*, F. *rappelable*, repealable; as *repeal* + *-able*.] Capable of being repealed; revocable, especially by the power that enacted.

Even that decision would have been *repealable* by a greater force. *Art of Contentment.* (*Latham.*)

repealableness (rẹ̄-pē'la-bl-nes), *n.* Same as *repealability*.

repealer (rẹ̄-pē'lėr), *n.* [< *repeal* + *-er*[1].] One who repeals; one who desires repeal; specifically, an agitator for repeal of the Articles of Union between Great Britain and Ireland.

In old days . . . [Separatists] would have been called *repealers*, and neither expression would to-day be repudiated by the Nationalist party in Ireland.
Edinburgh Rev., CLXIV. 580.

repealment (rẹ̄-pēl'mẹnt), *n.* [< *repeal* + *-ment*.] 1†. A calling back; recall, as from banishment.

Great is the comfort that a banished man takes at tidings of his *repealement*.
Wittes' Commonwealth, p. 220. (*Latham.*)

2. The act of abrogating or revoking; repeal. [Rare.]

repeat (rẹ̄-pēt'), *v.* [Early mod. E. *repete*; < OF. *repeter*, F. *répéter* = Pr. Sp. Pg. *repetir* = It. *repetere*, repeat, < L. *repetere*, attack again, seek again, resume, repeat, < *re-*, again, + *petere*, attack, seek: see *petition*. Cf. *appete, compete*.] **I.** *trans.* 1. To do, make, or perform again.

The thought or feeling a thousand times *repeated* becomes his at last who utters it best.
Lowell, Among my Books, 2d ser., p. 326.

2. To say again; iterate.

He that *repeateth* a matter separateth very friends.
Prov. xvii. 9.

No one can *repeat* any thing that Varilas has ever said that deserves repetition; but the man has that innate goodness of temper that he is welcome to every body.
Steele, Spectator, No. 100.

3. To say over; recite; rehearse.

The third of the five vowels, if you *repeat* them.
Shak., L. L. L., v. 1. 57.

He will think on her he loves,
Fondly he'll *repeat* her name.
Burns, Jockey 's ta'en the Parting Kiss.

4†. To seek again. [Rare.]

And, while through burning labyrinths they retire,
With loathing eyes *repeat* what they would shun.
Dryden, Annus Mirabilis, st. 257.

5. In *Scots law*, to restore; refund; repay, as money erroneously paid.—**To repeat one's self**, to say or do again what one has said or done before.—**To repeat signals** (*naut.*), to make the same signal which the senior officer has made, or to make a signal again.=**Syn.** 3. To relate. See *recapitulate*.

II. *intrans.* To perform some distinctive but unspecified function again or a second time. Specifically—(*a*) To strike the hour again when desired: said of watches that strike the hours, and will strike again the hour last struck when a spring is pressed. See *repeater*, 2. (*b*) To commit or attempt to commit the fraud of voting more than once for one candidate at one election. [U. S.]—**Repeating action**, in *pianoforte-making*, an action which admits of the repetition of the stroke of a hammer before its digital has been completely released.—**Repeating circle, decimal.** See *circle, decimal*.—**Repeating firearm**, a rifle or other firearm fitted with a magazine for cartridges, with an automatic feed to the barrel, or in some other way prepared for the rapid discharge of a number of shots without reloading. [This name was formerly applied to the revolver, but is now rarely so used.]—**Repeating instrument**, a geodetical or other optical instrument upon which the measurement of the angle can be repeated, beginning at the point of the limb where the last measurement ended, so as to eliminate in great measure the errors of graduation.—**Repeating rifle.** See *repeating firearm*, above.—**Repeating ship.** Same as *repeater*, 6 (*a*).

repeat (rẹ̄-pēt'), *n.* [< *repeat*, *v.*] 1. The act of repeating; repetition. [Rare.]

Of all whose speech Achilles first renew'd
The last part thus, . . .
And so of this *repeat* enough.
Chapman, tr. of Iliad, xvi. 57.

2. That which is repeated; specifically, in *music*, a passage performed a second time.

They [the Greek poets] called such linking verse Epimone, . . . and we may terme him the Loueburden, following the originall, or, if it please you, the long *repeate*.
Puttenham, Arte of Eng. Poesie, p. 188.

3. In *musical notation*, a sign that a passage or movement is to be twice performed. That which is to be repeated is usually included within the signs [sign] or [sign]. The sign 𝄋 is often added for greater distinctness. When the passage is not to be repeated entire, the terms *da capo* (*D. C.*) or *dal segno* (*D. S.*) are used, the former meaning 'from the beginning,' and the latter 'from the sign (𝄋),' and the end of the repeat is marked by *fine* or by a heavy bar with a hold, [sign]. A passage of only a measure or two which is to be repeated is sometimes marked [*bis.*].—**Double repeat†**, in *logic*, the middle term.

The *double repeat* (which is a woorde rehearsed in bothe proposicions) must not entre into the conclusion.
Wilson, Rule of Reason.

repeatedly (rẹ̄-pē'ted-li), *adv.* With repetition; more than once; again and again indefinitely.

repeater (rẹ̄-pē'tėr), *n.* 1. One who repeats; one who recites or rehearses.

Repeaters of their popular oratorious vehemencies.
Jer. Taylor (?), Artif. Handsomeness, p. 121.

2. A watch that, on the compression of a spring, strikes the last hour. Some also indicate the quarters, or even the hours, quarters, and odd minutes.—3. In *arith.*, an interminate decimal in which the same figure continually recurs. If this repetition goes on from the beginning, the decimal is called a *pure repeater*, as .3333, etc.; but if any other figure or figures intervene between the decimal point and the repeating figure, the decimal is called a *mixed repeater*, as .08333, etc. It is usual to indicate pure and mixed repeaters by placing a dot over the repeating figure: thus, the above examples are written $.\dot{3}$, and $.08\dot{3}$. A repeater is also called a *simple repetend*.

4. One who votes or attempts to vote more than once for one candidate at an election. [U. S.]

When every town and city in the United States is voting on the same day, and "colonists" and *repeaters* are needed at home, and each State is reduced for its voters to its own citizens.
The Nation, VI. 282.

5. A repeating firearm. (*a*†) A revolver. (*b*) A magazine-gun.

6. *Naut.*: (*a*) A vessel, usually a frigate, appointed to attend an admiral in a fleet, and to repeat any signal he makes, with which she immediately sails to the ship for which it is intended, or the whole length of the fleet when the signal is general. Also called *repeating ship*. (*b*) A flag which indicates that the first, second, or third flag in a hoist of signals is to be repeated.—7. In *teleg.*, an instrument for automatically retransmitting a message at an intermediate point, when, by reason of length of circuit, defective insulation, etc., the original line current becomes too feeble to transmit intelligible signals through the whole circuit.—8. In *calico-printing*, a figure which is repeated at equal intervals in a pattern.

repeating (rẹ̄-pē'ting), *n.* [Verbal n. of *repeat*, *v.*] The fraudulent voting, or attempt to vote, more than once for a single candidate in an election. [U. S.]

Repeating and personation are not rare in dense populations, where the agents and officials do not, and cannot, know the voters' faces.
Bryce, Amer. Commonwealth, II. 109.

repedation† (rep-ẹ̄-dā'shọn), *n.* [< LL. *repedare*, pp. *repedatus*, step back, < L. *re-*, back, + *pes* (*ped-*), foot: see *pedal, pedestrian*.] A stepping or going back; return.

To take notice of the directions, stations, and *repedations* of those erratick lights, and from thence most convincingly to inform himself of that pleasant and true paradox of the annual motion of the earth.
Dr. H. More, Antidote against Atheism, ii. 12.

repel (rẹ̄-pel'), *v.*; pret. and pp. *repelled*, ppr. *repelling*. [Formerly also *repell*; < ME. *repellen*, < OF. **repeller* = Sp. *repeler* = Pg. *repellir* = It. *repellere*, < L. *repellere*, pp. *repulsus*, drive back, < *re-*, back, + *pellere*, drive: see *pulse*[1]. Cf. *compel, expel, impel, propel*.] **I.** *trans.* 1. To drive back; force to return; check the advance of; repulse: as, to *repel* an assailant.

'Wyth this honde hast thou wryten many lettres by whiche thou *repellyd* moche folke fro doyng sacrefyse to our goddes. *Holy Rood* (E. E. T. S.), p. 159.

Foul words and frowns must not *repel* a lover.
Shak., Venus and Adonis, l. 573.

The Batavians . . . had enclos'd the Romans unawares behind, but that Agricola, with a strong Body of Horse which he reserv'd for such a purpose, *repell'd* them back as fast. *Milton*, Hist. Eng., ii.

But in the past a multitude of aggressions have occurred . . . which needed to be *repelled* by the speediest means. *Woolsey*, Introd. to Inter. Law, § 111.

2. To encounter in any manner with effectual resistance; resist; oppose; reject: as, to *repel* an encroachment; to *repel* an argument.—3. To drive back or away: the opposite of *attract*. See *repulsion*.—**Pleas proponed and repelled.** See *propone*.=**Syn.** 1 and 2. *Decline, Reject*, etc. (see *refuse*[1]), parry, ward off, defeat.

II. *intrans.* 1. To act with force in opposition to force impressed; antagonize.—2. In *med.*, to prevent such an afflux of fluids to any particular part as would render it tumid or swollen.

repellence (rẹ̄-pel'ẹns), *n.* [< *repellen(t)* + *-ce*.] Same as *repellency*.

repellency (rẹ̄-pel'ẹn-si), *n.* [As *repellence* (see *-cy*).] The character of being repellent; the property of repelling; repulsion.

repellent (rẹ̄-pel'ẹnt), *a.* and *n.* [= Sp. *repeliente* = Pg. It. *repellente*, < L. *repellen(t-)s*, ppr. of *repellere*, drive back: see *repel*.] **I.** *a.* 1. Having the effect of repelling, physically or morally; having power to repel; able or tending to repel; repulsive.

Why should the most *repellent* particles be the most attractive upon contact? *Bp. Berkeley*, Siris, § 237.

Its *repellent* plot deals with the love of a man who is more than half a monkey for a woman he saves from the penalty of murder. *Athenæum*, No. 2867, p. 474.

There are some men whom destiny has endowed with the faculty of external neatness, whose clothes are *repellent* of dust and mud. *Lowell*, Fireside Travels, p. 47.

2. Specifically, capable of repelling water; water-proof: as, *repellent* cloth or paper.

II. *n.* 1. In *med.*, an agent which is used to prevent or reduce a swelling. Astringents, ice, cold water, etc., are *repellents*.—2. A kind of water-proof cloth.

repeller (rẹ̄-pel'ẹ̄r), *n.* One who or that which repels.

repelless† (rẹ̄-pel'les), *a.* [< *repel* + *-less*.] Invincible; that cannot be repelled. [Rare.]

Two great Armados howrelie plow'd their way,
And by assaulte made knowne *repellesse* might.
G. Markham, Sir R. Grinuile (Arber rep.), p. 71.

repent[1] (rẹ̄-pent'), *v.* [< ME. *repenten*, < OF. (and F.) *repentir*, refl., = Pr. *repentir*, *repenedere* = Cat. *repenedir* = OSp. *repentir* (cf. mod. Sp. *arrepentir* = Pg. *ar-repender*, refl.) = It. *ripentire, ripentere*, repent, < ML. as if **repenitere*, repent (ppr. *repeniten(t-)s*, repentant), < L. *re-*, again, + *pænitere* (> OF. *pentir*), repent: see *penitent*.] **I.** *intrans.* 1. To feel pain, sorrow, or regret for something one has done or left undone.

Yef the myght thei wolde *repente* with gode will of the stryfe that thei hadde a-gein Merlin, but to late thei were to repente. *Merlin* (E. E. T. S.), ii. 176.

I never did *repent* for doing good,
Nor shall not now. *Shak.*, M. of V., iii. 4. 10.

Thus Grief still treads upon the Heels of Pleasure;
Marry'd in haste, we may *repent* at Leisure.
Congreve, Old Batchelor, v. 8.

2. Especially, to experience such sorrow for sin as produces amendment of life; be grieved over one's past life, and seek forgiveness; be penitent. See *repentance*.

Except ye *repent*, ye shall all likewise perish.
Luke xiii. 3.

Full seldom does a man *repent*, or use
Both grace and will to pick the vicious quitch
Of blood and custom wholly out of him,
And make all clean, and plant himself afresh.
Tennyson, Geraint.

3. To do penance.—4. To change the mind or course of conduct in consequence of regret or dissatisfaction with something that is past.

Sir knyght, so fer haste thow gon that late it is to *repente*, for he is longinge to me, and ther-fore I com hym for to chalenge. *Merlin* (E. E. T. S.), ii. 328.

Lest peradventure the people *repent* when they see war, and they return. Ex. xiii. 17.

5†. To express sorrow for something past.

For dead, I surely doubt, thou maist aread
Henceforth for ever Florimell to bee;
That all the noble knights of Maydenhead,
Which her ador'd, may sore *repent* with mee.
Spenser, F. Q., III. viii. 47.

Be witness to me, O thou blessed moon,
. . . poor Enobarbus did
Before thy face *repent!* *Shak.*, A. and C., iv. 9. 7.

=**Syn.** 1-4. See *repentance*.

II. *trans.* 1. To remember or regard with contrition, compunction, or self-reproach; feel self-accusing pain or grief on account of: as, to *repent* rash words; to *repent* an injury done to a neighbor.

Peraventur thu may *repent* it twyes,
That thu hast askid of this lande trevage.
Generydes (E. E. T. S.), l. 3342.

Confess yourself to heaven;
Repent what 's past; avoid what is to come.
Shak., Hamlet, iii. 4. 150.

My loss I mourn, but not *repent* it.
Burns, To Major Logan.

[Formerly often, and sometimes still, used reflexively and impersonally.

It *repenteth me* not of my cost or labor bestowed in the service of this commonwealth.
Winthrop, Hist. New England, I. 476.

This was that which *repented him*, to have giv'n up to just punishment so stout a Champion of his designes.
Milton, Eikonoklastes, ii.

Thou may'st *repent thee* yet
The giving of this gift.
William Morris, Earthly Paradise, II. 47.]

2†. To be sorry for or on account of.

"To that shalt thow come basicly," quod Gawein, "and that me *repenteth* sore, ffor moche wolde I love thy companye yef it the liked." *Merlin* (E. E. T. S.), iii. 592.

repent[1] (rē-pent'), *n.* [< *repent*[1], *v.*] Repentance. [Obsolete or archaic.]

Reproch the first, Shame next, *Repent* behinde.
Spenser, F. Q., III. xii. 24.

repent[2] (rē'pent), *a.* [< L. *repen(t-)s*, ppr. of *repere* (> It. *repere*), creep; akin to *serpere*, creep, Gr. ἕρπειν, creep: see *reptile* and *serpent*.] 1. In *bot.*, creeping; growing prostrate along the ground, or horizontally beneath the surface, and rooting progressively.—2. In *zoöl.*, creeping, as an animalcule; specifically, of or pertaining to the *Repentia*.

repentable (rē-pen'ta-bl), *a.* [< *repent*[1] + *-able*.] Capable of being repented of. [Rare.]

It seems scarce pardonable, because 'tis scarce a *repentable* sin or repairable malice.
Bp. Gauden, Tears of the Church, p. 65. (*Davies.*)

repentance (rē-pen'tans), *n.* [< ME. *repentance*, *repentaunce*, < OF. *repentance*, *repentaunce*, F. *repentance* = Pr. *repentensa* = It. *ripentenza*, < ML. as if **repenitentia*, < *repeniten(t-)s*, repentant: see *repentant*, and cf. *penitence*.] 1. The act of repenting; the state of being penitent; sorrow or contrition for what one has done or left undone.

For what is true *repentance* but in thought—
Not ev'n in inmost thought to think again
The sins that made the past so pleasant to us?
Tennyson, Guinevere.

2. In *theol.*, a change of mental and spiritual habit respecting sin, involving a hatred of and sorrow because of it, and a hearty and genuine abandonment of it in conduct of life.

John did . . . preach the baptism of *repentance* for the remission of sins. Mark i. 4.

As all sins deprive us of the favour of Almighty God, our way of reconciliation with him is the inward secret *repentance* of the heart. *Hooker*, Eccles. Polity, vi. 3.

Try what *repentance* can; what can it not?
Yet what can it when one can not repent?
Shak., Hamlet, iii. 3. 65.

=**Syn.** *Repentance, Penitence, Contrition, Compunction, Regret, Remorse*, may express the sorrowful feeling of the wrong-doer in view of his conduct. *Regret* is quite as often used of wishing that one had not done that which is unwise; as applied to misconduct, it expresses the feeblest degree of sorrow for doing wrong; but it may contain no element of real *repentance*. *Repentance* goes beyond feeling to express distinct purposes of turning from sin to righteousness; the Bible word most often translated *repentance* means a change of mental and spiritual attitude toward sin. Strictly, *repentance* is the beginning of amendment of life; the word does not imply any greater degree of feeling than is necessary to bring about a change, whether the turning be from a particular sin or from an attitude of sin. *Penitence* implies a large measure of feeling, and applies more exclusively than *repentance* to wrong-doing as an offense against God and right. *Contrition*, literally breaking or bruising, is essentially the same as *penitence*; it is a deep, quiet, and continued sorrow, chiefly for specific acts. *Compunction*, literally pricking, is a sharp pang of regret or self-reproach, often momentary and not always resulting in moral benefit. It is more likely than remorse to result in good. *Remorse*, literally gnawing, is naturally sharper mental suffering than *compunction*; the word often suggests a sort of spiritual despair or hopelessness, paralyzing one for efforts to attain repentance.

repentant (rē-pen'tant), *a.* and *n.* [< ME. *repentant*, < OF. *repentant*, repentant, penitent, < ML. *repeniten(t-)s*, ppr. of **repenitere*, repent: see *repent*[1].] **I.** *a.* 1. Experiencing repentance; sorrowful for past conduct or words; sorrowful for sin.

There is no sin so great but God may forgive it, and doth forgive it to the *repentant* heart.
Latimer, 2d Sermon bef. Edw. VI., 1550.

Thus they, in lowliest plight, *repentant* stood,
Praying. *Milton*, P. L., xi. 1.

2. Expressing or showing repentance.

After I have solemnly interr'd
At Chertsey monastery this noble king,
And wet his grave with my *repentant* tears.
Shak., Rich. III., i. 2. 216.

Relentless walls! whose darksome round contains
Repentant sighs and voluntary pains.
Pope, Eloisa to Abelard.

=**Syn.** See *repentance*.

II. *n.* One who repents; a penitent.

repentantly (rē-pen'tant-li), *adv.* In a repentant manner; with repentance.

To her I will myself address,
And my rash faults *repentantly* confess.
Fletcher, Faithful Shepherdess, v. 4.

repenter (rē-pen'tėr), *n.* One who repents.

Sentences from which a too-late *repenter* will suck desperation. *Donne*, Devotions, p. 221.

Repentia† (rē-pen'shi-ạ), *n. pl.* [NL., neut. pl. of L. *repen(t-)s*, creeping: see *repent*[2].] The limbless lacertilians as a division of squamate reptiles. *Merrem.*

repentingly (rē-pen'ting-li), *adv.* With repentance. *Imp. Dict.*

repentless (rē-pent'les), *a.* [< *repent*[1] + *-less*.] Without repentance; unrepenting. *Jodrell.*

repeople (rē-pē'pl), *v. t.* [< OF. *repeupler*, F. *repeupler*, also *repopuler* = Sp. *repoblar* = It. *ripopolare*; as *re-* + *people*.] To people anew; furnish again with a stock of people.

I send with this my discourse of ways and means for encouraging marriage and *repeopling* the island.
Steele, Tatler, No. 195.

repercept (rē-pėr'sept), *n.* [< *re-* + *percept*.] A represented percept. *Mind*, X. 122.

reperception (rē-pėr-sep'shon), *n.* [< *re-* + *perception*.] The act of perceiving again; a repeated perception.

Keats . . . writes to his publisher, . . . "No external praise can give me such a glow as my own solitary *reperception* and ratification of what is fine."
Lowell, Among my Books, 2d ser., p. 313.

repercolation (rē-pėr-kō-lā'shon), *n.* [< *re-* + *percolation*.] Repeated percolation; in *phar.*, the successive application of the same percolating menstruum to fresh parts of the substance to be percolated.

repercuss (rē-pėr-kus'), *v. t.* [< L. *repercussus*, pp. of *repercutere* (> It. *ripercuotere* = Sp. Pg. *repercutir* = Pr. *repercutir* = F. *répercuter*), strike, push or drive back, reflect, reverberate, < *re-*, back, + *percutere*, strike: see *percuss*.] To beat or drive back; send back; reflect.

Air in ovens, though . . . it doth . . . boil and dilate itself, and is *repercussed*, yet it is without noise.
Bacon, Nat. Hist., § 118.

Perceiving all the subjacent country, at so small an horizontal distance, to *repercuss* such a light as I could hardly look against. *Evelyn*, Diary, Oct. 4, 1641.

repercussion (rē-pėr-kush'on), *n.* [< OF. *repercussion*, F. *répercussion* = Pr. *repercussio* = Sp. *repercusion* = Pg. *repercussão* = It. *ripercussione*, < L. *repercussio(n-)*, a rebounding, reflecting, < *repercutere*, strike back, reflect: see *repercuss*.] 1. The act of driving back; a rebounding or reflection; the throwing back of a moving body by another upon which it impinges; reverberation.

In echoes (whereof some are as loud as the original voice) there is no new elision, but a *repercussion* only.
Bacon, Nat. Hist., § 124.

The streams . . . appearing, by the *repercussion* of the water in manie places, to be full of great stones in the bottome. *J. Brende*, tr. of Quintus Curtius, viii.

The peculiar style of this critic [Hazlitt] is at once sparkling and vehement. . . . The volcano of his criticism heaves; the short, irruptive periods clash with quick *repercussion*. *I. D'Israeli*, Amen. of Lit., II. 99.

2. In *music*: (*a*) That tone in a Gregorian mode which is most frequently repeated; the dominant. (*b*) The reappearance of the subject and answer of a fugue in regular order after the general development with its episodes. (*c*) Any reiteration or repetition of a tone or chord.

repercussive (rē-pėr-kus'iv), *a.* and *n.* [< OF. *repercussif*, F. *répercussif* = Pr. *repercussiu* = Sp. *repercusivo* = Pg. *repercussivo* = It. *ripercussivo*; as *repercuss* + *-ive*.] **I.** *a.* 1. Of the nature of repercussion; causing repercussion or reflection.

Whose dishevell'd locks,
Like gems against the *repercussive* sun,
Give light and splendour.
Middleton, Family of Love, iv. 2.

The huge Cyclops did with molding Thunder sweat,
And Massive Bolts on *repercussive* Anvils bear.
Congreve, Taking of Namure.

2†. Repellent.

Blood is stanched . . . by astringents and *repercussive* medicines. *Bacon*, Nat. Hist., § 66.

3. Driven back; reverberated.

Echo, fair Echo, speak, . . .
Salute me with thy *repercussive* voice.
B. Jonson, Cynthia's Revels, i. 1.

Amid Carnarvon's mountains rages loud
The *repercussive* Roar. *Thomson*, Summer, l. 1162.

II. *n.* A repellent.

repertoire (rep-ėr-twor'), *n.* [< F. *répertoire*: see *repertory*.] A repertory; specifically, in *music* and the *drama*, the list of works which a performer or company of performers has carefully studied, and is ready to perform.

repertor† (rẹ-pėr'tor), *n.* [< L. *repertor*, a finder, discoverer, < *reperire*, pp. *repertus*, find out, discover: see *repertory*.] A finder. [Rare.]

Let others dispute whether Anah was the inventor or only the *repertor* of mules, the industrious founder or the casual finder of them.
Fuller, Pisgah Sight, IV. ii. 32. (*Davies.*)

repertorium (rep-ėr-tō'ri-um), *n.*; pl. *repertoria* (-ạ). [LL.] Same as *repertory*.

repertory (rep'ėr-tọ-ri), *n.*; pl. *repertories* (-riz). [< OF. **repertorie*, later *repertoire*, F. *répertoire* = Sp. Pg. It. *repertorio*, < LL. *repertorium*, an inventory, list, repertory, < L. *reperire*, pp. *repertus*, find, find out, discover, invent, < *re-*, again, + *parire*, usually *parere*, produce: see *parent*.] 1. A place where things are so arranged that they can readily be found when wanted; a book the contents of which are so arranged; hence, an inventory; a list; an index.

Hermippus, who wrote of . . . the poëme of Zoroastes, containing a hundred thousand verses twentie times told, of his making; and made besides a *repertorie* or index to every book of the said poësie.
Holland, tr. of Pliny, xxx. 1.

2. A store or collection; a treasury; a magazine; a repository.

His [Homer's] writings became the sole *repertory* to later ages of all the theology, philosophy, and history of those which preceded his.
Bolingbroke, Essays, ii., Error and Superstition.

The revolution of France is an inexhaustible *repertory* of one kind of examples. *Burke.*

3. Same as *repertoire*.

A great academic, artistic theatre, . . . rich in its *repertory*, rich in the high quality and the wide array of its servants. *H. James, Jr.*, The Tragic Muse, xxix.

reperusal (rē-pẹ-rö'zạl), *n.* [< *reperuse* + *-al*.] A second or a repeated perusal.

reperuse (rē-pẹ-röz'), *v. t.* [< *re-* + *peruse*.] To peruse again. *Bulwer.*

repet. An abbreviation of the Latin word *repetatur* (let it be repeated), used in prescriptions.

repetend (rep'ẹ-tend), *n.* [< L. *repetendus*, to be repeated, gerundive of *repetere*, repeat: see *repeat*.] 1. In *arith.*, that part of a repeating decimal which recurs continually; the circulate. It is called a *simple repetend* when only one figure recurs, as .3333, etc., and a *compound repetend* when there are more figures than one in the repeating period, as .029029, etc. It is usual to mark the single figure or the first and last figures of the period by dots placed over them: thus, the repetends above mentioned are written $.\dot{3}$ and $.\dot{0}2\dot{9}$. See *repeater*, 3.

2. Something which is or has to be repeated, as the burden of a song. [Rare.]

In "The Raven," "Lenore," and elsewhere, he [Poe] employed the *repetend* also, and with still more novel results. *Stedman*, Poets of America, p. 251.

repetent (rep-ẹ-tent'), *n.* [G., < L. *repeten(t-)s*, pp. of *repetere*, repeat: see *repeat*.] In Germany, a tutor or private teacher; a repetitor.

He [Bleek] was recalled to Berlin to occupy the position of *Repetent* or tutor in theology. *Encyc. Brit.*, III. 824.

repetition (rep-ẹ-tish'on), *n.* [< OF. *repetition*, F. *répétition* = Pr. *repetitio* = Sp. *repeticion* = Pg. *repetição* = It. *ripetizione*, < L. *repetitio(n-)*, a demanding back, reclamation, repetition, < *repetere*, seek again, repeat: see *repeat*.] 1. The act of repeating, in any sense; iteration of the same act, word, sound, or idea.

Ye haue another sort of *repetition* when in one verse or clause of a verse ye iterate one word without any intermission, as thus:

It was Maryne, Maryne that wrought mine woe.
Puttenham, Arte of Eng. Poesie, p. 167.

All the neighbour caves . . .
Make verbal *repetition* of her moans.
Shak., Venus and Adonis, l. 831.

Every feeling tends to a certain extent to become deeper by *repetition*. *J. Sully*, Outlines of Psychol., p. 484.

2. That which is repeated.—3†. Remembrance; recollection.

> Call him hither;
> We are reconciled, and the first view shall kill
> All *repetition*: let him not ask our pardon;
> The nature of his great offence is dead,
> And deeper than oblivion we do bury
> The incensing relics of it.
> *Shak.*, All's Well, v. 3. 22.

4. In *Scots law*, repayment of money erroneously paid.—5. Specifically, in *music*, the rapid reiteration or repercussion of a tone or chord, so as to produce a sustained effect, as upon the pianoforte and other stringed instruments.—6. Same as *repeating action* (which see, under *repeat*).—Repetition of 1', in *math.*, a partition in which a number occurs r times. Thus, 2 + 2 + 2 + 5 is a repetition of 3.=Syn. 1 and 2. See *recapitulate* and *pleonasm*.

repetitional (rep-ẹ-tish'on-al), *a.* [< *repetition* + *-al.*] Of the nature of or containing repetition.

repetitionary (rep-ẹ-tish'on-ā-ri), *a.* [< *repetition* + *-ary.*] Same as *repetitional*.

repetitioner† (rep-ẹ-tish'on-ėr), *n.* [< *repetition* + *-er*[1].] One who repeats; a repeater.

> In 1665 he [Sam. Jemmat] was the Repeater or *Repetitioner*, in St. Mary's church, on Low Sunday, of the four Easter Sermons. *Wood*, Fasti Oxon., II. 141.

repetitious (rep-ẹ-tish'us), *a.* [< *repetiti(on)* + *-ous.*] Containing or employing repetition; especially, characterized by undue or tiresome iteration. [U. S.]

> The observation which you have quoted from the Abbé Raynal, which has been written off in a succession not much less *repetitious*, or protracted, than that in which school-boys of former times wrote.
> Quoted by Pickering from *Remarks on the Review of Inchiquin's Letters* in the Quarterly Rev., Boston, 1815.

> The whole passage, Hamlet, i. 4. 17–38, "This heavy-headed revel, east and west," etc., is diffuse, involved, and *repetitious*. *Proc. Amer. Phil. Ass.*, 1883, p. xxii.

> An irrelevant or *repetitious* speaker.
> *Harper's Mag.*, LXXV. 515.

repetitiously (rep-ẹ-tish'us-li), *adv.* In a repetitious manner; with tiresome repetition. [U. S.]

repetitiousness (rep-ẹ-tish'us-nes), *n.* The character of being repetitious. [U. S.]

repetitive (rẹ-pet'i-tiv), *a.* [= Sp. *repetitivo*, < L. *repetere*, pp. *repetitus*, repeat: see *repeat*.] Containing repetitions; repeating; repetitious.

repetitor (rẹ-pet'i-tor), *n.* [= F. *répétiteur* = Pr. *repeteire* = Sp. Pg. *repetidor* = It. *ripetitore*, *ripititore*, < L. *repetitor*, one who demands back, a reclaimer, ML. a repeater, < *repetere*, seek again, repeat: see *repeat*.] A private instructor or tutor in a university.

repicque, *n.* and *v.* See *repique*.

repine (rẹ-pīn'), *v. i.*; pret. and pp. *repined*, ppr. *repining*. [Early mod. E. *repyne*; < *re-* + *pine*[2]; perhaps suggested by OF. *repoindre*, prick again, or by *repent*[1].] 1. To be fretfully discontented; be unhappy and indulge in complaint; murmur: often with *at* or *against*.

> Lachesis thereat gan to *repine*,
> And sayd: . . .
> "Not so; for what the Fates do once decree,
> Not all the gods can chaunge, nor Jove himself can free!"
> *Spenser*, F. Q., IV. ii. 51.

> This Saluage trash you so scornfully *repine at*, being put in your mouthes, your stomackes can disgest.
> Quoted in *Capt. John Smith's* Works, I. 229.

> Our Men, seeing we made such great runs, and the Wind like to continue, *repined* because they were kept at such short allowance. *Dampier*, Voyages, I. 281.

> Thy rack'd inhabitants *repine*, complain,
> Tax'd till the brow of Labour sweats in vain.
> *Cowper*, Expostulation, l. 304.

2†. To fail; give way.

> *Repining* courage yields
> No foote to foe. *Spenser*, F. Q., I. ii. 17.

repine (rẹ-pīn'), *n.* [< *repine*, *v.*] A repining. [Rare.]

> Were never four such lamps together mix'd,
> Had not his [eyes] clouded with his brow's *repine*.
> *Shak.*, Venus and Adonis, l. 490.

> And ye, fair heaps, the Muses' sacred shrines
> (In spite of time and envious *repines*)
> Stand still, and flourish. *Bp. Hall*, Satires, II. ii. 8.

repiner (rẹ-pī'nėr), *n.* One who repines or murmurs.

> Let rash *repiners* stand appalled
> Who dare not trust in Thee. *Young.*

> Alas for maiden, alas for Judge,
> For rich *repiner* and household drudge!
> *Whittier*, Maud Muller.

repining (rẹ-pī'ning), *n.* [Verbal n. of *repine*, *v.*] Discontent; regret; complaint.

> He sat upon the rocks that edged the shore,
> And in continued weeping and in sighs
> And vain *repinings* wore the hours away.
> *The Atlantic*, LXVI. 79.

repiningly (rẹ-pī'ning-li), *adv.* With murmuring or complaint.

repique (re-pēk'), *n.* [Also *repicque*; < F. *repic*, repique, < *repiquer*, formerly *repicquer*, prick or thrust again, < *re-* + *piquer*, prick, thrust, < *pic*, a point, pike: see *pike*[1].] In *piquet*, the winning of thirty points or more from combinations of cards in one's hand, before the playing begins and before an opponent has scored at all.

repique (re-pēk'), *v.* [< *repique*, *n.*] **I.** *intrans.* In *piquet*, to score a repique.

II. *trans.* To score a repique over.

> "Your game has been short," said Harley. "I *repiqued* him," answered the old man, with joy sparkling in his countenance. *H. Mackenzie*, Man of Feeling, xxv.

Also *repicque*.

replace (rẹ-plās'), *v. t.*; pret. and pp. *replaced*, ppr. *replacing*. [< *re-* + *place*; prob. suggested by F. *remplacer* (see *remplace*).] 1. To put again in the former or the proper place.

> The earl . . . was *replaced* in his government. *Bacon.*

> The deities of Troy, and his own Penates, are made the companions of his flight; . . . and at last he *replaces* them in Italy, their native country. *Dryden*, Æneid, Ded.

> A hermit . . . *replac'd* his book
> Within its customary nook.
> *Cowper*, Moralizer Corrected.

2. To restore (what has been taken away or borrowed); return; make good: as, to *replace* a sum of money borrowed.—3. To substitute something competent in the place of, as of something which has been displaced or lost or destroyed.—4. To fill or take the place of; supersede; be a substitute for; fulfil the end or office of.

> It is a heavy charge against Peter to have suffered that so important a person as the successor of an absolute monarch must needs be should grow up ill-educated and unfit to *replace* him. *Brougham.*

> With Israel, religion *replaced* morality.
> *M. Arnold*, Literature and Dogma, p. 44.

> These compounds [organic acids] may be regarded as hydrocarbons in which hydrogen is *replaced* by carboxyl.
> *Encyc. Brit.*, V. 553.

> The view of life as a thing to be put up with *replacing* that zest for existence which was so intense in early civilisations. *T. Hardy*, Return of the Native, iii. 1.

Replaced crystal. See *crystal*.=Syn. 1. To reinstate, reëstablish, restore.

replaceable (rẹ-plā'sa-bl), *a.* Capable of being replaced; that may be replaced.

replacement (rẹ-plās'ment), *n.* [< *replace* + *-ment*. Cf. F. *remplacement*, < *remplacer*, replace.] 1. The act of replacing.

> The organic acids may likewise be regarded as derived from alcohols by the *replacement* of H_2 by O.
> *Encyc. Brit.*, V. 553.

2. In *crystal.*, the removal of an edge or angle by one plane or more.

Replacement of the solid angles of a cube by the planes of a trapezohedron.

replacer (rẹ-plā'sėr), *n.* 1. One who or that which replaces, or restores to the former or proper place.—2. One who or that which takes the place of another; a substitute.—**Car-replacer**, a device carried on nearly all American railway-trains for quickly replacing derailed wheels on the track. It is used in pairs, one for each rail, and consists of a short heavy bar of i n swiveling on a yoke which is placed over the railhead. A sharp pull of the locomotive pulls the derailed wheels up the replacer, whence they drop upon the rails.

Car-replacer.

a, rail; *b*, *c*, replacer. The part *c* embraces the head of the rail when in use. The derailed car-wheel rolls up the incline *b*.

replacing-switch (rẹ-plā'sing-swich), *n.* A device consisting of a united pair of iron plates hinged to shoes fitting over the rails, used as a bridge to replace on the track derailed railway rolling-stock. A second pair of plates may be hinged to the first to facilitate the placing of the bridge in position to receive the car-wheels.

replait (rē-plāt'), *v. t.* [Also *repleat*; < *re-* + *plait*, *v.*] To plait or fold again; fold one part of over another again and again.

> In his [Raphael's] first works, . . . we behold many small foldings often *repleated*, which look like so many whipcords. *Dryden*, Observations on Dufresnoy's Art [of Painting.

replant (rē-plant'), *v. t.* [< OF. (and F.) *replanter* = Sp. Pg. *replantar* = It. *ripiantare*, < ML. *replantare*, plant again, < L. *re-*, again, + *plantare*, plant: see *plant*[1].] 1. To plant again.

> Small trees upon which figs or other fruit grow, being yet unripe, . . . take . . . up in a warm day, and *replant* them in good ground. *Bacon*, Nat. Hist., § 443.

2. Figuratively, to reinstate.

> I will revenge his wrong to Lady Bona,
> And *replant* Henry in his former state.
> *Shak.*, 3 Hen. VI., iii. 3. 198.

replant (rē-plant'), *n.* [< *replant*, *v.*] That which is replanted. [Recent.]

> No growth has appeared in any of the *replants*.
> *Medical News*, LII. 488.

replantable (rē-plan'ta-bl), *a.* [< OF. *replantable*; as *replant* + *-able*.] Capable of being planted again. *Imp. Dict.*

replantation (rē-plan-tā'shon), *n.* [< F. *replantation*; as *replant* + *-ation*.] The act of planting again.

> Attempting the *replantation* of that beautiful image sin and vice had obliterated and defaced.
> *Hallywell*, Saving of Souls (1677), p. 100. (*Latham.*)

replead (rē-plēd'), *v. t.* and *i.* [< OF. **replaider*, *repledoier*, *reploider*, plead again; as *re-* + *plead*.] To plead again.

repleader (rē-plē'dėr), *n.* [< OF. **replaider*, inf. used as a noun: see *replead*.] In *law*, a second pleading or course of pleadings; the right or privilege of pleading again: a course allowed for the correction of mispleading.

repleat (rē-plēt'), *v. t.* Same as *replait*.

repledge (rē-plej'), *v. t.* [< OF. *replegier* (ML. *replegiare*), pledge again; as *re-* + *pledge*. Cf. *replevy*.] 1. To pledge again.—2. In *Scots law*, to demand judicially, as the person of an offender accused before another tribunal, on the ground that the alleged offense had been committed within the repledger's jurisdiction. This was formerly a privilege competent to certain private jurisdictions.

repledger (rē-plej'ėr), *n.* One who repledges.

replenish (rẹ-plen'ish), *v.* [< ME. *replenissen*, < *repleniss-*, stem of certain parts of OF. *replenir*, fill up again, < L. *re-*, again, + ML. **plenire*, < *plenus*, full: see *plenish*.] **I.** *trans.* 1. To fill again; hence, to fill completely; stock.

> Desertes *replenisshed* with wylde beastis and venimous serpentes. *Sir T. Elyot*, The Governour, ii. 9.

> Be fruitful, and multiply, and *replenish* the earth.
> Gen. i. 28.

> Ther was . . . a quantitie of a great sorte of flies, . . . which came out of holes in ye ground, and *replenished* all ye woods, and eate ye green things.
> *Bradford*, Plymouth Plantation, p. 315.

2†. To finish; complete; consummate; perfect.

> We smothered
> The most *replenished* sweet work of nature.
> *Shak.*, Rich. III., iv. 3. 18.

3†. To revive. *Palsgrave.* (*Halliwell.*)

II.† *intrans.* To recover former fullness.

> It is like . . . that the humours in men's bodies increase and decrease as the moon doth; and therefore it were good to purge some day or two after the full; for that then the humours will not *replenish* so soon.
> *Bacon*, Nat. Hist., § 894.

replenisher (rẹ-plen'ish-ėr), *n.* One who or that which replenishes; specifically, in *elect.*, a static influence- or induction-machine used for maintaining the charge of a quadrant electrometer.

replenishment (rẹ-plen'ish-mẹnt), *n.* [< *replenish* + *-ment*.] 1. The act of replenishing, or the state of being replenished.—2. That which replenishes; a supply. *Cowper.*

replete (rē-plēt'), *a.* [Early mod. E. also *repleat*; < ME. *replete*, *replet*, < OF. (and F.) *replet* = Pr. *replet* = Sp. Pg. It. *repleto*, < L. *repletus*, filled up, pp. of *replere*, fill again, < *re-*, again, + *plere*, fill: see *plenty*. Cf. *complete*.] Filled up; completely filled; full; abounding.

> Ware the sonne in his ascencioun
> Ne fynde yow not *replet* of humours hote.
> *Chaucer*, Nun's Priest's Tale, l. 137.

> The world's large tongue
> Proclaims you for a man *replete* with mocks.
> *Shak.*, L. L. L., v. 2. 853.

> O, that's a comedy on a very new plan; *replete* with wit and mirth, yet of a most serious moral!
> *Sheridan*, The Critic, i. 1.

replete (rẹ-plēt'), *v. t.*; pret. and pp. *repleted*, ppr. *repleting*. [< L. *repletus*, pp. of *replere*, fill up: see *replete*, *a.*] To fill to repletion or satiety; fill full.

> Such have their intestines *repleted* with wind and excrements. *Venner*, Treatise of Tobacco, p. 407. (*Encyc. Dict.*)

repleteness (rē-plēt'nes), *n.* The state of being replete; fullness; repletion. *Bailey*, 1727.

repletion (rẹ-plē'shon), *n.* [< ME. *replecioun*, < OF. *repletion*, *replecion*, F. *réplétion* = Pr. *replecio* = Sp. *replecion* = Pg. *repleção* = It. *re-*

plezione, < L. *repletio(n-)*, a filling up, < *replere*, fill up: see *replete*.] 1. The state of being replete; fullness; specifically, superabundant fullness; surfeit, especially of food or drink.

> *Replecciour* ne made hire nevere sik;
> Attempre dyete was al hire phisik.
> *Chaucer*, Nun's Priest's Tale, l. 17.

> Drowsiness followed *repletion*, as a matter of course, and they gave us a bed of skins in an inner room.
> *B. Taylor*, Northern Travel, p. 118.

2. In *med.*, fullness of blood; plethora.

repletive (rē-plē'tiv), *a.* [< OF. *repletif*; as *replete* + *-ive*.] Causing repletion. *Cotgrave.*

repletively† (rē-plē'tiv-li), *adv.* In a repletive manner; redundantly.

> It [*behold*] is like the hand in the margin of a book, pointing to some remarkable thing, and of great succeeding consequence. It is a direct, a reference, a dash of the Holy Ghost's pen; seldom used *repletively*, but to impart and import some special note.
> *Rev. T. Adams*, Works, II. 110.

repletory (rē-plē'tō-ri), *a.* [< *replete* + *-ory*.] Of or pertaining to repletion; tending to or producing repletion.

> A University, as an intellectual gymnasium, should consider that its "mental dietetic" is tonic, not *repletory*.
> *Sir W. Hamilton*, Discussions, App. iii., C.

repleviable (rē-plev'i-a-bl), *a.* [< *replevy* + *-able*.] Same as *replevisable*.

replevin (rē-plev'in), *n.* [< OF. *replevin*, **replevine* (ML. *replevina*), < *replevir*, warrant, pledge: see *replevy*. Cf. *plevin*.] 1. In *law*, a personal action which lies to recover possession of goods or chattels wrongfully taken or detained, upon giving security to try the right to them in a suit at law, and, if that should be determined against the plaintiff, to return the property replevied. Originally it was a remedy peculiar to cases for wrongful distress, but it may now be brought in all cases of wrongful taking or detention, with certain exceptions as to property in custody of the law, taken for a tax, or the like. 2. The writ by which goods and chattels are replevied.—3†. Bail.—**Replevin in the cepit**, an action of replevin in which the charge was that the defendant wrongfully took the goods.—**Replevin in the detinet**, an action in which the charge was only that the defendant wrongfully detained the goods. The importance of the distinction between this and replevin in the cepit was that the latter was appropriate in cases where an action of trespass might lie, and did not require any demand before bringing the action.

replevin (rē-plev'in), *v. t.* [< *replevin*, *n.*] To replevy.

> Me, who once, you know,
> Did from the pound *replevin* you.
> *S. Butler*, The Lady's Answer to the Knight, l. 4.

replevisable (rē-plev'i-sa-bl), *a.* [< OF. *replevissable*, < *replevir*, replevy: see *replevish*.] In *law*, capable of being replevied. Also *repleviable*.

> This is a case in which neither bail nor mainprize can be received, the felon who is liable to be committed on heavy grounds of suspicion not being *replevisable* under the statute of the 3d of King Edward. *Scott*, Rob Roy, viii.

replevish (rē-plev'ish), *v. t.* [< OF. *repleviss-*, stem of certain parts of *replevir*, replevy: see *replevy*.] In *law*, to bail out; replevy.

replevisor (rē-plev'i-sor), *n.* [NL., < *replevis(h)* + *-or*[1].] A plaintiff in replevin.

replevy (rē-plev'i), *v.*; pret. and pp. *replevied*, ppr. *replevying*. [Early mod. E. *replevie*; < ME. **replevien*, < OF. *replevir*, < ML. *replevire*, also *replegiare* (after Rom.), give bail, surety, < *re-* + *plevire*, *plegiare*, warrant, pledge: see *pledge* and *plevin*, and cf. *replevin*.] I. *trans.* 1. To recover possession of by an action of replevin; sue for and get back, pending the action, by giving security to try the right to the goods in a suit at law. See *replevin*.—2†. To take back or set at liberty upon security, as anything seized; bail, as a person.

> But yours the waift [waif] by high prerogative.
> Therefore I humbly crave your Majestie
> It to *replevie*, and my son reprive.
> *Spenser*, F. Q., IV. xii. 31.

II. *intrans.* To take possession of goods or chattels sued for by an action of replevin.

> The cattle-owner . . . might either apply to the King's Chancery for a writ commanding the Sheriff to "make replevin," or he might verbally complain himself to the Sheriff, who would then proceed at once to *replevy*.
> *Maine*, Early Hist. of Institutions, p. 264.

replevy (rē-plev'i), *n.* [< ME. *replevy*; < *replevy*, *v.* Cf. *replevin*, *n.*] Replevin.

> The baly of the hundred told me that Wharles spake to hym, in cas he had be distreyned, that he wold have gete hym a *replevy*; and the baly bad hym kete a *replevy* of his mayster and he wold serve it. *Paston Letters*, I. 104.

replica (rep'li-kä), *n.* [= F. *réplique*, a copy, a repeat, < It. *replica*, a repetition, reply, < *replicare*, repeat, reply: see *reply*, *v.* Cf. *reply*, *n.*] 1. A work of art made in exact likeness of another and by the same artist, differing from a copy in that it is held to have the same right as the first made to be considered an original work.—2. In *music*, same as *repeat*, 2.

replicant (rep'li-kant), *n.* [= F. *répliquant* = Sp. Pg. It. *replicante*, a replier, < L. *replican(t-)s*, ppr. of *replicare*, repeat, reply: see *replicate*, *reply*.] One who makes a reply.

replicate (rep'li-kāt), *v. t.*; pret. and pp. *replicated*, ppr. *replicating*. [< L. *replicatus*, pp. of *replicare*, fold or bend back, reply: see *reply*.] 1. To fold or bend back: as, a *replicated* leaf.—2†. To reply.

> They cringing in their neckes, like rats, smothered in the holde, poorely *replicated*, . . . "With hunger, and hope, and thirst, wee content oureselves."
> *Nashe*, Lenten Stuffe (Harl. Misc., VI. 180).

3. In *music*, to add one of its replicates to (a given tone).

replicate (rep'li-kāt), *a.* and *n.* [= F. *répliqué* = Sp. Pg. *replicado* = It. *replicato*, < L. *replicatus*, pp. of *replicare*, fold or bend back: see *replicate*, *v.*] I. *a.* Folded. Specifically—(*a*) In *bot.*, folded back upon itself, either outward as in vernation, or inward as in estivation. (*b*) In *entom.*, noting wings which have a joint in the costal margin by means of which the outer part folds or rather slides back on the base, as the posterior wings of most beetles. Sometimes there are more than one of such transverse folds, and the wing may be folded like a fan before it is bent, as in the earwigs.

II. *n.* In *music*, a tone one or more octaves distant from a given tone; a repetition at a higher or lower octave.

replicatile (rep'li-kā-til), *a.* [< *replicate* + *-ile*.] In *entom.*, that may be folded back on itself, as the wings of certain insects.

replication (rep-li-kā'shon), *n.* [< ME. *replication*, *replicacioun*, < OF. **replication* = Sp. *replicacion* = Pg. *replicação* = It. *replicazione*, < L. *replicatio(n-)*, a reply, < *replicare*, reply: see *replicate*, *reply*.] 1. An answer; a reply.

> My will is this, for plat conclusioun,
> Withouten eny *repplicacioun*.
> *Chaucer*, Knight's Tale, l. 988.

> Besides, to be demanded of a sponge! what *replication* should be made by the son of a king?
> *Shak.*, Hamlet, iv. 2. 13.

2. In *law*, the third step in the pleadings in a common-law action or bill in equity, being the reply of the plaintiff or complainant to the defendant's plea or answer.

> To that that he hath aunsuerd y have replyed yn such wyse that y trowe to be sure ynough that there shall no vayllable thyng be seyd to the contrarie of my seyd *replicacion*, and asmoch as he woold sey shall be but falsnesse and lesyngs. *Paston Letters*, I. 200.

3†. Return or repercussion of sound.

> Tiber trembled underneath her banks,
> To hear the *replication* of your sounds
> Made in her concave shores. *Shak.*, J. C., i. 1. 51.

> The echoes sighed
> In lulling *replication*. *Glover.*

4. In *logic*, the assuming or using of the same term twice in the same proposition.—5. Repetition; hence, a copy; a portrait.

> The notes on which he appeared to be so assiduously occupied mainly consisted of *replications* of Mr. Grayson's placid physiognomy. *Farrar*, Julian Home, vi.

6. A repeated folding or bending back of a surface.—7. In *music*, the repetition of a tone at a higher or lower octave, or a combination of replicates together.

replicative (rep'li-kā-tiv), *a.* [= F. *replicatif*; < *replicate* + *-ive*.] Of the nature of replication; containing replication.

replier (rē-plī'ėr), *n.* [Also *replyer*; < *reply* + *-er*[1].] One who replies or answers; one who makes a reply; specifically, in school disputations, one who makes a return to an answer; a respondent.

> At an act of the Commencement, the answerer gave for his question: That an aristocracy was better than a monarchy. The *replier*, who was a dissolute fellow, did tax him: That, being a private bred man, he would give a question of state. The answerer said: That the *replier* did much wrong the privilege of scholars; who would be much straitened if they should give questions of nothing but such things wherein they are practised.
> *Bacon*, Apophthegms (ed. Spedding, XIII. 349).

replum (rep'lum), *n.* [NL., < L. *replum*, a door-case.] In *bot.*, the frame-like placenta, across which the septum stretches, from which the valves of a capsule or other dehiscent fruit fall away in dehiscence, as in *Cruciferæ*, certain *Papaveraceæ*, *Mimosa*, etc.: sometimes incorrectly applied to the septum.

replume (rē-plöm'), *v. t.* [< *re-* + *plume*.] To rearrange; put in proper order again; preen, as a bird its feathers.

> The right hand *replumed*
> His black locks to their wonted composure.
> *Browning*, Saul, xv.

replunge (rē-plunj'), *v. t.* [< OF. *replongier*, F. *replonger*, plunge again; as *re-* + *plunge*.] To plunge again; immerse anew. *Milton.*

reply (rē-plī'), *v.*; pret. and pp. *replied*, ppr. *replying*. [< ME. *replyen*, *replien*, < OF. *replier*, reply, also lit. fold again, turn back, F. *replier*, fold again, turn, coil, *répliquer*, reply, = Pr. Sp. Pg. *replicar* = It. *replicare*, reply, < L. *replicare*, fold back, turn back, turn over, repeat, LL. (as a law-term) reply, < *re-*, back, + *plicare*, fold: see *ply*. Cf. *apply*.] I. *trans.* 1†. To fold back.

> The ouer nape [table-cloth] schalle dowbulle be layde,
> To the vttur syde the seluage brade;
> The ouer seluage he schalle *replye*,
> As towelle hit were. *Babees Book* (E. E. T. S.), p. 321.

2. To return for an answer.

> Perplex'd and troubled at his bad success
> The tempter stood, nor had what to *reply*.
> *Milton*, P. R., iv. 2.

II. *intrans.* 1. To make answer; answer; respond.

> O man, who art thou that *repliest* against God?
> Rom. ix. 20.

> *Reply* not to me with a fool-born jest.
> *Shak.*, 2 Hen. IV., v. 5. 59.

> Full ten years slander'd, did he once *reply*!
> *Pope*, Prol. to Satires, l. 374.

> He sang his song, and I *replied* with mine.
> *Tennyson*, Audley Court.

2. To do or give something in return for something else; make return or response; answer by suitable action; meet an attack: as, to *reply* to the enemy's fire.

> The nymph exulting fills with shouts the sky;
> The walls, the woods, and long canals *reply*.
> *Pope*, R. of the L., iii. 100.

> When I addressed her with my customary salutation, she only *replied* by a sharp gesture, and continued her walk. *R. L. Stevenson*, Olalla.

3. In *law*, to answer a defendant's plea. The defendant pleads in bar to the plaintiff's declaration; the plaintiff *replies* to the defendant's plea in bar.

reply (rē-plī'), *n.* [= F. *réplique* = Sp. *réplica* = Pg. *replica*, a reply; from the verb: see *reply*, *v.*] 1. An answer; a response.

> Quherat al laughed, as if I had bene dryven from al *replye*, and I fretted to see a frivolouse jest goe for a solid ansuer. *A. Hume*, Orthographie (E. E. T. S.), p. 18.

> I pause for a *reply*. *Shak.*, J. C., iii. 2. 37.

> Thus saying rose
> The monarch, and prevented all *reply*.
> *Milton*, P. L., ii. 467.

> I leave the quibbles by which such persons would try to creep out from under the crushing weight of these conclusions to the unfortunates who suppose that a *reply* is equivalent to an answer.
> *O. W. Holmes*, Med. Essays, p. 81.

2. The act or power of answering, especially with fitness or conclusiveness.

> In statement, the late Lord Holland was not successful; his chief excellence lay in *reply*.
> *Macaulay*, Lord Holland.

3. That which is done for or in consequence of something else; an answer by deeds; a counter-attack: as, his *reply* was a blow.—4. In *music*, the answer of a fugue. =**Syn.** 1 and 2. Rejoinder, retort.

repolish (rē-pol'ish), *v. t.* To polish again.

repone (rē-pōn'), *v. t.*; pret. and pp. *reponed*, ppr. *reponing*. [= OF. *repondre*, *repoure*, lay aside, conceal, also reply, = Sp. *reponer* = Pg. *repôr* = It. *riporre*, < L. *reponere*, lay, place, put, or set back, replace, lay aside, lay up, preserve; ML. (as a law-term) reply; < *re-*, back, + *ponere*, put: see *ponent*. Cf. *repose*.] 1. To replace; specifically, in *Scots law*, to restore to a position or a situation formerly held.—2. To reply. [Scotch in both uses.]

repopulate (rē-pop'ū-lāt), *v. t.* [< *re-* + *populate*. Cf. *repeople*.] To populate or people anew; supply with a new population; repeople.

> Temiragio returned to the city, and then beganne for to *repopulate* it. *Hakluyt's Voyages*, II. 220.

repopulation (rē-pop-ū-lā'shon), *n.* [= F. *repopulation* = Sp. *repoblacion*; as *re-* + *population*.] The act of repeopling, or the state of being repeopled.

report (rē-pōrt'), *v.* [< ME. *reporten*, < OF. (and F.) *reporter*, carry back, return, remit, refer, = Pr. Sp. *reportar*, carry back (cf. Pg. *reportar*, respect, honor, regard), = It. *riportare*, < L. *reportare*, carry back, bring back, carry off, get, obtain, bring back (an account), report, ML. also write (an account) for information or record, < *re-*, back, + *portare*, carry: see *port*[3]. Cf. *rapport*.] I. *trans.* 1. To bear or bring back as an answer; relate, as what has been discovered by a person sent to examine, explore, or investigate.

> But you, faire Sir, whose pageant next ensewes,
> Well mote yee thee, as well can wish your thought,
> That home ye may *report* thrise happy newes.
> *Spenser*, F. Q., II. i. 33.

> Tom, an arch, sly rogue. . . .
> Moves without noise, and, swift as an express,
> *Reports* a message with a pleasing grace.
> *Cowper*, Truth, l. 205.

2. To give an account of; make a statement concerning; say; make known; tell or relate from one to another.

> *Reporte* no slaunder, ne yet shew
> The fruites of flattery.
> *Babees Book* (E. E. T. S.), p. 97.

> It is *reported* among the heathen, and Gashmu saith it, that thou and the Jews think to rebel. Neh. vi. 6.

> Why does the world *report* that Kate doth limp?
> O slanderous world! *Shak.*, T. of the S., ii. 1. 254.

> Came
> The lord of Astolat out, to whom the Prince
> *Reported* who he was, and on what quest.
> *Tennyson*, Lancelot and Elaine.

3. To give an official or formal account or statement of: as, to *report* a deficit.

> A committee of the whole . . . has no authority to punish a breach of order, . . . but can only rise and *report* the matter to the assembly.
> *Cushing*, Manual of Parl. Practice, § 308.

4. To write out and give an account or statement of, as of the proceedings, debates, etc., of a legislative body, a convention, court, etc.; specifically, to write out or take down from the lips of the speaker: as, the debate was fully *reported*.—5. To lay a charge against; bring to the cognizance of: as, to *report* one to one's employer.—6†. To refer (one's self) for information or credit.

> I *report* me unto the consciences of all the land, whether he say truth or otherwise.
> *Tyndale*, Ans. to Sir T. More, etc. (Parker Soc., 1850), p. 14.

> Wherein I *report* me to them that knew Sir Nicholas Bacon Lord keeper of the great Seale.
> *Puttenham*, Arte of Eng. Poesie, p. 116.

7†. To return or reverberate, as sound; echo back.

> The care taking pleasure to heare the like tune *reported*, and to feele his returne.
> *Puttenham*, Arte of Eng. Poesie, p. 163.

> If you speak three words, it will (perhaps) some three times *report* you the whole three words.
> *Bacon*, Nat. Hist., § 249.

8†. To describe; represent.

> He shall know you better, sir, if I may live to *report* you.
> *Shak.*, M. for M., iii. 2. 172.

> Bid him
> *Report* the feature of Octavia, her years,
> Her inclination, let him not leave out
> The colour of her hair. *Shak.*, A. and C., ii. 5. 112.

To be reported, or (usually) **to be reported of**, to be (well or ill) spoken of; be mentioned.

> Timotheus . . . *was* well *reported of*. Acts xvi. 2.

To report one's self. (*a*) To make known one's own whereabouts or movements to any person, or in any designated place or office, so as to be in readiness to perform a duty, service, etc., when called upon. (*b*) To give information about one's self; speak for one's self.

> The chimney-piece
> Chaste Dian bathing; never saw I figures
> So likely to *report themselves*; the cutter
> Was as another nature.
> *Shak.*, Cymbeline, ii. 4. 83.

=**Syn.** I. To announce, communicate.—2. To rumor, bruit.

II. *intrans.* 1. To give in a report, or make a formal statement: as, the committee will *report* at twelve o'clock.—2. To give an account or description; specifically, to do the work of a reporter. See *reporter* (*b*).

> There is a gentleman that serves the count
> *Reports* but coarsely of her.
> *Shak.*, All's Well, iii. 5. 60.

> For two sessions he [Dickens] *reported* for the "Mirror of Parliament," . . . and in the session of 1835 became reporter for the "Morning Chronicle."
> *Leslie Stephen*, Dict. National Biog., XV. 21.

3. Same as *to report one's self* (*a*) (see under I.): as, to *report* at headquarters.

report (rẹ-pōrt'), *n.* [< ME. *report* = F. *report*, a bringing forward (*rapport*, relation, a statement, report), = It. *riporto*, report; from the verb.] 1. An account brought back or returned; a statement or relation of facts given in reply to inquiry, as the result of investigation, or by a person authorized to examine and bring or send information.

> Other service thanne this I myhte comende
> To yow to done, but, for the tyme is shorte,
> I putte theym nouhte in this lytyl *Reporte*.
> *Babees Book* (E. E. T. S.), p. 8.

> This is (quod he) the richt *report*
> Of all that I did heir and knaw.
> *Battle of Harlaw* (Child's Ballads, VII. 187).

> 'Tis greatly wise to talk with our past hours;
> And ask them what *report* they bore to heaven.
> *Young*, Night Thoughts, ii. 377.

> Geraint . . . woke . . . and call'd
> For Enid, and . . . Yniol made *report*
> Of that good mother making Enid gay.
> *Tennyson*, Geraint.

2. A tale carried; a story circulated; hence, rumor; common fame.

> It was a true *report* that I heard in mine own land of thy acts and of thy wisdom. 1 Ki. x. 6.

> My brother Jaques he keeps at school, and *report* speaks goldenly of his profit. *Shak.*, As you Like it, i. 1. 6.

3. Repute; public character.

> Cornelius the centurion, a just man, and one that feareth God, and of good *report* among all the nation of the Jews. Acts x. 22.

> A gentlewoman of mine,
> Who, falling in the flaws of her own youth,
> Hath blistered her *report*.
> *Shak.*, M. for M., ii. 3. 12.

4. An account or statement. (*a*) A statement of a judicial opinion or decision, or of a case argued and determined in a court of justice, the object being to present such parts of the pleadings, evidence, and argument, with the opinion of the court, as shall serve to inform the profession and other courts of the points of law in respect to which the case may be a precedent. The books containing such statements are also called *reports*. (*b*) The official document in which a referee, master in chancery, or auditor embodies his findings or his proceedings for the purpose of presentation to the court, or of filing as a part of its records. (*c*) In *parliamentary law*, an official statement of facts or opinions by a committee, officer, or board to the superior body. (*d*) A paper delivered by the masters of all ships arriving from parts beyond seas to the custom-house, and attested upon oath, containing a statement in detail of the cargo on board, etc. (*e*) An account or statement, more or less full and circumstantial, of the proceedings, debates, etc., of a legislative assembly, meeting, court, etc., or of any occurrence of public interest, intended for publication; an epitome or fully written account of a speech.

> Stuart occasionally took him [Coleridge] to the reporters' gallery, where his only effort appears to have been a *report* of a remarkable speech delivered by Pitt 17 Feb., 1800. *Leslie Stephen*, Dict. National Biog., XI. 308.

5. The sound of an explosion; a loud noise.

> Russet-pated choughs, many in sort,
> Rising and cawing at the gun's *report*.
> *Shak.*, M. N. D., iii. 2. 22.

> The lashing billows make a loud *report*,
> And beat her sides.
> *Dryden*, tr. of Ovid's Metamorph., x. 139.

6†. Relation; correspondence; connection; reference.

> The kitchen and stables are ill-plac'd, and the corridore worse, having no *report* to the wings they joyne to.
> *Evelyn*, Diary, Sept. 25, 1672.

Guard report. See *guard*.—**Pinion of report.** See *pinion*[2].—**Practice reports.** See *practice*.—**Sick report.** See *sick*. =**Syn.** 1. Narration, detail, description, recital, narrative, communication.—2. Hearsay.—4. (*a*), (*b*) *Verdict*, etc. See *decision*.

reportable (rẹ-pōr'tạ-bl), *a.* [< *report* + *-able*.] That may be reported; fit to be reported. *Imp. Dict.*

reportage (rẹ-pōr'tạj), *n.* [< F. *reportage*, reporter, report: see *report*.] Report.

> Lord Lytton says some sensible things both about poetry and about Proteus [his friend]; and he will interest the lovers of personal detail by certain *reportage*, in which he has exhibited the sentiments of an "illustrious poet, X."
> *The Academy*, Nov. 5, 1881, p. 347.

reporter (rẹ-pōr'tėr), *n.* [< ME. *reportour*, < OF. **reporteor*, *reportour*, one who reports a case, < ML. *reportator*, < *reportare*, report: see *report*.] One who reports or gives an account.

> And that he wolde bene oure governour,
> And of oure tales juge and *reportour*.
> *Chaucer*, Gen. Prol. to C. T., l. 814.

> There she appeared indeed; or my *reporter* devised well for her. *Shak.*, A. and C., ii. 2. 193.

> The mind of man, whereto the senses are but *reporters*.
> *Bacon*, Advancement of Learning, i. 8.

Specifically—(*a*) One who draws up official statements of law proceedings and decisions, or of legislative debates. (*b*) A member of the staff of a newspaper whose work is to collect and put in form for submission to the editors local information of all kinds, to give an account of the proceedings at public meetings, entertainments, etc., and, in general, to go upon any mission or quest for news, to interview persons whose names are before the public, and to obtain news for his paper in any other way that may be assigned to him by his chiefs.

> Among the *reporters* who sat in the Gallery, it is remarkable that two-thirds did not write short-hand; they made notes, and trusted to their memories; Charles Dickens sat with them in the year 1836.
> *W. Besant*, Fifty Years Ago, p. 210.

(*c*) One who makes or signs a report, as of a committee. *A. J. Ellis.*

reporterism (rẹ-pōr'tėr-izm), *n.* [< *reporter* + *-ism*.] The practice or business of reporting; work done by a reporter. [Rare.]

> Fraser . . . seems more bent on Toryism and Irish *reporterism*, to me infinitely detestable.
> *Carlyle*, in Froude, II.

reporterize (rẹ-pōr'tėr-īz), *v. t.*; pret. and pp. *reporterized*, ppr. *reporterizing*. [< *reporter* + *-ize*.] To submit to the influence of newspaper reporters; corrupt with the methods of reporters. [Rare and objectionable.]

> Our *reporterized* press is often truculently reckless of privacy and decency. *Harper's Mag.*, LXXVII. 314.

reporting (rẹ-pōr'ting), *n.* [Verbal n. of *report*, *v.*] The act or system of drawing up reports; the practice of making a report; specifically, newspaper reporting (see phrase below): also used attributively: as, the *reporting* style of phonography.

> At the Restoration all *reporting* was forbidden, though the votes and proceedings of the House were printed by direction of the Speaker. *Lecky*, Eng. in 18th Cent., iii.

Newspaper reporting, the system by which proceedings and debates of Congress or Parliament or other legislative bodies, and the proceedings of public meetings, the accounts of important or interesting events, etc., are taken down, usually in shorthand, by a body of reporters attached to various newspapers or to general news-agencies, and are afterward prepared for publication.

reportingly (rẹ-pōr'ting-li), *adv.* By report or common fame. [Rare.]

> For others say thou dost deserve, and I
> Believe it better than *reportingly*.
> *Shak.*, Much Ado, iii. 1. 116.

reportorial (rē-pọr-tō'ri-ạl), *a.* [Irreg. < *reporter*, taken as **reportor*, + *-ial*, in imitation of words like *editorial*, *professorial*, etc.] Of or pertaining to a reporter or reporters. [An objectionable word, not in good use.]

> The great newspapers of New York have capital, editorial talent, *reportorial* enterprise, and competent business management, and an unequalled field both for the collection of news and the extension of their circulation.
> *Harper's Mag.*, LXXVII. 687.

reportory† (rẹ-pōr'tọ-ri), *n.* [Irreg. < *report* + *-ory*.] A report.

> In this transcursive *reportory*, without some observant glaunce, I may not dully overpasse the gallant beauty of their haven. *Nashe*, Lenten Stuffe (Harl. Misc., VI. 149).

reposal (rẹ-pō'zạl), *n.* [< *repose* + *-al*.] 1. The act of reposing or resting.

> Dost thou think,
> If I would stand against thee, would the *reposal*
> Of any trust, virtue, or worth in thee
> Make thy words faith'd? *Shak.*, Lear, ii. 1. 70.

2†. That on which one reposes.

> The devil's cushion, as Gualter cals it, his pillow and chiefe *reposall*. *Burton*, Anat. of Mel., p. 85.

reposance† (rẹ-pō'zạns), *n.* [< *repose* + *-ance*.] The act of reposing; reliance. [Rare.]

> See what sweet
> *Reposance* heaven can beget.
> *Bp. Hall*, Poems, p. 92.

repose (rẹ-pōz'), *v.*; pret. and pp. *reposed*, ppr. *reposing*. [< ME. *reposen*, < OF. *reposer*, *repauser*, repose, rest, stay, F. *reposer* = Pr. *repausar* = Sp. *reposar* = Pg. *repousar* = It. *riposare*, < ML. *repausare*, lay at rest, quiet, also nourish, intr. be at rest, rest, repose, < L. *re-*, again, + *pausare*, pause, rest: see *pose*[2]. Cf. *repone*, *reposit*.] I. *trans.* 1†. To lay (a thing) at rest; lay by; lay up; deposit.

> Write upon the [almond] cornel . . . outetake,
> Or this or that, and faire aboute it close
> In cley and swynes doungo and so *repose*.
> *Palladius*, Husbondrie (E. E. T. S.), p. 56.

> Pebbles, *reposed* in those cliffs amongst the earth, being not so dissoluble and more bulky, are left behind.
> *Woodward.*

2. To lay at rest; refresh by rest: with reference to a person, and often used reflexively.

> Enter in the castle
> And there *repose you* for this night.
> *Shak.*, Rich. II., ii. 3. 161.

> I *reposed my selfe* all that night in a certaine Inne in the suburbes of the city. *Coryat*, Crudities, I. 132.

> Whose causeway parts the vale with shady rows?
> Whose seats the weary traveller *repose*?
> *Pope*, Moral Essays, iii. 260.

> The hardy chief upon the rugged rock, . . .
> Fearless of wrong, *repos'd* his wearied strength.
> *Cowper*, Task, i. 15.

3†. To cause to be calm or quiet; tranquilize; compose.

> All being settled and *reposed*, the lord archbishop did present his majesty to the lords and commons.
> *Fuller.* (*Webster.*)

4. To lay, place, or rest, as confidence or trust.

> The king *reposeth* all his confidence in thee.
> *Shak.*, Rich. II., ii. 4. 6.

> Mr. Godolphin requested me to continue the trust his wife had *reposed* in me in behalfe of his little sonn.
> *Evelyn*, Diary, Oct. 16, 1678.

> There are some writers who *repose* undoubting confidence in words. *Whipple*, Ess. and Rev., I. 60.

> The absolute control [of a society] is *reposed* in a committee. *Art Age*, VII. 51.

II. *intrans.* **1.** To lie or be at rest; take rest; sleep.

Yet must we credit that his [the Lord's] hand compos'd All in six Dayes, and that be then *Repos'd.*
Sylvester, tr. of Du Bartas's Weeks, i. 7.

When statesmen, heroes, kings, in dust *repose.*
Pope, Essay on Man, iv. 387.

The public mind was then *reposing* from one great effort, and collecting strength for another.
Macaulay, Lord Bacon.

2. To rest in confidence; rely: followed by *on* or *upon.*

I do desire thy worthy company,
Upon whose faith and honour I *repose.*
Shak., T. G. of V., iv. 3. 26.

The best of those that then wrote disclaim that any man should *repose on* them, and send all to the Scriptures.
Milton, Reformation in Eng., i.

The soul, *reposing on* assur'd relief,
Feels herself happy amidst all her grief.
Cowper, Truth, l. 55.

=**Syn. 1.** To recline, settle, slumber. See *rest*, *v. i.*

repose (rę̄-pōz'), *n.* [< OF. *repos*, *repaus*, F. *repos*, F. dial. *repous* = Pr. *repaus* = Cat. *repos* = Sp. *reposo* = Pg. *repouso* = It. *riposo*, repose; from the verb.] **1.** The act or state of reposing; inaction; a lying at rest; sleep; rest.

Shake off the golden slumber of *repose.*
Shak., Pericles, iii. 2. 23.

Black Melancholy sits, and round her throws
A death-like silence, and a dread *repose.*
Pope, Eloisa to Abelard, l. 166.

Absolute *repose* is, indeed, a state utterly unknown upon the earth's surface.
Huxley, Physiography, xx.

2. Freedom from disturbance of any kind; tranquillity.

The great civil and religious conflict which began at the Reformation seemed to have terminated in universal *repose.*
Macaulay, William Pitt.

A goal which, gain'd, may give *repose.*
M. Arnold, Resignation.

3. Settled composure; natural or habitual dignity and calmness of manner and action.

Her manners had not that *repose*
Which stamps the caste of Vere de Vere.
Tennyson, Lady Clara Vere de Vere.

That *repose* which is the ornament and ripeness of man is not American. That *repose* which indicates a faith in the laws of the universe, a faith that they will fulfil themselves, and are not to be impeded, transgressed, or accelerated.
Emerson, Fortune of the Republic.

4. Cause of rest; that which gives repose; a rest; a pause.

After great lights must be great shadows, which we call *reposes*, because in reality the sight would be tired if attracted by a continuity of glittering objects.
Dryden, tr. of Dufresnoy's Art of Painting.

5. In a work of art, dependence for effect entirely upon inherent excellence, all meretricious effect of gaudiness of color or exaggeration of attitude being avoided; a general moderation or restraint of color and treatment; an avoidance of obtrusive tints and of violent action.—**Angle of repose.** See *angle*[3].—**Repose of St. Anne,** in the Gr. *Ch.*, a festival observed on July 25th in memory of the death of St. Anne, the mother of the Virgin Mary.—**Repose of the Theotocos,** in the *Gr. Ch.*, a festival observed on August 15th in commemoration of the death and assumption of the Virgin Mary.=**Syn. 1-3.** *Quiet, Tranquillity*, etc. (see *rest*[1]), quietness.

reposed (rę̄-pōzd'), *p. a.* [Pp. of *repose*, *v.*] Exhibiting repose; calm; settled.

He was in feeding temperate, in drinking sober, in giuing liberall, in receiuing of consideration, in sleeping short, in his speech *reposed.*
Guevara, Letters (tr. by Hellowes, 1577), p. 20.

But *reposed* natures may do well in youth, as is seen in Augustus Cæsar . . . and others. *Bacon*, Youth and Age.

reposedly (rę̄-pō'zed-li), *adv.* In a reposed manner; quietly; composedly; calmly. *Imp. Dict.*

reposedness (rę̄-pō'zed-nes), *n.* The state of being reposed or at rest.

Of which [wishes] none rises in me that is not bent upon your enjoying of peace and *reposedness* in your fortunes, in your affections, and in your conscience.
Donne, Letters, xlviii.

reposeful (rę̄-pōz'fůl), *a.* [< *repose* + *-ful.*] **1.** Full of repose.—**2.** Affording repose or rest; trustworthy; worthy of reliance.

Though princes may take, above others, some *reposefull* friend, with whom they may participate their neerest passions. *Sir Robert B. Cotton*, A Short View, etc., in *J. Morgan's* Phœnix Britannicus, I. 68. (*F. Hall.*)

I know not where she can picke out a fast friend, or *reposefull* confident of such reciprocable interest.
Howell, Vocall Forrest, 28. (*Latham.*)

reposer (rę̄-pō'zėr), *n.* One who reposes. *Imp. Dict.*

reposit (rę̄-poz'it), *v. t.* [Formerly also *reposite*; < L. *repositus*, pp. of *reponere*, lay up: see *repone.*] To lay up; lodge, as for safety or preservation.

I caused his body to be coffin'd in lead, and *reposited* on the 30th at 8 o'clock that night in the church at Deptford.
Evelyn, Diary, Jan. 27, 1658.

reposit (rę̄-poz'it), *n.* [Formerly also *reposite*; < *reposit*, *v.*] That which is laid up; a deposit. *Encyc. Dict.*

reposition (rē-pō-zish'on), *n.* [< ML. *repositio(n-)*, < L. *reponere*, pp. *repositus*, lay up: see *reposit.*] **1.** The act of repositing, or laying up in safety.

That age which is not capable of observation, careless of *reposition.* *Bp. Hall*, Censure of Travell, § 4.

2. The act of replacing, or restoring to its normal position; reduction.

Being satisfied in the *reposition* of the bone, take care to keep it so by deligation. *Wiseman*, Surgery.

3. In *Scots law*, retrocession, or the returning back of a right from the assignee to the person granting the right.

repositor (rę̄-poz'i-tor), *n.* [< *reposit* + *-or*[1].] One who or that which replaces; specifically, in *surg.*, an instrument for restoring a displaced uterus to its normal position.

repository (rę̄-poz'i-tō-ri), *a.* and *n.* [L *a.* < L. **repositorius*, < *reponere*, pp. *repositus*, lay up: see *reposit.* II. *n.* < OF. **repositorie*, later *repositoire* = Sp. Pg. *repositorio* = It. *ripositorio*, < L. *repositorium*, a repository, neut. of *repositorius*: see I.] **I.** *a.* Pertaining to reposition; adapted or intended for deposition or storage.

If the bee knoweth when, and whence, and how to gather her honey and wax, and how to form the *repository* combs, and how to lay it up, and all the rest of her marvellous economy. Baxter, Dying Thoughts.

II. *n.*; pl. *repositories* (-riz). **1.** A place where things are or may be deposited for safety or preservation; a depository; a storehouse; a magazine.

The mind of man not being capable of having many ideas under view at once, it was necessary to have a *repository* to lay up those ideas. Locke.

2. A place where things are kept for sale; a shop: as, a carriage-*repository.*

She confides the card to the gentleman of the Fine Art *Repository*, who consents to 'allow it to lie upon the counter. *Thackeray.*

repossess (rē-po-zes'), *v. t.* [< *re-* + *possess.*] To possess again; regain possession of.

The resolution to die had *repossessed* his place in her mind. *Sir P. Sidney*, Arcadia, iv.

To repossess one's self of, to obtain possession of again.

repossession (rē-po-zesh'on), *n.* [< *re-* + *possession.*] The act or state of possessing again.

Whoso hath been robbed or spoiled of his lands or goods may lawfully seek *repossession* by force. *Raleigh.*

reposure (rę̄-pō'zhūr), *n.* [< *repose* + *-ure.*] Rest; quiet; repose.

In the *reposure* of most soft content. *Marston.*

It was the Franciscans antient Dormitory, as appeareth by the concavities still extant in the walls, places for their severall *reposure.* *Fuller*, Hist. of Camb., viii. 19. (*Davies.*)

repot (rē-pot'), *v. t.* [< *re-* + *pot*[1], *v.*] To replace in pots; specifically, in *hort.*, to shift (plants in pots) from one pot to another, usually of a larger size, or to remove from the pot and replace more or less of the old earth with fresh earth.

repour (rē-pōr'), *v. t.* [< *re-* + *pour*[1].] To pour again.

The horrid noise amazed the silent night,
Repouring down black darkness from the sky.
Mir. for Mags.

repoussage (rē-pö'säzh), *n.* [F., < *repousser*, beat back: see *repoussé.*] **1.** The beating out from behind of ornamental patterns upon a metal surface. See *repoussé*, *n.*—**2.** In *etching*, the hammering out from behind of parts of an etched plate which have been brought by charcoal or scraper below half its thickness, making hollows which would show as spots in printing, in order to bring them up to the required level. A spot to be thus treated is fixed by letting one of the points of a pair of calipers (compasses with curved legs) rest on the place, and marking the corresponding place on the back of the plate with the other point.

repoussé (rē-pö'sā), *a.* and *n.* [< F. *repoussé*, pp. of *repousser*, push back, beat back, repulse: see *repulse*, and cf. *push.*] **I.** *a.* Raised in relief by means of the hammer; beaten up from the under or reverse side.

In this tomb was a magnificent silver-gilt amphora, certainly the finest extant specimen of Greek *repoussé* work in silver. The body of this vase is richly ornamented with birds and floral arabesques.
C. T. *Newton*, Art and Archæol., p. 381.

II. *n.* Repoussé work; the art of shaping vessels and the like, and of producing ornament on the surface, by hammering thin metal on the reverse side, the artist watching the side destined to be exposed to follow the development of the pattern by the blows of the hammer; also, the articles thus produced. A hammer with an elastic handle screwed to a permanent support, and having many adjustable heads, is used for this work. Repoussé work is often finished by chasing; the chaser, working upon the right side of the metal, presses back or modifies the relief of the metal, which has taken shape from the hammer. For this purpose a bed of some resistant but soft material is provided to support the metal while in the chaser's hands: hollow silver vessels, for instance, are filled with pitch. Compare *chasing.*

Gold Étui, decorated with Repoussé work; time of Louis XV.

repp, *n.* See *rep*[1].

repped (rept), *a.* [< *rep* + *-ed*[2].] Ribbed or corded transversely: as, *repped* silk.

repr. An abbreviation (used in this work) of (*a*) *representing*; (*b*) *representative.*

repreeft, *n.* An obsolete form of *reproof.*

repreevet, *v.* An obsolete form of *reprove.*

reprefablet, *a.* A Middle English form of *reprovable.*

reprefet, *n.* A Middle English form of *reproof.*

reprehend (rep-rę̄-hend'), *v. t.* [< ME. *reprehenden* = OF. *reprendre*, F. *reprendre* = Pr. *reprehendre*, *reprendre*, *repreure*, *repenre* = Cat. *rependrer* = Sp. *reprender* = Pg. *reprehender* = It. *reprendere*, *riprendere*, < L. *reprehendere*, *reprendere*, hold back, check, blame, < *re-*, back, + *prehendere*, hold, seize: see *prehend.*] **1.** To charge with a fault; chide sharply; reprove: formerly sometimes followed by *of.*

Thow were ay wont eche lovere *reprehende*
Of thing fro which thow kanst the nat defende.
Chaucer, Troilus, i. 510.

Then pardon me for *reprehending* thee,
For thou hast done a charitable deed.
Shak., Tit. And., iii. 2. 69.

I bring an angry mind to see your folly,
A sharp one too to *reprehend* you for it.
Fletcher (*and another*), Elder Brother, iii. 3.

2. To take exception to; speak of as a fault; censure.

I have faults myself, and will not *reprehend*
A crime I am not free from.
Beau. and Fl., Little French Lawyer, i. 2.

Let men *reprehend* them [my labours], so they observe and weigh them.
Bacon, Advancement of Learning, ii. 359.

3†. To convict of fallacy.

This colour will be *reprehended* or encountered, by imputing to all excellencies in composition a kind of poverty.
Bacon. (*Latham.*)

=**Syn. 1.** To blame, rebuke, reprimand, upbraid. See *admonition.*

reprehender (rep-rę̄-hen'dėr), *n.* One who reprehends; one who blames or reproves.

To the second rancke of *reprehenders*, that complain of my boystrous compound wordes, and ending my Italionate coyned verbes all in ize, thus I replie: That no winde that blowes strong but is boystrous; no speech or wordes of any power or force to confute or perswade but must be swelling and boystrous.
Nashe, quoted in Int. to Pierce Penilesse, p. xxx.

reprehensibility (rep-rę̄-hen-si-bil'i-ti), *n.* [= Pg. *reprehensibilidade*, < LL. as if **reprehensibilita(t-)s*, < *reprehensibilis*, reprehensible: see *reprehensible.*] The character of being reprehensible.

reprehensible (rep-rę̄-hen'si-bl), *a.* [< OF. *reprehensible*, F. *répréhensible* = Sp. *reprensible*, *reprehensible* = Pg. *reprehensivel* = It. *riprensibile*, < LL. *reprehensibilis*, reprehensible, < L. *reprehendere*, pp. *reprehensus*, reprehend: see *reprehend.*] Deserving to be reprehended or censured; blameworthy; censurable; deserving reproof: applied to persons or things.

In a meane man prodigalitie and pride are faultes more *reprehensible* than in Princes.
Puttenham, Arte of Eng. Poesie, p. 34.

This proceeding appears to me wholly illegal, and *reprehensible* in a very high degree.
Webster, Speech in Senate, May 7, 1834.

=**Syn.** Blamable, culpable, reprovable. See *admonition.*

reprehensibleness (rep-rẹ̄-hen'si-bl-nes), *n.* The character of being reprehensible; blamableness; culpableness.

reprehensibly (rep-rẹ̄-hen'si-bli), *adv.* With reprehension, or so as to merit it; culpably; in a manner to deserve censure or reproof.

reprehension (rep-rẹ̄-hen'shọn), *n.* [< ME. *reprehension*, < OF. *reprehension*, F. *répréhension* = Pr. *reprehensio*, *reprencio* = Sp. *reprension*, *reprehension* = Pg. *reprehensão* = It. *riprensione*, < L. *reprehensio(n-)*, < *reprehendere*, pp. *reprehensus*, reprehend: see *reprehend*.] The act of reprehending; reproof; censure; blame.

> Let him use his harsh
> Unsavoury *reprehensions* upon those
> That are his hinds, and not on me.
> *Fletcher*, Spanish Curate, i. 1.

> We have . . . characterised in terms of just *reprehension* that spirit which shows itself in every part of his prolix work. *Macaulay*, Sadler's Ref. Refuted.

=**Syn.** *Monition*, etc. See *admonition*.

reprehensive (rep-rẹ̄-hen'siv), *a.* [= It. *riprensivo*; as L. *reprehensus*, pp. of *reprehendere*, reprehend, + *-ive*.] Of the nature of reprehension; containing reprehension or reproof.

> The said auncient Poets vsed . . . three kinds of poems *reprehensiue*: to wit, the Satyre, the Comedie, & the Tragedie. *Puttenham*, Arte of Eng. Poesie, p. 24.

> The sharpenesse
> Of *reprehensive* language.
> *Marston*, The Fawne, i. 2.

reprehensively (rep-rẹ̄-hen'siv-li), *adv.* With reprehension; reprovingly.

reprehensory (rep-rẹ̄-hen'sọ̄-ri), *a.* [< L. *reprehensus*, pp. of *reprehendere*, reprehend, + *-ory*.] Containing reproof; reproving.

> Of this, however, there is no reason for making any *reprehensory* complaint. *Johnson.*

repremiation†, *n.* [< OF. *repremiation*, rewarding, < L. *re-*, back, + *præmiari*, reward, < *præmium*, reward: see *premium*.] A rewarding. *Cotgrave.*

represent (rep-rẹ̄-zent'), *v. t.* [< ME. *representen*, < OF. *representer*, F. *représenter* = Pr. Sp. Pg. *representar* = It. *rippresentare*, *rappresentare*, < L. *repræsentare*, bring before one, show, manifest, exhibit, represent, pay in cash, do or perform at once, < *re-*, again, + *præsentare*, present, hold out: see *present*[2].] **1.** To present again; specifically, to bring again before the mind. *Sir W. Hamilton.*

> Reasoning grasps at — infers — *represents* under new circumstances what has already been presented under other circumstances.
> G. H. Lewes, Probs. of Life and Mind, II. 169.

> When we perceive an orange by sight we may say that its taste or feel is *represented*, when we perceive it by touch we may in like manner say that its colour is *represented*. *J. Ward*, Encyc. Brit., XX. 57.

2. To present in place of something else; exhibit the image or counterpart of; suggest by being like; typify.

> This fellow here, with envious carping tongue,
> Upbraided me about the rose I wear;
> Saying, the sanguine colour of the leaves
> Did *represent* my master's blushing cheeks.
> *Shak.*, 1 Hen. VI., iv. 1. 93.

> They have a kind of Cupboard to *represent* the Tabernacle. *Howell*, Letters, I. vi. 14.

> Before him burn
> Seven lamps, as in a zodiac *representing*
> The heavenly fires. *Milton*, P. L., xii. 255.

> The call of Abraham from a heathen state *represents* the gracious call of Christians to forsake the wickedness of the world. *W. Gilpin*, Works, II. xvi.

3. To portray by pictorial or plastic art.

> My wife desired to be *represented* as Venus, and the painter was requested not to be too frugal of his diamonds.
> *Goldsmith*, Vicar, xvi.

> The other bas-reliefs in the Raj Rani cave *represent* scenes of hunting, fighting, dancing, drinking, and love-making — anything, in fact, but religion or praying in any shape or form. *J. Fergusson*, Hist. Indian Arch., p. 142.

4. To portray, present, or exhibit dramatically. (*a*) To put upon the stage; produce, as a play.

> An Italian opera entitled Lucio Papirio Dittatore was *represented* four several times.
> *Burney*, Hist. Music, IV. 302.

(*b*) To enact; personate; present by mimicry or action.

> He so entirely associated himself with the characters he *represented* on the stage that he lost himself in them, or rather they were lost in him.
> J. H. *Shorthouse*, Countess Eve, i.

5. To state; describe or portray in words; give one's own impressions, idea, or judgment of; declare; set forth.

> This bank is thought the greatest load on the Genoese, and the managers of it have been *represented* as a second kind of senate. *Addison.*

> The Jesuits strongly *represented* to the king the danger which he had so narrowly escaped.
> *Macaulay*, Hist. Eng., vi.

6. To supply the place or perform the duties or functions of; specifically, to speak and act with authority on behalf of; be a substitute for, or a representative of or agent for.

> I . . . deliver up my title in the queen
> To your most gracious hands, that are the substance
> Of that great shadow I did *represent*.
> *Shak.*, 2 Hen. VI., i. 1. 14.

> Ye Irish lords, ye knights an' squires,
> Wha *represent* our brughs and shires,
> An' doucely manage our affairs
> In Parliament.
> *Burns*, Author's Cry and Prayer.

7. Specifically, to stand in the place of, in the right of inheritance.

> All the branches inherit the same share that their root, whom they *represent*, would have done.
> *Blackstone*, Com., II. xiv.

8. To serve as a sign or symbol of; stand for; be understood as: as, mathematical symbols *represent* quantities or relations; words *represent* ideas or things.

> But we must not attribute to them [constitutions] that value which really belongs to what they *represent*.
> *Macaulay*, Utilitarian Theory of Government.

> He [the farmer] *represents* continuous hard labor, year in, year out, and small gains. *Emerson*, Farming.

> Vortimer, the son of Vortigern, Aurelius Ambrosius, and Uther Pendragon *represent* in some respects one and the same person. *Merlin* (E. E. T. S.), Pref., p. iii.

9. To serve as a type or specimen of; exemplity; furnish a case or instance of: as, a genus *represented* by few species; a species *represented* by many individuals; especially, in *zoögeog.*, to replace; fill the part or place of (another) in any given fauna: as, llamas *represent* camels in the New World; the Old World starlings are *represented* in America by the *Icteridæ*. See *mimotype*.

> As we ascend in the geological series, vertebrate life has its commencement, beginning, like the lower forms, in the waters, and *represented* at first only by the fishes.
> J. W. *Dawson*, Nat. and the Bible, Lect. iv., p. 122.

10. To image or picture in the mind; place definitely before the mind.

> By a distinct, clear, or well-defined concept is meant one in which the several features or characters forming the concept-elements are distinctly *represented*.
> J. *Sully*, Outlines of Psychol., p. 363.

> Among these Fancy next
> Her office holds; of all external things,
> Which the five watchful senses *represent*,
> She forms imaginations, aery shapes.
> *Milton*, P. L., v. 104.

> To *represent* an object is to "envisage" it in time and space, and therefore in conformity with the conditions of time and space. *Caird*, Philos. of Kant, p. 437.

=**Syn. 2.** To show, express.—**3** and **4.** To delineate, depict, draw.

represent† (rep-rẹ̄-zent'), *n.* [< *represent*, *v.*] Representation. [Rare.]

> Their Churches are many of them well set forth, and painted with the *represents* of Saints.
> *Sandys*, Travailes (1652), p. 64.

representability (rep-rẹ̄-zen-tạ-bil'ị-ti), *n.* [< *representable* + *-ity* (see *-bility*).] The character of being representable, or of being susceptible of representation.

representable (rep-rẹ̄-zen'tạ-bl), *a.* [= F. *représentable* = Sp. *representable* = Pg. *representavel* = It. *rappresentabile*; as *represent* + *-able*.] Capable of being represented.

representamen (rep'rẹ̄-zen-tā'men), *n.* [< NL. **repræsentamen*, < L. *repræsentare*, represent: see *represent*.] In *metaph.*, representation; an object serving to represent something to the mind. *Sir W. Hamilton.*

representance† (rep-rẹ̄-zen'tans), *n.* [= It. *rappresentanza*; as *representan(t)* + *-ce*.] Representation; likeness.

> They affirm foolishly that the images and likenesses they frame of stone or of wood are the *representances* and forms of those who have brought something profitable, by their inventions, to the common use of their living.
> *Donne*, Hist. of the Septuagint, p. 93.

representant (rep-rẹ̄-zen'tạnt), *a.* and *n.* [< F. *représentant*, ppr. of *représenter*, represent, = Sp. Pg. ppr. *representante* = It. *ripresentante*, *rappresentante*, < L. *repræsentan(t-)s*, ppr. of *repræsentare*, represent: see *represent*.] **I.** *a.* Representing; having vicarious power.

II. *n.* A representative.

> There is expected the Count Henry of Nassau to be at the said solemnity, as the *representant* of his brother.
> *Wotton.*

representation (rep'rẹ̄-zen-tā'shọn), *n.* [< OF. *representation*, F. *représentation* = Pr. *representacio* = Sp. *representacion* = Pg. *representação* = It. *rappresentazione*, < L. *repræsentatio(n-)*, a showing, exhibiting, manifesting, < *repræsentare*, pp. *repræsentatus*, represent: see *represent*.] **1.** The act of presenting again.—**2.** The act of presenting to the mind or the view; the act of portraying, depicting, or exhibiting, as in imagination, in a picture, or on the stage; portrayal.

> The act of *Representation* is merely the energy of the mind in holding up to its own contemplation what it is determined to represent. I distinguish, as essentially different, the *Representation* and the determination to represent. *Sir W. Hamilton*, Metaphysics, xxiv.

> The author [Thomas Bently] . . . sent this piece ["The Wishes"] first to Garrick, who very properly rejected it as unfit for *representation*.
> *W. Cooke*, Memoirs of S. Foote, I. 63.

3. The image, picture, or scene presented, depicted, or exhibited. (*a*) A picture, statue, or likeness. (*b*) A dramatic performance or exhibition; hence, theatrical action; make-believe.

> The inference usually drawn is that his [a widower's] grief was pure mummery and *representation*.
> *Godwin*, Fleetwood, vii.

4. A statement or an assertion made in regard to some matter or circumstance; a verbal description or statement: as, to obtain money by false *representations*. Specifically—(*a*) In *insurance* and *law*, a verbal or written statement made on the part of the insured to the insurer, before or at the time of the making of the contract, as to the existence of some fact or state of facts tending to induce the insurer more readily to assume the risk, by diminishing the estimate he would otherwise have formed of it. It differs from a warranty and from a condition expressed in the policy, in being part of the preliminary proceedings which propose the contract, and its falsity does not vitiate the contract unless made with fraudulent intent or perhaps with respect to a material point; while the latter are part of the contract when completed, and non-compliance therewith is an express breach which of itself avoids the contract. (*b*) In *Scots law*, the written pleading presented to a lord ordinary of the Court of Session when his judgment is brought under review.

5. An expostulatory statement of facts, arguments, or the like; remonstrance.

> He threatened "to send his jack-boot to rule the country," when the senate once ventured to make a *representation* against his ruinous policy. *Brougham.*

6. In *psychol.*, the word chiefly used to translate the German *Vorstellung*, used in that language to translate the English word *idea*. See *idea*, 2 and 3. (*a*) The immediate object of cognition; anything that the soul is conscious of. This is now the commonest meaning of *Vorstellung*, and recent translators have most frequently rendered it by the word *idea*. (*b*) A reproduced perception.

> The word *representation* I have restricted to denote, what it only can in propriety express, the immediate object or product of imagination.
> *Sir W. Hamilton*, Logic, vii.

> If all reasoning be the *re-presentation* of what is now absent but formerly was present and can again be made present — in other words, if the test of accurate reasoning is its reduction to fact — then is it evident that Philosophy, dealing with transcendental objects which cannot be present, and employing a method which admits of no verification (or reduction to the test of fact), must be an impossible attempt. G. H. Lewes.

> It is quite evident that the growth of perception involves *representation* of sensations; that the growth of simple reasoning involves *representation* of perceptions; and that the growth of complex reasoning involves *representation* of the results of simple reasoning.
> *H. Spencer*, Prin. of Psychol., § 482.

> Assimilation involves retentiveness and differentiation, as we have seen, and prepares the way for *re-presentation*; but in itself there is no confronting the new with the old, no determination of likeness, and no subsequent classification. *J. Ward*, Encyc. Brit., XX. 53.

(*c*) A singular conception; a thought or idea of something as having a definite place in space at a definite epoch in time; the image of an object produced in consciousness. (*d*) A representative cognition; a mediate or vicarious cognition.

> A mediate cognition, inasmuch as the thing known is held up or mirrored to the mind in a vicarious *representation*, may be called a representative cognition.
> *Sir W. Hamilton*, Reid's Works, Note B, § 1.

7. In *law*: (*a*) The standing in the place of another, as an heir, or in the right of taking by inheritance; the personating of another, as an heir, executor, or administrator. (*b*) More specifically, the coming in of children of a deceased heir apparent, devisee dying before the testator, etc., to take the share their parent would have taken had he survived, not as succeeding as the heirs of the parent, but as together representing him among the other heirs of the ancestor. See *representative*, *n.*, 3. In Scots law the term is usually applied to the obligation incurred by an heir to pay the debts and perform the obligations incumbent upon his predecessor.

8. Share or participation, as in legislation, deliberation, management, etc., by means of regularly chosen or appointed delegates; or, the system by which communities have a voice in the direction of their own affairs, and in the making of their own laws, by means of chosen delegates: as, parliamentary *representation*.

> The reform in *representation* he uniformly opposed.
> *Burke.*

He [Daniel Gookin] was the originator and the prophet of that immortal dogma of our national greatness—no taxation without *representation*. M. C. *Tyler*, Amer. Lit., I. 154.

As for the principle of *representation*, that seems to have been an invention of the Teutonic mind; no statesman of antiquity, either in Greece or at Rome, seems to have conceived the idea of a city sending delegates armed with plenary powers to represent its interests in a general legislative assembly. *J. Fiske*, Amer. Pol. Ideas, p. 59.

In these small [Grecian] commonwealths *representation* is unknown: whatever powers may be entrusted to individual magistrates or to smaller councils, the supreme authority must rest with an assembly in which every qualified citizen gives his vote in his own person. *E. A. Freeman*, Amer. Lects., p. 246.

9. A representative or delegate, or a number of representatives collectively.

The *representations* of the people are most obviously susceptible of improvement. *J. Adams*, Works, IV. 284.

Proportional representation, representation, as in a political assembly, according to the number of electors, inhabitants, etc., in an electoral district or other unit. This principle is recognized in the United States House of Representatives and in many other bodies, especially those of a popular character.—**Pure representation.** See *pure*. =**Syn.** 3. Show; delineation, portraiture, likeness, resemblance.

representational (rep″rē̤-zen-tā′shọn-ạl), *a.* [< *representation* + *-al*.] Pertaining to or containing representation, in any sense; of the nature of representation.

We find that in "constructive imagination" a new kind of effort is often requisite in order to dissociate these *representational* complexes as a preliminary to new combinations. *J. Ward*, Encyc. Brit., XX. 57.

representationary (rep″rē̤-zen-tā′shọn-ạ̄-ri), *a.* [< *representation* + *-ary*.] Of or pertaining to representation; representative: as, a *representationary* system of government. [Rare.] *Imp. Dict.*

representationism (rep″rē̤-zen-tā′shọn-izm), *n.* [< *representation* + *-ism*.] The doctrine, held by Descartes and others, that in the perception of the external world the immediate object of consciousness is vicarious, or representative of another and principal object beyond the sphere of consciousness.—**Egoistical representationism.** See *egoistic*.

representationist (rep″rē̤-zen-tā′shọn-ist), *n.* [< *representation* + *-ist*.] One who holds the doctrine of representationism.

The *representationists*, as denying to consciousness the cognisance of aught beyond a merely subjective phenomenon, are likewise idealists: yet, as positing the reality of an external world, they must be distinguished as cosmothetic idealists. *Hamilton*, Reid's Works, Note C, § 1.

representative (rep-rē̤-zen′tạ-tiv), *a.* and *n.* [< F. *représentatif* = Pr. *representatiu* = Sp. Pg. *representativo* = It. *rappresentativo*, < ML. *repræsentativus*, < L. *repræsentare*, represent: see *represent*.] **I.** *a.* **1.** Representing, portraying, or typifying.

Representative [poesy] is as a visible history, and is an image of actions as if they were present, as history is of actions in nature as they are, (that is) past. *Bacon*, Advancement of Learning, ii.

They relieve themselves with this distinction, and yet own the legal sacrifices, though *representative*, to be proper and real. *Bp. Atterbury.*

Men have a pictorial or *representative* quality, and serve us in the intellect. Behmen and Swedenborg saw that things were *representative*. Men are also *representative*—first, of things, and, secondly, of ideas. *Emerson*, Representative Men, p. 14.

2. Acting as the substitute for or agent of another or of others; performing the functions of another or of others.

This council of four hundred was chosen, one hundred out of each tribe, and seems to have been a body *representative* of the people. *Swift.*

The more multitudinous a *representative* assembly may be rendered, the more it will partake of the infirmities incident to collective meetings of the people. *A. Hamilton*, Federalist, No. 58.

3. Pertaining to or founded on representation of the people; conducted by the agency of delegates chosen by or representing the people: as, a *representative* government.

A *representative* government, even when entire, cannot possibly be the seat of sovereignty—the supreme and ultimate power of a State. The very term *representative* implies a superior in the individual or body represented. *Calhoun*, Works, I. 190.

He [Cromwell] gave the country a constitution far more perfect than any which had at that time been known in the world. He reformed the *representative* system in a manner which has extorted praise even from Lord Clarendon. *Macaulay.*

4. In *biol.*: (*a*) Typical; fully presenting, or alone representing, the characters of a given class or group: as, in zoölogy and botany, the *representative* genus of a family.

No one human being can be completely the *representative* man of his race. *Palgrave.* (*Latham.*)

(*b*) Representing in any group the characters of another and different group: chiefly used in the quinarian system; also, pertaining to such supposed representation: as, the *representative* theory. (*c*) In zoögeography, replacing; taking the place of, or holding a similar position: as, the llama is *representative* of the camel in America.—5. In *psychol.* and *logic*, mediately known; known by means of a representation or object which signifies another object.

The chief merit or excellence of a *representative* image consists in its distinctness or clearness. *J. Sully*, Outlines of Psychol., p. 227.

Representative cognitions, or those in which consciousness is occupied with the relations among ideas or represented sensations, as in all acts of recollection. *H. Spencer*, Prin. of Psychol., § 480.

Representative being, being as an immediate object of consciousness.—**Representative faculty**, the faculty of representing images which the reproductive faculty has evoked; the imagination.—**Representative function**, a function having the properties of $\phi(a, n)$, stated below, under *representative integral*.—**Representative integral**, an integral of the form

$$\int_A^b fa \cdot \phi(a, n) \cdot da,$$

where fa is a function of limited variation between A and another limit, B, exceeding b, while $\phi(a, n)$ is (1) such a function of a and the parameter n that the integral of it between the same limits is less than an assignable finite quantity, whatever value between A and B be given to b, and whatever value be given to n; and (2) is such that when n tends toward infinity, the integral of $\phi(a, n)$ from A to b, where b is greater than A and less than B, tends toward a constant finite value. This is called a *representative integral*, because it is equal to the function fA multiplied by a constant.—**Representative knowledge**, knowledge of a thing by means of a mental image, but not as actually existing.—**Representative primogeniture.** See *primogeniture*.

II. *n.* **1.** One who or that which represents another person or thing; that by which anything is represented or exhibited.

This doctrine supposes the perfections of God to be *representatives* to us of whatever we perceive in the creatures. *Locke.*

A statue of Rumour, whispering an idiot in the ear, who was the *representative* of credulity. *Addison*, Freeholder.

This breadth entitles him [Plato] to stand as the *representative* of philosophy. *Emerson*, Representative Men, p. 44.

2. An agent, deputy, or substitute, who supplies the place of another or others, being invested with his or their authority: as, an attorney is the *representative* of his client or employer; specifically, a member of the British House of Commons, or, in the United States, of the lower branch of Congress (the House of Representatives) or of the corresponding branch of the legislature in some States.

Then let us drink the Stewartry,
Kerroughtree's laird, and a' that,
Our *representative* to be.
Burns, Election Ballads, I.

The tribunes of Rome, who were the *representatives* of the people, prevailed, it is well known, in almost every contest with the senate for life. *A. Hamilton*, Federalist, No. 63.

There are four essentials to the excellence of a representative system:—That the *representatives* . . . shall be *representatives* rather than mere delegates. *Bryce*, Amer. Commonwealth, I. 296.

3. In *law*: (*a*) One who occupies another's place and succeeds to his beneficial rights in such a way that he may also in some degree be charged with his liabilities. Thus, an heir or devisee, since, to the extent of the property to which he succeeds, he is liable for his ancestor's debts, is a *representative* of the ancestor; but the widow, who takes part of the estate as dower, without liability, is not deemed a *representative* of the deceased; nor is an officer or trustee who succeeds to the rights and powers of the office or trust a *representative* of his predecessor, for, though he comes under liability in respect of the office or trust as his predecessor did, he does not succeed to the liabilities which his predecessor had incurred. The executor or administrator is sometimes spoken of as the *representative* of the decedent, but is usually distinguished by being called the *personal representative*. (*b*) One who takes under the Statute of Descents or the Statute of Distributions, or under a will or trust deed, a share which by the primary intention would have gone to his parent had the parent survived to the time for taking. If a gift has vested in interest absolutely in the parent, then, upon the parent's death before it vests in possession, the child will take as successor in interest of the parent, but not as *representative* of the parent in this sense. But if the parent dies before acquiring any interest whatever, as where one of several heirs apparent dies before the ancestor, leaving a child or children, the other heirs take their respective shares as if the one had not died, and the child or children of the deceased take the share their deceased parent would have taken. In this case all who share are *representatives* of the ancestor in sense (*a*), and the child or children are also *representatives* of the deceased heir apparent in sense (*b*). See *representation*, 7.—**House of Representatives**, the lower branch of the United States Congress, consisting of members chosen biennially by the people. It consists at present (1890) of about 330 members. In many of the separate States, also, the lower branch of the legislature is called the *House of Representatives*.—**Personal representative.** See *personal*.—**Real representative**, an heir at law or devisee.

representatively (rep-rē̤-zen′tạ-tiv-li), *adv.* In a representative manner; as or through a representative.

Having sustained the brunt of God's displeasure, he [our Lord] was solemnly reinstated in favour and we *representatively*, or virtually, in him. *Barrow*, Works, V. 468.

representativeness (rep-rē̤-zen′tạ-tiv-nes), *n.* The character of being representative.

representer (rep-rē̤-zen′tėr), *n.* One who or that which represents. (*a*) One who or that which shows, exhibits, or describes.

Where the real works of nature or veritable acts of story are to be described, . . . art being but the imitator or secondary *representer*, it must not vary from the verity of the example. *Sir T. Browne*, Vulg. Err., v. 19.

(*b*) A representative; one who acts by deputation. [Rare.]

My Muse officious ventures
On the nation's *representers*. *Swift.*

representment (rep-rē̤-zent′mẹnt), *n.* [= It. *rappresentamento*; < *represent* + *-ment*.] Representation; renewed presentation. [Obsolete or archaic.]

Grant that all our praises, hymns, eucharistical remembrances, and *representments* of thy glories may be useful, blessed, and effectual. *Jer. Taylor*, Works (ed. 1835), I. 226.

So far approv'd as to have bin trusted with the *representment* and defence of your Actions to all Christendom against an Adversary of no mean repute. *Milton*, To the Parliament.

Turning to Alice, the soul of the first Alice looked out at her eyes with such a reality of *re-presentment* that I became in doubt which of them stood there before me. *Lamb*, Dream Children.

repress (rē̤-pres′), *v. t.* [< ME. *repressen* (cf. F. *represser*, press again), < L. *repressus*, pp. of *reprimere*, hold back, check, < *re-*, back, + *premere*, press: see *press*[1].] **1.** To press back or down effectually; crush; quell; put down; subdue; suppress.

All this while King Richard was in Ireland, where he performed Acts, in *repressing* the Rebels there, not unworthy of him. *Baker*, Chronicles, p. 150.

If your Spirit will not let you retract, yet you shall do well to *repress* any more Copies of the Satire. *Howell*, Letters, ii. 2.

And sov'reign Law, that state's collected will, . . .
Sits Empress, crowning good, *repressing* ill.
Sir W. Jones, Ode in Imit. of Alcæus.

This attempt at desertion he *repressed* at the hazard of his life. *Bancroft*, Hist. U. S., I. 102.

2. To check; restrain; keep under due restraint.

Such kings . . .
Favour the innocent, *repress* the bold.
Waller, Ruin of the Turkish Empire.

Though secret anger swell'd Minerva's breast,
The prudent goddess yet her wrath *represt*.
Pope, Iliad, viii. 573.

Sophia even *repressed* excellence, from her fears to offend. *Goldsmith*, Vicar, i.

=**Syn.** 1. To curb, smother, overcome, overpower.—1 and 2. *Restrict*, etc. See *restrain*.

repress† (rē̤-pres′), *n.* [< *repress*, *v.*] The act of subduing.

Loud outcries of injury, when they tend nothing to the *repress* of it, is a liberty rather assumed by rage and impatience than authorized by justice. *Government of the Tongue.* (*Encyc. Dict.*)

represser (rē̤-pres′ėr), *n.* One who represses; one who crushes or subdues. *Imp. Dict.*

repressible (rē̤-pres′i-bl), *a.* [< *repress* + *-ible*.] Capable of being repressed or restrained. *Imp. Dict.*

repressibly (rē̤-pres′i-bli), *adv.* In a repressible manner. *Imp. Dict.*

repressing-machine (rē̤-pres′ing-mạ-shēn″), *n.* 1. A machine for making pressed bricks, or for giving them a finishing pressing.—2. A heavy cotton-press for compressing cotton-bales into as compact form as possible for transportation.

repression (rē̤-presh′ọn), *n.* [< ME. *repression*, < OF. *repression*, F. *répression* = Sp. *represion* = Pg. *repressão* = It. *repressione*, *ripressione*, < ML. *repressio(n-)*, < L. *reprimere*, pp. *repressus*, repress, check: see *repress*.] 1. The act of repressing, restraining, or subduing: as, the *repression* of tumults.

We see him as he moved, . . .
With what sublime *repression* of himself,
And in what limits, and how tenderly.
Tennyson, Idylls, Dedication.

The condition of the papacy itself occupied the minds of the bishops too much . . . to allow time for elaborate measures of *repression*. *Stubbs*, Const. Hist., § 404.

2. That which represses; check; restraint.—3†. Power of repressing.

And som so ful of furie is and despite
That it surmounteth his *repression*.
Chaucer, Troilus, iii. 1038.

repressive (rẹ̄-pres'iv), *a.* [< F. *répressif* = Pg. *repressivo*; as *repress* + *-ive*.] Having power to repress or crush; tending to subdue or restrain.

Visible disorders are no more than symptoms which no measures, *repressive* or revolutionary, can do more than palliate. *Froude*, Cæsar, vi.

repressively (rẹ̄-pres'iv-li), *adv.* In a repressive manner; with repression; so as to repress. *Imp. Dict.*

repressor (rẹ̄-pres'ọr), *n.* [< ME. *repressour* = It. *ripressore*, < L. *repressor*, one who restrains or limits, < *reprimere*, pp. *repressus*, repress: see *repress*.] One who represses or restrains.

reprevable†, *a.* A Middle English form of *reproevable*.

repreve†, *n.* and *v.* A Middle English form of *reproof* and *reprove*.

repriet, **repryt**†, *v. t.* [A reduced form of *reprieve*.] Same as *reprieve*.

Wherupon they *repryede* me to prison cheynde. *Heywood's Spider and Flie* (1556). (*Nares.*)

repriet, **repryt**†, *n.* [A reduced form of *reprieve*. Cf. *reprie*, *v.*] Same as *reprieve*.

Why, master Vaux, is there no remedy
But instantly they must be led to death?
Can it not be deferrd till afternoon,
Or but two hours, in hope to get *repriet*?
Heywood, 2 Edw. IV. (Works, ed. Pearson, 1874, I. 135).

repriefe†, *n.* Same as *repreve* for *reproof*.

reprieval† (rẹ̄-prē'vạl), *n.* [< *reprieve* + *-al*.] Respite.

The *reprieval* of my life. *Bp. Hall*, Contemplations (ed. Tegg), IV. 125.

reprieve (rẹ̄-prēv'), *v. t.*; pret. and pp. *reprieved*, ppr. *reprieving*. [Early mod. E. also *repreeve*, *reprive*; a particular use of *reprove*: see *reprove*, of which *reprieve* is a doublet.] 1†. To acquit; set free; release.

It is by name
Proteus, that hath ordayn'd my sonne to die; . . .
Therefore I humbly crave your Majestie
It to replevie, and my sonne *reprive*.
Spenser, F. Q., IV. xii. 31.

He cannot thrive
Unless her prayers . . . *reprieve* him from the wrath
Of greatest justice. *Shak.*, All's Well, iii. 4. 28.

2. To grant a respite to; suspend or delay the execution of for a time: as, to *reprieve* a criminal for thirty days.

His Majesty had been graciously pleased to *reprieve* him, with several of his friends, in order, as it was thought, to give them their lives. *Addison*, Conversion of the Foxhunter.

3. To relieve for a time from any danger or suffering; respite; spare; save.

At my Return, if it shall please God to *reprieve* me in these dangerous Times of Contagion, I shall continue my wonted Service to your Lordship. *Howell*, Letters, I. iv. 20.

Vain, transitory splendours! Could not all
Reprieve the tottering mansion from its fall?
Goldsmith, Des. Vil., l. 238.

4. To secure a postponement of (an execution). [Rare.]

I *repriev'd*
Th' intended execution with entreaties
And interruption. *Ford*, Lover's Melancholy, i. 1.

=**Syn.** 2. See the noun.

reprieve (rẹ̄-prēv'), *n.* [< *reprieve*, *v.* Cf. *reproof*.] 1. The suspension of the execution of a criminal's sentence. Sometimes incorrectly used to signify a permanent remission or commutation of a capital sentence. In the United States reprieves may be granted by the President, by the governor of a State, governor and council, etc.; in Great Britain they are granted by the home secretary in the name of the sovereign. See *pardon*, 2.

Duke. How came it that the absent duke had not . . . executed him? . . .
Prov. His friends still wrought *reprieves* for him.
Shak., M. for M., iv. 2. 140.

The morning that Sir John Hotham was to die, a *reprieve* was sent . . . to suspend the execution for three days. *Clarendon*, Hist. of the Rebellion (1648), p. 589.

2. Respite in general; interval of ease or relief; delay of something dreaded.

I search'd the shades of sleep, to ease my day
Of griping sorrows with a night's *reprieve*.
Quarles, Emblems, iv. 14.

All that I ask is but a short *reprieve*,
Till I forget to love, and learn to grieve.
Sir J. Denham, Passion of Dido.

Their theory was despair; the Whig wisdom was only *reprieve*, a waiting to be last devoured. *Emerson*, Fugitive Slave Law.

=**Syn.** *Reprieve, Respite. Reprieve* is now used chiefly in the sense of the first definition, to name a suspension or postponement of the execution of a sentence of death. *Respite* is a free word, applying to an intermission or postponement of something wearying, burdensome, or troublesome: as, *respite* from work. *Respite* may be for an indefinite or a definite time: a *reprieve* is generally for a time named. A *respite* may be a *reprieve*.

reprimand (rep'ri-mȧnd), *n.* [< OF. *reprimande*, *reprimende*, F. *réprimande* = Sp. Pg. *reprimenda*, reprehension, reproof, < L. *reprimenda*, sc. *res*, a thing that ought to be repressed, fem. gerundive of *reprimere*, repress: see *repress*.] Severe reproof for a fault; reprehension, private or public.

Goldsmith gave his landlady a sharp *reprimand* for her treatment of him. *Macaulay*, Goldsmith.

=**Syn.** *Monition, Reprehension*, etc. See *admonition*.

reprimand (rep-ri-mȧnd'), *v. t.* [< OF. *reprimander*, F. *réprimander*, < *reprimande*, reproof: see *reprimand*, *n.*] To reprove severely; reprehend; chide for a fault.

Germanicus was severely *reprimanded* by Tiberius for travelling into Egypt without his permission. *Arbuthnot.*

The people are feared and flattered. They are not *reprimanded*. *Emerson*, Fortune of the Republic.

=**Syn.** *Rebuke*, etc. See *censure*.

reprimander (rep-ri-mȧn'dėr), *n.* One who reprimands.

Then said the owl unto his *reprimander*,
"Fair sir, I have no enemies to slander."
Quiver, 1867, p. 186. (*Encyc. Dict.*)

reprimer (rē-prī'mėr), *n.* [< *re-* + *primer*[2].] An instrument for setting a cap upon a cartridge-shell. It is one of a set of reloading-tools. *E. H. Knight.*

reprint (rẹ̄-print'), *v. t.* [< *re-* + *print*, *v.*] 1. To print again; print a second or any new edition of.

My bookseller is *reprinting* the "Essay on Criticism." *Pope.*

2. To renew the impression of. [Rare.]

The whole business of our redemption is . . . to *reprint* God's image upon the soul. *South*, Sermons, I. ii.

reprint (rẹ̄-print'), *n.* [< *reprint*, *v.*] 1. A second or a new impression or edition of any printed work; reimpression.—2. In *printing*, printed matter taken from some other publication for reproduction.

How are ye off for copy, Mike?" "Bad," answered the old printer. "I've a little *reprint*, but no original matter at all." *The Century*, XXXVII. 303.

reprisal (rẹ̄-prī'zal), *n.* [Early mod. E. also *reprisall*, *reprisel*; < OF. *represaille*, F. *représaille* (= Sp. *represalia*, *represaria* = Pg. *represalia* = It. *ripresaglia*; ML. reflex *reprisaliæ*, *repræsaliæ*, pl.), a taking, seizing, prize, booty, < *reprise*, a taking, prize: see *reprise*, *n.*] 1. In *international law*: (*a*) The recovering by force of what is one's own. (*b*) The seizing of an equivalent, or, negatively, the detaining of that which belongs to an adversary, as a means of obtaining redress of a grievance. (*Woolsey.*) A reprisal is the use of force by one nation against property of another to obtain redress without thereby commencing war; and the uncertainty of the distinction between it and war results from the uncertainty as to what degree of force can be used without practically declaring war or creating a state of war.

All this Year and the Year past sundry quarrels and complaints arose between the English and French, touching *reprisals* of Goods taken from each other by Parties of either Nation. *Baker*, Chronicles, p. 389.

Reprisals differ from retorsion in this, that the essence of the former consists in seizing the property of another nation by way of security, until it shall have listened to the just reclamations of the offended party, while retorsion includes all kinds of measures which do an injury to another, similar and equivalent to that which we have experienced from him. *Woolsey*, Introd. to Inter. Law, § 114.

2. The act of retorting on an enemy by inflicting suffering or death on a prisoner taken from him, in retaliation of an act of inhumanity.

The military executions on both sides, the massacre of prisoners, the illegal *reprisals* of Warwick and Clarence in 1469 and 1470, were alike unjustifiable. *Stubbs*, Const. Hist., § 373.

3. Any taking by way of retaliation; an act of severity done in retaliation.

This gentleman being very desirous, as it seems, to make *reprisals* upon me, undertakes to furnish out a whole section of gross misrepresentations made by me in my quotations. *Waterland*, Works, III. 70.

He considered himself as robbed and plundered, and took it into his head that he had a right to make *reprisals*, as he could find opportunity. *Scott*, Heart of Mid-Lothian, ii.

Who call things wicked that give too much joy,
And nickname the *reprisal* envy makes
Punishment. *Browning*, Ring and Book, II. 249.

4. Same as *recaption*.—5†. A prize.

I am on fire
To hear this rich *reprisal* is so nigh,
And yet not ours. Come, let me taste my horse,
Who is to bear me like a thunderbolt
Against the bosom of the Prince of Wales.
Shak., 1 Hen. IV., iv. 1. 118.

6. A restitution. [An erroneous use.]

He was able to refund, to make *reprisals*, if they could be fairly demanded. *George Eliot*, Felix Holt, ix.

Letters of marque and reprisal. See *marque*. =**Syn.** 1-3. *Retribution, Retaliation*, etc. See *revenge*.

reprise†, **reprize**[1]† (rẹ̄-prīz'), *v. t.* [< OF. (and F.) *repris*, pp. of *reprendre*, take again, retake (cf. Sp. Pg. *represar*, recapture), < L. *reprehendere*, seize again: see *reprehend*.] 1. To take again; retake.

He now begunne
To challenge her anew, as his own prize,
Whom formerly he had in battell wonne,
And proffer made by force her to *reprize*.
Spenser, F. Q., IV. iv. 8.

Ye might *reprise* the armes Sarpedon forfeited,
By forfeit of your rights to him. *Chapman*, Iliad, vii.

2. To recompense; pay.

If any of the lands so granted by his majesty should be otherwise decreed, his majesty's grantee should be *reprised* with other lands.
Grant, in Lord Clarendon's Life, ii. 252. (*Latham.*)

3. To take; arrest.

He was *repriz'd*.
Howell, Exact Hist. of the late Rev. in Naples, 1664.

reprise (rẹ̄-prīz'), *n.* [Early mod. E. also *reprize*; < ME. *reprise*, < OF. *reprise*, a taking back, etc., F. *reprise*, a taking back, recovery, recapture, resumption, return, repetition, revival (= Sp. *represa* = Pg. *represa*, *repreza* = It. *ripresa*, a retaking), < *repris*, pp. of *reprendre*, take; from the verb.] 1†. A taking by way of retaliation; reprisal.

If so, a just *reprise* would only be
Of what the land usurp'd upon the sea.
Dryden, Hind and Panther, iii. 862.

2. In *masonry*, the return of a molding in an internal angle.—3. In *maritime law*, a ship recaptured from an enemy or a pirate. If recaptured within twenty-four hours of her capture, she must be restored to her owners; if after that period, she is the lawful prize of those who have recaptured her.
4. *pl.* In *law*, yearly deductions, duties, or payments out of a manor and lands, as rent-charge, rent-seck, annuities, and the like. Also written *reprizes*.—5. In *music*: (*a*) The act of repeating a passage, or a passage repeated. (*b*) A return to the first theme or subject of a short work or section, after an intermediate or contrasted passage. (*c*) A revival of an obsolete or forgotten work.—6†. Blame; reproach. *Halliwell.*

That alle the world ne may suffise
To staunche of pride the *reprise*.
Gower, MS. Soc. Antiq. 134, f. 60.

repristinate (rē-pris'ti-nāt), *v. t.* [< *re-* + *pristinate*.] To restore to the pristine or first state or condition. [Rare.] *Imp. Dict.*

repristination (rē-pris-ti-nā'shọn), *n.* [< *repristinate* + *-ion*.] Restoration to the pristine form or state.

The *repristination* of the simple and hallowed names of early Hebrew history.
Smith's Dict. Bible (Amer. ed.), p. 2062.

reprive†, *v. t.* An obsolete form of *reprieve* and *reprove*.

reprize[1]†, *v.* and *n.* See *reprise*.

reprize[2], *v. t.* [< OF. *repriser*, set a new price on, prize again; as *re-* + *prize*[2], *v.*] To prize anew. *Imp. Dict.*

reproach (rẹ̄-prōch'), *v. t.* [< OF. *reprocher*, *reprochier*, F. *reprocher* = Pr. *repropchar* = Sp. Pg. *reprochar* = It. *rimprocciare* (ML. reflex *reprochare*), reproach, prob. < LL. **repropiare*, bring near to, hence cast in one's teeth, impute, object (cf. *approach*, < OF. *aprocher*, approach, < LL. **appropiare*), < *re-*, again, + **propiare*, < L. *propius*, nearer, compar. of *prope*, near: see *propinquity*, and cf. *approach*.] 1. To charge with a fault; censure with severity; upbraid: now usually with a personal object.

With a most inhumane cruelty they who have put out the peoples eyes *reproach* them of their blindnesse.
Milton, Apology for Smectymnuus.

Scenes which, never having known me free,
Would not *reproach* me with the loss I felt.
Cowper, Task, v. 490.

2†. To disgrace.

I thought your marriage fit; else imputation,
For that he knew you, might *reproach* your life,
And choke your good to come.
Shak., M. for M., v. 1. 426.

=**Syn.** 1. *Reprove, Rebuke*, etc. (see *censure*); revile, vilify, accuse.

reproach (rẹ̄-prōch'), *n.* [Early mod. E. also *reproch*, *reproche*; < OF. *reproche*, *reproce*, *reprocce*, F. *reproche* = Pr. *repropche* = Sp. Pg. *reproche* = It. *rimproccio*, reproach; from the verb.] 1. The act of reproaching; a severe expression of censure or blame.

A man's first care should be to avoid the *reproaches* of his own heart. *Addison*, Sir Roger at the Assizes.

In vain Thalestris with *reproach* assails,
For who can move when fair Belinda fails?
Pope, R. of the L., v. 3.

The name of Whig was never used except as a term of *reproach*. *Macaulay*, Hist. Eng., vi.

2. An occasion of blame or censure, shame, infamy, or disgrace; also, the state of being subject to blame or censure; a state of disgrace.

In any writer vntruth and flatterie are counted most great *reproches*. *Puttenham*, Arte of Eng. Poesie, p. 21.

Give not thine heritage to *reproach*. Joel ii. 17.

I know repentant tears ensue the deed,
Reproach, disdain, and deadly enmity;
Yet strive I to embrace mine infamy.
Shak., Lucrece, l. 503.

Many scandalous libells and invectives [were] scatter'd about the streets, to y^e *reproch* of government and the fermentation of our since distractions.
Evelyn, Diary, June 10, 1640.

Why did the King dwell on my name to me?
Mine own name shames me, seeming a *reproach*.
Tennyson, Lancelot and Elaine.

3. An object of contempt, scorn, or derision.

Come, and let us build up the wall of Jerusalem, that we may be no more a *reproach*. Neh. ii. 17.

I will deliver them . . . to be a *reproach* and a proverb, a taunt and a curse, in all places whither I shall drive them. Jer. xxiv. 9.

The Reproaches, in the *Rom. Cath. Ch.*, antiphons sung on Good Friday during the Adoration of the Cross. They follow the special prayers which succeed the Gospel of the Passion, and consist of sentences addressed by Christ to his people, reminding them of the great things he had done for them, in delivering them from Egypt, etc., and their ungrateful return for his goodness, as shown in the details of the passion and crucifixion. They are intermingled with the Trisagion ("Holy God . . .") in Greek and Latin, and succeeded by hymns and the bringing in of the presanctified host in procession, after which the Mass of the Presanctified is celebrated. The Reproaches are sometimes sung in Anglican churches before the Three Hours' service. Also called *Improperia*. =**Syn.** 1. *Monition, Reprehension*, etc. (see *admonition*), blame, reviling, abuse, invective, vilification, upbraiding. —2. Disrepute, discredit, dishonor, scandal, contumely.

reproachable (rẹ-prō'chạ-bl), *a.* [< ME. *reprochable*, < OF. *reprochable*, F. *reprochable*; as *reproach* + *-able*.] 1. Deserving reproach.

Nor, in the mean time, is our ignorance *reproachable*.
Evelyn, True Religion, I. 166.

2†. Opprobrious; scurrilous; reproachful; abusive. [Rare.]

Catullus the poet wrote againste him [Julius Cæsar] contumelious or *reproachable* verses.
Sir T. Elyot, The Governour, fol. 170 b. (*Latham.*)

reproachableness (rẹ-prō'chạ-bl-nes), *n.* The character of being reproachable. *Bailey*, 1727.

reproachably (rẹ-prō'chạ-bli), *adv.* In a reproachable manner; so as to be reproachable. *Imp. Dict.*

reproacher (rẹ-prō'chėr), *n.* One who reproaches. *Imp. Dict.*

reproachful (rẹ-prōch'fụl), *a.* [< *reproach* + *-ful.*] 1. Containing or expressing reproach or censure; upbraiding.

Fixed were her eyes upon his, as if she divined his intention,
Fixed with a look so sad, so *reproachful*, imploring, and patient,
That with a sudden revulsion his heart recoiled from its purpose. *Longfellow*, Miles Standish, v.

2†. Scurrilous; opprobrious.

Aar. For shame, put up.
Dem. Not I, till I have sheathed
My rapier in his bosom, and withal
Thrust these *reproachful* speeches down his throat.
Shak., Tit. And., ii. 1. 55.

The common People cast out *reproachful* Slanders against the Lord Treasurer Buckhurst, as the Granter of Licenses for transportation of Corn.
Baker, Chronicles, p. 389.

Bozon Allen, one of the deputies of Hingham, and a delinquent in that common cause, should be publicly convict of divers false and *reproachful* speeches published by him concerning the deputy governour.
Winthrop, Hist. New England, II. 265.

3. Worthy or deserving of, or receiving, reproach; shameful: as, *reproachful* conduct.

Thy punishment
He shall endure, by coming in the flesh
To a *reproachful* life and cursed death.
Milton, P. L., xii. 406.

=**Syn.** 1. Rebuking, censuring, upbraiding, censorious, contemptuous, contumelious, abusive.

reproachfully (rẹ-prōch'fụl-i), *adv.* 1. In a reproachful manner; with reproach or censure.

Give none occasion to the adversary to speak *reproachfully*. 1 Tim. v. 14.

2. Shamefully; disgracefully; contemptuously.

William Bussey, Steward to William de Valence, is committed to the Tower of London, and most *reproachfully* used. *Baker*, Chronicles, p. 86.

reproachfulness (rẹ-prōch'fụl-nes), *n.* The quality of being reproachful. *Bailey*, 1727.

reproachless (rẹ-prōch'les), *a.* [< *reproach* + *-less.*] Without reproach; irreproachable.

reprobable†, *a.* [< ML. *reprobabilis*, < L. *reprobare*, reprove: see *reprove*, *reprobate*. Cf. *reprovable*.] Reprovable.

No thynge ther in was *reprobable*,
But all to gedder true and veritable.
Roy and Barlow, Rede me and Be nott Wroth, p. 44.
(*Davies.*)

reprobacy (rep'rọ-bā-si), *n.* [< *reproba(te)* + *-cy.*] The state or character of being a reprobate; wickedness; profligacy. [Rare.]

Greater evils . . . were yet behind, and . . . were as sure as this of overtaking him in his state of *reprobacy*.
Fielding, Tom Jones, v. 2.

"I should be sorry," said he, "that the wretch would die in his present state of *reprobacy*."
H. Brooke, Fool of Quality, II. 134. (*Davies.*)

reprobance† (rep'rọ-bans), *n.* [< L. *reproban(t-)s*, ppr. of *reprobare*, disapprove, reject, condemn: see *reprobate*.] Reprobation.

This sight would make him do a desperate turne,
Yea, curse his better Angell from his side,
And fall to *reprobance*.
Shak., Othello (folio 1623), v. 2, 209.

reprobate (rep'rọ-bāt), *v. t.*; pret. and pp. *reprobated*, ppr. *reprobating*. [< L. *reprobatus*, pp. of *reprobare*, disapprove, reject, condemn: see *reprove*.] 1. To disapprove vehemently; contemn strongly; condemn; reject.

And doth he *reprobate*, and will he damn,
The use of his own bounty? *Cowper*, Task, v. 638.

If, for example, a man, through intemperance or extravagance, becomes unable to pay his debts, . . . he is deservedly *reprobated*, and might be justly punished.
J. S. Mill, On Liberty, iv.

Thousands who detested the policy of the New Englanders . . . *reprobated* the Stamp Act and many other parts of English policy. *Lecky*, Eng. in 18th Cent., xiv.

2. To abandon to vice or punishment, or to hopeless ruin or destruction. See *reprobation*, 3.

I believe many are saved who to man seem *reprobated*.
Sir T. Browne, Religio Medici, i. 57.

If he doom that people with a frown, . . .
Obduracy takes place; callous and tough,
The *reprobated* race grows judgment-proof.
Cowper, Table-Talk, l. 459.

To approbate and reprobate, in *Scots law*. See *approbate*. =**Syn.** 1. To reprehend, censure. See *reprobate*, *a.*

reprobate (rep'rọ-bāt), *a.* and *n.* [= F. *réprouvé* = Sp. *reprobado* = Pg. *reprovado* = It. *riprovato*, *reprobato*, < L. *reprobatus*, pp. of *reprobare*, reprobate, condemn: see *reprobate*, *v.*] **I.** *a.* 1†. Disallowed; disapproved; rejected; not enduring proof or trial.

Reprobate silver shall men call them, because the Lord hath rejected them. Jer. vi. 30.

2. Abandoned in sin; morally abandoned; depraved; characteristic of a reprobate.

By *reprobate* desire thus madly led.
Shak., Lucrece, l. 300.

So fond are mortal men,
Fallen into wrath divine,
As their own ruin on themselves to invite,
Insensate left, or to sense *reprobate*,
And with blindness internal struck.
Milton, S. A., l. 1685.

3. Expressing disapproval or censure; condemnatory. [Rare.]

I instantly reproached my heart . . . in the bitterest and most *reprobate* of expressions.
Sterne, Sentimental Journey, p. 44.

=**Syn.** 2. *Profligate*, etc. (see *abandoned*), vitiated, corrupt, hardened, wicked, base, vile, cast away, graceless, shameless.

II. *n.* One who is very profligate or abandoned; a person given over to sin; one lost to virtue and religion; a wicked, depraved wretch.

We think our selves the Elect, and have the Spirit, and the rest a Company of *Reprobates* that belong to the Devil.
Selden, Table-Talk, p. 67.

I fear
A hopeless *reprobate*, a hardened sinner,
Must be that Carmelite now passing near.
Longfellow, Golden Legend, i. 5.

reprobateness (rep'rọ-bāt-nes), *n.* The state or character of being reprobate. *Imp. Dict.*

reprobater (rep'rọ-bā-tėr), *n.* One who reprobates.

John, Duke of Argyle, the patriotic *reprobater* of French modes.
M. Noble, Cont. of Granger's Biograph. Hist., III. 490.

reprobation (rep-rọ-bā'shọn), *n.* [< OF. *reprobation*, F. *réprobation* = Sp. *reprobacion* = Pg. *reprovação* = It. *riprovazione*, *reprobazione*, < LL. (eccl.) *reprobatio(n-)*, rejection, reprobation, < L. *reprobare*, pp. *reprobatus*, reject, reprobate: see *reprobate*.] 1. The act of reprobating, or of vehemently disapproving or condemning.

The profligate pretenses . . . are mentioned with becoming *reprobation*. *Jeffrey.*

Among other agents whose approbation or *reprobation* are contemplated by the savage as consequences of his conduct, are the spirits of his ancestors.
H. Spencer, Prin. of Psychol., § 520.

2. The state of being reprobated; condemnation; censure; rejection.

You are empowered to . . . put your stamp on all that ought to pass for current, and set a brand of *reprobation* on clipt poetry and false coin. *Dryden.*

He exhibited this institution in the blackest colors of *reprobation*. *Sumner*, Speech, Aug. 27, 1846.

3. In *theol.*, the act of consigning or the state of being consigned to eternal punishment; the predestination by the decree and counsel of God of certain individuals or communities to eternal death, as election is the predestination to eternal life.

No sin at all but impenitency can give testimony of final *reprobation*. *Burton*, Anat. of Mel., p. 654.

What transubstantiation is in the order of reason, the Augustinian doctrine of the damnation of unbaptised infants, and the Calvinistic doctrine of *reprobation*, are in the order of morals. *Lecky*, European Morals, I. 98.

4. In *eccles. law*, the propounding of exceptions to facts, persons, or things.—5. Disqualification to bear office: a punishment inflicted upon military officers for neglect of duty. *Grose.*

reprobationer (rep-rọ-bā'shọn-ėr), *n.* In *theol.*, one who believes in the doctrine of reprobation.

Let them take heed that they mistake not their own fierce temper for the mind of God. . . . But I never knew any of the Geneva or Scotch model (which sort of sanctified *reprobationers* we abound with) either use or like this way of preaching in my life; but generally whips and scorpions, wrath and vengeance, fire and brimstone, made both top and bottom, front and rear, first and last, of all their discourses. *South*, Sermons, III. xi.

reprobative (rep'rọ-bā-tiv), *a.* [< *reprobate* + *-ive.*] Of or pertaining to reprobation; condemning in strong terms; criminatory. *Imp. Dict.*

reprobator (rep'rọ-bā-tọr), *n.* [Orig. adj., a form of *reprobatory*.] In *Scots law*, formerly, an action to convict a witness of perjury, or to establish that he was biased.

reprobatory (rep'rọ-bạ-tọ-ri), *a.* [= Sp. *reprobatorio*; as *reprobate* + *-ory*.] Reprobative. *Imp. Dict.*

reproduce (rē-prọ-dūs'), *v. t.* [= F. *reproduire* = Sp. *reproducir* = Pg. *reproduzir* = It. *riprodurre*, reproduce, < ML. **reproducere*, < L. *re-*, again, + *producere*, produce: see *produce*.] 1. To bring forward again; produce or exhibit anew.

Topics of which she retained details with the utmost accuracy, and *reproduced* them in an excellent pickle of epigrams. *George Eliot*, Middlemarch, vi.

2. To produce or yield again or anew; generate, as offspring; beget; procreate; give rise by an organic process to a new individual of the same species; propagate. See *reproduction*.

If horse-dung *reproduceth* oats, it will not be easily determined where the power of generation ceaseth.
Sir T. Browne.

The power of *reproducing* lost parts is greatest where the organization is lowest, and almost disappears where the organization is highest.
H. *Spencer*, Prin. of Biol., § 62.

In the seventeenth century Scotland *reproduced* all the characteristics and accustomed itself to the phrases of the Jewish theocracy, and the world saw again a covenanted people. *J. R. Seeley*, Nat. Religion, p. 181.

3. To make a copy or representation of; portray; represent.

Such a comparison . . . would enable us to *reproduce* the ancient society of our common ancestry in a way that would speedily set at rest some of the most controverted questions of institutional history.
Stubbs, Medieval and Modern Hist., p. 65.

From the Eternal Being among whose mountains he wandered there came to his heart steadfastness, stillness, a sort of reflected or *reproduced* eternity.
J. R. Seeley, Nat. Religion, p. 98.

A number of commendably quaint designs, however, are *reproduced* from the "Voyages Pittoresques."
N. and Q., 7th ser., III. 260.

reproducer (rē-prọ-dū'sėr), *n.* 1. One who or that which reproduces.

I speak of Charles Townshend, officially the *re-producer* of this fatal scheme. *Burke*, American Taxation.

Specifically—2. The diaphragm used in reproducing speech in the phonograph.

Consequently, there are two diaphragms, one a recorder and the other a *reproducer*. *Nature*, XXXIX. 108.

reproducible (rē-prọ-dū'si-bl), *a.* [< *reproduce* + *-ible*.] Susceptible or capable of reproduction.

reproduction (rē-prọ-duk'shọn), *n.* [= F. *reproduction* = Sp. *reproduccion* = Pg. *reproducção* = It. *riproduzione*, < ML. **reproductio(n-)*, < **reproducere*, reproduce: see *reproduce*.] 1. The act or process of reproducing, presenting, or yielding again; repetition.

The labourers and labouring cattle, therefore, employed in agriculture, not only occasion, like the workmen in manufactures, the *reproduction* of a value equal to their own consumption, or to the capital which employs them, together with its owners' profits, but of a much greater value. *Adam Smith*, Wealth of Nations, ii. 2.

2. The act or process of restoring parts of an organism that have been destroyed or removed.

The question of the *Reproduction* of Lost Parts is interesting from several points of view in biology. *Mind*, IX. 415.

Specifically—3. The process whereby new individuals are generated and the perpetuation of the species is insured; the process whereby new organisms are produced from those already existing: as, the *reproduction* of plants or animals. (*a*) The reproduction of plants is effected either vegetatively or by means of spores or of seeds. Vegetative reproduction consists in the individualizing of some part of the parent organism. In low unicellular plants this is simply a process of fission, one cell dividing into two or more, much as in the formation of tissue, save that the new cells become independent. In higher plants this method obtains by the shooting and rooting of some fraction of the organism, as a branch, a joint of a rootstock, in *Begonia* even a part of a leaf; or through specially modified shoots or buds, as the gemmæ of some algæ, mosses, etc., the bulblets of some mosses, ferns, the tiger-lily, etc., the corms, bulbs, and tubers of numerous annual plants. The cells engaged in this mode of reproduction are simply those of the ordinary tissues. Very many, but not all, plants propagate in this manner; but all are capable of reproduction in other methods included under the term *spore-reproduction*, which is reproduction most properly so called. This is accomplished through special reproductive cells, each of which is capable of developing into an individual plant. These are produced either independently, or through the conjunction of two separate cells by which their protoplasm coalesces. These may also in a less perfect sense be called reproductive cells. Reproduction through the union of two cells is sexual; through an independent cell, asexual. Sexual reproduction proceeds either by conjugation (that is, the union of two cells apparently just alike, which may be either common vegetative cells or specialized in form) or by fertilization, in which a smaller but more active sperm-cell or male cell impregnates a larger, less active germ-cell or female cell. In cryptogamous plants both methods are common, and the reproductive cells are termed *spores*, or when of the two sexes *gametes*, the male being distinguished as *antherozoids*, the female as *oöspheres*. In flowering plants spore-reproduction is always sexual, fertilization becoming pollination, the embryo-sac in the ovule affording the female cell and the pollen-grain the male cell. But the union of these cells produces, instead of a detachable spore, an embryo or plantlet, which, often accompanied by a store of nutriment, is inclosed within an integument, the whole forming a seed. The production of seeds instead of spores is the most fundamental distinction of phanerogams. Spore-reproduction is consummated by the germination of the spore or seed, which often takes place after a considerable interval. (*b*) Among the lowest animals, in which no sex is recognizable, reproduction takes place in various ways, which correspond to those above described for the lowest plants. (See *conjugation*, *fission*, *gemmation*, and *sporulation*.) Among sexed animals, reproduction results from the fecundation of an ovum by spermatozoa, with or without sexual copulation, and with many modifications of the details of the process. (See *genesis*, 2, and words there given.) Many animals are hermaphrodite, containing both sexes in one individual, and maturing the opposite sexual elements either simultaneously or successively: such are self-impregnating or reciprocally fecundating, as the case may be. Reproduction may be effected also by a detached part of an individual, constituting a separate person (see *generative person*, under *generative*). Sexual may alternate with asexual reproduction (see *parthenogenesis*); but in the vast majority of animals, invertebrate as well as vertebrate, permanent and perfect distinction of sex exists, in which cases reproduction always and only results from impregnation of the female by the male in a more or less direct or intimate act of copulation, and extends to but one generation of offspring. The organs or system of organs by which this is effected are known as the *reproductive organs* or *system*. *Reproduction* is always exactly synonymous with *generation* (def. 1); less precisely with *procreation* and *propagation* in their biological senses. See *sex*.

4. That which is produced or revived; that which is presented anew; a repetition; hence, also, a copy.

The silversmiths . . . sold to the pilgrims *reproductions* in silver of the temple and its sculptures. *The Century*, XXXIII. 138.

Butrinto was once a city no less than Corfu; to Virgil's eyes it was the *reproduction* of Troy itself. *E. A. Freeman*, Venice, p. 340.

5. In *psychol.*, the act of repeating in consciousness a group of sensations which has already been presented in perception.

All *Reproduction* rests on the impossibility of the resuscitated impression reappearing alone. *Lotze*, Microcosmus (trans.), I. 216.

Fear and anger have their rise in the mental *reproduction* of some organic pain. *J. Sully*, Outlines of Psychol., p. 477.

All knowledge is *reproduction* of experiences. *G. H. Lewes*, Probs. of Life and Mind, I. i. 33.

Asexual reproduction. See *asexual*, and def. 3, above.—**Empirical synthesis of reproduction**, an association by the principle of contiguity, depending on the association of ideas having been presented together or successively.—**Pure transcendental synthesis of reproduction**, an association of ideas such that one will suggest the other independent of experience, due to innate laws of the mind, and one of the necessary conditions of knowledge.—**Sexual reproduction.** See def. 3, and *sexual*.—**Synthesis of reproduction**, the name given by Kant to that association of ideas by which one calls up another in the mind.

reproductive (rē-prọ̄-duk'tiv), *a.* [= F. *reproductif* = Pg. *reproductivo*, < ML. **reproductivus*, < **reproducere*, reproduce: see *reproduce*.] Of the nature of, pertaining to, or employed in reproduction; tending to reproduce: as, the *reproductive* organs of an animal.

These trees had very great *reproductive* power, since they produced numerous seeds, not singly or a few together, as in modern yews, but in long spikes or catkins bearing many seeds. *Dawson*, Geol. Hist. of Plants, p. 133.

Rembrandt . . . never put his hand to any *reproductive* etching, not even after one of his own paintings. *Harper's Mag.*, LXXVI. 331.

Reproductive cells, in *bot.* See *reproduction*, 3 (*a*).—**Reproductive faculty**, in the psychology of Sir William Hamilton, the faculty of association of ideas, by virtue of which one suggests a definite other, but not including the faculty of apprehending an idea a second time.—**Reproductive function of order *n*.** See *function*.—**Reproductive imagination**, the elementary faculty by virtue of which one idea calls up another, of which memory and imagination, as popularly understood, are special developments. See *imagination*, 1.

Philosophers have divided *imagination* into two — what they call the *reproductive* and the productive. By the former they mean imagination considered simply as re-exhibition, representing the objects presented by perception — that is, exhibiting them without addition or retrenchment, or any change in the relations which they reciprocally held when first made known to us through sense. *Sir W. Hamilton*, Metaph., xxxiii.

Reproductive organs. (*a*) In *bot.*, the organs appropriated to the production of seeds or spores: in flowering plants, chiefly the stamens and pistils together with the accessory floral envelops; in cryptogams, mainly the antheridia and archegonia. (*b*) In *zoöl.*, those organs or parts of the body, collectively considered, whose function it is to produce and mature ova or spermatozoa or their equivalents, and effect the impregnation of the female by the male elements, or otherwise accomplish reproduction; the reproductive or generative system of any animal in either sex; the genitals, in a broad sense. The fundamental reproductive organ of all sexed animals is an indifferent genital gland, differentiated in the male as a testis, in the female as an ovary (or their respective equivalents); its ulterior modifications are almost endless. These organs are sometimes detached from the main body of the individual (see *person*, 8, and *hectocotylus*); they often represent both sexes in one individual; they are usually separated in two individuals of opposite sexes; they sometimes fail of functional activity in certain individuals of one sex (see *neuter*, *worker*).—**Reproductive system**, in *biol.*, the sum of the reproductive or generative organs in plants and animals; the generative system; the sexual system of those plants and animals which have distinction of sex. The term is a very broad one, covering not only all parts immediately concerned in generation, but others indirectly conducing to the same end, as devices for effecting fecundation, for protecting or nourishing the product of conception, for cross-fertilization (as of plants by insects), for attracting opposite sexes (as of animals by odorous secretions), and the like. See *secondary sexual characters*, under *sexual*.

reproductiveness (rē-prọ̄-duk'tiv-nes), *n.* The state or quality of being reproductive; tendency or ability to reproduce.

reproductivity (rē″prọ̄-duk-tiv'i-ti), *n.* [< *reproductive* + *-ity*.] In *math.*, a number, *a*, connected with a function, ψu, such that $\psi(\gamma u) = \gamma^a \psi u$.

reproductory (rē-prọ̄-duk'tọ̄-ri), *a.* [< *reproduct(ive)* + *-ory*.] Same as *reproductive*. *Imp. Dict.*

repromission† (rē-prọ̄-mish'on), *n.* [= F. *repromission* = Sp. *repromision* = Pg. *repromissão* = It. *repromissione*, *ripromissione*, < L. *repromissio(n-)*, a counter-promise, < *repromittere*, promise in return, engage oneself, < *re-*, back, + *promittere*, promise: see *promise*.] Promise.

And he blesside this Abraham which hadde *repromyssiouns*. *Wyclif*, Heb. vii. 6.

repromulgate (rē-prọ̄-mul'gāt), *v. t.* [< *re-* + *promulgate*.] To promulgate again; republish. *Imp. Dict.*

repromulgation (rē″prọ̄-mul-gā'shon), *n.* [< *repromulgate* + *-ion*.] A second or repeated promulgation. *Imp. Dict.*

reproof (rẹ̄-pröf'), *n.* [< ME. *reprofe*, *reproef*, *reprof*, *reproffe*, *reprove*, *repreve* (whence early mod. E. *repreef*, *reprief*, *repreve*); < *reprove*, *v.*] 1†. Reproach; blame.

The childe certis is noght myne,
That *reproffe* dose me pyne,
And gars me fle fra hame.
York Plays, p. 104.

The doubleness of the benefit defends the deceit from *reproof*. *Shak.*, M. for M., iii. 1. 269.

2. The act of one who reproves; expression of blame or censure addressed to a person; blame expressed to the face; censure for a fault; reprehension; rebuke; reprimand.

There is an oblique way of *reproof* which takes off from the sharpness of it. *Steele.*

Those best can bear *reproof* who merit praise. *Pope*, Essay on Criticism, l. 583.

3†. Disproof; confutation; refutation.

But men been evere untrewe,
And wommen have *repreve* of yow ay newe.
Chaucer, Merchant's Tale, l. 960.

The virtue of this jest will be the incomprehensible lies that this same fat rogue will tell us when we meet at supper, . . . what wards, what blows, what extremities he endured; and in the *reproof* of this lies the jest. *Shak.*, 1 Hen. IV., i. 2. 213.

=**Syn.** 2. *Monition*, *Reprehension*, etc. See *admonition* and *censure*.

reprovable (rẹ̄-prö'va-bl), *a.* [Also *reproveable*; < OF. *reprouvable*, F. *réprouvable* = Sp. *reprobable* = Pg. *reprovavel* = It. *reprobabile*, < ML. *reprobabilis*, < L. *reprobare*, disapprove, condemn, reject: see *reprove*.] Blamable; worthy of reproof.

The superfluitee or disordinat scantinesse of clothynge is *reprevable*. *Chaucer*, Parson's Tale.

A *reprovable* badness in himself. *Shak.*, Lear, iii. 5. 9.

We will endeavour to amend all things *reproveable*. *Marston*, Antonio and Mellida, Epil.

reprovableness (rẹ̄-prö'va-bl-nes), *n.* The character of being reprovable. *Bailey*, 1727.

reprovably (rẹ̄-prö'va-bli), *adv.* In a reprovable manner. *Imp. Dict.*

reproval (rẹ̄-prö'val), *n.* [< *reprove* + *-al*.] The act of reproving; admonition; reproof. *Imp. Dict.*

reprove (rẹ̄-pröv'), *v. t.*; pret. and pp. *reproved*, ppr. *reproving*. [< ME. *reproven*, *reprouen*, also *repreuen* (whence early mod. E. *reprieve*, *repreeve*), < OF. *reprover*, *repruever*, *reprouver*, F. *réprouver*, reprove, reject, = Pr. *reproar*, *reprobar* = Sp. *reprobar* = Pg. *reprovar* = It. *reprobare*, *riprovare*, < L. *reprobare*, disapprove, condemn, reject, < *re-*, again, + *probare*, test, prove: see *prove*. Cf. *reprieve*, a doublet of *reprove*, retained in a differentiated meaning; cf. also *reprobate*, from the same L. source.] 1. To disapprove; condemn; censure.

The stoon which men bildynge *repreueden*. *Wyclif*, Luke xx. 17.

There's something in me that *reproves* my fault;
But such a headstrong potent fault it is
That it but mocks reproof. *Shak.*, T. N., iii. 4. 225.

2. To charge with a fault; chide; reprehend: formerly sometimes with *of*.

And there also he was examyned, *repreved*, and scorned, and crouned eft with a whyte Thorn. *Mandeville*, Travels, p. 14.

Herod the tetrarch, being *reproved* by him . . . for all the evils which Herod had done, . . . shut up John in prison. Luke iii. 19.

There is . . . no railing in a known discreet man, though he do nothing but *reprove*. *Shak.*, T. N., i. 5. 104.

Our blessed Master *reproved* them *of* ignorance . . . of his Spirit, which had they but known . . . they had not been such abecedarii in the school of mercy. *Jer. Taylor*, Works (ed. 1835), II. 94.

3†. To convince, as of a fault; convict.

When he is come he will *reprove* [*convict*, R. V.] the world of sin [in respect of sin, R. V.], and of righteousness, and of judgment. John xvi. 8.

God hath never been deficient, but hath to all men that believe him given sufficient to confirm them; to those few that believed not, sufficient to *reprove* them. *Jer. Taylor*, Great Exemplar, Pref., p. 14.

4†. To refute; disprove.

Reprove my allegation if you can,
Or else conclude my words effectual.
Shak., 2 Hen. VI., iii. 1. 40.

D. Willet *reproueth* Philoes opinion, That the Chalde and Hebrew was all one, because Daniel, an Hebrew, was set to learne the Chalde. *Purchas*, Pilgrimage, p. 47.

=**Syn.** 1 and 2. *Rebuke*, *Reprimand*, etc. See *censure* and *admonition*.

reprover (rẹ̄-prö'vėr), *n.* One who reproves; one who or that which blames.

This shall have from every one, even the *reprovers* of vice, the title of living well. *Locke*, Education, § 38.

reproving (rẹ̄-prö'ving), *n.* [Early mod. E. also *repreving*; < ME. *repreving*; verbal n. of *reprove*, *v.*] Reproof.

And there it lykede him to suffre many *Reprevinges* and Scornes for us. *Mandeville*, Travels, p. 1.

reprovingly (rẹ̄-prö'ving-li), *adv.* In a reproving manner; with reproof or censure. *Imp. Dict.*

reprune (rē-prön'), *v. t.* [< *re-* + *prune*[2].] 1. To prune or trim again, as trees or shrubs.

Re-prune now abricots and peaches, saving as many of the young likeliest shoots as are well placed. *Evelyn*, Calendarium Hortense, July.

2. To dress or trim again, as a bird its feathers.

In mid-way flight imagination tires;
Yet soon *re-prunes* her wing to soar anew.
Young, Night Thoughts, ix.

reps (reps), *n.* Same as *rep*[1].

repsilver†, *n.* Same as *reap-silver*.

reptant (rep'tant), *a.* [< L. *reptan(t-)s*, ppr. of *reptare*, crawl, creep: see *repent*[2], *reptile*.]

Creeping or crawling; repent; reptatory; reptile; specifically, of or pertaining to the *Reptantia*.

Reptantia† (rep-tan'shi-ạ̈), *n. pl.* [NL., neut. pl. of L. *reptan(t-)s*, ppr. of *reptare*, crawl: see *reptant*.] 1. In Illiger's classification (1811), the tenth order and also the thirtieth family of mammals, composed of the monotremes together with a certain tortoise (*Pamphractus*).—2. In *Mollusca*, those azygobranchiate gastropods which are adapted for creeping or crawling by the formation of the foot as a creeping-disk. All ordinary gastropods are *Reptantia*, the term being used in distinction from *Natantia* (which latter is a name of the *Heteropoda*). The *Reptantia* were divided into *Holochlamyda*, *Pneumonochlamyda*, and *Siphonochlamyda*.

reptation (rep-tā'shọn), *n.* [= F. *reptation*, < L. *reptatio(n-)*, a creeping, crawling, < *reptare*, pp. *reptatus*, creep, crawl: see *reptant*.] 1. The act of creeping or crawling on the belly, as a reptile does. *Owen*.—2. In *math.*, the motion of one plane figure around another, so as constantly to be tangent to the latter while preserving parallelism between different positions of its own lines; especially, such a motion of one figure round another precisely like it so that the longest diameter of one shall come into line with the shortest of the other. This motion was applied by John Bernoulli in 1705 to the rectification of curves. Let AB be a curve whose length is required; let this be reversed about its normal, giving the curve ABC, and let this be reversed about the line between its extremities, giving the spindle-shaped figure ABCD; let DEFG be a similar and equal figure turned through a right angle—then, if the first has a reptatory motion about the second, its center will describe a four-humped or quadrigibbous figure OPQRSTUV, with humps at P, R, T, V. Let this be placed in contact with a similar and equal figure so that a maximum and minimum diameter shall coincide, and receive a reptatory motion, then its center will describe an octogibbous or eight-humped figure. By a similar process, this will describe a sixteen-humped figure, etc. Each of these figures will have double the periphery of the preceding, and they will rapidly approximate toward circles. Hence, by finding the diameters of each, we approximate to the length of the original curve.

Reptation.

Reptatores (rep-tạ̈-tō'rēz), *n. pl.* [NL., < L. *reptare*, pp. *reptatus*, creep, crawl: see *reptant*.] In *ornith.*, in Macgillivray's system of classification, an order of creeping birds, as creepers and nuthatches. [Not in use.]

reptatorial (rep-tạ̈-tō'ri-ạl), *a.* [< *reptatory* + *-ial*.] In *ornith.*, creeping, as a bird; belonging to the *Reptatores*.

reptatory (rep'tạ̈-tō-ri), *a.* [= F. *reptatoire*, < NL. **reptatorius*, < L. *reptare*, pp. *reptatus*, creep: see *reptant*.] 1. In *zoöl.*, creeping or crawling; repant; reptile; repent.—2. Of the nature of reptation in mathematics.

reptile (rep'til or -tīl), *a.* and *n.* [< F. *reptile* = Sp. Pg. *reptil* = It. *rettile*, < L. *reptilis*, creeping, crawling; as a noun, LL. *reptile*, neut. (sc. *animal*), a creeping animal, a reptile; < *repere*, pp. *reptus*, creep: see *repent*[2], and cf. *serpent*.] I. *a.* 1. Creeping or crawling; repent; reptant; reptatory; of or pertaining to the *Reptilia*, in any sense.—2. Groveling; low; mean: as, a *reptile* race.

> Man is a very worm by birth,
> Vile, *reptile*, weak, and vain.
> *Pope*, To Mr. John Moore.

There is a false, *reptile* prudence, the result not of caution, but of fear. *Burke.* (*Webster.*)

> Dislodge their *reptile* souls
> From the bodies and forms of men. *Coleridge.*

II. *n.* 1. A creeping animal; an animal that goes on its belly, or moves with small, short legs.

> Eve's tempter thus the Rabbins have express'd,
> A cherub's face, a *reptile* all the rest.
> *Pope*, Prol. to Satires, l. 331.

> An inadvertent step may crush the snail
> That crawls at ev'ning in the public path;
> But he that has humanity, forewarn'd,
> Will step aside and let the *reptile* live.
> *Cowper*, Task, vi. 567.

Specifically—2. An oviparous quadruped; a four-footed egg-laying animal: applied about the middle of the eighteenth century to the animals then technically called *Amphibia*, as frogs, toads, newts, lizards, crocodiles, and turtles; any amphibian.—3. By restriction, upon the recognition of the divisions *Amphibia* and *Reptilia*, a scaly or pholidote reptile, as distinguished from a naked reptile; any snake, lizard, crocodile, or turtle; a member of the *Reptilia* proper; a saurian.—4. A groveling, abject, or mean person: used in contempt.

It would be the highest folly and arrogance in the *reptile* Man to imagine that he, by any of his endeavours, could add to the glory of God. *Warburton*, Works, IX. vii.

Reptilia[1] (rep-til'i-ạ̈), *n. pl.* [NL., pl. of LL. *reptile*, a reptile: see *reptile*.] In *zoöl.*: (*a*†) In Linnæus's system of classification (1766), the first order of the third class *Amphibia*, including turtles, lizards, and frogs. See *Amphibia*, 2 (*a*). [Disused.] (*b*) A class of cold-blooded oviparous or ovoviviparous vertebrated animals whose skin is covered with scales or scutes; the reptiles proper. There are two pairs or one pair of limbs, or none. The skull is monocondylian. The mandible articulates with the skull by a tree or fixed quadrate bone. The heart has two auricles, generally not two completed ventricles; the ventricle gives rise to two arterial trunks, and the venous and arterial circulation are more or less mixed. Respiration is pulmonary, never branchial. No diaphragm is completed. There is a common cloaca of the digestive and urogenital systems, and usually two penes, sometimes one, seldom none. There are an amnion and an allantois. *Reptilia* thus defined were formerly associated with batrachians in a class *Amphibia*; but they are more nearly related to birds, and when brigaded therewith form their part of a superclass *Sauropsida*. The only living representatives of *Reptilia* are turtles or tortoises, crocodiles or alligators, lizards or saurians, and snakes or serpents, respectively constituting the four orders *Chelonia*, *Crocodilia*, *Lacertilia*, and *Ophidia*; and one living lizard, known as *Hatteria*, *Sphenodon*, or *Rhynchocephalus*, forming by itself an order *Rhynchocephalia*. In former times there were other orders of strange and huge reptiles, as the *Ichthyopterygia* or *Ichthyosauria*, the ichthyosaurs; *Anomodontia*; *Dinosauria*, by some ranked as a subclass and divided into several orders; *Ornithosauria* or *Pterosauria*, the pterodactyls; and *Plesiosauria* or *Sauropterygia*, the plesiosaurs. See the technical names, and cuts under *Crocodilia*, *Ichthyosauria*, *Ornithoscelida*, *Plesiosaurus*, *Pleurospondylia*, *pterodactyl*, and *Python*.

reptilia[2], *n.* Latin plural of *reptilium*.

reptilian (rep-til'i-ạn), *a.* and *n.* [< LL. *reptile*, a reptile, + *-ian*.] I. *a.* Of or pertaining to the *Reptilia*, in any sense; resembling or like a reptile.

It is an accepted doctrine that birds are organized on a type closely allied to the *reptilian* type, but superior to it. *H. Spencer*, Prin. of Biol., § 43.

He had an agreeable confidence that his faults were all of a generous kind—impetuous, warm-blooded, leonine; never crawling, crafty, *reptilian*. *George Eliot*, Adam Bede, xii.

Reptilian age, the Mesozoic age, era, or period, during which reptiles attained great development, as in the Triassic, Jurassic, or Cretaceous.

II. *n.* Any member of the *Reptilia*; a reptile.

reptiliferous (rep-ti-lif'ẹ-rus), *a.* [< LL. *reptile*, a reptile, + L. *ferre* = E. *bear*[1].] Producing reptiles; containing the remains of reptiles, as beds of rock. *Nature*, XXXIII. 311.

reptiliform (rep'til-i-fôrm), *a.* [< LL. *reptile*, reptile, + *forma*, form.] Having the form or structure of a reptile; related to reptiles; belonging to the *Reptilia*; saurian. Also, rarely, *reptiloid*.

reptilious (rep-til'i-us), *a.* [< LL. *reptile*, a reptile, + *-i-ous*.] Resembling or like a reptile. [Rare.]

The advantage taken . . . made her feel abject, *reptilious*; she was lost, carried away on the flood of the cataract. *G. Meredith*, The Egoist, xxi.

reptilium (rep-til'i-um), *n.*; pl. *reptiliums*, *reptilia* (-umz, -ạ̈). [NL., < LL. *reptile*, a reptile: see *reptile*.] A reptile-house, or other place where reptiles are confined and kept alive; a herpetological vivarium.

A special reptile-house, or *reptilium*, was built in 1882 and 1883 by the Zoological Society of London. *Smithsonian Report*, 1883, p. 728.

reptilivorous (rep-ti-liv'ọ̄-rus), *a.* [< LL. *reptile*, a reptile, + L. *vorare*, devour.] Devouring or habitually feeding upon reptiles, as a bird; saurophagous.

A broad triangular head and short tail, which sufficiently marks out the tribe of viperine poisonous snakes to *reptilivorous* birds and mammals. *A. R. Wallace*, Fortnightly Rev., N. S., XL. 305.

reptiloid (rep'ti-loid), *a.* [< LL. *reptile*, a reptile, + Gr. εἶδος, form.] Reptiliform. [Rare.]

The thrushes . . . are farthest removed in structure from the early *reptiloid* forms [of birds]. *Pop. Sci. Mo.*, XXXIII. 75.

Reptonize (rep'tọn-īz), *v. t.*; pret. and pp. *Reptonized*, ppr. *Reptonizing*. [< *Repton* (see def.) + *-ize*.] To lay out, as a garden, after the manner of or according to the rules of Humphry Repton (1752–1818), the author of works on the theory and practice of landscape-gardening.

Jackson assists me in *Reptonizing* the garden. *Southey*, Letters (1807), II. 4. (*Davies.*)

republic (rẹ̄-pub'lik), *n.* [Early mod. E. also *republick*, *republique* (= D. *republiek* = G. Dan. Sw. *republik*); < OF. *republique*, F. *république* = Sp. *república* = Pg. *republica* = It. *republica*, *repubblica*, < L. *res publica*, prop. two words, but commonly written as one, *respublica* (abl. *re publicā*, *republicā*), the commonwealth, the state, < *res*, a thing, + *publica*, fem. of *publicus*, public: see *real*[1] and *public*.] 1†. The commonwealth; the state.

> That by their deeds will make it known
> Whose dignity they do sustain;
> And life, state, glory, all they gain,
> Count the *republic's*, not their own.
> *B. Jonson*, Catiline, ii. (cho.).

2. A commonwealth; a government in which the executive power is vested in a person or persons chosen directly or indirectly by the body of citizens entitled to vote. It is distinguished from a monarchy on the one hand, and generally from a pure democracy on the other. In the latter case the mass of citizens meet and choose the executive, as is still the case in certain Swiss cantons. In a republic the executive is usually chosen indirectly, either by an electoral college as in the United States, or by the National Assembly as in France. Republics are oligarchic, as formerly Venice and Genoa, military, as ancient Rome, strongly centralized, as France, federal, as Switzerland, or, like the United States, may combine a strong central government with large individual powers for the several states in their particular affairs. See *democracy*.

We may define a *republic* to be . . . a government which derives all its powers directly or indirectly from the great body of the people, and is administered by persons holding their offices during pleasure, for a limited period, or during good behaviour. *Madison*, The Federalist, No. 39.

The constitution and the government [of the United States] . . . rest, throughout, on the principle of the concurrent majority; and . . . it is, of course, a *Republic*, a constitutional democracy, in contradistinction to an absolute democracy; and . . . the theory which regards it as a government of the mere numerical majority rests on a gross and groundless misconception. *Calhoun*, Works, I. 185.

Cisalpine, Cispadane, Helvetic Republic. See the adjectives.—**Grand Army of the Republic**, a secret society composed of veterans who served in the army or navy of the United States during the civil war. Its objects are preservation of fraternal feeling, strengthening of loyal sentiment, and aid to needy families of veterans. Its first "post" was organized at Decatur, Illinois, in 1866; its members are known as "comrades," and its annual meetings are "encampments." Abbreviated G. *A. R.*—**Republic of letters**, the collective body of literary and learned men.

republican (rẹ̄-pub'li-kạn), *a.* and *n.* [= F. *républicain* = Sp. Pg. *republicano* = It. *repubblicano* (cf. D. *republiekeinsch* = G. *republikanisch* = Dan. Sw. *republikansk*, a.; D. *republiekein* = G. Dan. Sw. *republikaner*, n.), < NL. *republicanus*, < L. *res publica*, republic: see *republic*.] I. *a.* 1. Of the nature of or pertaining to a republic or commonwealth: as, a *republican* constitution or government.—2. Consonant to the principles of a republic: as, *republican* sentiments or opinions; *republican* manners.—3. [*cap.*] Of or pertaining to or favoring the Republican party: as, a *Republican* senator. See below.—4. In *ornith.*, living in community; nesting or breeding in common: as, the *republican* or sociable grosbeak, *Philetærus socius*; the *republican* swallow, formerly called *Hirundo respublicana*. See cuts under *hive-nest*.—**Liberal-Republican party**, in *U. S. hist.*, a political party which arose in Missouri in 1870–1 through a fusion of Liberal Republicans and Democrats, and as a national party nominated Horace Greeley as a candidate for the Presidency in 1872. It opposed the southern policy of the Republican party, and advocated universal amnesty, civil-service reform, and universal suffrage. Its candidate was indorsed by the Democratic convention, but was defeated, and the party soon disappeared.—**Republican calendar.** See *calendar*.—**Republican era**, the era adopted by the French soon after the proclamation of the republic, and used for a number of years. It was September 22d, 1792, "the first day of the Republic."—**Republican party.** (*a*) Any party which advocates a republic, either existing or desired: as, the *Republican party* of France, composed chiefly of Opportunists, Radicals, and Conservative Republicans: the *Republican party* in Italy in which Mazzini was a leader. (*b*) In *U. S. hist.*: (1) The usual name of the Democratic party (in full *Democratic-Republican* party) during the years following 1792–3: it replaced the name *Anti-Federal*, and was replaced by the name *Democratic*. See *Democratic party*, under *democratic*. (2) A party formed in 1854, having as its original purpose opposition to the extension of slavery into the Territories. It was composed of Free-soilers, of antislavery Whigs, and of some Democrats (who unitedly formed the group known as Anti-Nebraska men), and was joined by the Abolitionists, and eventually by many Know-nothings. During the period of the civil war many war Democrats acted with it. It first nominated a candidate for President in 1856. It controlled the executive from 1861 to 1885 and again in 1889 and 1897 (Presidents Lincoln, Johnson, Grant, Hayes, Garfield, Arthur, Harrison, and McKinley), and both houses of Congress from 1861 to 1875 and again in 1889. It favors generally a broad construction of the Constitution, liberal expenditures, extension of the powers of the national government, and a high protective tariff. Among the measures with which it has been identified in whole or in part are the suppression of the rebellion, the abolition of slavery, reconstruction, and the resumption of specie payments.—**Republican swallow**, the cliff- or eaves-swallow. See def. 4, and cut under *eaves-swallow*.

II. *n.* 1. One who favors or prefers a republican form of government.

There is a want of polish in the subjects of free states which has made the roughness of a *republican* almost proverbial. *Brougham.*

2. A member of a republican party; specifically [*cap.*], in *U. S. hist.*, a member of the Republican party.—3. In *ornith.*, the republican swallow.—**Black Republican**, in *U. S. hist.*, an extreme or radical Republican: one who after the civil war advocated strong measures in dealing with persons in the States lately in rebellion. The term arose before the war; the epithet "black" was used intensively, in offensive allusion to the alleged friendliness of the party toward the negro.—**National Republican**, in *U. S. hist.*, a name assumed during the administration of J. Q. Adams (1825–9) by that wing of the Democratic party which sympathized with him and his measures, as distinguished from the followers of Jackson. The National Republicans in a few years took the name of Whigs. See *Whig*.—**Red republican**, an extreme or radical republican; specifically, in *French hist.*, one of the more violent republicans, especially in the first revolution, at the time of the ascendancy of the Mountain, about 1793, and at the time of the Commune in 1871. In the first period the phrase was derived from the red cap which formed part of the costume of the carmagnole.—**Stalwart Republican.** See *stalwart*.

republicanism (rē-pub'li-kan-izm), *n.* [= F. *républicanisme* = Sp. Pg. *republicanismo* = It. *repubblicanismo* = G. *republikanismus* = Dan. *republikanisme* = Sw. *republikanism*; as *republican* + *-ism*.] 1. A republican form or system of government.—2. Attachment to a republican form of government; republican principles: as, his *republicanism* was of the most advanced type.

Our young people are educated in *republicanism*; an apostacy from that to royalism is unprecedented and impossible. *Jefferson*, Correspondence, II. 443.

3. [*cap.*] The principles or doctrine of the Republican party, specifically of the Republican party in the United States.

republicanize (rē-pub'li-kan-īz), *v. t.*; pret. and pp. *republicanized*, ppr. *republicanizing*. [< F. *républicaniser*; as *republican* + *-ize*.] To convert to republican principles; render republican. Also spelled *republicanise*.

Let us not, with malice prepense, go about to *republicanize* our orthography and our syntax.
G. P. Marsh, Lects. on Eng. Lang., xxx.

republicarian† (rē-pub-li-kā'ri-an), *n.* [< *republic* + *-arian*.] A republican. [Rare.]

There were *Republicarians* who would make the Prince of Orange like a Stadtholder.
Evelyn, Diary, Jan. 15, 1688–9.

republicate† (rē-pub'li-kāt), *v. t.* [< ML. *republicatus*, pp. of *republicare*, publish, lit. republish: see *republish*.] To set forth afresh; rehabilitate.

The Cabinet-men at Wallingford-house set upon it to consider what exploit this lord should commence, to be the darling of the Commons and as it were to *republicate* his lordship, and to be precious to those who had the vogue to be the chief lovers of their country.
Bp. Hacket, Abp. Williams, i. 137. (*Davies.*)

republication (rē-pub-li-kā'shon), *n.* [< ML. **republicatio(n-)*, < *republicare*, publish: see *republish*.] 1. The act of republishing; a new publication of something before published; specifically, the reprint in one country of a work published in another: as, the *republication* of a book or pamphlet.

The Gospel itself is only a *republication* of the religion of nature. *Warburton*, Divine Legation, ix. 3.

2. In *law*, a second publication of a former will, usually resorted to after canceling or revoking, or upon doubts as to the validity of its execution, or after the termination of a suggested disability, in order to avoid the labor of drawing a new will, or in order that the will may stand if either the original execution or the republication proves to be valid.

If there be many testaments, the last overthrows all the former; but the *republication* of a former will revokes one of a later date, and establishes the first again.
Blackstone, Com., II. xxxii.

republish (rē-pub'lish), *v. t.* [< *re-* + *publish*, after OF. *republier*, republish, < ML. *republicare*, publish, lit. 'republish,' < L. *re-*, again, + *publicare*, publish: see *publish*.] To publish anew. (*a*) To publish a new edition of, as a book. (*b*) To print or publish again, as a foreign reprint. (*c*) In *law*, to revive, as a will revoked, either by reëxecution or by a codicil. *Blackstone*, Com., II. xxxii.

republisher (rē-pub'lish-ėr), *n.* One who republishes. *Imp. Dict.*

repudiable (rē-pū'di-a-bl), *a.* [< OF. *repudiable*, F. *répudiable* = Sp. *repudiable* = Pg. *repudiavel*, < ML. **repudiabilis*, < L. *repudiare*, repudiate: see *repudiate*.] Capable of being repudiated or rejected; fit or proper to be put away.

The reasons that on each side make them differ are such as make the authority itself the less authentic and more *repudiable*. *Jer. Taylor*, Works (ed. 1835), II. 339.

repudiate (rē-pū'di-āt), *v. t.*; pret. and pp. *repudiated*, ppr. *repudiating*. [< L. *repudiatus*, pp. of *repudiare*, put away, divorce (one's spouse), in gen. cast off, reject, refuse, repudiate (> It. *ripudiare* = Sp. Pg. *repudiar* = OF. *repudier*, F. *répudier*, repudiate), < L. *repudium*, a putting off or divorce of one's spouse or betrothed, repudiation, lit. a rejection of what one is ashamed of, < *re-*, away, back, + *pudere*, feel shame: see *pudency*.] 1. To put away; divorce.

His separation from Terentia, whom he *repudiated* not long afterward, was perhaps an affliction to him at this time. *Bolingbroke*, Exile.

2. To cast away; reject; discard; renounce; disavow.

He [Phalaris] is defended by the like practice of other writers, who, being Dorians born, *repudiated* their vernacular idiom for that of the Athenians.
Bentley, Works, I. 359.

In *repudiating* metaphysics, M. Comte did not interdict himself from analyzing or criticising any of the abstract conceptions of the mind.
J. S. Mill, Auguste Comte and Positivism, p. 15.

3. To refuse to acknowledge or to pay, as a debt; disclaim.

I petition your honourable House to institute some measures for . . . the repayment of debts incurred and *repudiated* by several of the States.
Sydney Smith, Petition to Congress.

When Pennsylvania and other States sought to *repudiate* the debt due to England, the witty canon of St. Paul's [Sydney Smith] took the field, and, by a petition and letters on the subject, roused all Europe against the *repudiating* States. *Chambers*, Eng. Lit., art. Sydney Smith.

repudiate† (rē-pū'di-āt), *a.* [< L. *repudiatus*, pp.: see the verb.] Repudiated.

To be debarred of that imperial state
Which to her graces rightly did belong,
Basely rejected, and *repudiate*.
Drayton, Barons' Wars, i. 30.

repudiation (rē-pū-di-ā'shon), *n.* [< OF. *repudiation*, F. *répudiation* = Sp. *repudiacion*, < L. *repudiatio(n-)*, repudiation, < *repudiare*, repudiate: see *repudiate*.] The act of repudiating, or the state of being repudiated. (*a*) The putting away of a wife, or of a woman betrothed; divorce.

Just causes for *repudiation* by the husband were [under Constantine]—1, adultery; 2, preparing poisons; 3, being a procuress. *Encyc. Brit.*, VII. 300.

(*b*) Rejection; disavowal or renunciation of a right or an obligation, as of a debt; specifically, refusal by a state or municipality to pay a debt lawfully contracted. Repudiation of a debt implies that the debt is just, and that its payment is denied, not because of sufficient legal defense, but to take advantage of the rule that a sovereign state cannot be sued by individuals.

Other states have been even more unprincipled, and have got rid of their debts at one sweep by the simple method of *repudiation*. *Encyc. Brit.*, XVII. 245.

(*c*) *Eccles.*, the refusal to accept a benefice.

repudiationist (rē-pū-di-ā'shon-ist), *n.* [< *repudiation* + *-ist*.] One who advocates repudiation; one who disclaims liability for debt contracted by a predecessor in office, etc.

Perhaps not a single citizen of the State [Tennessee] would have consented to be called a *repudiationist*.
The Nation, XXXVI. 58.

repudiator (rē-pū'di-ā-tor), *n.* [< LL. *repudiator*, a rejecter, contemner, < L. *repudiare*, repudiate: see *repudiate*.] One who repudiates; specifically, one who advocates the repudiation of debts contracted in good faith by a state. See *readjuster*, 2.

The people of the State [Virginia] appear now to be divided into two main parties by the McCulloch Bill, which the *Repudiators* desire repealed, and which is in reality, even as it stands, a compromise between the State and its creditors. *The Nation*, XXIX. 317.

repudiatory (rē-pū'di-ā-tō-ri), *a.* [< *repudiate* + *-ory*.] Pertaining to or of the nature of repudiation or repudiators. [Rare.]

They refused to admit . . . a delegate who was of known *repudiatory* principles. *The American*, IV. 67.

repugn (rē-pūn'), *v.* [< ME. *repugnen*, < OF. *repugner*, F. *répugner* = Pr. Sp. Pg. *repugnar* = It. *repugnare*, *ripugnare*, < L. *repugnare*, fight against, < *re-*, back, against, + *pugnare*, fight: see *pugnacious*. Cf. *expugn*, *impugn*, *propugn*.] **I.** *trans.* 1. To oppose; resist; fight against; feel repugnance toward.

Your will oft resisteth and *repugneth* God's will.
Tyndale, Ans. to Sir T. More, etc. (Parker Soc., 1850), p. 224.

Stubbornly he did *repugn* the truth
About a certain question in the law.
Shak., 1 Hen. VI., iv. 1. 94.

2. To affect with repugnance. [Rare.]

Man, highest of the animals—so much so that the base kinship *repugns* him. *Maudsley*, Body and Will, p. 24.

II. *intrans.* To be opposed; be in conflict with anything; conflict.

It semyth, quod I, to *repugnen* and to contraryen gretly that God knowit byforn alle thinges.
Chaucer, Boëthius, v. prose 3.

Be thou content to know that God's will, his word, and his power be all one, and *repugn* not.
Tyndale, Ans. to Sir T. More, etc. (Parker Soc., 1850), p. 232.

In many thinges *repugning* quite both to God and mans lawe. *Spenser*, State of Ireland.

repugnable† (rē-pū'- or rē-pug'na-bl), *a.* [< *repugn* + *-able*.] Capable of being resisted.

The demonstration proving it so exquisitely, with wonderfull reason and facility, as it is not *repugnable*.
North, tr. of Plutarch, p. 262.

repugnance (rē-pug'nans), *n.* [Early mod. E. also *repugnaunce*; < OF. *repugnance*, F. *répugnance* = Pr. Sp. Pg. *repugnancia* = It. *repugnanza*, < L. *repugnantia*, resistance, opposition, contradiction, repugnance, < *repugnan(t-)s*, resisting, repugnant: see *repugnant*.] 1†. Opposition; conflict; resistance, in a physical sense.

As the shotte of great artillerie is driuen furth by violence of fyre, euen so by the commixtion and *repugnaunce* of fyre, coulde, and brymstome, greate stones are here throwne into the ayer.
R. Eden, tr. of Jacobus Zieglerus (First Books on America, [ed. Arber, p. 300).

2. Mental opposition or antagonism; positive disinclination (to do or suffer something); in a general sense, aversion.

That which causes us to lose most of our time is the *repugnance* which we naturally have to labour. *Dryden.*

Chivalrous courage . . . is honorable, because it is in fact the triumph of lofty sentiment over an instinctive *repugnance* to pain. *Irving*, Sketch-Book, p. 350.

We cannot feel moral *repugnance* at an act of meanness or cruelty except when we discern to some extent the character of the action.
J. Sully, Outlines of Psychol., p. 558.

3. Contradictory opposition; in *logic*, disagreement; inconsistency; contradiction; the relation of two propositions one of which must be true and the other false; the relation of two characters such that every individual must possess the one and lack the other.

Those ill counsellors have most unhappily engaged him in . . . pernicious projects and frequent *repugnances* of workes and words. *Prynne*, Soveraigne Power, ii. 40.

I found in those Descriptions and Charts [of the South Sea Coasts of America] a *repugnance* with each other in many particulars, and some things which from my own experience I knew to be erroneous.
Dampier, Voyages, II., Pref.

Immediate or contradictory opposition is called likewise *repugnance*. *Sir W. Hamilton*, Logic, xi.

The principle of repugnance. Same as *the principle of contradiction* (which see, under *contradiction*).=**Syn.** 2. Hatred, *Dislike*, etc. (see *antipathy*), backwardness, disinclination. See list under *aversion*.

repugnancy (rē-pug'nan-si), *n.* [As *repugnance* (see *-cy*).] 1†. Same as *repugnance*.

Why do fond men expose themselves to battle, . . .
And let the foes quietly cut their throats,
Without *repugnancy*? *Shak.*, T. of A., iii. 5. 46.

Neuerthelesse without any *repugnancie* at all, a Poet may in some sort be said a follower or imitator, because he can expresse the true and liuely of euery thing is set before him. *Puttenham*, Arte of Eng. Poesie, p. 1.

2. In *law*, inconsistency between two clauses or provisions in the same law or document, or in separate laws or documents that must be construed together.—**Formal repugnancy.** See *formal*.

repugnant (rē-pug'nant), *a.* [< OF. *repugnant*, F. *répugnant* = Sp. Pg. It. *repugnante*, < L. *repugnan(t-)s*, ppr. of *repugnare*, oppose: see *repugn*.] 1†. Opposing; resisting; refractory; disposed to oppose or antagonize.

His antique sword,
Rebellious to his arm, lies where it falls,
Repugnant to command. *Shak.*, Hamlet, ii. 2. 493.

2. Standing or being in opposition; opposite; contrary; contradictory; at variance; inconsistent.

It seemeth *repugnant* both to him and to me, one body to be in two places at once.
Tyndale, Ans. to Sir T. More, etc. (Parker Soc., 1850), p. 234.

She conforms to a general fashion only when it happens not to be *repugnant* to private beauty.
Goldsmith, The Bee, No. 2.

3. In *law*, contrary to or inconsistent with another part of the same document or law, or of another which must be construed with it: generally used of a clause inconsistent with some other clause or with the general object of the instrument.

If he had broken any wholesome law not *repugnant* to the laws of England, he was ready to submit to censure.
Winthrop, Hist. New England, II. 312.

Sometimes clauses in the same treaty, or treaties between the same parties, are *repugnant*.
Woolsey, Introd. to Inter. Law, § 109.

4. Causing mental antagonism or aversion; highly distasteful; offensive.

There are certain national dishes that are *repugnant* to every foreign palate. *Lowell*, Don Quixote.

To one who is ruled by a predominant sentiment of justice, the thought of profiting in any way, direct or indirect, at the expense of another is *repugnant*. *H. Spencer*, Prin. of Sociol., § 579.

=Syn. 2. Opposed, irreconcilable.—4. Disagreeable. See *antipathy*.

repugnantly (rē-pug'nant-li), *adv.* In a repugnant manner; with opposition; in contradiction.

They speak not *repugnantly* thereto. *Sir T. Browne*, Vulg. Err.

repugnantness† (rē-pug'nant-nes), *n.* Repugnance. *Bailey*, 1727.

repugnate† (rē-pug'nāt), *v. t.* [< L. *repugnatus*, pp. of *repugnare*, fight against, oppose: see *repugn*.] To oppose; fight against. *Imp. Dict.*

repugnatorial (rē-pug'na-tō-ri-al), *a.* [< *repugnate* + *-ory* + *-al*.] Repugnant; serving as a means of defense by repelling enemies: specific in the phrase.—**Repugnatorial pores**, the openings of the ducts of certain glands which secrete prussic acid in most diplopod myriapods. The secretion poured out when the creature is alarmed has a strong odor, which may be perceived at a distance of several feet. The absence or presence of these pores, and their number or disposition when present, afford zoological characters in the classification of the chilognaths.

repugner (rē-pū'nėr), *n.* One who rebels or is opposed.

Excommunicating all *repugners* and rebellers against the same. *Foxe*, Martyrs, p. 264.

repullulate† (rē-pul'ū-lāt), *v. i.* [< L. *repullulatus*, pp. of *repullulare*, sprout forth again (> It. *ripullulare* = Sp. *repulular* = Pg. *repullular* = OF. *repulluler*, F. *repulluler*), < *re-*, again, + *pullulare*, put forth, sprout: see *pullulate*.] To sprout or bud again.

Vanisht man,
Like to a lilly-lost, nere can,
Nere can *repullulate*, or bring
His dayes to see a second spring.
Herrick, His Age.

Though Tares *repullulate*, there is Wheat still left in the Field. *Howell*, Vocall Forrest, p. 65.

With what delight have I beheld this tender and innumerable offspring *repullulating* at the feet of an aged tree. *Evelyn*, Silva.

repullulation (rē-pul-ū-lā'shon), *n.* [= F. *répullulation*, < L. as if **repullulatio(n-)*, < *repullulare*, sprout again: see *repullulate*.] The act of sprouting or budding again: used in pathology to indicate the return of a morbid growth.

Here I myselfe might likewise die,
And vtterly forgotten lye,
But that eternall poetrie
Repullulation gives me here
Unto the thirtieth thousand yeere,
When all now dead shall reappeare.
Herrick, Poetry Perpetuates the Poet.

repullulescent† (rē-pul-ū-les'ent), *a.* [< LL. *repullulescen(t-)s*, ppr. of *repullulescere*, begin to bud, sprout again, inceptive of L. *repullulare*, sprout again: see *repullulate*.] Sprouting or budding anew; reviving; springing up afresh.

One would have believed this expedient plausible enough, and calculated to obviate the ill use a *repullulescent* faction might make, if the other way was taken. *Roger North*, Lord Guilford, II. 190. (*Davies*.)

repulpit (rē-pùl'pit), *v. t.* [< *re-* + *pulpit*.] To restore to the pulpit; reinvest with authority over a church. *Tennyson*, Queen Mary, i. 5. [Rare.]

repulse (rē-puls'), *v. t.*; pret. and pp. *repulsed*, ppr. *repulsing*. [= OF. *repousser*, F. *repousser* = Sp. Pg. *repulsar* = It. *repulsare*, *ripulsare*, drive back, repulse, < ML. *repulsare*, freq. of L. *repellere*, pp. *repulsus*, drive back: see *repel*.] 1. To beat or drive back; repel: as, to *repulse* an assailant or advancing enemy.

Complete to have discover'd and *repulsed*
Whatever wiles of foe or seeming friend.
Milton, P. L., x. 10.

Near this mouth is a place called Comana, where the Privateers were once *repulsed* without daring to attempt it any more, being the only place in the North Seas they attempted in vain for many years. *Dampier*, Voyages, I. 63.

2. To refuse; reject.

She took the fruits of my advice;
And he, *repulsed*—a short tale to make—
Fell into a sadness. *Shak.*, Hamlet, ii. 2. 146.

Mr. Thornhill . . . was going to embrace his uncle, which the other *repulsed* with an air of disdain. *Goldsmith*, Vicar, xxxi.

repulse (rē-puls'), *n.* [= Sp. Pg. *repulsa* = It. *repulsa*, *ripulsa*, < L. *repulsa* (sc. *petitio*), a repulse in soliciting for an office, in gen. a refusal, denial, repulse, fem. of *repulsus*, pp. of *repellere*, drive back, > *repulsus*, a driving back. The E. noun includes the two L. nouns *repulsa* and *repulsus*, and is also in part directly from the E. verb.] 1. The act of repelling or driving back.

He received, in the *repulse* of Tarquin, seven hurts i' the body. *Shak.*, Cor., ii. 1. 166.

2. The condition of being repelled; the state of being checked in advancing, or driven back by force.

What should they do? if on they rush'd, *repulse*
Repeated, and indecent overthrow
Doubled, would render them yet more despised.
Milton, P. L., vi. 600.

3. Refusal; denial.

Take no *repulse*, whatever she doth say.
Shak., T. G. of V., iii. 1. 100.

I went to the Dominican Monastery, and made suit to see it [Christ's thorny crown]; but I had the *repulse*; for they told me it was kept under three or four lockes. *Coryat*, Crudities, I. 41, sig. D.

repulser (rē-pul'sėr), *n.* One who or that which repulses or drives back. *Cotgrave*.

repulsion (rē-pul'shon), *n.* [= OF. *repulsion*, F. *répulsion* = Sp. *repulsion* = Pg. *repulsão* = It. *repulsione*, *ripulsione*, < LL. *repulsio(n-)*, a refutation, < L. *repellere*, pp. *repulsus*, drive back, repulse: see *repulse* and *repel*.] 1. The act of repelling or driving back, or the state of being repelled; specifically, in *physics*, the action which two bodies exert upon each other when they tend to increase their mutual distance: as, the *repulsion* between like magnetic poles or similarly electrified bodies.

Mutual action between distant bodies is called attraction when it tends to bring them nearer, and *repulsion* when it tends to separate them. *Clerk Maxwell*, Matter and Motion, art. 56.

2. The act of repelling mentally; the act of arousing repellent feeling; also, the feeling thus aroused, or the occasion of it; aversion.

Poetry, the mirror of the world, cannot deal with its attractions only, but must present some of its *repulsions* also, and avail herself of the powerful assistance of its contrasts. *Gladstone*, Might of Right, p. 116.

If Love his moment overstay,
Hatred's swift *repulsions* play.
Emerson, The Visit.

Capillary repulsion. See *capillary*.

repulsive (rē-pul'siv), *a.* [= F. *répulsif* = Sp. Pg. *repulsivo* = It. *repulsivo*, *ripulsivo*; as *repulse* + *-ive*.] 1. Acting so as to repel or drive away; exercising repulsion; repelling.

Be not discouraged that my daughter here,
Like a well-fortified and lofty tower,
Is so *repulsive* and unapt to yield.
Chapman, Blind Beggar of Alexandria.

A *Repulsive* force by which they [particles of salt or vitriol floating in water] fly from one another. *Newton*, Optics, iii. query 31.

The foe thrice tugg'd and shook the rooted wood;
Repulsive of his might the weapon stood.
Pope, Iliad, xxi. 192.

2. Serving or tending to deter or forbid approach or familiarity; repellent; forbidding; grossly or coarsely offensive to taste or feeling; causing intense aversion with disgust.

Mary was not so *repulsive* and unsisterly as Elizabeth, nor so inaccessible to all influence of hers. *Jane Austin*, Persuasion, vi.

Our ordinary mental food has become distasteful, and what would have been intellectual luxuries at other times are now absolutely *repulsive*. *O. W. Holmes*, Old Vol. of Life, p. 2.

We learn to see with patience the men whom we like best often in the wrong, and the *repulsive* men often in the right. *Stubbs*, Medieval and Modern Hist., p. 95.

=Syn. 2. Offensive, disgusting, sickening, revolting, shocking.

repulsively (rē-pul'siv-li), *adv.* In a repulsive manner. *Imp. Dict.*

repulsiveness (rē-pul'siv-nes), *n.* The character of being repulsive or forbidding. *Imp. Dict.*

repulsory (rē-pul'sō-ri), *a.* and *n.* [= OF. *repoussoir*, n.; < L. *repulsorius*, driving or forcing back (LL. *repulsorium*, neut., a means of driving back), < *repellere*, pp. *repulsus*, repel, repulse: see *repulse*.] I. *a.* Repulsive; driving back. *Bailey*, 1727. [Rare.]

II.† *n.* Something used to drive or thrust out something else, as a punch, etc. *Cotgrave*. [Rare.]

repurchase (rē-pėr'chās), *v. t.* [< *re-* + *purchase*.] To purchase back or again; buy back; regain by purchase or expenditure.

Once more we sit in England's royal throne,
Re-purchased with the blood of enemies.
Shak., 3 Hen. VI., v. 7. 2.

repurchase (rē-pėr'chās), *n.* [< *repurchase*, *v.*] The act of buying again; the purchase again of what has been sold.

repure† (rē-pūr'), *v. t.* [< *re-* + *pure*.] To purify or refine again.

What will it be,
When that the watery palate tastes indeed
Love's thrice *repured* nectar?
Shak., T. and C., iii. 2. 23.

repurge (rē-pėrj'), *v. t.* [< OF. *repurger*, < L. *repurgare*, cleanse again, < *re-* + *purgare*, cleanse: see *purge*.] To purge or cleanse again.

All which haue, either by their priuate readings, or publique workes, *repurged* the errors of Arts, expelde from their puritie. *Nash*, Pref. to Greene's Menaphon, p. 11.

Repurge your spirits from euery hatefull sin.
Hudson, tr. of Du Bartas's Judith, i.

repurify (rē-pū'ri-fī), *v. t.* [< *re-* + *purify*.] To purify again.

The joyful bliss for ghosts *repurified*,
The ever-springing gardens of the bless'd.
Daniel, Complaint of Rosamond.

reputable (rep'ū-ta-bl), *a.* [< *repute* + *-able*.] 1. Being in good repute; held in esteem; estimable: as, a *reputable* man or character; *reputable* conduct.

Men as shabby have . . . stepped into fine carriages from quarters not a whit more *reputable* than the "Café des Ambassadeurs." *Thackeray*, Lovel the Widower, ii.

2. Consistent with good reputation; not mean or disgraceful.

In the article of danger, it is as *reputable* to elude an enemy as defeat one. *Broome*.

=Syn. Respectable, creditable, honorable.

reputableness (rep'ū-ta-bl-nes), *n.* The character of being reputable. *Bailey*, 1727.

reputably (rep'ū-ta-bli), *adv.* In a reputable manner; without disgrace or discredit: as, to fill an office *reputably*. *Imp. Dict.*

reputation (rep-ū-tā'shon), *n.* [< ME. *reputation*, *reputacioun*, < OF. *reputation*, F. *réputation* = Pr. *reputatio* = Sp. *reputacion* = Pg. *reputação* = It. *reputazione*, *riputazione*, < L. *reputatio(n-)*, a reckoning, a pondering, estimation, fame, < *reputare*, pp. *reputatus*, reckon, count over, compute: see *repute*.] 1. Account; estimation; consideration; especially, the estimate attached to a person by the community; character by report; opinion of character generally entertained; character attributed to a person, action, or thing; repute, in a good or bad sense. See *character*.

For which he heeld his glorie or his renoun
At no value or *reputacioun*.
Chaucer, Pardoner's Tale, l. 164.

Christ Jesus: . . . who . . . made himself of no *reputation*, and took upon him the form of a servant. Phil. ii. 7.

For to be honest is nothing; the *Reputation* of it is all. *Congreve*, Old Batchelor, v. 7.

The people of this province were in the very worst *reputation* for cruelty, and hatred of the Christian name. *Bruce*, Source of the Nile, II. 55.

2. Favorable regard; the credit, honor, or character which is derived from a favorable public opinion or esteem; good name; fame.

Cas. O, I have lost my *reputation!* I have lost the immortal part of myself, and what remains is bestial.
Iago. *Reputation* is an idle and most false imposition; oft got without merit, and lost without deserving.
Shak., Othello, ii. 3. 263.

My Lady loves her, and will come to any Composition to save her *Reputation*. *Congreve*, Way of the World, iii. 18.

Love of *reputation* is a darling passion in great men. *Steele*, Tatler, No. 92.

A third interprets motions, looks, and eyes;
At every word a *reputation* dies.
Pope, R. of the L., iii. 16.

Thus *reputation* is a spur to wit,
And some wits flag through fear of losing it.
Cowper, Table-Talk, l. 520.

Every year he used to visit London, where his *reputation* was so great that, if a day's notice were given, "the meeting-house in Southwark, at which he generally preached, would not hold half the people that attended." *Southey*, Bunyan, p. 55.

=Syn. 2. Esteem, estimation, name, fame, renown, distinction.

reputatively (rep'ū-tā-tiv-li), *adv.* [< **reputative* (< *repute* + *-ative*) + *-ly*[2].] By repute. [Rare.]

But this prozer Dionysius, and the rest of these grave and *reputatively* learned, dare undertake for their gravities the headstrong censure of all things. *Chapman*, Odyssey, Ep. Ded.

If Christ had suffered in our person *reputatively* in all respects, his sufferings would not have redeemed us. *Baxter*, Life of Faith, iii. 8.

repute (rē-pūt'), *v. t.*; pret. and pp. *reputed*, ppr. *reputing*. [< OF. *reputer*, F. *réputer* = Pr. Sp. Pg. *reputar* = It. *riputare*, *reputare*, < L. *reputare*, count over, reckon, calculate, compute, think over, consider, < *re-*, again, + *putare*, think: see *putation*. Cf. *ret*[2], from the same L. verb. Cf. also *compute*, *depute*, *impute*.] 1. To hold in thought; account; hold; reckon; deem.

Wherefore are we counted as beasts, and *reputed* vile in your sight? Job xviii. 3.

All in England did *repute* him dead.
Shak., 1 Hen. IV., v. 1. 54.

Hadst thou rather be a Faulconbridge . . .
Or the *reputed* son of Cœur-de-lion?
Shak., K. John, i. 1. 136.

She was generally *reputed* a witch by the country people. *Addison*, Freeholder, No. 22.

Most of the *reputed* saints of Egypt are either lunatics or idiots or impostors. *E. W. Lane*, Modern Egyptians, I. 291.

2. To estimate; value; regard.

I *repute* them [Surrey and Wyatt] . . . for the two chief lanternes of light to all others that have since employed their pennes vpon English Poesie. *Puttenham*, Arte of Eng. Poesie, p. 50.

How will the world *repute* me
For undertaking so unstaid a journey?
Shak., T. G. of V., ii. 7. 59.

We aim and intend to *repute* and use honours but as instrumental causes of virtuous effects in actions. *Ford*, Line of Life.

Reputed owner, in *law*, a person who has to all appearances the title to and possession of property: thus, according to the rule applied in some jurisdictions, if a *reputed owner* becomes bankrupt, all goods in his possession, with the consent of the true owner, may, in general, be claimed for the creditors.

repute (rẹ-pūt'), *n.* [< *repute*, *v.*] Reputation; character; established opinion; specifically, good character; the credit or honor derived from common or public opinion.

All these Cardinals have the *Repute* of Princes, and, besides other Incomes, they have the Annats of Benefices to support their Greatness. *Howell*, Letters, I. i. 38.

He who reigns
Monarch in heaven, till then as one secure
Sat on his throne, upheld by old *repute*.
Milton, P. L., i. 639.

You have a good *repute* for gentleness
And wisdom. *Shelley*, The Cenci, v. 2.

Habit and repute. See *habit*. =**Syn.** See list under *reputation*.

reputedly (rẹ-pū'ted-li), *adv.* In common opinion or estimation; by repute. *Imp. Dict.*

reputeless (rẹ-pūt'les), *a.* [< *repute* + *-less*.] Not having good repute; obscure; inglorious; disreputable; disgraceful.

In *reputeless* banishment,
A fellow of no mark nor likelihood.
Shak., 1 Hen. IV., iii. 2. 44.

Requa battery (rē'kwạ bat'ẹ-ri). [So called from its inventor, *Requa*.] A kind of machine-gun or mitrailleuse, consisting of a number of breech-loading rifle-barrels arranged in a horizontal plane on a light field-carriage.

requérant (rē-kā-roṅ'), *n.* [F., ppr. of *requérir*, require: see *require*.] In *French law*, an applicant; a petitioner.

requere, *v. t.* A Middle English form of *require*.

request (rẹ-kwest'), *n.* [< ME. *requeest*, *requeste*, < OF. *requeste*, F. *requête* = Pr. Pg. *requesta* = Sp. *requesta*, *recuesta* = It. *richiesta*, a request, < ML. *requista*, *requesta*, also neuter *requistum* (after Rom.), a request, < L. *requisita*, sc. *res*, a thing asked for, fem. of *requisitus*, ML. *requistus*, pp. of *requirere*, ask: see *require*, and cf. *requisite* and *quest*¹.] 1. The expression of desire to some person for something to be granted or done; an asking; a petition; a prayer; an entreaty.

I calle thee to me ȝeer and ȝeer,
ȝit wolt thou not come at my *requeest*.
Political Poems, etc. (ed. Furnivall), p. 187.

Haman stood up to make *request* for his life to Esther the queen. Esther vii. 7.

Put my Lord Bolingbroke in mind
To get my warrant quickly sign'd;
Consider, 'tis my first *request*.
Pope, Imit. of Horace, II. vi. 77.

2. That which is asked for or requested.

He gave them their *request*; but sent leanness into their soul. Ps. cvi. 15.

Let the *request* be fifty talents. *Shak.*, T. of A., ii. 2. 201.

3†. A question. [Rare.]

My prime *request*,
Which I do last pronounce, is, O you wonder!
If you be maid or no. *Shak.*, Tempest, i. 2. 425.

4. The state of being desired, or held in such estimation as to be sought after, pursued, or asked for.

Your noble Tullus Aufidius will appear well in these wars, his great opposer, Coriolanus, being now in no *request* of his country. *Shak.*, Cor., iv. 3. 37.

Even Guicciardine's silver history, and Ariosto's golden cantos, grow out of *request*. *G. Harvey*, Four Letters.

Knowledge and fame were in as great *request* as wealth among us now. *Sir W. Temple.*

Court of requests. (*a*) A former English court of equity for the relief of such persons as addressed the king by supplication. (*b*) An English tribunal of a special jurisdiction for the recovery of small debts.—**Letters of requests.** (*a*) In *Eng. eccles. law*, the formal instrument by which an inferior judge remits or waives his natural jurisdiction over a cause, and authorizes it to be instituted in the superior court, which otherwise could only exercise jurisdiction as a court of appeal. This may be done in some instances without any consent from or communication to the defendant. (*b*) Letters formerly granted by the Lord Privy Seal preparatory to granting letters of marque.—**Return request.** See *return*¹. =**Syn.** 1. *Petition, Suit*, etc. (see *prayer*¹), solicitation. See *ask*¹.

request (rẹ-kwest'), *v. t.* [< OF. *requester*, ask again, request, reclaim, F. *requêter*, search again, = Sp. *requestar*, *recuestar*, request, engage, = Pg. *requestar*, request; from the noun.] 1. To make a request for; ask; solicit; express desire for.

The weight of the golden ear-rings that he *requested* was a thousand and seven hundred shekels of gold. Judges viii. 26.

The drooping crests of fading flow'rs
Request the bounty of a morning rain.
Quarles, Emblems, v. 11.

2. To express a request to; ask.

I *request* you
To give my poor host freedom.
Shak., Cor., i. 9. 86.

I pray you, sir, let me *request* you to the Windmill.
B. *Jonson*, Every Man in his Humour, iv. 4.

=**Syn.** *Beg, Beseech*, etc. (see *ask*¹), desire, petition for.

requester (rẹ-kwes'tėr), *n.* One who requests; a petitioner.

A regard for the *requester* would often make one readily yield to a request, without waiting for arguments to reason one into it. *Jane Austen*, Pride and Prejudice, x.

request-note (rẹ-kwest'nōt), *n.* In the *inland revenue*, an application to obtain a permit for removing excisable articles. [Eng.]

request-program (rẹ-kwest'prō″gram), *n.* A concert program made up of numbers the performance of which has been requested by the audience.

requicken (rē-kwik'n), *v. t.* [< *re-* + *quicken*¹.] To reanimate; give new life to.

His doubled spirit
Re-quicken'd what in flesh was fatigate,
And to the battle came he. *Shak.*, Cor., ii. 2. 121.

Sweet Music *requickneth* the heaviest spirits of dumpish melancholy. *G. Harvey*, Four Letters, iii.

requiem (rē'kwi-em), *n.* [= F. *requiem*, so called from the first word of the introit of the mass for the dead, "*Requiem æternam dona eis*," etc.—a form which also serves as the gradual, and occurs in other offices of the departed: L. *requiem*, acc. of *requies*, rest, < *re-*, again, + *quies*, quiet, rest. Cf. *dirge*, similarly named from "*Dirige*."] 1. In the *Rom. Cath. Ch.*, the mass for the dead.

We should profane the service of the dead
To sing a *requiem* and such rest to her
As to peace-parted souls. *Shak.*, Hamlet, v. 1. 260.

The silent organ loudest chants
The master's *requiem*. *Emerson*, Dirge.

2. A musical setting of the mass for the dead. The usual sections of such a mass are the Requiem, the Kyrie, the Dies iræ (in several sections), the Domine Jesu Christe, the Sanctus, the Benedictus, the Agnus Dei, and the Lux æterna.

3. Hence, in popular usage, a musical service or hymn for the dead. Compare the popular use of *dirge*.

For pity's sake, you that have tears to shed,
Sigh a soft *requiem*, and let fall a bead
For two unfortunate nobles.
Webster, Devil's Law-Case, ii. 3.

4†. Rest; quiet; peace.

Else had I an eternal *requiem* kept.
Sandys, Paraphrase upon Job iii.

=**Syn.** *Dirge, Elegy*, etc. See *dirge*.

requiem-mass (rē'kwi-em-màs), *n.* Same as *requiem*, 1.

requiescat in pace (rek-wi-es'kat in pā'sē). [L.: *requiescat*, 3d pers. sing. subj. of *requiescere*, rest (see *requiescence*); *in*, in; *pace*, abl. of *pax*, peace: see *peace*.] May he (or she) rest in peace: a form of prayer for the dead, frequent in sepulchral inscriptions. Often abbreviated *R. I. P.*

requiescence (rek-wi-es'ẹns), *n.* [< L. *requiescen(t-)s*, ppr. of *requiescere*, rest, repose, < *re-* + *quiescere*, rest: see *quiesce*, *quiescence*.] A state of quiescence; rest; repose. [Rare.]

Such bolts . . . shall strike agitated Paris if not into *requiescence*, yet into wholesome astonishment.
Carlyle, French Rev., I. iii. 8.

requietory† (rẹ-kwī'e-tọ̄-ri), *n.* [< L. *requietorium*, a resting-place, sepulcher, < *requiescere*, rest: see *requiescence*.] A sepulcher.

Bodies digged up out of their *requietories*.
Weever, Ancient Funeral Monuments, p. 419.

requirable (rẹ-kwīr'ạ-bl), *a.* [< ME. *requerable*, < OF. *requerable*, < *requerre*, require: see *require* and *-able*.] 1. Capable of being required; fit or proper to be demanded.

The gentleman . . . is a man of fair living, and able to maintain a lady in her two coaches a day; . . . and therefore there is more respect *requirable*.
B. *Jonson*, Cynthia's Revels, iv. 1.

I deny not but learning to divide the word, elocution to pronounce it, wisdom to discern the truth, boldness to deliver it, be all parts *requirable* in a preacher.
Rev. T. Adams, Works, II. 256.

2†. Desirable; demanded.

Which is thilke yowre dereworthe power that is so cleer and so *requerable*? *Chaucer*, Boëthius, ii. prose 6.

require (rẹ-kwīr'), *v. t.*; pret. and pp. *required*, ppr. *requiring*. [Early mod. E. also *requyre*; < ME. *requiren*, *requyren*, *requeren*, < OF. *requirer*, *requerir*, *requerre*, F. *requérir* = Pr. *requerer*, *requerir*, *requerre* = Cat. *requirir* = Sp. *requerir* = Pg. *requerer* = It. *richiedere*, < L. *requirere*, pp. *requisitus*, seek again, look after, seek to know, ask or inquire after, ask for (something needed), need, want, < *re-*, again, + *quærere*, seek: see *querent*², *query*, *quest*¹. From the same L. verb are also ult. E. *requisite*, etc., *request*. Cf. *acquire*, *inquire*, etc.] 1†. To search for; seek.

The thirsty Trav'ler
In vain *requir'd* the Current, then imprison'd
In subterraneous Caverns.
Prior, First Hymn of Callimachus.

From the soft Lyre,
Sweet Flute, and ten-string'd Instrument *require*
Sounds of Delight. *Prior*, Solomon, ii.

2. To ask for as a favor; request. [Obsolete or archaic.]

Feire lordynges, me merveileth gretly of that ye haue me *requered*, that ye will not that noon know what ye be, ne what be youre names. *Merlin* (E. E. T. S.), ii. 204.

He sends an Agent with Letters to the King of Denmark *requiring* aid against the Parlament.
Milton, Eikonoklastes, x.

What favour then, not yet possess'd,
Can I for thee *require*?
Cowper, Poet's New-Year's Gift.

3. To ask or claim, as of right and by authority; demand; insist on having; exact.

The same wicked man shall die in his iniquity; but his blood will I *require* at thine hand. Ezek. iii. 18.

Doubling their speed, they march with fresh delight,
Eager for glory, and *require* the fight.
Addison, The Campaign.

We do not *require* the same self-control in a child as in a man. *Froude*, Sketches, p. 57.

4. To ask or order to do something; call on.

And I pray yow and *requyre*, telle me of that ye knowe my herte desireth so. *Merlin* (E. E. T. S.), i. 74.

In humblest manner I *require* your highness
That it shall please you to declare.
Shak., Hen. VIII., ii. 4. 144.

Let the two given extreams be 6 and 48, between which it is *required* to find two mean proportionals.
Hawkins, Cocker's Decimal Arithmetick (1685).

Shall burning Ætna, if a sage *requires*,
Forget to thunder, and recall her fires?
Pope, Essay on Man, iv. 123.

Persons to be presented for degrees (other than honorary) are *required* to wear not only a white necktie but also bands. *The Academy*, June 1, 1889, p. 376.

5. To have need or necessity for; render necessary or indispensable; demand; need; want.

But moist bothe erthe and ayer thai [grains] ther *require*,
Land argillose or drie hem sleth for yre.
Palladius, Husbondrie (E. E. T. S.), p. 106.

Beseech your highness,
My women may be with me, for you see
My plight *requires* it. *Shak.*, W. T., ii. 1. 118.

Poetry *requires* not an examining but a believing frame of mind. *Macaulay*, Dryden.

=**Syn.** 2–4. *Request, Beg*, etc. (see *ask*¹), enjoin (upon), prescribe, direct, command.

requirement (rẹ-kwīr'mẹnt), *n.* [= Sp. *requerimiento* = Pg. *requerimento*; as *require* + *-ment*.] 1. The act of requiring, in any sense; demand; requisition.

Now, though our actual moral attainment may always be far below what our conscience requires of us, it does tend to rise in response to a heightened *requirement* of conscience, and will not rise without it.
T. H. Green, Prolegomena to Ethics, § 251.

2. That which requires the doing of something; an authoritative or imperative command; an essential condition; claim.

The *requirement* that a wife shall be taken from a foreign tribe readily becomes confounded with the *requirement* that a wife shall be of foreign blood.
H. *Spencer*, Prin. of Sociol., § 293.

3. That which is required; something demanded or necessary.

The great want and *requirement* of our age is an earnest, thoughtful, and suitable ministry. *Eclec. Rev.*

=**Syn.** 2. *Requisite, Requirement* (see *requisite*), mandate, injunction, charge.

requirer (rẹ-kwīr'ėr), *n.* One who requires.

It was better for them that they shulde go and requyre batayle of their enemyes, rather than they shulde come on them; for they said they had sene and herde dyuers

ensamples of *requyrers* and nat *requyrers*, and euer of fyue four hath obtayned.
Berners, tr. of Froissart's Chron., II. xxxii.

requiring (rē-kwīr'ing), *n.* [Verbal n. of *require*, *v.*] Demand; requisition; requirement.

If *requiring* fail, he will compel.
Shak., Hen. V., ii. 4. 101.

requisite (rek'wi-zit), *a.* and *n.* [Formerly also *requisit*; = Sp. Pg. *requisito* = It. *requisito*, *riquisito*, < L. *requisitus*, pp. of *requirere*, seek or ask again: see *require*.] **I.** *a.* Required by the nature of things or by circumstances; necessary; so needful that it cannot be dispensed with; indispensable.

It is . . . *requisit* that leasure be taken in pronuntiation, such as may make our wordes plaine & most audible and agreable to the eare.
Puttenham, Arte of Eng. Poesie, p. 61.

God . . . sends his Spirit of truth henceforth to dwell
In pious hearts, an inward oracle
To all truth *requisite* for men to know.
Milton, P. R., i. 464.

To be witnesses of His resurrection it was *requisite* to have known our Lord intimately before His death.
J. H. Newman, Parochial Sermons, i. 286.

=**Syn.** *Essential*, etc. See *necessary*.

II. *n.* That which is necessary; something essential or indispensable.

The knave is handsome, young, and hath all those *requisites* in him that folly and green minds look after.
Shak., Othello, ii. 1. 251.

=**Syn.** *Requisite, Requirement.* That which is required by the nature of the case, or is only indirectly thought of as required by a person, is called a *requisite*; that which is viewed as required directly by a person or persons is called a *requirement*; thus, a certain study is in the one aspect a *requisite* and in the other a *requirement* for admission to college; we speak of the *requisites* to a great commander or to a successful life; of the *requirements* in a candidate for a clerkship. Hence, generally, a *requisite* is more absolutely necessary or essential than a *requirement*; a *requisite* is more often material than a *requirement*; a *requisite* may be a possession or something that may be viewed as a possession, but a *requirement* is a thing to be done or learned.

requisitely (rek'wi-zit-li), *adv.* So as to be requisite; necessarily. *Boyle.*

requisiteness (rek'wi-zit-nes), *n.* The state of being requisite or necessary; necessity. *Boyle.*

requisition (rek-wi-zish'on), *n.* [< OF. *requisition*, F. *réquisition* = Pr. *requisicio* = OSp. *requisicion* = Pg. *requisição* = It. *requisizione*, *riquisizione*, < L. *requisitio(n-)*, a searching, examination, < *requirere*, pp. *requisitus*, search for, require: see *require* and *requisite*.] **1.** The act of requiring; demand; specifically, the demand made by one state upon another for the giving up of a fugitive from law; also, an authoritative demand or official request for a supply of necessaries, as for a military or naval force; a levying of necessaries by hostile troops from the people in whose country they are.

To administer equality and justice to all, according to the *requisition* of his office. *Ford*, Line of Life.

The hackney-coach stand was again put into *requisition* for a carriage to convey this stout hero to his lodgings and bed. *Thackeray*, Vanity Fair, xxvi.

The wars of Napoleon were marked by the enormous *requisitions* which were levied upon invaded countries.
Woolsey, Introd. to Inter. Law, § 129.

2. In *Scots law*, a demand made by a creditor that a debt be paid or an obligation fulfilled.—**3.** A written call or invitation: as, a *requisition* for a public meeting.—**4.** The state of being required or desired; request; demand.

What we now call the alb . . . was of the sacred garments that one most in *requisition*.
Rock, Church of our Fathers, ii. 1.

requisition (rek-wi-zish'on), *v. t.* [= F. *réquisitionner*; from the noun.] **1.** To make a requisition or demand upon: as, to *requisition* a community for the support of troops.—**2.** To demand, as for the use of an army or the public service; also, to get on demanding; seize.

Twelve thousand Masons are *requisitioned* from the neighbouring country to raze Toulon from the face of the Earth. *Carlyle*, French Rev., III. v. 3.

The night before, the youth of Haltwhistle, who had forcibly *requisitioned* the best horses they could find, started for a secret destination. *N. and Q.*, 7th ser., III. 345.

3. To present a requisition or request to: as, to *requisition* a person to become a candidate for a seat in Parliament. [Eng.]

requisitive† (rē-kwiz'i-tiv), *a.* and *n.* [< *requisite* + *-ive*.] **I.** *a.* **1.** Expressing or implying demand.

Hence then new modes of speaking: if we interrogate, 'tis the interrogative mode; if we require, 'tis the *requisitive*. *Harris*, Hermes, i. 8.

2. Requisite.

Two things are *requisitive* to prevent a man's being deceived. *Stillingfleet*, Origines Sacræ, ii. 11. (*Latham.*)

II. *n.* One who or that which makes or expresses a requisition.

The *requisitive* too appears under two distinct species, either as it is imperative to inferiors, or precative to superiors. *Harris*, Hermes, i. 8.

requisitor (rē-kwiz'i-tor), *n.* [< ML. *requisitor*, a searcher, examiner, < L. *requirere*, pp. *requisitus*, search for, examine: see *require*.] One who makes requisition: specifically, one empowered by a requisition to investigate facts.

The property which each individual possessed should be at his own disposal, and not at that of any publick *requisitors*.
H. M. Williams, Letters on France (ed. 1796), IV. 18.

requisitory (rē-kwiz'i-tō-ri), *a.* [= Sp. *requisitorio* (cf. Pg. It. *requisitoria*, n., a warrant requiring obedience), < ML. *requisitorius*, < L. *requirere*, pp. *requisitus*, search for, require: see *requisite*, *require*.] **1.** Sought for; demanded. [Rare.]—**2.** Conveying a requisition or demand.

The Duke addressed a *requisitory* letter to the alcaldes. . . . On the arrival of the requisition there was a serious debate. *Motley*, Dutch Republic, II. 305.

requisitum (rek-wi-si'tum), *n.* [L., neut. of *requisitus*, pp. of *requirere*, search for, require: see *requisite*.] That which a problem asks for.

requit†, *v. t.* An obsolete form of *requite*.

requit (rē-kwit'), *n.* Same as *requite*.

The star that rules my luckless lot
Has fated me the russet coat,
And damn'd my fortune to the groat;
But, in *requit*,
Has blest me wi' a random shot
O' countra wit.
Burns, To James Smith.

requitable (rē-kwī'ta-bl), *a.* [< *requite* + *-able*.] Capable of being requited. *Imp. Dict.*

requital (rē-kwī'tal), *n.* [< *requite* + *-al*.] The act of requiting, or that which requites; return for any office, good or bad. (*a*) In a good sense, compensation; recompense; reward: as, the *requital* of services.

Such courtesies are real which flow cheerfully
Without an expectation of *requital*.
Ford, Broken Heart, v. 2.

(*b*) In a bad sense, retaliation or punishment.

Remember how they mangle our Brittish names abroad; what trespass were it, if wee in *requitall* should as much neglect theirs? *Milton*, On Def. of Humb. Remonst.

=**Syn.** Remuneration, payment, retribution. *Requital* differs from the other nouns indicating reward in expressing most emphatically either a full reward or a sharp retaliation. In the latter sense it comes near *revenge* (which see).

requite (rē-kwīt'), *v. t.*; pret. and pp. *requited*, ppr. *requiting*. [Early mod. E. also *requit*, with pret. *requit*; < *re-* + *quite*[1], *v.*, now only *quit*[1], *v.*] To repay (either good or evil). (*a*) In a good sense, to recompense; return an equivalent in good for or to; reward.

They lightly her *requit* (for small delight
They had as then her long to entertaine),
And eft them turned both againe to fight.
Spenser, F. Q., IV. iii. 47.

I give thee thanks in part of thy deserts,
And will with deeds *requite* thy gentleness.
Shak., Tit. And., i. 1. 237.

(*b*) In a bad sense, to retaliate; return evil for evil for or to; punish.

But warily he did avoide the blow,
And with his speare *requited* him againe.
Spenser, F. Q., III. v. 21.

Pearl felt the sentiment, and *requited* it with the bitterest hatred that can be supposed to rankle in a childish bosom. *Hawthorne*, Scarlet Letter, vi.

(c) To return. [Rare.]

I spent my time much in the visits of the princes, council of state, and great persons of the French kingdom, who did ever punctually *requite* my visits.
Lord Herbert *of Cherbury*, Life (ed. Howells), p. 135.

=**Syn.** *Remunerate, Recompense*, etc. (see *indemnify*), pay, repay, pay off.

requite (rē-kwīt'), *n.* [Also *requit*; < *requite*, *v.*] Requital. [Rare.]

For counsel given unto the king
Is this thy just *requite*!
T. Preston, Cambyses.

requiteful† (rē-kwīt'ful), *a.* [< *requite* + *-ful*.] Ready or disposed to requite.

Yet were you never that *requiteful* mistress
That grac'd me with one favour.
Middleton, Your Five Gallants, ii. 1.

requiteless† (rē-kwīt'les), *a.* [< *requite* + *-less*.] **1.** Without return or requital.

Why, faith, dear friend, I would not die *requiteless*.
Chapman, Gentleman Usher, iii. 1.

2. Not given in return for something else; free; voluntary.

For this His love *requiteless* doth approue,
He gaue her heeing meerly of free grace,
Before she was, or could His mercie moue.
Davies, Microcosmos, p. 68. (*Davies.*)

requitement† (rē-kwīt'ment), *n.* [< *requite* + *-ment*.] Requital.

The erle Douglas sore beyng greued with the losse of his nacion and frendes, entendyng a *requitement* if it were possible of the same, . . . did gather a houge armye.
Hall, Hen. IV., an. 1.

rerage†, *n.* See *rearage*.

rerail (rē-rāl'), *v. t.* [< *re-* + *rail*[1].] To replace on the rails, as a derailed locomotive. [Recent.]

They [interlocking bolts] are supposed to have prevented the rails being crowded aside, and thus to have made possible the *rerailing* of the engine. *Scribner's Mag.*, VI. 346.

rere†. An obsolete form of *rear*[1], *rear*[2], *rear*[3].

rere†, *v. t.* See *rear*[4].

re-read (rē-rēd'), *v. t.* [< *re-* + *read*[1].] To read again or anew.

rere-banquet† (rēr'bang"kwet), *n.* [Early mod. E. *rere-banket*; < *rere*, *rear*[4], + *banquet*.] A second course of sweets or desserts after dinner. Compare *rere-supper*. *Palsgrave.*

He came againe another day in the after noone, and finding the king at a *rere-banquet*, and to haue taken the wine somewhat plentifully, turned back againe.
Puttenham, Arte of Eng. Poesie (ed. Arber), p. 288.

rerebrace (rēr'brās), *n.* [< ME. *rerebrace*, < OF. **rerebras*, *arierebras*, F. *arrièrebras*; as *rere*, *rear*[3], + *brace*[1], *n.*] The armor of the upper arm from the shoulder to the elbow-joint, especially when it is of steel or leather worn over the sleeve of the hauberk, or replacing it by inclosing the arm in a complete cylinder. Also *arrière-bras*.

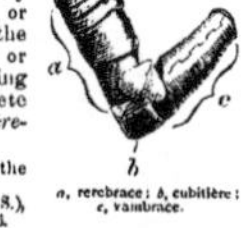

a, rerebrace; *b*, cubitière; *c*, vambrace.

Bristes the *rerebrace* with the bronde ryche.
Morte Arthure (E. E. T. S.), [l. 2566.

rere-brake (rēr'brāk), *n.* An appurtenance of a mounted warrior in the fifteenth century. It is said to have been the cushion forming a ball, or in some cases a ring, used in justs to break the shock to the knight when forced backward upon the crupper by the lance. Such contrivances are known to have been used at the time mentioned.

reredemain† (rēr'dē-mān), *n.* [ME., < OF. *rere*, back, + *de*, of, + *main*, hand: see *main*[3].] A back-handed stroke.

I shall with a *reredemayne* so make them rebounde . . . that the beste stopper that he hath at tenyce shal not well stoppe without a faulte.
Hall, Richard III., f. 11. (*Halliwell.*)

reredos (rēr'dos), *n.* [Early mod. E. *reredosse*, also *reredorse*, *reardorse* (see *reardorse*), < ME. **reredos*, *reredoos*, < OF. *reredos*, < *rere*, *riere*, rear (see *rear*[3]), + *dos*, *dors*, F. *dos*, < L. *dorsum*, back: see *dorse*[1].] **1.** In *arch.*, the back of a fireplace, or of an open fire-hearth, as commonly used in domestic halls of medieval times and the Renaissance; the iron plate often forming the back of a fireplace in which andirons are used.

Now haue we manie chimnies and yet our tenderlings complaine of rheumes, catarhs and poses. Then had we none but *reredosses*, and our heads did neuer ake.
Harrison, Descrip. of Eng., ii. 22.

The *reredos*, or brazier for the fire of logs, in the centre of the hall, continued in use [in the fifteenth century], but in addition to this large fireplaces were introduced into the walls. *J. H. Parker*, Domestic Arch. in Eng., iii.

2. A screen or a decorated part of the wall behind an altar in a church, especially when

Reredos and Altar of Lichfield Cathedral, England.

the altar does not stand free, but against the wall; an altarpiece. Compare *altarpiece* and *retable*.

It was usually ornamented with panelling, &c., especially behind an altar, and sometimes was enriched with a profusion of niches, buttresses, pinnacles, statues, and other decorations, which were often painted with brilliant colours: *reredoses* of this kind not unfrequently extended across the whole breadth of the church, and were sometimes carried up nearly to the ceiling. *Oxford Glossary.*

3. In *medieval armor*, same as *backpiece*.

reree (re-rē'), *n.* [E. Ind.] The narrow-leafed cattail, *Typha angustifolia*, whose leaves are used in northwest India for making mats and for other purposes.

rerefief (rēr'fēf), *n.* [< OF. *rierefief*, *rerefief*, abbr. of *arriere fief*, F. *arrière-fief*, < *arriere*, F. *arrière*, back (see *rear*[3]), + *fief*, fief: see *fief*.] In *Scots law*, a fief held of a superior feudatory; an under-fief, held by an under-tenant.

reremouse, rearmouse (rēr'mous), *n.*; pl. *reremice*, *rearmice* (-mīs). [Also *reermouse*; < ME. *reremous* (pl. *reremys*), < AS. *hrēremūs*, a bat, < *hrēran*, move, shake, stir (see *rear*[4], *v.*), + *mūs*, mouse: see *mouse*. Cf. *flittermouse*, *flindermouse*.] A bat. [Obsolete except in heraldic use.]

[Not] to rewle as *reremys* and rest on the daies,
And spende of the spicerie more than it nedid.
Richard the Redeless, iii. 272.

Some war with *rere-mice* for their leathern wings,
To make my small elves coats.
Shak., M. N. D., ii. 2. 4.

re-representative (rē-rep-rē-zen'tā-tiv), *a.* [< *re-* + *representative*.] See the quotation.

Re-representative cognitions; or those in which the occupation of consciousness is not by representations of special relations that have before been presented to consciousness; but those in which such represented special relations are thought of merely as comprehended in a general relation. *H. Spencer*, Prin. of Psychol., § 480.

rere-supper† (rēr'sup'ėr), *n.* [Also *rearsupper*; dial. *resupper*, as if < *re-* + *supper*; < ME. *reresouper*, *rere-soper*, *rere-sopere*, < OF. **rere-souper*, < *rere*, *riere*, behind, + *souper*, supper: see *rear*[3] and *supper*.] A late supper, after the ordinary meal so called.

Vse no surfetis neithir day ne nyght,
Neither ony *rere soupers*, which is but excesse.
Babees Book (E. E. T. S.), p. 56.

And also she wold haue *rere sopers* whanne her fader and moder was a bedde. *Book of the Knight of La Tour Landry*, p. 8.

The *rere-supper*, or banket where men syt downe to drynke and eate agayne after their meate. *Palsgrave*, Acolastus (1540). (*Halliwell.*)

If we ride not the faster the worthy Abbot Waltheoff's preparations for a *rere-supper* will be altogether spoiled. *Scott*, Ivanhoe, xviii.

rereward†, *n.* See *rearward*[1].

res (rēz), *n.* [< L. *res*, a thing, property, substance, affair, case; of doubtful origin; perhaps related to Skt. √ *rā*, give, *rāi*, property, wealth. Hence *rebus*, *real*[1], *realism*, etc.; also the first element in *republic*, etc.] A thing; a matter; a point; a cause or action. Used in sundry legal phrases: as, *res gestæ*, things done, material facts; as in the rule that the conversation accompanying an act or forming part of a transaction may usually be given in evidence as part of the *res gestæ*, when the act or transaction has been given in evidence, although such conversation would otherwise be incompetent because hearsay; *res judicata*, a matter already decided.

resail (rē-sāl'), *v. i.* [< *re-* + *sail*[1].] To sail back.

Before he anchors in his native port,
From Pyle *resailing*, and the Spartan court.
Fenton, in Pope's Odyssey, iv. 931.

resale (rē-sāl'), *n.* [< *re-* + *sale*[1].] A second sale; a sale of what was before sold to the possessor; a sale at second hand.

Monopolies, and coemption of wares for *resale*, where they are not restrained, are great meanes to enrich. *Bacon*, Riches.

resalgar†, *n.* [< ME. *resalgar*, *rysalgar*, *rosalgar*: see *realgar*.] Same as *realgar*.

Resalgar, and our materes enbibing.
Chaucer, Prol. to Canon's Yeoman's Tale, l. 261.

Our chirurgions and also ferrers do find both arsenicke and *resalgar* to be . . . sharpe, hotte, and burning things. *Topsell*, Beasts (1607), p. 429. (*Halliwell.*)

resalute (rē-sa-lūt'), *v. t.* [< *re-* + *salute*.] 1. To salute or greet anew.

To *resalute* the world with sacred light.
Milton, P. L., xi. 134.

2. To salute in return.

They of the Court made obeisance to him, . . . and he in like order *resaluted* them. *Hakluyt's Voyages*, II. 171.

res angusta domi (rēz an-gus'tā dō'mī). [L.: *res*, a thing, circumstance; *angusta*, fem. of *angustus*, narrow; *domi*, locative of *domus*, house: see *res*, *angust*, and *dome*[1].] Straitened or narrow circumstances.

resarcelé (re-sär-se-lā'), *a.* Same as *resarceled*.

resarceled, resarcelled (rē-sär'seld), *a.* In *her.*, separated by the field showing within. See *sarceled*.—**Cross sarceled, resarceled.** See *cross*[1].

resaunt†, *n.* Same as *ressaut*.

resawing-machine (rē-sâ'ing-ma-shēn"), *n.* [< *re* + *sawing*, verbal n. of *saw*[1], *v.*, + *machine*.] Any machine for cutting up squared timber into small stuff or boards. *E. H. Knight.*

resayve†, *v.* An obsolete variant of *receive*.

rescaille†, *n.* An obsolete variant of *rascal*.

rescate†, *v. t.* [Also *reescate*, *riscate* (?); < It. *riscattare*, redeem, ransom, rescue, = Sp. *rescatar* = Pg. *resgatar*, ransom (cf. OF. *rachater*, *racheter*, F. *racheter*, ransom, redeem, repurchase), < L. *re-*, back, + *ex*, out, + *captare*, take: see *capacious*.] To ransom.

The great Honour you have acquired by your gallant Comportment in Algier, in *re-escating* so many English Slaves. *Howell*, Letters, I. v. 30.

rescate†, *n.* [< It. *riscatto* = Sp. *rescate* = Pg. *resgate*, ransom, rescue; from the verb: see *rescate*, *v.*] Ransom; relief; rescue.

Euery day wee were taken prisoners, by reason of the great dissension in that kingdome; and euery morning at our departure we must pay *rescat* foure or fiue pagies a man. *Hakluyt's Voyages*, II. 222.

reschowe†, *v.* and *n.* A Middle English form of *rescue*.

rescind (rē-sind'), *v. t.* [< OF. (and F.) *rescinder* = Sp. Pg. *rescindir* = It. *rescindere*, cut off, cancel, < L. *rescindere*, cut off, annul, < *re-*, back, + *scindere*, pp. *scissus*, cut: see *scission*.] 1. To cut off; cut short; remove.

Contrarily, the great gifts of the king are judged void, his unnecessary expenses are *rescinded*, his superfluous cut off. *Prynne*, Treachery and Disloyalty, p. 168, App.

2. To abrogate; revoke; annul; vacate, as an act, by the enacting authority or by superior authority: as, to *rescind* a law, a resolution, or a vote; to *rescind* an edict or decree; to *rescind* a judgment.

Even in the worst times this power of parliament to repeal and *rescind* charters has not often been exercised.
Webster, Speech, March 10, 1818.

The sentence of exile against Wheelwright was *rescinded*.
Bancroft, Hist. U. S., I. 349.

3. To avoid (a voidable contract). *Bishop.*=**Syn.** 2. *Repeal*, *Revoke*, etc. (see *abolish*), reverse, take back.

rescindable (rē-sin'da-bl), *a.* [= F. *rescindable*; as *rescind* + *-able*.] Capable of being rescinded. *Imp. Dict.*

rescindment (rē-sind'ment), *n.* [= F. *rescindement*; as *rescind* + *-ment*.] The act of rescinding; rescission. *Imp. Dict.*

rescission (rē-sizh'on), *n.* [= F. *rescision* (for **rescission*) = Sp. *rescision* = Pg. *rescisão* = It. *rescissione*, < LL. *rescissio(n-)*, a making void, annulling, rescinding, < L. *rescindere*, pp. *rescissus*, cut off: see *rescind*.] 1. The act of rescinding or cutting off.

If any man infer upon the words of the prophets following (which declare this rejection and, to use the words of the text, *rescision* of their estate to have been for their idolatry) that by this reason the governments of all idolatrous nations should be also dissolved . . .; in my judgment it followeth not. *Bacon*, Holy War.

2. The act of abrogating, annulling, or vacating: as, the *rescission* of a law, decree, or judgment.

No ceremonial and pompous *rescision* of our fathers' crimes can be sufficient to interrupt the succession of the curse. *Jer. Taylor*, Works (ed. 1835), I. 778.

He [the daimio of Chôshiû] would communicate with the mikado, and endeavour to obtain the *rescission* of the present orders. *F. O. Adams*, Hist. Japan, I. 445.

3. The avoiding of a voidable contract.

He [the seller] was bound to suffer *rescission* or to give compensation at the option of the buyer if the thing sold had undisclosed faults which hindered the free possession of it. *Encyc. Brit.*, XXI. 206.

rescissory (rē-sis'ọ-ri), *a.* [= F. *rescisoire* = Sp. Pg. *rescisorio* = It. *rescissorio*, < LL. *rescissorius*, of or pertaining to rescinding, < L. *rescindere*, pp. *rescissus*, rescind: see *rescind*.] Having power to rescind, cut off, or abrogate; having the effect of rescinding.

To pass a general act *rescissory* (as it was called), annulling all the parliaments that had been held since the year 1633. *Bp. Burnet*, Hist. Own Times, an. 1661.

The general Act *rescissory* of 1661, which swept away the legislative enactments of the Covenanting Parliament.
Second General Council of the Presbyterian Alliance, 1880, [p. 970.

Rescissory actions, in *Scots law*, those actions whereby deeds, etc., are declared void.

rescore (rē-skōr'), *v. t.* [< *re-* + *score*.] In *music*, to score again; arrange again or differently for voices or instruments.

rescous†, *n.* [< ME. *rescous*, *rescouse*, < OF. *rescous*, *rescos*, also *rescousse*, F. *rescousse*, *recousse* = Pr. *rescossa* = It. *riscossa* (ML. reflex *rescussa*), a rescue, < ML. as if **reexcussa*, fem. pp. of **reexcutere*, rescue: see *rescue*, *v.*] Same as *rescue*.

For none hate he to the Greke hadde,
Ne also for the *rescous* of the town,
Ne made him thus in armes for to madde.
Chaucer, Troilus, i. 478.

rescribe (rē-skrīb'), *v. t.* [= OF. *rescrire* = Sp. *rescribir* = Pg. *rescrever* = It. *riscrivere*, < L. *rescribere*, write back or again, < *re-*, again, back, + *scribere*, write: see *scribe*.] 1. To write back.

Whenever a prince on his being consulted *rescribes* or writes back toleramus, he dispenses with that act otherwise unlawful. *Ayliffe*, Parergon.

2. To write again.

Calling for more paper to *rescribe* them, he showed him the difference betwixt the ink-box and the sand-box.
Howell.

rescribendary (rē-skrib'en-dā-ri), *n.*; pl. *rescribendaries* (-riz). [< ML. *rescribendarius*, < L. *rescribendus*, gerundive of *rescribere*, write back: see *rescribe*.] In the *Rom. Cath. Ch.*, an officer in the court of Rome who sets a value upon indulgences.

rescript (rē'skript), *n.* [< OF. *rescrit*, *rescript*, F. *rescrit* = Pr. *reschrich* = Cat. *rescrit* = Sp. *rescripto* = Pg. *rescripto*, *rescrito* = It. *rescritto*, < L. *rescriptum*, a rescript, reply, neut. of *rescriptus*, pp. of *rescribere*, write back: see *rescribe*.] 1. The written answer of an emperor or a pope to questions of jurisprudence officially propounded to him; hence, an edict or decree.

Maximinus gave leave to rebuild [the churches]. . . . Upon which *rescript* (saith the story) the Christians were overjoyed. *Jer. Taylor*, Works (ed. 1835), I. 156.

The society was established as soon as possible after the receipt of the Papal *rescript*.
E. A. Freeman, Norman Conquest, III. 74.

2. A counterpart. *Bouvier.*

rescription (rē-skrip'shon), *n.* [< OF. *rescription*, F. *rescription*, < LL. *rescriptio(n-)*, a rescript, < L. *rescribere*, pp. *rescriptus*, answer in writing: see *rescript* and *rescribe*.] A writing back; the answering of a letter.

You cannot oblige me more than to be punctual in *rescription*. *Loveday*, Letters (1662), p. 31. (*Latham.*)

rescriptive (rē-skrip'tiv), *a.* [< *rescript* + *-ive*.] Pertaining to a rescript; having the character of a rescript; decisive.

rescriptively (rē-skrip'tiv-li), *adv.* By rescript. *Burke.* [Rare.]

rescuable (res'kū-a-bl), *a.* [< OF. *rescouable*, < *rescorre*, *rescourre*, rescue: see *rescue* and *-able*.] Capable of being rescued.

Everything under force is *rescuable* by my function.
Gayton, Notes on Don Quixote, p. 116.

rescue (res'kū), *v.*; pret. and pp. *rescued*, ppr. *rescuing*. [Early mod. E. also *reskue*, *reskew*; < ME. *reskewen*, *rescouen*, *rescowen*, < OF. *rescorre*, *rescourre*, *reskeure*, *resquerre* (ML. reflex *rescuere*) = It. *riscuotere* (ML. reflex *rescutere*), rescue, < L. *re-*, again, + *excutere* (pp. *excussus*), shake off, drive away, < *ex-*, off, + *quatere*, shake: see *quash*[1]. Cf. *rescous*.] **I.** *trans.* 1. To free or deliver from any confinement, violence, danger, or evil; liberate from actual restraint; remove or withdraw from a state of exposure to evil: as, to *rescue* seamen from destruction by shipwreck.

Ercules *rescowed* hire, parde,
And brought hire out of helle agayne to blys.
Chaucer, Good Women, l. 515.

That was cleped the rescouse, for that Vortiger was *rescowed* whan Aungis the saisne was slain and chaced oute of the place. *Merlin* (E. E. T. S.), iii. 586.

Draw forth thy weapon, we are beset with thieves;
Rescue thy mistress, if thou be a man.
Shak., T. of the S., iii. 2. 238.

2. In *law*, to liberate or take by forcible or illegal means from lawful custody: as, to *rescue* a prisoner from a constable.=**Syn.** 1 and 2. To retake, recapture.

II.† *intrans.* To go to the rescue.

For when a chaumbere afire is or an halle,
Wel more nede is it sodenly *rescowe*
Than to dispute, and axe amonges alle,
How is this candele in the strow yfalle.
Chaucer, Troilus, iii. 857.

rescue (res'kū), *n.* [Early mod. E. also *reskue*, *reskew*; from the verb. The earlier noun was *rescous*, q. v.] 1. The act of rescuing; deliverance from restraint, violence, danger, or any evil.

Spur to the *rescue* of the noble Talbot.
Shak., 1 Hen. VI., iv. 3. 19.

Flights, terrors, sudden *rescues*, and true love
Crown'd after trial. *Tennyson*, Aylmer's Field.

2. In *law*, the forcible or illegal taking of a person or thing out of the custody of the law.

Fang. Sir John, I arrest you. . . .
Fal. Keep them off Bardolph.
Fang. A rescue! a rescue! *Shak.*, 2 Hen. IV., ii. 1. 61.

Rescue is the forcibly and knowingly freeing another from an arrest or imprisonment; and it is generally the same offence in the stranger so rescuing as it would have been in a gaoler to have voluntarily permitted an escape. *Blackstone*, Com., IV. x.

Rescue shot†, money paid for the rescue or assistance in the rescue of stolen or raided property. See *shot*.

Instead of his ain ten milk kye,
Jamie Telfer has gotten thirty and three.
And he has paid the *rescue shot*,
Baith wi' goud and white monie.
Jamie Telfer (Child's Ballads, VI. 115).

To make a rescue, to take a prisoner forcibly from the custody of an officer.

Thou gaoler, thou,
I am thy prisoner; wilt thou suffer them
To *make a rescue*? *Shak.*, C. of E., iv. 4. 114.

=**Syn.** 1. Release, liberation, extrication, redemption.

rescue-grass (res'kū-gràs), *n.* A species of brome-grass, *Bromus unioloides*. It is native in South America, perhaps also in Texas, and has been introduced with some favor as a forage-grass into several countries. In the warmest parts of the southern United States it is found valuable, as producing a crop in winter and early spring. See *prairie-grass*. Also called *Schrader's grass*.

rescuer (res'kū-ėr), *n.* One who rescues.

rescussee (res-ku-sē'), *n.* [< *rescuss(or)* + *-ee*[1].] In *law*, the party in whose favor a rescue is made.

rescussor (res-kus'ọr), *n.* [< ML. *rescussor*, < *rescutere*, pp. *rescussus*, rescue: see *rescue*, *rescous*.] In *law*, one who commits an unlawful rescue; a rescuer.

rese[1]†, *v.* A Middle English form of *raise*[1].

rese[2]†, *v.* A Middle English form of *race*[1].

research[1] (rē̦-sėrch'), *v. t.* [< OF. *recercher*, *recercer*, *rechercher*, F. *rechercher* (= It. *ricercare*), search diligently, inquire into, < *re-* + *cercher*, search: see *search*.] To search or examine with continued care; examine into or inquire about diligently. [Rare.]

It is not easy . . . to *research* with due distinction . . . in the Actions of Eminent Personages, both how much may have been blemished by the envy of others, and what was corrupted by their own felicity. *Sir H. Wotton*, Reliquiæ, p. 207.

research[1] (rē̦-sėrch'), *n.* [< OF. *recerche*, F. *recherche*, F. dial. *ressurche*, *resserche* = It. *ricerca*, diligent search; from the verb: see *research*[1], *v.*] 1. Diligent inquiry, examination, or study; laborious or continued search after facts or principles; investigation: as, microscopical *research*; historical *researches*.

Many medicinal remedys, cautious, directions, curiosities, and Arcans, which owe their birth or illustration to his indefatigable *recherches*. *Evelyn*, To Mr. Wotton.

He sucks intelligence in ev'ry clime,
And spreads the honey of his deep *research*
At his return — a rich repast for me.
Cowper, Task, iv. 112.

2. In *music*, an extemporaneous composition preluding the performance of a work, and introducing some of its leading themes. [Rare.]

=**Syn.** 1. *Investigation*, *Inquiry*, etc. (see *examination*), exploration.

research[2] (rē-sėrch'), *v.* [< *re-* + *search*.] To search again; examine anew.

researcher (rē̦-sėr'chėr), *n.* [< *research*[1] + *-er*[1]. Cf. F. *rechercheur* = It. *ricercatore*.] One who makes researches; one who is engaged in research.

He was too refined a *researcher* to lie open to so gross an imposition. *Sterne*, Tristram Shandy, ii. 19.

researchful (rē̦-sėrch'fůl), *a.* [< *research*[1] + *-ful*.] Full of or characterized by research; making research; inquisitive.

China, in truth, we find more interesting on the surface than to a more *researchful* study. *The American*, VII. 230.

reseat (rē-sēt'), *v. t.* [< *re-* + *seat*.] 1. To seat or set again.

What! will you adventure to *reseat* him
Upon his father's throne? *Dryden*, Spanish Friar, v. 2.

2. To put a new seat or new seats in; furnish with a new seat or seats: as, to *reseat* a church.

Trousers are *re-seated* and repaired where the material is strong enough.
Mayhew, London Labour and London Poor, II. 33.

réseau (rā-zō'), *n.* [F., a net or network, OF. *resel* = It. *reticello*, a net, < ML. **reticellum*, dim. of L. *rete*, a net: see *rete*.] In *lace-making*, the ground when composed of regular uniform meshes, whether of one shape only or of two or more shapes alternating.

The fine-meshed ground, or *réseau*, which has been held to be distinctive of "point d'Alençon."
Encyc. Brit., XIV. 186.

Réseau à brides, bride ground when the brides are arranged with great regularity so as to resemble a réseau properly so called, or net ground.

resect (rē̦-sekt'), *v. t.* [< L. *resectus*, pp. of *resecare* (> It. *risecare*, *risegare* = Sp. Pg. *resegar* = OF. *resequer*, F. *réséquer*), cut off, cut loose, < *re-*, back, + *secare*, cut: see *section*. Cf. *risk*.] To cut or pare off.

Perhaps the most striking illustration of the advanced surgery of the period [Roman empire] is the freedom with which bones were *resected*, including the long bones, the lower jaw, and the upper jaw. *Encyc. Brit.*, XXII. 675.

Resecting fracture, a fracture produced by a rifle-ball which has hit one of the two bones of the forearm or leg, or one or two of the metacarpal or metatarsal bones, and has taken a piece out of the bone hit without injury to the others.

resect† (rē̦-sekt'), *a.* and *n.* [< L. *resectus*, pp. of *resecare*, cut off: see *resect*, *v.*] **I.** *a.* Cut off; resected.

I ought reject
No soul from wished immortalitie,
But give them durance when they are *resect*
From organized corporeitie.
Dr. H. More, Psychathanasia, I. ii. 46.

II. *n.* In *math.*, the subtangent of a point on a curve diminished by the abscissa.

resection (rē̦-sek'shọn), *n.* [= F. *résection*, < LL. *resectio(n-)*, a cutting off, trimming, pruning, < L. *resecare*, pp. *resectus*, cut off: see *resect*.] The act of cutting or paring off; specifically, in *surg.*, the removal of the articular extremity of a bone, or of the ends of the bones in a false articulation; excision of a portion of some part, as of a bone or nerve.

Some surgeons reckoned their *resections* by the hundred.
Pop. Sci. Mo., XXVIII. 422.

Resection of the larynx, a partial laryngectomy.

resectional (rē̦-sek'shọn-al), *a.* [< *resection* + *-al*.] Of or pertaining to, or consisting in, resection.

Plastic and *resectional* operations.
Alien. and Neurol., X. 490.

Reseda (rē̦-sē'dạ̈), *n.* [NL. (Tournefort, 1700) (cf. F. *réséda* = D. *reseda* = G. *resede* = Sw. Dan. *reseda*), < L. *reseda*, a plant, < *resedare*, calm, < *re-*, back, + *sedare*, calm: see *sedative*. According to Pliny (XXVII. 12, 106), the plant was so called because it was employed to allay tumors by pronouncing the formula *reseda morbos*.] 1. A genus of polypetalous plants, type of the order *Resedaceæ*. It is characterized by cleft or dissected and unequal petals, by an urn-shaped receptacle dilated behind, bearing on one side the ten to forty stamens, and by a capsule three-lobed and open at the apex. There are about 30 species, or many more according to some authors, and all very variable. They are most abundant in the Mediterranean region, especially Spain and northern Africa, found also in Syria, Persia, and Arabia. They are erect or decumbent herbs, with entire or divided leaves, and racemed flowers. *R. luteola* is said to be diuretic and diaphoretic. See *mignonette*, and, for *R. lutea*, *base-rocket*. For *R. luteola*, see *dyer's-weed*, *weld*, *woad*, *yellow-weed*, and *ash of Jerusalem* (under *ash*[1]); also *gaude*.

2. [*l. c.*] A grayish-green tint.

Resedaceæ (res-ē̦-dā'sē̦-ē), *n. pl.* [NL. (A. P. de Candolle, 1813), < *Reseda* + *-aceæ*.] An order of dicotyledonous plants of the cohort *Parietales*, characterized by a curved embryo without albumen, a four- or eight-parted calyx, minute glands in place of stipules, an open estivation, small and commonly irregular petals, and usually numerous stamens. There are about 70 species, by some reduced to 45, belonging to 6 genera, all but 11 species being included in *Reseda*, the type. They are annual or perennial herbs, with scattered or clustered leaves, which are entire, three-parted, or pinnatifid; and with small bracted flowers in racemes or spikes. Their range is mainly that of *Reseda*, excepting *Oligomeris* with 3 species in Cape Colony and 1 in California.

reseek (rē-sēk'), *v. t.* and *i.* [< *re-* + *seek*.] To seek again. *Imp. Dict.*

reseize (rē-sēz'), *v. t.* [< *re-* + *seize*.] 1. To seize again; seize a second time.— 2. To put into possession of; reinstate: chiefly in such phrases as to be *reseized of* or *in* (to be repossessed of).

Next Archigald, who for his proud disdayne
Deposed was from princedome soverayne, . . .
And then therein *reseized* was againe.
Spenser, F. Q., II. x. 45.

3. In *law*, to take possession of, as of lands and tenements which have been disseized.

Whereupon the sheriff is commanded to *reseize* the land and all the chattels thereon, and keep the same in his custody till the arrival of the justices of assize.
Blackstone, Com., III. x.

reseizer (rē-sē'zėr), *n.* One who reseizes, in any sense.

reseizure (rē-sē'zụ̈r), *n.* [< *re-* + *seizure*.] A second seizure; the act of seizing again.

I moved to have a *reseizure* of the lands of George More, a relapsed recusant, a fugitive, and a practising traytor.
Bacon, To Cecil.

resell (rē-sel'), *v. t.* [< *re-* + *sell*[1].] To sell again; sell, as what has been recently bought.

I will not *resell* that heere which shall bee confuted heere-after. *Lyly*, Euphues and his England, p. 339.

resemblable† (rē̦-zem'blạ-bl), *a.* [< ME. *resemblable*, < OF. *resemblable*, < *resembler*, resemble: see *resemble*.] Capable or admitting of being compared; like.

These arowis that I speke of heere
Were alle fyve on oon manere,
And alle were they *resemblable*.
Rom. of the Rose, l. 985.

resemblance (rē̦-zem'blạns), *n.* [< ME. *resemblaunce*, < OF. *resemblance*, *ressemblance*, F. *ressemblance* = It. *rassembranza*; as *resemblan(t)* + *-ce*.] 1. The state or property of resembling or being like; likeness; similarity either of external form or of qualities.

Though with those streams he no *resemblance* hold,
Whose foam is amber, and their gravel gold.
Sir J. Denham, Cooper's Hill, l. 165.

It would be easy to indicate many points of *resemblance* between the subjects of Diocletian and the people of that Celestial Empire where, during many centuries, nothing has been learned or unlearned. *Macaulay*, History.

Very definite *resemblances* unite the lobster with the woodlouse, the kingcrab, the waterflea, and the barnacle, and separate them from all other animals.
Huxley, Lay Sermons, p. 102.

2. Something similar; a similitude; a point or detail of likeness; a representation; an image; semblance.

Fairest *resemblance* of thy Maker fair,
Thee all things living gaze on.
Milton, P. L., ix. 538.

He is then described as gliding through the Garden under the *resemblance* of a Mist.
Addison, Spectator, No. 351.

The soul whose sight all-quickening grace renews
Takes the *resemblance* of the good she views.
Cowper, Charity, l. 390.

3†. Likelihood; probability.

Prov. But what likelihood is in that?
Duke. Not a *resemblance*, but a certainty.
Shak., M. for M., iv. 2. 203.

4†. A simile.

Been ther none othere maner *resemblances*
That ye may likne your parables unto,
But if a sely wyf be oon of tho?
Chaucer, Prol. to Wife of Bath's Tale, l. 368.

I will set them all foorth by a triple diuision, exempting the generall Similitude as their common Auncestour, and I will cal him by the name of *Resemblance*.
Puttenham, Arte of Eng. Poesie, p. 201.

5†. Look; regard; show of affection.

With soft sighes and lovely semblaunces
He ween'd that his affection entire
She should aread; many *resemblaunces*
To her he made, and many kind remembraunces.
Spenser, F. Q., III. vii. 16.

Term of resemblance†, a general name.

resemblant (rē̦-zem'blạnt), *a.* [< F. *ressemblant*, ppr. of *ressembler*, resemble: see *resemble*.] Bearing or exhibiting resemblance; resembling. [Obsolete or rare.]

The Spanish woolls are grown originally from the English sheep, which by that soyle (*resemblant* to the Downs of England) . . . are come to that fineness.
Golden Fleece (1657). (*Nares.*)

What marvel then if thus their features were
Resemblant lineaments of kindred birth? *Southey*.

resemble (rē̦-zem'bl), *v.*; pret. and pp. *resembled*, ppr. *resembling*. [< ME. *resemblen*, < OF. *resembler*, *ressambler*, *ressembler*, F. *ressembler* = Pr. *ressemblar*, *ressemlar* = It. *risembrare*, < ML. as if **resimulare*, < L. *re-*, again, + *simulare*, simulate, imitate, copy, < *similis*, like: see *similar*, *simulate*, *semble*, and cf. *assemble*[2].] **I.** *trans.* 1. To be like to; have similarity to, in form, figure, or qualities.

Each one *resembled* the children of a king.
Judges viii. 18.

The soule, in regard of the spiritual and immortall substance, *resembleth* him which is a Spirit.
Purchas, Pilgrimage, p. 16.

The river, as it flows, *resembles* the air that flows over it.
Emerson, Nature.

2. To represent as like something else; liken; compare; note a resemblance.

Th' other, al yclad in garments light, . . .
He did *resemble* to his lady bright;
And ever his faint hart much earned at the sight.
Spenser, F. Q., III. x. 21.

Unto what is the kingdom of God like? and whereunto shall I *resemble* it? Luke xiii. 18.

3†. To imitate; simulate; counterfeit.

The Chinians . . . if they would *resemble* a deformed man, they paint him with short habite, great eyes and beard, and a long nose. *Purchas*, Pilgrimage, p. 437.

Then was I commanded to stand upon a box by the wall, and to spread my arms with the needle in them, and to *resemble* the death upon the cross.
Quoted in *S. Clarke's* Examples (1671), p. 270.

II.† *intrans.* To be like; have a resemblance; appear.

And Merlyn, that wel *resembled* to Bretel, cleped the porter, . . . and thei dought it was Bretel and Iurdan. *Merlin* (E. E. T. S.), i. 76.

An huge tablet this fair lady bar
In hir handes twain all this to declare,
Resembling to be fourged all of-new.
Rom. of Partenay (E. E. T. S.), l. 4521.

resembler (rę̄-zem'blėr), *n.* One who or that which resembles.

Tartar is a body by itself that has few *resemblers* in the world. *Boyle*, Works, I. 516.

resembling (rē-zem'bling), *a.* Like; similar; homogeneous; congruous.

They came to the side of the wood where the hounds were . . . many of them in colour and marks so *resembling* that it showed they were of one kind. *Sir P. Sidney*, Arcadia, i.

Good actions still must be maintained with good,
As bodies nourished with *resembling* food.
Dryden, To His Sacred Majesty, l. 78.

resemblingly (rę̄-zem'bling-li), *adv.* So as to resemble; with resemblance or verisimilitude.

The angel that holds the book, in the Revelations, describes him *resemblingly*. *Boyle*, Works, II. 402.

reseminate (rē-sem'i-nāt), *v. t.* [< L. *reseminatus*, pp. of *reseminare* (> It. *riseminare* = Sp. *resembrar* = Pg. *resemear* = OF. *resemer*, F. *ressemer*), sow again, beget again, < *re-*, again, + *seminare*, sow: see *seminate*. Cf. *disseminate*.] To p paga e again; beget or produce again by seedro t

Concerning its generation, that without all conjunction it [the phœnix] begets and *reseminates* itself, hereby we introduce a vegetable production in animals, and unto sensible natures transfer the propriety of plants. *Sir T. Browne*, Vulg. Err., iii. 12.

resend (rē-send'), *v. t.* [< *re-* + *send*.] To send again; send back; return.

My book of "The hurt of hearing," &c., I did give unto you; howbeit, if you be weary of it, you may *re-send* it again. *J. Bradford*, Letters (Parker Soc., 1853), II. 116.

I sent to her . . .
Tokens and letters which she did *resend*.
Shak., All's Well, iii. 6. 123.

resent (rę̄-zent'), *v.* [< OF. *resentir*, *ressentir*, F. *ressentir* = Pr. *resentir* = Cat. *ressentir* = Sp. Pg. *resentir* = It. *risentire*, < ML. **resentire*, feel in return, resent, < L. *re-*, again, + *sentire*, feel: see *scent*, *sense*. Cf. *assent*, *consent*, *dissent*.] **I.** *trans.* **1**†. To perceive by the senses; have a keen or strong sense, perception, or feeling of; be affected by.

'Tis by my touch alone that you *resent*
What objects yield delight, what discontent.
J. Beaumont, Psyche, iv. 156.

Our King Henry the Seventh quickly *resented* his drift. *Fuller.* (*Webster.*)

Hence, specifically—**2**†. To scent; perceive by the sense of smell.

Perchance, as vultures are said to smell the earthliness of a dying corpse; so this bird of prey [the evil spirit whom the writer supposes to have personated Samuel (1 Sam. xxviii. 14)] *resented* a worse than earthly savour in the soul of Saul,—as evidence of his death at hand. *Fuller*, Profane State, v. 4.

3†. To give the odor of; present to the sense of smell.

Where does the pleasant air *resent* a sweeter breath? *Drayton*, Polyolbion, xxv. 221.

4†. To have a certain sense or feeling at something; take well or ill; have satisfaction from or regret for.

He . . . began, though over-late, to *resent* the injury he had done her. *B. Jonson*, New Inn, Arg.

Many here shrink in their Shoulders, and are very sensible of his Departure, and the Lady Infanta *resents* it more than any. *Howell*, Letters, I. iii. 25.

5. To take ill; consider as an injury or affront; be in some degree angry or provoked at; hence, also, to show anger by words or acts.

Thou thyself with scorn
And anger wouldst *resent* the offer'd wrong.
Milton, P. L., ix. 300.

An injurious or slighting word is thrown out, which we think ourselves obliged to *resent*. *Bp. Atterbury*, Sermons, I. x.

Mankind *resent* nothing so much as the intrusion upon them of a new and disturbing truth. *Leslie Stephen*, Eng. Thought, i. § 17.

6†. To bear; endure.

Very hot—soultry hot, upon my honour—phoo, my lady Whimsey—how does your ladiship *resent* it? I shall be most horribly tann'd. *D'Urfey*, A Virtuous Wife (1680). (*Wright.*)

=**Syn. 5.** See *anger*[1].

II.† *intrans.* **1.** To have a certain flavor; savor.

Vessels full of traditionary pottage, *resenting* of the wild gourd of human invention. *Fuller*, Pisgah Sight, iii. 3.

2. To feel resentment; be indignant.

When he [Pompey] had carried the consulship for a friend of his, against the pursuit of Sylla, . . . Sylla did a little *resent* thereat. *Bacon*, Friendship (ed. 1887).

The town highly *resented* to see a person of Sir William Temple's character and merits roughly used. *Swift*, Battle of the Books, Bookseller to the Reader.

resenter (rę̄-zen'tėr), *n.* One who resents, in any sense of that word.

resentful (rę̄-zent'fůl), *a.* [< *resent* + *-ful*.] Inclined or apt to resent; full of resentment.

To soften the obdurate, to convince the mistaken, to mollify the *resentful*, are worthy of a statesman. *Johnson*, Works, II. 647.

Not for prud'ry's sake,
But dignity's, *resentful* of the wrong.
Cowper, Task, iii. 79.

=**Syn.** Irascible, choleric, vindictive, ill-tempered. See *anger*[1].

resentfully (rę̄-zent'fůl-i), *adv.* In a resentful manner; with resentment.

resentiment† (rę̄-zen'ti-ment), *n.* [< ML. **resentimentum*; < *resentment*.] **1.** Feeling or sense of anything; the state of being deeply affected by anything.

I . . . choose rather, being absent, to contribute what aydes I can towards its remedy, than, being present, to renew her sorrows by such expressions of *resentiment* as of course use to fall from friends. *Evelyn*, To his Brother, G. Evelyn.

2. Resentment.

Though this king might have *resentiment*
And will t' avenge him of this injury.
Daniel, Civil Wars, iv. 5.

resentingly (rę̄-zen'ting-li), *adv.* **1**†. With deep sense or strong perception.

Nor can I secure myself from seeming deficient to him that more *resentingly* considers the usefulness of that treatise in that I have not added another of superstition. *Dr. H. More*, Philosophical Writings, Gen. Pref.

2. With resentment, or a sense of wrong or affront.

resentive (rę̄-zen'tiv), *a.* [< *resent* + *-ive*.] Quick to feel an injury or affront; resentful.

From the keen *resentive* north,
By long oppression, by religion rous'd,
The guardian army came. *Thomson*, Liberty, iv.

resentment (rę̄-zent'ment), *n.* [Early mod. E. also *resentiment*, *ressentiment*; < OF. (and F.) *ressentiment* = Sp. *resentimiento* = Pg. *resentimento* = It. *risentimento*, < ML. **resentimentum*, perception, feeling, resentment, < *resentire*, feel, resent: see *resent* and *-ment*.] **1**†. The state of feeling or perceiving; strong or clear sensation, feeling, or perception; conviction; impression.

It is a greater wonder that so many of them die with so little *resentment* of their danger. *Jer. Taylor.*

You cannot suspect the reality of my *resentments* when I decline not so criminal an evidence thereof. *Parker*, Platonic Philosophy, Dedication.

2. The sense of what is done to one, whether good or evil. (*a*†) A strong perception of good; gratitude.

We need not now travel so far as Asia or Greece for instances to enhaunse our due *resentments* of God's benefits. *J. Walker*, Hist. Eucharist. (*Nares.*)

By a thankful and honourable recognition, the convocation of the church of Ireland has transmitted in record to posterity their deep *resentment* of his singular services and great abilities in this whole affair. *Jer. Taylor*, Works (ed. 1835), II. 74.

(*b*) A deep sense of injury; the excitement of passion which proceeds from a sense of wrong offered to one's self or one's kindred or friends; strong displeasure; anger.

In the two and thirtieth Year of his Reign, King Edward began to shew his *Resentment* of the stubborn Behaviour of his Nobles towards him in Times past. *Baker*, Chronicles, p. 99.

Not youthful kings in battle seized alive . . .
E'er felt such rage, *resentment*, and despair,
As thou, sad virgin! for thy ravish'd hair.
Pope, R. of the L., iv. 9.

Resentment is a union of sorrow and malignity; a combination of a passion which all endeavor to avoid with a passion which all concur to detest. *Johnson*, Rambler.

Although the exercise of *resentment* is beset with numerous incidental pains, the one feeling of gratified vengeance is a pleasure as real and indisputable as any form of human delight. *A. Bain*, Emotions and Will, p. 142.

=**Syn. 2.** (*b*) *Vexation*, *Indignation* (see *anger*[1]), irritation, rankling, grudge, heart-burning, animosity, vindictiveness.

reserate† (res'ę-rāt), *v. t.* [< L. *reseratus*, pp. of *reserare*, unlock, unclose, disclose (> It. *riserrare* = OF. (and F.) *resserrer*, shut up again), < *re-*, back, + *sera*, a bar for fastening a door (< *serere*, join, bind ?).] To unlock; open.

There appears no reason, or at least there has been none given that I know of, why the *reserating* operation (if I may so speak) of sublimate should be confined to antimony. *Boyle*, Works, III. 79.

reservance† (rę̄-zėr'vans), *n.* [= It. *riserbanza*, *riservanza*; as *reserve* + *-ance*.] Reservation.

We [Edward R.] are pleased that the *Reservance* of our Rights and Titles . . . be in general words. *Bp. Burnet*, Records, II. ii. No. 50.

reservation (rez-ėr-vā'shǫn), *n.* [< OF. *reservation*, F. *réservation* = Pr. *reservatio* = Sp. *reservacion* = Pg. *reservação* = It. *riserbazione*, *riservazione*, *reservazione*, < ML. *reservatio(n-)*, < L. *reservare*, reserve: see *reserve*.] **1.** The act of reserving or keeping back; reserve; concealment or withholding from disclosure.

I most unfeignedly beseech your lordship to make some *reservation* of your wrongs. *Shak.*, All's Well, ii. 3. 260.

2. Something withheld, either not expressed or disclosed, or not given up or brought forward.

He has some *reservation*,
Some concealed purpose, and close meaning sure.
B. Jonson, Every Man in his Humour, iii. 2.

3. In the United States, a tract of the public land reserved for some special use, as for schools, the use of Indians, etc.: as, the Crow *reservation*. Also *reserve*.

The first record [of Concord] now remaining is that of a *reservation* of land for the minister, and the appropriation of new lands as commons or pastures to some poor men. *Emerson*, Hist. Discourse at Concord.

4†. The state of being treasured up or kept in store; custody; safe keeping.

He will'd me
In heedfull'st *reservation* to bestow them [prescriptions].
Shak., All's Well, i. 3. 231.

5. In *law*: (*a*) An express withholding of certain rights the surrender of which would otherwise follow or might be inferred from one's act (*Mackeldey*); a clause or part of an instrument by which something is reserved.

I gave you all, . . .
Made you my guardians, my depositaries;
But kept a *reservation* to be follow'd
With such a number. *Shak.*, Lear, ii. 4. 255.

(*b*) Technically, in the law of conveyancing, a clause by which the grantor of real property reserves to himself, or himself and his successors in interest, some new thing to issue out of the thing granted, as distinguished from excepting a part of the thing itself. Thus, if a man conveys a farm, saving to himself a field, this is an *exception*; but if he saves to himself a right of way through a field, this is a *reservation*. (*c*) The right created by such a clause.—**6.** *Eccles.*: (*a*) The act or practice of retaining or preserving part of the consecrated eucharistic elements or species, especially that of bread, unconsumed for a shorter or longer period after the celebration of the sacrament. The practice has existed from early times, and is still in use in the Roman Catholic, the Greek, and other churches, especially to provide for the communion of the sick and prisoners. (*b*) In the Roman Catholic Church, the act of the Pope in reserving to himself the right to nominate to certain benefices.

On the 1st of October he [the Pope] appointed Reynolds by virtue of the *reservation*, and immediately filled up the see of Worcester which Reynolds vacated. *Stubbs*, Const. Hist., § 384.

Indian reservation, a tract of land reserved by the State or nation as the domain of Indians. [U. S.]—**Mental reservation**, the intentional withholding of some word or clause necessary to convey fully the meaning of the speaker or writer; the word or clause so withheld. Also called *mental restriction*.

Almost all [Roman Catholic] theologians hold that it is sometimes lawful to use a *mental reservation* which may be, though very likely it will not be, understood from the circumstances. Thus, a priest may deny that he knows a crime which he has only learnt through sacramental confession. *Rom. Cath. Dict.*, p. 572.

Reservation system, the system by which Indians have been provided for, and to some extent governed, by confining them to tracts of public lands reserved for the purpose, and excepting them from the rights and obligations of ordinary citizens. [U. S.]

reservative (rę̄-zėr'vą-tiv), *a.* [< *reserve* + *-ative*. Cf. *conservative*.] Tending to reserve or keep; keeping; reserving.

reservatory (rę̄-zėr'vą-tō-ri), *n.*; pl. *reservatories* (-riz). [= F. *réservoir* (> E. *reservoir*) = Sp. Pg. *reservatorio*, < ML. *reservatorium*, a storehouse, < L. *reservare*, keep, reserve: see *reserve*. Doublet of *reservoir*.] A place in which things are reserved or kept.

How I got such notice of that subterranean *reservatory* as to make a computation of the water now concealed therein, peruse the propositions concerning earthquakes. *Woodward.*

reserve (rę̄-zėrv'), *v. t.*; pret. and pp. *reserved*, ppr. *reserving*. [< ME. *reserven*, < OF. *reserver*, F. *réserver* = Pr. Sp. Pg. *reservar* = It. *riserbare*, *riservare*, *reservare*, < L. *reservare*, keep back, < *re-*, back, + *servare*, keep: see *serve*. Cf. *conserve*, *observe*, *preserve*.] **1.** To keep back; keep in store for future or other use; preserve; withhold from present use for another purpose; keep back for a time: as, a *reserved* seat.

Hast thou seen the treasures of the hail, which I have *reserved* against the time of trouble? Job xxxviii. 22, 23.

Take each man's censure, but *reserve* thy judgement. *Shak.*, Hamlet, i. 3. 69.

His great powers of painting he *reserves* for events of which the slightest details are interesting. *Macaulay*, History.

2†. To preserve; keep safe; guard.

One in the prison,
That should by private order else have died,
I have *reserved* alive. *Shak.*, M. for M., v. 1. 472.

In the other two destructions, by deluge and earthquake, it is farther to be noted that the remnant of people which hap to be *reserved* are commonly ignorant. *Bacon*, Vicissitudes of Things (ed. 1887).

At Alexandria, where two goodly pillars of Theban marble *reserve* the memory of the place. *Sandys*, Travailes, p. 90.

Farewel, my noble Friend, cheer up, and *reserve* your self for better Days. *Howell*, Letters, ii. 76.

3. To make an exception of; except, as from the conditions of an agreement.

War. Shall our condition stand?
Char. It shall;
Only *reserved*, you claim no interest
In any of our towns of garrison.
Shak., 1 Hen. VI., v. 4. 167.

The old Men, Women, and sicke Folkes were *reserved* from this Tribute. *Purchas*, Pilgrimage, p. 870.

=**Syn.** 1. *Reserve, Retain*, etc. See *keep*.

reserve (rẹ̄-zėrv'), *n.* [< OF. *reserve*, F. *réserve* = Sp. Pg. *reserva* = It. *riserba, riserva*, a store, reserve; from the verb: see *reserve, v.*] 1. The act of reserving or keeping back.—2. That which is reserved or kept for other or future use; that which is retained from present use or disposal.

Where all is due, make no *reserve*. *Sir T. Browne*, Christ. Mor., i. 1.

Still hoarding up, most scandalously nice,
Amidst their virtues, a *reserve* of vice.
Pope, Epil. to Rowe's Jane Shore.

3. Something in the mind withheld from disclosure; a reservation.

However any one may concur in the general scheme, it is still with certain *reserves* and deviations. *Addison*, Freeholder. (*Latham*.)

4. Self-imposed restraint of freedom in words or actions; the habit of keeping back or restraining the feelings; a certain closeness or coldness toward others; caution in personal behavior.

Upon my arrival I attributed that *reserve* to modesty, which I now find has its origin in pride. *Goldsmith*, Citizen of the World, iv.

Fasting and prayer sit well upon a priest,
A decent caution and *reserve* at least.
Cowper, Hope, l. 404.

Instead of scornful pity or pure scorn,
Such fine *reserve* and noble reticence.
Tennyson, Geraint.

5. An exception; something excepted.

Each has some darling lust, which pleads for a *reserve*. *Dr. J. Rogers*.

Is knowledge so despised,
Or envy, or what *reserve* forbids to taste?
Milton, P. L., v. 61.

In the minds of almost all religious persons, even in the most tolerant countries, the duty of toleration is admitted with tacit *reserves*. *J. S. Mill*, On Liberty, i.

6. In *law*, reservation.—7. In *banking*, that part of capital which is retained in order to meet average liabilities, and is therefore not employed in discounts or temporary loans. See *bank*[2], 4.

They [the precious metals] are employed as *reserves* in banks, or other hands, forming the guarantee of paper money and cheques, and thus becoming the instrument of the wholesale payments of society. *Nineteenth Century*, XXVI. 805.

8. *Milit.*: (*a*) The body of troops, in an army drawn up for battle, reserved to sustain the other lines as occasion may require; a body of troops kept for an exigency. (*b*) That part of the fighting force of a country which is in general held back, and upon which its defense is thrown when its regular forces are seriously weakened or defeated: as, the naval *reserve*. In countries where compulsory service exists, as Germany, the reserve denotes technically that body of troops in the standing army who have served in the line, before their entry into the landwehr. The period of service is about four years. (*c*) A magazine of warlike stores situated between an army and its base of operations.—9. In *theol.*, the system according to which only that part of the truth is set before the people which they are regarded as able to comprehend or to receive with benefit: known also as *economy*. Compare *discipline of the secret*, under *discipline*.—10. In *calico-printing* and other processes, same as *resist*, 2.—11. Same as *reservation*, 3.—**Connecticut Reserve, Connecticut Western Reserve**, or **Western Reserve**, the name given to the region, lying south of Lake Erie and in the present State of Ohio, which the State of Connecticut, in ceding its claims upon western lands, reserved to itself for the purposes of a school fund.—**Gold reserve**, the gold held by the United States treasury for the redemption of United States notes. This fund was first accumulated for the resumption of specie payments, and at that date (Jan. 1, 1879) amounted to over $114,000,000. By the provisions of the act of July 12, 1882, it was practically fixed at $100,000,000. In April, 1893, it first fell below this sum as a result of the policy of the treasury (under the "parity" clause of the act of July 14, 1890) in paying the treasury notes of 1890, on demand, in gold; and by January, 1894, fell to $65,650,000. To replenish the fund the government sold bonds—$50,000,000 of 5 per cent. bonds in January, 1894; $50,000,000 of 5 per cent. bonds in November, 1894; about $62,000,000 of 4 per cent. bonds in February, 1895; and $100,000,000 of 4 per cent. bonds in January, 1896.—**In reserve**, in store; in keeping for other or future use.—**Reserve air.** Same as *residual air* (which see, under *air*[1]).—**Without reserve.** See the quotation.

When a sale is announced as *without reserve*—whether the announcement be contained in the written particulars or be made orally by the auctioneer—that, according to all the cases, both at law and in equity, means not merely that the property will be peremptorily sold, but that neither the vendor nor any one acting for him will bid at the auction. *Bateman*.

=**Syn.** 1. Retention.—4. Restraint, distance.

reserved (rẹ̄-zėrvd'), *p. a.* 1. Kept for another or future use; retained; kept back.

He hath reasons *reserved* to himself, which our frailty cannot apprehend. *Burton*, Anat. of Mel., p. 657.

2. Showing reserve in behavior; backward in communicating one's thoughts; not open, free, or frank; distant; cold; shy; coy.

The man I trust, if shy to me,
Shall find me as *reserv'd* as he.
Cowper, Friendship.

New England's poet, soul *reserved* and deep,
November nature with a name of May.
Lowell, Agassiz, iii. 5.

3. Retired; secluded. [Rare.]

They [the pope or ruffe] will usually lie, abundance of them together, in one *reserved* place, where the water is deep and runs quietly. *I. Walton*, Complete Angler (ed. Major), p. 236, i. 15.

4. In *decorative art*, left of the color of the background, as when another color is worked upon the ground to form a new ground, the pattern being left of the first color.—**Case reserved.** See *case*[1].—**Reserved case**, in the *Rom. Cath. Ch.*, a sin the power to absolve from which is reserved to the Pope or his legate, the ordinary of the diocese, or a prelate of a religious order, other confessors not being allowed to give absolution. A sin, to be reserved, must be external (one of word or deed), and sufficiently proved. No sin is reserved in the case of a person *in articulo mortis*.—**Reserved list**, in the *British navy*, a list of officers put on half-pay, and removed from active service, but liable to be called out on the contingency of there being an insufficiency of officers for active service.—**Reserved power**, in *Scots law*, a reservation made in deeds, settlements, etc. Reserved powers are of different sorts: as, a *reserved power* of burdening a property; a *reserved power* to revoke or recall a settlement or other deed.—**Reserved powers**, in *U. S. const. law*, powers pertaining to sovereignty, but not delegated to a representative body; more specifically, those powers of the people which are not delegated to the United States by the Constitution of the country, but remain with the respective States. The national government possesses no powers but such as have been delegated to it. The States have all that they inherited from the British Parliament, except such as they have surrendered, either by delegation to the United States, or by prohibition, in their respective constitutions or in the Constitution of the United States. =**Syn.** 1. Excepted, withheld.—2. Restrained, cautious, uncommunicative, unsocial, unsociable, taciturn.

reservedly (rẹ̄-zėr'ved-li), *adv.* In a reserved manner; with reserve; without openness or frankness; cautiously; coldly.

He speaks *reservedly*, but he speaks with force. *Pope*.

reservedness (rẹ̄-zėr'ved-nes), *n.* The character of being reserved; closeness; lack of frankness, openness, or freedom.

A certain *reserv'dnesse* of naturall disposition, and morall discipline learnt out of the noblest Philosophy. *Milton*, Apology for Smectymnuus.

reservee (rez-ėr-vē'), *n.* [< F. *réservé*, pp. of *réserver*, reserve: see *reserve*.] In *law*, one to whom anything is reserved.

reserver (rẹ̄-zėr'vėr), *n.* One who or that which reserves.

reservist (rẹ̄-zėr'vist), *n.* [< F. **réserviste*; as *reserve* + *-ist*.] A soldier who belongs to the reserve. [Recent.]

The town was full of the military reserve, out for the French autumn manœuvres, and the *reservists* walked speedily and wore their formidable great-coats. *R. L. Stevenson*, Inland Voyage, p. 172.

reservoir (rez'ėr-vwor), *n.* [< F. *réservoir*, a storehouse, reservoir: see *reservatory*. Doublet of *reservatory*.] 1. A place where anything is kept in store: usually applied to a large receptacle for fluids or liquids, as gases or oils.

What is his [God's] creation less
Than a capacious *reservoir* of means
Form'd for his use, and ready at his will?
Cowper, Task, ii. 201.

The fly-wheel is a vast *reservoir* into which the engine pours its energy, sudden floods alternating with droughts; but these succeed each other so rapidly, and the area of the *reservoir* is so vast, that its level remains uniform. *R. S. Ball*, Exper. Mechanics, p. 207.

Specifically—2. A place where water collects naturally or is stored for use when wanted, as to supply a fountain, a canal, or a city, or for any other purpose.

There is not a spring or fountain but are well provided with huge cisterns and *reservoirs* of rain and snow water. *Addison*.

Here was the great basin of the Nile that received every drop of water, even from the passing shower to the roaring mountain torrent that drained from Central Africa toward the north. This was the great *reservoir* of the Nile. *Sir S. W. Baker*, Heart of Africa, p. 253.

3. In *anat.*, a receptacle. See *receptaculum*.—4. In *bot.*: (*a*) One of the passages or cavities found in many plant-tissues, in which are secreted and stored resins, oils, mucilage, etc. More frequently called *receptacle*. *De Bary*, Comp. Anat. (trans.), p. 202. (*b*) A seed or any organ of a plant in which surplus assimilated matter (reserve material) is stored up for subsequent use.—**Mucilage-reservoirs.** See *mucilage*.—**Reservoir of Pecquet.** Same as *receptaculum chyli* (which see, under *receptaculum*).

reservoir (rez'ėr-vwor), *v. t.* [< *reservoir, n.*] To furnish with a reservoir; also, to collect and store in a reservoir.

Millions of pools of oil have been lost, owing to the inefficient way in which it is *reservoired* and stored. *Sci. Amer.*, N. S., LVIII. 52.

reservor (rẹ̄-zėr'vọr), *n.* [< *reserve* + *-or*[1].] In *law*, one who reserves. *Story*.

reset[1] (rẹ̄-set'), *n.* [< ME. *reset*, etc., < OF. *recet, receit*, etc.: see *receipt, n.*] 1†. Same as *receipt*, 5, 6.—2. In *Scots law*, the receiving and harboring of an outlaw or a criminal.—**Reset of theft**, the offense of receiving and keeping goods knowing them to be stolen, and with an intention to conceal and withhold them from the owner.

reset[1] (rẹ̄-set'), *v. t.*; pret. and pp. *resetted*, ppr. *resetting*. [< ME. *reseten*, etc., < OF. *receter*, etc., receive: see *receipt, v.*] 1†. Same as *receipt*.—2. In *Scots law*, to receive and harbor (an outlaw or criminal); receive (stolen goods).

We shall see if an English hound is to harbour and *reset* the southrons here. *Scott*.

Gif ony ydill men, that has not to live of thare awin to left apon, be *resett* within the lande . . . Quoted in *Ribton-Turner's* Vagrants and Vagrancy, p. 338.

reset[2] (rē-set'), *v. t.* and *i.* [< *re-* + *set*[1].] To set again, in any sense of the word *set*.

reset[2] (rē-set'), *n.* [< *reset*[2], *v.*] 1. The act of resetting.—2. In *printing*, matter set over again.

resettable (rē-set'ạ-bl), *a.* [< *reset*[2] + *-able*.] Capable of being reset.

Cups . . . with gems . . .
Moveable and *resettable* at will.
Tennyson, Lover's Tale, iv.

resetter[1] (rẹ̄-set'ėr), *n.* [< *reset*[1] + *-er*[1].] In *Scots law*, a receiver of stolen goods; also, one who harbors a criminal.

I thought him an industrious, peaceful man—if he turns *resetter* of idle companions and night-walkers, the place must be rid of him. *Scott*, Abbot, xxxv.

Wicked thieves, oppressors, and peacebreakers and *resetters* of theft. *Ribton-Turner*, Vagrants and Vagrancy, p. 349.

resetter[2] (rē-set'ėr), *n.* [< *reset*[2] + *-er*[1].] One who resets or places again.

resettle (rē-set'l), *v.* [< *re-* + *settle*[2].] I. *trans.* To settle again; specifically, to install again, as a minister in a parish.

Will the house of Austria yield . . . the least article of strained and even usurped prerogative, to *resettle* the minds of those princes in the alliance who are alarmed at the consequences of . . . the emperor's death? *Swift*, Conduct of the Allies.

II. *intrans.* To become settled again; specifically, to be installed a second time or anew in a parish.

resettlement (rē-set'l-mẹnt), *n.* [< *resettle* + *-ment*.] The act of resettling, or the process or state of being resettled, in any sense.

resh[1] (resh), *a.* [Origin obscure. Cf. *rash*[1].] Fresh; recent. *Halliwell*.

resh[2] (resh), *n.* A frequent dialectal variant of *rush*[1].

reshape (rē-shāp'), *v. t.* [< *re-* + *shape*.] To shape again; give a new shape to.

reship (rē-ship'), *v. t.* [< *re-* + *ship*.] To ship again: as, goods *reshipped* to Chicago.

reshipment (rē-ship'mẹnt), *n.* [< *reship* + *-ment*.] 1. The act of shipping a second time; specifically, the shipping for exportation of what has been imported.—2. That which is reshipped.

resiance† (rez'i-ans), *n.* [< OF. **reseance*, **resiance*, *resseance*, < ML. *residentia*, residence: see *residence*, and cf. *séance*. Doublet of *residence*.] Residence; abode.

Resolved there to make his *resiance*, the seat of his principality. *Knolles*, 1174 G. (*Nares.*)

The King forthwith banished all Flemmings . . . out of his Kingdome, Commanding . . . (. . . his Merchant-Adventurers) which had a *Resiance* in Antwerp, to return. Bacon, Hist. Hen. VII., p. 130.

resiant† (rez'i-ant), *a.* and *n.* [< OF. *resiant*, *reseant*, *resseant*, < L. *residen(t-)s*, resident: see *resident*. Doublet of *resident*.] **I.** *a.* Resident; dwelling.

Articles conceiued and determined for the Commission of the Merchants of this company *resiant* in Prussia. *Hakluyt's Voyages*, I. 259.

I have already
Dealt by Umbrenus with the Allobroges
Here *resiant* in Rome. B. *Jonson*, Catiline, iv. 3.

Resiant rolls, in *law*, rolls naming the resiants or residents in a tithing, etc., called over by the steward on holding court-leet.

II. *n.* A resident.

Touching the custom of "suit and service" (i. e., grinding corn, &c.) of the "*resiants* and inhabitants of Whalley" to said antient mills . . . *Record Soc. Lancashire and Cheshire*, XI. 79.

All manner of folk, *resiants* or subjects within this his [the King of England's] realm.
Quoted in *R. W. Dixon's* Hist. Church of Eng., iii., note.

reside (rẹ-zīd'), *v. i.*; pret. and pp. *resided*, ppr. *residing*. [= D. *resideren* = G. *residiren* = Dan. *residere* = Sw. *residera*, < OF. *resider*, vernacularly *resier*, F. *résider* = Sp. Pg. *residir* = It. *risedere*, < L. *residere*, remain behind, reside, dwell, < *re-*, back, + *sedere*, sit (= E. *sit*): see *sit*. Cf. *preside*.] **1.** To dwell permanently or for a considerable time; have a settled abode for a time, or a dwelling or home; specifically, to be in official residence (said of holders of benefices, etc.).

To bathe in fiery floods, or to *reside*
In thrilling region of thick-ribbed ice;
To be imprison'd in the viewless winds.
Shak., M. for M., iii. 1. 122.

These Sirens *resided* in certain pleasant islands.
Bacon, Moral Fables, vi.

Thy crystal stream, Afton, how lovely it glides,
And winds by the cot where my Mary *resides*.
Burns, Flow Gently, sweet Afton.

2. To abide or be inherent in, as a quality; inhere.

Excellence, and quantity of energy, *reside* in mixture and composition. *Bacon*, Physical Fables, ii., Expl.

It is in man and not in his circumstances that the secret of his destiny *resides*. *Gladstone*, Might of Right, p. 21.

3†. To sink to the bottom, as of liquids; settle; subside, in general.

The madding Winds are hush'd, the Tempests cease,
And ev'ry rowling Surge *resides* in Peace.
Congreve, Birth of the Muse.

=**Syn. 1.** *Sojourn*, *Continue*, etc. (see *abide*1), be domiciled, be domiciliated, make a home.

residence (rez'i-dẹns), *n.* [< ME. *residence*, < OF. *residence*, F. *résidence* = Pr. *residensa*, *residencia* = Sp. Pg. *residencia* = It. *residenzia*, *residenza* (= D. *residentie* = G. *residenz* = Dan. *residents* = Sw. *residens*, < F.), < ML. *residentia*, < L. *residen(t-)s*, resident: see *resident*. Doublet of *resiance*.] **1.** The act of residing or dwelling in a place permanently or for a considerable time.

What place is this?
Sure, something more than human keeps *residence* here.
Fletcher (and another), Sea Voyage, ii. 2.

I upon my frontiers here
Keep *residence*. *Milton*, P. L., ii. 999.

Ambassadors in ancient times were sent on special occasions by one nation to another. Their *residence* at foreign courts is a practice of modern growth.
Woolsey, Introd. to Inter. Law, § 89.

2. A place of residing or abode; especially, the place where a person resides; a dwelling; a habitation.

Within the infant rind of this small flower
Poison hath *residence* and medicine power.
Shak., R. and J., ii. 3. 24.

What is man? . . .
Once the blest *residence* of truth divine.
Cowper, Truth, l. 387.

In front of this esplanade [Plaza de los Algibes] is the splendid pile commenced by Charles V., and intended, it is said, to eclipse the *residence* of the Moorish kings.
Irving, Alhambra, p. 57.

3. That in which anything permanently rests or inheres.

But when a king sets himself to bandy against the highest court and *residence* of all his regal power, he then, in the single person of a man, fights against his own majesty and kingship. *Milton.*

4. A remaining or abiding where one's duties lie, or where one's occupation is properly carried on; *eccles.*, the presence of a bishop in his diocese, a canon in his cathedral or collegiate church, or a rector or an incumbent in his benefice: opposed to *non-residence*.

He is ever in his parish; he keepeth *residence* at all times. *Latimer*, Sermon of the Plough.

Residence on the part of the students appears to have been sometimes dispensed with [at the university of Siena].
Encyc. Brit., XXIII. 837.

5. In *law*: (*a*) The place where a man's habitation is fixed without any present intention of removing it therefrom; domicile. (*b*) An established abode, fixed for a considerable time, whether with or without a present intention of ultimate removal. A man cannot fix an intentionally temporary domicile, for the intention that it be temporary makes it in law no domicile, though the abode may be sufficiently fixed to make it in law a residence in this sense. A man may have two residences, but only one can be his domicile. The bankruptcy law uses the term *residence* specifically, as contradistinguished from *domicile*, so as to free cases under it from the difficult and embarrassing presumptions and circumstances upon which the distinctions between *domicile* and *residence* rest. Residence is a fact easily ascertained, domicile a question difficult of proof. It is true that the two terms are often used as synonymous, but in law they have distinct meanings. (*Bump.*) See *resident*.

Residence is to be taken in its jural sense, so that a transient absence does not interrupt it.
Woolsey, Introd. to Inter. Law, App. iii., p. 438.

6†. (*a*) The settling or settlement of liquors; the process of clearing, as by the settling of sediment. (*b*) That which settles or is deposited, as the thick part of wine that has grown old in bottle.

Hipostasi [It.], a substance. Also *residence* in vrine flitting toward the bottom. *Florio.*

(*c*) Any residue or remnant.

When meate is taken quyte awaye,
And voyders in presence,
Put you your trenchour in the same,
And all your *resydence*.
Babees Book (E. E. T. S.), p. 80.

Divers *residences* of bodies are thrown away as soon as the distillation or calcination of the body that yielded them is ended. *Boyle.*

=**Syn. 1.** Domiciliation, inhabitancy, sojourn, stay.—**2.** Home, domicile, mansion. See *abide*1.

residencer (rez'i-dẹn-sėr), *n.* [< ME. *residencer*, < OF. *residencier*, < ML. *residentiarius*, a clergyman in residence: see *residentiary*.] A clergyman in residence.

Alle prechers, *residencers*, and persones that ar greable [of similar degree] . . .
They may be set semely at a squyers table.
Babees Book (E. E. T. S.), p. 189.

Their humanity is a legge [bow] to the *Residencer*, their learning a Chapter, for they learne it commonly before they read it.
Bp. Earle, Micro-cosmographie, The Common Singing-men [in Cathedrall Churches.

residency (rez'i-dẹn-si), *n.*; pl. *residencies* (-siz). [As *residence* (see *-cy*).] **1.** Same as *residence*.

That crime, which hath so great a tincture and *residency* in the will that from thence only it hath its being criminal.
Jer. Taylor, Works (ed. 1835), II. 415.

Specifically—**2.** The official residence of a British resident at the court of a native prince in India.

Sir Henry Lawrence immediately took steps to meet the danger [the mutiny in Lucknow] by fortifying the *residency* and accumulating stores. *Encyc. Brit.*, XV. 50.

3. A province or administrative division in some of the islands of the Dutch East Indies.

resident (rez'i-dẹnt), *a.* and *n.* [< ME. *resident*, < OF. *resident*, *residant* (vernacularly *reseant*, *resiant*: see *resiant*), F. *résident*, *résidant* = Pr. *resident* = Sp. Pg. It. *residente*, < L. *residen(t-)s*, ppr. of *residere*, remain behind, reside: see *reside*.] **I.** *a.* **1.** Residing; having a seat or dwelling; dwelling or having an abode in a place for a continuance of time.

The forain merchants here *resident* are for the most part English. *Sandys*, Travailes, p. 7.

Authority herself not seldom sleeps.
Though *resident*, and witness of the wrong.
Cowper, Task, iv. 594.

2†. Fixed; firm.

The watery pavement is not stable and *resident* like a rock. *Jer. Taylor*, Works (ed. 1835), I. 829.

3. In *zoöl.*: (*a*) Remaining in a place the whole year; not migratory: said especially of birds. (*b*) Pertaining to or consisting of residents: as, the *resident* fauna; a *resident* theory.—**4.** Having one's abode in a given place in pursuit of one's duty or occupation: as, he is minister *resident* at that court.

II. *n.* **1.** One who or that which resides or dwells in a place permanently or for a considerable time; one residing: as, the American *residents* of Paris.—**2.** In *law*, one who has a residence in the legal sense. See *residence*.

Resident and its contrary, *non-resident*, are more commonly used to refer to abode, irrespective of the absence of intention to remove.

3. A public minister who resides at a foreign court: the name is usually given to ministers of a rank inferior to that of ambassadors.

We have receiv'd two Letters from your Majesty, the one by your Envoy, the other transmitted to us from our *Resident* Philip Meadows.
Milton, Letters of State, Oct. 13, 1658.

This night, when we were in bed, came the *resident* of several princes (a serious and tender man) to find us out.
Penn, Travels in Holland, etc.

4. In *zoöl.*, an animal, or a species of animal, which remains in the same place throughout the year: distinguished from *migrant* or *visitant*: said especially of birds.—**5.** In *feudal law*, a tenant who was obliged to reside on his lord's land, and not to depart from it.—**6.** In India: (*a*) Previous to the organization of the civil service, a chief of one of the commercial establishments of the East India Company. (*b*) Later, a representative of the viceroy at an important native court, as at Lucknow or Delhi. —**7.** The governor of a residency in the Dutch East Indies.=**Syn. 1.** Inhabitant, inhabiter, dweller, sojourner.

residental (rez'i-den-tạl), *a.* [< *resident* + *-al*.] Residential. [Rare.]

The beautiful *residental* apartments of the Pitti Palace.
H. *James, Jr.*, Trans. Sketches, p. 303.

residenter (rez'i-den-tėr), *n.* [< late ME. *residenter*, < *resident* + *-er*1. Cf. *residencer*.] A resident. [Scotch and U. S.]

I write as a *residenter* for nearly three years, having an intimate acquaintance with "the kingdom" [of Fife] of some fifteen years' standing. *N. and Q.*, 7th ser., IX. 92.

residential (rez-i-den'shạl), *a.* [< *residence* (ML. *residentia*) + *-al*.] Relating or pertaining to residence or to residents; adapted or intended for residence.

Such I may presume roughly to call a *residential* extension. *Gladstone.*

It [a medical college for women] has no *residential* hall, nor is it desirable, perhaps, that it should have any.
Fortnightly Rev., N. S., XXXIX. 24.

It may be added that *residential* has been good English at least since 1690.
J. A. H. Murray, in N. and Q., 7th ser., VIII. 134.

residentiary (rez-i-den'shiạ̄-ri), *a.* and *n.* [< ML. *residentiarius*, being in residence, a clergyman in residence, < *residentia*, residence: see *residence*.] **I.** *a.* **1.** Having or keeping a residence; residing; especially (*eccles.*), bound to reside a certain time at a cathedral church: as, a canon *residentiary* of St. Paul's.

Christ was the conductor of the Israelites into the land of Canaan, and their *residentiary* guardian. *Dr. H. More.*

There was express power given to the bishops of Lincoln and London alone to create another *residentiary* canonry in their own patronage.
Edinburgh Rev., CLXIII. 180.

2. Of or pertaining to a residentiary.

Dr. John Taylor died 1766, at his *residentiary* house, Amen Corner. *N. and Q.*, 7th ser., II. 447.

II. *n.*; pl. *residentiaries* (-riz). **1.** One who or that which is resident.

Faith, temperance, patience, zeal, charity, hope, humility, are perpetual *residentiaries* in the temple of their [regenerate] souls. *Rev. T. Adams*, Works, II. 55.

The *residentiary*, or the frequent visitor of the favoured spot. *Coleridge.*

2. An ecclesiastic who keeps a certain residence.

It was not then unusual, in such great churches, to have many men who were temporary *residentiaries*, but of an apostolical and episcopal authority.
Jer. Taylor, Works (ed. 1835), II. 183.

residentiaryship (rez-i-den'shiạ̄-ri-ship), *n.* [< *residentiary* + *-ship*.] The station of a residentiary. *Imp. Dict.*

residentship (rez'i-dẹnt-ship), *n.* [< *resident* + *-ship*.] The functions or dignity of a resident; the condition or station of a resident.

The Prince Elector did afterwards kindly invite him [Theodore Haak] to be his Secretary, but he, loving Solitude, declined that employment, as he did the *Residentship* at London for the City of Hamburgh.
Wood, Athenæ Oxon., II. 845.

resider (rẹ-zī'dėr), *n.* One who resides or has residence.

residew†, *n.* An obsolete form of *residue*.

residual (rẹ-zid'ụ̄-al), *a.* and *n.* [= F. *résiduel*, < NL. **residualis*, < L. *residuum*, residue: see *residuum*, *residue*.] **I.** *a.* Pertaining to or having the character of a residuum; remaining.—**Residual abscess.** (*a*) A collection of pus forming in or around the cicatrix of a previous inflammation. (*b*) A chronic abscess in which the contents have been mostly absorbed.—**Residual air.** See *air*1.—**Residual analysis**†, the calculus of differences. This is the old designation, employed by Landen, 1764.—**Residual calculus**, the calculus of residuals or residues. See II.—**Residual charge**, a charge of electricity spontaneously acquired by coated glass, or any other coated dielectric arranged as a condenser after a discharge, apparently owing to the slow return to the surface of that part of the original charge which had penetrated within the dielectric, as in the Leyden jar. (*Faraday.*) In such cases there is said to be electric absorption. It is doubtless due to the fact that the solid dielectric does not immediately recover from the strain resulting from the electric stress. Also called *dielectric after-working*.—**Residual estate**, residuary estate.—**Residual figure**, in *geom.*, the figure remaining after subtracting a less from a greater.—**Residual magnetism.** See *magnetism*.—**Residual quantity**, in *alg.*, a binomial connected by the sign − (minus): thus, $a - b$, $a - \sqrt{b}$ are *residual quantities*.

II. *n.* 1. A remainder; especially, the remainder of an observed quantity, after subtracting so much as can be accounted for in a given way.—2. The integral of a function round a closed contour in the plane of imaginary quantity inclosing a value for which the function becomes infinite, this integral being divided by $2\pi i$. An earlier definition, amounting to the same thing, was the coefficient of x^{-1} in the development of the function *a* in a sum of two series, one according to ascending, the other according to descending powers of *x*. If the oval includes only one value for which the function becomes infinite, the residual is said to be taken for or with respect to that value. Also *residue*.

3. A system of points which, together with another system of points of which it is said to be the residual, makes up all the intersections of a given curve with a plane cubic curve.—**Integral residual**, the residual obtained by extending the integration round a contour including several values of the variable for which the function becomes infinite.—**Total residual**, the residual obtained by integrating round a contour including all the values of the variable for which the function becomes infinite. Also called *principal residual*.

residuary (rē̤-zid̤'ṳ̄-ā̤-ri), *a.* [= F. *résiduaire*, < NL. **residuarius*, < L. *residuum*, residue: see *residuum*, *residue*.] Of or pertaining to a residue or residuum; forming a residue, or part not dealt with: as, *residuary* estate (the portion of a testator's estate not devised specially).

'Tis enough to lose the legacy, or the *residuary* advantage of the estate left him by the deceased. *Ayliffe*, Parergon.

Residuary clause, that part of a will which in general language gives whatever may be left after satisfying the other provisions of the will.—**Residuary devisee** or **legatee**, in *law*, the legatee to whom is bequeathed the residuum.—**Residuary gum**, the dark residuary matter from the treatment of oils and fats in the manufacture of stearin, used in coating fabrics for the manufacture of roofing.—**Residuary legacy.** See *legacy*.

residuate (rē̤-zid̤'ṳ̄-āt), *v. t.*; pret. and pp. *residuated*, ppr. *residuating*. [< *residu(al)* + *-ate*[2].] In *math.*, to find the residual of, in the sense of the quotient of $2\pi i$ into the integral round one or more poles.

residuation (rē̤-zid̤-ṳ̄-ā'shon̤), *n.* [< *residuate* + *-ion*.] In *math.*, the act of finding the residual or integral round a pole divided by $2\pi i$; the process of finding residuals and co-residuals upon a cubic curve by linear constructions.—**Sign of residuation**, the sign $\mathcal{E}$ prefixed to the expression of a function to denote the residual. The rules for the use of this sign are not entirely consistent.

residue (rez'i-dṳ̄), *n.* [Early mod. E. also *residew*; < ME. *residue*, < OF. *residu*, F. *résidu* = Sp. Pg. It. *residuo*, < L. *residuum*, a remainder, neut. of *residuus*, remaining, < *residere*, remain, reside: see *reside*. Doublet of *residuum*.] 1. That which remains after a part is taken, separated, removed, or dealt with in some other way; what is left over; remainder; the rest.

John for his charge taking Asia, and so the *residue* other quarters to labour in. *Hooker*, Eccles. Polity, vii. 4.

The *residue* of your fortune
Go to my cave and tell me.
Shak., As you Like it, ii. 7. 196.

2. In *law*: (*a*) The residuum of a testator's estate after payment of debts and legacies. (*b*) That which remains of a testator's estate after payment of debts and particular legacies, and is undisposed of except it may be by a general clause or residuary legacy.—3. In the theory of numbers, the remainder after division, especially after division by a fixed modulus; in the integral calculus, the integral of a monodromic function taken round a pole or poles: same as *residual*, 2.—**Biquadratic residue**, the same as a *cubic residue*, except that it refers to a fourth power instead of to a cube. Thus, any fourth power of an integer divided by 5 gives as remainder either 0 or 1. These are, therefore, the *biquadratic residues* of 5.—**Cubic residue**, a number which, being added to a multiple of a number of which it is said to be a residue, gives a cube. Thus, every exact cube divided by 7 gives as remainder either 0, 1, or 6. These are, therefore, the *cubic residues* of 7.—**Method of residues.** See *method*.—**Quadratic residue.** See *quadratic*.—**Trigonal residue**, a number which, added to a multiple of another number of which it is said to be a residue, will give a trigonal number. Thus, 1, 3, 6, 10, 2, 8, are the *trigonal residues* of 13.=**Syn.** 1. *Rest*, etc. See *remainder*.

residuent (rē̤-zid̤'ṳ̄-ent), *n.* [< *residu(um)* + *-ent*.] In *chemical processes*, a by-product, or waste product, left after the removal or separation of a principal product.

residuous (rē̤-zid̤'ṳ̄-us), *a.* [< L. *residuus*, remaining, residual: see *residue*, *residuum*.] Remaining; residual. *Landor.* [Rare.]

residuum (rē̤-zid̤'ṳ̄-um), *n.* [< L. *residuum*, what remains: see *residue*. Doublet of *residue*.] 1. That which is left after any process; that which remains; a residue.

The metal [copper] is pronounced to be chemically pure, leaving no *residuum* when dissolved in pure nitric acid. *W. F. Rae*, Newfoundland to Manitoba, vi.

Residuum shall be understood to be the refuse from the distillation of Crude Petroleum, free from coke and water, and from any foreign impurities, and of gravity from 16° to 21° Beaumé. *New York Produce Exchange Report* (1888–9), p. 279.

2. Specifically, in *law*, that part of an estate which is left after the payment of charges, debts, and particular bequests; more strictly, the part so left which is effectively disposed of by a residuary clause. Sometimes the subject of a particular bequest which proves ineffectual passes by law to the heir or next of kin, instead of falling into the residuum.

resign[1] (rē̤-zīn'), *v.* [< ME. *resignen*, *resynen*, < OF. *resiner*, *resigner*, F. *résigner* (> G. *resigniren* = Dan. *resignere* = Sw. *resignera*) = Pr. Sp. Pg. *resignar* = It. *risegnare*, *rassegnare*, < L. *resignare*, unseal, annul, assign back, resign, lit. 'sign back or again,' < *re-*, back, + *signare*, sign: see *sign*.] **I.** *trans.* 1. To assign back: return formally; give up; give back, as an office or a commission, to the person or authority that conferred it; hence, to surrender; relinquish; give over; renounce.

As yow [Love] list, ye maken hertes digne;
Algates hem that ye wol sette a fyre,
They dreden shame and vices they *resigne*.
Chaucer, Troilus, iii. 25.

He [More] had *resigned* up his office, and the King had graciously accepted it.
Family of Sir T. More, Int. to Utopia, p. xv.

The Earl of Worcester
Hath broke his staff, *resign'd* his stewardship.
Shak., Rich. II., ii. 2. 59.

What sinners value I *resign*;
Lord! 'tis enough that thou art mine. *Watts.*

2. To withdraw, as a claim; give up; abandon.

Soon *resigned* his former suit. *Spenser.*

Passionate hopes not ill *resign'd*
For quiet, and a fearless mind!
M. Arnold, Resignation.

3. To yield or give up in a confiding or trusting spirit; submit, particularly to Providence.

What more reasonable than that we should in all things *resign* up ourselves to the will of God? *Tillotson.*

Then to the sleep I crave
Resign me. *Bryant*, A Sick-bed.

4. To submit without resistance; yield; commit.

Be that thou hop'st to be, or what thou art
Resign to death. *Shak.*, 2 Hen. VI., iii. 1. 334.

He, cruel and ungrateful, smil'd
When she *resign'd* her Breath.
Prior, The Viceroy, st. 32.

Æneas heard, and for a space *resign'd*
To tender pity all his manly mind.
Pope, Iliad, xiii. 590.

5†. To intrust; consign; commit to the care of.

Gentlemen of quality have been sent beyond the seas, *resigned* and concredited to the conduct of such as they call governors. *Evelyn.*

=**Syn.** 1. To abandon, renounce, abdicate. *Resign* differs from the words compared under *forsake* in expressing primarily a formal and deliberate act, in being the ordinary word for giving up formally an elective office or an appointment, and in having similar figurative use.

II. *intrans.* 1. To submit one's self; yield; endure with resignation.

O break, my heart! poor bankrupt, break at once! . . .
Vile earth, to earth *resign*; end motion here.
Shak., R. and J., iii. 2. 59.

Amazed, confused, he found his power expired,
Resign'd to fate, and with a sigh retired.
Pope, R. of the L., iii. 146.

2. To give up an office, commission, post, or the like.

resign[1]† (rē̤-zīn'), *n.* [< *resign*[1], *v.*] Resignation.

You have gain'd more in a royal brother
Than you could lose by your *resign* of Empire.
Shirley (*and Fletcher* ?), Coronation, iv. 2.

resign[2] (rē-sīn'), *v. t.* [< *re-* + *sign*.] To sign again.

resignal† (rē̤-zī'nal̤), *n.* [< *resign*[1] + *-al*.] Resignation.

A bold and just challenge of an old Judge [Samuel] made before all the people upon his *resignal* of the government into the hands of a new King.
Sanderson, Works, II. 330. (*Davies.*)

resignant (rez'ig-nant), *a.* [< F. *résignant*, ppr. of *résigner*, resign: see *resign*[1].] In *her.*, concealed: said of a lion's tail.

resignant† (rē̤-zī'nant), *n.* [< OF. *resignant* (= Sp. Pg. *resignante*), a resigner, ppr. of *resigner*, resign: see *resign*[1].] A resigner.

Upon the 25th of October Sir John Suckling brought the warrant from the King to receive the Seal; and the good news came together, very welcome to the *resignant*, that Sir Thomas Coventry should have that honour.
Bp. Hacket, Abp. Williams, ii. 27. (*Davies.*)

resignation (rez-ig-nā'shon̤), *n.* [< OF. *resignation*, *resignacion*, F. *résignation* = Pr. *resignatio* = Sp. *resignacion* = Pg. *resignação* = It. *rassegnazione*, *risegnazione*, < ML. (f) *resignatio(n-)*, < L. *resignare*, resign: see *resign*[1].] 1. The act of resigning or giving up, as a claim, office, place, or possession.

The *resignation* of thy state and crown
To Henry Bolingbroke.
Shak., Rich. II., iv. 1. 179.

2. The state of being resigned or submissive; unresisting acquiescence; particularly, quiet submission to the will of Providence; contented submission.

But on he moves to meet his latter end. . . .
Sinks to the grave with unperceiv'd decay,
While *resignation* gently slopes the way.
Goldsmith, Des. Vil., l. 110.

3. In *Scots law*, the form by which a vassal returns the feu into the hands of a superior. =**Syn.** 1. Relinquishment, renunciation.—2. *Endurance*, *Fortitude*, etc. See *patience*.

resigned (rē̤-zīnd'), *p. a.* 1. Surrendered: given up.—2. Feeling resignation; submissive.

What shall I do (she cried), my peace of mind
To gain in dying, and to die *resign'd*!
Crabbe, Works, I. 112.

=**Syn.** 2. Unresisting, yielding, uncomplaining, meek. See *patience*.

resignedly (rē̤-zī'ned-li), *adv.* With resignation; submissively.

resignee (rē̤-zī-nē'), *n.* [< F. *résigné*, pp. of *résigner*, resign: see *resign*[1].] In *law*, the party to whom a thing is resigned.

resigner (rē-zī'nėr), *n.* One who resigns.

resignment (rē̤-zīn'ment̤), *n.* [< *resign*[1] + *-ment*.] The act of resigning.

Here I am, by his command, to cure you,
Nay, more, for ever, by his full *resignment*.
Beau. and Fl., Mons. Thomas, iii. 1.

resile (rē̤-zīl'), *v. i.*; pret. and pp. *resiled*, ppr. *resiling*. [< OF. *resilir*, *resiler*, F. *résilier*, < L. *resilire*, jump back, recoil, < *re-*, back, + *salire*, jump, leap: see *salient*, and cf. *resilient*.] To start back; recede, as from a purpose; recoil.

If the Quene wold herafter *resile* and goo back from that she semeth nowe to be contented with, it shuld not be in her power soo to doo.
State Papers, i. 343. (*Halliwell.*)

The small majority . . . *resiling* from their own previously professed intention. *Sir W. Hamilton.*

resilement (rē̤-zīl'ment̤), *n.* [< *resile* + *-ment*.] The act of drawing back; a recoil; a withdrawal. *Imp. Dict.*, art. "back," adv., 7.

resilience (rē̤-zil'i-ens̤), *n.* [= It. *resilienza*; as *resilien(t)* + *-ce*.] 1. The act of resiling, leaping, or springing back; the act of rebounding.

If you strike a ball side-long, not full upon the surface, the rebound will be as much the contrary way; whether there be any such *resilience* in ecchos . . . may be tried.
Bacon, Nat. Hist., § 245.

2. In *mech.* See the quotation.

The word *resilience*, used without special qualifications, may be understood as meaning *extreme resilience*, or the work given back by the spring after being strained to the extreme limit within which it can be strained again and again without breaking or taking a permanent set.
Thomson and Tait, Nat. Phil., § 601, b.

Coefficient of resilience. Same as *coefficient of elasticity* (which see, under *coefficient*).

resiliency (rē̤-zil'i-en̤-si), *n.* [As *resilience* (see *-cy*).] Same as *resilience*.

The common *resiliency* of the mind from one extreme to the other. *Johnson*, Rambler, No. 110.

resilient (rē̤-zil'i-ent̤), *a.* [< L. *resilien(t-)s*, ppr. of *resilire*, leap back: see *resile*.] Having resilience; inclined to leap or spring back; leaping or springing back; rebounding.

Their act and reach
Stretch'd to the farthest is *resilient* ever.
And in resilience hath its plenary force.
Sir H. Taylor, Edwin the Fair, iii. 5.

A highly *resilient* body is a body which has large coefficients of resilience. Steel is an example of a body with large, and cork of a body with small, coefficients of resilience. *J. D. Everett*, Units and Phys. Const., p. 46.

Resilient stricture, a contractile stricture formed by elastic tissue, and making permanent dilatation impossible or difficult.

resilition (rez-i-lish'on), *n.* [Irreg. < *resile* + *-ition.*] The act of resiling or springing back; resilience. [Rare.]

The act of flying back in consequence of motion resisted: *resilition.* *Johnson's Dict.* (under *rebound*).

resiluation† (rē-zil-ū-ā'shon), *n.* [Prob. irreg. (in late ML. medical jargon?) < L. *resilire* (pp. *resultus*), spring back: see *resilient.*] Resilience; renewed attack.

There is, as phisicians saye, and as we also fynd, double the perell in the *resiluacion* that was in the fyrste sycknes. *Hall*, Edward V., f. 11. (*Halliwell.*)

The *resiluation* of an Ague is desperate, and the second opening of a veyne deadly. *Lyly*, Euphues and his England, p. 316.

resin (rez'in), *n.* [Also *rosin*, q. v.; early mod. E. also *rasin*; < ME. *recyn*, *recyne*, also *rosyn*, *rosyne*, < OF. *resine* (also *rosine*, *rasine*), F. *résine* = Sp. Pg. It. *resina*, < L. *resina*, prob. < Gr. ῥητίνη, resin (of the pine).] **1.** (*a*) A hardened secretion found in many species of plants, or a substance produced by exposure of the secretion to the air. It is allied to and probably derived from a volatile oil. The typical resins are oxidized hydrocarbons, amorphous, brittle, having a vitreous fracture, insoluble in water, and freely soluble in alcohol, ether, and volatile oils. They unite with alkalis to form soaps. They melt at a low heat, are non-volatile, and burn quickly with a smoky flame. The hardest resins are fossilized like amber and copal, but they show all gradations of hardness through oleoresins and balsams to essential oils. The *hard resins* are nearly inodorous, and contain little or no volatile oil; the *soft resins* owe their softness to the volatile oil associated with them. The common resin of commerce exudes in a semi-fluid state from several species of pine (in the United States, chiefly the long-leaved pine). From this the oil of turpentine is separated by distillation. Resins are largely used in the preparation of varnishes, and several are used in medicine. See *gum.* (*b*) The precipitate formed by treating a tincture with water.

2. See *rosin*, 2.—**Acaroid resin.** See *acaroid.*—**Aldehyde resin.** See *aldehyde.*—**Bile-resin**, a name given to the bile-acids.—**Blackboy resin.** Same as *blackboy gum.* See *blackboy.*—**Bon-nafa resin**, an amber-yellow resin prepared in Algeria from *Thapsia Garganica.*—**Botany Bay resin.** Same as *acaroid gum* (which see, under *acaroid*).—**Carbolized resin-cloth**, an antiseptic dressing made by steeping thin calico muslin in carbolic acid, 2 parts; castor-oil, 2; resin, 16; alcohol, 40.—**Fossil or mineral resins**, amber, petroleum, asphalt, bitumen, and other mineral hydrocarbons.—**Grass-tree resin.** Same as *acaroid resin.*—**Highgate resin**, fossil copal: named from Highgate, near London. See *copalin.*—**Kauri-resin.** Same as *kauri-gum.*—**Piny resin.** See *pinyl.*—**Resin cerate**, a cerate composed of 35 parts of resin, 15 of yellow wax, and 50 of lard.—**Resin core**, in *founding.* See *core*[1].—**Resin of copaiba**, the residue left after distilling the volatile oil from copaiba.—**Resin of copper**, copper protochlorid: so called from its resemblance to common resin.—**Resin of guaiac**, the resin of the wood of *Guaiacum officinale*: same as *guaiacum*, 3. Also called *guaiac* and *guaiaci resina.*—**Resin of jalap**, the resin obtained by treating the strong tincture of the tuberous root of *Ipomœa purga* with water. It is purgative in its action.—**Resin of Leptandra**, the resin obtained from *Veronica Virginica.*—**Resin of podophyllum**, the resin obtained by precipitation with water from a concentrated tincture of podophyllum. It is cathartic in its action.—**Resin of scammony**, the resin obtained from tincture of scammony by precipitation with water or by evaporation of the clarified tincture.—**Resin of thapsia**, a resin obtained from *Thapsia garganica* by evaporating the tincture: used as a counter-irritant. Also called *thapsia-resin* and *resina thapsiæ.*—**Resin of turpeth**, a resin obtained from the root-bark of *Ipomœa Turpethum.*—**Resin ointment, plaster**, etc. See *ointment*, *plaster*, etc.—**White resin.** See *rosin.*—**Yellow resin.** See *rosin.*

resin (rez'in), *v. t.* [< *resin*, *n.*] To treat, rub, or coat with resin.

resina (re-zī'nä), *n.* [L.: see *resin.*] Resin.

resinaceous (rez-i-nā'shius), *a.* [< L. *resinaceus*, < *resina*, resin: see *resin.*] Resinous; having the quality of resin. *Imp. Dict.*

resinata (rez-i-nā'tä), *n.* [< L. *resinata*, fem. of *resinatus*, resined: see *resinate.*] The common white wine used in Greece, which is generally kept in goat- or pig-skins, and has its peculiar flavor from the pine resin or pitch with which the skins are smeared on the inside.

resinate (rez'i-nāt), *v. t.*; pret. and pp. *resinated*, ppr. *resinating.* [< L. *resinatus*, resined (*vinum resinatum*, resined wine), < *resina*, resin: see *resin.*] To flavor or impregnate with resin, as the ordinary white wine of modern Greece.

resinate (rez'i-nāt), *n.* [= F. *résinate*, < NL. *resinatum*, neut. of *resinatus*, resined: see *resinate*, *v.*] A salt of the acids obtained from turpentine.

resin-bush (rez'in-bush), *n.* See *mastic* 2.

resin-cell (rez'in-sel), *n.* In *bot.*, a cell which has the office of secreting resin.

resin-duct (rez'in-dukt), *n.* In *bot.*, same as *resin-passage.*

resin-flux (rez'in-fluks), *n.* A disease in conifers characterized by a copious flow of resin, with the ultimate death of the tree, due to the attacks of a fungus, *Agaricus melleus.* *De Bary.*

resin-gland (rez'in-gland), *n.* In *bot.*, a cell or a small group of cells which secrete or contain resin.

resiniferous (rez-i-nif'e-rus), *a.* [= F. *résinifère* = It. *resinifero*, < L. *resina*, resin, + *ferre*, = E. *bear*[1].] Yielding resin: as, a *resiniferous* tree or vessel.

resinification (rez"i-ni-fi-kā'shon), *n.* [= F. *résinification*, < *résinifier*, treat with resin: see *resinify.*] The act or process of treating with resin.

The *resinification* of the drying oils may be effected by the smallest quantities of certain substances. *Ure*, Dict., III. 448.

resiniform (rez'i-ni-fôrm), *a.* [< F. *résiniforme*, < L. *resina*, resin, + *forma*, shape.] Having the character of resin; resinoid. *Imp. Dict.*

resinify (rez'i-ni-fī), *v.*; pret. and pp. *resinified*, ppr. *resinifying.* [< F. *résinifier*, < L. *resina*, resin, + *-ficare*, < *facere*, make: see *resin* and *-fy.*] **I.** *trans.* To change into resin; cause to become resinous.

II. *intrans.* To become resinous; be transformed into resin.

Exposed to the air, it [volatile oil obtained from hops by distillation with water] *resinifies.* *Encyc. Brit.*, XII. 157.

resinize (rez'i-nīz), *v. t.*; pret. and pp. *resinized*, ppr. *resinizing.* [< *resin* + *-ize.*] To treat with resin.

resino-electric (rez"i-nō-ē-lek'trik), *a.* Containing or exhibiting negative electricity: applied to certain substances, as amber, sealing-wax, etc., which become resinously or negatively electric under friction.

resinoid (rez'i-noid), *a.* and *n.* [= F. *résinoïde*, < L. *resina*, resin, + Gr. εἶδος, form. Cf. Gr. ῥητινώδης, resinoid.] **I.** *a.* Resembling resin.

Minute *resinoid* yellowish-brown granules. *W. B. Carpenter*, Micros., § 696.

II. *n.* A resinous substance, either a true resin or a mixture containing one.

resinous (rez'i-nus), *a.* [< OF. *resineux*, F. *résineux* = Sp. Pg. It. *resinoso*, < L. *resinosus*, full of resin, < *resina*, resin: see *resin.*] Pertaining to or obtained from resin; partaking of the properties of resin; like resin: as, *resinous* substances.—**Resinous electricity.** See *electricity.*—**Resinous luster.** See *luster*[2], 2.

resinously (rez'i-nus-li), *adv.* In the manner of a resinous body; also, by means of resin.

If any body become electrified in any way, it must become either vitreously or *resinously* electrified. *A. Daniell*, Prin. of Physics, p. 519.

resinousness (rez'i-nus-nes), *n.* The character of being resinous.

resin-passage (rez'in-pas"āj), *n.* In *bot.*, an intercellular canal in which resin is secreted.

resin-tube (rez'in-tūb), *n.* In *bot.*, same as *resin-passage.*

resiny (rez'i-ni), *a.* [< *resin* + *-y*[1].] Having a resinous character; containing or covered with resin.

resipiscence (res-i-pis'ens), *n.* [< OF. *resipiscence*, F. *résipiscence* = It. *resipiscenza*, < L. *resipiscentia*, a change of mind, repentance (tr. Gr. μετάνοια), < *resipiscere*, repent.] Change to a better frame of mind; repentance. The term is never used for that regret of a vicious man at letting pass an opportunity of vice or crime which is sometimes called *repentance.* [Rare.]

They drew a flattering picture of the *resipiscence* of the Anglican party. *Hallam.*

resipiscent (res-i-pis'ent), *a.* [< L. *resipiscen(t-)s*, ppr. of *resipiscere*, recover one's senses, come to oneself again, recover, inceptive of *resipere*, savor, taste of, < *re-*, again, + *sapere*, taste, also be wise: see *sapient.*] Restored to one's senses; right-minded. [Rare.]

Grammar, in the end, *resipiscent* and sane as of old, goes forth properly clothed and in its right mind. *F. Hall*, False Philol., p. 67.

resist (rē-zist'), *v.* [< OF. *resister*, F. *résister* = Pr. Sp. Pg. *resistir* = It. *resistere*, < L. *resistere*, stand back, stand still, withstand, resist, < *re-*, back, + *sistere*, make to stand, set, also stand fast, causative of *stare*, stand: see *stand.* Cf. *assist*, *consist*, *desist*, *exist*, *insist*, *persist.*] **I.** *trans.* **1.** To withstand; oppose passively or actively; antagonize; act against; exert physical or moral force in opposition to.

Either side of the bank being fringed with most beautiful trees, which *resisted* the sun's darts from over-much piercing the natural coldness of the river. *Sir P. Sidney*, Arcadia, ii.

Resist the devil, and he will flee from you. Jas. iv. 7.

The sword
Of Michael, from the armoury of God,
Was given him, temper'd so that neither keen
Nor solid might *resist* that edge.
Milton, P. L., vi. 323.

That which gives me most Hopes of her is her telling me of the many Temptations she has *resisted.* *Congreve*, Double-Dealer, iii. 5.

While self-dependent power can time defy,
As rocks *resist* the billows and the sky.
Goldsmith, Des. Vil., l. 430.

What 's done we partly may compute,
But know not what 's *resisted.*
Burns, To the Unco Guid.

2†. To be disagreeable or distasteful to; offend.

These cates *resist* me, she but thought upon. *Shak.*, Pericles, ii. 3. 29.

=**Syn.** 1. *Withstand*, etc. See *oppose.*

II. *intrans.* To make opposition; act in opposition.

Lay hold upon him; if he do *resist*,
Subdue him at his peril.
Shak., Othello, i. 2. 80.

resist (rē-zist'), *n.* [< *resist*, *v.*] **1.** Any composition applied to a surface to protect it from chemical action, as to enable it to resist the corrosion of acids, etc.

This latter metal [steel] requires to be preserved against the action of the cleansing acids and of the graining mixture by a composition called *resist.* *Workshop Receipts*, 1st ser., p. 199.

2. Specifically, in *calico-printing*, a sort of paste applied to a fabric to prevent color or mordant from fixing on those parts not intended to be colored, either by acting mechanically in preventing the color, etc., from reaching the cloth, or chemically in changing the color so as to render it incapable of fixing itself in the fibers. Also called *resist-paste*, *resistant*, and *reserve.*—**3.** A stopping-out; also, the material used for stopping out.—**Resist style**, in *calico-printing*, the process of dyeing in a pattern by the use of a resist.

resistal (rē-zis'tal), *n.* Resistance. [Rare.]

All *resistalls*,
Quarrels, and ripping up of injuries
Are smother'd in the ashes of our wrath,
Whose fire is now extinct.
Heywood, Fair Maid of the West (Works, ed. Pearson, 1874, [II. 401).

resistance (rē-zis'tans), *n.* [Also *resistence*; < ME. *resistence*, < OF. *resistence*, later *resistance*, F. *résistance* = Pr. Sp. Pg. *resistencia* = It. *resistenza*, < ML. **resistentia*, < L. *resisten(t-)s*, ppr. of *resistere*, resist: see *resist*, *resistant.*] **1.** The act of resisting; opposition; antagonism. Resistance is *passive*, as that of a fixed body which interrupts the passage of a moving body; or *active*, as in the exertion of force to stop, repel, or defeat progress or design.

Nae *resistans* durst they mak.
Battle of Harlaw (Child's Ballads, VII. 183).

He'll not swagger with a Barbary hen, if her feathers turn back in any show of *resistance.* *Shak.*, 2 Hen. IV., ii. 4. 109.

2. The force exerted by a fluid or other medium to retard the motion of a body through it; more generally, any force which always acts in a direction opposite to the residual velocity, or to any component of it: as, *resistance* to shearing. In a phrase like this, *resistance* may be defined as a stress produced by a strain, and tending to restoration of figure. But the resistance is not necessarily elastic—that is, it may cease, and as resistance does cease, when the velocity vanishes. In the older dynamical treatises, resistance is always considered as a function of the velocity, except in the case of friction, which does not vary with the velocity, or at least not much. In modern hydrodynamics the viscosity is taken into account, and produces a kind of resistance partly proportional to the velocity and partly to the acceleration. The theory of resistance still remains imperfect.

Energy, which is force acting, does work in overcoming *Resistance*, which is force acted on and reacting. *G. H. Lewes*, Probs. of Life and Mind, II. v. § 5.

3. In *elect.*, that property of a conductor in virtue of which the passage of a current through it is accompanied by a dissipation of energy; the transformation of electric energy into heat. It is one of the two elements upon which the strength of an electric current depends when the flow is steady; the other is electromotive force, and the relation between them is generally expressed by the equation $C = E/R$, which is Ohm's law. *Resistance* may therefore be defined as the ratio of the electromotive force to the current strength ($R = E/C$), the flow being assumed to be steady. For simple periodic alternate currents, the resistance increases as the rapidity of alternation increases, and it also depends on the form of the conductor. Resistance to such currents is sometimes called *impedance* and also *virtual resistance*, that for steady flow being named *ohmic resistance.* In general, resistance is proportional to the length of the conductor and inversely proportional to its cross-section. It also varies with the temperature of the conductor, the nature of the material of which it is composed, the stress to which it is subjected, and in some instances with other physical conditions, as in the case of selenium, the resistance of which diminishes as the intensity of the light to which it is exposed increases. It is the reciprocal of conductivity. The unit of resistance is the ohm (which see). The designation *resistance* is also applied to coils of wire or other material devices which are introduced into electric circuits on account of the resistance which they offer to the passage of the current. The resistance of a conductor may be measured by Wheatstone's bridge. This is a device for the accurate comparison of electric resistances, invented by Christie and brought into notice by Wheatstone. It consists essentially of a complex circuit of six conductors, arranged as shown in the cut. A current from the battery B enters at the junction of *a* and *c*, and, after dividing into parts depending on the relative resistances of the branches *a*, *b*, *c*, and *d*, returns to the battery through the junction of *b* and *d*. G is a galvanometer joined to the junctions *a b* and *c d*. When the relative resistances are such that *a* : *b* : : *c* : *d*, no current will flow through the galvanometer. If *a* and *b* are comparable and adjustable resistances, it is only necessary to establish this condition in order to know the ratio of *c* to *d*. Many modifications of the bridge have been devised.—**Center of resistance.** See *center*¹.—**Conduction resistance,** the resistance offered by a conductor to an electric current.—**Contact resistance.** See *contact*.—**Curve of elastic resistance.** See *curve*.—**Living resistance,** the work required to produce a sudden strain of a body, especially a sudden elongation of a solid.—**Magnetic resistance,** the reciprocal of magnetic conductivity or permeability. The magnetic flux, or total number of magnetic lines of force passing through a cross-section of any magnetic circuit, may be given in an expression analogous to that giving the strength of an electric current in terms of the electromotive force and resistance. The denominator of the fraction represents the magnetic resistance, sometimes called *magnetic reluctance*.—**Passive resistance,** a friction or similar force opposing the motion of a machine.—**Principle of least resistance,** the principle that when a structure is in equilibrium the passive forces, or stresses occasioned by minute strains, are the least that are capable of balancing the active forces, or those which are independent of the strains.—**Solid of least resistance,** in *mech.*, the solid whose figure is such that in its motion through a fluid it sustains less resistance than any other having the same length and base, or, on the other hand, being stationary in a current of fluid, offers the least interruption to the progress of that fluid. In the former case it has been considered the best form for the stem of a ship; in the latter, the proper form for the pier of a bridge. The problem of finding the solid of least resistance was first proposed and solved by Newton, but only for hypothetical conditions extremely remote from those of nature.—**Specific resistance,** the resistance offered by a conductor of any given material the length of which is one centimeter and the cross-section one square centimeter.—**Transition resistance,** the resistance to an electric current in electrolysis caused by the presence of the ions at the electrodes. = **Syn. 1.** Hindrance, antagonism, check. See *oppose*.

Wheatstone Bridge.

resistance-box (rę̄-zis'tąns-boks), *n.* A box containing one or more resistance-coils.

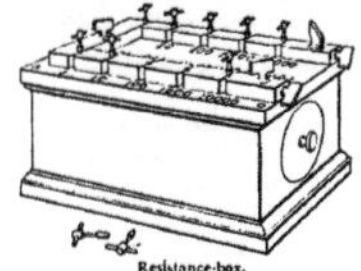

Resistance-box.

resistance-coil (rę̄-zis'tąns-koil), *n.* A coil of wire which offers a definite resistance to the passage of a current of electricity. Resistance-coils are generally of German-silver wire, on account of the low temperature coefficient of that alloy, and are usually multiples or submultiples of the unit of resistance, the ohm.

resistant (rę̄-zis'tąnt), *a.* and *n.* [Also *resistent*; < OF. *resistant*, F. *résistant* = Sp. Pg. It. *resistente*, < L. *resisten(t-)s*, ppr. of *resistere*, withstand, resist: see *resist*.] **I.** *a.* Making resistance; resisting.

> This Excommunication . . . simplified and ennobled the *resistant* position of Savonarola.
> *George Eliot*, Romola, lv.

II. *n.* **1.** One who or that which resists.

> According to the degrees of power in the agent and *resistant* is an action performed or hindered.
> *Bp. Pearson*, Expos. of Creed, vi.

2. Same as *resist*, 2.

> The first crops of citric acid crystals, which are brownish in colour, are used largely by the calico-printer as a *resistant* for iron and alumina mordants.
> *Spons' Encyc. Manuf.*, I. 50.

resistence (rę̄-zis'tęns), *n.* Same as *resistance*.

resistent (rę̄-zis'tęnt), *a.* Same as *resistant*.

resister (rę̄-zis'tėr), *n.* One who resists; one who opposes or withstands.

resistibility (rę̄-zis-ti-bil'į-ti), *n.* [= F. *résistibilité*; as *resistible* + *-ity* (see *-bility*).] **1.** The property of being resistible.

> Whether the *resistibility* of his reason did not equivalence the facility of her seduction.
> *Sir T. Browne*, Vulg. Err., i. 1.

2†. The property of resisting.

> The same body being the complex idea of extension and *resistibility* together in the same subject, these two ideas are not exactly one and the same. *Locke.*

resistible (rę̄-zis'ti-bl), *a.* [= F. *résistible* = Sp. *resistible* = Pg. *resistivel*; as *resist* + *-ible*.] Capable of being resisted: as, a *resistible* force.

resistibleness (rę̄-zis'ti-bl-nes), *n.* The property of being resistible; resistibility.

resistibly (rę̄-zis'ti-bli), *adv.* So as to be resistible.

resistingly (rę̄-zis'ting-li), *adv.* With resistance or opposition; so as to resist.

resistive (rę̄-zis'tiv), *a.* [< *resist* + *-ive*.] Having the power to resist; resisting.

> I'll have an excellent new fucus made,
> *Resistive* 'gainst the sun, the rain, or wind.
> *B. Jonson*, Sejanus, ii. 1.

resistively (rę̄-zis'tiv-li), *adv.* With or by means of resistance.

> Flexion and extension of the leg at the knee, either passively or *resistively*.
> *Buck's Handbook of Med. Sciences*, IV. 649.

resistivity (rē-zis-tiv'į-ti), *n.* The power or property of resistance; capacity for resisting.

> The *resistivity* of the wires. *Elect. Rev.* (Eng.), XXV. 641.

resistless (rę̄-zist'les), *a.* [< *resist* + *-less*.] **1.** Incapable of being resisted, opposed, or withstood; irresistible.

> Masters' commands come with a power *resistless*
> To such as owe them absolute subjection.
> *Milton*, S. A., l. 1404.

2. Powerless to resist; helpless; unresisting.

> Open an entrance for the wasteful sea,
> Whose billows, beating the *resistless* banks,
> Shall overflow it with their refluence.
> *Marlowe*, Jew of Malta, iii. 5. 17.
>
> *Resistless*, tame,
> Am I to be burn'd up? No, I will shout
> Until the gods through heaven's blue look out!
> *Keats*, Endymion, iii.

resistlessly (rę̄-zist'les-li), *adv.* In a resistless manner; so as not to be opposed or denied.

resistlessness (rę̄-zist'les-nes), *n.* The character of being resistless or irresistible.

resist-work (rę̄-zist'wėrk), *n.* Calico-printing in which the pattern is produced wholly or in part by means of resist, which preserves certain parts uncolored.

reskew, reskue†, *v.* and *n.* Obsolete forms of *rescue*.

resmooth (rē-smöᴛʜ'), *v. t.* [< *re-* + *smooth*.] To make smooth again; smooth out.

> And thus your pains
> May only make that footprint upon sand
> Which old-recurring waves of prejudice
> *Resmooth* to nothing. *Tennyson*, Princess, iii.

resolder (rē-sol'dėr), *v. t.* [< *re-* + *solder*.] To solder or mend again; rejoin; make whole again. *Tennyson*, Princess, v.

resoluble (rez'ǫ-lū-bl), *a.* [< OF. *resoluble*, F. *résoluble* = Sp. *resoluble* = It. *resolubile*, < LL. *resolubilis*, < L. *resolvere*, resolve: see *resolve*.] Capable of being resolved.

> The synthetic [Greek compounds] are organic, and, being made up of constituents modified, more or less, with a view to combination, are not thus *resoluble*.
> *F. Hall*, False Philol., p. 42, note.

resolute (rez'ǫ-lūt), *a.* and *n.* [< ME. *resolute* = OF. *resolu*, F. *résolu* = Sp. Pg. *resoluto* = It. *risoluto*, < L. *resolutus*, pp. of *resolvere*, resolve: see *resolve*.] **I.** *a.* **1†.** Separated; loose; broken up; dissolved.

> For bathes boote ammonyake is tolde
> Right goode with brymstone *resolute* ypitte
> Aboute in evry chynyng, clifte, or slitte.
> *Palladius*, Husbondrie (E. E. T. S.), p. 41.

2†. Convinced; satisfied; certain. *Imp. Dict.*—**3†.** Resolving; convincing; satisfying.

> Th[e] interpretour answered, . . . Wyllynge hym to take this for a *resolute* answere, that . . . if he rather desyred warre, he shoulde haue his handes full.
> *R. Eden*, tr. of Pigafetta (First English Books on America, [ed. Arber, p. 256).
>
> I [Luther] have giuen *resolute* answer to the first, in the which I persist, and shall persevere for evermore.
> *Foxe*, Acts, etc. (Cattley ed.), IV. 284.

4. Having a fixed resolve; determined; hence, bold; firm; steady; constant in pursuing a purpose.

> Edward is at hand,
> Ready to fight; therefore be *resolute*.
> *Shak.*, 3 Hen. VI., v. 4. 61.

= **Syn. 4.** Decided, fixed, unshaken, unwavering, staunch, undaunted, steadfast: the place of *resolute* among such words is determined by its fundamental idea, that of a fixed will or purpose, and its acquired idea, that of a firm front and bold action presented to opposers or resisters. It is therefore a high word in the field of will and courage. See *decision*.

II.† *n.* **1.** A resolute or determined person.

> Young Fortinbras . . .
> Hath in the skirts of Norway here and there
> Shark'd up a list of lawless *resolutes*.
> *Shak.*, Hamlet, i. 1. 98.

2. Repayment; redelivery.

> And ye shall enquire of the yearly *resolutes*, deductions, and paiements going forth of the same.
> *Bp. Burnet*, Records, II. i., No. 27.

resolutely (rez'ǫ-lūt-li), *adv.* In a resolute manner; with fixed purpose; firmly; steadily; with steady perseverance; boldly.

resoluteness (rez'ǫ-lūt-nes), *n.* The character of being resolute; fixity of purpose; firm determination; unshaken firmness.

resolution (rez-ǭ-lū'shǫn), *n.* [< OF. *resolution*, F. *résolution* = Pr. *rezolucio* = Sp. *resolucion* = Pg. *resolução* = It. *risoluzione*, < L. *resolutio(n-)*, an untying, unbinding, loosening, relaxing, < *resolvere*, pp. *resolutus*, loose, resolve: see *resolve*.] **1.** The act, operation, or process of resolving. Specifically—(*a*) The act of separating the component parts of a body, as by chemical means or (to the eye) under the lens of a microscope. (*b*) The act of separating the parts which compose a complex idea. (*c*) The act of unraveling a perplexing question, a difficult problem, or the like; explication; solution; answer.

> It is a question
> Needs not a *resolution*.
> *Beau. and Fl.*, Laws of Candy, iv. 1.

(*d*) The act of mathematically analyzing a velocity, force, or other vector quantity into components having different directions, whether these have independent causes or not.

2. The state or process of dissolving; dissolution; solution.

> In the hot springs of extreme cold countries, the first heats are unsufferable, which proceed out of the *resolution* of humidity congealed. *Sir K. Digby*, Bodies.

3. The act of resolving or determining; also, anything resolved or determined upon; a fixed determination of mind; a settled purpose: as, a *resolution* to reform our lives; a *resolution* to undertake an expedition.

> Your *resolution* cannot hold, when 'tis
> Opposed, as it must be, by the power of the king.
> *Shak.*, W. T., iv. 4. 36.
>
> *Resolution*, therefore, means the preliminary volition for ascertaining when to enter upon a series of actions necessarily deferred. *A. Bain*, Emotions and Will, p. 420.

4. The character of acting with fixed purpose; resoluteness; firmness, steadiness, or constancy in execution; determination: as, a man of great *resolution*.

> No want of *resolution* in me, but only my followers' . . . treasons, makes me betake me to my heels.
> *Shak.*, 2 Hen. VI., iv. 8. 65.
>
> Off with thy pining black!—it dulls a soldier—
> And put on *resolution* like a man.
> *Fletcher* (*and another*), False One, iv. 3.

5. A formal proposition brought before a deliberative body for discussion and adoption.

> If the report . . . conclude with *resolutions* or other specific propositions of any kind, . . . the question should be on agreeing to the *resolutions*.
> *Cushing*, Manual of Parliamentary Practice, § 296.

6. A formal determination or decision of a legislative or corporate body, or of any association of individuals, when adopted by vote. See *by-law*, 2, *ordinance*, 7, *regulation*, 2.—**7.** Determination of a cause, as in a court of justice. [Rare.]

> Nor have we all the acts of parliament or of judicial *resolutions* which might occasion such alterations.
> *Sir M. Hale.*

8†. The state of being settled in opinion; freedom from doubt; conviction; certainty.

> Ah, but the *resolution* of thy death
> Made me to lose such thought.
> *Heywood*, Four Prentices.
>
> *Edm.* You shall . . . by an auricular assurance have your satisfaction. . . .
> *Glou.* I would unstate myself, to be in a due *resolution*.
> *Shak.*, Lear, i. 2. 108.

9. In *music*: (*a*) Of a particular voice-part, the act, process, or result of passing from a discord to a concord. See *preparation* and *percussion*. (*b*) The concordant tone in which a discord is merged.—**10.** In *med.*, a removal or disappearance, as the disappearing of a swelling or an inflammation without coming to suppuration, the removal by absorption and expectoration of inflammatory products in pulmonary solidification, or the disappearance of fever.—**11.** In *math.*, same as *solution*.—**12.** In *anc. pros.*: (*a*) The use of two short times or syllables as the equivalent for one long; the division of a disemic time into the two semeia of which it is composed. (*b*) An equivalent of a time or of a foot in which two shorts are substituted for a long: as, the dactyl (– ⏑ ⏑) or anapest (⏑ ⏑ –) is a *resolution* of the spondee (– –). The resolution of a syllable bearing the ictus takes its ictus on the first of the two shorts representing the long (⏑́ ⏑ ⏑ for –́ ⏑, ⏑ ⏑́ ⏑ for ⏑ –́). Opposed to *contraction*.—**Joint resolution**, in *Amer. parliamentary law*, a resolution adopted by both branches of a legislative assembly. See *concurrent resolution*, under *concurrent*.—**Resolution of forces or of velocities**, the application of the principle of the parallelogram of forces or velocities to the mathematical separation of a force or velocity into parts, which, however, need have no independent reality. See *force*1, 8 (*a*).—**The Expunging Resolution.** See *expunge*.—**Virginia and Kentucky Resolutions**, in *U. S. hist.*, resolutions passed in 1798 and 1799 by the legislatures of Virginia and Kentucky, declaring the passage of the Alien and Sedition Acts to be an unconstitutional act of the federal government, and setting forth the States' rights theory as to the proper remedies in such cases. The Virginia Resolutions were prepared by Madison, and the Kentucky Resolutions of 1798 by Jefferson. The Kentucky Resolutions of 1799, in addition to declaring the Constitution a compact, affirmed the right of a State to nullify any Act of Congress which it deemed unconstitutional. =**Syn.** 1. Decomposition, separation, disentanglement.—4. *Determination*, etc. (see *decision*), perseverance, tenacity, inflexibility, fortitude, boldness, courage, resolve.

Resolutioner (rez-ǫ-lū'shǫn-ėr), *n.* One of a party in the Church of Scotland, in the seventeenth century, which approved the resolutions of the General Assembly admitting all except those of bad character, or hostile to the Covenant, to bear arms against Cromwell. See the quotation under *Protester*, 3.

> The church was, however, divided into two utterly antagonistic parties, the *Resolutioners* and the Remonstrants.
> *J. H. Burton*, Hist. Scotland, I. 194.

resolutionist (rez-ǫ-lū'shǫn-ist), *n.* [< *resolution* + *-ist*.] One who makes a resolution. *Quarterly Rev.* (*Imp. Dict.*)

resolutive (rez'ǫ-lū-tiv), *a.* and *n.* [= F. *résolutif* = Sp. Pg. *resolutivo* = It. *risolutivo*, *resolutivo*; as *resolute* + *-ive*.] **I.** *a.* Having the power to dissolve or relax. [Rare.]

> The ashes of the void [snail] shels . . . are of a *resolutive* and discutient facultie. *Holland*, tr. of Pliny, xxx. 8.

Resolutive clause or condition, in *Scots law*, a condition subsequent; a condition inserted in a deed or other contract, a breach of which will cause a forfeiture or cessation of that which is provided for by the instrument, as distinguished from a *suspensive* condition, or condition precedent, which prevents the instrument from taking effect until the condition has been performed.—**Resolutive method**, in *logic*, the analytic method. See *analytic*.

II. *n.* In *med.*, same as *discutient*.

> It has been recommended to establish a seton . . . as a derivative and *resolutive* [in metritis].
> *R. Barnes*, Dis. of Women, xl.

resolutory (rez'ǫ-lū-tǫ-ri), *a.* [= F. *résolutoire* = Sp. Pg. It. *resolutorio*, < L. as if **resolutorius*, < *resolvere*, pp. *resolutus*, loose, loosen: see *resolve*.] Having the effect of resolving, determining, or rescinding; giving a right to rescind.

resolvability (rē-zol-vạ-bil'į-ti), *n.* [< *resolvable* + *-ity* (see *-bility*).] The property of being resolvable; the capability of being separated into parts; resolvableness.

> Lord Rosse was able to get the suggestion of *resolvability* in . . . many bodies which had been classed as nebulæ by Sir William Herschel and others.
> *J. N. Lockyer*, Harper's Mag., LXXVIII. 589.

resolvable (rē-zol'vạ-bl), *a.* [< *resolve* + *-able*. Cf. *resoluble*.] Capable of being resolved, in any sense of that word.—**Resolvable nebula.** See *nebula*.

resolvableness (rē-zol'vạ-bl-nes), *n.* The property of being resolvable; resolvability. *Bailey*, 1727.

resolve (rē-zolv'), *v.*; pret. and pp. *resolved*, ppr. *resolving*. [< ME. *resolven*, < OF. *resolver*, vernacularly *resoudre*, F. *résoudre* = Sp. Pg. *resolver* = It. *risolvere*, *resolvere*, < L. *resolvere*, pp. *resolutus*, loosen, resolve, dissolve, melt, thaw, < *re-*, again, + *solvere*, loosen: see *solve*.] **I.** *trans.* 1†. To loosen; set loose or at ease; relax.

> It is a very hard work of continence to repell the paynting glose of flatterings whose words *resolue* the hart with pleasure. *Babees Book* (E. E. T. S.), p. 106.

> His limbs, *resolv'd* through idle leisour,
> Unto sweete sleepe he may securely lend.
> *Spenser*, Virgil's Gnat, l. 141.

> *Cat.* The city's custom
> Of being then in mirth and feast—
> *Len.* Loosed whole
> In pleasure and security—
> *Aut.* Each house
> *Resolved* in freedom. *B. Jonson*, Catiline, iii. 3.

2. To melt; dissolve.

> The weyghte of the snowe yharded by the colde is *resolved* by the brennynge hete of Phebus the soone.
> *Chaucer*, Boethius, iv. prose 6.

> I could be content to *resolve* myself into teares, to rid thee of trouble. *Lyly*, Euphues, p. 38. (*Nares*.)

> O, that this too too solid flesh would melt,
> Thaw, and *resolve* itself into a dew!
> *Shak.*, Hamlet, i. 2. 130.

3. To disintegrate; reduce to constituent or elementary parts; separate the component parts of.

> The see gravel is lattest for to drie,
> And lattest may thou therwith edifie.
> The salt in it thy werkes wol *resolve*.
> *Palladius*, Husbondrie (E. E. T. S.), p. 14.

> And ye, immortal souls, who once were men,
> And now, *resolved* to elements again.
> *Dryden*, Indian Emperor, ii. 1.

> It is no necessity of his [the musician's] art to *resolve* the clang of an instrument into its constituent tones.
> *Tyndall*, Sound, p. 120.

Specifically—4. In *med.*, to effect the disappearance of (a swelling) without the formation of pus.—5. To analyze; reduce by mental analysis.

> I cannot think that the branded Epicurus, Lucretius, and their fellows were in earnest when they *resolv'd* this composition into a fortuitous range of atoms.
> *Glanville*, Essays, i.

> *Resolving* all events, with their effects
> And manifold results, into the will
> And arbitration wise of the Supreme.
> *Cowper*, Task, ii. 163.

> They tell us that on the hypothesis of evolution all human feelings may be *resolved* into a desire for food, into a fear of being eaten, or into the reproductive instinct.
> *Mivart*, Nature and Thought, p. 128.

6. To solve; free from perplexities; clear of difficulties; explain: as, to *resolve* questions of casuistry; to *resolve* doubts; to *resolve* a riddle.

> After their publike praiers the Talby sits downe, and spends halfe an houre in *resolving* the doubts of such as shall moue any questions in matters of their Law.
> *Purchas*, Pilgrimage, p. 623.

> Here were also several foundations of Buildings, but whether there were ever any place of note situated hereabouts, or what it might be, I cannot *resolve*.
> *Maundrell*, Aleppo to Jerusalem, p. 12.

> I ask these sober questions of my heart; . . .
> The heart *resolves* this matter in a trice.
> *Pope*, Imit. of Horace, II. ii. 216.

7. In *math.*, to solve; answer (a question).—8. In *alg.*, to bring all the known quantities of (an equation) to one side, and the unknown quantity to the other.—9. In *mech.*, to separate mathematically (a force or other vector quantity) into components, by the application of the parallelogram of forces, or of an analogous principle. The parts need not have independent reality.—10. To transform by or as by dissolution.

> The form of going from the assembly into committee is for the presiding officer . . . to put the question that the assembly do now *resolve* itself into a committee of the whole. *Cushing*, Manual of Parliamentary Practice, § 297.

11†. To free from doubt or perplexity; inform; acquaint; answer.

> If Brutus will vouchsafe that Antony
> May safely come to him, and be *resolved*
> How Cæsar hath deserved to lie in death.
> *Shak.*, J. C., iii. 1. 131.

> Pray, sir, *resolve* me, what religion 's best
> For a man to die in? *Webster*, White Devil, v. 1.

> You shall be fully *resolved* in every one of those many questions you have asked me.
> *Goldsmith*, To Mrs. Anne Goldsmith.

12†. To settle in an opinion; make certain; convince.

> The word of God can give us assurance in anything we are to do, and *resolve* us that we do well.
> *Hooker*, Eccles. Polity, ii. 4.

> Long since we were *resolved* of your truth,
> Your faithful service, and your toil in war.
> *Shak.*, 1 Hen. VI., iii. 4. 20.

> I am *resolv'd* my Cloe yet is true.
> *Fletcher*, Faithful Shepherdess, ii. 4.

13. To fix in a determination or purpose; determine; decide: used chiefly in the past participle.

> Therefore at last I firmly am *resolved*
> You shall have aid. *Shak.*, 3 Hen. VI., iii. 3. 219.

> Rather by this his last affront *resolved*,
> Desperate of better course, to vent his rage.
> *Milton*, P. R., iv. 444.

> With phrenzy seized, I run to meet the alarms,
> *Resolved* on death, *resolved* to die in arms.
> *Dryden*, Æneid, ii. 424.

14. To determine on; intend; purpose.

> I am *resolved* that thou shalt spend some time
> With Valentinus in the emperor's court.
> *Shak.*, T. G. of V., i. 3. 66.

> They [the Longobards] *resolved* to goe into some more fertile country. *Coryat*, Crudities, I. 107.

> War then, war,
> Open or understood, must be *resolved*.
> *Milton*, P. L., i. 662.

15†. To make ready in mind; prepare.

> Quit presently the chapel, or *resolve* you
> For more amazement. *Shak.*, W. T., v. 3. 86.

> Tell me, have you *resolv'd* yourself for court,
> And utterly renounc'd the slavish country,
> With all the cares thereof?
> *Fletcher* (*and another*), Noble Gentleman, iv. 4.

16. To determine on; specifically, to express, as an opinion or determination, by or as by resolution and vote.

> He loses no reputation with us; for we all *resolved* him as an ass before. *B. Jonson*, Epicœne, iv. 2.

17. In *music*, of a voice-part or of the harmony in general, to cause to progress from a discord to a concord.

II. *intrans.* 1†. To melt; dissolve; become fluid.

> Even as a form of wax
> *Resolveth* from his figure 'gainst the fire.
> *Shak.*, K. John, v. 4. 25.

> May my brain
> *Resolve* to water, and my blood turn phlegm.
> *B. Jonson*, Catiline, iii. 3.

2. To become separated into component or elementary parts; disintegrate; in general, to be reduced as by dissolution or analysis.

> The spices are so corrupted . . . that theyr naturall sauour, taste, and qualitye . . . vanyssheth and *resolueth*.
> *R. Eden*, tr. of Paolo Giovio (First Books on America, [ed. Arber, p. 309).

> Subterraneous bodies, from whence all the things upon the earth's surface spring, and into which they again *resolve* and return. *Bacon*, Physical Fables, xi., Expl.

> These several quarterly meetings should digest the reports of their monthly meetings, and prepare one for each respective county, against the yearly meeting, in which all quarterly meetings *resolve*.
> *Penn*, Rise and Progress of Quakers, iv.

> I lifted up my head to look: the roof *resolved* to clouds, high and dim; the gleam was such as the moon imparts to vapors she is about to sever.
> *Charlotte Brontë*, Jane Eyre, xxvii.

3. To form an opinion, purpose, or resolution; determine in mind; purpose: as, he *resolved* on amendment of life.

> How yet *resolves* the governor of the town?
> *Shak.*, Hen. V., iii. 3. 1.

4. To be settled in opinion; be convinced.

> Let men *resolve* of that as they please. *Locke*.

5. In *music*, of a voice-part or of the harmony in general, to pass from a discord to a concord. =**Syn.** 3. To decide, conclude.

resolve (rē-zolv'), *n.* [< *resolve*, *v.*] 1†. The act of resolving or solving; resolution; solution. *Milton*.—2†. An answer.

> I crave but ten short days to give *resolve*
> To this important suit, in which consists
> My endless shame or lasting happiness.
> *Beau. and Fl.* (?), Faithful Friends, ii. 2.

3. That which has been resolved or determined on; a resolution.

> Now, sister, let us hear your firm *resolve*.
> *Shak.*, 3 Hen. VI., iii. 3. 129.

> 'Tis thus
> Men cast the blame of their unprosperous acts
> Upon the abettors of their own *resolve*.
> *Shelley*, The Cenci, v. 1.

4. Firmness or fixedness of purpose; resolution; determination.

> A lady of so high *resolve*
> As is fair Margaret. *Shak.*, 1 Hen. VI., v. 5. 75.

> Come, firm *Resolve*, take thou the van,
> Thou stalk o' carl-hemp in man!
> *Burns*, To Dr. Blacklock.

5. The determination or declaration of any corporation, association, or representative body; a resolution.

> I then commenced my career as a political writer, devoting weeks and months to support the *resolves* of Congress.
> *Noah Webster*, Letter, 1783 (Life, by Scudder, p. 112).

Peace resolves. See *peace*.

resolved (rē-zolvd'), *p. a.* Determined; resolute; firm.

> How now, my hardy, stout *resolved* mates!
> Are you now going to dispatch this deed?
> *Shak.*, Rich. III., i. 3. 340.

resolvedly (rē-zol'ved-li), *adv.* 1. In a resolved manner; firmly; resolutely; with firmness of purpose.

> Let us chearfully and *resolvedly* apply ourselves to the working out our salvation. *Abp. Sharp*, Sermons, II. v.

2. In such a manner as to resolve or clear up all doubts and difficulties; satisfactorily. [Rare.]

> Of that and all the progress, more or less,
> *Resolvedly* more leisure shall express.
> *Shak.*, All's Well, v. 3. 332.

> He that hath rightly and *resolvedly* determined of his end hath virtually resolved a thousand controversies that others are unsatisfied and erroneous in.
> *Baxter*, Divine Life, ii. 6.

resolvedness (rē-zol'ved-nes), *n.* Fixedness of purpose; firmness; resolution.

This *resolvedness*, this high fortitude in sin, can with no reason be imagined a preparative to its remission.
Decay of Christian Piety.

resolvend (rẹ-zol'vend), *n.* [< L. *resolvendus*, gerundive of *resolvere*, resolve: see *resolve*.] In *arith.*, a number formed by appending two or three figures to a remainder after subtraction in extracting the square or cube root.

resolvent (rẹ-zol'vent), *a.* and *n.* [= F. *résolvant* = Sp. Pg. *resolvente* = It. *risolvente*, *resolvente*, < L. *resolven(t-)s*, ppr. of *resolvere*: see *resolve*.] **I.** *a.* Having the power to resolve or dissolve; causing solution; solvent.—**Resolvent equation, product**, etc. See the nouns.

II. *n.* **1.** That which has the power of causing solution.—**2.** In *med.*, a remedy which causes the resolution of a swelling; a discutient.—**3.** In *alg.*, an equation formed to aid the resolution of a given equation having for its roots known functions of the roots of the given equation. Thus, if x, x', x'', x''' are the roots of a biquadratic, one method of solution begins by solving the cubic whose roots are of the form $xx' + x''x'''$.—**Differential resolvent**, a linear differential equation of the $(n-1)$th order which is satisfied by every root of an equation of the nth degree whose coefficients are functions of a single parameter.—**Galois resolvent**, that resolvent of an equation whose roots are unaltered for every permutation of the group of the primitive equation.

resolver (rẹ-zol'vėr), *n.* One who or that which resolves, in any sense of that word.

Thy resolutions were not before sincere; consequently God, that saw that, cannot be thought to have justified that unsincere *resolver*, that dead faith. *Hammond.*

It may be doubted whether or no the fire be the genuine and universal *resolver* of mixed bodies. *Boyle.*

reson[1]†, *n.* and *v.* A Middle English form of *reason*[1].

reson[2]†. A Middle English plural preterit of *rise*[1].

resonance (rez'ọ-nans), *n.* [< OF. *resonnance*, F. *résonnance* = Sp. Pg. *resonancia* = It. *risonanza*, < L. *resonantia*, an echo, < *resonan(t-)s*, ppr. of *resonare*, sound back, echo: see *resonant*.] **1.** The act of resounding, or the state or quality of being resonant.—**2.** In *acoustics*: (*a*) The prolongation or repetition of sound by reflection; reverberation; echo. (*b*) The prolongation or increase of sound by the sympathetic vibration of other bodies than that by which it is originally produced. Such sympathetic vibration is properly in unison either with the fundamental tone or with one of its harmonics. It occurs to some extent in connection with all sound. It is carefully utilized in musical instruments, as by means of the sounding-board of a pianoforte, the body of a violin, or the tube of a horn. In many wind-instruments, like the flute, and the flue-pipes of an organ, the pitch of the tone is almost wholly determined by the shape and size of the resonant cavity or tube. In the voice, the quality of both song and speech and the distinctions between the various articulate sounds are largely governed by the resonance of the cavities of the pharynx, mouth, and nose. **3.** In *med.*, the sound evoked on percussing the chest or other part, or heard on auscultating the chest while the subject of examination speaks either aloud or in a whisper.—**Amphoric resonance**, a variety of tympanitic resonance in which there is a musical quality.—**Bandbox resonance**, the vesiculotympanitic resonance occurring in vesicular emphysema.—**Bell-metal resonance**, a ringing metallic sound heard in auscultation in pneumothorax and over other large cavities, when the chest is percussed with two pieces of money, one being used as pleximeter.—**Cough resonance**, the sound of the cough as heard in auscultation.—**Cracked-pot resonance**, a percussion sound obtained sometimes over cavities, but also sometimes in health, resembling somewhat the sound produced by striking a cracked pot.—**Normal pulmonary resonance, normal vesicular resonance.** Same as *vesicular resonance*.—**Resonance globe**, a resonator tuned to a certain musical tone.—**Skodaic resonance**, resonance more or less tympanitic above a pleuritic effusion.—**Sympathetic resonance.** See *sympathetic*.—**Tympanitic resonance**, such resonance as is obtained on percussion over the intestines when they contain air. It may also be heard in the thorax over lung-cavities, in pneumothorax, and otherwise.—**Vesicular resonance**, resonance of such quality as is obtained by percussion over normal lung-tissue. Also called *normal vesicular resonance* and *normal pulmonary resonance*.—**Vesiculotympanitic resonance**, pulmonary resonance intermediate between vesicular and tympanitic resonance.—**Vocal resonance**, the sound heard on auscultation of the chest when the subject makes a vocal noise.—**Whispering resonance**, the sound of a whisper as heard in resonance.

resonance-box (rez'ọ-nans-boks), *n.* A resonant cavity or chamber in a musical instrument, designed to increase the sonority of its tone, as the body of a violin or the box attached to a tuning-fork for acoustical investigation. Also *resonance-body*, *resonance-chamber*, etc.

resonancy (rez'ọ-nan-si), *n.* [As *resonance* (see *-cy*).] Same as *resonance*. *Imp. Dict.*

resonant (rez'ọ-nant), *a.* and *n.* [< OF. *resonnant*, F. *résonnant* = Sp. Pg. *resonante* = It. *risonante*, < L. *resonan(t-)s*, ppr. of *resonare*, resound, echo: see *resound*[1].] **I.** *a.* **1.** Resounding; specifically, noting a substance, structure, or confined body of air which is capable of decided sympathetic vibrations; or a voice, instrument, or tone in which such vibrations are prominent.

His volant touch,
Instinct through all proportions, low and high,
Fled and pursued transverse the *resonant* fugue.
Milton, P. L., xi. 563.

Sometimes he came to an arcadian square flooded with light and *resonant* with the fall of statued fountains.
Disraeli, Lothair, lxix.

2. Sounding or ringing in the nasal passages: used by some authors instead of *nasal* as applied to articulate sounds.

II. *n.* A resonant or nasal sound.

resonantly (rez'ọ-nant-li), *adv.* In a resonant or resounding manner; with resonance.

resonate (rez'ọ-nāt), *v. i.* [< L. *resonatus*, pp. of *resonare*, resound: see *resound*[1].] To resound.—**Resonating circle**, in *elect.*, the circle used as a resonator.

resonator (rez'ọ-nā-tor), *n.* [NL., < L. *resonare*, resound: see *resound*[1].] **1.** An acoustical instrument used in the analysis of sounds, consisting of a chamber so formed as to respond sympathetically to some particular tone. It is used especially to detect the presence of that tone in a compound sound.—**2.** In *elect.*, an instrument devised by Hertz for detecting the existence of waves of electrical disturbance. It consists usually of a conductor in the form of a wire or rod bent into a circle or rectangle, leaving a short opening or break, the length of which can be regulated. The ends of the conductor are generally furnished with small brass knobs.

resorb (rẹ-sôrb'), *v. t.* [< F. *résorber* = Sp. *resorber* = It. *risorbire*, < L. *resorbere*, suck back, swallow again, < *re-*, back, again, + *sorbere*, suck up: see *absorb*.] To absorb or take back, as that which has been given out; reabsorb.

And when past
Their various trials, in their various spheres,
If they continue rational, as made,
Resorbs them all into himself again.
Young, Night Thoughts, iv.

resorbent (rẹ-sôr'bent), *a.* [= F. *résorbant* = Sp. *resorbente*, < L. *resorben(t-)s*, ppr. of *resorbere*, swallow up, resorb: see *resorb*.] Absorbing or taking back that which has been given out.

Again *resorbent* ocean's wave
Receives the waters which it gave
From thousand rills with copious currents fraught.
Wodhull.

resorcin, resorcine (rẹ-sôr'sin), *n.* [= F. *résorcine*; as *res(in)* + *orcin*.] A colorless crystalline phenol, $C_6H_4(OH)_2$. It is obtained by treating benzene with sulphuric acid, preparing a sodium salt from the disulphonic acid thus produced, heating with caustic soda, and finally dissolving in water and precipitating resorcin with hydrochloric acid. It yields a fine purple-red coloring matter, and several other dyes of commercial importance, and is also used in medicine as an antiseptic. Also *resorcinum*.—**Resorcin blue, brown**, etc. See *blue*, etc.

resorcinal (rẹ-sôr'si-nal), *a.* [< *resorcin* + *-al*.] Pertaining to resorcin.—**Fluorescent resorcinal blue.** See *blue*.—**Resorcinal yellow.** See *yellow*.

resorcine, *n.* See *resorcin*.

resorcinism (rẹ-sôr'sin-izm), *n.* Toxic symptoms produced by excessive doses of resorcin.

resorcinol-phthalein (rẹ-sôr'si-nol-thal'ẹ-in), *n.* A brilliant red dye ($C_{20}H_{12}O_5$) obtained by the action of phthalic anhydrid on resorcin at a temperature of 120° C. Generally known as *fluorescein*.

resorcinum (rẹ-sôr'si-num), *n.* [NL.: see *resorcin*.] Same as *resorcin*.

resorption (rẹ-sôrp'shon), *n.* [= F. *résorption*, < L. *resorbere*, pp. *resorptus*, resorb: see *resorb*.] **1.** Retrogressive absorption; specifically, a physiological process by which a part or organ, having advanced to a certain state of development, disappears as such by the absorption of its substance into that of a part or organ which replaces it.

The larval skeleton undergoes *resorption*, but the rest of the Echinopædium passes into the Echinoderm.
Huxley, Anat. Invert., p. 497.

2. Absorption of some product of the organism, as a tissue, exudate, or secretion.

An extensive hæmorrhage which had undergone *resorption*. *Ziegler*, Pathol. Anat. (trans.), I. § 114.

Lacunar resorption of bone, the resorption of bone by osteoclasts forming and occupying Howship's lacunæ.

resorptive (rẹ-sôrp'tiv), *a.* [< *resorpt(ion)* + *-ive*.] Pertaining to or characterized by resorption.

The *resorptive* phenomena of porphyritic quartz and other minerals in eruptive rocks is a consequence chiefly of the relief of pressure in the process of eruption.
Science, XIII. 232.

Resorptive fever, such a fever as the hectic of phthisis, due to the absorption of toxic material.

resort[1] (rẹ-zôrt'), *v.* [< ME. *resorten*, < OF. *resortir*, *ressortir*, fall back, return, resort, have recourse, appeal, F. *ressortir*, resort, appeal, < ML. *resortire*, resort, appeal (to a tribunal), *resortiri*, return, revert, < L. *re-*, again, + *sortiri*, obtain, lit. obtain by lot, < *sor(t-)s*, a lot: see *sort*.] **I.** *intrans.* **1**†. To fall back; return; revert.

When he past of his payne & his pale hete,
And *resort* to hym selle & his sight gate,
He plainted full pitiously, was pyn for to here.
Destruction of Troy (E. E. T. S.), l. 3553.

He faught with hem so fiercely that he made hem *resorte* bakke. *Merlin* (E. E. T. S.), iii. 414.

The quicke bloode somwhat *resorted* unto his visage.
Sir T. Elyot, The Governour, ii. 12.

The rule of descents in Normandy was . . . that the descent of the line of the father shall not *resort* to that of the mother. *Sir M. Hale*, Hist. Common Law of Eng., VI. 151.

2. To go; repair; go customarily or frequently.

The people *resort* unto him again. Mark x. 1.

The vault . . . where, as they say,
At some hours in the night spirits *resort*.
Shak., R. and J., iv. 3. 44.

Noah . . . entered the Arke at Gods appointment, to which by diuine instinct *resorted* both birds and beasts.
Purchas, Pilgrimage, p. 39.

Let us not think we have fulfilled our duty merely by *resorting* to the church and adding one to the number of the congregation. *Bp. Atterbury*, Sermons, II. xx.

Head waiter of the chop-house here,
To which I most *resort*.
Tennyson, Will Waterproof.

3. To have recourse; apply; betake one's self: with *to*: as, to *resort to* force.

The king thought it time to *resort to* other counsels.
Clarendon.

Th' expedients and inventions multiform,
To which the mind *resorts*, in chase of terms.
Cowper, Task, ii. 288.

That species of political animadversion which is *resorted to* in the daily papers. *Sydney Smith*, in Lady Holland, vi.

II. *trans.* To visit; frequent. [Rare.]

A pallace of pleasure, and daily *resorted*, and fill'd with Lords and Knights, and their Ladies.
Brome, The Sparagus Garden, ii. 2.

resort[1] (rẹ-zôrt'), *n.* [< ME. *resort*, < OF. *resort*, *ressort*, the authority or jurisdiction of a court, F. *ressort*, a place of refuge, a court of appeal, = Pr. *ressort* = It. *risorto*, resort; from the verb.] **1.** The act of going to some person or thing or making application; a betaking one's self; recourse: as, a *resort* to other means of defense; a resort to subterfuges or evasion.

Where we pass, and make *resort*,
It is our Kingdom and our Court.
Brome, Jovial Crew, i.

2. One who or that which is resorted to: as in the phrase *last resort* (see below).

In trouth always to do yow my servise,
As to my lady right and chief *resort*.
Chaucer, Troilus, iii. 134.

3. An assembling; a going to or frequenting in numbers; confluence.

Where there is such *resort*
Of wanton gallants, and young revellers.
B. Jonson, Every Man in his Humour, ii. 1.

Wisdom's self
Oft seeks to sweet retired solitude, . . .
She plumes her feathers, and lets grow her wings,
That in the various bustle of *resort*
Were all-to ruffled. *Milton*, Comus, l. 379.

The like places of *resort* are frequented by men out of place. *Swift.*

4. The act of visiting or frequenting one's society; company; intercourse.

She I mean is promised by her friends
Unto a youthful gentleman of worth,
And kept severely from *resort* of men.
Shak., T. G. of V., iii. 1. 108.

5. A place frequented; a place commonly or habitually visited; a haunt.

With vij. lyttle hamlettes therto belonging, whiche hathe no other *resort* but only to the same Chapelle and parisshe Chirche. *English Gilds* (E. E. T. S.), p. 222.

But chiefly the woods were her fav'rite *resort*.
Burns, Caledonia.

Her bright form kneels beside me at the altar,
And follows me to the *resort* of men.
Shelley, The Cenci, ii. 2.

6. In *law*, the authority or jurisdiction of a court. [Rare.]—**7**†. Those who frequent a place; those who assemble. [Rare.]

Of all the fair *resort* of gentlemen
That every day with parle encounter me,
In thy opinion which is worthiest love?
Shak., T. G. of V., i. 2. 4.

As Wiltshire is a place best pleas'd with that *resort*
Which spend away the time continually in sport.
Drayton, Polyolbion, iii. 359.

8†. Spring; active power or movement. [A Gallicism.]

Certainly some there are that know the *resorts* and falls of business, that cannot sink into the main of it. *Bacon*, Cunning (ed. 1887).

If you can enter more deeply than they have done into the causes and *resorts* of that which moves pleasure in a reader, the field is open, you may be heard. *Dryden*, State of Innocence, Pref.

Last resort, the last resource or refuge; ultimate means of relief; also, final tribunal; a court from which there is no appeal. Also, as French, *dernier ressort.*

Mercy, fled to as the *last resort*. *Cowper*, Hope, l. 373.

=**Syn.** 2. *Resource, Contrivance*, etc. See *expedient*, n.

resort² (rē-sôrt'), *v. t.* [< *re-* + *sort.*] To sort over again. Also written distinctively *re-sort*.

resorter (rẹ-zôr'tėr), *n.* One who resorts, in any sense of that word.

'Tis the better for you that your *resorters* stand upon sound legs. *Shak.*, Pericles, iv. 6. 27.

resount, *v.* A Middle English form of *resound¹*.

resound¹ (rẹ-zound'), *v.* [With excrescent *d*, as in *sound⁶*, *expound*, etc.; < ME. *resounen*, < OF. *resoner*, *resouner*, *ressouner*, F. *résonner*, dial. *ressouner*, *ressonner* = Sp. *resonar* = Pg. *resonar*, *resoar* = It. *risonare*, < L. *resonare*, sound or ring again, resound, echo, < *re-*, again, + *sonare*, sound: see *sound⁵*. Cf. *resount.*] **I.** *intrans.* 1. To sound back; ring; echo; reverberate; be filled with sound; sound by sympathetic vibration.

Swich sorwe he maketh that the grete tour
Resouneth of his youling and clamour.
Chaucer, Knight's Tale, l. 420.

He call'd so loud that all the hollow deep
Of hell *resounded*. *Milton*, P. L., i. 315.

The robin, the thrush, and a thousand other wanton songsters make the woods to *resound* with amorous ditties. *Irving*, Knickerbocker, p. 147.

The pavement stones *resound*,
As he totters o'er the ground
With his cane.
O. W. Holmes, The Last Leaf.

2. To sound loudly; give forth a loud sound.

His arms *resounded* as the boaster fell. *Pope*, Iliad, xiii. 470.

The din of War *resounds* throughout more than seven hundred years of Roman history, with only two short lulls of repose. *Sumner*, Orations, I. 97.

3. To be echoed; be sent back, as sound.

Common fame . . . *resounds* back to them. *South.*

4. To be much mentioned; be famed.

What *resounds*
In fable or romance of Uther's son.
Milton, P. L., i. 579.

Milton, a name to *resound* for ages.
Tennyson, Experiments, In Quantity.

II. *trans.* 1. To sound again; send back sound; echo.

And Albion's cliffs *resound* the rural lay.
Pope, Spring, l. 6.

2. To sound; praise or celebrate with the voice or the sound of instruments; extol with sounds; spread the fame of.

With her shrill trumpet never dying Fame
Vnto the world shall still *resound* his name.
Times' Whistle (E. E. T. S.), p. 130.

Orpheus, . . . by loudly chanting and *resounding* the praises of the gods, confounded the voices.
Bacon, Moral Fables, vi., Expl.

The man for wisdom's various arts renown'd,
Long exercis'd in woes, O muse, *resound*.
Fenton, in Pope's Odyssey, i. 2.

=**Syn.** 1. To reëcho, reverberate.

resound¹ (rẹ-zound'), *n.* [< *resound¹*, *v.*] Return of sound; echo.

Itis huge trunke sounded, and his armes did eccho the *resound*. *Chapman*, Iliad, v.

Virtuous actions have their own trumpets, and, without any noise from thyself, will have their *resound* abroad.
Sir T. Browne, Christ. Mor., i. 34.

resound² (rē-sound'), *v.* [< *re-* + *sound⁵*.] **I.** *trans.* To sound again or repeatedly: as, to *resound* a note or a syllable.

And these words in their next prayer they repeat, *resounding* that last word One by the halfe or the whole hour together, looking vp to Heauen.
Purchas, Pilgrimage, p. 197.

II. *intrans.* To sound again: as, the trumpet sounded and *resounded*.

Upon the *resounding* of the Eccho there seemed three to sound together. *Coryat*, Crudities, I. 36, sig. D.

resounder (rẹ-zoun'dėr), *n.* One who or that which resounds; specifically, a monotelephone.

resource (rọ̄-sōrs'), *n.* [< OF. *resource*, *ressourse*, *ressource*, F. *ressource*, dial. *resorse* (= It. *risorsa*), a source, spring, < OF. *resourdre* (pp. *resours*, fem. *resourse*), < L. *resurgere*, rise again, spring up anew: see *resourd*, *resurgent*, and cf. *source*.] 1. Any source of aid or support; an expedient to which one may resort; means yet untried; resort.

Pallas, who, with disdain and grief, had view'd
His foes pursuing, and his friends pursued,
Used threatenings mix'd with prayers, his last *resource*.
Dryden, Æneid, x. 512.

When women engage in any art or trade, it is usually as a *resource*, not as a primary object. *Emerson*, Woman.

2. *pl.* Pecuniary means; funds; money or any property that can be converted into supplies; means of raising money or supplies.

Scotland by no means escaped the fate ordained for every country which is connected, but not incorporated, with another country of greater *resources*.
Macaulay, Hist. Eng., i.

3. *pl.* Available means or capabilities of any kind.

He always had the full command of all the *resources* of one of the most fertile minds that ever existed.
Macaulay, Warren Hastings.

He was a man of infinite *resources*, gained in his barrack experience. *Mrs. Gaskell*, Cranford, ii.

=**Syn.** 1. *Resort*, etc. See *expedient*.

resourceful (rẹ-sōrs'fụl), *a.* [< *resource* + *-ful.*] 1. Abounding in resources.

The justness of his gradations, and the *resourceful* variety of his touch, are equally to be admired.
The Academy, No. 892, p. 402.

2. Good at devising expedients; shifty.

She was cheerful and *resourceful* when any difficulty arose. *A. Helps*, Casimir Maremma, xxxiii.

resourcefulness (rẹ-sōrs'fụl-nes), *n.* The state or character of being resourceful.

Here [in the Far West], if anywhere, settlers may combine the practical *resourcefulness* of the savage with the intellectual activity of the dweller in cities.
Quarterly Rev., CXXVI. 388.

resourceless (rẹ-sōrs'les), *a.* [< *resource* + *-less.*] Destitute of resources.

Mungo Park, *resourceless*, had sunk down to die under the Negro Village-Tree, a horrible White object in the eyes of all. *Carlyle*, Past and Present, iii. 13.

resourd†, *v. i.* [ME. *resourden*, < OF. *resourdre*, rise up, spring up, < L. *resurgere*, rise again: see *resurgent*. Cf. *resource*.] To spring up; rise anew.

Frowhens that the deth grew, frothens the lyf *resourded*.
Holy Rood (E. E. T. S.), p. 161.

resow (rē-sō'), *v. t.* [< *re-* + *sow¹*.] To sow again.

To *resow* summer corn. *Bacon.*

resownt, *v.* A Middle English form of *resound¹*.

resp (resp), *v. t.* Same as *risp*.

respet, *n.* An obsolete form of *rasp²*.

respeak (rē-spēk'), *v. t.* [< *re-* + *speak.*] 1. To answer; speak in return; reply. [Rare.]

And the king's rouse the heav'n shall bruit again,
Re-speaking earthly thunder. *Shak.*, Hamlet, i. 2. 128.

2. To speak again; repeat.

respect (rẹ-spekt'), *v. t.* [= OF. *respecter*, look back, respect, delay (also *respiter*, delay: see *respite*), F. *respecter* = Sp. *respetar*, *respectar* = Pg. *respeitar* = It. *rispettare*, < L. *respectare*, look back or behind, look intently, regard, respect, freq. of *respicere*, pp. *respectus*, look at, look back upon, respect, < *re-*, back, + *specere*, look at, see, spy: see *spectacle*, *spy*. Doublet of *respite*, *v.*] 1†. To look toward; front upon or in the direction of.

Palladius adviseth the front of his house should so *respect* the south. *Sir T. Browne.*

2†. To postpone; respite.

As touching the musters of all the soldiours upon the shore, we have *respected* the same tyll this tyme for lacke of money. *State Papers*, i. 832. (*Halliwell.*)

3. To notice with especial attention; regard as worthy of particular notice; regard; heed; consider; care for; have regard to in design or purpose.

Small difficulties, when exceeding great good is to ensue, . . . are not at all to be *respected*. *Hooker.*

But thou, O blessed soul! dost haply not *respect*
These tears we shed, though full of loving pure effect.
L. Bryskett (Arber's Eng. Garner, I. 271).

I am armed so strong in honesty
That they pass by me as the idle wind,
Which I *respect* not. *Shak.*, J. C., iv. 3. 69.

He that *respects* to get must relish all commodities alike. *B. Jonson*, Poetaster, ii. 1.

4. To have reference or regard to; relate to.

The knowledge which *respecteth* the faculties of the mind of man is of two kinds.
Bacon, Advancement of Learning, ii. 206.

I too am a degenerate Osbaldistone, so far as *respects* the circulation of the bottle. *Scott*, Rob Roy, x.

5. To hold in esteem, regard, or consideration; regard with some degree of reverence: as, to *respect* womanhood; hence, to refrain from interference with: as, to *respect* one's privacy.

Well, well, my lords, *respect* him:
Take him, and use him well, he 's worthy of it.
Shak., Hen. VIII., v. 3. 153.

In the excursions which they make for pleasure they [the English] are commonly *respected* by the Arabs, Curdeens, and Turcomen, there being very few instances of their having been plundered by them.
Pococke, Description of the East, II. i. 152.

To such I render more than mere respect
Whose actions say that they *respect* themselves.
Cowper, Task, ii. 377.

How could they hope that others would *respect* laws which they had themselves insulted?
Macaulay, Conversation between Cowley and Milton.

What I look upon as essential to their full utility is that those who enter into such combinations [trades-unions] shall fully and absolutely *respect* the liberty of those who do not wish to enter them.
Gladstone, Might of Right, p. 274.

To respect a person or **persons**, also **to respect the person of** (some one), to show undue bias toward or against a person, etc.; suffer the opinion or judgment to be influenced or biased by a regard to the outward circumstances of a person, to the prejudice of right and equity.

Thou shalt not *respect the person of* the poor, nor honour the person of the mighty. Lev. xix. 15.

Neither doth God *respect* any *person*. 2 Sam. xiv. 14.

As Solomon saith, *to respect persons* is not good, for such a man will transgress for a piece of bread. *Bacon.*

=**Syn.** 5. To honor, revere, venerate. See *esteem*, *n.*

respect (rẹ-spekt'), *n.* [= G. *respect* = D. Sw. Dan. *respekt*, < OF. *respect*, also *respit* (see *respite*), F. *respect* = Pr. *respiey*, *respiech*, *respieit*, *respcit* = Cat. *respecte* = Sp. *respecto* = Pg. *respeito* = It. *rispetto*, < L. *respectus*, a looking at, respect, regard, < *respicere*, pp. *respectus*, look at, look back upon: see *respect*, *v.* Doublet of *respite*, *n.*] 1. The act of looking at or regarding, or noticing with attention; regard; attention.

This maistyr sittith in the halle, next unto these Henxmen, at the same boarde, to have his *respecte* unto theyre demeanynges, howe manerly they ete and drinke.
Babees Book (E. E. T. S.), p. ii.

In writing this booke, I haue had earnest *respecte* to three speciall pointes. *Ascham*, The Scholemaster, p. 23.

But he it well did ward with wise *respect*,
And twixt him and the blow his shield did cast.
Spenser, F. Q., V. xii. 21.

At that day shall a man look to his Maker, and his eyes shall have *respect* to the Holy One of Israel. Isa. xvii. 7.

You have too much *respect* upon the world;
They lose it that do buy it with much care.
Shak., M. of V., i. 1. 74.

Hee sought a heav'nly reward which could make him happy, and never hurt him, and to such a reward every good man may have a *respect*.
Milton, Apology for Smectymnuus.

2†. Deliberation; reflection; consideration.

Thou wouldst have plunged thyself
In general riot; . . . and never learn'd
The icy precepts of *respect*, but follow'd
The sugar'd game before thee.
Shak., T. of A., iv. 3. 258.

Then is no child nor father; then eternity
Frees all from any temporal *respect*.
B. Jonson, Poetaster, iv. 6.

3†. Circumspect behavior or deportment; decency.

If I do not put on a sober habit,
Talk with *respect*, and swear but now and then.
Shak., M. of V., ii. 2. 200.

4. The feeling of esteem, regard, or consideration excited by the contemplation of personal worth, dignity, or power; also, a similar feeling excited by corresponding attributes in things.

Is there no *respect* of place, persons, nor time in you?
Shak., T. N., ii. 3. 98.

The natural effect
Of love by absence chill'd into *respect*.
Cowper, Tirocinium, l. 576.

A decent *respect* to the opinions of mankind requires that they should declare the causes which impel them to the separation. *Declaration of Independence.*

Milton's *respect* for himself and for his own mind and its movements rises wellnigh to veneration.
Lowell, Among my Books, 2d ser., p. 288.

5. Courteous or considerate treatment; that which is due, as to personal worth or power.

According to his virtue let us use him,
With all *respect* and rites of burial.
Shak., J. C., v. 5. 77.

6. *pl.* Expression or sign of esteem, deference, or compliment: as, to pay one's *respects* to the governor; please give him my *respects*.

Up comes one of Marsault's companions . . . into my chamber, with three others at his heeles, who by their *respects* and distance seemed to be his servants.
History of Francion (1655). (*Nares.*)

He had no doubt they said among themselves, "She is an excellent and beautiful girl, and deserving all respect"; and respect they accorded, but their *respects* they never came to pay. *G. W. Cable*, Old Creole Days, p. 89.

7. Good will; favor.

The Lord had *respect* unto Abel and to his offering.
Gen. iv. 4.

8. Partial regard; undue bias; discrimination for or against some one.

It is not good to have *respect* of persons in judgment.
Prov. xxiv. 23.

It is of the highest importance that judges and administrators should never be persuaded by money or otherwise to shew "*respect* of persons."
H. Sidgwick, Methods of Ethics, p. 239.

9. Reputation; repute.

Many of the best *respect* in Rome . . .
Have wish'd that noble Brutus had his eyes.
Shak., J. C., i. 2. 59.

10. Consideration; motive.

He was not moved with these worldly *respects*.
Latimer, Sermon of the Plough.

The end for which we are moved to work is sometimes the goodness which we conceive of the very working itself, without any further *respect* at all.
Hooker, Eccles. Polity, i. 7.

Master Scrivener, for some private *respect*, plotted in England to ruine Captaine Smith.
Quoted in *Capt. John Smith's* Works, I. 205.

For *respects*
Of birth, degrees of title, and advancement,
I nor admire nor slight them.
Ford, Perkin Warbeck, i. 2.

11. Point or particular; matter; feature; point of view.

I think she will be ruled
In all *respects* by me. *Shak.*, R. and J., iii. 4. 14.

Now, as we seem to differ in our ideas of expense, I have resolved she shall have her own way, and be her own mistress in that *respect* for the future.
Sheridan, School for Scandal, iv. 3.

India is governed bureaucratically, but this bureaucracy differs in more than one *respect* from ours in Europe.
Quarterly Rev., CLXII. 453.

12. Relation; regard; reference: used especially in the phrase *in* or *with respect to* (or *of*).

Church government that is appointed in the Gospel, and has chief *respect* to the soul.
Milton, Reformation in Eng., ii.

Shirtliff having his wife by the hand, and sitting by her to cheer her, *in respect* that the said storm was so fierce, he was slain, and she preserved.
N. Morton, New England's Memorial, p. 319.

In respect†, relatively; comparatively speaking.

He was a man; this, *in respect*, a child.
Shak., 3 Hen. VI., v. 5. 56.

In respect of. (*a*†) In comparison with; relatively to.

All paines are nothing *in respect of* this.
Spenser, Sonnets, lxiii.

In respect of a fine workman, I am but . . . a cobbler.
Shak., J. C., i. 1. 10.

(*b*) In consideration of.

The feathers of their [Ostriches'] wings and tailes are very soft and fine. *In respect whereof* they are much used in the fannes of Gentlewomen.
Coryat, Crudities, I. 40, sig. E.

They should depress their guns and fire down into the hold, *in respect of* the vessel attacked standing so high out of the water. *De Quincey.*

(*c*) In point of; in regard to.

If *in respect of* speculation all men are either Platonists or Aristotelians, *in respect of* taste all men are either Greek or German.
J. A. Symonds, Italy and Greece, p. 301.

=**Syn. 4.** *Estimate, Estimation*, etc. See *esteem*.

respectability (rẹ̄-spek-tạ-bil'i-ti), *n.*; pl. *respectabilities* (-tiz). [= F. *respectabilité* = Sp. *respetabilidad* = Pg. *respeitabilidade*; as *respectable* + *-ity* (see *-bility*).] **1.** The state or character of being respectable; the condition or qualities which deserve or command respect.

A gold-headed cane, of rare oriental wood, added materially to the high *respectability* of his aspect.
Hawthorne, Seven Gables, viii.

2. A respectable person or thing; a specimen or type of what is respectable.

Smooth-shaven *respectabilities* not a few one finds that are not good for much. *Carlyle.*

respectable (rẹ̄-spek'tạ-bl), *a.* [< OF. (and F.) *respectable* = Sp. *respetable* = Pg. *respeitavel* = It. *rispettabile*, < ML. *respectabilis*, worthy of respect, < L. *respectare*, respect: see *respect*.] **1.** Capable of being respected; worthy of respect or esteem.

In the great civil war, even the bad cause had been rendered *respectable* and amiable by the purity and elevation of mind which many of its friends displayed.
Macaulay, Hallam's Const. Hist.

She irritates my nerves, that dear and *respectable* Potts.
W. E. Norris, Matrimony, xxvii.

2. Having an honest or good reputation; standing well with other people; reputable: as, born of poor but *respectable* parents.

At this time . . . Mrs. Prior was outwardly *respectable*; and yet . . . my groceries were consumed with remarkable rapidity. *Thackeray*, Lovel the Widower, i.

3. Occupying or pertaining to a fairly good position in society; moderately well-to-do.

You mistake, my good Mrs. Bonnington! . . . You have lived in a quiet and most *respectable* sphere, but not, you understand, not ——.
Thackeray, Lovel the Widower, iv.

4. Mediocre; moderate; fair; not despisable.

The Earl of Essex, a man of *respectable* abilities and of some military experience, was appointed to the command of the parliamentary army.
Macaulay, Nugent's Hampden.

British writers, not of the highest grade, but of *respectable* rank. *R. G. White*, Words and Their Uses, iii.

5. Proper; decent: as, conduct that is not *respectable*. [Colloq.]

It will be necessary to find a milliner, my love. . . . Something must be done with Maggy, too, who at present is — ha — barely *respectable*. *Dickens*, Little Dorrit, i. 35.

respectableness (rẹ̄-spek'tạ-bl-nes), *n.* Respectability.

respectably (rẹ̄-spek'tạ-bli), *adv.* In a respectable manner. (*a*) In a manner to merit respect. (*b*) Moderately; pretty well; in a manner not to be despised.

respectant (rẹ̄-spek'tạnt), *a.* [< OF. *respectant*, < L. *respectan(t-)s*, ppr. of *respectare*, look at, respect: see *respect*.] In *her.*, looking at each other: said of two animals borne face to face. Rampant beasts of prey so borne are said to be *combatant*. Compare *affronté*. [Rare.]—**Respectant in triangle**, in *her.*, arranged in a triangle with the heads or beaks pointing inward or toward one another: said of three beasts or birds.

respecter (rẹ̄-spek'tėr), *n.* One who respects or regards: chiefly used in the phrase *respecter of persons*, a person who regards the external circumstances of others in his judgment, and suffers his opinion to be biased by them, to the prejudice of candor, justice, and equity.

I perceive that God is no *respecter of persons*.
Acts x. 34.

respectful (rẹ̄-spekt'fůl), *a.* [< *respect* + *-ful*.] **1.** Marked or characterized by respect; showing respect: as, *respectful* deportment.

With humble Joy, and with *respectful* Fear,
The listening People shall his Story hear.
Prior, Carmen Seculare, xxxviii.

His costume struck me with *respectful* astonishment.
Thackeray, Newcomes, vi.

2. Full of outward or formal civility; ceremonious.

From this dear Bosom shall I ne'er be torn?
Or you grow cold, *respectful*, or forsworn?
Prior, Celia to Damon.

3†. Worthy of respect; receiving respect. [Rare.]

And Mr. Miles, of Swansey, who afterwards came to Boston, and is now gone to his rest. Both of these have a *respectful* character in the churches of this wilderness.
C. Mather, Mag. Chris., iii., Int.

=**Syn.** Civil, dutiful, courteous, complaisant, deferential, polite.

respectfully (rẹ̄-spekt'fůl-i), *adv.* In a respectful manner; with respect; in a manner comporting with due estimation.

We relieve idle vagrants and counterfeit beggars, but have no care at all of these really poor men, who are, methinks, to be *respectfully* treated in regard of their quality.
Cowley, Avarice.

respectfulness (rẹ̄-spekt'fůl-nes), *n.* The character of being respectful.

respecting (rẹ̄-spek'ting), *prep.* [Ppr. of *respect*, *v.*] **1.** Considering.

There is none worthy,
Respecting her that 's gone.
Shak., W. T., v. 1. 35.

2. Regarding; in regard to; relating to.

Respecting man, whatever wrong we call
May, must be right, as relative to all.
Pope, Essay on Man, i. 51.

Respecting my sermons, I most sincerely beg of you to extenuate nothing. Treat me exactly as I deserve.
Sydney Smith, To Francis Jeffrey.

respection (rẹ̄-spek'shọn), *n.* [< LL. *respectio(n-)*, < L. *respicere*, pp. *respectus*, respect, regard: see *respect*.] The act of respecting; respect; regard. [Obsolete or colloq.]

Then sayd Christ, Goe thou and do likewise — that is, without difference or *respection* of persons.
Tyndale, Works, p. 78.

Now, mum, with *respections* to this boy.
Dickens, Great Expectations, xii.

respective (rẹ̄-spek'tiv), *a.* [< OF. (and F.) *respectif* = Pr. *respectiu* = Sp. Pg. *respectivo* = It. *rispettivo*, < ML. *respectivus*, < L. *respicere*, pp. *respectus*, look at, observe, respect: see *respect*.] **1.** Observing or noting with attention; regardful; hence, careful; circumspect; cautious; attentive to consequences. [Obsolete or archaic.]

Respective and wary men had rather seek quietly their own . . . than with pain and hazard make themselves advisers for the common good. *Hooker.*

Love that is *respective* for increase
Is like a good king, that keeps all in peace.
Middleton, Women Beware Women, i. 3.

To be virtuous, zealous, valiant, wise,
Learned, *respective* of his country's good.
Ford, Fame's Memorial.

2†. Relative; having relation to something else; not absolute.

Which are said to be relative or *respective*? Those that cannot be well understood of themselves without having relation to some other thing.
Blundeville, Arte of Logicke (1599), i. 11.

Heat, as concerning the humane sense of feeling, is a various and *respective* thing.
Bacon, Nat. and Exper. Hist. of Winds (trans. 1653), [p. 275.

3†. Worthy of respect; respectable.

What should it be that he respects in her
But I can make *respective* in myself?
Shak., T. G. of V., iv. 4. 200.

Win. Pray thee forbear, for my respect, somewhat.
Quar. Hoy-day! how *respective* you are become o' the sudden! *B. Jonson*, Bartholomew Fair, i. 1.

4†. Rendering respect; respectful.

The bold and careless servant still obtains;
The modest and *respective* nothing gains.
Chapman, All Fools, i. 1.

I doubt not but that for your noble name's sake (not their own merit), wheresoever they [sermons] light, they shall find *respective* entertainment, and do yet some more good to the church of God. *Rev. T. Adams*, Works, I. 14.

5†. Characterized by respect for special persons or things; partial.

Away to heaven *respective* lenity,
And fire-eyed fury be my conduct now!
Shak., R. and J., iii. 1. 128.

This is the day that must . . . reduce those seeming inequalities and *respective* distributions in this world to an equality and recompensive justice in the next.
Sir T. Browne, Religio Medici, i. § 47.

6. Relating or pertaining severally each to each; several; particular.

To those places straight repair
Where your *respective* dwellings are.
S. Butler, Hudibras, I. ii. 666.

They both went very quietly out of the court, and retired to their *respective* lodgings.
Addison, Trial of False Affronts.

Beyond the physical differences, there are produced by the *respective* habits of life mental differences.
H. Spencer, Prin. of Sociol., § 403.

Respective being, being which in its essential nature refers to something else, as action, passion, date, place, posture, and habit.—**Respective ens, locality**, etc. See the nouns.

respectively (rẹ̄-spek'tiv-li), *adv.* In a respective manner, in any sense.

The World hath nor East nor West, but *respectively*.
Raleigh, Hist. World, p. 36.

Sir, she ever
For your sake most *respectively* lov'd me.
Beau. and Fl., Laws of Candy, iv. 2.

respectiveness† (rẹ̄-spek'tiv-nes), *n.* The state or quality of being respective; regard or respect had to anything.

So that hee shall find neither a paraphrasticall, epitomized, or meere verball translation: but such a mixed *respectivenesse* as may shewe I indevoured nothing more then the true use, benefit, and delight of the reader.
Lomatius on Painting, by Haydock, 1598. (*Nares.*)

respectivist† (rẹ̄-spek'tiv-ist), *n.* [< *respective* + *-ist*.] A captious person or critic.

But what haue these our *respectiuists* to doe with the Apostle Paule? *Foxe*, Martyrs, p. 1173.

respectless (rẹ̄-spekt'les), *a.* [< *respect* + *-less*.] **1.** Having no respect; without regard; without reference; careless; regardless. [Rare.]

The Cambrian part, *respectless* of their power.
Drayton, Polyolbion, xii. 17.

I was not
Respectless of your honour, nor my fame.
Shirley, Maid's Revenge, ii. 5.

2†. Having no respect or regard, as for reputation, power, persons, etc.

He that is so *respectlesse* in his courses
Oft sells his reputation at cheap market.
B. Jonson, Every Man in his Humour, i. 1.

O, indignity
To my *respectless* free-bred poesy!
Marston, Scourge of Villanie, vi. 100.

respectuous† (rẹ̄-spek'tṳ̄-us), *a.* [< OF. (and F.) *respectueux* = Sp. *respetuoso*, *respetoso* = Pg. *respeitoso*, *respectuoso* = It. *rispettoso*, < L. *respectus*, respect: see *respect*, *n.*] **1.** Inspiring respect.

Neither is it to be marvelled . . . if they [princes] become *respectuous* and admirable in the eyes and sight of the common people. *Knolles*, Hist. Turks (1610). (*Nares.*)

2. Respectful.

I thought it pardonabler to say nothing by a *respectuous* silence than by idle words. *Boyle*, Works, VI. 44.

respell (rē-spel'), *v. t.* [< *re-* + *spell*[2].] To spell again; specifically, to spell again in another form, according to some phonetic system (as in this dictionary), so as to indicate the actual or supposed pronunciation.

Now a uniform system of representing sounds . . . would be of great use as a system to be followed for every word or name on the principle of phonetic *respelling*. *Nature*, XLII. 7.

resperse† (rẹ̄-spėrs'), *v. t.* [< L. *respersus*, pp. of *respergere*, sprinkle again or over, besprinkle, bestrew, < *re-*, again, + *spargere*, sprinkle: see *sparse*.] To sprinkle; scatter.

Those excellent, moral, and perfective discourses which with much pains and greater pleasure we find *repersed* and thinly scattered in all the Greek and Roman poets. *Jer. Taylor*, Great Exemplar, Pref.

respersion† (rẹ̄-spėr'shọn), *n.* [< L. *respersio(n-)*, a sprinkling, < *respergere* (pp. *respersus*), sprinkle: see *resperse*.] The act of sprinkling or spreading; scattering.

All the joys which they should have received in *respersion* and distinct emanations if they had kept their anniversaries at Jerusalem, all that united they received in the duplication of their joys at their return. *Jer. Taylor*, Works (ed. 1835), I. 80.

respirability (rẹ̄-spīr-ạ-bil'i-ti), *n.* [= F. *respirabilité*; as *respirable* + *-ity* (see *-bility*).] The property of being respirable. *Imp. Dict.*

respirable (rẹ̄-spīr'ạ-bl), *a.* [< OF. F. *respirable* = Sp. *respirable* = Pg. *respiravel* = It. *respirabile*, < NL. **respirabilis*, < L. *respirare*, respire: see *respire*.] 1†. That can respire. *Imp. Dict.*—2. Capable of or fit for being respired or breathed: as, *respirable* air.

respirableness (rẹ̄-spīr'ạ-bl-nes), *n.* Same as *respirability*. *Imp. Dict.*

respiration (res-pi-rā'shọn), *n.* [< OF. (and F.) *respiration* = Pr. *respiracio* = Sp. *respiracion* = Pg. *respiração* = It. *respirazione*, < L. *respiratio(n-)*, breathing, respiration, < *respirare*, pp. *respiratus*, breathe out, respire, take breath: see *respire*.] 1†. The act of breathing again or resuming life.

Till the day
Appear of *respiration* to the just,
And vengeance to the wicked.
Milton, P. L., xii. 540.

2. The inspiration and expiration of air.—3. That function by which there takes place an absorption of oxygen from the surrounding medium into the blood with a corresponding excretion of carbon dioxid. This is accomplished in the higher animal forms chiefly by the lungs and skin; the gills or branchiæ of aquatic animals and the tracheæ of insects perform the same function. In unicellular organisms these changes take place in the protoplasm of the cell itself. The number of respirations in the human adult is from 16 to 24 per minute. About 500 centimeters or one sixth of the volume of the air in the lungs is changed at each respiration, giving a daily income of about 744 grams of oxygen and an expenditure of 900 grains of carbon dioxid. Inspiration is slightly shorter than expiration.

Ev'ry breath, by *respiration* strong
Forc'd downward. *Cowper*, Task, iv. 348.

4. In *physiological bot.*, a process consisting in the absorption by plants of oxygen from the air, the oxidation of assimilated products, and the release of carbon dioxid and watery vapor. It is the opposite of *assimilation*, in which carbon dioxid (carbonic acid) is absorbed and oxygen given off—contrasted also as being the waste process in the plant economy, a part of the potential energy of a higher compound being converted into kinetic energy, supporting the activities of the plant, the resulting compound of lower potential being excreted. Respiration takes place in all active cells both by day and by night; assimilation only by daylight (then overshadowing the other process) and in cells containing chlorophyl.

5. The respiratory murmur.—6†. A breathing-spell; an interval.

Some meet *respiration* of a more full trial and enquiry into each others' condition. *Bp. Hall*, Cases of Conscience, iv. 6.

Abdominal respiration. See *abdominal*.—**Amphoric respiration**, respiratory murmur with musical intonation, such as might be produced by blowing across the mouth of a bottle. It occurs in some cases of pneumothorax and with some phthisical cavities.—**Artificial respiration**, respiration induced by artificial means. It is required in cases of drowning, the excessive inhalation of chloroform or of noxious gases, etc. In the case of a person apparently drowned, or in an asphyxiated condition, the following treatment has been recommended. After clearing the mouth and throat, the patient should be laid on his back on a plane inclined a little from the feet upward; the shoulders gently raised by a firm cushion placed under them; the tongue brought forward so as to project from the side of the mouth, and kept in that position by an elastic band or string tied under the chin. Remove all tight clothing from neck and chest. The arms should then be grasped just above the elbows, raised till they nearly meet above the head, and kept stretched upward for two seconds: this action imitates inspiration. The arms are then turned down and firmly pressed for two seconds against the sides of the chest, thus imitating a deep expiration. These two sets of movements should be perseveringly repeated at the rate of fifteen times in a minute. As soon as a spontaneous effort to breathe is perceived, cease the movements and induce circulation and warmth.—**Branchial respiration.** See *branchial*.—**Bronchial respiration**, respiration such as is heard immediately over bronchi, or over the trachea. The inspiratory sound is high in pitch and tubular; the expiratory sound is higher, tubular, and prolonged. It is heard in disease over consolidated lungs. Also called *tubular respiration*.—**Bronchocavernous respiration**, respiration intermediate in character between bronchial and cavernous respiration.—**Bronchovesicular respiration**, respiration intermediate in character between bronchial and vesicular respiration.—**Cavernous respiration.** See *cavernous*.—**Center of respiration**, the nervous center which regulates respiration. It is automatic in action, but is guided by incoming influences from the vagus, the skin, and elsewhere. The main center is limited in extent, and situated in the floor of the fourth ventricle, near the point of the calamus.—**Cerebral respiration**, shallow, quick, irregular, more or less sighing respiration, sometimes resulting from cerebral disease in children.—**Cheyne-Stokes respiration**, a rhythmic form of respiration described by Cheyne in 1818 and by Stokes in 1846. It consists of a series of cycles in every one of which the respirations pass gradually from feeble and shallow to forcible and deep, and then back to feeble again. A pause follows, and then the next cycle begins with a feeble inspiration. This symptom has been found associated with cardiac and brain lesions.—**Cogged or cog-wheel respiration.** Same as *interrupted respiration*.—**Costal respiration**, respiration in which the costal movements predominate over the diaphragmatic.—**Cutaneous respiration**, gaseous absorption and excretion by the skin.—**Diaphragmatic respiration.** Same as *abdominal respiration* (which see, under *abdominal*).—**Divided respiration**, respiration in which inspiration is separated from expiration by a well-marked interval.—**Facial respiration**, respiratory movements of the face, as of the alæ nasi.—**Harsh respiration.** Same as *rude respiration*.—**Indeterminate respiration.** Same as *bronchovesicular respiration*, especially its more vesicular grades.—**Interrupted respiration**, respiration in which the inspiratory, sometimes the expiratory, sound is broken into two or more parts. Also called *jerking*, *wavy*, and *cogged* or *cog-wheel respiration*.—**Jerking respiration.** Same as *interrupted respiration*.—**Laryngeal respiration**, laryngeal respiratory movements.—**Metamorphosing respiration**, respiration in which the first part of the inspiratory sound is tubular and the last part cavernous.—**Organs of respiration**, any parts of the body by means of which constituents of the blood are interchanged with those of air or water. In the higher vertebrates, all of which are air-breathers, such organs are internal, and of complex lobulated structure, called *lungs*. (See *lung*.) In lower vertebrates and many invertebrates respiration is effected by breathing water, and such organs are usually called *gills* or *branchiæ*. Most invertebrates, however (as nearly all the immense class of insects), breathe air by various contrivances for its admission to the body, generally of tubular or laminated structure, which may open by pores or spiracles on almost any part of the body. The organs of mollusks are extremely variable in form and position; they are commonly called *branchiæ* or *gills*, technically *ctenidia*. Some gastropods, called *pulmonate*, are air-breathers. Arachnidans are distinguished as *pulmonate* and *tracheate*, according to the laminate (or saccular) or the simply tubular character of their organs of respiration. The character of the lungs as offsets of the alimentary canal is somewhat peculiar to the higher vertebrates—being represented in the lower, as fishes, only by an air-bladder, if at all; and the various organs of respiration of lower animals are only analogous or functionally representative, not homologous or morphologically representative, of such lungs. (See *pneogaster*.) In birds the organs are distributed in most parts of the body, even in the interior of bones. (See *pneumatocyst*.) In embryos the allantois is an organ of respiration, as well as of digestion and circulation. See cuts under *Branchiostoma*, *gill*, and *Mya*.—**Puerile respiration.** See *puerile*.—**Rough respiration.** Same as *rude respiration*.—**Rude respiration**, a form of bronchovesicular respiration, the sounds being harsh.—**Supplementary respiration**, respiration with increased vesicular murmur, as heard over normal parts of the lungs when some other part of them is incapacitated, as from pneumonia or pleurisy.—**Thoracic respiration.** Same as *costal respiration*.—**Tubular respiration.** Same as *bronchial respiration*.—**Vesiculocavernous respiration**, respiration intermediate in character between vesicular and cavernous respiration.

respirational (res-pi-rā'shọn-ạl), *a.* [< *respiration* + *-al*.] Same as *respiratory*.

respirative (rẹ̄-spīr'ạ-tiv), *a.* [< *respirat(ion)* + *-ive*.] Performing respiration.

respirator (res'pi-rā-tọr), *n.* [NL., < L. *respirare*, pp. *respiratus*, respire: see *respire*.] An instrument for breathing through, fitted to cover the mouth, or the nose and mouth, over which it is secured by proper bandages or other appliances. It is mostly used to exclude the passage into the lungs of cold air, smoke, dust, and other noxious substances, especially by persons having delicate chests, by firemen, cutlers, grinders, and the like, and by divers in operations under water. Respirators for persons with weak lungs have several plies of fine gauze made of highly heat-conducting metal, which warms the air as it passes through. See *aërophore*.

respiratorium (res"pi-rạ-tō'ri-um), *n.*; pl. *respiratoria* (-ạ̈). [NL., neut. of *respiratorius*, respiratory: see *respiratory*.] In *entom.*, one of the laminiform gill-like organs or branchiæ found on the larvæ of certain aquatic insects, and used to draw air from the water. In dipterous larvæ they are commonly four in number, two near the head and two at the end of the abdomen.

respiratory (rẹ̄-spīr'ạ- or res'pi-rạ-tō-ri), *a.* [= F. *respiratoire*, < NL. *respiratorius*, < L. *respirare*, pp. *respiratus*, respire: see *respire*.] Pertaining to or serving for respiration.—**Bronchial respiratory murmur.** Same as *bronchial respiration* (which see, under *respiration*).—**Bronchovesicular respiratory murmur**, a murmur intermediate between a vesicular and a bronchial murmur. Also called *rude*, *rough*, and *harsh respiration*.—**Indeterminate respiratory murmur.** Same as *bronchovesicular respiratory murmur*.—**Respiratory bronchial tube, respiratory bronchiole.** Same as *lobular bronchial tube* (which see, under *lobular*).—**Respiratory bundle.** Same as *solitary funiculus* (which see, under *solitary*).—**Respiratory capacity.** Same as *extreme differential capacity* (which see, under *capacity*).—**Respiratory cavities**, a general name of the air-passages: used also to designate the body-cavities which contain the respiratory organs.—**Respiratory chamber**, a respiratory cavity.—**Respiratory column, respiratory fascicle.** Same as *solitary funiculus* (which see, under *solitary*).—**Respiratory filaments**, thread-like organs arranged in tufts near the head of the larva or pupa of a gnat.—**Respiratory glottis**, the posterior portion of the glottis, between the arytenoid cartilages.—**Respiratory leaflets**, the laminated organs of respiration, or so-called lungs, of the pulmonary arachnidans. See cut under *pulmonary*.—**Respiratory murmur.** See *respiratory sounds*.—**Respiratory nerve.** (*a*) *External*, the posterior thoracic nerve. See *thoracic*. (*b*) *Internal*, the phrenic nerve.—**Respiratory nerve of the face**, the facial nerve.—**Respiratory nerves of Bell**, the facial, phrenic, and posterior thoracic nerves.—**Respiratory orifice.** (*a*) A stigmatum or breathing-pore. (*b*) An orifice, generally at the end of a tubular process, through which some aquatic larvæ, or larvæ living in putrescent matter, under the skin of animals, etc., obtain air.—**Respiratory percussion**, the percussion of the chest in different phases of respiration, with regard to the variations of the sounds elicited.—**Respiratory period**, the time from the beginning of one inspiration to that of the next.—**Respiratory plate**, in *entom.*, a respiratorium, or false gill.—**Respiratory portion of the nose**, the lower portion of the nasal cavity, excluding the upper or olfactory portion.—**Respiratory pulse**, alternating condition of fullness and emptiness of the large vessels of the neck or elsewhere, synchronous with expiration and inspiration.—**Respiratory quotient**, the ratio of the oxygen excreted by the lungs (as carbon dioxid) to that absorbed by them in the same time (as free oxygen). It is usually in the neighborhood of 0.9.—**Respiratory sac**, a simple sac-like respiratory organ of various animals.—**Respiratory sounds**, the sounds made by the air when being inhaled or exhaled, especially as heard in auscultation over lung-tissue, normal or diseased. See *vesicular respiratory murmur* below, for description of normal sounds.—**Respiratory surface**, the surface of the lungs that comes in contact with the air. This surface is extended by minute subdivision of the lungs into small cavities or air-cells.—**Respiratory tract**, in *med.*, a general term denoting the sum of the air-passages.—**Respiratory tree**, in *zoöl.*, an organ found in some holothurians, consisting of two highly contractile, branched, and arborescent tubes which run up toward the anterior extremity of the body, and perform the function of respiration; the cloaca.—**Respiratory tube**, any tubular organ of respiration; a spiracle. See *spiracle* and *breathing-tube*.—**Vesicular respiratory murmur**, the normal murmur. The quality of the inspiratory sound is vesicular; the expiratory sound, absent in many cases, is continuous with the inspiratory, and is more blowing, lower, and much shorter.—**Vesiculobronchial respiratory murmur.** Same as *bronchovesicular respiratory murmur*.

respire (rẹ̄-spīr'), *v.*; pret. and pp. *respired*, ppr. *respiring*. [< OF. *respirer*, F. *respirer* = Pr. Sp. Pg. *respirar* = It. *respirare*, < L. *respirare*, breathe out, exhale, breathe, take breath, revive, recover, < *re-*, back, again, + *spirare*, breathe, blow: see *spirit*. Cf. *aspire*, *conspire*, *expire*, *inspire*, *perspire*.] **I.** *intrans.* 1†. To breathe again; hence, to rest or enjoy relief after toil or suffering.

Then shall the Britons, late dismayd and weake,
From their long vassalage gin to *respire*.
Spenser, F. Q., III. iii. 36.

Sooth'd with Ease, the panting Youth *respires*.
Congreve, To Sleep.

Hark! he strikes the golden lyre;
And see! the tortured ghosts *respire*;
See shady forms advance!
Pope, Ode on St. Cecilia's Day, l. 64.

2. To breathe; inhale air into the lungs and exhale it, for the purpose of maintaining animal life; hence, to live.

Yet the brave Barons, whilst they do *respire*, . . .
With courage charge, with comeliness retire.
Drayton, Barons' Wars, ii. 55.

II. *trans.* 1. To breathe in and out, as air; inhale and exhale; breathe.

Methinks, now I come near her, I *respire*
Some air of that late comfort I received.
B. Jonson, Poetaster, iv. 6.

But I, who ne'er was bless'd by Fortune's hand, . . .
Long in the noisy Town have been immur'd,
Respir'd its smoke, and all its cares endur'd.
Gay, Rural Sports, i.

2. To exhale; breathe out; send out in exhalations.

The air *respires* the pure Elysian sweets
In which she breathes. *B. Jonson*, Poetaster, i. 1.

As smoke and various substances separately issue from fire lighted with moist wood, so from this great being [Brahma] were *respired* the Rigveda, etc.
Colebroke, Asiatic Researches, VIII.

respiring (rẹ̄-spīr'ing), *n.* [Verbal n. of *respire*, *v.*] A breathing; a breath.

They could not stir him from his stand, although he wrought it out
With short *respirings*, and with sweat.
Chapman, Iliad, xvi. 102.

respirometer (res-pi-rom'e-tėr), *n.* [Irreg. < L. *respirare*, take breath, + Gr. μέτρον, measure.] 1. An instrument which is used to determine the condition of the respiration.—2. An apparatus for supplying air to a diver under water by means of a supply of compressed oxygen, which is caused to combine in due proportion with nitrogen chemically filtered from the air expired from his lungs in breathing.

respite (res'pit), *n.* [Early mod. E. *respit*; < ME. *respit*, *respyt*, *respyte*, < OF. *respit*, respect, delay, respite, F. *répit* = Pr. *respieg*, *respeit* = Sp. *respecto* = Pg. *respeito* = It. *rispitto*, *rispetto*, respect, delay, < L. *respectus*, consideration, respect, ML. delay, postponement, respite, prorogation: see *respect*.] 1†. Respect; regard. See *respect*.

> Out of more *respit*,
> Myn herte hath for to amende it grete delit.
> *Chaucer*, Troilus, v. 137.

2. Temporary intermission of labor, or of any process or operation; interval of rest; pause.

> With that word, withoute more *respite*,
> They fillen gruf and criden pitously.
> *Chaucer*, Knight's Tale, l. 90.

> Some pause and *respite* only I require.
> *Sir J. Denham*, Passion of Dido for Æneas.

> Byzantium has a *respite* of half a century, and Egypt of more than a hundred years, of Mameluke tyranny.
> *Stubbs*, Medieval and Modern Hist., p. 202.

3. A putting off or postponement of what was fixed; delay; forbearance; prolongation of time, as for the payment of a debt, beyond the fixed or legal time.

> To make you understand this. . . . I crave but four days' *respite*.
> *Shak.*, M. for M., iv. 2. 170.

4. In *law*: (*a*) A reprieve; temporary suspension of the execution of a capital offender. See *reprieve*.

> The court gave him *respite* to the next session (which was appointed the first Tuesday in August) to bethink himself, that, retracting and reforming his error, etc., the court might show him favor.
> *Winthrop*, Hist. New England, I. 205.

> Christian . . . had some *respite*, and was remanded back to prison. *Bunyan*, Pilgrim's Progress, p. 161.

> Why grant me *respite* who deserve my doom?
> *Browning*, Ring and Book, II. 247.

(*b*) The delay of appearance at court granted to a jury beyond the proper term. =**Syn. 2.** Stop, cessation, stay.—**4.** *Reprieve, Respite.* See *reprieve*.

respite (res'pit), *v. t.*; pret. and pp. *respited*, ppr. *respiting*. [< ME. *respiten*, *respite*, < OF. *respiter*, *respeiter*, respect, delay, postpone, < L. *respectare*, consider, respect, ML. delay, postpone: see *respect*.] 1. To delay; postpone; adjourn.

> Thanne to the Sowdon furth with all they went,
> The lordes and the knyghtes eueryehone,
> And prayed hym to *respite* the Iugement.
> *Generydes* (E. E. T. S.), l. 1641.

> They declared only their opinions in writing, and *respited* the full determination to another general meeting.
> *Winthrop*, Hist. New England, I. 383.

2. To relieve for a time from the execution of a sentence or other punishment or penalty; reprieve.

> It is grete harme that thow art no cristin, and fain I wolde that thow so were, to *respite* the fro deth.
> *Merlin* (E. E. T. S.), iii. 592.

> Jeffreys had *respited* the younger brother.
> *Macaulay*, Hist. Eng., vii.

3. To relieve by a pause or interval of rest.

> With a dreadful industry of ten days, not *respiting* his Souldiers day or night, [Cæsar] drew up all his Ships, and entrench'd them round within the circuit of his Camp.
> *Milton*, Hist. Eng., ii.

> Care may be *respited*, but not repealed;
> No perfect cure grows on that bounded field.
> *Wordsworth*, Evening Voluntaries, iv.

4†. To cease; forbear.

> Your manly resoun oghte it to *respite*,
> To slen your frende, and namely me,
> That never yet in no degre
> Offended you.
> *Chaucer*, Anelida and Arcite, l. 259.

=**Syn. 2.** See *reprieve, n.*

respiteless (res'pit-les), *a.* [< *respite* + *-less*.] Without respite or relief. *Baxter*.

resplend (rē-splend'), *v. i.* [< ME. *resplenden*, < OF. *resplendir*, also *resplandre*, F. *resplendir* = Pr. *resplandre*, *resplandir* (cf. Sp. Pg. *resplandecer*) = It. *risplendere*, < L. *resplendere*, shine brightly, glitter, < *re-*, again, back, + *splendere*, shine: see *splendid*.] To shine; be resplendent. *Lydgate*. [Rare.]

> Lieutenant-General Webb, . . . who *resplended* in velvet and gold lace. *Thackeray*, Henry Esmond, ii. 15.

resplendence (rē-splen'dens), *n.* [< LL. *resplendentia*, < L. *resplenden(t-)s*, resplendent: see *resplendent*.] Brilliant luster; vivid brightness; splendor.

> Son! thou in whom my glory I behold
> In full *resplendence*, heir of all my might.
> *Milton*, P. L., v. 720.

=**Syn.** See *radiance*.

resplendency (rē-splen'den-si), *n.* [As *resplendence* (see *-cy*).] Same as *resplendence*. *Cotgrave*.

resplendent (rē-splen'dent), *a.* [< ME. *resplendent*, < L. *resplenden(t-)s*, ppr. of *resplendere*, shine brightly: see *resplend*.] 1. Shining with brilliant luster; very bright; splendid.

> There all within full rich arayd he found,
> With royall arras, and *resplendent* gold.
> *Spenser*, F. Q., I. viii. 35.

> Bright
> As the *resplendent* cactus of the night,
> That floods the gloom with fragrance and with light.
> *O. W. Holmes*, Bryant's Seventieth Birthday.

2. In *her.*, issuing rays: said especially of the sun, sometimes of clouds. See *radiant*, 3.—**Resplendent feldspar.** Same as *adularia* or *moonstone*. =**Syn. 1.** Glorious, beaming. See *radiance*.

resplendently (rē-splen'dent-li), *adv.* In a resplendent manner; with brilliant luster; with great brightness.

resplendish† (rē-splen'dish), *v. i.* [< OF. *resplendiss-*, stem of certain parts of *resplendir*, shine brightly: see *resplend*.] To shine with great brilliancy; be resplendent.

> Vppon this said tombe was he ther ligging,
> *Resplendising* fair in this chambre sprad.
> *Rom. of Partenay* (E. E. T. S.), l. 4512.

> The heuyn visible is . . . garnisshed with planettes and sterres, *resplendisshinge* in the moste pure firmament.
> *Sir T. Elyot*, The Governour, iii. 2.

resplendishant† (rē-splen'di-shant), *a.* [< OF. *resplendissant*, ppr. of *resplendir*, shine brightly: see *resplend*.] Resplendent; brilliant.

> And thorowe yᵉ vertue of thy full myght
> Causest yᵉ world to be *resplendishaunt*.
> *Fabyan*, Chron., xlix.

resplendishing† (rē-splen'di-shing), *n.* Resplendence; splendor.

> And as the Sunne doth glorifie each thing
> (Howeuer base) on which he deigns to smile,
> So your cleare eyes doe giue *resplendishing*
> To all their objects, be they ne'er so vile.
> *Davies*, Muse's Sacrifice, p. 7. (*Davies.*)

respond (rē-spond'), *v.* [< OF. *respondre*, *respundre*, F. *répondre* = Pr. *respondre* = Sp. Pg. *responder* = It. *respondere*, *rispondere*, < L. *respondere*, pp. *responsus*, answer, < *re-*, again, back, + *spondere*, pp. *sponsus*, promise: see *sponsor*. Cf. *despond*, *correspond*.] **I.** *intrans.* 1. To make answer; give a reply in words; specifically, to make a liturgical response.

> I remember him in the divinity school *responding* and disputing with a perspicuous energy.
> *Oldisworth*, Edmund Smith, in Johnson's Lives of the Poets.

2. To answer or reply in any way; exhibit some action or effect in return to a force or stimulus.

> A new affliction strings a new chord in the heart, which *responds* to some new note of complaint within the wide scale of human woe. *Buckminster*.

> Whenever there arises a special necessity for the better performance of any one function, or for the establishment of some function, nature will *respond*.
> *H. Spencer*, Social Statics, p. 427.

3. To correspond; suit.

> To every theme *responds* thy various lay.
> *W. Broome*, To Mr. Pope, On His Works (1726).

4. To be answerable; be liable to make payment: as, the defendant is held to *respond* in damages.

II. *trans.* 1†. To answer to; correspond to. [Rare.]

> His great deeds *respond* his speeches great.
> *Fairfax*, tr. of Tasso's Godfrey of Boulogne, x. 40.

2. To answer; satisfy, as by payment: as, the prisoner was held to *respond* the judgment of the court.

respond (rē-spond'), *n.* [< ME. *responde*, *respounde*, *responne*, *respon*; from the verb.] 1†. An answer; a response.

> Whereunto the whole Armie answered with a short *respond*, and, at the same time, bowing themselues to the ground, saluted the Moone with great superstition.
> *Purchas*, Pilgrimage, p. 295.

2. In *liturgics*: (*a*) A versicle or short anthem chanted at intervals during the reading of a lection. In the Anglican Church the responses to the commandments (Kyries) are responds in this sense.

> The reader paused, and the choir burst in with *responds*, versicles, and anthems.
> *R. W. Dixon*, Hist. Church of Eng., xv.

(*b*) A response.

> The clerk answering in the name of all, Et cum spiritu tuo, and other *responds*.
> J. *Bradford*, Works (Parker Soc., 1853), II. 334.

3. In *arch.*, a half-pillar, pilaster, or any corresponding device engaged in a wall to receive the impost of an arch.

> The four *responds* have the four evangelistic symbols.
> *E. A. Freeman*, Venice, p. 208.

respondeat ouster. See *judgment*.

responde-book (rē-spon'dē-bůk), *n.* A book kept by the directors of chancery in Scotland for entering the accounts of all non-entry and relief duties payable by heirs who take precepts from chancery.

respondence (rē-spon'dens), *n.* [= It. *rispondenza*, conformity, < L. *responden(t-)s*, respondent: see *respondent*. Cf. *correspondence*.] 1. The state or character of being respondent; also, the act of responding or answering; response.

> Th' Angelicall soft trembling voyces made
> To th' instruments divine *respondence* meet.
> *Spenser*, F. Q., II. xii. 71.

2†. Correspondence; agreement.

> His rent in fair *respondence* must arise
> To double trebles of his one yeare's price.
> *Bp. Hall*, Satires, V. i. 57.

respondency (rē-spon'den-si), *n.* [As *respondence* (see *-cy*).] Same as *respondence*.

> Thus you see the *respondency* of the spiritual to the natural tool in their qualities. *Rev. T. Adams*, Works, I. 248.

respondent (rē-spon'dent), *a.* and *n.* [= OF. *respondant*, F. *répondant* = Sp. *respondiente* = Pg. *respondente* = It. *rispondente*, < L. *responden(t-)s*, ppr. of *respondere*, answer: see *respond*.] **I.** *a.* 1. Answering; responding.

> The wards *respondent* to the key turn round;
> The bars fall back. *Pope*, Odyssey, xxi. 49.

2. Conformable; corresponding.

> Wealth *respondent* to payment and contributions.
> *Bacon*.

> Well may this palace admiration claim,
> Great, and *respondent* to the master's fame!
> *Pope*, Odyssey, xvii. 315.

II. *n.* 1. One who responds; specifically, in a scholastic disputation, one who maintains a thesis, and defends it against the objections of one or more opponents. There was no burden of proof upon the respondent at the outset, but, owing to the admissions which he was obliged by the rules of disputation to make, it was soon thrown upon him.

> Let them [scholars] occasionally change their attitude of mind from that of receivers and *respondents* to that of enquirers. *Fitch*, Lectures on Teaching, p. 172.

Specifically—2. One who answers or is called on to answer a petition or an appeal.—3. In *math.*, a quantity in the body of a table: opposed to *argument*, or the regularly varying quantity with which the table is entered. Thus, in a table of powers, where the base is entered at the side, the exponent at the top, and the power is found in the body of the table, the last quantity is the *respondent*.

respondentia (res-pon-den'shi-ä), *n.* [NL.: see *respondence*.] A loan on the cargo of a vessel, payment being contingent on the safe arrival of the cargo at the port of destination—the effect of such condition being to except the contract from the common usury laws. See *bottomry*.

> Commissions on money advanced, maritime interest on bottomry and *respondentia*, and the loss on exchanges, etc., are apportioned relatively to the gross sums expended on behalf of the several interests concerned.
> *Encyc. Brit.*, III. 148.

responsal (rē-spon'sal), *a.* and *n.* [= F. *responsal*, < LL. *responsalis*, one who answers for another, a sponsor, apocrisiary, prop. adj., pertaining to an answer, < L. *responsum*, an answer, response: see *response*.] **I.†** *a.* Answerable; responsible.

> They were both required to find sureties to be *responsal*, etc., whereupon they were troubled.
> *Winthrop*, Hist. New England, II. 347.

II. *n.* 1. Response; answer; especially, a liturgical response.

> After some short praiers and *responsals*, the mass-priest begs at the hands of God this great . . . favor.
> *Brevint*, Saul and Samuel, xiv.

2. (*a*) In the Roman empire, a representative of a foreign church or prelate, who resided at the capital and conducted negotiations on ecclesiastical matters; an apocrisiary. (*b*) A proctor for a monastery or for a member of it before the bishop.

response (rē-spons'), *n.* [< ME. *responnse*, *respons*, < OF. *respons*, *respuns*, *responce*, F. *réponse* = Pr. *respos* = Cat. *respons* = Sp. Pg. *responso* = It. *risponso*, *responso*, < L. *responsum*, an answer, neut. of *responsus*, pp. of *respondere*, answer: see *respond*.] 1. An answer or reply, or something in the nature of an answer or reply.

> What was his *respons* written, I ne sauh no herd.
> *Rob. of Brunne*, tr. of Langtoft, p. 98. (*Latham.*)

> There seems a vast psychological interval between an emotional *response* to the action of some grateful stimulus and the highly complex intellectual and emotional devel-

opment implied in a distinct appreciation of objective beauty. *J. Sully*, Sensation and Intuition, p. 17.

More specifically—(*a*) An oracular answer.

Then did my *response* clearer fall:
"No compound of this earthly ball
Is like another, all in all."
Tennyson, Two Voices.

(*b*) In *liturgics*: (1) A verse, sentence, phrase, or word said or sung by the choir or congregation in sequence or reply to the priest or officiant. Among the most ancient responses besides the responsories (which see) are *Et cum spiritu tuo* after the Dominus vobiscum, *Habemus ad Dominum* after the Sursum Corda, *Amen*, etc. Sometimes the response is a repetition of something said by the officiant. A verse which has its own response subjoined, the two together often forming one sentence, is called a *versicle*. In liturgical books the signs ℣ and ℟ are often prefixed to the versicle and response respectively. Also (formerly) *responsal*. (2) A versicle or anthem said or sung during or after a lection; a respond or responsory. (*c*) Reply to an objection in formal disputation. (*d*) In *music*, same as *answer*, 2 (*b*).

2. The act of responding or replying; reply: as, to speak in *response* to a question.—**Consultary response.** See *consultary*.

responsibility (rē-spon-si-bil'i-ti), *n.*; pl. *responsibilities* (-tiz). [= F. *responsabilité* = Sp. *responsabilidad* = Pg. *responsabilidade* = It. *risponsabilità*; as *responsible* + *-ity* (see *-bility*).] 1. The state of being responsible, accountable, or answerable.

A *responsibility* to a tribunal at which not only ministers, . . . but even nations themselves, must one day answer. *Burke*, A Regicide Peace, iii.

Responsibility, in order to be reasonable, must be limited to objects within the power of the responsible party. *A. Hamilton*, The Federalist, No. 63.

Gen. Jackson was a man of will, and his phrase on one memorable occasion, "I will take the *responsibility*," is a proverb ever since. *Emerson*, Fortune of the Republic.

2. That for which one is responsible or accountable; a trust, duty, or the like: as, heavy *responsibilities*.

His wife persuaded him that he had done the best that any one could do with the *responsibilities* that ought never to have been laid on a man of his temperament and habits. *Howells*, A Fearful Responsibility, xiii.

3. Ability to answer in payment; means of paying contracts.

responsible (rē-spon'si-bl), *a.* [= OF. (and F.) *responsable* = Pr. Sp. *responsable* = Pg. *responsavel* = It. *risponsabile*, < ML. *responsabilis*, requiring an answer, < L. *responsum*, response: see *response*.] 1†. Correspondent; answering; responsive.

I have scarce collected my spirits, but lately scattered in the admiration of your form; to which if the bounties of your mind be any way *responsible*, I doubt not but my desires shall find a smooth and secure passage. *B. Jonson*, Every Man out of his Humour, ii. 1.

2. Answerable, as for an act performed or for its consequences, or for a trust reposed or a debt; accountable; specifically, in *ethics*, in general, having such a mental or moral character as to be capable of knowing and observing the distinction of right from wrong in conduct, and therefore morally accountable for one's acts; in particular (with reference to a certain act), acting or having acted as a free agent, and with knowledge of the ethical character of the act or of its consequences. With regard to the legal use of the word, two conceptions are often confused—namely, that of the potential condition of being bound to answer or respond in case a wrong should occur, and that of the actual condition of being bound to respond because a wrong has occurred. For the first of these *responsible* is properly used, and for the second *liable*.

With ministers thus *responsible*, "the king could do no wrong." *Sir E. May*, Const. Hist. Eng., I. i.

In this sense of the word we say that a man is *responsible* for that part of an event which was undetermined when he was left out of account, and which became determined when he was taken account of. *W. K. Clifford*, Lectures, II. 150.

3. Able to answer or respond to any reasonable claim or to what is expected; able to discharge an obligation, or having estate adequate to the payment of a debt.

He is a *responsible*-looking gentleman dressed in black. *Dickens*, Bleak House, xxviii.

4. Involving responsibility.

But it is a *responsible* trust, and difficult to discharge. *Dickens*.

Responsible business (*theat.*), rôles next in importance above those described as "utility."—**Responsible utility** (*theat.*), a minor actor who can be trusted with very small parts—who is also said to play "genteel business."

responsibleness (rē-spon'si-bl-nes), *n.* The state of being responsible; responsibility. *Bailey*, 1727.

responsibly (rē-spon'si-bli), *adv.* In a responsible manner.

responsion (rē-spon'shon), *n.* [= OF. *responsion*, an answer, surety, suretyship, = Pg. *responsão*, ground-rent, = It. *risponsione*, an answer, reply, < L. *responsio(n-)*, an answer, reply, refutation, < *respondere*, pp. *responsus*, answer: see *response*.] 1. The act of answering; answer; reply.

Responsions unto the questions. *Bp. Burnet*, Records, iii., No. 21.

Everywhere in nature, Whitman finds human relations, human *responsions*. *The Century*, XIX. 294.

2. In *anc. pros.*: (*a*) The metrical correspondence between strophe and antistrophe. (*b*) A formal correspondence between successive parts in dialogue.—3. *pl.* The first examination which those students at Oxford have to pass who are candidates for the degree of B. A.

responsive (rē-spon'siv), *a.* and *n.* [< OF. (and F.) *responsif* = It. *risponsivo*, < LL. *responsivus*, answering (ML. *responsiva*, f., an answering epistle), < L. *respondere*, pp. *responsus*, respond: see *respond*.] I. *a.* 1. Answering; correspondent; suited to something else; being in accord.

The vocal lay *responsive* to the strings. *Pope*.

2†. Responsible; answerable.

Such persons . . . for whom the church herself may safely be *responsive*. *Jer. Taylor*, Works (ed. 1835), II. 288.

3. Able, ready, or inclined to respond or answer; answering; replying.

A *responsive* letter, or letter by way of answer. *Ayliffe*, Parergon.

The swain *responsive* as the milk-maid sung. *Goldsmith*, Des. Vil., l. 117.

A may be more quickly *responsive* to a stimulus than B, and may have a wider range of sensibility, and yet not be more discriminative. *J. Sully*, Outlines of Psychol., p. 145.

4. Characterized by the use of responses: as, a *responsive* service of public worship.—5. In *law*, pertinent in answer; called for by the question: as, a party is not bound by an answer given by his own witness if it is not *responsive* to the question, but may have the irresponsive matter struck out.

II.† *n.* An answer; a response; a reply.

Responsives to such as ye wrote of the dates before rehearsed. *Bp. Burnet*, Records, ii. 23.

responsively (rē-spon'siv-li), *adv.* In a responsive manner.

responsiveness (rē-spon'siv-nes), *n.* The state of being responsive.

responsorial (res-pon-sō'ri-al), *a.* and *n.* [< *responsory* + *-al*.] I. *a.* Responsive; specifically, sung in response to or alternation with a lector or precentor.

II. *n.* An office-book formerly in use, containing the responsories or these and the antiphons for the canonical hours.

responsorium (res-pon-sō'ri-um), *n.*; pl. *responsoria* (-ä). [ML., neut. of **responsorius*: see *responsory*.] Same as *responsory*.

responsory (rē-spon'sō-ri), *a.* and *n.* [< ML. **responsorius*, adj. (as a noun, *responsorium*, neut., *responsoria*, f., eccl., a response), < L. *respondere*, pp. *responsus*, respond: see *respond*, *response*.] I. *a.* Containing answer.

II. *n.*; pl. *responsories* (-riz). In *liturgics*: (*a*) A psalm or portion of a psalm sung between the missal lections. Among the anthems representing this custom are the Greek prokeimenon, the Ambrosian psalmulus or psalmellus, the Gallican psalmus responsorius (responsory psalm), and the Mozarabic psalterium or psallendo—all these preceding the epistle, and the Roman and Sarum gradual preceding the gospel. The responsory was sung not antiphonally, but by a lector, precentor, or several cantors, the whole choir responding. The name *responsory* is often given specifically to the *gradual* (which see). (*b*) A portion of a psalm (originally, a whole psalm) sung between the lections at the canonical hours; a respond. Also *responsorium*.

responsure (rē-spon'sūr), *n.* [< *response* + *-ure*.] Response. [Rare.]

Fogs, damps, trees, stones, their sole encompassure,
To whom they mone, black todes giue *responsure*.
C. Tourneur, Transformed Metamorphosis, st. 87.

ressala (res'a-lä), *n.* See *risala*.

ressaldar (res'al-där), *n.* See *risaldar*.

ressant†, **ressaunt**†, *n.* Same as *ressaut*.

ressaut (res-ât'), *n.* [Also *ressault*, also erroneously *ressant*, *ressaunt*; < OF. *ressaut*, *ressault*, F. *ressaut* = Pr. *ressaut*, *resaut* = Cat. *ressalt* = Sp. Pg. *resalto* = It. *risalto*, a projection (in arch.), < ML. as if **resultus*, < L. *resilire*, pp. **resultus*, leap back: see *resile*, and cf. *result*.] In *arch.*, a projection of any member or part from or before another.

rest[1] (rest), *n.* [< ME. *rest*, *reste*, < AS. *rest*, *ræst*, rest, quiet, = OS. *resta*, *rasta*, resting-place, burial-place, = D. *rust* = MLG. *reste*, rest, = OHG. *rasta*, rest, also a measure of distance, *resti*, rest, MHG. *raste*, G. *rast*, rest, repose, = Icel. *röst*, a mile, i. e. the distance between two resting-places, = Sw. Dan. *rast*, rest, = Goth. *rasta*, a stage of a journey, a mile; with abstract formative *-st*, < √*ra*, rest, Skt. √*ram*, rest, rejoice at, sport, > *rati*, pleasure.] 1. A state of quiet or repose; absence or cessation of motion, labor, or action of any kind; release from exertion or action.

Whils forto sytte ye haue in komaundement,
Youre heede, youre hande, your feet, holde yee in *reste*.
Babees Book (E. E. T. S.), p. 4.

Our rural ancestors, with little blest,
Patient of labour when the end was *rest*.
Pope, Imit. of Horace, II. i. 242.

The working of a sea
Before a calm, that rocks itself to *rest*.
Cowper, Task, vi. 739.

2. Freedom or relief from everything that disquiets, wearies, or disturbs; peace; quiet; security; tranquillity.

Yef we may hem discounfite, we shall be riche and in *reste* alwey aftere. *Merlin* (E. E. T. S.), ii. 174.

The man will not be in *rest* until he have finished the thing this day. Ruth iii. 18.

Yet shall the oracle
Give *rest* to the minds of others.
Shak., W. T., ii. 1. 191.

Rest,
As deep as death, as soft as sleep,
Across his troubled heart did creep.
William Morris, Earthly Paradise, II. 48.

3. Sleep; slumber; hence, the last sleep; death; the grave.

After al this surfet and accesse he hedde,
That he slepte Seturday and Sonenday til sonne wente to
reste. *Piers Plowman* (A), v. 210.

One that thinks a man always going to bed, and says, "God give you good *rest!*" *Shak.*, C. of E., iv. 3. 33.

4. A place of quiet; permanent habitation.

In dust, our final *rest* and native home.
Milton, P. L., x. 1085.

5. Stay; abode.

That you vouchsafe your *rest* here in our court
Some little time. *Shak.*, Hamlet, ii. 2. 13.

6. That on or in which anything leans or lies for support.

He made narrowed *rests* round about, that the beams should not be fastened in the walls of the house. 1 Ki. vi. 6.

Specifically—(*a*) A contrivance for steadying the lance when couched for the charge: originally a mere loop or stirrup, usually of leather, perhaps passed over the shoulder, but when the cuirass or breastplate was introduced secured to a hook or projecting horn of iron riveted to this on the left side. This hook also is called *rest*. A similar hook was sometimes arranged so far at the side, and so projecting, as to receive the lance itself; but, this form being inconvenient, the projecting hook was arranged with a hinge. In the justs of the fifteenth and sixteenth centuries the heavy lance was found to require a counterpoise, and the rest was made double, the hook projecting sidewise, and a long tongue or bar projecting backward under the arm with a sort of spiral twist at the end to prevent the butt of the lance from rising, so that the lance was held firmly, and required from the juster only the exertion of directing its point.

When his staff was in his *rest*, coming down to meet with the knight, now very near him, he perceived the knight had missed his *rest*. *Sir P. Sidney*, Arcadia, iii.

Not like that Arthur who, with lance in *rest*, . . .
Shot thro' the lists at Camelot.
Tennyson, Passing of Arthur.

(*b*) A device of any kind for supporting the turning-tool or the work in a lathe. (c) A support for the barrel of a gun in aiming and firing.

Change love for arms; girt to your blades, my boys!
Your *rests* and muskets take, take helm and targe.
Peele, A Farewell.

(d) In *billiards*, a rod having fixed at its point a crosspiece on which to support the cue: used when the cue-ball cannot easily be reached in the usual way. Also called *bridge*. (*e*) A support or guide for stuff fed to a saw. *E. H. Knight*. (*f*) In *glyptics*, a support, somewhat resembling a vise in form, attached to the lathe-head, and serving to steady the arm while the edges of graving-tools are being shaped.

7. In *pros.*, a short pause of the voice in reading; a cesura.

So varying still their [bards'] moods, observing yet in all
Their quantities, their *rests*, their ceasures metrical.
Drayton, Polyolbion, iv. 186.

8. In *music*: (*a*) A silence or pause between tones. (*b*) In musical notation, a mark or sign denoting such a silence. Rests vary in form to indicate their duration with reference to each other and to the notes with which they occur; and they are named from the notes to which they are equivalent, as follows: breve rest, 𝄺; semibreve or whole-note rest, 𝄻; minim or half-note rest, 𝄼; crotchet or quarter-note rest, 𝄽 or 𝄽; quaver or eighth-note rest, 𝄾; semiquaver or sixteenth-note rest, 𝄿; demisemiquaver or thirty-second-note rest, 𝅀; hemidemisemiquaver or sixty-fourth-note rest, 𝅁. The duration of a rest, as of a note, may be extended one half by a dot, as 𝄾. (= 𝄾𝄿), or indefinitely by a hold, 𝄐𝄾. The semibreve rest is often used as a measure-rest, whatever may be the rhythmic signature (as *a* below); similarly, the two-measure rest is like *b*, the three-measure rest like

c, the four-measure rest like d; or a semibreve rest or similar character is used with a figure above to indicate the number of measures, as e or f.

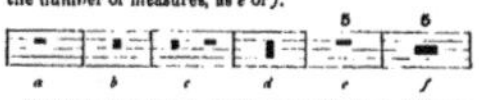

He fights as you sing prick-song, keeps time, distance, and proportion; rests me his minim *rest*, one, two, and the third in your bosom. *Shak.*, R. and J., ii. 4. 23.

9†. A syllable.

Two *rests*, a short and long, th' Iambic frame.
B. Jonson, tr. of Horace's Art of Poetry.

10. In *accounting*, the stopping to strike a balance or sum up the total, as for the purpose of computing commissions or compounding interest. Thus, an annual *rest* takes place where the rents received by the mortgagee in possession are more than sufficient to keep down the interest, and the surplus is directed to be employed in liquidation of the principal *pro tanto*.

11. In *her.*, same as *clarion* and *sufflue*.—**12.** Same as *mascl*, 3.—**13†.** In *court-tennis*, a quick and continued returning of the ball from one player to the other. *R. W. Lowe*, Note in Cibber's Apology, I. 148.

For a wit is like a *rest*
Held up at tennis, which men do the best
With the best gamesters.
F. Beaumont, To Ben Jonson.

Knock me down if ever I saw a *rest* of wit better played than that last, in my life. *Cibber*, Careless Husband, iv. 1.

14. In the game of primero, the highest or final stake made by a player; also, the hand of cards or the number of points held. See *to set up one's rest*, under *set*.

Each one in possibility to win,
Great *rests* were up and mightie hands were in.
Mir. for Mags., p. 528. (*Nares.*)

Absolute rest, a state of absence of motion, without reference to other bodies. No definite meaning can be attached to the phrase.—**Currents of rest.** See *current*¹.—**Equation of rest.** See *equation*.—**Friction of rest.** See *friction*.—**Large rest**, in *mediæval musical notation*, a rest or sign for silence equal in time-value to a large. It was either perfect (*a*), or imperfect (*b*). The former was equal to three longs, the latter to two.—**Relative rest**, the absence of motion relative to some body.—**To set one's heart at rest.** See *heart*.—**To set up one's rest†.** See *set*. =**Syn. 1.** *Pause, Stay*, etc. (see *stop*).—**2.** *Rest, Repose, Ease, Quiet, Tranquillity, Peace.* While these words are used with some freedom, *rest* and *repose* apply especially to the suspended activity of the body; *ease* and *quiet* to freedom from occupation or demands for activity, especially of the body; *tranquillity* and *peace* to the freedom of the mind from harassing cares or demands.

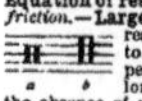

rest¹ (rest), *v.* [< ME. *resten*, < AS. *restan* = OS. *restian* = OFries. *resta* = D. *rusten* = MLG. *resten* = OHG. *rastên*, *restan*, *raston*, *resten*, MHG. *rasten*, *resten*, G. *rasten* = Sw. *rasta* = Dan. *raste*, rest; from the noun: see *rest*¹, *n.* The verb *rest*¹ in some uses mingles with the different verb *rest*².] **I.** *intrans.* **1.** To cease from action, motion, work, or performance of any kind; stop; desist; be without motion.

He *rested* on the seventh day from all his work which he had made. Gen. ii. 2.

Over the tent a cloud
Shall *rest* by day. *Milton*, P. L., xii. 257.

He hangs between; in doubt to act, or *rest*.
Pope, Essay on Man, ii. 7.

2†. To come to a pause or to an end; end.

But now *resteth* the tale of kynge Rion, . . . and returne for to speke of kynge Arthur. *Merlin* (E. E. T. S.), ii. 224.

3. To be free from whatever harasses or disturbs; be quiet or still; be undisturbed.

My lord shall never *rest*;
I'll watch him tame and talk him out of patience.
Shak., Othello, iii. 3. 22.

Woo'd an unfeeling statue for his wife,
Nor *rested* till the gods had giv'n it life.
Cowper, Progress of Error, l. 520.

4. To take rest; repose.

Eche yede to his ostell to *resten*, for therto hadde thei nede and gret myster, for many were they hurte.
Merlin (E. E. T. S.), ii. 138.

Old lord, I cannot blame thee,
Who am myself attach'd with weariness,
To the dulling of my spirits; sit down, and *rest*.
Shak., Tempest, iii. 3. 6.

5. To sleep; slumber.

Thick slumber
Hangs upon mine eyes; let me *rest*. [Sleeps.]
Shak., Pericles, v. 1. 236.

6. In *bot.*, to lie dormant. See *resting-spore*, *resting-state*, etc.—**7.** To sleep the final sleep; die, or be dead.

If in the world he live, we'll seek him out;
If in his grave he *rest*, we'll find him there.
Shak., Pericles, ii. 4. 30.

So peaceful *rests*, without a stone, a name,
What once had beauty, titles, wealth, and fame.
Pope, Elegy on an Unfortunate Lady.

8. To stand or lie, as upon a support or basis; be supported; have a foundation: literally or figuratively.

Flitting light
From spray to spray, where'er he *rests* he shakes
From many a twig the pendent drops of ice.
Cowper, Task, vi. 80.

Eloquence, like every other art, *rests* on laws the most exact and determinate. *Emerson*, Eloquence.

This abbatial staff often *rested*, like a bishop's, on the abbot's left side [when borne to church for his burial].
Rock, Church of our Fathers, ii. 215.

Belief *rests* upon knowledge as a house *rests* upon its foundation. *H. James*, Subs. and Shad., p. 98.

9. To be satisfied; acquiesce.

I was forced to *rest* with patience, while my noble and beloved country was so injuriously treated.
Swift, Gulliver's Travels, ii. 7.

10. To be fixed in any state or opinion; remain.

Neither will he *rest* content, though thou givest many gifts. Prov. vi. 35.

Thou Power Supreme, whose mighty scheme
These woes of mine fulfil,
Here, firm, I *rest*, they must be best,
Because they are thy will! *Burns*, Winter.

11. To lean; trust; rely; have confidence; depend for support.

Behold, thou art called a Jew, and *restest* in the law, and makest thy boast of God. Rom. ii. 17.

Help us, O Lord our God; for we *rest* on thee, and in thy name do we go against this multitude. 2 Chron. xiv. 11.

That spirit upon whose weal depend and *rest*
The lives of many. *Shak.*, Hamlet, iii. 3. 14.

They *rested* in the declaration which God had made in his church. *Donne*, Sermons, vi.

12. To be in a certain state or position, as an affair; stand.

Now thus it *rests*;
Her father means she shall be all in white.
Shak., M. W. of W., iv. 6. 34.

13. In *law*, to terminate voluntarily the adducing of evidence, in order to await the counter-evidence of the adverse party, or to submit the case, upon the evidence, to the tribunal for decision. After a party has rested he has no longer a legal right to put in evidence, unless to countervail new matter in the evidence thereafter adduced by his adversary, although the court, for cause shown, may in its discretion allow him to do so.—**To rest in.** (*a*†) To depend upon.

It *rested in* your grace
To unloose this tied-up justice when you pleased.
Shak., M. for M., i. 3. 31.

(*b*) To consist or remain in.

They [Utopians] think not felicity to *rest in* all pleasure, but only in that pleasure that is good and honest.
Sir T. More, Utopia (tr. by Robinson), ii. 7.

To rest with, to be in the power of; depend upon: as, it *rests with* time to decide. =**Syn. 1.** To stay, forbear.—**1, 3, and 4.** *Rest, Repose. Rest* signifies primarily to cease from action or work, but naturally by extension to be refreshed by doing so, and further to be refreshed by sleeping. *Repose* does not necessarily imply previous work, but does imply quietness, and generally a reclining position, while we may *rest* in a standing position. See *stop*, *n.*, and *rest*¹, *n.*—**11.** To depend.

II. *trans.* **1.** To give repose to; place at rest; refresh by repose: sometimes used reflexively: as, to *rest one's self* (that is, to cease from exertion for the purpose of recruiting one's energies).

By the renke [when the knight] hade *hym restid* ryses the sun. *Destruction of Troy* (E. E. T. S.), l. 814.

Enter Ferdinand, bearing a log.
Miranda. Pray, set it down and *rest you*: when this burns,
'Twill weep for having wearied you. *Shak.*, Tempest, iii. 1.

I pray you, tell me, is my boy, God *rest* his soul, alive or dead? *Shak.*, M. of V., ii. 2. 75.

2. To lay or place, as on a support, basis, or foundation: literally or figuratively.

This is my plea, on this I *rest* my cause—
What saith my counsel, learned in the laws?
Pope, Imit. of Horace, II. i. 141.

Straight he took his bow of ash-tree,
On the sand one end he *rested*.
Longfellow, Hiawatha, ix.

3. To leave; allow to stand.

Now how I haue or could preuent these accidents, hauing no more meanes, I *rest* at your censures [judgments].
Capt. John Smith, Works, II. 213.

rest² (rest), *v.* [= D. *resten*, *resteren* = G. *resten*, *restiren* = Dan. *restere* = Sw. *restera*, rest, remain, < OF. (and F.) *rester* = Pr. Sp. Pg. *restar* = It. *restare*, *ristare*, < L. *restare*, stop, rest, stand still, remain, < *re-*, behind, back, + *stare*, stand: see *stand*. Cf. *arrest*¹. The verb *rest*² is partly confused with some uses of *rest*¹.] **I.** *intrans.* **1.** To be left; remain.

Nought *rests*
But that she fit her love now to her fortune.
B. Jonson, Alchemist, iv. 2.

What *rests* of both, one Sepulchre shall hold.
Prior, Henry and Emma.

2. To continue to be; remain: as, *rest* assured that it is true.

He shal *reste* in stockes
As longe as ich lyue for hus luther werkes.
Piers Plowman (C), v. 104.

Nought shall make us rue,
If England to itself do *rest* but true.
Shak., K. John, v. 7. 118.

I *rest* Your dutiful Son, J. H. *Howell*, Letters, I. iv. 24.

II.† *trans.* To keep; cause to continue or remain: used with a predicate adjective following and qualifying the object.

God *rest* you merry, sir. *Shak.*, As you Like it, v. 1. 65.

Rest you fair, good signior. *Shak.*, M. of V., i. 3. 60.

rest² (rest), *n.* [= D. G. Sw. Dan. *rest*, < OF. and F. *reste*, rest, residue, remnant, = Pr. *resta* = Sp. *resto*, *resta* = Pg. *resto* = It. *resta*, rest, repose, pause; from the verb: see *rest*², *v.*] **1.** That which is left, or which remains after the separation of a part, either in fact or in contemplation; remainder.

Let us not daily with God when he offers us a full blessing, to take as much of it as wee think will serve our ends, and turne him backe the *rest* upon his hands.
Milton, Reformation in Eng., ii.

2. Those not included in a proposition or description; others. [In this sense *rest* is a collective noun taking a plural verb.]

Plato, and the *rest* of the philosophers, acknowledged the unity, power, wisdom, goodness, and providence of the supreme God. *Bp. Stillingfleet.*

The million flit as gay
As if created only like the fly, . . .
The *rest* are sober dreamers, grave and wise.
Cowper, Task, iii. 137.

3. Balance; difference; specifically, in the weekly reports of the Bank of England, the balance of assets above liabilities, forming a sort of reserve fund against contingencies. [In all uses *rest* is always preceded by the definite article.]—**Above the rest.** See *above*.—**For the rest**, as regards other matters; in fine. =**Syn. 1.** *Residue*, etc. See *remainder*.

rest³ (rest), *v. t.* [By apheresis from *arrest*¹.] To arrest. [Colloq.]

Fear me not, man; I will not break away;
I'll give thee, ere I leave thee, so much money,
To warrant thee, as I am '*rested* for.
Shak., C. of E., iv. 4. 3.

rest⁴†, *v.* An obsolete form of *reast*¹.

rest⁵ (rest), *v.* A dialectal variant of *roast*. *Halliwell.* [Prov. Eng.]

rest⁶†, *n.* An obsolete phonetic spelling of *wrest*.

restagnant† (rē-stag′nạnt), *a.* [= It. *ristagnante*, stanching, stopping; < L. *restagnan(t-)s*, overflowing, ppr. of *restagnare*, overflow: see *restagnate*.] Stagnant; remaining without a flow or current.

The nearer we come to the top of the atmosphere, the shorter and lighter is the cylinder of air incumbent upon the *restagnant* mercury. *Boyle*, Works, I. 151.

restagnate† (rē-stag′nāt), *v. i.* [= It. *ristagnare*, stop, solder with lime; < L. *restagnare*, overflow, run over, < *re-*, again, + *stagnare*, form a pool, overflow: see *stagnate*.] To stand or remain without flowing; stagnate.

The blood returns thick, and is apt to *restagnate*.
Wiseman, Surgery, i. 21.

restagnation† (rē-stag-nā′shọn), *n.* [< L. *restagnatio(n-)*, an overflow, inundation, < *restagnare*, overflow: see *restagnate*.] Stagnation.

The *restagnation* of gross blood.
Wiseman, Surgery, i. 14.

restant (res′tạnt), *a.* [< F. *restant*, ppr. of *rester*, remain: see *rest*².] **1†.** Remaining; being in possession.

With him they were *restant* all those things that the foolish virgins could wish for, beauty, daintie, delicates, riches, faire speech.
Holland, tr. of Camden, p. 302. (*Davies.*)

2. In *bot.*, same as *persistent*: sometimes applied specifically to a footstalk from which the fructification has fallen away. [Rare.]

restate (rē-stāt′), *v. t.* [< *re-* + *state*.] To state again: as, to *restate* a charge.

restatement (rē-stāt′mẹnt), *n.* A second statement, as of facts or opinions, in either the same or a new form.

restaur (res-târ′), *n.* [Also *restor*; < OF. *restors*, *restour*, F. *restaur* = It. *restauro*, *ristauro*, < ML. *restaurum*, a restoring: see *restore*¹.] In *law*: (*a*) The remedy or recourse which assurers have against each other, according to the date of their assurances, or against the master of a ship if the loss arose through his fault. (*b*) The remedy or recourse a person has against his guarantor or other person who is to indemnify him for any damage sustained.

restaurant (res'tạ-rant), *n.* [< F. *restaurant*, a restaurant, formerly also a restorative, = Sp. *restaurante*, a restorer, < ML. *restauran(t-)s*, restoring, ppr. of *restaurare*, restore, refresh: see *restore*.] An establishment for the sale of refreshments, both food and drink; a place where meals are served; an eating-house.

The substitution of the *Restaurant* for the Tavern is of recent origin. In the year 1837 there were *restaurants*, it is true, but they were humble places, and confined to the parts of London frequented by the French; for English of every degree there was the Tavern.
W. Besant, Fifty Years Ago, p. 160.

restaurant-car (res'tạ-rant-kär), *n.* A railway-car in which meals are cooked and served to passengers; a dining-car or hotel-car.

restaurate† (res'tạ-rāt), *v. t.* [< L. *restauratus*, pp. of *restaurare*, restore, repair, renew: see *restore*[1].] To restore.

If one repulse hath us quite ruinated,
And fortune never can be *restaurated*.
Vicars, tr. of Virgil (1632). (*Nares.*)

restaurateur (res-tō'ra-tėr), *n.* [< F. *restaurateur* = Pr. *restauraire*, *restaurador* = Sp. Pg. *restaurador* = It. *restauratore*, *ristoratore* = D. G. *restaurateur* = Dan. Sw. *restauratör*, the keeper of a restaurant, < ML. *restaurator*, one who restores or reëstablishes: see *restorator*.] The keeper of a restaurant.

The ticket merely secures you a place on board the steamer, but neither a berth nor provisions. The latter you obtain from a *restaurateur* on board, according to fixed rates.
B. Taylor, Northern Travel, p. 273.

restauration† (res-tạ-rā'shọn), *n.* An obsolete form of *restoration*.

restaurator†, *n.* See *restorator*.

restaure†, *v. t.* An obsolete form of *restore*[1].

restay†, *v. t.* [< ME. *restayen*, < OF. *restaier*, < *rester*, rest: see *rest*[2].] To keep back; restrain.

To touch her chyldor thay fayr him [Christ] prayed.
His dessypeleȝ with blame let be hym bede,
& wyth her resouneȝ ful fele *restayed*.
Alliterative Poems (ed. Morris), i. 715.

rest-cure (rest'kūr), *n.* The treatment, as of nervous exhaustion, by more or less prolonged and complete rest, as by isolation in bed. This is usually combined with over-feeding, massage, and electricity.

restem (rẹ-stem'), *v. t.* [< *re-* + *stem*.] To stem again; force back against the current.

Now they do *re-stem*
Their backward course, bearing with frank appearance
Their purposes toward Cyprus. *Shak.*, Othello, i. 3. 37.

restful (rest'fůl), *a.* [< late ME. *restefulle*; < *rest*[1] + *-ful*.] 1. Full of rest; giving rest.

Tired with all these, for *restful* death I cry.
Shak., Sonnets, lxvi.

2. Quiet; being at rest.

I heard you say, "Is not my arm of length
That reacheth from the *restful* English court
As far as Calais, to my uncle's head?"
Shak., Rich. II., iv. 1. 12.

restfully (rest'fůl-i), *adv.* [< late ME. *restfully*; < *restful* + *-ly*[2].] In a restful manner; in a state of rest or quiet.

They liuing *restfully* and in helth vnto extreme age.
Sir T. Elyot, The Governour, iii. 21.

restfulness (rest'fůl-nes), *n.* The state of being restful. *Imp. Dict.*

rest-harrow (rest'har"ō), *n.* [So called because the root of the plant 'arrests' or stops the harrow; < *rest*[3], *v.*, + obj. *harrow*[1]. Cf. equiv. F. *arrête-bœuf*, lit. 'stop-ox,' < *arrêter*, stop, arrest, + *bœuf*, ox.] 1. A common European under-shrub, *Ononis arvensis*, generally low, spreading, and much branched (often thorny), bearing pink papilionaceous flowers, and having tough matted roots which hinder the plow or harrow. The root is diuretic. Also *wild liquorice*, *cammock*, *whin*, etc.— 2. A small geometrid moth, *Aplasta ononaria*: popularly so called in England because the caterpillar feeds in April and September on *Ononis arvensis*, var. *spinosa*. The moth flies in May, July, and August.

Flowering Branch of Rest-harrow (*Ononis arvensis*).
a, a flower; *b*, the leaf.

resthouse (rest'hous), *n.* [< *rest*[1] + *house*[1].] Same as *dak-bungalow* (which see, under *bungalow*).

Restiaceæ (res-ti-ā'sē-ē), *n. pl.* [NL. (R. Brown, 1810), < *Restio* + *-aceæ*.] An order of monocotyledonous plants of the series *Glumaceæ*. It resembles the rushes (*Juncaceæ*) in its one- to three-celled ovary and dry, rigid, and glumaceous perianth of six equal segments; and the sedges (*Cyperaceæ*) in habit, in structure of spikelets, and in the three stamens, small embryo, and mealy or fleshy albumen. It is distinguished from both by its pendulous orthotropous ovules and its split sheaths. It includes about 240 species, belonging to 20 genera, of which *Restio* (the type), *Willdenovia*, and *Elegia* are the chief—all sedge-like plants of the southern hemisphere, mainly natives of South Africa and Australia, absent from America and Asia excepting one species in Chili and one in Cochin-China. They are generally perennials, tufted or with a hard horizontal or creeping, more often scaly rootstock, the stems rigid, erect or variously twisted, the leaves commonly reduced. They are almost always diœcious, and have a polymorphous inflorescence often extremely different in the two sexes.

restibrachial (res-ti-brā'ki-al), *a.* [< *restibrachium* + *-al*.] Pertaining to the restibrachium; postpeduncular.

restibrachium (res-ti-brā'ki-um), *n.*; pl. *restibrachia* (-ạ̈). [NL., < L. *restis*, a rope, + *brachium*, an arm.] The inferior peduncle of the cerebellum. Also called *myelobrachium*.

Restibrachium (Science, April 9, 1881, p. 165) is an admirable compound, and the same may be said of its correlatives, pontibrachium and tegmentibrachium.
Buck's Handbook of Med. Sciences, VIII. 525, note.

restie†, *a.* See *resty*[1].

restiff†, *a.* An obsolete form of *restive*.

restiffness†, *n.* An obsolete form of *restiveness*. *Imp. Dict.*

restiform (res'ti-fôrm), *a.* [= F. *restiforme*, < L. *restis*, a cord, rope, + *forma*, form.] Corded or cord-like: specifically, in *anat.*, noting a part of the medulla oblongata, called the *corpus restiforme*, or *restiform body*.—**Restiform body**, the inferior peduncle of the cerebellum, by which it connects with the oblongata and parts below. It contains the direct cerebellar-tract fibers, crossed and uncrossed from the posterior columns of the cord, and fibers from the contralateral (lower) olive.

restily (res'ti-li), *adv.* [< *resty*[1] + *-ly*[2].] In a sluggish manner; stubbornly; untowardly. *Imp. Dict.*

restinction (rẹ-stingk'shọn), *n.* [< L. *restinctio(n-)*, a quenching, < *restinguere*, put out, destroy, quench, < *re-*, again, + *stinguere*, extinguish: see *extinguish*.] The act of quenching or extinguishing. *E. Phillips*, 1706. [Rare.]

restiness† (res'ti-nes), *n.* [< *resty*[1] + *-ness*.] Tendency to rest or inaction; sluggishness.

The Snake, by *restinesse* and lying still all Winter, hath a certain membrane or filme growing ouer her whole body.
Holland, tr. of Pliny, viii. 27.

A tenuity and agility of spirits, contrary to that *restiness* of the spirits supposed in those that are dull.
Hobbes, Works, IV. 56.

resting-cell (res'ting-sel), *n.* Same as *resting-spore*.

resting-owing (res'ting-ō"ing), *a.* [< *resting*, ppr. of *rest*[2], *v.*, + *owing*, ppr. of *owe*[1], *v.*] In *Scots law*: (*a*) Resting or remaining due: said of a debt. (*b*) Indebted: said of a debtor.

resting-place (res'ting-plās), *n.* 1. A place for rest; a place to stop at, as on a journey: used figuratively for the grave.

Arise, O Lord God, into thy *resting place*, thou and the ark of thy strength. 2 Chron. vi. 41.

It was from Istrian soil that the mighty stone was brought which once covered the *resting-place* of Theodoric. *E. A. Freeman*, Venice, p. 100.

2. In *building*, a half- or quarter-pace in a staircase.

resting-sporangium (res'ting-spọ̄-ran"ji-um), *n.* A term applied by Pringsheim to certain dormant gonidia of *Saprolegnia* and related fungi which eventually produce swarm-spores.

resting-spore (res'ting-spōr), *n.* A spore which can germinate only after a period of dormancy. A majority of the spores of algæ and fungi are of this nature, and they are more largely of sexual production. Many of the same plants produce spores capable of immediate germination. Also *resting-cell*.

resting-stage (res'ting-stāj), *n.* In *bot.*, a period of dormancy in the history of a plant or germ.

resting-state (res'ting-stāt), *n.* In *bot.*, the periodic condition of dormancy in the history of woody plants, bulbs, etc.; also, the quiescence of some seeds and spores (resting-spores) between maturity and germination; in general, any state of suspended activity.

restinguish (rẹ-sting'gwish), *v. t.* [< L. *restinguere*, put out, < *re-*, again, + *stinguere*, extinguish. Cf. *extinguish*, *distinguish*.] To quench or extinguish. [Rare.]

Hence the thirst of languishing souls is *restinguished*, as from the most pure fountains of living water.
Field, Of Controversy (Life, 1716), p. 41.

resting-while† (res'ting-hwīl), *n.* [< ME. *restingwhile*; < *resting*, verbal n. of *rest*[1], *v.*, + *while*.] A moment of leisure; time free from business.

Thilke thinges that I hadde lerned of the among my secre *restingwhiles*. *Chaucer*, Boëthius, i. prose 4.

Restio (res'ti-ō), *n.* [NL. (Linnæus, 1767), so called from the tough stringy stems; < L. *restis*, a cord.] A genus of glumaceous plants, the type of the order *Restiaceæ* and tribe *Restioideæ*. It is characterized by one-celled anthers opening by a single chink, by two or three styles or branches and a compressed capsule with two or three cells and as many dehiscent angles, and by persistent sheaths, and commonly many-flowered and panicled spikelets with imbricated glumes. The two long linear stigmas are generally plumose. The staminate inflorescence is extremely polymorphous. There are over 100 species, natives of South Africa and Australia. They have erect and leafless stems from a scaly rootstock, very much branched or entirely without branches, with numerous scattered sheaths replacing the leaves, or sometimes in the young plant bearing a small and perishable leaf-blade. From their use *R. australis* is known as *Tasmanian rope-grass*.

Flowering Male Plant of *Restio complanatus*.
a, a male flower.

Restioideæ (res-ti-oi'dẹ̄-ē), *n. pl.* [NL. (Masters, 1878), < *Restio* + *-ideæ*.] A tribe of plants of the order *Restiaceæ*, characterized by an ovary of three, or sometimes two, cells, or reduced by abortion to a single one, and by a capsular fruit —the fruit of the other tribe, *Willdenovieæ*, being nut-like. It includes 7 genera, of which *Restio* is the type.

restipulate (rē-stip'ū-lāt), *v. i.* [< L. *restipulatus*, pp. of *restipulari*, promise or stipulate anew, < *re-*, back, + *stipulari*, promise: see *stipulate*.] To stipulate anew. *Imp. Dict.*

restipulation (rē-stip-ū-lā'shọn), *n.* [< L. *restipulatio(n-)*, a counter-engagement, < *restipulari*, pp. *restipulatus*, promise again: see *restipulate*.] The act of restipulating; a new stipulation.

But if the *restipulation* were absolute, and the withdrawing of this homage upon none but civil grounds, I cannot excuse the good king from a just offence.
Bp. Hall, Contemplations, xx. 9.

restitue†, *v. t.* [ME. *restituen*, < OF. *restituer*, restore: see *restitute*.] To restore; make restitution of.

Rather haue we no reste til we *restitue*
Our lyf to oure lord god for oure lykames [body's] gultes.
Piers Plowman (C), xi. 54.

restitute† (res'ti-tūt), *v. t.* [< L. *restitutus*, pp. of *restituere* (> It. *restituire*, *ristituire* = Sp. Pg. *restituir* = F. *restituer*, > E. *restitue*), reinstate, set up again, replace, restore, < *re-*, again, + *statuere*, set up: see *statute*. Cf. *constitute*, *institute*.] To bring back to a former state; restore.

Restituted trade
To every virtue lent his helping stores,
And cheer'd the vales around. *Dyer*, Fleece, ii.

restitute† (res'ti-tūt), *n.* [< L. *restitutus*, pp. of *restituere*, restore, reinstate: see *restitute*, *v.*] That which is restored or offered in place of something; a substitute. *Imp. Dict.* [Rare.]

restitutio in integrum (res-ti-tū'shi-ō in in'tẹ-grum). [L.: *restitutio* (see *restitution*); *in*, in; *integrum*, acc. of *integer*, whole: see *integer*.] In *Rom. law*, a restoration to the previous condition, effected by the pretor for equitable causes, on the prayer of an injured party, by annulling a transaction valid by the strict law, or annulling a change in the legal condition produced by an omission, and restoring the parties to their previous legal relations. After equitable defense and claim had been introduced in the ordinary proceeding, the importance of the institution diminished. In English and American law the phrase is used when a court of equity annuls a transaction or contract and orders the restoration of what has been received or given under it.

restitution (res-ti-tū'shọn), *n.* [< ME. *restitucion*, *restytucyon*, < OF. (and F.) *restitution* = Pr. *restitucio* = Sp. *restitucion* = Pg. *restituição* = It. *restituzione*, < L. *restitutio(n-)*, a restoring,

‹ *restituere*, pp. *restitutus*, set up again, restore: see *restitute*.] **1.** The act of returning or restoring what has been lost or taken away; the restoring to a person of some thing or right of which he has been deprived: as, the *restitution* of ancient rights to the crown.

> We yet crave *restitution* of those lands,
> Those cities sack'd, those prisoners, and that prey
> The soldier by your will stands master of.
> *Fletcher*, Humorous Lieutenant, i. 1.

2. The act of making good or of giving an equivalent for any loss, damage, or injury; indemnification.

> "Repentest thow neuere?" quath Repentaunce, "ne *restitucion* madest?" *Piers Plowman* (C), vii. 234.

> A free release
> From *restitution* for the late affronts.
> *Ford*, Perkin Warbeck, iv. 3.

> If a man shall cause a field or vineyard to be eaten, and shall put in his beast, and shall feed in another man's field; of the best of his own field, and of the best of his own vineyard, shall he make *restitution*. Ex. xxii. 5.

3. The putting of things back to their former relative positions.—**4.** In *law*: (*a*) The putting of a person in possession of lands or tenements of which he had been unlawfully disseized. (*b*) The restoration of what a party had gained by a judgment or order, upon the reversal of such adjudication by appeal or writ of error.—**5.** In *theol.*, the restoration of the kingdom of God, embracing the elevation, not only of all his sinful creatures, but also of all the physical creation, to a state of perfection. See *apocatastasis*.—**Coefficient of restitution**, the ratio of the relative velocity of two balls the instant after their impact to their relative velocity the instant before.—**Force of restitution**, a force tending to restore the relative positions of parts of a body.—**Interdict of restitution**. See *interdict*, 2 (*b*).—**Restitution Edict**, in *German hist.*, an edict issued A. D. 1629 by the Emperor Ferdinand II.: it required the Protestants to restore to the Roman Catholic authorities all ecclesiastical property and sees which they had appropriated at the peace of Passau in 1552.—**Restitution of conjugal rights**, in *law*, a species of matrimonial action which has been allowed in some jurisdictions, for redress against a husband or wife who lives apart from the other without a sufficient reason.—**Restitution of minors**, in *law*, a restoring of minors to rights lost by deeds executed during their minority.—**Writ of restitution**, in *law*, a writ which lies where judgment has been reversed, to restore to the defendant what he has been deprived of by the judgment. =**Syn. 1–3.** Restoration, return.

restitutive (res'ti-tū-tiv), *a.* [‹ *restitute* + *-ive*.] Pertaining to or characterized by restitution, in any sense.

> Under any given distortion within the limits of *restitutive* power, the restitution-pressure is equal to the product of the coefficient of restitution into the distortion.
> *A. Daniell*, Prin. of Physics, p. 235.

restitutor (res'ti-tū-tor), *n.* [= F. *restituteur* = Sp. Pg. *restituidor* = It. *restitutore*, ‹ L. *restitutor*, a restorer, ‹ *restituere*, restore: see *restitute*.] One who makes restitution; a restorer.

> Their rescuer, or *restitutor*, Quixote.
> *Gayton*, Notes on Don Quixote, p. 124.

restive (res'tiv), *a.* [Early mod. E. also *restiff*, and with loss of the terminal *f* (as in *jolly* ‹ *jolif*), *restie*, *resty* (see *resty*[1]); ‹ ME. *restif*, *restiff*, ‹ OF. *restif*, fem. *restive*, "restie, stubborn, drawing backward, that will not go forward" (Cotgrave), F. *restif*, fem. *restive* = Pr. *restiu* = It. *restio*, ‹ ML. as if **restivus*, disposed to rest or stay, ‹ L. *restare*, stay, rest: see *rest*[2]. By transition through the sense 'impatient under restraint' (def. 4), and partly by confusion with *restless*, the word has taken in present use the additional sense 'restless' (def. 5).] **1.** Unwilling to go or to move forward; stopping; balky; obstinate; stubborn. Compare def. 5.

> Since I haue shewed you by reason that obedience is just and necessary, by example that it is possible, be not *restive* in their weake stubburnness that will either keepe or lose all.
> *Certaine Learned and Elegant Workes*, etc. (1633), p. 286.

> The people remarked with awe and wonder that the beasts which were to drag him [Abraham Holmes] to the gallows became *restive* and went back.
> *Macaulay*, Hist. Eng., v.

2†. Not easily moved or worked; stiff.

> Farrage in *restyf* lande ydounged eck
> Is doone, X strike is for oon acre even.
> *Palladius*, Husbondrie (E. E. T. S.), p. 181.

3†. Being at rest; being less in motion.

> Palsies oftenest happen upon the left side; the most vigorous part protecting itself, and protruding the matter upon the weaker and *restive* side.
> *Sir T. Browne*, Vulg. Err. (*Latham*.)

4. Impatient under restraint or opposition; recalcitrant.

> The pampered colt will discipline disdain,
> Impatient of the lash, and *restiff* to the rein.
> *Dryden*, tr. of Virgil's Georgics, iii. 324.

> Socrates had as *restive* a constitution as his neighbours, and yet reclaim'd it, all by the strength of his philosophy.
> *Essays upon Several Moral Subjects*, iii. 77.

> The subject . . . becomes *restive*.
> *Gladstone*, State and Church, vi.

5. Refusing to rest or stand still; restless: said especially of horses.

> For maintaining his seat, the horseman should depend upon his thighs and knees: . . . at times, of course, when on a *restive* horse, every available muscle may have to be brought into play. *Encyc. Brit.*, XII. 196.

restively (res'tiv-li), *adv.* In a restive manner.

restiveness (res'tiv-nes), *n.* The state or character of being restive, in any sense.

> When there be not stonds and *restiveness* in a man's nature, . . . the wheels of his mind keep way with the wheels of his fortune. *Bacon*, Fortune.

restless (rest'les), *a.* [‹ ME. *restles*, *restelees*, ‹ AS. *restleás* (= D. *rusteloos* = G. *rastlos* = Sw. Dan. *rastlös*), ‹ *rest*, rest, + *-leás*, E. *-less*.] Without rest. (*a*) Deprived of repose or sleep; unable to sleep; sleepless.

> Better be with the dead . . .
> Than on the torture of the mind to lie
> In *restless* ecstasy. *Shak.*, Macbeth, iii. 2. 22.

> *Restless* he passed the remnants of the night.
> *Dryden*, Annus Mirabilis, st. 102.

(*b*) Unresting; unquiet; uneasy; continually moving or agitated.

> The courser pawed the ground with *restless* feet,
> And snorting foamed, and champed the golden bit.
> *Dryden*, Pal. and Arc., iii. 457.

> O mill-girl watching late and long the shuttle's *restless* play! *Whittier*, Mary Garvin.

> He lost his color, he lost his appetite, he was *restless*, incapable of keeping still.
> *Mrs. Oliphant*, Poor Gentleman, xxxvii.

(*c*) Marked by unrest: as, a *restless* night. (*d*) Unquiet; not satisfied to be at rest or in peace: as, a *restless* politician; *restless* ambition; *restless* passions.

> In a valey of this *restles* mynde
> I sou3te in mounteyne & in myde,
> Trustynge a trewe loue for to fynde.
> *Political Poems*, etc. (ed. Furnivall), p. 150.

> *Restless* was his soul, and wandered wide
> Through a dim maze of lusts unsatisfied.
> *William Morris*, Earthly Paradise, II. 12.

(*e*) Inclined to agitation; turbulent: as, *restless* subjects.

> Nature had given him [Sunderland] . . . a *restless* and mischievous temper. *Macaulay*, Hist. Eng., ii.

(*f*) Unsettled; disposed to wander or to change place or condition.

> She 's proud, fantastic, apt to change,
> *Restless* at home, and ever prone to range.
> *Dryden*, State of Innocence, v. 1.

> Alone he wanders by the murmuring shore,
> His thoughts as *restless* as the waves that roar.
> *O. W. Holmes*, The Disappointed Statesman.

(*g*) Not affording rest; uneasy. [Rare.]

> To be imprison'd in the viewless winds,
> And blown with *restless* violence round about
> The pendent world. *Shak.*, M. for M., iii. 1. 125.

> But *restless* was the chair; the back erect
> Distressed the weary loins, that felt no ease.
> *Cowper*, Task, i. 44.

Restless cavy. See *cavy*.—**Restless flycatcher**, *Seisura inquieta*, an Australian bird, called by the colonists *grinder*. See cut under *Seisura*. =**Syn.** (*a*–*c*) Disturbed, disquieted, agitated, anxious. (*f*) Roving, wandering, unstable, fickle.

restlessly (rest'les-li), *adv.* In a restless manner; unquietly.

restlessness (rest'les-nes), *n.* The state or character of being restless, in any sense.

restor, *n.* See *restaur*.

restorable (rē̤-stōr'a̤-bl), *a.* [‹ *restore*[1] + *-able*.] Capable of being restored, or brought to a former condition.

> I may add that absurd practice of cutting turf without any regularity; whereby great quantities of *restorable* land are made utterly desperate. *Swift*, Drapier's Letters, vii.

restorableness (rē̤-stōr'a̤-bl-nes), *n.* The state or character of being restorable. *Imp. Dict.*

restoral† (rē̤-stōr'al), *n.* [‹ *restore*[1] + *-al*.] Restitution; restoration.

> Promises of pardon to our sins, and *restoral* into God's favour. *Barrow*, Works, II. iv.

restoration (res-tō̤-rā'sho̤n), *n.* [Formerly also *restauration*; ‹ ME. *restauracion*, ‹ OF. *restoration*, *restauration*, F. *restauration* = Pr. *restauracio* = Sp. *restauracion* = Pg. *restauração* = It. *restaurazione*, *ristorazione*, ‹ LL. *restauratio(n-)*, a restoration, renewal, ‹ L. *restaurare*, pp. *restauratus*, restore: see *restore*[1].] **1.** The act of restoring. (*a*) The replacing in a former state or position; return: as, the *restoration* of a man to his office; the *restoration* of a child to its parents. Compare phrase below.

> Christ as the cause original of *restauration* to life.
> *Hooker*.

> Men's ignorance leads them to expect the renovation to *restauration* of things, from their corruption and remains.
> *Bacon*, Physical Fables, ix., Expl.

> The nation without regret and without enthusiasm recognized the Lancastrian *restoration*.
> *Stubbs*, Const. Hist., § 358.

(*b*) Renewal; revival; reëstablishment: as, the *restoration* of friendship between enemies; the *restoration* of peace after war; the *restoration* of a declining commerce.

> After those other before mentioned, followeth a prayer for the good sort, for proselytes, reedifying of the Temple, for sending the Messias and *restauration* of their Kingdome. *Purchas*, Pilgrimage, p. 197.

2. In *arch.* and *art*, the repair of injuries suffered. In restoration, even when most carefully done, the new work cannot reproduce the old exactly: however, when a monument must be restored for its preservation, correct practice demands that every fragment possible of the old be retained in the new work, so as to preserve as far as may be the artistic quality of the old, and that the original design be followed with the utmost care.

> Thence to the Sorbonne, an antient fabriq built by one Robert de Sorbonne, whose name it retains; but the *restauration* which the late Cardinal de Richlieu has made to it renders it one of the most excellent moderne buildings.
> *Evelyn*, Diary, Jan. 4, 1644.

> Christ Church Cathedral [Dublin] is now in course of *restoration*. *Encyc. Brit.*, VII. 500.

3. A plan or design of an ancient building, etc., showing it in its original state: as, the *restoration* of a picture; the *restoration* of a cathedral.—**4.** The state of being restored; recovery; renewal of health and soundness; recovery from a lapse or any bad state: as, *restoration* from sickness.

> O my dear father! *Restoration* hang
> Thy medicine on my lips; and let this kiss
> Repair those violent harms! *Shak.*, Lear, iv. 7. 26.

> Trust me the ingredients are very cordiall, . . . and most powerfull in *restauration*.
> *Marston and Webster*, Malcontent, ii. 4.

5. In *theol.*: (*a*) The recovery of a sinner to the divine favor.

> The scope of St. John's writing is that the *restoration* of mankind must be made by the Son of God.
> *J. Bradford*, Works (Parker Soc., 1853), II. 264.

(*b*) The doctrine of the final recovery of all men from sin and alienation from God to a state of blessedness; universal salvation: a form of Universalism.—**6.** That which is restored.—**7.** In *milit. service*, repayment for private losses incurred by persons in service, such as horses killed or arms destroyed.—**8.** In *paleon.*, the putting together in their proper places of the bones or other remains of an extinct animal; also, the more or less ideal representation of the external form and aspect of such an animal, as inferred from its known remains. See cuts under *Dinotherium*, *Iguanodon*, and *Labyrinthodon*.—**9.** In *musical notation*, the act, process, or result of canceling a chromatic sign, whether ♯, ♭, or ♮, and thus bringing a degree of the staff or a note on it back to its original signification.—**The Restoration.** (*a*) In *Eng. hist.*, the reëstablishment of the English monarchy with the return of King Charles II. in 1660; by extension, the whole reign of Charles II.: as, the dramatists of *the Restoration*. (*b*) In *Jewish hist.*, the return of the Jews to Palestine about 537 B. C.; also, their future return to and possession of the Holy Land as expected by many of the Jewish race, and by others. (*c*) In *French hist.*, the return of the Bourbons to power in 1814 and—after the episode of the "Hundred Days"—in 1815. =**Syn. 1** and **2.** Renovation, redintegration, reinstatement, return, restitution. See *restore*[1].

restorationer (res-tō̤-rā'sho̤n-ėr), *n.* [‹ *restoration* + *-er*[1].] A restorationist. *Imp. Dict.*

restorationism (res-tō̤-rā'sho̤n-izm), *n.* [‹ *restoration* + *-ism*.] The doctrines or belief of the restorationists.

> We cannot pause to dwell longer upon the biblical evidence which has in all ages constrained the evangelical church to reject all forms of *restorationism*.
> *Bibliotheca Sacra*, XLV. 717.

restorationist (res-tō̤-rā'sho̤n-ist), *n.* [‹ *restoration* + *-ist*.] One who believes in the temporary punishment of the impenitent after death, but in the final restoration of all to holiness and the favor and presence of God. See *Universalism*.

restorative (rē̤-stōr'a̤-tiv), *a.* and *n.* [‹ ME. *restoratyve*, *restauratife*, ‹ OF. *restauratif* = Pr. *restauratiu* = Sp. Pg. *restaurativo* = It. *ristorativo*, ‹ ML. *restaurativus* (in neut. *restaurativum*, a restorative), ‹ L. *restaurare*, restore: see *restore*[1].] **I.** *a.* Pertaining to restoration; specifically, capable of restoring or renewing vitality or strength.

> Your Presence would be a Cordial to me more *restorative* than exalted Gold. *Howell*, Letters, I. ii. 3.

II. *n.* That which is efficacious in restoring vigor; a food, cordial, or medicine which recruits the vital powers.

> I will kiss thy lips:
> Haply some poison yet doth hang on them,
> To make me die with a *restorative*.
> *Shak.*, R. and J., v. 3. 166.

restoratively (rẹ-stōr'ạ-tiv-li), *adv.* In a manner or degree that tends to renew strength or vigor. *Imp. Dict.*

restorator† (res'tọ-rā-tọr), *n.* [Also *restaurator*; = F. *restaurateur* = It. *ristoratore*, < LL. *restaurator*, restorer, < L. *restaurare*, restore: see *restore*[1].] 1. One who restores, reëstablishes, or revives.—2. The keeper of an eating-house; a restaurateur. *Ford.* (*Imp. Dict.*)

restoratory (rẹ-stōr'ạ-tọ-ri), *a.* [< *restore*[1] + *-at-ory.*] Restorative. [Rare.] *Imp. Dict.*

restore[1] (rē-stōr'), *v. t.*; pret. and pp. *restored*, ppr. *restoring*. [Formerly also *restaure*; < ME. *restoren*, < OF. *restorer*, *restaurer*, F. *restaurer* = Pr. Sp. Pg. *restaurar* = It. *ristorare*, *restaurare*, < L. *restaurare*, restore, repair, rebuild, renew, < *re-*, again, + **staurare* (not used), establish, make firm, < **staurus*, fixed, = Gr. σταυρός, that which is firmly fixed, a pole or stake, = Skt. *sthāvara*, fixed, stable, standing; as a noun, plants; from the root of L. *stare*, Skt. √ *sthā*, stand: see *state*, *stand*. Cf. *enstore*, *instore*, *store*[2].] 1. To bring back to a former and better state. (*a*) To bring back from a state of ruin, injury, or decay; repair; refresh; rebuild; reconstruct.

The Lord (saith Cyprian) dooth vouchsafe in manie of his seruants to forshew to come the *restauring* of his church, the stable quiet of our health and safeguard. *Foxe*, Acts, p. 62.

To *restore* and to build Jerusalem. Dan. ix. 25.

(*b*) To bring back from lapse, degeneracy, or a fallen condition to a former state.

If a man be overtaken in a fault, ye which are spiritual, *restore* such an one in the spirit of meekness. Gal. vi. 1.

He stablishes the strong, *restores* the weak. *Cowper*, Task, ii. 343.

(*c*) To bring back to a state of health or soundness; heal; cure.

Then saith he to the man, Stretch forth thine hand. And he stretched it forth; and it was *restored* whole, like as the other. Mat. xii. 13.

What, hast thou been long blind and now *restored?* *Shak.*, 2 Hen. VI., ii. 1. 76.

(d) In the *fine arts:* (1) To bring back from a state of injury or decay as nearly as may be to the primitive state, supplying any part that may be wanting, by a careful following of the original work: as, to *restore* a painting, a statue, etc. (2) To form a picture or model of, as of something lost or mutilated: as, to *restore* a ruined building according to its original state or design.

2. To bring back; renew or reëstablish after interruption.

That all their eyes may bear those tokens home
Of our *restored* love and amity.
Shak., 2 Hen. IV., iv. 2. 65.

By force to *restore* Laws abrogated by the Legislative Parlament is to conquer absolutely both them and Law it selfe. *Milton*, Eikonoklastes, xix.

A ghost of passion that no smiles *restore*.
Tennyson, Three Sonnets to a Coquette, ii.

3. To give or bring back; return to a person, as a specific thing which he has lost, or which has been taken from him and unjustly retained: as, to *restore* lost or stolen goods to the owner.

Now therefore *restore* the man his wife. Gen. xx. 7.

The kingdom shall to Israel be *restored*.
Milton, P. R., ii. 36.

4. To give in place of or as satisfaction for something; hence, to make amends for; compensate.

All that money that ye haue, & I to, wyll not *restore* the wronge that your fader hathe don.
Booke of Precedence (E. E. T. S., extra ser.), i. 78.

He shall *restore* five oxen for an ox, and four sheep for a sheep. Ex. xxii. 1.

But if the while I think on thee, dear friend,
All losses are *restored* and sorrows end.
Shak., Sonnets, xxx.

5. To bring or put back to a former position or condition; replace; return, as a person or thing to a former place.

So did the Romaines by their armes *restore* many Kings of Asia and Affricke expulsed out of their kingdoms.
Puttenham, Arte of Eng. Poesie, p. 206.

Within three days shall Pharaoh lift up thine head, and *restore* thee unto thy place. Gen. xl. 13.

Then spake Elisha unto the woman whose son he had *restored* to life. 2 Ki. viii. 1.

Release me, and *restore* me to the ground.
Tennyson, Tithonus.

6. To recover or renew, as passages of an author defective or corrupted; emend.—7. In *paleon.*, to represent (an extinct animal) from its existing remains. See *restoration*, 8.—8. In *musical notation*, to bring (a degree or note) back to its original signification by canceling a chromatic sign which had affected it temporarily.—9†. To store.

A park as it were.
That whilom with wilde beates was wel *restored*.
William of Palerne (E. E. T. S.), l. 2846.

To **restore to or in blood**. See *blood*. =**Syn.** 1 (*c*). To recover.—3 and 4. To refund, repay.—5. To reinstate.—1. *Return, Restore.* To *return* a thing to its former place; to *restore* it to its former condition; to *return* what has been borrowed; to *restore* what has been stolen; to be *restored* to health or prosperity.

restore[2]† (rẹ-stōr'), *n.* [Also *restour*; < OF. *restor*, *restour*, < *restorer*, restore: see *restore*[1], *v.*] Restoration; restitution.

His passage there to stay,
Till he had made amends, and full *restore*
For all the damage which he had him doen afore.
Spenser, F. Q., III. v. 18.

All sports which for life's *restore* variety assigns.
F. Greville (Arber's Eng. Garner, I. 296).

restore[3] (rē-stōr'), *v. t.* [< *re-* + *store*[2].] To store again or anew: as, the goods were *restored*.

restorement† (rẹ-stōr'ment), *n.* [< OF. *restorement* = It. *ristoramento*, < ML. *restauramentum*, < L. *restaurare*, restore: see *restore*[1].] The act of restoring; restoration.

Hengist, thus rid of his grand opposer, hearing gladly the *restorement* of his old favourer, returns again with great Forces. *Milton*, Hist. Eng., iii.

restorer (rẹ-stōr'ėr), *n.* One who or that which restores, in any sense.

Oh great *restorer* of the good old stage!
Pope, Dunciad, iii. 205.

Doubtless it was a fine work before the "effacing fingers" of *restorers* touched it.
Athenæum, Jan. 7, 1888, p. 21.

restority†, *n.* [Irreg. < *restore*[1] + *-ity.*] Restoration.

Well, said Camilla, let it goe, I must impute it to my ill fortune that, where I looked for *restority*, I found a consumption. *Lyly*, Euphues and his England. (*Nares.*)

restour†, *n.* See *restore*[2].

restrain (rẹ-strān'), *v. t.* [< ME. *restreinen*, *restreignen*, *restreynen*, < OF. *restraindre*, F. *restreindre* = Pr. *restrenher* = Cat. *restrenyer* = Sp. *restriñir* = Pg. *restringir* = It. *ristringere*, *ristrignere*, < L. *restringere*, draw back tightly, bind back, confine, check, restrain, restrict, < *re-*, back, + *stringere*, draw tight: see *stringent* and *restrict*. Cf. *constrain* and *strain*[2].] 1†. To draw tight; strain.

A half-checked bit and a head-stall of sheep's leather which, being *restrained* to keep him from stumbling, hath been often burst. *Shak.*, T. of the S., iii. 2. 59.

2. To hold back; hold in; check; confine; hold from action or motion, either by physical or moral force, or by any interposing obstacle; hence, to repress or suppress: as, to *restrain* a horse by a bridle; to *restrain* men from crimes and trespasses by laws; to *restrain* laughter.

Restreyne and kepe well thy tonge.
Booke of Precedence (E. E. T. S., extra ser.), i. 109.

Restrain in me the cursed thoughts that nature
Gives way to in repose. *Shak.*, Macbeth, ii. 1. 8.

Gums and pomatums shall his flight *restrain*,
While clogg'd he beats his silken wings in vain.
Pope, R. of the L., ii. 129.

3. To abridge; restrict; hinder from liberty of action.

Though they two were committed, at least *restrained* of their liberty, yet this discovered too much of the humour of the court. *Clarendon.*

4. To limit; confine; restrict in definition. [Obsolete or obsolescent.]

We do too narrowly define the power of God, *restraining* it to our capacities. *Sir T. Browne*, Religio Medici, i. 27.

And here I shall not *restrain* righteousness to the particular virtue of justice, . . . but enlarge it according to the genius and strain of the book of the Proverbs.
Tillotson, Works, I. 95.

5. To withhold; forbear.

Thou castest off fear, and *restrainest* prayer before God. Job xv. 4.

6†. To forbid; prohibit.

Restraining all manner of people to bear sail in any vessel or bottom wherein there were above five persons.
North, tr. of Plutarch, p. 7.

=**Syn.** 2. *Restrain, Repress, Restrict*; stop, withhold, curb, bridle, coerce. *Restrain* and *repress* are general words for holding or pressing back; *restrict* applies to holding back to a more definite degree: as, to *restrain* one's appetite; to *restrict* one's self in food or to a certain diet. That which we *restrain* we keep within limits; that which we *restrict* we keep within certain definite limits; that which we *repress* we try to put out of existence.

restrainable (rẹ-strā'nạ-bl), *a.* [< *restrain* + *-able.*] Capable of being restrained.

restrainedly (rẹ-strā'ned-li), *adv.* With restraint; with limitation.

restrainer (rẹ-strā'nėr), *n.* One who or that which restrains; specifically, in *photog.*, a chemical which is added to the developer for the purpose of retarding its action, especially in the case of an over-exposed plate, or in order to obtain greater contrast or intensity in a naturally weak plate. Acids, sodium sulphite, bromides, and other substances act as restrainers.

restraining (rẹ-strā'ning), *p. a.* Serving to restrain or restrict in any way. (*a*†) Binding; astringent.

Take hede that slippery meates be not fyrste eaten, nor that stiptik nor *restraining* meates be taken at the begynning, as quynces, peares, and medlars.
Sir T. Elyot, Castle of Health, fol. 45.

(*b*) Hampering; restrictive.

By degrees he acquired a certain influence over me that took away my liberty of mind; his praise and notice were more *restraining* than his indifference.
Charlotte Brontë, Jane Eyre, xxxiv.

restrainment (rẹ-strān'mẹnt), *n.* [< *restrain* + *-ment.*] The act of restraining.

restraint (rẹ-strānt'), *n.* [< OF. *restrainte*, *restraincte*, restraint, fem. of *restraint*, *restrainct*, pp. of *restraindre*, restrain: see *restrain*.] 1. The act of restraining, or of holding back or hindering from action or motion, in any manner; hindrance of any action, physical, moral, or mental.

Thus it shall befall
Him who, to worth in woman overtrusting,
Lets her will rule; *restraint* she will not brook.
Milton, P. L., ix. 1184.

Wherever thought is wholly wanting, or the power to act or forbear according to the direction of thought, there necessity takes place. This, in an agent capable of volition, when the beginning or continuation of any action is contrary to that preference of his mind, is called compulsion; when the hindering or stopping any action is contrary to his volition, it is called *restraint*.
Locke, Human Understanding, II. xxi. § 13.

2. The state of being repressed, curbed, or held back in any way; specifically, abridgment of liberty; confinement; detention.

I . . . heartily request
The enfranchisement of Arthur; whose *restraint*
Doth move the murmuring lips of discontent.
Shak., K. John, iv. 2. 52.

Restraint is for the savage, the rapacious, the violent; not for the just, the gentle, the benevolent.
H. Spencer, Social Statics, p. 25.

3. Repression of extravagance, exaggeration, or vehemence; constraint in manner or style; reserve.

She knew her distance and did angle for me,
Madding my eagerness with her *restraint*.
Shak., All's Well, v. 3. 213.

To yonder oak within the field
I spoke without *restraint*,
And with a larger faith appeal'd
Than Papist unto Saint.
Tennyson, Talking Oak.

4. That which restrains, limits, hinders, or represses; a limitation, restriction, or prohibition.

It pleaseth the care better, & sheweth more cunning in the maker by following the rule of his *restraint*.
Puttenham, Arte of Eng. Poesie, p. 62.

Say first, what cause
Moved our grand Parents, in that happy state,
Favour'd of heaven so highly, to fall off
From their Creator, and transgress his will,
For one *restraint*, lords of the world besides?
Milton, P. L., i. 32.

Whether they [*restraints*] be from God or Nature, from Reason or Conscience, as long as they are *restraints*, they look on them as inconsistent with their notion of liberty.
Stillingfleet, Sermons, II. iii.

5. Restriction; limitation, as in application or definition.

The positive laws which Moses gave, they were given for the greatest part with *restraint* to the land of Jewry.
Hooker, Eccles. Polity, iii. 11.

6. In *dynam.*, an absolute geometrical condition supposed to be precisely fulfilled: thus, a body moving upon an unyielding surface is subject to a *restraint*.—**Restraint bed and chair**, forms of apparatus used in controlling the insane, as when they exhibit suicidal or homicidal tendencies. =**Syn.** 1 and 4. *Constraint, Coercion*, etc. (see *force*[1], *n.*), repression, check, stop, curb, hold-back.

restriall (rẹ-stri'ạl), *a.* In *her.*, divided barwise, palewise, and pilewise: said of the field.

restrict (rẹ-strikt'), *v. t.* [< L. *restrictus*, pp. of *restringere*, restrict, restrain: see *restrain*.] 1. To prevent (a person or thing) from passing a certain limit in any kind of action; limit; restrain.

Neither shoulde we haue any more wherewith to vexe them with confessions, cares reserued, *restricted*, or amplified for our gaine. *Foxe*, Acts, etc., p. 1173, Hen. VIII.

If the canon law had *restricted* itself to really spiritual questions, . . . it is not likely that the kings would have been jealous of papal or archi-episcopal enactments.
Stubbs, Medieval and Modern Hist., p. 316.

2. To attach limitations to (a proposition or conception), so that it shall not apply to all the subjects to which it would otherwise seem to apply: as, a *restricted* sense of a word.

By *restricting* the omnitude or universality either of the subject or predicate. *Sir W. Hamilton*, Logic, App. iii.

=**Syn.** 1. *Repress*, etc. (see *restrain*), hedge in.

restrict† (rę-strikt'), *a.* [< L. *restrictus*, pp.: see the verb.] Limited; confined; restricted.

Men . . . in some one or two things demeaning themselves as exceedingly *restrict*, but in many others, or the most things, as remisse. *Gataker*, Just Man, p. 224. (*Latham.*)

Restrict or restricted. *Sir W. Hamilton*, Logic, App. iii.

restrictedly (rę-strik'ted-li), *adv.* In a restricted manner; with limitation.

restriction (rę-strik'shǫn), *n.* [< OF. *restriction*, F. *restriction* = Pr. *restriccio* = Sp. *restriccion* = Pg. *restricção* = It. *restrizione*, < LL. *restrictio(n-)*, a restriction, limitation, < L. *restringere*, pp. *restrictus*, restrain: see *restrict* and *restraint*.] **1.** The act of restricting, or the state of being restricted; limitation; confinement within bounds: as, grounds open to the public without *restriction*.

This is to have the same *restriction* with all other recreations, that it be made a divertisement, not a trade. *Government of the Tongue.*

There is, indeed, no power of the Government without *restriction*; not even that which is called the discretionary power of Congress. *Calhoun*, Works, I. 253.

2. That which restricts; a restraint: as, to impose *restrictions* on trade.

Wise politicians will be cautious about fettering the government with *restrictions* that cannot be observed. *A. Hamilton*, The Federalist, No. 25.

3. Reservation; reserve.—**4.** In *logic*: (*a*) The act of limiting a proposition by a restrictive particle. (*b*) The inference from a universal to a particular proposition, or to one in which the subject is narrower while the predicate remains the same: as, all crows are black, hence some white crows are black. The example illustrates the danger of such inference.—**Bilateral restriction.** See *bilateral*.—**Chinese Restriction Act.** See *act*.—**Mental restriction.** Same as *mental reservation* (which see, under *reservation*).—**Real restriction**, the use of words which are not true if strictly interpreted, but which contain no deviation from truth if the circumstances are considered: as in the statement that every particle of matter is present in every part of space, in so far as its gravitating power is concerned.

restrictionary (rę-strik'shǫn-ā-ri), *a.* [< *restriction* + *-ar-y*.] Exercising restriction; restrictive. *Athenæum.* [Rare.] (*Imp. Dict.*)

restrictionist (rę-strik'shǫn-ist), *n.* [< *restriction* + *-ist*.] In *U. S. hist.*, an advocate of the territorial restriction of slavery.

Lincoln . . . often had occasion . . . to show that he was not an abolitionist, but a slavery *restrictionist*. *N. A. Rev.*, CXL. 237.

restrictive (rę-strik'tiv), *a.* and *n.* [< ME. *restriktyve*, < OF. (and F.) *restrictif* = Pr. *restrictiu* = Sp. Pg. *restrictivo* = It. *restrittivo*, < ML. **restrictivus*, < L. *restringere*, pp. *restrictus*, restrict: see *restrict*.] **I.** *a.* **1**†. Serving to bind or draw together; astringent; styptic.

Medicyns comfortatyues, digestyues, laxatyues, *restriktyues*, and alle othere. *Book of Quinte Essence* (E. E. T. S.), p. 14.

I applied a plaister over it, made up with my common *restrictive* powder. *Wiseman*, Surgery.

2. Having the property of limiting or of expressing limitation: as, a *restrictive* particle or clause.—**3.** Imposing restrictions; operating through restrictions.

It were to be wished that we tried the *restrictive* arts of government, and made law the protector, but not the tyrant of the people. *Goldsmith*, Vicar, xxvii.

In the Senate so reconstituted was thus centred a complete *restrictive* control over the legislation and the administration. *Froude*, Cæsar, p. 87.

In the eighth year of Henry VI. was passed the *restrictive* act which . . . established the rule that only resident persons possessed of a freehold worth forty shillings a year should be allowed to vote. *Stubbs*, Const. Hist., § 368.

4. Expressing a restriction, or involving a restriction, in the logical sense.

Also *restringent*.

Restrictive enunciation. See *enunciation*.—**Restrictive indorsement.** See *indorsement*, 3.—**Restrictive proposition.** See *proposition*.

II.† *n.* A styptic or astringent.

I dressed that wound with the same digestive, . . . and some of the same *restrictive* over that. *Wiseman*, Surgery, vi. 6.

restrictively (rę-strik'tiv-li), *adv.* In a restrictive manner; with limitation. *Dr. H. More.*

restrictiveness (rę-strik'tiv-nes), *n.* The state or character of being restrictive. *Fuller.*

restrike (rē-strīk'), *v. t.* [< *re-* + *strike*.] To strike again, as a coin, in order to change its image and superscription to those current in place of the old.

These coins belong to the age of Timoleon, and are *restruck* over coins of Syracuse with the head of Zeus Eleutherios. *B. V. Head*, Historia Numorum, p. 125.

restringe† (rę-strinj'), *v. t.* [< L. *restringere*, confine; restrain: see *restrain*.] To confine; contract; astringe. *Bailey*, 1731.

restringency† (rē-strin'jen-si), *n.* [< *restringen(t)* + *-cy*.] The state, quality, or power of being restringent; astringency.

The dyers use this water in reds, and in other colours wanting *restringency*. *Sir W. Petty*, in Sprat's Hist. Roy. Soc., p. 293.

restringend (rę-strin'jend), *n.* A proposition destined to be restricted.

restringent (rę-strin'jent), *a.* and *n.* [= F. *restringent*, also *restreignant* = Sp. Pg. *restringente* = It. *ristringente*, < L. *restringen(t-)s*, ppr. of *restringere*, restrain: see *restrain*.] **I.** *a.* Same as *restrictive*.

II. *n.* An astringent or styptic.

The two latter indicate phlebotomy for revulsion, *restringents* to stanch, and incrassatives to thicken the blood. *Harvey.*

restryne†, *v.* A Middle English form of *restrain*. *Chaucer.*

resty[1]† (res'ti), *a.* [Formerly also *restic*, and by confusion *rusty*, a reduced form of *restive*, q. v.] A later form of *restive*, now obsolete. See *restive*.

Weariness
Can snore upon the flint, when *resty* sloth
Finds the down pillow hard.
Shak., Cymbeline, iii. 6. 34.

As one *restic* jade can hinder, by hanging back, more than two or three can . . . draw forward. *J. Robinson*, To Brewster, quoted in Leonard Bacon's Gen. [of N. E. Churches.

Where the Master is too *resty*, or too rich, to say his own Prayers. *Milton*, Eikonoklastes, § 24.

Restive or *resty*, drawing back instead of going forward, as some horses do. *E. Phillips*, New World of Words.

resty[2]†, *a.* Same as *reasty*[1] for *reasted*.

resty[3], *a.* An obsolete or dialectal form of *rusty*[1].

resublimation (rē-sub-li-mā'shǫn), *n.* [< *re-* + *sublimation*.] A second sublimation.

resublime (rē-sub-līm'), *v. t.* [< *re-* + *sublime*.] To sublime again: as, to *resublime* mercurial sublimate.

When mercury sublimate is *re-sublimed* with fresh mercury, . . . [it] becomes mercurius dulcis, which is a white tasteless earth scarce dissolvable in water; and mercurius dulcis, *re-sublimed* with spirit of salt, returns into mercury sublimate. *Newton*, Optics, iii. query 31.

resudation (rē-sū-dā'shǫn), *n.* [= Sp. *resudacion* = Pg. *resudação*, < L. *resudare*, pp. *resudatus*, sweat out, sweat again, < *re-*, again, + *sudare*, sweat: see *sudation*.] The act of sweating again. *Cotgrave.*

result (rę-zult'), *v.* [< OF. *resulter*, rebound or leap back, rise from, come out of, follow, result, F. *résulter*, follow, ensue, result, = Sp. Pg. *resultar* = It. *risultare*, result, < L. *resultare*, spring back, rebound, resound, reëcho, freq. of *resilire*, leap back: see *resile*, *resilient*. Cf. *insult*, *desultory*.] **I.** *intrans.* **1**†. To leap back; rebound; leap again.

Hee, like the glorious rare Arabian bird,
Will soon *result* from his incinderment.
Davies, Holy Roode, p. 20.

The huge round stone, *resulting* with a bound,
Thunders impetuous down, and smokes along the ground.
W. Broome, in Pope's Odyssey, xi. 737.

2. To proceed, spring, or rise as a consequence from facts, arguments, premises, combination of circumstances, etc.; be the outcome; be the final term in a connected series of events, operations, etc.

As music results out of our breath and a cornet. *Donne*, Letters, xxvii.

Good fortune in war *results* from the same prompt talent and unbending temper which lead to the same result in the peaceful professions. *Lowell*, Study Windows, p. 145.

3. To have an issue; terminate: followed by *in*.

The negotiations were not long in *resulting in* a definitive treaty, arranged to the mutual satisfaction of the parties. *Prescott*, Ferd. and Isa., ii. 12.

A soul shall draw from out the vast,
And strike his being into bounds,
And, moved thro' life of lower phase,
Result in man, be born and think.
Tennyson, In Memoriam, Conclusion.

Resulting force or **motion**, in *dynam.*, same as *resultant*.—**Resulting trust**, in *law*, a trust raised by implication in favor of the author of the trust himself, or his representatives; more specifically, the equitable title recognized in the person who pays the consideration for land conveyed to another person who pays nothing. See *trust*.—**Resulting use**, in *law*, a use returning by way of implication to the grantor himself, as where a deed is made, but for want of consideration or omission to declare the use, or a failure of its object, etc., the use cannot take effect. This doctrine is now generally obsolete.

II.† *trans.* To decree; determine, as an ecclesiastical council. [New Eng.]

According to Mr. Milner, the Council of Nice *resulted* in opposition to the views of Arius, "That the Son was peculiarly of the Father." *Rev. N. Worcester*, Bible News, p. 176.

result (rę-zult'), *n.* [= Sp. Pg. *resulta*, result; from the verb: see *result*, *v.*] **1**†. The act of leaping, springing, or flying back; resilience.

Sound . . . [is] produced between the string and the air . . . by the return or *result* of the string. *Bacon*, Nat. Hist., § 137.

2. Consequence; conclusion; outcome; issue; effect; that which proceeds naturally or logically from facts, premises, or the state of things: as, the *result* of reasoning; the *result* of reflection; the *result* of a consultation; the *result* of a certain procedure or effect.

If our proposals once again were heard,
We should compel them to a quick *result*.
Milton, P. L., vi. 619.

His Actions are the *result* of thinking. *Steele*, Conscious Lovers, ii. 1.

Resolving all events, with their effects
And manifold *results*, into the will
And arbitration wise of the Supreme.
Cowper, Task, ii. 164.

3. The final decision or determination of a council or deliberative assembly; resolution: as, the *result* of an ecclesiastical council.

Then of their session ended they bid cry
With trumpets' regal sound the great *result*.
Milton, P. L., ii. 515.

Four names, the *result* of this conclave, were laid before the assembled freeholders, who chose two by a majority of votes. *Stubbs*, Const. Hist., § 422.

4. In *math.*, a quantity, value, or expression ascertained by calculation.—**Tabular result**, one of a number of calculated numbers arranged in a tabular form; a quantity in the body of a mathematical table. =**Syn. 2.** *Consequence*, etc. (see *effect*), event, termination, end, upshot, consummation. See *resultant*.

resultance (rę-zul'tans), *n.* [= Sp. *resultancia*; as *resultan(t)* + *-ce*.] **1**†. A rebound; resilience; reflection.

For I confesse that power which works in me
Is but a weak *resultance* took from thee.
Randolph, Poems (1643). (*Halliwell.*)

Upon the wall there is a writing; a man sitting with his back to the wall, how should he read it? But let a looking-glass be set before him, it will reflect it to his eyes, he shall read it by the *resultance*. *Rev. T. Adams*, Works, II. 544.

2. The act of resulting; that which results; a result.

It is true that this conscience is the *resultance* of all other particular actions. *Donne*, Letters, xxxvii.

resultant (rę-zul'tant), *a.* and *n.* [< F. *résultant* = Sp. Pg. *resultante* = It. *risultante*, *resultante*, < L. *resultan(t-)s*, ppr. of *resultare*, spring back: see *result*.] **I.** *a.* Existing or following as a result or consequence; especially, resulting from the combination of two or more agents: as, a *resultant* motion produced by two forces. See diagram under *force*[1], 8.

The axis of magnetization at each point is parallel to the direction of the *resultant* force. *Atkinson*, tr. of Mascart and Joubert, I. 289.

Resultant diagram. See *diagram*.—**Resultant relation.** See *relation*.—**Resultant tone**, in *musical acoustics*, a tone produced or generated by the simultaneous sounding of any two somewhat loud and sustained tones. Two varieties are recognized, *differential* and *summational* tones, the former having a vibration-number equal to the difference between the vibration-numbers of the generating tones, and the latter one equal to their sum. It is disputed whether resultant tones, which are often perceptible, have a genuine objective existence, or are merely formed in the ear. Differential tones were first observed by Tartini in 1714, and are often called *Tartini's tones*. The entire subject has been elaborately treated by Helmholtz and recent investigators.

II. *n.* That which results or follows as a consequence or outcome. (*a*) In *mech.*, the geometrical sum of several vector quantities, as displacements, velocities, accelerations, or forces, which are said to be the components, and to the aggregate of which the resultant is equivalent. (*b*) In *alg.*, a function of the coefficients of two or more equations, the vanishing of which expresses that the equations have a common root: an eliminant.—**Topical resultant**, the resultant of a number of linear equations considered as implying the vanishing of matrices. =**Syn.** *Result*, *Resultant*. A result may proceed from one cause or from the combination of any number of causes. There has been of late a rapid increase in the use of *resultant* in a sense secondary to its physical one—namely, to represent that which is the result of a complex of moral forces, and would be precisely the result of no one of them acting alone.

resultate† (rę-zul'tāt), *n.* [= D. *resultaat* = G. Sw. Dan. *resultat*, < F. *résultat* = It. *risultato*, < ML. **resultatum*, a result, neut. of *resultatus*, pp. of *resultare*, spring back, ML. result: see *result*.] A result.

This work . . . doth disclaim to be tried by any thing but by experience, and the *resultats* of experience in a true way. *Bacon*, To the King, Oct. 20, 1620.

result-fee (rē̤-zult'fē), *n.* A fee for instruction, conditioned on or proportioned to the success or good progress of the pupil. [Eng.]

The national-school teachers showed a decided hostility to payment by *result-fees*, on the ground that it turned the pupil into a mere machine for getting money in the eyes of the master. *Athenæum*, Jan. 14, 1888, p. 52.

resultful (rē̤-zult'fụl), *a.* [< *result* + *-ful.*] Having or producing large or important results; effectual. [Rare.]

It (Concord) became . . . the source of our most *resultful* thought. *Stedman*, Poets of America, p. 139.

resultive† (rē̤-zul'tiv), *a.* [< *result* + *-ive.*] Resultant.

There is such a sympathy betwixt several sciences . . . that . . . a *resultive* firmness ariseth from their complication. *Fuller*, Ch. Hist., ii., Ded.

resultless (rē̤-zult'les), *a.* [< *result* + *-less.*] Without result: as, *resultless* investigations.

resultlessness (rē̤-zult'les-nes), *n.* The state or character of being resultless. *Encyc. Brit.*, XVI. 557.

resumable (rē̤-zū'ma̤-bl), *a.* [< *resume* + *-able.*] Capable of being resumed; liable to be taken back or taken up again.

This was but an indulgence, and therefore *resumable* by the victor, unless there intervened any capitulation to the contrary. *Sir M. Hale.*

resume (rē̤-zūm'), *v.*; pret. and pp. *resumed*, ppr. *resuming*. [< OF. *resumer*, F. *résumer* = Sp. Pg. *resumir* = It. *risumere*, *resumere*, < L. *resumere*, take again, resume, < *re-*, again, + *sumere*, take: see *assume*, and cf. *consume*, *desume*, *insume*, *presume.*] **I.** *trans.* 1. To take again; take back.

It pleased the diuine will to *resume* him vnto himselfe, whither both his and euery other high and noble minde haue alwayes aspired.
Quoted in *Booke of Precedence* (E. E. T. S., extra ser.), [Forewords, p. vii.

We that have conquered still, to save the conquered, . . .
More proud of reconcilement than revenge,
Resume into the late state of our love
Worthy Cordelius Gallus and Tibullus.
B. Jonson, Poetaster, v. 1.

2. To assume or take up again.

Thou shalt find
That I'll *resume* the shape which thou dost think
I have cast off for ever. *Shak.*, Lear, i. 4. 331.

Fortie yeares after he shall sound againe, and then the bones shall *resume* flesh and sinewes.
Purchas, Pilgrimage, p. 262.

The lessee [in New South Wales] was, however, given a preferential right of obtaining an annual occupation-license for the *resumed* area, which entitled him to use the land for grazing purposes, although not to the exclusion of any person who might be in a position to acquire a better tenure.
Sir C. W. Dilke, Probs. of Greater Britain, ii. 2.

3. To take up again after interruption; begin again: as, to *resume* an argument or a discourse; to *resume* specie payments.

Here the archangel paused, . . .
Then, with transition sweet, new speech *resumes*.
Milton, P. L., xii. 5.

The gods stand round him [Apollo] as he mourns, and pray
He would *resume* the conduct of the day,
Nor let the world be lost in endless night.
Addison, tr. of Ovid's Metamorph., ii.

4†. To take; assume. [Rare.]

Takes no account
How things go from him, nor *resumes* no care
Of what is to continue. *Shak.*, T. of A., ii. 2. 4

II. *intrans.* To proceed after interruption, as in a speech: chiefly used in the introductory phrase *to resume.*

résumé (rā-zü-mā'), *n.* [< F. *résumé*, a summary, < *résumé*, pp. of *résumer*, sum up, resume: see *resume.*] A summing up; a recapitulation; a condensed statement; a summary.

résumé (rā-zü-mā'), *v. t.* [< *résumé*, *n.*] To make an epitome or résumé of; summarize. [Rare.]

The work reveals this origin in a disjointedness of some of its portions that makes it difficult to read and still more so to *résumé*. *Amer. Jour. Psychol.*, I. 535.

resummon (rē-sum'on), *v. t.* [< *re-* + *summon.*] 1. To summon or call again.—2. To recall; recover. *Bacon.*

resummons (rē-sum'onz), *n.* [< *re-* + *summons.*] In *law*, a second summons or calling of a person to answer an action, as where the first summons is defeated by any occasion.

resumption (rē̤-zump'shon), *n.* [= F. *résomption* = Sp. *resuncion* = Pg. *resumpção* = It. *risunzione*, < LL. *resumptio(n-)*, a restoration, recovery (of a sick person), ML. lit. a taking up again, resumption, < L. *resumere*, pp. *resumptus*, take again, resume: see *resume.*] 1. The act of resuming, taking back, or taking again: as, the *resumption* of a grant; specifically, in *law*, the taking again by the state of such lands or tenements, etc., as on false suggestion or other error had been granted by letters patent.

This figure of retire holds part with the propounder of which we spake before (prolepsis), because of the *resumption* of a former proposition vttered in generalitie to explane the same better by a particular diuision.
Puttenham, Arte of Eng. Poesie, p. 184.

A general act of *resumption* was passed, by which all the grants made since the king's accession were annulled.
Stubbs, Const. Hist., § 345.

Specifically—2. In *U. S. hist.* and *politics*, the return to specie payments by the government.

The "more money" that is cried for, silver or shinplaster, is not the needed thing. It is . . . loanable capital, now paralyzed with distrust by delayed *resumption* and imminent silver swindles. *N. A. Rev.*, CXXVI. 170.

Act of Resumption, or Resumption Act, a title of several English statutes of Henry VI., by which he took and resumed possession of offices, property, etc., previously granted by him, and annulled such grants.—**Resumption Act**, a United States statute of 1875 (18 Stat., 296), providing for the payment of United States treasury notes in coin after January 1st, 1879.

resumptive (rē̤-zump'tiv), *a.* and *n.* [= F. *résomptif* = Sp. *resuntivo* = Pg. *resumptivo* = It. *resuntivo*, < LL. *resumptivus*, restorative, < L. *resumptus*, pp. of *resumere*, resume: see *resume.*] **I.** *a.* Taking back or again; tending to or of the nature of resumption. *Imp. Dict.*

II.† *n.* A restoring medicine; a restorative. *Bailey*, 1731. [Rare.]

resupinate (rē̤-sū'pi-nāt), *a.* [= F. *résupiné* = Sp. Pg. *resupinado*, < L. *resupinatus*, pp. of *resupinare*, bend or turn back, overthrow, < *re-*, back, + *supinare*, bend or lay backward: see *supine*, *supinate.*] 1. Inverted; reversed; appearing as if turned upside down.—2. In *bot.*, inverted: said specifically of flowers, like those of orchids, in which by a half-twist of the pedicel or ovary the posterior petal becomes lowermost; also of certain agaric fungi, in which the hymenium is on the upper instead of the under side of the pileus.—3. In *entom.*, same as *resupine.*

resupinated (rē̤-sū'pi-nā-ted), *a.* [< *resupinate* + *-ed*[2].] Same as *resupinate.*

resupination (rē̤-sū-pi-nā'shon), *n.* [= F. *résupination* = Pg. *resupinação*, < L. as if **resupinatio(n-)*, < *resupinare*, pp. *resupinatus*, bend back: see *resupinate.*] The state of being resupinate.

Our Vitruvius calleth this affection in the eye a *resupination* of the figure: for which word (being in truth his own, for ought I know) we are almost as much beholding to him as for the observation itself.
Sir H. Wotton, Reliquiæ, p. 62.

resupine (rē-sụ̄-pīn'), *a.* [= Pg. *resupino* = It. *risupino*, *resupino*, < L. *resupinus*, bent back or backward, lying on one's back, < *re-*, back, + *supinus*, lying on the back: see *supine.*] Lying on the back; supine. Also *resupinate.*

Then judge in what a tortured condition they must be of remorse and execrating themselves, for their most *resupine* and senseless madness.
Sir K. Digby, Observations. (*Latham.*)

He spake, and, downward sway'd, fell *resupine*,
With his huge neck aslant. *Cowper*, Odyssey, ix.

Specifically, in *entom.*, with the inferior surface upward, as when an insect lies on its back, or any part is twisted so that the lower surface is seen from above.

resurge (rē̤-sėrj'), *v. i.* [= OF. *resourdre* (> obs. E. *resourd*) = Sp. Pg. *resurgir* = It. *risurgere*, *risorgere*, *resurgere*, < L. *resurgere*, rise again, < *re-*, again, + *surgere*, rise: see *surge.* Cf. *resourd*, *resource*, *resurrection*, from the same source.] To rise again: in allusion to the motto *resurgam*, used on funeral hatchments. [Ludicrous.]

Hark at the dead jokes *resurging!* Memory greets them with the ghost of a smile.
Thackeray, Roundabout Papers, Letts's Diary.

resurgence (rē-sėr'jens), *n.* [< *resurgen(t)* + *-ce.*] The act of rising again; resurrection. *Coleridge.*

Night and day . . . the never-ending *resurgence* of the human spirit against the dead weight of oppression.
E. Dowden, Shelley, I. 44.

resurgent (rē-sėr'jent), *a.* and *n.* [< L. *resurgen(t-)s*, ppr. of *resurgere*, rise again: see *resurge.*] **I.** *a.* Rising again or from the dead. *Coleridge.*

The *resurgent* threatening past was making a conscience within him. *George Eliot*, Middlemarch, lxi.

A friend . . . whose bright temper, buoyant fancy, and generous heart ever leaped *resurgent* from the strokes of fortune. *E. Dowden*, Shelley, II. 59.

II. *n.* One who or that which rises again; especially, one who rises from the dead. *Sydney Smith.*

resurprise (rē-sėr-prīz'), *n.* [< *re-* + *surprise*, *n.*] A second or fresh surprise.

The process of this action drew on a *resurprise* of the castle by the Thebans. *Bacon*, War with Spain.

resurprise (rē-sėr-prīz'), *v. t.* [< *re-* + *surprise*, *v.*] To surprise again; retake unawares.

resurrect (rez-u-rekt'), *v. t.* [A back formation < *resurrection* assumed to be based on a transitive verb *resurrect*, as *connection*, *protection*, etc., are based on transitive verbs *connect*, *protect*, etc. The verb *resurrect*, if formed from the L. *resurrectus*, pp. of *resurgere*, would be intransitive, with the L. sense 'rise again': see *resurge.*] 1. To restore to life; reanimate; bring to public view, as what has been lost or forgotten. [Colloq.]

I *resurrect* the whole! put them in scene again on the living stage, every one with the best of his works in his hand.
Benton, Abridgement of Debates of Congress, VI. 712, note.

2. To take from the grave, as a dead body. [Colloq.]

resurrection (rez-u-rek'shon), *n.* [< ME. *resurreccioun*, *resurrectioun*, *resurexioun*, < OF. *resurrection*, F. *résurrection* = Pr. *resurrectio* = Sp. *resurreccion* = Pg. *resurreição* = It. *risurrezione*, *resurrezione*, < LL. (N. T. and eccles.) *resurrectio(n-)*, a rising again from the dead, < L. *resurgere*, pp. *resurrectus*, rise again, appear again, in LL. eccles. rise again from the dead, < *re-*, again, + *surgere*, rise: see *resurge.*] 1. In *theol.*: (*a*) A rising again from the dead. The doctrine of the resurrection has been held in three different forms: (1) As a literal resurrection of the self-same body which has been laid away in the grave: for example, "All the dead shall be raised up with the self-same bodies, and none other, although with different qualities, which shall be united again to their souls forever." *West. Conf. of Faith*, xxxii. 2. (2) As a resurrection from the dead, a coming forth from the place of the departed, but without the body with which the spirit was clothed in life, either with no body or with a new body given for the new life, and one either having no connection with the present earthly body or none that can be now apprehended: for example, "Resurrection of the Body, as taught in the New Testament, is not a Rising again of the same Body, but the Ascent into a higher Body." *J. F. Clarke*, Orthodoxy, its Truths and Errors, xii. § 6. (3) The doctrine of Swedenborg, that every man is possessed of two bodies, a natural and a spiritual, the latter within the former, and that at death the natural body is laid aside and the spiritual body rises at once from the death of the natural, resurrection thus taking place for every one immediately upon and simultaneously with death. The doctrine of the resurrection has been held in various other forms in detail, but they may all be classed under one of these three general heads.

There appeared first oure Lord to his Disciples, aftre his *Resurrexioun*. *Mandeville*, Travels, p. 91.

We therefore commit his body to the ground, . . . looking for the general *Resurrection* in the last day.
Book of Common Prayer, Burial of the Dead.

(*b*) The state which follows the resurrection; the future state.

In the *resurrection* they neither marry, nor are given in marriage. Mat. xxii. 30.

2. In general, a rising again; a springing again into life or to a previous mode of existence; a restoration.

Fix thyself firmly upon that belief of the general resurrection, and thou wilt never doubt of either of the particular *resurrections*, either from sin, by God's grace, or from worldly calamities, by God's power.
Donne, Sermons, xii.

3. Removal of a corpse from the grave for dissection; body-snatching. [Colloq.]

resurrectionary (rez-u-rek'shon-ā̤-ri), *a.* [< *resurrection* + *-ary.*] 1. Restoring to life; reviving.

Old men and women, . . . ugly and blind, who always seemed by *resurrectionary* process to be recalled out of the elements for the sudden peopling of the solitude!
Dickens, Uncommercial Traveller, vii.

2. Pertaining to or consisting in the act of resurrecting or digging up. [Colloq.]

A *resurrectionary* operation in quest of a presumed fault in the mains. *Elect. Rev.*, XXII. 288.

resurrectionist (rez-u-rek'shon-ist), *n.* [= F. *résurrectioniste* (< E.); as *resurrection* + *-ist.*] 1. One who makes a practice of stealing bodies from the grave for dissection: also used adjectively. [Colloq.]

He has emerged from his *resurrectionist* delvings in the graveyards of rhyme, without confounding moral distinctions, [or] vitiating his taste.
Whipple, Ess. and Rev., I. 32.

Hence—2. One who unearths anything from long concealment or obscurity. [Colloq.]

In short, . . . he was merely a *resurrectionist* of obsolete heresies. *Miss Edgeworth*, Helen, xi.

resurrectionize (rez-u-rek'shon-īz), *v. t.*; pret. and pp. *resurrectionized*, ppr. *resurrectionizing*. [< *resurrection* + *-ize.*] 1. To raise from the dead; resurrect. [Colloq. and rare.]

Half these gentlemen are not included in the common collection of the poets, and must be *resurrectionized* at Stationers' Hall. *Southey*, To Miss Barker, April 3, 1804.

2. To steal from the grave; dig up from the grave. [Colloq.]

The famous marble coffer in the king's chamber, which was doubtless also Cheops's coffin until his body was *resurrectionized* by the thieves who first broke into the pyramid. *Library Mag.*, III. 453.

Also spelled *resurrectionise*.

resurrection-man (rez-u-rek'shon-man), *n.* Same as *resurrectionist*. *Dickens*, Tale of Two Cities, ii. 14.

resurrection-plant (rez-u-rek'shon-plant), *n.* A name for several plants which, when dried, reëxpand if wetted. (*a*) The rose of Jericho. See *Anastatica*. (*b*) *Selaginella lepidophylla*, found from Texas and Mexico to Peru. It forms a nest-like ball when dry (whence called *bird's-nest moss*), but when moistened unfolds and displays its elegant, finely cut, fern-like branches radiating from a coiled central stem. (*c*) One of the fig-marigolds, *Mesembryanthemum Tripolium*. [The name has doubtless been applied to other hygrometric plants.]

resurvey (rē-sėr-vā'), *v. t.* [< *re-* + *survey*.] 1. To survey again or anew; review.—2. To read and examine again.

Once more *re-survey*
These poor rude lines of thy deceased lover.
Shak., Sonnets, xxxii.

resurvey (rē-sėr-vā'), *n.* [< *resurvey*, *v.*] A new survey.

resuscitable (rē-sus'i-ta-bl), *a.* [< OF. *ressuscitable*; as *resuscit(ate)* + *-able*.] Capable of being resuscitated or restored to life.

resuscitant (rē-sus'i-tant), *a.* and *n.* [= F. *ressuscitant*, < L. *resuscitan(t-)s*, ppr. of *resuscitare*, revive: see *resuscitate*.] I. *a.* Resuscitating.

II. *n.* One who or that which resuscitates.

resuscitate (rē-sus'i-tāt), *v.*; pret. and pp. *resuscitated*, ppr. *resuscitating*. [< L. *resuscitatus*, pp. of *resuscitare* (> It. *resuscitare*, *risuscitare* = Sp. *resucitar* = Pg. *resuscitar* = OF. *resusciter*, *ressusciter*, F. *ressusciter*), raise up again, revive, < *re-*, again, + *suscitare*, raise up, < *sus-*, *sub-*, up, under, + *citare*, summon, rouse: see *cite*[1].] I. *trans.* To stir up anew; revivify; revive; particularly, to recover from apparent death: as, to *resuscitate* a drowned person; to *resuscitate* withered plants.

After death we should be *resuscitated*.
Glanville, Pre-existence of Souls, xiv.

To wonder at a thousand insect forms,
These hatch'd, and those *resuscitated* worms,
Once prone on earth, now buoyant upon air.
Cowper, Retirement, l. 64.

It is difficult to *resuscitate* surprise when familiarity has once laid the sentiment asleep. *Paley*, Nat. Theol., xviii.

II. *intrans.* To revive; come to life again.

Our griefs, our pleasures, our youth, our sorrows, our dear, dear friends, *resuscitate*. *Thackeray*, Philip, xxviii.

As these projects, however often slain, always *resuscitate*, it is not superfluous to examine one or two of the fallacies by which the schemers impose on themselves. *J. S. Mill.*

resuscitate† (rē-sus'i-tāt), *a.* [< L. *resuscitatus*, pp.: see the verb.] Restored to life; revived.

Our mortall bodyes shal be *resuscitate*.
Bp. Gardiner, Exposition, The Presence, p. 65.

There is a grudge newly now *resuscitate* and revived in the minds of the people.
Abp. Warham, in Hallam's Const. Hist., I. 34, note 2.

resuscitation (rē-sus-i-tā'shon), *n.* [= OF. (and F.) *ressuscitation* = Pg. *resuscitação* = It. *risuscitazione*, < LL. *resuscitatio(n-)*, a resuscitation, < L. *resuscitare*, resuscitate: see *resuscitate*.] 1. The act of resuscitating, or the state of being resuscitated; revival; revivification; restoration to life; the restoring to animation of persons apparently dead, as in cases of drowning, or of suspended animation from exposure to cold or from disease.

The *resuscitation* of the body from its dust is a supernatural work. *Bp. Hall*, Temptations Repelled, i. § 5.

The extinction and *resuscitation* of arts.
Johnson, Rasselas, xxx.

2. Mental reproduction, or suggestion, in a sense which does not include the process of representation. *Sir W. Hamilton*.

resuscitative (rē-sus'i-tā-tiv), *a.* [< OF. *resuscitatif*, *ressuscitatif*, F. *ressuscitatif*; as *resuscitate* + *-ive*.] Tending to resuscitate; reviving; revivifying; raising from apparent death; reproducing.—**Resuscitative faculty**, a name given by Sir William Hamilton to the reproductive faculty of the mind.

resuscitator (rē-sus'i-tā-tor), *n.* [= F. *ressusciteur* = Sp. *resucitador* = Pg. *resuscitador* = It. *risuscitatore*, < LL. *resuscitator*, one who raises again from the dead, < L. *resuscitare*, raise up: see *resuscitate*.] One who resuscitates.

resveriet, *n.* See *reverie*.

ret[1] (ret), *v. t.*; pret. and pp. *retted*, ppr. *retting*. [< ME. *retten*, *reten*, < OD. OFlem. *reten*, *reeten*, ret (flax or hemp), break or heckle (flax), steep, soak, D. Flem. *reten*, ret (flax or hemp), = Sw. *röta*, putrefy, rot (flax or hemp), steep, soak; cf. *rot*.] To expose, as the gathered stems of fibrous plants, to moisture, in order, by partial fermentation or rotting, to facilitate the abstraction of the fiber. Retting is practised upon flax, hemp, jute, and other exogenous fiber-plants. *Dew-retting*, effected simply by exposing the material to the weather for a limited time, is largely applied to flax in Russia. *Water-retting*, the ordinary process, consists simply in steeping or macerating the stems in water, commonly in open ponds, sometimes in vats of warm water, the result being more speedily attained by the latter treatment.

A dam of 50 feet long, 9 feet broad, and 4 feet deep is sufficient to *ret* the produce of an acre of flax.
Encyc. Brit., IX. 294.

ret[2]†, *v. t.* [ME. *retten*, *reeten*, < OF. *retter*, *reter* (ML. reflex *rectare*, simulating L. *rectus*, right), repute, impute, charge, < L. *reputare*, repute, impute, ascribe: see *repute*, *v.*] To impute; ascribe.

I pray you of your curteisie,
That ye ne *rette* it nat my vileinye,
Though that I pleynly speke in this matere.
Chaucer, Gen. Prol. to C. T. (ed. Morris), l. 726.

ret[3]†. A Middle English contraction of *redeth* (modern *readeth*).

retable (rē-tā'bl), *n.* [< F. *retable*, OF. *retaule*, *restaule* (ML. reflex *retaule*), an altarpiece, reredos, retable, = Sp. *retablo* = Pg. *retabolo*, *retabulo*, a picture; of doubtful origin: (*a*) according to Scheler, < L. as if **restabilis*, fixed opposite (or in some other particular sense), < *restare*, rest, stay (see *rest*[2]); (*b*) according to Brachet, a contraction of OF. **riere-table*, **arriere-table*, a reredos, < *arriere*, rear, behind, + *table*, table: see *rear*[3] and *table*. In either view the Sp. and Pg. are prob. from the F.] A structure raised above an altar at the back, either independent in itself, or forming a decorative frame to a picture, a bas-relief, or the like, in which case the word includes the work of art itself. Usually that face only which looks toward the choir and nave of the church is called the *retable*, and the reverse is called the *counter-retable*. Sometimes the retable is a movable structure of hammered silver or other precious work, supported on the altar itself. This decorative feature is not found in the earliest ages of the Christian church. Many retables in Italy are made of Della Robbia ware, with figures in high relief, and richly colored in ceramic enamels. One of the most magnificent examples is the Pala d'Oro of the Basilica of St. Mark, in Venice. See *altar-ledge* and *reredos*.

retail[1] (rē'tāl), *n.* and *a.* [Early mod. E. *retaile*; < ME. *retaille*, < OF. *retail*, *retaille*, F. *retaille*, a piece cut off, a shred, paring (= Sp. *retal* = Pg. *retalho*, a shred, remnant, = It. *ritaglio*, a shred, piece, a selling by the piece, retail (*a ritaglio*, by retail)), < *retailler*, cut, shred, pare, clip, F. *retailler*, cut, recut, trim (a pen), prune (a tree) (= Pr. *retalhar*, recut, = Cat. *retallar* = Sp. *retajar*, cut around, recut, trim, = Pg. *retalhar* = It. *ritagliare*, slice, shred, pare, cut), < *re-*, again, + *tailler*, cut: see *tail*[2], *tally*, and cf. *detail*. The sense 'retail,' which does not appear in F., may have been derived from It.] I. *n.* The sale of commodities in small quantities or parcels, or at second hand; a dealing out in small portions: opposed to *wholesale*.

The Vintner's *retail* supports the merchant's trade.
Jer. Taylor, Works (ed. 1835), I. 851.

The duties on the *retail* of drinks made from tea, coffee, and chocolate. *S. Dowell*, Taxes in England, II. 44.

At (by, or formerly to) retail, in small quantities; a little at a time, as in the sale of merchandise.

And marchauntes yt be not in yt fraunshes of the for sayd cite yt they selle noo wyne ne ne noon oder marchaundisis *to retaille* wt in ye cite ne in ye subarbis of ye same. *Charter of London*, in Arnold's Chron., p. 25.

Now, all that God doth *by retail* bestowe
On perfect'st men to thee in grosse he giues.
Sylvester, tr. of Du Bartas's Triumph of Faith, Ded.

These, and most other things which are sold *by retail*. . . . are generally fully as cheap, or cheaper, in great towns than in the remoter parts of the country.
Adam Smith, Wealth of Nations, i. 8.

II. *a.* Of or pertaining to sale at retail; concerned with sale at retail: as, *retail* trade; a *retail* dealer.

But I find, in the present state of trade, that when the *retail* price is printed on books, all sorts of commissions and abatements take place, to the discredit of the author.
Ruskin.

retail[1] (rē-tāl'), *v. t.* [< *retail*[1], *n.*, in the phrase "to sell by *retail*." Cf. It. *ritagliare*, retail.] 1. To sell in small quantities or parcels.

He is wit's pedler, and *retails* his wares
At wakes and wassails, meetings, markets, fairs.
Shak., L. L. L., v. 2. 317.

The keepers of ale-houses pay for a licence to *retail* ale and spirituous liquors.
Adam Smith, Wealth of Nations, v. 2.

2. To sell at second hand.

The sage dame, experienced in her trade,
By names of toasts *retails* each batter'd jade.
Pope, Dunciad, ii. 134.

3. To deal out in small quantities; tell in broken parts; tell to many; tell again; hand down by report: as, to *retail* slander or idle reports.

Methinks the truth should live from age to age,
As 'twere *retail'd* to all posterity.
Shak., Rich. III., iii. 1. 77.

He could repeat all the observations that were *retailed* in the atmosphere of the play-houses.
Goldsmith, Vicar, xvi.

retail[2]† (rē-tāl'), *n.* [Irreg. (perhaps by confusion with *retail*[1]) < L. *retaliare*, retaliate: see *retaliate*.] Retaliation.

He that doth injury may well receive it. To look for good and do bad is against the law of *retail*.
Rev. T. Adams, Works, II. 116.

retailer (rē-tā'lėr or rē'tā-lėr), *n.* [< *retail*[1] + *-er*[1]. Cf. Pg. *retalhador*, one who shreds or clips; It. *ritagliatore*, a retail seller.] 1. A retail dealer; one who sells or deals out goods in small parcels or at second hand.

I was informed of late dayes that a certaine blinde *retayler*, called the Diuell, vsed to lend money vpon pawnes or anie thing. *Nashe*, Pierce Penilesse, p. 9.

From the Chapman to the *Retailer*, many whose ignorance was more audacious then the rest were admitted with all thir sordid Rudiments to bear no meane sway among them, both in Church and State.
Milton, Hist. Eng., iii.

2. One who tells at second hand; one who repeats or reports: as, a *retailer* of scandal.

retaillé (rē-ta-lyā'), *a.* [< F. *retaillé*, pp. of *retailler*, recut: see *retail*[1], *n.*] In *her.*, cut or divided twice: noting an escutcheon, especially when divided twice bendwise sinister.

retailment (rē-tāl'ment), *n.* [< *retail*[1], *v.*, + *-ment*.] The act of retailing.

retain (rē-tān'), *v.* [Early mod. E. *retayne*; < ME. *retaynen*, *reteynen*, < OF. F. *retenir*, *retanir* = Pr. *retener*, *retenir* = Sp. *retener* = Pg. *reter* = It. *ritenere*, < L. *retinere*, pp. *retentus*, hold back, < *re-*, back, + *tenere*, hold: see *tenant*.] I. *trans.* 1†. To hold back; restrain; hinder from action, departure, or escape; keep back; detain.

Ser, if it please your lordshepe for to here,
ffor your wurchippe yow most your self *reteyne*,
And take a good avise in this mater.
Generydes (E. E. T. S.), l. 1543.

For empty fystes, men vse to say,
Cannot the Hawke *retayne*.
Babees Book (E. E. T. S.), p. 102.

Whom I would have *retained* with me, that in thy stead he might have ministered unto me in the bonds of the gospel. Phile. 13.

2. To hold or keep in possession; reserve as one's own.

The Kingdome he *retain'd* against thir utmost opposition. *Milton*, Hist. Eng., ii.

Among debts of equal degree, the executor . . . is allowed to pay himself first, by *retaining* in his hands so much as his debt amounts to. *Blackstone*, Com., II. xxxii.

3. To continue in the use or practice of; preserve; keep up; keep from dying out: as, to *retain* a custom; to *retain* an appearance of youth.

Oh, you cannot be
So heavenly and so absolute in all things,
And yet *retain* such cruel tyranny!
Beau. and Fl., Laws of Candy, ii. 1.

William the Conqueror in all the time of his Sickness *retained* to the very last his Memory and Speech.
Baker, Chronicles, p. 31.

4. To keep in mind; preserve a knowledge or idea of; remember.

They did not like to *retain* God in their knowledge.
Rom. i. 28.

No Learning is *retained* without constant exercise and methodical repetition. *Milton*, Touching Hirelings.

5. To keep in pay; hire; take into service; especially, to engage by the payment of a preliminary fee: as, to *retain* counsel.

Sette no man a-worke that is *reteyignde* in any man-ys service. *English Gilds* (E. E. T. S.), p. 333.

They say you have *retained* brisk Master Practice
Here of your counsel.
B. *Jonson*, Magnetick Lady, ii. 1.

6†. To entertain.

Retayne a straunger after his estate and degree.
Babees Book (E. E. T. S.), p. 102.

=**Syn.** 2-4. *Reserve*, *Preserve*, etc. See *keep*.

II.† *intrans.* 1. To keep on; continue.

No more can impure man *retain* and move
In that pure region of a worthy love.
Donne, Epistles to the Countess of Huntingdon.

2. To pertain; belong; be a dependent or retainer.

In whose armie followed William Longespee, accompanied with a piked number of English warriors *retaining* vnto him. *Hakluyt's Voyages*, II. 34.

retainable (rẹ̄-tā'nạ-bl), *a.* [< *retain* + *-able.*] Capable of being retained.

retainal (rẹ̄-tā'nạl), *n.* [< *retain* + *-al.*] The act of retaining. *Annual Rev.*, II. (1804), p. 631. [Rare.]

retaindership† (rẹ̄-tān'dėr-ship), *n.* [For *retainership*: see *retainer* and *-ship.*] The state of being a retainer or dependent.

It was the policy of these kings to make them all [clergy and nobility] of their own livery or *retaindership*. *N. Bacon.* (*Imp. Dict.*)

retainer[1] (rẹ̄-tā'nėr), *n.* [Formerly also *retainour*; < ME. **retainour*; < *retain* + *-er*[1]. Cf. OF. *reteneur* (Sp. *retenedor*, It. *retenitore*), a retainer, detainer, < *retenir*, retain: see *retain*.] 1. One who or that which retains.

One that has forgot the common meaning of words, but an admirable *retainer* of the sound. *Swift*, Tale of a Tub, § 9.

2. One who is kept in service; a dependent; an attendant; especially, a follower who wears his master's livery, but ranks higher than a domestic.

In common law, *retainer* signifieth a servant not menial nor familiar — that is, not dwelling in his house, but only using or bearing his name and livery. *Cowell.*

If we once forsake the strict rules of Religion and Goodness, and are ready to yield our selves to whatever hath got *retainers* enough to set up for a custom, we may know where we begin, but we cannot where we shall make an end. *Stillingfleet*, Sermons, I. ii.

Kendall, a needy *retainer* of the court, who had, in obedience to the royal mandate, been sent to Parliament by a packed corporation in Cornwall. *Macaulay*, Hist. Eng., vi.

Another [abuse of maintenance], and that more directly connected with the giving of liveries, was the gathering round the lord's household of a swarm of armed *retainers* whom the lord could not control, and whom he conceived himself bound to protect. *Stubbs*, Const. Hist., § 470.

3. A sutler, camp-follower, or any person serving with an army who, though not enlisted, is subject to orders according to the rules and articles of war.—4. One who is connected with or frequents a certain place; an attendant.

That indulgence and undisturbed liberty of conscience . . . which the *retainers* to every petty conventicle enjoy. *Blackstone*, Com., IV. iv.

retainer[2] (rẹ̄-tā'nėr), *n.* [Formerly also *retainour*; < OF. *retenir*, retain, inf. used as a noun: see *retain*. Cf. *detainer*[2].] 1†. The act of retaining dependents; entrance into service as a retainer; the state of being a retainer.

The Kings Officers and Farmors were to forfeit their Places and Holds in case of unlawfull *Retainer*, or partaking in Routs and unlawfull Assemblies. *Bacon*, Hist. Hen. VII., p. 66.

2. That by which a person's services are secured; a fee.

The same Thomas Cromwell, earl of Essex, hath allured and drawn unto him by *retainours* many of your subjects. *Bp. Burnet*, Records, I. iii., No. 16.

3. Specifically, in *law*: (*a*) Same as *retaining fee* (which see, under *fee*[1]). (*b*) An authority given to an attorney or a solicitor to proceed in an action. (*c*) The unlawful taking or detention of a known servant from his master during the period of service. *Robinson.* (*d*) The act of an executor or administrator who is a creditor of the decedent, or whose estate he represents, in withholding from the fund so much as will pay what is due him: formerly allowed to be done even before any other creditors whose debts were of equal degree were paid.—**General retainer**, a fee given by a party to secure a priority of claim on the counsel's services for any case that he may have in any court which that counsel attends.—**Special retainer**, a fee for a particular case which is expected to come on.

retainership (rẹ̄-tā'nėr-ship), *n.* [< *retainer*[1] + *-ship.*] The state of being a retainer or follower; hence, a feeling of loyalty or attachment to a chief. [Rare.]

All the few in whom yet lingered any shadow of *retainership* toward the fast-fading chieftainship of Glenwarlock seemed to cherish the notion that the heir of the house had to be tended and cared for like a child. *G. MacDonald*, Warlock o' Glenwarlock, xiii.

retaining (rẹ̄-tā'ning), *p. a.* [Ppr. of *retain*, *v.*] Keeping in possession; serving to retain; keeping back; engaging.—**Retaining fee.** See *fee*[1].—**Retaining lien.** See *lien*[2].—**Retaining wall**, a wall built to prevent a bank, as of earth, from slipping down or being washed away; a revetment. See cut in next column.

retainment (rẹ̄-tān'mẹnt), *n.* [< *retain* + *-ment.*] The act of retaining; retention.

retain-wall (rẹ̄-tān'wâl), *n.* Same as *retaining wall* (which see, under *retaining*).

a, retaining wall; *b*, *c*, breast-walls.

retake (rē-tāk'), *v. t.* [< *re-* + *take.*] 1. To take again.

A day should be appointed when the remonstrance should be *retaken* into consideration. *Clarendon.*

Thy chair, a grief to all the brethren, stands
Vacant, but thou *retake* it, mine again!
Tennyson, Balin and Balan.

2. To take back; recapture.

retaker (rē-tā'kėr), *n.* [< *retake* + *-er*[1].] One who takes again what has been taken; a recaptor. *Imp. Dict.*

retaliate (rẹ̄-tal'i-āt), *v.*; pret. and pp. *retaliated*, ppr. *retaliating*. [< L. *retaliatus*, pp. of *retaliare*, requite, retaliate (cf. *talio*, retaliation in kind; *lex talionis*, law of retaliation), < *re-*, back, again, + *talis*, such: see *talion*. Cf. *retail*[2].] I. *trans.* To return in kind; repay or requite by an act of the same kind: now seldom or never used except in the sense of returning evil for evil: as, to *retaliate* injuries.

Our ambassador sent word . . . to the Duke's sonne his visit should be *retaliated*. *Sir T. Herbert*, Travels in Africa, p. 137.

The kindness which he has graciously shown them may be *retaliated* on those of his own persuasion. *Dryden*, Hind and Panther, To the Reader.

Let it be the pride of our writers, . . . disdaining to *retaliate* the illiberality of British authors, to speak of the English nation without prejudice. *Irving*, Sketch-Book, p. 78.

Our blood may boil at hearing of atrocities committed, without being able to ascertain how those atrocities were provoked, or how they may have been *retaliated*. *W. R. Greg*, Misc. Essays, 1st ser., p. 52.

II. *intrans.* To return like for like; especially (now usually), to return evil for evil.

Liberality . . . may lead the person obliged with the sense of the duty he lies under to *retaliate*. *Goldsmith*, Citizen of the World, lxvi.

=**Syn.** See *revenge*, *n.*

retaliation (rẹ̄-tal-i-ā'shọn), *n.* [< L. as if **retaliatio(n-)*, < *retaliare*, retaliate: see *retaliate*.] The act of retaliating; the return of like for like; the doing of that to another which he has done to us; especially (now usually), requital of evil; reprisal; revenge.

First, I will shew you the antiquity of these manors. Secondly, I will a little discuss the ancient honour of this manor of Levenham. Thirdly, I will give you a touch what respects you are likely to find from me; and fourthly, what *retaliation* I expect again from you. *MS. Harl.* 646. (*Halliwell.*)

The lex talionis, or law of *retaliation*, can never be in all cases an adequate or permanent rule of punishment. *Blackstone*, Com., IV. i.

=**Syn.** *Retribution*, *Reprisal*, etc. See *revenge*.

retaliative (rẹ̄-tal'i-ạ̄-tiv), *a.* [< *retaliate* + *-ive.*] Tending to or of the nature of retaliation; retaliatory; vindictive; revengeful. *Quarterly Rev.* (*Imp. Dict.*)

retaliatory (rẹ̄-tal'i-ạ̄-tọ̄-ri), *a.* [< *retaliate* + *-ory.*] Pertaining to or of the nature of retaliation.

The armed neutrality was succeeded by *retaliatory* embargoes, and on the 2d of April, 1801, the battle of Copenhagen prostrated the power of Denmark. *Woolsey*, Introd. to Inter. Law, § 191.

retama (re-tä'mạ̈ or re-tā'mạ̈), *n.* [< Sp. *retama*, Ar. *retama.*] Any one of a small group of plants forming the section *Retama* (sometimes considered a genus—*Boissier*, 1839), in the genus *Genista*. They are yellow-flowered shrubs with rush-like branches, which are leafless or bear a few unifoliate leaves. They are found in the Mediterranean region and the Canaries. Some species are useful for fixing sands.

The region of *retama*, the first bushes of which are met with at the pass which admits the traveller into the Llano de la Retama. *Encyc. Brit.*, IV. 798.

retard (rẹ̄-tärd'), *v.* [< OF. *retarder*, F. *retarder* = Pr. Sp. Pg. *retardar* = It. *ritardare*, < L. *retardare*, make slow, delay, < *re-*, back, + *tardare*, make slow, < *tardus*, slow: see *tardy*.] I. *trans.* 1. To make slow or slower; obstruct in motion or progress; delay; impede; clog; hinder.

This will *retard*
The work a month at least.
B. Jonson, Alchemist, iv. 3.

Accidental causes *retarded* at times, and at times accelerated, the progress of the controversy. *Webster*, Speech at Plymouth, Dec. 22, 1820.

While, however, the predatory activities have not prevented the development of sympathy in the directions open to it, they have *retarded* it throughout its entire range. *H. Spencer*, Prin. of Psychol., § 512.

2. To defer; postpone; put off.

Those relations which describe the tricks and vices only of mankind, by increasing our suspicion in life, *retard* our success. *Goldsmith*, Vicar, xxvi.

My friends, the time is coming when a State Church will be unknown in England, and it rests with you to accelerate or *retard* that happy consummation. *John Bright*, in G. Barnett Smith, ii.

Retarded motion, in *physics*, that motion which exhibits continual diminution of velocity, as the motion of a body projected upward. If the diminutions of velocity are equal in equal times, the motion is said to be *uniformly retarded*. The laws of retarded motion are the same as those of accelerated motion, only the order is reversed. See *acceleration*.—**Retarding ague**, a form of ague in which the paroxysm comes at a little later hour each day. =**Syn.** 1. To detain, delay.

II. *intrans.* To be delayed or later than usual.

Some years it [the inundation of the Nile] hath also *retarded*, and came far later then usually it was expected. *Sir T. Browne*, Vulg. Err., vi. 8.

retard (rẹ̄-tärd'), *n.* [= F. *retard* = Sp. *retardo* = It. *ritardo*; from the verb.] Retardation.—**In retard**, retarded; kept back; delayed in growth or progress.

A people of great natural capacities have been kept for centuries *in retard*. *The Atlantic*, LVIII. 516.

Retard of the tide, the interval between the transit of the moon at which a tide originates and the appearance of the tide itself.

retardant (rẹ̄-tär'dạnt), *a.* [< L. *retardan(t-)s*, ppr. of *retardare*, retard: see *retard*.] Retarding; tending to delay or impede motion, growth, or progress. [Rare.]

We know the *retardant* effect of society upon artists of exalted sensibility. *Stedman*, Poets of America, p. 468.

retardation (rē-tär-dā'shọn), *n.* [= OF. (and F.) *retardation* = Sp. *retardacion* = Pg. *retardação* = It. *ritardazione*, < L. *retardatio(n-)*, < *retardare*, pp. *retardatus*, retard: see *retard*.] 1. The act of retarding or making slower, or its effect; the hindering of motion, growth, or progress, or the hindrance effected; the act of delaying or impeding.

If the embryonic type were the offspring, then its failure to attain to the condition of the parent is due to the supervention of a slower rate of growth; to this phenomenon the term *retardation* was applied. *E. D. Cope*, Origin of the Fittest, p. 125.

2. In *physics*: (*a*) A continuous decrement of velocity; a negative acceleration.

The fall of meteoric dust on to the earth must cause a small *retardation* of the earth's rotation, although to an amount probably quite insensible in a century. *Thomson and Tait*, Nat. Phil., § 830.

It was generally supposed that the discrepancy between the theoretical and observed result is due to a *retardation* of the earth's rotation by the friction of the tides. *C. A. Young*, General Astronomy, § 461.

(*b*) In acoustics and optics, the distance by which one wave is behind another. Better called *retard*, being translation of French *retard*.

In reflexion at the surface of a denser medium the reflected ray undergoes a *retardation* in respect to the incident ray of a half wave-length. *Lommel*, Light (trans.), p. 240.

3†. Postponement; deferment.

Out of this ground a man may devise the means of altering the colour of birds, and the *retardation* of hoar hairs. *Bacon*, Nat. Hist., § 851.

4. Specifically, in *music*: (*a*) The act, process, or result of diminishing the speed or pace of the tempo. (*b*) The prolongation of a concordant tone into a chord where it is a discord which is resolved upward: opposed to *anticipation*, and distinguished from *suspension* by the upward resolution. [It would be well, however, if *retardation* were made the generic term, with *suspension* as a species.]

5. In *teleg.*, decrease in the speed of telegraph-signaling due to self-induction and induction from surrounding conductors.—6. That which retards; a hindrance; an obstruction; an impediment.

We find many persons who in seven years meet not with a violent temptation to a crime, but their battles are against impediments and *retardations* of improvement. *Jer. Taylor*, Works (ed. 1835), I. 99.

Retardation of mean solar time, the change of the mean sun's right ascension in a sidereal day, or the number of seconds by which mean noon comes later each successive sidereal day, as if the mean sun hung back in its diurnal revolution.—**Retardation of the tides.** See *acceleration*.

retardative (rẹ̄-tär'dạ̄-tiv), *a.* [= F. *retardatif* = It. *ritardativo*, < L. *retardatus*, pp. of *retardare*, retard.] Tending to retard; retarding.

The *retardative* effects would also be largely increased, to a serious extent, in fact, in the case of the telephones. *Pop. Sci. Mo.*, XXVII. 717.

retardatory (rẹ̄-tär'dạ̄-tọ̄-ri), *a.* [< *retard* + *-atory.*] Tending or having power to retard.

Instant promptitude of action, adequate *retardatory* power. *Athenæum*, No. 2802, p. 308.

retarder (rẹ̄-tär'dėr), *n.* One who retards; that which serves as a hindrance, impediment, or cause of retardation.

This disputing way of enquiry is so far from advancing science that it is no inconsiderable *retarder*. *Glanville.*

retardment (rẹ̄-tärd'mẹnt), *n.* [< OF. *retardement*, F. *retardement* = Pr. *retardamen* = Pg. *retardamento* = It. *ritardamento*, < ML. **retardamentum*, < L. *retardare*, retard: see *retard.*] The act of retarding; a retardation; delay.

Which Malice or which Art no more could stay
Than witches' charms can a *retardment* bring
To the resuscitation of the Day,
Or resurrection of the Spring.
Cowley, Upon His Majesty's Restoration and Return.

retaunt (rẹ̄-tänt'), *n.* [< *re-* + *taunt*, *n.*] The repetition of a taunt. [Rare.]

Wyth suche tauntes and *retauntes*, ye, in maner checke and checke mate to the uttermooste prote of my pacience. Hall, Richard III., f. 10. (*Halliwell.*)

retch[1] (rech), *v.* [(*a*) < ME. *recchen*, < AS. *reccan*, stretch, extend, hold forth (see under *rack*[1], *v.*); mixed in mod. dial. use with (*b*) *reach*, < ME. *rechen*, < AS. *rǣcan*, reach: see *reach*[1].] To reach. [Prov. Eng.]

I *retche* with a weapon or with my hande, je attains. *Palsgrave.* (*Halliwell.*)

retch[2] (rech), *v. i.* [Also formerly or dial. *reach*; < ME. **rechen*, < AS. *hrǣcan*, clear the throat, hawk, spit (cf. *hrāca*, spittle, expectoration, *hrǣcea*, hawking, clearing the throat, **hrǣcetan*, *hrǣctan*, eructate, retch, *hrǣcetung*, retching), = Icel. *hrækja*, hawk, spit (*hrāki*, spittle); cf. OHG. *rachisōn*, MHG. *rahsenen*, hawk; prob. ult. imitative (cf. *hawk*[3]). The AS. *hracu*, throat, = MD. *racke* = OHG. *rahho*, MHG. *rache*, G. *rachen*, throat, jaws, are prob. unrelated.] To make efforts to vomit.

The ashes of the said barke given in wine hote is greatly commended for the *reaching* and spitting of blood. *Holland*, tr. of Pliny, xxiv. 4.

"Beloved Julia, hear me still beseeching!"
(Here he grew inarticulate with *retching*.)
Byron, Don Juan, ii. 20.

retch[3]† (rech), *v. i.* and *t.* [An assibilated form of *reck.*] Same as *reck.*

retchless† (rech'les), *a.* [An assibilated form of *reckless.*] Same as *reckless.*

I left my natiue soile, full like a *retchlesse* man. *Hakluyt's Voyages*, I. 384.

They are such *retchless* flies as you are, that blow cutpurses abroad in every corner; your foolish having of money makes them. *B. Jonson*, Bartholomew Fair, iii. 1.

retchlessly† (rech'les-li), *adv.* Same as *recklessly.*

I do horribly and *retchlessly* neglect and lightly regard thy wrath hanging over my head. *J. Bradford*, Works (Parker Soc., 1853), II. 202.

retchlessness† (rech'les-nes), *n.* Same as *recklessness.*

A viper that hast eat a passage through me,
Through mine own bowels, by thy *retchlessness*.
B. Jonson, Magnetick Lady, iv. 1.

rete (rē'tē), *n.*; pl. *retia* (rē'shi-ạ̈). [NL., < L. *rete*, a net.] In *anat.*, a vascular network; a plexus, glomerulus, or congeries of small vessels; in *bot.*, a structure like network.

It sends out convoluted vessels (*retia*) from the large cerebral cleft, which are connected with the roof of the cleft. *Gegenbaur*, Comp. Anat. (trans.), p. 513.

Epidermal rete. Same as *rete mucosum.*—**Rete Halleri.** Same as *rete vasculosum testis.*—**Rete Malpighii.** Same as *rete mucosum.*—**Rete mirabile**, a network or plexus of small veins or arteries, formed by the immediate breaking up of a vessel of considerable size, terminating either by reuniting in a single vessel (bipolar), or in capillaries (unipolar).—**Rete mirabile geminum** or **conjugatum**, a plexus in which arteries and veins are combined.—**Rete mirabile of Galen**, a meshwork of vessels formed by the intracranial part of the internal carotid artery in some mammals.—**Rete mirabile simplex**, a plexus consisting of arteries only, or of veins only.—**Rete mucosum**, the deeper, softer part of the epidermis, below the stratum granulosum, consisting of prickle-cells. Also called *stratum spinosum*, *rete mucosum Malpighii*, *rete Malpighii*, *stratum Malpighii*, *corpus reticulare*, *corpus mucosum*, *Malpighian layer*, *epidermal rete*. See cuts under *skin* and *sweat-gland.*—**Rete vasculosum testis**, a network of vessels lying in the mediastinum testis, into which the straight tubules empty. It holds the accumulated secretion of the testis, discharging through the vasa deferentia. Also called *rete vasculosum Halleri*, *rete Halleri*, *rete testis*, *rete testis Halleri*, *spermatic rete.*

retecious (rẹ̄-tē'shus), *a.* [Irreg. < *rete* + *-cious.*] Same as *retiform.*

retection† (rẹ̄-tek'shọn), *n.* [< L. *retectus*, pp. of *retegere*, uncover, disclose, < *re-*, back, + *tegere*, cover: see *tegument.*] The act of disclosing or producing to view something concealed.

This may be said to be rather a restoration of a body to its own colour, or a *retection* of its native colour, than a change. *Boyle*, Works, I. 685.

retell (rē-tel'), *v. t.* [< *re-* + *tell.*] To tell again.

Whate'er Lord Harry Percy then had said . . .
At such a time, with all the rest *retold*,
May reasonably die, and never rise
To do him wrong. *Shak.*, 1 Hen. IV., i. 3. 73.

retent†, *n.* [ME., for *retenue*, retinue: see *retinue.*] Retinue.

Syre Degrivaunt ys whom [home] went,
And aftyr hys *reten* sent.
Sir Degrevant, 930. (*Halliwell.*)

retenance†, *n.* [ME., also *retenaunce*, *retenauns*, also *retainaunce*, < OF. *retenance*, < ML. **retinentia*, < L. *retinere*, retain: see *retain*. Cf. *retinue.*] Retinue.

Mede was ymaried in meteles me thouȝte;
That alle the riche *retenauns* that regneth with the false
Were boden to the bridale. *Piers Plowman* (B), ii. 52.

retent (rẹ̄-tent'), *n.* [< L. *retentus*, pp. of *retinere*, retain: see *retain.*] That which is retained. *Imp. Dict.*

retention (rẹ̄-ten'shọn), *n.* [< OF. *retention*, F. *rétention* = Pr. *retentio* = Sp. *retencion* = Pg. *retenção* = It. *ritenzione*, < L. *retentio(n-)*, a retaining, < *retinere*, pp. *retentus*, retain: see *retain.*] 1. The act of retaining or keeping back; restraint; reserve.

His life I gave him and did thereto add
My love, without *retention* or restraint.
Shak., T. N., v. 1. 84.

2. The act of retaining or holding as one's own; continued possession or ownership.

While no thoughtful Englishman can defend the acquisition of India, yet a thoughtful Englishman may easily defend its *retention*. *E. A. Freeman*, Amer. Lects., p. 350.

3. Continuance or perseverance, as in the use or practice of anything; preservation.

A froward *retention* of custom is as turbulent a thing as an innovation. *Bacon*, Advancement of Learning, vi.

Looked at from the outside, the work [western doorway of tower of Trail] is of the best and most finished kind of Italian Romanesque; and we have here, what is by no means uncommon in Dalmatia, an example of the late *retention* of the forms of that admirable style.
E. A. Freeman, Venice, p. 182.

4. The act of retaining or keeping in mind; especially, that activity of the mind by which it retains ideas; the retentive faculty: often used as synonymous with *memory*.

No woman's heart
So big, to hold so much; they lack *retention*.
Shak., T. N., ii. 4. 99.

The next faculty of the mind, whereby it makes a further progress towards knowledge, is that which I call *retention*, or the keeping of those simple ideas which from sensation or reflection it hath received.
Locke, Human Understanding, ii. 10.

Any particular acquisitive task will become easier, and . . . more difficult feats of *retention* will become possible.
J. Sully, Outlines of Psychol., p. 287.

Hence—5†. That which retains impressions, as a tablet. [Rare.]

That poor *retention* could not so much hold,
Nor need I tallies thy dear love to score;
Therefore to give them from me was I bold,
To trust those tables that receive thee more.
Shak., Sonnets, cxxii.

6. In *med.*: (*a*) The power of retaining, as in the stomach or bladder; inability to void or discharge: as, the *retention* of food or medicine by the stomach; *retention* of urine. Hence—(*b*) A morbid accumulation of solid or liquid matter in vessels of the body or cavities intended to contain it only for a time.—7†. The state of being confined; custody; confinement.

Sir, I thought it fit
To send the old and miserable king
To some *retention* and appointed guard.
Shak., Lear, v. 3. 47.

8. In *Scots law*, a lien; the right of withholding a debt or retaining property until a debt due to the person claiming this right is duly paid.—**Retention cyst**, a cyst which originates in the retention of some secretion, through obstruction in the efferent passage.—**Retention of urine**, in *med.*, a condition in which there is inability to empty the bladder voluntarily. =**Syn.** 2. Reservation, preservation. See *keep.*

retentive (rẹ̄-ten'tiv), *a.* and *n.* [< OF. *retentif* = Pr. *retentiu* = Sp. Pg. It. *retentivo*, < L. *retentus*, pp. of *retinere*, retain: see *retain.*] I. *a.* 1†. Serving to hold or confine; restraining; confining.

Nor airless dungeon, nor strong links of iron,
Can be *retentive* to the strength of spirit.
Shak., J. C., i. 3. 95.

2. Retaining; having the power to keep or preserve: as, a body *retentive* of heat or of magnetism; the *retentive* force of the stomach.—3. Specifically, in *psychol.*, retaining presentations or ideas; capable of preserving mental presentations.

As long as I have a *retentive* faculty to remember any thing, his Memory shall be fresh with me.
Howell, Letters, ii. 30.

Each mind . . . becomes specially *retentive* in the direction in which its ruling interest lies and its attention is habitually turned. *J. Sully*, Outlines of Psychol., p. 294.

Retentive faculty, the faculty of mental retention; the memory.

II.† *n.* That which restrains or confines; a restraint.

Those secret checks . . . readily conspire with all outward *retentives*. *Bp. Hall*, Nabal and Abigail.

retentively (rẹ̄-ten'tiv-li), *adv.* In a retentive manner.

retentiveness (rẹ̄-ten'tiv-nes), *n.* The property of being retentive; specifically, in *psychol.*, the capacity for retaining mental presentations: distinguished from *memory*, which implies certain relations existing among the presentations thus recorded. See *memory*.

Even the lowered vital activity which we know as great fatigue is characterized by a diminished *retentiveness* of impressions. H. *Spencer*, Prin. of Psychol., § 100.

Retentiveness is both a biological and a psychological fact; memory is exclusively the latter.
J. Ward, Encyc. Brit., XX. 47.

Magnetic retentiveness. Same as *coercive force* (which see, under *coercive*).

retentivity (rē-ten-tiv'i-ti), *n.* [= F. *rétentivité*; as *retentive* + *-ity.*] Retentiveness; specifically, in *magnetism*, coercive force (which see, under *coercive*).

This power of resisting magnetisation or demagnetisation is sometimes called coercive force; a much better term, due to Lamont, is *retentivity*.
S. P. Thompson, Elect. and Mag., p. 80.

retenue†, *n.* An obsolete form of *retinue*.

Retepora (rẹ̄-tep'ọ̄-rạ̈), *n.* [NL. (Lamarck, 1801), < L. *rete*, net, + *porus*, a pore: see *pore*[2].] The typical genus of *Reteporidæ*. *R. cellulosa* is known as *Neptune's ruffles*.

retepore (rē'tẹ̄-pōr), *n.* and *a.* [< NL. *Retepora.*] I. *n.* A member of the *Reteporidæ*.

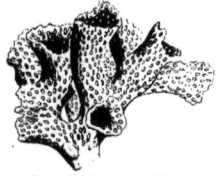

Retepore (*Retepora tubulata*), natural size.

II. *a.* Of or pertaining to the *Reteporidæ*.

Reteporidæ (rē-tẹ̄-por'i-dē), *n. pl.* [NL., < *Retepora* + *-idæ.*] A family of chilostomatous polyzoans, typified by the genus *Retepora*. The zoarium is calcareous, erect, fixed, foliaceous, and fenestrate (whence the name), unilaminar, reticulately or freely ramose in one plane; and the zoœcia are secund.

retetelarian (rē'tẹ̄-tẹ̄-lā'ri-ạn), *a.* and *n.* Same as *retitelarian*.

retex† (rẹ̄-teks'), *v. t.* [< L. *retexere*, unweave, unravel, break up, cancel, also weave again, < *re-*, back, again, + *texere*, weave: see *text.*] To unweave; unravel; hence, to undo; bring to naught; annul.

Neither King James, King Charles, nor any Parliament which gave due hearing to the frowardness of some complaints did ever appoint that any of his orders should be *retexed*. *Bp. Hacket*, Abp. Williams, i. 57. (*Davies.*)

retexture (rẹ̄-teks'tūr), *n.* [< *re-* + *texture*. Cf. *retex.*] The act of weaving again.

My Second Volume, . . . as treating practically of the Wear, Destruction, and *Retexture* of Spiritual Tissues or Garments, forms, properly speaking, the Transcendental or ultimate Portion of this my work on Clothes.
Carlyle, Sartor Resartus, iii. 2.

rethor†, *n.* A Middle English form of *rhetor*.

rethorice†, **rethoricke**†, *n.* Obsolete forms of *rhetoric*.

rethorien†, *a.* See *rhetorian*.

rethoriously†, *adv.* See *rhetoriously*.

retia, *n.* Plural of *rete*.

retial (rē'shi-ạl), *a.* [< *rete* + *-ial.*] Pertaining to a rete, or having its character.

Retiariæ (rē-shi-ā'ri-ē), *n. pl.* [NL., pl. of *retiaria*, fem. of *retiarius*, adj.: see *retiary*.] The spinning spiders; spiders which spin a web for the capture of their prey. See *Retitelæ*.

retiarius (rē-shi-ā'ri-us), *n.*; pl. *retiarii* (-ī). [L.: see *retiary*.] In *Rom. antiq.*, a gladiator who wore only a short tunic and carried a trident and a net. With these implements he endeavored to entangle and despatch his adversary, who was armed with helmet, shield, and sword.

retiary (rē'shi-ā-ri), *a.* and *n.* [= F. *rétiaire*, < L. *retiarius*, one who fights with a net, prop. adj., pertaining to a net, < *rete*, a net: see *rete*.] **I.** *a.* **1.** Net-like.

Retiary and hanging textures.
Sir T. Browne, Garden of Cyrus, ii.

2. Spinning a web, as a spider; of or pertaining to the *Retiariæ*.

We will not dispute the pictures of *retiary* spiders, and their position in the web. *Sir T. Browne*, Vulg. Err., v. 19.

3. Armed with a net; hence, skilful to entangle.

Scholastic *retiary* versatility of logic. *Coleridge*.

II. *n.*; pl. *retiaries* (-riz). **1.** Same as *retiarius*.—**2.** A retiary spider; a member of the *Retiariæ*.

reticence (ret'i-sens), *n.* [< OF. *reticence*, F. *réticence* = Sp. Pg. *reticencia* = It. *reticenza*, < L. *reticentia*, silence, < *reticen(t-)s*, silent, reticent: see *reticent*.] **1.** The fact or character of being reticent; a disposition to keep, or the keeping of, one's own counsel; the state of being silent; reservation of one's thoughts or opinions.

Many times, I wis, a smile, a *reticence* or keeping silence, may well express a speech, and make it more emphatical.
Holland, tr. of Plutarch, p. 841.

I found,
Instead of scornful pity or pure scorn,
Such fine reserve and noble *reticence*.
Tennyson, Geraint.

2. In *rhet.*, aposiopesis.=**Syn.** **1.** Reserve, taciturnity.

reticency (ret'i-sen-si), *n.* [As *reticence* (see *-cy*).] Reticence. *Imp. Dict.*

reticent (ret'i-sent), *a.* [< L. *reticen(t-)s*, ppr. of *reticere*, be silent, < *re-*, again, + *tacere*, be silent: see *tacit*.] Disposed to be silent; reserved; not apt to speak about or reveal any matters: as, he is very *reticent* about his affairs.

Upon this he is naturally *reticent*.
Lamb, To Coleridge. (*Latham*.)

Mr. Glegg, like all men of his stamp, was extremely *reticent* about his will. *George Eliot*, Mill on the Floss, i. 12.

reticle (ret'i-kl), *n.* [< F. *réticule*, a net: see *reticule*.] Same as *reticule*, 2.

The *reticle* [of the transit-telescope] is a network of fine spider lines placed in the focus of the objective.
Newcomb and Holden, Astron., p. 76.

reticula, *n.* Plural of *reticulum*.

reticular (rē-tik'ū-lär), *a.* [= F. *réticulaire* = Sp. Pg. *reticular* = It. *reticolare*, < NL. **reticularis*, < L. *reticulum*, a little net: see *reticule*.] **1.** Formed like a net or of network. Hence, by extension—**2.** Having many similar openings which are large in proportion to the solid parts. —**3.** Like a network; entangled; complicated.

The law [in England] is blind, crooked, and perverse, but sure and equal; its administration is on the practice of by-gone ages, slow, *reticular*, complicated.
The Century, XXVI. 822.

4. In *anat.*, forming or formed by reticulation; retial; full of interstices; cancellate; areolar; cellular: as, *reticular* substance, tissue, or membrane, which is the areolar or cellular or ordinary connective tissue. The rete mucosum of the skin is sometimes specifically called the *reticular body*. See *rete*.—**Reticular cartilage**, a cartilage in which the matrix is permeated with yellow elastic fibers. Also called *elastic fibrocartilage*, *yellow elastic cartilage*.—**Reticular formation**, the formatio reticularis, a formation occupying the anterior and lateral area of the oblongata dorsad of the pyramids and lower olives and extending up into the pons (and mesencephalon). The ninth, tenth, and eleventh nerves mark its lateral boundaries. It presents interlacing longitudinal and transverse fibers with interspersed ganglion-cells. These cells are more frequent in the lateral parts, or formatio reticularis grisea, which are marked off from the median parts, or formatio reticularis alba, by the hypoglossal nerve-roots.—**Reticular lamina.** See *lamina*.—**Reticular layer of skin**, the deeper-lying part of the corium, below the papillary layer.

reticulare (rē-tik-ū-lā'rē), *n.* [NL., neut. of **reticularis*: see *reticular*.] The reticular epidermal layer, more fully called *corpus reticulare*; the rete mucosum (which see, under *rete*).

Reticularia[1] (rē-tik-ū-lā'ri-ä), *n. pl.* [NL., neut. pl. of **reticularis*, reticular: see *reticule*.] Foraminiferous protozoans: a synonym of *Foraminifera*. Also *Reticulosa*. *W. B. Carpenter*, 1862.

Reticularia[2] (rē-tik-ū-lā'ri-ä), *n.* [NL. (Bulliard, 1791), < L. *reticulum*, a little net: see *reticule*.] A genus of myxomycetous fungi, giving name to the family *Reticulariaceæ*. The spores, capillitium, and columella are uniformly bright-colored, without lime.

Reticulariaceæ (rē-tik-ū-lā-ri-ā'sē-ē), *n. pl.* [NL. (Rostafinski, 1875), < *Reticularia*[2] + *-aceæ*.] A small family of myxomycetous fungi, taking its name from the genus *Reticularia*.

reticularian (rē-tik-ū-lā'ri-an), *a.* and *n.* [< *Reticularia*[1] + *-an*.] **I.** *a.* Having a reticulated or foraminated test; pertaining to the *Reticularia*, or having their characters.

II. *n.* A member of the *Reticularia*; a foraminifer.

reticularly (rē-tik'ū-lär-li), *adv.* So as to be reticulate; in a reticular manner.

The outer surface of the chorion is *reticularly* ridged.
Owen, Anat.

reticulary (rē-tik'ū-lā-ri), *a.* [< NL. *reticularis*: see *reticular*.] Same as *reticular*.

The Rhine, of a vile, reddish-drab color, and all cut into a *reticulary* work of branches, . . . was far from beautiful about Rotterdam. *Carlyle*, in Froude (Life in London, xx.).

reticulate (rē-tik'ū-lāt), *a.* [= F. *réticulé* = Pg. *reticulado* = It. *reticolato*, < L. *reticulatus*, made like a net, < *reticulum*, a little net: see *reticule*.] Netted; resembling network; having distinct lines or veins crossing as in network; covered with netted lines. Specifically—(*a*) In *zoöl.*, having distinct lines or veins crossing like network. (*b*) In *mineral.*, applied to minerals occurring in parallel fibers crossed by other fibers which are also parallel, so as to exhibit meshes like those of a net. (*c*) In *bot.*: (1) Resembling network; netted or mesh-like; retiform: said especially of a venation. (2) Netted-veined; retinerved: said of leaves or other organs. See *netted-veined*, and cuts 1 to 6 under *nervation*.—**Reticulate tarsus**, in *ornith.*, a tarsometatarsus covered with reticulations produced by numerous small plates separated by lines of impression. The reticulate tarsus is specially distinguished from the *scutellate tarsus*, and also from the *laminate* or *booted tarsus*. See *reticulation*, 2, and cuts under *booted* and *scutellate*.

reticulate (rē-tik'ū-lāt), *v.*; pret. and pp. *reticulated*, ppr. *reticulating*. [< *reticulate*, *a.*] **I.** *trans.* To form into network; cover with intersecting lines resembling network. [Rare.]

Spurs or ramifications of high mountains, making down from the Alps, and, as it were, *reticulating* these provinces, give to the vallies the protection of a particular inclosure to each. *Jefferson*, To La Fayette (Correspondence, II. 105).

II. *intrans.* In *zoöl.*, to cross irregularly so as to form meshes like those of a net: as, lines which *reticulate* on a surface.

reticulated (rē-tik'ū-lā-ted), *p. a.* [< *reticulate* + *-ed*[2].] Same as *reticulate*, *a.*—**Reticulated glass.** See *glass*.—**Reticulated head-dress.** Same as *crespine*.—**Reticulated line**, a line formed of a succession of loops or links, like a chain; a catenulated line. [Rare.]—**Reticulated masonry.** Same as *reticulated work*.—**Reticulated micrometer**, a reticule or network in equal squares, intended to be placed in the focus of a telescope and be viewed generally by a low power. Such an instrument is useful in some zone-work.—**Reticulated molding**, in *arch.*, a molding ornamented with

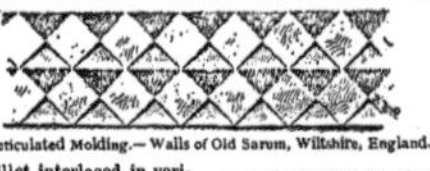

Reticulated Molding.—Walls of Old Sarum, Wiltshire, England.

a fillet interlaced in various ways like network, or otherwise formed so as to present a meshed appearance. It is found chiefly in buildings in the Byzantine and Romanesque styles. —**Reticulated work**, a variety of masonry wherein the stones are square and laid lozengewise, so that the joints resemble the meshes of a net. This form of masonry was very common among the

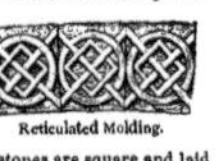

Reticulated Molding.

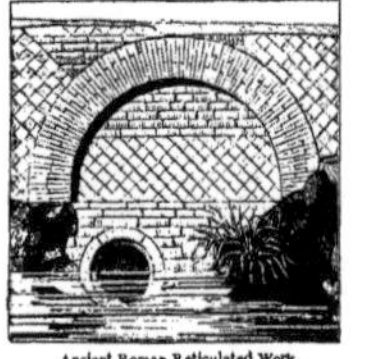

Ancient Roman Reticulated Work.

Romans, in Auvergne in France in the middle ages, and elsewhere. Also known as *opus reticulatum*. See also cut under *opus*.

reticulately (rē-tik'ū-lāt-li), *adv.* So as to form a network or reticulation.

Generally the sporangium contains, besides the spores, a structure called the Capillitium, consisting sometimes of small thin-walled tubes anastomosing *reticulately*.
Sachs, Botany (trans.), p. 275.

reticulate-veined (rē-tik'ū-lāt-vānd), *a.* Netted-veined.

reticulation (rē-tik-ū-lā'shon), *n.* [= F. *réticulation* = It. *reticulazione*; < *reticulate* + *-ion*.] **1.** The character of being reticulated or net-like; that which is reticulated; a network, or an arrangement of veins, etc., resembling one.

It is curious to observe the minute *reticulations* of tyranny which he had begun already to spin about a whole people, while cold, venomous, and patient he watched his victims from the centre of his web.
Motley, Dutch Republic, I. 279.

The Rhizomata [of *Calamites undulatus*] . . : are beautifully covered with a cellular *reticulation* on the thin bark, and show occasional round areoles marking the points of exit of the rootlets.
Dawson, Geol. Hist. Plants, p. 168.

2. In *ornith.*, one of the plates or small scales the assemblage of which makes the tarsus of a bird reticulate; also, the whole set of such plates, and the state of being reticulate: distinguished from *scutellation* and *lamination*. The individual reticulations may be quite regularly six-sided, like the cells of honeycomb, or of various other figures. Reticulation of the sides and back of the tarsus often concurs with scutellation on the front. The impressed lines may be mere creases in uniformly soft integument, somewhat like those of the human palm, or they may separate hard, roughened, or granulated reticulations. It is most characteristic of the feet of wading and swimming birds to show reticulation, and of those of land-birds to be scutellate or laminate, or both.

3. A method of copying a painting or drawing by the help of threads stretched across a frame so as to form squares, an equal number of proportional squares being made on the canvas or paper on which the copy is to be made.

reticule (ret'i-kūl), *n.* [< F. *réticule*, a net for the hair, a reticule, < L. *reticulum*, neut., also *reticulus*, m., a little net, reticule, double dim. of *rete*, a net: see *rete*. Doublet of *reticle*.] **1.** A bag, originally of network, but later of any formation or material, carried by women in the hand or upon the arm, and answering the purpose of a pocket.

There were five loads of straw, but then of those a lady could take no more than her *reticule* could carry.
De Quincey, Spanish Nun.

Dear Muse, 'tis twenty years or more
Since that enchanted, fairy time
When you came tapping at my door,
Your *reticule* stuffed full of rhyme.
T. B. Aldrich, At Twoscore.

2. An attachment to a telescope, consisting of a network of lines ruled on glass or of fine fibers crossing each other. These may form squares as in the reticulated micrometer, or they may be arranged meridionally, except two at right angles or perhaps one nearly at right angles, or otherwise. Also *reticle*.
3. Same as *reticulum*, 1.

Reticulosa (rē-tik-ū-lō'sä), *n. pl.* [NL., neut. pl. of **reticulosus*, < L. *reticulum*, a little net: see *reticule*.] Same as *Reticularia*[1].

reticulose (rē-tik'ū-lōs), *a.* In *entom.*, minutely or finely reticulate.

reticulum (rē-tik'ū-lum), *n.*; pl. *reticula* (-lä). [NL., < L. *reticulum*, a little net: see *reticule* and *reticle*.] **1.** A network. Also *reticule*.—**2.** Neuroglia. *Kölliker*.—**3.** The network which pervades the substance of the cell and nucleus inclosing the softer portions of the protoplasm. —**4.** The second stomach of a ruminant; that part of a quadripartite stomach which is between the rumen or paunch and the omasum, psalterium, or manyplies; the hood or honeycomb-bag: so called from the reticulation of the ridges into which the mucous membrane is thrown up. It makes the best part of tripe. See cuts under *ruminant* and *Tragulidæ*.—**5.** In *bot.*, any reticulated structure; sometimes, specifically, the fibrous web at the base of the petiole in some palms.—**6.** [*cap.*] A southern constellation, introduced by La Caille. Also *Reticulus Rhomboidalis*.

retiercé (rē-tyār-sā'), *a.* [Heraldic F., < OF. *retiers*, a third part of a third, < *re-*, again, + *tiers*, third: see *tierce*.] In *her.*, divided fessewise into three equal parts, each of which is subdivided fessewise and bears three tinctures, which are the same in their order in each of the three parts; barry of nine, of three successive tinctures thrice repeated, as gules, or, sable, gules, or, sable, gules, or, sable.

Retifera (rẹ̄-tif′e-rạ̈), *n. pl.* [NL., neut. pl. of *retiferus*: see *retiferous*.] A family of De Blainville's cervicobranchiate *Paracephalophora hermaphrodita*, based on the genus *Patella*; the true limpets. See *Patellidæ*.

retiferous (rẹ̄-tif′e-rus), *a.* [< NL. *retiferus*, < L. *rete*, a net, + *ferre* = E. *bear*[1].] Having a rete or retia; reticulate.

retiform (rē′ti-fôrm), *a.* [< OF. *retiforme*, F. *rétiforme* = Pg. It. *retiforme*, < NL. *retiformis*, < L. *rete*, a net, + *forma*, shape.] 1. In *anat.* and *zoöl.*, retial; like a network or rete in form or appearance; reticular: as, the *retiform* coat of the eyeball.—2. In *bot.*, net-like; reticulate.—**Retiform connective tissue.** See *adenoid tissue*, under *adenoid*.

retina (ret′i-nạ̈), *n.* [= OF. *retine*, *rectine*, F. *rétine* = Sp. Pg. It. *retina*, < NL. *retina*, retina: so called because resembling fine network, < L. *rete*, a net: see *rete*.] The innermost and chiefly nervous coat of the posterior part of the eyeball, between the choroid coat and the vitreous humor. It extends from the entrance into the eyeball of the optic nerve toward the crystalline lens, terminating in the ora serrata. A modified division of the retinal structure is, however, continued forward as the pars ciliaris retinæ. The retina consists of a delicate and complex expansion and modification of the optic nerve, supported by a network of connective tissue. It may be divided into ten layers: (1) internally, next the hyaloid membrane of the vitreous humor, the internal limiting membrane, formed of the expanded bases of the fibers of Müller; (2) the fibers of the optic nerve; (3) layer of ganglion-cells; (4) internal molecular or granular layer; (5) inner nuclear layer; (6) external molecular or granular layer; (7) external nuclear layer; (8) external limiting membrane, which is connected with the ends of Müller's fibers; (9) layer of rods and cones, or bacillary layer; (10) pigmentary layer. In the center of the back part of the retina, near the line of the optic axis, is the macula lutea, the most sensitive part of the retina; and in the center of the macula is a depression, the fovea centralis, in which the rods are absent. The color of the macula is due to a yellow pigment. About one tenth of an inch internally to the fovea is the point of entrance of the optic nerve with its central artery; the retina is incomplete at this point, and constitutes the "blind spot." The nerve-fibers have been estimated to number 400,000 broad and as many narrow fibers, and for each fiber there are 7 cones, 100 rods, and 7 pigment-cells. The retina serves the purpose of vision in being the organ through or by means of which vibrations of luminiferous ether excite the optic nerve to its appropriate activity. See *eye*[1]. —**Central artery and vein of retina.** See *central*.—**Coarctate retina**, a funnel-shaped condition of the retina, due to the accumulation of fluid between the retina and the choroid.—**Epilepsy of the retina.** See *epilepsy*. —**Pigmentary layer of the retina.** See *pigmentary*.—**Rod-and-cone layer of the retina**, a layer composed of minute elongated cylindrical and flask-shaped elements arranged vertically to the pigmentary layer of the retina, and parallel to one another. Also called *columnar layer*, *bacillar layer*, *bacillary layer*, *stratum bacillosum*, *stratum cylindrorum*, *Jacob's membrane*, *Jacobian membrane*.

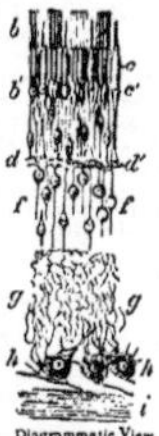

Diagrammatic View of a Section of the Nervous Elements of the Retina, the merely connective elements being not represented: magnified about 150 diameters: *b*, the rods; *c*, the cones; *b′*, *c′*, granules of the outer nuclear layer, with which these are connected; *d*, *d′*, interwoven very delicate nervous fibers of the outer molecular layer, from which fine nervous filaments bearing granules of the inner nuclear layer *f*, *f* proceed toward the front surface; *g*, *g*, continuation of these fine nerves in the inner molecular layer, which become convoluted and interwoven with the processes of the ganglionic corpuscles *h*, *h*; *i*, expansion of the fibers of the optic nerve.

retinaculum (ret-i-nak′ụ̄-lum), *n.*; pl. *retinacula* (-lạ̈). [= F. *rétinacle*, < L. *retinaculum*, a band, tether, halter, tie, < *retinere*, hold back: see *retain*.] 1. In *bot.*: (*a*) A viscid gland belonging to the stigma of orchids and asclepiads, and holding the pollen-masses fast. (*b*) The persistent and indurated hook-like funiculus of the seeds in most *Acanthaceæ*. *A. Gray*.—2. In *anat.*, a restraining band; a bridle or frenum: applied to such fibrous structures as those which bind down the tendons of muscles; also to the bridle of the ileocæcal valve.—3. In *entom.*, specifically, a small scale or plate which in some insects checks undue protrusion of the sting.—4. In *surg.*, an instrument formerly used in operations for hernia, etc.—**Retinacula of Morgagni**, or **retinacula of the ileocæcal valve**, the membranous ridge formed by the coalescence of the valvular segments at each end of the opening between the ileum and the colon. Also called *frena*.—**Retinaculum peroneorum**, a fibrous band which holds in place the tendons of the peroneal muscles as they pass through the grooves on the outer side of the calcaneum.—**Retinaculum tendineum**, a transverse band of fibrous tissue which in the region of joints passes over the tendons, and serves to hold them close to the bone, as the annular ligaments of the wrist and the ankle.

retinal (ret′i-nal), *a.* [< *retina* + *-al*.] Of or pertaining to the retina: as, *retinal* structure; *retinal* expansion; *retinal* images.

> Surely if form and length were originally *retinal* sensations, *retinal* rectangles ought not to become acute or obtuse, and lines ought not to alter their relative lengths as they do. — *W. James*, Mind, XII. 527.

Retinal apoplexy, hemorrhage into the tissues of the retina.—**Retinal horizon**, Helmholtz's term for the horizontal plane which passes through the transverse axis of the eyeball.—**Retinal image**, the image of external objects formed on the retina.—**Retinal ischemia**, partial or complete anemia of the retina, caused by contraction of one or more branches of the arteria centralis retinæ.—**Retinal purple.** Same as *rhodopsin*.

retinalite (rẹ̄-tin′a-līt), *n.* [Prop. **rhetinolite*, < Gr. ῥητίνη, resin (see *resin*), + λίθος, stone.] A green translucent variety of serpentine, from Canada, having a resinous aspect.

retinerved (rē′ti-nėrvd), *a.* [< L. *rete*, net, + *nervus*, nerve, + *-ed*[2].] In *bot.*, netted-veined; reticulate.

retinite (ret′i-nīt), *n.* [= F. *rétinite*, < Gr. ῥητίνη, resin (see *resin*), + *-ite*[2].] 1. Highgate resin.—2. One of the French names for pitchstone or obsidian, occasionally used in this sense by writers in English, especially in translating from the French. See cut under *fluidal*.

retinitis (ret-i-nī′tis), *n.* [NL., < *retina* + *-itis*.] Inflammation of the retina.—**Albuminuric retinitis**, retinitis caused by Bright's disease.—**Diabetic retinitis**, retinitis occurring in diabetes.—**Nephritic retinitis.** See *nephritic*.—**Retinitis pigmentosa**, a chronic interstitial connective-tissue proliferation of all the layers of the eye, with development of pigment due to a proliferation of the pigment-layer, and with final atrophy of the optic nerve.

retinochoroiditis (ret″i-nọ̄-kō-roi-dī′tis), *n.* [NL., < *retina* + *choroid* + *-itis*.] In *pathol.*, same as *chorioretinitis*.

retinogen (ret′i-nọ̄-jen), *n.* [< NL. *retina*, retina, + *-gen*, producing: see *-gen*.] The outer one of two layers into which the ectoderm of the embryonic eye of an arthropod may be differentiated: distinguished from *ganglogen*.

retinoid (ret′i-noid), *a.* [< Gr. ῥητίνη, resin, + εἶδος, form.] Resin-like or resiniform; resembling a resin.

retinophora (ret-i-nof′ọ̄-rạ̈), *n.*; pl. *retinophoræ* (-rē). [NL., < *retina*, retina, + Gr. -φόρος, < φέρειν = E. *bear*[1].] One of those cells of the embryonic eye of arthropods which secrete the chitinous crystalline cone on that surface which is toward the axis of the ommatidium. Also called *vitrella*.

retinoscopy (ret′i-nọ̄-skō-pi), *n.* [< NL. *retina* + Gr. σκοπια, < σκοπεῖν, view.] 1. Skiascopy.—2. Examination of the retina with an ophthalmoscope.

retinoskiascopy, *n.* Same as *skiascopy*.

Retinospora (ret-i-nos′pọ̄-rạ̈), *n.* [NL. (Siebold and Zuccarini, 1842), < Gr. ῥητίνη, resin, + σπορά, seed.] A former genus of coniferous trees, now united to *Chamæcyparis*, from which it has been distinguished by the conspicuous resin-ducts in the seed-coat. Several species are often cultivated in America under the name *retinospora*. They are also known as *Japanese cypress*—C. (*R.*) *obtusa* as the *Japanese tree-of-the-sun*, C. (*R.*) *pisifera* as *sawara*. They are in use for lawn-decoration, and for hedges, especially the golden retinospora, consisting of cultivated varieties (var. *aurea*) of both these species, with yellowish foliage.

retinue (ret′i-nū, formerly rẹ̄-tin′ū), *n.* [< ME. *retenue*, < OF. *retenue*, a retinue, F. *retenue*, reserve, modesty (= Pr. *retenguda*; ML. reflex *retenuta*), fem. of *retenu*, pp. of *retenir*, < L. *retinere*, retain: see *retain*.] 1. A body of retainers; a suite, as of a prince or other great personage; a train of persons; a cortège; a procession.

> Not only, sir, this your all-licensed tool,
> But other of your insolent *retinue*
> Do hourly carp and quarrel. — *Shak.*, Lear, i. 4. 221.

> To horse we got, and so
> Went forth in long *retinue* following up
> The river as it narrow'd to the hills. — *Tennyson*, Princess, iii.

2. An accompaniment; a concomitant. [Rare.]

> The long *retinue* of a prosperous reign,
> A series of successful years. — *Dryden*, Threnodia Augustalis, l. 507.

To have at one's retinue†, to have retained by one.

> He *hadde* eek wenches *at his retenue*. — *Chaucer*, Friar's Tale, l. 55.

retinula (rẹ̄-tin′ụ̄-lạ̈), *n.*; pl. *retinulæ* (-lē). [NL., dim. of *retina*, retina: see *retina*.] In *entom.*, a group of combined retinal cells, bearing a rhabdom. *Gegenbaur*, Comp. Anat. (trans.), p. 264.

retinular (rẹ̄-tin′ụ̄-lạ̈r), *a.* [< *retinula* + *-ar*[3].] Of or pertaining to a retinula.

retiped (rē′ti-ped), *a.* [< L. *rete*, a net, + *pes* (*ped-*) = E. *foot*.] Having reticulate tarsi, as a bird.

retiracy (rẹ̄-tīr′ạ̄-si), *n.* [Irreg. < *retire* + *-acy*, appar. after the analogy of *privacy*.] Retirement; seclusion. [Recent.]

> The two windows were draped with sheets, . . . the female mind cherishing a prejudice in favor of *retiracy* during the night-capped periods of existence. — *L. M. Alcott*, Hospital Sketches, p. 61.

> He, . . . in explanation of his motive for such remorseless *retiracy*, says: "I am engaged in a business in which my standing would be seriously compromised if it were known I had written a novel." — *The Critic*, March 1, 1884, p. 97.

retirade (ret-i-räd′), *n.* [< F. *retirade* (= Sp. Pg. (milit.) *retirada* = It. *ritirata*), < *retirer*, retire: see *retire*. Cf. *tirade*.] In *fort.*, a kind of retrenchment in the body of a bastion or other work, to which a garrison may retreat to prolong a defense. It usually consists of two faces, which make a reëntering angle.

retiral (rẹ̄-tīr′al), *n.* [< *retire* + *-al*.] The act of retiring or withdrawing; specifically, the act of taking up and paying a bill when due: as, the *retiral* of a bill. *Cotgrave.* (*Imp. Dict.*)

retire (rẹ̄-tīr′), *v.*; pret. and pp. *retired*, ppr. *retiring*. [< OF. *retirer*, F. *retirer* (= Pr. Sp. Pg. *retirar* = It. *ritirare*), retire, withdraw, < *re-*, back, + *tirer*, draw: see *tire*[2], and cf. *attire*.] I. *trans.* 1. To draw back; take or lead back; cause to move backward or retreat.

> He, our hope, might have *retired* his power,
> And driven into despair an enemy's hope. — *Shak.*, Rich. II., ii. 2. 46.

> The locks between her chamber and his will,
> Each one, by him enforced, *retires* his ward. — *Shak.*, Lucrece, l. 303.

2†. To take away; withdraw; remove.

> Where the sun is present all the year,
> And never doth *retire* his golden ray. — *Sir J. Davies*, Immortal. of Soul, Ded.

> I will *retire* my favorable presence from them. — *Leighton*, Works (ed. Carter), p. 306.

3†. To lead apart from others; bring into retirement; remove as from a company or a frequented place into seclusion: generally with a reflexive pronoun.

> Beseech you, give me leave to *retire myself*. — *Shak.*, Cor., i. 3. 30.

> Good Dioclesian,
> Weary of pomp and state, *retires himself*,
> With a small train, to a most private grange
> In Lombardy. — *Fletcher* (*and another* ?), Prophetess, v. (cho.).

4. To withdraw; separate; abstract.

> Let us suppose . . . the soul of Castor, while he is sleeping, *retired* from his body. — *Locke*, Human Understanding, II. i. § 12.

> So soon as you wake, *retire* your mind into pure silence from all thoughts and ideas of worldly things. — *Penn*, Advice to Children, ii.

5. Specifically, to remove from active service; place on the retired list, as of the army or navy.—6. To recover; redeem; regain by the payment of a sum of money; hence, specifically, to withdraw from circulation by taking up and paying: as, to *retire* the bonds of a railway company; to *retire* a bill.

> If he be furnished with supplies for the *retiring* of his old wardrobe from pawn. — *B. Jonson*, Cynthia's Revels, ii. 1.

> Many of these [State banks] were in being before the enactment of the national banking law, declined reorganization under its terms, and were obliged to *retire* their circulation. — *Harper's Mag.*, LXXX. 459.

II. *intrans.* 1. To draw back; go back; return.

> He'll say in Troy, when he *retires*,
> The Grecian dames are sunburnt, and not worth
> The splinter of a lance. — *Shak.*, T. and C., i. 3. 281.

> At his command the uprooted hills *retired*
> Each to his place. — *Milton*, P. L., vi. 781.

2. To draw back; fall back; retreat, as from battle or danger.

> The winter coming on, and sickness growing
> Upon our soldiers, we will *retire* to Calais. — *Shak.*, Hen. V., iii. 3. 56.

> Here Nature first begins
> Her farthest verge, and Chaos to *retire*
> As from her utmost works, a broken foe. — *Milton*, P. L., ii. 1038.

> At me you smiled, but unbeguiled
> I saw the snare, and I *retired*. — *Tennyson*, Lady Clara Vere de Vere.

3. To withdraw; go away or apart; depart; especially, to betake one's self, as from a company or a frequented place, into privacy; go into retirement or seclusion; in the army or navy, to go voluntarily on the retired list.

> If you be pleased, *retire* into my cell
> And there repose. — *Shak.*, Tempest, iv. 1. 161.

> The mind contracts herself, and shrinketh in,
> And to herself she gladly doth *retire*. — *Sir J. Davies*, Immortal. of Soul, Int.

> Q. Mary dying a little after, and he [Philip] *retiring*, there could be nothing done. — *Howell*, Letters, I. vi. 3.

> Banish'd therefore by his kindred, he *retires* into Greece. — *Milton*, Hist. Eng., i.

How oft we saw the sun *retire*,
And burn the threshold of the night.
Tennyson, The Voyage.

4. To withdraw from business or active life. —5. Specifically, to go to bed.

Satisfied that his wife had not been from home that evening, . . . he fell into raptures with her. . . . They then sat down to half an hour's cheerful conversation, after which they *retired* all in the most perfect good humour. *Fielding*, Amelia, x. 3.

Our landlady's daughter said, the other evening, that she was going to *retire*; whereupon . . . the schoolmistress [said] . . . in good plain English that it was her bed-time. *O. W. Holmes*, Autocrat, ix.

6. To slope back; recede; retreat.

The grounds which on the right aspire,
In dimness from the view *retire*.
T. Parnell, Night-Piece on Death.

=Syn. 1 and 2. To depart, recede. See *retreat*[1].

retire (rẹ̄-tīr'), *n.* [= It. *retiro*; from the verb: see *retire*, *v.*] 1. The act of retiring; withdrawal. Specifically—(*a*†) Return; removal to a former place or position.

She conjures him by high almighty Jove . . .
That to his borrow'd bed he make *retire*.
Shak., Lucrece, l. 573.

(*b*†) Retreat, especially in war.

From off our towers we might behold,
From first to last, the onset and *retire*
Of both your armies. *Shak.*, K. John, ii. 1. 326.

But chasing the enemie so farre for our recouerie as pouder and arrowes wanted, the Spaniardes perceiuing this returned and in our mens *retire* they slewe six of them. *Hakluyt's Voyages*, quoted in R. Eden's First [Books on America (ed. Arber), p. xx.

(*c*) Retirement; withdrawal into privacy or seclusion; hence, a state of retirement.

Eve . . . with audible lament
Discover'd soon the place of her *retire*.
Milton, P. L., xi. 267.

By some freakful chance he made *retire*
From his companions, and set forth to walk.
Keats, Lamia, i.

2†. A place of retirement or withdrawal.

This worlds gay showes, which we admire,
Be but vaine shadowes to this safe *retyre*
Of life, which here in lowlinesse ye lead.
Spenser, F. Q., VI. ix. 27.

And unto Calais (to his strong *retire*)
With speed betakes him.
Daniel, Civil Wars, vii. 18.

3†. Repair; resort.

All his behaviours did make their *retire*
To the court of his eye, peeping thorough desire.
Shak., L. L. L., ii. 1. 234.

retired (rẹ̄-tīrd'), *p. a.* [Pp. of *retire*, *v.*] 1. Secluded from society or from public notice; apart from public view.

Since the exile of Posthumus, most *retired*
Hath her life been. *Shak.*, Cymbeline, iii. 5. 36.

And add to these *retired* Leisure,
That in trim gardens takes his pleasure.
Milton, Il Penseroso, l. 49.

2. Withdrawn from public comprehension or knowledge; private; secret.

Language most shews a man: Speak, that I may see thee. It springs out of the most *retired* and inmost parts of us. *B. Jonson*, Discoveries, Oratio Imago Animi.

Those deepe and *retired* thoughts which, with every man Christianity instructed, ought to be most frequent. *Milton*, Reformation in Eng., i.

3. Withdrawn from business or active life; having given up business: as, a *retired* merchant.

Roanne seem'd to me one of the pleasantest and most agreeable places imaginable for a *retyred* person. *Evelyn*, Diary, Sept. 26, 1644.

The English lord is a *retired* shopkeeper, and has the prejudices and timidities of that profession. *Emerson*, W. I. Emancipation.

4. Given to seclusion; inclining to retirement; also, characteristic of a retired life.

There was one old lady of *retired* habits, but who had been much in Italy. *Bulwer*, My Novel, x. 2.

Retired flank, in *fort.*, a flank having an arc of a circle with its convexity turned toward the rear of the work.—**Retired list**, in the army and navy, a list on which the names of officers disabled for active service are placed. In the United States navy, all officers between the grades of vice-admiral and lieutenant-commander must be retired at the age of sixty-two, and any officer may be retired on application after forty years of service; in the United States army, any officer is retired on application after forty years of service, and any officer after forty-five years of service, or at the age of sixty-two, may be retired at the discretion of the President. Officers on the retired list can be ordered on duty only in case of war.

retiredly (rẹ̄-tīr'ed-li), *adv.* In a retired manner; in solitude or privacy. *Imp. Dict.*

retiredness (rẹ̄-tīr'ed-nes), *n.* The character or state of being retired; seclusion; privacy; reserve.

This king, with a toad-like *retiredness* of mind, had suffered, and well remembered what he had suffered, from the war in Thessalia. *Sir P. Sidney*, Arcadia, ii.

I am glad you make this right use of this sweetness,
This sweet *retiredness*.
Fletcher (*and another?*), Prophetess, v. 3.

retirement (rẹ̄-tīr'mẹnt), *n.* [< OF. (and F.) *retirement* = Sp. *retiramiento* = Pg. *retiramento* = It. *ritiramento*; as *retire* + *-ment*.] 1. The act of retiring or withdrawing from action, service, use, sight, public notice, or company; withdrawal: as, the *retirement* of an army from battle; the *retirement* of bonds; the *retirement* of invalid soldiers from service; *retirement* into the country.

I beseech your majesty, make up,
Lest your *retirement* do amaze your friends.
Shak., 1 Hen. IV., v. 4. 6.

With the *retirement* of General Scott came the executive duty of appointing in his stead a general-in-chief of the army. *Lincoln*, in Raymond, p. 178.

2. The state of being retired from society or public life; seclusion; a private manner of life.

His addiction was to courses vain, . . .
And never noted in him any study,
Any *retirement*, any sequestration
From open haunts and popularity.
Shak., Hen. V., i. 1. 58.

Men of such a disposition generally affect *retirement*, and absence from public affairs. *Bacon*, Moral Fables, iii., Expl.

Few that court *Retirement* are aware
Of half the toils they must encounter there.
Cowper, Retirement, l. 609.

3. The state of being abstracted or withdrawn.

Who can find it reasonable that the soul should, in its *retirement*, during sleep, have so many hours' thoughts, and yet never light on any of those ideas it borrowed not from sensation or reflection. *Locke*, Human Understanding, II. i. § 17.

4. A retired or sequestered place; a place to which one withdraws for privacy or freedom from public or social cares.

The King, sir, . . .
Is in his *retirement* marvellous distempered.
Shak., Hamlet, iii. 2. 312.

A prison is but a *retirement*, and opportunity of serious thoughts, to a person whose spirit is confined, and apt to sit still, and desires no enlargement beyond the cancels of the body. *Jer. Taylor*, Works (ed. 1835), I. 251.

5†. Recovery; retrieval.

There be a sort of moodie, hot-brain'd, and alwayes unedify'd consciences, apt to engage thir Leaders into great and dangerous affaires past *retirement*. *Milton*, Eikonoklastes, xxviii.

=Syn. 2. *Seclusion*, *Loneliness*, etc. See *solitude*.

retirer (rẹ̄-tīr'ėr), *n.* One who retires or withdraws.

retiring (rẹ̄-tīr'ing), *p. a.* [Ppr. of *retire*, *v.*] 1. Departing; retreating; going out of sight or notice.

There are few men so wise that they can look even at the back of a *retiring* sorrow with composure. *Lowell*, Fireside Travels, p. 85.

2. Fond of retirement; disposed to seclusion; shrinking from society or publicity; reserved.

Louis seemed naturally rather a grave, still, *retiring* man. *Charlotte Brontë*, Shirley, xxiii.

He [the rhinoceros] developed a nimbleness of limb and ferocity of temper that might hardly have been expected of so bulky and *retiring* an individual. *P. Robinson*, Under the Sun, p. 172.

3. Unobtrusive; modest; quiet; subdued: as, a person of *retiring* manners.

She seemed fluttered, too, by the circumstance of entering a strange house; for it appeared her habits were most *retiring* and secluded. *Charlotte Brontë*, Shirley, xii.

In general, colours which are most used for the expression of . . . shade have been called *retiring*. *Field's Chromatography*, p. 46.

4. Granted to or suitable for one who retires, as from public employment or service.

Binnie had his *retiring* pension, and, besides, had saved half his allowance ever since he had been in India. *Thackeray*, Newcomes, viii.

=Syn. 2 and 3. Coy, bashful, diffident, shy.

Retitelæ (ret-i-tē'lē), *n. pl.* [NL., < L. *rete*, a net, + *tela*, a web.] A tribe of sedentary spiders which spin webs whose threads cross irregularly in all directions. They are known as *line-weavers*. *Walckenaer*.

Retitelariæ (ret″i-tẹ̄-lā'ri-ē), *n. pl.* [NL., as *Retitelæ* + *-ariæ*.] Same as *Retitelæ*.

retitelarian (ret″i-tẹ̄-lā'ri-an), *a.* and *n.* I. *a.* Of or pertaining to the *Retitelariæ*.

II. *n.* A retitelarian spider; a retiary. Also *retetelarian*.

retoriant, *a.* and *n.* See *rhetorian*.

retorquet, *v. t.* [< OF. *retorquer*, < L. *retorquere*, turn back: see *retort*[1].] To turn back; cause to revert. [Rare.]

Shall we, in this detested guise,
With shame, with hunger, and with horror stay,
Griping our bowels with *retorqued* thoughts.
Marlowe, Tamburlaine the Great, v. 1. 237.

retorsion (rẹ̄-tôr'shọn), *n.* [= F. *rétorsion* = Sp. *retorsion* = Pg. *retorsão*, < ML. *retorsio(n-)*, *retortio(n-)*, a twisting or bending back, < L. *retorquere*, pp. *retortus*, twist back: see *retort*[1], *v.* Cf. *retortion*.] The act of retorting; retaliation; specifically, in *international law*, the adoption toward another nation or its subjects of a line of treatment in accordance with the course pursued by itself or them in the like circumstances. It implies peaceful retaliation. Also written *retortion*.

Reprisals differ from *retorsion* in this, that the essence of the former consists in seizing the property of another nation by way of security, until it shall have listened to the just reclamations of the offended party, while *retorsion* includes all kinds of measures which do an injury to another, similar and equivalent to that which we have experienced from him. *Woolsey*, Introd. to Inter. Law, § 114.

retort[1] (rẹ̄-tôrt'), *v.* [< ME. *retorten*, *retourten*, retort, return, < OF. *retort* (< L. *retortus*), *retordre*, F. *retordre*, also *rétorquer*, twist back, = Sp. Pg. *retorcer* = It. *ritorcere*, < L. *retorquere*, twist back, turn back, cast back (*argumentum retorquere*, retort an argument), < *re-*, back, + *torquere*, twist: see *tort*.] I. *trans.* 1†. To twist back; bend back by twisting or curving; turn back.

It would be tried, how . . . the voice will be carried in an horn, which is a line arched; or in a trumpet, which is a line *retorted*; or in some pipe that were sinuous. *Bacon*, Nat. Hist., § 132.

2†. To throw back; specifically, to reflect.

As when his virtues, shining upon others,
Heat them, and they *retort* that heat again
To the first giver. *Shak.*, T. and C., iii. 3. 101.

Dear sir, *retort* me naked to the world
Rather then lay those burdens on me, which
Will stifle me. *Brome*, Jovial Crew, i.

He pass'd
Long way through hostile scorn, . . .
And, with *retorted* scorn, his back he turn'd.
Milton, P. L., v. 906.

3†. To cast back; reject; refuse to accept or grant.

The duke 's unjust
Thus to *retort* your manifest appeal.
Shak., M. for M., v. 1. 303.

4. To return; turn back or repel, as an argument, accusation, manner of treatment, etc., upon the originator; retaliate: rarely applied to the return of kindness or civility.

We shall *retort* these kind favours with all alacrity of spirit. *B. Jonson*, Case is Altered, i. 2.

He . . . discovered the errors of the Roman church, *retorted* the arguments, stated the questions. *Jer. Taylor*, Works (ed. 1835), II. 76.

He was eminently calculated to exercise that moral pride which enables a poet to defy contemporary criticism, to *retort* contemporary scorn. *Whipple*, Ess. and Rev., I. 234.

5. To reply resentfully.

What if thy son
Prove disobedient, and, reproved, *retort*
Wherefore didst thou beget me? I sought it not.
Milton, P. L., x. 761.

II. *intrans.* 1†. To curve, twist, or coil back.

Her hairs as Gorgon's foul *retorting* snakes.
Greene, Ditty.

This line, thus curve and thus orbicular,
Render direct and perpendicular;
But so direct, that in no sort
It ever may in Rings *retort*.
Congreve, An Impossible Thing.

2. To retaliate; turn back an argument, accusation, or manner of treatment upon the originator; especially, to make a resentful reply; respond in a spirit of retaliation.

He took a joke without *retorting* by an impertinence. *O. W. Holmes*, Old Vol. of Life, p. 43.

Charles, who could not dissemble his indignation during this discourse, *retorted* with great acrimony when it was concluded. *Prescott*, Ferd. and Isa., ii. 1.

3†. To return.

ȝif they *retourte* agen by Jerusalem.
Lydgate, MS. Soc. Antiq. 134, f. 24. (*Halliwell.*)

retort[1] (rẹ̄-tôrt'), *n.* [< *retort*[1], *v.*] The act of retorting; the repelling of an argument, accusation, or incivility; hence, that which is retorted; a retaliatory act or remark; especially, a sharp or witty rejoinder; a repartee.

He sent me word, if I said his beard was not cut well, he was in the mind it was: this is called the *Retort* Courteous. *Shak.*, As you Like it, v. 4. 76.

The license of wit, the lash of criticism, and the *retort* of the libel suit, testified to the officiousness, as well as the usefulness, of the . . . "knights of the quill." *The Century*, XL. 314.

=Syn. See *repartee*.

retort[2] (rẹ̄-tôrt'), *n.* [< OF. *retorte* = Sp. Pg. *retorta*, < ML. **retorta*, a retort, lit. 'a thing bent or twisted,' being in form identical with OF. *reorte*, *riorte* = It. *ritorta*, a band, tie, < ML. *retorta*, a band, tie (of a vine); < L. *retorta*, fem. of *retortus*, pp. of *retorquere*, twist back: see *retort*[1].] In *chem.* and the *arts*, a vessel of glass, earthenware, metal, etc., employed for the purpose of distilling or effecting decomposition by the aid of heat. Glass retorts are commonly used for distilling liquids, and consist of a flask-shaped vessel, to which a long neck is attached. The liquid to be distilled is placed in the flask, and heat is applied. The products of distillation condense in the cold neck of the retort, and are collected in a suitable receiver. Retorts are sometimes provided with a stopper so placed above the bulb as to permit the introduction of liquids without soiling the neck. The name is also generally given to almost any apparatus in which solid substances, such as coal, wood, or bones, are submitted to destructive distillation, as retorts for producing coal-gas, which vary much both in dimensions and in shape.

Retort (*a*) and Receiver (*b*).

retort[2] (rẹ̄-tôrt'), *v. t.* [< *retort*[2], *n.*] In *metal.*, to separate by means of a retort, as gold from an amalgam. Gold is always obtained in the form of an amalgam in stamping quartz-rock, and frequently, also, in washing auriferous detritus with the sluice. The amalgam is placed in an iron retort, and then heated, when the mercury passes off in vapor and is condensed in a suitable receiver — the gold, always more or less alloyed with silver, remaining behind. See *gold*.

retorted (rẹ̄-tôr'ted), *p. a.* [Pp. of *retort*[1], *v.*] 1†. Twisted back; bent back; turned back.

He flies indeed, but threatens as he flies,
With heart indignant and *retorted* eyes.
Pope, Iliad, xvii. 120.

2. In *her.*, fretted or interlaced: said especially of serpents so arranged as to form a heraldic knot.

retorter (rẹ̄-tôr'tėr), *n.* One who retorts.

retort-holder (rẹ̄-tôrt'hōl"dėr), *n.* A device for holding flasks or retorts in applying heat to them, or for convenience at other times, or for holding a funnel, etc.

retort-house (rẹ̄-tôrt'hous), *n.* That part of a gas-works in which the retorts are situated.

retortion (rẹ̄-tôr'shọn), *n.* [< ML. *retortio*(*n*-), *retorsio*(*n*-), a twisting or bending back, < L. *retorquere*, pp. *retortus*, twist back: see *retort*[1], and cf. *retorsion*.] 1. The act of turning or bending back.

Our Sea, whose divers-brancht *retortions*
Divide the World in three vnequall Portions.
Sylvester, tr. of Du Bartas's Weeks, i. 3.

As for the seeming reasons which this opinion leads unto, they will appear, like the staff of Egypt, either to break under, or by an easy *retortion* to pierce and wound itself. *J. Spencer*, Prodigies, p. 253. (*Latham.*)

2. The act of giving back or retaliating anything, as an accusation or an indignity; a retort.

Complaints and *retortions* are the common refuge of causes that want better arguments.
Lively Gracies (1678), p. 24. (*Latham.*)

retortive (rẹ̄-tôr'tiv), *a.* [< *retort*[1] + *-ive.*] Retorting; turning backward; retrospective. [Rare.]

From all his guileful plots the veil they drew,
With eye *retortive* look'd creation thro.
J. Barlow, The Columbiad, v. 466.

retort-scaler (rẹ̄-tôrt'skā"lėr), *n.* An instrument for removing mechanically the incrustation from the interior of coal-gas retorts. The scale is sometimes removed by combustion.

retoss (rē-tos'), *v. t.* [< *re-* + *toss.*] To toss back or again.

Along the skies,
Tost and *retost*, the ball incessant flies.
Pope, Odyssey, vi. 112.

retouch (rē-tuch'), *v. t.* [< OF. (and F.) *retoucher* = Sp. Pg. *retocar* = It. *ritoccare*; as *re-* + *touch*.] To touch or touch up again; improve by new touches; revise; specifically, in the *fine arts*, to improve, as a painting, by new touches; go over a second time, as a work of art, in order to restore or strengthen a faded part, make additions, or remove blemishes, for its general improvement.

He sighs, departs, and leaves th' accomplish'd plan,
That he has touch'd, *retouch'd*, many a long day
Labor'd, and many a night pursu'd in dreams.
Cowper, Task, iii. 786.

That piece
By Pietro of Cortona — probably
His scholar Ciro Ferri may have *retouched*.
Browning, Ring and Book, I. 216.

These [frescos] are in very bad preservation — much faded and *retouched*. *The Century*, XXXVII. 543.

retouch (rē-tuch'), *n.* [< F. *retouche* = Sp. Pg. *retoque* = It. *ritocco*; from the verb: see *retouch*, *v.*] A repeated touch; an additional touch given in revision; specifically, in the *fine arts*, additional work done on that which might previously have been regarded as finished.

So many Touches and *Retouches*, when the Face is finished. *Steele*, Tender Husband, iv. 1.

To write con amore, . . . with perpetual touches and *retouches*, . . . and an unwearied pursuit of unattainable perfection, was, I think, no part of his character.
Johnson, Dryden.

retoucher (rē-tuch'ėr), *n.* One who retouches; specifically, in *photog.*, an operative employed to correct defects in both negatives and prints, whether such defects come from the process, or from spots, imperfections, etc., on the subject represented.

A first-class *retoucher* is a good artist.
The Engineer, LXVI. 280.

retouching (rē-tuch'ing), *n.* [Verbal n. of *retouch*, *v.*] 1. The act of adding touches, as to a work of art, after its approximate completion.

His almost invariable desire of *retouching* . . . at times amounted to repainting. *W. Sharp*, D. G. Rossetti, p. 154.

Afterthoughts, *retouchings*, finish, will be of profit only so far as they too really serve to bring out the original, initiative, germinating sense in them.
Fortnightly Rev., N. S., XLIII. 742.

Specifically—2. In *photog.*, the art and process of finishing and correcting negatives or positives, with the object of increasing the beauty of the picture or of obliterating defects of the sensitive film. The work is performed, according to the necessities of the case, by applying a pigment to the front or back of the negative, by shading with lead-pencils, by stippling with brushes, or by means of a mechanical sprayer, on the film, especially to stop out hard lines in the face, impurities on the skin, etc. In order to obtain dark lines or spots in the finished print, the film of the negative is sometimes carefully scraped away with a knife at the desired places. The retouching of the print or positive is done in water-colors or India ink.

retouching-desk (rē-tuch'ing-desk), *n.* Same as *retouching-frame*.

retouching-easel (rē-tuch'ing-ē"zl), *n.* In *photog.*, same as *retouching-frame*.

retouching-frame (rē-tuch'ing-frām), *n.* In *photog.*, a desk formed of fine ground glass set in a frame, adjustable in angle, used for retouching negatives. The negative is laid on the ground glass, a support being provided to hold it at a convenient height. A mirror under the desk reflects light upward through the ground glass and the negative, and the operator is often further aided by a hood over the desk to shade his eyes and prevent the interference of rays from above with the light reflected through the negative. Also called *retouching-easel* and *retouching-desk*. Compare *retouching-table*.

retouching-table (rē-tuch'ing-tā"bl), *n.* In *photog.*, a retouching-frame fixed on a stand with legs, so that it needs no independent support.

retouchment (rē-tuch'ment), *n.* [< *retouch* + *-ment.*] The act or process of retouching, or the state of being retouched.

The Death of Breuse sans Pitie — as it now appears, at any rate, after its *retouchment* — is the crudest in colour and most grotesque in treatment.
W. Sharp, D. G. Rossetti, p. 155.

retour (re-tör'), *n.* [< F. *retour*, OF. *retor*, *retur*, *retour*, a return: see *return*[1], *n.*] 1. A returning.—2. In *Scots law*, an extract from chancery of the service of an heir to his ancestor.

retoured (re-törd'), *a.* [< *retour* + *-ed*[2].] In *Scots law*, expressed or enumerated in a retour.—**Retoured duty**, the valuation, both new and old, of lands expressed in the retour to the chancery, when any one is returned or served heir.

retourn†, *v.* An obsolete form of *return*[1].

retrace (rẹ̄-trās'), *v. t.* [< OF. (and F.) *retracer* = Pr. *retrassar* = Sp. *retrasar* = Pg. *retraçor*; as *re-* + *trace*[1].] 1. To trace or track backward; go over again in the reverse direction: as, to *retrace* one's steps.

He *retraced*
His pathway homeward sadly and in haste.
Longfellow, Golden Legend, ii.

2. To trace back to an original source; trace out by investigation or consideration.

Then, if the line of Turnus you *retrace*,
He springs from Inachus of Argive race.
Dryden, Æneid, vii. 520.

The orthography of others eminent for their learning was as remarkable, and sometimes more eruditely whimsical, either in the attempt to *retrace* the etymology, or to modify exotic words to a native origin.
I. D'Israeli, Amen. of Lit., II. 22.

3. To trace again; renew the lines of: as, to *retrace* the defaced outline of a drawing.

This letter, traced in pencil-characters,
Guido as easily got *retraced* in ink
By his wife's pen, guided from end to end.
Browning, Ring and Book, I. 122.

4. To rehearse; repeat.

He regales his list'ning wife
With all th' adventures of his early life, . . .
Retracing thus his frolics.
Cowper, Tirocinium, l. 332.

retraceable (rẹ̄-trā'sa̤-bl), *a.* [< *retrace* + *-able.*] Capable of being retraced. *Imp. Dict.*

retract (rẹ̄-trakt'), *v.* [< OF. *retracter*, F. *rétracter* = Sp. Pg. *retractar* = It. *ritrattar*, < L. *retractare*, retract, freq. of *retrahere*, pp. *retractus*, draw back, < *re-*, back, + *trahere*, draw: see *tract*[1]. Cf. *retray*, *retrait*, *retreat*[1].] I. *trans.* 1. To draw back; draw in: sometimes opposed to *protract* or *protrude*: as, a cat *retracts* her claws.

The seas into themselves *retract* their flows.
Drayton, Of his Lady's not Coming to London.

From under the adductor a pair of delicate muscles runs to the basal edge of the labrum, so as to *retract* the whole mouth. *Darwin*, Cirripedia, p. 39.

The platform when *retracted* is adapted to pass over the floor proper, leaving, when extended, a surface over which things may be easily and safely moved.
Sci. Amer., N. S., LIX. 262.

2. To withdraw; remove.

Such admirable parts in all I spye,
From none of them I can *retract* myne eye.
Heywood, Dialogues (Works, ed. Pearson, 1874, VI. 240).

The excess of fertility, which contributed so much to their miscarriages, was *retracted* and cut off.
Woodward, Essay towards a Nat. Hist. of the Earth.

3. To take back; undo; recall; recant: as, to *retract* an assertion or an accusation.

Paris should ne'er *retract* what he hath done,
Nor faint in the pursuit. *Shak.*, T. and C., ii. 2. 141.

If thou pleasest to show me any error of mine, . . . I shall readily both acknowledge and *retract* it.
Life of Thomas Ellwood (ed. Howells), p. 300.

She began, therefore, to *retract* her false step as fast as she could. *Scott*, Heart of Mid-Lothian, xxvi.

4. To contract; lessen in length; shorten.=**Syn.** 3. *Recant*, *Revoke*, etc. (see *renounce*), disown, withdraw. See list under *abjure*.

II. *intrans.* 1. To draw or shrink back; draw in; recede.

The cut end of the bowel, muscular coat and mucous coat together, was seized with pressure forceps in the manner already described. It was thus held in position, was prevented from *retracting*, and all bleeding points were secured at once. *Lancet*, No. 3470, p. 454.

2. To undo or unsay what has been done or said before; recall or take back a declaration or a concession; recant.

She will, and she will not; she grants, denies,
Consents, *retracts*, advances, and then flies.
Granville, To Myra.

retract (rẹ̄-trakt'), *n.* [< LL. *retractus*, a drawing back, ML. retirement, retreat, < L. *retrahere*, pp. *retractus*, draw back: see *retract*, *v.* Cf. *retreat*[1], *retrait*.] 1†. A falling back; a retreat.

They erected forts and houses in the open plains, turning the Natives into the woods and places of fastnesse, whence they made eruptions and *retracts* at pleasure.
Howell, Vocall Forrest, p. 35.

2†. A retractation; recantation.

Saincte Augustyne . . . wrytte also at the lengthe a Booke of *retractes*, in whych he correcteth hys owne erroures. *R. Eden* (First Books on America, ed. Arber, p. 10).

3. In *farriery*, the prick of a horse's foot in nailing a shoe, requiring the nail to be withdrawn.

retractability (rẹ̄-trak-ta̤-bil'i̤-ti), *n.* [< *retractable* + *-ity* (see *-bility*).] The property of being retractable; capacity for being retracted. Also *retractibility*.

Tannin, which acts on the *retractability* of the mucous membrane, . . . might be useful in dilatation of the stomach. *Medical News*, LIII. 159.

retractable (rẹ̄-trak'ta̤-bl), *a.* [< *retract* + *-able.* Cf. *retractible.*] Capable of being retracted; retractile. Also *retractible*.

Its [a cuttlefish's] arms instead of suckers were furnished with a double row of very sharp talons, . . . *retractable* into a sheath of skin, from which they might be thrust at pleasure. *Cook*, First Voyage, i. 7.

retractate† (rẹ̄-trak'tāt), *v. t.* [< L. *retractare*, pp. *retractatus*, draw back: see *retract.*] To retract; recant.

St. Augustine was not ashamed to *retractate*, we might say revoke, many things that had passed him.
The Translatours of the Bible, To the Reader.

retractation (rē-trak-tā'shọn), *n.* [< OF. *retractation*, F. *rétractation* = Pr. *retractatio* = Sp. *retractacion* = Pg. *retractação* = It. *ritrattazione*, < L. *retractatio*(*n*-), a retouching, reconsideration, hesitation, refusal, < *retractare*, touch again, reconsider, draw back, retract: see *retract.*] The act of retracting or withdrawing; especially, the recall or withdrawal of an assertion, a claim, or a declared belief; a recantation.

The Dutch governour writes to our governour, . . . professing all good neighborhood to all the rest of the colonies, with some kind of *retractation* of his former claim to New Haven. *Winthrop*, Hist. New England, II. 384.

Praxeas, at one time, signed a *retractation* of his heresy, which *retractation* was in the hands of the Catholics.
Pusey, Eirenicon, p. 76.

There are perhaps no contracts or engagements, except those that relate to money or money's worth, of which one can venture to say that there ought to be no liberty whatever of *retractation*. *J. S. Mill*, On Liberty, v.

retracted (rẹ̄-trak'ted), *p. a.* **1.** In *her.*, couped by a line diagonal to their main direction: said of ordinaries or subordinaries: thus, three bars or pales are *retracted* when cut off bendwise or bendwise sinister.—**2.** In *entom.*, permanently received or contained in a hollow of another part.—**3.** In *bot.*, drawn back, as (sometimes) the radicle between the cotyledons; bent back. [Rare or obsolete.]—**Retracted abdomen**, an abdomen nearly hidden in the thorax or cephalothorax, as in the harvest-spiders.—**Retracted head**, a head, concealed in the thorax as far as the front, which cannot be protruded at will.—**Retracted mouth**, a mouth in which the trophi cannot be extended, as in most beetles: correlated with *retractile mouth*.=**Syn.** See *retractile*.

retractibility (rē-trak-ti-bil'i-ti), *n.* [< *retractible* + *-ity* (see *-bility*).] Same as *retractability*.

retractible (rẹ-trak'ti-bl), *a.* [< F. *rétractible*; as *retract* + *-ible*. Cf. *retractable*.] Same as *retractable*.

retractile (rẹ̄-trak'til), *a.* [= F. *rétractile*; as *retract* + *-ile*.] **1.** Retractable; capable of being retracted, drawn back, or drawn in after protraction or protrusion: correlated with *protractile* or *protrusile*, of which it is the opposite: as, the *retractile* claws of felines: the *retractile* head of a tortoise; the *retractile* horns or feelers of a snail: especially applied in entomology to parts, as legs or antennæ, which fold down or back into other parts which are hollowed to receive them.

Asterias, sea-star, covered with a coriaceous coat, furnished with five or more rays and numerous *retractile* tentacula. *Pennant*, British Zoöl. (ed. 1777), IV. 60.

The pieces in a telescope are *retractile* within each other. *Kirby and Spence*, Entomology, I. 151. (*Davies.*)

2. Retractive.

Cranmer himself published his Defence of the True and Catholic Doctrine of the Sacrament: a long treatise, with a characteristically *retractile* title. *R. W. Dixon*, Hist. Church of Eng., xvii.

Retractile cancer, mammary cancer with retraction of the nipple.=**Syn. 1.** *Retracted, Retractile*. A *retracted* part is permanently drawn in or back, and fixed in such position that it cannot be protracted or protruded. A *retractile* part is also protrusile or protrusile, and capable of retraction when it has been protracted.

retractility (rē-trak-til'i-ti), *n.* [= F. *rétractilité*, as *retractile* + *-ity*.] The quality of being retractile; susceptibility of retraction.

retraction (rẹ̄-trak'shọn), *n.* [< OF. *retraction*, F. *rétraction* = Sp. *retraccion* = Pg. *retracção* = It. *retrazione*, < L. *retractio(n-)*, a drawing back, diminishing, < *retrahere*, pp. *retractus*, draw back: see *retract*.] **1.** The act of retracting, or the state of being retracted or drawn back: as, the *retraction* of a cat's claws.—**2†.** A falling back; retreat.

They make bold with the Deity when they make him do and undo, go forward and backwards by such countermarches and *retractions* as we do not impute to the Almighty. *Woodward.*

3. The act of undoing or unsaying something previously done or said; the act of rescinding or recanting, as previous measures or opinions.

As soon as you shall do me the favour to make public a better notion of certainty than mine, I will by a public *retraction* call in mine.
Locke, Second Reply to Bp. of Worcester (Works, IV. 344).

=**Syn. 3.** See *renounce*.

retractive (rẹ̄-trak'tiv), *a.* and *n.* [= F. *rétractif* = It. *ritrattivo*; as *retract* + *-ive*.] **I.** *a.* Tending or serving to retract; retracting.

II. *n.* That which draws back or restrains.

The *retractives* of bashfulness and a natural modesty . . . might have hindered his progression.
Sir R. Naunton, Fragmenta Regalia, Lord Mountjoy.

We could make this use of it to be a strong *retractive* from any, even our dearest and gainfullest, sins.
Bp. Hall, Remains, p. 139.

retractively (rẹ̄-trak'tiv-li), *adv.* In a retractive manner; by retraction. *Imp. Dict.*

retractor (rẹ̄-trak'tọr), *n.*; pl. *retractors* or, as New Latin, *retractores* (rē-trak-tō'rēz). [= F. *rétracteur*, < NL. *retractor*, < L. *retrahere*, pp. *retractus*, draw back: see *retract*.] One who or that which retracts or draws back. Specifically—(*a*) In *anat.* and *zoöl.*, a muscle which draws an organ backward, or withdraws a protruded part, as that of the eye or ear of various animals, of the foot of a mollusk, etc.: the opposite of *protractor*. See *retrahens*. (*b*) In *surg.*: (1) A piece of cloth used in amputation for drawing back the divided muscles, etc., in order to keep them out of the way of the saw. (2) An instrument used to hold back some portion of tissue during an operation or examination. (*c*) In firearms, a device by which the metallic cartridge-cases employed in breech-loading guns are withdrawn after firing.—**Retractor bulbi**, or **retractor oculi**, the retractor muscle of the eyeball of various animals. See *choanoideus*.—**Retractores uteri**, small bundles of non-striped muscle passing from the uterus to the sacrum within the recto-uterine folds.

retrad (rē'trad), *adv.* [< L. *retro*, backward (see *retro-*), + *-ad*[3].] In *anat.*, backward; posteriorly; retrorsely; caudad: opposite of *prorsad*.

retrahens (rē'tra-henz), *n.*; pl. *retrahentes* (rē-tra-hen'tēz). [NL., sc. *musculus*, a muscle: see *retrahent*.] In *anat.*, a muscle which draws or tends to draw the human ear backward; one or two fleshy slips arising from the mastoid and inserted into the auricle: the opposite of *attrahens*: more fully called *retrahens aurem*, *retrahens auris*, or *retrahens auriculam*. See cut under *muscle*[1].—**Retrahentes costarum**, an extensive series of small oblique costovertebral muscles in lizards, etc., which draw the ribs backward.

retrahent (rē'tra-hent), *a.* [< L. *retrahen(t-)s*, ppr. of *retrahere*, draw back: see *retract*.] Drawing backward; retracting; having the function of a retrahens, as a muscle.

retrahentes, *n.* Plural of *retrahens*.

retraict†, *n.* See *retrait*[2].

retrair†, *n.* [ME., < OF. *retraire*, draw back: see *retray*.] Retreat; withdrawal.

At Montsarrant bide is my hole plesaunce,
Ther become hermite with-out any *retrayr*,
To Goddis honour and seruice repair.
Rom. of Partenay (E. E. T. S.), l. 5140.

retrait[1]†, *n.* An obsolete form of *retreat*[1].

retrait[1]†, *a.* [< OF. *retrait*, < L. *retractus*, pp. of *retrahere*, draw back: see *retract*, *retreat*[1].] Retired.

Some of their lodgings so obscure and *retrayte* as none but a priest or a devil could ever have sented it out.
Harsnett's Decl. of Popish Impostures, sig. I. 3. (*Nares.*)

retrait[2]† (rẹ̄-trāt'), *n.* [Also *retrate*; < Sp. Pg. *retrato* = It. *retratto*, a picture, effigy, < ML. **retractum*, a picture, portrait, neut. of L. *retractus*, pp. of *retrahere*, draw back (ML. draw, portray): see *retract*, *retray*. Cf. *retreat*[1] and *portrait*.] A drawing; picture; portrait; hence, countenance; aspect.

Shee is the mighty Queene of Faery
Whose faire *retraitt* I in my shield doe beare.
Spenser, F. Q., II. ix. 4.

More to let you know
How pleasing this *retrait* of peace doth seem,
Till I return from Palestine again,
Be you joint governors of this my realm.
Webster and Dekker (?), Weakest Goeth to the Wall, i. 1.

retral (rē'tral), *a.* [< L. *retro*, backward, + *-al*.] Back; hind or hinder; retrorse; posterior; caudal: the opposite of *prorsal*.

The furrows between the *retral* processes of the next segment. *W. B. Carpenter*, Micros., § 487.

retranché (rė-troṅ-shā'), *a.* [F., pp. of *retrancher*, cut off: see *retrench*.] In *her.*, divided bendwise twice or into three parts: said of the field. Compare *tranché*.

retransfer (rē-trȧns-fėr'), *v. t.* [< *re-* + *transfer*.] **1.** To transfer back to a former place or condition.—**2.** To transfer a second time.

retransfer (rē-trȧns'fėr), *n.* [< *retransfer*, *v.*] **1.** A transfer back to a previous place or condition.

It is by no means clear that at the next election there will not be a *retransfer* of such votes as did go over, and, in addition, such a number of Conservative abstentions as will give Mr. Gladstone a large majority.
Contemporary Rev., LIII. 147.

2. A second transfer.

If the *retransfer* has been perfectly done, the attachment of the print to the paper will be so strong that they cannot be separated (unless wet) without the face of the paper tearing. *Silver Sunbeam*, p. 342.

retransform (rē-trȧns-fôrm'), *v. t.* [< *re-* + *transform*.] **1.** To transform or change back to a previous state.

A certain quantity of heat may be changed into a definite quantity of work; this quantity of work can also be *retransformed* into heat, and, indeed, into exactly the same quantity of heat as that from which it originated.
Helmholtz, Pop. Sci. Lects. (tr. by Atkinson), p. 349.

2. To transform anew.

retransformation (rē-trȧns-fọr-mā'shọn), *n.* [< *retransform* + *-ation*.] The act of retransforming; transformation back again or anew.

retranslate (rē-trȧns-lāt'), *v. t.* [< *re-* + *translate*.] **1.** To translate back into the original form or language.

The "silver-tongued" Mansfield not only translated all of Cicero's orations into English, but also *retranslated* the English orations into Latin.
W. Mathews, Getting on in the World, p. 226.

2. To translate anew or again.

retranslation (rē-trȧns-lā'shọn), *n.* [< *retranslate* + *-ion*.] The act or process of retranslating; also, what is retranslated.

The final result of this sympathetic communication is the *retranslation* of the emotion felt by one into similar emotions in the others. *Pop. Sci. Mo.*, XXI. 824.

The critical student of Ecclesiasticus can only in occasional passages expect much help from the projected *retranslations*. *The Academy*, July 19, 1890, p. 51.

retransmission (rē-trȧns-mish'ọn), *n.* [< *re-* + *transmission*.] The act of retransmitting; a repeated or returned transmission.

The transmission and *retransmission* of electric power.
Elect. Rev. (Amer.), XV. v. 6.

retransmit (rē-trȧns-mit'), *v. t.* [< *re-* + *transmit*.] To transmit back or again.

Will . . . [a single] embossing point, upon being passed over the record thus made [by indentation], follow it with such fidelity as to *retransmit* to the disk the same variety of movement? *N. A. Rev.*, CXXVI. 528.

retrate[1]†, *n.* An obsolete form of *retreat*[1].

retrate[2]†, *n.* See *retrait*[2].

retraverse (rē-trav'ėrs), *v. t.* [< *re-* + *traverse*.] To traverse again.

But, not to *retraverse* once-trodden ground, shall we laugh or groan at the new proof of the Kantian doctrine of the ideality of time? *Athenæum*, No. 3203, p. 339.

Sir Henry Layard declines to *retraverse* the ground thus covered. *Quarterly Rev.*, CXLV. 88.

retraxit (rẹ-trak'sit), *n.* [< L. *retraxit*, 3d pers. sing. pret. ind. of *retrahere*, withdraw: see *retreat*[1], *retract*.] In *law*, the withdrawing or open renunciation of a suit in court, by which the plaintiff loses his action. *Blackstone.*

retray†, *v. i.* [ME. *retrayen*, < OF. *retraire*, < L. *retrahere*, draw back, withdraw: see *retract*, and cf. *retrait*[1], *retreat*[1]. For the form, cf. *extray*, *portray*.] To withdraw; retire.

Then euery man *retray* home.
English Gilds (E. E. T. S.), p. 422.

retreat[1] (rẹ̄-trēt'), *n.* [Early mod. E. also *retreit*, *retrait*, *retraict*, *retrate*; < ME. *retrete*, *retret* (= Sp. *retrete*, a closet, *retreta*, retreat or tattoo, = Pg. *retrete*, a closet, retreat), < OF. *retrete*, *retraite*, *retraicte*, f., retreat, a retreat, a place of refuge, F. *retraite*, retreat, a retreat, recess, etc. (OF. also *retrait*, *retraict*, m., a retreat, retired place, also, in law, redemption, withdrawal, F. *retrait*, in law, redemption, withdrawal, also shrinkage), = It. *ritratta*, a retreat, < ML. *retracta*, a retreat, recess (L. *retractus*, a drawing back, ML. retreat, recess, etc.), < L. *retractus*, pp. of *retrahere*, draw back, withdraw: see *retract* and *retray*.] **1.** The act of retiring or withdrawing; withdrawal; departure.

Into a chambre ther made he *retret*,
Hit unshit entring, the dore after drew.
Rom. of Partenay (E. E. T. S.), l. 3944.

Come, shepherd, let us make an honourable *retreat*.
Shak., As you Like it, iii. 2. 170.

Wisdom's triumph is well-timed *retreat*,
As hard a science to the fair as great!
Pope, Moral Essays, ii. 225.

2. Specifically, the retirement, either forced or strategical, of an army before an enemy; an orderly withdrawal from action or position: distinguished from a *flight*, which lacks system or plan.

They . . . now
To final battel drew, disdaining flight
Or faint *retreat*. *Milton*, P. L., vi. 799.

3. The withdrawing of a ship or fleet from action; also, the order or disposition of ships declining an engagement.—**4.** A signal given in the army or navy, by beat of drum or sound of trumpet, at sunset, or for retiring from exercise, parade, or action.

Here sound *retreat*, and cease our hot pursuit.
Shak., 1 Hen. VI., ii. 2. 3.

5. Retirement; privacy; a state of seclusion from society or public life.

I saw many pleasant and delectable Palaces and banqueting houses, which serve for houses of *retraite* for the Gentlemen of Venice, . . . wherein they solace themselves in sommer. *Coryat*, Crudities, I. 152.

The *retreat*, therefore, which I am speaking of is not that of monks and hermits, but of men living in the world, and going out of it for a time, in order to return into it; it is a temporary, not a total *retreat*.
Bp. Atterbury, Sermons, I. x.

'Tis pleasant, through the loopholes of *retreat*,
To peep at such a world; to see the stir
Of the great Babel, and not feel the crowd.
Cowper, Task, iv. 88.

6. Place of retirement or privacy; a refuge; an asylum; a place of security or peace.

Our firesides must be our sanctuaries, our refuges from misfortune, our choice *retreat* from all the world.
Goldsmith.

Here shall the shepherd make his seat,
To weave his crown of flow'rs;
Or find a shelt'ring safe *retreat*
From prone descending show'rs.
Burns, Humble Petition of Bruar Water.

Ah, for some *retreat*
Deep in yonder shining Orient.
Tennyson, Locksley Hall.

7. A period of retirement for religious self-examination, meditation, and special prayer. =**Syn.** 5. Seclusion, solitude, privacy.—6. Shelter, haunt, den.

retreat[1] (rē̤-trēt′), *v.* [< *retreat*[1], *n.*] **I.** *intrans.* 1. To retire; move backward; go back.

> The rapid currents drive
> Towards the *retreating* sea their furious tide.
> *Milton*, P. L., xi. 854.

2. Specifically, to retire from military action or from an enemy; give way; fall back, as from a dangerous position.

> Ask why from Britain Cæsar would *retreat*;
> Cæsar himself might whisper he was beat.
> *Pope*, Moral Essays, i. 129.

3. In *fencing*, to move backward in order to avoid the point of the adversary's sword: specifically expressing a quick movement of the left foot a few inches to the rear, followed by the right foot, the whole being so executed that the fencer keeps his equilibrium and is ready to lunge and parry at will.—4. To recede; withdraw from an asserted claim or pretension, or from a course of action previously undertaken.

As industrialism has progressed, the State has *retreated* from the greater part of those regulative actions it once undertook. *H. Spencer*, Prin. of Sociol., § 580.

5. To withdraw to a retreat; go into retirement; retire for shelter, rest, or quiet.

> Others, more mild,
> *Retreated* in a silent valley, sing,
> With notes angelical, to many a harp.
> *Milton*, P. L., ii. 547.

> But see, the shepherds shun the noonday heat,
> The lowing herds to murmuring brooks *retreat*.
> *Pope*, Summer, l. 86.

> When weary they *retreat*
> T' enjoy cool nature in a country seat.
> *Cowper*, Hope, l. 244.

6. To slope backward; have a receding outline or direction: as, a *retreating* forehead or chin. =**Syn.** To give way, fall back. All verbs of motion compounded with *re-* tend to express the idea of failure or defeat; but *retreat* is the only one that necessarily or emphatically expresses it.

II.† *trans.* To retract; retrace.

> His dreadfull voyce . . .
> Compelled Iordan to *retreat* his course.
> *Sylvester*, tr. of Du Bartas's Weeks, i. 3.

retreat[2]† (rē̤-trēt′), *v. t.* [ME. *retreten*, < OF. *retreter*, < L. *retractare*, *retrectare*, handle anew, reconsider: see *retract*.] To reconsider; examine anew.

He . . . *retretith* deepliche thinges iseyn byforn. *Chaucer*, Boëthius, v. meter 3.

retreater (rē̤-trē′tėr), *n.* One who retreats or falls back.

He stopt and drew the *retreaters* up into a body, and made a stand for an hower with them. *Prince Rupert's beating up the Rebels' Quarters at Post-combe [and Chenner*, p. 8. (*Davies*.)

retreatful† (rē̤-trēt′fůl), *a.* [< *retreat*[1] + *-ful*.] Furnishing or serving as a retreat. *Chapman*.

retreatment (rē̤-trēt′ment), *n.* [< *retreat*[1] + *-ment*.] Retreat. [Rare.]

> Our Prophet's great *retreatment* we
> From Mecca to Medina see.
> *D'Urfey*, Plague of Impertinence. (*Davies*.)

retree (rē̤-trē′), *n.* [Prob. < F. *retrait*, shrinkage: see *retreat*[1].] In *paper-making*, broken, wrinkled, or imperfect paper: often marked XX on the bundle or in the invoice.

The Fourdrinier machine may be relied on to give an evenly made sheet, with a freedom from hairs and irregularities of all kinds; also a small proportion of *retree*, quite unapproachable by hand making. *Art Age*, III. 100.

retrench (rē̤-trench′), *v.* [< OF. *retrencher*, *retrencer*, *retrancher*, F. *retrancher* (= Pr. *retrenchar* = It. *ritroncare*), cut off, diminish, < *re-*, back, + *trancher*, cut: see *trench*.] **I.** *trans.* 1. To cut off; pare away; prune.

> The pruner's hand, with letting blood, must quench
> Thy heat and thy exuberant parts *retrench*.
> *Sir J. Denham*, Old Age, iii.

2†. To deprive by cutting off; mutilate.

> Some hundreds on the place
> Were slain outright, and many a face
> *Retrenched* of nose, and eyes, and beard.
> *S. Butler*, Hudibras, II. ii. 23.

3. To cut down; reduce in size, number, extent, or amount; curtail; diminish; lessen.

As though they [the Faction] had said we appear only in behalf of the Fundamental Liberties of the people, both Civil and Spiritual; we only seek to *retrench* the exorbitances of power. *Stillingfleet*, Sermons, I. vii.

I must desire that you will not think of enlarging your expences, . . . but rather *retrench* them. *Swift*, Letter, June 29, 1725.

He [Louis XIV.] gradually *retrenched* all the privileges which the schismatics enjoyed. *Macaulay*, Hist. Eng., vi.

4. To cut short; abridge.

He told us flatly that he was born in the Low Countreys at Delft. This *retrenched* all farther examination of him; for thereby he was ineligible. *Sir H. Wotton*, Reliquiæ, p. 571.

5. To limit; restrict.

These figures, ought they then to receive a *retrenched* interpretation? *Is. Taylor*.

6. *Milit.*: (*a*) To furnish with a retrenchment or retrenchments. (*b*) To intrench.

That Evening he [Gustavus] appear'd in sight of the Place, and immediately *retrench'd* himself near the Chapel of St. Olans, with all the Care and Diligence of a Man that is afraid of being attacked. *J. Mitchel*, tr. of Vertot's Hist. Rev. in Sweden, p. 139.

II. *intrans.* 1. To make a reduction in quantity, amount, or extent; especially, to curtail expenses; economize.

> Can I *retrench*? Yes, mighty well,
> Shrink back to my paternal cell, . . .
> And there I'll die, nor worse nor better.
> *Pope*, Imit. of Horace, I. vii. 75.

2. To trench; encroach; make inroads.

He was forced to *retrench* deeply on his Japanese revenues. *Swift*, Account of the Court and Empire of Japan.

retrenchment (rē̤-trench′ment), *n.* [< OF. (and F.) *retranchement*; as *retrench* + *-ment*.] 1. The act of retrenching, lopping off, or pruning; the act of removing what is superfluous: as, *retrenchment* of words in a writing.—2. The act of curtailing, reducing, or lessening; diminution; particularly, the reduction of outlay or expenses; economy.

The *retrenchment* of my expenses will convince you that I mean to replace your fortune as far as I can. *H. Walpole*. (*Webster*.)

Retrenchment was exactly that form of amendment to which the Dandy was most averse. *Whyte Melville*, White Rose, II. xxvi.

There is also a fresh crop of difficulties caused for us by *retrenchment*. *Sir C. W. Dilke*, Probs. of Greater Britain, iv. 2.

3. *Milit.*: (*a*) An interior rampart or defensible line, comprising ditch and parapet, which cuts off a part of a fortress from the rest, and to which a garrison may retreat to prolong a defense, when the enemy has gained partial possession of the place. Also applied to a traverse or defense against flanking fire in a covered way or other part of a work liable to be enfiladed. A retrenchment is thrown across the gorge of a redan or bastion when there is danger that the salient angle will fall into the hands of the besiegers. (*b*) An intrenchment.

Numerous remains of Roman *retrenchments*, constructed to cover the country. *D'Anville* (trans.). (*Webster*.)

=**Syn.** 1 and 2. Reduction, curtailment, abridgment.

retrial (rē-trī′al), *n.* [< *re-* + *trial*.] A second trial; repetition of trial: as, the case was sent back for *retrial*.

Both [departments] hear appeals on points of law only, and do not reopen cases, but simply confirm or invalidate previous decisions, in the latter event sending them down for *retrial*. *Harper's Mag.*, LXXVI. 925.

retributary (rē̤-trib′ṳ̄-tā̤-ri), *a.* [< *retribute* + *-ary*.] Retributive.

The great wars of *retributary* conquest in the land of Naharina. *Jour. Anthrop. Inst.*, XIX. 193.

retribute† (rē̤-trib′ūt), *v.* [< L. *retribuere* (> It. *ritribuire*, *retribuire* = Sp. Pg. Pr. *retribuir* = F. *rétribuer*), give back, restore, repay, < *re-*, back, + *tribuere*, assign, give: see *tribute*. Cf. *attribute*, *contribute*.] **I.** *trans.* To restore; pay back; return; give in requital.

> I came to tender you the man you have made,
> And, like a thankful stream, to *retribute*
> All you, my ocean, have enrich'd me with.
> *Fletcher* (*and another*), Queen of Corinth, iii. 2.

In the state of nature, "one man comes by a power over another," but yet no absolute or arbitrary power to use a criminal according to the passionate heat or boundless extravagancy of his own will; but only to *retribute* to him, so far as calm reason and conscience dictate, what is proportionate to his transgression. *Locke*, Civil Government, ii. § 8.

II. *intrans.* To make compensation or requital, as for some past action, whether good or bad.

The gifts of mean persons are taken but as tributes of duty; it is dishonourable to take from equals, and not to *retribute*. *Bp. Hall*, Contemplations (ed. T. Tegg), III. 52.

retributer (rē̤-trib′ṳ̄-tėr), *n.* [< *retribute* + *-er*[1]. Cf. *retributor*.] Same as *retributor*. *Imp. Dict.*

retribution (ret-ri-bū′shon), *n.* [< OF. *retribution*, *retribucion*, F. *rétribution* = Pr. *retribucio* = Sp. *retribucion* = Pg. *retribuição* = It. *retribuzione*, < L. *retributio(n-)*, recompense, repayment, < *retribuere*, pp. *retributus*, restore, repay: see *retribute*.] 1. The act of retributing or paying back for past good or evil; hence, that which is given in return; requital according to merits or deserts, in present use generally restricted to the requital of evil, or punishment; retaliation.

> And lov'd to do good, more for goodness' sake
> Than any *retribution* man could make.
> *Webster*, Monuments of Honour.

The *retributions* of their obedience must be proportionable to their crimes. *Bp. Hall*, Contemplations (ed. T. Tegg), II. 396.

> If vice receiv'd her *retribution* due
> When we were visited, what hope for you?
> *Cowper*, Expostulation, l. 247.

2. In *theol.*, the distribution of rewards and punishments in a future life.

> All who have their reward on earth, the fruits
> Of painful superstition and blind zeal,
> Naught seeking but the praise of men, here find
> Fit *retribution*, empty as their deeds.
> *Milton*, P. L., iii. 454.

> Oh, happy *retribution*!
> Short toil, eternal rest;
> For mortals and for sinners
> A mansion with the blest!
> *J. M. Neale*, tr. of Bernard of Cluny.

Retribution theory, the theory that the condition of the soul after death depends upon a judicial award of rewards and punishments based upon the conduct pursued and the character developed in this life. It is distinguished from the theory that the future life is (*a*) simply a continuance of the present (continuance theory); (*b*) a life of gradual development by means of discipline (purgatory), or future redemptive influences (future probation).

On the whole, however, in the religions of the lower range of culture, unless where they may have been affected by contact with higher religions, the destiny of the soul after death seems comparatively seldom to turn on a judicial system of reward and punishment. Such difference as they make between the future conditions of different classes of souls seems often to belong to a remarkable intermediate doctrine, standing between the earlier continuance theory and the *retribution theory*. *E. B. Tylor*, Prim. Culture, II. 84.

=**Syn.** *Vengeance*, *Retaliation*, etc. (see *revenge*), repayment, payment.

retributive (rē̤-trib′ṳ̄-tiv), *a.* [< *retribute* + *-ive*.] Making or bringing retribution or requital; paying back; conferring reward or punishment according to desert; retaliative.

> I wait,
> Enduring thus, the *retributive* hour.
> *Shelley*, Prometheus Unbound, i. 1.

retributor (rē̤-trib′ṳ̄-tor), *n.* [= F. *rétributeur* = Pg. *retribuidor* = It. *retributore*, *retribuitore*, < LL. *retributor*, recompenser, requiter, < L. *retribuere*, recompense: see *retribute*.] One who dispenses retribution; one who requites according to merit or demerit.

God is a just judge, a *retributor* of every man his own. *Rev. T. Adams*, Works, I. 196.

They had learned that thankfulness was not to be measured of good men by the weight, but by the will of the *retributor*. *Bp. Hall*, Contemplations (ed. T. Tegg), II. 160.

retributory (rē̤-trib′ṳ̄-tō̤-ri), *a.* [< *retribute* + *-ory*.] Serving as a requital or retribution.

A price, not countervailable to what he seeks, but *retributory* to him of whom he seeks. *Bp. Hall*, Contemplations (ed. T. Tegg), III. 49.

God's design in constituting them was not that they should sin, and suffer either the natural or the *retributory* consequences of so doing. *Bibliotheca Sacra*, XLVI. 488.

retrieft, *n.* See *retrieve*.

retrievable (rē̤-trē′va̤-bl), *a.* [< *retrieve* + *-able*. Cf. It. *ritrovabile*.] Capable of being retrieved or recovered.

Still is sweet sleep *retrievable*; and still might the flesh weigh down the spirit, and recover itself of these blows. *Sterne*, Tristram Shandy, vii. 15.

I . . . wish somebody may accept it [the Laureateship] that will retrieve the credit of the thing, if it be *retrievable*. *Gray*, To Mr. Mason, Dec. 19, 1757.

retrievableness (rē̤-trē′va̤-bl-nes), *n.* The quality of being retrievable; susceptibility of being retrieved. *Bailey*, 1727.

retrievably (rē̤-trē′va̤-bli), *adv.* With a possibility of retrieval or recovery.

retrieval (rē̤-trē′val), *n.* [< *retrieve* + *-al*.] The act or process of retrieving; recovery; restoration.

Our continued coinage of standard silver dollars can accomplish nothing of itself for the *retrieval* of the metal's credit. *The American*, XII. 359.

retrieve (rē̤-trēv′), *v.*; pret. and pp. *retrieved*, ppr. *retrieving*. [Early mod. E. also *retrive*, *retreve*; < OF. *retreuver*, also *retrover*, *retrouver*, F. *retrouver* (= It. *ritrovare*), find again, recover, meet again, recognize, < *re-*, again, + *trouver*, find: see *trover*. Cf. *contrive*[1].] **I.** *trans.* 1. To find again; discover again; recover; regain.

Fire, Water, and Fame went to travel together (as you are going now); they consulted, that if they lost one another, how they might be *retrieved* and meet again. *Howell*, Letters, ii. 14.

I am sorry the original [of a letter] was not *retriev'd* from him. *Evelyn*, To Pepys.

To *retrieve* ourselves from this vain, uncertain, roving, distracted way of thinking and living, it is requisite to retire frequently, and to converse much with . . . ourselves. *Bp. Atterbury*, Sermons, I. x.

I'll . . . gloriously retrieve
My youth from its enforced calamity.
Browning, In a Balcony.

That which was lost might quickly be *retrieved*.
Crabbe, Works, VIII. 82.

2. Specifically, in *hunting*, to search for and fetch: as, a dog *retrieves* killed or wounded birds or other game to the sportsman.—3. To bring back to a state of well-being, prosperity, or success; restore; reëstablish: as, to *retrieve* one's credit.

Just Published. The Old and True Way of Manning the Fleet, Or how to *Retrieve* the Glory of the English Arms by Sea, as it is done by Land; and to have Seamen always in readiness, without Pressing.
Quoted in *Ashton's* Social Life in Reign of Queen Anne, [II. 209.

Not only had the poor orphan *retrieved* the fallen fortunes of his line. Not only had he repurchased the old lands, and rebuilt the old dwelling. He had preserved and extended an empire. *Macaulay*, Warren Hastings.

Melendez, who desired an opportunity to *retrieve* his honor, was constituted hereditary governor of a territory of almost unlimited extent. *Bancroft*, Hist. U. S., I. 57.

4. To make amends for; repair; better; ameliorate.

What ill news can come . . . which doth not relate to the badness of our circumstances? and those, I thank heaven, we have now a fair prospect of *retrieving*.
Fielding, Amelia, iv. 6.

II. *intrans.* To find, recover, or restore anything; specifically, in *sporting*, to seek and bring killed or wounded game: as, the dog *retrieves* well.

Virtue becomes a sort of *retrieving*, which the thus improved human animal practices by a perfected and inherited habit, regardless of self-gratification.
Mivart, Nature and Thought, p. 149.

retrieve† (rę̄-trēv'), *n.* [Also *retrief*; < *retrieve*, *v.*] A seeking again; a discovery; a recovery; specifically, in *hunting*, the recovery of game once sprung.

We'll have a flight at Mortgage, Statute, Bond,
And hard but we'll bring Wax to the *retrieve*.
B. Jonson, Staple of News, iii. 1.

Divers of these sermons did presume on the help of your noble wing, when they first ventured to fly abroad. In their *retrief*, or second flight, being now sprung up again in greater number, they humbly beg the same favour. *Rev. T. Adams*, Works, I. xiii.

retrievement (rę̄-trēv'mȩnt), *n.* [< *retrieve* + *-ment*.] The act of retrieving, or the state of being retrieved, recovered, or restored; retrieval.

Whether the seeds of all sciences, knowledge, and reason were inherent in pre-existency, which are now excited and stirred up to act by the suggestion, ministry, and *retreivement* of the senses.
Evelyn, True Religion, I. 239.

retriever (rę̄-trē'vėr), *n.* 1. One who retrieves or recovers.

Machiavel, the sole *retriever* of this antient prudence, is to his solid reason a beardless boy that has newly read Livy. *J. Harrington*, Oceana (ed. 1771), p. 49.

2. Specifically, a dog trained to seek and bring to hand game which a sportsman has shot, or a dog that takes readily to this kind of work. Retrievers are generally cross-bred, a large kind much in use being the progeny of the Newfoundland dog and the setter; a smaller kind is a cross between the spaniel and the terrier. Almost any dog can be trained to retrieve; most setters and pointers are so trained, and the term is not the name of any particular breed.

Retrieving is certainly in some degree inherited by *retrievers*. *Encyc. Brit.*, XIII. 150.

retriment (ret'ri-mȩnt), *n.* [< L. *retrimentum*, refuse, dregs, sediment of pressed olives, < *re-*, again, + *terere* (pret. *tri-vi*, pp. *tritus*), rub: see trite. Cf. *detriment*.] Refuse; dregs. *Imp. Dict.*

retro- (rē'trō or ret'rō). [= F. *rétro-* = Sp. Pg. It. retro-, < L. *retro-*, *retro*, backward, back, behind, formerly, < *re-* or *red-*, back (see *re-*), + *-tro*, abl. of a compar. suffix (as in *ultro*, *citro*, *intro*, etc.), = E. *-ther* in *nether*, etc. Hence ult. *rear*³.] A prefix of Latin origin, meaning 'back' or 'backward,' 'behind': equivalent to *post-*, and the opposite of *ante-* (also of *pre-* or *pro-*) with reference to place or position, rarely to time; sometimes also equivalent to *re-* and opposed to *pre-* or *pro-*. It corresponds to *opistho-* in words from the Greek.

retroact (rē-trō-akt'), *v. i.* [< L. *retroactus*, pp. of *retroagere*, drive, turn back (> F. *rétroagir*), < *retro*, backward, + *agere*, do: see *act*.] To act backward; have a backward action or influence; hence, to act upon or affect what is past. *Imp. Dict.*

retroaction (rē-trō-ak'shon), *n.* [= F. *rétroaction* = Sp. *retroaccion* = Pg. *retroacção* = It. *retroazione*; as *retroact* + *-ion*.] Action which is opposed or contrary to the preceding action; retrospective reference.

retroactive (rē-trō-ak'tiv), *a.* [= F. *rétroactif* = Sp. Pg. *retroactivo* = It. *retroattivo*; as *retroact* + *-ive*.] Retroacting; having a reversed or retrospective action; operative with respect to past circumstances; holding good for preceding cases.

If Congress had voted an increase of salary for its successor, it was said, the act would have been seemly; but to vote an increase for itself, and to make it *retroactive*, was sheer shameless robbery.
Harper's Mag., LXXIX. 148.

Retroactive law or statute, a law or statute which operates, or if enforced would operate, to make criminal or punishable or otherwise affect acts done prior to the passing of the law; a retrospective law. Compare *ex post facto*.

retroactively (rē-trō-ak'tiv-li), *a.* In a retroactive manner; with reversed or retrospective action.

retrobulbar (rē-trō-bul'bạr), *a.* [< L. *retro*, behind, + *bulbus*, bulb, + *-ar*³.] Being behind the eyeball; retroöcular.—**Retrobulbar neuritis**, inflammation of the optic nerve behind the eyeball.—**Retrobulbar perineuritis**, inflammation of the sheath of the optic nerve behind the eyeball.

retrocede (rē-trō-sēd'), *v.*; pret. and pp. *retroceded*, ppr. *retroceding*. [< F. *rétrocéder* = Sp. Pg. *retroceder* = It. *retrocedere*, < L. *retrocedere*, pp. *retrocessus*, go back, < *retro*, back, + *cedere*, go: see *cede*.] I. *intrans.* To go back; recede; retire; give place. *Blount*, Glossographia.

II. *trans.* To cede or grant back; restore to the former possession or control: as, to *retrocede* territory. [Rare.]

Jackson . . . always believed . . . that Texas was not properly *retroceded* to Spain by the Florida treaty.
The Century, XXVIII. 503.

retrocedent (rē-trō-sē'dȩnt), *a.* [= F. *rétrocédant*, < L. *retroceden(t-)s*, ppr. of *retrocedere*, go back: see *retrocede*.] Relapsing; going back.

retrocession (rē-trō-sesh'on), *n.* [< F. *rétrocession* = Sp. *retrocesion* = Pg. *retrocessão* = It. *retrocessione*, < LL. *retrocessio(n-)*, < L. *retrocedere*, pp. *retrocessus*, go backward: see *retrocede*.] 1. A going back or inward; relapse.

These transient and involuntary excursions and *retrocessions* of invention, having some appearance of deviation from the common train of nature, are eagerly caught by the lovers of a wonder. *Johnson*, Milton.

2. In *med.*, the disappearance or metastasis of a tumor, an eruption, etc., from the surface of the body inward. *Dunglison*.—3. A sloping backward; a backward inclination or progression; a retreating outline, form, or position.

The eye resumed its climbing, going next to the Gentiles' Court, then to the Israelites' Court, then to the Women's Court, . . . each a pillared tier of white marble, one above the other in terraced *retrocession*.
L. Wallace, Ben-Hur, vi. 3.

4. The act of retroceding or giving back; in *Scots law*, the reconveyance of any right by an assignee back to the assignor, who thus recovers his former right by becoming the assignee of his own assignee.—5. In *geom.*, inflection.—**Retrocession of the equinoxes.** Same as *precession of the equinoxes* (which see, under *precession*).

retrocessional (rē-trō-sesh'on-al), *a.* and *n.* [< *retrocession* + *-al*.] I. *a.* Pertaining to or involving retrocession; recessional: as, *retrocessional* motion; a *retrocessional* hymn.

II. *n.* Same as *recessional*.

retrochoir (rē'trō-kwīr), *n.* [< *retro-* + *choir*, after ML. *retrochorus*, < L. retro, back, behind, + *chorus*, choir: see *choir*.] In *arch.*, that part of the interior of a church or cathedral which is behind or beyond the choir, or between the choir and the lady-chapel.

The statue of his successor, Nicholas IV. (1288–1292), who was buried in the Lateran, may be seen in the *retrochoir*. C. C. *Perkins*, Italian Sculpture, Int., p. liv.

retroclusion (rē-trō-klö'zhon), *n.* [< L. *retro*, back, behind, + *-clusio(n-)*, in comp., < *claudere*, pp. *clausus*, in comp. *-clusus*, close: see *close*¹.] A method of acupressure in which the pin is passed into the tissue, over the artery, then, turning in a semicircle, is brought out behind the artery, the point of the pin coming out near its entrance.

retrocollic (rē-trō-kol'ik), *a.* [< L. *retro*, back, behind, + *collum*, neck: see *collar*.] Pertaining to the back of the neck.—**Retrocollic spasm**, spasm of the muscles on the back of the neck, tonic or clonic.

retrocopulant (rē-trō-kop'ū-lant), *a.* [< L. *retro*, back, behind, + *copulan(t-)s*, ppr. of *copulare*, copulate: see *copulate*.] Copulating backward or from behind.

retrocopulate (rē-trō-kop'ū-lāt), *v. i.* [< L. *retro*, back, behind, + *copulatus*, pp. of *copulare*, copulate: see *copulate*.] To copulate from behind or aversely and without ascension, as various quadrupeds the male of which faces in the opposite direction from the female during the act.

retrocopulation (rē-trō-kop-ū-lā'shon), *n.* [< *retrocopulate* + *-ion*.] The act of copulating from behind or aversely.

Now, from the nature of this position, there ensueth a necessity of *retrocopulation*, which also promoteth the conceit [that hares are hermaphrodite]: for some observing them to couple without ascension, have not been able to judge of male or female, or to determine the proper sex in either. *Sir T. Browne*, Vulg. Err., iii. 17.

retrocurved (rē'trō-kėrvd), *a.* [< *retro-* + *curve* + *-ed*².] Same as *recurved*.

retrodate (rē'trō-dāt), *v. t.* [< *retro-* + *date*¹.] To date back, as a book; affix or assign a date earlier than that of actual occurrence, appearance, or publication. Questions of retrodating have arisen in regard to scientific publications when priority of discovery, etc., has been concerned.

retrodeviation (rē-trō-dē-vi-ā'shon), *n.* [< L. *retro*, backward, + ML. *deviatio(n-)*, deviation: see *deviation*.] A displacement backward, especially of the uterus, as a retroflection or a retroversion.

retroduct (rē-trō-dukt'), *v. t.* [< L. *retroductus*, pp. of *retroducere*, bring back: see *retroduction*.] To lead, bring, or draw back; retract; withdraw.

retroduction (rē-trō-duk'shon), *n.* [< L. *retroducere*, pp. *retroductus*, bring or draw back, < *retro*, back, + *ducere*, lead: see *duct*.] The act of retroducting, drawing back, or retracting.

retroflected (rē'trō-flek-ted), *a.* [< L. *retroflectere*, bend back (see *retroflex*), + *-ed*².] Same as *reflexed*.

retroflection, retroflexion (rē-trō-flek'shon), *n.* [= F. *rétroflexion*; as *retroflex* + *-ion*.] A bending backward: especially applied in gynecology to the bending of the body of the uterus backward, the vaginal portion being but little or not at all changed in position.

retroflex (rē'trō-fleks), *a.* [< L. *retroflexus*, pp. of *retroflectere*, bend back, < *retro*, back, + *flectere*, bend: see *flex*¹.] Same as *reflexed*.

retroflexed (rē'trō-flekst), *a.* [< *retroflex* + *-ed*².] Bent backward; exhibiting retroflection.

retrofract (rē'trō-frakt), *a.* [< L. *retro*, back, + *fractus*, pp. of *frangere*, break: see *fragile*, *fraction*.] In *bot.*, same as *refracted*.

retrofracted (rē'trō-frak-ted), *a.* [< *retrofract* + *-ed*².] In *bot.*, same as *refracted*.

retrogenerative (rē-trō-jen'e-rā-tiv), *a.* [< *retro-* + *generative*.] Same as *retrocopulant*.

Retrogradæ (rē-trog'rā-dē), *n. pl.* [NL. (Sundevall, 1823), < L. *retrogradi*, go backward: see *retrograde*, *v.*] A group of spiders: same as *Laterigradæ*.

retrogradation (ret'rō- or rē'trō-grā-dā'shon), *n.* [< OF. *retrogradation*, F. *rétrogradation* = Pr. *retrogradacio* = Sp. *retrogradacion* = Pg. *retrogradação* = It. *retrogradazione*, < LL. *retrogradatio(n-)*, a going back, < *retrogradare*, pp. *retrogradatus*, a later form of L. *retrogradi*, go backward: see *retrograde*.] 1. The act of retrograding or moving backward; specifically, in *astron.*, the act of moving from east to west relatively to the fixed stars, or contrary to the order of the signs and the usual direction of planetary motion: applied to the apparent motion of the planets. Also *retrogression*.

Planets . . . have their stations and *retrogradations*, as well as their direct motion.
Cudworth, Sermons, p. 58. (*Latham.*)

2. The act of going backward or losing ground; hence, a decline in strength or excellence; deterioration.

retrograde (ret'rō- or rē'trō-grād), *v.* [< OF. *retrograder*, recoil, F. *rétrograder* = Pr. Sp. Pg. *retrogradar* = It. *retrogradare*, < LL. *retrogradare*, later form of L. *retrogradi*, go backward, < *retro*, backward, + *gradi*, go: see *grade*¹.] I. *intrans.* 1. To go backward; move backward.

Sir William Fraser says that the duke engaged a horse from Ducrow's Amphitheatre, which was taught to *retrograde* with proper dignity. *N. and Q.*, 7th ser., VII. 254.

2. To fall back or away; lose ground; decline; deteriorate; degenerate.

After his death, our literature *retrograded*; and a century was necessary to bring it back to the point at which he left it. *Macaulay*, Dryden.

Every thing *retrograded* with him [Dunover] towards the Verge of the miry Slough of Despond, which yawns for insolvent debtors. *Scott*, Heart of Mid-Lothian, i.

3. In *astron.*, to move westward relatively to the fixed stars.—4. In *biol.*, to undergo retrogression, as a plant or an animal; be retro-

grade or retrogressive; develop a less from a more complex organization; degenerate.

Of all existing species of animals, if we include parasites, the greater number have *retrograded* from a structure to which their remote ancestors had once advanced.
H. *Spencer*, Prin. of Sociol., § 50.

II. *trans.* To cause to go backward; turn back.

The Firmament shall *retrograde* his course,
Swift Euphrates goe hide him in his source.
Sylvester, tr. of Du Bartas's Weeks, ii., Eden.

retrograde (ret'rọ- or rē'trọ-grād), *a.* [< ME. *retrograd*, < OF. *retrograde*, F. *rétrograde* = Sp. Pg. It. *retrogrado*, < L. *retrogradus*, going backward (used of a planet), < *retrogradi*, go backward, retrograde: see *retrograde*, *v.*] 1. Moving backward; having a backward motion or direction; retreating.

A little above we entered the City at the gate of S. Stephen, where on each side a Lion *retrograde* doth stand.
Sandys, Travailes, p. 149.

Now, Sir, when he had read this act of American revenue, and a little recovered from his astonishment, I suppose he made one step *retrograde* (it is but one), and looked at the act which stands just before in the statute-book.
Burke, Amer. Taxation.

2. Specifically, in *astron.*, moving backward and contrary to the order of the signs relatively to the fixed stars: opposed to *direct*. The epithet does not apply to the diurnal motion, since this is not relative to the fixed stars.

I would have sworn some *retrograde* planet was hanging over this unfortunate house of mine.
Sterne, Tristram Shandy, iii. 23.

3. In *biol.*, characterized by or exhibiting degeneration or deterioration, as an organism or any of its parts which passes or has passed from a higher or more complex to a lower or simpler structure or composition; noting such change of organization: as, *retrograde* metamorphosis or development; a *retrograde* theory.—4. In *zoöl.*, habitually walking or swimming backward, as many animals: correlated with *laterigrade*, *gravigrade*, *saltigrade*, etc.—5. In *bot.*: (*a*) Going backward in the order of specialization, from a more to a less highly developed form: referring either to reversions of type or to individual monsters. (*b*†) Formerly used of hairs, in the sense of *retrorse*.—6. Losing ground; deteriorating; declining in strength or excellence.

It is good for princes, if they use ambitious men, to handle it so as they be still progressive and not *retrograde*.
Bacon, Ambition.

7†. Contrary; opposed; opposite.

For your intent
In going back to school to Wittenberg,
It is most *retrograde* to our desire.
Shak., Hamlet, i. 2. 114.

From instrumental causes proud to draw
Conclusions *retrograde*, and mad mistake.
Cowper, Task, iii. 239.

Retrograde cancer, a cancer which has become firmer and smaller, and so remains.—**Retrograde development** or **metamorphosis**, in *biol.*: (*a*) Degradation of the form or structure of an organism; reduction of morphological character to one less specialized or more generalized, as in parasites. See *parasitism*. (*b*) Change of tissue or substance from the more complex to the simpler composition; catabolism. See *metamorphosis*.—**Retrograde imitation** or **inversion**, in *contrapuntal music*, imitation in which the subject or theme is repeated backward: usually marked *recte e retro*. Compare *cancrizans*.—**Reversed retrograde imitation.** See *reversed*.

retrogradingly (ret'rọ- or rē'trọ-grā-ding-li), *adv.* By retrograde movement. *Imp. Dict.*

retrogress (rē'trọ-gres), *n.* [< L. *retrogressus*, a retrogression (of the sun), < *retrogradi*, pp. *retrogressus*, go backward: see *retrograde*.] Retrogradation; falling off; decline. [Rare.]

Progress in bulk, complexity, or activity involves *retrogress* in fertility; and progress in fertility involves *retrogress* in bulk, complexity, or activity.
H. Spencer, Prin. of Biol., § 327.

retrogression (rē-trọ-gresh'ọn), *n.* [= F. *rétrogression*, as if < L. **retrogressio(n-)*, < *retrogradi*, pp. *retrogressus*, go backward: see *retrograde*.] 1. The act of going backward; retrogradation.

In the body politic . . . it is the stoppage of that progress, and the commencement of *retrogression*, that alone would constitute decay.
J. S. Mill, Logic, V. v. § 6.

2. In *astron.*, same as *retrogradation*.—3. In *biol.*, backward development; degeneration; retrograde metamorphosis. When a plant, as it approaches maturity, becomes less perfectly organized than might be expected from its early stages and known relationships, it is said to undergo *retrogression*.

retrogressional (rē-trọ-gresh'ọn-ạl), *a.* [< *retrogression* + *-al*.] Pertaining to or characterized by retrogression; retrogressive.

Some of these [manipulations in glass-making], from a technical point of view, seem *retrogressional*.
Pop. Sci. Mo., XXXV. 23.

retrogressive (rē-trọ-gres'iv), *a.* [< *retrogress* + *-ive*.] Going backward; retrograde; declining in strength or excellence; degenerating.

We must have discovery, and that by licensing the fashions of successive times, most of them defective, many *retrogressive*, a few on the path to higher use and beauty.
The Century, XXIX. 503.

With regard to parasites, naturalists have long recognised what is called *retrogressive* metamorphosis; and parasitic animals are as a rule admitted to be instances of Degeneration.
E. R. Lankester, Degeneration, p. 30.

retrogressively (rē-trọ-gres'iv-li), *adv.* In a retrogressive manner; with retrogression or degeneration.

retroinsular (rē-trọ-in'sụ-lạr), *a.* [< L. *retro*, behind, + *insula*, an island: see *insular*, 5.] Situated behind the insula.—**Retroinsular convolutions**, two or three convolutions behind the insula, and wholly within the fissure of Sylvius. Also called *temporoparietal convolutions*.

retrojection (rē-trọ-jek'shọn), *n.* [< L. *retro*, back, behind, + *-jectio(n-)*, in comp., < *jacere*, throw: see *jet*[1].] In *med.*, the washing out of a cavity or canal from within outward.

retrolingual (rē-trọ-ling'gwạl), *a.* [< L. *retro*, back, behind, + *lingua*, tongue: see *lingual*.] Serving to retract the tongue.

The muscular and elastic elements of the *retrolingual* membrane of the frog.
Nature, XLI. 479.

retrolocation (rē'trọ-lọ-kā'shọn), *n.* [< L. *retro*, back, + *locatio(n-)*, location.] Same as *retroposition*.

retromammary (rē-trọ-mam'ạ-ri), *a.* [< L. *retro*, behind, + *mamma*, the breast: see *mammary*.] Situated behind the mammary gland: as, a *retromammary* abscess.

retromingency (rē-trọ-min'jen-si), *n.* [< *retromingen(t)* + *-cy*.] Backward urination; the habit of being retromingent, or the conformation of body which necessitates this mode of urinating.

The last foundation [for the belief that hares are hermaphrodite] was *retromingency*.
Sir T. Browne, Vulg. Err., iii. 17.

retromingent (rē-trọ-min'jent), *a.* and *n.* [< L. *retro*, back, behind, + *mingen(t-)s*, ppr. of *mingere*, urinate: see *micturition*.] I. *a.* Urinating backward; characterized by or exhibiting retromingency.

The long penis has a mushroom-shaped glans, and the animal [rhinoceros] is *retromingent*.
Huxley, Anat. Vert., p. 362.

II. *n.* A retromingent animal.

Except it be in *retromingents*, and such as couple backward.
Sir T. Browne, Vulg. Err., iii. 17.

retromingently (rē-trọ-min'jent-li), *adv.* So as to urinate backward; in a retromingent manner. *Imp. Dict.*

retromorphosed (rē-trọ-môr'fōzd), *a.* [< *retromorphos-is* + *-ed*[2].] Characterized by or exhibiting retromorphosis; affected by retrograde metamorphosis.

retromorphosis (rē'trọ-môr-fō'sis), *n.* [NL., < L. retro, backward, + *morphosis*, q. v.] Retrograde metamorphosis; catabolism.

retroöcular (rē-trọ-ok'ū-lạr), *a.* [< L. *retro*, back, behind, + *oculus*, eye.] Situated behind the eyeball; retrobulbar.

retroöperative (rē-trọ-op'e-rạ-tiv), *a.* [< L. *retro*, back, + LL. *operativus*, operative.] Retroactive; retrospective in effect: as, a *retroöperative* decree. *Kinglake.*

retroperitoneal (rē-trọ-per'i-tọ-nē'ạl), *a.* [< L. *retro*, back, behind, + *peritoneum*, peritoneum.] Situated or occurring behind the peritoneum.—**Retroperitoneal hernia**, hernia of the intestine into the iliac fossa behind the peritoneum.—**Retroperitoneal space**, the space behind the peritoneum along the spine, occupied by the aorta, vena cava, and other structures, with loose connective tissue.

retropharyngeal (rē'trọ-fạ-rin'jē-ạl), *a.* [< L. *retro*, back, + NL. *pharynx*, pharynx: see *pharynx*, *pharyngeal*.] Situated behind the pharynx. —**Retropharyngeal abscess**, an abscess forming in the connective tissue behind the pharynx.

Retropinna (rē-trọ-pin'ạ), *n.* [NL., < L. *retro*, back, + *pinna*, a feather: see *pinna*[1].] In *ichth.*, a genus of *Argentinidæ*. *R. richardsoni* is known as the *New Zealand smelt*.

retroposition (rē'trọ-pọ-zish'ọn), *n.* [< L. *retro*, back, + *positio(n-)*, position.] Displacement backward, but without flexion or version: said of the uterus.

retropulsion (rē-trọ-pul'shọn), *n.* [< L. *retro*, back, + LL. *pulsio(n-)*, a beating (pushing): see *pulsion*.] 1. A disorder of locomotion, seen sometimes in paralysis agitans, in which the patient is impelled to run backward as if in the endeavor to recover his balance.—2. A pushing or forcing of the fetal head backward in labor.

retropulsive (rē-trọ-pul'siv), *a.* [< L. *retro*, back, + *pulsus*, pp. of *pellere*, drive, push, + *-ive*. Cf. *pulsive*.] Driving back; repelling. *Smart.*

retrorse (rẹ-trôrs'), *a.* [< L. *retrorsus*, contracted form of *retroversus*, bent or turned backward, < *retro*, backward, + *versus*, pp. of *vertere*, turn: see *verse*.] 1. In *bot.* and *zoöl.*, turned back; directed backward; retral.—2. In *ornith.*, turned in a direction the opposite of the usual one, without reference to any other line or plane; antrorse. See the quotation.

Bristles or feathers thus growing forwards are called *retrorse*: here used in the sense of an opposite direction from the lay of the general plumage; but they should properly be called antrorse.
Coues, Key to N. A. Birds, p. 105.

retrorsely (rẹ-trôrs'li), *adv.* So as to be retrorse; in a backward direction; retrad.

retroserrate (rē-trọ-ser'āt), *a.* [< L. *retro*, back, + *serratus*, saw-shaped: see *serrate*.] In *entom.*, armed with retrorse teeth; barbed, as the sting of a bee.

retroserrulate (rē-trọ-ser'ọ-lāt), *a.* [< L. *retro*, back, + NL. *serrulatus*, < *serrula*, a little saw: see *serrulate*.] In *entom.*, finely retroserrate; armed with minute retrorse teeth, as the stings of some hymenopters.

Retrosiphonata (rē-trọ-si-fọ-nā'tạ), *n. pl.* [NL., neut. pl. of *retrosiphonatus*: see *retrosiphonate*.] A primary group of ammonitoid cephalopods whose partitions around the siphon were inclined backward, including the *Goniatitidæ*.

Retrosiphonatæ (rē-trọ-si-fọ-nā'tē), *n. pl.* [NL., fem. pl. of *retrosiphonatus*: see *retrosiphonate*.] A subdivision of belemnitoid cephalopods whose phragmacone had the siphon and partitions around it directed backward, including *Belemnites* and most other genera of the family *Belemnitidæ*.

retrosiphonate (rē-trọ-si'fọ-nāt), *a.* [< NL. *retrosiphonatus*, < L. retro, back, + *sipho(n-)*, a siphon: see *siphonate*.] In *conch.*, having the siphon and surrounding partitions directed backward, as in *Goniatitidæ* and most *Belemnitidæ*.

retrospect (ret'rọ- or rē'trọ-spekt), *v. t.* [< L. *retrospectus*, pp. (not used) of *retrospicere*, look back, < retro, backward, + *specere*, look: see *spectacle*.] To look back upon; consider retrospectively. [Rare.]

I will not sully the whiteness of it [my life] (pardon my vanity; I presume to call it so, on *retrospecting* it, regarding my intentions only), by giving way to an act of injustice.
Richardson, Sir Charles Grandison, III. lxxxviii.

retrospect (ret'rọ- or rē'trọ-spekt), *n.* [= Pg. *retrospecto*, < L. as if **retrospectus*, < *retrospicere*, pp. *retrospectus* (not used), look back: see *retrospect*, *v.*] 1. The act of looking backward; contemplation or consideration of the past; hence, a review or survey of past events.

Most of us take occasion to sit still and throw away the time in our possession by *retrospect* on what is past.
Steele, Spectator, No. 374.

He reviewed that grand and melancholy story, he gave them to see through that pictured *retrospect* how it had been appointed to them to act in the final extremity of Greece.
R. Choate, Addresses and Orations, p. 185.

Hence—2. That to which one looks back; the past; a past event or consideration.

This Instrument is executed by you, your Son, and my Niece, which discharges me of all *Retrospects*.
Steele, Tender Husband, v. 1.

"Know you no song of your own land," she said,
"Not such as moans about the *retrospect*,
But deals with the other distance and the hues
Of promise; not a death's-head at the wine."
Tennyson, Princess, iv.

retrospection (ret-rọ- or rē-trọ-spek'shọn), *n.* [< L. *retrospectus*, pp. (not used) of *retrospicere*, look back: see *retrospect*.] 1. The act of looking back on things past; reflection on the past.

Drooping she bends o'er pensive Fancy's urn,
To trace the hours which never can return;
Yet with the *retrospection* loves to dwell,
And soothe the sorrows of her last farewell!
Byron, Childish Recollections.

2. The faculty of looking back on the past; recollection.

Canst thou take delight in viewing
This poor isle's approaching ruin;
When thy *retrospection* vast
Sees the glorious ages past? *Swift.*

retrospective (ret-rē- or rē-trọ-spek'tiv), *a.* [= F. *rétrospectif* = Pg. *retrospectivo*; as retro-

spect + *-ive.*] 1. Looking backward; considering the past.

In vain the sage, with *retrospective* eye,
Would from the apparent what conclude the why.
Pope, Moral Essays, i. 99.

2. In *law*, retroactive; affecting matters which occurred before it was adopted: as, a *retrospective* act, law, or statute. In general, a penal statute, though expressed absolutely, is construed as applying only to offenses committed after it is passed. See *ex post facto.*

To annul by a *retrospective* statute patents which in Westminster Hall were held to be legally valid would have been simply robbery. *Macaulay*, Hist. Eng., xxiii.

Every statute which takes away or impairs vested rights acquired under existing laws, or creates a new obligation, imposes a new duty, or attaches a new liability in respect to transactions or considerations already past, must be deemed *retrospective.* *Story.*

3. Capable of being looked back to; occurring in the past; bygone.

I have sometimes wondered whether, as the faith of men in a future existence grew less confident, they might not be seeking some equivalent in the feeling of a *retrospective* duration, if not their own, at least that of their race.
Lowell, Harvard Anniversary.

retrospectively (ret-rō- or rē-trǫ-spek'tiv-li), *adv.* In retrospect; with reference to or with reflection upon the past; in *law*, ex post facto.

The law may have been meant to act *retrospectively*, to prevent a question being raised on the interpellations of Bibulus. *Froude*, Cæsar, p. 210.

retrosternal (rē-trǫ-stėr'nal), *a.* [< L. *retro*, back, behind, + NL. *sternum*, sternum.] Being behind the sternum.

retrotarsal (rē-trǫ-tär'sal), *a.* [< L. *retro*, behind, + NL. *tarsus*, the cartilage at the edges of the eyelids: see *tarsal.*] Being behind the tarsus of the eye.—**Retrotarsal fold**, the fornix of the conjunctiva.

retrotracheal (rē-trǫ-trā'kē-al), *a.* [< L. *retro*, back, behind, + NL. *trachea*, trachea.] Being at the back of the trachea.

retroussage (rē-trö-säzh'), *n.* [F., < *retrousser*, turn up: see *retroussé.*] In the *printing of etchings*, a method of producing effective tone, as in foregrounds, skies, or shadows, by skilful manipulation of ink in the parts to be treated, the ink being brought out from the filled lines, after careful wiping of the plate, by "pumping" with a soft cloth.

retroussé (rē-trö-sā'), *a.* [F., pp. of *retrousser*, turn up, < *re-* + *trousser*, tuck up, turn up: see *truss.*] Turned up, as the end of a nose; pug.

The four examples of Rehoboam's princes exhibit a more delicate and refined profile than any other type before us, and one has even a nose slightly *retroussé.*
Anthropological Jour., XVII. 239.

retro-uterine (rē-trǫ-ū'te-rin), *a.* [= F. *rétroutérin*, < L. *retro*, back, behind, + *uterus*, uterus: see *uterine.*] Situated behind the uterus.

retrovaccinate (rē-trǫ-vak'si-nāt), *v. t.* [< *retro-* + *vaccinate.*] 1. To vaccinate (a cow) with human virus.—2. To vaccinate with lymph from a cow which has been inoculated with vaccine matter from a human being.

retrovaccination (rē-trǫ-vak-si-nā'shon), *n.* [< *retrovaccinate* + *-ion.*] 1. Vaccination of a cow with human virus.—2. In *med.*, the act of vaccinating with lymph derived from a cow which has previously been inoculated with vaccine matter from the human subject; the act of passing vaccine matter through a cow.

retrovaccine (rē-trǫ-vak'sin), *n.* [< L. *retro*, back, + E. *vaccine.*] The virus produced by inoculating a cow with vaccine matter from the human subject.

retroversion (rē-trǫ-vėr'shon), *n.* [= F. *rétroversion*, < L. *retroversus* (*retrorsus*), turned or bent backward, < *retro*, backward, + *versio*(*n*-), a turning: see *version.*] A tilting or turning backward: as, *retroversion* of vertebral processes: especially applied in gynecology to an inclination of the uterus backward with the retention of its normal curve: opposed to *anteversion.*

retrovert (rē-trǫ-vėrt'), *v. t.* [< L. *retro*, backward, + *vertere*, turn: see *verse.*] To turn back.

retrovert (rē'trǫ-vėrt), *n.* [< *retrovert*, *v.*] 1. One who returns to his original creed. [Rare.]

The goats, if they come back to the old sheep-fold, . . . are now, in pious phrase, denominated *retroverts.*
F. Hall, Mod. Eng., p. 308.

2. That which undergoes retroversion, as a part or organ of the body.

retrovision (rē-trǫ-vizh'on), *n.* [< L. *retro*, backward, + *visio*(*n*-), vision: see *vision.*] The act, process, or power of mentally seeing past events, especially such as have not come within one's personal experience or observation. [Rare.]

Clairvoyance or second sight, including prevision and *retrovision.* *Pop. Sci. Mo.*, XIII. 337.

retrude (rē-tröd'), *v. t.*; pret. and pp. *retruded*, ppr. *retruding.* [< L. *retrudere*, thrust back, < *re-*, back, + *trudere*, thrust: see *threat.* Cf. *detrude*, *extrude*, *intrude*, *obtrude*, *protrude.*] To thrust back.

The term of latitude is breadthlesse line;
A point the line doth manfully *retrude*
From infinite processe.
Dr. H. More, Psychathanasia, II. ii. 6.

retruse† (rē-trös'), *a.* [< L. *retrusus*, pp. of *retrudere*, thrust back: see *retrude.*] Hidden; abstruse.

Let vs enquire no further into things *retruse* and hid than we have authoritie from the sacred Scriptures.
Heywood, Hierarchy of Angels, p. 50.

retrusion (rē-trö'zhon), *n.* [< L. *retrusus*, pp. of *retrudere*, thrust back: see *retrude.* Cf. *trusion.*] The act of retruding, or the state of being retruded.

In virtue of an endless re-motion or *retrusion* of the constituent cause. *Coleridge.*

rettet, *v. i.* See *ret*[1], *ret*[2].

rettery (ret'ėr-i), *n.*; pl. *retteries* (-iz). [< *ret*[3] + *-ery.*] A place where flax is retted.

retti (ret'i), *n. pl.* [< Hind. *ratti*, *rati.*] The hard smooth seeds of the red-bead vine, *Abrus precatorius*, used by East Indian jewelers and druggists for weights, and forming a standard. The weight so named varies in different parts of India from less than 2 to nearly 4 troy grains. See *Abrus.*

retting (ret'ing), *n.* [Verbal n. of *ret*[1], *v.*] 1. The process of steeping flax in open water, or its exposure, in thin layers, to dew, in which the woody part of the stalk is, by action of moisture and air, rendered easily separable from the fiber or harl. The principal change which the stalk undergoes is the conversion of insoluble pectose into soluble pectin, which is measurably removed by the water, and insoluble pectic acid, which is retained. Also called *rotting.*
2. The place where this operation is carried on; a rettery. *Ure.*

retund (rē-tund'), *v. t.* [< L. *retundere*, beat or pound back, blunt, dull (> It. *retundere*, dull, temper, = Sp. Pg. *retundir*, beat back, even up), < *re-*, back, + *tundere*, beat, strike. Cf. *contund*, *contuse*, *intuse.*] To blunt or turn, as the edge of a weapon; dull.

This [the skull] is covered with skin and hair, which serve . . . to quench and dissipate the force of any stroke that shall be dealt it, and *retund* the edge of any weapon.
Ray, Works of Creation.

return[1] (rē-tėrn'), *v.* [< ME. *returnen*, *retornen*, *retournen*, < OF. *returner*, *retorner*, *retourner*, F. *retourner* = Pr. Sp. Pg. *retornar* = It. *ritornare*, < ML. *retornare*, turn back, return, < L. *re-*, back, + *tornare*, turn: see *turn.*] **I.** *trans.* 1. To turn back. (*a*) To restore to a former position by turning.

We seeke . . . [the turtles] in the nights, where we finde them on shore, we turne them upon their backs, till the next day we fetch them home, for they can never *returne* themselves.
Quoted in *Capt. John Smith's* Works, II. 273.

(*b*) To fold back; turn or roll over, as a thing upon itself.

The attire of masquers was alike in all, . . . the colours azure and silver, but *returned* on the top with a scroll and antique dressing of feathers.
B. *Jonson*, Masque of Blackness.

(*c*) To reverse the position or direction of; turn backward.

Then dead through great affright
They both nigh were, and each bad other flye:
Both fled attonce, ne ever backe *retourned* eye.
Spenser, F. Q., II. iii. 19.

2. To cast back; reflect; reëcho.

In our passage we went by that famous bridge over ye Marne, where that renowned echo *returnes* the voice of a good singer 9 or 10 times. *Evelyn*, Diary, March 1, 1644.

Long Chancery-lane retentive rolls the sound,
And courts to courts *return* it round and round.
Pope, Dunciad, ii. 264.

3†. To turn over; revolve.

Retournynge in hir soule ay up and doun
The wordes of this sodeyn Diomede.
Chaucer, Troilus, v. 1023.

4. To send back; cause to go back to a former place.

Returninge his shyppes towarde the West, he [Columbus] found a more holesome ayre, and (as God woulde) came at the length to a lande well inhabyted.
R. Eden, tr. of Sebastian Munster (First Books on [America, ed. Arbor, p. 35).

Say that Marcius
Return me, as Cominius is *return'd*,
Unheard; what then? *Shak.*, Cor., v. 1. 42.

Cyrus, with relenting pity mov'd,
Return'd them happy to the land they lov'd.
Cowper, Expostulation, l. 76.

5†. To take with one when going back; bring or carry back.

The commodities which they *returned* backe were Silks, Chamlets, Rubarbe, Malmesies, Muskadels, and other wines. *Hakluyt's Voyages*, II. 96.

6. To give back; restore.

If she will *return* me my jewels, I will give over my suit, and repent my unlawful solicitation.
Shak., Othello, iv. 2. 200.

Restore, restore Eurydice to life;
Oh take the husband, or *return* the wife!
Pope, Ode for Music.

7. To give in repayment, requital, or recompense; make a return of: as, to *return* good for evil.

The Lord shall *return* thy wickedness upon thine own head. 1 Ki. ii. 44.

When, for some trifling present, you have bid me
Return so much, I have shook my head and wept.
Shak., T. of A., ii. 2. 146.

Thanks,
The slightest, easiest, readiest recompense
From them who could *return* him nothing else.
Milton, P. R., iii. 129.

8. To make a return for; repay; requite: as, to *return* kindness by ingratitude; to *return* a loan; to *return* a call.—9. To give back in response; reply.

The Dauphin, whom of succours we entreated,
Returns us that his powers are not yet ready
To raise so great a siege. *Shak.*, Hen. V., iii. 3. 46.

It was three moneths after ere hee *returned* vs any answer. Quoted in *Capt. John Smith's* Works, II. 14.

All the host of hell
With deafening shout *return'd* them loud acclaim.
Milton, P. L., ii. 520.

But Death *returns* an answer sweet:
"My sudden frost was sudden gain."
Tennyson, In Memoriam, lxxxi.

10. To retort.

Even in his throat—unless it be the king—
That calls me traitor, I *return* the lie.
Shak., Pericles, ii. 5. 57.

If you are a malicious reader, you *return* upon me that I affect to be thought more impartial than I am. *Dryden.*

11. To bring back and make known; report, tell, or communicate.

And Moses *returned* the words of the people unto the Lord. Ex. xix. 8.

Let the trumpets sound
While we *return* these dukes what we decree.
Shak., Rich. II., i. 3. 122.

12. To report officially; render as an official statement or account: as, to *return* a list of killed and wounded after a battle.

The borough members were often *returned* by the same sealers as the knights of the shire: not that they were chosen by them, but that the return was certified by their authority. *Stubbs*, Const. Hist., § 421.

13. In *law*, to bring or send back, as a process or other mandate, to the tribunal whence it issued, with a short statement (usually indorsed on the process) by the officer to whom it issued, and who returns it, stating what he has done under it, or why he has done nothing: as, to *return* an execution non est inventus; to *return* a commission with the depositions taken under it. The return is now usually made by filing the paper in the clerk's office, instead of by presenting it on a general return-day in open court.

14. To send; transmit; convey; remit.

Instead of a ship, he should levy money and *return* the same to the treasurer for His Majesty's use. *Clarendon.*

15. To elect as a member of Congress or of Parliament.

Upon the election of a new Parliament . . . Bolingbroke was not *returned.* *Goldsmith*, Bolingbroke.

In fact, only one papist had been *returned* to the Irish Parliament since the Restoration.
Macaulay, Hist. Eng., vi.

16. To yield; give a return or profit of.

I more then wonder they haue not fiue hundred Saluages to worke for them towards their generall maintenance, and as many more to *returne* some content and satisfaction to the Aduenturers.
Capt. John Smith, Works, II. 107.

17. In *card-playing*, to lead back, as a suit previously led; respond to by a similar lead: as, to *return* a lead or a suit.

At the end of every hand, Miss Bolo would inquire . . . why Mr. Pickwick had not *returned* that diamond or led the club. *Dickens*, Pickwick, xxxv.

=**Syn.** *Return*, *Restore* (see *restore*[1]), render.

II. *intrans.* 1†. To turn back.

The Saisnes were grete and stronge, and bolde and hardy, and full of grete prowesse, and often thei *returned* vpon hem that hem pursued. *Merlin* (E. E. T. S.), iii. 507.

2. To come back; come or go back to a former place or position: as, to *return* home.

As water that doun renneth ay,
But never droppe *returne* may.
Rom. of the Rose, l. 384.

Thursday, the vij Day of May, we *retornyed* by the same watir of Brent to Venese ageyne.
Torkington, Diarie of Eng. Travell, p. 9.

The undiscover'd country from whose bourn
No traveller *returns*. *Shak.*, Hamlet, iii. 1. 80.

She was so familiarly receiv'd [in heaven]
As one *returning*, not as one arriv'd.
Dryden, Eleonora, l. 133.

3. To go or come back to a former state; pass back; in general, to come by any process of retrogression.

The sea *returned* to his strength when the morning appeared. Ex. xiv. 27.

Alexander died, Alexander was buried, Alexander *returneth* into dust. *Shak.*, Hamlet, v. 1. 232.

4. To come again; come a second time or repeatedly; repeat a visit.

Thou to mankind
Be good and friendly still, and oft *return!*
Milton, P. L., viii. 651.

So sweetly she bade me adieu,
I thought that she bade me *return*.
Shenstone, A Pastoral Ballad, i. 5.

5. To appear or begin again after a periodical revolution.

The wind *returneth* again according to his circuits.
Eccles. i. 6.

Thus with the year
Seasons *return*, but not to me *returns*
Day, or the sweet approach of even or morn.
Milton, P. L., iii. 41.

6. To revert; come back to the original possessor; hence, to fall to the share of a person; become the possession of either a previous or a new owner.

In the year of the jubile the field shall *return* unto him of whom it was bought. Lev. xxvii. 24.

Had his necessity made use of me,
I would have put my wealth into donation,
And the best half should have *return'd* to him.
Shak., T. of A., iii. 2. 91.

7. To go back in thought or speech; come back to a previous subject of consideration; recur.

Now will I *retourne* azen, or I procede ony ferthere, for to declare zou the othere weyes, that drawen toward Babiloyne. *Mandeville*, Travels, p. 53.

But to *return* to the verses: did they please you?
Shak., L. L. L., iv. 2. 156.

8. To reappear; come back before the mind.

The scenes and forms of death with which he had been familiar in Naples *returned* again and again before his eyes. *J. H. Shorthouse*, John Inglesant, xxxvi.

9. To make reply; retort.

A plain-spoken and possibly high-thinking critic might here perhaps *return* upon me with my own expressions.
Scribner's Mag., IV. 126.

10. To yield a return; give a value or profit. [Rare.]

Allowing 25. men and boies to euery Barke, they will make 5000. persons, whose labours *returne* yeerely to about 135000. pound sterling.
Capt. John Smith, Works, II. 246.

11. In *fencing*, to give a thrust or cut after parrying a sword-thrust.

return[1] (rẹ̄-tėrn'), *n.* [< ME. *return*; cf. OF. *retor*, *retur*, *retour*, F. *retour* = Pr. *retorn* = Sp. Pg. *retorno* = It. *ritorno*; from the verb: see *return*[1], *v.*, and cf. *retour*.] **1.** The act of sending, bringing, rendering, or restoring to a former place, position, owner, or state; the act of giving back in requital, recompense, retort, or response; election, as of a member of Congress or of Parliament; also, the state of being returned. See *return*[1], *v. t.*

I'll pawn my victories, all
My honours to you, upon his good *returns*.
Shak., T. of A., iii. 5. 82.

Once the girl gave me a pair of beaded moccasons, in *return*, I suppose, for my bread and cider.
S. Judd, Margaret, ii. 4.

2. The act of going or coming back; resumption of a former place, position, state, condition, or subject of consideration; recurrence, reappearance, or reversion. See *return*[1], *v. i.*

At the *return* of the year, the king of Syria will come up against thee. 1 Ki. xx. 22.

In our *returnes* we visited all our friends, that reioyced much at our Victory against the Manahocks.
Quoted in *Capt. John Smith's* Works, I. 188.

To continue us in goodness there must be iterated *returns* of misery. *Sir T. Browne*, Christ. Mor., ii. 11.

The regular *return* of genial months,
And renovation of a faded world.
Cowper, Task, vi. 123.

3. That which is returned. (*a*) That which is given in repayment or requital; a recompense; a payment; a remittance.

Within these two months, that's a month before
This bond expires, I do expect *return*
Of thrice three times the value of this bond.
Shak., M. of V., i. 3. 160.

They export honour, and make him a *return* in envy.
Bacon, Followers and Friends.

Contempt instead, dishonour, obloquy?
Hard recompense, unsuitable *return*
For so much good, so much beneficence!
Milton, P. R., iii. 132.

(*b*) Profit, as arising from labor, effort, exertion, or use; advantage; a profitable result.

The fruit which comes from the many days of recreation and vanity is very little; . . . but from the few hours we spend in prayer and the exercises of a pious life the *return* is great. *Jer. Taylor*, Holy Living, i., Int.

Just Gods! shall all things yield *returns* but love?
Pope, Autumn, l. 76.

(*c*) A response; a reply; an answer.

Say, if my father render fair *return*,
It is against my will. *Shak.*, Hen. V., ii. 4. 127.

They neither appeared, nor sent satisfying reasons for their absence; but in stead thereof, many insolent, proud, railing, opprobrious *returns*.
N. Morton, New England's Memorial, p. 204.

(*d*) A report; a formal or official account of an action performed or a duty discharged, or of facts, statistics, and the like; especially, in the plural, a set of tabulated statistics prepared for general information: as, agricultural *returns*; census *returns*; election *returns*. The return of members of Parliament is, strictly speaking, the return by the sheriff or other returning officer of the writ addressed to him, certifying the election in pursuance of it.

No note was taken of the falsification of election *returns*, or the dangers peculiar to elective governments.
Bancroft, Hist. Const., II. 150.

Accordingly in some of the earlier *returns* it is possible that the sheriff, or the persons who joined with him in electing the knights of the shire, elected the borough members also. *Stubbs*, Const. Hist., § 422.

But a fairly adequate instrument of calculation is supplied by the Registrar-General's marriage-*returns*.
Quarterly Rev., CXLV. 50.

(*e*) In *fencing*, a thrust or cut given in answer to a sword-thrust: a more general term for *riposte*, which has a specific meaning, signifying the easiest and quickest return stroke available under given circumstances.

4. In *law*: (*a*) The bringing or sending back of a process or other mandate to the tribunal whence it issued, with a short statement (usually indorsed on the process) by the officer to whom it issued, and who returns it, stating what he has done under it, or why he has done nothing. The return is now usually made by filing the process, with indorsed certificate, in the clerk's office. (*b*) The official certificate so indorsed. (*c*) The day on which the terms of a process or other mandate require it to be returned. See *return-day*.

I must sit to bee kild, and stand to kill my selfe! I could vary it not so little as thrice ouer agen; 'tas some eight *returnes* like Michelmas Terme!
Tourneur, Revenger's Tragedy, v. 1.

5. *pl.* A light-colored mild-flavored kind of tobacco.—**6.** In *arch.*, the continuation of a molding, projection, etc., in an opposite or different direction; also, a side or part which falls away from the front of any straight work. As a feature of a molding, it is usual at the termination of the dripstone or hood of a window or door.

Returned Molding.—From Apse of a Romanesque Church at Agen, France.

I understand both these sides to be not only *returns*, but parts of the front. *Bacon*, Building (ed. 1887).

7. The air which ascends after having passed through the working in a coal-mine.—**8.** In *milit. engin.*, a short branch gallery for the reception of empty trucks. It enables loaded trucks to pass.—**9.** In *music*, same as *reprise*, 5. —**Clause of return**, in *Scots law*. See *clause*.—**False return.** See *false*.—**Return request**, in the postal system of the United States, a request, printed or written on the envelop of a letter, that, if not delivered within a certain time, it be returned to the writer's address, which is given.—**Returns of a mine**, in *fort.*, the turnings and windings of a gallery leading to a mine.—**Returns of a trench**, the various turnings and windings which form the lines of a trench.

return[2] (rē-tėrn'), *v.* [< *re-* + *turn*.] To turn again: as, to turn and *return*. Also written distinctively *re-turn*.

Face. O, you must follow, sir, and threaten him tame:
He'll turn again else.
Kas. I'll *re-turn* him then. *B. Jonson*, Alchemist, iv. 4.

returnability (rẹ̄-tėr-na-bil'i-ti), *n.* [< *returnable* + *-ity* (see *-bility*).] The character of being returnable.

returnable (rẹ̄-tėr'na-bl), *a.* [< *return*[1] + *-able*.] **1.** Capable of being returned.

Sins that disceit is ay *returnable*,
Of very force it is agreable
That therwithall be done the recompence.
Wyatt, Abused Lover.

2. In *law*, legally required to be returned, delivered, given, or rendered: as, a writ or precept *returnable* at a certain day; a verdict *returnable* to the court.

It may be decided in that court where the verdict is *returnable*. *Sir M. Hale*, Hist. Common Law of Eng., xii.

return-alkali (rẹ̄-tėrn'al"ka-li), *n.* In the manufacture of prussiate of potash (see *prussiate*) on a large scale, the salt obtained from the residual mother-liquor, which, after the lixiviation of the calcined cake, the second crystallization, and second concentration, yet contains about 70 per cent. of potassium carbonate. The salts crystallizing out are also called *blue salts*. They are utilized by mixing them with the charge for another calcining process.

return-ball (rẹ̄-tėrn'bâl), *n.* A ball used as a plaything, held by an elastic string which causes it to return to the hand from which it is thrown.

return-bead (rẹ̄-tėrn'bēd), *n.* In *arch.* and *carp.*, a double-quirk bead following an angle, and presenting the same profile on each face of the stuff. Also called *bead and double quirk*. See cut under *bead*.

return-bend (rẹ̄-tėrn'bend), *n.* A pipe-coupling in the shape of the letter U, used for joining the ends of two pipes in making pipe-coils, heat-radiators, etc.—**Open return-bend**, a return-bend having its branches separated in the form of the letter V. It differs from a *closed return-bend* in that the latter has its branches in contact.

return-cargo (rẹ̄-tėrn'kär"gō), *n.* A cargo brought back in return for or in place of merchandise previously sent out.

return-check (rẹ̄-tėrn'chek), *n.* A ticket for readmission given to one of the audience who leaves a theater between the acts.

return-crease (rẹ̄-tėrn'krēs), *n.* See *crease*[1], 2.

return-day (rẹ̄-tėrn'dā), *n.* In *law*: (*a*) The day fixed by legal process for the defendant to appear in court, or for the sheriff to return the process and his proceedings, or both. (*b*) A day in a term of court appointed for the return of all processes.

returner (rẹ̄-tėr'nėr), *n.* [< *return*[1] + *-er*[1].] One who or that which returns.

The chapmen that give highest for this [bullion from Spain] are . . . those who can make most profit by it; and those are the *returners* of our money, by exchange, into those countries where our debts . . . make a need of it. *Locke*, Obs. on Encouraging the Coining of Silver.

returning-board (rẹ̄-tėr'ning-bōrd), *n.* In some of the United States, a board consisting of certain designated State officers, who are by law empowered to canvass and declare returns of elections held within the State.

returning-officer (rẹ̄-tėr'ning-of"i-sėr), *n.* **1.** The officer whose duty it is to make returns of writs, precepts, juries, etc.—**2.** The presiding officer at an election, who returns the persons duly elected.

returnless (rẹ̄-tėrn'les), *a.* [< *return*[1] + *-less*.] Without return; admitting no return. [Rare.]

But I would neuer credit in you both
Least cause of sorrow, but well knew the troth
Of this thine owne returne; though all thy friends
I knew, as well should make *returnlesse* ends.
Chapman, Odyssey, xiii.

return-match (rẹ̄-tėrn'mach), *n.* A second match or trial played by the same two sets of opponents.

For this year the Wellesburn *return-match* and the Marylebone match played at Rugby.
T. *Hughes*, Tom Brown's School-Days, ii. 8.

returnment (rẹ̄-tėrn'ment), *n.* [< *return*[1] + *-ment*.] The act of returning; a return; a going back. [Rare.]

Sometimes we yeeld; but, like a ramme,
That makes *returnment* to redouble strength,
Then lore'd them yeeld.
Heywood, If you Know not me (Works, ed. Pearson, 1874, [I. 349).

return-piece (rẹ̄-tėrn'pēs), *n.* *Theat.*, a piece of scenery forming an angle of a building.

return-shock (rẹ̄-tėrn'shok), *n.* An electric shock, due to the action of induction, sometimes felt when a sudden discharge of electricity takes place in the neighborhood of the observer, as in the case of a lightning-flash.

return-tag (rẹ̄-tėrn'tag), *n.* A tag attached to a railway-car, usually by slipping it on to the shackle of the seal, serving as evidence of the due arrival of the car, or as a direction to what point the car is to be returned. *Car-Builder's Dict.*

return-ticket (rẹ-tėrn'tik"et), *n.* A ticket issued by a railway or steamboat company, coach proprietors, and the like, for a journey to some point and return to the place of starting, generally at a reduced charge.

An excursion opposition steamer was advertised to start for Boulogne—fares, half-a-crown; *return-tickets*, four shillings. *Mrs. H. Wood*, Mildred Arkell, xx.

return-valve (rẹ-tėrn'valv), *n.* A valve which opens to allow reflux of a fluid under certain conditions, as in the case of overflow.

retuse (rẹ-tūs'), *a.* [= F. *rétus*, < L. *retusus*, blunted, dull, pp. of *retundere*, blunt, dull: see *retund*.] 1. In *bot.*, obtuse at the apex, with a broad and very shallow sinus reëntering: as, a *retuse* leaf.—2. In *zoöl.*, ending in an obtuse sinus.

Retuse Leaf of *Salix retusa*.

Retzia (ret'si-ä), *n.* [NL. (King, 1850), named after *Retzius*, a naturalist.] A genus of brachiopods, typical of the subfamily *Retziinæ*. They flourished in the Paleozoic seas from the Silurian to the Upper Carboniferous.

Retziinæ (ret-si-ī'nē), *n. pl.* [NL., < *Retzia* + *-inæ*.] A subfamily of arthropomatous brachiopods, mostly referred to the family *Spiriferidæ*. Externally they much resemble the terebratulids.

Reuchlinian (rụ-klin'i-ạn), *a.* [< *Reuchlin* (see def.) + *-ian*.] Pertaining or relating to Johann Reuchlin (1455–1522), a celebrated German classical scholar.—**Reuchlinian pronunciation.** See *pronunciation*.

reul¹†, *n.* An obsolete form of *rule*¹.

reul²†, *v. i.* Same as *rule*². *Halliwell.*

reule†, *n.* and *v.* A Middle English form of *rule*¹.

reuliche†, *a.* A Middle English form of *ruly*¹.

reuly†, *a.* A Middle English form of *ruly*¹, *ruly*².

reume¹†, *n.* A Middle English form of *realm*.

reume²†, *n.* An obsolete form of *rheum*¹.

reumour†, *n.* A Middle English form of *rumor*. *Cath. Ang.*, p. 306.

reune (rẹ-ūn'), *v.*; pret. and pp. *reuned*, ppr. *reuning*. [< OF. *reunir*, F. *réunir* = Sp. Pg. *reunir* = It. *riunire*, < ML. *reunire*, make one again, unite again, < L. *re-*, again, + *unire*, unite: see *unite*.] **I.** *trans.* To reunite; bring into reunion and coherence. [Obsolete or rare.]

It pleased her Maiestie to call this Country of Wingandacoa, Virginia, by which name now you are to vnderstand how it was planted, disolued, *reuned*, and enlarged. Quoted in *Capt. John Smith's* Works, I. 85.

II. *intrans.* To be reunited; specifically, to hold a reunion. [American college slang.]

reunient (rẹ-ū'niẹnt), *a.* [< ML. *reunien(t-)s*, ppr. of *reunire*: see *reune*.] Uniting or connecting: as, the *reunient* canal of the ear, or canalis reuniens (which see, under *canalis*).

reunification (rẹ-ū"ni-fi-kā'shọn), *n.* [< *re-* + *unification*.] The act of reunifying, or reducing to unity; a state of reunion or reconciliation.

No scientific progress is possible unless the stimulus of the original unification is strong enough to clasp the discordant facts and establish a *reunification*. *Encyc. Brit.*, XI. 619.

reunify (rẹ-ū'ni-fī), *v. t.* [< *re-* + *unify*.] To bring back to a state of unity or union.

reunion (rẹ-ū'nyọn), *n.* [< OF. *reunion*, F. *réunion* = Sp. *reunion* = Pg. *reunião*, < ML. *reunire*, make one again, reunite: see *reune*. Cf. *union*.] 1. The act of reuniting, or bringing back to unity, juxtaposition, concurrence, or harmony; the state of being reunited.

She, that should all parts to *reunion* bow;
She, that had all magnetic force alone
To draw and fasten sundered parts in one.
Donne, Funeral Elegies, Anatomy of the World.

"The *reunion*, in a single invoice, of various parcels, every one of which does not amount to $20, but which in the aggregate exceed that quantity," remains subject to the tax. *Pop. Sci. Mo.*, XXIX. 294.

Mère Marchette struggled a moment, as if she could not yield to anything which delayed her *reunion* with Pierre. *The Century*, XL. 248.

Specifically—2. A meeting, assembly, or social gathering of familiar friends or associates after separation or absence from one another: as, a family *reunion*; a college *reunion*.—**Order of the Reunion**, an order founded by Napoleon in 1811 to commemorate the union of Holland with France. The badge was a silver star of twelve points, having the spaces filled with rays of gold, the whole surmounted by an imperial crown bearing the name *Napoléon*.

reunite (rẹ-ụ-nīt'), *v.* [< *re-* + *unite*. Cf. *reune*.] **I.** *trans.* 1. To unite again; join after separation.

By the which marriage the line of Charles the Great
Was *re-united* to the crown of France.
Shak., Hen. V., i. 2. 85.

I wander here in vain, and want thy hand
To guide and *re-unite* me to my Lord.
Rowe, Ambitious Stepmother, v. 2.

At length, after many eventful years, the associates, so long parted, were *reunited* in Westminster Abbey. *Macaulay*, Hist. Eng., vii.

2. To reconcile after variance.

A patriot king will not despair of reconciling and *re-uniting* his subjects to himself and to one another. *Bolingbroke*, Of a Patriot King.

II. *intrans.* To be united again; join and cohere again.

Yet not for this were the Britans dismaid, but *reuniteing* the next day fought with such a courage as made it hard to decide which way hung the Victorie. *Milton*, Hist. Eng., ii.

reunitedly (rē-ụ-nī'ted-li), *adv.* In a reunited manner.

reunition† (rē-ụ-nish'ọn), *n.* [< *reunite* + *-ion*.] A second or repeated uniting; reunion. [Rare.]

I believe the resurrection of the body, and its *reunition* with the soul. *Knatchbull*, On the New Testament Translation, p. 93.

reunitive (rẹ-ū'ni-tiv), *a.* [< *reunite* + *-ive*.] Causing reunion; tending toward or characterized by reunion. [Rare.]

Noon-time of a Sunday in a New England country town used to be, and even now is, a social and *reunitive* epoch of no small interest. *S. Judd*, Margaret, i. 14.

reurge (rē-ėrj'), *v. t.* [< *re-* + *urge*.] To urge again.

reus (rē'us), *n.*; pl. *rei* (-ī). [< L. *reus*, m., *rea*, f., orig. a party to an action, plaintiff or defendant, afterward restricted to the party accused, defendant, prisoner, etc.; also, a debtor (> It. *reo*, wicked, bad, = Sp. Pg. *reo*, a criminal, defendant), < *res*, a cause, action: see *res*.] In *law*, a defendant.

reuse (rē-ūz'), *v. t.* [< *re-* + *use*, *v.*] To use again.

It appears that large quantities of domestic distilled spirits are being placed upon the market as imported spirits and under *reused* imported spirit stamps. *Report of Sec. of Treasury*, 1886, I. 462.

reuse (rē-ūs'), *n.* [< *re-* + *use*, *n.*] Repeated use; use a second time.

The waste liquor is collected, and made up to the first strength for *re-use*. *Workshop Receipts*, 2d ser., p. 31.

reutilize (rē-ū'til-īz), *v. t.* [< *re-* + *utilize*.] To utilize again; make use of a second time. Also spelled *reutilise*.

After the white cells have lived their life and done their work, portions of their worn-out carcases may be *reutilised* in the body as nutriment. *Lancet*, No. 3447, p. 585.

reutter (rē-ut'ėr), *v. t.* [< *re-* + *utter*.] To utter again.

The truth of Man, as by God first spoken,
Which the actual generations garble,
Was *re-uttered*.
Browning, Old Pictures in Florence, st. 11.

rev. An abbreviation of (*a*) [*cap.*] *Revelation*; (*b*) *revenue*; (*c*) *reverend*; (*d*) *review*; (*e*) *revolution*; (*f*) *revised*; (*g*) *reverse*.

revalenta (rev-ạ-len'tä), *n.* [NL., transposed from *ervalenta*, < NL. *Ervum Lens*: see *Ervum* and *Lens*.] The commercial name of lentil-meal, introduced as a food for invalids. In full, *revalenta Arabica*. Also *ervalenta*. [Eng.]

revalescence (rev-ạ-les'ẹns), *n.* [< *revalescen(t)* + *-ce*.] The state of being revalescent. [Rare.]

Would this prove that the patient's *revalescence* had been independent of the medicines given him? *Coleridge.*

revalescent (rev-ạ-les'ẹnt), *a.* [< L. *revalescen(t-)s*, ppr. of *revalescere*, grow well again, < *re-*, again, + *valescere*, grow well: see *convalescent*.] Beginning to grow well. [Rare.] *Imp. Dict.*

revaluation (rē-val-ụ-ā'shọn), *n.* [< *revalue* + *-ation*.] A repeated valuation.

revalue (rē-val'ū), *v. t.* [< *re-* + *value*.] To value again.

revamp (rẹ-vamp'), *v. t.* [< *re-* + *vamp*.] To vamp, mend, or patch up again; rehabilitate; reconstruct.

Thenceforth he [Carlyle] has done nothing but *revamp* his telling things; but the oddity has become always odder, the paradoxes always more paradoxical. *Lowell*, Study Windows, p. 140.

The *revamping* of our own writings . . . after an interval so long that the mental status in which we composed them is forgotten, and cannot be conjured up and revivified, is a dangerous experiment. *Marsh*, Lects. on Eng. Lang., xxi. 447.

reve†, *v.* A Middle English form of *reave*. *Chaucer.*

reve²†, *n.* A Middle English form of *reeve*¹.

reve³† (rēv), *v. i.* [< F. *rêver*, OF. *resver*, dream: see *rave*¹.] To dream; muse.

I *reved* all night what could be the meaning of such a message. *Memoirs of Marshall Keith.*

reveal (rẹ-vēl'), *v. t.* [Early mod. E. *revele*, < OF. *reveler*, F. *révéler* = Pr. Sp. Pg. *revelar* = It. *revelare*, *rivelare*, < L. *revelare*, unveil, draw back a veil, < *re-*, back, + *velare*, veil, < *velum*, a veil: see *veil*.] 1. To discover; expose to sight, recognition, or understanding; disclose; divulge; make known.

I had . . . well played my first act, assuring myself that under that disguisement I should find opportunity to *reveal* myself. *Sir P. Sidney*, Arcadia, i.

I have not *revealed* it yet to any Soul breathing, but now I'll tell your Excellency, and so fell a relating the Passage in Flanders. *Howell*, Letters, I. iv. 28.

While in and out the verses wheel,
The wind-caught robes trim feet *reveal*.
Lowell, Dobson's "Old World Idylls."

Specifically—2. To disclose as religious truth; divulge by supernatural means; make known by divine agency.

The wrath of God is *revealed* from heaven against all ungodliness and unrighteousness of men. Rom. i. 18.

No Man or Angel can know how God would be worship't and serv'd unless God *reveal* it. *Milton*, True Religion.

I call on the souls who have left the light
To *reveal* their lot.
Whittier, My Soul and I.

3. In *metaph.*, to afford an immediate knowledge of.

Such is the fact of perception *revealed* in consciousness. *Sir W. Hamilton*, Edinburgh Rev., Oct., 1830.

=**Syn.** To unveil, uncover, communicate, show, impart.

reveal (rẹ-vēl'), *n.* [< *reveal*, *v.*] 1†. A revealing; disclosure.

In nature the concealment of secret parts is the same in both sexes, and the shame of their *reveal* equal. *Sir T. Browne*, Vulg. Err., iv. 7.

2. In *arch.*, one of the vertical faces of a window-opening or a doorway, included between the face of the wall and that of the window- or door-frame, when such frame is present.

revealable (rẹ-vē'lạ-bl), *a.* [< *reveal* + *-able*.] Capable of being revealed.

I would fain learn why treason is not as *revealable* as heresy? *Jer. Taylor*, Works (ed. 1835), II. 108.

revealableness (rẹ-vē'lạ-bl-nes), *n.* The state or character of being revealable. *Imp. Dict.*

revealed (rẹ-vēld'), *p. a.* 1. Brought to light; disclosed; specifically, made known by direct divine or supernatural agency.

Scripture teacheth all supernatural *revealed* truth, without the knowledge whereof salvation cannot be attained. *Hooker*, Eccles. Polity, iii. 8.

Undoubtedly the *revealed* law is of infinitely more authenticity than that moral system which is framed by ethical writers, and denominated the natural law. *Blackstone*, Com., Int., § 2.

2. In *entom.*, not hidden under other parts.—**Revealed alitrunk**, the posterior part of the thorax or alitrunk when it is not covered by elytra, hemielytra, or tegmina, as in *Hymenoptera*, *Diptera*, etc.—**Revealed religion.** See *religion*, and *evidences of Christianity* (under *Christianity*).

revealer (rẹ-vē'lėr), *n.* One who reveals or discloses; one who or that which brings to light, shows, or makes known.

A Lord of kings, and a *revealer* of secrets. Dan. ii. 47.

He brought a taper; the *revealer*, light,
Exposed both crime and criminal to sight.
Dryden.

revealment (rẹ-vēl'mẹnt), *n.* [< *reveal* + *-ment*.] The act of revealing; revelation. [Rare.]

This is one reason why he permits so many heinous impieties to be concealed here on earth, because he intends to dignify that day with the *revealment* of them. *South*, Sermons, VII. xiii.

revehent (rē'vẹ-hẹnt), *a.* [< L. *revehen(t-)s*, ppr. of *revehere*, carry back, < *re-*, back, + *vehere*, carry: see *vehicle*.] Carrying forth; taking away; efferent: applied in anatomy to sundry vessels: opposed to *advehent*.

reveille (re-vāl'ye, sometimes rev-e-lē'), *n.* [Also written incorrectly *reveillé* and *reveillée*, as if < F. *réveillé*, pp.; < F. *réveil*, OF. *reveil*, *resveil* (= Pr. *revelh*), an awaking, alarm, reveille, a hunt's-up, < *resveiller*, awake, < *re-*, again, + *esveiller*, waken, < L. *ex-*, out, + *vigilare*, watch, wake: see *vigilant*.] *Milit.* and *naval*, the beat of a drum, bugle-sound, or other signal given about break of day, to give notice that it is time for the soldiers or sailors to rise and for the sentinels to forbear challenging.

Sound a *reveille*, sound, sound,
The warrior god is come!
Dryden, Secular Masque, l. 63.

And all the bugle breezes blew
Reveillée to the breaking morn.
Tennyson, In Memoriam, lxviii.

revel¹ (rev'el), *n.* [< ME. *revel*, *revel*, *revell*, < OF. *revel* (= Pr. *revel*), pride, rebellion, sport, jest, disturbance, disorder, delay, < *reveler*, *rebeller*, F. *rebeller*, rebel, revolt, = Sp. *rebelar* = Pg. *rebellar* = It. *ribellare*, *rebellare*, < L. *rebellare*, rebel: see *rebel*, *v.* Hence, by contraction, *rule*².] 1. A merrymaking; a feast or festivity characterized by boisterous jollity; a carouse; hence, mirth-making in general; revelry.

When thei com in to the town thei fonde . . . ladyes and maydenes carollinge and daunsinge, and the most *revell* and disport that myght be made. *Merlin* (E. E. T. S.), iii. 448.

Revelle amangos thame was full ryfe.
Thomas of Ersseldoune (Child's Ballads, I. 106).

The brief night goes
In babble and revel and wine.
Tennyson, Maud, xxii. 5.

2. Specifically—(*a*) A kind of dance or choric performance often given in connection with masques or pageants; a dancing procession or entertainment: generally used in the plural.

Our *revels* now are ended. These our actors,
As I foretold you, were all spirits, and
Are melted into air, into thin air.
Shak., Tempest, iv. 1. 148.

We use always to have *revels*; which is indeed dancing, and makes an excellent shew in truth.
B. *Jonson*, Every Man out of his Humour, iii. 2.

The *Revels* were dances of a more free and general nature—that is, not immediately connected with the story of the piece under representation. In these many of the nobility of both sexes took part, who had previously been spectators. The *Revels*, it appears from other passages, were usually composed of galliards and corantos.
Gifford, Note on B. Jonson's Masque of Lethe.

(*b*) An anniversary festival to commemorate the dedication of a church; a wake. *Halliwell.* —**Master of the revels.** Same as *lord of misrule* (which see, under *lord*). =**Syn.** 1. *Debauch*, *Spree*, etc. See *carousal*¹.

revel¹ (rev'el), *v.*; pret. and pp. *reveled* or *revelled*, ppr. *reveling* or *revelling*. [< ME. *revelen*, *revelen*, < OF. *reveler*, also *reveller*, rebel, be riotous: see *revel*¹, *n.* The E. verb follows the noun.] **I.** *intrans.* 1. To hold or take part in revels; join in merrymaking; indulge in boisterous festivities; carouse.

See! Antony, that *revels* long o' nights,
Is notwithstanding up. *Shak.*, J. C., ii. 2. 116.

2. To dance; move with a light and dancing step; frolic.

Along the crisped shades and bowers
Revels the spruce and jocund Spring.
Milton, Comus, l. 985.

3. To act lawlessly; wanton; indulge one's inclination or caprice.

His father *revell'd* in the heart of France,
And tamed the king, and made the dauphin stoop.
Shak., 3 Hen. VI., ii. 2. 150.

The Nabob was *revelling* in fancied security: . . . it had never occurred to him . . . that the English would dare to invade his dominions. *Macaulay*, Lord Clive.

4. To take great pleasure; feel an ardent and keen enjoyment; delight.

Our kind host so *revelled* in my father's humour that he was incessantly stimulating him to attack him.
Lady Holland, Sydney Smith, vii.

II.† *trans.* To spend in revelry.

An age of pleasures *revell'd* out comes home
At last, and ends in sorrow.
Ford, Lover's Melancholy, iv. 3.

revel²†, *v. t.* [= It. *revellere*, draw away, < L. *revellere*, pp. *revulsus*, pluck or pull back, tear out, off, or away, < *re-*, back, + *vellere*, pluck. Cf. *avel*, *convulse*, *revulsion*.] To draw back or away; remove.

Those who miscarry escape by their flood *revelling* the humours from their lungs. *Harvey.*

reve-land† (rēv'land), *n.* [ME., repr. AS. *gerēf-land*, tributary land (*sundor-gerēf-land*, peculiar tributary land), < *gerēfa*, reeve, + *land*, land: see *reeve*¹ and *land*.] In *Anglo-Saxon law*, such land as, having reverted to the king after the death of his thane, who had it for life, was not afterward granted out to any by the king, but remained in charge upon the account of the reeve or bailiff of the manor.

revelate† (rev'ẹ-lāt), *v. t.* [< L. *revelatus*, pp. of *revelare*, reveal, disclose: see *reveal*.] To reveal. *Imp. Dict.*

revelation (rev-ẹ-lā'shon), *n.* [< ME. *revelacioun*, < OF. *revelation*, *revelacion*, F. *révélation* = Pr. *revelacio* = Sp. *revelacion* = Pg. *revelação* = It. *rivelazione*, revelation, < LL. *revelatio(n-)*, an uncovering, a revealing, < L. *revelare*, pp. *revelatus*, reveal: see *reveal*.] 1. The act of revealing. (*a*) The disclosing, discovering, or making known to others what was before unknown to them.

It was nothing short of a new *revelation*, when Scott turned back men's eyes on their own past history and national life, and showed them there a field of human interest and poetic creation which long had lain neglected.
J. C. Shairp, Aspects of Poetry, p. 104.

(*b*) The act of revealing or communicating religious truth, especially by divine or supernatural means.

The book of quintis essencijs . . . Hermys . . . hadde by *reuelacioun* of an aungil of God to him sende.
Book of Quinte Essence (ed. Furnivall), p. 1.

By *revelation* he made known unto me the mystery.
Eph. iii. 3.

A very faithful brother,
A botcher, and a man by *revelation*,
That hath a competent knowledge of the truth.
B. *Jonson*, Alchemist, iii. 2.

2. That which is revealed, disclosed, or made known; in *theol.*, that disclosure which God makes of himself and of his will to his creatures.

When God declares any truth to us, this is a *revelation*.
Locke, Human Understanding, IV. vii. 2.

More specifically—3. Such disclosure, communicated by supernatural means, of truths which could not be ascertained by natural means; hence, as containing such revelation, the Bible. Divine revelation may be afforded by any one of four media—(*a*) nature, (*b*) history, (*c*) consciousness, or (*d*) supernatural and direct communications. In theological writings the term, when properly used, signifies exclusively the last form of revelation. *Revelation* differs from *inspiration*, the latter being an exaltation of the natural faculties, the former a communication to or through them of truth not otherwise ascertainable, or at least not otherwise known.

The *Revelation* of Jesus Christ, which God gave unto him, to shew unto his servants things which must shortly come to pass. Rev. i. 1.

'Tis *Revelation* satisfies all doubts,
Explains all mysteries except her own,
And so illuminates the path of life.
Cowper, Task, ii. 527.

4. In *metaph.*, immediate consciousness of something real and not phenomenal.—**Book of Revelation, or The Revelation of St. John the Divine,** the last book of the New Testament, also called the *Apocalypse*. It is generally attributed by the church to the apostle John, and the date of its composition is often put near the end of the first century. There is a wide difference of opinion as to the interpretation and significance of this book. The schools of interpretation are of three principal kinds. The first school, that of the preterists, embraces those who hold that the whole or by far the greater part of the prophecy of this book has been fulfilled; the second is that of the historical interpreters, who hold that the prophecy embraces the whole history of the church and its foes, from the first century to the end of the world; the third view is that of the futurists, who maintain that the prophecy, with perhaps the exception of the first three chapters, relates entirely to events which are to take place at or near to the second coming of the Lord. Abbreviated *Rev.*

revelational (rev-ẹ-lā'shon-al), *a.* [< *revelation* + *-al*.] Pertaining to or involving revelation; admitting supernatural disclosure.

It seems, however, unnecessary to discuss the precise relation of different *Revelational* Codes to Utilitarianism.
H. Sidgwick, Methods of Ethics, p. 467.

revelationist (rev-ẹ-lā'shon-ist), *n.* [< *revelation* + *-ist*.] One who believes in supernatural revelation. [Rare.]

Gruppe's great work on Greek mythology . . . is likely in the immediate future to furnish matter for contention between evolutionists and *revelationists*.
Athenæum, No. 3149, p. 272.

revelator (rev'ẹ-lā-tor), *n.* [= F. *révélateur* = Sp. Pg. *revelador* = It. *rivelatore*, *revelatore*, < LL. *revelator*, < L. *revelare*, reveal: see *reveal*.] One who makes a revelation; a revealer. [Rare and objectionable.]

The forms of civil government were only to carry out the will of the Church, and this soon came to mean the will of Brigham Young, who from year to year was re-elected and installed "prophet, seer, and *revelator*."
New York Evening Post, March 8, 1890.

revelatory (rev'ẹ-lā-tō-ri), *a.* [< LL. *revelatorius*, of or belonging to revelation, < L. *revelare*, reveal: see *reveal*.] Having the nature or character of a revelation. *Imp. Dict.*

revel-coil†, *n.* [< *revel*¹ + *coil*², prob. originating as a sophisticated form of *level*-coil.] Loud and boisterous revelry; a wild revel; a carouse or debauch.

They all had leave to leave their endless toyles,
To dance, sing, sport, and to keepe *revell-coyles*.
John Taylor, Works (1630). (*Nares.*)

revel-dash†, *n.* Same as *revel*-coil.

Have a flurt and a crash,
Now play *reveldash*.
Greene, Dram. Works, I. 175.

reveler, reveller (rev'el-ėr), *n.* [< ME. *revelour*, *revelowre*, < OF. **revelcor*, *revelour*, < *reveler*, revel: see *revel*¹, *v.*] One who revels. (*a*) One who takes part in merrymakings, toasts, or carousals; hence, one who leads a disorderly or licentious life.

My fourthe housbonde was a *revelour* —
This is to seyn, he hadde a paramour.
Chaucer, Prol. to Wife of Bath's Tale, l. 453.

None a stranger there
So merry and so gamesome; he is call'd
The Briton *reveller*. *Shak.*, Cymbeline, i. 6. 61.

In the ears of the brutalized and drunken *revellers* there arose the sound of the clanking of British cavalry.
H. Kingsley, Stretton, liii.

Specifically—(*b*) One who dances in a revel; one who takes part in a choric entertainment.

It is no disgrace, no more than for your adventurous *reveller* to fall by some inauspicious chance in his galliard.
B. *Jonson*, Cynthia's Revels, iii. 1.

reveling†, *n.* Same as *riveling*².

revellent (rẹ-vel'ent), *a.* [= Pg. It. *revellente*, < L. *revellen(t-)s*, ppr. of *revellere*, pluck or tear back, off, away, or out: see *revel*².] Causing revulsion.

reveller, *n.* See *reveler*.

revel-master (rev'el-mȧs"tėr), *n.* The master or director of the revels at Christmas; the lord of misrule.

revelment (rev'el-ment), *n.* [< *revel*¹ + *-ment*.] The act of reveling.

revelour†, *n.* An obsolete form of *reveler*.

revelous†, *a.* [< ME. *revelous*, < OF. *reveleux*, full of revelry or jest, riotous, < *revel*, riot, revol: see *revel*1, *n.* Cf. *rebellious*.] Inclined to festivity and merrymaking.

A wyf he hadde of excellent beautee,
And compaignable and *revelous* was she.
Chaucer, Shipman's Tale, l. 4.

revel-rout†, *n.* 1. A troop of revelers; hence, any riotous throng; a mob; a rabble.

Ay, that we will, we'll break your spell,
Reply'd the *revel-rout*;
We'll teach you for to fix a bell
On any woman's snout.
The Fryar and the Boy, ii. (*Nares.*)

2. A lawless, uproarious revel; wild revelry; noisy merriment.

Then made they *revell route* and goodly glee.
Spenser, Mother Hub. Tale, l. 558.

The Sorcerers and Sorceresses make great lights, and incense all this visited house, . . . laughing, singing, dauncing in honour of that God. After all this *revel-rout* they demaund againe of the Demoniake if the God be appeased. *Purchas*, Pilgrimage, p. 430.

3. A dancing entertainment.

Wilt thou forsake us, Jeffrey? then who shall daunce
The hobby horse at our next *Revel rout?*
Brome, Queens Exchange, ii. 2.

To play revel-rout, to revel furiously; carouse; act the bacchanalian.

They chose a notable swaggering rogue called Puffing Dicke to reuell ouer them, who *plaid reuell-rout* with them indeede.
Rowlands, Hist. Rogues, quoted in Ribton-Turner's Vagrants and Vagrancy, p. 582.

revelry (rev'el-ri), *n.* [< ME. *revelrie*; as *revel*¹ + *-ry*.] The act of reveling; merrymaking; especially, boisterous festivity or jollity.

The swetnesse of her melodye
Made al myn herte in *revelrye* [var. *reverye*].
Rom. of the Rose, l. 720.

Meantime, forget this new-fall'n dignity,
And fall into our rustic *revelry*.—
Play, music! *Shak.*, As you Like it, v. 4. 183.

=**Syn.** See *carousal*¹.

revels†, *n.* Same as *revel*¹.

The huntress and queen of these groves, Diana, . . . hath . . . proclaimed a solemn *revels*.
B. Jonson, Cynthia's Revels, i. 1.

revenant (rev'ẹ-nant), *n.* [< F. *revenant*, ppr. of *revenir*, come back, < *re-*, back, again, + *venir*, < L. *venire*, come: see *come*. Cf. *revenue*.] 1. One who returns; especially, one who returns after a long period of absence or after death; a ghost; a specter; specifically, in *mod. spiritualism*, an apparition; a materialization. [Rare.]

The yellow glamour of the sunset, dazzling to Inglesant's eyes, fluttered upon its vestment of whitish gray, and clothed in transparent radiance this shadowy *revenant* from the tomb. *J. H. Shorthouse*, John Inglesant, xxxiii.

2. In *math.*, a form which continually returns as leading coefficient of irreducible covariants.

revendicate (rẹ-ven'di-kāt), *v. t.*; pret. and pp. *revendicated*, ppr. *revendicating*. Same as *revindicate*. *Imp. Dict.*

revendication (rẹ-ven-di-kā'shon), *n.* Same as *revindication*. *Imp. Dict.*—**Action of revendication,** in *civil law*, an action brought to assert a title to or some real right inherent in or directly attached to property.

revenge (rẹ-venj'), *v.*; pret. and pp. *revenged*, ppr. *revenging*. [< OF. *revenger*, *revencher*, F. *revancher*, F. dial. *revanger*, revenge, = Sp. *revindicar*, claim, = Pg. *revindicar*, claim, refl. be revenged, = It. *rivendicare*, revenge, refl. be revenged. < ML. **revindicare*, revenge, lit. vindicate again, < L. *re-*, again, + *vindicare* (> OF. *vengier*, *venger*), arrogate, lay claim to: see *vindicate*, *venge*, *avenge*. Cf. *revindicate*.]

I. *trans.* 1. To take vengeance on account of; inflict punishment because of; exact retribution for; obtain or seek to obtain satisfaction for, especially with the idea of gratifying a sense of injury or vindictiveness: as, to *revenge* an insult.

These injuries the king now bears will be *revenged* home. *Shak.*, Lear, iii. 3. 13.

I hope you are bred to more humanity
Than to *revenge* my father's wrong on me.
Fletcher (and another), Love's Cure, ii. 2.

2. To satisfy by taking vengeance; secure atonement or expiation to, as for an injury; avenge the real or fancied wrongs of; especially, to gratify the vindictive spirit of: as, to *revenge* one's self for rude treatment.

You do more for the obedience of your Lord the Emperour, then to be *reuenged* of the French Kinge. *Guevara*, Letters (tr. by Hellowes, 1577), p. 70.

O Lord, . . . visit me, and *revenge* me of my persecutors. Jer. xv. 15.

Come Antony, and young Octavius, come,
Revenge yourselves alone on Cassius.
Shak., J. C., iv. 3. 94.

=**Syn.** *Avenge, Revenge.* See *avenge.*

II. *intrans.* To take vengeance.

I wil *reuenge* (quoth she),
For here I shake off shame.
Gascoigne, Philomene (Steele Glas, etc., ed. Arber, p. 100).

The Lord *revengeth*, and is furious. Nahum i. 2.

revenge (rẹ̄-venj'), *n.* [Early mod. E. *revenge*, < OF. *revenche, revanche*, F. *revanche*, revenge, F. dial. *revainche, revenche*; from the verb.] 1. The act of revenging; the execution of vengeance; retaliation for wrongs real or fancied; hence, the gratification of vindictive feeling.

Revenge is a kind of wild justice. *Bacon*, Revenge.

Though now his mighty soul its grief contains;
He meditates *revenge* who least complains.
Dryden, Abs. and Achit., i. 446.

Sweet is *revenge* — especially to women.
Byron, Don Juan, i. 24.

2. That which is done by way of vengeance; a revengeful or vindictive act; a retaliatory measure; a means of revenging one's self.

I will make mine arrows drunk with blood . . . from the beginning of *revenges* upon the enemy. Deut. xxxii. 42.

And thus the whirligig of time brings in his *revenges*.
Shak., T. N., v. 1. 385.

3. The desire to be revenged; the emotion which is aroused by an injury or affront, and which leads to retaliation; vindictiveness of mind.

Not tied to rules of policy, you find
Revenge less sweet than a forgiving mind.
Dryden, Astræa Redux, l. 261.

The term *Revenge* expresses the angry passion carried to the full length of retaliation.
A. Bain, Emotions and Will, p. 136.

To give one his revenge, to play a return-match in any game with a defeated opponent; give a defeated opponent a chance to gain an equal score or standing.

Lady Smart. Well, miss, you'll have a sad husband, you have such good luck at cards. . . .
Miss. Well, my lady Smart, I'll *give you revenge* whenever you please. *Swift*, Polite Conversation, iii.

=**Syn.** 1. *Revenge, Vengeance, Retribution, Retaliation*, and *Reprisal* agree in expressing the visiting of evil upon others in return for their misdeeds. *Revenge* is the carrying out of a bitter desire to injure an enemy for a wrong done to one's self or to those who seem a part of one's self, and is a purely personal feeling. It generally has reference to one's equals or superiors, and the malignant feeling is all the more bitter when it cannot be gratified. *Vengeance* has an earlier and a later use. In its earlier use it may arise from no personal feeling, but may be visited upon a person for another's wrong as well as for his own. In the Scripture it means retribution with indignation, as in Rom. xii. 19: "*Vengeance* is mine; I will repay, saith the Lord," where it is a reservation for Jehovah of the offices of distributive and retributive justice. In its later use it involves the idea of wrathful retribution, whether just, unjust, or excessive; it is often a furious revenge: hence there is a general tendency to turn to other words to express just retribution, especially as an act of God. *Retribution* bears more in mind the amount of the wrong done, viewing it as a sort of loan whose equivalent is in some way paid back. Any evil result befalling the perpetrator of a bad deed in consequence of that deed is said to be a *retribution*, whether occurring by human intention or not; personal agency is not prominent in the idea of *retribution*. *Retaliation* combines the notion of equivalent return, which is found in *retribution*, with a distinctly personal agency and intention; sometimes, unlike the preceding words, it has a light sense for good-humored teasing or banter. *Reprisal* is an act of retaliation in war, its essential point being the capture of something in return or as indemnification for pecuniary damage from the other side. The word has also a looser figurative meaning, amounting essentially to retaliation of any sort. See *avenge, requital*, and the definition of *retortion*.

revengeable (rẹ̄-ven'ja-bl), *a.* [< *revenge* + *-able.*] Capable of or suitable for being revenged. [Rare.]

The buzzard, for he doted more
And dared lesse than reason,
Through blind bace loue induring wrong
Reuengeable in season.
Warner, Albion's England, vii. 342.

revengeance† (rẹ̄-ven'jans), *n.* [Early mod. E. *revengeaunce*; < *revenge* + *-ance*. Cf. *vengeance.*] Revenge; vengeance.

Hee woulde not neglecte to take *reuengeaunce* of so foule an act. *J. Brende*, tr. of Quintus Curtius, fol. 136.

revengeful (rẹ̄-venj'fụl), *a.* [< *revenge* + *-ful.*] 1. Full of revenge or a desire to inflict injury or pain for wrong received; harboring feelings of revenge; vindictive; resentful.

If thy *revengeful* heart cannot forgive,
Lo, here I lend thee this sharp-pointed sword.
Shak., Rich. III., i. 2. 174.

2. Avenging; executing revenge; instrumental to revenge.

'Tis a meritorious fair design
To chase injustice with *revengeful* arms.
Shak., Lucrece, l. 1693.

=**Syn.** 1. Unforgiving, implacable. See *revenge*, *n.*, and *avenge.*

revengefully (rẹ̄-venj'fụl-i), *adv.* In a revengeful manner; by way of revenge; vindictively; with the spirit of revenge.

He smiled *revengefully*, and leapt
Upon the floor; thence gazing at the skies,
His eye-balls fiery red, and glowing vengeance.
Dryden and Lee, Œdipus, v. 1.

revengefulness (rẹ̄-venj'fụl-nes), *n.* The quality of being revengeful; vindictiveness. *Bailey*, 1727.

revengeless (rẹ̄-venj'les), *a.* [< *revenge* + *-less.*] Without revenge; unrevenged. [Rare.]

We, full of heartie teares
For our good father's losse, . . .
Cannot so lightly over-jumpe his death
As leave his woes *revengelesse.*
Marston, Malcontent, iv. 3.

revengement (rẹ̄-venj'ment), *n.* [< *revenge* + *-ment.*] Revenge; retaliation for an injury. [Rare.]

Thinges of honour are so delicate that the same day that any confesseth to haue receiued an iniurie, from that day he bindeth himselfe to take *reuengement.*
Guevara, Letters (tr. by Hellowes, 1577), p. 218.

Murther . . . hath more shapes than Proteus, and will shift himselfe, vppon any occasion of *reuengement*, into a man's dish, his drinke, his apparell, his rings, his stirhops, his nosgay. *Nashe*, Pierce Penilesse, p. 34.

revenger (rẹ̄-ven'jėr), *n.* One who revenges; an avenger.

Now, darting Parthia, art thou struck; and now
Pleased fortune does of Marcus Crassus' death
Make me *revenger.* *Shak.*, A. and C., iii. 1. 3.

revengingly (rẹ̄-ven'jing-li), *adv.* With revenge; with the spirit of revenge; vindictively.

I have belied a lady,
The princess of this country, and the air on 't
Revengingly enfeebles me. *Shak.*, Cymbeline, v. 2. 4.

revenual (rev'ẹ-nụ̈-al), *a.* [< *revenue* + *-al.*] Pertaining to revenue: as, *revenual* expenditure. [Recent and rare.]

Admitting the restraint exercised to be due to a necessary caution in dealing with public funds, . . . the advantages of a more rapid advance might be secured without in the least involving *revenual* risks.
The Engineer, LXVI. 224.

revenue (rev'ẹ-nū, formerly and still occasionally rẹ̄-ven'ū), *n.* [Early mod. E. also *revenew*; < OF. *revenu*, m., also *revenue*, f., F. *revenu*, m. (ML. reflex *revenuta*, f., *revenutum*, n., also *revenuea*, f., also in pure L. form *reventus* and *reventio*), revenue, rent, < *revenu*, pp. of *revenir*, come back, return: see *revenant.* Cf. *avenue, parvenu.*] 1. The annual rents, profits, interest, or issues of any kind of property, real or personal; income.

She bears a duke's *revenues* on her back,
And in her heart she scorns our poverty.
Shak., 2 Hen. VI., i. 3. 83.

One that had more skill how to quaffe a can
Then manage his *revenewes.*
Times' Whistle (E. E. T. S.), p. 64.

I call it [a monastery of the Benedictine monks] . . . rich, because their yearly *revenew* amounteth to one hundred thousand Crowns. *Coryat*, Crudities, I. 177.

2. The annual income of a state, derived from the taxation, customs, excise, or other sources, and appropriated to the payment of the national expenses. [This is now the common meaning of the word, *income* being applied more generally to the rents and profits of individuals.]

The common charity,
Good people's alms and prayers of the gentle,
Is the *revenue* must support my state.
Ford, Perkin Warbeck, v. 1.

A complete power, therefore, to procure a regular and adequate supply of *revenue*, as far as the resources of the community will permit, may be regarded as an indispensable ingredient in every constitution.
A. Hamilton, The Federalist, No. 30.

3. Return; reward.

Neither doe I know any thing wherein a man may more improue the *reuenues* of his learning, or make greater shew with a little, . . . than in this matter of the Creation.
Purchas, Pilgrimage, p. 6.

Inland revenue, in Great Britain and Ireland, internal revenue, derived from excise, stamps, income-tax, and other taxes. The Board of Internal Revenue consists of a chairman, a deputy chairman, and three commissioners.—**Internal revenue**, that part of the revenue or income of a country which is derived from duties on articles manufactured or grown at home, on licenses, stamps, incomes, etc.; all the revenue of a country except that collected from export or import duties. In the United States the principal receipts are from spirits, tobacco, and fermented liquors. During the period of the civil war taxes were imposed on many other manufactures, but they were removed in great part in 1868.—**Revenue cadet, or cadet of the revenue-cutter service**, an officer of the junior grade in the United States revenue marine, undergoing instruction preparatory to examination for the position of third lieutenant. The appointment is made after a competitive examination, to which young men between the ages of 18 and 25 are eligible, by the Secretary of the Treasury. A term of two years' service aboard a practice-vessel is required, which is followed by the examination for promotion.—**Revenue cutter.** See *cutter*[1].—**Revenue-cutter school-ship**, a vessel used for the purpose of instructing cadets in the revenue-cutter service in the duties of their profession, previous to commissioning them as third lieutenants.—**Revenue-cutter service.** See *revenue marine.*—**Revenue ensign**, a distinctive flag, authorized March, 1798, for revenue cutters, to distinguish them from other armed vessels of the United States. Previous to that date, the revenue cutters sailed under the same flag as other United States vessels. The revenue flag is also used over custom-houses. It consists of sixteen vertical stripes of red and white alternately, with a white union in which is a blue eagle carrying in his beak the motto "E pluribus unum," a shield with red and white stripes on his breast, and in his talons a bundle of arrows and a branch of olive, the whole surrounded by a semicircle of thirteen blue stars.—**Revenue law.** See *law*[1].—**Revenue marine, or revenue-cutter service**, a corps organized in 1790, by Alexander Hamilton, then Secretary of the Treasury, for the purpose of guarding the coast and estuaries of the United States for the protection of the customs revenue. During the period of its existence, the duties of the service have necessarily undergone many changes. The corps, combining both civil and military features, is employed in assisting to maintain law and order throughout United States territory.—**Revenue pennant**, a pennant used on revenue vessels in commission, and in the bow of boats when carrying an officer on duty. It is made up of alternate vertical red and white stripes, and has a white field carrying thirteen blue stars. **Revenue tariff.** See *tariff.*—**To defraud the revenue.** See *defraud.* =**Syn.** *Profit*, etc. See *income.*

revenued (rev'ẹ-nūd, formerly rẹ̄-ven'ūd), *a.* [< *revenue* + *-ed*[2].] Endowed with a revenue or income.

Pray resolve me
Why, being a Gentleman of fortunes, meanes,
And well *revenude*, will you adventure thus
A doubtfull voyage.
Heywood, Fair Maid of the West (Works, ed. Pearson, [1874, II. 265).

revenue-officer (rev'ẹ-nū-of"i-sėr), *n.* An officer of the customs or excise.

revert, *n.* An obsolete form of *reaver.*

reverable (rẹ̄-vēr'ạ-bl), *a.* [< *revere* + *-able.*] Worthy of reverence; capable of being revered.

The character of a gentleman is the most *reverable*, the highest of all characters. H. *Brooke*, Fool of Quality, I. 167.

reverb† (rẹ̄-vėrb'), *v. t.* [Erroneously abbr. from *reverberate*: see *reverberate.*] To reverberate. [Rare.]

Nor are those empty-hearted, whose loud sound
Reverbs no hollowness. *Shak.*, Lear, i. 1. 156.

reverberant (rẹ̄-vėr'bėr-ạnt), *a.* [< L. *reverberan(t-)s*, ppr. of *reverberare*, repel: see *reverberate.*] Reverberating; causing reverberation; especially, returning sound; resounding.

Multitudinous echoes awoke and died in the distance,
Over the watery floor, and beneath the *reverberant* branches.
Longfellow, Evangeline, ii. 2.

reverberate (rẹ̄-vėr'bėr-āt), *v.*; pret. and pp. *reverberated*, ppr. *reverberating.* [< L. *reverberatus*, pp. of *reverberare* (> It. *riverberare* = Sp. Pg. *reverberar* = OF. *reverberer*, F. *réverbérer*), beat back, < *re-*, back, + *verberare*, beat: see *verberate.*] I. *trans.* 1†. To beat back; repel; repulse.

This banke . . . serveth in steed of a strong wall to repulse and *reverberate* the violence of the furious waves of the Sea. *Coryat*, Crudities, I. 199.

2. To return, as sound; echo.

Who, like an arch, *reverberates*
The voice again. *Shak.*, T. and C., iii. 3. 120.

3. To turn back; drive back; bend back; reflect: as, to *reverberate* rays of light or heat.—4. Specifically, to deflect (flame or heat) as in a reverberatory furnace.—5†. To reduce by reverberated heat; fuse.

Some of our chymicks facetiously affirm that at the last fire all shall be crystallized and *reverberated* into glass.
Sir T. Browne, Religio Medici, i. 50.

6†. To beat upon; fall upon.

The Sunne . . . goeth continually rounde about in circuite: so that his beames, *reuerberatyng* heauen, repre-

sente suche a maner of lyght as we haue in Sommer two houres before the Sunne ryse.
R. Eden (First Books on America, ed. Arber, p. xlii.).

How still your voice with prudent discipline
My Prentice ear doth oft *reverberate*.
Sylvester, tr. of Du Bartas's Weeks, ii., The Handy-Crafts.

II. *intrans.* **1.** To be driven back or reflected, as light or heat.

For the perpendicular beames reflect and *reuerberate* in themselves, so that the heat is doubled, euery beame striking twice. *Hakluyt's Voyages*, III. 49.

2. To echo; reëcho; resound.

And even at hand a drum is ready braced,
That shall *reverberate* all as well as thine.
Shak., K. John, v. 2. 170.

E'en for a demi-groat this opened soul . . .
Reverberates quick, and sends the tuneful tongue
To lavish music on the rugged walls
Of some dark dungeon. *Shenstone*, Economy, i.

Echoes die off, scarcely *reverberate*
Forever—why should ill keep echoing ill,
And never let our ears have done with noise?
Browning, Ring and Book, II. 27.

3. To apply reverberated heat; use reverberatory agency, as in the fusing of metals.

Sub. Out of that calx I have won the salt of mercury.
Mam. By pouring on your rectified water?
Sub. Yes, and *reverberating* in Athanor.
B. *Jonson*, Alchemist, ii. 1.

=**Syn.** *Recoil*, etc. See *rebound*.

reverberate (rē-vėr'bėr-āt), *a.* [< L. *reverberatus*, pp. of *reverberare*, cast back, repel: see the verb.] **1.** Reverberated; cast back; returned; reflected.

The lofty hills . . .
Sent forth such echoing shouts (which, every way so shrill,
With the *reverberate* sound the spacious air did fill),
That they were easily heard through the Vergivian main.
Drayton, Polyolbion, ix. 58.

2. Reverberant; causing reverberation.

Halloo your name to the *reverberate* hills.
Shak., T. N., i. 5. 291.

I was that bright face,
Reflected by the lake in which thy race
Read mystic lines, which skill Pythagoras
First taught to men by a *reverberate* glass.
B. *Jonson*, Masque of Blackness.

reverberation (rē-vėr-bė-rā'shon), *n.* [< ME. *reverberacioun*, < OF. *reverberation*, F. *réverbération* = Pr. *reverberatio* = Sp. *reverberacion* = Pg. *reverberação* = It. *reverberazione*, *riverberazione*, < L. *reverberare*, pp. *reverberatus*, beat back: see *reverberate*.] **1.** The act of reverberating, or of driving or turning back; particularly, the reflection of sound, light, or heat: now chiefly of sound.

Every soun
Nis but of eir *reverberacioun*.
Chaucer, Summoner's Tale, l. 520.

Also another maner of fier: sette youre vessel forseid to the strong *reuerberacioun* of the sunne in somer tyme, and lete it stonde there nyȝt and day.
Book of Quinte Essence (ed. Furnivall), p. 6.

The days are then very longe in that clime, and hot by reason of contynuall *reuerberation* of the beames of the soonne, and shorte nyghtes.
R. Eden, tr. of Sebastian Cabot (First Books on America, [ed. Arber, p. 287).

In these straights we frequently alighted, now freezing in the snow, and anon frying by the *reverberation* of the sun against the cliffs as we descend lower.
Evelyn, Diary, March 23, 1646.

My tub, which holds fifty-fold thy wisdom, would crack at the *reverberation* of thy voice.
Landor, Diogenes and Plato.

2. Resonance; sympathetic vibration.—**3.** That which is reverberated; reverberated light, heat, or sound: now chiefly sound.

Then through those realms of shade, in multiplied *reverberations*,
Heard he that cry of pain. *Longfellow*, Evangeline, ii. 5.

A . . . shed, . . . in strong contrast to the room, was painted with a red *reverberation*, as from furnace-doors.
R. L. Stevenson, The Dynamiter, p. 56.

4. The circulation of flame in a specially formed furnace, or its deflection toward the hearth of the furnace, as in the reverberatory furnace (which see, under *furnace*).

First ȝe moste the rigt hize erthe of oon hide nature [of vnkinde nature, Harl. 853], in the furneys of glas mon [made, Harl. 853], or ellis *reuerberacioun*, xx]. dayes calcyne. *Book of Quinte Essence* (ed. Furnivall), p. 13.

The evolved heat [in a rotative furnace] is . . . transmitted by *reverberation* and conduction to the mixture of ore, fluxes, and coal. *Ure*, Dict., II. 945.

reverberative (rē-vėr'bėr-ā-tiv), *a.* [< *reverberate* + *-ive*.] Tending to reverberate; reflecting; reverberant.

This *reverberative* influence is what we have intended above as the influence of the mass upon its centres.
I. Taylor.

reverberator (rē-vėr'bėr-ā-tor), *n.* [< *reverberate* + *-or*1.] That which reverberates; especially, that which reflects light; a reflecting lamp.

reverberatory (rē-vėr'bėr-ā-tō-ri), *a.* [= F. *réverbératoire* = Pg. *reverberatorio* = It. *riverberatorio*; as *reverberate* + *-ory*.] **1.** Characterized by or liable to reverberation; tending to reverberate.—**2.** Producing reverberation; acting by reverberation; reverberating: as, a *reverberatory* furnace or kiln. See *reverberation*, 4, and *furnace*, and cut under *puddling-furnace*.

Section of Reverberatory Furnace.

Reverdin's operation. See *operation*.

reverdure† (rē-vėr'dūr), *v. t.* [< *re-* + *verdure*.] To cover again with verdure. [Rare.]

The swete tyme of Marche was come, and the wyndes were apeased, and ye waters awaged of their rages, and the wodes *reverdured*. *Berners*, tr. of Froissart's Chron., II. clix.

revere1 (rē-vēr'), *v. t.*; pret. and pp. *revered*, ppr. *revering*. [< OF. *reverer*, F. *révérer* = It. *reverire*, *riverire*, < L. *revereri*, revere, fear, < *re-*, again, + *vereri*, fear, regard, feel awe of, akin to E. *ware*1.] To regard with deepest respect and awe; venerate; reverence; hold in great honor or high esteem.

Whose word is truth, as sacred and *revered*
As Heaven's own oracles from altars heard.
Pope, Imit. of Horace, II. i. 27.

I see men of advanced life, whom from infancy I have been taught to *revere*.
D. Webster, Speech at Concord, Sept. 30, 1834.

The war-god of the Mexicans (originally a conqueror), the most *revered* of all their gods, had his idol fed with human flesh. *H. Spencer*, Prin. of Sociol., § 259.

=**Syn.** *Worship*, *Reverence*, etc. See *adore*1.

revere2**†**, *n.* A Middle English form of *river*2.

reverence (rev'ẹ-rens), *n.* [< ME. *reverence*, < OF. *reverence*, F. *révérence* = Pr. *reverencia*, *reverensa* = Sp. Pg. *reverencia* = It. *reverenza*, *riverenza*, < L. *reverentia*, reverence, < *reveren(t-)s*, reverent: see *reverent*.] **1.** A feeling of mingled awe, respect, and admiration; veneration; esteem heightened by awe, as of a superior; reverent regard; especially, such a feeling toward deity.

They haue in more *reuerence* the triumphes of Petrarche than the Genesis of Moses.
Ascham, The Scholemaster, p. 82.

With what authority did he [Jesus] both speak and live, such as commanded a *reverence*, where it did not beget a love! *Stillingfleet*, Sermons, I. vi.

With all *reverence* I would say,
Let God do his work, we will see to ours.
Whittier, Abraham Davenport.

Reverence we may define as the feeling which accompanies the recognition of Superiority or Worth in others.
H. Sidgwick, Methods of Ethics, p. 225.

2. The outward manifestation of reverent feeling; respect, esteem, or honor, as shown by conduct. See *to do reverence*, below.

They give him the *reverence* of a master.
Sandys, Travailes, p. 52.

Honour due and *reverence* none neglects.
Milton, P. L., iii. 738.

3. An act or token of reverence. Specifically—(*a*) A bow; a courtesy; an obeisance.

The lamentation was so great that was made through out Spaine for the death of this good King Alonso that from thence forwarde euery time that any named his name, if he were a man he put off his cap, and if a woman she made a *reuerence*.
Guevara, Letters (tr. by Hellowes, 1577), p. 330.

With a low submissive *reverence*
Say, "What is it your honour will command?"
Shak., T. of the S., Ind., i. 53.

(*b*) The use of a phrase indicating respect. See *save your reverence*, below.

Not to be pronounced
In any lady's presence without a *reverence*.
B. *Jonson*, Tale of a Tub, i. 4.

4. Reverend character; worthiness of respect and esteem.

With him are the Lord Aumerle, Lord Salisbury,
Sir Stephen Scroop, besides a clergyman
Of holy *reverence*. *Shak.*, Rich. II., iii. 3. 29.

Hence—**5.** With a possessive personal pronoun, a title of respect, applied particularly to a clergyman.

Will Av'rice and Concupiscence give place,
Charm'd by the sounds—Your *Rev'rence*, or Your Grace?
Cowper, Progress of Error, l. 106.

Quoth I, "Your *reverence*, I believe you're safe."
Crabbe, Works, I. 134.

6†. Precedence; preëminence.

And some knyght is wedded to a lady of royal blode; she shal kepe the estate that she was before. And a lady of lower degree shal kepe the estate of her lordes blode, & therefore the royall blode shall haue the *reuerence*, as I haue shewed you here before.
Babees Book (E. E. T. S.), p. 285.

At the reverence of†, out of respect or regard for.

But I praye yow *at the reuerence of* God that ye hem now departe. *Merlin* (E. E. T. S.), iii. 492.

And, my Lord, hyt were to grete a thyng, and hyte laye yn my power, but y wold do *at the reverens of* your Lordschyp, yn las than hyt schold hurt me to gretly, wyche y wote wel your Lordschyp wol nevyr desyr.
Paston Letters, I. 75.

Save or **saving your reverence**, with all due respect to you: a phrase used to excuse an offensive expression or statement: sometimes contracted to *sir-reverence*.

To run away from the Jew, I should be ruled by the fiend, who, *saving your reverence*, is the devil himself.
Shak., M. of V., ii. 2. 27.

This Natatile Beet . . . grows in wet, stinking Places, and thrives no where so well as in Mud, or a Dunghill, *saving your Reverence*.
N. Bailey, tr. of Colloquies of Erasmus, II. 148.

To do reverence, to make reverence; show respect; do honor; specifically, to do homage; make a bow or obeisance.

Ech of hem doth al his diligence
To doon unto the feste *reverence*.
Chaucer, Clerk's Tale, l. 140.

"Apparaile the propirli," quod Pride, . . .
"Do no *reuerence* to foole ne wise."
Hymns to Virgin, etc. (E. E. T. S.), p. 62.

But yesterday the word of Cæsar might
Have stood against the world; now lies he there,
And none so poor to do him *reverence*.
Shak., J. C., iii. 2. 125.

To make reverence†, to perform an act of worship; worship.

Seynt John stered in his Modres Wombe, and *made reverence* to his Creatour, that he saughe not.
Mandeville, Travels, p. 94.

=**Syn. 1.** *Awe, Veneration, Reverence.* *Reverence* is nearly equivalent to *veneration*, but expresses something less of the same emotion. It differs from *awe* in that it is not akin to the feeling of fear, dread, or terror, while also implying a certain amount of love or affection. We feel *reverence* for a parent and for an upright magistrate, but we stand in *awe* of a tyrant.

reverence (rev'ẹ-rens), *v. t.*; pret. and pp. *reverenced*, ppr. *reverencing*. [< ME. *reverencen*, < OF. *reverencer*, *reverencier* = Sp. Pg. *reverenciar* = It. *riverenziare*, reverence, make a reverence; from the noun.] **1.** To regard with reverence; look upon with awe and esteem; respect deeply; venerate.

Those that I *reverence* those I fear, the wise.
Shak., Cymbeline, iv. 2. 95.

They too late *reverence* their advisers, as deep, foreseeing, and faithful prophets.
Bacon, Moral Fables, v., Expl.

The laws became ineffectual to restrain men who no longer *reverenced* justice.
C. E. Norton, Church-building in Middle Ages, p. 104.

2. To do reverence to; treat with respect; pay respect to; specifically, to salute with a reverence, bow, or obeisance.

Ich a-roos vp ryght with that and *reuerencede* hym fayre,
And yf hus wil were he wolde hus name telle?
Piers Plowman (C), xiv. 248.

Reuerence thi felawis; bigynne with hem no strijf;
To thi power kepe pees al thi lijf.
Babees Book (E. E. T. S.), p. 31.

Nor wanted at his end
The dark retinue *reverencing* death
At golden thresholds.
Tennyson, Aylmer's Field.

=**Syn. 1.** *Worship*, *Revere*, etc. See *adore*1.

reverencer (rev'ẹ-ren-sėr), *n.* [< *reverence* + *-er*1.] One who feels or displays reverence.

The Athenians, . . . quite sunk in their affairs, . . . were becoming great *reverencers* of crowned heads.
Swift, Nobles and Commons, ii.

reverend (rev'ẹ-rend), *a.* [= OF. *reverent*, F. *révérend* = Pr. *reverent* = Sp. Pg. It. *reverendo*, < L. *reverendus*, gerundive of *revereri*, revere: see *revere*1.] **1.** Worthy to be revered; worthy of reverence; entitled to veneration, esteem, or respect, by reason of one's character or sacred office, as a minister of religion; especially, deserving of respect or consideration on account of age; venerable.

If ancient sorrow be most *reverend*,
Give mine the benefit of seniory.
Shak., Rich. III., iv. 4. 35.

He is within, with two right *reverend* fathers,
Divinely bent to meditation.
Shak., Rich. III., iii. 7. 61.

His [Prosdocimus's] statue is made in free stone, . . . having a long *reverend* beard. *Coryat*, Crudities, I. 185.

At length a *reverend* sire among them came.
Milton, P. L., xi. 719.

The Duchess marked his weary pace,
His timid mien, and *reverend* face.
Scott, L. of L. M., Int.

I past beside the *reverend* walls
In which of old I wore the gown.
Tennyson, In Memoriam, lxxxvii.

2. Specifically, a title of respect given to clergymen or ecclesiastics: as, *Reverend* (or the *Reverend*) John Smith. In the Anglican Church deans are styled *very reverend*, bishops *right reverend*, and archbishops (also the Bishop of Meath) *most reverend*. In the Roman Catholic Church the members of the religious orders are also styled *reverend*, the superiors being styled *reverend fathers* or *reverend mothers*, as the case may be. In Scotland the principals of the universities, if clergymen, and the moderator of the General Assembly for the time being, are styled *very reverend*. Abbreviated *Rev.* (also, *the Rev.*) when used with the name of an individual.

The *reverend* gentleman was equipped in a buzzwig, upon the top of which was an equilateral cocked hat.
Scott, Antiquary, xvii.

3. Of or pertaining to ecclesiastics, or to the clerical office or profession.

Carlisle, this is your doom:
Choose out some secret place, some *reverend* room,
More than thou hast, and with it joy thy life.
Shak., Rich. II., v. 6. 25.

With all his humour and high spirits he [Sydney Smith] had always, as he said himself, fashioned his manners and conversation so as not to bring discredit on his *reverend* profession.
Encyc. Brit., XXII. 178.

4†. Reverent. [A misuse formerly common.]

With a joy
As *reverend* as religion can make man's,
I will embrace this blessing.
Middleton, The Witch, iv. 2.

Where-e'er you walk'd Trees were as *reverend* made
As when of old Gods dwelt in ev'ry shade.
Cowley, The Mistress, Spring.

There are, I find, to be in it [the drama] all the *reverend* offices of life (such as regard to parents, husbands, and honourable lovers), preserved with the utmost care.
Steele, Tatler, No. 182.

reverendly† (rev'ẹ-rend-li), *adv.* [< *reverend* + *-ly*[2].] Reverently.

Others ther be
Which doe indeed esteem more *reverendlie*
Of the Lords Supper.
Times' Whistle (E. E. T. S.), p. 18.

I am not the first ass, sir,
Has borne good office, and perform'd it *reverendly*.
Fletcher (*and another?*), Prophetess, i. 3.

reverent (rev'ẹ-rent), *a.* [< ME. *reverent*, < OF. *reverent* = Sp. Pg. *reverente* = It. *riverente*, *reverente*, < L. *reveren(t-)s*, ppr. of *revereri*, revere: see *revere*[1].] 1. Feeling or displaying reverence; impressed with veneration or deep respect; standing in awe with admiration, as before superior age, worth, capacity, power, or achievement.

Lowly *reverent*
Towards either throne they bow.
Milton, P. L., iii. 349.

The most awful, living, *reverent* frame I ever felt or beheld, I must say, was his [George Fox's] in prayer.
Penn, Rise and Progress of Quakers, v.

O sacred weapon! left for Truth's defence, . . .
Reverent I touch thee, but with honest zeal.
Pope, Epil. to Satires, ii. 216.

I have known
Wise and grave men, who . . .
Were *reverent* learners in the solemn school
Of Nature.
Bryant, Old Man's Counsel.

2. Proceeding from or characteristic of reverence; expressive of veneration or profound respect and awe: as, *reverent* conduct; a *reverent* attitude toward religious questions.

The *reverent* care I bear unto my lord
Made me collect these dangers in the duke.
Shak., 2 Hen. VI., iii. 1. 34.

3†. Reverend. [A misuse formerly common: compare *reverend*, 4.]

And I beseche your [mastership] that this sympil skrowe may recomaund me to my *reverant* and worshipful maistres your moder.
Paston Letters, I. 55.

A very *reverent* body; ay, such a one as a man may not speak of without he say, "sir-reverence."
Shak., C. of E., iii. 2. 91.

Yet, with good honest cut-throat usury,
I fear he'll mount to *reverent* dignity.
Marston, Scourge of Villanie, v. 67.

4. Strong; undiluted: noting liquors. *Trans. Amer. Philol. Ass.*, XVII. 46. [Local, U. S.]

reverential (rev-ẹ-ren'shal), *a.* [< OF. *reverential*, F. *révérenciel* = Sp. Pg. *reverencial* = It. *reverenziale*, *riverenziale*, < ML. *reverentialis*, reverential, < L. *reverentia*, reverence: see *reverence*.] Characterized by or expressive of reverence; humbly respectful; reverent.

Their *reverential* heads did all incline,
And render meek obeysance unto mine.
J. Beaumont, Psyche, i. 91.

All, all look up, with *reverential* awe,
At crimes that 'scape or triumph o'er the law.
Pope, Epil. to Satires, i. 167.

Rapt in *reverential* awe,
I sate obedient, in the fiery prime
Of youth, self-govern'd, at the feet of Law.
M. Arnold, Mycerinus.

reverentially (rev-ẹ-ren'shal-i), *adv.* In a reverential manner; with reverence.

reverently (rev'ẹ-rent-li), *adv.* [< ME. **reverently*, *reverentliche*; < *reverent* + *-ly*[2].] In a reverent manner; with reverence; with awe and deep respect.

Thauh he be here thyn vnderling, in heuene, parraunter,
He worth rather receyued and *reuerentloker* sette.
Piers Plowman (C), ix. 44.

Read the same diligently and *reverently* with prayer.
J. Bradford, Letters (Parker Soc., 1853), II. 9.

Chide him for faults, and do it *reverently*.
Shak., 2 Hen. IV., iv. 4. 37.

reverer (rẹ̄-vēr'ėr), *n.* [< *revere*[1] + *-er*[1].] One who reveres or venerates.

The Jews were such scrupulous *reverers* of them [the divine revelations] that it was the business of the Masorites to number not only the sections and lines, but even the words and letters of the Old Testament.
Government of the Tongue.

revergence (rẹ-vėr'jẹns), *n.* [< LL. *revergen(t-)s*, ppr. of *revergere*, incline toward, < L. *re-*, back, + *vergere*, bend, incline: see *verge*.] A tending toward a certain character. [Rare.]

The evernioid *revergence* of this subdivision is observable also in Parmelia perforata.
E. Tuckerman, Genera Lichenum, p. 22.

reverie, revery (rev'ẹ-ri or -rē), *n.*; pl. *reveries* (-riz). [Formerly also *resvery*; < OF. *resverie*, F. *rêverie*, delirium, raving, dream, day-dream, < *resver*, *rever*, also *raver*, F. dial. *raver*, > E. *rave*: see *rave*[1]. Cf. *ravery*.] 1. A state of mental abstraction in which more or less aimless fancy predominates over the reasoning faculty; dreamy meditation; fanciful musing. The mind may be occupied, according to the age, tastes, or pursuits of the individual, by calculations, by profound metaphysical speculations, by fanciful visions, or by such trifling and transitory objects as to make no impression on consciousness, so that the period of reverie is left an entire blank in the memory. The most obvious external feature marking this state is the apparent unconsciousness or imperfect perception of external objects.

When ideas float in our mind without any reflection or regard of the understanding, it is that which the French call *reverie*; our language has scarce a name for it.
Locke, Human Understanding, II. xix. 1.

Dream-forger, I refill thy cup
With *reverie's* wasteful pittance up.
Lowell, To C. F. Bradford.

In *reverie*, and even in understanding the communications of others, we are comparatively passive spectators of ideational movements, non-voluntarily determined.
J. Ward, Encyc. Brit., XX. 75.

2. A waking dream; a brown study; an imaginative, fanciful, or fantastic train of thought; a day-dream.

Defend me, therefore, common sense, say I,
From *reveries* so airy, from the toil
Of dropping buckets into empty wells,
And growing old in drawing nothing up!
Cowper, Task, iii. 188.

3. The object or product of reverie or idle fancy; a visionary scheme, plan, aim, ideal, or the like; a dream.

The principle of asceticism seems originally to have been the *reverie* of certain hasty speculators, who . . . took occasion to quarrel with every thing that offered itself under the name of pleasure.
Bentham, Introd. to Morals and Legislation, ii. 9.

4. In *music*, an instrumental composition of a vague and dreamy character.

reverist (rev'ẹ-rist), *n.* [< *reverie* + *-ist*.] One who is sunk in a reverie; one who indulges in or gives way to reverie. *Chambers's Encyc.*

Their religion consisted in a kind of sleepy, vaporous ascension of the thoughts into the ideal. They were *reverists*, idealists.
H. W. Beecher, Plymouth Pulpit, March 19, 1854, p. 483.

revers[1]†, *a.* An obsolete form of *reverse*.

revers[2] (rė-vãr', commonly rẹ̄-vēr'), *n.* [F.: see *reverse*.] In *dressmaking*, *tailoring*, etc.: (*a*) That part of a garment which is turned back so as to show what would otherwise be the inner surface, as the lapel of a waistcoat or the cuff of a sleeve. (*b*) The stuff used to cover or face such a turned-over surface, as a part of the lining exposed to view.

reversability (rẹ̄-vėr-sạ-bil'ị-ti), *n.* [< *reversable* + *-ity* (see *-bility*).] Same as *reversibility*.

reversable (rẹ̄-vėr'sạ-bl), *a.* [< *reverse* + *-able*.] Same as *reversible*.

reversal (rẹ̄-vėr'sạl), *n.* and *a.* [< F. *réversal*; as *reverse* + *-al*.] I. *n.* 1. The act of reversing, or of altering a position, direction, action, condition, or state to its opposite or contrary; also, the state of being reversed.

Time gives his hour-glass
Its due *reversal*;
Their hour is gone.
M. Arnold, Consolation.

It is assumed as possible that the astronomical conditions might be reversed without a *reversal* of the physical conditions.
J. Croll, Climate and Cosmology, p. 105.

2. In *physics*, specifically, the changing of a bright line in a spectrum, produced by an incandescent vapor, into a dark line (by absorption), and the reverse. The reversal of lines in the solar spectrum has been observed at the time of a total eclipse, when certain of the dark absorption-lines have suddenly become bright lines as the light from the body of the sun has been cut off. See *spectrum*.

3. The act of repealing, revoking, or annulling; a change or overthrowing: as, the *reversal* of a judgment, which amounts to an official declaration that it is erroneous and rendered void or terminated; the *reversal* of an attainder or of an outlawry.

She [Elizabeth] began her reign, of course, by a *reversal* of her sister's legislation; but she did not restore the Edwardian system. *Stubbs*, Medieval and Modern Hist., p. 323.

4. In *biol.*, reversion.—**Method of reversal.** See *method*.

II.† *a.* Causing, intending, or implying reverse action; reversing.

After his death there were *reversal* letters found among his papers. *Bp. Burnet*, Hist. Own Times, Charles II.

reversatile (rẹ̄-vėr'sạ-til), *a.* [< LL. *reversatus*, pp. of *reversare*, reverse, + *-ile*.] Reversible; capable of being reversed.

reverse (rẹ̄-vėrs'), *v.*; pret. and pp. *reversed*, ppr. *reversing*. [< ME. *reversen*, < OF. *reverser*, F. *reverser*, reverse, = Pr. *reversar* = Sp. *reversar*, *revesar*, *revezar*, vomit, = Pg. *revessar*, alternate, = It. *riversare*, upset, pour out, < LL. *reversare*, turn about, turn back, freq. of L. *revertere*, turn back, revert: see *revert*.] I. *trans.* 1. To turn about, around, or upside down; put in an opposite or contrary position; turn in an opposite direction, or through 180°; invert.

In her the stream of mild
Maternal nature had *revers'd* its course.
Cowper, Task, iii. 436.

Revers'd that spear, redoubtable in war.
Burns, Death of Sir J. H. Blair.

2. In *mach.*, to cause to revolve or act in a contrary direction; give an exactly opposite motion or action to, as the crank of an engine, or that part to which the piston-rod is attached.—3. In general, to alter to the opposite; change diametrically the state, relations, or bearings of.

With what tyranny custom governs men! It makes that reputable in one age which was a vice in another, and *reverses* even the distinctions of good and evil.
Dr. J. Rogers.

He that seem'd our counterpart at first
Soon shows the strong similitude *revers'd*.
Cowper, Tirocinium, l. 443.

4. To overturn; upset; throw into confusion.

Puzzling contraries confound the whole;
Or affectations quite *reverse* the soul.
Pope, Moral Essays, i. 66.

5. To overthrow; set aside; make void; annul; repeal; revoke: as, to *reverse* a judgment, sentence, or decree.

Yf the procés be erroneous, lete his concell *reverse* it.
Paston Letters, I. 125.

Is Clarence dead? The order was *reversed*.
Shak., Rich. III., ii. 1. 86.

When judgment pronounced upon conviction is falsified or *reversed*, all former proceedings are absolutely set aside, and the party stands as if he had never been at all accused.
Blackstone, Com., IV. xxx.

6†. To turn back; drive away; banish.

That old Dame said many an idle verse,
Out of her daughters hart fond fancies to *reverse*.
Spenser, F. Q., III. ii. 48.

7†. To cause to return; bring back; recall.

Well knowing trew all that he did reherse,
And to his fresh remembraunce did *reverse*
The ugly vew of his deformed crimes.
Spenser, F. Q., I. ix. 48.

Reversing counter-shaft. See *counter-shaft*.—**Reversing engine**, an engine provided with reversing valve-gear, by which it may be made to turn in either direction. Such engines are used on railways, for marine propulsion, in rolling-mills, and for other purposes. Compare *reversing-gear*.—**Reversing key.** See *telegraph*.—**To reverse a battery or current**, to turn the current in direction, as by means of a commutator or pole-changer. = **Syn.** 1. To invert.—5. To rescind, countermand.

II. *intrans.* 1. To change position, direction, motion, or action to the opposite; specifically, in round dances, to turn or revolve in a direction contrary to that previously taken: as, to *reverse* in waltzing.—2†. To be overturned; fall over.

The kyng presid fast away certayn,
Generides helde still the reane alway;
And so, betwix the striving of them twayn,
The horse *reversid* bak, and ther he lay.
Generydes (E. E. T. S.), l. 3476.

And happed that Boydas and Braundalis mette hym bothe attonys, and smote hym so on the shelde that he *reversed* on his horse croupe. *Merlin* (E. E. T. S.), iii. 551.

3†. To turn back; return; come back.

Boene they all dead, and laide in dolefull herse,
Or doen they onely sleepe, and shall againe reverse?
Spenser, F. Q., III. iv. 1.

reverse (rē-vėrs'), *a.* and *n.* [< ME. *reverse*, *revers*, < OF. *revers*, reverse, cross (as a noun *revers*, a back blow), = Pr. *revers* = Sp. Pg. *reverso* = It. *riverso*, < L. *reversus*, turned back, reversed, pp. of *revertere*, turn back, reverse: see *revert*.] **I.** *a.* **1.** Turned backward; opposite or contrary in position or direction; reversed: as, the *reverse* end of a lance; *reverse* curves; *reverse* motion.

The sword
Of Michael, . . . with swift wheel *reverse*, deep entering, shared
All his right side. *Milton*, P. L., vi. 326.

Two points are said to be *reverse* of each other, with reference to two fixed origins and two fixed axes, when the line through the first origin and the first point meets the first axis at the point where the line through the second origin and the second point meets the same axis, while the line through the first origin and the second point meets the second axis at the same point where the line through the second origin and the first point meets the same axis.

2. Contrary or opposite in nature, effects, or relations: as, a *reverse* order or method.

A vice *revers* unto this. *Gower*, Conf. Amant., ii.

He was troubled with a disease *reverse* to that called the stinging of the tarantula, and would run dog-mad at the noise of music. *Swift*, Tale of a Tub, xi.

3†. Overturned; overthrown.

Whan the kynge that was called le roy de Cent Chivalers saugh the kynge Tradelyuaunt *reuerse* to the erthe, he was right wroth, for he hym loved with grete love. *Merlin* (E. E. T. S.), ii. 157.

4†. Upset; tossed about; thrown into confusion.

He found the sea diuerse,
With many a windy storme *reverse*.
Gower, Conf. Amant., vi.

5. In *conch.*, same as *reversed*, 5.—**Reverse artillery fire.** See *fire*, 13.—**Reverse aspect** or **view**, in *entom.*, the appearance of an insect or any part of it when the posterior extremity is toward the observer.—**Reverse battery, current†, fault.** See the nouns.—**Reverse bearing**, in *surv.*, the bearing of a course taken from the course in advance, looking backward.—**Reverse curve**, in *rail.*, a double curve formed of two curves lying in opposite directions, like the letter S.—**Reverse imitation**, in *contrapuntal music*, imitation by inversion. See *inversion* (c), and *imitation*, 3.—**Reverse-jaw chuck.** See *chuck*4.—**Reverse motion**, in *music*, same as *contrary motion* (which see, under *motion*, 14 (*b*)).—**Reverse proof**, in *engraving*, a counter-proof.—**Reverse shell**, in *conch.*, a univalve shell which has the aperture opening on the left side when placed point upward in front of the spectator, or which has its volutions the reverse way of the common screw; a sinistral shell. The cut shows the reverse shell of *Chrysodomus antiquus*, variety *contrarius*.—**Reverse valve.** See *valve*.

Reverse Shell.

II. *n.* **1.** Reversal; a change to an opposite form, state, or condition; a complete alteration.

This pleasant and speedy *revers* of the former wordes holpe all the matter againe. *Puttenham*, Arte of Eng. Poesie, p. 231.

Base passion! said I, turning myself about, as a man naturally does upon a sudden *reverse* of sentiment. *Sterne*, Sentimental Journey, p. 17.

2. A complete change or turn of affairs; a vicissitude; a change of fortune, particularly for the worse; hence, adverse fortune; a misfortune; a calamity or blow; a defeat.

Violence, unless it escapes the *reverses* and changes of things by untimely death, is commonly unprosperous in the issue. *Bacon*, Moral Fables, vii., Expl.

My belief of this induces me to hope . . . that the same goodness will still be exercised toward me, in continuing . . . happiness, or enabling me to bear a fatal *reverse*. *B. Franklin*, Autobiography, p. 4.

3. In *fencing*, a back-handed stroke; a blow from a direction contrary to that usually taken; a thrust from left to right. [Obsolete or obsolescent.]

To see thee pass thy punto, thy stock, thy *reverse*, thy distance, thy montant. *Shak.*, M. W. of W., ii. 3. 27.

4. That which is presented when anything, as a lance, gun, etc., is reversed, or turned in the direction opposite to what is considered its natural position.

Any knight proposing to combat might . . . select a special antagonist from among the challengers, by touching his shield. If he did so with the *reverse* of his lance, the trial of skill was made with . . . the arms of courtesy. *Scott*, Ivanhoe, viii.

5. That which is directly opposite or contrary; the contrary; the opposite: generally with *the*.

"Out of wo in-to wele youre wyrdes shul chaunge."
Ac who so redeth of the riche *the reuers* he may fynde.
Piers Plowman (C), xiii. 210.

He . . . then mistook *reverse* of wrong for right.
Pope, Moral Essays, iii. 198.

They are called the Constituent Assembly. Never was a name less appropriate. They were not constituent, but *the* very *reverse* of constituent. *Macaulay*, Mirabeau.

6. In *numis.*, the back or inferior side of a coin or medal, as opposed to the *obverse*, the face or principal side. The reverse generally displays a design or an inscription; the obverse, a head. Usually abbreviated *Rev.* or ℞. See cuts under *numismatics*, *pie*6, and *pistole*.

A *reverse* often clears up the passage of an old poet, as the poet often serves to unriddle a *reverse*.
Addison, Ancient Medals, i.

7. In *her.*, the exact contrary of what has been described just before as an escutcheon or a quartering. An early form of heraldic difference is the giving to a younger branch the reverse of the arms of the elder branch: thus, if the original escutcheon is argent a chevron gules, a younger son takes the *reverse*, namely gules a chevron argent.

reversed (rē-vėrst'), *p. a.* **1.** Turned in a contrary or opposite position, direction, order, or state to that which is normal or usual; reverse; upside down; inside out; hind part before.

In all superstition wise men follow fools; and arguments are fitted to practice in a *reversed* order.
Bacon, Superstition.

And on the gibbet tree *reversed*
His foeman's scutcheon tied.
Scott, Marmion, i. 12.

2. Made void; overthrown or annulled: as, a *reversed* judgment or decree.—**3.** In *geol.*, noting strata which have been so completely overturned by crust-movements that older beds overlie those more recent, or occupy a reversed position.—**4.** In *bot.*, of flowers, resupinate (*Bigelow*); of leaves, having the lower surface turned upward (*Imp. Dict.*).—**5.** In *conch.*, sinistral, sinistrorse, or sinistrorsal; turning to the left; reverse; heterostrophic. See cut under *reverse*.—**6.** In *her.*, facing in a position the contrary of its usual position: said of any bearing which has a well-defined position on the escutcheon: thus, a chevron *reversed* is one which issues from the top of the escutcheon, and has its point downward. Also *renverse*, *reversie*.—**Gutté reversed.** See *gutté*.—**Regardant reversed.** See *regardant*.—**Reversed arch.** See *arch*1.—**Reversed motion**, in *music*, contrary motion. See *motion*, 14 (*b*).—**Reversed ogee.** See *ogee*.—**Reversed retrograde imitation**, in *contrapuntal music*, retrograde imitation by inversion, the subject or theme being repeated both backward and in contrary motion.—**Reversed wings**, in *entom.*, wings which are deflexed in repose, the upper wings lying closer to the body than the lower ones, which project beyond their anterior margins, as in certain *Lepidoptera*.

reversedly† (rē-vėr'sed-li), *adv.* Same as *reversely*. *Bp. Lowth*, Life of Wykeham, ix.

reverseless (rē-vėrs'les), *a.* [< *reverse* + *-less*.] Not to be reversed; unalterable.

E'en now thy lot shakes in the urn, whence Fate
Throws her pale edicts in *reverseless* doom!
A. Seward, To the Hon. T. Erskine.

reverse-lever (rē-vėrs'lev"ėr), *n.* In a steam-engine, a lever or handle which operates the valve-gear so as to reverse the action of the steam.

reversely (rē-vėrs'li), *adv.* **1.** In a reverse position, direction, or order.

Lourens . . . began to shape beechen bark first into figures of letters, by which, *reversely* impressed one by one on paper, he composed one or two lines to serve as an example. *Encyc. Brit.*, XXIII. 681.

2. On the other hand; on the contrary.

That is properly credible which is not . . . certainly to be collected, either antecedently by its cause, or *reversely* by its effect; and yet . . . hath the attestation of a truth.
Bp. Pearson, Expos. of Creed, i.

reverser (rē-vėr'sėr), *n.* **1.** One who reverses; that which causes reversal; specifically, a device for reversing or changing the direction of an electric current or the sign of an electrostatic charge.—**2.** In *law*, a reversioner.—**3.** In *Scots law*, a mortgagor of land.

reversi (rē-vėr'si), *n.* [OF. and F.: see *reversis*.] **1.** Same as *reversis*.—**2.** A modern game played by two persons with sixty-four counters, differently colored on opposite sides, on a board of sixty-four squares. A player, on placing a counter on a vacant square, "reverses" (that is, turns over, and thus appropriates) all his opponent's pieces lying in unbroken line in any direction between the piece thus placed and any other of his own pieces already on the board. A counter cannot be removed from its square, but may be reversed again and again.

reversibility (rē-vėr-si-bil'i-ti), *n.* [= F. *réversibilité* = It. *riversibilità*; as *reversible* + *-ity* (see *-bility*).] The property of being reversible; the capability of being reversed. Also *reversability*.

Reversibility is the sole test of perfection; so that all heat-engines, whatever be the working substance, provided only they be reversible, convert into work (under given circumstances) the same fraction of the heat supplied to them. *P. G. Tait*, Encyc. Brit., XXIII. 284.

reversible (rē-vėr'si-bl), *a.* and *n.* [= F. *réversible* = Sp. *reversible* = Pg. *reversivel* = It. *riversibile*; as *reverse* + *-ible*.] **I.** *a.* Capable of being reversed. Specifically—(*a*) Admitting, as a process, of change so that all the successive positions shall be reached in the contrary order and in the same intervals of time; thus, if the first process converts heat into work the second converts work into heat, and the like will be true of any other transformation of energy, form, state of aggregation, etc. See *reversible process*, below.

Although work can be transformed into heat with the greatest ease, there is no process known by which all the heat can be changed back again into work: . . . in fact, the process is not a *reversible* one.
W. L. Carpenter, Energy in Nature (1st ed.), p. 56.

(*b*) Admitting of legal reversal or annulment.

If the judgement be given by him that hath authority, and it be erroneous, it was at common law *reversible* by writ of error. *Sir M. Hale*, Hist. Pleas of the Crown, xxvi.

(*c*) Capable of being reversed, or of being used or shown with either side exposed: as, *reversible* cloth. Also *reversable*.—**Doubly reversible polyhedron.** See *polyhedron*.—**Reversible compressor, filter, lock.** See the nouns.—**Reversible engine.** See *Carnot's cycle*, under *cycle*1.—**Reversible factors**, commutable or interchangeable factors, as those of ordinary multiplication.—**Reversible pedal, plow**, etc. See the nouns.—**Reversible pendulum.** See *pendulum*, 2.—**Reversible process**, in *dynam.*, a motion which might, under the influence of the same forces, take place in either of two opposite directions, the different bodies running over precisely the same paths, with the same velocities, the directions only being reversed.

II. *n.* A textile fabric having two faces, either of which may be exposed; a reversible fabric. Reversibles usually have the two faces unlike, one of them being often striped or plaided while the other is plain.

reversibly (rē-vėr'si-bli), *adv.* In a reversible manner.

reversie (rē-vėr'si), *a.* [< OF. *reverse*, pp. of *reverser*, reverse: see *reverse*.] In *her.*, same as *reversed*, 6.

reversing-cylinder (rē-vėr'sing-sil"in-dėr), *n.* The cylinder of a small auxiliary steam-engine used to move the link or other reversing-gear of a large steam-engine, when the latter is too large to be quickly and easily operated by the hand: now much used in marine engines.

reversing-gear (rē-vėr'sing-gēr), *n.* Those parts of a steam-engine, particularly of a locomotive or marine engine, by which the direction of the motion is changed: a general term covering all such parts of the machine, including the reversing-lever, eccentrics, link-motion, and valves of the cylinders. The most widely used reversing-gear is that employing the link-motion. There are, however, many other forms in use. See *valve-gear*, *steam-engine*, and *locomotive*.

reversing-layer (rē-vėr'sing-lā"ėr), *n.* A hypothetical thin stratum of the solar atmosphere, containing in gaseous form the substances whose presence is shown by the dark lines of the solar spectrum, and supposed to be the seat of the absorption which produces the dark lines. The spectrum of this stratum, if it exists, must be one of bright lines—the negative of the ordinary solar spectrum—and should be seen at the moment when a solar eclipse becomes total. The observation of such a bright-line spectrum, first made by Professor C. A. Young in 1870, and since repeated more or less completely by several eclipse observers, led to the hypothesis. It still remains doubtful, however, whether all the Fraunhofer lines originate in such a thin stratum, or whether different regions of the solar atmosphere coöperate in their formation.

reversing-lever (rē-vėr'sing-lev"ėr), *n.* In a steam-engine, a lever which operates the slide-valve so as to reverse the action of the steam and thus change the direction of motion.

reversing-machine (rē-vėr'sing-ma-shēn"), *n.* In *founding*, a molding-machine in which the flask is carried on trunnions, so that it can be reversed and the sand rammed from either side.

reversing-motion (rē-vėr'sing-mō"shon), *n.* Any mechanism for changing the direction of motion of an engine or a machine. A common device of this nature for a steam-engine is a rock-shaft to operate the valves, having, on opposite sides, two levers to either of which may be connected the rod from an eccentric on the main shaft. The most usual form of reversing-motion for a locomotive is the link-motion.

reversing-shaft (rē-vėr'sing-shaft), *n.* A shaft connected with the valves of a steam-engine in such a manner as to permit a reversal of the order of steam-passage through the ports.

reversing-valve (rē-vėr'sing-valv), *n.* The valve of a reversing-cylinder. It is often a plain slide-valve, but in some forms of steam reversing-gear piston-valves have been used. See *reversing-cylinder*.

reversion (rē-vėr'shon), *n.* [Formerly also *revertion*; < OF. *reversion*, F. *réversion* = Pr. *reversio* = Sp. *reversion* = Pg. *reversão* = It. *riversione*, < L. *reversio(n-)*, < *revertere*, turn back: see *revert*, *reverse*.] **1.** The act of reverting or returning to a former position, state, frame of mind, subject, etc.; return; recurrence.

After his *reversion* home [he] was spoiled also of all that he brought with him. *Foxe*, Acts, etc., p. 152.

2. In *biol.*: (*a*) Return to some ancestral type or plan; exhibition of ancestral characters;

atavism; specifically, in botany, the conversion of organs proper to the summit or center of the floral axis into those which belong lower down, as stamens into petals, etc. Also *reversal*.

The simple brain of a microcephalous idiot, in as far as it resembles that of an ape, may in this sense be said to offer a case of *reversion*. *Darwin*, Descent of Man, I. 117.

(*b*) Return to the wild or feral state after domestication; exhibition of feral or natural characters after these have been artificially modified or lost.—3. In *law*: (*a*) The returning of property to the grantor or his heirs, after the granted estate or term therein is ended.

The rights of Guy devolved upon his brother; or rather Cyprus, for the *reversion* of which no arrangements had been made, fell to the lot of the possessor. *Stubbs*, Medieval and Modern Hist., p. 170.

Hence—(*b*) The estate which remains in the grantor where he grants away an estate smaller than that which he has himself. (*Digby*.) (See *estate*, 5, and *remainder*.) The term is also frequently, though improperly, used to include future estates in remainder. (c) In Scots law, a right of redeeming landed property which has been either mortgaged or adjudicated to secure the payment of a debt. In the former case the reversion is called *conventional*, in the latter case it is called *legal*. See *legal*.—4. A right or hope of future possession or enjoyment; succession.

As were our England in *reversion* his,
And he our subjects' next degree in hope.
Shak., Rich. II., i. 4. 35.

P. sen. My maid shall eat the relics.
Lick. When you and your dogs have dined! a sweet *reversion*. B. *Jonson*, Staple of News, ii. 1.

To London, concerning the office of Latine Secretary to his Maty, a place of more honour and dignitie than profit, the *revertion* of which he had promised me. *Evelyn*, Diary, May 5, 1670.

He knows . . . who got his pension rug,
Or quickened a *reversion* by a drug.
Pope, Satires of Donne, iv. 135.

5†. That which reverts or returns; the remainder.

The small *reversion* of this great army which came home might be looked on by religious eyes as relics. *Fuller*.

6. In *annuities*, a reversionary or deferred annuity. See *annuity*.—7. In *music*, same as *retrograde imitation* (which see, under *retrograde*).—8. In *chem.*, a change by which phosphates (notably such as are associated with oxid of iron and alumina) which have been made soluble in water by means of oil of vitriol, become again insoluble.—**Method of reversion**, a method of studying the properties of curves, especially conics, by means of points the reverse of one another.—**Principle of reversion**, the principle that, when any material system in which the forces acting depend only on the positions of the particles is in motion, if at any instant the velocities of the particles are reversed, the previous motion will be repeated in a reverse order.—**Reversion of series**, the process of passing from an infinite series expressing the value of one variable quantity in ascending powers of another to a second infinite series expressing the value of the second quantity in ascending powers of the first.

reversionary (rẹ̄-vėr'shọn-ā-ri), *a.* [< *reversion* + *-ary*.] 1. Pertaining to or involving a reversion; enjoyable in succession, or after the determination of a particular estate.

These money transactions—these speculations in life and death—these silent battles for *reversionary* spoil—make brothers very loving towards each other in Vanity Fair. *Thackeray*, Vanity Fair, xi.

2. In *biol.*, pertaining to or exhibiting reversion; tending to revert; reversive; atavic: as, *reversionary* characters; a *reversionary* process.—**Reversionary annuity.** See *annuity*.

reversioner (rẹ̄-vėr'shọn-ėr), *n.* [< *reversion* + *-er*¹.] One who has a reversion, or who is entitled to lands or tenements after a particular estate granted is determined: loosely applied in a general sense to any person entitled to any future estate in real or personal property.

Another statute of the same antiquity . . . protected estates for years from being destroyed by the *reversioner*. *Blackstone*, Com., IV. xxxiii.

reversis (rẹ̄-vėr'sis), *n.* [< OF. *reversis*, "*reversi*, a kind of trump (played backward, and full of sport) which the duke of Savoy brought some ten years ago into France" (Cotgrave), < *reverser*, reverse: see *reverse*.] An old French card game in which the player wins who takes the fewest tricks.

reversive (rẹ̄-vėr'siv), *a.* [< *reverse* + *-ive*.] 1. Causing or tending to cause reversal. [Rare.]

It was rather hard on humanity, and rather *reversive* of Providence, that all this care and pains should be lavished on cats and dogs, while little morsels of flesh and blood, ragged, hungry, and immortal, wandered up and down the streets. *R. T. Cooke*, Somebody's Neighbors, p. 47.

2. Reverting; tending toward reversion; specifically, in *biol.*, returning or tending to return to an ancestral or original type; reversionary; atavic.

There is considerable evidence tending to show that people who possess *reversive* characters are more common among those classes of society properly designated low. *Amer. Anthropologist*, I. 70.

reverso (rẹ̄-vėr'sō), *n.* [< It. **reverso*, *riverso*: see *reverse*, *n.*] 1†. In *fencing*, same as *reverse*, 3.

I would teach these nineteen the special rules, as your punto, your *reverso*, your stoccato, your imbroccato, your passada, your montanto, till they could all play very near or altogether as well as myself. B. *Jonson*, Every Man in his Humour, iv. 5.

2. In *printing*, any one of the left-hand pages in a book: the opposite of *recto*.

reversor (rẹ̄-vėr'sọr), *n.* [< *reverse* + *-or*¹.] A linkwork for reversing a figure.

revert (rẹ̄-vėrt'), *v.* [< ME. *reverten*, < OF. *revertir* = Pg. *reverter* = It. *rivertere*, < L. *revertere*, *revortere*, also deponent *reverti*, *revorti*, pp. *reversus*, *revorsus*, turn back, turn about, come back, return, < *re-*, back, + *vertere*, turn: see *verse*. Cf. *avert*, *advert*, *convert*, *invert*, etc.] I. *trans.* 1. To turn about or back; reverse the position or direction of.

Thane syr Priamous the prynce, in presens of lordes,
Presez to his penowne, and pertly it hentes;
Revertede it redily, and a-waye rydys
To the ryalle rowte of the rownde table.
Morte Arthure (E. E. T. S.), l. 2919.

The trembling stream . . . boils
Around the stone, or from the hollow'd bank
Reverted plays. *Thomson*, Spring, l. 405

With wild despair's *reverted* eye,
Close, close behind, he marks the throne.
Scott, The Wild Huntsman

Yet ever runs she with *reverted* face,
And looks and listens for the boy behind.
Coleridge, Time, Real and Imaginary

2†. To alter to the contrary; reverse.

Wretched her Subjects, gloomy sits the Queen
Till happy Chance *reverts* the cruel Scene.
Prior, Imit. of Passage in Moriæ Encomium of Erasmus.

3. To cast back; turn to the past. [Rare.]

Then, when you . . . chance to *revert* a look
Upon the price you gave for this sad thraldom,
You'le feel your heart stab'd through with many a woe.
Brome, Northern Lass, i. 7.

To **revert a series**, in *math.*, to transform a series by reversion. See *reversion of series*, under *reversion*.

II. *intrans.* 1. To turn back; face or look backward.

What half Januses are we, that cannot look forward with the same idolatry with which we for ever *revert*! *Lamb*, Oxford in Vacation.

2. To come back to a former place or position; return.

So that my arrows,
Too slightly timber'd for so loud a wind,
Would have *reverted* to my bow again.
Shak., Hamlet, iv. 7. 23.

Bid him [the goblin] labour, soon or late,
To lay these ringlets lank and straight; . . .
Th' elastic fibre, . . . dipt, new force exerts,
And in more vig'rous curls *reverts*.
Congreve, An Impossible Thing.

3. To return, as to a former habit, custom, or mode of thought or conduct.

Finding himself out of straits, he will *revert* to his customs. *Bacon*, Expense.

The Christians at that time had *reverted* to the habit of wearing the white turban. *E. W. Lane*, Modern Egyptians, II. 341.

4. In *biol.*, to go back to an earlier, former, or primitive type; reproduce the characteristics of antecedent stages of development; undergo reversion; exhibit atavism.

I may here refer to a statement often made by naturalists—namely, that our domestic varieties, when run wild, gradually but invariably *revert* in character to their aboriginal stocks. *Darwin*, Origin of Species, p. 28.

5. To go back in thought or discourse, as to a former subject of consideration; recur.

Permit me, in conclusion, gentlemen, to *revert* to the idea with which I commenced—the marvellous progress of the west. *Everett*, Orations, I. 213.

Each punishment of the extra-legal step
To which the high-born preferably revert
Is ever for some oversight, some slip
I' the taking vengeance, not for vengeance' self.
Browning, Ring and Book, II. 88.

My fancy, ranging thro' and thro',
To search a meaning for the song,
Perforce will still *revert* to you.
Tennyson, The Day-Dream, L'Envoi.

6. In *law*, to return to the donor, or to the former proprietor or his heirs.

If his tenant and patentee shall dispose of his gift without his kingly assent, the lands shall *revert* to the king. *Bacon*.

The earliest principle is that at a man's death his goods *revert* to the commonwealth, or pass as the custom of the commonwealth ordains. *E. A. Freeman*, Amer. Lects., p. 142.

7. In *chem.*, to return from a soluble to an insoluble condition: applied to a change which takes place in certain superphosphates. See *reversion*, 8.—**Reverting draft.** See *draft*¹.

revert† (rẹ̄-vėrt' or rē'vėrt), *n.* [< *revert*, *v.*] 1. One who or that which reverts; colloquially, one who is reconverted.

An active promoter in making the East Saxons converts, or rather *reverts*, to the faith. *Fuller*.

2. In *music*, return; recurrence; antistrophe.

Hath not musick her figures the same with rhetorick? What is a *revert* but her antistrophe? *Peacham*, Music.

3. That which is reverted. Compare *introvert*, *n.* [Rare.]

revertant (rẹ̄-vėr'tant), *a.* [< OF. *revertant*, < L. *reverten(t-)s*, ppr. of *revertere*, return: see *revert*.] In *her.*: (*a*) Flexed or reflexed—that is, bent in an S-curve. (*b*) Bent twice at a sharp angle, like a chevron and a half.—**Issuant and revertant.** See *issuant*.

reverted (rẹ̄-vėr'ted), *p. a.* 1. Reversed; turned back.—2. In *her.*, same as *revertant*.

reverter (rẹ̄-vėr'tėr), *n.* 1. One who or that which reverts.—2. In *law*, reversion.—**Formedon in the reverter**†. See *formedon*.

revertible (rẹ̄-vėr'ti-bl), *a.* [< *revert* + *-ible*.] Capable of reverting; subject to reversion.

A female fief *revertible* to daughters. *W. Coxe*, House of Austria, xliv.

revertive (rẹ̄-vėr'tiv), *a.* [< *revert* + *-ive*.] Turning back; retreating; retiring.

The tide *revertive*, unattracted, leaves
A yellow waste of idle sands behind.
Thomson, To the Memory of Sir Isaac Newton.

revertively (rẹ̄-vėr'tiv-li), *adv.* By way of reversion. *Imp. Dict.*

revery, *n.* See *reverie*.

revest (rẹ̄-vest'), *v.* [< ME. *revesten*, < OF. *revestir*, *ravestir*, F. *revêtir* = Pr. *revestir*, *rivestir* = Sp. Pg. *revestir* = It. *rivestire*, < LL. *revestire*, clothe again, < L. *re-*, again, + *vestire*, clothe: see *vest*. Doublet of *revet*².] I. *trans.* 1†. To reclothe; cover again as with a garment.

Right so as thise holtes and thise hay is,
That han in winter dede ben and drye,
Revesten hem in greene, when that May is.
Chaucer, Troilus, iii. 353.

Awaked all, shall rise, and all *revest*
The flesh and bones that they at first possest.
Sylvester, tr. of Du Bartas's Weeks, i. 1.

2†. To invest; robe; clothe, especially in the vestments of state or office.

Throly belles thay rynge, and Requiem syngys,
Dosse messes and matyns with mournande notes:
Relygeous *reveste* in theire riche copes,
Pontyficalles and prelates in precyouse wedys.
Morte Arthure (E. E. T. S.), l. 4335.

For the weale of the common wealth it is as necessarie that the Knight doe arme as the priest *reuest* himselfe: for, as prayers doe remoué sinnes, euen so doth armour defend from enimies.
Guevara, Letters (tr. by Hellowes, 1577), p. 42.

3. To reinvest; vest again with ownership or office: as, to *revest* a magistrate with authority.—4. To take possession of again; secure again as a possession or right.

If a captured ship escapes from the captor, or is retaken, or if the owner ransoms her, his property is thereby *revested*. *Kent*, Commentaries, v.

Like others for our spoils shall we return;
But not that any one may them *revest*,
For 'tis not just to have what one casts off.
Longfellow, tr. of Dante's Inferno, xiii. 104.

II. *intrans.* To take effect again, as a title; return to a former owner: as, the title or right *revests* in A after alienation.

revestiary† (rẹ̄-ves'ti-ā-ri), *n.* [= F. *revestiaire*, < ML. *revestiarium*, an apartment in or adjoining a church where the priests robed themselves for divine worship, the sacristy, vestry, < LL. *revestire*, revest: see *revest* and *vestiary*. Cf. *revestry*.] The apartment in a church or temple in which the ecclesiastical vestments are kept. Compare *vestry*.

The impious Jews ascribed all miracles to a name which was ingraved in the *revestiary* of the temple.
Camden, Remains.

"Nay," said the Abbot, "we will do more, and will instantly despatch a servant express to the keeper of our *revestiary* to send us such things as he may want, even this night." *Scott*, Monastery, xvi.

revestry† (rẹ̄-ves'tri), *n.* [< ME. *revestry*, *revestrie*, *revestre*, < OF. **revesterie*, *revestiere*, *revestiaire*, < ML. *revestiarium*, vestry: see *revestiary*. Cf. *vestry*.] Same as *revestiary*.

Then y[e] sayd Knight to bee convayd into the *revestre*, and there to bee vnarmyd.
Booke of Precedence (E. E. T. S., extra ser.), i. 35.

Bestrewe thine altars wth. flowers thicke,
Sente them w[t]. odours Arrabicque:
Perfuminge all the *revestryes*,
W[t]. muske, cyvett, and ambergries?
Puttenham, Partheniades, xvi.

revestu (rē-ves'tū), *a.* [OF., pp. of *revestir*, revest: see *revest*.] In *her.*, covered by a square set diagonally, or a lozenge, the corners of which touch the edges of the space covered by it: said of the field or of any ordinary, as a chief or fesse.

revesture† (rē-ves'tūr), *n.* [< *revest* + *-ure*. Cf. *vesture*.] Vesture.

The aultars of this chapell were hanged with riche *revesture* of clothe of gold of tissue, embroudered with pearles.
Hall, Hen. VIII., an. 12.

revet[1]†, *n.* and *v.* An obsolete form of *rivet*.

revet[2] (rē-vet'), *v. t.*; pret. and pp. *revetted*, ppr. *revetting*. [< F. *revêtir*, clothe again, face or line, as a fortification, foss, etc., < OF. *revestir*, clothe again: see *revest*.] To face, as an embankment, with masonry or other material.

All the principal apartments of the palace properly so called were *revetted* with sculptural slabs of alabaster, generally about 9 ft. in height, like those at Nimroud.
J. Fergusson, Hist. Arch., I. 168.

revetment (rē-vet'ment), *n.* [Also *revetement*; < F. *revêtement*, < *revêtir*, line, revet: see *revet*[2].] **1.** In *fort.*, a facing to a wall or bank, as of a scarp or parapet; a retaining wall (which see, under *retaining*). In permanent works the revetment is usually of masonry; in field-works it may be of sods, gabions, timber, hurdles, etc.
2. In *civil engin.*, a retaining wall or breast-wall; also, any method of protecting banks or the sides of a cut to preserve them from erosion, as the sheathing of a river-bank with mats, screens, or mattresses.

Back of all this rises a stone *revetement* wall, supporting the river street.
Harper's Mag., LXXIX. 92.

3. In *arch.*, any facing of stone, metal, or wood over a less sightly or durable substance or construction.

The absence of any fragments of columns, friezes, cornices, etc. (except terra-cotta *revetements*), confirms the theory that the Etruscan temple was built of wood.
New Princeton Rev., V. 141.

revict†, *v. t.* [< L. *revictus*, pp. of *revincere*, conquer, subdue, refute: see *revince*. Cf. *convict*.] To reconquer; reobtain. *Bp. Hall*, Autobiog., p. xxvii. (*Davies.*)

reviction† (rē-vik'shon), *n.* [< L. *revictus*, pp. *revivere*, live again, revive: see *revive*.] Return to life; revival.

Do we live to see a *reviction* of the old Sadduceeism, so long since dead and forgotten?
Bp. Hall, Mystery of Godliness, § 9.

revictual (rē-vit'l), *v.* [Formerly also *revittle*; < *re-* + *victual*.] **I.** *trans.* To victual again; furnish again with provisions.

We *revictualled* him, and sent him for England, with a true relation of the causes of our defailments.
Quoted in *Capt. John Smith's* Works, I. 232.

II. *intrans.* To renew one's stock of provisions.

He [Captain Giles de la Roche] had design'd to *revittle* in Portugal.
Milton, Letters of State, Aug., 1656.

revie† (rē-vī'), *v.* [Also *revye*; < *re-* + *vie*.] **I.** *trans.* **1.** To vie with again; rival in return; especially, at cards, to stake a larger sum against.

Thy game at weakest, still thou vy'st;
If seen, and then *revy'd*, deny'st
Thou art not what thou seem'st: false world, thou ly'st.
Quarles, Emblems, ii. 5.

To revie was to cover it [a certain sum] with a larger sum, by which the challenged became the challenger, and was to be *revied* in his turn, with a proportionate increase of stake.
Gifford, Note to B. Jonson's Every Man in his [Humour, iv. 1.

2. To surpass the amount of (a responsive challenge or bet): an old phrase at cards; hence, in general, to outdo; outstrip; surpass.

What shall we play for?—One shilling stake, and three rest. I vye it; will you hould it?—Yes, sir, I hould it, and *revye* it. *Florio*, Secret Frutes (1591). (*Latham.*)

Here 's a trick vied and *revied*!
B. Jonson, Every Man in his Humour, iv. 1.

True rest consists not in the oft *revying*
Of worldly dross. *Quarles*, Emblems, i. 6.

II. *intrans.* To respond to a challenge at cards by staking a larger sum; hence, to retort; recriminate.

We must not permit vying and *revying* upon one another.
Chief Justice Wright, in the Trial of the Seven Bishops.

review (rē-vū'), *n.* [< OF. *revue*, *reveue*, a reviewing or review, F. *revue*, a review, < *revu*, pp. of *revoir*, < L. *revidere*, see again, go to see again, < *re-*, again, + *videre*, see: see *view*, and cf. *revise*. Cf. Sp. Pg. *revista* = It. *rivista*, review, of similar formation: see *rista*.] **1.** A second or repeated view.

But the works of nature will bear a thousand views and *reviews*, and yet still be instructive and still wonderful.
Bp. Atterbury, Sermons, II. ii.

2. A view of the past; a retrospective survey.

Mem'ry's pointing wand,
That calls the past to our exact *review*.
Cowper, Task, iv. 184.

Is the pleasure that is tasted
Patient of a long *review*?
M. Arnold, New Sirens.

3. The process of going over again or repeating what is past: as, the *review* of a study; the class has monthly *reviews* in Latin.—**4.** A revision; a reëxamination with a view to amendment or improvement: as, an author's *review* of his works. [Obsolete or obsolescent.]

Great importunities were used to His Sacred Majesty that the said Book might be revised. . . . In which *review* we have endeavoured to observe the like moderation as we find to have been used in the like case in former times. *Book of Common Prayer* (Church of Eng.), Pref.

5. A critical examination; a critique; particularly, a written discussion of the merits and defects of a literary work; a critical essay.

If a *review* of his work was very laudatory, it was a great pleasure to him to send it home to his mother at Fairoaks. *Thackeray*, Pendennis, xli.

6. The name given to certain periodical publications, consisting of a collection of critical essays on subjects of public interest, literary, scientific, political, moral, or theological, together with critical examinations of new publications.

Novels (witness ev'ry month's *review*)
Belie their name, and offer nothing new.
Cowper, Retirement, l. 713.

7. The formal inspection of military or naval forces by a higher official or a superior in rank, with a view to learning the condition of the forces thus inspected, and their skill in performing customary evolutions and manœuvers.—**8.** In *law*, the judicial revision or reconsideration of a judgment or an order already made; the examination by an appellate tribunal of the decision of a lower tribunal, to determine whether it be erroneous.—**A bill of review**, in *law*, a bill filed to reverse or alter a decree in chancery if some error in law appears in the body of the decree, or if new evidence were discovered after the decree was made.—**Commission of review**, in *Eng. law*, a commission formerly granted by the sovereign to revise the sentence of the now extinct Court of Delegates.—**Court of Review**, the court of appeal from the commissioners in bankruptcy, established by 1 and 2 Wm. IV., lvi., but abolished by 10 and 11 Vict., cii., etc.

review (rē-vū'), *v.* [< *re-* + *view*; or < *review*, *n.*] **I.** *trans.* **1†.** To see again.

When thou *reviewest* this, thou dost *review*
The very part was consecrate to thee.
Shak., Sonnets, lxxiv.

Backe he was sent to Brasil; and long it was before his longing could be satisfied to *review* his Countrey and friends. *Purchas*, Pilgrimage, p. 842.

2. To look back upon; recall by the aid of memory.

Let me *review* the scene,
And summon from the shadowy Past
The forms that once have been.
Longfellow, A Gleam of Sunshine.

3. To repeat; go over again; retrace: as, to *review* a course of study.

Shall I the long, laborious scene *review*,
And open all the wounds of Greece anew?
Pope, Odyssey, iii. 127.

4. To examine again; go over again in order to prune or correct; revise.

Many hundred (Argus hundred) eyes
View, and *review*, each line, each word, as spies.
Times' Whistle (E. E. T. S.), p. 2.

I maturely thought it proper,
When a' my works I did *review*,
To dedicate them, Sir, to you.
Burns, Dedication to Gavin Hamilton.

5. To consider or discuss critically; go over in careful examination in order to bring out excellences and defects, and, with reference to established canons, to pass judgment; especially, to consider or discuss critically in a written essay.

How oft in pleasing tasks we wear the day, . . .
How oft our slowly-growing works impart. . . .
How oft *review*; each finding, like a friend,
Something to blame and something to commend!
Pope, To Mr. Jervas, l. 21.

See honest Hallam lay aside his fork,
Resume his pen, *review* his Lordship's work,
And, grateful for the dainties on his plate,
Declare his landlord can at least translate!
Byron, English Bards and Scotch Reviewers.

By-the-way, when we come by-and-by to *review* the exhibition at Burlington House, there is one painter whom we must try our best to crush.
Bulwer, Kenelm Chillingly, iv. 4.

6. To look carefully over; survey; especially, to make a formal or official inspection of: as, to *review* a regiment.

At the Mauchline muir, where they were *review'd*,
Ten thousand men in armour show'd.
Battle of Pentland Hills (Child's Ballads, VII. 241).

The skilful nymph *reviews* her force with care.
Pope, R. of the L., iii. 45.

7. In *law*: (*a*) To consider or examine again; revise: as, a court of appeal *reviews* the judgment of an inferior court. (*b*) To reëxamine or retax, as a bill of costs by the taxing-master or by a judge in chambers.

II. *intrans.* **1.** To look back.

His *reviewing* eye
Has lost the chasers, and his ear the cry.
Sir J. Denham, Cooper's Hill.

2. To make reviews; be a reviewer: as, he *reviews* for the "Times."

reviewable (rē-vū'a-bl), *a.* [< *review* + *-able*.] Capable of being reviewed; subject to review.

The proceedings in any criminal trial are *reviewable* by the full bench, whenever the judge who presides at the trial certifies that any point raised at it is doubtful.
The Nation, Dec. 20, 1883.

reviewage (rē-vū'āj), *n.* [< *review* + *-age*.] The act or art of reviewing or writing critical notices of books, etc.; the work of reviewing. [Rare.]

Whatever you order down to me in the way of *reviewage*, I shall of course execute.
W. Taylor, To R. Southey, Dec. 30, 1807.

reviewal (rē-vū'al), *n.* [< *review* + *-al*.] The act of reviewing; a review; a critique.

I have written a *reviewal* of "Lord Howe's Life."
Southey, To Mrs. J. W. Warter, June 5, 1838.

reviewer (rē-vū'ėr), *n.* **1.** One who revises; a reviser.

This rubric, being the same that we have in king Edward's second Common Prayer Book, may perhaps have slipt into the present book through the inadvertency of the *reviewers*.
Wheatly, Illus. of Book of Common Prayer, ii. § 5.

2. One who reviews or criticizes; especially, one who critically examines and passes judgment upon new publications; a writer of reviews.

Who shall dispute what the *reviewers* say?
Their word 's sufficient. *Churchill*, The Apology.

Those who have failed as writers turn *reviewers*.
Landor, Imaginary Conversations, Southey and Porson, i.

Between ourselves, I think *reviewers*,
When call'd to truss a crowing bard,
Should not be sparing of the skewers.
F. Locker, Advice to a Poet.

He has never, he says, been a *reviewer*. He confesses to wanting a *reviewer's* gift, the power of being "blind to great merits and lynx-eyed to minute errors."
Nineteenth Century, XXVI. 833.

revigorate (rē-vig'ọr-āt), *v. t.* [< L. *re-*, again, + *vigoratus*, pp. of *vigorare*, animate, strengthen, < *vigor*, vigor: see *vigor*. Cf. *invigorate*.] To give new vigor to. *Imp. Dict.*

revigorate (rē-vig'ọr-āt), *a.* [< *revigorate*, *v.*] Reinvigorated.

The fire which seem'd extinct
Hath risen *revigorate*. *Southey.*

revile (rē-vīl'), *v.*; pret. and pp. *reviled*, ppr. *reviling*. [< ME. *revilen*, *revylen*, < *re-* + OF. *aviler*, F. *avilir*, make vile or cheap, disprize, disesteem, < *a-*, to, + *vil*, vile, cheap: see *vile*.] **I.** *trans.* To cast reproach upon; vilify; especially, to use contemptuous or opprobrious language to; abuse; asperse.

Blessed are ye when men shall *revile* you, and persecute you, and shall say all manner of evil against you falsely, for my sake. Mat. v. 11.

His eye *reviled*
Me, as his abject object.
Shak., Hen. VIII., i. 1. 126.

No ill words: let his own shame first *revile* him.
Fletcher, Bonduca, ii. 4.

=**Syn.** To villify, abuse, malign, lampoon, defame. (See *asperse*.) The distinction of *revile* from these words is that it always applies to persons, is generally unjust and always improper, generally applies to what is said to or before the person affected, and makes him seem to others vile or worthless.

II. *intrans.* To act or speak abusively.

Christ, . . . when he was reviled, *reviled* not again.
1 Pet. ii. 23.

revile† (rē-vīl'), *n.* [< *revile*, *v.*] Revilement; abusive treatment or language; an insult; a reproach.

I have gain'd a name bestuck, or, as I may say, bedeckt with the reproaches and *reviles* of this modest Confuter.
Milton, Apology for Smectymnuus.

revilement† (rē̱-vil'mẹnt), *n.* [< *revile* + *-ment.*] The act of reviling; abuse; contemptuous or insulting language; a reproach.

> Yet n'ould she stent
> Her bitter rayling and foule *revilement.*
> *Spenser*, F. Q., II. iv. 12.

> Scorns, and *revilements*, that bold and profane wretches have cast upon him.
> *Dr. H. More*, Mystery of Godliness, p. 217. (*Latham.*)

reviler (rē̱-vī'lėr), *n.* One who reviles; one who acts or speaks abusively.

> Nor *revilers*, nor extortioners, shall inherit the kingdom of God. 1 Cor. vi. 10.

revilingly (rē̱-vī'ling-li), *adv.* With reproachful or contemptuous language; with opprobrium.

> The love I bear to the civility of expression will not suffer me to be *revilingly* broad. *Maine.*

revince† (rē̱-vins'), *v. t.* [= It. *rivincere*, < L. *revincere*, refute, overcome, < *re-*, again, + *vincere*, overcome: see *victor*. Cf. *convince*, *evince*, and *revict.*] To overcome; refute; disprove.

> Which being done, when he should see his error by manifest and sound testimonies of Scriptures *revinced*, Luther should find no favour at his hands.
> *Foxe*, Acts (ed. Cattley), IV. 280.

revindicate (rē̱-vin'di-kāt), *v. t.* [Also *revendicate*; < LL. *revindicatus*, pp. of *revindicare* (> Sp. Pg. *revindicar* = F. *revendiquer*), lay claim to, < L. *re-*, back, + *vindicare*, claim: see *vindicate.*] To vindicate again; reclaim; demand the surrender of, as goods taken away or detained illegally. *Mitford.* (*Imp. Dict.*)

revindication (rē̱-vin-di-kā'shọn), *n.* [Also *revendication*; = F. *revendication* = Pg. *revindicação*; as *revindicate* + *-ion.*] The act of revindicating, or demanding the restoration of anything taken away or retained illegally.

revire†, *v. i.* [< ME. *reviren*, < OF. *revivre*, revive: see *revive.*] To revive.

> Eke slitte and sonne-dried thou maist hem kepe,
> And when the list in water boote *revire*
> Thai wol, and taste even as the list desire.
> *Palladius*, Husbondrie (E. E. T. S.), p. 58.

revirescence (rev-i-res'ẹns), *n.* [< L. *revirescen(t-)s*, ppr. of *revirescere*, grow green again, inceptive of *revirere*, be green again, < *re-*, again, + *virere*, become green or strong: see *verdant.*] The renewal of youth or youthful strength. [Obsolete or archaic.]

> A serpent represented the divine nature, on account of its great vigour and spirit, its long age and *revirescence.*
> *Warburton*, Divine Legation, iv. 4.

> A faded archaic style trying as it were to resume a mockery of *revirescence.* *Swinburne*, Shakespeare, p. 126.

revisal (rē̱-vī'zạl), *n.* [< *revise* + *-al.*] The act of revising; examination with a view to correction or amendment; a revision.

> The *revisal* of these letters has been a kind of examination of conscience to me. *Pope.*

> The theory neither of the British nor the state constitutions authorizes the *revisal* of a judicial sentence by a legislative act. *A. Hamilton*, The Federalist, No. 81.

revise (rē̱-vīz'), *v. t.*; pret. and pp. *revised*, ppr. *revising.* [< OF. (and F.) *reviser* = Sp. *revisar*, < ML. as if **revisare* for L. *revisere*, look back on, revisit (cf. *revidere*, see again), < *re-*, again, back, + *visere*, survey, freq. of *videre*, pp. *visus*, see: see *vision*. Cf. *review.*] 1. To look carefully over with a view to correction; go over in order to suggest or make desirable changes and corrections; review: as, to *revise* a proof-sheet; to *revise* a translation of the Bible; specifically, in *printing*, to compare (a new proof-sheet of corrected composition) with its previously marked proof, to see that all marked errors have been corrected.

> He [Debendranath Tagore] *revised* the Brahmaic Covenant, and wrote and published his Brahma-dharma, or the religion of the one true God.
> *Max Muller*, Biog. Essays, p. 41.

2. To amend; bring into conformity with present needs and circumstances; reform, especially by public or official action.

> Fear for ages has boded and mowed and gibbered over government and property. That obscene bird is not there for nothing. He indicates great wrongs which must be *revised.* *Emerson*, Compensation.

Revised version of the Bible. See *version.*—**Revising barrister**, one of a number of barristers appointed to revise the list of voters for county and borough members of Parliament, and holding courts for this purpose throughout the country in the autumn. [Eng.]

revise (rē̱-vīz'), *n.* [< *revise*, *v.*] 1. A revision; a review and correction.

> Patiently proceed
> With oft *re-vises* Making sober speed
> In dearest business, and obserue by proof
> That What is well done is done soon enough.
> *Sylvester*, tr. of Du Bartas's Weeks, i. 1.

2. In *printing*, a proof-sheet to be examined by the reviser.

> I at length reached a vaulted room, . . . and beheld, seated by a lamp, and employed in reading a blotted *revise*, . . . the Author of Waverley!
> *Scott*, Fortunes of Nigel, Int. Ep., p. 5.

> I require to see a proof, a *revise*, a re-revise, and a double re-revise, or fourth proof rectified impression of all my productions, especially verse. *O. W. Holmes*, Autocrat, ii.

reviser (rē̱-vī'zėr), *n.* [< *revise* + *-er*1. Cf. *revisor.*] One who revises, reviews, or makes corrections or desirable changes, especially in a literary work; hence, specifically, in *printing*, one who revises proofs. Also *revisor.*

> The generality of my scheme does not admit the frequent notice of verbal inaccuracies . . . which he [Bentley] imputed to the obtrusions of a *reviser*, whom the author's blindness obliged him to employ. *Johnson*, Milton.

revision (rē̱-vizh'ọn), *n.* [< OF. *revision*, F. *révision* = Sp. *revision* = Pg. *revisão* = It. *revisione*, < LL. *revisio(n-)*, a seeing again, < L. *revidere*, pp. *revisus*, see again: see *revise*, *review.*] 1. The act of revising; reëxamination and correction: as, the *revision* of statistics; the *revision* of a book, of a creed, etc.

> I am persuaded that the stops have been misplaced in the Hebrew manuscripts, by the Jewish critics, upon the last *revision* of the text. *Bp. Horsley*, Sermons, I. viii.

> All male peasants in every part of the empire are inscribed in census lists, which form the basis of the direct taxation. These lists are revised at irregular intervals, and all males alive at the time of the *revision*, from the new-born babe to the centenarian, are duly inscribed.
> *D. M. Wallace*, Russia, p. 128.

2. That which is revised; a revised edition or version; specifically [*cap.*], the revised English version of the Bible.—**Council of Revision.** See *council.*

revisional (rē̱-vizh'ọn-ạl), *a.* [< *revision* + *-al.*] Revisionary.

revisionary (rē̱-vizh'ọn-ā̱-ri), *a.* [< *revision* + *-ary.*] Of or pertaining to revision; of the nature of a revision; revising: as, a *revisionary* work.

revisionist (rē̱-vizh'ọn-ist), *n.* [< *revision* + *-ist.*] 1. One who favors or supports revision, as in the case of a creed or a statute.—2. A reviser; specifically, one of the revisers of the English version of the Bible. See *revised version of the Bible*, under *version.*

> "I had rather speak," etc., 1 Corinthians xiv. 19. The Victorian *revisionists* are content with "had" there.
> *Amer. Jour. Philol.*, II. 281.

revisit (rē̱-viz'it), *v. t.* [< OF. *revisiter*, F. *revisiter* = Sp. Pg. *revistar* = It. *revisitare*, < L. *revisitare*, visit again, < *re-*, again, + *visitare*, visit: see *visit*, *v.*] 1. To visit again; go back for a visit to; return to.

> What may this mean,
> That thou, dead corse, again in complete steel
> *Revisit'st* thus the glimpses of the moon?
> *Shak.*, Hamlet, i. 4. 53.

> Thou
> *Revisit'st* not these eyes, that roll in vain
> To find thy piercing ray, and find no dawn.
> *Milton*, P. L., iii. 23.

2†. To revise; review.

> Also they saye that ye haue not dilygently *reuisyted* nor ouersene the letters patentes gyuen, accorded, sworne, and sealed by Kyng Johan.
> *Berners*, tr. of Froissart's Chron., II. ccxxii.

revisit (rē̱-viz'it), *n.* [< *re-* + *visit.*] A visit to a former place of sojourn; also, a repeated or second visit.

> I have been to pay a Visit to St. James at Compostella, and after that to the famous Virgin on the other Side the Water in England; and this was rather a *revisit*, for I had been to see her three Years before.
> *N. Bailey*, tr. of Colloquies of Erasmus, II. 2.

revisitant (rē̱-viz'i-tạnt), *a.* [< LL. *revisitan(t-)s*, ppr. of *revisitare*, revisit: see *revisit.*] Revisiting; returning, especially after long absence or separation.

> Catching sight of a solitary acquaintance, [I] would approach him amid the brown shadows of the trees—a kind of medium fit for spirits departed and *revisitant*, like myself. *Hawthorne*, Blithedale Romance, p. 242.

revisitation (rē̱-viz-i-tā'shọn), *n.* [< *re-* + *visitation.*] The act of revisiting; a revisit.

> A regular concerted plan of periodical *revisitation.*
> *J. A. Alexander*, On Mark vi. 6.

revisor (rē̱-vī'zọr), *n.* [= F. *réviseur* = Sp. Pg. *revisor* = It. *revisore*; as *revise* + *-or*1.] Same as *reviser.*

revisory (rē̱-vī'zō-ri), *a.* [= Pg. *revisorio*; as *revise* + *-ory*. Cf. Sp. *revisoria*, censorship.] Having power to revise; effecting revision; revising.

revitalization (rē-vī'tạl-i-zā'shọn), *n.* [< *revitalize* + *-ation.*] The act or process of revitalizing; the state of being revitalized, or informed with fresh life and vigor.

revitalize (rē-vī'tạl-īz), *v. t.* [< *re-* + *vitalize.*] To restore vitality or life to; inform again or anew with life; bring back to life.

> Professor Owen observes that "there are organisms . . . which we can devitalize and *revitalize*—devive and revive—many times." That such organisms can be revived, all will admit, but probably Professor Owen will be alone in not recognising considerable distinction between the words *revitalizing* and reviving. The animalcule that can be revived has never been dead, but that which is not dead cannot be *revitalized.*
> *Beale*, Protoplasm (3d ed.), p. 65.

revittle†, *v.* An obsolete spelling of *revictual.*

revivability (rē̱-vī-vạ-bil'i̱-ti), *n.* [< *revivable* + *-ity* (see *-bility*).] The character of being revivable; the capacity for being revived.

> The *revivability* of past feelings varies inversely as the vividness of present feelings.
> *H. Spencer*, Prin. of Psychol., § 98.

revivable (rē̱-vī'vạ-bl), *a.* [< *revive* + *-able.*] Capable of being revived.

> Nor will the response of a sensory organ . . . be an experience, unless it be registered in a modification of structure, and thus be *revivable*, because a statical condition is requisite for a dynamical manifestation.
> *G. H. Lewes*, Probs. of Life and Mind, I. i. § 12.

revivably (rē̱-vī'vạ-bli), *adv.* With a capacity for revival; so as to admit of revival.

> What kind of agency can it then be . . . that *revivably* stores up the memory of departed phenomena?
> *Mind*, IX. 350.

revival (rē̱-vī'vạl), *n.* [< *revive* + *-al.*] 1. The act of reviving, or returning to life after actual or apparent death; the act of bringing back to life; also, the state of being so revived or restored: as, the *revival* of a drowned person; the *revival* of a person from a swoon.—2. Restoration to former vigor, activity, or efficiency, after a period of languor, depression, or suspension; quickening; renewal: as, the *revival* of hope; the *revival* of one's spirits by good news; a *revival* of trade.

> "I've thought of something," said the Rector, with a sudden *revival* of spirits. *George Eliot*, Felix Holt, xxiii.

3. Restoration to general use, practice, acceptance, or belief; the state of being currently known or received: as, the *revival* of learning in Europe; the *revival* of bygone fashions; specifically [*cap.*], the Renaissance.

> The man to whom the literature of his country owes its origin and its *revival* was born in times singularly adapted to call forth his extraordinary powers. *Macaulay*, Dante.

4. Specifically, an extraordinary awakening in a church or a community of interest in and care for matters relating to personal religion.

> There ought not to be much for a *revival* to do in any church which has had the simple good news preached to it, and in which the heart and life and better motives have been affectionately and persistently addressed.
> *Scribner's Mo.*, XIV. 256.

> A *revival* of religion merely makes manifest for a time what religion there is in a community, but it does not exalt men above their nature or above their times.
> *H. B. Stowe*, Oldtown, p. 469.

5. The representation of something past; specifically, in *theatrical art*, the reproduction of a play which has not been presented for a considerable time.

> One can hardly pause before it [a gateway of the seventeenth century] without seeming to assist at a ten minutes' *revival* of old Italy.
> *H. James, Jr.*, Trans. Sketches, p. 145.

> Some of Mr. ——'s *revivals* have been beautifully costumed. *The Century*, XXXV. 544, note.

6. In *chem.*, same as *revivification.*—7. The reinstatement of an action or a suit after it has become abated, as, for instance, by the death of a party, when it may be revived by substituting the personal representative, if the cause of action has not abated.—8. That which is recalled to life, or to present existence or appearance. [Rare.]

> The place [Castle of Blois] is full of . . . memories, of ghosts, of echoes, of possible evocations and *revivals.*
> *H. James, Jr.*, Little Tour, p. 29.

Anglo-Catholic revival, Catholic revival, a revival of Catholic or Anglo-Catholic principles and practices in the Church of England (see *Anglo-Catholic*, and *Catholic*, I., 3 (*d*)), also known, because begun in the University of Oxford, as the *Oxford movement.* It began in 1833, in opposition to an agitation for the expulsion of the bishops from the House of Lords and for the disestablishment of the Church of England. Its founder was H. J. Rose, with whom were joined Arthur Percival, Hurrel Froude, and William Palmer, and, a little later, John Henry Newman (originally an Evangelical) and John Keble, the publication of whose "Christian Year" in 1827 has been regarded as an important precursor of the movement. In its earlier stage the promoters of the revival were known as *Tractarians.* (See *Tractarian.*) After Newman had, in 1845, abandoned the Church of England and joined the Church of Rome, Dr. Edward B. Pusey became generally recognized as the leader of the movement, and its adherents were nicknamed *Puseyites* by their opponents. The revival of doctrine was the main work of the movement, especially in its earlier stages, but this resulted afterward in a revival of ritual also, and this extension of the movement is known as *ritualism*. (See *ritualist*, 2.) The general object of the Catholic revival was to affirm and enforce the character of the Anglican Church as Catholic in the sense of unbroken historical derivation from and agreement in doctrine and organization with the ancient Catholic Church before the division between East and West.

revivalism (rē-vī'val-izm), *n.* [< *revival* + *-ism*.] That form of religious activity which manifests itself in revivals. [Recent.]

The most perfect example of *revivalism*, the one to which it constantly appeals for its warrant, was the mpt assembly at Pentecost, with its many-tongued psalmists and inspired prophets, its transports and fervors and miraculous conversions. *The Century*, XXXI. 80.

revivalist (rē-vī'val-ist), *n.* [< *revival* + *-ist*.] One who is instrumental in producing or promoting in a community a revival of religious interest and activity: specifically applied to an itinerant preacher who makes this his special work. [Recent.]

The conviction of enmity to God, which the *revivalist* assumes as the first step in any true spiritual life. *The American*, VIII. 126.

revivalistic (rē-vī-va-lis'tik), *a.* [< *revivalist* + *-ic*.] 1. Of or pertaining to a revivalist or revivalism.

Revivalistic success is seldom seen apart from a certain easily recognized type of man. *Religious Herald*, March 26, 1885.

2. Characterized by revivalism; of the nature of revivalism. [Recent and rare in both uses.]

Spiritual preaching is reviving; it is not necessarily *revivalistic*. *The Century*, XXXI. 438.

revive (rē-vīv'), *v.*; pret. and pp. *revived*, ppr. *reviving*. [< OF. F. *revivre* = Pr. *reviure* = Cat. *reviurer* = Sp. *revivir* = Pg. *reviver* = It. *rivivere*, < L. *revivere*, live again, revive (cf. ML. *revivare*, tr., revive), < *re-*, again, + *vivere*, live: see *vivid*. Cf. *revive*.] I. *intrans.* 1. To return to life after actual or seeming death; resume vital functions or activities: as, to *revive* after a swoon.

The soul of the child came into him again, and he *revived*. 1 Ki. xvii. 22.

Henry is dead, and never shall *revive*. *Shak.*, 1 Hen. VI., i. 1. 18.

She smiled to see the doughty hero slain,
But, at her smile, the beau *revived* again.
Pope, R. of the L., v. 70.

2. To live again; have a second life. [Rare.]

Emotionally we *revive* in our children: economically we sacrifice many of our present gratifications to the development of the race. *Pop. Sci. Mo.*, XXXIII. 380.

3. To gain fresh life and vigor; be reanimated or quickened; recover strength, as after languor or depression.

When he saw the wagons which Joseph had sent to carry him, the spirit of Jacob their father *revived*. Gen. xlv. 27.

A spirit which had been extinguished on the plains of Philippi *revived* in Athanasius and Ambrose. *Macaulay*, History.

4. To be renewed in the mind or memory: as, the memory of his wrongs *revived* within him; past emotions sometimes *revive*.—5. To regain use or currency; come into general use, practice, or acceptance, as after a period of neglect or disuse; become current once more.

Then Sculpture and her sister arts *revive*. *Pope*, Essay on Criticism, l. 701.

This heresy having *revived* in the world about an hundred years ago, . . . several divines . . . began to find out farther explanations of this doctrine of the Trinity. *Swift*, On the Trinity.

His [Clive's] policy was to a great extent abandoned; the abuses which he had suppressed began to *revive*. *Macaulay*, Lord Clive.

6. In *chem.*, to recover its natural or metallic state, as a metal.

II. *trans.* 1. To bring back to life; revivify; resuscitate after actual or seeming death or destruction; restore to a previous mode of existence.

To heale the sicke, and to *revive* the ded. *Spenser*, F. Q., II. iii. 22.

What do these feeble Jews? . . . will they *revive* the stones out of the heaps of the rubbish which are burned? Neh. iv. 2.

Is not this boy *revived* from death? *Shak.*, Cymbeline, v. 5. 120.

2. To quicken; refresh; rouse from languor, depression, or discouragement.

Those gracious words *revive* my drooping thoughts,
And give my tongue-tied sorrows leave to speak.
Shak., 3 Hen. VI., iii. 3. 21.

Your coming, friends, *revives* me. *Milton*, S. A., l. 157.

3. To renew in the mind or memory; recall; reawaken.

The mind has a power in many cases to *revive* perceptions which it has once had. *Locke*, Human Understanding, II. x. § 2.

With tempers too much given to pleasure, it is almost necessary to *revive* the old places of grief in our memory. *Steele*, Tatler, No. 181.

The beautiful specimens of pearls which he sent home from the coast of Paria *revived* the cupidity of the nation. *Prescott*, Ferd. and Isa., ii. 9.

When I describe the moon at which I am looking, I am describing merely a plexus of optical sensations with sundry *revived* states of mind linked by various laws of association with the optical sensations. *J. Fiske*, Evolutionist, p. 327.

4. To restore to use, practice, or general acceptance; make current, popular, or authoritative once more; recover from neglect or disuse: as, to *revive* a law or a custom.

After this a Parliament is holden, in which the Acts made in the eleventh Year of King Richard were *revived*, and the Acts made in his one and twentieth Yeare were wholly repealed. *Baker*, Chronicles, p. 157.

The function of the prophet was then *revived*, and poets for the first time aspired to teach the art of life, and founded schools. *J. R. Seeley*, Nat. Religion, p. 92.

5. To renovate. [Colloq.]

The boy . . . appeared . . . in a *revived* black coat of his master's. *Dickens*, Sketches, Tales, i.

6. To reproduce; represent after a lapse of time, especially upon the stage: as, to *revive* an old play.

A past, vamp'd, future, old, *reviv'd* new piece,
'Twixt Plautus, Fletcher, Shakespear, and Corneille,
Can make a Cibber, Tibbald, or Ozell.
Pope, Dunciad, i. 284.

Already in the latter days of the Republic the multitude (including even the knights, according to Horace) could only be reconciled to tragedy by the introduction of that species of accessories by which in our own day a play of Shakspere's is said to be *revived*. *A. W. Ward*, Eng. Dram. Lit., I. 8.

7. In *law*, to reinstate, as an action or suit which has become abated. See *revival*, 7.—8. In *chem.*, to restore or reduce to its natural state or to its metallic state: as, to *revive* a metal after calcination.=**Syn.** 1 and 2. To reanimate, reinvigorate, renew, reinspirit, cheer, hearten. See the quotation under *revitalize*.

revive†, *n.* Revival; return to life.

Hee is dead, and therefore grieue not thy memorie with the imagination of his new *reuiue*. *Greene*, Menaphon, p. 50. (*Davies*.)

revivement (rē-vīv'ment), *n.* [= It. *ravvivamento*; as *revive* + *-ment*.] The act of reviving; revivification.

We have the sacred Scriptures, our blessed Saviour, his apostles, and the purer primitive times, and the late Reformation, or *revivement* rather, all on our side. *Feltham*, Letters, xvii. (*Latham*.)

reviver (rē-vī'vėr), *n.* 1. One who revives or restores anything to use or prominence; one who recovers anything from inactivity, neglect, or disuse.

He saith it [learning] is the corrupter of the simple, the schoolmaster of sinne, the storehouse of treacherie, the *reuiuer* of vices, and mother of cowardize. *Nashe*, Pierce Penilesse, p. 30.

Giotto was not a *reviver*—he was an inventor. *The Century*, XXXVII. 67.

2. That which invigorates or revives.

"Now, Mr. Tapley," said Mark, giving himself a tremendous blow in the chest by way of *reviver*, "just you attend to what I've got to say." *Dickens*, Martin Chuzzlewit, xxiii.

3. A compound used for renovating clothes.

'Tis a deceitful liquid, that black and blue *reviver*. *Dickens*, Sketches, Characters, x.

4. In *law*. See *revivor*.

revivificate (rē-viv'i-fi-kāt), *v. t.* [< LL. *revivificatus*, pp. of (ML.) *revivificare*, restore to life: see *revivify*.] To revive; recall or restore to life. *Johnson*. [Rare.]

revivification (rē-viv"i-fi-kā'shon), *n.* [= F. *révivification* = Pg. *revivificação*, < ML. *revivificatio(n-)*, < *revivificare*, revivify: see *revivificate*, *revivify*.] 1. Renewal of life; restoration to life; resuscitation.

The resurrection or *revivification* (for the word signifies no more than so) is common to both. *Dr. H. More*, Mystery of Godliness, p. 225. (*Latham*.)

2. In *chem.*, the reduction of a metal from a state of combination to its metallic state.—3. In *surg.*, the dissection off of the skin or mucous membrane in a part or parts, that by the apposition of surfaces thus prepared union of parts may be secured.

revivify (rē-viv'i-fī), *v.* [< OF. *revivifier*, F. *révivifier* = Sp. Pg. *revivificar* = It. *revivificare*, < ML. *revivificare* (LL. in pp. *revivificatus*), restore to life, < L. *re-*, again, + LL. *vivificare*, restore to life: see *vivify*.] I. *trans.* 1. To restore to life after actual or apparent death.

This warm Libation . . . seemed to animate my frozen Frame, and to *revivify* my Body. *Wraxall*, Historical Memoirs, I. 369.

2. To give new vigor or animation to; enliven again.

Local literature is pretty sure, . . . when it comes, to have that distinctive Australian mark . . . which may even one day *revivify* the literature of England. *Sir C. W. Dilke*, Probs. of Greater Britain, ii. 1.

3. In *chem.*, to purify, as a substance that has been used as a reagent in a chemical process, so that it can be used again in the same way.

A description of the kiln in use for *revivifying* char will be found in the article on sugar. *Thorpe*, Dict. of Applied Chem., I. 171.

=**Syn.** See list under *revive*.

II. *intrans.* In *chem.*, to become efficient a second time as a reagent, without special chemical treatment, as by oxidation in the air, fermentation, etc.

revivingly (rē-vī'ving-li), *adv.* In a reviving manner. *Imp. Dict.*

reviviscence (rev-i-vis'ens), *n.* [= F. *réviviscence* = It. *reviviscenza*, < L. *reviviscen(t-)s*, ppr. of *reviviscere*, inceptive of *revivere*, revive: see *revive*.] Revival; reanimation; the renewal of life; in *nat. hist.*, an awakening from torpidity, especially in the case of insects after hibernation.

Neither will the life of the soul alone continuing amount to the *reviviscence* of the whole man. *Bp. Pearson*, Expos. of Creed, ii.

reviviscency (rev-i-vis'en-si), *n.* [As *reviviscence* (see *-cy*).] Same as *reviviscence*.

Since vitality has, somehow or other, commenced without a designing cause, why may not the same cause produce a *reviviscency*? *T. Cogan*, Disquisitions, iii.

reviviscent (rev-i-vis'ent), *a.* [= F. *réviviscent*, < L. *reviviscen(t-)s*, ppr. of *reviviscere*, revive, inceptive of *revivere*, revive: see *revive*.] Reviving; regaining life or animation.

All the details of the trial were canvassed anew with *reviviscent* interest. *The Atlantic*, LVIII. 390.

revivor (rē-vī'vor), *n.* [< *revive* + *-or*[1].] In *law*, the reviving of a suit which was abated by the death of a party, the marriage of a female plaintiff, or other cause. See *revival*, 7. Also spelled *reviver*.—**Bill of revivor**, a bill filed to revive a bill which had abated.—**Bill of revivor and supplement**, a bill of revivor filed where it was necessary not only to revive the suit, but also to allege by way of supplemental pleading other facts which had occurred since the suit was commenced.

revocability (rev"ō-ka-bil'i-ti), *n.* [= F. *révocabilité*; as *revocable* + *-ity* (see *-bility*).] The property of being revocable; revocableness. *Imp. Dict.*

revocable (rev'ō-ka-bl), *a.* [< OF. *revocable*, F. *révocable* = Pr. Sp. *revocable* = Pg. *revogavel* = It. *rivocabile*, < L. *revocabilis*, < *revocare*, revoke: see *revoke*.] Capable of being recalled or revoked: as, a *revocable* edict or grant. Compare *revokable*.

Howsoever you show bitterness, do not act anything that is not *revocable*. *Bacon*, Anger.

Treaties may . . . be *revocable* at the will of either party, or irrevocable. *Woolsey*, Introd. to Inter. Law, § 102.

revocableness (rev'ō-ka-bl-nes), *n.* The character of being revocable. *Bailey*, 1727.

revocably (rev'ō-ka-bli), *adv.* In a revocable manner; so as to be revocable. *Imp. Dict.*

revocate† (rev'ō-kāt), *v. t.* [< L. *revocatus*, pp. of *revocare*, revoke: see *revoke*.] To revoke; recall.

His successor, by order, nullifies
Many his patents, and did *revocate*
And re-assume his liberalities.
Daniel, Civil Wars, iii. 80.

revocate† (rev'ō-kāt), *a.* [< L. *revocatus*, pp. of *revocare*, call back: see *revoke*.] Repressed; checked; also, pruned.

But yf it axe to be *revocate*,
And yf the stok be holgh or concavate,
Purge of the dede [dead wood].
Palladius, Husbondrie (E. E. T. S.), p. 70.

revocation (rev-ō-kā'shon), *n.* [< OF. *revocacion*, *revocation*, F. *révocation* = Pr. *revocation* = Sp. *revocacion* = Pg. *revocação*, *revogação* = It. *rivocazione*, < L. *revocatio(n-)*, < *revocare*, revoke: see *revocate*, *revoke*.] 1. The act of revoking or recalling; also, the state of being recalled or summoned back.

One of the town ministers, that saw in what manner the people were bent for the *revocation* of Calvin, gave him notice of their affection in this sort. *Hooker*, Eccles. Polity, Pref., ii.

The faculty of which this act of *revocation* is the energy I call the reproductive. *Sir W. Hamilton*, Metaph., xxi.

2. The act of revoking or annulling; the reversal of a thing done by the revoker or his predecessor in the same authority; the calling back of a thing granted, or the making void of some deed previously existing; also, the state

of being revoked or annulled; reversal; repeal; annulment: as, the *revocation* of a will.—**Revocation of the edict of Nantes**, a proclamation by Louis XIV. of France, in 1685, annulling the edict of Nantes, and discontinuing religious toleration to the Huguenots. The Protestant emigration in consequence of this revocation and of previous persecutions greatly injured the industries of France. =**Syn. 2.** See *renounce, abolish.*

revocatory (rev'ǫ-kạ-tọ-ri), *a.* [< OF. *revocatoire*, F. *révocatoire* = Sp. *revocatorio* = Pg. *revocatorio, revogatorio* = It. *rivocatorio*, < LL. *revocatorius*, for calling or drawing back, < L. *revocare*, call back: see *revoke*.] Tending to revoke; pertaining to a revocation; revoking; recalling.

He granted writs to both parties, with *revocatory* letters one upon another, sometimes to the number of six or seven.
World of Wonders (1608), p. 137.

Revocatory action, in *civil law*, an action to set aside the real contracts of a debtor made in fraud of creditors and operating to their prejudice. *E. A. Cross*, Pleading, p. 251.

revoice (rē-vois'), *v. t.* [< *re-* + *voice*.] **1.** In *organ-building*, to voice again; adjust (a pipe) so that it may recover the voice it has lost or speak in a new way.—**2.** To call in return; repeat. [Rare.]

And to the winds the waters hoarsely call,
And echo back again *revoiced* all.
G. *Fletcher*, Christ's Triumph on Earth, st. 64.

revokable (rẹ-vō'kạ-bl), *a.* [< *revoke* + *-able*.] That can or may be revoked; revocable.

revoke (rẹ-vōk'), *v.*; pret. and pp. *revoked*, ppr. *revoking*. [< ME. *revoken*, < OF. *revoquer*, *revocquer*, F. *révoquer* = Pr. Sp. *revocar* = Pg. *revocar*, *revogar* = It. *rivocare*, < L. *revocare*, call back, revoke, < *re-*, back, again, + *vocare*, call: see *re-* and *vocation*. Cf. *avoke, convoke, evoke, provoke*.] **I.** *trans.* **1†.** To call back; summon back; cause to return.

Christ is the glorious instrument of God for the *revoking* of Man. G. *Herbert*, A Priest to the Temple, i.

What strength thou hast
Throughout the whole proportion of thy limbs,
Revoke it all into thy manly arms,
And spare me not.
Heywood, 1 Edw. IV. (Works, ed. Pearson, 1874, I. 55).

Mistress Anne Boleyn was . . . sent home again to her father for a season, whereat she smoked; . . . [but afterward she] was *revoked* unto the court.
G. *Cavendish*, Wolsey, p. 67.

How readily we wish time spent *revok'd*.
Cowper, Task, vi. 25.

2†. To bring back to consciousness; revive; resuscitate.

Hym to *revoken* she did al hire peyne,
And at the laste he gan his breth to drawe,
And of his swough sone eftir that adawe.
Chaucer, Troilus, iii. 1118.

3†. To call back to memory; recall to mind.

By *revoking* and recollecting . . . certain passages.
South.

4. To annul by recalling or taking back; make void; cancel; repeal; reverse: as, to *revoke* a will; to *revoke* a privilege.

Let them assemble,
And on a safer judgement all *revoke*
Your ignorant election. *Shak.*, Cor., ii. 3. 226.

That forgiveness was only conditional, and is *revoked* by his recovery. *Fielding*, Amelia, iii. 10.

A devise by writing . . . may be also *revoked* by burning, cancelling, tearing, or obliterating thereof by the devisor, or in his presence and with his consent.
Blackstone, Com., II. xxiii.

5†. To restrain; repress; check.

She with pitthy words, and counsell sad,
Still strove their stubborne rages to *revoke*.
Spenser, F. Q., II. ii. 28.

6†. To give up; renounce.

Nay, traitor, stay, and take with thee that mortal blow or stroke
The which shall cause thy wretched corpse this life for to *revoke*. *Peele*, Sir Clyomon and Sir Clamydes.

=**Syn. 4.** *Recant, Abjure*, etc. (see *renounce*); *Repeal, Rescind*, etc. (see *abolish*).

II. *intrans.* **1.** To recall a right or privilege conceded in a previous act or promise.

Thinke ye then our Bishops will forgoe the power of excommunication on whomsoever? No, certainly, unless to compasse sinister ends, and then *revoke* when they see their time. *Milton*, Reformation in Eng., ii.

I make a promise, and will not *revoke*.
Crabbe, Works, VII. 129.

2. In *card-playing*, to neglect to follow suit when the player can and should do so.

revoke (rẹ-vōk'), *n.* [< *revoke, v.*] **1.** Revocation; recall. [Rare.]

How callous seems beyond *revoke*
The clock with its last listless stroke!
D. G. Rossetti, Soothsay.

2. In *card-playing*, the act of revoking; a failure to follow suit when the player can and should do so. In whist the revoke is made when the wrong card is thrown; but it is not "established" (incurring a severe penalty) till the trick on which it was made is turned or quitted, or till the revoking player or his partner has again played.

She never made a *revoke*; nor ever passed it over in her adversary without exacting the utmost forfeiture.
Lamb, Mrs. Battle on Whist.

revokement (rẹ-vōk'mẹnt), *n.* [= It. *rivocamento*; as *revoke* + *-ment*.] The act of revoking; revocation; reversal.

Let it be noised
That through our intercession this *revokement*
And pardon comes. *Shak.*, Hen. VIII., i. 2. 106.

revoker (rẹ-vō'kėr), *n.* One who revokes.

revolt (rẹ-vōlt' or rẹ-volt'), *n.* [< OF. *revolte*, F. *révolte* = Sp. *revuelta* = Pg. *revolta*, < It. *rivolta*, *revolta*, a revolt, turning, overthrow, fem. of *rivolto*, *revolto* (< L. *revolutus*), pp. of *revolvere*, turn, overturn, overwhelm, revolve: see *revolve*.] **1.** An uprising against government or authority; rebellion; insurrection; hence, any act of insubordination or disobedience.

Their mutinies and *revolts*, wherein they show'd
Most valour, spoke not for them.
Shak., Cor., iii. 1. 126.

I doubt not but you have heard long since of the *Revolt* of Catelonia from the K. of Spain.
Howell, Letters, I. vi. 42.

On one side arose
The women up in wild *revolt*, and storm'd
At the Oppian law. *Tennyson*, Princess, vii.

2†. The act of turning away or going over to the opposite side; a change of sides; desertion.

He was greatly strengthened, and the enemy as much enfeebled by daily *revolts*. *Sir W. Raleigh.*

The blood of youth burns not with such excess
As gravity's *revolt* to wantonness.
Shak., L. L. L., v. 2. 74.

3†. Inconstancy; faithlessness; fickleness, especially in love.

Thou canst not vex me with inconstant mind,
Since that my life on thy *revolt* doth lie.
Shak., Sonnets, xcii.

4†. A revolter.

You ingrate *revolts*,
You bloody Neroes, ripping up the womb
Of your dear mother England.
Shak., K. John, v. 2. 151.

=**Syn. 1.** *Sedition, Rebellion*, etc. See *insurrection*.

revolt (rẹ-vōlt' or rẹ-volt'), *v.* [< OF. *revolter*, F. *révolter* = Pg. *revoltar* = It. *rivoltare*, *revoltare*; from the noun.] **I.** *intrans.* **1†.** To turn away; turn aside from a former cause or undertaking; fall off; change sides; go over to the opposite party; desert.

The stout Parisians do *revolt*,
And turn again unto the warlike French.
Shak., 1 Hen. VI., v. 2. 2.

Monsieur Arnaud . . . was then of the religion, but had promised to *revolt* to the King's side.
Life of Lord Herbert of Cherbury (ed. Howells), p. 146.

2. To break away from established authority; renounce allegiance and subjection; rise against a government in open rebellion; rebel; mutiny.

The Edomites *revolted* from under the hand of Judah.
2 Chron. xxi. 10.

Let the church, our mother, breathe her curse,
A mother's curse, on her *revolting* son.
Shak., K. John, iii. 1. 257.

3†. To prove faithless or inconstant, especially in love.

You are already Love's firm votary,
And cannot soon *revolt* and change your mind.
Shak., T. G. of V., iii. 2. 59.

Live happier
In other choice, fair Amidea, 'tis
Some shame to say my heart's *revolted*.
Shirley, Traitor, ii. 1.

4. To turn away in horror or disgust; be repelled or shocked.

Her mind *revolted* at the idea of using violence to any one. *Scott*, Heart of Mid-Lothian, xxxiv.

II. *trans.* **1†.** To roll back; turn back.

As a thonder bolt
Perceth the yielding ayre, and doth displace
The soring clouds into sad showres ymolt;
So to her yold the flames, and did their force *revolt*.
Spenser, F. Q., III. xi. 25.

2†. To turn away from allegiance; cause to rebel.

Whether of us is moste culpable, I in following and obeying the King, or you in altering and *revolting* ye kingdome. *Guevara*, Letters (tr. by Hellowes, 1577), p. 236.

3. To repel; shock; cause to turn away in abhorrence or disgust.

This abominable medley is made rather to *revolt* young and ingenuous minds. *Burke*, A Regicide Peace, iv.

Hideous as the deeds
Which you scarce hide from men's *revolted* eyes.
Shelley, The Cenci, i. 1.

Revolt, in the sense of 'provoke aversion in,' 'shock,' is, I believe, scarce a century old; it being a neoterism with Bishop Warburton, Horace Walpole, William Godwin, and Southey. *F. Hall*, Mod. Eng., p. 299.

=**Syn. 3.** To disgust, sicken, nauseate.

revolter (rẹ-vōl'tėr or rẹ-vol'tėr), *n.* One who revolts, or rises against authority; a rebel.

All their princes are *revolters*. Hos. ix. 15.

A murderer, a *revolter*, and a robber!
Milton, S. A., l. 1180.

revolting (rẹ-vōl'ting or rẹ-vol'ting), *p. a.* **1.** Given to revolt or sedition; rebellious.

Also they promise that his Maiestie shall not permit to be giuen from henceforth fortresse, Castell, bridge, gate, or towne . . . unto Gentlemen or knightes of power, which in *revolting* times may rise with the same.
Guevara, Letters (tr. by Hellowes, 1577), p. 271.

2. Causing abhorrence or extreme disgust; shocking; repulsive.

What can be more unnatural, not to say more *revolting*, than to set up any system of rights or privileges in moral action apart from duties?
Gladstone, Might of Right, p. 95.

=**Syn. 2.** Disgusting, nauseating, offensive, abominable.

revoltingly (rẹ-vōl'- or rẹ-vol'ting-li), *adv.* In a revolting manner; offensively; abhorrently.

revoluble (rev'ǫ-lū-bl), *a.* [< L. *revolubilis*, that may be revolved or rolled, < *revolvere*, revolve: see *revolve*.] Capable or admitting of revolution. [Rare.]

Us then, to whom the thrice three yeer
Hath fill'd his *revoluble* orb, since our arrival here,
I blame not to wish home much more.
Chapman, Iliad, ii. 256.

revolubly (rev'ǫ-lū-bli), *adv.* In a revoluble manner; so as to be capable of revolution. [Rare.]

The sight tube being clamped to the carriage [for transit-instruments], so as to be *revolubly* adjusted thereon.
Sci. Amer., N. S., LXIII. 35.

revolute (rev'ǫ-lūt), *a.* [= F. *révolu*, < L. *revolutus*, pp. of *revolvere*, revolve: see *revolve*.] Rolled or curled backward or downward; rolled back, as the tips or margins of some leaves, fronds, etc.; in vernation and estivation, rolled backward from both the sides. See also cuts under *Nothochlæna*, *Pteris*, and *Rafflesia*.—**Revolute antennæ**, in *entom.*, antennæ which in repose are rolled or coiled spirally outward and backward, as in certain *Hymenoptera*.

1. Revolute-margined Leaf of *Andromeda polifolia*. 2. The leaf as shown in transverse section.

revolute (rev'ǫ-lūt), *v. i.* To revolve. [Colloq.]

Then he frames a second motion
From thy *revoluting* eyes.
The Academy, March 1, 1890, p. 153.

revolution (rev-ǫ-lū'shǫn), *n.* [< ME. *revolucion*, < OF. *revolution*, F. *révolution* = Pr. *revolucio* = Sp. *revolucion* = Pg. *revolução* = It. *rivoluzione*, *revoluzione* = D. *revolutie* = G. Sw. Dan. *revolution*, < LL. *revolutio(n-)*, a revolving, < L. *revolvere*, pp. *revolutus*, revolve, turn over: see *revolve*.] **1.** The act of revolving or turning completely round, so as to bring every point of the turning body back to its first position; a complete rotation through 360°. Where the distinction is of importance, this is called a *rotation*.

She was probably the very last person in town who still kept the time-honored spinning-wheel in constant *revolution*. *Hawthorne*, Seven Gables, v.

2. The act of moving completely around a circular or oval course, independently of any rotation. In a revolution without rotation, every part of the body moves by an equal amount, while in rotation the motions of the different parts are proportional to their distances from the axis. But revolutions and rotations may be combined. Thus, the planets perform *revolutions* round the sun, and at the same time *rotations* about their own axes. The moon performs a *rotation* on its axis in precisely the same time in which it performs a *revolution* round the earth, to which it consequently always turns the same side.

So many nobler bodies to create,
Greater so manifold, . . . and on their orbs impose
Such restless *revolution* day by day.
Milton, P. L., viii. 31.

3. A round of periodic or recurrent changes or events; a cycle, especially of time: as, the *revolutions* of the seasons, or of the hours of the day and night.

O God! that one might read the book of fate,
And see the *revolution* of the times
Make mountains level. *Shak.*, 2 Hen. IV., iii. 1. 46.

The Duke of Buckingham himself flew not so high in so short a *Revolution* of Time. *Howell*, Letters, I. v. 32.

There must be a strange dissolution of natural affection, a strange unthankfulness for all that homes have given, . . . when each man would fain build to himself, and build for the little *revolution* of his own life only.
Ruskin, Seven Lamps of Architecture, Memory, § 3.

Hence—**4.** A recurrent period or moment in time. [Rare.]

Thither by harpy-footed furies haled,
At certain *revolutions* all the damn'd
Are brought. *Milton*, P. L., ii. 597.

5. A total change of circumstances; a complete alteration in character, system, or conditions.

Chapless, and knocked about the mazzard with a sexton's spade: here's a fine *revolution*, and we had the trick to see 't. *Shak.*, Hamlet, v. 1. 98.

Religions, and languages, and forms of government, and usages of private life, and modes of thinking, all have undergone a succession of *revolutions*.
Macaulay, Moore's Byron.

Specifically—**6.** A radical change in social or governmental conditions; the overthrow of an established political system, generally accompanied by far-reaching social changes. The term *Revolution*, in English history, is applied distinctively to the convulsion by which James II. was driven from the throne in 1688. In American history it is applied to the war of independence. See below. [In this sense the word is sometimes used adjectively.]

The elections . . . generally fell upon men of *revolution* principles. *Smollett*, Hist. Eng., i. 6.

The *revolution*, as it is called, produced no other changes than those which were necessarily caused by the declaration of independence. *Calhoun*, Works, I. 189.

A state of society in which *revolution* is always imminent is disastrous alike to moral, political, and material interests. *Lecky*, Eng. in 18th Cent., ii.

7. The act of rolling or moving back; a return to a point previously occupied.

Fear
Comes thundering back with dreadful *revolution*
On my defenceless head. *Milton*, P. L., x. 815.

8†. The act of revolving or turning to and fro in the mind; consideration; hence, open deliberation; discussion.

But, Sir, I pray you, howe some ever my maister rekeneth with any of his servaunts, bring not the matier in *revolution* in the open Courte. *Paston Letters*, I. 388.

9. The winding or turning of a spiral about its axis, as a spiral of a shell about the columella; one of the coils or whorls thus produced; a volution; a turn.—**American Revolution**, the series of movements by which the thirteen American colonies of Great Britain revolted against the mother country, and asserted and maintained their independence. Hostilities began in 1775, independence was declared in 1776, and the help of France was formally secured in 1778. The war was practically ended by the surrender of the chief British army at Yorktown in 1781, and the independence of the United States was recognized by treaty of peace in 1783.—**Anomalistic revolution.** See *anomalistic*.—**English Revolution**, the movements by which James II. was forced to leave England, and a purer constitutional government was secured through the aid of William of Orange, who landed with an Anglo-Dutch army in November, 1688. In 1689 William and Mary were proclaimed constitutional sovereigns, and Parliament passed the Bill of Rights.—**French Revolution**, the series of movements which brought about the downfall of the old absolute monarchy in France, the establishment of the republic, and the abolition of many abuses. The States General assembled in May, 1789, and the Third Estate at once took the lead. The Bastille was stormed by the people, and in the same year the Constituent Assembly overthrew feudal privileges and transferred ecclesiastical property to the state. Abolition of titles and of right of primogeniture, and other reforms, were effected in 1790. The next year a constitution was adopted and the Constituent was succeeded by the Legislative Assembly. In 1792 a coalition of nations was formed against France, the royal family was imprisoned, and in September the Convention replaced the Legislative Assembly and proclaimed the republic. Louis XVI. was executed in 1793, and the Reign of Terror followed in 1793–4; royalist risings were suppressed, and the foreign wars successfully prosecuted. The revolutionary period may be regarded as ending with the establishment of the Directory in 1795, or as extending to the founding of the Consulate in 1799, or even later. Other French revolutions in 1830, 1848, and 1870 resulted respectively in the overthrow of the Bourbon monarchy of the Restoration, of the monarchy of Louis Philippe, and of the Second Empire.—**Pole of revolution.** See *pole*2.—**Revolution-indicator.** Same as *operameter*.—**Solid of revolution**, a solid containing all the points traversed by a plane figure in making a revolution round an axis in its plane, and containing no others. The *ellipsoid, paraboloid, hyperboloid, etc., of revolution* are examples.=**Syn. 6.** See *insurrection*.

revolutionary (rev-ō-lū'shon-ā-ri), *a.* and *n.* [= F. *révolutionnaire* = Sp. Pg. *revolucionario* = It. *rivoluzionario*; as *revolution* + *-ary*.] **I.** *a.* **1.** Pertaining to a revolution in government, or [*cap.*] to any movement or crisis known as *the Revolution*: as, a *revolutionary* war; *Revolutionary* heroes; the *Revolutionary* epoch in American history.

In considering the policy to be adopted for suppressing the insurrection, I have been anxious and careful that the inevitable conflict for this purpose shall not degenerate into a violent and remorseless *revolutionary* struggle.
Lincoln, in Raymond, p. 176.

2. Tending to produce revolution; subversive of established codes or systems: as, *revolutionary* measures; *revolutionary* doctrines.

It is much less a reasoning conviction than unreasoning sentiments of attachment that enable Governments to bear the strain of occasional maladministration, *revolutionary* panics, and seasons of calamity.
Lecky, Eng. in 18th Cent., ii.

Revolutionary calendar. See *republican calendar*, under *calendar*.—**Revolutionary tribunal.** See *tribunal*.

II. *n.*; pl. *revolutionaries* (-riz). A revolutionist.

Dumfries was a Tory town, and could not tolerate a *revolutionary*. *J. Wilson.*

It is necessary for every student of history to know what manner of men they are who become *revolutionaries*, and what causes drive them to revolution.
Kingsley, Alton Locke, Pref. (1862). (*Davies.*)

revolutioner (rev-ō-lū'shon-ėr), *n.* [< *revolution* + *-er*2. Cf. *revolutionary*.] Same as *revolutionary*.

The people were divided into three parties, namely, the Williamites, the Jacobites, and the discontented *Revolutioners*. *Smollett*, Hist. Eng., i. 4.

revolutionise, *v.* See *revolutionize*.

revolutionism (rev-ō-lū'shon-izm), *n.* [< *revolution* + *-ism*.] Revolutionary principles. *North Brit. Rev.* (*Imp. Dict.*)

revolutionist (rev-ō-lū'shon-ist), *n.* [< *revolution* + *-ist*.] One who desires or endeavors to effect a social or political revolution; one who takes part in a revolution.

If all *revolutionists* were not proof against all caution, I should recommend it to their consideration that no persons were ever known in history, either sacred or profane, to vex the sepulchre. *Burke.*

Many foreign *revolutionists* out of work added to the general misunderstanding their contribution of broken English in every most ingenious form of fracture.
Lowell, Study Windows, p. 194.

revolutionize (rev-ō-lū'shon-īz), *v.*; pret. and pp. *revolutionized*, ppr. *revolutionizing*. [< *revolution* + *-ize*.] **I.** *trans.* **1.** To bring about a revolution in: effect a change in the political constitution of: as, to *revolutionize* a government.

Who, in his turn, was sure my father plann'd
To *revolutionise* his native land.
Crabbe, Tales of the Hall, x.

2. To alter completely; effect a radical change in.

We need this [absolute religion] to heal the vices of modern society, to *revolutionize* this modern feudalism of gold. *Theodore Parker*, Ten Sermons, v.

I even think that their [the rams'] employment will go as far to *revolutionize* the conditions of naval warfare as has the introduction of breech-loading guns and rifles those of fighting ashore. *N. A. Rev.*, CXXXIX. 434.

II. *intrans.* To undergo a revolution; become completely altered in social or political respects.

Germany is by nature too thorough to be able to *revolutionize* without *revolutionizing* from a fundamental principle, and following that principle to its utmost limits.
Marx, quoted in Rae's Contemporary Socialism, p. 124.

Also spelled *revolutionise*.

revolutive (rev'ō-lū-tiv), *a.* [< F. *révolutif* (in sense 2); as *revolute* + *-ive*.] **1.** Turning over; revolving; cogitating.

Being so concerned with the inquisitive and *revolutive* soul of man. *Feltham*, Letters, xvii. (*Latham.*)

2. In *bot.*, same as *revolute*, or sometimes restricted to the case of vernation and estivation.

revolvable (rē-vol'va-bl), *a.* [< *revolve* + *-able*.] Capable of being revolved.

The upper cap of the mill is *revolvable*. *Nature*, XL. 543.

revolve (rē-volv'), *v.*; pret. and pp. *revolved*, ppr. *revolving*. [< ME. *revolven*, < OF. *revolver* = Sp. Pg. *revolver*, stir, = It. *rivolvere*, < L. *revolvere*, roll back, revolve, < *re-*, back, + *volvere*, roll: see *voluble*, *volve*. Cf. *convolve*, *devolve*, *evolve*, *involve*.] **I.** *intrans.* **1.** To turn or roll about on an axis; rotate.

Beware
Lest, where you seek the common love of these,
The common hate with the *revolving* wheel
Should drag you down. *Tennyson*, Princess, vi.

2. To move about a center; circle; move in a curved path; follow such a course as to come round again to a former place: as, the planets *revolve* about the sun.

In the same circle we *revolve*. *Tennyson*, Two Voices.

Minds roll in paths like planets; they *revolve*,
This in a larger, that a narrower ring,
But round they come at last to that same phase.
O. W. Holmes, Master and Scholar.

3. To pass through periodic changes; return or recur at regular intervals; hence, to come around in process of time.

In the course of one *revolving* moon
Was chymist, fiddler, statesman, and buffoon.
Dryden, Absalom and Achitophel, i. 549.

To mute and to material things
New life *revolving* summer brings.
Scott, Marmion, i., Int.

4. To pass to and fro in the mind; be revolved or pondered.

Much of this nature *revolved* in my mind, thrown in by the enemy to discourage and cast me down.
T. Ellwood, Life (ed. Howells), p. 205.

5. To revolve ideas in the mind; dwell, as upon a fixed idea; meditate; ponder.

If this [letter] fall into thy hand, *revolve*.
Shak., T. N., ii. 5. 155.

Still
My mother went *revolving* on the word.
Tennyson, Princess, iii.

6†. To return; devolve again.

On the desertion of an appeal, the judgment does, ipso jure, *revolve* to the judge a quo. *Ayliffe*, Parergon.

II. *trans.* **1.** To turn or cause to roll round, as upon an axis.

Then in the east her turn she [the moon] shines,
Revolved on heaven's great axle. *Milton*, P. L., vii. 381.

2. To cause to move in a circular course or orbit: as, to *revolve* the planets in an orrery.

If the diurnal motion of the air
Revolves the planets in their destined sphere,
How are the secondary orbs impelled?
How are the moons from falling headlong held?
Chatterton, To Rev. Mr. Catcott.

3. To turn over and over in the mind; ponder; meditate on; consider.

The ancient authors, both in divinity and in humanity, which had long time slept in libraries, began generally to be read and *revolved*.
Bacon, Advancement of Learning, i. 30.

Long stood Sir Bedivere,
Revolving many memories.
Tennyson, Morte d'Arthur.

4†. To turn over the pages of; look through; search.

I remember, on a day I *revolued* the registers in the capitol, I red a right meruailous thyng. *Golden Book*, xii.

Straight I again *revolved*
The law and prophets, searching what was writ
Concerning the Messiah. *Milton*, P. R., i. 259.

revolve† (rē-volv'), *n.* [< *revolve*, *v.*] **1.** A revolution; a radical change in political or social affairs.

In all *revolves* and turns of state
Decreed by (what dee call him) fate.
D'Urfey, Colin's Walk, i. (*Davies.*)

2. A thought; a purpose or intention.

When Midelton saw Grinuill's hie *revolve*,
Past hope, past thought, past reach of all aspire,
Once more to moue him flie, he doth resolue.
G. Markham, Sir R. Grinuile, p. 59. (*Davies.*)

revolved (rē-volvd'), *a.* [< *revolve* + *-ed*2.] In *zoöl.*, same as *revolute*.

revolvement (rē-volv'ment), *n.* [= Sp. *revolvimiento* = Pg. *revolvimento*; as *revolve* + *-ment*.] The act of revolving or turning over, as in the mind; reflection. *Worcester.*

revolvency (rē-vol'ven-si), *n.* [< L. *revolven(t-)s*, ppr. of *revolvere*, revolve: see *revolve*.] The state, act, or principle of revolving; revolution.

Its own *revolvency* upholds the world.
Cowper, Task, i. 372.

revolver (rē-vol'vėr), *n.* [< *revolve* + *-er*1.] **1.** One who or that which revolves.—**2.** Specifical-

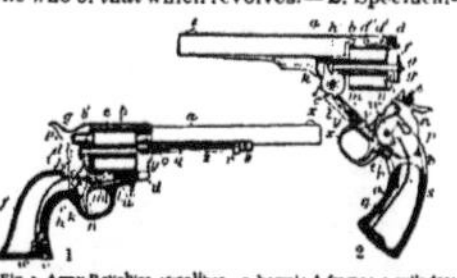

Fig. 1. Army Revolver, 45-caliber. *a*, barrel; *b*, frame; *c*, cylinder; *d*, center-pin; *e*, guard; *f*, back-strap; *g*, hammer; *h*, mainspring; *i*, hammer-roll and hammer-rivet; *j*, hammer-screw; *k*, hammer-cam; *l*, hand and hand-spring; *m*, stop-bolt and stop-bolt screw; *n*, trigger; *o*, center-pin bushing; *p*, firing-pin and firing-pin rivet; *q*, ejector-rod and spring; *r*, ejector-head; *s*, ejector-tube screw; *t*, guard-screw; *u*, sear and stop-bolt spring combined; *v*, back-strap screw; *w*, mainspring-screw; *x*, front sight; *y*, center-pin-catch screw; *z*, ejector-tube. By removing the center-pin *d*, the cylinder *c* may be taken out of the frame *b* for cleaning and reloading. In cocking the hand and hand-roll *l* revolve the cylinder through an arc limited by the stop, stop-bolt, and stop-bolt spring, bringing another cartridge into position for firing. The cylinder has six chambers. The stock (not shown) is fastened to the sides of the frame by screws. The recoil-plate is shown at *b'*.

Fig. 2. Partial Longitudinal Section of Common Revolver. *a*, barrel; *b*, frame; *c*, joint-pivot screw; *d*, cylinder-catch; *d'*, cylinder-catch-cam screw; *d''*, cylinder-catch screw; *e*, barrel-catch; *f*, cylinder; *g*, extractor; *g'*, extractor-stud; *h*, extractor-stem with coiled extractor-spring; *i*, steady-pin; *j*, friction-collar; *k*, lifter; *l*, pawl and pawl-pin; *m*, pawl-spring; *n*, hammer; *o*, mainspring; *p*, mainspring-swivel; *q*, strain-screw; *r*, hammer-stud; *s*, trigger; *t*, recoil-plate; *u*, stop, stop-pin, and stop-spring; *w*, hand, hand-spring, and hand-spring pin; *x*, guard; *y*, guard-screw; *z*, front sight.

ly—(*a*) A revolving firearm, especially a pistol, having a revolving barrel provided with a number of bores (as in earlier styles of the weapon), or (as in modern forms) a single barrel with a revolving cylinder at its base, provided with a number of chambers. When the barrel or cylinder revolves on its longitudinal axis, the several bores or chambers are brought in succession into relation with firing-mechanism for successive and rapid firing. In the modern forms of the arm the chambers of the cylinder are, by such revolution, brought successively into line with the bore in the barrel, which is also the firing position. In this position each chamber respectively forms a continuation of the bore in the barrel. Six is the common number of chambers. The most vital distinction between early and modern revolving firearms is that the barrels of the former were directly revolved by the hand; while in the latter the revolving-mechanism is connected with the firing-mechanism, the cocking of which automatically revolves the cylinder. Metal cartridges with conical bullets are used in all modern revolvers, the loading being done at the breech. Some are self-cocking—that is, are cocked by pulling the trigger which also discharges them. Some, by peculiar mechanism (though, for general use, they may be cocked in the ordinary way for taking deliberate aim), are by a quick adjustment changed into self-cocking pistols for more rapid firing in emergencies where accurate aim is of subordinate importance. Colonel Colt of the United States was the first to produce a really serviceable and valuable revolving arm, though the principle was known in the earlier part of the sixteenth century. (*b*) A revolving cannon.—3. A revolving horse-rake.

revolving (rę-vol'ving), *p. a.* Turning; rolling; moving round.—**Revolving brush, car, diaphragm, grate, harrow, light, mill, oven.** See the nouns.—**Revolving cannon.** See *machine-gun*.—**Revolving furnace**, a furnace used extensively in making ball-soda or black-ash, consisting of a large cylinder of iron hooped with solid steel tires shrunk on the shell, which is supported by and turns on friction-wheels or -rollers. Unlike the revolving furnace for chloridizing ores, this furnace has no interior partition. The heat is supplied by a Siemens regenerative gas-furnace, or by a coal-furnace, and the hot flame circulates longitudinally through the cylinder into a smoke-stack or chimney. The charging is done through a hole in the side of the cylinder, and the crude soda, rolled into balls by the motion of the cylinder, is discharged through the same opening.—**Revolving pistol.** Same as *revolver*.—**Revolving press.** See *press*[1].—**Revolving storm**, a cyclone.

revomit (rę-vom'it), *v. t.* [= It. *revomitare*; as *re-* + *vomit*. Cf. F. *revomir*, < L. *revomere*, vomit forth again, disgorge, < *re-*, again, + *vomere*, vomit: see *vomit*.] To vomit or pour forth again; reject from the stomach.

> They poure the wine downe the throate . . . that they might cast it vp againe and so take more in the place, vomiting and *revomiting* . . . that which they haue drunke.
> — *Hakewill*, Apology, iv. 3.

revulse† (rę-vuls'), *v. t.* [< F. *révulser*, < L. *revulsus*, pp. of *revellere*, pluck back: see *revel*[2].] 1. To affect by revulsion; pull or draw back; withdraw.

> Nothing is so effectual as frequent vomits to withdraw and *revulse* the peccant humours from the relaxed bowels.
> — *G. Cheyne*, Natural Method. (*Latham.*)

2. To draw away: applied to counter-irritation.

revulsent (rę-vul'sent), *a.* and *n.* [< *revulse* + *-ent.*] I. *a.* Same as *revellent*.

II. *n.* A counter-irritant.

revulsion (rę-vul'shǫn), *n.* [< OF. *revulsion*, F. *révulsion* = Sp. *revulsion* = Pg. *revulsão* = It. *rivulsione*, < L. *revulsio(n-)*, a tearing off or away, < *revellere*, pp. *revulsus*, pluck back: see *revel*[2].] 1. The act of pulling or drawing away; abstraction; forced separation.

> The *revulsion* of capital from other trades of which the returns are more frequent.
> — *Adam Smith*, Wealth of Nations, iv. 7.

2. In *med.*, the diminution of morbid action in one locality by developing it artificially in another, as by counter-irritation.—3. A sudden or violent change, particularly a change of feeling.

> A sudden and violent *revulsion* of feeling. — *Macaulay.*

> He was quite old enough . . . to have seen with his own eyes the conversion of the court, [and] its *revulsion* to the ancient worship under Julian the Apostate.
> — *The Atlantic*, LXV. 149.

revulsive (rę-vul'siv), *a.* and *n.* [= F. *révulsif* = Sp. Pg. It. *revulsivo*, < L. *revulsus*, pp. of *revellere*, pull away: see *revel*[2].] I. *a.* Having the power of revulsion; tending to revulsion; capable of producing revulsion.

> The way to cure the megrim is diverse, according to the cause; either by cutting a vein, purging, *revulsive* or local remedies.
> — *Rev. T. Adams*, Works, I. 473.

II. *n.* That which has the power of withdrawing; specifically, an agent which produces revulsion.

> Salt is a *revulsive*. Pass the salt.
> — *R. L. Stevenson*, The Dynamiter, p. 138.

revulsor (rę-vul'sǫr), *n.* [< *revulse* + *-or*.] An apparatus by means of which heat and cold can be alternately applied as curative agents.

Rev. Ver. An abbreviation of *Revised Version* (of the English Bible).

revyet, *v.* See *revie*.

rew[1], *n.* An obsolete or dialectal form of *row*[2].

rew[2]†, *v.* and *n.* An obsolete spelling of *rue*[1].

rew[3]† (rö). An obsolete preterit of *row*[1].

rewake, *v.* An erroneous form, found in the sixteenth-century editions of Chaucer, for *revoke*.

rewaken (rē-wā'kn), *v.* [< *re-* + *waken*.] To waken again.

> Love will . . . at the spiritual prime
> *Rewaken* with the dawning soul.
> — *Tennyson*, In Memoriam, xliii.

rewall†, *v.* A (perverted) Middle English form of *rule*[1]. *Lydgate.*

rewalt†, *v. t.* and *i.* [ME.; origin obscure.] To give up or surrender. *Halliwell.*

reward (rę-wârd'), *v.* [< ME. *rewarden*, < OF. *rewarder*, *reswarder*, an older form of *reguarder*, *regarder*, regard, < *re-*, back, + *warder*, *garder*, mark, heed: see *guard*. Doublet of *regard*.] I. *trans.* 1†. To mark; regard; observe; notice carefully.

> Hit you behouith *rewarde* and behold
> Ho shall doo gouerne and rule this contre.
> — *Rom. of Partenay* (E. E. T. S.), l. 2367.

2†. To look after; watch over; have regard or consideration for.

> Ac if ye riche haue reuthe and *rewarde* wel the pore, . . . Criste of his curteysie shal conforte ȝow atte laste.
> — *Piers Plowman* (B), xiv. 146.

3. To recompense; requite; repay, as for good or evil conduct (commonly in a good sense); remunerate, as for usefulness or merit; compensate.

> Kyng Auferius ther with he was contente,
> And hym *rewardid* well for his presente.
> — *Generydes* (E. E. T. S.), l. 2407.

> I'll follow, as they say, for reward. He that *rewards* me, God *reward* him! — *Shak.*, 1 Hen. IV., v. 4. 167.

4. To make return for; give a recompense for.

> *Reward* not hospitality
> With such black payment.
> — *Shak.*, Lucrece, l. 575.

5†. To give in recompense or return, as for either good or evil.

> Thou hast *rewarded* me good, whereas I have *rewarded* thee evil. — 1 Sam. xxiv. 17.

> A blessing may be *rewarded* into the bosom of the faithful and tender brother or sister that . . . admonisheth.
> — *Penn*, Travels in Holland, etc.

6. To serve as a return or recompense to; be a reward to.

> No petty post *rewards* a nobleman
> For spending youth in splendid lackey-work.
> — *Browning*, Ring and Book, I. 60.

7. To serve as return or recompense for.

> Still happier, if he till a thankful soil,
> And fruit *reward* his honourable toil.
> — *Cowper*, Hope, l. 761.

> The central court of the Hareem is one of the richest discoveries that *rewarded* M. Place's industry.
> — *J. Fergusson*, Hist. Arch., I. 173.

II. *intrans.* To make requital; bestow a return or recompense, especially for meritorious conduct.

> But you great wise persons have a fetch of state, to employ with countenance and encouragement, but *reward* with austerity and disgrace.
> — *Chapman*, Mask of Middle Temple and Lincoln's Inn.

reward (rę-wârd'), *n.* [< ME. *rewarde*, *reward*, < OF. *reward*, an earlier form of *reguard*, *regard*, regard, < *rewarder*, *regarder*, regard: see *reward*, *v.*, and cf. *regard*, *n.*] 1†. Notice; heed; consideration; respect; regard.

> Thanne Reson rod forth and tok *reward* of no man,
> And dude as Conscience kenned til he the kyng mette.
> — *Piers Plowman* (C), v. 40.

> Men take more *rewarde* to the nombre than to the sapience of persons. — *Chaucer*, Tale of Melibeus.

2. The act of rewarding, or the state of being rewarded; requital, especially for usefulness or merit; remuneration.

> The end for which all profitable laws
> Were made looks two ways only, the reward
> Of innocent good men, and the punishment
> Of bad delinquents.
> — *Fletcher* (*and another*), Queen of Corinth, v. 4.

> The hope of *reward* and fear of punishment, especially in a future life, are indispensable as auxiliary motives to the great majority of mankind.
> — *Fowler*, Shaftesbury and Hutcheson, p. 159.

3. That which is given in requital of good or evil, especially good; a return; a recompense; commonly, a gift bestowed in recognition of past service or merit; a guerdon.

> Now-a-days they call them gentle *rewards*: let them leave their coloring, and call them by their Christian name, bribes. — *Latimer*, 3d Sermon bef. Edw. VI., 1549.

> Now *rewards* and punishments do always presuppose something willingly done well or ill.
> — *Hooker*, Eccles. Polity, i. 9.

> A man that fortune's buffets and *rewards*
> Hast ta'en with equal thanks.
> — *Shak.*, Hamlet, iii. 2. 72.

> Hanging was the *reward* of treason and desertion.
> — *Stubbs*, Const. Hist., § 16.

4. The fruit of one's labor or works; profit; return.

> The dead know not any thing, neither have they any more a *reward*. — Eccl. ix. 5.

5. A sum of money offered for taking or detecting a criminal, or for the recovery of anything lost.—**In reward of**†, in comparison with.

> Yit of Daunger cometh no blame,
> *In reward of* my doughter Shame.
> — *Rom. of the Rose*, l. 3254.

=**Syn.** 3. Pay, compensation, remuneration, requital, retribution.

rewardable (rę-wâr'dạ-bl), *a.* [< *reward* + *-able*.] Capable of being rewarded; worthy of recompense.

> No good woorke of man is *rewardable* in heauen of his owne nature, but through the mere goodnes of God.
> — *Sir T. More*, Cumfort against Tribulation (1573), fol. 25.

> Rewards do always presuppose such duties performed as are *rewardable*. — *Hooker*, Eccles. Polity, i. 11.

rewardableness (rę-wâr'dạ-bl-nes), *n.* The character of being rewardable, or worthy of reward.

> What can be the praise or *rewardableness* of doing that which a man cannot chuse but do?
> — *J. Goodman*, Winter Evening Conferences, p. 2.

rewardably (rę-wâr'dạ-bli), *adv.* In a rewardable manner; so as to be rewardable. *Imp. Dict.*

rewarder (rę-wâr'dėr), *n.* One who rewards; one who requites or recompenses.

> A liberal *rewarder* of his friends.
> — *Shak.*, Rich. III., i. 3. 123.

rewardful (rę-wârd'fůl), *a.* [< *reward* + *-ful*.] Yielding reward; rewarding. [Rare.]

> Whose grace was great, and bounty most *rewardfull*.
> — *Spenser*, Colin Clout, l. 187.

rewardfulness (rę-wârd'fůl-nes), *n.* The quality of being rewardful; capability of yielding a reward.

> Of the beauty, the *rewardfulness*, of the place I cannot trust myself to speak. — *The Century*, VI. 30.

rewardless (rę-wârd'les), *a.* [< *reward* + *-less*.] Having no reward.

rewa-rewa (rā'wạ-rā'wạ), *n.* [New Zealand.] See *Knightia*.

rewbarb†, *n.* An obsolete form of *rhubarb*.

rewe†. An obsolete form of *rue*[1], *rue*[2], *row*[2].

reweigh (rē-wā'), *v. t.* [< *re-* + *weigh*.] To weigh a second time; verify the weight of by a second test or trial.

> It only remained now to remove the condensers, and *reweigh* them with all necessary precautions.
> — *Amer. Chem. Jour.*, X. 97.

rewel†, *n.* and *v.* An obsolete spelling of *rule*[1].

rewel-bone†, *n.* [< ME. *rewel-boon*, *rowel-boon*, *rewel-bone*, *ruelle-bone*, *reuylle-bone*, < *rewel*, *rowel* (of uncertain meaning, in form like *rowel*, lit. a little wheel, < OF. *rouelle*, a little wheel: see *rowel*), + *boon*, *bone*, appar. same as *bone*[1].] A word of unknown meaning, occurring in the line:

> His sadel was of *rewel-boon*. — *Chaucer*, Sir Thopas, l. 167.

> *Ruel-bone* is mentioned by Chaucer . . . as the material of a saddle. It is not, of course, to be thence supposed that *ruel-bone* was commonly or even actually used for that purpose. . . . In the Turnament of Tottenham Tibbe's garland is described as "fulle of *ruelle bones*," which another copy alters to *rounde bonys*. In the romance of Rembrun, p. 458, the coping of a wall is mentioned as made "of fin *ruwal*, that schon swithe brighte."
> — *Halliwell.*

rewet (rö'et), *n.* [< F. *rouet*, little wheel, gunlock, dim. of *roue*, a wheel, < L. *rota*, a wheel: see *rotary*, *rowel*.] 1. Originally, the revolving part of a wheel-lock. Hence—2. The wheel-lock itself.—3. A gun fitted with a wheel-lock. See *harquebus*.

rewful†, *a.* A Middle English form of *rueful*.

rewfulliche†, *adv.* A Middle English form of *ruefully*. *Chaucer.*

rewin (rē-win'), *v. t.* [< *re-* + *win*.] To win a second time; win back.

> The Palatinate was not worth the *rewinning*. — *Fuller.*

rewliche†, *a.* See *ruly*[1].

rewme†, *n.* A Middle English form of *realm*.

rewood (rē-wůd'), *v. t.* [< *re-* + *wood*[1].] To plant again with trees; reforest.

Rewooding the high lands where the streams take rise.
New York Semi-weekly Tribune, Dec. 24, 1880.

reword (rē-wėrd'), *v. t.* [< *re-* + *word*.] **1.** To put into words again; repeat.

It is not madness
That I have utter'd; bring me to the test,
And I the matter will *re-word*; which madness
Would gambol from. *Shak.*, Hamlet, iii. 4. 143.

2. To reëcho.

A hill whose concave womb *re-worded*
A plaintful story from a sistering vale.
Shak., Lover's Complaint, l. 1.

3. To word anew; put into different words: as, to *reword* a statement.

rewrite (rē-rīt'), *v. t.* [< *re-* + *write*.] To write a second time.

Write and *rewrite*, blot out, and write again,
And for its swiftness ne'er applaud your pen.
Young, To Pope.

rewthe†, *n.* An obsolete form of *ruth*.

rewthles†, *a.* An obsolete form of *ruthless*.

rex (reks), *n.* [< L. *rex* (*reg-*), a king (= OIr. *rig*, Ir. *righ* = Gael. *righ* = W. *rhi* = Skt. *rājan*, a king: see *Raja*[2]), < *regere* (Skt. √ *rāj*), rule: see *regent*, and rich, *riche*. Hence ult. *roy*, *royal*, *regal*, *real*[2], *ryale*[2], etc.] A king.—**To play rex†**, to play the king; act despotically or with violence; handle a person roughly; "play the mischief." This phrase probably alludes to the *Rex*, or king, in the early English plays, a character marked by more or less violence. The noun in time lost its literal meaning, and was often spelled *reaks*, *reeks* ("keep a *reaks*," etc.), and used as if meaning 'tricks.'

I . . . thinke it to be the greatest indignitie to the Queene that may be to suffer such a caytiff to *play* such *Rex*. *Spenser*, State of Ireland.

The sound of the hautboys and bagpipes *playing reeks* with the high and stately timber.
Urquhart, tr. of Rabelais, iii. 2.

Love with Rage *kept* such *a reakes* that I thought they would have gone mad together.
Breton, Dream of Strange Effects, p. 17.

Then came the English ordnance, which had been brought to land, to *play* such *reaks* among the horse that they were forced to fly.
Court and Times of Charles I., I. 256.

rexen, *n.* A plural of *resh*[2], a variant of *rush*[1]. *Halliwell.*

rex-player†, *n.* [Found only in the form *reaks-player*; < *rex*, in *to play rex* (*reaks*), + *player*.] One who plays rex.

Ribleur, a disordered roaver, jetter, swaggerer, outragious *reake-player*, a robber, ransaker, boothaler, preyer upon passengers, etc. *Cotgrave.*

rey†, *n.* An obsolete form of *ray*[4].

reyal†, *n.* An obsolete form of *royal*.

reyn†, *n.* A Middle English form of *rain*[1].

reynald†, *n.* An obsolete variant of *reynard*.

reynard (rā'närd or ren'ärd), *n.* [Formerly also *reynold*, *reynald*; < late ME. *reynard*, < OF. *reynard*, *regnard*, *regnar*, *regnart*, *renart*, *renard*, F. *renard* = Pr. *raynart* = OCat. *ranart*, a fox, < OFlem. (OLG.) *Reinaerd*, *Reinaert* (G. *Reinhart*, *Reinecke*), a name given to the fox in a famous epic of Low German origin ("Reynard the Fox"), in which animals take the place of men, each one having a personal name, the lion being called *Noble*, the cat *Tibert*, the bear *Bruin*, the wolf *Isegrim*, the fox *Reynard*, etc., and which became so popular that *renard* in the common speech began to take the place of the vernacular OF. *goulpil*, *goupil*, fox, and finally supplanted it entirely; < MHG. *Reinhart*, OHG. *Reginhart*, *Raginhart*, a personal name, lit. 'strong in counsel,' < *ragin-*, *regin-*, counsel (cf. Icel. *regin*, pl., the gods: see *Ragnarök*, and cf. AS. *regn-* (= Icel. *regin-*), intensive prefix in *regn-heard*, very hard, etc., *regn-meld*, a solemn announcement, *regn-theóf*, an arch-thief, etc., and in personal names such as *Regen-here*, etc., = Goth. *ragin*, an opinion, judgment, decree, advice), + *hart*, strong, hard, = E. *hard*: see *hard* and *-ard*.] A name of the fox in fable and poetry, in which the fox figures as cunning personified.

Hyer [here] begynneth th[e h]ystorye of *reynard* the foxe. *Caxton*, tr. of *Reynard* the Fox (ed. 1481), p. 16.

Now read, Sir *Reynold*, as ye be right wise,
What course ye weene is best for us to take.
Spenser, Mother Hub. Tale.

Reynosia (rā-nō'si-ạ̈), *n.* [NL. (Grisebach, 1866); after Alvaro *Reynoso* of Havana.] A genus of imperfectly known polypetalous plants, assigned to the order *Rhamnaceæ*, consisting of a single Cuban species, *R. latifolia*, extending into Florida, where it is known as *red ironwood*.

reyoung (rē-yung'), *v. t.* [< *re-* + *young*.] To make young again. [Rare.]

With rapid rush,
Out of the stone a plentious stream doth gush,
Which murmurs through the Plain; proud, that his glass,
Gliding so swift, so soon *re-youngs* the grass.
Sylvester, tr. of Du Bartas's Weeks, ii., The Lawe.

reyse[1]†, *v.* A Middle English form of *raise*[1].

reyse[2]†, *v.* A Middle English form of *race*[1].

rezbanyite (rez-ban'yīt), *n.* [< *Rez-Bánya* (see def.) + *-ite*[2].] A sulphid of bismuth and lead, occurring in massive forms having a metallic luster and light lead-gray color. It is found at Rez-Bánya, Hungary.

rezed†, *a.* Same as *reasted*.

rf., rfz. Abbreviations of *rinforzando* or *rinforzato*.

rh. [L., etc., *rh-*, used for *hr-*, a more exact rendering of the Gr. *ῥ*, the aspirated *p* (*r*).] An initial sequence, originally an aspirated *r*, occurring in English, etc., in words of Greek origin. In early modern and Middle English, as well as in Spanish, Italian, Old French, etc., it is also or only written *r*. When medial, as it becomes in composition, the *r* is doubled, and is commonly written *rrh*, after the Greek form *ῤῥ*, which, however, is now commonly written *ρρ*. In modern formations medial *rrh* is often reduced to *rh*. (For examples of *rh*, see the words following, and *catarrh*, *diarrhea*, *hemorrhage*, *myrrh*, *pyrrhic*, etc.) The combination *rh* properly occurs only in Greek words: other instances are due to error or confusion, or are exceptional, as in *rhyme* for *rime*[1], *rhine* for *rine*, *rhone* for *rone*, etc.

Rh. The chemical symbol of *rhodium*.

rha† (rä), *n.* [NL., < L. *rha* (*barbarum*), < Gr. *ῥᾶ*, rhubarb, so called, it is said, from the river *Rha*, Ῥᾶ, now called *Volga*. See *rhubarb* and *Rheum*[2].] Rhubarb.

Neere unto this is the river Rha, on the sides whereof groweth a comfortable and holsom root so named [*rha*], good for many uses in physick.
Holland, tr. of Ammianus Marcellinus, xxii. 8. 28.

rhabarbarate† (ra-bär'ba-rāt), *a.* [< NL. *rhabarbaratus*, < *rhabarbarum*, rhubarb: see *rhabarbarum*.] Impregnated or tinctured with rhubarb.

The salt humours must be evacuated by the sennate, *rhabarbarate*, and sweet manna purgers, with acids added, or the purging waters.
Floyer, Preternatural State of Animal Humours. [(*Latham*.)

rhabarbarin, rhabarbarine (ra-bär'ba-rin), *n.* [< *rhabarbarum* + *-in*[2], *-ine*[2].] Same as *chrysophanic acid*. See *chrysophanic*.

rhabarbarum (ra-bär'ba-rum), *n.* [NL., < L. *rha barbarum*, rhubarb: see *rhubarb* and *rha*.] Rhubarb.

rhabd (rabd), *n.* [Also *rabd*; < NL. *rhabdus*, < Gr. *ῥάβδος*, a rod: see *rhabdus*.] A rhabdus.

Rhabdammina (rab-da-mī'nạ̈), *n.* [NL., < Gr. *ῥάβδος*, a rod, + *ἄμμος*, sand, + *-ina*[1].] The typical genus of *Rhabdamminina*. *O. Sars*, 1872.

Rhabdamminina (rab-dam-i-nī'nạ̈), *n. pl.* [NL., < *Rhabdammina* + *-ina*[2].] A group of marine imperforate foraminiferous protozoans, typified by the genus *Rhabdammina*. The test, composed of cemented sand-grains often mixed with sponge-spicules, is of some tubular form, free or fixed, with one or a few apertures, and sometimes segmented. The genus *Haliphysema*, supposed to be a sponge, and made by Haeckel the type of a class *Physemaria*, has been assigned to this group. Also *Rhabdamminine*, as a subfamily of *Astrorhizidæ*.

rhabdi, *n.* Plural of *rhabdus*.

rhabdia, *n.* Plural of *rhabdium*, 1.

rhabdichnite (rab-dik'nīt), *n.* [< NL. *Rhabdichnites*, < Gr. *ῥάβδος*, a rod, + *ἴχνος*, a track, + *-ite*[2]. Cf. *ichnite*.] A fossil trace or track of uncertain character, such as may have been made by various animals in crawling or otherwise.

Rhabdichnites (rab-dik-nī'tēz), *n.* [NL., also *Rabdichnites* (J. W. Dawson, 1875): see *rhabdichnite*.] A hypothetical genus of no definition, covering organisms which are supposed to have left the traces called *rhabdichnites*.

Rhabdichnites and Eophyton belong to impressions explicable by the trails of drifting sea-weeds, the tail-markings of Crustacea, and the ruts ploughed by bivalve mollusks, and occurring in the Silurian, Erian, and Carboniferous rocks. *Dawson*, Geol. Hist. of Plants, p. 30.

rhabdite (rab'dīt), *n.* [< Gr. *ῥάβδος*, a rod, + *-ite*[2].] **1.** One of the three pairs of appendages of the abdominal sternites which unite to form the ovipositor of some insects.—**2.** A refractive rod-like body of homogeneous structure and firm consistency, found in numbers in the cells of the integument of most turbellarian worms. They may be entirely within these cells, or protrude from them, are readily pressed out, and often found in abundance in the mucus secreted and deposited by the worms. The function of the rhabdites seems related to the tactile sense. They vary in size and form, and also in their local or general dispersion on the body of the worm. They are produced in the ordinary epidermic cells, or in special formative cells beneath the integument, whence they work their way to the surface. Some similar bodies, of granular instead of homogeneous structure, are distinguished as *pseudo-rhabdites*. See *sagittocyst*.

3. A member of the genus *Rhabditis*.—**4.** A phosphide of iron, occurring in minute tetragonal prisms in some meteoric irons.

rhabditic (rab-dit'ik), *a.* [< *rhabdite* + *-ic*.] Of or pertaining to a rhabdite, in any sense.

Rhabditis (rab-dī'tis), *n.* [NL. (Dujardin), < Gr. *ῥάβδος*, a rod.] A generic name of minute nematoid worms of the family *Anguillulidæ*, under which various species of different genera of this family have been described in certain stages of their transformations. Worms of this form develop from the embryo in damp earth, where they lead an independent life till they migrate into their host, where, after further transformations, they acquire the sexually mature condition, though this is sometimes attained while they are still free. Members of the genera *Leptodera*, *Pelodera*, *Rhabdonema*, and others have been referred to *Rhabditis* under various specific names.—**Rhabditis genitalis**, a small round worm which has been found in the urine.

rhabdium (rab'di-um), *n.* [NL., < Gr. *ῥάβδος*, a rod.] **1.** Pl. *rhabdia* (-ạ̈). A striped muscular fiber. [Rare.]

The voluntary muscles of all vertebrates and of many invertebrates consist of fibers, the contents of which are perfectly regularly disposed in layers and transversely striped. For shortness, this striped mass may be called *rhabdia*. *Nature*, XXXIX. 48.

2. [*cap.*] A genus of coleopterous insects. *Schaum*, 1861.

Rhabdocarpus (rab-dō-kär'pus), *n.* [NL., < Gr. *ῥάβδος*, a rod, + *καρπός*, fruit.] A generic name given by Göppert and Berger, in 1848, to a fossil fruit of very uncertain affinities. Specimens referred to this genus have been described by various authors as occurring in the coal-measures of France, Germany, England, and various parts of the United States.

rhabdocœl (rab'dō-sēl), *a.* Same as *rhabdocœlous*.

Rhabdocœla (rab-dō-sē'lạ̈), *n. pl.* [NL., < Gr. *ῥάβδος*, a rod, + *κοῖλος*, hollow.] A prime division of turbellarian worms, forming a suborder of *Turbellaria*, contrasted with *Dendrocœla* (which see), containing small forms whose intestine, when present, is straight and simple. The body is cylindric (as compared with other flatworms), but more or less flattened; the sexual organs are usually hermaphrodite; there is no anus (see *Aprocta*), but a mouth, the position of which varies extremely in different genera, and usually a protrusile pharynx or buccal proboscis. In most forms the alimentary canal is distinct; in others (see *Acœla*) it is not fairly differentiated from the general digestive parenchyma. There are numerous forms of this group, mostly inhabiting fresh water, though some are marine. They live on the juices of small worms, crustaceans, and insects, which they suck after enveloping their prey in a sort of mucus secreted by the skin and containing rhabdites. (See *rhabdite*, 2.) The group is divided, mainly upon the character of the intestine, into three sections: (1) *Acœla*, without differentiated intestine, represented by the family *Convolutidæ*; (2) *Rhabdocœla* proper, with definite intestinal tract, a nervous system and excretory organs present, compact male and female generative glands, complicated pharynx, and generally no otoliths—embracing numerous forms of several different families, both of fresh and salt water; (3) *Allœocœla*, resembling (2), but with otoliths, represented by one family, *Monotidæ*. Another division, based mainly upon the position or other character of the mouth, is directly into a number of families, as *Convolutidæ*, *Opisthomidæ*, *Derostomidæ*, *Mesostomidæ*, *Prostomidæ*, and *Microstomidæ*. Also called *Rhabdocœlida*.

A Species of *Opisthomum*, illustrating the structure of *Rhabdocœla*.

a, central nervous system, close to which are seen ramifications of the water-vascular vessels; *b*, mouth; *c*, proboscis; *d*, testes; *e*, Vasa deferentia; *f*, Vesicula seminalis; *g*, penis; *h*, sexual aperture; *i*, Vagina; *k*, spermatheca; *l*, germarium; *m*, vitellarium; *n*, uterus with two ova, inclosed in hard shells.

rhabdocœlan (rab-dō-sē'lạn), *n.* and *a.* [< *Rhabdocœla* + *-an*.] **I.** *n.* A member of the *Rhabdocœla*.

II. *a.* Same as *rhabdocœlous*.

Rhabdocœlida (rab-dō-sē'li-dạ̈), *n. pl.* [NL., < *Rhabdocœla* + *-ida*.] Same as *Rhabdocœla*.

rhabdocœlidan (rab-dō-sē'li-dan), *a.* and *n.* [< *Rhabdocœlida* + *-an*.] **I.** *a.* Of or pertaining to the *Rhabdocœlida*.

II. *n.* A member of the *Rhabdocœlida*.

rhabdocœlous (rab-dō-sē'lus), *a.* [< Gr. *ῥάβδος*, a rod, + *κοῖλος*, hollow.] Having, as a turbellarian, a simple straight digestive cavity; of or pertaining to the *Rhabdocœla*.

Rhabdocrepida (rab-dō-krep'i-dạ̈), *n. pl.* [NL., < Gr. *ῥάβδος*, a rod, + *κρηπίς* (*κρηπιδ-*), a foundation.] A suborder or other group of lithistidan tetractinellidan sponges, with diversiform desmas produced by the various growth of silica over uniaxial spicules. The families *Megamorinidæ* and *Micromorinidæ* represent this group.

rhabdoid (rab'doid), *n.* [Also *rabdoid;* < Gr. ῥαβδοειδής, like a rod, < ῥάβδος, a rod, + εἶδος, form.] In *bot.*, a spindle-shaped or acicular body, chemically related to the plastids, which occurs in certain cells of plants exhibiting irritability, such as *Drosera, Dionæa*, etc., and which probably plays an important part in this function. The position in the cell is such that it stretches diagonally across the cell from end to end.

rhabdoidal (rab-doi'dal), *a.* [Also *rabdoidal;* < *rhabdoid* + *-al.*] Rod-like; specifically, in *anat.*, sagittal: as, the *rhabdoidal* suture.

rhabdolith (rab'dọ-lith), *n.* [< Gr. ῥάβδος, a rod, + λίθος, a stone.] A minute rhabdoidal concretion of calcareous matter occurring in globigerina-ooze—one of the elements which cover a rhabdosphere.

The clubs of the *rhabdoliths* get worn out of shape, and are last seen, under a high power, as minute cylinders scattered over the field.
Sir C. W. Thomson, Voyage of Challenger, I. iii.

rhabdolithic (rab-dọ-lith'ik), *a.* [< *rhabdolith* + *-ic.*] Concreted in rhabdoidal form, as calcareous matter; of or pertaining to rhabdoliths.

rhabdology (rab-dol'ọ-ji), *n.* [Also *rabdology;* < F. *rhabdologie*, < Gr. ῥάβδος, a rod, + -λογία, < λέγειν, speak: see *-ology.*] The act or art of computing by Napier's rods or Napier's bones. See *rod.*

rhabdom (rab'dom), *n.* [< LGr. ῥάβδωμα, a bundle of rods: see *rhabdome.*] In *entom.*, a special structure in the eye, consisting of a concrescence of the rods developed on the cells of the retina, when these cells are themselves united in a retinula.

The rods also become united, and form a special structure, the *rhabdom*, in the long axis of a group of combined retinal cells. *Gegenbaur*, Comp. Anat. (trans.), p. 264.

rhabdomal (rab'dọ-mal), *a.* [< *rhabdome* + *-al.*] Having the character of a rhabdome; pertaining to a rhabdome.

rhabdomancer (rab'dọ-man-sėr), *n.* [Also *rabdomancer;* < *rhabdomancy* + *-er*[1].] One who professes or practises rhabdomancy; a romancer of the divining-rod; a bletonist; a douser.

rhabdomancy (rab'dọ-man-si), *n.* [Also *rabdomancy;* < F. *rhabdomancie, rhabdomance* = Pg. *rhabdomancia* = It. *rabdomanzia*, < Gr. ῥαβδομαντεία, divination by means of a rod, < ῥάβδος, a rod, + μαντεία, divination.] Divination by a rod or wand; specifically, the attempt to discover things concealed in the earth, as ores, metals, or springs of water, by a divining-rod; bletonism; dousing.

Agreeably to the doctrines of *rhabdomancy*, formerly in vogue, and at the present moment not entirely discarded, a twig, usually of witchhazel, borne over the surface of the ground, indicates the presence of water, to which it is instinctively alive, by stirring in the hand.
S. Judd, Margaret, i. 9.

rhabdomantic (rab-dọ-man'tik), *a.* [Also *rabdomantic;* < *rhabdomancy* (*-mant-*) + *-ic.*] Pertaining to rhabdomancy, or the use of the divining-rod.

rhabdome (rab'dōm), *n.* [< LGr. ῥάβδωμα, a bundle of rods, < Gr. ῥάβδος, a rod. Cf. *rhabdom.*] In sponges, the shaft of a cladose rhabdus, bearing the cladome.

The rhabdus then [*i. e.*, when cladose] becomes known as the shaft or *rhabdome*, and the secondary rays are the arms or cladi, collectively the head or cladome of the spicule. *W. J. Sollas*, Encyc. Brit., XXII. 417.

rhabdomere (rab'dọ-mēr), *n.* [< Gr. ῥάβδος, a rod, + μέρος, a part.] One of the chitinous rods which, when united, form a rhabdom. *Amer. Naturalist*, XXIV. 373.

Rhabdomesodon (rab-dọ-mes'ọ-don), *n.* [NL., < Gr. ῥάβδος, a rod, + μέσος, middle, + ὀδούς (ὀδοντ-) = E. *tooth.*] A genus of polyzoans, typical of the family *Rhabdomesodontidæ*. *R. gracile* is a characteristic species.

Rhabdomesodontidæ (rab-dọ-mes-ọ-don'ti-dē), *n. pl.* [NL., < *Rhabdomesodon* (*-odont-*) + *-idæ.*] A family of polyzoans, typified by the genus *Rhabdomesodon*. They had a ramose polyzoary composed of slender cylindrical solid or tubular branches with the cell-apertures on all sides. The cell-mouth was below the surface, and opened into a vestibule or outer chamber which constituted the apparent cell-aperture on the surface. The species lived in the Carboniferous seas.

rhabdomyoma (rab"dọ-mī-ō'mạ̈), *n.*; pl. *rhabdomyomata* (-mạ-tạ̈). [NL., < Gr. ῥάβδος, a rod, + NL. *myoma*, q. v.] A myoma consisting of striated muscular fibers.

Rhabdonema (rab-dọ-nē'mạ̈), *n.* [NL., < Gr. ῥάβδος, a rod, + νῆμα, a thread.] A genus of small nematoid worms referred to the family *Anguillulidæ*, containing parasitic species, some of which are known to pass through the *Rhabditis* form. Such is *R. nigrovenosum*, a viviparous parasite of the lungs of batrachians, half to three quarters of an inch long, whose embryos make their way into the intestine and thence to the exterior, being passed with the feces into water or mud, where they acquire the *Rhabditis* form. These have separate sexes, and the females produce living young, which finally migrate into the batrachian host. Another species, which occurs in the intestine of various animals, including man, is *R. strongyloides*, formerly known as *Anguillula intestinalis*.

rhabdophane (rab'dọ-fān), *n.* [< Gr. ῥάβδος, a rod, + -φανής, appearing, < φαίνεσθαι, appear.] A rare phosphate of the yttrium and cerium earths from Cornwall in England, and also from Salisbury in Connecticut, where the variety called *scovillite* is found.

Rhabdophora (rab-dof'ọ-rạ̈), *n. pl.* [NL., neut. pl. of **rhabdophorus:* see *rhabdophorous.*] A group of fossil organisms: same as *Graptolithina:* so called by Allman from the chitinous rod which supports the perisarc.

rhabdophoran (rab-dof'ọ-ran), *a.* and *n.* [< *Rhabdophora* + *-an.*] **I.** *a.* Of or pertaining to the *Rhabdophora;* graptolithic.

II. *n.* A member of the *Rhabdophora;* a graptolite.

rhabdophorous (rab-dof'ọ-rus), *a.* [< NL. **rhabdophorus*, < Gr. ῥάβδος, a rod, + φέρειν = L. *ferre* = E. *bear*[1].] Same as *rhabdophoran.*

Rhabdopleura (rab-dọ-plö'rạ̈), *n.* [NL. (Allman, 1869), < Gr. ῥάβδος, a rod, + πλευρόν, a rib.] The typical genus of *Rhabdopleuridæ*, having the tentacles confined to a pair of outgrowths of the lophophore containing each a cartilaginoid skeleton. *R. normani* is a marine form found in deep water of the North Atlantic, off the coasts of Shetland and Normandy. It is a small branching organism, apparently a molluscoid of polyzoan affinities, living in a system of delicate membranous tubes, each of which contains its polypide, free to crawl up and down the tube by means of a contractile stalk or cord called the *gymnocaulus*.

Rhabdopleuræ (rab-dọ-plö'rē), *n. pl.* [NL., pl. of *Rhabdopleura.*] An order of marine polyzoans, represented by the family *Rhabdopleuridæ*. Also *Rhabdopleurea.*

Rhabdopleuridæ (rab-dọ-plö'ri-dē), *n. pl.* [NL., < *Rhabdopleura* + *-idæ.*] The family represented by the genus *Rhabdopleura*. Together with *Cephalodiscidæ* the family forms a particular group of molluscoids, related to polyzoans, and named by Lankester *Pterobranchia*. It forms the type of the suborder *Aspidophora* of Allman.

rhabdopleurous (rab-dọ-plö'rus), *a.* Pertaining to the *Rhabdopleuridæ*, or having their characters.

rhabdosphere (rab'dọ-sfēr), *n.* [< Gr. ῥάβδος, a rod, + σφαῖρα, a sphere: see *sphere.*] A minute spherical body bristling with rhabdolithic rods, found in the depths of the Atlantic, whose nature is not yet determined. *Sir C. W. Thomson*, Voyage of Challenger, I. 220.

Rhabdosteidæ (rab-dos-tē'i-dē), *n. pl.* [NL., < *Rhabdosteus* + *-idæ.*] A family of fossil toothed cetaceans, typified by the genus *Rhabdosteus*, having the rostrum prolonged like a sword, and maxillary bones bearing teeth on their proximal portion. By some paleontologists it is referred to the family *Platanistidæ*. The only known species lived in the Eocene of eastern North America.

Rhabdosteoidea (rab-dos-tẹ-oi'dẹ-ạ̈), *n. pl.* [NL., < *Rhabdosteus* + *-oidea.*] The *Rhabdosteidæ* rated as a superfamily of *Denticete*. *Gill.*

Rhabdosteus (rab-dos'tẹ-us), *n.* [NL. (Cope, 1867), < Gr. ῥάβδος, a rod, + ὀστέον, a bone.] The typical genus of *Rhabdosteidæ*.

Rhabdostyla (rab-dọ-stī'lạ̈), *n.* [NL., < Gr. ῥάβδος, a rod, + στῦλος, a pillar.] A genus of peritrichous ciliate infusorians, related to *Vorticella*, but having a rigid instead of a contractile pedicel. Six species are described, all of fresh water.

rhabdous (rab'dus), *a.* [Also *rabdous;* < *rhabd*, *rhabdus*, + *-ous.*] Having the character of a rhabdus; exhibiting the uniaxial biradiate type of structure, as a sponge-spicule.

rhabdus (rab'dus), *n.*; pl. *rhabdi* (-dī). [NL., < Gr. ῥάβδος, a rod, stick, staff, wand, twig, switch.] 1. A sponge-spicule of the monaxon biradiate type; a simple straight spicule. There are several kinds of rhabdi, named according to their endings. A rhabdus sharp at both ends is an *oxea;* blunt at both ends, a *strongyle;* knobbed at both ends, a *tylote;* knobbed at one end and pointed at the other, a *tylotoxea;* blunt at one end and sharp at the other, a *strongyloxea*. The last two forms are scarcely distinguishable from the stylus.
2. In *bot.*, the stipe of certain fungi.

rhachial, rhachialgia, etc. See *rachial*, etc.

rhachilla, *n.* See *rachilla.*

Rhachiodon, rhachiodont, etc. See *Rachiodon*, etc.

rhachiomyelitis (rā"ki-ọ-mī-e-lī'tis), *n.* [NL., < Gr. ῥάχις, the spine, + μυελός, marrow, + *-itis.*] Inflammation of the spinal cord, usually called *myelitis.*

rhachiotome (rā'ki-ọ-tōm), *n.* Same as *rachitome.*

rhachiotomy (rā-ki-ot'ọ-mi), *n.* [< Gr. ῥάχις, the spine, + -τομία, < τέμνειν, ταμεῖν, cut.] Incision into an opening of the spinal canal.

rhachipagus, rhachis, *n.* See *rachipagus*, etc.

rhachischisis (rạ-kis'ki-sis), *n.* [NL., < Gr. ῥάχις, the spine, + σχίσις, a cleaving, < σχίζειν, cleave: see *schism.*] In *pathol.*, incomplete closure of the spinal canal, commonly called *spina bifida.*

rhachitic, rhachitis. See *rachitic*, etc.

rhachitome, rhachitomous. See *rachitome*, etc.

Rhacochilus (rak-ọ-kī'lus), *n.* [NL. (Agassiz, 1854), < Gr. ῥάκος, a rag, rags, + χεῖλος, lip.] In *ichth.*, a genus of embiotocoid fishes. *R. toxotes* is the alfiona. See cut under *alfiona.*

Rhacophorus (rạ-kof'ọ-rus), *n.* [NL., < LGr. ῥακοφόρος, wearing rags, < Gr. ῥάκος, a rag, rags, + φέρειν = E. *bear*[1].] A genus of batrachians of the family *Ranidæ*, containing arboreal frogs with such long and so broadly webbed toes that the feet serve somewhat as parachutes by means of which the creature takes long flying leaps. *R. reinhardti* is one of the largest tree-frogs, with the body three inches in length, the hind legs six inches. See cut under *flying-frog.*

Rhacophyllum (rak-ọ-fil'um), *n.* [NL., < Gr. ῥάκος, a rag, rags, + φύλλον, leaf.] A generic name given by Schimper (1869) to certain fossil plants found in the coal-measures of England and Germany, and supposed to be related to the ferns, but of very uncertain and obscure affinities. Lesquereux has described under this generic name a large number of species from the Carboniferous of various parts of the United States.

Rhadamanthine, Rhadamantine (rad-a-man'thin, -tin), *a.* [< L. *Rhadamanthus*, < Gr. Ῥαδάμανθυς, Rhadamanthus (see def.).] Pertaining to or resembling Rhadamanthus, in Greek mythology one of the three judges of the lower world, son of Zeus and Europa, and brother of Minos: applied to a solemn and final judgment.

Your doom is *Rhadamantine.* *Carlyle*, Dr. Francia.

To conquer in the great struggle with the devil, with incarnate evil, and to have the sentence pronounced by the *Rhadamanthine* voice of the past — Well done!
J. F. Clarke, Self-Culture, p. 73.

Rhadinosomus (rad"i-nọ-sō'mus), *n.* [NL. (Schönherr, 1840), < Gr. ῥαδινός, Æolic βραδινός, slender, taper, + σῶμα, body.] A genus of weevils or *Curculionidæ*. Formerly called *Leptosomus*, a name preoccupied in ornithology.

Rhætian (rē'shian), *a.* and *n.* [Also *Rhetian;* < F. *Rhétien*, < L. *Rhætius*, prop. *Rætius*, < *Rhæti*, *Ræti*, the Rhætians, *Rhætia*, *Rætia*, their country.] **I.** *a.* Of or pertaining to the ancient Rhæti or their country Rhætia, corresponding nearly to the modern Grisons, Vorarlberg, and western Tyrol: as, the *Rhætian* Alps.

II. *n.* A native of Rhætia.

Rhætic (rē'tik), *a.* [Also *Rhetic;* < L. *Rhæticus*, prop. *Ræticus*, < *Rhæti*, *Ræti*, the Rhætians: see *Rhætian.*] Of or belonging to the Rhætian Alps.—**Rhætic beds**, in *geol.*, certain strata, particularly well developed in the Swiss and Tyrolese Alps, which are regarded as being beds of passage between the Trias and the Jura. One of the most important divisions of the Rhætic series in England is the so-called *bone-bed*, which abounds in bones and teeth of fish, coprolites, and other organic remains.

rhætizite (rē'ti-zit), *n.* [Prop. **Rhæticite*, irreg. < *Rhætic* + *-ite*[2].] A white variety of cyanite, found at Greiner in Tyrol. Also *rhetizite.*

Rhæto-Romanic (rē'tō-rọ-man'ik), *a.* and *n.* [< *Rhætic* + *Romanic.*] Belonging to, or a member of, the group of Romance dialects spoken in southeastern Switzerland, part of Tyrol, and in the districts to the north of the Adriatic. Also *Rheto-Romanic.*

rhagades (rag'a-dēz), *n. pl.* [NL., < L. *rhagades*, < Gr. ῥαγάς, pl. ῥαγάδες, a chink, crack, rent, a crack of the skin, < ῥηγνύναι, ῥαγῆναι, break: see *break.*] Fissures of the skin; linear excoriations.

rhagite (rag'īt), *n.* [< Gr. ῥαγή, a crack (< ῥηγνύναι, ῥαγῆναι, break), + *-ite*[2].] A hydrous arseniate of bismuth occurring in yellow or yellowish-green crystalline aggregates at Schneeberg in Saxony.

Rhagodia (rạ-gō'di-ạ̈), *n.* [NL. (R. Brown, 1810), named from the resemblance of the clustered fruit to grapes; < Gr. ῥαγώδης, like grapes,

< ῥάξ (ῥαγ-), a grape.] A genus of apetalous plants of the order *Chenopodiaceæ* and tribe *Chenopodieæ*, characterized by glomerate flowers, a horizontal seed, and fleshy fruit crowning the persistent five-lobed calyx. The 13 species are all Australian. They are shrubs or rarely herbs, either slender or robust, mealy or minutely woolly, bearing chiefly alternate leaves and small greenish flowers which are spiked or panicled, and are followed by globose or flattened berries, often red. General names for the species are *red-berry* and *seaberry*. *R. Billardieri* is a sea-side shrub with somewhat fleshy shoots and leaves, straggling or 5 or 6 feet high, of some use in binding sands. *R. hastata* is the saloop-bush, an undershrub with small soft leaves, introduced at Hong-Kong and elsewhere as food for cattle.

rhagon (rag'on), *n.* [NL., < Gr. ῥάξ (ῥαγ-), a grape.] A type of sponge-structure resulting from the modification of a primitive form, as an olynthus, by the outgrowth of the endoderm into a number of approximately spherical chambers communicating with the exterior by a prosopyle and with the paragastric cavity by an apopyle (see *prosopyle*), with conversion of the flagellated into pavement epithelium except in the chambers. The rhagon occurs as a stage in the early development of some sponges, and others exhibit it in the adult state. The structure is named from the grape-like form of the spherical chambers. The term is correlated with *ascon*, *leucon*, and *sycon*. Also called *dysyeus*.

This may be termed the aphodal or racemose type of the *Rhagon* system, since the chambers at the ends of the aphodi radiating from the excurrent canal look like grapes on a bunch. *W. J. Sollas*, Encyc. Brit., XXII. 415.

rhagonate (rag'ọ-nāt), *a.* [< *rhagon* + *-ate*[1].] Having the character of a rhagon; of or pertaining to a rhagon; rhagose.

rhagose (rag'ōs), *a.* [< Gr. ῥάξ (ῥαγ-), a grape, + *-ose*.] Racemose, as the rhagon type of sponge-structure; rhagonate. *W. J. Sollas.*

Rhamnaceæ (ram-nā'sẹ-ē), *n. pl.* [NL. (Lindley, 1835), < *Rhamnus* + *-aceæ*.] An order of polypetalous plants of the series *Disciflorœ*. It is unlike the rest of its cohort *Celastrales* in its valvate calyx-lobes, and resembles the related *Ampelidaceæ*, or grape family, in its superior ovary and the position of its stamens opposite the petals; it is distinguished by its habit, strongly perigynous stamens, concave petals which are not caducous, larger and valvate sepals, and fruit not a berry. It includes about 475 species, classed in 5 tribes and 42 genera, widely diffused through warm countries. They are commonly erect trees or shrubs, often thorny, bearing undivided alternate or opposite stipulate leaves, which are often coriaceous and three- to five-nerved. The small flowers are greenish or yellow, commonly in axillary cymes, which are followed by three-celled capsules or drupes, sometimes edible, sometimes hard and indehiscent. It is often called the *buckthorn family*, from the common name of *Rhamnus*, the type genus. See cut under *Rhamnus*.

rhamnaceous (ram-nā'shius), *a.* [< NL. *Rhamnus* + *-aceous*.] Of or pertaining to the order *Rhamnaceæ*.

Rhamneæ (ram'nẹ-ē), *n. pl.* [NL. (A. P. de Candolle, 1825), < *Rhamnus* + *-eæ*.] The principal tribe of the order *Rhamnaceæ*, characterized by a dry or drupaceous fruit containing three stones which are indehiscent or two-valved. Although this name was originally employed for the order, it is better to restrict it to the tribe, and adopt the later form *Rhamnaceæ* of Lindley for the ordinal term, as is very generally done. See *Rhamnus*, *Ceanothus*, *Sageretia*, and *Pomaderris* for the chief among its 21 genera.

rhamnegin (ram'ne-jin), *n.* [< *Rhamnus* + *-eg-*, an arbitrary syllable, + *-in*[2].] A glucoside ($C_{24}H_{32}O_{14}$) found in buckthorn-berries.

rhamnetin (ram'ne-tin), *n.* [< *Rhamnus* + *-et-*, an arbitrary syllable, + *-in*[2].] A decomposition-product ($C_{12}H_{10}O_5$) formed from rhamnin.

rhamnin (ram'nin), *n.* [< *Rhamnus* + *-in*[2].] A crystallizable glucoside found in buckthorn-berries.

rhamnoxanthin (ram-nok-san'thin), *n.* [< NL. *Rhamnus* + Gr. ξανθός, yellow, + *-in*[2].] Same as *frangulin*.

Rhamnus (ram'nus), *n.* [NL. (Tournefort, 1700), < L. *rhamnos*, < Gr. ῥάμνος, the buckthorn, Christ's-thorn.] A genus of polypetalous shrubs and trees, including the buckthorn, type of the order *Rhamnaceæ* and of the tribe *Rhamneæ*. It is characterized by a thin disk sheathing the bell-shaped calyx-tube and bearing the four or five stamens on its margin; by a free ovary often immersed within the disk; and by its fruit, an oblong or spherical drupe, surrounded at its base by the small calyx-tube, and containing two, three, or four hard one-seeded stones. There are about 60 species, natives of warm and temperate regions, frequent in Europe, Asia, and America, rare in the tropics. They bear alternate petioled and feather-veined leaves, which are either entire or toothed, deciduous or evergreen, and are furnished with small deciduous stipules. The flowers are in axillary racemes or cymes, and are commonly diœcious in the typical section, but not so in the principal American species (the genus *Frangula* of Brongniart), which also differ in their unfurrowed seeds and flat fleshy seed-leaves. A general name for the species is *buckthorn*, the common buckthorn being *R. catharticus* of the northern Old World, planted and sparingly naturalized in the United States. It is used as a hedge-plant. Its bark is medicinal, like that of *R. Frangula*; its black berries afford a now nearly disused cathartic, and with

Branch of Common Buckthorn (*Rhamnus catharticus*) with Fruit. *a*, female flower; *b*, male flower; *c*, leaf, showing the nervation.

those of some other species yield by treatment the pigment known as *sap-green*. *R. Frangula*, of the same nativity, called *black* or *berry-bearing alder*, *alder-buckthorn*, and (*black*) *dogwood*, affords one of the very best gunpowder-charcoals, while its bark is an official cathartic. (See *frangula*, *frangulin*.) The fruit of *R. infectorius* and other species forms the French, Turkey, or Persian berries of the dyers. (See under *Persian*.) In China the bark of *R. tinctorius* (*R. chlorophorus*) and *R. Davuricus* (*R. utilis*) affords the famous green indigo, or lokao, there used to dye silks, also introduced at Lyons. (For other Old World species, see *alaternus* and *lotus-tree*, 3.) *R. Carolinianus* of the southern United States is a shrub or small tree, bearing a sweet and agreeable fruit. The berries of *R. croceus* of California are much eaten by the Indians. *R. Californicus*, the California coffee-tree, yields an unimportant coffee-substitute. *R. Purshianus* of the western coast yields the cascara sagrada bark (see under *bark*[2]), sometimes called *chittam-bark*, whence probably, in view of the hard fine wood, the name *shittim-wood*. See *bearberry*, 2, and *redwood*, 2.

Rhamphalcyon (ram-fal'si-on), *n.* [NL., < Gr. ῥάμφος, a curved beak, + ἀλκυών, the kingfisher: see *alcyon*, *halcyon*.] A genus of *Alcedininæ*: same as *Pelargopsis*. *Reichenbach*, 1851.

Rhamphastidæ (ram-fas'ti-dē), *n. pl.* [NL., < *Rhamphastos* + *-idæ*.] A family of picarian birds, typified by the genus *Rhamphastos*; the toucans. They have a bill of enormous size, though very light, the interior bony structure being highly cancellous and pneumatic; the tongue is long, slender, and feathery; the toes are four, yoked in pairs; there are ten tail-feathers; the vomer is truncate; the manubrium sterni is pointed; the clavicles are separate; the carotid is single; the oil-gland is tufted; and there are no cæca. The legs are homalogonatous, and the feet are antiopelmous. The tail can be thrown up on the back in a peculiar manner. The cutting edges of the bill are more or less serrate, and there is a naked space about the eye. The coloration is bold and varied. There are upward of 60 species, confined to the warmer parts of continental America. The leading genus besides *Rhamphastos* is *Pteroglossus*. See *toucan*, *toucanet*, and cuts under *Rhamphastos*, *Selenidera*, and *aracari*.

Rhamphastinæ (ram-fas-ti'nē), *n. pl.* [NL., < *Rhamphastos* + *-inæ*.] 1†. The *Rhamphastidæ* as a subfamily of some other family.—2. A subfamily of *Rhamphastidæ*, contrasted with *Pteroglossinæ*.

Rhamphastos (ram-fas'tos), *n.* [NL. (Linnæus, 1766, after Aldrovandus, 1599), more prop. *Rhamphestes* (Gesner, 1560) (cf. Gr. ῥαμφηστής, a fish, prob. the pike), < Gr. ῥάμφος, a curved beak.] The typical genus of *Rhamphastidæ*, formerly coextensive with the family, now restricted to large species having the bill at a maximum of size, as *R. picatus*, the toco toucan, or *R. ariel*. Usually written *Ramphastos*.

Ariel Toucan (*Rhamphastos ariel*).

Rhamphobatis (ram-fob'a-tis), *n.* [NL., < Gr. ῥάμφος, a curved beak, + βατίς, a flat fish.] Same as *Rhina*, 1 (*b*).

Rhamphocelus (ram-fọ-sē'lus), *n.* [NL. (Desmarest, 1805, as *Ramphocelus*), < Gr. ῥάμφος, a curved beak, + κήλη, tumor; altered to *Rhamphocœlus* (Sclater, 1886), on the presumption that the second element is < Gr. κοῖλος, hollow.] A remarkable genus of tanagers, having the rami of the under mandible peculiarly tumid and colored, and the plumage brilliant scarlet or yellow and black in the male. There are about 12 species, all of South America, especially Brazil, as *R. brasilius* and *R. jacapa*.

Rhamphocottidæ (ram-fọ-kot'i-dē), *n. pl.* [NL., < *Rhamphocottus* + *-idæ*.] A family of mail-cheeked acanthopterygian fishes, represented by the genus *Rhamphocottus*. The body is compressed, and the head also compressed and with a projecting snout; there are a short spinous and oblong soft dorsal fins, and the ventrals are subabdominal and imperfect.

Rhamphocottinæ (ram"fọ-ko-ti'nē), *n. pl.* [NL., < *Rhamphocottus* + *-inæ*.] The *Rhamphocottidæ* considered as a subfamily of *Cottidæ*.

Rhamphocottoidea (ram"fọ-ko-toi'dẹ-ä), *n. pl.* [NL., < *Rhamphocottus* + *-oidea*.] A superfamily of mail-cheeked acanthopterygian fishes, represented by the family *Rhamphocottidæ*, and distinguished by the development of the post-temporal bones.

Rhamphocottus (ram-fọ-kot'us), *n.* [NL. (Günther, 1874), < Gr. ῥάμφος, a curved beak, + κόττος, a river-fish, perhaps the bullhead or miller's-thumb: see *Cottus*.] A genus of mail-cheeked fishes having a projecting snout, typical of the family *Rhamphocottidæ*. The only known species, *R. richardsoni*, is an inhabitant of the colder waters of the Pacific coast of North America.

Rhamphodon (ram'fọ-don), *n.* [NL. (Lesson, 1831, as *Ramphodon*), < Gr. ῥάμφος, a curved beak, + ὀδούς (ὀδοντ-) = E. *tooth*.] A genus of *Trochilidæ*, so called from the serration of the bill of the male; the saw-billed humming-birds, as the Brazilian *R. nævius*: synonymous with *Grypus*, 1.

rhamphoid (ram'foid), *a.* [< Gr. ῥαμφώδης, beak-shaped, < ῥάμφος, a curved beak, + εἶδος, form.] Beak-shaped.—**Rhamphoid cusp**, a cusp on a plane curve, where the two branches lie on the same side of the tangent at the cusp; the union of an ordinary cusp; an inflexion, a binode, and a bitangent.

Rhampholeon (ram-fō'lẹ-on), *n.* [NL., < Gr. ῥάμφος, a curved beak, + λέων, a lion: see *lion*, and cf. *chameleon*.] A genus of chameleons, having the tail non-prehensile. *R. spectrum* is a Madagascan species. *Günther*, 1874.

Rhamphomicron (ram-fọ-mik'ron), *n.* [NL., < Gr. ῥάμφος, a curved beak, + μικρός, little.] A notable genus of *Trochilidæ*, including large humming-birds with short weak bill, no crest, and a beard of pendent metallic feathers, ranging from the United States of Colombia to Bolivia. *R. stanleyi* and *R. herrani* are examples. They are known as *thornbills*.

Rhamphorhynchinæ (ram"fọ-ring-ki'nē), *n. pl.* [NL., < *Rhamphorhynchus* + *-inæ*.] A subfamily of pterodactyls, typified by the genus *Rhamphorhynchus*.

rhamphorhynchine (ram-fọ-ring'kin), *a.* Of or pertaining to the *Rhamphorhynchinæ*.

Rhamphorhynchus (ram-fō-ring'kus), *n.* [NL., < Gr. ῥάμφος, a curved beak, + ῥύγχος, a beak, snout.] A genus of pterodactyls, differing from *Pterodactylus* in having the tail very long with immobile vertebræ, the metacarpus less than half as long as the forearm, and the ends of the jaw produced into a toothless beak which was probably sheathed in horn. One of the species is *R. gemmingi*.

Rhamphosidæ (ram-fos'i-dē), *n. pl.* [NL., < *Rhamphosus* + *-idæ*.] A family of extinct hemibranchiate fishes, represented by the genus *Rhamphosus*. They had normal anterior vertebræ, plates on the nape and shoulders only, a tubiform mouth, subthoracic ventrals, and a dorsal spine behind the nuchal plates. They lived in the Eocene seas.

Rhamphosus (ram'fọ-sus), *n.* [NL. (Agassiz), with term. *-osus* (see *-ose*), < Gr. ῥάμφος, a curved beak.] An extinct genus of hemibranchiate fishes, representing the family *Rhamphosidæ*.

rhamphotheca (ram-fọ-thē'kä), *n.*; pl. *rhamphothecæ* (-sē). [NL., < Gr. ῥάμφος, a curved beak, + θήκη, a sheath.] In *ornith.*, the integument of the whole beak, of which the rhinotheca, dertrotheca, and gnathotheca are parts.

rhamphothecal (ram-fọ̄-thē'kal), *a.* [< *rhamphotheca* + *-al.*] Sheathing or covering the beak, as integument; of or pertaining to the rhamphotheca.

Rhamphus (ram'fus), *n.* [NL. (Clairville, 1798, as *Ramphus*), < Gr. ῥάμφος, a curved beak.] A genus of coleopterous insects, giving name to the *Rhamphidæ*, but usually placed in the family *Curculionidæ*, having a few European species.

rhaphe, *n.* See *raphe*.

Rhaphidia, Rhaphidiidæ. See *Raphidia*, etc.

Rhaphidopsis (raf-i-dop'sis), *n.* [NL. (Gerstaecker, 1855), < Gr. ῥαφίς (ῥαφιδ-), needle, + ὄψις, face, aspect.] A genus of exclusively African longicorn beetles, of eleven known species, generally of handsome coloration.

Rhaphiosaurus (raf"i-ō-sâ'rus), *n.* [NL., < Gr. ῥάφιον, a little needle or pin (dim. of ῥαφίς, needle, pin), + σαῦρος, a lizard.] A genus of fossil lizards of the Cretaceous period, so called from the acicular teeth. Usually *Raphiosaurus*.

rhaphis, *n.* See *raphis*.

Rhapidophyllum (rap"i-dọ̄-fil'um), *n.* [NL. (Wendland and Drude, 1876), < Gr. ῥαπίς (ῥαπιδ-), a rod, + φύλλον, leaf.] A genus of palms of the tribe *Corypheæ*. It is characterized by globose, partly diœcious flowers, with three broad and imbricated petals, six stamens with large linear and versatile anthers, and an ovary of three free ovoid carpels, tapering into a short recurved stigma, only one carpel usually ripening, forming a one-seeded nut tipped by a persistent subterminal stigma and composed of a hard crust covered with a fibrous pericarp which is clad in a loose wool. It is distinguished from the allied and well-known genus *Chamærops* by the fruit and by its spines. The only species, *R. Hystrix* (*Chamærops Hystrix*), is the blue palmetto of Florida, etc., a low palm with the leaves deeply plaited and cut, and the minute saffron flowers sessile on the branches of the two to five spadices, which are surrounded by woolly spathes. See *blue palmetto*, under *palmetto*.

Rhapis (rā'pis), *n.* [NL. (Linnæus filius, 1789), so called in allusion to the wand-like stem; < Gr. ῥαπίς, a rod.] A genus of palms of the tribe *Corypheæ*. It is characterized by a fruit of one to three small obovoid one-seeded carpels, each tipped by a terminal style, with a fleshy pericarp which is fibrous within, and with a soft endocarp, and by flowers mostly diœcious, sessile and solitary on the slender branches of a leafy spadix, with a three-cleft valvate corolla, anthers opening outward, and three distinct ovary-carpels borne on an elongated pedicel or carpophore. There are 4 or 5 species, natives of China and Japan. They are low palms with reed-like stems springing up in dense tufts from the same root, each stem wrapped in a network of fibers which are the remnants of leaf-sheaths. They bear alternate and terminal roundish leaves, irregularly and radiately parted into linear, wedge-shaped, or elliptical segments with conspicuous transverse veins. The yellowish flowers are borne on a spadix which is shorter than the leaves and is sheathed along its axis with deciduous bracts, the whole at first inclosed within two or three membranous spathes. The slender stems of *R. flabelliformis*, the ground-ratan, are available for numerous uses (see *ratan*), and the plant is one of the best for table decoration. *R. humilis* is a beautiful species, rare in collections.

rhapontic (rạ̄-pon'tik), *n.* [= OF. *rheupontique* = Sp. *rapóntico* = Pg. *ruiponto* = It. *rapontico*, < L. *rhaponticum*, orig. *rha Ponticum*, rhubarb, lit. 'Pontic rha': see *rha* and *Pontic*, and cf. *rhubarb*.] Rhubarb: chiefly in *phar.* in composition, *rhapontic*-root.

rhapsode (rap'sōd), *n.* [= F. *rapsode*, *rhapsode* = Sp. *rapsoda* = It. *rapsodo*, < Gr. ῥαψῳδός, a writer of epic poetry, a bard who recites poetry, lit. 'one who strings or joins songs together,' < ῥάπτειν (ῥαψ-), stitch together, fasten together, + ᾠδή, song, ode: see *ode*[1].] A rhapsodist.

> I venture to think that the *rhapsodes* incurred the displeasure of Kleisthenês by reciting, not the Homeric Iliad, but the Homeric Thebais and Epigoni.
> *Grote*, Hist. Greece, I. 21, note.

rhapsoder† (rap'sọ̄-dėr), *n.* [< *rhapsode* + *-er*[2].] A rhapsodist.

> By this occasion [printing my own poems] I am made a *rhapsoder* of mine own rags, and that cost me more diligence to seek them than it did to make them.
> *Donne*, Letters, li.

rhapsodic (rap-sod'ik), *a.* [= F. *rapsodique*, *rhapsodique*, < Gr. ῥαψῳδικός, < ῥαψῳδία, rhapsody: see *rhapsody*.] Same as *rhapsodical*.

rhapsodical (rap-sod'i-kal), *a.* [< *rhapsodic* + *-al.*] Of, pertaining to, or consisting of rhapsody; of the nature of rhapsody; hence, enthusiastic to extravagance; exaggerated in sentiment and expression; gushing.

> They [Prynne's works] . . . by the generality of Scholars are looked upon to be rather *rapsodical* and confused than any way polite or concise. *Wood*, Athenæ Oxon., II. 439.

> The odes of Jean Baptiste Rousseau . . . are animated, without being *rhapsodical*. H. *Blair*, Rhetoric, xxxix.

rhapsodically (rap-sod'i-kal-i), *adv.* In the manner of rhapsody.

rhapsodise, *v.* See *rhapsodize*.

rhapsodist (rap'sọ̄-dist), *n.* [= F. *rapsodiste*, *rhapsodiste* = Sp. Pg. It. *rapsodista*; as *rhapsode* + *-ist.*] 1. Among the ancient Greeks, one who composed, recited, or sang rhapsodies; especially, one who made it his profession to recite or sing the compositions of Homer and other epic poets.

> While the latter [the poet] sang, solely or chiefly, his own compositions to the accompaniment of his lyre, the *rhapsodist* . . . rehearsed . . . the poems of others.
> *W. Mure*, Lang. and Lit. of Anc. Greece, II. ii. § 4.

> The *rhapsodist* did not, like the early minstrel, use the accompaniment of the harp; he gave the verses in a flowing recitative, bearing in his hand a branch of laurel, the symbol of Apollo's inspiration. *Encyc. Brit.*, XI. 137.

2. One who recites or sings verses for a livelihood; one who makes and recites verses extempore.

> As to the origin of this [harvest] song — whether it came in its actual state from the brain of a single *rhapsodist*, or was gradually perfected by a school or succession of *rhapsodists* — I am ignorant. *George Eliot*, Adam Bede, liii.

3. One who speaks or writes with exaggerated sentiment or expression; one who expresses himself with more enthusiasm than accuracy or logical connection of ideas.

> Let me ask our *rhapsodist*,—"If you have nothing . . . but the beauty and excellency and loveliness of virtue to preach, . . . and . . . no future rewards or punishments . . .—how many . . . vicious wretches will you ever reclaim?" *Watts*, Improvement of Mind, I. x. § 11.

rhapsodistic (rap-sọ̄-dis'tik), *a.* [< *rhapsodist* + *-ic.*] Same as *rhapsodical*.

rhapsodize (rap'sọ̄-dīz), *v.*; pret. and pp. *rhapsodized*, ppr. *rhapsodizing*. [< *rhapsode* + *-ize.*] I. *intrans.* To recite rhapsodies; act as a rhapsodist; hence, to express one's self with poetic enthusiasm; speak with an intenseness or exaggeration due to strong feeling.

> You will think me *rhapsodizing*; but . . . one cannot fix one's eyes on the commonest natural production without finding food for a rambling fancy.
> *Jane Austen*, Mansfield Park, xxii.

> Walter, the young Franconian knight, with his *rhapsodizing* and love-making, needs a representative with a good voice and a good appearance.
> *The Academy*, No. 898, p. 46.

II. *trans.* To sing or narrate or recite as a rhapsody; rehearse in the manner of a rhapsody.

> Upon the banks of the Garonne, . . . where I now sit *rhapsodizing* all these affairs.
> *Sterne*, Tristram Shandy, vii. 28.

Also spelled *rhapsodise*.

rhapsodomancy (rap'sọ̄-dọ̄-man-si), *n.* [< F. *rhapsodomancie* = Sp. Pg. *rapsodomancia*, < Gr. ῥαψῳδός, a rhapsodist (see *rhapsode*), + μαντεία, divination.] Divination by means of verses.

> There were various methods of practising this *rhapsodomancy*. Sometimes they wrote several verses or sentences of a poet on so many pieces of wood, paper, or the like, shook them together in an urn, and drew out one. . . . Sometimes they cast dice on a table on which verses were written, and that on which the die lodged contained the prediction. A third manner was by opening a book, and pitching on some verse at first sight. This method they particularly called the Sortes Prænestinæ, and afterwards, according to the poet thus made use of, Sortes Homericæ, Sortes Virgilianæ, &c. *Rees*, Cyclopædia.

rhapsody (rap'sọ̄-di), *n.*; pl. *rhapsodies* (-diz). [Formerly also *rhapsodie*, *rapsodie*; < OF. *rapsodie*, F. *rapsodie*, *rhapsodie* = Sp. Pg. It. *rapsodia*, < L. *rhapsodia*, < Gr. ῥαψῳδία, the reciting of epic poetry, a part of an epic recited at a time, a rhapsody, a tirade, < ῥαψῳδός, a rhapsodist: see *rhapsode*.] 1. The recitation of epic poetry; hence, a short epic poem, or such a part of a longer epic as could be recited at one time: as, the Homeric *rhapsodies*.

> A *rhapsody*
> Of Homer's.
> B. *Jonson*, tr. of Horace's Art of Poetry, l. 184.

> *Rhapsody*, originally applied to the portions of the poem habitually allotted to different performers in the order of recital, afterwards transferred to the twenty-four books into which each work [the Iliad and the Odyssey] was permanently divided by the Alexandrian grammarians.
> *W. Mure*, Lang. and Lit. of Anc. Greece, II. ii. § 5.

2. The exaggerated expression of real or affected feeling or enthusiasm; an outburst of extravagant admiration or regard; especially, a poetic composition marked rather by exaggerated sentiment or fancy than by sober, connected thought.

> Then my breast
> Should warble airs whose *rhapsodies* should least
> The ears of seraphims. *Quarles*, Emblems, iv. 15.

> Spend all the pow'rs
> Of rant and *rhapsody* in virtue's praise.
> *Cowper*, Task, v. 677.

3. In *music*, an instrumental composition in irregular form, somewhat like a caprice, impromptu, or improvisation, though properly more important: as, Liszt's Hungarian *rhapsodies*.—4†. Any rambling composition; a cento; hence, a medley; a jumble.

> O, such a deed
> As from the body of contraction plucks
> The very soul, and sweet religion makes
> A *rhapsody* of words. *Shak.*, Hamlet, iii. 4. 48.

> He was very light-headed, and had uttered nothing but a *rhapsody* of nonsense all the time he stayed in the room.
> *Fielding*, Joseph Andrews, i. 13.

rhatany, *n.* See *ratany*.

rhaw, *n.* [W. *rhaw*, a shovel, spade.] A measure of peat in Wales, 140 or 120 cubic yards.

Rhe (rē), *n.* A variant of *Ra*.

Rhea[1] (rē'ạ̈), *n.* [= F. *Rhée*, < L. *Rhea*, < Gr. Ῥέα, Rhea (see def. 1).] 1. In *anc. myth.*, a daughter of Uranus and Ge, or Heaven and Earth, wife and sister of Kronos, and mother of various divinities.

> However intimate the connection, however inextricable the confusion between the Great Mother and *Rhea*, even down to late days the memory remained that they were not in origin one and the same.
> *Harrison and Verrall*, Ancient Athens, p. 51.

2. [NL.] In *ornith.*: (*a*) The only genus of *Rheidæ*; the only American genus of living ratite birds; the only three-toed ostriches. *R. americana* is the common American ostrich, avestruz, or

South American Ostrich (*Rhea americana*).

nandu. *R. darwini* is a second very distinct species, sometimes placed in another genus, *Pterocnemis*, owing to the extensive feathering of the legs. *R. macrorhyncha* is a third species, which is closely related to the first. (*b*) [*l. c.*] An American ostrich.—3. The fifth satellite of Saturn.

rhea[2] (rē'ạ̈), *n.* [Also *rheea*; E. Ind.] The ramie-plant or -fiber.

Rheæ (rē'ē), *n. pl.* [NL., pl. of *Rhea*[1], 2.] A superfamily group, by Newton made an order, of extant ratite birds, including only the *Rheidæ*, or family of the American ostriches.

rhea-fiber (rē'ạ̈-fī"bėr), *n.* Same as *ramie*.

rhea-grass (rē'ạ̈-gràs), *n.* The ramie-plant. See *ramie*.

rheebok, *n.* A corrupt spelling of *reebok*.

rheic (rē'ik), *a.* [< F. *rhéique*; as *Rheum*[2] + *-ic.*] Pertaining to or derived from rhubarb.—**Rheic acid**, $C_{15}H_{10}O_4$, the yellow crystalline granular matter of rhubarb, procured from the plant by extraction with potash solution, precipitation with hydrochloric acid, and purification by crystallizing from a solution in chloroform. Also called *rheumic acid* and *chrysophanic acid*.

Rheidæ (rē'i-dē), *n. pl.* [NL., < *Rhea*[1] + *-idæ.*] A family of living ratite birds confined to America and having three toes, typified by the genus *Rhea*; the nandus or American ostriches. There is an ischiac symphysis beneath the sacral vertebræ, but no pubic symphysis; the maxillopalatines are free from the vomer; the carotid is single, sinistral; the lower larynx is specialized and has a pair of intrinsic syringeal muscles; the ambiens is present; the gall-bladder is absent; the wing-bones are unusually well developed for ratite birds; and the manus has three digits.

rhein (rē'in), *n.* [< *Rheum*[2] + *-in*[2].] Same as *rheic acid* (which see, under *rheic*).

Rhein-berry (rīn'ber"i), *n.* [Also *Rhine-berry*; early mod. E. *rheyn-berrie*; appar. accom. < MD. *reyn-besie*, also *rijn-besie*, D. *rijn-bezie*, blackberry, = G. *rheinbeere* (Webster), as if 'Rhine-berry' (berry growing along the Rhine ?); < MD. *reyn-*, *rijn-*, occurring also, appar., in other plant-names, namely *reyn-bloeme*, *rijn-bloeme* (D. *rijnbloeme*), cudweed; *reynweyde*, also *reynwilghe*, *rijnwilghe*, privet; *reynvaeren*, *reynvaer* (D. *reinvaar*), tansy; the element *reyn-*, *rijn-*, being uncertain.] The common buckthorn.

rhematic (rẹ̄-mat'ik), *a.* and *n.* [< Gr. ῥηματικός, belonging to a verb, < ῥῆμα, a word, a verb, lit. 'that which is said or spoken,' < ἐρεῖν, εἴρειν, say, speak: see *rhetor* and *verb*.] I. *a.* Pertaining to or derived from a verb.

Such [adjectives in *-able*] as are derived from verbs deserve the precedence. And these, to avoid the ambiguousness of the term verbal, I shall take leave to denominate *rhematic*. *F. Hall*, Adjectives in *-able*, p. 47.

II. *n.* The doctrine of propositions or sentences. *Coleridge.*

Rhemish (rē'mish), *a.* [< *Rheims* + *-ish*[1].] Pertaining to Rheims or Reims, a city of northeastern France.—**Rhemish version**, the version of the New Testament in the Douay Bible. See *Bible*.

rhenet†, *n.* An erroneous form of *rine*[3].

Rhenish (ren'ish), *a.* and *n.* [< G. *rheinisch*, MHG. *rînisch*, *rînesch*, *rînsch* (= D. *rijnsch* = Dan. *rhinsk* = Sw. *rhensk*), < *Rhein*, MHG. *Rîn*, OHG. *Rîn*, *Hrîn* (= D. *Rijn* = ME. *Rin*) (L. *Rhenus*, Gr. 'Ῥῆνος), the Rhine; a name prob. of Celtic origin.] **I.** *a.* Of or pertaining to the Rhine, a river of Europe which rises in Switzerland, traverses Germany and the Netherlands, and empties into the North Sea.—**Rhenish architecture**, the local form assumed by Romanesque or round-arched architecture in the eleventh and twelfth centuries in the regions bordering upon the Rhine. The earliest churches seem to have

Rhenish Architecture.—Apse of the Church of the Apostles, Cologne.

been circular; the circular original in the later rectangular type may perhaps be represented by the semicircular western apse in addition to that at the east end, characteristic of those regions. In buildings of this style small circular or octagonal towers are frequent. Arcaded galleries beneath the eaves, and richly carved capitals, often resembling Byzantine work, are among the most beautiful features. The Rhenish buildings are, however, despite much dignity and manifest suitability to their purpose, inferior in both design and ornament to those of the French Romanesque.—**Rhenish wine.** See *wine*.

II. *n.* Rhine or Rhenish wine. See *wine*.

A' poured a flagon of *Rhenish* on my head once. *Shak.*, Hamlet, v. 1. 197.

rheochord (rē'ǫ-kôrd), *n.* [< Gr. ῥεῖν, flow, + χορδή, a chord: see *chord*.] A metallic wire used in measuring the resistance or varying the strength of an electric current, in proportion to the greater or less length of it inserted in the circuit.

Rheoideæ (rę-oi'dę-ē), *n. pl.* [NL., < *Rhea*[1] + *-oideæ*.] The *Rheidæ* rated as a superfamily: same as *Rheæ*.

rheometer (rę-om'e-tėr), *n.* [Also *reometer*; = F. *rhéomètre*; irreg. < Gr. ῥεῖν, flow, + μέτρον, a measure.] **1.** An instrument for measuring an electric current; an electrometer or galvanometer.—**2.** An instrument for measuring the velocity of the blood-flow.

rheometric (rē-ǫ-met'rik), *a.* [< *rheometer* + *-ic*.] Pertaining to a rheometer or its use; galvanometric.

rheometry (rę-om'e-tri), *n.* [As *rheometer* + *-y*[3].] **1.** In *math.*, the differential and integral calculus; fluxions.—**2.** The measurement of electric currents; galvanometry.

rheomotor (rē'ǫ-mō-tor), *n.* [< Gr. ῥεῖν, flow, + L. *motor*, a mover.] Any apparatus, as an electric battery, by which an electric current is originated.

rheophore (rē'ǫ-fōr), *n.* [Also *reophore*; < Gr. ῥεῖν, flow, + -φόρος, < φέρειν = E. *bear*[1].] A general name given by Ampère to the conductor joining the poles of a voltaic cell.

rheoscope (rē'ǫ-skōp), *n.* [< Gr. ῥεῖν, flow, + σκοπεῖν, view.] An instrument by which the existence of an electric current may be ascertained; an electroscope.

rheoscopic (rē-ǫ-skop'ik), *a.* [< *rheoscope* + *-ic*.] Same as *electroscopic*.—**Rheoscopic limb**, the gastrocnemius of the frog with sciatic nerve attached, used to show the variations of electric currents, as in another similar preparation when its nerve is stimulated.

rheostat (rē'ǫ-stat), *n.* [< Gr. ῥεῖν, flow, + στατός, verbal adj. of ἱστάναι, stand: see *static*.] In *electromagnetism*, an instrument for regu-

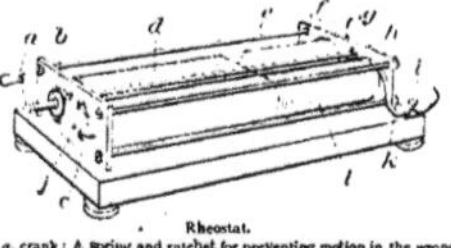

Rheostat.

a, crank; *b*, spring and ratchet for preventing motion in the wrong direction; *c*, spring for other barrel or cylinder; *d*, non-conducting cylinder; *e*, wire; *f* and *k*, contact-springs for carrying current to and from binding-posts *g* and *i*; *h*, scale for showing number of revolutions; *l*, conducting cylinder; *j*, pin for crank when reversing motion.

lating or adjusting a circuit so that any required degree of resistance may be maintained; a resistance-coil. See *resistance*, 3.

rheostatic (rē-ǫ-stat'ik), *a.* [< *rheostat* + *-ic*.] Pertaining or relating to a rheostat: incorrectly used to note a device of Planté's, which is essentially a commutator, by means of which the grouping of a number of secondary cells can be rapidly changed.

In the second class naturally figure induction coils, Planté's *rheostatic* machine, and the secondary batteries. *E. Hospitalier*, Electricity (trans.), p. 104.

rheostatics (rē-ǫ-stat'iks), *n.* [Pl. of *rheostatic* (see *-ics*).] The statics of fluids; hydrostatics.

rheotannic (rē-ǫ-tan'ik), *a.* [< *Rheum*[2] + *tannic*.] Used only in the phrase below.—**Rheotannic acid**, $C_{26}H_{26}O_{14}$, a variety of tannic acid found in rhubarb.

rheotome (rē'ǫ-tōm), *n.* [< Gr. ῥεῖν, flow, + -τομος, < τέμνειν, ταμεῖν, cut.] A device by means of which an electric circuit can be periodically interrupted; an interrupter.

rheotrope (rē'ǫ-trōp), *n.* [Also *reotrope*; < Gr. ῥεῖν, flow, + -τροπος, < τρέπειν, turn.] An instrument for periodically changing the direction of an electric current. *Faraday.*

rheotropic (rē-ǫ-trop'ik), *a.* [< Gr. ῥεῖν, flow, + τροπικός, < τρέπειν, turn: see *tropic*.] In *bot.*, determined in its direction of growth by a current of water. See *rheotropism*.

rheotropism (rę-ot'rǫ-pizm), *n.* [< *rheotrop(ic)* + *-ism*.] In *bot.*, a term introduced by Jönsson to denote the effect of a current of water upon the direction of plant-growth. In some cases the plant grows with the current, then exhibiting positive rheotropism; in some cases against the current, exhibiting negative rheotropism.

rhesian (rē'shi-ạn), *a.* [< *rhesus* + *-ian*.] Characteristic of the rhesus; monkey-like: as, *rhesian* antics. *Literary World*, Oct. 31, 1885.

rhesus (rē'sus), *n.* [NL., < L. *Rhesus*, < Gr. 'Ῥῆσος, a king of Thracia, a river of the Troas, a river in Bithynia, etc.] **1.** A macaque, *Macacus rhesus*, one of the sacred monkeys of India. It is 18 inches long, the tail 7 or 8 inches, and mostly of a yellowish-brown color. It is a near relative of the common Javan macaque, *M. cynomolgus*, of the Malay bruh, *M. nemestrinus*, and of the bonnet-macaque or munga, *M. sinicus*, and in some respects, as length of tail and formation of the "bonnet," holds an intermediate position between the extremes in this large and varied genus. The rhesus is widely distributed in India, both in the hill-country and on the plains, where it is known by the native name *bunder*. It runs into several varieties, which have received technical specific names, and is among the monkeys commonly seen in zoological gardens and menageries.

Rhesus Monkey (*Macacus rhesus*).

2. [*cap.*] [NL.] In *mammal.*, same as *Macacus*.—**3.** [*cap.*] In *entom.*, a genus of coleopterous insects. *Lacordaire*, 1869.

Rhetian, *a.* and *n.* See *Rhætian*.

Rhetic, *a.* Same as *Rhætic*.

rhetizite, *n.* See *rhætizite*.

rhetor (rē'tǫr), *n.* [< ME. *rethor*, < OF. *retor*, F. *rhéteur* = It. *retore*, < L. *rhetor*, a teacher of oratory, a rhetorician, also an orator, < Gr. ῥήτωρ, a speaker, orator, < ἐρεῖν, εἴρειν (pret. εἴρηκα; √Fερ), say, speak: see *verb*.] **1.** A rhetorician; a master or teacher of rhetoric.

Myn English eek is insufficient;
It moste ben a *rethor* excellent,
That coude his colours longing for that art,
If he sholde hir discriven every part.
Chaucer, Squire's Tale, l. 30.

Your hearing, what is it but as of a *rhetor* at a desk, to commend or dislike? *Hammond*, Works, IV. 514. (*Latham.*)

2. Among the ancient Greeks, an orator. Specifically—(*a*) One who made it his occupation to speak in the ecclesia or public assembly, and often to devote himself unofficially to some particular branch of the administration; a political orator or statesman. (*b*) One who made it his occupation to prepare speeches for other citizens to deliver in their own cases in court, and to teach them how to deliver them, act as an advocate, give instruction in the art of rhetoric, and deliver panegyrics or epideictic orations; hence, a professor of rhetoric; a rhetorician.

They are (and that cannot be otherwise) of the same profession with the *rhetorics* [read *rhetores*?] at Rome, as much used to defend the wrong as to protect and maintain the most upright cause. *Bp. Hacket*, Abp. Williams, i. 72.

When a private citizen had to appear before court, the *rhetor* who wrote the speech for him often tried to make him appear at his best. *Amer. Jour. of Philol.*, VI. 341.

rhetorian†, *a.* [ME. *rethoryen*; < *rhetor* + *-ian*.] Rhetorical.

The suasion of swetenesse *rethoryen*. *Chaucer*, Boëthius, ii. prose 1.

rhetoric (ret'ǫr-ik), *n.* [Early mod. E. *rhetorick*, *rethoryck*; < ME. *retorike*, *rethoryke*, *retoryke*, *retoryk* (also *rethorice*, after L. *rhetorice*), < OF. *rhetorique*, *rectorique*, F. *rhétorique* = Pr. *rethorica* = Sp. *retórica* = Pg. *rhetorica* = It. *retorica*, *rettorica*, < L. *rhetorica* (sc. *ars*), also *rhetorice*, < Gr. ῥητορική (sc. τέχνη), the rhetorical art, fem. of ῥητορικός (> L. *rhetoricus*), of or pertaining to a speaker or orator, rhetorical, < ῥήτωρ, a speaker, orator: see *rhetor*.] **1.** The art of discourse; the art of using language so as to influence others. Rhetoric is that art which consists in a systematic use of the technical means of influencing the minds, imaginations, emotions, and actions of others by the use of language. Primarily, it is the art of oratory, with inclusion of both composition and delivery; secondarily, it also includes written composition and recitation. It is also used in narrower senses, so as to present the idea of composition alone, or the idea of oratorical delivery (elocution) alone. Etymologically, rhetoric is the art, or rather the technics (τέχνη, somewhat different in scope from our *art*), of the rhetor—that is, either the popular (political) orator or the judicial and professional rhetor. Accordingly, ancient writers regarded it mainly as the art of persuasion, and something of this view almost always attaches to the word even in modern use, so that it appears to be more or less inappropriate to use *rhetoric* of mere scientific, didactic, or expository composition. The element of persuasion, or at least of influence of thought, belongs, however, to such composition also in so far as accurate and well-arranged statement of views leads to their adoption or rejection, the very object of instruction involving this. On the other hand, poetry and epideictic oratory chiefly address the imagination and emotions, while the most important branches of oratory (deliberative and judicial oratory) appeal especially to the mind and emotions with a view to influencing immediate action. The theory or science underlying the art of rhetoric, and sometimes called by the same name, is essentially a creation of the ancient Greeks. Rhetoric was cultivated on its more practical side first of all by the earlier rhetors (so-called "sophists") and orators (Empedocles—considered the inventor of rhetoric—Gorgias, Isocrates, etc.), many of whom wrote practical treatises (τέχναι) on the art. The philosophers, on the other hand, among them Aristotle, treated the subject from the theoretical side. The system of rhetoric which finally became established, and has never been superseded, though largely mutilated and misunderstood in medieval and modern times, is that founded upon the system of the Stoic philosophers by the practical rhetorician Hermagoras (about 60 B. C.). Its most important extant representatives are Hermogenes (about A. D. 165) among the Greeks, and Quintilian (about A. D. 95) among the Latins. This theory recognizes three great divisions of oratory. (See *oratory*.) The art of rhetoric was divided into five parts: invention, disposition, elocution (not in the modern sense, but comprising diction and style), memory (mnemonics), and action (delivery, including the modern elocution).

With *rethorice* com forth Musice, a damsel of oure hows. *Chaucer*, Boethius, ii. prose 1.

Generall report, that surpasseth my praise, condemneth my *rethoricke* of dulnesse for so colde a commendation. *Nashe*, quoted in Int. to Pierce Penilesse, p. xxv.

For *rhetoric*, he could not ope
His mouth, but out there flew a trope.
Butler, Hudibras, I. i. 81.

2. Skill in discourse; artistic use of language. —**3.** Artificial oratory, as opposed to that which is natural and unaffected; display in language; ostentatious or meretricious declamation.

Enjoy your dear wit, and gay *rhetorick*,
That hath so well been taught her dazzling fence.
Milton, Comus, l. 790.

Like quicksilver, the *rhet'ric* they display
Shines as it runs, but, grasp'd at, slips away.
Cowper, Progress of Error, l. 21.

4. The power of persuasion; persuasive influence.

Every part of the Tragedy of his [the Son of God's] life, every wound at his death, every groan and sigh which he uttered upon the Cross, were designed by him as the most prevailing *Rhetorick*, to perswade men to forsake their sins, and be happy. *Stillingfleet*, Sermons, I. iii.

She was long deaf to all the sufferings of her lovers, till . . . the *rhetoric* of John the hostler, with a new straw hat and a pint of wine, made a second conquest over her. *Fielding*, Joseph Andrews, i. 18.

Chambers of rhetoric. See *chamber*.=**Syn.** *Elocution, Eloquence*, etc. See *oratory*.

rhetorical (rē-tor'i-kal), *a.* [Early mod. E. *rethoricall*; < *rhetoric* + *-al*.] Pertaining to, of the nature of, or containing rhetoric; oratorical: as, the *rhetorical* art; a *rhetorical* treatise; a *rhetorical* flourish.

A telling quotation, when the whole point lies perhaps in some accidental likeness of words and names, is perfectly fair as a *rhetorical* point, as long as it does not pretend to be an argument. *E. A. Freeman*, Amer. Lects., p. 224.

Rhetorical accent, in *music*. See *accent*, 8 (a).—**Rhetorical algebra**, algebra without a special notation; an analysis of problems in the manner of algebra, but using only ordinary language.—**Rhetorical figure.** See *figure*, 16.—**Rhetorical question.** See *question*.—**Rhetorical syllogism**, a probable argumentation: so called by Aristotle, from the ancient notion that science should rest on demonstrative and not on probable reasoning—an opinion which constituted the great fault of ancient science.

rhetorically (rē-tor'i-kal-i), *adv.* In a rhetorical manner; according to the rules of rhetoric: as, to treat a subject *rhetorically*; a discourse *rhetorically* delivered.

rhetoricate† (rē-tor'i-kāt), *v. i.* [< LL. *rhetoricatus*, pp. of *rhetoricari*, speak rhetorically, < L. *rhetorica*, rhetoric: see *rhetoric*.] To play the orator.

A person ready to sink under his wants has neither time nor heart to *rhetoricate*, or make flourishes. *South.*

rhetorication† (rē-tor-i-kā'shon), *n.* [< *rhetoricate* + *-ion*.] Rhetorical amplification.

"When I consider your wealth I doe admire your wisdome, and when I consider your wisdome I doe admire your wealth." It was a two-handed *rhetorication*, but the citizens [of London] tooke it in the best sense. *Aubrey*, Lives, Sir M. Fleetwood.

Their *rhetorications* and equivocal expressions. *Waterland*, Charge (1732), p. 9.

rhetorician (ret-ọ-rish'an), *n.* and *a.* [< OF. *rhetoricien*, *rethoricien*, F. *rhétoricien*; as *rhetoric* + *-ian*.] **I.** *n.* **1.** A teacher of rhetoric or oratory; one who teaches the art of correct and effective speech or composition.

The ancient sophists and *rhetoricians*, who had young auditors, lived till they were a hundred years old. *Bacon.*

All a *rhetorician's* rules
Teach nothing but to name his tools.
S. Butler, Hudibras, I. i. 89.

2. One who is versed in the art and principles of rhetoric; especially, one who employs rhetorical aid in speech or written composition; in general, a public speaker, especially one who speaks for show; a declaimer.

He speaks handsomely;
What a rare *rhetorician* his grief plays!
Fletcher, Mad Lover, iii. 4.

Or played at Lyons a declaiming prize,
For which the vanquish'd *rhetorician* dies.
Dryden, tr. of Juvenal's Satires, i. 66.

A man is held to play the *rhetorician* when he treats a subject with more than usual gaiety of ornament; and perhaps we may add, as an essential element in the idea, with conscious ornament. *De Quincey*, Rhetoric.

The "understanding" is that by which a man becomes a mere logician, and a mere *rhetorician*. *F. W. Robertson.*

II. *a.* Belonging to or befitting a master of rhetoric.

Boldly presum'd, with *rhetorician* pride,
To hold of any question either side.
Sir R. Blackmore, Creation, iii.

rhetoriously†, *adv.* [ME. *rethoriously*; < **rhetorious* (< *rhetor* + *-ious*) + *-ly*².] Rhetorically.

Now ye all that shall thys behold or rede,
Remembreth myn uncomyng simplesse:
Thought *rethoriously* peinted be not in-dede,
As other han don by ther discretnesse.
Rom. of Partenay (E. E. T. S.), l. 6611.

rhetorize† (ret'ọr-īz), *v.* [< OF. *rhetoriser*, < LL. *rhetorissare*, < Gr. ῥητορίζειν, speak rhetorically, < ῥήτωρ, an orator: see *rhetor*.] **I.** *intrans.* To play the orator. *Cotgrave.*

II. *trans.* To represent by a figure of oratory; introduce by a rhetorical device.

No lesse was that before his book against the Brownists to write a Letter to a prosopopoea, a certain *rhetoriz'd* woman whom he calls mother. *Milton*, Apology for Smectymnuus.

Rheto-Romanic, *a.* and *n.* Same as *Rhæto-Romanic*.

rheum¹ (röm), *n.* [Early mod. E. also *reume*, *reume*; < ME. *rewme*, *reem*, < OF. *reume*, *rheume*, F. *rhume* = Pr. Sp. *reuma* = Pg. *rheuma* = It. *reuma*, *rema*, a cold, catarrh, rheum, < L. *rheuma*, < Gr. ῥεῦμα, a flow, flood, flux, rheum, < ῥεῖν (√ ῥευ, orig. σρεϝ), flow, = Skt. √ *sru*, flow: see *stream*. Hence *rheumatism*, etc.; from the same Gr. verb are ult. E. *catarrh*, *diarrhea*, *rhythm*, etc.] **1.** A mucous discharge, as from the nostrils or lungs during a cold; hence, catarrhal discharge from the air-passages, nose, or eyes.

Your Lordship doth write that by sleeping upon the ground you haue taken a pestilent *Rheum*. *Guevara*, Letters (tr. by Hellowes, 1577), p. 134.

I have a *rheum* in mine eyes too.
Shak., T. and C., v. 3. 105.

A mist falling as I returned gave me such a *rheume* as kept me within doores neere a whole moneth after. *Evelyn*, Diary, Jan. 18, 1656.

2. A thin serous fluid, secreted by the mucous glands, etc., as in catarrh; humid matter which collects in the eyes, nose, or mouth, as tears, saliva, and the like.

Reume of the hed or of the breste. *Prompt. Parv.*, p. 432.

You that did void your *rheum* upon my beard.
Shak., M. of V., i. 3. 118.

Flows a cold sweat, with a continual *rheum*,
Forth the resolved corners of his eyes.
B. Jonson, Volpone, i. 1.

3†. Spleen; choler.

Nay, I have my *rheum*, and I can be angry as well as another, sir. B. *Jonson*, Every Man in his Humour, iii. 2.

Rheum² (rē'um), *n.* [NL. (Linnæus, 1737), < ML. *rheum*, < Gr. ῥῆον, the rhubarb; according to some, so named from its purgative properties, < ῥεῖν, flow (see *rheum*¹), but prob. an accom. form of ῥᾶ, rhubarb: see *rha*, *rhubarb*.] A genus of apetalous plants of the order *Polygonaceæ* and tribe *Rumiceæ*. It is characterized by its (usually) nine stamens, and its six-parted perianth which remains unchanged in fruit, around the three-winged and exserted fruit. There are about 20 species, natives of Siberia, the Himalayas, and western Asia. They are stout herbs from thick and somewhat woody rootstocks, with large toothed or lobed and wavy leaves, and loose dry stipular sheaths. The small white or greenish pedicelled bractless flowers are in racemed fascicles, the racemes panicled. The floral leaves are in some species small, in others large and colored, as in *R. nobile*, a remarkable species of the Sikhim Himalayas. For this and other species, see *rhubarb*, the common name of the genus. See also cuts under *plumule* and *rhubarb*.

rheuma (rö'mạ̈), *n.* [NL., < L. *rheuma*, < Gr. ῥεῦμα, a flow, flood, flux: see *rheum*¹.] Same as *rheum*¹.—**Rheuma epidemicum.** Same as *influenza*.

rheumarthritis (rö-mär-thrī'tis), *n.* [NL., < Gr. ῥεῦμα, flux (see *rheum*¹), + ἄρθρον, joint, + *-itis*. Cf. *arthritis*.] Acute articular rheumatism (see *rheumatism*), and such chronic forms as have the same ætiology.

rheumarthrosis (rö-mär-thrō'sis), *n.* [NL., < Gr. ῥεῦμα, flux (see *rheum*¹), + ἄρθρον, joint, + *-osis*. Cf. *arthrosis*.] Same as *rheumarthritis*.

rheumatalgia (rö-mạ-tal'ji-ạ̈), *n.* [NL., < Gr. ῥεῦμα, flux (see *rheum*¹), + ἄλγος, pain.] Rheumatic pain.

rheumatic (rọ̈-mat'ik, formerly rö'mạ-tik), *a.* and *n.* [Early mod. E. *rheumatick*, *reumatick*, *rewmatick*, *rumatike*; < OF. *rumatique*, *rhumatique*, F. *rhumatique* = Pr. *reumatic* = Sp. *reumático* = Pg. *rheumatico* = It. *reumatico*, *rematico*, < L. *rheumaticus*, < Gr. ῥευματικός, of or pertaining to a flux or discharge, < ῥεῦμα, a flux, rheum: see *rheum*¹.] **I.** *a.* **1**†. Pertaining to a rheum or catarrhal affection; of the nature of rheum.

The moon, the governess of floods,
Pale in her anger, washes all the air,
That *rheumatic* diseases do abound.
Shak., M. N. D., ii. 1. 105.

2†. Having a rheum or cold; affected by rheum.

By sleeping in an ayrie place you haue bene very *rumatike*, . . . [but] it is lesse euil in Summer to sweate then to cough. *Guevara*, Letters (tr. by Hellowes, 1577), p. 122.

3†. Causing rheum; unhealthy; damp.

The sun with his flame-coloured wings hath fanned away the misty smoke of the morning, and refined that thick tobacco-breath which the *rheumatick* night throws abroad. *Dekker*, Gull's Hornbook, p. 62.

Now time is near to pen our sheep in fold,
And evening air is *rheumatick* and cold.
Peele, An Eclogue.

4. Pertaining to or caused by rheumatism; of the nature of rheumatism: as, *rheumatic* symptoms.

The patched figure of good Uncle Venner was now visible, coming slowly from the head of the street downward, with a *rheumatic* limp, because the east wind had got into his joints. *Hawthorne*, Seven Gables, xvi.

5. Affected by rheumatism; subject to rheumatism: as, a *rheumatic* patient.

O'erworn, despised, *rheumatic*, and cold.
Shak., Venus and Adonis, l. 135.

The electrical sensibility of the skin connected with an acutely *rheumatic* joint has been described by Drosdoff as being remarkably diminished. *Quain*, Med. Dict., p. 1357.

6†. Splenetic; choleric.

You two never meet but you fall to some discord; you are both, i' good troth, as *rheumatic* as two dry toasts. *Shak.*, 2 Hen. IV., ii. 4. 62.

Acute rheumatic polyarthritis. Same as *acute articular rheumatism*. See *rheumatism*.—**Chronic rheumatic arthritis.** Same as *rheumatoid arthritis* (which see, under *rheumatoid*), or as *chronic articular rheumatism* (which see, under *rheumatism*).—**Eruptive rheumatic fever**, dengue.—**Rheumatic amygdalitis**, amygdalitis of rheumatic origin.—**Rheumatic anæsthesia**, anæsthesia associated with rheumatism.—**Rheumatic apoplexy**, the stupor or coma sometimes developing in the course of acute rheumatism.—**Rheumatic atrophy**, loss of size and strength of muscles after rheumatism.—**Rheumatic bronchitis**, an attack of bronchitis which is supposed to depend on a rheumatic diathesis or an attack of acute rheumatism.—**Rheumatic contraction.** Same as *tetany*.—**Rheumatic diathesis**, the condition of body tending to the development of rheumatism.—**Rheumatic dysentery**, dysentery accompanied by rheumatic inflammation of one or several joints, with synovial effusion, pleurodynia, and catarrh of the bronchial mucous membranes.—**Rheumatic fever.** Same as *acute articular rheumatism*. See *rheumatism*.—**Rheumatic gout.** Same as *rheumatoid arthritis* (which see, under *rheumatoid*).—**Rheumatic inflammation**, inflammation due to rheumatism.—**Rheumatic iritis**, inflammation of the iris resulting from cold, especially in weak subjects.

II. *n.* **1.** One who suffers from or is liable to rheumatism: as, a confirmed *rheumatic*.—**2.** *pl.* Rheumatic pains; rheumatism. [Colloq.]

When fevers burn, or ague freezes,
Rheumatics gnaw, or cholic squeezes,
Our neighbour's sympathy may ease us.
Burns, To the Toothache.

rheumatical (rọ̈-mat'i-kạl), *a.* [< *rheumatic* + *-al*.] Same as *rheumatic*.

rheumaticky (rọ̈-mat'i-ki), *a.* [< *rheumatic* + *-y*¹.] Rheumatic. [Colloq.]

rheumatism (rö'mạ-tizm), *n.* [= F. *rhumatisme* = Sp. It. *reumatismo* = Pg. *rheumatismo*, < L. *rheumatismus*, < Gr. ῥευματισμός, liability to rheum, a humor or flux, < ῥευματίζεσθαι, have a flux, < ῥεῦμα, a flux: see *rheum*¹.] The disease specifically known as *acute articular rheumatism* (see below)—the name including also subacute and chronic forms apparently of the same causation. The word is used with a certain and unfortunate freedom in application to joint pains of various origins and anatomical forms.—**Acute articular rheumatism**, an acute febrile disease, with pain and inflammation of the joints as the prominent symptom. It is to be separated as of distinct, possibly bacterial, origin from joint affections caused by gout, plumbism, scarlatina, gonorrhea, septicemia, tuberculosis, or syphilis. It often begins suddenly; a number of joints are usually attacked one after the other; the fever is irregular; there is apt to be profuse sweating; endocarditis, pericarditis, pleuritis, sudamina, erythema nodosum, hyperpyrexia, and delirium are more or less frequent features of the cases. Its duration is from one to six weeks or more. It is most frequent between 15 and 35, but may occur in the first year of life or after 50. One attack does not protect, but, as in pneumonia and erysipelas, is often succeeded by others. It almost always issues in recovery, but frequently leaves permanent cardiac lesions. Also called *acute rheumatism*, *rheumarthritis*, *rheumatic fever*, *acute rheumatic polyarthritis*.—**Chronic articular rheumatism**, the result, commonly, of one or more attacks of acute rheumatism, characterized by a chronic inflammation of one or more joints without profound structural alteration.—**Gonorrheal rheumatism**, an inflammation of the joints occurring in persons having gonorrhea.—**Muscular rheumatism**, a painful disorder of the muscles, characterized by local pain, especially on use of the muscles affected: same as *myalgia*.—**Progressive chronic articular rheumatism.** Same as *rheumatoid arthritis* (which see, under *rheumatoid*).

rheumatismal (rö-mạ-tiz'mạl), *a.* [< *rheumatism* + *-al*.] Rheumatic.

rheumatism-root (rö'mạ-tizm-röt), *n.* **1.** The twinleaf. See *Jeffersonia*.—**2.** The wild yam, *Dioscorea villosa*. See *yam*.

rheumatiz, rheumatize (rö'mạ-tiz), *n.* Rheumatism. [Vulgar.]

I did feel a *rheumatize* in my back-spauld yestreen.
Scott, Pirate, vii.

rheumatizy (rö'mạ-tiz-i), *n.* Same as *rheumatiz*. [Vulgar.]

Eh, my *rheumatizy* be that bad howiver be I to win to the burnin'. *Tennyson*, Queen Mary, iv. 3.

rheumatoceles (rọ̈-mat-ọ̄-sē'lēz), *n.* [NL., < Gr. ῥεῦμα, flux (see *rheum*¹), + κήλη, tumor.] Same as *purpura rheumatica* (which see, under *purpura*).

rheumatoid (rö'mạ-toid), *a.* [< Gr. ῥευματώδης, like a flux, < ῥεῦμα, flux, + εἶδος, form.] Resembling rheumatism or some of its characters: as, *rheumatoid* pains.—**Rheumatoid arthritis**, a disease of the joints characterized by chronic inflammatory and degenerative changes, which involve the structure of the various articulations, resulting in rigidity and deformity. Also called *chronic rheumatic arthritis*, *rheumatic gout*, *progressive chronic articular rheumatism*, *chronic osteo-arthritis*.

Chronic rheumatism of the most severe degree thus merges into, if it be not actually identical with, the class of diseases known as *rheumatoid* or "rheumatic" *arthritis*. *Quain*, Med. Dict., p. 1367.

rheumatoidal (rö-mạ-toi'dạl), *a.* Same as *rheumatoid*.

rheumic (rö'mik), *a.* [irreg. < *Rhrum*[2] + *-ic.*] Related to rhubarb.—**Rheumic acid** ($C_{20}H_{16}O_{9}$), a product of the treatment of rheotannic acid with dilute acids.

rheumophthalmia (rö-mof-thal'mi-ä), *n.* [NL., < Gr. ῥεῦμα, flux (see *rheum*[1]), + ὀφθαλμία, ophthalmia.] Rheumatic ophthalmia.

rheumy (rö'mi), *a.* [< *rheum*[1] + *-y*[1].] 1. Affected by rheum; full of rheum or watery matter.

> So, too-much Cold couors with hoary Fleece
> The head of Age, . . . hollowes his *rheumy* eyes,
> And makes himselfe euen his owne selfe despise.
> *Sylvester*, tr. of Du Bartas's Weeks, i. 2.

2. Causing rheum.

> And tempt the *rheumy* and unpurged air
> To add unto his sickness? *Shak.*, J. C., ii. 1. 266.

Rhexia (rek'si-ä), *n.* [NL., in def. 1 (Linnæus, 1753), < L. *rhexia*, a plant, prob. *Echium rubrum*; in def. 2 (Stål, 1867), directly from the Gr.; < Gr. ῥῆξις, a breaking, rent, rupture, < ῥηγνύναι, break, burst forth: see *break*.] 1. A genus of polypetalous plants of the order *Melastomaceæ*, type of the tribe *Rhexieæ*. It is characterized by the four obovate petals, the smooth ovary, and the eight equal anthers with a thickened or spurred connective, each anther long and slender, incurved, and opening by a single terminal pore. The 7 species are natives of North America, and are the only members of their large family which pass beyond the tropics, except the 2 species of *Bredia* in eastern Asia. Three or four species extend to the Middle Atlantic States, and one is found in New England. They are herbs or erect undershrubs, branched and usually set with conspicuous, dark, gland-bearing bristles. Their leaves are oblong, short-petioled, three-nerved, entire or bristle-toothed, the flowers solitary or cymose, commonly of a purplish-red color with yellow stamens, and very pretty.

The Inflorescence of Meadow-beauty (*Rhexia Virginica*). *a*, the fruit; *b*, a stamen; *c*, a leaf.

They bear the names *deer-grass* and *meadow-beauty*, the latter applying especially to *R. Virginica*, the best-known and most northern species, sometimes cultivated.

2. In *zoöl.*, a genus of hemipterous insects.

Rhexieæ (rek-si'ē-ē), *n. pl.* [NL. (A. P. de Candolle, 1838), < *Rhexia* + *-eæ*.] A tribe of plants of the order *Melastomaceæ*. It is characterized by a four-celled ovary with numerous ovules fixed upon a placenta projecting from the inner angle of the cell, a capsular fruit, spirally coiled seeds, and anthers with their connective commonly produced behind into a spur or tail. It includes about 37 species, belonging to 3 genera, of which *Rhexia* is the type and *Monochætum* the largest genus, containing 28 species of unimportant plants of western tropical America.

rhigolene (rig'ō-lēn), *n.* [< Gr. ῥῖγος, cold (prob. = L. *frigus*, cold, < *frigere*, be cold: see *frigid*), + *oleum*, oil, < Gr. ἔλαιον: see *oil*.] A product obtained in the distillation of petroleum. It is probably the most volatile fluid known, and one of the very best for use in producing intense cold; when atomized it gives a temperature of −9° C. Its specific gravity is .600 to .629 (105° to 95° B.); it boils at 18° C. It is used as a local anesthetic. Also *rhigoline*.

rhime†, **rhimer**†, etc. See *rime*[1], etc.

Rhina[1] (rī'nä), *n.* [NL., < L. *rhina*, < Gr. ῥίνη, a file or rasp, a shark with a rough skin.] In *ichth.*: (*a*†) An old generic name (Klein, 1745) of the angel-fish or monk-fish: now called *Squatina*. See *Rhinæ*. (*b*) A genus of rays of the family *Rhinobatidæ*, having a broad and obtuse snout, as *R. ancylostomus*. Also called *Rhamphobatis*. *Bloch and Schneider*, 1801.

Rhina[2] (rī'nä), *n.* [< Gr. ῥίς (ῥιν-), nose.] In *entom.*, a genus of coleopterous insects.

Rhinacanthus (rī-na-kan'thus), *n.* [NL. (Nees von Esenbeck, 1832), so called in allusion to the shape of the flower; < Gr. ῥίς (ῥιν-), nose, + ἄκανθος, acanthus.] A genus of gamopetalous plants of the order *Acanthaceæ*, tribe *Justicieæ*, and subtribe *Eujusticieæ*. It is characterized by its two anthers, each having two blunt cells without spurs, one cell placed higher than the other; and by the slenderly cylindrical elongated corolla-tube, with a linear and recurved upper lip, the lower broad, flat, and spreading. The 4 species are natives of tropical and southern Africa, India, and the Moluccas. They are next allied to *Dianthera*, the water-willow of the United States, but are readily distinguished by their inflorescence and shrubby habit. They bear entire leaves, and small axillary clusters of flowers which often form a large loose-branched panicle or dense terminal thyrsus of crowded cymes. *R. communis* is a slender shrub, whose root and leaves are used in India and China as an application for ringworm and other cutaneous diseases, whence called *ringworm-root*.

Rhinæ (rī'nē), *n. pl.* [NL. (Gill, 1861), pl. of *Rhina*, q. v.] In *ichth.*, one of the main divisions of sharks, represented only by the angel-sharks or *Squatinidæ*. Also called *Squatinoidea*, as a superfamily.

rhinæsthesia (rī-nes-thē'si-ä), *n.* [NL., < Gr. ῥίς (ῥιν-), nose, + αἴσθησις, perception: see *æsthesia*.] Sense of smell; olfaction.

rhinæsthesis (rī-nes-thē'sis), *n.* [NL.: see *rhinæsthesia*.] Same as *rhinæsthesia*.

rhinæsthetics (rī-nes-thet'iks), *n.* [As *rhinæsthesia* (*-æsthet-*) + *-ics*. Cf. *esthetics*.] The science of sensations of smell.

rhinal (rī'nal), *a.* [< Gr. ῥίς (ῥιν-), later also ῥίν, the nose, + *-al*.] Of or pertaining to the nose; nasal; narial: as, the *rhinal* cavities (that is, the nasal passages).

> To make the laryngeal and *rhinal* mirrors available, the artificial illumination of these parts [hidden behind and above the palate] is necessary. *Pop. Sci. Mo.*, XII. 170.

rhinalgia (rī-nal'ji-ä), *n.* [NL., < Gr. ῥίς (ῥιν-), nose, + ἄλγος, pain.] Pain, especially neuralgic pain, in the nose.

Rhinanthaceæ (rī-nan-thā'sē-ē), *n. pl.* [NL. (Jussieu, 1805), < *Rhinanthus* + *-aceæ*.] An order of dicotyledons established by Jussieu, but now incorporated with the *Scrophularineæ*.

Rhinanthus (rī-nan'thus), *n.* [NL. (Linnæus, 1737), named from the compressed and beaked upper lip of a former species; < Gr. ῥίς (ῥιν-), nose, + ἄνθος, flower.] A genus of gamopetalous plants of the order *Scrophularineæ* and tribe *Euphrasieæ*. It is characterized by a long two-lipped corolla, the upper lip entire, straight, compressed, and helmet-like; by a swollen and compressed four-toothed calyx, inflated in fruit; by four unequal stamens with equal anther-cells; and by a roundish capsule containing few winged seeds. The 2 or 3 very variable species are natives of temperate and northern regions in Europe, Asia, and America. They are annual erect herbs, more or less parasitic on the roots of grasses. They bear opposite crenate leaves, and yellow, violet, or bluish flowers sessile in the axils of deep-cut floral leaves, the upper flowers condensed into a spike. *R. Crista-galli* of the northern Old World is the common rattle, yellow rattle, or rattlebox of Great Britain: also called *penny-grass* and *cockscomb*. It is often injurious to herbage on account of its parasitic habit.

rhinarium (rī-nā'ri-um), *n.*; pl. *rhinaria* (-ä). [NL., < Gr. ῥίς (ῥιν-), nose, + *-arium*.] In *entom.*, the nostril-piece; the front part of the nasus, or clypeus, or its equivalent when reduced in size: used in the classification of the *Neuroptera*. In certain lamellicorn beetles it forms a large sclerite between the clypeus and the labrum. *Kirby and Spence.*

rhinaster (rī-nas'tėr), *n.* [NL., < Gr. ῥίς (ῥιν-), nose, + ἀστήρ, a star.] 1. The common two-horned African rhinoceros, *R. bicornis*.—2. [*cap.*] [NL.] (*a*) The genus of two-horned rhinoceroses. See *Rhinocerotidæ*. (*b*) The genus of star-nosed moles: synonymous with *Condylura*. *Wagner*, 1843.

rhind-mart†, *n.* See *rindmart*.

rhine, *n.* A spelling of *rine*[1].

Rhine-berry (rīn'ber"i), *n.* Same as *Rheinberry*.

rhinencephal (rī-nen'se-fal), *n.* Same as *rhinencephalon*.

rhinencephala, *n.* Plural of *rhinencephalon*.

rhinencephali, *n.* Plural of *rhinencephalus*.

rhinencephalic (rī-nen-se-fal'ik or -sef'a-lik), *a.* [< *rhinencephal* + *-ic*.] Pertaining to the rhinencephalon; olfactory, as a lobe or segment of the brain.—**Rhinencephalic segment** of the brain, the rhinencephalon.—**Rhinencephalic vertebra**, the foremost one of four cranial vertebræ or segments of which the skull has been theoretically supposed by some anatomists, as Owen, to consist.

rhinencephalon (rī-nen-sef'a-lon), *n.*; pl. *rhinencephala* (-lä). [NL., < Gr. ῥίς (ῥιν-), nose, + ἐγκέφαλος, brain: see *encephalon*.] The olfactory lobe of the brain; the foremost one of the several morphological segments of the encephalon, preceding the prosencephalon. In the lower vertebrates the rhinencephalon is relatively large, and evidently a distinct part of the brain. In the higher it gradually diminishes in size, becoming relatively very small, and apparently a mere outgrowth of the cerebrum. Thus, in man the rhinencephalon is reduced to the so-called pair of olfactory nerves, from their roots in the cerebrum to the olfactory bulbs whence are given off the numerous filaments, the proper olfactory nerves, which pierce the cribriform plate of the ethmoid, and ramify in the nose. The rhinencephalon, like other encephalic segments, is paired or double—that is, consists of right and left halves. It is primitively hollow, or has its proper ventricle, which, however, is entirely obliterated in the adults of the higher vertebrates. This hollow is a prolongation of the system of cavities common to the other encephalic segments, and known as the *rhinocœle*. Also *rhinencephal*. See cuts under *Petromyzontidæ*, *Rana*, *brain* (cut 2), and *encephalon*.

rhinencephalous (rī-nen-sef'a-lus), *a.* [< *rhinencephal* + *-ous*.] Same as *rhinencephalic*.

rhinencephalus (rī-nen-sef'a-lus), *n.*; pl. *rhinencephali* (-lī). [NL., < Gr. ῥίς (ῥιν-), the nose, + ἐγκέφαλος, the brain: see *encephalon*.] In *teratol.*, a cyclops. Also *rhinocephalus*.

rhinestone (rīn'stōn), *n.* [Tr. F. *cailloux du Rhin*, rhinestones, so called from the river Rhine, in allusion to the origin of strass, invented at Strasburg in 1680.] An imitation stone made of paste or strass (a lead glass), generally cut in the form of a brilliant and made and cut to imitate the diamond, set usually in silver or other inexpensive mounting. Rhinestones were extensively worn in the latter part of the eighteenth century, and are now much used in shoe-buckles, clasps, and ornaments for the hair.

rhineurynter (rī-nū-rin'tėr), *n.* [< Gr. ῥίς (ῥιν-), nose, + *εὐρυντήρ (an assumed form), < εὐρύνειν, widen, < εὐρύς, wide.] A small inflatable elastic bag used for plugging the nose.

Rhinichthys (rī-nik'this), *n.* [NL. (Agassiz, 1838), < Gr. ῥίς (ῥιν-), nose, + ἰχθύς, a fish.] In *ichth.*, a genus of cyprinoid fishes from the fresh waters of North America. They are known

Black-nosed Dace (*Rhinichthys atronasus*).

as *long-nosed* or *black-nosed dace*. They are abundant in clear fresh streams and brooks of the United States, and include some of the prettiest minnows, as *R. cataractæ* and *R. atronasus*.

Rhinidæ (rin'i-dē), *n. pl.* [NL., < *Rhina*[1] + *-idæ*.] A family of plagiostomous fishes, named from the genus *Rhina*: same as *Squatinidæ*.

rhinitis (rī-nī'tis), *n.* [NL., < Gr. ῥίς (ῥιν-), nose, + *-itis*.] Inflammation of the nose, especially of the nasal mucous membrane.

rhino (rī'nō), *n.* [Also *rino*; of obscure cant origin, perhaps a made word.] Money; cash. [Slang.]

> "The Seaman's Adieu," an old ballad dated 1670, has the following:
>
> Some as I know
> Have parted with their ready *rino*.
> N. *and* Q., 7th ser., V. 417.
>
> To sum up the whole, in the shortest phrase I know,
> Beware of the Rhine, and take care of the *rhino*.
> *Barham*, Ingoldsby Legends, II. 45.
>
> No doubt you might have found a quarry,
> Perhaps a gold-mine, for aught I know,
> Containing heaps of native *rhino*.
> *Lowell*, Biglow Papers, 1st ser., Int.

Rhinobatidæ (rī-nō-bat'i-dē), *n. pl.* [NL., < *Rhinobatus*[1] + *-idæ*.] A family of selachians, typified by the genus *Rhinobatus*; the shark-rays or beaked rays. They are shark-like rays, whose trunk gradually passes into the long strong tail, which is provided with two well-developed dorsal fins, a caudal fin, and a conspicuous dermal fold on each side. The rayed part of the pectoral fins is not extended to the snout. Three to five genera are recognized, with about 15 species, of warm seas.

rhinobatoid (rī-nob'a-toid), *a.* and *n.* [< *Rhinobatus*[1] + *-oid*.] I. *a.* Of or relating to the *Rhinobatidæ*.

II. *n.* A selachian of the family *Rhinobatidæ*.

Rhinobatus[1] (rī-nob'a-tus), *n.* [NL. (Bloch and Schneider, 1801), < Gr. ῥινόβατος, also ῥινοβάτης, a rough-skinned fish, perhaps *Raia rhinobatos*, < ῥίνη, a shark, + βάτος, a ray.] The typical genus of *Rhinobatidæ*, having the first dorsal fin much behind the ventrals, and the anterior nasal valves not confluent. *R. productus* is the long-nosed ray of California. Also *Rhinobatis*.

Rhinobatus[2] (rī-nob'a-tus), *n.* [NL., < Gr. ῥίς (ῥιν-), nose.] In *entom.*, a genus of coleopterous insects. *Germar*, 1817.

rhinoblennorrhea, rhinoblennorrhœa (rī-nō-blen-ō-rē'ä), *n.* [NL., < Gr. ῥίς (ῥιν-), nose, + βλέννος, mucus, + ῥοία, a flow. Cf. *blennorrhea*.] Mucous or mucopurulent discharges from the nose.

rhinocaul (rī'nō-kâl), *n.* [< Gr. ῥίς (ῥιν-), nose, + καυλός, a stalk: see *caulis*.] In *anat.*, the crus, peduncle, or support of the olfactory bulb. *Buck's Handbook of Med. Sciences*, VIII. 525.

rhinocephalus (rī-nǫ-sef′ạ-lus), *n.* [NL., < Gr. ῥίς (ῥιν-), nose, + κεφαλή, head.] Same as *rhinencephalus*.

rhinocerial (rī-nǫ-sē′ri-ạl), *a.* [< *rhinoceros* + *-ial*.] 1. Same as *rhinocerotic*.—2. Pug or retroussé, as the nose. [Rare.]

rhinocerical (rī-nǫ-ser′i-kạl), *a.* [< *rhinoceros* + *-ic-al*.] Same as *rhinocerial*, 2. [Rare.]

These gentlemen were formerly marked out and distinguished by the little *rhinocerical* nose, . . . which they were used to cock, toss, or draw up in a contemptuous manner, upon reading the works of their ingenious contemporaries. *Addison*, Tatler, No. 260.

Rhinoceridæ (rī-nǫ-ser′i-dē), *n.* [NL.] Same as *Rhinocerotidæ*.

rhinocerine (rī-nos′ẹ-rin), *a.* [< *rhinoceros* + *-ine*[1].] Same as *rhinocerotic*.

rhinoceroid (rī-nos′ẹ-roid), *a.* [< *rhinoceros* + *-oid*.] Same as *rhinocerotoid*.

Rhinocerontidæ (rī-nos-ẹ-ron′ti-dē), *n. pl.* [< *Rhinoceros* (*-ot-*) + *-idæ*.] An erroneous form of *Rhinocerotidæ*. *W. H. Flower.*

Rhinocerontina (rī-nos″ẹ-ron-tī′nạ̈), *n. pl.* [< *Rhinoceros* (*-ot-*) + *-ina*[2].] Same as *Rhinocerotidæ*.

rhinocerontine (rī-nos-ẹ-ron′tin), *a.* [Irreg. < *rhinoceros* (*-ot-*) + *-ine*[1].] Of or pertaining to a rhinoceros or the *Rhinocerotidæ*; rhinocerotic.

In the manner practiced by others of the *rhinocerontine* family.
Livingstone, Missionary Travels and Researches, i., note.

rhinoceros (rī-nos′ẹ-ros), *n.* [Formerly also *rhinocerot*, *rhinocerote*; = OF. *rhinoceros*, F. *rhinocéros* = Sp. It. *rinoceronte* = Pg. *rhinoceros*, *rhinoceronte*, < L. *rhinoceros*, < Gr. ῥινόκερως (-κερωτ-), a rhinoceros, lit. 'nose-horned,' < ῥίς (ῥιν-), the nose, + κέρας, a horn.] 1. A large pachydermatous perissodactyl mammal with a horn on the nose; any member of the genus *Rhinoceros* or family *Rhinocerotidæ*. There are several living as well as many fossil species. They are huge ungainly quadrupeds, having an extremely thick and tough or hard skin, thrown into various buckler-like plates and folds. The legs are short, stout, and clumsy, with odd-toed feet, whose three digits are incased in separate hoofs. The tail is short; the ears are high and rather large; the head is very large and unshapely, supported upon a thick stocky neck; the muzzle is blunt, and the upper lip freely movable. The head is especially long in the nasal region, and there are usually one or two massive upright horns, without any bony core, the substance of the horn being epidermal only. When two horns are present they are one behind the other in the median line, and the hinder one rests over the frontal bone, the front one being in any case borne upon the nasal bones. Rhinoceroses live mainly in marshy places, in thick or rank vegetation, and subsist entirely upon vegetable food. The living species are now confined to the warmer parts of Africa and Asia, and are hairless or nearly so; but these animals formerly had a much more extensive range, not only in the Old World, but also in America. The best-known of the extinct species is *R. tichorhinus*, the woolly rhinoceros, which formerly ranged over Europe, including the British Isles. Of the existing one-horned

One-horned Rhinoceros (*Rhinoceros unicornis*).

species are the Indian rhinoceros, *R. indicus* or *R. unicornis*, which inhabits the warmer parts of Asia, attains a height of 5 feet, and has the horn short and stout; the Javan rhinoceros, *R. sondaicus*, or *R. javanus*, distinct from the Indian species, inhabiting Java, the Malay peninsula, etc.; the hairy-eared rhinoceros, *R. lasiotis*; and the African kobaoba, *R. simus*. The two-horned species include the Sumatran or Malaccan rhinoceros, *R. sumatrensis*; and the African keitloa, *R. keitloa* or *bicornis*. See also cut under *Perissodactyla*.

Approach thou like the rugged Russian bear,
The arm'd *rhinoceros*, or the Hyrcan tiger.
Shak., Macbeth, iii. 4. 101.

2. [*cap.*] [NL. (Linnæus, 1758).] The typical genus of *Rhinocerotidæ*, containing all the living and some of the extinct forms. See above.—**Rhinoceros leg**, pachydermia or elephantiasis.

rhinoceros-auk (rī-nos′ẹ-ros-âk), *n.* The bird *Ceratorhina monocerata*, belonging to the family *Alcidæ*, having an upright deciduous horn on the base of the beak. See *Ceratorhina*, and cut in next column.

rhinoceros-beetle (rī-nos′ẹ-ros-bē″tl), *n.* A beetle of the genus *Dynastes*, having in the

Rhinoceros-auk (*Ceratorhina monocerata*): left-hand figure in winter, after molting the horn and plumes.

male sex a large up-curved horn on the head, resembling somewhat the horn of the rhinoceros, as well as a more or less developed prothoracic horn. The common rhinoceros-beetle of the United States, *Dynastes tityus*, the largest of the North American beetles, has two large horns directed forward, one arising from the thorax and one from the head, in the male beetle only. The general color is greenish-gray with black markings, and between this form and a uniform brown there are many gradations. The larva feeds in decaying stumps and logs. Both beetle and larva have a peculiarly disagreeable odor, which, when they are present in any number, becomes insupportable. *D. hercules* of South America is another rhinoceros-beetle, specifically called the *Hercules-beetle*, whose prothoracic horn is immensely long. See also cut under *Hercules-beetle*.

Rhinoceros-beetle (*Dynastes tityus*), half natural size.

rhinoceros-bird (rī-nos′ẹ-ros-bėrd), *n.* 1. The rhinoceros-hornbill.—2. A beef-eater or ox-pecker. See *Buphaga*.

rhinoceros-bush (rī-nos′ẹ-ros-bu̇sh), *n.* A composite shrub, *Elytropappus Rhinocerotis*, a rough much-branching bush with minute scale-like leaves, and heads disposed singly. It abounds in the South African karoo lands—a plant of dry ground, but said to be a principal food of the rhinoceros.

rhinoceros-chameleon (rī-nos′ẹ-ros-kạ-mē″lẹ-ọn), *n.* The Madagascar *Chamæleon rhinoceratus*, having a horn on the snout.

rhinoceros-hornbill (rī-nos′ẹ-ros-hôrn″bil), *n.* The bird *Buceros rhinoceros*, a large hornbill of the family *Bucerotidæ*, having the horn on the bill enormously developed. See cut under *hornbill*.

rhinoceros-tick (rī-nos′ẹ-ros-tik), *n.* The tick *Ixodes rhinocerinus*, which infests rhinoceroses.

rhinocerot†, **rhinocerote†** (rī-nos′e-rot, -rōt), *n.* [< *rhinoceros* (*-ot-*): see *rhinoceros*.] A rhinoceros.

For a Plough he got
The horn or tooth of som *Rhinocerot*.
Sylvester, tr. of Du Bartas's Weeks, ii., The Handy-Crafts.

He speaks to men with a *rhinocerote's* nose,
Which he thinks great, and so reads verses too.
B. Jonson, Epigrams, xxviii.

rhinocerotic (rī-nos-ẹ-rot′ik), *a.* [< *rhinoceros* (*-ot-*) + *-ic*.] Of or pertaining to the rhinoceros; resembling or characteristic of a rhinoceros; rhinocerotiform.

In these respects the Tapir is Horse-like, but in the following it is more *Rhinocerotic*. *Huxley*, Anat. Vert., p. 310.

Rhinocerotic section, an incongruous series of extinct and extant perissodactyl quadrupeds, having teeth substantially like those of the rhinoceros. The families *Rhinocerotidæ*, *Hyracodontidæ*, *Macraucheniidæ*, *Chalicotheriidæ*, *Menodontidæ*, and *Palæotheriidæ* are by Flower ranged in this section.

Rhinocerotidæ (rī-nos-e-rot′i-dē), *n. pl.* [NL., < *Rhinoceros* (*-ot-*) + *-idæ*.] A family of perissodactyl ungulate mammals, for the most part extinct, typified by the genus *Rhinoceros*. The nasal region is expanded or thrown backward, the supramaxillary bones forming a considerable part of the border of the anterior nares, and the nasal bones being contracted forward or atrophied. The neck is comparatively abbreviated. The molar crowns are traversed by continuous ridges, more or less well defined, the upper ones having a continuous outer wall without complete transverse crests; the incisors are reduced in number or entirely suppressed. The basioccipital is comparatively broad behind and narrow forward; the tympanic and periotic bones are ankylosed and wedged in between the squamosal, exoccipital, and other contiguous bones. The only living genus is *Rhinoceros*, from which *Rhinaster* and *Atelodus* are sometimes separated. There are several extinct genera, as *Cœlodonta*, *Acerotherium*, *Badactherium*, and *Hyracodon*. The family is one of only three which now represent the once numerous and diversified suborder *Perissodactyla*, the other two being the *Tapiridæ* or tapirs and the *Equidæ* or horses. See cuts under *Perissodactyla* and *rhinoceros*.

rhinocerotiform (rī-nos-ẹ-rot′i-fôrm), *a.* [< NL. *rhinocerotiformis*, < L. *rhinoceros* (*-ot-*) + *forma*, form.] Shaped like a rhinoceros; having the structure of the *Rhinocerotidæ*; belonging to the *Rhinocerotiformia*.

Rhinocerotiformia (rī-nos-ẹ-rot-i-fôr′mi-ạ̈), *n. pl.* [NL., neut. pl. of *rhinocerotiformis*: see *rhinocerotiform*.] One of two series of *Rhinocerotoidea*, containing only the family *Rhinocerotidæ*. *Gill.*

rhinocerotoid (rī-nǫ-ser′ǫ-toid), *a.* and *n.* [< Gr. ῥινόκερως (-ωτ-), rhinoceros, + εἶδος, form.] I. *a.* Resembling a rhinoceros; rhinocerotiform in a broad sense; belonging to the *Rhinocerotoidea*.

II. *n.* A member of the *Rhinocerotoidea*.

Rhinocerotoidea (rī-nos″ẹ-rǫ-toi′dẹ-ạ̈), *n. pl.* [NL., < *Rhinoceros* (*-ot-*) + *-oidea*.] A superfamily of *Perissodactyla*, containing two series, *Rhinocerotiformia* and *Macraucheniiformia*, the former corresponding to the single family *Rhinocerotidæ*, the latter containing the two families *Macraucheniidæ* and *Palæotheriidæ*. The superfamily is characterized by the continuous crests of the upper molars. *Gill.*

rhinocerotoidean (rī-nos″ẹ-rǫ-toi′dẹ-ạn), *a.* and *n.* [< *rhinocerotoid* + *-e-an*.] Same as *rhinocerotoid*.

Rhinochetidæ (rī-nǫ-ket′i-dē), *n. pl.* [NL., < *Rhinochetus* + *-idæ*.] A Polynesian family of precocial wading birds, related to the South American *Eurypygidæ* and the Madagascar *Mesitidæ*, typified by the genus *Rhinochetus*. The family is an isolated one, and represents in some respects a generalized type of structure now shared to any great extent by only the other two families named. It is confined, as far as known, to New Caledonia.

Rhinochetus (rī-nok′e-tus), *n.* [NL. (Vorreaux and Des Murs, 1860, in the erroneous form *Rhynochetos*); also, erroneously, *Rhinochætus*, *Rhinocœtus*, etc., prop. *Rhinochetus* (Hartlaub, 1862) or *Rhinochetos*, < Gr. ῥίς (ῥιν-), nose, + ὀχετός, a conduit, channel, duct, pore, < ὀχεῖν, hold, carry, < ἔχειν, hold: see *scheme*.] The only genus of *Rhinochetidæ*: so called from the lid-like character of the nasal opercle or scale, which automatically closes the nostrils. *R. jubatus* is the only species known. See cut under *kagu*.

Rhinochilus (rī-nǫ-kī′lus), *n.* [NL. (S. F. Baird and C. Girard, 1853), in form *Rhinocheilus*, < Gr. ῥίς (ῥιν-), nose, + χεῖλος, a lip.] A genus of harmless serpents of the family *Colubridæ* and subfamily *Calamariinæ*, having the body cylindric and rigid, with smooth scales, postabdominal and subcaudal scutella entire, vertical plate broad, rostral produced, a loreal, a preocular, and two nasals. *R. lecontei* is a Californian snake, blotched with pale red and black.

rhinocleisis (rī-nǫ-klī′sis), *n.* [NL., < Gr. ῥίς (ῥιν-), nose, + κλεῖσις, κλῆσις, a shutting up, closing, < κλείειν, close: see *close*[1].] Nasal obstruction.

rhinocœle (rī′nǫ-sēl), *n.* The rhinocœlia.

rhinocœlia (rī-nǫ-sē′li-ạ̈), *n.*; pl. *rhinocœliæ* (-ē). [NL., < Gr. ῥίς (ῥιν-), nose, + κοιλία, the cœlia: see *cœlia*.] The cœlia of the rhinencephalon; the ventricle or proper cavity of the olfactory lobe of the brain, primitively communicating with the lateral ventricle of the cerebrum. It persists distinctly in many animals, but in man it grows so small as to escape notice, or becomes entirely obliterated.

Rhinocrypta (rī-nǫ-krip′tạ̈), *n.* [NL. (G. R. Gray, 1841), < Gr. ῥίς (ῥιν-), nose, nostril, + κρυπτός, hidden.] A remarkable genus of rock-wrens, belonging to the family *Pteroptochidæ*, and characteristic of the Patagonian subregion, where they represent the genus *Pteroptochus* of the Chilian. Like others of this family, they have the nostrils covered by a membrane; in general appearance and habits they resemble wrens. Two species are described, *R. lanceolata* and *R. fusca*. The former is 8 inches long, the wing and tail each 3½, olivaceous-brown above, with the head crested and its feathers marked with long white shaft-stripes, the tail blackish, the under parts cinereous, whitening on the breast and belly, and a chestnut patch on each side; the feet are large and strong, in adaptation to terrestrial habits.

Rhinoderma (rī-nǫ-dėr′mạ̈), *n.* [NL. (Duméril and Bibron), < Gr. ῥίς (ῥιν-), nose, + δέρμα, skin.] A genus of batrachians, of the family *Engystomatidæ*, or made type of the family *Rhinodermatidæ*. *R. darwini* of Chili has an enormous brood-pouch, formed by the extension of a gular sac along the ventral surface beneath the integument, in which the young are retained for a time, giving rise to a former belief that the animal is viviparous. As many as 10 or 15 young with the legs well developed have been found in the pouch.

Rhinodermatidæ (rī″nǫ-dėr-mat′i-dē), *n. pl.* [NL., < *Rhinoderma*(*t-*) + *-idæ*.] A family of salient batrachians, typified by the genus *Rhinoderma*.

Rhinodon (rī'nō-don), *n.* [NL. (Smith, 1841), < Gr. ῥίνη, shark, + ὀδούς (ὀδοντ-) = E. *tooth*.] In *ichth.*, the typical genus of *Rhinodontidæ*, having very numerous small teeth. *R. typicus* is an immense shark, occasionally reaching a length of 40 feet or more, found in the Indian ocean, called *whale-shark* from its size.

Rhinodontidæ (rī-nō-don'ti-dē), *n. pl.* [NL., < *Rhinodon(t-)* + *-idæ*.] A family of selachians, typified by the genus *Rhinodon*; the whale-sharks. There are two dorsals, neither with spines, and a pit at the root of the caudal fin, whose lower lobe is well developed; the sides of the tail are keeled; there are no nictitating membranes; the spiracles are very small, the teeth small and many, the gill-slits wide, and the mouth and nostrils subterminal. Besides *R. typicus* the family contains *Micristodus punctatus* of California.

rhinodynia (rī-nō-din'i-ä), *n.* [< Gr. ῥίς (ῥιν-), nose, + ὀδύνη, pain.] Pain in the nose or nasal region.

Rhinogale (rī-nō-gā'lē), *n.* [NL. (J. E. Gray, 1864), < Gr. ῥίς (ῥιν-), nose, + γαλῆ, weasel.] The typical genus of *Rhinogalinæ*. The species is *R. melleri* of eastern Africa.

Rhinogalidæ (rī-nō-gal'i-dē), *n. pl.* A family of viverrine quadrupeds, named by Gray from the genus *Rhinogale*, corresponding to the two subfamilies *Rhinogalinæ* and *Crossarchinæ*.

Rhinogalinæ (rī"nō-gā-lī'nē), *n. pl.* [NL., < *Rhinogale* + *-inæ*.] The typical subfamily of *Rhinogalidæ*.

rhinolith (rī'nō-lith), *n.* [< Gr. ῥίς (ῥιν-), nose, + λίθος, stone.] A stony concretion formed in the nose.

> Mr. M—— showed a *Rhinolith* weighing 105 grains. It had been extracted without much difficulty from the nasal fossa of a woman aged about forty-five.
> *Lancet*, No. 3421, p. 582.

rhinolithiasis (rī"nō-li-thī'a-sis), *n.* [NL., < *rhinolith* + *-iasis*.] The condition characterized by the formation of rhinoliths.

rhinological (rī-nō-loj'i-kal), *a.* [< *rhinolog-y* + *-ic-al*.] Pertaining to or of the nature of rhinology.

rhinologist (rī-nol'ō-jist), *n.* [< *rhinolog-y* + *-ist*.] One versed in rhinology; a specialist in diseases of the nose.

rhinology (rī-nol'ō-ji), *n.* [< Gr. ῥίς (ῥιν-), nose, + -λογία, < λέγειν, speak: see *-ology*.] The sum of scientific knowledge concerning the nose.

Rhinolophidæ (rī-nō-lof'i-dē), *n. pl.* [NL., < *Rhinolophus* + *-idæ*.] A family of the vespertilionine alliance of the suborder *Microchiroptera* and order *Chiroptera*, typified by the genus *Rhinolophus*; the horseshoe, leaf-nosed, or rhinolophine bats. They have a highly developed nose-leaf, large ears with no tragus, rudimentary inarticulate premaxillary bones, minute upper incisors, the tail long and inclosed in the interfemoral membrane, and a pair of prepubic teat-like appendages in the female. These bats inhabit temperate and tropical regions of both hemispheres. The family is divided into *Rhinolophinæ* and *Phyllorhininæ*. See cut under *Phyllorhina*.

Rhinolophinæ (rī"nō-lō-fī'nē), *n. pl.* [NL., < *Rhinolophus* + *-inæ*.] The typical subfamily of *Rhinolophidæ*, containing the horseshoe-bats proper, having the pedal digits with the normal number of phalanges, and the iliopectineal spine distinct from the antero-inferior surface of the ilium.

rhinolophine (rī-nol'ō-fin), *a.* and *n.* **I.** *a.* Of or belonging to the *Rhinolophinæ*.

II. *n.* A horseshoe-bat.

Rhinolophus (rī-nol'ō-fus), *n.* [NL. (Geoffroy), < Gr. ῥίς (ῥιν-), nose, + λόφος, crest.] The typical and only genus of horseshoe-bats. It contains upward of 20 species, having the dental formula 1 incisor, 1 canine, 2 premolars, and 3 molars in each upper half-jaw, and 2 incisors, 1 canine, 3 premolars, and 3 molars in each lower half-jaw, and the nose-leaf lanceolate behind. *R. hipposideros* of Europe is the best-known species. *R. ferrum-equinum* is widely distributed in Europe, Africa, and Asia. *R. luctus* is a large Indian and Malayan species.

Rhinomacer (rī-nom'a-sėr), *n.* [NL. (Fabricius, 1787), < Gr. ῥίς (ῥιν-), nose, + μακρός, long.] A small genus of rhynchophorous beetles, typical of the family *Rhinomaceridæ*, comprising only 5 species, 4 of which are North American and 1 European.

Rhinomaceridæ (rī"nō-ma-ser'i-dē), *n. pl.* [NL., < *Rhinomacer* + *-idæ*.] A family of rhynchophorous coleopterous insects named by Leach in 1817 from the genus *Rhinomacer*, having the fold on the inner surface of the elytra near the edge obsolete or null, the pygidium alike in both sexes, and the labrum distinct. It is a small family, inhabiting the north temperate zone, and feeding upon the male flowers of conifers, in which also the eggs are laid.

rhinopharyngitis (rī-nō-far-in-jī'tis), *n.* [NL., < Gr. ῥίς (ῥιν-), nose, + φάρυγξ (φαρυγγ-) + *-itis*.] Inflammation of the mucous membrane of the nose and pharynx.

Rhinophidæ (rī-nof'i-dē), *n. pl.* [NL., < *Rhinophis* + *-idæ*.] A family of tortricine serpents, named from the genus *Rhinophis*: synonymous with *Uropeltidæ*. *E. D. Cope*, 1886.

Rhinophis (rī'nō-fis), *n.* [NL. (Hemprich), < Gr. ῥίς (ῥιν-), nose, + ὄφις, a serpent.] A genus of shield-tailed serpents, of the family *Uropeltidæ*, and giving name to the *Rhinophidæ*, having the rostral plate produced between and separating the nasals, and the tail ending in a large shield, as in *Uropeltis*. They are small serpents, under 2 feet long, and live under ground or in ant-hills, feeding upon worms and insect-larvæ. The tail is short, the mouth not distensible, and the eyes are small. Several Ceylonese species are described, as *R. oxyrhynchus* and *R. punctatus*, sharing with those of *Uropeltis* the name *shieldtail*.

rhinophore (rī'nō-fōr), *n.* [< Gr. ῥίς (ῥιν-), nose, + φέρειν = E. *bear*[1].] In *Mollusca*, one of the hinder pair of tentacles of opisthobranchiate gastropods, supposed to function as olfactory organs; in general, an organ bearing an olfactory sense. Also spelled *rhinophor*.

> The *rhinophores* are a pair of tentacles placed near the anterior end of the body, on the dorsal surface of the head.
> *Micros. Sci.*, N. S., XXXI. i. 41.

Rhinophryne (rī-nō-frī'nē), *n.* [NL., also *Rhinophrynus* (Duméril and Bibron), < Gr. ῥίς (ῥιν-), nose, + φρύνη, a toad.] A genus of spade-footed toads, typical of the family *Rhinophrynidæ*, having the skull remarkably ossified. *R. dorsalis* of Mexico, the only species, lives under ground, being capable of making extensive excavations with the "spades" with which the hind feet are furnished.

Rhinophrynidæ (rī-nō-frin'i-dē), *n. pl.* [NL., < *Rhinophryne* + *-idæ*.] A family of arciferous salient batrachians, represented by the genus *Rhinophryne*, without maxillary teeth, with dilated sacral diapophyses, and the tongue free in front (proteroglossate). These toads are among a number known as *spade-footed*.

Rhinophylla (rī-nō-fil'ạ), *n.* [NL. (W. Peters, 1865), < Gr. ῥίς (ῥιν-), nose, + φύλλον, a leaf.] A genus of very small South American phyllostomine bats, having no tail. *R. pumilio* is the least in size of the family, having a forearm only 1¼ inches long.

rhinophyma (rī-nō-fī'mạ), *n.* [NL., < Gr. ῥίς (ῥιν-), nose, + φῦμα, a tumor: see *Phymata*.] Hyperemia of the skin of the nose, with hypertrophy of its connective tissue and more or less inflammation of its glands, forming a well-developed grade of acne rosacea: restricted by some to cases presenting extraordinary enlargement, sometimes regarded as distinct from acne rosacea.

rhinoplast (rī'nō-plast), *n.* [Irreg. < *rhinoplast-ic*.] One who undergoes a rhinoplastic operation; one who has an artificial nose.

rhinoplastic (rī-nō-plas'tik), *a.* [< Gr. ῥίς (ῥιν-), nose, + πλάσσειν, form, mold: see *plastic*.] Pertaining to or of the nature of rhinoplasty.—**Rhinoplastic operation**, a surgical operation for forming an artificial nose, or restoring a nose partly lost. It generally consists in bringing down a triangular piece of skin from the forehead, twisting it round, and causing it to adhere by its under surface and edges to the part of the nose remaining. The skin may also be taken from another part of the body. The extreme joint of one of the fingers has been used in supporting such an artificial nose. Sometimes called *Taliacotian operation*, from Taliacotius, an Italian surgeon, who first performed it. See *Carpue's rhinoplastic operation*, under *operation*.

rhinoplasty (rī'nō-plas-ti), *n.* [= F. *rhinoplastie*; as *rhinoplast-ic* + *-y*[3].] Plastic surgery of the nose.

Rhinopoma (rī-nō-pō'mạ), *n.* [NL. (Geoffroy), < Gr. ῥίς (ῥιν-), nose, + πῶμα, a lid, cover.] A remarkable genus of Old World emballonurine bats, with one species, *R. microphyllum*, having a long slender tail produced far beyond the narrow interfemoral membrane, two joints of the index-finger, united premaxillary bones, and very weak incisors. The genus exhibits cross-relationships between *Emballonuridæ* and *Nycteridæ* (of another section of *Microchiroptera*), and is sometimes made type of a supergeneric group (*Rhinopomata*). This bat is found in Egyptian tombs and similar dusky retreats of Africa and India.

Rhinopomastes (rī"nō-pō-mas'tēz), *n.* [NL. (Sir Andrew Smith, 1828, in the form *Rhinopomastus*), irreg. < Gr. ῥίς (ῥιν-), nose, + πωμαστήριον, dim. of πῶμα, a lid, cover.] A genus of African wood-hoopoes of the family *Irrisoridæ*. There are several species, as *R. cyanomelas*. See *Irrisoridæ*.

Rhinoptera (rī-nop'te-rä), *n.* [NL. (Kuhl, 1836), < Gr. ῥίς (ῥιν-), nose, + πτερόν, wing, = E. *feather*.] In *ichth.*, a genus of rays of the family *Myliobatidæ*, having the snout emarginate, teeth in several series, and cephalic fins below the level of the disk. *R. quadriloba* is a cow-nosed ray, of great size, common on the Atlantic coast of the United States from Cape Cod southward.

rhinorrhagia (rī-nō-rā'ji-ä), *n.* [NL., < Gr. ῥίς (ῥιν-), nose, + -ραγία, < ῥηγνύναι, break, burst.] Hemorrhage from the nose; epistaxis.

rhinorrhea, rhinorrhœa (rī-nō-rē'ä), *n.* [NL. *rhinorrhœa*, < Gr. ῥίς (ῥιν-), nose, + ῥοία, a flow, < ῥεῖν, flow.] Mucous or mucopurulent discharge from the nose. Also called *rhinoblennorrhea*.

rhinorrheal, rhinorrhœal (rī-nō-rē'al), *a.* [< *rhinorrhea* + *-al*.] Pertaining to or affected with rhinorrhea.

Rhinortha (rī-nôr'thä), *n.* [NL., < Gr. ῥίς (ῥιν-), nose, + ὀρθός, straight.] **1.** In *ornith.*, a genus of cuckoos, of the family *Cuculidæ* and subfamily *Phœnicophæinæ*, founded by Vigors in 1830, characteristic of the Malaccas. *R. chlorophæa* is the only species.—**2.** In *entom.*, a genus of hemipterous insects.

rhinoscleroma (rī"nō-sklē-rō'mä), *n.* [NL., < Gr. ῥίς (ῥιν-), nose, + σκληρός, hard, + *-oma*.] A disease affecting principally the nose, but also the nasal passages, lips, and the pharynx, characterized by smooth nodular swellings of a red color and of a stony induration. It is of slow growth, without inflammation of surrounding parts, and without pain except on pressure; a short bacillus seems to be invariably present in the growth. Rhinoscleroma is a rare disease, the accounts of which have come mainly from Austrian observers.

rhinoscope (rī'nō-skōp), *n.* [< Gr. ῥίς (ῥιν-), nose, + σκοπεῖν, view.] An instrument for examining the nose. The common rhinoscope is a small plane mirror like a laryngoscopic mirror, but smaller, for introduction into the pharynx, with a concave head-mirror or other device for throwing the light upon it; with this the posterior nares are examined. An instrument for holding the nostrils open and the hairs out of the way, so that the nasal passages may be inspected from in front, is usually called a *nose-speculum*.

rhinoscopic (rī-nō-skop'ik), *a.* [< *rhinoscope* + *-ic*.] Of or pertaining to the rhinoscope or rhinoscopy; made with or effected by the use of the rhinoscope.

rhinoscopy (rī'nō-skō-pi), *n.* [< *rhinoscope* + *-y*[3].] The inspection of the nares with a rhinoscope from behind (posterior rhinoscopy), or with a nasal speculum from in front (anterior rhinoscopy).

rhinotheca (rī-nō-thē'kä), *n.*; pl. *rhinothecæ* (-sē). [NL., < Gr. ῥίς (ῥιν-), nose, + θήκη, a sheath.] In *ornith.*, the integument of the upper mandible of a bird, exclusive of the dertrotheca.

rhinothecal (rī-nō-thē'kal), *a.* [< *rhinotheca* + *-al*.] Of or pertaining to the rhinotheca.

Rhiphiptera† (rī-fip'te-rä), *n. pl.* Same as *Rhipiptera*.

Rhipicera (rī-pis'e-rä), *n.* [NL. (Latreille, 1817), < Gr. ῥιπίς, a fan, + κέρας, horn.] A genus of serricorn beetles, typical of the family *Rhipiceridæ*. The species are all South American and Australian. Also called *Rhipidocera*.

Rhipiceridæ (rip-i-ser'i-dē), *n. pl.* [NL. (Latreille, 1834), < *Rhipicera* + *-idæ*.] A small family of serricorn beetles, having the front coxæ transverse and the onychium large and hairy, comprising 9 genera of few species, widely distributed except in Europe. Also called *Rhipidoceridæ*.

rhipidate (rip'i-dāt), *a.* [< Gr. ῥιπίς (ῥιπιδ-), a fan, + *-ate*[1].] Fan-shaped; flabelliform.

rhipidion (ri-pid'i-on), *n.*; pl. *rhipidia* (-ä). [Gr. ῥιπίδιον: see *rhipidium*.] In the *Gr. Ch.*, the eucharistic fan, or flabellum. Also *rhipis*.

Rhipidistia (rip-i-dis'ti-ä), *n. pl.* [NL., < Gr. ῥιπίς (ῥιπιδ-), a fan, + ἱστίον, a sail.] An order of rhipidopterygian fishes, having special basal bones to the dorsal and anal fins, comprising the extinct family *Tristichopteridæ*.

rhipidistious (rip-i-dis'ti-us), *a.* [< *Rhipidistia* + *-ous*.] Of or relating to the *Rhipidistia*. See quotation under *rhipidopterygian*.

rhipidium (ri-pid'i-um), *n.*; pl. *rhipidia* (-ä). [NL., < Gr. ῥιπίδιον, dim. of ῥιπίς, a fan.] In *bot.*, a fan-shaped cymose inflorescence, in which the successive branches or relative axes are in the same plane, and each from the back of the preceding: a form, according to Eichler (the author of the name), occurring only in monocotyledons.

Rhipidoglossa (rip"i-dō-glos'ä), *n. pl.* [NL., < Gr. ῥιπίς (ῥιπιδ-), a fan, + γλῶσσα, the tongue.] Rhipidoglossate mollusks; a large group, variously called order, suborder, or division, of prosobranchiate gastropods, characterized by a heart with two auricles and a ventricle, and teeth of the odontophore in many marginal rows; the other teeth are generally a median, several admedian, and numerous marginal on each side. It includes numerous marine forms of the families *Turbinidæ*, *Trochidæ*, *Neritidæ*, etc., and terrestrial species of the families *Helicinidæ*, *Hydrocenidæ*, and *Proserpinidæ*.

Rhipidoglossata (rip″i-dọ-glo-sā′tä), *n. pl.* [NL.: see *rhipidoglossate.*] Same as *Rhipidoglossa*.

rhipidoglossate (rip″i-dọ-glos′āt), *a.* [< NL. **rhipidoglossatus*, < Gr. ῥιπίς (ῥιπιδ-), a fan, + γλῶσσα, the tongue: see *glossate.*] In *Mollusca*, having upon the radula, in any one of the many cross-rows of teeth, generally one median tooth, three or more admedian teeth, and numerous marginal teeth. See cut under *radula*.

Rhipidogorgia (rip″i-dọ-gôr′ji-ä), *n.* [NL., < Gr. ῥιπίς (ῥιπιδ-), a fan, + γοργός, grim, fierce, terrible.] A genus of alcyonarian polyps of the family *Gorgoniidæ*, expanded in a regularly reticulate flabelliform shape. They are known as *fan-corals* and *sea-fans*, and have often been referred to the more comprehensive genus *Gorgonia*. *R. flabellum* is one of the commonest corals of tropical and subtropical waters, found in most collections of such objects for ornamental purposes. It varies much in size and contour (compare cut under *coral*), but preserves its flatness and finely netted structure; it is generally of a purplish color.

Fan-coral (*Rhipidogorgia flabellum*).

Rhipidophoridæ, Rhipidophorus. Same as *Rhipiphoridæ*, etc.

Rhipidoptera (rip-i-dop′te-rä), *n. pl.* [NL., neut. pl. of *rhipidopterus*: see *rhipidopterous.*] Fan-winged insects, a group of abnormal *Coleoptera*, regarded as an order: synonymous with *Strepsiptera*. The usual form is *Rhipiptera*, after Latreille, 1817.

rhipidopterous (rip-i-dop′te-rus), *a.* [< NL. *rhipidopterus*, < Gr. ῥιπίς (ῥιπιδ-), a fan, + πτερόν, wing, = E. *feather.*] Fan-winged, as an insect; specifically, of or pertaining to the *Rhipidoptera*; strepsipterous. Also *rhipipterous*.

Rhipidopterygia (rip-i-dop-te-rij′i-ä), *n. pl.* [NL., < Gr. ῥιπίς (ῥιπιδ-), a fan, + πτέρυξ (πτερυγ-), a wing.] A superorder of teleostomous fishes, having special fin-supports to the pectorals and ventrals as well as to the dorsal and anal. It is subdivided into the orders *Rhipidistia* and *Actinistia*.

rhipidopterygian (rip-i-dop-te-rij′i-an), *a.* and *n.* **I.** *a.* Of or relating to the *Rhipidopterygia*.

As I have already pointed out, there are two types of the *Rhipidopterygian* fin, the Rhipidistious, where bascosts are present (teste Traquair), and the Actinistious.
Amer. Nat., May, 1890.

II. *n.* One of the *Rhipidopterygia*.

rhipidura (rip-i-dū′rä), *n.* [NL., < Gr. ῥιπίς (ῥιπιδ-), a fan, + οὐρά, tail.] **1.** Pl. *rhipiduræ* (-rē). The posterior pair of pleopods of a crustacean, together with the telson, when these are developed, as in macrurous crustaceans. For example, the flat shelly plates or swimmerets of the end of a lobster's tail form a rhipidura. See *c* in cut under *pereiopod*. *C. Spence Bate.*

The scaphocerite and *rhipidura* are both present as well-developed appendages, the latter of which they never entirely lose.
Nature, XXXVIII. 339.

Fan-tailed Flycatcher (*Rhipidura flabellifera*).

2. [*cap.*] An extensive genus of *Muscicapidæ*, ranging through the Oriental and Australian regions; the fan-tailed flycatchers. *R. flabellifera* is an example. *Vigors and Horsfield*, 1825.

Rhipiphoridæ (rip-i-for′i-dē), *n. pl.* [NL. (Gerstaecker, 1855), < *Rhipiphorus* + *-idæ.*] A family of heteromerous beetles, having the anterior coxal cavities open behind, the head strongly constricted at the base and suddenly narrowed behind, and the prothorax at the base as wide as the elytra. The family is represented in all parts of the globe, but comprises only 14 genera, none of them very rich in species. North America has 4 genera and 23 species. The beetles are found upon flowers, and the larvæ, so far as known, are parasitic upon other insects. *Rhiphidius pectinicornis* is parasitic in Europe upon the croton-bug, or German roach, *Ectobia germanica*. Also called *Rhipidophoridæ*.

Rhipiphorus (ri-pif′ọ-rus), *n.* [NL. (Fabricius, 1792), < Gr. ῥιπίς, a fan, + -φορος, < φέρειν = E. *bear*[1].] A genus of heteromerous beetles, typical of the family *Rhipiphoridæ*, having the elytra shorter than the body, the mouth-organs perfect, the middle coxæ contiguous, and the vertex depressed, not projecting above the anterior border of the pronotum. It is represented in all parts of the world, although only about 50 species have been described; 11 are known in North America. Also *Rhipidophorus*.

rhipipter (ri-pip′tėr), *n.* [< NL. *Rhipiptera.*] A member of the *Rhipiptera*; a strepsipter, as a stylops.

Rhipiptera (ri-pip′te-rä), *n. pl.* [NL. (Latreille, 1817), neut. pl. of **rhipipterus*: see *rhipipterous*, and cf. *Rhipidoptera.*] In Latreille's classification, the eleventh order of insects, composed of degraded parasitic forms, corresponding to Kirby's order *Strepsiptera*, and now considered to form a family of heteromerous *Coleoptera* under the name *Stylopidæ*. Also *Rhipidoptera*. See cut under *stylops*.

rhipipteran (ri-pip′te-ran), *n.* and *a.* **I.** *n.* A rhipipter.

II. *a.* Same as *rhipipterous* or *rhipidopterous*.

rhipipterous (ri-pip′te-rus), *a.* [< NL. **rhipipterus* for *rhipidopterus*: see *rhipidopterous.*] Same as *rhipidopterous*.

Rhipsalis (rip′sa-lis), *n.* [NL. (Gaertner, 1788), irreg. < Gr. ῥίψ (ῥιπ-), plaited work of osiers or rushes, a mat, crate.] A genus of cacti of the tribe *Opuntieæ*. It is characterized by small flat flowers, six to ten spreading oblong petals, a cylindrical, angled, and dilated stem, and a smooth ovary bearing in fruit a smooth pea-like berry containing somewhat pear-shaped seeds. There are about 30 species, natives of tropical America, with one in South Africa, Mauritius, Madagascar, and Ceylon, the only cactus native to those regions. They are unlike any other cactus genus in their great variety of form and habit of stems, some resembling mistletoe, some the marsh-samphire, some the ice-plant, others the *Epiphyllum*, etc. They are fleshy shrubs with a woody axis, jointed branches, and lateral flowers, which project from notches on the edges of the flat-branched species. Their leaves are reduced to minute scales, which appear at the notches, mixed with wool and stiff needles. Most of the species are epiphytes, pendent from the branches of trees, often for many feet; whence sometimes called *mistletoe-cactus*, some species also having white berries. Also called *willow-cactus*, in conformity with the genus name. In cultivation they are reared in pots and baskets.

Rhiptoglossa (rip-tọ-glos′ä), *n. pl.* [NL., < Gr. ῥιπτός, thrown out (< ῥίπτειν, throw), + γλῶσσα, the tongue.] A suborder of *Lacertilia*, or lizards, represented by the family *Chamæleontidæ* alone, characterized by the vermiform protrusile tongue, well-developed limbs, but no clavicle, pterygoid not reaching the quadrate bone, and nasal bones not bounding the nasal apertures: contrasted with *Eriglossa*. Also *Rhiptoglossæ*. *Gill*, 1885.

rhiptoglossate (rip-tọ-glos′āt), *a.* Pertaining to the *Rhiptoglossa*, or having their characters.

rhizanth (rī′zanth), *n.* [< *rhizanth-ous.*] A plant of the class *Rhizantheæ*; a plant that flowers or seems to flower from the root, as *Rafflesia*.

Rhizantheæ (rī-zan′thē-ē), *n. pl.* [NL. (Blume, 1828), < Gr. ῥίζα, root, + ἄνθος, flower, + *-eæ.*] A class of plants proposed by Lindley. See *rhizogen*.

rhizanthous (rī-zan′thus), *a.* [< Gr. ῥίζα, root, + ἄνθος, flower.] Flowering from the root or seeming root. *A. Gray.*

rhizantoicous (rī-zan-toi′kus), *a.* [Irreg. < Gr. ῥίζα, root, + ἀντί, opposite, + οἶκος, dwelling. Cf. *antæci*, *antecians.*] In *bryol.*, having both male and female inflorescence on the same plant, the former on a very short branch cohering with the latter by the rhizome.

rhizic (rī′zik), *a.* [< Gr. ῥιζικός, of or pertaining to the root, < ῥίζα, root: see *root*[1].] Pertaining to the root of an equation.—**Rhizic curve**, a curve expressed by $P = 0$ or $Q = 0$, where $P + Q\sqrt{-1} = z^n + p_1z^{n-1} + \text{etc.}$, and $z = x + y\sqrt{-1}$.

rhizina (rī-zī′nä), *n.*; pl. *rhizinæ* (-nē). [NL., < Gr. ῥίζα, a root, + *-ina*[1].] In *bot.*, same as *rhizoid*.

rhizine (rī′zin), *a.* [< Gr. ῥίζα, root, + *-ine*[1].] In *bot.*, same as *rhizoid*.

rhizinous (rī-zī′nus), *a.* [< *rhizine* + *-ous.*] In *bot.*, having rhizoids.

rhizocarp (rī′zọ-kärp), *n.* A plant of the order *Rhizocarpeæ*.

Rhizocarpeæ (rī-zọ-kär′pẹ-ē), *n. pl.* [NL. (Batsch, 1802), < Gr. ῥίζα, root, + καρπός, fruit.] A class or group of cryptogamous plants, the heterosporous *Filicineæ*, embracing the families *Salviniaceæ* and *Marsileaceæ*. This name is not much used at the present time, the two families being embraced in the *Hydropterideæ*, or heterosporous ferns. See *Hydropterideæ*, *Marsileaceæ*, and *Salviniaceæ* for special characterization.

rhizocarpean (rī-zọ-kär′pẹ-an), *a.* [< *Rhizocarpeæ* + *-an.*] In *bot.*, of or pertaining to the *Rhizocarpeæ*.

rhizocarpian (rī-zọ-kär′pi-an), *a.* Same as *rhizocarpean*.

rhizocarpic (rī-zọ-kär′pik), *a.* [< *rhizocarp-ous* + *-ic.*] In *bot.*, characterized as a perennial herb; having the stem annual but the root perennial. *De Candolle.*

rhizocarpous (rī-zọ-kär′pus), *a.* [< Gr. ῥίζα, root, + καρπός, fruit.] Same as *rhizocarpic*.

rhizocaul (rī′zọ-kâl), *n.* [< NL. *rhizocaulus*, < Gr. ῥίζα, root, + καυλός, stalk.] The rootstock of a polyp; that part of a polypidom by which it is affixed as if rooted to some support.

rhizocaulus (rī-zọ-kâ′lus), *n.*; pl. *rhizocauli* (-lī). [NL.: see *rhizocaul.*] A rhizocaul.

Rhizocephala (rī-zọ-sef′a-lä), *n. pl.* [NL., neut. pl. of *rhizocephalus*: see *rhizocephalous.*] A group of small parasitic crustaceans, having a cylindroid, sac-like, or disciform unsegmented body, without organs of sense, intestine, limbs, or cement-organs, but with an oral and an anal opening, and the sexual organs well developed. The species are hermaphroditic, and the young go through a nauplius stage and a cypris stage. The *Rhizocephala* are by some made an order of a subclass *Cirripedia*; others class them with *Cirripedia* as a division, *Pectostraca*, of *Entomostraca*; by others again they are referred to the *Epizoa* (*Ichthyophthiria* or fish-lice). These parasites attach themselves by their modified antennæ, resembling a number of root-like processes, which bury themselves in the substance of the host, whence the name. They are represented by two principal genera, *Sacculina* and *Peltogaster*, each made by some the type of a family. They are parasites of crabs. Also called *Centrogonida*.

Forms of *Rhizocephala*.
A, nauplius stage of *Sacculina purpurea*. *B*, cypris stage of *Lernæodiscus porcellanæ*. *C*, adult of *Peltogaster paguri*; *a*, anterior end; *b*, aperture through which pass the root-like processes, *c*.

rhizocephalon (rī-zọ-sef′a-lon), *n.* [NL., sing. of *Rhizocephala.*] Any member of the order *Rhizocephala*. [Rare.]

rhizocephalous (rī-zọ-sef′a-lus), *a.* [< NL. *rhizocephalus*, < Gr. ῥιζοκέφαλος, having the flower growing straight from the root, < ῥίζα, root, + κεφαλή, head.] Rooted by the head; specifically, of or pertaining to the *Rhizocephala*.

rhizoconin (rī-zọ-kō′nin), *n.* [< Gr. ῥίζα, root, + NL. *conium* + *-in*[2].] A crystallizable proximate principle found in the root of *Conium maculatum*.

rhizoconolein (rī″zọ-kọ-nō′lẹ-in), *n.* [< *rhizocon(in)* + L. *oleum*, oil, + *-in*[2].] A crystallizable body found in *Conium maculatum*.

rhizocrinoid (rī-zok′ri-noid), *n.* [< *Rhizocrinus* + *-oid* (cf. *crinoid*).] A crinoid of the genus *Rhizocrinus*; an apiocrinite.

Rhizocrinus (rī-zok′ri-nus), *n.* [NL., < Gr. ῥίζα, a root, + κρίνον, lily: see *crinoid.*] A genus of crinoids of the family *Encrinidæ*, one of the few living forms of *Crinoidea*. *R. lofotensis*, the typical species, is a kind of lily-star or sea-lily, about 3 inches in length, living at a depth of from one hundred to three hundred fathoms in the sea, rooted to the bottom. Its structure is fully illustrated in the figure given under *Crinoidea*.

rhizodont (rī′zọ-dont), *a.* and *n.* [< Gr. ῥίζα, root, + ὀδούς (ὀδοντ-) = E. *tooth.*] **I.** *a.* Having teeth rooted by fangs which ankylose with the jaw, as crocodiles.

II. *n.* A rhizodont reptile.

Rhizodonta (rī-zọ-don′tä), *n. pl.* [NL.: see *rhizodont.*] The rhizodont reptiles.

Rhizodus (rī′zọ-dus), *n.* [NL., < Gr. ῥίζα, root, + ὀδούς = E. *tooth.*] In *ichth.*, a genus of fossil ganoid fishes of the coal-measures, referred to the family *Cyclodipteridæ*. They were of large size, with huge teeth. *R. hibberti* is one of the species.

Rhizoflagellata (rī-zọ-flaj-e-lā′tä), *n. pl.* [NL., < Gr. ῥίζα, root, + NL. *flagellum*: see *flagellum*, 3.] An order of flagellate *Infusoria*, having pseudopodial as well as flagelliform appendages. These animalcules move by means of pseudopodia, like ordinary rhizopods, but also have a flagellum or flagella; the ingestive area is diffuse. In W. S. Kent's system of classification the order consists of the genera *Mastigamœba*, *Reptomonas*, *Rhizomonas*, and *Podostoma*.

rhizoflagellate (rī-zǫ-flaj'e-lāt), *a.* Of or pertaining to the *Rhizoflagellata*.

rhizogen (rī'zǫ-jen), *n.* [< Gr. ῥίζα, root, + -γενής, producing (see *-gen*).] A parasitic plant growing on the roots of other plants; specifically, a member of a division of plants (the class *Rhizantheæ*) proposed by Lindley, composed of flowering plants of a fungoid habit, parasitic upon rootstocks and stems. It embraced the present orders *Balanophoreæ* and *Cytinaceæ*, now regarded as belonging to the apetalous dicotyledons. The genus *Rafflesia* is an illustration.

rhizogenic (rī-zǫ-jen'ik), *a.* [As *rhizogen* + *-ic*.] In *bot.*, root-producing: said of cells in the pericambium of a root, just in front of a xylem-ray of a fibrovascular bundle, which give origin to root-branches.

rhizogenous (rī-zoj'e-nus), *a.* [As *rhizogen* + *-ous*.] Same as *rhizogenic*.

rhizoid (rī'zoid), *a.* and *n.* [< Gr. ῥιζοειδής, contr. ῥιζώδης, like a root, < ῥίζα, root, + εἶδος, form.] **I.** *a.* In *bot.* and *zoöl.*, root-like; resembling a root.

II. *n.* In *bot.*, a filamentous organ resembling a root, but of simple structure, found on compound thalli of all kinds, and on the stems of the *Muscineæ*. Rhizoids are numerously produced, and their function is the attachment of the plant to the substratum. The older term was *rhizina*. See cut under *prothallium*.

rhizoidal (rī'zoi-dal), *a.* [< *rhizoid* + *-al*.] In *bot.*, rhizoid-like; resembling or characteristic of a rhizoid.

The *rhizoidal* tubes are segmented by only a few septa which lie far below the growing apex.
Sachs, Botany (trans.), p. 282.

rhizoideous (rī-zoi'dē-us), *a.* [< *rhizoid* + *-eous*.] 1. In *bot.*, like or resembling a rhizoid. —2. Same as *rhizoid*.

rhizoma (rī-zō'mä), *n.*; pl. *rhizomata* (-ma-tä). [NL.: see *rhizome*.] A rhizome: used chiefly with reference to the rhizomes of medicinal plants.

rhizomania (rī-zǫ-mā'ni-ä), *n.* [NL., < Gr. ῥίζα, a root, + μανία, madness.] In *bot.*, an abnormal development of adventitious roots peculiar to many plants, as ivy, screw-pines, and figs, which send out roots from various parts, just as trees produce adventitious buds. In some plants rhizomania is an indication that there is some defect in the true root, in consequence of which it cannot supply sufficient nourishment to the plant. In such cases rhizomania is an effort of nature to supply the deficiency. This is the case in common laurel, in which plant rhizomania generally forebodes death. The phenomenon is also frequently seen in apple-trees, from the stems of which bundles of roots are sent out; these, absorbing moisture and finally decaying, are a cause of canker on the tree.

rhizome (rī'zōm), *n.* [= F. *rhizome*, < NL. *rhizoma*, < Gr. ῥίζωμα, root, < ῥιζοῦν, cause to take root, in pass. take root, < ῥίζα, root: see *root*[1].] In *bot.*, a stem of root-like appearance, horizontal or oblique in position, lying on the ground or subterranean, bearing scales instead of leaves, and usually producing from its apex a leafy shoot or scape. Rhizomes may be slender, with well-marked nodes, as in mints, couch-grass, etc., or thickened with stores of nutriment, as in species of iris, Solomon's-seal, etc.—in the latter case producing at the apex an annual bud which furnishes the aërial shoot of the next season, and gradually dying at the old end. Rhizomes shade off gradually into corms and bulbs on the one hand, and into tubers on the other. See these terms. Also *rhizoma*. See also cuts under *arrowroot* and *moniliform*.

Forms of Rhizome.
1, *Polygonatum giganteum* (Solomon's-seal); 2, *Arisæma triphyllum* (Indian turnip); 3, *Trillium sessile*.

Rhizomonadidæ (rī"zǫ-mō-nad'i-dē), *n. pl.* [NL., < *Rhizomonas* (*-monad-*) + *-idæ*.] A family of rhizoflagellate infusorians, typified by the genus *Rhizomonas*. These animalcules are repent or sedentary, with a single anterior flagellum. The family includes *Reptomonas* and *Mastigamœba*.

Rhizomonas (rī-zom'ǫ-nas), *n.* [NL. (Kent, 1880–1), < Gr. ῥίζα, root, + μονάς, a unit: see *monad*.] The typical genus of *Rhizomonadidæ*. The species are monadiform, uniflagellate, sedentary, with radiating digitiform pseudopodial prolongations. *R. verrucosa* is found in hay-infusions.

rhizomorph (rī'zǫ-môrf), *n.* [< NL. *rhizomorpha*.] In *bot.*, a comprehensive term for certain subterranean mycelial growths associated with or preying upon the roots of the higher plants, especially trees, the cultivated vine, etc. They are produced by a considerable variety of fungi, as *Agaricus melleus*, *Dematophora necatrix*, etc.

Rhizomorpha (rī-zǫ-môr'fä), *n.* [NL., < Gr. ῥίζα, root, + μορφή, form.] A supposed genus of fungi, characterized by fibrous bundles of mycelial filaments, now known to belong to *Agaricus melleus*, *Dematophora necatrix*, and other forms.

rhizomorphoid (rī-zǫ-môr'foid), *a.* [< *rhizomorph* + *-oid*.] Rhizomorphous.

rhizomorphous (rī-zǫ-môr'fus), *a.* [< Gr. ῥίζα, root, + μορφή, form.] 1. Root-like in form.—2. In *zoöl.*, same as *rhizoid*.

Rhizomys (rī'zǫ-mis), *n.* [NL. (J. E. Gray, 1830), < Gr. ῥίζα, root, + μῦς, a mouse.] A notable genus of mole-rats of the family *Spalacidæ*, having the eyes open, though very small, ears naked and very short, thumb rudimentary, tail short and partially haired, and general form robust. The upper incisors arch forward, and there is no premolar: the upper molars have one deep internal and two or more external enamel-folds; the lower molars reverse this pattern. There are several Asiatic and African species, as the bay bamboo-rat of Asia, *R. badius*, which is of large size and very destructive to the bamboo, on the roots of which it feeds.

Bamboo-rat (*Rhizomys badius*).

rhizonychial (rī-zǫ-nik'i-al), *a.* [< *rhizonychium* + *-al*.] Rooting or giving root to a nail or claw; of or pertaining to a rhizonychium.

rhizonychium (rī-zǫ-nik'i-um), *n.*; pl. *rhizonychia* (-ä). [NL., < Gr. ῥίζα, root, + ὄνυξ (ὀνυχ-), a claw.] A claw-joint; the ungual or last phalanx of a digit; that phalanx which bears a claw.

Rhizophaga (rī-zof'a-gä), *n. pl.* [NL., neut. pl. of *rhizophagus*: see *rhizophagous*.] One of five sections in Owen's classification of marsupials, including those which feed on roots. The wombat is a characteristic example.

rhizophagan (rī-zof'a-gan), *a.* and *n.* **I.** *a.* Same as *rhizophagous*.

II. *n.* A member of the *Rhizophaga*.

rhizophagous (rī-zof'a-gus), *a.* [< NL. *rhizophagus*, < Gr. ῥιζοφάγος, eating roots (ῥιζοφαγεῖν, eat roots), < ῥίζα, root, + φαγεῖν, eat.] Root-eating; habitually feeding on roots; specifically, of or pertaining to the *Rhizophaga*.

All Poor-Slaves are *Rhizophagous* (or Root-eaters).
Carlyle, Sartor Resartus, iii. 10.

Rhizophora (rī-zof'ǫ-rä), *n.* [NL. (Linnæus, 1737), named with ref. to the aërial roots; neut. pl. of *rhizophorus*: see *rhizophorous*.] A genus of polypetalous trees, the mangroves, type of the order *Rhizophoraceæ*, and of the tribe *Rhizophoreæ*. It is characterized by a four-parted calyx, surrounded with a cupule or involucre of partly united bractlets, by its four petals and eight to twelve elongated and nearly sessile anthers, which are at first many-celled, and by a partly inferior ovary which is prolonged above into a fleshy cone and bears two pendulous ovules in each of its two cells. There are 2 (or, as some regard them, 5) species, frequent on muddy or coral shores in the tropics, there forming dense and almost impassable jungles known as mangrove-swamps. They are trees with thick cylindrical and scarred branchlets, bearing opposite thick and smooth coriaceous leaves, which are ovate or elliptical and entire. Their large rigid flowers are borne in axillary clusters, followed by a nut-like one-seeded fruit. The seed is remarkable for germinating while yet in the long-persistent fruit. It contains a large embryo with a very long club-shaped radicle, which soon pierces the point of the hard pericarp and lengthens till it reaches the mud, or becomes a foot long before falling. The mangrove is also remarkable for spreading by aërial roots. The ordinary species is *R. mucronata*, which reaches to semitropical Florida, the delta of the Mississippi, and Texas. See *mangrove*, 1.

Rhizophoraceæ (rī"zǫ-fǫ-rā'sę-ē), *n. pl.* [NL. (Lindley, 1845), < *Rhizophora* + *-aceæ*.] An order of dicotyledonous trees and shrubs of the cohort *Myrtales* and series *Calyciforæ*; the mangrove family. It is characterized by a two- to six-celled ovary with its ovules pendulous from the apex of the cell, and by a valvate calyx, and two, three, or four times as many stamens as petals. It includes about 50 species in 17 genera and 3 tribes, all tropical, and most of them forming dense and malarious jungles about river-mouths and along shores. They are usually extremely smooth, with round and nodose branchlets, and opposite thick and rigid leaves, which are commonly entire and have elongated and very caducous interpetiolar stipules. They bear axillary cymes, panicles, spikes, or racemes of rather inconspicuous flowers.

rhizophore (rī'zǫ-fōr), *n.* [< NL. *rhizophorum*, neut. of *rhizophorus*, root-bearing: see *rhizophorous*.] In *bot.*, a structure, developed in certain species of the genus *Selaginella*, which bears the true roots. It has the external appearance of a root, but has no root-cap, and the true roots are produced from its interior when it deliquesces into a homogeneous mucilage.

Rhizophoreæ (rī-zǫ-fō'rę-ē), *n. pl.* [NL. (R. Brown, 1814), < *Rhizophora* + *-eæ*.] A tribe of plants of the order *Rhizophoraceæ*. It is characterized by extremely smooth opposite entire and stipulate leaves, and by an interior ovary with a single style and an embryo without albumen. It includes about 17 species, all tropical maritime trees, belonging to 4 genera, of which *Rhizophora*, the mangrove, is the type.

rhizophorous (rī-zof'ǫ-rus), *a.* [< NL. *rhizophorus*, < MGr. ῥιζοφόρος, root-bearing, < Gr. ῥίζα, root, + -φορος, < φέρειν = E. *bear*[1].] In *bot.*, root-bearing; specifically, of or pertaining to the natural order *Rhizophoraceæ*.

rhizophydial (rī-zǫ-fid'i-al), *a.* [< *Rhizophydium* + *-al*.] In *bot.*, belonging to or characteristic of the genus *Rhizophydium*.

Rhizophydium (rī-zǫ-fid'i-um), *n.* [NL. (Schenk), supposed to stand for **Rhizophidium*, alluding to the deficiency of roots; irreg. < Gr. ῥίζα, root, + φειδός, sparing.] A small genus of unicellular zygomycetous fungi of the suborder *Cladochytrieæ*, parasitic on certain of the larger algæ. The parasitic cells enter the cells of the host plant at a very early stage of their existence, and gradually develop at the expense of the protoplasmic contents of the latter. *R. Dicksonii* is parasitic on species of *Ectocarpus*.

rhizopod (rī'zǫ-pod), *a.* and *n.* [< NL. **rhizopus* (*-pod-*) (as a noun, in def. 2, *rhizopodium*), < Gr. ῥίζα, root, + πούς (ποδ-) = E. *foot*.] **I.** *a.* Provided with pseudopods, as an animalcule; having processes of sarcode, as if roots, by means of which the animalcule is attached or moves; root-footed; specifically, of or pertaining to the *Rhizopoda*, in any sense. Also *rhizopodous*.

II. *n.* 1. A member of the *Rhizopoda*, in any sense.—2. In *bot.*, same as *rhizopodium*.

Rhizopoda (rī-zop'ǫ-dä), *n. pl.* [NL.: see *rhizopod*.] 1†. In Dujardin's system of classification (1841), the third family of "diversiform infusorians without visible locomotory appendages"—that is, without permanent appendages, as cilia or flagella. This is the original meaning of the word, since much extended. Dujardin included in his *Rhizopoda* the 8 genera *Arcella*, *Difflugia*, *Trinema*, *Euglypha*, *Gromia*, *Miliola*, *Cristellaria*, and *Vorticella*. 2. The lowest class of *Protozoa*, composed of simple or multiple animalcules without definite or permanent distinction of external parts, and provided with diversiform temporary or permanent pseudopodial prolongations of the body-substance, by means of which locomotion, fixation, and ingestion are effected. There is no mouth or special ingestive area; the sarcode may be distinguishable into an outer ectoplasm and an inner endoplasm; a nucleus and nucleolus (endoplast and endoplastule) may be present; and most of these animalcules secrete a shell or test, often of great beauty and complexity. The rhizopods are minute, usually microscopic organisms, some or other forms of which abound in both salt and fresh waters. The characteristic pseudopodia are highly diverse in form, and constantly change, but occur in two principal forms, coarse lobate or digitate processes and fine slender rays, both of which may run together or interlace. The valuation and limitation of the *Rhizopoda* have varied with different authors. A normal amœboid protozoan is a characteristic example of this class. Other forms included under *Rhizopoda* are the so-called moners of the order *Monera*; the *Foraminifera*, with a calcareous shell; and the *Radiolaria*, with a silicious shell. By common consent the sponges, which have been classed with *Rhizopoda*, are now excluded, even by those who still consider these organisms as protozoans. See cuts under *Amœba*, *Foraminifera*, and *Radiolaria*.

rhizopodal (rī-zop'ǫ-dal), *a.* [< *rhizopod* + *-al*.] Same as *rhizopod*. *W. B. Carpenter*, Micros., xii. § 474.

rhizopodan (rī-zop'ǫ-dan), *a.* and *n.* [< *rhizopod* + *-an*.] Same as *rhizopod*.

rhizopodium (rī-zǫ-pō'di-um), *n.* [NL.: see *rhizopod*.] In *bot.*, the mycelium of fungi. Also *rhizopod*.

rhizopodous (rī-zop'ǫ-dus), *a.* [< *rhizopod* + *-ous*.] Same as *rhizopod*.

rhizoristic (ri-zǭ-ris'tik), *a.* [< Gr. *ῥίζα*, root, + *ὁριστός*, verbal adj. of *ὁρίζειν*, limit, define (see *horizon*, *aorist*), + *-ic*.] In *math.*, pertaining to the separation of roots of an equation.—**Rhizoristic series**, a series of disconnected functions which serve to fix the number of real roots of a given function lying between any assigned limits. *Sylvester.*

Rhizostoma (ri-zos'tǭ-mạ̈), *n.* [NL., < Gr. *ῥίζα*, root, + *στόμα*, mouth.] The typical genus of *Rhizostomidæ*. *R. pulmo* is an example.

Rhizostomata (ri-zǭ-stō'mạ-tạ̈), *n. pl.* [NL., < Gr. *ῥίζα*, root, + *στόμα(τ-)*, mouth.] An order of discomedusans, or suborder of *Discomedusæ*, having the parts arranged in fours or multiples of four, and the single primitive mouth closed up and replaced by several secondary oral apertures, whence several long root-like processes or so-called polypites depend (whence the name), and provided with four subgenital pouches, distinct (*Tetragameliæ*) or fused in one (*Monogameliæ*). *Rhizostoma*, *Cassiopeia*, *Cephea*, and *Crambessa* are leading genera. See cuts under *acaleph* and *Discophora*.

Rhizostomatidæ (ri″zǭ-stǭ-mat'i-dē), *n. pl.* [NL., < *Rhizostoma* (*-stomat-*) + *-idæ*.] A family of acalephs; the root-mouthed jellyfishes: the emended form of *Rhizostomidæ*.

rhizostomatous (ri-zǭ-stom'ạ-tus), *a.* [< Gr. *ῥίζα*, root, + *στόμα(τ)*, mouth.] Having root-like processes depending from the mouth; specifically, pertaining to the *Rhizostomata*, or having their characters.

rhizostome (ri'zǭ-stōm), *n.* A member of the *Rhizostomata*.

rhizostomean (ri-zǭ-stō'mē-ạn), *a.* [< *rhizostome* + *-an*.] Same as *rhizostomatous*.

Rhizostomidæ (ri-zǭ-stom'i-dē), *n. pl.* [NL., < *Rhizostoma* + *-idæ*.] A family of monogamelian rhizostomatous discomedusans, represented by the genus *Rhizostoma*. They are huge jellyfishes, which may attain a diameter of 3 feet, possess powerful stinging-organs proportionate to their size, and are found chiefly in tropical seas. See cut under *acaleph*.

rhizostomous (ri-zos'tǭ-mus), *a.* Same as *rhizostomatous*.

Rhizota (ri-zō'tạ̈), *n. pl.* [NL., neut. pl. of *rhizotus*: see *rhizote*.] An order of *Rotifera*, containing the rooted or fixed wheel-animalcules, as the families *Flosculariidæ* and *Melicertidæ*. *C. T. Hudson*, 1884. It is one of 4 orders, contrasting with *Ploïma*, *Bdelloïda*, and *Scirtopoda*. See cut under *Floscularia*.

rhizotaxis (ri-zǭ-tak'sis), *n.* [NL., < Gr. *ῥίζα*, root, + *τάξις*, order.] In *bot.*, the arrangement or disposition of roots. Compare *phyllotaxis*.

rhizotaxy (ri'zǭ-tak-si), *n.* Same as *rhizotaxis*.

rhizote (ri'zōt), *a.* [< NL. *rhizotus*, < Gr. **ῥιζωτός*, rooted, < *ῥιζοῦν*, root, < *ῥίζα*, root.] Rooted, as a rotifer; of or pertaining to the *Rhizota*.

Rhizotrogus (ri-zǭ-trō'gus), *n.* [NL. (Latreille, 1825), < Gr. *ῥίζα*, root, + *τρώγειν*, gnaw, nibble, munch.] A genus of melolonthine beetles. *R. solstitialis* is a European species known as the *midsummer chafer*.

rhizula (riz'ū-lạ̈), *n.* [NL., dim. of Gr. *ῥίζα*, root: see *root*[1].] The root-like prothallium of mosses (protonema) and of some other cryptogams. [Disused.]

rho (rō), *n.* The Greek letter *ρ*, corresponding to the English *r*.

rhodalose (rō'dạ-lōs), *n.* [< Gr. *ῥόδον*, rose (see *rose*[1]), + *ἅλς* (*ἁλ-*), salt, + *-ose*.] Red or cobalt vitriol; cobalt sulphate.

rhodanic (rǭ-dan'ik), *a.* [< Gr. *ῥόδον*, rose, + *-an* + *-ic*.] Noting an acid which produces a red color with persalts of iron. Rhodanic acid is also called *sulphocyanic acid*.

Rhodanthe (rǭ-dan'thē), *n.* [NL. (Lindley, 1834), < Gr. *ῥόδον*, rose, + *ἄνθος*, flower.] A former genus of *Compositæ* found in western Australia. The only species is *R. Manglesii*, of which there are several varieties, differing from each other mainly in the size and color of the flower-heads, which have the dry character of the flowers commonly called "everlastings." It is an annual, rising from 1 to 1½ feet high, with an erect branching stem, oblong blunt entire stem-clasping leaves of a glaucous green, and flower-heads, varying from deep rose to deep purple, supported on stalks arranged in a corymbose manner. It is now made a section of *Helipterum*.

Rhodeina (rō-dẹ̄-ī'nạ̈), *n. pl.* [NL., < *Rhodeus* + *-ina*[2].] A group of cyprinoid fishes, typified by the genus *Rhodeus*. They have a moderate anal (commencing under the dorsal), and the lateral line running midway between the upper and lower edges of the caudal peduncle. They are confined to Europe and Asia.

rhodeoretin (rō-dẹ̄-or'e-tin), *n.* [< Gr. *ῥόδεος*, of roses (< *ῥόδον*, rose), + *ῥητίνη*, resin.] One of the elements of resin of jalap, identical with jalapin and convolvulin. It is hard, and insoluble in ether.

rhodeoretinic (rō-dẹ̄-or-e-tin'ik), *a.* [< *rhodeoretin* + *-ic*.] Obtained from rhodeoretin.—**Rhodeoretinic acid**, an acid produced by treating rhodeoretin with alkalis.

rhodes-wood (rōdz'wůd), *n.* The wood of the West Indian tree *Amyris balsamifera*: so called from its resemblance to rhodium-wood, and used for a similar purpose. See *rhodium-wood*. Also called *candlewood*.

Rhodeus (rō'dẹ̄-us), *n.* [NL. (Agassiz, 1836), < Gr. *ῥόδεος*, of roses, < *ῥόδον*, rose: see *rose*[1].] The typical genus of *Rhodeina*. *R. amarus* (the *bitterling* in German) is the typical species.

Rhodian (rō'di-ạn), *a.* and *n.* [= F. *Rhodien*, < L. *Rhodius*, Rhodian, < *Rhodus*, *Rhodos*, < Gr. *Ῥόδος*, the isle of Rhodes.] **I.** *a.* Pertaining to Rhodes, an island of the Mediterranean, southwest of Asia Minor.—**Rhodian laws**, the earliest system of marine law known to history, said to have been compiled by the Rhodians after they had by their commerce and naval victories obtained the sovereignty of the sea.—**Rhodian pottery.** See *pottery*, and cut under *amphora*.—**Rhodian school of sculpture**, an important school of Hellenistic sculpture, of which the celebrated group known as the Laocoön is the capital work. The artists of this school sought their inspiration in the works of Lysippus. The intensity of expression attained in the Laocoön has never been surpassed, and its exaggerations are redeemed by its real power. The group, however, falls far short of the supreme excellence attributed to it by Pliny and by the art amateurs of the end of the eighteenth century. The Rhodian school is intimately connected with that of Pergamum.

Rhodian School of Sculpture.—The Laocoön, in the Vatican. (The existing incorrect restorations of arms, etc., are omitted.)

II. *n.* A native or an inhabitant of Rhodes.

rhoding (rō'ding), *n.* *Naut.*, either of the brass boxes for the brake of a ship's pump.

rhodiochlorid, rhodiochloride (rō″di-ǭ-klō'-rid, -rid or -rīd), *n.* [< *rhodium* + *chlorid*, *chloride*.] In *chem.*, a double chlorid of rhodium and the alkali metals.

Rhodiola (rǭ-dī'ǭ-lạ̈), *n.* [NL. (Linnæus, 1737), < Gr. *ῥόδον*, rose, + dim. *-i-ola*.] A former genus of alpine plants belonging to the natural order *Crassulaceæ*, now made a section of *Sedum* (which see).

Rhodites (rǭ-dī'tēz), *n.* [NL. (Hartig, 1840), < Gr. *ῥοδίτης*, pertaining to a rose (applied to wine flavored with roses), < *ῥόδον*, rose: see *rose*[1].] A notable genus of gall-flies of the hymenopterous family *Cynipidæ*, having the hypopygium shaped like a plowshare, the marginal cell of the fore wings completely closed, and the claws of the hind tarsi entire. All of the species make galls on the rose. *R. rosæ* produces the mossy rose-gall, or bedegar. (See *bedegar*.) *R. radicum* produces root-galls. Seven species are known in North America, and five in Europe.

rhodium (rō'di-um), *n.* [NL., < Gr. *ῥόδιος*, made of roses, rose-like, < *ῥόδον*, a rose: see *rose*.] Chemical symbol, Rh; atomic weight, 103 (Jörgensen). A metal discovered in the beginning of the nineteenth century by Wollaston, associated with palladium in the ore of platinum. Rhodium fuses in the flame of the oxyhydrogen blowpipe, but with greater difficulty than platinum. When fused it is grayish-white, resembling aluminium in luster and color, and has a specific gravity of 12.1. When pure it is almost insoluble in acids, but if in the state of an alloy it is dissolved by aqua regia. Of all the metals of the platinum group rhodium is the one most easily attacked by chlorin.—**Oil of rhodium.** See *oil*.

rhodium-gold (rō'di-um-gōld), *n.* A doubtful variety of native gold, said to contain a considerable amount of rhodium.

rhodium-wood (rō'di-um-wůd), *n.* [NL. *lignum rhodium*, rosewood: see *rhodium* and *rosewood*.] A sweet-scented wood from the root and stem of two shrubs, *Convolvulus scoparius* and *C. floridus*, found in the Canaries. It has been an article of commerce, and from it was distilled an essential oil used in perfumery, liniments, etc., but now replaced by artificial compounds. The name is applied also, at least in the form *rhodes-wood*, to the similar wood of *Amyris balsamifera* of the West Indies, etc., also called *candlewood*.

rhodizite (rō'di-zīt), *n.* [So called because it colors the blowpipe-flame red; < Gr. *ῥοδίζειν*, be like a rose (< *ῥόδον*, rose), + *-ite*[2].] A rare borate of aluminium and potassium, occurring in minute isometric crystals resembling boracite in form. It is known only from the vicinity of Ekaterinburg in the Urals.

rhodochrome (rō'dǭ-krōm), *n.* [< Gr. *ῥόδον*, rose, + *χρῶμα*, color.] A mineral of a compact or granular structure and reddish color. Like the related crystallized mineral kämmererite, it is classed as a chromiferous variety of the chlorite penninite.

rhodochrosite (rē-dǭ-krō'sīt), *n.* [< Gr. *ῥόδον*, rose, + *χρῶσις*, a coloring, + *-ite*[2].] Native manganese protocarbonate, a mineral occurring in rhombohedral crystals, or massive with rhombohedral cleavage; usually of a delicate rose-red color. It is isomorphous with the other rhombohedral carbonates, calcite or calcium carbonate, siderite or iron carbonate, etc. Also called *dialogite*.

Rhodocrinidæ (rō-dǭ-krin'i-dē), *n. pl.* [NL., < *Rhodocrinus* + *-idæ*.] A family of *Crinoidea*, typified by the genus *Rhodocrinus*, having five basals, five parabasals or subradials, and ten or twenty branched rays; the rose-encrinites, chiefly of the Carboniferous formation.

rhodocrinite (rō-dok'ri-nīt), *n.* [< NL. *Rhodocrinus* + *-ite*[2].] An encrinite of the genus *Rhodocrinus*; a rose-encrinite.

Rhodocrinus (rǭ-dok'ri-nus), *n.* [NL., < Gr. *ῥόδον*, rose, + *κρίνον*, lily.] A genus of Paleozoic encrinites, or fossil crinoids, with a cylindric or slightly pentagonal column of many joints, perforated by a pentagonal alimentary canal; the rose-encrinites.

Rhododendron (rō-dǭ-den'dron), *n.* [NL. (Linnæus, 1753), < Gr. *ῥοδόδενδρον*, the oleander, < *ῥόδον*, rose, + *δένδρον*, tree.] **1.** A large genus of shrubs of the order *Ericaceæ* and tribe *Rhodoreæ*. It is characterized by a broad, spreading, and oblique corolla, usually with five imbricating lobes; eight to ten stamens, the anthers opening by pores; and a five- to twenty-celled ovary with numerous ovules in many crowded rows, the seeds appendaged. There are about 170 species, natives of the mountains of Europe, Asia, the Malay archipelago, and North America, most abundant in the Himalayas. They are commonly shrubs, less often trees, smooth, hairy, woolly, or scurfy, and often with whorled branches. They bear alternate entire leaves, most often crowded at the ends of the branches. Their handsome flowers are commonly borne in corymbs, and have conspicuous, more or less unequal, long, slender, and curving stamens, with long hairs clothing their base.

Rhododendron grande (Himalayas).

The fruit is a woody pod, splitting septicidally from the apex into valves, and filled with seeds like fine sawdust, each containing a cylindrical embryo and fleshy albumen. Most of the species, and all of those best known, produce their new growths below the flowers, which form a terminal inflorescence destitute of leaves, and developed from a large scaly bud. The leaves in the typical species, forming the section *Rhododendron* proper, are evergreen and coriaceous; but they are deciduous in the sections *Azalea* and *Tsusia*, which include the American species commonly known as *azaleas*, and produce leaves closely encircling the flowers, or, in *Tsusia*, mixed with them. The flowers, nearly or quite 2 inches across, often reach in *R. Aucklandiæ* a breadth of 6 inches. See *pinkster-flower*.

2. [*l. c.*] Any one of the many species of the above genus, belonging to the section *Rhododendron*; the rose-bay. The rhododendrons are handsome shrubs, much cultivated for their evergreen leathery leaves and profusion of beautifully formed and colored flowers. The ordinary species of American outdoor plantations is *R. Catawbiense*, the Catawba or Carolina rhododendron, hybridized with the more tender exotics *R. Ponticum* and *R. arboreum*. The Catawba species grows from 3 to 6, rarely 20, feet high, has oval or oblong leaves and broadly bell-shaped lilac-purple or (in culture) variously colored flowers. It is native in the Alleghanies from Virginia southward. It has also been largely cultivated in Europe, and there are hundreds of varieties. The great rhododendron (or laurel), *R. maximum*, abounds in the Alleghanies, and is found as far north as Maine and Canada. It is commonly taller than *R. Catawbiense*, with narrower leaves, and flowers pink or nearly white with a greenish throat. It is a fine species, but much less cultivated than the last; it affords some hybrids. The Californian rhododendron, *R. Californicum*, resembles the Catawba rhododendron, but has more showy flowers. It deserves cultivation, and has proved hardy in England. The Pontic rhododendron, *R. Ponticum*, is the most common species of European gardens, hardy only as a low shrub in the northern United States. *R. arboreum*, the tree rhododendron, is a fine Himalayan species, 25 feet high, with the leaves silvery-white beneath, and the flowers scarlet varying to white. The Lapland rhododendron, *R. Lapponicum*, is a dwarf arctic and alpine species of both hemispheres, growing prostrate in broad tufts. The Siberian or Dahurian rhododendron, *R. Dauricum*, a dwarf species, somewhat cultivated, bears its bright rose-purple flowers on naked shoots in early spring.—**Indian rhododendron.** See *Melastoma*.

Flowering Branch of the Great Laurel (*Rhododendron maximum*).

Rhodomela (rō-dom'e-lạ̈), *n.* [NL. (Agardh, 1824), < Gr. ῥόδον, rose, + μέλας, black.] A genus of marine algæ of the class *Florideæ* and type of the suborder *Rhodomeleæ*. The fronds are dark-red, filiform or subcompressed and pinnately decompound, with filiform branches, the tetraspores tripartite, the cystocarps sessile or pedicellate, and the spores pyriform. The genus is small, and mostly confined to high latitudes in both hemispheres. There are two species or forms on the New England coast.

Rhodomelaceæ (rō''dọ-mẹ-lā'sẹ̄-ē), *n. pl.* [NL. (Harvey, 1849), < *Rhodomela* + *-aceæ*.] Same as *Rhodomeleæ*.

Rhodomeleæ (rō-dọ-mē'lẹ̄-ē), *n. pl.* [NL. (Agardh, 1841), < *Rhodomela* + *-eæ*.] A suborder of floridean algæ, named from the genus *Rhodomela*. This is the largest suborder of the *Florideæ*, and contains many of the most beautiful seaweeds. It is characterized mainly by the cystocarpic fruit, which is external and has the spores borne separately on short stalks. The fronds are usually filiform and branching.

rhodomontade, *n.* and *v.* See *rodomontade*.

rhodonite (rō'dọ-nīt), *n.* [Irreg. < Gr. ῥόδον, rose, + *-ite*[2].] Native manganese silicate, sometimes containing zinc or calcium: a mineral occurring massive, rarely in distinct crystals, of a fine rose-red or pink color. It is sometimes used as an ornamental stone.

Rhodope (rō'dọ-pē), *n.* [NL. (Kölliker, 1847), prob. < Gr. Ῥοδόπη, Rhodope, a Thracian nymph.] A remarkable genus, type of the family *Rhodopidæ*, based on *R. veranyi*. This little creature exhibits such equivocal characters that it has been considered by some as a planarian worm, by others as an abranchiate mollusk, though it has no odontophore.

Rhodope veranyi.
a, top view; *b*, side view; *c*, longitudinal section (enlarged).

rhodophane (rō'dọ-fān), *n.* [< Gr. ῥόδον, rose, + -φανής, appearing, < φαίνεσθαι, appear.] A red pigment found in the retinal cones of the eyes of certain fishes, reptiles, and birds. The pigment is held in solution by a fatty body.

rhodophyl, rhodophyll (rō'dọ-fil), *n.* [< Gr. ῥόδεος, red, + φύλλον, a leaf.] The compound pigment of the red algæ.

rhodophyllite (rē-dọ-fil'īt), *n.* [< Gr. ῥόδον, rose, + φύλλον, leaf, + *-ite*[2].] In *mineral.*, a variety of penninite from Texas in Pennsylvania, of a reddish color, and peculiar in containing a small percentage of chromium sesquioxid.

rhodophyllous (rō-dọ-fil'us), *a.* [< *rhodophyll* + *-ous*.] In *bot.*, containing rhodophyl; like rhodophyl.

Cytioplasm mostly *rhodophyllous*.
H. C. Wood, Fresh-Water Algæ, p. 213.

Rhodopidæ (rō-dop'i-dē), *n. pl.* [NL., < *Rhodope* + *-idæ*.] A family of simple marine invertebrates of uncertain relationship, typified by the genus *Rhodope*. They are of an elongate flattened form, somewhat convex dorsally, and destitute of mantle, dorsal appendages, tentacles, branchiæ, and odontophore. The digestive tube is very simple, and there is no pharynx, kidney, or heart. The family has been referred to the nudibranchiate gastropods and to the turbellarians. See cut under *Rhodope*.

rhodopsin (rọ-dop'sin), *n.* [< Gr. ῥόδον, rose, + ὄψις, view, + *-in*[2].] Visual purple; a pigment found in the outer segments of the retinal rods. It is quickly bleached by light, but the purple color is regained by placing the pigment in the dark. In the normal retina it is restored by the action of the pigmentary layer of cells.

Rhodora (rọ-dō'rạ̈), *n.* [NL. (Duhamel du Monceau, 1767), so called from the rose-colored flowers; < Gr. ῥόδον, rose (see *rose*[1]), the NL. word being based, as to form, on the L. *rhodora*, a plant, *Spiræa Ulmaria* or *Aruncus*, and said to be a Gallic word.] 1. A former genus of *Ericaceæ*, now included in *Rhododendron*, section *Azalea*, but still giving name to the tribe *Rhodoreæ*. It was set apart chiefly on account of its prominently two-lipped flower, of which the lower lip consists of two petals, completely separate, or much more nearly so than the three divisions of the upper lip. There was but one species. See def. 2.

2. [*l. c.*] A low deciduous shrub, *Rhododendron Rhodora* (*Rhodora Canadensis*), a native of cold and wet wooded places from Pennsylvania northward, often covering acres with its delicate rosy flowers, which appear before the leaves.

In May, when sea-winds pierced our solitudes,
I found the fresh *Rhodora* in the woods,
Spreading its leafless blooms in a damp nook; . . .
The purple petals, fallen in the pool,
Made the black water with their beauty gay.
Emerson, The *Rhodora*.

Rhodoreæ (rọ-dō'rẹ-ē), *n. pl.* [NL. (Don, 1834), < *Rhodora* + *-eæ*.] A tribe of plants of the order *Ericaceæ*, characterized by a septicidal capsular fruit, deciduous, imbricated, and commonly gamopetalous corolla, and shrubby habit. It includes 16 genera, chiefly of northern regions and mountains, often very showy in blossom, as in the genera *Rhododendron*, *Kalmia*, *Ledum*, and *Rhodothamnus*. See *Rhodora* and *Azalea*.

rhodosperm (rō'dọ-spėrm), *n.* [< *Rhodospermeæ*.] An individual alga of the class *Rhodospermeæ*.

Rhodospermeæ (rē-dọ-spėr'mẹ-ē), *n. pl.* [NL. (Harvey), < Gr. ῥόδον, rose, + σπέρμα, seed.] A name employed by Harvey for the red or purple algæ, which are now placed under Agardh's older name *Florideæ*.

rhodospermin (rō-dọ-spėr'min), *n.* [< Gr. ῥόδον, rose, + σπέρμα, seed, + *-in*[2].] Crystalloids of proteid bodies found in the *Florideæ*, forming the red coloring matter.

Rhodosporeæ (rō-dọ-spō'rẹ-ē), *n. pl.* [NL., < Gr. ῥόδον, rose, + σπόρος, seed, + *-eæ*.] Same as *Rhodospermeæ*.

Rhodostaurotic† (rō'dọ-stâ-rot'ik), *a.* [Intended as a translation into Gr. form of *Rosicrucian*; < Gr. ῥόδον, rose, + σταυρός, cross, + -otic. Cf. Gr. σταυρωτικός, crossed, cruciform.] Rosicrucian.

Outis, . . .
The good old hermit, that was said to dwell
Here in the forest without trees, that built
The castle in the air, where all the brethren
Rhodostaurotic live.
B. Jonson, Masque of Fortunate Isles.

Rhodostethia (rē-dọ-stē'thi-ạ̈), *n.* [NL. (Macgillivray, 1842), < Gr. ῥόδον, rose, + στῆθος, the breast.] A genus of *Laridæ*, so called from the rose-tint of the breast, unique in the family in having the tail cuneate: the wedge-tailed gulls. Ross's rosy gull, *R. rosea*, is the only species, inhabiting the arctic regions. It was long regarded as one of the rarest of birds, but has lately been found abundantly on the arctic coast of Alaska. It is white, rose-tinted, with black collar, wing-tips, and bill, red feet, and pearl-blue mantle; the length is 14 inches. Also called *Rossia*. See cut in next column.

Rhodothamnus (rō-dọ-tham'nus), *n.* [NL. (Reichenbach, 1830), < Gr. ῥόδον, rose, + θάμνος, bush.] A genus of small shrubs of the order *Ericaceæ* and tribe *Rhodoreæ*. It is characterized by having a wheel-shaped corolla and ten long stamens, and terminal, solitary, and long-peduncled flowers. The only species, *R. Chamæcistus*, is a native of the Austrian and Italian Alps. It is a low branching shrub with scattered short-petioled leaves, which are elliptical-lanceolate, entire, evergreen, and shining. It bears rose-colored flowers, large for the size of the plant, with spreading and curving stamens, the long slender peduncles and the calyx glandular-hairy. The whole plant in habit and flower resembles an azalea. The fruit is an erect five-furrowed globose capsule. Sometimes called *ground-cistus*, translating the specific name.

Rosy or Wedge-tailed Gull (*Rhodostethia rosea*).

rhodotilite (rọ-dot'i-līt), *n.* [< Gr. ῥόδον, rose, + τίλος, down, + *-ite*[2].] A mineral found at Pajsberg in Sweden, having the same composition as inesite.

Rhodymenia (rō-di-mē'ni-ạ̈), *n.* [NL. (Greville, 1830), < Gr. ῥόδον, rose, + ὑμήν, membrane: see *hymen*[2].] A genus of marine algæ of the class *Florideæ*, giving its name to the order *Rhodymeniaceæ* (which see for characters). See *dulse*, *dillisk*.

Rhodymeniaceæ (rē-di-mē-ni-ā'sẹ-ē), *n. pl.* [NL., < *Rhodymenia* + *-aceæ*.] An order of floridous seaweeds of purplish or blood-red color. The root is disk-like or branched, much matted; the frond, which is composed of polygonal cells, is either leafy or filiform, and much branched, never articulate. The species are widely dispersed. *Rhodymenia palmata*, or dulse, is a well-known example. Many of the species of the genus *Gracilaria* are largely used in the East as ingredients in soups, jellies, etc., and as substitutes for glue. One of them is the *agar-agar* of the Chinese.

rhœadic (rẹ-ad'ik), *a.* [< NL. *Rhœas* (*Rhœad-*) (see def.) (< Gr. ῥοιάς (ῥοιαδ-), a kind of poppy) + *-ic*.] Contained in or derived from the poppy *Papaver Rhœas*.—**Rhœadic acid**, one of the coloring principles in the petals of *Papaver Rhœas*.

rhœadine (rē'ạ-din), *n.* [< *rhœad*(*ic*) + *-ine*[2].] A crystallizable alkaloid ($C_{21}H_{21}NO_6$) found in *Papaver Rhœas*. It is non-poisonous.

rhœagenine (rẹ-aj'e-nin), *n.* [< NL. *Rhœas* (see *rhœadic*) + *-gen* + *-ine*[2].] A base, isomeric with rhœadine, found in acidified solutions of rhœadine.

rhomb (romb), *n.* [< OF. *rhombe*, F. *rhombe* = Sp. It. *rombo* = Pg. *rhombo*, < L. *rhombus*, ML. also *rhumbus*, *rumbus*, a magician's circle, a kind of fish, in LL. a rhomb in geometry, ML. also a point of the compass, < Gr. ῥόμβος, ῥύμβος, a spinning-top or -wheel, a magic wheel, a spinning or whirling motion, also a rhomb in geometry, a lozenge, < ῥέμβειν, revolve, totter, nasalized form of ῥέπειν, sink, fall, be unsteady. Doublet of *rhumb*, *rumb*.] 1. In *geom.*, an oblique-angled equilateral parallelogram; a quadrilateral figure whose sides are equal, and the opposite sides parallel, but the angles unequal, two being obtuse and two acute.

Rhomb.

See how in warlike muster they appear,
In *rhombs*, and wedges, and half-moons, and wings.
Milton, P. R., iii. 309.

2. In *crystal.*, a solid bounded by six equal and similar rhombic planes; a rhombohedron.—3. In *zoöl.*, a pair of semirhombs forming a rhombic figure, as certain plates of cystic crinoids. —4. A material circle. [Rare.]

That swift
Nocturnal and diurnal *rhomb* suppos'd,
Invisible else above all stars, the wheel
Of day and night; which needs not thy belief
If earth, industrious of herself, fetch day
Travelling east, and with her part averse
From the sun's beam meet night, her other part
Still luminous by his ray. *Milton*, P. L., viii. 134.

Fresnel's rhomb, a rhomb of crown-glass, so cut that a ray of light entering one of its faces at right angles shall emerge at right angles at the opposite face, after undergoing within the rhomb, at its outer faces, two total reflections. It is used to produce a ray circularly polarized, which becomes plane-polarized again on being transmitted through a second Fresnel's rhomb.—**Pectinated rhomb**, in crinoids, a hydrospire.

rhombarsenite (rom-bär′se-nīt), *n.* [< Gr. ῥόμβος, rhomb, + E. *arsenite.*] Same as *claudetite.*

rhombi, *n.* Plural of *rhombus.*

rhombic (rom′bik), *a.* [= F. *rhombique*; as *rhomb* + *-ic.*] 1. Having the figure of a rhomb.—2. In *zoöl.*, approaching the form of a rhomb or diamond, usually with the angles a little rounded.—3. In *crystal.*, often used as an equivalent of *orthorhombic*: as, the *rhombic* pyroxenes (that is, those crystallizing in the orthorhombic system).—4. In *bot.*, oval, but somewhat angular at the sides.—**Longitudinally rhombic**, having, as a rhomb, the longer diameter in a postero-anterior direction.—**Rhombic dodecahedron, octahedron**, etc. See the nouns.—**Rhombic pyroxenes.** See *pyroxene.*—**Transversely rhombic**, having the longer diameter of the rhomb across the length of the body or organ.

rhombical (rom′bi-kal), *a.* [< *rhombic* + *-al.*] Same as *rhombic.*

rhombicosidodecahedron (rom-bī″kō-si-dō″-dek-a-hē′dron), *n.* [< Gr. ῥόμβος, rhomb, rhombus, + εἴκοσι, twenty, + δωδεκάεδρον, a dodecahedron. Cf. *icosidodecahedron.*] A solid having sixty-two faces—twelve belonging to the regular dodecahedron, twenty to the icosahedron, and thirty to the semi-regular triacontahedron. Among the thirteen Archimedean solids there are two such solids: one, usually so called, has its dodecahedral faces pentagonal, its icosahedral faces triangular, and its triacontahedral faces square; while the other has the dodecahedral faces decagons, the icosahedral faces hexagons, and the triacontahedral faces squares. The latter is commonly called a *truncated icosidodecahedron*, a misleading designation.

rhombicuboctahedron (rom″bi-kū-bok-ta-hē′-dron), *n.* [< Gr. ῥόμβος, rhomb, + κύβος, cube, + ὀκτάεδρον, neut. of ὀκτάεδρος, eight-sided (see *octahedron*).] A solid having twenty-six faces, formed by the surfaces of the coaxial cube, octahedron, and rhombic dodecahedron. Among the thirteen Archimedean solids there are two such solids: one, usually so called, has the cubic and dodecahedral faces squares, and the octahedral faces triangles; while the other has the cubic faces octagons, the octahedral faces hexagons, and the dodecahedral faces squares. The latter is commonly called a *truncated cuboctahedron*, a misleading designation.

rhombiform (rom′bi-fôrm), *a.* [< L. *rhombus*, rhomb, + *forma*, form.] Shaped like a rhomb; rhombic; rhomboid. In *entom.*, noting parts which are of the same thickness throughout, the horizontal section being a rhomb: as, *rhombiform* joints of the antennæ.

Rhombigena (rom-bij′e-nā), *n. pl.* [NL.] A variant of *Rhombogena.*

rhombo-atloideus (rom″bō-at-loi′dē-us), *n.*; pl. *rhombo-atloidei* (-ī). [< Gr. ῥόμβος, rhomb, + NL. *atl(as)* (see *atlas*[1], 3) + *-oideus.*] A muscular slip, occasionally arising from one or two lower cervical or upper dorsal spines, and inserted into the transverse process of the atlas.

Rhombochirus (rom-bō-kī′rus), *n.* [NL. (Gill, 1863), < Gr. ῥόμβος, rhomb, + χείρ, hand (with ref. to the pectoral fin).] A genus of *Echeneididæ* or remoras, differing from *Remora* in the structure

Rhombochirus osteochir.

of the pectoral fins, which are short and broad, somewhat rhombic in outline, and with flat, stiff, partially ossified rays. There is but one species, *R. osteochir* (so named from the bony pectoral rays), occurring from the West Indies to Cape Cod.

rhombocœle (rom′bō-sēl), *n.* [< NL. *rhombocœlia.*] Same as *rhombocœlia.* *Wilder*, N. Y. Med. Jour., March 21, 1885, p. 326.

rhombocœlia (rom-bō-sē′li-ā), *n.*; pl. *rhombocœliæ* (-ē). [NL., < Gr. ῥόμβος, rhomb, + κοιλία, cavity: see *cœlia.*] The sinus rhomboidalis of the myelon: a dilatation of the cavity of the spinal cord in the sacral region. This is a sort of ventricle, or enlargement of the hollow of the primitively tubular spinal cord, observable in many vertebrate embryos, representing to some extent the complicated and persistent system of ventricles in the opposite end of the same neural axis; but it is not often well marked in adults. It is most notable and persistent in birds, in which class it presents the figure which has suggested the term *sinus rhomboidalis* and its later synonym *rhombocœlia* or *rhombocœle*, applied conformably with a recent system of naming the several cœliæ of the cerebrospinal axis. See cut under *protovertebra.*

rhombocœlian (rom-bō-sē′li-an), *a.* [< *rhombocœlia* + *-an.*] Pertaining to the rhombocœlia, or having its characters.

Rhomboganoidei (rom″bō-ga-noi′dē-ī), *n. pl.* [NL., < Gr. ῥόμβος, rhomb, + NL. *Ganoidei.*] An order of fishes: same as *Ginglymodi.*

rhombogen (rom′bō-jen), *n.* [< NL. *rhombogenus*: see *rhombogenous.*] The infusoriform embryo of a nematoid worm: one of the phases or stages of a nematoid embryo: distinguished from *nematogen.* See cut under *Dicyema.*

Rhombogena (rom-boj′e-nā), *n. pl.* [NL., neut. pl. of *rhombogenus*: see *rhombogenous.*] Those *Dicyemida* which give rise to infusoriform embryos. See cut under *Dicyema.*

rhombogenic (rom-bō-jen′ik), *a.* [< *rhombogen-ous* + *-ic.*] Same as *rhombogenous.*

rhombogenous (rom-boj′e-nus), *a.* [< NL. *rhombogenus*, < Gr. ῥόμβος, rhomb, + -γενής, producing: see *-gen.*] Producing infusoriform embryos, as a nematoid worm; having the character of a rhombogen.

rhombohedral (rom-bō-hē′dral), *a.* [< *rhombohedron* + *-al.*] 1. In *geom.*, of or pertaining to a rhombohedron; having forms derived from the rhombohedron.—2. In *crystal.*, relating to a system of forms of which the rhombohedron is taken as the type. They are embraced in the rhombohedral division of the hexagonal system. See *hexagonal.*—**Rhombohedral carbonates**, the isomorphous group of the native carbonates of calcium (calcite), of magnesium (magnesite), of iron (siderite), of manganese (rhodochrosite), of zinc (smithsonite), and the intermediate compounds, as the double carbonate of calcium and magnesium (dolomite), etc. These all crystallize in rhombohedrons and related forms with closely similar angles, the angle of the cleavage rhombohedron varying from 105° to 107½°.—**Rhombohedral tetartohedrism.** See *tetartohedrism.*

rhombohedrally (rom-bō-hē′dral-i), *adv.* In a rhombohedral form; as a rhombohedron.

It [nordenskjoldite] crystallizes *rhombohedrally* with $c : c = 1 : 0.8221$, and is tabular in habit.
American Naturalist, XXIV. 364.

rhombohedric (rom-bō-hē′drik), *a.* [< *rhombohedron* + *-ic.*] Same as *rhombohedral.* *Lommel*, Light (trans.), p. 290.

rhombohedron (rom-bō-hē′dron), *n.* [< Gr. ῥόμβος, rhomb, + ἕδρα, base.] In *geom.* and *crystal.*, a solid bounded by six rhombic planes. In crystallography a rhombohedron is usually regarded as a hemihedral form of the double hexagonal pyramid. It may be obtuse or acute, according as the terminal angle—that is, the angle over one of the edges which meet in the vertex—is greater or less than 90°.

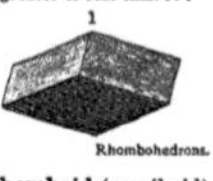

Rhombohedrons. 1, obtuse; 2, 3, acute.

rhomboid (rom′boid), *a.* and *n.* [= OF. *rhomboide*, F. *rhomboïde* = Sp. It. *romboide* = Pg. *rhomboide*, < L. *rhomboides*, < Gr. ῥομβοειδής, rhomboid-shaped, < ῥόμβος, rhomb, + εἶδος, form.] I. *a.* Having a form like or approaching that of a rhomb; having the shape of a rhomboid (see II., 1); rhomboidal. Specifically—(*a*) In *anat.*, rhombiform, as a muscle or ligament; pertaining to the rhomboidei or rhomboideum. (*b*) In *bot.*, imperfectly rhombic with obtuse angles, as some leaves.—**Rhomboid ligament.** Same as *rhomboideum.*—**Rhomboid muscle.** Same as *rhomboideus.*

II. *n.* 1. In *geom.*, a quadrilateral figure whose opposite sides and angles are equal, but which is neither equilateral nor equiangular; a non-equilateral oblique parallelogram.—2. In *crystal.*, a solid having a rhomboidal form with three axes of unequal lengths, two of which are at right angles to each other, while the third is so inclined as to be perpendicular to one of the two axes, and oblique to the other.—3. In *anat.*, a rhomboideus.

Rhomboid, 1.

rhomboidal (rom-boi′dal), *a.* [= F. *rhomboïdal* = Sp. It. *romboidale*; as *rhomboid* + *-al.*] Having the shape of a rhomboid.

A rhomb of Iceland spar, a solid bounded by six equal and similar *rhomboidal* surfaces whose sides are parallel.
Brewster, Treatise on Optics, ii. 22.

Rhomboidal fossa, the fourth ventricle of the brain.—**Rhomboidal porgy.** See *porgy.*—**Rhomboidal sinus**, the fourth ventricle.

rhomboidea, *n.* Plural of *rhomboideum.*

rhomboidei, *n.* Plural of *rhomboideus.*

rhomboides (rom-boi′dēs), *n.* [< L. *rhomboides*, < Gr. ῥομβοειδής, neut. of ῥομβοειδής, rhomboid-shaped: see *rhomboid.*] 1. A rhomboid. [Rare.]

See them under sail in all their lawn and sarcenet, with a geometrical *rhomboides* upon their heads.
Milton, Reformation in Eng., ii.

2†. [*cap.*] [NL.] An old genus of fishes. *Klein*, 1745.—3. [*cap.*] [NL.] A genus of mollusks. *De Blainville*, 1824.

rhomboideum (rom-boi′dē-um), *n.*; pl. *rhomboidea* (-ā). [NL.: see *rhomboid.*] In *anat.*, the ligament which unites the sternal end of the clavicle with the cartilage of the first rib; the rhomboid ligament: so called from its rhombic form in man.

rhomboideus (rom-boi′dē-us), *n.*; pl. *rhomboidei* (-ī). [NL. (sc. *musculus*, muscle): see *rhomboid.*] Either of two muscles, major and minor, which connect the last cervical vertebra and several upper dorsal vertebræ with the vertebral border of the scapula.—**Rhomboideus occipitalis**, an additional muscle sometimes found running parallel with the rhomboideus minor, from the scapula to the occipital bone.

rhomb-solid (romb′sol″id), *n.* A solid generated by the revolution of a rhomb on a diagonal. It consists of two equal right cones joined at their bases.

rhomb-spar (romb′spär), *n.* A variety of dolomite occurring in rhombohedral crystals.

rhombus (rom′bus), *n.*; pl. *rhombi* (-bī). [L.: see *rhomb.*] 1. Same as *rhomb.*—2. [*cap.*] An obsolete constellation, near the south pole.—3. [NL.] In *ichth.*: (*a*) [*cap.*] A genus of *Stromateidæ*, generally united with *Stromateus.* *Lacépède*, 1800. (*b*) The Linnean specific name of the turbot (as *Pleuronectes rhombus*), and later [*cap.*] a generic name of the same (as *Rhombus maximus*), and of various other flatfishes now assigned to different genera. *Cuvier*, 1817.

rhonchal (rong′kal), *a.* [< *rhonchus* + *-al.*] Relating or pertaining to rhonchus.—**Rhonchal fremitus**, a vibration or thrill felt in palpating the chest-wall when there is mucus or other secretion in the bronchial tubes or a cavity.

rhonchial (rong′ki-al), *a.* Same as *rhonchal.*

rhonchisonant (rong′ki-sō-nant), *a.* [< LL. *rhonchisonus*, snorting (said of the rhinoceros), < L. *rhonchus*, a snoring, snorting, + *sonare*, sound: see *sonant.*] Snorting. [Rare.] *Imp. Dict.*

rhonchus (rong′kus), *n.* [= F. *rhoncus* = Sp. Pg. *ronco*, < L. *rhonchus*, < Gr. *ῥόγχος, ῥέγχος, prop. ῥέγκος, a snoring, snorting, < ῥέγκειν, rarely ῥέγχειν, snore, snort.] A râle, usually a bronchial or cavernous râle.—**Cavernous rhonchus**, a cavernous râle.—**Cavernulous rhonchus**, a small cavernous râle.—**Rhonchus sibilans**, a sibilant râle.—**Rhonchus sonorus**, a sonorous râle.

rhone (rōn), *n.* An erroneous spelling of *rone*[2].

rhopalic (rō-pal′ik), *a.* [= F. *rhopalique*, < LL. *rhopalicus*, < Gr. ῥοπαλικός, lit. like a club (increasing gradually in size from one end to the other), < ῥόπαλον (> ML. *rhopalum*), a club, < ῥέπειν, incline.] In *anc. pros.*, noting a hexameter in which each succeeding word contains one syllable more than that preceding it. Also spelled *ropalic.*

Rhopalocera (rō-pa-los′e-rā), *n. pl.* [NL. (Boisduval, 1840), neut. pl. of *rhopalocerus*: see *rhopalocerous.*] One of two suborders of *Lepidoptera*, characterized by the clubbed or knobbed antennæ (whence the name); the butterflies, or diurnal lepidopterous insects: contrasted with *Heterocera*, the nocturnal lepidopterous insects, or moths. In a few exceptional cases the antennæ are filiform, pectinate, or otherwise modified. The wings are elevated when at rest, and there is no bristle connecting the two wings of the same side. The larvæ are very variable, but are generally not hairy, and never spin cocoons. Five families are usually recognized, the *Nymphalidæ*, *Erycinidæ* (or *Lemoniidæ*), *Lycænidæ*, *Papilionidæ*, and *Hesperiidæ*. The genera (including synonyms) are 1,100 or more in number; the species are estimated at 7,000. About 460 species inhabit Europe, while about 625 are known in America north of Mexico.

rhopaloceral (rō-pa-los′e-ral), *a.* [< *rhopalocer-ous* + *-al.*] Same as *rhopalocerous.*

A wealth of illustration to which *rhopaloceral* literature was hitherto a stranger. *Athenæum*, No. 3141, p. 19.

rhopalocerous (rō-pa-los′e-rus), *a.* [< NL. *rhopalocerus*, < Gr. ῥόπαλον, a club, + κέρας, a horn.] Having clubbed antennæ, as a butterfly; of or pertaining to the *Rhopalocera*, or having their characters.

Rhopalodina (rō″pa-lō-dī′nā), *n.* [NL., < Gr. ῥόπαλον, a club, + *-d-* (meaningless) + *-ina.*] The only genus of *Rhopalodinidæ*. *R. lageniformis* is the only species. *J. E. Gray*, 1848.

Rhopalodinidæ (rō″pa-lō-din′i-dē), *n. pl.* [NL., < *Rhopalodina* + *-idæ.*] A family of diœcious tetrapneumonous holothurians, represented by the genus *Rhopalodina.* They have separate sexes, four water-lungs or respiratory trees, a lageniform body with the mouth and anus at the same end of it, five oral and five anal ambulacra, ten oral tentacles and calcareous plates, ten anal papillæ and plates, and two-rowed pedicels. They are sometimes called *sea-gourds*.

Rhopalodon (rō-pal'ō-don), *n.* [NL., < Gr. ῥόπαλον, a club, + ὀδούς (ὀδοντ-) = E. *tooth*.] A genus of fossil dinosaurs from the Permian of Russia, based on remains exhibiting club-shaped teeth, as *R. wangenheimi*. *Fischer*.

Rhopalonema (rō'pa-lō-nē'mą̈), *n.* [NL., < Gr. ῥόπαλον, a club, + νῆμα, a thread.] A notable genus of trachymedusans of the family *Trachynematidæ*, represented by such species as *R. velatum* of the Mediterranean. *Gegenbaur*.

rhotacise, *v. i.* See *rhotacize*.

rhotacism (rō'ta-sizm), *n.* [= F. *rhotacisme*, < LL. *rhotacismus*, < LGr. *ῥωτακισμός, < ῥωτακίζειν, rhotacize: see *rhotacize*.] 1. Too frequent use of *r*.—2. Erroneous pronunciation of *r*; utterance of r with vibration of the uvula.

Neither the Spaniards nor Portuguese retain in their speech that strong *Rhotacism* which they denoted by the double *rr*, and which Camden and Fuller notice as peculiar to the people of Carlton in Leicestershire.
Southey, The Doctor, ccxxiii.

3. Conversion of another sound, as *s*, into r.

That too many exceptions to the law of *rhotacism* in Latin exist has been felt by many scholars, but no one has ventured a theory that would explain them en masse.
Amer. Jour. Philol., IX. 492.

Also spelled *rotacism*.

rhotacize (rō'ta-sīz), *v. i.*; pret. and pp. *rhotacized*, ppr. *rhotacizing*. [< LGr. ῥωτακίζειν, make overmuch or wrong use of r, < ῥῶ, rho, the letter ρ, r.. Cf. *iotacism*.] 1. To use r too frequently.—2. To make wrong use of *r*; pronounce r with vibration of the uvula instead of the tip of the tongue.—3. To convert other sounds, as *s*, into *r*; substitute r in pronunciation.

Latin, Umbrian, and other *rhotacizing* dialects.
The Academy, Feb. 4, 1888, p. 82.

Also spelled *rhotacise*, *rotacize*, *rotacise*.

rhubarb (rö'bärb), *n.* and *a.* [Early mod E. also *rheubarb*, *reubarbe*, *rubarbe*, *rewbarbe*; < OF. *rubarbe*, *reobarbe*, *rheubarbe*, *reubarbare*, F. *rhubarbe* = Pr. *reubarba* = Cat. *ruibarbarro* = Sp. *ruibarbo* = Pg. *reubarbo*, *ruibarbo* = It. *reobarbaro*, *rabarbaro*, formerly *rabbarbaro* = D. *rabarber* = G. *rhabarber* = Dan. Sw. *rabarber* (Turk. *rubris*), < ML. *rheubarbarum*, *rhabarbarum*, also *reubarbarum*, for *rheum barbarum*, < Gr. ῥῆον βάρβαρον, rhubarb, ῥῆον, rhubarb (ῥῆον, ML. *rheum*, being appar. a deriv. or orig. an adj. form of 'Pᾶ, the *Rha*, or Volga river, whence rhubarb was also called *rha Ponticum*, 'Pontic rha' (see *rhapontic*), and *rha barbarum*, 'barbarous (i. e. foreign) rha'): see *rha*, *Rheum*[2], and *barbarous*.] **I.** *n.* 1. The general name for plants of the genus *Rheum*, especially for species affording the drug rhubarb and the culinary herb of that name. The specific source of the officinal rhubarb is still partially in question; but it is practically

Medicinal Rhubarb (*Rheum officinale*).

settled that *R. officinale* is one of the probably several species which yield it. *R. palmatum*, *R. Franzenbachii*, and *R. hybridum* also have some claims. The article is produced on the high table-lands of western China and eastern Tibet, and formerly reached the western market by the way of Russia and Turkey, being named accordingly. It is now obtained from China by sea (Chinese rhubarb), but is more mixed in quality, from lack of the rigorous Russian inspection. Various species, especially *R. Rhaponticum* and *R. palmatum*, have been grown in England and elsewhere in Europe for the root, but the product is inferior, from difference either of species or of conditions. The common garden rhubarb is *R. Rhaponticum* and its varieties. It is native from the Volga to central Asia, and was introduced into England about 1573. Its leaves were early used as a pot-herb, but the now common use of its tender acidulous leafstalks as a spring substitute for fruit in making tarts, pies, etc., is only of recent date. Attempts to use it as a wine-plant have not been specially successful. Some other species have a similar acid quality. From their stature and huge leaves, various rhubarbs produce striking scenic effects, especially *R. Emodi*, the Nepal rhubarb, which grows 5 feet high and has wrinkled leaves veined with red; and still more the better-formed *R. officinale*. A finer and most remarkable species is *R. nobile*, the Sikhim rhubarb, which presents a conical tower of imbricating foliage a yard or more high, the ample shining-green root-leaves passing into large straw-colored bracts which conceal beautiful pink stipules and small green flowers. The root is very long, winding among the rocks. This plant is not easily cultivated.

2. The root of any medicinal rhubarb, or some preparation of it. Rhubarb is a much-prized remedy, remarkable as combining a cathartic with an astringent effect, the latter succeeding the former. It is also tonic and stomachic. It is administered in substance or in various preparations.

The patient that doth determine to receiue a little *Rheubarb* suffereth the bitternesse it leaueth in the throte for the profite it doth him against his feuer.
Guevara, Letters (tr. by Hellowes, 1577), p. 242.

What *rhubarb*, cyme, or what purgative drug,
Would scour these English hence?
Shak., Macbeth, v. 3. 55.

3. The leafstalks of the garden rhubarb collectively; pie-plant.—**Bog-rhubarb.** See *Petasites*.—**Compound powder of rhubarb.** See *powder*.—**False rhubarb**, *Thalictrum flavum*.—**Monk's rhubarb**, the patience-dock, *Rumex Patientia*, probably from the use of its root like rhubarb; also, a species of meadow-rue, *Thalictrum flavum*.—**Poor man's rhubarb**, *Thalictrum flavum*.

II.† *a.* Resembling rhubarb; bitter.

But with your *rubarbe* words ye must contend
To grieue me worse.
Sir P. Sidney, Astrophel and Stella, xiv.

rhubarbative†, *a.* [< *rhubarb* + *-ative*.] Like rhubarb; hence, figuratively, sour. [Rare.]

A man were better to lye vnder the hands of a Hangman than one of your *rhubarbatiue* faces.
Dekker, Match Me in London, iii.

rhubarby (rö'bärb-i), *a.* [< *rhubarb* + *-y*[1].] Like rhubarb; containing, or in some way qualified by, rhubarb.

rhumb, rumb (rumb or rum), *n.* [Formerly also *rhume*, *roomb*, *roumb*, *roumbe*; prob. < OF. *rhomb*, *rumb*, *rhombe*, a point of the compass, < Sp. *rumbo*, a course, point of the compass, = Pg. *rumbo*, *rumo*, a ship's course (*quarto do rumo*, a point of the compass), = It. *rombo*, < L. *rhombus*, a magician's circle, a rhombus, < Gr. ῥόμβος, a spinning-top, a magic wheel, a whirling motion, a rhomb in geometry: see *rhomb*.] 1. A vertical circle of the celestial sphere. So says Hutton; but if so, it is difficult to understand how Kepler (*Epitom. Astron.*, ii. 10), in order to explain def. 2, is driven to the trapezoidal figure of the points on the compass-card.

2. A point of the compass, a thirty-second part of the circle of the horizon, 11° 15′ in azimuth.—3. The course of a ship constantly moving at the same angle to its meridian; a rhumb-line.

rhumb-line (rumb'līn), *n.* The curve described upon the terrestrial spheroid by a ship sailing on one course—that is, always in the same direction relatively to the north point. For long courses, especially in high latitudes, the rhumb-line is not the shortest or geodetical line, which is substantially a great circle: for the rhumb-line evidently goes round and round the pole, approximating to the equiangular spiral. Also called *loxodromic curve*.

rhumb-sailing (rumb'sā'ling), *n.* In *navig.*, the course of a vessel when she keeps on the rhumb-line which passes through the place of departure and the place of destination. See *sailing*.

rhumet, *n.* See *rhumb*.

Branch of Poison-ivy (*Rhus Toxicodendron*) with Male Flowers.
a, male flower; *b*, fruits.

Rhus (rus), *n.* [NL. (Tournefort, 1700), < L. *rhus*, < Gr. ῥοῦς, sumac.] A genus of shrubs and trees, belonging to the tribe *Spondieæ* of the order *Anacardiaceæ*, the cashew-nut family. It is characterized by flowers with from four to ten stamens, a solitary ovule pendulous from a basilar stalk, a small four- to six-cleft calyx, and four to six imbricated petals unchanged after flowering. The leaves are pinnate, one- to three-foliolate, or sometimes simple; the flowers are small, in axillary or terminal panicles; the fruit is a small compressed drupe. The plant often abounds in a caustic poisonous juice, sometimes exudes a varnish. There are about 120 species, found throughout subtropical and warm climates, but infrequent in the tropics. They are especially abundant at the Cape of Good Hope, also in eastern Asia; 4 species are found in southern Europe, a few in the East Indies and the Andes, and 13 in the United States. Several species, some useful for tanning, are known as *sumac*. (For poisonous American species, see *poison-ivy*, *poison-oak*, and *poisonwood*.) *R. Cotinus* is the smoke-tree, mist-tree, or purple fringe-tree. (See *smoke-tree*; also *young fustic*, under *fustic*.) A somewhat similar species, *R. cotinoides*, is known as *chittam-wood*. *R. vernicifera* is the Japanese lacquer-tree or varnish-tree. (See *lacquer-tree*.) The kindred black-varnish tree is of the genus *Melanorrhœa*. *R. succedanea* is the Japanese wax-tree. *R. semialata* bears the Chinese galls. *R. caustica*, the lithy-tree of Chili, is a small tree with very hard useful wood. *R. integrifolia*, though often but a shrub, is said to be the local "mahogany" in Lower California. See cut in preceding column.

rhusma (rus'mą̈), *n.* [Also *rusma*; origin unknown.] A depilatory composed of lime, orpiment, and water, and called in the United States Dispensatory "Atkinson's depilatory." It is used not only for removing superfluous human hair, but also to some extent in tanning and tawing for removing hair from skins.

rhyacolite (rī-ak'ō-līt), *n.* [< Gr. ῥύαξ (ῥυακ-), a stream (< ῥεῖν, flow), + λίθος, a stone.] A name given to the glassy feldspar (orthoclase) from Monte Somma in italy. Also spelled *ryacolite*.

Rhyacophila (rī-a-kof'i-lą̈), *n.* [NL., < Gr. ῥύαξ (ῥυακ-), a stream, + φιλεῖν, love.] The typical genus of *Rhyacophilidæ*.

Rhyacophilidæ (rī'a-kō-fil'i-dē), *n. pl.* [NL., < *Rhyacophila* + *-idæ*.] A family of trichopterous neuropterous insects, typified by the genus *Rhyacophila*. The larvæ inhabit fixed stone cases in torrents, and the pupæ are inclosed in a silken cocoon. The forms are numerous, and are mostly European.

Rhyacophilus (rī-a-kof'i-lus), *n.* [NL. (Kaup, 1829), < Gr. ῥύαξ (ῥυακ-), a stream, + φιλεῖν, love.] A genus of *Scolopacidæ*, belonging to the totanine section, having a slender bill little longer than the head and grooved to beyond the middle, legs comparatively short, a moderate basal web between the outer and middle toes, the plumage dark-colored above with small whitish spots, and the tail rounded, fully barred with black and white; the green sandpipers or solitary tattlers. The green sandpiper of Europe, *R. ochropus*, is the type. The similar American species is *R.*

Solitary Sandpiper (*Rhyacophilus solitarius*).

solitarius, commonly called the *solitary sandpiper*, abundant about pools and in wet woods and fields throughout the greater part of the United States. It is 8½ inches long and 16 in extent of wings.

rhyme, rhymeless, etc. See *rime*[1], etc.

Rhynchæa (ring-kē'ą̈), *n.* [NL. (Cuvier, 1817), also *Rhynchea*, *Rynchæa*, *Rynchea*, *Rynchæn*; prop. *Rhynchæna* (Gloger, 1849), < LGr. ῥυγχαινα, with a large snout, < Gr. ῥύγχος, snout,

South American Painted Snipe (*Rhynchæa semicollaris*).

muzzle (of swine, dogs, etc.), also a beak, bill (of birds), < ῥύζειν, growl, snarl; cf. L. *rugire*, roar, bray, rumble: see *rut*[2].] 1. A peculiar genus of *Scolopacidæ*, having the plumage highly variegated in both sexes, and the windpipe of the female singularly convoluted; the painted snipes. The female is also larger and handsomer than the male, to whom the duty of incubation is relegated. There are 4 widely distributed species—*R. capensis* of Africa, *R. bengalensis* of Asia, *R. australis* of Australia, and *R. semicollaris* of South America. More properly called by the prior name *Rostratula*.

2. A genus of dipterous insects. *Zetterstedt*, 1842.

rhynchæan (ring-kē'an), *a.* and *n.* [< *Rhynchæa* + *-an*.] I. *a.* In *ornith.*, pertaining to the genus *Rhynchæa*.

II. *n.* A snipe of the genus *Rhynchæa*.

Also *rhynchean*.

Rhynchæna (ring-kē'nä), *n.* An emended form of *Rhynchæa*. *Gloger*, 1849.

Rhynchænus (ring-kē'nus), *n.* [NL. (Fabricius, 1801), < Gr. ῥύγχαινα, with a large snout: see *Rhynchæa*.] A genus of coleopterous insects, belonging to the family of snout-beetles or *Curculionidæ*, having twelve-jointed antennæ.

Rhynchaspis (ring-kas'pis), *n.* [NL., < Gr. ῥύγχος, snout, + ἀσπίς, a shield.] A genus of *Anatidæ*; the shovelers: same as *Spatula*. *Leach*, 1824.

Rhynchea, *n.* See *Rhynchæa*.

rhynchean, *a.* and *n.* See *rhynchæan*.

Rhyncheta (ring-kē'tä), *n.* [NL., for **Rhynchochæta*, < Gr. ῥύγχος, snout, + χαίτη, mane, cilium.] The typical genus of *Rhynchetidæ*, containing free naked forms with only one tentacle, as *R. cyclopum*, an epizoic species.

Rhynchetidæ (ring-ket'i-dē), *n. pl.* [NL., < *Rhyncheta* + *-idæ*.] A family of suctorial tentaculiferous infusorians, represented by the genera *Rhyncheta* and *Urnula*, illoricate or loricate, with one or two tentacles and of parasitic habit.

Rhynchites (ring-kī'tēz), *n.* [NL. (Herbst, 1796), < Gr. ῥύγχος, snout.] A genus of weevils, typical of the family *Rhynchitidæ*, having the pygidium exposed and the elytra with striæ of punctures. It is a large and wide-spread genus, comprising about 75 species, and represented in all parts of the world except in Polynesia. They are of a coppery-bronze, bluish, or greenish color, and are found upon the flowers and leaves of shrubs. Thirteen species are known in the United States. *R. bacchus* is a handsome European species, which does great damage to the vine.

Rhynchitidæ (ring-kit'i-dē), *n. pl.* [NL. (Le Conte, 1874), < *Rhynchites* + *-idæ*.] A family of rhynchophorous beetles or weevils, having the labrum wanting and the mandibles flat and toothed on inner and outer sides. It is a small but rather widely distributed group.

Rhynchobdella[1] (ring-kob-del'ä), *n.* [NL. (Bloch and Schneider, 1801), < Gr. ῥύγχος, snout, + βδέλλα, leech.] A genus of opisthomous fishes, typical of the family *Rhynchobdelloidei*.

Rhynchobdella[2] (ring-kob-del'ä), *n. pl.* [NL., < Gr. ῥύγχος, snout, + βδέλλα, leech.] One of two orders of *Hirudinea*, contrasting with *Gnathobdella*: so named in some systems when the *Hirudinea* are raised to the rank of a class.

Rhynchobdelloidei (ring"kob-de-loi'dē-ī), *n. pl.* [NL., < *Rhynchobdella*[1] + *-oidei*.] A family of opisthomous fishes, typified by the genus *Rhynchobdella*: same as *Mastacembelidæ*.

Rhynchocephala (ring-kō-sef'a-lä), *n. pl.* [NL. (Goldfuss, 1820), < Gr. ῥύγχος, snout, + κεφαλή, head.] 1†. A family of abdominal fishes having a produced snout, including *Centriscus*, *Mormyrus*, and *Fistularia*.—2. In *herpet.*, same as *Rhynchocephalia*.

Rhynchocephalia (ring"kō-se-fā'li-ä), *n. pl.* [NL., < Gr. ῥύγχος, snout, + κεφαλή, head.] An order of *Reptilia*, having the skull monimostylic and cionocranial (with fixed quadrate bone and a columella), united mandibular rami, amphicœlian vertebræ, and no organs of copulation: named by Günther in 1867 from the genus *Rhynchocephalus* (or *Hatteria* or *Sphenodon*). See cut under *Hatteria*.

rhynchocephalian (ring"kō-se-fā'li-an), *a.* and *n.* [< *Rhynchocephalia* + *-an*.] I. *a.* Pertaining to the *Rhynchocephalia*, or having their characters: as, a *rhynchocephalian* type of structure; a *rhynchocephalian* lizard.

II. *n.* A member of the *Rhynchocephalia*.

rhynchocephalous (ring-kō-sef'a-lus), *a.* Same as *rhynchocephalian*.

Rhynchoceti (ring-kō-sē'tī), *n. pl.* [NL., pl. of *Rhynchocetus*, q. v.] The ziphioid whales: so called from the genus *Rhynchocetus*. See *Ziphiidæ*.

Rhynchocetus (ring-kō-sē'tus), *n.* [NL. (Eschricht, 1849), < Gr. ῥύγχος, snout, + κῆτος, a whale: see *cetaceous*.] A genus of odontocete cetaceans; the toothed whales. See *Ziphius*.

Rhynchocœla (ring-kō-sē'lä), *n. pl.* [NL., < Gr. ῥύγχος, snout, + κοῖλος, hollow.] A group of proctuchous turbellarians, consisting of the nemerteans, and including all the *Proctucha* excepting the lowest forms called *Arhynchia*. The name was contrasted with *Dendrocœla* and *Rhabdocœla* when the nemerteans were included under *Turbellaria*, from which they are now generally excluded. See also figure of *Tetrastemma* under *Proctucha*, and cut under *Pilidium*.

Fore End of Everted Frontal Proboscis of *Tetrastemma*, one of the *Rhynchocœla*, showing the principal chitinous style and the reserve stylets.

rhynchocœlan (ring-kō-sē'lan), *a.* and *n.* [< *Rhynchocœla* + *-an*.] I. *a.* Of or pertaining to the *Rhynchocœla*; nemertean.

II. *n.* A member of the *Rhynchocœla*; a nemertean.

rhynchocœle (ring'kō-sēl), *a.* Of or pertaining to the *Rhynchocœla*; nemertean.

rhynchocœlous (ring-kō-sē'lus), *a.* Same as *rhynchocœlan*.

Rhynchocyon (ring-kos'i-on), *n.* [NL. (W. Peters, 1847), < Gr. ῥύγχος, snout, + κύων, dog.] The typical genus of *Rhynchocyonidæ*. There are several species, which share with the macroscelidans the name *elephant-shrew*. *R. cernei* of Mozambique is about 8 inches long without the rat-like tail. *R. petersi* is another example.

Rhynchocyon petersi.

Rhynchocyonidæ (ring"kō-si-on'i-dē), *n. pl.* [NL., < *Rhynchocyon* + *-idæ*.] A family of small saltatorial insectivorous mammals of eastern Africa, typified by the genus *Rhynchocyon*. They are closely related to *Macroscelididæ*, but differ in having the ulna distinct from the radius, the skull broad between the orbits, distinct postorbital processes, all the feet four-toed, and the teeth thirty-six or thirty-four. The teeth are, in each half-jaw, 1 or no incisors above and 3 below, 1 canine, 3 premolars, and 3 molars above and below.

rhynchodont (ring'kō-dont), *a.* [< Gr. ῥύγχος, snout, + ὀδούς (ὀδοντ-) = E. *tooth*.] In *ornith.*, having the beak toothed, as a falcon.

Rhynchoflagellata (ring-kō-flaj-e-lā'tä), *n. pl.* [NL., neut. pl. of *rhynchoflagellatus*: see *rhynchoflagellate*.] Lankester's name of the *Noctilucidæ*, regarded as the fourth class of corticate protozoans: so named from the large beak-like flagellum. See cut under *Noctiluca*. *Encyc. Brit.*, XIX. 860.

rhynchoflagellate (ring-kō-flaj'e-lāt), *a.* [< Gr. ῥύγχος, snout, + NL. *flagellum*: see *flagellate*[1].] Having a flagellum like a snout; of or pertaining to the *Rhynchoflagellata*.

rhyncholite (ring'kō-līt), *n.* [< Gr. ῥύγχος, snout, beak, + λίθος, a stone.] The fossil beak of a tetrabranchiate cephalopod. Several pseudogenera have been based upon these beaks, as *Palæoteuthis* and *Rhyncholeuthis* of D'Orbigny, and *Conchorhynchus* of De Blainville.

Rhyncholophidæ (ring-kō-lof'i-dē), *n. pl.* [NL., < *Rhyncholophus* + *-idæ*.] A family of arachnidans. *Koch*.

Rhyncholophus (ring-kol'ō-fus), *n.* [NL., < Gr. ῥύγχος, snout, + λόφος, crest.] The typical genus of *Rhyncholophidæ*.

Rhynchonella (ring-kō-nel'ä), *n.* [NL., < Gr. ῥύγχος, snout, beak, + *-on-* + dim. suffix *-ella*.] The typical genus of the family *Rhynchonellidæ*. It is characterized by an acutely beaked trigonal shell, whose dorsal valve is elevated in front and depressed at the sides, the ventral valve being flattened or hollowed toward the middle, the hinge-plates supporting two slender curved lamellæ, and the dental plates diverging. Six living species and a number of fossil ones represent the genus, which was founded by Fischer-Waldheim in 1809. *R. psittacea* is a common North Atlantic species. See also cut under *brachial*.

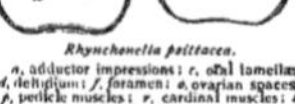

Rhynchonella psittacea.

a, adductor impressions; *c*, oral lamellæ; *d*, deltidium; *f*, foramen; *o*, ovarian spaces; *p*, pedicle muscles; *r*, cardinal muscles; *s*, septum; *t*, teeth; *t'*, sockets.

rhynchonella-bed (ring-kō-nel'ä-bed), *n.* Any bed of rock containing a large proportion of specimens of the genus *Rhynchonella*: for example, a bed in the Middle Lias in Lincolnshire, England; a bed in the Middle Chalk, etc.

Rhynchonellidæ (ring-kō-nel'i-dē), *n. pl.* [NL., < *Rhynchonella* + *-idæ*.] A family of arthropomatous brachiopods. They have the brachial appendages flexible and spirally coiled toward the center of the shell, supported only at the base by a pair of short-curved shelly processes; the valves more or less trigonal; the foramen beneath a usually produced beak, completed by a deltidium; and the shell-substance fibrous and impunctate. They first appear in the Silurian, and continue to the present time.

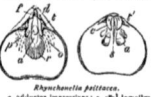

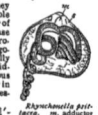

Rhynchonella psittacea. *m*, adductor muscles; *s*, sockets.

rhynchonelloid (ring-kō-nel'oid), *a.* [< *Rhynchonella* + *-oid*.] Of or relating to the *Rhynchonellidæ*.

Rhynchonycteris (ring-kō-nik'te-ris), *n.* [NL. (W. Peters, 1867), < Gr. ῥύγχος, snout, + νυκτερίς, a bat: see *Nycteris*.] A genus of emballonurine bats with prolonged snout, containing one South and Central American species, *R. naso*.

Rhynchophora (ring-kof'ō-rä), *n. pl.* [NL., neut. pl. of *rhynchophorus*: see *rhynchophorous*.] A section of tetramerous coleopterous insects, characterized by the (usual) prolongation of the head into a snout or proboscis (whence the name); the weevils, curculios, or snout-beetles. In Latreille's classification (1807), the *Rhynchophora* were the first family of the *Coleoptera tetramera*. They have the palpi typically rigid, without distinct palpariæ, the maxillary four-jointed and the labial three-jointed; labrum typically absent; gular sutures confluent on the median line; prosternum cut off behind by the epimera, and prosternal sutures wanting; and the epipleuræ of the elytra generally wanting. The characteristic beak or rostrum varies from a mere vestige in some of these insects to three times the length of the body. The antennæ are generally elbowed or geniculate, with the basal joint or scape received into a groove or scrobe. The larvæ are legless grubs; some spin a cocoon in which to pupate. This suborder is divided into 3 series, and contains 13 families. The species are all vegetable-feeders except *Brachytarsus*, which is said to feed on bark-lice. They are very numerous, being estimated at 30,000, and many are among the most injurious insects to farm, garden, and orchard. See also cuts under *Anthonomus*, *Balaninus*, *Brenthus*, *Calandra*, *Conotrachelus*, *diamond-beetle*, *Epicærus*, *Pissodes*, and *plum-gouger*.

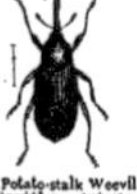

Potato-stalk Weevil (*Baridius trinotatus*). (Line shows natural size.)

rhynchophoran (ring-kof'ō-ran), *a.* and *n.* I. *a.* Of or belonging to the *Rhynchophora*; rhynchophorous.

II. *n.* A member of the *Rhynchophora*; a rhynchophore.

rhynchophore (ring'kō-fōr), *n.* Same as *rhynchophoran*.

rhynchophorous (ring-kof'ō-rus), *a.* [< NL. *rhynchophorus*, < Gr. ῥύγχος, snout, + -φόρος, < φέρειν = E. *bear*[1].] Having a beak or proboscis, as a weevil or curculio; rhynchophoran: as, a *rhynchophorous* coleopter.

Rhynchophorus (ring-kof'ō-rus), *n.* [NL.: see *rhynchophorous*.] A genus of weevils, of the family *Curculionidæ*, giving name to the order *Rhynchophora*.

Rhynchopinæ (ring-kō-pī'nē), *n. pl.* [NL., < *Rhynchops* + *-inæ*.] A subfamily of *Laridæ*, typified by the genus *Rhynchops*; the skimmers or scissorbills. Also *Rhynchopsinæ*, and, as a family, *Rhynchopidæ*.

Rhynchoprion† (ring-kop'ri-on), *n.* [NL., < Gr. ῥύγχος, snout, + πρίων, saw.] 1. A genus of ticks, of the family *Ixodidæ*. *Herman*, 1804.—2. A genus of fleas, containing the chigoe: same as *Sarcopsylla*. *Oken*, 1815. Also *Rhyncoprion*.

Rhynchops (ring'kops), *n.* [NL. (Linnæus, in the form *Rynchops*); also *Ryncops*, *Rhyncops* (also *Rhynchopsalia*, orig. in the corrupt form *Rygchopsalia*, also *Rhygchopsalia*), < Gr. ῥύγχος, snout, + ὤψ (ὠπός), eye, face.] The only genus of *Rhynchopinæ*; the skimmers or scissorbills. These birds are closely related to the terns or sea-swallows, *Sterninæ*, except in the extraordinary conformation of the beak, which is hypognathous, with the under mandible longer than the upper one, compressed like a knife-blade in most of its length, with the upper edge as sharp as the under, and the end obtuse. The upper mandible is less compressed, with light spongy tissue within like a toucan's, and freely movable by means of an elastic hinge at the forehead. The tongue is very short, and there are cranial peculiarities, conformable to the shape of the mandibles: thus, the lower jaw-bone has the shape of a

Black Skimmer (*Rhynchops nigra*).

short-handled pitchfork. There are 3 species, *R. nigra* of America, and *R. flavirostris* and *R. albicollis* of Asia. See *skimmer*. Also called *Anisorhamphus*.

Rhynchopsitta (ring-kop-sit'ạ̈), *n.* [NL. (Bonaparte, 1854), < Gr. ῥύγχος, snout, + ψιττα(κός), a parrot.] A Mexican genus of *Psittacidæ*; the beaked parrots. The thick-billed parrot is *R. pachyrhyncha*, found on or near the Mexican border of the United States, probably to be added to the fauna of the latter.

rhynchosaurian (ring-kọ̄-sâ'ri-an), *a.* and *n.* I. *a.* Pertaining to the genus *Rhynchosaurus*.

II. *n.* A member of the *Rhynchosauridæ*.

Rhynchosauridæ (ring-kọ̄-sâ'ri-dē), *n. pl.* [NL., < *Rhynchosaurus* + *-idæ*.] A family of fossil rhynchocephalian reptiles, typified by the genus *Rhynchosaurus*.

Rhynchosaurus (ring-kọ̄-sâ'rus), *n.* [NL. (Owen), < Gr. ῥύγχος, snout, + σαῦρος, lizard.] A genus of fossil reptiles, discovered in the New Red Sandstone of Warwickshire, England, having edentulous jaws with distinct produced premaxillaries. The species is *R. articeps*.

Rhynchosia (ring-kō'si-ạ̈), *n.* [NL. (Loureiro, 1790), named from the keel-petals; irreg. < Gr. ῥύγχος, snout.] A genus of leguminous plants, of the tribe *Phaseoleæ* and subtribe *Cajaneæ*. It is characterized by its two ovules with central funiculus, by its compressed and often falcate pod, and by papilionaceous flowers with beardless style and terminal stigma. There are about 82 species, natives of warm regions, with some extratropical species in North America and South Africa. They are herbs or undershrubs, usually twining or prostrate. They bear compound resinous-dotted leaves of three leaflets, with ovate or lanceolate stipules, and sometimes with additional minute bristle-shaped stipels. The flowers are yellow, rarely purple, often with brown stripes on the keel, and are borne singly or in pairs along axillary racemes. *R. phaseoloides* of tropical America, a high-climbing vine, has the seeds black with a scarlet-yellow ring around the hilum, and from the use made of them is named *Mexican rosary-plant*. This and other species in the West Indies are included under the name *red bead-vine*. *R. minima*, a low twining tropical weed of both hemispheres, reaching into the United States, has the West Indian name of *wart-herb*.

Rhynchospora (ring-kos'pọ̄-rạ̈), *n.* [NL. (Vahl, 1806), < Gr. ῥύγχος, snout, beak, + σπόρος, seed.] A genus of sedge-like plants, known as *beak-rush* or *beak-sedge*, belonging to the order *Cyperaceæ*, type of the tribe *Rhynchosporeæ*. It is characterized by commonly narrow or acuminate spikelets in many and close clusters, which are terminal or apparently axillary; by an undivided or two-cleft style; and by a nut beaked at its top by the dilated and persistent base of the style. There are about 200 species, widely scattered through tropical and subtropical regions, especially in America, where many extend into the United States; in the Old World only two similarly extend into Europe and Asiatic Russia. They are annual or perennial, slender or robust, erect or rarely diffuse or floating, often with leafy stems. The spikelets are disposed in irregular umbels or sessile heads, which are clustered, corymbed, or panicled. Most of the species of tropical America (*Haplostyleæ*) have capitate spikelets, commonly one-seeded, and a long undivided slender style; the typical species (*Dichostyleæ*) have two- to four-seeded polymorphous spikelets, and a style deeply divided into two branches. *R. corniculata*, a species of the interior United States, from 3 to 6 feet high, has the special name of *horned rush*. A slender species, *R. Vahliana*, of the warm parts of America, has in the West Indies the name of *star-grass*. See cut under *rostrate*.

Rhynchosporeæ (ring-kō-spō'rē-ē), *n. pl.* [NL. (Nees von Esenbeck, 1834), < *Rhynchospora* + *-eæ*.] A tribe of monocotyledonous plants of the order *Cyperaceæ*, characterized by fertile flowers with both stamens and pistils, most often only one or two in a spikelet, the two or more inferior glumes being empty. The perianth is here absent, or represented either by bristles or flat and filiform scales under the ovary. It includes 21 genera, of which *Rhynchospora* (the type), *Schœnus*, *Cladium*, and *Remirea* are widely distributed, and the others are chiefly small genera of the southern hemisphere, especially Australian.

Rhynchostoma† (ring-kos'tọ̄-mạ̈), *n. pl.* [NL., < Gr. ῥύγχος, snout, + στόμα, mouth.] In Latreille's classification, the fifth tribe of stenelytrous heteromerous beetles, having the head prolonged in a flattened rostrum, with antennæ at its base and in front of the eyes, which are entire. Also *Rhyncostoma*.

Rhynchota (ring-kō'tạ̈), *n. pl.* [NL.: see *rhynchote*.] An order of *Insecta*, or true hexapod insects, named by Fabricius in the form *Rhyngota*, otherwise called *Hemiptera*.

rhynchote (ring'kōt), *a.* [< NL. *rhynchotus*, < Gr. ῥύγχος, snout, beak: see *Rhynchæa*.] Beaked, as a hemipterous insect; specifically, relating or belonging to the *Rhynchota*; hemipterous.

Rhynchoteuthis† (ring-kọ̄-tū'this), *n.* [NL., < Gr. ῥύγχος, snout, + τευθίς, a cuttlefish.] A pseudogenus of fossil cephalopods, based by D'Orbigny on certain rhyncholites.

rhynchotous (ring-kō'tus), *a.* [< *rhynchote*, *Rhynchota*, + *-ous*.] Of or pertaining to the *Rhynchota*; hemipterous.

Descriptions will be appended relating to the curious organs possessed by some species, and other subjects connected with the economy of this interesting but difficult group of *Rhynchotous* insects. *Nature*, XLI. 302.

Rhynchotus (ring-kō'tus), *n.* [NL. (Spix, 1825), < Gr. ῥύγχος, snout, beak: see *rhynchote*.] A genus of South American tinamous of the family *Tinamidæ*, containing a number of spe-

Tinamou (*Rhynchotus rufescens*).

cies of large size, with variegated plumage, short soft tail-feathers, well-developed hind toe, and rather long bill. One of the best-known is the ynambu, *R. rufescens*, among those known to South American sportsmen as *partridges*.

rhyncho-. For words so beginning, see *rhyncho-*.

rhyne (rin), *n.* The best quality of Russian hemp.

Rhyngota (ring-gō'tạ̈), *n. pl.* The original improper form of the word *Rhynchota*. *Fabricius*, 1766.

rhyolite (rī'ọ̄-līt), *n.* [Irreg. < Gr. ῥύαξ, a stream, esp. a stream of lava from a volcano (< ῥεῖν, flow: see *rheum*[1]), + λίθος, a stone.] The name given by Richthofen to certain rocks occurring in Hungary which resemble trachyte, but are distinguished from it by the presence of quartz as an essential ingredient, and also by a great variety of texture, showing more distinctly than rocks usually do that the material had flowed while in a viscous state. The name *liparite* was given later by J. Roth to rocks of similar character occurring on the Lipari Islands. Non-vitreous rocks of this kind had previously been called *trachytic porphyries*, and they have also been designated as *quartz-trachytes*. Later Richthofen proposed the name of *nevadite* (also called *granitic rhyolite* by Zirkel) for the variety in which large macroscopic ingredients, like quartz and sanidine, predominated over the ground-mass, retaining the name *liparite*, and applying it to the varieties having a porphyritic or felsitic structure, and limiting the term *rhyolite* to the lithoidal and hyaline modifications, such as obsidian, pumice-stone, and perlite; and nearly the same nomenclature was adopted by Zirkel. Rosenbusch recognizes as structural types of the rhyolitic rocks nevadite, liparite proper, and glassy liparite, remarking that these names correspond closely to Zirkel's nevadite, rhyolite, and glassy rhyolite respectively. These rocks are abundant in various countries, especially in the Cordilleran region, and are interesting from their connection and association with certain important metalliferous deposits. See cut under *axiolite*.

rhyolitic (rī-ọ̄-lit'ik), *a.* [< *rhyolite* + *-ic*.] Composed of or related to rhyolite. *Quart. Jour. Geol. Soc.*, XLV. 198.

rhyparographic (rip'ạ-rọ̄-graf'ik), *a.* [< *rhyparograph-y* + *-ic*.] Pertaining to or involved in rhyparography; dealing with commonplace or low subjects.

She takes a sort of naturalist delight in describing the most sordid and shabbiest features of the least attractive kind of English middle-class life, and in doing this never misses a *rhyparographic* touch when she can introduce one. *The Academy*, April 3, 1886, p. 234.

rhyparography (rip-ạ-rog'rạ-fi), *n.* [= F. *rhyparographie*; < L. *rhyparographos*, < Gr. ῥυπαρογράφος, a painter of low or mean subjects, < ῥυπαρός, foul, dirty, mean, + γράφειν, write.] Genre or still-life pictures, including all subjects of a trivial, coarse, or common kind: so called in contempt. *Fairholt.*

Rhyphidæ (rif'i-dē), *n. pl.* [NL., < *Rhyphus* + *-idæ*.] A family of nematocerous dipterous insects, based on the genus *Rhyphus*, allied to the fungus-gnats of the family *Mycetophilidæ*, but differing from them and from all other nematocerous flies by their peculiar wing-venation, the second longitudinal vein having a sigmoid curve. Only the typical genus is known. They are called *false crane-flies*.

Rhyphus (rī'fus), *n.* [NL. (Latreille, 1804).] A genus of gnats, typical of the family *Rhyphidæ*. Five European and the same number of North American species are known, two of them, *R. fenestralis* and *R. punctatus*, being common to both hemispheres.

Rhypophaga (rī-pof'ạ-gạ̈), *n. pl.* [NL., < MGr. ῥυποφάγος, dirt-eating, < Gr. ῥύπος, dirt, filth, + φαγεῖν, eat.] In some systems, a legion of predaceous water-beetles. Also *Rypophaga*.

rhypophagous (rī-pof'ạ-gus), *a.* Of or pertaining to the *Rhypophaga*.

Rhypticidæ (rip-tis'i-dē), *n. pl.* [NL., < *Rhypticus* + *-idæ*.] A family of acanthopterygian fishes, typified by the genus *Rhypticus*; the soapfishes. They have an oblong compressed body with smooth scales, dorsal fin with only two or three spines, and anal unarmed. They are inhabitants of the warm American seas. Also *Rhypticinæ*, as a subfamily of *Serranidæ*.

Rhypticinæ (rip-ti-sī'nē), *n. pl.* [NL., < *Rhypticus* + *-inæ*.] The *Rhypticidæ* as a subfamily of *Serranidæ*.

Rhypticus (rip'ti-kus), *n.* [NL. (Cuvier, 1829), also *Rypticus*, < Gr. ῥυπτικός, fit for cleansing from dirt, < ῥύπτειν, cleanse from dirt, < ῥύπος, dirt, filth.] In *ichth.*, a genus of serranoid fishes, having only two or three dorsal spines. They are known as the *soap-fishes*, from their soapy skins. Some have three dorsal spines, as *R. arenatus*. Those

Soap-fish (*Rhypticus arenatus*).

having only two dorsal spines are sometimes placed in a different genus, *Promicropterus*; they are such as *R. decoratus*, *R. maculatus*, and *R. pituitosus*, found along the Atlantic coast of the United States.

rhysimeter (rī-sim'e-tėr), *n.* [< Gr. ῥύσις, a flow, flowing, stream (< ῥεῖν, flow: see *rheum*[1]), + μέτρον, a measure.] An instrument for measuring the velocity of fluids or the speed of ships. It presents the open end of a tube to the impact of the current, which raises a column of mercury in a graduated tube.

Rhysodes, Rhysodidæ. See *Rhyssodes*, etc.

Rhyssa (ris'ạ̈), *n.* [NL. (Gravenhorst, 1829), < Gr. ῥυσσός, prop. ῥυσός, drawn up, wrinkled, < *ῥύειν, ἐρύειν, draw.] A notable genus of long-tailed ichneumon-flies of the subfamily *Pimplinæ*. They are of large size, and the females are furnished with very long ovipositors, with which they pierce to considerable depth the trunks of trees, in order to lay their eggs in the tunnels of wood-boring larvæ, upon which their larvæ are external parasites. A number of European and North American species are known. The most prominent American long-stings, formerly placed in this genus, are now considered to belong to *Thalessa*.

Rhyssodes (ri-sō'dēz), *n.* [NL. (Dalman, 1823), < Gr. ῥυσσώδης, prop. ῥυσώδης, wrinkled-looking, < ῥυσσός, prop. ῥυσός, wrinkled (see *Rhyssa*), + εἶδος, form.] A genus of clavicorn beetles, typical of the family *Rhyssodidæ*, having the eyes lateral, rounded, and distinctly granulated. Although only 9 species are known, they are found in India, South Africa, North and South America, and Europe. Also spelled *Rhysodes*.

Rhyssodidæ (ri-sod'i-dē), *n. pl.* [NL. (Erichson, 1845), < *Rhyssodes* + *-idæ*.] A small family of clavicorn beetles, typified by the genus *Rhyssodes*. They have the first three ventral abdominal segments connate, the tarsi five-jointed, the last joint moderate in length, and the claws not large. They live under bark, and to some extent resemble the *Carabidæ*. Only 3 genera of very few species are known. Also spelled *Rhysodidæ*.

rhyta, *n.* Plural of *rhyton*.

rhythm (riᴛʜm or rithm), *n.* [Formerly also *rhithm*, *rithme*; < OF. *rithme*, *rhythme*, F. *rhythme* = Sp. It. *ritmo* = Pg. *rhythmo*, < L. *rhythmus*, ML. also *rhithmus*, *ritmus*, rhythm, < Gr. ῥυθμός, Ionic ῥυσμός, measured motion, time, measure, proportion, rhythm, a metrical measure or foot (cf. ῥύσις, a stream, ῥύμα, a stream, ῥυτός, flowing), < ῥεῖν (√ ῥευ, ῥυ), flow:

see *rheum*1. The word *rhythm*, variously spelled, was formerly much confused with *rime*, which thus came to be spelled *rhyme*: see *rime*1.] 1. Movement in time, characterized by equality of measures and by alternation of tension (stress) and relaxation. The word *rhythm* (ῥυθμός) means 'flow,' and, by development from this sense, 'uniform movement, perceptible as such, and accordingly divisible into measures, the measures marked by the recurrence of stress.' Examples of rhythm, in its stricter sense, in nature are respiration and the beating of the pulse, also the effect produced on the ear by the steady dripping of water. The three arts regulated by rhythm are music, metrics, and, according to the ancients, orchestic, or the art of rhythmical bodily movement. Rhythm in language is *meter*. The term was further extended to sculpture, etc. (compare def. 5), as when a writer speaks of "the *rhythm* of Myron's Discobolus."

We have here the three principal applications of *rhythm*, three principal domains in which *rhythm* manifests its nature and power—dancing, music, poetry.
J. Hadley, Essays, p. 81.

2. In *music*: (*a*) That characteristic of all composition which depends on the regular succession of relatively heavy and light accents, beats, or pulses; accentual structure in the abstract. Strictly speaking, the organic partition of a piece into equal measures, and also the distribution of long and short tones within measures, in addition to the formation of larger divisions, like phrases, sections, etc., are matters of *meter*, because they have to do primarily with time-values; while everything that concerns accent and accentual groups is more fitly arranged under *rhythm*. But this distinction is often ignored or denied, *meter* and *rhythm* being used either indiscriminately, or even in exactly the reverse sense to the above. (See *meter*2.) In any case, in musical analysis, *rhythm* and *meter* are coördinate with *melody* and *harmony* in the abstract sense. (*b*) A particular accentual pattern typical of all the measures of a given piece or movement. Such patterns or rhythms are made up of accents, beats, or pulses of equal duration, but of different dynamic importance. A rhythm of two beats to the measure is often called a two-part rhythm; one of three beats, a three-part rhythm, etc. Almost all rhythms may be reduced to two principal kinds: *duple* or two-part, consisting of a heavy accent or beat and a light one (often called *march rhythm* or *common time*); and *triple* or three-part, consisting of a heavy accent or beat and two light ones (*waltz rhythm*). The accent or beat with which a rhythm begins is called the *primary accent*. Its place is marked in written music by a bar, and in conducting by a down-beat. Each part of a rhythm may be made compound by subdivision into two or three secondary parts, which form duple or triple groups within themselves. Thus, if each part of a duple rhythm is replaced by duple secondary groups, a four-part or *quadruple* rhythm is produced, or if by triple secondary groups, a six-part or *sextuple* rhythm (first variety). By a similar process of replacement, from a triple rhythm may be derived a six-part or *sextuple* rhythm (second variety) and a nine-part or *nonuple* rhythm; and from a quadruple rhythm, an eight-part or *octuple* rhythm and a twelve-part or *dodecuple* rhythm. The constituent groups of compound rhythms always retain the relative importance of the simple part from which they are derived. The above eight rhythms are all that are ordinarily used, though quintuple, septuple, decuple, and other rhythms occasionally appear, usually in isolated groups of tones. (See *quintuplet, septuplet, decimole*, etc.) In ancient music a measure did not necessarily begin with a beat, and the rhythms were the same as those indicated in metrics below (3 (*b*)). While all music is constructed on these patterns, the pattern is not always shown in the tones or chords as sounded. The time-value of one or more parts may be supplied by a silence or rest. A single tone or chord may be made to include two or more parts, especially in compound rhythms; and thus every possible combination of long and short tones occurs within each rhythm. When a weak accent is thus made to coalesce with a following heavier one, especially if the latter is a primary accent, the rhythm is syncopated. (See *syncopation*.) The regularity of a rhythm is maintained by counting or beating time—that is, marking each part by a word or motion, with a suitable difference of emphasis between the heavy and the light accents. In written music the rhythm of a piece or movement is indicated at the outset by the *rhythmical signature* (which see, under *rhythmical*). The speed of a rhythm in a given case—that is, the time-value assigned to each measure and part—is called its *tempo* (which see). Rhythm and tempo are wholly independent in the abstract, but the tempo of a given piece is approximately fixed. Although regularity and definiteness of rhythm are characteristic of all music, various influences tend to modify and obliterate its form. The metrical patterns of successive measures often differ widely from the typical rhythmic pattern and from each other. Except in very rudimentary music, purely rhythmic accents are constantly superseded by accents belonging to figures and phrases—that is, to units of higher degree than measures. Indeed, in advancing from rudimentary to highly artistic music, rhythmic patterns become less and less apparent, though furnishing everywhere a firm and continuous accentual groundwork. Rhythm is often loosely called *time*. Also called *proportion*. 3. In *metrics*: (*a*) Succession of times divisible into measures with theses and arses; metrical movement. Theoretically, all spoken language possesses rhythm, but the name is distinctively given to that which is not too complicated to be easily perceived as such. Rhythm, so limited, is indispensable in metrical composition, but is regarded as inappropriate in prose, except in elevated style and in oratory, and even in these only in the way of vague suggestion, unless in certain passages of special character.

Rhythm . . . is of course governed by law, but it is a law which transcends in subtlety the conscious art of the metricist, and is only caught by the poet in his most inspired moods.
Encyc. Brit., XIX. 262.

(*b*) A particular kind or variety of metrical movement, expressed by a succession of a particular kind or variety of feet: as, iambic *rhythm*; dactylic *rhythm*. In ancient metrics, rhythm is *isorrhythmic*, *direct*, or *dochmiac* (see the phrases below), or belongs to a subdivision of these. (*c*) A measure or foot. (*d*) Verse, as opposed to prose. See *rime*1.—4. In *physics* and *physiol.*, succession of alternate and opposite or correlative states.

The longer astronomic *rhythm*, known as the earth's annual revolution, causes corresponding *rhythms* in vegetable and animal life: witness the blossoming and leafing of plants in the spring, the revival of insect activity at the same season, the periodic flights of migratory birds, the hybernating sleep of many vertebrates, and the thickened coats or the altered habits of others that do not hybernate.
J. Fiske, Cosmic Philos., I. 307.

5. In the *graphic* and *plastic arts*, a proper relation and interdependence of parts with reference to each other and to an artistic whole.—**Ascending rhythm**. See *ascending*.—**Descending** or **falling rhythm**. See *descending*.—**Direct rhythm**, in *anc. metrics*, rhythm in which the number of times or moræ in the thesis of the foot differs from that in the arsis by one. Direct rhythm includes diplasic, hemiolic, and epitritic rhythm, these having a pedal ratio (proportion of moræ in arsis and thesis) of 1 to 2, 2 to 3, and 3 to 4 respectively: opposed to *dochmiac rhythm*.—**Dochmiac rhythm**, in *anc. metrics*, rhythm in which the number of times in the arsis differs from that in the thesis by more than one. Dochmiac rhythm in this wider sense includes *dochmiac rhythm* in the narrower sense (that is, the rhythm of the dochmius, which has a pedal ratio of 3 to 5), and triplasic *rhythm*, characterized by a pedal ratio of 1 to 3.—**Double rhythm**. Same as *duple rhythm*. See def. 2.—**Equal rhythm, isorrhythmic rhythm**, in *anc. metrics*, rhythm in which the number of times in the thesis and arsis is equal. Also called *dactylic rhythm*.—**Imperfect rhythm**. Same as *imperfect measure*. See *imperfect*.—**Oblique rhythm**. Same as *dochmiac rhythm*. =**Syn. 2.** *Melody, Harmony*, etc. See *euphony*.

rhythmer† (riᴛʜ′- or rith′mėr), *n*. [< *rhythm* + *-er*1.] A rimer; a poetaster.

One now scarce counted for a *rhythmer*, formerly admitted for a poet. *Fuller*. (*Imp. Dict.*)

rhythmic (rith′mik), *a*. and *n*. [= F. *rhythmique* = Pr. *rithmic, rithimic* = Sp. *rítmico* = Pg. *rhythmico* = It. *ritmico*, < ML. *rhythmicus*, rhythmic, in L. only as a noun, one versed in rhythm, < Gr. ῥυθμικός, pertaining to rhythm (as n., ἡ ῥυθμική, sc. τέχνη), < ῥυθμός, rhythm: see *rhythm*.] **I.** *a*. Same as *rhythmical*.

The working of the law whence springs
The *rhythmic* harmony of things.
Whittier, Questions of Life.

Rhythmic chorea, that form of chorea in which the movements take place at definite intervals.

II. *n*. Same as *rhythmics*.

The student of ancient *rhythmic* is not oppressed by the extent of his authorities. *J. Hadley*, Essays, p. 86.

rhythmical (rith′mi-kal), *a*. [< *rhythmic* + *-al*.] 1. Pertaining to rhythm in art, or to a succession of measures marked by regularly recurrent accents, beats, or pulses; noting any succession so marked; hence, musical, metrical, or poetic: as, the *rhythmical* movement of marching or of a dance.

Honest agitators have been moved, by passionate zeal for their several causes, to outbursts of *rhythmical* expression. *Stedman*, Vict. Poets, p. 29.

2. In *physics* and *physiol.*, pertaining to or constituting a succession of alternate and opposite or correlative states.

This *rhythmical* movement, impelling the filaments in an undeviating onward course, is greatly influenced by temperature and light. *W. B. Carpenter*, Micros., vi. § 246.

3. In *med.*, periodical.—4. In the *graphic* and *plastic arts*, properly proportioned or balanced.—**Rhythmical signature**, in *musical notation*, a sign placed at the beginning of a piece, after the key-signature, to indicate its rhythm or time. (Also called *time-signature*.) It consists of two numerals placed one above the other on each staff, the upper numeral indicating the number of principal beats or pulses to the measure, and the lower the kind of note which in the given piece is assigned to each beat. (See *rhythm* and *note*1, 13.) Thus, $\frac{4}{4}$ indicates quadruple rhythm, four beats to the measure, each beat marked by a quarter-note, ♩, or its equivalent. Difference of rhythm is unfortunately not always indicated by difference of rhythmic signature; and difference of signature often means only an unessential difference of notes rather than of rhythm. Thus, duple rhythm may be marked either by $\frac{2}{1}$, $\frac{2}{2}$, $\frac{2}{4}$, $\frac{2}{8}$, or $\frac{4}{4}$; triple rhythm, by $\frac{3}{1}$, $\frac{3}{2}$, $\frac{3}{4}$, $\frac{3}{8}$, $\frac{3}{16}$; quadruple rhythm, by $\frac{4}{1}$, $\frac{4}{2}$, $\frac{4}{4}$, $\frac{4}{8}$; sextuple rhythm (first variety), by $\frac{6}{4}$, $\frac{6}{8}$; sextuple rhythm (second variety), by $\frac{3}{2}$, $\frac{3}{4}$, $\frac{3}{8}$; octuple rhythm, by $\frac{4}{2}$, $\frac{4}{4}$, $\frac{4}{8}$; nonuple rhythm, by $\frac{9}{8}$, $\frac{9}{16}$; dodecuple rhythm, by $\frac{12}{8}$. Most of the varieties of duple and quadruple signatures are often written simply C, common; when duple rhythm is to be distinguished from quadruple, this sign is changed to ₵, or the words *alla breve* are added. The rhythmical signature is not repeated on successive braces. A decided change of rhythm is marked by a new signature; but the isolated intrusion of a foreign rhythm, especially in a short melodic group, is usually marked by a curve and an inclosed numeral, as 3, 5. See *triplet, quartole, quintuplet*, etc.

rhythmicality (rith-mi-kal′i-ti), *n*. [< *rhythmical* + *-ity*.] Rhythmic property; the fact or property of being regulated by or exemplifying rhythm. *G. J. Romanes*, Jelly-fish, etc., p. 186.

rhythmically (rith′mi-kal-i), *adv*. In a rhythmical manner; with regularly recurrent accents of varying emphasis.

rhythmics (rith′miks), *n*. [Pl. of *rhythmic* (see *-ics*).] The science of rhythm and of rhythmical forms.

rhythming† (riᴛʜ′- or rith′ming), *a*. [Appar. < *rhythm*, used as a verb, + *-ing*2, but perhaps a mere variant spelling of *rhyming, riming*.] Riming.

Witness that impudent lie of the *rhythming* monk.
Fuller. (*Imp. Dict.*)

rhythmist (rith′mist), *n*. [< *rhythm* + *-ist*.] 1. One who composes in rhythm; a rhythmical composer.

I have a right to reaffirm, and to show by many illustrations, that he [Swinburne] is the most sovereign of *rhythmists*. *Stedman*, Vict. Poets, p. 381.

2. One versed in the theory of rhythm; a writer on the science of rhythmics.

rhythmize (rith′mīz), *v*. [< *rhythm* + *-ize*.] **I.** *trans*. To subject to rhythm; use in rhythmic composition: as, to *rhythmize* tones or words.

II. *intrans*. To observe rhythm; compose in rhythm. *Trans. Amer. Philol. Assoc.*, XVI. 100.

rhythmizomenon (rith-mi-zom′e-non), *n*.; pl. *rhythmizomena* (-nä). [< Gr. ῥυθμιζόμενον, that which is rhythmically treated, prop. neut. of pass. part. of ῥυθμίζειν, arrange, order, scan: see *rhythm*.] In *anc. rhythmics*, the material of rhythm; that which is rhythmically treated. Three rhythmizomena were recognized by ancient writers—tones as the rhythmizomenon of music, words as that of poetry, and bodily movements and attitudes as that of orchestic.

rhythmless (riᴛʜm′les), *a*. [< *rhythm* + *-less*.] Destitute of rhythm. *Coleridge*. (*Imp. Dict.*)

rhythmometer (rith-mom′e-tėr), *n*. [< Gr. ῥυθμός, rhythm, + μέτρον, measure.] A machine for marking rhythm for music; a metronome. *Mind*, XLI. 57.

rhythmopœia (rith-mọ-pē′yä), *n*. [NL., < Gr. ῥυθμοποιία, making of time or rhythm, < ῥυθμός, rhythm, + ποιεῖν, make.] The act of composing rhythmically; the art of rhythmic composition.

The fixing of 2 to 1 as the precise numerical relation was probably the work of *rhythmopœia*, or of *rhythmopœia* and melopœia together. *J. Hadley*, Essays, p. 264.

rhythmus (rith′mus), *n*. [L.] Same as *rhythm*.

rhytidoma (rī-tid′ọ-mä), *n*. [NL., < Gr. ῥυτίδωμα, the state of being wrinkled, < ῥυτιδοῦσθαι, be wrinkled, < ῥυτίς, a wrinkle, < *ῥύειν, ἐρύειν, draw.] In *bot.*, a formation of plates of cellular tissue within the liber or mesophlœum.

Rhytina (rī-tī′nä), *n*. [NL. (Steller), < Gr. ῥυτίς, a wrinkle, + *-ina*1.] The typical and only genus of the family *Rhytinidæ*, containing Steller's or the arctic sea-cow, *R. stelleri* or *R. gigas*, which has no teeth, but horny plates functioning as such. The head is small; the tail has lateral lobes; the fore limbs are small; the hide is very rugged; the cæcum is simple, and there are no pyloric cæca; the cervical vertebræ are 7, the dorsal 19, the lumbar and caudal 34 to 37, without any sacrum. See *sea-cow*. Also called *Stellerus* and *Nepus*.

Skull of Steller's Sea-cow (*Rhytina stelleri*).

Rhytinidæ (rī-tin′i-dē), *n. pl.* [NL., < *Rhytina* + *-idæ*.] A family of sirenians, typified by *Rhytina*, having no teeth, manducation being effected by large horny plates; the sea-cows.

rhyton (rī′ton), *n*.; pl. *rhyta* (-tä). [< Gr. ῥυτόν, a drinking-cup, < ῥεῖν, flow: see *rheum*1.] In *Gr. antiq.*, a type of drinking-vase, usually with one handle. In its usually curved form, pointed below, it corresponds to the primitive cup of horn. The lower part of the rhyton is generally molded into the form of a head of a man or, more often, of an animal, and is often pierced with a small hole through which the beverage was allowed to flow into the mouth.

Rhyton.

Rhyzæna (ri-zē'nä), *n.* [NL. (Illiger, 1811, in form *Ryzæna*), < Gr. ῥύζειν, growl, snarl.] A genus of viverrine quadrupeds; the suricates: synonymous with *Suricata*.

rhyzo-. For words beginning thus, see *rhizo-*.

ri (rē), *n.* [Jap., = Chinese *li*, mile.] A Japanese mile. It is divided into 36 cho, and is equal to about 2.45 English miles. See *cho*.

rial[1]†, *a.* Same as *real*[2].

rial[2]†, *n.* Same as *real*[3].

rial[3], *n.* See *ryal*.

riallyt, riallichet, *adv.* Middle English obsolete variants of *royally*. *Chaucer.*

rialtet, *n.* A Middle English form of *royalty*.

Rialto (ri-al'tō), *n.* [It., < *rio*, also *rivo*, brook, stream (= Sp. Pg. rio, < L. *rivus*, a stream, river: see *rivulet*), + *alto*, deep, high, < L. *altus*, deep, high: see *altitude*.] A bridge, noted in literature and art, over the Grand Canal in Venice.

> On the *Rialto* ev'ry night at twelve
> I take my evening's walk of meditation.
> *Otway*, Venice Preserved, I.

riancy (ri'an-si), *n.* [< *rian(t)* + *-cy*.] The state or character of being riant; cheerfulness; gaiety.

> The tone, in some parts, has more of *riancy*, even of levity, than we could have expected!
> *Carlyle*, Sartor Resartus, ii. 9.

riant (ri'ant), *a.* [< F. *riant* (< L. *riden(t-)s*), laughing, ppr. of *rire*, laugh, = Pr. *rire*, *rir* = Sp. *reir* = Pg. *rir* = It. *ridere*, < L. *ridere*, laugh: see *rident*.] Laughing; gay; smiling: as, a *riant* landscape.

> Goethe's childhood is throughout of *riant*, joyful character.
> *Carlyle*, Essays, Goethe's Works.

riata, *n.* See *reata*.

rib[1] (rib), *n.* [< ME. *rib*, *ribbe*, < AS. *ribb* = OFries. *rib*, *reb* = MD. *ribbe*, D. *rib* = MLG. LG. *ribbe* = OHG. *rippi*, *ribbi*, *ribi*, MHG. *rippe*, *ribe*, G. *rippe*, *riebe* (obs.) = Icel. *rif* = Sw. *ref* (in *ref-ben*, rib-bone, rib) = Dan. *rib* (*rib-ben*, rib-bone, rib) = Goth. **ribi* (not recorded); akin to OBulg. Russ. *rebro*, rib, and prob., as 'that which incloses or envelops,' to G. *rebe*, a tendril, vine (cf. OHG. *hirni-reba*, MHG. *hirnrebe*, that which envelops the brain, the skull).] **1.** In *anat.* and *zoöl.*, a costa; a pleurapophysis, with or without a hemapophysis; the pleurapophysial element of a vertebra, of whatever size, shape, or mode of connection with a vertebra. In ordinary language the term *rib* is restricted to one of the series of long slender bones which are movably articulated with or entirely disconnected from the vertebræ, occur in pairs, and extend to or toward the sternum or middle ventral line of the body. In many vertebrates such ribs are characteristic of or confined to the thoracic or dorsal region, and form, together with the corresponding vertebræ and with the sternum, a kind of bony cage for the thoracic viscera—the chest or thorax. Such ribs are called *thoracic* or *dorsal*, and are often the only free ribs an animal may possess, as is usually the case in mammals. In man there are twelve pairs of such ribs. The first of these articulates with the upper part of the side of the body of the first dorsal vertebra; the second to the ninth inclusive articulate at an intervertebral space, and consequently with two vertebræ apiece; the tenth, eleventh, and twelfth articulate with the single vertebra to which they correspond. The first to the tenth ribs articulate by their heads with bodies of vertebræ as above stated, and also by their shoulders with transverse processes, which latter articulations are lacking to the eleventh and twelfth ribs. The first seven ribs reach the sternum by means of costal cartilages, and are called *true ribs*; the last five ribs do not, and are called *false ribs*: of these last the first three join one another by means of their costal cartilages, while the last two are entirely free or "floating" at their ends. Only the bony part of a rib is a pleurapophysis; the gristly part, or costal cartilage, is a hemapophysis. Parts of a bony rib commonly distinguished are the *head* or *capitulum*, the *neck* or *cervix*, the *shoulder* or *tuberculum*, and the *shaft*. Most of the ribs are not only curved as a whole, but also somewhat bent at a point called the *angle*, and, moreover, twisted on their own axis. In man there are occasionally supernumerary cervical or lumbar ribs of ordinary character, that are extended from and freely jointed to their vertebræ; and all the human cervical vertebræ have rudimentary ribs ankylosed with their respective vertebræ, represented by that part of the transverse process which bounds the vertebrarterial foramen in front. Mammals have frequently more or fewer than twelve pairs of thoracic ribs. Ribs occurring in any part of the vertebral column are named from that part: as, *cervical*, *thoracic* or *dorsal*, *dorsolumbar*, *lumbar*, or *sacral* ribs. In birds and reptiles the number of ribs is extremely variable, and their situation may extend from head to tail. Frequently they are jointed in the middle, or at the point where in a mammal the bony part joins the cartilaginous. Some of them may be free or floating at the vertebral as well as at the sternal end. Some ribs in birds bear peculiar splint-bones called *uncinate processes*. (See cut under *epipleura*.) In chelonians the ribs are fixed, and consolidated with broad plate-like dermal bones to form the carapace. The greatest number of ribs is found in some serpents, which have more than two hundred pairs. In some fishes, ribs are apparently doubled in number by forking; this is the principal reason why the bones of a shad, for example, seem so numerous. See also cuts under *carapace* and *skeleton*.

Human Ribs, left side (rear view), the first, second, seventh, ninth, and twelfth shaded in detail, the others in outline—all without their costal cartilages.

> U't of his side he toc a *rib*,
> And made a wimman him ful sib,
> And heled him that side wel.
> *Genesis and Exodus* (E. E. T. S.), l. 227.

> Dainty bits
> Make rich the *ribs*, but bankrupt quite the wits.
> *Shak.*, L. L. L., i. 1. 27.

2. That which resembles a rib in use, position, etc.; a strip, band, or piece of anything when used as a support, or as a member of a framework or skeleton.

> Thirdly, in settyng on of your tether [a question may be asked], whether it be pared or drawen with a thicke *rybbe*, or a thinne *rybbe* (the *rybbe* is ye hard quill whiche deuydeth the fether).
> *Ascham*, Toxophilus, ii.

> We should have been in love with flames, and have thought the gridiron fairer than the spondæ, the *ribs* of a marital bed.
> *Jer. Taylor*, Holy Dying, iii. 9.

> He consulted to remove the whole wall by binding it about with *ribs* of iron and timber, to convey it into France.
> *Evelyn*, Diary, March 23, 1646.

Specifically—(*a*) Some part or organ of an animal like or likened to a rib; a costate or costiform process; a long narrow thickening of a surface; a ridge; a strip or stripe: as, (1) one of the veins or nerves of an insect's wing; (2) one of a set or series of parallel or radiating ridges on a shell; (3) one of the ciliated rays or ctenophores of a ctenophoran. (*b*) In *ship-building*, one of the bent timber or metallic bars which spring from the keel, and form or strengthen the side of the ship.

> How like the prodigal doth she return,
> With over-weather'd *ribs* and ragged sails!
> *Shak.*, M. of V., ii. 6. 18.

(*c*) In *arch.*: (1) In vaulting, a plain or variously molded and sculptured arch, properly, supporting a vault, or, in combination with other ribs, the filling of a groined vault. In pointed vaults the groins typically rest upon or are covered by ribs; and secondary ribs connecting the main ribs, especially in late and less pure designs, are sometimes applied, usually as a mere decoration, to the plain surfaces of the vaulting-cells. The three main vaulting-ribs are designated as (α) groin-ribs or ogives, (β) doubleaux, and (γ) formerets. (See plan under *arc*[1].) Ribs upon the surfaces of the cells are known as *surface-ribs*. The groin-rib or ogive is also called the *diagonal rib*, because it occupies the diagonal of the plan of a quadripartite vault. See *arch*[1] and *arc*[1].

> All these *ribs* [of Notre Dame Cathedral, Paris] are independent arches, which determine the forms of, and actually sustain, the vault shells.
> C. H. *Moore*, Gothic Architecture, p. 52.

(2) An arch-formed piece of timber for supporting the lath-and-plaster work of pseudo-domes, vaults, etc. (*d*) In *coal-mining*, a narrow strip or block of solid coal left to support the workings. (*e*) One of the curved extension rods on which the cover of an umbrella is stretched.

> Let Persian Dames th' Umbrella's *Ribs* display,
> To guard their Beauties from the sunny Ray.
> *Gay*, Trivia, i.

(*f*) In *bot.*: (1) One of the principal vascular bundles, otherwise called *nerves* or *veins*, into which the primary bundle divides on entering the blade to form the framework of a leaf, commonly salient on its lower surface; a primary nerve: contrasted with *vein* and *veinlet*, the branches to which it gives origin. See *midrib* and *nervation*. (2) A prominent line on the surface of some other organ, as the fruit. (*g*) In cloth or knitted work, a ridge or stripe rising from the groundwork of the material, as in corduroy. (*h*) In *bookbinding*, one of the ridges on the back of a book, which serve for covering the tapes and for ornament. (*i*) One of the narrow tracks or ways of iron in which the bed of a printing-press slides to and from impression. (*j*) In *mach.*, an angle-plate cast between two other plates, to brace and strengthen them, as between the sole and wall-plate of a bracket. (*k*) In a violin or similar instrument, one of the curved sides of the body, separating the belly from the back. (*l*) In *gun-making*, either of the longitudinally extending upper or lower projections of the metal which join the barrels of a double-barreled gun, and which in fine guns are often ornamented or of ornamental shape. The upper rib is called the *top rib*; the lower, the *bottom rib*.

3. A piece of meat containing one or more ribs; a rib-piece: as, a *rib* of beef.—**4.** A wife: in allusion to Eve, who, according to the account in Genesis, was formed out of one of Adam's ribs. [Humorous.]

> Punch and his *rib* Joan. *Scott*, Pirate, xxvii.

5. A strip; a band or ribbon; a long and narrow piece of anything.

> A small *rib* of land, that is scarce to be found without a guide.
> *J. Echard*, Contempt of the Clergy, p. 104. (*Latham.*)

Abdominal ribs, in *herpet.* See *abdominal*.—**Back of a rib**, in *arch.*, the upper surface of a vaulting rib.—**Built rib**, in *arch.*, for bridges or roofs, a rib constructed of several layers of planks set on edge, breaking joints, and united by bolts.—**Diagonal rib**, in *arch.* See def. 2 (*c*) (1).—**False rib.** See def. 1.—**Floating rib**, a rib unattached at one or both ends; a free or false rib, as the eleventh or twelfth of man.—**Laminated rib**, in *arch.*, a rib constructed of layers of plank, laid flat, one over another, and bolted together.—**Longitudinal rib**, in *arch.*, a formeret, or arc formeret. See plan under *arc*[1].—**Rib and pillar.** See *pillar*.—**Ribs of a parrel** (*naut.*), a name formerly given to short pieces of wood having holes through which are reeved the two parts of the parrel-rope.—**Rib-top machine**, a special form of knitting-machine for making ribbed hosiery.—**Ridge rib**, in *arch.*, a rib in the axis of a vault and extending along its ridge. It is of rare occurrence except in English medieval vaulting, and is not used in vaults of the most correct and scientific design.—**Sacral rib**, the pleurapophysis of a sacral vertebra, of whatever character. The very complex sacrarium of a bird often bears articulated or ankylosed ribs of ordinary character, called *sacral*, though these may be really lumbosacral, or dorsolumbar. No mammal has such sacral ribs; but the whole "lateral mass," so called, of a mammalian sacrum, as in man, which ossifies from several independent centers, is regarded by some anatomists as pleurapophysial, and therefore as representing a consolidation of sacral ribs.—**Surface-rib**, in *arch.*, a rib without constructive office, applied to the surface of vaulting merely for ornament; a lierne, tierceron, etc. Such ribs, as a rule, were not used until after the best time of medieval vaulting.—**To give a rib of roast**†, to rib-roast; thrash soundly. See *rib-roast*.

> Though the skorneful do mocke me for a time, yet in the ende I hope to *giue* them al *a rybbe of roste* for their paynes.
> *Gascoigne*, Steele Glas (ed. Arber), Ep. Ded.

Transverse rib, in *arch.*, a doubleau or arc doubleau. See plan under *arc*[1].—**Wall-rib**, in *arch.*, same as *arc formeret* (which see, under *arc*[1]).

rib[1] (rib), *v. t.*; pret. and pp. *ribbed*, ppr. *ribbing*. [< *rib*[1], *n.*] **1.** To furnish with ribs; strengthen or support by ribs: as, to *rib* a ship.

> Was I by rocks engender'd, *ribb'd* with steel,
> Such tortures to resist, or not to feel?
> *Sandys*, Paraphrase upon Job, vi.

2. To form into ribs or ridges; mark with alternate channels and projecting lines; ridge: as, to *rib* a field by plowing; to *rib* cloth.

> The long dun wolds are *ribb'd* with snow.
> *Tennyson*, Oriana.

> The print of its first rush-wrapping,
> Wound ere it dried, still *ribbed* the thing.
> *D. G. Rossetti*, Burden of Nineveh.

3. To inclose as with ribs; shut in; confine.

> It were too gross
> To *rib* her cerecloth in the obscure grave.
> *Shak.*, M. of V., ii. 7. 51.

> And by the hand of Justice, never arms more
> Shall *rib* this body in, nor sword hang here, sir.
> *Fletcher*, Loyal Subject, i. 1.

rib[2] (rib), *n.* [< ME. *ribbe*, *rybbe*, < AS. *ribbe*, hound's-tongue, *Cynoglossum officinale*.] **1.** Hound's-tongue.—**2.** Costmary. *Cath. Ang.*, p. 306.—**3.** Water-cress. *Halliwell.*

rib[3] (rib), *v. t.* [< ME. *ribben*, *rybbyn*, dress; cf. D. *repelen*, beat (flax), = Sw. *repa*, ripple flax: see *rip*[1], *ripple*[1].] To dress (flax); ripple.

rib[3]† (rib), *n.* [< ME. *rybbe*, *ryb*: see *rib*[3], *v.*, and *ripple*[1].] An instrument for cleaning flax. *Halliwell.*

ribadoquin (ri-bad'ọ-kin), *n.* **1.** See *ribaudequin*.

> The clash of arms, the thundering of *ribadoquines* and arquebuses, . . . bespoke the deadly conflict waging.
> *Irving*, Granada, p. 455.

2. Same as *organ-gun*.

ribald (rib'ald), *n.* and *a.* [< ME. *ribald*, *ribold*, *rebald*, *ribaud*, *rybaud*, *ribaut* = Icel. *ribbaldi* = MHG. *ribalt*, < OF. *ribald*, *ribaud*, *ribauld*, *ribaut*, F. *ribaud* = Pr. *ribaut* = Sp. Pg. *ribaldo* = It. *ribaldo*, *rubaldo* (ML. *ribaldus*) (fem. OF. *ribaude*, ML. *ribalda*), a lewd, base person, a ruffian, ribald, also, without moral implication, a stout fellow, a porter, guard, soldier, etc. (see *ribaud*[2]); of uncertain origin: perhaps (with suffix *-ald*) < OHG. *hrîpâ*, MHG. *ribe*, a prostitute; cf. OF. *riber*, toy, wanton.] **I.** *n.* A low, base fellow; a profligate; a ruffian; a person of lewd habits: applied particularly to one who is coarse, abusive, or obscene in language.

> Ephistafus hym presit with his proude wordes,
> As a *ribald* with reuersy in his Roide speche.
> *Destruction of Troy* (E. E. T. S.), l. 7651.

> A wise man seide, as we may seen,
> Is no man wrecched, but he it wene,
> Be he kyng, knyght or *ribaude*;
> And many a *ribaude* is mery and baude,
> That swynkith and berith, bothe day and nyght,
> Many a burthen of grete myght.
> *Rom. of the Rose*, l. 5673.

> As for that proverb, the Bishops foot hath been in it, it were more fit for a Scurra in Trivio, or som *Ribald* upon an Ale-bench.
> *Milton*, On Def. of Humb. Remonst.

> In the last year of this reign (1376) we find the Commons petitioning the King "that *Ribalds* . . . and Sturdy Beggars may be banished out of every town."
> *Ribton-Turner*, Vagrants and Vagrancy, p. 52.

II. *a.* Licentious; profligate; obscene; coarse; abusive or indecent, especially in language; foul-mouthed.

> The busy day,
> Waked by the lark, hath roused the *ribald* crows.
> *Shak.*, T. and C., iv. 2. 9.

Me they seized and me they tortured, me they lash'd and humiliated,
Me the sport of *ribald* Veterans, mine of ruffian violators!
Tennyson, Boadicea.

Instead of having the solemn countenance of the average English driver, his face was almost *ribald* in its conviviality of expression.
T. C. Crawford, English Life, p. 37.

=**Syn.** Gross, coarse, filthy, indecent.

ribaldish (rib'al-dish), *a.* [< *ribald* + *-ish*[1].] Disposed to ribaldry.

They have a *ribaldish* tongue.
Bp. Hall, Estate of a Christian.

ribaldrous† (rib'al-drus), *a.* [Also *ribaudrous*; < *ribaldr(y)* + *-ous*.] Ribald; licentious; obscene; indecent.

A *ribaudrous* and filthie tongue, os incestum, obscaenum, impurum, et impudicum. *Baret*, Alvearie. (*Nares*.)

ribaldry (rib'al-dri), *n.* [< ME. *ribaldrie*, *ribaudrie*, *ribawdrye*, *rybaudrie*, *rybaudry*, etc., < OF. *ribauderie*, F. *ribauderie* (= Sp. *ribalderia* = Pg. *ribaldaria* = It. *ribalderia*, ML. *ribaldria*), < *ribald*, *ribaud*, a ribald: see *ribald*.] The qualities or acts of a ribald; licentious or foul language; ribald conversation; obscenity; indecency.

On fastingdais by-fore none ich fedde me with ale,
Out of reson, a-mong rybaudes here *rybaudrye* to huyre.
Her-of, good god, graunte me forȝeuenesse.
Piers Plowman (C), vii. 435.

Abstayn euer from wordes of *rybaudry*.
Babees Book (E. E. T. S.), p. 105.

Satire has long since done his best; and curst
And loathsome *Ribaldry* has done its worst.
Cowper, Table-Talk, l. 729.

He softens down the language for which the river was noted, and ignores the torrent of licentious *ribaldry* with which every boat greeted each other, and which was known as "River Wit."
J. Ashton, Social Life in Reign of Queen Anne, II. 144.

ribaldy†, *n.* [ME. *ribaudie*, < OF. *ribaudie*, equiv. to *ribaudric*, ribaldry: see *ribaldry*.] Same as *ribaldry*.

riban†, *n.* An obsolete form of *ribbon*.

riband, *n.* and *v.* An obsolete or archaic form of *ribbon*.

riband-fish, riband-gurnard, etc. See *ribbon-fish*, etc.

ribaning†, *n.* See *ribboning*.

ribattuta (rē-bät-tö'tä), *n.* [It., prop. fem. pp. of *ribattere*, beat again, beat back, reverberate, = F. *rebattre*, beat down, rebate: see *rebate*[1].] In *music*, a melodic embellishment consisting in an alternation of two adjacent tones, gradually increasing in rapidity until it becomes a shake or trill.

ribaud[1]†, *n.* A Middle English form of *ribald*.

ribaud[2] (rē-bō'), *n.* [OF., a soldier, porter, etc., a particular use of *ribaud*, a base fellow: see *ribald*.] In *French hist.*, one of a bodyguard created by Philip Augustus (1180–1223) of France.—**King of the ribauds,** the chief of the old French royal guard known as the ribauds. In the field, his station was at the door of the sovereign's quarters, and he permitted to enter only those who had the right. He had jurisdiction of crimes and misdemeanors committed within the king's abode, as well as of gaming and debauchery, executed his own sentences, and enjoyed various privileges and perquisites. The title disappeared after the fifteenth century, and the office became merged in that of the executioner.

ribaudequin (ri-bâ'de-kin), *n.* [Also *ribadoquin* (< Sp. *ribadoquin*); < OF. *ribaudequin*, *ribaudequien*, *ribausdesquin* (OFlem. *rabaudcken*) (see def.); origin uncertain.] 1. (*a*) Originally, a cart or barrow plated with iron or other material to protect it from fire, and armed with long iron-shod pikes; a movable cheval-de-frise. *Hewitt.* (*b*) A similar cart armed with a large crossbow, or with a small cannon in the fifteenth century. Hence—(*c*) The cannon itself so used.

ribaudour†, *n.* [ME., < OF. *ribaudour*, < *ribaud*, ribald: see *ribald*.] A ribald.

I schal fynden hem heore fode that feithfulliche lyuen;
Save Jacke the logelour, and Ionete of the stuyues,
And Robert the *ribaudour* for his rousti wordes.
Piers Plowman (A), vii. 66.

ribaudrous†, *a.* Same as *ribaldrous*.

ribaudry†, *n.* An obsolete form of *ribaldry*.

ribaudy†, *n.* See *ribaldy*.

Ribbail's bandage. A spica bandage for the instep.

ribband, *n.* An obsolete or archaic form of *ribbon*.

rib-band (rib'band), *n.* In *ship-building*: (*a*) A piece of timber extending the length of the square body of a vessel, used to secure the frames in position until the outside planking is put on. (*b*) A square timber of the slip fastened lengthwise in the bilgeways to prevent the timbers of the cradle from slipping outward during launching. See cut under *launching-ways*. (*c*) A scantling of wood, about 15 feet long and 4 inches square, used in rack-lashing gun-platforms to keep the platform secure: also used for mortar-platforms. Two rib-bands accompany every platform.—**Rib-band line,** in *ship-building*, one of the diagonal lines on the body-plan, by means of which the points called *surmarks*, where the respective bevelings are to be applied to the timbers, are marked off upon the mold.—**Rib-band nail,** in *ship-building*, a nail having a large round head with a ring to prevent the head from splitting the timber or being drawn through: used chiefly for fastening rib-bands. Also written *ribbing-nail*.

rib-baste (rib'bāst), *v. t.* To baste the ribs of; beat severely; rib-roast. *Halliwell.* [Prov. Eng.]

ribbed (ribd), *a.* [< *rib*[1] + *-ed*[2].] 1. Furnished with ribs; strengthened or supported by ribs, in any sense of the word.

Ribbed vaulting was the greatest improvement which the Mediæval architects made on the Roman vaults, giving not only additional strength of construction, but an apparent vigour and expression to the vault which is one of the greatest beauties of the style.
J. Fergusson, Hist. Arch., I. 525.

2. Formed into ribs or ridges; having alternate lines of projection and depression; ridged: as, *ribbed* cloth; *ribbed* hose.

And thou art long, and lank, and brown,
As is the *ribbed* sea-sand.
Wordsworth, Lines contributed to Coleridge's Ancient [Mariner.

This *ribbed* mountain structure . . . always wears a mantle of beauty, changeable purple and violet.
C. D. Warner, Their Pilgrimage, p. 205.

3. In *anat.* and *zoöl.*, having a rib or ribs, in any sense; costal; costate; costiferous.—**Ribbed arch.** See *arch*[1].—**Ribbed armor,** armor consisting of ridges alternating with sunken bands, which are usually set with studs. It is described in the tourney-book of René of Anjou as composed of cuir-bouilli upon which small bars, apparently of metal, are laid, and either sewed to the leather, or covered by an additional thickness of leather, which is glued to the background.—**Ribbed-fabric machine,** a knitting-machine for making the rib-stitch. It has special adjustments in both power- and hand-machines, and can be set to make different forms or combinations of stitches, as the polka-rib, one-and-one rib, etc. *E. H. Knight.*—**Ribbed form, plate, velveteen,** etc. See the nouns.

ribbing (rib'ing), *n.* [Verbal n. of *rib*[1], *v.*] 1. An assemblage or arrangement of ribs, as timberwork sustaining a vaulted ceiling, ridges on cloth, veins in the leaves of plants, etc.—2. In *agri.*, a kind of imperfect plowing, formerly common, by which stubbles were rapidly turned over, every alternate strip only being moved. By this method only half the land is raised, the furrow being laid over quite flat, and covering an equal space of the level surface. A similar operation is still in use in some places, after land has been pulverized by clean plowings and is ready for receiving the seed, and the mode of sowing upon land thus prepared is also called *ribbing*.

ribbing-nail (rib'ing-nāl), *n.* Same as *rib-band nail* (which see, under *rib-band*).

ribble-rabble (rib'l-rab"l), *n.* [A varied reduplication of *rabble*[2].] 1. A rabble; a mob.

A *ribble-rabble* of gossips.
John Taylor, Works (1630). (*Nares*.)

2. Idle and low talk; lewd or indecent language: sometimes used adjectively.

I cry God mercy (quoth the woman with much disdain in her countenance) if thou gratest my cares any more with thy *ribble-rabble* discourse.
History of Francion (1655). (*Nares*.)

Such wicked stuff, such poys'nous babble,
Such uncouth, wretched *ribble rabble*.
Hudibras Redivivus (1706). (*Nares*.)

ribble-row† (rib'l-rē), *n.* [A burlesque name, after analogy of *rigmarole*. Cf. *ribble-rabble*.] A list of rabble.

This witch of *ribble-row* rehearses,
Of scurvy names in scurvy verses.
Cotton, Works (1734), p. 119. (*Halliwell*.)

ribbon (rib'on), *n.* and *a.* [Formerly also *ribon*, *riban*, also *riband*, *ribband* (appar. simulating *band*, and still used archaically); < ME. *riban*, *riband*, < OF. *riban*, *ruben*, *rubant*, F. *ruban*, dial. *rebant*, *riban* (ML. *rubanus*), a ribbon; perhaps of Celtic origin: cf. Ir. *ribin*, a ribbon, *ribean*, a ribbon, fillet, = W. *rhibin*, a streak; Ir. *ribe*, a flake, hair, ribbon, = Gael. *rib*, *ribe*, a hair, rag, clout, = W. *rhib*, a streak. The Bret. *ruban* is prob. < F.] I. *n.* 1. Originally, a stripe in a material, or the band or border of a garment, whether woven in the stuff or applied.—2. A strip of fine stuff, as silk, satin, or velvet, having two selvages. Ribbons in this sense seem to have been introduced in the sixteenth century. Ordinarily ribbons are made of widths varying from one fourth of an inch, or perhaps even less, to seven or eight inches, but occasionally sash-ribbons or the like are made of much greater widths. According to the fashion of the day, ribbons are made richly figured or brocaded, of corded silk with velvet and satin stripes, satin-faced on each side, the two sides being of different colors, each perfect, and in many other styles.

Get your apparel together, good strings to your beards, new *ribbons* to your pumps. *Shak.*, M. N. D., iv. 2. 37.

Sweet-faced Corinna, deign the *riband* tie
Of thy cork-shoe, or else thy slave will die.
Marston, Scourge of Villanie, viii. 7.

She 's torn the *ribbons* frae her head,
They were baith thick and narrow.
The Braes o' Yarrow (Child's Ballads, III. 71).

It was pretty to see the young, pretty ladies dressed like men, in velvet coats, caps with *ribbands*, and with laced bands, just like men. *Pepys*, Diary, July 27, 1665.

Just for a handful of silver he left us;
Just for a *riband* to stick in his coat.
Browning, Lost Leader.

3. Specifically, the honorary distinction of an order of knighthood, usually in two forms: first, the broad ribbon, denoting the highest class of such an order (for which see *cordon*, 7); second, the small knot of ribbon worn in the buttonhole by members of an order when not wearing the cross or other badge. *Blue ribbon* and *red ribbon* are often used to denote the orders of the Garter and Bath respectively. A blue ribbon was also a badge of the Order of the Holy Ghost in France. Compare *cordon bleu*, under *cordon*.

4. That which resembles a ribbon in shape; a long and narrow strip of anything.

The houses stood well back, leaving a *ribbon* of waste land on either side of the road.
R. L. Stevenson, Inland Voyage, p. 68.

These [spiral nebulæ] are usually elongated strings or *ribbons* of nebulous matter twisted about a central nucleus and seen by us in the form of a spiral curve.
The Century, XXXIX. 458.

5. *pl.* Reins for driving. [Colloq.]

He [Egalité] drove his own phaeton when it was decidedly low for a man of fashion to handle the *ribands*.
Phillips, Essays from the Times, I. 76.

If he had ever held the coachman's *ribbons* in his hands, as I have in my younger days—a—he would know that stopping is not always easy.
George Eliot, Felix Holt, xvii.

6. A strip; a shred: as, the sails were torn to *ribbons*.

They're very naked; their things is all to *ribbins*.
Mayhew, London Labour and London Poor, II. 84.

7. In *spinning*, a continuous strand of cotton or other fiber in a loose, untwisted condition; a sliver.—8. In *metal-working*, a long, thin strip of metal, such as (*a*) a watch-spring; (*b*) a thin steel band for a belt, or an endless saw; (*c*) a thin band of magnesium for burning; (*d*) a thin steel strip for measuring, resembling a tape-line.—9. One of the stripes painted on arrow-shafts, generally around the shaftment. Also called *clan-mark*, *owner-mark*, *game-tally*, etc. *Amer. Nat.*, July, 1886, p. 675.—10. A narrow web of silk for hand-stamps, saturated with free color, which is readily transferred by pressure to paper.—11. In *stained-glass work* and the like, a strip or thin bar of lead grooved to hold the edges of the glass. See *lead*[2], 7.—12. In *her.*, a bearing considered usually as one of the subordinaries. It is a diminutive of the bend, and one eighth of its width.—13. In *carp.*, a long thin strip of wood, or a series of such strips, uniting several parts. Compare *rib-band*.—14. *Naut.*, a painted molding on the side of a ship.—**Autophyte ribbon,** a Swiss ribbon printed in a lace pattern by means of zinc plates produced by a photo-engraving process from a real lace original. *E. H. Knight.*—**Blue ribbon.** (*a*) A broad, dark-blue ribbon, the border embroidered with gold, worn by members of the Order of the Garter diagonally across the breast.

Ribbon (*a*).

They get invited . . . to assemblies . . . where they see stars and *blue ribbons*. *Disraeli*, Sybil, iv. 3.

(*b*) Figuratively, anything which marks the attainment of an object of ambition; also, the object itself.

In Germany the art of emending is no longer the chief art of the scholar. A brilliant and certain conjecture is no longer the *blue ribbon* of his career.
Fortnightly Rev., N. S., XLIII. 47.

(*c*) A member of the Order of the Garter.

Why should dancing round a May-pole be more obsolete than holding a Chapter of the Garter? asked Lord Henry. The Duke, who was a *blue-ribbon*, felt this a home thrust. *Disraeli*, Coningsby, iii. 3.

(*d*) The badge of a society pledged to total abstinence from the use of intoxicating drinks: it consists of a bit of blue ribbon worn in a buttonhole.—**China ribbon,** a ribbon, about an eighth of an inch wide, formerly used in the toilet, but now for markers inserted in bound books and the like, and also in a kind of embroidery which takes its name from the employment of this material.—**China-ribbon embroidery,** a kind of embroidery much in favor in the early years of the nineteenth century, and recently revived. The needle is threaded with a ribbon, which is drawn through the material as well as applied upon it.—

A, rachiglossate lingual ribbon, or radula, of a whelk (*Buccinum undatum*): *a*, anterior end; *b*, posterior end. *B*, a transverse row of radular teeth: *c*, central; *l, l*, lateral.

Lingual ribbon, in *Mollusca*, the surface that bears the teeth; the radula. See *odontophore*, and *radula* (with cut).—**Nidamental ribbon.** See *nidamental*.—**Petersham ribbon**, a ribbon of extra thickness, usually watered on both sides, used in women's dress to strengthen the skirt at the waist, etc., and also as a belt-ribbon when belt-ribbons are in fashion. Compare *pad*[3], 7.—**Red ribbon.** (*a*) The ribbon of the Order of the Bath, used to denote the decoration of that order, or the order itself: as, he has got the *red ribbon*. (*b*) The ribbon of a knight of the Legion of Honor.

II. *a.* 1. Made of ribbon: as, a *ribbon* bow; *ribbon* trimming.—2. In *mineral.*, characterized by parallel bands of different colors: as, *ribbon* agate.—3. [*cap.*] Pertaining to the Ribbon Society or to Ribbonism: as, a *Ribbon* lodge.—**Ribbon isinglass, letter.** See the nouns.—**Ribbon sections**, a series or chain of microtome-cut sections which remain attached to each other, edge to edge, by means of the embedding material.—**Ribbon Society**, in *Irish hist.*, a secret association formed about 1808 in opposition to the Orange organization of the northern Irish counties, and so named from the green ribbon worn as a badge by the members. The primary object of the society was soon merged in a struggle against the landlord class, with the purpose of securing to tenants fixity of tenure, or of inflicting retaliation for real or supposed agrarian oppression. The members were bound together by an oath, had passwords and signs, and were divided locally into lodges.

ribbon (rib'on), *v. t.* [Formerly (and still archaically) also *riband, ribband*; early mod. E. also *reband*; < ME. *ribanen, rybanen*, < *riban*, a ribbon: see *ribbon, n.*] 1. To border with stripes resembling ribbons; stripe; streak.

> It is a slowe may not forbere
> Ragges *ribaned* with gold to were.
> *Rom. of the Rose*, l. 4752.

I could see all the inland valleys *ribboned* with broad waters. *R. D. Blackmore*, Lorna Doone, xlviii.

When imitations of *ribboned* stones are wished, . . . pour each of the colors separately upon the Marble, taking care to spread them in small pools over the whole surface: then, with a wooden spatula, form the *ribboned* shades which are wished by lightly moving the mixture. *Marble-Worker*, § 128.

2. To adorn with ribbons.

> Each her *ribbon'd* tambourine
> Flinging on the mountain-sod,
> With a lovely frighten'd mien
> Came about the youthful god.
> *M. Arnold*, Empedocles on Etna.

Herrick gaily assimilated to his antique dream these pleasant pastoral survivals, *ribbanding* the may-pole as though it were the cone-tipped rod of Dionysus. *E. W. Gosse*, in Ward's Eng. Poets, II. 126.

3. To form into long narrow strips; cause to take the shape of ribbon.

When it [wax in bleaching] . . . still continues yellow upon the fracture, it is remelted, *ribboned*, and again bleached. *Workshop Receipts*, 1st ser., p. 354.

ribbon-bordering (rib'on-bôr'dėr-ing), *n.* In *hort.*, the use of foliage-plants set in ribbons or stripes of contrasting shades as a border; also, a border thus formed.

Whether it [the garden] went in for *ribbon-bordering* and bedding-out plants, or essayed the classical, with marble statues. *Miss Braddon*, Hostages to Fortune, ii.

ribbon-brake (rib'on-brāk), *n.* A brake having a band which nearly surrounds the wheel whose motion is to be checked.

rib-bone (rib'bōn), *n.* [< ME. *ribbebon* (= Sw. *ribben* = Dan. *ribben*); < *rib*[1] + *bone*[1].] A rib.

> And [he] made man likkest to hym-self one,
> And Eue of his *ribbe-bon* with-outen eny mene.
> *Piers Plowman* (B), ix. 34.

ribbon-fish (rib'on-fish), *n.* One of sundry fishes of long, slender, compressed form, like a ribbon, as those of the genera *Cepola, Trichiurus, Trachypterus*, and *Regalecus*: especially applied to those of the suborder *Tæniosomi*. See the technical names, and cut under *hairtail*.

ribbon-grass (rib'on-gràs), *n.* A striped green and white garden variety of the grass *Phalaris arundinacea*. Also called *painted-grass*.

ribbon-gurnard (rib'on-gėr'nārd), *n.* A fish of the family *Macruridæ* or *Lepidosomatidæ*. *A. Adams.*

ribboning† (rib'on-ing), *n.* [Also *ribbaning, ribaning*; < ME. *ribanyng*; verbal n. of *ribbon, v.*] 1. A striped or ornamented border.

> It [the robe] ful wel
> With orfrays leyd was everydel,
> And portraied in the *ribanynges*
> Of dukes storyes and of kynges.
> *Rom. of the Rose*, l. 1077.

2. An ornament made of ribbon.

> What gloves we'l give and *ribanings*.
> *Herrick*, To the Maids, to Walke Abroad.

Ribbonism (rib'on-izm), *n.* [< *Ribbon* + *-ism*.] The principles and methods of the Ribbon Society of Ireland. See under *ribbon, a.*

There had always smouldered *Ribbonism*, Whiteboyism, some form of that protean Vehmgericht which strove, too often by unmanly methods, to keep alive a flicker of manly independence. *Contemporary Rev.*, LI. 243.

ribbon-line (rib'on-līn), *n.* In *hort.*, a long, generally marginal, bed of close-set plants in contrasted colors. *Henderson*, Handbook of Plants.

Ribbonman (rib'on-man), *n.*; pl. *Ribbonmen* (-men). [See *Ribbonism*.] A member of an Irish Ribbon lodge; an adherent of Ribbonism.

Orangemen and *Ribbonmen* once divided Ireland. *The American*, VII. 133.

ribbon-map (rib'on-map), *n.* A map printed on a long strip which winds on an axis within a case.

ribbon-pattern (rib'on-pat'ėrn), *n.* A decorated design imitating interlacing and knotted ribbons.

ribbon-register (rib'on-rej'is-tėr), *n.* Same as *register*[1], 11.

ribbon-saw (rib'on-sâ), *n.* Same as *band-saw*.

ribbon-seal (rib'on-sēl), *n.* A seal of the genus *Histriophoca, H. fasciata*, the male of which is

Ribbon-seal (*Histriophoca fasciata*).

curiously banded with whitish on a dark ground, as if adorned with ribbons. It inhabits the North Pacific.

ribbon-snake (rib'on-snāk), *n.* A small slender striped snake, *Eutænia saurita*, abundant in the United States: a kind of garden snake, having several long yellow stripes on a dark variegated ground. It is a very pretty and quite harmless serpent. See *Eutænia*.

ribbon-stamp (rib'on-stamp), *n.* A small and simple form of printing-press which transfers to paper the free color in a movable ribbon which covers the stamp.

ribbon-tree (rib'on-trē), *n.* See *Plagianthus*.

ribbon-wave (rib'on-wāv), *n.* A common European geometrid moth, *Acidalia aversata*: an English collectors' name.

ribbonweed (rib'on-wēd), *n.* The ordinary form of the seaweed *Laminaria saccharina*, whose frond has a long flat blade, sometimes membranaceous and waved on the margin. [Prov. Eng.] *Treas. of Bot.*

ribbon-wire (rib'on-wīr), *n.* A kind of tape in which several fine wires are introduced, running in the direction of the length of the stuff. It is employed by milliners for strengthening or stiffening their work.

ribbonwood (rib'on-wụ̈d), *n.* A small handsome malvaceous tree, *Hoheria populnea*, of New Zealand. Its bark affords a demulcent drink, and also serves for cordage. It is doubtless named from the ribbon-like strips of its bark.

ribbon-worm (rib'on-wėrm), *n.* 1. Same as *tapeworm*.—2. A nemertean or nemertine worm; one of the *Nemertea*: so called from the extraordinary length and flattened form of some of them, as the long sea-worms of the family *Lineidæ*, which attain a length of many feet, as *Lineus marinus*.

ribebat, ribecat, *n.* Same as *rebec*.

ribes[1]† (ribz), *n. sing.* and *pl.* [= Dan. *ribs*, currant; < OF. *ribes*, "red gooseberries, beyond-sea gooseberries, garden currans, bastard currans" (Cotgrave), F. *ribes* = It. *ribes*, "red gooseberies, bastard corans, or common ribes" (Florio), prop. sing., = Sp. *ribes*, currant-tree, < ML. *ribes, ribus, ribesium, ribasium*, < Ar. *rībās, rībās*, Pers. **ribāj*, gooseberry.] A currant; generally as plural, currants.

Red Gooseberies, or *ribes*, do refresh and coole the hote stomacke and liuer, and are good against all Inflammations. *Langham*, Garden of Health, p. 289.

Ribes[2] (rī'bēz), *n.* [NL. (Linnæus, 1737), < ML. *ribesium*, currant: see *ribes*[1].] A genus of polypetalous shrubs, constituting the tribe *Ribesieæ* in the order *Saxifragaceæ*, and producing small flowers with four or five scale-like petals, four or five stamens, two styles, and an ovoid calyx-tube united to the ovary, continued above into a tubular or bell-shaped four- or five-cleft limb, which is often colored. There are about 75 species, natives of temperate Europe, Asia, and America, and of the Andes. Several species extend northward in Alaska nearly or quite to the arctic circle. The plants of this genus are often covered with resinous glands, and the stems are sometimes sparingly armed with spines below the axils. They bear scattered and often clustered leaves, which are petioled and entire or crenately lobed or cut, plicate or convolute in the bud. The flowers are often unisexual by abortion, are white, yellow, red, or green, rarely purple, in color, and occur either singly or few together, or, in the currants, in racemes. The fruit is an oblong or spherical pulpy berry, containing one cell and few or many seeds, and crowned with the calyx-lobes. Several species, mostly with thorny and often also prickly stems, the flowers single or few together, the fruit often spiny, are known as gooseberries; other species, wholly unarmed, with racemed flowers and smooth fruit, are grouped as currants. *R. Grossularia* is the common garden or English gooseberry. (See *gooseberry*.) *R. speciosum* is the showy flowering gooseberry or fuchsia-flowered gooseberry of California, much prized in cultivation for its bright-red drooping flowers with far-exserted red stamens. *R. gracile* of the central United States, its fruit bearing long red spines, is called *Missouri gooseberry*. *R. rubrum*, the common red currant (see *currant*[2], 2), is native in Europe, Asia, and northern North America. *R. nigrum* is the garden black currant, a native of the northern Old World; *R. floridum* is the wild black currant of America.

1, Branch with Flowers of Missouri Currant (*Ribes aureum*). 2, fruits of red currant (*R. rubrum*); 3, fruit of English gooseberry (*R. Grossularia*); 4, fruit of wild gooseberry (*R. Cynosbati*).

R. aureum, the golden, buffalo, or Missouri currant, wild in the western United States, is in common cultivation for its early bright-yellow spicy-scented flowers. *R. sanguineum*, the red-flowered currant of California and Oregon, is another well-known ornamental species. *R. prostratum*, the fetid currant of northern woods in America, emits a nauseous odor when bruised.

Ribesieæ (rī-bẹ̄-sī'ẹ̄-ē), *n. pl.* [NL. (A. Richard, 1823), < *Ribes*[2] + *-eæ*.] A tribe of polypetalous plants of the order *Saxifragaceæ*. It is characterized by a one-celled ovary, seeds immersed in pulp, alternate undivided leaves, without free stipules, and commonly racemed or clustered flowers. It consists of the genus *Ribes*.

rib-faced (rib'fāst), *a.* Having the face ribbed or ridged; rib-nosed.

rib-grass (rib'gràs), *n.* The English or ribwort plantain, *Plantago lanceolata*.

The rich infield ground produced spontaneously *rib grass*, white, yellow, and red clover, with the other plants of which cattle are fondest. *Edinburgh Rev.*, CXLV. 196.

ribibe†, *n.* [Also *ribible*; < ME. *ribibe*, < OF. *ribibe, rubebe, rebube*, etc.: see *rebec*.] 1. A musical instrument; a rebec.

The *ribibe* is said to have had three strings, to have been played with a bow, and to have been introduced into Spain by the Moors. *Skeat*, Piers Plowman, II. 426.

2. A shrill-voiced old woman.

> This somnpnour, ever waityng on his pray,
> Rod forth to sompne a widewe, an old *ribibe*,
> Fynyng a cause, for he wolde bribe.
> *Chaucer*, Friar's Tale, l. 79.

> There came an old *rybybe*,
> She halted of a kybe.
> *Skelton*, Elynour Rummyng, l. 42.

> Or some good *ribibe* about Kentish town
> Or Hogsden, you would hang now for a witch.
> *B. Jonson*, Devil is an Ass, i. 1.

ribibe† (ri-bib'), *v. i.* [ME. *rybyben*; < *ribibe, n.*] To play on a ribibe.

Tho ratton *rybybyd*. *Rel. Antiq.*, i. 81. (*Halliwell*.)

ribible† (ri-bib'l), *n.* [ME. *ribible, rubible:* see *ribibe, rebec.*] Same as *ribibe.*

> In twenty manere koude he trippe and daunce, . . .
> And pleyen songes on a smal *rubible.*
> Chaucer, Miller's Tale, l. 145.

> Where, my friend, is your fiddle, your *ribible,* or such-like instrument belonging to a minstrel?
> Quoted in *Strutt's* Sports and Pastimes, p. 271.

ribibour†, *n.* [ME. *ribibour,* < OF. **ribibour,* < *ribibe,* a ribibe: see *ribibe.*] One who plays on the ribibe.

> A *ribibour,* a ratonere, a rakyer of Chepe.
> *Piers Plowman* (B), v. 322.

ribless (rib'les), *a.* [< *rib*[1] + *-less.*] 1. Having no ribs.—2. So fat that the ribs cannot be felt.

> Where Toil shall call the charmer Health his bride,
> And Laughter tickle Plenty's *ribless* side!
> *Coleridge,* To a Young Ass.

riblet (rib'let), *n.* [< *rib*[1] + *-let.*] A little rib; a rudimentary rib; a vertebral pleurapophysis not developed into a free and functional rib: as, a cervical *riblet* of man. See *pleurapophysis.*

> The surface has longitudinal ridges, which on the hinder moiety of the valve are connected by transverse *riblets.*
> Geol. *Mag.,* IV. 451.

rib-like (rib'lik), *a.* [< *rib*[1] + *like.*] Resembling a rib; of the nature of a rib.

> *Riblike* cartilaginous rods appear in the first, second, and more or fewer of the succeeding visceral arches in all but the lowest Vertebrata. *Huxley,* Anat. Vert., p. 22.

rib-nosed (rib'nōzd), *a.* Having the side of the snout ribbed; rib-faced, as a baboon. See *mandrill,* and cut under *baboon.*

ribon†, *n.* An obsolete form of *ribbon.*

ribosa (ri-bō'sä), *n.* Same as *rebozo.*

rib-piece (rib'pēs), *n.* A rib-roast.

rib-roast (rib'rōst), *n.* 1. A joint of meat for roasting which includes one or more ribs of the animal.—2. A beating or drubbing; a cudgeling.

> Such a peece of filching is as punishable with *ribroast* among the turne-spits at Pie Corner.
> *Maroccus Extaticus* (1595). (*Halliwell.*)

rib-roast (rib'rōst), *v. t.* [< *rib*[1] + *roast, v.*] To beat soundly; cudgel; thrash.

> Tom, take thou a cudgell and *rib-roast* him.
> Let me alone, quoth Tom, I will be-ghost him.
> *Rowland,* Night-Raven (1620). (*Nares.*)

> But much I scorne my fingers should be foule
> With beating such a durty dunghill-owle.
> But I'll *rib-roast* thee and bum-bast thee still
> With my enraged muse and angry quill.
> *John Taylor,* Works (1630). (*Nares.*)

> I have been pinched in flesh, and well *rib-roasted* under my former masters; but I'm in now for skin and all.
> *Sir R. L'Estrange.*

rib-roaster (rib'rōs"tėr), *n.* A heavy blow on the ribs; a body-blow. [Colloq.]

> There was some terrible slugging. . . . In the fourth and last round the men seemed afraid of each other. Cleary planted two *rib-roasters,* and a tap on Langdon's face.
> *Philadelphia Times,* May 6, 1886.

rib-roasting (rib'rōs"ting), *n.* A beating or drubbing; a cudgeling.

> That done, he rises, humbly bows,
> And gives thanks for the princely blows;
> Departs not meanly proud, and boasting
> Of his magnificent *rib-roasting.*
> *S. Butler,* Hudibras, II. i. 248.

> Every day or two he was sure to get a sound *rib-roasting* for some of his misdemeanors.
> *Irving,* Knickerbocker, p. 335.

rib-roost†, *v. t.* See *rib-roast.*

ribskin†, *n.* [Early mod. E. *rybskyn,* < ME. *rybschyn* (also *rybbynge-skin*); < *rib*[3] + *skin.*] A piece of leather worn in flax-dressing. Compare *trip-skin.* *Halliwell.*

> Theyr *rybskyn* and theyr spyndell.
> *Skelton,* Elynour Rummyng, l. 209.

rib-stitch (rib'stich), *n.* In *crochet-work,* a stitch or point by which a fabric is produced having raised ridges alternately on the one side and the other.

Ribston pippin. [From *Ribston,* in Yorkshire, where Sir Henry Goodricke planted three pips obtained from Rouen in Normandy. Two died, but one survived to become the parent of all the Ribston apples in England. (Brewer.)] A fine variety of winter apple.

rib-vaulting (rib'vâl"ting), *n.* In *arch.,* vaulting having ribs projecting below the general surface of the ceiling for support or ornament.

ribwort (rib'wėrt), *n.* See *plantain*[1].

-ric. [< ME. *-riche, -ricke,* used in comp., as in *bischop-, kine-, king-, weoreld-, eorth-, heovenriche,* realm, jurisdiction, power, of a bishop, king, the world, earth, heaven, etc.: same as ME. *riche,* < AS. *rice,* reign, realm, dominion: see *riche*[1], *n.*] A termination denoting jurisdiction, or a district over which government is exercised. It occurs in *bishopric,* and a few words now obsolete.

Ricania (ri-kā'ni-ä), *n.* [NL. (Germar, 1818).] The typical genus of *Ricaniidæ.*

Ricaniidæ (rik-a-nī'i-dē), *n. pl.* [NL., < *Ricania* + *-idæ.*] A large family of homopterous insects, typified by the genus *Ricania,* belonging to the group *Fulgorida.* It includes many beautiful and striking tropical and subtropical forms. Also, as a subfamily, *Ricaniida, Ricaninæ.*

Ricardian (ri-kär'di-an), *a.* and *n.* [< *Ricardo* (see def.) + *-ian.*] I. *a.* Pertaining to or characteristic of David Ricardo, an English political economist (1772–1823), or his theories.

> It is interesting to observe that Malthus, though the combination of his doctrine of population with the principles of Ricardo composed the creed for some time professed by all the "orthodox" economists, did not himself accept the *Ricardian* scheme. *Encyc. Brit.,* XIX. 376.

II. *n.* An adherent or follower of Ricardo.

> Though in his great work he [Rau] kept clear of the exaggerated abstraction of the *Ricardians,* and rejected some of their a priori assumptions, he never joined the historical school. *Encyc. Brit.,* XX. 294.

ricasso (ri-kas'ō), *n.* [Origin obscure.] That part of the blade of a rapier which is included between the outermost guard (see *cup-guard, counter-guard*) and the cross-guard, or the point of connection between the blade and the hilt. In the rapier of the sixteenth century this part was narrower and thicker than the blade proper, and usually rectangular in section. Compare *heel*[1], 2 (*e*), and *talon,* and see cut under *hilt.*

Riccati's equation. [Named after Count Jacopo *Riccati* (1676–1754).] Properly, the equation $ax^m dx + by^2 dx = dy$, but usually the equation $dy/dx + by^2 = cx^m$, an equation always solvable by Bessel's functions, and often in finite terms.

Riccia (rik'si-ä), *n.* [NL. (Micheli, 1729), named after P. Francisco *Ricci,* an Italian botanist.] A genus of cryptogamous plants of the class *Hepaticæ,* typical of the order *Ricciaceæ.* They are delicate little terrestrial or pseudo-aquatic, chiefly annual, plants with thallose vegetation. The thallus is at first radiately divided from the center, which often soon decays; the divisions are bifid or ditrichotomous; the fruit is immersed in the thallus, sessile; and the spores are alveolate or muriculate, flattish, and angular. There are 20 North American species.

Ricciaceæ (rik-si-ā'sē-ē), *n. pl.* [NL. (Endlicher, 1836), < *Riccia* + *-aceæ.*] An order of thallose cryptogamous plants of the class *Hepaticæ,* typified by the genus *Riccia.* By Leitgeb they are regarded as forming a connecting-link between the *Jungermanniaceæ* and the *Marchantiaceæ;* but they are in some respects of simpler structure than either of these orders. The thallus is usually flat, branching dichotomously, and floating on water or rooting in soil. The fruit is short-pedicelled or sessile on the thallus or immersed in it; the capsule is free or connate with the calyptra, globose, rupturing irregularly; the spores are usually angular; and elaters are wanting.

rice[1] (rīs), *n.* [Early mod. E. also *ryce, rize;* < late ME. *ryce* = D. *rijst* = MLG. *ris* = MHG. *ris,* G. *reis* = Sw. Dan. *ris,* < OF. *ris,* F. *riz* = Pr. *ris* = It. *riso* (ML. *risus, risum*), < ML. *orysum,* L. *oryza,* rice, = Ar. *uruzz, aruzz, ruzz* (> Sp. Pg. *arroz*), < Gr. ὄρυζα, ὄρυζον, rice (plant and grain); from an OPers. form preserved in the Pushtu (Afghan) *wrijzey, wrijey,* pl., rice, *wrijza'h,* a grain of rice; cf. Skt. *vrīhi,* rice.] 1. The grain of the rice-plant. It forms a larger part of human food than the product of any other one plant, being often an almost exclusive diet in India, China, and the Malayan islands, and abundantly used elsewhere. Over 75 per cent. of its substance consists of starchy matter, but it is deficient in albuminoids, the flesh-forming material, and is thus best adapted for use in warm climates. It is commonly prepared by boiling; in warm countries it is much employed in curries. Rice-flour, rice-glue, rice-starch, rice-sugar, and rice-water are made from it; the *sake* of the Japanese is brewed from rice, and one kind of true arrack is distilled from it.

The Panicle of Rice (*Oryza sativa*).
a, a spikelet; *b,* the empty glumes; *c,* the flowering glume; *d,* the palet; *e,* the lodicules, the stamens, and the pistil.

2. The rice-plant, *Oryza sativa.* It is a member of the grass family (see *Oryza*), native in India, also in northern Australia; extensively cultivated in India, China, Malaysia, Brazil, the southern United States, and somewhat in Italy and Spain. It has numerous natural and cultivated varieties, and ranges in height from 1 to 6 feet. It requires for ripening a temperature of from sixty to eighty degrees, and in general can be grown only on irrigable land (but see *mountain-rice*). Rice is one of the most prolific of all crops. It was introduced into South Carolina about 1700—it is said by chance. The finest quality is produced in the United States, South Carolina and Georgia leading in amount; but the production has considerably declined since the civil war.—**Canada rice.** Same as *Indian rice.*—**False rice,** a grass of the rice-like genus *Leersia.*—**Hungary rice,** a corruption of *hungry rice.*—**Hungry rice.** Same as *fundi.*—**Indian rice.** (*a*) A reed-like grass, *Zizania aquatica,* common in shallow water in eastern North America, and especially abundant northwestward. The seeds, which are slender and half an inch long, are farinaceous, much eaten by birds, and largely gathered by the Indians in canoes; but they fall so easily as to render the plant unfit for cropping, even if otherwise worthy. The straw has been recommended as a paper-stock. Its height and large monœcious panicle render it a striking plant. A more southerly species, *Z. miliacea,* is included under the name. Also called *Canada* or *wild rice,* and *Indian oats* or *water-oats.* (*b*) Rice produced in India.—**Millet-rice,** the East Indian *Panicum colonum.*—**Petty-rice.** See *Quinoa.*—**Rice cut-grass.** See *cut-grass.*—**Rice-grain decoration,** in *ceram.,* a kind of decoration used in porcelain, especially Chinese, and in fine earthenware, as sometimes in Persian work. The paste of a cup or bowl is cut through with a stamp bearing small leaf-shaped or oval openings; the vessel being dipped in the glaze and then fired, the glaze fills these openings completely, leaving translucent spots in the opaque vessel. Occasionally the openings are of different shapes, as small stars, crosses, etc.—**Rough rice,** the common name for the East Indian paddy or unhusked rice.—**Water-rice, wild rice.** Same as *Indian rice.*

rice[2], *n.* Another spelling of *rise*[2]. *Cotgrave.*

rice-bird (rīs'bėrd), *n.* 1. Another name of the reed-bird: applied to the bobolink in the fall, when it is in yellowish plumage and feeds largely on wild rice (*Zizania aquatica*), or, in the southern United States, upon cultivated rice, to which it does much damage. The name is little used north of the States where rice is cultivated. Also called *rice-bunting* and *rice-troopial.* See *reed-bird,* and cut under *bobolink.*
2. The paddy-bird, *Padda oryzivora,* well known in confinement as the *Java sparrow,* and common in China, etc.

rice-bunting (rīs'bun"ting), *n.* Same as *rice-bird,* 1.

rice-corn (rīs'kôrn), *n.* Same as *pampas-rice.*

rice-drill (rīs'dril), *n.* In *agri.,* a force-feed machine, for planting rice in drills: same as *rice-planter.* See *drill*[1], 3. *E. H. Knight.*

rice-dust (rīs'dust), *n.* The refuse of rice which remains when it is cleaned for the market, consisting of the husk, broken grains, and dust. It is a valuable food for cattle. Also *rice-meal.*

rice-embroidery (rīs'em-broi"dėr-i), *n.* Embroidery in which rice-stitch is used either exclusively or to a great extent, so as to produce the appearance of grains of rice scattered over the surface.

rice-field (rīs'fēld), *n.* A field on which rice is grown.—**Rice-field mouse,** an American sigmodont murine rodent, the rice-rat, *Hesperomys* (*Oryzomys*) *palustris,* abounding in the rice-fields of the southern United States. It is the largest North American species of its genus, and has the general appearance of a half-grown house-rat. It is 4 inches long, the scaly tail as much more.

Rice-field Mouse (*Oryzomys palustris*).

The pelage is hispid and glossy. The color is that of the common rat. In habits this animal is the most aquatic of its kind, resembling the European water-rat (*Arvicola amphibius*) in this respect. It is a nuisance in the rice-plantations.

rice-flour (rīs'flour), *n.* Ground rice, used for making puddings, gruel for infants, etc., and as a face-powder.

rice-flower (rīs'flou"ėr), *n.* See *Pimelea.*

rice-glue (rīs'glö), *n.* A cement made by boiling rice-flour in soft water. It dries nearly transparent, and is used in making many paper articles; when made sufficiently stiff it can be molded into models, busts, etc.

rice-grain (rīs'grān), *n.* 1. A grain of rice.—2. A mottled appearance upon the sun, resembling grains or granules.

rice-hen (rīs'hen), *n.* The common American gallinule, *Gallinula galeata.* [Illinois.]

rice-huller (rīs'hul"ėr), *n.* Same as *rice-pounder.*

rice-meal (rīs'mēl), *n.* Same as *rice-dust.*

rice-milk (rīs'milk), *n.* Milk boiled and thickened with rice.

> There are fifty street-sellers of *rice-milk* in London. Saturday night is the best time of sale, when it is not uncommon for a *rice-milk* woman to sell six quarts.
> *Mayhew,* London Labour and London Poor, I. 203.

rice-mill (rīs′mil), *n.* A mill for removing the husk from rough rice or paddy; a rice-huller.

rice-paper (rīs′pā″pėr), *n.* 1. Paper made from the straw of rice, used in China and Japan and elsewhere.—2. A name commonly but erroneously applied to a delicate white film prepared in China from the pith of a shrub, *Fatsia papyrifera*. The pith freed from the stem is an inch or an inch and a half in diameter, and is cut into lengths of about three inches. These by the use of a sharp blade are pared into thin rolls which are flattened and dried under pressure, forming sheets a few inches square. The Chinese draw and paint upon these, and they are much used in the manufacture of artificial flowers, some pith being imported in the stem for the same purpose. In the Malay archipelago the pith of *Scævola Kœnigii* furnishes the rice-paper. See *Fatsia*.—**Rice-paper tree**, a small tree, *Fatsia papyrifera*, native in the swamps of Formosa, and cultivated in China, whose pith forms the material of so-called rice-paper. It grows 20 feet high or less, has leaves a foot across, palmately five- to seven-lobed, and clusters of small greenish flowers on long peduncles. From its ample leaves and stately habit, it is a favorite in subtropical planting. The Malayan rice-paper plant, *Scævola Kœnigii*, is a sea-shore shrub found from India to Australia and Polynesia. Its young stems are stout and succulent, and yield a pith used like that of *Fatsia*, though smaller. It is the taccada of India and Ceylon.

rice-planter (rīs′plan″tėr), *n.* An implement for sowing or planting rice; a special form of grain-drill. The seed falls through the tubular standard of a plow which opens a furrow for it, is deflected by a board or plate, and covered by a serrated or ribbed follower-plate. Also called *rice-sower* and *rice-drill*. *E. H. Knight.*

rice-pounder (rīs′poun″dėr), *n.* A rice-mill; a machine for freeing rice from its outer skin or hull. This is effected by placing the rice in mortars which have small pointed elevations to prevent the pestles from crushing the rice, while their action causes the grains to rub off the red skin against one another.

rice-pudding (rīs′půd″ing), *n.* A pudding made of rice and milk, with sugar, and often enriched with eggs and fruit, as currants, raisins, etc.

rice-rat (rīs′rat), *n.* The rice-field mouse.

ricercare (rē-cher-kä′re), *n.* [It. *ricercare*, a prelude, flourish, < *ricercare*, seek out, request, etc.: see *research*.] In *music*, same as *ricercata*.

ricercata (rē-cher-kä′tạ), *n.* [It., a prelude, search, < *ricercare*, search: see *ricercare*.] In *music*: (*a*) Originally, a composition in fugal style, like a toccata. (*b*) Now, a fugue of specially learned character, in which every contrapuntal device is utilized; or a fugue without episodes, subject and answer recurring continually.

rice-shell (rīs′shel), *n.* A shell of the genus *Olivella*, of about the size and whiteness of a grain of rice: sometimes extended to similar shells of the family *Olividæ*. See cut under *olive-shell*.

rice-soup (rīs′söp), *n.* A soup made with rice and thickened with flour, enriched with veal, chicken, or mutton stock.

rice-sower (rīs′sō″ėr), *n.* Same as *rice-planter*.

rice-stitch (rīs′stich), *n.* An embroidery-stitch by which a loop an eighth of an inch long and pointed at each end is made on the surface of the foundation. This, when done in white thread, resembles a grain of rice.

rice-stone (rīs′stōn), *n.* Stone mottled as with rice-grains.—**Rice-stone glass.** Same as *alabaster glass* (which see, under *alabaster*).

rice-sugar (rīs′shůg″ạr), *n.* A confection made from rice in Japan, and there called *ame*.

rice-tenrec (rīs′ten″rek), *n.* A species of the genus *Oryzorycles*. Also *rice-tendrac*.

rice-troopial (rīs′trö″pi-ạl), *n.* Same as *rice-bird*, 1. [A book-name.]

rice-water (rīs′wâ″tėr), *n.* Water which has been thickened with the substance of rice by boiling. It is administered as a drink to the sick, either plain, or sweetened and flavored.—**Rice-water evacuations**, watery evacuations passed by cholera patients, containing albuminous flakes, epithelial cells, bacteria, salts, and organic substances.

rice-weevil (rīs′wē″vl), *n.* The cosmopolitan beetle, *Calandra oryzæ*, which feeds on rice and other stored grains in all parts of the world. It is an especial pest in the corn-cribs of the southern United States, and in the rice-granaries of India. See cut under *Calandra*.

rice-wine (rīs′win), *n.* A name given to the fermented liquor made from rice, used by the Chinese and Japanese. See *samshoo* and *sake*[2].

rich[1] (rich), *a.* [< ME. *rich, riche, ryche*; (*a*) partly < AS. *rīce*, rich, powerful, = OS. *rīki* = OFries. *rike, rīk* = D. *rijk* = MLG. LG. *rīk, rike* = OHG. *rīhhi*, MHG. *riche*, G. *reich* = Icel. *rīkr* = Sw. *rik* = Dan. *rig* = Goth. *reiks*, powerful; and (*b*) partly < OF. *riche*, F. *riche* = Pr. *ric* = Sp. Pg. *rico* = It. *ricco*, rich (all from Teut.); with adj. formative, < Goth. *reiks*, ruler, king, < OCelt. *rig* (Ir. *righ*, Gael. *righ*), a king, = L. *rex* (*reg-*), a king (= Skt. *rājan*, a king), < *regere*, Skt. √ *rāj*, rule: see *regent*, *rex*, *Raja*[2]. Cf. *riche*[1], *n.*] 1†. Ruling; powerful; mighty; noble.

> This kyng lay at Camylot vpon krystmasse,
> With mony luflych lorde, ledez of the best,
> Rekenly of the rounde table alle tho *rich* brether.
> *Sir Gawayne and the Green Knight* (E. E. T. S.), l. 39.

> O rightwis *riche* Code, this rewthe thow be-holde!
> *Morte Arthure* (E. E. T. S.), l. 3990.

2. Having wealth or large possessions; possessed of much money, goods, land, or other valuable property; wealthy; opulent: opposed to poor.

> This *riche* man hadde grete plente of bestes and of othir richesse. *Merlin* (E. E. T. S.), i. 3.

> Why, man, she is mine own,
> And I as *rich* in having such a jewel
> As twenty seas, if all their sand were pearl,
> The water nectar, and the rocks pure gold.
> *Shak.*, T. G. of V., ii. 4. 169.

3. Amply supplied or equipped; abundantly provided; abounding: often followed by *in* or *with*.

> God, who is *rich in* mercy, . . . hath quickened us together with Christ. Eph. ii. 4.

> The King of Scots . . . she did send to France,
> To fill King Edward's fame with prisoner kings,
> And make her chronicle as *rich with* praise
> As is the ooze and bottom of the sea
> With sunken wreck and sumless treasuries.
> *Shak.*, Hen. V., i. 2. 163.

> Foremost captain of his time,
> *Rich* in saving common-sense.
> *Tennyson*, Death of Wellington.

4. Abundant in materials; producing or yielding abundantly; productive; fertile; fruitful: as, a *rich* mine; *rich* ore; *rich* soil.

> Let us not hang like roping icicles
> Upon our houses' thatch, whiles a more frosty people
> Sweat drops of gallant youth in our *rich* fields!
> *Shak.*, Hen. V., iii. 5. 25.

> After crossing a small ascent, we came into a Very *rich* Valley called Rooge.
> *Maundrell*, Aleppo to Jerusalem, p. 3.

> Where some refulgent sunset of India
> Streams o'er a *rich* ambrosial ocean isle.
> *Tennyson*, Experiments in Quantity, Milton.

5. Of great price or money value; costly; expensive; sumptuous; magnificent: as, *rich* jewels; *rich* gifts.

> Forthi I rede ȝow *riche* reueles whan ȝe maketh
> For to solace ȝoure soules suche ministrales to haue.
> *Piers Plowman* (B), xiii. 442.

> The next day they came to the Savoy, the Duke of Lancaster's House, which they set on Fire, burning all his *rich* Furniture. *Baker*, Chronicles, p. 138.

> Yet some of the Portuguese, fearing the worst, would every Night put their *richest* Goods into a Boat, ready to take their flight on the first Alarm.
> *Dampier*, Voyages, II. i. 145.

> He took me from a goodly house,
> With store of *rich* apparel, sumptuous fare,
> And page, and maid, and squire, and seneschal.
> *Tennyson*, Geraint.

6. Of great moral worth; highly esteemed; invaluable; precious.

> As frendes be a *rich* and ioful possession, so be foes a continuall torment and canker to the minde of man.
> *Puttenham*, Arte of Eng. Poesie, p. 46.

> Ah! but those tears are pearl which thy love sheds,
> And they are *rich*, and ransom all ill deeds.
> *Shak.*, Sonnets, xxxiv.

> A faith once fair
> Was *richer* than these diamonds.
> *Tennyson*, Lancelot and Elaine.

7. Ample; copious; abundant; plentiful; luxuriant.

> In shorte tyme shull oure enmyes be put bakke, and fayn to take flight, for I se ther my baners that brynge vs *riche* socour. *Merlin* (E. E. T. S.), iii. 400.

> Our duty is so *rich*, so infinite,
> That we may do it still without accompt.
> *Shak.*, L. L. L., v. 2. 199.

> Down on her shoulders falls the brown hair, in *rich* liberal clusters.
> *Thackeray*, Fitz-Boodle Papers, Dorothea.

> With the figure sculpture of French architecture is associated a *rich* profusion of carved leafage.
> *C. H. Moore*, Gothic Architecture, p. 266.

8. Abounding in desirable or effective qualities or elements; of superior quality, composition, or potency.

> The hatayle was so stronge,
> At many a betyr wownde
> The *ryche* blod out spronge.
> *Holy Rood* (E. E. T. S.), p. 151.

> Bees, the little almsmen of spring-bowers,
> Know there is *richest* juice in poison-flowers.
> *Keats*, Isabella, st. 13.

Hence, specifically—9. Having a pleasing or otherwise marked effect upon the senses by virtue of the abundance of some characteristic quality. (*a*) As applied to articles of food, highly seasoned, or containing an excess of nutritive, saccharine, or oily matter; pleasing to the palate; or to articles of drink, highly flavored, stimulating, or strong: as, *rich* wine; *rich* cream; *rich* cake; *rich* gravy; *rich* sauce.

> That jelly 's *rich*, this malmsey healing.
> *Pope*, Imit. of Horace, II. vi. 202.

> Who now will bring me a beaker
> Of the *rich* old wine that here,
> In the choked-up vaults of Windeck,
> Has lain for many a year?
> *Bryant*, Lady of Castle Windeck.

(*b*) Pleasing to the ear; full or mellow in tone; harmonious; sweet.

> Let *rich* music's tongue
> Unfold the imagined happiness that both
> Receive in either by this dear encounter.
> *Shak.*, R. and J., ii. 6. 27.

> What . . . voice, the *richest*-toned that sings,
> Hath power to give thee as thou wert?
> *Tennyson*, In Memoriam, lxxv.

(*c*) Pleasing to the eye, through strength and beauty of hue; pure and strong; vivid: applied especially to color.

> Ther myght oon haue seyn many a riche garnement and many a fressh banere of *riche* colour wave in the wynde.
> *Merlin* (E. E. T. S.), iii. 384.

> A sudden splendour from behind
> Flush'd all the leaves with *rich* gold-green.
> *Tennyson*, Arabian Nights.

> A colour is said to be *rich* or "pure" when the proportion of white light entering into its composition is small.
> *Field's Chromatography*, p. 41.

[*Rich* as applied to colors in zoölogy has a restricted meaning, which, however, is very difficult to define. A metallic, lustrous, or iridescent color is not rich; the word is generally applied to soft and velvety colors which are pure and distinct, as a *rich* black, a *rich* scarlet spot, etc., just as we speak of *rich* velvets, but generally of bright or glossy silks. *Vivid* is very rich or very distinct.] (*d*) Pleasing to the sense of smell; full of fragrance; sweet-scented; aromatic.

> No *rich* perfumes refresh the fruitful field,
> Nor fragrant herbs their native incense yield.
> *Pope*, Winter, l. 47.

10. Excessive; extravagant; inordinate; outrageous; preposterous: commonly applied to ideas, fancies, fabrications, claims, demands, pretensions, conceits, jests, tricks, etc.: as, a *rich* notion; a *rich* idea; *rich* impudence; a *rich* joke; a *rich* hoax. [Colloq.]

> "A capital party, only you were wanted. We had Beaumanoir and Vere, and Jack Tufton and Spraggs."—"Was Spraggs *rich*?"—"Wasn't he! I have not done laughing yet. He told us a story about the little Biron, who was over here last year. . . . Killing! Get him to tell it you. The *richest* thing you ever heard."
> *Disraeli*, Coningsby, viii. 1.

The rich, the rich man; more frequently, in the plural, people of wealth.

> *The rich* hath many friends. Prov. xiv. 20.

> Vicissitude wheels round the motley crowd,
> *The rich* grow poor, the poor become purse-proud.
> *Cowper*, Hope, l. 18.

> *The rich*, on going out of the mosque, often give alms to the poor outside the door.
> *E. W. Lane*, Modern Egyptians, I. 107.

[This word is often used in the formation of compounds which are self-explanatory: as, *rich*-colored, *rich*-fleeced, *rich*-haired, *rich*-laden, etc.]=**Syn.** 2 and 3. Affluent.—4. *Fertile*, etc. (see *fruitful*), luxuriant, teeming.—5 and 6. Splendid, valuable.—7. Copious, plenteous.—9. Savory, delicious.

rich[1]† (rich), *v.* [Also sometimes *ritch*; < ME. *richen, rechen, rychen* (= OD. *rijken* = OHG. *richan, rihhan, richen*, rule, control), < *rich*[1], *a.* Cf. *rich*[1], *a.*] **I.** *trans.* To enrich.

> To *ritch* his country, let his words lyke flowing water fall.
> *Drant*, tr. of Horace. (*Nares.*)

> *Rich'd* with the pride of nature's excellence.
> *Greene and Lodge*, Looking Glass for Lond. and Eng.

> Of all these bounds, even from this line to this,
> With shadowy forests and with champains *rich'd*.
> *Shak.*, Lear, i. 1. 65.

II. *intrans.* To grow rich.

> Thei *rychen* thorw regratorye and rentes hem buggen
> With that the pore people shulde put in here wombe.
> *Piers Plowman* (B), iii. 83.

rich[1]†, *adv.* [< ME. *riche*; < *rich*[1], *a.*] Richly.

> Ful *riche* he was astored prively.
> *Chaucer*, Gen. Prol. to C. T., l. 609.

rich[2]†, *v.* [ME. *richen, ricchen*, a var. of **recchen*, < AS. *reccan*, stretch, direct, rule: see *retch*[1], *rack*[1].] **I.** *trans.* 1. To stretch; pull.

> Ector *richit* his reyne, the Renke for to mete,
> ffor to wreike of his wound, & the wegh harme.
> *Destruction of Troy* (E. E. T. S.), l. 6693.

2. To direct.

> ȝe schal not rise of your bedde, I *rych* yow better,
> I schal happe yow here that other half als,
> And sythen karp wyth my knyȝt that I kaȝt haue.
> *Sir Gawayne and the Green Knight* (E. E. T. S.), l. 1223.

3. To adjust; set right.

> There launchit I to laund, a litle for ese,
> Restid me rifely, *ricchit* my seluyn.
> *Destruction of Troy* (E. E. T. S.), l. 13149.

4. To address; set (one's self to do a thing).

> (He) *riches* him radly to ride and remowis his ost.
> *Alliterative Poems* (ed. Morris), Gloss., p. 186. (K. Alex., p. 172.)

5. To dress.

> When he watz gon, syr G. gerez hym sone,
> Rises, and riches hym in araye noble.
> *Sir Gawayne and the Green Knight* (E. E. T. S.), l. 1873.

6. To mend; improve.

> Then comford he caght in his cole hert,
> Thus hengit in hope, and his hele meudit;
> More redy to rest, *ricchit* his chere.
> *Destruction of Troy* (E. E. T. S.), l. 9257.

7. To avenge.

> Than he purpost plainly with a proude ost
> Ffor to send of his sonnes and other sibbe fryndes,
> The Grekes for to greve, if hom grace telle;
> To wreke hym of wrathe and his wrong *riche*.
> *Destruction of Troy* (E. E. T. S.), l. 2059.

II. *intrans.* To take one's way.

> As he herd the howndes, that hasted hym swythe,
> Renaud com *richchande* thurz a roze greue,
> And alle the rabel in a res, ryzt at his heles.
> *Sir Gawayne and the Green Knight* (E. E. T. S.), l. 1898.

Richardia (ri-chär'di-ä), *n.* [NL. (Kunth, 1815), named from the French botanists L. C. M. *Richard* (1754–1821) and his son Achille *Richard* (1794–1859).] 1. A genus of monocotyledonous plants of the order *Araceæ*, suborder *Philodendroideæ*, and tribe *Richardieæ* (of the last the only genus). It comprises perennial stemless herbs, with monœcious flowers without perianth, the two sexes borne close together on the same spadix. The male flowers bear two or three stamens, the female three staminodia. The ovoid ovary ripens into a berry of from two to five cells, each containing one or two anatropous albuminous seeds. The leaves are sagittate, and the spadix is surrounded with an open white or yellow spathe, the persistent base of which adheres to the fruit. *R. Africana* is the common calla (the *Calla Æthiopica* of Linnæus), often called *calla-lily* on account of its pure-white spathe. Also called *African* or *Ethiopian lily*, and *lily of the Nile*, though it is native only in South Africa. *R. albo-maculata*, having the leaves variegated with translucent white spots, is also cultivated. There are in all 5 species.
2. In *entom.*, a genus of dipterous insects. *Desvoidy*, 1830.

Richardieæ (rich-är-di'ē-ē), *n. pl.* [NL. (Schott, 1856), < *Richardia*, q. v., + *-eæ*.] A plant tribe of the order *Araceæ*, and suborder *Philodendroideæ*, formed by the single genus *Richardia*, and marked by its leading characters.

Richardsonia (rich-ärd-sō'ni-ä), *n.* [NL. (Kunth, 1818), named from Richard *Richardson*, an English botanist, who wrote (1699) on horticulture.] A genus of gamopetalous plants, belonging to the order *Rubiaceæ*, the madder family, and to the tribe *Spermacoceæ*, characterized by three to four ovary-cells, as many style-branches, and a two- to four-celled fruit crowned with from four to eight calyx-lobes, the summit finally falling away from the four lobes or nutlets which constitute its base, and so discharging the four oblong and furrowed seeds. There are 5 or 6 species, natives of warm parts of America. They are erect or prostrate hairy herbs, with a perennial root and round stems, bearing opposite nearly or quite sessile ovate leaves, stipules forming bristly sheaths, and small white or rose-colored flowers in dense heads or whorls. *R. scabra*, with succulent spreading stems and white flowers, has been extensively naturalized from regions further south in the southern United States, where it is known as *Mexican clover*, also as *Spanish* or *Florida clover*, *water-parsley*, etc. Though often a weed, it appears to be of some value as a forage-plant, and perhaps of more value as a green manure. The roots of this species, as also of several others, are supplied to the market from Brazil as a substitute for ipecacuanha.

Richardson's bellows. An apparatus for injecting vapors into the middle ear.

Richardson's grouse. See *dusky grouse*, under *grouse*.

richdomt, *n.* [Early mod. E. *rychedome*; < ME. *richedom*, < AS. *rīcedōm*, power, rule, dominion (= OS. *rīkidōm*, *rīcdōm*, power, = OFries. *rīkedōm* = D. *rijkdom* = MLG. *rīkedōm* = OHG. *rīchiduam*, *rīhtuom*, power, riches, MHG. *rīchtuom*, G. *reichthum* = Icel. *rīkdómr*, power, riches, = Sw. *rikedom* = Dan. *rigdom*, riches, wealth), < *rīce*, rule (in later use taken as if *rīce*, rich), + *dōm*, jurisdiction: see *rich*[1], *a.*, *richel*, *n.*, and *-dom*.] Riches; wealth.

> They of Indyen hath one prynce, and that is pope Iohn, whose myghtynes and *rychedome* amounteth aboue all prynces of the world.
> *R. Eden*, tr. of Amerigo Vespucci (First Books on America, (ed. Arber, p. xxx).

riche[1]†, *a.* and *adv.* See *rich*[1].

riche[1]†, *n.* [ME. *riche*, *ryche*, *rike*, < AS. *rīce*, power, authority, dominion, empire, a kingdom, realm, diocese, district, nation, = OS. *rīki* = OFries. *rīke*, *rīk* = D. *rijk* = MLG. *rīke* = OHG. *rīchi*, *rīhhi*, MHG. *rīche*, G. *reich* = Icel. *rīki* = Sw. *rike* = Dan. *rige* = Goth. *reiki*, power, authority, rule, kingdom; with orig. formative *-ja*, from the noun represented only by Goth. *reiks*, ruler, king: see *rich*[1]. Cf. *-ric*.] A kingdom.

> Comforte thi careful, Cryst, in thi *ryche*,
> For how thow confortest all creatures clerkes hereth witnesse.
> *Piers Plowman* (B), xiv. 179.

> Ihesu Crist con calle to hym hys mylde
> & sayde hys *ryche* no wyz myzt wynne,
> Bot he com thyder ryzt as a chylde.
> *Alliterative Poems* (ed. Morris), i. 721.

riche[2], *v.* See *rich*[2].

richel-bird (rich'el-bėrd), *n.* The least tern, *Sterna minuta*. [Prov. Eng.]

richellest, *n.* A form of *rekels*.

richellite (ri-shel'īt), *n.* [< *Richelle* (see def.) + *-ite*[2].] A hydrated fluophosphate of iron and calcium, occurring in compact masses of a yellow color. It is found at Richelle, near Visé, in Belgium.

richen (rich'n), *v. i.* [< *rich*[1] + *-en*[1].] To become rich; become superior in quality, composition, or effectiveness; specifically, to gain richness of color; become heightened or intensified in brilliancy. [Rare.]

> As the afternoon wanes, and the skies *richen* in intensity, the wide calm stretch of sea becomes a lake of crimson fire.
> *W. Black*, In Far Lochaber, xxiii.

riches (rich'ez), *n. sing.* or *pl.* [Prop. *richess* (with term. as in *largess*), the form *riches* being erroneously used as a plural; early mod. E. *richesse*, < ME. *richesse*, *ritchesse*, *richeise*, *riches*, *ryches* (pl. *richesses*, *ricchessis*), < OF. *richesse*, also *richeise*, *richoise*, F. *richesse* (= Pr. *riquesa* = Sp. Pg. *riqueza* = It. *ricchezza*), riches, wealth; with suffix *-esse*, < *riche*, rich: see *rich*[1], *a.*] 1. The state of being rich, or of having large possessions in land, goods, money, or other valuable property; wealth; opulence; affluence: originally a singular noun, but from its form now regarded as plural.

> In one hour so great *riches* is come to nought.
> Rev. xviii. 17.

> *Riches* do not consist in having more gold and silver, but in having more in proportion than . . . our neighbours.
> *Locke*, Consequences of the Lowering of Interest.

2. That which makes wealthy; any valuable article or property; hence, collectively, wealth; abundant possessions; material treasures. [Formerly with a plural *richesses*.]

> Coupes of clene gold and coppis of siluer,
> Rynges with rubies and *ricchesses* manye.
> *Piers Plowman* (B), iii. 23.

> Alle the *richesses* in this world ben in aventure and passen as a shadowe on the wal.
> *Chaucer*, Parson's Tale.

> In living Princes court none ever knew
> Such endlesse *richesse*, and so sumpteous shew.
> *Spenser*, F. Q., I. iv. 7.

> I bequeath . . .
> My *riches* to the earth from whence they came.
> *Shak.*, Pericles, i. 1. 52.

> Through the bounty of the soile he [Macarius] acquired much *riches*.
> *Sandys*, Travailes, p. 13.

> The writings of the wise are the only *riches* our posterity cannot squander.
> *Landor*, Imag. Conv., Milton and Andrew Marvel.

3. That which has a high moral value; any object of high regard or esteem; an intellectual or spiritual treasure: as, the *riches* of knowledge.

> On her he spent the *riches* of his wit.
> *Spenser*, Astrophel, l. 62.

> If therefore ye have not been faithful in the unrighteous mammon, who will commit to your trust the true *riches*?
> Luke xvi. 11.

> It is not your riches of this world, but your *riches* of grace, that shall do your souls good.
> *Rev. T. Adams*, Works, I. 141.

> His best companions innocence and health,
> And his best *riches* ignorance of wealth.
> *Goldsmith*, Des. Vil., l. 62.

4†. The choicest product or representative of anything; the pearl; the flower; the cream.

> For grace hath wold so ferforth him avaunce
> That of knighthode he is parfit *richesse*.
> *Chaucer*, Complaint of Venus, l. 12.

5†. An abundance; a wealth: used as a hunting term, in the form *richess* or *richesse*. *Strutt.*

> The foresters . . . talk of . . . a *richesse* of martens to be chased.
> *The Academy*, Feb. 4, 1888, p. 71.

=Syn. 1. *Wealth*, *Affluence*, etc. (see *opulence*), wealthiness, plenty, abundance.

richesst, **richesset**, *n.* Obsolete forms of *riches*.

rich-left (rich'left), *a.* Inheriting great wealth. [Rare.]

> O ill, sore-shaming
> Those *rich-left* heirs that let their fathers lie
> Without a monument!
> *Shak.*, Cymbeline, iv. 2. 226.

richly (rich'li), *adv.* [< ME. *richeliche*, *richelike*, < AS. *rīclīce* (= D. *rijkelijk* = MLG. *rīkelik* = OHG. *rīchlīcho*, *rīhlīcho*, MHG. *rīchlīche*, *rīlīche*, G. *reichlich* = Icel. *rīkuliga* = Sw. *riklig* = Dan. *rigelig*), richly, < *rīce*, rich: see *rich*[1] and *-ly*[2].] With riches; with wealth or affluence; sumptuously; amply or abundantly; with unusual excellence of quality; finely.

> She was faire and noble, . . . and *richly* married to Sinatus the Tetrarch.
> *Purchas*, Pilgrimage, p. 321.

> Oh thou, my Muse! guid auld Scotch drink:
> Whether thro' wimplin' worms thou jink,
> Or, *richly* brown, ream o'er the brink
> In glorious faem.
> *Burns*, Scotch Drink.

Richmond herald. One of the six heralds of the English heralds' college: an office created by Henry VII., in memory of his previous title of Earl of Richmond.

richness (rich'nes), *n.* [< ME. *richnesse*; < *rich*[1] + *-ness*.] The state or quality of being rich.

> The country-girl, willing to give her utmost assistance, proposed to make an Indian cake, . . . which she could vouch for as possessing a *richness*, and, if rightly prepared, a delicacy, unequalled by any other mode of breakfast-cake.
> *Hawthorne*, Seven Gables, vii.

richterite (rich'tėr-īt), *n.* [Named after Dr. R. *Richter*, of Saxony.] In *mineral.*, a variety of amphibole or hornblende, containing a small percentage of manganese, found in Sweden.

Richter's collyrium. A mixture of rose-water and white of egg beaten to a froth.

richweed (rich'wēd), *n.* 1. See *horse-balm*.— 2. Same as *clearweed*.

ricinelaidic (ris-i-nel-a-id'ik), *a.* [< *ricinelaïd(in)* + *-ic*.] Related to elaïdin; derived from castor-oil.—**Ricinelaidic acid**, an acid derived from and isomeric with ricinolic acid.

ricinelaidin (ris″in-e-lā'i-din), *n.* [< NL. *Ricinus* (see *Ricinus*[1]) + Gr. ἔλαιον, oil, + *-id*[1] + *-in*[2].] A fatty substance obtained from castor-oil by acting on it with nitric acid.

ricinia, *n.* Plural of *ricinium*.

Riciniæ† (rī-sin'i-ē), *n. pl.* [NL., < L. *ricinus*, a tick: see *Ricinus*[1].] In Latreille's classification, a division of mites or acarines, including such genera of ticks as *Ixodes*, *Argas*, etc. The name indicates the common tick of the dog, *Ixodes ricinus*.

ricinium (rī-sin'i-um), *n.*; pl. *ricinia* (-ä). [L., cf. *ricinus*, veiled, < *rica*, a veil to be thrown over the head.] A piece of dress among the ancient Romans, consisting of a mantle, smaller and shorter than the pallium, and having a cowl or hood for the head attached to it. It was worn especially by women, particularly as a morning garment, and by mimes on the stage.

> The *ricinium*—in the form of a veil, as worn by the Arval Brothers.
> *Encyc. Brit.*, VI. 457.

ricinoleic (ris-i-nō'lē-ik), *a.* [< NL. *Ricinus* (see *Ricinus*[1]) + L. *oleum*, oil, + *-ic*.] Same as *ricinolic*.

> It [purging-nut oil] is a violent purgative, and contains, like castor oil, *ricinoleic* acid.
> *Encyc. Brit.*, XVII. 746.

ricinolein (ris-i-nē'lē-in), *n.* [< NL. *Ricinus* (see *Ricinus*[1]) + L. *ole(um)*, oil, + *-in*[2].] In *chem.*, a fatty substance obtained from castor-oil, of which it is the chief constituent. It is a glyceride of ricinolic acid.

ricinolic (ris-i-nol'ik), *a.* [< NL. *Ricinus* (see *Ricinus*[1]) + L. *ol(eum)*, oil, + *-ic*.] In *chem.*, pertaining to or obtained from castor-oil. Also *ricinoleic*.—**Ricinolic acid**, $C_{18}H_{34}O_3$, an acid obtained from castor-oil, in which it exists in combination with glycerin. It is an oily, colorless liquid.

Ricinula (rī-sin'ū-lä), *n.* [NL. (Lamarck, 1812), so called from a supposed resemblance to the castor-oil bean; dim. of L. *ricinus*, the castor-oil plant: see *Ricinus*[1].] In *conch.*, a genus of gastropods of the family *Muricidæ*, inhabiting the Indian and Pacific oceans. Also called *Pentadactylus* and *Sistrum*.

Ricinula arachnoides.

Ricinus[1] (ris'i-nus), *n.* [NL. (Tournefort, 1700), < L. *ricinus*, a plant, also called *cici* and *croton*; perhaps orig. an error for **cicinus*, < Gr. κίκινος, of the castor-oil plant (κίκινον ἔλαιον, castor-oil), < κίκι (> L. *cici*), the castor-oil plant.] A genus of apetalous plants of the order *Euphorbiaceæ*, tribe *Crotoneæ*, and subtribe *Acalypheæ*. It is characterized by monœcious flowers, the calyx in the staminate flowers closed in the bud, in the pistillate sheath-like and cleft and very caducous; by very numerous (sometimes 1,000) stamens, with their crowded filaments repeatedly branched, each branch bearing two separate and roundish anther-cells; and by a three-celled ovary with two-cleft plumose styles, ripening into a capsule with three two-valved cells, each containing one smooth ovoid hard-crusted seed with fleshy albumen and two broad and flat cotyledons. The only species, *R. communis*, the well-known castor-oil plant, is a native probably of Africa, often naturalized in warm climates, and possibly indigenous in America and Asia. It is a tall annual herb, smooth and often glaucous, becoming arborescent in warm regions, and bearing large alternate leaves palmately lobed and peltate. The conspicuous terminal inflorescence is composed of somewhat panicled racemes, the upper part of each formed of crowded staminate flowers, the lower part of pistillate flowers, each short-pedicelled. The plant is very variable in its capsules, which are either smooth or prickly, and in the seeds, which are often mottled with gray and brown markings, and appendaged with a large whitish caruncle. The castor-oil plant is not only of medicinal value, as the source of a mild and speedy cathartic, but is one of the most imposing of ornamental plants, and thrives as an annual in temperate climates. It has several garden varieties. Also called *castor-bean* and *palma Christi*. See *castor-oil*; also *arillode* and *caruncle*.

Ricinus[2] (ris'i-nus), *n.* [NL., < L. *ricinus*, a tick on sheep, dogs, etc.] In *entom.*, an old genus of bird-lice. *De Geer*, 1778.

rick[1] (rik), *n.* [Also dial. *ruck*; < ME. **rykke*, < AS. *hrycce*, in comp. *corn-hrycce*, a corn-rick, a derivative form of *hrodc*, a rick, E. *reek*: see *reek*[2].] A heap or pile; specifically, a pile of hay or grain, generally cylindrical, with the top rounded or conical, and sometimes thatched for protection from rain.

> Great King, whence came this Courage (Titan-like)
> So many Hils to heap upon a *rick*?
> *Sylvester*, tr. of Du Bartas's Weeks, ii., The Magnificence.

> When the wild peasant rights himself, the *rick*
> Flames, and his anger reddens in the heavens.
> *Tennyson*, Princess, iv.

=**Syn.** *Shock*, etc. See *sheaf*.

rick[1] (rik), *v. t.* [< *rick*[1], *n.*] To pile up in ricks.

rick[2] (rik), *v.* See *wrick*.

ricker (rik'ėr), *n.* [< *rick*[1], *v.*, + *-er*[1].] An implement, drawn by a horse or mule, for cocking up or shocking hay. It has long teeth, and operates like an earth-scraper while collecting the hay; and inclining the handle upward causes the ricker to turn over and discharge its load where a shock is to be formed. Also called *shocker*. More properly called *hay-ricker*.

rickers (rik'ėrz), *n. pl.* [Perhaps so called as used in making a base or props for ricks; < *rick*[1], *n.*, + *-er*[1].] The stems or trunks of young trees cut up into lengths for stowing flax, hemp, and the like, or for spars for boat-masts and -yards, boat-hook staves, etc. [Eng.]

ricket-body†, *n.* A body affected with the rickets; a rickety body.

> Both may be good; but when heads swell, men say,
> The rest of the poor members pine away,
> Like *ricket-bodies*, upwards over-grown,
> Which is no wholsome constitution.
> *Wilson*, James I. (1653). (*Nares.*)

ricketily (rik'et-i-li), *adv.* In a rickety manner; feebly; shakily; unsteadily.

> At least this one among all her institutions she has succeeded in setting, however *ricketily*, on its legs again.
> *R. Broughton*, Second Thoughts, iii. 4.

ricketiness (rik'et-i-nes), *n.* The state or character of being rickety; hence, in general, shakiness; unsteadiness.

ricketish (rik'ot-ish), *a.* [< *ricket(s)* + *-ish*[1].] Having a tendency to rickets; rickety. [Rare.]

> Surely there is some other cure for a *ricketish* body than to kill it. *Fuller*, Worthies, xi.

ricketly† (rik'ot-li), *a.* [< *ricket(s)* + *-ly*[1].] Rickety; shaky; weak.

> No wonder if the whole constitution of Religion grow weak, *ricketly*, and consumptuous.
> *Bp. Gauden*, Tears of the Church, p. 262. (*Davies.*)

rickets (rik'ets), *n.* [Prop. **wrickets*, < *wrick*, twist, + *-et-s*. The NL. term *rachitis* is of Gr. formation, but was suggested by the E. word: see *rachitis*.] A disease, technically called *rachitis*. See *rachitis*, 1.

> The new disease.—There is a disease of Infants, and an infant-disease, having scarcely as yet got a proper name in Latin, called the *rickets*; wherein the head waxeth too great, whilst the legs and lower parts wain too little.
> *Fuller*, Meditation on the Times (1647), xx. 103, quoted in [Notes and Queries, 6th ser., II. 219.

rickety (rik'ot-i), *a.* [< *ricket(s)* + *-y*[1].] 1. Affected with rickets.

> But in a young Animal, when the Solids are too Lax (the Case of *rickety* Children), the Diet ought to be gently Astringent. *Arbuthnot*, Aliments, II. vii. § 5.

2. Feeble in the joints; tottering; infirm; hence, in general, shaky; liable to fall or collapse, as a table, chair, bridge, etc.; figuratively, ill-sustained; weak.

> Crude and *rickety* notions, enfeebled by restraint, when permitted to be drawn out and examined, may . . . at length acquire health and proportion.
> *Warburton*, Works, I. 146.

rickle (rik'l), *n.* [< *rick*[1] + dim. *-le* (*-el*).] 1. A heap or pile, as of stones or peats, loosely thrown together; specifically, a small rick of hay or grain. [Scotch or prov. Eng.]

> May Boreas never thrash your rigs,
> Nor kick your *rickles* aff their legs.
> *Burns*, Third Epistle to J. Lapraik.

2. A quantity of anything loosely and carelessly put together; a loose or indiscriminate mass: as, the man is a *rickle* of bones. [Scotch.]

> The proud Percy caused bang five of the Laird's henchmen at Alnwick for burning a *rickle* of houses some gate beyond Fowberry. *Scott*, Monastery, xiii.

rick-rack (rik'rak), *n.* [A varied redupl. of *rack*[1].] A kind of openwork trimming made by hand, with needle and thread, out of a narrow zigzag braid.

> The young hostess sat placidly making *rick-rack* on the . . . porch at the side of the house.
> *The Christian Union*, Aug. 11, 1887.

rickshaw (rik'shâ), *n.* An abbreviated form of *jinrikisha*, in current colloquial use throughout the East.

rick-stand (rik'stand), *n.* A basement of timber or iron, or sometimes wholly or partly of masonry, on which corn-ricks or -stacks are built.

rickyard (rik'yärd), *n.* A farm-yard containing ricks of hay or corn. [Rare in U. S.]

ricochet (rik-ō-shā' or -shet'), *n.* [< OF. *ricochet*; cf. F. *ricocher*, ricochet, make ducks and drakes; origin uncertain.] The motion of an object which rebounds from a flat surface over which it is passing, as in the case of a stone thrown along the surface of water.—**Ricochet battery.** See *battery*.—**Ricochet fire, ricochet firing.** See *fire*, 13.—**Ricochet shot**, a shot made by ricochet fire.

ricochet (rik-ō-shā' or -shet'), *v. i.*; pret. and pp. *ricochetted*, ppr. *ricochetting*. [< *ricochet*, *n.*] To bound by touching the earth or the surface of water and glancing off, as a cannon-ball.

> The round-shot, which seemed to pitch into the centre of a squadron of the Carabineers, *ricochetted* through the fields. *W. H. Russell*, Diary in India, II. 4.

> The pioneer sunbeam . . . flashed into Richard Wade's eyes, waked him, and was off, *ricochetting* across the black ice of the river. *T. Winthrop*, Love and Skates.

ricolite (rē'kō-līt), *n.* [< *Rico*, in New Mexico, + Gr. λίθος, stone.] A stratified ornamental stone, made up of successive layers of white limestone and olive and snuff-green serpentine, found in New Mexico.

rictal (rik'tal), *a.* [< *rict(us)* + *-al*.] In *ornith.*, of or pertaining to the rictus: as, *rictal* vibrissæ. See *rictus*, 1.

ricture† (rik'tūr), *n.* [< L. *rictus*, pp. of *ringi*, open the mouth wide, gape, grin (> It. *ringhiare*, grin, frown): see *ringent*.] A gaping. *Bailey*.

rictus (rik'tus), *n.*; pl. *rictus*. [< L. *rictus*, a gaping, distention of the jaws of animals, < *ringi*, pp. *rictus*, gape: see *ringent*.] 1. In *ornith.*, the gape of the bill; the cleft between the upper and the lower mandible when the mouth is open.—2. In *bot.*, the throat, as of a calyx, corolla, etc.; the opening between the lips of a ringent or personate flower. [Rare.]

rid[1] (rid), *v. t.*; pret. and pp. *rid*, formerly also *ridded*, ppr. *ridding*. [Also dial. (and orig.) *red*; < ME. *ridden*, *rydden*, *redden* (pret. *redde*, pp. *red*), < AS. *hreddan*, take away, save, liberate, deliver, = OFries. *hredda*, *reda* = D. MLG. LG. *redden* = OHG. *rettan*, *retten*, MHG. G. *retten* = Norw. *rædda* = Sw. *rädda* = Dan. *redde*, save, rescue, forms not found in Icel. or Goth. (the Scand. forms are modern, < LG. or E.); perhaps = Skt. √ *çrath*, loosen.] 1†. To take away; remove, as from a position of trouble or danger; deliver.

> Why thow has *redyne* and raymede, and raunsound the pople,
> And kyllyde doune his cosyns, kyngys ennoynttyde.
> *Morte Arthure* (E. E. T. S.), l. 100.

> Take you your keen bright sword,
> And *rid* me out of my life.
> *The West-Country Damosel's Complaint* (Child's Ballads, [II. 384).

> We thought it safer to *rid* ourselves out of their hands and the trouble we were brought into, and therefore we patiently layd down the mony.
> *Evelyn*, Diary, March 23, 1646.

2. To separate or free from anything superfluous or objectionable; disencumber; clear.

> Thi fader in fuerse with his fre will
> *Rid* me this Rewme out of ronke Enmys.
> *Destruction of Troy* (E. E. T. S.), l. 5343.

> I must
> *Rid* all the sea of pirates.
> *Shak.*, A. and C., ii. 6. 36.

> That is a light Burthen which *rids* one of a far harder.
> *Stillingfleet*, Sermons, III. iii.

3†. To send or drive away; expel; banish.

> I will *rid* evil beasts out of the land. Lev. xxvi. 6.

> And, once before deceiv'd, she newly cast about
> To *rid* him out of sight. *Drayton*, Polyolbion, ii. 295.

4†. To clear away; disencumber or clear one's self of; get rid of.

> But if I my cage can *rid*,
> I'll fly where I never did.
> *Wither*, The Shepherd's Hunting.

Specifically—(*a*) To part from; dispose of; spend.

> Hee [any handicraft man] will haue a thousand florishes, which before hee neuer thought vpon, and in one day *rid* more out of hand than erst he did in ten.
> *Nashe*, Pierce Penilesse, p. 28.

(*b*) To get through or over; accomplish; achieve; despatch.

> As they are woont to say, not to stand all day trifling to no purpose, but to *rid* it out of the way quickly.
> *Puttenham*, Arte of Eng. Poesie, p. 195.

> We, having now the best at Barnet field,
> Will thither straight, for willingness *rids* way.
> *Shak.*, 3 Hen. VI., v. 3. 21.

> The Printer in one day shall *rid*
> More Books then yerst a thousand Writers did.
> *Sylvester*, tr. of Du Bartas's Weeks, ii., The Columnes.

(*c*) To put out of the way; destroy; kill.

> I *rid* her not: I made her not away,
> By heaven I swear! traitors
> They are to Edward and to England's Queen
> That say I made away the Mayoress.
> *Peele*, Edward I.

> But if you ever chance to have a child,
> Look in his youth to have him so cut off
> As, deathsmen, you have *rid* this sweet young prince!
> *Shak.*, 3 Hen. VI., v. 5. 67.

> Such mercy in thy heart was found,
> To *rid* a lingering wretch.
> *Beau. and Fl.*, Maid's Tragedy, ii. 1.

5†. To part; put asunder; separate.

> We ar in this valay, verayly oure one,
> Here are no renkes vs to *rydde*, rele as vus likez.
> *Sir Gawayne and the Green Knight* (E. E. T. S.), l. 2246.

To rid house, to remove all the furniture from a house. *Halliwell*. [Prov. Eng.]

rid[1] (rid), *p. a.* [< *rid*[1], *v.*] Free; clear; quit; relieved: followed by *of*.

> Surely he was a wicked man; the realm was well *rid of* him. *Latimer*, 4th Sermon bef. Edw. VI., 1549.

> I would we were well *rid of* this knavery.
> *Shak.*, T. N., iv. 2. 73.

> The townesmen remaining presently fraughted our Barge to be *rid of* our companies.
> Quoted in *Capt. John Smith's* Works, I. 219.

> Thence I rode all-shamed, hating the life
> He gave me, meaning to be *rid of* it.
> *Tennyson*, Geraint.

To get rid of. See *get*.

rid[2] (rid). An obsolete or dialectal preterit of *ride*.

rid[3] (rid), *v. t.* A dialectal variant of *red*[3].

rid[4] (rid), *n.* A variant of *red*[5].

> Favorite grounds where the trout make their *rids*.
> *Report of the Maine Fisheries Commission*, 1875, p. 12.

rida (rē'dä), *n.* That part of the ihram, or Moslem pilgrim's dress, which is thrown over the left shoulder and knotted at the right side.

ridable, rideable (rī'da-bl), *a.* [< *ride* + *-able*.] 1. Capable of being ridden, as a saddle-horse.

> I rode everything *rideable*.
> *M. W. Savage*, Reuben Medlicott, ii. 3. (*Davies.*)

2. Passable on horseback; capable of being ridden through or over: as, a *ridable* stream or bridge.

> For at this very time there was a man that used to trade to Hartlepool weekly, and who had many years known when the water was *rideable*, and yet he ventured in as I did, and he and his horse were both drowned at the very time when I lay sick. *Lister*, Autobiog., p. 45. (*Halliwell.*)

riddance (rid'ans), *n.* [< *rid*[1] + *-ance*.] 1. The act of ridding or getting rid, as of something superfluous, objectionable, or injurious; the state of being thus relieved; deliverance; specifically, the act of clearing or cleaning out.

> Some [things] which ought not to be desired, as the deliverance from sudden death, *riddance* from all adversity, and the extent of saving mercy towards all men.
> Hooker, Eccles. Polity, v. 27.

> Thou shalt not make clean *riddance* of the corners of thy field when thou reapest, neither shalt thou gather any gleaning of thy harvest; thou shalt leave them unto the poor. Lev. xxiii. 22.

> They have a great care to keep them [the Streets] clean; in Winter, for Example, upon the melting of the Ice, by a heavy drag with a Horse, which makes a quick *riddance* and cleaning the Gutters. *Lister*, Journey to Paris, p. 24.

2. The act of putting out of the way; specifically, destruction.

> The whole land shall be devoured by the fire of his jealousy; for he shall make even a speedy *riddance* of all them that dwell in the land. Zeph. i. 18.

> Those blossoms also, and those dropping gums,
> That lie bestrown, unsightly and unsmooth,
> Ask *riddance*, if we mean to tread with ease.
> *Milton*, P. L., iv. 632.

3. The earth thrown out by an animal, as a fox, badger, or woodchuck, in burrowing into the ground.—**A good riddance**, a welcome relief from unpleasant company or an embarrassing connection or complication; hence, something of which one is glad to be quit.

> *Ther.* I will see you hanged, like clotpoles, ere I come any more to your tents. . . . [Exit.]
> *Patr. A good riddance.* *Shak.*, T. and C., ii. 1. 132.

> What *a good riddance* for Ainslie! Now the weight is taken off, it is just possible he may get a fresh start, and make a race of it after all.
> *Whyte Melville*, White Rose, I. xxvii.

Riddance salts. See the quotation.

A group of salts chiefly magnesic and potassic, and formerly called *riddance salts* (Abraumsalze), because they were at first without industrial application, and were merely extracted to reach the rock-salt below.
Ure, Dict., III. 593.

riddel†, *n.* See *riddle*[3].

ridden (rid'n). Past participle of *ride*.

ridder[1] (rid'ėr), *n.* [< ME. *ridder*, *rydder*, < AS. *hridder*, orig. *hridder* = OHG. *ritera*, MHG. *ritere*, *riter*, G. *reiter*, a sieve, = L. *cribrum* for **crithrum*, a sieve, = Ir. *criathar*, *creathair* = Gael. *criathar* = Corn. *croider* = Bret. *krouer*, a sieve; with formative *-der* (*-ther*), < √ *hri*, sift, = L. √ *cri*, in *cernere*, separate, sift, *cretura*, a sifting, etc., Gr. √ *κρι*, in *κρίνειν*, separate: see *concern*, *critic*, etc. The G. *räder*, *rädel*, a sieve, is of diff. origin, < MHG. *reden*, OHG. *redan*, sift.] A sieve: now usually *riddle*. [Prov. Eng.]

ridder[1] (rid'ėr), *v. t.* [< ME. *riddren*, < AS. *hridrian* (= OHG. *hriturōn*, *riterōn*, MHG. *riteren*, *ritern*, G. *reitern*), sift, winnow, < *hridder*, a sieve: see *ridder*[1], *n.*] To sift; riddle. *Wyclif*, Luke xxii. 31.

ridder[2] (rid'ėr), *n.* [= D. *redder* = G. *retter*, saver, savior; as *rid*[1] + *-er*[1].] One who or that which rids, frees, or relieves.

riddle[1] (rid'l), *n.* [< ME. *ridil*, *rydyl*, *redel* (pl. *redeles*), earlier *rydels*, *redels*, *rædels* (pl. *rædelses*), < AS. *rǣdels* (pl. *rǣdelsas*), m., *rǣdelse*, *rēdelse* (pl. *rǣdelsan*), f., counsel, consideration, debate, conjecture, interpretation, imagination, an enigma, riddle (= D. *raadsel* = MLG. *radelse*, LG. *redelse*, *rudelse* = OHG. **rātisal*, MHG. *rǣtsal*, *raetsel*, G. *rätsel*, *räthsel*, a riddle), < *rǣdan*, counsel, consider, interpret, read: see *read*[1].] 1. A proposition so framed as to exercise one's ingenuity in discovering its meaning; an ambiguous, complex, or puzzling question offered for solution; an enigma; a dark saying.

"What?" quod Clergye to Conscience, "ar ȝe coueitouse nouthe
After ȝeresȝyues or ȝiftes, or ȝernen to rede *redeles?*"
Piers Plowman (B), xiii. 184.

We dissemble againe vnder couert and darke speaches, when we speake by way of *riddle* (Enigma), of which the sence can hardly be picked out but by the parties owne assoile.
Puttenham, Arte of Eng. Poesie, p. 157.

Life presented itself to him like the Sphinx with its perpetual *riddle* of the real and the ideal.
Longfellow, Kavanagh, i.

2. Anything abstruse, intricate, paradoxical, or puzzling; a puzzle.

I would not yet be pointed at, as he is,
For the fine courtier, the woman's man,
That tells my lady stories, dissolves *riddles*.
Fletcher (and another), Queen of Corinth, i. 2.

3. A person who manifests ambiguities or contradictions of character or conduct.

She could love none but only such
As scorned and hated her as much.
'Twas a strange *riddle* of a lady.
S. Butler, Hudibras, I. iii. 337.

Great lord of all things, yet a prey to all;
Sole judge of truth, in endless error hurled:
The glory, jest, and *riddle* of the world!
Pope, Essay on Man, ii. 18.

Riddle canon. Same as *enigmatical canon* (which see, under *canon*[1]).

riddle[1] (rid'l), *v.*; pret. and pp. *riddled*, ppr. *riddling*. [= G. *räthseln*, *rätseln*; from the noun: see *riddle*[1], *n.*] I. *trans.* 1. To explain; interpret; solve; unriddle.

Riddle me this, and guess him if you can:
Who bears a nation in a single man?
Dryden, tr. of Juvenal's Satires, iii. 135.

2. To understand; make out.

What, do you *riddle* me? Is she contracted?
And can I by your counsell attaine my wishes?
Carlell, Deserving Favorite (1629). (*Nares*.)

3. To puzzle; perplex.

I think it will *riddle* him or he gets his horse over the Border again.
Scott, Rob Roy, xviii.

II. *intrans.* To speak in riddles, ambiguously, or enigmatically.

Lys. Lying so, Hermia, I do not lie.
Her. Lysander *riddles* very prettily.
Shak., M. N. D., ii. 2. 53.

riddle[2] (rid'l), *n.* [< ME. **riddel*, *ryddel*, *rydel*, *ridil*, *rydyl*, for earlier *ridder*: see *ridder*[1].] 1. A sieve, especially a coarse one for sand, grain, and the like.

So this young gentleman, who had scarcely done a day's work in his life, made his way to the modern El Dorado, to cook, and dig, and wield a pickaxe, and shake a *riddle* till his back ached.
Whyte Melville, White Rose, I. xxx.

2. In *founding*, a sieve with half-inch mesh, used in the molding-shop for cleaning and mixing old floor-sand.—3. In *hydraul. engin.*, a form of river-weir.—4. In *wire-working*, a flat board set with iron pins sloped in opposite directions. It is used to straighten wire, which is drawn in a zigzag course between the pins. *E. H. Knight*.—**A riddle of claret.** See the quotation.

A *riddle of claret* is thirteen bottles, a magnum and twelve quarts. The name comes from the fact that the wine is brought in on a literal riddle—the magnum in the center surrounded by the quarts. A *riddle of claret* thus displayed duly appeared recently at the Edinburgh arrow dinner of the Royal Company of Archers.
N. and Q., 7th ser., VIII. 13.

riddle[2] (rid'l), *v.*; pret. and pp. *riddled*, ppr. *riddling*. [< ME. *riddlen*, *ridlen*, *ridelen*, *rydelen*, for earlier *riddren*: see *ridder*[1], *v.* Cf. *riddle*[2], *n.*] I. *trans.* 1. To sift through a riddle or sieve: as, to *riddle* sand.—2. To sift by means of a coarse-netted dredge, as young oysters on a bed.—3. To reduce in quantity as if by sifting; condense.

For general use the book . . . wants *riddling* down into a single volume or a large essay.
Athenæum, No. 3207, p. 467.

4. To fill with holes; especially, to perforate with shot so as to make like a riddle; hence, to puncture or pierce all over as if with shot; penetrate.

His moral feelings . . . were regularly fusilladed by the Major . . . and *riddled* through and through. *Dickens*.

II. *intrans.* 1. To use a riddle or sieve; pass anything through a riddle.

Robin Goodfellow, he that sweeps the hearth and the house clean, *riddles* for the country maids, and does all their other drudgery. *B. Jonson*, Love Restored.

2. To fall in drops or fine streams, as through a riddle or sieve.

The rayn rueled adoun, *ridlande* thikke,
Of felle flaunkes of fyr and flakes of soufre.
Alliterative Poems (ed. Morris), ii. 958.

riddle[3]†, *n.* [< ME. *riddel*, *ridel*, *redel*, *rudel*, < OF. *ridel*, F. *rideau* (ML. *ridellus*), a curtain, orig. a plaited stuff, < *rider*, wrinkle, plait, < MHG. *riden*, wrinkle, = E. *writhe*: see *writhe*.] A curtain; a bed-curtain; in a church, one of the pair of curtains inclosing an altar on the north and south, often hung from rods driven into the wall.

That was a mervelle thynge
To se the *riddels* hynge
With many red golde rynge
That thame up bare.
MS. Lincoln A. i. 17, f. 136. (*Halliwell.*)

Rudeleȝ rennande on ropeȝ, red golde rynges.
Sir Gawayne and the Green Knight (E. E. T. S.), l. 857.

Item ij *ridelles* of the same suyte, wt aungell.
Inventory of St. Peter Cheap (Cheapside), 1431, in Jour. [Brit. Archæol. Ass., XXIV.

riddle[3]†, *v. t.* [< ME. *ridlen*; appar. < *riddle*[3], *n.*, in its orig. sense, a plaited stuff. Cf. *raddle*[1].] To plait.

Lord, it was *ridled* fetysly!
Ther nas not a poynt trewely
That it nas in his right assise.
Rom. of the Rose, l. 1235.

Riddleberger Act. See *act*.

riddle-cake (rid'l-kāk), *n.* A thick sour oaten cake. *Halliwell*.

riddle-like (rid'l-līk), *a.* Like a riddle; enigmatical; paradoxical.

O, then, give pity
To her, whose state is such that cannot choose
But lend and give where she is sure to lose;
That seeks not to find that her search implies,
But *riddle-like* lives sweetly where she dies!
Shak., All's Well, i. 3. 223.

riddlemeree (rid'l-me-rē'), *n.* [A fanciful word, based on *riddle*, as if *riddle my riddle*, explain my enigma.] Same as *rigmarole*.

This style, I apprehend, Sir, is what the learned Scriblerus calls rigmarol in logic—*Riddlemeree* among School-boys. *Junius*, Letters (ed. Woodfall), II. 316.

riddler[1] (rid'lėr), *n.* [< *riddle*[1] + *-er*[1].] One who speaks in riddles or enigmatically.

Each songster, *riddler*, every nameless name,
All crowd, who foremost shall be damn'd to fame.
Pope, Dunciad, iii. 157.

riddler[2] (rid'lėr), *n.* [< *riddle*[2] + *-er*[1].] One who works with a riddle or sieve.

riddling (rid'ling), *p. a.* [Ppr. of *riddle*[1], *v.*] 1. Speaking in riddles or ambiguously.

This is a *riddling* merchant for the nonce;
He will be here, and yet he is not here:
How can these contrarieties agree?
Shak., 1 Hen. VI., ii. 3. 57.

2. Having the form or character of a riddle; enigmatical; puzzling.

Every man is under that complicated disease, and that *riddling* distemper, not to be content with the most, and yet to be proud of the least thing he hath.
Donne, Sermons, v.

He laugh'd as is his wont, and answer'd me
In *riddling* triplets of old time.
Tennyson, Coming of Arthur.

3. Divining; interpreting; guessing.

Much she mus'd, yet could not construe it
By any *ridling* skill, or commune wit.
Spenser, F. Q., III. xi. 54.

riddlingly (rid'ling-li), *adv.* In the manner of a riddle; enigmatically; mysteriously.

Though, like the pestilence and old fashion'd love,
Riddlingly it catch men. *Donne*, Satires, ii.

riddlings (rid'lingz), *n. pl.* [Pl. of *riddling*, verbal n. of *riddle*[2], *v.*] The coarser part of anything, as grain or ashes, which is left in the riddle after sifting; siftings; screenings.

She . . . pointed to the great bock of wash, and *riddlings*, and brown hulkage (for we ground our own corn always). *R. D. Blackmore*, Lorna Doone, xxxii.

ride (rīd), *v.*; pret. *rode* (formerly also *rid*), pp. *ridden* (formerly also *rid*), ppr. *riding*. [< ME. *riden* (pret. *rod*, *rood*, earlier *rad*, pl. *riden*, *reden*, pp. *riden*), < AS. *rīdan* (pret. *rād*, pl. *ridon*, pp. *riden*), ride on horseback, move forward (as a ship or a cloud), rock (as a ship at anchor), swing (as one hung on a gallows), = OFries. *rīda* = D. *rijden*, ride on horseback or in a vehicle, slide, as on skates, = MLG. LG. *riden* = OHG. *rītan*, move forward, proceed, ride on horseback or in a vehicle, MHG. *rīten*, G. *reiten*, ride, = Icel. *rītha* = Sw. *rida* = Dan. *ride*, ride; orig. prob. simply 'go,' 'travel' (as in the derived noun *road*, in the general sense 'a way'); cf. OIr. *riad*, ride, move, *riadami*, I ride, Gaulish *rēda* (> L. *rheda*, *reda*, *ræda*), a wagon. Hence ult. *road*[1], *raid*, bed-*ridden*.] I. *intrans.* 1. To be carried on the back of a horse, ass, mule, camel, elephant, or other animal; specifically, to sit on and manage a horse in motion.

Beves an hakenai bestrit,
And in his wei forth a *rit*.
Beves of Hamtoun, p. 51. (*Halliwell.*)

And yet was he, whereso men wente or *riden*,
Founde on the beste. *Chaucer*, Troilus, i. 473.

And lastly came cold February, sitting
In an old wagon, for he could not *ride*.
Spenser, F. Q., VII. vii. 43.

Brutus and Cassius
Are *rid* like madmen through the gates of Rome.
Shak., J. C., iii. 2. 274.

2. To be borne along in a vehicle, or in or on any kind of conveyance; be carried in or on a wagon, coach, car, balloon, ship, palanquin, bicycle, or the like; hence, in general, to travel or make progress by means of any supporting and moving agency.

So on a day, hys fadur and hee
Redyn yn a schyppe yn the see.
MS. Cantab. Ff. ii. 38, f. 144. (*Halliwell.*)

Wise Cambina, . . .
Unto her Coch remounting, home did *ride*.
Spenser, F. Q., IV. iii. 51.

Be 't to fly,
To swim, to dive into the fire, to *ride*
On the curl'd clouds, to thy strong bidding task
Ariel and all his quality. *Shak.*, Tempest, i. 2. 191.

3. To be borne in or on a fluid; float; specifically, to lie at anchor.

Thanks to Heaven's goodness, no man lost!
The ship *rides* fair, too, and her leaks in good plight.
Fletcher (and another), Sea Voyage, i. 3.

This we found to be an Ile, where we *rid* that night.
Capt. John Smith, Works, II. 224.

They shall be sent in the Ship Lion, which *rides* here at Malamocco. *Howell*, Letters, I. i. 26.

I walk unseen . . .
To behold the wandering moon
Riding near her highest noon.
Milton, Il Penseroso, l. 68.

4. To move on or about something.

Strong as the axletree
On which heaven *rides*.
Shak., T. and C., i. 3. 67.

5. To be mounted and borne along; hence, to move triumphantly or proudly.

Disdain and scorn *ride* sparkling in her eyes.
Shak., Much Ado, iii. 1. 51.

6†. To be carted, as a convicted bawd.

I'll hang you both, you rascals!
I can but *ride*. *Massinger*, City Madam, iii. 1.

7. To have free play; have the upper hand; domineer.

A brother noble,
. . . on whose foolish honesty
My practices *ride* easy! *Shak.*, Lear, i. 2. 198.

8. To lap or lie over: said especially of a rope when the part on which the strain is brought lies over and jams the other parts. *Hamersly*.

Care must be taken not to raise the headle, or headles too high, or too much strain will be thrown upon the raised threads, and the result will be that the weft threads will

overlap or *ride* over each other, and the evil effect will be observable on both surfaces of the cloth.
A. Barlow, Weaving, p. 414.

9. To serve as a means of travel; be in condition to support a rider or traveler: as, that horse *rides* well under the saddle.

Honest man, will the water *ride?*
Jock o' the Side (Child's Ballads, VI. 86).

10. In *surg.*, said of the ends of a fractured bone when they overlap each other.

When a fracture is oblique there will probably be some shortening of the limb from the drawing up of the lower portion of the limb, or *riding*, as it is called, of one end over the other. *Bryant*, Surgery (3d Amer. ed.), p. 817.

11. To climb up or rise, as an ill-fitting coat tends to do at the shoulders and the back of the neck.—**Riding committee.** See *committee*.—**Riding interests**, in *Scots law*, interests saddled or dependent upon other interests: thus, when any of the claimants in an action of multiplepoinding, or in a process of ranking and sale, have creditors, these creditors may claim to be ranked on the fund set aside for their debtor; and such claims are called *riding interests*.—**The devil rides on a fiddlestick.** See *devil*.—**To ride and tie**, to ride and go on foot alternately: said of two persons. See the first quotation.

Mr. Adams discharged the bill, and they were both setting out, having agreed to *ride and tie:* a method of travelling much used by persons who have but one horse between them, and is thus performed. The two travellers set out together, one on horseback, the other on foot. Now as it generally happens that he on horseback outgoes him on foot, the custom is that when he arrives at the distance agreed on, he is to dismount, tie his horse to some gate, tree, post, or other thing, and then proceed on foot, when the other comes up to the horse, unties him, mounts, and gallops on; till, having passed by his fellow-traveller, he likewise arrives at the place of tying.
Fielding, Joseph Andrews, ii. 2. (*Davies.*)

Both of them [Garrick and Johnson] used to talk pleasantly of this their first journey to London. Garrick, evidently meaning to embellish a little, said one day in my hearing, "We *rode and tied*."
Boswell, Johnson, I. v. (1737), note.

To ride a portlast (*naut.*), to lie at anchor with the lower yards lowered to the rail: an old use.—**To ride at anchor** (*naut.*). See *anchor*.

After this Thomas Duke of Clarence, the King's second Son, and the Earl of Kent, with competent Forces, entred the Haven of Sluice, where they burnt four Ships *riding at Anchor*. *Baker*, Chronicles, p. 162.

To ride at the ring. See *ring*1.—**To ride bodkin.** See *bodkin*1.—**To ride easy** (*naut.*), said of a ship when she does not pitch, or strain her cables.—**To ride hard**, said of a ship when she pitches violently, so as to strain her cables and masts.—**To ride in the marrow-bone coach**, to go on foot. [Slang.]—**To ride out†**, to go upon a military expedition; enter military service.

From the tyme that he first bigan
To *riden out*, he lovede chyvalrie.
Chaucer, Gen. Prol. to C. T., l. 45.

To ride over, to domineer over as if trampling upon: override or overpower triumphantly, insolently, or roughly.

Thou hast caused men to *ride over* our heads.
Ps. lxvi. 12.

Let thy dauntless mind
Still *ride* in triumph *over* all mischance.
Shak., 3 Hen. VI., iii. 3. 18.

To ride roughshod, to pursue a violent, stubborn, or selfish course, regardless of consequences or of the pain or distress that may be caused to others.

Henry [VIII.], in his later proceedings, *rode roughshod* over the constitution of the Church.
Nineteenth Century, XXVI. 894.

The Chamber had again been *riding roughshod* over His Majesty's schemes of army reform.
Lowe, Bismarck, I. 283.

To ride rusty. See *rusty*3.—**To ride to hounds**, to take part in a fox-hunt; specifically, to ride close behind the hounds in fox-hunting.

He not only went straight as a die, but *rode to hounds* instead of over them. *Lawrence*, Guy Livingstone, iii.

To ride upon a cowlstaff†. See *cowlstaff*. =**Syn. 1** and **2.** The effort has been made, in both England and America, to confine *ride* to progression on horseback, and to use *drive* for progression in a vehicle, but it has not been altogether successful, being checked by the counter-tendency to use *drive* only where the person in question holds the reins or where the kind of motion is emphasized.

We have seen that Shakespeare, and Milton, and the translators of the Bible, use *drive* in connection with chariot when they wish to express the urging it along; but, when they wish to say that a man is borne up and onward in a chariot, they use *ride*.
R. G. White, Words and Their Uses, p. 193.

The practice of standard authors is exhibited in a liberal list of citations, and proves the imputed Americanism to *ride* (instead of to *drive*) in a carriage to be "Queen's English," although there remains a nice distinction — not a national one — established by good usage, between *riding* in a carriage and *driving* in a carriage.
Amer. Jour. Philol., IX. 498.

II. *trans.* 1. To sit on and drive; be carried along on and by: used specifically of a horse.

Neither shall he that *rideth* the horse deliver himself.
Amos ii. 15.

He dash'd across me — mad,
And maddening what he *rode*.
Tennyson, Holy Grail.

Not infrequently the boys will *ride* a log down the current as fearlessly, and with as little danger of upsetting into the water, as an old and well-practiced river-driver.
St. Nicholas, XVII. 584.

2. To be carried or travel on, through, or over.

Others . . . *ride* the air
In whirlwind. *Milton*, P. L., ii. 540.

The rising waves . . .
Thunder and flash upon the stedfast shores,
Till he that *rides* the whirlwind checks the rein.
Cowper, Retirement, l. 535.

This boat-shaped roof, which is extremely graceful and is repeated in another apartment, would suggest that the imagination of Jacques Cœur was fond of *riding* the waves.
H. James, Jr., Little Tour, p. 85.

3. To do, make, or execute by riding: as, to *ride* a race; to *ride* an errand.

Right here seith the frensch booke that, whan the kynge Arthur was departed fro Bredigan, he and the kynge Ban of Benoyk, and the kynge boors of Gannes, his brother, that thei *rode* so her iournes till thei com to Tarsaide. *Merlin* (E. E. T. S.), ii. 202.

And we can neither hunt nor *ride*
A foray on the Scottish side.
Scott, Marmion, i. 22.

4. To hurry over; gallop through.

He hath *rid* his prologue like a rough colt; he knows not the stop. *Shak.*, M. N. D., v. 1. 119.

5. To control and manage, especially with harshness or arrogance; domineer or tyrannize over: especially in the past participle *ridden*, in composition, as in *priest-ridden*.

He that suffers himself to be *ridden*, or through pusillanimity or sottishness will let every man baffle him, shall be a common laughing stock.
Burton, Anat. of Mel., p. 384.

And yet this man [Ambrose], such as we hear he was, would have the Emperor *ride* other people, that himself might *ride* him, which is a common trick of almost all ecclesiastics. *Milton*, Ans. to Salmasius, iii.

But as for them [scorners], they know better things than to fall in with the herd, and to give themselves up to be *ridden* by the tribe of Levi. *Bp. Atterbury*, Sermons, I. v.

What chance was there of reason being heard in a land that was king-*ridden*, priest-*ridden*, peer-*ridden!*
Charlotte Brontë, Shirley, iv.

6. To carry; transport. [Local, U. S.]

The custom-house license Nos. of the carts authorized to *ride* the merchandise.
Laws and Regulations of Customs Inspectors, etc., p. 48.

Riding the fair, the ceremony of proclaiming a fair, performed by the steward of a court-baron, who rode through the town attended by the tenants.—**Riding the marches.** See *march*1.—**To ride a hobby**, to pursue a favorite theory, notion, or habit on every possible occasion. See *hobby*1.

It may look like *riding a hobby* to death, but I cannot help suspecting a wooden origin for it [Raj Rani temple].
J. Fergusson, Hist. Indian Arch., p. 425.

He must of course be naturally of a rather attitudinizing turn, fond of brooding and spouting and *riding a* theological *hobby*. *N. A. Rev.*, CXX. 189.

To ride circuit or **the circuit.** See *circuit*.—**To ride down**, to overthrow, trample on, or drive over in riding; hence, to treat with extreme roughness or insolence.

We hunt them for the beauty of their skins;
They love us for it, and we *ride* them *down*.
Tennyson, Princess, v.

To ride down a sail, to stretch the head of a sail by bearing down on the middle.—**To ride down a stay** or **backstay** (*naut.*), to come down on the stay for the purpose of tarring it.—**To ride out**, to keep afloat during, as a gale; withstand the fury of, as a storm: said of a vessel or of her crew.

He bears
A tempest, which his mortal vessel tears,
And yet he *rides* it *out*. *Shak.*, Pericles, iv. 4. 31.

The fleet *rode out* the storm in safety.
Prescott, Ferd. and Isa., ii. 8.

To ride shanks' mare, to walk. [Colloq.]—**To ride the broose†.** See *broose*.—**To ride the great horse†**, to practise horsemanship in the fashion of the time.

Then comes he [Prince of Orange] abroad, and goes to his Stables, if it be no Sermon-day, to see some of his Gentlemen or Pages (of whose Breeding he is very careful) *ride the great horse*. *Howell*, Letters, I. i. 10.

He told me he did not know what travelling was good for but to teach a man to *ride the great horse*, to jabber French, and to talk against passive obedience.
Addison, Tory Foxhunter.

To ride the high horse. See *to mount the high horse*, under *horse*1.—**To ride the line.** See *line-riding*.

Even for those who do not have to look up stray horses, and who are not forced to *ride the line* day in and day out, there is apt to be some hardship and danger in being abroad during the bitter weather.
T. Roosevelt, The Century, XXXV. 669.

To ride the Spanish mare (*naut.*), to be put astride of a boom with the guys eased off when the vessel is in a seaway: a punishment formerly in vogue.—**To ride the wild mare†**, to play at see-saw.

With that, bestriding the mast, I gat by little and little towards him, after such manner as boys are wont, if ever you saw that sport, when they *ride the wild mare*.
Sir P. Sidney, Arcadia, ii.

A' . . . *rides the wild-mare* with the boys.
Shak., 2 Hen. IV., ii. 4. 268.

ride (rīd), *n.* [< ME. *ride* = G. *ritt* = Icel. *reith* = Sw. Dan. *ridt;* from the verb: see *ride*, *v.* Cf. *road*1, *raid*.] 1. A journey on the back of a horse, ass, mule, camel, elephant, or other animal; more broadly, any excursion, whether on the back of an animal, in a vehicle, or by some other mode of conveyance: as, a *ride* in a wagon or a balloon; a *ride* on a bicycle or a cow-catcher.

To Madian lond wente he [Balaam] his *ride*.
Genesis and Exodus (E. E. T. S.), l. 3950.

"Alas," he said, "your *ride* has wearied you."
Tennyson, Lancelot and Elaine.

2. A saddle-horse. *Grose*. [Prov. Eng.]—3. A road intended expressly for riding; a bridle-path; a place for exercise on horseback. Also called *riding*.

This through the *ride* upon his steed
Goes slowly by, and this at speed.
M. Arnold, Epilogue to Lessing's Laocoon.

4. A little stream or brook. [Prov. Eng.]—5. A certain district patrolled by mounted excise officers.—6. In *printing*, a fault caused by overlapping: said of leads or rules that slip and overlap, of a kerned type that overlaps or binds a type in a line below, also of a color that impinges on another color in prints of two or more colors.

rideable, *a.* See *ridable*.

rideau (rē-dō'), *n.* [< F. *rideau*, a curtain: see *riddle*3.] In *fort.*, a small elevation of earth extended lengthwise on a plain, serving to cover a camp from the approach of the enemy, or to give other advantage to a post.

ridelt, *n.* See *riddle*3.

rident. An obsolete preterit plural of *ride*.

rident (rī'dent), *a.* [< L. *riden(t-)s*, ppr. of *ridere* (> It. *ridere* = Sp. *reir* = Pg. *rir* = Cat. *riurer* = Pr. *rir*, *rire* = F. *rire*), laugh. Hence (from L. *ridere*) *arride*, *deride*, *ridiculous*, *risible*, etc., also *riant* (a doublet of *rident*).] Smiling broadly; grinning.

A smile so wide and steady, so exceedingly *rident*, indeed, as almost to be ridiculous, may be drawn upon the buxom face, if the artist chooses to attempt it.
Thackeray, Newcomes, xxiv.

ride-officer (rīd'of"i-sėr), *n.* An excise-officer who makes his rounds on horseback; the officer of a ride.

rider (rī'dėr), *n.* [< ME. *ridere*, *rydare*, < AS. *ridere*, a rider, cavalryman, knight (= OFries. *ridder* = D. *rijder* = MLG. *ridder* = OHG. *ritāre*, MHG. *ritære*, *riter*, *ritter*, a rider, knight, G. *reiter*, a rider, *ritter*, knight, = Icel. *rithari*, *ritheri*, later *riddari* = Sw. *riddare*, knight, *ryttare*, horseman, trooper, = Dan. *ridder*, knight, *rytter*, horseman, rider, knight), < *ridan*, ride: see *ride*. Cf. *ritter*, *reiter* (< G.).] 1. One who rides; particularly, one who rides on the back of a horse or other animal; specifically, one who is skilled in horsemanship and the manège.

Ac now is Religioun a *ridere* and a rennere aboute.
Piers Plowman (A), xi. 208.

The horse and his *rider* hath he thrown into the sea.
Ex. xv. 1.

Well could he ride, and often men would say,
"That horse his mettle from his *rider* takes."
Shak., Lover's Complaint, l. 107.

The weary steed of Pelleas floundering flung
His *rider*. *Tennyson*, Pelleas and Ettarre.

2†. A mounted reaver or robber.

In Ewsdale, Eight and Forty notorious *Riders* are hung on growing Trees, the most famous of which was John Armstrong. *Drummond*, Works, p. 99.

3. Formerly, one who traveled for a mercantile house to collect orders, money, etc.: now called a *traveler* or (in the United States) *drummer*.

They come to us as *riders* in a trade,
And with much art exhibit and persuade.
Crabbe, Works, II. 53.

4. In *hort.*, a budded or grafted standard or stock branching from a main or parent trunk or stem.—5. A knight. [Archaic.]

He dubbed his youngest son, the Ætheling Henry, to *rider* or knight. *Freeman*, Norman Conquest, IV. 471.

6. Any device straddling something; something mounted upon or attached to something else. Especially – (*a*) A small piece of platinum or aluminium set astride of the beam of a balance, and moved from or toward the fulcrum in determining results requiring weights of the utmost delicacy. (*b*) A small piece of paper or other light substance placed on a wire or string to measure or mark distance.

We measure the distance between the two [nodes], and cut the wire so that its total length shall be a multiple of this length, and then we proceed to find all the nodes, and mark them by paper *riders*. *Pop. Sci. Mo.*, XXXV. 573.

(*c*) Anything saddled upon or attached to a record, document, statement, etc., after its supposed completion; specifically, an additional clause, as to a bill in Congress.

Vholes finally adds, by way of *rider* to this declaration of his principles, that as Mr. Carstone is about to rejoin his regiment, perhaps Mr. C. will favour him with an order on his agent for twenty pounds.
Dickens, Bleak House, xxxix.

The proposed amendment had been given by the previous action of the House, a *rider* providing for compensation to distillers. *The American*, VI. 36.

But the Pacific Mail and its friends in Congress did not despair, and success came at last by a *rider* to the General Post-Office appropriation bill passed by Congress, February 18, 1867. *Congressional Record*, XXI. 7770.

(d) In *printing*, a cylindrical rod of iron which in use rests on the top of an ink-roller, and aids in evenly distributing the ink on this roller. (*e*) A supplementary part of a question in an examination, especially in the Cambridge mathematical tripos, connected with or dependent on the main question.

Though the *riders* were joined to the propositions on which their solution depended, and though all these *riders* were easy, very few of the papers were satisfactory. *Science*, XI. 75.

(*f*) In a snake fence, a rail or stake one end of which rests on the ground, while the other end crosses and bears upon the fence-rails at their angle of meeting, and thus holds them in place. [Local, U. S.]
7. In *mining*, a ferruginous veinstone, or a similar impregnation of the walls adjacent to the vein. [North of Eng. mining districts.]

In Alston the contents of the unproductive parts of veins are chiefly described as dowk and *rider*. The former is a brown, friable, and soft soil; the latter a hard stony matter, varying much in colour, hardness, and other characteristics. *Sopwith*, Mining Districts of Alston Moor, Weardale, and Teesdale, p. 108.

8. One of a series of interior ribs fixed occasionally in a ship's hold, opposite to some of the principal timbers, to which they are bolted, and reaching from the keelson to the beams of the lower deck, to strengthen the frame.—9. A piece of wood in a gun-carriage on which the side pieces rest.—10. A gold coin formerly current in the Netherlands: so called from its obverse type being the figure of a horseman. The specimen here illustrated was struck by Charles of Eg-

Obverse. Reverse.
Rider of Charles of Egmont, Duke of Gelderland.—British Museum. (Size of the original.)

mont, Duke of Gelderland (sixteenth century), and weighs nearly 50 grains. The name was also given to a gold coin of Scotland, issued by James VI., worth about $2.

His mouldy money! Half-a-dozen *riders*,
That cannot sit, but stampt fast to their saddles.
Beau. and Fl.

Bush-rider, in Australia, a cross-country rider; one who can ride horses over rough or dangerous ground; also, one who can ride imperfectly broken horses.

An excellent *bushrider*, if not a first-class rough-rider, there were few horses he could not back with a fair chance of remaining in the saddle. *A. C. Grant*, Bush Life in Queensland, I. 262.

Rider keelson. See *keelson*.—**Rider's bone**, an exostosis at the origin of the adductor longus. Also called *drill bone*.—**Rider truss**, an early form of tram truss, composed of a cast-iron upper chord, wrought-iron lower chord, and vertical posts of cast-iron, and diagonal braces of wrought-iron.

ridered (rī'dėrd), *a.* [< *rider* + *-ed*[2].] Carrying a rider; specifically, having riders or stakes laid across the bars, as a snake fence. [Local, U. S.]

The fences are generally too high to jump, being usually what are called staked and *ridered* fences. *Tribune Book of Sports*, p. 49.

riderless (rī'dėr-les), *a.* [< *rider* + *-less*.] Having no rider.

He caught a *riderless* horse, and the cornet mounted. *H. Kingsley*, Ravenshoe, liv.

rider-roll (rī'dėr-rōl), *n.* A separate addition made to a roll or record. See *rider*, 5 (c).

ridge (rij), *n.* [< ME. *rigge*, *rygge*; also without assibilation *rig*, *ryg*, *rug* (> E. dial. *rig*), < AS. *hrycg*, the back of a man or beast, = MD. *rugge*, D. *rug* = OLG. *ruggi*. MLG. *rugge* = OHG. *hrucci*, *hrucki*, *rucki*, MHG. *rucke*, *rücke*, G. *rücken* = Icel. *hryggr* = Sw. *rygg* = Dan. *ryg*, the back; cf. Ir. *crocan*, skin, back.] 1. The back of any animal; especially, the upper or projecting part of the back of a quadruped.

All is rede, Ribbe and *rigge*,
The bak bledeth agens the borde.
Holy Rood (E. E. T. S.), p. 202.

His ryche robe he to rof of his *rigge* naked,
And of a hope of askes he hitte in the myddez.
Alliterative Poems (ed. Morris), iii. 370.

There the pore preseth bifor the riche with a pakke at his *rugge*. *Piers Plowman* (B), xiv. 212.

On the other side of the aloes, not fifteen paces from us, I made out the horns, neck, and the *ridge* of the back of a tremendous old bull. *Harper's Mag.*, LXXVII. 180.

2. Any extended protuberance; a projecting line or strip; a long and narrow pile sloping at the sides; specifically, a long elevation of land, or the summit of such an elevation; an extended hill or mountain.

Even to the frozen *ridges* of the Alps,
Or any other ground inhabitable.
Shak., Rich. II., i. 1. 64.

The snow-white *ridge*
Of carded wool, which the old man had piled.
Wordsworth, The Brothers.

3. In *agri.*, a strip of ground thrown up by a plow or left between furrows; a bed of ground formed by furrow-slices running the whole length of the field, varying in breadth according to circumstances, and divided from another by gutters or open furrows, parallel to each other, which last serve as guides to the hand and eye of the sower, to the reapers, and also for the application of manures in a regular manner. In wet soils they also serve as drains for carrying off the surface-water. In Wales, formerly, a measure of land, 20½ feet.

Lete se the litel plough, the large also,
The *rigges* forto enhance.
Palladius, Husbondrie (E. E. T. S.), p. 42.

Thou waterest the *ridges* thereof abundantly: thou settlest the furrows thereof. Ps. lxv. 10.

4. The highest part of the roof of a building; specifically, the meeting of the upper ends of the rafters. When the upper ends of the rafters abut against a horizontal piece of timber, it is called a *ridge-pole*. *Ridge* also denotes the internal angle or nook of a vault. See cut under *roof*.
5. In *fort.*, the highest portion of the glacis, proceeding from the salient angle of the covered way.—6. In *anat.* and *zoöl.*, a prominent border; an elevated line, or crest; a lineal protuberance: said especially of rough elevations on bones for muscular or ligamentous attachments: as, the superciliary, occipital, mylohyoid, condylar, etc., *ridges*.—7. A succession of small processes along the small abaft the hump of a sperm-whale, or the top of the back just forward of the small. The ridge is thickest just around the hump. See *scrag-whale*.—8. One of the several linear elevations of the lining membrane of the roof of a horse's mouth, more commonly called *bars*. Similar ridges occur on the hard palate of most mammals.—**Bicipital ridges.** See *bicipital*.—**Dental ridge** a thick ridge of epithelium just over the spot where the future dental structures are to be formed.—**Frontal, genital, gluteal, interantennal ridge.** See the adjectives.—**Maxillary ridge.** Same as *dental ridge*.—**Mylohyoid ridge.** See *mylohyoid*.—**Neural ridge**, a series of enlargements along the borders of the medullary plates, from which the dorsal spinal nerves originate. More commonly called *neural crest*.—**Oblique ridge of the trapezium, of the ulna.** See *oblique*.—**Palatine, pectineal, pectoral, pterygoid ridge.** See the adjectives.—**Ridge rib.** See *rib*[1].—**Ridge-roll**, a batten with a rounded face, over which the sheathing of lead or other metal is bent on the ridges and hips of a roof. Also called *ridge-batten*.—**Sagittal, superciliary ridge.** See the adjectives.—**Temporal ridges.** See *temporal lines* (under *line*[2]), and cut under *parietal*.

ridge (rij), *v.*; pret. and pp. *ridged*, ppr. *ridging*. [< ME. *ryggen*; from the noun: see *ridge*, *n.*] I. *trans.* To cover or mark with ridges; rib.

Though all thy hairs
Were bristles ranged like those that *ridge* the back
Of chaf'd wild boars, or ruffled porcupines.
Milton, S. A., l. 1137.

A north-midland shire, dusk with moorland, *ridged* with mountain: this I see. *Charlotte Brontë*, Jane Eyre, xxviii.

Ridged sleeve, a sleeve worn by women at the middle of the seventeenth century, puffed in longitudinal ridges.
II. *intrans.* To rise or stretch in ridges.

The Biscay, roughly *ridging* eastward, shook
And almost overwhelm'd her.
Tennyson, Enoch Arden.

ridge-band (rij'band), *n.* That part of the harness of a cart-, wagon-, or gig-horse which goes over the saddle on the back.

ridge-beam (rij'bēm), *n.* In *carp.*, a beam at the upper ends of the rafters, below the ridge; a crown-plate. *E. H. Knight.*

ridge-bone† (rij'bōn), *n.* [< ME. *rygge-bone*, *rigbone*, < AS. *hrycg-bān* (= D. *ruggebeen*, *rugbeen* = OHG. *hruckipein*, *ruccipeini*, MHG. *rückebein* = Sw. *ryggben* = Dan. *rygben*), backbone, spine, < *hrycg*, back, + *bān*, bone.] The spine or backbone.

So ryde thay of by resoun bi the *rygge bonez*
Euenden to the haunche.
Sir Gawayne and the Green Knight (E. E. T. S.), l. 1344.

I would fain now see them rolled
Down a hill, or from a bridge
Headlong cast, to break their *ridge*-
Bones. *B. Jonson*, Masque of Oberon.

ridged (rijd), *a.* [< *ridge* + *-ed*[2].] 1. Having a ridge or back; having an angular, projecting backbone.

The tinners could summarily lodge in Lydford Gaol those who impeded them; consequently two messengers, sent from Plymouth to protect the leat on Roborough Down, were set up on a bare *ridged* horse, with their legs tied under his belly, and trotted off to gaol. *N. and Q.*, 7th ser., VII. 443.

2. In *zoöl.*, carinate; costate; having ridges or carinæ on a surface, generally longitudinal ones. When the ridges run crosswise, the surface is said to be *transversely ridged*.—3. Rising in a ridge or ridges; ridgy.

The sharp clear twang of the golden chords
Runs up the *ridged* sea. *Tennyson*, Sea-Fairies.

ridge-drill (rij'dril), *n.* In *agri.*, a seed-drill adapted to sowing seeds upon the ridges of a listed field. Compare *list*[4], *n.*, 10, and *listing-plow*.

ridge-fillet (rij'fil″et), *n.* 1. In *arch.*, a fillet between two depressions, as between two flutes of a column.—2. In *founding*, the runner, or principal channel. *E. H. Knight.*

ridge-harrow (rij'har″ō), *n.* In *agri.*, a harrow hinged longitudinally so that it can lap upon the sides of a ridge over which it passes. *E. H. Knight.*

ridge-hoe (rij'hō), *n.* A horse-hoe operating on the same principle as a ridge-plow.

ridgel, ridgil (rij'el, -il), *n.* [Also *rig* (of which *ridgel* may be a dim. form), *rigsie*; origin uncertain; cf. Sc. *riglan*, *rigland*, *rig-widdie*, a nag, a horse half-castrated, *riggot*, an animal half-castrated.] A male animal with one testicle removed or wanting. Also *ridgeling*, *ridgling*.

O Tityrus, tend my herd, and see them fed,
To morning pastures, evening waters, led;
And 'ware the Libyan *ridgil's* butting head.
Dryden, tr. of Virgil's Pastorals, ix. 31.

Ridgling or *ridgil* . . . is still used in Tennessee and the West, . . . but has been corrupted into *riginal*, and would-be correct people say *original*. *Trans. Amer. Philol. Ass.*, XVII. 42.

ridgelet (rij'let), *n.* [< *ridge* + *-let*.] A little ridge. *Encyc. Brit.*, I. 368.

ridgeling (rij'ling), *n.* [Also *ridgling*; appar. < *ridgel* + *-ing*[3].] Same as *ridgel*.

ridge-piece (rij'pēs), *n.* Same as *ridge-pole*.

ridge-plate (rij'plāt), *n.* Same as *ridge-pole*.

ridge-plow (rij'plou), *n.* In *agri.*, a plow having a double mold-board, used to make ridges for planting or cultivating certain crops and for opening water-furrows. Also called *ridging-plow*.

ridge-pole (rij'pōl), *n.* The board or timber at the ridge of a roof, into which the rafters are fastened. Also called *ridge-plate* or *ridge-piece*. See cut under *roof*.—**Ridge-pole pine.** See *pine*[1].

ridger (rij'ėr), *n.* 1. That which makes a ridge or ridges.

A small *ridger* or subsoiler extending below to form a small furrow into which the seed is dropped. *Sci. Amer.*, N. S., LXII. 181.

2. Same as *ridge-band*. *Halliwell.*

ridge-roof (rij'röf), *n.* A raised or peaked roof.

ridge-rope (rij'rōp), *n.* 1. *Naut.*: (*a*) The central rope of an awning, usually called the *backbone*. (*b*) The rope along the side of a ship to which an awning is stretched. (*c*) One of two ropes running out on each side of the bowsprit for the men to hold on by.—2. A ridge-band.

Surselle, a broad and great band or thong of strong leather, &c., fastned on either side of a thill, and bearing upon the pad or saddle of the thill-horse: about London it is called the *ridge-rope*. *Cotgrave.*

ridge-stay (rij'stā), *n.* Same as *ridge-band*. *Halliwell.*

ridge-tile (rij'tīl), *n.* In *arch.*, same as *crown-tile*, 2.

ridgil, *n.* See *ridgel*.

ridging-grass (rij'ing-gràs), *n.* A coarse grass, *Andropogon* (*Anatherum*) *bicornis*, of tropical America. [West Indies.]

ridging-plow (rij'ing-plou), *n.* Same as *ridge-plow*.

ridgling (rij'ling), *n.* Same as *ridgel*.

ridgy (rij'i), *a.* [< *ridge* + *-y*[1].] Rising in a ridge or ridges; ridged.

Faint, lazy waves o'ercreep the *ridgy* sand. *Crabbe*, Works, II. 10.

Scant along the *ridgy* land
The beans their new-born ranks expand.
T. Warton, The First of April.

ridicule[1]† (rid'i-kūl), *a.* [< OF. (and F.) *ridicule* = Sp. *ridículo* = Pg. *ridiculo* = It. *ridicolo*, < L. *ridiculus*, laughable, comical, amusing, absurd, ridiculous, < *ridere*, laugh: see *rident*. Cf. *ridiculous*.] Ridiculous.

That way (e. g. Mr. Edm. Waller's) of quibling with sence will hereafter growe as much out of fashion and be as *ridicule* as quibling with words. *Aubrey*, Lives, Samuel Butler.

ridicule[1] (rid'i-kūl), *n.* [Early mod. E. *ridicle*; = Sp. *ridiculo* = It. *ridicolo*, mockery, < L. *ridiculum*, a jest, neut. of *ridiculus*, ridiculous: see *ridiculous*.] 1. Mocking or jesting words intended to excite laughter, with more or less contempt, at the expense of the person or thing of whom they are spoken or written; also, action or gesture designed to produce the same effect.

> Whoe'er offends, at some unlucky time
> Slides into verse, and hitches in a rhyme,
> Sacred to *ridicule* his whole life long,
> And the sad burthen of some merry song.
> *Pope*, Imit. of Horace, II. i. 79.

> Foote possessed a rich talent for *ridicule*, which tinted vividly the genius for satire that shone within him.
> *Jon Bee*, Essay on Samuel Foote, p. v.

2. An object of mockery or contemptuous jesting.

> They began to hate me likewise, and to turn my equipage into *ridicule*. *Fielding*, Amelia, iii. 12.

3†. Ridiculousness.

> It does not want any great measure of sense to see the *ridicule* of this monstrous practice.
> *Addison*, Spectator, No. 18.

> At the same time that I see all their *ridicules*, there is a douceur in the society of the women of fashion that captivates me. *H. Walpole*, To Chute, Jan., 1766.

=**Syn.** 1. Derision, mockery, gibe, jeer, sneer. See *satire*, *ludicrous*, and *banter*, *v.*

ridicule[1] (rid'i-kūl), *v.*; pret. and pp. *ridiculed*, ppr. *ridiculing*. [< *ridicule*[1], *n.*] **I.** *trans.* To treat with ridicule; treat with contemptuous merriment; represent as deserving of contemptuous mirth; mock; make sport or game of; deride.

> I've known the young, who *ridicul'd* his rage,
> Love's humblest vassals, when oppress'd with age.
> *Grainger*, tr. of Tibullus, i. 5.

=**Syn.** *Deride*, *Mock*, etc. (see *taunt*), jeer at, scoff at, scout; rally, make fun of, lampoon. See the noun.

II. *intrans.* To bring ridicule upon a person or thing; make some one or something ridiculous; cause contemptuous laughter.

> One dedicates in high heroic prose,
> And *ridicules* beyond a hundred foes.
> *Pope*, Prologue to Satires, l. 110.

ridicule[2] (rid'i-kūl), *n.* [= F. *ridicule*, corruption of *réticule*.] A corruption of *reticule*, formerly common.

ridiculer (rid'i-kū-lėr), *n.* [< *ridicule*[1] + *-er*[1].] One who ridicules. *Bp. Atterbury*, Sermons, I. ix.

ridiculize† (ri-dik'ū-līz), *v. t.* [< F. *ridiculiser*, turn into ridicule, = Sp. Pg. *ridiculizar*; as *ridicule*[1] + *-ize*.] To make ridiculous; ridicule.

> My heart still trembling lest the false alarms
> That words oft strike-up should *ridiculize* me.
> *Chapman*, Odyssey, xxiii. 333.

ridiculosity (ri-dik-ū-los'i-ti), *n.*; pl. *ridiculosities* (-tiz). [= It. *ridicolosità*; < L. *ridiculosus*, laughable, facetious (see *ridiculous*), + *-ity*.] The character of being ridiculous; ridiculousness; hence, anything that arouses laughter; a jest or joke.

> Shut up your ill-natured Muses at Home with your Business, but bring your good-natured Muses, all your witty Jests, your By-words, your Banters, your Pleasantries, your pretty Sayings, and all your *Ridiculosities*, along with you. *N. Bailey*, tr. of Colloquies of Erasmus, I. 120.

ridiculous (ri-dik'ū-lus), *a.* [< L. *ridiculus*, laughable, ridiculous: see *ridicule*[1], *n.*] 1. Worthy of ridicule or contemptuous laughter; exciting derision; amusingly absurd; preposterous.

> Those that are good manners at the court are as *ridiculous* in the country as the behaviour of the country is most mockable at the court.
> *Shak.*, As you Like it, iii. 2. 47.

2†. Expressive of ridicule; derisive; mocking.

> He that sacrificeth of a thing wrongfully gotten, his offering is *ridiculous*: and the gifts of unjust men are not accepted. Ecclus. xxxiv. 18.

> The heaving of my lungs provokes me to *ridiculous* smiling. *Shak.*, L. L. L., iii. 1. 78.

3. Abominable; outrageous; shocking. [Obsolete or provincial.]

> A Nazarite in place abominable
> Vaunting my strength in honour to their Dagon!
> Besides, how vile, contemptible, *ridiculous*!
> What act more execrably unclean, profane?
> *Milton*, S. A., l. 1361.

> In the South we often say, "That's a *ridiculous* affair," when we really mean outrageous. It seems to be so used sometimes in the North.
> *Trans. Amer. Philol. Ass.*, XVII. 43.

> This [*ridiculous*] is used in a very different sense in some counties from its original meaning. Something very indecent and improper is understood by it: as, any violent attack upon a woman's chastity is called "very *ridiculous* behaviour"; a very disorderly and ill-conducted house is also called a "*ridiculous* one." *Halliwell.*

> A man once informed me that the death by drowning of a relative was "most *ridiculous*."
> *N. and Q.*, 7th ser., IX. 453.

=**Syn.** 1. *Funny*, *Laughable*, etc. (see *ludicrous*), absurd, preposterous, farcical.

ridiculously (ri-dik'ū-lus-li), *adv.* In a ridiculous manner; laughably; absurdly.

ridiculousness (ri-dik'ū-lus-nes), *n.* The character of being ridiculous, laughable, or absurd.

riding[1] (rī'ding), *n.* [< ME. *ridinge*, *rydynge*; verbal n. of *ride*, *v.*] 1. The act of going on horseback, or in a carriage, etc. See *ride*, *v.* Specifically—2†. A festival procession.

> Whan ther any *ridyng* was in Chepe,
> Out of the shoppe thider wolde he lepe,
> Til that he hadde al the sighte yseyn.
> *Chaucer*, Cook's Tale, l. 13.

> On the return of Edward I. from his victory over the Scots in 1298 occurred the earliest exhibition of shows connected with the City trades. These processions were in England frequently called *ridings*.
> *A. W. Ward*, Eng. Dram. Lit., I. 80.

3. Same as *ride*, 3.

> The lodge is . . . built in the form of a star, having round about a garden framed into like points; and beyond the garden *ridings* cut out, each answering the angles of the lodge. *Sir P. Sidney*, Arcadia, i.

The riding of the witch, the nightmare. *Halliwell.*

riding[2] (rī'ding), *n.* [Prop. **thriding*, the loss of *th* being prob. due to the wrong division of the compounds *North-thriding* (corrupted to *North-riding*), *South-thriding*, *East-thriding*, *West-thriding*; < Icel. *thrithjungr* (= Norw. *tridjung*), the third part of a thing, third part of a shire, < *thrithi* (= Norw. *tridje*) = E. *third*: see *third*.] One of the three districts, each anciently under the government of a reeve, into which the county of York, in England, is divided. These are called the *North*, *East*, and *West Ridings*. The same system of division exists also in Lincolnshire. Pennsylvania also, in the earliest portion of its colonial history, was divided into ridings.

> Gisborne is a market town in the west *riding* of the county of York, on the borders of Lancashire.
> Quoted in Child's Ballads, V. 159.

> The most skilled housewife in all the three *Ridings*.
> *Mrs. Gaskell*, Sylvia's Lovers, v.

> Lincolnshire was divided into three parts, Lindsey, Kesteven, and Holland; Lindsey was subdivided into three *ridings*, North, West, and South.
> *Stubbs*, Const. Hist., § 45.

riding-bitts (rī'ding-bits), *n. pl.* The bitts to which a ship's cable is secured when riding at anchor.

riding-boot (rī'ding-böt), *n.* A kind of high boot worn in riding.

> With such a tramp of his ponderous *riding-boots* as might of itself have been audible in the remotest of the seven gables, he advanced to the door, which the servant pointed out. *Hawthorne*, Seven Gables, i.

riding-clerk† (rī'ding-klėrk), *n.* 1. A mercantile traveler. *Imp. Dict.*—2. Formerly, one of six clerks in Chancery, each of whom in his turn, for one year, kept the controlment-books of all grants that passed the great seal. The six clerks were superseded by the clerks of records and writs. *Rapalje and Lawrence.*

riding-day (rī'ding-dā), *n.* A day given up to a hostile incursion on horseback. *Scott.*

riding-glove (rī'ding-gluv), *n.* A stout, heavy glove worn in riding; a gauntlet.

> The walls were adorned with old-fashioned lithographs, principally portraits of country gentlemen with high collars and *riding-gloves*. *The Century*, XXXVI. 123.

riding-graith (rī'ding-grāth), *n.* See *graith*.

riding-habit (rī'ding-hab"it), *n.* See *habit*, 5.

riding-hood (rī'ding-hůd), *n.* A hood used by women in the eighteenth century, and perhaps earlier, when traveling or exposed to the weather, the use of it depending on the style of head-dress or coiffure in fashion of the time.

> Good housewives all the winter's rage despise,
> Defended by the *riding-hood's* disguise.
> *Gay*, Trivia, i. 210.

riding-house† (rī'ding-hous), *n.* Same as *riding-school*.

riding-light (rī'ding-līt), *n.* A light hung out in the rigging at night when a vessel is riding at anchor. Also called *stay-light*.

riding-master (rī'ding-mås"tėr), *n.* A teacher of the art of riding; specifically (*milit.*), one who instructs soldiers and officers in the management of horses.

riding-rime† (rī'ding-rīm), *n.* A form of verse, the same as the rimed couplet that goes now under the name *heroic verse*. It was introduced into English versification by Chaucer, and in it are composed most of the "Canterbury Tales." From the fact that it was represented as used by the pilgrims in telling these tales on their journey, it received the name of *riding-rime*; but it was not much used after Chaucer's death till the close of the sixteenth century. In the sixteenth century it is frequently contrasted with *rime-royal* (which see).

> I had forgotten a notable kinde of ryme, called *ryding rime*, and that is suche as our Mayster and Father Chaucer vsed in his Canterburie Tales, and in diuers other delectable and light enterprises.
> *Gascoigne*, Notes on Eng. Verse (ed. Arber), § 16.

riding-robe (rī'ding-rōb), *n.* A robe worn in riding; a riding-habit.

> But who comes in such haste in *riding-robes*?
> What woman-post is this? *Shak.*, K. John, i. 1. 217.

riding-rod (rī'ding-rod), *n.* A switch or light cane used as a whip by equestrians.

> And if my legs were two such *riding-rods*, . . .
> And, to his shape, were heir to all this land,
> Would I might never stir from off this place,
> I would give it every foot to have this face.
> *Shak.*, K. John, i. 1. 140.

riding-sail (rī'ding-sāl), *n.* A triangular sail bent to the mainmast and sheeted down aft, to steady a vessel when head on to the wind.

riding-school (rī'ding-sköl), *n.* A school or place where the art of riding is taught; specifically, a military school to perfect troopers in the management of their horses and the use of arms.

riding-skirt (rī'ding-skėrt), *n.* 1. The skirt of a riding-habit.—2. A separate skirt fastened around the waist over the other dress, worn by women in riding.

riding-spear† (rī'ding-spēr), *n.* A javelin. *Palsgrave.* (*Halliwell.*)

riding-suit (rī'ding-sūt), *n.* A suit adapted for riding.

> Provide me presently
> A *riding-suit*, no costlier than would fit
> A franklin's wife. *Shak.*, Cymbeline, iii. 2. 78.

riding-whip (rī'ding-hwip), *n.* A switch or a whip with a short lash, used by riders.

ridotto (ri-dot'ō), *n.* [= F. *ridotte*, < It. *ridotto*, a retreat, resort, company, etc.: see *redout*[2].] 1. A house or hall of public entertainment.

> They went to the *Ridotto*;—'tis a hall
> Where people dance, and sup, and dance again;
> Its proper name, perhaps, were a masqued ball,
> But that 's of no importance to my strain;
> 'Tis (on a smaller scale) like our Vauxhall,
> Excepting that it can't be spoilt by rain.
> *Byron*, Beppo, lviii.

2†. A company of persons met together for amusement; a social assembly.—3. A public entertainment devoted to music and dancing; a dancing-party, often in masquerade.

> The masked balls or *Ridottos* in Carnival are held in the Imperial palace. *Wraxall*, Court of Berlin, II. 289.

> To-night there is a masquerade at Ranelagh for him, a play at Covent Garden on Monday, and a *ridotto* at the Haymarket. *Walpole*, Letters, II. 24.

4. In *music*, an arrangement or reduction of a piece from the full score.

ridotto (ri-dot'ō), *v. i.* [< *ridotto*, *n.*] To frequent or hold ridottos. [Rare.]

> And heroines, whilst 'twas the fashion,
> *Ridotto'd* on the rural plains.
> *Cowper*, Retreat of Aristippus.

rie†, *n.* An old spelling of *rye*[1]. Ex. ix. 32.

riebeckite (rē'bek-īt), *n.* [Named after E. *Riebeck*.] A silicate of iron and sodium, belonging to the amphibole group, and corresponding to acmite among the pyroxenes.

riedel, *n.* A Middle English variant of *reed*[1].

rief, *n.* See *reef*[3].

rie-grass†, *n.* Same as *rye-grass*.

riem (rēm), *n.* [< D. *riem*, a thong: see *rim*[2].] A rawhide thong, about 8 feet long, used in South Africa for hitching horses, for fastening yokes to the trek-tow, and generally as a strong cord or binder. Also spelled *reim*.

> He rose suddenly and walked slowly to a beam from which an ox *riem* hung. Loosening it, he ran a noose in one end and then doubled it round his arm.
> *Olive Schreiner*, Story of an African Farm, i. 12.

Riemann's function, surface. See *function*, *surface*.

riesel-iron (rē'zel-ī"ėrn), *n.* A sort of claw or nipper used to remove irregularities from the edges of glass where cut by the dividing-iron (which see, under *iron*).

Riesling (rēs'ling), *n.* [G. *riessling*, a kind of grape.] Wine made from the Riesling grape, and best known in the variety made in Alsace and elsewhere on the upper Rhine. It keeps many years, and is considered exceptionally wholesome. A good Riesling wine is made in California.

rietbok (rēt'bok), *n.* [< D. *rietbok*, < *riet*, = E. *reed*[1], + *bok* = E. *buck*[1].] The reedbuck of South Africa, *Eleotragus arundinaceus*.

riever, *n.* Same as *reaver*.

rifacimento (rē-fä-chi-men'tō), *n.*; pl. *rifacimenti* (-ti). [< It. *rifacimento*, < *rifare*, make over again, < ML. *refacere* (L. *reficere*), make over again, < L. *re-*, again, + *facere*, make: see *fact.* Cf. *refect.*] A remaking or reëstablishment: a term most commonly applied to the process of recasting literary works so as to adapt them to a changed state or changed circumstances; an adaptation, as when a work written in one age or country is modified to suit the circumstances of another. The term is applied in an analogous sense to musical compositions.

What man of taste and feeling can endure *rifacimenti*, harmonies, abridgments, expurgated editions?
Macaulay, Boswell's Johnson.

Shakespeare's earliest works were undoubtedly *rifacimenti* of the plays of his predecessors.
Dyce, Note to Greene, Int., p. 37.

rife^{1} (rīf), *a.* [< ME. *rif*, *rife*, *rive*, < AS. *rīfe* (occurs but once), abundant, = OD. *rijf*, *rijve*, abundant, copious, = MLG. LG. *rive*, abundant, munificent, = Icel. *rīfr*, abundant, munificent, *rifligr*, large, munificent, = OSw. *rif*, rife. Cf. Icel. *reifa*, bestow, *reifir*, a giver.] **1.** Great in quantity or number; abundant; plentiful; numerous.

That citie wer sure men sett for too keepe,
With mich riall araie redy too fight,
With atling of areblast & archers *ryfe*.
Alisaunder of Macedoine (E. E. T. S.), l. 268.

The men who have given to one character life
And objective existence are not very *rife*.
Lowell, Fable for Critics.

2. Well supplied; abounding; rich; replete; filled: followed by *with*.

Whose life was work, whose language *rife*
With rugged maxims hewn from life.
Tennyson, Death of Wellington.

Our swelling actions want the little leaven
To make them *with* the sighed-for blessing *rife*.
Jones Very, Poems, p. 74.

3†. Easy.

With Gods it is *rife*
To geue and bereue breath.
Puttenham, Arte of Eng. Poesie, p. 78.

Hath utmost Inde aught better than his own?
Then utmost Inde is near, and *rife* to gone.
Bp. Hall, Satires, III. i. 55.

4. Prevalent; current; in common use or acceptance.

To be cumbrid with couetous, by custome of old,
That rote is & rankist of all the *rif* syns.
Destruction of Troy (E. E. T. S.), l. 11775.

Errors are infinite; and follies, how universally *rife!* even of the wisest sort. *G. Harvey*, Four Letters.

That grounded maxim,
So *rife* and celebrated in the mouths
Of wisest men. *Milton*, S. A., l. 866.

5†. Publicly or openly known; hence, manifest; plain; clear.

Adam abraid, and sag that wif,
Name he gaf hire dat is ful *rif*;
Issa was hire drste name.
Genesis and Exodus (E. E. T. S.), l. 232.

Even now the tumult of loud mirth
Was *rife*, and perfect in my listening ear.
Milton, Comus, l. 203.

rife^{1}† (rīf), *adv.* [< ME. *rife*; < *rife*^{1}, *a.*] **1.** Abundantly; plentifully.

I presse a grape with stork and stryf,
The Rede wyn renneth *ryf*.
Holy Rood (E. E. T. S.), p. 136.

In tribulacioun y regne moore *rijf*
Ofttymes than in disport.
Political Poems, etc. (ed. Furnivall), p. 158.

2. Plainly; clearly.

Bi thi witt thou maist knowe *rijf*
That merci passith rigtwisnes.
Hymns to Virgin, etc. (E. E. T. S.), p. 98.

3. Currently; commonly; frequently.

The Pestilence doth most *rifest* infect the clearest complection, and the Caterpiller cleaueth vnto the ripest fruite. *Lyly*, Euphues, Anat. of Wit (ed. Arber), p. 39.

rife^{2}†, *v.* An obsolete form of *rive*^{1}.

rifely (rīf'li), *adv.* [< ME. *rifli*, *rifliche* (= Icel. *rifligа*); < *rife*^{1} + *-ly*^{2}.] In a rife manner. (*a*) Plentifully; abundantly.

There launchit I to laund, a litle for ese,
Restid me *rifely*, ricchit my seluyn.
Destruction of Troy (E. E. T. S.), l. 13149.

(*b*) Prevalently; currently; widely.

The word went wide how the mayde was geue
Rifliche thurth-out rome.
William of Palerne (E. E. T. S.), l. 1472.

rifeness (rīf'nes), *n.* The state of being rife.

riff^{1}† (rif), *n.* [< ME. **rif*, < AS. *hrif* = OS. *hrif* = OFries. *rif*, *ref* = OHG. *href*, *ref*, belly. Cf. *midriff*.] The belly; the bowels.

Then came his good sword forth to act his part,
Which pierc'd skin, ribs, and *riffe*, and rove her heart.
The head (his trophy) from the trunk he cuts,
And with it back unto the shore he struts.
Legend of Captain Jones. (Halliwell.)

riff^{2} (rif), *n.* [See *reef*^{1}.] **1†.** An obsolete form of *reef*^{1}.—**2.** A rapid or riffle. See *riffle*^{2}. [Local, U. S.]

The lower side of large, loose stones at the *riffs* or shallow places in streams; the rock amid the foaming water; . . . in all these places they [fresh-water sponges] have been found in great abundance.
Pop. Sci. Mo., XXXIV. 711.

riff^{3}†, *n.* An obsolete form of *reef*^{2}.

riffle^{1} (rif'l), *n.* [< Dan. *rifle*, a groove, channel: see *rifle*^{2}, *n.*] **1.** In *mining*, the lining of the bottom of a sluice, made of blocks or slats of wood, or stones, arranged in such a manner that chinks are left open between them. In these chinks more or less quicksilver is usually placed, and it is by the aid of this arrangement that the particles of gold, as they are carried downward by the current of water, are arrested and held fast. The whole arrangement at the bottom of the sluices is usually called *the riffles*. In the smaller gold-saving machines, formerly much used, as the cradle, the slats of wood nailed across the bottom for the purpose of detaining the gold are called *riffle-bars* or simply *riffles*.

2. A piece of plank placed transversely in, and fastened to the bottom of, a fish-ladder. The riffles do not extend from side to side, but only about two thirds across. If the first riffle is fastened on the right side of the box at right angles to its side, it will extend about 30 inches across the box; the next, about 4 feet above, will be fastened on the left side of the box; the next, about 4 feet above, on the right side; and so on alternately until the top is reached. The water passing into the top is caught by the riffles and turned right and left by them until it reaches the stream below. Riffles furnish the fish a resting-place in scaling a dam.

3. In *seal-engraving*, a very small iron disk at the end of a tool, used to develop a high polish.

riffle^{2} (rif'l), *n.* [Appar. a dim. of *riff*^{2}, prob. associated with *ripple*^{2}.] A ripple, as upon the surface of water; hence, a rapid; a place in a stream where a swift current, striking upon rocks, produces a boiling motion in the water. [Local, U. S.]

riffle-bars (rif'l-bärz), *n. pl.* In *mining*, slats of wood nailed across the bottom of a cradle or other small gold-washing machine, for the purpose of detaining the gold; riffles.

riffler (rif'lėr), *n.* [< *riffle*^{1}, *rifle*^{2}, groove, + *-er*^{1}. Cf. G. *riffel-feile*, a riffle-file, a curved file grooved for working in depressions: see *riffle*^{1}.] **1.** A kind of file with a somewhat curved extremity, suitable for working in small depressions.

Riffler.

The *rifflers* of sculptors and a few other files are curvilinear in their central line. *Encyc. Brit.*, IX. 160.

2. A workman who uses such a file, especially in metal-work.

riffraff (rif'raf), *n.* [Early mod. E. *rifferaffe*; < ME. *rif and raf*, every particle, things of small value, < OF. *rif et raf* ("*il ne luy lairra rif ny raf*, he will leave him neither *rif* nor *raf*"—Cotgrave), also *rifle rafle* ("*on n'y a laisse ne rifle ne rafle*, they have swept all away, they have left no manner of thing behind them"—Cotgrave), *rif* and *raf* being half-riming quasi-nouns reduced respectively from OF. *rifler*, rifle, ransack, spoil (see *rifle*^{1}, *v.*), and *raffler* (F. *rafler*), rifle, ravage, snatch away: see *raffle*^{1}. Cf. OIt. *raffola*, *ruffola*, "by *riffraffe*, by hooke or crooke, by pinching or scraping" (Florio).] **1.** Scraps; refuse; rubbish; trash.

It is not Ciceroes tongue that can peerce their armour to wound the body, nor Archimedes prickes, and lines, and circles, and triangles, and rhombus, and *riffe-raffe* that hath any force to drive them backe.
Gosson, Schoole of Abuse (1579). (Halliwell.)

You would inforce upon us the old *riffe-raffe* of Sarum, and other monasticall reliques.
Milton, On Def. of Humb. Remonst.

"La, yes, Miss Matt," said she after seating me in her splint-bottom chair before a *riff-raff* fire.
The Century, XXXVII. 939.

2. The rabble.

Like modern prize fights, they drew together all the scum and *riff-raff*, as well as the gentry who were fond of so-called sport.
J. Ashton, Social Life in Reign of Queen Anne, I. 315.

Almack's, for instance, was far more exclusive than the Court. *Riff-raff* might go to Court; but they could not get to Almack's, for at its gates there stood, not one angel with a fiery sword, but six in the shape of English ladies, terrible in turbans, splendid in diamonds, magnificent in satin, and awful in rank.
W. Besant, Fifty Years Ago, p. 114.

3. Sport; fun. *Halliwell.* [Prov. Eng.]

rifle^{1} (rī'fl), *v.*; pret. and pp. *rifled*, ppr. *rifling*. [< ME. *riflen*, < OF. *rifler*, rifle, ransack, spoil; with freq. suffix, < Icel. *hrifa*, *rifa*, grapple, seize, pull up, scratch, grasp, akin to *hrifsa*, rob, pillage, *hrifs*, plunder.] **I.** *trans.* **1.** To seize and bear away by force; snatch away.

Till Time shall *rifle* ev'ry youthful Grace.
Pope, Iliad, i. 41.

2. To rob; plunder; pillage: often followed by *of*.

"Ones," quath he, "ich was yherborwed with an hep of chapmen;
Ich a-ros and *rifled* here males [bags] whenne thei a reste were." *Piers Plowman* (C), vii. 236.

H. said, as touchyng the peple that *rifled* yow, and the doyng thereof, he was not privy therto.
Paston Letters, I. 158.

The city shall be taken, and the houses *rifled*.
Zech. xiv. 2.

The roadside garden and the secret glen
Were *rifled of* their sweetest flowers.
Bryant, Sella.

3†. To raffle; dispose of in a raffle.

I have at one throw
Rifled away the diadem of Spain.
Lust's Dominion, v. 1.

II. *intrans.* **1.** To commit robbery or theft.

Thither repair at accustomed times their harlots, . . . not with empty hands, for they be as skilful in picking, *rifling*, and filching as the upright men.
Harman, Caveat for Cursetors, p. 21.

2†. To raffle; play at dice or some other game of chance wherein the winner secures stakes previously agreed upon.

A *rifling*, or a kind of game wherein he that in casting doth throw most on the dyce takes up all the monye that is layd downe. *Nomenclator* (1585), p. 293. (*Halliwell.*)

We'll strike up a drum, set up a tent, call people together, put crowns apiece, let 's *rifle* for her.
Chapman, Blind Beggar of Alexandria.

rifle^{2} (rī'fl), *v.*; pret. and pp. *rifled*, ppr. *rifling*. [< Dan. *rifle*, rifle, groove (*riflede söiler*, fluted columns; cf. *rifle*, a groove, flute), = Sw. *reffla*, rifle (*reffelbössa*, a rifled gun), < *rive* (for **rife*), tear, = Sw. *rifva*, scratch, tear, grate, grind, = Icel. *rifa*, rive: see *rive*^{1}, and cf. *rivel*. Cf. G. *riefe*, a furrow (< LG.), *riefen*, rifle; and see *riffle*^{1}.] **I.** *trans.* **1.** In *gun-making*, to cut spiral grooves in (the bore of a gun-barrel). Grooves are now in universal use for small-arms, and for the most part are used in ordnance. Small-arms are rifled by a cutting-tool attached to a rod and drawn through the barrel, while at the same time a revolution on the longitudinal axis is imparted to the tool. Rifled cannon are rifled by pushing through their bores a cutting-tool mounted on an arbor that exactly fits the bore. See *rifling-machine*.

2. To whet, as a scythe, with a rifle. [Local, Eng. and New Eng.]

II. *intrans.* To groove firearms spirally along the interior of the bore.

The leading American match-rifle makers all *rifle* upon the same plan—viz., a sharp continual spiral and very shallow grooves. *W. W. Greener*, The Gun, p. 148.

rifle^{2} (rī'fl), *n.* [Short for *rifled gun*: see *rifle*^{2}, *v.* Cf. Sw. *reffelbössa*, a rifled gun. The Dan. *riffel*, Sw. *rifle*, a rifle, are < E.] **1.** A firearm or a piece of ordnance having a barrel (or barrels) with a spirally grooved bore. Spirally grooved gun-barrels are of German origin; some authorities think they were invented by Gaspard Kollner of Vienna, in 1498; others regard Augustus Kotter of Nuremberg as the originator, the invention, according to these writers, dating between 1500 and 1520. Straight grooves were used in the fifteenth century, but their purpose was simply to form recesses for the reception of dirt and to aid in cleaning the gun. Spiral grooving has a distinct object beyond this, namely, to impart to the projectile a rotation whereby its flight is rendered more nearly accurate—the principle being that, when the center of gravity in the bullet does not exactly coincide with its longitudinal axis, as is nearly always the case, any tendency to deviate from the vertical plane including that axis will, by the constant revolution of the bullet, be exerted in all directions at right angles with its geometrical axis. A variety of shapes in the cross-sections of the grooves have been and are still used. The number of grooves is also different for different rifles, as is the pitch of the spiral—that is, the distance, measured on the axis of the bore, included by a single turn of the spiral. The variation in small-arms in this particular is wide—from one turn in 17 inches to one turn in 7 feet. In ordnance the pitch is much greater. Breech-loading guns began to appear in the first half of the sixteenth century, and were probably either of French or German origin. Such guns were made in Italy in the latter half of the sixteenth century. During the war of independence in America, a breech-loading rifle invented by Major Patrick Ferguson, and known as the Ferguson rifle, was used; it was the first breech-loading carbine used in the British regular army. A great many breech-loading rifles have since appeared. Muzzle-loading rifles have been superseded as military arms by these guns, and to a large extent the latter have supplanted muzzle-loaders for sporting arms. Many breech-loaders once of importance in American and European warfare have in their turn been superseded by improved arms. Among them is the once justly celebrated Prussian needle-gun. These improvements have culminated in the Winchester and other repeating arms, which admit of refined accuracy of aim with great rapidity of firing. The tendency in modern rifles is toward smaller bores and chambers. The most recent advance in this direction of improvement is of German origin (1889–90), and consists in making rifles of much smaller bore and less weight than have hitherto been used, with bullets of lead and wolfram alloy having a specific gravity 50 per cent. greater than that of the lead and antimony alloy of the common hardened rifle-bullets. The bores of guns with which experiments have been made are less than 8 millimeters in diameter. Some having bores only 4 millimeters (about $\frac{1}{6}$ inch) in diameter have been tried with surprising increase of range and effectiveness, on account of the diminished air-resistance. Exclusive of repeating rifles or magazine-guns, the principal differences between modern rifles are in their breech-actions and their firing-mechanism. Some of the more important of these arms are described below.

2. A soldier armed with a rifle: so named at a time when the rifle was not the usual weapon of the infantry: as, the Royal Irish *Rifles*—that is, the 83d and 86th regiments of British infantry.—**Albini-Braendlin rifle**, prior to 1889 the firearm of the Belgian government.—**Berdan rifle**, a combination of the Albini-Braendlin and the Chassepot rifles (which see). It is named after its inventor, an American, General Berdan. It has a hinged breech-block, which, when turned forward over the barrel, extracts the spent cartridge. A new cartridge having been inserted, the block is closed, and fastened by a bolt analogous to the cock of the Chassepot rifle. The lock has a spiral mainspring which drives the locking-bolt against a striker working in the center of the breech-block, instead of at the side as in the Albini-Braendlin gun. This rifle was used in the American civil war, and was at one time the adopted arm of the Russian government, which manufactured an improved pattern of the gun at its arsenal at Tula. The arm is hence called in Europe the Berdan-Russian rifle.—**Berthier rifle**, a rifle (carbine) invented by M. Berthier, adopted for the French cavalry in 1890. It is a bolt-gun with a box-magazine, capable of containing three cartridges, which is filled by means of clips or chargers, which are then thrown away. The caliber of the carbine is 8 millimeters (.315 inch), the weight of the bullet 208 grains, and the muzzle velocity about 2,000 feet per second.—**Breech-loading rifle**, in distinction from *muzzle-loading rifle*, a rifle that is charged at the breech instead of at the muzzle.—**Chassepot rifle**, a French modification of the Prussian needle-gun (which see). The barrel has four deep grooves with a left-handed instead of a right-handed spiral, this direction being chosen to counteract the disturbing effect of the pull-off on the aim. The self-consuming cartridge was originally used, but, this causing the gun to foul quickly, the arm has been adapted to the use of metallic cartridges.—**Double rifle**, a double-barreled rifle. Such rifles have hitherto been used only as sporting guns.—**Enfield rifle**, a muzzle-loading gun formerly manufactured by the English government at Enfield. The gun in its original form is still used by native regiments in India, but it has been converted into a breech-loader, and is called the "Snider Enfield" or "Snider rifle." It is, except in India, now superseded.—**Express-rifle.** See *express*, n., 5.—**Francotte-Martini rifle**, a gun having the Martini breech-action with an important modification by M. Francotte of Liège, whereby the lock-mechanism may be, for cleaning, all removed at once from below, by taking out a single pin from the trigger-plate and guard to which the lock-work is wholly attached, and by which it is supported in the breech-action body.—**Henry repeating rifle**, a gun in which a magazine for cartridges extends under the entire length of the barrel, and holds fifteen cartridges. It can be fired thirty times per minute, including the time necessary to supply the magazine. The Winchester rifle has superseded this arm, which was one of the weapons used in the United States army during the American civil war.—**High-powered, low-powered rifles.** See *powered*.—**Krag-Jorgensen rifle**, the military small-arm used by Denmark and Norway and, in an improved form, by the United States. See *United States magazine-rifle*.—**Lebel rifle**, the rifle adopted for the French infantry in 1886. It is a bolt-gun with a tubular magazine holding eight cartridges under the barrel. The caliber is 8 millimeters (.315 inch), the weight of the bullet 208 grains, and the initial velocity 2,073 feet per second. The ammunition supply for each man is 120 rounds.—**Lee-Metford rifle**, the magazine-gun adopted in 1889 for use in the English army. It is also known as the Lee-Speed, and is nearly identical with the Remington-Lee. It is a bolt-gun, and has a detachable box-magazine, which, however, is not entirely separated from the gun, but when withdrawn from its seat is secured to the guard-swivel by a short chain. The magazine has a cut-off, so that the gun may be used as a single-loader and the magazine held in reserve. The magazine of the Mark I gun holds eight cartridges, and that of the Mark II ten cartridges. The caliber of the Lee-Metford is .303 inch, the weight of the bullet 216 grains, and the muzzle velocity 2,100 feet per second.—**Lee straight-pull rifle.** See *United States navy rifle*.—**Mannlicher rifle**, a repeating rifle adopted by Austria, Peru, and Chile in 1888, and by Holland and Rumania in 1893. It is a bolt-gun having a fixed magazine-box into which is introduced from above, through the receiver, a metal packet holding five cartridges. After the cartridges have been fed into the chamber, the packet falls to the ground through a cut in the bottom of the box. There is no cut-off, and the gun can be used only as a single-loader when the magazine is empty. The caliber of the model of 1896 is 6 millimeters (.234 inch), and the gun gives an initial velocity of 2,526 feet per second.—**Martini-Henry rifle**, a rifle adopted by the English government, rifled on the Henry principle described under *rifling*², and having its breech-action that of Martini, in which the breech-block is hinged, and opened backward by pushing downward and forward a lever pivoted just back of the trigger-guard, which movement also automatically extracts the cartridge-case. The gun has been slightly improved since its adoption. It is now used with a coiled brass bottle-necked cartridge carrying a large charge of powder. It shoots accurately at 800 yards, but has a range of 1,800 yards. It was superseded by the Lee-Metford in 1889.—**Match-rifle**, a fine, well-made arm used for match-shooting.—**Mauser rifle**, a military rifle adopted by Belgium in 1889 and by the Argentine Republic in 1891. It is a bolt-gun, and the magazine-box, having a capacity of five cartridges, is underneath the receiver and in front of the trigger-guard. The magazine is of the fixed type, but so arranged that it can readily be removed for cleaning. It can be charged through the receiver with single cartridges, or the five can be stripped at once from a metal clip. The clip is pushed out to the right as the bolt is closed, and does not form any part of the magazine mechanism. The gun has no cut-off, but a single-loading fire can be maintained, retaining four cartridges in the magazine, by replacing the top cartridge after each discharge. The caliber of the Belgian Mauser is .301 inch, the weight of the bullet 219 grains, and the initial velocity 1,968 feet per second.—**Minié rifle**, a rifle using the Minié ball.—**Muzzle-loading rifle**, a rifle which is charged or loaded at the muzzle, as distinguished from a breech-loading rifle.—**Peabody-Martini rifle**, a breech-loading military firearm, made at Providence, Rhode Island. It is a modification of the English Martini-Henry rifle, and was used by the armies of Turkey and Rumania.—**Peabody rifle**, the first breech-loader which used a dropping breech-block pivoted at the rear end above the axis of the bore. The operating lever is also the trigger-guard, and is connected with the block in such manner that pressing it forward pulls downward the front end of the block, thus rendering it impossible to jam the block by any expansion of the cartridge at the base, as sometimes has occurred in rifles wherein the whole block slides downward below the bore. This breech-action appears to have been the forerunner of the breech-actions of the Martini, Westley-Richards, Swinburne, Stahl, Field, and other arms that have appeared since 1862 (the year in which the Peabody rifle was first submitted to military tests at the United States arsenal in Watertown).—**Remington rifle**, an arm once extensively used in the armies of the United States, France, Denmark, Austria, Italy, China, Egypt, and many South American governments. The bore has been made either to take a bottle-necked cartridge, as do the Martini-Henry and some express-rifles, or a Berdan cartridge. The breech-action of the earlier patterns has been criticized as lacking solidity, but no other military rifle has ever proved more generally satisfactory in use. The construction is remarkably simple. The breech-action of earlier patterns consisted mainly of two pieces—a combined breech-piece and extractor, and a hammer breech-bolt. Each of these parts works upon a strong center-pin with a breech-bolt to back up the breech-piece, and a spring holds the latter till the hammer falls. The action has, however, been much improved in later models, and the earlier defects removed. The breech-block is actuated by a side-lever, and it is locked independently of the hammer. It is provided with a powerful and durable extractor, and the lock-mechanism is both simple and strong. The principle of the Remington-Lee rifle was adopted by the government of Great Britain in 1889 in the Lee-Metford.—**Repeating rifle**, a rifle which can be repeatedly fired without stopping to load.—**Rook and rabbit rifle**, a small breech-loading sporting rifle, used only for short ranges.—**Saloon rifle**, a small, smooth-bore, breech-loading gun, incongruously named, having a strong heavy barrel, and used for ranges of from 50 to 100 feet. The cartridge is a small copper case charged with a fulminate. Such guns are principally used in shooting-galleries or rifle-saloons. The best of these guns shoot with remarkable accuracy, and hence are called by the French "carabines de précision."—**Schneider repeating rifle**, a gun having a reciprocating block like the Sharps rifle, the block moving down vertically, instead of being pivoted on hinges and turning downward as in actions of rifles of the Peabody type. It has a tubular magazine with a spring-coil feed extending under the barrel. The breech-block is depressed by moving an under lever downward and forward, and at the lowest position of the lever a cartridge is delivered rearward upon the top of the block. The lever is then moved back, thus lifting the cartridge into line with the bore, on arriving at which it is automatically thrust into the breech by a swinging cam on the left side of the breech-block. This cam also acts as the extractor when the breech is again opened. A link connecting the lever and hammer cocks the gun.—**Schulhof repeating rifle**, a gun having a striker of the bolt form, resembling that of the Chassepot and other guns of that class, a spacious and handy magazine in the stock-butt, a peculiar and efficient cartridge-carrier, and a trigger unlike that in any other rifle. The trigger is on the top of the grip of the stock, and is pressed instead of pulled in firing. Turning over the breech-block and drawing it rearward cocks the gun, and at the same time brings a cartridge into position for insertion; closing the block thrusts in the cartridge, leaving the gun cocked: pressing the trigger fires it. This is one of the most simple and rapid of repeating arms. Twenty-five well-aimed shots can be fired with it by an expert in thirty seconds.—**Sharps rifle**, a rifle having a nearly vertical breech-block sliding in a mortise behind the fixed chamber in the barrel, and operated from below by a lever, which forms the trigger-guard. This gun was used in the American civil war, and was also used to a very limited extent in the British cavalry. It has now only historical importance.—**Snider rifle**, an Enfield rifle converted into a breech-loader. (Compare *Enfield rifle*.) In the change, two inches in length of the breech was cut away at the top, and a slightly tapered chamber made for the reception of the cartridge. A breech-block hinged on the right-hand side was used to close the opening thus made. This block closes down behind the cartridge and receives the recoil. The block is opened, and the cartridge pushed in by the thumb. A striker passes through the breech-block, and transmits the blow of the hammer to the fulminate. The general principle of the breech-action is among the earliest known in the history of breech-loading arms.—**Soper rifle**, an arm having a side-hinged swinging block like the Wendl (Austrian) breech-loading rifle. The block is, however, operated by a lever situated on the side of the stock in a position where it can be depressed by the thumb of the right hand, while the gun is at the shoulder, without moving the hand from the grip of the stock. The movement of the lever simultaneously opens the breech-block, extracts the cartridge, carries back the striker in the breech-block, and places the hammer at full cock. The cartridge is then inserted with the left hand, and on releasing the lever from pressure the breech-block closes. The gun is then ready to fire. The possible rapidity of firing with this gun is probably greater than that of any other breech-loader not of the repeating class.—**Springfield rifle**, a single breech-loader adopted and manufactured (at Springfield in Massachusetts) by the United States government prior to 1892. The breech-fermeture consists of a rotating breech-block and a locking-cam. It is fired by means of a side-lock and firing-pin.—**United States magazine-rifle**, the rifle adopted for the United States military service in 1892. It is constructed upon the Krag-Jorgensen system, and is the same in principle as the gun used by the Danish army, but is a great improvement upon that arm. The magazine is of the fixed type, and is wrapped partly around the receiver. (See the cuts.) It holds five cartridges, which are dropped in on the right and are driven to the left and finally upward into the receiver by a spring. There is a cut-off which converts the rifle into an excellent single-loader, so that the cartridges in the magazine can be held in reserve. The bolt is a hollow cylindrical piece of steel, having an operating handle, and combines within itself the firing and extracting mechanism and the support for the cartridge-head. The bolt slides to the rear in a guide groove, and the firing-apparatus is automatically cocked in the process. The caliber of the United States magazine-rifle is .30 inch, the weight

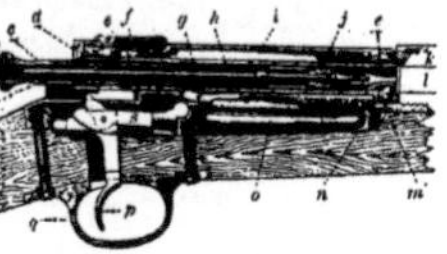

United States Magazine-rifle (cross-section).

a, mainspring; *b*, firing-pin; *c*, bolt; *d*, guide-rib; *e*, gate; *f*, follower; *g*, carrier; *h*, hinge-bar; *i*, magazine-spring; *j*, magazine; *k*, side-plate; *l*, cut-off; *m*, receiver; *n*, extractor.

United States Magazine-rifle.

a, firing-pin; *b*, thumb-piece; *c*, cocking-piece; *d*, safety-lock; *e*, *e*, bolt; *f*, sleeve; *g*, ejector; *h*, mainspring; *i*, extractor; *j*, striker; *k*, barrel; *l*, chamber; *m*, locking-lug; *n*, receiver; *o*, magazine; *p*, trigger; *q*, guard; *r*, sear.

of the bullet is 220 grains, and the initial velocity obtained is 2,000 feet per second. The penetration in oak at three feet from the muzzle is from 16 to 24 inches. The rifle is furnished with a knife-bayonet.—**United States navy rifle**, the rifle adopted for the United States naval service in 1895. It is also known as the Lee straight-pull rifle. It is a bolt-gun with the peculiarity that the bolt is drawn directly to the rear in loading without being turned. The magazine is of the fixed type, and is placed in front of the

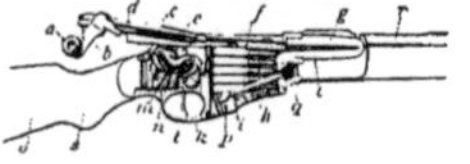

United States Navy Rifle.

a, cam-lever handle; *b*, cam-lever; *c*, bolt; *d*, firing-pin; *e*, mainspring; *f*, receiver; *g*, barrel; *h*, follower; *i*, elevator-arm; *k*, trigger-guard; *l*, trigger; *m*, sear; *n*, sear-spring; *o*, stock; *p*, magazine; *q*, elevator-spring; *r*, barrel-cover; *s*, pistol-grip; *t*, chamber.

guard under the receiver. The magazine is charged from a clip holding five cartridges, and there is no cut-off. The gun is therefore rather a repeating than a magazine arm. If the magazine be not charged the gun can be used as a single-loader. The caliber of the United States navy rifle is 6 millimeters (.236 inch), the weight of the bullet is 135 grains, and the velocity at 60 feet from the muzzle is 2,460 feet per second.—**Vetterlin repeating rifle**, a Swiss arm, of which its inventor, Vetterlin, has produced several patterns. Its firing-mechanism acts on the same principle as that of the Chassepot, but it has a magazine placed longitudinally under the barrel. The cartridges are respectively delivered rearward into a carriage which is moved upward into proper relation with the barrel by a bell-crank connected with the sliding-block when the latter is pulled backward, and descends again for another cartridge when the breech-block is closed. The extractor is similar to that of the Winchester rifle (see cut below). A coiled mainspring drives the needle against the base of the cartridge.—**Winchester rifle**, a rifle the main features of which were invented by Horace Smith and D. B.

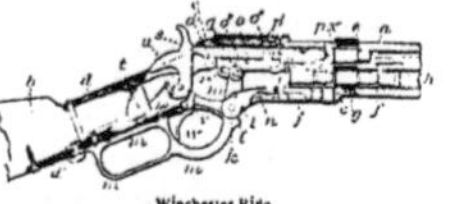

Winchester Rifle.

a, rifled barrel; *b*, stock; *c*, *c'*, receiver, which contains all the internal lock-mechanism, and is attached to the barrel by a screw-thread as shown at *c*, and to the wooden stock *b* by the tangs *d* and *d'*, through which screws pass, one passing entirely through and binding both tangs tightly against the stock; *f*, the magazine, containing cartridges *g*, which are pressed toward the rear by the long coiled spring *h* into a recess in a vertically moving carrier-block *i* in the receiver *c*; *j*, the carrier-lever, pivoted at *k* to the finger-lever *m*, *m*, *m*, *m*, which is also pivoted to the receiver by the same pivot *k*; *l* and *l'* are abutments respectively on the carrier-lever and finger-lever, whose action is explained below; *n*, the carrier-lever spring, which holds it downward when not lifted by the finger-lever; *o*, one of the two links or toggles pivoted to the receiver at *o'*, to the breech-block *p* at *o''*, and toggle-joined at *o'''*; *q*, a pin attached to the finger-lever and working in the slot *r* of the link *o*; *p'*, the firing-pin, which slides in the breech-pin and whose point is driven against the cartridge by the hammer *s* at the instant of firing; *t*, the mainspring, connected by a link with the hammer below the hammer-pivot *u*; *v*, the sear with sear-spring and safety-catch mechanism (not lettered) situated behind it; *w*, the trigger; *x*, extractor and extractor-mechanism, the extractor engaging the rim of the cartridge in the barrel and pulling the spent cartridge-shell out when the breech-block is moved rearward. Turning the finger-lever *m*, *m*, *m*, *m* downward toward the front forces the breech-block, breech-pin, and hammer rearward, cocking the hammer and extracting the spent cartridge-shell. At the same time the ledge or abutment *l* on the finger-lever presses against the ledge *l* on the carrier-lever, forcing up the carrier *j*, with its contained cartridge. When moved back to its original position the finger-lever permits the carrier to return to its original position and receive another cartridge from the magazine *f*, and also forces the breech-block *p* forward, pressing the cartridge into the breech of the barrel. The hammer remains cocked until the trigger is pulled. The loading of the gun and cocking for firing are thus effected by the single motion forward and rearward of the finger-lever *m*. The opening of a side plate (not shown) permits the charging of the magazine by successive insertions of cartridges.

Wesson about 1854, and which has been improved by B. T. Henry and others. Since 1866 it has been manufactured in substantially its present form by the Winchester Repeating Arms Co., whence its name.

rifle³ (rī'fl), *n.* [Origin uncertain.] 1. A bent stick standing on the butt of the handle of a scythe. *Halliwell.*—2. An instrument used after the manner of a whetstone for sharpening scythes, and consisting of a piece of wood coated with sharp sand or emery, with a handle at one end. [Local, Eng. and New Eng.]

rifle-ball (rī'fl-bâl), *n.* A bullet designed to be fired from a rifle. Such balls are not now made spherical, as formerly, but generally cylindrical, with a conoidal head, the base being usually hollowed and fitted with a plug, which causes the bullet to expand into the grooves of the bore of the weapon. See *rifle*², *v. t.*, and cut under *bullet*.

rifle-bird (rī'fl-bėrd), *n.* An Australian bird of paradise, *Ptilorhis paradisea*, belonging to the slender-billed section (*Epimachinæ*) of the family *Paradiseidæ*: said to have been so named by the early colonists from suggesting by its colors the uniform of the Rifle Brigade. This bird is 11 or 12 inches long, the wing 6, the tail 4½, the bill 2; the male is black, splendidly iridescent with fiery,

Rifle-bird (*Ptilorhis paradisea*).

purplish, violet, steel-blue, and green tints, which change like burnished metal when viewed in different lights; the female is plain brown, varied with buff, white, and black. The rifle-bird inhabits especially New South Wales. There are 3 or 4 other species of *Ptilorhis*, of other parts of Australia and some of the adjacent islands, of which the best-known is *P. magnifica* of New Guinea.

rifle-corps (rī'fl-kōr), *n.* A body of soldiers armed with rifles. Especially, in England, since about 1857, a body of volunteers wearing a self-chosen uniform and undergoing drill by their own officers as part of a body of citizen-soldiers formed for the defense of the country.

rifleman (rī'fl-man), *n.*; pl. *riflemen* (-men). [< *rifle*² + *man*.] A man armed with a rifle; a man skilled in shooting with the rifle; *milit.*, formerly, a member of a body armed with the rifle when most of the infantry had muskets.

rifleman-bird (rī'fl-man-bėrd), *n.* Same as *rifle-bird*. *Encyc. Brit.*, XX. 553.

rifle-pit (rī'fl-pit), *n.* A pit or short trench in front of an army, fort, etc., generally about 4 feet long and 3 feet deep, with the earth thrown up in front so as to afford cover to two skirmishers. Sometimes they are loopholed by laying a sand-bag over two other bags on the top of the breastwork, so that the head and shoulders of the rifleman are covered.

rifler (rī'flėr), *n.* [ME. *rifler*, *riffler*, *riflowr*; < *rifle*¹ + *-er*¹.] 1. One who rifles; a robber.

> And eke repreue robbers and *rifleris* of peple.
> *Richard the Redeless*, iii. 197.

> Parting both with cloak and coat, if any please to be the *rifler*. *Milton*, Divorce.

2. A hawk that does not return to the lure.

> *Fran.* Your Hawke is but a *Rifler*.
> *Heywood*, Woman Killed with Kindness.

> However well trained, these birds [falcons] were always liable to prove *riflers*, that is, not to return to the lure.
> *Encyc. Brit.*, XI. 700.

rifle-range (rī'fl-rānj), *n.* 1. A place for practice in shooting with the rifle.—2. A specific distance at which rifle-shooting is practised.

rifle-shell (rī'fl-shel), *n.* In *ordnance*, a shell adapted for firing from a rifled cannon.

rifle-shot (rī'fl-shot), *n.* 1. A shot fired with a rifle.—2. One who shoots with a rifle.

> The scientific knowledge required to become a successful *rifle-shot* necessitates much study, and continual practice with the weapon is also called for.
> *W. W. Greener*, The Gun, p. 157.

rifling¹ (rī'fling), *n.* [Verbal n. of *rifle*¹, *v.*] 1. The act of plundering or pillaging.—2. *pl.* The waste from sorting bristles.

rifling² (rī'fling), *n.* [Verbal n. of *rifle*², *v.*] 1. The operation of cutting spiral grooves in the bore of a gun.—2. A system or method of spiral grooving in the bore of a rifle. Whatever may be the form of cross-section in the grooves, the modern practice is to make them, for small-arms, extremely shallow; and, though the rectangular form with sharp angles is still retained, the angles are commonly rounded, this being an easier form to keep clean. Henry's system of rifling, used in most military rifles, has seven grooves; and the grooves make one turn in 22 inches. The grooves are broad, rectangular, and very shallow, with rounded angles, the lands being much narrower than the grooves. This is the system used in the Martini-Henry rifle. The system most in vogue in America for match-rifles is that of a uniform spiral, one turn in 18 inches, with very shallow grooves. With shallow grooves, hardened bullets are required; and the method of shallow grooving, with hardened bullets, is now taking the place of deep grooves and soft bullets, which were characteristic of Whitworth's and Henry's system of rifling. In express-rifles the rifling is very shallow with a slow spiral (one turn in 4 feet to one turn in 6 feet); and six is considered the best number of grooves. The so-called "Metford system" of rifling, used in England for fine match-rifles, employs five extremely shallow grooves, each including about 32° of the circumference of the bore, the twist of the spiral increasing toward the muzzle, generally finishing with one turn in 17 inches; but it is part of this system to vary the spiral in different guns according to the character of the powder to be used. In large-bore rifles with shallow circular-arc-bottomed grooves, the grooves are often ten in number, with one turn in 7 feet. A system, still of doubtful expediency, has been introduced, called the *non-fouling system*. In this method the barrel is rifled in its front half only. Some very fine shooting has been done by guns thus rifled. The Whitworth system of rifling is that of a hexagonal bore with spiral faces. It is still retained for ordnance. The projectiles for such rifles are also hexagonal with twisted sides. The Haddan system of rifling for ordnance consists of three spiral grooves of deep elliptical cross-section, into which fit three wings on the front of the shot or shell. Other shapes of grooves are also used for ordnance.—**Ratchet-rifling**, a kind of grooving in gun-barrels in which the grooves have a cross-section closely approximating a right-angled triangle with the hypotenuse at the bottom of the groove, like the spaces between the teeth of a ratchet. It is now used only for inferior guns.

rifling-machine (rī'fling-ma-shēn"), *n.* A machine serving to cut spiral grooves or rifles in the surface of the bore of a small-arm or cannon. For small-arms, the cutter-head is armed with two or more cutters, and the grooves are cut in the pulling stroke of the rifling rod to prevent bending, no work being done on the return stroke. After every stroke the cutter-head or barrel is revolved a certain angular distance (depending on the number of grooves to be cut) by the automatic rotation of the rifling bar, so that the several grooves are successively occupied by each cutter. For cannon, the cutter-head fits the bore exactly, and the cutter projects above its cylindrical surface to a height equal to the depth of the chip to be taken out at each stroke, cutting but one groove at a time. The twist is obtained automatically by means of a rack and pinion. The pinion-wheel is made fast to the cutter-bar, and gears into a rack carrying two or three friction-wheels at one end. These friction-wheels roll upon an inclined guide, curved or straight according as the twist is to be increasing or uniform.

rifling-tool (rī'fling-töl), *n.* An instrument for rifling firearms.

rift¹ (rift), *n.* [< ME. *rift*, *ryfte*, < Dan. *rift* = Norw. *rift*, a rift, crevice, rent, = Icel. *ript*, a breach of contract; with formative *-t*, < Dan. *rive* = Norw. *riva*, tear, rive: see *rive*¹.] 1. An opening made by riving or splitting; a fissure; a cleft or crevice; a chink.

> The grete barrez of the abyme he barst vp at enez,
> That alle the regioun to-rof in *riftes* ful grete,
> & clouen alle in lyttel cloutes the clyffez aywhere.
> *Alliterative Poems* (ed. Morris), ii. 964.

> He pluckt a bough, out of whose *rifte* there came
> Smal drops of gory bloud, that trickled down the same.
> *Spenser*, F. Q., I. ii. 30.

> It is the little *rift* within the lute
> That by and by will make the music mute.
> *Tennyson*, Merlin and Vivien (song).

2†. A riving or splitting; a shattering.

> The remnond, that rode by the rugh bonkis,
> Hord the rurde and the *rifte* of the rank schippis,
> The frusshe and the fare of folke that were drounet.
> *Destruction of Troy* (E. E. T. S.), l. 12697.

rift¹ (rift), *v.* [< *rift*¹, *n.*] I. *trans.* 1. To rive; cleave; split.

> To the dread rattling thunder
> Have I given fire, and *rifted* Jove's stout oak
> With his own bolt. *Shak.*, Tempest, v. 1. 45.

> The *rifted* crags that hold
> The gathered ice of winter. *Bryant*, Song.

2. To make or effect by cleavage.

> The intellect is a cleaver; it discerns and *rifts* its way into the secret of things. *Thoreau*, Walden, p. 106.

II. *intrans.* To burst open; split.

> I'ld shriek, that even your ears
> Should *rift* to hear me. *Shak.*, W. T., v. 1. 66.

rift¹ (rift), *p. a.* Split; specifically, following the general direction of the splitting or checking: said of a log: as, *rift* pine boards. Compare *quartered*, 4.

rift²†, *n.* [ME. *rift*, < AS. *rift*, a veil, curtain, cloak, = Icel. *ript*, *ripti*, a kind of cloth or linen jerkin.] A veil; a curtain. *Layamon.*

rift³ (rift), *v. i.* [< ME. *riften*, *ryften*, < Icel. *rypta*, belch; cf. *ropi*, a belching, *ropa*, belch.] To belch. [Obsolete or dialectal.]

rift⁴ (rift), *n.* [Prob. an altered form, simulating *rift*¹, of *riff*²: see *riff*², *reef*¹, *n.*] A shallow place in a stream; a fording-place; also, rough water indicating submerged rocks. [Local.]

rig¹ (rig), *n.* An obsolete or dialectal form of *ridge*.

rig² (rig), *v.*; pret. and pp. *rigged*, ppr. *rigging*. [Early mod. E. *rygge*; < Norw. *rigga*, bind up, wrap round, rig (a ship) (cf. *rigg*, rigging of a ship), = Sw. dial. *rigga*, in *rigga på*, harness (rig up) (a horse); perhaps allied to AS. **wrīhan*, *wreón* (pp. *wrigen*), cover: see *wry*².] I. *trans.* 1. To fit (a ship) with the necessary tackle; fit, as the shrouds, stays, braces, etc., to their respective masts and yards.

> I *rygge* a shyppe, I make it redye to go to the see.
> *Palsgrave*, p. 691.

> Our ship . . .
> Is tight and yare and bravely *rigg'd* as when
> We first put out to sea. *Shak.*, Tempest, v. 1. 224.

> Now Patrick he *rigg'd* out his ship,
> And sailed ower the faem.
> *Sir Patrick Spens* (Child's Ballads, III. 339).

2. To dress; fit out or decorate with clothes or personal adornments: often with *out* or *up*. [Colloq.]

> She is not *rigged*, sir; setting forth some lady
> Will cost as much as furnishing a fleet.
> *B. Jonson*, Staple of News, ii. 1.

> Jack was *rigged out* in his gold and silver lace, with a feather in his cap. *Sir R. L'Estrange.*

> You shall see how I *rigg'd* my Squire *out* with the Remains of my shipwreck'd Wardrobe.
> *Wycherley*, Plain Dealer, iv. 1.

> Why, to show you that I have a kindness for you and your Husband, there is Ten Guineas to *rig* you for the Honours I design to prefer you to.
> *Mrs. Centlivre*, Gotham Election, i. 1.

3. To fit out; furnish; equip; put in condition for use: often followed by *out* or *up*. [Colloq.]

> She insisted upon being stabbed on the stage, and she had *rigged up* a kitchen carving-knife with a handle of gilt paper, ornamented with various breastpins, . . . as a Tyrian dagger. *H. B. Stowe*, Oldtown, p. 501.

> I was aroused by the order from the officer, "Forward there! *rig* the head-pump!" . . . Having called up the "idlers," . . . and *rigged* the pump, we began washing down the decks. *R. H. Dana, Jr.*, Before the Mast, p. 8.

Cat-rigged, rigged as a cat-boat. See cut under *cat-rig*.—**To rig in a boom**, to draw in a boom which is rigged out.—**To rig out a boom**, to run out a studdingsail-boom on the end of a yard, or a jib-boom or flying-jib boom on the end of a bowsprit, in order to extend the foot of a sail.—**To rig the capstan.** See *capstan*.—**To rig the cast**, in *angling*, to fix the hooks on the leader by their snells.—**To rig the market**, to raise or lower prices artificially in order to one's private advantage; especially, in the stock exchange, to enhance fictitiously the value of the stock or shares in a company, as when the directors or officers buy them up out of the funds of the association. The market is also sometimes rigged by a combination of parties, as large shareholders, interested in raising the value of the stock.

> The gold *market* may *be rigged* as well as the iron or any other special market.
> *Jevons*, Money and Mech. of Exchange, p. 214.

II. *intrans.* To make or use a rig, as in angling: as, to *rig* light (that is, to use a light fishing-tackle).

rig² (rig), *n.* [= Norw. *rigg*, rigging: see the verb.] 1. *Naut.*, the characteristic manner of fitting the masts and rigging to the hull of any vessel: thus, schooner-*rig*, ship-*rig*, etc., have reference to the masts and sails of those vessels, without regard to the hull.—2. Costume; dress, especially of a gay or fanciful description. [Colloq.]—3. An equipage or turnout; a vehicle with a horse or horses, as for driving. [Colloq., U. S.]

> One part of the team [in Homer] (or *rig*, as they say west of the Hudson) had come to include by metonymy the whole. *Trans. Amer. Philol. Ass.*, XVI. 110.

4. Fishing-tackle collectively; an angler's cast. [Colloq.]—**Cat rig.** See *cat-rig*.—**Gunter rig** (*naut.*), a method of rigging boats in which the topmast is made to slide up and down alongside of the lower mast. When hoisted, the topmast stretches up the head of the three-cornered sail. This rig is largely used in the United States navy, and takes its name from the sliding scale known as Gunter's scale, on account of the sliding up and down of the topmast. Also *sliding-gunter rig*.—**Square rig**, that rig in which the sails are bent to horizontal yards.

rig³† (rig), *v.* [Early mod. E. *rigge*; prob. for **wrig*, and akin to *wriggle*, *wrick*: see *wriggle*, *wrick*.] I. *intrans.* To romp; play the wanton.

To *Rigge*, lasciuire puellam.
Levins, Manip. Vocab., p. 119.

II. *trans.* To make free with.

Some prowleth for fewel, and some away *rig*
Fat goose and the capon, duck, hen, and the pig.
Tusser, September's Husbandry, st. 30.

rig[3] (rig), *n.* [< *rig*[3], *v.*] **1**†. A romp; a wanton; a strumpet.

Wantonis is a drab!
For the nonce she is an old *rig*.
Mariage of Witt and Wisdome (1579). (*Halliwell.*)

Nay, fy on thee, thou rampe, thou *ryg*, with al that take thy part. *Bp. Still*, Gammer Gurton's Needle, iii. 3.

2. A frolic: a trick. [Prov. Eng. and Scotch.]

The one expressed his opinion that it was a *rig*, and the other his conviction that it was a "go." *Dickens.*

To **run a rig**, to play a trick or caper.

Away went Gilpin, neck or nought,
Away went hat and wig;
He little dreamt, when he set out,
Of *running* such a *rig*. *Cowper*, John Gilpin.

To **run the rig** (or **one's rig**) **upon**, to practise a sportive trick on.

I am afraid your goddess of bed-making has been *running her rig upon* you. *Smollett.*

rig[4] (rig), *n.* Same as *ridgel*.

Riga balsam. The essential oil or turpentine distilled from the cones and young shoots of *Pinus Cembra*. Also called *Carpathian oil*, *Carpathian balsam*, *German-oil*.

rigadoon (rig-a-dön'), *n.* [= D. *rigodon*, < F. *rigaudon*, *rigodon* = Sp. *rigodon* = It. *rigodone*, a dance; origin unknown.] **1.** A lively dance for one couple, characterized by a peculiar jumping step. It probably originated in Provence. It was very popular in England in the seventeenth century.

Dance she would, not in such court-like measures as she had learned abroad, but some high-paced jig, or hop-skip *rigadoon*, befitting the brisk lasses at a rustic merry-making. *Hawthorne*, Seven Gables, xiii.

2. Music for such a dance, the rhythm being usually duple (occasionally sextuple) and quick. —**3.** Formerly, in the French army, a beat of drum while men condemned to be shelled were, previous to their punishment, paraded up and down the ranks.

Riga fir. Same as *Riga pine*.

rigal, *n.* Same as *regal*[2], 1.

Riga pine. A variety of the Scotch pine or fir, *Pinus sylvestris*, which comes from Riga, a seaport of Russia. See *Scotch pine*, under *pine*[1].

rigation (ri-gā'shon), *n.* [< L. *rigatio*(*n*-), a watering, wetting, < *rigare* (> It. *rigare*), water, wet. Cf. *irrigation*.] The act of watering; irrigation.

In dry years, every field that has not some spring, or aqueduct, to furnish it with repeated *rigations*, is sure to fall in its crop.
H. *Swinburne*, Travels through Spain, xvi. (*Latham.*)

rigescent (ri-jes'ent), *a.* [< L. *rigescen*(*t*-)*s*, ppr. of *rigescere*, grow stiff or numb, < *rigere*, stiffen: see *rigid*.] In *bot.*, approaching a rigid or stiff consistence. *Cooke.*

rigged† (rigd), *a.* [< *rig*[1] + *-ed*[2]; var. of *ridged*.] Ridged; humped.

The young elephant, or two-tailed steer,
Or the *rigg'd* camel, or the fiddling frere.
Bp. Hall, Satires, IV. ii. 96.

rigger (rig'ėr), *n.* [< *rig*[2] + *-er*[1].] **1.** One who rigs; specifically, one whose occupation is the fitting of the rigging of ships.—**2.** In *mach.*: (*a*) A band-wheel having a slightly curved rim. (*b*) A fast-and-loose pulley. *E. H. Knight.* —**3.** A long-pointed sable brush used for painting, etc. *Art Jour.*, 1887, p. 341.—**Riggers' screw**, a screw-clamp for setting up shrouds and stays.

rigging[1] (rig'ing), *n.* [< *rig*[1] + *-ing*[1].] A ridge, as of a house; also, a roof. [Scotch and prov. Eng.]

They broke the house in at the *rigging*.
Lads of Wamphray (Child's Ballads, VI. 170).

By some auld houlet-haunted biggin',
Or kirk deserted by its *riggin'*,
It 's ten to ane ye'll find him snug in
Some eldritch part.
Burns, Captain Grose's Peregrinations.

rigging[2] (rig'ing), *n.* [Verbal n. of *rig*[2], *v.*] The ropes, chains, etc., which are employed to support and work all masts, yards, sails, etc., in a ship; tackle. Rigging is of two kinds: *standing rigging*, or rigging set up permanently, as shrouds, stays, backstays, etc.; and *running rigging*, which comprises all the ropes hauled upon to brace yards, make and take in sail, etc., such as braces, sheets, clue-lines, buntlines, and halyards. See cut under *ship*.—**Lower rigging.** See *low*[2]. —**Rigging-cutter.** See *cutter*[1].

rigging-loft (rig'ing-lôft), *n.* **1.** A large room where rigging is fitted and prepared for use on shipboard.—**2.** *Theat.*, the space immediately under the roof and over the stage of a theater; the place from which the scenery is lowered or raised by means of ropes.

Looking upward from the floor of the stage, he would call them [the beams] the gridiron; standing on them, he would speak of them as the *rigging-loft*.
Scribner's Mag., IV. 438.

rigging-screws (rig'ing-skröz), *n. pl.* A machine formed of a clamp worked by a screw, used to force together two parts of a stiff rope, in order that a seizing may be put on.

rigging-tree (rig'ing-trē), *n.* [Also *riggin-tree*; < *rigging*[1] + *tree*.] A roof-tree. [Scotch and prov. Eng.]

riggish (rig'ish), *a.* [< *rig*[3] + *-ish*[1].] Having the characteristics of a rig or romp; wanton; lewd.

For vilest things
Become themselves in her; that the holy priests
Bless her when she is *riggish*.
Shak., A. and C., ii. 2. 245.

The wanton gesticulations of a virgin in a wild assembly of gallants warmed with wine, could be no other than *riggish*, and unmaidenly.
Bp. Hall, John Baptist Beheaded.

riggite (rig'īt), *n.* [< *rig*[3], a frolic, a prank, + *-ite*[1].] One who plays rigs; a joker; a jester.

This and my being esteem'd a pretty good *riggite*—that is, a jocular verbal satirist—supported my consequence in the society. *Franklin*, Autobiog., p. 149.

rigglet, *v. i.* An obsolete spelling of *wriggle*.

riggle (rig'l), *n.* [< *riggle*, *wriggle*, *v.*] A species of sand-eel, the *Ammodytes lancea*, or small-mouthed lance.

Rigg's disease. Pyorrhœa alveolaris, or alveolar abscess.

right (rīt), *a.* and *n.* [Also dial. *richt*, *reet*; < ME. *right*, *ryght*, *ryth*, *ryt*, *rict*, *rigt*, *rizt*, *riht*, *ryht*, < AS. *riht* = OS. *reht* = OFries. *riucht* = MD. *recht*, *regt*, D. *regt* = MLG. LG. *recht* = OHG. MHG. *reht*, G. *recht*, straight, right, just, = Icel. *réttr* (for **rehtr*) = Sw. *rätt* = Dan. *ret* = Goth. *raihts*, straight, right, just, = L. *rectus* (for **regtus*) (> It. *retto*, *ritto* = Sp. Pg. *recto*), right, direct, = Zend *rashta*, straight, right, just; orig. pp. of a verb represented by AS. *reccan*, stretch, etc., also direct, etc. (see *rack*[1]), and L. *regere*, pp. *rectus*, direct, rule, Skt. √ *rij*, stretch, *rāj*, rule: see *regent*, and cf. *rail*[1], *rule*[1], a straight piece of wood, etc., from the same L. source.] **I.** *a.* **1.** Straight; direct; being the shortest course; keeping one direction throughout: as, a *right* line.

For crokid & creplis he makith *rigt*.
Hymns to Virgin, etc. (E. E. T. S.), p. 46.

Than with al his real route he rides on gate,
Redili to-wardes Rome tho *riztes* gates.
William of Palerne (E. E. T. S.), l. 5322.

To Britaigne tooke they the *righte* way.
Chaucer, Franklin's Tale, l. 512.

Circles and *right* lines limit and close all bodies.
Sir T. Browne, Urn-burial, v.

2. In conformity with the moral law; permitted by the principle which ought to regulate conduct; in accordance with truth, justice, duty, or the will of God; ethically good; equitable; just.

Goodness in actions is like unto straightness; wherefore that which is done well we term *right*.
Hooker, Eccles. Polity, i. 8.

When the son hath done that which is lawful and *right*, and hath kept all my statutes, . . . he shall surely live.
Ezek. xviii. 19.

Cousin of Hereford, as thy cause is *right*,
So be thy fortune in this royal fight!
Shak., Rich. II., i. 3. 55.

He
Who now is Sovran can dispose and bid
What shall be *right*. *Milton*, P. L., i. 247.

The adjective *right* has a much wider signification than the substantive Right. Everything is *right* which is conformable to the Supreme Rule of human action; but that only is a Right which, being conformable to the Supreme Rule, is realized in Society, and vested in a particular person. Hence the two words may often be properly opposed. We may say that a poor man has no Right to relief, but it is *right* he should have it. A rich man has a Right to destroy the harvest of his fields, but to do so would not be *right*. *Whewell*, Elements of Morality, § 84.

3. Acting in accordance with the highest moral standard; upright in conduct; righteous; free from guilt or blame.

A God of truth and without iniquity, just and *right* is he. Deut. xxxii. 4.

I made him just and *right*,
Sufficient to have stood, though free to fall.
Milton, P. L., iii. 98.

If I am *right*, Thy grace impart,
Still in the right to stay;
If I am wrong, oh teach my heart
To find that better way!
Pope, The Universal Prayer.

4. Rightful; due; proper; fitting; suitable.

Aren none rather yrauysshed fro the *rigte* byleue
Than ar this cunnynge clerkes that conne many bokes.
Piers Plowman (B), x. 456.

Put your bonnet to his *right* use; 'tis for the head.
Shak., Hamlet, v. 2. 95.

The *right* word is always a power, and communicates its definiteness to our action.
George Eliot, Middlemarch, xxxi.

Hence—**5.** Most convenient, desirable, or favorable; conforming to one's wish or desire; to be preferred; fortunate; lucky.

If he should offer to choose, and choose the *right* casket, you should refuse to perform your father's will, if you should refuse to accept him. *Shak.*, M. of V., i. 2. 100.

The lady has been disappointed on the *right* side.
Addison, Guardian, No. 113.

6. True; actual; real; genuine. [Obsolete or archaic.]

My *ryghte* doghter, tresoure of myn herte.
Chaucer, Good Women, l. 2629.

The Poet is indeed the *right* Popular Philosopher, whereof Esops tales giue good proofe.
Sir P. Sidney, Apol. for Poetrie.

O this false soul of Egypt! this grave charm, . . .
Like a *right* gipsy, hath, at fast and loose,
Beguiled me to the very heart of loss.
Shak., A. and C., iv. 12. 28.

In truth, sir, if they be not *right* Granado silk— . . .
You give me not a penny, sir.
B. *Jonson*, Cynthia's Revels, v. 2.

She filled the one [glass] brimful for her guest, . . . repeating, as the rich cordial trickled forth in a smooth oily stream—"*Right* rosa solis as ever washed mulligrubs out of a moody brain!" *Scott*, Fortunes of Nigel, xxi.

7†. Precise; exact; very. Compare *right*, *adv.*, 5.

With that ich seyh an other
Rappliche renne the *righte* wey we wente.
Piers Plowman (C), xix. 291.

8. In conformity with truth or fact or reason; correct; not erroneous.

If there be no prospect beyond the grave, the inference is certainly *right*, "Let us eat and drink, for to-morrow we die." *Locke.*

Some praise at morning what they blame at night;
But always think the last opinion *right*.
Pope, Essay on Criticism, l. 431.

9. Recognizing or stating truth; correct in judgment or opinion.

You are *right*, justice, and you weigh this well.
Shak., 2 Hen. IV., v. 2. 102.

A fool must now and then be *right* by chance.
Cowper, Conversation, l. 96.

The world will not believe a man repents;
And this wise world of ours is mainly *right*.
Tennyson, Geraint.

10. Properly done, made, placed, disposed, or adjusted; orderly; well-regulated; well-performed; correct: as, the sum is not *right*; the drawing is not *right*.

But most by numbers judge a poet's song:
And smooth or rough, with them, is *right* or wrong.
Pope, Essay on Criticism, l. 338.

11. In good health or spirits; well in body or mind; in good condition; comfortable.

Nae treasures nor pleasures
Could mak' us happy lang;
The heart aye 's the part aye
That makes us *right* or wrang.
Burns, First Epistle to Davie.

"Oh," said Mr. Winkle the elder, . . . "I hope you are well, sir." "*Right* as a trivet, sir," replied Bob Sawyer.
Dickens, Pickwick, l.

12. Most finished, ornamental, or elaborate; most important: chief; front: as, the *right* side of a piece of cloth.

What the street medal-sellers call the *right* side . . . presents the Crystal Palace, raised from the surface of the medal, and whitened by the application of aqua fortis.
Mayhew, London Labour and London Poor, I. 388.

13. Belonging to or located upon that side which, with reference to the human body, is on the east when the face is toward the north; dexter or dextral: as, the *right* arm; the *right* cheek: opposed to *left*.

Hee raught forthe his *right* hand & his rigge frotus,
And coies hym as he kan with his clene handes.
Alisaunder of Macedoine (E. E. T. S.), l. 1175.

He set up the *right* pillar, and called the name thereof Jachin, and he set up the left pillar, and called the name thereof Boaz. 1 Ki. vii. 21.

If I forget thee, O Jerusalem, let my *right* hand forget her cunning. Ps. cxxxvii. 5.

14. Formed by or with reference to a line drawn to another line or surface by the shortest course: as, a *right* angle; a *right* cone; *right* ascension.—**All right.** See *all*, *adv.*—**At right angles**, so as to form a right angle or right angles; perpendicular.—**Directed right line.** See *direct*.—**Order of multiplicity of a right line.** See *multiplicity*.—**Right angle**, an angle equal to a quarter of a complete rotation, or subtending at the center of a circle one fourth of the circumference; an angle formed by a line let fall upon another line by the shortest way.—**Right ascension.** See *ascension.*—**Right bower.** See *bower*[3].—**Right camphor,** the camphor produced from the *Lauraceæ,* which gives a right polarization.—**Right circle,** in the stereographic projection, a circle represented by a right line.—**Right descension,** in *old astron.* See *descension,* 4.—**Right hand.** See *hand.*—**Right hand of fellowship.** See *fellowship.*—**Right helicoid, money†, reason.** See the nouns.—**Right-line pen.** See *pen*[2].—**Right solid,** a solid whose axis is perpendicular to its base, as a right prism, pyramid, cone, cylinder, etc.—**Right sphere,** a sphere so placed with regard to the horizon or plane of projection that the latter is parallel to a meridian or to the equator.—**Right tensor,** a dyadic of a form suitable to represent a pure strain.—**Right whale.** See *whale.*—**To put the saddle on the right horse.** See *saddle.* =**Syn. 2** and **3.** Upright, honest, lawful, rightful.—**4.** Correct, meet, appropriate.

II. *n.* 1. Rightness; conformity to an authoritative standard; obedience to or harmony with the rules of morality, justice, truth, reason, propriety, etc.; especially, moral rightness; justice; integrity; righteousness: opposed to *wrong.*

> Shall even he that hateth *right* govern? and wilt thou condemn him that is most just? Job xxxiv. 17.

> But *right* is might through all the world.
> *Emerson,* Centennial Poem, Boston.

2. That which is right, or conforms to rule. (*a*) Right conduct; a just and good act, or course of action; anything which justly may or should be done.

> Wrest once the law to your authority:
> To do a great *right,* do a little wrong.
> *Shak.,* M. of V., iv. 1. 216.

> For a patriot too cool; for a drudge disobedient;
> And too fond of the *right* to pursue the expedient.
> *Goldsmith,* Retaliation.

> With firmness in the *right* as God gives us to see the *right.* *Lincoln,* Second Inaugural Address.

(*b*) The person, party, or cause which is sustained by justice.

> Receive thy lance; and God defend the *right!*
> *Shak.,* Rich. II., i. 3. 101.

(*c*) That which accords with truth, fact, or reason; the truth.

> *Nym.* The king hath run bad humours on the knight; that's the even of it.
> *Pist.* Nym, thou hast spoke the *right.*
> *Shak.,* Hen. V., ii. 1. 129.

3. A just claim or title; a power or privilege whereby one may be, do, receive, or enjoy something; an authoritative title, whether arising through custom, courtesy, reason, humanity, or morality, or conceded by law.

> Yey schal saue ye kynge hys *rythe,* and non prejudys don a-geyn his lawe in yes ordenaunce.
> *English Gilds* (E. E. T. S.), p. 30.

> The *right* of the needy do they not judge. Jer. v. 28.

> The people have a *right* supreme
> To make their kings; for kings are made for them.
> *Dryden,* Absalom and Achitophel, l. 409.

> The *right* divine of kings to govern wrong.
> *Pope,* Dunciad, iv. 188.

> And why is it, that still
> Man with his lot thus fights?
> 'Tis that he makes his will
> The measure of his *rights.*
> *M. Arnold,* Empedocles on Etna.

4. In *law,* that which any one is entitled to have, or to do, or to require from others, within the limits prescribed by law (*Kent*); any legal consequence which any person, natural or artificial, is entitled to insist attaches to a given state of facts; the power recognized by law in a person by virtue of which another or others are bound to do or forbear toward or in regard of him or his interests; a legally protectable interest. In this sense things possess no rights; but every person has some rights irrespective of power to act or to compel the acts of others, as, for instance, an idiot, etc.; and even the obligations of persons in being, in view of the possibility of the future existence of one not yet in being, are the subject of what are termed *contingent rights.* In this general meaning of *right* are included—(*a*) the just claim of one to whom another owes a duty to have that duty performed; (*b*) the just freedom of a person to do any act not forbidden or to omit any act not commanded; (*c*) the title or interest which one person has in a thing exclusive of other persons; and (*d*) a power of a person to appoint the disposition of a thing in which he has no interest or title. *Right* has also been defined as a legally protected interest. A distinction is made between *personal* and *real rights.* The former term is often used in English law for a right relating to personal, the latter for a right relating to real property. But in the language of writers on general jurisprudence and on civil law, a personal right is a right exclusively against persons specifically determined, and a real right is a right availing against all persons generally. By some writers a distinction is taken between *primary rights* and *sanctioning rights,* by the latter being meant the rights of action which the law gives to protect the primary rights, such as ownership, or contracts.

5. That which is due by just claim; a rightful portion; one's due or deserts.

> I shall fast the this forward all with tyne othes,
> All the londis to leue that longyn to Troy,
> And our ground to the Grekes graunt as for *right.*
> *Destruction of Troy* (E. E. T. S.), l. 7986.

> Moderate lamentation is the *right* of the dead.
> *Shak.,* All's Well, i. 1. 64.

> Honour and admiration are her *rights.*
> *Fletcher* (*and another*), Nice Valour, v. 3.

> Grief claimed his *right,* and tears their course.
> *Scott,* L. of the L., iii. 18.

6†. A fee required; a charge.

> Qwo-so entrez in-to thys fraternite, he xal paye ye *rytes* of ye hows, at his entre, viij. d.
> *English Gilds* (E. E. T. S.), p. 54.

7. The outward, front, or most finished surface of anything: as, the *right* of a piece of cloth, a coin, etc: opposed to the *reverse.*—8. The right side; the side or direction opposite to the left.

> On his *right*
> The radiant image of his glory sat,
> His only Son. *Milton,* P. L., iii. 62.

9. Anything, usually one member of a pair, shaped or otherwise adapted for a right-hand position or use.

> Those [bricks] . . . are termed *rights* and lefts when they are so moulded or ornamented that they cannot be used for any corner. C. T. *Davis,* Bricks and Tiles, p. 78.

> The instrument is made in *rights* and lefts, so that the convex bearing surface may always be next the gum of the patient. *Sci. Amer.,* N. S., LXII. 342.

10. [*cap.*] In the politics of continental Europe, the conservative party: so named from their customary position on the right of the president in the legislative assembly.

> The occupation of Rome by the Italian troops in 1870, and the removal of the Chamber of Deputies from Florence to the new capital of united Italy, to a great extent removed the political differences between the two great parties, the parliamentary *Right* and Left.
> *Harper's Mag.,* LXXVI. 180.

Absolute rights, those rights which belong to human beings as such; those rights to which corresponds a negative obligation of respect on the part of every one. They are usually accounted to be three—the right of a personal security, of personal liberty, and of private property. The right of freedom of conscience, if not involved in these three, should be added. They are termed *absolute,* in contradistinction to those to which corresponds the obligation of a particular person to do or forbear from doing some act, which are termed *relative.*—**At all rights†,** at all points; in all respects.

> Everich of you shal brynge an hundred knightes,
> Armed for lystes up *at alle rightes.*
> *Chaucer,* Knight's Tale, l. 994.

Base right, in *Scots law,* the right which a disponer or disposer of feudal property acquires when he dispones it to be held under himself and not under his superior.—**Bill of Rights.** See *bill*[3].—**By right.** (*a*) In accordance with right; rightfully; properly. Also *by rights.*

> For swich lawe as man yeveth another wyghte,
> He sholde himselven usen it *by ryghte.*
> *Chaucer,* Prol. to Man of Law's Tale, l. 44.

> I should have been a woman *by right.*
> *Shak.,* As you Like it, iv. 3. 177.

(*b*) By authorization; by reason or virtue; because: followed by *of.* Also *in right.*

> The first Place is yours, Timothy, *in Right of* your Grey Hairs. *N. Bailey,* tr. of Colloquies of Erasmus, I. 168.

> Then of the moral instinct would she prate,
> And of the rising from the dead,
> As hers *by right of* full-accomplish'd Fate.
> *Tennyson,* Palace of Art.

Civil Rights Act, Bill, cases. See *civil.*—**Commonable Rights Compensation Act.** See *compensation.*—**Conjunct rights.** See *conjunct.*—**Contingent rights,** such rights as are only to come into certain existence on an event or a condition which may not happen or be performed until some other event may prevent their vesting: as distinguished from *vested rights,* or those in which the right to enjoyment, present or prospective, has become the property of a particular person or persons as a present interest. *Cooley.*—**Corporeal rights.** See *corporeal.*—**Cottage right.** See *cottage.*—**Declaration of rights,** a document setting forth the personal rights of individual citizens over against the government.—**Divine right.** See *divine.*—**Equal Rights party.** See *Locofoco,* 3.—**Free trade and sailors' rights.** See *free.*—**Inchoate right of dower.** See *dower*[2].—**Indivisible rights.** See *pro indiviso.*—**Innominate right.** See *innominate.*—**In one's own right,** by absolute right; by inherent or personal rather than acquired right: as, a peeress *in her own right* (that is, as distinguished from a peeress by marriage).

> A bride who had fourteen thousand a year *in her own right.* *Trollope,* Doctor Thorne, xlvii.

In the right, right; free from error. (*a*) Upright; righteous.

> For modes of faith let graceless zealots fight;
> His can't be wrong whose life is *in the right.*
> *Pope,* Essay on Man, iii. 306.

(*b*) Correct; not deceived or mistaken as to the truth of a matter.

> Now how is it possible to believe that such devout persons as these are mistaken, and the Sect of the Nazarenes only *in the right?* *Stillingfleet,* Sermons, II. i.

> I believe you're *in the right,* major!
> I see you're *in the right.* *Colman,* Jealous Wife, i.

Joint rights in rem, in *civil law,* same as *condominium.*—**Mere right.** See *mere*[3].—**Mineral right or rights,** the right to seek for and possess all the mineral products of a given territory: distinguished, in mining regions, from the *surface right,* the privilege of using the surface of land, as in farming, building, etc.—**Natural rights,** those rights which exist by virtue of *natural law,* such as liberty and security of person and property, as distinguished from those which arise out of conventional relations or *positive law.*—**Nominate right.** See *nominate.*—**Of right,** matter of right; demandable as a right, as distinguished from that which is allowable or not in the discretion of the court: as, in an action for damages for a tort, jury trial is *of right.*—**Personal rights.** See *personal,* and def. 4.—**Petition of right,** in *Eng. law,* a proceeding resembling an action by which a subject vindicates his rights against the crown. See *petition.*—**Petitions of Rights Act.** See *Bovill's Act* (*a*), under *act.*—**Pretensed right.** See *pretensed.*—**Private rights, private rights of way.** See *private.*—**Public right,** in *Scots feudal law.* See *public.*—**Public rights,** those rights which the state possesses over its own subjects, and which subjects, in their turn, possess in or against the state. *Robinson.*—**Real right,** in *law,* a right of property in a subject, or, as it is termed, a *jus in re,* in virtue of which the person vested with the real right may claim possession of the subject.—**Redeemable rights.** See *redeemable.*—**Rental right.** See *rental.*—**Restitution of conjugal rights.** See *restitution.*—**Right about!** See *about.*—**Right-and-left coupling,** a turnbuckle.—**Right in rem,** the legal relation between a person and a thing in which he has an interest or over which he has a power, as distinguished from a *right in personam,* or the legal relation of a person to another who owes him a duty. (But see, for the meaning implied in the civil law, the distinction between *real right* and *personal right,* indicated under def. 4.)—**Right of action,** a right which will sustain a civil action; a right and an infringement or danger of infringement of it such as to entitle the possessor of the right to apply to a court of justice for relief or redress.—**Right of drip, of eminent domain, of expatriation.** See *drip, domain,* etc.—**Right of entry.** See *entry,* 10.—**Right of feud, forest, petition, search, succession.** See *feud*[1], *forest,* etc.—**Riparian rights.** See *riparian.*—**To do one right.** (*a*) To do one justice.

> I doo adiure thee (O great King) by all
> That in the World we sacred count or call,
> To *doe me Right.*
> *Sylvester,* tr. of Du Bartas's Weeks, ii., The Magnificence.

> In earnest, Sir, I am ravished to meet with a friend of Mr. Izaac Walton's, and one that *does him* so much *right* in so good and true a character.
> *Cotton,* in Walton's Angler, ii. 225.

(*b*†) To pledge one in a toast. [Compare the French phrase *faire raison à.*]

> Why, now you have *done me right.* [To Silence, seeing him take off a bumper.] *Shak.,* 2 Hen. IV., v. 3. 76.

> *Ero.* Sighing has made me something short-winded. I'll pledge y' at twice.
> *Lys.* 'Tis well done; *do me right.*
> *Chapman,* Widow's Tears, iv.

> These glasses contain nothing;—*do me right,* [Takes the bottle.
> As e'er you hope for liberty.
> *Massinger,* Bondman, ii. 3.

To have a right, to have a good right. (*a*) To have a moral obligation; be under a moral necessity: equivalent to *ought.* [Colloq.]

> Luvv? what's luvv? thou can luvv thy lass an' 'er munny too,
> Maakin' 'em goä togither as they've *good right* to do.
> *Tennyson,* Northern Farmer, O. S.

> As for spinning, why, you've wasted as much as your wage i' the flax you've spoiled learning to spin. And you've *a right* to feel that, and not to go about as gaping and as thoughtless as if you was beholding to nobody.
> *George Eliot,* Adam Bede, vi.

> I'm thinkin' . . . that thim Germans have declared a war, and we've *a right* to go home.
> *Harper's Weekly,* XXXIV. 86.

(*b*) To have good reason or cause. Hence—(*c*) To come near; have a narrow escape from: as, I'd *a good right* to be run over by a runaway horse this morning; I *had a right* to get lost going through the woods. [Colloq. and local.]—**To have right†,** to be right.

> For trewely that swete wyght,
> Whan I *had* wrong and she the *ryght,*
> She wolde alway so goodely
> Forgive me so debonairely.
> *Chaucer,* Death of Blanche, l. 1282.

> "Sir," seide Gawein, "thei *haue right* to go, for the abidinge here for hem is not goode."
> *Merlin* (E. E. T. S.), iii. 409.

To put to rights, to arrange in an orderly condition; bring into a normal state; set in proper order.

> *Putting* things *to rights*—an occupation he performed with exemplary care once a-week.
> *Bulwer,* My Novel, ii. 3.

To rights. (*a*†) In a direct line; directly; hence, straightway; immediately; at once.

> These strata failing, the whole tract sinks down *to rights* into the abyss. *Woodward.*

> [The hull], by reason of many breaches made in the bottom and sides, sunk *to rights.*
> *Swift,* Gulliver's Travels, ii. 8.

(*b*) In the right or proper order; properly; fittingly: now rarely used except with the verbs *put* and *set:* as, to *put* a room *to rights* (see above).

> The quen er the day was dizt wel *to riztes*
> Hendli in that hiude-skyn as swiche bestes were.
> *William of Palerne* (E. E. T. S.), l. 3066.

To set to rights. Same as *to put to rights.*

> A scamper o'er the breezy wolds
> *Sets* all *to-rights.* *Browning,* Stafford, v. 2.

Vested rights. See *contingent rights.*—**Writ of right,** an action which had for its object to establish the title to real property. It is now abolished, the same object being secured by the order of ejectment. =**Syn. 2** and **3.** *Equity, Law,* etc. See *justice.*—**3.** Prerogative.

right (rīt), *adv.* [Also dial. *reet,* Sc. *richt;* < ME. *right, ryght, rizt, rit, righte, ryghte, rizte,* < AS. *rihte, ryhte,* straight, directly, straightway, rightly, justly, correctly (= OS. *rehto, reht,* MD. *recht,* D. *regt* = OHG. *rehto,* MHG. *rehte, reht,* G. *recht* = Icel. *rētt* = Sw. *rätt* = Dan. *ret,* straight, directly), < *riht,* right: see *right, a.*] 1. In a right or straight line; straight; directly.

> Unto Dianes temple goth she *right,*
> And hente the ymage in hir handes two.
> *Chaucer,* Franklin's Tale, l. 662.

> So to his graue I went ful *rythe,*
> And pursuyd after to wetyn an ende.
> *Political Poems,* etc. (ed. Furnivall), p. 208.

> Let thine eyes look *right* on. Prov. iv. 25.

> Clark went *right* home, and told the captain that the governour had ordered that the constable should set the watch. *Winthrop,* Hist. New England, I. 89.

> *Right* up Ben-Lomond could he press,
> And not a sob his toil confess.
> *Scott,* L. of the L., ii. 25.

2. In a right manner; justly; according to the law or will of God, or to the standard of truth and justice; righteously.

> Thise zeues uirtues loketh and ledeth wel *rigte* and wel zikerliche thane goat of wytte thet hise let be the waye of rigtuolnesse. *Ayenbite of Inwyt* (E. E. T. S.), p. 100.

> Thou satest in the throne judging *right* [Heb. in righteousness]. Ps. ix. 4.

3. In a proper, suitable, or desirable manner; according to rule, requirement, or desire; in order and to the purpose; properly; well; successfully.

> Alack, when once our grace we have forgot,
> Nothing goes *right.* *Shak.,* M. for M., iv. 4. 37.

> Direct my course so *right* as with thy hand to show
> Which way thy Forests range, which way thy Rivers flow.
> *Drayton,* Polyolbion, i. 13.

> The lines, though touch'd but faintly, are drawn *right.*
> *Pope,* Essay on Criticism, l. 22.

4. According to fact or truth; truly; correctly; not erroneously.

> He sothli thus sayde, schortly to telle,
> That it was Alphicuns his sone anon *rigt* he wist.
> *William of Palerne* (E. E. T. S.), l. 4248.

> You say not *right,* old man. *Shak.,* Much Ado, v. 1. 73.

> The clock that stands still points *right* twice in the four-and-twenty hours; while others may keep going continually and be continually going wrong.
> *Irving,* Knickerbocker, p. 270.

5. Exactly; precisely; completely; quite; just: as, *right* here; *right* now; to speak *right* out.

> Sche swelt for sorwe and swoned *rit* there.
> *William of Palerne* (E. E. T. S.), l. 4268.

> And be hem turnethe alle the Firmament, *righte* as dothe a Wheel that turnethe be his Axille Tree.
> *Mandeville,* Travels, p. 181.

> Her waspish-headed son has broke his arrows,
> Swears he will shoot no more, but play with sparrows,
> And be a boy *right* out. *Shak.,* Tempest, iv. 1. 101.

> I am *right* of mine old master's humour for that.
> *B. Jonson,* Poetaster, i. 1.

> *Right* across its track there lay,
> Down in the water, a long reef of gold.
> *Tennyson,* Sea Dreams.

6. In a great degree; very: used specifically in certain titles: as, *right* reverend; *right* honorable.

> Thei asked yef thei hadde grete haste; and thei ansuerde, "Ye, *right* grete." *Merlin* (E. E. T. S.), ii. 129.

> *Right* truly it may be said, that Anti-christ is Mammons Son. *Milton,* Reformation in Eng., ii.

7. Toward the right hand; to the right; dextrad.

> She's twisted *right,* she's twisted left,
> To balance fair in ilka quarter.
> *Burns,* Willie Wastle.

All right. See *all.*—**Guide right.** See *guide.*—**Right aft.** See *aft.*—**Right and left,** to the right and to the left; on both sides; on all sides; in all directions: as, the enemy were dispersed *right and left.*

> Miracils of the crossis migt
> Has oft standen in stede and rigt,
> Ouer and vnder, *rigt and left,*
> In this compas god has al weft.
> *Holy Rood* (E. E. T. S.), p. 116.

> When storm is on the heights, and *right and left* . . . roll
> The torrents, dash'd to the vale. *Tennyson,* Princess, v.

Right away. See *away.*—**Right down,** downright; plainly; bluntly.

> The wisdom of God . . . can speak that pleasingly by a prudent circumlocution which *right down* would not be digested. *Bp. Hall,* Contemplations (ed. Tegg), V. 176.

Right Honorable. See *honorable.*—**Right off,** at once; immediately. [Colloq., U. S.]

right (rīt), *v.* [< ME. *righten, rihten, rigten, rigten, ryȝten,* < AS. *rihtan,* ONorth. *rehta* (= OS. *rihtian* = OFries. *riuchta* = MD. *rechten,* D. *regten* = MLG. *richten* = OHG. *rihtan,* MHG. *rihten,* G. *richten* = Icel. *rētta* = Sw. *rätta* = Dan. *rette* = Goth. **raihtjan,* in *ga-raihtjan,* and *at-ga-raihtjan*), make right, set right, restore, amend, correct, keep right, rule, < *riht,* right: see *right, a.*] **I.** *trans.* 1. To set straight or upright; restore to the normal or proper position.

> At this moment the vessel ceased rolling, and *righted* herself. *Everett,* Orations, II. 130.

2. To set right; adjust or correct, as something out of the proper order or state; make right.

> Henrri was entrid on the est half,
> Whom all the londe loued, in lengthe and in brede,
> And ros with him rapely to *rigtyn* his wronge.
> *Richard the Redeless,* Prol., l. 13.

> Your mother's hand shall *right* your mother's wrong.
> *Shak.,* Tit. And., ii. 3. 121.

3. To do justice to; relieve from wrong; vindicate: often used reflexively.

> So just is God, to *right* the Innocent.
> *Shak.,* Rich. III., i. 3. 182.

> Here let our hate be buried; and this hand
> Shall *right* us both.
> *Beau. and Fl.,* Maid's Tragedy, iv. 2.

4†. To direct; address.

> When none wolde kepe hym with carp he coged ful hyȝe,
> Ande rimed him ful richley, and *ryȝt* him to speke.
> "What, is this Arthures hous," quoth the hathel thenne.
> *Sir Gawayne and the Green Knight* (E. E. T. S.), l. 308.

To right the helm, to put the helm amidships—that is, in a line with the keel.

II. *intrans.* To resume an upright or vertical position: as, the ship *righted.*

> With Crist than sall thai *right* vp ryght,
> And wende to won in last and light.
> *Holy Rood* (E. E. T. S.), p. 67.

right-about (rīt'a-bout'), *n.* [< *right about,* adverbial phrase.] The opposite direction: used only in the phrase *to send* or *turn to the right-about,* to send or turn in the opposite direction; pack off; send or turn off; dismiss.

> Six grenadiers of Ligonier's . . . would have *sent* all these fellows *to the right about.* *Scott,* Waverley, xxxv.

> "Now, I tell you what, Gradgrind," said Mr. Bounderby. "*Turn* this girl *to the right-about,* and there's an end of it."
> *Dickens,* Hard Times, iv.

right-angled (rīt'ang'gld), *a.* Containing a right angle or right angles; rectangular: as, a *right-angled* triangle; a *right-angled* parallelogram.

right-drawn (rīt'drân), *a.* Drawn in a just cause. [Rare.]

> What my tongue speaks my *right-drawn* sword may prove.
> *Shak.,* Rich. II., i. 1. 46.

right-edge (rīt'ej), *n.* In a flat sword-blade, that edge which is outward, or turned away from the arm and person of the holder, when the sword is held as on guard. See *false edge,* under *false.*

righten (rī'tn), *v. t.* [< *right* + *-en*[1]. Cf. *right, v.*] To set right; right.

> Relieve [margin, *righten*] the oppressed. Isa. i. 17.

> We shut our eyes, and muse
> How our own minds are made,
> What springs of thought they use,
> How *righten'd,* how betray'd.
> *M. Arnold,* Empedocles on Etna.

righteous (rī'tyus), *a.* [Early mod. E. also *rightuous,* the termination *-u-ous,* later *-e-ous,* being a corruption of the second element of the orig. compound (appar. simulating *ingenuous, bounteous, plenteous,* etc.), the proper form existing in early mod. E. as *rightwise,* < ME. *rightwise, rightwis, richtwisr, rigtwis, ryȝtwys, rihtwis,* < AS. *rihtwis* (cf. OHG. *rehtwisic,* Icel. *rēttviss*), righteous, just; heretofore explained as lit. 'wise as to what is right,' < *riht,* n., right, + *wis,* a., wise; but such a construction of ideas would hardly be expressed by a mere compound, and the explanation fails when applied to the opposite adj. **wrangwis,* ME. *wrangwis, wrongwise, wrongwis,* mod. E. *wrongous,* which cannot well mean 'wise as to what is wrong' (though this adj. may have been formed merely on the external model of *rihtwis*). The formation is, no doubt, as the cognate OHG. form *rehtwisic,* which has an additional adj. suffix, also indicates, < AS. *riht,* a., right, just, + *wise,* n., way, manner, wise (reduced to *-wis* in comp., as also in Icel. *ödhurvis* = E. *otherwise;* the Icel. *rēttviss,* prop. **rēttvis,* simulates *viss* = E. *wise*); the compound meaning lit. 'right-way,' 'acting in just wise': see *right, a.,* and *wise*[2], *n.*] 1. Upright; incorrupt; virtuous; conforming in character and conduct to a right standard; free from guilt or sin; obedient to the moral or divine law.

> It is reuth to rede how *rigtwis* men lyued,
> How thei defouled her flessh, forsoke her owne wille,
> Fer fro kitth and fro kynne yuel-yclothed geden.
> *Piers Plowman* (B), xv. 495.

> Aristides, who for his vertue was surnamed *rightwise.*
> *Sir T. Elyot,* The Governour, iii. 5.

> And if any man sin, we have an advocate with the Father, Jesus Christ the *righteous.* 1 John ii. 1.

> Rome and the *righteous* heavens be my judge.
> *Shak.,* Tit. And., i. 1. 426.

2. In accordance with right; authorized by moral or divine law; just and good; right; worthy.

> We lefte hym there for man moste wise,
> If any rebelles wolde ought rise
> Oure *rightwise* dome for to dispise,
> Or it offende,
> To sese thame till the nexte assise.
> *York Plays,* p. 397.

> I will keep thy *righteous* judgments. Ps. cxix. 106.

> I love your daughter
> In such a *righteous* fashion.
> *Shak.,* M. W. of W., iii. 4. 83.

> Faithful hath been your warfare, and of God
> Accepted, fearless in his *righteous* cause.
> *Milton,* P. L., vi. 804.

3. Proper; fitting: as, *righteous* indignation.

> Is this *ryȝt-wys,* thou renk, alle thy ronk noyse,
> So wroth for a wodbynde to wax so sone,
> Why art thou so waymot [sorrowful] wyȝe for so lyttel?
> *Alliterative Poems* (ed. Morris), iii. 490.

=**Syn.** 1. *Righteous, Rightful, Upright, Just;* honest, equitable, fair; godly, holy, saintly. The first three of the italicized words go back directly to the first principles of right, while *just,* though expressing quite as much conformity to right, suggests more of the intricate questions arising out of the relations of men. *Upright* gets force from the idea of physical perpendicularity, a standing up straight by the standard of right; *righteous* carries up the idea of right to the standards, motives, and sanctions of religion; *rightful* applies not to conduct, but to claims by right: as, he is the *rightful* owner of the land; *just* suggests by derivation a written law, but presumes that the law is a right one, or that there is above it, and if necessary overruling it, a law of God. This last is the uniform Biblical usage. *Just* generally implies the exercise of some power or authority. See *justice* and *honesty.*

righteous† (rī'tyus), *v. t.* [< ME. *rightwisen,* < *rightwis,* righteous: see *righteous, a.*] To make righteous; justify.

> Can we meryte grace with synne? or deserve to be *ryghteoused* by folye?
> *Bp. Bale,* A Course at the Romyshe Foxe, fol. 62, b. (*Latham.*)

righteously (rī'tyus-li), *adv.* [< ME. **rightwisly, ryȝtwysly,* < AS. *rihtwislīce* (= Icel. *rēttvisliga*), rightly, justly, < *rihtwislīc* (= OHG. *rehtwislih*), right, righteous, < *rihtwis,* right, righteous, + *-lic,* E. *-ly*[1]; or rather orig. < *riht,* a., right, + *wise,* way, manner, wise, + *-lic,* E. *-ly*[1]: see *righteous.*] 1. In a righteous or upright manner; rightly; worthily; justly.

> Thou shalt judge the people *righteously.* Ps. lxvii. 4.

> We should live soberly, *righteously.* Tit. ii. 12.

2†. Aright; properly; well.

> *Ryȝt-wysly* quo con rede,
> He loke on bok & be awayed
> How Ihesu Crist hym welke in are thede [country],
> & burneȝ [men] her barneȝ [children] vnto hym brayde
> [brought]. *Alliterative Poems* (ed. Morris), i. 708.

> I could have taught my love to take thy father for mine; so wouldst thou, if the truth of thy love to me were so *righteously* tempered as mine is to thee.
> *Shak.,* As you Like it, i. 2. 14.

3. Rightfully; deservedly; by right. [Archaic.]

> Turn from us all those evils that we most *righteously* have deserved.
> *Book of Common Prayer* (Church of England), Litany.

righteousness (rī'tyus-nes), *n.* [< ME. *rightwisenes, ryȝtwisnesse, rigtwisnesse, ryghtwisnesse, rihtwisnesse,* < AS. *rihtwisnes,* rightness, righteousness, reasonableness, < *rihtwis,* righteous: see *righteous* and *-ness.*] 1. The character of being righteous; purity of heart and rectitude of life; the being and doing right; conformity in character and conduct to a right standard.

> Ihesu fro the realme of *rightwysnes* descended down
> To take the moke clothyng of our humanyte.
> *Joseph of Arimathie* (E. E. T. S.), p. 37.

> Pure religion, I say, standeth not in wearing of a monk's cowl, but in *righteousness,* justice, and well-doing.
> *Latimer,* Misc. Sel.

> If this we swore to do, with what *Righteousness* in the sight of God, with what Assurance that we bring not by such an Oath the whole Sea of Blood-guiltiness upon our own Heads? *Milton,* Free Commonwealth.

> Justification is an act of God's free grace wherein he pardoneth all our sins, and accepteth us as righteous in his sight, only for the *righteousness* of Christ imputed to us, and received by faith alone.
> *Shorter Catechism,* ans. to qu. 33.

Hence, also—2. In *theol.,* a coming into spiritual oneness with God, because for Christ's sake the believer in Christ is treated as righteous.—3. A righteous act or quality; anything which is or purports to be righteous.

> All our *righteousnesses* are as filthy rags. Isa. lxiv. 6.

4. Rightfulness; justice. [Rare.]

> "Catching bargains," as they are called, throw on the persons claiming the benefit of them the burden of proving their substantial *righteousness.* *Encyc. Brit.,* XIII. 2.

Active righteousness, passive righteousness. Luther ("Commentary on the Epistle to the Galatians," Introd.) and other Protestant theologians following him distinguish between *active* and *passive righteousness*, the former consisting in what is right because it is right, the latter in accepting for Christ's sake by faith the free gift of righteousness as defined in the second definition above.—**Original righteousness**, in *scholastic theol.*, the condition of man as made in the image of God before the fall.—**Proselytes of righteousness.** See *proselyte*.—**The righteousness of God** (Rom. i. 17), a phrase defined antagonistically by Biblical interpreters as "Righteousness which proceeds from God, the relation of being right into which man is put by God—that is, by an act of God declaring him righteous" (*Meyer*), and as "The attribute of God, embodied in Christ, manifested in the world, revealed in the Gospel, communicated to the individual soul, the righteousness not of the law, but of faith" (*Jowett*). The former is the general Protestant view; the latter comes near the view of the Roman Catholic Church, Greek Church, etc. The one regards *righteousness* as indicating a relation, the other as descriptive of character; the one as something bestowed by God and imputed to man, the other as something inherent in God and spiritually communicated to man. =**Syn.** 1. See *righteous*.

righter (rī'tėr), *n.* [< AS. *rihtere*, a ruler, director, = OFries. *riuchtere*, *riuchter* = D. *regter* = MLG. *richter* = OHG. *rihtari*, MHG. *rihtære*, G. *richter*, ruler, judge, = Icel. *réttari*, a justiciary; as *right*, *v.*, + *-er*[1].] One who sets right; one who adjusts or redresses that which is wrong.

> I will pay thee what I owe thee, as that *righter* of wrongs hath left me commanded.
> *Shelton*, tr. of Don Quixote, i. 4. (*Latham*.)

rightful (rīt'fůl), *a.* [< ME. *rightful*, *riȝtful*, *ryȝtfol*, *reȝtful*; < *right*, *n.*, + *-ful*.] 1†. Righteous; upright; just and good.

> The laborer schulde truly traueile than,
> And be *riȝtful* bothe in worde & deede.
> *Hymns to Virgin*, etc. (E. E. T. S.), p. 38.

> Were now the bowe bent in swich mansere
> As it was first, of justice and of ire,
> The *rightful* God nolde of no mercy heere.
> *Chaucer*, A. B. C., l. 31.

2. Just; consonant to justice: as, a *rightful* cause; a *rightful* war.

> My bloody judge forbade my tongue to speak;
> No *rightful* plea might plead for justice there.
> *Shak.*, Lucrece, l. 1649.

3. Having the right or just claim according to established laws: as, the *rightful* heir to a throne or an estate.

> Some will mourn in ashes, some coal-black,
> For the deposing of a *rightful* king.
> *Shak.*, Rich. II., v. 1. 50.

> The legitimate and *rightful* lord
> Is but a transient guest, newly arriv'd,
> As soon to be supplanted. *Cowper*, Task, iii. 749.

4. Being or belonging by right or just claim: as, one's *rightful* property.

> Wink at our advent: help my prince to gain
> His *rightful* bride. *Tennyson*, Princess, iii.

5. Proper; suitable; appropriate.

> The hand and foot that stir not, they shall find
> Sooner than all the *rightful* place to go.
> *Jones Very*, Poems, p. 42.

=**Syn.** 2-4. *Just*, *Upright*, etc. (see *righteous*), true, lawful, proper.

rightfully (rīt'fůl-i), *adv.* [< ME. *ryghtefully*; < *rightful* + *-ly*[2].] 1†. In a righteous manner; righteously.

> Whate are all thi werkes worthe, whethire thay be bodyly or gastely, bot if thay be done *ryghtefully* and resonably, to the wirchipp of Godde, and at His byddynges?
> *Hampole*, Prose Treatises (E. E. T. S.), p. 27.

2. In a rightful manner; according to right, law, or justice; legitimately: as, a title *rightfully* vested.

> Plain and right must my possession be:
> Which I with more than with a common pain
> 'Gainst all the world will *rightfully* maintain.
> *Shak.*, 2 Hen. IV., iv. 5. 225.

3. Properly; fittingly.

> Books, the oldest and the best, stand naturally and *rightfully* on the shelves of every cottage.
> *Thoreau*, Walden, p. 112.

rightfulness (rīt'fůl-nes), *n.* [< ME. *riȝtfulnesse*, *riȝtfulnes*, *riȝtvolnesse*: see *rightful* and *-ness*.] 1†. Righteousness.

> Ouerweninge . . . maketh to moche sprede the merci of oure lhorde, and litel prayzeth his *riȝtuolnesse*.
> *Ayenbite of Inwyt* (E. E. T. S.), p. 29.

> But still, although we fail of perfect *rightfulness*,
> Seek we to tame these superfluities,
> Nor wholly wink though void of purest sightfulness.
> *Sir P. Sidney.*

2. The character or state of being rightful; justice; accordance with the rules of right: as, the *rightfulness* of a claim to lands or tenements.

right-hand (rīt'hand), *a.* [< ME. *ryghte-hande*, < AS. *riht-hand*, *ryht-hand*, the right hand, < *riht*, right, + *hand*, hand: see *right*, *a.*, and *hand*, *n.*] 1. Belonging or adapted to the right hand.

> The *right-hand* glove must always be worn when practicing throwing [in base-ball], in order that this also shall offer no unusual difficulty in the later work.
> *St. Nicholas*, XVII. 828.

2. Situated on the right hand, or in a direction from the right side; leading to the right: as, a *right-hand* road.

> Sir Jeoffrey Notch, who is the oldest of the club, has been in possession of the *right-hand* chair time out of mind. *Steele*, Tatler, No. 132.

3. Serving as a right hand; hence, foremost in usefulness; of greatest service as an assistant.

> O wha has slain my *right-hand* man,
> That held my hawk and hound?
> *Earl Richard* (Child's Ballads, III. 8).

Right-hand file†, patricians; aristocrats.

> Do you two know how you are censured here in the city, I mean of us o' the *right-hand file*? *Shak.*, Cor., ii. 1. 26.

Right-hand rope. See *rope*[1].

right-handed (rīt'han"ded), *a.* 1. Using the right hand more easily and readily than the left. See *dexterous*.

> A left-handed pitcher [in base-ball] is able to make much more of what to a *right-handed* batsman is an incurve, . . . while its opposite, or the out-curve to a *right-handed* batsman, is correspondingly weak.
> *St. Nicholas*, XVII. 827.

2. Turning so as to pass from above or in front to the right hand; clockwise: thus, an ordinary screw is driven in by a *right-handed* rotation; specifically, in *conch.*, dextral, as the spiral shell of a univalve (see cut under *purpura*). The rotation of the plane of polarization by certain substances showing circular polarization is called *right-handed* when, to an observer looking in the direction in which the ray is moving, the rotation is clockwise—that is, in the same direction as that of the hands of a clock; if in the opposite direction (counter-clockwise), the rotation is called *left-handed*. These terms are also applied to the substances themselves which produce these effects: as, a *right-handed* quartz-crystal. 3. In *bot.*, of twining plants or circumnutating parts, properly, rising or advancing in the direction of a right-handed screw or spiral, or that of the hands of a watch. Certain authors, neglecting the notion of forward growth and conceiving the plant as viewed from above, have used the term in the opposite sense, which is quite unnatural. 4. Laid from left to right, as the strands of a rope.—5. Executed by the right hand.

> The Slogger waits for the attack, and hopes to finish it by some heavy *right-handed* blow.
> *T. Hughes*, Tom Brown at Rugby, ii. 5.

6. On the right side; of a favorable, convenient, or easily pardoned character.

> St. Paul tells us of divisions and factions and "schisms" that were in the Church of Corinth; yet these were not about the essentials of religion, but about a *right-handed* error, even too much admiration of their pastors.
> *Abp. Bramhall*, Works, II. 28.

right-handedness (rīt'han"ded-nes), *n.* The state or property of being right-handed; hence, skill; dexterity. *Imp. Dict.*

right-hander (rīt'han"dėr), *n.* 1. One who is right-handed; one who uses the right hand more skilfully than the left.

> There are, however, some *right-handers* (if this useful abbreviative term may be allowed) who, if they try to write with their left hands, instinctively produce Spiegel-Schrift. *Proc. Soc. Psych. Research*, III. 42.

2. A blow with the right hand. [Colloq.]

> Tom gets out-and-out the worst of it, and is at last hit clean off his legs, and deposited on the grass by a *right-hander* from the Slogger.
> *T. Hughes*, Tom Brown at Rugby, ii. 5.

right-hearted (rīt'här"ted), *a.* [< *right* + *heart* + *-ed*[2]. Cf. AS. *riht-heort*, *reht-heort* = OHG. *reht-herze*, upright in heart: see *right* and *heart*.] Having a right heart or disposition. *Imp. Dict.*

rightleche†, *v. t.* [ME. *riȝtlechen*, *ryȝtloken*; < AS. *rihtlǣcan*, make right, correct, < *riht*, right, + *-lǣcan*, ME. *-lechen*, as in *cnawlechen*, later E. *knowledge*, q. v.] To set right; direct.

> Thei sente with hem sondes to saxoyne that time,
> And nomen omage in his name nouȝt forto layne,
> Forto *riȝtleche* that reaume real of riche & of pore.
> *William of Palerne* (E. E. T. S.), l. 1310.

rightless (rīt'les), *a.* [< *right* + *-less*.] Destitute of rights; without right.

> Whoso enters (*Right-less*)
> By Force, is forced to go out with shame.
> *Sylvester*, tr. of Du Bartas's Weeks, ii., The Captaines.

> Thou art liable to the Ban of the Empire—hast deserved to be declared outlawed and fugitive, landless and *rightless*. *Scott*, Quentin Durward, xxii.

rightly (rīt'li), *adv.* [< ME. *rightly*, *riȝtli*, *rihtliche*, < AS. *rihtlīce*, rightly, justly, < *rihtlic*, right, just, < *riht*, right, + *-lic*, E. *-ly*[1]: see *right* and *-ly*[2].] 1†. In a straight or right line; directly.

> Like perspectives which *rightly* gazed upon
> Show nothing but confusion, eyed awry
> Distinguish form. *Shak.*, Rich. II., ii. 2. 18.

2. According to justice, duty, or the divine will; uprightly; honestly; virtuously.

> Master, we know that thou sayest and teachest *rightly*.
> Luke xx. 21.

3. Properly; fitly; suitably: as, a person *rightly* named.

> Descend from heaven, Urania, by that name
> If *rightly* thou art call'd. *Milton*, P. L., vii. 2.

4. According to truth or fact; not erroneously; correctly: as, he has *rightly* conjectured.

> He it was that might *rightly* say Veni, vidi, vici.
> *Shak.*, L. L. L., iv. 1. 68.

> No man has learned anything *rightly*, until he knows that every day is Doomsday.
> *Emerson*, Society and Solitude.

right-minded (rīt'mīn"ded), *a.* Having a right mind; well or properly disposed.

right-mindedness (rīt'mīn"ded-nes), *n.* The state of being right-minded.

> While Lady Elliot lived, there had been method, moderation, and economy, . . . but with her had died all such *right-mindedness*. *Jane Austen*, Persuasion, i.

rightness (rīt'nes), *n.* [< ME. *rigtnesse*, < AS. *rihtness* (= OS. *rehtnussi* = OHG. *rehtnissa*), < *riht*, right: see *right* and *-ness*.] 1. The state or character of being right. (*a*) Straightness; directness: as, the *rightness* of a line.

> They [sounds] move strongest in a right line: which nevertheless is not caused by the *rightness* of the line, but by the shortness of the distance. *Bacon*, Nat. Hist., § 201.

(*b*) Conformity with the laws regulating conduct; uprightness; rectitude; righteousness.

> *Ryȝ[t]nesse* zayth, Lybbe we sobreliche, ryuolyche, an bonayrelyche. *Ayenbite of Inwyt* (E. E. T. S.), p. 265.

> *Rightness* expresses of actions what straightness does of lines; and there can no more be two kinds of right action than there can be two kinds of straight line.
> *H. Spencer*, Social Statics (ed. 1884), xxxii. § 4.

(*c*) Propriety; appropriateness; fittingness.

> Sir Hugo's watch-chain and seals, his handwriting, his mode of smoking, . . . had all a *rightness* and charm about them to the boy. *George Eliot*, Daniel Deronda, xvi.

(*d*) Correctness; truth: as, the *rightness* of a conjecture.
2. The state or attribute of being on the right hand; hence, in *psychol.*, the sensation or perception of such a position or attribute.

> *Rightness* and leftness, upness and downness, are again pure sensations, differing specifically from each other, and generically from everything else.
> *W. James*, in Mind, XII. 14.

rights† (rīts), *adv.* [< ME. *rightes*, *riȝtes*, adv. gen. of *right*, *a.*] Right; rightly; properly.

> Alle anon *riȝtes* there omage him dede.
> *William of Palerne* (E. E. T. S.), l. 1306.

rightward (rīt'wärd), *adv.* [< *right* + *-ward*.] To or on the right hand. [Rare.]

> *Rightward* and leftward rise the rocks,
> And now they meet across the vale. *Southey.*

right-whaler (rīt'hwā"lėr), *n.* One who pursues the right whale. Also *right-whaleman*.

right-whaling (rīt'hwā"ling), *n.* The practice, method, or industry of capturing the right whale: opposed to *sperm-whaling*.

rightwise† (rīt'wīz), *a.* and *v.* Same as *righteous*.

rightwisely† (rīt'wīz"li), *adv.* Same as *righteously*.

rightwiseness† (rīt'wīz"nes), *n.* Same as *righteousness*.

rigid (rij'id), *a.* [= F. *rigide*, vernacularly *roide*, *raide* (> ME. *roid*) = Pr. *rege*, *rede*, *rot* = Sp. *rigido* = Pg. It. *rigido*, < L. *rigidus*, stiff, < *rigere*, be stiff; prob. orig. 'be straight'; cf. *rectus*, straight, < *regere*, taken in sense of 'stretch': see *regent* and *right*. Cf. *rigor*.] 1. Stiff; not pliant or easily bent; not plastic or easily molded; resisting any change of form when acted upon by force; hard.

> The earth as a whole is much more *rigid* than any of the rocks that constitute its upper crust.
> *Thomson and Tait*, Nat. Phil., § 832.

2. Not easily driven back or thrust out of place; unyielding; firm.

> Bristled with upright beams innumerable
> Of *rigid* spears. *Milton*, P. L., vi. 83.

3. Not easily wrought upon or affected; inflexible; hence, harsh; severe; rigorous; rigorously framed or executed: as, a *rigid* sentence; *rigid* criticism.

> Witness also his Harshness to our Ambassadors, and the *rigid* Terms he would have tied the Prince Palsgrave to. *Howell*, Letters, I. vi. 6.

> Thy mandate *rigid* as the will of Fate.
> *Bryant*, Death of Slavery.

> The absurdities of official routine, *rigid* where it need not be and lax where it should be *rigid*, occasionally become glaring enough to cause scandals.
> *H. Spencer*, Man vs. State, p. 57.

4. Strict in opinion, conduct, discipline, or observance; uncompromising; scrupulously exact or exacting: as, a *rigid* disciplinarian; a *rigid* Calvinist.

Soft, debonaire, and amiable Prue
May do as well as rough and *rigid* Prue.
B. Jonson, New Inn, ii. 2.

The *rigid* Jews were wont to garnish the sepulchres of the righteous. *Sir T. Browne*, Urn-burial, iii.

David was a *rigid* adherent to the church of Alexandria, and educated by his mother in the tenets of the monks of Saint Eustathius. *Bruce*, Source of the Nile, II. 579.

He was one of those rare men who are *rigid* to themselves and indulgent to others.
George Eliot, Middlemarch, xxiii.

5. Stiff in outline or aspect; harsh; hard; rugged; without smoothness, softness, or delicacy of appearance.

The broken landscape, by degrees
Ascending, roughens into *rigid* hills.
Thomson, Spring, l. 958.

But still the preaching cant forbear,
An' ev'n the *rigid* feature.
Burns, Epistle to a Young Friend.

Pale as the Jephtha's daughter, a rough piece
Of early *rigid* colour. *Tennyson*, Aylmer's Field.

6. Sharp; severe; bitter; cruel.

Sealed up and silent, as when *rigid* frosts
Have bound up brooks and rivers.
B. Jonson, Catiline, i. 1.

Cressy's plains
And Agincourt, deep ting'd with blood, confess
What the Silures vigour unwithstood
Could do in *rigid* fight. *J. Philips*, Cider, i.

7. In *dynam.*: (*a*) Absolutely incapable of being strained. (*b*) Resisting stresses.—**Rigid antennæ**, those antennæ that do not admit of motion, either at the base or at any of the joints, as of the dragon-flies.—**Rigid atrophy**, muscular atrophy combined with rigidity.—**Rigid dynamics**. See *dynamics*.=**Syn.** 3 and 4. *Severe, Rigorous*, etc. (see *austere*), inflexible, unbending, unyielding.

rigidity (ri-jid'i-ti), *n.* [= F. *rigidité* = It. *rigidità*, < L. *rigidita(t-)s*, < *rigidus*, rigid: see *rigid*.] 1. The quality of being rigid; stiffness; inflexibility; absence of pliancy; specifically, in *mech.*, resistance to change of form. In all theoretical discussions respecting the application of forces through the intervention of machines, those machines are assumed to be perfectly rigid so far as the forces employed are able to affect their integrity of form and structure. *Rigidity* is directly opposed to *flexibility*, and only indirectly to *malleability* and *ductility*, which depend chiefly on relations between the tenacity, the rigidity, and the limit of elasticity.

Whilst there is some evidence of a tidal yielding of the earth's mass, that yielding is certainly small, and . . . the effective *rigidity* is at least as great as that of steel.
Thomson and Tait, Nat. Phil., § 848.

The restraint of the figure [statue of the west portal of Chartres Cathedral] is apparently self-imposed in obedience to its architectural position. The *rigidity* of the example from St. Trophime appears, on the other hand, to be inherent in its nature.
C. H. *Moore*, Gothic Architecture, p. 254.

2. Strictness; severity; harshness: as, *rigidity* of principles or of censure.—**Cadaveric rigidity**. Same as *rigor mortis* (which see, under *rigor*).—**Modulus of rigidity**, the amount of stress upon a solid per unit of area divided by the corresponding deformation of a right angle in that area.=**Syn. 2.** Inflexibility. See *austere*, *rigor*.

rigidly (rij'id-li), *adv.* In a rigid manner. (*a*) Stiffly; unpliantly; inflexibly.

Be not too *rigidly* censorious;
A string may jar in the best master's hand.
Roscommon, tr. of Horace's Art of Poetry.

(*b*) Severely; strictly; exactingly; without allowance, indulgence, or abatement: as, to judge *rigidly*; to execute a law *rigidly*.

He was a plain, busy man, who wrought in stone and lived a little *rigidly*. The granite of his quarries had got into him, one might say. *Harper's Mag.*, LXXVI. 127.

rigidness (rij'id-nes), *n.* Rigidity.

Many excellent men, . . . wholy giving themselves over to meditation, to prayer, to tasting, to all severity and *rigidness* of life. *Hales*, Remains, Sermon on Peter's Fall.

=**Syn.** See *rigor*.

Rigiduli (ri-jid'ū-li), *n. pl.* [NL., pl. of *rigidulus*: see *rigidulous*.] In Lamarck's classification (1801–12), an order of his *Vermes*, containing the nematoids or threadworms.

rigidulous (ri-jid'ū-lus), *a.* [< NL. *rigidulus*, dim. of L. *rigidus*, rigid: see *rigid*.] Rather stiff.

rigleen (rig-lēn'), *n.* [< Ar. *rijlin*, pl. of *rijl*, foot.] An ear-ring having five main projections. See the quotation.

The *Rigleen* or "feet" earrings, which are like fans with five knobs or balls at the edge, to each of which a small coin is sometimes attached.
C. G. *Leland*, Egyptian Sketch-Book, xviii.

riglet (rig'let), *n.* Same as *reglet*.

rigmarole (rig'ma-rōl), *n.* and *a.* [Formerly also *rig-my-roll*; corrupted from *ragman-roll*.] I. *n.* A succession of confused or foolish statements; an incoherent, long-winded harangue; disjointed talk or writing; balderdash; nonsense.

A variety of other heart-rending, soul-stirring tropes and figures, . . . of the kind which even to the present day form the style of popular harangues and patriotic orations, and may be classed in rhetoric under the general title of *Rigmarole*. *Irving*, Knickerbocker, p. 444.

=**Syn.** *Chat, Jargon*, etc. See *prattle*.

II. *a.* Consisting of or characterized by rigmarole; long-winded and foolish; prolix; hence, formal; tedious.

You must all of you go on in one *rig-my-roll* way, in one beaten track. *Richardson*, Sir Charles Grandison, IV. iv.

rigol[1]† (rig'ol), *n.* [< It. *rigolo*, < OHG. *ringilā*, MHG. *ringel*, G. *ringel*, a little ring, dim. of *ring*, a ring: see *ring*[1].] A circle; a ring; hence, a diadem; a crown.

This is a sleep
That from this golden *rigol* hath divorced
So many English kings.
Shak., 2 Hen. IV., iv. 5. 36.

rigol[2]†, *n.* An obsolete form of *regal*[2].

rigole†, *n.* Same as *regal*[2], 1.

rigolette (rig-ọ-let'), *n.* A light wrap sometimes worn by women upon the head; a head-covering resembling a scarf rather than a hood, and usually knitted or crocheted of wool.

rigor, rigour (rig'ọr), *n.* [< ME. *rigour*, < OF. *rigour*, *rigueur*, F. *rigueur* = Pr. *rigor* = Sp. Pg. *rigor* = It. *rigore*, < L. *rigor*, stiffness, rigidness, rigor, cold, harshness, < *rigere*, be rigid: see *rigid*.] 1. The state or property of being stiff or rigid; stiffness; rigidity; rigidness.

The rest his look
Bound with Gorgonian *rigour* not to move.
Milton, P. L., x. 297.

2. The property of not bending or yielding; inflexibility; stiffness; hence, strictness without allowance, latitude, or indulgence; exactingness: as, to execute a law with *rigor*; to criticize with *rigor*.

To me and other Kings who are to govern the People belongs the *Rigour* of Judgment and Justice.
Baker, Chronicles, p. 83.

3. Severity of life; austerity.

All the *rigour* and austerity of a Capuchin.
Addison, Remarks on Italy, etc.

4. Sternness; harshness; cruelty.

Such as can punishe sharpely with pacience, and not with *rygour*. *Babees Book* (E. E. T. S.), p. 64.

We shall be judged by the grace and mercy of the Gospel, and not by the *rigours* of unrelenting justice.
Bp. Atterbury, Sermons, I. xv.

I tell you
'Tis *rigour* and not law.
Shak., W. T., iii. 2. 115.

5. Sharpness; violence; asperity; inclemency: as, the *rigor* of winter.

Like as *rigour* of tempestuous gusts
Provokes the mightiest hulk against the tide.
Shak., 1 Hen. VI., v. 5. 5.

They defy
The rage and *rigour* of a polar sky,
And plant successfully sweet Sharon's rose
On icy plains, and in eternal snows.
Cowper, Hope, l. 462.

6. That which is harsh or severe; especially, an act of injustice, oppression, or cruelty.

The cruel and insupportable hardships which those forest laws created to the subject occasioned our ancestors to be as jealous for their reformation as for the relaxation of the feodal *rigours* and the other exactions introduced by the Norman family.
Blackstone, Com., II. xxvii.

Slavery extended, with new *rigors*, under the military dominion of Rome. *Sumner*, Orations, I. 214.

7 (rī'gor). [NL.] In *pathol.*, a sudden coldness, attended by shivering more or less marked, which ushers in many diseases, especially fevers and acute inflammation: commonly called *chill*. It is also produced by nervous disturbance or shock. [In this sense always spelled *rigor*.]—**Rigor mortis**, the characteristic stiffening of the body caused by the contraction of the muscles after death. It comes on more or less speedily according to temperature or climate, and also after death by different diseases, both of which circumstances also influence its intensity and duration. In hot countries, and after some diseases, the rigor is slight or brief, or may hardly be appreciable. The relaxation of the body as the rigor passes off is one of the earliest signs of incipient decomposition. See *stiff*, *n.* Also called *cadaveric rigidity*.=**Syn.** 1 and 2. *Rigor, Rigidity, Rigidness*, inclemency. There is a marked tendency to use *rigidity* of physical stiffness. *Rigidity* seems to take also the passive, while *rigor* takes the active, of the moral senses: as, *rigidity* of manner, of mood; *rigor* in the enforcement of laws. *Rigidness* perhaps holds a middle position, or inclines to be synonymous with *rigidity*. *Rigor* applies also to severity of cold. See *austere*.

rigore (ri-gō're), *n.* [It.: see *rigor*.] In *music*, strictness or regularity of rhythm.

rigorism, rigourism (rig'ọr-izm), *n.* [< F. *rigorisme* = Sp. Pg. It. *rigorismo*; as *rigor* + *-ism*.] 1. Rigidity in principles or practice; exactingness; strictness; severity, as of style, conduct, etc.; especially, severity in the mode of life; austerity.

Your morals have a flavour of *rigorism*; they are sour, morose, ill-natur'd, and call for a dram of Charity.
Gentleman Instructed, p. 69. (*Davies.*)

Basil's *rigorism* had a decided influence on the later Greek Church. A council of Constantinople, in 920, discouraged second, imposed penance for third, and excommunication for fourth marriage. *Cath. Dict.*, p. 550.

2. In *Rom. Cath. theol.*, the doctrine that one must always in a case of doubt as to right and wrong take the safer way, sacrificing his freedom of choice, however small the doubt as to the morality of the action: the opposite of *probabilism*. Also *tutiorism*.

rigorist, rigourist (rig'ọr-ist), *n.* and *a.* [< F. *rigoriste* = Sp. Pg. It. *rigorista*; as *rigor* + *-ist*.] I. *n.* 1. A person of strict or rigid principles or manners; in general, one who adheres to severity or purity in anything, as in style.

The exhortation of the worthy Abbot Trithemius proves that he was no *rigorist* in conduct. *Sir W. Hamilton.*

2. One who maintained the doctrine of rigorism: a term sometimes applied to Jansenists. Also *tutiorist*.

Rigorists . . . lay down that the safer way, that of obedience to the law, is always to be followed.
Encyc. Brit., XIV. 636.

II. *a.* 1. Characterized by strictness or severity in principles or practice; rigid; strict; exacting.

They [certain translations] are a thought too free, perhaps, to give satisfaction to persons of very *rigourist* tendencies, but they admirably give the sense.
N. and Q., 7th ser., VII. 240.

2. Specifically, pertaining to rigorism in theology: as, *rigorist* doctrines.

rigorous (rig'ọr-us), *a.* [< OF. *rigoureux*, *rigoreux*, F. *rigoureux* = Pr. *rigoros* = Sp. *rigoroso*, *riguroso* = Pg. It. *rigoroso*, < ML. *rigorosus*, rigorous, < L. *rigor*, rigor: see *rigor*.] 1. Acting with rigor; strict in performance or requirement.

They have no set rites prescribed by Law, . . . although in some of their customs they are very *rigorous*.
Purchas, Pilgrimage, p. 412.

2. Marked by inflexibility or severity; stringent; exacting; hence, unmitigated; merciless.

Merchants, our well-dealing countrymen,
Who, wanting guilders to redeem their lives,
Have seal'd his *rigorous* statutes with their bloods.
Shak., C. of E., i. 1. 9.

The ministers are obliged to have recourse to the most *rigorous* methods to raise the expenses of the war.
Goldsmith, Citizen of the World, v.

Religion curbs indeed its [wit's] wanton play,
And brings the trifler under *rig'rous* sway.
Cowper, Conversation, l. 596.

3. Exact; strict; precise; scrupulously accurate: as, a *rigorous* definition or demonstration.

It is absurd to speak, as many authors have recently done, of a *rigorous* proof of the equality of absorption and emissivity. *Tait*, Light, § 314.

4. Hard; inclement; bitter; severe: as, a *rigorous* winter.

At a period comparatively recent almost the entire Northern hemisphere down to tolerably low latitudes was buried under snow and ice, the climate being perhaps as *rigorous* as that of Greenland at the present day.
J. Croll, Climate and Cosmology, p. 12.

=**Syn.** 1 and 2. *Severe, Rigid*, etc. (see *austere*), inflexible, unbending, unyielding.

rigorously (rig'ọr-us-li), *adv.* In a rigorous manner. (*a*) Severely; without relaxation, mitigation, or abatement; relentlessly; inexorably; mercilessly: as, a sentence *rigorously* executed.

I am derided, suspected, accused, and condemned: yea, more than that, I am *rygorously* reiected when I proffer amendes for my harme.
Gascoigne, Steele Glas (ed. Arber), Ep. Ded., p. 43.

Joan of Arc, . . .
Whose maiden blood, thus *rigorously* effused,
Will cry for vengeance at the gates of heaven.
Shak., 1 Hen. VI., v. 4. 52.

They faint
At the sad sentence *rigorously* urged.
Milton, P. L., xi. 109.

(*b*) Strictly; severely; exactly; precisely; with scrupulous nicety.

Nothing could be more *rigorously* simple than the furniture of the parlor. *Poe*, Landor's Cottage.

I have endeavoured to make the "Chronology of Steele's Life" as *rigorously* exact as possible.
A. Dobson, Pref. to Steele.

rigorousness (rig'ọr-us-nes), *n.* The quality or state of being rigorous; severity without allowance or mitigation; strictness; exactness; rigor. *Bailey*, 1727.

rigour, rigourism, etc. See *rigor*, etc.

rig-out (rig'out), *n.* A rig; an outfit; a suit of clothes; a costume. [Colloq.]

I could get a goodish *rig-out* in the lane for a few shillings. A pair of boots would cost me 2*s*., and a coat I get for 2*s*. 6*d*.
Mayhew, London Labour and London Poor, II. 89.

Despres, who had exchanged his toilette for a ready-made *rig-out* of poor materials, . . . sank speechless on the nearest chair. *R. L. Stevenson*, Treasure of Franchard.

Rigsdag (rigz'däg), *n.* [Dan. (= Sw. *riksdag* = G. *reichstag* = D. *rijksdag*), < *rige*, kingdom, + *dag*, day: see *riche*[1], *n.*, and *day*[1].] The parliament or diet of Denmark. It is composed of an upper house (Landsthing) and a lower house (Folkething).

rigsdaler (rigz'dä"lėr), *n.* [Dan.: see *rix-dollar*.] Same as *rix-dollar*.

rigsie (rig'si), *n.* Same as *ridgel*.

Rig-Veda (rig-vä'dạ̈), *n.* [Skt., < *rich*, a hymn of praise, esp. a stanza spoken, as distinguished from *sâman*, a stanza sung (√ *rich*, praise), + *veda*, knowledge (the general name for the Hindu sacred writings, esp. the four collections called *Rig-Veda*, *Yajur-Veda*, *Sâma-Veda*, and *Atharva-Veda*): see *Veda*.] The first and principal of the Vedas, or sacred books of the Hindus. See *Veda*.

rigwiddie (rig-wid'i), *n.* [< *rig*[1], the back, + *widdie*, a Sc. form of *withy*, a rope, withy: see *withy*.] The rope or chain that goes over a horse's back to support the shafts of a vehicle. Burns uses it adjectively in the sense of resembling a rigwiddie, and hence ill-shaped, thrawn, weazen. [Scotch.]

Wither'd beldams, auld and droll,
Rigwoodie hags, wad spean a foal.
Burns, Tam o' Shanter.

rikk (rik), *n.* A small form of tambourine, used in Egypt.

rilasciando (rē-lä-shian'dō), *a.* [It., ppr. of *rilasciare*, relax: see *relax*.] In *music*, same as *rallentando*.

rile (ril), *v. t.* A dialectal variant of *roil*[2].

rilievo (rē-lyā'vō), *n.* [< It. *rilievo*, pl. *rilievi*: see *relief*.] Same as *relief*, in sculpture, etc.: the Italian form, often used in English. Sometimes spelled *relievo*.

Shallow porticoes of columns . . . supported statues, or rather, to judge from the coins representing the building, *rilievos*, which may have set off, but could hardly have given much dignity to, a building designed as this was. *J. Fergusson*, Hist. Arch., I. 318.

rill (ril), *n.* [= LG. *rille*, *rile*, a channel, a rill, G. *rille*, a small furrow, chamfer; origin uncertain. Cf. W. *rhill*, a trench, drill, row, contr. < *rhigol*, a trench, groove, dim. of *rhig*, a notch, groove, hence a shallow trench, channel. Cf. F. *rigole*, > G. *rigole*, *riole*, a trench, furrow. Cf. *rillet*, *rivulet*.] 1. A small brook; a rivulet; a streamlet.

May thy brimmed waves for this
Their full tribute never miss
From a thousand petty *rills*,
That tumble down the snowy hills.
Milton, Comus, l. 926.

2. A deep, winding valley on the moon. [Little used.]

rill (ril), *v. i.* [< *rill*, *n.*] To flow in a small stream or rill; run in streamlets; purl. [Rare.]

The wholesome Draught from Aganippe's Spring
Genuine, and with soft Murmurs gently *rilling*
Adown the Mountains where thy Daughters haunt.
Prior, Second Hymn of Callimachus.

rillet (ril'et), *n.* [< *rill* + *-et*. Cf. *rivulet*; cf. also F. *rigolet*, an irrigation ditch, < *rigole*, a rill: see *rill*.] A little rill; a brook; a rivulet.

The water which in one poole hath abiding
Is not so sweet as *rillets* ever gliding.
W. Browne, Britannia's Pastorals, ii. 3.

From the green rivage many a fall
Of diamond *rillets* musical, . . .
Fall'n silver-chiming, seem'd to shake
The sparkling flints beneath the prow.
Tennyson, Arabian Nights.

rill-mark (ril'märk), *n.* A marking or tracery formed upon any surface by the action of water trickling over it in little rills.

Another kind of markings not even organic, but altogether depending on physical causes, are the beautiful branching *rill-marks* produced by the oozing of water out of mud and sand-banks left by the tide.
Dawson, Geol. Hist. of Plants, p. 32.

rim[1] (rim), *n.* [< ME. *rim*, *rym*, *rime*, < AS. *rima*, rim, edge, border (*sǣ-rima*, sea-coast); cf. Icel. *rim*, a rail, *rimi*, a strip of land; prob. from the same root (√ *ram*) as *rind*[1] and *rand*[1], q. v. The W. *rhim*, with the secondary forms *rhimp*, *rhimyn*, a rim, edge, *rhimpyn*, an extremity, is appar. from the E.] 1. The border, edge, or margin of anything, whether forming part of the thing itself, or separate from it and surrounding or partly surrounding it, most commonly a circular border, often raised above the inclosed surface: as, the *rim* of a hat.

The moon lifting her silver *rim*
Above a cloud, and with a gradual swim
Coming into the blue with all her light.
Keats, I stood Tiptoe upon a Little Hill.

A large caldron lined with copper, with a *rim* of brass.
H. James, Jr., Little Tour, p. 165.

We have observed them [whales] just "under the *rim* of the water" (as whalemen used to say).
C. M. Scammon, Marine Mammals, p. 42.

Specifically—2. In a wheel, the circular part furthest from the axle, connected by spokes to the hub, nave, or boss. In a carriage- or wagon-wheel the rim is built up of bent or sawed pieces called *fellies*, and is encircled by the tire. See cut under *felly*.

The *rim* proper appears to have been bent into shape; the wooden tire was cut out from the solid timber.
E. M. Stratton, World on Wheels, p. 67.

= **Syn.** 1. The *rim* of a vessel; the *brim* of a cup or goblet; the *brink*, *verge*, or *edge* of a precipice; the *margin* of a brook or a book; the *border* of a garment or a country.

rim[1] (rim), *v. t.*; pret. and pp. *rimmed*, ppr. *rimming*. [< *rim*[1], *n.*] 1. To surround with a rim or border; form a rim round.

A length of bright horizon *rimm'd* the dark.
Tennyson, Gardener's Daughter.

All night they ate the boar Serimner's flesh,
And from their horns, with silver *rimm'd*, drank mead.
M. Arnold, Balder Dead.

2. To plow or slash the sides of, as mackerel, to make them seem fatter.

rim[2] (rim), *n.* [Early mod. E. also *rimme*, *rymme*; < ME. *rim*, *rym*, *ryme*, earlier *reme*, a membrane, < AS. *reóma*, a membrane, ligament, = OS. *riomo*, *reomo*, a thong, latchet, = D. *riem*, a thong (see *riem*), = OHG. *riomo*, *riumo*, thong, band, girdle, rein, etc., MHG. *rieme*, G. *riemen*, a thong, band, etc., = Sw. Dan. *rem*, thong, a strap, = Gr. ῥῦμα, a tow-line, < *ῥύειν, ἐρύειν, draw. No connection with *rim*[1].] 1. A membrane. [Prov. Eng.]

As is the walnutte, so is this fruite [nutmeg] defended with a double couering, as fyrste with a grene huske, voder the whiche is a thinne skinne or *rimme* like a nette, encompassing the shell of a nutte.
R. Eden, tr. of Sebastian Munster (First Books on America, ed. Arber, p. 35).

2. The membrane inclosing the intestines; the peritoneum; hence, loosely, the intestines; the belly. [Obsolete or provincial.]

Alle the *rymes* by the rybbes radly thay lance.
Sir Gawayne and the Green Knight (E. E. T. S.), l. 1343.

I will fetch thy *rim* out at thy throat
In drops of crimson blood.
Shak., Hen. V., iv. 4. 15.

We may not affirm that . . . ruptures are confinable unto one side; whereas the peritoneum or *rim* of the belly may be broke, or its perforations relaxed in either.
Sir T. Browne, Vulg. Err., iv. 3.

Struck through the belly's *rim*, the warrior lies
Supine, and shades eternal veil his eyes.
Pope, Iliad, xiv. 521.

rima (rī'mạ̈), *n.*; pl. *rimæ* (-mē). [< L. *rima*, a crack, cleft, opening: see *rime*[6].] 1. In *biol.*, an opening, as a fissure or cleft; a long or narrow aperture.—2. In *conch.*, the fissure or aperture between the valves of a bivalve shell when the hymen is removed.—**Rima glottidis**, the opening between the vocal cords in front and the arytenoid cartilages behind.—**Rima glottidis cartilaginea**, that part of the rima glottidis which lies between the arytenoid cartilages. Also called *respiratory glottis*.—**Rima oris**, the orifice of the mouth; in *ornith.*, the rictus; the gape. See *rictus*.—**Rima vocalis**, that part of the rima glottidis which lies between the vocal cords. Also called *rima glottidis membranacea* and *vocal glottis*.

rimbase (rim'bās), *n.* [< *rim*[1] + *base*[2], *n.*] In *gun.*: (*a*) A short cylinder connecting a trunnion with the body of a cannon. (*b*) The shoulder on the stock of a musket against which the breech of the barrel rests.

rime[1] (rim), *n.* [Also and more commonly *rhyme*, a spelling first used, alternating with *rhime*, about the year 1550, and due to the erroneous notion that the word is identical with *rhythm* (indeed even the spellings *rhythm* and *rhithm* were sometimes used for the proper word *rime*); prop. only *rime*, a spelling which has never become wholly obsolete and is now widely used by persons who are aware of the blunder involved in the spelling *rhyme*. Early mod. E. *rime*, *ryme*, < ME. *rime*, *ryme*, *rim*, *rym*, number, rime, verse, < AS. *rīm*, number (not in the senses 'verse' or 'rime,' which appear to be of Rom. origin), = OS. *rīm*, number (in comp. *unrim* = AS. *unrim*, "numbers without number," a great number), = OFries. *rīm*, tale, = MD. *rijm*, *rijme*, D. *rijm* = MLG. *rīm*, LG. *riem*, *rim*, rime, = OHG. *rīm*, erroneously *hrīm*, number, series, row, MHG. *rīm*, verse, rime, G. *reim*, rime, = Icel. *rīm*, also *rīma* = Sw. Dan. *rim*, rime; hence (< OHG.) OF. *rime*, F. *rime* = Pr. *rim*, *rima* = OCat. *rim* = Sp. Pg. It. *rima* (ML. *rima*), verse, rime. The sense of 'poetic number,' whence 'verse,' 'a tale in verse,' 'agreement of terminal sounds,' seems to have arisen in Rom., this meaning, with the thing itself, being unknown to the earlier Teut. tongues. The transition of sense, though paralleled by a similar development of *number* and *tale*, was prob. due in part to association with L. *rhythmus*, ML. also *rhithmus*, *rithmus*, *ritmus*, which, with the Rom. forms, and later the E. form *rhythm*, seems to have been constantly confused with *rime*, the two words having the sense 'verse' in common. Connection of AS. *rim*, etc., with Gr. ἀριθμός, number (see *arithmetic*), Ir. Gael. *aireamh*, number, = W. *eirif*, number, Ir. *rimh* = W. *rhif*, number, is improbable.] 1†. Number.

Thurh tale and *rime* of fowertig. *Ormulum*, l. 11248.

2. Thought expressed in verse; verse; meter; poetry; also, a composition in verse; a poem, especially a short one; a tale in verse.

Horn sede on his *rime*:
"Iblessed beo the time
I com to Suddenne
With mine irisse men."
King Horn (E. E. T. S.), p. 39.

Other tale certes can I noon,
But of a *ryme* I lerned longe agoon.
Chaucer, Prol. to Sir Thopas, l. 19.

Things unattempted yet in prose or *rhyme*.
Milton, P. L., i. 16.

3. Agreement in the terminal sounds of two or more words, namely in the last accented vowel and the sounds following, if there be any, while the sounds preceding differ; also, by extension, such agreement in the initial sounds (*initial rime*, usually called *alliteration*). See *homœoteleuton*, and compare *assonance*.

Rime is the rhythmical repetition of letters. Nations who unite arsis and prose accent need to mark off their verses plainly. They do it by *rime*. Other nations shun *rime*. When the riming letters begin their words, it is called *alliteration*. When the accented vowels and the following letters are alike, it is called *perfect rime*. When only the consonants are alike, it is called *half rime*.
F. A. March, Anglo-Sax. Gram., p. 223.

The clock-work tintinnabulum of *rhyme*.
Cowper, Table-Talk, l. 529.

4. A verse or line agreeing with another in terminal sounds: as, to string *rimes* together.

The *rhymes* are dazzled from their place,
And order'd words asunder fly.
Tennyson, The Day-Dream, Prol.

5. A word answering in sound to another word.

They ring round the same unvaried chimes,
With sure returns of still expected *rhymes*;
Where'er you find "the cooling western breeze,"
In the next line it "whispers through the trees."
Pope, Essay on Criticism, l. 349.

Caudate rime, rime at the end of successive lines: opposed to *leonine* (which see) or other rime between the ends of sections of the same line. Also *tailed rime*.—**Female** or **feminine rimes**. See *female*.—**Male** or **masculine rimes**. See *male*[1].—**Neither rime nor reason**, neither consistency nor rational meaning; neither sound nor sense; hence, with no mitigating feature or excuse. The phrase occurs under various forms, and especially in plays upon words.

I would exhorte you also to beware of *rime without reason*: my meaning is hereby that your rime leade you not from your firste Inuention.
Gascoigne, Notes on Eng. Verse (ed. Arber), § 6.

I was promis'd on a time
To have reason for my rhyme;
From that time unto this season,
I receiv'd *nor rhyme nor reason*.
Spenser, Lines on his Promised Pension, Int. to Works, [p. xiv.

Thus sayd one in a meeter of eleuen very harshly in mine care, whether it be for lacke of good *rime or* of good *reason*, or of both, I wot not.
Puttenham, Arte of Eng. Poesie, p. 59.

Was there ever any man thus beaten out of season
When in the why and the wherefore is *neither rhyme nor reason?*
Shak., C. of E., ii. 2. 49.

These fellows of infinite tongue, that can *rhyme* themselves into ladies' favours, they do always *reason* themselves out again. *Shak.*, Hen. V., v. 2. 164.

And every one super-aboundeth in his own humour, even to the annihilating of any other *without rhyme or reason*.
G. Harvey, Four Letters.

rime[1] (rim), *v.*; pret. and pp. *rimed*, ppr. *riming*. [Also and more commonly *rhyme* (formerly also *rhime*), an erroneous spelling as with the noun; early mod. E. *rime*, *ryme*, < ME. *rimen*, *rymen*, rime, < AS. *rīman*, number, count, reckon, = D. *rijmen*, rime, = OHG. *rīman*, number, count, count up, MHG. *rīmen*, rime, fig. bring together, unite, G. *reimen*, rime, = Sw. *rimma* = Dan. *rime* = OF. and F. *rimer* = Pr. Sp. Pg. *rimar* = It. *rimare* (ML. *rimare*), rime; from the noun: see *rime*[1], *n.*] **I.** *trans.* 1†. To number; count; reckon.—2. To compose in verse; treat in verse; versify.

But alle shal passen that men prose or *ryme*,
Take every man hys turn as for his tyme.
Chaucer, Envoy of Chaucer to Scogan, l. 41.

3. To put into rime: as, to *rime* a story.—4. To bring into a certain condition by riming; influence by rime.

Fellows of Infinite tongue, that can *rhyme* themselves into ladies' favours. *Shak.*, Hen. V., v. 2. 164.

To **rime to death**, to destroy by the use of riming incantations; hence, to kill off in any manner; get rid of; make an end of.

And my poets
Shall with a satire, steep'd in gall and vinegar,
Rhyme 'em *to death*, as they do rats in Ireland.
Randolph, Jealous Lovers, v. 2.

Were the brute capable of being *rhymed to death*, Mr. Creech should do it genteely, and take the widow with her jointure. *R. Parsons*, in Letters of Eminent Men, from [Bodl. Coll. (Lond., 1813), I. 54.

II. *intrans.* **1.** To compose verses; make verses.

There march'd the bard and blockhead side by side,
Who *rhymed* for hire, and patronized for pride.
Pope, Dunciad, iv. 102.

2. To accord in the terminal sounds; more widely, to correspond in sound; assonate; harmonize; accord; chime.

But fagotted his notions as they fell,
And, if they *rhymed* and rattled, all was well.
Dryden, Abs. and Achit., ii. 420.

Riming delirium, a form of mania in which the patient speaks in verses.

rime[2] (rīm), *n.* [< ME. *rime*, *rim*, *ryme*, < AS. *hrīm* = OD. D. *rijm* = OHG. **hrīm*, **rīm*, *rīme*, MHG. **rīm* (in verb *rīmeln*), G. dial. *reim*, *rein* = Icel. *hrīm* = Sw. Dan. *rim*, frost; cf. D. *rijp* = OHG. *hrīfo*, *rīfo*, MHG. *rīfe*, G. *reif*, frost. Some erroneously connect the word with Gr. κρυμός, κρύος, frost, κρύσταλλος, ice, < √ *kru*, be hard: see *crystal*, *crude*.] White frost, or hoar-frost; congealed dew or vapor: same as *frost*, 3.

Frosty *rime*,
That in the morning whitened hill and plain
And is no more. *Wordsworth*, Eccles. Sonnets, iii. 34.

My grated casement whitened with Autumn's early *rime*.
Whittier, Cassandra Southwick.

rime[2] (rīm), *v. i.*; pret. and pp. *rimed*, ppr. *riming*. [< *rime*[2], *n.*] To freeze or congeal into hoar-frost.

rime[3] (rīm), *v. t.* Same as *ream*[2].

rime[4], *n.* A Middle English or modern dialectal form of *rim*[1].

rime[5]†, *n.* A Middle English form of *rim*[2].

rime[6] (rīm), *n.* [< OF. *rime*, < L. *rima*, a crack, fissure, cleft, chink.] A chink; a fissure; a rent or long aperture. *Sir T. Browne.*

rime-frost (rīm'frôst), *n.* [< ME. *rymefrost*, *rimfrost* (= Sw. Dan. *rimfrost*), < *rime*[2] + *frost*.] Hoar-frost; rime.

On morgen fel hem a dew a-gein. . . .
It lai thor, quit as a *rim frost*.
Genesis and Exodus (E. E. T. S.), l. 3328.

rime-frosted (rīm'frôs″ted), *a.* Covered with hoar-frost or rime.

The birch-trees delicately *rime-frosted* to their finest tips. *Harper's Mag.*, LXXVIII. 643.

rimeless (rīm'les), *a.* [< *rime*[1] + *-less*.] Having no rime; not in the form of rime. Also *rhymeless*.

Too popular is Tragic Poesy,
Straining his tip-toes for a farthing fee,
And doth beside on *rhymeless* numbers tread,
Unbid Iambics flow from careless head.
Bp. Hall, Satires, I. iv. 3.

rime-letter (rīm'let″ėr), *n.* A recurring letter, as in alliteration.

The repeated letter [in alliteration] is called the *rime-letter*. *F. A. March*, Anglo-Sax. Gram., p. 224.

rimer[1] (rī'mėr), *n.* [Also and more commonly *rhymer*, an erroneous spelling (see *rime*[1], *n.*); early mod. E. *rimer*, *rymer*, < ME. **rimer*, *rymare*, a rimer (used in a depreciative sense) (cf. AS. *rīmere*, a computer, reckoner, calculator), = D. *rijmer* = MHG. *rīmære*, G. *reimer* = Icel. *rīmari* = Sw. *rimmare* = Dan. *rimer*, a rimer, versifier; as *rime*[1], *v.*, + *-er*[1]. Cf. ML. *rimarius*, a rimer; F. *rimeur* = Pg. *rimador* = It. *rimatore*, a rimer.] One who makes rimes or verses; especially, a maker of verses wherein rime or metrical form predominates over poetic thought or creation; hence, an inferior poet; in former use, also, a minstrel.

To eschew many Diseases and mischiefs, which have happened before this time in the Land of Wales, by many Wasters, *Rhymers*, Minstrels, and other Vagabonds: It is ordained, etc.
Laws of Hen. IV. (1402), in Ribton-Turner's Vagrants and [Vagrancy, p. 64.

Sawcie Lictors
Will catch at vs like Strumpets, and scald *Rimers*
Ballad vs out a Tune.
Shak., A. and C. (folio 1623), v. 2. 215.

I am nae poet in a sense,
But just a *rhymer*, like, by chance.
Burns, First Epistle to J. Lapraik.

rimer[2] (rī'mėr), *n.* Same as *reamer*. Also *rimmer*. [Eng.]

rimer[2] (rī'mėr), *v. t.* [< *rimer*[2], *n.*] To ream. Also *rimmer*. [Eng.]

When . . . the rivet cannot be inserted without recourse to some means for straightening the holes, it is best to *rimer* them out and use a larger rivet.
R. Wilson, Steam Boilers, p. 67.

The lower end of each column is bolted by turned bolts in *rimered* holes to cast iron girders 20 in. deep.
The Engineer, LXVI. 530.

rimer[3] (rī'mėr), *n.* In *fort.*, a palisade.

rime-royal† (rīm'roi″al), *n.* A seven-line stanza which Chaucer introduced into English versification. There are in it three rimes, the first and third lines riming together, the second, fourth, and fifth also riming, and the sixth and seventh. It is generally supposed that this form of verse received the name of *rime-royal* from the fact that it was used by King James I. of Scotland in his poem of the "Kinges Quair." It was a favorite form of verse till the end of the sixteenth century. The following stanza is an example:

And first, within the porch and jaws of hell,
Sat deep Remorse of Conscience, all besprent
With tears; and to herself oft would she tell
Her wretchedness, and, cursing, never stent
To sob and sigh, but ever thus lament
With thoughtful care, as she that, all in vain,
Would wear and waste continually in pain.
Sackville, Induction to Mir. for Mags.

rimery (rī'mėr-i), *n.* [< *rime*[1] + *-ery*.] The art of making rimes. *Eclec. Rev.* [Rare.] (*Imp. Dict.*)

rimester (rīm'stėr), *n.* [Also and more commonly *rhymester* (see *rime*[1]); < *rime*[1] + *-ster*.] A rimer; a maker of rimes, generally of an inferior order; a would-be poet; a poetaster.

Railing was the ypocras of the drunken *rhymester*, and Quipping the marchpane of the mad libeller.
G. Harvey, Four Letters.

But who forgives the senior's ceaseless verse,
Whose hairs grow hoary as his rhymes grow worse?
What heterogeneous honours deck the peer!
Lord, *rhymester*, petit-maître, and pamphleteer!
Byron, Eng. Bards and Scotch Reviewers.

rimeyt, *v. t.* [ME. *rimeyen*, < OF. *rimeier*, *rimaier*, *rimoier*, *rimoyer*, < *rime*, rime: see *rime*[1].] To compose in rime; versify.

This olde gentil Britons in hir dayes
Of diverse aventures maden layes,
Rymeyed in hir firste Briton tonge.
Chaucer, Prol. to Franklin's Tale, l. 39.

rim-fire (rim'fīr), *a.* **1.** Noting a cartridge which has a detonating substance placed in some part of the rim of its base: distinguished from *center-fire*. Such cartridges have the defect (from which center-fire cartridges are free) that, unless the detonating substance is distributed all around the base, particular care must be used in their insertion to obtain the proper position for it relatively to the hammer of the lock. **2.** Pertaining to or adapted for the use of a rim-fire cartridge: as, a *rim-fire* gun (a gun in which rim-fire cartridges are used).

rimic (rī'mik), *a.* [< *rime*[1] + *-ic*.] Pertaining to rime. Also *rhymic*. [Rare.]

His [Mitford's] remarks are on the verbal, grammatical, and *rhymic* (why not rhymical?) inaccuracies to be met with in the Elegy. *N. and Q.*, 7th ser., VII. 517.

rimiform (rī'mi-fôrm), *a.* [< L. *rima*, a chink, + *forma*, form.] In *bot.*, having a longitudinal chink or furrow. *Leighton*, Brit. Lichens, glossary.

rimist (rī'mist), *n.* [< *rime*[1] + *-ist*.] A rimer. Also *rhymist*. [Rare.]

His [Milton's] character of Dryden, who sometimes visited him, was that he was a good *rhymist*, but no poet.
Johnson, Milton.

rimless (rim'les), *a.* [< *rim*[1] + *-less*.] Having no rim.

The other wore a *rimless* crown,
With leaves of laurel stuck about.
Wordsworth, Beggars.

rim-line (rim'līn), *n.* A rope which extends from the top of one stake to that of another in the pound-nets used on the Great Lakes. These ropes serve the double purpose of holding the stakes firmly and affording a means of hauling a boat along the net when the crib is lifted.

rim-lock (rim'lok), *n.* A lock having a metallic case, intended to be affixed to the outside of a door, etc., instead of being inserted within it. See *mortise-lock*.

rimmer[1] (rim'ėr), *n.* [< *rim*[1], *v.*, + *-er*[1].] **1.** An implement used in impressing ornamental figures upon the margins of the paste or crust of pies, etc. It may have the nature either of a hand-stamp or of an embossed roller.—**2.** An instrument used in rimming mackerel; a plow; a rimming-knife.

rimmer[2] (rim'ėr), *n.* and *v.* Same as *reamer*, *rimer*[2].

rimose (rī'mōs), *a.* [= Sp. Pg. It. *rimoso*, < L. *rimosus*, full of chinks, < *rima*, a chink, fissure: see *rime*[6].] Full of chinks, clefts, or crevices; chinky, like the bark of a tree: specifically said, in entomology, of the sculpture of insects when the surface shows many minute narrow and generally parallel excavations. Also *rimous*.

rimosely (rī'mōs-li), *adv.* In a rimose manner.

rimosity (rī-mos'i-ti), *n.* [< *rimose* + *-ity*.] The state of being rimose or chinky.

rimous (rī'mus), *a.* [< L. *rimosus*, full of chinks: see *rimose*.] Same as *rimose*.

rim-planer (rim'plā″nėr), *n.* A machine for dressing wheel-fellies, planing simultaneously one flat and one curved surface.

rimple (rim'pl), *v.*; pret. and pp. *rimpled*, ppr. *rimpling*. [Also (now more commonly) *rumple*; < ME. *rimplen*, < AS. **hrimpelian* (cf. *hrympelle*, a rimple), wrinkle, freq. of **hrimpan*, *rimpan* (pp. *gerumpen*) = MD. D. *rimpelen* = MLG. *rimpen*, wrinkle, = OHG. *hrimfan*, *rimphan*, *rimpfan*, *rimpfen*, MHG. *rimpfen*, *rümphen*, G. *rümpfen*, crook, bend, wrinkle; perhaps (assuming the Teut. root to be *hramp*) a nasalized form of √ *hrap* = Gr. κάρφειν, wrinkle; otherwise (assuming the initial *h* to be merely casual), akin to Gr. ῥάμφος, a curved beak, ῥομφή, a curved sword.] **I.** *trans.* To wrinkle; rumple. See *rumple*.

A *rympled* vekke, ferre ronne in age.
Rom. of the Rose, l. 4495.

He was grete and longe, and blakke and rowe *rympled*.
Merlin (E. E. T. S.), ii. 168.

No more by the banks of the streamlet we'll wander,
And smile at the moon's *rimpled* face on the wave.
Burns, O'er the Mist-shrouded Cliffs.

II. *intrans.* To wrinkle; ripple.

As glids the moon the *rimpling* of the brook.
Crabbe, Parish Register (ed. 1807), i.

rimple (rim'pl), *n.* [Also (now more commonly) *rumple*; < ME. *rimple*, *rympyl*, *rimpel*, < AS. **hrimpele*, *hrympelle* = MD. D. *rimpel* = MLG. *rimpel* (also *rimpe*), a wrinkle; from the verb.] A wrinkle; rumple. See *rumple*.

rim-rock (rim'rok), *n.* In *mining*, parts still remaining of the edges of the channels which the old or Tertiary rivers wore away in the bed-rock, and within which the auriferous detritus was accumulated. [California.]

rim-saw (rim'sâ), *n.* A saw the cutting part of which is annular and is mounted upon a central circular disk. *E. H. Knight.*

Rim-saw.
a, central disk upon which the cutting part *b* is mounted, attached to the disk by rivets.

rim-stock (rim'stok), *n.* A clog-almanac. *Chambers's Encyc.*

rimu (rim'ö), *n.* [Maori.] Same as *imou-pine*.

Rimula (rim'ū-lạ̈), *n.* [NL., < L. *rimula*, dim. of *rima*, a crack: see *rime*[6].] In *conch.*, a genus of fossil keyhole-limpets, or *Fissurellidæ*. *Defrance*, 1819.

rimuliform (rim'ū-li-fôrm), *a.* [< L. *rimula*, a little crack, + *forma*, form.] Shaped like a crack or fissure; specifically, in *conch.*, resembling or related to the genus *Rimula*.

rimulose (rim'ū-lōs), *a.* [< NL. **rimulosus*, < L. *rimula*, a little crack: see *Rimula*.] In *bot.*, full of small cracks or chinks: said chiefly of lichens and fungi.

rimy[1]† (rī'mi), *a.* [Usually *rhymy*; < *rime*[1] + *-y*[1].] Riming.

Playing *rhimy* plays with scurvy heroes.
Tom Brown, Works, III. 30. (*Davies.*)

rimy[2] (rī'mi), *a.* [< ME. **rimy*, < AS. *hrīmig*, rimy, frosty, < *hrīm*, rime, frost: see *rime*[2].] **1.** Covered with rime or hoar-frost.

But now the clear bright Moon her zenith gains,
And *rimy* without speck extend the plains.
Wordsworth, Evening Walk.

2. Frosty; cold.

In little more than a month after that meeting on the hill—on a *rimy* morning in departing November—Adam and Dinah were married. *George Eliot*, Adam Bede, lv.

rin[1] (rin), *v.* and *n.* An obsolete or Scotch variant of *run*[1].

rin[2] (rin), *n.* [Jap., = Chinese *li*, the thousandth part of a liang or ounce.] A Japanese bronze or brass coin, exactly similar in form to the Chinese cash, and equal in value to the thousandth part of a yen. See *li*[1] and *yen*.

rinabout (rin'a-bout), *n.* [Sc. form of *run-about*, < *run*[1] + *about*.] One who runs about through the country; a vagabond. [Scotch.]

rind[1] (rind), *n.* [< ME. *rind*, *rinde*, < AS. *rind*, *rinde*, bark of a tree, crust, = MD. *rinde*, the bark of a tree, D. *rinde*, oak-bark, tan, = MLG. *rinde* = OHG. *rinta*, *rinda*, MHG. *rinte*, *rinde*, G. *rinde*, rind, crust, crust of bread; prob. akin to AS. *rand*, E. *rand*, edge, border, and to AS. *rima*, E. *rim*, border: see *rand*[1] and *rim*[1].] 1. A thick and firm outer coat or covering, as of animals, plants, fruits, cheeses, etc.; a thick skin or integument; specifically, in *bot.*, same as *cortex*: applied to the outer layer or layers of a fungus-body, to the cortical layer (see *cortical*) of a lichen, as well as to the bark of trees.

His sheide todasshed was with swerds and maces,
In which men myghte many an arwe tynde,
That thyrled hadde horn and nerf and *rynde*.
Chaucer, Troilus, ii. 642.

Whoso takithe from the tre the *rinde* and the levis,
It wer better that he in his bed lay long.
Song of Roland, 152 (quoted in Cath. Ang., p. 308).

Sweetest nut hath sourest *rind*.
Shak., As you Like it, iii. 2. 115.

Leviathan . . .
The pilot of some small night-founder'd skiff
Deeming some island, oft, as seamen tell,
With fixed anchor in his scaly *rind*
Moors by his side under the lee. *Milton*, P. L., i. 206.

Hard wood I am, and wrinkled *rind*,
But yet my sap was stirr'd.
Tennyson, Talking Oak.

2. The skin of a whale; whale-rind: a whalers' term.—3†. Edge; border.

Thane they roode by that ryver, that rynnyd so swythe,
Thare the *ryndez* overrechez with realle bowghez.
Morte Arthure (E. E. T. S.), l. 921.

= Syn. 1. *Peel*, etc. See *skin*.

rind[1] (rind), *v. t.* [< *rind*[1], *n.*; cf. AS. *be-rindan*, strip the rind off.] To take the rind from; bark; decorticate.

All persons were forbidden . . . to set fire to the woods of the country, or work detriment to them by "*rinding* of the trees." *W. F. Rae*, Newfoundland to Manitoba, i.

rind[2], *n.* See *rynd*.

rinded (rin'ded), *a.* [< *rind*[1] + *-ed*[2].] Having a rind or outer coat: occurring chiefly in composition with a descriptive adjective: as, smooth-*rinded* trees.

Summer herself should minister
To thee, with fruitage golden-*rinded*
On golden salvers. *Tennyson*, Eleänore.

The soft-*rinded* smoothening facile chalk,
That yields your outline to the air's embrace,
Half-softened by a halo's pearly gloom.
Browning, Pippa Passes.

rinderpest (rin'dėr-pest), *n.* [< G. *rinderpest* (= D. *rinder-pest*), cattle-plague, < *rinder*, pl. of *rind*, horned cattle (= E. dial. *rother*, a horned beast: see *rother*[2]), + *pest*, plague (= E. *pest*): see *pest*.] An acute infectious disease of cattle, appearing occasionally among sheep, and communicable to other ruminants. In western Europe the disease has prevailed from time to time since the fourth century in extensive epizoötics. From its home on the steppes of eastern Russia and central Asia it has been carried westward by the great migrations and later by the transportation of cattle. The losses in Europe have been enormous. Thus, in 1711–14 1,500,000 beeves are said to have perished, and in 1870–1 30,000 beeves in France alone. The infection (the precise nature of which has not yet been definitely determined) may be transmitted directly by sick animals or indirectly by manure, or by persons and animals going from the sick to the well. It may be carried a short distance in the air. Its vitality is retained longest in the moist condition. The disease, after a period of incubation of from three to six days, begins with high temperature, rapid pulse, and cessation of milk-secretion. This latent period is followed by a congestion of all the visible mucous membranes, on which small erosions or ulcers subsequently develop. About 90 per cent. of all attacked die in from four to seven days after the appearance of the disease. If the animal survives, one attack confers a lasting immunity.

rind-gall (rīnd'gâl), *n.* A defect in timber caused by a bruise in the bark which produces a callus upon the wood over which the later layers grow without consolidating. *Laslett*, Timber and Timber Trees.

rind-grafting (rīnd'gráf"ting), *n.* See *grafting*, I.

rind-layer (rīnd'lā"ėr), *n.* Same as *cortical layer* (which see, under *cortical*).

rindle (rin'dl), *n.* A dialectal form of *runnel*.

rindmart (rind'märt), *n.* [Erroneously *rhindmart*, *rynmart*; < *rind, prob. < G. *rind*, horned cattle (see *rinderpest*), + *mart*, said to be shortened < *Martinmas*, because such carcasses were deliverable then for rent or feu-duty: see *Martinmas*, *mart*[3].] In *Scots law*, a word of occasional occurrence in the reddendo of charters in the north of Scotland, signifying any species of horned cattle given at Martinmas as part of the rent or feu-duty. *Bell*.

rine[1] (rīn), *n.* [Also erroneously *rhine*, and in var. form *rone*, *rune*; < ME. *rune*, < AS. *ryne*, a run, course, flow, watercourse, orbit, course of time (= OFries. *rene*, a flow (in comp. *blōd-rene*), = G. *ronne*, a channel, = Icel. *ryne* (in comp.), a flow, stream, = Goth. *runs*, a flow, flux), < *rinnan*, run: see *run*[1], *v.*, and cf. *run*[1], *n.*, in part identical with *rine*; cf. also *runnel*.] A watercourse or ditch. [Prov. Eng.]

This plain [Sedgemoor], intersected by ditches known as *rhines*, and in some parts rich in peat, is broken by isolated hills and lower ridges. *Encyc. Brit.*, XXII. 257.

rine[2], *v. t.* [< ME. *rinen* (pret. *ran*), also *rynde*, < AS. *hrīnan* = OS. *hrīnan* = OHG. *hrīnan*, touch, etc., = Icel. *hrīna*, cleave, hurt.] 1. To touch. [Prov. Eng.]—2†. To concern. *Jamieson*.

rine[2] (rīn), *n.* A dialectal form of *rind*[1].

rine[3]†, *n.* Same as *rim*[2].

rinforzando (rin-fôr-tsän'dō), *a.* [< It. *rinforzando*, ppr. of *rinforzare*, strengthen, reinforce: see *reinforce*.] In *music*, with special or increased emphasis: usually applied to a single phrase or voice-part which is to be made specially prominent. Abbreviated *rinf.*, *rf.*, and *rfz.*

rinforzato (rin-fôr-tsä'tō), *a.* [It., pp. of *rinforzare*, strengthen: see *rinforzando*.] Same as *rinforzando*.

ring[1] (ring), *n.* [< ME. *ring*, *ryng*, also *rink*, *rynk*, < AS. *hring* = OS. *hring* = OFries. *hring*, *ring* = D. *ring* = MLG. *rink*, LG. *ring*, *rink* = OHG. *hring*, *ring*, MHG. *rinc* (*ring-*), G. *ring* = Icel. *hringr* = Sw. Dan. *ring* (= Goth. **hriggs*, not recorded), a ring, circle; cf. F. *rang*, a row, rank (see *rank*[2]), F. *harangue* = Sp. Pg. *arenga* = It. *aringa*, harangue, etc. (see *harangue*), < OHG.; = OSlav. *kragŭ*, circle, *kraglŭ*, round, = Russ. *krugŭ*, a circle, round; supposed to be akin also to L. *circus* = Gr. κρίκος, κίρκος (see *circus*), Skt. *chakra* (for **kakra*), a wheel, circle. Hence ult. *rink*[2], *rank*[2], *range*, *arrange*, *derange*, *harangue*.] 1. A circular body with a comparatively large central circular opening. Specifically—(*a*) A circular band of any material or size, or designed for any purpose; a circlet; a hoop: as, a key-*ring*; a napkin-*ring*; an umbrella-*ring*; a *ring*-bolt; a *ring*-dial; especially, a circlet of gold or other material worn as an ornament upon the finger, in the ear, or upon some other part of the body.

Ho ragt hym a riche *rynk* of red golde werkez,
Wyth a starande ston, stondande alofte,
That bere blusschande bemez as the bryȝt sunne.
Sir Gawayne and the Green Knight (E. E. T. S.), l. 1817.

With this *Ring* I thee wed.
Book of Common Prayer, Solemnization of Matrimony.

Hangings fastened with cords of fine linen and purple to silver *rings* and pillars of marble. Esther i. 6.

There 's a French lord coming o'er the sea
To wed me wi' a *ring*.
Fair Janet (Child's Ballads, II. 87).

Hence—(*b*) A circular group; a circular disposition of persons or things.

Then make a *ring* about the corpse of Cæsar,
And let me show you him that made the will.
Shak., J. C., iii. 2. 162.

Ranks wedg'd in ranks; of arms a steely *ring*
Still grows, and spreads, and thickens round the king.
Pope, Iliad, xvi. 254.

A cottage . . . perch'd upon the green hill top, but close
Environ'd with a *ring* of branching elms.
Cowper, Task, i. 223.

(*c*) One of the circular layers of wood acquired periodically by many growing trees. See *annual ring*, below.

Huge trees, a thousand *rings* of Spring
In every bole. *Tennyson*, Princess, v.

2. In *geom.*: (*a*) The area or space between two concentric circles. (*b*) An anallagmatic surface; an anchor-ring.—3. A circle or circular line. Hence—(*a*) A circular course; a revolution; a circuit.

Ere twice the horses of the sun shall bring
Their fiery torcher his diurnal *ring*.
Shak., All's Well, ii. 1. 165.

(*b*) A limiting boundary; compass.

But life, within a narrow *ring*
Of giddy joys comprised.
Cowper, On the Bill of Mortality for 1793.

4. A constantly curving line; a helix.

Oft, as in airy *rings* they skim the heath,
The clamorous lapwings feel the leaden death.
Pope, Windsor Forest, l. 131.

Woodbine . . .
In spiral *rings* ascends the trunk, and lays
Her golden tassels on the leafy sprays.
Cowper, Retirement, l. 231.

5. A circular or oval or even square area; an arena. (*a*) An area in which games or sports are performed. (*b*) The arena of a hippodrome or circus.

"Your father breaks horses, don't he?" "If you please, sir, when they can get any to break, they do break horses in the *ring*, sir." *Dickens*, Hard Times, ii.

(*c*) The inclosure in which pugilists fight, usually a square area marked off by a rope and stakes.

And being powerfully aided by Jenkin Vincent . . . with plenty of cold water, and a little vinegar applied according to the scientific method practised by the bottle-holders in a modern *ring*, the man began to raise himself. *Scott*, Fortunes of Nigel, ii.

(*d*) The betting-arena on a race-course. (*e*) The space in which horses are exhibited or exercised at a cattle-show or market, or on a public promenade.

One day, in the *ring*, Rawdon's stanhope came in sight. *Thackeray*, Vanity Fair, xix.

6. A combination of persons for attaining such objects as the controlling of the market in stocks, or the price of a commodity, or the effecting of personal and selfish (especially corrupt) ends, as by the control of political or legislative agencies.

A [political] *Ring* is, in its common form, a small number of persons who get possession of an administrative machine, and distribute the offices or other good things connected with it among a band of fellows, of greater or less dimensions, who agree to divide with them whatever they make. *The Nation*, XIII. 333.

Those who in great cities form the committees and work the machine are persons whose chief aim in life is to make their living by office. . . . They cement their dominion by combination, each placing his influence at the disposal of the others, and settle all important measures in secret conclave. Such a combination is called a *Ring*. *Bryce*, Amer. Commonwealth, II. 75.

7. In the language of produce-exchanges, a device to simplify the settlement of contracts for delivery, where the same quantity of a commodity is called for by several contracts, the buyer in one being the seller in another, the object of the ring being to fill all contracts by delivery made by the first seller to the last buyer. *T. H. Dewey*, Contracts, etc., p. 66.—8. In *arch.*: (*a*) A list, cincture, or annulet round a column. (*b*) An archivolt, in its specific sense of the arch proper.

They [old arches of stone or brick] differ from metal or wooden arches, inasmuch as the compressed arc of materials called the *ring* is built of a number of separate pieces having little or no cohesion. *Encyc. Brit.*, IV. 806.

9. An instrument formerly used for taking the sun's altitude, etc., consisting of a ring, usually of brass, suspended by a swivel, with a hole in one side, through which a solar ray entering indicated the altitude upon the inner graduated concave surface. Compare *ring-dial*.—10. In *angling*, a guide.—11. In *anat.* and *zoöl.*, an annulus; any circular part or structure like a ring or hoop: as, a tracheal *ring* (one of the circular hoop-like cartilages of the windpipe); a somitic *ring* (an annular somite, as one of the segments of a worm); a *ring* of color.—12. In *bot.*, same as *annulus*.—13. A commercial measure of staves, or wood prepared for casks, containing four shocks, or 240 pieces.—**Abdominal ring.** See *abdominal*.—**Annual ring**, in *bot.*, one of the concentric layers of wood produced yearly in exogenous trunks. Such rings result from the more porous structure of the wood formed in spring as compared with the autumn growth, a difference attributed to less and greater tension of the bark at the two seasons. In the exogens of temperate regions, on account of the winter rest, these zones are strongly marked; in those of the tropics they are less obvious, but the same difference of structure exists in them with few if any exceptions, save in cases of individual peculiarity. In temperate climates a double ring is exceptionally produced in one season, owing to a cessation and resumption of growth, caused, for example, by the stripping of the leaves. It is a question whether some, especially tropical, trees do not normally form semiannual rings corresponding to two growing seasons. Somewhat similar rings are formed, several in a season, in such roots as the beet. These have no reference to seasons, but result, according to De Bary, from the successive formation of cambium-zones in the peripheral layer of parenchyma. Also *annual layer* or *zone*.—**A ring! a ring!** See *a hall! a hall!* under *hall*.—**Arthritic ring**, the zone of injected blood-vessels surrounding the corneal margin, seen in iritis.—**Auriculoventricular ring**, the margin of the auriculoventricular opening.—**Benzene ring**, a circular group of six carbon and six hydrogen atoms which is regarded as representing the constitution of benzene, and by which its relations to its derivatives may be most conveniently expressed.—**Bishop's ring.** See *bishop*.—**Broadwell ring**, a gas-check for use in heavy breech-loading guns, invented by L. W. Broadwell. See *gas-check* and *fermeture*.—**Bronchial rings**, cartilaginous hoops in the walls of the bronchi, serving to distend those air-passages. They are often incomplete in a part (about half) of their circumference, in which case they are more precisely called *bronchial half-rings*. Such is the rule in birds.—**Chinese rings**, a set of seven rings used by prestigiators.—**Ciliary ring**, the inner circular part of the ciliary muscle.—**Circumesophageal ring.** See *circumesophageal*.—**Clearing ring**, in *angling*, a ring or ring-shaped sinker used for clearing a foul hook. Such rings are of brass or iron, comparatively heavy, opening with a hinge to be put on the line, and having a cord attached to recover them. In case the hook gets fast, the ring is run down to dislodge it; or if a salmon or striped-bass sulks,

the ring is slid down on the line to his nose.—**Colored rings**, in *optics*. See *Newton's rings*.—**Columns** or **pillars of the abdominal ring**. See *column*.—**Cornice-ring**. See *cornice*.—**Crural ring**. See *crural*.—**Decad ring**. See *decad*.—**Diaphragmatic ring**, a name given by Chaussier to the irregularly quadrilateral aperture by which the inferior vena cava passes through the diaphragm to the heart. Also called *foramen quadratum*. See cut under *diaphragm*.—**Dicket ring**. Same as *decad ring*.—**Douglas ring**, a name given in Scotland and the north of England to a ring decorated with a heart or hearts, or having a heart-shaped seal or stone: in allusion to the "bloody heart," the bearing of the Douglas family.—**Episcopal ring**. Same as *bishop's ring*.—**Esophageal, fairy, femoral ring**. See the adjectives.—**Fisherman's ring**. See *fisherman*.—**Gemow ring**. Same as *gemel-ring*.—**Hernial ring**, the constricted opening of a hernial sac.—**Inguinal rings**. Same as *abdominal rings*.—**Investiture ring**. See *investiture*.—**Linked ring**, a ring composed of two or more hoops hinged or linked together in such a way that it shuts up as a solid ring or can be opened and the parts broken asunder.—**Live, mandibular, medicinable, meteoric ring**. See the adjectives.—**Newton's rings**, a series of colored rings produced by pressing a convex lens of very long focus against a plane surface of glass. The rings are due to interference. (See *interference*, 5.) These rings, in the case of white light, may be seven in number, and the order of color follows that known as Newton's scale of colors. Sir Isaac Newton was the first to investigate them (whence the name).—**Nobili's rings**, concentric colored rings formed on a flat surface about a pointed electrode by the electrolysis of certain salts. Nobili used a solution of lead upon a sheet of polished metal, the cathode being a platinum wire.—**Ocellary, ophthalmic, parheliacal rings**. See the adjectives.—**Open ring**, a coupling-link which is left open on one side, the ends passing each other but not touching. It is used in agricultural machines. Also called *cap-ring* and *open link*.—**Pixy ring**. See *pixy*.—**Polarized rings**. See *interference figures*, under *interference*, 5.—**Reinforce-rings**. See *reinforce*.—**Ring-and-staff investiture**. See *ecclesiastical investiture*, under *investiture*.—**Ring course**. See *course*[1].—**Ring nebula**. See *nebula*.—**Ring of an anchor**, that part of an anchor to which the cable is fastened.—**Ring of Venus**, in *palmistry*, a curved line running below the mounts of Apollo and Saturn. See *mount*[1], 5.—**Ring settlement**, in business transactions, a settlement made by means of a ring. See def. 7.

Where it appears that several parties have contracts between each other, corresponding in all respects (except as to p e), and that a *ring settlement* can be made, the party finding said "ring" shall notify all parties thereto, leaving with each a copy thereof, and get their acknowledgment, from which time the said ring shall be in force.
New York Produce Exchange Report, 1888-9, p. 180.

Rings of a gun, in *gun.*, circles of metal, of which there are five kinds, namely, the *base-ring*, *reinforce-ring*, *trunnion-ring*, *cornice-ring*, and *muzzle-ring*; but these terms do not in general apply to modern ordnance.—**Rings of the trachea**. See *tracheal rings*, below.—**Rosary ring**. Same as *decad ring*.—**Saturn's ring**. See *Saturn*.—**Sclerotic ring** of birds and various reptiles, the circlet of small bones which surround the cornea, embedded in the sclerotic coat of the eye. See cut under *sclerotal*, *n*.—**Split ring**, a metallic ring split spirally, on which keys or other objects required to be kept together may be suspended by passing part of them through the spiral, so that they hang loose on the ring.—**St. Martin's rings**, rings of copper or brass, in imitation of gold. They may have been so called because the makers or venders of them resided within the collegiate church of St. Martin's-le-Grand. *Halliwell*.

I doubt whether all be gold that glistereth, sith *saint Martins rings* be but copper within, though they be gilt without, sayes the Goldsmith.
Plaine Percevall, in Brand's Pop. Antiq., II. 27, note.

The ring, the prize-ring, pugilism and those connected with pugilism.

The Ring was his chief delight, and a well-fought battle between two accomplished bruisers caused his heart to leap with joy. *W. Besant*, Fifty Years Ago, p. 73.

To come on the ring†, to take one's turn.

Judge infernal Mynos, of Crete Kynge,
Now cometh thy lotte! now *comestow on the rynge!*
Nat oonly for thy sake writen ys this story.
Chaucer, Good Women, l. 1887.

To ride, run, or **tilt at the ring**, an exercise much in vogue in the sixteenth century in Europe, and replacing to a certain extent the justs or tilts of armed knights one against another. It was for the nobility nearly what the quintain or similar games of tilting were for the people. A ring was suspended at a height, and the horsemen rode at it with a light spear with which they tried to carry it off.

'Tis not because the ring they ride,
And Lindesay *at the ring rides* well.
Scott, L. of L. M., vi. 23.

To take the mantle and ring. See *mantle*.—**Tracheal rings**, in *anat.* and *zoöl.*, the rings or hoops of cartilage (sometimes of bone) which are situated in the walls of the windpipe and serve to keep that air-passage permanently distended. Such rings are usually of hyaline cartilage and very elastic, but may ossify more or less completely. They are numerous, closely succeeding one another along the course of the trachea. They are frequently incomplete in a part of their circumference, or otherwise irregular, when, like the corresponding bronchial rings, they are known as *half-rings*. In animals whose necks undergo notable lengthening and shortening in different attitudes of the head, the rings provide for a corresponding extension and contraction of the trachea, as notably in birds, whose tracheal rings are regularly beveled alternately on the right and left sides, so as to slide over one another when the windpipe is contracted in retraction of the neck. (See cut under *tracheal*.) Tracheal rings are normally much alike in most of the length of the windpipe, but commonly undergo special modifications at each end of that tube (see *cricoid*, *n.*, and cut under *pessulus*); less frequently several rings are enlarged and consolidated in a dilatation called the *tympanum*. Several ordinary rings are shown in the cuts under *larynx* and *mouth*.—**Tweed Ring**, an association of corrupt politicians belonging to the Tammany Society, which from about 1863 to 1871 controlled nearly all the departments of administration in New York city, and plundered the city of many millions of dollars. The principal leaders were William M. Tweed (commissioner of public works, chairman of the executive committee of Tammany Hall, and grand sachem of the Tammany Society), Connolly (comptroller of the city), and Sweeny (park commissioner). The ring was overthrown in 1871, and Tweed died in jail.—**Vortex ring**. See *vortex*.—**Widow's ring**, a ring assumed by one who vows perpetual widowhood, a custom followed in the fourteenth century and later. Compare *widow's mantle*, under *mantle*. (See also *cramp-ring*, *mourning-ring*, *posy-ring*, *thumb-ring*.)

ring[1] (ring), *v.* [< ME. *ringen*, < AS. *hringian* (also in comp. *ymb-hringian*, surround, encircle) = D. *ringen*, ring, wear a ring, = OHG. *gehringen*, MHG. *ringen*; cf. G. (*um-*)*ringen*, surround, = Icel. *hringa* = Sw. *ringa* = Dan. *ringe*, furnish with a ring; from the noun: see *ring*[1], *n.*] **I.** *trans.* **1.** To be round about in the form of a circle; form a ring about; encircle; encompass; gird.

Lord Talbot,
. . . *ring'd* about with bold adversity,
Cries out for noble York and Somerset.
Shak., 1 Hen. VI., iv. 4. 14.

We are left as scorpions *ringed* with fire.
Shelley, The Cenci, ii. 2.

2. To take a position around; surround; hence, to hem in; specifically, in Australia, to keep (cattle) together, by riding around them in a circle.

My followers *ring* him round;
He sits unarm'd. *Tennyson*, Geraint.

I'll tell you what, West, you'll have to *ring* them — pass the word for all hands to follow one another in a circle at a little distance apart.
A. C. Grant, Bush Life in Queensland, II. 126.

3. In the *manège*, to exercise by causing to run round in a ring while being held by a long rein; lunge.

She caught a glimpse, through the glass door opening on the park, of the General, and a fine horse they were *ringing*, and she hurried out. *Miss Edgeworth*, Helen, vi.

4. To provide with a ring or rings; mark or decorate with rings; especially, to fit with a metallic ring, as the finger, or as an animal or its nose; also, to furnish with rings, or attach rings to, for the line to run in, as an anglers' rod.

On alle hure fyue fyngres rycheliche *yrynged*,
And ther-on rede rubies and other riche stones.
Piers Plowman (C), iii. 12.

Ring these fingers with thy household worms.
Shak., K. John, iii. 4. 31.

5. To wed with a marriage-ring. [Rare.]

I was born of a true man and a *ring'd* wife.
Tennyson, Queen Mary, i. 1.

6. In *hort.*, to cut out a ring of bark from, as from a branch or root, in order to obstruct the return of the sap and oblige it to accumulate above the part operated on.

One of the expedients for inducing a state of fruitfulness in trees is the *ringing* of the branches or stem.
Encyc. Brit., XII. 244.

Gaunt trunks of trees, which had been *rung* [erroneously used for *ringed*] and allowed to die slowly, stood like white skeletons waiting to be felled and burned.
Mrs. Campbell Praed, The Head Station, p. 2.

To ring a quoit, to throw it so that it encircles the pin.—**To ring up cattle**. See def. 2.—**To ring up the anchor**, to pull the ring of an anchor close up to the cathead.

II. *intrans.* **1.** To form a ring.

The rest which round about you *ring*,
Faire Lords and Ladies which about you dwell.
Spenser, F. Q., VI., Int., st. 7.

2. To move in rings or in a constantly curving course.

A bird is said to *ring* when it rises spirally in the air.
Encyc. Brit., IX. 7.

ring[2] (ring), *v.*; pret. *rang* (sometimes *rung*), pp. *rung*, ppr. *ringing*. [< ME. *ringen*, *ryngen* (pret. *ringde*, pl. *ringden*, *ringeden*; also (by conformity with *sang*, *sung*, etc.) pret. *rang*, *rong*, pl. *rungen*, *rongen*, *ronge*, pp. *rungen*, *i-rungen*, *i-runge*), < AS. *hringan* (weak verb, pret. *hringde*), clash, ring, = MD. *ringhen*, D. *ringen* = Icel. *hringja* = Sw. *ringa* = Dan. *ringe*, ring; cf. Icel. *hrang*, a din, Dan. *rangle*, rattle; prob. orig. imitative, or later considered so; perhaps akin to L. *clangere*, sound, clang: see *clang*, *clank*, and cf. *clink*, *ting*[1], *tink*, *tinkle*, etc.] **I.** *trans.* **1.** To cause (a bell or other sonorous body, usually metallic) to sound, particularly by striking. In the United States *ring* and *toll* are sometimes distinguished, the former being applied to swinging a bell so as to throw the clapper against it, and the latter to striking it while at rest with a hammer. See *toll*.

Religiouse reuerencede hym and *rongen* here belles.
Piers Plowman (C), xxiii. 59.

The statue of Mars bigan his hauberk *rynge*.
Chaucer, Knight's Tale, l. 1573.

Rejoice, you men of Angiers, *ring* your bells;
King John, your king and England's, doth approach.
Shak., K. John, ii. 1. 312.

Whene'er the old exchange of profit *rings*
Her silver saints' bell of uncertain gains,
My merchant-soul can stretch both legs and wings.
Quarles, Emblems, iv. 3.

"Give no credit!"—these were some of his golden maxims,—"Never take paper-money! Look well to your change! *Ring* the silver on the four-pound weight!"
Hawthorne, Seven Gables, iv.

2. To produce by or as by ringing, as a sound or peal.

Ere to black Hecate's summons
The shard-borne beetle with his drowsy hums
Hath *rung* night's yawning peal.
Shak., Macbeth, iii. 2. 43.

Ere the first cock his matin *rings*.
Milton, L'Allegro, l. 114.

3. To announce or celebrate by ringing; usher with ringing, as of bells; hence, to proclaim or introduce musically: often followed by *in* or *out*.

He hade morthired this mylde be myddaye war *rongene*,
With-owttyne mercy. *Morte Arthure* (E. E. T. S.), l. 976.

No mournful bell shall *ring* her burial.
Shak., Tit. And., v. 3. 197.

The same considerations, supported by religious motives, caused the strict prohibition of work on Sundays and festivals, and "on Saturday, or the eve of a double feast, after noon has been *rung*."
English Gilds (E. E. T. S.), Int., p. cxxxi.

Wild bird, whose warble, liquid sweet,
Rings Eden thro' the budded quicks.
Tennyson, In Memoriam, lxxxviii.

Hear the mellow wedding-bells— . . .
How they *ring out* their delight!
Poe, The Bells.

4. To utter sonorously; repeat often, loudly, or earnestly; sound: as, to *ring* one's praises.

I would *ring* him such a lesson.
Fletcher, Humorous Lieutenant, v. 1.

To ring bells backward. See *backward*.—**To ring changes** or **the changes on**. See *change*.—**To ring in**. (*a*) To usher in by ringing.

Ring out the old, *ring in* the new,
Ring, happy bells, across the snow.
Tennyson, In Memoriam, cvi.

Hence—(*b*) (also **to ring into**). To introduce or bring in or into. [Slang.]

They want to *ring* me *into* it [the performance of Bulwer's "Money"], but I do not see anything in it I can do.
Lester Wallack, Memories (Scribner's Mag., IV. 723).

To ring the change, to swindle in the changing of money by a complicated system of changing and rechanging, in order to produce confusion and deception.—**To ring the changes**. See *change*.—**To ring the hallowed bell**. See *bell*[1].—**To ring up**, to summon or rouse by the ringing of a bell: as, to *ring up* a person at the telephone; to *ring up* a doctor in the middle of the night. [Colloq.]

II. *intrans.* **1.** To give forth a musical, resonant, and metallic sound; resound, as a bell or other sonorous body when set in sudden vibration by a blow or otherwise: as, the anvil *rang*.

Hys armour *ryngis* or clattirs horribly.
G. Douglas, in Sir Gawayne and the Green Knight [(E. E. T. S.), p. 112, Gloss.

Now *ryngen* trompes loude and clarioun.
Chaucer, Knight's Tale, l. 1742.

Duke. Who call'd here of late?
Prov. None, since the curfew *rung*.
Shak., M. for M., iv. 2. 78.

And the ancient Rhyme *rang* strange, with its passion and its change,
Here where all done lay undone.
Mrs. Browning, Rhyme of the Duchess May.

The silken gauntlet that is thrown
In such a quarrel *rings* like steel.
Whittier, To Friends under Arrest for Treason against the [Slave Power.

2. To ring a bell; especially, to give a signal with a bell: as, to *ring* for a servant or a messenger.

Bull. A cough, sir, which I caught with ringing in the king's affairs upon his coronation-day, sir. . . .
Fal. I will take such order that thy friends shall *ring* for thee. *Shak.*, 2 Hen. IV., iii. 2. 198.

We . . . shall have no need of Mr. Bowls's kind services. Mr. Bowls, if you please, we will *ring* when we want you.
Thackeray, Vanity Fair, xiv.

3. To sound loudly and clearly, like the tone of a bell; be distinctly audible: as, the music still *rings* in our ears.

Thene herde he of that hyge hil . . . a wonder breme noyse, . . .
What! hit wharred, & whette, as water at a mulne,
What! hit rusched, & *ronge*, rawthe to here.
Sir Gawayne and the Green Knight (E. E. T. S.), l. 2204.

Thy old groans *ring* yet in my ancient ears.
Shak., R. and J., ii. 3. 74.

Ere the sound of an axe in the forest had *rung*.
Whittier, The Merrimack.

4. To resound; reverberate; echo.

The silver roof of the Olympian palace *rung* again with applause of the fact. *B. Jonson*, Cynthia's Revels, i. 1.

Ten thousand harps . . . tuned
Angelic harmonies; the earth, the air, . . .
The heavens, and all the constellations rung.
Milton, P. L., vii. 563.

5. To have the sensation of a continued humming or buzzing sound: as, to make one's head *ring*.

My ears still *ring* with noise; I'm vext to death,
Tongue-kill'd, and have not yet recovered breath.
Dryden, Aurengzebe, ii. 1.

With both his ears
Ringing with clink of mail and clash of spears,
The messenger went forth upon his way.
William Morris, Earthly Paradise, II. 287.

6. To exercise or follow the art of bell-ringing. —7. To be filled with report or talk: as, the whole town *rings* with his fame.

What supports me, dost thou ask?
The conscience, friend, to have lost them overplied
In liberty's defence, my noble task,
Of which all Europe *rings* from side to side.
Milton, Sonnets, xvii.

Hear of him! . . . all our country *rings* of him.
Bunyan, Pilgrim's Progress, p. 228.

8. To be widely heard of or known; be celebrated.

Fairfax, whose name in arms through Europe *rings*,
Filling each mouth with envy or with praise.
Milton, Sonnets, x.

To ring backward, in *bell-ringing*, to sound a peal or change in an order the reverse of the usual one: formerly used as an alarm-signal.

It generally concerneth all, and particularly behooveth every one to look about him when he heareth the bells *ringing backward*, and seeth the fire running forward.
G. Harvey, Four Letters.

To ring down, to conclude; end at once: a theatrical phrase, alluding to the custom of ringing a bell to give notice for the fall of the curtain.

It is time to *ring down* on these remarks. *Dickens*.

To ring in (*theat.*), to signal the conductor to begin the overture.—**To ring off**, to signal the close of a communication by telephone. [Colloq.]—**To ring up** (*theat.*), to give the signal for raising the curtain.

ring[2] (ring), *n.* [< *ring*[2], *v.*] 1. The sound of a bell or other sonorous body, usually metallic; the sound produced by striking metal; a clang; a peal.

In vain with cymbals' *ring*
They call the grisly king.
Milton, Nativity, l. 208.

Good were the days of yore, when men were tried
By *ring* of shields, as now by *ring* of words.
Lowell, Voyage to Vinland.

2. Any loud sound, or the sounds of numerous voices; sound continued, repeated, or reverberated.

The King, full of confidence and assurance, as a Prince that had beene victorious in Battaile, and had prevailed with his Parliament in all that he desired, and had the *Ring* of Acclamations fresh in his eares, thought the rest of his Raigne should be but Play.
Bacon, Hist. Hen. VII., p. 17.

3. Characteristic sound.

Finally, the inspiration of all three has a literary source; for, while two professedly revive the practice of ancient masters, the third, though dealing with contemporary interests, expresses himself in a borrowed style, which gives his verse all the *ring* of ancient rhetoric.
Quarterly Rev. (*Imp. Dict.*)

Washington's letter of "homage to his Catholic majesty" for this "gift of jackasses," sent through the Prime Minister of Spain in 1785, has a diverting *ring*.
The Century, XXXVII. 839.

4. A set of bells tuned to each other; a chime, peal, or carillon.

I am like a famous cathedral with two *ring* of bells, a sweet chime on both sides. *Shirley*, Bird in a Cage, ii. 1.

Here is also a very fine *ring* of six bells, and they mighty tuneable. *Pepys*, Diary, III. 462.

Cracked in or **within the ring**, cracked in sound; failing of the true ring, as money when tested by striking against something else; hence, in general, flawed; marred by defects.

Pray God, your voice, like a piece of uncurrent gold, be not *cracked within the ring*. *Shak.*, Hamlet, ii. 2. 448.

ring-armature (ring'är"ma-tūr), *n.* An armature in which the coils of wire are wound round a ring. The Gramme armature is the best-known type of this form.

ring-armor (ring'är"mor), *n.* (*a*) Same as *ring-mail*. (*b*) Armor made by sewing rings of metal on a background of leather or cloth. See cut in next column.

ring-banded (ring'ban"ded), *a.* Encircled or ringed with a band of color.—**Ring-banded soldier-bug.** See *Perillus*.

ring-bark (ring'bärk), *v. t.* To girdle, as a tree.

ring-barker (ring'bär"kėr), *n.* One who barks trees circularly about the trunk, in order to kill them.

ring-barking (ring'bär"king), *n.* The practice of barking trees in rings about the trunk, in order to kill them.

Ring-armor. (From Viollet-le-Duc's "Dict. du Mobilier français.")

ringbill (ring'bil), *n.* The ring-necked scaup or duck, *Fulix collaris* or *Fuligula rufitorques*; the moonbill. *G. Trumbull; J. J. Audubon.* [Illinois and Kentucky.]

ring-billed (ring'bild), *a.* Having the bill ringed with color: as, the *ring-billed* gull (which see, under *gull*[2]).

ring-bird (ring'bėrd), *n.* Same as *ring-bunting*.

ring-bit (ring'bit), *n.* In *harness*, a bit with a ring-check, which may be either loose or fixed.

ring-blackbird (ring'blak"bėrd), *n.* The ring-ouzel, *Merula torquata*. See cut under *ouzel*.

ring-bolt (ring'bōlt), *n.* [= D. *ring-bout* = G. *ring-bolzen* = Dan. *ringebolt* = Sw. *ring-bult*; as *ring*[1] + *bolt*[1].] In ships, a metallic bolt with an eye to which is fitted a ring.

ring-bone (ring'bōn), *n.* [< Dan. *ring-ben*, ringbone; cf. AS. *hring-bān*, a circular bone; as *ring*[1] + *bone*[1].] 1. In *farriery*, a bony callus or exostosis, the result of inflammation, on one or both pastern-bones of a horse, which sometimes extends to the interphalangeal joints and causes immobility and lameness.—2. The disease or disordered condition in horses which is caused by ring-bone: as, a horse affected by *ring-bone* and spavin.

Heaves, curb, spavin, sidebone, and *ringbone* are the most ordinary ailments in horses.
A. B. Allen, in Amer. Agriculturist, 1886.

ring-boot (ring'böt), *n.* A ring of caoutchouc placed on the fetlock of a horse to cause him to travel wider, and thus prevent interfering.

ring-brooch (ring'brōch), *n.* A brooch the body of which consists of a bar bent to a ring form, but not joined. The ends terminate in a ball, or globular or acorn-shaped ornament; and the pin or acus is secured to the curved bar by being bent round it, but moving freely upon it. This form of brooch was common among the northern nations of Europe in the early middle ages.

ring-bunting (ring'bun"ting), *n.* The reed-bunting, *Emberiza schœniclus*: so called from its collar. Also *ring-bird*, *ring-fowl*. [Local, British.]

ring-bush (ring'bůsh), *n.* A socket having anti-friction rings or rolls on its interior perimeter, as in some forms of rope-block. *E. H. Knight.*

ring-canal (ring'ka-nal"), *n.* 1. The circular peripheral enteric cavity of cœlenterates, opening upon the exterior and continued by processes into the radiated parts of the animal; an annular enterocœle.

The peripheral portion of the lumen of the original enteric cavity forms the *ring-canal*, which runs all round the margin of the disc, and is continued into the hollow tentacles. *Encyc. Brit.*, XII. 550.

2. A circular canal of the water-vascular system of an echinoderm.

The only trace of the water-system is to be found in the *ring-canal* round the gullet. *Stand. Nat. Hist.*, I. 176.

ring-carrier (ring'kar"i-ėr), *n.* A go-between; one who transacts business between parties.

Wid. Marry, hang you!
Mar. And your courtesy, for a *ring-carrier*!
Shak., All's Well, iii. 5. 95.

ring-chuck (ring'chuk), *n.* A chuck or appendage to a lathe with a brass ring fitted over the end.

ring-cross (ring'krôs), *n.* A figure representing a Greek cross in a circle, incised or carved in relief on many works of prehistoric art: the figure is thought to indicate the sun and also the active or masculine principle in creation. *Worsaa*, S. K. Handbook, Danish Arts, p. 33.

ring-dial (ring'dī"al), *n.* A kind of portable sun-dial, consisting of a metal ring, broad in proportion to its diameter, and having slits in the direction of its circumference, which can be partially closed or covered by a sliding appliance on the outside of the ring. There are divisions on the outside denoting the months of the year, and figures on the inside denoting the hour of the day. By partly closing the slit, so as to let the rays of the sun pass through that part of it belonging to the current month (as in the direction *ab* in the cut), the hour of the day is approximately denoted by the point where the beam of light strikes the inside of the ring.

Ring-dial, 17th century.

ring-dog (ring'dog), *n.* An iron implement for hauling timber, made by connecting two common dogs by means of a ring through the eyes. When united with cordage they form a sling-dog. See cut under *dog*.

ring-dotterel (ring'dot"ėr-el), *n.* The ringed plover, *Ægialites hiaticula*. Also called *sea-dotterel*, *ringlestone*, *sea-* or *sand-lark*, and by many other names. See *ring-plover*, and cut under *Ægialites*.

ring-dove (ring'duv), *n.* [= Dan. *ringdue* = Sw. *ringdufva*; as *ring*[1] + *dove*[1]. Cf. equiv. D. *ringel-duif* = G. *ringeltaube* (< G. *ringel*, dim. of *ring*, a circle, + *taube* = E. *dove*[1]).] 1. The ringed dove, wood-pigeon, or cushat, *Columba palumbus*, a common European bird, distinguished by this name from the stock-dove (*C. œnas*) and rock-dove (*C. livia*), the only other British members of this genus. It is about 17 inches long and 30 inches in extent of wings. The plumage of the upper parts is grayish-blue, tinged with brown on the wings and scapulars; the back and sides of the neck are bright-green and purplish-red, with two cream-colored patches; the fore-neck and breast are reddish-purple; there is a white patch on the wing, including four outer secondary coverts; the bill is partly red; the iris is yellow; and the feet are carmine. The ring-dove subsists on grains, acorns, ivy-berries, and other wild fruits, and lays two white eggs on a nest which may be described as a platform of sticks so loosely put together that often the eggs may be seen through it.

2. A small dove, *Turtur risorius*, now known only in confinement, having the general plumage of a pale dull creamy color, with a black half-ring around the nape of the neck.

ring-dropper (ring'drop"ėr), *n.* One who practises ring-dropping.

Some *ring-droppers* write out an account and make a little parcel of jewellery, and when they pick out their man they say, "If you please, sir, will you read this for me and tell me what I shall do with these things, as I've just found them?"
Mayhew, London Labour and London Poor, I. 389.

ring-dropping (ring'drop"ing), *n.* A trick practised upon simple people by rogues in various ways. One mode is described in the quotation.

In *ring-dropping* we pretend to have found a ring, and ask some simple-looking fellow if it's good gold, as it's only just picked up. Sometimes it is immediately pronounced gold: "Well, it's no use to me," we'll say, "will you buy it?" Often they are foolish enough to buy, and . . . they give you only a shilling or two for an article which if really gold would be worth eight or ten.
Mayhew, London Labour and London Poor, I. 351.

ringe (rinj), *n.* [Supposed to be used for **rinse*, < *rinse*, *v.*] A whisk made of heath.—**Ringe-heather**, the heath-plant, *Erica Tetralix*, used in making ringes. *Jamieson.*

ringed (ringd), *p. a.* [< ME. *ringed*, < AS. *hringed*, furnished with or formed of rings, pp. of *hringian*, encircle, surround: see *ring*[1].] 1. Surrounded with or as with a ring; having a ring or rings; encircled.

He cautiously felt the weight of the *ringed* and polished rod. *The Century*, XXXI. 31.

2. In *bot.*, surrounded by elevated or depressed circular lines or bands, as the roots or stems of some plants.—3. In *zoöl.*: (*a*) Annular; circular; formed into or shaped like a ring. (*b*) Having an annulus; annulated; marked with a ring or with rings; collared: as, a *ringed* plover; the *ringed* dove; the *ringed* snake. (*c*) Composed of rings; annulose, annulate, or annuloid; formed of a series of annulations: as, the *ringed* type of structure; a *ringed* worm.—**Ringed animals**, the *Annulosa*.—**Ringed guard**, a modification of the cup-guard or shell-guard, in which the ricasso is nearly covered by a series of rings of steel forming a deep hollow cup, its mouth toward the grip of the hilt. A common modification of this is where a steel bar, forming a continuous helix, replaces the rings.—**Ringed guillemot.** See *guillemot*.—**Ringed plover.** See *ring-plover*.—**Ringed seal**, the fetid seal, or fiord-seal, *Pagomys hispida*. See cut under *Pagomys*.—**Ringed snake.** See *snake*.—**Ringed worms**, the annelids or *Annelida*.

ringed-arm (ringd'ärm), *n.* One of the *Colobrachia.*

ringed-carpet (ringd'kär"pet), *n.* A British geometrid moth, *Boarmia cincturia.*

ringent (rin'jent), *a.* [= F. *ringent*, < L. *ringen(t-)s*, ppr. of *ringi*, gape open-mouthed. Cf. *rictus*, *rima*, *rime*[1].] 1. In *bot.*, gaping: noting a bilabiate corolla with the lips widely spread and the throat open, as in the dead-nettle, *Lamium.*—2. In *zoöl.*, gaping irregularly, as parts of some zoöphytes and the valves of some shells.

ringer[1] (ring'ėr), *n.* [< *ring*[1] + *-er*[1].] In *quoits*, a throw by which the quoit is cast so as to encircle the pin.

Each player attempts to make his quoit pitch on the hob or pin so that the head of the latter passes through the circular opening in the center of the missile. Such a success is termed a *ringer*, and two is scored.
Encyc. Brit., XX. 189.

ringer[2] (ring'ėr), *n.* [< *ring*[2] + *-er*[1].] 1. One who rings; specifically, a bell-ringer.

The *ringers* rang with a will, and he gave the *ringers* a crown. *Tennyson*, The Grandmother.

2. Any apparatus for ringing chimes, or a bell of any kind.

A novel feature of this bell is that the *ringer* and gongs are inside of the case. *Elect. Rev.* (Amer.), XV. xvi. 3.

3. In *mining*, a crowbar.

ring-faller† (ring'fâ"lėr), *n.* Same as *ring-dropper. Nares.*

ring-fence (ring'fens), *n.* A fence continuously encircling an estate or some considerable extent of ground; hence, any bounding or inclosing line; a limit or pale.

In that Augustan era we descry a clear belt of cultivation, . . . running in a *ring-fence* about the Mediterranean. *De Quincey*, Roman Meals. (*Davies.*)

The union of the two estates, Tipton and Freshitt, lying charmingly within a *ring-fence*, was a prospect that flattered him for his son and heir.
George Eliot, Middlemarch, lxxxiv.

ring-finger (ring'fing"gėr), *n.* [< AS. *hring-finger* = D. *ring-vinger* = G. Dan. Sw. *ring-finger*; as *ring*[1] + *finger.*] The third finger of the left hand, on which the marriage-ring is placed; in *anat.*, the third finger of either hand, technically called the *annularis.*

ring-fish (ring'fish), *n.* A kind of cobia, *Elacate nigra*, probably not different from *E. canada.* See cut under *cobia.* [New South Wales.]

ring-footed (ring'füt"ed), *a.* Having ringed or annulated feet: as, the *ring-footed* gnat, *Culex annulatus*, of Europe.

ring-formed (ring'fôrmd), *a.* [= Dan. *ringformet*; as *ring*[1] + *form* + *-ed*[2].] Shaped like a ring; annular; circular.

ring-fowl (ring'foul), *n.* Same as *ring-bunting.*

ring-frame (ring'frām), *n.* Any one of a class of spinning-machines with vertical spindles, now extensively used, in which the winding of each thread is governed by passing through the eye of a small steel loop called a *traveler*, one of which revolves around each spindle in an annular way called the *ring.* These rings are supported by a horizontal bar, which moves up and down in such manner as to give a shape to the cap on the spindle that adapts it for use in a shuttle. Also called *ring-throstle*, *ring-throstle frame*, *ring-and-traveler spinner*, and *ring-spinner.*

ring-gage (ring'gāj), *n.* 1. A measure, consisting of a ring of fixed size, used for measuring spherical objects, and also for the separating or classifying of objects of irregular form. Thus, oysters have been sorted by two or three rings of different sizes through which they are allowed to drop.
2. A piece of wood, ivory, or the like, generally conical in form, but usually having minute steps or offsets: it is used for measuring finger-rings, a number being affixed to every offset.

ring-handle (ring'han"dl), *n.* A handle, as of a jar or other vessel, formed by a ring, especially a free ring hanging loose in a socket or eyelet attached to the body of the vessel.

ring-head (ring'hed), *n.* An instrument used for stretching woolen cloth.

ring-hedge (ring'hej), *n.* Same as *ring-fence.*

Lo, how Apollo's Pegasses prepare
To rend the *ring-hedge* of our Horizon.
Davies, Summa Totalis, p. 11. (*Davies.*)

Ringicula (rin-jik'ū-lạ), *n.* [NL., irreg., with dim. suffix, < L. *ringi*, gape: see *ringent.*] A genus of tectibranchiates with a narrow ringent mouth, typical of the family *Ringiculidæ.*

Ringiculidæ (rin-ji-kū'li-dē), *n. pl.* [NL., < *Ringicula* + *-idæ.*] A family of tectibranchiate gastropods, typified by the genus *Ringicula.* The animal has a reflected cephalic disk developed backward in a siphon-like manner, and teeth in few series. The shell is ventricose with a narrow ringent aperture. The species live in warm seas.

ringing[1] (ring'ing), *n.* [Verbal n. of *ring*[1], *v.*] 1. Decoration by means of rings or circlets; rings collectively.

The *ringing* on the arms, which the natives call bracelets. *H. O. Forbes*, Eastern Archipelago, p. 203.

2. In *hort.*, the operation of cutting out a circle of bark. See *ring*[1], *v. t.*, 6.

ringing[2] (ring'ing), *n.* [< ME. *ringinge*; verbal n. of *ring*[2], *v.*] 1. The act of sounding or of causing to sound, as sonorous metallic bodies; the art or act of making music with bells.

The Talipois euery Monday arise early, and by the *ringing* of a Bason call together the people to their Sermons.
Purchas, Pilgrimage, p. 470.

2. A ringing sound; the hearing of a sound as of ringing.—**Ringing in** (or **of**) **the ears**, ringing sounds not caused by external vibrations; tinnitus aurium.

Thou shalt hear the "Never, never," whisper'd by the phantom years,
And a song from out the distance in the *ringing of* thine *ears.* *Tennyson*, Locksley Hall.

ringing[2] (ring'ing), *p. a.* Having or giving the sound of a bell or other resonant metallic body; resounding: as, a *ringing* voice; *ringing* cheers.

Aungelles with instrumentes of organes & pypes,
& rial *ryngande* rotes [lyres] & the reken fythel, . . .
Aboutte my lady watz lent.
Alliterative Poems (ed. Morris), ii. 1082.

ringing-engine (ring'ing-en"jin), *n.* A simple form of pile-driver in which the weight is raised between timber guides by a rope manned by a gang of men. *E. H. Knight.*

ringingly (ring'ing-li), *adv.* With a ringing sound; resonantly, like the sound of a bell.

ringing-out (ring'ing-out'), *n.* In the language of produce-exchanges, the settlement of a number of contracts which call for the delivery of the same quantity of a commodity, the buyer in one being the seller in another, and the operation consisting in bringing the seller in the first contract and the buyer in the last together and dropping the intermediate parties. *T. H. Dewey*, Contracts, etc.

ring-joint (ring'joint), *n.* 1. A joint formed by means of circular flanges.

From these reservoirs start the distributing mains, all of which are of cast iron with *ring joints.*
Sci. Amer., N. S., LV. 163.

2. In *entom.*, a very short, disk-like joint; specifically, such a joint in the geniculate antennæ of certain small *Hymenoptera*, between the pedicel or third joint and the flagellum.

ring-keeper (ring'kē"pėr), *n.* A small thin piece of brass or copper that holds a ring or guide to an anglers' rod. *Norris.*

ringle (ring'l), *n.* [= MD. **ringhel* = MLG. *ringel* (in comp.), a ring, *ringele*, a sunflower, = G. *ringel*, a ring; dim. of *ring*[1].] A little ring. [Obsolete or prov. Eng.]

Some clogge, cheine, collers of iron, *ringle*, or manacle.
Harl. MS., quoted in Ribton-Turner's Vagrants and [Vagrancy, p. 117.

ringle (ring'l), *v. t.* [= MD. *ringhelen*; < *ringle*; from the noun.] To ring; fit with a ring, as the snout of a hog. [Obsolete or prov. Eng.]

From rooting of pasture, ring hog ye had need,
Which being well *ringled*, the better do feed.
Though young with their elders will lightly keep best,
Yet spare not to *ringle* both great and the rest.
Tusser, September's Husbandry, st. 29.

As a hot proud horse highly disdains
To have his head controlled, but breaks the reins,
Spits forth the *ringled* bit, and with his hoves
Checks the submissive ground.
Marlowe, Hero and Leander, ii. 143.

ringleader (ring'lē"dėr), *n.* [< *ring*[1] + *leader*[1].] 1†. One who leads a ring, as of dancers; one who opens a ball.

Upon such grounds it may be reasonable to allow St. Peter a primacy of order; such a one as the *ringleader* hath in a dance. *Barrow*, Works, VII. 70.

Hence—2. The leader or chief in any enterprise; particularly, one who leads and incites others to the violation of the law or the recognized rules of society: as, the *ringleader* in a riot or a mutiny.

Lady Eleanor, the protector's wife,
The *ringleader* and head of all this rout.
Shak., 2 Hen. VI., ii. 1. 170.

We have found this man a pestilent fellow, . . . and a *ringleader* of the sect of the Nazarenes. Acts xxiv. 5.

ringless (ring'les), *a.* [< *ring*[1] + *-less.*] Having or wearing no ring: as, a *ringless* finger.

ringlestone (ring'l-stōn), *n.* Same as *ring-dotterel. Sir T. Browne.* [Norfolk, Eng.]

ringlet (ring'let), *n.* [< *ring*[1] + *-let.*] 1. A circle, in a poetical or unusual sense; a ring other than a finger-ring: used loosely.

To dance our *ringlets* to the whistling wind.
Shak., M. N. D., ii. 1. 86.

Who first Ulysses' wond'rous bow shall bend,
And thro' twelve *ringlets* the fleet arrow send,
Him will I follow. *Pope*, Odyssey, xxi. 76.

2. A curl of hair; usually, a long and spirally curled lock, as distinguished from one of the small naturally curled locks of short hair.

She . . .
Her unadorned golden tresses wore
Dishevel'd, but in wanton *ringlets* waved
As the vine curls her tendrils. *Milton*, P. L., iv. 306.

No longer shall thy comely Tresses break
In flowing *Ringlets* on thy snowy Neck.
Prior, Henry and Emma.

3. An English collectors' name for certain satyrid butterflies: thus, *Epinephele hyperanthus* is the ringlet, and *Cœnonympha tiphon* is the small ringlet.

ringleted (ring'let-ed), *a.* [< *ringlet* + *-ed*[2].] 1. Adorned with ringlets; wearing the hair in ringlets.

Thither at their will they haled the yellow-*ringleted* Britoness. *Tennyson*, Boadicea.

2. Curled; worn in ringlets or curls.

A full-blown, very plump damsel, fair as waxwork, with handsome and regular features, languishing blue eyes, and *ringleted* yellow hair. *Charlotte Brontë*, Jane Eyre, xxi.

ring-lock (ring'lok), *n.* A form of letter- or puzzle-lock which has several movable rings surrounding the bolt. The grooves of these rings must be brought into a straight line with one another before the bolt can be passed through them.

ring-locket (ring'lok"et), *n.* A locket, as of a sword-scabbard, which has a loose ring through which the hook of the sword-belt can be passed.

ring-mail (ring'māl), *n.* [< *ring*[1] + *mail*[1].] (*a*) Chain-mail. (*b*) In some writers, mail having unusually large links or rings: in attempted discrimination of different styles of chain-mail.

Ring-mail differs from chain-mail in the rings of the latter being interlaced with each other, and strongly fastened with rivets. *Fairholt.*

ring-mallet (ring'mal"et), *n.* A mallet the head of which is strengthened by means of rings driven on it.

ring-man (ring'man), *n.* [< ME. *rynge man*, the ring-finger; < *ring*[1] + *man.*] 1†. The third finger of the hand; the ring-finger.

And when a man shooteth, the might of his shoot lieth on the foremost finger and on the *ringman*; for the middle finger, which is the strongest, like a lubber, starteth back, and beareth no weight of the string in a manner at all. *Ascham*, Toxophilus (ed. 1864), p. 101.

2. One interested in matters connected with the ring—that is, with prize-fighting; a sporting or betting man.

No *ringmen* to force the betting and deafen you with their blatant proffers. *Lawrence*, Guy Livingstone, ix.

ring-master (ring'mås"tėr), *n.* One who has charge of the performances in a circus-ring.

ring-money (ring'mun"i), *n.* 1. Rudely formed rings and ring-shaped or pen-annular bodies of bronze and other materials found among the remains of ancient peoples of Europe, and generally thought to have been used, at least in some cases, as money.—2. In modern times, same as *manilla*[1].

Gaulish Ring-money, gold.—British Museum. (Size of the original.)

ring-mule (ring'mūl), *n.* An occasional name for the ring-frame.

ringneck (ring'nek), *n.* 1. One of several kinds of ring-plovers. In the United States the name is chiefly given to *Ægialites semipalmatus*, the semipalmated plover; also to *Æ. melodus*, the piping-plover. See *Ægialites*, and cut under *piping-plover.*
2. The ring-necked duck or bastard broadbill, *Fuligula rufitorques*, having a reddish ring around the black neck in the male.

ring-necked (ring'nekt), *a.* Having a ring of color around the neck; collared; torquate.—**Ring-necked loon, pheasant.** See the nouns.

ring-net (ring'net), *n.* [< *ring*[1] + *net*[1]. Cf. AS. *hringnet*, 'a net of rings,' coat of mail.] A net whose mouth is stretched upon a hoop or ring, as the ordinary butterfly-net used by entomologists. Such a ring-net consists of leno, muslin, or other very light fabric, stretched upon a hoop of wood or metal attached to a short wooden handle, and is made baggy rather than pointed, that the insects may not get jammed.

ring-ouzel (ring'ö"zl), *n.* A bird of the thrush kind, *Turdus torquatus* or *Merula torquata*, resembling and closely related to the blackbird, *Turdus merula* or *Merula vulgaris*, but having a white ring or bar on the breast; the ring-blackbird. See cut under *ouzel.*

ring-parrot (ring'par"ọt), *n.* A common Indian parrot, *Palæornis torquatus*, having a ring or collar on the neck; also, any species of the

Ring-parrot (*Palæornis torquatus*).

same genus, in which this coloration is a characteristic feature. The species named is the one commonly represented as the vâhana or 'vehicle' of the Hindu god Kama, corresponding to the classic Eros or Cupid, and is more fully called *rose-ringed parrakeet*. See *Palæornis*.

ring-perch (ring'pėrch), *n.* The common yellow perch of North America, *Perca flavescens*.

ring-plain (ring'plān), *n.* One of the nearly level circular areas upon the moon's surface which are surrounded by high ridges or walls, and which have no central crater. Also called *walled plain* and *ramparted plain*.

ring-plover (ring'pluv"ėr), *n.* A ring-necked plover; any one of the many small plovers of the genus *Ægialites*, which have the head, neck, or breast annulated, collared, or ringed with color. There are many species, of nearly all parts of the world. The European ring-dotterel and the American ringneck are familiar examples. See cuts under *killdee*, *piping-plover*, and *Ægialites*.

ring-rope (ring'rōp), *n.* *Naut.*: (*a*) A rope rove through the ring of the anchor to haul the cable through it, in order to bend or make it fast in rough weather. It is first rove through the ring, and then through the hawse-holes, when the end of the cable is secured to it. (*b*) A rope by which, after the anchor is catted, the ring of the anchor is hauled close up to the cat-head.

ringsail (ring'sāl), *n.* Same as *ringtail*, 2.

ring-saw (ring'sâ), *n.* A form of scroll-saw the web of which is annular. It runs upon guides which maintain its tension and prevent it from being deformed.

ring-shaped (ring'shāpt), *a.* Having the shape of a ring.

ring-small (ring'smâl), *a.* and *n.* **I.** *a.* Small enough to pass through a ring of some fixed size.

II. *n.* Broken stones (especially pieces of granite) of a size that will pass through a ring 2 inches in diameter. [Eng.]

> List of tenders for the following works and supply of materials. . . . 6. For the supply of granite kerb, setts, squares, *ringsmall*, rammel, gravel, etc.
> *The Engineer*, LXVII. 117.

ring-snake (ring'snāk), *n.* **1.** The common snake of Europe, *Coluber* or *Tropidonotus natrix*. See cut under *Tropidonotus*.—**2.** The collared snake, *Diadophis punctatus*, a small, pretty, and harmless serpent of the United States, of a blackish color above, with a distinct yellow collar just behind the head.

ring-sparrow (ring'spar"ō), *n.* The rock-sparrow, *Petronia stulta*. *Latham*, 1783.

ring-spinner (ring'spin"ėr), *n.* Same as *ring-frame*.

ring-stand (ring'stand), *n.* A stand with a projecting pin for holding finger-rings.

ringster (ring'stėr), *n.* [< *ring*[1] + *-ster*.] A member of a ring or band of persons uniting for personal or selfish ends. See *ring*[1], *n.*, 7. [Colloq.]

> An attempt should also be made to displace the *ringsters* whose terms expire this year with better men.
> *Science*, XI. 279.

ring-stopper (ring'stop"ėr), *n.* *Naut.*: (*a*) A piece of rope or chain by which the ring of an anchor is secured to the cat-head. In anchoring, one end of the ring-stopper is let go, thus dropping the anchor. Also called *cat-head stopper*. See *shank-painter*. (*b*) A stopper for cable secured to a ring-bolt in the deck.

ringstraked (ring'strākt), *a.* Same as *ring-streaked*.

ring-streaked (ring'strēkt), *a.* Having circular streaks or lines on the body. Also *ring-straked*.

> He removed that day the he goats that were *ringstraked* and spotted. Gen. xxx. 35.

ringtail (ring'tāl), *n.* **1.** A ring-tailed bird of prey: especially, the female or young male harrier, *Circus cyaneus*.

> Thou royal *ring-tail*, fit to fly at nothing
> But poor men's poultry!
> *Beau. and Fl.*, Philaster, v. 4.

2. A small quadrilateral sail, set on a small mast on a ship's taffrail; also, a studdingsail set upon the gaff of a fore-and-aft sail. Also called *ring-sail*.

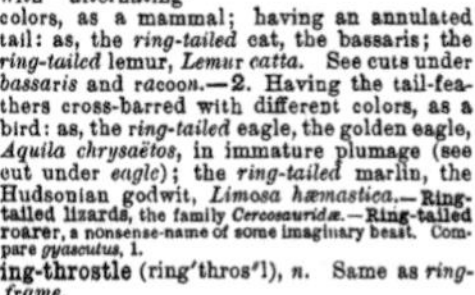

a, Ringtail, or Studdingsail set upon the Gaff.

> He was going aloft to fit a strap round the main topmast head, for *ringtail* halyards.
> *R. H. Dana, Jr.*, Before the Mast, p. 39.

Ringtail-boom, a boom extending beyond a spanker-boom or main-boom, for spreading a ringtail.

ring-tailed (ring'tāld), *a.* **1.** Having the tail ringed with alternating colors, as a mammal; having an annulated tail: as, the *ring-tailed* cat, the bassaris; the *ring-tailed* lemur, *Lemur catta*. See cuts under *bassaris* and *racoon*.—**2.** Having the tail-feathers cross-barred with different colors, as a bird: as, the *ring-tailed* eagle, the golden eagle, *Aquila chrysaëtos*, in immature plumage (see cut under *eagle*); the *ring-tailed* marlin, the Hudsonian godwit, *Limosa hæmastica*.—**Ring-tailed lizards**, the family *Cercosauridæ*.—**Ring-tailed roarer**, a nonsense-name of some imaginary beast. Compare *gyascutus*, 1.

ring-throstle (ring'thros"l), *n.* Same as *ring-frame*.

ring-thrush (ring'thrush), *n.* The ring-ouzel.

ring-time (ring'tīm), *n.* The time for exchanging rings, or for betrothal or marriage. [Rare.]

> In the spring time, the only pretty *ring time*,
> When birds do sing, hey ding a ding, ding;
> Sweet lovers love the spring.
> *Shak.*, As you Like it, v. 3. 20.

ring-tongue (ring'tung), *n.* A short bar or tongue of metal having a ring or eye at one end for the engagement of a hook, a bolt, or other attachment: as, the *ring-tongue* of a lewis. See cut under *lewis*.

ring-top (ring'top), *a.* Having an annular top.—**Ring-top furnace.** See *furnace*.

ring-tumbler (ring'tum"blėr), *n.* In a lock, a tumbler of annular shape.

ring-valve (ring'valv), *n.* A hollow cylindrical valve sliding in a chamber of corresponding form, and having openings for the passage of the fluid. The passage is free when the valve is raised, and closed when the cylinder is screwed down. The valve has a vertical slit at one side, and when nearly closed the inner edge bears against a wedge, which presses the cylinder outward against its seat.

ring-vortex (ring'vôr"teks), *n.* Same as *vortex-ring*.

ring-wad (ring'wod), *n.* Same as *gromet-wad*.

ring-wall (ring'wâl), *n.* In *metal.*, the inner lining of a blast-furnace, composed of fire-bricks.

ringwise (ring'wīz), *adv.* In rings or circles; so as to make or be a ring; annularly. *Encyc. Brit.*

> Their foreheads are tattoed *ringwise*, with singularly shaped cuttings in the skin. *Lancet*, No. 3440, p. 244.

ring-work (ring'wėrk), *n.* A material or surface composed of rings interlinked, or held together by being secured to another substance, or in other ways.

> The interior of the garment [hauberk] . . . exhibits the *ring-work* exactly in the same manner as it is seen on the outside of others. *J. Hewitt*, Ancient Armour, I. 63.

ringworm (ring'wėrm), *n.* [< ME. *rynge wyrme*, *ring-worm*, *rynge worme* (= D. *ringworm* = G. *ringwurm*, tetter, = Sw. *ringorm*, an annulated snake, the amphisbæna, = Dan. *ringorm*); < *ring*[1] + *worm*.] **1.** A milleped of the genus *Julus* in a broad sense: so called from the way it curls up in a ring.—**2.** A name sometimes given to certain dermatophytic diseases. See *tinea* and *favus*.—**Bald ringworm**, tinea tonsurans.—**Bowditch Island ringworm**, tinea imbricata.—**Chinese, Indian, or Oriental ringworm**, tinea circinata tropica. Also called *dhobie's itch*.—**Honeycomb ringworm**, favus.—**Ringworm of the body**, tinea circinata.—**Ringworm of the scalp**, tinea tonsurans.

ringworm-root (ring'wėrm-röt), *n.* See *Rhinacanthus*.

ringworm-shrub (ring'wėrm-shrub), *n.* The shrub *Cassia alata* of tropical America, whose leaves are used as a remedy for ringworm and kindred diseases. [West Indies.]

ringy (ring'i), *a.* [< *ring*[1] + *-y*[1].] Presenting a ringed appearance of discoloration: applied to elephants' teeth.

rink[1]† (ringk), *n.* [ME., also *renk*, < AS. *rinc* = OS. *rink* = Icel. *rekkr*, a man: a poetical word, not found in other languages.] A man; especially, a warrior or hero.

> To a riche raunson the *rinkes* they putt,
> That amounted [to] more than they might paye.
> *Alisaunder of Macedoine* (E. E. T. S.), l. 356.

> The ryealle *renkys* of the rowunde table.
> *Morte Arthure* (E. E. T. S.), l. 17.

rink[2] (ringk), *n.* [< ME. *rink*, *rynk* (cf. LG. *rink* = MHG. *rinc*, a ring), a var. of *ring*[1].] **1.** A ring; a circle. [Prov. Eng. or Scotch.]—**2.** A section of a sheet of ice, generally from 32 to 45 yards in length and 8 or 9 feet in breadth, measured off for playing the game of curling.—**3.** The persons playing any one game on such a curling-rink.

> Games [of curling] can be played by two persons, but usually matches are arranged for with numerous competitors formed into *rinks* of four players a side.
> *Encyc. Brit.*, VI. 713.

4. A sheet of artificially prepared ice, usually under cover, for skating on; or a smooth flooring, generally of asphalt or wood, on which roller-skating is practised.—**5.** The building or inclosure containing such a surface prepared for skating.

> In March 1876 a *rink* was opened in Chelsea, the floor thereof being formed of real ice. *Ure*, Dict., IV. 408.

rink[2] (ringk), *v. i.* [< *rink*[2], *n.*] To skate on or in a rink.

rinkite (ring'kīt), *n.* [Named after Dr. *Rink*, a writer on the geology of Greenland.] A titanosilicate of cerium, calcium, and sodium, related in form to pyroxene.

Rinman's green. See *green*[1].

rino, *n.* See *rhino*.

rino-. For words so beginning, see *rhino-*.

rinse (rins), *v. t.*; pret. and pp. *rinsed*, ppr. *rinsing*. [Also dial. *rense*, *rench*; early mod. E. also *reinse*, *rynse*, *rince*, *rynce*; < ME. *rinsen*, *rincen*, *ryncen*, *rensen*, *rencen*, *ryneshen*, < OF. *rinser*, *renser*, *raincer*, *rainser*, *rincer*, *reinser*, F. *rincer*, rinse, < Icel. *hreinsa* = Sw. *rensa* = Dan. *rense*, make clean, cleanse; with verb-formative *-s* (as in *cleanse* and *mince*), < Icel. *hreinn* = Sw. Dan. *ren* = OHG. *hreini*, *reini*, MHG. *reine*, *rein*, G. *rein*, pure, clean, G. dial. *rein*, sifted, fine (of flour), = OS. *hrêni* = OFries. *rene*, North Fries. *rian* (not in AS. or E.) = Goth. *hrains*, pure, clean; prob. orig. 'sifted,' with pp. formative *-n*, ult. < √ *hri*, sift: see *ridder*[2], *riddle*[2].] **1.** To wash lightly, as by laving or bathing rather than rubbing; wash out or off with any cleansing liquid; especially, to subject to a fresh application of water in order to remove stains or impurities that may have been left from a former washing.

> She toke the Shirte withoute wordes moo,
> And weaht it onys, and *rynsshed* it so clene
> That afterward was noo spotte on it seen.
> *Generydes* (E. E. T. S.), l. 1182.

> Every vessel of wood shall be *rinsed* in water.
> Lev. xv. 12.

> Every bottle must be first *rinced* with wine, for fear of any moisture left in the washing; some, out of a mistaken thrift, will *rince* a dozen bottles with the same wine.
> *Swift*, Advice to Servants (Butler).

> They went to the cistern on the back side of the house, washed and *rinsed* themselves for dinner.
> *S. Judd*, Margaret, i. 2.

2. To remove by rinsing: with *out*, *away*, *off*, etc.

rinse (rins), *n.* [< *rinse*, *v.*] A rinsing or light washing; specifically, a renewed or final application of water or some other liquid in order to remove any impurities still remaining from a former washing.

> A thorough *rinse* with fresh cold water should be given.
> *Sci. Amer.*, N. S., LVI. 297.

rinser (rin'sėr), *n.* [< *rinse* + *-er*[1].] One who or that which rinses.

rinsing (rin'sing), *n.* [Verbal n. of *rinse*, *v.*] **1.** The act of one who rinses.

The Interview,
That swallow'd so much treasure, . . . like a glass
Did break i' the *rinsing*. *Shak.*, Hen. VIII., i. 1. 167.

2. That in which anything is rinsed; the liquid left from washing off.

The beadle bolted in haste his last mouthful of fat bacon, [and] washed down the greasy morsel with the last *rinsings* of the pot of ale. *Scott*, Heart of Mid-Lothian, xxxii.

The very pigs and white ducks seeming to wander about the uneven neglected yard as if in low spirits from feeding on a too meagre quality of *rinsings*.
George Eliot, Middlemarch, xxxix.

rinsing-machine (rin'sing-ma-shēn"), *n.* 1. In *cotton-manuf.*, a series of tanks fitted with rollers, through which fabrics are passed in the process of dyeing, to free them from dirt or surplus color.—2. A form of centrifugal drier for use in laundries.

rin-thereout (rin'THār-öt), *n.* and *a.* [< Sc. *rin*, = E. *run*, + *thereout*.] I. *n.* A needy, houseless vagrant; a vagabond. [Scotch.]

II. *a.* Vagrant; vagabond; wandering without a home. [Scotch.]

Ye little *rin-there-out* de'il that ye are, what takes you raking through the gutters to see folk hangit?
Scott, Heart of Mid-Lothian, v.

rio, riyo (rē-ō'), *n.* [Jap., = Chin. *liang*: see *liang*.] A Japanese ounce, of the same value as the Chinese liang; especially, an ounce of silver; a tael.

Riolani's muscle. See *ciliary muscle of Riolanus*, under *ciliary*.

rionite (rī'on-īt), *n.* [Formation not ascertained.] A massive metallic mineral, allied to tetrahedrite in composition, but peculiar in containing a considerable amount of bismuth. It is found in Switzerland.

riot (rī'ot), *n.* [Early mod. E. also *riotte*; < ME. *riot*, *ryot*, *ryott*, *riote*, *ryote*, *riotte*, < OF. *riot*, *ryot*, usually *riote*, *riotte*, F. *riotte*, quarreling, brawling, confusion, riot, revelry, feasting, wrangling, = Pr. *riota* = It. *riotta* (ML. reflex **riota*, *riotta*), quarrel, dispute, uproar, riot; origin unknown. Cf. OD. *revot*, *ravot*, "caterua nebulonum et lupanar, luxus, luxuria" (Kilian).] 1. A disturbance arising from wanton and disorderly conduct; a tumult; an uproar; a brawl.

Horse harneys tyte, that thei be tane,
This *ryott* rudly sall tham rewe. *York Plays*, p. 90.

Other of your insolent retinue
Do hourly carp and quarrel, breaking forth
In rank and not-to-be-endured *riots*.
Shak., Lear, i. 4. 223.

Now were all transform'd
Alike, to serpents all, as accessories
To his bold *riot*. *Milton*, P. L., x. 521.

Specifically—2. In *law*, an unlawful assembly which has actually begun to execute the purpose for which it assembled by a breach of the peace, and to the terror of the public, or a lawful assembly proceeding to execute an unlawful purpose. A riot cannot take place unless three persons at least are present. *Stephen.* Compare *rout*[3], 4, and *unlawful assembly* (under *unlawful*).—3. A luxurious and loose manner of living; boisterous and excessive festivity; revelry.

For sikerly a prentys revelour,
That haunteth dys, *riot*, or paramour,
His maister shal it in his shoppe abye,
Al han he no part of the mynstralcye;
For thefte and *riot* they been convertible.
Chaucer, Cook's Tale, l. 28.

All now was turn'd to jollity and game,
To luxury and *riot*, feast and dance.
Milton, P. L., xi. 715.

4. Confusion; a confused or chaotic mass; a jumble; a medley.

Brute terrors, like the scurrying of rats in a deserted attic, filled the more remote chambers of his brain with *riot*. *R. L. Stevenson*, Markheim.

No-popery or **Gordon riots.** See *no-popery*.—**Riot Act**, an English statute of 1714 (1 Geo. I., st. 2, c. 5), designed to prevent tumults and riotous assemblies, and providing for the punishment of rioters who do not disperse upon proclamation made. Any one who continues to riot after this proclamation is made (called *reading the Riot Act*) is guilty of felony.—**To run riot** (adverbial use of the noun). (*a*) To act or move without control or restraint.

One man's head *runs riot* upon hawks and dice.
Sir R. L'Estrange.

(*b*) To grow luxuriantly, wildly, or in rank abundance.

And overhead the wandering ivy and vine,
This way and that, in many a wild festoon,
Ran riot. *Tennyson*, Œnone.

=**Syn.** 1 and 2. *Mutiny, Sedition*, etc. See *insurrection*, *quarrel*.

riot (rī'ot), *v.* [< ME. *rioten*, *ryoten*, *riotten*, *ryotten*, < OF. *rioter* (= It. *riottare*; ML. *riotare*, **riottare*), quarrel, revel, < *riote*, quarrel, riot: see *riot*, *n.*] I. *intrans.* 1. To act in a wanton and disorderly manner; rouse a tumult or disturbance; specifically, to take part in a riot (see *riot*, *n.*, 2), or outbreak against the public peace.

Under this word *rioting* . . . many thousands of old women have been arrested and put to expense, sometimes in prison, for a little intemperate use of their tongues.
Fielding, Amelia, i. 2, note.

2. To be in a state of disorder or confusion; act irregularly.

Thy life a long dead calm of fix'd repose;
No pulse that *riots*, and no blood that glows.
Pope, Eloisa to Abelard, l. 252.

3. To revel; run to excess in feasting, drinking, or other sensual indulgences; act in an unrestrained or wanton manner.

Now lat him *riote* al the nyght or leve.
Chaucer, Cook's Tale, l. 50.

Let us walk honestly, as in the day; not in *rioting* [*revelling*, R. V.] and drunkenness, not in chambering and wantonness. Rom. xiii. 13.

It may well be conceived that, at such a time, such a nature as that of Marlborough would *riot* in the very luxury of baseness. *Macaulay*, Hallam's Const. Hist.

II. *trans.* 1†. To throw into tumult or confusion; disturb; harass; annoy.

Sir, and we wyste ȝour wylle, we walde wirke ther-aftyre;
ȝif this journee suldo halde, or be arouwede [doubtful reading] forthyre,
To ryde one ȝone Romaynes and *ryott* theire landez.
Morte Arthure (E. E. T. S.), l. 340.

Indeed, perjury is but scandalous words; and I know a man cannot have a warrant for those, unless you put for *rioting* them into the warrant. *Fielding*, Amelia, i. 2.

2†. To indulge in pleasure or sensual enjoyment; satiate: used reflexively.

The roo and the rayne-dere reklesse thare rounene,
In ranez and in rosers to *ryotte thame selvene*.
Morte Arthure (E. E. T. S.), l. 923.

3. To pass in riot; destroy or put an end to by riotous living: with *out*. [Rare.]

And he,
Thwarted by one of these old father-fools,
Had *rioted* his life *out*, and made an end.
Tennyson, Aylmer's Field.

rioter (rī'ot-ėr), *n.* [< ME. *riotour*, *rioter*, *ryotour*, < OF. *riotour*, F. *rioteur*, a rioter, < *rioter*, riot: see *riot*, *v.*] One who riots. (*a*) A person who originates an uproar or disturbance or takes part in one; specifically, in *law*, one guilty of uniting with others in a riot.

Any two justices, together with the sheriff or under-sheriff of the county, may come with the posse comitatus, if need be, and suppress any such riot, assembly, or rout, [and] arrest the *rioters*. *Blackstone*, Com., IV. xi.

In 1411 a statute against *rioters* was passed.
Stubbs, Const. Hist., § 372.

(*b*) A reveler; a roisterer.

Thise *ryotoures* three, of which I telle, . . .
Were set hem in a taverne for to drinke.
Chaucer, Pardoner's Tale, l. 199.

He 's a sworn *rioter*; he has a sin that often
Drowns him, and takes his valour prisoner.
Shak., T. of A., iii. 5. 68.

riotise† (rī'ot-is), *n.* [Early mod. E. also *riotyze*; < *riot* + *-ise*[1].] 1. Turbulence; riot; uproar.

They come at last, who, with the warders cryes
Astonisht, to the tumult preaseth neere,
Thinking t' appease the broyle and *riotyze*.
Heywood, Troia Britannica (1609). (*Nares.*)

2. Luxury; dissoluteness; debauchery.

His life he led in lawlesse *riotise*.
Spenser, F. Q., I. iv. 20.

riotous (rī'ot-us), *a.* [< ME. *riotous*, < OF. **riotos*, *riotoux*, *rioteux* = It. *riottoso* (ML. *riotosus*); as *riot* + *-ous*.] 1. Tumultuous; of the nature of an unlawful assembly; seditious; guilty of riot: as, a *riotous* mob; a *riotous* demagogue.

The forfeit, sovereign, of my servant's life;
Who slew to-day a *riotous* gentleman
Lately attendant on the Duke of Norfolk.
Shak., Rich. III., ii. 1. 100.

2. Indulging in riot or revelry; accompanied by or consisting in revelry or debauchery; wanton or licentious.

The younger son . . . wasted his substance with *riotous* living. Luke xv. 13.

All our offices have been oppress'd
With *riotous* feeders. *Shak.*, T. of A., ii. 2. 168.

Be sumptuous, but not *riotous*; be bounteous,
But not in drunken bacchanals.
Fletcher, Pilgrim, v. 3.

He devoted himself to the expression of sensuous, even *riotous* beauty. *Stedman*, Vict. Poets, p. 392.

3. Boisterous; uproarious: as, *riotous* glee.—**Riotous assembling**, in *law*, the unlawful assembling of twelve or more persons to the detriment of the peace. If such persons refuse to disperse after proclamation, they are accounted felons. A *riot* may be made by three persons (see *riot*, 2), while it takes at least twelve persons to constitute a *riotous assembly*. =**Syn.** 1. See *insurrection*.

riotously (rī'ot-us-li), *adv.* In a riotous manner. (*a*) In the manner of an unlawful assembly; tumultuously; turbulently; seditiously.

If any persons so *riotously* assembled begin, even before proclamation, to pull down any church, chapel, meeting-house, dwelling-house, or out-houses, they shall be felons without benefit of clergy. *Blackstone*, Com., IV. xi.

(*b*) With licentious revelry or debauchery.

He that gathereth by defrauding his own soul gathereth for others that shall spend his goods *riotously*.
Ecclus. xiv. 4.

riotousness (rī'ot-us-nes), *n.* The state or condition of being riotous.

Excess includeth *riotousness*, expence of money, prodigal housekeeping.
Raleigh, Arts of Empire, xix. (*Latham.*)

riotry (rī'ot-ri), *n.* [< *riot* + *-ry*.] Riot; the practice of rioting; riotousness.

I hope your electioneering *riotry* has not, nor will mix in these tumults.
Walpole, Letters, To Rev. W. Cole, June 15, 1780.

They at will
Entered our houses, lived upon our means
In *riotry*, made plunder of our goods.
Sir H. Taylor, Ph. van Artevelde, I., i. 3.

rip[1] (rip), *v.*; pret. and pp. *ripped*, ppr. *ripping*. [Early mod. E. *ryppe*, *rype*, < ME. *rippen*, *ripen*, *rypen*, rip up, search into, seek out (AS. **rypan*, **ryppan*, rip, break in pieces, not authenticated), = F. *riper*, scrape, drag, < Norw. *ripa*, scratch, score with the point of a knife, = Sw. dial. *ripa*, scratch, also pluck asunder, rip open, Sw. *repa*, scratch, rip (in *repa upp*, rip up), = Dan. *rippe*, rip (in *oprippe*, rip up); appar. a secondary form, from the root of Icel. *rīfa*, rive (*rīfa upp*, pull up, *rīfa aptr*, rip up): see *rive*[1]. The word has prob. been confused with others of similar form, and has thus taken on an unusual variety of meanings; cf. *rip*[3], *rip*[4], *ripe*[2], *ripple*[1], *reap*.] I. *trans.* 1. To separate or divide the parts of by cutting or tearing; tear or cut open or off; split: as, to *rip* open a sack; to *rip* off the shingles of a roof; to *rip* up the belly; especially, to undo (a seam, as of a garment), either by cutting the threads of it or by pulling the two pieces of material apart, so that the sewing-thread is drawn out or broken.

Poor I am stale, a garment out of fashion;
And, for I am richer than to hang by the walls,
I must be *ripp'd*:—to pieces with me.
Shak., Cymbeline, iii. 4. 55.

Tell me thy thoughts; for I will know the least
That dwells within thee, or will *rip* thy heart
To know it. *Beau. and Fl.*, Philaster, iii. 1.

Multitudes of the Jews (2000 in one night) had their bowels *ript* up by the Roman Souldiers, in hopes to have found the gold and silver there which they were supposed to have swallowed. *Stillingfleet*, Sermons, I. viii.

Sails *ripp'd*, seams op'ning wide, and compass lost.
Cowper, My Mother's Picture.

2. To drag or force out or away, as by cutting or rending.

Macduff was from his mother's womb
Untimely *ripped*. *Shak.*, Macbeth, v. 8. 16.

He'll *rip* the fatal secret from her heart. *Granville.*

3. Figuratively, to open or reopen for search or disclosure; lay bare; search out and disclose: usually with *up*. See *ripe*[2].

Certes, sir Knight, ye seemen much to blame
To *rip up* wrong that battell once hath tried.
Spenser, F. Q., IV. ix. 37.

I shall not need
To *rip* the cause *up* from the first to you.
Fletcher (and another), Noble Gentleman, iv. 3.

It was printed, he saith, by his own hand, and *rips* all the faults of the kingdom in king and people.
Court and Times of Charles I., I. 367.

They *ripped up* all that had been done from the beginning of the rebellion. *Clarendon.*

4. To saw (wood) in the direction of the grain. See *rip-saw*.—5†. To rob; pillage; plunder.

To *rippenn* hemm and refenn. *Ormulum*, l. 10212.

=**Syn.** 1. *Tear, Cleave*, etc. See *rend*[1].

II. *intrans.* 1. To be torn or split open; open or part: as, a seam *rips* by the breaking or drawing out of the threads; the *ripping* of a boiler at the seams.—2. To rush or drive headlong or with violence. [Colloq.]—**Let her rip.** See *let*[1].—**To rip and tear**, to be violent or furious, as with excitement or rage. [Colloq.]

rip[1] (rip), *n.* [< *rip*[1], *v.*] 1. A rent made by ripping or tearing; a laceration; the place so ripped.

A *rip* in his flesh-coloured doublet.
Addison, Spectator, No. 13.

2. A rip-saw. [Colloq.]

rip[2] (rip), *n.* [< ME. *rip*, *rippe*, a basket, < Icel. *hrip*, a basket or box of laths to carry peat, etc.] A wicker basket in which to carry fish.

Astirte til him with his *rippe*,
And bigan the fish to kippe.
Havelok (ed. Madden-Skeat), l. 893.

Yet must you have a little *rip* beside,
Of willow twigs, the finest you can wish;
Which shall be made so handsome and so wide
As may contain good store of sundry fish.
J. Dennys (Arber's Eng. Garner, I. 155).

rip[3] (rip), *v.*; pret. and pp. *ripped*, ppr. *ripping*. [Appar. a particular use of *rip*[1], like *rap*[1] in "to *rap* out an oath."] **I.** *intrans.* To break forth with violence; explode: with *out.* [Colloq.]

I *rip out* with an oath every now and then.
H. B. Stowe, Dred, xx.

"You may leave the table," he added, his temper *ripping out.* *R. L. Stevenson*, Prince Otto, ii. 7.

II. *trans.* To utter with sudden violence; give vent to, as an oath: with *out.* [Colloq.]

Here I *ripped out* something, perhaps rather rash,
Quite innocent, though.
Wm. Allen Butler, Nothing to Wear.

rip[4] (rip), *n.* [Of obscure origin; prob. in all uses < *rip*[1], *v.*, in the general sense of 'act violently, recklessly, rudely,' hence 'go to ruin or decay.'] **1.** A vicious, reckless, and worthless person; a "bad lot": applied to a man or woman of vicious practices or propensities, and more or less worn by dissipation. [Colloq.]

"If it's ever broke to him that his *Rip* of a brother has turned up, I could wish," says the trooper, . . . "to break it myself." *Dickens*, Bleak House, lv.

I've been robbed before, and I've caught young *rips* in the act. *Mayhew*, London Labour and London Poor, II. 49.

2. A worthless or vicious animal, as a horse or a mule. [Colloq.]

"There's an old *rip* down there in the stable; you may take him and ride him to hell, if you want to," said an irate Carolina farmer to a foraging party during the war.
Trans. Amer. Phil. Ass., XIV. 52.

rip[5] (rip), *v. t.*; pret. and pp. *ripped*, ppr. *ripping.* A dialectal form of *reap.* *Halliwell.*

rip[5] (rip), *n.* [A var. of *reap*, a sheaf.] A handful of grain not thrashed. [Scotch.]

A guid New-Year I wish thee, Maggie!
Hae, there's a *ripp* to thy auld baggie.
Burns, Auld Farmer's Salutation to his Auld Mare.

rip[6] (rip), *n.* [Cf. *ripple*[3].] **1.** A ridge of water; a rapid.

We passed through a very heavy overfall or *rip.*
Quoted in *R. Tomes's* Americans in Japan, p. 369.

2. A little wave; a ripple; especially, in the plural, ripples or waves formed over a bar or ledge, as when the wind and tide are opposed.

The tide *rips* began to show in the distance.
Salem (Mass.) Gazette, July 5, 1887.

rip[7] (rip), *n.* [Also *ripe*, *ripple*; origin uncertain.] An implement for sharpening a scythe. Compare *rifle*[3]. [Prov. Eng. and New Eng.]

Ripe, *rifle*, vel *ripple*, a short wooden dagger with which the mowers smooth their scythes after they have used the coarse whetstone.
MS. Devon Glossary. (*Halliwell.*)

R. I. P. An abbreviation of the Latin phrase *requiescat in pace*, may he (or she) rest in peace.

ripa (rī'pä), *n.*; pl. *ripas*, *ripæ* (rī'pāz, -pē). [NL., < L. *ripa*, the bank of a stream: see *rive*[3].] A line of reflection of the endyma of the brain upon any tela or plexus. *Wilder and Gage*, Anat. Tech., p. 488.

riparial (rī-pā'ri-al), *a.* [< L. *riparius*, of or belonging to the bank of a river (see *riparian*), + *-al.*] **1.** Same as *riparian.*

At both these points in the river's course chalk came to the surface, and formed the rock base of the soil of these four *riparial* districts. *Lancet*, No. 3446, p. 535.

2. In *zoöl.*, living on a shore; shore-loving; riparious: said of terrestrial animals which frequent the shores of streams, ponds, etc.: as, insects of *riparial* habits.

riparian (rī-pā'ri-an), *a.* and *n.* [< L. *riparius*, of or belonging to the bank of a river (< *ripa*, bank: see *rive*[3], *river*[2]), + *-an.*] **I.** *a.* **1.** Pertaining to or situated on the bank of a river.

As long as the Oise was a small rural river, it took us near by people's doors, and we could hold a conversation with natives in the *riparian* fields.
R. L. Stevenson, Inland Voyage, p. 212.

Staines, in Middlesex, that quiet but quaint and pretty *riparian* town. *N. and Q.*, 7th ser., IV. 142.

2. In *anat.*, of or pertaining to a ripa of the brain; marginal, as a part of the brain.

The *riparian* parts of the cerebrum are the tænia and the fimbria. *Buck's Handbook of Med. Sciences*, VIII. 120.

Riparian nations, nations possessing opposite banks or different parts of banks of the same river. *Wharton.*—**Riparian proprietor**, an owner of land bounded by water, generally on a stream, who, as such, has a qualified property in the soil to the thread of the stream, with the privileges annexed thereto by law. *Shaw, C. J.*—**Riparian rights**, the right of fishery, of ferry, and any other right which is properly appendant to the owner of the soil bordering a river. *Angell.*

II. *n.* One who dwells or owns property on the banks of a river.

Annoyances to *riparians* and danger to small craft on the river. *The Field*, July 24, 1886. (*Encyc. Dict.*)

riparious (rī-pā'ri-us), *a.* [< L. *riparius*, of or belonging to the bank of a river: see *riparian.*] In *zoöl.* and *bot.*, riparial; riparian; living or growing along the banks of rivers.

ripe[1] (rīp), *a.* [< ME. *ripe*, *rype*, < AS. *rīpe* = OS. *rīpi* = D. *rijp* = MLG. *ripe*, LG. *riep* = OHG. *rifi*, MHG. *rīfe*, *rīf*, G. *reif*, ripe, mature: usually explained as 'fit for reaping,' < AS. *rīpan*, reap; but this verb, not found outside of AS., is unstable in form (see *reap*), and would hardly produce an adj. derivative like *ripe*; if connected at all, it is more likely to be itself derived from the adjective (the reg. verb from the adj. *ripe* exists in *ripe*[1], *v.*). The verb applies only to cutting grain; the adj. applies not only to mature grain, but to all mature fruit.] **1.** Ready for reaping, gathering, or using; brought to completion or perfection; mature: usually said of that which is grown and used for food: as, *ripe* fruit; *ripe* corn.

If it [the fruit] be not *ripe*, it will draw a mans mouth awry. *Capt. John Smith*, Works, I. 122.

Cherrie-*ripe*, *Ripe*, *Ripe*, I cry,
Full and fair ones; come and buy.
Herrick, Cherrie-ripe.

Through the *ripe* harvest lies their destin'd road.
Cowper, Heroism.

Nature . . .
Fills out the homely quickset-screens,
And makes the purple lilac *ripe*.
Tennyson, On a Mourner.

2. Advanced to the state of being fit for use, or in the best condition for use: said of mutton, venison, game, cheese, beer, etc., which has acquired a peculiar and approved flavor by keeping.

When the *ripe* beer is to be drawn from the fermenting tun, the contaminations swimming upon it are first skimmed off. *Thausing*, Beer (trans.), p. 598.

3. Resembling ripe fruit in ruddiness, juiciness, or plumpness.

O, how *ripe* in show
Thy lips, those kissing cherries, tempting grow!
Shak., M. N. D., iii. 2. 139.

An underlip, you may call it a little too *ripe*, too full.
Tennyson, Maud, ii.

4. Full-grown; developed; finished; having experience, knowledge, or skill; equipped; accomplished; wise; clever: as, a *ripe* judgment; a *ripe* old age.

A man ful *ripe* in other clerigie
Off the right Canoun and Ciuile also.
Rom. of Partenay (E. E. T. S.), l. 7.

He than beinge of *ripe* yeres; . . . his frendes . . . exhorted hym busely to take a wyfe.
Sir T. Elyot, The Governour, ii. 12.

This exercise may bring moch profite to *ripe* heads.
Ascham, The Scholemaster, p. 109.

He was a scholar, and a *ripe* and good one.
Shak., Hen. VIII., iv. 2. 51.

5. Mature; ready for some change or operation, as an ovum for discharge from the ovary, an abscess for lancing, a cataract for extraction, or a fish for spawning.—**6.** Ready for action or effect: often preceded by a specific word: as, *bursting ripe*, *fighting ripe*—that is, ready to burst, or to fight.

The toole . . . in an envious spleene *smarting ripe* runnes after him. *Armin*, Nest of Ninnies (1608). (*Nares.*)

Our legions are brim-full, our cause is *ripe.*
Shak., J. C., iv. 3. 215.

I've sounded my Numidians, man by man,
And find 'em *ripe* for a revolt. *Addison*, Cato, i. 3.

The man that with me trod
This planet was a noble type,
Appearing ere the times were *ripe.*
Tennyson, In Memoriam, Conclusion.

Ripe fish. See *fish*[1].=**Syn.** *Mature*, *Ripe.* See *mature.*

ripe[1] (rīp), *v.*; pret. and pp. *riped*, ppr. *riping.* [< ME. *ripen*, *rypen*, < AS. *rīpian*, *ge-rīpian* (= OS. *rīpōn* = D. *rijpen* = MLG. *ripen* = OHG. *rīfēn*, *riphen*, MHG. *rīfen*, G. *reifen*), become ripe, < *ripe*, ripe: see *ripe*[1], *a.*] **I.** *intrans.* **1.** To ripen; grow ripe; be matured. See *ripen.*

Wheate sowne in the grounde . . . spryngeth, groweth, and *rypeth* with woonderfull celeritie.
R. Eden, tr. of Sebastian Munster (First Books on America, ed. Arber, p. 293).

The *riping* corn grows yellow in the stalk.
Greene, Palmer's Verses.

And so, from hour to hour, we *ripe* and *ripe*,
And then, from hour to hour, we rot and rot.
Shak., As you Like it, ii. 7. 26.

'Till death us lay
To *ripe* and mellow here, we're stubborn clay.
Donne, Elegy on Himself.

2. To grow old. *Halliwell.* [Prov. Eng.]

II. *trans.* To mature; ripen; make ripe.

Theyr corne and other grayne, by reason of longe coulde, doo seldome waxe rype on the ground; by reason wherof they are sumtimes inforced to *rype* and dry them in theyr stooues and hottes houses.
R. Eden, tr. of Sebastian Munster (First Books on America, ed. Arber, p. 292).

Yon green boy shall have no sun to *ripe*
The bloom that promiseth a mighty fruit.
Shak., K. John, ii. 1. 472.

ripe[2] (rīp), *v. t.*; pret. and pp. *riped*, ppr. *riping.* [< ME. *ripen*, search: see *rip*[1], *v.*] **1.** To search (especially, pockets); rummage; hence, to plunder.

Now if ye have suspowse to Gille or to me,
Com and *rype* oure howse, and then may ye se
Who had hir. *Towneley Mysteries*, p. 112.

And loose the strings of all thy pocks,
I'll *ripe* them with my hand.
Robin Hood and the Beggar (Child's Ballads, V. 190).

I was amaist feared to look at him [a corpse]; however, I thought to hae turn about wi' him, and sae I e'en *riped* his pouches. *Scott*, Old Mortality, xxiii.

2. To poke.

Then fling on coals, and *ripe* the ribs [grate].
Ramsay, Poems, II. 205. (*Jamieson.*)

3. To sweep or wipe clean; clean.

The shaking of my pocks [of meal] I fear
Hath blown into your eyne;
But I have a good pike-staff here
Can *ripe* them out full clean. . . .
In the thick wood the beggar fled
E'er they *riped* their eyne.
Robin Hood and the Beggar (Child's Ballads, V. 202).

4. To examine strictly.

His Highnes delyvered me the boke of his said wil in many pointes refourmed, wherin His Grace *riped* me.
State Papers, i. 295. (*Halliwell.*)

5. To break up (rough ground). *Halliwell.* [Obsolete or prov. Eng. in all uses.]

ripe[3]†, *n.* [< L. *ripa*, a bank. Cf. *rive*[3], *river*[2].] A bank.

Whereof the principall is within a butt shoote of the right *ripe* of the river that there cometh downe.
Leland, Itinerary (1769), iv. 110. (*Halliwell.*)

ripe[4] (rīp), *n.* Same as *rip*[7].

ripely (rīp'li), *adv.* [< ME. *rypely* (= D. *rijpelijk* = MLG. *riplik* = G. *reiflich*); < *ripe*[1], *a.*, + *-ly*[2].] In a ripe manner; maturely; fully; thoroughly; fittingly.

Shew the chieff wrytynges . . . to Master Paston, that he may be more *rypelyer* grounded yn the seyd mater.
Paston Letters, I. 254.

It fits us therefore *ripely*
Our chariots and our horsemen be in readiness.
Shak., Cymbeline, iii. 5. 22.

ripe-man†, *n.* Same as *reapman.*

ripen (rī'pn), *v.* [< *ripe*[1] + *-en*[1].] **I.** *intrans.* **1.** To grow ripe; come to maturity, as grain or fruit: used by extension of the maturing of anything, as of a boil.

Wholesome berries thrive and *ripen* best
Neighbour'd by fruit of baser quality.
Shak., Hen. V., i. 1. 61.

The unnetted black-hearts *ripen* dark.
Tennyson, The Blackbird.

2. To become fit for some particular use by lying or resting.

After *ripening*, the cream is churned.
Sci. Amer., N. S., LIV. 40.

It [Indian-ink paste] is then poured out in the form of flat cakes, . . . and is left in that condition for many days to *ripen.* *Workshop Receipts*, 2d ser., p. 335.

3. To approach or come to completeness or perfection; come to a state of fitness or readiness; be prepared or made ready: as, the project is *ripening* for execution.

While villains *ripen* gray with time,
Must thou, the noble, gen'rous, great,
Fall in bold manhood's hardy prime?
Burns, Lament for Glencairn.

It was not till our acquaintance had *ripened* . . . that these particulars were elicited.
Barham, Ingoldsby Legends, I. 190.

But woman *ripen'd* earlier, and her life
Was longer. *Tennyson*, Princess, ii.

=**Syn.** See *mature*, *a.*

II. *trans.* **1.** To mature; make ripe, as grain or fruit.

Bid her steal into the pleached bower,
Where honeysuckles, *ripen'd* by the sun,
Forbid the sun to enter.
Shak., Much Ado, iii. 1. 8.

The Sun that *ripeneth* your Pippins and our Pomgranates. *Howell*, Letters, I. i. 24.

2. To bring to maturity, perfection, or completion; develop to a desired or desirable state.

Were growing time once *ripen'd* to my will.
Shak., 1 Hen. VI., ii. 4. 99.

Come not, sir,
Until I send, for I have something else
To *ripen* for your good, you must not know 't.
B. Jonson, Volpone, ii. 3.

The magistrates should (as far as might be) *ripen* their consultations beforehand, that their vote in public might bear (as the voice of God).

Winthrop, Hist. New England, I. 213.

He did not *ripen* his plans, and in the rapidity of his work he was too easily contented with helping himself from the novels or the histories from which he took his plays to the scenes in the order in which he found them.

The Century, XXXVIII. 828.

3. To make fit or ready for use.

They [pottery-clays] are worked by shallow pits, and are *ripened*, ground, and washed, as the other clays.

Spons' Encyc. Manuf., I. 640.

ripeness (rip'nes), *n.* [< ME. **ripnes*, < AS. *ripnes*, *ripnys*, < *ripe*, ripe: see *ripe*¹.] The state of being ripe, in any sense.

In man, the *ripeness* of strength of the body and mind cometh much about an age.

Bacon, Advancement of Learning, I. 16.

Thou gav'st that *ripeness* which so soon began,
And ceased so soon, he ne'er was boy nor man.

Pope, Dunciad, iv. 287.

When love is grown
To *ripeness*, that on which it throve
Falls off, and love is left alone.

Tennyson, To J. S.

rip-fishing (rip'fish"ing), *n.* See *fishing*.

Ripi-. For words so beginning, see *Rhipi-*.

ripicolous (rī-pik'ọ-lus), *a.* [< L. *ripa*, a bank, + *colere*, inhabit.] In *zoöl.*, riparian or riparious.

ripidolite (rī-pid'ọ-līt), *n.* [< Gr. ῥιπίς (ῥιπιδ-), a fan, + λίθος, a stone.] The commonest member of the chlorite family of minerals, occurring in monoclinic crystals with micaceous cleavage, also scaly and granular, usually of a deep-green color, rarely rose-red. It is a hydrous silicate of aluminium and magnesium. Also called *clinochlore*.

ripienist (ri-pyā'nist), *n.* [= F. *ripiéniste*; as *ripieno* + *-ist*.] In *music*, one who plays a ripieno part; a supplementary or assisting instrumentalist.

ripieno (ri-pyā'nọ), *a.* and *n.* [It., < L. *re-* + *plenus*, full: see *plenty*.] **I.** *a.* In *music*, supplementary. Specifically, noting an instrument or a performer who assists in tutti passages, merely doubling or reinforcing the part of the leading performers.

II. *n.* Pl. *ripieni* (-nē). Such an instrument or performer. In an orchestra, all the first violins, except the leader or concert-master, are ripieni. Opposed to *principal* or *solo*.

ripier¹† (rip'i-ėr), *n.* See *ripper*².

ripier² (rip'i-ėr), *n.* See *ripper*¹, 3.

ripon, rippon (rip'on), *n.* [< *Ripon*: see def.] 1. A spur: so called from the excellence attributed to the spurs made at Ripon, Yorkshire, England. *Fairholt.*—2. A sword or sword-blade named from Ripon.

riposte (ri-pōst'), *n.* [< F. *riposte*, < It. *risposta*, a response, reply, < *rispondere*, respond: see *respond*.] 1. In *fencing*, a quick, short thrust by a swordsman after parrying a lunge from his opponent: usually given without moving from the spot, before the opponent has time to recover his position or guard.

The *riposte* in its simplest form is exactly analogous to a war of words—a short, smart answer to an attack.

H. A. C. Dunn, Fencing, vi.

Hence—2. A quick, smart reply; a repartee.

ripper¹ (rip'ėr), *n.* [< *rip*¹ + *-er*¹.] 1. One who or that which rips, tears, or cuts open; a ripping-tool. (*a*) A tool used in shaping roofing-slates. (*b*) An implement for ripping seams in fabrics by cutting the stitches without injury to the cloth. (*c*) A machine with circular knives for cutting the millboards used in the making of cloth cases or covers for books.

2. A very efficient person or thing; one who does great execution: as, he is a regular *ripper*. [Slang.]—3. A robber. *Halliwell* (in the form *ripier*). See *rip*¹, *v. t.*, 5. [Prov. Eng.]

ripper²† (rip'ėr), *n.* [Also *rippar*, *rippier*, *ripier*, < OF. **ripier* (?), < L. *riparius*, of or pertaining to the bank or coast: see *riparian* and *river*². By some derived < *rip*², a basket, + *-er*¹.] One who brings fish inland from the coast to market.

But what 's the action we are for now, ha?
Robbing a *ripper* of his fish?

Fletcher, Beggars' Bush, v. 1.

I can send you speedier advertisement of her constancy by the next *ripier* that rides that way with mackrel.

Chapman, Widow's Tears, ii.

Also that all *Ripiers*, and other Fishers from any of the Sea-coasts, should sell their Fish in Cornhill and Cheapside themselves, and not to Fishmongers that would buy to sell again.

Baker, Chronicles, p. 164.

ripper³ (rip'ėr), *n.* [Perhaps a particular use of *ripper*¹.] A fog-horn. Also called *lipper*. [Newfoundland.]

ripping-bed (rip'ing-bed), *n.* A machine for dividing stones by passing them on a traveling bed under a gang of saws. The saws have no teeth, but act by abrasion, which is facilitated by the use of sand.

ripping-chisel (rip'ing-chiz"el), *n.* In *wood-working*, a bent chisel used in clearing out mortises, or for ripping the old oakum out of seams which need calking.

ripping-iron (rip'ing-ī"ėrn), *n.* A hook used by calkers for tearing old oakum out of seams.

ripping-saw (rip'ing-sâ), *n.* Same as *rip-saw*.

ripple¹ (rip'l), *n.* [Early mod. E. or dial. also *reeple*, *riple*; = D. *repel* = MLG. *repel*, LG. *repel*, *reppel*, a ripple, = OHG. *rifilā*, a saw, MHG. *riffel*, a ripple, hoe, G. *riffel*, a ripple (G. *riffel*, *rüffel*, a reproof, lit. a 'combing over,' is from the verb); with formative *-le* (*-el*, equiv. to *-er*¹), denoting an agent (as in *ladle*, *stopple*, *beetle*¹, etc.), and equiv. to the simple form MD. MLG. LG. *repe*, a ripple, from the verb represented by MD. D. *repen* = MLG. *repen*, LG. *repen*, *reppen* = G. *reffen*, beat or ripple (flax), = Sw. *repa* (cf. MHG. *reffen*, pluck, pick, a secondary form of *raffen*, pluck, snatch, = E. *rap*²); prob. connected with *rap*², but in part at least associated with *rip*¹, *v.* Hence *ripple*¹, *v.*] A large comb or hatchel for separating the seeds or capsules from flax; also, in the United States, a toothed instrument for removing the seeds from broom-corn.

Ripple.

a, toothed wheel; *b*, chute into which the heads of unthreshed material are put; *c* and *d*, treadle and pitman by which the wheel is revolved.

ripple¹ (rip'l), *v. t.*; pret. and pp. *rippled*, ppr. *rippling*. [< ME. *ripplen*, *rypelen* = D. *repelen* = MLG. *repelen*, LG. *repeln* = MHG. *rifeln*, G. *riffeln*, ripple (flax); from the noun: see *ripple*¹, *n.*] To clean or remove the seeds or capsules from, as from the stalks of flax.

There must be . . . *rippling*, braking, wingling, and heckling of hemp.

Howell, Party of Beasts, p. 14. (*Davies*, under *brake*.)

ripple²† (rip'l), *v. t.* [< ME. **ripelen*, *repulen*; dim. or freq. (prob. confused with *ripple*¹): see *rip*¹.] To scratch or break slightly; graze.

And smote Gye wyth envye,
And *repulde* hys face and hys chynne,
And of hys cheke all the skynne.

MS. Cantab. Ff. ii. 38, f. 209. (*Halliwell.*)

A horseman's javelin, having slightly *rippled* the skin of his (Julian's) left arm, pierced within his short ribs.

Holland, tr. of Ammianus, p. 264. (*Trench*, Select Gloss.)

ripple³ (rip'l), *v.*; pret. and pp. *rippled*, ppr. *rippling*. [A mod. var. of *rimple*, wrinkle, due appar. to confusion with *rip*¹, *ripple*²: see *rimple*.] **I.** *intrans.* 1. To assume or wear a ruffled surface, as water when agitated by a gentle wind or by running over a stony bottom; be covered with small waves or undulations.

Left the Keswick road, and turned to the left through shady lanes along the vale of [the] Eeman, which runs . . . *rippling* over the stones.

Gray, To Dr. Wharton, Oct. 18, 1769.

Thine eddy's *rippling* race
Would blur the perfect image of his face.

D. G. Rossetti, The Stream's Secret.

2. To make a sound as of water running over a rough bottom: as, laughter *rippling* pleasantly.

Thy slender voice with *rippling* trill
The budding April bowers would fill.

O. W. Holmes, An Old-Year Song.

II. *trans.* 1. To fret or agitate lightly, as the surface of water; form in small waves or undulations; curl.

Anon she shook her head,
And shower'd the *rippled* ringlets to her knee.

Tennyson, Godiva.

Like the lake, my serenity is *rippled* but not ruffled.

Thoreau, Walden, p. 140.

2. To mark with or as with ripples. See *ripple-mark*.

Some of the *rippled* rain-pitted beds contain amphibian foot-prints.

A. Geikie, Encyc. Brit., X. 350.

ripple³ (rip'l), *n.* [< *ripple*³, *v.*] 1. The light fretting or ruffling of the surface of water; a little curling wave; an undulation.

He sees . . . a tremor pass across her frame, like a *ripple* over water.

Dickens, Bleak House, xxix.

To watch the crisping *ripples* on the beach.

Tennyson, The Lotos-Eaters, Choric Song.

2. A sound like that of water running over a stony bottom: as, a *ripple* of laughter.=**Syn.** 1. See *wave*.

ripple⁴ (rip'l), *n.* [Origin obscure.] A small coppice. *Halliwell.* [Prov. Eng.]

ripple⁵ (rip'l), *n.* [Origin obscure.] A weakness in the back and loins, attended with shooting pains: a form of tabes dorsualis, the same as *Friedrich's ataxia* (which see, under *ataxia*). [Scotch.]

For warld's wasters, like poor cripples,
Look blunt with poverty and *ripples*.

Ramsay, Works, I. 143. (*Jamieson.*)

ripple⁶ (rip'l), *n.* Same as *rip*⁷.

ripple-barrel (rip'l-bar"el), *n.* *Theat.*, a drum covered with tinsel, which revolves behind a perforated drop, to produce the effect of light on water.

ripple-grass (rip'l-gràs), *n.* [Sc. *ripple-girse*, also *ripplin-gurss*; appar. < *ripple*³ + *grass*, but cf. *rib-grass*.] The rib-grass or ribwort-plantain, *Plantago lanceolata*. See *plantain*¹.

ripple-mark (rip'l-märk), *n.* A wavy surface such as is often seen on sand, where it has been formed by the action of the wind, and which may have its origin in the motion of water as well as of air, or which is often a result of the combined action of the two. Examples of the former action of winds and waves may often be seen among the older sandy deposits where they happen to have been preserved by the consolidation of the material. These ripple-marks, with which are frequently associated sun-cracks and prints of rain or surf-drops, afford evidence of tidal and river action along gently sloping shores, and with markings of this kind are occasionally found traces of former life in the form of trails and tracks, as in the case of the Triassic sandstones of the Connecticut valley.

ripple-marked (rip'l-märkt), *a.* Having ripple-marks.

rippler (rip'lėr), *n.* 1. One who ripples flax or hemp.

Two *ripplers* sitting opposite each other, with the machine between them, work at the same time.

Encyc. Brit., IX. 294.

2. An apparatus for rippling flax or hemp.

The best *rippler* . . . consists of a kind of comb having, set in a wooden frame, iron teeth . . . 18 inches long.

Encyc. Brit., IX. 294.

ripplet (rip'let), *n.* [< *ripple*³ + *-et*.] A small ripple.

rippling (rip'ling), *n.* [Verbal n. of *ripple*³, *v.*] An eddy caused by conflicting currents or tides; a tide-rip.

ripplingly (rip'ling-li), *adv.* In an undulating manner; so as to ripple: as, the stream ran *ripplingly*.

ripply (rip'li), *a.* [< *ripple*³ + *-y*¹.] Rippling; characterized by ripples. [Rare.]

And whatever of life hath ebbed away
Comes flooding back with a *ripply* cheer,
Into every bare inlet and creek and bay.

Lowell, Sir Launfal, i.

rippon, *n.* See *ripon*.

riprap (rip'rap), *n.* [Usually in plural (orig. appar. sing.) *ripraps*; appar. < Dan. *rips-raps*, riffraff, rubbish, refuse, a form prob. due to the same source as E. *riffraff*: see *riffraff*.] In *engin.*: (*a*) Broken stones used for walls, beds, and foundations: sometimes used attributively.

After the vertical piles are driven, cobble stones, gravel, and *riprap* are put in place around them.

Sci. Amer., N. S., LX. 261.

The shore below the landing is a line of broken, ragged, slimy rocks, as if they had been dumped there for a *riprap* wall.

C. D. Warner, Their Pilgrimage, p. 120.

(*b*) A foundation or parapet of stones thrown together without any attempt at regular structural arrangement, as in deep water or on a soft bottom.

riprapped (rip'rapt), *a.* [< *riprap* + *-ed*².] Formed of or strengthened with riprap.

The dam is made of clay, and is 720 feet long. . . . The front is *riprapped*.

Sci. Amer., N. S., LXII. 167.

ripsack (rip'sak), *n.* The California gray whale, *Rachianectes glaucus*: so called from the manner of flensing.

ripsack (rip'sak), *v. i.* [< *ripsack*, *n.*] To pursue or capture the ripsack.

rip-saw (rip'sâ), *n.* A hand-saw the teeth of which have more rake and less set than a cross-cut saw, used for cutting wood in the direction of the grain. [U. S.]

ript (ript). Another spelling of *ripped*, preterit and past participle of *rip*[1].

ripuarian (rip-ū-ā'ri-an), *a.* [< F. *ripuaire* = Sp. Pg. *ripuario*, < ML. *ripuarius*, pertaining to a shore, < L. *ripa*, shore: see *ripe*[3]. Cf. *riparian*.] Pertaining to or dwelling near a shore.—**Ripuarian Franks**, one of the great divisions of the ancient Franks: so called because they dwelt near the banks of the Rhine, in the neighborhood of Cologne.

risala (ris'a-lä), *n.* [Also *ressala, rissala*; < Hind. *risālā*, Beng. *resālā*, a troop of horse, cavalry, also a treatise, pamphlet, < Ar. *risāla*, a mission, despatch, letter.] In the British Indian army, a troop of native irregular cavalry.

risaldar (ris-al-där'), *n.* [Also *ressaldar*; < Hind. *risāldār*, the commander of a troop of horse, < *risālā*, a troop of horse (see *risala*), + *dār*, one who holds.] The native commander of a risala.

risban (ris'ban), *n.* [Also *risband*; < F. *risban*, < G. *rissbank*, risban, < *riss*, gap, rent (< *reissen*, tear, split, draw: see *write* and *rit*), + *bank*, bank, bench: see *bank*[1].] 1. Any flat piece of ground upon which a fort is constructed for the defense of a port.—2. The fort itself.

risberm (ris-bėrm'), *n.* [Also *risberme*; < F. *risberme*, < G. **rissberme*, < *riss*, gap, + *berme*, a narrow ledge: see *berm*. Cf. *risban* and *berm*.] 1. A work composed of fascines, constructed at the bottom of an earth wall.—2. A sort of glacis of fascine-work used in jetties to withstand the violence of the sea.

rise[1] (rīz), *v.*; pret. *rose*, pp. *risen*, ppr. *rising*. [< ME. *risen, rysen* (pret. *ros, roos*, earlier *ras*, pl. *risen, rise, resin, reson*, pp. *risen, risin*), < AS. *risan* (pret. *rās*, pl. *rison*, pp. *risen*), rise, = OS. *risan* = OFries. *risa*, rise, = D. *rijzen*, rise or fall, = MLG. LG. *risen* = OHG. *rīsan*, MHG. *rīsen*, rise or fall, = Icel. *rīsa* = Goth. **reisan* (pret. **rais*, pp. *risans*), in comp. *urreisan* (= AS. *ārīsan*, E. *arise*); orig. expressive of vertical motion either up or down, but in E. confined to upward motion. The OHG. *reisôn*, MHG. G. *reisen* (= Sw. *resa* = Dan. *reise*), travel, is from the noun, OHG. *reisa*, MHG. *reise*, a setting out, expedition, journey, G. *reise* (= Sw. *resa* = Dan. *reise*), a journey, < OHG. *rīsan*, MHG. *rīsen*, rise.] **I.** *intrans.* 1. To move or pass from a lower position to a higher; move upward; ascend; mount up: as, a bird *rises* in the air; a fog *rises* from the river; the mercury *rises* in the thermometer (or, as commonly expressed, the thermometer *rises*).

> I saw young Harry, with his beaver on, . . .
> *Rise* from the ground like feather'd Mercury.
> *Shak.*, 1 Hen. IV., iv. 1. 106.

> In happier fields a *rising* town I see,
> Greater than what e'er was, or is, or e'er shall be.
> *Dryden*, tr. of Ovid's Metamorph., l. 653.

> Dark and voluminous the vapors *rise*,
> And hang their horrors in the neighb'ring skies.
> *Cowper*, Heroism.

> The falconer is frightening the fowls to make them *rise*, and the hawk is in the act of seizing upon one of them.
> *Strutt*, Sports and Pastimes, p. 89.

2. Specifically, to change from a lying, sitting, or kneeling posture to a standing one; stand up; assume an upright position: as, to *rise* from a chair; to *rise* after a fall.

> With that word they *rysen* sodeynly.
> *Chaucer*, Merchant's Tale, l. 330.

> Iden, kneel down. [He kneels.] *Rise* up a knight.
> *Shak.*, 2 Hen. VI., v. 1. 78.

> *Risse* [pret.] not the consular men, and left their places,
> So soon as thou sat'st down? *B. Jonson*, Catiline, iv. 2.

> Go to your banquet then, but use delight
> So as to *rise* still with an appetite.
> *Herrick*, Connubii Flores.

> And all the men and women in the hall
> *Rose* when they saw the dead man *rise*, and fled.
> *Tennyson*, Geraint.

Hence—(*a*) To bring a sitting or a session to an end: as, the house *rose* at midnight.

> It is then moved by some member . . . that the committee *rise*, and that the chairman or some other member make their report to the assembly.
> *Cushing*, Manual of Parliamentary Practice, § 285.

> When Parliament *rises* for the vacation the work of the circuit begins. *Fortnightly Rev.*, N. S., XXXIX. 208.

(*b*) To get up from bed.

> Go to bed when she list, *rise* when she list, all is as she will. *Shak.*, M. W. of W., ii. 2. 124.

> About two o'clock in the morning, letters came from London by our coxon. . . . I *rose* and carried them in to my Lord, who read them a-bed.
> *Pepys*, Diary, March 25, 1660.

> With early dawn Lord Marmion *rose*.
> *Scott*, Marmion, i. 31.

3. To grow or stretch upward; attain an altitude or stature; stand in height: as, the tower *rises* to the height of 60 feet.

> In sailing round Caprea we were entertained with many rude prospects of rocks and precipices, that *rise* in several places half a mile high in perpendicular.
> *Addison*, Remarks on Italy (ed. Bohn), I. 446.

> Where Windsor-domes and pompous turrets *rise*.
> *Pope*, Windsor Forest, l. 352.

> She that *rose* the tallest of them all,
> And fairest. *Tennyson*, Passing of Arthur.

4. To swell upward. Specifically—(*a*) To reach a higher level by increase of bulk or volume: as, the river *rises* in its bed.

> He told a boding dream,
> Of *rising* waters, and a troubled stream.
> *Dryden*, Hind and Panther, iii. 481.

> The olde sea wall (he cried) is downe,
> The *rising* tide comes on apace.
> *Jean Ingelow*, High Tide on the Coast of Lincolnshire.

(*b*) To swell or puff up, as dough in the process of fermentation.

> Generally in from four to five hours the [bread] sponge *rises*; fermentation has been going on, and carbonic acid steadily accumulating within the tenacious mass, till it has assumed a puffed out appearance. *Encyc. Brit.*, III. 253.

5. To slope or extend upward; have an upward direction: as, a line, a path, or a surface *rises* gradually or abruptly.

> There, lost behind a *rising* ground, the wood
> Seems sunk. *Cowper*, Task, i. 305.

6. To appear above the horizon; move from below the horizon to above it, in consequence of the earth's diurnal rotation; hence, to move from an invisible to a visible position.

> Whiles these renkes thus rest than *rises* the sun,
> Bredis with his beames all the brode vales.
> *Destruction of Troy* (E. E. T. S.), l. 1172.

> He maketh his sun to *rise* on the evil and on the good.
> Mat. v. 45.

> Till the star, that *rose* at evening bright,
> Toward heaven's descent had sloped his westering wheel.
> *Milton*, Lycidas, l. 30.

> *Risest* thou thus, dim dawn, again?
> *Tennyson*, In Memoriam, lxxii.

7. To come into existence; emerge into sight; arise. (*a*) To become apparent; come into view; stand out; emerge; come forth; appear: as, an eruption *rises* on the skin; the color *rose* on her cheeks.

> There chaunst to them a dangerous accident.
> A Tigre forth out of the wood did *rise*.
> *Spenser*, F. Q., VI. x. 34.

> Go to; does not my coulour *rise*?
> It shall *rise*; for I can force my blood
> To come and go. *Marston*, The Fawne, ii. 1.

> I [stake] this bowl, where wanton ivy twines, . . .
> Four figures *rising* from the work appear.
> *Pope*, Spring, l. 37.

(*b*) To become audible.

> Heroes' and heroines' shouts confusedly *rise*.
> *Pope*, R. of the L., v. 41.

> There *rose* a noise of striking clocks.
> *Tennyson*, Day-Dream, The Revival.

(*c*) To have a beginning; originate; spring; come into existence; be produced.

> A nobler gratitude
> *Rose* in her soul: for from that hour she lov'd me.
> *Otway*, Venice Preserved, i. 1.

> 'Tis very rare that Tornadoes arise from thence [the sea]; for they generally *rise* first over the Land, and that in a very strange manner. *Dampier*, Voyages, II. iii. 87.

> Honour and shame from no condition *rise*;
> Act well your part; there all the honour lies.
> *Pope*, Essay on Man, iv. 193.

> The river Blackwater *rises* in the county Kerry.
> *Trollope*, Castle Richmond, i.

8. To increase in force, intensity, spirit, degree, value, or the like. (*a*) To increase in force or intensity; become stronger: as, his anger *rises*.

> He blewe hys horne in that tyde,
> Hertys *reson* on eche a syde.
> *MS. Cantab.* Ff. ii. 38, f. 64. (*Halliwell.*)

> Sunday, the wynde began to *ryse* in the north.
> *Torkington*, Diarie of Eng. Travell, p. 59.

> His spirits *rising* as his toils increase.
> *Cowper*, Table-Talk, l. 279.

> The power of the Crown was constantly sinking, and that of the Commons constantly *rising*.
> *Macaulay*, Sir William Temple.

(*b*) To increase in degree or volume, as heat or sound.

> The day was raw and chilly, and the temperature *rose* very little. *B. Taylor*, Northern Travel, p. 43.

> The music . . . *rose* again, . . .
> Storm'd in orbs of song, a growing gale.
> *Tennyson*, Vision of Sin.

(*c*) To increase in value; become higher in price; become dearer.

> Poor fellow, never joyed since the price of oats *rose*; it was the death of him. *Shak.*, 1 Hen. IV., ii. 1. 14.

> Bullion is *risen* to six shillings and five pence the ounce.
> *Locke*.

(*d*) To increase in amount: as, his expenses *rose* greatly.

9. To stand up in opposition; become opposed or hostile; take up arms; rebel; revolt: as, to *rise* against the government.

> The commons haply *rise*, to save his life.
> *Shak.*, 2 Hen. VI., iii. 1. 240.

> To hinder this prowd enterprise,
> The stout and michty Erle of Marr
> With all his men in arms did *ryse*.
> *Battle of Harlaw* (Child's Ballads, VII. 184).

> At our heels all hell should *rise*
> With blackest insurrection.
> *Milton*, P. L., ii. 136.

10. To take up a higher position; increase in wealth, dignity, or power; prosper; thrive; be promoted or exalted: as, he is a *rising* man.

> Some *rise* by sin, and some by virtue fall.
> *Shak.*, M. for M., ii. 1. 38.

> His fortune is not made,
> You hurt a man that 's *rising* in the trade.
> *Pope*, Epil. to Satires, ii. 35.

11. To become more forcible or impressive; increase in power, dignity, or interest: said of thought, discourse, or manner.

> *Dangle.* The interest rather falls off in the fifth act.
> *Sir Fretful.* *Rises*, I believe you mean, sir.
> *Sheridan*, The Critic, i. 1.

12. To come by chance; turn up; occur.

> There chaunced to the Princes hand to *rize*
> An auncient booke. *Spenser*, F. Q., II. ix. 59.

13. To arise from the grave or from the dead; be restored to life: often with *again*.

> Thou ne woldest leue thomas
> That oure lord fram deth *ras*.
> *King Horn* (E. E. T. S.), p. 98.

> Deed & lijf bigunne to striuen
> Whether myȝt be maister there;
> Liif was slayn, & *roos a-ȝen*.
> *Hymns to Virgin*, etc. (E. E. T. S.), p. 20.

> And vpon Ester day erely our blessyd Sauyoure come to hym and brought hym mete, sayenge, "Iames, nowe ete, for I am *rysyn*." *Sir R. Guylforde*, Pylgrymage, p. 33.

> Awake, ye faithful! throw your grave-clothes by,
> He whom ye seek is *risen*, bids ye *rise*.
> *Jones Very*, Poems, p. 77.

14. Of sound, to ascend in pitch; pass from a lower to a higher tone.

> Miss Abercrombie had a soft voice with melancholy cadences; her tones had no *rising* inflections; all her sentences died away. *Harper's Mag.*, LXXVIII. 243.

15. In *mining*, to excavate upward: the opposite of *sink*. Thus, a level may be connected with one above it by either sinking from the upper level to the lower one, or by *rising* from the lower to the upper.

16. To come to the surface or to the baited hook, as a whale or a game-fish.

> Where they have so much choice, you may easily imagine they will not be so eager and forward to *rise* at a bait.
> *Cotton*, in Walton's Angler, ii. 263.

17. *Milit.*, to be promoted; go up in rank.—**The curtain rises.** See *curtain*.—**To have the gorge rise.** See *gorge*.—**To rise from the ranks**, to win a commission, after serving in the ranks as a private soldier or a non-commissioned officer.—**To rise to the fly.** See *fly*[2].—**To rise to the occasion**, or **to the emergency**, to feel, speak, or act as an emergency demands; show one's self equal to a difficult task or to mastering a dilemma.

> "I should have walked over there every day, on the chance of seeing your pretty face!" answered the Dandy, *rising*, as he flattered himself, *to the occasion*.
> *Whyte Melville*, White Rose, I. vi.

=**Syn.** *Arise, Rise.* See *arise*.

II. *trans.* 1. To ascend; mount; climb.

> The carriage that took them to the station was *rising* a little hill the top of which would shut off the sight of the Priory. *R. G. White*, Fate of Mansfield Humphreys, viii.

2. In *angling*, to cause or induce to rise, as a fish.

> Some men, having once *risen* a fish, are tempted to flog the water in which he is with fly after fly.
> *Quarterly Rev.*, CXXVI. 349.

3. *Naut.*, to cause, by approaching, to rise into view above the horizon. Compare *raise*[1], 11.

> She was heading S. E., and we were heading S. S. W., and consequently before I quitted the deck we had *risen* her hull. *W. C. Russell*, Sailor's Sweetheart, v.

rise[1] (rīz), *n.* [First in mod. E.; < *rise*[1], *v.*] 1. The act of rising; ascent: as, the *rise* of vapor in the air; the *rise* of water in a river; the *rise* of mercury in a barometer.

> The steed along the drawbridge flies,
> Just as it trembled on the *rise*.
> *Scott*, Marmion, vi. 15.

2. Elevation; degree of ascent: as, the *rise* of a hill or a road.

> The approach to the house was by a gentle *rise* and through an avenue of noble trees.
> *Mark Lemon*, Wait for the End, I. 29.

3. Any place elevated above the common level; a rising ground: as, a *rise* of land.

> I turning saw, throned on a flowery *rise*,
> One sitting on a crimson scarf unroll'd.
> *Tennyson*, Fair Women.

> Laramie Jack led slightly, riding straight towards a tall branchless tree on the crest of the *rise* up which they were racing. *The Century*, XXXIX. 527.

4. Spring; source; origin; beginning: as, the *rise* of a stream in a mountain.

He observes very well that musical instruments took their first *rise* from the notes of birds and other melodious animals. *Addison*, The Cat-Call.

The Stories that Apparitions have been seen oftner than once in the same Place have no Doubt been the *Rise* and Spring of the walking Places of Spirits. *Bourne's Pop. Antiq.* (1777), p. 100.

It is true that genius takes its *rise* out of the mountains of rectitude. *Emerson*, Conduct of Life.

5. Appearance above the horizon: as, the *rise* of the sun or a star.

From the *rise* to set
Sweats in the eye of Phœbus, and all night
Sleeps in Elysium. *Shak.*, Hen. V., iv. 1. 289.

Long Isaac proposed waiting until midnight for moon-*rise*, as it was already dark, and there was no track beyond Lippajarvi. *B. Taylor*, Northern Travel, p. 118.

6. Increase; advance: said of price: as, a *rise* in (the price of) stocks or wheat.

Eighteen bob a-week, and a *rise* if he behaved himself. *Dickens*, Pickwick, liii.

7. Elevation in rank, reputation, wealth, or importance; mental or moral elevation.

Wrinkled benchers often talk'd of him
Approvingly, and prophesied his *rise*. *Tennyson*, Aylmer's Field.

8. Increase of sound; swell.

His mind
. . . borne perhaps upon the *rise*
And long roll of the Hexameter. *Tennyson*, Lucretius.

9. Height to which one can rise mentally or spiritually; elevation possible to thought or feeling.

These were sublimities above the *rise* of the apostolic spirit. *South.*

10. In *sporting*, the distance from the score-line to the traps in glass-ball- or pigeon-shooting matches.—11. In *arch.*, the perpendicular height of an arch in the clear, from the level of impost to the crown. See *arch*1, 2.—12. In *music*: (*a*) Increase of sound or force in a tone. (*b*) Ascent in pitch; passage from a lower to a higher tone.—13. In *coal-mining*, the inclination of strata considered from below upward. Thus, a seam of coal is said to be worked "to the *rise*" when it is followed upward on its inclination.—14. In *mining*, an excavation begun from below and carried upward, as in connecting one level with another, or in proving the ground above a level. Also called *rising*.—15. In *carp.*, the height of a step in a flight of stairs.—16. The action of a game-fish in coming to the surface to take the hook.

If you can attain to angle with one hair, you shall have more *rises*, and catch more fish. *I. Walton*, Complete Angler, p. 102.

Rise of strata, in *geol.* See *dip*, *n.*, 4 (*a*).—**To get** or **take a rise out of** (a person), to take the conceit out of a person, or to render him ridiculous. [Colloq. or slang.]

Possibly *taking a rise out of* his worship the Corregidor, as a repeating echo of Don Quixote. *De Quincey*, Spanish Nun.

To give rise. See *give*1.

rise2 (ris), *n.* [Also rice, Sc. *reise*; < ME. *ris*, *rys*, < AS. *hris*, a twig, branch, = D. *rijs* = OHG. *hrīs*, *ris*, MHG. *ris*, G. reis = Icel. *hrīs* = Sw. Dan. *ris*, a twig, branch, rod.] 1. A branch of a tree; a twig.

And therupon he hadde a gay sarplys,
As whit as is the blosme upon the *rys*. *Chaucer*, Miller's Tale, l. 138.

Anone he lokyd hym besyde,
And say syxty ladés on palferays ryde,
Gentyll and gay as bryd on *ryse*. *MS. Ashmole* 61, 15th Cent. (*Halliwell.*)

Among Lydgate's cries are enumerated "Strawberries ripe and cherries in the *rise*"; the *rise* being a twig to which the cherries were tied, as at present. *Mayhew*, London Labour and London Poor, I. 10.

2. A small bush.

"It was that deevil's buckie, Callum Beg," said Alick; "I saw him whisk away through amang the *reises*." *Scott*, Waverley, lviii.

rise-bush (ris'bûsh), *n.* [< *rise*2 + *bush*1.] A fagot; brushwood.

The streets were barricaded up with chaines, harrowes, and waggons of bavins or *rise-bushes*. *Relation of Action before Cyrencester* (1642), p. 4. (*Davies.*)

rise-dike (ris'dik), *n.* [< rise2 + *dike*.] A hedge made of boughs and brushwood. *Halliwell.*

risel, *n.* A support for a climbing or running vine.

The blankest, barest wall in the world is good enough for ivy to cling to. . . . But the healthiest hop or scarlet runner won't grow without what we call a *risel*. *D. Christie Murray*, The Weaker Vessel, xxxvi.

risen (riz'n). 1. Past participle of *rise*1.—2†. An obsolete preterit plural of *rise*1.

riser (rī'zėr), *n.* One who or that which rises. Specifically—(*a*) One who leaves his bed: generally with a qualifying word.

Th' early *riser* with the rosy hands,
Active Aurora. *Chapman*, Odyssey, xii. 4.

Such picturesque objects . . . as were familiar to an early *riser*. *Sir E. Brydges*, Note on Milton's L'Allegro, l. 67.

(*b*) One who revolts; a rebel or rioter.

The noyse that was telde of zow, that ze schuld a be on of the capetayns of the *ryserse* in Norfolk. *Paston Letters*, I. 86.

(*c*) In *angling*, a fish considered with reference to its manner of rising.

All the fish, to whichever class of *risers* they might belong. *Three in Norway*, p. 123.

(*d*) In *founding*: (1) An opening in a molding-flask into which the molten metal rises as the flask is filled; a head.

It is well known that, to obtain a sound casting in steel, with most methods in use, a very high *riser* is necessary, which also means a high gate, and consequent waste of labor and material. *Sci. Amer.*, N. S., LIX. 88.

(2) Same as *feed-head*, 2. (*e*) The vertical face of a stair-step. Also *raiser* and *lift*.

The *risers* of these stairs . . . are all richly ornamented, being divided generally into two panels by figures of dwarfs, and framed by foliaged borders. *J. Fergusson*, Hist. Indian Arch., p. 198.

(*f*) *pl.* In *printing*, blocks of wood or metal upon which electrotype plates are mounted to raise them to the height of type. [Eng.]

rise-wood (ris'wůd), *n.* [< *rise*2 + *wood*1.] Small wood cut for hedging. *Halliwell.* [Prov. Eng.]

rish1 (rish), *n.* and *v.* An obsolete or dialectal form of *rush*1.

rish2†, *n.* [Origin obscure.] A sickle. *Nominale MS.* (*Halliwell.*)

rishi (rish'i), *n.* [Skt. *rishi*; derivation unknown.] In *Skt. myth.*, an inspired sage or poet; the author of a Vedic hymn.—**The seven rishis**, the stars of the Great Bear.

risibility (riz-i-bil'i-ti), *n.*; pl. *risibilities* (-tiz). [= F. *risibilité* = Sp. *risibilidad* = Pg. *risibilidade* = It. *risibilità*, < LL. as if **risibilita(t-)s*, < *risibilis*, risible: see *risible*.] 1. The property of being risible; disposition to laugh.

To be religious is, therefore, more adequate to his character than either polity, society, *risibility*, without which he were no reasonable creature, but a mere brute, the very worst of the kind. *Evelyn*, True Religion, I. 200.

Her too obvious disposition to *risibility*. *Scott*, Guy Mannering, xx.

2. *pl.* The faculty of laughing; a sense of the ludicrous. Also *risibles*.

risible (riz'i-bl), *a.* and *n.* [< OF. (and F.) *risible* = Sp. *risible* = Pg. *risivel* = It. *risibile*, laughable, < LL. *risibilis*, that can laugh, < L. *ridere*, pp. *risus*, laugh: see *rident*, *ridicule*.] I. *a.* 1. Having the faculty or power of laughing.

We are in a merry world; laughing is our business, as if, because it has been made the definition of man that he is *risible*, his manhood consisteth of nothing else. *Government of the Tongue.*

2. Laughable; capable of exciting laughter; ridiculous.

For a terse point, a happy surprise, or a *risible* quibble, there is no man in this town can match little Laconic. *Foote*, An Occasional Prelude.

A few wild blunders, and *risible* absurdities, from which no work of such multiplicity was ever free. *Johnson*, Pref. to Dictionary.

The denunciations of Leicester . . . would seem almost *risible*, were it not that the capricious wrath of the all-powerful favorite was often sufficient to blast the character . . . of honest men. *Motley*, Hist. Netherlands, II. 279, note.

3. Of or pertaining to laughter; exerted to produce laughter: as, the *risible* faculty.

The obstreperous peals of broad-mouthed laughter of the Dutch negroes at Communipaw, who, like most other negroes, are famous for their *risible* powers. *Irving*, Knickerbocker, p. 98.

II. *n. pl.* Same as *risibilities*. See *risibility*, 2. [Jocular.]

Something in his tone stirred the *risibles* of the convention, and loud laughter saluted the Illinoisan. *The Century*, XXXVIII. 285.

risibleness (riz'i-bl-nes), *n.* Same as *risibility*. *Bailey*, 1727.

risibly (riz'i-bli), *adv.* In a risible manner; laughably.

risilabialis (ri-si-lā-bi-ā'lis), *n.*; pl. *risilabiales* (-lēz). [NL., < L. *ridere*, pp. *risus*, laugh, + *labium*, lip: see *labial*.] Same as *risorius*.

rising (rī'zing), *n.* [< ME. *risinge*, *rysynge*; verbal n. of *rise*1, *v.*] 1. The act of one who or that which rises.

Men that are in hopes and in the way of *rising* keep in the Channel. *Selden*, Table-Talk, p. 96.

A Saxon nobleman and his falconer, with their hawks, upon the bank of a river, waiting for the *rising* of the game. *Strutt*, Sports and Pastimes, p. 88.

Specifically—(*a*) The appearance of the sun or a star above the horizon. In astronomy the sun or a planet is said to rise when the upper limb appears in the horizon; and in calculating the time allowance must be made for refraction, parallax, and the dip of the horizon. Primitive astronomers defined the seasons by means of the risings and settings of certain stars relatively to the sun. These, called by Kepler "poetical risings and settings," are the acronychal, cosmical, and heliacal (see these words).

We alone of all animals have known the *risings*, settings, and courses of the stars. *Derham*, Astrotheology, viii. 3.

(*b*) The act of arising from the dead, or of coming to life again; resurrection.

Questioning one with another what the *rising* from the dead should mean. Mark ix. 10.

Then of the moral instinct would she prate,
And of the *rising* from the dead. *Tennyson*, Palace of Art.

(*c*) A hostile demonstration of people opposed to the government; a revolt; an insurrection; sedition: as, to call out troops to quell a *rising*.

There was a *rising* now in Kent, my Lord of Norwich being at the head of them. *Evelyn*, Diary, May 30, 1648.

In 1536, even a great religious movement like the Pilgrimage of Grace sinks into a local and provincial *rising*, an abortive tumult. *Stubbs*, Medieval and Modern Hist., p. 253.

The futile *risings*, the cruel reprisals, the heroic deaths, kept alive among the people the belief in the cause of Italy. *E. Dicey*, Victor Emmanuel, p. 63.

2. That which rises; a prominence, elevation, or swelling; specifically, a tumor on the body, as a boil or a wen. [Now colloq. or dialectal.]

When a man shall have in the skin of his flesh a *rising*, a scab, or bright spot, and it be in the skin of his flesh like the plague of leprosy, then he shall be brought unto Aaron the priest, or unto one of his sons the priests. Lev. xiii. 2.

On each foot there are five flat horny *risings*, which seem to be the extremities of the toes. *Goldsmith*, Hist. of Earth (ed. 1790), IV. 254. (*Jodrell.*)

3. In *mining*, same as *rise*1, 14.—4. A giving way in an upward direction from pressure exerted from beneath.

The only danger to be feared [in domes] is what is technically called a *rising* of the haunches; and to avoid this it might be necessary, where large domes were attempted, to adopt a form more nearly conical than that used at Mycenæ. *J. Fergusson*, Hist. Arch., I. 236.

5. That which is used to make dough rise, as yeast or leaven. See *salt-rising*. [Prov. Eng. and U. S.]

It behoveth my wits to worke like barme, alias yeast, alias sizing, alias *rising*. *Lyly*, Mother Bombie, ii. 1.

So strong is it [alkali] that the earth when wet rises like bread under yeast. It taints the water everywhere, and sometimes so strongly that bread mixed with it needs no other *rising*. *S. Bowles*, Our New West, xiv.

6. In *bread-making*, the quantity of dough set to rise at one time.—7. A defect sometimes occurring in casting crucible steel, which is said to "boil" in the mold after teeming, producing a honeycomb structure of the metal.

The *rising* of steel, and consequently the formation of blow-holes, is attributed to hydrogen and nitrogen, and to a small extent to carbonic oxide. *The Ironmonger*, quoted in Science, IV. 331.

8. A water-swelling: said of ova by fish-culturists.—9. *Naut.*, the thick planking laid fore and aft, on which the timbers of the deck bear; also, the narrow strake inside a boat just under the thwarts.—**The rising of the sun**, in *Scrip.*, the place where the sun appears to rise; the extreme eastern limit of the world; the orient.

From *the rising of the sun* even to the going down of the same, my name shall be great among the Gentiles. Mal. i. 11.

rising (rī'zing), *p. a.* [Ppr. of *rise*1, *v.*] 1. Increasing in possessions, importance, power, or distinction: as, a *rising* town; a *rising* man.

Feign what I will, and paint it e'er so strong,
Some *rising* genius sins up to my song. *Pope*, Epilogue to Satires, ii. 9.

2. Growing; advancing to adult years, and to the state of active life: as, the *rising* generation.—3. Growing so as to be near some specified or indicated amount: used loosely in an awkward quasi-adverbial construction: (*a*) reaching an amount greater than that specified: sometimes with *of*: as, *rising* three years old; *rising of* a thousand men were killed; the colt is *rising of* two this grass [U. S.]; (*b*) reaching an amount which is at least that specified and may be greater: as, a horse *rising* fourteen hands; (*c*) approaching but not yet reaching the specified amount: as, a colt *rising* two years old [Eng.].

A house is never perfectly furnished for enjoyment unless there is a child in it *rising* three years old, and a kitten *rising* three weeks. *Southey*, quoted in Allibone's Dict. of Quots., p. 102.

Rising butt. See *butt*2.—**Rising hinge.** See *hinge*.—**Rising line**, an incurvated line drawn on the plane of elevations or sheer drafts of a ship, to determine the height of the ends of all the floor-timbers.—**Rising timbers**, or **rising floors**, the floor-timbers in the forward and after parts of a ship.

rising-anvil (rī'zing-an'vil), *n.* In *sheet-metal working*, a double-beak iron.

rising-lark (rī'zing-lärk), *n.* The skylark, *Alauda arvensis.* [Prov. Eng.]

rising-line (rī'zing-līn), *n.* An elliptical line drawn upon the sheer-plan to determine the sweep of the floor-heads throughout the ship's length. *Hamersly,* Naval Encyc.

rising-main (rī'zing-mān), *n.* In a mine, the column of pumps through which water is lifted or forced to the surface or adit: usually made of cast-iron pipes joined together.

rising-rod (rī'zing-rod), *n.* A rod operating the valves in a Cornish pumping-engine.

rising-seat (rī'zing-sēt), *n.* In a Friends' meeting-house, one of a series of three or four seats, each raised a little above the one before it, and all facing the body of the congregation. These seats are usually occupied by ministers and elders. They are often collectively called "the gallery." Also *facing-seat, high seat.*

In the sing-song drawl once peculiar to the tuneful exhortations of the *rising seat* he thus held forth.
M. C. Lee, A Quaker Girl of Nantucket, p. 28.

rising-square (rī'zing-skwãr), *n.* In *ship-building,* a square upon which is marked the height of the rising-line above the keel. [Eng.]

rising-wood (rī'zing-wụd), *n.* In *ship-building,* timber placed under the flooring when the extremities of a vessel are very fine and extend beyond the cant-body.

risk1 (risk), *n.* [Formerly also *risque;* < OF. *risque,* F. *risque* = Pr. *rezegue* = Sp. *riesgo* = Pg. *risco* = It. *risico* (> D. G. Sw. Dan. *risiko*), formerly also *risigo,* dial. *resega* (ML. *risigus, riscus*), risk, hazard, peril, danger; perhaps orig. Sp., < Sp. *risco,* a steep, abrupt rock, = Pg. *risco,* a rock, crag (cf. It. *risega,* f., a jutting out) (hence the verb, Sp. *arriesgar,* formerly *arriscar,* venture into danger (pp. *arriscado,* bold, forward), = It. *arrischiarsi,* risk (pp. *arrischiato,* hazardous)); from the verb represented by It. *resegare, risecare,* cut off, = Pr. *rezega,* cut off, = Pg. *riscar,* erase, < L. *resecare,* cut off, < *re-,* back, + *secare,* cut: see *secant.*] 1. Hazard; danger; peril; exposure to mischance or harm; venture: as, at the *risk* of one's life; at the *risk* of contagion. Common in the phrase *to run a (the) risk,* to incur hazard; take the chance of failure or disaster.

If you had not performed the Vow, what *Risque had you run?* *N. Bailey,* tr. of Colloquies of Erasmus, II. 3.

If he [the Arab] had left me, I should have *run a great risque* of being stript, for people came to the gate before it was open. *Pococke,* Description of the East, II. i. 7.

Where there is *risk,* there may be loss.
Sterne, Sentimental Journey, p. 44.

Indulging their passions in defiance of divine laws, and at the *risk* of awful penalties. *Macaulay,* Hist. Eng., vi.

2. In *com.:* (*a*) The hazard of loss of ship, goods, or other property. (*b*) The degree of hazard or danger upon which the premiums of insurance are calculated.

It would take a great many years to determine tornado *risks* with sufficient accuracy to estimate the amount of premium needed; but we can make a comparison with the *risks* and losses by fire, and thus arrive at an approximate solution of the question. *Science,* XVI. 19.

(*c*) Hence, by extension, insurance obligation: as, our company has no *risks* in that city. =**Syn.** 1. *Exposure, Venture, Risk, Hazard,* jeopardy, peril. The first four words are in the order of strength. They imply voluntary action more often than *danger,* etc. (see *danger*): as, he ran a great *risk;* it was a bold *venture,* involving the *exposure* of his health and the *hazard* of his fortunes. They generally imply also that the chances are unfavorable rather than favorable. *Exposure* is, literally, a putting out, as into a dangerous place; the word is generally followed by that to which one is exposed: as, *exposure* to attack.

risk1 (risk), *v. t.* [Formerly *risque;* < OF. (and F.) *risquer,* risk; cf. Sp. *arriesgar,* formerly *arriscar,* venture into danger, = Pg. *arriscar* = It. *arrischiare,* run a risk; from the noun: see *risk1, n.*] 1. To hazard; expose to the chance of injury or loss.

There is little credit among the Turks, and it is very rare they trust one another to negotiate any business by bills, or *risque* their money in the hands of any one.
Pococke, Description of the East, I. 39.

This one fallen amongst them, who could make
The rich man *risk* his life for honour's sake.
William Morris, Earthly Paradise, III. 235.

2. To venture upon; take the chances of: as, to *risk* a surgical operation.

The other [party] must then *risque* an amercement.
Sir W. Jones, Dissertations and Miscell. Pieces, p. 388.

Nor had Emana Christos forces enough to *risk* a battle with an officer of the known experience of Af Christos.
Bruce, Source of the Nile, II. 335.

=**Syn.** 1. To peril, jeopard, stake. See *risk1, n.*

risk2 (risk), *n.* Same as *reesk* and *risp3.* [Scotch.]

risker (ris'kėr), *n.* One who risks, ventures, or hazards.

Hither came t' observe and smoke
What courses other *riskers* took;
And to the utmost do his best
To save himself, and hang the rest.
S. Butler, Hudibras, III. ii. 418.

riskful (risk'fụl), *a.* [< *risk1* + *-ful.*] Full of risk or danger; hazardous; risky. [Rare.]

At the first glance such an attempt to reverse the relationship between population and railways appears a *riskful* undertaking. *Fortnightly Rev.,* N. S., XXXIX. 55.

risky (ris'ki), *a.* [< *risk1* + *-y1.*] 1. Attended with risk; hazardous; dangerous: as, a very *risky* business.

No young lady in Miss Verinder's position could manage such a *risky* matter as that by herself.
W. Collins, Moonstone, i. 20.

2. Running a risk; venturesome; bold; audacious.

I am no mortal, if the *risky* devils haven't swam down upon the very pitch, and, as bad luck would have it, they have hit the head of the island.
Cooper, Last of the Mohicans, vii.

In spite of all his *risky* passages and all his tender expressions, Galiani wrote for posthumous publication, to the terror of Madame d'Epinay, who had made him her confidant. *Fortnightly Rev.,* N. S., XLIII. 350.

risoluto (rē-zọ-lö'tọ̄), *a.* [It., = E. *resolute.*] In *music,* with resolution or firmness.

risorial (rī-sō'ri-al), *a.* [< NL. *risorius,* laughing (< L. *risor,* laugher, mocker, < *ridere,* laugh: see *rident*), + *-al.*] Of or pertaining to laughter; causing laughter, or effecting the act of laughing; exciting risibility; risible: as, the *risorial* muscle.

risorius (rī-sō'ri-us), *n.;* pl. *risorii* (-ī). [NL. (sc. *musculus*) *risorial.*] The laughing-muscle, some transverse fibers of the platysma that are inserted into the angle of the mouth: more fully called *risorius Santorini.* Also *risilabialis.*

risp1 (risp), *v. t.* [Also *resp;* < Icel. *rispa,* scratch. Cf. *rasp1, v.*] 1. To rasp; file.—2. To rub or grate (hard bodies, as the teeth) together. [Scotch in both uses.]

risp1 (risp), *n.* [< *risp1, v.* Cf. *rasp1, n.*] A rasp. [Scotch.]

risp2 (risp), *n.* [Appar. a var. of *rise2;* cf. *risp3.*] 1. A bush or branch; a twig. *Halliwell.* [Prov. Eng.]—2. The green stalks collectively of growing peas or potatoes. *Halliwell.* [Prov. Eng.]

risp3 (risp), *n.* [Var. of *risk2, reesk.*] Coarse grass that grows on marshy ground.

The hay-rope . . . was made of *risp,* a sort of long sword-grass that grows about marshes and the sides of lakes.
Blackwood's Mag., XIV. 190.

risposta (ris-pos'tä), *n.* [It., < *rispondere,* respond: see *respond, response.*] In *contrapuntal music,* same as *answer.*

risque†, *n.* and *v.* An obsolete spelling of *risk1.*

Rissa (ris'ä), *n.* [NL. (Leach's MSS., Stephens, in Shaw's "General Zoölogy," 1825).] A genus of *Laridæ,* having the hind toe rudimentary or very small; the kittiwakes. There are at least two species, *R. tridactyla,* the common kittiwake of the arctic and North Atlantic oceans, and the very different red-legged kittiwake, *R. brevirostris,* of the North Pacific. See cut under *kittiwake.* Also called *Gavia.*

risse†. An obsolete past participle of *rise1.*

Rissoa (ris'ọ̄-ä), *n.* [NL., after *Risso,* a naturalist of Nice.] A genus of small shells, typical of the family *Rissoidæ.* Also *Rissoia.*

Rissoella (ris-ọ̄-el'ä), *n.* [NL., < *Risso* + dim. *-ella.*] A genus of gastropods. Also called *Jeffreysia.*

Rissoellidæ (ris-ọ̄-el'i-dē), *n. pl.* [NL., < *Rissoella* + *-idæ.*] A family of tænioglossate gastropods, typified by the genus *Rissoella.* Also called *Jeffreysiidæ.*

rissoid (ris'oid), *a.* and *n.* I. *a.* Of or related to the *Rissoidæ.*

II. *n.* A gastropod of the family *Rissoidæ.*

Rissoidæ (ri-sō'i-dē), *n. pl.* [NL., < *Rissoa* + *-idæ.*] A family of tænioglossate gastropods, typified by the genus *Rissoa.* The animal has long tentacles with the eyes external at their base, and the central tooth multicuspidate and with basal denticles; the shell is turbinate or turreted, with an oval or semilunate aperture, and the operculum is corneous and paucispiral. The species are phytophagous and abound in seaweed.

rissole (ris'ōl), *n.* [< F. *rissole,* F. dial. *risole, rezole,* a rissole, formerly *rissolle,* "a Jews ear, or mushrom that's fashioned like a demi-circle, and grows cleaving to trees; also a small and delicate minced pie, made of that fashion" (Cotgrave); cf. *rissole,* browuness from frying; < *rissoler,* fry brown, F. dial. *roussoler* = It. *rosolare,* fry, roast; origin uncertain.] In *cookery,* an entrée consisting of meat or fish compounded with bread-crumbs and yolk of eggs, all wrapped in a fine puff-paste, so as to resemble a sausage, and fried.

rist (rist), *v.* 1. An obsolete or dialectal preterit of *rise1.*—2†. Third person singular present indicative of *rise1* (contracted from *riseth*). *Chaucer.*

riste†, *n.* and *v.* A Middle English form of *rest1.*

ristori (ris-tō'ri), *n.* [So named from Madame *Ristori,* an Italian tragic actress.] A loose open jacket for women, usually of silk or some rather thick material.

risus (rī'sus), *n.* [NL., < L. *risus,* laughter, < *ridere,* pp. *risus,* laugh: see *rident.*] A laugh, or the act of laughing; a grin.—**Risus sardonicus** or **caninus,** a spasmodic grin seen in tetanus.

rit1 (rit), *v. t.* or *i.* [< ME. *ritte, ritten* (pret. *ritte*), tear, break, split (*to-ritten,* tear apart), < D. *ritten,* tear, = OHG. *rizzân, rizzōn,* MHG. G. *ritzen,* tear, wound, lacerate; a secondary verb, akin to AS. *wrītan,* E. *write:* see *write.*] 1†. To tear; break; rend; strike.

Young Johnstone had a nut-brown sword, . . .
And he *ritted* it through the young Col'nel,
That word he ne'er spake mair.
Young Johnstone (Child's Ballads, II. 292).

2. To make an incision in the ground, with a spade or other instrument, as a line of direction for future delving or digging; rip; scratch; cut. [Scotch.]

rit1 (rit), *n.* [< *rit1, v.*] A slight incision made in the ground, as with a spade; a scratch made on a board, etc. [Scotch.]

Ye scart the land with a bit thing ye ca' a pleugh—ye might as weel give it a *ritt* with the teeth of a redding-kame. *Scott,* Pirate, xv.

rit2 (rit), *v. t.* [Prob. a var. of *ret1.*] To dry (hemp or flax). *Halliwell.* [Prov. Eng.]

rit3†, *v.* A Middle English form of the third person singular present indicative of *ride* (contracted from *rideth*). *Chaucer.*

ritardando (rē-tär-dän'dọ̄), *a.* [< It. *ritardando,* ppr. of *ritardare,* retard: see *retard.*] In *music,* becoming gradually slower; diminishing in speed: same as *rallentando* and (usually) *ritenuto* (but see the latter). Abbreviated *rit.* and *ritard.*

ritardo (ri-tär'dọ̄), *a.* [It., < *ritardare,* retard: see *retard.*] Same as *ritardando.*

ritch (rich), *n.* The Syrian bear, *Ursus syriacus.*

rite (rīt), *n.* [= F. *rit, rite* = Sp. Pg. It. *rito,* < L. *ritus,* a custom, esp. religious custom; cf. Skt. *rīti,* a going, way, usage, < √ *ri,* flow, let flow.] 1. A formal act or series of acts of religious or other solemn service, performed according to a manner regularly established by law, precept, or custom.

Every Church hath Authority to appoint and change Ceremonies and Ecclesiastical *Rites,* so they be to Edification. *Baker,* Chronicles, p. 328.

When the prince her funeral *rites* had paid,
He ploughed the Tyrrhene seas.
Dryden, Æneid, vii. 7.

2. The manner or form prescribed for such an act; a ceremonial. Hence—3. Any ceremony or due observance.

Time goes on crutches till love have all his *rites.*
Shak., Much Ado, ii. 1. 373.

How shall I
Pass, where in piles Carnavian cheeses lie;
Cheese, that the table's closing *rites* denies,
And bids me with th' unwilling chaplain rise?
Gay, Trivia, ii. 255.

Ambrosian rite, the Ambrosian office and liturgy.—**Congregation of Rites.** See *congregation,* 6 (*a*).—**Mozarabic rite.** See *Mozarabic.* =**Syn.** *Form, Observance,* etc. See *ceremony.*

ritely† (rīt'li), *adv.* [< *rite* + *-ly2.*] With all due rites; in accordance with the ritual; in due form.

After the minister of the holy mysteries hath *ritely* prayed. *Jer. Taylor,* Real Presence. (*Latham.*)

ritenuto (rē-te-nö'tọ̄), *a.* [< It. *ritenuto,* pp. of *ritenere,* retain: see *retain, re-, tenable.*] In *music,* at a slower tempo or pace. *Ritenuto* sometimes has the same sense as *rallentando* and *ritardando,* but is used more exactly to mark an abrupt instead of a gradual change of speed. Also *ritenendo, ritenente.* Abbreviated *riten.*

rith1†, *n.* A Middle English form of *rithe1.*

rith2†, *a.* An awkward Middle English spelling of *right.* *Chaucer.*

rithe1 (riᴛʜ), *n.* [Formerly also *ryth;* < ME. *rithe,* < AS. *rith, rithe,* a stream (*eá-rith,* a stream of water; *wæter-rithe,* water-stream), also *rithig,* a stream, = North Fries. *ride, rie,* the bed of a stream, = OLG. *rith,* a stream (used in proper names).] A stream; a small stream, usually one occasioned by heavy rain. *Halliwell.* [Prov. Eng.]

rithe2 (riᴛʜ), *n.* [Perhaps a corruption of *rise2.*] A stalk of the potato. *Halliwell.* [Prov. Eng.]

rither[1] (riᴛʜ'ėr), *n.* A dialectal form of *rudder*[1].

He jumpeth and courseth this way and that way, as a man roving without a mark, or a ship fleeting without a *rither*. *Bp. Jewell*, Works (Parker Soc.), III. 156.

rither[2] (riᴛʜ'ėr), *n.* A dialectal form of *rother*[2].

ritling (rit'ling), *n.* Same as *reckling*.

ritornelle, ritornello (rē-tôr-nel', rē-tôr-nel'lō), *n.* [= F. *ritournelle*, < It. *ritornello*, dim. of *ritorno*, a return, a refrain: see *return*[1].] In *music*, an instrumental prelude, interlude, or refrain belonging to a vocal work, like a song, aria, or chorus; also, one of the tutti passages in an instrumental concerto. Also formerly called a *symphony*.

ritratto† (ri-trat'tō), *n.* [It.: see *retrait*.] A picture.

Let not this *ritratto* of a large landscape be thought trifling. *Roger North*, Examen, p. 251. (*Davies.*)

ritter (rit'ėr), *n.* [< G. *ritter*, a rider, knight: see *rider*.] A knight.

Your Duke's old father
Met with th' assailants, and their grove of *ritters*
Repulsed so fiercely.
Chapman, Byron's Conspiracy, ii. 1.

The *Ritter's* colour went and came.
Campbell, The Ritter Bann.

Ritteric (rit'ėr-ik), *a.* [< *Ritter* (see def.) + *-ic*.] Pertaining to or named after Dr. J. W. Ritter (1776–1810).—**Ritteric rays**, the invisible ultra-violet rays of the spectrum. See *spectrum*.

Ritter-Valli law. The statement of the centrifugal progress of an initial increase followed by loss of irritability in the distal part of a divided nerve.

rittingerite (rit'ing-ėr-īt), *n.* [< *Rittinger*, the name of an Austrian mining official, + *-ite*[2].] A rare mineral occurring in small tabular monoclinic crystals of a nearly black color. It contains arsenic, sulphur, selenium, and silver, but its exact composition is not known.

Rittinger's side-blow percussion-table. See *jogging-table*.

ritt-master (rit'mås'tėr), *n.* [< G. *rittmeister*, a captain of cavalry, < *ritt*, a riding, + *meister*, master: see *master*[1].] A captain of cavalry.

Duke Hamilton was only *Ritt-master* Hamilton, as the General used to call him; . . . Linlithgow was Colonel Livingstone. *Wodrow*, I. 271. (*Jamieson.*)

"If I understand you, Captain Dalgetty—I think that rank corresponds with your foreign title of *ritt-master* —." "The same grade preceesely," answered Dalgetty. *Scott*, Legend of Montrose, ii.

rittock (rit'ok), *n.* The common tern or sea-swallow. Also *rippock*. [Orkney.]

ritual (rit'ū-al), *a.* and *n.* [< OF. *ritual*, F. *rituel* = Sp. Pg. *ritual* = It. *rituale* = D. *ritual* = G. Sw. Dan. *ritual*, < L. *ritualis*, relating to rites (LL. neut. pl. *ritualia*, rites), < *ritus*, a rite: see *rite*.] **I.** *a.* Pertaining to, consisting of, or prescribing a rite or rites.

The first Religion that ever was reduced to exact Rules and *ritual* Observances was that of the Hebrews. *Howell*, Letters, ii. 8.

The *ritual* year
Of England's Church.
Wordsworth, Eccles. Sonnets, iii. 19.

II. *n.* **1.** A book containing the rites or ordinances of a church or of any special service. Specifically, in the Roman Catholic Church, the ritual is an office-book containing the offices to be used by a priest in administering the sacraments (baptism, marriage, penance, extreme unction, communion out of mass), together with the offices for the visitation of the sick, burial of the dead, benedictions, etc. The corresponding book in the medieval church in England was called the *manual*.

2. (*a*) A prescribed manner of performing religious worship or other devotional service in any given ecclesiastical or other organization.

Bishop Hugh de Nonant . . . enlarged the body of statutes which he found in his church for the government of its chapter and the regulation of its services and *ritual*. *Rock*, Church of our Fathers, i. 7.

(*b*) The external form prescribed for religious or other devotional services.

And come, whatever loves to weep,
And hear the *ritual* of the dead.
Tennyson, In Memoriam, xviii.

3. Any ceremonial form or custom of procedure.

False are our Words, and fickle is our Mind;
Nor in Love's *Ritual* can we ever find
Vows made to last, or Promises to bind.
Prior, Henry and Emma.

Ambrosian ritual. See *Ambrosian*[2].

ritualism (rit'ū-al-izm), *n.* [= F. *ritualisme*; as *ritual* + *-ism*.] **1.** A system of public worship which consists in forms regularly established by law, precept, or custom, as distinguished from that which is largely extemporaneous and therefore variable and left to the judgment of the conductor of the worship.

The typical Illustration of *ritualism*, and that to which it naturally reverts for its model, was the medieval cathedral, with its supposed reenactment of the great tragedy of the Cross, amid all the æsthetical influences of architecture, sculpture, painting, music, and eloquence. *The Century*, XXXI. 80.

2. Observance of prescribed forms in religious worship or in reverence of anything.

The Troubadour hailed the return of spring; but with him it was a piece of empty *ritualism*. *Lowell*, Study Windows, p. 280.

3. Specifically—(*a*) The science of ritual; the systematic study of liturgical rites. (*b*) An observance of ritual in public worship founded upon a high estimate of the value of symbolism and a belief in the practical importance of established rites, and particularly in the efficacy of sacraments, as having been divinely appointed to be channels of spiritual grace to those who use them; more especially, the principles and practices of those Anglicans who are called Ritualists.

ritualist (rit'ū-al-ist), *n.* and *a.* [= F. *ritualiste* = Sp. Pg. It. *ritualista*; as *ritual* + *-ist*.] **I.** *n.* **1.** One versed in or devoted to ritual; a specialist in the systematic study of liturgical rites and ceremonies; especially, a writer upon this subject.—**2.** One who advocates or practises distinctive sacramental and symbolic ritual, especially that inherited or revived from ancient usage; specifically [*cap.*], one of that branch of the High-church party in the Anglican Church which has revived the ritual authoritatively in use in the second year of King Edward VI. (see *ornaments rubric*, under *ornament*). The ritualistic movement is an extension of the Anglo-Catholic revival. (See *revival*.) The points especially insisted on by the Ritualists are the eastward position (declared legal in England), and the use of vestments, lights, wafer-bread, and the mixed chalice, to which some add that of incense.

II. *a.* Ritualistic.

ritualistic (rit'ū-a-lis'tik), *a.* [< *ritualist* + *-ic*.] **1.** Pertaining or according to ritual.—**2.** Adhering to rituals: often used to designate a devotion to external forms and symbols as of great importance in religious worship. Hence —**3.** Pertaining to or characteristic of the party called Ritualists in the Anglican Church. See *ritualist*, 2.

ritually (rit'ū-al-i), *adv.* By rites, or by a particular rite; by or with a ritual.

Whereto in some parts of this kingdom is joined also the solemnity of drinking out of a cup, *ritually* composed, decked, and filled with country liquor.
Selden, Illust. of Drayton's Polyolbion, ix. 417.

We can no ways better, or more solemnly and *ritually*, give glory to the holy Trinity than by being baptized.
Jer. Taylor, Works (ed. 1835), II. 255.

riva (rī'vä), *n.* [< Icel. *rifa*, a rift, cleft, fissure (*bjarg-rifa*, cleft in a mountain): see *rive*[1].] A rift or cleft. [Orkney and Shetland.]

He proceeded towards a *riva*, or cleft in a rock, containing a path, called Erick's steps. *Scott*, Pirate, vii.

rivage[1] (riv'āj), *n.* [< F. *rivage*, OF. *rivaige*, *rivage* = Pr. Cat. *ribatge* = It. *rivaggio*, < ML. *ripaticum* (also, after Rom., *rivaticus*, *ribaticus*), shore, < L. *ripa*, shore, bank: see *rive*[3], *river*[2].] **1.** A bank, shore, or coast.

And sir Gawein made serche all the *ryvages*, and take shippes and assembled a grete navie.
Merlin (E. E. T. S.), ii. 378.

Do but think
You stand upon the *rivage*, and behold
A city on the inconstant billows dancing.
Shak., Hen. V., iii. (cho.).

From the green *rivage* many a fall
Of diamond rillets musical.
Tennyson, Arabian Nights.

2. A toll formerly paid to the crown on some rivers for the passage of boats or vessels.

rivage[2]†, *n.* [ME. *ryvage*; an aphetic form of, or an error for, *arrivage*. Cf. *rive*[5].] Same as *arrivage*.

He . . . privoly toke a *ryvage* (var. *arryvage*)
In the contre of Cartage.
Chaucer, House of Fame, l. 223.

rivaille†, *n.* [ME., < OF. **rivaille*, < L. *ripa*, bank: see *rivage*[1].] A harbor.

And they in sothe comen to the *ryvaille*
At Suncourt, an havens of gret renoun.
MS. Digby 230. (*Halliwell.*)

rival (rī'val), *n.* and *a.* [< OF. (and F.) *rival*, a rival, competitor, = Sp. Pg. *rival* = It. *rivale* = D. G. Sw. Dan. *rival*, a rival, competitor, < L. *rivalis*, a rival in love, orig., in the pl. *rivales*, one who uses the same brook as another, prop. adj. *rivalis*, belonging to a brook, < *rivus*, a brook, stream: see *rivulet*.] **I.** *n.* **1**†. One having a common right or privilege with another; an associate; an alternating partner or companion in duty.

Well, good night:
If you do meet Horatio and Marcellus,
The *rivals* of my watch, bid them make haste.
Shak., Hamlet, i. 1. 12.

2. One who is in pursuit of the same object as another; one who strives to reach or obtain something which another is attempting to obtain, and which only one can possess; a competitor: as, *rivals* in love; *rivals* for a crown.

Oh, love! thou sternly dost thy pow'r maintain,
And wilt not bear a *rival* in thy reign. *Dryden.*

My lovers are at the feet of my *rivals*.
Steele, Spectator, No. 306.

3. One who emulates or strives to equal or exceed another in excellence; a competitor; an antagonist: as, two *rivals* in eloquence.

You both are rivals, and love Hermia;
And now both *rivals* to mock Helena.
Shak., M. N. D., iii. 2. 156.

=**Syn.** 2 and 3. See *emulation*.

II. *a.* Having the same pretensions or claims; standing in competition for superiority: as, *rival* lovers; *rival* claims or pretensions.

Even *rival* wits did Voiture's death deplore.
Pope, To Miss Blount.

I do not recommend German reviews as models for English ones; too often they seem to me to be written by *rival* competitors in the same field with the author.
Stubbs, Medieval and Modern Hist., p. 53.

rival (rī'val), *v.*; pret. and pp. *rivaled* or *rivalled*, ppr. *rivaling* or *rivalling*. [< *rival*, *n.*] **I.** *trans.* **1.** To stand in competition with; seek to gain something in opposition to: as, to *rival* one in love.—**2.** To strive to equal or excel; emulate.

To *rival* thunder in its rapid course.
Dryden, Æneid, vi. 798.

But would you sing, and *rival* Orpheus' strain,
The wondering forests soon should dance again.
Pope, Summer, l. 81.

II. *intrans.* To be a competitor; act as a rival. [Obsolete or archaic.]

My lord of Burgundy,
We first address towards you, who with this king
Hath *rivall'd* for our daughter. *Shak.*, Lear, i. 1. 194.

There was one giant on the staff (a man with some talent, when he chose to use it) with whom I very early perceived it was in vain to *rival*.
R. L. Stevenson, Scribner's Mag., IV. 124.

rivaless (rī'val-es), *n.* [< *rival* + *-ess*.] A female rival. [Rare.]

Oh, my happy *rivaless*! if you tear from me my husband, he is in his own disposal, and I cannot help it.
Richardson, Pamela, IV. 153. (*Davies.*)

rival-hating (rī'val-hā'ting), *a.* Hating any competitor; jealous.

Rival-hating envy. *Shak.*, Rich. II., i. 3. 131.

rivality (rī-val'i-ti), *n.* [< F. *rivalité* = Sp. *rivalidad* = Pg. *rivalidade* = It. *rivalità* = G. *rivalität*, < L. *rivalita(t-)s*, rivalship, < *rivalis*, rival: see *rival*.] **1**†. Association; equality; copartnership.

Cæsar, having made use of him in the wars 'gainst Pompey, presently denied him *rivality*, would not let him partake in the glory of the action.
Shak., A. and C., iii. 5. 8.

2. Rivalry. [Rare.]

I need fear
No check in his *rivality*, since her virtues
Are so renown'd, and he of all dames hated.
Chapman, Bussy d'Ambois, ii. 1.

Some, though a comparatively small, space must still be made for the fact of commercial *rivality*. *J. S. Mill.*

rivalize (rī'val-īz), *v. i.*; pret. and pp. *rivalized*, ppr. *rivalizing*. [= F. *rivaliser* = Sp. Pg. *rivalizar*; as *rival* + *-ize*.] To enter into rivalry; contend; compete. [Rare.]

Declaring himself a partisan of General Jackson, to *rivalize* with Mr. Calhoun for the Vice-Presidency.
John Quincy Adams, Diary, 1828.

rivalry (rī'val-ri), *n.*; pl. *rivalries* (-riz). [< *rival* + *-ry*.] The act of rivaling; competition; a strife or effort to obtain an object which another is pursuing: as, *rivalry* in love; an endeavor to equal or surpass another in some excellence; emulation: as, *rivalry* for superiority at the bar or in the senate.

And now commenced a tremendous *rivalry* between these two doughty commanders—striving to outstrut and outswell each other, like a couple of belligerent turkey-cocks. *Irving*, Knickerbocker, p. 322.

=**Syn.** *Competition*, etc. See *emulation*.

rivalship (rī'val-ship), *n.* [< *rival* + *-ship*.] The state or character of a rival; competition; contention for superiority; emulation; rivalry.

Rivalships have grown languid, animosities tame, inert, and inexcitable.
Landor, Imaginary Conversations, Southey and Porson, ii.

rivaye†, *v. i.* [ME., appar. < OF. **riveier*, hawk by the bank of a river, < *rive*, bank: see *rive*[4], *rive*[5], *river*[2].] To hawk.

I salle never *ryvaye*, ne racches un-cowpylle,
At roo ne rayne dere that rynnes apponne erthe.
Morte Arthure (E. E. T. S.), l. 4000.

rive[1] (rīv), *v.*; pret. *rived*, pp. *rived* or *riven*, ppr. *riving*. [< ME. *riven*, *ryven* (pret. *rof*, *roof*, *raf*, *ref*, pp. *riven*, *rifen*, *reven*), < Icel. *rifa* (pret. *rif*, pp. *rifinn*), rive, = Sw. *rifva* = Dan. *rive*, scratch, tear, = D. *rijven* = MLG. *riven*, grate, rake, = OHG. *riban*, MHG. *riben*, G. *reiben*, rub, grate (but the OHG. form may be for **wriban* = D. *wrijven* = MLG. *wriven*, LG. *wriven*, rub). Hardly allied to Gr. ἐρείπειν, throw or dash down, tear down, or ἐρείκειν, tear, break, rend, rive, = Skt. √ *rikh*, scratch. Hence *rive*[1], *n.*, *rift*[1], and ult. *rivel*, *rifle*[2], and perhaps *ribald*. Cf. *rip*[1], *ripple*[1].] **I.** *trans.* **1.** To split; cleave; rend asunder by force: as, to *rive* timber for rails, etc., with wedges; the oak is *riven*.

And [he] lifte vp the serpentes skyn, and *rof* hym thourgh the body with the swerde. *Merlin* (E. E. T. S.), iii. 649.

But it would have made your heart right sair . . .
To see the bridegroom *rive* his hair.
The Cruel Brother (Child's Ballads, II. 256).

The scolding winds
Have *rived* the knotty oaks.
Shak., *J. C.*, i. 3. 6.

2†. To cause to pierce; thrust.

This swerde thurgh thyn herte shal I *ryve*.
Chaucer, Good Women, l. 1793.

3†. To pierce; stab.

She *rof* [var. *roof*] hirselven to the herte.
Chaucer, House of Fame, l. 373.

But Guyon drove so furious and tell
That seemed both shield and plate it would have *riv'd*.
Spenser, F. Q., III. i. 6.

4. To explode; discharge. [Rare.]

Ten thousand French have ta'en the sacrament
To *rive* their dangerous artillery
Upon no Christian soul but English Talbot.
Shak., 1 Hen. VI., iv. 2. 29.

=**Syn. 1.** See *rend*[1].

II. *intrans.* **1.** To be split or rent asunder; fall apart.

Nought allone the sonne was mirke,
But howe youre vaile *raffe* in youre kirke,
That witte I wolde. *York Plays*, p. 401.

The soul and body *rive* not more in parting
Than greatness going off.
Shak., A. and C., iv. 13. 5.

There is such extreame colde in those parts that stones and trees doe euen *riue* asunder in regarde thereof.
Hakluyt's Voyages, I. 111.

The captain, . . . seeing Tinlinn . . . floundering in the bog, used these words of insult: "Sutor Watt, ye cannot sew your boots, the heels risp, and the seams *rive*."
Scott, L. of L. M., iv. 4, note.

rive[1] (rīv), *n.* [= Icel. *rifa*, a cleft, fissure; from the verb. Cf. *riva*.] **1.** A place torn; a rent; a tear. *Brockett.* [Prov. Eng.]—**2.** That which is torn, as with the teeth.

Our horses got nothing but a *rive* o' heather.
Hogg, Perils of Man, II. 246. (*Jamieson.*)

rive[2]**†**, *n.* [ME., < MD. *rijve* (= MHG. *rive*), a rake, < *rijven*, scrape, scratch: see *rive*[1].] A rake. *Nominale MS.* (*Halliwell.*)

rive[3] (rīv), *a.* An obsolete or dialectal form of *rife*[1].

rive[4] (rīv), *n.* [ME. *rive*, < OF. *rive*, < L. *ripa*, a bank of a stream, rarely the shore of the sea; of doubtful origin. Cf. Gr. ἐρίπνη, a broken cliff, scar, a steep edge or bank, < ἐρείπειν, tear down. From the L. *ripa* are also ult. E. *ripe*[3], *rive*[5], *arrive*, *rivage*[1], etc. See *river*[2].] Bank; shore.

Now bringeth me atte *rive*
Schip and other thing.
Sir Tristrem, p. 34. (*Jamieson.*)

rive[5]**†** (rīv), *v. i.* [< ME. *riven*, aphetic form of *ariven*, arrive: see *arrive*. Cf. OF. *river*, follow the edge or border of a stream, road, or wood, < *rive*, bank, edge: see *rive*[4].] **1.** To land; arrive.

That iche, lef and dere,
On londe am *rived* here.
MS. Laud. 108, f. 220. (Halliwell.)

2. To go; travel.

Then they *rived* east and they *rived* west
In many a strange country.
King Arthur and the King of Cornwall (Child's Ballads, I. [233).

rivel (riv'el), *v. t.*; pret. and pp. *riveled* or *rivelled*, ppr. *riveling* or *rivelling*. [< ME. *rivelen*, a freq. form, < AS. **rifian*, wrinkle, in pp. *ge-rifod* (in Somner also erroneously **gerifiod*, **gerifled*), wrinkled; prob. connected with *rive*: see *rive*[1] and cf. *rifle*[2].] To wrinkle; corrugate; shrink: as, *riveled* fruit; *riveled* flowers.

He lefte vp his heed, that was lothly and *rivelid*, and loked on high to hym with oon eye open and a-nother clos, . . . grennynge with his teth as a man that loked a-gein the sonne. *Merlin* (E. E. T. S.), ii. 262.

I'll give thee tackling made of *rivelled* gold,
Wound on the barks of odoriferous trees.
Marlowe and Nashe, Dido, iii. 1. 115.

Griefe, that sucks veines drie,
Rivels the skinne, casts ashes in mens faces.
Marston and Webster, Malcontent, ii. 3.

Ev'ry worm industriously weaves
And winds his web about the *rivell'd* leaves.
Cowper, Tirocinium, l. 596.

rivel† (riv'el), *n.* [< ME. *rivel*; < *rivel*, *v.*] A wrinkle. *Wyclif*, Job xvi. 8; *Huloet.*

riveling[1]**†** (riv'el-ing), *n.* [< ME. *riveling*; verbal n. of *rivel*, *v.*] A wrinkle.

To ghyue the chyrche glorious to hymsilf that it hadde no wem ne *ryueling* or ony such thing. *Wyclif*, Eph. v. 27.

riveling[2]**†**, *n.* [Also *reveling*, and dial. *rivlin*; OSc. *rewelyn*, etc.; < ME. *riveling*, *reviling* (> AF. *rivelings*), < AS. *rifeling*, a kind of shoe.] **1.** A rough kind of shoe or sandal of rawhide, formerly worn in Scotland.

Sum es left na thing
Boute his rivyn *riveling*.
Wright, Political Songs, p. 307. (*Encyc. Dict.*)

2. A Scotchman. [Contemptuous.]

Rugh-fute *reviling*, now kindels thi care,
Bere-bag with thi boote, thi biging es bare.
Wright, Polit. Poems and Songs, I. 62.

riven (riv'n), *p. a.* [Pp. of *rive*[1], *v.*] Split; rent or burst asunder.

The well-stack'd pile of *riven* logs and roots.
Cowper, Task, iv. 444.

river[1] (rī'vėr), *n.* [< *rive*[1] + *-er*[1].] One who rives or splits.

An honest block *river*, with his beetle, heartily calling.
J. Echard, Obs. on Ans. to Contempt of Clergy, p. 23.
[(*Latham.*)

river[2] (riv'ėr), *n.* [< ME. *river*, *rivere* (= D. *rivier*, river, = MHG. *rivier*, brook, *riviere*, *rivier*, *revier*, district), < OF. *riviere*, F. *rivière*, a river, stream, = Pr. *ribeira*, *ribayra*, shore, bank, plain, river, = Sp. *ribera*, shore, strand, sea-coast, = Pg. *ribeira*, a meadow near the bank of a river (*ribeiro*, a brook), = It. *riviera*, the sea-shore, a bank, also a river, < ML. *riparia*, a sea-shore or river-bank, a river, fem. of L. *riparius*, of or belonging to a bank, < *ripa*, a bank of a stream (rarely the coast of the sea): see *rive*[3]. The word *river* is not connected with the word *rivulet*.] **1.** A considerable body of water flowing with a perceptible current in a certain definite course or channel, and usually without cessation during the entire year. Some watercourses, however, are called *rivers* although their beds may be almost, or even entirely, dry during more or less of the year. As water must find its way downward, under the influence of gravity, wherever the opportunity is offered, most rivers reach the ocean, which is the lowest attainable level, either independently or by uniting with some other stream; but this process of joining and becoming merged in another river may be repeated several times before the main stream is finally reached. As a general rule, the river which heads furthest from the sea, or which has the longest course, retains its name, while the affluents entering it lose their identity when merged in the larger stream. There are various exceptions to this, one of the most remarkable of which is the Mississippi, which retains that name to its mouth, although the affluent called the Missouri is much longer than the Mississippi and somewhat larger at the junction. Asia, North America, and South America have "closed basins," or regions in which the surplus water does not find its way to the sea, for the reason that there evaporation is in excess of precipitation, so that the water cannot accumulate to a height sufficient to allow it to run over at the lowest point in the edge of the basin, and thus reach the sea. The water carried by rivers is rain or melted snow, a part of which runs on the surface to the nearest rivulet while the rain is falling, or immediately after it has fallen, while a larger part consists of that rain-water which, falling upon a permeable material, such as sand and gravel, sinks beneath the surface for a certain distance, and then makes its way to the nearest available river, more or less slowly according to the permeability of the superficial material, the extent to which it is saturated with water, and the nature and position of the impermeable beds, as of clay or crystalline rocks, which may underlie it. Were the surface everywhere entirely impermeable, the rainfall would be carried at once to the nearest rivers, and disastrous freshets would be the rule rather than the exception in regions of large rainfall. It is a matter of great importance that many of the largest rivers head in high mountain regions, where the precipitation is chiefly or entirely in the form of snow, which can melt only gradually, so that disastrous floods are thus prevented, while the winter's precipitation in many regions is stored away for summer's use, extensive tracts being thus made available for habitation which otherwise would be deserts. The size of a river depends chiefly on the orographical features and the amount of rainfall of the region through which it flows. Thus, the Amazon is the largest river in the world because the peculiar topography of South America causes the drainage of a vast region (over a million and a half square miles) to converge toward one central line, and because throughout the whole course of that river and its branches there is a region of very large rainfall. The Orinoco, although draining an area less than one fifth of that of the Amazon, is navigable for fully 1,000 miles, and is, when full, over three miles wide at 560 miles from its mouth, because it drains a region of extraordinarily large precipitation. The Missouri-Mississippi, on the other hand, although draining an area nearly as large as that of the Amazon, is very much inferior to that river in volume at its mouth, because it flows for a considerable part of its course through a region where the precipitation is very small, while it is not extraordinarily large in any part of the Mississippi basin. The area drained by any river is called its *basin*; but this term is not generally used except with reference to a river of considerable size, and then includes the main river and all its affluents. The edge of a river-basin is the watershed, in the United States frequently called the *divide*, and this may be a mountain-range or an entirely inconspicuous elevation of the surface. Thus, for a part of the distance, the divide between the Mississippi basin and that of the Great Lakes is quite imperceptible topographically. Exceptionally some large rivers (as the Amazon and Orinoco) inosculate with each other.

The *river* Rhine, it is well known,
Doth wash your city of Cologne.
Coleridge, Cologne.

In speaking of *rivers*, Americans commonly put the name before the word *river*, thus: Connecticut *river*, Charles *river*, Merrimack *river*; whereas the English would place the name after it, and say, the *river* Charles, &c. And when English writers copy from our geographers, they commonly make this alteration, as will be seen by referring to any of the English Gazetteers. *Pickering*, Vocab.

2. In *law*, a stream of flowing water, of greater magnitude than a rivulet or brook. It may be navigable or not; the right to use it may be purely public, or it may be private property; it may arise from streams, or constitute the outlet of a lake; it may be known by the appellation of *river* or by some other name — these particulars not being material to its legal character as a river. *Bishop.*

3. A large stream; copious flow; abundance: as, *rivers* of oil.

Rivers of blood I see, and hills of slain,
An Iliad rising out of one campaign.
Addison, The Campaign.

Flash, ye cities, in *rivers* of fire!
Tennyson, Welcome to Alexandra.

River and Harbor Bill, an appropriation bill generally passed in recent years by the United States Congress, for the improvement of navigable waters, the development of streams, etc., alleged to be suitable for navigation. In 1882, and again in 1896, such a bill was vetoed by the President on account of its extravagance, but it was passed over the veto. The amount appropriated increased from less than $4,000,000 in 1870 to about $25,000,000 in 1891; the average for the six years ending June 30, 1896, was $16,700,000.—**River Brethren**, a denomination of Baptists in the United States, which arose during the Revolution, and derived its origin from the Mennonites. It recognizes three orders of clergy, rejects infant baptism, and baptizes adults by a threefold immersion. Its other church ordinances are the communion, feet-washing, and the love-feast.—**To set the river on fire.** See *fire*.

riverain (riv'ėr-ān), *a.* [< F. *riverain*, pertaining to or dwelling on the banks of a river, < *rivière*, a river: see *river*[2].] Riparian.

Turkish authorities do not attempt to run their steamers up and down throughout the year, but content themselves with a few trips between Beles and Hillah while the river remains in flood from April to August, with the political object of controlling the *riverain* tribes rather than for purposes of commerce. *Encyc. Brit.*, VIII. 671.

98 per cent. of the entries in the tables were correct within 8 inches of actual heights at open coast stations, and 69 per cent. at *riverain* stations. *Nature*, XLI. 140.

river-bass (riv'ėr-bås), *n.* Any bass of the genus *Micropterus*.

river-bed (riv'ėr-bed), *n.* The channel in which a river flows.

river-birch (riv'ėr-bėrch), *n.* A moderate-sized tree, *Betula nigra*, common southward in the eastern half of the United States, growing chiefly along streams. Its wood is used in the manufacture of furniture, wooden ware, etc. Also *red birch*.

river-bottom (riv'ėr-bot"um), *n.* The alluvial land along the margin of a river. See *bottom*, 3. [U. S.]

river-bullhead (riv'ėr-bůl"hed), *n.* The miller's-thumb, *Cottus* or *Uranidea gobio*.

river-carp (riv'ėr-kärp), *n.* The common carp, *Cyprinus carpio*, as living in rivers: distinguished from *pond-carp*.

river-chub (riv'ėr-chub), *n.* A cyprinoid fish, the hornyhead or jerker, *Ceratichthys biguttatus*, widely distributed and abundant in the

River-chub (*Ceratichthys biguttatus*).

United States, attaining a length of from 6 to 9 inches. There are numerous fishes of the same genus which share the name.

river-crab (riv'ėr-krab), *n.* A fresh-water crab of the family *Thelphusidæ*, inhabiting rivers and lakes. It has a quadrate carapace and very short antennæ. *Thelphusa depressa* is a river-crab of southern Europe, much esteemed for food. It is often found figured on ancient Greek coins. See cut under *Thelphusa*.

river-craft (riv'ėr-kråft), *n.* Small vessels or boats which ply on rivers and are not designed to go to sea.

river-crawfish (riv'ėr-krâ'fish), *n.* A fluviatile long-tailed crustacean, as *Astacus fluviatilis* and related forms; a crawfish proper—of either of the genera *Astacus* and *Cambarus*. Such crawfish common in the United States are of the latter genus, as *C. affinis*. See *crawfish*, and cuts under *Astacidæ* and *Astacus*.

River-crawfish (*Cambarus affinis*).

river-dolphin (riv'ėr-dol'fin), *n.* A Gangetic dolphin; any member of the *Platanistidæ*. See cut under *Platanista*.

river-dragon (riv'ėr-drag'on), *n.* A crocodile; a name given by Milton to the King of Egypt, in allusion to Ezek. xxix. 3.

> With ten wounds
> The *river-dragon* tamed at length submits
> To let his sojourners depart. *Milton*, P. L., xii. 191.

river-driver (riv'ėr-drī'vėr), *n.* In *lumbering*, a man who drives logs down streams, and prevents their lodging on shoals or being otherwise detained in their passage. [Local, U. S.]

river-duck (riv'ėr-duk), *n.* A fresh-water duck; any member of the subfamily *Anatinæ*: distinguished from *sea-duck*. See cuts under *Chaulelasmus*, *mallard*, *teal*, and *widgeon*.

riverett (riv'ėr-et), *n.* [< OF. *rivierette* (cf. equiv. *riverotte*), dim. of *riviere*, a river: see *river*².] A small river; a rivulet.

> How Arden of her Rills and *Riverets* doth dispose. *Drayton*, Polyolbion, xiii. 237.

> May not he justly disdain that the least *riveret* should be drained another way? *Rev. S. Ward*, Sermons, p. 77.

river-flat (riv'ėr-flat), *n.* The alluvial plain adjacent to a river; bottom; interval; intervale. [New Eng.]

river-god (riv'ėr-god), *n.* A deity supposed to preside over a river as its tutelary divinity: in

River-god.—Tiberis, the River Tiber, in the Louvre Museum.

art generally represented as a reclining figure, often with an urn from which water flows, and other distinguishing attributes.

riverhead (riv'ėr-hed), *n.* The spring or source of a river.

> In earth it first excessive saltness spends,
> Then to our springs and *riverheads* ascends.
> *Dryden*, Misc. (ed. 1685), ii. 408. (*Jodrell.*)

river-hog (riv'ėr-hog), *n.* 1. The capibara.—2. An African swine of the genus *Potamochærus*; a bush hog. *P. penicillatus* is known as the *red river-hog*. See cut under *Potamochærus*.

riverhood (riv'ėr-hůd), *n.* [< *river*² + *-hood*.] The state of being a river. [Rare.]

> Useful *riverhood*. *Hugh Miller*. (*Imp. Dict.*)

river-horse (riv'ėr-hôrs), *n.* [Tr. L. *hippopotamus*, Gr. ἵππος ποτάμιος: see *hippopotamus*.] The hippopotamus.

> The *river-horse*, and scaly crocodile. *Milton*, P. L., vii. 474.

riverine (riv'ėr-in), *a.* [< *river*² + *-ine*¹. Cf. *riverain*.] Of or pertaining to a river; resembling a river in any way.

> Timbuktu, . . . 9 miles north of its [Mossina's] *riverine* port Kabara, on the left bank of the Niger. *Encyc. Brit.*, XXIII. 391.

> His face . . . deeply rutted here and there with expressive valleys and *riverine* lines of wrinkle. *E. Jenkins*, Week of Passion, xiii.

riverish (riv'ėr-ish), *a.* [< *river*² + *-ish*¹.] Rivery.

> Easie ways are made by which the zealous philosophers may win neer this *riverish* Ida, this mountain of contemplation. *Dr. John Dee*, Preface to Euclid (1570).

river-jack (riv'ėr-jak), *n.* 1. The common water-snake of Europe, *Tropidonotus natrix*.—2. A venomous African serpent, *Clotho nasicornis*.

river-lamprey (riv'ėr-lam'pri), *n.* A fresh-water lamprey, *Ammocœtes fluviatilis*, and others of the same genus.

river-limpet (riv'ėr-lim'pet), *n.* A fluviatile gastropod of the genus *Ancylus*.

riverling (riv'ėr-ling), *n.* [< *river*² + *-ling*¹.] A little river; a stream. [Rare.]

> Of him she also holds her Siluer Springs,
> And all her hidden Crystall *Riverlings*.
> *Sylvester*, tr. of Du Bartas's Weeks, i. 3.

river-man (riv'ėr-man), *n.* One who frequents a river and picks up a livelihood about it, as by dragging for sunken goods.

> The oil floated into the Thames, and offered a rich booty to a number of the *river-men*, who were busy all day scooping it into their crazy old boats from the surface of the water. *First Year of a Silken Reign*, p. 82.

river-meadow (riv'ėr-med'ō), *n.* A meadow on the bank of a river.

river-mussel (riv'ėr-mus'l), *n.* A fresh-water mussel; a unio; one of the *Unionidæ*, of several different genera. See cut under *Anodonta*.

river-otter (riv'ėr-ot'ėr), *n.* The common European otter, *Lutra vulgaris*; a land-otter: in distinction from *sea-otter*.

river-perch (riv'ėr-pėrch), *n.* A Californian surf-fish, *Hysterocarpus traski*; one of the embiotocoids, which, contrary to the rule in this family, is found in fresh waters.

river-pie (riv'ėr-pī), *n.* The water-ouzel, *Cinclus aquaticus*. [Ireland.]

river-plain (riv'ėr-plān), *n.* A plain by a river.

river-shrew (riv'ėr-shrö), *n.* An African aquatic insectivorous animal, the only representative of the genus *Potamogale* and family *Potamogalidæ*. See these words.

riverside (riv'ėr-sīd), *n.* The bank of a river: often used attributively.

> This animal therefore seldom ventures from the *riverside*. *Goldsmith*, Hist. Earth (ed. 1790), IV. 296. (*Jodrell.*)

> A poor man, living in a small, muddy, *riverside* house. *Mrs. Oliphant*, Poor Gentleman, vi.

river-smeltt (riv'ėr-smelt), *n.* The gudgeon. *Day*. [Local, Eng.]

river-snail (riv'ėr-snāl), *n.* A fresh-water gastropod of the family *Viviparidæ* or *Paludinidæ*; a pond-snail.

river-swallow (riv'ėr-swol'ō), *n.* The sand-swallow or sand-martin, *Cotile* or *Clivicola riparia*. [Local, British.]

river-terrace (riv'ėr-ter'ās), *n.* In *geol.* See *terrace*.

river-tortoise (riv'ėr-tôr'tis), *n.* A tortoise of the family *Trionychidæ*; a snapping-turtle; a soft-shelled turtle; any fresh-water chelonian.

river-turtle (riv'ėr-tėr'tl), *n.* Same as *river-tortoise*.

river-wall (riv'ėr-wâl), *n.* In *hydraul. engin.*, a wall made to confine a river within definite bounds, either to prevent denudation or erosion of the banks, or overflow of the adjacent land, or to concentrate the force of the stream within a smaller area for the purpose of deepening a navigable channel.

river-water (riv'ėr-wâ'tėr), *n.* The water of a river, as distinguished from *rain-water*, *spring-water*, etc.

river-weed (riv'ėr-wēd), *n.* See *Podostemon*.

river-weight (riv'ėr-wāt), *n.* The weight set upon a fish by guess; the estimated weight, which is apt to exceed the actual weight. [Colloq.]

river-wolf (riv'ėr-wůlf), *n.* The nutria, or Brazilian otter: translating *lobo da rio*. See cut under *coypou*.

rivery (riv'ėr-i), *a.* [< *river*² + *-y*¹.] 1. Of or pertaining to rivers; resembling rivers.

> Thy tall and youthful breasts, which in their meadowy pride
> Are branch'd with *rivery* veins, meander-like that glide.
> *Drayton*, Polyolbion, x. 94.

2. Abounding in rivers: as, a *rivery* district.

> A *rivery* country. *Drayton*.

[Rare in both senses.]

Rivesaltes (rēv'salt), *n.* [< *Rivesaltes*, a town in southern France.] A sweet wine made from Muscat grapes in the neighborhood of Perpignan in France.

rivet¹ (riv'et), *n.* [Early mod. E. also *ryvet*, *revet*; < OF. *rivet*, *rivect*, a rivet, also the welt of a shoe, < *river*, clench, rivet, tuck in (bedclothes), F. *river*, clench, rivet; cf. Sc. dial. *riv*, clench (Aberdeen), sew coarsely (Shetland), < Icel. *rifa*, tack together, stitch together (Skeat). Cf. *rivet*¹, *v.*] A short metallic malleable pin or bolt passing through a hole and so fastened as to keep pieces of metal (or sometimes other substances) together; especially, a short bolt or pin of wrought-iron, copper, or of any other malleable material, formed with a head and inserted into a hole at the junction of two or more pieces of metal, the point after insertion being hammered broad so as to keep the pieces closely bound together. Large rivets are usually hammered or closed up (riveted) when they are in a heated state, so as to draw the pieces more firmly together by the contraction of the rivet when cool. It is in this manner that boilers, tanks, etc., are made. Small rivets are frequently riveted cold. Instead of being closed by hammering, rivets are now often riveted by means of powerful machinery, which makes better joints than can be made by hand, and executes the work far more quickly. In some kinds of metal-work, as armor, the metal pin is movable in a slot, allowing one of the plates of metal to slide over the other for a certain distance. Compare *Almain-rivet*.

Rivets and Hand-riveting Tools.
a, round-headed rivets, one riveted and the other inserted ready for riveting; *c*, round-headed rivet, with washer *d* under the riveted end; *b*, riveting-hammer; *c*, chisel for trimming off the ends of rivets before riveting.

Rivet with Countersink.
a, countersink head; *b*, washer; *c*, riveted end.

> The armourers, accomplishing the knights,
> With busy hammers closing rivets up,
> Give dreadful note of preparation.
> *Shak.*, 1 Hen. V., iv. (cho.).

rivet¹ (riv'et), *v. t.*; pret. and pp. *riveted* or *rivetted*, ppr. *riveting* or *rivetting*. [Early mod. E. *ryvet*, *revet*, < late ME. *revet*, *revett*; prob. (like Pg. *rebitare* = It. *ribadire*, clench, rivet, appar. from the F.) from an unrecorded OF. **riveter* (equiv. to *river*), clench, rivet, < *rivet*, a rivet: see *rivet*¹, *n.*] 1. To fasten with a rivet or with rivets: as, to *rivet* two pieces of iron.

> Riding further past an armourer's,
> Who, with back turn'd, and bow'd above his work,
> Sat *riveting* a helmet on his knee. *Tennyson*, Geraint.

2. To clench: as, to *rivet* a pin or bolt.—3. Figuratively, to fasten firmly; make firm, strong, or immovable: as, to *rivet* friendship.

> For I mine eyes will *rivet* to his face. *Shak.*, Hamlet, iii. 2. 90.

> If a man . . . takes pains to vitiate his mind with lewd principles, . . . he may at last root and *rivet* them so fast till scarce any application whatsoever is able to loosen them. *Bp. Atterbury*, Sermons, II. xvi.

> Her elbows were *rivetted* to her sides, and her whole person so ordered as to inform every body that she was afraid they should touch her. *Swift*, Tatler, No. 5.

rivet² (riv'et), *n.* [Origin obscure.] Bearded wheat. *Halliwell*. [Prov. Eng.]

> White wheat or else red, red *rivet* or white,
> Far passeth all other, for land that is light.
> *Tusser*, October's Husbandry, st. 16.

rivet³ (riv'et), *n.* [Origin obscure.] The roe of a fish. *Halliwell*. [Prov. Eng.]

rivet-clipper (riv'et-klip'ėr), *n.* A tool for cutting off, before swaging, the ends of rivets which are too long.

rivet-cutter (riv'et-kut'ėr), *n.* A tool with powerful jaws for cutting off the stub-ends of bolts or rivets.

riveter (riv'et-ėr), *n.* One who or that which rivets.

rivet-hearth (riv'et-härth), *n.* A light, portable furnace fitted with a blower, which is worked by hand, and has a fireplace arranged for heating rivets. Also *riveting-forge*.

riveting, rivetting (riv'et-ing), *n.* [Verbal n. of *rivet*¹, *v.*] 1. The act or method of joining with rivets.—2. Rivets taken collectively.

riveting-bur (riv'et-ing-bėr), *n.* A washer upon which a rivet-head is swaged down: sometimes used with small rivets.

riveting-forge (riv'et-ing-fōrj), *n.* A portable forge used in heating rivets.

riveting-hammer (riv'et-ing-ham"ėr), *n.* A hammer with a long head, flat face, and narrow peen, used for swaging down rivets. See cuts under *hammer* and *peen*.

riveting-machine (riv'et-ing-ma-shēn"), *n.* A power-machine for forcing hot rivets into position in metal-work and heading them. Such machines consist essentially of a die and anvil; and in typical forms of the machine the work to be riveted is supported over the anvil, the hot rivet is put in place in the hole, its end resting in a die-socket in the anvil, and the horizontal die advances, squeezes the rivet into place, and shapes both heads at the same time. Riveting-machines are made in a great variety of forms for both light and heavy work. In some the anvil and die are both movable and are operated by hydraulic power. Some recent machines are portable, and are suspended by chains from a crane, so that the machine can be brought to the work instead of carrying the work to the machine. A recent American machine employs an anvil and a riveting-hammer operated by compressed air and delivering a series of rapid blows instead of a direct pressure, and thus more nearly copies hand-work. Riveting-machines are sometimes called by special names, as the *girder riveter*, *keel riveter*, etc.

riveting-plates (riv'et-ing-plāts), *n. pl.* In *gun.*, small square pieces of iron on gun-carriages, through which bolts pass, the heads being riveted down upon them.

riveting-set (riv'et-ing-set), *n.* A hollow-faced punch for swaging rivet-heads. The concavity is made of the shape which it is desired to give to the head of the rivet.

rivet-joint (riv'et-joint), *n.* A joint formed by a rivet or by rivets.

rivet-knob (riv'et-nob), *n.* A form of swaging-tool used for closing down the heads of rivets.

rivet-machine (riv'et-ma-shēn"), *n.* A machine for making rivets from rod-iron; a rivet-making machine. It is essentially a form of nail-machine, cutting off the piece from the rod, stamping the head to shape, and finishing the rivets in quick succession.

rivetting, *n.* See *riveting*.

rivière (rē-viãr'), *n.* [F., a river (*une rivière de diamants*, a string of diamonds): see *river*2.] A necklace of precious stones, especially diamonds; particularly, such a piece of jewelry consisting of more than one string.

Rivina (ri-vi'nā), *n.* [NL. (Plumier, 1703), named after A. Q. *Rivinus*: see *Rivinian*.] A genus of apetalous plants of the order *Phytolaccaceæ*, the pokeweed family, type of the tribe *Rivineæ*. It is characterized by a globose and compressed fleshy fruit, and by flowers with a calyx of four small equal segments, four stamens, a short curved style, and capitate stigma. The five enumerated species are reducible perhaps to one, *R. lævis*, a native of tropical and subtropical America, extending into Texas and Florida, introduced in Asia and some African islands. It is an erect smooth or hairy herb with shrubby base, 6 or 8 feet high, or in some forms much smaller, producing many two-forked and two-furrowed branches. It bears alternate slender-petioled thin ovate leaves, and slender pendulous racemes of small reddish-white flowers, followed by red pea-like berries. In the West Indies it is called *hoop-withe*. The smaller variety, *humilis*, is known as *blood-berry*, also as *rouge-berry* or *rouge-plant*, from a use made of its fruit before it becomes dry. Both plants, especially the latter, are somewhat cultivated for ornament.

Rivineæ (ri-vin'ē-ē), *n. pl.* [NL. (K. A. Agardh, 1825), < *Rivina* + *-eæ*.] A tribe of plants of the order *Phytolaccaceæ*, characterized by a four- or five-parted calyx, a one-celled ovary, and an indehiscent dry or fleshy fruit, containing a single seed with two plicate-convolute seed-leaves. It includes 10 genera, mainly South American, for the chief of which see *Petiveria* and *Rivina* (the type).

riving (rī'ving), *n.* [Verbal n. of *rive*1, *v.*] 1. The act of cleaving or separating.—2. Refuse of corn. *Halliwell.* [Prov. Eng.]

riving-knife (rī'ving-nīf), *n.* A tool for splitting shingles, staves, etc.: same as *frow*1.

riving-machine (rī'ving-ma-shēn"), *n.* A machine for splitting wood with the grain to make hoops, staves, splints, shingles, etc.

Rivinian (ri-vin'i-an), *a.* [< *Rivinus* (see def.) + *-an*.] Of or pertaining to A. Q. Rivinus (1652–1723), a German anatomist and botanist.—**Rivinian ducts.** See *ducts of Rivinus*, under *duct*.—**Rivinian or Rivini's gland.** Same as *sublingual gland* (which see, under *gland*).—**Rivinian notch.** See *notch of Rivini*, under *notch*.

rivo† (rī'vō), *interj.* [Of obscure origin; by some supposed to be an imitation (with parasitic r) of L. *evoe* (= Gr. εὐοῖ), a shout in the festival of Bacchus.] An exclamation in drinking-bouts.

> *Rivo!* says the drunkard. *Shak.*, 1 Hen. IV., ii. 4. 124.
>
> *Rivo*, heer 's good juice, fresh burrage, boy!
> *Marston*, What you Will, v. 1.

rivose (rī'vōs), *a.* [< NL. **rivosus*, < L. *rivus*, a stream, channel, groove: see *rivulet*.] Furrowed; specifically, marked with furrows which do not run in parallel directions, but are somewhat sinuate: used especially in zoölogy.

Rivularia (riv-ū-lā'ri-ā), *n.* [NL. (Roth, 1797), < L. *rivulus*, a small stream: see *rivulet*.] A genus of mostly fresh-water algæ of the class *Cyanophyceæ* and type of the order *Rivulariaceæ*. The filaments are radiately arranged, agglutinated by a more or less firm mucilage, and unitedly forming hemispherical or bladdery well-defined forms; the heterocysts are basal. They occur in both running and standing fresh water—*R. fluitans*, for example, forming a blue-green scum on stagnant pools; and there are a few species in brackish or salt water.

Rivulariaceæ (riv-ū-lā-ri-ā'sē-ē), *n. pl.* [NL., < *Rivularia* + *-aceæ*.] An order of usually minute algæ of the class *Cyanophyceæ*, typified by the genus *Rivularia*. The cells of which each filament is composed form a continuous thread divided by transverse septa, and the filaments grow attached in tufts to a solid substratum, or make small green floating disks or cushions, often embedded in copious mucilage. The ordinary mode of multiplication is by means of hormogones, but quiescent resting-spores have been observed in some species.

Rivularieæ (riv"ū-lā-ri'ē-ē), *n. pl.* [NL., < *Rivularia* + *-eæ*.] Same as *Rivulariaceæ*.

rivulet (riv'ū-let), *n.* [Formerly also *rivolet*; with dim. suffix *-et*, < L. *rivulus*, a small stream, dim. of *rivus*, a stream, brook, channel, gutter (> It. *rivo*, *rio* = Sp. Pg. *rio*, a river); akin to Skt. √ *ri*, run, ooze, flow. Hence (< L. *rivus*) ult. E. *derive*, *rival*, *corrival*, etc. (but not *river*2).] 1. A small stream or brook; a streamlet.

> Some clear *rivolet* on land.
> *Times' Whistle* (E. E. T. S.), p. 116.
>
> By fountain or by shady *rivulet*
> He sought them. *Milton*, P. L., ix. 420.

2. In *entom.*: (*a*) One of certain geometrid moths of the genus *Emmelesia* or *Cidaria*: a collectors' name in England. The small rivulet is *E.* or *C. alchemillata*; the grass-rivulet is *E.* or *C. albulata*; the heath-rivulet is *E. ericetata*; and the single-barred rivulet is *E.* or *C. unifasciata*. (*b*) A narrow and more or less tortuous colored band on a transparent wing: a translation of the Latin *rivulis*, so used in Loew's monographs of the *Diptera*.

rivulet-tree (riv'ū-let-trē), *n.* A low evergreen euphorbiaceous shrub, *Phyllanthus australis*, of Australia and Tasmania.

rivulose (riv'ū-lōs), *a.* [< NL. **rivulosus*, < L. *rivulus*, a small stream: see *rivulet*.] In *bot.*, marked with lines like the rivers in a map. *Phillips*, British Discomycetes, Gloss.

rix1 (riks), *n.* [A form of *rish*1, *rush*1.] A reed. *Halliwell.* [Prov. Eng.]

rix2†, *v. i.* [< ME. *rixien*, < AS. *ricsian*, *rixian* (= OHG. *richisōn*, also *rihhisōn*, *richsenōn*, MHG. *richesen*, *richsen*, also *richsenen*), reign, < *rice*, kingdom: see *riche*1, *n.*] To reign. *Saxon Chron.*, 265. (*Stratmann.*)

rixation (rik-sā'shon), *n.* [< L. **rixatio(n-)*, < *rixari*, pp. *rixatus*, brawl, quarrel (> It. *rissare*, scold, quarrel), < *rixa* (> It. *rissa* = Sp. *rija* = Pg. *reixa*, *rixa* = F. *rixe*), a quarrel.] A brawl or quarrel. *Bailey*, 1731. [Rare.]

rixatrix (rik-sā'triks), *n.* [NL., fem. of L. *rixator*, a brawler, wrangler, < *rixari*, brawl: see *rixation*.] A quarrelsome woman; a common scold. *Bouvier.* [Rare.]

rix-dollar (riks'dol"ār), *n.* [Also (Dan.) *rigsdaler*; = F. *rixdale* = Sp. *risdala*, < D. *rijksdaalder*, earlier *rijcksdaelder*, = Dan. *rigsdaler* = Sw. *riksdaler*, < G. *reichsthaler*, a rix-dollar, lit. 'a dollar of the kingdom,' < G. *reichs*, gen. of *reich*, kingdom, + *thaler*, a dollar: see *riche*1, *n.*, and *dollar*.] A name given to large silver coins current, chiefly during the eighteenth and the beginning of the nineteenth century, in several European countries (Germany, Sweden, Denmark, etc.). The value varied between

Obverse. Reverse.
Rigsdaler of Denmark, 1854, silver.—British Museum. (Size of the original.)

Obverse.

Reverse.
Rix-dollar of Utrecht, 1805.—British Museum. (Size of the original.)

$1.15 and 60 cents United States money, but was usually a little over $1.

> He accepted of a *rix-dollar*.
> *Evelyn*, Diary, Aug. 28, 1641.

rixy1 (rik'si), *n.*; pl. *rixies* (-siz). [Origin obscure.] The common tern or sea-swallow. [Prov. Eng.]

rixy2 (rik'si), *a.* [Appar. < **rix*, < F. *rixe*, < L. *rixa*, quarrel (see *rixation*), + *-y*1; but no noun **rix*, quarrel, appears.] Quarrelsome. *Halliwell.* [Prov. Eng.]

riyo, *n.* See *rio*.

rize†, *v.* A former spelling of *rise*1.

rizom (riz'om), *n.* [Also *ruzzom*; cf. Sc. *rizzim*, a stalk of corn, corrupted < *raceme*: see *raceme*.] A plume, as that of oats or millet. [Prov. Eng.]

rizomed (riz'omd), *a.* [< *rizom* + *-ed*2.] In *her.*, having grains, as an oat-stalk used as a bearing: a term used when the grains are of a different tincture from that of the stalk: as, an oat-stalk vert, *rizomed* or.

rizzar, *v.* and *n.* See *rizzer*1, *rizzer*2.

rizzer1 (riz'ėr), *v. t.* [Also *rizzar*; prob. < OF. *ressorer*, dry in the sun. Less prob., as suggested by the var. *rizzle* (see *rizzle*1), < F. *rissoler*, fry brown (see *rissole*), or a freq. form of *reeze*, for *reast*1: see *reast*1.] To dry in the sun; dry partly: as, "*rizzered* fish," *Scott.* [Scotch.]

> The substantialities consisted of *rizzared* haddies, eggs, ham, wheaten bread. *The Smugglers*, II. 75. (*Jamieson.*)

rizzer1 (riz'ėr), *n.* [Also *rizzar*; < *rizzer*1, *v.*] A rizzered haddock. [Scotch.]

> Leave a moderate fringe of unoystered timber, which strew with *rizzars*, interspersed at intervals.
> *Noctes Ambrosianæ*, Feb., 1832.

rizzer2 (riz'ėr), *n.* [Also *rizzar*, *rizard*; perhaps a var. of *reason*, *resin*, *raisin*: see *raisin*1.] A red currant. [Scotch.]

rizzle1 (riz'l), *v. t.*; pret. and pp. *rizzled*, ppr. *rizzling*. [Var. of *rizzer*: see *rizzer*1.] To warm; dry, as in the sun; roast imperfectly. *Halliwell.* [Prov. Eng.]

rizzle2 (riz'l), *v. i.*; pret. and pp. *rizzled*, ppr. *rizzling*. [Perhaps lit. 'branch,' freq. from *rise*2, *n.*] To creep, as ivy, etc. *Halliwell.* [Prov. Eng.]

R. M. An abbreviation of (*a*) *Royal Marines*; (*b*) *Royal Mail*; (*c*) *Resident Magistrate*.

R. N. An abbreviation of *Royal Navy*.

ro†, *n.* A Middle English form of *roe*1.

Ro. An abbreviation of *recto*, meaning 'right-hand,' 'right-side.'

roach1 (rōch), *n.* [< ME. *roche*, < OF. *roche*, *rosse*, F. dial. *roche* (ML. *roche*, *rochia*), a roach, < MD. *roch*, a roach (?), skate, D. *rog*, a ray, = MLG. *roche*, *ruche*, LG. *ruche*, > G. *roche*, a roach, ray, thornback, = Sw. *rocka*, a ray, thornback, = Dan. *rokke*, a ray, = AS. *reohhe*, *reohche*, a fish, prob. a roach, ME. *rohge*, *rouhe*, *rohge*, *reihe*, a roach, = L. *rāia* (for **ragia*), a roach, ray, thornback (> It. *raja* = Sp. *raya* = Pg. *raia* = F. *raie*, a skate, > E. *ray*: see *ray*2).] 1. A common cyprinoid fish of Europe, *Leuciscus rutilus*. It inhabits the lakes, ponds, and slow-running rivers of England and of the south of Scot-

Roach (*Leuciscus rutilus*).

land, and is common in most other rivers in temperate parts of Europe. Its color is a grayish-green, the abdomen being silvery-white, and the fins reddish. It is gregarious, and the shoals are often large. Its average weight is under a pound, and, though a favorite with anglers, it is not much esteemed for the table.

> Kodlynges, konger, or suche queyse fysche
> As wolwyche *roches* that be not worth a rusche.
> *Piers of Fullham*, quoted in Babees Book (E. E. T. S.), [index, p. 112.

2. In the United States, one of many different fishes like or mistaken for the roach, as (*a*) some sunfish of the genus *Lepomis* or *Pomotis*; (*b*) the spot or lafayette; (*c*) the American chub, *Semotilus atromaculatus*.

roach2, **roche**2 (rōch), *n.* [< ME. *roche*, < OF. *roche*, F. *roche*, a rock: see *rock*1.] 1†. A rock. *Palsgrave.*

> Like betynge of the se,
> Quod I, agen the *roches* holowe.
> *Chaucer*, House of Fame, l. 1035.

> Whan the marches ben garnysshed, than moste we take counseile of oon stronge Castell that thei haue in this contrey, that is cleped the *roche* of saxons.
> *Merlin* (E. E. T. S.), ii. 176.

2. Refuse gritty stone. *Halliwell.* [Prov. Eng.] —**As sound as a roach**, perfectly sound. [The word *roach*, a rock, being obsolete, no definite meaning is now attached to *roach* in this phrase. It is often referred to *roach*1.]

roach2†, **roche**2† (rōch), *v. t.* [< *roach*2, *n.*] To make hard like a rock.

> Thee winters coldnesse thee riuer hardlye *roching*.
> *Stanihurst*, Conceites (ed. Arber), p. 136.

roach3 (rōch), *n.* [Origin obscure.] 1. *Naut.*, a concave curve in the leech or foot of a square sail, to improve the fit of the sail. A convex curve used in the head and foot of fore-and-aft sails is called a *sweep*.

2. An upstanding curl or roll of hair over the forehead, like the roach of a sail. [Colloq.]

roach3 (rōch), *v. t.* [See *roach*3, *n.*] 1. To cause to stand up or arch; make projecting or convex: as, his hair was *roached* up over his forehead. [Colloq.]

> An arched loin is desirable, but not to the extent of being *roached* or "wheel-backed," a defect which generally tends to slow up-and-down gallop.
> *Dogs of Great Britain and America*, p. 100.

2. To cut short so as to cause to stand up straight; hog: said of horses' manes.

> I *roached* his mane and docked his tail, and put him in a warm stall with half a foot of straw underneath.
> *The Century*, XXXVII. 335.

roach4 (rōch), *n.* [Origin obscure.] A rash, or eruption on the skin. *Halliwell.* [Prov. Eng.]

roach5 (rōch), *n.* [Abbr. for *cockroach*, assumed to be a compound, < *cock* + **roach*: but see *cockroach*.] A cockroach.

roach-backed (rōch'bakt), *a.* Having a roached or arched back.

roach-dace (rōch'dās), *n.* The roach. See *roach*1. [Local, Eng.]

road (rōd), *n.* [Early mod. E. also *rode*; also dial. (Sc.) *raid*, now in general use (see *raid*); < ME. *rode*, *roode*, *rade*, a road, raid, foray, < AS. *rād*, riding expedition, a journey, road (= MD. D. *reede* = MLG. *rēde*, *reide*, LG. *rede* (> G. *rhede*), roadstead for ships, = It. Sp. *rada* = F. *rade*, roadstead, = Icel. *reithi*, preparations of ship, ride, raid, vehicle, *reitha*, implements, outfit, *reithi*, rigging, = Sw. *redd* = Dan. *red*, a road, roadstead), < *rīdan* (pret. *rād*), ride: see *ride*. Cf. *raid*, *inroad*, and *ready*.] 1. A ride; journey; expedition.

> At last, with easy *roads*, he came to Leicester.
> *Shak.*, Hen. VIII., iv. 2. 17.

> I set out towards the Euphrates, in company with two Turks, who were going that way, there being some danger in the *road*. *Pococke*, Description of the East, II. i. 155.

> Our *road* was all the way in an open plain, bounded by hillocks of sand and fine gravel, perfectly hard, and not perceptibly above the level of the plain country of Egypt.
> *Bruce*, Source of the Nile, I. 171.

> I never get spoken to on my *roads*, only some people say, "Good morning," "There you are, old lady."
> *Mayhew*, London Labour and London Poor, II. 542.

2. A hostile expedition; an incursion; an inroad; a raid. See *raid*.

> Therefore, sothely me semys, yf ye so wille,
> That we dresse to our dede when the day sprynges;
> All redy to *rode*, aray for our shippes.
> *Destruction of Troy* (E. E. T. S.), l. 5680.

> Him he named who at that time was absent making *roads* upon the Lacedæmonians.
> *Sir P. Sidney*, Arcadia, i.

> In these wylde deserts where she now abode
> There dwelt a salvage nation, which did live
> Of stealth and spoile, and making nightly *rode*
> Into their neighbours borders.
> *Spenser*, F. Q., VI. viii. 35.

> And Achish said, Whither have ye made a road to-day? And David said, Against the south of Judah.
> 1 Sam. xxvii. 10.

> Lay down our proportions to defend
> Against the Scot, who will make *road* upon us.
> *Shak.*, Hen. V., i. 2. 138.

3. A public way for passage or travel; a strip of ground appropriated for travel, forming a line of communication between different places; a highway; hence, any similar passage for travel, public or private; by extension, a railroad or railway. See *street*. Hence—4. Any means or way of approach or access; a course; a path.

> To be indifferent whether we embrace falsehood or truth is the great *road* to error. *Locke.*

> There is one *road*
> To peace — and that is truth, which follow ye.
> *Shelley*, Julian and Maddalo.

5. A place near the shore where vessels may anchor, differing from a harbor in not being sheltered. Also called *roadstead*.

> Harbours they have none, but exceeding good *Rodes*, which with a small charge might bee very well fortified; it doth ebbe and flow foure or five foot.
> Quoted in *Capt. John Smith's* Works, II. 276.

> The anchorage, however, is an open *road*, and in stormy weather it is impossible for a boat to land.
> *B. Taylor*, Lands of the Saracen, p. 30.

> At anchor in Hampton *Roads* we lay.
> *Longfellow*, The Cumberland.

Accommodation road. See *accommodation*.—**By road**, by the highway, as distinguished from the railway or waterway.

> The journey had been fatiguing, for a great part of it was *by road*. *George MacDonald*, What's Mine's Mine, ii.

Corduroy, Dunstable, Flaminian road. See the qualifying words.—**Knight of the road.** See *knight*.—**Occupation road.** See *occupation*.—**On the road**, passing; traveling; specifically, traveling on business, as making sales for a firm, peddling, etc.: also, in *theat. slang*, making a provincial tour.—**Parallel roads.** See *parallel*.—**Plank road**, a road formed of planks laid transversely, used in somewhat primitive districts in America.—**Royal road to knowledge.** See *royal*.—**Rule of the road.** (*a*) The custom of a country with regard to the passing of those who meet on a highway. In the United States, and generally in continental Europe, teams or riders approaching each other on the highway are expected to keep to the right of the center of the traveled part of the highway. In Great Britain the reverse obtains. (*b*) The regulations embodied in a code of rules for the safe handling of vessels meeting or passing each other.—**The road**, the highway: used figuratively for highway robbery.

> There is always some little Trifle given to Prisoners, they call Garnish; we of *the Road* are above it, but o' t'other side of the House, Silly Rascals that come voluntarily hither . . . may perhaps want it.
> Quoted in *Ashton's* Social Life in Reign of Queen Anne, [II. 242.

To break a road. See *break*.—**To take the road**, to set out on a journey.—**To take to the road**, to become a highway robber. =**Syn.** 3. *Street*, *Passage*, etc. (see *way*), lane, route, course, thoroughfare.

road (rōd), *v. t.* [< *road*, *n.*] 1. To furnish with a road or with roads. [Rare.]

> One of the most Extensive and Complete Establishments in the Kingdom, well *roaded*, and situate in the Borough of Leeds. *The Engineer*, LXIX.

2. To follow the trail of by scent; track or pursue on foot, as game: said of dogs.

> When pursued or *roaded* by a dog, they [Virginian rail] may be raised once, but the second time will be a task of more difficulty. *Wilson and Bonaparte*, Amer. Ornithol- [ogy (ed. 1877), II. 406, note.

3. To jostle (one) off the road by riding against him. *Halliwell.* [Prov. Eng.]—**To road up**, to flush, or cause to rise on the wing, by roading.

> The Prairie Chicken always goes to feed on foot, and may thus be *roaded up* by a dog.
> *Sportsman's Gazetteer*, p. 119.

road-agent (rōd'ā"jent), *n.* One who collects dues from travelers on private roads; hence, jocosely, a highwayman. [Slang, western U. S.]

> A band of concealed marauders or *road agents*, whose purpose was to preserve their haunts from intrusion.
> *Bret Harte*, A Ghost of the Sierras (Argonauts, p. 366).

road-bed (rōd'bed), *n.* 1. The bed or foundation on which the superstructure of a railway rests.—2. The whole material laid in place and ready for traffic in ordinary roads.

road-book (rōd'bůk), *n.* A travelers' guide-book of towns, distances, etc. *Simmonds.*

road-car (rōd'kär), *n.* A low-hung omnibus with slatted seats placed crosswise on the roof, and with a curving staircase for reaching the top. It is commonly drawn by three horses abreast, and is used in London, and to some extent in New York. [Eng.]

> What is it but pride that makes us on a fine day prefer a hansom cab to the box seat of an Omnibus or the garden-seated top of a *road-car*?
> *Nineteenth Century*, XXIII. 240.

road-drift (rōd'drift), *n.* See *drift*.

roader (rō'dėr), *n.* *Naut.*, same as *roadster*, 5.

> I caused the Pinnesse to beare in with the shore, to see whether she might find an harborough for the ships or not, and that she found and saw two *roaders* ride in the sound. *Hakluyt's Voyages*, I. 275.

road-harrow (rōd'har"ō), *n.* A machine for dragging over roads much out of repair, to bring back to the proper profile the stones or gravel disturbed by the traffic.

roading (rō'ding), *n.* [< *road* + *-ing*1.] 1. The act of running races on the road with teams. *Halliwell.* [Prov. Eng.]—2. The continuous or ordinary travel of a horse on the road, as distinguished from *speeding*. [Colloq.]

> On another occasion she [a mare] accomplished forty-three miles in three hours and twenty-five minutes. This was great *roading*. *The Atlantic*, LXV. 524.

3. See the quotation.

> This characteristic flight [of the woodcock] is in some parts of England called "*roading*," and the track taken by the bird a "cock-road." *Encyc. Brit.*, XXIV. 651.

road-level (rōd'lev"el), *n.* 1. A species of plumb-level used in the construction of roads.—2. A level surface; a surface such that no work is gained or lost by any displacement of a particle remaining within the surface; an equipotential surface.

road-leveler (rōd'lev"el-ėr), *n.* A form of scraper used to level a road-bed and bring it to shape; a road-grader or road-scraper. It is set obliquely to the line of direction in which it is dragged.

road-locomotive (rōd'lō-kō-mō"tiv), *n.* A locomotive adapted to run on common roads; a road-steamer.

road-machine (rōd'ma-shēn"), *n.* A scraper mounted on wheels, used to excavate earth, transport it, and dump it where it is needed; a road-scraper. It is used in road-making to take earth from the sides of the way and throw it up in a ridge in the middle.

road-maker (rōd'mā"kėr), *n.* One who makes a road or roads.

roadman (rōd'man), *n.*; pl. *roadmen* (-men). [< *road* + *man*.] A man who keeps roads in repair. Also *roadsman*.

road-measurer (rōd'mezh"ūr-ėr), *n.* An odometer.

road-metal (rōd'met"al), *n.* Broken stone, etc., used for making roads: same as *metal*, 6.

> The coal being broken up into fragments like *road-metal*.
> *Pop. Sci. Mo.*, XXXI. 115.

road-plow (rōd'plou), *n.* A strong plow designed especially for throwing up embankments, loosening earth to be moved by a scraper, etc.

road-roller (rōd'rō"lėr), *n.* A heavy roller used to compact the material on a macadamized road. Such rollers may be drawn by horses or driven by steam-power. In the latter case they are a form of traction-engine mounted on large and broad tread-wheels.

road-runner (rōd'run"ėr), *n.* The paisano or chaparral-cock, *Geococcyx californianus*, a large ground-cuckoo. See cut under *chaparral-cock*.

road-scraper (rōd'skrā"pėr), *n.* An implement used for leveling roads and moving loose soil or gravel. The name is applied to two distinct implements. One is practically a plow with a broad scraper set obliquely beneath the beam in place of a share, and is used on roads to level ruts and bring the road-bed to a good surface. The other is a shovel or scraper, drawn by a horse, for removing mud, lifting earth for transport, etc. When loaded, this scraper can be moved any distance with its burden and then tilted over to discharge it. A road-scraper mounted on wheels is a *road-machine*.

roadside (rōd'sīd), *n.* and *a.* I. *n.* The side of a road; border of a road; footpath; wayside.

> By the *roadside* fell and perished,
> Weary with the march of life!
> *Longfellow*, Footsteps of Angels.

II. *a.* Situated by the side of a road.

> The coach pu s up at a little *road-side* inn with huge stables behind. *T. Hughes*, Tom Brown at Rugby, i. 4.

roadsman (rōdz'man), *n.* Same as *roadman*.

> We have had *roadsmen* for many weeks gravelling the front . . . and thoroughly repairing the old road.
> *Carlyle*, in Froude, II.

roadstead (rōd'sted), *n.* [Formerly also *road-sted*; < *road* + *-stead*.] Same as *road*, 5.

Our barke did ride such a *road sted* that it was to be marueiled . . . how she was able to abide it. *Hakluyt's Voyages*, I. 276.

road-steamer (rōd'stē"mėr), *n.* A locomotive with broad wheels suitable for running on common roads.

roadster (rōd'stėr), *n.* [< *road* + *-ster.*] 1. A horse driven or ridden on the road, used in driving for pleasure and for light work rather than for draft.

The brown mare was as good a *roadster* as man might back. *Barham*, Ingoldsby Legends, I. 129.

2. A person much accustomed to driving; a coach-driver.

I . . . entered into conversation with Walter, the "whip," a veteran *roadster*. *Kimball*, St. Leger, I. 7.

3. In *hunting*, one who keeps to the road instead of riding across country. [Slang.]

Once in a way the *roadsters* and shirkers are distinctly favoured. *The Field*, April 4, 1885. (*Encyc. Dict.*)

4. A tricycle or bicycle built strongly for road use, as distinguished from one intended for racing.—5. *Naut.*, a vessel which works by tides, and seeks some known road to await turn of tide and change of wind. Also *roader*. *Admiral Smyth*. [Eng.]

road-sulky (rōd'sul"ki), *n.* A light conveyance, which can accommodate only one person (whence the name). Also called *sulky*.

road-surveyor (rōd'sėr-vā"or), *n.* A person who supervises roads and sees to their being kept in good order.

roadway (rōd'wā), *n.* [< *road* + *way*.] A highway; a road; particularly, the part of a road used by horses, carriages, etc.; the road-bed.

Thou art a blessed fellow to think as every man thinks: never a man's thought in the world keeps the *road-way* better than thine. *Shak.*, 2 Hen. IV., ii. 2. 63.

Such a path as I doubt not ye will agree with me to be much fairer and more delightfull than the *rode way* I was in. *Milton*, Apology for Smectymnuus.

"My caution has misled me," he continued, pausing thoughtfully when he was left alone in the *roadway*. *W. Collins*, The Yellow Mask, ii. 3.

roadweed (rōd'wēd), *n.* A plant of the genus *Plantago*.

Plantago major, minor, and lanceolata, called plantains, or *road-weeds*, are among the commonest of our weeds on roadsides, in meadows, and all undisturbed ground where the soil is not very light. *Henfrey*, Elem. Botany. (*Latham.*)

road-work (rōd'wėrk), *n.* Work done in the making of roads.

roadworthy (rōd'wėr"ᵺi), *a.* Fit for the road; likely to go well: applied to horses.

I conclude myself *road-worthy* for fourteen days. *Carlyle*, in Froude, II. 188.

roak (rōk), *n.* [Perhaps same as *roke*. Cf. *roaky* for *roky*.] See the quotation.

The [steel] bar, if it was not burnt up in the fire, would be so full of the imperfections technically called "seams" or *roaks* as to be perfectly useless. *Michaelis*, tr. of Monthaye's Krupp and De Bange, p. 21.

roaky, *a.* See *roky*.

roam (rōm), *v.* [Also dial. *rome*, ramble, *rame*, *roam*, *raum*, *rawm*, reach after; < ME. *romen*, *rowmen*, *ramen*, roam; cf. AS. *rōmigan*, strive after (occurring but once, in a passage imitated from OS.), = OS. *rōmōn*, aim at, strive after, = OFries. *ramia*, strive after; OD. *ramen*, stretch (cloth), D. *ramen*, hit, plan, aim, = OHG. *rāmēn*, MHG. *rāmen*, aim at, strive after (*rām*, an aim), = Dan. *ramme*, hit, strike; erroneously associated with *Rome* (cf. ME. *Rome-rennere*, a runner to Rome, a pilgrim; OF. *romier* = Sp. *romero* = It. *romeo*, one who goes to Rome, a pilgrim). Hence ult. *ramble*.] I. *intrans.* 1†. To walk; go; proceed.

He *rometh* to the carpenteres hous,
And stille he stant under the shot wyndow.
Chaucer, Miller's Tale, l. 508.

Win. Rome shall remedy this.
War. *Roam* thither, then.
Shak., 1 Hen. VI., iii. 1. 51.

2. To wander; ramble; rove; walk or move about from place to place without any certain purpose or direction.

Ac he may renne in arrerage, and *rowme* so fro home,
And as a reneyed caityf recchelesly gon aboute.
Piers Plowman (B), xi. 125.

Up and down and side and slant they *roamed*.
M. Arnold, Balder Dead.

=Syn. 2. *Rove*, *Wander*, etc. See *ramble*.

II. *trans.* To range; wander over: as, to *roam* the woods.

My imagination would conjure up all that I had heard or read of the watery world beneath me; of the finny herds that *roam* its fathomless valleys. *Irving*, Sketch-Book, p. 19.

roam (rōm), *n.* [< *roam*, *v.*] The act of wandering; a ramble.

The boundless space, through which these rovers take
Their restless *roam*, suggests the sister thought
Of boundless time. *Young*, Night Thoughts, ix.

roamer (rō'mėr), *n.* [< ME. **romere*, *romare*, *rowmer*; < *roam* + *-er*[1].] One who roams; a rover; a rambler; a vagrant.

Ac now is Religioun a ryder, a *rowmer* bi stretes, . . .
A priker on a palfray fro manere to manere.
Piers Plowman (B), x. 306.

roan[1] (rōn), *a.* and *n.* [Early mod. E. also *roen*; < OF. *roan*, *roen*, *rouen*, roan (*cheval rouën*, a roan horse), F. *rouan* = Sp. *ruano* = Pg. *ruão* = It. *roano*, *rovano*, roan, prob. < LL. or ML. **rufanus*, reddish, < L. *rufus*, red: see *rufous*.] I. *a.* Of a bay, sorrel, or chestnut color, with gray or white hairs more or less thickly interspersed: said chiefly of horses. A bright-red mixture is called *strawberry-roan* or *red-roan*.

Give my *roan* horse a drench. *Shak.*, 1 Hen. IV., ii. 4. 120.

And the bridegroom led the flight on his *red-roan* steed of might. *Mrs. Browning*, Rhyme of Duchess May.

He rode ahead, on his *blue-roan* Indian pony. *Mary Hallock Foote*, St. Nicholas, XIV. 733.

Roan antelope, the blauwbok.—**Roan fleuk**, the turbot. See *fluke*[2], 1 (c).

II. *n.* 1. An animal, especially a horse, of a roan color.

What horse? a *roan*, a crop-ear, is it not?
Shak., 1 Hen. IV., ii. 3. 72.

As quaint a four-in-hand
As you shall see—three pyebalds and a *roan*.
Tennyson, Walking to the Mall.

2. A roan color; the color of a roan horse.

Y schalle yeve the a nobylle stede,
Also redd as ony *roone*.
MS. Cantab. Ff. ii. 38, f. 66. (*Halliwell.*)

3. A soft and flexible sheepskin, largely used by bookbinders, and often made in imitation of morocco.

roan[2] (rōn), *n.* Same as *rowan*.

roan[3] (rōn), *n.* [Origin obscure.] A clump of whins. *Halliwell*. [Prov. Eng.]

roaned† (rōnd), *a.* [ME. *ronyd*; perhaps for *roined*, scabbed (?), < *roin* + *-ed*[2].] Scabbed; scurvy.

A *ronyd* colte. *Bury Wills* (ed. Tymms), p. 132. (*Skeat.*)

[He] had euer more pitty on one good paced mare then two *roaned* curtalles. *Breton*, Merry Wonders, p. 6. (*Davies.*)

roanoke, **roenoke** (rē-a-nōk', rō-e-nōk'), *n.* [Amer. Ind.] A kind of shell-money formerly used by the Indians in New England and Virginia. See the quotation, and compare *peag*.

They have also another sort [of money] which is as current among them, but of far less value; and this is made of the Cockle shell, broke into small bits with rough edges, drill'd through in the same manner as Beads; and this they call *Roenoke*, and use it as the Peak.
Beverley, Virginia, iii. ¶ 46.

Roanoke chub. See *Micropterus*, 1.

roan-tree (rōn'trē), *n.* [< *roan*[2] + *tree*.] Same as *rowan-tree*.

A branch of the *roan-tree* is still considered good against evil influences in the Highlands of Scotland and Wales.
Sir T. Dick Lauder.

roapy, *a.* See *ropy*.

roar (rōr), *v.* [Early mod. E. *rore*; < ME. *roren*, *rooren*, *raren*, < AS. *rārian*, roar, wail, lament, = MLG. *rāren*, *rēren*, LG. *reren* = OHG. *rērēn*, MHG. *rēren*, G. *röhren*, bellow; an imitative word, a reduplication of √ *rā*, Skt. √ *rā*, bark; cf. L. *latrare*, bark.] I. *intrans.* 1. To cry with a full, loud, continued sound; bellow, as a beast.

Will a lion roar in the forest when he hath no prey?
Amos iii. 4.

2. To cry aloud, as in distress or anger.

He bygan benedicite with a bolke, and his brest knocked,
And roxed and *rored*. *Piers Plowman* (B), v. 398.

I am feeble and sore broken; I have roared by reason of the disquietness of my heart. Ps. xxxviii. 8.

If you winna rock him, you may let him *rair*.
Burd Ellen and Young Tamlane (Child's Ballads, I. 272).

3. To make a loud, continued, confused sound, as winds, waves, a multitude of people shouting together, etc.; give out a full, deep sound; resound.

When it was day he broghte him to the halle,
That *roreth* of the crying and the soun.
Chaucer, Knight's Tale, l. 2023.

Th' Atlantic billows roared. *Cowper*, The Castaway.

Down all the rocks the torrents roar,
O'er the black waves incessant driven.
Scott, Marmion, ii., Int.

4. To laugh out loudly and continuously; guffaw.

And to hear Philip roar with laughter! . . . You might have heard him from the Obelisk to the Etoile.
Thackeray, Philip, xxiii.

5†. To behave in a riotous and bullying manner. [Old London slang.]

The gallant *roares*; roarers drinke oathes and gall.
Dekker, Londons Tempe.

6. To make a loud noise in breathing, as horses in a specific disease. See *roaring*, *n.*, 2.

Cox's most roomy fly, the mouldy green one, in which he insists on putting the *roaring* gray horse.
Thackeray, Sketches, etc., in London, A Night's Pleasure, i.

=Syn. 1 and 2. To bawl, howl, yell.—3. To boom, resound, thunder, peal.

II. *trans.* To cry aloud; proclaim with loud noise; utter in a roar; shout: as, to *roar* out one's name.

And that engenders thunder in his breast,
And makes him roar these accusations forth.
Shak., 1 Hen. VI., iii. 1. 40.

roar (rōr), *n.* [< ME. *rore*, *rar*, < AS. *gerār*, < *rārian*, roar: see *roar*, *v.*] 1. A full, loud, and deep cry, as of the larger beasts.

It was the *roar*
Of a whole herd of lions.
Shak., Tempest, ii. 1. 315.

The great creature [a mastiff] does nothing but stand still . . . and roar—yes, roar; a long, serious, remonstrative roar. *Dr. J. Brown*, Rab.

2. A loud, continued, confused sound; a clamor; tumult; uproar.

Why nyl I make at ones riche and pore
To have ynough to done or that she go?
Why nyl I brynge al Troie upon a *rore*?
Chaucer, Troilus, v. 45.

If by your art, my dearest father, you have
Put the wild waters in this *roar*, allay them.
Shak., Tempest, i. 2. 2.

I hear the far-off curfeu sound,
Over some wide-water'd shore,
Swinging slow with sullen *roar*.
Milton, Il Penseroso, l. 76.

Arm! arm! it is—it is—the cannon's opening *roar*!
Byron, Childe Harold, iii. 22.

3. The loud, impassioned cry of a person in distress, pain, anger, or the like; also, a boisterous outcry of joy or mirth: as, a *roar* of laughter.

Where be your gibes now? . . . your flashes of merriment, that were wont to set the table on a *roar*?
Shak., Hamlet, v. 1. 211.

Staniford gave a sort of roar of grief and pain to know how her heart must have been wrung before she could come to this. *Howells*, The Lady of the Aroostook, xxvi.

roarer (rōr'ėr), *n.* One who or that which roars.

Gon. Nay, good, be patient.
Boats. When the sea is. Hence! What care these *roarers* for the name of king? *Shak.*, Tempest, i. 1. 18.

Specifically—(*a*†) A noisy, riotous person; a roaring boy or girl. See *roaring*, *p. a.* [Old London slang.]

O strange!
A lady to turn *roarer*, and break glasses!
Massinger, Renegado, i. 3.

A Gallant all in scarlet, . . . a brave man, in a long horsemans Coat (or gown rather) down to his heels, daub'd thicke with gold Lace; a huge Feather in his spangled hat, a Lock to his shoulders playing with the Winde, a Steeletto hanging at his girdle; Belt and Sword embracing his body; and the ring of Bells you heare are his gingling Cathern-wheele spurs. He presently says: "I am a man of the Sword, a Battoon Gallant, one of your Dammees, a bouncing Boy, a kicker of Bawdes, a tyrant over Puncks, a terrour to Fencers, a mewer of Playes, a jeerer of Poets, a gallon-pot flinger—in rugged English, a *Roarer*." *The Wandering Jew* (1640).

(*b*) One who shouts or bawls.

The *Roarer* is an enemy rather terrible than dangerous. He has no other qualification for a champion of controversy than a hardened front and strong voice.
Johnson, Rambler, No. 144.

(*c*) A broken-winded horse. See *roaring*, *n.*, 2.

If you set him cantering, he goes on like twenty sawyers. I never heard but one worse *roarer* in my life, and that was a roan. *George Eliot*, Middlemarch, xxiii.

Ring-tailed roarer. See *ring-tailed*.

roaring (rōr'ing), *n.* [< ME. *roryng*e, *rarunge*, < AS. *rārung*, verbal n. of *rārian*, roar: see *roar*, *v.*] 1. A loud, deep cry, as of a lion; an outcry of distress, anger, applause, boisterous mirth, or the like; loud continued sound, as of the billows of the sea or of a tempest.

My *roarings* are poured out like the waters. Job iii. 24.

I hear the *roaring* of the sea. *Tennyson*, Oriana.

2. A disease of horses which causes them to make a singular noise in breathing under exertion; the act of making the noise so caused; also, this noise. The disease is due to paralysis and wasting of certain laryngeal muscles, usually of the left side; this results in a narrowing of the glottis, giving rise to an unnatural inspiratory sound, manifested chiefly under exertion.

Mr. —— has recently operated upon two army horses which were to have been cast for *roaring*.
Sci. Amer., N. S., LIX. 7.

roaring (rôr'ing), *p. a.* [Ppr. of *roar, v.*] **1.** Making or characterized by a noise or disturbance; disorderly; riotous.

A mad, *roaring* time, full of extravagance. *Burnet.*

That every naig was ca'd a shoe on
The smith and thee gat *roaring* fou on.
Burns, Tam o' Shanter.

2. Going briskly; highly successful. [Colloq.]

People who can afford to smother themselves in roses like this must be driving a *roaring* trade.
W. E. Norris, Miss Shafto, xxv.

Roaring boys†, roaring lads†, swaggerers; ruffians: slang names applied, about the beginning of the seventeenth century, to the noisy, riotous roisterers who infested the taverns and the streets of London, and, in general, acted the part of the Mohocks of a century later. *Roaring girls* are also alluded to by the old dramatists, though much less frequently.

Ther were 4 *roring boyes*, they say,
That drunk a hogshead dry in one poor day.
Times' Whistle (E. E. T. S.), p. 62.

Shamelesse double sex'd hermaphrodites, Virago *roaring girles*.
Taylor, Works (1630). (*Nares.*)

A very unthrift, master Thorney; one of the Country *roaring Lads*; we have such, as well as the city, and as arrant rakehells as they are, though not so nimble at their prizes of wit. *Ford and Dekker*, Witch of Edmonton, i. 2.

Roaring buckie. See *buckie*, 1.—**Roaring Meg.** (*a*†) A cannon. (*Nares.*)

Beates downe a fortresse like a *roaring Meg*.
Whiting, Albino and Bellama (1638). (*Nares.*)

(*b*) A kind of humming-top. *Halliwell.*—**The roaring forties.** See *forty*.—**The roaring game,** curling. [Scotch.]

roaringly (rôr'ing-li), *adv.* [< *roaring* + *-ly*[2].] In a roaring manner; noisily.

Ferdinand snored *roaringly* from his coiled position among the traps. *T. Winthrop*, Canoe and Saddle, xii.

roary†, *a.* See *rory*.

roast (rōst), *v.* [Early mod. E. also *rost*; < ME. *rosten, roosten*, partly (*a*) < AS. **rōstian, gerōstian*, also *gerōscian* (only in glosses), roast, = MD. D. *roosten* = MLG. *rōsten*, LG. *rosten* = OHG. *rōstan*, MHG. *ræsten*, later *roschten*, G. *rösten*, roast; orig. cook on a grate or gridiron, < AS. **rōst* (not found) = MLG. *rōste*, LG. *roste* = OHG. *rōst, rōsta*, gridiron, MHG. *rōste*, a grate, also heap of coals, glow, fire, G. *rost*, a grate, gridiron; and partly (*b*) < OF. *rostir*, F. *rôtir*, dial. *roûtir* = Pr. *raustir* = Cat. OSp. *rostir* = It. *arrostire*, roast, < OHG. *rōstan*, roast (as above). Perhaps orig. Celtic: cf. Ir. *roistin*, a gridiron, *rosdaim*, I roast, *rost*, roast meat, Gael. *rost, roist*, W. *rhostio*, Bret. *rosta*, roast; but these words may be from E. and F.] **I.** *trans.* **1.** To cook, dress, or prepare (meats) for eating, originally on a grate or gridiron over or beneath a fire (broiling), but now by exposure to the direct action of dry heat (toasting). Roasting is generally performed by revolving the article on a spit or a string before a fire, with a reflector or Dutch oven to concentrate the heat: in primitive cookery hot ashes serve a similar purpose. Meat cooked over or beneath a fire, on a gridiron, is now said to be *broiled*; and meat cooked in a stove- or range-oven, where it does not receive the direct action of the fire, is properly said to be *baked* (though generally said to be *roasted*).

Maistir, the custome wele we knawe,
That with ouro cithers euer has bene,
How like man with his meyne awe
To *roste* a lambe, and ete it clene.
York Plays, p. 233.

Davie [an idiot] . . . lay with his nose almost in the fire . . . turning the eggs as they lay in the hot embers, as if to confute the proverb that "there goes reason to *roasting* of eggs." *Scott*, Waverley, lxiv.

2. To heat to excess; heat violently.

Roasted in wrath and fire, . . .
With eyes like carbuncles, the hellish Pyrrhus
Old grandsire Priam seeks. *Shak.*, Hamlet, ii. 2. 483.

He shakes with cold — you stir the fire and strive
To make a blaze — that's *roasting* him alive.
Cowper, Conversation, l. 334.

3. To dry and parch by exposure to heat: as, to *roast* coffee.

The fruit of it not scabby, *rosted* drie.
Palladius, Husbondrie (E. E. T. S.), p. 4.

4. In *metal.*, to heat with access of air. The objects of roasting substances are various: (*a*) to expel from them something which can be separated by heat alone, as when calamin (carbonate of zinc) is roasted in order to expel the carbonic acid; (*b*) to expel some ingredient capable of being got rid of by the agency of heat and air, oxygen being substituted for the material thus expelled, as when sulphuret of lead is roasted to expel the sulphur; (*c*) to raise to a higher stage of oxidation, as when tap-cinder (silicate of the protoxid of iron) is roasted in order to convert it into a silicate of the peroxid. See *calcination*.

5. To expose (a person) to scathing ridicule or jesting, as by a company of persons, or for the amusement of a company. [Slang.]

On bishop Atterbury's *roasting* lord Coningsby about the topick of being priest-ridden.
Bp. Atterbury, Epist. Correspondence, II. 417. (*Latham.*)

II. *intrans.* **1.** To perform the act of cooking by the direct action of dry heat.

He coude *roste*, and sethe, and broille, and frye.
Chaucer, Prol. to C. T., l. 383.

2. To become roasted or fit for eating by exposure to fire; hence, to be overheated or parched.

In some places we did find
Pye baking in the oven,
Meat at the fire *roasting*.
The Winning of Cales (Child's Ballads, VII. 127).

Tales! for never yet on earth
Could dead flesh creep, or bits of *roasting* ox
Moan round the spit. *Tennyson*, Lucretius.

roast (rōst), *a.* [Early mod. E. also *rost*; < ME. *rost, frost*, contr. pp. of *rosten*, roast: see *roast, v.*] Roasted: as, *roast* beef; *roast* meat.

Plutus has put me out of commons. Yet my nose
Smells the delicious odour of *roast-beef*.
Randolph, Hey for Honesty, iv. 1.

O the *roast* beef of Old England!
R. Leveridge, The *Roast* Beef of Old England.

Roast-beef plant, an iris of western Europe, *Iris fœtidissima*, whose leaves when bruised emit an odor which, though very unpleasant, is often likened to that of roast beef.—**To cry roast meat**, to betray or make known one's good fortune.

The foolish beast, not able to fare well but he must *cry roast meat*, . . . waxing fat and kicking in the fulness of bread, . . . would needs proclaim his good fortune to the world below. *Lamb*, Christ's Hospital.

roast (rōst), *n.* [Early mod. E. also *rost*; < ME. *rost, roost* = MD. *roost* (OF. *rost*), a roast; from the verb.] That which is roasted, specifically a piece of beef; that part of a slaughtered animal which is selected for roasting, as a sirloin of beef or a shoulder of mutton.

A fat swan lovede he best of any *roost*.
Chaucer, Prol. to C. T., l. 206.

I tell you that we have a Course of *Roast* a coming, and after that some small Desert.
N. Bailey, tr. of Colloquies of Erasmus, I. 174.

Cold roast†. See *cold*.—**To give a rib of roast†.** See *rib*[1].—**To rule the roast**, to have the chief direction of affairs; have the lead; domineer. [The phrase is by some supposed to stand for *to rule the roost*, in allusion to the domineering manner of a cock.]

In cholerick bodies, fire doth govern moste;
In sanguine, aire doth chiefly *rule the rost*.
Times' Whistle (E. E. T. S.), p. 117.

Suffolk, the new-made duke that *rules the roast*.
Shak., 2 Hen. VI., i. 1. 109.

In the Kitchin he will domineere, and *rule the roste*, in spight of his Master, and Curses is the very Dialect of his Calling. *Bp. Earle*, Micro-cosmographie, A Cooke.

To smell of the roast†, to be prisoners. *Nares.*

My souldiers were slayne fast before mine owne eyes,
Or forc'd to flie, yeelde, and *smell of the rost*.
Mir. for Mags.

roast-bitter (rōst'bit"ėr), *n.* A peculiar bitter principle contained in the crust of baked bread, similar to that produced by the roasting of other organic compounds.

roaster (rōs'tėr), *n.* [= D. *rooster* = LG. *röster* = G. *röster*, a gridiron, grate; as *roast* + *-er*[1].] **1.** One who or that which roasts: as, a meat-*roaster*.—**2.** Specifically, the finishing-furnace in the Leblanc process of making ball-soda. It is a large reverberatory of brickwork, with a detachable casing of iron plates held in place by upright iron binders and tightening-rods.

3. A pig or other animal or article fit for roasting.

Here Loolowcan presented me the three birds plucked. . . . The two *roasters* we planted carefully on spits before a sultry spot of the fire.
T. Winthrop, Canoe and Saddle, viii.

When we keep a *roaster* of the sucking pigs, we choose, and praise at table most, the favourite of its mother.
R. D. Blackmore, Lorna Doone, l.

Blind roaster, a furnace for completing the roasting of the sodium sulphate in the ball-soda process, in which the sulphate is confined in a chamber or large muffle, and the hydrochloric acid set free in the process is conducted away by itself, instead of mixing with the air and the gases of combustion in the chimney.

roaster-slag (rōs'tėr-slag), *n.* Slag from the fifth stage of the English copper-smelting process, which consists in the calcination of the so-called white metal, and the product of which is blister-copper and roaster-slag.

roasting-cylinder (rōs'ting-sil"in-dėr), *n.* A furnace for roasting ores, for amalgamation, lixiviation, or smelting, which is provided with a revolving cylindrical chamber in which the roasting takes place. The name is chiefly used with reference to the particular furnace invented by W. Brückner.

roasting-ear (rōs'ting-ēr), *n.* An ear of maize or Indian corn in the green and milky state, and fit for roasting. [Colloq., U. S.]

They [the Indians] delight much to feed on *Roasting-ears*: that is, the Indian corn, gathered green and milky, before it is grown to its full bigness, and roasted before the Fire, in the Ear. . . . And indeed this is a very sweet and pleasing Food. *Beverley*, Virginia (1705), iii. ¶ 16.

roasting-furnace (rōs'ting-fėr"nās), *n.* Any furnace in which the operation of roasting is performed. See *roast, v. t.*, 4.

roasting-iron† (rōs'ting-ī"ėrn), *n.* [< ME. *rostynge-yrne.*] Same as *roast-iron*.

roasting-jack (rōs'ting-jak), *n.* [< *roasting* + *jack*[1].] An apparatus for turning the spit on which meat is roasted before an open fire. See *smoke-jack*.

roasting-kiln (rōs'ting-kil), *n.* A kiln used in roasting ores.

roasting-oven (rōs'ting-uv"n), *n.* An oven in which any substance is roasted; specifically, in *metal.*, an oven for roasting or calcining ores, the purpose being to expel sulphur, arsenic, etc., by the action of heat, which volatilizes these substances. Also called *ore-calcining furnace* and *roasting-furnace*.

roast-iron† (rōst'ī"ėrn), *n.* [Early mod. E. *rost-iron*; < ME. *rostyren, rostyryn*; < *roast* + *iron*.] A gridiron. *Cath. Ang.*, p. 312.

Item, j. *roste iren* with vij. staves and j. foldyng stele of silver, weiyng lxxiiij. unces. *Paston Letters*, I. 468.

roast-stall (rōst'stâl), *n.* A peculiar form of roasting-furnace, built in compartments or stalls open in front, with flues running up the wall at the back for the purpose of creating a draft: used at Mansfeld in Prussia. Iron ores are also sometimes calcined between closed walls in stall-like chambers open in front. If closed in front, these chambers would more properly be called *kilns*.

roat†, *v.* See *rote*[2].

rob[1] (rob), *v.*; pret. and pp. *robbed*, ppr. *robbing*. [< ME. *robben*, < OF. *robber, rober* = Sp. *robar* = Pg. *roubar* = It. *rubare*, < ML. *raubare*, rob, steal, plunder, < OHG. *roubôn*, MHG. *rouben*, G. *rauben* = OS. *rôbhôn* = AS. *reáfian*, E. *reave* = Goth. *bi-raubôn*, rob, bereave: see *reave*, of which *rob* is thus a doublet, derived through OF. and ML. from the OHG. cognate of the E. *reave*. Cf. *robe*.] **I.** *trans.* **1†.** To steal; take away unlawfully.

That our fos, with no faulshed in the fyght tyme,
Sese not our Cité, our seluyn to pyne,
Ne *rob* not our ryches, ne our ryf godys.
Destruction of Troy (E. E. T. S.), l. 6209.

An empty casket, where the jewel of life
By some damn'd hand was *robb'd* and ta'en away.
Shak., K. John, v. 1. 41.

2. To plunder or strip by force or violence; strip or deprive of something by stealing; deprive unlawfully; commit robbery upon. See *robbery*.

To socour the kynge de Cent Chyualers, that hadde herde tydinges that the saisnes com *robbinge* the contrey.
Merlin (E. E. T. S.), ii. 233.

Rob not the poor, because he is poor. Prov. xxii. 22.

Like a thief, to come to *rob* my grounds.
Shak., 2 Hen. VI., iv. 10. 36.

3. To deprive.

This concern for futurities *robs* us of all the ease and the advantages which might arise from a proper and discreet use of the present moment.
Bp. Atterbury, Sermons, II. xxii.

I care not, Fortune, what you me deny:
You cannot *rob* me of free Nature's grace.
Thomson, Castle of Indolence, ii. 3.

4. To carry away; ravish. [Rare.]

The eyes of all, allur'd with close delight,
And hearts quite *robbed* with so glorious sight.
Spenser, F. Q., IV. iv. 16.

5. To hinder; prevent. [Rare.]

What is thy sentence then but speechless death,
Which *robs* my tongue from breathing native breath?
Shak., Rich. II., i. 3. 173.

6. In *metal-mining*, to remove ore from (a mine) with a view to immediate profit rather than to the permanent safety and development of the property.—**7.** In *coal-mining*, to cut away or reduce in size, as the pillars of coal left for the support of the mine.—**Robbing Peter to pay Paul**, taking what is due one person to satisfy the claim of another; sacrificing one interest for the advancement of another.

By *robbing Peter* he *paid Paul*, . . . and hoped to catch larks if ever the heavens should fall.
Urquhart, tr. of Rabelais, i. 11.

=**Syn. 2** and **3.** To despoil, fleece. See *pillage, n.*

II. *intrans.* To commit robbery.

I am accursed to *rob* in that thief's company.
Shak., 1 Hen. IV., ii. 2. 10.

Of Highway-Elephants at Ceylan,
That *rob* in Clans, like Men o' th' Highland.
Prior, To Fleetwood Shephard.

rob[2] (rob), *n.* [< F. *rob*, < Sp. *rob*, *arrope* = Pg. *robe*, *arrobe* = It. *rob*, *robbo*, < Ar. *robb*, Pers. *rubb*, inspissated juice, syrup, fruit-jelly.] The inspissated juice of ripe fruit, mixed with honey or sugar to the consistence of a conserve; a conserve of fruit. [Now prov. Eng. and pharmaceutical.]

The *Rob* [margin, *Rob* of Ribes]—that is, the juyce of the berries boyled with a third part or somewhat more of Sugar added unto it, till it become thick, . . . is . . . preferred before the raw berries themselves.
Venner, Via Recta ad Vitam Longam (1637), p. 167.

The Infusion and Decoction . . . passeth into a Jelly, Defrutum, sapa *Rob* extract which contain all the virtues of the Infusion or Decoction freed only from some of the watery parts. *Arbuthnot*, Aliments, III. v. § 7.

robalo (rob'a-lō), *n.* [Sp. *róbalo* = Pg. *robalo* = Cat. *llobarro*, a fish so called; said to be < L. *labrus*, *labros*, < Gr. λάβραξ, a fish, the sea-wolf: see *Labrax*.] A fish of the genus *Centropomus*, represented by many species in tropical America. C. *undecimalis* is abundant in the West Indian and adjacent waters. It is a large and important food-fish, of a silvery color, greenish above, with sharp black lateral line, dusky dorsal and caudal fins, the other fins yellowish. See cut under *Centropomus*.

rob-altar (rob'âl″tär), *n.* [< *rob*[1], *v.*, + obj. *altar*.] A plunderer of what is consecrated or sacred.

"Will a man rob God?" . . . But, alas! what law can be given to *rob-altars*? *Rev. T. Adams*, Works, I. 179.

roband (rob'and), *n.* Same as *robbin*[1].

All hands were . . . kept on deck hour after hour in a drenching rain, . . . picking old rope to pieces, or laying up gaskets and *robands*.
R. H. Dana, Before the Mast, p. 105.

robber (rob'ėr), *n.* [< ME. *robber*, *robbere*, *robbare*, earlier *robbour*, *robbeour*, < OF. *robeor*, *robbeur*, *robeur* = Sp. *robador* = Pg. *roubador* = It. *rubatore*, < ML. **raubator*, *robator*, < *raubare*, rob: see *rob*[1]. Doublet of *reaver*.] One who robs; one who commits a robbery; in a looser sense, one who takes that to which he has no right; one who steals, plunders, or strips by violence and wrong.

Robbours and reuers that riche men dispoilen.
Piers Plowman (C), xiv. 58.

The Bandits, which are the murdering *robbers* upon the Alpes, and many places of Italy. *Coryat*, Crudities, I. 141.

Robber council or **synod.** Same as *Latrocinium*, 2. = **Syn.** *Robber, Thief, Pilferer, Freebooter, Marauder, Brigand, Bandit, Pirate*, depredator, despoiler, rider, highwayman, footpad. (See *pillage, n.*) A *thief* takes other people's property without their knowledge; a *robber* takes it openly, whether or not resistance is offered: in a looser sense, *thief* is often applied to one who takes a small amount, and *robber* to one who takes a large amount. A *pilferer* takes very small amounts by stealth. A *freebooter* and a *marauder* rove about, robbing and plundering: the word *freebooter* emphasizes the fact that the man helps himself at his pleasure, while *marauder* suggests the loss, inconvenience, fright, or distress produced. A *brigand* or *bandit* is one of an organized band of outlaws and robbers, especially in certain countries long known as infested with such bands; *bandit* is rather a poetic or elevated word; *brigand* is more common in prose. A *pirate* is a brigand of the sea. All these words have considerable extension by metonymy or hyperbole.

robber-crab (rob'ėr-krab), *n.* A hermit-crab; a member of the family *Paguridæ*, especially *Birgus latro*: so called from its habit of stealing cocoanuts. See cut under *palm-crab*.

robber-fly (rob'ėr-flī), *n.* Any dipterous insect of the family *Asilidæ*. They are large swift flies with strong proboscis, and prey upon other insects. They are also called *hornet-flies* and *hawk-flies*. The term *robber-fly* is taken direct from the German *raubfliege*. See cuts under *Asilus*, *hawk-fly*, and *Promachus*.

robber-gull (rob'ėr-gul), *n.* The skua, or other jäger. See *Lestridinæ*, *Lestris*.

robbery (rob'ėr-i), *n.*; pl. *robberies* (-iz). [< ME. *robberie*, *robry*, *roberie*, < OF. *roberie*, *robberie*, robbery, < *robber*, rob: see *rob*[1]. Cf. *reavery*.] The act or practice of robbing; a plundering; a pillaging; a taking away by violence, wrong, or oppression; the act of unjustly and forcibly depriving one of anything; specifically, in *law*, the felonious and forcible taking of the property of another from his person, or in his presence, against his will, by violence or by putting him in fear (*Wharton*). It is a more serious offense than larceny, by reason of the element of force or fear entering into it.

Thieves for their *robbery* have authority
When judges steal themselves.
Shak., M. for M., ii. 2. 176.

Highway robbery, robbery committed in or near a highway. At common law no other robbery was punishable with death. = **Syn.** Depredation, spoliation, despoilment. See *robber*.

robbin[1] (rob'in), *n.* [Also *roband*; appar. contr. of *rope-band*. In sense 2 appar. of same origin.] 1. A short piece of spun-yarn, rope-yarn, or sennit, used to fasten the head of a sail to the yard or gaff by passing several turns through the eyelet-hole in the sail and around the jack-stay.—2. The spring of a carriage. *Simmonds.*

robbin[2] (rob'in), *n.* [< F. *robin*; appar. of E. Ind. origin.] In *com.*, the package in which Ceylonese and other dry goods, as pepper, are imported. The Malabar robbin of rice weighs 84 pounds. *Simmonds.*

robbin[3] (rob'in), *n.* An occasional spelling of *robin*[1].

rob-Davy†, *n.* See *rob-o-Davy*.

robe[1] (rōb), *n.* [< ME. *robe*, *roobe*, < OF. *robe*, *robbe*, *reube*, F. *robe*, a robe, = Pr. *rauba* = Cat. *roba* = Sp. *ropa* = Pg. *roupa* = It. *roba*, dress, merchandise, goods, < ML. *rauba*, spoil, < OHG. *roub*, robbery, breakage, MHG. *roup*, robbery, booty, spoil, garment, G. *raub* = D. *roof* = OS. *rōf* = AS. *reáf*, spoil, clothing, = Icel. *rauf*, spoil: see *reaf* and *reave*. Cf. *rob*[1].] 1. A gown or long loose garment worn over other dress; a gown or dress of a rich, flowing, or elegant style or make.

A womman wortheli yclothed, . . .
Hire *robe* was ful riche of red scarlet engreyned,
With ribanes of red golde and of riche stones.
Piers Plowman (B), ii. 15.

2. An official vestment; a flowing garment symbolizing honor, dignity, or authority.

The *robes* of a judge do not add to his virtue; the chiefest ornament of kings is justice.
Hooker, Eccles. Polity, vii. 20.

Thou shalt take the garments, and put upon Aaron the coat, and the *robe* of the ephod, and the ephod.
Ex. xxix. 5.

I am sorry one I esteemed ever the first of his *robe* should so undeservedly stain me. *Penn*, To Dr. Tillotson.

3. Any garment; apparel in general; dress; costume.

Bion. Petruchio is coming in a new hat and an old jerkin, a pair of old breeches thrice turned. . . .
Tra. [To Petruchio.] See not your bride in these unreverent *robes*. *Shak.*, T. of the S., iii. 2. 114.

Say, have you got no armour on?
Have you no under *robe* of steel?
Duel of Wharton and Stuart (Child's Ballads, VIII. 262).

4. Hence, that which covers or invests; something resembling or suggesting a robe.

She tore the azure *robe* of night,
And set the stars of glory there.
Drake, The American Flag.

Another [cottage] wore
A close-set *robe* of jasmine sown with stars.
Tennyson, Aylmer's Field.

5. A woman's gown of any cut or fabric, with trimmings, usually in the form of bands or borders, woven in or embroidered on the material. [Trade and dressmakers' term.]—6. A dressed skin or pelt: first applied to that of the American bison, but now to that of any animal when used for a carriage- or sleigh-rug, and by extension to any protecting wrap used in driving: as, a linen lap-*robe*. [U. S.]

The large and roomy sleigh decked with buffalo, black bear, and lynx *robes*.
The Upper Ten Thousand, p. 4. (Bartlett.)

Under the head of *robes* was included all [buffalo] cow skins taken during the proper season, from one year old upward, and all bull skins from one to three years old. Bull skins over three years of age were classed as hides, and while the best of them were finally tanned and used as *robes*, the really poor ones were converted into leather.
W. T. Hornaday, Smithsonian Report, 1887, ii. 443.

7. The largest and strongest tobacco-leaves, which are used as covers for the thicker kinds of pigtail. [U. S.]—8. *Eccles.*, specifically, the early chasuble, a large garment covering the body. Compare *garment*, 2.—9. *pl.* Garments of state or ceremony, forming together an entire costume. Thus, coronation robes may include all the garments worn by a prince at the time of his coronation, and always include the outer or decorative pieces, as the dalmatic, the mantle, etc.—**Guarded robe**†. See *guard*.—**Master of the robes**, an officer in the royal household of Great Britain charged with ordering the sovereign's robes, and having several officers under him, as a clerk of the robes, wardrobe-keepers, etc. Under a queen this office is performed by a lady, designated *mistress of the robes*, who holds the highest rank among the ladies in the service of the queen.—**Pack of robes**, ten robes of buffalo-hide packed together for transportation to market. [U. S.]—**The robe**, or **the long robe**, the legal profession: as, gentlemen of *the long robe*.

Far be it from any Man's Thought to say there are not Men of strict Integrity of *the Long Robe*, tho' it is not every Body's good Fortune to meet with them.
Steele, Grief A-la-Mode, Pref.

Rich advocates, and other gentlemen of *the robe*.
Motley, Dutch Republic, I. 377.

robe[1] (rōb), *v.*; pret. and pp. *robed*, ppr. *robing*. [< ME. *roben*; < *robe*[1], *n.*] **I.** *trans.* 1. To put a robe on; clothe in a robe; especially, to clothe magnificently or ceremoniously: as, to *robe* a sovereign for a coronation.

Thou *robed* man of justice, take thy place.
Shak., Lear, iii. 6. 38.

2. To clothe or dress in general.

Thus *robed* in russett, ich romede a-boute.
Piers Plowman (C), xi. 1.

Here and there a tall Scotch fir, completely *robed* in snow. *B. Taylor*, Northern Travel, p. 117.

The elms have *robed* their slender spray
With full-blown flower and embryo leaf.
O. W. Holmes, Spring has Come.

II. *intrans.* To put on a robe or robes; assume official vestments: as, the judges are *robing*; the clergy *robed* in the vestry.

robe[2] (rōb), *n.* An abbreviation of *arroba*.

robe-de-chambre (rōb-dė-shom'br), *n.* [F.: *robe*, robe; *de*, of; *chambre*, chamber.] 1. A dressing-gown or morning dress, whether for men or for women—the exact signification varying with the fashion and habits of the day.—2†. A dress cut in a certain negligée style: thus, a *robe-de-chambre* is mentioned as worn at a party in 1732.

robe-maker (rōb'mā″kėr), *n.* A maker of official robes, as for clergymen, university dignitaries, and others.

The modern Anglican rochet is sleeveless, the bulbous sleeves having been wholly detached from it by the Caroline tailors or *robe-makers*. *Lee*, Eccles. Gloss., p. 336.

roberd (rob'ėrd), *n.* [A familiar use of *Roberd*, a form of the personal name *Robert*. Cf. *robin*[1], *robinet*.] The chaffinch. Also *robinet*.

Roberdsman†, *n.* See *Robertsman*.

robert (rob'ėrt), *n.* Same as *herb-robert*.

Robertman†, *n.* Same as *Robertsman*.

Robertsman†, **Roberdsman**† (rob'ėrts-man, rob'ėrdz-man), *n.* [Also *Robartsman*, *Robertman*; ME. *roberdesman* (also *Roberdes knave*), supposed to be so called because regarded or feigned to be one of Robin (Robert) Hood's men.] A bold, stout robber or night thief.

Robartes men, or *Roberdsmen*, were a set of lawless vagabonds, notorious for their outrages when Pierce Plowman was written. . . . The statute of Edward the Third (an. reg. 5, c. xiv.) specifies "divers manslaughters, felonies, and robberies, done by people that be called *Roberdesmen*, Wastours, and drawlatches." And the statute of Richard the Second (an. reg. 7, c. v.) ordains that the statute of King Edward concerning *Roberdesmen* and Drawlacches shall be rigorously observed. Sir Edward Coke (Instit. iii. 197.) supposes them to have been originally the followers of Robin Hood in the reign of Richard the First. See Blackstone's Comm., B. iv. ch. 17.
T. Warton, Hist. Eng. Poetry (1840), II. 94, 95.

Roberts's pelvis. See *pelvis*.

Robervallian (rob-ėr-val'i-an), *a.* Pertaining to G. P. de Roberval (1602–75), a noted French mathematician.—**Robervallian line**, a curve of infinite length but of finite area.

Roberval's balance. See *balance*.

roberycht†, *n.* A Middle English form of *rubric*. *Halliwell.*

robin[1] (rob'in), *n.* [Short for *robin-redbreast*, early mod. E. *robyn redbrest*, < ME. **robin redbreast*, *robinet redbrest*, in which the first element was orig. a quasi-proper name, *Robin*, < OF. *Robin*, Robin (a name also given to the sheep), a familiar dim. of *Robert*, Robert (a name early known in England, as that of the oldest son of William I.), = Sp. Pg. It. *Roberto*, also *Ruperto* (> E. *Rupert*), < OHG. *Ruodpert*, MHG. G. *Ruprecht*, lit. 'fame-bright,' illustrious in fame, < OHG. *ruod* (= AS. **hrōth*- (in proper name *Hrōthgar* = G. *Rudiger*, > ult. E. *Roger*: see *Roger*) = Icel. *hrōthr*, praise, fame, = Goth. **hrōth*, in *hrōtheigs*, victorious, triumphant) + *perht*, *peraht*, MHG. *berht* = E. *bright*[1]: see *bright*[1].] 1. A small sylviine bird of Europe, *Erythacus rubecula*, more fully called *robin-redbreast*, and also *redbreast*, *robinet*, and *ruddock*. It is more like a warbler than like a thrush, only about 5½ inches long and 9 in extent of wings; the upper parts are olive-green; the forehead, sides of the head, front of the neck, and fore part of the breast are yellowish-red (whence the name *redbreast*). It is an abundant and familiar British bird, widely distributed in other parts of the Palearctic region. The song is rich, mellow, and finely modulated. The nest is placed on the ground, in herbage or moss, generally under a hedge or bush. The eggs are usually five or six in number, pinkish-white freckled with purplish-red. This robin is a common figure in English nursery tales and folk-lore.

Robin-redbreast (*Erythacus rubecula*).

Art thou the bird whom Man loves best,
The pious bird with the scarlet breast,
Our little English Robin?
Wordsworth, Redbreast Chasing the Butterfly.

A strange world where the *robin* was a little domestic bird that fed at the table, instead of a great fidgety, jerky, whooping thrush. *O. W. Holmes*, Old Vol. of Life, p. 172.

2. The red-breasted or migratory thrush of North America, *Turdus migratorius* or *Merula migratoria*, one of the most abundant and fa-

American Robin (*Merula migratoria*).

miliar of North American birds: so called from the reddish-brown color of the under parts, which, however, is very different, both in hue and in extent, from that of the European redbreast. This robin is 10 inches long and 16 in extent of wings. The upper parts are slate-color with an olive shade; most of the under parts are chestnut-red; the vent-feathers are white, with dusky markings; the head is black, with white marks about the eyes and white streaks on the throat; and the tail is blackish, usually marked with white at the ends of the outer feathers. The bill is mostly yellow. The robin inhabits the whole of North America; it is migratory, feeds on insects, worms, berries, and other fruits, and breeds at large throughout its range, building a large strong nest of hay and mud on a bough, and laying from four to six uniform greenish-blue eggs, 1¼ inches long by ⅞ inch broad. Also, familiarly, *robin-redbreast.*

3. With a qualifying term, one of numerous warbler-like or thrush-like birds, more or less nearly related to or resembling either of the foregoing: as, the blue-throated *robin*. (See *Cyanecula*, and cut under *bluethroat*.) Some of these terms are book-names, others are casual transfers of the word *robin* by English residents in various parts of the world, especially India and Australia. In the latter region are various flycatchers (*Muscicapidæ*) of the genus *Petrœca* and its subdivisions, some of which are called *robins*, as the scarlet-breasted, *P. multicolor*, peculiar to Norfolk Island. Some of the Asiatic chats of the genus *Pratincola* are known as *Indian robins*; these are related to the British whinchat and stonechat, and do not particularly resemble the true robin of England. Others, recently separated generically under the name *Erythromyias*, inhabit Java, Sumatra, Borneo, and other islands of the same zoogeographical region, and resemble the true robin, as *E. dumetoria* and *E. muelleri*. The red-breasted flycatcher, *Muscicapa* (*Erythrosterna*) *parva*, which ranges from central Europe into India, bears a striking resemblance to the true robin. Among other Indian robins, loosely so called, may be noted one sometimes specified as the *water-robin*. This is a flycatcher, *Xanthopygia fuliginosa*, originally described by Vigors in 1831 as *Phœnicura fuliginosa*, and commonly catalogued as *Ruticilla fuliginosa* (after G. R. Gray); but it does not belong to the same family as the robin, nor to the same genus as the redstart. It inhabits the Himalayan region, and ranges widely in China and India. It has been placed in 5 different genera, two of which, *Rhyacornis* of Blanford and *Nymphæus* of A. O. Hume, were specially framed for its reception.

4. The robin-snipe or red-breasted sandpiper, *Tringa canutus*: a clipped name among gunners. Also *beach-robin*. See *knot*[2], 1.—5. The sea-robin or red-breasted merganser, *Mergus serrator*. [Massachusetts.]—6. In *ichth.*, a sea-robin or flying-robin; one of several kinds of *Triglidæ*.—7. A local name of the pinfish. [U.S.]—8. A name variously applied (commonly as part of a compound) to the herb-robert, to species of *Lychnis*, and to some other plants. *Red-robin* denotes, besides the wheat-rust, the herb-robert, the *Lychnis diurna*, etc. See *ragged-robin* and *wake-robin*. [Prov. Eng.]—**Golden robin**, the Baltimore oriole, *Icterus galbula*.—**Ground robin**, the chewink. See *marsh-robin*, and cut under *Pipilo*. [Local, U. S.]—**Magpie robin**, a dayal. See cut under *Copsichus*.—**Oregon robin**, the varied thrush, *Turdus nævius* or *Hesperocichla nævia*.—**Red robin**, the scarlet tanager. [Local, U. S.]—**Robin redbreast.** See *robin-redbreast*.—**Robin's-egg blue**, a greenish blue, like that of the American robin's egg.—**Round robin.** See *round-robin*, 5.—**Sea robin.** See *sea-robin*.—**St. Lucas robin**, *Turdus* or *Merula confinis*, much like but specifically distinct from the common American robin, inhabiting Lower California.—**Water-robin.** See def. 3.—**Yellow robin**, an Australian bird of the genus *Eopsaltria*.

robin[2]† (rob'in), *n.* [Appar. ult. due to the F. name *Robin*: see *robin*[1].] A trimming on the front of a dress. *Davies.*

Several pieces of printed calico, remnants of silk, and such like, that . . . would serve for *robins* and facings.
Richardson, Pamela, I. xxix.

robin[3], *n.* Same as *robbin*[2].

robin-accentor (rob'in-ak-sen'tor), *n.* A small sylviine bird of Asia, *Accentor rubeculoides*: an occasional book-name, translating the specific designation bestowed by Moore in 1854 from Hodgson's MSS. This bird belongs to the same genus as the common hedge-sparrow of Europe, *A. modularis*, but resembles the British robin in the color of the breast. It inhabits the Himalayas and southward, Cashmere, Sikhim, etc.

robin-breast (rob'in-brest), *n.* The robin-snipe, or red-breasted sandpiper.

robin-dipper (rob'in-dip'ėr), *n.* The buffle, or buffle-headed duck. [New Eng.]

robinet (rob'in-et), *n.* [< ME. *robinet*, a chaffinch, < OF. *Robinet*, 'little Robin,' dim. of *Robin*, Robin; as a common noun, OF. *robinet*, a pipkin, tap, cock, F. *robinet*, a tap, cock.] 1. A chaffinch. Also *roberd*. *Cath. Ang.*, p. 310.—2. A little robin. See *robin*[1], 1. *Drayton*, Muses' Elysium, viii.—3. A tap or faucet.—4†. A military engine for throwing darts and stones. *Grose.*

robing (rō'bing), *n.* [Verbal n. of *robe*[1], *v.*] 1. The act of putting on a robe or ceremonious apparel.—2. Material for women's gowns and the like: a term of the eighteenth century.—3. A kind of trimming like a flounce or ruffle, used on women's and children's garments. *Dict. of Needlework.*

Robin Goodfellow. 1. A domestic spirit or fairy, said to be the offspring of a mortal woman and Oberon, king of Fairyland. He is analogous to the brownie of Scotland. It was from the popular belief in this spirit that Shakspere's Puck was derived.

2. As a general name, an elf; a fairy.

Kottri, or Kibaldi; such as wee
Pugs and Hob-goblins call. Their dwellings bee
In corners of old houses least frequented,
Or beneath stacks of wood: and these conuented,
Make fearefull noise in Buttries and in Dairies;
Robin good-fellowes some, some call them Fairies.
Heywood, Hierarchy of Angels, p. 574.

robing-room (rō'bing-röm), *n.* A room where robes of ceremony are put on and off; a vestiary: as, the peers' *robing-room* in the House of Lords.

Robinia (rọ-bin'i-ạ̈), *n.* [NL. (Linnæus, 1737), named after the royal gardeners at Paris, Jean *Robin* (1550–1629) and his son Vespasien *Robin*; the latter introduced this genus into Europe, under the name *Pseudacacia*, in 1635.] A genus of leguminous trees and shrubs of the tribe *Galegeæ*, type of the subtribe *Robinieæ*; the locusts. It is characterized by a legume with thin valves, winged on its upper margin, and by papilionaceous flowers with a broad reflexed standard, an awl-

Flowering Branch of Locust (*Robinia Pseudacacia*).
a, pod; *b*, flower.

shaped inflexed style terminating a stalked and many-ovuled ovary, and surrounding these a long sheath of ten diadelphous stamens, one of them partly, or at length wholly, free. The branchlets and leafstalks are nearly smooth, bristly, or viscid-hairy. The leaves are unequally pinnate with stipulate leaflets, and are furnished with a pair of bristle-shaped stipules, or of short stout spines in their place. The flowers are white or rose-purple, borne in conspicuous racemes. There are 5 or 6 species, 2 of them little-known Mexican trees, the others native in the southern and central United States. Of the latter the chief is *R. Pseudacacia*, the common locust or false acacia, widely planted and naturalized in the Northern States, also much planted in Europe, where it presents several varieties. For this and other species, see *locust*[2], 1, and *rose-acacia*; also *acacia*, 3.

Robinieæ (rob-i-nī'ẹ̄-ē), *n. pl.* [NL. (Bentham and Hooker, 1862), < *Robinia* + *-eæ*.] A subtribe of leguminous plants of the tribe *Galegeæ*. It is characterized by racemed flowers from the axils or fascicled at the older nodes, commonly free banner-stamen, blunt anthers, numerous ovules, somewhat rigid style, and usually flat and two-valved pod. It includes 16 genera, of which 11 are American, 1 African, 3 Australasian, and 1 (*Sesbania*) of general distribution. They are either herbs, shrubs, or trees, rarely shrubby climbers. For important genera, see *Robinia* (the type), *Sesbania*, and *Olneya*.

robin-redbreast (rob'in-red'brest), *n.* [Early mod. E. *robyn redbrest*: see *robin*[1].] 1. Same as *robin*[1], 1.

Robyn redbrest,
He shall be the preest
The requiem masse to synge.
Skelton, Phyllyp Sparowe, l. 399.

No burial this pretty pair
Of any man receives,
Till *Robin-red-breast* piously
Did cover them with leaves.
Children in the Wood (Child's Ballads, III. 133).

2. Same as *robin*[1], 2.—3. The American bluebird, *Sialia sialis*: an occasional misnomer. See *bluebird*, and cut under *Sialia*.—4. The old-time Bow street runner: in allusion to the color of his waistcoat. [Slang, Eng.]—**Robin-redbreast's pincushion.** Same as *bedegar*.

robin-ruddock (rob'in-rud'ọk), *n.* Same as *robin*[1], 1.

Dyd you ever see two suche little *Robin ruddockes*
So laden with breeches?
R. Edwards, Damon and Pythias.

robin-run-in-the-hedge (rob'in-run'in-thẹ̄-hej), *n.* The ground-ivy, *Nepeta Glechoma*; the bedstraw, *Galium Aparine*; rarely the bindweed, *Convolvulus sepium*; and the bittersweet, *Solanum Dulcamara*. [Prov. Eng.]

robin-sandpiper (rob'in-sand'pi-pėr), *n.* Same as *robin-snipe*, 1.

robin-snipe (rob'in-snīp), *n.* 1. The red-breasted or ash-colored sandpiper; the canute or knot, *Tringa canutus*. In plain gray plumage it is also called *white robin-snipe*. See *knot*[2], 1.—2. Same as *red-breasted snipe* (*a*) (which see, under *red-breasted*). [New Eng.]

robin's-plantain (rob'inz-plan'tạn), *n.* See *plantain*[1].

robin's-rye (rob'inz-rī), *n.* The haircap-moss, *Polytrichum juniperinum*: so called, perhaps, as suggesting a miniature grain-field. Also *robin-wheat*. See *haircap-moss*.

robin-wheat (rob'in-hwēt), *n.* Same as *robin's-rye*.

The birds are not the only harvesters of the pretty moss known as *robin-wheat*. *Pop. Sci. Mo.*, XXIX. 368.

roble (rō'bl), *n.* [< Sp. *roble*, oak-tree, < L. *robur*, oak, oak-tree: see *robust*.] 1. In California, one of the white oaks, *Quercus lobata*, also called *weeping oak*. It is a majestic tree with very widely spreading branches; its wood is of little value except for fuel.—2. In the West Indies, *Platymiscium platystachyum* and *Catalpa longisiliqua*, trees yielding ship-timber.—3. In Chili, a species of beech, *Fagus obliqua*, which affords a durable hard-wood building-material.

rob-o-Davy†, *n.* [Prob. orig. *rob-of-Davy*, 'Davy's syrup' (see *rob*[2]); *Davy* being a familiar term for a Welshman, and *metheglin* a Welsh name for mead.] Metheglin.

Sherry, nor *Rob-o-Davy* here could flow,
The French frontiniacke, claret, red nor white,
Graves nor high-country, could our hearts delight.
Taylor's Works (1630). (*Nares.*)

roborant (rob'ọ̄-rant), *a.* and *n.* [= F. *roborant* = Sp. Pg. It. *roborante*, < L. *roboran(t-)s*, ppr. of *roborare*, strengthen: see *roborate*.] I. *a.* Tonic; strengthening.

II. *n.* A medicine that strengthens; a tonic.

roborate† (rob'ọ̄-rāt), *v. t.* [< L. *roboratus*, pp. of *roborare*, strengthen (> It. *roborare* = Sp. Pg. *roborar* = OF. *roborer*), < *robur* (*robor-*), strength: see *robust*. Cf. *corroborate*.] To give strength to; strengthen; confirm; establish.

This Bull also relateth to ancient priviledges of popes and princes, bestowed upon her; which herein are *roborated* and confirmed.
Fuller, Hist. of Cambridge Univ., ii. 37.

roboration (rob-ọ̄-rā'shọn), *n.* [= OF. *roboration* = Sp. *roboracion* = Pg. *roboração*, < ML. *roboratio(n-)*, a strengthening, < L. *roborare*, strengthen: see *roborate*. Cf. *corroboration*.] A strengthening. *Bailey*, 1731. [Rare.]

roborean (rọ-bō'rẹ̄-an), *a.* [< L. *roboreus*, of oak (see *roboreous*), + *-an*.] Same as *roboreous*. *Bailey*, 1731. [Rare.]

roboreous (rọ-bō'rẹ̄-us), *a.* [< L. *roboreus*, made of oak, < *robur*, an oak: see *robust*.] Made of oak; hence, strong. *Bailey*, 1727. [Rare.]

Robulina (rō-bū-lī'nạ̈), *n.* [NL. (D'Orbigny, 1826, as a genus of supposed cephalopods), < L. *robur*, strength, + a dim. *-ina*, the reg. term. with this author for his genera of microscopic cephalopods.] A genus of foraminifers. Also called *Lampas*.

Robur Caroli (rō'bėr kar'ọ̄-lī). [NL., Charles's Oak (see def.): L. *robur*, oak; ML. *Caroli*, gen. of *Carolus*, Charles: see *carl*.] A now obsolete constellation, introduced by Halley in 1677, between Argo and Centaurus, to represent the royal oak in which Charles II. was hidden after the battle of Worcester.

robust (rọ̄-bust'), *a.* [< OF. (and F.) *robuste* = Sp. Pg. It. *robusto*, < L. *robustus*, strong, < *robur*, OL. *robus* (*robor-*), hardness, strength, a hard wood, oak, an oak-tree; = Skt. *rabhas*, violence, force, < √ *rabh*, seize.] 1. Having or indicating great strength; strong; lusty; sinewy; muscular; sound; vigorous: as, a *robust* body; *robust* youth; *robust* health.

> A *robust* boisterous Rogue knocked him down.
> *Howell*, Letters, I. iii. 22.

> Survey the warlike horse! didst thou invest
> With thunder his *robust* distended chest?
> *Young*, Paraphrase of Job.

> I said, "How is Mr. Murdstone?" She replied, "My brother is *robust*, I am obliged to you."
> *Dickens*, David Copperfield, xxvi.

> One can only respect a *robust* faith of this sort.
> *Saturday Rev.*, May, 1874, p. 674.

2. Violent; rough; rude.

> Romp-loving miss
> Is haul'd about, in gallantry *robust*.
> *Thomson*, Autumn, l. 529.

3. Requiring vigor or strength: as, *robust* employment. *Imp. Dict.*—4. In *zoöl.*, stout; thick: as, a *robust* joint; *robust* antennæ. =**Syn.** 1. *Strong, Robust, Lusty, Sturdy, Stalwart, Stout*, hale, hearty, brawny, mighty, powerful. *Strong* is the generic term among these, and is the most widely used in figurative applications. By derivation it means having the power of exerting great muscular force. *Robust* suggests an oaken strength, hence compactness, toughness, soundness of constitution, blooming health, and good size if not largeness of frame. *Lusty* characterizes the kind of strength that one enjoys possessing, abounding health, strength, vitality, and spirits. *Sturdy* suggests compactness and solidity even more than *robust* does; it expresses a well-knit strength that is hard to shake or resist, standing strongly upon its feet. *Stalwart* suggests tallness or largeness with great strength or sturdiness. *Stout* is little different from *strong*; it sometimes means strong to do or to support burdens: as, a *stout* defender; a *stout* porter carrying a heavy trunk.

robustious (rọ̄-bus'tyus), *a.* [Formerly also *robusteous*, *robustuous*; < L. *robusteus*, oaken (*robustus*, oaken, strong): see *robust*.] Robust; rough; violent; rude. [Obsolete or archaic.]

> Violent and *robustuous* seas.
> *Heywood*, Jupiter and Io (Works, ed. Pearson, 1874, [VI. 258).

> These redundant locks,
> *Robustious* to no purpose, clustering down,
> Vain monument of strength.
> *Milton*, S. A., l. 569.

> Poh! you are so *robustious*, you had like to put out my eye; I assure you, if you blind me, you must lead me.
> *Swift*, Polite Conversation, i.

robustiously (rọ̄-bus'tyus-li), *adv.* In a robustious manner. [Obsolete or archaic.]

> The multitude commend writers as they do fencers or wrestlers; who if they come in *robustiously*, and put for it with a deal of violence, are received for the braver fellows.
> *B. Jonson*, Discoveries.

robustiousness (rọ̄-bus'tyus-nes), *n.* Vigor; muscular size and strength. [Obsolete or archaic.]

> That *robustiousness* of body, and puissance of person, which is the only fruit of strength.
> *Sir E. Sandys*, State of Religion, sig. S. 2.

robustly (rọ̄-bust'li), *adv.* In a robust manner; with great strength; muscularly.

robustness (rọ̄-bust'nes), *n.* The quality of being robust; strength; vigor, or the condition of the body when it has full firm flesh and sound health.

roc[1] (rok), *n.* [Also *rock, rok, ruc, ruck, rukh*; = G. *roc* = Sw. *roc*, *rok* = Dan. *rok* = It. *ruch*, *rochi* (Florio), < Ar. Pers. *rukh*, a roc. Cf. *rook*[2].] A fabulous bird of prey of monstrous size, famous in Arabian mythology, and corresponding to the Persian simurg. There is no certain basis of fact upon which the myth of the roc rests. The most colossal birds of which we have any knowledge are the dinornithic moas of New Zealand and the Madagascar æpyornithic elephant-birds. The largest known rapacious bird (the roc figures as a bird of prey) is the *Harpagornis*, which may have been able to kill a moa, though certainly not to fly away with one. The most plausible speculation bases the roc on the *Æpyornis*. See the quotation.

> On the 27th of January, 1851, Isidore Geoffroy Saint-Hilaire read before the Parisian Academy of Sciences a paper, in which he described two enormous eggs and part of the metatarsus of a bird which he called *Æpyornis maximus*. . . . This brought again to mind the old story of the famous Venetian traveller, Marco Polo, who located the *ruc* or *roc*, the giant bird of the Arabian tales, upon Madagascar, and related that the great Khan of the Tartars, having heard of the bird, sent messengers to Madagascar, who brought back a feather nine spans long, and two palms in circumference.
> *Stand. Nat. Hist.*, IV. 47.

Roc's egg, something marvelous or prodigious, having no foundation in fact; a mare's nest.

roc[2]†, *n.* A Middle English form of *rock*[1].

rocaille (rọ̄-kaly'), *n.* [F., rockwork, formerly also *rochaille*, < *roche*, a rock: see *roach*[2].] The scroll ornament of the eighteenth century, and especially of the epoch of Louis XV., combining forms apparently based on those of water-worn rocks and those of shells or deduced from them. See *rococo*.

rocambole (rok'am-bōl), *n.* [Also *rokambole*, and formerly also *rocombole*; < F. *rocambole*, < G. *rockenbollen*, *roggenbollen* (so called because it grows among rye), < *rocken*, *roggen*, rye, + *bolle*, a bulb: see *rye* and *boll*[1].] A plant of the onion kind, *Allium Scorodoprasum*, native through the middle latitudes of Europe, and there somewhat cultivated. Its uses resemble those of garlic and the shallot, like which, also, it has a compound bulb composed of bulblets or cloves.

> Insipid taste, old friend, to them who Paris know,
> Where *rocombole*, shallot, and the rank garlic grow.
> *W. King*, Art of Cookery, l. 336.

Roccella (rok-sel'ạ̈), *n.* [NL. (A. P. de Candolle, 1805), an accom. form (based on ML. *rocca*, *roca*, a rock) of It. *orcella*, F. *orseille*, etc., orchil: see *orchil*, *archil*.] A genus of parmeliaceous lichens of the tribe *Usneei*. The thallus is fruticulose or finally pendulous, alike on both sides, and cartilaginous-coriaceous; the medullary layer is loosely cottony. The species are few and closely related, growing especially in the warmer maritime regions of the earth, and furnishing the famous archil or orchil of dyers. *R. tinctoria* and *R. fuciformis*, the best-known species, are the chief sources of the dye. See cut under *archil*; see also *canary-moss*, *cape-weed*, *dyer's-moss*, *flat-orchil*, *litmus*, *Mauritius-weed*.

roccellic (rok-sel'ik), *a.* [< *Roccella* + *-ic*.] Related to or derived from *Roccella*.—**Roccellic acid**, $C_{17}H_{32}O_4$, a crystalline acid which occurs uncombined in *Roccella tinctoria*.

roccellin (rok-sel'in), *n.* [< *roccell(ic)* + *-in*[2].] A coal-tar color: same as *orseillin*.

roccelline (rok-sel'in), *a.* [< *Roccella* + *-ine*[1].] In *bot.*, of or pertaining to the genus *Roccella*.

Roccus (rok'us), *n.* [NL. (S. L. Mitchell, 1814), < ML. *rocca*, E. *rock*: see *rock*[1].] A genus of serranoid fishes. It contains *R. lineatus*, the common rockfish or striped-bass of the United States, and *R. chrysops*, the white-bass. Both are well-known game-fish, of some economic importance. See cut under *bass*.

roche[1]†, *n.* A Middle English form of *roach*[1].

roche[2], *n.* and *v.* See *roach*[2].

Rochea (rō'kē-ạ̈), *n.* [NL. (A. P. de Candolle, 1799), named after François *Laroche*, who wrote on the genera *Ixia* and *Gladiolus*.] A genus of plants of the order *Crassulaceæ*. It is characterized by a salver-shaped corolla with its tube much longer than the small five-cleft calyx, the five stamens united to the petals, and five free carpels, attenuated into elongated and exserted converging styles. The 4 species are natives of South Africa, and are fleshy undershrubs, bearing thick opposite leaves with united bases. The flowers are showy and rather large, white, yellow, scarlet, or rose-colored, and clustered in dense cymes. For these and the singular leaves the species are somewhat cultivated as house-plants. *R. coccinea*, with scarlet flowers, has the name of *coral*, and *R. falcata* is sometimes called *ice-plant*.

Rochelle powder (rọ̄-shel' pou″dėr). [< *La Rochelle*, a city in France, + *powder*.] Same as *Seidlitz powder*, or *compound effervescing powder* (which see, under *powder*).

Rochelle salt. See *salt*[1].

roches moutonnées (rosh mö-to-nā'). [F.: *roche*, rock (see *roach*[2], *rock*[1]); *moutonnée*, fem. of *moutonné*, rounded like the back of a sheep: see *mutton*.] Scattered knobs of rock rounded and smoothed by glacial action: fancifully so called from their resemblance, as seen rising here and there or in groups above a surface, to a flock of sheep lying down: sometimes Englished as "sheep-backs."

> The surface of rock, instead of being jagged, rugged, or worn into rugged defiles, is even and rounded, often dome-shaped or spheroidal. . . . Such surfaces were called *Roches Moutonnées* by De Saussure.
> *J. D. Forbes*, Travels in the Alps, p. 53.

rochet[1] (roch'et), *n.* [Also dial. *rocket*; < ME. *rochet*, *rochette*, also *roket*, *rokette*, < OF. *rochet*, *roquet*, a frock, a prelate's rochet, F. dial. *rochet*, a blouse, mantle, = Sp. Pg. *roquete* = It. *rocchetto*, *roccetto* (ML. *rochetum*), a rochet, dim. of ML. *roccus*, *rocus*, < OHG. *roch*, MHG. *roc* (rock), G. *rock* = MLG. D. *rok* = OFries. *rokk* = AS. *roc*, *rocc* = Icel. *rokkr*, a frock, coat; cf. Ir. *rocan*, a mantle, cloak, Gael. *rochall*, a coverlet.] 1. Originally, a short cloak worn by men of all degrees, also by women (in this case frequently a white linen outer garment).

> A *Roket* full rent & Ragget aboue,
> Cast ouer his corse.
> *Destruction of Troy* (E. E. T. S.), l. 13525.

> A womman wel more fetys is
> In *roket* than in cote, ywis.
> *Rom. of the Rose*, l. 1242.

> Superior vestis mulierum, Anglice a *rochet*.
> *MS. Bibl. Reg.*, 12 B. i. f. 12. (*Halliwell.*)

2. *Eccles.*, a close-fitting vestment of linen or lawn, worn by bishops and some others. It reaches to the knees or lower, and has close sleeves extending to the wrists, or is sleeveless. The rochet is a variety of the alb or surplice, the latter differing from both alb and rochet by the fullness of its sleeves. In the Roman Catholic Church the rochet is worn by bishops and abbots, usually under a manteletta, and, as a choir vestment, by some canons. In the Anglican Church the rochet is worn under the chimere—these vestments constituting the distinctive episcopal habit as ordinarily worn in church and in Parliament and Convocation. The lawn sleeves are now made very full, and attached to the chimere, not to the rochet.

> And an Arm men seyn is ther
> Of seint Thomas the holy Marter, . . .
> And a *Rochet* that is good,
> Al be-spreint with his blod.
> *Stacions of Rome* (ed. Furnivall), l. 501.

> The Elected Bishop, vested with his *Rochet*, shall be presented . . . unto the Presiding Bishop.
> *Book of Common Prayer* [American], Consecration of [Bishops.

3†. Hence, a bishop: also used attributively.

> They would strain us out a certain figurative prelate, by wringing the collective allegory of those seven angels into seven single *rochets*.
> *Milton*, Church-Government, i. 5.

4. A mantelet worn by the peers of England during ceremonies.

rochet[2] (roch'et), *n.* [< F. *rouget*, a gurnard.] A kind of fish, the roach or piper gurnard.

> The whiting, known to all, a general wholesome dish,
> The gurnet, *rochet*, mayd, and mullet, dainty fish.
> *Drayton.*

> Slit thy nose,
> Like a raw *rochet!*
> *B. Jonson*, Volpone, iii. 6.

> *Rochets*, whitings, or such common fish.
> *W. Browne.*

roching-cask (roch'ing-kȧsk), *n.* A tank lined with lead, used for crystallizing alum.

rock[1] (rok), *n.* [< ME. *rocke*, *rokke*, < AS. **roc* (in *stān-rocc*, 'stone-rock') = OF. *roc*, m. (= It. *rocco*, m.), *roke*, usually assibilated *roche* (> ME. *roche*, E. obs. *roach*[2], q. v.), F. *roche*, f., = Pr. *roca*, *rocha* = Sp. *roca* = Pg. *roca*, *rocha* = It. *rocca*, *roccia*, < ML. *roca*, *rocca*, a rock; prob. of Celtic origin: Ir. Gael. *roc* = Bret. *roch*, a rock. According to Diez, prob. < LL. **rupica*, or *rupea*, < L. *rupes*, a rock.] 1. The mass of mineral matter of which the earth, so far as accessible to observation, is made up; a mass, fragment, or piece of that crust, if too large to be designated as a *stone*, and if spoken of in a general way without special designation of its nature. When there is such special designation, the term *stone* is more generally adopted, as in *building-stone*, *paving-stone*, *limestone*, *freestone*; or the special designation of the material itself may be used without qualification, as *granite*, *slate*, *marble*, etc. The unconsolidated stony materials which form a considerable part of the superficial crust, or that which is at or near the surface, such as sand, gravel, and clay, are not commonly designated as *rock* or *rocks*; the geologist, however, includes under the term *rock*, for the purpose of general description, all the consolidated materials forming the crust, as well as the fragmental or detrital beds which have been derived from it. Rocks are ordinarily composed of two or more mineral species, but some rocks are made up almost entirely of one species: thus, granite is essentially an aggregate of quartz, feldspar, and mica, while marble usually consists chiefly of carbonate of lime, and sandstone and quartzite chiefly of quartz. The number of varieties of rock, according to the classification and description of lithologists, is very great. The number of names popularly in use for rocks is small: *granite*, *porphyry*, *lava*, *sandstone* or *freestone*, *limestone*, *marble*, and *slate* are terms under one or the other of which by far the largest part of the rocks are commonly classed. (See these words.) More than 600 distinct species of minerals have been described, but a very small number of them occur as essential constituents of rocks: of these, quartz, the feldspars, the micas, the minerals of the augite and hornblende group, talc, chlorite, olivin, and carbonate of lime, with which often more or less of carbonate of magnesia is associated, form the great bulk of the rocks. But there are several other minerals which are quite commonly found as accessory constituents, and sometimes in masses large enough to be worthy of the designation of *rock*: such are garnet, epidote, various oxids of iron, pyrites, apatite, andalusite, leucite, tourmalin, and a few others. Some mineral substances occur in masses of great extent and thickness, but do not play the part of rock-forming minerals: such are salt, gypsum, and the varieties of coal. Rocks are variously classed by geologists. The most general subdivision of them is into *igneous* and *aqueous*: the former are divided into *plutonic* and *volcanic*, according as they have been formed under conditions of depth and pressure, like granite, or have been poured out upon the surface in the manner of lava. The aqueous rocks are also designated as *sedimentary*, *fossiliferous*, or *stratified*. The sedimentary rocks in general are believed to be made up of material resulting from the decay and abrasion of igneous masses, since almost all geologists admit that the crust of the earth has cooled from a state of fusion. Part of the stratified deposits, however, have been formed through the agency of life, as in the case of the limestones, most of which have been secreted from an aqueous solution by various organisms, and of coal, which is the result of a peculiar kind of decay of vegetable matter. Some rocks have been formed by the simple evaporation of a solution: for instance, rock-salt. The sedimentary rocks are classified for lithological description according to the nature and texture of the materials of which they are made up: they are arranged in the chronological order of their deposition according to the nature of the fossils which they contain. Sedimentary rocks have frequently been greatly changed in character by metamorphosis, by which they have been rendered crystalline, and sometimes made so closely to resemble igneous rocks that their true character can only with the greatest difficulty be made out.

> Whan ye han maad the coost so clene
> Of rokkes that ther nys no stoon ysene.
> *Chaucer*, Franklin's Tale, l. 15772.

A *rock* may be defined as a mass of mineral matter, composed of one, more usually of several, kinds of minerals, having, as a rule, no definite external form, and liable to vary considerably in chemical composition.
A. Geikie, Encyc. Brit., X. 229.

2. A stone of any size, even a pebble. [Vulgar, U. S.]

I put a hot *rock* to his feet, and made him a large bowl o' catmint tea. *Georgia Scenes*, p. 193.

> Now I hold it is not decent for a scientific gent
> To say another is an ass,—at least, to all intent;
> Nor should the individual who happens to be meant
> Reply by heaving *rocks* at him to any great extent.
> *Bret Harte*, The Society upon the Stanislaus.

3. A mass of stone forming an eminence or a cliff.

And he [Samson] went down and dwelt in the top of the *rock* Etam. *Judges* xv. 8.

> When he sees afar
> His country's weather-bleached and battered *rocks*
> From the green wave emerging. *Cowper*, Task, v. 834.

4. Hence, in *Scrip.*, figuratively, foundation; strength; asylum; means of safety; defense.

The Lord is my *rock*. 2 Sam. xxii. 2.

5. A cause or source of peril or disaster: from the wrecking of vessels on rocks: as, this was the *rock* on which he split.

> Lo, where comes that *rock*
> That I advise your shunning.
> (Enter Cardinal Wolsey.)
> *Shak.*, Hen. VIII., i. 1. 113.

Either we must say every Church govern'd itself, or else we must fall upon that old foolish *Rock*, that St. Peter and his Successours govern'd all. *Selden*, Table-Talk, p. 57.

6. A kind of hard sweetmeat, variously flavored.

Around a revolving dial were arranged various-sized pieces of peppermint *rock*, closely resembling putty, but prized by youthful gourmands.
Harper's Mag., LXXVI. 625.

7. Same as *rockfish*, 1 (*a*). [Southern U. S.] —**8.** The rock-dove, *Columba livia*, more fully called *blue-rock*.—**9.** A kind of soap. See the quotation.

The action of lime upon the constituents of tallow decomposes them, glycerin being set at liberty, while calcium stearate and oleate are formed. . . . These salts, . . . when mixed together, constitute an insoluble soap, technically called *rock*.
W. L. Carpenter, Soap and Candles, p. 254.

10. A piece of money: commonly in the plural: as, a pocketful of *rocks*. [Slang, U. S.]

Here I am in town without a *rock* in my pocket.
New Orleans Picayune. (*Bartlett.*)

11. A very hard kind of cheese, made from skimmed milk, used in Hampshire, England. *Halliwell*.—**Acidic** (or **acid**) **rock**. See *acidic*.—**Æolian, aqueous, argillaceous rocks.** See the adjectives.—**Aërial rocks.** Same as *æolian rocks*.—**Band of rock.** See *band*[2] and *blackband*.—**Blue, clay, coltsfoot, conglomerate rock.** See the qualifying words.—**Cock of the rock.** See *cock*[1].—**Country rock.** See *country*, 8, and *country-rock*.—**Denuded rocks.** See *denuded*.—**Detrital rock.** See *detrital*.—**Dressed rocks,** ice-worn bosses of rock, usually called *roches moutonnées* or *sheep-back rocks*.—**Dudley rock.** See *Dudley limestone*, under *limestone*.—**Farewell rock.** See *farewell*.—**Gibraltar rock,** rock-candy.—**Intrusive rocks.** See *intrusive*.—**Kellaways rocks,** in *geol.*, the lower of the two zones into which the Oxfordian is divided, the latter being a division of the Middle or Oxford Oolite. The Oxfordian is the lowest division of the Upper Jura or White Jura of the Continental geologists. The name *Kellaways* is frequently spelled *Kelloway*. It is a locality in Wiltshire, England.—**Littoral rocks.** See *littoral*.—**Ludlow rocks,** in *geol.*, a portion of the Upper Silurian rocks, 2,000 feet in thickness. It is composed of three groups, the lower Ludlow rock or mudstone, the Aymestry limestone, and the upper Ludlow rock. They have their name from Ludlow in Shropshire, England, where they are characteristically developed.—**Metamorphic rocks.** See *metamorphism*.—**On the rocks,** quite out of funds; in great want of money. [Slang.]—**Rock-drilling machine,** a power-drill for boring rock or mineral substances. It operates either by percussion or by rotation. The usual motive power, in confined situations, is compressed air.—**Rock ice-cream.** Same as *granite*, 2.—**Rock-onion.** Same as *cibol*, 2, and *stone-leek* (see *leek*).—**Rocks of mechanical origin.** See *mechanical*. =**Syn.** It is an error to use *rock* for a stone so small that a man can handle it: only a fabulous person or a demi-god can lift a *rock*.

> When Ajax strives some *rock's* vast weight to throw,
> The line too labours, and the words move slow.
> *Pope*, Essay on Criticism, l. 370.

> The Douglas rent an earth-fast *stone*
> From its deep bed, then heaved it high,
> And sent the fragment through the sky.
> *Scott*, L. of the L., v. 23.

rock[1] (rok), *v. t.* [‹ *rock*[1], *n.* Cf. OF. *rocher*, stone, ‹ *roche*, a stone, rock.] To throw stones at; stone. [U. S.]

It used to be said that if an unknown landsman showed himself in the streets [of Marblehead, Massachusetts] the boys would follow after him, crying, "*Rock* him! *Rock* him! He's got a long-tailed coat on!"
O. W. Holmes, Poet at the Breakfast Table, xii.

rock[2] (rok), *v.* [‹ ME. *rokken*, also *roggen* (cf. OF. *rocquer*), ‹ AS. **roccian* (in a gloss) = Dan. *rokke* = Sw. freq. *rockera*, shake, rock; cf. OHG. *rucchen*, MHG. *rucken*, *rücken*, G. *rücken*, pull, = Dan. *rykke* = Sw. *rycka*, pull, = Icel. *rykkja*, pull roughly and hastily; from the noun, OHG. *ruc* (gen. *rucch-*), MHG. *ruc* (gen. *ruck-*), G. *ruck*, a pull, jolt, jerk, = Sw. *ryck* = Dan. *ryk*, a pull.] **I.** *trans.* **1.** To move backward and forward, as a body supported below (especially on a single point, a narrow line, or a curved base); cause to sway upon a support: as, to *rock* a cradle; to *rock* a chair; sometimes, to cause to reel or totter.

> The cradel at hir beddes feet is set,
> To *rokken*. *Chaucer*, Reeve's Tale, l. 237.

> The god whose earthquakes *rock* the solid ground.
> *Pope*, Iliad, xiii. 68.

2. To move backward and forward in a cradle, chair, etc.

> High in his hall, *rocked* in a chair of state,
> The king with his tempestuous council sate.
> *Dryden*, tr. of Ovid's Epistles, xi.

3. To lull; quiet, as if by rocking in a cradle.

> Sleep *rock* thy brain. *Shak.*, Hamlet, iii. 2. 237.

> Blow, Ignorance; O thou, whose idle knee
> *Rocks* earth into a lethargy.
> *Quarles*, Emblems, i. 14.

4. In *engraving*, to abrade the surface of, as a copper or steel plate, preparatory to scraping a mezzotinto. See *cradle*, *n.*, 4 (*e*).—**5†.** To cleanse by rocking or shaking about in sand.

> His other harnays, that holdely watz keped,
> Bothe his paunce, & his platez piked ful clene,
> The ryngez *rokked* of the roust, of his riche bruny;
> And al watz fresch as vpon fyrst.
> *Sir Gawayne and the Green Knight* (E. E. T. S.), l. 2018.

6. To affect by rocking in a manner indicated by a connected word or words: as, to *rock* one into a headache; the earthquake *rocked* down the houses.

> Tyl Resoun hadde reuthe on me and *rokked* me aslepe.
> *Piers Plowman* (B), xv. 11.

II. *intrans.* To move backward and forward; be moved backward and forward; reel.

> How her hand, in my hand being lock'd,
> Forced it to tremble with her loyal fear!
> Which struck her sad, and then it faster *rock'd*.
> *Shak.*, Lucrece, l. 262.

During the whole dialogue, Jonas had been *rocking* on his chair. *Dickens*, Martin Chuzzlewit, xliv.

> The blind wall *rocks*, and on the trees
> The dead leaf trembles to the bells.
> *Tennyson*, In Memoriam, Conclusion.

Rocking bob. Same as *balance-bob*.—**Rocking stone,** a large block of stone poised so nicely upon its point that a moderate force applied to it causes it to rock or oscillate. Such stones are most common in regions of granite, and especially where it has a marked cuboidal jointing. The quadrangular masses resulting from the weathering of this granite assume spherical forms, since the edges and angles waste away more rapidly than the sides, and a rocking stone is not infrequently the result. There are several rocking stones in the granite region of Devonshire and Cornwall, where they are known as *loggans*, *loggan-stones*, or *loggan-rocks*. The best-known of these is near Castle Treryn, St. Levan; it is about 17 feet long, and weighs about 65 tons. "There are seven loggan-rocks in the parish of Zennor." *Woodward*, Geol. of Eng. and Wales (2d ed.), p. 606.

The same cause affects granitic cliffs, rounding the surfaces formed by the "joints," and often leaving detached blocks on the brow of the cliff; and they also give rise to the *Rocking Stones* common in granite districts.
Prestwich, Geol., I. 56.

=**Syn. 1** and **2.** *Rock, Shake, Swing, Roll.* *Shake* expresses a quicker, more sudden, and less uniform motion than the others: as, to *shake* a tree or a carpet; his knees *shook*. *Rock* expresses the slow and regular motion to and fro of a body supported below—as a cradle upon *rockers*, or a *rocking* stone—or at the sides. *Swing* expresses the regular and generally slow motion to and fro, or around and around, of a body supported or held at one end, generally above: as, the *swinging* of a pendulum, a censer, a sword. *Roll* is sometimes used of an irregular motion to and fro, suggesting the *rolling* over of a round log: as, a *rolling* walk; the *rolling* of a ship in the trough of the sea. The figurative uses of these words are akin to their literal meanings: a ship *rocks* when the wind is steady on the aft quarter; it *swings* about its anchor with the change of the tide; it *shakes* with each blow from a heavy wave.

rock[2] (rok), *n.* [‹ *rock*[2], *v.*] The act of rocking; specifically, a step in fancy dancing.

rock[3] (rok), *n.* [‹ ME. *rokke*, *rocke*, *rok*, ‹ AS. **rocca* (not recorded) = MD. *rocke*, D. *rok*, *rokken* = OHG. *rocco*, *roccho*, *rocho*, MHG. *rocke*, G. *rocken* = Icel. *rokkr* = Sw. *rock* = Dan. *rok*, a distaff (cf. It. *rocca* = Sp. *rueca* = Pg. *roca*, a distaff; OF. *rocquet*, *rochet*, F. *rochet*, a spinning-wheel; ‹ Teut.); root unknown.] A distaff used in hand-spinning; the staff or frame about which the flax or wool is arranged from which the thread is drawn in spinning.

> Sad Clotho held the *rocke*, the whiles the thrid
> By griesly Lachesis was spun with paine.
> *Spenser*, F. Q., IV. ii. 48.

> Herself a snowy fleece doth wear,
> And these her *rock* and spindle bear.
> *B. Jonson*, Masque of Hymen.

Rock Monday, the Monday after Twelfth Day: so called because spinning, interrupted by the Christmas sports, was then resumed. Also called *Plow Monday*.

rock[4] (rok), *n.* [Perhaps a dial. var. of *rough*.] A young hedgehog. *Halliwell*. [Prov. Eng.]

rock[5], *n.* See *roc*[1].

rockahominie†, *n.* [Amer. Ind.] Same as *hominy*.

Sometimes also in their travels each man takes with him a pint or quart of *rockahomonie*—that is, the finest Indian corn parched and beaten to powder.
Beverley, Virginia, iii. ¶ 19.

rock-alum (rok'al'um), *n.* **1.** Same as *alum-stone*.—**2.** The solid residue obtained from potash crystals on their liquefaction by heat and subsequent cooling. *Spons' Encyc. Manuf.*, p. 326.—**3.** A factitious article made by coloring small crystalline fragments of alum with Venetian red.

rock-alyssum (rok'a-lis'um), *n.* See *Alyssum*.

rockaway (rok'a-wā), *n.* A four-wheeled pleasure-carriage with two or three seats (each for two persons) and a standing top. It is a distinctly American type of vehicle.

rock-badger (rok'baj'ėr), *n.* **1.** Parry's ground-squirrel, *Spermophilus parryi*, of northwestern North America.—**2.** See *Hyrax*, 1.

rock-barnacle (rok'bär'na-kl), *n.* A sessile cirriped which adheres to rocks, as any species of *Balanus* proper: not specific.

rock-basin (rok'bā'sn), *n.* In *phys. geog.*, a basin or hollow in a rock. Such cavities are common on the exposed surface of the rocks in various countries, and they are most frequently met with in granitic regions, especially in Cornwall and Devonshire, where they have been worn out by atmospheric erosion, assisted by the tendency to a concentric structure which granite frequently exhibits. These rock-basins have been, and still are by some, ascribed to the Druids. On the Scilly Islands such cavities are common; some are called *devil's kettles* and *devil's punch-bowls*, and one group is known as the *Kettle and Pans*. There are multitudes of them, of all dimensions, in the Sierra Nevada, but few have received names. See *kettle*[1], 4 (*b*).

rock-bass (rok'bås), *n.* **1.** A centrarchoid fish, *Ambloplites rupestris*; the redeye or goggle-

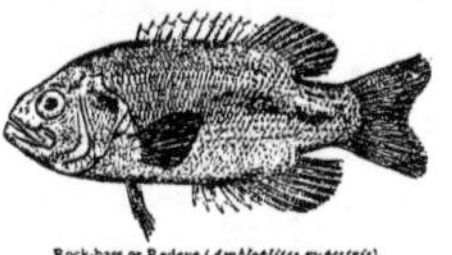

Rock-bass or Redeye (*Ambloplites rupestris*).

eye. It is found from the Great Lake region to Louisiana, attains a length of a foot, and is of an olive-green color with brassy tints and much dark mottling.

2. The striped-bass. See *Roccus*, and cut under *bass*[1].—**3.** A serranoid fish, *Serranus* or *Paralabrax clathratus*; the cabrilla: found off the coast of California, attaining a length of 18 inches.

rock-beauty (rok'bū'ti), *n.* A plant of the Pyrenees and Alps, *Draba* (*Petrocallis*) *Pyrenaica*, forming dense cushions 2 or 3 inches high, with pale-lilac sweet-scented flowers in early spring. With care it can be cultivated on rock-work.

rock-bird (rok'bėrd), *n.* **1.** A bird of the genus *Rupicola* or subfamily *Rupicolinæ*; a cock of the rock. See cut under *Rupicola*.—**2.** The rock-snipe.

rock-blackbird (rok'blak'bėrd), *n.* Same as *rock-ouzel*. [Local, Eng.]

rock-borer (rok'bōr'ėr), *n.* A bivalve mollusk of the family *Petricolidæ*.

rock-bound (rok'bound), *a.* Hemmed in by rocks.

> The breaking waves dash'd high
> On a stern and *rock-bound* coast.
> *Mrs. Hemans*, Landing of the Pilgrim Fathers.

rock-brake (rok'brāk), *n.* Same as *parsley-fern.*

rock-breaker (rok'brā″kėr), *n.* A machine for breaking rock and stones, in which the material to be broken passes between two jaws, one or both of which are movable. It is by machinery of this kind that stones are usually broken for road-metal.

rock-butter (rok'but″ėr), *n.* In *mineral.* See *butter*[1].

rock-candy (rok'kan″di), *n.* Pure sugar in cohering crystals of considerable size and hardness. Also called *candy-sugar*, and sometimes *Gibraltar rock.*

rock-cavy (rok'kā″vi), *n.* A South American quadruped of the family *Caviidæ, Kerodon moco* or *Cavia rupestris;* the moco.

rock-cist (rok'sist), *n.* [Shortened from *rock-cistus* (the plants were once included in the genus *Cistus*).] A book-name for plants of the genus *Helianthemum.*

rock-cod (rok'kod), *n.* See *cod*[2] and *rockfish.*

rock-cook (rok'kůk), *n.* The small-mouthed wrasse, *Centrolabrus exoletus*, about 4 inches long. [Cornwall, Eng.]

rock-cork (rok'kôrk), *n.* Mountain-cork, a white- or gray-colored variety of asbestos: so called from its lightness and fibrous structure. Also called *rock-leather.*

rock-crab (rok'krab), *n.* One of several different crabs found on rocky sea-bottoms, as the

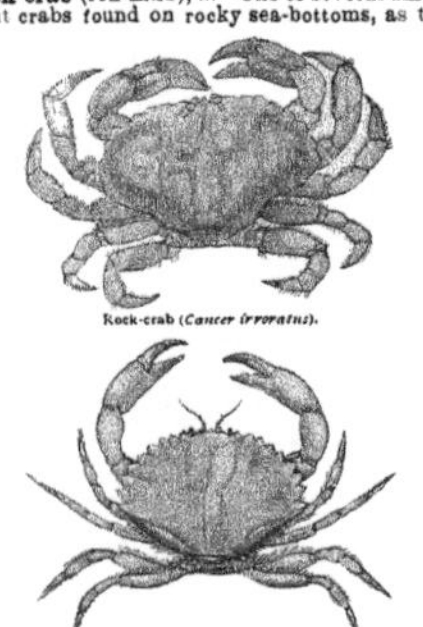

Rock-crab (*Cancer irroratus*).

California Rock-crab (*Cancer antennarius*).

common *Carcinus mænas, Cancer irroratus, C. antennarius, Panopæus depressus*, and related species. [Eng. and U. S.]

rock-cress (rok'kres), *n.* See *Arabis.*

rock-crowned (rok'kround), *a.* Crowned or surmounted with rocks: as, a *rock-crowned* height.

rock-crusher (rok'krush″ėr), *n.* A stone-breaker or stone-crusher.

rock-crystal (rok'kris″tạl), *n.* See *crystal*, and cut under *pokal.*

Rock-day (rok'dā), *n.* [< *rock*[3] + *day*[1].] A popular name for St. Distaff's day, or the day after Twelfth Day.

rock-demon (rok'dē″mọn), *n.* One of certain spirits or demons worshiped by the Huron Indians, and conceived of as dwelling in some famed, renowned, or dangerous rock.

> An early missionary account of a *rock-demon* worshipped by the Huron Indians will show with what absolute personality savages can conceive such a being.
> *E. B. Tylor*, Prim. Culture, II. 180.

rock-doe† (rok'dō), *n.* A species of Alpine deer.

> The *rock-doe* breeds chiefly upon the Alps: a creature of admirable swiftness. *N. Grew*, Museum.

rock-dolphin (rok'dol″fin), *n.* A local name at Brighton, England, of the sea-scorpion, *Cottus scorpius.*

rock-doo (rok'dö), *n.* A Scotch form of *rock-dove.*

rock-dove (rok'duv), *n.* 1. The rock-pigeon or blue-rock, *Columba livia:* in distinction from the other two British pigeons of the same genus, the ring-dove (*C. palumbus*) and the stock-dove (*C. œnas*). It is widely distributed throughout the western part of the Palearctic region, and is the reputed wild stock or original of the domestic pigeon. The commonest varieties of the latter retain close resem-

Rock-dove (*Columba livia*).

blance to the wild bird, as may be seen by comparing the figure here given with that under *pigeon.* 2. The sea-dove, sea-pigeon, or black guillemot, *Uria grylle:* so called because it breeds in the rocks. [Ireland.]

rock-drill (rok'dril), *n.* A machine-drill; a drill worked by steam-, water-, or horse-power: distinguished from a drill worked by hand. In the accompanying figures A, A are the legs which support the working parts shown in the section. The legs form a tripod stand which is pivoted at C to the bed-plate D.

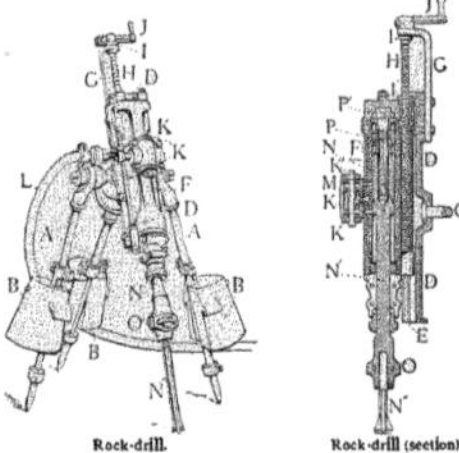

Rock-drill. Rock-drill (section).

The legs are weighted at B to hold the machine firmly when at work. The bed-plate has guideways E formed on its upper surface, one of which is shown in the section. To these ways are fitted guides on the cylinder F. A standard G is bolted to the back of the bed-plate, and at its upper end has a fixed bearing I for the feed-screw H. A winch *J* is used to turn the feed-screw, which, as the latter cannot move vertically, operates in the nut I′ to raise or lower the cylinder F together with all its attachments; K is the steam-chest and valve-box with bonnets K′. Steam is supplied to K by a steam-hose L; M (in the section) is the steam-thrown induction-valve, which also controls exhaust after the manner of the common slide-valve, but is cylindrical in form and is moved by the action of the steam admitted to K; N is the piston; N′, the piston-rod; N″, the drill, fitted to a socket O in the exterior end of N; P and P′ are parts of the mechanism which turns the piston, piston-rod, and drill a short distance on their vertical axis at each stroke of the piston.

rock-duck (rok'duk), *n.* The harlequin duck. *J. H. Langille.* [Nova Scotia.]

rock-eel (rok'ēl), *n.* A fish, *Murænoides gunnellus*, of the family *Xiphidiontidæ*, with an elongated smooth body, nearly eighty dorsal spines, and two spines and thirty-eight rays in dorsal. It inhabits the northern seas.

rockelt†, *n.* [Cf. *roquelaure.*] A woman's cloak. *Halliwell.* [Prov. Eng.]

rockelay (rok'e-lā), *n.* Same as *roquelaure.*

rock-elm (rok'elm), *n.* An American elm, *Ulmus racemosa*, highly valued for its heavy, hard, and strong timber, which is used in making agricultural implements, for railroad-ties, etc. Also *cork-elm, hickory-elm*, etc.

rocker[1] (rok'ėr), *n.* [< *rock*[1] + *-er*[1].] The rock-dove, *Columba livia. Montagu.* Also *rockier, rock.*

rocker[2] (rok'ėr), *n.* [< ME. *rokker;* < *rock*[2], *v.*, + *-er*[1].] One who or that which rocks. Specifically — (*a*) One who rocks a cradle.

> His majesty was graciously pleased that there should neither be nurse, *rocker*, nor any other officer belonging to the queen's nursery . . . save only Protestants.
> *Court and Times of Charles I.*, II. 63.

> His fellow, who the narrow bed had kept,
> Was weary, and without a *rocker* slept.
> *Dryden*, Cock and Fox, l. 228.

(*b*) The curved piece of wood on which a cradle or rocking-chair rocks. (c) A rocking-horse.

> There were beasts of all sorts; horses, in particular, of every breed, from the spotted barrel on four pegs . . . to the thoroughbred *rocker* on his highest mettle.
> *Dickens*, Cricket on the Hearth, ii.

(d) A rocking-chair. (*e*) In *engraving*, same as *cradle*, 4 (*e*). (*f*) A rocker-shaft. (*g*) In *mining*, same as *cradle* 4 (*i*) (1). (*h*) In an electric-lamp regulator, a lever, pivoted in the middle, carrying at its extremities the armatures of two electromagnets, by the alternate attraction of which the carbon rods are made to separate or to approach each other.

> The armatures of the two electro-magnets were placed at the two extremities of a *rocker*, carrying a lever for the release of the mechanisms used for the approach or withdrawal of the carbons.
> *Hospitalier*, Electricity (trans.), p. 170.

(*i*) A boat or yacht having a rocker keel.

> When a fast sloop of the straight-keel type came out, the *rockers* were beaten. *Tribune Book of Sports*, p. 251.

(*j*) A skate in which the bottom of the runner is not straight, but is convex from toe to heel. (*k*) A vessel for freezing chemical mixtures, essentially a freezer mounted on rockers. (*l*) In a railway gravel tip-car, a curved iron casting which supports the car-body, and on which the body rocks when the load is dumped. (*m*) One of two beams used in the body-frame of a carriage to support the floor-boards. See cut under *barouche.*—**Boston rocker**, a rocking-chair with a plain wooden seat shaped slightly to the person, and back and arms supported on slender uprights, usually turned. This form has persisted nearly unchanged for two centuries. [U. S.]—**Rocker keel**, a keel curved upward both forward and aft of the midship line.

rocker-cam (rok'ėr-kam), *n.* A cam keyed to a rock-shaft. It does not make successive complete revolutions, but has a reciprocating rotary movement through an arc of generally less than 180°. Such cams are much used in the valve-gear of steam-engines on river-boats propelled by paddle-wheels, in the valve-gear of some stationary engines, and also in the construction of other machinery. Also called *wiper.*

rockered (rok'ėrd), *a.* [< *rocker*[2] + *-ed*[1].] Shaped like a rocker; curved or bellied downward: as, a *rockered* keel.

rocker-shaft (rok'ėr-shȧft), *n.* Same as *rock-shaft.*

rocker-sleeve (rok'ėr-slēv), *n.* A part of the breech-action of a magazine-gun.

rockery (rok'ėr-i), *n.*; pl. *rockeries* (-iz). [< *rock*[1] + *-ery.*] An artificial mound formed of stones or fragments of rock, earth, etc., for the cultivation of particular kinds of plants, as ferns.

rocket[1] (rok'et), *n.* [= D. *raket* = G. *rakete* = Dan. Sw. *raket* = F. *roquet, roquette, racquette* (> Sp. *raquete*), < OIt. *rocchetto* (ML. *rochetus, rocheta*), a rocket, so named from its shape, lit. 'a bobbin,' It. *rocchetto*, a bobbin (*rochetta*, a distaff) (= F. *rochet, roquet*, a bobbin), dim. of *rocca*, a distaff: see *rock*[3].] 1. A cylindrical tube of pasteboard or metal filled with a mixture of niter, sulphur, charcoal, etc., which, on being ignited at the base, propels the tube forward by the impact of the liberated gases against the atmosphere. Rockets are used for various purposes. (*a*) In war, when the apparatus generally consists of a sheet-iron case filled with a composition such as is described above, and a head which may be solid, or hollow and filled with a bursting-charge. (*b*) Life-rockets, used for carrying a line over a wreck, and thus establishing communication between the ship and the shore. The Russian rocket has a short stick attached to the base and armed with a hook which slides in a groove on the under side of the rocket-stand and engages the ring of the chain attached to the line as the rocket leaves the stand. The German system comprises five-centimeter and eight-centimeter rockets and eight-centimeter anchor-rockets, all of which have long chains attached to the rocket-stick at one end and to the line at the other. The English system consists of double Boxer rockets placed end to end in a single metallic case, having a stick fastened to one side of the case. The Hooper rocket is a modification of the Hale war-rocket, and was very unsatisfactory in its results. All these rockets have metallic cases, and are fired by means of fuses. The uncertainty of their flight and their liability to deterioration by transportation and storage have prevented their adoption for life-saving purposes in the United States. (c) Signal- or sky-rockets, pasteboard cylinders filled with nearly

Fig. 1 Fig. 3 Fig. 4 Fig. 2

Life-saving Rocket.

Fig. 1. Rocket before firing: *a*, rocket proper; *c*, metal rod connecting rocket with a float *d* carrying a torch *e*, which burns after the rocket strikes the water, showing at night position of line *f*; *g*, rod to which line *f* is attached; *h*, fuse. Fig. 2. Rocket after firing: lettering as above. Fig. 3. Rocket proper: *a*, metallic shell filled with a slow-burning composition *b*, around a wooden core *k*, and supplied with symmetrically arranged vents as shown in fig. 4.

the same composition, but with a conical head containing stars of various ingredients and colors, and a quantity of powder which, when the rocket has attained its greatest height, bursts the cylinder, when the ignited stars spread through the air and cast a brilliant or colored light producing a beautiful effect. These rockets are used in signaling or for mere pyrotechnic display. Rockets are kept point foremost in their flight by means of a stick projecting behind, which acts in the same way as the shaft of an arrow.

To the head of such *rockets* may be placed petards, balls of fire, granadoes, etc., and so may be applied to warlike affairs. *Mathematical Recreations* (1674).

And the final event to himself [Burke] has been that, as he rose like a *rocket*, he fell like the stick. T. *Paine*, Letters to the Addressers. (*Bartlett.*)

2. The lever by which a forge-bellows is inflated.—**Congreve rocket**, a large rocket having a shell of sheet-iron and carrying charges of canister-shot, bullets, and other missiles. Sir William Congreve, who first introduced this weapon into warfare, and from whom its name is derived, caused sizes to be constructed ranging from 12 to 32 pounds, with sticks for the larger sizes 20 feet in length. The first notable use of Congreve rockets was at Copenhagen in 1807, and among the then-existing means of attack it proved a very formidable weapon. The composition used in these rockets is saltpeter, sulphur, and charcoal; and they sometimes have a metal head loaded with a bursting-charge very destructive in a fortress or town. Modern improvements in ordnance have supplied more efficient means of attack, and rockets are now used in warfare chiefly as a means for signaling.

rocket^{1} (rok'et), *v. i.* [< *rocket*^{1}, *n.*] To fly straight up rapidly when flushed, as a pheasant.

The driven partridge and the *rocketing* pheasant are beyond the skill of many a man who considers himself a very fair shot. Quarterly *Rev.*, CXXVII. 387.

Presently an old cock-pheasant came *rocketing* over me, looking as though the feathers were all being blown out of his tail. *Harper's Mag.*, LXXVII. 182.

rocket^{2} (rok'et), *n.* [Early mod. E. *rokat*; < OF. *roquette*, F. *roquette* = Sp. *roqueta*, *ruqueta*, < It. *ruchetta*, the herb rocket, dim. of *ruca*, garden-rocket, < L. *eruca*, a species of colewort: see *Eruca*.] 1. In old usage, the salad-plant *Eruca sativa*. See *Eruca*.—2. In modern usage, a plant of the genus *Hesperis*, chiefly *H. matronalis*, also called *dame's-violet* or *-rocket*, *garden-rocket*, or *white rocket*. This is a somewhat coarse standard garden plant with racemes of rather large flowers, which are fragrant after dark. They are naturally pinkish and single, but in cultivation have double varieties both white and purple. *H. tristis* is the night-scented rocket or stock. 3. One of various other plants, chiefly *Cruciferæ*. See phrases.—**Bastard rocket**, a European weed, *Brassica Erucastrum*.—**Crambling rocket**, the name in some old herbals of *Reseda lutea*, probably with the sense of 'scrambling rocket,' translating the old name Eruca peregrina. *Britton and Holland*, Eng. Plant-Names.—**Cress-rocket**, any of the three species of *Vella*, a Spanish cruciferous genus.—**Dame's-rocket**. See def. 2, above.—**Dyer's rocket**. Same as *dyer's-weed*.—**Night-scented rocket**. See def. 2, above.—**Wall-rocket**, *Diplotaxis tenuifolia*, a bushy mustard-plant on old walls, etc. —**White rocket**. See def. 2, above.—**Winter rocket**. See *yellow-rocket*. (See also *base-rocket*, *London-rocket*, *sea-rocket*, and *yellow-rocket*.)

The Inflorescence of Rocket (*Hesperis matronalis*).

rocket^{3} (rok'et), *n.* An obsolete or dialectal form of *rochet*^{1}.

rocket^{4} (rok'et), *n.* [Origin not ascertained.] A portion. *Halliwell.* [Prov. Eng.]

rocket-bird (rok'et-bėrd), *n.* [< *rocket*^{1} + *bird*.] The Indian paradise flycatcher, *Terpsiphone* (formerly *Tchitrea*) *paradisi*. See cut under *Terpsiphone*. [Anglo-Indian.]

In the mango topes were procured examples of the Paradise flycatcher (Tchitrea paradisi), generally yclept the *rocket-bird* by our countrymen. *The Field* (London), April 4, 1885.

rocket-case (rok'et-kās), *n.* A stout case, made of cardboard or cartridge-paper, for holding the materials of a rocket.

rocket-drift (rok'et-drift), *n.* In *pyrotechny*, a copper-tipped wooden rammer which is driven by a mallet in packing the composition in the cases of rockets.

rocketer (rok'et-ėr), *n.* [< *rocket*^{1} + *-er*^{1}.] A bird that rises rapidly and flies straight up when flushed, as a pheasant may do. [Eng.]

rocket-harpoon (rok'et-här-pön), *n.* In *whaling*, a harpoon propelled by a rocket. It carries at its point a shell, which is exploded by a time-fuse. The projectile is fired from a tube, or from the shoulder by means of a special form of gun.

rocket-larkspur (rok'et-lärk'spėr), *n.* See *larkspur*.

rock-faced (rok'fāst), *a.* In *masonry*, same as *quarry-faced*. See *ashler*, 3.

rock-falcon (rok'fâ'kn), *n.* See *falcon*.

rock-fever (rok'fē'vėr), *n.* Intermittent fever.

rock-fire (rok'fīr), *n.* In *pyrotechny*, a composition of resin (three parts), sulphur (four parts), niter (ten parts), and regulus of antimony and turpentine (each one part). It burns slowly and is extinguished with difficulty. It is used in military operations for setting fire to ships, buildings, magazines, etc., and can be charged in cases or shells to be thrown from artillery, or it may be used with rockets.

rockfish (rok'fish), *n.* 1. A name of several fishes which are found about rocks. (*a*) The striped-bass, *Roccus lineatus*, a fine game-fish highly esteemed for the table. See *Roccus*, and cut under *bass*^{1}. [U. S.] (*b*) One of several different wrasses. [Eng.] (*c*) The black goby. [Eng.] (*d*) The killifish or May-fish, *Hydrargyra majalis*. [Local, U. S.] (*e*) The log-perch or hog-fish, *Percina caprodes*. [Local, U. S.] (*f*) Any scorpænoid fish of the genus *Sebastodes* or *Sebastichthys* and related genera; as a collective name, the *Scorpænidæ* in general. These rockfish are especially numerous on the Pacific coast of North America, on rocky bottoms, and are economically important. Some specific names into which *rockfish* enters are S. *flavidus*, the yellow-tailed, also called *rock-cod*; S. *mystinus*, the black; S. *pinniger*, the orange; S. *ruber*, the red; S. *rastrelliger*, the grass-rockfish. See also *boccaccio*, *jack*^{1}, 9 (*c*), *priest-fish*, *viuva*, *garrupa*, *floum*, *rasher*^{2}, *tambor*, *corsair*, *fly-fish*, *rena*, *tree-fish*, *Spanish-flag*. (*g*) One of various species of serranids. [Local, U. S.] 2. A codfish split, washed, and dried on the rocks.—**Banded rockfish**, *Sebastomus fasciatus*.—**Black rockfish**, *Sebastichthys melanops*, the priest-fish. See cut under *priest-fish*. [Pacific coast, U. S.]—**Grass-rockfish**, one of several species of *Sebastichthys* or rock-

Grass-rockfish (*Sebastichthys nigrocinctus*).

cod, as S. *nigrocinctus*. [Pacific coast.]—**Green rockfish**, the cultus-cod.—**Red rockfish**, a serranoid, *Trisotropis guttatus*. [Bermudas.]—**Rosy rockfish**, *Sebastomus rosaceus*. [California.]

rockfishing (rok'fish'ing), *n.* [< *rockfish* + *-ing*^{1}.] The act or art of taking rockfish.

rock-flint (rok'flint), *n.* Same as *chert*.

rock-flour (rok'flour), *n.* Same as *rock-meal*.

rock-gas (rok'gas), *n.* See *gas*.

rock-goat (rok'gōt), *n.* A goat which makes its home among rocks; an ibex. *Holland.*

rock-goose (rok'gös), *n.* Same as *kelp-goose*.

rockhair (rok'hãr), *n.* A rock-loving lichen, *Alectoria jubata*. See *Alectoria*^{2}.

rock-harmonicon (rok'här-mon'i-kon), *n.* A musical instrument consisting of a graduated series of pieces of rock-crystal, which are sounded by blows from hammers. Compare *lapideon*.

rock-hawk (rok'hâk), *n.* The merlin or stone-falcon, *Falco æsalon* or *F. lithofalco*. See cut under *merlin*.

rock-head (rok'hed), *n.* Bed-rock. [Rare, Eng.]

It is seldom that the geologist has an opportunity of seeing a complete section down to the *rock-head* in such a place. Croll, Climate and Time, p. 467.

rock-hearted (rok'här'ted), *a.* Hard-hearted; unfeeling.

rock-hopper (rok'hop'ėr), *n.* A curl-crested penguin; a penguin of the genus *Eudyptes*, as *E. chrysocome* or *E. chrysolopha*; a macaroni: so called by seamen from the way they hop over the rocks in places where they congregate to breed. See cut under *Eudyptes*.

rock-hopping (rok'hop'ing), *n.* See the quotation.

The end of the rope is thrown to a boat just outside the breakers, and the raft of blubber is towed to the tender or vessel. This rafting process is called by the sealers *rock hopping*. *Fisheries of U. S.*, V. ii. 437.

rockie (rok'i), *n.* The rock-lintie or twite. [Scotch.]

rockier (rok'i-ėr), *n.* Same as *rocker*^{1}.

rockiness^{1} (rok'i-nes), *n.* [< *rocky*^{1} + *-ness*.] The state of being rocky, or abounding with rocks.

rockiness^{2} (rok'i-nes), *n.* [< *rocky*^{2} + *-ness*.] The condition or sensations of one who is rocky, as from drinking. See *rocky*^{2}. [Slang.]

rocking^{1} (rok'ing), *n.* [< *rock*^{1} + *-ing*^{1}.] The mass of stone or ballast laid to form the understratum of a road.

rocking^{2} (rok'ing), *n.* [ME. **rockynge*, *roggynge*; verbal n. of *rock*^{2}, *v.*] 1. The act of one who or of that which rocks; the act of swaying backward and forward.—2. The abrading of the surface of a copper or steel plate with a rocker, preparatory to scraping a mezzotint. —3. The motion by which the design on a steel mill is transferred to a copper cylinder to be used in calico-printing. Compare *mill*^{1}, 7.

rocking^{3} (rok'ing), *n.* [< *rock*^{3} + *-ing*^{1}.] An evening party in the country: so called from the practice once prevalent among the women of taking their rocks (distaffs) with them and spinning. [Scotch.]

On Fasten-e'en we had a *rockin'*,
To ca' the crack and weave our stockin'.
Burns, First Epistle to J. Lapraik.

rocking-bar (rok'ing-bär), *n.* A bar supporting a grate in a furnace, so arranged that, when desired, the grate will rock or tip over.

rocking-beam (rok'ing-bēm), *n.* In Wheatstone's automatic transmitter, an oscillating beam by the motion of which momentary contacts between the battery and the line-wire are made.

rocking-chair (rok'ing-chãr), *n.* A chair mounted upon rockers.

He has extracted a particularly important one, and leaning back in his *rocking-chair*—that cradle for grown-up babies—is obeying my Lord Bacon and inwardly digesting the same. *W. M. Baker*, New Timothy, p. 32.

rocking-horse (rok'ing-hôrs), *n.* A wooden horse mounted on rockers for the recreation of children; a hobby-horse.

rocking-pier (rok'ing-pēr), *n.* In *metallic-bridge construction*, a pier which is fastened by a movable joint to the truss which it supports, and has its lower end supported by a hinged shoe, so that it may rock slightly from the vertical position as the superstructure expands or contracts when exposed to changes of temperature. The device obviates the necessity of supporting metal trusses on rollers or sliding plates resting on rigid piers.

rocking-shaft (rok'ing-shȧft), *n.* Same as *rock-shaft*.

A pair of those levers, to act on the two link motions at once, project from the *rocking-shaft*. *Rankine*, Steam Engine, § 388.

rocking-tree (rok'ing-trē), *n.* In *weaving*, the axle from which the lay of a loom is suspended. *E. H. Knight.*

rockish (rok'ish), *a.* [< *rock*^{1} + *-ish*^{1}.] Rocky. [Rare.]

His carcasse on *rockish* pinnacle hanged.
Stanihurst, Æneid, ii. 714. (*Davies.*)

rock-kangaroo (rok'kang-ga-rö'), *n.* A general name for the whallabees, or small kangaroos of the genus *Halmaturus* and (especially) of the genus *Petrogale*. See cut under *Petrogale*.

rock-kelp (rok'kelp), *n.* Same as *rockweed*.

rock-knotweed (rok'not'wēd), *n.* See *Polygonum*.

rock-lark (rok'lärk), *n.* See *lark*^{1} and *rock-pipit*.

rocklay (rok'lā), *n.* Same as *roquelaure*.

rock-leather (rok'leᴛʜ'ėr), *n.* Same as *rock-cork*.

rockless (rok'les), *a.* [< *rock*^{1} + *-less*.] Destitute of rocks.

I'm clear by nature as a *rockless* stream.
Dryden and Lee, Duke of Guise, iii. 1.

rocklet (rok'let), *n.* [< *rock*^{1} + *-let*.] A small rock. *Bulwer.* (*Imp. Dict.*)

rock-lever (rok'lev'ėr), *n.* An equalizing-bar with a knuckle-joint in the middle of the rear. *Car-Builder's Dict.* See cut under *ratchet-wheel*.

rocklier (rok'li-ėr), *n.* Same as *roquelaure*.

rock-lily (rok'lil'i), *n.* 1. A tropical American cryptogamous plant, *Selaginella convoluta*: so called from its rosette of densely tufted stems. —2. In Australia, a showy white-flowered orchid, *Dendrobium speciosum*, growing on rocks. It has large pseudobulbs, said to be eaten by the natives.

rock-limpet (rok'lim'pet), *n.* A limpet which adheres to rocks; a patella, as *Patella vulgaris*, the common limpet. See cuts under *patella* and *patelliform*.

rockling (rok'ling), *n.* [< *rock*^{1} + *ling*^{1}.] A gadoid fish of the genus *Onos* or *Motella*; a whistlefish; a sea-loach. Several species are distinguished by the number of their barbels, as three-bearded, four-bearded, five-bearded. Also called *gade*.

rock-lintie (rok'lin'ti), *n.* 1. The twite, *Linota flavirostris*. Also *rockie*.—2. The rock-lark or rock-pipit, *Anthus obscurus*. [Scotch in both senses.]

rock-lobster (rok'lob'stėr), *n.* See *lobster*, 2, and cut under *Palinurus*.

rocklow (rok'lō), *n.* Same as *roquelaure*.

rock-lychnis (rok'lik'nis), *n.* Any one of certain species of *Lychnis*, once considered to form a genus *Viscaria*.

rock-manikin (rok'man"i-kin), *n.* A manikin of the genus *Rupicola;* a rock-bird or cock of the rock. See cut under *Rupicola.*

rock-maple (rok'mā"pl), *n.* See *maple*[1].

rock-meal (rok'mēl), *n.* In *mineral.*, a white, cotton-like variety of calcite occurring as an efflorescence, as at the quarries of Nanterre, near Paris.

rock-milk (rok'milk), *n.* [Tr. G. *bergmilch.*] A name given to a cryptocrystalline mixture of aragonite, with calcite in a condition resembling chalk, and some organic matter.

rock-moss (rok'môs), *n.* The lichen *Lecanora tartarea*, which yields archil; perhaps also one of some other lichens. It is much used in the Highlands of Scotland as a dyestuff, and is so called from abounding on rocks in alpine districts. See cut under *cudbear.*

rock-mouse (rok'mous), *n.* A South African rodent, *Petromys typicus.* See cut under *Petromys.*

rock-nosing (rok'nō"zing), *n.* See the quotation.

> Whilst the good ship lies secure in these unsurveyed and unauthorized harbors (each master mariner according to his predilection), the boats go outside to watch for whales. If they succeed in capturing one, frequently, if possible, the vessel goes out and assists in securing it. Though they are supposed to return to the ship every night, yet at this time the men are often subjected to great hardship and danger. This is known as the "autumn" or "fall fishing," and this method of pursuing it as *rock-nosing.*
> *Fisheries of U. S.*, V. ii. 203.

rock-oil (rok'oil), *n.* Petroleum.

rock-ouzel (rok'ö"zl), *n.* The ring-ouzel. See cut under *ouzel.* Also called *rock-blackbird.* [Local, Eng.]

rock-oyster (rok'ois"tėr), *n.* 1. An oyster growing upon a rock, as distinguished from oysters found in beds. [Delaware.]—2. An oyster-like bivalve, *Placunanomia macroschisma*, inhabiting the Pacific coast of North America from Alaska to California.

rock-parrakeet (rok'par"a-kēt), *n.* One of the Australian grass-parrakeets, *Euphema petrophila*, so called from nesting in rocks.

rock-pigeon (rok'pij"on), *n.* 1. The common pigeon, rock-dove, or rock, *Columba livia*, the wild original of the domestic pigeon or dove. See cut under *rock-dove.*—2. The sand-pigeon or sand-grouse. See *Pteroclidæ.*

rock-pipit (rok'pip"it), *n.* The British titlark, water-pipit, or sea-lark, whose two most frequent technical names are *Anthus aquaticus* and *A. obscurus.* It has several others, as *A. petrosus*, *A. rupestris*, *A. campestris* (of Bewick), *A. littoralis* (Brehm), and *A. immutabilis* (Degland). This bird is the titlark of Pennant (1766), and its earliest recognized scientific designation is *Alauda obscura* of Latham (1790).

> The resident *rock-pipit* of the British Islands is certainly distinct from the Scandinavian bird, but whether it is confined to Great Britain or inhabits also some part of continental Europe, I have not been able to determine with certainty.
> *R. B. Sharpe*, Cat. Birds British Museum (1885), X. 601.

rock-plant (rok'plant), *n.* A plant habitually growing on or among rocks.—**Rock-plant of St. Helena.** See *Petrobium.*

rock-plover (rok'pluv"ėr), *n.* 1. See *plover.*—2. The rock-snipe.

rock-ptarmigan (rok'tär"mi-gan), *n.* The ptarmigan *Lagopus rupestris*, of circumpolar and subarctic distribution, in winter white with a black tail and a black stripe from bill to eye. See cut under *ptarmigan.*

rock-pulverizer (rok'pul"ve-rī-zėr), *n.* A mill or machine for breaking stone or ore. See *stone-mill*, *stone-crusher.*

rock-punch (rok'punch), *n.* Same as *granite*, 2.

rock-rabbit (rok'rab"it), *n.* A hyrax, as the Cape cony, *Hyrax capensis*, called by the Dutch colonists *klipdas.*

rock-rat (rok'rat), *n.* An African rodent of the genus *Petromys*, *P. typicus.* See cut under *Petromys.*

rock-ribbed (rok'ribd), *a.* Having ribs of rock.

> The hills,
> *Rock-ribbed*, and ancient as the sun.
> *Bryant*, Thanatopsis.

rock-rose (rok'rōz), *n.* A plant of either of the genera *Cistus* and *Helianthemum.* These genera are closely allied, and were both (with others) included in the Linnean genus *Cistus.* The species of *Helianthemum* are now often distinguished as *sun-rose.* See cut in next column, and cut under *Cistus.*—**Australian rock-rose.** See *Hibbertia.*

rock-ruby (rok'rö"bi), *n.* A ruby-red garnet.

rock-salmon (rok'sam"on), *n.* 1. The coalfish. [Eng.]—2. A carangoid fish of the genus *Seriola*, such as *S. rivoliana*, found from Brazil to Florida, and *S. falcata* of the Gulf of Mexico; an amber-fish.

rock-salt (rok'sâlt), *n.* Salt existing in nature in the solid form, as distinguished from salt in solution, either in sea-water or in salt springs or lakes. Rock-salt made into prisms and lenses is invaluable in the study of the distribution of heat in the spectrum of the sun or other spectra, and in similar investigations, since it is very highly diathermanous even to the rays of long wave-length, which are largely absorbed by glass. See *salt*[1].

rock-samphire (rok'sam"fīr), *n.* A plant, *Crithmum maritimum.* See *samphire.*

rock-scorpion (rok'skôr"pi-on), *n.* A name given to natives of Gibraltar. [Slang.]

rock-seal (rok'sēl), *n.* The common harbor-seal, *Phoca vitulina*, as commonly seen basking on tide-rocks. See cut under *Phoca.*

Rock-rose (*Helianthemum vulgare*).
a, longitudinal section of the flower, petals and sepals removed; *b*, calyx; *c*, fruit.

rock-serpent (rok'sėr"pent), *n.* 1. A rock-snake.—2. A venomous serpent of the genus *Bungarus*, family *Elapidæ* (or *Najidæ*), native of India, and closely allied to the cobra, though the neck is not so dilatable. See *Bungarus.*

rock-shaft (rok'shâft), *n.* In steam-engines, a shaft that oscillates or rocks on its journals instead of revolving; specifically, a vibrating shaft with levers which works the slide-valves of some engines. This mode was generally adopted before the introduction of the direct-action mode of working them. Also *rocker-shaft*, *rocking-shaft.*

rock-shell (rok'shel), *n.* A species of *Purpura.* The common rock-shell is *P. lapillus.* Some writers loosely extend the name to various related shells. See cut under *Purpura.*

rock-shrike (rok'shrīk), *n.* Same as *rock-thrush. Latham*, 1781.

rock-slater (rok'slā"tėr), *n.* A slater or wood-louse of the genus *Ligia*, found on rocky coasts.

rock-snake (rok'snāk), *n.* A snake that frequents rocks or rocky places; a rock-serpent; specifically, a very large snake of the family *Pythonidæ;* a python or anaconda, as *Python molurus*, or an Australian member of the genus *Morelia.* The true pythons are confined to the warmer parts of the Old World; but the term *rock-snake* has often been extended, as *anaconda* had been transferred, to the great boas of America, belonging to the family *Boidæ.* See *Morelia*, and cuts under *Python* and *Pythonidæ.*

rock-snipe (rok'snip), *n.* The purple sandpiper, *Tringa* (*Arquatella*) *maritima*, which haunts rocky shores; the rock-bird or rock-plover: a gunners' name in New England.

rock-soap (rok'sōp), *n.* A mineral of a pitch-black or bluish-black color, having a somewhat greasy feel and adhering strongly to the tongue, used for crayons and for washing cloth. It is a hydrated silicate of aluminium containing some iron, and is properly a variety of halloysite.

rock-sparrow (rok'spar"ō), *n.* A finch of the genus *Petronia.* There are 6 species, ranging through the greater part of Europe, Asia, and Africa. The best-known is *P. stulta* (originally *Fringilla petronia* of Linnæus), known to the early English ornithologists also as the *ring-sparrow*, *speckled*, *white-tailed*, and *foolish sparrow*, the last designation giving rise to the technical term *stulta*, bestowed by Gmelin in 1788. This sparrow occurs from central Europe to China and cis-Saharic Africa.

rock-staff (rok'stâf), *n.* The lever of a forge-bellows, or other vibrating bar in a machine.

rock-starling (rok'stär"ling), *n.* The rock-ouzel. [Local, Scotland.]

rock-sturgeon (rok'stėr"jon), *n.* Same as *lake-sturgeon.* [Local, U. S.]

rock-sucker (rok'suk"ėr), *n.* A lamprey. See *Petromyzon.*

rock-swallow (rok'swol"ō), *n.* A swallow which affixes its nest to rocks: not specific.

> Lark and chat and *rock-swallow* leaped to wing.
> *L. Wallace*, Ben-Hur, p. 7.

rock-swift (rok'swift), *n.* A bird of the family *Cypselidæ* and genus *Panyptila*, as *P. saxatilis* (or *melanoleuca*), the white-throated rock-swift of western North America. It abounds in some places in the Rocky and other mountains, frequenting the most inaccessible cliffs and precipices, where it nests, and usually flies at a great height and with amazing celerity. It is blackish, mostly white underneath, with white tips of the secondaries, and is from 6½ to 7 inches long and 14 inches in extent of wings. See cut under *Panyptila.*

rock-tar (rok'tär), *n.* Rock-oil; petroleum.

rock-temple (rok'tem"pl), *n.* A temple hewn

Rock-temple.—An interior at Ellora, India, with figure of Oudra.

out of the solid rock, as at Ellora in Hindustan, and elsewhere.

rock-thrush (rok'thrush), *n.* Any bird of the genus variously called *Monticola*, *Petrocincla*, *Petrocossyphus*, or *Petrophila.* The species are 10 or 12 in number, and range from southern Europe through Africa and to China and Japan. The sexes are quite unlike; the males of nearly all have blue throats and chestnut breasts, with black bills and feet. The best-known, and the one to which the English name *rock-shrike* was given by Latham in 1781, is *M.* or *P. saxatilis* of southern Europe and many parts of Asia and Africa, prettily variegated with cobalt-blue, bluish-black, white, and chestnut. The blue rock-thrush, also of southern Europe, and with an extensive Asiatic and African range, is *M.* or *P. cyanea*, the blue or solitary thrush of Latham (1783), with about thirty other names, and mostly of a dark slaty-blue color. Its oriental congener is the solitaire, or pensive thrush, *M.* or *P. solitaria*, ranging from Japan and China through the Malay archipelago. All these birds are saxicoline, nest in holes, lay blue eggs, and are fair songsters. They appear to be the nearest Old World representatives or allies of the American bluebirds of the genus *Sialia.*

rock-tools (rok'tölz), *n. pl.* Tools used in drilling rock. See *cable-tools.*

rock-tripe (rok'trīp), *n.* [Tr. F. *tripe de roche.*] Lichens of the genus *Umbilicaria.* They grow upon rocks in high northern latitudes, and have been the means of preserving for weeks or months the lives of arctic travelers. The name is suggested by the expanded and seemingly blistered thallus.

rock-trout (rok'trout), *n.* 1. The common American brook-trout, *Salvelinus fontinalis*, as occurring in Lake Superior.—2. A chiroid fish of the genus *Hexagrammus;* especially, the boregat or bodieron, *H. decagrammus*, abundant on the North Pacific coast of North America, about 18 inches long. Also called *sea-trout* and *starling.* See cut under *Hexagrammus.*

rock-turquoise (rok'tėr-koiz'), *n.* See *turquoise.*

rock-violet (rok'vī"ọ-let), *n.* An alga, *Chroölepus Iolithus*, growing on moist rocks in the Alps, the White Mountains, etc. Stones overgrown with it emit, especially when moistened, a strong fragrance of violets.

rock-warbler (rok'wâr"blėr), *n.* A small Australian bird, so named by Lewin in 1822, respecting the affinities of which there is much difference of opinion. It was described as the ruddy warbler by Latham in 1801, and a genus was framed for its reception by Gould in 1837. It is now technically known as *Origma rubricata*, and placed by the latest authority in the ornithological waste-basket (*Timeliidæ*). It is 5¾ inches long and of a sooty-brown color varied with ruddy hues, and chiefly inhabits New South Wales. It is said to haunt rocky watercourses, and is sometimes called *cataract-bird.*

rock-water (rok'wâ"tėr), *n.* Water issuing from a rock.

> It [the Rhone] was extremely muddy at its entrance, when I saw it, though as clear as *rockwater* at its going out.
> *Addison*, Remarks on Italy, Geneva, and the Lake.

> The river Wherfe . . . runs in a bed of stone, and looks as clear as *rock-water.*
> *Defoe*, Tour through Great Britain, III. 124. (*Davies.*)

rockweed (rok'wēd), *n.* A seaweed of the genera *Fucus*, *Sargassum*, etc., common on the rocks exposed at low tide. *Fucus vesiculosus* and *F. nodosus* are especially abundant on the New England coast. See *Fucus* (for description and cut) and *kelp*[2], 1 (*a*). Also called *rock-kelp.*

rock-winkle (rok'wing"kl), *n.* A periwinkle, *Littorina subtenebrosa*, frequenting rocks.

rock-wood (rok'wůd), *n.* Ligniform asbestos. It is of a brown color, and in its general appearance greatly resembles fossil wood.

rockwork (rok'wėrk), *n.* 1. Stones fixed in mortar in imitation of the irregular surface of natural rocks, and arranged to form a mound, or constructed as a wall.—2. A rockery; a design formed of fragments of rocks or large stones in gardens or pleasure-grounds: often forming a kind of grotto.—3. A natural wall or mass of rock.—4. Rock-faced or quarry-faced masonry. See *quarry-faced* (with cut).

rock-wren (rok'ren), *n.* **1.** A wren of the genus *Salpinctes*, as *S. obsoletus*: so called from its habit of frequenting rocks. The species named is common in the western parts of the United States; it is of active, restless habits, and has a loud song. The eggs

Rock-wren (*Salpinctes obsoletus*).

are from five to eight in number, crystal-white sparsely dotted with reddish-brown. The bird is 5½ inches long, and of varied blended brownish colors, the most conspicuous markings being black and white dots on the brownish-gray of the upper parts. It is a near relative of the cañon-wren and cactus-wren.

2. The barking-bird of South America, *Hylactes tarnii*. The name is also given to other members of the family *Pteroptochidæ*. See cut under *Scytalopus*.

rocky¹ (rok'i), *a.* [< *rock*¹ + *-y*¹.] **1.** Full of rocks; abounding in rocks: as, a *rocky* mountain.

> Listening to the doubling roar,
> Surging on the rocky shore.
> *Burns*, How can my poor heart be glad?

2. Consisting of rock or rocks.

> Betwixt these rocky pillars Gabriel sat.
> *Milton*, P. L., iv. 549.

3. Resembling a rock; hence, hard; stony; obdurate; insusceptible of impression; hard as a rock: as, a *rocky* bosom.

> A rocky heart, killing with cruelty.
> *Massinger*, Virgin-Martyr, ii. 3.

rocky² (rok'i), *a.* [< *rock*² + *-y*¹.] Disposed to rock or reel; hence, giddy; tipsy; dizzy. [Slang, prov. Eng. and U. S.]

Rocky Mountain bluebird, locust. See *bluebird, locust*¹.

Rocky Mountain garrot. *Clangula* or *Bucephala islandica*, otherwise called *Barrow's goldeneye*. See *garrot*¹.

Rocky Mountain goat. See *goat*, and cut under *Haploceros*.

Rocky Mountain pika. *Lagomys princeps*, the little chief hare.

Rocky Mountain rat. The pack-rat. See *Neotoma* and *rat*¹.

Rocky Mountain sheep. See *sheep*, and cut under *bighorn*.

rococo (rộ-kō'kō), *n.* [< F. rococo, appar. a made word, based perhaps, as usually explained, on *rocaille*, rockwork (on account of the

Rococo.—An Interior in Schloss Bruchsal, Baden, Germany. (From "L'Art pour Tous.")

rockwork which figures in the style), < *roche* (ML. *roca*), a rock: see *rock*¹.] A variety of ornament originating in the Louis-Quatorze style and continuing with constantly increasing inorganic exaggeration and extravagance throughout the artistic degeneracy of the Louis-Quinze. It is generally a meaningless, though often a very rich, assemblage of fantastic scrolls and crimped conventional shell-work, wrought into irregular and indescribable forms, without individuality and without expression apart from its usually costly material and surroundings. The style has a certain interest from its use in a great number of sumptuous European residences, and from its intimate association with a social life of great outward refinement and splendor. Much of the painting, engraving, porcelain-work, etc., of the time has, too, a real decorative charm, though not of a very high order in art. Hence *rococo* is used attributively in contempt to note anything feebly pretentious and tasteless in art or literature. Compare *baroque*.

> The jumble called rococo is, in general, detestable. A parrot seems to have invented the word; and the thing is worthy of his tawdriness and his incoherence.
> *Leigh Hunt*, Old Court Suburbs, iv.

Rococo embroidery, ornamental needlework and other fancy work of different sorts, the application of the term varying at different times. Especially—(*a*) A kind of China-ribbon embroidery. (*b*) A kind of Roman work.

rocou (rō'kö), *n.* [F. *rocou*, *roucou*, arnotto; of Braz. origin.] Same as *arnotto*, 2.

rocta (rok'tä), *n.* [ML.: see *rote*³.] A medieval musical instrument, much used by the minstrels and troubadours of the thirteenth century. It was somewhat like the modern violin. *O. Shipley*.

rod¹ (rod), *n.* [< ME. *rod*, *rodde* (with short vowel; orig. with long vowel, *rôd*, *rôde*, > E. *rood*), < AS. *rōd*, a rod, pole, also a measure of land, a cross, the (holy) rood, a crucifix, = OS. *rōda*, *ruoda*, a cross, = OFries. *rōde*, a gallows, = D. *roede*, a rod, measuring-pole, perch, = MLG. *rôde*, *rūde*, LG. *rode*, *roode* = OHG. *ruota*, MHG. *ruote*, G. *ruthe*, *rute*, a rod, pole, a rod of land, = Icel. *rōtha*, a rood, crucifix (ML. *roda*); perhaps akin to L. *rudis*, a rod, staff, *radius*, staff, spoke, ray (see *radius*, *ray*¹), Skt. √ *rudh*, Zend √ *rud*, grow. Doublet of *rood*.] **1.** A shoot or slender stem of any woody plant, more especially when cut off and stripped of leaves or twigs; a wand; a straight slender stick; a cane; also, anything of similar form: as, a brass *rod*.

> Ye relyques yt Titus caryed to Rome—that is to say, the .x. commaundements, Aarons rodde, Moyses *rod*, a vessell of gold full of manna.
> *Sir R. Guylforde*, Pylgrymage, p. 45.

> Wi' walkin' *rod* intill his hand,
> He walked the castle roun'.
> *Heir of Linne* (Child's Ballads, VIII. 74).

> There shall come forth a *rod* out of the stem of Jesse, and a Branch shall grow out of his roots. Isa. xi. 1.

Specifically—(*a*) An instrument of punishment or correction; a single switch or stick, or a bundle of switches; hence, chastisement.

> M. Peter, as one somewhat seuere of nature, said plainlie that the *Rodde* onelie was the sworde that must keepe the Schole in obedience. *Ascham*, The Scholemaster, p. 18.

> Thrice was I beaten with *rods*. 2 Cor. xi. 25.

> A light to guide, a *rod*
> To check the erring, and reprove.
> *Wordsworth*, Ode to Duty.

(*b*) The badge of office of certain officials who are in a sense guardians or controllers of others, or ushers, marshals, and the like. The use of rods of certain colors gives names to their bearers: as, in England, *black-rod*, *green-rod*, etc. See *black-rod*.

> About this Time John Duke of Lancaster was created Duke of Aquitain, receiving at the King's Hands the *Rod* and the Cap, as Investitures of that Duchy.
> *Baker*, Chronicles, p. 146.

(*c*) A scepter; hence, figuratively, authority; sway.

> She had all the royal makings of a queen;
> As holy oil, Edward Confessor's crown,
> The *rod*, and bird of peace, and all such emblems
> Laid nobly on her. *Shak.*, Hen. VIII., iv. 1. 89.

> Hands that the *rod* of empire might have sway'd.
> *Gray*, Elegy.

(*d*) An enchanter's wand, or a wand possessing the power of enchantment.

> Ye should have snatch'd his wand,
> And bound him fast; without his *rod* reversed,
> And backward mutters of dissevering power,
> We cannot free the Lady. *Milton*, Comus, l. 816.

(*e*) A long, light, tapering, elastic pole used in angling, to which the line is attached, now usually made in adjustable sections or joints, and fitted with guides and a reel. There are eight woods commonly used for rods, of which four are solid (greenheart, hickory, ash, and willow) and four are hollow (East Indian bamboo, Carolina and West Indian cane, white cane, and jungle-cane). Rods have also been made of hard rubber and of steel. Jointed rods are made in three or four pieces, of which the largest and heaviest is the butt, and the slenderest is the tip. The joints are fitted with metal rings or ferrules, and with small rings called *guides* to receive the line. The reel is stepped into the butt, near its end, or otherwise suitably attached, as by a reel-plate. The special makes of rods are very numerous, and their names almost equally so. Besides being named and classed according to the material of which they are composed, as *bamboo rod*, etc., they are commonly identified with the name of the fish for which they are specially designed: as, *salmon-rod*, *trout-rod*, *bass-rod*, etc. All rods are, however, divisible into three classes, according to their make and purpose. These are (1) the *fly-rod*, which is long, slender, tapering, tough, and highly elastic; (2) the *trolling-rod*, which is comparatively short, stout, and stiff; and (3) the *bait-rod*, which is a mean between the other two. Fly-rods are most used, with artificial flies. Split-bamboo rods are now manufactured for all kinds of angling. See *fly-rod*, and cut under *reel*. (*f*) An instrument for measuring.

2. In *mech.*, any bar slender in proportion to its length, particularly such a bar used as a brace or a tie between parts for connecting them, or for strengthening a connection between them. The term is used in a very indefinite manner, depending entirely upon individual judgment or caprice. What some would call a rod would by others be called a bar.

> The *rod* in the shaft, known as the main *rod* or spear *rod*, is usually made of strong balks of timber butted together and connected by strapping plates fastened by bolts. *Encyc. Brit.*, XVI. 458.

3. Specifically, in a steam-engine, the pitman which connects the cross-head with the crank: also and more generally called *connecting-rod*. The connection is made at the cross-head to the cross-head pin, and at the crank to the crank-wrist. See cut under *steam-engine*.—**4.** A measure of length equal to 5½ yards, or 16½ feet. (Also called *pole* and *perch*.) A square rod is the usual measure of brickwork, and is equal to 272¼ square feet.—**5.** A shoot or branch of a family; a tribe or race.

> Remember thy congregation, which thou hast purchased of old; the *rod* of thine inheritance, which thou hast redeemed. Ps. lxxiv. 2.

6. In *anat.*, one of numerous slender rod-like or bacillary structures which collectively form, together with similar but conical bodies called *cones*, one of the layers of which the retina of the eye is composed, called the *layer of rods and cones*, essential to the function of vision. See cut under *retina*.—**7.** In *entom.*, specifically, any differentiation of the anterior end of a retinal cell of the eye, which may unite to form a rhabdom. See *rhabdomere*.—**Bait-rod**, a fishing-rod used with natural bait.—**Binding-rod**, a tie-rod.—**Boning-rod.** See *boning*.—**Cortian rods.** Same as *rods of Corti*.—**Crystalline rods.** See *crystalline*.—**Divining rod.** See *divining-rod*.—**Lengthening rod**, an extension-rod fitted with screws at the ends and used as a long shank for an auger or a drill in deep boring, as for a tube-well.—**Meckelian rod**, in *embryol.*, the cartilaginous basis of the mandibular or first postoral visceral arch of the embryo of most vertebrates, about the greater distal section of which the ossification of the lower jawbone takes place, the proximal end being converted into the malleus of a mammal, the quadrate bone of a bird or reptile, or the corresponding bones of lower vertebrates. See cut under *palatoquadrate*. Also called *Meckel's cartilage*.—**Napier's rods** (or **bones**), a contrivance, commonly attributed to John Napier (1550–1617), but in fact described in the Arithmetic of Oronce Finée (1532), for facilitating large calculations in multiplication or division for those who do not perfectly know the multiplication table. It consists of a number of rods made of bone, ivory, horn, wood, pasteboard, or other convenient material, the face of each of which is divided into nine equal parts in the form of little squares, and each part, with the exception of the top compartment, subdivided by a dexter diagonal line into two triangles. These nine little squares contain the successive multiples of the number in the

Napier's Bones or Rods.

first, the figures in the tens' place being separated by the diagonal line from that in the units' place. A sufficient number of rods must be provided for each of the headings 0, 1, 2, 3, 4, 5, 6, 7, 8, 9, so that by placing the proper rods side by side any number may be seen at the top, while the several multiples occupy, in order, the eight lower compartments; when the multiple consists of two figures these are placed one on each side of the diagonal line. There is also a rod called the *index-rod*, the squares on which are not subdivided into triangles. To multiply, for example, the number 6789 by 56: Place four of the rods together, so that the top numbers form the multiplicand; then look on the index-rod for 5, the first number of the multiplier, and on the corresponding compartments of the four rods the following disposition of figures will be found ranged in the two lines formed by the triangles of each

square	6254	
	3445	
These added together make		40734
Against 5, on the index-rod, the figures are	0505	
	3344	33945
The products when added give the sum required		380184

Division is performed in an analogous manner. Napier's rods are still made, though they are of little use.—**Parallel rod**, in locomotives having more than one pair of driving-wheels, a rod connecting the crank-pins of all the driving-wheels on one side of the engine, so that when one is moved by the piston-rod all will be moved equally. Also called *coupling-rod*.—**Pedal rod.** See *pedal*.—**Perforating rods of Sharpey.** Same as *Sharpey's fibers* (which see, under *fiber*).—**Rod-and-cone layer of the retina.** See *retina*.—**Rod license.** See *license*.—**Rods of Corti**, the pillars of the arches of the organ of Corti. The external rods which form the outer pillars are shorter and less numerous than the inner rods. They consist of a cylindrical striated body with an expanded base; the upper extremity is curved, and has somewhat the shape of the head of a bird; the back part fits into a cavity between the heads of two or more inner rods; while the bill-like process projects toward the reticular membrane. The inner rods have a striated body and an expanded base; the heads have a concavity which receives the outer rods, and a process entering into the composition of the membrana reticularis. The arches thus formed support the outer and inner hair-cells. Also called *pillars of Corti*.—**Setting-out rod**, a guide or gage used in making window-frames, doors, etc.—**Split rod.** (*a*) One of the rods into which plates of wrought-iron are cut by means of slitting rollers, to be afterward made into nails. (*b*) A fishing-rod made in sections of split bamboo strips.—**To have a rod in pickle for one.** See *pickle*[2].—**To kiss the rod.** See *kiss*.

rod[1] (rod), *v. t.*; pret. and pp. *rodded*, ppr. *rodding*. [< *rod*[1], *n.*] 1. To furnish with a rod or rods; specifically, in recent use, to furnish or equip with lightning-rods.

Several other houses in the town were rodded in the same way. *Sci. Amer.*, N. S., LVIII. 358.

2. To operate upon with a rod, in any way.

In most of the systems the cable is inserted by a process technically called *rodding*—that is, pushing rods through the duct from one manhole to the next. *Elect. Rev.* (Amer.), XVI. i. 14.

rod[2]†, *n.* A Middle English form of *road*[1].

rod[3]†. A Middle English form of *rode*[1], preterit of *ride*.

rod-bacterium (rod′bak-tē″ri-um), *n.* A bacillus.

rod-bayonet (rod′bā″o̤-net), *n.* See *bayonet*.

rod-chisel (rod′chiz″el), *n.* A smiths' chisel fixed to the end of a rod, used for cutting hot metal. *E. H. Knight.*

rod-coupling (rod′kup″ling), *n.* A coupling, clasp, or other device for uniting the rods which carry the tools used in boring artesian wells, oil-wells, etc.

roddin (rod′in), *n.* A Scotch form of *rowan*.

roddin-tree (rod′in-trē), *n.* A Scotch form of *rowan-tree*.

roddy (rod′i), *a.* [< *rod*[1] + *-y*[1].] Full of rods or twigs. [Rare.]

rode[1] (rōd). Preterit of *ride*.

rode[2]†, *n.* An obsolete form of *road*[1].

rode[3]†, *n.* A Middle English form of *rood*.

rode[4]†, *n.* A Middle English form of *rud*[1].

rode[5] (rōd), *n.* [Origin obscure.] A rope attached to a boat-anchor or killock. *Perley.* [Bay of Fundy.]

rod-end (rod′end), *n.* One of the ends of a connecting-rod of an engine. Rod-ends are variously fitted. A common method is to fit them each with a strap and brasses, and a key for tightening the brasses when the latter wear loose. Sometimes called *pitman-box*.

rodent (rō′de̤nt), *a.* and *n.* [< L. *roden(t-)s*, ppr. of *rodere* (> It. *rodere* = Sp. Pg. roer = OF. *roder*, gnaw); akin to *radere*, scratch: see *rase*[1], *raze*[1]. From the L. *rodere* are also ult. *corrode*, *erode*, *rostrum*, etc. Cf. Skt. *rada*, a tooth.] I. *a.* Gnawing, as certain mammals; habitually feeding upon vegetable substances, which are gnawed or bitten first with the front teeth; pertaining to the *Rodentia*, *Rosores*, or *Glires*, or having their characters; gliriform.—**Rodent dentition.** See *dentition*, 3.

II. *n.* A member of the order *Rodentia*, *Rosores*, or *Glires*; a rodent mammal; a gnawer.

In temperate climates prolonged sleep is not unknown among *rodents*. *Science*, VI. 408.

Rodentes† (ro̤-den′tēz), *n. pl.* [NL.] Same as *Rodentia*.

Rodentia (ro̤-den′shi-ä̤), *n. pl.* [NL., < L. *rodentia* (sc. *animalia*), neut. pl. of *roden(t-)s*, ppr. of *rodere*, gnaw: see *rodent*.] An order of ineducabilian placental diphyodont *Mammalia*; the gnawers. The brain has a relatively small cerebrum, leaving much of the cerebellum and olfactory lobes exposed, and the corpus callosum has no well-defined rostrum in front. The placentation is discoidal-deciduate. The limbs are ambulatorial, variously modified for running, leaping, climbing, or swimming. The condyle of the lower jaw has its long axis longitudinal, and is not confined in a special socket, but glides back and forth, so that the lower jaw can be put forward and backward as well as moved up and down. The molar teeth are typically ridged on their crowns in various patterns; they are nearly always 3 in number above and below on each side. The premolars are small or few, often none. There are no canines. The incisors are large, strong, heavily enameled on their front surface, scalpriform or beveled to a sharp edge, and grow continually from persistently open pulps; their roots traverse much or nearly all of the bones of either jaw, in the arc of a circle. The typical number of incisors is 2 above and below, or one pair of upper and under front teeth; exceptionally, as in the rabbit tribe, there are small supplementary upper incisors, crowded together and concealed behind the functional pair. In some groups, as *Arvicolinæ*, the molar teeth are perennial, like the incisors. There being no canines, and the premolars being few and small, if any, there is a great gap between the front and the back teeth. The typical number of teeth is 16, which obtains with few exceptions throughout the murine series of rodents; in one genus there are only 12. In the hystricine series there are normally 20 teeth, in one genus 16. In the sciurine series the teeth are always either 20 or 22; in the leporine series there are 26 or 28. This order is by far the largest one among mammals, and of world-wide distribution; its numerous members are adapted to every kind of life. They are mostly of small size, a rabbit being far above the average; the beaver, porcupine, or coypou is a very large rodent, and the capibara is a giant. The order is divisible into 3 suborders: (1) *Hebetidentata*, enormal or blunt-toothed rodents, exceptional in having 4 lower incisors, and extinct; (2) *Duplicidentata*, subnormal or double-toothed rodents, with 4 upper incisors: these are the hares, rabbits, and pikas; and (3) *Simplicidentata*, normal or simple-toothed rodents, with only 2 incisors above and below. The last fall in 3 series: (1) *Hystricomorpha*, the hystricine series, including the porcupines and very numerous related forms, chiefly South American, as the capibara, coypou, cavies, viscachas, chinchillas, octodonts, etc. (see cuts under *capibara*, *coypou*, *rabbit-squirrel*, *porcupine*, and *Plagiodon*); (2) *Myomorpha*, the murine series, including rats and mice of all kinds (see cuts under *mouse*, *Muridæ*, and *rice-field*); and (3) *Sciuromorpha*, the sciurine series, or the squirrels, spermophiles, marmots, beaver, etc. (see cuts under *Arctomys*, *beaver*, and *prairie-dog*). In addition, the duplicident rodents are (4) *Lagomorpha*, the leporine series, the same as the suborder *Duplicidentata*. (See cut under *Lagomys*.) Many fossils of all these groups are known. There are 20 or 21 families of living rodents, and 100 genera. The order corresponds to the Linnean *Glires*, and is still often called by that name. Also called *Rosores*. See cuts under *castor*, *Leporidæ*, and *scalpriform*.

rodential (ro̤-den′sha̤l), *a.* Of or pertaining to the *Rodentia*. *Nature*, XLII. 193. [Rare.]

rodeo (ro̤-dā′ō), *n.* [Sp. *rodeo*, a place for cattle at a market or fair, also a going round, a roundabout road, < *rodar*, go round, < L. *rotare*, go round, wheel: see *rotate*.] A gathering of cattle to be branded or marked; a round-up. [California.]

The ranch owner who gives the *rodeo* takes his own cattle . . . and drives them in with the ones to be branded, leaving in the *rodeo*-ground the cattle bearing the brands of all other rancheros. K. D. *Wiggin*, A Summer in a Cañon, p. 255.

rod-fish (rod′fish), *n.* A fish that may be taken with a rod; any game-fish.

rod-fisher (rod′fish″ėr), *n.* One who fishes with a rod; a rodster.

rod-fishing (rod′fish″ing), *n.* The art or practice of fishing with a rod; fly-fishing; angling.

rod-fructification (rod′fruk-ti-fi-kā″sho̤n), *n.* In *bot.*, a special simple gonidiophore in *Basidiomycetes*, consisting of a short branch of the mycelium from which small gonidia-like rods are abscised—fertile, however, only in the *Tremellineæ*. *Goebel.*

rodge (roj), *n.* [Formerly also *radge*; origin obscure.] The gadwall, or gray duck, *Chaulelasmus streperus*. See cut under *Chaulelasmus*. [Prov. Eng.]

The *Radge* is next unto the Teale in goodnesse: but yet there is great difference in the nourishment which they make. *Venner*, Via Recta ad Vitam Longam, p. 84.

rod-granule (rod′gran″ūl), *n.* One of the granules in the outer nuclear layer of the retina which are connected with the rods.

rod-holder (rod′hōl″dėr), *n.* One who holds or uses a fishing-rod.

They thus decrease the rental of waters either from net or *rod-holders*. Cassell, Technical Educator, xii. 356. (*Encyc. Dict.*)

rod-iron (rod′ī″ėrn), *n.* Rolled round iron for nails, fences, etc.

rod-knight†, *n.* One of a class of servitors who held their land by serving their lords on horseback. *Minsheu.*

rodlet (rod′let), *n.* [< *rod*[1] + *-let*.] A bacillus or rod-bacterium.

Billroth and Klebs assert that micrococci may grow into *rodlets* or bacilli. *Ziegler*, Pathol. Anat. (trans.), i. 184.

rod-line (rod′līn), *n.* A fishing-line not wound on a reel: used by anglers in distinction from *reel-line*.

rod-machine (rod′ma̤-shēn″), *n.* In *wood-working*, a machine for cutting out cylindrical sticks, such as pins, dowels, chair-rounds, and broom-handles. It has a cutter on the principle of a hollow auger, and operates on squared stuff.

rodman (rod′ma̤n), *n.*; pl. *rodmen* (-men). A man whose duty it is to carry the rod used in surveying.

Rodman gun. See *gun*[1].

rodomel (rod′o̤-mel), *n.* [= Sp. *rodomel*, < Gr. ῥόδον, a rose, + μέλι = L. *mel*, honey: see *rose* and *mell*[2].] The juice of roses mixed with honey.

XL dayes to beholde on heven
In juce of rose a sester [sextarius] that weel smelle
A pounde hony, and name it *rodomelle*.
Palladius, Husbondrie (E. E. T. S.), p. 156.

rodomont (rod′o̤-mont), *n.* and *a.* [< F. *rodomont*, < It. *rodomonte*, a bully, < *Rodomonte*, the name of the brave but somewhat boastful leader of the Saracens against Charlemagne, in Ariosto's "Orlando Furioso," xiv., earlier (in Boiardo's "Orlando Innamorato") *Rodamonte*, lit. 'one who rolls away mountains,' < *rodare* (< L. *rotare*), wheel, roll, + *monte* (< L. *mons*), a mountain: see *rotate* and *mount*.] I. *n.* A vain boaster; a braggart; a bombastic fellow; a bully.

He vapoured; [but] being pretty sharply admonished, he quickly became mild and calm, a posture ill-becoming such a *rodomont*. *Sir T. Herbert*, Memorials of King Charles I. (*Todd.*)

II. *a.* Bragging; vainly boasting.

He had thought to have ben the leader
Had the match gone on,
And triumpht our whole nation
In his *rodomont* fashion.
B. *Jonson*, Masque of Owls.

rodomontade (rod″o̤-mon-tād′), *n.* and *a.* [Formerly also *rhodomontade*, *rodomontado*; = G. *rodomontade*, < OF. *rodemontade*, *rodomontade*, *rotomontade*, F. *rodomontade*, < It. *rodomontata*, a boast, brag, < *rodomonte*, a boaster: see *rodomont*.] I. *n.* Vain boasting; empty bluster or vaunting; rant.

I could shew that the *rhodomontades* of Almanzor are neither so irrational as his, nor so impossible to be put in execution. *Dryden*, Of Heroic Plays.

Poor Phil used to bore me after dinner with endless *rhodomontades* about his passion and his charmer. *Thackeray*, Philip, viii.

II. *a.* Bragging.

I don't know what's the matter with the boy all this day; he has got into such a *rhodomontade* manner all this morning. *Goldsmith*, Good-natured Man, ii.

rodomontade (rod″o̤-mon-tād′), *v. i.*; pret. and pp. *rodomontaded*, ppr. *rodomontading*. [< *rodomontade*, *n.*] To boast; brag; bluster; rant.

Abuse which Pitt in his free-lance days heaped upon the "desperate *rhodomontading* minister." *Edinburgh Rev.*, CXLV. 235.

rodomontadist† (rod″o̤-mon-tā′dist), *n.* [< *rodomontade* + *-ist*.] A blustering boaster; one who brags or vaunts.

When this *Rhodomontadist* had ended his perilous story, it was dinner time. *E. Terry*, Voyage to East India, p. 157.

rodomontado† (rod″o̤-mon-tā′dō), *n.* and *a.* [See *rodomontade*.] I. *n.* 1. Rodomontade; also, a piece of rodomontade; a brag.

I have heard a Biscayner make a *Rodomantado* that he was as good a Gentleman as Don Philippo himself. *Howell*, Letters, I. iii. 32.

"So," says he, "if a *rhodomontado* will do any good, why do you not say 100 ships?" *Pepys*, Diary, III. 350.

2. A blusterer; a braggart.

Most terribly he comes off; like your *rodomontado*. B. *Jonson*, Cynthia's Revels, v. 2.

II. *a.* Bragging; blustering.

A huge *rodomontado* Picture of the Duke of Lerma, wherein he is painted like a Giant, bearing up the Monarchy of Spain, that of France, and the Popedom upon his Shoulders. *Howell*, Letters, I. iii. 11.

rodomontador (rod″ō-mon-tā′do̤r), *n.* [< *rodomontade* + *-or*[1].] Same as *rodomontadist*.

rod-planer (rod′plā″nėr), *n.* A machine-tool especially designed for planing the connecting-rods of locomotives, guide-bars, etc., and for similar work. *E. H. Knight.*

Rodrigues's aneurism. A varicose aneurism in which the sac is formed in the tissue immediately contiguous to the artery.

Rodrigues's coördinates. See *coördinate*.

rod-ring (rod′ring), *n.* One of the small rings or guides through which the line passes along an angler's rod. The caliber is generally about six times that of the line.

rods-gold† (rodz′gōld), *n.* An old name of the marigold. *Gerarde.*

rodsman (rodz′ma̤n), *n.*; pl. *rodsmen* (-men). Same as *rodman*.

rodster (rod′stėr), *n.* [< *rod*[1] + *-ster*.] One who uses a fishing-rod; a rod-fisher; an angler.

It is the intention of a number of our local *rodsters* to leave the city for different streams. *Daily Telegraph*, Sept. 2, 1882. (*Encyc. Dict.*)

rodwood (rod′wụd), *n.* One of several West Indian shrubs or trees: *Lætia Thamnia* of the *Bixineæ*, several species of *Eugenia* (as *E. pallens*, the black rodwood, and *E. axillaris*, the red rodwood), and *Calyptranthes Chytraculia* of the *Myrtaceæ*, the white rodwood.

rody†, *a.* A Middle English form of *ruddy*.

roe[1] (rō), *n.* [< ME. *ro, roo, ra*, < AS. *rā, rāh, rāha, raa*, m. (also, in comp., *rāh-deór*), a roe, *rāge, rǣge*, f., a wild she-goat, a roe, = D. *ree*, roe, roebuck, = OLG. *rēho*, MLG. *rē* = OHG. *rēh* (*rēh-*), n., *rēho*, m., *reia*, f., MHG. *rēch* (*rēh-*), G. *reh*, n., OHG. *reia*, f., also **riccha*, MHG. **ricke*, G. *ricke*, f., = Icel. *rā*, f., = Sw. *rå* = Dan. *raa*, roe, roebuck.] 1. The roe-deer.

I is ful wight [swift], God wast, as is a *raa*.
Chaucer, Reeve's Tale, l. 166.

Now than am I light as a *roo*. *York Plays*, p. 281.

Asahel was as light of foot as a wild *roe*. 2 Sam. ii. 18.

2. Improperly, the adult female of the hart; the doe of the stag or red deer.

roe[2] (rō), *n.* [Oftener in pl. *roes*; early mod. E. also *roughes*, pl.; prop. *roan* or *rone*, as still in E. dial. use (the terminal *-n* being mistaken for the pl. suffix *-n, -en*[4], as in *eyne, kine*[1], *shoon*); E. dial. *roan, rone, roun, rown, rawn*, and with excrescent *-d*, *round*, early mod. E. also *roughne*; < ME. *rowne, rawne*, < AS. **hrogn* (not recorded) = MLG. *rogen, rogel*, LG. *rōgen* = OHG. **hrogan, rogan, rogo*, MHG. *rogen, roge*, G. *rogen* = Icel. *hrogn* = Sw. *rom* = Dan. *rogn* and *ravn*, roe. Root unknown; some compare Gr. *κρόκη*, *κροκάλη*, a rounded pebble, L. *calx*, lime, a stone, dim. *calculus*, a pebble, Skt. *çarkara*, gravel, W. *careg*, a stone, etc.: see *calx*[1].] 1. The spawn of a fish. That of the male is sperm, called *milt* or *soft roe*; that of the female is the mass of eggs, distinguished as *hard roe*. Roe is much eaten, either in its natural state or variously prepared. See *botargo, caviar*.

From fountains small Nilus flude doith flow,
Even so of *rawnis* do michty fisches breid.
K. James VI. Chron. S. P., iii. 489. (*Jamieson.*)

The hie fische [he-fish] spawnis his meltis. And the scho fische [she-fish] hir *rounis*.
Bellenden, Descr. Alb., xi. (*Jamieson.*)

2. The spawn of various crustaceans, used for food, as the berry, coral, or mass of eggs of the female lobster.—3. A mottled appearance in wood, especially in mahogany, being the alternate streak of light and shade running with the grain, or from end to end of the log.

roebuck (rō'buk), *n.* [< ME. *roobukke, raabuke, rabuke* = D. *reebok* = G. *rehbock* = Icel. *rābukkr* = Sw. *råbock* = Dan. *raabuk*; as *roe*[1] + *buck*[1]. Cf. *roe-deer*.] The male of the roe-deer; less properly, the roe-deer.

Roebuck (*Capreolus capræa*).

roebuck-berry (rō'buk-ber″i), *n.* A low herbaceous bramble, *Rubus saxatilis*, of the northern Old World; the stone-bramble; also, its fruit, which consists of a few rather large red grains.

roed (rōd), *a.* [< *roe*[2] + *-ed*[2].] Having roe, as a fish; containing spawn developed to the stage in which it is known as roe.

The female or *roed* fish.
Pennant, Brit. Zool. (ed. 1776), III. 197.

roe-deer (rō'dēr), *n.* [< ME. *roodeer*, < AS. *rāh-deór* = Icel. *raudhdýri* = Sw. *rådjur* = Dan. *raadyr*; as *roe*[1] + *deer*.] A species of the genus *Capreolus*, *C. capræa* or *caprea*, formerly *Cervus capreolus*, of small size, elegant form, and very agile, inhabiting most parts of Europe, including Great Britain, and parts of Asia; a roebuck or roe. The animal is only about 2 feet 3 inches high at the shoulder, and weighs 50 or 60 pounds; it is of a reddish-brown or grayish-brown color, with a large white disk on the rump, and very short tail. The antlers of the male are about a foot long, erect, cylindric, and branching toward the tip. See cut under *roebuck*.

roe-fish (rō'fish), *n.* A fish heavy with roe; a ripe fish, or spawner.

Rœmeria (rē-mē'ri-ä), *n.* [NL. (A. P. de Candolle, 1821), named after J. J. *Roemer*, 1763–1819, a Swiss naturalist.] A genus of polypetalous plants of the order *Papaveraceæ*, the poppy family, and of the tribe *Eupapavereæ*. It is characterized by a linear, usually three-valved capsule opening down nearly to the base, by pitted seeds destitute of a crest, and by flowers with two sepals, four petals, many stamens, and a sessile stigma with deflexed lobes. The 3 species are natives of the Mediterranean region, naturalized in fields in temperate parts of Europe and Asia. They are annuals resembling poppies, but readily distinguished by their long and valvular fruit, and by their less dilated stigmas. They bear dissected leaves and long-stalked violet flowers. *R. hybrida* has a pretty flower, and is sometimes planted, but the petals fall very quickly. It receives the names *purple horned poppy* and *wind-rose*.

roemerite (rėm'ėr-it), *n.* [Named after F. A. *Roemer*, a German geologist.] A basic sulphate of iron, occurring in tabular triclinic crystals of a brownish-yellow color. Also written *römerite*.

roenoke, *n.* See *roanoke*.

roepperite (rėp'ėr-it), *n.* [Named after W. T. *Roepper* of Bethlehem in Pennsylvania.] A variety of chrysolite from the zinc-mines in Sussex county, New Jersey. It is peculiar in containing, besides iron and magnesium, considerable amounts of zinc and manganese. Also spelled *ropperite*.

roesslerite (rės'lėr-it), *n.* [Named after Dr. C. *Roessler* of Hanau in Prussia.] A rare mineral consisting of hydrous arseniate of magnesium, and occurring in white crystalline plates. Also spelled *rösslerite*.

roe-stone (rō'stōn), *n.* A rock having the appearance of the roe of a fish; oölite.

roft. An obsolete preterit of *rive*[1].

roff†, *n.* A Middle English form of *roof*[1].

roffia, rofia, *n.* See *raffia*.

rog†, *v. t.* [ME. *roggen, ruggen*; a var. of *rock*[2], q. v.] To shake.

Hym she *roggeth* and awaketh softe.
Chaucer, Good Women, l. 2708.

He romede, he rarede, that *roggede* alle the erthe,
So ruydly he rappyd at to ryot hymselvene.
Morte Arthure (E. E. T. S.), l. 784.

rogament†, *n.* [< LL. *rogamentum*, something asked, a question, < L. *rogare*, ask: see *rogation*.] A postulate or axiom.

Rogate Sunday. Same as *Rogation Sunday*.

rogation (rọ-gā'shọn), *n.* [< OF. *rogation, rogasion* (pl. *rogations*, Rogation days), F. *rogation* = Pr. *rogazo, roazo* = Sp. *rogacion* = Pg. *rogações*, pl., prayers in Rogation week, = It. *rogazione*, < L. *rogatio(n-)*, a supplication, an asking, < *rogare*, pp. *rogatus*, ask. Cf. *abrogate, interrogate, supererogation, prerogative, prorogue*, etc.] 1. In *Rom. jurisprudence*, the demand by the consuls or tribunes of a law to be passed by the people.—2. Litany; supplication: especially as said in procession.

He [Bishop Mamercus] perfecteth the *Rogations* or Litanies before in use. Hooker, Eccles. Polity, v. 41.

Rogation days, the Monday, Tuesday, and Wednesday before Ascension day. The special observance of these days with fasting and rogations (litanies and public processions) was first introduced by Mamertus or Mamercus, bishop of Vienne in southern France, about A. D. 470, at a time of general distress arising from earthquakes, volcanic eruptions, floods, and other troubles. It soon became general in Gaul, and spread to England. In the Roman Catholic Church (which adopted the observance about 800) the Litany of the Saints is said in procession on these days. In the Anglican Church the Rogation days are appointed days of fasting or abstinence, and it was formerly the custom to say the Litany, to read the homily and exhortation given in the Book of Homilies, and to perambulate the parish. The custom of perambulation (which see) is still observed in some places in England. Also called *gang-days*.—**Rogation Sunday**, the Sunday preceding Ascension day.—**Rogation-tide**, the time of Rogation days.—**Rogation week**, the week in which the Rogation days occur. Also called *procession week, cross-week, gang-week*.

rogation-flower (rọ-gā'shọn-flou″ėr), *n.* An Old World milkwort, *Polygala vulgaris*, which blooms during Rogation week and was carried in processions. See *milkwort*.

rogatory (rog'ạ-tọ-ri), *a.* [= F. *rogatoire* = It. *rogatorio*, < L. *rogator*, an asker, solicitor: see *rogation*.] Seeking information; authorized to collect or engaged in collecting information.

Many countries aid one another's judicial proceedings by consenting that their judges may accept *rogatory* commissions, or act as agents of foreign courts for the purpose of examining witnesses or otherwise ascertaining facts. *Woolsey*, Introd. to Inter. Law, § 76.

Letters rogatory. See *letter*[3].

roger (roj'ėr), *n.* [A familiar use of the personal name *Roger*, < OF. *Roger*, < OHG. *Ruodiger*, G. *Rudiger*. Cf. *robin*[1].] 1. A ram. See *Collins Miscellanies* (1742), p. 116. (*Halliwell.*) [Prov. Eng.]—2†. A rogue. [Old cant.]—**Roger of the buttery**, a goose. *Halliwell.*

Roger de Coverley (roj'ėr dẹ kuv'ėr-li). [Named after Sir *Roger de Coverley*, one of the members of the club under whose direction the "Spectator" professed to be edited.] An English country-dance, corresponding to the Virginia reel. Also called *Sir Roger de Coverley*.

After . . . dinner . . . comes dancing, . . . reels and flings, and strathspeys and *Roger de Coverleys*.
Motley, Correspondence, I. 353.

rogerian† (rọ-jē'ri-ạn), *n.* [Appar. < *Roger*, a person's name, + *-ian*.] A wig. [Rare.]

The unruly wind blows off his periwink. . . .
The sportful wind, to mock the headless man,
Tosses apace his pitch'd *Rogerian*.
Bp. Hall, Satires, III. v. 16.

rogersite (roj'ėrz-it), *n.* [Named after Prof. W. B. *Rogers*.] An imperfectly known mineral occurring in the form of a thin white crust upon the samarskite of North Carolina: it is essentially a hydrated niobate of the yttrium metals.

roggan (rog'ạn), *n.* [Cf. *rog*.] A rocking stone. See *rocking*. *Halliwell.* [Prov. Eng.]

roggenstein (rog'en-stīn), *n.* [G., lit. 'rye-stone,' < *roggen*, = E. *rye*, + *stein* = E. *stone*.] A kind of oölite in which the grains are cemented by argillaceous matter. The roggenstein anticlinal is the uplift in which are the important mines of Stassfurt in Prussia, and its vicinity.

roggle (rog'l), *v. t.* and *i.* [Freq. of *rog*.] To shake; jumble. *Brockett.* [Prov. Eng.]

roghtlesse†, *a.* [ME., appar. an erroneously formed word, equiv. to *reckless* (after *roghte*, pret. of *reck*): see *reck, reckless*.] Reckless; careless.

Dreding ye were of my woos *roghtlesse*;
That was to me a grevous hevinesse.
MS. Cantab. Ff. ii. 6, f. 116. (*Halliwell.*)

rogue (rōg), *n.* [Early mod. E. also *roag, roge*; < OF. *rogue*, presumptuous, malapert, rude, hence used in E. as a noun, a surly fellow, a vagabond; prob. < Bret. *rok, rog*, arrogant, proud, haughty, brusk; cf. Ir. Gael. *rucas*, pride, arrogance.] 1. A vagrant; a sturdy beggar; a tramp. Persons of this character were, by the old laws of England, to be punished by whipping and having the ear bored with a hot iron.

Wast thou fain, poor father,
To hovel thee with swine, and *rogues* forlorn,
In short and musty straw? *Shak.*, Lear, iv. 7. 39.

Roe. Methinks 'tis pity such a lusty fellow
Should wander up and down, and want employment.
Bel. She takes me for a *rogue*!—You may do well, madam,
To stay this wanderer, and set him a-work, forsooth.
Fletcher, Wildgoose Chase, ii. 3.

2. A knave; a dishonest person; a rascal: applied generally to males.

We're bought and sold for English gold—
Such a parcel of *rogues* in a nation.
Burns, Farewell to a' our Scottish Fame.

3. A sly fellow; a wag.

The satirical *rogue* says here that old men have grey beards, . . . and that they have a plentiful lack of wit.
Shak., Hamlet, ii. 2. 197.

4. A mischievous or playful person: applied in slight endearment to children or women. Compare *roguish*, 3.

Ah, you sweet little *rogue*, you!
Shak., 2 Hen. IV., ii. 4. 233.

What, rob your boys? those pretty *rogues*!
Pope, Imit. of Horace, I. vii. 27.

5. A rogue elephant (which see, under *elephant*).—6. A plant that falls short of a standard required by nurserymen, gardeners, etc.

When a race of plants is once pretty well established, the seed-raisers do not pick out the best plants, but merely go over their seed-beds, and pull up the *rogues*, as they call the plants that deviate from the proper standard.
Darwin, Origin of Species, p. 42.

Rogue elephant. See *elephant*.—**Rogue-money**, in Scotland, an assessment laid on each county for defraying the expense of apprehending offenders, maintaining them in jail, and prosecuting them.—**Rogues and vagabonds**, an appellation under which, in English law, fall various classes of persons who may be summarily committed, such as fortune-tellers, persons collecting alms under false pretenses, persons deserting their families and leaving them chargeable to the parish, persons wandering about as vagrants without visible means of subsistence, persons found on any premises for an unlawful purpose, and others. Rogues and vagabonds may be summarily committed to prison for three months with hard labor. See *vagrant*.—**Rogues' gallery**, a collection of photographs of notorious law-breakers, kept at police headquarters.—**Rogue's march.** See *march*[2].—**Rogue's yarn**, a rope-yarn distinguishable from the rest of the yarns in a rope, serving to identify rope made in government dock-yards. In rope made in United States navy-yards the rogue's yarn is twisted in a contrary direction to the others, and is of manila in hemp rope and of hemp in manila rope.—**Wild rogue**†, a vagrant by family inheritance.

A *wilde Roge* is he that is borne a Roge: he is more subtil and more geuen by nature to all kinde of knauery than the

other. . . . I once rebuking a wyld roge because he went idelly about, he shewed me that he was a begger by enheritance — his Grandfather was a begger, his father was one, and he must nedes be one by good reason.
Warning for Common Cursetors (1567), quoted in Ribton-[Turner's Vagrants and Vagrancy, p. 597.

=Syn. 2. Cheat, sharper, scamp, swindler.

rogue (rōg), *v.*; pret. and pp. *rogued*, ppr. *roguing*. [Early mod. E. also *roge*; < *rogue*, *n.*] I. *intrans.* 1. To play the rogue; play knavish tricks. [Rare.]

And *roguing* virtue brings a man defame,
A packstaff epithet, and scorned name.
Marston, Scourge of Villanie, v. 101.

2†. To wander; tramp; play the vagabond.

Yf he be but once taken soe idlye *roging*, he may punnish him more lightlye, as with stockes or such like.
Spenser, State of Ireland.

II. *trans.* 1†. To call (one) a rogue; denounce as a rogue; stigmatize as a cheat or impostor.

It may be thou wast put in office lately,
Which makes thee *rogue* me so, and rayle so stately.
John Taylor, Works (1630).

2. To cheat; injure by roguery.

That envious Scotchman, Sandy Macraw (a scurvy limb of the coast-guards, who lived by poaching on my born rights), had set himself up with a boat, forsooth, on purpose to *rogue* me and rob me the better.
R. D. Blackmore, Maid of Sker, v.

3. To uproot or destroy, as plants which do not conform to a desired standard.

The destruction of horses under a certain size was ordered, and this may be compared to the *roguing* of plants by nurserymen. *Darwin*, Origin of Species, p. 43.

rogue-house (rōg'hous), *n.* A prison; a lock-up. *Halliwell.* [Prov. Eng.]

roguery (rō'gėr-i), *n.*; pl. *rogueries* (-iz). [< *rogue* + *-ery.*] 1†. The life of a vagrant; vagabondism.—2. Knavish tricks; cheating; fraud; dishonest practices.

You rogue, here 's lime in this sack too: there is nothing but *roguery* to be found in villanous man.
Shak., 1 Hen. IV., ii. 4. 138.

Peter had lately done some *rogueries* that forced him to abscond. *Swift*, Tale of a Tub, xi.

3. Waggery; arch tricks; mischievousness.

rogue's-gilliflower† (rōgz'jil'i-flou-ėr), *n.* An old name of the rocket *Hesperis matronalis*. *Lyte.*

rogueship (rōg'ship), *n.* [< *rogue* + *-ship.*] The character or state of a rogue; also, a roguish person. [Rare.]

Ramb. Rank and rotten, is she not?
Shave. Your spittle *rogueships*
Shall not make me so.
Massinger, City Madam, iii. 1.

roguish (rō'gish), *a.* [< *rogue* + *-ish*[1].] 1†. Vagrant; vagabond.

Let 's follow the old earl, and get the Bedlam
To lead him where he would: his *roguish* madness
Allows itself to any thing. *Shak.*, Lear, iii. 7. 104.

2. Knavish; fraudulent; dishonest.

The law of evidence; a law very excellently calculated for the preservation of the lives of His Majesty's *roguish* subjects. *Fielding*, Amelia, xi. 3.

3. Mischievous; playful.

An' she has twa sparkling *roguish* een.
Burns, On Cessnock Banks.

roguishly (rō'gish-li), *adv.* In a roguish manner; like a rogue; knavishly; mischievously.

roguishness (rō'gish-nes), *n.* The state or character of being roguish. (*a*) Knavery. (*b*) Mischievousness; archness; sly cunning: as, the *roguishness* of a look.

roguy† (rō'gi), *a.* [< *rogue* + *-y*[1].] Knavish; dishonest. [Rare.]

Car. Gipsies, and yet pick no pockets?
Alv. Infamous and *roguy!*
Middleton, Spanish Gypsy, ii. 1.

rohan (rō'han), *n.* [Also *rohun*, *rohuna*; E. Ind.] A large East Indian tree, *Soymida febrifuga*, also called *red* or *bastard cedar*, *red-wood*, and *East Indian mahogany*. Its bark is tonic and astringent; its wood is heavy, dark, and durable, and is used for purposes of construction.

roi (rō'i), *n.* [Maori.] The rootstock of the brake, *Pteris aquilina*, var. *esculenta*, which when roasted was formerly a staple article of food with the aborigines of New Zealand.

roicond†, *a.* [ME., < OF. **roicond*, < L. *rubicundus*, red, ruddy: see *rubicund*.] Ruddy; rubicund.

Wele colouret by course, clene of his face,
Redo *roicond* in white, as the Roose fresshe.
Destruction of Troy (E. E. T. S.), l. 3771

roid†, *a.* [ME. *roid*, *ruyd*, < OF. *roide*, F. *raide*, < L. *rigidus*, stiff: see *rigid*. Cf. *redour*.] Stiff; stout; violent.

That bemoth in Ebrew ys opunly to say —
"A *Roid* beste vnreasonable, that no Rule holdes."
Destruction of Troy (E. E. T. S.), l. 4428.

roidly†, *adv.* [ME., < *roid* + *-ly*[2].] Violently.

Hit the hathill o the hede in his hote angur,
And rent hym doun *roidly* ryght to the sadill.
Destruction of Troy (E. E. T. S.), l. 6988.

roignet, *n.* See *roin*.

roil[1]† (roil), *v. i.* [< ME. *roilen*, *roylen*, prob. a var. of *roulen*, roll, used in the same sense: see *roll* (I., 12), and cf. *roil*[2].] To run; wander; roll; rove.

Rigt so, quod Gregorie, religioun *roileth*,
Sterueth and stynketh and steleth lordes almesses,
That oute of couent and cloystre coueyten to libbe.
Piers Plowman (B), x. 297.

The fletynge strem that *royleth* doun diversly fro hy mountaygnes is arested and resisted ofte tyme by the encountrynge of a stoon. *Chaucer*, Boëthius, i. meter 7.

roil[2] (roil), *v. t.* [Formerly also *royle*; also dial. *rile* (sometimes spelled *ryle*), the common colloq. form in the U. S. (cf. *oil*, dial. *ile*, *point*, dial. *pint*, etc.). (*a*) According to Stratmann, < OF. *roeler*, *roler*, *roller*, vex, disturb, beat, particular uses of the orig. sense 'roll': see *roil*[1], *roll*. (*b*) In another view, prop. *rile*, and orig. as a noun, ME. *ryal*, *riall*, foam, fermentation; perhaps < OF. *roille*, *rouille*, F. *rouille* = Pr. *roill*, rust, mildew, fungous growth, ult. < L. *robigo*, rust: see *roin*.] 1. To render turbid by stirring up the dregs or sediment: as, to *roil* wine, cider, or other liquor in casks or bottles.

The lamb down stream *roiled* the wolf's water above.
Roger North, Examen, p. 359. (*Davies.*)

I had dug out the spring and made a well of clear gray water, where I could dip up a pailful without *roiling* it.
Thoreau, Walden, p. 245.

I thirst for one cool cup of water clear,
But drink the *riled* stream of lying breath.
Jones Very, Poems, p. 78.

2. To excite to some degree of anger; annoy; vex: now more commonly, in colloquial use, *rile*.

His spirits were very much *roiled*.
Roger North, Lord Guilford, II. 69. (*Davies.*)

You have always been one of the best fellows in the world, . . . and the most generous, and the most cordial — that you have; only you do *rile* me when you sing that confounded Mayfair twang. *Thackeray*, Philip, xvii.

3. To perplex. [Local.]—4. To salt (fish) by means of a roiler.

roil[3]†, *n.* [Early mod. E. *royle*; < ME. *roile*, *royle*; origin uncertain.] A Flemish horse.

Polidamas the prise horse presit vnto,
Raght to the Reyne, and the *Roile* toke.
Destruction of Troy (E. E. T. S.), l. 8337.

By the good swimminge of horses many men haue ben saued, and contrary wise, by a timorouse *royle*, where the water hath uneth come to his bely, his legges hath foltred, wherby many a good and propre man hath perisshed.
Sir T. Elyot, The Governour, i. 17.

roiler (roi'lėr), *n.* [< *roil*[2] + *-er*[1].] A machine for salting small fish, as a revolving box turned by means of a crank. [North Carolina.]

roily (roi'li), *a.* [Also dial. *rily*, *riley*; < *roil*[2] + *-y*[1].] Muddy; turbid: as, *roily* water.

Then flow away, my sweety sap,
And I will make you boily;
Nor catch a woodman's hasty nap,
For fear you should get *roily*.
J. F. Cooper, Pioneer, xx.

The streams full and *roily*. *The Century*, XXVII. 107.

roin† (roin), *n.* [Also *royne*; < ME. *roine*, *roigne*, < OF. *roingne*, *rogne*, *rongne*, scurf, mange, scabbiness, itch, F. *rogne*, itch, = Pr. *ronha*, *runha* = Cat. *ronya* = Sp. *roña* = Pg. *ronha* = It. *rogna*, itch; perhaps < L. *robigo*, *rubigo* (*-gin-*), rust, mildew, also sore, ulcer, scab: see *ronion*.] A scab or scurf.

Hir nekke was of good fasoun
In lengthe and gretnesse by resoun,
Withoute bleyne, scabbe, or *royne*.
Rom. of the Rose, l. 553.

roinish† (roi'nish), *a.* [Also *roynish*; < *roin* + *-ish*[1]. Cf. *roinous*.] Mangy; scabby; hence, mean; paltry; scurvy.

My lord, the *roynish* clown, at whom so oft
Your grace was wont to laugh, is also missing.
Shak., As you Like it, ii. 2. 8.

roinous† (roi'nus), *a.* [Also *roynous*; < ME. *roinous*, *roignous*, < OF. *roigneux*, *roingneux*, *rongneux* (= Pr. *rognos*, *ronhos*, *runhos* = Cat. *ronyos* = Sp. *roñoso* = Pg. *ronhoso* = It. *rognoso*), mangy, scabby; perhaps < L. *robiginosus*, rusty, mangy, etc., < *robigo* (*robigin-*), rust: see *roin*.] Scabby; rough; crooked; worthless.

The foule croked bowe bidous,
That knotty was and al *roynous*.
Rom. of the Rose, l. 988.

This argument is al *roignous*;
It is not worth a croked brere.
Rom. of the Rose, l. 6190.

roint† (roint), *v.* See *aroint*.

roist† (roist), *v. i.* [Early mod. E. *royst*; cf. *roister*.] Same as *roister*. *Cotgrave.*

The vayne glorious, . . .
Whose humour the *roysting* sort continually doth feede.
Udall, Roister Doister, Prol.

I have a *roisting* challenge sent amongst
The dull and factious nobles of the Greeks.
Shak., T. and C., ii. 2. 208.

roister (rois'tėr), *n.* [Also *royster*; < OF. *rustre*, a ruffian, roister, a particular use (with unoriginal *r*) of OF. *ruste*, *ruiste*, a rustic, F. *rustique*: see *rustic*.] 1. A rioter; a blusterer; a roisterer. [Obsolete or archaic.]

They must not part till they have drunk a barrell,
Or straight this *royster* will begin to quarrel.
Times' Whistle (E. E. T. S.), p. 60.

The natives were an honest, social race of jolly *roysters*, who had no objection to a drinking bout, and were very merry in their cups. *Irving*, Knickerbocker, p. 92.

2. [< *roister*, *v.*] A drunken or riotous frolic; a spree.

roister (rois'tėr), *v. i.* [Also *royster*; < *roister*, *n.*] To bluster; swagger; bully; be bold, noisy, vaunting, or turbulent.

A gang of merry *roistering* devils, frisking and curveting on a flat rock. *Irving*, Knickerbocker, p. 348.

Her brother lingers late
With a *roystering* company.
Tennyson, Maud, xiv. 2.

The wind is *roistering* out of doors.
Lowell, To Charles Eliot Norton.

roister-doister† (rois'tėr-dois'tėr), *n.* [First recorded in the title of the first English comedy, Udall's "Ralph *Roister-Doister*" (1553); a varied redupl. of *roister*.] A roisterer.

I have . . . seen the mad-brainest *roister-doister* in a country dashed out of countenance.
G. Harvey, Four Letters.

roisterer (rois'tėr-ėr), *n.* [Also *roysterer*; < *roister* + *-er*[1].] One who roisters; a bold, blustering, or turbulent fellow.

Midmost of a rout of *roisterers*,
Femininely fair and dissolutely pale.
Tennyson, Geraint.

roistering (rois'tėr-ing), *p. a.* Swaggering; rude.

She again encounters "Dick" Talbot, now grown more *roystering* and bloated than ever, and marries the lover of her youth. *The Academy*, March 1, 1890, p. 148.

roisterly† (rois'tėr-li), *a.* [< *roister* + *-ly*[1].] Like a roisterer; blustering; violent.

A mad world, where such shameful stuff is bought and sold; and where such *roisterly* varlets may be suffered to play upon whom they lust, and how they lust.
G. *Harvey*, Four Letters.

roisterly (rois'tėr-li), *adv.* [< *roisterly*, *a.*] In a bullying, violent manner.

roisterous (rois'tėr-us), *a.* [< *roister* + *-ous*.] Violent; blustery; uproarious. [Rare.]

Was the like ever heard of? The *roysterous* young dogs; carolling, howling, breaking the Lord Abbot's sleep!
Carlyle, Past and Present, ii. 15.

roitelet (roi'te-let), *n.* [Also *roytelet*; < F. *roitelet*, a petty king, a wren (Cotgrave), dim. of *roi*, a king: see *roy*.] 1†. A little or petty king; a royalet.

Causing the American *roytelets* to turn all homagers to that king and the crown of England. *Heylin.*

2. In *ornith.*, a kinglet or goldcrest; a small bird of the genus *Regulus*.

rok, *n.* See *roc*[1].

roka (rō'kä), *n.* A large East African tree, *Trichilia emetica*, whose fruit is considered emetic, and whose seeds yield a fatty oil.

rokambole, *n.* See *rocambole*.

roke (rōk), *n.* [< ME. *roke*, a var. of *reke* (= OD. *roke*, etc.): see *reek*[1].] Mist; smoke; damp.

Roke, myste. Nebula. *Prompt. Parv.*, p. 436.

rokeage, rokee (rō'kāj, rō'kē), *n.* [Also *roucheage*, *yokeage*, *yokeague*; Amer. Ind.; orig. form uncertain. Cf. *nocake*.] Indian corn parched, pulverized, and mixed with sugar: commonly called *pinole*. [Local, U. S.]

rokelay (rok'e-lā), *n.* Same as *roquelaure*.

roker (rō'kėr), *n.* [Prob. connected with *roach*[1], and thus ult. with *ray*[2].] A species of *Raia*; especially, the thornback ray.

The English word *roker* in most cases signifies thornback, but is occasionally employed to denote any species of the ray family, with the exception of the skate.
N. and Q., 7th ser., VII. 146.

Into lobsters and crabs which have become by reason of age of lighter weight are introduced portions of fresh haddock or roker. *Lancet*, No. 3455, p. 1025.

roket†, **rokette**[1]†, *n.* Middle English forms of *rochet*[1]. *Destruction of Troy* (E. E. T. S.), l. 13525.

rokket. A Middle English form of *rock*[1], *rock*[2], etc.

roky (rō'ki), *a.* [Also *roaky, rooky;* < ME. *roky*, misty, < *roke*, mist: see *roke* and *reek*[1].] Misty; foggy; cloudy. *Ray.*

Roky, or mysty. Nebulosus. *Prompt. Parv.*, p. 436.

He . . . in a *roky* hollow, belling, heard
The hounds of Mark.
Tennyson, Last Tournament.

Rolandic (rọ̄-lan'dik), *a.* [< *Rolando* (see def.) + *-ic.*] Pertaining to Rolando, an Italian anatomist and physiologist (died 1831). Compare *postrolandic* (*prerolandic* is also used).—**Rolandic fissure.** Same as *fissure of Rolando* (which see, under *fissure*).—**Rolandic funiculus.** See *funiculus of Rolando*, under *funiculus*.—**Rolandic line,** a line on the surface of the skull (or head) marking the position of the fissure of Rolando beneath.—**Rolandic point,** the intersection of the Rolandic lines with the median plane and with each other on the surface of the skull. It is about half an inch behind the middle of the line passing over the skull from the glabella to the inion.

rolet, *v.* An obsolete form of *roll*.

rolet, *n.* [A var. of *roll*.] A unit of quantity formerly in use in England, defined by a statute of Charles II. as seventy-two sheets of parchment.

rôle (rōl), *n.* [< F. *rôle:* see *roll* and *rotary*.] A part or character represented by an actor; any conspicuous part or function assumed by any one, as a leading public character.—**Title rôle,** the part in a play which gives its name to the play, as Hamlet in the play of "Hamlet," or Macbeth in that of "Macbeth."

roll (rōl), *v.* [Early mod. E. also *rowl, rowle, roule;* < ME. *rollen, rolen* (= D. *rollen* = MHG. *rolen*, G. *rollen* = Icel. *rolla* = Dan. *rulle* = Sw. *rulla*), < OF. *roler, roller, rueler, roeler, rouler*, F. *rouler*, F. dial. *roler, roller*, roll, roll up, roll along, go on wheels, = Pr. *rolar, rotlar* = Cat. *rotolar* = Sp. *rollar, rular* = Pg. *rolar* = It. *rotolare, rullare*, < ML. *rotulare*, roll, revolve, < L. *rotula*, a little wheel, dim. of *rota*, a wheel: see *rota*[1]. Cf. *roll, n.*] **I.** *intrans.* **1.** To move like a carriage-wheel; move along a surface without slipping by perpetually turning over the foremost point of contact as an instantaneous axis: as, a ball or wheel *rolls* on the earth; a body *rolls* on an inclined plane.

The fayre hede fro the halce hit [fell] to the erthe,
That fele hit foyned [spurned] wyth her fete, there hit forth *roled*.
Sir Gawayne and the Green Knight (E. E. T. S.), l. 428.

The *rolling* stone never gathereth mosse.
Heywood, Proverbs (ed. Sharman).

That goddess [Fortune] blind,
That stands upon the *rolling* restless stone.
Shak., Hen. V., iii. 6. 31.

2. To run or travel on wheels.

The wealthy, the luxurious, by the stress
Of business roused, or pleasure, ere their time,
May *roll* in chariots. *Wordsworth*, Excursion, ii.

3. To revolve; perform a periodical revolution.

The *rolling* Year
Is full of Thee. *Thomson*, Hymn, l. 2.

Sleep, holy spirit, blessed soul,
While the stars burn, the moons increase,
And the great ages onward *roll*.
Tennyson, To J. S.

4. To turn; have a rotatory motion, generally reciprocating and irregular, especially in lateral directions: as, the ship *rolls* (that is, turns back and forth about a longitudinal axis).

His eyen steepe, and *rollynge* in his heede.
Chaucer, Prol. to C. T., l. 201.

The poet's eye, in a fine frenzy *rolling*,
Doth glance from heaven to earth, from earth to heaven.
Shak., M. N. D., v. 1. 12.

Twice ten tempestuous nights I *rolled*, resigned
To roaring billows and the warring wind.
Pope, Odyssey, vi. 205.

The ship *rolled* and dashed, . . . now showing us the whole sweep of her deck, . . . now nothing but her keel.
Dickens, David Copperfield, lv.

5. To move like waves or billows; also, to move like a considerable body of water, as a river. Each particle of water in a wave revolves in a circle, and though this cannot be seen, there is a vague appearance of a wheel-like movement.

Wave *rolling* after wave, where way they found,
If steep, with torrent rapture. *Milton*, P. L., vii. 298.

The *rolling* smoke involves the sacrifice.
Pope, Dunciad, l. 248.

6. To fluctuate; move tumultuously.

What diff'rent Sorrows did within thee *roll!*
Prior, Solomon, ii.

7. To tumble or fall over and over.

Down they fell
By thousands, angel on archangel *roll'd*.
Milton, P. L., vi. 594.

8. To emit a deep prolonged sound, like the roll of a ball or the continuous beating of a drum.

Near and more near the thunders *roll*.
Burns, Tam o' Shanter.

A *rolling* organ-harmony
Swells up, and shakes and falls.
Tennyson, Sir Galahad.

9. To enroll one's self; be enrolled.

He lends at legal value considerable sums, which he might highly increase by *rolling* in the public stocks.
Steele, Spectator, No. 49.

Papillion. Right honourable sharpers; and Frenchmen from the county of York.
Wilding. In the last list, I presume, you *roll*.
Foote, The Liar, i. 1.

10. To trill: said of certain singing birds.

The continuous roll is possessed almost exclusively by the canary, and the nightingale is one of the very few birds that share to some degree the faculty of *rolling* at any pitch of the voice uninterruptedly.
Appleton's Ann. Cyc., 1886, p. 87.

11. To lend itself to being coiled up in a cylindrical form: as, cloth that *rolls* well.—**12†.** To ramble; wander abroad; gad about. Compare *roil*[1].

That like proverbe of Ecclesiaste,
Where he comandeth and forbedeth faste
Man shal nat suffre his wyf go *roule* aboute.
Chaucer, Prol. to Wife of Bath's Tale, l. 653.

These unruly rascals in their *rolling* disperse themselves into several companies, as occasion serveth, sometime more and sometime less.
Harman, Caveat for Cursetors, p. 20.

II. *trans.* **1.** To cause to rotate; whirl or wheel.

When thou shalt speake to any man, *role* not to fast thyne eye. *Babees Book* (E. E. T. S.), p. 76.

Rolling his greedy eyeballs in his head.
Shak., Lucrece, l. 368.

Now heaven in all her glory shone, and *roll'd*
Her motions. *Milton*, P. L., vii. 499.

We have had enough of action, and of motion we,
Roll'd to starboard, *roll'd* to larboard, when the surge was seething free. *Tennyson*, Lotos-Eaters, Choric Song.

2. To cause to move like a carriage-wheel; cause to move over a surface without sliding, by perpetually turning over the foremost point of contact: as, to *roll* a cask or a ball.

Who shall *roll* us away the stone from the door of the sepulchre? Mark xvi. 3.

3. To turn over in one's thoughts; revolve; consider again and again.

The yongest, which that wente unto the toun,
Ful ofte in herte he *rolleth* up and doun
The beautee of thise florins newe and bryghte.
Chaucer, Pardoner's Tale, l. 376.

I came home *rolling* resentments in my mind, and framing schemes of vengeance.
Swift, Letter, Sept. 9, 1710. (*Seager.*)

4. To wrap round and round an axis, so as to bring into a compact cylindrical form: as, to *roll* a piece of cloth; to *roll* a sheet of paper; to *roll* parchment; to *roll* tobacco.

As the snake, *roll'd* in a flowering bank,
With shining checker'd slough, doth sting a child.
Shak., 2 Hen. VI., iii. 1. 228.

He lies like a hedgehog *roll'd* up the wrong way,
Tormenting himself with his prickles.
Hood, Miss Kilmansegg, Her Dream.

The bed, in the day-time, is *rolled* up, and placed on one side. *E. W. Lane*, Modern Egyptians, I. 20.

5. To bind or infold in a bandage or wrapper; inwrap.

Their Kings, whose bodies are . . . lapped in white skinnes, and *rowled* in mats. *Purchas*, Pilgrimage, p. 765.

What time the foeman's line is broke,
And all the war is *roll'd* in smoke.
Tennyson, Two Voices.

6. To press or level with a roller; spread out with a roller or rolling-pin: as, to *roll* a field; to *roll* pie-crust.

It is passed between cylinders often, and *rolled*.
Cowper, Flatting Mill, l. 3.

7. To drive or impel forward with a sweeping, easy motion, as of rolling.

And chalky Wey, that *rolls* a milky wave.
Pope, Windsor Forest, l. 344.

Where Afric's sunny fountains
Roll down their golden sand.
Bp. Heber, Missionary Hymn.

8. To give expression to or emit in a prolonged deep sound.

They care for no understanding: it is enough if thou canst *roll* up a pair of matins, or an even-song, and mumble a few ceremonies. *Tyndale*, Doctrinal Treatises, p. 243.

Man, her last work, who seem'd so fair,
Such splendid purpose in his eyes,
Who *roll'd* the psalm to wintry skies,
Who built him fanes of fruitless prayer.
Tennyson, In Memoriam, lvi.

9. To utter with vibration of the tongue; trill.

Don't, like a lecturer or dramatic star,
Try over hard to *roll* the British R.
O. W. Holmes, A Rhymed Lesson.

10. In *printing*, to make (paper) smooth by passing it under calendering rollers. [Eng.]—**11.** To turn over by degrees, as a whale when cutting in. At first the whale is rolled carefully and gently, then more quickly, as the blubber is hove up, and the head is cut off at last.

12. In *drum-playing*, to beat with rapid blows so as to produce a continuous sound.—**Rolled chop.** See *chop*[1], 2.—**Rolled cod,** boneless cod, prepared by rolling several slices into parcels which are packed in boxes. [Trade-name.]—**Rolled glass.** See *glass*.—**Rolled plating.** See *plate, v. t.*—**Rolled rail.** See *rail*[1]. =**Syn. 2.** *Swing*, etc. See *rock*[2], *v. t.*

roll (rōl), *n.* [Early mod. E. also *rowl, rowle, roule;* < ME. *rolle* = MD. *rol*, D. *rol* = MLG. *rol* = MHG. *rolle, rulle*, G. *rolle* = Sw. *rulla* = Dan. *rulle*, < OF. *rolle, roole, roule*, F. *rôle* (see *rôle*) = Pr. *rolle, rotlle, rutle* = Cat. *rotllo* = Sp. *rol*, a list, roll, *rollo*, a roll, record, = Pg. *rolo, rol* = It. *ruolo, rullo, ruotolo, rotolo*, a roll, list, < ML. *rotulus*, a roll, list, catalogue, schedule, record, prop. a paper or parchment rolled up (cf. *volume*, ult. < L. *volvere*, roll); cf. *rotulare*, roll up: see *roll, v.* The ML. *rotulus*, a roll, is partly from the verb, and not wholly identical with L. *rotulus*, also *rotula*, a little wheel, from which the verb is derived. In the later senses directly from the mod. verb.] **1.** A cylinder formed by winding something round and round; that which is rolled up: as, a *roll* of wool; a *roll* of paper.

The gentlemen . . . hauing theyr heades bounde aboute with listes and *rowles* of sundry coloures after the maner of the Turkes.
R. Eden, tr. of Sebastian Munster (First Books on America, [ed. Arber, p. 14).

Take thee a roll of a book, and write therein.
Jer. xxxvi. 2.

Specifically—(*a*) A document of paper, parchment, or the like which is or may be rolled up; hence, an official document; a list; a register; a catalogue; a record: as, a muster-*roll;* a class-*roll;* a court-*roll*.

Nis nou so lutel thing of theos thet the deouel naueth enbrened ou his *rolle*. *Ancren Riwle*, p. 344.

I am not in the *roll* of common men.
Shak., 1 Hen. IV., iii. 1. 43.

Then thundered forth a *roll* of names:
The first was thine, unhappy James!
Scott, Marmion, v. 26.

(*b*) A long piece of cloth, paper, or the like, usually of uniform width throughout, and rolled upon either a round stick or a thin board, or upon itself merely, as the most convenient form of making a package. See *roller*, 2. (*c*) In *cookery*, something rolled up: as, a veal *roll;* a jelly *roll*. Specifically—(1) A small cake of bread rolled or doubled on itself before baking: as, a French *roll*. (2) Same as *roly-poly*, 2. (*d*) A cylindrical twist of tobacco. (*e*) In *carding*, a slender, slightly compacted cylinder or sliver of carded wool, delivered from hand-cards or from the doffing-cylinder of a carding-machine. Such rolls were formerly much used in the hand-spinning of wool. For machine-spinning the sliver is extended into a continuous roving. (*f*) Part of the head-dress of a woman, a rounded cushion or mass of hair usually laid above the forehead, especially in the sixteenth century.

Antiæ, the heare of a woman that is layed over hir forheade; gentilwomen dyd lately call them their *rolles*.
Elyot, ed. 1559. (*Halliwell.*)

2. A revolving cylinder employed in any manner to operate upon a material, as in forming metals into bars, plates, or sheets, smoothing the surfaces of textures, as in paper-making, laundering, etc., or in comminuting substances, as in grinding grain, crushing ores, etc.

Where land is clotty, and a shower of rain comes that soaks through, use a *roll* to break the clots.
Mortimer, Husbandry.

(*a*) One of a pair of cylinders in a rolling-mill, between which metals are passed to form them into bars, plates,

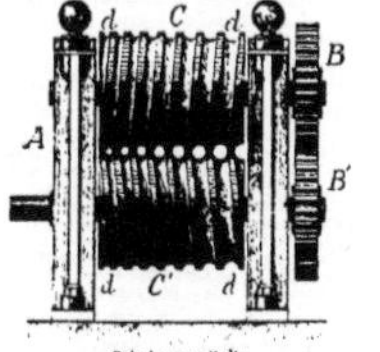

Spiral-groove Rolls.

A, frame: *B, B'*, intermeshed gears: *C, C'*, spirally grooved rolls, having the grooves *d* gradually diminishing in size from right to left, and driven by the gears.

or sheets. See *rolling-mill*. (*b*) In *engraving*, the cylindrical die of a transferring-press. (*c*) In *metal.*, one of a pair of hard and strong metallic cylinders between which ores are crushed. (d) In *paper-making*, one of the cylinders of a calender; also, the cylinder of a pulping-engine. See *calender*[1], 1, and *pulp-engine*. (e) In *high milling*, one of a pair of metal cylinders through a series of which pairs grain is passed for successively crushing it to the requisite fineness. See *high milling*, under *milling*. (f) In *calico-printing*, a cylinder of a calico-printing machine. (g) The impression-cylinder of a printing-machine. (h) In a great variety of machines, one of the cylinders over which an endless apron extends, and upon which it is moved, as in the feed-aprons of carding-machines, pickers for opening cotton as taken from the bale, machines for manufacturing shoddy from rags, etc. (i) Either of a pair of plain or fluted cylinders between which material is passed to feed it into a machine, as in feeding rags to a shoddy-machine, paper to printing-presses, calico to calico-printing machines, etc. Such rolls are also called *feed-rolls*. (j) A hand-tool used by bookbinders for embossing book-covers, or forming thereon embossed gilded lines. It consists of either a plain or an embossed cylinder with a handle adapted to rest (when in use) against the shoulder of the workman. The roller is heated for use in embossing. (k) In the manufacture of plate-glass, a heavy metallic cylinder which spreads the "metal" on the table, and which, being supported on ways on opposite sides of the table, produces a sheet or plate of uniform thickness. (The distinction between *roll* and *roller* is exceedingly indefinite. The term *roller* is, however, more generally applied to a revolving cylinder working in movable bearings, as in an agricultural roller for smoothing the surface of land, or the roller of a lawn-mower; while *roll* is more commonly used for a cylinder working in fixed bearings, as in a rolling-mill for working metals, or in a calender, or in a grinding-mill.)

Bookbinders' Roll.
a, roll, pivoted to furcated handle *b* at *c*.

3. In *building*: (a) A rounded strip fastened upon and extending along the ridge of a roof. (b) In a leaden roof, one of a number of rounded strips placed under the lead at intervals, whereby crawling of the metal through alternate expansion and contraction is prevented. —4. The act of rolling, or the state of being rolled; a rotatory movement: as, the *roll* of a ball; the *roll* of a ship.

> These larger hearts must feel the *rolls*
> Of stormier-waved temptation.
> *Lowell*, At the Burns Centennial.

5. A deep, prolonged, or sustained sound: as, the *roll* of thunder. Also *rolling*.

> A *roll* of periods, sweeter than her [the Muse's] song.
> *Thomson*, Autumn, l. 17.

> Fancy, borne perhaps upon the rise
> And long *roll* of the Hexameter.
> *Tennyson*, Lucretius.

Specifically—(a) The prolonged sound produced by a drum when rapidly beaten, or the act of producing such a sound.

> Now, to the *roll* of muffled drums,
> To thee the greatest soldier comes.
> *Tennyson*, Death of Wellington, vi.

The *roll* [on the side-drum] . . . is made by alternately striking two blows with the left hand and two with the right, very regularly and rapidly, so as to produce one continuous tremolo. *Grove*, Dict. Music, I. 466.

(b) A trill: applied to the notes of certain birds, as the canary and nightingale.

The *roll* is the most characteristic of all the canary-notes. . . . This even and continuous roll is as perfect as the trill of any instrument, and can be produced at any pitch within the range of the voice. *Appleton's Ann. Cyc.*, XI. 87.

6. In *organ-playing*, the act or result of taking the tones of a chord in quick succession, as in an arpeggio.—7†. Round of duty; particular office; function; duty assigned or assumed; rôle.

In human society every man has his *roll* and station assigned him. *Sir R. L'Estrange.*

8. A swell or undulation of surface: as, the *roll* of the prairie.—9. A rotatory or sidelong movement of the head or body; a swagger; a rolling gait.

That grave, but confident, kind of *roll*, peculiar to old boys in general. *Dickens*, Sketches, Characters, vii.

10. In *mining*, an inequality in the roof or floor of a mine. *Gresley*.—**Bagimont's Roll**, the rent-roll of Scotland, made up in 1275 by Benemund or Baiamund de Vicci, vulgarly called *Bagimont*, who was sent from Rome by the Pope, in the reign of Alexander III., to collect the tithe of all the church livings in Scotland for an expedition to the Holy Land. It remained the statutory valuation, according to which the benefices were taxed, till the Reformation. A copy of it as it existed in the reign of James V. is in the Advocates' Library, Edinburgh. Also spelled *Bajimont's Roll*.—**Burgess roll**. See *burgess*.—**Close rolls**. See *close*[2].—**Great roll**. Same as *pipe-roll*.—**Judgment roll**. See *judgment*.—**Liberate roll**. See *liberate*.—**Long roll** (*milit.*), a prolonged roll of the drums: a signal of an attack by the enemy, or for the troops to assemble rapidly in line.—**Master of the Rolls**. See *master*[1].—**Merchant rolls**. See *merchant*.—**Oblate roll**. See *oblate*.—**Poor's roll**. (a) In England, a roll or list of paupers, or persons entitled to parochial relief or those who have received such aid. (b) In *Scots law*, the roll of litigants who, by reason of poverty, are privileged to sue or defend in forma pauperis, their cause being conducted gratuitously by the counsel and agents for the poor.—**Ragman's roll**†. Same as *ragman-roll*, 1.—**Resiant roll**†. See *resiant*.—**Ridge-roll**. See *ridge*.—**Roll-and-fillet molding**, a round molding with a square fillet on the face of it. It is most usual in the Early Decorated style of English Pointed architecture.—**Roll latten**. See *latten*.—**Roll-molding**, in *arch.*, a molding resembling a segment of a scroll with its end overlapping. It occurs often in the Early Pointed style, in which it is used for dripstones, string-courses, etc.—**Roll of arms**, a document containing written lists of persons entitled to bear arms, with descriptions of their armorial bearings: usually a parchment of medieval origin. The earliest of these important documents dates from about 1245. They are of great value historically and for questions of genealogy.—**Rolls of court, of parliament**, or of any public body, the parchments, kept in rolls, on which are engrossed by the proper officer the acts and proceedings of the body in question, and which constitute the official records of that body.—**Roughing-down rolls**. Same as *roughing-rolls*.—**Scavenger roll**. See *scavenger*.—**To call the roll**. See *call*[1]. =**Syn.** 1. (a) *Catalogue*, etc. See *list*[5].

1. Roll-molding. 2. Roll-and-fillet molding.

rollable (rō'la̤-bl), *a.* [< *roll* + *-able*.] Capable of being rolled.

roll-about (rōl'a̤-bout), *a.* Thick or pudgy, so as to roll when walking. [Colloq.]

A little fat *roll-about* girl of six. *Scott*, Guy Mannering, xxvi.

roll-boiling (rōl'boi"ling), *n.* In *woolen-manuf.*, a process for giving a luster to cloth by scalding it, while tightly wound upon a roller, in a vessel filled with hot water or steam. *E. H. Knight.*

roll-box (rōl'boks), *n.* In *spinning*, the rotary can or cylinder of a jack-frame, in which revolve the bobbin and the carrier-cylinder for the rovings. *E. H. Knight.*

roll-call (rōl'kâl), *n.* 1. The act of calling over a list of names, as of a school or society, or of men who compose a military or legislative body. In the United States military service there are at least three roll-calls daily by the first sergeants under a commissioned officer of the company—namely, at reveille, at retreat, and at tattoo.
2. The military signal given by the drum, trumpet, or other musical instrument for soldiers to attend the calling of the roll.

roll-cumulus (rōl'kū"mụ̄-lus), *n.* A form of strato-cumulus cloud in which the component masses of cloud at a distance from the zenith present the appearance of long bars, while overhead there is seen only the irregular flat base of scattered clouds. The linear arrangement increases toward the horizon, and is simply the effect of perspective. [Eng.]

roller (rō'lėr), *n.* [Early mod. E. also *rowler*; < *roll* + *-er*[1].] 1. One who or that which rolls, especially a cylinder which turns on its axis, used for various purposes, as smoothing, crushing, and spreading out. (a) A heavy cylinder of wood, stone, or (now more usually) metal set in a frame, used in agriculture, gardening, road-making, etc., to break lumps of earth, press the ground compactly about newly sown seeds, compress and smooth the surface of grass-fields, level the surface of walks or roads, etc. Land-rollers are also constructed of a series of disks or a series of rings with serrated edges placed side by side. Such rollers are used for breaking up clods and cutting up rough grass-land, and are known as *disk-rollers* and *clod-crushers*. Heavy road-rollers are often combined with steam traction-engines. Agricultural rollers are also combined with other tools, as with a seeder or a harrow. See *roll*, *n.*, 2.

Pope's [page] is a velvet lawn, shaven by the scythe, and levelled by the *roller*. *Johnson*, Pope.

(b) A rolling-pin. (c) In *printing*, a cylindrical rod of iron covered with a thick composition of glue and molasses, or glue, sugar, and glycerin, which takes ink on its surface by rolling on a table or against other rollers, and which deposits this ink on types when it is rolled over them. (d) In *etching*, a cylinder, about three inches in diameter, covered with soft leather, and used for revarnishing an imperfectly bitten plate. The ground is applied to the roller with a palette-knife on which a little has been taken up. When the ground has, by repeated passing, been evenly spread over all parts of the roller, this is carefully passed with slight pressure over the etched plate so as to cover its surface with varnish, without allowing it to enter the furrows. (e) In *organ-building*, a wooden bar with pins in the ends upon which it may be rolled or rocked, and two projecting arms, usually at some distance from each other, one of which is pulled by a tracker from the keyboards, while the other pulls a tracker attached to a valve. Rollers are primarily designed to transfer motion from side to side, but they also often change it from a horizontal to a vertical plane, or vice versa. The rollers belonging to a single keyboard are usually placed together on a common roller-board, and the entire mechanism is called a *roller-board action* or *movement*. See cut under *organ*. (f) Any cylindrical tool or part of a machine serving to press, flatten, guide, etc., as the cylinders of a paper-making machine, the impression-cylinders in calico-printing, the roller-die by means of which patterns are transferred to such cylinders, etc. (g) The barrel of a musical box or of a chime-ringing machine.

2. That upon which something may be rolled up, as a wooden cylinder, or pasteboard rolled up, usually with a circular section.—3. A cylindrical or spherical body upon which a heavy body can be rolled or moved along: used to lessen friction.

> What mighty *Rowlers*, and what massie Cars,
> Could bring so far so many monstrous Quars?
> *Sylvester*, tr. of Du Bartas's Weeks, ii., The Magnificence.

Specifically—(a) A cylindrical piece of wood put under a heavy stone to facilitate moving it. (b) A wheel in a roller-skate. (c) The wheel of a caster. (d) Same as *roller-towel*. [Colloq.] (e) A stout heavy sheave which revolves and saves a rope that passes over it from wear by friction.

4. A go-cart for a child.

He could run about without a *rowler* or leading-strings. *Smith*, Lives of Highwaymen, II. 50. (*Encyc. Dict.*)

5. That in which something may be rolled; a bandage; specifically, a long rolled bandage used in surgery. It is unrolled as it is used.

I have broken the arm of Pharaoh king of Egypt: and, lo, it shall not be bound up to be healed, to put a *roller* to bind it. Ezek. xxx. 21.

6. In *saddlery*, a broad padded surcingle, serving as a girth to hold a heavy blanket in place. *E. H. Knight.*—7. A long, heavy, swelling wave, such as sets in upon a coast after the subsiding of a storm.

From their feet stretched away to the westward the sapphire *rollers* of the vast Atlantic, crowned with a thousand crests of flying foam. *Kingsley*, Westward Ho, xxxii.

> The league-long *roller* thundering on the reef.
> *Tennyson*, Enoch Arden.

8. In *ornith.*: (a) Any bird of the family *Coraciidæ*: so called from the way they roll or tumble about in flight. The common roller of Europe, Asia, and Africa is *Coracias garrula*. There are many other species, of several different genera. The Madagascar ground-rollers are birds of the genera *Brachypteracias* and *Atelornis*. See cut under *Coracias*. (b) A kind of domestic pigeon; one of the varieties of tumblers.—9. In *herpet.*, a snake of the family *Tortricidæ*; a shorttail.—10. The rockfish or striped-bass, *Roccus lineatus*. [Maryland.]—**Breaking-down rollers**, in *metal-working*, rollers used to roll the metal while it is hot, for the purpose of consolidating it.—**Damping-roller**. See *damping*.—**Delivery-roller**. See *delivery*.—**Diluting roller**, in a paper-making machine, a roller which carries water into the pulp-cistern to reduce the density of the pulp.—**Distributing-roller**, a roller in the inking-apparatus of a printing-press between the ductor and the inking-rolls; a waver.—**Drawing-rollers**, in a drawing-machine, the fluted rollers by which the sliver is elongated.—**Dutch roller**, a kind of domestic pigeon, a variety of the tumbler. *Darwin*.—**Fancy roller**. See *fancy*.—**Lithographic roller**. See *lithographic*.—**Printers' roller**. See *inking-roller*.—**Roller bandage**. Same as *roller*, 5.—**Roller bolt**. See *bolt*[1].—**Roller handspike**. See *handspike*.—**Side roller**, in *sugar-manuf.*, one of the side cylinders of the press. See *king-roller* and *macasse*.—**The rollers**, the local name of a heavy surf peculiar to St. Helena and the Island of Ascension. Rollers prevail on the leeward side of the island after a period of strong trades, and are due to the confluence of the swell passing around the island by the right with that passing around by the left, the swell being also heightened by the surrounding shoals. The resulting surf is so dangerous to shipping that single and double roller-flags are displayed to warn small craft against making for land while the rollers prevail.

roller-bar (rō'lėr-bär), *n.* The sharp-edged bar or knife in the bed of a rag-cutting machine. *E. H. Knight.*

roller-barrow (rō'lėr-bar"ō), *n.* A barrow traveling on a roller of some width, instead of on the ordinary small front wheel, so that it can pass over smooth turf without cutting into it.

roller-bearing (rō'lėr-bãr"ing), *n.* A journal-socket which has antifriction rollers on its interior perimeter; a ring-bush.

roller-bird (rō'lėr-bėrd), *n.* Same as *roller*, 8.

roller-board (rō'lėr-bōrd), *n.* In *organ-building*. See *roller*, 1 (*e*).

roller-bowl (rō'lėr-bōl), *n.* In *woolen-manuf.*, a device used with a carding-machine to roll the detached slivers into cardings or rolls ready for the slubbing-machine.

roller-box (rō'lėr-boks), *n.* In *printing*, a chest or closet of wood in which inking-rollers are kept. Also *roller-closet*.

roller-composition (rō'lėr-kom-pọ̄-zish"ọn), *n.* In *printing*, the composition of which inking-rollers are made. See *composition*, 5.

roller-die (rō'lėr-dī), *n.* A cylindrical die for transferring steel-plate engravings, as for printing bank-notes, and also for the transfer of patterns to calico-printing rolls. The design is engraved on a plate of soft steel, which is afterward hardened, and subjected to strong pressure upon the soft steel die, to which the incised lines of the plate are thus transferred in relief. The die is then hardened, and is used in turn to transfer the design to a plate, a roller, or another die.

roller-flag (rō'lėr-flag), *n.* A signal displayed, as at St. Helena and the Island of Ascension, to warn boats against attempting to land during the prevalence of the rollers.

roller-forks (rō'lėr-fôrks), *n. pl.* In a printing-press, slotted or forked supports, of the nature of uncapped journal-boxes, in which the journals of the composition rollers are fitted, and in which they turn.

roller-gin (rō'lėr-jin), *n.* A machine for separating cotton-seeds from cotton-fiber, in the best form of which the separation is effected by leather rollers acting in conjunction with a knife or knives. The rollers are set at a distance from each other too narrow for the passage of the seeds, while the fiber is forced in and carried through between the rollers. The knife is blunt-edged, and sometimes has a longitudinal motion, its action assisting the separation of the seeds, which drop down behind the rollers while the detached fiber passes through. Such gins are slower in action than saw-gins, but they injure the fiber less. Compare *gin*1, 6.

roller-grip (rō'lėr-grip), *n.* A device for clutching a traveling-rope, used as a means of traction for railroad-cars. It consists of a set of binding-rollers or -wheels controlled by special mechanism so as to grasp or let loose the traveling-rope or -cable at will.

roller-lift (rō'lėr-lift), *n.* In some printing-machines, a small cam which raises the ink-distributing roller from the surface of the inking-plate.

roller-mill (rō'lėr-mil), *n.* 1. Any form of mill for the coarse grinding of grain for feed. Specifically—2. A mill in which wheat is made into flour by a cracking process, passing between sets of rollers arranged consecutively at fixed distances apart.—3. A machine for bruising flaxseed before grinding under edge-stones and pressing. *E. H. Knight.*

roller-mold (rō'lėr-mōld), *n.* In *printing*, a metallic mold into which, in the casting of composition rollers, the melted composition is poured.

roller-skate (rō'lėr-skāt), *n.* A skate mounted on small wheels or rollers, instead of the usual iron or steel runner, and used for skating upon asphalt or some other smooth surface. Also called *parlor-skate.*

roller-stock (rō'lėr-stok), *n.* The cylindrical rod of iron, sometimes covered with wood, which serves as the axis of a printer's roller, and gives it its needed stiffness.

roller-stop (rō'lėr-stop), *n.* An apparatus for arresting or limiting the motion of the ductor inking-roller on a printing-machine.

roller-towel (rō'lėr-tou'el), *n.* An endless towel arranged to roll over a cylinder of wood bracketed to the wall, so that all parts of it may be conveniently used. Also called *jack-towel* and *roller.*

Rolle's plane. In *anat.*, the plane passing through the alveolar and the two auricular points.

rolley (rō'li), *n.* [Prob. < *roll* + dim. *-ey.*] A kind of truck drawn by a horse, used in coal-mines for carrying tubs or corfs along underground ways. [North. Eng.]

rolley-polley, *n.* See *roly-poly.*

rolleyway (rō'li-wā), *n.* Any underground road along which rolleys are conveyed. [Prov. Eng.]

rollichie (rol'i-chi), *n.* [Also *rullichie*; < D. *rolletje*, "a truckle" (Sewel), sheave of a pulley, lit. 'little roll,' dim. of MD. *rolle*, D. *rol*, a roll: see *roll, n.*] Chopped meat stuffed into small bags of tripe, which are then cut into slices and fried: an old and favorite dish among the Dutch in New York. *Bartlett.*

> They [the burghers of New Amsterdam] ate their supaen and *rolliches* of an evening, smoked their pipes in the chimney-nook, and upon the Lord's Day waddled their wonted way to the Gereformeerde Kerche.
> *E. L. Bynner*, Begum's Daughter, i.

rollick (rol'ik), *v. i.* [Perhaps < *roll* + dim. *-ick*, equiv. to *-ock.*] To move in a careless, swaggering manner, with a frolicsome air; swagger; be jovial in behavior.

> He described his friends as *rollicking* blades, evidently mistaking himself for one of their set.
> T. Hook, Jack Brag. (*Latham.*)

> There was something desperately amusing to him in the thought that he had not even money enough to pay the cabman, or provide for a repast. He *rollicked* in his present poverty.
> *G. Meredith*, Rhoda Fleming, xxix.

rolling (rō'ling), *n.* [< ME. *rollynge*; verbal n. of *roll, v.*] 1. A reciprocating rotary motion about a fore-and-aft axis, more or less irregular, as of a ship at sea.—2. (*a*) Ornamenting, by means of a bookbinders' roll, the edges or inner covers of a full-bound book. (*b*) Smoothing or polishing paper by means of calendering rollers.—3. A method of taking trout. When the streams are at their lowest stage in summer, a dam of logs, stones, and brush is roughly built at the lower end of some pool in which the fish have congregated. This rolling-dam being constructed, the stream for some distance above the pool is beaten with poles, and the fish are driven down to the deepest water, out of which they are swept with a net. [New Brunswick.]

4. Same as *roll*, 5.—5. A twist or partial knot by which the thread is secured to the bobbin in lace-making. *Dict. of Needlework.*—**Friction of rolling.** See *friction.*—**Instantaneous center of rolling.** See *center*1.

rolling (rō'ling), *p. a.* 1. Moving on wheels, or as if on wheels.

> He next essays to walk, but, downward pressed,
> On four feet imitates his brother beast:
> By slow degrees he gathers from the ground
> His legs, and to the *rolling* chair is bound.
> *Dryden*, tr. of Ovid's Metamorph., xv. 340.

2. Making a continuous noise resembling the roll of a drum: as, a *rolling* fire of musketry.—3. Wavy; undulating; rising and falling in gentle slopes.

> The country was what was termed *rolling*, from some fancied resemblance to the surface of the ocean when it is just undulating with a long "ground-swell."
> *Cooper*, Oak Openings, i.

4. Turned over or down with the effect of a roll, or that may be so turned down.

> Solemn old Thoresby records how he and his cousin "bought each a pair of black silk *rolling* stockings in Westminster Hall."
> Quoted in *Ashton's* Social Life in Reign of Queen Anne, [I. 153.

> A black and red velvet tartan [waistcoat] with white stripes and a *rolling* collar. *Thackeray*, Vanity Fair, lix.

Rolling bridge, a drawbridge or a ferry bridge which rolls upon wheels; or a swing bridge supported upon balls moving in a circular path.—**Rolling-cam press.** See *press*1.—**Rolling circle** of a paddle-wheel, the circle described by a point in the paddle-wheel which moves with the speed with which the vessel passes through the water. If the vessel were traveling upon land upon wheels of the size of this circle and with the same speed of engine, her velocity would remain unaffected.—**Rolling colter.** See *colter.*—**Rolling curve**, a roulette.—**Rolling fire.** See *fire*, 13.—**Rolling friction.** See *friction.*—**Rolling globe**, a large ball on which acrobats stand and ascend inclined planes.—**Rolling hitch**, a hitch made with the end of one rope round another rope under tension, or round a spar, in such a way that when drawn on in the direction of the length of the rope or spar the hitch will jam.—**Rolling pendulum**, a pendulum carrying cylindrical bearings which roll upon a plane or other surface. A special case of a rolling pendulum is a cylinder loaded at one side; another and extreme case is a pendulum turning on knife-edges.—**Rolling-pressure press.** See *press*1.—**Rolling purchase**, an arrangement of pulleys with one or more movable blocks: a phrase having application especially to the mechanical appliance used for bending the great arbalist of the fourteenth and fifteenth centuries. It was an apparatus which could be applied to the stock when required, and then detached and carried in the belt. See cut under *moulinet.*—**Rolling reef**, a method of shortening sail by rolling the canvas about a roller underneath the yard, thereby doing away with the use of reef-points.—**Rolling resistance**, that resistance to the rolling of a body over a surface which is caused by cohesion.—**Rolling topsail, rolling topgallantsail**, sails reduced in area by being rolled up on a roller underneath the yard.

rolling-barrel (rō'ling-bar'el), *n.* In *gunpowder-manuf.* See *barrel.*

rolling-chock (rō'ling-chok), *n.* *Naut.*, a piece of wood fastened to the middle of an upper yard, with a piece cut out of its center so that it may half encircle the mast, to which it is secured by an iron or rope parrel inclosing the other half of the mast. Its purpose is to steady the yard.

rolling-cleat (rō'ling-klēt), *n.* Same as *rolling-chock.*

rolling-dam (rō'ling-dam), *n.* The rough dam used in rolling for trout. See *rolling*, 3.

rolling-frame (rō'ling-frām), *n.* In *dyeing*, an arrangement of rollers for drawing cloth through the dye-beck. Also called *galloper.* *E. H. Knight.*

rolling-machine (rō'ling-ma-shēn'), *n.* Any machine which performs its functions essentially by means of rollers. Specifically—(*a*) A machine for making brass fender-moldings and brasswork for grates. (*b*) A machine for smoothing out a cotton-bat and working it into fiber like flax ready for carding. (*c*) A rolling-mill.

rolling-mill (rō'ling-mil), *n.* 1. A metal-working establishment using, in connection with heating-furnaces, systems of steel rollers for forming metal into sheets, bars, rods, or wires. Such rolling-mills sometimes bear special names, as a rail-mill, wire-rolling mill, etc. The essential feature of a rolling-mill is a set or train of steel rollers placed either in pairs one over the other, as in a two-high train, or in a group of three, as in a three-high train. The heated metal direct from the furnaces is presented to these rollers and is drawn through between the trains. It is at once caught on the other side and repassed between the rollers, each passage between them being called a *pass.* In a two-high train the rollers are stopped and reversed at each pass. In a three-high train the rollers turn constantly in one direction, the return pass being between a different pair of rollers from the pair first passed through, the middle roller, however, always being one of either pair. The distance between the rollers is regulated by screws at the ends. The section given to the metal in passing through the rollers is determined by the shape of the rollers, whether flat or grooved, it being possible to produce in this way bars having a great variety of sections, adapted for independent or structural uses. The rolling-mill serves also to some extent to clear the metal passed through it from impurities. Small rolling-mills with tapering rollers are used to roll short flat metal bars into rings, the passage between the rollers expanding the outside more than the inside edge, and thus causing the strip to assume a curved form. See cut under *roll*, 2 (*a*).

2. One of the trains of rolls with its framework and driving-mechanism used in rolling metal bars, plates, or sheets in a rolling-mill. They are also called *rolls*, and *two-high* and *three-high rolls* according to the number of superimposed rolls in the machine.

3. A rolling-machine for making sheet-glass by rolling the hot metal.—4. A form of leather-rolling machine.

rolling-pin (rō'ling-pin), *n.* A cylindrical piece of wood, marble, or copper, having a projecting handle at each end, with which dough, paste, confectioners' sugar, etc., are molded and reduced to a proper thickness.

rolling-plant (rō'ling-plant), *n.* Same as *rolling-stock.*

rolling-press (rō'ling-pres), *n.* 1. A copper-plate-printers' press in which impression is made by passing the plate under a rolling cylinder.—2. A calendering-machine, which consists of two or more closely geared cylinders of smooth surface, used for smoothing and polishing the surface of paper.—3. A machine with two or more steam-heated iron rollers, which removes indentations from printed sheets.

rolling-rope (rō'ling-rōp), *n.* Same as *rolling-tackle.*

rolling-stock (rō'ling-stok), *n.* In *railways*, the cars, locomotive engines, etc. Also called *rolling-plant.*

rolling-tackle (rō'ling-tak'l), *n.* A tackle used to steady a yard when the ship rolls heavily. It is hooked to the weather-quarter of the yard and to a strap around the mast, and hauled taut. Also called *rolling-rope.*

Rollinia (ro-lin'i-ä), *n.* [NL. (A. St. Hilaire, 1825), named after Charles *Rollin* (1661–1741), a French historian, who aided the botanist Tournefort in his work the "Institutiones."] A genus of trees and shrubs of the order *Anonaceæ*, the custard-apple family, and of the tribe *Xylopieæ.* It is characterized by its globose corolla with six lobes in two series, the three outer concave at the base and produced into a thick, laterally flattened dorsal wing, the three inner small, sometimes minute or obsolete. It is readily distinguished from the next related genus, *Anona*, the custard-apple, by its appendaged petals. There are about 20 species, all natives of warmer parts of America. They bear either thin or rigid leaves, and flowers in small clusters which are either terminal or opposite the leaves. The fruit is composed of many sessile berries borne on a broad convex receptacle, either separate or more often united into one roundish and many-celled fruit. *R. multiflora* and *R. longifolia* furnish a light tough wood, a kind of lancewood. *R. Sieberi* is called *sugar-apple* in the West Indies.

roll-joint (rōl'joint), *n.* 1. A method of joining metal sheets by rolling one edge over the other and pressing the joining flat.—2. A joint made by this method.

roll-lathe (rōl'lāᴛʜ), *n.* In *mach.*, a lathe for turning off massive rolls for rolling-mills, calendering-machines, etc. The centers are relieved from strain in such lathes by rests which support the journals of the rolls during the process.

roll-molding (rōl'mōl'ding), *n.* See *roll.*

rollock (rol'ok), *n.* Same as *rowlock.*

roll-top (rōl'top), *a.* Having a rolling top.—**Roll-top desk.** Same as *cylinder-desk.*

roll-train (rōl'trān), *n.* A rolling-mill train. See *rolling-mill* and *train.*

Rollulidæ (ro-lū'li-dē), *n. pl.* [NL., < *Rollulus* + *-idæ.*] The *Rollulinæ* raised to family rank.

Rollulinæ (rol-ū-lī'nē), *n. pl.* [NL., < *Rollulus* + *-inæ.*] A subfamily of *Perdicidæ* or *Tetraonidæ*, represented by the genus *Rollulus.* *Bonaparte*, 1850. Also called *Cryptonychinæ.*

rolluline (rol'ū-lin), *a.* Of or pertaining to the *Rollulinæ.*

Rollulus (rol'ū-lus), *n.* [NL. (Bonnaterre, 1790), < *roulroul*, native name.] A genus of gallinaceous birds, type of the subfamily *Rollulinæ*, having the hind claw rudimentary; the roulrouls or wood-quail. The species inhabit Java, Sumatra, Borneo, Malacca, and Tenasserim. The red-crested wood-quail is *R. cristatus* or *roulroul*, of a rich green color, with a long red crest; it lives in the woods in small flocks from the sea-level to a height of 4,000 feet. The female is lighter-colored, and lacks the red crest. Another roulroul is *R. niger*, sometimes generically separated as *Melanoperdix* (Jerdon, 1864). The genus is also called *Cryptonyx* and *Liponyx.* See cut on following page.

Roulroul (*Rollulus cristatus*).

roll-up (rōl'up), *n.* **1.** Same as *roly-poly*, 2.

> I know what the pudden 's to be—apricot *roll-up*—O my buttons! *George Eliot*, Mill on the Floss, i. 6.

2. A clogging of machinery in cotton-carding or the like. *F. Wilson*, Cotton Carder's Companion, p. 90.

rollway (rōl'wā), *n.* **1.** A natural incline (as the bank of a stream), or an inclined structure, down which heavy bodies, especially logs, are propelled by their own weight; a shoot.

> This appliance for swinging logs from stump to *rollway*, car, or boat is to be the chief means for placing this North Carolina cypress where it will do the most good. *Sci. Amer.*, N. S., LVIII. 152.

2. In *lumbering*, a mass of logs piled up for rolling down to or into a stream, or placed upon the ice to await spring freshets.

> The logs are drawn to the nearest river, where they are piled in great *roll-ways*, either on the ice or on a high bank, there to remain until the spring floods launch them. *Scribner's Mag.*, IV. 655.

roloway (rol'ǫ-wā), *n.* [Origin obscure.] The Diana monkey, *Cercopithecus diana.* See cut under *Diana.*

roly-poly (rō'li-pō"li), *n.* and *a.* [Also spelled *rowly-powly*, *rolley-polley*, *rolly-poly*, etc.; a riming compound, with dim. effect, appar. < *roll* + *bowl*[2] (the game having formerly been called *half-bowl*).] **I.** *n.* **1†.** An old game, somewhat resembling bowls, played with pins and a half-sphere of wood on a floor or smooth plot of ground.—**2.** A sheet of paste spread with jam and rolled up, to form a pudding.

> As for the *roly-poly*, it was too good. *Thackeray*, Book of Snobs, i.

3. A low, vulgar person. *Halliwell.* [Prov. Eng.]

> I'll have thee in league first with these two *rollypoolies*. *Dekker*, Satiromastix.

4. A short, stout person. [Colloq.]

II. *a.* Of or pertaining to a roly-poly; shaped like a roly-poly; round; pudgy.

> You said I make the best *roly-poly* puddings in the world. *Thackeray*, Great Hoggarty Diamond, xii.

> It [plum-duff] is sometimes made in the rounded form of the plum-pudding; but more frequently in the *roly-poly* style. *Mayhew*, London Labour and London Poor, I. 207.

> Cottages, in the doors of which a few *rolypoly*, open-eyed children stood. *Mrs. Craik*, Agatha's Husband, xii.

Rom (rom), *n.* [Gipsy *rom*, a man, husband; prob. < Hind. *dom*, also *domrā* (with initial cerebral *d*, which confuses with r), a man of a low caste who, in eastern India, make ropes, mats, baskets, fans, etc., and are also employed in removing dead bodies and carcasses, and are generally thieves, but who, in western India, are musicians or singers; < Skt. *domba* (with cerebral *d*), a man of a low caste who make their living by singing and dancing. Cf. *Romany*, *rum*[2].] A Gipsy; a Romany.

> She [the Gipsy queen] had known the chiefs of her people in the days . . . when the *Rom* was a leader in the prize-ring, or noted as a highwayman. C. G. Leland, The Century, XXV. 900.

Rom. An abbreviation (*a*) [*cap.* or *l. c.*] of *Roman*; (*b*) of *Romance* (languages).

Romæan (rǫ-mē'an), *n.* [< Gr. Ῥωμαῖος, Roman; after Constantinople became the capital of the empire also applied to the Greeks.] An inhabitant of one of the countries included in the eastern Roman (Byzantine) empire; a subject of the Greek emperor. *Robertson*, Hist. Christ. Church, viii. 95.

romage†, *v.* and *n.* An obsolete form of *roomage*, *rummage*.

Romaic (rǫ-mā'ik), *a.* and *n.* [= F. *romaïque* = Sp. Pg. It. *romaico*, < ML. *Romaicus*, < Gr. Ῥωμαϊκός, belonging to Rome, Roman, Latin (later applied to the Greeks when the Roman capital was transferred to Constantinople) (NGr. Ῥωμαϊκός, Roman, Latin, Ῥωμαΐικος, Romaic, modern Greek), < Gr. Ῥώμη, L. *Roma*, Rome: see *Roman*.] **I.** *a.* Relating to the vernacular language of modern Greece, or to those who use it.

II. *n.* The vernacular language of modern Greece, the popular modern form of ancient Greek, written in the ancient character. The literary language of modern Greece is Romaic more or less conformed to classical Greek; it is styled *Hellenic*.

romaika (rǫ-mā'i-kạ̈), *n.* [NGr. ῥωμαϊκή, fem. of Ῥωμαϊκός, Roman: see *Romaic*.] A modern Greek dance, characterized by serpentine figures and a throwing of handkerchiefs among the dancers.

romal[1] (rǫ-mâl'), *n.* See *rumal*.

romal[2] (rǫ-mal'), *n.* [Prop. **rumal*, < Sp. *ramal*, a halter, rope's end, pendant, branch, < L. *ramale*, a branch, < *ramus*, branch: see *ramus*, *rammel*.] A round braided thong of leather, rawhide, or horsehair looped to the ends of the reins, and serving as a horseman's whip. [Western U. S.]

> He rode ahead, on his blue-roan Indian pony, twirling his *romal*, a long leathern strap attached to the saddle, the end divided like a double whip-lash. *Mary Hallock Foote*, St. Nicholas, XIV. 33.

Romalea (rǫ-mā'lẹ-ạ̈), *n.* [NL. (Serville, 1831), prop. *Rhomalea*, < Gr. ῥωμαλέος, strong of body, < ῥώμη, bodily strength.] A notable genus of large-bodied short-winged locusts, or short-horned grasshoppers. *R. microptera* is the lubber-grasshopper of the southern United States, sharing the English name with a similar but quite distinct species, *Brachystola magna* of the western States.

Lubber-grasshopper (*Romalea microptera*).

Roman (rō'man), *a.* and *n.* [Early mod. E. also *Romayne*; < ME. *Romayne*, < OF. *romain*, F. *romain* = Sp. Pg. It. *romano*, < L. *Romanus*, Roman, < *Roma*, Rome. Cf. *Romish*.] **I.** *a.* **1.** Of or pertaining to ancient or modern Rome, or the people, institutions, or characteristics of Rome.

> To every *Roman* citizen he gives,
> To every several man, seventy-five drachmas.
> *Shak.*, J. C., iii. 2. 246.

> Judea now, and all the Promised Land,
> Reduced a province under *Roman* yoke,
> Obeys Tiberius. *Milton*, P. R., iii. 158.

Hence—**2.** Having some attribute deemed especially characteristic of the ancient Romans; noble; distinguished; brave; hardy; patriotic; stern.

> What 's brave, what 's noble,
> Let 's do it after the high *Roman* fashion,
> And make death proud to take us.
> *Shak.*, A. and C., iv. 15. 87.

> There is something fine, something *Roman* in the best sense, in the calm way in which the British Government of India looks upon itself as virtually eternal. *Fortnightly Rev.*, N. S., XLIII. 7.

3. Pertaining to Rome ecclesiastically; of or pertaining to the Church of Rome; papal.

> The chief grounds upon which we separate from the *Roman* communion. *Burnet.*

4. [*l. c.* or *cap.*] Noting a form of letter or type of which the text of this book is an example. It is the form preferred for books and newspapers by the Latin races and by English-speaking peoples. Three series are used conjointly in printing: (1) capitals, which are copies of Old Latin lapidary letters; (2) small capitals, a medieval Italian fashion, first made in type by Aldus Manutius in 1501; and (3) minuscule or lower-case letters, first made in type by Sweinheim and Pannartz at Subiaco in 1465, and afterward, of better form, by Jenson at Venice in 1471.—**Holy Roman Empire.** See *empire*.—**Roman alum.** See *alum*.—**Roman architecture**, the architecture of the ancient Romans, characterized by admirable development and application of the round arch and vault, and of stone and particularly brick masonry of all varieties, especially in small materials and with proper use of excellent cements and mortar, and by adoption of the Greek orders in general as mere exterior ornaments in lavishness of redundant and artificial decoration, and without understanding of their delicately studied proportions and logical arrangement. The true Roman architecture, considered apart from its Hellenistic decoration, was not artistic, though the boldness and great span of its arches and vaults very frequently produce a grand and majestic effect; it was, however, a thoroughly practical architecture, flexible to all requirements, and admitting of the quick and solid construction, by great numbers of soldiers or other unskilled workmen, of even the greatest structures, as aqueducts, bridges, amphitheaters, basilicas, thermæ, and fortresses, under the direction of a small number of trained engineers. From the Roman arched and vaulted construction medieval architecture was developed, and back to it can be traced most that is best in modern masonry. The interior decoration of Roman architecture under the empire was evolved from Greek models, without the Greek moderation and refinement; mosaic and molded stucco were profusely used, and wall-painting on a surface of mortar was universal. The artisans of this decoration were in large measure of Greek birth. See cuts under *amphitheater*, *Colosseum*, *octastyle*, *Pantheon*.—**Roman art**, the art of ancient Rome. Under the republic there was practically no Roman art. During the last two centuries of the republic the spoils of Greece, the masterpieces of the Greek sculptor and painter, accumulated in Rome. Greek art became fashionable, and Greek artists began to flock to Rome. The Greek taste became modified to accord with the love of the Romans for lavish richness and display. Under the empire there was developed from this Greek source a sculpture of truly Roman style, characteristic especially in its portrait-statues, in which the person represented is often idealized as a god, and which are often highly naturalistic and skilful in treatment, and many of them excellent art as portraiture. Another chief development of Roman sculpture is the historical relief, illustrating all phases of Roman imperial life and triumphs. Though these reliefs are seldom artistic, the episodes which they present are precise in detail, and strikingly true to life. *Roman painting* in its origin, and with Fabius Pictor and Pacuvius, was Etruscan; in its development under the empire, when it was profuse in quantity, covering in general the interior walls of all buildings of any pretension, it was Greek, of the degenerated but clever and light style of Alexandria. At its best, as seen in many of the wall-paintings of Pompeii and of Rome, it is highly decorative; and it is especially valuable as preserving the chief material that survives for the study of the great Greek painters of the fifth and fourth centuries B. C. See *Pasitelean*.—**Roman balance.** See *steelyard*.—**Roman camomile**, a cultivated form of the common camomile.—**Roman candle**, a kind of firework, consisting of a tube, which discharges a succession of white or colored stars or balls.—**Roman Catholic**, of or pertaining to the Church of Rome; hence, as a noun, a member of the Roman Catholic Church. Abbreviated *R. C.*—**Roman Catholic Church**, the popular designation of the church of which the Pope or Bishop of Rome is the head, and which holds him, as the successor of St. Peter and heir of his spiritual authority,

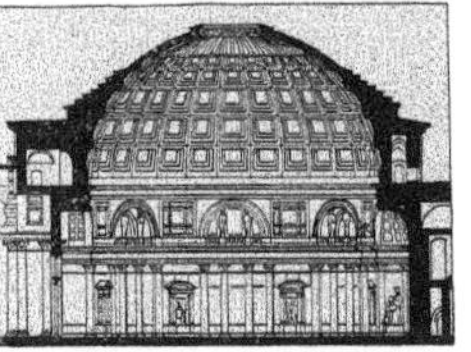

Roman Architecture.—Section of the Pantheon, illustrating the use of vaulting, arches, and columns.

Roman Art.—Bust of the Empress Faustina, wife of Antoninus Pius.

privileges, and gifts, as the supreme ruler, pastor, and teacher of the whole Catholic Church. Ecclesiastically, it is a hierarchy consisting of priests, bishops, and archbishops, presided over by the Pope, who is the supreme head of the church, and who is elected for life by the College of Cardinals from their own number. Every priest receives his consecration from a bishop or archbishop, and every bishop and archbishop holds his appointment from the Pope, by whose permission he must be consecrated. Celibacy is strictly enforced on the clergy. The doctrines of the church are contained in the decrees of the Council of Trent, and in a briefer form in the creed of Pius IV. (1564). This creed contains twelve articles, including an acceptance of the traditions and constitutions of the church and of the Scriptures as interpreted by the church; seven sacraments, necessary for the salvation of mankind, though not all for every individual—namely, baptism, confirmation, eucharist, penance, extreme unction, orders, and matrimony; the doctrines concerning original sin and justification defined by the decrees of the Council of Trent; the mass as a true propitiatory sacrifice; the real presence and transubstantiation; purgatory; the invocation of the saints; the veneration of images; indulgences; and the supremacy of the Pope. The last article, as since defined by the Vatican Council, involves the infallibility of the Pope. The worship of the Roman Catholic Church is an elaborate ritual, the central feature of it being the sacrifice of the mass, in which the real body and blood of Christ are believed to be corporeally present, each repetition of the mass being regarded as a real sacrifice for sin and as exercising a real efficacy in securing the salvation of those who in faith assist at and partake of it. These doctrines and usages are, with some differences, largely also those of the Greek and some other churches. The most distinctive doctrines of the Roman Catholic Church are the papal supremacy and infallibility, the immaculate conception, and the purgatorial fire. Communion is given in one kind only.—**Roman Catholicism**, the principles, doctrines, rules, etc., of the Roman Catholic Church collectively.—**Roman Catholic Relief Acts**, a series of English statutes of 1829, 1833, 1834, 1843, 1844, and 1846, removing the political disabilities of Roman Catholics.—**Roman cement.** See *cement*.—**Roman collar** (*eccles.*), a straight collar of lawn or linen, bound and stitched. It is worn by priests and clerics over a black collar, by bishops and prelates over a purple, and by cardinals over a scarlet one. It is modern and secular in its origin.—**Roman empire**, the ancient empire of Rome, the beginning of which is generally placed at 31 B. C. Its division into Eastern and Western empires began in the fourth century. See *Eastern Empire*, *Holy Roman Empire*, and *Western Empire*, under *empire*.—**Roman fever.** See *fever*1.—**Roman hyacinth.** See *Hyacinthus*.—**Roman indiction.** See *indiction*, 3.—**Roman laurel**, the true laurel, *Laurus nobilis*.—**Roman law**, the civil law; the system of jurisprudence finally elaborated in the ancient Roman empire. The principles of the Roman law have exerted an extraordinary influence over most systems of jurisprudence in continental Europe, and are incorporated in a remarkable degree with the law of Scotland. See *civil law*, under *civil*.—**Roman lock, mosaic, nettle, nose, ocher.** See the nouns.—**Roman order**, in *arch.*, same as *composite order*. See *composite*, 3.—**Roman pearl.** See *pearl*.—**Roman pitch.** See *pitch of a roof*, under *pitch*1.—**Roman pottery.** See *pottery*.—**Roman pronunciation.** See *pronunciation*.—**Roman punch**, a water-ice, flavored usually with lemon, and mixed with rum or other spirit.—**Roman red ware.** Same as *Samian ware* (which see, under *Samian*).—**Roman school**, in *art*, the style of painting which prevailed at Rome in the beginning of the sixteenth century, and was developed from the art of Raphael (1483–1520), who in his later manner was the founder of the school. It was in no way a native school, being based on the art of Florence, and counting foreigners, for the most part, among its painters. Among the most prominent names of this school are Giulio Romano, Caravaggio, and the later Sassoferrato and Maratta.—**Roman string**, a peculiarly fine variety of catgut string for violins and similar instruments, made in Italy.—**Roman surface**, a surface invented by the geometer Steiner in Rome. See *Steiner's surface*, under *surface*.—**Roman vitriol, white**, etc. See the nouns.—**Roman wormwood**, one of the ragweeds, *Ambrosia artemisiæfolia*. See *ragweed*.=**Syn. 1.** *Roman, Latin*. *Roman* naturally applies to that which is especially associated or connected with the city, Rome; *Latin* to that which similarly belongs to the district, Latium. Hence, we speak of *Roman* power, fortitude, administration; the *Roman* church: the *Latin* language. Nearly all the use of *Latin* has grown out of its application to the language: as, *Latin* grammar; a *Latin* idiom; the *Latin* Church. The words are not interchangeable.

II. *n.* **1.** A native or an inhabitant of Rome, the capital of Italy, and chief city of the ancient Roman empire.

Thei assemble and somowne on alle partes, and now be meved the *romaynes* with an hugo peple, and theire lorde and gouernoure is Pounce, Antony, tweyne of the counsellours of Rome. *Merlin* (E. E. T. S.), ii. 303.

The last of all the *Romans*, fare thee well!
It is impossible that ever Rome
Should breed thy fellow. *Shak.*, *J. C.*, v. 3. 99.

2. A person enjoying the freedom or citizenship of ancient Rome. [An old use.]

Then the chief captain came, and said unto him, Tell me, art thou a *Roman*? He said, Yea. And the chief captain answered, With a great sum obtained I this freedom. And Paul said, But I was free born. Acts xxii. 28.

3. A member or an adherent of the Church of Rome; a Romanist. [Now mostly colloq.] —**4.** [*l. c.*] A roman letter or type, in distinction from an *italic*.—**Epistle to the Romans**, an epistle written by the apostle Paul to a Christian community at Rome consisting partly of Jews and partly of Gentile converts. It was composed before the apostle had visited Rome, and is generally supposed to have been written from Corinth about A. D. 58. Its main subject is the doctrine of justification by faith, with special reference to the relative position of the *Jews* and Gentiles to the law of God (natural and revealed), the rejection of the *Jews*, and the admission of the Gentiles. Abbreviated *Rom.*

romance (rọ̄-mans′), *n.* and *a.* [L *n.* Early mod. E. also *romaunce*; < ME. *romance*, *romaunce*, *romans* (also *romant*, *romaunt*, q. v.), = D. G. Dan. Sw. *roman*, < OF. *romans*, *romanz*, *roumans*, also *roman*, *romant*, *roumant*, a story, history, romance, also the Romance language, = Pr. *romans*, a romance, the Romance or (vulgar) Roman language, = Sp. *romance*, a romance, tale, ballad, the common Spanish language, = Pg. *romance*, the vulgar tongue, = It. *romanzo*, a romance, fable, = Romansh *romansch* (ML. reflex *Romancium*, the Romance language; also *romagium*, a romance); < L. *Romanicus*, Roman (through the adverb, ML. *Romanice*, in Roman or Latin fashion; *Romanice loqui*, F. *parler romans*, speak in Romance, or the vulgar Latin tongue), < *Romanus*, Roman: see *Romanic*, *Roman*. Cf. *romant*. II. *a.* (and I., *n.*, 7). In form after the noun. < ML. *Romanicus*, Romanic, Romance: see above. Cf. *Romansh*.] **I.** *n.* **1.** Originally, a tale in verse, written in one of the Romance dialects, as early French or Provençal; hence, any popular epic belonging to the literature of modern Europe, or any fictitious story of heroic, marvelous, or supernatural incidents derived from history or legend, and told in prose or verse and at considerable length: as, the *romance* of Charlemagne; the Arthurian *romances*.

He honoured that hit hade, euer-more after,
As hit is breued in the best boke of *romaunce*.
Sir Gawayne and the Green Knight (E. E. T. S.), l. 2521.

Upon my bedde I sat upright,
And bad oon reche me a book,
A *romaunce*, and hit me took
To rede and dryve the night away;
For me thoghte it better play
Than playe either at chesse or tables.
And in this boke were written fables
That clerkes hadde, in olde tyme,
And other poets, put in ryme.
Chaucer, Death of Blanche, l. 48.

And yf any man demaunde hou certain,
What me shall call thys *romans* souerain,
Hit name the *Romans* as of Partenay,
And so som it call certes at this day.
Rom. of Partenay (E. E. T. S.), l. 6417.

Upon these three columns—chivalry, gallantry, and religion—repose the fictions of the middle ages, especially those usually designated as *romances*. These, such as we now know them, and such as display the characteristics above mentioned, were originally metrical, and chiefly written by natives of the north of France.
Hallam, Introd. to Lit. of Europe, I. ii. § 59.

History commenced among the modern nations of Europe, as it had commenced among the Greeks, in *romance*.
Macaulay, History.

2. In Spain and other Romanic countries—either (*a*) a short epic narrative poem (historic ballad), or, later, (*b*) a short lyric poem.

The *romance* . . . is a composition in long verses of fourteen syllables ending with one rhyme, or assonance, which have been generally, but wrongly, divided into two short lines, the first of which, naturally, is rhymeless.
Encyc. Brit., XXII. 354.

3. A tale or novel dealing not so much with real or familiar life as with extraordinary and often extravagant adventures, as Cervantes's "Don Quixote," with rapid and violent changes of scene and fortune, as Dumas's "Count of Monte Cristo," with mysterious and supernatural events, as R. L. Stevenson's "Strange Case of Dr. Jekyll and Mr. Hyde," or with morbid idiosyncrasies of temperament, as Godwin's "Caleb Williams," or picturing imaginary conditions of society influenced by imaginary characters, as Fouqué's "Undine." Special forms of the romance, suggested by the subject and the manner of treatment, are the historical, the pastoral, the philosophical, the psychological, the allegorical, etc. See *novel*, *n.*, 4.

The narrative manner of Defoe has a naturalness about it beyond that of any other novel or *romance* writer. His fictions have all the air of true stories.
Lamb, Estimate of Defoe.

Others were much scandalized. It ["The Pilgrim's Progress"] was a vain story, a mere *romance*, about giants, and lions, and goblins, and warriors. *Macaulay*, John Bunyan.

Sir Philip Sidney's The Countess of Pembroke's Arcadia, which appeared in 1590, after the author's death, is the most brilliant prose fiction in English of the century, and a genuine pastoral and heroic *romance*.
Encyc. Brit., XX. 600.

4. An invention; fiction; falsehood: used euphemistically.

This knight was indeeds a valiant gentleman, but not a little given to *romance* when he spake of himselfe.
Evelyn, Diary, Sept. 6, 1651.

A Staple of *Romance* and Lies,
False Tears and real Perjuries.
Prior, An English Padlock.

5. A blending of the heroic, the marvelous, the mysterious, and the imaginative in actions, manners, ideas, language, or literature; tendency of mind to dwell upon or give expression to the heroic, the marvelous, the mysterious, or the imaginative.

The splendid phantoms of chivalrous *romance*, the trophied lists, the embroidered housings, the quaint devices, the haunted forests, the enchanted gardens, the achievements of enamoured knights, and the smiles of rescued princesses. *Macaulay*, Milton.

The hardships of the journey and of the first encampment are certainly related by their contemporary with some air of *romance*, yet they can hardly be exaggerated.
Emerson, Hist. Discourse at Concord.

The age of *Romance* has not ceased; it never ceases; it does not, if we think of it, so much as very sensibly decline. *Carlyle*, Diamond Necklace, i.

6. In *music*: (*a*) A setting of a romantic story or tale; a ballad. (*b*) Any short, simple melody of tender character, whether vocal or instrumental; a song, or song without words. Also *romanza*.—**7.** [*cap.*] A Romance language, or the Romance languages. See II.

Did not the Norman Conquest . . . bring with it a settlement of strangers, of *Romance*-speaking strangers, enough to destroy all pretence on the part of the English nation to pure Teutonic descent?
E. A. Freeman, Amer. Lects., p. 155.

=**Syn. 3.** *Tale*, etc. See *novel*.

II. *a.* [*cap.*] Pertaining to or denoting the languages which arose, in the south and west of Europe, out of the Roman or Latin language as spoken in the provinces at one time subject to Rome. The principal Romance languages are the Italian, French, Provençal, Spanish, Portuguese, Wallachian, and Rhæto-Romanic. Also *Romanic*. Abbreviated *Rom.*

romance (rọ̄-mans′), *v.*; pret. and pp. *romanced*, ppr. *romancing*. [= OF. *romancier*, *roumancer* = Pr. *romansar* = Sp. Pg. *romancear*, translate into the vulgar tongue, = It. *romanzeggiare*, write romances; from the noun: see *romance*, *n.*] **I.** *intrans.* **1.** To invent and relate fictitious stories; deal in extravagant, fanciful, or false recitals; lie.

I hear others *romancing* about Things they never heard nor saw; nay, and that they do with that Assurance that, when they are telling the most ridiculous and impossible Things in Nature, they persuade themselves they are speaking Truth all the While.
N. Bailey, tr. of Colloquies of Erasmus, I. 53.

2. To be romantic; behave romantically or with fanciful or extravagant enthusiasm; build castles in the air.

That I am a "*romancing* chit of a girl" is a mere conjecture on your part; I never *romanced* to you.
Charlotte Brontë, Shirley, xxiii.

II. *trans.* To treat, present, or discuss in a romantic manner. [Recent, and a Gallicism.]

At the end Mr. B. does not *romance* us. His last words, where he treats of our social and economic future, embody the thoughts of every enlightened American.
Harper's Mag., LXXVIII. 663.

romancer (rọ̄-man′sėr), *n.* [< F. *romancier*, a romancer, novelist, = Sp. *romancero*, one who sings or recites romances or ballads (cf. *romancero* = Pg. *romanceiro*, a collection of romantic ballads), = It. *romanziere*, a romancer, novelist; as *romance* + *-er*2.] **1.** A writer of romance.

In the civill warres [he was] colonel of horse. . . . Good sword-man; admirable extempore orator; great memorie; great historian and *romanceer*. *Aubrey*, Lives, Sir J. Long.

Illustrious *romancer* [Cervantes]! were the "fine frenzies" which possessed the brain of thy own Quixote a fit subject . . . to be exposed to the jeers of duennas?
Lamb, Barrenness of the Imaginative Faculty.

2. One who romances; one who invents fictitious or extravagant stories.

The allusion of the daw extends to all impostors, vain pretenders, and *romancers*. *Sir R. L'Estrange.*

romancical (rọ̄-man′si-kạl), *a.* [< *romance* + *-ic-al*.] Relating to or dealing in romance, particularly the romances of chivalry. [Rare.]

The poets and *romancical* writers (as dear Margaret Newcastle would call them). *Lamb*, Decay of Beggars.

romancist (rọ̄-man′sist), *n.* [= Sp. Pg. *romancista*, one who writes in the vernacular tongue, Pg. also a romancer; as *romance* + *-ist*.] A writer of romance; a romancer.

A story! what story? Père Silas is no *romancist*.
Charlotte Brontë, Villette, xxxv.

Slow, determined, sure, artistic work . . . made the successful careers of the earlier generation of American poets, *romancists*, and essayists. *The Century*, XL. 313.

romancy† (rọ̄-man′si), *a.* [< *romance* + *-y*1.] Romantic. [Rare.]

An old house, situated in a *romancy* place.
Life of A. Wood, p. 118.

Romanée Conti. A wine of Burgundy, grown on the Côte d'Or, in a very small district in the commune of Vosne. It is considered by many the chief of all the red wines of Burgundy.

Romanée St. Vivant. A wine of Burgundy of the highest class, grown on the Côte d'Or, a very small amount being produced.

romanesca (rō-ma-nes'kä), *n.* [It., fem. of *Romanesco*, Romanesque: see *Romanesque*.] A dance: same as *galliard*, 2.

Romanese (rē-man-ēs' or -ēz'), *n.* [< L. *Romanensis*, Roman, < *Romanus*, Roman: see *Roman*.] Same as *Wallachian*.

Romanesk† (rō-ma-nesk'), *a.* and *n.* Same as *Romanesque*. *Imp. Dict.*

Romanesque (rō-ma-nesk'), *a.* and *n.* [Formerly also *Romanesk*; < F. *romanesque*, < Sp. *romanesco* = Pg. *romanisco* = It. *romanesco*, Roman, Romanish, < ML. *Romaniscus*, Roman, < L. *Romanus*, Roman: see *Roman* and *-esque*.] **I.** *a.* **1.** Roman or Romance. Specifically, in *art*: (*a*) Belonging to or designating the early medieval style of art and ornament developed in western Europe from those of the later Roman empire.

The name *Romanesque*, which has been given to this style, very nearly corresponds with the term Romance as applied to a group of languages. It signifies the derivation of the main elements, both of plan and of construction, from the works of the later Roman Empire. But *Romanesque* architecture was not, as it has been called, "a corrupted imitation of the Roman architecture," any more than the Provençal or the Italian language was a corrupted imitation of the Latin. It was a new thing, the slowly matured product of a long period and of many influences.
C. E. Norton, Church-building in Middle Ages, p. 22.

Hence — (*b*) Same as *romantic*, 5.

2. Noting the dialect of Languedoc. See II., 2.— **3.** [*l. c.*] Pertaining to romance; romantic. [A Gallicism.]—**Romanesque architecture**, a general and rather vague phrase including the styles of round-arched and -vaulted architecture which prevailed in the West from the fifth to the middle of the twelfth century.

Romanesque.— Great Doorway of the Abbey Church of Vézelay, 12th century. (From Viollet-le-Duc's "Dict. de l'Architecture.")

The Romanesque can be separated into two distinct divisions: (*a*) that but little removed from debased Roman, prevalent from the fifth to the eleventh century; and (*b*) the late, fully developed Romanesque of the eleventh and twelfth centuries, which comprises the advanced and differentiated Lombard, Rhenish, Saxon, Norman, and Burgundian styles. The latter division, while retaining the semicircular arch and other characteristic features of Roman architecture, is in every sense an original style of great richness and dignity, always inferior, however, to the succeeding Pointed style in the less perfect stability of its round arch and vault, the greater heaviness and less organic quality of its structure (the Romanesque architect, like the old Roman, still trusting for stability rather to the massiveness of his walls than, like his successor in the thirteenth century, to the scientific combination of a skeleton framework of masonry), the inferior flexibility of its design, and the archaic character of its figure-sculpture, of which much, however, is admirable in the best examples, particularly in France. See *medieval architecture* (under *medieval*), and compare cuts under *Norman*, *Rhenish*, and *modillion*.

II. *n.* **1.** The early medieval style of architecture and ornament founded in the West upon those of the later Roman empire, and the varieties into which it is subdivided, known as *Lombard*, *Norman*, *Rhenish*, etc. See I.

There existed a transitional style, properly called the *Romanesque*, which may be described as that modification of the classical Roman form which was introduced between the reigns of Constantine and Justinian, and was avowedly an attempt to adapt classical forms to Christian purposes. *J. Fergusson*, Hist. Arch., I. 396.

2. The common dialect of Languedoc and some other districts in the south of France. [Rare.]

romaney†, *n.* See *rumney*. *Redding*, Wines, i.

Romanic (rǫ-man'ik), *a.* [< L. *Romanicus*, Roman, < *Romanus*, Roman: see *Roman*. Cf. *Romance*, *Romansh*.] **1.** Pertaining to the Romance languages or dialects, or to the races or nations speaking any of the Romance tongues; Romance.

They [the Provençaux] are interesting as showing the tendency of the *Romanic* races to a scientific treatment of what, if it be not spontaneous, becomes a fashion and erelong an impertinence. *Lowell*, Study Windows, p. 241.

2. Being in or derived from the Roman alphabet.

Romaniform (rē-man'i-fôrm), *a.* [< L. *Romanus*, Roman, + *forma*, form.] Formed on the model of the Romance languages, as a phrase or term. Compare *Latiniform*. [Rare.]

The relative positions of the substantive and adjective are too inconstant in Latin to admit of generalization; but in the derivative Romance languages . . . the adjective almost invariably follows, while in the Germanic tongues it as commonly precedes; hence, strictly speaking, the two combinations should be called *Romaniform* and Germaniform, respectively.
Buck's Handbook of Med. Sciences, VIII. 518, note.

Romanisation, Romanise, etc. See *Romanization*, etc.

Romanish (rō'man-ish), *a.* [< ME. *romanishe*, *romanisce*; < *Roman* + *-ish*[1].] **1**†. Roman. *Ormulum*, l. 8327.—**2.** Pertaining to the customs, ceremonies, doctrines, or polity peculiar to the Roman Catholic Church: used invidiously.

Romanism (rō'man-izm), *n.* [= F. *romanisme* = Pg. *romanismo*; as *Roman* + *-ism*.] The polity, doctrine, ceremonies, and customs peculiar to the Church of Rome.

Romanism is medieval Christianity in conflict with modern progress. *Schaff*, Christ and Christianity, p. 127.

Romanist (rō'man-ist), *n.* and *a.* [< F. *romaniste* = Sp. *Romanista*; as *Roman* + *-ist*.] **I.** *n.* A Roman Catholic; an adherent of the Church of Rome: used chiefly by opponents of that church.

To these Oratories the people repair with their Vows and Prayers, in their several distresses, much after the same manner as the *Romanists* do to the shrines of their Saints. *Maundrell*, Aleppo to Jerusalem, p. 10.

Those slight velitations he had with Bellarmin and the *Romanists*. *Harrington*, Oceana (ed. 1771), p. 28. (*Jodrell*.)

II. *a.* Belonging or relating to Romanism; Roman Catholic: as, the *Romanist* and the Protestant systems.

Romanization (rō"man-i-zā'shon), *n.* [< *Romanize* + *-ation*.] A making Roman; the act or system of causing to conform to Roman standards and institutions. Also spelled *Romanisation*.

He [Cæsar] completed the *Romanization* of Italy by his enfranchisement of the Transpadane Gauls.
Encyc. Brit., XX. 768.

Romanize (rō'man-īz), *v.*; pret. and pp. *Romanized*, ppr. *Romanizing*. [< F. *romaniser* = Sp. *Romanizar*; as *Roman* + *-ize*; cf. ML. *romanizare*, write in Romance, or make romances: see *romance*, *v.*] **I.** *trans.* **1.** To make Roman; specifically, to Latinize; fill with Latin words or modes of speech.

They [the Gallo-Romans of the South] had been thoroughly *romanized* in language and culture.
Lowell, Study Windows, p. 240.

2. To convert or proselytize to the Roman Catholic Church; imbue with Roman Catholic ideas, doctrines, or observances.—**3.** [*l. c.*] To represent in writing or printing by roman letters or types.

A society for *Romanizing* the [Japanese] language.
Missionary Herald, July, 1886, p. 262.

II. *intrans.* **1.** To use Latin words or idioms.

So apishly *Romanizing* that the word of command still was set down in Latine. *Milton*, Areopagitica, p. 12.

2. To conform to or tend toward Roman Catholic polity, doctrine, ceremonies, or observances. Also spelled *Romanise*.

Romanizer (rō'man-ī-zėr), *n.* One who Romanizes, especially in religion. Also spelled *Romaniser*.

Romano-Byzantine (rō'man-ō-biz'an-tin), *a.* In *art*: (*a*†) Noting the style usually known as Romanesque. (*b*) Noting an early medieval architectural style of much of northeastern Italy, in which Byzantine elements are modified by the influence of distinctively Romanesque or Western elements. It was due to the influence of the Byzantine Church of San Vitale at Ravenna, completed about A. D. 550.

As it [the Byzantine style] was gradually blended with the classical Roman, with which it was then first brought face to face, a third great style was formed, known as the Romanesque, *Romano-Byzantine*, Lombard, or Comacine.
C. C. *Perkins*, Italian Sculpture, Int., p. x.

Romansh (rō-mansh'), *a.* and *n.* [Also *Romansch*, *Rumansch*, *Roumansch*, *Rumonsch* (G. *Romanisch*); < Romansh *romansch*, *rumansch*, *rumonsch*, *romonsch*, the Romansh language, lit. Romance: see *Romance*.] Same as *Rhæto-Romanic*.

romant (rǫ-mänt'), *n.* [< ME *romant*, *romaunt*, < OF. *romant*, *roumant*, a var., with excrescent *t*, of *roman*, *romans*, a romance: see *romance*.] Same as *romance*. *Florio*; *Cotgrave*. [Obsolete, but used archaically, in the Middle English form *romaunt*, as in the title of the "*Romaunt* of the Rose."]

Or else some *romant* unto us areed,
By former shepherds taught thee in thy youth,
Of noble lords' and ladies' gentle deed.
Drayton, Pastorals, Ecl. vi.

O, hearken, loving hearts and bold,
Unto my wild *romaunt*.
Mrs. Browning, Romaunt of Margret.

romant† (rǫ-mänt'), *v. t.* and *i.* [Also *romaunt*; < *romant*, *romaunt*, *n.*] To romance; exaggerate. *Halliwell*.

romantic (rǫ-man'tik), *a.* and *n.* [Formerly *romantick*; = Sp. *romántico* = Pg. It. *romantico* (= D. *romantiek* = G. *romantik* = Dan. Sw. *romantik*, n.; D. G. *romantisch* = Dan. Sw. *romantisk*, a.), < F. *romantique*, pertaining to romance, < OF. *romant*, a romance: see *romance* and *romant*.] **I.** *a.* **1.** Pertaining to or resembling romance, or an ideal state of things; partaking of the heroic, the marvelous, the supernatural, or the imaginative; chimerical; fanciful; extravagantly enthusiastic: as, *romantic* notions; *romantic* expectations; *romantic* devotion.

So fair a place was never seen
Of all that ever charm'd *romantic* eye.
Keats, Imitation of Spenser.

A *romantic* scheme is one which is wild, impracticable, and yet contains something which captivates the young.
Whately.

The poets of Greece and Rome . . . do not seem to have visited their great battle-fields, nor to have hung on the scenery that surrounded them with that *romantic* interest which modern poets do.
Shairp, Poetic Interpretation of Nature, p. 110.

2. Pertaining to romances or the popular literature of the middle ages; hence, improbable; fabulous; fictitious.

Their feigned and *romantic* heroes.
Dr. J. Scott, Works, II. 124.

I speak especially of that imagination which is most free, such as we use in *romantick* inventions.
Dr. H. More, Immortal. of Soul, ii. 11.

3. Wildly or impressively picturesque; characterized by poetic or inspiring scenery; suggesting thoughts of romance: as, a *romantic* prospect; a *romantic* glen.

Such dusky grandeur clothed the height
Where the huge Castle holds its state, . . .
Mine own *romantic* town!
Scott, Marmion, iv. 30.

4. In *music*, noting a style, work, or musician characterized by less attention to the formal and objective methods of composition than to the expression of subjective feeling; sentimental; imaginative; passionate: opposed to *classical*. *Romantic* in music, as elsewhere, is a relative word; it denotes especially the style, tendency, or school represented by Von Weber, Schumann, Chopin, Wagner, and others, and by certain works or characteristics of Beethoven, Mendelssohn, and Schubert.

5. In *arch.* and *art*, fanciful; fantastic; not formal or classical; characterized by pathos. See *pathos*, 2.

There was nothing of classic idealism in his [the medieval church-builder's] work; it was modern and *romantic* in the sense that in it the matter predominated over the form.
C. E. Norton, Church-building in Middle Ages, p. 29.

Romantic school, a name assumed by a number of young poets and critics in Germany—the Schlegels, Novalis, Tieck, and others—to designate a combination of writers whose efforts were directed to the overthrow of the artificial rhetoric and unimaginative pedantry of the French school of poetry. The name is also given to a similar school which arose in France between twenty and thirty years later, and engaged in a long struggle for supremacy with the older *classic school*; Victor Hugo and Lamartine were among the leaders. From literature the name passed into music as the designation of a class of musicians having many of the characteristics of the romantic school of authors. See def. 4.=**Syn.** 1. *Romantic*, *Sentimental*. *Sentimental* is used in reference to the feelings, *romantic* in reference to the imagination. *Sentimental* is used in a sense unfavorable, but in all degrees: as, an amiably *sentimental* person; the *sentimental* pity that would surround imprisoned criminals with luxuries. "The *sentimental* person is one of wrong or excessive sensibility, or who imports mere sentiment into matters worthy of more vigorous thought." (*C. J. Smith*, Syn. Disc., p. 680.) *Romantic*, when applied to character, is generally unfavorable, but in all degrees, implying that the use of the imagination is extravagant. A *romantic* person indulges his imagination in the creation and contemplation of scenes of ideal enterprise, adventure, and enjoyment.

A *romantic* tendency is often a part of the exuberance of youthful vitality, and may be disciplined into imaginative strength; *sentimentality* is a sort of mental sickliness or degeneration, and is not easily recovered from.

II. *n.* An adherent of the romantic school. See *romantic school*, under I.

Indeed, Chateaubriand had been a *romantic* before the time, and André Chénier had already written verse too warm and free for the classic mould.
New Princeton Rev., III. 2.

He [Balzac] includes in himself a mystic, a "realist," a classic, a *romantic*, and a humourist after the mediæval fashion of Rabelais. *The Academy*, March 1, 1890, p. 144.

romantical (rọ̄-man'ti-kal), *a.* [‹ *romantic* + *-al.*] Same as *romantic.* [Rare.]

But whosoever had the least sagacity in him could not but perceive that this theology of Epicurus was but *romantical*. *Cudworth*, Intellectual System, I. 2.

romantically (rọ̄-man'ti-kal-i), *adv.* In a romantic manner; fancifully; extravagantly.

romanticism (rọ̄-man'ti-sizm), *n.* [‹ *romantic* + *-ism.*] 1. The state or quality of being romantic; specifically, in *lit.*, the use of romantic forms shown in the reaction from classical to medieval models which originated in Germany in the last half of the eighteenth century. Similar reactions took place at a later period in France and England. See *romantic school*, under *romantic*.

In poetic literature there came that splendid burst of *Romanticism* in which Coleridge was the first and most potent participant. *Shairp*, D. G. Rossetti, ii.

2. Romantic feeling, expression, action, or conduct; a tendency to romance.

Romanticism, which has helped to fill some dull blanks with love and knowledge, had not yet penetrated the times with its leaven, and entered into everybody's food.
George Eliot, Middlemarch, xix.

You hope she has remained the same, that you may renew that piece of *romanticism* that has got into your head.
W. Black, Princess of Thule.

romanticist (rọ̄-man'ti-sist), *n.* [‹ *romantic* + *-ist.*] One imbued with romanticism; a romantic.

There is a story . . . that Spenser was half-bullied into re-writing the "Fairy Queen" in hexameters, had not Raleigh, a true *romanticist*, . . . persuaded him to follow his better genius. *Kingsley*, Westward Ho, ix.

Julian was a *romanticist* in wishing to restore the Greek religion and its spirit, when mankind had entered on the new development. *George Eliot*, in Cross, I. iii.

Hugo had already, in the preface to the "Odes et Ballades," planted the flag of the *romanticists*.
Edinburgh Rev., CLXIII. 128.

romanticly (rọ̄-man'tik-li), *adv.* Romantically. [Rare.]

He tells us *romanticly* on the same argument, that many posts went to and fro, between Peter Martyr and Cranmer. *Strype*, Cranmer, iii. 38.

romanticness (rọ̄-man'tik-nes), *n.* The state or character of being romantic.

Having heard me often praise the *romanticness* of the place, she was astonished . . . that I should set myself against going to a house so much in my taste.
Richardson, Clarissa Harlowe, I. liii.

Romany, Rommany (rom'ạ-ni), *n.* and *a.* [‹ Gipsy *Romani*, Gipsy; cf. *rom*, man, husband: see *Rom.*] I. *n.*; pl. *Romanies*, *Rommanies* (-niz). 1. A Gipsy.

Very nice, deep, old-fashioned *Romanies* they are.
C. G. Leland, The Century, XXV. 905.

2. The language spoken by the Gipsies. Originally a dialect brought from India and allied to the Hindustani, it has been much corrupted by the tongues of the peoples among whom the Gipsies have sojourned. The corrupt broken dialect now used by British Gipsies is called by them *posh-romany* or *romanes*; the purer, "*deep*" *romanes*. See *Gipsy*.

"We were talking of languages, Jasper. . . . Yours must be a rum one?" "'Tis called *Rommany*."
G. Borrow, Lavengro, xvii.

II. *a.* Belonging or relating to the Romanies or Gipsies: as, *Romany* songs; a *Romany* custom.

"And you are what is called a Gypsy King?" "Ay, ay; a *Rommany* Kral." *G. Borrow*, Lavengro, xvii.

Also *Roman*.

romanza (rọ̄-man'zạ̈), *n.* [It. *romanzo*: see *romance.*] Same as *romance*, 6.

romanzovite (rọ̄-man'zọv-īt), *n.* [Named after Count *Romanzoff.*] A variety of garnet, of a brown or brownish-yellow color.

romaunt†, *n.* and *v.* See *romant.*

rombelt, *n.* An obsolete form of *rumble*.

Romberg's symptom, trophoneurosis. See *symptom*, *trophoneurosis*.

romblet, *v. i.* A Middle English form of *ramble*.

rombonelli (rom-bọ-nel'i), *n.* In South America, a breed of sheep having long fine wool.

The horses and cattle looked small, but there were some good specimens of sheep — especially the *rombonellis*.
Lady Brassey, Voyage of Sunbeam, I. v.

rombowline, rumbowline (rom-, rum-bō'lin), *n.* [Origin obscure.] Condemned canvas, rope, etc. *Dana.*

rome[1]†, *v.* A Middle English form of *roam*.

rome[2]†, *v. i.* [E. dial. *raum*, shout, cry; ‹ ME. *romen*, roar, growl; prob. ‹ Sw. *råma*, low. Cf. *reem*[3].] To growl; roar.

He comanded that thay solde take a onge damesele, and nakkene hir, and sett hir bifore hym, and thay did soo; and onane he ranne apone hir *romyand*, as he hadd bene wodd. *MS. Lincoln* A. i. 17, f. 37. (*Halliwell.*)

rome[3]†, *n.* A Middle English form of *room*[1].

Rome-feet (rōm'fē), *n.* Same as *Rome-scot*.

romeine (rō'mẹ-in), *n.* [‹ *Romé* (*Romé* de Lisle, a mineralogist, 1736–90) + *-ine*[2].] A mineral of a hyacinth or honey-yellow color, occurring in square octahedrons. It is an antimoniate of calcium. Also called *romeite*.

romekint, *n.* See *rumkin*[1].

rome-mort†, *n.* [‹ *rom* (*rum*[2]) + *mort*[4].] A queen. *Harman*, Caveat for Cursetors, p. 115. [Old cant.]

Rome-penny (rōm'pen"i), *n.* [ME. **Rome-peny*, ‹ AS. *Rōm-pening*, *Rōm-penig*, *Rōmpænig*, ‹ *Rōm*, Rome, + *pelling*, *penig*, *pænig*, penny: see *penny.*] Same as *Rome-scot*.

romert, *n.* A Middle English form of *roamer*.

romerillo (rō-mėr-il'ō), *n.* [Perhaps Sp., dim. of *romero*, a pilgrim: see *romero.*] A plant, *Heterothalamus brunioides*, whose flowers yield a yellow dye; also, the dye thus produced. See *Heterothalamus*.

romero (rọ̄-mā'rō), *n.* [‹ Sp. *romero*, a pilot-fish, a pilgrim, = OF. *romier*, traveling as a pilgrim, a pilgrim, ‹ ML. **romarius*, *romerius*, a pilgrim (orig. to Rome), ‹ L. *Roma*, Rome. Cf. *roamer.*] The pilot-fish, *Naucrates ductor*.

Rome-runner† (rōm'run"ėr), *n.* [ME. *rome-renner*; ‹ *Rome* + *runner.*] One who runs to or seeks Rome; specifically, an agent at the court of Rome.

And [that] alle *Rome-renners* for [the benefit of] robbers in Fraunce
Bere no suluer ouer see. *Piers Plowman* (C), v. 125.

And thus thes *rome renneris* beren the kyngys gold out of oure lond, & bryngen agen deed leed and heresie and symonye and goddis curse.
Wyclif, Eng. Works (E. E. T. S.), p. 23.

Rome-scot†, **Rome-shot**† (rōm'skot, -shot), *n.* [Late AS. *Rōme-scot*, *Rōm-gescot*, ‹ *Rōm*, Rome, + *scot*, *gescot*, payment: see *scot*[2].] Same as *alms-fee*, and *Peter's pence* (which see, under *penny*).

This was the course which the Romains used in the conquest of England, for they planted some of theyr legions in all places convenient, the which they caused the countrey to maintayne, cutting upon everye portion of lande a reasonable rent, which they called *Romescott*, the which might not surcharge the tenaunte or freeholder, and defrayed the pay of the garrison.
Spenser, State of Ireland.

Romescot, or Peter's Penny, was by as good Statute Law paid to the Pope. *Milton*, Touching Hirelings.

Romeward (rōm'wạ̈rd), *adv.* [‹ *Rome* (see def.) + *-ward.*] To or toward Rome or the Roman Catholic Church.

Romic (rō'mik), *n.* [‹ *Rom*(*an*) + *-ic*; a distinctive form of *Roman.*] A system of phonetic notation devised by Henry Sweet, consisting of the ordinary letters of the English alphabet used so far as possible with their original Roman values, and supplemented by ligatures, digraphs, and turned letters. In a stricter scientific form called *Narrow Romic*; in a more general practical form called *Broad Romic*. It is in part a recasting of Ellis's Glossic (which see). *H. Sweet*, Handbook of Phonetics, pp. 102, 105, 202.

Romish (rō'mish), *a.* [‹ ME. **Romish* = D. *roomsch* = MHG. *ræmesch*, *ræmisch*, *ræmsch*, G. *römisch*; as *Rome* + *-ish*[1].] Belonging or relating to Rome; specifically, belonging to the Roman Catholic Church: commonly used in a slightly invidious sense.

A saucy stranger in his court to mart
As in a *Romish* stew.
Shak., Cymbeline, i. 6. 152.

Romish Methodists. Same as *dialectic Methodists* (which see, under *Methodist*). = **Syn.** See *papal*.

Romist† (rō'mist), *n.* [‹ *Rome* + *-ist.*] A Roman Catholic.

The *Romists* hold fast the distinction of mortal and venial sins. *South*, Sermons, VII. v.

romite (rō'mīt), *n.* [Orig. Sw. *romit*; ‹ Gr. ῥώμη, strength, + *-ite*[2].] An explosive of Swedish origin, composed of a mixture of ammonium nitrate and naphthalene with potassium chlorate and potassium nitrate. The reaction of the nitrates and chlorate render the compound unstable, and on this account a license for its manufacture in England has been refused.

Romize† (rō'mīz), *v. t.* [‹ *Rome* + *-ize.*] To Romanize.

The *Romiz'd* faction were zealous in his behalf.
Fuller, Ch. Hist., III. iv. 16. (*Davies.*)

romkint, *n.* See *rumkin*[1].

Rommany, *n.* and *a.* See *Romany*.

rommle (rom'l), *v.* A dialectal form of *rumble*.

romney†, *n.* Same as *Romany*.

romp (romp), *v. i.* [‹ ME. *rompen*; a var. of *ramp*: see *ramp*, *v.*] To play rudely and boisterously; leap and frisk about in play.

The air she gave herself was that of a *romping* girl: . . . she would . . . snatch off my periwig, try it upon herself in the glass, clap her arms a-kimbo, draw my sword, and make passes on the wall.
Steele, Spectator, No. 187.

romp (romp), *n.* [A var. of *ramp*: see *ramp*, *n.*, *romp*, *v.*] 1. A rude girl who indulges in boisterous play.

My cousin Betty, the greatest *romp* in nature: she whisks me such a height over her head that I cried out for fear of falling. *Steele*, Tatler, No. 15.

First, giggling, plotting chamber-maids arrive,
Hoydens and *romps*, led on by Gen'ral Clive.
Churchill, Rosciad.

2. Rude play or frolic: as, a game of *romps*.

Romp-loving miss
Is haul'd about, in gallantry robust.
Thomson, Autumn, l. 528.

romping (rom'ping), *n.* [Verbal n. of *romp*, *v.*] The act of playing in a boisterous manner; a game of romps.

A stool, a chair, or a table is the first weapon taken up in a general *romping* or skirmish.
Swift, Advice to Servants, General Directions.

rompingly (rom'ping-li), *adv.* In a romping manner; rompishly.

rompish (rom'pish), *a.* [‹ *romp* + *-ish*[1]. Cf. *rampish.*] Given to romp; inclined to romp.

rompishly (rom'pish-li), *adv.* In a rompish, rude, or boisterous manner.

rompishness (rom'pish-nes), *n.* The quality of being rompish; disposition to rude, boisterous play, or the practice of romping.

She would . . . take off my cravat, and seize it to make some other use of the lace, or run into some other unaccountable *rompishness*. *Steele*, Spectator, No. 187.

rompu (rom-pū'), *a.* [‹ F. *rompu*, pp. of *rompre*, break, ‹ L. *rumpere*, break: see *rupture.*] In *her.*, same as *fracted*.

ron[1]†, *v.* An obsolete form of *run*[1].

ron[2]†. An obsolete strong preterit of *rain*[1]. *Chaucer.*

ron[3]†, *n.* An obsolete form of *rune*[1].

roncador (rong'kạ-dôr), *n.* [‹ Sp. *roncador*, a snorer, grunter, ‹ *roncar*, snore, roar, ‹ LL. *rhonchare*, snore, ‹ L. *rhonchus*, a snoring: see *rhonchus.*] 1. One of several sciænoid fishes of the Pacific coast of North America. (*a*) The *Sciæna*

Roncador (*Roncador stearnsi*).

or *Roncador stearnsi*, a large and valuable food-fish of the coast of California, attaining a weight of from 5 to 6 pounds, of a silvery bluish or grayish color, with darker markings, and especially a black pectoral spot. (*b*) The *Sciæna* or *Rhinoscion saturna*, distinguished as the *red* or *black roncador*. (*c*) The yellow-finned or yellow-tailed roncador, *Umbrina xanti*. (d) The little roncador, *Genyonemus lineatus*.

2. [*cap.*] [NL.] A section of *Sciæna*, or a genus of sciænoids, represented by the roncador (see 1 (*a*)). *Jordan and Gilbert*, 1880.

ronceval†, *n.* See *rounceval*.

ronchil, *n.* Same as *ronquil*.

roncho (rong'kō), *n.* [‹ Sp. *ronco*, snoring, *roncador*, snorer: see *roncador.*] The croaker, *Micropogon undulatus*. [Galveston, Texas.]

rondache (ron-dash'), *n.* [= D. *rondas*, ‹ OF. *rondache*, a buckler, ‹ *rond*, round: see *round.*] A buckler, or small round shield. Also called *roundel*.

Caspar . . . carries, for decorative purposes, the round buckler or *rondache* of the foot-soldier.
Harper's Mag., LXXVIII. 68.

Rondache.—Roundhand buckler of the 16th and 17th centuries. (From Viollet-le-Duc's "Dict. du Mobilier français.")

ronde (rond), *n.* [‹ F. *ronde*, round-hand writing: see *round*[1].] In *printing*, an angular form of script or writing-type, of which the following is an example:

This is one form of Ronde.

rondeau (ron'dō), *n.* [< F. *rondeau*, < OF. *rondel*, a roundel: see *roundel*.] **1.** A poem in a fixed form, borrowed from the French, and consisting either of thirteen lines on two rimes with an unriming refrain, or of ten lines on two rimes with an unriming refrain. It may be written in octosyllabic or decasyllabic measure. The refrain is usually a repetition of the first three or four words, sometimes of the first word only. The order of rimes in the thirteen-line rondeau, known technically as the "rondeau of Voiture" (that is, Vincent Voiture, 1598–1648), is *a, a, b, b, a; a, a, b* (and refrain); *a, a, b, b, a* (and refrain); that of the ten-line rondeau, known technically as the "rondeau of Villon" (that is, François Villon, 1431–1461 ?), is *a, b, b, a; a, b* (and refrain); *a, b, b, a* (and refrain). These are the strict rules; but, as in the case of the sonnet, both in France and England, they are not always observed. There is also a form called the *rondeau redoublé*. It consists of six quatrains, *a, b, a, b*, on two rimes. The first four lines form in succession the last lines of the second, third, fourth, and fifth quatrains. At the end of the final quatrain, the first words of the poem are added as an unriming and independent refrain. Sometimes the final quatrain is styled the *envoi* or *envoy*.

This sort of writing, called the *rondeau*, is what I never knew practised in our nation. *Pope.*

2. In *music*. See *rondo*.

rondel (ron'del), *n.* [< OF. *rondel*: see *roundel*.] A poem in a fixed form, borrowed from the French, and consisting of thirteen lines on two rimes. It may be written in octosyllabic or decasyllabic measure. The first line is repeated at the close, and the first two lines are repeated as the seventh and eighth lines. Thus, the whole poem, like the rondeau (which see), falls into three divisions or stanzas—two of four, and one of five—arranged as follows: *a, b, b, a; a b, a, b; a, b, b, a, a*. It is permissible to repeat the first couplet at the close, making the last division *a, b, b, a. a, b*, and fourteen lines in all. Rondels in English were written by Charles of Orleans, Chaucer, Occleve, Lydgate, and others.

In its origin the *rondel* was a lyric of two verses, each having four or five lines, rhyming on two rhymes only. In its eight (or ten) lines, but five (or six) were distinct, the others being made by repeating the first couplet at the end of the second stanza, sometimes in an inverse order, and the first line at the end of its first stanza. The eight-lined *rondel* is thus to all intents and purposes a triolet. . . . With Charles d'Orléans the *rondel* took the distinct shape we now assign to it, namely of fourteen lines on two rhymes, the first two lines repeating for the seventh and eighth and the final couplet. . . . By the time of Octavien de Saint Gelais (1466–1502) the *rondel* has nearly become the rondeau as we know it.
Gleeson White, Ballades and Rondeaus, Int., p. lviii.

rondelet (ron'de-let), *n.* [< OF. *rondelet*, dim. of *rondel*, a roundel: see *rondel*, *roundel*, and cf. *rundlet*.] A poem of five lines and two refrains. The refrains repeat the first line, generally two words, the rime-scheme being *a, b* (and refrain); *a, b, b* (and refrain). It has been written in English, but not much.

Then haue you also a *rondlette*, the which doth alwayes end with one self same foote or repeticion, and was thereof (in my iudgment) called a *rondelet*.
Gascoigne, Notes on Eng. Verse (Steele Glas., etc., ed. Arber), § 14.

Rondeletia (ron-de-let'i-ä), *n.* [NL. (Plumier, 1703), named after Guillaume *Rondelet* (1507–1566?), a French professor of medicine.] A genus of gamopetalous shrubs and trees of the order *Rubiaceæ*, type of the tribe *Rondeletieæ*. It is characterized by a globose calyx bearing four or five narrow, persistent, and nearly equal lobes, by a wheel-shaped or salver-form corolla with a long slender tube and four or five obovate broadly imbricating lobes, and by the loculicidal capsule, which is small, rigid, globose, two-furrowed, and two-valved. There are about 60 species, natives of the West Indies and tropical America from Mexico to the United States of Colombia, rarely extending into Guiana and Peru. They bear opposite or whorled leaves, which are thin or coriaceous and sessile, furnished with broad stipules between the petioles. Their small flowers are white, yellow, or red, and usually in axillary flattened, rounded, or panicled cymes. Various handsome species are cultivated under glass, among them *R. odorata*, with fragrant scarlet flowers, and *R. versicolor*, whose deep rose-colored flowers become paler after expansion. Some species are still known as *Rogiera*, the name of a former genus, including species with connate stipules and corolla hairy in the throat.

Rondeletieæ (ron"de-le-tī'ē-ē), *n. pl.* [NL. (A. P. de Candolle, 1830), < *Rondeletia* + *-eæ*.] A tribe of gamopetalous plants of the order *Rubiaceæ*, characterized by the exceedingly numerous minute albuminous wingless seeds which fill the two cells of the dry capsule, and by the regular corolla with imbricated or contorted lobes. It includes 14 genera of shrubs and trees, with stipulate leaves and cymose, spiked, or variously clustered flowers, and 2 genera of herbs, without stipules, bearing terminal three-forked cymes. The species are tropical and mainly American. See *Rondeletia*, the type.

rondelle (ron-del'), *n.* [< OF. *rondelle*, dim. of *rond*, round: see *rondel*, *roundel*.] **1.** Something round.

A *rondelle* of firwood is fixed normally to the tube by its centre, and gives a larger surface for the voice to act against. *G. B. Prescott*, Elect. Invent., p. 288.

2. In *metal.*, one of successive crusts which form upon the surface of molten metal while cooling, and which as they form are removed for further treatment. In copper-working these disks are also called *rose-copper* and *rosettes*. Suboxid of copper contained in them is removed by further refining.
3. *Milit.*: (*a*) A small shield (15 inches in length) formerly used by pikemen and archers. (*b*) One of the iron disks, each having an opening in the center for the passage of a bolt, placed between the cheeks and stock of a field-gun carriage in bolting these parts together. (*c*) A semicircular bastion introduced by Albert Dürer. It was about 300 feet in diameter, and contained spacious casemates.—**Rondelle à poing**, a name given to the very small round buckler of the sixteenth century, often fitted with a long and pointed spike, and serving, when held in the left hand, to parry the thrusts of a rapier instead of a dagger of any description. See cuts under *buckler* and *rondache*.

rondle (ron'dl), *n.* [< OF. *rondel*, a round, roundel: see *round*, *roundel*.] **1.** Same as *rondelle*.—**2.** The step of a ladder; a round.

Yea, peradventure in as ill a case as hee that goes up a ladder, but slippeth off the *rondells*, or, when one breakes, falls downe in great danger.
Rich Cabinet furnished with Varietie of Excellent Descriptions (1616). (*Nares.*)

rondo (ron'dō), *n.* [It. *rondò*, < F. *rondeau*: see *rondeau*.] **1.** In *music*: (*a*) Same as *round*[1], 7 (*e*). (*b*) A setting of a rondeau or similar poem. (*c*) A work or movement in which a principal phrase or section is several times repeated in its original key in alternation with contrasted phrases or sections in the same or other keys. The succession of principal and subordinate phrases is often exactly regulated, but the form is open to wide variations. In a sonata the last movement is often a rondo. **2.** A game of hazard played with small balls on a table.

With card and dice, roulette wheels and *rondo* balls, he fooled himself to the top of his bent.
J. W. Palmer, The New and the Old, p. 229.

Rondo form, in *music*, the form or method of composition of a rondo: often opposed to *sonata form*.

rondoletto (ron-dọ-let'ō), *n.* [Dim. of *rondo*, q. v.] In *music*, a short or simple rondo.

rondure (ron'dụ̄r), *n.* [< F. *rondeur*, roundness, < *rond*, round: see *round*[1].] A round; a circle; a curve; a swell; roundness. Also *roundure*. [Obsolete or archaic.]

All things rare
That heaven's air in this huge *rondure* hems.
Shak., Sonnets, xxi.

The shape [of a ring] remains,
The *rondure* brave, the lilied loveliness,
Gold as it was. *Browning*, Ring and Book, I. 8.

High-kirtled for the chase, and what was shown,
Of maiden *rondure*, like the rose half-blown.
Lowell, Endymion, iv.

rone[1] (rōn), *n.* An earlier, now only dialectal, form of *roe*[2].

rone[2], *n.* [< ME. *rone*, < Icel. *runnr*, older *rudhr*, a bush, grove.] **1.** A shrub.—**2.** A thicket; brushwood. *Jamieson*. [Scotch in both senses.]

The lorde on a lyȝt horce launces hym after,
As burne bolde vpon bent his bugle he blowez,
He rechated, & r[ode] thurȝ *ronez* ful thyk,
Suande this wylde swyn til the sunne schafted.
Sir Gawayne and the Green Knight (E. E. T. S.), l. 1466.

rone[3] (rōn), *n.* An obsolete or dialectal form of *rine*[1], *run*[1].

rone[4], *n.* Another form of *roan*[2].

rone[5]†. A Middle English preterit of *rain*[1].

rong[1]†. An obsolete preterit and past participle of *ring*[2].

rong[2]† (rong), *n.* A Middle English form of *rung*[1].

rongeur (rôṅ-zhėr'), *n.* [< F. *rongeur*, gnawer, < *ronger*, gnaw, nibble, OF. also chew the cud, = Pr. *romiar* = Sp. *rumiar*, < L. *rumigare*, chew the cud, ruminate, < *rumen*, throat, gullet: see *ruminate*.] A surgical forceps for gnawing or gouging bones.

ronin (rō'nin), *n.*; pl. *ronin* or *ronins*. [Jap., < *rō* (= Chin. *lang*), wave, + *nin* (= Chin. *jin*), man; lit. 'wave-man.'] A Japanese samurai, or two-sworded military retainer, who for any cause had renounced his clan, or who for some offense against his superior had been dismissed from service, and dispossessed of his estate, revenue, or pay; a masterless man; an outcast; an outlaw.

ronion†, **ronyon**† (run'yọn), *n.* [Perhaps < OF. **roignon*, < *roingne*, F. *rogne*, itch, scab, mange: see *roin*.] A mangy, scabby animal; also, a scurvy person. Also *runnion*.

Out of my door, you witch, you hag, you baggage, you polecat, you *ronyon*! *Shak.*, M. W. of W., iv. 2. 195.

ronnet, *v.* An obsolete form of *run*[1].

ronnen†. A Middle English past participle of *run*[1].

ronquil (rong'kil), *n.* [Also *ronchil*; < Sp. *ronquillo*, slightly hoarse, dim. of *ronco*, hoarse, < L. *raucus*, hoarse; see *raucous*.] **1.** A fish of the North Pacific, *Bathymaster signatus*, of an elongate form with a long dorsal having only the foremost two or three rays inarticulate, frequenting moderately deep water with rocky grounds.—**2.** One of a group or family of fishes of which *Bathymaster* has been supposed to be a representative—namely, the *Icosteidæ*.

Ronsdorfer (ronz'dôrf-ėr), *n.* [So called from *Ronsdorf*, a town in Prussia.] A member of a sect of German millenarians of the eighteenth century: same as *Ellerian*.

Ronsdorfian (ronz-dôr'fi-ạn), *n.* [< *Ronsdorf* (see *Ronsdorfer*) + *-ian*.] Same as *Ronsdorfer*.

ront†, *n.* Same as *runt*[1].

Röntgen rays. See *ray*.

ronyon†, *n.* See *ronion*.

roo[1]†, *n.* [ME. roo, *ro*, < AS. *rōw* = OHG. *rōa*, MHG. *ruo*, G. *ruhe* = Icel. *rō* = Dan. *ro*, rest, = Sw. *ro*, fun, amusement.] Peace; quietness.

Allas! for doole what shall y doo?
Now mon I neuer haue rest ne *roo*.
York Plays, p. 31.

roo[2]†, *n.* A Middle English form of *roe*[1].

roo[3]†, *n.* [ME., < OF. *roe*, *roue*, < L. *rota*, a wheel: see *rota*[1].] A wheel.

And I salle redily rolle the *roo* at the gayneste,
And reche the riche wyne in rynsede coupes.
Morte Arthure (E. E. T. S.), l. 3375.

rood (röd), *n.* [< ME. *rood*, *rode*, *rod*, < AS. *rōd*, a rod, rood, cross: see *rod*[1].] **1**†. A rod. See *rod*[1], 1.—**2.** A cross or crucifix; especially, a large crucifix placed at the entrance to the choir in medieval churches, often supported on the rood-beam or rood-screen. Usually, after the fifteenth century, images of the Virgin Mary and St. John were placed the one on the one side and the other on the other side of the image of Christ, in allusion to John xix. 26. See cut under *rood-loft*.

Of the appeltre that our uerste fader then luther [evil] appel nom
In the manere that ichulle ȝou telle the swete *rode* com.
Holy Rood (E. E. T. S.), p. 18.

No, by the *rood*, not so. *Shak.*, Hamlet, iii. 4. 14.

3. A name of various measures. (*a*) A measure of 5½ yards in length; a rod, pole, or perch; also, locally, a measure of 6, 7, or 8 yards, especially for hedging and ditching. (*b*) A square measure, the fourth part of a statute acre, equal to 40 square rods or square poles, or 1,210 square yards. This is the sense in which *rood* is generally used as a measure. See *acre*.

A terrace-walk, and half a *rood*
Of land, set out to plant a wood.
Pope, Imit. of Horace, II. vi. 5.

(*c*) A square pole, or 30¼ square yards, used in estimating masons' work; also, locally, a measure of 36, 42¼, 44, 49, or 64 square yards. (*d*) A cubic measure for masons' work of 64, 72, etc., cubic yards.—**Holy rood**, the cross of Christ; a crucifix.

The *holi rode* the swete tre riȝt is to habbe in munde,
That hath fram stronge deth ibroȝt to lyue al mankunde.
Holy Rood (E. E. T. S.), p. 18.

The English answered [the Normans] with their own battle-cry, "God's Rood! *Holy Rood!*"
Dickens, England, vii.

Holy-rood day. (*a*) The feast of the Finding of the Cross, celebrated on May 3d.

The knights . . . vpon *holy Rood day* in May made their musters before the Commissioners ordained.
Hakluyt's Voyages, II. 76.

(*b*) Same as *Holy-cross day* (which see, under *day*[1]).

The holi Roode was i-founde as ȝe witeth in May,
Honoured he was seththe in Septembre the *holi Rode day*.
Holy Rood (E. E. T. S.), p. 49.

On *Holy-rood day*, the gallant Hotspur there,
Young Harry Percy, and brave Archibald . . .
At Holmedon met. *Shak.*, 1 Hen. IV., i. 1. 52.

Rood's body†, the body on the cross—that is, Christ's body.

I'le be even with him; and get you gone, or, I sweare by the *rood's body*, I'le lay you by the heeles.
Lyly, Mother Bombie, v. 3.

rood-arch (röd'ärch), *n.* The arch in a church between the nave and the choir: so called from the rood being placed over it.

rood-altar (röd'âl"tär), *n.* An altar standing against the outer side of the rood-screen.

rood-beam (röd'bēm), *n.* [< ME. *roode beem*; < *rood* + *beam*.] A beam extending across the entrance to the choir of a church for supporting the rood. Also called *beam*.

He deyde whan I cam fro Jerusalem,
And lith ygrave under the *roode beem*.
Chaucer, Prol. to Wife of Bath's Tale, l. 496.

Rood-day (röd'dā), *n.* Holy-rood day. See under *rood*.

roodebok (rö'de-bok), *n.* [< D. *rood*, red, + *bok*, buck: see *red*[1] and *buck*[1].] The Natal bushbuck, *Cephalophus natalensis*. It is of a deep reddish brown in color, stands about 2 feet high, has large ears, and straight, pointed horns about 3 inches long. It

Roodebok (*Cephalophus natalensis*).

is solitary in its habits, and rarely leaves dense forests except in the evening or during rainy weather.

rood-free (röd'frē), *a.* Exempt from punishment. [Rare.] *Imp. Dict.*

roodhout (röd'hout), *n.* [D., < *rood*, red (= E. *red*), + *hout*, wood (= E. *holt*).] The Cape red-wood. See *Ochna*.

rood-loft (röd'lôft), *n.* [< ME. *rode lofte*; < *rood* + *loft*.] A gallery in a church where the rood and its appendages were placed. This loft or gallery was commonly situated between the nave and

Rood-loft (now destroyed) of the Abbey of St. Denis. 13th century. (From Viollet le Duc's "Dict. de l'Architecture.")

the chancel, or over the rood-screen. The front of the loft, like the screen below, was usually richly ornamented with tracery and carvings, either in wood or in stone. It was often approached by a small staircase in the wall of the building. This feature does not appear in modern churches, and has now been removed from a large proportion of the medieval churches. The rood-lott originated from a combination of the rood-beam and ambo. The center was used as ambo (jube), and the epistle and gospel were read and announcements made from it. It was placed over the entrance to the choir, so that both could stand in the middle line (longitudinal axis) of the church, and the approach to it was made from the side of the church along a broadened rood-beam or loft crowning the rood-screen. See also diagram under *cathedral*.

And then to zee the *rood-loft*
Zo bravely zet with zaints.
Plain Truth and Blind Ignorance (Percy's Reliques, p. 275).

The priest formerly stood in the *rood-loft* to read the Gospel and Epistle, and occasionally to preach the sermon at High Mass. *F. G. Lee*, Gloss. Eccles. Terms.

Rood-steeple.—Cathedral of Notre Dame, Paris, from the southeast.

Roodmas-day†, *n.* Holy-rood day. Also *Rood-day (Rode-day)*, *Rudmas-day*.

rood-screen (röd'skrēn), *n.* A screen or ornamental partition separating the choir of a church from the nave, and (properly) supporting the rood or crucifix. See cuts under *rood-loft* and *cathedral*.

The western limit of the quire [in Salisbury Cathedral] was shut in by the *rood-screen*, . . . a solid erection of stone. *G. Scott*, Hist. Eng. Church Architecture, p. 148.

rood-spire (röd'spīr), *n.* Same as *rood-steeple*.

rood-steeple (röd'stē'pl), *n.* A steeple or spire built over the entrance to the chancel, especially at the crossing of a cruciform church. See cut in preceding column.

rood-tower (röd'tou'ėr), *n.* A tower occupying the position described under *rood-steeple*.

rood-tree† (röd'trē), *n.* [< ME. *roodetre*, *rode-tre*; < *rood* + *tree*.] The cross.

I leue and trust in Christes feith,
Whiche died vpon the *roode tre*.
Gower, Conf. Amant., ii.

roody (rö'di), *a.* [Appar. a var. of *rooty*.] Rank in growth; coarse; luxuriant. [Prov. Eng.]

roof[1] (röf), *n.* [< ME *rof*, < AS. *hrōf*, a roof, = OFries. *hrōf*, a roof, = OD. *roef*, a roof, ceiling, shelter, cover, D. *roef*, a cabin, a wooden cover, = MLG. *rōf*, LG. *rof*, a roof, = Icel. *hrōf*, a shed under which ships are kept or built. Cf. Icel. *rāf*, also *rāfr*, mod. *ræfr*, a roof; Russ. *krovŭ*, a roof; perhaps akin to Gr. κρύπτειν, hide (see *crypt*).] **1.** The external upper covering of a house or other building. Roofs are distinguished (1) by the materials of which they are mainly formed, as thatch, stone, wood, slate, tile, iron, etc., and (2) by their form and mode of construction, in great variety, as shed, curb, hip, gable, pavilion, ogee, and flat roofs.

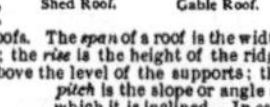

Shed Roof. Gable Roof.

The *span* of a roof is the width between the supports; the *rise* is the height of the ridge of the highest part above the level of the supports; the *pitch* is the slope or angle at which it is inclined. In carpentry, *roof* signifies the timber framework by which the roofing or covering materials of the building are supported. This consists in general of the principal rafters, the purlins, and the common rafters.

Conical Roof. Ogee Roof.

The principal rafters, or principals, as they are commonly termed, are placed so as to span the building at intervals usually of 10 or 12 feet; the purlins lie horizontally upon these, and sustain the common rafters, which carry the covering of the roof. The accompanying figure shows one of

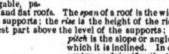

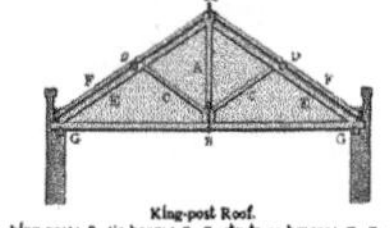

King-post Roof.
A, king-post; B, tie-beam; C, C, struts or braces; D, D, purlins; E, E, principal rafters; F, F, common rafters; G, G, wall-plates; H, ridge-pole.

the two varieties of principals which are in common use (the king-post principal), with the purlins and common rafters in position. (For a diagram of the second, the queen-post principal, see *queen-post*.) Each of these modes of framing constitutes a truss. Sometimes, when the width of the building is not great, common rafters are used alone to support the roof. They are in that case joined together in pairs, nailed where they meet at the top, and connected by means of a tie at the bottom. They are then termed *couples*, a pair forming a *couple-close*. See also cuts under *hammer-beam*, *hip-roof*, *jerkin-head*, *M-roof*, *pendent*, and *pendentive*.

Goodly buildings left without a *roof*
Soon fall to ruin. *Shak.*, Pericles, ii. 4. 36.

2. Anything which in form or position corresponds to or resembles the covering of a house, as the arch or top of a furnace or oven, the top of a carriage or coach or car, an arch or the interior of a vault, the ceiling of a room, etc.; hence, a canopy or the like.

Ffor tristith, als trewly as tyllinge us helpeth,
That iche rewme vndir *roff* of the reyne-bowe
Sholde stable and stonde be these thre degrees.
Richard the Redeless, iii. 248.

This brave o'erhanging firmament, this majestical *roof* fretted with golden fire. *Shak.*, Hamlet, ii. 2. 313.

Under the shady *roof*
Of branching elm star-proof.
Milton, Arcades, l. 88.

3. A house.

My dwelling, sir?
'Tis a poor yeoman's *roof*, scarce a league off.
Fletcher and Rowley, Maid in the Mill, ii. 2.

4. The upper part of the mouth; the hard palate.

Swearing till my very *roof* was dry.
Shak., M. of V., iii. 2. 206.

5. Figuratively, the loftiest part.

Why should we only toil, the *roof* and crown of things?
Tennyson, Lotos-Eaters, Choric Song.

6. In *geol.*, the overlying stratum.—**7.** In *mining*, the top of any subterranean excavation: little used except in coal-mining.—**False roof**, in *arch.*, the ceiling of an upper room or garret where it is shaped like a roof: but a space is, in fact, left between the ceiling and the rafters of the roof proper.—**Flat roof**. (*a*) A roof the upper surface of which is horizontal. Such roofs are frequent in the East, where they are usually thickly covered with clay or mortar. (*b*) A roof but slightly inclined for the discharge of water. Roofs of this form are common in city buildings, especially in the United States, and are usually covered with sheet-metal.—**French roof**, a form of roof with almost vertical sides, sometimes concave or even convex, and the top usually flat or sloping toward the rear. The sides are commonly pierced with dormer or other windows. This form of roof spread through-

French Roof.—Pavilion of Women's Hospital, New York City.

out the United States about 1870 and in succeeding years. It has its name from its fancied resemblance to the French Mansard roof—its object, like that roof, being to gain space in the topmost story.—**Imperial roof**. See *imperial dome*, under *imperial*.—**Mansard roof**, a form of curb-roof the lower slope of which approaches the vertical, while the upper slope is variable, but much more nearly flat than in the typical curb-roof. The lower section of the roof is pierced with windows. A roof of this type permits the establishment of an upper story, but little inferior to the others, in place of an ordinary garret. It was

Mansard Roof.—Château of Maisons Laffitte, France, by François Mansart.

first used in the Louvre by Pierre Lescot, about 1550, but has its name from François Mansart (1598–1662), a French architect (uncle of the better-known Jules Hardouin Mansart, the architect of Versailles and of the dome of the Invalides), who brought these roofs into a vogue which they have since retained in France.—**Ogee roof**. See *ogee*.—**Packsaddle-roof, saddle-back roof**. Same as *saddle-roof*.—**Pavilion roof**. See *pavilion*.—**Pitch of a roof**. See *pitch*[1].—**Raised roof**, in *car-building*, a car-roof the middle part of which is raised to form a clear-story.—**Roof of the mouth**, the hard palate; the upper wall of the mouth, as far as the bone extends. Compare def. 4.—**Square roof**, a roof in which the principal rafters meet at a right angle. (See also *curb-roof*, *gambrel-roof*, *hip-roof*.)

roof[1] (röf), *v. t.* [< *roof*[1], *n.*] **1.** To cover with a roof, in any sense of that word.

I have not, indeed, seen the remains of any ancient Roman buildings that have not been *roofed* with either vaults or arches.
Addison, Remarks on Italy (Works, ed. Bohn, I. 444).

Every winter in the Arctic regions the sea freezes, *roofing* itself with ice of enormous thickness and vast extent. *Tyndall*, Forms of Water, p. 133.

2. To inclose in a house; shelter.

Here had we now our country's honour *roof'd*,
Were the graced person of our Banquo present.
Shak., Macbeth, iii. 4. 40.

3. To arch or form like a roof. [Rare.]

And enter'd soon the shade
High *roof'd*, and walks beneath, and alleys brown.
Milton, P. R., ii. 293.

roof[2]†. An obsolete preterit of *rive*[1].

roof-cell (röf'sel), *n.* A nerve-cell found in the roof-nucleus.

roofer (rö'fėr), *n.* One who roofs, or makes and repairs roofs.

roof-gradation (röf'grā-dā'shon), *n.* In *salt-manuf.*, the system of utilizing the roofs of the large tanks containing the brine as evaporating-surfaces, by causing the contents of the tanks to flow in a thin and constant stream over the roofs.

roof-guard (röf'gärd), *n.* A board or an ornamental edging of ironwork placed just above the eaves of a roof to prevent snow from sliding off.

roofing (rö'fing), *n.* [< ME. **rofing, roving;* < *roof*[1] + *-ing*[1].] 1. The act of covering with a roof.—2. The materials of which a roof is composed, or materials for a roof.—3. The roof itself; hence, shelter.

Lete hem [walls] drie er thou thi bemes bent,
Or *rovyng* sette uppon, lest all be shent
For lacke of crafte.
Palladius, Husbondrie (E. E. T. S.), p. 15.

Which forme of *roofing* [flat] is generally used in all those Italian Cities. *Coryat*, Crudities, I. 204.

Fit *roofing* gave. *Southey.* (*Imp. Dict.*)

4. The ridge-cap of a thatched roof. *Halliwell.* [Prov. Eng.]—**Bay of roofing.** See *bay*[3].—**Carcass-roofing.** See *carcass*.—**Common roofing**, a roof-frame composed only of common rafters, with no principals.—**Roofing-felt.** See *felt*.—**Roofing-paper.** See *paper*.

roofless (röf'les), *a.* [< *roof*[1] + *-less.*] 1. Having no roof: as, a *roofless* house.

I, who lived
Beneath the wings of angels yesterday,
Wander to-day beneath the *roofless* world.
Mrs. Browning, Drama of Exile.

The great majority of the houses [in Sebastopol] were still *roofless* and in ruins. *D. M. Wallace*, Russia, p. 436.

2. Having no house or home; unsheltered.

roofiet (röf'let), *n.* [< *roof*[1] + *-let.*] A small roof or covering.

roof-like (röf'lik), *a.* Like a roof.

roof-nucleus (röf'nū"klē-us), *n.* The nucleus fastigii in the white matter of the cerebellum which forms the roof of the fourth ventricle. It lies close to the middle line.

roof-plate (röf'plāt), *n.* A wall-plate which receives the lower ends of the rafters of a roof.

roof-rat (röf'rat), *n.* A white-bellied variety of the black rat, specifically called *Mus tectorum*. See *black rat*, under *rat*[1].

roof-shaped (röf'shāpt), *a.* In *entom.*, shaped like a gable-roof; having two slanting surfaces meeting in a ridge.

roof-staging (röf'stā"jing), *n.* A scaffold used in working on an inclined roof. It holds fast to the roof automatically by means of barbed rods and claw-plates.

roof-stay (röf'stā), *n.* In boilers of the locomotive type, one of the stays which bind the arch or roof of the boiler to the crown-sheet of the fire-box, for the support of the crown-sheet against internal pressure.

roof-tree (röf'trē), *n.* [< ME. *roof-tree, ruff-tree;* < *roof*[1] + *tree.*] 1. The beam at the ridge of a roof; the ridge-pole.

Her head hat the *roof-tree* o' the house.
King Henry (Child's Ballads, I. 148).

Hence—2. The roof itself.

Phil blessed his stars that he had not assaulted his father's guest then and there, under his own *roof-tree*.
Thackeray, Philip, x.

To your roof-tree, in Scotland, a toast expressive of a wish for prosperity to one's family, because the roof-tree covers the house and all in it.

roof-truss (röf'trus), *n.* In *carp.*, the framework of a roof, consisting of thrust- and tie-pieces. *E. H. Knight.* See cuts under *roof* and *pendent*.

roof-winged (röf'wingd), *a.* In *entom.*, stegopterous: as a descriptive epithet, applied to many insects which hold their wings in the shape of a roof when at rest. See *Stegoptera*.

roofy (rö'fi), *a.* [< *roof*[1] + *-y*[1].] Having a roof.

Whether to *roofy* houses they repair,
Or sun themselves abroad in open air
Dryden, tr. of Virgil's Georgics, iii. 634.

rook[1] (rùk), *n.* [< ME. *rook, rok, roc,* < AS. *hrōc* = MD. *roeck*, D. *roek* = MLG. *rōk, rōke*, LG. *rok, rock* = OHG. *hruoh*, MHG. *ruoch* (cf. G. *ruchert*, a jackdaw) = Icel. *hrōkr* = Sw. *råka* = Dan. *raage* = Ir. Gael. *rocas*, a rook; cf. *rook*[1], *v.*, Gael. *roc*, croak, Goth. *hrūkjan*, crow as a cock, Skt. √ *kruc*, cry out: of imitative origin; cf. *croak, crow*[1], *crow*[2], etc.] 1. A kind of crow, *Corvus frugilegus*, abundant in Europe. It is entirely black, with the parts about the base of the bill more or less bare of feathers in the adult. The size is nearly or about that of the common crow; it is thus much smaller than the raven, and larger than the jackdaw. It is of a gregarious and sociable disposition, preferring to nest in rookeries about buildings, and feeding on insects and grain.

Rook (*Corvus frugilegus*).

The halle was al ful ywis
Of hem that writen olde gestes,
As ben on trees *rokes* nestes.
Chaucer, House of Fame, l. 1516.

He . . . saw the tops of the great elms, and the *rooks* circling about, and cawing remonstrances.
T. Hughes, Tom Brown at Rugby, i. 7.

2. The ruddy duck, *Erismatura rubida*. [Local, U. S.]—3. A cheat; a trickster or swindler; one who practises the "plucking of pigeons." See *pigeon*, 2.

Your city blades are cunning *rookes*,
How rarely you collogue him!
Songs of the London Prentices, p. 91. (*Halliwell.*)

The Butcherly execution of Tormentors, *Rooks*, and Rakeshames sold to lucre.
Milton, Reformation in Eng., ii.

4†. A simpleton; a gull; one liable to be cheated.

An arrant *rook*, by this light, a capable cheating-stock; a man may carry him up and down by the ears like a pipkin. *Chapman*, May-Day, iii. 2.

What! shall I have my son a Stager now? . . . a Gull, a *Rooke*, . . . to make suppers, and bee laughed at?
B. Jonson, Poetaster, i. 1.

5. [Cf. *crow*[2], 6, *crowbar.*] A crowbar. *Halliwell.* [Prov. Eng.]

rook[1] (rùk), *v.* [< *rook*[1], *n.*] **I.** *intrans.* 1. To caw or croak as a crow or raven. [Scotch.]—2. To cheat; defraud.

A band of *rooking* Officials, with cloke bagges full of Citations and Processes, to be serv'd by a corporalty of griffonlike Promooters and Apparitors.
Milton, Reformation in Eng., i.

II. *trans.* To cheat; defraud by cheating.

He was much *rooked* by gamesters, and fell acquainted with that unsanctified crew to his ruine.
Aubrey, Lives, Sir J. Denham.

His hand having been transfixed to a table, only because it innocently concealed a card, with which he merely meant to "*rook* the pigeon" he was then playing against.
Jon Bee, Essay on Samuel Foote.

rook[2] (rùk), *n.* [< ME. *rook, roke, rok* = MHG. *roch*, G. *roche*, < OF. (and F.) *roc* = Pr. *roc* = Sp. Pg. *roque* = It. *rocco* (ML. *rocus*) = Ar. Hind. *rukh*, < Pers. *rokh*, the rook or tower at chess: said to have meant 'warrior, hero'; cf. Pers. *rukh*, a hero, knight errant (also a rhinoceros, and a roc, a fabulous bird: see *roc*[1]).] In *chess*, one of the four pieces placed on the corner squares of the board; a castle. The rook may move along the ranks or the files the whole extent of the board unless impeded by some other piece. See *chess*[1].

After chec for the *roke* ware fore the mate,
For ȝif the foudment be false, the werke most nede falle.
MS. Douce 302, f. 4. (*Halliwell.*)

rook[3] (rùk), *v.* Same as *ruck*[1].

rooker[1]† (rùk'ėr), *n.* [< *rook*[1] + *-er*[1].] A sharper; a cheat; a swindler.

Rookers and sharpers work their several ends upon such as they make a prey of.
Kennet, tr. of Erasmus's Praise of Folly, p. 76. (*Davies.*)

rooker[2] (rùk'ėr), *n.* [< **rook, ruck*[3], + *-er*[1].] An L-shaped implement used by bakers to withdraw ashes from the oven.

rookery (rùk'ėr-i), *n.*; pl. *rookeries* (-iz). [< *rook*[1] + *-ery.*] 1. A place where rooks congregate to breed.

Its gray front stood out well from the background of a *rookery*, whose cawing tenants were now on the wing.
Charlotte Brontë, Jane Eyre, xi.

2. The rooks that breed in a rookery, collectively.

The many-winter'd crow that leads the clanging *rookery* home. *Tennyson*, Locksley Hall.

3. A place where birds or other animals resort in great numbers to breed. (*a*) The resort of various sea-birds, as auks, murres, guillemots, puffins, petrels, penguins, and cormorants, generally a rocky sea-coast or island. (*b*) The breeding-grounds of the fur-seal and other pinnipeds.

Millions of live seals to be seen hauled up on the *rookeries* [in the Pribylof Islands].
Arc. Cruise of the Corwin (1881), p. 18.

4. A cluster of mean tenements inhabited by people of the lowest class; a resort of thieves, tramps, ruffians, and the like.

All that remained, in the autumn of 1849, of this infamous *Rookery* (so called as a place of resort for sharpers and quarrelsome people) was included and condensed in ninety-five wretched houses in Church-lane and Carrier-street. *Murray*, London as it is (1860), p. 282. (*Hoppe.*)

The misery, the disease, the mortality in *rookeries*, made continually worse by artificial impediments to the increase of fourth-rate houses. *H. Spencer*, Man vs. State, p. 54.

5. A brothel. [Slang.]—6. A disturbance; a row. [Prov. Eng.]

rookle (rö'kl), *v. i.*; pret. and pp. *rookled*, ppr. *rookling*. [Irreg. var. of *routle.*] To rummage about; poke about with the nose, like a pig; root. [Prov. Eng.]

What 'll they say to me if I go a routing and *rookling* in their drains, like an old sow by the wayside?
Kingsley, Two Years Ago, xiv.

rookler (rök'lėr), *n.* [< *rookle* + *-er*[1].] One who or that which goes rookling or rooting about; a pig. [Prov. Eng.]

High-withered, furry, grizzled, game-flavoured little *rooklers*, whereof many a sounder still grunted about Swinley down. *Kingsley*, Westward Ho, viii.

rooky[1] (rùk'i), *a.* [< *rook*[1] + *-y*[1].] Abounding in rooks; inhabited by rooks: as, a *rooky* tree.

Light thickens; and the crow
Makes wing to the *rooky* wood.
Shak., Macbeth, iii. 2. 51.

[The above quotation is by some commentators held to bear the meaning of *rooky*[2].]

rooky[2] (rùk'i), *a.* Same as *roky*. *Brockett.* [Prov. Eng.]

rool (röl), *v. t.* and *i.* [Perhaps a contr. of *ruffle*[1].] To ruffle; rumple; pucker. [Prov. Eng.]

Whenever the balsam begins to *rool* or cause hitching of the specimen, add a few drops of the soap solution.
Jour. Roy. Micros. Soc., 2d ser., VI. i.

room[1]† (röm), *a.* [Early mod. E. **roum*, **rowm;* < ME. *roum, rom, rum,* < AS. *rūm* = OFries. *rum* = D. *ruim* = MLG. *rūm* = OHG. *rūmi*, MHG. *rūme, rūm* (also *gerūme, gerūm*, G. *geraum*) = Icel. *rūmr* = Goth. *rūms*, spacious, wide; perhaps akin to L. *rūs* (*rur-*), open country (see *rural*), OBulg. *ravĭnŭ* = Serv. *ravan* = Bohem. *rovný* = Pol. *rowny* = Russ. *rovnuĭ*, plain, even, Pol. *rownia* = Russ. *raviina*, a plain, etc., Zend *ravanh*, wide, free, open, *ravan*, a plain.] Wide; spacious; roomy.

Ye konne by argumentez make a place
A myle brood of twenty foot of space,
Lat se now if this place may suffise,
Or make it *rowm* [var. *rom*] with speche as is your gise.
Chaucer, Reeve's Tale, l. 205.

Ther was no *rommer* herberwe in the place.
Chaucer, Reeve's Tale, l. 225.

A renke in a rownde cloke, with right *rowmme* clothes.
Morte Arthure (E. E. T. S.), l. 3471.

Jhesu that made the planettes vij,
And all the worlde undur hevyn,
And made thys worlde wyde and *rome*.
MS. Cantab. Ff. ii. 38, f. 105. (*Halliwell.*)

room[1] (röm), *adv.* [< ME. *rome*, < AS. *rūme* (= D. *ruim*), wide, far, < *rūm*, wide: see *room*[1], *a.*] Far; at a distance; wide, in space or extent; in nautical use, off from the wind. [Obsolete except in nautical use.]

The geaunt was wonder strong,
Rome thretti fote long.
Beves of Hamtoun, l. 1860.

Rowse, quoth the ship against the rocks; *roomer* cry I in the cocke; my Lord wept for the company, I laught to comfort him. *Tragedy of Hoffman* (1631). (*Halliwell.*)

To go, steer, put, or **bear roomer**, to go off with the wind free; sail wide.

Yet did the master by all meanes assay
To *steare* out *roomer*, or to keepe aloofe.
Sir J. Harington, tr. of Orlando Furioso (1591), p. 343.
[(*Halliwell.*)

I have (as your Highnesse sees) past already the Godwins [Bishop Godwin], if I can as well passe over this Edwin Sands [another bishop], I will *goe roomer* of Greenwiche rocke.
Sir J. Harington, Addition to the Catalogue of Bishops
[(Nugæ Ant., II. 233).

We thought it best to returne vnto the harbor which we had found before, and so we *bare roomer* with the same.
Hakluyt's Voyages, I. 236.

The wind vering more Northerly, we were forced to *put roomer* with the coast of England againe.
Hakluyt's Voyages, I. 310.

room[1] (röm), *n.* [Early mod. E. also *rome, roum, rowm;* < ME. *roum, rowm, rum, rom,* < AS. *rūm*, room, = OS. *rūm* = D. *ruim* = MLG. LG. *rūm* = OHG. *rūmi, rūmin, rūm, rūn*, MHG. *rūm, rūn*, G. *raum*, space, room, = Icel. *rūm* = Sw. Dan. *rum* = Goth. *rūms*, space; from the adj.: see *room*[1], *a.* Cf. Pol., Sorbian, and Little Russ. *rum*, space, < OHG. *rūm*. Hence *roomy, rummage*, etc.] 1. Space; compass; extent of space, great or small: as, here is *room* enough for an army.

So he rid hym a *rowme* in a rad hast,
Of tho tulkes, with tene, that hym take wold.
Destruction of Troy (E. E. T. S.), l. 6478.

And, as their wealth increaseth, so inclose
Infinite riches in a little *room*.
Marlowe, Jew of Malta, i. 1.

Thou . . . hast not shut me up into the hand of the enemy; thou hast set my feet in a large *room*. Ps. xxxi. 8.

So doth the Circle in his Circuit span
More room then any other Figure can.
Sylvester, tr. of Du Bartas's Weeks, ii., The Columnes.

2. Space or place unoccupied or unobstructed; place for reception of any thing or person; accommodation for entering or for moving about: as, to make *room* for a carriage to pass.

There was no *room* for them in the inn. Luke ii. 7.

Now to sea we go,
Fair fortune with us, give us *room*, and blow.
Fletcher, Mad Lover, Prol.

There was no *room* for other pictures, because of the books which filled every corner.
Mrs. Oliphant, Poor Gentleman, i.

3. Fit occasion; opportunity; freedom to admit or indulge: as, in this case there is no *room* for doubt or for argument.

Men have still *room* left for commiseration.
Bacon, Moral Fables, vii., Expl.

He allowed your crimes to be great, but that still there was *room* for mercy. *Swift*, Gulliver's Travels, i. 7.

In his [the Prince Consort's] well-ordered life there seemed to be *room* for all things.
Gladstone, Gleanings, I. 5.

4. Place or station once occupied by another; stead, as in succession or substitution: as, one magistrate or king comes in the *room* of a former one.

After two years Porcius Festus came into Felix' *room*.
Acts xxiv. 27.

Poore silly groome,
Which tother day wouldst faine have had the *roome*
Of some base trencher-scraper.
Times' Whistle (E. E. T. S.), p. 27.

Like the valet, [he] seems to have entirely forgot his master's message, and substituted another in its *room* very unlike it. *Goldsmith*, Criticisms, xii.

The inland counties had not been required to furnish ships, or money in the *room* of ships.
Macaulay, Nugent's Hampden.

5. Any inclosure or division separated by partitions from other parts of a house or other structure; a chamber; an apartment; a compartment; a cabin, or the like: as, a drawing-*room*; a bedroom; a state-*room* in a ship; an engine-*room* in a factory; a harness-*room* in a stable.

Up from my cabin,
My sea-gown scarf'd about me, in the dark
Groped I, . . . and in fine withdrew
To mine own *room* again. *Shak.*, Hamlet, v. 2. 16.

Others adde that this Moloch had seuen *Roomes*, Chambers, or Ambries therein. *Purchas*, Pilgrimage, p. 97.

The central hall with its 16 columns, around which were arranged smaller *rooms* or cells.
J. Fergusson, Hist. Arch., I. 193.

6†. Particular place or station; a seat.

It behoveth every man to live in his own vocation, and not to seek any higher *room* than that whereunto he was at the first appointed.
Sir T. Wilson (Arber's Eng. Garner, I. 460).

And let an happie *roome* remaine for thee
'Mongst heavenly ranks, where blessed soules do rest.
Spenser, tr. of Virgil's Gnat, l. 57.

When thou art bidden of any man to a wedding, sit not down in the highest *room*. Luke xiv. 8.

7†. A box or seat in a theater.

I beg it with as forced a looke as a player that, in speaking an epilogue, makes love to the two-pennie *roume* for a plaudite.
Hospit. of Incurable Fooles (1600), Ded. (*Nares.*)

As if he had . . . ta'en tobacco with them over the stage, in the lords' *room*.
B. Jonson, Every Man out of his Humour, ii. 1.

8†. Family; company.

For offerd presents come,
And all the Greeks will honour thee, as of celestiall *roome*.
Chapman, Iliad, ix. 568.

9†. Office; post; position.

In consecrations and ordinations of men unto *rooms* of divine calling, the like [imposition of hands] was usually done from the time of Moses to Christ.
Hooker, Eccles. Polity, v. 66.

Euery man, according to his *roome*, bent to performe his office with alacritie and diligence.
Hakluyt's Voyages, II. 288.

He exercised his high *rome* of Chauncellorship, as he was accustomed. *G. Cavendish*, Wolsey.

10. A fishing-station; also, an establishment for curing fish. [British North America.]—11. A heading or working-place in a coal-mine.—**Blubber-room.** (*a*) In a whaling-ship, a place down the main hatch between decks where blubber is stowed away. It is merely a hold, which, when not used for stowing blubber, is usually filled up with oil-casks, fire-wood, etc. (*b*) The stomach: as, to fill the *blubber-room* (to take a hearty meal). [Whalers' slang.]—**Combination-room.** See *combination*.—**Commercial, common, dark room.** See the adjectives.—**Muniment-room.** See *muniment*.—**Pillar and room, stoop and room.** Same as *pillar and bread* (which see, under *pillar*).—**Room and space,** in *ship-building*, the distance from the joint of one frame to that of the adjoining one.—**To make room,** to open a way or passage; make space or place for any person or thing to enter or pass.=**Syn.** 3. Capacity, scope, latitude, range, sweep, swing, play.

room[1] (röm), *v. i.* [< *room*[1], *n.*] To occupy a room or rooms; lodge: as, he *rooms* at No. 7. [Colloq.]

I don't doubt I shall become very good, for just think what a place I am in—living at the minister's! and then I *room* with Esther! *H. B. Stowe*, Oldtown, p. 418.

room[2] (röm), *n.* [Also *roum*; Assamese.] A deep-blue dye like indigo, obtained by maceration from the shrub *Strobilanthes flaccidifolius* (*Ruellia indigotica*, etc.); also, the plant itself, which is native and cultivated in India, Burma, and China.

room[3] (röm), *n.* Dandruff. *Halliwell.* [Prov. Eng.]

roomage (rö'māj), *n.* [< *room*[1] + *-age.*] 1. Space; capacity.

Pile my ship with bars of silver, pack with coins of Spanish gold,
From keel piece up to deck-plank, the *roomage* of her hold!
Whittier, Cassandra Southwick.

2†. An obsolete form of *rummage*.

roomal, *n.* See *rumal*.

roomed (römd), *a.* [< *room*[1] + *-ed*[2].] Containing rooms; divided into rooms: used in composition: as, a ten-*roomed* house.

roomer (rö'mėr), *n.* One who hires a room; a lodger.

The mother . . . occupies herself more with the needs of the *roomers*, or tenants, and makes more money.
The Standard, VII. 4.

roomful (röm'fůl), *a.* [< *room*[1] + *-ful*, 1.] Abounding with rooms; roomy; spacious.

Now in a *roomful* house this soul doth float,
And, like a prince, she sends her faculties
To all her limbs, distant as provinces.
Donne, Progress of the Soul.

roomful (röm'fůl), *n.* [< *room*[1] + *-ful*, 2.] As much or as many as a room will hold: as, a *roomful* of people.

roomily (rö'mi-li), *adv.* [< *roomy* + *-ly*[2].] Spaciously.

roominess (rö'mi-nes), *n.* [< *roomy* + *-ness.*] The state of being roomy; spaciousness.

The oaken chair, to be sure, may tempt him with its *roominess*. *Hawthorne*, Seven Gables, xviii.

room-keeper (röm'kē"pėr), *n.* One who occupies a room in a house, with or without a family.

roomless (röm'les), *a.* [< *room*[1] + *-less.*] Without room or rooms; not affording space; contracted.

The shyppe wherein Jesus preached is very narowe and *roumles* to vncleane and synfull persons.
J. Udall, On Mark iii.

room-mate (röm'māt), *n.* One who shares a room with another or others.

We two Americans join company with our *room-mate*, an Alexandrian of Italian parentage.
B. Taylor, Lands of the Saracen, p. 28.

room-paper (röm'pā"pėr), *n.* Same as *wall-paper*.

room-ridden (röm'rid"n), *a.* Confined to one's room. Compare *bedridden*. [Rare.]

As the *room-ridden* invalid settled for the night.
Dickens, Little Dorrit, i. 15.

roomsome† (röm'sum), *a.* [< *room*[1] + *-some.*] Roomy.

In a more vnruly, more vnvveildie, and more *roomesome* vessell then the biggest hulke on Thames.
Florio, It. Dict., Ep. Ded., p. [11].

Not only capable but *roomsome*. *Evelyn.*

roomstead (röm'sted), *n.* [< *room*[1] + *stead.*] A lodging.

His greens take up six or seven houses or *roomsteads*.
Archæologia, XII. 188 (Account of Gardens near London, (1691).

roomth† (römth), *n.* [< ME. *rumthe*, *rymthe*, < AS. **rȳmth* (Lye), *rȳmet*, space (= MD. *ruimte*), < *rūm*, spacious: see *room*[1], *a.*] 1. Room or place, in any sense.

And when his voyce failed him at any time, Mecœnas supplied his *roomth* in reading.
Phaer, tr. of Virgil (1600). (*Nares.*)

The Seas (then wanting *roomth* to lay their boist'rous load)
Upon the Belgian Marsh their pamp'red stomachs cast.
Drayton, Polyolbion, v. 244.

2. Roominess; spaciousness.

A monstrous paunch for *roomth*, and wondrous wide.
Mir. for Mags., p. 100.

roomthsome† (römth'sum), *a.* [< *roomth* + *-some.*] Roomy; spacious.

By the sea-side, on the other side, stoode Heroe's tower; . . . a cage or pigeon-house, *roomthsome* enough to comprehend her. *Nashe*, Lenten Stuffe (Harl. Misc., VI. 167).

roomthy† (röm'thi), *a.* [< *roomth* + *-y*[1].] Spacious.

And her [Atre] not much behind
Comes Kensey; after whom, clear Bnian in doth make,
In Tamer's *roomthier* banks their rest that scarcely take.
Drayton, Polyolbion, i. 210.

roomy (rö'mi), *a.* [< *room*[1] + *-y*[1].] Having ample room; spacious; large.

Indeed, the city of glory is capacious and *roomy*; "In my Father's house there are many mansions."
Rev. T. Adams, Works, II. 252.

With *roomy* decks, her guns of mighty strength,
Whose lowlaid mouths each mounting billow laves.
Dryden, Annus Mirabilis, st. 153.

A very antique elbow-chair, with a high back, carved elaborately in oak, and a *roomy* depth within its arms.
Hawthorne, Seven Gables, ii.

roon[1]†, *a.* An obsolete form of *roan*[1].

roon[2] (rön), *n.* [A dial. form of *rund*, < Icel. *rönd*, rim, border, stripe, = E. *rand*: see *rand*[1].] A border; edge; selvage. [Scotch.]

In thae auld times, they thought the moon . . .
Wore by degrees, till her last *roon*
Gaed past their viewing.
Burns, To W. Simpson (Postscript).

Her face was like the lily *roon*
That veils the vestal planet's hue.
J. R. Drake, Culprit Fay.

[*Roon* in this passage is usually explained as 'vermilion,' apparently after Halliwell, who defines the Middle English *roone*, properly 'roan,' in one passage as 'vermilion.']

roop (röp), *v. i.* [Also dial. (Sc.) *roup*; < ME. *ropen*, < AS. *hrōpan* (pret. *hreóp*) = OS. *hrōpon* = OFries. *hrōpa* = D. *roepen* = MLG. *ropen* = OHG. *hruofan*, *ruofan*, MHG. *ruofen*, G. *rufen*, cry out; also in weak form, OHG. *ruofen*, MHG. *rüefen*, cry out, = Icel. *hrōpa*, call, cry out, in old use slander, = Sw. *ropa* = Dan. *raabe*, cry out, = Goth. *hrōpjan*, cry out. Cf. *roup.*] 1. To cry; shout. [Obsolete or prov. Eng. and Scotch.]—2. To roar; make a great noise.

And a *ropand* rayne raiked fro the heuyn.
Destruction of Troy (E. E. T. S.), l. 4631.

roop (röp), *n.* [Also (Sc.) *roup*; < ME. *rōp*, < AS. *hrōp* = OHG. **hruof*, *ruof*, MHG. *ruof*, G. *ruf*, a cry, = Icel. *hrōp*, crying, in old use caviling, scurrility, = Sw. *rop* = Dan. *raab*, a cry, a call, crying; cf. Goth. *hrōpei*, a cry; from the verb.] 1. A cry; a call.—2. Hoarseness.

O may the *roup* ne'er roust thy weason!
Beattie's Address (Ross's Helenore), st. 3. (*Jamieson.*)

roopit (rö'pit), *a.* [Also (Sc.) *roupit*, *roupet*; < *roop*, *n.*, + *-it* = *-ed*[2].] Hoarse; husky. [Scotch.]

Alas! my *roopit* Muse is hoarse!
Burns, Prayer to the Scotch Representatives.

roopy (rö'pi), *a.* [Also (Sc.) *roupy*; < *roop* + *-y*[1].] Hoarse.

He said he had observed I was sometimes hoarse—a little *roopy* was his exact expression.
Dickens, David Copperfield, vii.

roorback (rör'bak), *n.* [So called in allusion to certain fictions, published in the United States in 1844, devised for political purposes, but purporting to be taken from the "Travels of Baron *Roorbach*."] A fictitious story published for political effect; a "campaign lie." [U. S.]

Roosa (rö'sä), *n.* See *Rusa*.

roosa-oil (rö'sä-oil), *n.* See *rusa-oil*.

roose (röz), *v. t.*; pret. and pp. *roosed*, ppr. *roosing*. [Also dial. *rose*, *ruse*; < ME. *rosen*, < Icel. *hrōsa*, praise, extol, boast, = Sw. *rosa* = Dan. *rose*, praise.] To extol; commend highly. [Now only Scotch.]

To *rose* him [the king] in his rialty rych men soʒtten [sought]. *Alliterative Poems* (ed. Morris), ii. 1371.

To *roose* you up, and ca' you guid.
Burns, Dedication to Gavin Hamilton.

roost[1] (röst), *n.* [< ME. **rost*, < AS. *hrōst*, given by Somner ("*hrost*, al. *henna hrost*, petaurum, a hen-roost"), and contained also in the compound *hrōst-beág*, a poetical term of uncertain meaning, explained as 'the woodwork of a circular roof'; = OS. *hrōst*, roof, = MD. *roest*, a hen-roost, = Icel. *hraust*, roof, ceiling, = Norw. *rost*, *raust*, *röst*, roof, roofing, space under the roof; prob. orig. the inner framework of a roof (as in Sc.); prob., with formative *-st*, from the same root (√ *hro*) as Icel. *hrōt*, a roof, *rōt*, the inner part of the roof of a house where fish are hung up to dry, = Norw. *rot*, a roof, the inner part of a roof, a cockloft, = Goth. *hrōt*, a roof. The Sc. sense (def. 4) is prob. of Scand. origin (< Norw. *rost*, see above).] 1. A pole or perch upon which fowls rest at night; any place upon which a bird may perch to rest; also, a locality where birds, as pigeons, habitually spend the night.

Who [the cock] daily riseth when the Sun doth rise,
And when Sol setteth, then to *roost* he hies.
Sylvester, tr. of Du Bartas's Weeks, i. 5.

He clapp'd his wings upon his *roost*.
Dryden, Cock and Fox, l. 46.

Thousands of white gulls, gone to their nightly *roost*, rested on every ledge and cornice of the rock.
B. *Taylor*, Northern Travel, p. 304.

These *roosts* [of wild pigeons] have been known to extend for a distance of forty miles in length and several miles in breadth.
Stand. Nat. Hist., IV. 251.

Hence—2. A temporary abiding- or resting-place.

No, the world has a million *roosts* for a man, but only one nest.
O. W. Holmes, Autocrat, vi.

3. The fowls which occupy such a roost, collectively. A somewhat special application of the word (like *rookery*, 2) is to the roosts of some perching birds, which assemble in vast numbers, but not to breed, and for no obvious purpose that would not be as well attained without such congregation. Among conspicuous instances may be noted the roosts of the passenger-pigeon, sometimes several miles in extent, and the winter roosts of many thousands of crows (see *crow*, 2), which in the breeding season are dispersed. It is not generally known that the common robin of the United States sometimes forms such roosts in summer.
4. The inner roof of a cottage, composed of spars reaching from one wall to the other; a garret. *Jamieson.* [Scotch.]—**At roost**, roosting; hence, in a state of rest or sleep.

A fox spied out a cock *at roost* upon a tree.
Sir R. L'Estrange.

roost[1] (röst), *v.* [= MD. *roesten*, roost; from the noun.] I. *intrans.* 1. To occupy a roost; perch, as a bird.

O let me, when Thy roof my soul hath hid,
O let me *roost* and nestle there.
G. *Herbert*, The Temper.

So [I] sought a Poet, *roosted* near the skies.
Burns, Address spoken by Miss Fontenelle.

The peacock in the broad ash-tree
Aloft is *roosted* for the night.
Wordsworth, White Doe of Rylstone, iv.

2. To stick or stay upon a resting-place; cling or adhere to a rest, as a limpet on a rock.

The larger number of limpets *roost* upon rocks.
Nature, XXXI. 200.

II. *trans.* To set or perch, as a bird on a roost: used reflexively.

I wonder,
How that profane nest of pernicious birds
Dare *roost themselves* there in the midst of us,
So many good and well-disposed persons.
O impudence! *Randolph*, Muses' Looking-glass, i. 1.

roost[2] (röst), *n.* and *v.* See *roust*[2].
roost-cock (röst'kok), *n.* A cock; a rooster. [Prov. Eng.]

Gallus, that greatest *roost-cock* in the rout.
The Mous-Trap (1606). (*Halliwell*, under *porpentine*.)

rooster (rös'tėr), *n.* 1. The male of the domestic hen; a cock, as distinguished from the female or hen. [U. S.]

A huge turkey gobbling in the road, a *rooster* crowing on the fence, and ducks quacking in the ditches.
S. Judd, Margaret, ii. 1.

2. Any bird that roosts; a percher. See *Insessores*.

Almost all birds are *roosters*.
R. G. White, Words and their Uses, p. 182.

root[1] (röt or rût), *n.* [< ME. *roote*, *rote*, < late AS. *rōt* (acc. pl. *rota*, occurring in connection with *barc* (see *bark*[2]) in a fragment printed in AS. Leechdoms, I. 378), < Icel. *rōt* = Sw. Norw. *rot* = Dan. *rod*, a root, the lower part of a tree, a root in mathematics; prob. orig. with initial *w* (Icel. *v*, reg. lost before *r*), Icel. **vrōt* = AS. **wrōt*, a collateral form of *wyrt* = OHG. MHG. *wurz*, G. *wurz*, a plant, = Goth. *waurts*, a root; prob. akin to W. *gwreiddyn* = OCorn. *grueiten*, a root, L. *rādix* (√ *vrad*), a root, = Gr. ῥάδιξ (√ Ϝραδ), a branch, a root, ῥίζα (for *Ϝρίδya, √ Ϝριδ), a root: see *wort*[1], and cf. *radix*, *rhizome*. See also *root*[2].] 1. (*a*) In *bot.*, a part of the body of a plant which, typically, grows downward into the soil, fixes the plant, and absorbs nutriment. A root may be either a descending axis originating in germination from the lower end of the caulicle, and persisting as a *tap-root*, or one of a group of such roots—in either case called *primary*; or a branch of such a root, the ultimate ramifications forming rootlets or *root-fibrils*; or a similar organ developed from some other part of the plant (adventitious), sometimes with special functions—in the latter cases called *secondary*. The root differs from the stem in having no nodes and internodes, its branches appearing in no regular order, and, normally, in giving rise to no other organs, though, as in the pear and poplar, it may develop buds and thence suckers. In mode of growth the root is peculiar in elongating only or chiefly at the extremity, and at the same time in not building upon the naked apex, but in a stratum (the growing-point) just short of the apex under the protection of a cover or sheath—the *root-cap* (which see). Aside from securing the plant in position, the ordinary function of roots is the absorption of water with nutritive matter in solution from the soil, or, in the case of aquatics, wholly or partly from the water. This office is performed by imbibition through the cell-walls of the fresher root-surface, except that of the extreme tip, the absorbent surface being greatly increased by the production of root-hairs. (See *root-hair*.) Many roots, however—chiefly the tap-roots of biennials—serve the special purpose of storing nutriment for a second season, becoming thus much enlarged, as in the beet and turnip. Roots of this class must be distinguished from the rhizome, bulb, etc., which, though subterranean, are modifications of the stem. Numerous plants put forth aërial roots, eventually reaching the soil (banian, mangrove),

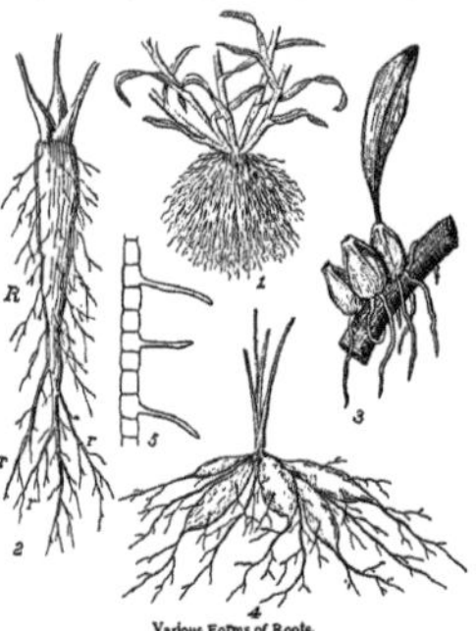

Various Forms of Roots.
1. Fibrous Roots of *Poa annua*. 2. Root of *Daucus Carota*; *R*, tap-root; *r*, *r*, rootlets. 3. Aërial Roots of *Oncidium ciliatum*. 4. Tuberous Roots of *Anemone thalictroides*. 5. Root-hairs of *Yucca gloriosa* (highly magnified).

serving as means of climbing (ivy, poison-ivy), or, in the case of epiphytes, part fastening the plant to a bough, part free in the air, whence they are capable of absorbing some moisture. The roots of a parasitic plant penetrate the tissues of the host-plant and draw their nutritive matter from it. True roots are confined to flowering plants and vascular cryptogams, the rhizoids of many lower plants in part taking their place. See *annual*, *biennial*, *perennial*. See also cuts under *ivy*, *monocotyledonous*, *prothallium*, and *rhizome*.

An oak whose antique root peeps out
Upon the brook that brawls along this wood.
Shak., As you Like it, ii. 1. 31.

(*b*) Specifically, an esculent root, as a beet or a carrot.

But his neat cookery! he cut our roots
In characters. *Shak.*, Cymbeline, iv. 2. 49.

2. That which resembles a root in shape, position, or function; that from which anything springs. (*a*) The part of anything that resembles the root of a plant in manner of growth, or as a source of nourishment, support, or origin; specifically, in *anat.* and *zoöl.*, some part or organ like or likened to the root of a plant; the deepest or most fixed part of something embedded in another; a base, bottom, or supporting part: technically called *radix*: as, the root of a finger-nail or a tooth; the root of a nerve or a hair: often used in the plural, though the thing in fact is singular: as, to drag out a nail by the roots.

The oolde blode that was at our lordes herte *rote*
Fell within Iosephes sherte & lay on his chest.
Joseph of Arimathie (E. E. T. S.), p. 38.

Each false [word]
Be as a cauterizing to the *root* o' the tongue.
Shak., T. of A., v. 1. 136.

Hence—(*b*) The bottom or lower part of anything; foundation.

Ther is at the west syde of Itaille,
Doun at the *roote* of Vesulus the colde,
A lusty playne, abundant of vitaille.
Chaucer, Clerk's Tale, l. 2.

The Mount, which was a frame of wood built by Master More for a Watch-tower to looke out to Sea, was blowne up by the *roots*.
Quoted in *Capt. John Smith's* Works, II. 150.

In the Domdaniel caverns,
Under the *Roots* of the Ocean,
Met the Masters of the Spell.
Southey, Thalaba, ii. 2.

(*c*) The origin or cause of anything; source.

Whan that Aprille with his shoures soote
The droghte of Marche hath perced to the *roote*.
Chaucer, Gen. Prol. to C. T., l. 2.

The love of money is the root of all [all kinds of, R. V.] evil. 1 Tim. vi. 10.

(*d*) The basis of anything; ground; support.

The *root* of his opinion. *Shak.*, W. T., ii. 3. 89.

With a courage of unshaken *root*.
Cowper, Table-Talk, l. 15.

(*e*) In *philol.*, an elementary notional syllable; that part of a word which conveys its essential meaning, as distinguished from the formative parts by which this meaning is modified: an element in a language, whether arrived at by analysis of words or existing uncombined, in which no formative element is demonstrable: thus, *true* may be regarded as the root of un-*tru*-th-ful-ness.

But we must beware of pushing the figure involved in *root* to the extent of regarding *roots* thus set up as the elements out of which the language containing them has grown. A given root may be more modern than certain or than all of the formative elements with which it is combined.
Whitney, Trans. Amer. Philol. Ass., XVII., App., p. xx.

Equity and equal are from the same *root*; and equity literally means equalness.
H. Spencer, Social Statics, p. 109.

(*f*) The first ancestor; an early progenitor.

Myself should be the *root* and father
Of many kings. *Shak.*, Macbeth, iii. 1. 5.

(*g*) In *math.*: (1) The root of any quantity is such a quantity as, when multiplied into itself a certain number of times, will exactly produce that quantity. Thus, 2 is a root of 4, because when multiplied into itself it exactly produces 4. *Power* and root are correlative terms: the power is named from the number of the factors employed in the multiplication, and the root is named from the power. Thus, if a quantity be multiplied once by itself, the product is called the *second power*, or *square*, and the quantity itself the *square root*, or second root of the product; if the quantity be multiplied twice by itself, we obtain the *third power*, or *cube*, and the quantity is the *cube* root or third root; and so on. The character marking a root is $\sqrt{}$ (a modification of r for *radix*, which has been used probably since the middle of the sixteenth century), and the particular root is indicated by placing above the sign the figure which expresses the number of the root, which figure is called the *index* of the root. Thus, $\sqrt[4]{16}$ indicates the fourth root of 16 (that is, 2), and $\sqrt{4}$ the square root of 4 (that is, 2)—the index in the case of the square root being usually omitted. The same is the case with algebraic quantities, as $\sqrt[3]{(a^3 + 3a^2b + 3ab^2 + b^3)} = a + b$. See *power*[1], *index*, *involution*, *evolution*. (2) The root of an equation is a quantity which, substituted for the unknown quantity, satisfies the equation: thus, $2 + \sqrt{2}$ is a root of the equation $x^3 - 5x^2 + 6x - 2 = 0$; for

$$\begin{aligned} (2+\sqrt{2})^3 &= 20 + 14\sqrt{2} \\ -5(2+\sqrt{2})^2 &= -30 - 20\sqrt{2} \\ +6(2+\sqrt{2}) &= 12 + 6\sqrt{2} \\ -2 &= -2, \end{aligned}$$

the sum of which is 0. Another root of the same equation is obviously 1; and the third root will be found to be $2 - \sqrt{2}$. (*h*) In *music*: (1) With reference to a compound tone or a series of harmonics, the fundamental, generator, or ground tone. (2) With reference to a chord, the fundamental tone—that is, the tone from whose harmonics the tones of the chord are selected, or the tone on which they are conceived to be built up. Theorists are not agreed as to what constitutes a root of a chord, or whether a chord may have two roots; and in many cases the term is used merely to designate the lowest tone of a chord when arranged in its simplest or normal position. (*i*) In *chron.*, the earliest time at which an event can take place, as a movable feast; also, the time at which any progressive change begins. (*j*) In *astrol.*, the state of things at the beginning of any time; particularly, the figure of the heavens at the instant of birth, specifically called the *root of nativity*, a term also applied to the horoscope, or ascendant. Chaucer, in the passage below, has in mind the introduction to Zahel's treatise on Elections, where it is stated that elections of fortunate times for undertakings are not much to be depended upon, except in the case of kings, who have their *roots of nativity* (that is, in their case there is no doubt as to the precise aspect of the heavens at the moment of birth), which roots strengthen the inferences to be drawn, especially (at least so Chaucer understands the words) in the case of a journey. When the horoscope of birth was not known, astrologers were accustomed to determine elections chiefly by the place and phase of the moon, whose influence was, however, considered debile. It appears that in the case of the lady of the story, the moon was impedited in the *root of nativity* (see Almansor, Prop. 35: "Cum in radice nativitatis impedietur luna," etc.), and Mars, a planet most unfavorable to journeys, was at azir, or lord of the ascendant, at her birth, and was in the fourth, or darkest, house; so that the omens of the journey were as gloomy as they well could be.

Of viage is ther non eleccioun,
Namely to folk of hey condicioun,
Not whan a *rote* is of a birthe yknowe?
Chaucer, Man of Law's Tale, l. 216.

(*k*) In *hydraul. engin.*, the end of a weir or dam where it is joined to the natural bank. *E. H. Knight.*
3. In *hort.*, a growing plant with its root; also, a tuber or bulb.

Your herb-woman; she that sets seeds and *roots*.
Shak., Pericles, iv. 6. 93.

Perhaps the pleasantest of all cries in early spring is that of "All a-growing—all a-blowing," heard for the first time in the season. It is that of the root-seller, who has stocked his barrow with primroses, violets, and daisies.
Mayhew, London Labour and London Poor, I. 138.

4. Gross amount; sum total. *Halliwell.*—**Aërial roots.** See def. 1.—**Bear's-paw root**, the rhizome of the male fern, *Aspidium Filix-mas*.—**Bengal root**, the root of a species of ginger, *Zingiber Cassumunar*.—**Biquadratic root.** See *biquadratic*.—**Commensurable root**, a root of an equation equal to a whole number or fraction.—**Conjugate roots.** See *conjugate*.—**Continuity of roots**, the fact that the values of the roots of an algebraic equation vary continuously with the coefficients.—**Criterion for roots**, a rule for deciding whether a solution is multiple or not, how many solutions are imaginary, and the like.—**Crop and root.** See *crop*.—**Crown of a root.** See *crown*.—**Cubocubic root.** See *cubocubic*.—**Demonstrative root.** See *demonstrative*.—**Double root**, in *music*, two tones assumed as the generators of one chord.—**Dutch roots or bulbs**, a trade-name of certain ornamental flowering bulbs, especially tulips and hyacinths, exported from Holland.—**Equal roots**, two or more roots of an equation having the same value. That is, if x_1 is such a root, the equation is not only satisfied by putting x_1 for x, the unknown quantity, but this is also true after the equation (with all its terms equated to zero) has been divided by $x - x_1$.—**Fibrous roots**, roots in the form of fibers—the

regular form of roots except so far as they are thickened for strength as holdfasts or by the accumulation of nutriment.—**Horizontal root**, in *bot.*, a root that lies horizontally on the ground.—**Latent roots of a matrix**, in *math.* See *latent*.—**Lateral root of the auditory nerve**, the root which passes on the outer side of the restiform tract. Also called *superficial*, *inferior*, or *posterior root*; also sometimes *radix cochlearis*.—**Limit of the roots.** See *limit*.—**Mechoacan root**, a jalap-tuber of very feeble properties, obtained from Mexico, apparently identical with the *Ipomœa Jalapa* (*I. macrorhiza*) found in the southern United States from South Carolina to Florida.—**Medial root of the auditory nerve**, the root which passes on the inner side of the restiform tract, between the latter and the ascending root of the trigeminus. Also called *deep*, *anterior*, or *upper root*; sometimes *radix vestibularis*.—**Musquash-root.** Same as *beaver-poison*.—**Primary root.** See *primary*, and def. 1, above.—**Primitive root**, a root of an equation or congruence which satisfies no lower equation that implies the truth of the former. Thus, 9 is a root of the congruence $x^4 \equiv 1$ (mod 10), but not a primitive root, since it also satisfies $x^2 \equiv 1$ (mod 10). For *primitive root* in various specific phrases, see *primitive*.—**Quadratocubic root, quadratoquadratic root.** See the adjectives.—**Root and branch.** (a) As a whole; wholly; completely.

He was going and leaving his malison on us, *root and branch*. I was never so becursed in all my days.
C. Reade, Cloister and Hearth, xlviii.

(b) In *Eng. hist.*, the extremists of the Parliamentary party who about 1641 favored the overthrow of Episcopacy; also, the policy of these extremists.—**Root of a hair**, the portion contained in the follicle, the lower portion being the bulb.—**Root of a lung**, the place where the bronchi and large vessels enter a lung.—**Root of an equation.** See *equation*, and def. 2 (g) (2).—**Root of bitterness.** See *bitterness*.—**Root of the mesentery**, the junction of the mesentery with the body-wall.—**Root of the tongue**, the posterior basal part of the tongue.—**Secondary root.** See def. 1 (a).—**Separation of the roots of an equation**, the separation of the whole field of quantity into such parts that there shall be only one root at most in each part.—**The root of the matter**, that which is fundamental or essential.

But ye should say, Why persecute we him, seeing *the root of the matter* is found in me? Job xix. 28.

To **extract the root.** See *extract*.—To **take root**, or to **strike root.** (a) To begin rooting in germination or (more frequently) as a layer, cutting, or transplanted plant. (b) To become fixed; become established.

If we shall stand still,
In fear our motion will be mock'd or carp'd at,
We should *take root* here where we sit.
Shak., Hen. VIII., i. 2. 87.

Deep *strike* thy *roots*, O heavenly Vine,
Within our earthly sod. *Whittier*, Our Master.

(See also *bloodroot*, *bowman's-root*, *cancer-root*, *colic-root*, *musk-root*, *orris-root*, *rattlesnake-root*, and *snakeroot*.)

root[1] (röt or rụ̈t), *v.* [= Sw. *rota*, take root; from the noun. Cf. *root*[2].] **I.** *intrans.* **1.** To fix the root; strike root; enter the earth, as roots.

In deep grounds the weeds *root* the deeper.
Mortimer, Husbandry.

2. To be firmly fixed; be established.

There rooted betwixt them then such an affection which cannot choose but branch now. *Shak.*, W. T., i. 1. 25.

If any error chanced . . . to cause misapprehensions, he gave them not leave to root and fasten by concealment.
Bp. Fell.

II. *trans.* **1.** To fix by the root or as if by roots; plant and fix deep in the earth: as, a tree *roots* itself; a deeply *rooted* tree.

The fat weed
That *roots* itself in ease on Lethe wharf.
Shak., Hamlet, i. 5. 33.

2. To plant deeply; impress deeply and durably: used chiefly in the past participle.

Canst thou not minister to a mind diseased,
Pluck from the memory a *rooted* sorrow?
Shak., Macbeth, v. 3. 41.

root[2] (röt or rụ̈t), *v.* [Also *rout*, early mod. E. *wroot*, *wrout*; < ME. *roten*, *routen*, prop. *wroten*, < AS. *wrōtan*, root or grub up, as a hog, = NFries. *wrotten* = MD. D. *wroeten* = MLG. *wrōten*, LG. *wrōten*, root or grub in the earth, = OHG. *ruozjan*, *ruozzan*, root up (cf. G. *rotten*, *reuten*, *roden*, root out), = Icel. *rōta* = Sw. Norw. *rota* = Dan. *rode*, root, grub up; connected with the noun, AS. *wrōt* = OFries. **wrōte*, snout, = OHG. dim. **ruozil*, MHG. *rüezel*, G. *rüssel*, snout; perhaps allied to L. *rodere*, gnaw, nag, and to *radere*, scratch: see *rodent*, *rase*[1], *raze*[1]. The verb is commonly associated with the noun root[1] as if root *up* or *up*root meant 'pull up the roots of,' 'pull up by the roots'; but it means rather 'raise or plow up with the snout,' and is orig. applied to swine.] **I.** *trans.* **1.** To dig or burrow in with the snout; turn up with the snout, as a swine.

Alas, he [the boar] nought esteems that face of thine, . . .
Would root these beauties as he roots the mead.
Shak., Venus and Adonis, l. 636.

2. To tear up or out as if by rooting; eradicate; extirpate; remove or destroy utterly; exterminate: generally with *up*, *out*, or *away*.

Er that eight dais were ended fully,
Al the wodys were *roted up* and gon.
Rom. of Partenay (E. E. T. S.), l. 1112.

I will go *root away*
The noisome weeds. *Shak.*, Rich. II., iii. 4. 37.

He's a rank weed, Sir Thomas,
And we must *root* him *out*.
Shak., Hen. VIII., v. 1. 53.

II. *intrans.* **1.** To turn up the earth with the snout, as swine.

Al swa that wilde swin
That *wroteth* zeond than grouen.
Layamon, l. 469.

Doo heestes smale in hit [earth] to stere and stonde,
And make hem *route* aboute, and trede.
Palladius, Husboudrie (E. E. T. S.), p. 158.

The kyng that had grete plente
Off mete and drinke, withoutene le,
Long he may dyge and *wrote*,
Or he have hys tyll of the rote.
MS. Ashmole 61. (*Halliwell*.)

Thou elvish-mark'd, abortive, *rooting* hog!
Shak., Rich. III., i. 3. 228.

2†. To push with the snout.

Delphyns knowe by smello yf a deed man that is in the see ete euer of Delphyns kynde, and yf the deed hath ete therof he etyth hym anone, and yf be dyde not he kepyth and defendyth hym fro etynge and bytynge of other fisshe, and showyth hym and bryngyth him to the clyffe with his own *wrotynge*.
Glanvil, De Propr. Rerum, XIII. xxvi. 460 (Cath. Ang., p. 425).

root[3] (röt), *n.* A form of *rut*[1]. *Halliwell.* [Prov. Eng.]

root[4] (rọ̈t), *v.* A dialectal form of *rot*.

rootage[1] (rö'tāj or rụ̈t'āj), *n.* [< *root*[1] + *-age*.] The act of striking root; the growth or fixture of roots; the hold obtained by means of a root or roots. [Rare.]

Ours is, scarcely less than the British [government], a living and fecund system. It does not, indeed, find its *rootage* so widely in the hidden soil of unwritten law; its tap-root at least is the Constitution.
W. Wilson, Cong. Gov., i.

rootage[2] (rö'tāj or rụ̈t'āj), *n.* [< *root*[2] + *-age*.] Extirpation. *Halliwell.*

root-alcohol (röt'al'kō-hol), *n.* See *alcohol*, 1.

root-barnacle (röt'bär'na-kl), *n.* A root-headed cirriped. See *Rhizocephala*.

root-beer (röt'bēr), *n.* A drink containing the extracted juices of various roots, as of dock, dandelion, sarsaparilla, and sassafras.

No less than five persons, during the forenoon, inquired for ginger-beer, or *root-beer*, or any drink of a similar brewage. *Hawthorne*, Seven Gables, iii.

root-borer (röt'bōr'ėr), *n.* An insect which perforates the roots of plants; as, the clover *root-borer*, *Hylesinus trifolii*.

root-bound (röt'bound), *a.* Fixed to the earth by roots; firmly fixed, as if by the root; immovable.

And you a statue, or, as Daphne was,
Root-bound, that fled Apollo.
Milton, Comus, l. 662.

root-breaker (röt'brā'kėr), *n.* A machine for breaking potatoes, turnips, carrots, or other raw roots into small or moderate-sized pieces, in order to prepare them as food for cattle or horses.

root-bruiser (röt'brö'zėr), *n.* Same as *root-breaker*.

root-built (röt'bilt), *a.* Built of roots.

Philosophy requires
No lavish cost; to crown its utmost prayer
Suffice the *root-built* cell, the simple fleece,
The juicy viand, and the crystal stream.
Shenstone, Economy, i.

root-cap (röt'kap), *n.* A cap-like layer of parenchymatous cells which occurs at the tip of growing roots. It may be several or many or only two or three layers of cells thick, the cells composing it being older, firmer, and in part effete, and serving to protect the active growing-point, which is immediately behind it.

At the very end of the radicle they [the cells] are relatively large, and form a sort of cap-like covering (*root-cap*) for the smaller cells lying directly back (the growing point). *Goodale*, Physiol. Bot., p. 106.

root-cellar (röt'sel'ạ̈r), *n.* A cellar or part of a cellar set apart for the storage of roots or tubers, as potatoes. Compare root-*house*, 2.

root-crop (röt'krop), *n.* A crop of plants with esculent roots, especially of plants having single roots, as turnips, beets, or carrots.

root-digger (röt'dig'ėr), *n.* In *agri.*, a form of tongs with curved jaws for raising carrots and beets from the ground.

root-eater (röt'ē'tėr), *n.* A rhizophagous marsupial; a member of the *Rhizophaga*; any root-eating animal.

root-eating (röt'ē'ting), *a.* Feeding habitually upon roots; rhizophagous.

rooted (rö'ted or rụ̈t'ed), *a.* [< *root*[1] + *-ed*[2].] **1.** Fixed by a root or roots; firmly planted or embedded.—**2.** In *zoöl.* and *anat.*: (a) Fixed by the roots; embedded and attached as if rooted, as a hair, feather, nail, or tooth. (b) Specifically, fixed so by the root as to cease to grow, as a tooth: the opposite of root*less*.—**3.** Provided with roots.

rootedly (rö'ted-li or rụ̈t'ed-li), *adv.* [< *rooted* + *-ly*[2].] Deeply; from the heart.

They all do hate him
As *rootedly* as I. *Shak.*, Tempest, iii. 2. 103.

rootedness (rö'ted-nes or rụ̈t'ed-nes), *n.* [< *rooted* + *-ness*.] The state or condition of being rooted.

rooter[1] (rö'tėr or rụ̈t'ėr), *n.* [< root[1] + *-er*[1].] A plant (or, figuratively, some other thing, or a person) which takes root.

They require dividing and planting on fresh soil frequently, being strong *rooters*. *The Field*, LXVII. 338.

rooter[2] (rö'tėr or rụ̈t'ėr), *n.* [< root[2] + *-er*[1].] One who or that which roots or roots up, or tears up by the roots; one who eradicates or destroys.

The strongest champion of the Pagan gods,
And *rooter* out of Christians.
Massinger, Virgin-Martyr, i. 1.

rootery (rö'tėr-i or rụ̈t'ėr-i), *n.*; pl. *rooteries* (-iz). [< root[1] + *-ery*.] A mound or pile formed with the roots of trees, in which plants are set as in a rockery. *Imp. Dict.*

rootfast (röt'fast), *a.* [< ME. *rotfest* (= Icel. *rōtfastr*); < *root*[1] + *fast*[1].] Firmly rooted.

root-fibril (röt'fī'bril), *n.* One of the fine ultimate divisions of a root; a rootlet; less properly, same as root-*hair*.

root-footed (röt'fụ̈t'ed), *a.* Provided with pseudopodia. See *pseudopodium* and *rhizopod*.

root-forceps (röt'fôr'seps), *n.* In *dentistry*, a forceps for extracting roots of teeth.

root-form (röt'fôrm), *n.* A form assumed by an insect when radicicolous or living on roots, if different from some other form of the same insect: thus, the grape-vine pest, *Phylloxera vastatrix*, is most destructive in its root-*form*.

root-grafting (röt'graf'ting), *n.* In *hort.*, the process of grafting scions directly on a small part of the root of some appropriate stock, the grafted root being then potted.

root-hair (röt'hãr), *n.* A delicate filament developed from a single cell (thus distinguished from a root-fibril) on the epidermis of the young parts of a root; a unicellular trichome borne on a root. The office of root-hairs is absorption, and they are often so numerous as greatly to enlarge the absorbent capacity of the root. As the surface ripens, they shrivel and disappear. See cut under *root*.

root-headed (röt'hed'ed), *a.* Fixed as if rooted by the head; having a head like roots; rhizocephalous: as, the root-*headed* cirripeds.

root-house (röt'hous), *n.* **1.** A rustic house or lodge built ornamentally of roots.

Winding forward down the valley, you pass beside a small *root-house*, where on a tablet are these lines.
Shenstone, Works (ed. 1791), II. 289.

2. A house for storing up or depositing potatoes, turnips, carrots, cabbages, or other roots or tops, for the winter feed of cattle.

root-knot (röt'not), *n.* A knot or excrescence of a root; specifically, an abnormal irregular growth of the subcortical layer of tissue of roots and underground stems of various plants, shrubs, and trees, resulting from the attack of a nematoid worm, as a species of *Anguillulidæ*.

rootle (rö'tl), *v. t.*; pret. and pp. root*led*, ppr. root*ling*. [Freq. of root[2].] To root up, as swine. *Halliwell.* [Prov. Eng.]

root-leaf (röt'lēf), *n.* A radical leaf. See *radical leaves*, under *radical*.

rootless (röt'- or rụ̈t'les), *a.* [< *root*[1] + *-less*.] **1.** Having no root.

But by a long continuance, a stronge depe roted habitte, not lyke a *rooteles* tree, scante vp an end in a lose heape of light sand, that wil with a blast or two be blowen down.
Sir T. More, Works, p. 1:0.

2. In *zoöl.*, having a persistently open pulp-cavity and growing perennially, as the incisor teeth of rodents, and the molar teeth of many of these animals; not rooted so as to stop growing. See *Rodentia*.

rootlet (röt'- or rụ̈t'let), *n.* [< *root*[1] + *-let*.] A little root; a radicle; a root-fibril: specifically applied to the fine roots put forth by certain plants, by which they cling to their supports, as in *Rhus Toxicodendron*.

The tree whose *rootlets* drink of every river.
Kingsley, Saint's Tragedy, v. 2.

root-loop (röt'löp), *n.* An arch or bow in a root, standing out of the ground.

root-louse (röt'lous), *n.* One of a number of radicicolous or root-feeding plant-lice of the family *Aphididæ*, and usually of the subfamily *Pemphiginæ*. The grape-vine root-louse is an example. (See *Phylloxera*.) The root-louse of the apple is *Schizo-*

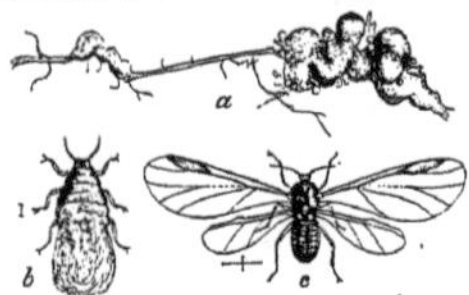

Root-louse of the Apple (*Schizoneura lanigera*).
a, apple-root, showing swellings caused by lice; *b*, wingless stem-mother, or first spring generation; *c*, winged agamic female. (Line and cross show natural sizes.)

neura lanigera, apparently indigenous to America, but now occurring in Europe, New Zealand, and Australia, where it is known as the *American blight*. It passes the winter under ground in the wingless condition, and also as a winter egg on the trunk. It spreads by means of an occasional generation of winged agamic females. It has an above-ground summer form which is furnished with a flocculent excretion of white wax.

root-mouthed (röt'moutht), *a.* In *zoöl.*, rhizostomous.

root-parasite (röt'par″a-sīt), *n.* A plant which grows upon the root of another plant, as plants of the order *Orobanchaceæ*, or broom-rapes.

root-pressure (röt'presh″ụ̈r), *n.* In *bot.*, a hydrostatic pressure exerted in plants, which manifests itself by causing, especially in the spring, a more or less copious flow of watery fluid from the cut surface of a part of the stem which is directly connected with the root. This flow of sap is the so-called "bleeding" of plants, and is found to be the result of the absorbent activity of the root-hairs.

In a vine, for example, before its leaves have grown in the spring, this process, called *root-pressure*, causes a rapid ascent of fluid (sap) absorbed from the soil.
Huxley and Martin, Elementary Biology, p. 469.

root-pulper (röt'pul″pėr), *n.* A mill for grinding roots or reducing them to pulp for industrial uses or for preparing them as food for farm-stock. Also called *root-grinder*, *root-shredder*, and *root-rasp*.

root-sheath (röt'shēth), *n.* The sheath of the root of a hair or feather, an invert of epidermis lining the follicle in which a hair or feather grows. See second cut under *hair*.

rootstock (röt'stok), *n.* 1. In *bot.*, same as *rhizome*.—2. The original ground or cause of anything; a root.

The Egyptians being really the oldest civilized people that we certainly know, and therefore, if languages have one origin, likely to be near its *root-stock*.
Dawson, Origin of the World, p. 272.

3. In *zoöl.*, a cormus, as of a zoöphyte; a rhizocaulus.

root-tree (röt'trē), *n.* An aspect of a geometrical tree in which it is regarded as springing from a given knot.

root-vole (röt'vōl), *n.* A vole or meadow-mouse of Siberia, *Arvicola œconomus*, which feeds on roots like other animals of its kind.

rooty (rö'ti or rụ̈t'i), *a.* [Also dial. *rutty*; < *root*¹ + *-y*¹.] 1. Abounding in roots; containing many roots: as, *rooty* ground.

Along the shoare of siluer streaming Themmes,
Whose *rutty* Bancke, the which his Riuer hemmes.
Spenser, Prothalamion (ed. Grosart).

Yet as a syluane hill
Thrusts back a torrent that hath kept a narrow channell still, . . .
Nor can [it] with all the confluence break through his *rooty* sides.
Chapman, Iliad, xvii.

2. Rank, as grass. *Halliwell*. [Prov. Eng.]

root-zone (röt'zōn), *n.* A region of the spinal cord traversed by or immediately adjacent to the roots of the spinal nerves.—**Posterior root-zone**, the postero-external column of the spinal cord, especially its lateral portions.

rooye-bok (rö'ye-bok), *n.* [< D. *rooije-bok*, < *rooijen*, regulate, order (< *rooi*, regular order, rule), + *bok* = E. *buck*¹.] The African pallah, *Æpyceros melampus*: so called by the Dutch colonists from its habit of walking in single file. See cut under *pallah*.

rop†, *n.* [Also *rope* (in pl. *ropes*); < ME. *rop* (pl. *roppes*), < AS. *rop*, irreg. *roop* (i. e. *rōp*), also *hrop*, an intestine, the colon, = MD. *rop*, intestine.] An intestine: commonly in the plural.

His talowe also servythe for plastyrs mo than one;
For harpe stryngis his *Ropys* seruythe Ichoone.
Political Poems, etc. (ed. Furnivall), p. 17.

ropalic, *a.* See *rhopalic*.

rope¹ (rōp), *n.* [< ME. *rop*, *roop*, *rope*, *rape*, < AS. *rāp*, a rope, = OFries. *rāp* (in *silrap*), cord, = D. *reep*, also *roop* = MLG. *rēp*, *reep* = OHG. MHG. *reif*, a cord, string, circular band, fetter, circle, G. *reif*, ring, a rope, circular band, circle, wheel, hoop, ferrule, = Icel. *reip* = Sw. *rep* = Dan. *reb*, a rope, = Goth. *raips*, a string (in comp. *skauda-raips*), shoe-string: root uncertain. The word *rope* exists disguised in the second element of *stirrup*.] 1. A cord of considerable thickness; technically, a cord over one inch in circumference. Ropes are usually made of hemp, manila, flax, cotton, coir, or other vegetable fiber, or of iron, steel, or other metallic wire. A hempen rope is composed of a certain number of yarns or threads, which are first spun or twisted into strands, and the finished ropes have special names according to the number and arrangement of the strands, and the various sizes are indicated by the circumference in inches. The ropes in ordinary use on board a vessel are composed of three strands, laid right-handed, or, as it is called (though this is not correct for southern latitudes), "with the sun." Occasionally a piece of large rope will be found laid up in four strands, also with the sun. This is generally used for standing rigging, tacks, sheets, etc., and is sometimes called *shroud-laid*. In nautical language a rope is usually called a *line*.

Furste to murte [broke] mony *rop* & the mast after.
Alliterative Poems (ed. Morris), iii. 150.

If they bind me fast with new *ropes* that never were occupied, then shall I be weak. Judges xvi. 11.

2. A row or string consisting of a number of things united so as to form a cord more or less thick: as, a *rope* of onions; a *rope* of pearls.

Car. . . . Let's choke him with Welsh parsley [hemp].
Never. Good friend, be merciful; choke me with puddings and a *rope* of sausages.
Randolph, Hey for Honesty, iv. 1.

This King was at Chawonock two yeares agoe to trade with blacke pearle, his worst sort, whereof I had a *rope*, but they were naught.
Quoted in *Capt. John Smith's* Works, I. 88.

What lady
I' the primitive times wore *ropes* of pearl or rubies?
Jasper Mayne, City Match, ii. 2.

3. Anything glutinous or gelatinous which is drawn out in long strings.

A pickled minnow is very good, . . . but I count him no more than the *ropes* in beer compared with a loach done properly. *R. D. Blackmore*, Lorna Doone, vii.

4. A local linear measure, twenty feet; in Devonshire, a measure of stonework, 20 feet in length, 1 foot in height, and 18 inches in thickness.—**Cable-laid rope**, a rope composed of nine strands. It is made by first laying the strands into three ropes of three strands each, right-handed; and then laying the three ropes up together into one, left-handed. Thus, cable-laid rope is like three small common ropes laid up into one large one. Formerly the ordinary three-stranded right-hand rope was called *hawser-laid*, and the nine-stranded *cable-laid*, and they will be found so distinguished in books; but among seafaring men now the terms *hawser-laid* and *cable-laid* are applied indiscriminately to nine-stranded rope, and the three-stranded, being the usual kind of rope, has no particular name, or is called *right-hand rope*. See cut under *cable-laid*.—**Cat-block rope**. See *cat-block*.—**Clue-rope**, a rope fastened to the clue of a course and used as a temporary tack or sheet.—**Flat rope**, a rope the strands of which are not twisted, but plaited together.—**Hawser-rope, hawser-laid rope**. See *cable-laid rope*.—**Holy rope**†. See *holy*.—**In the rope**, in the original twist or braid as delivered by the factory: said of horsehair used in upholstery, and of similar fibers which are put up in this form.—**Laid rope**, a rope that is twisted in strands. See *cable-laid rope*.—**Left-hand rope**, rope which is laid up and twisted from right to left, or "against the sun," as it is termed (see def. 1). Also called *backhanded rope*, *water-laid rope*.—**Locked-wire rope**, wire rope having the outer layer or layers of wires so made that they interlock each other. It is intended to prevent broken wires from springing out of place; the adjoining wires are supposed to hold them down.—**Manila rope**, rope made from Manila hemp. See *manila*, 2.—**On or upon the high ropes**. (*a*) Elated; in high spirits. (*b*) Haughty; arrogant.

He is one day humble, and the next day *on the high ropes*. *Swift*, Journal to Stella, xxxvi.

Plain-laid rope, rope made by twisting three strands together right-handed, or from left to right.—**Right-hand rope**, the three-stranded rope ordinarily used, which generally bears this name: it is laid "with the sun" (see def. 1). See *cable-laid rope*, above.—**Rope bridge**. See *bridge*¹.—**Rope driving-gear**. See *gear*.—**Rope ladder**, a ladder made by connecting two long pieces of rope at regular intervals by shorter pieces, or by rounds of wood or metal.—**Rope of sand**, proverbially, a feeble union or tie; a band easily broken.—**Rope's end**, the end of a rope; a short piece of rope, often used as an instrument of punishment.

Buy a *rope's end*; that will I bestow
Among my wife and her confederates
For locking me out of my doors by day.
Shak., C. of E., iv. 1. 16.

Shroud-laid rope, rope made by laying four strands together right-handed: it takes its name from the use to which it is frequently applied. All four-stranded rope is made with a central strand called a *heart*, which assists in keeping the others in place.—**Straw rope**, a rope made of straw twisted. It is used to secure the thatch of corn-ricks and -stacks, and also the thatch of poor cottages.—**Tapered rope**, rope made larger at one end than the other, used where there is considerable travel to the rope, and where much strain is brought on only one end, such as the fore- and main-tacks and -sheets.—**To back a rope**. See *back*¹.—**To be at the end of one's rope**, to have exhausted one's powers or resources.—**To cap a rope**. See *cap*¹.—**To give a person rope**, to let him go on without check, usually to his own defeat or injury.—**To know the ropes**. See *know*¹.—**To lay, overhaul, point a rope**. See the verbs.—**Twice-laid rope**, rope made from yarns that have already been used in other ropes.—**White rope**, rope not saturated with tar; untarred rope.—**Wire rope**, a collection of wires of iron, steel, etc., twisted, or (less usually) bound together so as to act in unison in resisting a strain. They are extensively used in raising and lowering apparatus in coal-mines, as standing rigging for ships, as substitutes for chains in suspension-bridges, for telegraph-cables, etc.

rope¹ (rōp), *v.*; pret. and pp. *roped*, ppr. *roping*. [< *rope*¹, *n.*] **I.** *intrans.* To be drawn out or extended into a filament or thread by means of any glutinous or adhesive element.

Their poor jades
Lob down their heads, . . .
The gum down-*roping* from their pale-dead eyes.
Shak., Hen. V., iv. 2. 48.

II. *trans.* 1. To draw by or as by a rope; tie up or fasten together with a rope or ropes: as, to *rope* a bale of goods; specifically, to connect by means of ropes fastened to the body, for safety in mountain-climbing: as, the guides insisted that the party should be *roped*.—2. To pull or curb in; restrain, as a rider his horse, to prevent him from winning a race; pull: a not uncommon trick on the turf.

The bold yeomen, in full confidence that their favourite will not be *roped*, back their opinions manfully for crowns.
Lawrence, Guy Livingstone, ix.

3. To catch with a noosed rope; lasso. [Western U. S.]

Californians use the Spanish word "lasso," which has with us been entirely dropped, no plainsman with pretensions to the title thinking of any word but *rope* either as noun or verb. *T. Roosevelt*, The Century, XXXV. 506.

4. To tether, as a horse. *Halliwell*. [Prov. Eng.]—5. To inclose or mark off with a rope: as, a space in front of the pictures was *roped* off to prevent injury to them; a circle was *roped* out for the games.—6. To sew a bolt-rope on, as on a sail or an awning.—**To rope in**, to secure for some business, social, or other enterprise: frequently with the idea of entanglement or disadvantage: as, I was *roped in* for this excursion before I knew it. [Slang, U. S.]

rope²†, *v.* and *n.* A Middle English form of *roop*.

rope³†, *n.* See *rop*.

rope⁴ (rōp), *n.* [Origin obscure.] A dwarf. *Halliwell*. [Prov. Eng.]

rope-band (rōp'band), *n.* A small piece of two- or three-yarn spun-yarn or marline, used to confine the head of a sail to the yard or gaff. Also *roband*. *Dana*.

ropebark (rōp'bärk), *n.* The shrub leatherwood, *Dirca palustris*. See cut under *leatherwood*.

rope-clamp (rōp'klamp), *n.* 1. A device consisting of a pair of clamping-jaws carrying a ring and hook, used for securing or attaching

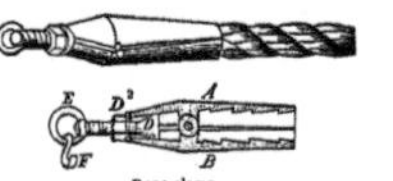

Rope-clamp.

The clamping-jaws are formed by two half-tubes *A*, *B*, made with teeth on their inner faces to hold the rope and prevent it from slipping out. An inclined groove is cut in the ends of the clamping-jaws to receive a wedge *D*, which is formed on the end of the screw-threaded stem, on which is a nut *D²*, resting against a washer. *E* is a swivel-ring on the end of the stem; *F*, a hook on the ring for attachment. The wedge is tightened by turning the nut *D²*.

the end of a cord, as a round lathe-belt or a railroad-car signal-cord.—2. A device by which a rope can be compressed to check its motion. *E. H. Knight*.

rope-clutch (rōp'kluch), *n.* A device for grasping and holding a rope. It usually consists of a pair of movable jaws, or of one fixed and one movable jaw, which are made to seize the rope either automatically or by pulling a cord. *E. H. Knight*.

rope-cord (rōp'kôrd), *n.* In *upholstery*, an ornamental cord of large diameter.

rope-dancer (rōp'dàn″sėr), *n.* One who walks, dances, or performs acrobatic feats on a rope extended at a considerable height above the floor or ground; a funambulist. Also *rope-walker*.

A daring *rope-dancer*, whom they expect to fall every moment. *Addison*, Guardian, No. 115.

Terence, in the prologue to Hecyra, complains that the attention of the public was drawn from his play by the exhibitions of a *rope-dancer*.
Strutt, Sports and Pastimes, p. 302.

rope-dancing (rōp'dàn"sing), *n.* The act or profession of a rope-dancer. *Arbuthnot.*

rope-drilling (rōp'dril"ing), *n.* A method of drilling or boring holes, in which a rope or cable is used, for any purpose connected with prospecting or mining, or more especially for obtaining petroleum. The rope forms the connection between the drilling-tools proper (see *cable-tools*) and the walking-beam, which, driven by a steam-engine, gives the reciprocating motions to the drilling-tools. These are lowered as the hole deepens by letting out the so-called "temper-screw," and they are rotated constantly by the driller by means of a short lever. The jars, by means of the vibrations communicated through the rope, show the driller how the tools are working. Also called *cable-drilling.*

rope-end (rōp'end), *v. t.* Same as *rope's-end.*

The roof all frayed with cobwebs, and the corners such as, in the navy, we should have been *rope-ended* for.
R. D. Blackmore, Maid of Sker, vi.

rope-grass (rōp'gràs), *n.* See *Restio.*

rope-house (rōp'hous), *n.* In *salt-manuf.*, an evaporating-house. It is a shed with open sides for free circulation of air, and with a number of ropes depending from the roof, to each of which leads a conduit: through this flows brine from a reservoir. The brine trickles slowly down the ropes, and the evaporation of the water leaves upon them a deposit of salt.

rope-machine (rōp'ma-shēn"), *n.* **1.** A machine for making rope from yarn. It consists essentially of a series of bobbins arranged in a frame and made to revolve as they deliver the yarns to a revolving reel, which compacts and unites them into the twisted rope. For large ropes, as cables, etc., a traveling rope-machine is used, the bobbins of yarn being made to revolve by a sun-and-planet motion as they deliver the yarns to the forming-reel, and the entire mechanism advancing along the ropewalk as fast as the cable is formed. Compare *rope-winch.*
2. A machine for laying up the strands of a rope: same as *laying-machine.*—**3.** Same as *rope-winch.*

rope-maker (rōp'mā"kėr), *n.* One whose occupation is the making of ropes or cordage.

rope-making (rōp'mā"king), *n.* The art or business of manufacturing ropes or cordage.

ropen†. A Middle English past participle of *reap.*

rope-pattern (rōp'pat"ėrn), *n.* An ornamental design in which twisted or spiral lines combine to form a decorative pattern.

rope-porter (rōp'pōr"tėr), *n.* A pulley mounted on a frame, over which the ropes of steam-plows are borne off the ground so as to prevent wear and tear from friction.

rope-pull (rōp'pu̇l), *n.* In *athletics*, same as *tug of war* (which see, under *tug*).

rope-pulling (rōp'pu̇l"ing), *n.* The sport of pulling at a rope, the contending parties endeavoring to pull one another over a line marked on the ground between them. See *tug of war*, under *tug*, and also the quotation.

The ancient custom of *rope-pulling* is always strictly observed in Ludlow on Shrove Tuesday. At about four o'clock in the afternoon the rope is given out from the town-hall by the Mayor, on whom this important duty by right devolves. Immediately on the rope being let down from a window, an indescribable struggle and trial of strength commences between the denizens of the different wards, which is not concluded without an obstinate contention. There are afterwards ordinaries at the various inns, and pleasure and conviviality are the order of the day.
Halliwell.

rope-pump (rōp'pump), *n.* A machine for raising water, consisting of an endless rope or ropes passing over a pulley fixed at the place to which the water is to be raised, and under another pulley fixed below the surface of the water. The upper pulley being turned rapidly by a winch, motion is given to the rope, and the water rises along with the ascending part of the rope, partly by the momentum it acquires when in motion, and partly by capillary attraction.

roper (rō'pėr), *n.* [< ME. *ropere*, a rope-maker; < *rope*1 + *-er*1.] **1.** A rope-maker.

Robyn the *ropere* arose. *Piers Plowman* (B), v. 336.

We will send you such things as you write to haue for the *ropers*; and wee would they should make more store of small cables and ropes. *Hakluyt's Voyages*, I. 307.

2. One who ropes or cords parcels, bales, and the like.—**3.** One who deserves a halter; a crafty fellow; a rogue. *Halliwell.* (*Douce.*) [Prov. Eng.]—**4.** One who throws the lasso. [Western U. S.]

Once a cowboy is a good *roper* and rider, the only other accomplishment he values is skill with his great army revolver. T. *Roosevelt*, The Century, XXXV. 506.

rope-railway (rōp'rāl"wā), *n.* A railway on which the cars are moved by means of ropes wound upon drums actuated by stationary engines; a cable-railway. Such railways are common in mining districts. Also *ropeway.*

rope-ripe (rōp'rīp), *a.* Fit for being hanged; deserving punishment by hanging. [Rare.]

Lord, how you roll in your *rope-ripe* terms!
Chapman, May-Day, iii. 1.

rope-roll (rōp'rōl), *n.* In *mach.*, a drum on which to wind a rope.

rope-runner (rōp'run"ėr), *n.* See the quotation.

I was what is called *rope-runner* on as neat a little tipping-engine as you need to see. A *rope-runner* is pretty much the same as a breakman on a goods-train — that is, he has to see to coupling and uncoupling the wagons that run with his engine, and to drive the engine at a pinch.
All the Year Round, quoted in N. Y. Evening Post, April [10, 1886.

ropery (rō'pėr-i), *n.*; pl. *roperies* (-iz). [< *rope*1 + *-ery.* In def. 2, cf. *roper*, 3.] **1.** A place where ropes are made.

In Riley's Memorials of London (an. 1310) . . . where mention is also made of a *roperie* or rope-walk, situate in the parish of Allhallows' the Great, Thames Street.
Piers Plowman (ed. Skeat), Notes, p. 91.

2†. Knavery; roguery.

I pray you, sir, what saucy merchant was this, that was so full of his *ropery?* *Shak.*, R. and J., ii. 4. 154.

Thou art very pleasant, and full of thy *ropery.*
Three Ladies of London. (*Nares.*)

rope's-end (rōps'end), *v. t.* [< *rope's end.*] To punish by beating with a rope's end.

rope-shaped (rōp'shāpt), *a.* Same as *funiliform.*

rope-socket (rōp'sok"et), *n.* Same as *rope-clamp.*

rope-spinner (rōp'spin"ėr), *n.* One who makes ropes in a ropewalk by means of a revolving wheel.

rope-spinning (rōp'spin"ing), *n.* The operation of twisting ropes by means of a revolving wheel.

rope-stitch (rōp'stich), *n.* In *embroidery*, a kind of work in which the separate stitches are laid diagonally side by side so as to produce the appearance of a rope or twist.

rope-trick (rōp'trik), *n.* **1†.** A trick that deserves the halter.

Why, that's nothing; an he begin once, he'll rail in his *rope-tricks.* *Shak.*, T. of the S., i. 2. 112.

2. A juggling trick performed with ropes.

ropewalk (rōp'wâk), *n.* A long low building or shed prepared for making ropes, and furnished with machinery for that purpose.

rope-walker (rōp'wâ"kėr), *n.* Same as *rope-dancer.*

ropeway (rōp'wā), *n.* Same as *rope-railway.*

Rope railways, as they were called, or *rope-ways* for transmitting minerals and goods, seem to be rapidly growing in favour, especially for mining purposes.
The Engineer, LXVIII. 454.

rope-winch (rōp'winch), *n.* In *rope-making*, a set of three whirlers, actuated by a belt or band, each making the same number of turns per minute, for simultaneously twisting the three yarns which are to be laid up into a rope. By this arrangement the same twist is given to each of the three yarns, which can hardly be done by separate and independent twisting, and the uniformity of twisting secures a perfectly even rope.

rope-work (rōp'wėrk), *n.* Decorative work imitating the twisted or spiral form of cordage.

rope-yarn (rōp'yärn), *n.* A yarn composed of many fibers, as of hemp, loosely twisted, several of which twisted together make a strand.

The owners of a vessel buy up incredible quantities of old junk, which the sailors unlay, and, after drawing out the yarns, knot them together, and roll them up in balls. These *rope-yarns* are constantly used for various purposes.
R. H. Dana, Jr., Before the Mast, p. 16.

ropily (rō'pi-li), *adv.* [< *ropy* + *-ly*2.] In a ropy or viscous manner; so as to be capable of being drawn out like a rope. *Imp. Dict.*

ropiness (rō'pi-nes), *n.* [< *ropy* + *-ness.*] The state or property of being ropy, or of containing ropes; stringiness, or capability of being drawn out in a string or thread without breaking, as of glutinous substances; viscosity; adhesiveness.

roping (rō'ping), *n.* [< *rope*1 + *-ing*1.] A collection of ropes; ropes in general.

Coil all the remainder of the *roping.*
Luce, Seamanship, p. 332.

roping (rō'ping), *a.* [< ME. *ropynge*, ropy, viscous: see *rope*1, *v.*] Ropy; viscous.

Let us not hang like *roping* icicles
Upon our houses' thatch, whiles a more frosty people
Sweat drops of gallant youth in our rich fields!
Shak., Hen. V., iii. 5. 23.

roping-needle (rō'ping-nē"dl), *n.* A large needle used in sewing bolt-rope on the edges of sails and awnings.

roping-palm (rō'ping-päm), *n.* *Naut.*, a heavy palm or piece of leather used in sewing bolt-rope on the edge of sails. See *palm*1, 4.

ropish (rō'pish), *a.* [< *rope*1 + *-ish*1.] Tending to ropiness; ropy.

ropy (rō'pi), *a.* [Formerly also *roapy*; < ME. *ropy*; < *rope*1 + *-y*1.] **1.** Resembling a rope or cord; cord-like. [Rare.]

In vain
Their lax'd and *ropy* sinews sorely strain
Heap'd loads to draw. *J. Baillie.*

2. Capable of being drawn into a thread, as a glutinous substance; stringy; viscous; tenacious; glutinous: as, *ropy* wine; *ropy* lees. Wine is called *ropy* when it shows a milky or flaky sediment and an oily appearance when poured out.

Ropy as ale, . . . Viscosus. *Prompt. Parv.*, p. 436.

Roquefort cheese. See *cheese*1.

roquelaure (rok'e-lōr), *n.* [Also *rocklay*, *rockelay*, *rokelay*, *rocklow*, rocolo, *roquelo*, *rocklier*, *roclier*; < F. *roquelaure*; so called from the Duc de *Roquelaure.* Hence *rocklay*, etc.] A form of short cloak much worn in the earlier part of the eighteenth century.

Within the *roquelaure's* clasp thy hands are pent.
Gay, Trivia, i. 51.

It is not the firmest heart (and Jeanie, under her russet *rokelay*, had one that would not have disgraced Cato's daughter) that can most easily bid adieu to these soft and mingled emotions.
Scott, Heart of Mid-Lothian, xiv.

Roquelaure, time of George II.

Scarlet seems to have been the favourite colour for the *roquelaure* or cloak, and some must have been "exceedingly magnifical," scarlet *rocklowe* and *rocliere*, with gold buttons and loops, being advertised as lost.
J. Ashton, Social Life in Reign of Queen Anne, I. 160.

roquelo (rok'e-lō), *n.* Same as *roquelaure.*

She then saw, parading up and down the hall, a figure wrapped round in a dark blue *roquelo.*
Mme. D'Arblay, Camilla, ix. 4. (*Davies.*)

roquet1 (rō-kā'), *v. t.* [Appar. an arbitrary alteration of *croquet*, to express a special meaning.] In the game of croquet, to cause one's ball to strike (another ball), entitling the player to place his own ball beside that he has struck and to continue in play.

roquet1 (rō-kā'), *n.* [< *roquet*1, *v.*] In the game of croquet, a stroke by which a player roquets another ball.

roquet2 (rō'ket), *n.* [Origin obscure.] A lizard of the genus *Liocephalus.*

roquet-croquet (rō-kā'krō-kā'), *n.* In the game of croquet, the act of a player, after roqueting a ball, of putting his own in contact with it and driving both away by a blow of the mallet against his own ball.

roquet-croquet (rō-kā'krō-kā'), *v. t.* [< *roquet-croquet*, *n.*] In the game of croquet, to move by a roquet-croquet, as one's own and another ball.

roral† (rō'ral), *a.* [< L. *ros* (ror-), dew, + *-al.*] Pertaining to dew, or consisting of dew; dewy.

These see her from the dusky plight . . .
With *roral* wash redeem her face.
M. Green, The Spleen.

roration† (rō-rā'shon), *n.* [< L. *roratio(n-)*, a falling of dew, < *rorare*, pp. *roratus*, distil dew, < *ros* (ror-), dew: see *rore*3.] A falling of dew. *Bailey*, 1727.

rore1†, *v.* A Middle English form of *roar.*

rore2†, *v. i.* [ME. *roren*, *rooren*; origin obscure; perhaps a use of rore1, roar, cry (cf. *roop*, cry out, auction).] To barter or exchange merchandise.

Rooryn or chaungyne on chaffare fro a nother.
Prompt. Parv., p. 71, note 4.

rore3 (rōr), *n.* [< L. *ros* (ror-), dew. Cf. *rorid*, *rory*, *honey-rore*, *rosemary.*] Dew. Compare *honey-rore.*

roric (rō'rik), *a.* [< L. *ros* (ror-), dew, + *-ic.*] Pertaining to or resembling dew; dewy: specifically applied to certain curious figures or appearances seen on polished solid surfaces after breathing on them, also to a class of related phenomena produced under various conditions. See *cohesion figures*, under *cohesion.*

Roricrucian (rē-ri-krö'shi-an), *n.* and *a.* [As if < L. *ros* (*ror-*), dew, + *crux* (*cruc-*), a cross.] Same as *Rosicrucian*: an occasional spelling adopted by those who take the implied view of the derivation of the word.

rorid† (rō'rid), *a.* [< L. *roridus*, dewy, < *ros* (ror-), dew: see *rore*3.] Dewy.

A loose and *rorid* vapour.
Marlowe and Chapman, Hero and Leander, Sestiad 3.

Roridula (rō-rid'ū-lä), *n.* [NL. (Linnæus, 1767), named from the dewy appearance of the glandular hairs covering the plant; dim. of L. *roridus*, dewy: see *rorid*.] A genus of polypetalous plants of the order *Droseraceæ*, the sundew family. It is unlike the rest of the order in its three-celled ovary, and is further characterized by a five-parted calyx, five petals, five stamens, their anthers with thickened connectives and dehiscent by terminal pores facing outward, and by the ovoid three-angled septifragal capsules, containing three large pendulous seeds. The 2 species are natives of the Cape of Good Hope. They are very leafy and glandular-hairy undershrubs, bearing narrow entire or pinnatifid leaves, circinately coiled in the bud, and rather large red or white two-bracted flowers forming a terminal raceme or spike. *R. dentata* is a shrubby herb 3 feet high, with the leaves so viscid that it is hung up as a flycatcher in Cape country-houses.

roriferous (rō-rif'e-rus), *a.* [< L. *rorifer*, dew-bringing (> F. *rorifère*), < *ros* (*rōr-*), dew, + *ferre* = E. *bear*[1].] Generating or producing dew.

rorifluent† (rō-rif'lō-ent), *a.* [< L. *ros* (*ror-*), dew, + *fluen(t-)s*, flowing. Cf. L. *rorifluus*, honey-flowing.] Flowing with dew.

rorqual (rôr'kwal), *n.* [= F. *rorqual* (NL. *Rorqualus*): (*a*) Prob. < Sw. *rörhval*, 'the round-headed cachalot,' < rör (= Dan. *rœr* = Icel. *reyrr* = G. *rohr* = D. *roer* = Goth. *raus*), reed, + *hval* = E. *whale*. (*b*) According to Bugge (Romania, X. 157), < Norw. *reydhr-hval*, < (Icel.) *raudhr*,

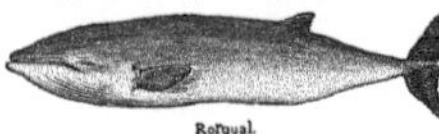

Rorqual.

red, + *hvalr*, whale.] A finner-whale of the genus *Balænoptera*, having short flippers, a dorsal fin, and the throat plicated. There are several species, and the name is sometimes extended to other cetaceans of the subfamily *Balænopterinæ*. Some of these whales attain great size, the common rorqual, B. *musculus*, reaching a length of 60 or 70 feet, while the blue rorqual, B. *sibbaldi* or *Sibbaldius maximus*, is sometimes 80 feet, being thus the longest known mammal. Rudolphi's rorqual, B. *borealis*, is about 50 feet long; the lesser rorqual, B. *rostrata*, 30 feet. These four are well-established species in North Atlantic waters, though their synonymy has been much confused by the introduction and cross-use of various generic names. The sulphur-bottomed whale of the Pacific is a rorqual, B. *sulphureus*.

rorulent (rō'rō-lent), *a.* [< L. *rorulentus*, full of dew, < *ros* (*ror-*), dew: see *rory*.] **1†.** Full of dew.—**2.** In *entom.*, covered with a kind of bloom which may be rubbed off, like that of a plum.

rory† (rō'ri), *a.* [< rore[3] + *-y*[1]. Cf. *rorid*.] Dewy. Also *roary*.

> On Libanon at first his foot he set,
> And shook his wings, with *rory* May-dews wet.
> *Fairfax*, tr. of Tasso's Godfrey of Boulogne, i. 14.

Rosa (rō'zä), *n.* [NL. (Tournefort, 1700), < L. *rosa*, a rose: see *rose*[1].] A genus of polypetalous plants, comprising all the genuine roses, type of the order *Rosaceæ* and sole genus of the tribe *Roseæ*. It is characterized by an urn-shaped calyx-tube with constricted mouth, bearing five leaf-like imbricated lobes, destitute of the intermediate bractlets which are frequent in related genera, but often furnished with similar smaller leaf-like lobes on their sides. It is also distinguished by the broad and open corolla of five obovate petals, numerous stamens in many rows, and many free carpels each with one pendulous ovule, a ventral style, and a somewhat dilated stigma, and each forming in fruit a one-seeded bony achene, the whole mass of achenes inclosed in a fleshy fruiting receptacle, known as the *hip* or *hep*. (See *Rosaceæ*.) The species are polymorphous and variable, and though 600 have been enumerated (exclusive of garden varieties), they are believed to be reducible to 50 or 55. They inhabit temperate and subalpine regions through a large part of the northern hemisphere, being limited southward by India, Abyssinia, and Mexico, and being less numerous in America than in the Old World. *R. cinnamomea* is said to be found as far north as Point Barrow in Alaska (71° 27'). Ten species are native in the northeastern United States, of which one, *R. blanda*, extends to Hudson's Bay. Five species are found in Great Britain, or, as they are sometimes classified, 20. They are erect or climbing shrubs, commonly with prickly stems, the leaves smooth, silky, or downy, or (in *R. rubiginosa*, the sweetbrier) beset with copious minute glands beneath and fragrant. The leaves are alternate and unequally pinnate, with adherent wing-like stipules and serrate leaflets; in *R. berberifolia*, a small yellow-flowered Persian species, they are reduced to a single leaflet or are replaced wholly by stipules. The flowers are large and beautiful, often fragrant, made double in cultivation by the transformation of part or all of the stamens into petals, and also so occurring rarely in the wild state. They are of numerous shades of red, white, and yellow, and often over 2 inches across, in *R. gigantea*, of Upper Burma, reaching 6 inches. The scarlet or crimson fruit is often ornamental and sometimes edible. See *rose*[1].

Rosaceæ (rō-zā'sē-ē), *n. pl.* [NL. (Jussieu, 1789), fem. pl. of L. *rosaceus*: see *rosaceous*.] An order of polypetalous plants, of the cohort *Rosales*; the rose family. It is characterized by a calyx of five lobes often alternating with five bractlets; by a calyx-tube sheathed by a disk which bears the five uniform petals and the one or more complete circles of numerous stamens; and by the usually several or many separate carpels inserted at the base or throat of the calyx-tube, each with a basilar or ventral style, and usually with two anatropous ovules which are pendulous or ascending. Some yellow- or white-flowered species suggest by their appearance the buttercup family, *Ranunculaceæ*, but their numerous stamens and pistils are inserted on the calyx or disk, not on the receptacle. The rose family is closely allied to the *Leguminosæ*; but in that order the fifth petal, in this the fifth sepal, is nearest the axis of the plant. The resemblance is most strongly marked between the drupaceous *Rosaceæ* and the acacias. The order passes gradually, through the spiræas, into the saxifrage family, but is distinguished in general by its inflorescence, its exalbuminous seeds, and its commonly numerous pistils. Its species are properly about 1,000, though over 2,000 have been enumerated. They are classed in 71 genera composing 10 tribes (*Chrysobalaneæ*, *Pruneæ*, *Spiræeæ*, *Quillaieæ*, *Rubeæ*, *Potentilleæ*, *Poterieæ*, *Roseæ*, *Neuradeæ*, and *Pomeæ*). These are often grouped in 3 subfamilies, *Drupaceæ*, *Pomaceæ*, and *Rosaceæ* proper. They are natives both of temperate and of tropical regions, extending southward principally in the tribes *Chrysobalaneæ* and *Quillaieæ*; 4 genera reach Australia, 4 South Africa, and 4 or 5 Chili. The chief home of the order, however, is the north temperate zone, whence it extends into the extreme north. More than 25 species occur in Alaska, while the genera *Alchemilla*, *Potentilla*, and especially *Dryas*, furnish characteristic arctic plants, the last affording the most common plant found by the Greely arctic expedition, forming beds covering acres in the interior of Grinnell Land, and flourishing on Lockwood's island, latitude 83° 24' N. The order includes herbs, trees, and shrubs, either erect or prostrate, rarely climbing. Their leaves are generally alternate, either simple or compound, often with glandular teeth, accompanied by stipules, these being free or adherent to the petiole, which is frequently dilated at the base and gland-bearing at the summit. The flowers are very often showy, commonly red, white, or yellow, but not blue, of very various inflorescence, either solitary or in racemes, spikes, panicles, or cymes. The order offers examples of widely different types of fruit, as the drupe, pome, follicle, and achene, with many specialized fruiting-bodies, as the rose-hip, the fleshy receptacle of the strawberry, and the drupe-tum or collection of small drupes found in the raspberry, and, with the addition of a fleshy receptacle, in the blackberry. The true berry and the capsule are, however, but seldom produced in this family. Many of the most valued fruit-trees belong here, as the apple, pear, plum, cherry, peach, and apricot; and many of the most common ornamental flowering shrubs of cultivation, for which see *Rosa* (the type), *Spiræa*, *Kerria*, *Photinia*, *Pyrus*, *Prunus*, etc.; together with many weedy plants, as *Agrimonia*, *Geum*, *Potentilla*.

rosaceous (rō-zā'shius), *a.* [< L. *rosaceus*, made of roses, < *rosa*, a rose: see *rose*[1].] **1.** In *bot.*: (*a*) Rose-like; having a corolla composed of several wide-spreading roundish petals, with the claws very short or almost wanting. (*b*) Of or pertaining to the order *Rosaceæ*.—**2.** In *zoöl.*, of a rosy color; rose-red; rosy; roseate.

rosal (rō'zal), *a.* [< L. **rosalis*, of roses (> Sp. *rosal*, rose-bush, = Pg. *rosal*, bed of roses), < *rosa*, a rose: see *rose*[1].] **1†.** Rosy.

> While thus from forth her *rosall* gate she sent
> Breath form'd in words, the marrow of content.
> *Beedome*, Poems (1641). (*Nares*.)

2. In *bot.*, typified by the order *Rosaceæ*: used by Lindley in his class name *rosal alliance*.—**3.** Belonging to the cohort *Rosales*.

Rosales (rō-zā'lēz), *n. pl.* [NL. (Lindley, 1833), pl. of L. **rosalis*: see *rosal*.] A cohort of dicotyledonous plants, of the polypetalous series *Calycifloræ*, characterized by distinct styles and solitary or numerous and separate carpels, not united into a syncarpic ovary as in the other cohorts of the series. The leaves are either compound or simple, and the flowers either regular or irregular, but commonly unisexual. It includes 9 orders, 3 of which are small families with a pendulous apical ovule—the *Hamamelideæ*, trees and shrubs, *Bruniaceæ*, heath-like shrubs, and *Haloragеæ*, chiefly aquatics; 1, a small family with parietal ovules—the *Droseraceæ*, glandular herbs; and the 5 others, families with ovules ascending or affixed to the central angle—the large orders *Leguminosæ*, *Rosaceæ*, and *Saxifragaceæ*, together with the *Connaraceæ*, tropical trees and shrubs, and the *Crassulaceæ*, fleshy herbs.

rosalia (rō-zā'li-ä), *n.* [< It. *rosalia* (> F. *rosalie*): see def.] **1.** In *music*, a form of melody in which a phrase or figure is repeated two or three times, each time being transposed a step or half-step upward. The term is derived from the first word of an old Italian song in which such repetition was used. It is sometimes applied to repetitions in which the progression is downward or is by longer intervals than a step. **2.** A kind of marmoset, the marikina.—**3.** [*cap.*] [NL.] In *entom.*, a genus of cerambycid beetles. *Serville*, 1833.

Rosalina (rō-za-lī'nä), *n.* [NL., < L. *rosa*, a rose: see *rose*[1].] A fossil genus of many-chambered *Foraminifera*: so named because the cells are disposed in a circular or rose-like form.

rosaniline (rō-zan'i-lin), *n.* [< *rose*[1] + *aniline*. See *rose-aniline*.] An organic base ($C_{20}H_{21}N_3O$), a derivative of aniline, crystallizing in white needles, capable of uniting with acids to form salts, which are the well-known rosaniline coloring matters of commerce; also, the color thus produced. Thus, fuchsin is the monohydrochlorid and azalein the nitrate of rosaniline. Silk and wool dipped into aqueous solutions of any of the salts withdraw them from solution and become dyed at once. Cotton, on the other hand, does not withdraw the coloring matter, but must be first treated with a mordant of some animal substance, such as albumen. Also called *aniline red*, *roseine*, *magenta*, *azalein*.—**Diphenyl rosaniline**, an aniline dye giving a blue-violet color.—**Rosaniline-blue.** Same as *spirit-blue*.

rosaria, *n.* A plural of *rosarium*.

rosarian (rō-zā'ri-an), *n.* [< L. *rosarium*, a rose-garden (see *rosary*), + *-an*.] **1.** A cultivator of roses; a rose-grower; a rose-fancier.

> The Rev. Reynolds Hole, Canon of Lincoln, the genial pastor and *rosarian*, who formulated the aphorism that "he who would grow beautiful roses in his garden must first of all have beautiful roses in his heart."
> *Harper's Mag.*, LXXVI. 14.

2. [*cap.*] A member of the Fraternity of the Rosary.

> Another *Rosarian* recommends a special temporal intention. *Rosarian*, I. 378. (*Encyc. Dict.*)

rosarium (rō-zā'ri-um), *n.*; pl. *rosariums*, *rosaria* (-umz, -ä). [L., a rose-garden: see *rosary*.] A rose-garden.

> The *rosarium* must be both open and sheltered, a place both of sunshine and shade. *Quarterly Rev.*, CXLV. 360.

rosary (rō'za-ri), *n.*; pl. *rosaries* (-riz). [< ME. *rosarie*, < OF. *rosarie*, later *rosaire* = Sp. Pg. It. *rosario*, a rosary, < ML. *rosarium*, a garland of roses to crown the image of the Virgin, a chaplet of beads used in prayers in honor of the Virgin, instituted by St. Dominic, a rosary, also a rose-bush, and, as in L., a rose-garden (hence used in ML. as a fanciful title for treatises or anthologies); neut. of *rosarius*, of roses, < *rosa*, a rose: see *rose*[1]. In def. 8, < ML. *rosarius* (sc. *nummus*), a coin so called, < L. *rosarius*, adj., as above.] **1†.** A rose-garden.

> This moone is eke the *rosaries* to make
> With setes, or me may here sedes sowe.
> *Palladius*, Husbondrie (E. E. T. S.), p. 80.
>
> Is there a Hercules that dare to touch,
> Or enter the Hesperian *rosaries*?
> *Machin*, Dumb Knight, iv. 1.

2†. A rose-bush.

> The ruddy *rosary*,
> The souerayne rosemary,
> The praty strawbery.
> *Skelton*, Garland of Laurel, l. 970.
>
> The sweetest and the fairest blossom that ever budded, either out of the white or red *rosary*.
> *Proceedings against Garnet*, etc., sig. D. d. 3 (1606). [(*Latham*.)

3. A garland of roses; any garland; a chaplet.

> Every day propound to yourself a *rosary* or chaplet of good works, to present to God at night.
> *Jer. Taylor*, Holy Dying. (*Latham*.)

4. Hence, an anthology; a book culled from various authors, like a garland of flowers: formerly often given as a title to works of such a character.—**5.** A string of beads carried about the person, either for mere pastime, as to occupy the fingers, or for reckoning, especially in numbering the prayers offered up at fixed times of the day. Mohammedans carry rosaries with them for both these purposes, wearing them in the girdle or carrying them in the hand at all hours of the day.

6. Specifically, in the *Rom. Cath. Ch.*: (*a*) A series of devotions consisting of a specified number of aves (that is, salutations to the Virgin Mary), of paternosters (that is, repetitions of the Lord's Prayer), and of glorias (or doxologies).

> Our Lady's Psalter . . . is now better known as the *Rosary*. *Rock*, Church of our Fathers, III. i. 320.

(*b*) A string of beads of various sizes representing the same number of aves, paternosters, and glorias respectively, used for marking off these prayers. Each bead receives the name of the prayer it represents. The rosary is divided into decads of aves, each decad being preceded by a paternoster and followed by a gloria. The ordinary rosary, sometimes called the *Dominican rosary*, consists of fifteen decads—that is, of one hundred and fifty aves (corresponding to the number of psalms in the Psalter), fifteen paternosters, and fifteen glorias. In this rosary each decad is devoted to the contemplation of a mystery of the life of Christ, the first five being joyful mysteries (such as the annunciation and the nativity), the second five being the sorrowful mysteries (such as the passion), the third five being the glorious mysteries (such as the resurrection and ascension). This regular use of the rosary of one hundred and fifty aves was first instituted by St. Dominic (1170–1221), although the devotional use of beads, etc., was already familiar. The term *rosary* also applies to a similar instrument of devotion in use among the Greeks, Armenians, and other Eastern communions. See *chaplet*, 5.

7. A string of eggs of a batrachian wound about the body or limbs, as of the nurse-frog or obstetrical toad, *Alytes obstetricans*. See cut under *Alytes*. *E. D. Cope*.—**8.** A counterfeit coin of base metal, illegally introduced into England in the reign of Edward I. It probably bore a general resemblance to the silver penny or sterling current at the time, and may have derived its name from having a rose or rosette as part of its reverse type.—**Festival of the Rosary**, a festival celebrated in the Roman Catholic Church on the first Sunday in October, in commemoration of the victory of the Christian forces over the Turks at Lepanto (1571).—**Fraternity of the Rosary**, a Roman Catholic order established in the fourteenth or fifteenth century for the purpose of averting public evils by means of prayer to God. To its prayers was ascribed the victory at Lepanto (see above).—**Rosary-peas.** See *peal* and *rosary-plant*.—**Rosary ring.** Same as *decad ring* (which see, under *decad*).

rosary-plant (rō'za-ri-plant), *n.* A vine, the Indian licorice, *Abrus precatorius*, whose seeds are known as *crabs'-eyes*, *rosary-peas*, etc. See *Abrus*.—**Mexican rosary-plant.** See *Rhynchosia*.

rosary-shell (rō'za-ri-shel), *n.* A gastropod of the genus *Monodonta*. See cut under *Monodonta*.

rosa solis (rō'zä sō'lis). [NL., 'rose of the sun': L. *rosa*, rose; *solis*, gen. of *sol*, the sun. Cf. *rosolio*.] A cordial made with spirits and various flavorings, as orange-flower and cinnamon, and formerly much esteemed.

> We abandon all ale,
> And beer that is stale,
> *Rosa-solis*, and damnable hum.
> *Wits' Recreations* (1654). (*Nares.*)

Repeating, as the rich cordial trickled forth in a smooth oily stream—"Right *rosa solis* as ever washed mulligrubs out of a moody brain!" *Scott*, Fortunes of Nigel, xxi.

rosated† (rō'zā-ted), *a.* [‹ *rosate (= F. *rosat* = Sp. Pg. *rosado* = It. *rosato*; as *rose*[1] + *-ate*[1]) + *-ed*[2].] Crowned or adorned with roses. [Rare.]

He (Gower) appeareth there neither the laureated nor hederated poet, . . . but only *rosated*, having a Chaplet of four roses about his head. *Fuller*, Worthies, Yorkshire, III. 426.

Rosicrucian, *n.* and *a.* See *Rosicrucian*.

roscid (ros'id), *a.* [= Pg. *roscido*; ‹ L. *roscidus*, dewy, ‹ *ros* (*ror-*), dew: see *rore*[3], *rorid*.] Dewy; containing dew, or consisting of dew.

> These relicks dry suck in the heavenly dew,
> And *roscid* Manna rains upon her breast.
> *Dr. H. More*, Infinity of Worlds, st. 100.

roscoelite (ros'kō-lit), *n.* [‹ *Roscoe* (Prof. H. E. Roscoe) + Gr. λίθος, stone.] A mineral of a green color and micaceous structure, in composition a silicate of aluminium and potassium, remarkable for containing nearly 30 per cent. of vanadium pentoxid. It has been found in California associated with gold.

rose[1] (rōz), *n.* and *a.* [‹ ME. *rose*, *roose* (pl. *roses*, *rosen*), ‹ AS. *rōse* (pl. *rōsan*) = MD. *rose*, D. *roos* = OHG. *rōsa*, MHG. *rōse*, G. *rose* = Icel. *rōs* = Sw. *ros* = Dan. *rose* = F. *rose* = Pr. Sp. Pg. It. *rosa* = OBulg. *rosa* = Bulg. Serv. *ruzha* = Bohem. *ruzhe* = Pol. *rozha* = Little Russ. *ruzha* = White Russ. *rozha* = Russ. *roza* = Lith. *rozhe* = Lett. *roze* = Hung. *rózsa* = Ir. *ros* = Gael. *ros* = W. *rhosyn*, pl. *rhos*, ‹ L. *rosa*, ‹ Gr. *ῥοδία (not found), ῥόδον, Æolic Gr. βρόδον, a rose, of Eastern origin: cf. Ar. Pers. *ward*, a rose, flower, petal, flowering shrub, Armen. *ward*, a rose. The AS. *rōse* (ME. *rose*, *roose*) would reg. produce a mod. E. **roose*; the mod. E. *rose* is due partly to the F. form.] **I.** *n.* **1.** A shrub of the genus *Rosa*, or its flower, found wild in numerous species, and cultivated from remote antiquity. In the wild state the rose is generally single, its corolla consisting of one circle of round-

Flowering Branch of Prairie-rose (*Rosa setigera*). *a*, the fruit.

ish spreading petals. Under cultivation the petals commonly multiply at the expense of the stamens, the flower thus doubling into a cushion-, nest-, or cabbage-shaped body. Starting with a few natural species, cultivation has obtained, through selection and complex intercrossing, many hundred varieties, whose parentage frequently cannot be conjectured. Some, however, remain near their originals, and very many can be referred to certain general stocks. For practical purposes the roses of culture have been loosely grouped as follows: (1) Climbing roses. Here belong the prairie-rose, and its offspring the queen-of-the-prairies, Baltimore belle, etc., and the evergreen, Ayrshire, musk, many-flowered, and Banksian stocks (see below). (2) Garden roses, non-climbers, blooming but once in the season; summer or June roses. Among these are the Scotch roses, derived from the burnet-rose, *R. spinosissima* (*R. pimpinellifolia*), a low bush of temperate Europe and Asia; the cinnamon- and damask-roses; the Provins, hundred-leaved, or cabbage rose, *R. centifolia*, among whose numerous varieties are most of the moss-roses; and the French or red rose, *R. Gallica*, prolific of variegated and other varieties. These are old favorites, now giving way to the next class. (3) The so-called hybrid perpetuals or autumn roses, best called *remontants* (see *remontant*), as blooming not perpetually, but a second time after rest. The characteristic element in this group is from the China or Indian rose, *R. Indica*. They are large, brilliant, and hardy, afford the great fancy roses of the rosarians, and include such varieties as the *Baronne Prévost*, *General Jacqueminot*, and *giant-of-battles*. The Jacqueminot is forced in immense quantities for the market. (4) Roses blooming continuously. Here may be classed the *Bourbons*, originating in a cross between the China and a damask variety, a rather tender race, including the *Souvenir de Malmaison*, a famous standard. More constant bloomers are varieties of the China rose known popularly as *monthly roses*, also called Bengal *roses*; the flowers are brilliant and abundant; the plant multiplies readily, and is the best for house culture. Another race of perpetuals is the *noisette*, derived from the musk- and the tea-rose, mostly climbers. Lastly, here belong the tea-roses, or tea-scented roses, descended from var. *odorata* of the China rose, a race of numerous and increasing varieties, most extensively cultivated. The large yellow Maréchal (or Marshal) Niel, highly popular for forcing, is by some classed as a tea-rose, by others as a Noisette. In England roses called *standards* are produced by budding the desired variety on the stock of the common dogrose, or of a vigorous variety known as *Manetti*; in the American climate most sorts do better on their own stock. The rose in culture has numerous enemies, as the rose-aphis or greenfly, the rose-beetle, the rose-slug, and the red-spider. The most important economical use of the rose is in the manufacture of attar or oil of roses. (See *attar* and *rose-water*.) The petals of the red or French rose are slightly astringent and tonic, and are used in various officinal preparations, chiefly as a vehicle for stronger tonic astringents. The petals of the cabbage-rose are slightly laxative, but are used chiefly in making rose-water. The bright-red hip of some wild roses is ornamental and sometimes edible: that of the dogrose is used to make a confection. The rose is a national emblem of England.

> As the *Roose* in his Radness is Richest of floures.
> *Destruction of Troy* (E. E. T. S.), l. 624.

> Like the red *rose* on triumphant brier.
> *Shak.*, M. N. D., iii. 1. 96.

2. One of various other plants so named from some resemblance to the true rose. See the phrases below.—**3.** A knot of ribbon in the form of a rose, used as an ornamental tie of a hat-band, garter, shoe, etc.

> My heart was at my mouth
> Till I had viewed his shoes well; for those *roses*
> Were big enough to hide a cloven foot.
> B. *Jonson*, Devil is an Ass, i. 2.

> The heir, with *roses* in his shoes,
> That night might village partner choose.
> *Scott*, Marmion, vi., Int.

4. Figuratively, full flush or bloom.

> He wears the *rose*
> Of youth upon him. *Shak.*, A. and C., iii. 13. 20.

5. A light crimson color. Colors ordinarily called crimson are too dark to receive the name of *rose*. See II.

> Her cheek had lost the *rose*. *Tennyson*, Œnone.

6. In *her.*, a conventional representation of the flower, composed of five leaves or lobes, or, in other words, a kind of cinquefoil: when the five spaces between the leaves are filled by small pointed leaves representing the calyx, it is said to be *barbed*. (See *barb*[1], *n.*, 8.) The center is usually a circle with small dots or points of a different tincture, usually or. These may be supposed to represent the stamens, but they are called in heraldry *seeds*, and when they are of a different tincture the rose is said to be *seeded*.

7. In *arch.* and *art*: (*a*) A rose-window. (*b*) Any ornamental feature or work of decorative character having a circular outline: properly a larger and more important feature or work than a rosette or a circular boss.—**8.** A rosette, as of lace.—**9.** In *zoöl.*, a formation suggestive of a rose; a radiating disposition or arrangement of parts; a rosette, as that formed at the parting of feathers on the heads of domestic pigeons of different breeds, or that represented by caruncles about the eyes or beak. Compare *rose-comb*, under *comb*[1], 3.

It [tetronerythrin] was first found in the so-called *roses* around the eyes of certain birds by Dr. Wurm. *Micros. Sci.*, XXX. 90.

10. A perforated nozle of a pipe, spout, etc., to distribute water in fine shower-like jets; a rose-head; also, a plate similarly perforated covering some aperture.

The acid enters the cistern . . . through a leaden *rose*, which detains all solid bodies which may have accidentally got into the acid. *Spons' Encyc. Manuf.*, I. 73.

11. An ornamental annular piece of wood or metal surrounding the spindle of a door-lock or a gas-pipe at the point where it passes through a wall or ceiling.—**12.** The disease erysipelas: so named, popularly, from its color.

Among the hot swellings, whereof commonly the foresaid imposthumes are caused, is also the *rose*, or erysipelas, which is none other thing but an inflammation of the skin, which in this country we call the *rose*. *Moxan's Physic* (4th ed.), p. 595. (*Nares.*)

13. In *Eng. hist.*, one of the two rival factions, York and Lancastrian. See *Wars of the Roses*, below.

Henry VII., combining the interests of the rival *Roses*, combines the leading characteristics of their respective policies. *Stubbs*, Const. Hist., § 373.

14. A circular card or disk, or a diagram with radiating lines: as, the compass-card or *rose* of the compass; the barometric *rose*, which shows the barometric pressure, at any place, in connection with the winds blowing from different points of the compass; a wind-*rose*.—**15.** In musical instruments like flutes, guitars, dulcimers, and harpsichords, an ornamental device set in the sound-hole of the belly, and often serving as a trade-mark as well as a decoration.—**16.** A form in which precious stones, especially small diamonds, are frequently cut. Large rose diamonds were much used from the sixteenth to the eighteenth century, but are now quite obsolete. The characteristic of the rose is that it is flat below, and forms a hemisphere or low pyramid above, covered with small facets. When, as is usually the case, these facets are 24 in number, the cut is called a *Dutch rose*; when 36, a *rose recoupée*. The *Brabant rose* has also 24 facets, but they are flatter or less raised than in the Dutch rose. The rose cut is selected when the loss to the stone in cutting would be too great if the brilliant cut were selected. Rose diamonds are generally cut from plates cleaved from the crystals of diamonds while being cleaved into brilliant form. See *brilliant*.

17. A very small diamond, scarcely more than a splinter, of which as many as 400 are sometimes necessary to make a carat, or 60,000 to make an ounce. These are seldom regularly cut, 6 to 8 facets only being the usual number.—**Alpine rose**, *Rosa alpina* of European mountains, to which are commonly referred the Boursault roses. The name has also been applied to certain species of *Rhododendron*, as *R. ferruginea*, etc.—**Ashes of roses.** See *red*[1], 1.—**Attar of roses.** See *attar*.—**Austrian rose.** See *yellow rose*.—**Ayrshire rose**, a group of climbing roses derived from *Rosa sempervirens*, the evergreen rose of southern Europe.—**Banksian rose**, *Rosa Banksiæ* of China, a climber, producing large clusters, not hardy.—**Bengal rose.** See def. 1.—**Blue rose**, an impossibility.

The niece of the prince-bishop of Wilna strikes us as in many respects a typical Pole, and . . . we can only think of Hélène Massalska as one who was, in her way, a seeker after *blue roses*. *N. and Q.*, 7th ser., V. 120.

Blush-rose, a delicate pink rose of the damask and other stocks.—**Bourbon rose.** See def. 1.—**Brier-rose**, the dogrose; also, a sweetbrier.—**Burgundy rose**, a small variety of *Rosa centifolia*.—**Burnet-rose** or **burnet-leafed rose.** See def. 1.—**Canker-rose**, the corn-poppy, *Papaver Rhœas*. [Prov. Eng.]—**Cayenne rose.** See *Licania*.—**Chaplet of roses**, in *her.* See *chaplet*, 3.—**Cherokee rose**, *Rosa lævigata* (*R. Sinica*), a climber once supposed to be indigenous in the southeastern United States, where it abounds, but now known to be from China, whence it was early introduced. Its flowers are single, pure-white, large, and profuse. It makes an excellent hedge-plant.—**China rose.** See def. 1.—**Chinese rose.** (*a*) The China rose. (*b*) A rose-mallow, *Hibiscus Rosa-sinensis*. See *shoeblack-plant*.—**Christmas rose.** See *Christmas* and *Helleborus*.—**Cinnamon-rose**, an old-fashioned sweet-scented rose, *Rosa cinnamomea* of Europe.—**Collar of roses**, an ornamental or honorary collar worn in the time of the Tudor sovereigns as emblematic of the union of the houses of York and Lancaster.—**Corn-rose.** See *poppy* and *cockle*[1].—**Cotton-rose.** See *Filago*.—**Crown of the rose, of the double rose.** See *crown*, 13.—**Crucified rose**, an emblem of the Rosicrucians; a rose-cross.—**Damask rose.** See def. 1 and *damask*.—**Dogrose**, *Rosa canina*, the most common wild rose of Europe and Russian Asia. The stems are commonly erect the first year, 2 or 3 feet high, later elongated and rather straggling, armed with curved prickles; the flowers are pink or white, three or four together. It is sparingly naturalized in Pennsylvania, etc.—**Double rose**, in *her.*, a bearing consisting of a smaller cinquefoil laid upon another larger one, the leaves or lobes of the one coming opposite the divisions between the leaves of the other. The double rose may be barbed and seeded like the rose.—**Egyptian rose**, *Scabiosa arvensis* and *S. atropurpurea*, the latter also known as *mourning-bride*.—**Evergreen rose**, *Rosa sempervirens* of southern Europe. It is the parent of many varieties of free-growing, hardy climbers, including the Ayrshires, evergreen in mild climates.—**Fairy rose**, a miniature rose known as *Rosa Lawrenceana*, doubtless derived from the China rose.—**Field-rose**, *Rosa arvensis*, a trailing rose of western Europe, with white scentless flowers.—**French rose.** See def. 1.—**Golden rose.** See *golden*.—**Holland rose.** See *rose-cut*.—**Holly-rose.** (*a*) The rock-rose, *Helianthemum*. (*b*) Same as *sage-rose*.—**Hundred-leaved rose**, *Rosa centifolia*, a stock of uncertain origin. See def. 1.—**Indian rose**, the China rose, *R. Indica*.—**Jamaica rose**, the name of species of *Meriania*, also of *Blakea trinervis* of the *Melastomaceæ* (Jamaica wild rose), a pretty greenhouse climber.—**Ja-**

pan or **Japanese rose**, one of various true roses, as *Rosa multiflora*, the many-flowered rose, and *R. rugosa*. The name is also applied to plants of the genus *Camellia*.—**Macartney rose**, *Rosa bracteata*, introduced from China, an evergreen climber, the source of a small group of varieties. It is not hardy in the northern United States, but in the South is used for hedges and is sometimes spontaneous.—**Malabar rose**, a shrubby East Indian rose-mallow, *Hibiscus hirtus* (*H. Rosa-malabarica*).—**Many-flowered rose**, a Japanese species, *Rosa multiflora*, the source of several varieties: not hardy in the northern United States.—**Michigan rose.** Same as *prairie-rose*.—**Monthly rose**, one of a class of perpetuals derived from the China rose; a Bengal rose.—**Musk-rose**, *Rosa moschata*, found in southern Europe, Abyssinia, and in Asia to China: a tall climber and profuse bloomer with strongly scented flowers, long known in cultivation, but not hardy.—**Mystic rose**, a vague phrase empty of real meaning, frequent in Rosicrucian literature, especially in the phrase *crucifixion of the mystic rose*. See *Rosicrucian*.—**Noisette rose.** See def. 1.—**Nutka rose**, *Rosa Nutkana* of northwestern North America, the most showy western wild rose, with larger flowers and fruit than any other American species.—**Oil of roses.** See *oil* and *attar*.—**Pale rose**, in the pharmacopœias, same as *hundred-leaved rose*.—**Pompon-rose**, the name of miniature varieties of *Rosa centifolia* or of *R. Indica* (Bengal pompons).—**Prairie-rose**, *Rosa setigera*, common in the interior of the United States. It is the only American climber, a vigorous grower, the flowers large and abundant in corymbs. Also *climbing* and *Michigan rose*. See cut under def. 1.—**Provence, Provins rose.** Same as *cabbage-rose*.—**Provincial rose.** See *provincial*[2].—**Red rose.** (*a*) The badge of the house of Lancaster. (*b*) Specifically, the French rose.—**Rose bengale.** Same as *Bengal red* (which see, under red[1]).—**Rose cut.** See *cut*.—**Rose drill.** See *drill*[1].—**Rose du Barry**, in *ceram.*, a pink or light-crimson color in porcelain-decoration, named from Madame du Barry, mistress of Louis XV. See *rose Pompadour*.—**Rose family.** (*a*) A name given by some writers to a division of the porcelain of China in which red prevails, and which is marked by the abundant use of enameled color in perceptible relief above the background. (*b*) In *bot.*, the order *Rosaceæ*.—**Rose of Jericho.** See *Anastatica*.—**Rose of Plymouth.** See *Sabbatia*.—**Rose of Sharon.** (*a*) In *Scrip.* (Cant. ii. 1), the autumn crocus (so explained in R. V. margin); perhaps *Colchicum autumnale*. (*b*) A St.-John's-wort, *Hypericum calycinum*. *Britten and Holland*, Eng. Plant-names. [Prov. Eng.] (*c*) Same as *althæa*, 2. [U. S.]—**Rose Pompadour**, a rose-pink or light-crimson color of the Sèvres porcelain, imitated by other factories: a name derived from the Marquise de Pompadour: called later *rose du Barry*, as a compliment to Madame du Barry. The second name is more commonly heard in England, though it is less correct, the name *rose Pompadour* having been given when the color was first introduced.—**Scotch rose.** See def. 1.—**South-sea rose**, the oleander. [Jamaica.]—**Sun-rose**, the rock-rose, *Helianthemum*.—**Swamp-rose**, *Rosa Carolina*, common in the eastern United States, forming thickets in swampy ground.—**Tea-rose**, or **tea-scented rose.** See def. 1.—**Tudor rose**, in *her.*, a combination of two heraldic roses, one gules and the other argent. Sometimes one of these is set upon the other, the upper being the smaller; in other instances it is divided, as per cross or per saltier, alternately red and white.—**Under the rose** (a translation of Latin *sub rosa*), in secret; privately; in a manner that forbids disclosure.

> *Under the rose*, since here are none but friends,
> (To own the truth) we have some private ends.
> *Swift*, Epil. to a Benefit Play, for the Distressed Weavers.

Wars of the Roses, in *Eng. hist.*, the prolonged armed struggle between the houses of Lancaster and York: so called from the red rose and white rose, badges respectively of the adherents of the two families. The wars commenced with the first battle of St. Albans in 1455; the Yorkist claimant was killed in 1460, but his son Edward IV. supplanted the Lancastrian king Henry VI. in 1461; the Yorkist kings (Edward IV., Edward V., and Richard III.) continued in power in spite of the repeated efforts of Queen Margaret (wife of Henry VI.), except for a brief period in 1470-71, when Henry VI. was restored. The contest was ended in 1485 with the death of Richard III. at Bosworth, and the succession of Henry VII., a Lancastrian, who, by his marriage with a Yorkist princess, united the conflicting interests.—**White rose.** (*a*) The badge of the house of York. (*b*) Specifically, *Rosa alba*, a garden rose, native in the Caucasus.—**Wild rose**, any native species.—**Wind-rose.** (*a*) An old name of *Papaver Argemone*. (*b*) See *Rœmeria*.—**Yellow rose.** Specifically—(*a*) *Rosa lutea* (*R. Eglanteria*), the Austrian brier or yellow eglantine, sometimes distinguished as *single yellow rose*, though often double. It is a summer rose of many varieties, with a habit like that of sweetbrier (eglantine); native from Asia Minor to the Himalayas and northward. (*b*) *R. sulphurea*, the double yellow rose, beautiful in warm climates, native from Asia Minor to Persia.—**York-and-Lancaster rose**, a variegated variety of the French, also of the damask rose. (See also *cabbage-rose, eglantine, guelder-rose*, Lent-rose, *moss-rose, mountain-rose*, rock-rose, *sage-rose, sweetbrier*.)

II. *a.* Of an extremely luminous purplish-red color. Some *rose* colors are deficient in chroma, and are therefore varieties of pink, *rose-pink*; others have the most intense chroma, *rose-reds*; others incline so much toward purple as to be called *rose-purple*.

> The lights, *rose*, amber, emerald, blue.
> *Tennyson*, Palace of Art.

Bengal rose, a coal-tar color used in dyeing, somewhat similar to eosin, but producing bluer shades. It is the sodium salt of tetra-iodo-dichlor-fluoresceïn.—**Rose elder, finch, lake, linnet.** See the nouns.—**Rose madder.** See *madder lakes*, under *madder*[1].—**Rose pink, porcelain.** See the nouns.

rose[1] (rōz), *v. t.*; pret. and pp. *rosed*, ppr. *rosing*. [‹ *rose*[1], *n.*] 1. To render rose-colored; redden; cause to flush or blush.

> A maid yet *rosed* over with the virgin crimson of modesty.
> *Shak.*, Hen. V., v. 2. 323.

2. To perfume as with roses.

> A *rosed* breath from lips rosie proceeding.
> *Sir P. Sidney*, Arcadia, p. 234.

rose[2] (rōz). Preterit of *rise*[1].

rose[3] (rōz), *v. t.* An obsolete or dialectal form of *roose*.

rose-acacia (rōz-a-kā'shiạ̈), *n.* The bristly or moss locust, *Robinia hispida*, from the southern Alleghanies, an admired shrub or small tree with large deep rose-colored inodorous flowers in racemes.

Roseæ (rō'zẹ̄-ē), *n. pl.* [NL. (A. P. de Candolle, 1825), ‹ *Rosa* + *-eæ*.] A tribe of rosaceous plants consisting of the genus *Rosa*.

roseaker†, *n.* Blue vitriol.

> To have a man chased to death in such manner by poison after poison, first *roseaker*, then arsenick, then mercury sublimate, then sublimate again, it is a thing would astonish man's nature to hear it.
> *Bacon*, Accusation of Wentworth, 1615 (Works, ed. Spedding, XII. 218).

roseal† (rō'zẹ̄-al), *a.* [Also *rosial*; ‹ L. *roseus*, rosy (‹ *rosa*[1], rose), + *-al*.] Like a rose, especially in color; roseate.

> Beholding the *rosiall* colour, which was wont to be in his visage, tourned in to salowe.
> *Sir T. Elyot*, The Governour, ii. 12.

> The *roseal* cross is spread within thy field,
> A sign of peace, not of revenging war.
> *Greene*, James IV., v.

> From the West returning,
> To th' honored Cradle of the *rosiall* Morning.
> *Sylvester*, tr. of Du Bartas's Weeks, i. 2.

> His *roseal* cheeks ten thousand Graces swell'd.
> *J. Beaumont*, Psyche, i. 58.

rose-aniline (rōz'an″i-lin), *n.* Same as *rosaniline*.

rose-aphis (rōz'ā″fis), *n.* Any aphid which infests roses; a greenfly; specifically, *Siphonophora rosæ*.

rose-apple (rōz'ap″l), *n.* An East Indian tree, *Eugenia Jambos*, widely cultivated in the tropics, beautiful in flower, foliage, and fruit. The fruit is of the size of a hen's egg, heavily rose-scented, only moderately palatable, wanting juice. Related species are to some extent included under the name. Also *jam-rosade* and *Malabar plum*.

rose-a-ruby† (rōz'ạ̈-rö'bi), *n.* [L. *rosa rubea*, red rose: *rosa*, rose; *rubea*, fem. of *rubeus*, red: see *ruby*.] The pheasant's-eye, *Adonis autumnalis*.

roseate (rō'zẹ̄-āt), *a.* [‹ L. *roseus*, rosy, + *-ate*[1]. Cf. *rosated*.] 1. Full of roses; consisting of roses; prepared from roses.

> I come, I come! prepare your *roseate* bowers,
> Celestial palms, and ever-blooming flowers.
> *Pope*, Eloisa to Abelard, l. 317.

> Celestial Venus hover'd o'er his head,
> And *roseate* unguents, heav'nly fragrance! shed.
> *Pope*, Iliad, xxiii. 229.

2. Of a rose color; blooming: as, *roseate* beauty.

> The wind-stirred robe of *roseate* gray,
> And rose-crown of the hour that leads the day.
> *D. G. Rossetti*, The Stream's Secret.

Roseate spoonbill, *Ajaja rosea*, the common spoonbill of America. See cut under *Ajaja*.—**Roseate tern**, *Sterna paradisea* or *S. dougalli*, the paradise tern, the under parts of which, in the breeding-season, are white with a delicate rosy blush. The mantle is pale pearl-blue; the cap is black, the bill is black, and the feet are coral-red. The tail is long and deeply forked. The length is 14 or 15 inches, the extent 30. This bird is common along the Atlantic coast of the United States, and in many other regions of both hemispheres. It was named in 1813 by Colonel Montagu in compliment to one of its discoverers, Dr. McDougall; though often called *S. paradisea*, the latter name, brought into use by Keyserling and Blasius in 1840, rests upon a questionable identification of a tern so called by Brünnich in 1764. Montagu's specific name was "emended" *macdougalli* by Macgillivray in 1842.

Roseate Tern (*Sterna dougalli* or *paradisea*).

rose-back (rōz'bak), *a.* In *ceram.*, having the back or outside decorated richly in red, either plain or with an incised pattern or some peculiarity of texture, as some fine Oriental porcelain.

rose-bay (rōz'bā), *n.* A name of several plants. (*a*) The oleander. (*b*) The willow-herb, *Epilobium angustifolium*. (*c*) Any rhododendron; somewhat specially, *Rhododendron maximum*.—**Lapland rose-bay**, the Lapland rhododendron. See *rhododendron*, 2.

rose-beetle (rōz'bē″tl), *n.* 1. A coleopterous insect which affects or frequents roses; especially, *Cetonia aurata*, the common rose-chafer of Great Britain. Also called *rose-fly* and *rose-bug*.—2. A curculionid beetle, *Aramigus fulleri*,

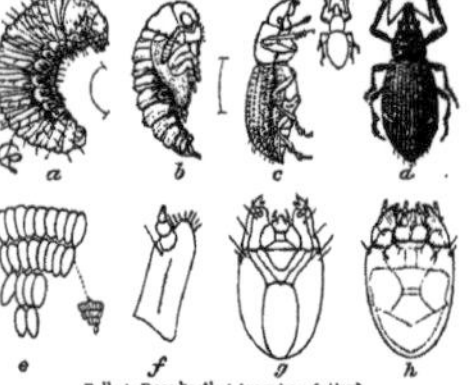

Fuller's Rose-beetle (*Aramigus fulleri*).
a, full-grown larva; *b*, pupa (lines showing natural sizes of *a* and *b*); *c*, adult beetle, from side; *d*, same, from above (outline between them showing natural size); *e*, eggs, enlarged and natural size; *f*, left maxilla with palpus, enlarged; *g*, head of larva, from below, enlarged; *h*, same, from above, enlarged.

more fully called *Fuller's rose-beetle*.—3. The rose-chafer of the United States, *Macrodactylus subspinosus*. See cut under *rose-bug*.

roseberry (rōz'ber″i), *n.*; pl. *roseberries* (-iz). The fruit of the rose; a hip. [Colloq.]

rose-bit (rōz'bit), *n.* A cylindrical bit, terminating in a truncated cone, the oblique surface of which is cut into teeth. It is often used for enlarging holes of considerable depth in metals and hard woods.

rose-blanket (rōz'blang″ket), *n.* A blanket of fine quality, having a rose, or a conventional device resembling a rose, worked in one corner.

rosebone (rōz'bōn), *n.* A fish with a deformity of the backbone; a humpbacked fish, as a cod.

rose-box (rōz'boks), *n.* A plant of the genus *Cotoneaster*.

rose-breasted (rōz'bres″ted), *a.* Having rose color on the breast, as a bird: as, the *rose-breasted* grosbeak, *Zamelodia* (or *Habia*) *ludoviciana*. This is one of the most beautiful birds of the United States, abundant from the Atlantic to the Mississippi and somewhat beyond. It is a fine songster. The male is black, much varied with white on the wings, tail, and under parts; the bill is white; and a patch on the breast and the lining of the wings are rose-red or carmine. It is 8 inches long and 12½ in extent of wings.—**Rose-breasted godwit**, the Hudsonian or red-breasted godwit, *Limosa hæmastica*.

Rose-breasted Grosbeak (*Habia ludoviciana*).

rosebud (rōz'bud), *n.* 1. The bud of a rose.

> Let us crown ourselves with *rosebuds*, before they be withered.
> *Wisdom of Solomon*, ii. 8.

Hence—2. A young girl in her first bloom; a débutante; a bud. [Colloq.]

> A *rosebud* set with little wilful thorns,
> And sweet as English air could make her, she.
> *Tennyson*, Princess, Prol.

> They flutter their brief hour in society, and if they fail to marry as they or their friends expect, they're so deplorably de trop. Some of them hold on like grim death to *rosebud* privileges.
> *The Century*, XL. 582.

rose-bug (rōz'bug), *n.* A rose-beetle. A common species which infests roses in the United States is a melolonthid, *Macrodactylus subspinosus*, a pest in gardens and vineyards.

> Crop injured by attacks of *rose-bug* in the spring. Whether Noah was justifiable in preserving this class of insects?
> *Lowell*, Biglow Papers, 1st ser., Int.

Rose-bug (*Macrodactylus subspinosus*), natural size.

rose-burner (rōz'bėr″nėr), *n.* A gas-burner in which the gas issues from a series of openings disposed radially around a center, so that the flames resemble the petals of a flower. Also called *rosette-burner*.

rose-bush (rōz'bủsh), *n.* A shrub which bears roses, commonly of a bushy habit.

rose-camphor (rōz'kam"fėr), *n.* One of the two volatile oils composing attar of roses. It is a stearoptene, and is solid.

rose-campion (rōz'kam"pi-on), *n.* A pretty garden flower, *Lychnis coronaria*. The plant is a branching woolly herb, covered in summer and autumn with rosy-crimson blossoms. Also *mullen-pink*.

rose-carnation (rōz'kär-nā'shon), *n.* A carnation the ground-color of whose petals is striped with rose-color.

> And many a *rose-carnation* feed
> With summer spice the humming air.
> *Tennyson*, In Memoriam, ci.

rose carthame. A color used in water-color painting. See *Carthamus*.

rose-catarrh (rōz'ka-tär"), *n.* Same as *rose-cold*.

rose-chafer (rōz'chā"fėr), *n.* Same as *rose-beetle* or *rose-bug*.

rose-cheeked (rōz'chēkt), *a.* 1. Having rosy or ruddy cheeks.

> *Rose-cheek'd* Adonis hied him to the chase.
> *Shak.*, Venus and Adonis, l. 3.

2. Having rose-red on the cheeks, as a bird: as, the *rose-cheeked* kingfisher, *Ispidina picta*, of Africa.

rose-cold (rōz'kōld), *n.* A form of hay-fever developing early in the summer. Also called *rose-catarrh*, *rose-fever*.

rose-color (rōz'kul"or), *n.* 1. The color of a rose; specifically, a deep and vivid pink, a color common in roses. See rose[1], *a.* Hence— 2. Beauty or attractiveness, as of a rose; often, fancied beauty or attractiveness; couleur de rose: as, life appears to the young all *rose-color*.

rose-colored (rōz'kul"ord), *a.* 1. Having the color of a rose; rosy: as, the *rose-colored* pastors, the starlings of the genus *Pastor*. See cut under *Pastor*.—2. Uncommonly beautiful; hence, extravagantly fine or pleasing: as, *rose-colored* views of the future.

> She believed her husband was a hero of a *rose-colored* romance, and he turns out to be not even a hero of very sad-colored reality. *H. James, Jr.*, Pass. Pilgrim, p. 425.

rose-comb (rōz'kōm), *n.* See *comb*[1], 3.

rose-copper (rōz'kop"ėr), *n.* Same as *rosette-copper*.

rose-cross (rōz'krôs), *n.* and *a.* I. *n.* 1. [*cap.*] [See *Rosicrucian*.] A Rosicrucian.—2. A rosy cross, the alleged symbol of the Rosicrucians, supposed to denote the union of a rose with a cross: indicated by a cross within a circle, a rose on a cross, and otherwise. See *crucified rose* and *mystic rose*, under rose[1]. Also called *rosic-cross*, *rosy cross*, *rosicrux*, *rosecroix*, etc.

II. *a.* [*cap.*] Rosicrucian.

> That stone of which so many have us told, ...
> The great Elixir, or . . .
> The *Rose-Cross* knowledge.
> *Drayton*, To Master William Jeffreys.

rose-cut (rōz'kut), *a.* Cut with a series of triangular facets, the whole surface rounding up from the girdle. The number of triangular faces on the upper side of the girdle is usually twenty-four. The back is usually flat—that is, the girdle is at one extreme of the stone, having no base projecting beyond it. In some cases, however, there is a base resembling a crown; then the cut is called the *double* or *Holland rose*.

rose-drop (rōz'drop), *n.* 1. A lozenge flavored with rose-essence.—2. An ear-ring.—3. A pimple on the nose caused by drinking ardent spirits; a grog-blossom; acne.

rose-ear (rōz'ēr), *n.* A dog's ear which hangs so as to show the flesh-colored inside.

rose-encrinite (rōz'en"kri-nīt), *n.* A rhodocrinite.

rose-engine (rōz'en"jin), *n.* A form of lathe in which the rotary motion of the mandrel may be combined with a radial movement of the tool-rest, the result being a movement of eccentric character. An eccentric chuck is also used with a stationary tool-rest, or the work in the lathe is, by means of suitable mechanism, made to oscillate slightly. Whatever the method used, the result is the tracing on a flat surface, such as the back of a watch-case, of a series of waved or circular lines which may be considered to bear some resemblance to a full-blown rose. The rose-engine is used to make complicated ornamental tracings on the engraved plates used for printing bank-notes, bonds, etc., and in decorating watch-cases and other metal-work. The work performed by it is called *engine-turning*. Also called *geometrical lathe*.

Specimen of Engine-turning.

rose-festival (rōz'fes"ti-val), *n.* A festival celebrated on June 8, which had its origin at the village of Salency, near Noyon, in France. A girl is selected from three most distinguished for feminine virtues, her name being announced from the pulpit to give an opportunity for objections. She is then conducted to church, where she hears service in a place of honor, after which she formerly used to open a ball with the seigneur. She is called *La Rosière*, because she is adorned with roses held together by a silver clasp presented by Louis XIII. The festival has been imitated at other places in France, at many of which the rosière receives a purse or a dower from a foundation established for the purpose.

rose-fever (rōz'fē"vėr), *n.* Same as *rose-cold*.

rose-fish (rōz'fish), *n.* A scorpænoid fish, the Norway haddock, *Sebastes marinus*. It inhabits both coasts of the North Atlantic; it is mostly orange-red. Also called *snapper*, *bergylt*, *redfish*, etc. See cut under *Sebastes*.

rose-fly (rōz'flī), *n.* Same as *rose-beetle*, 1, or *rose-bug*.

rose-flycatcher (rōz'flī"kach-ėr), *n.* One of the American fly-catching warblers of the genus *Cardellina*, as *C. rubra* and *C. rubrifrons*. They are small insectivorous birds related to the redstart (*Setophaga*), of rich or varied coloration, of which rose-red is one tint. Those named reach the border of the United States from Mexico.

rose-gall (rōz'gâl), *n.* A gall produced on roses by an insect, as the cynipid *Rhodites rosæ*.

rose-geranium (rōz'jē-rā"ni-um), *n.* A common house-plant, *Pelargonium capitatum*, with rose-scented leaves and small rose-purple flowers.

rose-haw (rōz'hâ), *n.* The fruit of the wild rose; a rose-hip. [Colloq.]

> Redly gleam the *rose-haws*, dripping with the wet,
> Fruit of sober autumn, glowing crimson yet.
> *Celia Thaxter*, May Morning.

rose-house (rōz'hous), *n.* In *hort.*, a glass house for the propagation of roses, or for the forcing of roses into bloom.

rose-hued (rōz'hūd), *a.* Of the hue or color of the rose; rose-colored.

> Many a dark delicious curl,
> Flowing beneath her *rose-hued* zone.
> *Tennyson*, Arabian Nights.

roseine (rō'zē-in), *n.* [< *rose*[1] + *-ine*[2].] Same as *fuchsin*.

rose-knot (rōz'not), *n.* A rosette of ribbon, worsted, or other soft material.

Rose-lashing.

rose-lashing (rōz'lash"ing), *n.* *Naut.*, a kind of lashing or seizing employed in binding anything on a spar: so termed from the rose-like form in which the end of the seizing is secured.

rose-lathe (rōz'lāᴛʜ), *n.* A lathe fitted with a rose-engine.

rose-leaf (rōz'lēf), *n.* [< ME. *rose-lēf*; < rose[1] + *leaf*.] One of the petals of a rose.

roselet (rōz'let), *n.* [< F. *roselet*, the stoat or ermine in summer when brown, not white, < *rose*, rose: see *rose*[1].] The fur of the ermine, *Putorius erminea*, as taken from the animal in the summer.

roselette (rōz'let), *n.* [< OF. **roselette*, dim. of *rose*, a rose: see rose[1].] In *her.*, a rose, when many are used on a field at once. Compare *lioncel*.

rose-lip (rōz'lip), *n.* A lip of a rosy or red-ripe color. *Tennyson*, Adeline, i.

rose-lipped (rōz'lipt), *a.* Having red or rosy lips. [Rare.]

> Thou young and *rose-lipp'd* cherubin.
> *Shak.*, Othello, iv. 2. 63.

roselite (rō'ze-līt), *n.* [=G. *roselith*; named after Gustav *Rose*, a German naturalist (1798–1873).] A hydrous arseniate of cobalt and calcium, occurring in small red triclinic crystals at Schneeberg in Saxony.

rosella (rō-zel'ä), *n.* [NL., < L. *rosa*, rose: see *rose*[1].] A beautiful Australian parrot, *Platycercus eximius*, the rose-parrakeet. This is a favorite cage-bird, elegantly varied with scarlet, green, blue, yellow, white, and other colors. There are many similar birds of the same genus. See cut in next column.

rosella-fiber (rō-zel'ä-fī"bėr), *n.* See *roselle*.

rosellate (rō-zel'āt), *a.* [< NL. **rosella*, dim. of L. *rosa*, rose (see *rose*[1]), + *-ate*[1].] In *bot.*, disposed like the petals of a rose, or in rosettes: said of leaves.

roselle (rō-zel'), *n.* [Also *rozelle*, *rouselle*; < NL. *rosella*; cf. F. *oseille*, sorrel.] An East Indian rose-mallow, *Hibiscus Sabdariffa*, widely cultivated in the tropics, where its pleasantly acidulous calyxes are used for tarts, jellies, etc., and for making a cool refreshing drink. It yields also a fiber sparingly substituted for hemp, known as *roselle-hemp* or *rosella-fiber*. In the West Indies the plant is called *Indian* or *red sorrel*. Also called *sabdariffa*.

Rosella (*Platycercus eximius*).

rose-mallow (rōz'mal"ō), *n.* See *mallow*.

rose-maloes (rōz'mal"ōz), *n.* [An Anglo-Malayan modification of *rasamala*, q. v.] A kind of liquid storax obtained from the East Indian *Altingia excelsa*.

rosemarinet, *n.* Same as *rosemary*.

rosemary (rōz'mā-ri), *n.* [Formerly also *rosmary*; < ME. *rosemary*, altered (in simulation of *rosa Mariæ*, 'Mary's rose') from *rosemarine*, *rosemaryne*, *rosemaryn*, *rosmarin*, < OF. *rosmarin*, *romarin*, F. *romarin* = Pr. *romani*, *romanin* = Sp. *rosmarino*, *romero* = Pg. *rosmaninho* = It. *rosmarino*, *ramerino* = D. *rozemarijn*, *rosmarijn* = G. Dan. Sw. *rosmarin*, < L. *rosmarinus*, *rosmarinum*; prop. two words, *ros marinus* or *marinus ros*, rosemary, lit. 'marine dew,' sea-dew (called *ros maris*, 'dew of the sea,' by Ovid): *ros* (*ror-*), dew; *marinus*, marine: see *rore*[3] and *marine*.] An evergreen shrub, *Rosmarinus officinalis*, native in southern Europe, widely cultivated. (See *Rosmarinus*.) It has a fragrant smell, and a warm, pungent, bitterish taste. It yields by distillation a light pale essential oil of great fragrance, which is extensively employed in the manufacture of pomatums for the hair. Its leaves are gently stimulant, and are used to some extent in European medicine.

Rosemary (*Rosmarinus officinalis*).
1, the upper part of the stem, with flowers; 2, the lower part of the stem; *a*, a flower; *b*, a leaf, seen from below, showing the revolute margin.

> There's *rosemary*, that's for remembrance.
> *Shak.*, Hamlet, iv. 5. 175.

> Some sign of mourning was shown by every one, down to the little child in its mother's arms, that innocently clutched the piece of *rosemary* to be thrown into the grave "for remembrance."
> *Mrs. Gaskell*, Sylvia's Lovers, vi.

Rosemary-moorwort. Same as *wild rosemary* (*a*).—**Rosemary-pine.** See *loblolly-pine*.—**Wild rosemary.** (*a*) A plant, the *Andromeda polifolia*. (*b*) See *Ledum*.

rose-molding (rōz'mōl"ding), *n.* In *arch.*, a molding ornamented with roses. Very beautiful examples with conventionalized yet naturalistic treatment of the flowers and climbing vine occur in French work of the thirteenth century.

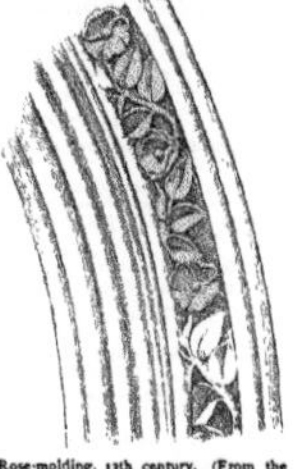
Rose-molding, 13th century. (From the Porte Rouge, Notre Dame de Paris.)

rose-money (rōz'mun"i), *n.* A name sometimes given to screw-dollars or screw-medals.

rosen† (rō'zn), *a.* [< ME. *rosen*, < AS. *rōsen*, made of roses, < *rōse*, a rose: see rose[1] and *-en*[2].] 1. Roseate; rose-colored; ruddy.

Phebus the sonne with his golden chariet bryngeth forth the rosene day. *Chaucer*, Boëthius, ii. meter 8.

2. Consisting of roses.

His leef a rosyn chapelet
Hadde made, and on his heed it set.
Rom. of the Rose, l. 845.

rose-nail (rōz'nāl), *n.* A nail with a conical head which is hammered into triangular facets.

Rosenbach's sign. See *sign*.

rosenbuschite (rō'zn-bùsh-īt), *n.* [Named after Prof. H. *Rosenbusch* of Heidelberg.] A silicate of calcium and sodium, containing also zirconium and titanium: it occurs in monoclinic crystals and in fibrous forms of a pale orange color. It is found in the elæolite-syenite of southern Norway.

Rosendale cement. See *cement*, 2.

Rosenhain's function. See *function*.

Rosenmüller's fossa. A somewhat triangular depression in the pharynx on either side behind the openings of the Eustachian tubes.

Rosenmüller's gland. The inferior or palpebral portion of the lacrymal gland.

Rosenmüller's organ. See *organ*.

rose-noble (rōz'nō"bl), *n.* An English gold coin first issued by Edward IV., and worth at the time ten shillings: same as *ryal*.

2. Hunt. What haue they giuen vs?
1. Hunt. Six *rose-nobles* just.
Heywood, 1 Edw. IV. (Works, ed. Pearson, 1874, I. 43).

Rosen's liniment. A liniment composed of oil of nutmeg, spirit of juniper, and oil of cloves.

Rosenstrehl's green. See *green*[1].

Rosenthal's canal. The spiral canal of the modiolus.

Rosenthal's test. See *test*.

rose-of-heaven (rōz'ov-hev'n), *n.* A pretty garden plant, *Lychnis Cœli-rosa*.

rose-oil (rōz'oil), *n.* Same as *oil of rose* (which see, under *oil*).

roseola (rō-zē'ō-lạ̈), *n.* [= F. *roséole*; < NL., < L. *roseus*, rosy (< *rosa*, rose: see *rose*[1]), + dim. *-ola*.] In *pathol.*, a kind of rash or rose-colored efflorescence, mostly symptomatic, occurring in connection with different febrile complaints. Also called *rose-rash* and *scarlet rash*.

roseolar (rō-zē'ō-lạ̈r), *a.* [< *roseola* + *-ar*[2].] Of, pertaining to, or exhibiting roseola.

roseoloid (rō-zē'ō-loid), *a.* [< *roseola* + *-oid*.] Same as *roseolous*.

roseolous (rō-zē'ō-lus), *a.* [< *roseola* + *-ous*.] Of, pertaining to, or resembling roseola: as, *roseolous* rash.

rose-ouzel (rōz'ö"zl), *n.* The rose-colored pastor, *Pastor roseus*.

rose-parrakeet (rōz-par"ạ-kēt), *n.* The rosella.

rose-pink (rōz'pingk), *n.* and *a.* **I.** *n.* **1.** A chromatic crimson-pink color.—**2.** A pigment prepared by dyeing chalk or whiting with a decoction of Brazil-wood and alum.

Clean faces appeared in lieu of black ones smeared with *rose pink*. *Dickens*, Sketches.

3. The American centaury, *Sabbatia angularis*. [Rare or obsolete.]

II. *a.* Of a rosy-pink color or hue; roseate; having a delicate bloom: also used figuratively: as, "*rose-pink* piety," *Kingsley*. (*Imp. Dict.*)

rose-point (rōz'point), *n.* See *point*[1].

rose-quartz (rōz'kwârts), *n.* A translucent and at times almost transparent variety of quartz, varying in color from light rose-red to dark-pink. The coloring matter is due to the presence of oxid of manganese, which is more or less affected by the action of the sunlight. Fine examples are found in Oxford county, Maine, and in other localities.

roser† (rō'zėr), *n.* [Early mod. E. also *rosier*, *rosyer*; < ME. *roser*, *roseere*, < OF. *rosier*, *rozier*, F. *rosier*, a rose-bush, = Pr. *roser*, *rosier*, < L. *rosarium*, a rose-garden, ML. also a rosebush: see *rosary*.] **1.** A rose-garden.—**2.** A rose-bush.

An hound whan he cometh to a *roser*.
Chaucer, Parson's Tale.

The third was a *rosyer*, with the armes of England; the fourth a braunche of lylies, bearing the armes of France.
Hall, Hen. VIII., fol. 59, quoted in Strutt's Sports and [Pastimes, p. 240.

rose-rash (rōz'rash), *n.* Same as *roseola*.

rose-red (rōz'red), *a.* and *n.* [< ME. *rose-red*; < *rose*[1] + *red*[1].] **I.** *a.* Red as a red rose.

Two corones han we,
Snow-whyte and *rose-reed*.
Chaucer, Second Nun's Tale, l. 254.

From thy *rose-red* lips my name
Floweth. *Tennyson*, Eleänore.

II. *n.* A luminous and chromatic crimson.

rose-ringed (rōz'ringd), *a.* Having a collar of rose-red feathers: noting a collared parrot, *Palæornis torquatus*, known as the *rose-ringed parrakeet*. See cut under *ring-parrot*.

roseroot (rōz'röt), *n.* A succulent herb, *Sedum Rhodiola*, having simple leafy stems 5 to 10 inches high, broad thick leaves, yellowish or purplish flowers in a close cyme, and a rose-scented root. It grows on cliffs in northern Europe and Asia, and in North America in eastern Pennsylvania, Maine, and northward. Also *rosewort*.

rose-rowel (rōz'rou"el), *n.* See *rowel*.

rosery (rō'zėr-i), *n.*; pl. *roseries* (-iz). [< *rose*[1] + *-ery*. Cf. *rosary*, and also F. *roseraie*, < *rosier*, a rose-bush: see *roser*.] A place where roses grow; a nursery of rose-bushes; a rosary.

rose-ryal (rōz'rī"al), *n.* An English gold coin of the reign of James I. See *ryal*.

rose-sawfly (rōz'sâ"flī), *n.* A sawfly which affects the rose. (*a*) In Europe, *Hylotoma rosarum*. (*b*) In America, *Monostegia rosæ*, whose larva is called *rose-slug*.

American Rose-sawfly (*Monostegia rosæ*).
a, female fly (cross shows natural size); *b*, her saws; *c*, antenna (*b* and *c* enlarged).

rose-slug (rōz'slug), *n.* The larva of the American rose-sawfly, *Monostegia rosæ*, which skeletonizes the leaves of the rose in the United States.

Rose's metal. See *metal*.

rose-steel (rōz'stēl), *n.* A cement-steel the interior of which exhibits on fracture a different structure from the exterior.

roset[1] (rō'zet), *n.* [Also *rosette*; < OF. (and F.) *rosette*, a kind of red coloring matter, < *rose*, rose: see *rose*[1].] A red color used by painters.

roset[2] (roz'et), *n.* [A corrupt form of *rosin*.] Rosin. [Scotch.]

roseta, *n.* Latin plural of *rosetum*.

rose-tanager (rōz'tan"ạ-jėr), *n.* The summer redbird, *Piranga æstiva*: distinguished from the scarlet tanager, *P. rubra*.

rose-tangle (rōz'tang"gl), *n.* Red or brown-red seaweeds of the suborder *Ceramieæ*.

rose-topaz (rōz'tō"paz), *n.* An artificial color of the true topaz produced by heating the crystals of yellow Brazilian topaz to a red heat. A chemical change results which, if prolonged too great a time, would change the topaz into the colorless white variety, the color ranging from light rose-red to sherry-red.

rose-tree (rōz'trē), *n.* A standard rose; a rose-bush.

Rosetta stone. See *stone*.

rosetta-wood (rō-zet'ạ̈-wùd), *n.* A handsome wood, of an orange-red color with very dark veins, from the East Indies, used in fine cabinet-making. It is of durable texture, but the colors become dark by exposure. The tree yielding it is not known.

rosette (rō-zet'), *n.* [< F. *rosette*, a rosette, a little rose (= Pr. Sp. *roseta*, tassel, = Pg. *roseta*, the rowel of a spur, = It. *rosetta*, a rosette), dim. of *rose*, < L. *rosa*, rose: see *rose*[1].] **1.** Any circular ornament having many small parts in concentric circles, or regularly arranged around the center.

She lifted Suzanne's hair to the middle of the head in two *rosettes* that she called riquettes, and fastened them with a silver comb. *G. W. Cable*, Stories of Louisiana, x.

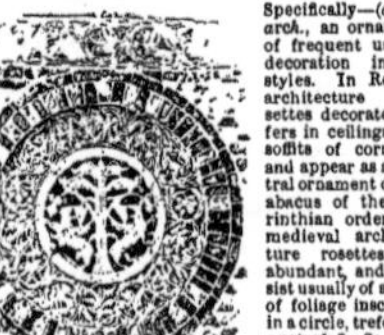

Rosette.—Early Italian medieval work.

Specifically—(*a*) In *arch.*, an ornament of frequent use in decoration in all styles. In Roman architecture rosettes decorate coffers in ceilings and soffits of cornices, and appear as a central ornament of the abacus of the Corinthian order. In medieval architecture rosettes are abundant, and consist usually of a knot of foliage inscribed in a circle, trefoil, or quatrefoil. See also cut under *patera*. (*b*) A knot of ribbon or a bunch of colored worsted used as an ornament of costume, especially one of the two bunches of ribbons attached to the loops by which an officer's gorget was suspended on his chest.

2. Any object or arrangement resembling in form a full-blown rose. (*a*) A rose gas-burner, in which the jets of flame are disposed radially about a center. (*b*) A particular arrangement of the sails of a windmill. (*c*) The pattern produced by a rose-engine lathe. (*d*) In *bot.*, a circle of leaves or fronds.

3. Same as *roset*[1].—**4.** In *zoöl.* and *anat.*, a natural formation of parts resembling a rose. See *rose*, 9. (*a*) The anal bunch of gills of a nudibranchiate gastropod. (*b*) The central plate which occupies the space between the apices of the first five radials of *Comatula*, and is formed from the confluence of five basals. *Carpenter; Huxley*. (*c*) The set of live petaloid ambulacra of some sea-urchins. See cut under *Petalosticha*. (*d*) A spot of color which resembles a flower, as a broken-up ocellus. See cut under *jaguar*. (*e*) A rosette-cell. (*f*) A rosette-plate.

5. A curve whose polar equation is $r = a + \sin m\theta$, which presents a great variety of forms symmetrical about a center.—**6.** *Naut.*, a form of knot.—**7.** In *metal.*, a disk or plate formed by throwing water on melted metal. See *rosette-copper*, and compare *quenching*, 2.—**Red rosette**, or **red button**, the rosette worn in the buttonhole by officers and higher dignitaries of the Legion of Honor.

Rosette, 5.

rosette-burner (rō-zet'bėr"nėr), *n.* Same as *rose-burner*.

rosette-cell (rō-zet'sel), *n.* One of the small spheroidal clusters or masses of usually eight or sixteen cells which are developed in sponges, in the cavity both of the adult sponge and of its free-swimming ciliated gemmules. *W. S. Kent.*

rosette-copper (rō-zet'kop"ėr), *n.* A product of copper made by throwing water on the surface of the melted metal (after the refining process), which is then removed in the form of a disk, the operation being repeated as often as is necessary. These disks or rosettes are colored bright-red by the action of the water on the copper, by which a suboxid is formed. This process has been followed at Chessy in France, chiefly, and also at Mansfeld in Prussia. Also called *rose-copper*.

rosette-cutter (rō-zet'kut"ėr), *n.* A rotary cutting-tool for making wooden rosettes or circular ornaments in which different moldings are combined. Its cutting edge is of the inverse form of the ornament desired. Such tools are used in cabinet-making and carpentry.

rosetted (rō-zet'ed), *a.* [< *rosette* + *-ed*[2].] **1.** Furnished or ornamented with a rosette.

The low-cut and *rosetted* shoe. *The Atlantic*, LXIV. 614.

2. Formed or arranged in rosettes: as, the decorations were of looped and *rosetted* ribbons.

rosette-plate (rō-zet'plāt), *n.* In *Polyzoa*, a communication-plate.

rosetum (rō-zē'tum), *n.*; pl. *rosetums*, *roseta* (-tumz, -tạ̈). [< L. *rosetum*, a garden or bed of roses, < *rosa*, a rose: see *rose*[1].] A garden or parterre devoted to the cultivation of roses.

rose-vinegar (rōz'vin"ē-gạ̈r), *n.* An infusion made by steeping the petals of roses in vinegar, used as an external application in headaches, also to dispel unpleasant odors. *Chambers's Encyc.*, art. Rose.

rose-water (rōz'wâ"tėr), *n.* and *a.* **I.** *n.* Water tinctured with oil of roses by distillation.

Euery morning their Priestes (called Bramini) washe the Image of the deuyll with *rose water*, or such other swete liquoure, and perfume hym with dyuerse swete sauours.
R. Eden, tr. of Sebastian Munster (First Books on Amer- [ica, ed. Arber, p. 17).

Let one attend him with a silver basin
Full of *rose-water* and bestrew'd with flowers.
Shak., T. of the S., Ind., i. 56.

II. *a.* Having the odor or character of rose-water; hence, affectedly delicate or sentimental: as, *rose-water* religion.

Rose-water philanthropy. *Carlyle*. (*Imp. Dict.*)

Rose-water dish. (*a*) A dish with perforated top, for pouring or sprinkling rose-water over the hands. (*b*) The plateau for a rose-water ewer.—**Rose-water ewer**, a name given to the aftaba, or spouted aiguière, used in Persia and other parts of the East for pouring water over the hands after eating. See cut under *aftaba*.—**Rose-water ointment.** See *ointment*.

rose-willow (rōz'wil"ō), *n.* See *willow*.

rose-window (rōz'win"dō), *n.* In *arch.*, a circular window divided into compartments by mullions or tracery radiating or branching from a center. Such windows are especially fine and numerous in French medieval architecture, and often attain very considerable dimensions, as in the cathedrals of

Rose-window in North Transept of Abbey Church of Saint Denis, France.

Paris, Chartres, Rheims, Amiens, etc. Also called *catharine-wheel* and, rarely, *marigold-window*.

> Nothing can exceed the majesty of its deeply-recessed triple portals, the beauty of the *rose-window* that surmounts them, or the elegance of the gallery that completes the façade.
> *J. Fergusson*, Hist. Arch., I. 541.

rosewood (rōz'wụd), *n.* **1.** The wood of various Brazilian trees, especially of *Dalbergia nigra.* It is a fine hard cabinet-wood of a chestnut color streaked with black, or varying in the different sorts, and used chiefly in veneers. The name is due to the faint rose-scent of some kinds when freshly cut. Other species of *Dalbergia*, species of *Jacaranda*, and perhaps of *Machærium*, produce the rosewood of commerce. The woods known as *kingwood* and *violet-wood* may be considered as varieties. See *palisander*, the several generic names, and the phrases below.
2. A wood, lignum rhodium, the source of oil of rhodium, or rosewood-oil; Canary rosewood. It is obtained in pieces a few inches thick from the root and stem of *Convolvulus scoparius* and *C. floridus*, small trees of the Canaries. See *rosewood-oil*.
3. Any of the trees producing rosewood.—**African rosewood**, the molompi, *Pterocarpus erinaceus*.—**Australian rosewood**, a moderate-sized tree, *Synoum glandulosum* of the *Meliaceæ*.—**Burmese rosewood.** See *Pterocarpus*.—**Canary rosewood.** See def. 2.—**Dominica rosewood**, *Cordia Gerascanthus*, a boraginaceous tree of the West Indies.—**East Indian rosewood.** See *blackwood*, 1, and *Dalbergia*.—**Jamaica rosewood**, *Linociera ligustrina* and *Amyris balsamifera*, West Indian trees not botanically related—the latter also called *candlewood* and *rhodes-wood*.—**Moulmein rosewood**, a Burmese species of *Millettia*.

rosewood-oil (rōz'wụd-oil), *n.* A pale-yellow, viscid, volatile oil, having an odor resembling that of sandalwood or rosewood, and obtained by distillation with water from a kind of rosewood. (See *rosewood*, 2.) It has been used in perfumery, liniments, etc., but is now wholly or mostly replaced by artificial compounds.

rose-worm (rōz'wėrm), *n.* The larva of a common tortricid moth, *Cacœcia rosaceana*, which folds the leaves of the rose and skeletonizes them. It feeds also on many other plants, as the apple, peach, plum, birch, clover, strawberry, and cotton.

rosewort (rōz'wėrt), *n.* **1.** A plant of the order *Rosaceæ*. *Lindley*.—**2.** Same as *roseroot*, 1.

rose-yard (rōz'yärd), *n.* [< ME. *rosegerde*; < *rose*¹ + *yard*².] A rose-garden.

rosial†, *a.* See *roseal*.

rosicler (rō-si-kler'), *n.* [Sp.] The Spanish term for the ores of silver embraced under the general English name *ruby silver*. It includes the light-red silver ore proustite (rosicler claro) and the dark-red silver ore pyrargyrite (rosicler oscuro); besides these, the mineral stephanite is sometimes called *rosicler negro*.

Rosicrucian (rō-zi-krö'shi-ạn), *n.* and *a.* [Said to be a Latinized form of *Rosenkreuz*, 'rose-cross,' the mythical name of the mythical founder of the sect, identified with L. *rosa*, a rose, + *crux* (*cruc-*), a cross, whence F. *rose-croix*, a Rosicrucian, E. *rose-cross*, the Rosicrucian symbol: see *rose*¹ and *cross*¹. Others alter the name to *Roscicrucian* or *Roricrucian*, in order to derive it < L. *roscidus*, dewy (see *roscid*), or *ros* (*ror-*), dew (see *rore*³), + *crux* (*cruc-*), cross, the emblem of light.] **I.** *n.* A member of a supposed secret society, said to have originated in the fifteenth century, which combined pretensions to the possession of occult wisdom and gifts with so-called mysteries of physic, astronomy, alchemy, etc. The book describing the Rosicrucians ("Fama Fraternitatis," published in 1614) is generally regarded as merely an elaborate satire on the charlatanry and credulity of the times. Books of Rosicrucian pretensions were formerly numerous in England as well as in Germany, and several have lately reappeared in the United States. The sect were also styled *Brethren* or *Knights of the Rosy-cross*, *Rosy-cross Philosophers*, etc.

II. *a.* Pertaining to the Rosicrucians or their arts.

Rosicrucianism (rē-zi-krö'shi-ạn-izm), *n.* [< *Rosicrucian* + *-ism*.] The doctrines, arts, or practices of the Rosicrucians.

rosicrux (rō'zi-kruks), *n.*; pl. *rosicruces* (rē-zi-krö'sēz). Same as *rose-cross*, 2.

rosied (rō'zid), *a.* [< *rosy* + *-ed*².] Adorned with roses or rose-color; made rosy.

rosier†, *n.* See *roser*.

rosière (rō-ziãr'), *n.* [F., the young girl who wins the rose, emblem of virtue, < L. *rosaria*, fem. of *rosarius*, of roses: see *rosary*.] See *rose-festival*.

rosily (rō'zi-li), *adv.* With a rosy color or effect.

> The white Olympus-peaks
> *Rosily* brighten, and the soothed gods smile.
> *M. Arnold*, Empedocles on Etna, ii.

rosin (roz'in), *n.* [Formerly also *rozin*; a var. of *resin*: see *resin*.] **1.** Same as *resin*. Specifically—**2.** Resin as employed in a solid state for ordinary purposes. It is obtained from turpentine by distillation. In this process the oil of the turpentine comes over, and the rosin remains behind. Rosin varies in color from dark brown or black to white, according to its purity and the degree of heat used in its preparation. Chemically it is the anhydrid of abietic acid. It has the physical and chemical properties common to all resins. It is used in common varnishes, is combined with tallow to make common candles, is used by founders to give tenacity to their cores, by tinmen and plumbers as a flux for their solder, for rubbing on violin-bows, and for many other purposes. Also called *colophony*.

> Suddainly Aucrous Gulf did swim
> With *Rozin*, Pitch, and Brimstone to the brim.
> *Sylvester*, tr. of Du Bartas's Weeks, ii., The Furies.

rosin (roz'in), *v. t.* [< *rosin*, *n.*] To cover or rub with rosin.

> Black Cæsar had that afternoon *rosined* his bow, and tuned his fiddle, and practised jigs and Virginia reels.
> *H. B. Stowe*, Oldtown, p. 349.

rosined (roz'ind), *a.* [< *rosin* + *-ed*².] Treated with rosin.

rosiness (rō'zi-nes), *n.* [< *rosy* + *-ness*.] The quality of being rosy, or of resembling the rose in color.

> The *rosiness* of glowing embers tinted the walls of Jouaneaux's house.
> *M. H. Catherwood*, Romance of Dollard, xvii.

rosing (rō'zing), *n.* [Verbal n. of *rose*¹, *v.*] The operation of imparting a pink tint to raw white silk.

rosin-oil (roz'in-oil), *n.* An oil manufactured from pine-resin, used for lubricating machinery, etc., and in France for printers' ink. See *London oil*, under *oil*.

rosin-plant (roz'in-plant), *n.* Same as *rosin-weed*.

rosin-soap (roz'in-sōp), *n.* A soap made of rosin and an alkali, as soda or potash, or by boiling with an alkaline carbonate and evaporating to dryness. It is worthless except when mixed with tallow soap, or palm-oil soap, or with both, as in the common yellow soap of commerce. See *soap*.

rosin-tin (roz'in-tin), *n.* A pale-colored native oxid of tin with a resinous luster.

rosin-weed (roz'in-wēd), *n.* Any plant of the genus *Silphium*; especially, *S. laciniatum*. See *compass-plant*, 1, and *prairie burdock* (under *burdock*).

Rosin-weed (*Silphium laciniatum*).
1, the upper part of the stem with the head; 2, a leaf; *a*, one of the involucral scales.

rosiny (roz'in-i), *a.* [< *rosin* + *-y*¹.] Resembling rosin; abounding with rosin.

rosland (ros'lạnd), *n.* [Prop. **rossland*, < *ross*² + *land*¹.] Moorish or watery land; heathy land. [Prov. Eng.]

rosmart (ros'mär), *n.* [< Dan. *rosmar*, a walrus, < Norw. *rossmaar*, *rossmaal*, *rossmul*, < Icel. *rosmhvalr*, a walrus, < *rosm*, of unknown meaning (appar. connected with *rostungr*, a walrus), + *hvalr* = E. *whale*: see *whale*. Cf. *horse-whale*, *walrus*, and *rorqual*.] The morse or walrus. See cuts under *rosmarine*² and *walrus*.

Rosmaridæ (ros-mar'i-dē), *n. pl.* [NL., < *Rosmarus* + *-idæ*.] A family of *Pinnipedia*, named from the genus *Rosmarus*: now usually called *Trichechidæ* and sometimes *Odobænidæ*.

rosmarine¹† (roz'mạ-rēn or -rin), *n.* [< L. *ros marinus*, 'sea-dew,' rosemary: see *rosemary*.] **1.** Sea-dew.

> You shall . . . steep
> Your bodies in that purer brine
> And wholesome dew called *rosmarine*.
> *B. Jonson*, Masque of Blackness.

2. Rosemary.

> Cold Lettuce, and refreshing *Rosmarine*.
> *Spenser*, Muiopotmos, l. 200.

rosmarine² (roz'mạ-rēn or -rin), *n.* and *a.* [Appar. an altered form of Dan. *rosmar*, a walrus (see *rosmar*), simulating *rosmarine*¹, whence the fable of its feeding on dew.] **I.** *n.* The walrus: formerly imagined as a sea-monster which climbed cliffs to feed on dew. Some of the early representations of this animal are extremely curious (as

Rosmarine (*Vacca marina* of Gesner, 1560).

that from Gesner here reproduced), and to them is probably traceable the heraldic creation known as the *marine wolf* (which see, under *marine*). Gesner's figure is clearly the walrus, though the tusks point upward from the lower jaw, instead of downward from the upper jaw, and though it is provided with hind feet besides a tail, instead of hind limbs forming a tail. Many zoölogical illustrations of the sixteenth century are not more accurate. Compare the cut under *walrus*.

> Greedy *Rosmarines* with visages deforme.
> *Spenser*, F. Q., II. xii. 24.

II. *a.* Pertaining or relating to the walruses.

Rosmarinus (ros-mạ-rī'nus), *n.* [< L. *ros marinus*, sea-dew: see *rosemary*.] A genus of gamopetalous plants, of the order *Labiatæ* and tribe *Monardeæ*. It is characterized by an ovoid and slightly two-lipped calyx, beardless within; by an exserted corolla-tube enlarged in the throat, the limb two-lipped, the large middle lobe of the lower lip declined and concave; and by having two stamens, each with a single anther-cell, the connective being continuous with the filament and the other cell represented by a slender reflexed tooth. The only species, *R. officinalis*, the rosemary (which see), is native through the Mediterranean region, and cultivated elsewhere, but is not hardy in America north of Virginia. It is a low-branched evergreen aromatic shrub, 4 or 5 feet high, bearing linear entire opposite leaves which are sessile, thickish, about one inch long, smooth and green above, with revolute margins, and white with stellate hairs beneath. The pale-blue flowers are produced throughout the year; they are nearly sessile among the upper leaves, and form loosely few-flowered and axillary bracted verticillasters clustered in a few short racemes.

rosmaroid (ros'mạ-roid), *a.* Belonging to the *Rosmaroidea*.

Rosmaroidea (ros-mạ-roi'dẹ̄-ạ̈), *n. pl.* [NL., < *Rosmarus* + *-oidea*.] A superfamily of *Pinnipedia*, represented by the *Rosmaridæ* alone, having the lower canines atrophied and the upper ones enormously developed as tusks protruding far from the mouth. Also called *Trichechoidea*.

Rosmarus (ros'mạ-rus), *n.* [NL. (Scopoli, 1777, after Klein, 1751), < Dan. *rosmar*, a walrus: see *rosmar*, *rosmarine*².] The typical genus of *Rosmaridæ*; the walruses: also called *Trichechus* and *Odobænus*.

Rosminian (ros-min'i-ạn), *n.* [< *Rosmini* (see def.) + *-an*.] A member of a Roman Catholic congregation, entitled the Fathers of the Institute of Charity, founded by the Italian philosopher Antonio Rosmini Serbati in 1828, for the purpose of pursuing charitable work.

Rosminianism (ros-min'i-ạn-izm), *n.* [< *Rosminian* + *-ism*.] The philosophical system of Antonio Rosmini Serbati. Its fundamental proposition is that every idea involves the idea of being.

rosolic (rọ-zol'ik), *a.* [< *rose* + *-ol* + *-ic*.] Related to rosaniline.—**Rosolic acid**, an acid closely related to rosaniline, and differing from it in that the amide groups of the latter are replaced by hydroxyl groups in rosolic acid, with elimination of one molecule of water.

rosolio (rọ-zō'liō), *n.* [Also *rosoglio* (and *rosoli*, *rosolis*, < F.); < It. *rosolio* = Sp. *rosoli* = Pg. *rossoli* = F. *rossolis*, rosolio, appar., like *rossolis*, sundew, a plant, < L. *ros solis*, sundew (*ros*, dew; *solis*, gen. of *sol*, the sun); but perhaps orig. It., < It. *rosso*, red, < L. *russus*, red: see *russet*[1].] A red wine of Malta; also, a sweet cordial made from raisins, popular throughout the Levant.

> Rogue Hyacinth . . .
> Shall have a small full glass
> Of manly red *rosolio* to himself.
> *Browning*, Ring and Book, II. 117.

Rosores (rọ̄-sō'rēz), *n. pl.* [NL., pl. of *rosor*, gnawer, < L. *rodere*, pp. *rosus*, gnaw: see *rodent*.] In *zoöl.*, the gnawing mammals: a synonym of *Glires* and of *Rodentia*. [Now rare.]

Rosoria (rō-sō'ri-ạ̈), *n. pl.* [NL.: see *Rosores*.] Same as *Rosores*. *Bonaparte*, 1837.

rosorial (rọ̄-sō'ri-ạl), *a.* [< *Rosores* + *-al*.] Belonging to the *Rosores* or *Rosoria*; rodent.

ross[1] (ros), *n.* [< Norw. *ros*, *rus*, *rös*, *rys*, shell, rind, peel, scale (usually of that which falls off of itself), = Dan. *ros*, shavings, chips; prob. connected with Norw. *ros*, f., a fall, landslide, etc., < *rusa* = AS. *hreósan*, etc., fall: see *ruse*[1].] 1. The rough scaly matter on the surface of the bark of certain trees.—2. Branches of trees lopped off; the refuse of plants. [Scotch.]

ross[1] (ros), *v. t.* [< *ross*[1], *n.*] 1. To strip the ross from; strip bark from.—2. To cut up (bark) for boiling, etc.

ross[2] (ros), *n.* [< W. *rhos*, a moor, heath, morass. Cf. *rosland*.] A morass. *Halliwell*. [Prov. Eng.]

rossel† (ros'el), *n.* [Cf. *ross*[2], *rosland*.] Light land; rosland.

> A true *rossel* or light land, whether white or black, is what they are usually planted in.
> *Mortimer*, Husbandry.

Rossella (ro-sel'ạ̈), *n.* [NL.] The typical genus of *Rossellidæ*. *Carter*.

Rossellidæ (ro-sel'i-dē), *n. pl.* [NL., < *Rossella* + *-idæ*.] A family of lyssacine silicious sponges whose dermal spicules have no centripetal ray, typified by the genus *Rossella*. The other genera are numerous.

rosselly† (ros'el-i), *a.* [< *rossel* + *-y*[1].] Loose; light: said of soil.

> In Essex, moory land is thought to be the most proper; that which I have observed to be the best soil is a *rosselly* top, and a brick earthy bottom. *Mortimer*, Husbandry.

rosset (ros'et), *n.* Same as *roussette*.

Ross Herald. One of the six heralds of the Scottish Heralds' College.

Rossia (ros'i-ạ̈), *n.* [NL., named after Sir John *Ross* (1777–1856), an Arctic explorer.] 1. In *ornith.*, same as *Rhodostethia*. *Bonaparte*, 1838. —2. In *Mollusca*, a genus of decapod cephalopods of the family *Sepiolidæ*. *R. Owen*, 1838.

rossignol (ros'i-nyol), *n.* [< F. *rossignol*, OF. *lousseignol*, *louseignol* = Pr. *rossignol*, *rossinhos*, *rossignola* = Cat. *rossinyol* = Sp. *ruiseñor* = Pg. *rouxinol*, *roxinol* = It. *rusignuolo*, < L. *lusciniola*, *lusciniolus*, nightingale, dim. of *luscinia*, nightingale: see *luscinia*.] The nightingale.

rossing-machine (ros'ing-mạ-shēn"), *n.* 1. A machine for removing the ross or rough exterior part of bark; a bark-rossing machine. —2. A rossing attachment to a sawmill for removing the bark from the log just before it meets the saw.—3. A machine for cutting up bark preparatory to boiling or steeping, for purposes of tanning, medicine, dyeing, etc. *E. H. Knight*.

rosso antico (ros"ọ̄ an-tē'kọ̄). [It., < *rosso*, red, + *antico*, antique, ancient: see *russet* and *antique*.] See *marble*, 1.

rossoli (ros'ọ̄-li), *n.* [It., < L. *ros*, dew, + *sol*, the sun.] An Italian liquor in the preparation of which the sundew (*Drosera rotundifolia*) is used.

Ross's rosy gull. See *gull*[2], and cut under *Rhodostethia*.

rost[1]†, *v.* and *n.* An obsolete spelling of *roast*.

rost[2]†, *n.* A Middle English form of *roust*[2].

rostel (ros'tel), *n.* [= F. *rostelle*, < L. *rostellum*, a little beak or snout, dim. of *rostrum*, a beak: see *rostrum*.] Same as *rostellum*.

rostella, *n.* Plural of *rostellum*.

rostellar (ros'te-lär), *a.* [< *rostel(l)* + *-ar*[3].] Of or pertaining to a rostellum.

Rostellaria (ros-te-lā'ri-ạ̈), *n.* [NL., < L. *rostellum*, a little beak or snout: see *rostel*.] A genus of marine univalves belonging to the family *Strombidæ*; the spindlestrombs. It is found both recent and fossil. The shell is fusiform or subturriculate, with an elevated pointed spire; the aperture is oval, with canal projecting, and terminating in a pointed beak. The species are found in the Indian ocean and neighboring seas.

Rostellaria curta.

rostellarian (ros-te-lā'ri-ạn), *a.* and *n.* I. *a.* Resembling a spindlestromb; pertaining or belonging to the genus *Rostellaria*.

II. *n.* A member of the genus *Rostellaria*.

rostellate (ros'te-lāt), *a.* [= F. *rostellé*, < NL. **rostellatus*, < L. *rostellum*, a little beak or snout: see *rostel*.] Having a rostellum; diminutively rostrate or beaked.

rostelliform (ros-tel'i-fôrm), *a.* [< L. *rostellum*, a little beak or snout, + *forma*, form.] Having the form of a rostel; shaped like a rostellum.

rostellum (ros-tel'um), *n.*; pl. *rostella* (-ạ̈). [L.: see *rostel*.] 1. In *bot.*: (*a*) Any small beak-shaped process, as in the stigma of many violets; specifically, a modification of the stigma in many orchids, which bears the glands to which the pollen-masses are attached.

> The upper stigma is modified into an extraordinary organ, called the *rostellum*, which in many Orchids presents no resemblance to a true stigma.
> *Darwin*, Fertil. of Orchids by Insects, p. 4.

(*b*) A Linnean term for the caulicle or radicle. —2. In *zoöl.*, the fore part of the head of tapeworms or other cestoids, bearing spines or hooklets which are said to be *rostellar*. See cut under *Cestoidea*.—3. [*cap.*] [NL.] In *conch.*, same as *Rostellaria*.

roster[1]†, *n.* An obsolete form of *roaster*.

roster[2] (ros'tėr), *n.* [Also dial. *royster*, an inventory; < D. *rooster*, a list, table; prob. a particular use, in allusion to the crossing lines and columns in a table, of *rooster*, a grate, gridiron, = E. *roaster* (see *roaster*). The word is commonly supposed to be a corruption of *register*[1].] 1. In the British and the United States regular armies, a list showing the turn or rotation of service or duty of those who relieve or succeed each other; specifically, a military list or register showing or fixing the rotation in which individuals, companies, or regiments are called into service.—2. In Massachusetts and Connecticut, a list of the officers of a division, brigade, regiment, etc., containing, under several heads, their names, rank, corps, place of abode, etc. These are called *division rosters*, *brigade rosters*, *regimental* or *battalion rosters*. *Bartlett*.—3. Hence, any roll, list, or register of names. [Colloq.]

rosterite (ros'tėr-īt), *n.* A variety of beryl of a pale rose-red color, found in the granite of the island of Elba, Italy.

rostle†, *n.* [Appar. an error for **rostre*, < F. *rostre* = Sp. Pg. It. *rostro*, < L. *rostrum*, beak: see *rostrum*.] The beak of a ship.

> Vectis rostratus, a barre or leaver with an iron point or end; a *rostle*. *Nomenclator*, 1585. (*Nares*.)

rostra, *n.* Latin and New Latin plural of *rostrum*.

rostral (ros'trạl), *a.* [= F. *rostral* = Sp. Pg. *rostral* = It. *rostrale*, < LL. *rostralis*, < L. *rostrum*, a beak, snout: see *rostrum*.] 1. Of, pertaining to, or resembling a rostrum. —2. In *zoöl.*: (*a*) Of or pertaining to a rostrum in any sense; rostellar; rostriform. (*b*) Having a rostrum or beak of this or that kind; rostrate: usually in composition with a qualifying epithet: as, *lamellirostral*, *longirostral*, *fissirostral*, *conirostral*, *cultrirostral*, *curvirostral*, *rectirostral*, *dentirostral*, *recurvirostral*, *pressirostral*, *tenuirostral*, *serratirostral*, etc. See the compounds.

> Thus for a day or two in the chick there are two "basi-temporal" and one *rostral* center.
> *Nature*, XXXVII. 501.

Rostral channel or **canal**, in the *Hemiptera*, a hollow on the lower surface of the thorax, in which the rostrum is received.—**Rostral column**, a column in honor of a naval triumph: it was ornamented with the rostra or prows of ships (whence the name).

Rostral Column, Grand Opera, Paris.

> At each angle of the esplanade rises a *rostral column* of rose-colored granite 100 feet high.
> *Harper's Mag.*, LXXIX. 192.

Rostral crown. Same as *naval crown* (which see, under *crown*).

> The monuments of their admirals . . . are adorned with *rostral crowns* and naval ornaments, with beautiful festoons of seaweed, shells, and coral.
> *Addison*, Thoughts in Westminster Abbey.

Rostral groove or **furrow**, a groove or furrow on the lower surface of the body of a weevil, in which the rostrum is received in repose or when the insect feigns death. Its extension and form (shallow or deep, open or closed behind, etc.) are of great use in the classification of these insects.—**Rostral sheath**, in *Hemiptera*, a jointed organ formed by an extension of the labium, and deeply grooved on its upper surface for the reception of the needle-like mandibles and maxillæ: generally simply called *rostrum*.

rostrate (ros'trāt), *a.* [= F. *rostré* = Sp. Pg. *rostrado* = It. *rostrato*, < L. *rostratus*, having a beak, hook, or crooked point, < *rostrum*, a beak: see *rostrum*.] 1. Furnished or adorned with beaks: as, *rostrated* galleys.—2. In *bot.*, beaked; having a process resembling the beak of a bird.—3. In *conch.*, having a beak-like extension of the shell, in which the canal is situated; canaliculate; rostriferous. See cuts under *murex* and *Rostellaria*.—4. In *entom.*, provided with a rostrum or snout-like prolongation of the head, as the weevils; rhynchophorous.

Rostrate Fruit of *Rhynchospora macrostachya*.

rostrated (ros'trā-ted), *a.* [< *rostrate* + *-ed*[2].] Same as *rostrate*.

Rostratula (ros-trat'ụ̄-lạ̈), *n.* [NL. (Vieillot, 1816), < L. *rostrum*, a beak: see *rostrum*.] The proper name of the genus usually called *Rhynchæa* (Cuvier, 1817), and the type of the subfamily *Rostratulinæ*.

Rostratulinæ (ros-trat-ụ̄-lī'nē), *n. pl.* [NL. (Coues, 1888), < *Rostratula* + *-inæ*.] A subfamily of *Scolopacidæ*, typified by the genus *Rostratula*, characterized by the formation of the windpipe, which makes one or more subcutaneous convolutions; the painted snipes, usually called *Rhynchæinæ* (see *Rhynchæa*).

Rostrhamus (ros-trā'mus), *n.* [NL. (Lesson, 1831), irreg. < L. *rostrum*, beak, + *hamus*, hook.] An American genus of *Falconidæ*, having the slender bill extremely hooked, the upper mandible being almost like a reaping-hook; the sickle-billed kites. There are 2 or 3 species, of the warmer parts of America, among them the well-known everglade kite of Florida, *R. sociabilis*. See cut under *everglade*.

rostrifacture (ros-tri-fak'tụ̄r), *n.* [Formed on the model of *manufacture*; < L. *rostrum*, beak, + *factura*, a making, < *facere*, pp. *factus*, make: see *rostrum* and *facture*.] That which is constructed or fabricated by means of the bill or beak of a bird, as a nest. [Rare.]

> The dexterity and assiduity they [orioles] display in their elaborate textile *rostrifactures*.
> *Coues*, Key to N. A. Birds, p. 408.

Rostrifera (ros-trif'ẹ-rạ̈), *n. pl.* [NL., neut. pl. of *rostriferus*: see *rostriferous*.] A suborder or otherwise denominated group of gastropods having a contractile rostrum or snout, and supposed to be phytophagous. It includes most of the holostomatous shells and various others. The name is contrasted with *Proboscidifera*.

rostriferous (ros-trif'ẹ-rus), *a.* [< NL. *rostriferus*, < L. *rostrum*, beak, + *ferre* = E. *bear*[1].] Having a beak or rostrum; belonging to the *Rostrifera*, or having their characters.

rostriform (ros'tri-fôrm), *a.* [= F. *rostriforme*, < L. *rostrum*, a beak, + *forma*, form.] Formed like or as a rostrum; shaped like a beak.

rostro-antennary (ros"trō-an-ten'ạ-ri), *a.* [< L. *rostrum*, beak, + NL. *antenna*, antenna, + *-ary*. Cf. *antennary*.] Pertaining to the rostrum and antennæ of a crustacean. *Huxley and Martin*, Elementary Biology, p. 225. [Rare.]

rostrobranchial (ros-trō-brang'ki-ạl), *a.* [< L. *rostrum*, beak, + *branchiæ*, gills, + *-al*. Cf. *branchial*.] Pertaining to or representing the extent of the rostral and branchial parts of a fish. *Gill*. [Rare.]

rostroid (ros'troid), *a.* [< L. *rostrum*, beak, + Gr. εἶδος, form.] Resembling a rostrum, beak, or snout; rostrate; rostriform. [Rare.]

> The head [of *Macrotus*, a genus of bats] has the same long *rostroid* appearance. *H. Allen*, Smiths. Misc. Coll., VII. 2.

rostrolateral (ros-trọ̄-lat'ẹ-rạl), *a.* [< L. *rostrum*, beak, + *latus* (*later-*), side: see *lateral*.] 1. Lateral with reference to the rostrum: applied to a part of the shell of a cirriped: see *rostrum*, 3 (*f*).—2. Situated alongside the rostrum, as of the skull of a fish.

> Infraorbital chain with its anterior bones excluded from the orbit and functional as *rostrolateral*.
> *Gill*, Amer. Nat., 1888, p. 357.

rostrular (ros'trọ̄-lạ̈r), *a.* [< *rostrul(um)* + *-ar*[3].] Pertaining to the rostrulum of fleas.

rostrulate (ros'trö-lāt), *a.* [< *rostrul(um)* + *-ate*1.] In *entom.*: (*a*) Having the form of a rostrulum, as the oral organs of a flea. (*b*) Provided with a rostrulum, as the *Pulicidæ*.

rostrulum (ros'trö-lum), *n.*; pl. *rostrula* (-lä). [NL., dim. of L. *rostrum*, a beak, snout: see *rostrum*.] The peculiar rostrum, beak, or mouth-parts of fleas.

rostrum (ros'trum), *n.*; pl. *rostrums*, *rostra* (-trumz, -trä). [< L. *rostrum*, the beak or bill of a bird, the snout or muzzle of a beast, a curved point, as of a bill-hook, hammer, plow, etc., the curved end of a ship's prow, the beak of a ship; orig. *rodtrum, with formative *-trum* (*-tro-*) (= E. *-ther*, *-der*, in *rother*1, *rudder*1), < *rodere*, gnaw, peck: see *rodent*.] 1. The beak or bill of a bird.—2. The snout, muzzle, or sometimes the face of an animal, especially when protrusive.—3. In *anat.* and *zoöl.*, any beaked or rostrate part, or part likened to a beak. Hence—(*a*) In *anat.*: (1) The forward median projection from the body of the sphenoid bone, received between the lips of the vomer, and effecting articulation with that bone; the beak of the sphenoid. See cuts under *parasphenoid* and *Acipenser*. (2) The reflected anterior part of the corpus callosum of a mammalian brain below the genu. (*b*) In *ornith.*: (1) The beak of the skull; the narrow spike-like projection forward of the basisphenoid bone in the middle line of the base of the skull, along which play the movable palatal parts, and upon which the vomer is supported in some cases: its lower border, especially if thickened, is commonly formed by a parasphenoid. (2) The beak of the sternum; the manubrium. *Coues*, 1884. (*c*) In *Crustacea*, the anterior termination of the carapace, especially when prominent or protrusive. For example, see cut of *Libinia*, under *Oxyrhyncha*; see also cuts under *Amphithoë*, *cephalothorax*, *Copepoda*, and *stalk-eyed*. (*d*) In *entom.*: (1) The beak or suctorial organ formed by the appendages of the mouth in certain insects, as *Hemiptera*. More fully called *rostral sheath* (which see, under *rostral*). (2) The proboscis, snout, or elongated anterior part of the head of a rhynchophorous beetle. The parts of the mouth are situated at the end of the rostrum, and the antennæ generally lie in grooves at the sides. See *Rhynchophora*. (3) A more or less cylindrical anterior prolongation of the head of certain *Diptera*, not to be confounded with the proboscis or sucking-mouth, which in these flies is a prolongation from the front of the rostrum, though *rostrum* is incorrectly applied by some authors to the proboscis of any fly. (*e*) In *Cirripedia*, as an acorn-shell, the median one of three compartments of the fixed conical shell, into which the movable valves may be retracted, situated on the same side of the animal as the opening between the valves, between the two rostrolateral compartments. See cut under *Balanus*. (*f*) In *conch.*: (1) The anterior extension of the head or snout when simply contractile (not retractile) and transversely annulated: opposed to *proboscis*. (2) The beak or beak-like extension of the shell, in which the canal is situated. See cuts under *murex* and *Rostellaria*. (3) A strong solid process behind the apex of the phragmacone of a cephalopod, formed by its investing layers. In *Belemnites* it is a conical calcified laminated structure, the guard, inclosing the straight phragmacone of these Mesozoic cephalopods. It is continued forward into the prostracum, the rostrum and prostracum together representing the pen of the *Teuthidæ*. See cut under *belemnite*.
4. The beak of a ship: an ancient form of ram, consisting of a beam to which were attached heavy pointed irons, fixed to the bows, sometimes just above and sometimes below the water-line, and used for the purpose of sinking other vessels. See cut under *rostral*.

> A man would expect, in so very ancient a town of Italy [Genoa], to find some considerable antiquities; but all they have to show of this nature is an old *rostrum* of a Roman ship that stands over the door of their arsenal.
> *Addison*, Remarks on Italy (Works, ed. Bohn, I. 363).

5. *pl.* A platform or elevated place in the Roman forum, whence orations, pleadings, funeral harangues, etc., were delivered: so called because it was adorned with the rostra or beaks of the ships taken in the first naval victory gained by the republic. Hence—6. A pulpit or any platform or elevated spot from which a speaker addresses his audience. See cut under *pulpit*.

> The things that mount the *rostrum* with a skip,
> And then skip down again; pronounce a text.
> *Cowper*, Task, ii. 409.

7. In *bot.*, an elongated receptacle with the styles adhering: also applied generally to any rigid process of remarkable length, or to any additional process at the end of any of the parts of a plant.—8. A trestle used in supporting platforms in a theater.—9. In an ancient lamp, the beak or projection in which the wick lies.—10. In *distilling*, that part of the still which connects the head with the worm and forms a passage for vapor from the head to the worm; the beak. It has a very marked taper from the head to the worm, and a downward inclination which gives it somewhat the appearance of a beak. See *still*2.

rosula (roz'ū-lä), *n.* [NL., dim. of L. *rosa*, a rose: see *rose*1.] 1. A small rose; a rosette.—2. [*cap.*] A genus of echinoderms.

rosular (roz'ū-lär), *a.* [< *rosula* + *-ar*2.] In *bot.*, same as *rosulate*.

rosulate (roz'ū-lāt), *a.* [< *rosula* + *-ate*1.] In *bot.*, having the leaves arranged in little rosettes or rose-like clusters.

rosy (rō'zi), *a.* [< ME. *rosy, < AS. *rôsig*, rosy, < *rôse*, rose: see *rose*1.] 1. Resembling a rose in color or qualities; red; blushing; blooming.

> That sweet *rosy* lad
> Who died, and was Fidele.
> *Shak.*, Cymbeline, v. 5. 121.

> Celestial *rosy* red, love's proper hue.
> *Milton*, P. L., viii. 619.

> And every *rosy* tint that lay
> On the smooth sea hath died away.
> *Moore*, Lalla Rookh, The Fire-Worshippers.

2. Consisting of roses; made of roses.

> I sent thee late a *rosy* wreath.
> B. *Jonson*, To Celia.

> And we shall meet once more in happier days,
> When death lurks not amidst of *rosy* ways.
> *William Morris*, Earthly Paradise, III. 230.

3†. Made in the form of a rose.

> His *rosy* ties and garters so o'erblown.
> B. *Jonson*, Epigrams, xcvii.

Rosy cross [also *rosie cross*, an accommodated form of rose cross, F. rose *croix*, NL. *rosicrux*, etc.: see *Rosicrucian*]. Same as *rose-cross*, 2.—**Rosy finch, gull, minor, rock-fish,** etc. See the nouns. =**Syn. 1.** See *ruddy*.

rosy-bosomed (rō'zi-bůz'umd), *a.* Having the bosom rosy in color or filled with roses.

> Lo! where the *rosy-bosom'd* hours,
> Fair Venus' train, appear,
> Disclose the long-expecting flowers,
> And wake the purple year!
> *Gray*, Ode on the Spring.

rosy-colored (rō'zi-kul'ord), *a.* Having a rosy color.

> *Rosy-coloured* Helen is the pride
> Of Lacedemon, and of Greece beside.
> *Dryden*, tr. of Theocritus's Idylls, xviii.

rosy-crowned (rō'zi-kround), *a.* Crowned with roses. *Gray*.

rosy-drop (rō'zi-drop), *n.* Acne rosacea; grog-blossoms; brandy-face.

rosy-fingered (rō'zi-fing'gėrd), *a.* Having rosy fingers: Homer's favorite epithet of the dawn, ῥοδοδάκτυλος Ἠώς.

rosy-footman (rō'zi-fůt'man), *n.* The red-arches, a British moth, *Calligenia miniata*.

rosy-kindled (rō'zi-kin'dld), *a.* Suffused with a rosy color; blushing.

> Her bright hair blown about the serious face,
> Yet *rosy-kindled* with her brother's kiss.
> *Tennyson*, Lancelot and Elaine.

rosy-marbled (rō'zi-mär'bld), *a.* Marbled with rosy color: as, the *rosy-marbled* moth.

rosy-marsh (rō'zi-märsh), *n.* A British noctuid moth, *Noctua subrosea*.

rosy-rustic (rō'zi-rus'tik), *n.* A British noctuid moth, *Hydræcia micacea*.

rosy-tinted (rō'zi-tin'ted), *a.* Having rose-tints.

> All about the thorn will blow
> In tufts of *rosy-tinted* snow.
> *Tennyson*, Two Voices.

rosy-wave (rō'zi-wāv), *n.* A British geometrid moth, *Acidalia emutaria*.

rot (rot), *v.*; pret. and pp. *rotted*, ppr. *rotting*. [< ME. *roten*, *rotien* (pret. *rotede*, pp. *roted*), < AS. *rotian* (pret. *rotede*, *rotode*, pp. *rotod*) = OS. *rotôn* = D. *rotten* = MLG. *roten*, *raten*, *rotten*, LG. *rotten* (> G. *rotten*, *verrotten*), rot, = OHG. *rôzên*, *rozên*, MHG. *rozen*, *roezen*, *ræzen*, become or make rotten, G. *rösten*, rot or ret (hemp, flax, etc.); cf. D. *rot* = MHG. *roz*, rotten; Icel. *rotna* = Sw. *ruttna* = Dan. *raadne*, become rotten: see *rotten*1. Cf. *ret*.] **I.** *intrans.* 1. To undergo natural decomposition; fall into a course or a state of elemental dissolution; suffer loss of coherence from decay: used of organic substances which either do or do not putrefy in the process, and sometimes, by extension, of inorganic substances.

> I *root*, he seyde, fro the boon;
> Jhesu Cryste, what schall y done?
> *MS. Cantab.* Ff. ii. 38, f. 114. (*Halliwell.*)

> For Cedre may not, in Erthe ne in Watre, *rote*.
> *Mandeville*, Travels, p. 10.

> Ay, but to die; . . .
> To lie in cold obstruction, and to *rot*.
> *Shak.*, M. for M., iii. 1. 119.

2. To become morally corrupt; deteriorate through stagnation or indulgence; suffer loss of stamina or principle.

> Wither, poor girl, in your garret; *rot*, poor bachelor, in your Club.
> *Thackeray*, Book of Snobs, xxxiii.

3. To become morally offensive or putrid; be nauseous or repulsive; excite contempt or disgust. [Rare.]

> The memory of the just is blessed; but the name of the wicked shall rot.
> Prov. x. 7.

> Cutthroats by the score abroad, come home, and *rot* in fripperies.
> *Ford*, Lady's Trial, iii. 1.

4. To become affected with the disease called rot.

> The hungry sheep look up, and are not fed;
> But, swoln with wind, and the rank mist they draw,
> *Rot* inwardly, and foul contagion spread.
> *Milton*, Lycidas, l. 127.

=**Syn. 1.** *Rot*, *Decay*, *Putrefy*, *Corrupt*, *Decompose*. *Rot* is, by its age and brevity, so energetic a word that it is often considered inelegant, and *decay* is used as a softer word. That which *rots* or *decays* may or may not emit a foul odor, as an egg or an apple; *putrefy* by derivation implies such foulness of odor, and hence is especially applied to animal matter when it is desired to emphasize that characteristic result of its rotting. *Corrupt* is sometimes used as a strong but not offensive word for thorough spoiling, that makes a thing repulsive or loathsome. To *decompose* is to return to the original elements; the word is sometimes used as a euphemism for *rot* or *putrefy*. The moral uses of the first four words correspond to the physical.

II. *trans.* 1. To cause decomposition in; subject to a process of rotting; make rotten: as, dampness *rots* many things; to *rot* flax. See *ret*1. Sometimes used imperatively in imprecation. Compare *rat*3, *drat*2.

> Wel bet is roten appul out of hoord,
> Than that it rotie al the remenaunt.
> *Chaucer*, Cook's Tale, l. 43.

> I would my tongue could rot them [your hands] off!
> *Shak.*, T. of A., iv. 3. 370.

> "What are they fear'd on? fools! 'od *rot* 'em!"
> Were the last words of Higginbottom.
> H. *Smith*, Rejected Addresses, ix.

2. To produce a rotting or putrefactive disease in; specifically, to give the rot to, as sheep or other animals. See *rot*, *n.*, 2.

> The other [sheep] *rotted* with delicious feed.
> *Shak.*, Tit. And., iv. 4. 93.

rot (rot), *n.* [Early mod. E. also *rott*; < ME. *rot*, *rott*, *rote*, *rotte* = MD. *rot*, rottenness: see *rot*, *v.*] 1. The process of rotting, or the state of being rotten; also, rotted substance; matter weakened or disintegrated by rotting.

> I will not kiss thee; then the *rot* returns
> To thine own lips again. *Shak.*, T. of A., iv. 3. 63.

2. A condition of rottenness to which certain animals and plants are liable, as the sheep and the potato (see *potato*), attended by more or less putrescence. (*a*) The rot in sheep, which sometimes affects other animals also, is a fatal distemper caused by the presence of a great number of entozoa, called liver-flukes (*Distoma hepaticum*), in the liver, developed from germs swallowed with the food. The disease is promoted also by a humid state of atmosphere, soil, and herbage. It has different degrees of rapidity, but is generally fatal. (*b*) In botany rot is a general term somewhat loosely applied to cases of the breaking down of the tissues of plants by the destructive agencies of fungi, especially saprophytic fungi and bacteria, but also parasitic fungi. The attacks of parasitic forms, the punctures of insects, and mechanical injuries to plants are frequently followed by decay or rot, since these accidents permit the introduction of bacteria, which are very active agents. The rot may be either "dry" (see *dry-rot*) or "wet"—that is, it may or may not be accompanied by moisture: both kinds may be seen in the potato-rot, which is caused by the fungus *Phytophthora infestans*. The so-called black rot of the grape is caused by *Phoma uvicola*, the white rot by *Coniothyrium diplodiella*, the brown rot by *Peronospora viticola*, and the bitter rot by *Greeneria fuliginea*. The brown rot of the cherry is caused by *Monilia fructigena*. See *potato-rot*, *Phytophthora*, *grape-rot*, *Phoma*, *Peronospora*.

> They have a *Rott* some Years like Sheep.
> *Congreve*, Husband his own Cuckold, Prol.

3. Disgusting stuff; nauseating nonsense; unendurable trash; rant; twaddle; bosh. [Slang.]

> Immediately upon the conclusion of the second act Sir Christopher charged out, muttering something, as he passed, about . . . having had enough of this *rot*.
> *W. E.* Norris, Miss Shafto, vi.

> The accomplished stenographer . . . restored the awful volume of unmitigated *rot*. *N. A. Rev.*, CXLII. 477.

Grinders' rot. See *grinder*.—**Saltpeter rot.** See *saltpeter*.—**White rot,** hydrocotyle, a small herb belonging to the natural order *Umbelliferæ*; pennywort; sheep-rot.

rota1 (rō'tä), *n.* [= OF. roe, *roue* (> ME. roo), F. *roue*, dial. *reue* = Pr. *roda* = Sp. *rueda* = Pg. *roda* = It. *rota*, *ruota*, a wheel, < L. *rota*, a wheel of a vehicle, a potters' wheel, a wheel for torture, poet. a car, chariot, the disk of the sun, etc., ML. a circle, circular garment, a round cake, etc., = Ir. Gael. *roth* = W. *rhod*, a wheel, = D. *rad* = MLG. *rat*, LG. *rad* = OHG. *rad*, MHG. *rat* (*rad-*), G. *rad*, a wheel, = Lith. *ratas*, a wheel, pl. *ratai*, a cart, wheeled vehicle, = Skt. *ratha*, wagon, war-chariot, prob. < √ *ar*, go. From L. *rota* are ult. E. *rotate*, *rotary*, *rotatory*, *rotund*, *round*, *roundel*, *rondel*, *rondeau*, *rundlet*, *roué*, *roll*, *rowel*, *roulade*, *rouleau*, *roulette*, *control*, etc.] 1. A wheel.—2. A course, turn, or routine.

> Fifty years' service of our country had familiarized the whole *rota* of duty in every office and department.
> *E. Styles*, Sermon, 1788.

The experience of those managers who have taken their *rota* of duty in the office.
Ribton-Turner, Vagrants and Vagrancy, p. 254.

3. A roll or list; a school-roll, a military roll, a roll of jurors, or the like, showing the order of call or of turns of duty.

"Whose turn for hot water?" . . . "East's and Tadpole's," answered the senior fag, who kept the *rota*.
T. *Hughes*, Tom Brown at Rugby, i. 7.

Its [the county court's] ordinary judicial work . . . required the attendance of the parties to suits and the *rota* of qualified jurors, and of none others.
Stubbs, Const. Hist., § 420.

4. In *music*, same as *round*[1], or any variety of piece in which repeats are frequent.—5. A reliquary or other receptacle of circular form, ornamented with a cross whose arms reach the outer rim so that the whole resembles a wheel.—6. [*cap.*] An ecclesiastical tribunal in the Roman Catholic Church, having its seat at the papal court. It is composed of twelve prelates, called *auditors*, and was formerly the supreme court of justice and universal court of appeal. It is now divided into two colleges or senates, and has jurisdiction, in the territory of the church, of all suits by appeal and of all matters beneficiary and patrimonial. Owing to the present political position of the papacy, its power is very greatly diminished. There is no appeal from its decisions except to the Pope.

rota[2] (rō'tạ̈), *n.* [ML., also *rotta*: see *rote*[3].] Same as rote[3], in either of its senses.

rotacism, rotacize, etc. See *rhotacism*, etc.

rotal (rō'tạl), *a.* [< LL. *rotalis*, having wheels, < L. *rota*, a wheel: see *rota*[1].] 1. Pertaining to a wheel or wheels, or to wheeled vehicles. [Rare.]

The Cannebière is in a chronic state of vocal and *rotal* tumult.
G. A. *Sala*, in Illustrated London News, Nov. 5, 1881, [p. 439. (*Encyc. Dict.*)

2. Rotary; pertaining to circular or rotary motion. [Rare.] *Imp. Dict.*

Rotalia (rọ̄-tā'li-ạ̈), *n.* [NL. (Lamarck, 1809), neut. pl. of LL. *rotalis*, having wheels: see *rotal*.] The typical genus of *Rotaliidæ*, formerly used with great latitude, now much restricted.

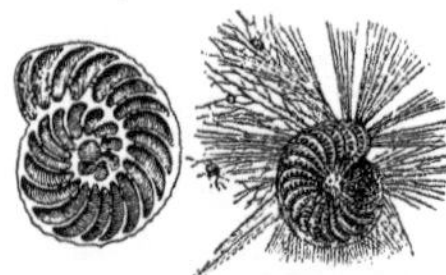

Rotalia.—On the right, with extended filamentous pseudopodia; on the left, more enlarged section of the chambered shell.

The shells or tests of these foraminifers are extremely minute, and of a rotate, turbinate, or nautiloid figure. They abound from the Chalk onward.

rotalian (rọ̄-tā'li-ạn), *a.* and *n.* [< *Rotalia* + *-an*.] I. *a.* Pertaining to the genus *Rotalia*, in a broad sense; rotaline; rotaliform.

In the *Rotalian* series the chambers are disposed in a turbinoid spire. *W. B. Carpenter*, Micros., § 483.

II. *n.* A member of the genus *Rotalia* in a broad sense.

Rotalidea (rō-tạ-lid'ẹ̄-ạ̈), *n. pl.* [NL., < *Rotalia* + *-idea*.] A group of perforate foraminifers, regarded as an order. It contains groups called families and named *Spirillinina*, *Rotalina*, and *Tinoporina*, and corresponds to the family *Rotaliidæ*.

rotalidean (rō-tạ-lid'ē-an), *a.* and *n.* [< *Rotalidea* + *-an*.] I. *a.* Rotaline or rotaliform, in a broad sense; of or pertaining to the *Rotalidea*.

II. *n.* A rotalidean foraminifer.

rotaliform (rọ̄-tal'i-fôrm), *a.* [< NL. *Rotalia* + L. *forma*, form.] Shaped like the test of members of the genus *Rotalia*; rotaline in form. The peculiarity is that the shell is coiled so as to show all the segments on the upper surface, but only those of the last convolution on the lower surface, where the aperture is situated. Also *rotaliiform*.

Rotaliidæ (rō-tạ-li'i-dē), *n. pl.* [NL., < *Rotalia* + *-idæ*.] A family of rhizopods whose test is calcareous, perforate, free or adherent, typically spiral, and rotaliform—that is to say, coiled in such a manner that the whole of the segments are visible on the superior surface, those of the last convolution only on the inferior or apertural side, sometimes one face being more convex, sometimes the other. Aberrant forms are evolute, outspread, acervuline, or irregular. Some of the higher modifications have double chamber-walls, supplemental skeleton, and a system of canals. See cut under *Rotalia*.

rotaliiform (rọ̄-tā'li-i-fôrm), *a.* Same as *rotaliform*.

Rotaliinæ (rọ̄-tā-li-ī'nē), *n. pl.* [NL., < *Rotalia* + *-inæ*.] A subfamily of *Rotaliidæ* with the test spiral, rotaliform, rarely evolute, and very rarely irregular or acervuline.

Rotalina (rō-tạ-lī'nạ̈), *n. pl.* [NL., < *Rotalia* + *-ina*[2].] A group of *Rotalidea*: same as *Rotaliinæ*.

rotaline (rō'tạ-lin), *a.* and *n.* [< NL. *Rotalina*.] I. *a.* Of or pertaining to the *Rotalina* or *Rotalidea*; rotalidean.

II. *n.* A member of the *Rotalina*, *Rotaliidæ*, or *Rotalidea*.

rotalite (rō'tạ-līt), *n.* [< L. *rota*, a wheel, + Gr. λίθος, a stone.] A fossil rotalian or rotaline.

rotamant (rō'tạ̈-mạn), *n.* [< *rota*[1] + *man*.] One who belongs to a rota. [Rare.]

Sidrophel, as full of tricks
As *Rota-men* of politicks,
Straight cast about to over-reach
Th' unwary conqueror with a fetch.
S. Butler, Hudibras, II. iii. 1108.

rotang (rō'tang), *n.* [< F. (NL.) *rotang*: see *ratan*.] One of the ratan-palms, *Calamus Rotang*. See *ratan*.

rotary (rō'tạ-ri), *a.* [< ML. **rotarius*, pertaining to wheels (found as a noun, a wheelwright), < L. *rota*, a wheel: see *rota*[1].] 1. Rotating; turning round and round, as a wheel on its axis; having or characterized by rotation: as, *rotary* animalcules; *rotary* motion.—2. Acting or held in rotation, as officers or an office; turn-about; rotating. [Rare.]

Several years since they . . . became an Independent Presbyterian church with a *rotary* board of elders.
The Congregationalist, May 30, 1862.

Danks rotary furnace. See *furnace*.—**Rotary battery**, a peculiar arrangement of the stamps in a stamping-mill, in which they are grouped in circular form instead of standing in a straight line as is ordinarily the case.—**Rotary blower, brush, crane.** See the nouns.—**Rotary cutter.** (*a*) A milling-tool. (*b*) In *metal-working*, a serrated rotary steel tool used on a mandrel in a lathe for operating upon a piece of metal presented to it and fed toward it on a slide-rest or other analogous movable support. (*c*) In *wood-working*: (1) A rotary chisel-edged cutter fastened to a cutter-head, or one of a gang of cutters so attached, used to cut away superfluous wood in shaping irregular forms, as in the manufacture of hames for harness, of fellies for wagon-wheels, of curved chair-legs, etc. (2) A solid steel tool having rotating cutting edges, in the nature of a burring-tool or router, used in carving-machines for cutting ornamental figures in intaglio. In working upon wood with rotary cutters, the cutter-head shafts or cutter-spindles are sometimes carried by movable bearings, and guided after the manner of a tracing-point or stylus in a pantograph. In other machines the bearings of the cutter-head shafts or spindles are stationary, and the work is itself guided and moved to produce the required shape or pattern. See *burl*, 4 (c), and *router*. Compare also *shaper* and *shaping-machine*.—**Rotary fan**, in *pneumatic engin.*, a blowing-machine consisting of a rotary shaft with vanes or fans that rotate in a case to which the shaft-bearings are usually attached, the air entering the case through central annular openings around the shaft, and being driven by centrifugal force against the inside periphery of the case, whence it issues under pressure corresponding with the centrifugal force generated, and for any given diameter of the fan-wheel depending upon the velocity of rotation. Also called *fan-blower*, *fan-wheel*, or simply *fan*.—**Rotary gatherer**, in *printing*, a revolving circular table on which the sections of a book are put, and successively brought to the gatherer. [Eng.]—**Rotary-hearth oven, rotary oven.** See *oven*.—**Rotary press, rotary machine**, in *printing*, a printing-press or -machine in which the types or plates to be printed are fastened upon a rotating cylinder, and are impressed on a continuous roll of paper. See *printing-machine*.—**Rotary puddler, pump, steam-engine.** See the nouns.—**Rotary shears**, shears having circular overlapping blades, provided with mechanism for rotating the blades, which cut at the point of intersection of their overlapping edges.—**Rotary tubular steam-boiler**, a tubular boiler with a cylindrical shell supported on trunnions to permit revolution.—**Rotary valve.** (*a*) A valve that acts by partial rotation, after the manner of a rock-shaft, thus alternately bringing its port or ports into continuity and discontinuity with the port or ports in the valve-seat, to which it is accurately fitted. Such valves were used in the earliest forms of steam-engines to which automatic valve-gear was applied, and are now used in the automatic valve-gear of some of the finest variable cut-off engines. (See *steam-engine* and *valve-gear*.) When a single rotary valve is used both for induction and for eduction, and actuated by an eccentric rod connected with a rocker-arm rigidly attached to the body of the valve, the principles of this valve-motion are precisely the same as those of the common slide-valve motion, the point of cut-off depending upon angular advance of the eccentric and lap, and the admission being influenced by lead as in the slide-valve. Also called *rock-valve*. See *slide-valve*, *cut-off*, *angular advance* (under *angular*), *lap*[3], 3, and *lead*[1], 8. (*b*) A valve which makes complete and successive revolutions, thus alternately bringing its port or ports into continuity and discontinuity with a port or ports in its seat. This kind of valve has been but little used.

Rotary Shears.

a, *a*, cutting edges of one form; *b*, *b*, cutting edges of another form; *c*, a series of rotary-shear blades formed in a single piece of the form shown at *a*; they operate simultaneously to cut a sheet of metal into parallel strips of uniform width.

rotascope (rō'tạ-skōp), *n.* [< L. *rota*, a wheel (see *rota*[1]), + Gr. σκοπεῖν, view.] Same as *gyroscope*.

rotatable (rō'tā-tạ-bl), *a.* [< *rotate* + *-able*.] Capable of being rotated; admitting of rotation or rotatory movement.

The improvement consists in the *rotatable* nozzle.
The Engineer, LXV. 359.

The *rotatable* blade is designed to do the general work of the pressman in making forms ready.
Sci. Amer., N. S., LX. 306.

rotatably (rō'tā-tạ-bli), *adv.* In a rotatable manner; so as to be rotated.

Pocketed valve *rotatably* supported in said casing.
The Engineer, LXVI. 212.

rotate (rō'tāt), *v.*; pret. and pp. *rotated*, ppr. *rotating*. [< L. *rotatus*, pp. of *rotare* (> It. *rotare* = Pg. Sp. *rodar* = Pr. *rodar*, *rogar* = F. *rouer*), revolve like a wheel, < *rota*, a wheel: see *rota*[1].] I. *intrans.* 1. To revolve or move round a center or axis; turn in a circle, as or like a wheel; have a continuous circular motion.—2. To turn in a curve upon a center or support; have a revolving motion from side to side or up and down; specifically, in *anat.*, to be rotated; execute one or any of the movements of rotation.

In convergence the eyes *rotate* on the optic axis in opposite directions. *G. T. Ladd*, Physiol. Psychology, p. 438.

3. To go round in succession, as in or among a revolving or a repeating series; alternate serially; especially, to act or pass in rotation, as a set of office-holders or an office.—**Rotating fires.** See *firework*, 2.

II. *trans.* 1. To cause to revolve upon an axis or upon a support; give a circular or curvilinear movement to; turn in a curve: as, to *rotate* a cylinder by hand; to *rotate* the head or the eyes.—2. To move or change about in a series or in rotation; cause to succeed in a serial or recurrent order: as, to *rotate* certain men in the tenure of an office.

The best men would be sooner or later *rotated* out of office, and inferior men would take their places.
Amer. Nat., June, 1890, p. 549.

rotate (rō'tāt), *a.* [< L. *rotatus*, pp. of *rotare*, turn: see *rotate*, *v.*] 1. In *bot.*, wheel-shaped; spreading out nearly flat like a wheel: as, the limb of a *rotate* corolla, calyx, etc.: usually applied to a gamopetalous corolla with a short tube.—2. In *zoöl.*, wheel-shaped; rotiform; specifically, in *entom.*, noting hairs, spines, etc., when they form a ring around any organ or part, projecting at right angles to the axis.

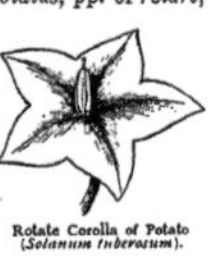

Rotate Corolla of Potato (*Solanum tuberosum*).

rotated (rō'tā-ted), *a.* [< *rotate* + *-ed*[2].] Same as *rotate*.

rotate-plane (rō'tāt-plān), *a.* In *bot.*, wheel-shaped and flat, without a tube: as, a *rotate-plane* corolla. Also *rotato-plane*.

rotating-ring (rō'tā-ting-ring), *n.* In *gun.*, a band of brass or copper placed around a projectile to take the grooves in the bore of a cannon and give rotation to the projectile.

A single *rotating ring* of copper is used for all calibers.
Gun Foundry Board Report, p. 33.

rotation (rọ̄-tā'shọn), *n.* [= F. *rotation* = Sp. *rotacion* = Pg. *rotação* = It. *rotazione*, < L. *rotatio(n-)*, < *rotare*, pp. *rotatus*, rotate: see *rotate*.] 1. The act of rotating or turning, or the state of being whirled round; the continuous motion of a solid body, as a wheel or sphere, about an axis, its opposite sides moving relatively to one another, as distinguished from the forward motion of the whole body in a circle or an ellipse independent of any relative motion of its parts, as that of the planets. Thus, the daily turning of the earth on its axis is a *rotation*; its annual motion round the sun is a *revolution*.

In *rotations* a little force toward the circumference is equal to a greater force towards the centre.
Bacon, Works (ed. Spedding), IX. 447.

The axle-trees of chariots . . . [take] fire by the rapid *rotation* of the wheels. *Newton*, Opticks, iii., query 8.

She has that everlasting *Rotation* of Tongue that an Echo must wait till she dies before it can catch her last Words. *Congreve*, Way of the World, ii. 4.

The *rotation* of the plane of polarization is proportional to the strength of the magnetic action.
J. E. H. Gordon, Elect. and Mag., II. 221.

2. A peculiar spiral movement of fluids observed within the cavity of certain vegetable

cells, as in *Chara* and *Vallisneria*. See below.—3. Serial or recurrent order; a round or sequence of one after another; a fixed or definite routine of succession; regularly recurring change.

I have often observed particular words and phrases come much into vogue. . . . This has lately been remarkable of the word *rotation*. . . . Nothing is done now but by *rotation*. . . . [In] whist, they play the rubbers by *rotation*; a fine lady returns her visits by *rotation*; and the parson of our parish declared yesterday that . . . he, his curate, the lecturer, and now and then a friend, would for the future preach by *rotation*.
British Mag., 1763, p. 542, quoted in N. and Q., 7th ser., [VII. 164.

Angular velocity of rotation. When a solid body revolves about an axis, its different particles move with a velocity proportional to their respective distances from the axis, and the velocity of the particle whose distance from the axis is unity is the angular velocity of rotation. It is often expressed as in turns per second.—**Axial rotation.** See *axial*.—**Axis of rotation.** See *axis*[1].—**Center of rotation,** the point about which a body revolves. It is the same as the center of motion.—**Center of spontaneous rotation,** the point about which a body all whose parts are at liberty to move, and which has been struck in a direction not passing through its center of gravity, begins to turn. If any force is impressed upon a body or system of bodies in free space, and not in a direction passing through the center of gravity of the body or system, a rotatory motion will ensue about an axis passing through the center of gravity, and the center about which this motion is performed is called the *center of spontaneous rotation*.—**Circular rotation of the eyeball,** rotation about the visual axis.—**Congruency of rotations.** See *congruency*.—**Couple of rotations.** See *couple*.—**Energy of rotation.** See *energy*.—**Magnetic rotation of currents.** See *magnetic*.—**Magnetic rotation of the plane of polarization.** See *magnetic rotatory polarization*, under *rotatory*.—**Method of rotations,** a method used in descriptive geometry, consisting in turning a part of the given geometrical system about an axis, usually perpendicular to a plane of projection.—**Principal axes of rotation.** If a point which is not the center of gravity be taken in a solid body, all the axes which pass through that point (and they may be infinite in number) will have different moments of inertia, and there must exist one in which the moment is a maximum, and another in which it is a minimum. Those axes in respect of which the moment of inertia is a maximum or minimum are called the *principal axes of rotation*. In every body, however irregular, there are three principal axes of rotation, at right angles to each other, on any one of which, when the body revolves, the opposite centrifugal forces counterbalance each other, and hence the rotation becomes permanent.—**Principle of the composition of rotations,** the proposition that three rotations about axes which meet in one point are equivalent to one rotation round an axis through the same point, the measure of the rotations being taken upon the axes, and the axis of the resultant rotation being the diagonal of the parallelepiped of which the others are sides.—**Pure rotation,** rotation without translation; a screw-motion where the pitch of the screw vanishes.—**Rotation in office,** the holding of the same office by different persons in succession; specifically, in *politics*, the transfer of offices, especially those filled by appointment, to new incumbents at more or less regular intervals, without regard to the manner in which their duties have been discharged. In the United States the principle of rotation in appointive offices has been both advocated and condemned with great urgency on grounds of public advantage and partisan or personal right.

Jefferson would have *rotation in office*.
Theodore Parker, Historic Americans, p. 260.

Rotation of crops, a recurring series of different crops grown on the same ground; the order of recurrence in cropping. It is found that the same kind of crop cannot be advantageously cultivated on the same soil through a succession of years, and hence one kind of crop is made to succeed another in repeated series. Different soils and climates require different systems of rotation, but it is a recognized rule in all cases that culmiferous crops ripening their seeds should not be repeated without the intervention of pulse, roots, herbage, or fallow.—**Rotation of protoplasm,** in *bot.*, the circulation or streaming movement of the protoplasmic contents of active vegetable cells. Under a moderately high power of the microscope the protoplasm of vitally active cells is seen to be in a state of constant activity or rotation—that is, it flows or moves about in steady streams or bands in various directions inside the cell. These moving protoplasmic bands have embedded in them minute granules. The rate of the movements varies in different plants, being (at a temperature of 15° C.) only .009 millimeter per minute in the leaf-cells of *Potamogeton crispus*, and 10 millimeters per minute in the plasmodium of *Didymium Serpula*. See *protoplasm*.—**Rotation of the plane of polarization.** See *rotatory polarization*, under *rotatory*.

rotational (rō̤-tā'shon-al̤), *a.* [< *rotation* + *-al*.] Pertaining to or consisting in rotation; of the nature of rotation: as, *rotational* velocity.

We should thus be led to find an atom, not in the *rotational* motion of a vortex-ring, but in irrotational motion round a re-entering channel.
W. K. Clifford, Lects., I. 242.

Rotational motion of a fluid. See *cortex-motion*.

rotation-area (rō̤-tā'shon-ā'rē-ạ̈), *n.* Double the sum of the products obtained by multiplying each element of mass of a material system by the differential coefficient relative to the time of the area described by the radius vector upon the plane perpendicular to the axis of rotation. If all the external forces which act upon a system are directed toward an axis, the rotation-area for that axis will be described with a uniform motion, which is the principle of the conservation of areas.

The *rotation-area* for an axis may be exhibited geometrically by a portion of the axis which is taken proportional to the area, and it is evident from the theory of projections that *rotation-areas* for different axes may be combined by the same laws with which forces applied to a point and rotations are combined, so that there is a corresponding parallelopiped of *rotation-areas*. There is, then, for every system, an axis of resultant *rotation-area*, with reference to which the rotation is a maximum, and the *rotation-area* for any other axis is the corresponding projection of the resultant *rotation-area*. The *rotation-area* vanishes for an axis which is perpendicular to the axis of resultant *rotation-area*.
B. Peirce, Analytical Mechanics, § 754.

rotative (rō'tā̤-tiv), *a.* [< F. *rotatif*, < L. *rotatus*, pp. of *rotare*, rotate: see *rotate*.] 1. Causing something to rotate; producing rotation.

The *rotative* forces acting on A and B are, as it were, distributed by the diurnal rotation around NS.
Newcomb and Holden, Astronomy, p. 211.

2. Pertaining to rotation; rotational.

This high *rotative* velocity of the sun must cause an equatorial rise of the solar atmosphere.
Siemens, New Theory of the Sun, p. 21.

rotatively (rō'tā̤-tiv-li), *adv.* So as to rotate; in a rotatory manner.

An internally-toothed wheel *c*, *rotatively* connected with the said shaft. *The Engineer*, LXIX. 290.

rotato-plane (rō'tā̤-tō-plān), *a.* Same as *rotate-plane*.

rotator (rō̤-tā'tor̤), *n.* [= F. *rotateur* = Sp. *rodador* = Pg. *rolador* = It. *rotatore*, < L. *rotator*, a whirler, < *rotare*, whirl, rotate: see *rotate*.] 1. One who or that which rotates, or causes rotation; any rotational agency or instrument.

This is mounted on the *rotator*, so that it can be turned around quickly. *Mayer*, Sound, p. 110.

2. Specifically, in *anat.*, a muscle that produces a rolling or rotatory motion of a part; a muscle which rotates a part upon its own axis. [In this sense usually as New Latin, with plural *rotatores*.]—3. In *metal-working*, a revolving or rotary furnace.—**Rotatores dorsi.** Same as *rotatores spinæ*.—**Rotatores femoris,** six muscles which in the human subject rotate the femur and evert the thigh: they are the pyriformis, quadratus, obturator externus and internus, with the gemellus superior and inferior.—**Rotatores spinæ,** several (about eleven) small deep-seated muscles of the thoracic region of the spine beneath the multifidus, passing obliquely from the transverse process of a vertebra to the lamina of the next vertebra above. Also called *rotispinales*.—**Rotator fibulæ,** the rotator of the fibula, a muscle of the leg of some animals, as lemurs, from the back of the tibia obliquely downward and outward to the front of the fibula.

Rotatoria (rō-tā̤-tō'ri-ā̤), *n. pl.* [NL., fem. of L. *rotatorius, < *rotare*, rotate: see *rotary*.] The wheel-animalcules: same as *Rotifera*.

rotatorial (rō-tā̤-tō'ri-al̤), *a.* [< *Rotatoria* + *-al*.] In *zoöl.*, of or pertaining to the *Rotatoria* or *Rotifera*; rotiferal.

rotatorian (rō-tā̤-tō'ri-an̤), *n.* [< *Rotatoria* + *-an*.] A member of the *Rotatoria*; a rotifer or wheel-animalcule.

The tiny creature, as it develops, shows itself a *rotatorian*. *The Century*, XIV. 154.

rotatory (rō'tā̤-tō̤-ri), *a.* and *n.* [= F. *rotatoire*, < NL. **rotatorius*, < L. *rotator*, a whirler, < *rotare*, whirl, rotate: see *rotate*.] I. *a.* 1. Of, pertaining to, or effecting rotation; turning or causing to turn about or upon an axis or support; relating to motion from or about a fixed point or center: opposed to *reciprocatory*.

The ball and socket joint allows . . . of a *rotatory* or sweeping motion. *Paley*, Nat. Theol., ix.

Verdet demonstrated that when a salt is dissolved in water the water and the salt each bring into the solution their special *rotatory* power.
Atkinson, tr. of Mascart and Joubert, I. 576.

My lady with her fingers interlock'd,
And *rotatory* thumbs on silken knees.
Tennyson, Aylmer's Field.

2. Going about in a recurrent series; moving from point to point; following in succession: as, *rotatory* assemblies. *Burke*. (*Imp. Dict.*)—3. In *zoöl.*, rotatorial or rotiferal, as a wheel-animalcule.—4. In *anat.*, causing rotation: as, a *rotatory* muscle.—**Magnetic rotatory polarization,** that rotation of the plane of polarization, + or —, which takes place when a plane-polarized beam of light is transmitted through a transparent medium in a powerful magnetic field, and similarly when it is reflected from the pole of a powerful electromagnet.—**Magnetic rotatory power.** See *magnetic*.—**Rotatory diarthrosis.** Same as *cyclarthrosis*.—**Rotatory muscle,** a rotator.—**Rotatory polarization,** the change of plane to the right or to the left (of an observer looking in the direction the ray is moving) which a ray of plane-polarized light undergoes when passed through quartz, sugar, etc.: if the rotation is to the right, the substance is said to be *dextrorotatory* (or positive), as cane-sugar and glucose; if to the left, it is called *levorotatory* (or negative), as starch-sugar, quinine, etc. See also *magnetic rotatory polarization*, above.—**Rotatory power,** the property which is possessed by some crystalline bodies, and a great number of liquids and solutions, of rotating the plane of polarization. See *rotatory polarization*.—**Rotatory steam-engine.** See *steam-engine*.—**Specific rotatory power,** the angle of rotation which a layer of unit thickness would give to a certain light-ray; practically, an assumed color called the *transition-tint*.

II. *n.*; pl. *rotatories* (-riz). In *zoöl.*, a rotatorian or rotifer.

The *rotatories* fix the posterior extremity of the body.
Van der Hoeven, Zoöl. (trans.), I. 196.

rotch (roch), *n.* Same as *roach*[2], 2. [Prov. Eng.]

rotche (roch), *n.* [Said to be < D. *rotje*, a petrel; cf. G. dial. *rätsche*, G. *rätsch-ente*, the common wild duck, < *rätschen*, *rätschen*, splash like a duck.] The little auk, auklet, dovekie, or sea-dove, *Mergulus alle* or *Alle nigricans*. See *Mergulus*, *Alle*, and cut under *dovekie*. Also *rotchie*.

rotchet†, *n.* Same as *rochet*[2].

rotchie, *n.* Same as *rotche*.

rote[1] (rōt), *n.* [< ME. *rot*, *root*, *rote*, < OF. *rote*, *route*, *route*, a way through a forest, a way, road, track, rut, F. *route*, a way, road, track, = Sp. *ruta* = Pg. *rota*, track, course of a ship at sea (ML. reflex *rotta*, *rota*), < ML. *rupta*, a way through a forest, a way, road, street; prop. adj., sc. *via*, a way broken or cut through a forest; < L. *rupta*, fem. of *ruptus*, pp. of *rumpere*, break: see *rupture*. *Rote*[1] is thus a doublet of *route*[1], *rout*[5], *rut*[1], q. v. Cf. *routine*.] 1. A fixed or unchanging round, as in learning or reciting something; mechanical routine in learning, or in the repetition of that which has been learned; exact memorizing, or reproduction from memory, as of words or sounds, with or without attention to their significance: chiefly in the phrase *by rote*.

Loke a ribaut of hem that can nougt wel reden
His rewle ne his respondes but be pure *rote*,
Als as he were a connynge Clerke he casteth the lawes.
Piers Plowman's Crede (E. E. T. S.), l. 377.

First, rehearse your song *by rote*,
To each word a warbling note.
Shak., M. N. D., v. 1. 404.

He rather saith it *by rote* to himself, as that he would have, than that he can thoroughly believe it, or be persuaded of it. *Bacon*, Atheism (ed. 1887).

The lazy manner of reading sermons, or speaking sermons *by rote*. *Goldsmith*, The Bee, No. 7.

2. A part mechanically committed to memory. [Rare.]

A *rote* of buffoonery that serveth all occasions. *Swift*.

3. A row or rank. [Prov. Eng.]

We'll go among them when the barley has been laid in *rotes*. *R. D. Blackmore*, Lorna Doone, xxix. (song).

rote[1]† (rōt), *v. t.* [< *rote*[1], *n.* Cf. *rote*[2].] 1. To learn by rote or by heart.

Speak
To the people; not by your own instruction, . . .
But with such words that are but *roted* in
Your tongue. *Shak.*, Cor., iii. 2. 55.

2. To repeat from memory.

And if by chance a tune you *rote*,
'Twill foot it finely to your note.
Drayton, Muses' Elysium, ii.

rote[2]† (rōt), *v. i.* [< L. *rotare*, whirl, rotate: see *rotate*.] To rotate; change by rotation.

Now this modell upon rotation was that the third part of the House should *rote* out by ballot every yeare, so that every ninth yeare the House would be wholly altered. No magistrate to continue above 3 yeares.
Aubrey, Lives, J. Harrington.

A third part of the senate, or Parliament, should *rote* out by ballot every year, and new ones to be chosen in their room. *Z. Grey*, Note on Hudibras, II. iii. 1108.

rote[3] (rōt), *n.* [< ME. *rote*, *roote*, < OF. *rote* (= Pr. OSp. *rota*) = OHG. *hrottā*, *rottā*, *rotā*, *roddā*, MHG. *rotte*, < ML. *rotta*, *rota*, *rocta*, earlier *chrotta*, a kind of fiddle, a crowd; of Celtic origin: < W. *crwth* = OIr. *crot* = Gael. *cruit*, a fiddle, crowd: see *crowd*[2].] A musical instrument with strings, and played either by a bow, like a crowd or fiddle, or by a wheel, like a hurdy-gurdy. See *crowd*[2]. Also called *rota*.

Wel couthe he synge and pleyen on a *rote*.
Chaucer, Gen. Prol. to C. T., l. 236.

There were two sets of instruments in the middle ages very similar to each other, the one played with the fingers, the other with a bow. The term *Rote* may perhaps have been applied to both classes.
W. K. Sullivan, Introd. to O'Curry's Anc. Irish, p. ii.

rote[4]† (rōt), *v. i.* An obsolete dialectal form of *rout*[1].

rote[4] (rōt), *n.* [A dial. var. of *rout*[1] or *rut*[2].] The sound of surf, as before a storm. [Local, Eng. and U. S.]

Then all amaz'd shriekes out confused cries,
While the seas *rote* doth ring their doleful knell.
Mir. for Mags. (England's Eliza, st. 270), II. 895.

I hear the sea very strong and loud at the north. . . . They call this the *rote* or *rut* of the sea.
D. Webster, Private Correspondence (ed. Fletcher Webster), II. 262.

The rote of the surf on Menimsha Bight
Murmurs its warning.
Walter Mitchell, In the Vineyard Sound, Harper's Weekly, [XXXIV. 743.

Within sound of the rote of the sea.
Stedman, Poets of America, p. 224.

rote[5]†, *n.* A Middle English form of *root*[1].

rote[6]†, *v.* A Middle English form of *root*[2].

rotella (rō-tel'ä), *n.*; pl. *rotellæ* (-ē). [ML., dim. of L. *rota*, a wheel: see *rota*[1]. Cf. *rowel*, from the same source.] **1.** A disk; a round plate.—**2.** A round shield.—**3.** [*cap.*] [NL.] A genus of gastropods of the family *Rotellidæ*, containing small polished highly colored shells, as *R. suturalis*.—**4.** Any member of this genus.

Rotellidæ (rō-tel'i-dē), *n. pl.* [NL., < *Rotella* + *-idæ*.] A family of scutibranchiate gastropods, typified by the genus *Rotella*, united generally with the *Trochidæ*.

roten†, *a.* A Middle English form of *rotten*[1].

rote-song (rōt'sông), *n.* A song to be taught by rote, or by frequent repetition to the learner, as a child before it is able to read.

rot-grass (rot'gràs), *n.* The soft-grass, *Holcus lanatus* and *H. mollis*; also, the butterwort, *Pinguicula vulgaris*, and the pennywort or penny-rot, *Hydrocotyle vulgaris*: so called as being supposed to cause rot in sheep. [Prov. Eng.]

rotgut (rot'gut), *n.* and *a.* [< *rot*, *v.*, + obj. *gut*.] **I.** *n.* Bad or adulterated liquor, injurious to the stomach and bowels; in the United States, specifically, whisky adulterated with deleterious substances to cheapen it while increasing its apparent strength. [Colloq. and low.]

They overwhelm their paunch daily with a kind of flat *rotgut*; we with a bitter dreggish small liquor. *Harvey.*

Rot-gut: cheap whiskey; the word occurs in Heywood's "English Traveller" and Addison's "Drummer" for a poor kind of drink. *Lowell*, Biglow Papers, 2d ser., Int.

II. *a.* Injurious and corrosive: said of bad liquor. [Colloq. and low.]

Then there's fuddling about in the public-house, and drinking bad spirits, and punch, and such *rot-gut* stuff.
T. Hughes, School Days at Rugby, i. 6.

rötheln (rė'teln), *n.* [G.] Same as *rubella*.

rother[1], *n.* An obsolete or dialectal form of *rudder*[1].

rother[2] (roᴛʜ'ėr), *n.* [< ME. *rother*, *reother*, *rither*, *rether* (pl. *rotheres*, *retheren*, *rutheren*, *ritheren*), < AS. *hrīther*, *hr̄ȳther*, a horned beast, an ox, bull, cow, pl. *hritheru*, *hrytheru*, *hrythera*, *hrutheru*, *hrythro*, earlier with long vowel *hrīther*, etc., horned cattle, oxen, = OFries. *hrither*, *rither*, *reder* = D. *rund* = OHG. *hrind*, *rind*, MHG. *rint* (*rind-*), G. *rind* (the formative *-er* being retained in the plural *rinder*), a horned beast, an ox, etc., pl. *rinder*, horned cattle (> *rinderpest*, > E. *rinderpest*, a cattle-plague), = Goth. **hrinthis* or **hrunthis* (not recorded). Connection with *horn* is doubtful: see *horn*.] A bovine animal; a cow, or an animal of the cow kind. [Obsolete or prov. Eng.]

Foure *rotheren* hym by-forn that feble were [worthen];
Men myȝte reken ich a ryb, so reufull they weren.
Piers Plowman's Crede (E. E. T. S.), l. 431.

It is the pasture lards the *rother's* sides,
The want that makes him lean.
Shak., T. of A., iv. 3. 12.

[In this passage *rother's* is an emendation of *brother's*, which is given in most editions.]

rother[3] (roᴛʜ'ėr), *n.* [Abbr. of *rother-soil*.] Cattle-dung; manure. [Obsolete or local, Eng.]

rother-beast (roᴛʜ'ėr-bēst), *n.* A bovine or rother.

Bucerum pecus, an hearde of *rother beastes*.
Elyot, ed. 1559. (*Halliwell.*)

rothermuck (roᴛʜ'ėr-muk), *n.* The barnacle-goose, *Anser bernicla* or *Bernicla leucopsis*. *Montagu.* [Local, British.]

rother-nail (roᴛʜ'ėr-nāl), *n.* [That is, *rudder-nail*.] In *ship-building*, a nail with a very full head, used for fastening the rudder-irons. [Eng.]

rother-soil (roᴛʜ'ėr-soil), *n.* [< *rother*[2] + *soil*[3].] Cattle-dung; manure. [Obsolete or prov. Eng.]

In Herefordshire the dung of such [horned] beasts is still called *rother soyl*.
Kennett, MS. Lansd. 1033. (*Halliwell.*)

Rothesay herald. One of the six heralds of the Scottish Heralds' College.

rothoffite (rot'hof-īt), *n.* [< *Rothoff* (?) + *-ite*[2].] A variety of garnet, brown or black in color, found in Sweden.

Rotifer (rō'ti-fėr), *n.* [NL. (Leeuwenhoek, 1702), having a wheel, < L. *rota*, a wheel (see *rota*[1]), + *ferre* = E. *bear*[1].] **1.** The name-giving genus of *Rotifera*, based upon a species called *R. vulgaris*, and now placed in the family *Philodinidæ*, including forms which swim or creep like a leech, and have a forked, jointed, telescopic foot. Hence—**2.** [*l. c.*] One of the *Rotifera* (which see); any wheel-animalcule. Rotifers are found all over the world, in salt as well as fresh water, though chiefly in the latter; they often swarm in infusions with other animalcules; a few are parasitic. Many rotifers can be desiccated and kept in a dry state for months and still be revived by the application of moisture.

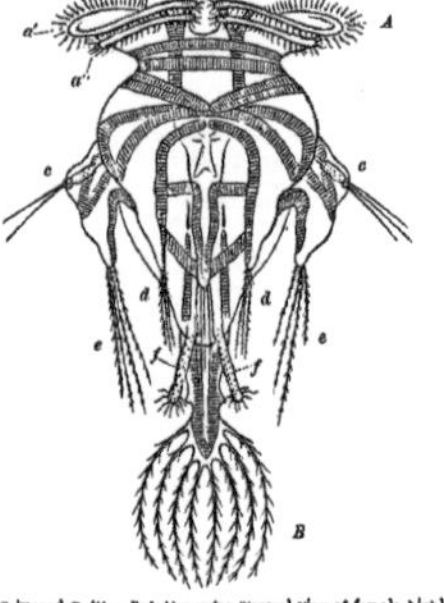

A Scirtopod Rotifer, *Pedalion mira* (ventral view of female, highly magnified).
A, head with trochal disk of a double wreath: *a'*, the cephalotroch; *a''*, the branchiotroch; *B*, appendaged foot, or pseudopodium; *c c*, *d d*, *e e*, *f f*, four pairs of appendages. The dark bands are the muscles.

Rotifera (rō-tif'e-rä), *n. pl.* [NL., neut. pl. of *Rotifer*: see *Rotifer*.] A class of animalcules, usually classified with or near the lowest worms, distinguished by their circles of cilia, sometimes single, sometimes double, which through the microscope appear like revolving wheels, whence they have been called *wheel-animalcules* and *Rotatoria*. They are a small but well-marked group, whose true position in the evolutionary series is much questioned. Some of the forms have been known for nearly two centuries, and many others have only recently been brought to light. Being all of microscopic size, and often appearing in infusions, the rotifers that were known up to about 1838, the period of Ehrenberg's researches, were considered to be protozoan, and they were placed with some vegetable organisms in the old-fashioned infusories. (See *Infusoria*, 1.) Their readily discernible complex organization gave one of the reasons for supposing that infusorians reach a comparatively high grade of development. Rotifers present great attractions to the microscopist, and have been much studied; and the organization of few of the low invertebrates is better known. They are true metazoans, of microscopic size, bilaterally symmetrical, usually without metameric segmentation, always with an intestinal canal and a body-cavity or cœlom, and with an anus as well as a mouth (except in one group). Head and tail are generally well marked; the former bears, under many modifications, the characteristic wheel-organ which gives name to the group, and is technically called the *trochal disk* (see cut under *trochal*); the tail or foot-body, called *pseudopodium*, is variously modified as a locomotory organ for swimming, skipping, creeping, or rooting (see *pseudopodium*, 2, and cut under *Rotifer*); in a few genera it is wanting. The body is covered with a firm cuticle, and sometimes also sheathed in a protective case (see *urceolus*); it often presents peculiar spinose or setose appendages. The muscular system may be quite highly developed, as in *Pedalion*, where it consists of several symmetrically disposed bands. In the alimentary canal may usually be distinguished a mouth, pharynx, esophagus, stomach, intestine, and anus. The pharynx contains the *mastax* with its teeth or *trophi*, among which are parts called *malleus*, *incus*, *uncus*, *fulcrum*, *ramus*, and *manubrium* (see these names, and cut under *uncus*). All true rotifers have a mastax; its homologies are disputed. Both the pharynx and the esophagus are chitinized. The intestine is lined with ciliated epithelium. Nephridia are present; a nervous system is demonstrable; and various sense-organs, as eye-spots, are recognized. Rotifers were supposed to be hermaphroditic; but separation of sex has been determined for most members of the class, the males being in all such cases small and degenerate in comparison with the females. Details of the reproductive process vary in different cases. The classification of *Rotifera*, as well as the taxonomic rank and systematic position of the group, is not yet settled, as some equivocal or aberrant forms remain to be accounted for. Exclusive of these, a reclassification given by C. T. Hudson in 1884, and generally accepted, is into four orders: (1) *Rhizota*, rooted rotifers, with families *Flosculariidæ* and *Melicertidæ*; (2) *Bdelloida* (or *Bdelligrada*), creeping rotifers, with one family, called *Philodinidæ*, though containing the original genus *Rotifer*; (3) *Scirtopoda*, skipping rotifers, the *Pedalionidæ*, with one genus (see cut under *Rotifer*); and (4) *Ploima*, or swimming rotifers, the rest of the class. These are either illoricate (the *Hydatinidæ*, *Synchætidæ*, *Notommatidæ*, *Triarthridæ*, and *Asplanchnidæ*) or loricate (the *Brachionidæ*, *Pterodinidæ*, and *Euchlanidæ*). Ranked as a superclass or phylum, the rotifers have also been divided into two classes: *Parapodiata*, represented alone by the genus *Pedalion*; and *Lipopoda*, all the rest. One of the commonest rotifers is *Hydatina senta*, belonging to the illoricate ploimate group.

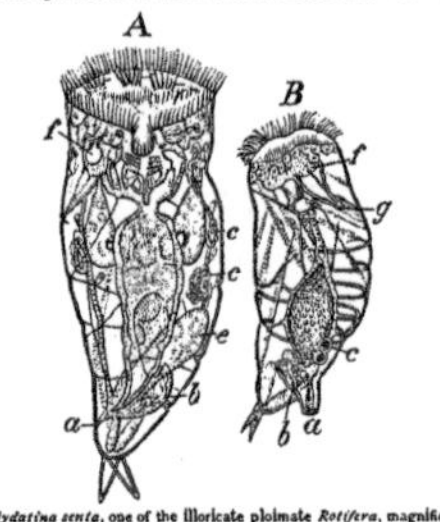

Hydatina senta, one of the illoricate ploimate *Rotifera*, magnified.
A, female: *a*, anus; *b*, contractile vacuole; *c*, water-vessels; *e*, ovary; *f*, ganglion. *B*, male: *a*, penis; *b*, contractile vacuole; *c*, testis; *f*, ganglion; *g*, setigerous pit. In both figures the conspicuous wheel or wreath and the forked foot are unmarked.

rotiferal (rō-tif'e-ral), *a.* [< *rotifer* + *-al*.] Bearing a wheel—that is, having a wheel-organ; pertaining to the *Rotifera* or wheel-animalcules, or having their characters; rotatorial or rotatory, as an animalcule. *Encyc. Brit.*, XXI. 8.

rotiferan (rō-tif'e-ran), *n.* [< *rotifer* + *-an*.] An individual member of the *Rotifera*; a rotifer. *Nature*, XLI. 378. [Rare.]

rotiferous (rō-tif'e-rus), *a.* [< *rotifer* + *-ous*.] Having a wheel, as a wheel-animalcule; provided with a trochal disk or wheel-organ; relating to rotifers.

rotiform (rō'ti-fôrm), *a.* [= F. *rotiforme*, < L. *rota*, a wheel (see *rotary*), + *forma*, form.] Wheel-shaped; rotate.

rotispinalis (rō"ti-spī-nā'lis), *n.*; pl. *rotispinales* (-lēz). [NL., < L. *rota*, a wheel, + *spina*, spine: see *spinal*.] A muscle of the back which assists in rotating the vertebræ; one of the rotatores spinæ. *Coues and Shute*, 1887.

rotl (rot'l), *n.* [Ar.] An Arabian pound of twelve ounces. Each city has its own rotls for different commodities, so that the number of these units is great. Few weigh less than a troy pound, about one third of them have weights between one and two, another third between two and five, and the remainder between five and ninety troy pounds. The following are a few of the rotls now in use:

	Grams.	Pounds Avoirdupois.
Egypt	444	0.98
Tripoli, market	1817	4.01
" large	2180	4.81
Tunis, for metals	507	1.12
" " fruit, etc.	568	1.17
" " vegetables	639	1.41
Abyssinia	311	0.69
Morocco	508	1.12
Acre, for raw cotton	2207	4.87
" " yarn	2037	4.49
Aleppo, for figs, etc.	2280	5.03
" " silk	2220	4.89
" " Persian silk	2154	4.75
" " drugs	1902	4.19
Damascus	1787	3.94

rotonde (rō-tond'), *n.* [F., < *rotonde*, round: see *rotund*.] **1.** A ruff of the kind worn during the early years of the seventeenth century by both men and women. Compare *ruff*[1], 1.—**2.** A cope, the ecclesiastical garment especially so called when considered as an object of decorative art.

rotondo (rō-ton'dō), *a.* [< It. *rotondo*, round: see *round*[1], *rotund*.] In *music*, round; full.

rotor (rō'tor), *n.* [Short for *rotator*.] A quantity having magnitude, direction, and position.

In analogy with this [Hamilton's use of the word *vector*], I propose to use the name *rotor* (short for rotator) to mean a quantity having magnitude, direction, and position, of which the simplest type is a velocity of rotation about a certain axis. A *rotor* will be geometrically represented by a length proportional to its magnitude measured upon its axis in a certain sense.
W. K. Clifford, Lond. Math. Soc. Proc., 1873, p. 381.

rotour†, *n.* [ME., < OF. **rotour*, < *rote*, a rote: see *rote*[3].] A player on the rote.

He is a persone, she thynkethe, of fair figure,
A yong *rotour*, redy to hir pleasier.
Lydgate, Minor Poems, p. 35. (*Halliwell.*)

rot-steep (rot'stēp), *n.* The process of steeping cotton fabrics in water to remove impurities, preparatory to bleaching. See the quotation.

The *rot steep*, so called because the flour or size with which the goods were impregnated was formerly allowed to ferment and putrefy, is intended to thoroughly wet the cloth. *W. Crookes*, Dyeing and Calico-printing, p. 45.

rottat, *n.* Same as *rota*[2].

rottan†, *n.* An occasional spelling of *ratan*.

Rottbœllia (rot-bel'i-ä), *n.* [NL. (Linnæus filius, 1779), named after C. F. *Rottbøll* (1727–1797), professor of botany at Copenhagen, author of botanical works.] A genus of grasses, of the series *Panicaceæ* and tribe *Andropogoneæ*, type of the subtribe *Rottbœllieæ*. It is marked by spikelets spiked in pairs, one of each pair sterile and pedicelled, the other fertile and sessile, and, further, by the cylindrical form of the spike, by the spikelets being embedded in excavations of the axis, by the absence of long hairs or awns, and by the single unisexual flower which commonly forms the fertile spikelet, containing four obtuse glumes, three stamens, and two distinct styles. The 27 species inhabit warm or temperate regions in both hemispheres; one species, *R. rugosa*, is found in pine-barrens from Delaware southward. They are generally tall grasses with flat leaves, either rough or smooth. Some species bear a cluster of spikes, others a single one, or, as in *R. digitata*, a handsome Asiatic species, an elongated spike is sometimes set with a few short branches at its base, with often an additional male flower in each spikelet. Some are forage-grasses, as the tropical *R. compressa*, valued by graziers in Australia.

rotten[1] (rot'n), *a.* [< ME. *roten*, *roton*, *rotin*, < Icel. *rotinn* = Sw. *rutten* = Dan. *raaden*, rotten; in form pp. of a lost verb, Icel. as if **rjōta*, rot: see *rot*.] 1. Undergoing natural decomposition; affected by rot or organic dissolution; putrid (as animal and some vegetable matters), soft (as fruits, etc.), or weak (as vegetable fibers, fabrics, etc.) from elemental decay: as, a *rotten* carcass or egg; a *rotten* log or plank; *rotten* cloth.

The seed is rotten under their clods. Joel i. 17.

Breaking his oath and resolution like
A twist of rotten silk. *Shak.*, Cor., v. 6. 96.

2. Putrid from organic decay, or from the presence of decomposing matter; hence, of a putrid quality; ill-smelling; fetid.

You common cry of curs! whose breath I hate
As reek o' the rotten fens. *Shak.*, Cor., iii. 3. 121.

3. Affected with the disease called rot, as sheep or other animals.

Many of those that got safe on the Island, for want of being accustomed to such hardships, died like *rotten* Sheep. *Dampier*, Voyages, I. 50.

4. Unsound as if from rotting; in a loose or disintegrated state; soft or friable; yielding: as, *rotten* iron or stone.

They were left moiled with dirt and mire, by reason of the deepness of the *rotten* way. *Knolles*, Hist. Turks.

His principal care was to have many Bridges laid over Bogs and *rott'n* Moars. *Milton*, Hist. Eng., ii.

We were obliged to leave the river on account of *rotten* ice, and took to the open plains, where our deers sank to their bellies in the loose snow. B. Taylor, Northern Travel, p. 144.

5. Unsound in character or quality; in a corrupt or untrustworthy state; destitute of stability or integrity.

Never did base and *rotten* policy
Colour her working with such deadly wounds.
Shak., 1 Hen. IV., i. 3. 108.

Leauing these Antiquities [Babylonian legends], *rotten* with age, let vs come to take better view of this stately Cittie. *Purchas*, Pilgrimage, p. 55.

Our condition is not sound but *rotten*, both in religion and civil prudence. *Milton*, Free Commonwealth.

6. In *printing*, said of bad prints from woodcuts, that show holes and broken lines.—**Rotten borough.** See *borough*[1].

rotten[2] (rot'n), *n.* A dialectal variant of *ratten*.

rotten-egg (rot'n-eg'), *v. t.* [< *rotten egg*.] To pelt with rotten or putrid eggs; throw rotten eggs at: done as a manifestation of extreme anger or disgust.

Rev. ——— and Bishop ——— . . . were *rotten-egged* and "rocked," but San Antonio is bitterly ashamed of it. *Congregationalist*, Aug. 11, 1887.

rottenly (rot'n-li), *adv.* In a rotten manner; hence, fetidly; putridly; unsoundly; defectively.

rottenness (rot'n-nes), *n.* The state of being rotten, decayed, or putrid; unsoundness; corruptness.

A sound heart is the life of the flesh; but envy the *rottenness* of the bones. Prov. xiv. 30.

What's gained by falsehood? There they stand
Whose trade it is, whose life it is! How vain
To gild such *rottenness*! *Browning*, Strafford, iv. 1.

rottenstone (rot'n-stōn), *n.* An argillaceous or silicious limestone which by weathering has become soft and friable, the calcareous part having been wholly or in part removed. This material when pulverized forms a cheap and efficient substance for use in polishing the softer metals.

rottenstone (rot'n-stōn), *v. t.*; pret. and pp. *rottenstoned*, ppr. *rottenstoning*. [< *rottenstone*, *n.*] To polish with rottenstone.

rotting (rot'ing), *n.* [Verbal n. of *rot*, *v.*] Same as *retting*, 1.

Rottlera (rot'lėr-ä), *n.* [NL., named after Dr. *Rottler*, a Danish missionary.] A genus of plants, now placed under *Mallotus*.

rottolo (rot'ọ-lō), *n.* [< It. *rotolo*, a certain weight, also a round wheel, < L. *rotulus*, a little wheel, ML. a certain weight: see *rotula*, *roll*.] A weight used in parts of the Mediterranean.

rotton (rot'on), *n.* Same as *ratten*.

rotula (rot'ū-lä), *n.*; pl. *rotulæ* (-lē). [< L. *rotula*, a little wheel, dim. of *rota*, a wheel: see *rota*[1]. Cf. *roll*.] 1. In *anat.* and *zoöl.*: (*a*) Same as *patella*, 2. (*b*) One of the five radial pieces entering into the composition of the dentary apparatus of a sea-urchin, serving to connect the epiphyses of each of the five alveoli, and to furnish an articulation for each of the five radii or compasses. See *lantern of Aristotle* (under *lantern*), and cut under *Clypeastridæ*. (*c*) A small hard nodule embedded in soft parts of other echinoderms, as the calcareous rotulæ of some holothurians (*Chirodotæ*). (*d*) [*cap.*] [NL.] A genus of flat rotiform sea-urchins of the family *Mellitidæ*, having the test perforate and digitate.—2. In *music*, a little rota or round; especially, a carol or song for Christmas.

rotular (rot'ū-lär), *a.* [< L. *rotula*, a little wheel (see *rotula*), + *-ar*[3].] 1. Of or pertaining to a rotula; resembling a rotula; rotuliform; nodular; patellar: as, a *rotular* groove; the *rotular* bone of a limb.—2. Specifically, noting that aspect or surface of the hind limb on which the rotula is situated: as, the *rotular* aspect of the foot, the dorsum of the foot, as opposed to the sole or plantar surface: opposed to *popliteal*, and corresponding to *anconal* in the fore limb, and to *epaxial* in either limb, when the limb is in its morphological position, extended at right angles with the axis of the body.

rotulet (rot'ū-let), *n.* [< ML. *rotulus*, a roll, + *-et*.] A roll.

There is every probability that the handy-book or register called Doomesday followed the Court whenever important business was to be transacted, the original *rotulets* usually remaining in the Winchester treasury. *Athenæum*, No. 3083, p. 707.

rotuliform (rot'ū-li-fôrm), *a.* [< L. *rotula*, a little wheel, + *forma*, form.] Shaped like a rotula; patelliform.

rotund (rọ-tund'), *a.* [= F. *rond*, OF. *roond*, *roont* = Pr. *redon*, *redun* = Cat. *redó*, *rodó* = Sp. Pg. *rotundo*, *redondo* = It. *rotondo*, *ritondo*, round, < L. *rotundus*, like a wheel, round, circular, spherical, < *rota*, a wheel: see *rota*[1], and cf. *round*[1], an earlier form of the word.] 1. Round or roundish; spherical or globular; rounded out; convexly protuberant; bulbous: as, a *rotund* paunch or figure.

It was a little too exasperating to look at this pink-faced *rotund* specimen of prosperity, to witness the power for evil that lay in his vulgar cant. *George Eliot*, Felix Holt, xxx.

2. In *bot.* and *entom.*, circumscribed by one unbroken curve, or without angles: as, a *rotund* leaf or wing.

rotund† (rọ-tund'), *n.* [< F. *rotonde*, < It. *rotonda*, a rotunda: see *rotunda*.] A rotunda. [Rare.]

I must confess the eye is better filled at first entering the *rotund*, and takes in the whole beauty and magnificence of the temple [the Pantheon at Rome] at one view. *Addison*, Remarks on Italy (Works, ed. Bohn, I. 418).

rotunda (rọ-tun'dä), *n.* [Formerly also *rotundo* (also *rotund*, < F. *rotonde*); < It. *rotonda* = Sp. Pg. *rotunda*, < ML. **rotunda* (sc. *domus*), a round building, < L. *rotunda*, fem. of *rotundus*, round: see *rotund*, *round*[1].] 1. A round building, especially one with a dome; any building that is round both outside and inside. The most celebrated edifice of this kind is the Pantheon at Rome. See cuts under *octastyle* and *pantheon*.—2. A circular hall in a large building, generally surmounted by a dome: as, the *rotunda* of the Capitol in Washington.

rotundate (rọ-tun'dāt), *a.* [< L. *rotundatus*, rounded, pp. of *rotundare*, make round, < *rotundus*, round: see *rotund*, and cf. *round*[1], *v.*] Rounded off; specifically, in *bot.* and *zoöl.*, noting bodies which are rounded off at their ends; also, in *bot.*, same as *rotund*.

rotundifolious (rọ-tun-di-fō'li-us), *a.* [< L. *rotundifolius*, round-leafed, < *rotundus*, round, + *folium*, leaf.] Having round leaves.

rotundious† (rọ-tun'di-us), *a.* [Irreg. for **rotundous*, < L. *rotundus*, round: see *rotund*.] Rotund; rounded out. [Rare.]

So your rare wit, that 's ever at the full,
Lyes in the cave of your *rotundious* skull.
John Taylor, Works (1630). (*Nares.*)

rotundity (rọ-tun'di-ti), *n.* [< OF. (and F.) *rotondité* = Pr. *rotonditat* = Sp. *rotundidad* = Pg. *rotundidade* = It. *rotondità*, < L. *rotundita(t-)s*, roundness, < *rotundus*, rotund, round: see *round*[1], *rotund*.] 1. Roundness; sphericity; globular form.

And thou, all-shaking thunder,
Strike flat the thick *rotundity* o' the world!
Shak., Lear, iii. 2. 7.

The usual French scenery, with its fields cut up by hedges, and a considerable *rotundity* in its trees. *H. James, Jr.*, Little Tour, p. 97.

2†. Rounded fullness; integral entireness.

For the mere *rotundity* of the number and grace of the matter it passeth for a full thousand. *Fuller*.

=Syn. 1. See *roundness*.

rotundness (rọ-tund'nes), *n.* Same as *rotundity*.

rotundo† (rọ-tun'dō), *n.* Same as *rotunda*.

rotund-ovate (rọ-tund'ō″vāt), *a.* In *bot.*, roundly egg-shaped.

rotund-pointed (rọ-tund'poin″ted), *a.* In *entom.*, having the point rounded off or blunt; bluntly pointed.

roture (rọ-tür'), *n.* [F., < ML. *ruptura*, land broken up by the plow, cleared land capable of being used for sowing, etc., < LL. *ruptura*, a breaking: see *rupture*.] 1. In France, plebeian rank; the state of being a roturier.

Indeed he himself always signed the name Delabruyère in one word, thus avowing his *roture*. *Encyc. Brit.*, XIV. 177.

2. In *French-Canadian law*, a grant made of feudal property, part of a fief, subject to a ground-rent or annual charge, and with no privilege attached.

roturer†, *n.* Same as *roturier*.

roturier (rọ-tü-ri-ā'), *n.* [F., a plebeian, < ML. *rupturarius*, that cultivates a field, < *ruptura*, a field: see *roture*.] 1. In France, a person not of noble birth; a plebeian.

He required all persons, noble as well as *roturier*, to furnish so many soldiers in proportion to their revenues. *Brougham*.

2. In *French-Canadian law*, one who holds real property subject to an annual rent or charge.

Roubaix blue. See *blue*.

rouble, *n.* See *ruble*.

rouche, *n.* See *ruche*.

roucheage†, *n.* Same as *rokeage*.

rouched (roucht), *a.* [An assibilated form, with lengthened vowel, of *rucked*, < *ruck*[2] + *-ed*[2].] 1. Wrinkled. *Halliwell*. [Prov. Eng.]—2. Puckery; puckering the mouth, as sour beer. [Prov. Eng.]

Beer is said to be *rouched* when it acquires a tartness. *Halliwell*.

roucou (rö'kö), *n.* [F. *roucou*, *rocou* = Pg. *rucú*, < Braz. *urucú*, arnotto.] A dye: same as *arnotto*.

roué (rö-ā'), *n.* [< F. *roué*, an epithet applied by the Duke of Orleans, regent of France from 1715 to 1723, to his companions in dissipation, and usually explained as 'broken on a wheel,' implying that his companions deserved to be broken on the wheel; but it is prob. to be taken in the other fig. use, 'jaded,' 'worn out'; pp. of *rouer*, break on the wheel, run over, beat, bang (*roué*, *roué de fatigue*, jaded), < *roue*, a wheel, < L. *rota*, a wheel: see *rota*[1].] A man devoted to a life of pleasure and sensuality, especially in his relation to women; a debauchee; a rake.

rouelle-guard (rọ-el'gärd), *n.* [F., a little wheel, < ML. *rotella*, a little wheel: see *rotella*[1], *rowel*.] A guard having the shape of a disk, the plane of it at right angles with the grip. In some daggers of the fourteenth century both pommel and guard are of this form, the whole hilt resembling a spool or reel for thread. See *dague à roelle*, under *dague*.

rouen, *n.* See *rowen*.

Rouen cross. A jewel, worn either as a brooch or as a pendant, or sometimes in the form of a pendant hanging from a brooch, composed of a somewhat elaborate piece of fretwork in the general shape of a cross, usually of gold. These crosses are often set with small crystals cut like diamonds, or with diamonds of small value, the stones and the chief decoration being gathered up into four or five bosses marking the form of the cross.

Rouen duck. See *duck*[2].

Rouen pottery. See *pottery*.

rouerie (rö'ė-rē), *n.* [F., < *roué*, a profligate: see *roué*.] The character or conduct of a roué; rakishness; debauchery.

Certain young English gentlemen from the age of fifteen to twenty . . . ape all sorts of selfishness and *rouerie*.
Thackeray, Fitz-Boodle's Confessions.

rouet (rö-ā'), *n.* [< F. *rouet*, a little wheel, dim. of *roue*, a wheel: see *rota*[1].] Same as *rewet*.

rouge (rözh), *a.* and *n.* [< F. *rouge*, red, as a noun rouge, OF. *roge*, *rouge* = Pr. *rog*, fem. *roja* = Cat. *roig* = Sp. *rojo*, *rubio* = It. *roggio*, *robbio*, < ML. L. *rubius*, L. *rubeus*, red; akin to *ruber*, *rufus*, red: see *red*[1].] **I.** *a.* Red: as in the French *rouge croix*, *rouge et noir*, etc.—**Rouge Croix**, one of the pursuivants of the English heraldic establishment: so called from the red cross of St. George, the patron saint of England.—**Rouge Dragon**, in *her.*, one of the pursuivants of the Heralds' College of England. The name is taken from the red dragon, one of the supporters of the arms of Henry VII., and said to have been taken by him from the badge or device of some Welsh ancestor.

II. *n.* **1.** Any red cosmetic or coloring for the skin. There are many coloring matters used for this purpose. That obtained from the safflower, *Carthamus tinctorius*, is rather a stain than a paint, and is thought to be harmless to the skin. Rouge has been used at many epochs by women, and even by men. The custom was carried to a great extent in Europe in the eighteenth century, at which time, at least in court circles, there was little attempt at imitating the natural blush of the cheek, but the red was applied, as patches were, to produce a supposed decorative effect.

Doth riotous laughter now replace
Thy smile, and *rouge*, with stony glare,
Thy cheek's soft hue?
Matthew Arnold, Switzerland.

To see the *rouge* and the powder on the face of a young woman still playing her part was one thing; to mark the traces of them on the vulgarized and faded countenance of one whose day was over was quite another.
Mrs. Oliphant, Poor Gentleman, xl.

2. A scarlet, bright-crimson, or dark-red polishing-powder (peroxid of iron, sometimes intermingled with black oxid) made by a variety of processes, and varying in color according to the mode of production. Common rouge is made by calcining iron sulphate (copperas), its color being lighter or darker according to the prolongation of the heating. The darker product is called *crocus* and the lighter *rouge*. A general name for both rouge and crocus is *colcothar*. A fine scarlet rouge used by jewelers for polishing gold and silver is made from iron oxalate either by calcination or precipitation. Rouge obtained from the sulphate of iron is much used for polishing glass, metals, and other hard substances. A polishing-powder for plate is a mixture of prepared chalk and fine rouge.—**Jewelers' rouge.** See *jeweler* and *plate-powder*.

rouge (rözh), *v.*; pret. and pp. *rouged*, ppr. *rouging*. [< *rouge*, *n.*] **I.** *trans.* **1.** To color (the skin, especially the cheeks) with rouge.

There was not a lady at the bull-fight who was not highly *rouged* and powdered. *The Century*, XXVII. 5.

2. To cause to become red, as from blushing. [Rare.]

Madame d'Hénin, though *rouged* the whole time with confusion, never ventured to address a word to me.
Mme. D'Arblay, Diary and Letters, IV. 284.

II. *intrans.* **1.** To use rouge, especially on the cheeks.

Rouging and making-up [in a theater] are largely dependent upon the size of the house.
The Century, XXXV. 539.

2. To become red; redden; blush. [Rare.]

They all stared, and to be sure I *rouged* pretty high.
Mme. D'Arblay, Diary and Letters, I. 228.

rouge-berry (rözh'ber"i), *n.* A shrub, *Rivina lævis* (including *R. humilis*), of tropical America, often grown in hothouses. It bears racemes of bright-red berries whose juice affords an evanescent scarlet color, used in the West Indies as a cosmetic. Also *rouge-plant*.

rouge-dish (rözh'dish), *n.* A small saucer containing a thin layer of dry rouge for use as a cosmetic. Such saucers, as prepared in Portugal, usually contain genuine carmine.

rouge-et-noir (rözh-ā-nwor'), *n.* [F., red and black: *rouge*, red (see *rouge*); *et* (< L. *et*), and; *noir* (< L. *niger*), black (see *negro*).] A game at cards, played between a "banker" and an unlimited number of persons, at a table marked with four spots of a diamond shape, two colored black and two red. A player may stake his money upon *rouge* (red) or *noir* (black) by placing it on the outer ring of the table. Two rows of cards are placed upon the table, one for *noir*, the other for *rouge*: the spots on the cards in each row are counted, the face-cards being considered as ten-spots, and the players betting on that row the spots on which come nearest to 31 are winners. Also called *trente-et-quarante*.

rouge-plant (rözh'plant), *n.* Same as *rouge-berry*.

rouge-pot (rözh'pot), *n.* A small covered pot for rouge, intended to form part of a toilet-set.

rouge-powder (rözh'pou'dėr), *n.* See *rouge* and *plate-powder*.

Rouge's operation. An operation by which the upper lip and the lower part of the nose are cut away from the upper jaw, to aid in removing growths or necrosed bone from the nasal cavity.

rouget (rö-zhā'), *n.* [< F. *rouget*, < *rouge*, red: see *rouge*.] An acute infectious disease (septicemia) of swine: so called on account of more or less redness of skin accompanying it. It is caused by the multiplication, in the blood and various vital organs, of a specific bacillus, and is fatal in about one half of the cases. It is not known to prevail outside of France and Germany.

To investigate the disease known as swine fever, which is unfortunately prevalent in several counties at the present moment, with a view to ascertain the truth of the alleged identity of that disease and *rouget*.
Daily Chronicle, Aug. 12, 1886. (*Encyc. Dict.*)

rough[1] (ruf), *a.* and *n.* [< ME. *rough*, *rogh*, *roge*, *row*, *rou*, *rugh*, *ru*, *rug*, *ruh*, < AS. *rūh*, rarely *rūg* (in inflection *rūh-*, *rūg-*, *rūw-*, rarely *rūch-*), rough, hairy, shaggy, untrimmed, uncultivated, knotty, undressed, = OD. *ruch*, *ru*, MD. *ruych*, *ruygh*, D. *ruig*, *ruw* = MLG. *rūch*, *rūw*, *rū*, LG. *rug* = OHG. *rūh*, MHG. *rūch*, G. *rauh*, also *rauch* (in *rauch-werk*, peltries, furs, *rauch-handel*, trade in furs, etc.), rough, shaggy, = Dan. *ru*, rough; cf. Lith. *raukas*, a fold, wrinkle, *rukti*, wrinkle. Cf. *rug*[1], *rugged*.] **I.** *a.* **1.** Not smooth to the touch or to the sight; uneven, from projections, ridges, wrinkles, or the like; broken in outline or continuity by protruding points or lines, irregularities, or obstructions; shaggy: as, a *rough* surface of any kind; *rough* land; a *rough* road; *rough* cloth.

His browes reade and *rowe*, and his berde reade and longe, that henge down to his breste.
Merlin (E. E. T. S.), iii. 635.

These high wild hills and *rough* uneven ways
Draws out our miles, and makes them wearisome.
Shak., Rich. II., ii. 3. 4.

She sped
Through camp and cities *rough* with stone and steel.
Shelley, Adonais, xxiv.

At the end of the file Irene noticed a gentleman clad in a perfectly-fitting *rough* travelling suit.
C. D. Warner, Their Pilgrimage, p. 4.

2. Not smoothed or formed by art; existing or left in a natural or an incomplete state; crude; unwrought; uneven; untrimmed: as, the *rough* materials of manufacture.

She is very honest,
And will be hard to cut as a *rough* diamond.
Fletcher, Wife for a Month, iv. 2.

3. Rugged in form, outline, or appearance; harsh or unpleasing to the eye; irregular.

A ropy chain of rheums: a visage *rough*,
Deformed, unfeatured, and a skin of buff.
Dryden, tr. of Juvenal's Satires, x.

4. Crudely done or considered; indefinitely approximate; vague; partial; careless; hasty: as, to make a *rough* estimate or calculation; at a *rough* guess.

There is not a subscription goes forward in which Tom is not privy to the first *rough* draught of the proposals.
Addison, Tatler, No. 158.

A *rough* census was taken at the time of the Armada.
Froude, Sketches, p. 138.

At the same time, for carrying conviction in the first instance, it is only necessary to use large masses, and for this a *rough* count will answer.
Amer. Jour. Philol., IX. 146.

5. Characterized by harshness or asperity; disagreeably severe or coarse; discordant: used of things and actions with reference to their effects upon the senses or feelings, actions, sounds, etc.: as, *rough* weather; a *rough* remedy; *rough* treatment.

Your reproof is something too *rough* [in some editions, *round*]. *Shak.*, Hen. V., iv. 1. 216.

I am glad to find that the *rough* Clime of Russia agrees so well with you. *Howell*, Letters, I. vi. 33.

6. Lacking refinement; rude in character or action; unpolished; untrained; uncouth; awkward: as, *rough* kindness or attendance; a *rough* backwoodsman.

For I am *rough*, and woo not like a babe.
Shak., T. of the S., ii. 1. 138.

Brom, who had a degree of *rough* chivalry in his nature, would fain have carried matters to open warfare.
Irving, Sketch-Book, p. 433.

7. Characterized by violent or disorderly action or movement; rudely agitated or disturbed; boisterously violent; unrestrained: as, *rough* water; *rough* play.

The winds grew contrary, and seas too *rough* to be brooked by so small a vessel. *Sandys*, Travailes, p. 14.

When I was a Boy, the Prince of Salmona, riding a *rough* Horse at Naples, . . . held Reals under his Knees and Toes. *Montaigne*, Essays (tr. by Cotton, 1693), I. 501.

The town was *rough* with a riot between the press-gang and the whaling-folk. *Mrs. Gaskell*, Sylvia's Lovers, iv.

Nor is that wind less *rough* which blows a good man's barge. *M. Arnold*, Empedocles on Etna.

8. Coarse; stale: as, *rough* bread; *rough* fish. [Slang.]

The poorer classes live mostly on fish, and the "dropped" and *rough* fish is bought chiefly for the poor.
Mayhew, London Labour and London Poor, I. 53.

9. Astringent: said of wines or other beverages: as, a *rough* claret.

The *rougher* the drink [cider] the farther it will go, and the more acceptable it is to the working man.
Spons' Encyc. Manuf., I. 417.

10. In *bot.*, same as *scabrous*.—**11.** In *Gr. gram.*, accompanied by, constituting, or marking the stronger aspiration, equivalent to our *h*; aspirated (in a narrower sense): as, a *rough* mute; the *rough* breathing. The *rough breathing* (*spiritus asper*) is our *h*. The *rough mutes* are θ (*th*), φ (*ph*), and χ (*ch*), equivalent in earlier times to t + *h*, p + *h*, and *k* + *h*, but in later times to English *th* (in *thin*), *f*, and German *ch* (ch), respectively. *Rough* translates Greek δασύς, and is opposed to *smooth* (ψιλός).—**Perfectly rough**, in *theoretical dynam.*, so rough that a body will not slip over the surfaces so characterized.—**Rough-and-ready.** (*a*) Rough in character or manner, but prompt in action or ready for emergencies: as, a *rough-and-ready* workman.

He was not going to hang back when called upon—he had always been *rough and ready* when wanted—and then he was now ready as ever, and *rough* enough, too, God knows. *Trollope*, Dr. Thorne, xxii.

(*b*) Rough, harsh, or crude in kind, but ready or prompt in action or use.

He [Rousseau] could not have been the mere sentimentalist and rhetorician for which the *rough-and-ready* understanding would at first glance be inclined to condemn him. *Lowell*, Among My Books, 1st ser., p. 353.

Teutons or Celtic we were to be, and in this *rough-and-ready* fashion we were enlisted under one or other of the banners. *Contemporary Rev.*, LIII.

Rough-and-tumble, consisting of or characterized by rough and tumbling action; carried on with, requiring, or employing indiscriminate blows, falls, or struggles: used of a method of free fighting in which all means are allowable, and extended to other subjects involving similar conditions. [Colloq.]—**Rough arch, bindweed, cicely, coat, diamond.** See the nouns.—**Rough breathing.** See def. 11.—**Rough-cut margin.** See *margin*, 1.—**Rough-faced rustic work**, masonry in which the faces of the blocks are left rough, and the joints are chiseled, either plain or chamfered.—**Rough file, fish, log, parsnip, plate-glass.** See the nouns.—**Rough oak.** Same as *post-oak*.—**Rough-pointed stone**, in *stone-cutting*, stone from the face of which an inch or more has been removed by the pick, or by heavy points, leaving projections of from half an inch to an inch in height. Blocks of stone are thus treated as the first operation in dressing limestone and granite.—**Rough respiration, rice, setter**, etc. See the nouns.—**Short and rough.** See *short*. =**Syn.** 1. Rugged, jagged.—2. Unhewn, unwrought.—5. Hirsute, bristly.—6. Indelicate, ungracious, bluff, blunt, bearish, churlish, gruff, impolite, brusk.

II. *n.* **1.** Rough or roughened state or condition; crudeness; rawness; vehemence; exacerbation: with *the*: as, materials or work in *the rough*; *the rough* of a storm.

I knew a King that, being crossed in his Game, would amid his Oaths fall on the Ground, and bite the very Earth in *the Rough* of his Passion. *Howell*, Letters, I. v. 11.

Contemplating the people in *the rough*.
Mrs. Browning, Aurora Leigh, vi.

2. A projecting piece inserted in a horse's shoe, to keep him from slipping.

If this steel *rough* [a spike inserted in a square hole in each heel of a horseshoe] be made to fit the hole exactly, it remains firm in its place.
E. H. Knight, New Mech. Dict., p. 770.

3†. Rough weather.

In calms, you fish; in *roughs*, use songs and dances.
P. Fletcher, Piscatory Eclogues, vii. 32.

4. *pl.* In *mining*, a poor grade of tin ore, or that which has been only roughly dressed. Also *rows*. [Cornwall, Eng.]

rough[1] (ruf), *v.* [< ME. *ruhen*, *rouwen* = OHG. *gi-rūhan*, make rough; from the adj.: see *rough*[1], *a.*] **I.** *trans.* **1.** To make rough; give a rough condition or appearance to; roughen: as, to *rough* a horse's shoes to prevent slipping.

The *roughing* of bottle-neck interiors is done by iron tools fixed on a lathe and moistened with sand and water.
Harper's Mag., LXXIX. 261.

2. To execute or shape out roughly; finish partially or in the rough; prepare for a finishing operation: as, to *rough* out building-stones.

The bowlders . . . were thrown to the surface to be *roughed* out and trimmed. *Amer. Anthrop.*, III. 224.

In the grinding of a lens, the first operation consists in *roughing* it, or bringing it approximately to the curvature it is ultimately to assume.
E. L. Wilson, Quarter Century in Photography, p. 35.

Roughing-down rolls. Same as *roughing-rolls*.—**Roughing-in** or **roughing-up coat.** See *coat*[2].—**To rough a horse.** (*a*) To make a horse's shoes rough in order to keep him from slipping. See *rough*[1], *n.*, 2.

A simple mode of *roughing horses*, practised in Russia. *E. H. Knight*, New Mech. Dict., p. 770.

(*b*) To break in a horse, especially for military use.—**To rough in**, in *plastering*, to spread roughly upon brick, as the first of three coats.

When three coats are used, it [the laying on of the first coat of plaster] is called pricking up when upon laths, and *roughing in* when upon brick. *De Colange*, Dict. Commerce, I. 378.

To rough it, to live in a rough, haphazard manner; put up with coarse or casual food and accommodations; endure hardship or inconvenience.

Take care of Fanny, mother. She is tender, and not used to *rough it* like the rest of us. *Jane Austen*, Mansfield Park, xxxix.

Molly Corney was one of a large family of children, and had to *rough it* accordingly. *Mrs. Gaskell*, Sylvia's Lovers, ii.

II. *intrans.* To behave roughly; specifically, to break the rules in boxing by too much roughness.

That no wrestling, *roughing*, or hugging on the ropes [in boxing] be allowed. *Encyc. Brit.*, XXIV. 691.

rough[1] (ruf), *adv.* [< *rough*[1], *a.*] Roughly; in a coarse, crude, or harsh manner.

Abb. You should for that have reprehended him.
Adr. Why, so I did.
Abb. Ay, but not *rough* enough.
Shak., C. of E., v. 1. 58.

To cut up rough. See *cut*.

My jealous Pussy *cut up rough*
The day before I bought her muff
With Sable trimming. *F. Locker*, Mabel.

rough[2] (ruf), *n.* [Also formerly *ruff*; appar. an abbr. of *ruffian*, but now associated with *rough*[1] and accordingly conformed to it in spelling. It is not probable that the adj. *rough* alone would give rise to such substantive use.] A rowdy; a ruffian; a rude, coarse fellow; one given to riotous violence; a bully.

The great queen, moody, despairing, dying, wrapt in the profoundest thought, with eyes fixed upon the ground or already gazing into infinity, was besought by the counsellors around her to name the man to whom she chose that the crown should devolve. "Not to a *rough*," said Elizabeth, sententiously and grimly. *Motley*, United Netherlands, IV. 138.

[In a foot-note Scaramelli is quoted to the effect that the word signifies in English "persona bassa e vile."]

I entertain so strong an objection to the euphonious softening of ruffian into *rough*, which has lately become popular, that I restore the right word to the heading of this paper. *Dickens*, All the Year Round, Oct. 10, 1868. (*Latham.*)

A lady living in the suburbs of London had occasion to make complaint because a *rough* climbed on to her garden wall and broke off a branch from one of her fruit trees. *T. C. Crawford*, English Life, p. 188.

rough[3] (ruf), *v. t.* A bad spelling of *ruff*[4].

roughage (ruf'ąj), *n.* [< *rough*[1] + *-age*.] Rough or course material; something for rough use, as straw for bedding animals. [Local, U. S.]

Bedding or *roughage* is scarce, especially in the milk- and the fancy-butter-producing regions near our great cities. *Encyc. Amer.*, I. 98.

rough-backed (ruf'bakt), *a.* Having a rough back: as, the *rough-backed* cayman, *Alligator* or *Caiman trigonatus*, of South America.

rough-billed (ruf'bild), *a.* Having a rough horny excrescence on the beak: specific in the phrase *rough-billed pelican*, *Pelecanus trachyrhynchus* (or *erythrorhynchus*). This remarkable formation is deciduous, and is found only on adult birds during the breeding-season.

Rough-billed Pelican (*Pelecanus trachyrhynchus*).

rough-bore (ruf'bōr), *v. t.* In *metal-working*, to make, with a boring-tool, a heavy, coarse cut in, preparatory to a lighter and smooth finishing cut.

rough-cast (ruf'kȧst), *n.* A kind of plastering for an external wall, composed of an almost fluid mixture of clean gravel and lime, dashed on the wall, to which it adheres.

Let him have some plaster, or some loam, or some *rough-cast* about him, to signify wall. *Shak.*, M. N. D., iii. 1. 71.

Gorgon. 'Twas my invention.
Gasp. But I gave it polish, Gorgon.
Gorg. I confess you took off the *rough-cast*.
Shirley, Love Tricks, i. 1.

rough-cast (ruf'kȧst), *v. t.* 1. To form roughly or crudely; compose or shape in a rudimental manner; block out in the rough: as, to *rough-cast* a model; to *rough-cast* a story or an essay.

Nor bodily nor ghostly negro could
Roughcast thy figure in a sadder mould.
Cleaveland.

This *rough-cast*, unhewn poetry was instead of stage-plays, for the space of an hundred and twenty years together. *Dryden*, Essay on Satire.

2. To cover with a coarse semi-fluid plaster by casting or throwing it: as, to *rough-cast* a wall. See the noun.—**Rough-cast pottery.** See *pottery*.

rough-caster (ruf'kȧs'tėr), *n.* One who rough-casts.

rough-clad (ruf'klad), *a.* Having rough or coarse apparel. *Thomson.*

rough-cull (ruf'kul), *v. t.* To cull (oysters) hastily or for the first time, throwing out only dead shells and other large trash.

rough-dab (ruf'dab), *n.* A pleuronectid fish, *Hippoglossoides limandoides.*

rough-draft (ruf'drȧft), *v. t.* To draft or draw roughly; make a rough sketch of.

rough-draw (ruf'drâ), *v. t.* To draw or delineate coarsely; trace rudely.

His victories we scarce could keep in view,
Or polish 'em so fast as he *rough-drew*. *Dryden.*

rough-dry (ruf'drī), *v. t.* To dry by exposure to the air without rubbing, smoothing, ironing, etc.

The process of being washed in the night air, and *rough-dried* in a close closet, is as dangerous as it is peculiar. *Dickens*, Pickwick, xvii.

rough-dry (ruf'drī), *a.* Dry but not smoothed or ironed: as, *rough-dry* clothes.

roughen (ruf'n), *v.* [< *rough*[1] + *-en*. Cf. *rough*[1], *v.*] I. *trans.* To make rough; bring into a rough condition.

Such difference there is in tongues that the same figure which *roughens* one gives majesty to another; and that it was which Virgil studied in his verses. *Dryden*, Ded. of the Æneid.

Her complexion had been freckled and *roughened* by exposure to wind and weather. *The Century*, XXXVI. 513.

II. *intrans.* To grow or become rough.

The broken landscape, by degrees
Ascending, *roughens* into rigid hills.
Thomson, Spring, l. 958.

rougher (ruf'ėr), *n.* 1. One who roughens or roughs out; specifically, a workman who shapes or makes something roughly, preparatory to finishing operations.

When the glass [for a lens] is handed to the *rougher*, it is round in shape. *E. L. Wilson*, Quarter Century in Photography, p. 35.

2. A piece of woolen cloth as taken from the loom, previous to its preparation for fulling by the operation called *perching*.

Woollen cloth from the loom, called *roughers*, has an irregular, slack aspect, very different from the same web when it comes to be sold as, say, broad-cloth. *Encyc. Brit.*, XXIV. 661.

3. A percher.

rough-footed (ruf'fůt'ed), *a.* Having feathered feet, as a grouse, pigeon, or hawk; feather-footed; rough-legged.

rough-grained (ruf'grānd), *a.* Same as *coarse-grained*, as qualifying things or persons. [Rare.]

She became quite a favourite with her *rough-grained* hostess. *Cornhill Mag.*

rough-grind (ruf'grīnd), *v. t.* To grind roughly, or so as to leave the surface rough or unpolished, as with a coarse grindstone or with the aid of a rougheuing material.

The Duke of Wellington ordered his Scots Greys to *rough-grind* their swords, as at Waterloo. *W. Phillips*, Speeches, etc., p. 83.

Cast-iron is used by . . . opticians, with sand or emery, for *rough-grinding*. *O. Byrne*, Artisan's Handbook, p. 433.

rough-head (ruf'hed), *n.* 1. The iguanoid lizard of the Galapagos, *Trachycephalus subcristatus*.—2. Same as *red-dace*.—3. The common shiner, *Luxilus cornutus*. [Local, U. S.]

rough-hew (ruf'hū), *v. t.* [Early mod. E. *roughe-hewe*; < *rough*[1] + *hew*[1].] To hew coarsely without smoothing, as timber; hence, to give a rough or crude form to, as if by hewing.

There's a divinity that shapes our ends,
Rough-hew them how we will.
Shak., Hamlet, v. 2. 11.

A *rough-hewn* seaman, being brought before a wise just-ass for some misdemeanour, was by him sent away to prison. *Bacon*, Spurious Apophthegms, 6.

This *roughhewen*, ill-timber'd discourse. *Howell*, Vocall Forrest, Pref.

rough-hewer (ruf'hū'ėr), *n.* [< *rough-hew* + *-er*[1].] One who rough-hews.

rough-hound (ruf'hound), *n.* The rough hound-fish or dogfish, a kind of shark.

roughie (ruf'i), *n.* [Dim. of *rough*[1].] Brushwood; dried heath. [Scotch.]

Laying the *roughies* to keep the cauld wind frae you. *Scott*, Guy Mannering, liv.

roughing-drill (ruf'ing-dril), *n.* See *drill*[1].

roughing-hole (ruf'ing-hōl), *n.* In *metal.*, a hole into which iron from the blast-furnace is sometimes allowed to run.

roughing-mill (ruf'ing-mil), *n.* A circular plate or wheel, made of lead or iron, charged with emery wet with water, and usually revolved in a horizontal position, for roughing and grinding any gem except the diamond.

roughing-rolls (ruf'ing-rōlz), *n. pl.* In a rolling-mill, the first pair of rolls between which prepared blooms are passed, for working them into approximate shape. Also called *roughing-down rolls*.

roughings (ruf'ingz), *n. pl.* [< *rough*[1] (cf. *roughie*) + *-ing*[1].] See *rowen*. [Prov. Eng.]

roughleg (ruf'leg), *n.* A rough-legged hawk.

rough-legged (ruf'leg'ed or -legd), *a.* Having the tarsi feathered; feather-footed, as a hawk: specifically noting the members of the genus *Archibuteo*. The common rough-legged hawk or buzzard is *A. lagopus*. See cuts under *Archibuteo* and *squirrel-hawk*.

roughly (ruf'li), *adv.* 1. In a rough manner; with physical roughness or coarseness; without smoothness or finish; in an uneven or irregular manner as to surface or execution.

A portrait of a stern old man, in a Puritan garb, painted *roughly*, but with a bold effect and a remarkably strong expression of character. *Hawthorne*, Seven Gables, xiii.

2. With asperity of manner or effect; coarsely; harshly; gruffly; rudely; gratingly; austerely.

Joseph saw his brethren, and knew them, but . . . spake *roughly* unto them. Gen. xlii. 7.

3. Without precision or exactness; approximately; in a general way.

Six miles, speaking *roughly*, are 30,000 feet. *Huxley*, Amer. Addresses, p. 35.

rough-necked (ruf'nekt), *a.* Having the neck rough: as, the *rough-necked* jacare, *Jacare hirticollis*, of South America.

roughness (ruf'nes), *n.* [< ME. **roughnes*, *rownes*; < *rough*[1] + *-ness*.] 1. The state or property of being rough, in any sense of that word; physical, mental, or moral want of smoothness or equability; asperity, coarseness, harshness, rudeness, etc.

This is some fellow
Who, having been praised for bluntness, doth affect
A saucy *roughness*. *Shak.*, Lear, ii. 2. 103.

Divers plants contain a grateful sharpness, as lemons; or an austere and inconcocted *roughness*, as sloes. *Sir T. Browne.*

The *roughness* of a surface, as that of a piece of undressed stone, may be recognized to some extent by merely laying the outspread hand on the surface. *J. Sully*, Outlines of Psychol., p. 168.

2. Fodder for animals, consisting of dried corn-stalks cut into short pieces. [Southern and western U. S.]

She slipped off her horse, pulled the saddle from him, and threw it inside the door, then turned the animal loose. "Ef he gits ter thur *roughness*, I shan't blame him noan," she remarked. *On a North Carolina Mountain*, N. Y. Tribune, Oct. 28, 1888.

= **Syn.** See *rough*[1].

rough-perfect (ruf'pėr'fekt), *a.* Approximately perfect in the memorizing of a part: said of an actor when he can begin rehearsing from memory. [Theatrical slang.]

rough-rider (ruf'rī'dėr), *n.* 1. One who breaks young or wild horses to the saddle; in the army, a non-commissioned cavalry or artillery officer detailed to assist the riding-master, one being allowed to each troop or battery.—2. Loosely, a horseman occupied with hard, rough work.

The *rough-rider* of the plains, the hero of rope and revolver, is first cousin to the backwoodsman of the southern Alleghanies. *T. Roosevelt*, The Century, XXXV. 505.

rough-scuff (ruf'skuf), *n.* A rough, coarse fellow; a rough; collectively, the lowest class of the people; the riffraff; the rabble. [Colloq., U. S.]

rough-setter (ruf'set'ėr), *n.* A mason who builds rough walls, as distinguished from one who hews also.

roughshod (ruf'shod), *a.* Shod with shoes armed with points or calks: as, a horse is said to be *roughshod* when his shoes are roughed or sharpened for slippery roads.—**To ride roughshod.** See *ride*.

rough-slant (ruf'slȧnt), *n.* A lean-to; a shelter made of canvas, blankets, bark, or boards laid on poles supported on crotches, and sloping from a ridge-pole to the ground. *Sportsman's Gazetteer.*

rough-spun (ruf'spun), *a.* Rude; unpolished; blunt. *Halliwell.*

rough-string (ruf'string), *n.* In *carp.*, one of the generally unplaned inclined supports for the steps of a wooden stairway, usually concealed from view.

rough-stuff (ruf'stuf), *n.* In *painting*, coarse paint applied next after the priming, to be covered by the final coat or coats.

Paint has less tendency to crack where *rough-stuff* is left off. *Workshop Receipts*, 2d ser., p. 439.

rought†. An obsolete preterit of *reck*.

roughtail (ruf'tāl), *n.* Any snake of the family *Uropeltidæ*; a shieldtail.

rough-tailed (ruf'tāld), *a.* Having a rough tail, as a snake: specifically said of the *Uropeltidæ*.

rough-tree (ruf'trē), *n.* *Naut.*: (*a*) A rough unfinished mast or spar. (*b*) The part of a mast above the deck.—**Rough-tree rails**, a timber forming the top of the bulwark.

roughwing (ruf'wing), *n.* 1. A British moth, *Phtheochroa rugosana*.—2. A rough-winged swallow.

rough-winged (ruf'wingd), *a.* Having the outer web of the first primary retrorsely serrulate, as a swallow of the subfamily *Psalidoprocninæ*. The common rough-winged swallow of the United States is *Stelgidopteryx serripennis*. It closely resembles the bank-swallow.

Rough-winged. Magnified outer web of part of first primary of *Stelgidopteryx serripennis*.

rough-work (ruf'wėrk), *v. t.* To work over coarsely, without regard to nicety, smoothness, or finish.

Thus you must continue till you have *rough-wrought* all your work from end to end. *J. Moxon*, Mechanical Exercises.

rouket†, *v.* A Middle English form of *ruck*[1].

roulade (rö-läd'), *n.* [< F. *roulade*, < *rouler*, roll, trill: see *roll*.] In *vocal music*, a melodic embellishment consisting in a rapid succession of tones sung to a single syllable; a run.

roulet†, *v.* An obsolete form of *roll*.

rouleau (rö-lō'), *n.*; pl. *rouleaux* (rö-lōz', F. rö-lō'). [< F. *rouleau*, a roll, a roll of paper, dim. of OF. *roule*, a roll: see *roll*.] 1. A roll. Specifically—(*a*) A roll of paper containing a specified number of coins of the same denomination.

In bright confusion open *rouleaux* lie.
Pope, The Basket-Table, l. 81.

Wer. (showing a *rouleau*). Here's gold—gold, Josephine,
Will rescue us from this detested dungeon.
Byron, Werner, i. 1.

(*b*) In *millinery*, a large piping or rounded fluting: generally used in the plural: as, a trimming of *rouleaux*.
2. *Milit.*, one of a collection of round bundles of fascines tied together, which serve to cover besiegers or to mask the head of a work.—**Rouleau of blood-corpuscles**, the peculiar arrangement that the red blood-corpuscles tend to assume when drawn from the system, forming cylindrical columns, like rolls or piles of coins.

roulet†, *n.* An obsolete form of *roulette*.

roulette (rö-let'), *n.* [< F. *roulette*, a little wheel, a caster, etc., also a game so called, fem. dim. of OF. *roule*, a wheel, a roll, etc.: see *roll*.] 1. An engravers' tool, used for producing a series of dots on a copperplate, and in mezzotint to darken any part which has been too much burnished. Roulettes are of two kinds: one is shaped like the rowel of a spur; the other has the rowel at right angles with the shaft, thick in the middle and diminishing toward the sides, which are notched and sharpened to a series of fine points. A similar instrument is used in mechanical drawing, and in plotting. It is dipped into India ink, so that the points imprint a dotted line as the wheel is passed over the paper.
2. A cylindrical object used to curl hair upon, whether of the head or of a wig.—3. In *geom.*, a curve traced by any point in the plane of a

Roulette.

given curve when this plane rolls on this curve over another curve.—4. A game of chance, played at a table, in the center of which is a cavity surmounted by a revolving disk, the circumference of which is generally divided into 38 compartments colored black and red alternately, and numbered 1 to 36, with a zero and double zero. The person in charge of the table (the banker or tailleur) sets the disk in motion, and causes a ball to revolve on it in an opposite direction. This ball finally drops into one of the compartments, thus determining the winning number or color. The players, of whom there may be any number, may stake on a figure or a group of figures, on even or odd number, or on the black or red. Should the player stake on a single figure and be successful, he wins 35 times his stake. The amount varies in the event of success on other chances.

roulroul, *n.* [Native name. See *Rollulus*.] A bird of the genus *Rollulus*.

rouly-pouly†, *n.* An obsolete form of *roly-poly*.

roum[1]**†**, *a.* and *n.* An obsolete form of *room*[1].

roum[2], *n.* Same as *room*[2].

Roumanian, *a.* and *n.* See *Rumanian*.

Roumansh, *a.* and *n.* Same as *Romansh*.

Roumelian, *a.* and *n.* Same as *Rumelian*.

rount†, *v.* See *round*[2].

rount†, *n.* See *round*[2].

Herkne to my *roun*.
Morris and Skeat, Spec. of Early English, II. iv. (A) 44.

Lenten ys come with love to toune,
With blosmen ant with briddes *roune* [birds' song].
Ritson, Ancient Songs (ed. 1829), I. 63. (*Halliwell*.)

rounce (rouns), *n.* [Origin uncertain.] 1. In *printing*, a wheel-pulley in a hand-press, which winds and unwinds girths that draw the type-form on the bed to and from impression under the platen. See cut under *printing-press*.—2. A game of cards, played with a full pack by not more than nine persons. Each player starts with fifteen points, and for every trick he takes subtracts one from the score; the player who first reaches zero wins.

rounce-handle (rouns'han"dl), *n.* In *printing*, the crank attached to the rounce, by which it is turned. See *printing-press*.

rounceval†, rouncival† (roun'se-val, -si-val), *n.* and *a.* [Also *ronceval*, *runcival*; so called in allusion to the gigantic bones, believed to be those of Charlemagne's heroes, said to have been dug up at *Roncesvalles* (F. *Roncevaux*), a town at the foot of the Pyrenees, where, according to the old romances, the army of Charlemagne was routed by the Saracens.] I. *n.* 1. A giant; hence, anything very large and strong.

Hereof I take it comes that seeing a great woman we say she is a *Rouncevall*. *Fol.* 22. b. (ed. 1600). (*Nares*.)

2. The marrowfat pea: so called from its large size.

And set, as a dainty, thy *runcival* pease.
Tusser, January's Husbandry, st. 8.

Another [serving-man], stumbling at the Threshold, tumbled in his Dish of *Rouncevals* before him.
Brome, Jovial Crew, v.

From Cicero, that wrote in prose,
So call'd from *rounceval* on 's nose.
Musarum Deliciæ (1656). (*Nares*.)

In Staffordshire, garden-*rouncivals* sown in the fields kernel well. *Mortimer*, Husbandry.

II. *a.* Large; strong; robustious.

Dost roare, bulchin? dost roare? th' ast a good *rouncivall* voice to cry Lanthorne & Candle-light.
Dekker, Humorous Poet (Works, ed. Pearson, I. 243).

rouncey†, rouncie†, *n.* See *rouncy*.

rouncle†, *v. t.* An obsolete form of *runkle*.

rouncy† (roun'si), *n.* [Also *rouncey*, *rouncie*; < ME. *rouncy*, *rounsie*, *rounce*, *rounse*, *rouncin*, < OF. *roncin*, *runcin*, *ronci*, F. *roussin* = Pr. *rossi*, *roci*, *roncin* = Cat. *roci* = Sp. *rocin* = Pg. *rocim* = It. *ronciono*, *ronzino*, a nag, hack (whence Sp. *rocinante* = OF. *rossinante*, a miserable hack, the name of Don Quixote's horse), < ML. *runcinus*; origin uncertain; perhaps < G. *ross*, a horse (> F. *rosse*, a poor horse, sorry jade), = E. *horse*[1]: see *horse*[1]. The W. *rhwnsi*, a rough-coated horse, is perhaps < E.] 1. A common hackney-horse; a nag.

He rood upon a *rouncy* as he couthe.
Chaucer, Gen. Prol. to C. T., l. 390.

The war horse is termed dextrarius, as led by the squire with his right hand; the runcinus, or *rouncey*, was the horse of an attendant or servant.
S. Dowell, Taxes in England, I. 74, note.

2. A vulgar, coarse woman. *Halliwell.*

round[1] (round), *a.* and *n.* [Early mod. E. also *rownd*; < ME. *round*, *rownd*, *ronde* = D. *rond* = MHG. *runt*, G. *rund* = Dan. Sw. *rund*, < OF. *rond*, *roont*, *roond*, F. *rond* = Pr. *redon*, *redun* = Cat. *redó*, *rodó* = Sp. Pg. *rotundo*, *redondo* = It. *rotondo*, *ritondo*, < L. *rotundus*, like a wheel, round, circular, spherical, < *rota*, a wheel: see *rota*[1], and cf. *rotund*. Hence ult. *roundel*, *roundelay*, *rondeau*, *rundlet*, etc.] I. *a.* 1. Circular, or roughly so; plane, without angles, and having no axis much longer than any other.

Round was his face, and camuse was his nose.
Chaucer, Miller's Tale, l. 14.

This yle of Mylo is an c. myle northe from Candy; it was called Melos, and is *roundest* of all yles.
Sir R. Guylforde, Pylgrymage, p. 62.

For meals, a *round* tray is brought in, and placed upon a low stool. *E. W. Lane*, Modern Egyptians, I. 20.

2. Having circular sections: as, *round* columns; *round* chambers. See *round bodies*, below.—3. Spherical; globular; compressed about a center; collected into a shape more or less exactly spherical.

Upon the firm opacous globe
Of this *round* world. *Milton*, P. L., iii. 419.

4. Without corners or edges; convex, not elongated, and unwrinkled; bounded by lines or surfaces of tolerably uniform curvature.

And yet it irks me, the poor dappled fools [deer] . . .
Should . . . have their *round* haunches gored.
Shak., As you Like it, ii. 1. 25.

In person he was not very tall, but exceedingly *round*; neither did his bulk proceed from his being fat, but windy; being blown up by a prodigious conviction of his own importance. *Irving*, Knickerbocker, p. 312.

He [the King of Saxony] is of medium height, with sloping, *round* shoulders. *T. C. Crawford*, English Life, p. 87.

5. Proceeding with an easy, smooth, brisk motion, like that of a wheel: as, a *round* trot.

A *round* and flowing utterance. *Baret*, Alvearie, 1580.

Round was their pace at first, but slacken'd soon.
Tennyson, Geraint.

6. Well-filled; full; liberal or large in amount or volume: as, "good *round* sum," *Shak.*, M. of V., i. 3. 104.

I lay ye all
By the heels and suddenly, and on your heads
Clap *round* fines for neglect.
Shak., Hen. VIII., v. 4. 84.

7. Not descending to unworthy and vexatious stickling over small details.

Clear and *round* dealing is the honour of man's nature.
Bacon, Truth (ed. 1887).

8. Not prevaricating; candid; open.

I will a *round* unvarnish'd tale deliver.
Shak., Othello, i. 3. 90.

9. Without much delicacy or reserve; plain-spoken: as, a *round* oath.

What shall be done? He will not hear, till feel:
I must be *round* with him. *Shak.*, T. of A., ii. 2. 8.

The kings interposed in a *round* and princely manner; not only by way of request and persuasion, but also by way of protestation and menace. *Bacon.* (*Johnson.*)

10†. Severe; harsh.

Your reproof is something too *round*.
Shak., Hen. V., iv. 1.

The deputy began to be in passion, and told the governour that, if he were so *round*, he would be *round* too.
Winthrop, Hist. New England, I. 99.

11. Periodic; beginning and ending at the same position or state of things, and that without reversal of the direction of advance: as, a *round* journey.

The *round* year
Will bring all fruits and virtues here.
Emerson, Conduct of Life.

12. Filled out roundly or symmetrically; made complete in sense, symmetrical in form, and well-balanced in cadence; well-turned: said of a sentence or of literary style.

His style, though *round* and comprehensive, was incumbered sometimes by parentheses, and became difficult to vulgar understandings. *Bp. Fell*, Life of Hammond.

If sentiment were sacrific'd to sound,
And truth cut short to make a period *round*,
I judged a man of sense could scarce do worse
Than caper in the morris-dance of verse.
Cowper, Table-Talk, l. 517.

13. Written, as a number, with one or more "round figures," or ciphers, at the end. See *round number*, below.—14. In *anat.* and *zoöl.*: (*a*) Circular; annular. (*b*) Cylindric; terete. (*c*) Rotund; globose or globular; spherical.—15. In *arch.*, round-arched or -vaulted; characterized by the presence of round arches or a barrel-vault.

The distinctly Gothic type of capital, which finds one of its earliest illustrations in the *round* portion of the choir of the Cathedral of Senlis.
C. H. Moore, Gothic Architecture, p. 201.

In round numbers, considered in the aggregate; with disregard of the smaller elements of a number or numbers, or of minute calculation: as, *in round numbers* a population of 90,000.

She [the United States] has risen, during one simple century of freedom, *in round numbers* from two millions to forty-five. *Gladstone*, Might of Right, p. 175.

The earth in its motion round the sun moves in *round numbers* 20 miles in a second. *Stokes*, Light, p. 228.

Round arch, belting, cardamom. See the nouns.—**Round bodies**, in *geom.*, the sphere, right cone, and right cylinder.—**Round clam**, one of many different edible clams of rounded or subcircular figure, as of the families *Veneridæ* and *Mactridæ*: distinguished from *long clam*, as *Myidæ*, *Solenidæ*, etc.; especially, the quahog, *Venus mercenaria* of the eastern United States, and *Cuneus staminea* of the Pacific coast. See *quahog*, *little-neck*.—**Round corn.** See corn[1], 2.—**Round dance**, a dance in which the dancers are arranged in a circle or ring, or one in which they move in circular or revolving figures, as in a waltz, polka, etc.: opposed to *square dance*.—**Round dock.** See *dock*[1], 2.—**Round-edge file, round file.** See *file*[1].—**Round fish, game.** See the nouns.—**Round herring**, a clupeoid fish of the genus *Etrumeus.* The species so called in the United States is *E. teres,* of the Atlantic coast, of a terete or fusiform figure, olivaceous above and silvery on the sides and belly, with small mouth and fins and large eyes.—**Round jack.** See *jack*[1].—**Round jacket.** Same as *roundabout*, 5.

When he wore a *round jacket*, and showed a marvelous nicety of aim in playing at marbles.
George Eliot, Middlemarch, Finale.

Round-joint file. See *file*[1].—**Round knife, ligament, mackerel, meal.** See the nouns.—**Round number,** a number evenly divisible by tens, hundreds, etc., or a number forming an aliquot part of one so divisible, as 10, 25, 75, 100, 750, 1,000, etc.: used especially with reference to approximate or indefinite statement.

Nor is it unreasonable to make some doubt whether, in the first ages and long lives of our fathers, Moses doth not sometime account by full and *round numbers* . . . as in the age of Noah it is delivered to be just five hundred when he begat Sem; whereas perhaps he might be somewhat above or below that *round* and complete *number*.
Sir T. Browne, Vulg. Err., vi. 1.

This, still pursuing the *round-number* system, would supply nearly five articles of refuse apparel to every man, woman, and child in this, the greatest metropolis of the world.
Mayhew, London Labour and London Poor, II. 626.

Round O. (*a*) See *O*[1]. (*b*) A corruption of the word *rondo*, common in English music-books of the early part of the eighteenth century.—**Round ore.** Same as *leap-ore*.—**Round plane.** See *plane*[2].—**Round pound.** See *pound*[2].—**Round pronator,** the pronator radii teres (which see, under *pronator*).—**Round robin.** See *round-robin*, 5.—**Round shore-herring.** See *herring*.—**Round shot, seam, table, tower,** etc. See the nouns.—**Round tool.** (*a*) In *wood-working*, a chisel with a round nose, used for making concave moldings. (*b*) In *seal-engraving*, a tool with a round bead-like end, used for purposes very similar to those of the bead-tool.—**Round turn,** the passing of one end of a rope, attached by the other end to some moving object, completely around a post or timber-head, so as to give a strong hold. This is commonly done to check the movement of a vessel coming into her berth, or the like: hence the saying *to bring a person up with a round turn*, to stop him suddenly in doing or saying something: administer an effectual check to him.—**Round zedoary.** See *zedoary*.=**Syn.** See *roundness*.

II. *n.* **1.** That which has roundness; a round (spherical, circular, cylindrical, or conical) object or group of objects; a round part or piece of something: as, a *round* of beef.

We'll dress [some children]
Like urchins, ouphes, and fairies, green and white,
With *rounds* of waxen tapers on their heads.
Shak., M. W. of W., iv. 4. 50.

Over their sashes the men wear *rounds* of stiffened russet, to defend their brains from the piercing fervor.
Sandys, Travailes, p. 85.

As this pale taper's earthly spark,
To yonder argent *round* [the moon].
Tennyson, St. Agnes' Eve.

The arches of the *round* [circular stage] rest on heavy rectangular piers of truly Roman strength.
E. A. Freeman, Venice, p. 133.

Specifically—(*a*) A rung of a ladder or a chair, or any similar round or spindle-shaped piece joining side- or corner-pieces by its ends.

That lowliness is young ambition's ladder; . . .
But, when he once attains the utmost *round*,
He then unto the ladder turns his back.
Shak., J. C., ii. 1. 24.

Where all the *rounds* like Jacob's ladder rise.
Dryden, Hind and Panther, ii. 220.

(*b*) In *arch.*, a molding the section of which is a segment of a circle or of a curved figure differing but little from a circle.

2. In *art*, form rounded or curved and standing free in nature or representation; specifically, the presentation in sculpture of complete

Figure in the Round.
The Sleeping Ariadne, in the Vatican Museum.

roundness, represented with its projection on all sides, as in nature, free from any ground, as distinguished from *relief*: used with the definite article, especially with reference to sculptures of human and animal figures.

The progress of sculpture in *the round* from the Branchidæ statues to the perfect art of Pheidias may be traced through a series of transition specimens.
C. T. Newton, Art and Archæol., p. 81.

To the training in this school, and the habit of drawing from *the round*, . . . we may be indebted for the careful drawing and modeling of the details of his pictures which distinguish Mantegna from all his contemporaries.
The Century, XXXIX. 390.

3. A circle; a ring or coil; a gathering in a circle or company, as of persons. [Rare.]

Him [the serpent] fast sleeping soon he found
In labyrinth of many a *round* self-roll'd.
Milton, P. L., ix. 183.

Sometimes I am seen thrusting my head into a *round* of politicians at Will's.
Addison, Spectator, No. 1.

4. A circuit of action or progression; a going about from point to point or from one to another in a more or less definite series; a range or course through a circle of places, persons, things, or doings: as, a *round* of travel or of visits; a *round* of duties or pleasures; the story went the *rounds* of the papers.

Come, ladies, shall we take a *round*? as men
Do walk a mile, women should talk an hour
After supper; 'tis their exercise.
Beau. and Fl., Philaster, ii. 4.

He walks the *round* up and down, through every room o' the house.
B. Jonson, Epicœne, iv. 2.

Thro' each returning Year, may that Hour be
Distinguish'd in the *Rounds* of all Eternity.
Congreve, To Cynthia.

The trivial *round*, the common task,
Would furnish all we ought to ask;
Room to deny ourselves; a road
To bring us daily nearer God.
Keble, Christian Year, Morning.

5. A fixed or prescribed circuit of going or doing, supposed to be repeated at regular intervals; a course or tour of duty: as, a policeman's or a sentinel's *round*; the *rounds* of postmen, milkmen, newsmen, etc.; a *round* of inspection by a military officer or guard.

We must keep a *round*, and a strong watch to-night.
Fletcher, Humorous Lieutenant, iii. 5.

They accompany the military guards in their nightly *rounds* through the streets of the metropolis.
E. W. Lane, Modern Egyptians, I. 143.

The wise old Doctor went his *round*.
Whittier, Snow-Bound.

6. A complete or continuous circuit or course; revolution or range from beginning to end, or without limit; sweep; scope; sphere: as, the *rounds* of the planets; the whole *round* of science.

They hold that the Blood, which hath a Circulation, and fetcheth a *Round* every 24 Hours about the Body, is quickly repaired again.
Howell, Letters, I. ii. 21.

In the Glorious *Round* of Fame,
Great Marlbro, still the same,
Incessant runs his Course.
Congreve, Pindaric Odes, i.

Thy pinions, universal Air, . . .
Are delegates of harmony, and bear
Strains that support the Seasons in their *round*.
Wordsworth, Power of Sound, xii.

He seems, indeed, to have run the whole *round* of knowledge.
Sumner, Hon. John Pickering.

So runs the *round* of life from hour to hour.
Tennyson, Circumstance.

7. A bout or turn of joint or reciprocal action; a course of procedure by two or more, either complete in itself, or one of a series with intermissions or renewals: as, *rounds* of applause; a *round* at cards; a *round* of golf (a course of play round the whole extent of the golfing-ground).

Women to cards may be compar'd; we play
A *round* or two, when us'd, we throw away.
Granville, Epigrams and Characters.

The simultaneous start with which they increased their distance by at least a fathom, on hearing the door-bell jingling all over the house, would have ensured a *round* of applause from any audience in Europe.
Whyte Melville, White Rose, I. iii.

Specifically—(*a*) In *pugilism*, one of the series of bouts constituting a prize-fight or a sparring-match. A round may last for a certain specified length of time, as three minutes, or until one of the combatants is down.

He stood up to the Banbury man for three minutes, and polished him off in four *rounds*.
Thackeray, Vanity Fair, xxxiv.

The second *round* in this diplomatic encounter closed with the British government fairly discomfited.
H. Adams, Albert Gallatin, p. 540.

(*b*) A bout of shooting, as at a target, in saluting, or in battle, either with firearms or with bows, in which a certain number of shots are delivered, or in which the participants shoot or fire by turns.

The first time I reviewed my regiment they . . . would salute with some *rounds* fired before my door.
B. Franklin, Autobiog., p. 239.

The "National *Round*," shot by the ladies of Great Britain at all public meetings, consists of 48 arrows at 60 yards, and 24 arrows at 50 yards.
M. and W. Thompson, Archery, p. 12.

(*c*) A bout of toast-drinking; the drinking of a toast or of a set of toasts by the persons round a table; also, a toast to be drunk by the company.

Them that drank the *round*, when they crowned their heads with folly and forgetfulness, and their cups with wine and noises.
Jer. Taylor, Works (ed. 1835), I. 615.

The Tories are forced to borrow their toasts from their antagonists, and can scarce find beauties enough of their own side to supply a single *round* of October.
Addison, Freeholder, No. 8.

(*d*) A bout of drinking participated in by a number of persons; a treat all round: as, to pay for the *round*. (*e*) In *vocal music*, a short rhythmical canon at the unison, in which the several voices enter at equal intervals of time: distinguished from a *catch* simply in not being necessarily humorous. Rounds have always been very popular in England. The earliest specimen is the famous "Sumer is i-cumen in," which dates from the early part of the thirteenth century, and is the oldest example of counterpoint extant. Also called *rondo*, *rota*.

Some jolly shepherd sung a lusty *round*.
Fairfax, tr. of Tasso's Godfrey of Boulogne, vii. 6.

A *Round*, a *Round*, a *Round*, Boyes, a *Round*,
Let Mirth fly aloft, and Sorrow be drown'd.
Brome, Jovial Crew, iv. 1.

In the convivial *Round*, in which each voice chases, so to speak, the different movements in the same order.
J. Sully, Sensation and Intuition, p. 213.

(*f*) Same as *round dance* (which see, under I.).

A troupe of Faunes and Satyres far away
Within the wood were dauncing in a *rownd*.
Spenser, F. Q., I. vi. 7.

Tread we softly in a *round*,
Whilst the hollow murmuring ground
Fills the music with her sound.
Fletcher, Faithful Shepherdess, i. 2.

8. Same as *roundel*.—**9.** Ammunition for a single shot or volley: as, to supply a marksman or a company with forty *rounds*.—**10.** In the *manège*, a volt, or circular tread.—**11.** A brewers' vessel for holding beer while undergoing the final fermentation.

It was at one time the practice amongst the Scotch brewers to employ the fermenting *rounds* only, and to cleanse from these directly into the casks.
Spons' Encyc. Manuf., I. 406.

Cog and round. See *cog*[2].—**Gentleman of the round.** See *gentleman*.—**Hollows and rounds.** See *hollow*[1].—**In the round,** in *art*. See def. 2, above.—**Round of beef,** a cut of the thigh through and across the bone.

Instead of boiling or stewing a piece of the *round of beef*, for example, the Mount Desert cooks broil or fry it.
The Century, XL. 562.

To cut the round. See *volt*.

round[1] (round), *adv.*[1] [< ME. *round*; < *round*[1], *a.*] Roundly; vigorously; loudly.

I peyne me to han an hauteyn speche,
And ringe it oute as *round* as goth a belle.
Chaucer, Prol. to Pardoner's Tale, l. 45.

round[1] (round), *adv.*[2] and *prep.* [Prop. an aphetic form of *around*: see *around*.] **I.** *adv.* **1.** On all sides; so as to surround or make the circuit of. See *round about*, below.

Thine enemies shall cast a trench about thee, and compass thee *round*, and keep thee in on every side.
Luke xix. 43.

When he alighted, he surveyed me *round* with great admiration.
Swift, Gulliver's Travels, i. 2.

2. With a revolving or rotating movement or course; in a circular or curvilinear direction; around: as, to go *round* in a circle; to turn *round* and go the other way.

He that is giddy thinks the world turns *round*.
Shak., T. of the S., v. 2. 20.

3. In or within a circuit; round about.

The longest way *round* is the shortest way home.
Popular saying.

Round and around the sounds were cast,
Till echo seemed an answering blast.
Scott, L. of the L., i. 10.

A brutal cold country this. . . . Never . . . a stick thicker than your finger for seven mile *round*.
H. Kingsley, Geoffry Hamlyn, v.

4. To or at this place or time through a circuit or circuitous course.

Time is come *round*,
And where I did begin, there shall I end.
Shak., J. C., v. 3. 23.

Tally-ho coach for Leicester 'll be *round* in half-an-hour, and don't wait for nobody.
T. Hughes, Tom Brown at Rugby, i. 4.

Once more the slow, dumb years
Bring their avenging cycle *round*.
Whittier, Mithridates at Chios.

5. In circumference: as, a tree or a pillar 40 inches *round*.—**6.** In a circling or circulating course; through a circle, as of persons or things: as, there was not food enough to go *round*; to pass *round* among the company.

The invitations were sent *round*. *Scott.*

7. In a complete round or series; from beginning to end.

She named the ancient heroes *round*. *Swift.*

The San Franciscans now eat the best of grapes, cherries, and pears almost the year *round*.
Dublin Univ. Mag., Feb., 1872, p. 224.

All round. (*a*) Over the whole place: in every direction. (*b*) In all respects; for all purposes: also used adjectively: as, a clever *all-round* writer or actor; a good horse for *all-round* work.

One of the quietest, but, *all round*, one of the brainiest merchants and financiers in the United States.
Harper's Mag., LXXVII. 241.

Luff round. See *luff*2.—**Round about.** (*a*) [*About*, adv.] (1) In an opposite direction; with reversed position; so as to face the other way.

She 's turned her richt and *round about*,
And the kembe fell frae her han'.
Lady Maisry (Child's Ballads, II. 82).

(2) All around; in every direction.

When he giveth you rest from all your enemies *round about*, so that ye dwell in safety. Deut. xii. 10.

Round about are like Tombes for his wiues and children, but not so great and faire. *Purchas*, Pilgrimage, p. 288.

On the other side . . . stood a great square Tower, and *round about* the rubbish of many other Buildings.
Maundrell, Aleppo to Jerusalem, p. 17.

(*b*) [*About*, prep.] On every side of; all round.

And he made darkness pavilions *round about* him, dark waters, and thick clouds of the skies. 2 Sam. xxii. 12.

The skins hanging *round about* his head, backe, and shoulders.
Quoted in *Capt. John Smith's* True Travels, I. 161.

And hears the Muses in a ring
Aye *round about* Jove's altar sing.
Milton, Il Penseroso, l. 48.

To bring round. See *bring*.

"What 's the matter, Mother?" said I, when we had *brought* her a little *round*. *Dickens*, Little Dorrit, i. 2.

To come round. See *come*.

He was about as glib-tongued a Jacobin as you'd wish to see; but now my young man has *come round* handsomely.
H. B. *Stowe*, Oldtown, p. 495.

To fly, get, go, turn round. See the verbs.—**To pass round the hat.** See *hat*1.

II. *prep.* 1. On every side of; surrounding; encircling: as, the people stood *round* him; to put a rope *round* a post.

O thou, my love, whose love is one with mine,
I, maiden, *round* thee, maiden, bind my belt.
Tennyson, Holy Grail.

2. Circuitously about: as, a ramble *round* the park; to sail *round* Cape Horn; a journey *round* the world.

He led the hero round
The confines of the blest Elysian ground.
Dryden, Æneid, vi. 1227.

The successful expedition round Cape Bojador, being soon spread abroad through Europe, excited a spirit of adventure in all foreigners.
Bruce, Source of the Nile, II. 99.

To come round, get round, etc. See the verbs.

round1 (round), *v.* [= D. *ronden*, round, = G. *runden*, become round, *ründen*, make round, = Sw. *runda* = Dan. *runde*, make round, = F. *rondir*, become round; from the adj. (in defs. I., 4, 5, and II., 2, 3, 5, rather from the adverb): see *round*1, *a.*, *round*1, *adv.*2.] I. *trans.* 1. To give roundness or rotundity to; make circular, spherical, cylindrical, conical, convex, or curved; form with a round or curved outline: as, to *round* the edges of anything; the *rounded* corners of a piano or of a book.

Ye shall not *round* the corners of your heads.
Lev. xix. 27.

The figures on several of our modern medals are raised and *rounded* to a very great perfection.
Addison, Ancient Medals, iii.

Bull, the dog, lies *rounded* on the hearth, his nose between his paws, fast asleep. *S. Judd*, Margaret, i. 17.

Remains of Roman architecture . . . controlled the minds of artists, and induced them to adopt the *rounded* rather than the pointed arch.
J. A. Symonds, Italy and Greece, p. 101.

2. To fill out roundly or symmetrically; complete or perfect in form or substance.

A quaint, terse, florid style, *rounded* into periods and cadencies. *Swift*, Misc.

General ideas are essences; they are our gods; they *round* and ennoble the most partial and sordid way of living. *Emerson*, Nominalist and Realist.

He has lived to *round* a personality that will be traditional. *Stedman*, Poets of America, p. 302.

3. To fill out the circle or term of; bring to completion; finish off.

We are such stuff
As dreams are made on, and our little life
Is *rounded* with a sleep. *Shak.*, Tempest, iv. 1. 158.

I like your picture, but I fain would see
A sketch of what your promised land will be
When . . .
The twentieth century *rounds* a new decade.
Whittier, The Panorama.

4. To encircle; encompass; surround.

Am I not he that rules great Nineveh,
Rounded with Lycas' silver-flowing streams?
Greene and Lodge, Looking Glass for Lond. and Eng.

I would to God that the inclusive verge
Of golden metal that must *round* my brow
Were red-hot steel. *Shak.*, Rich. III., iv. 1. 60.

With garlands of great pearl his brow
Begirt and *rounded*.
Fletcher (*and another*), False One, iii. 4.

5. To go, pass, or get round; make a course round the limit or terminus of: as, the ship *rounded* Cape Horn; to *round* the corner of a street.—**To round down**, to overhaul downward, as a rope or tackle.—**To round in**, or **round in on** (*naut.*), to haul in the slack of: as, to *round in* a rope; to *round in on* a weather-brace.—**To round off.** (*a*) To finish off in a curved or rounded form; give a rounding finish to: as, to *round off* the corners of a table or a marble slab. See *round-off file*, under *file*1. (*b*) To finish completely; bring into a completed or perfected state.

Just as little in the course of its development in time as in space is the body *rounded off* into strict unity.
Lotze, Microcosmos (trans.), I. 136.

Positive science, like common-sense, treats objects as *rounded-off* totals, as "absolutes." *Mind*, XLI. 124.

To round out. (*a*) To expand, distend, or fill out in a rounded form: as, a paunch or a bust well *rounded out*. (*b*) To fill out symmetrically or completely: as, to *round out* a speech with apt illustrations.—**To round to**, to haul by the wind when sailing free; bring (a vessel) head up to the wind preparatory to letting go the anchor.—**To round up.** (*a*) To heap or fill up so as to make round at top: as, to *round up* a measure of grain. (*b*) In grazing regions, to drive or bring together in close order: as, to *round up* a scattered herd of cattle. (*c*) *Naut.*, to haul up, as the slack of a rope through its leading-block, or a tackle which hangs loose by its fall. (*d*) To scold or reprove roundly; bring to account.

II. *intrans.* 1. To grow or become round; acquire curvature, plumpness, roundness, or rounded bigness.

The queen your mother *rounds* apace.
Shak., W. T., ii. 1. 16.

All the jarring notes of life
Seem blending in a psalm,
And all the angles of the strife
Slow *rounding* into calm.
Whittier, My Psalm.

The fair pink blooms . . . gave way to small green spheres *rounding* daily to full-orbed fruit.
R. T. Cooke, Somebody's Neighbors, p. 217.

2. To go round about; make a circuit; go the rounds, as a guard.

While they keep watch, or nightly *rounding* walk.
Milton, P. L., iv. 685.

So *rounds* he to a separate mind,
From whence clear memory may begin.
Tennyson, In Memoriam, xlv.

The stream goes *rounding* away through the sward, bending somewhat to the right, where the ground gradually descends. *The Century*, XXXVI. 806.

3. To turn around or about; make a turn.

The men who met him *rounded* on their heels,
And wonder'd after him.
Tennyson, Pelleas and Ettarre.

4. To become full or finished; develop into a completed or perfected type: as, the girl *rounds* into the woman.—5. To bend or turn downward, as a whale; make ready to dive, as a whale, by curving its small. Also *round out*.—**To round on**, to turn upon or against; abuse; assail; beset: as, he *rounded on* me in a rage.

round2 (round), *v.* [With excrescent *d*, as in *sound*, *pound*2, etc.; < ME. *rounen*, *rownen*, *runen*, < AS. *rūnian* (= OD. *rūnen*, MD. *ruinen*, *ruynen* = OLG. *runōn* = OHG. *rūnēn*, MHG. *rūnen*, G. *raunen*, > OF. *runer*), whisper, murmur, < *rūn*, mystery: see *rune*1.] I.† *intrans.* To speak low; whisper; speak secretly; take counsel.

The steward on knees him set adown,
With the emperour for to *rown*.
Richard Coer de Lion (Weber's Metr. Rom., II. 84).

Another *rowned* to his felawe lowe.
Chaucer, Squire's Tale, l. 208.

II. *trans.* To address or speak to in a whisper; utter in a whisper.

One *rounded* another in the ear, and said "Erat dives," He was a rich man: — a great fault.
Latimer, 5th Sermon bef. Edw. VI., 1549.

They 're here with me already, whispering, *rounding*,
"Sicilia is a so-forth." *Shak.*, W. T., i. 2. 217.

At the same time he [April Fool] slyly *rounded* the first lady in the ear that an action might lie against the Crown for bi-geny. *Lamb*, On the New-Year's Coming of Age.

How often must I *round* thee in the ears —
All means are lawful to a lawful end?
Browning, Ring and Book, II. 104.

round2†, *n.* [< ME. *roun*, < AS. *rūn*, a whisper, secret, mystery: see *round*2, *v.*, and *rune*1.] A whisper or whispering; discourse; song.

ix. and nigneti ger he [Abraham] was old,
Quuanne him cam bode [message] in sunder [diverse] *run*,
Fro gode of circumcicioun.
Genesis and Exodus (E. E. T. S.), l. 991.

roundabout (round'a-bout″), *a.* and *n.* [< *round about*, adverbial phrase: see *round*1, *adv.*, and *about*, *adv.*] I. *a.* 1. Circuitous; tortuous; indirect.

Girls have always a *round-about* way of saying yes before company. *Goldsmith*, Good-natured Man, ii.

The inferences of political economy are true only because they are discoveries by a *roundabout* process of what the moral law commands. H. *Spencer*, Social Statics, p. 502.

2. Comprehensive; taking a wide range.

Those sincerely follow reason, but, for want of having large, sound, *roundabout* sense, have not a full view of all that relates to the question.
Locke, Human Understanding.

3. Encircling; surrounding; encompassing. *Tatler.* (*Imp. Dict.*)

II. *n.* 1. A large horizontal revolving frame, carrying small wooden horses and carriages, sometimes elephants, etc., on or in which children ride; a merry-go-round.—2. A round dance.

The Miss Flamboroughs . . . understood the jig and the *roundabout* to perfection. *Goldsmith*, Vicar, ix. 1.

3. A scene of incessant revolution, change, or vicissitude. [Rare.]

He sees that this great *roundabout*,
The world, with all its motley rout,
Church, army, physic, law,
Its customs, and its bus'nesses,
Is no concern at all of his,
And says — what says he? — "Caw!"
Cowper, The Jackdaw (trans.).

4. An arm-chair with rounded back and sides. —5. A short coat or jacket for men and boys, without skirts, which fits the body closely. Also *round jacket*.

He sauntered about the streets in a plain linen *roundabout*. *The Century*, XXV. 176.

6. A cyclonic storm. [Bermudas.]

roundaboutly (round'a-bout″li), *adv.* [< *roundabout*, *a.*, + *-ly*2.] In a roundabout manner; circuitously; indirectly. [Rare.]

He said it much more lengthily and *roundaboutly*.
R. Broughton, Joan, i.

roundaboutness (round'a-bout″nes), *n.* [< *roundabout*, *a.*, + *-ness*.] Circuitousness of course or manner; the quality of being roundabout or tortuous. [Rare.]

Coleridge's prose writings have the same "vice of *roundaboutness*," as Southey called it, as his talk, but without its charm; the same endless interpolations, digressions, and apologies — with the same superabundance of long, strange, and hard words. *Quarterly Rev.*, CXLV. 77.

round-all (round'âl), *n.* An acrobatic feat. See the quotation.

Doing . . . *round-alls* (that's throwing yourself backwards on to your hands and back again to your feet).
Mayhew, London Labour and London Poor, III. 104.

round-arched (round'ärcht), *a.* In *arch.*, characterized by semicircular arches, as a style or a building, as ancient Roman, Byzantine, Romanesque, and other construction, and the edifices in those styles; also, having the form of a round arch, as an architectural member.

Round-arched Construction.—A pier with perspective of nave, aisle, and vaulting of the Abbey Church of Vézelay, France.

The transverse ribs [choir of Noyon Cathedral] alone are pointed, and the *round-arched* longitudinal ribs are . . . much stilted.
C. H. Moore, Gothic Architecture, p. 49.

round-arm (round'ärm), *a.* In *cricket*, swinging the arm round more or less horizontally, or done with the arm so used: as, a *round-arm* bowler; *round-arm* bowling. *Encyc. Dict.*

round-armed (round'ärmd), *a.* In *boxing*, given with a horizontal swing of the arm.

And the clumsy *round-armed* hit, even though it does more harm to the recipient, is not esteemed so highly as a straight hit made directly from the shoulder.
Saturday Rev., No. 1474.

round-backed (round'bakt), *a.* Having a round or curved back; showing unusual convexity of back, especially between the shoulders; round-shouldered.

round-bend (round'bend), *a.* Bent in a certain curve: specifically said of fly-hooks.

round-crested (round'kres"ted), *a.* Having a round crest; fan-crested: specific in the phrase *round-crested duck*, the hooded merganser, *Lophodytes cucullatus.* *Catesby*, 1731. See cut under *merganser*.

roundel (roun'del), *n.* [Also *roundle, rondel, rondle, rundle*, in obsolete, technical, or dialectal uses; < ME. *roundel, rundel, rondel*, < OF. *rondel*, later *rondeau*, anything round and flat, a round plate, a round cake, etc., a scroll, dim. of *rond*, round: see *round*[1]. Cf. Sp. *redondilla* = Pg. *redondilha*, a roundel: see *redondilla*. Cf. *rondeau, rondel*.] 1. Anything round; a round form or figure; a circle, or something of circular form. [Archaic except in some technical uses.]

A *roundel* to set dishes on for soiling the tablecloth.
Baret, 1580. (*Halliwell.*)

The Spaniardes, vniting themselues, gathered their whole Fleete close together into a *roundell*.
Hakluyt's Voyages, I. 598.

Come, put in his leg in the middle *roundel* [round hole of stocks]. *B. Jonson*, Bartholomew Fair, iv. 4.

Scales and *roundles* to mount the pinnacles and highest pieces of divinity. *Sir T. Browne*, Religio Medici, i. 12.

Those *roundels* of gold fringe, drawn out with cypress.
Scott, Kenilworth, xx.

The *roundels* or "bulls'-eyes," so largely used in domestic glazing. *Glass-making*, p. 92.

Specifically—(*a*) In *her.*, a circular figure used as a bearing, and commonly blazoned, not roundel, but by a special name according to the tincture. Also *roundle, roundlet*. (*b*) In *medieval armor*: (1) A round shield made of osiers, wood, sinews, or ropes covered with leather, or plates of metal, or stuck full of nails in concentric circles or other figures: sometimes made wholly of metal, and generally convex, but sometimes concave, and both with and without the umbo or boss. (2) A piece of metal of circular or nearly circular form. (*a*) A very small plate sewed or riveted to cloth or leather as part of a coat of fence. (*β*) A larger plate, used to protect the body at the défaut de la cuirasse, where that on the left side was fixed, that on the right side movable to allow of the couching of the lance, and at the knee-joint, usually one on each side, covering the articulation. Also called *disk*. (*c*) In *fort.*, a bastion of a semicircular form, introduced by Albert Dürer. It was about 300 feet in diameter, and contained roomy casemates for troops. (*d*) In *arch.*, a molding of semicircular profile. *J. T. Clarke.* (*e*) A fruit-trencher of circular form.

Per pale gules and argent three roundels counterchanged.

2†. A dance in which the dancers form a ring or circle. Also called *round*.

Come, now a *roundel* and a fairy song.
Shak., M. N. D., ii. 2. 1.

3. Same as *rondel*: specifically applied by Swinburne to a form apparently invented by himself. This consists of nine lines with two refrains, arranged as follows: *a, b, a* (and refrain); *b, a, b*; *a, b, a* (and refrain)—the refrain, as in the rondeau and rondel, being part of the first line. The measure is unrestricted, and the refrain generally rimes with the *b* lines.

Many a himpne for your holy daies
That highten balades, *roundels*, virelaies.
Chaucer, Good Women.

All day long we rode
Thro' the dim land against a rushing wind,
That glorious *roundel* echoing in our ears.
Tennyson, Merlin and Vivien.

roundelay (roun'de-lā), *n.* [< OF. *rondelet*, dim. of *rondel*, a roundel: see *roundel*. The spelling *roundelay* appar. simulates E. *lay*[3].] 1. Any song in which an idea, line, or refrain is continually repeated.

Per. It fell upon a holy eve,
Wil. Hey, ho, hallidaye!
Per. When holy fathers went to shrieve;
Wil. Now ginneth this *roundelay*.
. . . .
Wil. Now endeth our *roundelay*.
Cud. Sicker, sike a *roundle* never heard I none.
Spenser, Shep. Cal., August.

Loudly sung his *roundelay* of love. *Dryden.*

While linnet, lark, and blackbird gay
Sing forth her nuptial *roundelay*.
Scott, Rokeby, ii. 16.

The breath of Winter . . . plays a *roundelay*
Of death among the bushes and the leaves.
Keats, Isabella, st. 32.

2. Same as *rondeau*, 1.

The *roundelay*, in which, after each strophe of the song, a chorus interposes with the same refrain.
J. Sully, Sensation and Intuition, p. 214.

3. A dance in a circle; a round or roundel.

The fawns, satyrs, and nymphs did dance their *roundelays*. *Howell.*

As doth the billow there upon Charybdis,
That breaks itself on that which it encounters,
So here the folk must dance their *roundelay*.
Longfellow, tr. of Dante's Inferno, vii. 24.

roundeleer (roun-de-lēr'), *n.* [< *roundel* + *-eer*.] A writer of roundels or roundelays. [Rare.]

In this path he must thus have preceded . . . all contemporary *roundeleers*. *Scribner's Mag.*, IV. 250.

rounder (roun'dėr), *n.* [< *round*[1], *v.*, + *-er*[1].] 1. One who or that which rounds or makes round; specifically, a tool for rounding, or rounding out or off, as a cylindrical rock-boring tool with an indented face, a plane used by wheelwrights for rounding off tenons, etc.—2. One who habitually goes round, or from point to point and back, for any purpose; especially, one who continually goes the round of misdemeanor, arrest, trial, imprisonment, and release, as a habitual drunkard or petty thief.

G—— had made himself conspicuous as a *rounder*, . . . and occupied much of his time in threatening employes of the various railroad companies.
Philadelphia Times, 1886.

A very large proportion of the inmates [of the workhouse on Blackwell's Island] are "old *rounders*" who return to the Island again and again.
Christian Union, Aug. 25, 1887.

During our civil war the regiments which were composed of plug-uglies, thugs, and midnight *rounders*, with noses laid over to one side as evidence of their prowess in bar-room mills and paving-stone riots, were generally cringing cowards in battle. *The Century*, XXXVI. 249.

3. Something well rounded or filled out; a round or plump oath, or the like. [Colloq.]

Though we can all swear a *rounder* in the stockyard or on the drafting camp, as a rule we are a happy-go-lucky, peaceable lot. *Mrs. Campbell Praed*, Head Station, p. 33.

4. A round; an act or instance of going or passing round. Specifically—(*a*) A round of demonstrative speech or procedure: as, they gave him a *rounder* (a round of applause).

Mrs. Cork . . . was off amid a *rounder* of "Thank'e ma'am, thank'e." *R. D. Blackmore*, Christowell, II. viii.

(*b*) A complete run in the game of rounders.

A *rounder* was when a player struck the ball with such force as to enable him to run all four bases and "get home." *The Century*, XXXIX. 637.

5. *pl.* (*a*) A game played with a soft and small ball and a bat of about 2 feet in length. About four or five players are on each side. The game is played on a ground in the form of a rectangle or pentagon with a base at each angle; on one of these bases, called the "home," the batsman stands. When the ball is thrown toward the batter he tries to drive it away as far as he can and secure a run completely round the boundary, or over any of the parts of it, before he can be hit by the ball secured and thrown at him by one of the opposite party. In some forms of the game the batter is declared out if he fails to strike the ball, if he drives it too short a distance to secure a run, or if the ball from his bat is caught in the air by one of the opposite party. From rounders the game of base-ball has been developed. (*b*) In England, a game like fives, but played with a football.

round-faced (round'fāst), *a.* Having a round face: as, the *round-faced* macaque, *Macacus cyclopis*.

I can give no other account of him but that he was pretty tall, *round-faced*, and one, I'm sure, I ne'er had seen before. *Wycherley*, Plain Dealer, v. 1.

roundfish (round'fish), *n.* 1. The common carp, *Cyprinus carpio*.—2. The shad-waiter or pilot-fish, *Coregonus quadrilateralis*; the Menomonee whitefish, abundant in the Great Lake region and northward. See cut under *shad-waiter*.

roundhand (round'hand), *n.* [< *round*[1] + *hand*.] 1. A style of penmanship in which the letters are round and full.—2. A style of bowling in cricket in which the arm is brought round horizontally. See *round-arm*. *Imp. Dict.*

Roundhead (round'hed), *n.* [< *round*[1] + *head*.] 1. In *Eng. hist.*, a member of the Parliamentarian or Puritan party during the civil war: so called opprobriously by the Royalists or Cavaliers, in allusion to the Puritans' custom of wearing their hair closely cut, while the Cavaliers usually wore theirs in long ringlets. The Roundheads were one of the two great parties in English politics first formed about 1641, and continued under the succeeding names of Whigs and Liberals, as opposed to the Cavaliers, Tories, and Conservatives respectively.

But our Scene's London now; and by the rout
We perish, if the *Roundheads* be about.
Cowley, The Guardian, Prol.

2. [*l. c.*] The weakfish or squeteague, *Cynoscion regalis*. [Virginia.]

round-headed (round'hed"ed), *a.* [< *round*[1] + *head* + *-ed*[2].] 1. Having a round head or top: as, a *round-headed* nail or rivet.

Roundheaded arches and windows.
Bp. Louth, Life of Wykeham, § 6. (*Latham.*)

Above was a simple *round-headed* clerestory, and outside are the same slight beginnings of ornamental arcades.
E. A. Freeman, Venice, p. 104.

2. Hence, having the hair of the head cut short; close-cropped; specifically, belonging or pertaining to the Roundheads or Parliamentarians. [Rare.]

The *round-headed* rebels of Westminster Hall.
Scott, Rokeby, v. 20 (song).

roundhouse (round'hous), *n.* 1†. A lockup; a station-house; a watch-house. *Foote.*—2. *Naut.*: (*a*) A cabin or apartment on the after part of the quarter-deck, having the poop for its roof: formerly sometimes called the *coach*; also, the poop itself.

Our captain sent his skiff and fetched aboard us the masters of the other two ships, and Mr. Pynchon, and they dined with us in the *round house*.
Winthrop, Hist. New England, I. 14.

(*b*) An erection abaft the mainmast for the accommodation of the officers or crew of a vessel.—3. On American railroads, a building, usually round and built of brick, having stalls for the storage of locomotives, with tracks leading from them to a central turn-table. In Great Britain called *engine-house* or *engine-shed*.—4. A privy. [Southwestern U. S.]

rounding (roun'ding), *n.* [Verbal n. of *round*[1], *v.*] 1. In *bookbinding*, the operation of shaping the folded and sewed sheets into a slightly convex form at the back. It is done either by hand-tools or by machinery.—2. The action or attitude of a whale when curving its small in order to dive. Also *rounding-out*.—3. *Naut.*, old rope or strands wound about a rope to prevent its chafing.

rounding-adz (roun'ding-adz), *n.* A form of adz having a curved blade for hollowing out timber.

rounding-machine (roun'ding-ma-shēn"), *n.* One of several kinds of machines for producing round forms or roundness of form. Especially—(*a*) A machine for sawing out circular heads for casks and barrels. (*b*) A machine for rounding the backs of books. (*c*) A machine for forming the rounded depressions in shoe-sole blanks; a sole-stamping machine. (*d*) A machine for making rods and spindles; a rod-machine or dowel-machine. (*e*) A cornering-machine for chamfering off the angles of stuff in tool-making and carriage-work.

rounding-out (roun'ding-out), *n.* Same as *rounding*, 2.

rounding-plane (roun'ding-plān), *n.* A wood-working tool for rounding and finishing the handles of rakes or brooms, chair-rounds, and other round pieces. It has a plane-bit placed parallel to the axis of a circular hole, and projecting slightly. The rough stuff is passed through the hole, and rotated against the cutting edge.

Rounding-plane or Witchet.
a, plane-iron; *b*, stock; *c*, piece to be rounded; *d*, *d*, handles.

rounding-tool (roun'ding-tōl), *n.* 1. In *forging*, a top- or bottom-tool having a semicylindrical groove, used as a swage for rounding a rod, the stem of a bolt, and the like. *E. H. Knight.*—2. In *saddlery*, a kind of draw-plate for shaping round leather straps. It consists of a pair of jaws with corresponding semicylindrical grooves of various sizes on both sides. The jaws can be locked shut in order that the strap may be passed through the cylindrical openings thus formed.

round-iron (round'ī"ėrn), *n.* A plumbers' tool with a bulbous head, for finishing soldered work.

Round-iron.
a, head, in use made red-hot and passed over the joint to be smoothed until the latter is sufficiently heated for the application of the solder; *b b*, handle.

roundish (roun'dish), *a.* [< *round*[1] + *-ish*[1].] Somewhat round; nearly round; inclining to roundness: as, a *roundish* seed or leaf.

roundishness (roun'dish-nes), *n.* The state of being roundish. *Imp. Dict.*

roundle (roun'dl), *n.* Same as *roundel*.

round-leaved (round'lēvd), *a.* Having round leaves.—**Round-leaved cornel, horsemint, spinach.** See the nouns.

roundlet (round'let), *n.* [< F. *rondelet*, dim. of OF. *rondel*, roundel: see *roundel*. Cf. *rundlet*, *runlet*[2], *roundelay*.] 1. A little circle; a roundel.

Like *roundlets* that arise
By a stone cast into a standing brook.
Drayton, Barons' Wars, v. 60.

2†. Same as *rundlet*.—3. In *her.*, same as *roundel*.—4. *pl.* The fuller rounded part of the hood worn as a head-dress in the middle ages. See *hood*.

roundly (round'li), *adv.* [< *round*[1] + *-ly*[2].] 1. In a round form. [Rare.]—2. In a round or positive manner; frankly, bluntly, vigorously, earnestly, energetically, or the like. See *round*[1], *a.*, 9.

What a bold man of war! he invites me *roundly*. *Beau. and Fl.*, Little French Lawyer, iii. 2.

He *roundly* and openly avows what most others studiously conceal. *Bacon*, Political Fables, ii., Expl.

Not to weary you with long preambles, . . . I will come *roundly* to the matter. *R. Peeke* (Arber's Eng. Garner, I. 625).

Let me beg you, Mrs. Malaprop, to enforce this matter *roundly* to the girl. *Sheridan*, The Rivals, i. 2.

3. In round numbers; without formal exactness; approximately.

The destructors now consumed, *roundly*, about 500 loads of refuse a week. *Lancet*, No. 3454, p. 984.

4. Briskly; hastily; quickly.

She has mounted on her true love's steed, . . .
And *roundly* she rade frae the toun.
Sir Roland (Child's Ballads, I. 224).

Two of the outlaws . . . walked *roundly* forward. *Scott*, Ivanhoe, xi.

To come off roundly†. See *come*.

roundmouth (round'mouth), *n.* In *zoöl.*, a lamprey or a hag: a book-name translating the technical name of the order, *Cyclostomi*.

round-mouthed (round'moutht), *a.* In *zoöl.*, having a mouth without any lower jaw; cyclostomous: specifically noting the *Cyclostomi*, or lampreys and hags.

roundness (round'nes), *n.* [< ME. *rowndnes*, *rowndenesse*; < *round*[1] + *-ness*.] 1. The state of being round, or circular, spherical, globular, cylindrical, curved, or convex; circularity; sphericity; cylindrical form; rotundity; convexity: as, the *roundness* of the globe, of the orb of the sun, of a ball, of a bowl, of a hill, etc.

Egges they may eate in the night for their *roundnesse*. *Purchas*, Pilgrimage, p. 211.

2. The quality of being well filled or rounded out metaphorically; fullness, completeness, openness, positiveness, boldness, or the like.

The whole periode and compasse of this speache so delightsome for the *roundnesse*, and so grave for the straungenesse. *Spenser*, To Gabriell Harvey.

Albeit *roundness* and plain dealing be most worthy praise. *Raleigh*, Arts of Empire, xx. (*Latham*.)

=Syn. 1. *Roundness*, *Rotundity*, plumpness, globularity. *Roundness* applies with equal freedom to a circle, a sphere, a cylinder, or a cone, and, by extension, to forms that by approach suggest any one of these: as, *roundness* of limb or cheek. *Rotundity* now applies usually to spheres and to forms suggesting a sphere or a hemisphere: as, the *rotundity* of the earth or of a barrel; *rotundity* of abdomen.

round-nosed (round'nōzd), *a.* Having a full blunt snout, as a female salmon before spawning; not hook-billed.—**Round-nosed chisel, plane,** etc. See the nouns.

round-ridge (round'rij), *v. t.* [< *round*[1] + *ridge*.] In *agri.*, to form into round ridges by plowing.

round-robin (round'rob″in), *n.* 1. A pancake. *Halliwell.* [Prov. Eng.]—2. A kind of ruff, apparently the smaller ruff of the latter part of the sixteenth century.—3. Same as *cigar-fish*.—4. The angler, *Lophius piscatorius*.—5. A written paper, as a petition, memorial, or remonstrance, bearing a number of signatures arranged in a circular or concentric form. This device, whereby the order of signing is concealed, is used for the purpose of making all the signers equally responsible for it. Also written as two words, *round robin*.

I enclose the *Round Robin*. This jeu d'esprit took its rise one day [in 1776] at dinner at our friend Sir Joshua Reynolds's. All the company present, except myself, were friends and acquaintance of Dr. Goldsmith. The Epitaph written for him by Dr. Johnson became the subject of conversation, and various emendations were suggested, which it was agreed should be submitted to the Doctor's consideration. But the question was, who should have the courage to propose them to him? At last it was hinted that there could be no way so good as that of a *Round Robin*, as the sailors call it, which they make use of when they enter into a conspiracy, so as not to let it be known who puts his name first or last to the paper. *Sir W. Forbes*, in Boswell's Life of Johnson (ed. Hill), III. 83.

round-shouldered (round'shōl″dėrd), *a.* Having the shoulders carried forward, giving the upper part of the back a rounded configuration.

roundsman (roundz'man), *n.*; pl. *roundsmen* (-men). A police officer, of a rank above patrolmen and below sergeants, who goes the rounds within a prescribed district to see that the patrolmen or ordinary policemen attend to their duties properly, and to aid them in case of necessity. [U. S.]

roundstone (round'stōn), *n.* Small round or roundish stones collectively, used for paving; cobblestone. [Local, U. S.]

Gangs of street paviors were seen and heard here, there, and yonder, swinging the pick and ramming the *roundstone*. *G. W. Cable*, Creoles of Louisiana, xxix.

round-tailed (round'tāld), *a.* 1. Having a cylindric or terete tail: as, the *round-tailed* spermophile, *Spermophilus tereticauda*.—2. Having the end of the tail rounded by gradual shortening of the lateral feathers in succession, as a bird.

roundtop† (round'top), *n.* 1. *Naut.*, a platform at the masthead; a top.—2. In *her.*, an inclosed circular platform, like a large flat tub, set upon the top of a pole, which pole is shown to be a mast by having a small yard with furled sail attached put across it, usually at an angle—the whole being a conventional representation of an ancient round top of a ship.

round-up (round'up), *n.* [< *round up*: see *round*[1], *v.*] 1. A rounding up; the forming of upward curves; curvature upward.

These curves are used in drawing the frames, the *round-up* of the forefoot, the rudder, and the other quick curves in the boat. *Tribune Book of Sports*, p. 204.

2. In grazing regions, the herding or driving together of all the cattle on a range or ranch, for inspection, branding, sorting, etc.; also, the beating up or gathering of any animals, as those of the chase.

His [a ranchman's] hardest work comes during the spring and fall *round-ups*, when the calves are branded or the beeves gathered for market. *T. Roosevelt*, Hunting Trips, p. 11.

3. A rounding off or finishing, as of an arrangement or undertaking; a bringing round to settlement or completion. [Colloq.]

That exception . . . will probably be included in the general *round-up* [of an agreement among railroads] to-morrow. *Philadelphia Times*, May 3, 1886.

4. In *ship-building*, the convexity of a deck; crown; camber. [Eng.]

roundure (roun'dūr), *n.* Same as *rondure*.

'Tis not the *roundure* of your old-faced walls
Can hide you from our messengers of war.
Shak., K. John, ii. 1. 259.

round-winged (round'wingd), *a.* Having rounded wings, as an insect or a bird: as, the *round-winged* muslin, a British moth, *Nudaria senex*; the *round-winged* white-wave, another moth, *Cabera exanthemaria*; the *round-winged* hawks, as of the genera *Astur* and *Accipiter*.

roundworm (round'wėrm), *n.* 1. An intestinal parasitic worm, *Ascaris lumbricoides*, several inches long, infesting the human intestine: distinguished from the similar but much smaller pinworms or threadworms, and from the larger and more formidable flatworms, jointworms, or tapes. Hence—2. Any member of the class *Nematelmintha*; a nematoid worm: distinguished from cestoid and trematoid worms, or tapeworms and flukes.

roundy (roun'di), *a.* [< *round*[1] + *-y*[1].] Rounding; curving; rounded out. [Rare.]

Her *roundy*, sweetly-swelling lips a little trembling, as though they kissed their neighbour Death. *Sir P. Sidney*, Arcadia, iii.

rounet†, *v.* See *round*[2].

roun-tree (roun'trē), *n.* Same as *rowan-tree* or *roan-tree*. *Halliwell.* [Prov. Eng.]

roup[1] (röp), *v.* and *n.* Same as *roop*.

roup[2] (roup), *v. t.* [A particular use, in another pronunciation, of *roup*[1], *roop*: see *roop*.] To sell by outcry for bids; sell at public auction; auction. [Scotch.]

They had *rouped* me out of house and hold. *Carlyle*, in Froude, Life in London, ii.

roup[2] (roup), *n.* [< *roup*[2], *v.*] A sale of goods by outcry; a public auction. [Scotch.]

The tenements are set by *Roup*, or auction. *Pennant*, Tour in Scotland (1772), p. 201. (*Jamieson*.)

roup[3] (röp), *n.* [Also *roop*; < *roup*[1], *roop*, *v.*] An infectious disease of the respiratory passages of poultry, closely similar in character and origin to catarrh in man, but more virulent and rapid in its progress, and very commonly fatal. It begins with a slight cough or a discharge from the nostrils; the discharge quickly becomes fetid, and frequently fills the eyes. The head swells, the eyes are closed, and sight is often destroyed. Cheesy cankers of diphtheritic character often form in the throat and mouth, frequently causing death by choking. As a remedy, injection of a weak solution of copper sulphate (¼ ounce to 1 quart water) gives good results.

roupit, roupet (rö'pit, -pet), *a.* See *roopit*.

roupy, *a.* See *roopy*.

rousant (rou'zant), *a.* [< *rouse*[1] + *-ant*.] In *her.*, starting up, as from being roused or alarmed: noting a bird in the attitude of rising, as if preparing to take flight. When applied to a swan it is understood that the wings are indorsed. Also spelled *roussant*.

Swan Rousant.

rouse[1] (rouz), *v.*; pret. and pp. *roused*, ppr. *rousing*. [Early mod. E. also *rowse*, *rouze*, *rowze*; < ME. *rowsen*, *rouzen*, < Sw. *rusa* = Dan. *ruse*, rush; cf. AS. *hreósan*, fall, rush down or forward, come down with a rush: see *ruse*[1]. Cf. *rush*[2], *v.*, and *arouse*.] I. *trans.* 1. To cause to start up by noise or clamor, especially from sleep; startle into movement or activity; in *hunting*, to drive or frighten from a lurking-place or covert.

The night outwatched made us make a night of the morning, untill *rouz'd* from our groundbeds by the report of the Canon. *Sandys*, Travailes, p. 69.

We find them [the ladies] . . . in the open fields winding the horn, *rousing* the game, and pursuing it. *Strutt*, Sports and Pastimes, p. 70.

Your rough voice
(You spoke so loud) has *roused* the child again.
Tennyson, Sea Dreams.

2. To raise or waken from torpor or inaction by any means; provoke to activity; wake or stir up: said of animate beings.

This rebalde he *rowses* hym it rathely to rayse. *York Plays*, p. 264.

He stooped down, he couched as a lion; . . . who shall *rouse* him up? Gen. xlix. 9.

"For the heavens, *rouse* up a brave mind," says the fiend, "and run." *Shak.*, M. of V., ii. 2. 12.

3. To evoke a commotion in or about: said of inanimate things.

He should have found his uncle Gaunt a father,
To *rouse* his wrongs and chase them to the bay.
Shak., Rich. II., ii. 3. 128.

Blustering winds, which all night long
Had *roused* the sea. *Milton*, P. L., ii. 287.

Hence—4. To move or stir up vigorously by direct force; use energetic means for raising, stirring, or moving along. In this sense still sometimes written *rowse*.

We were obliged to sit down and slide about in the close hold, passing hides, and *rowsing* about the great steeves, tackles, and dogs. *R. H. Dana, Jr.*, Before the Mast, p. 308.

5†. To raise up; erect; rear; fix in an elevated position.

Being mounted and both *roused* in their seats,
Their neighing coursers daring of the spur.
Shak., 2 Hen. IV., iv. 1. 118.

6. To put and turn over or work about in salt, as fish in the operation of rousing; roil.

Another carries them [fish] off to be *roused*, as it is called: that is, cast into vats or barrels, then sprinkled with salt, then more herrings and more salt, and next a brawny arm plunged among them far above the elbow, thus mingling them together. *Encyc. Brit.*, IX. 259.

7. *Naut.*, to haul heavily.

The object is that the hawser mayn't slip as we *rouse* it taut. *W. C. Russell*, A Strange Voyage, xlvii.

To rouse out, to turn out or call up (hands or the crew) from their berths to the deck. =Syn. 1 and 2. To animate, kindle, stimulate, provoke, stir up.

II. *intrans.* 1. To start or rise up, as from sleep, repose, or inaction; throw off torpor or quietude; make a stir or movement.

Night's black agents to their preys do *rouse*.
Shak., Macbeth, iii. 2. 53.

Melancholy lifts her head;
Morpheus *rouses* from his bed.
Pope, Ode on St. Cecilia's Day, l. 31.

2†. To rise; become erect; stand up.

My fell of hair
Would at a dismal treatise *rouse* and stir
As life were in 't. *Shak.*, Macbeth, v. 5. 12.

3. *Naut.*, to haul with great force, as upon a cable or the like.—**Rouse-about block.** See *block*[1].

rouse[1] (rouz), *n.* [< *rouse*[1], *v.*] An arousing; a sudden start or movement, as from torpor or inaction; also, a signal for arousing or starting up; the reveille. [Rare.]

These fowles in their moulting time, . . . their feathers be sick, and . . . so loase in the flesh that at any little *rowse* they can easilie shake them off. *Puttenham*, Arte of Eng. Poesie, p. 222.

At five on Sunday morning the *rouse* was sounded, breakfast at seven, and church parade at eight. *City Press*, Sept. 30, 1885. (*Encyc. Dict.*)

rouse[1]† (rouz), *adv.* [An exclamatory use of *rouse*[1], *v.*] As if suddenly aroused; rousingly; vehemently.

What, Sir! 'Slife, sir! you should have come out in choler, *rous* upon the Stage, just as the other went off. *Buckingham*, Rehearsal (ed. Arber), iii. 2.

rouse[2]† (rouz), *n.* [Early mod. E. *rowze*, also *rowza*; < Sw. *rus* = Dan. *rus*, drunkenness, a drunken fit, = Icel. *rúss*, drunkenness (Haldorsen), = D. *roes*, drunkenness (*eenen roes drinken*, drink a rouse, drink till one is fuddled; cf. G. *rausch*, intoxication, adapted from D. *roes*); connections uncertain.] 1. Wine or other liquor considered as an inducement to mirth or drunkenness; a full glass; a bumper.

Cas. 'Fore God, they have given me a *rouse* already.
Mon. Good faith, a little one; not past a pint, as I am a soldier. *Shak.*, Othello, ii. 3. 66.

I have took, since supper,
A *rouse* or two too much, and, by [the gods],
It warms my blood.
Beau. and Fl., Knight of Malta, iii. 4.

Fill the cup and fill the can,
Have a *rouse* before the morn.
Tennyson, Vision of Sin.

Hence—2. Noise; intemperate mirth. *Halliwell.* [Prov. Eng.]

rouse³ (röz), *v. t.* Same as *roose.*

rousement (rouz'ment), *n.* [‹ *rouse*¹ + *-ment.*] Arousal; a rousing up; specifically, an arousing religious discourse; an awakening appeal or incitement. [Colloq.]

Deep strong feeling, but no excitement. They are not apt to indulge in any more *rousements.* *The Congregationalist*, Sept. 27, 1883.

Dr. ——— was also present to add the *rousements.* *The Advance*, Dec. 9, 1886.

rouser (rou'zėr), *n.* [‹ *rouse*¹ + *-er*¹.] 1. One who or that which rouses or excites to action.

All this which I have depainted to thee are incitors and *rousers* of my mind. *Shelton*, tr. of Don Quixote, iii. 6. (*Latham.*)

2. That which rouses attention or interest; something exciting or astonishing: as, the speech was a *rouser;* that's a *rouser* (an astonishing lie). [Colloq.]—3. Something to rouse with; specifically, in *brewing*, a stirrer in the hop-copper.

rousey† (rou'zi), *a.* [Also *rowsey;* ‹ *rouse*² + *-y*¹.] Carousing; noisy; riotous.

I thought it good, necessary, and my bounden duty to acquaint your goodness with the abominable, wicked, and detestable behaviour of all these *rowsey*, ragged rabblement of rake-hells. *Harman*, Caveat for Cursetors, p. ii.

rousing (rou'zing), *n.* [Verbal n. of *rouse*¹, *v.*] A method of curing herring; roiling. See *rouse*¹, *v. t.*, 6.

rousing (rou'zing), *p. a.* [Ppr. of *rouse*¹, *v.*] Having power to rouse, excite, or astonish; surprisingly great, swift, violent, forcible, lively, or the like: as, a *rousing* fire; a *rousing* pace; a *rousing* meeting; a *rousing* lie or oath.

A Jew, who kept a sausage-shop in the same street, had the ill-luck to die of a stranguary, and leave his widow in possession of a *rousing* trade. *Sterne*, Tristram Shandy, ix. 5.

rousingly (rou'zing-li), *adv.* In a rousing manner; astonishingly; excitingly.

roussant (rö'sant), *a.* In *her.*, same as *rousant.*

Rousseauism (rö-sō'izm), *n.* [‹ *Rousseau* (see def.) + *-ism.*] That which distinguishes or is characteristic of the writings of the French author Jean Jacques Rousseau (1712–78), especially in regard to social order and relations, or the social contract (which see, under *contract*).

Rousseauist (rö-sō'ist), *n.* [‹ *Rousseau* (see *Rousseauism*) + *-ist.*] A follower or an admirer of J. J. Rousseau; a believer in Rousseau's doctrines or principles.

Rousseauite (rö-sō'īt), *n.* [‹ *Rousseau* (see *Rousseauism*) + *-ite*².] Same as *Rousseauist.*

Rousseau's laudanum. A fermented aqueous solution of opium, to which is added very weak alcohol: seven drops contain about one grain of opium.

Rousselot's caustic. A caustic composed of one part of arsenious acid, five parts of red sulphuret of mercury, and two parts of burnt sponge. Also called *Frère Come's caustic.*

roussette (rö-set'), *n.* [Also *rosset;* ‹ F. *roussette*, ‹ *rousset*, reddish: see *russet*¹.] 1. A fruit-eating bat of a russet or brownish-red color; hence, any fox-bat of the genus *Pteropus* or family *Pteropodidæ.* See cuts under *fruit-bat* and *Pteropus.*—2. Any shark of the family *Scylliidæ;* a dogfish.

Roussillon (rö-sē-lyôn'), *n.* [‹ *Roussillon*, a former province in southern France.] A strong wine of very dark-red color, made in southern France. It is used for mixing with light-colored and weaker wines, a few of the better varieties being used as dessert-wines. It appears, too, that a great deal goes into the Spanish peninsula, where it is flavored and sold as port-wine.

roust¹ (roust), *v.* [Appar. ‹ *rouse*¹ (with excrescent *t*).] I. *trans.* To rouse or disturb; rout out: stir or start up.

II. *intrans.* To stir or act briskly; move or work energetically. Compare *roustabout.* [Colloq. in both uses.]

roust², **roost**² (röst), *n.* [Also *rost;* ‹ Icel. *röst* (pl. *rostir*), a current, a stream in the sea, = Norw. *röst*, a current, a line of billows.] A tidal current.

This lofty promontory is constantly exposed to the current of a strong and furious tide, . . . called the *Roost* of Sumburgh. *Scott*, Pirate, i.

roust², **roost**² (röst), *v. i.* [‹ *roust*², *n.*] To drive fiercely, as a current. [Rare.]

And in the .vi. degrees wee mette northerly wyndes and greate *roostynge* of tydes. *R. Eden* (First Books on America, ed. Arber, p. 382).

roustabout (roust'a-bout*), *n.* [Cf. E. dial. *rousabout*, a restless, fidgety person; ‹ *rouse*¹ or *roust*¹ + *about.*] A common wharf-laborer or deck-hand, originally one on the Mississippi or other western river. [U. S.]

In the middle of the group was an old Mississippi *roustabout* singing the famous old river song called "Limber Jim." *New York Sun*, March 23, 1890.

rouster (rous'tėr), *n.* Same as *roustabout.*

Men . . . who used to be *rousters*, and are now broken down and played out. *The American*, VI. 40.

rousty (rös'ti), *a.* A Scotch form of *rusty*¹.

rout¹ (rout), *v.* i. [‹ ME. *routen*, *rowten*, *ruten*, ‹ AS. *hrūtan*, also **hreótan*, *reótan* (pret. *reát*), make a noise, snore, = OFries. *hrûta*, *rûta* = OD. *rūten*, MD. *ruyten*, make a noise, chatter, as birds, = OHG. *riuzan*, make a noise, weep, etc., = Icel. *rjóta*, *hrjóta*, roar, rattle, snore; cf. OHG. *rūzan*, *rūzzan*, *rūzōn*, MHG. *rūzen*, *rūssen*, make a noise, rattle, buzz, snore, = Icel. *rauta* = Sw. *ryta*, roar, secondary forms of the orig. verb.] 1. To make a noise; roar; bellow, as a bull or cow; snort, as a horse. [Obsolete or Scotch.]

Sax poor ca's stand in the sta',
A' *routing* loud for their minnie.
Jamie Telfer (Child's Ballads, VI. 108).

The bum-clock humm'd wi' lazy drone,
The kye stood *rowtin'* i' the loan.
Burns, The Twa Dogs.

Some of the bulls keep traveling up and down, bellowing and *routing*, or giving vent to long, surly grumblings as they paw the sand. *T. Roosevelt*, The Century, XXXV. 665.

2†. To snore.

Longe tyme I slepte; . . .
Reste me there, and *rutte* taste.
Piers Plowman (B), xviii. 7.

For travaille of his goost he groneth sore,
And eft he *routeth*, for his heed myslay.
Chaucer, Miller's Tale, l. 461.

3†. To howl, as the wind; make a roaring noise.

The sterne wynde so loude gan to *route*
That no wight other noyse myghte here.
Chaucer, Troilus, iii. 743.

The stormy winds did roar again,
The raging waves did *rout.*
The Lowlands of Holland (Child's Ballads, II. 214).

rout¹ (rout), *n.* [‹ ME. *rowt*, *rowte;* from the verb.] 1. A loud noise; uproar; tumult.

Give me to know
How this foul *rout* began, who set it on.
Shak., Othello, ii. 3. 210.

They haue many professed Phisicians, who with their charmes and Rattles, with an infernal *rout* of words and actions, will seeme to sucke their inward griefe from their navels. *Capt. John Smith*, Works, I. 137.

Not school boys at a barring out
Rais'd ever such incessant *rout.*
Swift, Journal of a Modern Lady.

Sir Robert, who makes as much *rout* with him [a dog] as I do, says he never saw ten people show so much real concern. *H. Walpole*, To Mann, Oct. 8, 1742.

2†. Snoring. *Chaucer* (ed. Morris).—3. A stunning blow.

rout² (rout), *v.* [Formerly *wrout;* a var. of *root*², formerly *wroot:* see *root*².] I. *trans.* 1. To turn up with the snout; root, as a hog: same as *root*², 1.

Winder of the horn
When snouted wild-boars, *routing* tender corn,
Anger our huntsman. *Keats*, Endymion, i.

2. In *mech.*, to deepen; scoop out; cut out; dig out, as moldings, the spaces between and around block-letters, bookbinders' stamps, etc.

II. *intrans.* To root; rummage or poke about.

What 'll they say to me if I go a *routing* and rookling in their drains, like an old sow by the wayside? *Kingsley*, Two Years Ago, xiv.

rout³ (rout), *n.* [Formerly also *rowt;* ‹ ME. *route*, *rute* = MD. *rote*, D. *rot* = MHG. *rote*, *rotte*, G. *rotte* = Icel. *rotti* = Sw. *rote* = Dan. *rode*, a troop, band, ‹ OF. *route*, *route*, *rote* = Pr. *rota*, a troop, band, company, multitude, flock, herd, ‹ ML. *rupta*, also, after Rom., *rutta*, *ruta*, *rota*, a troop, band, prop. a division of an army, ‹ L. *rupta*, fem. of *ruptus* (› It. *rotto* = OF. *rout*, *roupt*), broken, divided, pp. of *rumpere*, break: see *rupture.* Cf. *rout*⁴, *rout*⁵, *route*, *rote*, *rut*¹, from the same ult. source.] 1. A troop; a band; a company in general, either of persons or of animals; specifically, a pack of wolves; any irregular or casual aggregation of beings; a crowd.

Al the englene *rute.* *Ancren Riwle*, p. 92, note.

Tukked he was, as is a frere, aboute,
And evere he rood the hyndreste of our *route.*
Chaucer, Gen. Prol. to C. T., l. 622.

Alle the *route* [of ants]
A trayne of chalk or askes holdeth oute.
Palladius, Husbondrie (E. E. T. S.), p. 31.

The foresters . . . talk of the chase of the boar and bull, of a *rout* of wolves, etc. *The Academy*, Feb. 4, 1888, p. 71.

2. A disorderly or confused crowd of persons; a tumultuous rabble; used absolutely, the general or vulgar mass; the rabble.

You shall be cast
Into that pitt, with the ungodlie *rout*,
Where the worm dies not, the fire ne're goes out.
Times' Whistle (E. E. T. S.), p. 18.

Whence can sport in kind arise,
But from the rural *routs* and families?
B. Jonson, Sad Shepherd, Prol.

A *rout* of saucy boys
Brake on us at our books, and marr'd our peace.
Tennyson, Princess, v.

3. A large social assemblage; a general gathering of guests for entertainment; a crowded evening party.

I have attended a very splendid *rout* at Lord Grey's. *Macaulay*, in Trevelyan, I. 265.

He found everybody going away from his house, and all to Mrs. Dumplin's *rout;* upon which . . . he painted and described in such glowing colors the horrors of a Dumplin *rout*—the heat, the crowd, the bad lemonade, the ignominy of appearing next day in the Morning Post—that at last, with one accord, all turned back. *Lady Holland*, Sydney Smith, iv.

4. At *common law*, an assemblage of three or more persons breaking or threatening to break the peace; a company which is engaged in or has made some movement toward unlawful action.

rout³† (rout), *v. i.* [‹ ME. *routen*, *ruten* (= Sw. *rota* = Dan. *rotte*), assemble; ‹ *rout*³, *n.*] To collect together; assemble in a company.

In al that lond no Cristen men durste *route.* *Chaucer*, Man of Law's Tale, l. 442.

The meaner sort *routed* together, and, suddenly assailing the earl [of Northumberland] in his house, slew him. *Bacon*, Hist. Hen. VII.

rout⁴ (rout), *n.* [Formerly also *rowt;* ‹ ME. *route*, *rute*, ‹ OF. *route*, *rote*, *rute* = Pr. Sp. Pg. *rota* = It. *rotta*, formerly also *rotto*, a defeat, rout, ‹ ML. *rupta*, defeat, overthrow, rout, ‹ L. *rupta*, fem. of *ruptus*, broken: see *rout*³, which is in form and source identical with *rout*⁴, though differently applied.] A defeat followed by confused or tumultuous retreat; disorderly flight caused by defeat, as of an army or any body of contestants; hence, any thorough repulse, overthrow, or discomfiture: as, to put an army to rout.

Shame and confusion! all is on the *rout.* *Shak.*, 2 Hen. VI., v. 2. 21.

I hope this bout to give thee the *rout*,
And then have at thy purse.
Robin Hood and the Beggar (Child's Ballads, V. 253).

Such a numerous host
Fled not in silence through the frighted deep,
With ruin upon ruin, *rout* on *rout*,
Confusion worse confounded. *Milton*, P. L., ii. 995.

rout⁴ (rout), *v.* [‹ *rout*⁴, *n.*] I. *trans.* 1. To put to rout; drive into disordered flight by defeat, as an armed force; hence, to defeat or repulse thoroughly; drive off or dispel, as something of an inimical character.

Spur through Media,
Mesopotamia, and the shelters whither
The *routed* fly. *Shak.*, A. and C., iii. 1. 9.

Come, come, my Lord, we're *routed* Horse and Foot. *Steele*, Grief A-la-Mode, ii. 1.

O sound to *rout* the brood of cares,
The sweep of scythe in morning dew!
Tennyson, In Memoriam, lxxxix.

They were *routed* in the house, *routed* in the Courts, and *routed* before the people. *Theodore Parker*, Historic Americans, iii.

2. To drive or force, as from a state of repose, concealment, or the like; urge or incite to movement or activity; hence, to draw or drag (forth or out): generally with *out* or *up:* as, to rout *out* a lot of intruders; to rout *up* a sleeper; to rout *out* a secret hoard or a recondite fact. See *router-out.*

Routed out at length from her hiding place. *Barham*, Ingoldsby Legends, I. 123.

=**Syn.** 1. *Overwhelm*, *Overthrow*, etc. See *defeat.*

II. *intrans.* 1†. To crowd or be driven into a confused mass, as from panic following defeat, or from any external force.—2. To start up hurriedly; turn out suddenly or reluctantly, as from a state of repose. [Colloq.]

We have *routed* night after night from our warm quarters, in the dead of winter, to make fires, etc.
Good Housekeeping, quoted in The Advance, Sept. 2, 1886.

rout[5] (rout), *n.* See *route*[1].

rout[6] (rout), *n.* [< Icel. *hrota*, the barnacle-goose, in comp. *hrotgas* = Norw. *rotgaas* = Dan. *rodgaas* (> E. dial. (Orkneys) *roodgoose*), the barnacle-goose. Cf. *routherock*.] The brent- or brant-goose, *Bernicla brenta*. *Encyc. Dict.*

rout-cake (rout'kāk), *n.* A rich sweet cake made for evening parties. [Eng.]

The audience . . . waited . . . with the utmost patience, being enlivened by an interlude of *rout-cakes* and lemonade. *Dickens*, Sketches, Mrs. Joseph Porter.

route[1] (röt or rout), *n.* [Now spelled *route* and usually pron. röt, after mod. F.; historically the proper spelling is *rout* (rout), or, shortened, *rut* (rut), now used in a restricted sense (cf. *rote*[1], a fourth form of the same word); < ME. *route*, *rute*, a way, course, track (see *rut*[1]), < OF. *route*, *rote*, *rute*, a way, path, street, course, a glade in a wood, F. *route*, a way, course, route, = Sp. *rota*, *ruta* = Pg. *rota* (naut.), a way, course, < ML. *rupta*, also, after Rom., *rutta*, *rotta*, *rota*, a way, path, orig. (sc. *via*) a way broken or cut through a forest, fem. of L. *ruptus*, broken: see *rout*[3], *rout*[4].] 1. A way; road; path; space for passage.

He gave the *route* to the blue-bloused peasant.
Shand, Shooting the Rapids, I. 07.

2. A way or course of transit; a line of travel, passage, or progression; the course passed or to be passed over in reaching a destination, or (by extension) an object or a purpose; as a legal or engineering term, the horizontal direction along and near the surface of the earth of a way or course, as a road, a railway, or a canal, occupied or to be occupied for travel.

Wide through the furzy field their *route* they take,
Their bleeding bosoms force the thorny brake.
Gay, Rural Sports, ii. 100.

Ocean-lane route. See *lane-route*.—**Overland route.** See *overland*.—**Star route,** in the United States, a post-route over which the mail is carried, under contract, by other means than steam: so called because the blank contracts for transportation of the mail over such routes have printed upon them three groups of four stars or asterisks each, to identify them as coming under the terms of the act, which refers only to "celerity, certainty, and security" in the mode of transportation—for which words the groups of stars respectively stand. The name became famous from the discovery of extensive frauds in the procurement and execution of star-route contracts, which led in 1881–2 and in 1883 to the indictment and trial of many persons, of whom a few were convicted.—**To get the route** (*milit.*), to receive orders to quit one station for another.

The Colonel calls it [a rose] "Marching Orders." . . . Whenever it settled and began to flower the regiment *got the route*. *J. H. Ewing*, Story of a Short Life, iii.

route[2]† (rout), *v.* and *n.* An obsolete form of *rout*[1], *rout*[2], *rout*[3], *rout*[4].

router (rou'tėr), *n.* [< *rout*[2] + *-er*[1].] In *carp.*, a sash-plane made like a spokeshave, to work on sashes.—**Router-gage,** in inlaid work, a gage used in cutting out the narrow channels in which metal or colored woods are to be laid. It is similar to a common marking-gage, but instead of the marking-point has a narrow chisel as a cutter.—**Router-plane,** a kind of plane used for working out the bottoms of rectangular cavities. The sole of the plane is broad, and carries a narrow cutter which projects from it as far as the intended depth of the cavity. This plane is vulgarly called *old woman's tooth*.—**Router-saw,** a saw used for routing. In setting it, every alternate tooth is left in the plane of the saw. In filing it, the teeth which are set are filed much like those of the cross-cut hand-saw, while the teeth not set are filed more chisel-edged.

Router-plane.
a, stock; *b*, plane-iron or cutter.

router (rou'tėr), *v. t.* [< *router*, *n.*] In *wood-working*, to cut away, or cut out, as material below a general surface, leaving some parts, figures, or designs in relief; rout.

router-out (rou'tėr-out'), *n.* One who routs out, or drives or draws forth, as from repose, concealment, or the like. [Colloq.]

He is a fair scholar, well up in Herodotus, and a grand *router-out* of antiquities. *Quarterly Rev.*, CXLV. 110.

route-step (röt'step), *n.* An order of march in which soldiers are not required to keep step or remain silent, and may carry their arms at will, provided the muzzles are elevated.

routh[1]†, *n.* An obsolete form of *ruth*.

routh[2] (routh), *a.* [Also *rowth*; cf. W. *rhwth*, wide, gaping, *rhwth*, loose, hollow.] Plentiful; abundant. *Jamieson.* [Scotch.]

routh[2] (routh), *n.* [Also *rowth*: see *routh*[2], *a.*] Plenty; abundance. [Scotch.]

Lat never a man a wooing wend
That lacketh thingis three:
A *routh* o' gould, an open heart,
Ay fu' o' charity.
King Henry (Child's Ballads, I. 147).

routherock, *n.* [Also *routhurrock*. Cf. *rout*[6].] The barnacle-goose, *Bernicla leucopsis*.

routhie (rou'thi), *a.* [Also *rowthie*; < *routh*[2] + *-ie* (*-y*[1]).] Plentiful; well-filled; abundant. [Scotch.]

Wait a wee, an' cannie wale [choose]
A *routhie* butt, a *routhie* ben; . . .
It 's plenty beets the luver's fire.
Burns, The Country Lassie.

routier (rö-ti-ā'), *n.* [F., < OF. *routier*, < ML. *ruptarius*, *rutarius*, a trooper, mercenary soldier, a mounted freebooter, < *rupta*, a troop, band: see *rout*[3]; see also *rutter*[1], from the same source.] 1. One of a class of French brigands of about the twelfth century, who infested the roads in companies on horse or foot, and sometimes served as military mercenaries. They differed little from earlier and later organizations of the same kind throughout Europe, under various names.—2. Hence, any undisciplined, plundering soldier, or brigand.

routinary (rö-tē'nạ-ri), *a.* [< *routine* + *-ary*. Cf. F. *routinier*, routinist.] Involving or pertaining to routine; customary; ordinary. [Rare.]

He retreats into his *routinary* existence, which is quite separate from his scientific. *Emerson*, Works and Days.

routine (rö-tēn'), *n.* and *a.* [= Sp. *rutina* = Pg. *rotina*, < F. *routine*, OF. *routine*, *rotine*, *rottine*, a beaten path, usual course of action, dim. of *route*, *rote*, a way, path, course, route: see *route*[1] and *rote*[1].] **I.** *n.* 1. A customary course of action or round of occupation; a way or method systematically followed; regular recurrence of the same acts or kind of action: as, the *routine* of official duties; to weary of a monotonous *routine*.

The very ordinary *routine* of the day.
Brougham, Lord Chatham.

2. Fixed habit or method in action; the habitual doing of the same things in the same way; unvarying procedure or conduct.

A restlessness and excitement of mind hostile to the spirit of *routine*. *Buckle*, Hist. Civilization, I. xiv.

That beneficent harness of *routine* which enables silly men to live respectably and unhappy men to live calmly.
George Eliot, Middlemarch, lxvi.

II. *a.* Habitually practised or acting in the same way; following or consisting in an unvarying round: as, *routine* methods or duties; a *routine* official.

The tendency of such a system is to make mere *routine* men. *J. R. Soley*, Blockade and Cruisers, p. 5.

routineer (rö-ti-nēr'), *n.* [< *routine* + *-eer*.] One who follows routine; an adherent of settled custom or opinion. [Rare.]

The mere *routineer* in gas-making has been shaken out of his complacency. *Sci. Amer.*, N. S., LXII. 259.

routing-machine (rou'ting-mạ-shēn"), *n.* A shaping-machine or shaper for wood, metal, or stone. It works by means of cutting apparatus revolving above a bed with universal horizontal adjustment, and

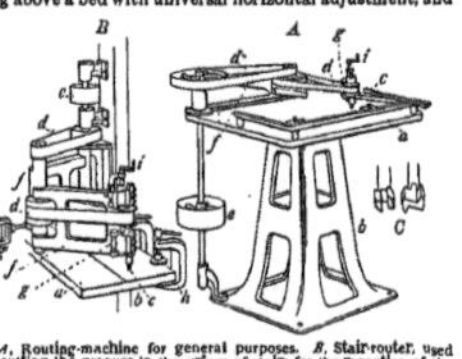

A, Routing-machine for general purposes. *B*, Stair-router, used in cutting the grooves in the strings of stairs for the reception of the ends of the steps and risers. *C*, Router-tools.

a, table; *b*, pedestal; *c*, cutter, whose spindle is driven by the belts *d*, *d*; *e*, main driving-pulley; *f*, *f*, swinging arms or frames by means of which the cutter can be moved to any place on the table; *g*, handle by which *f*, *f* are operated by a workman who follows with the cutter a guiding former or pattern; *g'*, handle sometimes used in manipulating the machine; *h*, clamp which binds the work to the table; *i*, adjusting screw, for regulating depth of cut.

cuts the work to a shape or grooves it to a fixed depth. It executes paneling in relief or intaglio, lettering, slotting, key-seating, beveling, bordering, etc. *E. H. Knight.*

routing-tool (rou'ting-töl), *n.* In *metal-working*, a revolving cutter used for cutting or scraping out scores, channels, and depressions.

routinism (rö-tē'nizm), *n.* [< *routine* + *-ism*.] The spirit or practice of routine; a rigid and unvarying course of action or opinion; routine method or manner.

He deprecated *routinism*, automatism, mechanical prescription in medicine, and vindicated the value of living personal observation and opinion.
Lancet, No. 3449, p. 703.

routinist (rö-tē'nist), *n.* [< *routine* + *-ist*.] An adherent of routine; a follower of unvarying methods or prescribed principles: as, a *routinist* in medicine, in education, etc.

The mere *routinists* and unthinking artisans in most callings dislike whatever shakes the dust out of their traditions. *O. W. Holmes*, Med. Essays, Pref.

routish† (rou'tish), *a.* [< *rout*[1] + *-ish*[1].] Characterized by routing; clamorous; disorderly.

The Common Hall . . . became a *routish* assembly of sorry citizens. *Roger North*, Examen, p. 93. (*Davies.*)

routle (rou'tl), *v. t.*; pret. and pp. *routled*, ppr. *routling*. [Var. of *rootle*, freq. of *root*[2], var. *rout*[2].] To rout out; disturb. *Davies.* [Prov. Eng.]

A misdoubt me if there were a felly there as would ha' thought o' *routling* out yon wasps' nest.
Mrs. Gaskell, Sylvia's Lovers, xxiii.

routous (rou'tus), *a.* [< *rout*[1] + *-ous*.] Noisy. *Halliwell.* [Prov. Eng.]

routously (rou'tus-li), *adv.* [< *routous* + *-ly*[2].] Noisily. *Imp. Dict.*

roux (rö), *n.* [< F. *roux*, a sauce made with brown butter or fat, < *roux*, red, reddish, < L. *russus*, red: see *russet*[1].] In *cookery*, a material composed of melted butter and flour, used to thicken soups and gravies.

Roux's operation. See *operation*.

rouze† (rouz), *v.* An obsolete form of *rouse*[1].

rove[1] (rōv), *v.*; pret. and pp. *roved*, ppr. *roving*. [A back formation, < *rover*, a robber, used generally in the sense of 'a wandering robber,' and hence taken as simply 'a wanderer.' The Icel. *rāfa*, rove, stray about, is not related.] **I.** *intrans.* 1. To wander at pleasure or without definite aim; pass the time in going about freely; range at random, or as accident or fancy may determine; roam; ramble.

The Fauns forsake the Woods, the Nymphs the Grove,
And round the Plain in sad Distractions *rove*.
Congreve, Death of Queen Mary.

I view'd th' effects of that disastrous flame,
Which, kindled by th' imperious queen of love,
Constrain'd me from my native realm to *rove*.
Fenton, in Pope's Odyssey, iv. 360.

Let us suppose a *roving* crew of these soaring philosophers, in the course of an aerial voyage of discovery among the stars, should chance to alight upon this outlandish planet. *Irving*, Knickerbocker, p. 76.

2. To aim, as in archery or other sport, especially at some accidental or casual mark. See *roving mark*, below.

Faire Venus sonne, that with thy cruell dart
At that good knight so cunningly didst *rove*.
Spenser, F. Q., I., Prol., st. 3.

Mont. How now, are thy arrows feather'd?
Vel. Well enough for *roving*.
Shirley, Maid's Revenge, i. 2.

And if you *rove* for a Perch with a minnow, then it is best to be alive. *I. Walton*, Complete Angler, p. 157.

This *roving* archery was far prettier than the stationary game, but success in shooting at variable marks was less favored by practice. *George Eliot*, Daniel Deronda, xiv.

3. To act the rover; lead a wandering life of robbery, especially on the high seas; rob.

To *Roue*, robbe, rapère. *Levins*, Manip. Vocab., p. 179.

And so to the number of forescore of them departed with a barke and a pinnesse, spoiling their store of victuall, and taking away a great part thereof with them, and so went to the Islands of Hispaniola and Jamaica a *roving*.
Hakluyt's Voyages, III. 517.

4. To have rambling thoughts; be in a delirium; rave; be light-headed; hence, to be in high spirits; be full of fun and frolic. [Scotch.]—**Roving mark,** in *archery*, an accidental mark, in contradistinction to butts and targets: trees, bushes, posts, mounds of earth, landmarks, stones, etc., are *roving marks*. *Hansard*, Archery. =**Syn. 1.** *Roam*, *Wander*, etc. See *ramble*, *v.*

II. *trans.* 1. To wander over; roam about.

For Arthur, long before they crown'd him King,
Roving the trackless realms of Lyonnesse,
Had found a glen. *Tennyson*, Lancelot and Elaine.

2†. To discharge or shoot, as an arrow, at rovers, or in roving. See *rover*, 5.

And well I see this writer *roves* a shaft
Nere fairest marke, yet happily not hit it.
Harington, Ep. iv. 11. (*Nares.*)

3. To plow into ridges, as a field, by turning one furrow upon another. [Prov. Eng. and U. S.]

rove[1] (rōv), *n.* [< *rove*[1], *v.*] The act of roving; a ramble; a wandering.

In thy nocturnal *rove*, one moment halt.
Young, Night Thoughts, ix.

Sordello's paradise, his roves
Among the hills and valleys, plains and groves.
Browning, Sordello.

rove[2] (rōv), *v. t.*; pret. and pp. *roved*, ppr. *roving*. [Perhaps an irreg. var. of *reeve*[3] (< *reef*[2]), due to confusion with the pret. *rove*, or of *rive*[1], due to the former pret. *rove*: see *reeve*[3], *rive*[1]. Some take *rove* to be a form of *roll*[1] through Sc. *row*. Others refer to *ruff*[1] = D. *ruif*, a fold.] 1. To draw through an eye or aperture; bring, as wool or cotton, into the form which it receives before being spun into thread; card into flakes, as wool, etc.; slub; sliver.—2. To draw out into thread; ravel out.

rove[2] (rōv), *n.* [Cf. *rove*[2], *v.*] 1. A roll of wool, cotton, etc., drawn out and slightly twisted; a slub.—2. A diamond-shaped washer placed over the end of a rove clench-nail, which is riveted down upon it.—**Rove clench-nail.** See *clench-nail*.

rove[3] (rōv). Preterit and past participle of *reeve*[3].

rove[4]†, *n.* An obsolete form of *roof*[1]. *Chaucer.*

rove[5]†, *n.* [A reduced form of *arroba*.] A unit of weight, the arroba, formerly used in England. The arroba was 25 pounds of Castile, and in England 25 pounds avoirdupois was called a *rove*. The arroba in Portugal contained 32 pounds.

Fotein wool, to wit, French, Spanish, and Estrich, is also sold by the pound or hundredweight, but most commonly by the *rove*, 25 pound to a *rove*.
Recorde, Grounde of Artes (1543), iii. 17.

rove-beetle (rōv'bē″tl), *n.* A brachelytrous coleopterous insect of the family *Staphylinidæ*, especially one of the larger species, such as the devil's coach-horse. The name is sometimes extended to all the brachelytrous beetles, when several of the leading forms are distinguished by qualifying terms. Large-eyed rove-beetles are *Stenidæ*; burrowing rove-beetles, *Oxytelidæ*; broad-bodied rove-beetles, *Omaliidæ*; small-headed rove-beetles, *Tachyporidæ*. The *Pselaphidæ* are sometimes known as *moss-loving rove-beetles*. See also cuts under *devil's coach-horse* (at *devil*), *Homalium*, and *Pselaphus*.

Rove-beetles.
a, larva of *Goerius olens*, enlarged thrice; *b*, pupa of *Quedius molochinus*; *c*, imago of *Philonthus apicalis*. (Lines show natural sizes of *b* and *c*.)

rover (rō'vėr), *n.* [Early mod. E. also *roaver*; < ME. *rover*, *roware*, a var. < D. *roover*, a robber, a pirate, = AS. *reáfere*, ME. *revere*, E. *reaver*, a robber. Doublet of *reaver*.] 1. A robber, especially a sea-robber; a freebooter; a pirate; a forager.

Robare, or robbar yn the see (*rovare*, or thef of the se, K., *rowar*, as thyf on the see, P.), Pirata. *Prompt. Parv.*, p. 437.

And they helped David against the band of the *rovers*; for they were all mighty men of valour. 1 Chron. xii. 21.

The Maltese *rovers* take away every thing that is valuable both from Turks and Christians.
Pococke, Description of the East, II. i. 51.

She may be neither more nor less than the ship of that nefarious pirate the Red *Rover*. *Cooper*, Red Rover, ii.

2. One who roves; a wanderer; one who rambles about, or goes at random from point to point.

Next to thyself and my young *rover*, he 's
Apparent to my heart. *Shak.*, W. T., i. 2. 176.

I'd be a Butterfly; living, a *rover*,
Dying when fair things are fading away!
T. H. Bayly, I'd be a Butterfly.

Hence—3. A fickle or inconstant person.

Man was formed to be a *rover*,
Foolish women to believe.
Mendez, Song in the Chaplet. (*Latham.*)

4. In *archery*: (*a*) A person shooting at a mark with a longbow and arrow, or shooting merely for distance, the position of the archer being shifted with every shot, and not confined to a staked-out ground. The flight-arrow was used by the rover. (*b*) An arrow used by a rover. See *flight-arrow*.

O yes, here be of all sorts—flights, *rovers*, and butt-shafts. B. Jonson, Cynthia's Revels, v. 3.

(*c*) An irregular or uncertain point to be aimed at; also, a mark at an uncertain or indefinite distance.

The Bowar is a marke incertaine, sometimes long, sometimes short, and therefore must haue arrowes lighter or heauier, according to the distance of the place.
G. Markham, Country Contentments (ed. 1615), p. 108.

6. In *arch.*, any member, as a molding, that follows the line of a curve.—7. In *croquet*: (*a*) A ball that has gone through all the hoops, and only needs to strike the winning-stake to be out of the game. (*b*) A player whose ball is in the above condition.—**To shoot at rovers**, in *archery*: (*a*) To shoot an arrow for distance or at a mark, but with an elevation, not point-blank; or to shoot an arrow at a distant object, not the butt, which was nearer. (*b*) To shoot at random, or without any particular aim.

Providence never *shoots at rovers*. *South*, Sermons.

rover (rō'vėr), *v. i.* [< *rover*, *n.*] To shoot at rovers; shoot arrows at other marks than the butt; shoot for height or distance.

rover-beetle (rō'vėr-bē″tl), *n.* A salt-water insect, *Bledius cordatus*.

rovery† (rō'vėr-i), *n.* [< *rove*1 + *-ery*. Cf. *reavery*, *robbery*.] The action of a rover; piratical or predatory roving.

These Norwegians, who with their manifold robberies and *roveries* did most hurt from the Northern Sea, took up their haunt into this Iland.
Holland, tr. of Camden, II. 205. (*Davies.*)

rovescio (rọ̄-vesh'iō), *n.* [It., var. of *rivescio*, the reverse, the wrong side, = Sp. Pg. *reves* = F. *revers*, < L. *reversus*, reverse: see *reverse*. The It. Sp. Pg. forms are irregular, and indicate confusion or borrowing from the F.] In *music*, imitation either by reversion or by inversion. See *imitation*, 3.

roving[1] (rō'ving), *n.* [Verbal n. of *rove*[1], *v.*] 1. The act of rambling or wandering.

The numberless *rovings* of fancy, and windings of language. *Barrow*, Sermons, I. 177. (*Latham.*)

2. Archery as practised by a rover. See *rover*, 4.

roving[2] (rō'ving), *n.* [Verbal n. of *rove*[2], *v.*] 1. The process of giving the first twist to yarn, or of forming a rove.—2. A slightly twisted sliver of carded fiber, as wool or cotton; a rove.

roving-frame (rō'ving-frām), *n.* 1. In *cotton-manuf.*, a machine in which a number of slivers from the carder are taken from the cans and united, stretched, and compacted into rovings. Sometimes called *roving-machine*. See *drawing-frame*.—2. In *worsted-manuf.*, a machine which takes two slivers from the cans of the drawing-frame, elongates them four times, and twists them together. Also called *roving-head*. *E. H. Knight.*

roving-head (rō'ving-hed), *n.* Same as *roving-frame*, 2.

rovingly (rō'ving-li), *adv.* In a roving or wandering manner.

roving-machine (rō'ving-ma̤-shēn″), *n.* A machine for winding slubbings on bobbins for creels of spinning-machines.

rovingness (rō'ving-nes), *n.* A state of roving; disposition to rove.

roving-plate (rō'ving-plāt), *n.* An iron or steel scraper which is held at an inclination against the grinding-surface of a rotating grindstone, for giving it a true circular form, scraping off ridges, or obliterating grooves that may be formed in it by the grinding of pointed or curvilinear-edged tools.

roving-reel (rō'ving-rēl), *n.* A device for measuring the length of a roving, sliver, or hank of yarn, etc. It consists essentially of two flat-faced wheels, between which the yarn is made to pass, the revolutions of one of the wheels, as turned by a crank, being recorded by a dial and serving to measure the yarn.

row[1] (rō), *v.* [< ME. *rowen*, *rouwen* (pret. *rowede*, earlier (and still as a survival) *rew*, *reow*), < AS. *rōwan* (pret. *reów*) = D. *roeijen* = MLG. *rōien*, *rōjen*, *rōen*, LG. *rojen* = MHG. *rūon*, *rūgen*, *rūen*, *rüejen* = Icel. *rōa* = Sw. *ro* = Dan. *roe*, row; akin to OIr. *rām*, an oar, L. *rēmus*, an oar, Gr. ἐρετμόν, an oar, ἐρέτης, a rower, Skt. *aritra*, a rudder, paddle, etc., √ *ar*, drive, push. Hence ult. *rudder*[1].] **I.** *trans.* 1. To impel (a boat) along the surface of water by means of oars. In ancient times rowing was the chief means of propulsion for vessels of all sizes then existing; and large galleys in the Mediterranean continued to be rowed till the nineteenth century. The service on the galleys, both ancient and modern, was very laborious. In later times it was generally performed by slaves or criminals chained to the bars or benches.

Row the boat, my mariners,
And bring me to the land!
The Lass of Lochroyan (Child's Ballads, II. 108).

2. To transport by rowing: as, to *row* one across a stream.

II. *intrans.* 1. To labor with the oar; use oars in propelling a boat through the water; be transported in a boat propelled by oars.

Merie sungen the muneches binnen Ely
Tha [when] Cnut Ching *rew* thare by.
Historia Eliensis, quoted in Chambers's Eng. Lit., I. 8.

And thei *rowiden* to the cuntree of Gerasenus, which is agens Galilee. *Wyclif*, Luke viii. 26.

Propostrous Wits, that cannot *rowe* at ease
On the smooth Chanell of our common Seas.
Sylvester, tr. of Du Bartas's Weeks, i. 4.

2. To be moved by means of oars: as, the boat *rows* easily.—**Rowed of all**, an order given to oarsmen to stop rowing and unship the oars.—**To row dry.** (*a*) To handle the oars in rowing so as to avoid splashing water into the boat. (*b*) To go through the motions of rowing in a boat swung at the davits of a ship, as a sailor in punishment for some offense connected with boats or rowing. The forced exercise is called a *dry row*. [Colloq. in both uses.]

row[1] (rō), *n.* [< *row*[1], *v.*] An act of rowing; also, an excursion taken in a rowboat.

Wondering travelers go for an evening *row* on the Caspian, to visit the submarine oil-springs to the south of the town of Baku. *Pop. Sci. Mo.*, XXVI. 254.

row[2] (rō), *n.* [Also dial. *rew*, < ME. *rowe*, *rewe*, *raw*, *rawe*, < AS. *rāw*, *rǣw*, a row, line; akin to (*a*) OD. *rijge*, *rijg*, D. *rij* = MLG. *rige*, LG. *rige*, *reoe* = OHG. *rīga*, *rīga*, MHG. *rige*, a row; (*b*) MHG. *rihe*, G. *reihe*, a series, line, row; from the verb, OHG. *rīhan*, MHG. *rīhen*, string together (Teut. √ *rihw*); cf. Skt. *rēkhā*, line, stroke.] 1. A series of things in a line, especially a straight line; a rank; a file: as, a *row* of houses or of trees; *rows* of benches or of figures; the people stood in *rows*; to plant corn in *rows*.

To hakke and hewe
The okes olde and leye hem on a *rewe*.
Chaucer, Knight's Tale, l. 2008.

My wretchedness unto a *row* of pins,
They'll talk of state. *Shak.*, Rich. II., iii. 4. 26.

The bright Seraphim, in burning *row*,
Their loud uplifted angel trumpets blow.
Milton, Solemn Music.

2†. A line of writing.

Which whoso willeth for to knowe,
He moste rede many a *rowe*
In Virgile or in Claudian,
Or Daunte, that it telle can.
Chaucer, House of Fame, l. 448.

3†. A streak, as of blood. Compare *rowy*.

The bloody *rowes* stremed doune over al,
They him assayled so maliciously.
Lamentation of Mary Magdalene, l. 120.

4. A hedge. *Halliwell.* [Local, Eng.]—5. A continuous course or extent; a long passage. [This sense, now obsolete in general use, appears in the unique *Rows* of Chester in England, which are open public galleries or lines of passage running along the fronts of the houses in the principal streets, generally over the first stories, covered by the projecting upper stories, lined with shops on the inner side, and reached by stairs from the street.]

6. A line of houses in a town, standing contiguously or near together; especially, such a line of houses nearly or quite alike, or forming an architectural whole: sometimes used as part of the name of a short street, or section of a street, from one corner to the next.—7. In *organ-building*, same as *bank*[1], 7, or *keyboard*.—**A hard or a long row to hoe.** See *hoe*[1].—**Harmonic row.** See *harmonic*.—**To hoe one's own row.** See *hoe*[1].

row[2] (rō), *v. t.* [< *row*[2], *n.*] To arrange in a line; set or stud with a number of things ranged in a row or line.

Bid her wear thy necklace *row'd* with pearl.
Parnell, Elegy to an Old Beauty.

row[3] (rou), *n.* [Of obscure slang origin; vaguely associated with *rowdy*, *rowdydow*, and perhaps due in part to *rout*[1]. The Icel. *hrjā*, a rout, struggle, can hardly be related.] A noisy disturbance; a riot; a contest; a riotous noise or outbreak; any disorderly or disturbing affray, brawl, hubbub, or clatter: a colloquial word of wide application.

Next morning there was a great *row* about it [the breaking of a window].
Barham, in Mem. prefixed to Ingoldsby Legends, I. 35.

They began the *row*, . . . and then opened upon Germany a career of scepticism, which from the very first promised to be contagious. *De Quincey*, Homer, i.

We turned in about eleven o'clock, it not being possible to do so before on account of the *row* the men made talking. *E. Sartorius*, In the Soudan, p. 92.

To kick up a row. Same as *to kick up a dust* (which see, under *dust*[1]).=**Syn.** Uproar, tumult, commotion, broil, affray.

row[3] (rou), *v.* [< *row*[3], *n.*] **I.** *trans.* 1. To injure by rough and wild treatment: as, to *row* a college room (that is, to damage the furniture in wild behavior). [Slang.]—2. To scold; abuse; upbraid roughly or noisily. [Colloq.]

Tell him [Campbell] all this, and let him take it in good part; for I might have rammed it into a review and *rowed* him. *Byron*, To Mr. Murray, May 20, 1820.

II. *intrans.* To behave in a wild and riotous wi y; engage in a noisy dispute, affray, or the like.

If they are found out, the woman is not punished, but they *row* (probably a mild kind of fight).
Anthrop. Jour., XIX. 420.

More disposed to *rowing* than reading.
Bristed, Five Years in an English Univ.

row[4], *v.* A Scotch form of *roll*.

row[5], *a.* and *v.* An obsolete or dialectal form of *rough*[1].

To certifie vs whether our set clothes be vendible there or not, and whether they be *rowed* and shorne; because ofttimes they goe vndrest. *Hakluyt's Voyages*, I. 298.

rowable† (rō'a-bl), *a.* [< *row*[1] + *-able*.] Capable of being rowed or rowed upon. [Rare.]

That long barren fen,
Once *rowable*, but now doth nourish men
In neighbour towns, and feels the weighty plough.
B. Jonson, tr. of Horace's Art of Poetry.

rowan (rou'an), *n.* [Also *roan, roun*; < OSw. *rönn, runn*, Sw. *rönn* = Dan. *rön* = Icel. *reynir*, the service, sorb, mountain-ash; cf. L. *ornus*, the mountain-ash.] 1. The rowan-tree.—2. The fruit or berry of the rowan-tree.

rowan-berry (rou'an-ber"i), *n.* Same as *rowan*, 2.

rowan-tree (rou'an-trē), *n.* The mountain-ash of the Old World, *Pyrus aucuparia*; also, less properly, either of the American species *P. Americana* and *P. sambucifolia*. See *mountain-ash*, 1. Also *roan-tree, roun-tree*.

rowboat (rō'bōt), *n.* [< *row*[1] + *boat*.] A boat fitted for propulsion by means of oars; a boat moved by rowing.

row-cloth (rō'klôth), *n.* [< *row*[5] + *cloth*.] A folding cloak, made of a kind of warm but coarse cloth completely dressed after weaving. *Halliwell*. [Prov. Eng.]

row-de-dow (rou'dē-dou), *n.* Same as *rowdydow*.

row-dow (rou'dou), *n.* The sparrow, *Passer domesticus*. Also *roo-doo*. [Prov. Eng.]

rowdy (rou'di), *n.* and *a.* [Perhaps an abbr. of *rowdydow*, noise, confusion, an imitative word transferred to a noisy, turbulent person: see *rowdydow*. Cf. *row*[3].] I. *n.*; pl. *rowdies* (-diz). A riotous, turbulent fellow; a person given to quarreling and fighting; a rough.

"A murderer?" "Yes; a drunken, gambling cut-throat *rowdy* as ever grew ripe for the gallows."
Kingsley, Two Years Ago, x.

II. *a.* Having the characteristics of a rowdy; given to rowdyism; rough; coarse-grained; disreputable.

For a few years it [Victoria] was a very *rowdy* and noisy colony indeed. *W. Besant*, Fifty Years Ago, p. 8.

rowdydow (rou'di-dou), *n.* [Also *row-de-dow*; an imitative word, prob. orig. formed, like *rub-a-dub*, in imitation of the beat of a drum. Cf. *row*[3], *rowdy*.] A continuous noise; a rumpus; a row. [Colloq.]

rowdy-dowdy (rou'di-dou"di), *a.* [< *rowdydow* + *-y*[1]; the two parts being made to rime.] Making a rowdydow; uproarious. [Colloq.]

rowdyish (rou'di-ish), *a.* [< *rowdy* + *-ish*[1].] Belonging to or characteristic of a rowdy; characterized by or disposed to rowdyism: as, *rowdyish* conduct; *rowdyish* boys.

They give the white people very little trouble, being neither *rowdyish* nor thievish. *The Century*, XXIX. 835.

rowdyism (rou'di-izm), *n.* [< *rowdy* + *-ism*.] The conduct of a rowdy or rough; coarse turbulence; vulgar disorderliness.

The presence of women in these places [barrooms] appears to have the effect of eliminating the element of *rowdyism*. You hear no loud conversation, oaths, or coarse expressions. *T. C. Crawford*, English Life, p. 121.

rowed (rōd), *a.* [< *row*[2] + *-ed*[2].] 1. Having rows; formed into rows.

In 1869 he sowed . . . seed from an 18-*rowed* ear [of maize]. *Amer. Jour. Psychol.*, I. 178.

2. Striped: same as *rayed*, 3.

rowel (rou'el), *n.* [< ME. *rowel, rowelle, rowell*, < OF. *rouelle, roiele, roele, rouele*, a little wheel or flat ring, a roller on a bit, F. *rouelle*, a slice, = Pr. Sp. *rodela*, a shield, target, = Cat. *rodella* = Pg. *rodella*, a round target, = It. *rotella*, a little wheel, a buckler, round spot, kneepan, < ML. *rotella*, a little wheel, dim. of L. *rota*, a wheel: see *rota*[1]. Cf. *rotella*.] 1†. A small wheel, ring, or circle.

The *rowelle* whas rede golde with ryalle stones.
Morte Arthure (E. E. T. S.), l. 3263.

And then, for wings, the golden plumes she wears
Of that proud Bird [the peacock] which starry *Rowells* bears.
Sylvester, tr. of Du Bartas's Weeks, ii., The Columnes.

2. The wheel of a horseman's spur, armed with pointed rays.

Not having leisure to put off my silver spurs, one of the *rowels* catched hold of the ruffle of my boot.
B. Jonson, Every Man out of his Humour, iv. 4.

Lord Marmion turn'd — well was his need —
And dash'd the *rowels* in his steed.
Scott, Marmion, vi. 14.

3. A roller on the mouthpiece of an old form of bit for horses.

The yron *rowels* into frothy fome he bitt.
Spenser, F. Q., I. vii. 37.

4. In *farriery*, a seton inserted in the flesh of an animal. Rowels are made of horsehair, leather, and sometimes of silk, as is the practice with setons inserted in the human body.
5. The spiked wheel of some forms of soil-pulverizers and wheel-harrows.—**Foliated rowel**, a rowel without points, or very blunt, as distinguished from a *star-rowel* and *rose-rowel*.—**Rose-rowel**, a rowel having short points, taking about one sixth of the diameter.—**Star-rowel**, a rowel having long points, taking at least one third of the total diameter of the circle.

rowel (rou'el), *v. t.*; pret. and pp. *roweled* or *rowelled*, ppr. *roweling* or *rowelling*. [< *rowel*, *n.*] 1. To use the rowel on; put spurs to.—2. In *farriery*, to apply a rowel to.

Rowel the horse in the chest. *Mortimer*, Husbandry.

He has been ten times *rowell'd*.
Beau. and Fl., Scornful Lady, iii. 2.

3. To furnish with a rowel, as a spur.

rowel-bone†, *n.* A variant of *rewel-bone*.

rowel-head (rou'el-hed), *n.* The axis on which the rowel of a spur turns.

Bending forward, [he] struck his armed heels
Against the panting sides of his poor jade
Up to the *rowel-head*. *Shak.*, 2 Hen. IV., i. 1. 46.

roweling, rowelling (rou'el-ing), *n.* [Verbal n. of *rowel*, *v.*] The act of inserting a rowel.

roweling-needle (rou'el-ing-nē"dl), *n.* A needle with a large eye, for carrying the bundle of horsehair, silk, or the leather thong forming a rowel, and either straight or curved according to the nature of the part in which the rowel is required to be inserted.

roweling-scissors (rou'el-ing-siz"orz), *n. sing.* and *pl.* A farriers' instrument for inserting rowels in the flesh of horses, for cutting the silk or other material forming the seton.

rowel-spur (rou'el-spėr), *n.* A spur having a rowel of several radiating points, as distinguished from the *goad-spur*. This appears in mediæval monuments during the thirteenth century, as in the

Rowel-spur, 14th century.

first great seal of King Henry III. of England, but is extremely rare before the beginning of the fourteenth; it is probable that the earliest rowels did not turn upon a pivot. Pivoted rowel-spurs with very long spikes, not very sharp, are in common use in western parts of the United States and in Spanish-American countries generally. They are fastened to the heel of the riding-boot by a broad leather strap passing over the instep, and often have special devices to make them clank or jingle.

rowen (rou'en), *n.* [A dial. form, also *rouen, rowings* (and *rowet, rowett*), of *roughings*: see *roughings*.] 1. The lattermath, or second crop of hay cut off the same ground in one year.—2. A stubble-field left unplowed till late autumn, and furnishing a certain amount of herbage. [Prov. Eng.; usually in plural form.]

Turn your cows that give milk into your *rowens* till snow comes. *Mortimer*, Husbandry.

rower[1] (rō'ėr), *n.* [< ME. *rowere, roware*; < *row*[1] + *-er*[1].] One who rows, or manages an oar in rowing.

The whole party being embarked, therefore, in a large boat, . . . the exertions of six stout *rowers* sped them rapidly on their voyage. *Scott*, Heart of Mid-Lothian, xlv.

rower[2] (rou'ėr), *n.* [< *row*[3] + *-er*[1].] One given to rows; a quarrelsome or disorderly fellow.

rower[3]† (rou'ėr), *n.* [< *row*[5] + *-er*[1].] A workman who roughens cloth preparatory to shearing; a rougher.

rowet, rowett (rou'et), *n.* Same as *rowen*. [Prov. Eng.]

rowet-work (rou'et-wėrk), *n.* [< F. *rouet*, a wheel-lock, spinning-wheel, dim. of *roue*, a wheel: see *rowel*.] The lock and appurtenances of a wheel-lock gun. See the quotation under *snapwork*, and cut under *wheel-lock*.

rowey, *a.* See *rowy*.

rowiness (rō'i-nes), *n.* The state of being rowy; streakiness; striation. [Now only technical.]

A process [skimming] which demands very careful attention in the case of curd soaps, lest any portions of lye should be accidentally entangled in the soap, producing want of homogeneity, called *rowiness*.
W. L. Carpenter, Soap and Candles, p. 174.

The Karanee Teak has alternate shades of dull brown and yellow colour, the grain being close and long, with occasionally a *rowiness* or figure in it, and is also very free from defects. *Laslett*, Timber, p. 116.

rowing (rō'ing), *n.* [< ME. *rowynge*, < AS. **rōwung, rōwing*, verbal n. of *rōwan*, row: see *row*[1], *v.*] The act or practice of propelling a boat by means of oars. See *row*[1], *v. t.*

rowing-feather (rō'ing-feᴛʜ"ėr), *n.* See *feather*.

rowing-gear (rō'ing-gēr), *n.* Any device or contrivance used in rowing; especially, a mechanical device for facilitating the handling of the oars.

rowl†, **rowlet**, *v.* and *n.* Obsolete forms of *roll*.

Rowland gratings. In *optics*. See *diffraction*, 1.

rowler†, *n.* An obsolete form of *roller*.

rowlet (rou'let), *n.* [< F. *roulette*, a little wheel, fem. of *roulet*, dim. of OF. *roule*, a roll, a little wheel: see *roll, rowel, roulette*. Doublet of *roulette*.] A small broad wheel; a wheel like a roller. [Now only dialectal.]

Rails of timber, laid down from the collieries to the river, . . . were worked with bulky carts made with four *rowlets* fitting the rails.
S. Dowell, Taxes in England, III. 64.

Rowley rag. See *rag*[1].

rowlock (rō'lok), *n.* [Also *rollock, rullock*; prob. a transposition (as if < *row*[1] + *lock*[1]) of *oarlock*, < ME. *orlok*, < AS. *ārlōc*, an oarlock, < *ār*, oar, + *loc*, a lock, bolt, bar, inclosed place (cf. E. *oarhole*, an oarlock): see *oar*[1] and *lock*[1].] A contrivance on a boat's gunwale in or on which the oar rests and swings freely in rowing. The principal kinds of rowlocks are—(1) a notch in the gunwale (as in the first illustration), which may be either square or rounded, and is usually lined with metal; (2) two short pegs, called *thole-pins*, projecting from the gunwale, between which the oar is placed; (3) a stirrup-shaped swivel of metal pivoted in the gunwale (as in the second illustration), or on an outrigger. Sometimes a single pin set into the gunwale is used instead of a rowlock, the oar having a hole through which the pin passes, or vice versa, or being fastened to it by means of a thong or gromet.

Ship's Boat. *a a*, Rowlocks (notched).

Rowlock.

rowly-powly†, *n.* Same as *roly-poly*.

row-marker (rō'mär"kėr), *n.* In *agri.*, an implement for marking out the ground for crops to be planted in rows.

rowne†, *n.* An obsolete form of *roe*[2].

row-port (rō'pōrt), *n.* A little square hole in the side of small vessels, near the water-line, for the passage of a sweep for rowing in a calm.

rows (rōz), *n. pl.* In *mining*, same as *roughs*. See *rough*[1], *n.*, 4.

rowsandt, rowsant†, *a.* In *her.*, obsolete forms of *rousant*.

rowse, *v.* See *rouse*[1].

rowt†, *v.* and *n.* An obsolete spelling of *rout*[1], *rout*[2], etc.

rowth, rowthie. See *routh*[2], *routhie*.

rowy (rō'i), *a.* [< *row*[2], *n.*, + *-y*[1].] Having rows or lines; streaked or striped; striated. Also spelled, improperly, *rowey*. [Now only technical. See the second quotation.]

Rowy or stricky [streaky], as some stuffs are.
Howell. (*Halliwell*.)

Is there such a word in the English language as *rowey*? . . . Frequently, through some fault in weaving, a piece of cloth will be thinner in some places than others; this occurs at regular intervals through the whole piece, for which reason it is styled *rowey*, as the thin places extend across the piece similar to the lines on writing-paper. In the several mills with which I have been connected, *rowey* was the technical term applied to such goods. . . . I have examined all the books at my disposal, but have been unable to find it. *Cor. Boston Evening Transcript*, June 4, 1883.

roxburghe (roks'bur-ǫ), *n.* [See def.] A binding for books, first used by the third Duke of Roxburghe (1740–1804), having a plain leather back lettered in gold near the top, and cloth or paper sides, with the leaves gilt at the top and uncut at the edge.

Printed at the Chiswick Press, on laid paper, with wide margins, in limp covers, 10s. 6d. net; in *roxburghe*, 12s. 6d. net. *The Academy*, May 24, 1890, p. ii.

Roxburghia (roks-bėr'gi-ạ), *n.* [NL. (Sir Joseph Banks, 1795), named after W. *Roxburgh*, a British botanist in India.] A genus of plants, now known as *Stemona*.

Roxburghiaceæ (roks-bėr-gi-ā′sē-ē), *n. pl.* [NL. (Wallich, 1832), < *Roxburghia* + *-aceæ*.] An order of monocotyledonous plants, now known as *Stemonaceæ*.

Roxbury waxwork. See *waxwork*.

royt, *n.* [< ME. *roy*, also *ray*, < OF. *roy*, *rei*, F. *roi* = Pr. *roi*, *rey*, *re* = Sp. *rey* = Pg. *rey*, *rei* = It. *re*, < L. *rex* (*reg-*), a king, = OIr. *rig*, Ir. Gael. *righ*, a king, = Skt. *rājan*, a king: see *rex*, *raja*[1], *regent*, and *rich*[1], *riche*[1], *n.*] A king.

This *roy* with his ryalle mene of the rownde table.
Morte Arthure (E. E. T. S.), l. 3174.

royal (roi′al), *a.* and *n.* [Early mod. E. also *roial* (also dial. or technically *rial*, *ryal*); < ME. *roial*, *roiall*, *reyal*, *real*, *rial*, *ryal*, *ryall*, *rioll*, < OF. *roial*, *royal*, *real*, F. *royal* = Pr. *reial*, *rial* = Sp. Pg. *real* = It. *reale*, *reale*, < L. *regalis*, regal, royal, kingly, < *rex* (*reg-*), a king: see *roy*, and cf. *regal*[1] and *real*[2], doublets of *royal*.] **I.** *a.* **1.** Of or pertaining to a king; derived from or cognate to a king; belonging to or connected with the crown of a kingdom; regal: as, the *royal* family; a *royal* prince; *royal* domains; a *royal* palace.

And seide that he wolde holde court open and enforced, and sente by his messangers that alle sholde come to his court *roiall*. *Merlin* (E. E. T. S.), iii. 479.

Why should thy servant dwell in the *royal* city with thee? 1 Sam. xxvii. 5.

Thou camest not of the blood *royal*, if thou darest not stand for ten shillings. *Shak.*, 1 Hen. IV., i. 2. 157.

2. Pertaining or relating to the sovereign power of a king; acting under, derived from, or dependent upon regal authority, aid, or patronage: as, a *royal* parliament or government; the *royal* army or navy; *royal* purveyors. *Royal* enters into the names of many literary, scientific, artistic, and other associations in monarchical countries, implying their existence under royal charter or patronage: *e. g.*, the Royal Academy of Arts in London, whose members are distinguished by the title R. A. (Royal Academician), and the associate members by the title A. R. A.; the Royal Institution of London, for the promotion of and instruction in scientific and technical knowledge; the Royal Society of London for Improving Natural Knowledge (usually designated specifically *the Royal Society*), which takes charge of many scientific matters with which the government is concerned, and whose members or fellows are styled F. R. S.; the Royal Societies of Edinburgh and of Dublin, the Royal Antiquarian, Asiatic, Astronomical, and Geographical Societies, etc.

3. Of kingly character or quality; proper for or suitable to kingship; ideally like or characteristic of a king or royalty; royally eminent, excellent, or the like: used either literally or figuratively: as, *royal* state or magnificence; he proved a *royal* friend; a right *royal* welcome.

And thei made the teste of the mariage so *riall* that neuer in that londe was seyn soche.
Merlin (E. E. T. S.), ii. 320.

A kyng shold *roiall* obsequy haue.
Rom. of Partenay (E. E. T. S.), l. 1538.

Hath she forgot already that brave prince, . . .
Young, valiant, wise, and, no doubt, right *royal*?
Shak., Rich. III., i. 2. 245.

As at this day, to the Tartars, Horseflesh is *royall* fare; to the Arabians, Camels; to some Americans, Serpents.
Purchas, Pilgrimage, p. 39.

Her step was *royal*, queen-like, and her face
As beautiful as a saint's in Paradise.
Longfellow, Spanish Student, i. 1.

4. Large or superior of its kind; of more than ordinary size, excellence, or the like: used as a specific qualification, as in *royal* quarto or *royal* octavo in printing, a *royal* antler or stag, etc., or as an assertion of superiority for that to which it is applied, as in the names of some articles of trade.—**Amercement, antler, astronomer, ballade, battle, beast, chapel, cygnet royal.** See the nouns.—**Convention of royal burghs.** See *convention*.—**Coroner of the royal household.** See *coroner*.—**Dean of the chapel royal, gentleman of the chapel royal.** See *dean*[2], *gentleman*.—**Hart royal.** See *hart*[1] and *hartroyal*.—**Pair royal.** See *pair*[1].—**Peer of the blood royal.** See *peer*[2].—**Prince royal, princess royal.** See *prince*, *princess*.—**Royal abbey.** See *abbey*[1], 1.—**Royal agate**, a mottled variety of obsidian.—**Royal American Order.** Same as *Order of Isabella the Catholic* (which see, under *order*).—**Royal assent, bark.** See the nouns.—**Royal bay.** (*a*) An East Indian bay-tree, *Machilus odoratissima* (*Laurus Indica*). (*b*) The bay-laurel, *Laurus nobilis*.—**Royal Bengal tiger.** See *tiger*.—**Royal bistoury**, a narrow, curved, probe-pointed bistoury: so called because used in an operation on Louis XIV.—**Royal blue.** See *blue* and *smalt*.—**Royal bounty**, in England, a fund from which the sovereign grants money to the female relatives of officers who die of wounds received when on duty.—**Royal burgh, cement, glove.** See the nouns.—**Royal cashmere**, a thin material, generally made of pure wool, used for garments for women and summer garments for men.—**Royal charter.** See *charter*, 1.—**Royal domains.** Same as *crown lands* (which see, under *crown*).—**Royal fern.** See *Osmunda*.—**Royal fishes.** See *royal fishes*, under *regal*[1].—**Royal flush.** See *flush*[5].—**Royal folio.** See *folio*, 4.—**Royal grant**, a grant by letters patent from the crown.—**Royal horned caterpillar**, the larva of *Citheronia regalis*, a large bombycid moth of beautiful olive and crimson colors, which inhabits the United States. The larva feeds on the foliage of the black walnut, persimmon, butternut, hickory, and sumac,

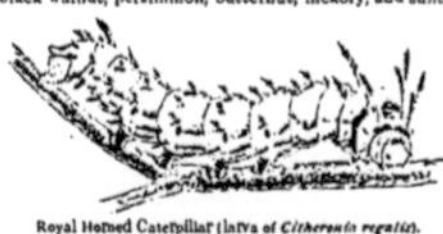

Royal Horned Caterpillar (larva of *Citheronia regalis*).
(About half natural size.)

and is the largest of all North American lepidopterous larvæ. The moth is popularly known as the *royal walnut-moth*.—**Royal household**, the body of persons employed about the court or in the personal service of a reigning king or queen. In former times the royal household included all the chief officers of state, who were regarded as merely the king's servants, and often performed menial duties toward him; afterward, only persons who had special functions relating to the royal needs, dignity, or prerogatives. In the British royal household, as it has existed for several centuries, the chief officers are the lord steward, lord chamberlain, and master of the horse, who are always peers and members of the government of the time. Under each of them are many subordinate officers, among whom the different branches of their duty are distributed. Independent of them are the private secretary and the keeper of the privy purse to the sovereign, modern additions to the household, with their subordinates. When there is a queen consort, the queen's household is a separate establishment, similarly though less elaborately organized. On the accession of Queen Victoria the expenses of the royal household were permanently fixed at £303,760 per annum.—**Royal letter.** See *letter*[3].—**Royal marines.** See *marine*.—**Royal merchant.** (*a*) One of those merchants of the middle ages who combined mercantile pursuits with princely power, as those of Venice who founded principalities in the Archipelago, the Grimaldi of Genoa, or the Medici of Florence. (*b*) A merchant who managed the mercantile affairs of or purveyed for a sovereign or state.—**Royal mine**, in monarchical countries, a mine of gold or silver—all such mines being by prescription the property of the crown.—**Royal oak.** (*a*) See *oak*. (*b*) [*caps.*] Another name for the constellation Robur Caroli.—**Royal palm, palmetto.** See the nouns.—**Royal peacock-flower.** See *Poinciana*.—**Royal peculiar, prerogative, purple.** See the nouns.—**Royal regiment of artillery.** See *artillery*.—**Royal road to knowledge**, a direct and easy method of attaining knowledge: so called because the royal roads were straighter and better than ordinary roads.—**Royal Society.** See def. 2.—**Royal standard.** See *standard*.—**Royal stitch**, an old operation for the cure of inguinal hernia.—**Royal tern, touch, water-lily**, etc. See the nouns.—**Royal Vienna**, a name frequently given to Vienna porcelain.—**Royal Worcester porcelain.** See *porcelain*[1].—**The royal doors** or **gates.** See *door*.=**Syn.** *Royal*, *Regal*, *Kingly*. *Regal* is applicable primarily to what pertains to a king in virtue of his office, and hence to what is proper to or suggestive of a king, and as now frequently used is nearly synonymous with *princely*, *magnificent*: as, *regal* state or pomp; *regal* power. *Royal* notes what pertains to the king as an individual, or is associated with his person: as, his *royal* highness (applied to a prince of the blood); the *royal* family; the *royal* presence; the *royal* robes; a *royal* salute. It does not, like *regal*, necessarily imply magnificence. Thus, a *royal* residence may not be *regal* in its character, while on the other hand any magnificent mansion belonging to a subject may be described as *regal*, though it is not *royal*. The sway of a great Highland chief of old was *regal*, but not *royal*. Hence, in figurative use, *royal* is applied to qualities, actions, or things which are conceived of as superlatively great, noble, or admirable in themselves, or as worthy of a king: as, a *royal* disposition, *royal* virtues, a *royal* entertainment, etc.; *regal*, to those which make an impression of the highest grandeur, stateliness, ascendancy, or the like: as, a *regal* bearing, *regal* munificence, *regal* commands, etc. *Kingly* seems to be intermediate. It signifies literally like a king, hence proper to or befitting a king, and in its more general use resembling or suggestive of a king. Like *royal*, it has reference to personal qualities: as, a *kingly* bearing, presence, disposition, and the like; while, like *regal*, it is not restricted to the monarch or members of his house.—**3.** Imperial, august, majestic, superb, splendid, magnificent, illustrious.

II. *n.* **1**†. A royal person; a member of a royal family; a king or prince.

And also wythout the forsayde cyte metyng vs our moder oure wyff our chyldren or oure cyrs or other *reyals* to the same cyte comyng, etc.
Charter of London, in Arnold's Chronicle, p. 36.

He araiet for that *Rioll*, all of Riche stones,
A faire toumbe & a fresshe, all of fre marbill.
Destruction of Troy (E. E. T. S.), l. 7150.

2†. A gold coin formerly current in England: same as *ryal*.

The prieste, purposyng to gratifie the dead, and with dewe praise to commende his liberalitie, saieth: surely he was a goode manne, a verteous man, yea, he was a noble gentleman. I thinke if it hadde been his happe to have had a *roiall*, he had called him a roiall gentleman to.
Wilson, Rule of Reason.

Roials of Spaine are currant mony there.
Hakluyt's Voyages, II. 177.

They are incompetent witnesses, his own creatures,
And will swear any thing for half a *royal*.
Fletcher, Spanish Curate, iii. 3.

3. *Naut.*, a small square sail, usually the highest on a ship, carried on the royalmast only in a light breeze.—**4.** One of the tines of a stag's antlers; an antler royal, or royal antler. See *antler*, 3.—**5.** A stag which has the antler royal.

A *royal* differs only in having an extra point on each horn. *W. W. Greener*, The Gun, p. 510.

6. In *artillery*, a small mortar.—**7.** That part of the beard which grows below the under lip and above the point of the chin, especially when the beard around it is shaved. This with the mustache has long formed the trim of the beard most in favor for military men, etc., on the continent of Europe. The term *royal* prevailed until the second French empire, when the name *imperial* was given to it, as it was worn by Napoleon III.

8. A writing-paper of the size 19 × 24 inches; also, a printing-paper of the size 20 × 25 inches. A royal folio has a leaf about 12 × 20 inches; a royal quarto is about 10 × 12½ inches; a royal octavo, about 6¼ × 10 inches.—**Double royal.** See *double*.—**Quadruple royal.** See *quadruple*.—**The Royals.** (*a*) A name formerly given to the first regiment of foot in the British army, now called the *Royal Scots* (Lothian Regiment). (*b*) A name sometimes given to other regiments in whose title the word *royal* occurs: as, the King's *Royal* Rifle Corps; the *Royal* Scots Fusiliers, etc.

royalet (roi′al-et), *n.* [< *royal* + *-et*. Cf. *roitelet*.] A petty king or prince. [Rare.]

There were, indeed, at this time two other *royalets*, as onely kings by his leave. *Fuller*, Ch. Hist., II. iv. 10.

Pallas and Jove! defend me from being carried down the stream of time among a shoal of *royalets*, and the rootless weeds they are hatched on!
Landor, Epicurus, Leontion, and Ternissa.

royalise, *v.* See *royalize*.

royalism (roi′al-izm), *n.* [= F. *royalisme* = Sp. Pg. *realismo*; as *royal* + *-ism*. Cf. *regalism*.] The principles or cause of royalty; attachment to a royal government or cause.

royalist (roi′al-ist), *n.* and *a.* [= F. *royaliste* = Sp. Pg. *realista* = It. *realista*, *regalista*; as *royal* + *-ist*.] **I.** *n.* A supporter of a king or of royal government; one who adheres to or upholds the cause of a king against its opponents or assailants. Specifically [*cap.*]—(*a*) In *Eng. hist.*, one of the partizans of Charles I. and of Charles II. during the civil war and the Commonwealth; a Cavalier, as opposed to a Roundhead.

Where Ca'ndish fought, the *royalists* prevail'd.
Waller, Epitaph on Colonel Charles Cavendish.

(*b*) In *Amer. hist.*, an adherent of the British government during the revolutionary period. (*c*) In *French hist.*, a supporter of the Bourbons as against the revolutionary and subsequent governments.

II. *a.* Of or pertaining to Royalists or royalism; adhering to or supporting a royal government.

Royalist Antiquarians still show the rooms where Majesty and suite, in these extraordinary circumstances, had their lodging. *Carlyle*, French Rev., II. i. 1.

The battle of Marston Moor, with the defeat of the *Royalist* forces, . . . was the result. *Encyc. Brit.*, VIII. 347.

royalize (roi′al-īz), *v.*; pret. and pp. *royalized*, ppr. *royalizing*. [< F. *royaliser*; as *royal* + *-ize*.] **I.** *trans.* To make royal; bring into a royal state or relation.

Royalizing Henry's Albion
With presence of your princely mightiness.
Greene, Friar Bacon and Friar Bungay.

To *royalize* his blood I spilt my own.
Shak., Rich. III., i. 3. 125.

II. *intrans.* To exercise kingly power; bear royal sway. [Rare.]

Euen He (my Son) must be both Iust and Wise,
If long he look to Rule and *Royalize*.
Sylvester, tr. of Du Bartas's Weeks, ii., The Magnificence.

Also spelled *royalise*.

royally (roi′al-i), *adv.* [< ME. **roially*, *rially*, *riolly*, *realliche*; < *royal* + *-ly*[2].] In a royal or kingly manner; like a king; as becomes a king.

In Ensample of this Cite, sothely to telle,
Rome on a Riuer *rially* was set.
Destruction of Troy (E. E. T. S.), l. 1610.

Did I not tell thee
He was only given to the book, and for that
How *royally* he pays?
Fletcher, Spanish Curate, ii. 4.

royalmast (roi′al-mȧst), *n.* The highest part of a full-rigged ship's mast, the fourth from the deck, above and now generally in one piece with the topgallantmast, for carrying the sail called the royal. See cut under *ship*.

royalty (roi′al-ti), *n.*; pl. *royalties* (-tiz). [< ME. **roialte*, *realtee*, *realte*, *reaute*, *rialte*, < OF. *roialte*, *royaulte*, *royaute*, *reialte*, F. *royauté* = It. *realtà*, < ML. *regalita(t-)s*, < L. *regalis*, royal, regal: see *royal*, *regal*[1]. Cf. *regality*, *realty*[2], doublets of *royalty*.] **1.** The state or condition of being royal; royal rank or extraction; existence as or derivation from a king or a royal personage.

Setting aside his high blood's *royalty*,
And let him be no kinsman to my liege,
I do defy him. *Shak.*, Rich. II., i. 1. 58.

2. Royal personality; concretely, a royal personage, or member of a royal family; collectively, an aggregate or assemblage of royal persons: as, *royalty* absented itself; discrowned *royalties*.

As a branch and member of this *royalty*, . . .
We do salute you, Duke of Burgundy.
Shak., Hen. V., v. 1. 5.

3. Royal authority; sovereign state; kingly rule or majesty; kingship, either as an attribute or as a principle.

Now, hear our English king;
For thus his *royalty* doth speak in me.
Shak., K. John, v. 2. 129.

England, notwithstanding the advantages of politic *royalty*, had fallen into trouble. *Stubbs*, Const. Hist., § 365.

4. The character of being kingly, or proper to a king; royal quality, literally or figuratively; kingliness.

In his *royalty* of nature
Reigns that which would be fear'd.
Shak., Macbeth, iii. 1. 50.

There is no true *royalty* but in the rule of our own spirits. *Channing*, Perfect Life, p. 114.

5. That which pertains or is proper to a king or sovereign; a sovereign right or attribute; regal dominion or prerogative; a manifestation or an emblem of kingship.

You were crown'd before,
And that high *royalty* was ne'er pluck'd off.
Shak., K. John, iv. 2. 5.

Wherefore do I [Satan] assume
These *royalties* and not refuse to reign?
Milton, P. L., ii. 451.

6. A royal domain; a manor or possession belonging to the crown.

The titles of the several *royalties* which thus came to an end [when Cyprus was conquered by the Turks] were claimed, as titles easily may be claimed, by other competitors. *Stubbs*, Medieval and Modern Hist., p. 204.

7. A royal due or perquisite; especially, a seigniorage due to a king from a manor of which he is lord; a tax paid to the crown, or to a superior as representing the crown, as on the produce of a royal mine.

For to my Muse, if not to me,
I'm sure all game is free;
Heaven, earth, all are but parts of her great *royalty*.
Randolph, Ode to Master Anthony Stafford.

With the property [an estate in Denbighshire] were inseparably connected extensive *royalties*. *Macaulay*, Hist. Eng., xxi.

Hence—8. (*a*) A compensation paid to one who holds a patent for the use of the patent, or for the right to act under it, generally at a certain rate for each article manufactured. (*b*) A proportional payment made on sales, as to an author or an inventor for each copy of a work or for each article sold.—9. In Scotland, the area occupied by a royal burgh, or (in the plural) the bounds of a royal burgh.—**Ensigns of royalty.** See *regale*[2], 3.

royal-yard (roi al-yärd), *n.* *Naut.*, the yard of the royalmast, on which the royal is set.

Royena (roi'e-nä), *n.* [NL. (Linnæus, 1753), named after Adrian van *Royen*, a Dutch botanist of the 18th century.] A genus of gamopetalous trees and shrubs of the order *Ebenaceæ*, the ebony family. It is characterized by flowers which are commonly bisexual (the family being chiefly diœcious), with a broad urn-like or bell-shaped five-lobed calyx enlarging under the fruit, five contorted and reflexed corolla-lobes, stamens commonly ten and in one row, anthers and ovary usually hirsute, styles two to five, and the ovary-cells twice as many and one-ovuled. The 13 species are natives of southern Africa in and beyond the tropics. They bear small leaves which are nearly or quite sessile, and axillary solitary or clustered urn-shaped flowers, followed by a coriaceous roundish or five-angled fruit. The wood of *R. pseudebenus* and other species resembles ebony, but the trees are small. *R. lucida*, known as *African snowdrop*, or *African bladder-nut*, is a pretty greenhouse species with white flowers and shining leaves.

roylet, *v. t.* An obsolete form of *roil*[2].

roynet, *n.* See *roin*.

roynisht, *a.* See *roinish*.

roynoust, *a.* See *roinous*.

royster, roysterer, etc., *n.* See *roister*, etc.

Royston crow. [Formerly also *Roiston crow*.] The gray crow, *Corvus cornix*.

Corneille emmantelée, the *Roiston Crow*, or Winter Crow, whose back and belly are of an ashie colour. *Cotgrave*.

roytelett, *n.* An obsolete form of *roitelet*.

roytisht (roi'tish), *a.* [Perhaps for **riotish* or *routish*.] Wild; irregular.

No Weed presum'd to show its *roytish* face.
J. Beaumont, Psyche, vi. 140.

rozelle, *n.* See *roselle*.

R. S. V. P. An abbreviation of the French phrase *Répondez s'il vous plaît* ('answer, if you please'), appended to a note of invitation or the like.

Rt. Hon. An abbreviation of the title *Right Honorable*.

Rt. Rev. An abbreviation of the title *Right Reverend*.

Ru. The chemical symbol of *ruthenium*.

ruana (rö-an'ä), *n.* A variety of viol used in India.

rub (rub), *v.*; pret. and pp. *rubbed*, ppr. *rubbing*. [< ME. *rubben*; origin uncertain; cf. Dan. *rubbe* (< E.?); Gael. *rub*, rub, Ir. Gael. *rubadh*, a rubbing, Ir. *ruboir*, Gael. *rubair*, a rubber, W. *rhwbio*, rub, *rhwb*, a rub. The Celtic forms may be original.] **I.** *trans.* 1. To apply pressure with motion to the surface of; apply friction to by chafing or fretting with something else: as, to *rub* the face with a towel; to *rub* one hand with the other.

Sone this doctour,
As rody as a rose, *rubbed* his chekes,
Coughed and carped. *Piers Plowman* (B), xiii. 99.

His disciples plucked the ears of corn, and did eat, *rubbing* them in their hands. Luke vi. 1.

2. To smooth, polish, clean, or coat by means of friction or frictional applications: as, to *rub* brasses or silver; to *rub* a floor; to *rub* furniture.

Go, sir, *rub* your chain with crums. *Shak.*, T. N., ii. 3. 128.

Let but these fits and flashes pass, she will shew to you
As jewels *rubb'd* from dust, or gold new burnish'd.
Fletcher, Wildgoose Chase, iv. 1.

As bees . . . on the smoothed plank,
The suburb of their straw-built citadel,
New *rubb'd* with balm, expatiate, and confer
Their state affairs. *Milton*, P. L., i. 774.

3. To treat, act upon, or remove by frictional pressure; act with or upon by friction: with *out, off, in*, etc.: as, to *rub out* marks, spots, or stains; to *rub off* rust; to *rub in* a liniment; to *rub up* an ointment in a mortar.

In such cases, the painter's deep conception of his subject's inward traits . . . is seen after the superficial coloring has been *rubbed off* by time. *Hawthorne*, Seven Gables, iv.

4. To take an impression of by friction; apply frictional pressure to, as an engraved or sculptured figure or inscription, for the purpose of copying. See *rubbing*, 2.

I believe that . . . nearly all of them [monumental brasses in England] have been *rubbed*, so that if, by any untoward chance, the originals should perish, a memorial of them will still remain. *N. and Q.*, 6th ser., X. 26.

5. Figuratively, to affect in any way as if by frictional contact or pressure; furbish; fret: as, to *rub* (usually *rub up*) one's memory; to *rub* one the wrong way. See phrases below.

'Tis the duke's pleasure,
Whose disposition, all the world well knows,
Will not be *rubb'd* nor stopp'd.
Shak., Lear, ii. 2. 161.

6. To cause to move over another body with friction: as, to *rub* one's hand over a mirror.—**Rubbed tints**, in *chromolithography*, tints produced on the stone by rubbing freely upon it colored inks formed into blocks or masses. The ink is distributed, the superfluous part removed, or in parts softened down as required, by means of a cloth or stump. Where more force or detail is required, inks in crayon form are used.—**Rubbed work**, in *building*, work in stone or brick smoothed by rubbing with gritstone aided by sand and water.—**To rub a thing in**, to make a disagreeable thing still more disagreeable by repeating it or emphasizing it. [Colloq.]—**To rub down.** (*a*) To rub from top to bottom, from head to foot, or all over, for any purpose: as, to *rub down* a horse after a hard run.

Opportunities for petty thefts occur . . . which necessitate the large body of dock police, with the custom of *rubbing down* each labourer [for the detection of stolen articles] as he passes the dock gates.
Nineteenth Century, XXII. 487.

(*b*) To reduce or bring to smaller dimensions by friction; smooth or render less prominent by rubbing.

We *rub* each other's angles *down*.
Tennyson, In Memoriam, lxxxix.

To **rub elbows**. See *elbow*.—To **rub off**, to clean or clear off, or get rid of, by or as if by rubbing: as, to *rub off* dust; to *rub off* one's rusticity. See def. 3.—To **rub out**. (*a*) To erase or remove by rubbing: as, to *rub out* figures on a slate. (*b*) To spread by rubbing; diffuse over a surface with a rubbing instrument: as, to *rub out* paint. —**To rub the hair** (or **fur**) **the wrong way**, to excite or irritate by petty opposition or bickering or by an inopportune or indiscreet remark: in allusion to the effect produced on a cat by such a rubbing of its hair. Sometimes, by contraction, to *rub the wrong way* (with or without a person as object).

It is no unusual drawback to married life, this same knack of *rubbing the hair the wrong way*; and I think it helps to bring a very large proportion of cases into the "Court of Probate, &c."
Whyte Melville, White Rose, I. xxv.

"Your ladyship is kind to forewarn me," said Philip, who was always *rubbed the wrong way* by Lady Flanders.
J. Hawthorne, Dust, p. 291.

To **rub up**. (*a*) To burnish; furbish, polish, or clean by rubbing. (*b*) To blend or otherwise prepare by trituration: as, to *rub up* an ointment. (*c*) To awaken or excite by effort; rouse; freshen: as, to *rub up* the memory.

But, David, has Mr. De-la-grace been here? I must *rub up* my balancing, and chasing, and boring.
Sheridan, The Rivals, iii. 4.

II. *intrans.* 1. To move or act with friction; exert frictional pressure in moving: as, to *rub* against or along something.

This last allusion gall'd the Panther more,
Because indeed it *rubb'd* upon the sore.
Dryden, Hind and Panther, iii. 132.

2. Figuratively, to proceed with friction or collision; do anything with more or less effort or difficulty: commonly with *on, along, through*, etc.

We had nearly consumed all my pistoles, and now just *rubbed on* from hand to mouth.
Franklin, Autobiog., p. 73.

People now seem to think that they will *rub on* a little longer. *Walpole*, Letters, II. 231.

They *rubb'd through* yesterday
In their hereditary way,
And they will *rub through*, if they can,
To-morrow on the self-same plan.
M. Arnold, Resignation.

Most of us learn to be content if we can *rub along* easily with our life-partners.
R. T. Cooke, Somebody's Neighbors, p. 103.

3. In the old game of bowls, to touch or graze the jack or another ball with the bowl or played ball.

Cost. Challenge her to bowl.
Boyet. I fear too much *rubbing*.
Shak., L. L. L., iv. 1. 141.

rub (rub), *n.* [< *rub*, *v.*; cf. W. *rhwb*, a rub.] 1. An act or the action of rubbing; an application or occurrence of frictional contact: as, to ake a *rub* with a towel; to give something a *rub*.

The surgeon had been sitting with his face turned towards the fire, giving the palms of his hands a warm and a *rub* alternately. *Dickens*, Oliver Twist, i.

The bolsters between the cheeks, to take the *rub* of the cable. *Thearle*, Naval Arch., § 232.

The relief is to be onely water, the *rub* [of race-horses] but half an hour, and then the Judge is to bid them mount.
Quoted in *N. and Q.*, 7th ser., VI. 421.

2. A metaphorical rubbing or chafing; an irritating or disturbing act or expression; interference; affront; sarcasm, gibe, or the like.

Bristol can literary *rubs* despise;
You'll wonder whence the wisdom may proceed;
'Tis doubtful if her aldermen can read.
Chatterton, Kew Gardens.

I had the management of the paper; and I made bold to give our rulers some *rubs* in it.
Franklin, Autobiog., p. 31.

3. That which opposes or checks, as if from friction; any chafing or disturbing circumstance or predicament; an impediment, embarrassment, or stumbling-block; a pinch.

To die, to sleep;
To sleep: perchance to dream: ay, there's the *rub*.
Shak., Hamlet, iii. 1. 65.

Perceiuing that their power and authoritie would be a perillous *rub* in his way. *Purchas*, Pilgrimage, p. 243.

I have no crosse, no *rub* to stop my sute.
Marston, What you Will, i. 1.

They are well inclined to marry, but one *rub* or other is ever in the way. *Burton*, Anat. of Mel., p. 555.

Upon the death of a prince among us, the administration goes on without any *rub* or interruption.
Swift, Sentiments of Ch. of Eng. Man, ii.

We sometimes had those little *rubs* which Providence sends to enhance the value of its favours.
Goldsmith, Vicar, i.

4†. An unevenness of surface or character; a roughness or inequality; an imperfection; a flaw; a fault.

To leave no *rubs* nor botches in the work.
Shak., Macbeth, iii. 1. 134.

A gentleman, excepting some few *rubs*, . . .
Fraughted as deep with noble and brave parts . . .
As any he alive. *Fletcher*, Wit without Money, i. 2.

My floor is not so flat, so fine,
And has more obvious *rubs* than thine.
Quarles, Emblems, ii. 11.

5†. Inequality of the ground in a bowling-green.

A *rub* to an overthrown bowl proves a help by hindering it. *Fuller*, Holy State, i. 11.

6. In *card-playing*, same as *rubber*, 6. [Colloq.]

"Can you one?" inquired the old lady. "I can," replied Mr. Pickwick. "Double, single, and the *rub*."
Dickens, Pickwick, vi.

7. A rubstone. [Prov. Eng.]

rubadub, rub-a-dub (rub'a-dub), *n.* [Imitative of the sound of the drum; cf. *rataplan*, etc.] The sound of a drum when beaten; a drumming sound; hence, any disturbing clatter.

The drum advanced, beating no measured martial tune, but a kind of *rub-a-dub-dub*, like that with which the fire-drum startles the slumbering artizans of a Scotch burgh.
Scott, Waverley, xxxiv.

No drum-head, in the longest day's march, was ever more incessantly beaten and smitten than public sentiment in the North has been, every month, and day, and hour, by the din, and roll, and *rub-a-dub* of Abolition writers and Abolition lecturers.
D. Webster, Speech, Senate, July 17, 1850.

rubarb†, *n.* An obsolete spelling of *rhubarb*.

rubasse (rö-bas′), *n.* [< F. *rubace*, *rubasse*, also dim. *rubacelle*, colored quartz, < L. *rubeus*, red, reddish: see *ruby*, *red*[1].] A lapidaries' name for a beautiful variety of rock-crystal, limpid or slightly amethystine, speckled in the interior with minute spangles of specular iron, which reflect a bright red color. The best rubasse comes from Brazil. An artificial kind is made by heating rock-crystal red-hot, and then plunging it into a coloring liquid. The crystal becomes full of cracks, which the coloring matter enters. Also called *Ancona ruby* and *Mont Blanc ruby*.

rubato (rö-bä′tō), *a.* [< It. *rubato*, lit. 'stolen' (time), pp. of *rubare*, steal, rob: see *rob*[1].] In *music*, in modified or distorted rhythm: especially used of the arbitrary lengthening of certain notes in a measure and the corresponding shortening of others, for the purpose of bringing some tone or chord into decided prominence without altering the total duration of the measure.

rubbage (rub′āj), *n.* An obsolete or dialectal form of *rubbish*.

rubbee (rub′ē), *n.* Same as *rabi*[2].

rubber (rub′ėr), *n.* and *a.* [< *rub* + *-er*[1]. Cf. Ir. *ruboir*, Gael. *rubair*, a rubber.] **I.** *n.* **1.** A person who rubs, or who practises rubbing of any kind as a business, as one employed in rubbing or polishing stone, one who attends and rubs down horses (as those used for racing), one who practises massage, etc.

The strike of the stone-workers . . . began . . . when the *rubbers* and mill men made a demand.
New York Semi-weekly Tribune, Sept. 23, 1888.

All the great trotters have had grooms, or *rubbers*, as they are technically called. *The Atlantic*, LXIII. 701.

2. An instrument, substance, or stuff used for rubbing, or cleaning or polishing by friction. Specifically—(*a*) A towel or piece of cloth for rubbing the body after bathing, rubbing down horses, cleaning or polishing household articles, etc.

The retiring bower,
So furnish'd as might force the Persian's envy,
The silver bathing-tub, the cambric *rubbers*,
The embroider'd quilt. *Massinger*, Guardian, ii. 5.

Clean your plate, wipe your knives, and rub the dirty tables with the napkins and tablecloths used that day; for . . . it will save you wearing out the coarse *rubbers*.
Swift, Advice to Servants (Butler).

(*b*) A piece of caoutchouc used to erase pencil-marks from paper, etc. From this, the first use to which caoutchouc was put, it came to be called *rubber*, or *India rubber* (now *india-rubber*). See def. 3. (*c*) A brush consisting of wool, felt, chamois-skin, or other substance fastened to a back, used for erasing chalk from a blackboard or slate. (*d*) In *stone-work*: (1) An implement used in grinding or polishing. In the moldings of stone, an iron rubber mounted on a wooden stock is employed for fillets, heads, and astragals. These rubbers have convex or concave faces, according to the required contour of the work. A stone or wooden block covered with thick felt is used for polishing stone and marble. *E. H. Knight.* (2) An implement for polishing marble, consisting of a mass of rags compressed by screws in an iron frame. (*e*) A tool for rubbing or flattening down the seams of a sail in sail-making. (*f*) The cushion of an electric machine, by friction against which the plate becomes charged with one kind of electricity and the rubber with the opposite kind. The rubber is made of horsehair, and covered with leather overlaid with a metallic preparation, sometimes consisting of the bisulphid of tin, or an amalgam, usually of zinc, tin, and mercury. (*g*) A whetstone, rubstone, or rubbing-stone. (*h*) A coarse file, or the rough part of it. (*i*) A device for applying French polish to furniture, etc. It consists of a small ball of wadding covered with a linen rag. This is saturated with the varnish, and then covered with another rag moistened with oil. The varnish oozes gradually through the outside rag as the rubber is passed over the work with a uniform circular motion. (*j*) A grinding or abrading agent, as emery-cloth or glass-paper for surfacing plates. (*k*) The part of a wagon-lock which presses against the wheels.

3. India-rubber; caoutchouc. See def. 2 (*b*), and *india-rubber*.—**4.** Something made partly or wholly of india-rubber or caoutchouc. (*a*) An overshoe: usually in the plural. [U. S.] (*b*) A tire for the wheel of a bicycle.

5. An inequality of the ground in a bowling-green; a rub; hence, obstruction; difficulty; unpleasant collision in the business of life.

A man who plays at bowls . . . must expect to meet with *rubbers*. *Thackeray*, Virginians, xxix.

6. *pl.* In the game of bowls, a contact or collision of two bowls. *Halliwell.*—**7.** A limited series of games, usually three, as at whist, in which the contest is decided by the winning of the greater number of games; also, the decisive game in such a series.

It is the trade of man, and ev'ry sinner
Has play'd his *rubbers*; every soul 's a winner.
Quarles, Emblems, i. 10.

Brazilian or **Ceara rubber.** See *india-rubber*.—**Hard rubber**, hardened india-rubber of which solid articles are made. See *ebonite* and *vulcanite*.—**Para rubber.** See *india-rubber*.—**White rubber**, a preparation of hard rubber colored by mixture of a white pigment. See *artificial ivory*, under *ivory*.

II. *a.* Made of caoutchouc or india-rubber; having caoutchouc as the principal component.

The feet and legs as high up as the hips [were] incased in *rubber* boots. . . . *Rubber* coats completed the outfit.
New York Tribune, Feb. 2, 1890.

Rubber cement. See *cement*.—**Rubber cloth.** (*a*) A fabric coated with caoutchouc. (*b*) Caoutchouc in sheets.—**Rubber dam**, a thin sheet of flexible caoutchouc, used by dentists to keep a tooth free from saliva while it is being filled.—**Rubber mold**, in *dentistry*, a vulcanite mold in which plates for artificial dentures are shaped. *E. H. Knight.*—**Rubber mop.** See *mop*[3].—**Rubber mounting**, in *saddlery*, harness-mounting in which the metal is covered with vulcanized india-rubber in imitation of leather-covered work. *E. H. Knight.*—**Rubber stamp**, an instrument for stamping by hand with ink, having words or figures cast in slightly flexible vulcanized rubber.—**Rubber type**, a separate type cast in rubber, usually mounted on a metal body for use in stamping.

rubber-file (rub′ėr-fīl), *n.* A heavy file of square, triangular, or half-round section, used for the coarsest work.

rubber-gage (rub′ėr-gāj), *n.* A device for measuring the amount of india-rubber needed to make a given article. It is a vessel in which a model of the article is submerged in water to ascertain its displacement, which is measured by an index or read off on a scale.

rubberide (rub′ėr-id), *n.* [< *rubber* + *-ide*[1].] A trade-name for an imitation of vulcanized rubber. The principal ingredient in this imitation is said to be shellac.

rubberite (rub′ėr-īt), *n.* [< *rubber* + *-ite*[2].] A trade-name for an imitation of vulcanite or vulcanized rubber.

rubber-knife (rub′ėr-nīf), *n.* Same as *rubber-saw*.

rubber-mold (rub′ėr-mōld), *n.* A flask or form for shaping plastic rubber.

rubberoid (rub′ėr-oid), *n.* A trade-name for an imitation of hard rubber.

rubbers (rub′ėrz), *n. pl.* [Pl. of *rubber*.] **1.** A disease in sheep characterized by heat and itching. Also called *scab*, *shab*, or *ray*.—**2.** Same as *rubber*, 4 (*a*).

rubber-saw (rub′ėr-sâ), *n.* An incongruous name for a circular rotary knife used for cutting caoutchouc. In use it is rotated at high speed, and is kept constantly wet by a jet or spray of water. Also called *rubber-knife*.

rubber-tree (rub′ėr-trē), *n.* Same as *india-rubber tree* (which see, under *india-rubber*).

rubber-vine (rub′ėr-vīn), *n.* Same as *india-rubber vine* (which see, under *india-rubber*).

rubbidge (rub′ij), *n.* An obsolete, dialectal, or vulgar form of *rubbish*.

rubbing (rub′ing), *n.* [< ME. *rubbynge*; verbal n. of *rub*, *v.*] **1.** An application of friction by any means; a frictional movement, as of the hand over the surface of the body for remedial purposes.

There is, however, the scar of an old injury. . . . This is not to be reached by our *rubbings*, frictions, and electricity. *Lancet*, No. 3495, p. 889.

He was hardened sufficiently for a Northern winter by trunk and spine *rubbings* twice a day.
Sci. Amer., N. S., LXI. 296.

2. A copy of an inscribed, engraved, or sculptured surface procured by rubbing superimposed paper with something, as heel-ball or plumbago, that reproduces the outlines and saliences on its exposed side. Compare *squeeze*, *n.*

The walls at the head of the staircase . . . are now occupied by a fine series of *rubbings* of foreign brasses and incised slabs. *Athenæum*, No. 3244, p. 902.

The drawing is a copy of a *rubbing*, and is therefore correct. *Amer. Antiq.*, IX. 366.

rubbing-batten (rub′ing-bat″n), *n.* Same as *rubbing-panch*. See *panch*.

rubbing-bed (rub′ing-bed), *n.* In *marble-working*, a bench with a stone or marble surface, on which a slab of marble is placed to be subdivided by a grub-saw.

rubbing-block (rub′ing-blok), *n.* In *marble-polishing*: (*a*) A block of sandstone with which the preliminary operation of smoothing is done by hand. (*b*) A marble-polisher, marble-rubber, or marble-scourer.

rubbing-machine (rub′ing-ma-shēn″), *n.* In *linen-bleaching*, a machine in which the cloth is subjected to friction between the corrugated surfaces of two planks, of which the upper is moved back and forth over the lower by a crank-shaft.

rubbing-panch (rub′ing-pânch), *n.* *Naut.* See *panch*.

rubbing-post (rub′ing-pōst), *n.* A post of wood or stone set up for cattle to rub themselves against.

These Kistvaens are numerous, but they have been generally deprived of their long covering stones, which have been converted to *rubbing-posts* (as they are termed in the west of England) for the cattle.
Archæologia, XXII. 434.

rubbing-stone (rub′ing-stōn), *n.* In *building*, a gritstone for polishing or erasing the tool-marks on a stone, or on which bricks for gaged work, after they have been rough-shaped by the ax, are rubbed smooth.

rubbish (rub′ish), *n.* [Formerly or dial. also *rubbidge*, *rubbage*; early mod. E. *rubyes*, also *rubbrysshe*, *robrisshe* (with intrusive r, prob. due to confusion with similar forms of *rubric*); < ME. **robous*, *robows*, *robeux* (ML. *rubbosa*), < OF. *robous*, *robouse*, **robeux*, rubbish, pl. of **robel* (> E. *rubble*), dim. of *robe*, *robbe*, rubbish, trash, = OIt. *roba*, *robba*, It. *roba*, rubbish, trash, lit. 'spoil' (> *robaccia*, old goods, trifles, trash, rubbish, *robiccia*, trifles, rubbish): see *rube*, *rob*[1], *rubble*. Not connected with *rub*.] **1.** Waste, broken, or worn-out material; useless fragments or remains collectively, especially of stone; refuse in general.

Will they revive the stones out of the heaps of the *rubbish* which are burned? Neh. iv. 2.

The reprobate . . . are but the *rubbish* wherewith the vessels of honour are scoured.
Rev. T. Adams, Works, II. 392.

The earth is raised up very much about this gate, and all over the south end of the island, probably by the *rubbish* of a town of the middle ages.
Pococke, Description of the East, I. 118.

2. Any useless or worthless stuff; that which serves no good purpose, or is fit only to be thrown away; trash; trumpery; litter: used of both material and immaterial things.

What trash is Rome,
What *rubbish* and what offal, when it serves
For the base matter to illuminate
So vile a thing as Cæsar! *Shak.*, J. C., i. 3. 109.

Such conceits as these seem somewhat too fine among this *rubbage*, though I do not produce them in sport.
Sir H. Wotton, Reliquiæ, p. 12.

There was enough of splendid *rubbish* in his life to cover up and paralyze a more active and subtile conscience than the judge was ever troubled with.
Hawthorne, Seven Gables, xv.

That not one life shall be destroy'd,
Or cast as *rubbish* to the void,
When God hath made the pile complete.
Tennyson, In Memoriam, liv.

rubbish-heap (rub′ish-hēp), *n.* A pile of rubbish; a mass of worthless or rejected material.

The idol of to-day is often destined to find its place in the *rubbish-heap* of the future.
Nineteenth Century, XXVI. 781.

He yet found no difficulty in holding that the fragments of pottery accumulated in that great *rubbish-heap* in Rome, the Monte Testaccio, were works of nature, not of human art. *Quarterly Rev.*, CXLV. 116.

rubbishing (rub′ish-ing), *a.* [< *rubbish* + *-ing*[2].] Rubbishy; trashy; worthless; paltry.

This is the hend, is it, . . . of my taking notice of that *rubbishing* creature, and demeaning myself to patronize her? *Dickens*, Nicholas Nickleby, xlii.

Listen to the ringing this or that—sometimes a *rubbishing* proclamation, etc.
The Nation, Oct. 24, 1872, p. 257.

rubbish-pulley (rub′ish-pụ̈l″i), *n.* A simple form of tackle-block used with a rope in hoisting materials from a foundation or excavation; a gin-block. *E. H. Knight.*

rubbishy (rub′ish-i), *a.* [< *rubbish* + *-y*[1].] Worthless; trashy; paltry; full of rubbish; containing rubbish.

Rome disappoints me much; . . .
Rubbishy seems the word that most exactly would suit it.
All the foolish destructions, and all the sillier sayings,
All the incongruous things of past incompatible ages,
Seem to be treasured up here to make fools of present and future. *Clough*, Amours de Voyage, i. 1.

On one side is a *rubbishy* church that has on the balustrade of the steps four plaster figures cut off at the waist and planted on posts.
C. D. Warner, Roundabout Journey, p. 112.

rubble (rub′l), *n.* [Early mod. E. *rubble*, *rubbell*; < ME. **robel*, < OF. **robel*, in pl. **robeux*, dim. of *robe*, *robbe*, rubbish, trash, = OIt. *roba*, *robba*, It. *roba*, trash: see *rubbish*.] **1.** Rough stones of irregular shapes and sizes, broken from larger masses either naturally or artificially, as by geological action, in quarrying, or in stone-cutting or blasting. Rubble is used in masonry both for rough, uncoursed work and for filling in between outer courses of squared stone. See *rubble-work*.

Cary away *rubbell* or brokele of olde decayed houses.
Huloet, 1552.

The sub-soil is the disintegrated portion of the rock below, and this often forms a "brash," a term applied to the *rubble* formed on the limestones, especially in the Oölitic strata. *Woodward*, Geol. of Eng. and Wales (2d ed.), p. 51.

2. Masonry of rubble; rubble-work.—3. By extension, any solid substance in irregularly broken pieces. (*a*) A mass or aggregation of irregular pieces of ice broken off by the action of heavy floes, as in the arctic seas.

By dint of extraordinary exertions the sledge was got through the *rubble* to a palæocrystic floe, but the rough work necessitated the relashing of the boat on the sledge. *A. W. Greely*, Arctic Service, p. 230.

(*b*) The whole of the bran of wheat before it is sorted into pollard, bran, etc. [Prov. Eng.]—**Random rubble.** See *rubble-work*.—**Rubble drain.** See *drain*.—**Snecked rubble**, masonry laid up with rough or irregular stones, but so fitted as to preserve a strong bond. See *rubble-work*, *snecking*.

rubble-ice (rub'l-īs), *n.* Fragmentary ice; rubble. See *rubble*, 3 (*a*).

Stopped by dense *rubble-ice*, which extended as far south as could be seen. *Schley and Soley*, Rescue of Greely, p. 210.

rubble-stone (rub'l-stōn), *n.* Same as *rubble*, 1.

rubble-walling (rub'l-wâ″ling), *n.* Same as *rubble-work*.

rubble-work (rub'l-wėrk), *n.* Masonwork built of rubble-stone. Rubble walls are either coursed or uncoursed: in the former the stones are roughly dressed and laid in courses, but without regard to equality in the height of the courses; in the latter (called *random rubble*) the stones are used as they occur, the interstices between them being filled in with smaller pieces, or with mortar or clay, etc.

rubbly (rub'li), *a.* [< *rubble* + *-y*1.] Abounding in small irregular stones; containing or consisting of rubble.

The *rubbly* lavas of the basal series. *Darwin*, Geol. Observations, i. 87.

Rubeæ (rö'bẹ̄-ē), *n. pl.* [NL. (Bentham and Hooker, 1865), < *Rubus* + *-eæ*.] A tribe of rosaceous plants, consisting of the genus *Rubus* (which see for characters).

Rubecula (rọ̈-bek'ū̦-lạ̈), *n.* [NL., dim., < L. *rubere*, be red: see *ruby*.] A name of the genus of birds of which *Erythacus rubecula*, the European robin-redbreast, is the typical species: same as *Erythacus*. *Brehm*, 1828.

rubedinous (rọ̈-bed'i-nus), *a.* [< L. *rubedo* (*rubedin-*), redness (< *rubere*, be red), + *-ous*: see *ruby*, *red*1.] Reddish.

rubedity (rọ̈-bed'i̦-ti), *n.* [Irreg. L. *rubedo*, redness (see *rubedinous*), + *-ity*.] Ruddiness; reddishness; rubiginous coloration.

rubefacient (rö-bẹ̄-fā'shient), *a.* and *n.* [< L. *rubefacien(t-)s*, ppr. of *rubefacere*, make red: see *rubify*.] **I.** *a.* Making red; producing redness, as a medicinal application on the skin.

II. *n.* An application which causes redness or hyperemia of the skin where it is applied, as a mustard plaster.

rubefaction (rö-bẹ̄-fak'shọn), *n.* [Also *rubifaction*; < F. *rubéfaction* = Sp. *rubefaccion*, < L. *rubefacere*, make red: see *rubify* and *rubefacient*.] Redness of the skin produced by a rubefacient; also, the action of a rubefacient.

rubelet† (rö'be-let), *n.* [As *ruby* + *-let*.] A little ruby.

About the cover of this book there went
A curious-comely, clean compartiment;
And, in the midst, to grace it more, was set
A blushing, pretty-peeping *rubelet*.
Herrick, To his Closet-Gods.

rubella (rọ̈-bel'ạ̈), *n.* [NL., fem. of L. *rubellus*, reddish, dim. of *ruber*, red: see *ruby*.] A usually insignificant contagious disease, with a rose-colored eruption, slight catarrhal symptoms in the mucous membranes of the head and larger air-passages of the chest, and usually slight pyrexia and cervical lymphadenitis. The incubation period is from one to three weeks; there is no prodromal period, or it is only for a few hours. The rash, which migrates, lasts in one place not more than half a day, but is present on the body somewhere from two to four days. Rubella protects against second attacks, but not against measles or scarlet fever, with one or the other of which it is sometimes confused. Also called *rubeola* and *German measles*.

rubellane (rö'bel-ān), *n.* [< L. *rubellus*, reddish (see *rubella*), + *-ane*.] A kind of mica having a reddish color.

rubellite (rö'bel-īt), *n.* [< L. *rubellus*, reddish, (see *rubella*), + *-ite*2.] A red or pink variety of tourmalin found on the island of Elba, in Siberia, in Brazil, and at Paris in Maine. The ruby in the imperial crown of Russia is believed to be a rubellite.

Rubensian (rọ̈-ben'si-an), *a.* and *n.* [< *Rubens* (see def.) + *-ian*.] **I.** *a.* Of or pertaining to, or characteristic of, the Flemish painter Peter Paul Rubens (1577-1640).

The composition is distinguished by the true *Rubensian* swing and emphatic movement. *Athenæum*, No. 3247, p. 90.

II. *n.* A follower or an admirer of Rubens; one who belongs to the school or who imitates the style of Rubens, described by Fuseli as "a florid system of mannered magnificence."

Rubens's madder. See *madder lakes*, under *madder*1.

rubeola (rọ̈-bē'ọ̄-lạ̈), *n.* [NL., dim., < L. *rubeus*, red: see *ruby*.] In *med.*: (*a*) Same as *measles*, 1. (*b*) Rubella.

rubeolar (rọ̈-bē'ō-lạ̈r), *a.* [< *rubeola* + *-ar*3.] Pertaining to, of the nature of, or characteristic of rubeola or measles.

rubeoloid (rọ̈-bē'ọ̄-loid), *a.* [< *rubeola* + *-oid*.] Resembling rubeola.

ruberite (rö'bėr-īt), *n.* [< L. *ruber*, red (see *red*1), + *-ite*2.] Same as *cuprite*.

ruberythric (rö-be-rith'rik), *a.* [< L. *rubia*, madder, + Gr. ἐρυθρός, red, + *-ic*.] Derived from madder-root.—**Ruberythric acid.** Same as *rubianic acid*.

rubescence (rọ̈-bes'ẹns), *n.* [< *rubescen(t)* + *-ce*.] A growing rubescent or red; the state of becoming or being red; a blush. *Roget*.

rubescent (rọ̈-bes'ẹnt), *a.* [= F. *rubescent*, < L. *rubescen(t-)s*, ppr. of *rubescere*, become red, < *rubere*, be red: see *ruby*, *red*1.] Growing or becoming red; tending to a red color; blushing.

Rubia (rö'bi-ạ̈), *n.* [NL. (Tournefort, 1700), < L. *rubia* (> It. *robbia* = Sp. *rubia* = Pg. *ruiva*), madder, < *rubeus*, red, < *rubere*, be red: see *ruby*.] A genus of gamopetalous plants, including the madder, type of the order *Rubiaceæ*, belonging to the tribe *Galieæ*, distinguished from the closely related and well-known genus *Galium*, the bedstraw, by flowers with parts in fives instead of fours. It is further characterized by the absence of an involucre from the flowers, by a roundish calyx-tube without border, a wheel-shaped corolla, five stamens, a minute disk, and an ovary commonly two-celled and two-ovuled, forming a small fleshy twin fruit. There are about 38 species, natives of the Mediterranean region, tropical and temperate Asia, South Africa, and tropical and temperate South America. They are herbs with elongated angled stems, which are commonly rigid or minutely prickly, and with large thickened roots sometimes 3 feet long. They bear whorled lanceolate or obovate leaves, usually four at a node, and small flowers in axillary or terminal cymes, with their pedicels each jointed under the calyx. See *madder*1 and *munjeet*.

Rubiaceæ (rö-bi-ā'sẹ̄-ē), *n. pl.* [NL., < *Rubia* + *-aceæ*.] A very natural and distinct order of gamopetalous plants, of the cohort *Rubiales*, typified by the genus *Rubia*. The flowers are commonly perfect, regular, and symmetrical, the corolla most frequently salverform or wheel-shaped, often funnelform or bell-shaped, usually with equal valvate lobes; the stamens borne upon the corolla-tube, of the same number as its lobes and alternate with them, the anthers two-celled and usually oblong-linear; the ovary, which is crowned with a disk, one- to ten-celled, with one or more, commonly very numerous, ovules in each cell. The fruit is from one- to ten-celled, capsular or fleshy, or separating into nutlets, the seeds with fleshy or corneous albumen. The order is one of the largest among flowering plants, containing about 4,500 species of 373 genera and 25 tribes, and surpassed only by the *Compositæ*, *Leguminosæ*, and *Orchideæ*. The most important tribes are *Cinchoneæ*, *Naucleæ*, *Rondeletieæ*, *Hedyotideæ*, *Mussændeæ*, *Gardenieæ*, *Ixoreæ*, *Morindeæ*, *Psychotrieæ*, *Pæderieæ*, *Spermacoceæ*, and *Galieæ*. The species are more abundant in America, and are all tropical except two tribes, the *Galieæ* of the northern and the *Anthospermeæ* of the southern hemisphere. They are trees, shrubs, or herbs, and exhibit great variety of habit, being either erect, prostrate, or climbing, and sometimes thorny, but have remarkable uniformity of leaf-structure, varying from the entire- and opposite-leafed type in but very few cases. Stipules are well-nigh universal, and very various, being inter- or intra-petiolar, simple or two-cleft or -divided, free or united with the petiole, etc.; in the tribe *Galieæ* resembling the leaves, and with them making out a whorl. The flowers are very often dimorphous or trimorphous in the length of their stamens and pistils; and in some genera they are capitately disposed, giving rise to a syncarpous fruit through the union of their calyxes. Some genera—as *Bouvardia* and *Gardenia*—contain ornamental plants, and several supply important products, *Coffea* yielding coffee, and *Cinchona* the cinchona-bark; while *Rubia* (the type) contains the madder-plant, whence the order is often called the *madder family*.

rubiaceous (rö-bi-ā'shius), *a.* In *bot.*, belonging to or characteristic of the *Rubiaceæ*.

rubiacin (rö'bi-ạ-sin), *n.* [< *Rubiac(eæ)* + *-in*2.] A yellow crystallizable coloring matter ($C_{32}H_{22}O_{10}$) found in madder-root.

Rubiales (rö-bi-ā'lēz), *n. pl.* [NL. (Lindley, 1845), < L. *rubia*, madder: see *Rubia*.] A cohort of gamopetalous plants. They are characterized by opposite leaves, a calyx-tube adherent to the inferior ovary, a calyx-border toothed, lobed, or rarely obsolete, stamens fixed upon the corolla, alternate with and commonly equal to its lobes, the anthers separate, the ovary commonly two- to eight-celled, each cell sometimes with one, more often with two or more ovules, the seeds with copious fleshy albumen. It includes the two orders *Rubiaceæ* and *Caprifoliaceæ*, the madder and honeysuckle families, the former commonly with and the latter without stipules.

rubian (rö'bi-ạn), *n.* [< L. *rubia*, madder (see *Rubia*), + *-an*.] A bitter principle and coloring matter ($C_{28}H_{34}O_{15}$) of madder. It is a glucoside, amorphous, very soluble in water and alcohol, and has a yellow color and a slightly bitter taste. It is a very weak dye by itself, but is decomposed on boiling with an acid, and deposits insoluble yellow flocks, which, after being separated by filtration and well washed, serve as dye for the same colors as those given by madder. The tinctorial power of these flocks is due to alizarin.

rubianic (rö-bi-an'ik), *a.* [< *rubian* + *-ic*.] Pertaining to or derived from rubian.—**Rubianic acid**, $C_{20}H_{28}O_{14}$, a weak acid obtained from madder, *Rubia tinctorum*.

rubiate (rö'bi-āt), *n.* [< L. *rubia*, madder (see *Rubia*), + *-ate*1.] A pigment obtained from madder.—**Liquid rubiate**, a concentrated tincture of madder, very transparent and of a fine rose-color. Combined with all other madder colors, it works well in water and produces beautiful effects. It acts as a drier in oil. Also called *liquid madder lake*.—**Purple rubiate.** See *purple*.

rubible†, *n.* Same as *ribible* for *ribibe*.

rubican (rö'bi-kan), *a.* [< F. *rubican* = Sp. *rubican* = Pg. *rubicão*, *rubicano*, rubican, = It. *rabicano*, roan, a roan horse (cf. "*rabbicane*, a horse that is fashioned in the bodie like a greyhound, or that hath a white taile or rump"—Florio, 1611); perhaps (irreg.) < L. *rubricare*, color red: see *rubricate*.] Noting the color of a bay, sorrel, or black horse with light gray or white upon the flanks, but not predominant there. *Bailey*, 1727.

rubicative† (rö'bi-kā-tiv), *n.* [Appar. for **rubricative*, or for **rubificative* = It. *rubificativo*, < *rubificare*: see *rubify*.] That which produces a reddish or ruby color. *Imp. Dict.*

rubicel, rubicelle (rö'bi-sel), *n.* [< F. *rubicelle*, also *rubacelle*, dim. of *rubace*, a species of ruby: see *rubasse*.] An orange or flame-colored variety of spinel.

A pretty *rubicelle* of three quarters of a carat. *Pop. Sci. Mo.*, XXVIII. 825.

rubicund (rö'bi-kund), *a.* [< OF. *rubicunde*, *rubicond*, F. *rubicond* = Sp. Pg. *rubicundo* = It. *rubicondo*, < L. *rubicundus*, very red, < *rubere*, be red: see *ruby*.] Inclining to redness; ruddy; blood-red: said especially of the face; in *bot.*, turning rosy-red.

He had, indeed, all the outward signs of a sot: a sleepy eye, a *rubicund* face, and carbuncled nose. *Smollett*, Travels, ii.

Falstaff alludes to Pistol's *rubicund* nose. *Douce*, Illustrations of Shakspeare, p. 26.

=**Syn.** *Rosy*, etc. See *ruddy*.

rubicundity (rö-bi-kun'di-ti), *n.* [< ML. *rubicundita(t-)s*, redness, < *rubicundus*, red: see *rubicund*.] The state of being rubicund; redness. [Rare.]

I do not wish you to parade your *rubicundity* and gray hairs. *H. Walpole.* (*Imp. Dict.*)

rubidic (rọ̈-bid'ik), *a.* [< *rubidium* + *-ic*.] Of or pertaining to rubidium.

rubidin (rö'bi-din), *n.* [< L. *rubidus*, red, reddish, + *-in*2.] A basic coal-tar product ($C_{11}H_{17}N$), which is also found as a product in tobacco-smoke.

rubidium (rọ̈-bid'i-um), *n.* [NL., < L. *rubidus*, red, reddish, < *rubere*, be red: see *ruby*.] Chemical symbol, Rb; atomic weight, 85.25. A metal belonging to the group of elements which includes lithium, sodium, potassium, and cæsium: so named from the reddish tint of its salts. It is very soft, is silver-white in color, has a specific gravity of 1.52, and melts at about 101° F. When thrown into water it burns, forming rubidium hydrate, RbOH. Rubidium was first detected by the spectroscope, together with cæsium, in the mineral water of Dürkheim, in which it exists to the amount of two parts in ten million. It has since been found in considerable quantity, together with cæsium and lithium, in several other saline waters, and most abundantly in that of Bourbonne-les-Bains in France. It is also found in several lepidolites: that of Rozena, in Moravia, contains 0.24 per cent. of rubidium, with only a trace of cæsium; that of Hebron, in the State of Maine, 0.24 per cent. of rubidium and 0.3 per cent. of cæsium. The two metals likewise occur, though in smaller quantity, in the lepidolite of Prague, the petalite of Utö in Finland, the lithia-mica of Zinnwald in the Erzgebirge, and other lithia minerals. It has been found also in the ashes of many plants, and in the saline or crude potash obtained from the residue of the beet-sugar manufacture. It has been found in tobacco-leaves, and in coffee, tea, cocoa, and crude tartar. In minerals and mineral waters rubidium and cæsium are always associated with lithium, and generally also with potassium and sodium; but plants have the power of assimilating two or three of these metals to the exclusion of the rest; thus, tea, coffee, and the saline of beet-root contain potassium, sodium, and rubidium, but not a trace of lithium.

rubied (rö'bid), *a.* [< *ruby* + *-ed*2.] Having the color of the ruby; ruby-red: as, a *rubied* lip.

Twin with the *rubied* cherry. *Shak.*, Pericles, v., Prol., l. 8.

rubifaction (rö-bi-fak'shọn), *n.* Same as *rubefaction*.

rubific (rọ̈-bif'ik), *a.* [< L. *rubere*, be red, + *facere*, make. Cf. *rubify*.] Making red; communicating redness.

The several species of rays, as the rubifick, cerulifick, and others. *N. Grew*, Cosmologia Sacra, ii. 2.

rubification (rö″bi-fi-kā′shon), *n.* [< *rubify* + *-ation* (see *-fication*). Cf. *rubefaction*.] The act of making red.

All the Degrees and Effects of Fire, as distillation, sublimation, . . . *rubification*, and fixation. *Howell*, Letters, ii. 42.

rubiform (rö′bi-fôrm), *a.* [< *ruby* + *-form*.] Having or exhibiting some shade of red; characterized by redness. [Rare.]

Of those rays which pass close by the snow the *rubiform* will be the least refracted. *Newton.*

rubify (rö′bi-fī), *v. t.*; pret. and pp. *rubified*, ppr. *rubifying*. [< F. *rubéfier* = Sp. *rubificar* = It. *rubificare*, < L. as if **rubificare*, for *rubefacere*, make red, redden, < *rubere*, be red, + *facere*, make.] To make red; redden.

Deep-scarleted, *rubified*, and carbuncled faces. *Massinger*, Virgin-Martyr, ii. 1.

rubiginose (rö-bij′i-nōs), *a.* [< LL. *rubiginosus*, rusty: see *rubiginous*.] Having the color of iron-rust; brown-red; rubiginous; in *bot.*, usually, noting a surface whose peculiar color is due to glandular hairs. *Treas. of Bot.*

rubiginous (rö-bij′i-nus), *a.* [< F. *rubigineux* (= Sp. *ruginoso* = It. *rugginoso*), < LL. *rubiginosus*, *robiginosus*, < L. *rubigo*, *robigo* (*-gin-*), rust: see *rubigo*. Cf. *roinous*.] 1. Rusty; having a rusty appearance, as the sputa in some cases of pneumonia. *Dunglison*.—2. In *bot.* and *zoöl.*, rust-colored; brownish-red; ferruginous.—3. Affected by rubigo, as a plant.

rubigo (rö-bī′gō), *n.* [= It. *rubigine*, < L. *rubigo*, *robigo*, rust, < *rubere*, be red: see *ruby*, *red*[1]. Cf. *roin*.] A kind of rust on plants, consisting of a parasitic fungus; mildew.

rubijervine (rö-bi-jėr′vin), *n.* [< L. *rubeus*, red, + E. *jervine*, q. v.] An alkaloid ($C_{26}H_{43}NO_2$) found in *Veratrum album*.

rubin†, **rubine**[1]† (rö′bin), *n.* [= D. *robijn* = MHG. G. Dan. Sw. *rubin* = Sp. *rubin* = Pg. *rubim* (= Russ. *rubinŭ* = NGr. ῥουβῖνι, ῥουμπῖνι), < It. *rubino*, *robino*, < ML. *rubinus*, a ruby: see *ruby*, the older and now exclusive E. form.] Same as *ruby*.

rubine[2] (rö′bin), *n.* [< L. *rub-eus*, *rub-er*, red, + *-ine*[2].] An aniline dye: same as *fuchsin*.—**Rubine S.** Same as *acid-magenta*.

rubineous (rö-bin′ē-us), *a.* [< *rubine*[1] + *-ous*.] In *entom.*, of a glassy or semi-transparent deep-crimson red, resembling a ruby, as the eyes of an insect; less exactly, in *zoöl.*, of any bright, rich, or vivid red: as, the *rubineous* flycatchers (*Pyrocephalus*).

rubious† (rö′bi-us), *a.* [More prop. **rubeous*; = Sp. *rubio* = Pg. *ruivo* = It. *robbio*, < L. *rubeus*, ML. also *rubius*, red, reddish: see *red*[1]. Cf. *rouge*.] Red.

Diana's lip
Is not more smooth and *rubious*.
Shak., T. N., i. 4. 32.

rubiretin (rö-bi-ret′in), *n.* [< L. *rubeus*, red, + Gr. ῥητίνη, resin: see *resin*.] A resinous coloring matter ($C_7H_6O_2$), isomeric with benzoic acid, existing in madder, and formed from rubian under the influence of acids or of a soluble ferment found in madder.

rub-iron (rub′ī″ėrn), *n.* A plate attached to a carriage- or wagon-bed to protect it from abrasion by a fore wheel when making a sharp turn; a wheel-guard or wheel-guard plate.

ruble (rö′bl), *n.* [Also *rouble* (as F.); early mod. E. also *rubble*, *roble*; = F. *rouble* = G. Dan. Sw. *rubel* = NGr. ῥούβλιον, < Russ. *rubli*, a ruble (100 copecks); generally explained as lit. 'a piece cut off,' < *rubiti*, cut; but perhaps derived, through Turk., < Pers. *rūpiya*, rupee: see *rupee*.] A silver coin of Russia, current since the seventeenth century. The ruble of the present day, the legal unit of money in Russia, is equal to about 3*s.* 2*d.* English, or 77 United States cents. Little actual coin, however, now circulates in Russia, paper money of the nominal value of 100, 25, 10, 5, 3, and 1 rubles taking its place. The paper ruble is discounted at about 60 cents.

Obverse.

Reverse.

Ruble, 1862 — British Museum. (Size of the original.)

rubric (rö′brik), *n.* and *a.* [< ME. *rubricke*, *rubrik*, *rubrike*, *rubryke*, *robryk*, *rubriche*, *roberych*, *rubryce*, *rubrysshe*, < OF. *rubriche*, *rebriche*, *rubrique*, F. *rubrique* (= Pr. Sp. Pg. It. *rubrica* = D. *rubriek* = G. Sw. Dan. *rubrik*), < L. *rubrica*, red ocher, red earth, the title of a law written in red, a law, ML. (eccl.) a rubric; fem. (sc. *terra*, earth) of **rubricus*, red, < *ruber*, red: see *red*[1].] **I.** *n.* 1. Red ocher; red chalk; reddle. [Obsolete or archaic.]

Take *rubrik* poured in sum litel shelle,
And therwithall the bak of every bee
A pensel touche as thai drynk atte the welle.
Palladius, Husbondrie (E. E. T. S.), p. 146.

The same in sheeps milke with *rubricke* and soft pitch, drunke every day or eaten to your meate, helpeth the ptisicke and obstructions.
Topsell, Beasts (1607), p. 132. (*Halliwell.*)

Once a dwelling's doorpost marked and crossed
In *rubric* by the enemy on his rounds
As eligible, as fit place of prey,
Baffle him henceforth, keep him out who can!
Browning, Ring and Book, I. 74.

2. In old manuscripts and printed books, and still sometimes in the latter, some small part distinguished from the rest of the matter by being written or printed in red, as an initial letter, a title or heading, a liturgical direction, etc.

These *rubrics* [initial letters written with minium or red lead], as they were called, gradually received many fanciful adornments at the hands of the illustrators.
Amer. Cyc., XI. 590.

3. Anything of a kind which in manuscripts or books it was formerly customary to put in red, as the title of a subject or division, the heading of a statute, a guiding rule or direction, the first letter of a chapter, etc.

After thy text, ne after thy *rubriche*,
I wol not wirche as mochel as a gnat.
Chaucer, Prol. to Wife of Bath's Tale, l. 346.

They [Flacius's "Centuries"] divide the material by centuries, and each century by a uniform Procrustean scheme of not less than sixteen *rubrics*.
Schaff, Hist. Christ. Ch., I. § 7.

Specifically—4. A liturgical direction or injunction in an office-book such as a prayer-book, missal, or breviary; a rule prescribed for the conduct of religious worship, or of any part of a religious service, printed in the Roman Catholic, Greek, and sometimes other office-books in red characters; also, collectively, the body of such rules.

They had their particular prayers, according to the several days and months; and their tables or *rubricks* to instruct them. *Stillingfleet.*

Our obligations to observe the *rubric*, how indispensable soever, are subject to this proviso.
Hook, Church Dict., p. 668.

For processions, . . . the *rubrics* according to the Salisbury Use direct the chief celebrant, at least, to have on a cope. *Rock*, Church of our Fathers, ii. 45.

5. A flourish after a signature; a paraph.

Madre de Dios! the other day she makes me a *rubric* of the Governor, Pio Pico, the same, identical.—[Foot-note.] The Spanish *rubric* is the complicated flourish attached to a signature, and is as individual and characteristic as the handwriting. *Bret Harte*, Story of a Mine, p. 39.

Ornaments rubric. See *ornament*.

II. *a.* 1. Red; of a red or reddish color.

What though my name stood *rubric* on the walls,
Or plaster'd posts, with claps, in capitals?
Pope, Prol. to Satires, l. 215.

2. Pertaining to rubrics; made the subject of a rubric; rubrical; marked in red characters.

I don't know whether my father won't become a *rubric* martyr, for having been persecuted by him.
Walpole, To Mann, Dec. 1, 1754.

Rubric lakes, the pigments of various colors commonly known as *madder lakes*.

rubric (rö′brik), *v. t.*; pret. and pp. *rubricked*, ppr. *rubricking*. [ME. **rubrichen*, *rubrisshen*, *rubryeen*, < OF. *rubricher*, F. *rubriquer* = Sp. Pg. *rubricar* = It. *rubricare*; < L. *rubricare*, color red, < *rubrica*, red earth, red ocher: see *rubric*, *n.*] 1. To adorn with red; rubricate. *Johnson.*

Item, for *rubrissheyng* of all the booke, . . . iiis. iiijd.
Paston Letters, II. 335.

2. To make the subject of a rubric; enjoin observances regarding, as a saint of the calendar.

Stretching his [the Pope's] arm to heaven, in *rubricking* wha saints he list; to hell, in freeing what prisoners he list. *Rev. T. Adams*, Works, II. 255.

rubrical (rö′bri-kal), *a.* [< *rubric* + *-al*.] 1. Same as *rubric*, 1.

You thus persecute ingenuous men over all your booke, with this one over-tir'd *rubricall* conceit still of blushing.
Milton, On Def. of Humb. Remonst.

2. Of, pertaining to, or contained in a rubric or rubrics: as, a *rubrical* direction.

rubricality (rö-bri-kal′i-ti), *n.*; pl. *rubricalities* (-tiz). [< *rubrical* + *-ity*.] The character of being rubrical; that which is rubrical; a matter having relation to rubrics or ritual; agreement with a rubric or rubrics.

"Where have you been staying?" "With young Lord Vieuxbois, among high art and painted glass, spade farms and model smell-traps, *rubricalities* and sanitary reforms."
Kingsley, Yeast, vi. (*Davies.*)

rubrically (rö′bri-kal-i), *adv.* In a rubrical manner; according to a rubric or the rubrics; over-conventionally or -formally. [Rare.]

A lady-like old woman, . . . slight of figure, and *rubrically* punctual in her uprisings and downsittings.
J. S. Le Fanu, Tenants of Mallory, i.

rubricate (rö′bri-kāt), *v. t.*; pret. and pp. *rubricated*, ppr. *rubricating*. [< L. *rubricatus*, pp. of *rubricare*, color red: see *rubric*, *v.*] 1. To mark or distinguish with red; illuminate with red letters, words, etc., as a manuscript or book. See *rubrication* and *rubricator*.

Curroone *rubricates* this in the Kalendar of his greatest dangers and deliverances.
Sir T. Herbert, Travels into Africa (ed. 1638), p. 90.

There [on an old map of Burma] we see *rubricated* not only Ava, but Pochang. *Quarterly Rev.*, CLXII. 217.

2. To formulate as a rubric; arrange as rubrics or precepts; provide with rubrics.

A system . . . according to which the thoughts of men were to be . . . *rubricated* forever after. *Hare.* (*Webster.*)

Rubricated letters or **matter**, capital letters or separate words or lines written or printed in red.

rubricate (rö′bri-kāt), *a.* [< L. *rubricatus*: see the verb.] Represented in red; having red coloring, in whole or in part.

Other festivals I enquire not after, as of St. Dunstan's, and the rest that stand *rubricate* in the old Kalendars.
Spelman, Orig. of Terms, ii.

rubrication (rö-bri-kā′shon), *n.* [= Sp. *rubricacion* = It. *rubricazione*; < ML. **rubricatio(n-)*, < L. *rubricare*, color red: see *rubricate*.] 1. A making red; specifically, the act of illuminating with red or colored letters, words, etc., as old manuscripts and books.—2. That which is rubricated, or done in red; a letter, word, or other part of a text separately executed in red, or, in general, in color.

These are but a few of the subjects of these fine *rubrications* of the "Book of Wedding Days."
Athenæum, No. 3236, p. 603.

3. The act of formulating, as a rubric; arranging as or with rubrics.

rubricator (rö′bri-kā-tor), *n.* [= F. *rubricateur* = Pg. *rubricador* = It. *rubricatore*; < ML. **rubricator*, < L. *rubricare*, color red: see *rubricate*.] One who rubricates; formerly, a person employed to insert red or otherwise colored letters, words, etc., in the text of a manuscript or book.

The *rubricator's* work consists of the names of the speakers, . . . a rule between every speech, and a touch upon the initial letter of every line of poetry.
York Plays, Int., p. xvi.

We find in a good many MSS. as well as early printed books small letters written either in the margin or in the blank left for the initial, to guide the *rubricator*.
Encyc. Brit., XXIII. 686.

rubrician (rö-brish′an), *n.* [< *rubric* + *-ian*.] One who is versed in or who adheres to the rubric. *Quarterly Rev.* (*Imp. Dict.*)

rubricist (rö′bri-sist), *n.* [< *rubric* + *-ist*.] Same as *rubrician*.

rubricity (rö-bris′i-ti), *n.* [< L. **rubricus*, red (see *rubric*), + *-ity*.] 1†. Redness.

The *rubricity* of the Nile. *Geddes.* (*Encyc. Dict.*)

2. The character of being rubrical; accordance with the rubrics; rubricality.

Rubricity . . . is the sheet-anchor of the Church. . . . The rubric is explicit here, and settles the case.
W. A. Butler, Mrs. Limber's Raffle, iv.

rubricose (rö′bri-kōs), *a.* [< L. *rubricosus*, full of red earth or red ocher, < *rubrica*, red earth, red ocher: see *rubric*.] In *bot.*, marked with red, as the thallus of some lichens; rubricate.

rubrisher† (rö′brish-ėr), *n.* [ME., < *rubrisshe* (*rubric*), *v.*, + *-er*[1].] A painter of ornamental or directing letters in early manuscripts.

Thus in Bruges we find there were . . . Verlichters or *Rubrishers* who probably confined their attention to illuminated capitals. *Blades*, William Caxton, ix.

rubrisshe†, *v.* See *rubric*, *v.*

rübsen-cake (rüb'sen-kāk), *n.* [< G. *rübsen*, *rüb-samen*, rape-seed (< G. *rübe*, rape: see *rape*[4], + *samen*, seed, = L. *semen*: see *semen*), + *cake* (see *cake*[1]).] An oil-cake much used on the continent of Europe, made from the seeds of the summer rape. *Imp. Dict.*

rubstone (rub'stōn), *n.* 1. A kind of close-grained sandstone or gritstone used for sharpening instruments and for polishing metallic surfaces. A hard variety is made into whetstones for scythes and similar tools, and is also used for smoothing engravers' copperplates, etc. A softer variety, distinguished as *carpenters' rubstone*, is cut into suitable pieces for quickly giving a rough edge to knives or the like, to be finished on finer stones.

2†. A whetstone; a rub.

A cradle for barley, with *rubstone* and sand.
Tusser, September's Husbandry, st. 14.

Rubus (rö'bus), *n.* [NL. (Malpighi, 1675), < L. *rubus*, a bramble-bush, blackberry-bush (> It. Sp. Pg. *rubo*, bramble), so called with ref. to the color of the fruit of some species, < *rubere*, be red: see *ruby*, *red*[1].] A genus of rosaceous plants, constituting the tribe *Rubeæ*. It has flowers with a broad flattened five-lobed calyx, five petals, numerous subterminal filiform styles, and a fleshy fruit (a drupetum) consisting of small drupes on a common receptacle. Nearly 500 species have been described, of which about 100 may be admitted as valid. They are most abundant in Europe, northern Africa, and Asia, are moderately numerous in North America and the West Indies, and occur in nearly all other regions, but less commonly in southern tropical Africa, Madagascar, Australia, New Zealand, and the Pacific islands. About 10 species are found in the eastern United States, 5 in California, and 6 in Alaska. They are commonly prickly shrubs, sometimes creeping herbs, either with or without hairs, sometimes glandular, woolly or hoary. Their leaves are scattered and alternate, sometimes simple and either undivided or lobed, generally compound, with five or three leaflets. The flowers are white, pink, or purplish, usually disposed in terminal or axillary corymbs or panicles. A section in which the drupelets fall from the receptacle at maturity, together or separately, is represented by the raspberry; a second, in which they remain attached, comprises the blackberries. Various species produce the well-known fruits of these names; the roots of *R. Canadensis* and *R. villosus* afford a useful tonic astringent; some are ornamental plants. See *raspberry*, *blackberry*, *blackcap*, 4, *bramble*, *cloudberry* (with cut), *roebuck-berry*, and *dewberry*.

Branch with Flowers of Common or High Blackberry (*Rubus villosus*).
a, the fruit; *b*, leaf from the first year's shoot.

ruby (rö'bi), *n.* and *a.* [Early mod. E. also *rubie*; < ME. *ruby*, *rubi*, *rubeye*, < OF. *rubi*, also *rubis*, F. *rubis* = Pr. *robi*, *robina*, = Sp. *rubi*, *rubin* = Pg. *rubi*, *rubim* = It. *rubino* (> E. *rubin*), < ML. *rubinus*, also *rubius*, *rubium*, a ruby, so called from its red color, < L. *rubeus*, red, < *rubere*, be red: see *red*[1]. Cf. *rubin*.] I. *n.*; pl. *rubies* (-biz). 1. The clear rich-red variety of corundum. (See *corundum*.) It is highly prized as a gem, and ranks even above the diamond, fine examples of from one to five carats selling at a price from three to ten times greater than that of a diamond of corresponding size and quality. The finest rubies, those of a pigeon's-blood color, are found in Upper Burma, near Mogok, north of Mandalay; they occur there in place in a crystalline limestone, also in gem-bearing gravels; the spinel ruby is a common associate. Rubies of a dark-red color, sometimes with a tinge of brown, are found in the region about Chantibun, Siam; others, of a dark-pink or purplish tint, in Ceylon. A magenta-colored ruby from Victoria, in Australia, is locally known as *barklyite*. In Great Britain rubies of a dark-red or beef's-blood color are highly prized. The red variety of corundum described above is the true or Oriental ruby, but the name *ruby* is also sometimes given to a red variety of spinel; this spinel ruby varies in color from the deep-red to the rose-red balas ruby and the yellow or orange-red rubicel. The pale-red topaz from Brazil is also sometimes called Brazilian ruby, and a red variety of garnet, *rock-ruby*.

Fetislich hir fyngres were fretted with gold wyre,
And there-on red *rubyes* as red as any glede.
Piers Plowman (B), ii. 12.

Of fine *rubies* [var. *rubins*, Tyrwhitt] and of diamants.
Chaucer, Knight's Tale, l. 1280.

Paled pearls and *rubies* red as blood.
Shak., Lover's Complaint, l. 198.

2. A pure or somewhat crimson red color.

You can behold such sights,
And keep the natural *ruby* of your cheeks,
When mine is blanch'd with fear.
Shak., Macbeth, iii. 4. 115.

3. Something resembling a ruby; a blain; a blotch; a carbuncle.—4. In *her.*, the tincture red or gules, when blazoning is done by means of precious stones. See *blazon*, *n.*, 2.—5. In *printing*, a type smaller than nonpareil and larger than pearl, about the size of American agate, or 5½ points in the new system of sizes. [Eng.]—6. In *horol.*: (*a*) Any variety of ruby used as jewels in watchmaking, as in the finest watches. Hence—(*b*) The jewel of the roller of the balance-staff of a watch, irrespective of the material of which it is made. Compare *jewel*, *n.*, 4.—7. In *ornith.*: (*a*) The red bird of paradise, *Paradisea rubra* or *sanguinea*. (*b*) The ruby hummer, *Clytolæma rubineus* of Brazil, and some related humming-birds with ruby gorget.—**Cape ruby**, one of the rich ruby-red garnets found associated with diamonds in the South African diamond-mines. These are larger than the so-called *Arizona*, *New Mexico*, and *Colorado rubies*, all of which are identical with the so-called *Australian rubies*, which are a variety of pyrope garnet.—**Cat's-eye ruby**, a variety of ruby exhibiting more or less distinctly the chatoyant effect of the cat's-eye.—**Ruby of arsenic** or **sulphur**, the protosulphid of arsenic, or red compound of arsenic and sulphur.—**Ruby of zinc**, the sulphid of zinc, or red blende.

II. *a.* Of a color resembling that of the ruby; of a rich red color inclining toward crimson.

Over thy wounds now do I prophesy—
Which, like dumb mouths, do ope their *ruby* lips,
To beg the voice and utterance of my tongue.
Shak., J. C., iii. 1. 260.

Butler, fetch the *ruby* wine,
Which with sudden greatness fills us.
Emerson, From Hafiz.

Ruby glass. See *glass*.—**Ruby luster**, one of the varieties of metallic luster. The name is given to all lusters of any shade of red, even approaching purple or maroon.—**Ruby silver.** Same as *proustite* and *pyrargyrite*.—**Ruby spinel.** See def. 1, above.—**Ruby sulphur.** Same as *realgar*.

ruby (rö'bi), *v. t.*; pret. and pp. *rubied*, ppr. *rubying*. [< *ruby*, *n.*] To make red.

With sanguine drops the walls are *rubied* round.
Fenton, in Pope's Odyssey, xx. 426.

ruby-blende (rö'bi-blend), *n.* 1. A clear red variety of zinc sulphid, or sphalerite.—2. Ruby silver; a red silver ore, or sulphid of arsenic (as antimony) and silver. These ores include the mineral species proustite and pyrargyrite.

ruby-copper (rö'bi-kop"ėr), *n.* Same as *cuprite*.

ruby-crowned (rö'bi-kround), *a.* Having a red patch on the poll: as, the *ruby-crowned* kinglet, *Regulus calendula*.

ruby-mica (rö'bi-mī'kạ̈), *n.* Same as *goethite*.

rubytail (rö'bi-tāl), *n.* A gold wasp or cuckoo-fly of the hymenopterous family *Chrysididæ*, as *Chrysis ignita*, having the abdomen of a ruby color.

ruby-tailed (rö'bi-tāld), *a.* Having the abdomen red: specifically noting the rubytails or *Chrysididæ*. See cut under *Chrysididæ*.

ruby-throated (rö'bi-thrō"ted), *a.* Having a ruby gorget of feathers like metallic scales, as a humming-bird. The common ruby-throated humming-bird is *Trochilus colubris*, the only member of the *Trochilidæ* which is generally distributed in the eastern part of the United States. The male is 3¼ inches long and 5 inches in extent of wings, golden-green above, white below with green sides and ruby throat, the wings and tail dark-purplish. The female is smaller, and has no gorget, and the tail-feathers are varied with black and white. See cut under *humming-bird*.

ruby-tiger (rö'bi-tī"gėr), *n.* A beautiful British moth, *Phragmatobia fuliginosa*.

ruby-wood (rö'bi-wůd), *n.* The red sanders-wood or sandalwood, *Pterocarpus santalinus*. See *sandalwood*.

ruc† (ruk), *n.* Same as *roc*[1].

rucervine (rö-sėr'vin), *a.* [< *Rucervus* + *-ine*[1].] Relating or belonging to the genus *Rucervus*; having characteristics of *Rucervus*.

Its antlers are large, and of the intermediate *rucervine* type. *Cassell's Nat. Hist.*, III. 61. (*Encyc. Dict.*)

Rucervus (rö-sėr'vus), *n.* [NL., < *Ru*(*sa*) + *Cervus*.] A genus of East Indian *Cervidæ*, having doubly dichotomous antlers with a large brow-tine. There are several species. *C. schomburgki* inhabits Siam; *C. duvaucelii* is the Barasingha deer of Asia; *C. eldi*, the thamyn, is found in Burma.

ruche (rōsh), *n.* [Also *rouche*; < F. *ruche*, quilling; cf. F. *rouche*, the hull of a ship, < OF. *rouche*, *rousche*, *rusche*, *rucque*, a beehive, = Pr. *rusca*, a beehive; prob. of Celtic origin, and so called as once made of bark, < Bret. *rusk* = W. *rhisg* = Gael. *rusg* = Ir. *rusc*, bark.] 1. A full quilling, frilling, or plaiting of ribbon, muslin, grenadine, net, lace, or other material, used as a trimming for women's garments, or worn at the neck and wrists.—2. A loose pile of arched tiles to catch and lodge oyster-spawn.

ruching (rö'shing), *n.* [< *ruche* + *-ing*.] Same as *ruche*.

ruck[1] (ruk), *v.* [Also *rook*, *rouk*; < ME. *rouken*, *rukken*, crouch, bend, lie close; cf. Dan. *ruge*, brood.] I. *intrans.* To squat, like a bird on its nest or a beast crouching; crouch down; cower; hence, to huddle together; lie close, as sheep in a fold. [Obsolete or prov. Eng.]

What is mankynde more unto yow holde
Than is the scheep that *rouketh* in the folde?
Chaucer, Knight's Tale, l. 450.

But now they *rucken* in hire neste,
And resten as hem liken beste.
Gower, MS. Soc. Antiq. 134, f. 114. (*Halliwell.*)

The furies made the bride-groomes bed, and on the house did *rucke*
A cursed owle, the messenger of ill successe and lucke.
Golding, tr. of Ovid (ed. 1603), p. 73. (*Nares.*)

II. *trans.* To perch; seat, as a bird when roosting: used reflexively.

The raven *rook'd her* on the chimney's top.
Shak., 3 Hen. VI., v. 6. 47.

ruck[2] (ruk), *n.* [< Icel. *hrukka*, a wrinkle on the skin or in cloth; cf. Icel. *hrokkin*, curled, wrinkled, pp. of *hrökkva*, recoil, give way, curl; cf. Sw. *rynka*, Dan. *rynke*, a wrinkle (see *runkle*, *wrinkle*); Gael. *roc*, a wrinkle.] 1. A fold, crease, or pucker in the material of a garment, resulting from faults in the making.

The leather soon stretched and then went into *rucks* and folds which hardened, and, as a natural consequence, produced great discomfort. *Bury and Hillier*, Cycling, p. 238.

2. In *printing*, a crease or wrinkle made in a sheet of paper in passing from the feed-board to impression.

ruck[2] (ruk), *v.* [= Icel. *rykkja*, draw into folds: see *ruck*[2], *n.*] I. *trans.* 1. To wrinkle; crease; pucker: usually with *up*: as, to *ruck up* cloth; to *ruck up* a silk skirt. [Colloq.]

A *rucked* barke oregrewe their bodye and face,
And all their lymbes grewe starke and stiffe also.
The Newe Metamorphosis (1600), MS.

2. To ruffle the temper of; annoy; vex: followed by *up*. [Colloq.]

II. *intrans.* 1. To become creased and wrinkled; draw up in wrinkles or puckers: as, this stuff *rucks* easily.

The paper . . . *rucked* up when inserting the cartridge in the chamber of the gun, and has been superseded by coil brass. *W. W. Greener*, The Gun, p. 296.

2. To be ruffled in temper; be annoyed, vexed, or excited: followed by *up*. [Colloq.]

ruck[3] (ruk), *n.* [A var. of *rick*[1].] 1. Same as *rick*[1].

Your nowt may die; the spate may bear away
Frae aff the howms your dainty *rucks* of hay.
Ramsay, Gentle Shepherd, i. 2.

2. A vague unit of volume, a stack, about 5¾ cubic yards of bark. [Prov. Eng.]

ruck[4] (ruk), *n.* [< ME. *rok*, *ruke*; < OSw. *ruka*, a heap, prob. connected with Icel. *hraukr* = AS. *hreác*, a heap, rick: see *reek*[2], *rick*[1], *ruck*[3].] 1. A crowd or throng; especially, a closely packed and indiscriminate crowd or mass of persons or things; a jam; a press.

There watȝ rynging, on ryȝt, of ryche metalles
Quen renkkes in that ryche *rok* rennen hit to cache.
Alliterative Poems (ed. Morris), ii. 1514.

Now for the spurs! and as these, vigorously applied, screwed an extra stride out of Tétel, I soon found myself in the *ruck* of men, horses, and drawn swords.
Sir S. W. Baker, Heart of Africa, p. 112.

2. The common run of persons or things; the commonplace multitude, as contrasted with the distinguished or successful few: specifically said of the defeated horses in a race.

One [story] however, if true, is somewhat out of the ordinary *ruck*, and it is told of the same Lord Mohun ("Dog Mohun," as Swift calls him) who fought the Duke of Hamilton.
J. Ashton, Social Life in Reign of Queen Anne, II. 218.

3. Trash; rubbish; nonsense. [Colloq.]

He 's stuck up and citified, and wears gloves, and takes his meals private in his room, and all that sort of *ruck*.
Scribner's Mag., VIII. 159.

ruck[4] (ruk), *v. t.* [< *ruck*[4], *n.*] To gather together into heaps. *Halliwell.* [Prov. Eng.]

ruck[5] (ruk), *n.* [Origin obscure.] A small heifer. *Halliwell.* [Prov. Eng.]

ruck[6] (ruk), *n.* [A var. of *rut*[1].] A rut in a road. *Halliwell.* [Prov. Eng.]

ruck[7]† (ruk), *n.* Same as *roc*[1].

ruckerize† (ruk'ėr-īz), *v. i.* [‹ *Rucker* (the name of a citizen of Tennessee who, being in Baltimore at the time of the Democratic convention in 1835, took it upon himself to represent his State in it) + *-ize*.] To assume a position or function without credentials. [U. S. political slang of about 1835 and later.]

ruckle (ruk'l), *n.* [Cf. D. *rogchelen*, clear the throat, spit out; MHG. *ruohelen*, *ruhelen*, *rüchelen*, *rühelen*, *rüchelen*, *rüchelu*, whinny, roar, rattle, G. *röcheln*, rattle, freq. of OHG. *rohôn*, MHG. *rohen*, roar, grunt; Icel. *hrygla*, a rattling in the throat, Sw. *rackla*, hawk, or clear the throat; L. *rugire*, roar, Gr. ὠρυγμός, a roar; all prob. more or less imitative.] A rattling noise in the throat, as from suffocation. See *death-ruckle*. [Scotch.]

ruckle (ruk'l), *v. i.*; pret. and pp. *ruckled*, ppr. *ruckling*. [‹ *ruckle*, *n.*] To make a rattling noise; rattle. [Scotch.]

> The deep *ruckling* groans of the patient satisfied every one that she was breathing her last.
> Scott, St. Ronan's Well, xxxviii.

ruckling (ruk'ling), *n.* and *a.* Same as *reckling*.

ructation (ruk-tā'shon), *n.* [‹ LL. *ructatio(n-)*, ‹ L. *ructare*, belch: see *eructate*.] The act of belching; eructation. *Cockeram.*

> Absteyne from meate[s] that ingendre botches, inflammations, fumous *ructations*, or vapours.
> *Sir T. Elyot*, Castle of Health, iv. 12. (*Richardson.*)

> There are some little symptoms of this inordination, by which a man may perceive himself to have transgressed his measures; "*ructation*, uneasy loads, singing, looser pratings."
> *Jer. Taylor*, Works (ed. 1835), I. 701.

ruction (ruk'shon), *n.* [Prob. a dial. perversion of *eruption*.] A vexation or annoyance; also, a disturbance; a row or rumpus. [Slang.]

rud[1] (rud), *n.* [Also *rudd*; ‹ ME. *rud*, *rudde*, *rude*, *rode*, redness, ‹ AS. *rudu*, redness (of complexion), ‹ *reódan*, be red: see *red*[1]. Cf. *ruddy*.] 1†. Redness; blush; flush.

> Her chekes full choise, as the chalke white,
> As the rose was the *rud* that raiked hom in.
> *Destruction of Troy* (E. E. T. S.), l. 3048.

2†. Complexion; face.

> His *rode* was reed, his eyen greye as goos.
> *Chaucer*, Miller's Tale, l. 131.

> Olympias the onorable ouer all hue hyght,
> Rose red was hur *rode*, full riall of schape.
> *Alisaunder of Macedoine* (E. E. T. S.), l. 178.

3. Red ocher; reddle for marking sheep. [Prov. Eng.]

rud[1]† (rud), *a.* [An adj. use of *rud*[1], *n.*, or var. of *red*[1]: see *rud*[1], *n.*, *red*[1], and cf. *ruddy*.] Red; ruddy.

> Sweet blushes stayn'd her *rud*-red checke,
> Her eyen were blacke as sloe.
> *Percy's Reliques*, p. 327.

rud[1]† (rud), *v.* [‹ ME. *rudden*, *ruden*, *rodden*, *rotlen*, a secondary form or a var. of *red*[1], *v.*, ‹ AS. *reódian*, be or become red, *reódan*, redden, stain with blood: see *red*[1], *v.*] **I.** *trans.* To make red.

> Her checkes lyke apples which the sun hath *rudded*.
> *Spenser*, Epithalamion, l. 173.

II. *intrans.* To redden.

> As rody as a rose *roddede* hus chekes.
> *Piers Plowman* (C), xvi. 108.

> The apple *rodded* from its palie greene.
> *Chatterton*, An Excellente Balade of Charitie.

rud[2] (rud), *n.* A dialectal variant of *reed*[1].

rud[3] (rud), *v. t.* [A var. of *red*[3], *rid*[3] (?).] To rub; polish. *Halliwell.* [Prov. Eng.]

rudas (rö'das), *n.* and *a.* [Also *roudes*; cf. Sc. *roudoch*, *roodyoch*, sulky-looking.] **I.** *n.* A foul-mouthed old woman; a randy; a beldam; a hag. [Scotch.]

II. *a.* Bold; coarse; foul-mouthed: applied to women. [Scotch.]

> But what can ail them to bury the auld carlin (a *rudas* wife she was) in the night time?
> *Scott*, Antiquary, xxvi.

Cone-flower (*Rudbeckia hirta*).
1. Upper part of the stem with the heads. 2. Lower part of the stem. *a*, the achenium.

Rudbeckia (rud-bek'i-ä), *n.* [NL. (Linnæus, 1737), named after Olaus *Rudbeck* (1630–1702), his son Olaus (1660–1740), and a relative, Olaus John, all Swedish botanical writers, the first the founder (1657) of the Botanical Garden of Upsala.] A genus of composite plants of the tribe *Helianthoideæ* and subtribe *Verbesineæ*, consisting of rigid, mostly perennial herbs with large or middle-sized (often showy) heads borne on long stalks. The heads are marked by a hemispherical involucre, commonly with two rows of partly or wholly herbaceous bracts, long spreading sterile ray-flowers, and a conical or cylindrical receptacle, with concave chaff embracing the numerous disk-flowers. The fruit consists of many long compressed or four-angled smooth achenes, often tipped with an irregular crown-like pappus. The species now classed in this genus, including those of *Echinacea*, number about 25, natives chiefly of the eastern and central United States, with a few in California and Mexico. They are tall or low plants, sparingly branched, rough and often bristly, the leaves alternate, simple and divided or otherwise, or compound. The rays are in some species purple or violet, in one species crimson, but in many, including the most familiar, yellow or orange, contrasting with a commonly dark purple-brown disk. A general name for the species is *cone-flower* (which see). The most common is *R. hirta*, a coarse but brilliant plant of meadows and pastures. *R. speciosa* is a similar plant long cultivated in gardens, often wrongly called *R. fulgida*, which name belongs to a more southern species with shorter rays.

rudd[1], *n.* and *a.* Another spelling of *rud*[1].

rudd[2] (rud), *n.* [A particular use of *rud*[1], *rudd*[1].] The redeye, a cyprinoid fish of Europe, *Leuciscus* or *Scardinius erythrophthalmus*.

Rudd (*Leuciscus* or *Scardinius erythrophthalmus*).

It has a high back, deep body, and comparatively small head. The back is olivaceous, the sides and belly are yellowish marked with red, and the ventral and anal fins are deep-red. It is common in Great Britain and on the Continent, and attains a length of a foot or more.

rudder[1] (rud'ėr), *n.* [‹ ME. *roder*, *rother*, ‹ AS. *rōther*, *rōthor*, *rōthr*, an oar, a paddle (*rōthres blæd*, 'rudder-blade,' *steór-rōther*, 'a steering-rudder' or paddle, *scip-rōther*, 'a ship-rudder'); (cf. *rōther*, *rōthra*, *rēthra*, *gerēthra*, a rower, sailor, *gerēthru*, helm, rudder) (= MD. *roeder*, roer, D. roer, an oar, rudder (MD. *roeder*, a rower), = MLG. *roder*, LG. *roeder*, roer = OHG. *ruodar*, MHG. *ruoder*, G. *ruder* = Icel. *ræthri* = Sw. *roder*, ror = Dan. ror, rudder), with formative *-der*, *-ther*, of agent, ‹ *rōwan*, row: see *row*[1].] 1. That part of the helm which is abaft the stern-post, and is turned

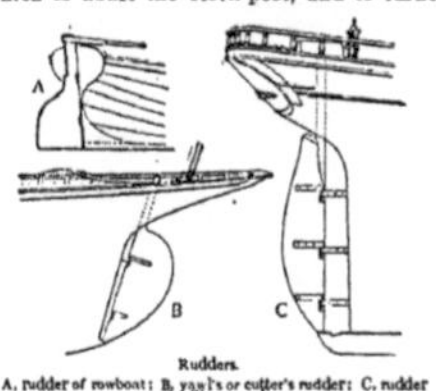

Rudders.
A, rudder of rowboat; B, yawl's or cutter's rudder; C, rudder of sailing vessel.

by the tiller so as to expose its side more or less to the resistance of the water and thus direct the ship's course. It is usually hinged on the stern-post by pintles and gudgeons.

> Discrecion . . . is the cartere of uirtues, ase zayth sant bernard, and the *rother* of the ssipe of the zaule.
> *Ayenbite of Inwyt* (E. E. T. S.), p. 160.

> In daunger hit [Noah's ark] semed,
> With-outen . . . hande-helme hasped on *rother*.
> *Alliterative Poems* (ed. Morris), ii. 419.

> The Antoniad, the Egyptian admiral,
> With all their sixty, fly and turn the *rudder*.
> *Shak.*, A. and C., iii. 10. 3.

2. That which guides or governs the course.

> For rhyme the *rudder* is of verses,
> With which, like ships, they steer their courses.
> *S. Butler*, Hudibras, I. i. 463.

3†. A kind of paddle to stir with.

> A *rudder* or instrument to stirre the meash fat with, motaculum. *Withals' Dict.* (ed. 1608), p. 173. (*Nares.*)

4. A bird's tail-feather; a rectrix: as, "rectrices, *rudders*, or true tail-feathers," *Coues*, Key to N. A. Birds, p. 115.—**Chocks of the rudder.** See *chock*[4].—**Equipoise-rudder.** Same as *balance-rudder*.

rudder[2] (rud'ėr), *n.* [A dial. form of *ridder*[1].] A riddle or sieve.

rudder[3]† (rud'ėr), *n.* An obsolete form of *rother*[2].

> *Boote*, a serpent liuing by milk of rudder beasts.
> *Florio.*

rudder-band (rud'ėr-band), *n.* A gearing with which the rudder is braced or made fast while the ship lies at anchor.

> They committed themselves unto the sea, and loosed the *rudder bands*. Acts xxvii. 40.

rudder-brace (rud'ėr-brās), *n.* A strap to receive a pintle of the rudder; a gudgeon.

rudder-brake (rud'ėr-brāk), *n.* A kind of compressor for controlling the rudder in a seaway or in case of accident to the wheel-ropes.

rudder-breeching† (rud'ėr-brē"ching), *n.* A rope for lifting the rudder to ease the motion of the pintles in their gudgeons. *Encyc. Dict.*

rudder-case (rud'ėr-kās), *n.* Same as *rudder-trunk*.

rudder-chain (rud'ėr-chān), *n.* *Naut.*, one of two strong chains often shackled to the after part of a rudder, near the water-line. Each chain is about 6 feet long, and into its end is spliced a rope pendant, which is stopped to eyebolts along the ship's counter, some slack being allowed for the working of the rudder. In case of damage to the rudder-head, the ship can be steered by these pendants worked by tackles.

rudder-chock (rud'ėr-chok), *n.* See *chocks of the rudder*, under *chock*[4].

rudder-coat (rud'ėr-kōt), *n.* A piece of canvas put round the rudder-head to keep the sea from rushing in at the tiller-hole.

rudder-duck (rud'ėr-duk), *n.* A duck of the subfamily *Erismaturinæ*: so called from the narrow stiff rectrices, denuded to their bases. See cut under *Erismatura*.

rudder-feather (rud'ėr-feᴛʜ"ėr), *n.* See *feather*, and *rudder*, 4.

rudder-fish (rud'ėr-fish), *n.* 1. A stromateid fish, *Lirus perciformis*; the log- or barrel-fish. —2. A carangoid fish, *Naucrates ductor*; the pilot-fish.—3. A carangoid fish (nearly related to the pilot-fish), *Seriola zonata*, or allied species; the amber-fish.

rudder-hanger (rud'ėr-hang"ėr), *n.* A device for hanging or shipping a rudder.

rudder-head (rud'ėr-hed), *n.* The upper end of the rudder, into which the tiller is fitted.

rudder-hole (rud'ėr-hōl), *n.* A hole in a ship's deck through which the head of the rudder passes.

rudder-iron (rud'ėr-ī"ėrn), *n.* *Naut.*, same as *pintle*, 1 (*d*). *Fallows.*

rudderless (rud'ėr-les), *a.* [‹ *rudder* + *-less*.] Having no rudder: as, a *rudderless* craft.

rudder-nail (rud'ėr-nāl), *n.* A nail used in fastening the pintle to the rudder.

rudder-pendant (rud'ėr-pen"dant), *n.* See *pendant* and *rudder-chain*. *Thearle*, Naval Arch., § 233.

rudder-perch (rud'ėr-pėrch), *n.* Same as *rudder-fish*, 1.

rudder-port (rud'ėr-pōrt), *n.* See *port*[2].

rudder-post (rud'ėr-pōst), *n.* *Naut.*, in a screw ship, an after stern-post, on which the rudder is hung, abaft of the propeller.

> A pair of legs short and sturdy as *rudder-posts*.
> *The Century*, XXXIX. 225.

rudder-stock (rud'ėr-stok), *n.* The main piece or broadest part of the rudder, attached to the stern-post by the pintles and gudgeons.

rudder-tackle (rud'ėr-tak"l), *n.* Tackle attached to the rudder-pendants.

rudder-trunk (rud'ėr-trungk), *n.* A casing of wood, fitted or boxed firmly into a round hole called the port, through which the rudder-stock is inserted.

rudder-wheel (rud'ėr-hwēl), *n.* In *agri.*, a small wheel sometimes placed at the rear end of a plow to bear part of the weight and to aid in steering or guiding the plow.

ruddied (rud'id), *a.* [‹ *ruddy* + *-ed*[2].] Made ruddy or red. *Scott.*

ruddily (rud'i-li), *adv.* In a ruddy manner; with a reddish appearance. *Imp. Dict.*

ruddiness (rud'i-nes), *n.* The state of being ruddy; redness; rosiness; especially, that degree of redness of complexion which denotes good health: as, the *ruddiness* of the cheeks or lips.

> The *ruddiness* upon her lip is wet. *Shak.*, W. T., v. 3. 81.

ruddle[1] (rud'l), *n.* [Also *reddle*, *raddle*, ‹ ME. *rudel*, **rodel* (in comp. *rodelwort*), ‹ AS. *rudu*, redness, ‹ *redd*, red: see *rud*[1], *red*[1].] 1. Same as *reddle*.

Of all other sorts of red earth, the *ruddle* of Ægypt and Affricke is fittest for carpenters; for if they strike their line upon timber with it . . . it will take colour and be marked verie well. *Holland*, tr. of Pliny, xxxv. 6.

2†. Ruddiness; redness.

His skin, like blushes which adorn
The bosom of the rising morn,
All over *ruddle* is, and from
His flaming eyes quick glances come.
Baker's Poems (1697), p. 11. (*Halliwell.*)

Lemnian ruddle. See *Lemnian.*

ruddle[1] (rud'l), *v. t.*; pret. and pp. *ruddled*, ppr. *ruddling*. [< *ruddle*[1], *n.*] To mark with ruddle.

Over the trap-doors to the cellars were piles of market-gardeners' sieves, *ruddled* like a sheep's back with big red letters. *Mayhew*, London Labour and London Poor, II. 570.

ruddle[2] (rud'l), *n.* A dialectal variant of *riddle*[2].

The holes of the sieve, *ruddle*, or try.
Holland, tr. of Plutarch, p. 86. (*Trench.*)

ruddle[2] (rud'l), *v. t.* [See *ruddle*[2], *n.*] To sift together; mix as through a sieve.

ruddle[3]† (rud'l), *v. t.* [A var. of *raddle*[1]; prob. due to *ruddle*[2].] To raddle; interweave; cross-plait, as twigs or split sticks in making lattice-work or wattles. [Obsolete or prov. Eng.]

ruddleman (rud'l-man), *n.*; pl. *ruddlemen* (-men). Same as *reddleman.*

Besmeared like a *ruddleman.*
Burton, Anat. of Mel., p. 467.

ruddock (rud'ok), *n.* [Formerly also *ruddoc*, *rudock*; also dial. *reddock*, *raddock*; < ME. *ruddocke*, *ruddok*, *roddok*, < AS. *rudduc*, *ruduc*, a ruddock; appar. with dim. suffix *-uc*, E. *-ock*, < *rudu*, redness (see *rud*[1], *n.*); otherwise < W. *rhuddog* = Corn. *ruddoc*, a redbreast; but these may be from the AS., and are in any case ult. connected with *rud*[1], *ruddy*.] 1. The bird *Erythacus rubecula*, the robin-redbreast of Europe. See *robin*[1], 1.

The tame *ruddok* and the coward kyte.
Chaucer, Parliament of Fowls, l. 349.

The *ruddock* would,
With charitable bill, . . . bring thee all this.
Shak., Cymbeline, iv. 2. 224.

That lesser pelican, the sweet
And shrilly *ruddock*, with its bleeding breast.
Hood, Plea of the Midsummer Fairies, st. 55.

2†. A gold coin: also called *red ruddock* or *golden ruddock*. [Old slang.]

In the second pocket he must have his *red ruddockes* ready, which he must give unto his lawier, who will not set penne to paper without them.
Choise of Change (1585). (*Nares.*)

If one bee olde, and have silver haires on his beard, so he have *golden ruddocks* in his bagges, hee must bee wise and honourable. *Lyly*, Midas, ii. 1.

The greedie Carle came there within a space
That ownd the good, and saw the Pot behinde
Where *Ruddocks* lay, . . . but *Ruddocks* could not finde.
Turberville, Of Two Desperate Men.

There be foure Sea-captaines. I believe they be little better then pirats, they are so flush of their *rudocks*.
Heywood, Fair Maid of the West (Works, II. 277).

3. A kind of apple. *Howell.* (*Halliwell.*)

ruddy (rud'i), *a.* [< ME. *ruddy*, *rody*, *rodi*, *rudi*, < AS. **rudig*, *rudi*, reddish, ruddy, < *rudu* (= Icel. *rothi*, redness), red, redness, < *reódan* (pret. pl. *rudon*), make red, < *reád*, red: see *rud*[1], *red*[1].] 1. Of a red color; reddish; inclining to red; rosy: as, a *ruddy* blaze; *ruddy* clouds; *ruddy* gold; *ruddy* cheeks.

Than hadde the lady grete shame, and wax all rody, but noon ne knewe the cause. *Merlin* (E. E. T. S.), ii. 181.

Now he [David] was *ruddy*, and withal of a beautiful countenance, and goodly to look to. 1 Sam. xvi. 12.

You are my true and honourable wife,
As dear to me as are the *ruddy* drops
That visit my sad heart. *Shak.*, J. C., ii. 1. 289.

Like a furnace mouth
Cast forth redounding smoke and *ruddy* flame.
Milton, P. L., ii. 889.

The *ruddier* orange and the paler lime.
Cowper, Task, iii. 573.

His face was *ruddy*, his hair was gold.
Tennyson, The Victim.

2. Glowing; cheery; bright.

With the best will, no man can be twenty-five for ever. The old *ruddy* convictions deserted me, and, along with them, the style that fits their presentation and defence.
R. L. Stevenson, Virginibus Puerisque, Ded.

Ruddy diver. Same as *ruddy duck.*—**Ruddy duck.** See *duck*[2].—**Ruddy gold,** gold so alloyed as to be reddish in color, used in the jewelry and goldsmiths' work of Cashmere and Burma. *S. K. Handbook*, Indian Arts.—**Ruddy plover.** See *plover.* =**Syn. 1.** *Ruddy, Rubicund, Rosy. Ruddy* indicates a fresh and healthy red upon the human skin, or, by extension, upon skies, etc. *Rubicund* indicates an unnatural red in the face or some part of it, as the cheeks or the nose; it is especially associated with high living or intemperance in drink. *Rosy* generally indicates a charming, blooming red: as, *rosy* cheeks; but it is occasionally used in a bad sense.

ruddy (rud'i), *v. t.*; pret. and pp. *ruddied*, ppr. *ruddying*. [< *ruddy*, *a.*] To make red or ruddy. [Rare.]

O'er Roslin all that dreary night
A wondrous blaze was seen to gleam; . . .
It glared on Roslin's castled rock,
It *ruddied* all the copse-wood glen.
Scott, L. of L. M., vi. 23.

ruddy-rudder (rud'i-rud″ėr), *n.* The long-eared sunfish, *Lepomis auritus:* so called from the red color of the tail. [New Jersey and Delaware.]

rude (röd), *a.* [< ME. *rude*, < OF. *rude*, F. *rude* = Pr. Pg. It. *rude* = Sp. *rudo*, < L. *rudis*, rough, raw, rude, wild, untilled; root unknown. From the same source are *rudiment*, *erudite*, *erudition*, etc.] 1. Rough; crude; unwrought; unfashioned; ill-fashioned; without finish or shapeliness: as, a *rude* mass of material.

And I my selfe sawe a masse of *rude* goulde (that is to say, such as was neuer molten), lyke vnto suche stones as are founde in the bottomes of ryuers, weighinge nyne ownces.
Peter Martyr, tr. in Eden's First Books on America [(ed Arber), p. 72.

Be of good comfort, prince; for you are born
To set a form upon that indigest
Which he hath left so shapeless and so *rude*.
Shak., K. John, v. 7. 27.

This *rude* plot, which blind chance (the ape
Of counsel and advice) hath brought forth blind.
Chapman, All Fools, i. 1.

It was the winter wild,
While the heaven-born child
All meanly wrapt in the *rude* manger lies.
Milton, Nativity, l. 31.

2. Lacking cultivation, refinement, or elegance; clumsy; uncouth: as, *rude* verses; *rude* art.

He sung, in *rude* harsh-sounding rhymes.
Shak., K. John, iv. 2. 150.

One example may serve, till you review the Æneis in the original, unblemished by my *rude* translation.
Dryden.

His *rude* oratory roused and melted hearers who listened without interest to the labored discourses of great logicians and Hebraists. *Macaulay*, Hist. Eng., vii.

With untaught *rudest* skill
Vexing a treble from the slender strings
Thin as the locust sings.
O. W. Holmes, Even-Song.

3. Mean; humble; little known or regarded; hence, as said of persons, low by birth or position.

Al were it that myne auncestres weren *rude*,
Yet may the hye God, and so hope I,
Grante me grace to lyven vertuously.
Chaucer, Wife of Bath's Tale, l. 316.

Jest not with a *rude* man, lest thy ancestors be disgraced. Ecclus. viii. 4.

From a rude isle his *ruder* lineage came.
Scott, Vision of Don Roderick, The Vision, st. 39.

4. Barbarous; uncivilized; unpolished; ignorant.

The Spanyard that nowe is is come from as *rude* and savage nations as they [the Irish].
Spenser, State of Ireland.

Though I be *rude* in speech, yet not in knowledge.
2 Cor. xi. 6.

When men were but *rude* in sea-causes in regard of the great knowledge which we now haue.
Hakluyt's Voyages, To the Reader.

Among the *rudest* savages personal interests are very vaguely distinguished from the interests of others.
H. *Spencer*, Data of Ethics, § 91.

Over the seas
With a crew that is neither *rude* nor rash.
Tennyson, The Islet.

5. Having a fierce or cruel disposition; ferocious; sanguinary; savage; brutal.

Strength should be lord of imbecility,
And the *rude* son should strike his father dead.
Shak., T. and C., i. 3. 115.

O but the Johnstones were wondrous *rude*,
When the Biddes-burn ran three days blood!
Lads of Wamphray (Child's Ballads, VI. 172).

Now timely sing, ere the *rude* bird of hate
Foretell my hopeless doom. *Milton*, Sonnets, i.

6. Marked by or expressing fierceness or savageness; ferocious, fierce, or cruel in quality.

The werwolf ful wiȝtli went to him euene,
With a *rude* roring as he him rende wold.
William of Palerne (E. E. T. S.), l. 1851.

He leide a-boute hym so grym strokes and *rude* that noon durste hym a-bide, but disparbled a-brode fro hym as from a wode lyon in rage. *Merlin* (E. E. T. S.), ii. 196.

Even thy song
Hath a *rude* martial tone, a blow in every thought!
Whittier, To J. P.

7. Ill-bred; boorish; uncivil; discourteous; impolite.

A *rude* despiser of good manners.
Shak., As you Like it, ii. 7. 92.

There was, indeed, in far less polish'd days,
A time when rough *rude* man had naughty ways.
Burns, Rights of Woman.

Young Branghton, who had been apparently awed by the presence of so fine a gentleman, was again himself, *rude* and familiar. *Miss Burney*, Evelina, xlvii.

8. Marked by incivility; contrary to the requirements of courtesy: as, *rude* conduct; a *rude* remark.

Ruffian, let go that *rude* uncivil touch!
Shak., T. G. of V., v. 4. 60.

I'm quite ashamed—'tis mighty *rude*
To eat so much—but all 's so good.
Pope, Imit. of Horace, II. vi. 206.

9. Rough; tempestuous; stormy: as, a *rude* gale; *rude* weather.

The *rude* sea grew civil at her [a mermaid's] song.
Shak., M. N. D., ii. 1. 152.

The storm
Of his *rude* misfortunes is blown over.
Middleton (*and others*), The Widow, iii. 3.

The *rude* inclemency of wintry skies.
Cowper, Truth, l. 138.

10. Robust; sturdy; rugged; vigorous.

Here and there smiled a plump rosy face enough; but the majority seemed under-sized, under-fed, utterly wanting in grace, vigour, and what the penny-a-liners call "*rude* health." *Kingsley*, Yeast, xiii.

How it disgusts when weakness, false-refined,
Censures the honest *rude* effective strength.
Browning, Ring and Book, II. 149.

When people in the *rudest* physical health are sick of life, they go to her for the curative virtue of her smiles.
S. Lanier, The English Novel, p. 55.

Rude respiration. See *respiration.* =**Syn. 1.** Ill-shaped, raw, uncouth, unformed.—7 and 8. Vulgar, loutish, boorish, ill-bred, insolent, surly, churlish, gruff, brusk.—9. Harsh, inclement, violent, turbulent.

rude (röd), *adv.* [< ME. *rude*; < *rude*, *a.*] Rudely.

Then to the abbot, which that balled was,
Hath Gaffray spokyn *rude* and bustealy.
Rom. of Partenay (E. E. T. S.), l. 3257.

And Caledon threw by the drone,
And did her whittle draw, man;
And swoor fu' *rude*, thro' dirt and blood,
To mak' it guid in law, man.
Burns, American War.

rude-growing (röd'grō″ing), *a.* Rough; wild.

Whose mouth is cover'd with *rude-growing* briers.
Shak., Tit. And., ii. 3. 199.

rudely (röd'li), *adv.* [< ME. *rudely*, *ruidly*, *rudeliche*; < *rude* + *-ly*[2].] In a rude manner. (*a*) Roughly; clumsily; unskilfully: as, work *rudely* done; an object *rudely* formed.

Thai war full grete and *rudely* wroght,
Bot tharfore thai forsuke tham noght,
Bot sone, when thai thir nailes had,
Furth thai went with hert ful glad.
Holy Rood (E. E. T. S.), p. 86.

I, that am *rudely* stamp'd, and want love's majesty.
Shak., Rich. III., i. 1. 16.

The savage who in his nocturnal prowlings guides himself by the stars has *rudely* classified these objects in their relations of position. *J. Fiske*, Cosmic Philos., I. 28.

(*b*) Inelegantly; awkwardly.

If yow be borne or brought vp in a rude co[u]ntrie, ye shall not chose but speake *rudelie*.
Ascham, The Scholemaster, p. 117.

(*c*) With offensive bluntness or roughness; uncivilly; impolitely.

Who spekithe to the in any maner place,
Rudely cast nat thyn ye adowne,
But with a sadde chiere loke hym in the face.
Babees Book (E. E. T. S.), p. 26.

You ne'er consider whom you shove,
But *rudely* press before a duke.
Pope, Imit. of Horace, II. vi. 59.

(*d*) Impetuously; fiercely; savagely.

He romed, he rared, that roggede alle the erthe!
So *ruydly* he rappyd at to ryot hym selvene!
Morte Arthure (E. E. T. S.), l. 785.

They found the king's army in order to receive them, and were so *rudely* attacked that most of those who had penetrated into the camp were left dead upon the spot.
Bruce, Source of the Nile, II. 123.

(*e*) Violently; stormily; boisterously: as, the wind blew *rudely*.

Ther com rennynge so grete a water, . . . so depe and brode and ther-to blakke, that com down fro the sides of the mounteynes so *rudely*, that ther was noon so hardy but he ther-of hadde drede. *Merlin* (E. E. T. S.), ii. 350.

(*f*†) Vulgarly; broadly; coarsely.

Al speke he never so *rudeliche* or large.
Chaucer, Gen. Prol. to C. T., l. 734.

rudeness (röd'nes), *n.* [< ME. *rudenesse*; < *rude* + *-ness*.] The state or quality of being rude. (*a*) Crudeness; roughness; clumsiness.

I thought he slept, and put
My clouted brogues from off my feet, whose *rudeness*
Answer'd my steps too loud.
Shak., Cymbeline, iv. 2. 214.

(*b*) Inelegance; lack of refinement or polish; uncouthness; awkwardness.

The *rudenes* of common and mother tonges is no bar for wise speaking. *Ascham*, The Scholemaster, p. 117.

All the antique fashions of the street were dear to him; even such as were characterized by a *rudeness* that would naturally have annoyed his fastidious senses.
Hawthorne, Seven Gables, xi.

(*c*) Humble position; rusticity; low life.

God hath swich favour sent hir of his grace,
That it ne semed nat by lyklinesse
That she was born and fed in *rudenesse*.
Chaucer, Clerk's Tale, l. 341.

(*d*) Barbarism; lack of civilization or enlightenment; ignorance.

"Hermit poore" and "Chiny Chese" was all the musique we had; and yet no ordinary fiddlers get so much money as our's do here, which speaks our *rudenesse* still.
Pepys, Diary, III. 62.

(*e*) Coarseness of manners or conduct; boorishness; churlishness; discourtesy; incivility.

The *rudeness* that hath appeared in me have I learned from my entertainment.
Shak., T. N., i. 5. 230.

He chooses company, but not the squire's,
Whose wit is *rudeness*, whose good breeding tires.
Cowper, Retirement, l. 438.

(*f*) Roughness of weather; tempestuousness; storminess; inclemency.

The *rudeness* of the Winter Season kept me in for some time.
Lister, Journey to Paris, p. 5.

(*g*) Impetuosity; brunt; fierceness: as, the *rudeness* of a conflict.

The ram that batters down the wall,
For the great swing and *rudeness* of his poise,
They place before his hand that made the engine.
Shak., T. and C., i. 3. 207.

=**Syn.** (*a*) Ruggedness. (*e*) *Impertinence, Effrontery*, etc. (see *impudence*), surliness, impoliteness, uncouthness.

rudented (rǫ-den'ted), *a.* [Accom. ‹ F. *rudenté*, rudented, ‹ L. *ruden(t-)s*, a rope, cord, appar. orig. ppr. of *rudere*, roar, rattle (with ref. to the noise made by cordage).] In *arch.*, same as *cabled*.

rudenture (rǫ-den'tūr), *n.* [‹ OF. (and F.) *rudenture*, ‹ *rudenté*, rudented: see *rudented*.] In *arch.*, the figure of a rope or staff, plain or carved, with which the flutings of columns are sometimes filled. Also called *cabling*.

ruderal (rö'de-ral), *a.* [‹ L. *rudus* (*ruder-*), rubbish, stones broken small and mixed with lime, for plastering walls.] In *bot.*, growing in waste places or among rubbish.

ruderary† (rö'de-rā-ri), *a.* [‹ L. *ruderarius*, of or belonging to rubbish, ‹ *rudus* (*ruder-*), rubbish: see *ruderal*.] Belonging to rubbish. *Bailey*, 1727.

ruderation† (rö-de-rā'shon), *n.* [‹ OF. *ruderation*, F. *rudération*, ‹ L. *ruderatio(n-)*, a paving with rubbish, ‹ *ruderare*, cover or pave with rubbish, ‹ *rudus* (*ruder-*), rubbish: see *ruderal*.] The act of paving with pebbles or small stones and mortar. *Bailey*.

rudesby† (rödz'bi), *n.* [‹ *rude* + *-s-* + *-by*, a termination, found also in *idlesby*, *sneaksby*, and *suresby* (also *sureby*), by some taken to be a reduced form of *boy*, but prob. an arbitrary addition, suggested perhaps by such surnames as *Catesby*, *Rigby*, etc., which are orig. local names (see *by*[2]).] A rude, boisterous, or turbulent fellow.

To give my hand, opposed against my heart,
Unto a mad-brain *rudesby* full of spleen.
Shak., T. of the S., iii. 2. 10.

Rüdesheimer (rü'des-hī-mėr), *n.* [‹ G. *Rüdesheimer*, ‹ *Rüdesheim*, name of a town in Prussia on the right bank of the Rhine, near Bingen.] One of the white Rhine wines, most highly esteemed after Johannisberger. It is made near Rüdesheim. The wine-growing district is very large, and there are many varieties and qualities of the wine.—**Rüdesheimer Berg**, wine produced in the vineyard of that name on the hillside facing the south, and considered the best of the vineyards of Rüdesheim.

rudge (ruj), *n.* [Origin obscure.] A partridge. *Halliwell*. [Prov. Eng.]

rudge-gown†, *n.* See *rug-gown*.

rudge-wash (ruj'wosh), *n.* [‹ **rudge*, var. of *ridge*, back, + *wash*.] Kersey cloth made of fleece-wool worked as it comes from the sheep's back, and not cleansed after it is shorn. *Halliwell*.

rudiment (rö'di-ment), *n.* [‹ OF. (and F.) *rudiment* = Sp. Pg. *rudimento* = It. *rudimento*, rudiments, elements, ‹ L. *rudimentum*, a first attempt, a beginning, pl. *rudimenta*, the elements, ‹ *rudis*, rude: see *rude*.] **1.** Anything which is in an undeveloped state; the principle which lies at the beginning or bottom of any development; an unformed or unfinished beginning.

When nature makes a flower or living creature, she formeth *rudiments* of all the parts at one time.
Bacon, Advancement of Learning, ii. 301.

But first I mean
To exercise him in the wilderness;
There he shall first lay down the *rudiments*
Of his great warfare.
Milton, P. R., i. 157.

The sappy boughs
Attire themselves with blooms, sweet *rudiments*
Of future harvest.
J. Philips, Cider, ii.

2. An element or first principle of any art or science; especially, in the plural, the beginning, first steps, or introduction to any branch of knowledge; the elements or elementary notions.

Beware lest any man spoil you through philosophy and vain deceit, . . . after the *rudiments* of the world, and not after Christ.
Col. ii. 8.

To learn the order of my fingering,
I must begin with *rudiments* of art.
Shak., T. of the S., iii. 1. 66.

3. In *biol.*: (*a*) That which is rudimentary; that which is in its first or an early stage of development, which may or may not be continued; the beginning or foundation of any part or organ: as, the *rudiment* of the embryo which is to go on to maturity; the *rudiment* of an organ whose further development has been arrested or aborted. (*b*) That which is vestigial; a vestigial or aborted part, organ, or structure; an abortion; a vestige. =**Syn.** 3. *Fœtus, Germ*, etc. See *embryo*.

rudiment (rö'di-ment), *v. t.* [‹ *rudiment*, *n.*] To furnish with first principles or rules; ground; settle in first principles.

It is the right discipline of knight-errantry to be *rudimented* in losses at first, and to have the tyrocinium somewhat tart.
Gayton, Notes on Don Quixote, p. 37.

rudimental (rö-di-men'tal), *a.* [‹ *rudiment* + *-al*.] Pertaining to or of the nature of rudiments; rudimentary.

Your first *rudimental* essays in spectatorship were made in my shop, where you often practised for hours.
Spectator.

rudimentarily (rö-di-men'ta-ri-li), *adv.* In a rudimentary manner or state; elementarily.

Every such event brings him [man] into relation with the unknown, and arouses in him a feeling which must be called *rudimentarily* religious.
Mind, X. 22.

rudimentary (rö-di-men'ta-ri), *a.* [= F. *rudimentaire* = Sp. *rudimentario* = Pg. *rudimentar*; as *rudiment* + *-ary*.] **1.** Pertaining to rudiments or first principles; consisting in or dealing with first principles; elementary; initial: as, *rudimentary* teachings; *rudimentary* laws.—**2.** Of the nature of a rudiment; elementary; undeveloped.

It ["Gammer Gurton's Needle"] is a capital example of farce, just as Ralph Roister Doister is of a rather *rudimentary* kind of regular comedy.
Saintsbury, Hist. Elizabethan Literature, iii.

The revelation of a *rudimentary* and imperfect science would be unworthy of God, and would require continual correction as knowledge advanced.
Dawson, Nature and the Bible, p. 21.

3. Specifically, in *biol.*: (*a*) Pertaining to or of the nature of a rudiment; rudimental; beginning to be formed; elementary; embryonic. (*b*) Vestigial; abortive; aborted or arrested in development; having no functional activity.

Organs, however little developed, if of use, should not be considered as *rudimentary*; they may be called nascent, and may hereafter be developed by natural selection to any further extent.
Darwin, Origin of Species, p. 406.

=**Syn.** 3. *Rudimentary, Vestigial, Abortive*. These three words, in their biological application, are commonly used interchangeably, and may mean exactly the same thing. But there is a clear and proper distinction in most cases, since that which is *rudimentary* in one organism may be fully developed in another organism, and that which is *rudimentary* in a given organism may or may not proceed to develop in that organism. So that which is developed in one organism but remains *rudimentary* in another is *vestigial* for the latter—that is, it affords a mere trace or hint of the former; and that which might have developed but did not develop in the same organism is *abortive*. Thus, all embryonic parts and organs are properly *rudimentary*; all functionless organs are *vestigial* which in another case have become functional; those which are normally functional but fail to become so in a given case are *abortive*. *Rudimentary* is the most general and comprehensive term for that which is rude, raw, crude, unformed, in an absolute sense; *vestigial* is a relative term, implying comparison with something else, of which that which is *vestigial* is a mere trace; *abortive* is likewise a relative term, but one implying arrest or failure of development in the thing itself, without reference to any other thing. Few if any organs can be described with equal accuracy by all three terms, though the distinctions are often ignored. *Vestigial* is a more technical term than either of the other two, implying a broad view of the thing described, derived from comparative anatomy and physiology, according to the theory of evolution. *Abortive* is specially applicable to pathological and teratological cases. A harelip or cleft palate is *abortive*, but neither *vestigial* nor *rudimentary*. The thymus of the adult is *vestigial*, but neither *abortive* nor *rudimentary*. The brain-bladders of the embryo are *rudimentary*, but neither *vestigial* nor *abortive*. Most of the functionless and apparently useless organs of adults of the higher animals are most properly to be designated as *vestigial*.

rudimentation (rö'di-men-tā'shon), *n.* [‹ *rudiment* + *-ation*.] The making rudimentary; reduction to or representation by mere rudiments. [Rare.]

Rudista (rǫ-dis'tä), *n. pl.* [NL.] In De Blainville's classification (1825), the second order of his *Acephalophora*, composed of the genera *Sphærulites*, *Hippurites*, *Radiolites*, *Birostrites*, and *Calceola*. These have been mostly referred next to the *Chamidæ* or to the superfamily *Chamacea* by most modern writers, and to the families *Hippuritidæ*, *Radiolitidæ*, and *Caprinidæ*. *Calceola* is a coralligenous zoantharian. Also called *Rudistæ*, *Rudistes*.

rudistan (rǫ-dis'tan), *a.* and *n.* **I.** *a.* Of or relating to the *Rudista*.

II. *n.* One of the *Rudista*.

rudity (rö'di-ti), *n.* [= It. *rudità*, ‹ L. *ruditа(t-)s*, ignorance, ‹ *rudis*, rude: see *rude*.] Rudeness. [Rare.] *Imp. Dict.*

Rudmas-day†, *n.* [ME. **rodmasse-day*; ‹ rood + *mass*[1] + *day*[1].] Holy-rood day (May 3d or September 14th). See *rood*.

Rudolphine (rǫ-dol'fin), *a.* [‹ *Rudolph* (see def.) + *-ine*[1].] Of or pertaining to the emperor Rudolph (Rudolf) II. (1576–1612): an epithet applied to a set of planetary and other astronomical tables composed by Kepler, and founded on the observations of Tycho Brahe.

rue[1] (rö), *v.*; pret. and pp. *rued*, ppr. *ruing*. [Early mod. E. also *rew*; ‹ ME. *rewen*, *reowen*, *ruwen*, *ruen* (pret. *rew*, *reu*, also *rewede*, *rewide*, *rewed*, *reude*), ‹ (*a*) AS. *hreówan* (a strong verb, pret. *hreáw*), make sorry, grieve (often used impersonally, like L. *pœnitet*), = OS. *hreuwan* (pret. *hrau*) = D. *rouwen* = MLG. *ruwen*, LG. *ruwen*, *rouwen*, *ruen* (the D. and LG. forms being weak, but orig. strong) = OHG. *hriuwan*, MHG. *riuwen*, make sorry, grieve; (*b*) also weak, AS. *hreówian* = OS. *hriwōn* = OHG. *hriuwōn*, MHG. *riuwen*, G. *reuen*, feel pain or sorrow, = Icel. *hryggja*, make sorry, grieve, refl. rue; (c) with formative *-s*, AS. *hreówsian* = OHG. **hriuwisōn*, *riuwisōn*, intr., be sorry, repent; cf. AS. *hreówe*, sad, mournful (= Icel. *hryggr*, grieved, afflicted), *hreów*, sorrow, grief (see *rue*[1], *n.*). Connection with L. *crudelis*, cruel, *crudus*, crude, etc., is improbable: see *crude*, *cruel*. Hence ult. *ruth*.] **I.** *trans.* **1**†. To cause to grieve; make repentant, compassionate, or sorrowful; afflict: often used impersonally with a personal pronoun.

Bot we find thi tales trew,
Ful sare it sall *thi seluen rew*.
Holy Rood (E. E. T. S.), p. 85.

By seint Thomas!
Me reweth score of hende Nicolas.
Chaucer, Miller's Tale, l. 276.

Deare dame, your suddein overthrow
Much *rueth me*.
Spenser, F. Q., I. ii. 21.

2. To repent of; feel remorse for; regret; hence, to suffer in expiation of: as, to *rue* one's folly or mistakes.

France, thou shalt *rue* this treason with thy tears,
If Talbot but survive thy treachery.
Shak., 1 Hen. VI., iii. 2. 36.

I came
Breathing self-murder, frenzy, spite,
To *rue* my guilt in endless flame.
M. Arnold, St. Brandan.

3. To feel sorrow or suffering on account of; suffer from or by; experience loss or injury from.

Gonys he bad me "go, foule Sathan!"
Euere-more that repreef y *rewe*.
Hymns to Virgin, etc. (E. E. T. S.), p. 47.

Orphans, for their parents' timeless death,
Shall *rue* the hour that ever thou wast born.
Shak., 3 Hen. VI., v. 6. 43.

I am bound to *rue* such knaves as you.
The Kings Disguise (Child's Ballads, V. 377).

Whose Crowns lay all before his Helmet broke;
Whose lopped Sceptres *ru'd* his faulchion's stroke.
J. Beaumont, Psyche, v. 84.

4. To have or take pity on; feel sorry for; compassionate.

Al folk hem migte *rewe*
That loueden hem so trewe.
Nu bene hi bothe dede.
King Horn (E. E. T. S.), l. 1521.

Who shall him *rew* that swimming in the maine
Will die for thirst, and water doth refuse?
Spenser, F. Q., II. vi. 17.

Victorious Titus, *rue* the tears I shed.
Shak., Tit. And., i. 1. 105.

5. To repent of and withdraw, or try to withdraw, from: as, to *rue* a bargain. See *rue-bargain*. [Colloq.]

II. *intrans.* **1.** To be sorrowful; experience grief or harm; suffer; mourn.

ȝit muste y *rue* til that he rise,
Quia amore langueo.
Political Poems, etc. (ed. Furnivall), p. 148.

Come the three corners of the world in arms,
And we shall shock them. Nought shall make us *rue*,
If England to itself do rest but true.
Shak., K. John, v. 7. 117.

2. To repent; feel remorse or regret.

To late is now for me to *rewe*.
Chaucer, Troilus, v. 1070.

O gin ye winna pay me,
I here sall mak a vow,
Before that ye come hame again,
Ye sall ha'e cause to *rue*.
Lamkin (Child's Ballads, III. 95).

3. To have pity; have compassion or mercy: often followed by *on* or *upon*.

In bittir bale nowe art thou boune,
Out-castyn shal thou be for care,
No man shal *rewe* of thy misfare.
York Plays, p. 39.

Therfor axe thou merci, & y schal thee saue,
With pitee y *rue upon* thee so.
Political Poems, etc. (ed. Furnivall), p. 150.

Reweth on this olde caytif in distresse.
Chaucer, Troilus, iv. 104.

Rue on thy despairing lover!
Canst thou break his faithful heart?
Burns, Turn again, thou fair Eliza.

rue[1] (rö), *n.* [< ME. *rewe*, *reowe*, < AS. *hreów*, sorrow, regret, penance, repentance, = D. *rouw* = OHG. *hriuwa*, *riuwa*, MHG. *riuwe*, G. *reue*, sorrow, regret, repentance; from the verb: see *rue*[1], *v.*] Sorrow; repentance. [Obsolete or prov. Eng.]

"I'm a man that, when he makes a bad trade, makes the most of it until he can make better. I'm for no *rues* and after-claps." *A. B. Longstreet*, Georgia Scenes, p. 29.

rue[2] (rö), *n.* [< ME. *rue*, *ruwe*, later *rewe*, < OF. (and F.) *rue* = Pr. *ruda*, *rutha* = Sp. *ruda* = Pg. *ar-ruda* = It. *ruta* = AS. *rūde* = D. LG. *ruit* = OHG. *rūta*, MHG. *rūte*, G. *raute* = Sw. *ruta* = Dan. *rude*, rue, < L. *rūta*, < Gr. ῥυτή, rue, a Peloponnesian word for the common Gr. πήγανον, rue.] Any plant of the genus *Ruta*, especially *R. graveolens*, the common or garden rue, a native of the Mediterranean region and western Asia, and elsewhere common in cultivation. It is a woody herb of bushy habit, 2 or 3 feet high, with decompound leaves, the leaflets of a bluish-green color, strongly dotted. The flowers are greenish-yellow and corymbed, and are produced all summer. The plant has a strong disagreeable odor, and the leaves are extremely acrid, even producing blisters. In antiquity and the middle ages rue was highly esteemed as a medicine, and was believed to ward off contagion. It has the properties of a stimulant and antispasmodic, but accompanied by excitant and irritant tendencies. It is not now officinal, but continues somewhat in popular use. In medieval folk-lore it was a common witches' drug. From its supposed virtues, or by association with the word *rue*, repentance, it was formerly called *herb-of-grace*.

Rue (*Ruta graveolens*).

Here in this place
I'll set a bank of *rue*, sour herb of grace:
Rue, even for ruth, here shortly shall be seen,
In the remembrance of a weeping queen.
Shak., Rich. II., iii. 4. 105.

African rue. Same as *Syrian rue*.—**Black rue,** the conifer *Podocarpus spicata* of New Zealand. See *matai*.—**Fen-rue,** a European meadow-rue, *Thalictrum flavum*.—**Goat's rue,** *Galega officinalis* (see *Galega*); also, the related *Tephrosia Virginiana* or catgut in the United States, and *T. cinerea* in the West Indies.—**Oil of rue.** See *oil*.—**Syrian rue.** See *harmel* and *Peganum*.—**Wall rue.** See *Asplenium*.

rue-anemone (rö'ạ-nem″ọ-nẹ), *n.* A little American wild flower, *Anemone thalictroides*, resembling both anemone and meadow-rue.

rue-bargain (rö'bär″gạn), *n.* 1. A bad bargain. *Halliwell*. [Prov. Eng. and Scotch.]—2. A forfeit paid for withdrawing from a bargain.

He said it would cost him a guinea of *rue-bargain* to the man who had bought his pony, before he could get it back again. *Scott*, Rob Roy, xxvii.

rue-fern (rö'fėrn), *n.* Same as *wall-rue*.

rueful (rö'fůl), *a.* [< ME. *ruful*, *rewful*, *reuful*, *reufol*; < *rue*[1], *n.*, + *-ful*.] 1†. Full of pity or compassion; pitying.

Criste of his curteysie shal conforte ȝow atte laste,
And rewarde alle dowble riccheuse that *reuful* hertes habbeth. *Piers Plowman* (B), xiv. 148.

2. Worthy of pity or sorrow; lamentable; pitiable; deplorable; sorry.

"That was a *reufol* restitucion," quath Repentaunce, "for sothe;
Thow wolt hongy [hang] heye ther-fore her other in helle!"
Piers Plowman (C), vii. 237.

A *ruefull* spectacle of death and ghastly drere.
Spenser, F. Q., I. viii. 40.

"Alas!" said I, "what *ruefu'* chance
Has twin'd ye o' your stately trees?"
Burns, Destruction of the Woods near Drumlanrig.

3. Expressive of regret, sorrow, or misfortune; mournful; sad; melancholy; lugubrious.

The accident was loud, and here before thee
With *rueful* cry, yet what it was we hear not.
Milton, S. A., l. 1553.

The wo-begone heroes of Communipaw eyed each other with *rueful* countenances. *Irving*, Knickerbocker, p. 121.

=Syn. 3. Doleful, lugubrious, regretful.

ruefully (rö'fůl-i), *adv.* [< ME. *rufully*, *rewfullich*, *rewfulliche*; < *rueful* + *-ly*[2].] In a rueful manner. Specifically—(*a*†) Compassionately; pityingly; mercifully.

Cryst ȝiueth heuene
Bothe to riche and to nouȝte riche that *rewfullich* lybbeth.
Piers Plowman (B), xiv. 152.

(*b*) Pitiably; lamentably; deplorably.

To see this ferly foode
Thus *rufully* dight,
Rugged and rente on a roode,
This is a rewfull sight. *York Plays*, p. 425.

(*c*) Sorrowfully; mournfully; lugubriously.

Troylus hym cladde
And *rewfulliche* his lady gan byholde.
Chaucer, Troilus, iv. 1691.

Dejected all, and *rufully* dismayed.
Dryden and Tate, Abs. and Achit., ii. 929.

ruefulness (rö'fůl-nes), *n.* [< ME. *reowfulnesse*, *reoufulnesse*; < *rueful* + *-ness*.] The quality or state of being rueful.

ruell-bone†, *n.* Same as *rewel-bone*.

ruelle (rē-el'), *n.* [ME. *ruel*, < OF. *ruelle*, F. *ruelle*, older *rule*, a little street, path, lane; *ruelle du lict*, or later simply *ruelle*, the space left between a bed and the wall; hence later an alcove in a bedroom; dim. of *rue*, street, path, = Pr. Sp. Pg. *rua* = OIt. *ruga*, < ML. *ruga*, also *rua*, place, street, path, perhaps < L. *ruga*, wrinkle: see *ruga*, *ruge*. The ML. *ruta*, *rutta*, a way, is a reflex of the Rom. forms of *rupta*, a way, path: see *rut*[1], *route*[1].] 1†. The space between a bed and the wall.

And wo in winter-tyme with wakynge a nyghtes
To ryse to the *ruel* to rocke the cradel.
Piers Plowman (C), x. 70.

The space thus left between the bed and the curtains was perhaps what was originally called in French the *ruelle* . . . of the bed, a term which was afterwards given to the space between the curtains of the bed and the wall.
Wright, Homes of Other Days, quoted by Skeat, [Notes on Piers Plowman, p. 122.

2. Hence, a bedchamber in which persons of quality, especially ladies, in France during the seventeenth and eighteenth centuries held receptions in the morning, to which persons distinguished for learning, wit, etc., as well as those constituting society, were invited; hence, such a reception, where the events of the day, etc., were discussed. In the seventeenth century the character of the ruelles was distinctively literary and artistic; but in the following century they degenerated into mere occasions for gossip and frivolity.

The poet who flourished in the scene is damned in the *ruelle*. *Dryden*, Ded. of the Æneid.

A Voice persuades.
Whether on Theatres loud Strains we hear,
Or in *Ruelles* some soft Egyptian Air.
Congreve, tr. of Ovid's Art of Love.

The lady received her visitors reposing on that throne of beauty, a bed placed in an alcove; the toilet was magnificently arranged. The space between the bed and the wall was called the *Ruelle*, the diminutive of la Rue; and in this narrow street, or "Fop's alley," walked the favoured. *I. D'Israeli*, Lit. Char. Men of Genius, p. 413.

Ruellia (rö-el'i-ạ̈), *n.* [NL. (Plumier, 1703), named after Jean *Ruel*, a French botanist of the 16th century.] A large genus of gamopetalous plants, of the order *Acanthaceæ*, type of the tribe *Ruellieæ* and subtribe *Euruellieæ*. It is characterized by a corolla with slender base, enlarged throat, and five lobes above, which are equal or posteriorly united, by a style recurved at the awl-shaped apex, and by a two-celled ovary with three to ten ovules in each cell, followed by an oblong-linear or club-shaped capsule, which is roundish or furrowed, and often contracted at the base into a long solid stalk. There are about 150 species, principally tropical and American, with a few extratropical in North and South America, 2 species extending into the northern United States. They are herbs or shrubs, generally hairy, bearing opposite and usually entire leaves. Their flowers are often of large size and are nearly or quite sessile in the axils of leaves or bracts, sometimes forming a scattered cyme or panicle. They are commonly violet, lilac, white, or red, rarely yellow or orange. Some species are desirable in greenhouses. *R. tuberosa* is the *manyroot*, also called *spiritleaf* and (*Jamaica*) *snapdragon*. *R. paniculata*, a trailing plant with blue corollas an inch long, is found in Mexico, etc., and in Jamaica, where it is called *Christmas-pride*. *R. ciliosa* is a pretty-flowered hardy species of the interior and southern United States. For the plant formerly called *R. indigotica*, see *room*[2].

Ruellieæ (rö-e-lī'ẹ̄-ē), *n. pl.* [NL. (Nees von Esenbeck, 1832), < *Ruellia* + *-eæ*.] A large tribe of gamopetalous plants, of the order *Acanthaceæ*, characterized by contorted corolla-lobes, by ovules commonly from two to eight in number in each ovary-cell, and by compressed seeds. It embraces 37 genera, containing about 533 species, three fifths of which belong to the large genus *Strobilanthes* or to the type, *Ruellia*.

ruer (rö'ėr), *n.* [< ME. *rewere*; < *rue*[1] + *-er*[1].] One who rues or pities.

ruet†, *n.* [ME. *ruet*, *ruett*, *ruwet*, *rewet*, < AF. *ruet*, a trumpet; prob. for OF. *rouet*, which is found in the sense of 'a spring of a gun,' lit. 'a little wheel'; cf. *rouette*, f., a little wheel, dim. of *roue*, a wheel: see *rowel*.] A small trumpet.

He . . . blew hus rounde *rewet*.
Piers Plowman (C), vii. 400.

ruewort (rö'wėrt), *n.* A plant of the rue family, or *Rutaceæ*. *Lindley*.

rufescence (rọ̈-fes'ẹns), *n.* [< *rufescen(t)* + *-ce*.] Tendency to be rufous; reddishness; a reddish color.

rufescent (rọ̈-fes'ẹnt), *a.* [< L. *rufescen(t-)s*, ppr. of *rufescere*, become reddish, < *rufus*, red: see *rufous*.] Tending to be rufous; somewhat rufous, or verging toward a dull-red color.

ruff[1] (ruf), *n.* [Early mod. E. *ruffe*; not found in earlier use, and prob. an abbr. of *ruffle*: see *ruffle*[1], *n.*] 1. A projecting band or frill, plaited or bristling, especially one worn around the neck. In the sixteenth century ruffs of muslin or lawn, often edged with lace, plaited or goffered, and stiffly starched, were worn by both men and women, some of them very broad, projecting six inches or more in all directions; narrower ruffs of similar material have formed a part of the costume of women at different epochs, down to the present day.

Ruff.—Close of 16th century.

Our bombast hose, our treble double *ruffes*,
Our sutes of Silke, our comely garded capes.
Gascoigne, Steele Glas (ed. Arber), p. 60.

We shall have him here to-morrow with his best *ruff* on.
Shak., Pericles, iv. 2. 111.

Ruffs, often of exaggerated amplitude and of a painfully severe stiffness, were worn by both sexes; sometimes open in front and rising like an expanded fan around the throat and head; more generally they completely encircled the throat, and rested, nearly at right angles to it, on the shoulders. *Encyc. Brit.*, VI. 472.

2. Something resembling a ruff in form or position. Specifically—(*a*) In *ornith.*, a packet, collar, or other set of lengthened, loosened, peculiarly colored, or otherwise distinguished feathers on the neck of a bird, as the condor, the ruff, certain grebes and grouse, etc. Also called *ruffle*. (*b*) A band of long hair growing round the neck of certain dogs.

A *ruff*, as the loose skin covered with long hair round the neck [of the English pointer] is called.
Dogs of Great Britain and America, p. 88.

(*c*) The loose top of the boot worn in the seventeenth century turned over and made somewhat ornamental: same as *boot-top*, 2 (*b*). Sometimes the top was of a different leather from the rest of the boot. Spanish leather is especially mentioned, and the edge was sometimes ornamented with gold lace or similar passement.

He will look upon his boot and sing; mend the *ruff* and sing. . . . I know a man that had this trick of melancholy sold a goodly manor for a song. *Shak.*, All's Well, iii. 2. 7.

(*d*) In *mach.*, an annular ridge formed on a shaft or other piece, commonly at a journal, to prevent motion endwise. Thus, in the cut, *a*, *a* are ruffs limiting the length of the journal *b*, to which the pillows or brasses are exactly fitted, so that the shaft is prevented from moving on end. Ruffs sometimes consist of separate rings fixed in the positions intended by set-screws, etc. They are then called *loose ruffs*.

Ruffs on a Shaft.

3†. Figuratively, that which is outspread or made public; an open display; a public exhibition, generally marked by pride or vanity.

It were not greatly amiss a little to consider that he, which in the *ruff* of his freshest jollity was fain to cry M. Churchyard a mercy in print, may be orderly driven to cry more peccavis than one. *G. Harvey*, Four Letters.

4. A breed of domestic pigeons; a kind of Jacobin having a ruff.

ruff[1] (ruf), *v. t.* [< *ruff*[1], *n.*, or abbr. of *ruffle*[1], *v.* Cf. It. *arruffare*, disorder, ruffle the hair.] 1†. To plait, pucker, or wrinkle; draw up in plaits or folds.

His uppergarment is of cloth of golde, . . . the sleeues thereof very long, which he weareth on his arme, *ruffed* vp. *Hakluyt's Voyages*, I. 314.

2†. To ruffle; disorder.

Thenceforth the tether in her lofty crest,
Ruffed of love, gan lowly to availe.
Spenser, F. Q., III. ii. 27.

3. In *falconry*, to hit without trussing. *E. Phillips*, 1706.—4. To applaud by making a noise with hands or feet. [Scotch.]

ruff[2] (ruf), *n.* [Formerly also *ruffe*; said to be < *ruff*[1], *n.*, and so named because the male has a ruff round its neck in the breeding season; but this is doubtful. The female is called a *reeve*, a name supposed to be formed from *ruff* by some change left unexplained, but prob. from a different source.] The bird *Pavoncella* or *Machetes pugnax* (the female of which is

Ruff (*Pavoncella* or *Machetes pugnax*).

called a *reeve*), a kind of sandpiper belonging to the family *Scolopacidæ*, having in breeding-plumage an enormous frill or ruff of feathers of peculiar texture on the neck, and noted for its pugnacity. It is widely distributed in the Old World, and occurs as a straggler in America. The length is about 12 inches. Besides the curious ruff, the bird has at the same season a pair of ear-tufts and the face studded with fleshy tubercles. The general plumage is much variegated, and the feathers of the ruff sport in several colors and endlessly varied patterns. When these feathers are erected in fighting, they form a sort of shield or buckler. Also called *combatant* and *fighting sandpiper*.

It has often been said that no one ever saw two *Ruffs* alike. This is perhaps an over-statement; but . . . fifty examples or more may be compared without finding a very close resemblance between any two of them.
A. Newton, Encyc. Brit., XXI. 54.

ruff[3] (ruf), *n.* [< ME. *ruffe*, a fish, glossed by L. *sparrus* for *sparus*; origin obscure.] *Acerina* or *Gymnocephalus cernua*, a fish of the family *Percidæ*, distinguished by the muciferous channels of the head, the villiform teeth of the jaws, and the connected dorsal fins. It is a fresh-water fish of Europe, living in families or schools, and mostly frequenting rather deep and cold waters. In habits and food it much resembles the common perch.

There is also another fish called a Pope, and by some a *Ruffe*, a fish that is not known to be in some Rivers; it is much like the Pearch for his shape, but will not grow to be bigger than a Gudgion; he is an excellent fish, no fish that swims is of a pleasanter taste.
I. Walton, Compleat Angler (ed. 1653), xi.

ruff[4] (ruf), *n.* [Prob. accom. < It. *ronfa*, "a game at cardes called *ruffo* or trump" (Florio) (whence also F. *ronfle*, "hand-ruff, at cards"—Cotgrave); prob. a reduced form of *trionfo* "a trump at cards, or the play called trump or ruff" (Florio): see *trump*[2]. The Pg. *rufa*, *rifa*, a set of cards of the same color, a sequence, is perhaps < E.] 1. An old game at cards, the predecessor of whist.

And to confounde all, to amende their badde games, having never a good carde in their handes, and leaving the ancient game of England (Trumpe), where every coate and sute are sorted in their degree, are running to *Ruffe*, where the greatest sorte of the sute carrieth away the game.
Martins Months Minde (1589), Ep. to the Reader, quoted in [Peele's Old Wives Tale, note.

What, shall we have a game at trump or *ruff* to drive away the time? how say you? *Peele*, Old Wives Tale.

2. In *card-playing*, the act of trumping when the player has no cards of the suit led.

ruff[4] (ruf), *v. t.* [< *ruff*[4], *n.*] In *card-playing*, to trump when holding none of the suit led. Also, erroneously, *rough*.

Miss Bolo would inquire . . . why Mr. Pickwick had not returned that diamond, or led the club, or *roughed* the spade, or finessed the heart. *Dickens*, Pickwick, xxxv.

ruff[5]† (ruf), *a.* and *n.* [An obs. spelling of *rough*[1].] I. *a.* Same as *rough*[1]. *Palsgrave*.

II. *n.* A state of roughness; ruggedness; hence, rude or riotous procedure or conduct.

To ruffle it out in a riotous *ruff*. *Latimer*.

As fields set all their bristles up, in such a *ruff* wert thou.
Chapman, Iliad. (*Imp. Dict.*)

ruff[5] (ruf), *v. t.* [A phonetic spelling of *rough*[1], *v.*] 1. To heckle (flax) on a coarse heckle called a *ruffer*.

The *ruffed* work is taken to the tool called a "common 8," the pins of which are much closer placed than those of the ruffer, and are only 4 or 5 inches long.
Ure, Dict., II. 421.

2. In *hat-manuf.*, to nap.

The known impossibility of napping or *ruffing* a hat by any means with machinery.
J. Thomson, Hats and Felting, p. 37.

ruff[6]†, *n.* An obsolete form of *rough*[2].

ruff[7] (ruf), *n.* A low vibrating beat of a drum; a ruffle. See *ruffle*[3].

The drum beats a *ruff*, and so to bed; that's all, the ceremony is concise. *Farquhar*, Recruiting Officer, v. 2.

ruff[8], *n.* A dialectal form of *roof*[1].

ruff-band (ruf'band), *n.* Same as *ruff*[1], 1.

What madnesse did possesse you? did you thinke that none but citizens were marked for death, that onely a blacke or civill suit of apparell, with a *ruffe-band*, was onely the plagues livery? *John Taylor*, Works (1630). (*Nares.*)

ruff-cuff (ruf'kuf), *n.* A ruffle for the wrist.

ruffe†, *n.* An obsolete form of *roughie*[2].

ruffed[1] (ruft), *a.* [< *ruff*[1] + *-ed*[2].] In *zoöl.*, having a ruff or ruffle: as, the *ruffed* grouse. See *ruff*[1], 2 (*a*), (*b*).—**Ruffed grouse**, *Bonasa umbella*, a common gallinaceous game-bird of North America, nearly related to the hazel-grouse of Europe (*B. betulina*), called *partridge* in the northern and *pheasant* in the middle and southern United States, having a pair of ruffs, one on each side of the neck. This grouse, either in its typical form or in some of its varieties, inhabits nearly all the woodland of North America. It ranks high as a game-bird; the flesh of the breast is white when cooked, like the bobwhite's. The head has a full soft crest; each ruff is composed of from fifteen to thirty broad soft feathers, glossy-black in the adult male, overlying a rudimentary tympanum. The wings are short and rounded; the tail is long, fan-shaped, normally of eighteen broad soft feathers; the tarsi are partly feathered, partly scaly. The plumage is intimately varied with brown, gray, and other shades; it is nearly alike in both sexes. This grouse is 17 inches long, and 23 in extent, the wings and tail from 7 to 8 inches each. It lays creamy or buff eggs, usually immaculate, sometimes speckled, 1½ inches long by 1¼ broad, of pyriform shape. The characteristic drumming sound for which this bird is noted is not vocal, but is produced by rapidly beating the wings. See *grouse*, *pheasant*, *partridge*, and *quail*[3] for other names, and cut under *Bonasa*.—**Ruffed lemur**, the black and white lemur, *Lemur varius*. See cut under *lemur*.—**Ruffed moufion.** Same as *aoudad*.

ruffed[2] (ruft), *p. a.* [Pp. of *ruff*[5], *v.*] Heckled on a ruffer.

ruffen†, *n.* An obsolete form of *ruffian*.

ruffer (ruf'ėr), *n.* [< *ruff*[5] + *-er*[1].] A coarse heckle, formed of a board sheathed with tin plate, and studded with round and pointed teeth about 7 inches long. Compare *heckle*, *n.* and *v. t.*

The teeth or needles of the rougher or *ruffer* heckle.
Encyc. Brit., XIV. 665.

ruffian (ruf'ian), *n.* and *a.* [Early mod. E. also *rufyan*, *ruffen*, *ruffin*; = MD. *ruffiaen*, *roffiaen*, < OF. *ruffian*, *ruffien*, *rufien*, F. *rufien* = Wall. *rouffian* = Pr. *rufian*, *rofian* = Sp. *rufian* = Pg. *rufião* = It. *ruffiano*, OIt. *roffiano* (ML. *ruffianus*), a pander, bully, ruffian; with Rom. suffix, < OD. *roffen*, *roffelen* = LG. *ruffeln*, a pander; cf. LG. *ruffeler*, a pander, intrigant, = Dan. *ruffer*, a pander (see *ruffler*[2]): see *ruffle*[2]. Cf. *ruff*[6], *rough*[2].] I. *n.* 1†. A pimp; a pander; a paramour.

He [her husband] is no sooner abroad than she is instantly at home, revelling with her *ruffians*.
Reynolds, God's Revenge against Murther, iii. 11.

2. A boisterous, brutal fellow; a fellow ready for any desperate crime; a robber; a cutthroat; a murderer.

Have you a *ruffian* that will swear, drink, dance,
Revel the night, rob, murder?
Shak., 2 Hen. IV., iv. 5. 125.

See that your polish'd arms be primed with care,
And drop the night-bolt; *ruffians* are abroad.
Cowper, Task, iv. 568.

3†. The devil. [Old slang.]

The *ruffian* cly thee, the devil take thee!
Harman, Caveat for Cursetors, p. 116.

II. *a.* 1†. Licentious; lascivious; wanton.

How dearly would it touch thee to the quick,
Shouldst thou but hear I were licentious,
And that this body, consecrate to thee,
By *ruffian* lust should be contaminate!
Shak., C. of E., ii. 2. 135.

2. Lawless and cruel; brutal; murderous; inhuman; villainous.

The chief of a rebellious clan,
Who in the Regent's court and sight
With *ruffian* dagger stabbed a knight.
Scott, L. of the L., v. 5.

3. Violent; tumultuous; stormy.

In the visitation of the winds,
Who take the *ruffian* billows by the top.
Shak., 2 Hen. IV., iii. 1. 22.

So may no *ruffian*-feeling in thy breast
Discordant jar thy bosom-chords among.
Burns, To Miss Graham of Fintry.

ruffian (ruf'ian), *v. i.* [= It. *ruffianare*, OIt. *roffianare* = Pg. *rufiar* = Sp. *rufianar*, act as a pander or ruffian; from the noun.] To play the ruffian; rage; raise tumult.

Bechewe disobedience and sedicious assembling, repent of light *ruffianyng* and blasphemous carnal gospelling.
Udal, Peter (John Olde to the Duchesse of Somerset).
[(*Richardson.*)

If it [the wind] hath *ruffian'd* so upon the sea,
What ribs of oak, when mountains melt on them,
Can hold the mortise? *Shak.*, Othello, ii. 1. 7.

ruffianage (ruf'ian-āj), *n.* [< *ruffian* + *-age*.] The state of being a ruffian; rascaldom; ruffians collectively.

Rufus never moved unless escorted by the vilest *ruffianage*. *Sir F. Palgrave.*

Driven from their homes by organized *ruffianage*.
The American, XIII. 214.

ruffianhood (ruf'ian-hůd), *n.* [< *ruffian* + *-hood*.] Ruffianage; ruffianism. *Literary Era*, II. 148.

ruffianish (ruf'ian-ish), *a.* [< *ruffian* + *-ish*[1].] Having the qualities or manners of a ruffian.

ruffianism (ruf'ian-izm), *n.* [< *ruffian* + *-ism*.] The character, habits, or manners of ruffians. *Sir J. Mackintosh.*

The lasagnone is a loafer, as an Italian can be a loafer, without the admixture of *ruffianism* which blemishes most loafers of northern race. *Howells*, Venetian Life, xx.

ruffianly (ruf'ian-li), *a.* [< *ruffian* + *-ly*[1].] 1. Having the character of a ruffian; bold in crime; brutal; violent; rough.

The *ruffianly* Tartar, who, sullen and impracticable to others, acquired a singular partiality for him.
C. Brontë, Shirley, xxvi.

2. Characteristic of or befitting a ruffian. (*a*†) Lascivious; wanton; unseemly.

Who in London hath not heard of his [Greene's] dissolute and licentious living; his fond disguising of a Master of Art with *ruffianly* hair, unseemly apparel, and more unseemly company? *G. Harvey*, Four Letters.

Some frenchified or outlandish monsieur, who hath nothing else to make him famous, I should say infamous, but an effeminate, *ruffianly*, ugly, and deformed lock.
Prynne, Unloveliness of Love-Locks, p. 27. (*Trench.*)

(*b*) Villainous; depraved: as, *ruffianly* conduct; *ruffianly* crimes.

ruffin[1]†, *n.* and *a.* An obsolete form of *ruffian*.

ruffin[2]† (ruf'in), *n.* [< *ruff*[3] + dim. *-in*.] Same as *ruff*[3]. [Rare.]

Him followed Yar, soft washing Norwitch wall,
And with him brought a present joyfully
Of his owne fish unto their festivall,
Whose like none else could shew, the which they *Ruffins* call.
Spenser, F. Q., IV. xi. 33.

ruffing (ruf'ing), *n.* [Verbal n. of *ruff*[5], *v.*] In *hat-manuf.*, same as *napping*.

ruffinous† (ruf'i-nus), *a.* [< *ruffin*[1] + *-ous*.] Ruffianly; outrageous.

To shelter the sad monument from all the *ruffinous* pride
Of stormes and tempests. *Chapman*, Iliad, vi. 456.

ruffle[1] (ruf'l), *v.*; pret. and pp. *ruffled*, ppr. *ruffling*. [Early mod. E. *ruffle*, < ME. *ruffelen*, < MD. *ruyffelen*, D. *ruifelen*, wrinkle, rumple, ruffle; cf. *ruyffel*, a wrinkle, ruffle. Cf. *ruff*[1].] I. *trans.* 1. To wrinkle; pucker; draw up into gathers, folds, or plaits.

I *ruffle* clothe or sylked, I bring them out of their playne foldynge, Je plionne. *Palsgrave*, p. 695.

2. To disorder; disturb the arrangement of; rumple; derange; disarrange; make uneven by agitation: as, *ruffled* attire; *ruffled* hair.

Where Contemplation prunes her *ruffled* wings.
Pope, Satires of Donne, iv. 186.

Thou wilt not gash thy flesh for him; for thine
Fares richly, in fine linen, not a hair
Ruffled upon the scarfskin.
Tennyson, Aylmer's Field.

3. To disturb the surface of; cause to ripple or rise in waves.

The Lake of Nemi lies in a very deep bottom, so surrounded on all sides with mountains and groves that the surface of it is never *ruffled* with the least breath of wind.
Addison, Remarks on Italy (Works, ed. Bohn, I. 486).

As the sharp wind that *ruffles* all day long
A little bitter pool about a stone
On the bare coast. *Tennyson*, Guinevere.

4†. To throw together in a disorderly manner.

I *ruffled* up fall'n leaves in heap.
Chapman, Odyssey, vii. 396.

5. To disquiet; discompose; agitate; disturb; annoy; vex: as, to *ruffle* the spirits or the temper.

Business must necessarily subject them to many neglects and contempts, which might disturb and *ruffle* their minds. *Bacon*, Moral Fables, iii., Expl.

Lord Granby's temper had been a little *ruffled* the night before. *Walpole*, Letters, II. 214.

But fortunately his ill tidings came too late to *ruffle* the tranquillity of this most tranquil of rulers.
Irving, Knickerbocker, p. 206.

As I sat between my cousins, I was surprised to find how easy I felt under the total neglect of the one and the semi-sarcastic attentions of the other — Eliza did not mortify, nor Georgiana *ruffle* me.
Charlotte Brontë, Jane Eyre, xxi.

6. To furnish or adorn with ruffles: as, to *ruffle* a shirt.

A thousand lamd heteroclites more, that cozen the world with a gilt spur and a *ruffled* boot.
Dekker, Gull's Hornbook.

To ruffle one's feathers or plumage. (*a*) To irritate one; make one angry; disturb or fret one. (*b*) To get irritated, angry, or fretted. *Farrar.*

II. *intrans.* To be in disorder; be tossed about; hence, to flutter.

On his right shoulder his thick mane reclined,
Ruffles at speed, and dances in the wind.
Dryden, tr. of Virgil's Georgics, iii. 136.

ruffle[1] (ruf'l), *n.* [< MD. *ruyffel*, wrinkle, a ruffle, < *ruyffelen*, wrinkle, rumple, ruffle: see *ruffle*[1], *v.* Cf. *ruff*[1], *n.*] 1. A strip of any textile material drawn up at one edge in gathers or plaits, and used as a bordering or trimming; a full, narrow flounce; a frill; a ruff. The term is used for such a plaited strip when much narrower than a ruff, even when worn around the neck, but it especially applies to the wrist and to the front of the shirt-bosom, as in men's dress of the early part of the eighteenth century.

Such dainties to them [poets], their health it might hurt,
It's like sending them *ruffles* when wanting a shirt.
Goldsmith, Haunch of Venison.

2. Something resembling a ruffle in form or position. (*a*) The top of a boot.

Not having leisure to put off my silver spurs, one of the rowels catched hold of the *ruffle* of my boot, and, being Spanish leather, and subject to tear, overthrows me.
B. Jonson, Every Man out of his Humour, iv. 4.

(*b*) In *ornith.*, same as *ruff*[1], 2 (*a*). (*c*) The string of egg-capsules of the periwinkles, whelks, and related gastropods. (*d*) In *mech.*, a series of projections, often connected by a web, formed on the inner face of a flange of a metal gudgeon for a wooden shaft or roller, and fitted to a corresponding series of recesses in the end of such shaft or roller, to secure a rigid attachment of the flange and prevent its turning except as the shaft or roller turns with it.

3. Disquietude or discomposure, as of the mind or temper; annoyance; irritation.

Make it your daily business to moderate your aversions and desires, and to govern them by reason. This will guard you against many a *ruffle* of spirit, both of anger and sorrow.
Watts, Doctrine of the Passions, § 23.

In this state of quiet and unostentatious enjoyment there were, besides the ordinary rubs and *ruffles* which disturb even the most uniform life, two things which particularly chequered Mrs. Butler's happiness.
Scott, Heart of Mid-Lothian, xlvii.

Neptune's ruffles, a retepore.

ruffle[2]† (ruf'l), *v.* [< ME. *ruffelen*, be quarrelsome, < MD. *roffelen* = LG. *ruffeln* = G. dial. *ruffeln*, pander, pimp; freq. of MD. *roffen*, pander; cf. *ruffian*. In some senses this verb is confused with fig. uses of *ruffle*[1].] I. *intrans.* 1. To act turbulently or lawlessly; riot; play the bully; hence, to bluster.

To Britaine I addrest an army great, perdy,
To quaile the Picts, that *ruffled* in that ile.
Mir. for Mags., I. 317.

A valiant son-in-law thou shalt enjoy;
One fit to bandy with thy lawless sons,
To *ruffle* in the commonwealth of Rome.
Shak., Tit. And., i. 1. 313.

2. To put on airs; swagger: often with an indefinite *it*.

Lady, I cannot *ruffle it* in red and yellow.
B. Jonson, Cynthia's Revels, iii. 3.

In a handsome suit of Tressilian's livery, with a sword by his side, and a buckler on his shoulder, he looked like a gay *ruffling* serving-man.
Scott, Kenilworth, xiii.

3. To be rough or boisterous: said of the weather.

Alack, the night comes on, and the bleak winds
Do sorely *ruffle*. *Shak.*, Lear, ii. 4. 304.

II. *trans.* To bully; insult; annoy.

Can I not go about my private meditations, ha!
But such companions as you must *ruffle* me?
Fletcher, Wit without Money, v. 3.

Now the gravest and worthiest Minister, a true Bishop of his fold, shall be revil'd and *ruff'd* by an insulting and only-Canon-wife Prelate, as if he were some slight paltry companion.
Milton, Reformation in Eng., i.

ruffle[2]† (ruf'l), *n.* [< *ruffle*[2], *v.*] A brawl; a quarrel; a tumult.

Sometime a blusterer, that the *ruffle* knew
Of court, of city. *Shak.*, Lover's Complaint, l. 58.

The captain was so little out of humour, and our company was so far from being soured by this little *ruffle*, that Ephraim and he took a particular delight in being agreeable to each other for the future.
Steele, Spectator, No. 132.

ruffle[3] (ruf'l), *n.* [Also *ruff*; origin uncertain; cf. Pg. *rufla*, *rufo*, the roll of a drum.] *Milit.*, a low vibrating beat of the drum, less loud than the roll, and used on certain occasions as a mark of respect.

The very drums and fifes that played the *ruffles* as each battalion passed the President had called out the troops to numberless night alarms, had sounded the onset at Vicksburg and Antietam. *The Century*, XXXIX. 570.

ruffle[3] (ruf'l), *v. t.*; pret. and pp. *ruffled*, ppr. *ruffling*. [See *ruffle*[3], *n.*] To beat the ruffle on: as, to *ruffle* a drum.

ruffled (ruf'ld), *a.* [< *ruffle*[1] + *-ed*[2].] Having a ruffle; ruffed: as, the *ruffled* grouse.

ruffleless (ruf'l-les), *a.* [< *ruffle*[1] + *-less.*] Having no ruffles. *Imp. Dict.*

rufflement (ruf'l-ment), *n.* [< *ruffle*[1] + *-ment.*] The act of ruffling. *Imp. Dict.*

ruffler[1] (ruf'lėr), *n.* [< *ruffle*[1] + *-er*[1].] A machine for making ruffles, sometimes forming an attachment to a sewing-machine.

ruffler[2] (ruf'lėr), *n.* [Early mod. E. also *ruffeler*; < LG. *ruffeler* (cf. Dan. *ruffer*), a pander, pimp, < *ruffeln*, pander, pimp: see *ruffle*[2].] 1. A bully; a swaggerer; a ruffian; a violent and lawless person.

Here's a company of *rufflers*, that, drinking in the tavern, have made a great brawl.
Greene, Friar Bacon and Friar Bungay.

Both the Parlament and people complain'd, and demanded Justice for those assaults, if not murders, don at his own dores by that crew of *Rufflers*.
Milton, Eikonoklastes, iv.

Specifically — 2†. A bullying thief or beggar; a blustering vagabond.

A *Ruffeler* goeth wyth a weapon to seeke seruice, saying he hath bene a Seruitor in the wars, and beggeth for his reliefe. But his chiefest trade is to robbe poore wayfaring men and market women.
Fraternity of Vagabonds (1561).

The *Ruffler* . . . is first in degree of this odious order: and is so called in a statute made for the punishment of vagabonds. *Harman*, Caveat for Cursetors, p. 14.

ruffler[3] (ruf'lėr), *n.* Same as *ruffer*.

ruffiered†, *a.* [< *ruffler*[2] + *-ed*[2].] Rough; boisterous. [Rare.]

Three wheru's fyerd glystring, with Soutwynds *ruffered* buffing. *Stanihurst*, Conceites (ed. Arber), p. 137.

ruffiery†, *n.* [< *ruffler*[2] + *-y* (see *-ery*).] Turbulence; violence. [Rare.]

But neere loynctlye brayeth with *rufflerye* rumboled Ætna. *Stanihurst*, Æneid, iii.

ruffling (ruf'ling), *n.* [Verbal n. of *ruffle*[1], *v.*] Ruffles in general; also, a length of manufactured ruffle, as prepared for sale: as, three yards of *ruffling*.—**Dimity ruffling**, a cotton textile, usually white, crinkled or plaited in weaving, the plaits following the length of the stuff. It is cut across and hemmed, then cut again to the width desired for the ruffle, and sewed fast with the plaits retained.

ruffmans†, *n. pl.* [Cf. *ruffe*, *roughie*[1].] Woods or bushes. *Harman*, Caveat for Cursetors, p. 115. [Thieves' slang.]

ruff-peck†, *n.* Bacon. [Thieves' slang.]

Here's *ruffpeck* and casson, and all of the best,
And scraps of the dainties of gentry cofe's feast.
Brome, Jovial Crew, ii.

ruff-wheel (ruf'hwēl), *n.* An ore-crushing mill for the pieces which will not feed into the usual crusher: now superseded by the more modern stone-breakers or ore-crushers. See *stone-breaker*.

ruffy-tuffy (ruf'i-tuf″i), *a.* [Formerly also *ruftie-tuftie*, *rufty-tufty*, a varied redupl. of *ruff*[5] for *rough*[1].] Disordered; rough.

Were I as Vince is, I would handle you
In *rufty-tufty* wise, in your right kind.
Chapman, Gentleman Usher, v. 1.

Powder'd bag-wigs and *ruffy-tuffy* heads
Of cinder wenches meet and soil each other.
Keats, Cap and Bells, st. 86.

ruffy-tuffy (ruf'i-tuf″i), *adv.* [Also *rufty-tufty*; cf. *ruffy-tuffy*, *a.*] In disorder; helter-skelter; pell-mell.

To sweare and stare until we come to shore,
Then *rifty tufty* each one to his skore.
Breton, Pilgrimage of Paradise, p. 16. (*Davies.*)

rufous (rö'fus), *a.* [= Sp. *rufo* = Pg. *ruivo* = It. *ruffo*, < L. *rufus*, red, reddish: see *red*[1].] Of a dull-red color; red but somewhat deficient in chroma: thus, a bay or chestnut horse is *rufous*; Venetian red is *rufous*. It enters into the specific name of many animals, technically called *rufus*, *rufescens*, etc.—**Rufous-chinned finch**†. See *finch*[1].—**Rufous-headed falcon.** See *falcon*.

ruft (ruft), *n.* A dialectal form of *rift*[3]. *Dunglison.*

ruftie-tuftie†, **rufty-tufty**†, *a.* Same as *ruffy-tuffy*.

rufulous (rö'fụ̈-lus), *a.* [< L. *rufulus*, rather red, dim. of *rufus*, red: see *rufous*.] In *zoöl.* and *bot.*, somewhat rufous.

One or two of the younger plants (which had not acquired a *rufulous* tinge).
Jour. of Bot., Brit. *and For.*, 1883, p. 214.

Rufus's pills. Pills of aloes and myrrh.

rug[1] (rug), *n.* [Formerly also *rugg*, *rugge*; < Sw. *rugg*, rough entangled hair; prob. from an adj. cognate with AS. *rūh*, E. *rough*: see *rough*[1]. Cf. *ruggy*, *rugged*. The Icel. *rögg*, coarse hair, goes with *rag*, not with *rug*.] 1†. A rough, heavy woolen fabric; a kind of coarse, nappy frieze, used especially for the garments of the poorer classes.

To cloathe Summer matter with Winter *Rugge* would make the Reader sweat. *N. Ward*, Simple Cobler, p. 87.

As they distill the best aqua-vitæ, so they spin the choicest *rug* in Ireland. *Holinshed*, Chron.

Let me come in, you knaues; how dare you keepe me out? 'Twas my gowne to a mantle of *rugge* I had not put you all to the pistoll.
Chapman, Blind Beggar of Alexandria.

2. A thick, heavy covering, ordinarily woolen, and having a shaggy nap; a piece of thick nappy material used for various purposes. (*a*) A cover for a bed; a blanket or coverlet.

I wish'd 'em then get him to bed; they did so,
And almost smother'd him with *ruggs* and pillows.
Fletcher and Shirley, Night-Walker, v. 1.

(*b*) A covering for the floor; a mat, usually oblong or square, and woven in one piece. Rugs, especially those of Oriental make, often show rich designs and elaborate workmanship, and are hence sometimes used for hangings.

I stood on the *rug* and warmed my hands, which were rather cold with sitting at a distance from the drawing-room fire. *Charlotte Brontë*, Jane Eyre, xix.

Is it a polished floor with *rugs*, or is it one of those great carpets woven in one piece?
Mrs. Oliphant, Poor Gentleman, xliii.

3. A lap-robe; a thick shawl or covering used in driving, traveling, etc., as a protection against the cold.—4. A rough, woolly, or shaggy dog.

Shoughs, water-*rugs*, and demi-wolves are clept
All by the name of dogs. *Shak.*, Macbeth, iii. 1. 94.

5. A kind of strong liquor or drink.

And (in a word) of all the drinks potable
Rug is most puisant, potent, notable.
Rug was the Capitall Commander there,
And his Lievtenant Generall was strong Beere.
John Taylor, The Certain Travailes of an Uncertain Journey (1653).

Braided rug. See *braid*[1].

rug[2] (rug), *v. t.* [< ME. *ruggen*, *roggen*, a secondary form of *rokken*, shake, rock: see *rog*, *rock*[2].] To pull roughly or hastily; tear; tug. [Obsolete or Scotch.]

No ruthe were it to *rug* the and ryue the in ropes.
York Plays, p. 286.

The gude auld times of *rugging* and riving . . . are come back again. *Scott*, Waverley, xlii.

rug[2] (rug), *n.* [< *rug*[2], *v.*] A rough or hasty pull; a tug.—**To get a rug**, to get a chance at something desirable; make a haul. [Colloq.]

He knows . . . who *got* his pension *rug*,
Or quickened a reversion by a drug.
Pope, Satires of Donne, iv. 134.

Sir John . . . sat in the last Scots Parliament and voted for the Union, having *gotten*, it was thought, *a rug* of the compensations. *Scott*, Redgauntlet, letter xi.

rug[3] (rug), *a.* [Perhaps < *rug*[1].] Snug; warm. *Halliwell.* [Prov. Eng.]

rug[4]†, *n.* Another form of *rig*[1], a dialectal variant of *ridge*.

ruga (rö'gạ̈), *n.*; pl. *rugæ* (-jē). [< L. *ruga*, a wrinkle, fold (> It. Sp. Pg. *ruga*, a wrinkle), = Ir. Gael. *rug*, a wrinkle: see *rugose*. Cf. *ruelle*.] In *zoöl.*, *anat.*, and *bot.*, a fold, ridge, or wrinkle; a crease or plait; a corrugation: variously applied, as to folds of mucous membrane or skin, the cross-bars of the hard palate, the wrinkles on a shell or a bird's bill or an insect's wing-covers, etc.: usually in the plural.—**Rugæ of the stomach.** See *stomach*.—**Rugæ of the vagina**, numerous small transverse folds of the vaginal mucous membrane, extending outwardly from the columns.

rugate (rö'gāt), *a.* [= Sp. *rugado*, < NL. *rugatus*, wrinkled, < L. *ruga*, a wrinkle, fold: see *ruga*.] Having rugæ; rugous or rugose; corrugated; wrinkled.

ruge[1]†, *n.* [< L. *ruga*, a wrinkle: see *ruga*.] A wrinkle. [Rare.]

Nowe [none] *ruge* on hem [fruits] puldde new olde wyne ysprонge
Wol suffre be.
Palladius, Husbondrie (E. E. T. S.), p. 144.

ruge[2] (röj), *v.* [Prob. for **rudge*, var. of *ridge*; not < *ruge*[1], *n.*, which was never in vernacular use.] To wrinkle. *Halliwell.* [Prov. Eng.]

rugge†, *n.* An obsolete variant of *ridge*.

rugged (rug'ed), *a.* [< ME. *rugged*, *roggyd*, *ruggyd*, < Sw. *rugg*, shaggy hair (see *rug*[1]), + *-ed*[2]. Cf. *ruggy*.] 1. Having a rough, hairy surface or nap; shaggy; bristly; ragged.

His well-proportion'd beard made rough and *rugged*,
Like to the summer's corn by tempests lodged.
Shak., 2 Hen. VI., iii. 2. 175.

Some of them have Jackets made of Plantain-leaves, which was as rough as any Bear's skin; I never saw such *rugged* Things. *Dampier*, Voyages, I. 427.

Like tears dried up with *rugged* huckaback,
That sets the mournful visage all awrack.
Hood, Irish Schoolmaster, st. 20.

2. Covered with rough projections; broken into sharp or irregular points or prominences; rough; uneven: as, a *rugged* mountain; *rugged* rocks.

The Wheel of Life no less will stay
In a smooth than *rugged* way.
Cowley, Anacreontics, ix.

Nooks and dells, beautiful as fairy land, are embosomed in its most *rugged* and gigantic elevations.
Macaulay, Milton.

Vast rocks, against whose *rugged* feet
Beats the mad torrent with perpetual roar.
Whittier, Bridal of Pennacook, Int.

3. Wrinkled; furrowed; corrugated; hence, ruffled; disturbed; uneasy.

The *rugged* forehead that with grave foresight
Welds kingdomes causes and affaires of state.
Spenser, F. Q., IV., Prol.

Gentle my lord, sleek o'er your *rugged* looks;
Be bright and jovial among your guests to-night.
Shak., Macbeth, iii. 2. 27.

The most deplorable-looking personage you can imagine; his face the colour of mahogany, rough and *rugged* to the last degree, all lines and wrinkles.
Jane Austen, Persuasion, iii.

4. Rough to the ear; harsh; grating.

But ah! my rymes too rude and *rugged* arre
When in so high an object they do lyte.
Spenser, F. Q., III. ii. 3.

Colkitto, or Macdonnel, or Galasp?
Those *rugged* names to our like mouths grow sleek.
Milton, Sonnets, vi.

5. Unsoftened by refinement or cultivation; rude; homely; unpolished; ignorant.

Even Frederic William, with all his *rugged* Saxon prejudices, thought it necessary that his children should know French. *Macaulay*, Frederic the Great.

Deafen'd by his own stir,
The *rugged* labourer
Caught not till then a sense . . .
Of his omnipotence.
M. Arnold, The World and the Quietist.

6. Rough in temper; harsh; hard; austere.

Signior Alphonso, you are too *rugged* to her,
Believe, too full of harshness.
Fletcher, Pilgrim, i. 1.

Stern *rugged* nurse! thy rigid lore
With patience many a year she bore:
What sorrow was, thou bad'st her know.
Gray, Hymn to Adversity.

7. Marked by harshness, severity, or anger; fierce; rough; ungentle.

Though he be stubborn,
And of a *rugged* nature, yet he is honest.
Fletcher, Wife for a Month, v. 1.

With words of sadness soothed his *rugged* mood.
Shelley, Revolt of Islam, v. 25.

8. Rough; tempestuous: said of the sea or weather.

Every gust of *rugged* wings
That blows from off each beaked promontory.
Milton, Lycidas, l. 93.

A rough sea, accompanied with blowing weather, is termed by whalers "*rugged* weather."
C. *M. Scammon*, Marine Mammals (Glossary), p. 311.

9. Vigorous; robust; strong in health. [Colloq., U. S.]

I'm getting along in life, and I ain't quite so *rugged* as I used to be. *O. W. Holmes*, Poet at Breakfast-Table, xii.

ruggedly (rug'ed-li), *adv.* In a rough or rugged manner; especially, with harshness or severity; sternly; rigorously.

Some spake to me courteously, with appearance of compassion; others *ruggedly*, with evident tokens of wrath and scorn. *T. Ellwood*, Life (ed. Howells), p. 244.

ruggedness (rug'ed-nes), *n.* The character or state of being rugged.

rugging (rug'ing), *n.* [< *rug*[1] + *-ing*[1].] 1. Heavy napped cloth for making rugs, wrapping blankets, etc.—2. A coarse cloth used for the body of horse-boots.

rug-gown† (rug'goun), *n.* [Also *rudge-gown*; < *rug*[1] + *gown*.] One who wears a gown of rug; hence, a low person.

Thousands of monsters more besides there be
Which I, fast hoodwink'd, at that time did see;
And in a word to shut up this discourse,
A *rudg-gowns* ribs are good to spur a horse.
Witts Recreations (1654). (*Nares.*)

rug-gowned (rug'gound), *a.* Wearing a gown made of rug, or coarse nappy frieze.

I had rather meet
An enemy in the field than stand thus nodding
Like to a *rug-gown'd* watchman.
Fletcher (*and another*?), Prophetess, ii. 2.

ruggy (rug'i), *a.* [< ME. *ruggy*, < Sw. *ruggig*, rough, hairy, rugged, < *rugg*, rough hair: see *rug*[1], and cf. *rugged*.] Rugged; rough; uneven.

With flotery berd and *ruggy* asshy heeres.
Chaucer, Knight's Tale, l. 2025.

It's a mighty *ruggy* trail, Mister, up the Shasta Mountain. *Scenes in the Far West*, p. 119, quoted in De Vere's [Americanisms, p. 536.

rug-headed (rug'hed"ed), *a.* Shock-headed.

Now for our Irish wars:
We must supplant those rough *rug-headed* kerns,
Which live like venom where no venom else
But only they have privilege to live.
Shak., Rich. II., ii. 1. 156.

rugin†, *n.* See *rugine*.

rugine (rö'jin), *n.* [Formerly also *rugin*; < F. *rugine*, a surgeons' scraper or rasp; perhaps < L. *runcina*, a plane, = Gr. ῥυκάνη, a plane.] 1. A surgeons' rasp.—2†. A nappy cloth. *Johnson.*

The lips grew so painful that she could not endure the wiping the ichor from it with a soft *rugin* with her own hand. *Wiseman*, Surgery.

rugine (rö'jin), *v. t.*; pret. and pp. *rugined*, ppr. *rugining*. [< F. *ruginer*, scrape, < *rugine*, a scraper: see *rugine*, *n.*] 1. To scrape with a rugine.—2†. To wipe with a rugine or nappy cloth.

Where you shall find it moist, there you are to *rugine* it.
Wiseman, Surgery, v. 9.

Rugosa (rö-gō'sä), *n. pl.* [NL. (Edwards and Haime, 1850), neut. pl. of L. *rugosus*, full of wrinkles: see *rugose*.] An order or other group of sclerodermatous stone-corals, exhibiting tetramerous arrangement of parts and a well-developed corallum, with true thecæ and generally septa and tabulæ; the rugose corals. The septa are mostly in multiples of four, and one septum is commonly predominant or represented by a vacant fossula. Some of the *Rugosa* are simple, others compound. All are extinct. They have been divided into the families *Cyathophyllidæ*, *Zaphrentidæ*, and *Cystiphyllidæ*. *Stauridæ* and *Cyathaxonidæ*, formerly referred to the group, are now considered to be aporose corals.

rugose (rö'gōs), *a.* [< L. *rugosus*, wrinkled: see *rugous*.] 1. Having rugæ; rugate or rugous; corrugated; wrinkled.

The internal *rugose* coat of the intestine.
Wiseman, Surgery.

Above you the woods climb up to the clouds, a prodigious precipitous surface of burning green, solid and *rugose* like a cliff. *Harper's Mag.*, LXXVII. 334.

2. In *bot.*, rough and wrinkled: applied to leaves in which the reticulate venation is very prominent beneath, with corresponding creases on the upper side, and also to lichens, algæ, etc., in which the surface is reticulately roughened. —3. Specifically, of or pertaining to the *Rugosa*.

rugosely (rö-gōs'li), *adv.* 1. In a rugose manner; with wrinkles.—2. In *entom.*, roughly and intricately; so as to present a rugose appearance: as, *rugosely* punctured.

rugosity (rö-gos'i-ti), *n.*; pl. *rugosities* (-tiz). [= OF. *rugosite*, F. *rugosité* = Pr. *rugozitat* = Sp. *rugosidad* = Pg. *rugosidade* = It. *rugosità*, < L. *rugosita(t-)s*, the state of being wrinkled: see *rugose*.] 1. The state or property of being rugose, corrugated, or wrinkled.

In many cases the wings of an insect not only assume the exact tint of the bark or leaf it is accustomed to rest on, but the form and veining of the leaf or the exact *rugosity* of the bark is imitated.
A. R. Wallace, Nat. Select., p. 48.

2. A wrinkle or corrugation.

An Italian Oak . . . wrinkles its bark into strange *rugosities*, from which its first scattered sprouts of yellow green seem to break out like a morbid fungus.
H. James, Jr., Trans. Sketches, p. 162.

rugous (rö'gus), *a.* [= OF. (and F.) *rugueux* = Pr. *rugos* = Sp. Pg. It. *rugoso*, < L. *rugosus*, wrinkled, < *ruga*, a wrinkle: see *ruga*.] Same as *rugose*.

In the rhinoceros . . . the trachea has thirty-one rings; they are close-set, cleft behind, the ends meeting; the lining membrane is longitudinally *rugous*, as is that of the bronchial ramifications for some way into the lung.
Owen, Anat., § 354.

rugulose (rö'gū-lōs), *a.* [< NL. *rugulosus, full of small wrinkles, < **rugula*, dim. of L. *ruga*, a wrinkle: see *ruga*.] Finely rugose; full of little wrinkles.

Ruhmkorff coil. A form of induction-coil or inductorium (see *induction-coil*): so called because constructed by H. D. Ruhmkorff (1803–1877).

ruin (rö'in), *n.* [Early mod. E. *ruine*, *ruyne*; < ME. *ruine*, < OF. *ruine*, F. *ruine* = Pr. *roina*, *ruina* = Sp. Pg. *ruina* = It. *rovina*, *ruina* = G. D. *ruine* = Dan. Sw. *ruin*, < L. *ruina*, overthrow, ruin, < *ruere*, fall down, tumble, sink in ruin, rush.] 1†. The act of falling or tumbling down; violent fall.

Immediately it fell; and the *ruin* of that house was great. Luke vi. 49.

His *ruin* startled the other steeds.
Chapman. (*Imp. Dict.*)

2. A violent or profound change of a thing, such as to unfit it for use, destroy its value, or bring it to an end; overthrow; downfall; collapse; wreck, material or moral: as, the *ruin* of a government; the *ruin* of health; financial *ruin*.

A flattering mouth worketh *ruin*. Prov. xxvi. 28.

And spread they shall be, to thy foul disgrace,
And utter *ruin* of the house of York.
Shak., 3 Hen. VI., i. 1. 254.

Priam's powers and Priam's self shall fall,
And one prodigious *ruin* swallow all.
Pope, Iliad, iv. 199.

3. That which promotes injury, decay, or destruction; bane.

And he said, Because the gods of the kings of Syria help them, therefore will I sacrifice to them that they may help me. But they were the *ruin* of him and of all Israel.
2 Chron. xxviii. 23.

Staumrel, corky-headed, graceless gentry,
The herryment and *ruin* of the country.
Burns, Brigs of Ayr.

4. That which has undergone overthrow, downfall, or collapse; anything, as a building, in a state of destruction, wreck, or decay; hence, in the plural, the fragments or remains of anything overthrown or destroyed: as, the *ruins* of former beauty; the *ruins* of Nineveh.

This Jaff was Sumtyme a grett Citee, as it appereth by the *Ruyne* of the same.
Torkington, Diarie of Eng. Travell, p. 24.

Thou art the *ruins* of the noblest man
That ever lived in the tide of times.
Shak., J. C., iii. 1. 256.

Through your *ruins* hoar and gray—
Ruins, yet beauteous in decay—
The silvery moonbeams trembling fly.
Burns, Ruins of Lincluden Abbey.

Alas, poor Clifford! . . . You are partly crazy, and partly imbecile; a *ruin*, a failure, as almost everybody is.
Hawthorne, Seven Gables, x.

5. The state of being ruined, decayed, destroyed, or rendered worthless.

Repair thy wit, good youth, or it will fall
To cureless *ruin*. *Shak.*, M. of V., iv. 1. 142.

Princely counsel in his face yet shone,
Majestic, though in *ruin*. *Milton*, P. L., ii. 305.

It was the Conservative, or rather the Agrarian, party which brought this bill to ruin.
Contemporary Rev., L. 285.

=**Syn.** 2. Subversion, wreck, shipwreck, prostration.

ruin (rö'in), *v.* [= F. *ruiner*, F. dial. *rouiner* = Pr. *reunar* = Sp. *ruinar* (Pg. *arruinar*) = It. *rovinare*, *ruinare* = D. *ruineren* = G. *ruiniren* = Dan. *ruinere* = Sw. *ruinera*, ruin, < ML. *ruinare*, ruin, fall in ruin, < L. *ruina*, ruin: see *ruin*, *n.*] I. *trans.* 1. To bring to ruin; cause the downfall, overthrow, or collapse of; damage essentially and irreparably; wreck the material or moral well-being of; demolish; subvert; spoil; undo: as, to *ruin* a city or a government; to *ruin* commerce; to *ruin* one's health or reputation.

Jerusalem is *ruined*, and Judah is fallen. Isa. iii. 8.

Mark but my fall, and that that *ruin'd* me.
Cromwell, I charge thee, fling away ambition.
Shak., Hen. VIII., iii. 2. 440.

All men that are *ruined* are *ruined* on the side of their natural propensities. *Burke*, A Regicide Peace, i.

The rain has *ruined* the ungrown corn.
Swinburne, Triumph of Time.

2. Specifically, to bring to financial ruin; reduce to a state of bankruptcy or extreme poverty.

The freeman is not to be amerced in a way that will *ruin* him; the penalty is to be fixed by a jury of his neighbourhood. *Stubbs*, Const. Hist., § 155.

=**Syn.** 1. To destroy, overthrow, overturn, overwhelm.—2. To impoverish.

II. *intrans.* 1. To fall headlong and with violence; rush furiously downward. [Rare.]

Headlong themselves they threw
Down from the verge of heaven; . . .
Hell heard the insufferable noise; hell saw
Heaven *ruining* from heaven.
Milton, P. L., vi. 868.

Torrents of her myriad universe,
Ruining along the illimitable inane,
Fly on to clash together again.
Tennyson, Lucretius.

2. To fall into ruins; run to ruin; fall into decay; be dilapidated.

Though he his house of polish'd marble build, . . .
Yet shall it *ruin* like the moth's frail cell.
Sandys, Paraphrase upon Job, xxvii.

3†. To be overwhelmed by loss, failure, suffering, or the like; be brought to misery or poverty.

They then perceive that dilatory stay
To be the causer of their ruining.
Drayton, Barons' Wars, i. 54.

Unless these things, which I have above proposed, one way or another, be once settl'd, in my fear, which God avert, we may instantly *ruin*.
Milton, Ruptures of the Commonwealth.

4. To inflict ruin; do irreparable harm.

He was never,
But where he meant to *ruin*, pitiful.
Shak., Hen. VIII., iv. 2. 40.

ruinable (rö'in-a-bl), *a.* [< *ruin* + *-able.*] Capable of being ruined.

Above these *ruinable* skies
They make their last retreat.
Watts, The Atheist's Mistake.

ruin-agate (rö'in-ag″āt), *n.* A variety of agate of various shades of brown, the color so arranged as to give to a polished slab a fancied resemblance to a ruined building.

ruinate (rö'i-nāt), *v.*; pret. and pp. *ruinated*, ppr. *ruinating*. [< ML. *ruinatus*, pp. of *ruinare*, ruin, fall in ruin: see *ruin*, *v.*] **I.** *trans.* **1**†. To hurl violently down; thrust or drive headlong.

On thother side they saw that perilous Rocke,
Threatning it selfe on them to *ruinate*.
Spenser, F. Q., II. xii. 7.

2. To bring to ruin; overthrow; undo. [Archaic or prov. Eng.]

I will not *ruinate* my father's house,
Who gave his blood to lime the stones together.
Shak., 3 Hen. VI., v. 1. 83.

I saw two Churches grievously demolished, . . . and two Monasteries extremely *ruinated*.
Coryat, Crudities, I. 9.

II. *intrans.* To fall; be overthrown; go to ruin. [Rare.]

We see others *ruinating* for want of our incomparable system of constitutional government.
S. H. Cox, Interviews Memorable and Useful, p. 115.

ruinate† (rö'i-nāt), *a.* [= Sp. Pg. *ruinado* = It. *rovinato*, *ruinato*, ruined, < ML. *ruinatus*, pp. of *ruinare*, fall in ruin, ruin: see *ruin*, *v.*] Brought to ruin; ruined; in ruins.

Shall love, in building, grow so *ruinate*?
Shak., C. of E., iii. 2. 4.

My brother Edward lives in pomp and state;
I in a mansion here all *ruinate*.
Dekker and Webster, Sir Thomas Wyatt, p. 11.

ruination (rö-i-nā'shon), *n.* [< ML. **ruinatio(n-)*, < *ruinare*, ruin: see *ruinate*.] The act of ruinating, or the state of being ruinated; ruin.

Roman coynes . . . were . . . ouercouered in the ground, in the sodaine *ruination* of tounes by the Saxons.
Camden, Remains, Money.

It was left for posterity, after three more centuries of Irish misery, to meet public necessity by private *ruination*.
R. W. Dixon, Hist. Church of Eng., xix.

ruiner (rö'i-nėr), *n.* [< OF. *ruineur*, < It. *rovinatore*, < ML. **ruinator*, < *ruinare*, ruin: see *ruin*.] One who ruins or destroys.

They [bishops] have been the most certain deformers and *ruiners* of the church. *Milton*, On Def. of Humb. Remonst.

ruing (rö'ing), *n.* [< ME. *ruynge*; verbal n. of *rue*[1], *v.*] Repentance; regret.

ruiniform (rö'i-ni-fôrm), *a.* [= F. *ruiniforme*, < L. *ruina*, ruin, + *forma*, form.] Having the appearance of ruins: noting various minerals.

ruin-marble (rö'in-mär″bl), *n.* Marble showing markings resembling vaguely the forms of ruined or dilapidated buildings.

ruinous (rö'i-nus), *a.* [< ME. *ruinous*, *ruynous*, < OF. *ruineux*, *ruyneux*, F. *ruineux* = Pr. *ruynos* = Sp. Pg. *ruinoso* = It. *rovinoso*, *ruinoso*, < L. *ruinosus*, ruinous, < *ruina*, overthrow, ruin: see *ruin*.] **1.** Fallen to ruin; decayed; dilapidated.

Somwhat bynethe that village we come to an olde, forleten, *ruynous* churche, somtyme of seynt Marke.
Sir R. Guylforde, Pylgrymage, p. 33.

Leave not the mansion so long tenantless,
Lest, growing *ruinous*, the building fall.
Shak., T. G. of V., v. 4. 9.

2. Composed of ruins; consisting in ruins.

Behold, Damascus is taken away from being a city, and it shall be a *ruinous* heap. Isa. xvii. 1.

3. Destructive; baneful; pernicious; bringing or tending to bring ruin.

Machinations, hollowness, treachery, and all *ruinous* disorders follow us disquietly to our graves.
Shak., Lear, i. 2. 123.

The favourite pressed for patents, lucrative to his relations and to his creatures, *ruinous* and vexatious to the body of the people. *Macaulay*, Lord Bacon.

ruinously (rö'i-nus-li), *adv.* In a ruinous manner; destructively.

ruinousness (rö'i-nus-nes), *n.* The state or character of being ruinous; mischievousness; banefulness.

ruit†, *n.* A Middle English form of *rut*[2].

rukh, *n.* Same as *roc*[1].

rulable (rö'la-bl), *a.* [< *rule*[1], *v.*, + *-able.*] **1.** Capable of being ruled; governable.

For the removing the impression of your nature to be opiniastre and not *rulable*, first and above all things I wish that all matters past, which cannot be revoked, your lordship would turn altogether upon insatisfaction, and not upon your nature or proper disposition.
Bacon, To Lord Essex, Oct., 1596.

2. Permissible according to rule; allowable. [Colloq.]

In all sales of Butter above "low grades" it shall be *rulable* to reject any package or packages varying widely in color or quality from the bulk of the lot.
New York Produce Exchange Report (1888–9), p. 305.

rule[1] (röl), *n.* [< ME. *rule*, *reule*, *rewle*, *ruell*, *riule*, *riwle* (as in *Ancren Riwle*, 'Anchoresses' Rule'), < OF. *reule*, *rieule*, *riule*, *reigle*, *riegle*, F. dial. (Norm.) *ruile*, F. *règle* = Pr. Sp. *regla* = Pg. *regra* = It. *regola* = AS. *regol*, *regul*, a rule, = D. *regel* = MLG. *reggele*, *regule* = OHG. *regula*, monastic rule, MHG. *regele*, *regel*, G. *regel* = Icel. *regla*, *regula* = Sw. Dan. *regel*, rule, < L. *regula* (ML. also *regula*), a rule, etc., < *regere*, keep straight, direct, govern, rule: see *regent*. See *rail*[1], a bar, etc., and *regle*, doublets of *rule*[1].] **1.** An instrument with an edge approximately straight, subserving purposes of measurement. A mere straight-edge is usually called a *ruler*. *Rules* are mostly of three kinds—(1) those with a scale of long measure on the edge, (2) parallel rules, and (3) sliding rules. See *ruler*, and cut under *caliper*.

Thes yefthe [gift, *i. e.* righteousness] is the maister of workes, thet is to zigge, of the uirtues of man; uor he doth al to wylle, and to the line, and to the *reule*, and to the leade, and to the leuele.
Ayenbite of Inwyt (E. E. T. S.), p. 150.

Mechanic slaves
With greasy aprons, *rules*, and hammers, shall
Uplift us to the view. *Shak.*, A. and C., v. 2. 210.

2. A formula to which conduct must be conformed; a minor law, canon, or regulation, especially a regulation which a person imposes upon himself: as, the *rules* of whist.

Now hath vche riche a *reule* to eten bi hym-selue
In a pryue parloure for pore mennes sake,
Or in a chambre with a chymneye.
Piers Plowman (B), x. 96.

If thou well observe
The *rule* of—Not too much, by temperance taught, . . .
So mayst thou live. *Milton*, P. L., xi. 531.

His Example still the *Rule* shall give,
And those it taught to Conquer, teach to Live.
Congreve, Birth of the Muse.

Specifically—(*a*) In monasteries or other religious societies, the code of laws required to be observed by the society and its individual members: as, the *rule* of St. Benedict, the *rule* of St. Basil, etc. (*b*) In *law:* (1) A statement of a principle of law propounded as controlling or entitled to control conduct; the principle thus stated: as, the *rule* against perpetuities (see *perpetuity*, 3). In this sense some rules are *statutory* or *constitutional*—that is, created by or embodied in statutes or a constitution; some are *common-law rules*, as many of the rules of evidence; and some are *equitable*—that is, introduced by the courts of equity. (2) More specifically, regulations (generally, if not always, promulgated in writing) prescribed by a court or judges for the conduct of litigation, being either *general rules*, applicable to whole classes of cases (commonly called *rules of court*), or *particular rules*, or orders in particular causes: as, a *rule* for a new trial, a *rule* nisi, etc. (*c*) *pl.* In American parliamentary law, the regulations adopted by a deliberative body for the conduct of its proceedings, corresponding to the standing orders of the British House of Commons. (*d*) In *gram.*, an established form of construction in a particular class of words, or the expression of that form in words. Thus, it is a *rule* in English that *s* or *es* added to a noun in the singular number forms the plural of that noun; but *man* forms its plural *men*, and so is an exception to the *rule*.

O Grammar *rules!* O now your virtues show!
So children still read you with awful eyes.
Sir P. Sidney (Arber's Eng. Garner, I. 534).

3. A form of words embodying a method for attaining a desired result; also, the method itself: as, the *rules* of art; especially, in *arith.*, the description of a process for solving a problem or performing a calculation; also, the method itself.

Led by some *rule* that guides but not constrains.
Pope, Epistle to Jervas.

The representation of a general condition according to which something manifold can be arranged [with uniformity] is called a *rule*; if it must be so arranged, a law.
Kant, Critique of Pure Reason, tr. by Müller, p. 113.

4. The expression of a uniformity; a general proposition; especially, the statement that under certain circumstances certain phenomena will present themselves: as, failure is the general *rule*, success the exception.

Arch. Against ill chances men are ever merry;
But heaviness foreruns the good event. . . .
Believe me, I am passing light in spirit.
Mowb. So much the worse, if your own *rule* be true.
Shak., 2 Hen. IV., iv. 2. 86.

For 'tis a *rule* that holds forever true:
Grant me discernment, and I grant it you.
Cowper, Progress of Error.

And first it [law] is a *rule:* . . . something permanent, uniform, and universal.
D. Webster, Speech, March 10, 1818.

5. In *law:* (*a*) Jail limits. See *rules of a prison*, below. (*b*) The time and place appointed in a court, or in the office of its clerk, for entering rules or orders such as do not require to be granted by the court in term time. Hence the phrase *at rules*, at the session so appointed.—6. Conformity to rule; regularity; propriety: as, to be out of *rule*.

[They] bowet euyn to the banke or thai bide wold;
Out of *rule* or aray raungit on lenght.
Destruction of Troy (E. E. T. S.), l. 5677.

He cannot buckle his distemper'd cause
Within the belt of *rule*. *Shak.*, Macbeth, v. 2. 15.

7. The possession and exertion of guiding and controlling power; government; sway; dominion; supreme command or authority.

He gouernyd the contre bothe lesse and more,
Also he badde the *Rule* of euery towne,
And namely tho that longyd to the crowne.
Generydes (E. E. T. S.), l. 25.

Though usurpers sway the *rule* awhile,
Yet heavens are just, and time suppresseth wrongs.
Shak., 3 Hen. VI., iii. 3. 76.

Deep harm to disobey,
Seeing obedience is the bond of *rule*.
Tennyson, Morte d'Arthur.

8. In *printing*, a thin strip of rolled brass, cut type-high, used for the printing of continuous lines. (See *composing*.) Rules are made in many forms; those in general use are shown here.

Single rule
Parallel "
Double "
Waved "
Dotted "

9. In *plastering*, a strip of wood placed on the face of a wall as a guide to assist in keeping the plane surface.—10. In *musical notation*, same as *line*[2], 2 (*b*) (1).—**Antepredicamental rule**, one of two rules laid down by Aristotle in the introductory part of his treatise on the categories. See *antepredicament*.—**A rule to show cause, or a rule nisi**, a rule which is conditional, so that, unless the party against whom it has been obtained shows sufficient cause to the contrary, it will become absolute.—**As a rule**, as a general thing; on the whole.—**Bevel plumb-rule**, an instrument used by engineers in testing the slope of an embankment. One limb of it can be set to any angle with the other, which is held plumb, to determine whether the slope has the proper angle or not.—**Brass rule.** See def. 8.—**Cardan's rule**, a rule for the solution of cubic equations, first published by Jerome Cardan, to whom it had been confidentially communicated by the Italian mathematician Tartaglia (died 1559). But the first discoverer is said to have been Scipione dal Tesso (died about 1525). The rule is that the solution of the equation $x^3 + qx + r = 0$ is

$$x = \sqrt[3]{-\tfrac{1}{2}r + \sqrt{\tfrac{1}{4}r^2 + \tfrac{1}{27}q^3}} + \sqrt[3]{-\tfrac{1}{2}r - \sqrt{\tfrac{1}{4}r^2 + \tfrac{1}{27}q^3}}.$$

The rule is applicable in all cases; but if there are three real roots, it is not convenient, on account of imaginaries.—**Carpenter's rule**, in the common form, a two-foot rule, folding in four, graduated to eighths and sixteenths of an inch. Sometimes a pivoted index with a scale or a graduated slider is added to adapt the instrument for a greater number of uses and to aid in making certain computations.—**Cross-rule paper.** See *paper*.—**De Gua's rule** [named after the French mathematician Jean Paul *de Gua* de Malves, who gave it in 1741], the proposition that if any even number of successive terms is wanting from an equation there are as many imaginary roots, and if any odd number of terms is wanting there are one more or one less imaginary roots according as the two terms adjoining the gap have like or unlike signs.—**Descartes's rule of signs**, otherwise called *Descartes's theorem*, the proposition that in a numerical algebraic equation the number of positive roots cannot surpass the number of variations in the series of signs of the successive terms after these have all been brought to the same side of the equation and arranged according to the powers of the unknown quantity; and, further, that the excess of the number of variations over the number of positive roots cannot be an odd number.—**Dotted rule.** See def. 8.—**Double rule.** See def. 8.—**Figure of the golden rule**, a line shaped like a Z, with the terms of a proposition at its ends and angles, thus:

as 4——is to——12
so 18——is to——54.

Figure of the rule of false†, a cross like an X, with the two false positions at its upper corners, and the errors of the result respectively under them, the difference of the errors under the middle of the cross, and the answer over the middle of the cross.—**French rule**, in *printing*, a dash, generally of brass, thus: ——◆——.—**Gag-rule.** Same as *gag-law*.

The legislature of Massachusetts pronounced the *gag rule* unconstitutional, and asserted that Congress had power to abolish slavery in the District of Columbia.
The Century, XXXVII. 875.

Gauss's Rule for finding the date of Easter. See *Easter*1.—**Golden rule.** See *golden*.—**Guldin's rule**, one of two rules, one giving the volume and the other the surface of any ring formed by the revolution of any plane closed curve about an axis lying in its plane. The rules are named after the Swiss mathematician Paul Guldin (1577–1643), but he obtained them from the collections of Pappus, a geometer of the fourth century.—**Home rule.** See *home*1.—**Home-Rule Bill.** See *bill*3.—**Inverse rule of three.** See *inverse*.—**Joint rule**, a rule adopted by both houses of Congress or a legislature for the conduct of transactions between them.—**Labor-saving rule**, in *printing*, brass rules cut by system to graduated lengths, so that they may be easily combined.—**Minding's rule**, a rule for the determination of the degree of an equation resulting from elimination, given by the Prussian mathematician E. F. A. Minding in 1841.—**Napier's rule**, one of two mnemonic rules given by Napier, the inventor of logarithms, for the solution of right-angled spherical triangles. The two legs and the complements of the hypotenuse and of the angles are called the *parts*. An angle and one of the sides going to form it are said to be *adjacent*; so, also, are the two legs. A part adjacent to both or neither of two parts is called, relatively to them, the *middle* part; and if the other two are not adjacent to it, they are called *opposite*. Then, the two rules are that the sine of the middle part is equal to the product of the tangents of the adjacent parts and to the product of the cosines of the opposite parts. These are equivalent to six equations of different forms.—**Newton's rule**, a certain rule for determining a superior limit to the number of positive roots of an algebraic equation, and another for the negative roots. Let the equation be

$$a_0 x^n + n a_1 x^{n-1} + \frac{n(n-1)}{1.2} a_2 x^{n-2} + \text{etc.} = 0.$$

Form a series of quantities $A_0, A_1 \ldots A_n$ by the formula $A_r = a^2_r - a_{r-1} a_{r+1}$. Write down the two rows

$$a_0, a_1, a_2, \ldots a_n$$
$$A_0, A_1, A_2, \ldots A_n.$$

If two successive numbers in the upper row have like signs while the numbers under them also have like signs, this is called a *double permanence*. But if two successive numbers in the upper row have different signs while the numbers under them have like signs, this is called a *variation-permanence*. The rule is that the number of negative roots cannot be greater than the number of double permanences, nor the number of positive roots greater than the number of variation-permanences.—**One-hour rule**, a standing rule of the United States House of Representatives, first adopted in 1847, in accordance with which no member, except one who reports a measure from a committee, may, without unanimous consent or permission given by vote, speak for more than one hour in debate on any subject.—**Parallel rule.** (a) A rule for drawing parallel lines. The old form of parallel rule consisted of two rulers connected by two bars turning upon pivots at the vertices of a parallelogram. For accurate work, a triangle and a straight-edge are used. (b) See def. 8.—**Rule day**, in legal proceedings, motion day; the regularly appointed day on which to make orders to show cause returnable.—**Rule of cossl.** See *coss*2.—**Rule of faith** (*regula fidei*), the sum of Christian doctrine as accepted by the orthodox church in opposition to heretical sects; the creed: a phrase used from the second century onward.—**Rule of false** (*regula falsi*), or **rule of double position.** See *position*, 7.—**Rule of intersection, rule of six quantities**, the proposition that, if a spherical triangle be cut by a transversal great circle, the product of the chords of the doubles of three segments which do not cut one another is equal to the product of the chords of the doubles of the other three segments. This rule was discovered by Menelaus, about A. D. 100.—**Rule of mixtures.** Same as *alligation*, 2.—**Rule of Nicomachus** (named from *Nicomachus*, a Greek arithmetician who flourished about A. D. 100, and who is said to have been the author of this rule), a rule for finding the square of a small number, as follows: subtract the number from 10 and to the square of the difference add 10 times the number diminished by the difference. Thus, to find the square of 9, subtract 9 from 10, which gives 1 as the difference, the square of which is 1, and adding to this 10 times the excess of the original number, 9, over the difference, 1, which excess is 8, we have 81 as the answer.—**Rule of philosophizing**, a rule for constructing theories. Newton propounded certain rules of this kind.—**Rule of signs**, the rule that any arrangement is positive or negative according as it contains an even or odd number of displacements.—**Rule of speech** (*regula sermonis*), the rule of false, so called because in the use of it we "say" a quantity has a value which is false.—**Rule of supposition**, the rule of false. See *position*, 7.—**Rule of the double sign**, the principle that zero may be regarded either as positive or negative at pleasure, which has important applications under Budan's theorem.—**Rule of the octave.** See *octave*.—**Rule of the road.** See *road*.—**Rule of three**, the method of finding the fourth term of a proportion when three are given. The numbers being so arranged that the first is to the second as the third is to the fourth, which last is the term required to be found, then this is found by multiplying the second and third terms together, and dividing the product by the first.—**Rule of thumb**, a rule suggested by a practical rather than a scientific knowledge: in allusion to a use of the thumb in marking off measurements roughly.

> We'll settle men and things by *rule of thumb*,
> And break the lingering night with ancient rum.
> *Sydney Smith*, To Francis Jeffrey, Sept. 3, 1809.

Rule of trial and error, the rule of false. See *position*, 7.—**Rules of a prison**, certain limits outside the walls of a prison, within which prisoners in custody were sometimes allowed to live, on giving security not to escape. The phrase is sometimes extended to mean the space so inclosed, and also the freedom thus accorded to the prisoner.

> To aid these, the prisoners took it in turns to perambulate the *rules*, and solicit help in money or kind.
> *J. Ashton*, Social Life in Reign of Queen Anne, II. 247.

> Both at the King's Bench and the Fleet debtors were allowed to purchase what were called the *Rules*, which enabled them to live within a certain area outside the prison, and practically left them free.
> *W. Besant*, Fifty Years Ago, p. 77.

Rules of course, rules which are drawn up by the proper officers on the authority of the mere signature of counsel; or, in some instances, as upon a judge's fiat, or allowance by the master, etc., without any signature by counsel. Rules which are not of course are grantable on the motion either of the party actually interested or of his counsel.—**Rules of practice**, general rules prescribed by a court or other authority for the regulation of legal or other official procedure. See def. 2, above.—**Single rule.** See def. 8.—**Sliding rule**, a rule having one or more scales which slide over others for the purpose of facilitating calculations.—**Stationers' rule**, a rule of considerable length, made of hard wood about half an inch in thickness, usually marked with inches, and having its edges sheathed with brass strips. It is used for measuring, and as a straight-edge to guide a knife in cutting thick paper, as drawing-paper, pasteboard, etc.—**The rule in Shelley's case**, a much-quoted doctrine of the common law, to the effect that wherever there is a limitation to a man which if it stood alone would convey to him a particular estate of freehold, followed by a limitation to his heirs or to the heirs of his body (or equivalent expressions) either immediately or after the interposition of one or more particular estates, the apparent gift to the heir or heirs of the body is to be construed as a limitation of the estate of the ancestor, and not as a gift to the heir.—**To buy in under the rule.** See *buy*.—**Twenty-first rule**, in *U. S. hist.*, a rule adopted by the House of Representatives in 1840, and dropped in 1844, prescribing that no abolition petitions should be received by the House.—**Waved rule.** See def. 8. =**Syn.** 2. *Precept*, etc. (see *principle*), law, regulation, formula, criterion, standard.—7. Direction, regulation, dominion, lordship, authority, mastery, domination.

rule1 (röl), *v.*; pret. and pp. *ruled*, ppr. *ruling*. [< ME. *rulen*, *reulen*, *rewlen*, *riulen*, < OF. *ruiler*, *rieuler*, *rieler*, *reguler*, *reigler*, *regler*, F. *régler* = Pr. *reglar* = Sp. *reglar*, *regular* = Pg. *regrar*, *regular* = It. *regolare* = D. *regelen* = G. *regeln* = Dan. *regulere* = Sw. *reglera*, < LL. *regulare*, regulate, rule, < L. *regula*, a rule: see *rule*1, *n.*, and cf. *rail*1, *v.*, and *regulate*.] **I.** *trans.* **1.** To make conformable to a rule, pattern, or standard; adjust or dispose according to rule; regulate; hence, to guide or order aright.

> Be thise uirtue [prudence] al thet man deth and zayth and thength, al he digt and let and *reuleth* to the lyne of scele [reason]. *Ayenbite of Inwyt* (E. E. T. S.), p. 124.

> Yet Pitee, through his stronge gentil might,
> Forgaf, and made Mercy passen Right,
> Through innocence and *ruled* curtesye.
> *Chaucer*, Good Women, l. 163.

> His actions seemed *ruled* with a ruler.
> *Lamb*, South-Sea House.

2. To settle as by a rule; in *law*, to establish by decision or rule; determine; decide: thus, a court is said to *rule* a point. *Burrill.*

> Had he done it with the pope's licence, his adversaries must have been silent; for that's a ruled case with the schoolmen. *Bp. Atterbury.*

3. To have or exercise authority or dominion over; govern; command; control; manage; restrain.

> Let reason *rule* thy wyt. *Babees Book* (E. E. T. S.), p. 79.

> We'll do thee homage and be *ruled* by thee,
> Love thee as our commander and our king.
> *Shak.*, T. G. of V., iv. 1. 66.

> Being not able to *rule* his horse and defend himselfe, he was throwne to the ground.
> *Capt. John Smith*, True Travels, I. 17.

4. To prevail on; persuade; advise: generally or always in the passive, so that *to be ruled by* is to take the advice or follow the directions of.

> I think she will *be ruled*
> In all respects *by* me; nay, more, I doubt it not.
> *Shak.*, R. and J., iii. 4. 13.

> Nay, master, *be ruled by* me a little; so, let him lean upon his staff. *Marlowe*, Jew of Malta, iv. 2.

5. To dominate; have a predominant influence or effect upon or in.

> And God made two great lights; the greater light to *rule* the day, and the lesser light to *rule* the night.
> Gen. i. 16.

> Soft undulating lines *rule* the composition; yet dignity of attitude and feature prevails over mere loveliness.
> *J. A. Symonds*, Italy and Greece, p. 65.

6. To mark with lines by means of a ruler; produce parallel straight lines in, by any means: as, to *rule* a blank book. See *ruled paper*, under *paper*.

> A singing-man had the license for printing music-books, which he extended to that of being the sole vendor of all *ruled* paper, on the plea that, where there were *ruled* lines, musical notes might be pricked down.
> *I. D'Israeli*, Amen. of Lit., II. 437.

7. To mark with or as with the aid of a ruler or a ruling-machine: as, to *rule* lines on paper.

> Age *rules* my lines with wrinkles in my face.
> *Drayton*, Idea, xliv.

Ruled surface. (a) A surface generated by the motion of a line; a locus of lines indeterminate in one degree. (b) Any surface, as of paper or metal, upon which a series of parallel lines has been marked or cut.—**To rule the roast.** See *roast*. =**Syn.** 1 and 3. *Control*, *Regulate*, etc. See *govern*.

II. *intrans.* **1.** To have power or command; exercise supreme authority.

> By me princes *rule*, and nobles, even all the judges of the earth. Prov. viii. 16.

> Let them obey that know not how to *rule*.
> *Shak.*, 2 Hen. VI., v. 1. 6.

2. To prevail; decide.

> Away with scrupulous wit! now arms must *rule*.
> *Shak.*, 3 Hen. VI., iv. 7. 61.

3. In *law*: (a) To decide. (b) To lay down and settle a rule or order of court; order by rule; enter a rule.—**4.** In *com.*, to stand or maintain a level.

> Prices generally *rule* low.
> *The Academy*, July 5, 1890, p. 15.

rule2 (röl), *n.* [A contracted form of *revel*; perhaps in part associated with *rule* in *misrule* ("lord of *misrule*," etc.): see *revel*.] Revel; revelry.

> What night-*rule* now about this haunted grove?
> *Shak.*, M. N. D., iii. 2. 5.

> And at each pause they kiss; was never seen such *rule*
> In any place but here, at Boon-fire, or at Yule.
> *Drayton*, Polyolbion, xxvii. 251.

rule2 (röl), *v. i.* [Also *reul*; a contr. of *revel*. Cf. *rule*2, *n.*] To revel; be unruly. *Halliwell* (under *reul*). [Prov. Eng.]

rule-case (röl'kās), *n.* In *printing*, a tray or case with partitions provided for rules.

rule-cutter (röl'kut″ėr), *n.* In *printing*, a machine for cutting brass rule to short lengths: usually a shears one blade of which is fixed and the other is moved by a strong lever.

rule-driller (röl'dril″ėr), *n.* A teacher who drills his pupils upon rules, or by rote, without teaching them the underlying principles.

> I speak to the teacher, not the *rule-driller*.
> *De Morgan*, Arith. Books, Int., p. xxii.

rule-joint (röl'joint), *n.* A pivoted joint in the nature of a hinge-joint, whereby two thin flat strips may be so united that each will turn edgewise toward or from the other, and in no other direction: so called from its general employment in folding rules and scales used by surveyors, engineers, and mechanics. Also called *prop-joint*.

Rule- or Prop-joint.
a and *b*, prop-rods; *c*, rule-joint.

ruleless (röl'les), *a.* [Early mod. E. also *rulesse*; < *rule*1 + *-less*.] Being without rule; lawless.

> A *rulesse* rout of yongmen which her woo'd,
> All slaine with darts, lie wallowed in their blood.
> *Spenser*, Virgil's Gnat, l. 431.

rulelessness (röl'les-nes), *n.* [< *ruleless* + *-ness*.] The state or quality of being ruleless, or without rule or law.

> Its [the Star-Chamber's] *rulelessness*, or want of rules that can be comprehended, is curiously illustrated here.
> *The Academy*, July 19, 1879, p. 43.

ruler (rö'lėr), *n.* [< *rule*1 + *-er*1.] **1.** One who rules or governs; one who exercises dominion or controlling power over others; a person who commands, manages, restrains, or has part in the making or administration of law; one in authority.

> *Rewlers* of rewmes around all the erthe
> Were not yffoundid at the ffrist tyme
> To lene al at likynge and lust of the world,
> But to laboure on the lawe as lewde men on plowes.
> *Richard the Redeless*, iii. 264.

> Who made thee a *ruler* and a judge over us?
> Acts vii. 27.

2. A rule; an instrument made of wood, brass, ivory, or the like, with straight edges or sides, by means of which, as a guide, straight lines may be drawn on paper, parchment, or other substance, by passing a pen or pencil along the edge. (See *rule*1, and *parallel ruler*, under *parallel*.) When a ruler has the lines of chords, tangents, sines, etc., it is called a *scale*. See *scale*3.—**3.** In *engraving*, a workman who operates a ruling-machine for ruling in flat tints, etc. See *ruling-machine*.—**4.** In *line-engraving*, a straight steel bar supported on cleats, to which a socket is so fitted that it slides evenly and steadily backward and forward. A perpendicular tube fixed to the side of the socket holds a sharp diamond-pointed graver which is pressed down by a spring. When the socket is drawn along the bar, the graver cuts a straight line across the plate; but by a slight motion of the hand lines can be formed to suit the shape of any object.—**Marquoi's rulers**, a mathematical instrument for drawing parallel lines at determinate distances from one another.

rulership (rö'lėr-ship), *n.* [< *ruler* + *-ship*.] The office or power of a ruler. [Rare.]

Much more unlikely things have come to pass than that this languid young man should be called to the helm of affairs, the virtual *rulership* of the British Empire.
T. W. Higginson, Eng. Statesmen, p. 288.

rulesset, *a.* An obsolete form of *ruleless*.

rule-work (röl'wėrk), *n.* In *printing*, composition in which many rules are used, as in tables of figures.

ruling (rö'ling), *n.* [Verbal n. of *rule*[1], *v.*] 1. The determination by a judge or court of a point arising in the course of a trial or hearing.—2. The act of making ruled lines; also, such lines collectively.

ruling (rö'ling), *p. a.* [Ppr. of *rule*[1], *v.*] Having control or authority; governing; reigning; chief; prevalent; predominant.

The *ruling* passion, be it what it will,
The *ruling* passion conquers reason still.
Pope, Moral Essays, iii. 153.

Ruling elder. See *elder*[1], 5.=**Syn.** *Prevailing, Predominant*, etc. (see *prevalent*), controlling.

ruling-engine (rö'ling-en'jin), *n.* A machine for ruling diffraction gratings. The ruling is performed by a fine diamond-point, the spacing of the lines being accomplished by the most refined micrometer-screw mechanism. (See *grating*[2], 2, and *micrometer*.) The new ruling-engine at Johns Hopkins University has produced gratings ruled with from 10,000 to 20,000 lines per inch, 6 inches in diameter, with faces formed on a radius of more than 21 feet, and having better definition than any ever before made. Such engines must be placed in as nearly equable a temperature as can be attained, as any sensible expansion or contraction during their operation defeats their purpose.

rulingly (rö'ling-li), *adv.* In a ruling manner; so as to rule; controllingly. *Imp. Dict.*

ruling-machine (rö'ling-ma-shēn'), *n.* 1. A machine used by engravers for ruling in flat tints, etc. The cutting of the lines is done by a tool with a diamond-shaped point. Mechanism for spacing and for lifting the cutting-tool when the carriage which supports the tool is to be shifted in its parallel ways are the other features of the machine.
2. A machine used for ruling parallel colored lines upon writing-paper, or upon paper for the manufacture of blank-books; a paper-ruler. Fountain-pens with mechanism for spacing and for drawing them simultaneously upon the surface to be ruled, or in some cases endless bands (each a fine thread passing through coloring material) arranged so that a part of each band is brought into contact with the paper to be ruled, mechanism for spacing the lines, intermittent feed for the paper, and mechanism for lifting the ruling-bands from the paper when the latter is fed forward are characteristics of such machines. In ruling columns on pages for blank-books ruling-pens are employed.

ruling-pen (rö'ling-pen), *n.* A form of pen used for drawing lines of even thickness. It commonly consists of two blades which hold the ink between

Ruling-pen.
a, fixed blade; *b*, adjustable blade; *c*, adjusting-screw; *e*, handle, which screws into a socket at *d*.

them, the distance apart of the points being adjusted by a screw to conform to the desired width of line. Some ruling-pens consist of three needle-points brought close together at their ends; others are formed of a point of glass with channels to hold and conduct the ink along the sides.

rullichie (rul'i-chi), *n.* See *rollichie*.

rullion (rul'yon), *n.* [Also *rewelyns, rowlyngis, rillings*, a contr. of ME. *rivcling*, < AS. *rifeling*, a kind of shoe or sandal: see *riveling*[2].] 1. A shoe made of untanned leather.

The dress of the lad was completely in village fashion, yet neat and handsome in appearance. He had a jerkin of grey cloth slashed and trimmed, with black hose of the same, with deer-skin *rullions* or sandals, and handsome silver spurs.
Scott, Monastery, xxix.

2. A coarse, masculine woman; also, a rough, ill-made animal. [Scotch.]

rullock, *n.* A variant of *rowlock*.

ruly[1]† (rö'li), *a.* [< ME. *ruly, rewly, rewely, rewliche*, < AS. *hreówlic*, pitiable, < *hreów*, pity: see *ruel*, *n.*] Pitiable; miserable.

With that cam a knaue with a confessoures face,
Lene and *rewlyche* with leggys ful smale.
Piers Plowman (A), xii. 78.

This *rewlych* Creaus was caught of Cyrus and lad to the fyr to ben brent. *Chaucer*, Boëthius, ii. prose 2.

ruly[1]† (rö'li), *adv.* [< ME. *rewly, reoly*; < *ruly*[1], *a.*] Pitiably; miserably.

Thynk on god al-mygt,
And on his wowndys smerte,
How *rewly* he was a-dygt.
Holy Rood (E. E. T. S.), p. 151.

ruly[2]† (rö'li), *a.* [< ME. *ruly*: < *rule*[1] + *-y*[1] or *-ly*[1]. Cf. *unruly*.] 1. Conforming to rule; not unruly; acting rightly; righteous.

Ruly & rightwise, a roghe man of hors,
He spake neuer dispituosly, ne spiset no man:
Ne warpit neuer worde of wrang with his mowthe.
Destruction of Troy (E. E. T. S.), l. 3888.

2. Orderly; well-regulated.

I meane the sonnes of such rash sinning sires
Are seldome sene to runne a *ruly* race.
Gascoigne, Complaynt of Phylomene (Steele Glas, etc., [ed. Arber, p. 118).

rum[1] (rum), *n.* [Abbr. of *rumbullion* or *rumbooze*. The F. *rhum, rum* = Sp. *ron* = Pg. *rom* = It. *rum* = D. G. Dan. *rum* = Sw. *rom*, rum, are all from E.] 1. Spirit distilled from the juice of the sugar-cane in any form, commonly from the refuse juice left from sugar-making, but often from molasses, as especially in countries where the sugar-cane is not produced. Rum has always been especially an American product, the most esteemed varieties being made in the West Indies and named from the place of manufacture, as *Jamaica rum, Antigua, Grenada*, or *Santa Cruz rum*. It is also made in New England.

Rum is a spirit extracted from the juice of sugar-canes, . . . called Kill-Devil in New England!
G. Warren, Description of Surinam (1661) (quoted in [The Academy, Sept. 5, 1885, p. 155).

2. Any distilled liquor or strong alcoholic drink: much used in reprobation, with reference to intemperance: as, the evils of *rum*.

Rum I take to be the name which unwashed moralists apply alike to the product distilled from molasses and the noblest juices of the vineyard. Burgundy "in all its sunset glow" is *rum*. Champagne, "the foaming wine of Eastern France," is *rum*. *O. W. Holmes*, Autocrat, viii.

Pineapple rum. See *pineapple*. *Dickens*, Pickwick.

rum[2] (rum), *a.* and *n.* [Early mod. E. *rome*; supposed to be of Gipsy origin: cf. Gipsy *rom*, a husband, *Rommani*, a Gipsy: see *Rom, Rommany*.] I. *a.* Good; fine; hence, satirically, in present use, queer; odd; droll. [Slang.]

And the neighbours say, as they see him look sick,
"What a *rum* old covey is Hairy-faced Dick!"
Barham, Ingoldsby Legends, I. 158.

"*Rum* creeters is women," said the dirty-faced man.
Dickens, Pickwick, xiv.

"We were talking of language, Jasper." . . . "Yours must be a *rum* one?" "'Tis called Rommany."
G. *Borrow*, Lavengro, xvii.

II. *n.* Any odd, queer person or thing; an oddity. [Slang.]

No company comes
But a rabble of tenants, and rusty, dull *rums*.
Swift, The Grand Question Debated.

It seems that though the books which booksellers call *rums* appear to be very numerous, because they come oftener in their way than they like, yet they are not really so, reckoning only one of a sort.
Nichols, Literary Anecdotes, V. 471.

rumal (rö'mal), *n.* [Also *roomal, romal*; < Hind. *rūmāl*, Pers. *rūmāl*, a handkerchief.] A handkerchief; a small square shawl or veil. Especially—(*a*) A silk square used as a head-dress, etc. (*b*) A square shawl of goat's hair.

They [Thugs] had arranged their plan, which was very simple. If the darkness suited, Shumshoodeen Khan was to address a question to Rowley Mellon, who would stoop from his horse to listen; Pershad Sing was then to cast the *roomal* over his head, and drag him from his horse into the Mango tope, when the holy pick-axe would soon do the rest. *J. Grant.*

Rumanian (rö-mā'ni-an), *a.* and *n.* [Also *Roumanian*; < *Rumania*, also written *Roumania* (F. *Roumanie*) (see def.), + *-an*.] I. *a.* Of or pertaining to Rumania, a kingdom (since 1881) of southeastern Europe, consisting of the former Turkish dependencies Wallachia and Moldavia, the Danubian principalities. In 1859 the two principalities were united under a single tributary prince, made independent in 1878.

II. *n.* 1. One of the members of a race in southeastern Europe, Latinized in the second century, or perhaps later. Called by the Slavs *Vlachs* (Welsh, Wallachs).—2. A Romance language spoken in Rumania, the neighboring parts of the Austrian empire, Bessarabia, the Pindus region, etc.

Rumansh (rö-mänsh'), *a.* and *n.* [See *Romansh*.] Same as *Rhæto-Romanic*.

rumb, *n.* See *rhumb*.

rum-barge (rum'bärj), *n.* [Cf. *rumbooze*.] A warm drink. *Halliwell.* [Prov. Eng.]

rumble (rum'bl), *v.*; pret. and pp. *rumbled*, ppr. *rumbling*. [E. dial. *rummle, rommle*; < ME. *rumblen, romblen, rummelyn* (= D. *rommelen* = LG. *rummeln* = MHG. G. *rumpeln*, be noisy, = Dan. *rumle*, rumble; cf. Sw. *ramla*, Dan. *ramle*, rattle), freq. of *romen*, roar: see *rome*[2].] I. *intrans.* 1. To make a deep, heavy, continued and more or less jarring sound: as, the thunder *rumbles*.

But whan they cam to wan water,
It now was *rumbling* like the sea.
Billie Archie (Child's Ballads, VI. 96).

The wild wind rang from park and plain,
And round the attics *rumbled*.
Tennyson, The Goose.

2†. To murmur.

The people cryed and *rombled* up and down.
Chaucer, Monk's Tale, l. 545.

3. To move with a deep, hoarse, thundering or jarring sound; roll heavily and noisily.

Greta, what fearful listening! when huge stones
Rumble along thy bed, block after block.
Wordsworth, To the River Greta.

Old women, capped and spectacled, still peered through the same windows from which they had watched Lord Percy's artillery *rumble* by to Lexington.
Lowell, Cambridge Thirty Years Ago.

4†. To roll about; hence, to create disorder or confusion.

When love so *rumbles* in his pate, no sleep comes in his eyes. *Suckling*, Love and Debt.

II. *trans.* To cause to make a deep, rattling or jarring sound; rattle.

And then he *rumbled* his money with his hands in his trowsers' pockets, and looked and spoke very little like a thriving lover. *Trollope.*

rumble (rum'bl), *n.* [< ME. *rombel*; < *rumble*, *v.*] 1. A deep, heavy, continuous, and more or less rattling or jarring sound, as of thunder; a low, jarring roar.

Clamour and *rumble*, and ringing and clatter.
Tennyson, Maud, xxvii.

2†. Confused reports; rumor.

O stormy peple! unsad and ever untrewe!
Ay undiscreet and chaunging as a vane,
Delyting ever in *rombel* that is newe.
Chaucer, Clerk's Tale, l. 941.

3†. Confusion; disorder; tumult.

Aboute whome he found muche heauinesse, *rumble*, haste and businesse, carriage and conueyaunce of her stuffe into sainctuary. *Sir T. More*, Works, p. 43.

4. A revolving cylinder or box in which articles are placed to be ground, cleaned, or polished by mutual attrition. Grinding- or polishing-material is added according to the need of the case.—5. A seat for servants in the rear of a carriage. Also *rumble-tumble*.

A travelling chariot with a lozenge on the panels, a discontented female in a green veil and crimped curls on the *rumble*, and a large and confidential man on the box.
Thackeray, Vanity Fair, xiv.

rumble-gumption (rum'bl-gump'shon), *n.* Same as *rumgumption*.

Ye sud hae stayed at hame, an' wantit a wife till ye gathered mair *rummelgumption*.
Hogg, Perils of Man, I. 78. (*Jamieson*.)

rumbler (rum'blėr), *n.* [< *rumble* + *-er*[1].] A person who or a thing which rumbles. *Imp. Dict.*

rumble-tumble (rum'bl-tum'bl), *n.* Same as *rumble*, 5.

From the dusty height of a *rumble-tumble* affixed to Lady Selina Vipont's barouche . . . Vance caught sight of Lionel and Sophy.
Bulwer, What will he Do with it? i. 15.

rumbling (rum'bling), *n.* [< ME. *rumlynge, romelynge* (= MD. *rommeling*); verbal n. of *rumble*, *v.*] A low, heavy, continued rattling or jarring sound; a rumble. The peculiar rumbling of the bowels is technically called *borborygmus*.

At the noise of the stamping of the hoofs of his strong horses, at the rushing of his chariots, and at the *rumbling* of his wheels, the fathers shall not look back to their children for feebleness of hands. Jer. xlvii. 3.

rumblingly (rum'bling-li), *adv.* In a rumbling manner; with a rumbling sound.

rum-blossom (rum'blos'um), *n.* A pimple on the nose caused by excessive drinking; a rum-bud; acne rosacea. Compare *grog-blossom, toddy-blossom*. [Slang.]

rumbo[1]† (rum'bō), *n.* [Prob. short for *rumbooze*: see *rumbooze*. Cf. *rumbullion*.] A strong liquor: same as *rum*[1] or *rumbullion*.

Hawkins the boatswain and Derrick the quartermaster . . . were regaling themselves with a can of *rumbo*, after the fatiguing duty of the day. *Scott*, Pirate, xxxix.

rumbo[2] (rum'bō), *n.* [Cf. *rumbowline*.] Rope stolen from a dockyard. *Admiral Smyth.*

rumbooze (rum-böz'), *n.* [Early mod. E. also *rumbowse, rombowse, rome bowse*, also *rambooze, ramboozs, rambuze, rambuse*; prob. < *rum*[2] (altered in some forms to *ram*: see *ram*[3]) + *booze, boose*[2], drink: see *booze*.] Originally, any alcoholic drink; a tipple; specifically, a mixed drink: a fanciful name given to several combinations.

This bowse is as good as *Rome bowse*.
Harman, Caveat for Cursetors, p. 118.

This Bowse is better then *Rum-bowse*,
It sets the Gan a gigling.
Brome, Jovial Crew, ii.

Piot, a common cant word used by French clowns, and other tippling companions; it signifies *rum-booze*, as our gipsies call good-guzzle, and comes from *rum*, bibo.
Urquhart, tr. of Rabelais, ii. 1, note.

Rambooz. A compound drink, in most request at Cambridge, and is commonly made of eggs, ale, wine, and sugar; but in summer of milk, wine, sugar, and rose-water. *Blount's Glossography.*

rumbowline, *n.* See *rombowline*.

rumbowling, *n.* [Cf. *rumbullion*.] Grog: so called by sailors.

rum-bud (rum'bud), *n.* A rum-blossom. [Slang.]

Redness and eruptions generally begin with the nose; . . . they have been called *rum-buds* when they appear in the face.
Dr. Rush, Effects of Ardent Spirits. (*Encyc. Dict.*)

rumbullion (rum-bul'yon), *n.* [Appar. an extended form of *rumble*, imitatively varied, and in sense 2 confused with other words, as *rumbooze* or *rumbol*. Hence *rum*[1]. Cf. *rumbowling*.] 1. A great tumult. *Halliwell.* [Prov. Eng.]—2. A strong distilled liquor. See the quotation, and *rum*[1].

The chief fudling they make in the island is *Rumbullion*, alias Kill-Divil, and this is made of sugar canes distilled, a hot, hellish, and terrible liquor.
MS. Description of Barbados (1651), quoted in [The Academy, Sept. 5, 1885, p. 155.

rumbustical (rum-bus'ti-kal), *a.* Same as *rambustious*. *Halliwell.* [Prov. Eng.]

rumbustious (rum-bus'tyus), *a.* Same as *rambustious*. [Prov. Eng.]

The sea has been rather *rumbustious*, I own; but then, . . . the land makes us ample amends.
Foote, Trip to Calais, i.

rum-cherry (rum'cher"i), *n.* The wild black or cabinet cherry, *Prunus serotina*, of eastern North America. In the forest it grows from 60 to 90 feet high, and affords a fine, hard, light-brown or red timber, turning darker with exposure, much esteemed for cabinet-work, inside finish, etc., and now becoming scarce. This tree, sometimes wrongly called *P. Virginiana*, is the source of the official wild-cherry bark. Its small, black, sweetish, and bitter astringent fruit is used to flavor liquors (whence the name).

Rumelian (rö-mē'lian), *a.* and *n.* [Also *Roumelian*; ‹ *Rumelia*, also *Roumelia* (F. *Roumélie*), + *-an*.] I. *a.* Of or pertaining to Rumelia (originally, in a loose sense, the European possessions of the Sultan, sometimes excepting Rumania, Servia, and Bosnia; in a restricted sense, the region south of Bulgaria). A Turkish eyalet of Rumelia was formed about 1836 from parts of Albania and Macedonia. Eastern Rumelia was an autonomous province on the Black Sea, formed in 1878, and united to Bulgaria in 1885.

II. *n.* A native or an inhabitant of Rumelia, especially in the restricted sense. [Rare.]

rumen (rö'men), *n.*; pl. *rumina* (rö'mi-nạ̈). [‹ L. *rumen*, the throat, gullet: see *ruminate*.] 1. The cud of a ruminant.—2. The paunch or first stomach of a ruminant; the largest of the four compartments of the ruminant stomach. It is the one which, with the reticulum or honeycomb, is eaten under the name of *tripe*. Also called *farding-bag*. See cuts under *Ruminantia* and *Tragulus*.

Rumex (rö'meks), *n.* [NL. (Linnæus, 1737), ‹ L. *rumex*, f., sorrel (*R. acetosa*, etc.), so called from the shape of the leaves, ‹ *rumex*, m., a kind of lance.] A genus of apetalous plants of the order *Polygonaceæ*, type of the tribe *Rumiceæ*. It is characterized by its six stamens and its six- or rarely four-parted perianth, with the outer segments unchanged in fruit, but the three inner ones erect and very much enlarged, often bearing a conspicuous grain or tubercle resulting from a thickening of the midrib. The included nut is sharply three-angled, but without wings. About 150 species have been enumerated, but the real number is much less. They are widely scattered through north temperate regions, with a few native to the tropics and southern hemisphere. Many are common weeds of cultivated grounds, and some are almost cosmopolitan. They are usually perennial deep-rooting herbs, rarely tall shrubs. They bear united stipules (ocreæ), which are often transparent, at first sheathing, soon torn and vanishing. The flowers are in small bracted clusters at the nodes, often forming terminal racemes or panicles. In the section *Lapathum*, the dock, the leaves are commonly large, undivided, and cordate or rounded at the base; in *Acetosa*, known as *sorrel*, they are small, commonly hastate, and permeated by an acid juice. The root is astringent, and has tonic, alterative, and antiscorbutic properties. Besides *dock* and *sorrel*, see *canaigre*, *wild pie-plant* (under *pie-plant*), *bloodwort*, *butter-dock*, *greensauce*, *monk's-rhubarb*, *mountain-rhubarb*; also cuts under *atropal* and *obtuse*.

Female Flowering Plant of Field-sorrel (*Rumex Acetosella*). *a*, a male flower; *b*, a female flower.

rumfustian (rum-fus'tyan), *n.* A hot drink made of eggs, beer, gin, sherry, cinnamon, nutmeg, sugar, etc.

rumgumption (rum-gump'shon), *n.* [Also *rumblegumption*, *rummelgumption*, *rummilgumption*; perhaps ‹ *rum*[2], good, excellent, + *gumption*: see *gumption*.] Rough common sense; keenness of intellect; understanding. [Prov. Eng. and Scotch.]

They need not try thy jokes to fathom,
They want *rumgumption*.
Beattie, Address. (*Jamieson.*)

rumgumptious (rum-gump'shus), *a.* [‹ *rumgumpti(on)* + *-ous*.] Sturdy in opinion; rough and surly; bold; rash. [Prov. Eng. and Scotch.]

rum-hole (rum'hōl), *n.* A grog-shop; a gin-mill: so called in opprobrium. [Colloq., U. S.]

Rumiceæ (rö-mis'ē-ē), *n. pl.* [NL. (Carl Anton Meyer, 1840), ‹ *Rumex* (*Rumic-*) + *-eæ*.] A tribe of apetalous plants of the order *Polygonaceæ*. It is characterized by a six-parted or rarely four-parted perianth, six or nine stamens, short recurved styles dilated into broadly peltate or fringed stigmas, flowers in clusters at the nodes, attended by a sheathing or concave bract, and leaves alternate on the stem or radicle. It includes the 4 genera *Rheum*, *Oxyria*, *Rumex*, and *Emex*, plants mainly of the northern hemisphere, sometimes shrubby, and generally with conspicuous or very large radical leaves. See cuts under *Rumex* and *rhubarb*.

rumina, *n.* Plural of *rumen*.

ruminal (rö'mi-nal), *a.* [= F. *ruminal*, ‹ L. *ruminalis*, ruminating, ‹ *rumen* (*-in-*), the throat, gullet: see *ruminate*.] Same as *ruminant*. [Rare.] *Imp. Dict.*

ruminant (rö'mi-nant), *a.* and *n.* [= F. *ruminant* = Sp. *rumiante* = Pg. It. *ruminante*, ‹ L. *ruminan(t-)s*, ppr. of *ruminare*, chew the cud: see *ruminate*.] I. *a.* 1. Ruminating; chewing the cud; belonging to the *Ruminantia*, or having their characters.—2. Hence, thoughtful; meditative; quiet.

Marriage . . . had not even filled her leisure with the *ruminant* joy of unchecked tenderness.
George Eliot, Middlemarch, xxviii.

II. *n.* An animal that chews the cud; any member of the *Ruminantia*.

Ruminantes (rö-mi-nan'tēz), *n. pl.* [NL., pl. of L. *ruminan(t-)s*, chewing the cud: see *ruminant*.] The original form of *Ruminantia*. *Vicq-d'Azyr*, 1792.

Ruminantia (rö-mi-nan'shi-ạ̈), *n. pl.* [NL., neut. pl. of L. *ruminan(t-)s*, chewing the cud: see *ruminant*.] A series or section of artiodactyl ungulate mammals; the ruminants or ruminating animals, or hoofed quadrupeds that chew the cud. All are even-toed and cloven-footed, and have a complex stomach of several compartments, in the largest one of which food is received without being chewed, to be afterward regurgitated or thrown up into the mouth, there chewed at the animal's leisure, and then swallowed again. In nearly all living ruminants the stomach has four compartments, or is quadripartite: these are the *rumen*, *paunch*, or *plain tripe*; the *reticulum*, or *honeycomb tripe*; the *omasum*, *psalterium*, or *manyplies*; and the *abomasum* or *rennet-bag*, succeeding one another in the order here given. The two former belong to the cardiac division of the stomach, the two latter to the pyloric. The families of living ruminants whose stomachs are thus perfectly quadrilocular are—(1) the *Giraffidæ*, or camelopards; (2) the *Saigidæ* (if regarded as distinct from the *Bovidæ*); (3) the *Bovidæ*, or cattle, including also sheep and goats and all kinds of antelopes excepting (4) the *Antilocapridæ*; and (5) the *Cervidæ*, or deer family. In the *Camelidæ*, or camels and llamas, the stomach is imperfectly four-parted. In the *Tragulidæ* it is tripartite, no psalterium being developed. Several extinct families are believed on other grounds (their stomachs being unknown) to have belonged to the *Ruminantia*. The ruminants are collectively contrasted with those ungulates which, though artiodactyl, do not ruminate, and are known as *Omnivora*, as the swine and hippopotamus. The average size of ruminants among mammals is large, a sheep being one of the smaller species; they are perfectly herbivorous, and have in addition to the peculiarities of the digestive system certain characteristic dental and cranial features; thus, there are no upper incisors, except in the camel family, in any of the living ruminants, and the under incisors bite against a callous pad. At the present time these animals are found in nearly all parts of the world (not, however, in the Australian); they are comparatively poorly represented in America, and occur in the greatest numbers, both of individuals and of species, in Africa. Also called *Pecora*. See also cut under *Tragulus*.

Typical Ruminant Stomach (Sheep).
Ru, rumen or paunch; *Ret*, reticulum or honeycomb, showing alveoli; *Ps*, omasum, psalterium, or manyplies; *A*, abomasum or rennet-bag; *œ*, esophagus; *Du*, duodenum. (*Ru* unopened; other divisions in section.)

Typical Ruminant Dentition (Sheep).
mx, maxilla; *px*, toothless premaxilla; *i*[1], *i*[2], *i*[3], three incisors of left side; *c*, left lower canine, like an incisor and usually called one; *pm*, upper and lower premolars; *m*, *m*, upper and lower molars.

ruminantly (rö'mi-nant-li), *adv.* In the manner of a ruminant; by means of rumination.

ruminate (rö'mi-nāt), *v.*; pret. and pp. *ruminated*, ppr. *ruminating*. [‹ L. *ruminatus*, pp. of *ruminare* or *ruminari* (› It. *ruminare* = Sp. *rumiar* = Pg. *ruminar* = Pr. *romiar*, *rominar* = OF. F. *ruminer*, F. dial. *roumir*, *rouinger*, *runger*, *roincer*, *roinger*, *runger*), chew the cud, ruminate, ‹ *rumen* (*rumin-*), the throat, gullet.] I. *intrans.* 1. To chew the cud, as a ruminant; practise rumination.

Ruminating flocks enjoy the shade.
Cowper, Heroism, l. 32.

2. To muse; meditate; think again and again; ponder: as, to *ruminate* on misfortunes.

This is that I iudge of that text of the Psalmist, about the whiche (maye it please the King of Heauen) that euen as my penne hath written, my soule may alwayes *ruminate*. *Guevara*, Letters (tr. by Hellowes, 1577), p. 108.

He . . . *ruminates* like an hostess that hath no arithmetic but her brain to set down her reckoning.
Shak., T. and C., iii. 3. 252.

II. *trans.* 1. To chew again.—2. To turn over in the mind; muse on; meditate over and over.

Conduct me where, from company,
I may revolve and *ruminate* my grief.
Shak., 1 Hen. VI., v. 5. 101.

If in debt, let him *ruminate* how to pay his debts.
Burton, Anat. of Mel., p. 535.

ruminate (rö'mi-nāt), *a.* [‹ L. *ruminatus*, pp. of *ruminare* or *ruminari*: see *ruminate*, *v.*] In *bot.*, appearing as if chewed: noting a structure of the endosperm (albumen) of a seed which gives a mottled appearance to its section, and which results from the infolding of a dark inner layer of the seed-coat into the lighter-colored matter of the endosperm, as in the nutmeg. *Goebel.*

ruminated (rö'mi-nā-ted), *a.* [‹ *ruminate* + *-ed*[2].] Same as *ruminate*.

ruminatingly (rö'mi-nā-ting-li), *n.* In a ruminating manner; ruminantly.

rumination (rö-mi-nā'shon), *n.* [= F. *rumination* = Pg. *ruminação* = It. *ruminazione*, ‹ L. *ruminatio(n-)*, chewing the cud: see *ruminate*.] 1. The act or process of ruminating, or chewing the cud. The food of ruminants is entirely herbaceous, and consists chiefly of grass. This is rapidly cropped by grazing, and hastily swallowed, mixed with saliva. When its appetite is satisfied, the ruminant stands still, or oftener lies down, generally on its side. Then occurs a spasmodic action of the abdominal muscles and of the diaphragm, like a hiccup, which forces a bolus of grass, sodden in the fluids of the paunch, up the gullet and into the mouth, to be masticated or chewed at leisure. During this second chewing the cud is mixed with more saliva, thoroughly ground to pulp, and in this semi-fluid state it is finally swallowed. The cropped grass, when first swallowed, passes indifferently into either the rumen or the reticulum (which are in fact only two compartments of the cardiac division of the stomach, the gullet entering the stomach just at their junction), and in the ordinary peristaltic action of the stomach the fodder passes back and forth from one to the other. But there is an arrangement of muscular folds by means of which a canal may be formed that leads directly from the gullet past the rumen and reticulum into the psalterium, and by this channel the food, when returned after the rumination, may be conducted directly to the third stomach. Water drunk passes easily into any of the four stomachs according to circumstances. Neither the paunch nor the honeycomb is ever completely emptied of food; they have been found partly filled with sodden fodder in animals which have starved to death. It does not appear, as has been supposed, that the reticulum is specially concerned in modeling the boluses which are to be regurgitated. The regurgitation is effected by the reversed peristaltic action of the gullet. During the spasmodic action by which the sodden mass is driven against the opening of the gullet, and some of it forced into the gullet to be thrown up, it is prevented from passing into the psalterium partly by the narrowness of the opening between the reticulum and the psalterium, and partly by the resistance offered to the coarse mass by the close-pressed psalterial leaves or layers, which act like a fine grating. But when the mass is swallowed again in its now pulpified and semi-fluid state, and is directed to the psalterium by the conformation of the parts, it readily soaks in through the psalterial layers, and thus reaches the abomasum or fourth stomach, where it is finally chymified by the action of the gastric juice, to which it is not before subjected. Rumination in man, when it is pathological, is also called *merycism*.

2. The act of ruminating or meditating; a musing or continued thinking on a subject; meditation or reflection.

It is a melancholy of mine own, . . . extracted from many objects, and indeed the sundry contemplation of my travels, in which my often *rumination* wraps me in a most humorous sadness. *Shak.*, As you Like it, iv. 1. 19.

ruminative (rö'mi-nạ̄-tiv), *a.* [‹ *ruminate* + *-ive*.] 1. Ruminant; disposed to rumination;

especially, given to meditation or thought.— 2. Marked by rumination or careful reflection; well-considered.

Such a thing as philosophical analysis, of calm, *ruminative* deliberation upon the principles of government, . . . seems unknown to them. *The Atlantic*, LXIV. 810.

ruminator (rö'mi-nā-tor), *n.* [= Sp. *rumiador* = It. *ruminatore*, < LL. *ruminator*, < L. *ruminare* or *ruminari*, ruminate: see *ruminate*.] One who ruminates or muses on any subject; one who pauses to deliberate and consider.

rumine† (rö'min), *v. t.* [< OF. *ruminer*, < L. *ruminare*, ruminate: see *ruminate*.] To ruminate.

As studious scholar, he self-*rumineth*
His lessons giv'n.
Sylvester, tr. of Du Bartas's Weeks, i. 6.

rumkin[1]† (rum'kin), *n.* [Also *rumken*, *romkin*, *romekin*; perhaps for **rummerkin*, < *rummer* + *-kin*.] A kind of drinking-vessel; a rummer. *Gayton.*

Wine ever flowing in large Saxon *romekins*
About my board.
Sir W. Davenant, The Wits, iv. 2.

rumkin[2] (rum'kin), *n.* [Perhaps < *rump* + *-kin*.] A tailless fowl. *Halliwell.* [Prov. Eng.]

rumly (rum'li), *adv.* [< *rum*[2] + *-ly*[2].] In a rum manner; finely; well: often used ironically. See *rum*[2], *a.* [Slang.]

We straight betook ourselves to the Boozing ken; and, having bubb'd *rumly*, we concluded an everlasting friendship. *R. Head*, English Rogue (1665), quoted in Ribton-Turner's Vagrants and Vagrancy, p. 621.

rummage (rum'āj), *v.*; pret. and pp. *rummaged*, ppr. *rummaging*. [Early mod. E. *rummage*, **rommage*, *roummidge*, *romage*, *roomage*; < *roomage*, *n.*: see *roomage*.] I. *trans.* 1†. To adjust the roomage or capacity of (a ship) with reference to the cargo; arrange or stow the cargo of (a ship) in the hold; especially, to clear by the removal of goods: as, to *rummage* a ship.

Vse your indeuour and faithfull diligence in charging, discharging, lading againe, and *roomaging* of the same shippe. *Hakluyt's Voyages*, I. 234.

2. To move to and fro the contents of, as in a search; ransack; hunt through; explore: as, to *rummage* a trunk.

By this time the English knew the Logwood Trees as growing; and, understanding their value, began to *rummage* other Coasts of the Main in search of it.
Dampier, Voyages, II. ii. 47.

Upon this they fell again to *romage* the will.
Swift, Tale of a Tub, ii.

At low water I went on board; and though I thought I had *rummaged* the cabin so effectually as that nothing more could be found, yet I discovered a locker with drawers in it. *Defoe*, Robinson Crusoe, iv.

Hortense was *rummaging* her drawers up-stairs — an unaccountable occupation, in which she spent a large portion of each day, arranging, disarranging, re-arranging, and counter-arranging. *Charlotte Brontë*, Shirley, vi.

3. To set in motion; stir; hence, specifically, to mix by stirring or some other form of agitation: as, to *rummage* a liquid.

The Feuer . . . now posting, sometimes pawsing,
Euen as the matter, all these changes causing,
Is *rommidged* with motions slowe or quick
In feeble bodies of the Ague sick.
Sylvester, tr. of Du Bartas's Weeks, ii., The Furies.

When finings are put into casks of wine, and are stirred round and round with great velocity by a stick introduced at the shive-hole, that is called *rummaging* a cask; and if the cask is quite full to the bung a little will overflow in so doing. *C. A. Ward*, N. and Q., 6th ser., IX. 478.

If *rummaged* well together, the whole [mixture] should be clear and bright in one day's time.
Spons' Encyc. Manuf., I. 223.

4. To bring to light by searching.

We'll go in a body and *rummage* out the badger in Birkenwood-bank. *Scott*, Rob Roy, xii.

The two ladies *rummaged* up, out of the recesses of their memory, such horrid stories of robbery and murder that I quite quaked in my shoes. *Mrs. Gaskell*, Cranford, x.

II. *intrans.* 1†. To arrange or stow the cargo of a ship in the hold.

Giue the master or Boatswaine, or him that will take upon him to *romage*, a good reward for his labour to see the goods well romaged. *Hakluyt's Voyages*, I. 300.

2. To search narrowly, especially by moving about and looking among the things in the place searched; execute a search.

I'll merely relate what, in spite of the pains
I have taken to *rummage* among his remains,
No edition of Shakspeare I've met with contains.
Barham, Ingoldsby Legends, II. 58.

So they found at Babylon, . . .
In *rummaging* among the rarities,
A certain coffer. *Browning*, Sordello.

3†. To make a stir, bustle, or disturbance.

I speak this the rather to prevent . . . the imprudent *romaging* that is like to be in England, from Villages to Townes, from Townes to Cities, for Churches sake, to the undoing of Societies, Friendships, Kindreds, Families.
N. Ward, Simple Cobler, p. 45.

rummage (rum'āj), *n.* [< *rummage*, *v.*] 1. The act of rummaging, in any sense; the act of searching a place, especially by turning over the contents.— 2. A stirring or bustling about; a disturbance; an upheaval.

The source of this our watch, and the chief head
Of this post-haste and *romage* in the land.
Shak., Hamlet, i. 1. 107.

There is a new bill which, under the notion of preventing clandestine marriages, has made . . . a general *rummage* and reform in the office of matrimony.
Walpole, Letters, II. 334.

3. Lumber; rubbish. *Halliwell.* [Prov. Eng.] — **Rummage sale**, a clearing-out sale of unclaimed goods at docks, or of miscellaneous articles left in a warehouse.

rummager (rum'āj-ėr), *n.* [Early mod. E. *romager*, *roomager*; < *rummage*, *v.*, + *-er*[1].] 1†. One who arranges or stows the cargo on a ship.

The master must prouide a perfect mariner called a *Romager*, to raunge and bestow all marchandize in such place as is conuenient. *Hakluyt's Voyages*, III. 862.

2. One who searches.

The smuggler exercises great cunning, and does his utmost to outwit the customs *rummager*.
Sci. Amer., N. S., LIX. 372.

rummer (rum'ėr), *n.* [< D. *roemer*, formerly also *romer*, = G. *römer* = Sw. *remmare*, a drinking-glass; said to be orig. G. (used for Rhenish wine according to Phillips; cf. "Rhenish rummers" in the first quot.), and so called because used in the *Römer-saal* at Frankfort (Skeat), lit. 'hall of the Romans': *Römer*, < *Rom*, Rome; *saal*, hall (see *sale*[2]). Cf. *rumkin*[1].] A drinking-glass or -cup; also, a cupful of wine or other liquor. The name is especially given to the tall and showy glasses, nearly cylindrical in form and without stem, which are identified with German glassware of the seventeenth century.

Then Rhenish *rummers* walk the round,
In bumpers every king is crown'd.
Dryden, To Sir George Etherege, l. 45.

Ordered in a whole bottle of the best port the beggarly place could afford — tossed it off in an ecstacy of two *rummers*, and died on the spot of sheer joy.
Noctes Ambrosianæ, Sept., 1832.

rummilgumption (rum'il-gump'shon), *n.* Same as *rumblegumption*.

rummle (rum'l), *v.* A dialectal form of *rumble*.

rummy[1] (rum'i), *a.* [< *rum*[1] + *-y*[1].] Of or pertaining to rum: as, a *rummy* flavor.

rummy[2] (rum'i), *a.* [< *rum*[2] + *-y*[1].] Rum; queer. [Slang.]

Although a *rummy* codger,
Now list to what I say.
Old Song, in N. and Q., 7th ser., IX. 97.

rumney†, **romney**† (rum'ni), *n.* [< ME. *rumney*, *romney*, *romnay*, < OF. **romenie*, < It. *romania*, "a kind of excellent wine in Italy, like malmesie" (Florio), so called from Napoli di *Romania*, in the Morea, where it was orig. produced.] A kind of sweet wine.

Larkys in hot schow, ladys for to pyk,
Good drynk therto, lycyus and fyne,
Blwet of allmayne, *romnay* and wyin.
Rel. Antiq., ii. 30. (*Halliwell.*)

All black wines, over-hot, compound, strong, thick drinks, as muscadine, malmsie, allegant, *rumny*, brown bastard, metheglen, and the like, . . . are hurtful in this case. *Burton*, Anat. of Mel., p. 70.

Malmsey, *romney*, sack, and other sweet wines.
S. Dowell, Taxes in England, IV. 80.

rumor, rumour (rö'mor), *n.* [< ME. *rumour*, *romour*, *reumor*, < OF. *rumour*, *rumor*, *remour*, *rumeur*, F. *rumeur* = Pr. *rimor*, *rumor* = Sp. Pg. *rumor* = It. *rimore*, *romore*, noise, rumor, = D. *rumoer* = G. Dan. Sw. *rumor*, noise, uproar, < L. *rumor*, a noise, rumor, murmur; cf. L. *rumificare*, proclaim, LL. *rumitare*, spread reports; Skt. √ *ru*, hum, bray. Cf. *rumble*.] 1. A confused and indistinct noise; a vague sound; a murmur.

And whan these com on ther was so grete toile and *romour* of noyse that wonder it was to heere, and therwith a-roos so grete a duste that the cleir sky wax all derk. *Merlin* (E. E. T. S.), iii. 393.

I pray you, hear me hence
From forth the noise and *rumour* of the field.
Shak., K. John, v. 4. 45.

For many a week
Hid from the wide world's *rumour* by the grove
Of poplars with their noise of falling showers,
And ever-tremulous aspen-trees, he lay.
Tennyson, Lancelot and Elaine.

2. Flying or popular report; the common voice.

Rumour doth double, like the voice and echo,
The numbers of the fear'd.
Shak., 2 Hen. IV., iii. 1. 97.

Fame is no plant that grows on mortal soil,
Nor in the glistering foil
Set off to the world, nor in broad *rumour* lies.
Milton, Lycidas, l. 80.

That talkative maiden, *Rumor*, though . . . figured as a youthful winged beauty, . . . is in fact a very old maid, who puckers her silly face by the fireside, and really does no more than chirp a wrong guess or a lame story into the ear of a fellow-gossip. *George Eliot*, Felix Holt, viii.

3. A current report, with or without foundation; commonly, a story or statement passing from one person to another without any known authority for its truth; a mere report; a piece of idle gossip.

When ye shall hear of wars and *rumours* of wars, be ye not troubled. Mark xiii. 7.

I find the people strangely fantasied;
Possess'd with *rumours*, full of idle dreams.
Shak., K. John, iv. 2. 145.

What record, or what relic of my lord
Should be to aftertime, but empty breath
And *rumours* of a doubt?
Tennyson, Morte d'Arthur.

4. Fame; reported celebrity; reputation.

Great is the *rumour* of this dreadful knight.
Shak., 1 Hen. VI., ii. 3. 7.

Go forth, and let the *rumor* of thee run
Through every land that is beneath the sun.
William Morris, Earthly Paradise, II. 277.

5†. A voice; a message.

I have heard a *rumour* from the Lord, and an ambassador is sent unto the heathen, saying, Gather ye together.
Jer. xlix. 14.

=**Syn.** 2 and 3. Talk, gossip, hearsay.

rumor, rumour (rö'mor), *v. t.* [< *rumor*, *n.*] To report; tell or circulate by report; spread abroad.

Rumour it abroad
That Anne, my wife, is sick and like to die.
Shak., Rich. III., iv. 2. 51.

Where nothing is examined, weighed,
But as 'tis *rumoured*, so believed.
B. Jonson, The Forest, iv., To the World.

rumorer, rumourer (rö'mor-ėr), *n.* [< *rumor* + *-er*[1].] One who rumors; a spreader of reports; a teller of news. [Rare.]

Go see this *rumourer* whipp'd. *Shak.*, Cor., iv. 6. 47.

rumorous (rö'mor-us), *a.* [Formerly also *rumourous*; < OF. *rumoreux* = Sp. It. *rumoroso*, noisy, < ML. *rumorosus*, < L. *rumor*, noise, rumor: see *rumor*.] 1. Of the nature of rumor; circulated by popular report. [Rare.]

This bearer will tell you what we hear of certain *rumorous* surmises at N. and the neighbouring towns.
Sir H. Wotton, Reliquiæ, p. 377.

2. Confused or indistinct in sound; vaguely heard; murmuring. [Rare.]

Clashing of armours, and the *rumorous* sound
Of the stern billows, in contention stood.
Drayton, Moses, iii.

rump (rump), *n.* [< ME. *rumpe*, appar. < Icel. *rumpr* = Sw. *rumpa* = Dan. *rumpe*, rump (the Scand. forms appar. from the D. or LG.), = MD. *rompe*, D. *romp*, a body or trunk, = MLG. LG. *rump* = MHG. G. *rumpf*, the bulk or trunk of a body, a trunk, carcass, hull.] 1. The tail-end of an animal; the hinder parts; the backside or buttocks; technically, the gluteal or uropygial region; the uropygium. See *sacrum* and *uropygium*.— 2. Figuratively, the fag-end of a thing. Specifically [*cap.*], in *Eng. hist.*, the fag-end of the Long Parliament, after the expulsion of the majority of its members, or Pride's Purge, by Cromwell in 1648. The Rump was forcibly dissolved by Cromwell in 1653, but was afterward reinstated on two different occasions for brief periods. Also called *Rump Parliament*.

rump (rump), *v. t.* [< *rump*, *n.*] To turn one's back upon. [Rare.]

This mythologick Deity was Plutus,
The grand Divinity of Cash,
Who, when he *rumps* us quite, and won't salute us,
If we are men of Commerce, then we smash.
Colman, Poetical Vagaries, p. 129. (*Davies.*)

rump-bone (rump'bōn), *n.* Same as *sacrum*.

rumper† (rum'pėr), *n.* [< *rump* + *-er*[1].] One who was favorable to, or was a member of, the Rump Parliament. See *rump*, 2.

This day, according to order, Sir Arthur appeared at the House; what was done I know not, but there was all the *rumpers* almost come to the House today.
Pepys, Diary, March 7, 1660.

Neither was the art of blasphemy or free-thinking invented by the court, . . . but first brought in by the fanatick faction, towards the end of their power, and, after the restoration, carried to Whitehall by the converted *rumpers*, with very good reason. *Swift*, Polite Conversation, Int.

rump-fed† (rump'fed), *a.* [< *rump* + *fed*, pp. of *feed*.] Fed on offal or scraps from the kitchen (according to Nares, fed, or fattened, in the rump; fat-bottomed). [Rare.]

Aroint thee, witch! the *rump-fed* ronyon cries.
Shak., Macbeth, i. 3. 6.

rumple (rum'pl), *v. t.*; pret. and pp. *rumpled*, ppr. *rumpling*. [A var. of *rimple*, q. v.] To wrinkle; make uneven; form into irregular inequalities.

The peremptory Analysis, that you will call it, I beleeve will be so hardy as once more to unpinne your spruce fas-

tidious oratory, to *rumple* her laces, her frizzles, and her bobins, though she wince and fling never so Peevishly.
Milton, On Def. of Humb. Remonst.

We all know the story of the princess and her *rumpled* rose-leaf felt through half-a-score of blankets.
Whyte Melville, White Rose, II. xi.

rumple (rum'pl), *n.* [A var. of *rimple*, q. v. Cf. *rumple*, *v.*] A wrinkle; a fold; a ridge.

And yet Lucretia's fate would bar that vow;
And fair Virginia would her fate bestow
On Rutila, and change her faultless make,
For the foul *rumple* of her camel-back.
Dryden, tr. of Juvenal's Satires, x.

rumpless (rump'les), *a.* [< *rump* + *-less*.] Having no tail: specifically noting male or female specimens of the common hen so characterized. The lack is not only of the tail-feathers, but of muscular and bony parts of the rump.

Rumpless fowls are those in which the coccygeal vertebræ are absent; there is consequently no tail. By crossing, *rumpless* breeds of any variety can be produced.
Encyc. Brit., XIX. 646.

rumply (rump'li), *a.* [< *rumple* + *-y*[1].] Rumpled. [Colloq.]

rump-post (rump'pōst), *n.* The share-bone or pygostyle of a bird. *Coues.* See cut under *pygostyle*.

rump-steak (rump'stāk), *n.* A beefsteak cut from the thigh near the rump.

After dinner was over he observed that the steak was tough; "and yet, sir," returns he, "bad as it was, it seemed a *rump-steak* to me." *Goldsmith*, Essays, xiii.

rumpus (rum'pus), *n.* [Perhaps imitative, based on *rumble*, *rumbustical*, *rumbustious*, etc.] An uproar; a disturbance; a riot; a noisy or disorderly outbreak. [Colloq.]

My dear Lady Bab, you'll be shock'd, I'm afraid,
When you hear the sad *rumpus* your Ponies have made.
Moore, Twopenny Post-Bag, letter i.

She is a young lady with a will of her own, I fancy. Extremely well-fitted to make a *rumpus*.
George Eliot, Daniel Deronda, xii.

rumseller (rum'sel'ėr), *n.* One who sells rum; hence, one who sells intoxicating liquors of any kind; specifically, the keeper of a rumshop. [U. S.]

rumshop (rum'shop), *n.* A shop where intoxicating liquors are sold. [U. S.]

rum-shrub (rum'shrub), *n.* A liquor of which rum is a principal ingredient. (*a*) Rum flavored with orange-juice and sweetened and allowed to stand for a long time before use: a kind of home-made cordial. (*b*) A drink made by mixing rum with orange-, lemon-, or lime-juice, the peel of the same fruit, milk, and sometimes other ingredients: this is strained and usually bottled for keeping.

rumswizzle (rum'swiz'l), *n.* [Perhaps < *rum*[2], good, excellent, + *swizzle*, a drink made of ale and beer mixed (fancifully applied to cloth that possesses the quality of resisting wet).] A cloth made in Ireland from pure wool undyed, and valuable because of its power of repelling moisture.

run[1] (run), *v.*; pret. *ran* (sometimes *run*), pp. *run*, ppr. *running*. [E. dial. or Sc. also *rin*, *ren*; < ME. *rinnen*, *rynnen*, *rennen* (pret. *ran*, *ron*, pl. and pp. *runnen*, *ronnen*, *runne*, *ronne*; the mod. E. having taken the vowel of the pp. also in the inf.), < AS. *rinnan* (pret. *ran*, pl. *runnon*, pp. *gerunnen*), usually transposed *eornan*, *irnan*, *iernan*, *yrnan* (pret. *arn*, *orn*, pl. *urnon*, pp. *urnen*) (> ME. *ernen*, etc.: see *earn*[3]), run, flow, = OS. *rinnan* = OFries. *rinna*, *ronna* = MD. *rinnen*, *rennen*, *runnen* = MLG. *rinnen*, flow, *rennen*, run, = OHG. *rinnan*, flow, swim, run, MHG. *rinnen*, G. *rinnen*, run, flow (pret. *rann*, pp. *geronnen*), = Icel. *rinna*, later *renna* = Sw. *rinna* = Dan. *rinde*, flow, *rende*, run, = Goth. *rinnan*, run; also causative, OS. *rennian* = OHG. *rennan*, MHG. G. *rennen* = Goth. *rannjan*, cause to run; prob., with present formative *-n*, < √ *ren*, run (cf. *rine*[1]), perhaps akin to Skt. √ *ar* or *ri*, go. Hence ult. *run*, *n.*, *runaway*, *runnel*, *rennet*[1], *rine*[1].] **I.** *intrans.* **1.** To move swiftly by using the legs; go on the legs more rapidly than in walking; hence, of animals without legs, to move swiftly by an energetic use of the machinery of locomotion: as, a *running* whale. In bipedal locomotion the usual distinction between *running* and *walking* is, that in running each foot in turn leaves the ground before the other reaches it. In zoölogy, usually, to *run* means to move the legs of each side alternately, whether fast or slow—being thus distinguished, not from *walk*, but from any locomotion in which the opposite legs move together, as in jumping, leaping, or hopping.

Freres and faitours that on here fete *rennen*.
Piers Plowman (B), ii. 182.

And as she *runs*, the bushes in the way,
Some catch her by the neck, some kiss her face.
Shak., Venus and Adonis, l. 871.

Thou dost float and *run*,
Like an unbodied joy whose race is just begun.
Shelley, To a Skylark.

Specifically—(*a*) Of the horse, to move with the gait distinctively called a *run*. See *run*[1], *n.*, 1 (*a*). (*b*) To take part in a race: as, to *run* for the stakes, or for a place: said of horses or athletes.

Know ye not that they which *run* in a race *run* all, but one receiveth the prize? So *run* that ye may obtain.
1 Cor. ix. 24.

(*c*) To take part in a hunt or chase: as, to *run* with the hounds.

2. To make haste; hasten; hurry, often with suddenness or violence; rush.

Thanne thei lete blowe an horn in the maister toure, and than *ronne* to armes thourgh the town.
Merlin (E. E. T. S.), ii. 197.

A kind heart he hath; a woman would *run* through fire and water for such a kind heart.
Shak., M. W. of W., iii. 4. 107.

What need a man forestall his date of grief,
And *run* to meet what he would most avoid?
Milton, Comus, l. 363.

'Tis habitual to them to *run* to the Succour of those they see in Danger. *Steele*, Grief A-la-Mode, Pref.

3. To flee; retreat hurriedly or secretly; steal away; abscond; desert: often followed by *away* or *off*.

The paens that er were so sturne,
Hi gunne *awei urne*.
King Horn (E. E. T. S.), p. 25.

That same man that *renneth awaie*
Male again fight, an other daie.
Udall, tr. of Erasmus's Apophthegms, p. 372.

My conscience will serve me to *run* from this Jew, my master. *Shak.*, M. of V., ii. 2. 2.

I forgot to say Carrat *run off* a month ago. . . . Mr. Grierson has expell him for *running away*.
Hood, School for Adults.

4. To move, especially over a definite course: said of inanimate things, and with the most varied applications; be propelled or borne along; travel; pursue a course; specifically, of a ship, to sail before the wind.

And *running* under a certain island which is called Clauda, we had much work to come by the boat.
Acts xxvii. 16.

Thou . . . think'st it much to tread the ooze
Of the salt deep,
To *run* upon the sharp wind of the north.
Shak., Tempest, i. 2. 254.

Far *ran* the naked moon across
The houseless ocean's heaving field.
Tennyson, The Voyage.

Squalls
Ran black o'er the sea's face.
M. Arnold, Balder Dead.

5. To perform a regular passage from place to place; ply: as, the boats *run* daily; a train *runs* every hour.—**6.** To flow. (*a*) To flow in any manner, slowly or rapidly; move, as a stream, the sand in an hour-glass, or the like.

In the tur ther is a welle
Suthe cler hit is with alle,
He *urneth* in o pipe of bras
Whider so hit ned was.
King Horn (E. E. T. S.), p. 57.

In the dede See *rennethe* the Flom Jordan, and there it dyethe; for it *rennethe* no furthermore.
Mandeville, Travels, p. 102.

The fourth [current of lava], at la Torre, is that which *run* at the great eruption on the fifth of May.
Pococke, Description of the East, II. ii.

(*b*) To spread on a surface; spread and blend together: as, colors *run* in washing.

An Arcadian hat of green sarcenet, . . . not so very much stained, except where the occasional storms of rain, incidental to a military life, had caused the green to *run*.
T. *Hardy*, The Trumpet-Major, ii.

7. To give passage to or discharge a fluid or a flowing substance, as tears, pus, the sand of an hour-glass, etc.

Mine eyes shall weep sore, and *run* down with tears, because the Lord's dock is carried away captive.
Jer. xiii. 17.

I should not see the sandy hour-glass *run*
But I should think of shallows and of flats.
Shak., M. of V., i. 1. 25.

The jest will make his eyes *run*, i' faith.
B. Jonson, Poetaster, iii. 1.

Reekin' red *ran* mony a sheugh.
Burns, Battle of Sheriff-Muir.

Specifically—(*a*) In *founding*, said of a mold when the molten metal works out through the parting or through some interstice, crevice, or break: as, the mold *runs*. (*b*) In *organ-building*, said of the air in a wind-chest when it leaks into a channel.

8. To become fluid; fuse; melt.

As wax dissolves, as ice begins to *run*,
And trickle into drops before the sun,
So melts the youth.
Addison, tr. of Ovid's Metamorph., iii.

If the arches are fired too hot, they will *run* or stick together. *C. T. Davis*, Bricks and Tiles, p. 147.

9. To extend from point to point; spread by growth, or expansion, or development of any kind: as, the flames *run* through the grass.

The fire *ran* along upon the ground. Ex. ix. 23.

10. To creep or trail; spread by runners; overrun; twine or climb in any manner: said of plants: as, the vine *ran* up the porch.

Beneath my feet
The ground-pine curled its pretty wreath,
Running over the club-moss burrs.
Emerson, Each and All.

11. To go through normal or allotted movements; be in action, motion, or operation; operate; work: as, the machines *run* night and day; the hotel is *running* again.

Rudelez [curtains] *rennande* on ropez.
Sir Gawayne and the Green Knight (E. E. T. S.), l. 857.

Wert thou not brother to great Edward's son,
This tongue that *runs* so roundly in thy head
Should run thy head from thy unreverent shoulders.
Shak., Rich. II., ii. 1. 122.

You've been *running* too fast, and under too high pressure. You must take these weights off the safety valve. . . . Bank your fires and *run* on half steam.
Bret Harte, Gabriel Conroy, xxvi.

A storage, or secondary, battery makes it possible to have a reservoir of electricity, from which a supply can be obtained when the dynamos are not *running*.
Sci. Amer., N. S., LIV. 308.

12. To strive for any end; especially, to enter a contest for office or honors; specifically, to stand as a candidate for election: as, three candidates are *running* for the presidency.

He has never failed in getting such offices as he wanted, the record of his *running* being about as good as that of any man in the country. *The Nation*, XI. 1.

Z., who has written a few witty pieces, and who, being rich and an epicure, is *running* for the Academy on the strength of his good dinners.
Harper's Mag., LXXVIII. 518.

13. To go on; go by; pass or glide by; elapse.

Since she is living, let the time *run* on
To good or bad. *Shak.*, Cymbeline, v. 5. 128.

She does well and wisely
To ask the counsel of the ancient'st, madam;
Our years have *run* through many things she knows not.
Fletcher, Rule a Wife, i. 4.

How *runs* the time of day?
Ford, Perkin Warbeck, iii. 1.

Merrily *ran* the years, seven happy years.
Tennyson, Enoch Arden.

14. To pass; proceed; advance; take a certain course or direction. Specifically—(*a*) To advance in a given line of change, development, growth, conduct, experience, etc.; especially, to proceed from one state to another: as, to *run* to seed; to *run* to waste; to *run* to weeds (said of land); to *run* into danger; hence, to become: as, to *run* mad: often followed by a predicate adjective, or by *in*, *into*, or *to*.

They think it strange that ye *run* not with them *to* the same excess of riot. 1 Pet. iv. 4.

At his own shadow let the thief *run* mad,
Himself himself seek every hour to kill!
Shak., Lucrece, l. 997.

We have *run*
Through ev'ry change that Fancy, at the loom
Exhausted, has had genius to supply.
Cowper, Task, ii. 607.

He *ran* headlong *into* the boisterous vices which prove fatal to so many of the ignorant and the brutal.
Southey, Bunyan, p. 13.

It is not only possible but quite probable that these last two [cows] were more influenced by the individual tendency to "*run* dry" than by the extra grain feed in the ration. *Science*, XV. 24.

Hence—(*b*) To tend or incline; have a proclivity or general tendency; be favorable: as, his inclinations *run* to public life: followed by *in*, *into*, *to*, or *toward*.

That spot of spysez mygt nedez sprede,
Ther such rychez *to* rot [root] is *runnen*.
Alliterative Poems (ed. Morris), i. 26.

Revenge is a kind of wild justice which the more Man's nature *runs to*, the more ought law to weed it out.
Bacon, Revenge (ed. 1887).

A man's nature *runs* either *to* herbs or weeds; therefore let him seasonably water the one, and destroy the other.
Bacon, Nature in Men (ed. 1887).

The temperate climates usually *run into* moderate governments, and the extremes *into* despotic power.
Swift, Sentiments of Ch. of Eng. Man, ii.

A birthplace
Where the richness *ran to* flowers.
Browning, Paracelsus.

(*c*) To pass in thought or notice; go cursorily, as in a hasty inspection, review, or summary: as, to *run* from one topic to another; to *run* through a list or a bill: generally followed by *through* or *over*.

The eyes of the Lord *run* to and fro throughout the whole earth. 2 Chron. xvi. 9.

So of the rest, till we have quite *run through*,
And wearied all the fables of the gods.
B. Jonson, Volpone, iii. 6.

If I write anything on a black Man, I *run over* in my Mind all the eminent Persons in the Nation who are of that Complection. *Addison*, Spectator, No. 262.

(*d*) To continue to think or speak of something; dwell in thought or words; harp: as, his mind or his talk *runs* continually on his troubles: followed by *on* or *upon*.

If they see a stage-play, they *run upon* that a week after. *Burton*, Anat. of Mel., p. 238.

When we desire anything, our minds *run* wholly *on* the good circumstances of it; when it is obtained, our minds *run* wholly on the bad ones. *Swift.*

(*e*) To pass by slight gradations or changes; blend or merge gradually: with *into*: as, colors that *run into* one another.

Observe how system *into* system *runs.*
Pope, Essay on Man, i. 25.

(*f*) To migrate, as fish; go in a school.

Salmon *run* early in the year.
Fortnightly Rev., N. S., XLI. 406.

15. To have a certain direction, course, or track; extend; stretch: as, the street *runs* east and west.

The ground cloath of siluer, richly embroidered with golden Sunns, and about euery Sunne *ran* a traile of gold, imitating Indian worke.
Chapman, Masque of Middle Temple and Lincoln's Inn.

Searching the ulcer with my probe, the sinus *run* up above the orifice. *Wiseman*, Surgery.

And thro' the field the road *runs* by
To many-tower'd Camelot.
Tennyson, Lady of Shalott, i.

16. To have a certain form, tenor, or purport; be written or expressed: as, the argument *runs* as follows.

They must— . . .
For so *run* the conditions—leave those remnants
Of fool and feather that they got in France.
Shak., Hen. VIII., i. 3. 24.

Once on a time (so *runs* the fable)
A country mouse, right hospitable,
Received a town mouse at his board.
Pope, Imit. of Horace, II. vi. 157.

That Matthew's numbers *run* with ease
Each man of common sense agrees!
Cowper, Epistle to Robert Lloyd.

17. In *law*: (*a*) To have legal authority or effect; be in force.

It cannot be said that the Emperor's writs *run* in it except in some few settled districts.
Athenæum, No. 3068, p. 202.

The Queen's writ, it has been remarked, cannot be said to *run* in large parts of Ireland, while in every part of the United States the Federal writ is implicitly obeyed.
Nineteenth Century, XIX. 793.

(*b*) To pass in connection with or as an incident to. Thus, a covenant restricting the use or enjoyment of land is said to *run* with the land, alike if the burden it imposes is to continue on the land burdened, into whatsoever hands that land passes, or if the right to claim its enforcement is to pass with the land intended to be benefited, into whosesoever hands the latter land may pass. If the covenant does not run with the land, it is merely personal, binding and benefiting only the parties to it and their personal representatives.

Covenants are said to "*run* with the land" when the liabilities and rights created by them pass to the assignees of the original parties. *Encyc. Brit.*, XIV. 275.

18. To be current; circulate publicly. (*a*) To be in current use or circulation.

And whan that Money hathe *ronne* so longe that it begynnethe to waste, than men beren it to the Emperoures Tresorye. *Mandeville*, Travels, p. 239.

Are not these the Spanish "pillar dollars"; and did they not *run* current in England as crown pieces?
N. and Q., 7th ser., VI. 338.

(*b*) To be publicly heard or known; be spread abroad; pass from one to another.

"What, is this Arthures hous," quoth the hathel thenne,
"That all the rous [fame] *rennes* of, thurg ryalmes so mony?"
Sir Gawayne and the Green Knight (E. E. T. S.), l. 310.

There *ran* a rumor
Of many worthy fellows that were out.
Shak., Macbeth, iv. 3. 182.

One day the story *ran* that Hamilton had given way, and that the government would carry every point.
Macaulay, Hist. Eng., vi.

A murmuring whisper thro' the nunnery *ran.*
Tennyson, Guinevere.

19. To keep going; be kept up; extend through a period of time; continue (used specifically of a play or other theatrical exhibition); hence, specifically, to continue so long before expiring or being paid or becoming payable: as, a subscription that has three months to *run;* the account *ran* on for a year.

She saw, with joy, the line immortal *run*,
Each sire impress'd and glaring in his son.
Pope, Dunciad, i. 99.

Learning that had *run* in the family like an heirloom!
Sheridan, School for Scandal, iii. 3.

No question had ever been raised as to Mr. Nolan's extraction on the strength of his hooked nose, or of his name being Baruch. Hebrew names *ran* in the best Saxon families; the Bible accounted for them.
George Eliot, Felix Holt, xx.

Yet I doubt not thro' the ages one increasing purpose *runs.* *Tennyson*, Locksley Hall.

The play on this occasion . . . only *ran* three days, and then Sir John Vanbrugh produced his comedy called "The Confederacy."
J. Ashton, Social Life in Reign of Queen Anne, II. 8.

20. To reach a certain pitch, extent, importance, quality, or value; hence, to average; rule.

"Bad this year, better the next."—We must take things rough and smooth as they *run.*
Foote, Mayor of Garratt, i. 1.

The disputes between the King and the Parliament *run* very high. *Walpole*, Letters, II. 511.

An age when Saurians *run* ridiculously small.
George Eliot, Theophrastus Such, iii.

In 1795 and 1796 . . . the price of wheat *ran* far beyond the statutory 54*s.*, viz., to 75*s.* the quarter.
S. Dowell, Taxes in England, IV. 11.

When Barrels are sold as they *run*, the term "as they *run*" shall be understood to refer to the condition as to cooperage only.
New York Produce Exchange Report (1888–9), p. 279.

21. To rest, as on a foundation or basis; turn; hinge.

Much upon this riddle *runs* the wisdom of the world.
Shak., M. for M., iii. 2. 242.

It is a confederating with him to whom the sacrifice is offered; for upon that the apostle's argument *runs.*
Bp. Atterbury.

22. In *music*, to perform a run or similar figure.

As when a maide, taught from her mother's wing
To tune her voyce unto a silver string,
When she should *run*, she rests; rests, when should *run.*
W. Browne, Britannia's Pastorals, i. 5.

23. In a variety of technical uses, to go awry; make a fault; slip: as, a thread *runs* in knitting when a stitch is dropped.

A common drill may *run*, as it is usually termed, and produce a hole which is anything but straight.
Farrow, Mil. Encyc., III. 524.

Lace made without this traversing motion would, in case a thread was broken, *run* or become undone.
A. Barlow, Weaving, p. 360.

24. To press with numerous and urgent demands: as, to *run* upon a bank.—**25.** To keep on the move; go about continually or uneasily; be restless, as a rutting animal; be in rut.—**To cut and run.** See *cut.*—**To let run**, to allow to pass freely or easily; slacken, as a rope, cable, or the like.—**To run across**, to come across; meet by chance; fall in with: as, to *run across* a friend in London.—**To run after**, to seek after; of persons, to pursue, especially for social purposes; hence, to court the society of.

The mind, upon the suggestion of any new notion, *runs after* similes, to make it the clearer to itself. *Locke.*

If he wants our society, let him seek it. . . . I will not spend my hours in *running after* my neighbours.
Jane Austen, Pride and Prejudice, liii.

To run against. (*a*) To come into collision with.

This man of God had his share of suffering from some that were convinced by him, who, through prejudice or mistake, *ran against* him.
Penn, Rise and Progress of Quakers, v.

(*b*) Same as *to run across.* (*c*) To result unfavorably or adversely to.

The owner hath incurred the forfeiture of eight years' profits of his lands before he cometh to the knowledge of the process that *runneth against* him. *Bacon.*

Had the present war indeed *run against* us, and all our attacks upon the enemy been vain, it might look like a degree of frenzy . . . to be determined on so impracticable an undertaking. *Addison*, Present State of the War.

To run ahead of one's reckoning. See *reckoning.*—**To run amuck.** See *amuck.*—**To run at**, to assail suddenly; rush upon.

Jack Stamford would have *run at* him [Felton], but he was kept off by Mr. Nicholas. *Howell*, Letters, I. v. 7.

To run at the ring. See *ring*[1].—**To run away or off with.** (*a*) To carry off in sudden or hurried flight: as, a horse *runs away with* a carriage; the mutineers *ran away with* the ship.

Now in Iames Towne they were all in combustion, the strongest preparing once more to *run away with* the Pinnace. Quoted in Capt. *John Smith's* Works, I. 163.

(*b*) To abscond or elope with.

Now, my dear sir, between you and I, we know very well, my dear sir, that you have *run off with* this lady for the sake of her money. *Dickens*, Pickwick, x.

(*c*) To carry too far; lead beyond bounds; transport.

His desires *run away with* him through the strength and force of a lively imagination. *Steele*, Tatler, No. 27.

To run awry. See *awry.*—**To run before.** (*a*) To run from in flight; flee before: as, the troops *ran before* the enemy. (*b*) To outstrip; surpass; excel.

But the scholar *ran*
Before the master, and so far, that Bleys
Laid magic by. *Tennyson*, Coming of Arthur.

To run counter. See *counter*[3], *adv.*, 1.—**To run deep**, to swim far under water, as fish or a whale.—**To run down.** (*a*) To have its motive power exhausted; stop working: as, the clock or the musical box *ran down.* (*b*) To become weakened or exhausted; deteriorate; fall off: as, his health has *run down.*

Here was, evidently, another case of an academy having *run down*, and its operations discontinued.
Supreme Court Reporter, X. 809.

To run down a coast, to sail along it.—**To run foul of.** Same as *to fall foul of* (which see, under *foul*[1]).—**To run idle.** See *idle.*—**To run in.** (*a*) In *printing*: (1) Same as *to run on.* (2) To occupy a smaller space in type than was expected: said of copy. (*b*) In the refining of iron as followed in Yorkshire, England, to run the molten pig directly from the furnace into the refinery: distinguished from *melting down*, when the refinery is charged with unmelted pig, scrap, etc.—**To run in debt**, to incur pecuniary obligations; make a debt.

Our long stay here hath occasioned the expense of much more money than I expected, so as I am *run* much *in* Mr. Goffe's debt. *Winthrop*, Hist. New England, I. 446.

To run in one's head or mind, to linger in one's memory; haunt one's mind.

These courtiers *run in my mind* still.
B. *Jonson*, Poetaster, ii. 1.

Heigh ho!—Though he has used me so, this fellow *runs* strangely *in my head.* I believe one lecture from my grave cousin will make me recall him.
Sheridan, The Rivals, v. 1.

To run in the blood. See *blood.*—**To run into**, to run against; collide with.—**To run in trust.** See *trust.*—**To run in with.** (*a*) To agree, comply, or close with. (*b*) *Naut.*, to sail close to: as, to *run in with* the land.—**To run mad.** See *mad*[1].—**To run of (or on) a gargett.** See *garget.*—**To run off with.** See *to run away with.*—**To run on.** (*a*) To keep on; continue without pause or change; especially, to keep on talking; keep up a running stream of conversation; ramble on in talking.

Even so must I *run on*, and even so stop.
What surety of the world, what hope, what stay,
When this was now a king, and now is clay?
Shak., K. John, v. 7. 67.

Even Boswell could say, with contemptuous compassion, that he liked very well to hear honest Goldsmith *run on.* "Yes, sir," said Johnson, "but he should not like to hear himself." *Macaulay*, Oliver Goldsmith.

(*b*) Specifically, in *printing*, to continue in the same line without making a break or beginning a new paragraph. (*c*) To carry on; behave in a lively, frolicsome manner; laugh and jest, as from high spirits. [Colloq.]—**To run on all fours.** See *four, n.*—**To run on pattens**†. See *patten*[2].—**To run on sorts**, in *printing*, to require an unusual or disproportionate quantity of one or more characters or types: said of copy.—**To run out.** (*a*) To stop after running to the end of its time, as a watch or a sand-glass.

Every Tuesday I make account that I turn a great hourglass, and consider that a week's life is *run out* since I writ. *Donne*, Letters, xx.

(*b*) To come to an end; expire: as, a lease *runs out* at Michaelmas. (*c*) To be wasted or exhausted: as, his money will soon *run out.*

Th' estate *runs out*, and mortgages are made,
Their fortune ruin'd, and their fame betray'd.
Dryden.

(*d*) To become poor by extravagance.

Had her stock been less, no doubt
She must have long ago *run out.* *Dryden.*

(*e*) To grow or sprout; spread exuberantly. [Prov. Eng.] (*f*†) To expatiate; run on.

She *ran out* extravagantly in praise of Hocus.
Arbuthnot.

(*g*) In *printing*, to occupy a larger space in type than was expected: said of copy.—**To run out of**, to come to the end of; run short of; exhaust.

When we had *run out of* our money, we had no living soul to befriend us. *Steele*, Guardian, No. 141.

To run over. (*a*) [*Over*, adv.] To overflow.

Good measure, pressed down, and shaken together, and *running over*, shall men give into your bosom.
Luke vi. 38.

Excessive Joys so swell'd her Soul, that she
Runs over with delicious tears.
J. Beaumont, Psyche, iii. 204.

(*b*) [*Over*, prep.] (1) To go over, examine, recapitulate, or recount cursorily.

I *ran over* their cabinet of medals [at Zurich], but do not remember to have met with any in it that are extraordinary rare.
Addison, Remarks on Italy (Works, ed. Bohn, I. 522).

(2) To ride or drive over: as, to *run over* a child.—**To run riot.** See *riot.*—**To run rusty.** See *rusty*[3].—**To run through**, to spend quickly; dissipate: as, he soon *ran through* his fortune.

For a man who had long ago *run through* his own money, servitude in a great family was the best kind of retirement after that of a pensioner. *George Eliot*, Felix Holt, xxv.

To run together. (*a*) To mingle or blend, as metals fused in the same vessel. (*b*) In *mining*, to fall in, as the walls of a lode, so as to render the shafts and levels impassable. *Ansted.* (*c*) To keep in a pod or school, as whales when one of their number has been struck.—**To run to seed.** (*a*) To shoot or spindle up, become stringy, and yield flowers, and ultimately seed, instead of developing the leaves, head, root, etc., for which they are valued: said of herbaceous plants. Such plants, if not required for seed, are pulled up and rejected as refuse.

Better to me the meanest weed
That blows upon its mountain,
The vilest herb that *runs to seed*
Beside its native fountain.
Tennyson, Amphion.

Hence—(*b*) To become impoverished, exhausted, or worn out; go to waste.—**To run under**, to swim under water near the surface after being struck, as a whale.—**To run up.** (*a*) [*Up*, adv.] (1) To rise; grow; increase: as, accounts *run up* very fast. (2) To draw up; shrink, as cloth when wet.

In working woollen cloths, they are, as is well known, liable to *run up* or contract in certain dimensions, becoming thicker at the same time.
W. Crookes, Dyeing and Calico-printing, p. 83.

(*b*) [*Up*, prep.] To count rapidly from bottom to top of in calculating, as a column of figures.—**To run upon**, to quiz; make a butt of. [U. S.]

He is a quiet, good-natured, inoffensive sort of chap, and will stand *running upon* as long as most men, but who is a perfect tiger when his passions are roused.
A. B. Longstreet, Southern Sketches, p. 137. (*Bartlett.*)

To run wide, to school at a considerable distance from the shore, or out of easy reach of the seine, as fish. [Beaufort, North Carolina.]—**To run with the machine.** See *machine.*

II. *trans.* 1. To cause to run. Specifically—(a) To cause to go at a rapid pace (especially in the gait known as the *run*), as a horse; also, to enter, as a horse, for a race; hence, colloquially, to put forward as a candidate for any prize or honor.

Beggars mounted *run* their horse to death. *Shak.*, 3 Hen. VI., i. 4. 127.

It was requisite in former times for a man of fashion, . . . using the words of an old romance writer, "to *runne* horses and to approve them." *Strutt*, Sports and Pastimes, p. 100.

If any enterprising burglar had taken it into his head to "chuck" that particular "crib" . . . and got clear off with the "swag," he . . . might have been *run* . . . for Congress in a year or two. *H. Kingsley*, Ravenshoe, xxxvii.

(b) To direct the course of; cause to go or pass as by guiding, forcing, driving, thrusting, pushing, etc.: as, to *run* one's head against a wall; to *run* a train off the track; to *run* a thread through a piece of cloth; to *run* a dagger into one's arm.

And falling into a place where two seas met, they *ran* the ship aground. Acts xxvii. 41.

In peril every hour to split,
Some unknown harbour suddenly [they] must sound,
Or *run* their fortunes desp'rately on ground.
Drayton, Barons' Wars, i. 55.

The glass was so clear that she thought it had been open, and so *ran* her head through the glass. Quoted in *S. Dowell's* Taxes in England, IV. 303.

(c) To cause to operate, work, ply, or perform the usual functions; keep in motion or operation, as a railway, a mill, or an engine: extended in the United States to the direction and management of any establishment, enterprise, or person: as, to *run* a mill, a hotel, or a school; that party is *running* the State.

The Democratic State Conventions have been largely *run* by the office-holding element. *The American*, XII. 307.

It is often said of the President that he is ruled—or, as the Americans express it, *run*—by his secretary. *Bryce*, American Commonwealth, I. 84.

A small knot of persons . . . pull the wires for the whole city, controlling the primaries, selecting candidates, "*running*" conventions. *Bryce*, American Commonwealth, II. 75.

(d) To pour forth, as a stream; let flow; discharge; emit.

Even at the base of Pompey's statua,
Which all the while *ran* blood, great Cæsar fell.
Shak., J. C., iii. 2. 193.

(e) To melt; fuse; shape by melting and molding: as, to *run* lead or silver.

The Tonquinese understand how to *run* Metals, and are very expert in tempering the Earth wherewith they make their mould. *Dampier*, Voyages, II. i. 70.

Hence—(f) To form by molding; mold; cast: as, to *run* bullets. (g) To cause to pass or change into a particular state; transform; cause to become.

These wild woods, and the fancies I have in me,
Will *run* me mad. *Fletcher*, Pilgrim, iii. 3.

Others, accustomed to retired speculations, *run* natural philosophy into metaphysical notions. *Locke.*

(h) To extend; stretch; especially, in *surveying*, to go over, observe, and mark by stakes, bench-marks, and the like: as, to *run* parallel lines; to *run* a line of levels from one point to another; to *run* a boundary-line (that is, to mark it upon the ground in accordance with an agreement).

We . . . rounded by the stillness of the beach
To where the bay *runs* up its latest horn.
Tennyson, Audley Court.

2. To accomplish or execute by running; hence, in general, to go through; perform; do: as, to *run* a trip or voyage; to *run* an errand.

Sesounez schal yow neuer sese of sede ne of heruest, . . .
Bot euer *renne* restlez rengnezze [courses] ther-inne.
Alliterative Poems (ed. Morris), ii. 527.

If thy wits *run* the wild-goose chase, I have done.
Shak., R. and J., ii. 4. 75.

What course I *rune*, Mr. Beachamp desireth to doe ye same. *Sherley*, quoted in Bradford's Plymouth Plantation, p. 229.

The Prince's grandfather . . . *ran* errands for gentlemen, and lent money. *Thackeray*, Vanity Fair, lxiv.

The year
Runs his old round of dubious cheer.
M. Arnold, Resignation.

3. To run after; pursue; chase; hunt by running down.

Alate we *ran* the deer. *Greene*, Friar Bacon and Friar Bungay.

Next to the still-hunt the method called "running buffalo" was the most fatal to the race, and the one most universally practiced. *Smithsonian Report*, 1887, ii. 470.

4. To pursue in thought; trace or carry in contemplation from point to point, as back along a series of causes or of antecedents.

To *run* the world back to its first original . . . is a research too great for mortal enquiry. *South.*

I would gladly understand the formation of a soul, and *run* it up to its punctum saliens. *Jeremy Collier.*

5. To pass rapidly along, over, through, or by; travel past or through, generally with the idea of danger or difficulty successfully overcome; hence, to break through or evade: as, to *run* the rapids; to *run* a blockade. Hence—6. To cause to pass or evade official restrictions; smuggle; import or export without paying duties.

Yorke had *run* his kegs of spirits ashore duty-free. *E. Dowden*, Shelley, I. 157.

All along the coasts of Kent and Sussex, and the districts most favourably situated for *running* spirits, almost the whole of the labouring population were every now and then withdrawn from their ordinary employments to engage in smuggling adventures. *S. Dowell*, Taxes in England, IV. 218.

7. To be exposed to; incur: as, to *run* a hazard, a risk, or a danger.

He must have *run* the risque of the Law, and been put upon his Clergy. *Congreve*, Way of the World, v. 1.

During an absence of six years, I *run* some risk of losing most of the distinction, literary and political, which I have acquired. *Macaulay*, in Trevelyan, I. 310.

8. To venture; hazard; risk.

He would himself be in the Highlands to receive them and *run* his fortune with them. *Clarendon.*

9. To pierce; stab: as, to *run* a person through with a rapier.

I'll *run* him up to the hilts, as I am a soldier.
Shak., Hen. V., ii. 1. 68.

I was *run* twice through the body, and shot i' th' head with a cross arrow. *Beau. and Fl.*, King and No King, ii. 1.

10. To sew by passing the needle through in a continuous line, generally taking a row of stitches on the needle at the same time: as, to *run* a seam; also, to make a number of such rows of stitches, in parallel lines, as in darning; hence, to darn; mend: as, to *run* stockings.—11. To tease; chaff; plague; nag: as, she was always teasing and *running* him. [Colloq.]—12. To fish in: as, to *run* a stream.—**Hard run.** See *hard*.—**Run net.** See *net*[1].—**Run up**, in *bookbinding*, said of a book-back in which a fillet is run from head to tail without being mitered in each cross-band.—To **run a bead**, in *carp.* and *joinery*, to form a bead, as on the edge or angle of a board.—To **run a blockade.** See *blockade*.—To **run a levanti.** See *levant*[3].—To **run a match**, to contend with another in running.—To **run and fell**, to make (as a seam) by running and felling. See *fell*[1], *n.*, 2.—**To run a rig, a risk**, etc. See the nouns.—**To run down.** (a) In *hunting*, to chase till exhausted: as, to *run down* a stag; hence, figuratively, to pursue and overtake, as a criminal; hunt down; persecute.

Must great offenders, once escaped the crown,
Like royal harts be never more *run down?*
Pope, Epil. to Satires, ii. 29.

My being hunted and *run down* on the score of my past transactions with regard to the family affairs is an abominably unjust and unnatural thing. *George Eliot*, Felix Holt, xiii.

(b) *Naut.*, to collide with (a ship); especially, to sink (a ship) by collision. (c) To overthrow; overwhelm.

Religion is *run down* by the license of these times.
Bp. Berkeley.

(d) To depreciate; disparage; abuse.

It was Cynthio's humour to *run down* everything that was rather for ostentation than use.
Addison, Ancient Medals, i.

No person should be permitted to kill characters and *run down* reputations, but qualified old maids and disappointed widows. *Sheridan*, School for Scandal, ii. 2.

(e) To reduce in health or strength: as, he was *run down* by overwork.—To **run hard.** (a) To press hard in a race or other competition.

Livingstone headed the list, though Fallowfield *ran* him *hard*. *Lawrence*, Guy Livingstone, xii.

(b) To urge or press importunately. [Colloq. in both uses.]—To **run in.** (a) In *printing*: (1) To cause to follow without break, as a word, clause, etc., after other matter in type. (2) To make room for (a small woodcut or other form of illustration) by overrunning or rearranging composed types; sometimes, conversely, the type thus arranged is said to be *run in* beside the woodcut. (b) To take into custody; arrest and confine; lock up, as a culprit or criminal. [Slang.]

The respectable gentleman [the consul] who in a foreign seaport town takes my part if I get *run in* by the police. *N. and Q.*, 7th ser., VIII. 49.

(c) To confine; inclose; corral: as, to *run in* cattle.—**To run into the ground**, to carry to an extreme; overdo. [Colloq., U. S.]—To **run off.** (a) To cause to flow out: as, to *run off* a charge of molten metal from a furnace. (b) *Theat.*, to move or roll off, as scenes from the stage. (c) In *printing*, to take impressions of; print: as, this press will *run off* ten thousand every hour; to *run off* an edition. (d) To tell off; repeat; count: as, he *ran off* the list or the figures from memory.—To **run on.** (a) In *printing*, to carry on or continue, as matter to fill up an incomplete line, without break. (b) *Theat.*, to move or bring upon the stage by means of wheels or rollers.

Nearly all scenes which are not raised or lowered by ropes from the "rigging-loft," or space under the roof above the stage, are mounted on wheels which enable them to be easily moved upon the stage, hence the compound verbs *run on* and *run off*, which are in universal use in the theatre. The word "move" is scarcely ever heard. *New York Tribune*, July 14, 1889.

(d) In *mach.*, to start (a machine or an apparatus) by connecting it or some part of it with a prime motor, or by some other adjustment necessary to set it in motion or action.—**To run one's face.** See *face*[1].—**To run one's letters.** See *letter*[3].—**To run out.** (a) To run to completion; make an end of; exhaust: as, we had *run out* all our line.

Fly, envious Time, till thou *run out* thy race.
Milton, Ode on Time.

(b) To cause to depart suddenly and by force; banish: as, to *run* a thief *out* of town or camp; *run* him out. [Slang, U. S.] (e) To carry out the end of, as a warp, hawser, cable, or the like, for the purpose of mooring or warping it to any object. (d) To cause to project beyond the ports by advancing the muzzles by means of the side-tackles: said of guns.—To **run** (something) **over**, to hurry over; go through cursorily and hastily.

And because these praiers are very many, therefore they *run* them *over*. *Purchas*, Pilgrimage, p. 196.

But who can *run* the British triumphs *o'er*,
And count the flames disperst on every shore?
Addison, To the King.

To **run the bath**, in canning fish or lobsters, to take the cans out of the first bath, prick or probe them to let out gas, and seal them up again.—**To run the foil, the gantlet, the hazard, the net.** See the nouns.—**To run the rig upon.** See *rig*[3].—**To run the stage.** See the quotation.

Before the scene can be set it is necessary to *run the stage*—that is, to get everything in the line of properties, such as stands of arms, chairs and tables, and scenery, ready to be put in place. *Scribner's Mag.*, IV. 444.

To **run the works**, in *whaling*, to try out oil.—**To run through**, in *founding*, to permit (the molten metal) to flow through the mold long enough to remove all air-bubbles, in order to insure a casting free from the defects resulting from such bubbles: expressed also by *to flow*.—**To run to cover** or **ground.** Same as *to run to earth*.—**To run to earth.** See *earth*[1].—**To run together**, to join by sewing, as the edges of stuff in making a seam.—**To run up.** (a) To raise in amount or value; increase by gradual additions; accumulate.

Between the middle of April and the end of May she *ran up* a bill of a hundred and five livres.
Fortnightly Rev., N. S., XLII. 288.

(b) To sew up with a running stitch, especially in mending; hence, to repair quickly or temporarily.

I want you to *run up* a tear in my flounce.
C. Reade, Love me Little, xiv.

(c) To put up, erect, or construct hastily: as, to *run up* a block of buildings.

What signifies a theatre? . . . just a side wing or two *run up*, doors in flat, and three or four scenes to be let down; nothing more would be necessary.
Jane Austen, Mansfield Park, xiii.

Nature never *ran up* in her haste a more restless piece of workmanship. *Lamb*, My Relations.

(d) To execute by hanging: as, they dragged the wretch to a tree and *ran* him *up*. [Western U. S.]

run[1] (run), *n.* [Partly < ME. *rune*, *rene*, *ren*, a course, run, running, < AS. *ryne*, course, path, orbit, also flow, flux (see *rine*[3], *runnel*), partly directly from the verb: see *run*[1], *v.*] 1. The act of running.

The wyf cam lepyng inward with a *ren*.
Chaucer, Reeve's Tale, l. 159.

Thou mayst slide from my shoulder to my heel with no greater a *run* but my head and my neck. A fire, good Curtis. *Shak.*, T. of the S., iv. 1. 16.

They . . . were in the midst of a good *run*, and at some distance from Mansfield, when, his horse being found to have flung a shoe, Henry Crawford had been obliged to give up, and make the best of his way back.
Jane Austen, Mansfield Park, xxv.

Specifically—(a) A leaping or springing gait, of horses or other quadrupeds, consisting in most animals of an acceleration of the action of the gallop, with two, three, or

Run.—Consecutive positions, after instantaneous photographs by Eadweard Muybridge.

all the feet off the ground at the same time during the stride. (b) In bipedal locomotion, as of man, a gait in which each foot in turn leaves the ground before the other reaches it. (c) A race: as, the horses were matched for a *run* at Newmarket. (d) A chase; a hunt: as, a *run* with the hounds. (e) *Milit.*, the highest degree of quickness in the marching step: on the same principle as the double-quick, but with more speed.

2. A traveling or going, generally with speed or haste; a passage; a journey; a trip; also,

the conducting of a journey or passage from start to finish: as, to take a *run* to Paris; the engineer had a good *run* from the west. Seamen are said to be engaged for the *run* when they are shipped for a single trip out or homeward, or from one port to another.
3. The act of working or plying; operation; activity, as of a machine, mill, etc.; also, a period of operation, or the amount of work performed in such a period.

Of the trial on Oct. 8, Dr. W. says that, during a *run* of about 21 hours, 70 cells, of about 1,400 pounds of cane apiece, or 49 tons, were diffused, giving from 65 cells 96,140 pounds of juice. *Science*, VI. 524.

The inquiry is admissible whether sufficient current could not be stored up from the average nightly *run* of a station with a spare or extra dynamo to feed a day circuit profitably. *Sci. Amer.*, N. S., LVII. 138.

4. A flowing or pouring, as of a liquid; a current; a flow.

This past spring an oil-man . . . was suffocated in one of these tank-sheds while making a *run* of oil: viz., running the oil from the receiving-tank to the transportation or pipe-line company's tanks. *Science*, XII. 172.

Already along the curve of Sandag Bay there was a splashing *run* of sea that I could hear from where I stood. *R. L. Stevenson*, The Merry Men.

5. Course; progress; especially, an observed or recorded course; succession of occurrences or chances; account: as, the *run* of events.

She hed the in and out o' the Sullivan house, and kind o' kept the *run* o' how things went and came in it. H. B. *Stowe*, Oldtown, p. 29.

Even if I had had time to follow his fortunes, it was not possible to keep the *run* of him. *J. W. Palmer*, The New and the Old, p. 62.

6. Continuance in circulation, use, observance, or the like; a continued course, occurrence, or operation: as, a *run* of ill luck; the *run* of a play or a fashion.

Now (shame to Fortune!) an ill *run* at play
Blank'd his bold visage. *Pope*, Dunciad, i. 113.

If the piece ["The Reformed Housebreaker"] has its proper *run*, I have no doubt but that bolts and bars will be entirely useless by the end of the season. *Sheridan*, The Critic, i. 1.

It is amusing to think over the history of most of the publications which have had a *run* during the last few years. *Macaulay*, Montgomery's Poems.

7. A current of opinion; tendency of thought; prejudice.

You cannot but have already observed what a violent *run* there is among too many weak people against university education. *Swift*, To a Young Clergyman.

8. A general or extraordinary pressure or demand; specifically, a pressure on a treasury or a banking-house for payment of its obligations.

"Busy just now, Caleb?" asked the Carrier. "Why, pretty well, John. . . . There's rather a *run* on Noah's Arks at present." *Dickens*, Cricket on the Hearth, i.

When there was a great *run* on Gottlib's bank in '16 I saw a gentleman come in with bags of gold, and say, "Tell Mr. Gottlib there's plenty more where that come from." It stopped the *run*, gentleman — it did, indeed. *George Eliot*, Felix Holt, xx.

9. *Naut.*: (*a*) The extreme after part of a ship's bottom or of the hold: opposed to *entrance*. (*b*) A trough for water that is caught by a coaming, built across the forecastle of a steamer to prevent the seas rushing aft. The run conducts the water overboard.—10. A small stream of water; a rivulet; a brook. See *rine*[1].

Out of the south-est parte of the said mountayne springeth and descendeth a lytle *ryn*. *MS. Cot. Calig.* B. viii. (*Halliwell*, under *rin.*)

"Do any of my young men know whither this *run* will lead us?" A Delaware . . . answered: "Before the sun could go his own length, the little water will be in the big." *Cooper*, Last of Mohicans, xxxii.

11. In *base-ball*, the feat of running around all the bases without being put out. See *base-ball*.

An earned *run* is one that is made without the assistance of fielding errors — that is, in spite of the most perfect playing of the opponents. *The Century*, XXXVIII. 835.

12. In *cricket*, one complete act of running from one wicket to the other by both the batsmen without either being put out. See *cricket*. —13. Power of running; strength for running.

They have too little *run* left in themselves to pull up for their own brothers. *T. Hughes*, Tom Brown at Rugby, i. 7.

14. The privilege of going through or over; hence, free access, as to a place from which others are excluded; freedom of use or enjoyment.

There is a great Peer in our neighborhood, who gives me the *run* of his library while he is in town. *Sydney Smith*, To Francis Jeffrey.

The contractor for the working of the railway was pleased to agree that I should have the "*run* of the shops." *The Engineer*, LXIX. 387.

15. That in or upon which anything runs or may run; especially, a place where animals may or do run, range, or move about. Compare *runway*. Specifically—(*a*) A stretch or range of pasturage, open or fenced, where cattle or sheep graze.

A wool-grower . . . could not safely venture on more than 9,000 sheep; for he might have his *run* swept by a fire any January night, and be forced to hurry his sheep down to the boiling-house. *H. Kingsley*, Hillyars and Burtons, lix.

If the country at the far end of the *run* is well grassed it will be occupied by a flock of sheep or two. *A. C. Grant*, Bush Life in Queensland, I. 61.

(*b*) An extensive underground burrow, as of a mole or gopher.

The mole has made his *run*,
The hedgehog underneath the plantain bores.
Tennyson, Aylmer's Field.

(*c*) The play-house of a bower-bird. See cut under *bower-bird*. (*d*) A series of planks laid down as a surface for rollers in moving heavy objects, or as a track for wheelbarrows. (*e*) *Theat.*, an incline; a sloping platform representing a road, etc.
16. A pair of millstones.

Every plantation, however, had a *run* of stone, propelled by mule power, to grind corn for the owners and their slaves. *U. S. Grant*, Personal Memoirs, II. 493.

17. In *music*, a rapid succession of consecutive tones constituting a single melodic figure; a division or roulade. In vocal music a run is properly sung to a single syllable.—18. In *mining*: (*a*) The horizontal distance to which a level can be carried, either from the nature of the formation or in accordance with agreement with the proprietor. (*b*) The direction of a vein. (*c*) A failure caused by looseness, weakness, slipping, sliding, giving way, or the like; a fault.

The working has been executed in the most irregular manner, and has opened up enormous excavations; whence disastrous *runs* have taken place in the mines. *Ure*, Dict., III. 294.

19. Character; peculiarities; lie.

Each . . . was entirely of the opinion that he knew the *run* of the country better than his neighbours. *The Field*, LXVII. 91.

20. The quantity run or produced at one time, as in various mechanical operations.

Where large quantities [of varnish] are required, it will always be found best to boil off the three *runs* in the boiling pot. *Workshop Receipts*, 1st ser., p. 65.

Woollen yarns are weighed in lengths or *runs* of 1600 yards. *A. Barlow*, Weaving, p. 330.

21. (*a*) A herd; a number of animals moving together, as a school of fish. (*b*) The action of such a school; especially, the general movement of anadromous fish up-stream or in-shore from deep water. *Sportsman's Gazetteer.*—22. A straight net, running out at right angles to the shore, and connecting with an inner pound; a leader. See cut under *pound-net*.—23. In *physics*, the value of a mean division of a circle or scale in revolutions of a micrometer-scale, divisions of a level, etc. When a microscope with a micrometer is employed to read a circle or linear scale, it is convenient to have a certain whole number of revolutions equal to a mean division of the circle or scale, and the amount by which the division exceeds or falls short of that whole number of revolutions, expressed in circular or linear measure, is called the *error of runs*, or, loosely, the *run*. It is taken as positive when the circle- or scale-division is greater than the intended whole number of turns.—**By the run**, suddenly; quickly; all at once; especially, by a continuous movement: said of a fall, descent, and the like: as, the wall came down *by the run*.—**Earned run.** See quotation under def. 11, above.—**Home run**, in *base-ball*, a continuous circuit of the bases made by a batsman as a consequence of a hit, and not due to any fielding errors of the opponents. —**In or at the long run**, after a long course of experience; at length; as the ultimate result of long trial.

I might have caught him [a trout] *at the long-run*, for so I use always to do when I meet with an overgrown fish. *I. Walton*, Complete Angler, p. 115.

I am sure always, *in the long run*, to be brought over to her way of thinking. *Lamb*, Mackery End.

Often it is seen that great changes which *in the long-run* turn to the good of the community bring suffering and grievous loss on their way to many an individual. *Shairp*, Culture and Religion, p. 129.

Run to clear, in *lumber-manuf.*, the proportion of clear sawed lumber in the output of a plant, or in the lumber-product of a quantity of logs when sawed: opposed to *run to culls*, which is the proportion of culls or defective pieces.—**Strawberry run**, a run of fish in the season of the year when strawberries are ripe. Compare *dandelion fleet*, vessels sailing when dandelions are in bloom. [Local, U. S.]—**The common run** (or, simply, **the run**), that which passes under observation as most usual or common; the generality.

In *the common run* of mankind, for one that is wise and good you find ten of a contrary character. *Addison*, Spectator, No. 287.

To get the run upon, to turn the joke upon; turn into ridicule. [U. S.]

run[1] (run), *p. a.* [Pp. of *run*[1], *v.*] **1.** Liquefied; melted: as, *run* butter. See *butter*[1]. [Colloq.] —**2.** Smuggled ashore or landed secretly; contraband: as, *run* brandy; a *run* cargo. [Colloq.]

She boasted of her feats in diving into dark dens in search of *run* goods, charming things—French warranted—that could be had for next to nothing. *Miss Edgeworth*, Helen, xxv. (*Davies.*)

3. Having migrated or made a run, as a fish; having come up from the sea. Compare *run-fish*.

Your fish is strong and active, fresh *run*, as full soon you see. *Quarterly Rev.*, CXXVI. 341.

run[2], *n.* See *runn*.

runabout (run'a̤-bout″), *n.* **1.** A gadabout; a vagabond.

A *runne-about*, a skipping French-man. *Marston*, What you Will, iii. 1.

2. Any light open wagon for ready and handy use.

runagate (run'a̤-gāt), *a.* and *n.* [Formerly also *runnagate*; a corruption of E. *renegade* (< ME. *renegat*), confused with *run* (ME. *renne*) *a gate*, i. e., 'run on the way,' and perhaps with *runaway*: see *renegate*, *renegade*.] **I.** *a.* **1.** Renegade; apostate.

To this Mahomet succeeded his sonne called Amurathes. He ordeyned first the Ianissaryes, *runnagate* Christians, to defend his person. *Guevara*, Letters (tr. by Hellowes, 1577), p. 331.

He [William Tyndale, the translator of the Scriptures] was a *runagate* friar living in foreign parts, and seems to have been a man of severe temper and unfortunate life. *R. W. Dixon*, Hist. Church of Eng., i.

2. Wandering about; vagabond.

Where they dare not with their owne forces to inuade, they basely entertaine the traitours and vacabonds of all Nations; seeking by those and by their *runnagate* Jesuits to winne parts. *Hakluyt's Voyages*, II. ii. 174.

II. *n.* **1.** A renegade; an apostate; hence, more broadly, one who deserts any cause; a turncoat.

He . . . letteth the *runagates* continue in scarceness. *Book of Common Prayer*, Psalter, Ps. lxviii. 6.

Traitor, no king, that seeks thy country's sack,
The famous *runagate* of Christendom!
Peele, Edward I.

Hence, hence, ye slave! dissemble not thy state,
But henceforth be a turncoat, *runagate*.
Marston, Satires, i. 122.

2. One who runs away; a fugitive; a runaway.

Dido I am, unless I be deceiv'd.
And must I rave thus for a *runagate*?
Must I make ships for him to sail away?
Marlowe and Nash, Dido, Queen of Carthage, v. 1. 265.

Thus chaind in wretched servitude doth live
A *runagate*, and English fugitive.
Times' Whistle (E. E. T. S.), p. 52.

3. A runabout; a vagabond; a wanderer.

He now cursed Cain from the earth, to be a *runagate* and wanderer thereon. *Purchas*, Pilgrimage, p. 33.

A vagabond and straggling *runnagate*; . . .
That vagrant exile, that vile bloody Cain.
Drayton, Queen Isabel to Rich. II.

runaway (run'a̤-wā″), *n.* and *a.* [< *run*[1] + *away*.] **I.** *n.* **1.** One who flees or departs; a fugitive; a deserter.

Thou *runaway*, thou coward, art thou fled?
Shak., M. N. D., iii. 2. 405.

My son was born a freeman; this, a slave
To beastly passions, a fugitive
And *run-away* from virtue.
Fletcher (and another), Queen of Corinth, v. 2.

The night hath plaid the swift-foot *runne-away*.
Heywood, Fair Maid of the Exchange (Works, II. 21).

2. A running away, as by a horse when breaking away from control and bolting.

If the driver is standing against one of the ultra-sloping driving cushions, a *runaway* will be found impossible. *New York Tribune*, May 11, 1890.

3. One who runs in the public ways; one who roves or rambles about.

Spread thy close curtain, love-performing night,
That *runaways'* eyes may wink, and Romeo
Leap to these arms untalk'd of and unseen.
Shak., R. and J., iii. 2. 6.

II. *a.* **1.** Acting the part of a runaway; escaping or breaking from control; defying or overcoming restraint: as, a *runaway* horse.

Shakspeare . . . was a *runaway* youth, . . . who obtained his living in London by holding horses at the door of the theatre for those who went to the play. *E. Everett*, Orations, I. 319.

2. Accomplished or effected by running away or eloping.

We are told that Miss Michell's guardian would not consent to his ward's marriage [with Bysshe Shelley], that it was a *runaway* match, and that the wedding was celebrated in London by the parson of the Fleet. *E. Dowden*, Shelley, I. 3.

runcation† (rung-kā'shọn), *n.* [< L. *runcatio(n-)*, a weeding, weeding out, < *runcare* (> It. *roncare*), weed.] A weeding. *Evelyn.* (*Imp. Dict.*)

runch (runch), *n.* [Origin obscure.] The charlock, *Brassica Sinapistrum*; also, the wild radish (jointed charlock), *Raphanus Raphanistrum.* [Prov. Eng.]

runch-balls (runch'bâlz), *n.* Dried charlock. [Prov. Eng.]

Runcina (run-sī'nạ̈), *n.* [NL., < L. *Runcina*, a rural goddess presiding over weeding, < *runcare*, weed: see *runcation.*] The typical genus of *Runcinidæ. Pelta* is a synonym.

runcinate (run'si-nāt), *a.* [= F. *runciné*, < NL. *runcinatus*, < L. *runcina*, a plane, = Gr. ῥυκάνη, a plane. Cf. *rugine.*] In *bot.*, irregularly saw-toothed or pinnately incised, with the lobes or teeth hooked backward: said chiefly of leaves, as those of the dandelion.

Runcinate Leaf of *Taraxacum officinale* (dandelion).

Runcinidæ (run-sin'i-dē), *n. pl.* [NL., < *Runcina* + *-idæ.*] A family of notaspidean nudibranchiate gastropods, typified by the genus *Runcina*. They have a distinct mantle, no tentacles, three or four branchial leaflets, and triserial lingual teeth. They mostly inhabit the European seas.

runcival†, *n.* See *rounceval.*

rund (rund), *n.* A dialectal form of *rand*[1].

rundale (run'dāl), *n.* A system of land-holding, in which single holdings consisted of detached pieces. Runrig (which see) was a form of rundale.

> There certainly seem to be vestiges of ancient collective enjoyment in the extensive prevalence of *rundale* holdings in parts of the country.
> *Maine*, Early Hist. of Institutions, p. 101.

rundle[1], **rundel** (run'dl, -del), *n.* [A var. of *runnel.*] 1†. A small stream: same as *runnel.*

> The river is enriched with many goodly brookes, which are maintained by an infinit number of small *rundles* and pleasant springs.
> *Capt. John Smith*, Works, I. 116.

2. A moat with water in it. *Halliwell.*

rundle[2] (run'dl), *n.* [A var. of *roundel*, *rondel*[2]. Hence *rundlet*, *runlet*, q. v.] 1†. A circular line or path; a ring; an orbit.

> Euery of the Planettes are carried in their *rundels* or circles by course.
> *R. Eden*, First Books on America (ed. Arber), p. xlviii.

2. Something disposed in circular form; a circular or encircling arrangement; specifically, a peritrochium.

> The third mechanical faculty, stiled "axis in peritrochio," consists of an axis or cylinder having a *rundle* about it, wherein are fastened divers spokes, by which the whole may be turned about.
> *Bp. Wilkins*, Math. Magick.

3†. A ball.

> An other Serpent hath a *rundle* on his Taile like a Bell, which also ringeth as it goeth.
> *Purchas*, Pilgrimage, p. 550.

4. A rung of a ladder; a round.—5. That part of a capstan round which a rope is wound in heaving.—6. One of the bars of a lantern-wheel; a rung.

rundled† (run'dld), *a.* [< *rundle*[2] + *-ed*[2].] Round; circular. *Chapman.*

rundlet, **runlet**[2] (rund'let, run'let), *n.* [Early mod. E. also *rundelet*, *roundlet*; < OF. **rondelet*, dim. of *rondele*, *rondelle*, a little tun or barrel, a round shield, etc.: see *rundle*[2]. Cf. *roundelay.*] A small barrel; a unit of capacity, equal, according to statutes of 1439 and 1483, to 18½ gallons, but in modern times usually reckoned at 18 gallons. The often-repeated statement that the rundlet varies from 3 to 20 gallons appears to be a blunder.

> *Roundlet*, a certayne measure of wine, oyle, &c., containing 18½ gallons; an. 1. Rich. III. cap. 13; so called of his roundness.
> *Minsheu.*

> Of wine and oyl the *rundlet* holdeth 18½ gallons.
> *Recorde*, Grounde of Artes.

> A catch or pinck no capabler than a *rundler* [read *rundlet*] or washing bowle.
> *Nashe*, Lenten Stuffe (Harl. Misc., VI. 163). (*Davies.*)

> Would you drink a cup of sack, father? here stand some with *runlets* to fill it out.
> *The Great Frost* (Arber's Eng. Garner, I. 85).

> It were good to set a *rundlet* of verjuice over against the sun in summer . . . to see whether it will ripen and sweeten.
> *Bacon*, Nat. Hist., § 898.

> A stoup of sack, or a *runlet* of Canary. *Scott.*

rune[1] (rön), *n.* [= F. *rune* = G. *rune* (LL. *runa*), a rune, a mod. book-form representing the AS. and Scand. word *rūn*, a letter, a writing, lit. a secret, mystery, secret or confidential speech, counsel (a letter being also called *rūnstæf* (= Icel. *rūnastafr*), a letter, < *rūn*, mystery, + *stæf*, staff; cf. *bōcstæf*, a letter: see *book*), = Icel. *rūnc* = Sw. *runa* = Dan. *rune*, a letter, rune (applied to the old Northern alphabet, and sometimes to the Latin), = OHG. *runa*, a secret, counsel, MHG. *rune*, a whisper, = Goth. *rūna*, a secret, mystery, counsel. Cf. Ir. Gael. *rūn*, a secret, mystery, craft, deceit, purpose, intention, desire, love, etc., = W. *rhin*, a secret, charm, virtue. The E. form descended from the AS. is *roun*, *round*, whisper: see *roun*, *round*[2].] 1. A letter or character used by the peoples of northern Europe from an early period to the eleventh century; in the plural, the ancient Scandinavian alphabets, believed to be derived from a Greek source; especially, the letters carved on stones, weapons, etc., found in Scandinavia, Scotland, and Ireland. Runes are found in almost all the maritime parts of Europe.

Runes.—Part of runic cross at Ruthwell, Dumfriesshire, Scotland.

Runes.—Runic alphabet, from MSS. at Friesengen and St. Gallen (9th century).

> The somewhat similar Scandinavian "tree *runes*," which were a sort of cryptograms, constructed on the plan of indicating, by the number of branches on the tree, the place occupied in the Futhorc by the corresponding ordinary *rune*.
> *Isaac Taylor*, The Alphabet, II. 226.

> Odhinn taught mankind the great art of *runes*, which means both writing and magic, and many other arts of life.
> *Keary*, Prim. Belief, vii. 337.

2. A short mystic sentence embodying the wisdom of the old Northern philosophers.

> Of the Troll of the Church they sing the *rune*
> By the Northern Sea in the harvest moon.
> *Whittier*, Kallundborg Church.

3. A secret; mystery; obscure saying.

> For wise he was, and many curious arts,
> Postures of *runes*, and healing herbs he knew.
> *M. Arnold*, Balder Dead, i.

4. Early rimes or poetry expressed, or which might be expressed, in runic characters.—5. Any song, poem, verse, or the like, which is mystically or obscurely expressed.

> For Nature beats in perfect tune,
> And rounds with rhyme her every *rune*.
> *Emerson*, Woodnotes, ii.

rune[2]†, *n.* An obsolete variant of *rine*[1], *run*[1].

runecraft (rön'krȧft), *n.* Knowledge of runes; skill in deciphering runic characters.

> Modern Swedish *runecraft* largely depends upon his [Dybeck's] many and valuable publications.
> *Archæologia*, XLIII. 98.

runed (rönd), *a.* [< *rune*[1] + *-ed*[2].] Bearing runes; inscribed with runes.

> The middenstead from which a leaden bulla of Archdeacon Boniface and a *runed* ivory comb, to mention nothing else, have been obtained.
> *N. and Q.*, 7th ser., II. 50.

runer (rö'nėr), *n.* [< *rune*[1] + *-er*[1]. Cf. *rounder*[2].] A bard or learned man among the ancient Goths.

> The Gothic *Runers*, to gain and establish the credit and admiration of their rhymes, turned the use of them very much to incantations and charms.
> *Sir W. Temple*, Of Poetry.

runesmith (rön'smith), *n.* A worker at runes. [Rare.]

> No one has workt with more zeal than Richard Dybeck of Stockholm; no one has publisht half so many Runic stones, mostly in excellent copies, as that energetic *runesmith*.
> *Archæologia*, XLIII. 98.

rune-stone (rön'stōn), *n.* A stone having runic inscriptions.

run-fish (run'fish), *n.* A salmon on its way to the sea after spawning. *Sir J. Richardson.*

rung[1] (rung), *n.* [Formerly also *reng*; < ME. *rong*, < AS. *hrung*, a rod or bar (found only once, with ref. to a wagon), = MD. *ronge*, *ronghe*, the beam of a plow or of a wagon, D. *rong*, a rundle, = MLG. LG. *runge* = OHG. *runga*, MHG. G. *runge*, a short thick piece of iron or wood, a pin, bolt, = Icel. *röng*, a rib of a ship, = Goth. *hrugga*, a staff; cf. Ir. *ronga*, a rung, joining spar, = Gael. *rong*, a joining spar, rib of a boat, staff (perhaps < E.). The OSw. *rangr*, *vrängr*, pl. *vränger*, sides of a vessel (> F. *varangue*, Sp. *varenga*, sides of a vessel), seems to be of diff. origin, connected with Sw. *vränga*, Dan. *vrange*, twist, and with E. *wring* (pp. *wrung*).] 1. A rod or bar; a heavy staff; hence, a cudgel; a club. [Prov. Eng. and Scotch.]

> Than up scho gat ane mekle *rung*,
> And the gudman maid to the doir.
> *Wyf of Auchtirmuchty* (Child's Ballads, VIII. 121).

> Till slap come in an unco loon
> An wi' a *rung* decide it.
> *Burns*, Does Haughty Gaul Invasion Threat?

Specifically—2. A round or step of a ladder.

> Thanne fondeth the Fende my fruit to destruye, . . .
> And leith a laddre there-to, of lesynges aren the *ronges*,
> And feccheth away my floures sumtyme afor bothe myn eyhen.
> *Piers Plowman* (B), xvi. 44.

> His owene hande made laddres three
> To clymber by the *ronges* [var. *renges*] and the stalkes,
> Into the tubbes, hangynge in the balkes.
> *Chaucer*, Miller's Tale, l. 439.

> There have been brilliant instances of persons stepping at once on to the higher *rungs* of the ladder [of success] in virtue of their audacity and energy.
> *Bryce*, American Commonwealth, II. 76.

3. One of the bars of a windmill-sail.—4. A spoke or bar of a wallower or lantern-wheel; a rundle.—5. *Naut.*: (*a*) One of the projecting handles of a steering-wheel. (*b*) A floor-timber in a ship.

rung[2]. Preterit and past participle of *ring*[2].

rung[3] (rung), *p. a.* [Prop. *ringed*, < *ring*[1]; erroneously conformed to *rung*[2], pp. of *ring*[2].] Ringed; having a ring through the snout, as a hog. [Prov. Eng.]

> A cramp-ring
> Will be reward enough; to wear like those
> That hang their richest jewels in their nose,
> Like a *rung* bear or swine.
> *B. Jonson*, Underwoods, lxxvii.

rung-head (rung'hed), *n.* *Naut.*, the upper end of a floor-timber.

runic (rö'nik), *a.* [= F. *runique* = Sp. *rúnico* = Pg. It. *runico*, < NL. *runicus*, < *runa*, a rune: see *rune*[1].] 1. Pertaining to, consisting in, or characteristic of runes.

> Keeping time, time, time,
> In a sort of *Runic* rhyme. *Poe*, The Bells.

> No graven line,
> Nor Druid mark, nor *Runic* sign
> Is left me here. *Whittier*, The Norsemen.

2. Inscribed with runes.

> Thinking of his own Gods, a Greek
> In pity and mournful awe might stand
> Before some fallen *Runic* stone—
> For both were faiths, and both are gone.
> *M. Arnold*, Stanzas from the Grande Chartreuse.

3. Resembling in style the work of the early civilization of the north of Europe.

> Three brooches, reproductions of *Runic* art.
> *Rev. C. Boutell*, Art Jour., 1867.

Runic knots, a form of interlaced ornament occurring in jewels and the like of early Teutonic manufacture.—**Runic wand, brooch**, etc., names given to articles found inscribed with runic characters: the inscriptions are considered generally to give the owner's and maker's name, or the like.

runish†, **runishly**†. Obsolete forms of *rennish*, *rennishly*.

runkle (rung'kl), *v. t.* or *i.*; pret. and pp. *runkled*, ppr. *runkling*. [< ME. *rounclen*; a form of *wrunkle*, var. of *wrinkle*: see *wrunkle*, *wrinkle*. The *w* is lost as in *root*[2].] To wrinkle; crease. [Obsolete or prov. Eng. and Scotch.]

> Than waxes his gast seke and sare,
> And his face *runcles*, ay mare & mare.
> *Specimens of Early English* (ed. Morris and Skeat), [II. x. 773.

> Gin ye'll go there, yon *runkl'd* pair,
> We will get famous laughin'
> At them this day.
> *Burns*, Holy Fair.

run-lace (run'lās), *n.* Lace made by embroidering with the needle upon a rēseau ground. It has been in fashion at different times, and was made especially in England in the eighteenth century.

runlet[1] (run'let), *n.* [< *run*[1], a stream, + dim. suf. *-let*. Cf. *runnel.*] A little rivulet or stream; a runnel.

> And the *runlet* that murmurs away [seems]
> To wind with a murmur of wo.
> *Wolcot* (Peter Pindar), Orson and Ellen, iv.

> The biographer, especially of a literary man, need only mark the main currents of tendency, without being officious to trace out to its marshy source every *runlet* that has cast in its tiny pitcherful with the rest.
> *Lowell*, Among my Books, 2d ser., p. 255.

> And *runlets* babbling down the glen.
> *Tennyson*, Mariana in the South.

runlet[2], *n.* See *rundlet.*

run-man (run'mạn), *n.* A runaway or deserter from a ship of war. [Eng.]

runn (run), *n.* [Also *run*, *ran*, *rann*; Hind. *rān*, a waste tract, a wood, forest.] In India, a tract of sand-flat or salt-bog, which is often covered by the tides or by land floods: as, the *Runn* of Cutch.

runnel (run'el), *n.* [Also dial. *rundle, rundel, rindle, rindel*; < ME. *runel, rinel*, a streamlet, < AS. *rynel*, a running stream (cf. *rynel*, a runner, messenger, courier), dim. of *ryne*, a stream, < *rinnan*, run: see *run*1 and *rine*3.] A rivulet or small brook.

> The *Runels* of red blode ran doun his chekes.
> *Destruction of Troy* (E. E. T. S.), l. 7506.

> As a trench the little valley was,
> To catch the *runnels* that made green its grass.
> *William Morris*, Earthly Paradise, II. 9.

> A willow Pleiades, . . .
> Their roots, like molten metal cooled in flowing,
> Stiffened in coils and *runnels* down the bank.
> *Lowell*, Under the Willows.

runner (run'ėr), *n.* [< ME. *runnere, rennere* (= MHG. *rennore, renner*); < *run*1 + *-er*1.] 1. One who or that which runs. Specifically—(*a*) A person who or an animal which moves with the gait called a *run*, as in a running-match or race.

> Forspent with toil, as *runners* with a race.
> *Shak.*, 3 Hen. VI., ii. 3. 1.

(*b*) One who is in the act of running, as in any game or sport.

> The other side are scouting and trying to put him out, either by hitting the batsman (or *runner*) as he is running, or by sending the ball into the hole, which is called grounding. *Tribune Book of Sports*, p. 69.

(*c*) One who frequents or runs habitually to a place.

> And fle farre from besy tungges as bytter as gall,
> And *rynnars* to howsis wher good ale is.
> *MS. Laud.* 416, f. 39. (*Halliwell.*)

(*d*) A runaway; a fugitive; a deserter.

> Let us score their backs,
> And snatch 'em up, as we take hares, behind:
> 'Tis sport to maul a *runner*.
> *Shak.*, A. and C., iv. 7. 14.

> If I finde any more *runners* for Newfoundland with the Pinnace, let him assuredly looke to ariue at the Gallows.
> Quoted in *Capt. John Smith's* Works, I. 229.

(*e*) One who risks or evades dangers, impediments, or legal restrictions, as in blockade-running or smuggling; especially, a smuggler.

> By merchants I mean fair traders, and not *runners* and trickers, as the little people often are that cover a contraband trade. *Roger North*, Examen, p. 490. (*Davies.*)

(*f*) An operator or manager, as of an engine or a machine.

> Every locomotive *runner* should . . . have an exact knowledge of the engine intrusted to him, and a general knowledge of the nature and construction of steam engines generally. *Forney*, Locomotive, p. 547.

> There are two classes of *runners*, and a second-class man must run an engine two years before he can be promoted to first-class. *The Engineer*, LXVIII. 349.

(*g*) One who goes about on any sort of errand; a messenger; specifically, in Great Britain and in the courts of China, a sheriff's officer; a bailiff; in the United States, one whose business it is to solicit passengers for railways, steamboats, etc.

> A somonour is a *rennere* up and doun
> With mandementz for fornicacioun,
> And is ybet at every townes ende.
> *Chaucer*, Prol. to Friar's Tale, l. 19.

> *Runner* [of a gaming-house], one who is to get Intelligence of the Meetings of the Justices, and when the Constables are out. *Bailey*, 1731.

> He was called the Man of Peace on the same principle which assigns to constables, Bow-street *runners*, and such like, who carry bludgeons to break folk's heads, and are perpetually and officially employed in scenes of riot, the title of peace-officers. *Scott*, St. Ronan's Well, iii.

> For this their *runners* ramble day and night,
> To drag each lurking deep to open light.
> *Crabbe*, The Newspaper (Works, I. 181).

> "It's the *runners!*" cried Brittles, to all appearance much relieved. "The what?" exclaimed the doctor, aghast in his turn. "The Bow Street officers, sir," replied Brittles. *Dickens*, Oliver Twist, xxx.

(*h*) A commercial traveler. [U. S.] (*i*) A running stream; a run.

> When they [trout] are going up the *runners* to spawn.
> *The Field*, LXVI. 560.

(*j*) *pl.* In *ornith.*, specifically, the Cursores or *Brevipennes*. (*k*) *pl.* In *entom.*, specifically, the cursorial orthopterous insects; the cockroaches. See *Cursoria*. (*l*) A carangoid fish, the leather-jacket, *Elagatis pinnulatus*.
2. In *bot.*, a slender prostrate stem, having a bud at the end which sends out leaves and roots, as in the strawberry; also, a plant that spreads by such creeping stems. Compare *run*1, *v. i.*, 10.

> In every root there will be one *runner* which hath little buds on it. *Mortimer*, Husbandry.

3. In *mach.*: (*a*) The tight pulley of a system of fast-and-loose pulleys. (*b*) In a grinding-mill, the stone which is turned, in distinction from the fixed stone, or bedstone. See cuts under *mill*1, 1.

> And somtimes whirling, on an open hill,
> The round-flat *runner* in a roaring mill.
> *Sylvester*, tr. of Du Bartas's Weeks, i. 2.

(*c*) In a system of pulleys, a block which moves, as distinguished from a block which is held in a fixed position. Also called *running block*. See cut under *pulley*. (*d*) A single rope rove through a movable block, having an eye or thimble in the end of which a tackle is hooked.

> There are . . . all kinds of Shipchandlery necessaries, such as blocks, tackles, *runners*, etc.
> *Defoe*, Tour through Great Britain, I. 147. (*Davies.*)

4. In *saddlery*, a loop of metal, leather, bone, celluloid, ivory, or other material, through which a running or sliding strap or rein is passed: as, the *runners* for the gag-rein on the throat-latch of a bridle or head-stall.—5. In *optical-instrument making*, a convex cast-iron support for lenses, used in shaping them by grinding.

> The cast-iron *runner* is heated just sufficiently to melt the cement, and carefully placed upon the cemented backs of the lenses. *Ure*, Dict., III. 106.

6. That part of anything on which it runs or slides: as, the *runner* or keel of a sleigh or a skate.

> The sleds, although so low, rest upon narrow *runners*, and the shafts are attached by a hook.
> *B. Taylor*, Northern Travel, p. 35.

7. In *molding*: (*a*) A channel cut in the sand of a mold to allow melted metal to run from the furnace to the space to be filled in the mold.

> The crucibles charged with molten steel direct from the melting-holes pour their contents into one of the *runners*.
> *W. H. Greenwood*, Steel and Iron, p. 427.

(*b*) The small mass of metal left in this channel, which shows, when the mold is removed, as a projection from the casting. See *jet*1, 4 (*b*).—8. In *bookbinding*, the front board of the plow-press, used in cutting edges. [Eng.]—9. *pl.* In *printing*: (*a*) The friction-rollers in the ribs of a printing-press, on which the bed slides to and from impression. [Eng.] (*b*) A line of corks put on a form of type to prevent the inking-rollers from sagging, and over-coloring the types. [Eng.]—10. The slide on an umbrella-stick, to which the ribs or spreaders are pivoted.—11. In *gunpowder-manuf.*, same as *runner-ball*.—12. In *iron-founding, soda-manuf.*, and other industries in which fusion is a necessary operation, a congealed piece of metal or material which in the molten state has run out of a mold or receptacle, and become waste until remelted.—13. In *rope-making*, a steel plate having three holes concentrically arranged, and used to separate the three yarns in laying up (twisting) a rope. The yarns are passed through the holes, and the plate is kept at a uniform distance from the junction of the twisted and untwisted parts, rendering the twist uniform.
14. A market-vessel for the transportation of fish, oysters, etc.—**Brook-runner.** Same as *velvet runner*.—**Double-runner.** Same as *bob-sled*.—**Runner of a trawl.** See *trawl*.—**Scarlet runner**, the scarlet-flowered form of the Spanish bean, *Phaseolus multiflorus*, native in South America: a common high-twining ornamental plant with showy, casually white blossoms. Also called *scarlet bean*.—**Velvet runner**, the water-rail, *Rallus aquaticus*: so called from its stealthy motions. [Local, British.]

runner-ball (run'ėr-bâl), *n.* In *gunpowder-manuf.*, a disk of hard wood used to crush the mill-cake through the sieves in order to granulate the powder.

runner-stick (run'ėr-stik), *n.* In *founding*, a cylindrical or conical piece of wood extending upward from the pattern and having the sand of the cope packed about it. When withdrawn, it leaves a channel called the *runner* leading to the interior of the mold.

runnet (run'et), *n.* A dialectal form of *rennet*1.

running (run'ing), *n.* [Verbal n. of *run*1, *v.*] 1. The act of one who or that which runs.—2. Specifically, the act of one who risks or evades dangers or legal restrictions, as in *running* a blockade or smuggling.

> It was hoped that the extensive smuggling that prevailed would be mitigated by heavy penalties, which were now imposed upon custom-house officers for neglect of duty in preventing the *running* of brandy.
> *S. Dowell*, Taxes in England, IV. 216.

3. The action of a whale after being struck by the harpoon, when it swims but does not sound.—4. In *racing*, etc., power, ability, or strength to run; hence, staying power.

> He thinks I've *running* in me yet; he sees that I'll come out one of these days in top condition.
> *Lever*, Davenport Dunn, xii.

> He [Kingston] was not only full of *running* throughout the race, but finished second, and just as strong as Hanover. *New York Evening Post*, June 28, 1889.

5. The ranging of any animals, particularly in connection with the rut, or other actions of the breeding season: also used attributively: as, the *running* time of salmon or deer.

> The history of the buffalo's daily life and habits should begin with the "*running* season."
> *Smithsonian Report*, 1887, ii. 415.

6. In *organ-building*, a leakage of the air in a wind-chest into a channel so that a pipe is sounded when its digital is depressed, although its stop is not drawn; also, the sound of a pipe thus sounded. Also called *running of the wind*.—7. That which runs or flows; the quantity run: as, the first *running* of a still, or of cider at the mill.

> And from the dregs of life think to receive
> What the first sprightly *running* could not give.
> *Dryden*, Aurengzebe, iv. 1.

> It [Glapthorne's work] is exactly in flavour and character the last not sprightly *runnings* of a generous liquor.
> *Saintsbury*, Hist. Elizabethan Lit., xi.

8. Course, direction, or manner of flowing or moving.

> All the rivers in the world, though they have divers risings and divers *runnings*, . . . do at last find and fall into the great ocean. *Raleigh*, Hist. World, Pref., p. 47.

In the running, out of the running, competing or not competing in a race or other contest; hence, qualified or not qualified for such a contest, or likely or not likely to take part in or to succeed in it. [Colloq.]—**Running off**, in *founding*, the operation of opening the tap-hole in a blast-furnace, so that the metal can flow through the channels to the molds.—**To make good one's running**, to run as well as one's rival; keep abreast with others; prove one's self a match for a rival.

> The world had esteemed him when he first *made good his running* with the Lady Fanny.
> *Trollope*, Small House at Allington, ii.

To make the running, to force the pace at the beginning of a race, by causing a second-class horse to set off at a high speed, with the view of giving a better chance to a staying horse of the same owner.

> Ben Caunt was to *make the running* for Haphazard.
> *H. Kingsley*, Ravenshoe, xxxvi.

To take up the running, to go off at full speed from a slower pace; take the lead; take the most active part in any undertaking.

> But silence was not dear to the heart of the honourable John, and so he *took up the running*.
> *Trollope*, Dr. Thorne, v.

running (run'ing), *p. a.* [Ppr. of *run*1, *v.*] 1. That runs; suited for running, racing, etc. See *run*1, *n.*, 1 (*a*).

> A concourse . . . of noblemen and gentlemen meet together, in mirth, peace, and amity, for the exercise of their swift *running*-horses, every Thursday in March. The prize they run for is a silver and gilt cup, with a cover, to the value of seven or eight pounds.
> *Butcher*, quoted in Strutt's Sports and Pastimes, p. 103.

> In the reign of Edward III. the *running*-horses purchased for the king's service were generally estimated at twenty marks, or thirteen pounds, six shillings, and eightpence each. *Strutt*, Sports and Pastimes, p. 104.

Specifically, in *zoöl.*, cursorial; gressorial; ambulatory; not salient or saltatory.
2†. Capable of moving quickly; movable; mobilized.

> The Indians did so annoy them by sudden assaults out of the swamps, etc., that he was forced to keep a *running* army to be ready to oppose them upon all occasions.
> *Winthrop*, Hist. New England, II. 117.

3. Done, made, taken, etc., in passing, or while hastening along; hence, cursory; hasty; speedy.

> The fourth Summer [A. D. 82], Domitian then ruling the Empire, he spent in settling and confirming what the year before he had travail'd over with a *running* Conquest. *Milton*, Hist. Eng., ii.

> When you step but a few doors off to tattle with a wench, or take a *running* pot of ale, . . . leave the street door open. *Swift*, Advice to Servants (Footman).

4. Cursive, as manuscript: as, *running* hand (see below).—5. Proceeding in close succession; without intermission: used in a semi-adverbial sense after nouns denoting periods of time: as, I had the same dream three nights *running*.

> How would my Lady Ailesbury have liked to be asked in a parish church for three Sundays *running*?
> *Walpole*, Letters, II. 334.

> Legislation may disappoint them fifty times *running*, without at all shaking their faith in its efficiency.
> *H. Spencer*, Social Statics, p. 422.

6. Continuous; unintermittent; persistent.

> The click-click of her knitting-needles is the *running* accompaniment to all her conversation.
> *George Eliot*, Amos Barton, i.

7. In *bot.*, repent or creeping by runners, as the strawberry. See *runner*, 2.—**Running banquet**†. See *banquet*, 3.—**Running block.** See *block*1, 11.—**Running board.** (*a*) A narrow platform extending along the side of a locomotive. (*b*) A horizontal board along the ridge of a box freight-car or the side of an oil-car, to form a passage for the trainmen.—**Running bond.** See *bond*1.—**Running bowline**, a bowline-knot made round a part of the same rope, so as to make a noose.—**Running bowsprit.** See *bowsprit*.—**Running buffalo-clover**, an American clover, *Trifolium stoloniferum*, closely related to *T. reflexum*, the buffalo-clover, but spreading by runners.—**Running days**, a chartering term for consecutive days occupied on a voyage, etc., including Sundays, and not therefore limited to working-days.—**Running dustman.** See *dustman*.—**Running fight**, a fight kept up by the party pursuing and the party pursued.—

Running fire. See *fire*.—**Running footman**†. See *footman*, 3.—**Running hand**, the style of handwriting or penmanship in which the letters are formed without lifting the pen from the paper.—**Running head.** See *head*, 13.—**Running knot**, a knot made in such a way as to form a noose which tightens as the rope is pulled on.—**Running lights**, the lights shown by vessels between sunset and sunrise, in order to guard against collision when under way. They are a green light on the starboard side and a red light on the port side. If the vessel is under steam, a bright white light is also hoisted at the foremast-head; a vessel towing another carries two white lights at the foremast-head.—**Running myrtle.** See *myrtle*.—**Running ornament**, any ornament in which the design is continuous, in intertwined or flowing

Running Ornament.—Medieval Architectural Sculpture.

lines, as in many medieval moldings carved with foliage, etc.—**Running patterer.** See *patterer*.—**Running pine.** See *Lycopodium*.—**Running rigging.** See *rigging*2.—**Running stationer.** See *stationer*.—**Running swamp-blackberry**, *Rubus hispidus*, an almost herbaceous species, with short flowering shoots, bearing a fruit of a few sour grains, and with long and slender prickly runners.—**Running title**, in *printing*, a descriptive headline put continuously at the top of pages of type. Also called *running head-line*.—**Running toad.** Same as *natterjack*.

running (run'ing), *prep.* [Prop. ppr., with *on* or *toward* understood. Cf. *rising*, *p. a.*, 3, in a somewhat similar use.] Approaching; going on. [Colloq.]

> I hae been your gudwife
> These nine years, *running* ten.
> *Laird of Wariestoun* (Child's Ballads, III. 112).

running-gear (run'ing-gēr), *n.* 1. The wheels and axles of a vehicle, and their attachments, as distinguished from the body; all the working parts of a locomotive.—2. Same as *running rigging*. See *rigging*2.

runningly (run'ing-li), *adv.* Continuously; without pause or hesitation.

> Played I not off-hand and *runningly*,
> Just now, your masterpiece, hard number twelve?
> *Browning*, Master Hugues of Saxe-Gotha.

running-rein (run'ing-rān), *n.* A driving-rein which is passed over pulleys on the headstall to give it increased freedom of motion. Such reins are sometimes passed over sheaves on the bit, and made to return up the cheek, in order to pull the bit up into the angle of the mouth.

running-roll (run'ing-rōl), *n.* In *plate-glass manuf.*, a brass cylinder used to spread the plastic glass over the casting-table.

running-string (run'ing-string), *n.* A cord, tape, or braid passed through an open hem at the top of a bag or anything which it is desirable to draw tight at pleasure.

running-thrush (run'ing-thrush), *n.* A disease in the feet of horses. See *thrush*2.

running-trap (run'ing-trap), *n.* A depressed U-shaped section in a pipe, which allows the free passage of fluid, but always remains full whatever the state of the pipe, so that it forms a seal against the passage of gases.

runnion†, *n.* Same as *ronion*.

runologist (rö-nol'ō-jist), *n.* [< *runology* + *-ist*.] One who is versed in runology; a student of runic remains.

> The advanced school of Scandinavian *runologists* holds that the Runic Futhork of twenty-four letters is derived from the Latin alphabet as it existed in the early days of Imperial Rome. *Athenæum*, June 28, 1879, p. 818.

runology (rö-nol'ō-ji), *n.* [< NL. *runa*, rune, + Gr. -λογία, < λέγειν, speak: see *-ology*.] The study of runes.

> Of late, however, great progress has been made in *runology*. *Archæologia*, XLIII. 98.

run-out (run'out), *n.* The extent of a run of fish: as, the *run-out* reaches 20 miles. *J. W. Milner.* [Lake Michigan.]

runrig (run'rig), *n.* [< *run*1 + *rig*1.] A ridge or rig (that is, a strip of ground) in land so divided that alternate rigs belong to different owners; hence, the system of land-holding by alternate rigs.

> We may assume that wherever in Ireland the land was cultivated in modern times according to the rundale or *runrig* system, the custom arose from the previous existence of co-partnerships.
> *W. K. Sullivan*, Introd. to O'Curry's Anc. Irish, p. clix.

> The face of a hill-side in Derbyshire was laid out in strips of garden land with ridges of turf dividing. These the holders of the land called "rigs"; the long narrow ones *run-rigs*; and one, wide, which intersected the rise at a right angle, the "cart-rig."
> *N. and Q.*, 7th ser., V. 374.

Runrig lands, in Scotland and Ireland, lands held by runrig.

runt1 (runt), *n.* [Early mod. E. also *ront*; a dial. word, perhaps orig. a var. of *rind*, a Sc. form (= D. *rund* = G. *rind*) of *rither*, *rother*: see *rother*2. The later senses may be of different origin.] 1. A young ox or cow; a steer or heifer; also, a stunted ox or cow, or other undersized animal; one below the usual size and strength of its kind; especially, the smallest or weakest one of a litter of pigs or puppies. Compare def. 4.

> *Giouenco*, a steere, a *runt*, a bullocke, a yeereling, a weanling. *Florio.*

> They say she has mountains to her marriage,
> She's full of cattle, some two thousand *runts*.
> *Middleton*, Chaste Maid, iv. 1.

> He was mounted on a little *runt* of a pony, so thin and woe-begone as to be remarkable among his kind.
> *The Century*, XXXVII. 909.

Hence—2. A short, stockish person; a dwarf.

> This overgrown *runt* has struck off his heels, lowered his foretop, and contracted his figure, that he might be looked upon as a member of this new-erected society [The Short Club]. *Addison*, Spectator, No. 108.

3†. A rude, ill-bred person; a boor or hoiden.

> Before I buy a bargain of such *runts*,
> I'll buy a college for bears, and live among 'em.
> *Fletcher*, Wit without Money, v. 2.

4. A breed of domestic pigeons. A single bird may weigh as much as 2¼ pounds.

> There are tame and wild pigeons; and of the tame, there be . . . *runts*, and carriers and croppers.
> *I. Walton*, Complete Angler, p. 112.

> While the *runt* is the weakest and most forlorn of pigs, by the contrariness which characterizes our fancier it is the name given to the largest and most robust among pigeons. *The Century*, XXXII. 107.

5. A stump of underwood; also, the dead stump of a tree. *Halliwell.* [Prov. Eng.]—6. The stalk or stem of a plant. [Prov. Eng. and Scotch.]

> For lapfu's large o' gospel kail
> Shall fill thy crib in plenty,
> An' *runts* of grace the pick an' wale,
> No gi'en by way o' dainty,
> But ilka day.
> *Burns*, The Ordination.

runt2 (runt), *n.* [A var. of *rump*.] The rump. *Halliwell.* [Prov. Eng.]

runtee†, *n.* [Amer. Ind.] A disk of shell used as an ornament by the Indians of Virginia in the seventeenth and eighteenth centuries.

> The boy wears a necklace of *runtees*.
> *Beverley*, Virginia, iii. ¶ 5.

runty (run'ti), *a.* [< *runt*1 + *-y*1.] 1. Stunted; dwarfish; little. [Prov. Eng. and U. S.]

> A brood of half-grown chickens picking in the grass, . . . and a *runty* pig tied to a "stob," were the only signs of thrift. *Harper's Mag.*, LXXIII. 696.

2. Boorish; surly; rude. *Halliwell.* [Prov. Eng.]

run-up (run'up), *n.* In *bookbinding*, the act of putting on a line, in finishing, by means of a roll running along the side of the back from the top to the bottom of the book.

runway (run'wā), *n.* The path or track over which anything runs; a passageway. Specifically—(*a*) The bed of a stream of water. (*b*) The beaten track of deer or other animals; a trail. Also *runaway*.

> The line of mounds overlooks the Grant river to the north, and Snake Hollow or Potosi to the south, and has a commanding position. It may have been used as an elevated *runway* or graded road designed for the pursuit of game.
> *Amer. Antiquarian*, XI. 385.

> Oftentimes drivers go out with dogs and make a wide circuit, while the hunters post themselves along the *runways* or beaten trails of the deer.
> *Tribune Book of Sports*, p. 431.

(*c*) A path made by domestic animals in going to and from an accustomed place of feeding, watering, etc. (*d*) In *lumbering*, a trough or channel on the surface of a declivity, down which logs are slid or run in places more or less inaccessible to horses or oxen. (*e*) One of the ways in the casing of a window for vertically sliding sashes. (*f*) *Theat.*, in the setting of scenery, a path or road, as upon a mountain-side or the face of a rock.

> If there is a "*runway*," which is an elevation like the rocky ascent in the second act of "Die Walküre," . . . it is "built" by the stage carpenters.
> *Scribner's Mag.*, IV. 444.

rupee (rö-pē'), *n.* [Formerly also *roopee*; = F. *roupie* = Sp. Pg. *rupia* = G. Dan. Sw. *rupie* =

Obverse. Reverse.
Rupee, 186-.—British Museum. (Size of the original.)

NGr. ῥούπι = Pers. *rūpiya*, < Hind. *rūpiya*, *rupiya*, *rupayā*, *rupaiya*, *rupaiyā*, a rupee, also coin, cash, specie, < *rūpā* (Pali *rūpi*), silver, < Skt. *rūpya*, silver, wrought silver or wrought gold, as adj. handsome, < *rūpa*, natural state, form, beauty (> Hind. *rūp*, form, beauty).] The standard unit of value in India; also, a current silver coin of India, valued normally at 2s., or about 48 United States cents. The relative value of Indian and English money varies with the price of silver, the rupee being sometimes worth 52 cents, sometimes only 38 cents or less, as has been the case for several years.

> They call the peeces of money *roopees*, of which there are some of divers values, the meanest worth two shillings and threepence, and the best two shillings and ninepence sterling. *Terry*, in Purchas, Pilgrimes, II. 1471.

> The nabob . . . is neither as wealthy nor as wicked as the jaundiced monster of romances and comedies, who purchases the estates of broken-down English gentlemen with *rupees* tortured out of bleeding rajahs.
> *Thackeray*, Newcomes, viii.

Rupelian (rö-pē'li-an), *n.* A division of the Oligocene in Belgium. It includes a series of clays and sands partly of marine and partly of brackish-water origin. The Rupelian lies above the Tongrian, which latter is a marine deposit, and is of the same age as the Egeln belt of the German Lower Oligocene.

rupellary† (rö'pe-lā-ri), *a.* [< L. **rupellus*, dim. of *rupes*, a rock, + *-ary*.] Rocky.

> In this *rupellary* nidary do the fowle lay eggs and breede. *Evelyn*, Diary, Feb. 27, 1644.

rupeoptereal (rö"pē-op-tē'rē-al), *n.* [Irreg. < L. *rupes*, a rock, + Gr. πτερόν, wing, + *-e-al*.] A bone of the batrachian skull, supposed to correspond to the proötic.

Rupert's drop (rö'pėrts drop). Same as *detonating bulb* (which see, under *detonating*).

rupestrine (rö-pes'trin), *a.* [< L. *rupes*, a rock, + *-trine*, as in *lacustrine*, *palustrine*, etc.] In *zoöl.* and *bot.*, rock-inhabiting; living or growing on or among rocks; rupicoline; saxicoline.

rupia (rö'pi-ä), *n.* [NL., prop. *rhypia*, < Gr. ῥύπος, dirt, filth.] A variety of the large flat pustular syphiloderm in which the crust is more or less distinctly conical and stratified: a use now obsolete.

rupial (rö'pi-al), *a.* [< *rupia* + *-al*.] Pertaining to, characterized by, or affected with rupia.

Rupicapra (rö-pi-kap'rä), *n.* [NL. (De Blainville), < L. *rupicapra*, a chamois, lit. 'rock-goat,' < *rupes*, a rock, + *capra*, a goat: see *caper*1.] A genus of antelopes, sometimes giving name to a subfamily *Rupicaprinæ*; the chamois. There is only one species, *R. tragus*. See *chamois*.

Rupicaprinæ (rö"pi-kap-rī'nē), *n. pl.* [NL., < *Rupicapra* + *-inæ*.] The chamois as a subfamily of *Bovidæ*. *Sir V. Brooke.*

rupicaprine (rö-pi-kap'rin), *a.* Pertaining to the chamois; belonging to the *Rupicaprinæ*, or having their characters.

> Chamois (Rupicapra tragus), the Gemse of the Germans, is the only Antelope found in Western Europe, and forms the type of the *Rupicaprine* or goat-like group of that family. *Encyc. Brit.*, V. 384.

Rupicola (rö-pik'ō-lä), *n.* [NL., < L. *rupes*, a rock, + *colere*, inhabit: see *culture*.] A genus

Cock of the Rock (*Rupicola crocea*).

of *Cotingidæ* or of *Pipridæ*, founded by Brisson in 1760, type of the subfamily *Rupicolinæ*; the rock-manikins, rock-cocks, or cocks of the rock, having the outer primary emarginate and attenuate toward the end. These singular birds have an erect compressed semicircular crest, and the plumage of the male is mostly flaming orange or blood-red. They are about 12 inches long, of large size for the group to which they belong, and very showy. They are confined to northern parts of South America. Three species have been recognized—*R. crocea*, *R. peruviana*, and *R. sanguinolenta*.

Rupicolinæ (rö"pi-kō-lī'nē), *n. pl.* [NL., < *Rupicola* + *-inæ*.] A subfamily of *Cotingidæ* or of *Pipridæ*, founded by Sclater in 1862 upon the genus *Rupicola*. It is a small group, combining to some extent characters of cotingas and pipras. The feet are syndactylous, and the tarsi pycnaspidean. The genus *Phœnicercus* is now commonly placed under *Rupicolinæ*.

rupicoline (rö-pik'ō-lin), *a.* [As *Rupicola* + *-ine*[1].] In *zoöl.* and *bot.*, rock-inhabiting; growing on rocks; living among rocks; saxicoline; rupestrine.

rupicolous (rö-pik'ō-lus), *a.* [As *Rupicola* + *-ous.*] Same as *rupicoline.*

Rüppell's griffin. See *griffin.*

Ruppia (rup'i-ä), *n.* [NL. (Linnæus, 1737), named after H. B. *Ruppius*, author (1718) of a flora of Jena.] A genus of monocotyledonous plants of the order *Naiadaceæ* and tribe *Potameæ.* It is distinguished from *Potamogeton*, the other genus of the tribe, by the absence of a perianth, and by the long-stalked fruits, and is characterized by spiked flowers composed of two opposite stamens or four one-celled and nearly sessile anthers, and four or more carpels each containing a single pendulous ovule. The carpels, at first nearly or quite sessile, become elevated on slender spirally twisted pedicels radiating from a long peduncle, each making in fruit an obliquely ovoid truncate nutlet with fleshy surface. The only certain species, *R. maritima*, known in America as *ditch-grass*, in Great Britain as *tassel-grass*, etc., is one of the very few flowering plants of marine waters, and is found throughout temperate and subtropical regions in salt-marshes, brackish ditches, and inlets of the sea. It grows in submerged tufts of thread-like forking and wiry stems from a filiform rootstock. It bears opposite and alternate leaves, which are long and bristle-shaped with a sheathing base, and inconspicuous flowers, usually two, in a terminal spike, at first covered by the sheathing leaf.

ruptile (rup'til), *a.* [< NL. **ruptilis*, < L. *rumpere*, pp. *ruptus*, break: see *rupture.*] In *bot.*, dehiscent by an irregular splitting or breaking of the walls; rupturing: said of seed-vessels.

ruption (rup'shon), *n.* [< OF. *ruption*, < L. *ruptio(n-)*, a breaking, < *rumpere*, pp. *ruptus*, break: see *rupture.*] A breach; a bursting open; rupture. *Cotgrave.*

> Plethora causes an extravasation of blood, by *ruption* or apertion. *Wiseman*, Surgery.

ruptive (rup'tiv), *a.* [< L. *rumpere*, pp. *ruptus*, break: see *rupture.*] Causing or tending to cause breakage. [Rare.]

> Certain breakages of this class may perhaps to some extent be accounted for by the action of a torsional *ruptive* force on rounding curves. *The Engineer*, LXIX. 492.

ruptuary (rup'tū-ā-ri), *n.*; pl. *ruptuaries* (-riz). [< ML. *rupturarius*, < *ruptura*, a field, a form of feudal tenure; cf. *roturier*, and see *rupture.*] A roturier; a member of the plebeian class, as contrasted with the nobles. [Rare.]

> The exclusion of the French *ruptuaries* ("roturiers," for history must find a word for this class when it speaks of other nations) from the order of nobility. *Chenevix.*

rupture (rup'tūr), *n.* [< OF. *rupture*, *rouppture*, *routure*, a rupture, breach, F. *rupture* = Sp. *ruptura*, *rotura* = Pg. *ruptura* = It. *rottura*, < L. *ruptura*, a breaking, rupture (of a limb or vein), in ML. also a road, a field, a form of feudal tenure, a tax, etc., < *rumpere*, pp. *ruptus*, break, burst; cf. Lith. *rupas*, rough, AS. *reófan*, Icel. *rjúfa*, break, reave, Skt. √ *rup*, *lup*, break, destroy, spoil. From the L. *rumpere* are also ult. E. *abrupt*, *corrupt*, *disrupt*, *erupt*, *interrupt*, *irruption*, *rote*[1], *rout*[3], *rout*[4], *route*[1], *routine*, *rut*[1]. To the same ult. root belong *reave*, *rob*[1], *robe*, *rove*[1], *rover*, etc., *loot.*] 1. The act of breaking or bursting; the state of being broken or violently parted: as, a *rupture* of the skin; the *rupture* of a vessel or fiber.

> Their brood as numerous hatch, from the egg that soon
> Bursting with kindly *rupture* forth disclosed
> Their callow young. *Milton*, P. L., vii. 419.

2. In *pathol.*, hernia, especially abdominal hernia.—3. A breach of peace or concord, either between individuals or between nations; open hostility or war between nations; a quarrel.

> Thus then wee see that our Ecclesiall and Politicall choyses may content and sort as well together without any *rupture* in the State as Christians and Freeholders. *Milton*, Reformation in Eng., ii.

> When the parties that divide the commonwealth come to a *rupture*, it seems every man's duty to choose a side. *Swift.*

> In honest words, her money was necessary to me; and in a situation like mine any thing was to be done to prevent a *rupture*. *Jane Austen*, Sense and Sensibility, xliv.

Moment of rupture. See *moment.*—**Plane of rupture**, the plane along which the tendency of a body (especially a mass of loose earth) under pressure to give way by sliding is the greatest.—**Radius of rupture.** See *mine*[2], 2 (*b*).—**Rupture of the choroid**, a rent of the choroidal tunic, due usually to mechanical injuries, as a blow, a gunshot wound, etc.=**Syn.** 1. *Breach*, etc. See *fracture.*

rupture (rup'tūr), *v.*; pret. and pp. *ruptured*, ppr. *rupturing.* [< *rupture*, *n.*] **I.** *trans.* 1. To break; burst; part by violence: as, to *rupture* a blood-vessel.—2. To affect with or cause to suffer from rupture or hernia.—3. To cause a break or severance of: as, to *rupture* friendly relations.

II. *intrans.* 1. To suffer a break or rupture; break.—2. In *bot.*, specifically, to dehisce irregularly; dehisce in a ruptile manner.

> When ripe the antheridia *rupture* or dehisce transversely at the top. *Le Maout and Decaisne*, Botany (trans.), p. 933.

rupturewort (rup'tūr-wėrt), *n.* A plant of the genus *Herniaria*, especially *H. glabra* of Europe and Asiatic Russia (see *burstwort*); also, an amarantaceous plant of the West Indies, *Alternanthera polygonoides*, somewhat resembling *Herniaria.*

rural (rö'ral), *a.* and *n.* [< OF. (and F.) *rural* = Pr. Sp. Pg. *rural* = It. *rurale*, < L. *ruralis*, rural, < *rūs* (*rūr-*), the country, perhaps contr. from **rovus* or **ravus*, and akin to Russ. *raviina*, a plain, Zend *ravan*, a plain, E. *room*: see *room*[1]. Hence ult. (from L. *rus*) also *rustic*, *rusticate*, etc., *roister*, *roist*, etc.] **I.** *a.* 1. Of or pertaining to the country, as distinguished from a city or town; belonging to or characteristic of the country.

> He spied his lady in rich array,
> As she walk'd ower a *rural* plain.
> *John Thomson and the Turk* (Child's Ballads, III. 352).

> The smell of grain, or tedded grass, or kine,
> Or dairy, each *rural* sight, each *rural* sound.
> *Milton*, P. L., ix. 451.

> The traveller passed rapidly . . . into a *rural* region, where the neighborhood of the town was only felt in the advantages of a near market for corn, cheese, and hay. *George Eliot*, Felix Holt, Int.

2. Pertaining to agriculture or farming: as, *rural* economy.—3. Living in the country; rustic.

> Where vertue is in a gentyl man, it is commonly myxte with more sufferance, more affabilitie and myldenes, than for the more parte it is in a person *rurall* or of a very base lynage. *Sir T. Elyot*, The Governour, i. 15.

> Here is a *rural* fellow,
> That will not be denied your highness' presence.
> *Shak.*, A. and C., v. 2. 233.

Rural dean, deanery, Dionysia, lock, etc. See the nouns.=**Syn.** 1. *Rural, Rustic, Pastoral, Bucolic.* *Rural* is always used in a good sense, and is applied chiefly to things: as, *rural* pleasures; *rural* scenery. *Rustic* is used in a good sense, but also has a sense implying a lack of the refinements of the town or city: as, *rustic* gallantry. *Pastoral* means belonging to a shepherd or his kind of life; *bucolic*, belonging to the care of cattle or to that kind of life. *Pastoral* is always used in a good sense; *bucolic* is now often used with a shade of contempt.

> For I have lov'd the *rural* walk through lanes
> Of grassy swarth, close cropp'd by nibbling sheep,
> And skirted thick with intertexture firm
> Of thorny boughs. *Cowper*, Task, i. 109.

> The *rural* lass,
> Whom once her virgin modesty and grace,
> Her artless manners and her neat attire,
> So dignified, that she was hardly less
> Than the fair shepherdess of old romance,
> Is seen no more. *Cowper*, Task, iv. 536.

[Cowper applies *rural* to persons as well as things.]

> What at first seemed *rustic* plainness now appears refined simplicity. *Goldsmith*, She Stoops to Conquer, v.

> Might we but hear
> The folded flocks penn'd in their wattled cotes,
> Or sound of *pastoral* reed with oaten stops.
> *Milton*, Comus, l. 345.

II.† *n.* A countryman; a rustic.

> Amongst *rurals* verse is scarcely found.
> *Middleton*, Father Hubbard's Tales.

> Beckon the *Rurals* in; the Country-gray
> Seldom ploughs treason.
> *Dekker and Ford*, Sun's Darling, ii.

Ruralest (rö-rā'lēz), *n. pl.* [NL. (Linnæus, 1758), pl. of L. *ruralis*, rural: see *rural.*] A family of butterflies, coming between the *Papilionidæ* and the *Nymphalidæ*, and including the *Lycæninæ* and the *Erycininæ.* They have six perfect legs in the females and four in the males.

Ruralia† (rö-rā'li-ä), *n. pl.* Same as *Rurales.*

ruralise, *v.* See *ruralize.*

ruralism (rö'ral-izm), *n.* [< *rural* + *-ism.*] 1. The state of being rural.—2. An idiom or expression peculiar to the country as opposed to the town. *Imp. Dict.*

ruralist (rö'ral-ist), *n.* [< *rural* + *-ist.*] One who leads a rural life.

> You have recalled to my thoughts an image which must have pleaded strongly with our Egyptian *ruralists* for a direct and unqualified adoration of the solar orb.
> *Coventry*, Philemon to Hydaspes, iii.

rurality (rö-ral'i-ti), *n.* [< F. *ruralité*, < ML. *ruralita(t-)s*, < L. *ruralis*, rural: see *rural.*] 1. The state or quality of being rural; ruralness. [Rare.]

> To see the country relapse into a state of arcadian *rurality*. *The American*, V. 97.

2. That which is rural; a characteristic of rural life; a rusticity. [Rare.]

> The old almanac-makers did well in wedding their pages with *ruralities.* *D. G. Mitchell*, Bound Together, iii.

ruralize (rö'ral-īz), *v.*; pret. and pp. *ruralized*, ppr. *ruralizing.* [< *rural* + *-ize.*] **I.** *trans.* To render rural; give a rural character or appearance to.

> The curling cloud
> Of city smoke, by distance *ruralized.*
> *Wordsworth*, Prelude, i.

> This tardy favorite of fortune, . . . with not a trace that I can remember of the sea, thoroughly *ruralized* from head to foot, proceeded to escort us up the hill.
> *The Century*, XXVII. 29.

II. *intrans.* To go into the country; dwell in the country; rusticate. *Imp. Dict.*

Also spelled *ruralise.*

rurally (rö'ral-i), *adv.* In a rural manner; as in the country: as, the cottage is *rurally* situated at some distance from the body of the town.

ruralness (rö'ral-nes), *n.* The character of being rural.

rurd†, *n.* A variant of *reard.*

ruricolist† (rö-rik'ō-list), *n.* [< L. *ruricola* (> F. *ruricole*), a dweller in the country (< *rus* (*rur-*), the country, + *colere*, dwell, inhabit, till), + *-ist.*] An inhabitant of the country; a rustic. *Bailey.*

ruridecanal (rö-ri-dek'a-nal), *a.* [< L. *rus* (*rur-*), the country, + LL. *decanus*, dean: see *decanal.*] Of or belonging to a rural dean or a rural deanery.

> My contention was, in a *ruridecanal* chapter lately held, that bishops suffragan ought thus to be addressed in virtue of their spiritual office. *N. and Q.*, 7th ser., VIII. 467.

rurigenous† (rö-rij'e-nus), *a.* [< L. *rurigena*, born in the country, < *rus* (*rur-*) + *-gena*, < *gignere*, be born: see *-genous.*] Born in the country. *Bailey*, 1727.

Rusa[1] (rö'sä), *n.* [NL. (Hamilton Smith, 1827), < Malay *rūsa*, a deer. Cf. *babirussa.*] 1. A genus of *Cervidæ* or subgenus of *Cervus*, containing the large East Indian stags, with cylindric antlers forked at the top and developing a

Sambur Deer (*Rusa aristotelis*).

brow-tine, and a tuft of hair on the hind legs; the rusine deer. They are related to such species as the elk or wapiti of America, and the hart or red deer of Europe. One of these large deer was known to Aristotle; but the species now called *Cervus* or *Rusa aristotelis* is the sambur, that commonly known as the rusa being *Cervus* or *Rusa hippelaphus.* Both are of great size and have a mane.

2. [*l. c.*] A species of this genus, especially *R. hippelaphus.*

rusa[2] (rö'sä), *n.* The lemon-grass or ginger-grass, *Andropogon Schœnanthus*, yielding rusa-oil. [East Indian.]

rusalka, *n.* [Russ.] In Russian folk-lore, a water-nymph.

> Mermaids and mermen . . . have various points of resemblance to the vodyany or water-sprite and the *rusalka* or stream-fairy of Russian mythology.
> *Encyc. Brit.*, XVI. 39.

> Rivers . . . are supposed to be the especial resort of the *Rusalkas* or water-nymphs. Dressed in green leaves, they will sit on the banks combing out their flowing locks. Their strength is in their hair, and if it becomes dry, they die. *A. J. C. Hare*, Studies in Russia, viii.

rusa-oil (rö'sä-oil), *n.* The oil of ginger-grass. See *ginger-grass* and *Andropogon.*

Ruscus (rus'kus), *n.* [NL. (Tournefort, 1700), < L. *ruscum*, also *rustum*, butcher's-broom: see rush1.] A genus of monocotyledonous plants of the order *Liliaceæ* and tribe *Asparageæ*. It is characterized by diœcious flowers, with the segments separate, the stamens with their filaments united into an urn-like body which bears three sessile anthers, and a roundish or oblong and one-celled ovary with two ovules, maturing two hemispherical seeds, or only a single globose one. There are 3 species, natives of Europe and the whole Mediterranean region, extending from Madeira to the Caucasus. They are erect, branching, half-woody plants, bearing, instead of leaves, alternate or scattered acute ovate and leaf-like branches (cladodia), which are rigidly coriaceous and lined with numerous parallel or somewhat netted veins, and are solitary in the axils of small dry scales which represent the true leaves. The small flowers are clustered upon the upper faces, or by twisting the lower faces, of the cladodia at the end of a rib-like adnate pedicel, and are followed by globose pulpy berries. *R. aculeatus* is the common butcher's-broom, also called *kneeholly* or *kneeholder*, *Jews'-* or *shepherd's-myrtle*, etc., an evergreen bush ornamental when studded with its red berries. *R. Hypophyllum* and *R. Hypoglossum* are dwarf species, also called *butcher's-broom*, and sometimes *double-tongue*. The rhizome is diuretic.

ruse1 (röz), *v. i.* [Also *roose (in dial. deriv. *roozeling*, sloping down), < ME. *reosen* (pret. *reas*, pl. *ruren*), < AS. *hreósan* (pret. *hreás*, pl. *hruron*, pp. *hroren*), fall, fall headlong, = Icel. *hrjósa* = Norw. *rysja* = Sw. *rysa*, shudder. For the form, cf. *chuse*, a spelling of *choose*, < AS. *ceósan*.] 1†. To fall. *Layamon*.—2. To slide down a declivity with a rustling noise. [Prov. Eng.]

ruse2† (röz), *v. i.* [< ME. *rusen*, < OF. *ruser*, *reüser*, refuse, recoil, retreat, escape, use tricks for escaping, F. *ruser* = Pr. *rahusar* (ML. *rusare*), < L. *recusare*, refuse: see *recuse*.] To give way; fall back; retreat; use tricks for the purpose of escaping.

As soone as Gawein was come he be-gan to do so well that the Saisnes *rused* and lefte place. *Merlin* (E. E. T. S.), ii. 288.

At the laste
This harte *rused* and staal away
Fro alle the houndes a prevy way.
Chaucer, Death of Blanche, l. 381.

ruse2 (röz), *n.* [< F. *ruse*, OF. *ruse*, a trick, < *ruser*, trick: see *ruse2*, *v.*] The use of artifice or trickery; also, a stratagem.

I might . . . add much concerning the Wiles and *Ruses* which these timid Creatures make use of to save themselves. *Ray*, Works of Creation, p. 137.

The effective action of cavalry as cavalry depends on *ruse*, on surprise, on skilful manœuvring, and on the impetuous power and moral effect of the man and horse, glued to one another as though they together formed the old ideal of the arm, the centaur. *Encyc. Brit.*, XXIV. 358.

Colonel Deveaux . . . secured the capitulation of the Spanish garrison by a boldly designed and well-executed military *ruse*. *Fortnightly Rev.*, N. S., XXXIX. 175.

She has only one string of diamonds left, and she fears that Chárudatta [her husband] will not accept it. . . . She sends for Maitreya, and induces him to palm it off on Chárudatta as a gift which he [Maitreya] had himself received in alms. The *ruse* was successful. Chárudatta accepts the diamonds, but with great reluctance. *Wheeler*, Hist. India, iii. 293.

Ruse de guerre, a trick of war; a stratagem. =**Syn.** *Manœuver*, *Trick*, etc. See *artifice* and *stratagem*.

ruse3, *v. t.* A Middle English or dialectal form of roose. *Cath. Ang.*

ruset-offal (rö'set-of"al), *n.* Kip or calf-curried leather. *Simmonds.*

rush1 (rush), *n.* [E. dial. also *rish*, *resh*, transposed *rix*; < ME. *rusche*, *rische*, *risshe*, *resche*, *reshe*, *resse*, < AS. *risce*, *resce*, *rysc*, *risc*, transposed *rixe* = D. *rusch* = MLG. *rusch*, *risch*, LG. *rusch*, *rusk*, *risch* = MHG. *rusche*, *rusch*, G. *rausch*, *rusch*, *risch*, a rush; prob. < L. *ruscum*, also *rustum*, butcher's-broom; perhaps, with formative *-cum* (see *-ic*), < *rus-* = Goth. *raus*, a reed (> OF. *ros*, dim. *rosel*, F. *roseau* = Pr. *raus*, dim. *rauzel*, *rauzeu*, a reed), = OHG. *rôr*, MHG. *rôr*, G. *rohr* = D. *roer* = Icel. *reyr* = Sw. Dan. *rör* (not in AS.), a reed. Cf. *bulrush*.] 1. Any plant belonging to the order *Juncaceæ*, especially a plant of the genus *Juncus*; also extended to some sedges (*Carex*), horsetails (*Equisetum*), and a few other plants. The typical rush is *Juncus effusus*, the common or soft rush, marked by its dense clump of slender cylindrical leafless stems, 2 or 3 feet high, from matted creeping rootstocks, some of the stems barren, the others producing from one side a close panicle of greenish or brownish flowers. It is found in wet places nearly throughout the northern hemisphere and in many parts of the southern. Very common in North America is *J. tenuis*, a smaller wiry species growing among grass, and especially in old roads and cow-paths. (See *Juncus*, and phrases below.) Rushes were formerly used to strew floors by way of covering.

Let wantons light of heart
Tickle the senseless *rushes* with their heels.
Shak., R. and J., i. 4. 36.

Why, pretty soul, tread softly, and come into this room; here be *rushes*, you need not fear the creaking of your cork shoes. *Dekker and Webster*, Westward Ho, ii. 2.

From the indelicate and filthy habits of our forefathers, carpets would have been a grievous nuisance; whereas *rushes*, which concealed the impurities with which they were charged, were, at convenient times, gathered up and thrown into the streets, where they only bred a general plague, instead of a particular one.
Gifford, Note to B. Jonson's Every Man out of his [Humour, iii. 3.

A flat malarian world of reed and *rush!*
Tennyson, Lover's Tale, iv.

2†. A wick. Compare *rush-candle*. *Baret.* (*Halliwell*).—3. Figuratively, anything weak, worthless, or of trivial value; the merest trifle; a straw.

Heo that ben curset in constorie counteth hit not at a *rusche*. *Piers Plowman* (A), iii. 137.

And if he myght stonde in so good a case,
Hir to reioyse and haue hir atte his wissh,
Of all his payne he wold not sett a *rissh*.
Generydes (E. E. T. S.), l. 1680.

I would not, my good people! give a *rush* for your judgment. *Sterne*, Tristram Shandy, ix. 17.

4. A small patch of underwood. *Halliwell.* [Prov. Eng.]—**Bald rush**, a plant of the American cyperaceous genus *Psilocarya*.—**Dutch rush.** See *scouring-rush*.—**Field-rush.** See *wood-rush*.—**Flowering rush**, an aquatic plant, *Butomus umbellatus*, of the *Alismaceæ*, found through temperate Europe and Asia. It has long narrow triangular leaves, and a scape from 2 to 4 feet high, bearing an umbel of twenty or thirty showy pink flowers, each an inch in diameter. An old name is *water-gladiole*.—**Hare's-tail rush.** See *hare's-tail*.—**Heath-rush**, an Old World species, *Juncus squarrosus*, growing on moors and heaths.—**Horned rush.** See *Rhynchospora*.—**Spike-rush.** See *Eleocharis*.—**Sweet-rush.** (*a*) Any plant of the genus *Cyperus*. (*b*) The lemon-grass or ginger-grass, *Andropogon Schœnanthus*.—**Toad-rush**, a low, tufted, pale-colored species, *Juncus bufonius*, distributed over a great part of the world.—**To wed** or **marry with a rush ring**, to marry in jest, but sometimes implying an evil purpose.

And Tommy was so [kind] to Katty,
And *wedded* her *with a rush ring*.
Winchest. Wedding, Pills to Purge Mel., I. 276. (*Nares.*)

I'll crown thee with a garland of straw then,
And I'll *marry* thee *with a rush ring*.
Sir W. Davenant, The Rivals, v.

(See *nut-rush*, *scouring-rush*, and *wood-rush*.)

rush1† (rush), *v. i.* [Early mod. E. also *ryshe*; < *rush1*, *n.*] To gather rushes.

I *ryshe*, I gather russhes; . . . Go no more a *ryshynge*.
Palsgrave, L'Éclaircissement de la Langue Française, [p. 692.

rush2 (rush), *v.* [< ME. *rushen*, *ruschen* = MLG. *rûschen*, LG. *rusken*, rush, clatter, rustle, = D. *ruischen*, rush, = MHG. *rûschen*, *riuschen*, G. *rauschen*, rush, roar, = OSw. *ruska*, rush, shake, Sw. *ruska*, shake, tremble, = Icel. *ruska*, shake violently, = Dan. *ruske*, shake, pull, twitch; cf. AS. *hriscan*, make a noise; appar., with formative *-k*, from a simple verb represented by OSw. *rusa*, rush, shake; perhaps ult. from the root of L. *rudere*, make a noise, etc.; cf. *rumor*.] I. *intrans.* 1. To move or drive forward with impetuosity, violence, or tumultuous rapidity.

The ryalle raunke stele to his hertte rynnys,
And he *rusches* to the erthe, rewthe es the more!
Morte Arthure (E. E. T. S.), l. 2241.

Every one turned to his course, as the horse *rusheth* into the battle. *Jer.* viii. 6.

They all *rush* by,
And leave you hindmost.
Shak., T. and C., iii. 3. 150.

The combat deepens. On, ye brave,
Who *rush* to glory or the grave!
Campbell, Hohenlinden.

2. To move or act with undue eagerness, or without due deliberation and preparation; hurry: as, to *rush* into business or politics.

O that my head were a fountain of tears, to weep for and bewail the stupidity, yea, the desperate madness of infinite sorts of people that *rush* upon death, and chop into hell blindling. *Rev. S. Ward*, Sermons, p. 57.

Fools *rush* in where angels fear to tread.
Pope, Essay on Criticism, l. 625.

3. In *foot-ball*, to fill the position of a rusher.

In *rushing*, as well as in following or heading off, when the "backs" or "half-backs" come together, the front lines get the most shocks. *Sci. Amer.*, N. S., LIX. 304.

4. To take part in a college rush. See *rush2*, *n.*, 5. [U. S.]

"Hazing," *rushing*, secret societies, society initiations and badges, . . . are unknown at Oxford and Cambridge.
N. A. Rev., CXXVI. 236.

II. *trans.* 1. To cause to rush; cause to go swiftly or violently; drive or thrust furiously; hence, to force impetuously or hastily; hurry; overturn.

Of alle his ryche castelles *rusche* doune the wallez;
I salle noghte lete in Paresche, by processe of tyme.
Morte Arthure (E. E. T. S.), l. 1330.

He pull'd him down upon his knee,
And *rushed* off his helm.
Sir Lancelot du Lake (Child's Ballads, I. 60).

When the whole force of the wind driveth to one place, there being no contrary motion to let or hinder it, many hills and buildings have been *rushed* down by this kind of earthquake. *N. Morton*, New England's Memorial, p. 392.

You present rather a remarkable spectacle, inasmuch as you are *rushing* a bill through here without knowing what it contains. *Congressional Record*, XXI. 7758.

Specifically—2. In *foot-ball*, to force by main strength toward the goal of one's opponents: said of the ball.—3. To secure by rushing. [Colloq.]

Peeresses . . . occupied every seat, and even *rushed* the reporters' gallery, three reporters only having been fortunate enough to take their places before the rush.
W. Besant, Fifty Years Ago, p. 137.

4. To cause to hasten; especially, to urge to undue haste; drive; push. [Colloq.]

Nearly all [telegraph] operators, good and bad, are vain of their abilities to send rapidly, and nearly all are ambitious to send faster than the operator at the receiving station can write it down, or in other words to *rush* him.
Elect. Rev. (Amer.), XV. xiv. 10.

rush2 (rush), *n.* [< *rush2*, *v.*] 1. A driving forward with eagerness and haste; a motion or course of action marked by violent or tumultuous haste: as, a *rush* of troops; a *rush* of winds.

A train of cars was just ready for a start; the locomotive was fretting and fuming, like a steed impatient for a headlong *rush*. *Hawthorne*, Seven Gables, xvii.

His panting breath told of the *rush* he had actually made. *Mrs. Oliphant*, Poor Gentleman, xxviii.

2. An eager demand; a run.

There was a slight boom in the mining market, and a bit of a *rush* on American rails.
Nineteenth Century, XXVI. 854.

3. In *foot-ball*, a play by which one of the contestants forces his way with the ball through the line of his opponents toward their goal.—4. A very successful passing of an examination, or a correct recitation. [College slang, U. S.]—5. A scrimmage between classes or bodies of students, such as occurs at some American colleges. [U. S.]—6. Extreme urgency of affairs; urgent pressure; such a quantity or quality of anything as to cause extraordinary effort or haste: as, a *rush* of business. [Colloq.]—7. A stampede, as of cattle, horses, etc. [Australian.]

As they discuss the evening meal they discuss also the likelihood of a quiet camp or a *rush* of it.
A. C. Grant, Bush Life in Queensland, II. 124.

8. A company; a flock or flight, as of birds.

The wild-fowler's and sportsman's terms for companies of various birds are as under:— . . . Of Dunbirds, a "flight," or "*rush*." *W. W. Greener*, The Gun, p. 538.

9. In *mining* or *blasting*, same as *spire*.—10. A feast or merrymaking. *Halliwell.* [Prov. Eng.]—**Cane-rush**, a rush between the freshmen and sophomores of an American college or academy for the possession of a cane, carried in defiance of custom by one of the freshmen. That class wins which, after a given time, has possession of the cane, or has the larger number of men with their hands on it.—**Rush of blood to** (the head, etc.), sudden hyperemia of.

rush-bearing (rush'bãr"ing), *n.* A country wake or feast of dedication, when the parishioners strew the church with rushes and sweet-smelling flowers; also, the day of the festival, and the rushes and flowers themselves. [Prov. Eng.]

In Westmoreland, Lancashire, and districts of Yorkshire, there is still celebrated between hay-making and harvest a village fête called the *Rush-bearing*.
Quoted in *Chambers's Book of Days*, I. 506.

rush-bottomed (rush'bot"omd), *a.* Having a bottom or seat made with rushes: as, a *rush-bottomed* chair.

rush-broom (rush'bröm), *n.* See *Viminaria* and *Spartium*.

rush-buckler† (rush'buk"lėr), *n.* A bullying, violent fellow; a swash-buckler.

Take into this number also their [gentlemen's] servants: I mean all that flock of stout bragging *rushbucklers*.
Sir T. More, Utopia (tr. by Robinson), ii. 4.

rush-candle (rush'kan"dl), *n.* A light made by stripping a dried rush of all its bark except one small strip, which holds the pith together, and dipping it repeatedly in tallow. Rush-candles, being long and slender, are used with the clip-candlestick. Also *rushlight*.

And be it moon, or sun, or what you please:
An if you please to call it a *rush-candle*,
Henceforth I vow it shall be so for me.
Shak., T. of the S., iv. 5. 14.

Some gentle taper,
Though a *rush-candle* from the wicker hole
Of some clay habitation. *Milton*, Comus, l. 338.

rush-daffodil (rush'daf"ō-dil), *n.* See *daffodil*.

rushed (rusht), *a.* [< *rush1*, *n.*, + *-ed2*.] Strewed with or abounding in rushes.

As slow he winds in museful mood,
Near the *rush'd* marge of Cherwell's flood.
T. Warton, Odes, xi.

And *rushed* floors, whereon our children play'd.
J. Baillie.

rusher[1]† (rush'ėr), *n.* [< *rush*[1] + *-er*[1].] One who strews rushes on the floors at dances.

Their pipers, fiddlers, *rushers*, puppet-masters,
Jugglers, and gipsies. *B. Jonson*, New Inn, v. 1.

rusher[2] (rush'ėr), *n.* [< *rush*[2] + *-er*[1].] 1. One who rushes; one who acts with undue haste and violence.—2. Specifically, in *foot-ball*, a player whose special function it is to force the ball toward his opponents' goal, prevent it from being kicked or brought toward his own, and protect the backs while they kick or run with the ball. When eleven players are on each side, the rushers are known, according to their positions in the rush-line, as *right end, right tackle, right guard, center rusher, left guard, left tackle, left end.* See *foot-ball.* Also called *forward.*
3. A go-ahead person; a rustler. [Colloq.]

The pretty girl from the East is hardly enough of a *rusher* to please the young Western masculine taste. *The Century*, XXXVIII. 874.

rush-grass (rush'grȧs), *n.* Any one of certain grasses formerly classed as *Vilfa*, now included in *Sporobolus.* They are wiry grasses, with their panicles more or less included in the leaf-sheaths, thus having a slightly rush-like appearance.

rush-grown (rush'grōn), *a.* Overgrown with rushes.

As by the brook, that ling'ring laves
Yon *rushgrown* moor with sable waves.
T. Warton, Odes, vi.

rush-holder (rush'hōl"dėr), *n.* A clip-candlestick used for rushlights. It is sometimes made small to stand upon the table, sometimes arranged to hang upon the wall, and sometimes made four feet or more high and intended to stand upon the floor.

rushiness (rush'i-nes), *n.* The state of being rushy, or abounding with rushes.

rushing[1] (rush'ing), *n.* [Compare *rush*[2], 10.] A refreshment. *Halliwell.* [Prov. Eng.]

rushing[2] (rush'ing), *n.* [Verbal n. of *rush*[2], *v.*] A rush.

All down the valley that night there was a *rushing* as of a smooth and steady wind descending towards the plain. *R. L. Stevenson*, Will o' the Mill.

rushlight (rush'līt), *n.* A rush-candle.

He had a great red pipe in his mouth, and was smoking, and staring at the *rushlight*, in a state of enviable placidity. *Dickens*, Pickwick, xliv.

Day had not yet begun to dawn, and a *rushlight* or two burned in the room. *Charlotte Brontë*, Jane Eyre, v.

rush-like (rush'līk), *a.* Resembling a rush; hence, weak.

Who thought it not true honour's glorious prize,
By nimblie cap'ring in a daintie dance, . . .
Ne yet did seeke their glorie to aduance
By only tilting with a *rush-like* lance.
Mir. for Mags., p. 788.

rush-lily (rush'lil"i), *n.* A plant of the more showy species of blue-eyed grass, *Sisyrinchium*, especially *S. grandiflorum*, a species with bright-yellow flowers, native in northwestern America, occasionally cultivated.

rush-line (rush'līn), *n.* The line or row in which the rushers in foot-ball stand when in position; the rushers collectively.

rush-nut (rush'nut), *n.* A plant, *Cyperus esculentus.* The tubers, called by the French *souchet comestible* or *amande de terre*, are used as food in the south of Europe, and have been proposed as a substitute, when roasted, for coffee and cocoa.

rush-stand (rush'stand), *n.* Same as *rush-holder.*

rush-stick (rush'stik), *n.* Same as *rush-holder.*

rush-toad (rush'tōd), *n.* The natterjack, *Bufo calamita.*

rushy (rush'i), *a.* [< *rush*[1] + *-y*[1].] 1. Abounding with rushes.

Met we on hill, in dale, forest, or mead,
By paved fountain or by *rushy* brook.
Shak., M. N. D., ii. 1. 84.

Beside some water's *rushy* brink
With me the Muse shall sit.
Gray, Ode on the Spring.

2. Made of rushes.

My *rushy* couch and frugal fare.
Goldsmith, The Hermit.

rushy-fringed (rush'i-frinjd), *a.* Fringed with rushes; rushy.

By the *rushy-fringed* bank,
Where grows the willow, and the osier dank,
My sliding chariot stays.
Milton, Comus, l. 890.

rushy-mill† (rush'i-mil), *n.* A toy mill-wheel made of rushes and placed in running water.

The god . . . solemnely then swore
His spring should flow some other way: . . .
Nor drive the *rushy-mills* that in his way
The shepheards made: but rather for their lot,
Send them red waters that their sheepe should rot.
W. Browne, Britannia's Pastorals, i. 1.

rusine (rö'sin), *a.* [< *Rusa*[1] + *-ine*[1].] Resembling or related to the rusa, or having its kind of antler; belonging to the group of deer which *Rusa* represents. See cut under *Rusa*[1].

rusk (rusk), *n.* [Prob. < Sp. *rosca*, a screw, anything round and spiral (*rosca de pan*, or simply *rosca*, a roll or twist of bread; cf. *rosca de mar*, sea-rusk, a kind of biscuit; dim. *rosquete*, a pancake, *rosquilla*, roll of bread, etc.), = Pg. *rosca*, a screw, the winding or wriggling of a serpent; origin unknown.] 1†. A kind of light, hard cake or bread, as for ships' stores. [Eng.]

I . . . filled a basket full of white *Ruske* to carie a shoare with me, but before I came to the Banio the Turkish boyes had taken away almost all my bread.
Hakluyt's Voyages, II. 186.

The lady sent me divers presents of fruit, sugar, and *rusk.* *Raleigh.*

2. Bread or cake dried and browned in the oven, and reduced to crumbs by pounding, the crumbs being usually eaten with milk. [New Eng.]—3. A kind of light cake; a kind of soft, sweetened biscuit.

It is pleasant to linger on the hills and enjoy stakantchai and fresh *rusks* and butter with the natives, till the blue shadows have gathered over the glorious distant city.
A. J. C. Hare, Studies in Russia, vi.

rusk (rusk), *v. t.* [< *rusk*, *n.*] To make rusk of; convert, as bread or cake, into rusk. See *rusk*, *n.*, 2. [New Eng.]

ruskie (rus'ki), *n.* [Perhaps of Celtic origin (see *ruche*), or akin to *rush*[1].] Any receptacle or utensil made of twigs, straw, or the like, as a basket, a hat, or a beehive.

rusma (ruz'mạ̈), *n.* See *rhusma.*

rusot, ruswut (rus'ọt, rus'wut), *n.* In India, an extract from the wood or roots of different species of *Berberis*, used with opium and alum as an application in conjunctivitis. It is supposed to be the same as the lycium of the ancients. See *Berberis.*

Russ (rus), *a.* and *n.* [Early mod. E. *Russe*; < F. *Russe* = Sp. *Ruso* = Pg. It. *Russo* = G. *Russe* = D. *Rus* = Icel. (pl.) *Russar* = Dan. *Russer* = Sw. *Ryss* (NL. *Russus*), Russ, Russian, < Russ. *Rusi*, the Russ, Russia (cf. *Rossiya*, Russia), = Pol. *Rus*; Hung. *Orosz*, Russ; Finn. *Ruotsi*, Sweden.] I. *a.* Of or pertaining to the Russ or Russians.

II. *n.* 1. The language of the Russ or Russians.—2. *sing.* and *pl.* A native or the natives of Russia. See *Russian*, which is the customary form.

The Tartar sent the *Russe* a knife, therewith to stab himselfe. *Purchas*, Pilgrimage, p. 420.

The *Russe* of better sort goes not out in Winter but on his Sled. *Milton*, Hist. Moscovia, i. 481.

Russ. An abbreviation of *Russia* or *Russian.*

russell (rus'el), *n.* [< OF. *roussel*, F. *rousseau*, reddish, dim. of *roux*, reddish, russet, < L. *russus*, red: see *red*[1], and cf. *russet*, *russeting.* *Russel*, like F. *rousseau*, has become a name (*Russel*, *Russell*; cf. *Lovel*, < OF. *lovel*, a wolf).] 1. A fox: in allusion to its reddish color.

Daun *Russel*, the fox, sterte up at oones,
And by the garget hente Chauntecleer.
Chaucer, Nun's Priest's Tale, l. 514.

2. *pl.* A stuff. (*a*) In the sixteenth century, a material mentioned as made out of England from English wool. (*b*) In the eighteenth century, a twilled woolen material, used for garments. *Dict. of Needlework.*

russel-cord (rus'el-kôrd), *n.* A kind of rep made of cotton and wool, or sometimes wholly of wool. *Dict. of Needlework.*

Russell's process. See *process.*

russet (rus'et), *a.* and *n.* [< ME. *russet*, < OF. *rousset* (= It. *rossetto*), russet, brown, ruddy, hence also red wheat, etc., fem. *roussette*, a russet apple, a coarse brown cloth, russet (ML. *russetum*), dim. of *roux*, fem. *rousse*, reddish, = Pr. Cat. *ros* = Pg. *ruço* = It. *rosso*, < L. *russus*, reddish (cf. L. *russatus*, clothed in red); put for **rudtus*, < √ *rudh*, red: see *red*[1].] I. *a.* 1. Of a reddish-brown color: applied also to some light browns not reddish. When said of leather, it includes nearly every variety browner than red Russia; but it does not include gray, nor pure buff. When applied to armor, a coppery red is generally meant—a kind of finish common in the sixteenth century.

But, look, the morn, in *russet* mantle clad,
Walks o'er the dew of yon high eastward hill.
Shak., Hamlet, i. 1. 166.

His attire was a doublet of *russet* leather, like those worn by the better sort of country folk.
Scott, Kenilworth, iii.

The mellow year is hasting to its close; . . .
The *russet* leaves obstruct the straggling way
Of oozy brooks. *H. Coleridge*, November.

2. Made of russet; hence, coarse; homespun; rustic: a use derived from the general color of homespun cloth.

Though we be very poor and have but a *russet* coat, yet we are well. *Latimer*, Misc. Sel.

In *russet* yeas, and honest kersey noes.
Shak., L. L. L., v. 2. 413.

His Muse had no objection to a *russet* attire; but she turned with disgust from the finery of Guarini, as tawdry and as paltry as the rags of a chimney-sweeper on May-day. *Macaulay*, Milton.

3. Made of russet leather.

The minstrel's garb was distinctive. It was not always the short laced tunic, tight trousers, and *russet* boots, with a well plumed cap—which seems to be the modern notion of this tuneful itinerant.
Mayhew, London Labour and London Poor, I. 296.

Russet gown, a homespun or rustic gown; hence, one who wears such a gown; a country girl.

Squires come to Court some fine Town Lady, and Town Sparks to pick up a *Russet Gown*.
Quoted in *Ashton's* Social Life in Reign of Queen Anne, [II. 112.

She clad herself in a *russet gown*, . . .
With a single rose in her hair.
Tennyson, Lady Clare.

Russet leather. See *leather.*

II. *n.* 1. A reddish-brown color: a broad and vague term, formerly applied to various shades of gray and brown or ash-color, sometimes used restrictively, but in no well-settled sense.

Grigietto, a fine graie or sheepes *russet*.
Florio, Worlde of Wordes (1598).

Russet was the usual colour of hermits' robes; Cutts, Scenes and Characters of the Middle Ages, p. 97.
Piers Plowman, (ed. Skeat), II. 132, notes.

Blacks, *russets*, and blues obtain in place of the clear silvery greys, pure whites, and fine scarlet reds of other days. *Athenæum*, No. 3246, p. 56.

2. Coarse cloth, country-made and often homespun, used for the garments of peasantry and even of country people of some means: a term originally derived from the reddish-brown color of much cloth of this quality, and retained when the color was different, as gray or ash-colored.

Thei vsen *russet* also somme of this freres,
That bitokneth trauaile & trewthe opon erthe.
Piers Plowman's Crede (E. E. T. S.), l. 719.

Though your clothes are of light Lincolne green,
And mine gray *russet*, and torne,
Yet it doth not you beseme
To doe an old man scorne.
Robin Hood and the Old Man (Child's Ballads, V. 258).

Her country *russet* was turn'd to silk and velvet,
As to her state agreed.
Patient Grissel (Child's Ballads, IV. 209).

3†. *pl.* Clothes of russet; especially, the garb of a shepherd.

There was many a frolic swain,
In fresh *russets* day by day,
That kept revels on the plain.
Drayton, Shepherd's Sirena.

He borrowed on the working daies
His holie *russets* oft.
Warner, Albion's England, iv. 27.

Let me alone to provide *russets*, crook, and tar-box.
Shirley, Love Tricks, iv. 5.

4. In *leather-manuf.*, leather finished, but not polished or colored, except as colored by the tanning liquor; russet leather.

They [skins] can be kept best in the state of finished *russet*, as it is called, previous to waxing.
Encyc. Brit., XIV. 387.

5. A kind of winter apple having a brownish color, rough skin, and characteristic flavor. Though no doubt named from its color, this is rather buff than russet, with a greenish bronze-like luster, very striking in some varieties.

Folks used to set me down among the simple ones, in my younger days. But I suppose I am like a Roxbury *russet*—a great deal the better, the longer I can be kept.
Hawthorne, Seven Gables, xxi.

russet (rus'et), *v. t.* [< *russet*, *a.*] To give a russet hue to; change into russet. [Rare.]

The summer ray
Russets the plain, inspiring Autumn gleams.
Thomson, Hymn, l. 96.

russeting† (rus'et-ing), *n.* [Also *russetting*, and in def. 3 *russetin*; < *russet* + *-ing*[1].] 1. Russet cloth.

He must chaunge his *russeting*
For satin and silke,
And he must weare no linnen shirt
That is not white as milke,
To come of a well borne familie.
Tarlton, Horse-loade of Fooles. (*Halliwell*.)

2. A person clothed in russet; a rustic; usually, an ignorant, clownish person. [Rare.]

Let me heare it, my sweet *russeting*.
Heywood, Fair Maid of the Exchange (Works, II. 57).

3. A russet apple.

Nor pippin, which we hold of kernel-fruits the king;
The apple orendge; then the savoury *russetting*.
Drayton, Polyolbion, xviii. 647.

I have brought thee . . . some of our country fruit, half a score of *russetings*. *Randolph*, Hey for Honesty, iii. 3.

russet-pated† (rus′et-pā″ted), *a.* Having a gray or ash-colored head or pate: used only in the following passage.

Russet-pated choughs, many in sort,
Rising and cawing at the gun's report.
Shak., M. N. D., iii. 2. 21.

russety (rus′et-i), *a.* [< *russet* + *-y*[1].] Of a russet color.

Russia (rush′ạ̈), *n.* [NL. *Russia* (Russ. *Rossiya*): see *Russ*.] Short for *Russia leather*.

Russia braid. 1. A kind of braid of mohair, or of wool and silk in imitation of it.—2. A fine silk braid used to decorate articles of dress.

Russia duck, leather, matting. See *duck*[4], *leather*, etc.

Russian (rush′ạn), *a.* and *n.* [< F. *russien*, < NL. *Russianus*, < *Russia* (Russ. *Rossiya*), Russia: see *Russia*, *Russ*.] **I.** *a.* Of or pertaining to Russia, an empire in eastern Europe with large possessions in northern and central Asia, or the Russians or their language.—**Russian architecture.** See *Russo-Byzantine*.—**Russian ashes**, a commercial name for crude potassium carbonate imported from Russia.—**Russian band.** See *Russian horn-band*.—**Russian bath.** See *bath*[1].—**Russian castor**, castor obtained from the Russian beaver, and considered as more valuable than the American product.—**Russian Church**, the national church of the Russians, and the dominant form of Christianity in the Russian empire. The Russian Church is a branch of the Orthodox Eastern Church, in full communion and doctrinal agreement with the Greek Church, but not subject to any Greek patriarchate. Christianity existed to some extent in earlier times in Russia, but was first permanently introduced, from Constantinople, by the great prince St. Vladimir, in 988. The seat of the metropolitans was at first at Kieff; it was transferred to Vladimir in 1299, and in 1388 to Moscow. In 1589 the metropolitan of Moscow was made patriarch, with the consent of the rest of the Eastern Church. In 1721, with the approval of the Greek patriarchs, the Holy Governing Synod succeeded to the power of the patriarch. The members of this synod are appointed by the emperor. Among them are a metropolitan as president, several other metropolitans and prelates, secular priests, and the procurator-general, a layman, representing the civil power. The bishops are all virtually equal in p we , though ranking as metropolitans, archbishops, and ordinary bishops. The Russian Church is the established church of the country; dissenters (see *Raskolnik*), as well as adherents of other religions, are tolerated, but are not allowed to proselytize. Sometimes called the *Russo-Greek Church*.—**Russian diaper**, diaper having a diamond pattern rather larger or more elaborate than the ordinary: it is made in both cotton and linen.—**Russian embroidery**, embroidery in simple and formal patterns, zigzags, frets, etc., especially that which is applied to washable materials, as towels, etc. Such embroidery, as originally practised by the Russian peasants, includes also the insertion of openwork patterns, strips of bright-colored material, and needlework representations of animals and the like—conventional but very decorative.—**Russian horn-band.** See *horn-band*.—**Russian isinglass**, isinglass prepared from the swimming-bladders of the Russian sturgeon, *Acipenser huso*.—**Russian musk**, musk obtained from Russia, and inferior to that which comes from China.—**Russian porcelain**, porcelain made in Russia, especially that of the imperial factory established by the czarina Elizabeth in 1756, and maintained by the sovereigns since that time. The mark is the initial of the reigning sovereign with a crown above it. The paste is very hard and of a bluish tinge.—**Russian sable.** See *sable*.—**Russian stitch**, in *crochet*. See *stitch*.—**Russian tapestry**, a stout material of hemp or of coarse linen, used for window-curtains, etc.—**Russian-tapestry work**, embroidery in crewels or other thread on Russian tapestry as a foundation. It is done rapidly, and is used for the borders of window-curtains, etc.

II. *n.* 1. A native or a citizen of Russia; a member of the principal branch of the Slavic race, forming the chief part of the population of European Russia, and the dominant people in Asiatic Russia.—2. A Slavic language, belonging to the southeastern branch (which includes also the Bulgarian). Its chief form is the Great Russian; other important dialects are Little Russian and White Russian. Abbreviated *Russ*.—**Great Russian.** (*a*) A member of the main stock of the Russian people, forming the bulk of the population in the northern and central parts of European Russia; the Great Russians have spread, however, into all regions of the empire. (*b*) The principal dialect of Russia, and the basis of the literary language.—**Little Russian.** (*a*) One of a race dwelling in southern and southwestern Russia, numbering about 14,000,000, and allied to the Great Russians. Members of this race in the Austrian empire are called *Ruthenians*. (*b*) The Russian dialect spoken by the Little Russians and Ruthenians.—**Red Russian.** (*a*) A member of a branch of the Little Russians dwelling in Galicia and the neighboring parts of Hungary and Russia. (*b*) The dialect of the Red Russians.—**White Russian.** (*a*) A member of a branch of the Russian family whose seat is in the western part of the empire, east of Poland. (*b*) The dialect of this branch.

Russianism (rush′an-izm), *n.* [< *Russian* + *-ism*.] Russian influence, tendencies, or characteristics *The American*, XII. 219.

Russianize (rush′an-īz), *v. t.*; pret. and pp. *Russianized*, ppr. *Russianizing*. [< *Russian* + *-ize*.] To impart Russian characteristics to.

The Tartar may learn the Russian language, but he does not on that account become *Russianized*.
D. M. Wallace, Russia, p. 157.

Russification (rus″i-fi-kā′shon), *n.* [< *Russify* + *-ation* (see *-fication*).] The act or process of Russianizing, or of bringing over to Russian forms, habits, or principles; also, annexation to the Russian empire.

The process of *Russification* may be likewise observed in the manner of building the houses and in the methods of farming, which plainly show that the Finnish races did not obtain rudimentary civilization from the Slavonians.
D. M. Wallace, Russia, p. 152.

The school is the great means used by the Russian Government for the so-called *Russification* of Poland.
Encyc. Brit., XIX. 311.

That the Turk has got to go is now hardly open to doubt, and in as far as British statesmanship can promote the Germanisation, as opposed to the *Russification*, of Turkey in Europe, our policy should be directed to that end. *Nineteenth Century*, XXI. 556.

Russify (rus′i-fī), *v. t.*; pret. and pp. *Russified*, ppr. *Russifying*. [< *Russ* (NL. *Russus*) + *-fy*.] To Russianize.

The aboriginal Meryas have been completely *Russified*.
Encyc. Brit., XXIV. 731.

Russniak (rus′ni-ak), *n.* [Little Russ. *Rusnak* (Hung. *Rusznják*): see *Russ*.] Same as *Ruthenian*, 1.

Russo-Byzantine (rus′ō-biz″an-tin), *a.* Noting the national art of Russia, and especially the characteristic architecture of Russia, which is

Russo-Byzantine Architecture.—Cathedral of the Assumption, Kremlin, Moscow.

based on the Byzantine, but evolved and differentiated in obedience to race characteristics. There is much sound art and construction in Russian architecture, despite the grotesque and fantastic characteristics of some examples.

Russo-Greek (rus′ō-grēk′), *a.* Of or pertaining to both the Russians and the Greeks.—**Russo-Greek Church.** See *Russian Church*, under *Russian*.

Russophile (rus′ō-fil), *n.* and *a.* [= F. *russophile*, < NL. *Russus*, Russ (see *Russ*), + Gr. φιλεῖν, love.] **I.** *n.* One who favors Russia or the Russians, or Russian policy, principles, or enterprises.

The offer is totally hollow, and one which cannot be accepted, even by the most willing *Russophile*.
C. Marvin, Gates of Herat, viii.

II. *a.* Favoring Russian methods or enterprises.

The so-called *Russophile* traders in politics.
C. Marvin, Russian Advance towards India, i.

Russophilism (rus′ō-fil-izm), *n.* [< *Russophile* + *-ism*.] The doctrines, sentiments, or principles of a Russophile.

Russophilist (rus′ō-fil-ist), *n.* [< *Russophile* + *-ist*.] Same as *Russophile*.

Russophobe (rus′ō-fōb), *n.* [NL., < *Russus*, Russ, + Gr. -φοβος, < φοβεῖσθαι, fear.] Same as *Russophobist*.

The unanimity of the condemnation of Russia on the part of the representative organs of public opinion indicates clearly enough that the union of Russophiles and *Russophobes* . . . has not been disrupted by the wrangles at home. *Contemporary Rev.*, L. 267.

Russophobia (rus-ō-fō′bi-ä), *n.* [< NL. *Russus*, Russ, + Gr. -φοβία, < φοβεῖσθαι, fear.] A dread of Russia or of Russian policy; a strong feeling against Russia or the Russians.

For some reason or other the *Russophobia* which prevalled so largely when first I began to take an interest in foreign affairs has gone out of fashion.
Nineteenth Century, XXI. 543.

Russophobism (rus′ọ-fō-bizm), *n.* [< *Russophobe* + *-ism*.] Same as *Russophobia*.

Equally guilty would be a blind, unreasoning *Russophobism* attributing sinister designs to every Russian advance. *Brit. Quarterly Rev.*, LXXXIII. 346.

Russophobist (rus′ō-fō-bist), *n.* [< *Russophobe* + *-ist*.] One who dreads the Russians or their policy; one whose feelings are strongly against Russia, its people, or its policy.

These opinions cannot but be so many red rags to English *Russophobists*. *C. Marvin*, Gates of Herat, p. 98.

russud (rus′ud), *n.* [< Hind. *rasad*, a progressive increase or diminution of tax, also the amount of such increase or diminution, orig. a store of grain provided for an army, < Pers. *rasad*, a supply of provisions.] In India, a progressively increasing land-tax.

Russula (rus′ụ-lạ̈), *n.* [NL. (Fries, 1836), so called in allusion to the color of the pileus in some species; fem. of LL. *russulus*, reddish, dim. of L. *russus*, red: see *russet*.] A genus of hymenomycetous fungi of the class *Agaricini*, differing from *Agaricus* by having the trama vesiculose and the lamellæ fragile, not filled with milk. The pileus is fleshy and convex; the stem is stout, polished, and spongy within; the veil is obsolete; the spores are white or pale-yellow, usually echinulate. There are many species, all growing on the ground. A few of the species are edible, but most are noxious.

rust[1] (rust), *n.* [< ME. *rust*, *rost*, *roust*, < AS. *rust* = OS. *rost* = D. *roest* = MLG. *rost*, *rust* = OHG. MHG. G. *rost* = Sw. *rost* = Dan. *rust* (not found in Goth., where *nidwa* is used), rust; with formative *-st*, < *rud-*, root of AS. *redd*, red, *rudu*, redness: see *red*[1]. Cf. Icel. *ryth*, rust, MHG. *rot*, rust, etc., OSlav. *rŭzda*, Lith. *rūdis*, Lett. *rūsa*, rust, L. *rubigo*, *robigo*, rust; all from the same root.] 1. The red or orange-yellow coating which is formed on the surface of iron when exposed to air and moisture; red oxid of iron; in an extended sense, any metallic oxid forming a coat on the metal. Oil-paint, varnish, plumbago, a film of caoutchouc, or a coating of tin may be employed, according to circumstances, to prevent the rusting of iron utensils.

And that (yer long) the share and coultar should
Rub off their *rust* vpon your Roofs of gold.
Sylvester, tr. of Du Bartas's Weeks, i. 2.

Go home, and hang your arms up; let *rust* rot 'em.
Fletcher, Bonduca, iv. 3.

A pound of metal produces considerably more than a pound of its *rust*. In point of fact, every 100 lbs. of quicksilver will produce not less than 108 lbs. of red *rust*.
Huxley, Physiography, vi.

2. In *metal-working*, a composition of iron-filings and sal ammoniac, with sometimes a little sulphur, moistened with water and used for filling fast joints. Oxidation rapidly sets in, and the composition, after a time, becomes very hard, and takes thorough hold of the surfaces between which it is placed. A joint formed in this way is called a *rust-joint*.

3. In *bot.*, a fungous growth on plants which resembles rust on metal; plant-disease caused by fungi of the class *Uredineæ* (which see, for special characterization): same as *brand*, 6. See *Fungi*, *mildew*, *Puccinia*, and *Trichobasis*; also *black rust* and *red rust*, below.

From the observations of Prof. Henslow, it seems certain that *rust* is only an earlier form of mildew.
W. B. Carpenter, Micros., § 319.

High farming encourages the development of *rust*, especially if the wheat is rank and it becomes lodged or fallen.
Science, III. 457.

4. Any foul extraneous matter; a corrosive, injurious, or disfiguring accretion.

A haunted house,
That keeps the *rust* of murder on the walls.
Tennyson, Guinevere.

5. Any growth, influence, or habit tending to injure the mental or moral faculties; a habit or tendency which clogs action or usefulness; also, the state of being affected with such a habit.

But, lord, thouȝ y haue ben vniust,
ȝit thoruȝ the help of thi benignite
I hope to rubbe aweye the *rust*,
With penaunce, from my goostli yȝe.
Political Poems, etc. (ed. Furnivall), p. 189.

How he glisters
Thorough my *rust*! and how his piety
Does my deeds make the blacker!
Shak., W. T., iii. 2. 172.

Those Fountains and Streams of all Polite Learning [the universities] have not yet been able to wash away that slavish *Rust* that sticks to you.
Milton, Ans. to Salmasius, iii. 96.

I should have endured in silence the rust and cramp of my best faculties. *Charlotte Brontë*, Professor, iv.

Just so much work as keeps the brain from rust. *Browning*, Ring and Book, II. 66.

Black rust, a fungus with dark-colored spores which attacks the leaves and stems of wheat and other cereals and of various grasses; the final or teleutospore stage of *Puccinia graminis*, or grain-blight.—**Red rust**, a common fungus, *Puccinia graminis*, which attacks wheat, oats, and other kinds of grain. See *barberry-fungus*, *Puccinia*.

rust[1] (rust), *v.* [< ME. *rusten*, < AS. **rustian* (not authenticated, the one instance cited by Lye involving the adj. *rustig*, rusty) = D. *roesten* = MLG. *rosten*, *rusten* = OHG. *rostên*, MHG. G. *rosten* = Sw. *rosta* = Dan. *ruste*, rust; from the noun.] **I.** *intrans.* **1.** To contract or gather rust; be oxidized.

Adieu, valour! rust, rapier! be still, drum! for your manager is in love. *Shak.*, L. L. L., i. 2. 187.

It is especially notable that during the *rusting* of quicksilver, as indeed of all other metals, there is a very appreciable increase of weight in the substance operated on. *Huxley*, Physiography, p. 76.

2. To assume an appearance of rust, or as if coated with rust.

This thy son's blood cleaving to my blade
Shall rust upon my weapon, till thy blood,
Congeal'd with this, do make me wipe off both.
Shak., 3 Hen. VI., i. 3. 51.

But, when the bracken *rusted* on their crags,
My suit had wither'd. *Tennyson*, Edwin Morris.

3. To degenerate in idleness; become dull through inaction.

Then must I *rust* in Egypt, never more
Appear in arms, and be the chief of Greece?
Dryden, Cleomenes, i. 1.

My Youth may wear and waste, but it shall never *rust* in my Possession. *Congreve*, Way of the World, ii. 1.

Neglected talents *rust* into decay.
Cowper, Table-Talk, l. 546.

II. *trans.* **1.** To cause to contract rust.

Keep up your bright swords, for the dew will *rust* them. *Shak.*, Othello, i. 2. 59.

Laid hand
Upon the *rusted* handle of the gate.
William Morris, Earthly Paradise, II. 175.

2. To impair by time and inactivity.

rust[2]†, *v. i.* An obsolete variant of *roost*[1]. *Palsgrave.* (*Halliwell.*)

rust-ball (rust'bâl), *n.* One of the yellow lumps of iron ore that are found among chalk near Foulmire, in Cambridgeshire, England. *Halliwell.*

rust-colored (rust'kul"ọrd), *a.* Of the color of iron-rust; ferruginous.

rustful (rust'fůl), *a.* [< *rust*[1] + *-ful.*] Rusty; tending to produce rust; characterized by rust: as, "*rustful* sloth," *Quarles.*

rust-fungus (rust'fung"gus), *n.* See *rust-mite*.

rustic (rus'tik), *a.* and *n.* [Early mod. E. *rustick*; < OF. *rustique* (vernacularly *ruiste*, *rustre*, > E. *roister*), F. *rustique* = Pr. *rustic*, *rostic*, *ruste* = Sp. *rústico* = Pg. It. *rustico*, < L. *rusticus*, belonging to the country, < *rūs* (*rur-*), the country: see *rural.*] **I.** *a.* **1.** Of or belonging to the country or to country people; characteristic of rural life; hence, plain; homely; inartificial; countrified: as, *rustic* fare; *rustic* garb.

Forget this new-fall'n dignity,
And fall into our *rustic* revelry.
Shak., As you Like it, v. 4. 183.

He once was chief in all the *rustic* trade;
His steady hand the straightest furrow made.
Crabbe, Works, I. 10.

Ye think the *rustic* cackle of your bourg
The murmur of the world! *Tennyson*, Geraint.

2. Living in the country; rural, as opposed to town-bred; hence, unsophisticated; artless; simple; sometimes in a depreciatory sense, rude; awkward; boorish.

Yield, *rustic* mountaineer. *Shak.*, Cymbeline, iv. 2. 100.

As the Turks sit crosse-legged, so doe they on their heels: differing little in habit from the *rustick* Ægyptians. *Sandys*, Travailes, p. 100.

And many a holy text around she strews,
That teach the *rustic* moralist to die.
Gray, Elegy.

3. Made of rustic work, especially in wood. See *rustic work*, below.

I would have everything as complete as possible in the country, shrubberies and flower gardens, and *rustic* seats innumerable. *Jane Austen*, Mansfield Park, vi.

4. In *anc. Latin manuscript*, noting letters of one of the two oldest forms, the other being the *square*. The rustic letters are as accurately formed as the square or lapidary letters, but are lighter and more slender, with the horizontal strokes more or less oblique and curved. These letters, being easier to form, were more generally used than the square in Roman manuscripts from the first to the fifth century, at which time both forms were generally superseded by the uncial writing.

The earliest application of the *rustic* hand appears in the papyrus rolls recovered from the ruins of Herculaneum (Exempla, tabb. 1–3), which must necessarily be earlier than 79 A. D. *Encyc. Brit.*, XVIII. 152.

Prison rustic ashler. See *ashler*, 3.—**Rough-faced rustic work.** See *rough*[1].—**Rustic joint**, in *masonry*, a square or chamfered sunken joint between blocks.—**Rustic moth**, one of certain noctuid moths; any noctuid: an English collectors' name: as, the rosy *rustic moth*, *Hydrœcia micacea*. See II., 4.—**Rustic pieces**, in *decorative art*, a phrase employed in various uses to note close imitation of nature, and also decoration outside of the received canons of the day. In the first sense, the pottery of Palissy, decorated with lizards, fish, and the like, molded from nature, is known as *rustic pottery* (*figulines rustiques*).—**Rustic quoins.** See *quoin*, 1.—**Rustic shoulder-knot**, a British moth, *Apamea basilinea*.—**Rustic ware**, in *modern ceram. manuf.*, a terra-cotta of a buff or light-brown paste having a brown glaze, sometimes mottled with green: used especially for balustrades, cornices, and similar architectural ornaments, fountains, flower-vases, etc.—**Rustic work.** (*a*) In *masonry*: (1) Stonework of which the face is hacked or picked in holes, or of which the courses and the separate blocks are marked by deep cham-

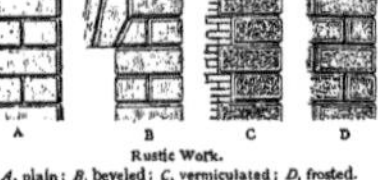

A B C D

Rustic Work.
A, plain; *B*, beveled; *C*, vermiculated; *D*, frosted.

fered or rectangular grooves. Work of the former class is sometimes termed *rockwork*, and the phrase *rustic work* is by some restricted to masonry of the latter class. The varieties of rustic work are named according to the way in which the face is treated, or from peculiarities of the salient edge. *Chamfered rustic work* has the edge of the salient panel beveled to an angle of 135° with the face, so that the beveling of two adjacent blocks forms a right angle at the joint. *Frosted work* displays a fine and even roughness. *Punctured work* is characterized by irregular holes or lines of holes. *Stalactited work* is formed by an ornamentation resembling agglomerated icicles. *Vermiculated work* is tooled in contorted or worm-shaped lines. (2) Any wall built of stones of different sizes and shapes fitted together. (*b*) In *woodwork*, summer-houses, garden furniture, etc., made from rough limbs and roots of trees arranged in fanciful forms.—**Sussex rustic ware.** See *ware*[2]. =**Syn. 1** and **2.** *Pastoral*, *Bucolic*, etc. See *rural*.—**2.** Countrified.

II. *n.* **1.** One who lives in the country; a countryman; a peasant; in a contemptuous use, a clown or boor.

While words of learned length and thundering sound
Amazed the gazing *rustics* ranged around.
Goldsmith, Des. Vil., l. 214.

You must not, madam, expect too much from my pupil: she is quite a little *rustic*, and knows nothing of the world. *Miss Burney*, Evelina, iv.

2. Rustic work.

Then clap four slices of pilasters on 't,
That, laced with bits of *rustic*, makes a front.
Pope, Moral Essays, iv. 34.

3. In *ceram.*, a ground picked with a sharp point so as to have the surface roughened with hollows having sharp edges, sometimes waved, as if imitating slag.—**4.** In *entom.*, a noctuid or rustic moth: as, the northern *rustic*, *Agrotis lucernea*; the unarmed *rustic*, *A. inermis*.

Unarmed Rustic (*Agrotis inermis*).
a, egg, greatly enlarged; *b*, eggs, natural size, in position upon twig.

rustical† (rus'ti-kạl), *a.* and *n.* [= Sp. *rustical* = It. *rusticale*; as *rustic* + *-al.*] **I.** *a.* Rustic.

He is of a *rustical* cut, I know not how: he doth not carry himself like a gentleman of fashion.
B. Jonson, Every Man in his Humour, iii. 1.

Our English courtiers . . . have infinitely refined upon the plain and *rustical* discourse of our fathers. *Scott*, Monastery, xiv.

II. *n.* A rustic.

Let me intreat you not to be wroth with this *rustical*—Credit me, the north wind shall as soon puff one of your rocks from its basis as . . . the churlish speech of an untaught churl shall move the spleen of Piercie Shafton. *Scott*, Monastery, xix.

rustically (rus'ti-kạl-i), *adv.* In a rustic manner; in a manner characteristic of or befitting a peasant; hence, rudely; plainly; inelegantly.

He keeps me *rustically* at home.
Shak., As you Like it, i. 1. 7.

The pulpit style [in Germany] has been always either *rustically* negligent, or bristling with pedantry.
De Quincey, Rhetoric.

rusticalness (rus'ti-kạl-nes), *n.* The character of being rustical; rudeness; coarseness; want of refinement. *Bailey*, 1727.

rusticate (rus'ti-kāt), *v.*; pret. and pp. *rusticated*, ppr. *rusticating*. [< L. *rusticatus*, pp. of *rusticari* (> It. *rusticare* = Pg. *rusticar* = F. *rustiquer*), live in the country, < *rusticus*, of the country: see *rustic.*] **I.** *intrans.* To dwell or reside in the country.

My lady Scudamore, from having *rusticated* in your company too long, pretends to open her eyes for the sake of seeing the sun, and to sleep because it is night. *Pope.*

II. *trans.* **1.** To send to the country; induce or (especially) compel to reside in the country; specifically, to suspend from studies at a college or university and send away for a time by way of punishment. See *rustication*.

The monks, who lived *rusticated* in their scattered monasteries, sojourners in the midst of their conquered land, often felt their Saxon blood tingle in their veins.
I. D'Israeli, Amen. of Lit., I. 83.

At school he was flogged and disgraced, he was disgraced and *rusticated* at the university, he was disgraced and expelled from the army.
Thackeray, Fitz-Boodle's Confessions.

2. In *masonry*, to form into rustic work.

If . . . a tower is to be built, the lower storey should not only be square, but should be marked by buttresses or other strong lines, and the masonry *rusticated*, so as to convey even a greater appearance of strength.
J. Fergusson, Hist. Arch., I. 26.

rusticated (rus'ti-kā-ted), *p. a.* [Pp. of *rusticate*, *v.*] In *building*, rustic.

To the south of the west entrance, the earth has been dug away, and I saw a *rusticated* wall three feet eight inches thick, built with two rows of stone in breadth, clamped together with irons.
Pococke, Description of the East, I. 23.

Rusticated ashler. See *ashler*, 3.

rustication (rus-ti-kā'shọn), *n.* [= Sp. *rusticacion*, < L. *rusticatio*(*n-*), a living in the country, < *rusticari*, live in the country: see *rusticate.*] **1.** The act of rusticating, or the state of being rusticated; residence, especially forced residence, in the country; in universities and colleges, the punishment of a student for some offense by compelling him to leave the institution, and sometimes also compelling him to reside for a time in some other specified place.

Mrs. Sydney is delighted with her *rustication*. She has suffered all the evils of London, and enjoyed none of its goods. *Sydney Smith*, To Francis Jeffrey.

To have touched upon this this spring . . . would either have been the means of abridging my exile, or at least would have procured me a change of residence during my *rustication*. *Scott*, Rob Roy, xiii.

And then came demand for an apology; refusal on my part; appeal to the dean; convocation; and *rustication* of George Savage Fitz-Boodle.
Thackeray, Fitz-Boodle's Confessions.

2. In *arch.*, that species of masonry called *rustic work* (which see, under *rustic*).—**Prismatic rustication**, in Elizabethan architecture, rusticated masonry with diamond-shaped projections worked on the face of every stone. *T. R. Smith*, Handbook of Architecture, Gloss.

rusticity (rus-tis'i-ti), *n.*; pl. *rusticities* (-tiz). [< OF. *rusticite*, F. *rusticité* = Pr. *rusticitat*, *rustat* = Sp. *rusticidad* = Pg. *rusticidade* = It. *rusticità*, < L. *rusticita*(*t-*)*s*, rusticity, < *rusticus*, rustic: see *rustic.*] **1.** The state or character of being rustic; rural existence, flavor, appearance, manners, or the like; especially, simplicity or homeliness of manner; and hence, in a bad sense, ignorance, clownishness, or boorishness.

Honestie is but a defect of Witt,
Respect but meere *Rusticitie* and Clownerie.
Chapman, All Fools (Works, 1873, I. 134).

The sweetness and *rusticity* of a pastoral cannot be so well expressed in any other tongue as in the Greek, when rightly mixed and qualified with the Doric dialect.
Addison, On Virgil's Georgics.

I . . . have alone with this right hand subdued barbarism, rudeness, and *rusticity*.
Swift, Polite Conversation, Int.

2. Anything betokening a rustic life or origin; especially, an error or defect due to ignorance of the world or of the usages of polite society.

The little *rusticities* and awkwardnesses which had at first made grievous inroads on the tranquillity of all . . . necessarily wore away. *Jane Austen*, Mansfield Park, ii.

rusticize (rus'ti-sīz), *v. t.*; pret. and pp. *rusticized*, ppr. *rusticizing*. [< *rustic* + *-ize.*] To make rustic; transform to a rustic.

Rusticized ourselves with uncouth hat,
Rough vest, and goatskin wrappage.
Browning, Ring and Book, II. 104.

rusticly (rus'tik-li), *adv.* [< *rustic* + *-ly*[2].] In a rustic manner; rustically.

To you it seemes so (*rusticly*) Aiax Oïleus said;
Your words are suited to your eyes. Those mares leade still that led.
Chapman, Iliad, xxiii. 416.

rusticola (rus-tik'ọ-lạ), *n.* [NL., supposed to be a mistake for *rusticula*, fem. dim. of L. *rusticus*, rustic: see *rustic*. Otherwise an error for *ruricola*, < L. *rus* (*rur-*), the country, + *colere*, inhabit.] **1.** An old book-name of the European woodcock, now called *Scolopax rusticola*, or *S. rusticula*.—2. [*cap.*] A genus of *Scolopacidæ*, containing only the rusticola: synonymous with *Scolopax* in the strictest sense.

Rusticolæ (rus-tik'ō-lē), *n. pl.* [NL., pl. of *Rusticola*, q. v.] In *ornith.*, in Merrem's classification of birds (1813), a group of birds, including the precocial grallatores, and approximately equivalent to the modern order *Limicolæ*. It was divided into two groups—(*a*) *Phalarideæ*, including the rails, coots, and jacanas; and (*b*) *Limosugæ*, nearly coextensive with the plover-snipe group, shore-birds, or *Limicolæ* proper of modern authors.

rustily (rus'ti-li), *adv.* [< *rusty*[1] + *-ly*[2].] In a rusty state; in such a manner as to suggest rustiness.

Lowten . . . was in conversation with a *rustily*-clad, miserable-looking man, in boots without toes, and gloves without fingers. *Dickens*, Pickwick, xxxi.

rustiness (rus'ti-nes), *n.* [< ME. *rustynes*; < *rusty*[1] + *-ness*.] The state or condition of being rusty.

The *rustiness* and infirmity of age gathered over the venerable house itself. *Hawthorne*, Seven Gables, i.

rust-joint (rust'joint), *n.* See *rust*[1], 2.

rustle (rus'l), *v.*; pret. and pp. *rustled*, ppr. *rustling*. [Formerly also *russle*; prob. freq. of Sw. *rusta*, stir, make a noise, var. of OSw. *ruska*, rustle, shake, = Dan. *ruske*, pull, shake, twitch, = Icel. *ruska*, shake rudely: see *rush*[2]. Cf. Icel. *rysla*, clatter, as money, and G. *rascheln*, freq. of *raschen*, rustle. Cf. AS. **hristlan*, rustle (in Lye, not authenticated), appar. freq. of **hristan*, in ppr. *hristenda* (verbal n. *hristung*), shake, = Icel. *hrista* = Dan. *ryste* = Sw. *rysta*, *rista*, shake, tremble.] **I.** *intrans.* **1.** To make a wavering, murmuring sound when set in motion and rubbed one part upon another or against something else; give out a slightly sibilant sound when shaken: as, a *rustling* silk; *rustling* foliage; *rustling* wings.

When the gust hath blown his fill,
Ending on the *rustling* leaves.
Milton, Il Penseroso, l. 129.

Now and then, sweet Philomel would wail,
Or stock-doves plain amid the forest deep,
That drowsy *rustled* to the sighing gale.
Thomson, Castle of Indolence, i. 4.

Her hand shook, and we heard
In the dead hush the papers that she held
Rustle. *Tennyson*, Princess, iv.

2. To move about or along with a rustling sound.

O, this life
Is nobler than attending for a check,
Richer than doing nothing for a bauble,
Prouder than *rustling* in unpaid-for silk.
Shak., Cymbeline, iii. 3. 24.

The breeze blows fresh; we reach the island's edge,
Our shallop *rustling* through the yielding sedge.
O. W. Holmes, The Island Ruin.

Madame Bourdon *rustled* from upper to lower hall, repeating instructions to her charges.
The Century, XXXVII. 87.

3. To stir about; bestir one's self; struggle or strive, especially against obstacles or difficulties; work vigorously or energetically; "hustle." [Slang, western U. S.]

Rustle now, boys, *rustle!* for you have a long and hard day's work before you. *Harper's Mag.*, LXXI. 190.

II. *trans.* **1.** To cause to rustle.

The wind was scarcely strong enough to *rustle* the leaves around. *T. C. Grattan.*

Where the stiff brocade of women's dresses may have *rustled* autumnal leaves.
H. James, Jr., Pass. Pilgrim, p. 59.

2. To shake with a murmuring, rustling sound.

The air-swept lindens yield
Their scent, and *rustle* down their perfumed showers
Of bloom on the bent grass where I am laid.
M. Arnold, The Scholar-Gipsy.

3. To make, do, secure, obtain, etc., in a lively, energetic manner. [Slang, western U. S.]

When the cow-boy on the round up, the surveyor, or hunter, who must camp out, pitches his tent in the grassy coulée or narrow creek-bottom, his first care is to start out with his largest gunning-bag to "*rustle* some buffalo chips" for a camp-fire. *Smithsonian Report*, 1887, ii. 451.

rustle (rus'l), *n.* [< *rustle*, *v.*] **1.** The noise made by one who or that which rustles; a rustling.

In the sweeping of the wind your ear
The passage of the Angel's wings will hear,
And on the lichen-crusted leads above
The *rustle* of the eternal rain of love.
M. Arnold, Church of Brou, iii.

2. A movement accompanied by a rustling sound.

The soft *rustle* of a maiden's gown
Fanning away the dandelion's down.
Keats, I Stood Tiptoe upon a Little Hill.

rustler (rus'lėr), *n.* [< *rustle* + *-er*[1].] **1.** One who or that which rustles.

The fairy hopes of my youth I have trodden under foot like those neglected *rustlers* [fallen oak-leaves].
Scott, Monastery, viii.

2. One who works or acts with energy and promptness; an active, efficient person; a "hustler"; originally, a cowboy. [Slang, western U. S.]

A horde of *rustlers* who are running off stock.
The Vindicator (Los Lunas, New Mexico), Oct. 27, 1883.

They're a thirsty crowd, an' it comes explosive; but they're worth it, for they're *rustlers*, ivery wan of thim.
The Century, XXXVII. 770.

rustless (rust'les), *a.* [< *rust*[1] + *-less*.] Free from rust; that will not rust.

I have known her fastidious in seeking pure metal for clean uses; and, when once a bloodless and *rustless* instrument was found, she was careful of the prize, keeping it in silk and cotton wool. *Charlotte Brontë*, Villette, viii.

"Polarite"—a *rustless* magnetic oxide of iron in a highly porous condition. *The Engineer*, LXIX. 486.

rustlingly (rus'ling-li), *adv.* With a rustling sound.

On Autumn-nights, when rain
Doth *rustlingly* above your heads complain
On the smooth leaden roof.
M. Arnold, Church of Brou, iii.

rust-mite (rust'mīt), *n.* One of certain mites of the family *Phytoptidæ*, or gall-mites, which do not produce galls properly speaking, but live in a rust-like substance which they produce upon the leaves or fruit of certain plants. Many of these rusts have been described by botanists as *rust-fungi*. *Phytoptus oleivorus* is the rust-mite of the orange, which produces the brownish discoloration often noticed on oranges.

rust-proof (rust'pröf), *a.* Proof against rust; free from the danger of rusting.

This tank is costly, for its joints and bearings must be *rust-proof*. *Jour. Franklin Inst.*, CXXI. 284.

rustre (rus'tėr), *n.* [< F. *rustre*, a lozenge pierced round in the center, also a sort of lance, prob. lozenge-shaped; prob. (with unorig. *s* and r) < OHG. **hrûta*, *rûta*, MHG. *rûte*, G. *raute*, a quadrangle, square, rhomboid, facet, pane, lozenge in heraldry, = D. ruit = Sw. *ruta* = Dan. *rude*, square, lozenge, pane; perhaps < Indo-Eur. **krûta*, **ktrûta*, and so connected with L. *quattuor*, Gr. *τέτταρες*, *πίσυρες*, etc., G. *vier*, E. *four*: see *four*.] **1.** A scale in early armor. See under *rustred*. Hence —**2.** In *her.*, a lozenge pierced with a circular opening, large in proportion to the whole surface, the field appearing through it. Compare *mascle*.

Rustre, a.

rust-red (rust'red), *a.* In *zoöl.*, same as *ferruginous*.

rustred (rus'tėrd), *a.* [< *rustre* + *-ed*[2].] Having rustres.—**Rustred armor**, armor composed of scales lapping one over another, and differing from mascled armor in the curved form of the scales, which make an imbricated pattern.

Rust's collyrium. A mixture of liquor plumbi, elder-water, and tincture of opium.

rusty[1] (rus'ti), *a.* [< ME. *rusti*, *rusty*, < AS. *rustig*, *rusteg* (= D. *roestig* = OHG. *rostag*, MHG. *rostec*, *rustic*, G. rostig = Sw. rostig), rusty, < *rust*[1], rust: see *rust*[1], *n.* In some senses partly confused with *resty*[1], *restive*, and *resty*[2], *reasty*[1]: see *rusty*[2], *rusty*[3], *resty*[1], *resty*[2].] **1.** Covered or affected with rust: as, a *rusty* knife or sword.

Yea, distaff-women manage *rusty* bills
Against thy seat. *Shak.*, Rich. II., iii. 2. 118.

Bars and bolts
Grew *rusty* by disuse. *Cowper*, Task, ii. 746.

Armies waned, for magnet-like she drew
The *rustiest* iron of old fighters' hearts.
Tennyson, Merlin and Vivien.

2. Consisting of rust; hence, having the appearance or effect of rust: as, *rusty* stains.

By that same way the direfull dames doe drive
Their mournefull charett, fild with *rusty* blood.
Spenser, F. Q., I. v. 32.

Not a ship's hull, with its rusty iron links of cable run out of hawse-holes long discolored with the iron's *rusty* tears, but seemed to be there with a fell intention.
Dickens, Our Mutual Friend, i. 14.

3. Covered, incrusted, or stained with a dirty substance resembling rust; hence, filthy; specifically, as applied to grain, affected with the rust-disease: as, *rusty* wheat.

Shew your *rusty* teeth
At every word. *B. Jonson*, Poetaster, Ind.

4. In *bot.* and *zoöl.*, of the color of rust; rubiginous; ferruginous.—**5.** Red or yellow, as fish when the brine in which they are prepared evaporates. Fat fish, like herrings, mackerel, or halibut-fins, often turn rusty.—**6.** Having lost the original gloss or luster; time-worn; shabby: as, a *rusty* black; clothes *rusty* at the seams.

Some there be that have pleasure only in old *rusty* antiquities, and some only in their own doings.
Sir T. More, Utopia, Ded. to Peter Giles, p. 12.

The hens were now scarcely larger than pigeons, and had a queer, *rusty*, withered aspect, and a gouty kind of movement, and a sleepy and melancholy tone throughout all the variations of their clucking and cackling.
Hawthorne, Seven Gables, vi.

Mordecai had no handsome Sabbath garment, but instead of the threadbare *rusty* black coat of the morning he wore one of light drab.
George Eliot, Daniel Deronda, xxxiv.

7. Out of practice; dulled in skill or knowledge through disuse or inactivity.

Hector . . . in this dull and long-continued truce
Is *rusty* grown. *Shak.*, T. and C., i. 3. 263.

One gets *rusty* in this part of the country, you know. Not you, Casaubon; you stick to your studies.
George Eliot, Middlemarch, ix.

8†. Causing rust; rendering dull or inactive.

I deeme thy braine emperished bee
Through *rusty* elde, that hath rotted thee.
Spenser, Shep. Cal., February.

9. Rough; hoarse; harsh; grating: as, a *rusty* voice.

The old parishioners . . . wondered what was going to happen, taking counsel of each other in *rusty* whispers as the door was shut. *Harper's Mag.*, LXXVI. 596.

Rusty blackbird or **grackle**, *Scolecophagus ferrugineus*, abundant in eastern North America, found in the United

Rusty Grackle (*Scolecophagus ferrugineus*).

States chiefly in the fall, winter, and early spring, when it is mostly of a reddish-brown color (whence the name). In full plumage the male is entirely iridescent black, with yellow eyes. It is from 9 to 9½ inches long, and 14½ in extent of wings.—**Rusty dab**, a flatfish of the genus *Platessa*, found in deep water on the coast of Massachusetts and New York.

rusty[1]† (rus'ti), *v. t.* [< *rusty*[1], *a.*] To make rusty; rust.

Th' vngodly Prince . . .
Reacht out his arm; but instantly the same
So strangely withered and so num became,
And God so *rustied* every ioynt, that there
(But as the Body stird) it could not stir.
Sylvester, tr. of Du Bartas's Weeks, ii., The Schisme.

rusty[2] (rus'ti), *a.* [A var. of *resty*[2], *reasty*[1], confused with *rusty*[1].] Same as *reasty*[1] for *reasted*.

You *rusty* piece of Martlemas bacon, away!
Middleton and Rowley, Fair Quarrel, iv. 1.

rusty[3] (rus'ti), *a.* [A var. of *resty*[1], confused with *rusty*[1].] Stubborn: same as *resty*[1] for *restive*.

In the mean time, there is much urging and spurring the parliament for supply and expedition, in both which they will prove somewhat *rusty*.
Court and Times of Charles I., I. 36.

To **ride, run,** or **turn rusty**, to become contumacious; rebel in a surly manner; resist or oppose any one ill-naturedly.

He [the monkey] takes her [the cat] round the neck, and tries to pull her down, and if then she *turns rusty*, . . . he'll . . . give her a nip with his teeth.
Mayhew, London Labour and London Poor.

And how the devil am I to get the crew to obey me? Why, even Dick Fletcher *rides rusty* on me now and then.
Scott, Pirate, xxxix.

Company that's got no more orders to give, and wants to *turn up rusty* to them that has, had better be making room than filling it. *George Eliot*, Felix Holt, xi.

They paraded the street, and watched the yard till dusk, when its proprietor *ran rusty* and turned them out.
C. Reade, Hard Cash, xlv.

rustyback (rus'ti-bak), *n.* A fern, *Ceterach officinarum*: so named in allusion to the rusty scales which cover its lower surface. [Eng.]

rusty-crowned (rus'ti-kround), *a.* Having a chestnut spot on the top of the head: specifically said of the *rusty-crowned* falcon, *Falco* (*Tinnunculus*) *sparverius*. See *sparrow-hawk*.

rusure (rö'zhūr), *n.* [Irreg., < *ruse*¹ + *-ure.*] The sliding down of a hedge, mound of earth, bank, or building. [Prov. Eng.]

ruswut, *n.* See *rusot.*

rut¹ (rut), *n.* [Formerly also *rutt;* with shortened vowel, < ME. *rute, route,* < OF. *route,* way, path, street, trace, track, etc., < ML. *rupta,* a way, path: see *route*¹, the same word, partly adapted to the mod. F. form *route.*] 1. A narrow track worn or cut in the ground; especially, the hollow track made by a wheel in passing over the ground.

> And as from hills raine waters headlong fall,
> That all waies eate huge *ruts.*
> *Chapman,* Iliad, iv. 480.

> A sleepy land where under the same wheel
> The same old *rut* would deepen year by year.
> *Tennyson,* Aylmer's Field.

2†. A wrinkle.

> To behold thee not painted inclines somewhat neere
> A miracle; these in thy face here were deep *ruts.*
> *Webster,* Duchess of Malfi, iii. 1.

> These many *ruts* and furrows in thy cheeks
> Proves thy old face to be but champion-ground,
> Till'd with the plough of age.
> *Randolph,* Hey for Honesty, iv. 3.

3. Any beaten path or mode of procedure; an established habit or course.

> War? the worst that follows
> Things that seem jerk'd out of the common *rut*
> Of Nature is the hot religious fool,
> Who, seeing war in heaven, for heaven's credit
> Makes it on earth. *Tennyson,* Harold, i. 1.

> The *ruts* of human life are full of healing for sick souls. We cannot be always taking the initiative and beginning life anew. *J. F. Clarke,* Self-Culture, Lect. xvii., p. 375.

> The disciples of a great master take the husk for the grain; they harden into the *ruts* of scholarship.
> *The Century,* XL. 250.

rut¹ (rut), *v. t.;* pret. and pp. *rutted,* ppr. *rutting.* [< *rut*¹, *n.*] To mark with or as with ruts; trace furrows in; also, to wrinkle: as, to *rut* the earth with a spade, or with cart-wheels.

> The two in high glee started behind old Dobbin, and jogged along the deep-*rutted* plashy roads.
> *T. Hughes,* Tom Brown at Rugby, i. 3.

> His face . . . deeply *rutted* here and there with expressive valleys and riverine lines of wrinkle.
> *E. Jenkins,* Week of Passion, xiii.

rut² (rut), *n.* [Formerly also *rutt;* < ME. **rut, ruit,* < OF. *ruit, rut,* a roaring, the noise of deer, etc., at the time of sexual excitement, rut, F. *rut,* rut, = Sp. *ruido* = Pg. *rugido* = It. *ruggito,* a roaring, bellowing, < L. *rugitus,* a roaring as of lions, a rumbling, < *rugire* (> It. *ruggire* = Pr. Sp. Pg. *rugir* = OF. *ruir,* F. *rugir*), roar, < √ *ru,* make a noise, Skt. √ *ru,* hum, bray: see *rumor.* In the lit. sense ('a roaring') the word appears to have merged in *rout*¹, *rote*⁴.] 1†. A roaring noise; uproar.

> Theues that loueden ryot and *ruit.*
> *Holy Rood* (ed. Morris), p. 132.

> And there arose such *rut,* th' unruly rout among,
> That soon the noise thereof through all the ocean rong.
> *Drayton,* Polyolbion, ii. 445.

2. The noise made by deer at the time of sexual excitement; hence, the periodical sexual excitement or heat of animals; the period of heat.

rut² (rut), *v.;* pret. and pp. *rutted,* ppr. *rutting.* [< ME. *rutien, rutyen;* < *rut*², *n.*] I. *intrans.* To be in heat; desire copulation.

II. *trans.* To copulate with. [Rare.]

> What piety forbids the lusty ram,
> Or more salacious goat, to *rut* their dam?
> *Dryden,* tr. of Ovid's Metamorph., x.

rut³ (rut), *v. i.* An obsolete or dialectal form of *rout*¹.

Ruta (rö'tä), *n.* [NL. (Tournefort, 1700), < L. *ruta,* < Gr. ῥυτή, rue: see *rue*².] A genus of polypetalous plants, type of the order *Rutaceæ* and tribe *Ruteæ.* It is characterized by a sessile four- or five-celled ovary, and eight or ten stamens alternately shorter, their filaments dilated at the base, and by four or five arched and toothed petals growing from a thick urn-shaped receptacle. There are about 50 species, widely scattered through the Mediterranean region and western and central Asia. They are herbs with perennial or somewhat shrubby base, dotted with glands and emitting a heavy odor. They bear alternate leaves, either simple, divided, trifoliate, or decompound, and many-flowered terminal corymbs or panicles of yellow or greenish flowers. The general name of the species is *rue* (which see). See cut under *Octandria.*

rutabaga (rö-ta-bā'gä), *n.* [= F. *rutabaga;* of Sw. or Lapp. origin (?).] The Swedish turnip, a probable derivative, with the rape and common turnip, of *Brassica campestris.* The leaves are smooth and covered with a bloom, and the roots are longer than broad. The rutabaga is more nutritious than the common turnip. There are numerous varieties.

Rutaceæ (rö-tā'sē-ē), *n. pl.* [NL. (A. P. de Candolle, 1824), fem. pl. of L. *rutaceus,* of or belonging to rue: see *rutaceous.*] An order of polypetalous plants of the cohort *Geraniales* and series *Disciflorœ.* It is characterized by flowers with four or five sepals and as many broadly imbricated petals, by an ovary of four or five carpels, either wholly connate or united only by their basilar or ventral styles or their stigmas, or rarely entirely free, the ovules commonly two in each cell, and usually by an annular or bowl-shaped disk within the circle of stamens. The seeds are oblong or reniform, most often sessile and solitary in the cell, often with a shining crust, with or without fleshy albumen. The order includes about 780 species, of 101 genera and 7 tribes, scattered through the warm and temperate parts of the globe, most abundant in South Africa and Australia, least frequent in tropical Africa. They are shrubs or trees, rarely herbs, dotted with glands and often exhaling a heavy odor. They bear leaves without stipules, which are usually opposite, sometimes simple, but more often compound, and of one, three, or five leaflets, or variously pinnate. The flowers are most often in axillary cymes; the fruit is very various. There are two well-marked series, of which the larger and typical, having the ovary deeply lobed and the fruit capsular, contains the tribes *Cusparieæ, Ruteæ, Diosmeæ, Boronieæ,* and *Xanthoxyleæ;* and the smaller, having the ovary little if at all lobed, and the fruit coriaceous, drupaceous, or a berry, contains the tribes *Toddalieæ* and *Aurantieæ.* The last includes, in the genus *Citrus,* the orange and the lemon, which depart from the type in their numerous carpels, ovules, and stamens. For some of the important genera, see *Ruta* (the type), *Ptelea, Xanthoxylum, Citrus, Murraya, Peganum,* and *Dictamnus.*

rutaceous (rö-tā'shius), *a.* [< L. *rutaceus,* < *ruta,* rue: see *rue*².] Of, belonging to, or characterizing the plant-order *Rutaceæ;* resembling rue.

rute¹, *v.* and *n.* An obsolete or dialectal form of *rout*¹.

rute²†, *n.* and *v.* A Middle English form of *root*¹.

rute³ (röt), *n.* [Cf. W. *rhwtws,* broken parts, dregs, *rhwtion, rhytion,* particles rubbed off.] In *mining,* very small threads of ore.

Ruteæ (rö'tē-ē), *n. pl.* [NL. (Adrien de Jussieu, 1825), < *Ruta* + *-eæ.*] A tribe of plants of the order *Rutaceæ,* characterized by free and spreading petals and stamens, a free and thickened disk, three or more ovules in a cell, fleshy albumen, and a curved embryo. It includes 6 genera, of which *Ruta* is the type. The species are herbs, often with a shrubby base, with perfect, mostly regular flowers, their parts commonly in fours, and often with pinnately divided leaves. They are widely scattered through most northern temperate regions.

Rutela (rö'te-lä), *n.* [NL. (Latreille, 1817), an error for *Rutila,* fem. of L. *rutilus,* red: see *rutile.*] A genus of lamellicorn beetles, giving name to the *Rutelinæ* or *Rutelidæ,* having the claws entire and the scutellum longer than broad. They are beetles of a moderate size and short and stout form, and are ornamented with striking and variable colors. They are confined to South America and the West Indies, but one Cuban species, *R. formosa,* has been seen in the United States. They are found on flowers.

Rutelidæ (rö-tel'i-dē), *n. pl.* [NL. (MacLeay, 1819), < *Rutela* + *-idæ.*] A family of lamellicorn beetles, usually ranking as a tribe or subfamily of *Scarabæidæ:* a little-used term.

Rutelinæ (rö-te-lī'nē), *n. pl.* [NL., < *Rutela* + *-inæ.*] A subfamily of *Scarabæidæ,* typified by the genus *Rutela;* the goldsmith-beetles or tree-beetles. They are splendid metallic beetles, mostly of the warmer parts of America. The body is shorter, rounder, and more polished than is usually the case with scarabs, and the tarsi are thick, enabling the insects to cling closely to trees. One of the commonest and most beautiful species is *Areoda (Cotalpa) lanigera,* the goldsmith-beetle, $\frac{9}{10}$ inch long, of a yellow color glittering like gold on the head and thorax. They appear in New England about the middle of May. *Plusiotis gloriosa* is pale-green, with the margins of the body and broad stripes on the elytra of pure polished gold-color. Also *Rutelidæ* as a family and *Rutelini* as a tribe. See cut under *Cotalpa.*

ruth (röth), *n.* [< ME. *ruthe, reuthe, rewth, rewthe, routh, reouthe, reowthe,* < Icel. *hryggth, hrygth,* ruth, sorrow, < *hryggr,* grieved, sorrowful: see *rue*¹, *v.* The equiv. noun in AS. was *hreów:* see *rue*¹, *n.*] 1. Sorrow; misery; grief.

> Of the quenes profer the puple badde *reuthe,*
> For sche fel to-fore the best flat to the grounde;
> Ther was weping & wo wonderli riue.
> *William of Palerne* (E. E. T. S.), l. 4413.

> Reign thou above the storms of sorrow and *ruth*
> That roar beneath; unshaken peace hath won thee.
> *Tennyson,* Sonnet, Though Night hath climbed, etc.

2. That which brings ruth; cruel or barbarous conduct.

> No *ruthe* were it to rug the and ryue the in ropes.
> *York Plays,* p. 286.

> The Danes with *ruth* our realme did ouerrunne,
> Their wrath inwrapte vs all in wretchednesse.
> *Mir. for Mags.,* I. 445.

> I come not here to be your foe!
> I seek these anchorites, not in *ruth,*
> To curse and to deny your truth.
> *M. Arnold,* Stanzas from the Grande Chartreuse.

3. Sorrow for the misery of another; compassion; pity; mercy; tenderness.

> For-thi I rede the riche haue *reuthe* on the pore.
> *Piers Plowman* (A), i. 149.

> Tho can she weepe, to stirre up gentle *ruth*
> Both for her noble blood and for her tender youth.
> *Spenser,* F. Q., I. i. 50.

> Vouchsafe of *ruth*
> To tell us who inhabits this fair town.
> *Marlowe and Nash,* Dido, Queen of Carthage, ii. 1. 41.

4. Repentance; regret.

> Of worldly pleasure it is a treasure, to say truth,
> To wed a gentle wyfe; of his bargayne he needes no *ruth.*
> *Babees Book* (E. E. T. S.), p. 86.

5. A pitiful sight; a pity.

> I trowe that to a norice in this case
> It had been hard this *rewthe* for to see;
> Wel myhte a moder than han cryed allas!
> *Chaucer,* Clerk's Tale, l. 506.

> For the principil of this text hath he contynued in dayly experiens sithe bifore the Parlement of Bury; but the conclusion of this text came neuer zet to experiens, and that is gret *rewthe.* *Paston Letters,* I. 536.

[*Ruth* in all its various senses is obsolete or archaic.]

Ruthenian (rö-thē'ni-an), *a.* and *n.* [< *Ruthenia,* a name of Russia, + *-an.*] I. *a.* Of or pertaining to the Ruthenians.—**Ruthenian Catholics.** Same as *United Ruthenians.*—**Ruthenian sturgeon,** *Acipenser ruthenus.* See *sterlet.*

II. *n.* 1. A member of that part of the Little Russian race dwelling in the eastern part of the Austrian empire. Also called *Russniak.* See *Little Russian,* under *Russian.*—2. The language spoken by the Ruthenians: same as *Little Russian.* See *Russian.*—**United Ruthenians,** those Ruthenians in Russian Poland and Austria-Hungary, belonging to communities formerly of the Orthodox Eastern Church, who acknowledge the supremacy of the Pope, but still continue to use the Old Slavonic liturgy. They have a married secular clergy, and a religious order which follows the rule of St. Basil. Also called *Ruthenian Catholics.*

ruthenic (rö-then'ik), *a.* [< *ruthen-ium* + *-ic.*] Pertaining to or derived from ruthenium.

ruthenious (rö-thē'ni-us), *a.* [< *ruthenium* + *-ous.*] Pertaining to or derived from ruthenium: noting compounds having a lower valence than ruthenic compounds.

ruthenium (rö-thē'ni-um), *n.* [NL., < *Ruthenia,* a name of Russia, whence it was originally obtained.] Chemical symbol, Ru; atomic weight, 103.5 (*Claus*). A metal of the platinum group. The name was given by Osann, in 1828, to one of three supposed new metals found in platinum ores from the Ural mountains. Most of what is known of it is due to Claus, who, in 1845, proved the existence of one of Osann's new metals, and retained his name (*ruthenium*) for it, because there was really a new metal in the substance called by Osann "ruthenium oxide," although, in point of fact, this was made up chiefly of various other substances—silica, zirconia, etc. Ruthenium is found in native platinum as well as in osmiridium, and in laurite, which is a sesqui-sulphuret of ruthenium, and occurs in Borneo and Oregon. It is a hard, brittle metal, fusing with more difficulty than any metal of the platinum group, with the exception of osmium. It is very little acted on by aqua regia, but combines with chlorin at a red heat. Its specific gravity, at 32°, is 12.261.

rutherfordite (rö'thėr-ford-īt), *n.* [< *Rutherford* (see def.) + *-ite*².] A rare and imperfectly known mineral found in the gold-mines of Rutherford county, North Carolina: it is supposed to contain titanic acid, cerium, etc.

ruthful (röth'fůl), *a.* [< ME. *reuthful, reouthful, reowthful;* < *ruth* + *-ful.*] 1. Full of sorrow; sorrowful; woful; rueful.

> What sad and *ruthful* faces!
> *Fletcher,* Double Marriage, iii. 2.

2. Causing ruth or pity; piteous.

> In Aust eke if the vyne yerde be lene,
> And she, thi vyne, a *ruthful* thing to se.
> *Palladius,* Husbondrie (E. E. T. S.), p. 171.

> O that my death would stay these *ruthful* deeds!
> *Shak.,* 3 Hen. VI., ii. 5. 95.

> Say a *ruthful* chance broke woof and warp.
> *Browning,* Sordello.

3. Full of ruth or pity; merciful; compassionate.

> Biholt, thou man with *routhful* herte,
> The sharpe scourge with knottes smerte.
> *Political Poems,* etc. (ed. Furnivall), p. 226.

> He [God] *ruthful* is to man. *Turberville,* Eclogues, iii.

ruthfully (röth'fůl-i), *adv.* [< ME. *reowthfulliche;* < *ruthful* + *-ly*².] Wofully; sadly; piteously; mournfully.

> The flower of horse and foot . . . *ruthfully* perished.
> *Knolles,* Hist. Turks.

ruthless (röth'les), *a.* [< ME. *reutheles, rewtheless, routheles;* < *ruth* + *-less.*] 1. Having no ruth or pity; cruel; pitiless; barbarous; insensible to the miseries of others.

> She loketh bakward to the londe,
> And seyde, "farwel, housbond *reutheless.*"
> *Chaucer,* Man of Law's Tale, l. 765.

See, *ruthless* queen, a hapless father's tears.
Shak., 3 Hen. VI., i. 4. 156.

2. Unmodified or unrestrained by pity; marked by unfaltering rigor; relentless; merciless: as, *ruthless* severity.

With *ruthless* joy the happy hound
Told hill and dale that Reynard's track was found.
Cowper, Needless Alarm.

A high morality and a true patriotism . . . must first be renounced before a *ruthless* career of selfish conquest can begin. *E. Everett*, Orations and Speeches, I. 521.

=**Syn.** Unpitying, hard-hearted.

ruthlessly (röth'les-li), *adv.* [< *ruthless* + *-ly*².] In a ruthless manner; without pity; cruelly; barbarously.

That the Moslems did *ruthlessly* destroy Jaina temples at Ajmir, Delhi, Canouge, and elsewhere may be quite true, but then it was because their columns served so admirably for the construction of their mosques.
J. Fergusson, Hist. Indian Arch., p. 409.

ruthlessness (röth'les-nes), *n.* The state or character of being ruthless; want of compassion; mercilessness; insensibility to the distresses of others.

rutic (rö'tik), *a.* [< L. *ruta*, rue, + *-ic*.] Pertaining to or derived from rue.—**Rutic acid**, a crystalline coloring matter found in the leaves of the common rue. Also called *rutin*.

ruticilla (rö-ti-sil'ä), *n.* [NL., < L. *rutilus*, red, + dim. term. *-cilla*, taken to mean 'tail' (cf. *Motacilla*).] 1. An old book-name of some small bird having a red tail, or having red on the tail; a redstart. It is the specific name of (*a*) the redstart of Europe, *Phœnicura ruticilla*, and of (*b*) the redstart of America, *Setophaga ruticilla*. See cuts under *redstart*.
2. [*cap.*] The genus of Old World redstarts, of which there are about 20 species. The common redstart is *R. phœnicura*. The black redstart is *R. tithys*. Also called *Phœnicura*.

Ruticillinæ (rö"ti-si-lī'nē), *n. pl.* [NL., < *Ruticilla* + *-inæ*.] A subfamily of Old World sylviine birds, named from the genus *Ruticilla*.

rutil, *n.* See *rutile*.

Rutila (rö'ti-lä), *n.* The amended form of *Rutela*.

rutilant (rö'ti-lant), *a.* [< F. *rutilant* = Sp. Pg. It. *rutilante*, < L. *rutilan(t-)s*, ppr. of *rutilare*, be or color reddish: see *rutilate*.] Shining; glittering. [Rare.]

Parchments coloured with this *rutilant* mixture.
Evelyn, II. iv. 1. (*Richardson.*)

Somehow the Abate's guardian eye—
Scintillant, *rutilant*, fraternal fire—
Roving round every way, had seized the prize.
Browning, Ring and Book, I. 110.

rutilate† (rö'ti-lāt), *v. i.* [< L. *rutilatus*, pp. of *rutilare* (> It. *rutilare* = Sp. Pg. *rutilar* = OF. *rutiler*, shine, glitter), be or color reddish, glow red, < *rutilus*, red, yellowish-red: see *red*¹.] To shine; emit rays of light. *Coles*, 1717.

rutile (rö'til), *n.* [Also *rutil*; < F. *rutile*, shining; < L. *rutilus*, red, yellowish-red: see *rutilant*.] One of the three forms in which titanium dioxid occurs in nature. (See also *octahedrite* and *brookite*.) It crystallizes in tetragonal crystals, generally in square prisms, often in geniculated twins. It has a brilliant metallic-adamantine luster, and reddish-brown to black color. The crystals are often black by reflected and deep-red by transmitted light. They are sometimes cut for jewels. Nigrin is a black ferriferous variety, and sagenite a variety consisting of acicular crystals often penetrating transparent quartz. The latter is also called *Venus's-hair stone* and *love's-arrows*.

rutilite (rö'ti-līt), *n.* [< *rutile* + *-ite*².] Native oxid of titanium.

rutin (rö'tin), *n.* [< L. *ruta*, rue, + *-in*².] Rutic acid.

rutter¹† (rut'ėr), *n.* [= D. *ruiter* = G. *reuter*, a trooper, horseman (partly confused with G. *reiter*, a rider, and *ritter*, knight: see *reiter*, *ritter*, *rider*), < OF. *routier*, *routtier*, a highwayman, roadsman, an experienced soldier, a veteran, < ML. *ruptarius*, *rutarius*, one of a band of irregular soldiers or mercenaries of the eleventh century, a trooper, < *rupta*, a troop, band, company: see *rout*³.] 1. A trooper; a dragoon; specifically, a mercenary horse-soldier in the seventeenth and eighteenth centuries.

Neither shal they be accompanied wyth a garde of rufelynge *rutters*. *Bp. Bale*, Image, ii.

Like Almain *rutters* with their horsemen's staves.
Marlowe, Faustus, i. 1.

True it is, a squadron of *rutters*, meaning pistoliers, ought to beat a squadron of launtiers.
Williams, Brief Discourse of War.

2. A dashing gallant; a man of fashion.

Some authors have compared it to a *rutter's* cod-piece, but I like not the allusion so well by reason the tylings have no correspondence; his mouth is allwaies mumbling, as if hee were at his muttons; and his beard is bristled here and there like a sow.
Lodge, Wit's Miserie (1596). (*Halliwell.*)

rutter²† (rut'ėr), *n.* [Also *ruttier*, *routtier*; < OF. *routier*, a chart, or directory of roads or courses, a road-chart, itinerary, a marine chart, < *route*, a way, road: see *route*¹.] A direction for the road or course, especially for a course by sea.

I, Mr. Awdrian Gilbert, and John Davis, went by appointment to Mr. Secretary to Mr. Beale his howse, where onely we four were secret, and we made Mr. Secretarie privie of the N. W. passage, and all charts and *rutters* were agreed uppon in generall.
Dr. Dee, Diary, p. 18. (*Halliwell.*)

rutter³ (rut'ėr), *n.* [< *rut*², *v.*, + *-er*¹.] One that ruts.

rutterkin† (rut'ėr-kin), *n.* [< *rutter*¹ + *-kin*.] A diminutive of *rutter*¹.

Such a rout of regular *rutterkins*, some bellowing in the quire, some muttering, and another sort jetting up and down!
Confutation of N. Shaxton (1546), sig. G. vi. (*Latham.*)

ruttier† (rut'i-ėr), *n.* Same as *rutter*².

rut-time (rut'tīm), *n.* The season of rut. *Cotgrave.*

rutting-time (rut'ing-tīm), *n.* Same as *rut-time*. *Halliwell.*

ruttish (rut'ish), *a.* [< *rut*² + *-ish*¹.] Lustful; libidinous.

Count Rousillon, a foolish idle boy, but for all that very *ruttish*. *Shak.*, All's Well, iv. 3. 243.

ruttishness (rut'ish-nes), *n.* The state or quality of being ruttish.

ruttle (rut'l), *v. i.*; pret. and pp. *ruttled*, ppr. *ruttling*. [< ME. *rotelen*, *rutelen*, var. of *ratelen*, rattle: see *rattle*¹. Cf. G. *rütteln*, shake, rattle.] To rattle; make a rattling sound, especially in breathing; gurgle. [Obsolete or prov. Eng.]

Then was *rutlynge* in Rome, and rubbynge of helmes.
MS. Cott. Calig. A. ii. f. 111. (*Halliwell.*)

When she was taken in her coffin to Dr. Petty, the professor of anatomy, "she was observed to breathe, and obscurely to *ruttle*."
J. Ashton, Social Life in Reign of Queen Anne, II. 216.

ruttle (rut'l), *n.* [< *ruttle*, *v.*; a var. of *rattle*¹, *n.*] Rattle. [Obsolete or prov. Eng.]

The last agonies, the fixed eyes, and the dismal *ruttle*.
Burnet, Sermons, p. 175. (*Latham.*)

rutton-root (rut'on-röt), *n.* [Prob. < Hind. *ratan*, a jewel, gem.] An Indian dye-plant, *Onosma Emodi*, or its root, which affords a stain for wood. It is the maharanga of the natives.

rutty¹ (rut'i), *a.* [< *rut*¹ + *-y*¹.] Full of ruts; cut by wheels.

The road was *rutty*. *C. Rowcroft.*

rutty² (rut'i), *a.* [< *rut*² + *-y*¹.] Ruttish; lustful.

rutty³ (rut'i), *a.* An obsolete or dialectal variant of *rooty*. *Spenser.*

rutula (rut'ū-lä), *n.* Same as *rotula*, 1 (*a*).

ruty†, *a.* A late Middle English form of *rooty*.

ruvid (rö'vid), *a.* [< It. *ruvido*, rough, rugged, rude, < L. *ruidus* (rare), rough.] Rough. [Rare.]

On passing my hand over the body . . . there was a *ruvid* feel, as if the two surfaces met with resistance, or as if a third body, slightly rough, like the finest sand or powder, lay between them.
A. B. Granville, Spas of Germany, p. 172.
[(*N. and Q.*, 6th ser., X. 368.)

Ruyschian (ris'ki-an), *a.* [< *Ruysch* (see def.) + *-ian*.] Pertaining to the Dutch anatomist Ruysch (1638–1731).—**Ruyschian tunic** (tunica Ruyschiana). Same as *choriocapillaris*.

Ruysch's glomerule. A Malpighian corpuscle.

Ruysch's map-projection. See *projection*.

ruzzom, *n.* Same as *rizom*.

R. V. An abbreviation of *Revised Version* (of the Bible).

R. W. An abbreviation of (*a*) *Right Worshipful*; (*b*) *Right Worthy*.

ry†, *n.* A late Middle English form of *rye*¹.

Ry. An abbreviation of *railway*.

ryacolite, *n.* See *rhyacolite*.

ryal†, *a.* An obsolete form of *royal*.

ryal, rial³ (rī'al), *n.* [A var. of *royal*.] 1. A gold coin formerly current in England, first coined by Edward IV., and worth at the time 10 shillings (about $2.40). It was also called the *rose-noble*, from its bearing a general resemblance to the older English nobles (see *noble*, *n.*, 2), and from its having a rose represented upon it. The *rose-ryal* was an English gold coin first coined by James I., and worth at the time about $7.20 or $7.90. On the obverse was the king enthroned; on the reverse, a large double rose with the shield of arms in the center. The *spur-ryal* was an English gold coin also first coined by James I., and worth at that time about $3.60 or $4.00.
2. Same as *pavilion*, 11.

Obverse.

Reverse.

Ryal or Rose-noble of Edward IV.—British Museum. (Size of original.)

ryally†, **ryalliche**†, *adv.* Obsolete forms of *royally*.

ryb†, *n.* A Middle English form of *rib*².

rybaud†, *n.* A Middle English form of *ribald*.

ryche†, *a.* A Middle English form of *rich*¹.

ryddel†, *n.* A Middle English form of *riddle*².

rydder†, *n.* A Middle English form of *ridder*¹.

ryde†, *v.* A Middle English form of *ride*.

rydelle†, *n.* A Middle English form of *ridel* for *riddle*³.

ryder†, *n.* An obsolete spelling of *rider*.

rye¹ (rī), *n.* [Early mod. E. also *rie*; < ME. *rye*, *ry*, *reye*, *ruge*, < AS. *ryge* = OS. *roggo* = D. *rogge* = OHG. *rocco*, *rocko*, MHG. *rogge*, *rocke*, G. *rocke*, *rocken*, usually (< D.) *roggen* = Icel. *rūgr* (orig. *rugr*) = Sw. *råg* = Dan. *rug*, rye, = OBulg. *rŭzhĭ*, Bulg. *rŭzh* = Serv. *rzh* = Bohem. Pol. *rezh* = Polabian *râz* = Russ. *rozhĭ* = OPruss. *rugis* = Lith. *rugis* = Lett. *rudzi*, rye. The Finn. *ruis* is from OPruss. or Lith.; W. *rhyg*, rye, is appar. from E.] 1. The cereal plant *Secale cereale*, or its seeds. Its nativity appears to have been in the region between the Black Sea and the Caspian. Its culture has been chiefly in the north, and, though ancient, is not of the highest antiquity. It bears more cold than any other grain, thrives on light and otherwise barren soils, and can be grown continuously on the same spot. It is most extensively produced in central and northern Europe, where it forms the almost exclusive breadstuff of large populations, furnishing the black bread of Germany and Russia, and the rye-cakes which in Sweden are baked twice in a year and preserved by drying. Rye is less nutritious than wheat, though in that respect standing next to it. The black bread has a sour taste, owing to the speedy acetous fermentation of the sugar contained in it. A sweet bread is also made from rye. The roasted grains have long been used as a substitute for coffee. Rye enters in Russia into the national drink, kvass, in Holland into gin, and in the United States it is the source of much whisky. When affected with ergot (see *ergot*¹, 2, and *spurred rye* below) rye becomes poisonous. The young plant affords a useful green fodder; the straw is valued for thatching, for filling mattresses, for the packing of horse-collars, etc. Rye is often planted with grass-seed in the United States as a protection during the first season, and similarly with pine-seeds in the Alpine region. It has spring and fall varieties, one of the latter being known as *Wallachian*; in general it has less varieties than other much-cultivated plants. The *rie* of Exodus ix. 32 and Isaiah xxviii. 25 is probably spelt.

1. Rye (*Secale cereale*). 2. The spike. *a*, a spikelet; *b*, the empty glumes; *c*, the flowering glume; *d*, the palet; *e*, one of the lodicles, highly magnified.

2. In *her.*, a bearing representing a stalk of grain with the ear bending downward, thus distinguished from wheat, in which the ear is erect. —3. Whisky made from rye. [Colloq., U. S.] —**Spurred rye**, rye affected with ergot, causing the ovary to assume a spurred form. In pharmacy it is called *secale cornutum*. See *ergot*¹, 2, and *St. John's bread*.—**Wild rye**, a grass of the genus *Elymus*.

rye² (rī), *n.* [Origin obscure.] A disease in hawks which causes the head to swell. *Halliwell.*

rye³ (rī), *n.* [Gipsy.] A gentleman; a superior person: as, a Rommany *rye*.

rye-grass (rī'gràs), *n.* [An altered form of *ray-grass*, simulating *rye*¹.] 1. The ray-grass, *Lolium perenne*.

On Desmonds mouldering turrets slowly shake
The trembling *rie-grass* and the hare-bell blue.
Mickle, Sir Martin, i.

2. Lyme-grass. See *Elymus*.—**Italian rye-grass**, the variety *Italicum* of the rye-grass, a meadow-grass

esteemed as highly in England as timothy-grass is in the United States.

Rye House plot. See *plot*[1].

rye-moth (rī'môth), *n.* A European insect whose larva feeds on stems of rye. It is referred to by Curtis as *Pyralis secalis*, but is probably *Orobena frumentalis.*

rye-straw (rī'strâ), *n.* A wisp of the straw of rye; hence, figuratively, a weak, insignificant person.

> Thou wouldst instruct thy master at this play;
> Think'st thou this *Rye-straw* can ore-rule my arme?
> *Heywood*, Four Prentises of London (Works, II. 203).

rye-wolf (rī'wůlf), *n.* [Tr. G. *roggen-wolf.*] A malignant spirit supposed by the German peasantry to infest rye-fields. *Dyer*, Folk-lore of Plants.

rye-worm (rī'wėrm), *n.* A European insect, the larva of the dipteran *Oscinis pumilionis*, which feeds on the stems of rye.

ryftet, *n.* A Middle English form of *rift*[1].

rygbanet, *n.* A Middle English form of *ridge-bone.*

Rygchopsalia (rig-kop-sā'li-ạ), *n.* The corrupt original form of *Rhynchopsalia.* See *Rhynchops.*

ryghtt, *a.*, *n.*, and *v.* A Middle English form of *right.*

ryghtwyst, *a.* A Middle English form of *righteous.*

ryke[1] (rīk), *v. i.* [A var. of *reach*[1].] To reach. [Scotch.]

> Let me *ryke* up to dight that tear,
> And go wi' me and be my dear.
> *Burns*, Jolly Beggars.

ryke[2]†, *n.* A Middle English variant of *riche*[1].

rymet, *n.* An obsolete form of *rime*[1].

rymourt, *n.* An obsolete form of *rimer*[1].

Rynchæa, Rynchea, Rynchœa, *n.* See *Rhynchæa.*

ryncho-. For words so beginning, see *rhyncho-.*

Ryncops, *n.* See *Rhynchops.*

rynd (rind), *n.* [Cf. E. *rind-spindle*, a mill-rynd; perhaps ult. < AS. *hrindan* (= Icel. *hrinda*), push, thrust, or *hrīnan*, touch, strike: see *rine*[2].] In a burstone mill, the iron which supports the upper stone, and upon which it is nicely balanced or trammed. At the middle of the rynd is a bearing called the *cockeye*, which is adapted to rest upon the pointed upper end of the mill-spindle, called the *cockhead.* See *mill*[1] and *mill-spindle.* Also spelled *rind.*

ryndet, *n.* A Middle English form of *rind*[1].

ryngt. A Middle English form of *ring*[1], *ring*[2].

Ryngota (ring-gō'tạ), *n.* [NL.] An erroneous form of *Rhynchota.* Compare *Rhyngota.*

rynnet, *v.* A Middle English form of *run*[1].

rynt, *v.* See *aroint.*

ryot (rī'ot), *n.* [Also *riot*, *rayat*; < Hind. *raiyat*, prop. *ra'iyat*, < Ar. *ra'iya*, a subject, tenant, a peasant, cultivator. Cf. *raya*[1].] In India, a peasant; a tenant of the soil; a cultivator; especially, one holding land as a cultivator or husbandman.

> He was not one of our men, but a common *ryot*, clad simply in a dhoti or waist-cloth, and a rather dirty turban.
> *F. M. Crawford*, Mr. Isaacs, x.

> In Bengal there are no great land-owners, but numerous *ryots*, or cultivators who have fixity of tenure and rent.
> *British Quarterly Rev.*, LXXXIII. 271.

> It is suggested that Government might by degrees undertake the advances required by the *ryots*, which they now raise under the disastrous village usurer's loan system, which, far from really helping them, only lands them deeper and deeper in the mire of debt each year.
> *A. G. F. Eliot James*, Indian Industries, i.

ryotwar, ryotwari (rī'ot-wär, -wä-ri), *n.* [Also *ryotwary*, *rayatwari*; < Hind. *raiyatwārī*, < *raiyat*, a ryot: see *ryot.*] The stipulated arrangement in regard to land-revenue or -rent made annually in parts of India, especially in the Madras presidency, by the government officials with the ryots or actual cultivators of the soil, and not with the village communities, or any landlord or middleman.

> Its [the United States land system's] nearest surviving relative in Europe is the metayage of France; but it is more like the zemeendaree and *ryotwar* of Britishized India than any land system now in existence.
> *N. A. Rev.*, CXLII. 54.

rype[1]†, *a.* and *v.* A Middle English form of *ripe*[1].

rype[2] (rīp), *n.* [< Dan. *rype*, a ptarmigan.] A ptarmigan. See *dalripa.*

> The *rype* must be regarded as the most important of Norwegian game birds, on account of its numbers no less than of its flavour. *Encyc. Brit.*, XVII. 581.

rypeck (rī'pek), *n.* [Also *ripeck*, *repeck*, *rypeg*; origin obscure.] A pole used to moor a punt while fishing, or in some similar way. [Local, Eng.]

> He ordered the fishermen to take up the *rypecks*, and he floated away down stream. H. *Kingsley*, Ravenshoe, lxiv.

> It is the name for a long pole shod with an iron point. Thames fishermen drive two of these into the bed of the river and attach their punts to them. . . . A single pole is sometimes called a *rypeck*, but the custom among fishermen in this part of the world [Halliford-on-Thames] is to speak of "a *rypecks.*" *N. and Q.*, 7th ser., II. 168.

Rypo-. For words so beginning, see *Rhypo-.*

Rypticus, *n.* See *Rhypticus.*

ryschet, *n.* A Middle English form of *rush*[1].

rysét. A Middle English form of *rise*[1], *rise*[2].

rysht, *n.* A Middle English form of *rush*[1].

rytht, *n.* An obsolete form of *rithe*[1].

rythmt, *v. i.* An obsolete spelling of *rhythm* and of *rime*[1].

rythmert, *n.* An obsolete spelling of *rimer*[1].

ryvet. A Middle English form of *rive*[1], *rive*[2], *rife*[1].

ryvert, *n.* A Middle English form of *river*[1], *river*[2].

Ryzæna, *n.* See *Rhyzæna.*

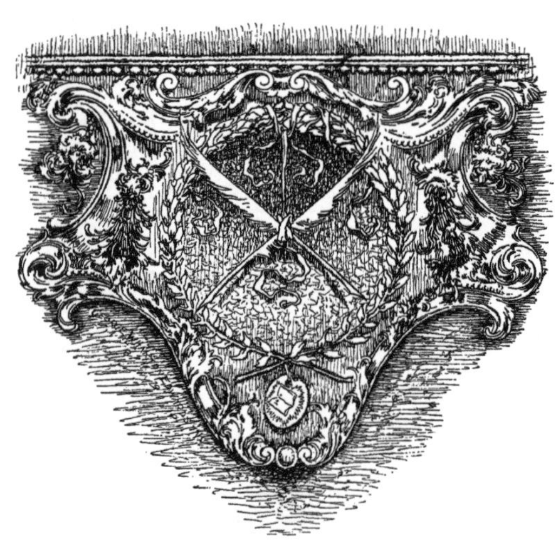

1. The nineteenth letter and fifteenth consonant of the English alphabet, having a corresponding place also in the alphabets from which that is derived (the twenty-first, or last but one, in Phenician). The historical exhibit of related forms, as given for the other letters (see especially *A*), is as follows:

Egyptian. Hieroglyphic. Hieratic. Phenician. Early Greek and Latin.

The Phenician system had more than one sibilant sign, and the Greek choice wavered at first between two of them, until it settled upon this one. Of all the signs here given the value was the same — namely, our normal *s*-sound, as in *so*, *us*. This is a surd or breathed utterance, a fricative or continuable consonant, of a peculiar character, to which we give the name of *sibilant* or *hissing*. Its sonant or voiced counterpart (related to it as d to *t*, as *v* to *f*, and so on) is *z*, as in *zeal*, *dizzy* (the buzzing sound). They are produced between the tongue, at or near its tip, and a point on the roof of the mouth either close behind the front teeth or at a further remove from them. Probably no other of our alphabetic sounds are producible through so wide a range of (slightly) varying positions, or actually produced, in different districts and individuals, in so different a manner. None, also, are more freely combinable with other consonant-sounds into intricate groups, as in *strands*, *twelfths*, *splints*, *sixths*. In virtue of their mode of production, they are akin with t and d, and, like them, are often called dental, or lingual, or tongue-tip sounds. The proper or hissing *s* is one of the most common elements of English utterance, forming more than 4½ per cent. of it. But its sign has also other values. As *s* is one of our most used endings — for example, of plural number, of possessive case, of third person singular present — it comes extremely often at the end of a word, and there, after any sonant sound, it is pronounced as *z*: for example, *loves*, *love's*, *he loves*; *flies*, *fly's*, *he flies*; and it has the same sound often in the interior of words, especially between sonants: for example, *use*, *nose*, *dismal*. The *s*-sound, on the other hand, is represented to a considerable extent by c before *e*, *i*, *y* (see C); and by double *s*, or *ss*, which is frequent in the middle and at the end of words, and has the hissing sound, save in a few exceptional cases, like *dissolve*, *possess* (between the o and e). Another sound often represented by *s* is the *sh*-sound (see below) — namely, in very numerous cases where the *s* is followed by a consonantal *y*-sound, whether written with *i*, as in *passion*, or implied in "long *u*," as in *sure*, *fissure*: since the combination *sy* in English pronunciation has a strong tendency to fuse into *sh*, and in ordinary free utterance often does so, even in cases where theory and extra-careful usage require the separation of the two sounds. This fused sound is represented by the important digraph *sh* (also by *ch* in a few French words, as *machine*). It is a second sibilant, a more palatal one — as simple an utterance as the *s*-sibilant, but very much less frequent (less than 1 per cent., or one fifth of *s*; but about 1½ per cent. if its presence in the *ch*-sound is included). It is made with nearly the same part of the tongue as *s*, and against the roof of the mouth, but generally a little further back, and especially (it would seem) with an opener cavity immediately behind the point of closest approximation of the organs. Its compound sign (Middle English and German *sch*) marks it as coming historically from the fusion of an *s* with a following guttural spirant. It has a rare sonant counterpart in the *zh*-sound of *azure*, *pleasure*, and the like (as to which, see *Z*). The *sh*- and *zh*-sounds also constitute the concluding element in the compound *ch*- and *j*- or soft *g*-sounds (see *ch* and *G* and *J*) combined with a somewhat modified *t* and *d* respectively (made by a contact at the *sh*-point) as first element.

2. As a medieval Roman numeral, 7; also 70; with a dash over it (S̄), 70,000.—**3.** In *chem.*, the symbol of *sulphur*.—**4.** An abbreviation: (*a*) Of *Society* in such combinations as *F. R. S.* (Fellow of the Royal Society), *F. L. S.* (Fellow of the Linnean Society), etc. (*b*) Of *Surgery*, as in *D. D. S.* (Doctor of Dental Surgery). (*c*) Of *Science*, as in *B. S.* (Bachelor of Science). (*d*) Of *South* or *Southern*. (*e*) Of *Sunday* and *Saturday*. (*f*) [*l. c.*] Of Latin *solidum*, equivalent to English *shilling*: as, £ *s. d.*, pounds, shillings, pence. (*g*) In *anat.* and *zoöl.*, of *sacral*: used in vertebral formulæ: as, *S.* 5, five sacral vertebræ. (*h*) [*l. c.*] Of *second* (sixtieth part of a minute), *substantive* (a noun), *snow* (in a ship's log-book), of Latin *semi*, half (used in medical prescriptions after a quantity which is to be divided into two), and of *spherical* (of a lens). (*i*) [*l. c.*] In *her.*, of *sable*. (*j*) In *meteor.*, of *stratus*. (*k*) In *musical notation* (1), of *senza*; (2) in the form :S:, of *segno* (see *D. S.* and *segno*).—**5.** An operative symbol in quaternions, signifying the operation of taking the scalar part of a quaternion. It is also used in algebra for certain varieties of summation. The lower-case *s* usually denotes space, or the length of the arc of a curve. An *s* below the line, in enumerative geometry, refers to a plane pencil of rays. Σ (Greek *S*) signifies the sum of successive values of a function; the variable which is to take successive integral values in the terms to be added may be written below the line after the Σ, and the lower and upper limit of the summation may be written below and above the Σ. Thus,

$$a^x = \sum_n^\infty \frac{1}{n!} (\log. x)^n.$$

In the calculus of finite differences Σ is used like a sign of indefinite integration, the lower limit being replaced by an arbitrary constant, while the upper is supposed to be 1 less than the value of the variable. Thus, Σ F*x* = F (*x*−1) + F (*x*−2) + etc., down to a constant value of the variable, and then an arbitrary constant is to be added to the series. σ is used in the integral calculus to denote the area of a surface. A modified long *s*, ∫, is the sign of integration.—**Light green S.** Same as *acid-green*.—**Magenta S., rubine S.** Same as *acid-magenta*.

-s[1]. The suffix of the possessive or genitive case singular, earlier *-es*, by syncope *-s*, now regularly written with an apostrophe, *'s*. See *-es*[1].

-s[2]. The suffix of the plural form of nouns, earlier *-es*, which is now retained in pronunciation only after a sibilant, being otherwise reduced by syncope to *-s*. See *-es*[2].

-s[3]. The suffix of the third person singular of the present indicative of verbs, earlier *-es*, more originally *-eth*, *-th*. See *-eth*[3], *-th*[3].

S. A. An abbreviation of Latin *secundum artem*, according to the rules of art: used in medical prescriptions.

s. a. An abbreviation of Latin *sine anno* (without year), without date.

sa, *adv.* An obsolete or Scotch form of *so*[2].

sa. In *her.*, an abbreviation of *sable*[1].

saat, *n.* A Middle English form of *soe*.

sab (sab), *v.* and *n.* A Scotch form of *sob*.

sabadilla (sab-a̤-dil'ä̤), *n.* See *cevadilla*, and *caustic barley* (under *barley*[1]).

Sabæan[1] (sa̤-bē'a̤n), *n.* and *a.* See *Sabean*[1], *Sabean*[2].

Sabæan[2] (sa̤-bē'a̤n), *a.* and *n.* See *Sabian*[1], *Sabian*[2].

Sabæanism (sa̤-bē'a̤n-izm), *n.* See *Sabaism*.

Sabaism (sā'ba̤-izm), *n.* [See *Sabian*[2].] The doctrines of the Sabians or Mandæans. Also *Sabæism*, *Sabianism*, *Sabeism*, and sometimes, incorrectly, *Sabæanism*.

Palmetto (*Sabal Palmetto*).

Sabal (sā'bal), *n.* [NL. (Adanson, 1763); said to be from a S. Amer. or Mex. name.] A genus of fan-palms of the tribe *Corypheæ*, including several palmettos. It is distinguished from the genera next akin, *Washingtonia* and *Corypha*, by its dorsal embryo, and is further characterized by bisexual flowers with a cup-shaped calyx and a deep-lobed imbricate corolla persistent unchanged after blossoming, by its six united stamens forming at their dilated bases a ring attached to the corolla-tube, and by its three-lobed and three-celled ovary, tapering into a robust columnar style which is basilar in fruit. The fruit is usually globose and one-celled, with a loose fleshy pericarp, and a single shining dark-brown roundish and depressed seed, with hard corneous albumen which is deeply hollowed in at the base. The 7 species are natives of tropical America, from Venezuela and Trinidad northward into Florida and South Carolina and the Bermuda Islands. They are thornless palms, some species low and almost stemless, others with a tall robust trunk ringed at the base and covered above with the remains of sheaths. The leaves are terminal, roundish, and deep-cleft; the flowers are small and smooth, white or greenish, and the fruit is small and black, borne on a large and elongated spadix which is at first erect, and inclosed in a long tubular spathe, from which hang many long and slender branches and branchlets. See *palmetto* and *cabbage-tree*, and cut in preceding column.

sabalo (sab'a̤-lō), *n.* [< Sp. *sábalo*, a shad.] The tarpon, *Megalops atlanticus*.

Sabaoth (sab'ā-oth or sa-bā'oth), *n. pl.* [= F. *Sabaoth*, < L. *Sabaoth*, < Gr. Σαβαώθ, < Heb. *tsebāōth*, armies, pl. of *tsābā*, an army, < *tsābā*, attack, fight.] **1.** In *Scrip.*, armies; hosts: used as part of a title of God.

The cries of them which have reaped are entered into the ears of the Lord of *sabaoth*. Jas. v. 4.

Holy, Holy, Holy, Lord God of *Sabaoth*.
Book of Common Prayer, Te Deum.

2†. Same as *Sabbath*. [An error.]

But thence-forth all shall rest eternally
With him that is the God of *Sabaoth* hight:
O! that great *Sabaoth* God, grant me that *Sabaoths* sight!
Spenser, F. Q., VII. viii. 2.

Sacred and inspired Divinity, the *Sabaoth* and port of all men's labours and peregrinations.
Bacon, Advancement of Learning, ii.

Sabathian (sa-bā'thi-a̤n), *n.* Same as *Sabbatian*.

sabatoun†, sabatyn†, *n.* Middle English forms of *sabbaton*.

Sabbat, *n.* See *Sabbath*.

Sabbatarian (sab-a̤-tā'ri-a̤n), *a.* and *n.* [< L. *sabbatarius* (> Sp. *sabatario* = Pg. *sabbatario* = F. *sabbataire*), of or belonging to the Sabbath (*sabbatarii*, pl., the Sabbath-keepers, i. e. the Jews), < *sabbatum*, Sabbath: see *Sabbath*.] **I.** *a.* Pertaining to the Sabbath or its observance.

II. *n.* One who maintains the observance of the Sabbath (in the original sense) as obligatory on Christians. Hence—(*a*) One who observes the seventh day of the week as the Sabbath, as the Jews do, instead of the first (Sunday), as do Christians generally. A denomination of Baptists are called *Sabbatarians*, or *Seventh-day Baptists*, because they maintain that the Jewish Sabbath has not been abrogated. The Seventh-day Adventists hold the same views.

And because some few *sabbatarians* among ourselves do keep the old sabbath only, and call still for Scripture proof for the institution of the Lord's day, let me briefly tell them that which is enough to evince their error.
Baxter, Life of Faith, ii. 7.

(*b*) One who observes the Sabbath (whether Saturday or Sunday) according to the real or supposed Jewish rules for its observance; hence, one who observes it with more than the usual strictness. In the Puritan controversies of the sixteenth century the church party maintained that the obligation to observe one day in seven as a day of rest and devotion rested not upon the fourth commandment, but upon church usage and the beneficent results arising therefrom; the Puritans maintained that the obligation was based upon the Jewish law, and that the nature of the obligation was to be deduced from the Jewish regulations. They interdicted every sort of worldly occupation and every form of pastime and recreation, and were termed *Sabbatarians* by their opponents; hence the later use of the term as one of reproach.

We have myriads of examples in this kinde amongst those rigid *Sabbatarians*. *Burton*, Anat. of Mel., p. 650.

We left Lillehammer on a heavenly Sabbath morning. . . . Rigid *Sabbatarians* may be shocked at our travelling on that day; but there were few hearts in all the churches of Christendom whose hymns of praise were more sincere and devout than ours. *B. Taylor*, Northern Travel, p. 254.

Sabbatarianism (sab-ạ-tā'ri-ạn-izm), *n.* [‹ *Sabbatarian* + *-ism.*] The tenets or practices of the Sabbatarians.

Sabbath (sab'ạth), *n.* and *a.* [Also dial. (or archaically in def. 5) *Sabbat*; ‹ ME. *sabat, sabbat, sabot, sabote*, rarely *saboth*, ‹ AS. *sabat* = D. *sabbath* = MHG. *sabbatus, sabbato*, G. *sabbat* = Sw. Dan. *sabbat* = OF. *sabbat, sabat* = Pr. *sabbat, sabat, sapte, sabte* (also *dissapte*, ‹ L. *dies sabbati*, day of the Sabbath) = Sp. *sábado* = Pg. *sabbado* = It. *sabato, sabbato* = W. *sabath, sabboth*, ‹ L. *sabbatum*, usually in pl. *sabbata*, the Jewish sabbath, ML. also any feast-day, the solstice, etc., = Goth. *sabbatō, sabbatus*, the Sabbath, ‹ Gr. *σάββατον*, usually in pl. *σάββατα*, the Jewish sabbath, in sing. Saturday, ‹ Heb. *shabbāth*, rest, sabbath, sabbath day, ‹ *shābath*, rest from labor. For other forms of the word, see etymology of *Saturday*.] **I.** *n.* **1.** In the Jewish calendar, the seventh day of the week, now known as Saturday, observed as a day of rest from secular employment, and of religious observance.

Thou ne sselt do ine the daye of the *sabat* [Zeterday] thine nyedes, ne thine workes thet thou migt do ine othre dayes. *Ayenbite of Inwyt* (E. E. T. S.), p. 7.

How could the Jewish congregations of old be put in mind by their weekly *Sabbaths* what the world reaped through his goodness which did of nothing create the world? *Hooker*, Eccles. Polity, v. 71.

> He would this *Sabbath* should a figure be
> Of the blest Sabbath of Eternity.
> *Sylvester*, tr. of Du Bartas's Weeks, i. 7.

> Glad we return'd up to the coasts of light
> Ere *sabbath* evening. *Milton*, P. L., viii. 246.

The Christian festival [Sunday] was carefully distinguished from the Jewish *Sabbath*, with which it never appears to have been confounded till the close of the sixteenth century. *Lecky*, Europ. Morals, II. 258.

2. The first day of the week, similarly observed by most Christian denominations: more properly designated *Sunday*, or *the Lord's Day*. The seventh day of the week, appointed by the fourth commandment, is still commonly observed by the Jews and by some Christian denominations. (See *Sabbatarian*.) But the resurrection of the Lord, on the first day of the week, being observed as a holy festival by the early church, soon supplanted the seventh day, though no definite law, either divine or ecclesiastical, directed the change. A wide difference of opinion exists among divines as regards both the grounds and the nature of this observance. On the one hand it is maintained that the obligation of Sabbath observance rests upon positive law as embodied in the fourth commandment; that the institution, though not the original day, is of perpetual obligation; that the day, but not the nature of its requirements, was providentially changed by the resurrection of Jesus Christ and the consequent action of the Christian church; and that, to determine what is the nature of the obligations of the day, we must go back to the original commandment and the additional Jewish laws. This may be termed the Puritan view, and it defines thus the nature of the Sabbath obligation: "This Sabbath is then kept holy unto the Lord, when men, after a due preparing of their hearts, and ordering of their common affairs beforehand, do not only observe an holy rest all the day from their own works, words, and thoughts about their worldly employments and recreations; but also are taken up the whole time in the public and private exercises of His worship, and in the duties of necessity and mercy." (*West. Conf. of Faith*, xxi. § 8.) The other view is that the fourth commandment is, strictly speaking, a part of the Jewish law, and not of perpetual obligation, though valuable as a guide to the Christian church; that this commandment, like the rest of the Jewish ceremonial law, is abrogated in the letter by Christ; and that the obligation of the observance of one day in seven as a day of rest and devotion rests upon the resurrection of the Lord, the usage of the church, the apostolic practice, and the blessing of God which has evidently followed such observance. This is the view of the Roman Catholic Church, of the Greek Church, of many Anglicans, and of others, including the Protestants of the European continent. It naturally involves a much less strict regulation of the day. Between these two opinions there are a variety of views, the more common one probably being that the obligation to observe one day in seven as a day of holy rest is grounded upon the fourth commandment and is of perpetual obligation, but that the day to be observed and the nature of the observance are left to the determination of the Christian church in the exercise of a Christian liberty and discretion. Other terms for the Sabbath are *Sunday, the Lord's Day*, and *First-day*. *Sabbath* designates the institution as well as the day, and is still in vogue in Jewish and Puritan usage and literature, but properly indicates an obligation based upon the fourth commandment and a continuance of the Jewish observance. *Sunday* (the Sun's day) is originally the title of a pagan holiday which the Christian holiday supplanted, and is the common designation of the day. *The Lord's Day* (the day of the Lord's resurrection) is of Christian origin, but is chiefly confined to ecclesiastical circles and religious literature. *First-day* is the title employed by the Friends to designate the day, their object being to avoid both pagan and Jewish titles.

The *Sabbath* he [Mr. Cotton] began the evening before; for which keeping of the *Sabbath*, from evening to evening, he wrote arguments before his coming to New England; and I suppose 'twas from his reason and practice that the Christians of New-England have generally done so too. C. *Mather*, Mag. Chris., iii. 1.

There were as many people as are usually collected at a muster, or on similar occasions, lounging about, without any apparent enjoyment; but the observation of this may serve me to make a sketch of the mode of spending the *Sabbath* by the majority of unmarried, young, middling class people near a great town. *Hawthorne*, Amer. Note Book, p. 18.

The Lord's Day was strictly observed as a *Sabbath*, according to the Puritan view that its observance was enjoined in the decalogue. The *Sabbath* extended from the sunset of Saturday to the sunset of Sunday, according to the Jewish method of reckoning days. G. *P. Fisher*, Hist. Christian Church, p. 468.

3. [*l. c.*] A time of rest or quiet; respite from toil, trouble, pain, sorrow, etc.

> The branded slave that tugs the weary oar
> Obtains the *sabbath* of a welcome shore.
> *Quarles*, Emblems, iii. 15.

> A silence, the brief *sabbath* of an hour,
> Reigns o'er the fields. *Bryant*, Noon.

The picture of a world covered with cheerful homesteads, blessed with a *sabbath* of perpetual peace. *J. Fiske*, Amer. Pol. Ideas, p. 152.

4. [*l. c.*] The sabbatical year among the Israelites.

But in the seventh year shall be a *sabbath* of rest unto the land, a *sabbath* for the Lord. Lev. xxv. 4.

5. A midnight meeting supposed in the middle ages to have been held annually by demons, sorcerers, and witches, under the leadership of Satan, for the purpose of celebrating their orgies. More fully called *Witches' Sabbath*. Also, archaically, *Sabbat*.

Pomponaccio points out that part of the functions of the *Witches' Sabbath* consisted in dancing round a goat, a remnant of the worship of Pan, and that it is in memory of this that the wearing and setting up in the house of a horn as a counter charm is common in Italy. *N. and Q.*, 6th ser., IX. 21.

It [witchcraft] became . . . a social body, and had a mystery uniting its members. . . . This mystery is known to us as the *Witches' Sabbath*. *Keary*, Prim. Belief, p. 513.

The very source of witch-life may be said to have been the *Sabbat*. *The Atlantic*, LVIII. 467.

Great Sabbath, Holy Sabbath, Easter Even. The name *Great Sabbath* was given to this day in the early church. Similarly, in John xix. 31, the Sabbath before Christ's resurrection is called *great* (Authorized Version, "an high day"). This name is still the official one in the Greek Church (in the fuller form, *The Great and Holy Sabbath*). In the Roman Catholic Church it is *Sabbatum Sanctum*, 'Holy Sabbath or Saturday.'

II. *a.* Of, pertaining to, or characteristic of the Sabbath (or, by common but less proper use, Sunday): as, *Sabbath* duties; *Sabbath* observance; *Sabbath* stillness.—**Sabbath-day's journey.** See *journey*.

Sabbathaic (sab-ạ-thā'ik), *a.* [‹ *Sabbathai* (see *Sabbathaist*) + *-ic.*] Of or pertaining to the Sabbathaists.

Sabbathaist (sab-ạ-thā'ist), *n.* [‹ *Sabbathai* (see def.) + *-ist.*] **1.** A follower of Sabbathai Sevi of Smyrna, a seventeenth-century Jew, who claimed to be the Messiah.—**2.** Same as *Sabbatian*.

Sabbatharian (sab-ạ-thā'ri-ạn), *n.* [‹ *Sabbath* + *-arian*. Cf. *Sabbatarian*.] **1**†. A Sabbatarian.

These *Sabbatharians* are so call'd because they will not remove the Day of Rest from Saturday to Sunday. They leave off Work betimes on Friday Evening, and are very rigid Observers of their Sabbath.
Quoted in *Ashton's* Social Life in Reign of Queen Anne, [II. 135.

2. Same as *Southcottian*.

Sabbathary†, *a.* [‹ *Sabbath* + *-ary*[2].] Pertaining to or characteristic of the Sabbath.

For they are of opinion that themselues haue a superfluous *Sabbatharie* soule, which on that day is plentifully sent in to them, to inlarge their heart and to expell care and sorrow. *Purchas*, Pilgrimage, p. 204.

Sabbath-breaker (sab'ạth-brā"kėr), *n.* One who breaks or profanes the Sabbath, or Sunday.

They say . . . that the usurer is the greatest *Sabbath-breaker*, because his plough goeth every Sunday. *Bacon*, Usury (ed. 1887).

Sabbath-breaking (sab'ạth-brā"king), *n.* and *a.* **I.** *n.* The act of breaking or profaning the Sabbath, or Sunday; in the law of a number of the United States, a violation of the laws which forbid specified immoral, disturbing, or unnecessary labors or practices on Sunday.

II. *a.* Given to breaking the Sabbath, or Sunday.

Sabbathian (sa-bā'thi-ạn), *n.* Same as *Sabbatian*.

sabbathless (sab'ạth-les), *a.* [‹ *sabbath* + *-less.*] Having no sabbath; without intermission of labor.

This incessant and *sabbathless* pursuit of a man's fortune leaveth not that tribute which we owe to God of our time. *Bacon*, Advancement of Learning, ii. 351.

Sabbath-school (sab'ạth-sköl'), *n.* Same as *Sunday-school*.

Sabbatia (sa-bā'ti-ặ), *n.* [NL. (Adanson, 1763), named after Liberatus *Sabbati*, an Italian botanist, who wrote a "Synopsis of the Plants of Rome" (1745).] A genus of gamopetalous plants of the order *Gentianeæ*, tribe *Chironieæ*, and subtribe *Erythræeæ*. It is characterized by flowers with from five to ten narrow calyx-lobes, a five- to twelve-lobed wheel-shaped corolla, as many stamens with short filaments inserted on its throat, their anthers erect and afterward recurved but not twisted, and a one-celled ovary with projecting placentæ and a thread-shaped style and stigma, the latter with two entire and linear lobes. The 15 species are natives of the United States, extending into Cuba. They are annual or biennial herbs, erect and unbranched or panicled above, bearing opposite sessile leaves, and white or rose-colored flowers, disposed in loose cymes. The flowers are usually numerous and handsome, marked by a small central yellow star, and in the largest species, *S. chloroides*, are about 2 inches across. This species, from its color and locality, is known as the *rose of Plymouth*. The various species are called most often by the generic name *Sabbatia*, and sometimes by the book-name *American centaury*. The plant is a simple bitter tonic. *S. chloroides, S. campestris*, and *S. angularis* are introduced into flower-gardens. See *bitter-bloom* and *rose-pink*, 3.

American Centaury (*Sabbatia angularis*).
1. Upper part of the stem with the flowers. 2. Lower part of the stem with the root. *a*, a flower before anthesis, showing the stamens and style declined in opposite directions.

Sabbatian (sa-bā'tiạn), *n.* [‹ *Sabbatius* (see def.) + *-an.*] A member of a Novatian sect of the fourth century, followers of Sabbatius, who adopted the Quartodeciman rule. See *Quartodeciman*. Also *Sabathian, Sabbathaist, Sabbathian*.

Sabbatic (sa-bat'ik), *a.* [= F. *sabbatique* = Sp. *sabático* = Pg. *sabbatico* = It. *sabatico*, ‹ LL. **sabbaticus*, ‹ Gr. *σαββατικός*, of or belonging to the Sabbath, ‹ *σάββατον*, Sabbath: see *Sabbath*.] Of, pertaining to, or resembling the Sabbath (Jewish or Christian); characteristic of or befitting the Sabbath; enjoying or bringing an intermission of labor.

They found themselves disobliged from that strict and necessary rest which was one great part of the *sabbatic* rites. *Jer. Taylor*, Works (ed. 1835), I. 210.

This salutary view is only effectually pursued by due attendance on *sabbatic* duty.
Stukely, Palæographia Sacra, p. 99. (*Latham.*)

sabbatical (sa-bat'i-kạl), *a.* [‹ *Sabbatic* + *-al.*] **1.** Sabbatic; characterized by rest or cessation from labor or tillage: as, the *sabbatical* years (see below).

Likewise their seuenth yeare was *Sabbathicall*. *Purchas*, Pilgrimage, p. 122.

2. Recurring in sevens, or on every seventh (day, month, year, etc.).

The *sabbatical* pool in Judea, which was dry six days, but gushed out in a full stream upon the sabbath. *Jer. Taylor*, Works (ed. 1835), I. 273.

Taking the Semitic letters in their final order, we find that they fall into three groups, . . . the three sibilants or *sabbatical* letters occupying the three *sabbatical* places as the 7th, 14th, and 21st letters. Remembering the importance attached among all Semitic races to the sacred planetary number seven, it seems probable that it was not by mere accident that the sibilants came to occupy these positions. *Isaac Taylor*, The Alphabet, I. 192.

Sabbatical year, every seventh year among the ancient Jews, during which no cultivation of the soil was to be practised, all spontaneous growth of the soil was common property, and all but foreign debtors were to be, at least for the year, released from their debts.

Sabbatically (sa-bat'i-kạl-i), *adv.* In a Sabbatic manner.

Sabbatine (sab'a-tin), *a.* [‹ ML. *sabbatinus*, ‹ L. *sabbatum*, Sabbath: see *Sabbath*.] Pertaining to the Sabbath (Saturday): as, *Sabbatine* preachers.

Sabbatism (sab'ạ-tizm), *n.* [= F. *sabbatisme* = It. *sabbatismo*, ‹ LL. *sabbatismus*, ‹ Gr. *σαββατισμός*, ‹ *σαββατίζειν*, keep the Sabbath: see *Sabbatize*.] Observance of the Sabbath or of a sabbath; a rest; intermission of labor.

That *sabbatisme* or rest that the author to the Hebrews exhorts them to strive to enter into through faith and obedience. *Dr. H. More*, Def. of Moral Cabbala, ii.

What an eternal *sabbatism*, then, when the work of redemption, sanctification, preservation, glorification, are all finished, and his [God's] work more perfect than ever, and very good indeed! *Baxter*, Saints' Rest, i. 4.

Christ, having entered into his *Sabbatism* in heaven, gives us a warrant for the Christian Sabbath or Lord's day, which has the same relation to Christ's present *Sab-*

batism in heaven that the old Sabbath had to God's rest from his work of creation.
Dawson, Origin of World, p. 132.

Sabbatize (sab'a-tiz), *v.*; pret. and pp. *Sabbatized*, ppr. *Sabbatizing*. [< LL. *sabbatizare*, < Gr. σαββατίζειν, keep the Sabbath, < σάββατον, the Jewish Sabbath: see *Sabbath*.] **I.** *intrans.* To keep the Sabbath; rest on the seventh day.

A *Sabbatizing* too much, by too many Christians imitated, which celebrate the same rather as a day of Bacchus then the Lords day. *Purchas*, Pilgrimage, p. 122.

Let us not therefore keep the sabbath (or *sabbatize*) Jewishly, as delighting in idleness (or rest from labour). *Baxter*, Divine Appointment of the Lord's Day, vii.

If he who does not rest out of regard to the Lord does not truly *Sabbatize*, his resting is only an empty form or a blasphemous pretense. *Pop. Sci. Mo.*, XXIX. 708.

II. *trans.* To convert into or observe as a sabbath, or day of rest.

The tendency to *sabbatize* the Lord's day is due chiefly to the necessities of legal enforcement.
Smith and Cheetham, Dict. of Christ. Antiq., p. 1052.

sabbaton† (sab'a-ton), *n.* [< ME. *sabatoun* (ML. *sabbatum*), a shoe. Cf. *sabot*.] **1.** A shoe or half-boot of the kind worn by persons of wealth in the fifteenth century, mentioned as made of satin, cloth of gold, etc.

Thenne set thay the *sabatoun3* vpon the segge fotes.
Sir Gawayne and the Green Knight (E. E. T. S.), l. 574.

2. The solleret of the sixteenth century, having a form broad and blunted at the toes.

Sabbaton, 2. (From Viollet-le-Duc's "Dict. du Mobilier français.")

sabdariffa (sab-da-rif'ä), *n.* Same as *roselle*.

Sabean1 (sa-bē'an), *n.* [Also *Sabæan*; < LL. *Sabæi* (Vulgate), in form same as L. *Sabæi*, the people of Saba (see *Sabean2*), but variously regarded as the descendants of Seba or Sheba (see def.).] A member of some obscure tribes mentioned in the authorized version of the Bible, and regarded as the descendants (1) of Seba, son of Cush; (2) of Seba, son of Raamah; or (3) of Sheba, son of Joktan. Compare *Sabian2*.

Sabean2 (sa-bē'an), *a.* and *n.* [Also *Sabæan*; < L. *Sabæus*, of Saba (pl. *Sabæi*, the people of Saba), < Gr. Σαβαῖος, of Saba (pl. Σαβαῖοι, the people of Saba), < Σάβα, L. *Saba*, the capital of Yemen in Arabia.] **I.** *a.* Of or pertaining to Saba in Arabia; Arabian.

Sabæan odours from the spicy shore
Of Araby the bless'd. *Milton*, P. L., iv. 162.

II. *n.* A native or an inhabitant of that part of Arabia now called Yemen, the chief city of which was Saba. The Sabeans were extensive merchants of spices, perfumes, precious stones, etc., which they imported from India.

Sabean3 (sa-bē'an), *a.* and *n.* Same as *Sabian1*.

Sabean4 (sa-bē'an), *n.* Same as *Sabian2*.

Sabeism (sa-bē'izm), *n.* [Also *Sabæism*; = F. *Sabéisme* = Sp. Pg. *sabeismo*: see *Sabian2*.] Same as *Sabaism*.

sabeline (sab'e-lin), *a.* and *n.* [ME. *sabeline*, n.; < OF. *sabelin*, *sebelin*, adj., *sabeline*, *sebeline*, n., F. *zibeline* = Pr. *sebelin*, *sembelin* = Sp. *cebellina* = Pg. *zebelina* = It. *zibellino*, the sable-fur, < ML. *sabelinus*, of the sable, as a noun sable-fur, < *sabelum*, sable: see *sable1*.] **I.** *a.* Of or pertaining to the sable; zibeline.

II.† *n.* The skin of the sable used as a fur.

Ne scal ther beo fou ne grei, ne cunig, ne ermine, ne ocquerne, ne martres cheole, ne beuer, ne *sabeline*.
Old Eng. Homilies (ed. Morris), 1st ser., p. 181.

They should wear the silk and the *sabelline*.
The Cruel Mother (Child's Ballads, II. 270).

sabelize (sab'e-līz), *v. t.*; pret. and pp. *sabelized*, ppr. *sabelizing*. [< *sable* (ME. *sabel*) + *-ize*.] Same as *sable*.

Sabella (sa-bel'ä), *n.* [NL. (Linnæus, 1758), dim. of L. *sabulum*, sand, gravel: see *sabulous*.] **1.** The typical genus of *Sabellidæ*, containing large tubicolous cephalobranchiate marine annelids or sea-worms, with feathery or fan-like gills of remarkable delicacy and brilliancy, and greenish blood. See cut under *cerebral*.—**2.** [*l. c.*] A worm of this genus, or any member of the *Sabellidæ*: as, the fan-sabella, *S. penicillus*.

sabellan (sa-bel'an), *a.* [< *sabella* + *-an*.] Gritty or gravelly; coarsely sabulous.

sabelliana (sab-e-lä'nä), *n.* [NL., < *sabella*, < L. *sabulum*, gravel: see *sabulous*.] In *geol.*, coarse sand or gravel.

Sabellaria (sab-e-lā'ri-ä), *n.* [NL. (Lamarck, 1812), < *Sabella* + *-aria*.] A genus of tubicolous worms, typical of the *Sabellariidæ*. *S. anglica* is a leading species, of the British Islands, forming massive irregular tubes of sand at and below low-water mark.

Sabellariidæ (sab"o-lā-ri'i-dē), *n. pl.* [NL., < *Sabellaria* + *-idæ*.] A family of cephalobranchiate annelids, typified by the genus *Sabellaria*. The body is subcylindric, of two distinct portions—an anterior segmented, with setigerous and uncinate appendages, and a posterior narrow, unsegmented, and unappendaged, like a tail. Those worms live between tidemarks, among seaweeds (especially *Laminaria*), and are oviparous. Also called *Hermellacea*.

Sabellian1 (sa-bel'i-an), *a.* and *n.* [< L. *Sabelli*, the Sabellians (see def.): see *Sabine2*.] **I.** *a.* Of or pertaining to the Sabellians.

II. *n.* One of a primitive Italian people which included the Sabines, Samnites, Lucanians, etc.

Sabellian2 (sa-bel'i-an), *a.* and *n.* [< *Sabellius* (see def.) + *-an*.] **I.** *a.* Of or pertaining to Sabellius or his doctrines or followers. See *Sabellianism*.

II. *n.* A follower of Sabellius, a philosopher of the third century. See *Sabellianism*.

Sabellianism (sa-bel'i-an-izm), *n.* [< *Sabellian* + *-ism*.] The doctrinal view respecting the Godhead maintained by Sabellius and his followers. Sabellianism arose out of an attempt to explain the doctrine of the Trinity on philosophical principles. It agrees with orthodox Trinitarianism in denying the subordination of the Son to the Father, and in recognizing the divinity manifested in Christ as the absolute deity; it differs therefrom in denying the real personality of the Son, and in recognizing in the Father, Son, and Holy Spirit not a real and eternal Trinity, but one only temporal and modalistic. According to Sabellianism, with the cessation of the manifestation of Christ in time the Son also ceases to be Son. It is nearly allied to *Modalism*.

Sabellidæ (sa-bel'i-dē), *n. pl.* [NL., < *Sabella* + *-idæ*.] A family of tubicolous cephalobranchiate polychætous annelids, typified by the genus *Sabella*.

sabelline (sa-bel'in), *a.* [< *Sabella* + *-ine1*.] Pertaining to *Sabella* or to the *Sabellidæ*.

sabellite (sa-bel'it), *n.* [< *Sabella* + *-ite3*.] A fossil sabella, or some similar worm.

sabelloid (sa-bel'oid), *a.* and *n.* [< *Sabella* + *-oid*.] **I.** *a.* Of or resembling the *Sabellidæ*.

II. *n.* One of the *Sabellidæ*.

saber, sabre (sā'bėr), *n.* [< F. *sabre* = Sp. *sable* = It. *sciabla*, *sciabola*, dial. *sabala*; prob. < late MHG. *sabel*, *sebel*, G. *säbel* (> D. Dan. Sw. *sabel*), a saber; cf. OBulg. Serv. Russ. *sablya* = Bohem. *shavle* = Pol. *szabla* = Hung. *száblya* = Lith. *shoble*, *shoblis*, a saber; origin uncertain; the Teut. forms are appar. from the Slavic, but the Slavic forms themselves appear to be unoriginal.] **1.** A heavy sword having a single edge, and thickest at the back of the blade, tapering gradually toward the edge. It is usually slightly curved; but some cavalry sabers are perfectly straight. The saber may be considered as a modification of the Oriental simitar increased in weight and diminished in curvature, and differs from the typical sword, which is double-edged, with its greatest thickness in the middle of the blade.

United States Light-cavalry Saber, as used in 1864.

2. A soldier armed with a saber.

saber, sabre (sā'bėr), *v. t.*; pret. and pp. *sabered*, *sabred*, ppr. *sabering*, *sabring*. [< *saber*, *n.*] **1.** To furnish with a saber.

There are persons whose loveliness is more formidable to me than a whole regiment of *sabred* hussars with their fierce-looking moustaches.
Brooke, Fool of Quality, II. 90. (*Davies.*)

2. To strike or cut with a saber.

Flash'd all their sabres bare,
Flash'd as they turn'd in air,
Sabring the gunners there.
Tennyson, Charge of the Light Brigade.

saberbill (sā'bėr-bil), *n.* **1.** A South American dendrocolaptine bird of the genus *Xiphorhynchus*, as *X. procurvus* or *X. trochilirostris*: so called from the shape of the bill. See cut in next column.—**2.** A curlew: same as *sicklebill*. *Sportsman's Gazetteer*.

saber-billed (sā'bėr-bild), *a.* Having a bill resembling a saber in shape; sickle-billed. See cuts under *saberbill* and *Eutoxeres*.

saber-fish (sā'bėr-fish), *n.* The hairtail or silver-eel, *Trichiurus lepturus*. [Texas, U. S.]

sabertooth (sā'bėr-töth), *n.* A saber-toothed fossil cat of the genus *Machærodus*.

Saberbill (*Xiphorhynchus procurvus*).

saber-toothed (sā'bėr-tötht), *a.* Having extremely long upper canine teeth; machærodont: applied to the fossil cats of the genus *Machærodus* and some related genera.

Dentition of Saber-toothed Cat (*Machærodus*), showing the very long upper canine.

saberwing (sā'bėr-wing), *n.* A humming-bird of the genus *Campylopterus* and some related genera, having strongly falcate primaries.

saber-winged (sā'bėr-wingd), *a.* Having falcate primaries, as a humming-bird.

Sabia (sā'bi-ä), *n.* [NL. (Colebrooke, 1818), < Beng. *sabjalät*, name of one of the species.] **1.** A genus of polypetalous plants, type of the order *Sabiaceæ*. It is characterized by flowers with all the stamens perfect and the sepals and petals nearly equal, by the number of parts in each of these sets (four or five), and by their peculiar arrangement, which is opposite throughout, contrary to the usual law of alternation. There are about 12 species, natives of tropical and temperate parts of Asia. They are climbing or twiggy shrubs, with roundish branchlets, around the base of which bud-scales remain persistent. They bear alternate and entire petioled leaves, and small axillary flowers, which are solitary, cymose, or panicled.
2. In *zoöl.*, a genus of mollusks. *J. E. Gray*, 1839.

Sabiaceæ (sā-bi-ā'sẹ-ē), *n. pl.* [NL. (Blume, 1851), < *Sabia* + *-aceæ*.] A small order of polypetalous plants of the cohort *Sapindales* and series *Disciflorœ*. It is characterized by stamens which are as many as the petals and opposite them, and, except in *Sabia*, unequal or in part imperfect, by an ovary two- or three-celled and compressed or with two or three lobes, and by a fruit of one or two dry or drupaceous one-seeded nutlets, usually with a deflexed apex. It includes about 40 species, belonging to 4 genera, of which *Sabia* is the type, natives of tropical and subtropical regions, chiefly northern. They are smooth or hairy shrubs or trees, bearing alternate simple or pinnate feather-veined leaves without stipules, and usually small flowers in panicles.

Sabian1 (sā'bi-an), *a.* and *n.* [Also *Sabæan*, *Sabean*; < Heb. *tsābā*, an army, host (sc. of heaven) (see *Sabaoth*), + *-ian*.] **I.** *a.* Pertaining to the religion and rites of the Sabians.

II. *n.* A worshiper of the host of heaven; an adherent of an ancient religion in Persia and Chaldea, the distinctive feature of which was star-worship. Also called *Tsabian*.

Sabian2 (sā'bi-an), *n.* [Also *Sabean*, *Sabæan*; usually identified with *Sabian1*, but otherwise derived from *Sabo*, one of the epithets bestowed on John, the supposed founder of the sect.] A Mandæan (which see).

Sabianism (sā'bi-an-izm), *n.* [< *Sabian2* + *-ism*.] Same as *Sabaism*.

sabicu (sab-i-kö'), *n.* [< Cuban *sabicú*, *saricú*.] The horse-flesh mahogany, *Lysiloma Sabicu*. Also *saracu*.

sabicu-wood (sab-i-kö'wůd), *n.* Same as *sabicu*.

sabin1 (sab'in), *n.* [F., < L. *Sabina* (*herba*), < *Sabini*, the Sabines.] Same as *savin*.

Sabin2†, *n.* [Origin obscure.] A conceited or fanciful person.

Grimsby, which our *Sabins*, or conceited persons, dreaming what they list and following their own fansies, will have to be so called of one Grimes a merchant.
Holland, tr. of Camden, p. 542. (*Davies.*)

sabina (sa-bī'nä), *n.* In *phar.*, the savin, *Juniperus Sabina*.

sabine1 (sab'in), *n.* Same as *savin*.

Sabine2 (sā'bīn), *a.* and *n.* [= F. *sabin* (> Sp. Pg. It. *sabino*), < L. *Sabinus*, Sabine, *Sabini*, the Sabines. Cf. *Sabelli*, the Sabellians. Hence ult. *savin*.] **I.** *a.* Of or pertaining to the Sabines.

II. *n.* One of an ancient people of Italy, dwelling in the central Apennines. The Sabines formed an important element in the colonization of ancient Rome. According to tradition, the Romans took their wives by force from among the Sabines, this incident being known as the "Rape of the Sabine Women."

sable (sā'bl), *n.* and *a.* [Early mod. E. also *sabell*; < ME. *sable*, the sable, the color black, = D. *sabel* = Icel. *safal*, *safali*, the sable, = Sp. Pg. *sable*, black, < OF. *sable*, the sable, also the color black, F. *sable*, black (ML. *sabelum*, *sabellum*), = G. *zobel* = Dan. Sw. *sobel*, the sable, < Russ. *soboli* = Bohem. Pol. *sobol* = Lith. *sabalas* = Hung. *czoboly*, the sable; cf. Turk. Hind. *samūr*, < Ar. *samūr*, the sable.] **I.** *n.* **1.** A digitigrade carnivorous quadruped, *Mustela zibellina*, of the family *Mustelidæ* and subfamily *Mustelinæ*, closely related to the martens. It inhabits arctic and subarctic regions of the Old World, especially Russia and Siberia, having a copious lustrous pelage, of a dark-brown or blackish color, yielding one of the most highly prized of pelts. The animal is about 18 inches long, with a full bushy tail nearly a foot long; the limbs are short and stout, with small paws. The nose is sharp, and the ears are pricked. There are three kinds of hairs in the pelage—a short soft dense under-fur,

Sable (*Mustela zibellina*).

a second set of longer hairs, kinky like the first but coming to the surface, and fewer longer glistening hairs, bristly to the very roots. The pursuit of the sable forms an important industry in Siberia. The pelt is in the best order in winter. The darkest furs are the most valuable. None are dead-black, nor is the animal ever uniformly dark-colored, the head being quite gray or even whitish, and there is usually a large tawny space on the throat, which color may be found also in blotches over much of the under surface. Some other martens, resembling the true sable, receive the same name. Thus, the American marten, *M. americana*, is a sable hardly distinguishable from that of Siberia, except in some technical dental characters. Its fur is very valuable, though usually not so dark as that of the Siberian sable. *M. melanopus* of Japan is a kind of sable. See also cut under *marten*[1].

2. The dressed pelt or fur of the sable.—**3.** The color black in a general sense, and especially as the color of mourning: so called with reference to the general dark color of the fur of the sable as compared with other furs, or from its being dyed black as sealskin is dyed.

> Quhen thai tak honour othir or sic thingis, thai sit in *sable* and siluer that euery bringis.
> *Booke of Precedence* (E. E. T. S., extra ser.), i. 96.

4. A black cloth or covering of any kind; mourning-garments in general; a suit of black: often in the plural.

> Now have ye cause to clothe yow in *sable*.
> *Chaucer*, Complaint of Mars, l. 284.

> To clothe in *sable* every social scene.
> *Cowper*, Conversation, l. 872.

> At last Sir Edward and his son appeared in their *sables*, both very grave and preoccupied.
> *Mrs. Oliphant*, Poor Gentleman, xxx.

5. A fine paint-brush or pencil made of hair from the tail of the sable.—**6.** In *her.*, black; one of the tinctures, represented when the colors are not given, as in engraving, by a close network of vertical and horizontal lines. Abbreviated *S.*, *sa.* See also cut under *pall*.—**7.** A British collectors' name of certain pyralid moths. *Botys nigrata* is the wavy-barred sable, and *B. lingulata* is the silver-barred sable.

Sable.

—**Alaska sable**, the fur of the common American skunk, *Nephitis americana*, as dressed for commercial purposes. [Trade-name.]

> Audubon and Bachman's statement that the fur [of the skunk] "is seldom used by the hatters, and never, we think, by the furriers; and, from the disagreeable task of preparing the skin, it is not considered an article of commerce," was wide of the mark, unless it was penned before "*Alaska sable*" became fashionable.
> *Coues*, Fur-bearing Animals (1877), p. 217.

American sable, the American marten, *Mustela americana*. See *marten*[1].—**Red** or **Tatar sable**, the chorok or Siberian mink, *Putorius sibiricus*; also, the fur or pelt of this animal. See *kolinsky*.—**Siberian** or **Russian sable**. See def. 1.

II. *a.* **1.** Made of sable: as, a *sable* muff or tippet.—**2.** Of the color of a sable; dark-brown; blackish.—**3.** Black, especially as applied to mourning, or as an attribute.

> Her riding-suit was of *sable* hew black,
> Cypress over her face.
> *Robin Hood and the Stranger* (Child's Ballads, V. 411).

> He whose *sable* arms,
> Black as his purpose, did the night resemble.
> *Shak.*, Hamlet, ii. 2. 474.

> Was I deceived, or did a *sable* cloud
> Turn forth her silver lining on the night?
> *Milton*, Comus, l. 221.

> The hues of bliss more brightly glow,
> Chastised by *sabler* tints of woe.
> *Gray*, Ode on Vicissitude.

Sable antelope, an antelope, *Hippotragus* (or *Ægocerus*) *niger*.—**Sable mouse**, the lemming, *Myodes lemmus*. See cut under *lemming*.

sable (sā'bl), *v. t.*; pret. and pp. *sabled*, ppr. *sabling*. [< *sable*, *n.*] To make like sable in color; darken; blacken; hence, figuratively, to make sad or dismal; sadden.

> And *sabled* all in black the shady sky.
> G. *Fletcher*, Christ's Triumph over Death.

sable-fish (sā'bl-fish), *n.* The hilsah of the Ganges.

sableize (sā'bl-īz), *v. t.*; pret. and pp. *sableized*, ppr. *sableizing*. [< *sable* + *-ize*.] To make black; blacken; darken. Also *sabelize*.

> Some chroniclers that write of kingdomes states
> Do so absurdly *sableize* my White
> With Maskes and Enterludes by day and night.
> *Davies*, Paper's Complaint, l. 241. (*Davies*.)

sable-stoled (sā'bl-stōld), *a.* Wearing a black stole; hence, clothed or robed in black.

> The *sable-stoled* sorcerers bear his worshipt ark.
> *Milton*, Nativity, l. 220.

sable-vested (sā'bl-ves″ted), *a.* Clothed with black.

> With him [Chaos] enthroned
> Sat *sable-vested* Night, eldest of things,
> The consort of his reign. *Milton*, P. L., ii. 962.

sablière[1] (sab-li-ãr'), *n.* [< F. *sablière*, sand-pit, < *sable*, sand, < L. *sabulum*, sand: see *sabulous*.] A sand-pit. [Rare.]

sablière[2] (sab-li-ãr'), *n.* [< F. *sablière*, a raising-piece; origin unknown.] In *carp.*, same as *raising-piece*. *Imp. Dict.*

sabot (sa-bō'), *n.* [< F. *sabot*, a wooden shoe, in mech. a socket, shoe, skid, etc., OF. *sabot*, *çabot*, F. dial. *sibot*, *chabou*, *chabot*, *cabou*, a wooden shoe; perhaps related to F. *savate*, OF. *cavate*, *chavate* = Pr. *sabata* = Sp. *zapata*, *zabata*, *zapato* = Pg. *sapato* = It. *ciavatta*, *ciabatta*, an old shoe, < ML. *sabbatum*, a shoe: see *sabbaton*.] **1.** (*a*) A wooden shoe, made of one piece hollowed out by boring-tools and scrapers, worn by the peasantry in France, Belgium, etc. (*b*) In parts of France, a sort of shoe consisting of a thick wooden sole with sides and top of coarse leather; a sort of clog worn in wet weather.—**2.** A thick circular wooden disk to which a projectile is attached so as to maintain its proper position in the bore of a gun; also, a metallic cup or disk fixed to the bottom of an elongated projectile so as to fill the bore and take the rifling when the gun is discharged.—**3.** A pointed iron shoe used to protect the end of a file.—**4.** In *harp-making*, one of the little disks with projecting pins by which a string is shortened when a pedal is depressed.

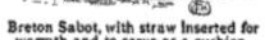

Breton Sabot, with straw inserted for warmth and to serve as a cushion.

sabotier (sa-bo-tiā'), *n.* [F. *sabotier*, a maker of sabots, < *sabot*, a wooden shoe: see *sabot*.] A wearer of sabots or wooden shoes; hence, contemptuously, one of the Waldenses.

sabre, *n.* and *v.* See *saber*.

sabretash (sā'bėr-tash), *n.* [Also *sabretache*, *sabretasche*; < F. *sabretache*, < G. *säbeltasche*, a loose pouch hanging near the saber, worn by hussars, < *säbel*, a saber, + *tasche*, a pocket.] A case or receptacle, usually of leather, suspended from the sword-belt by straps, and hanging beside the saber: it is worn by officers and men of certain mounted corps. See cut in next column.

> Puttenham's Art of Poetry . . . might be compared to an Art of War, of which one book treated of barrack drill, and the other of busbies, *sabre-tasches*, and different forms of epaulettes and feathers. *R. W. Church*, Spenser, ii.

sabrina-work (sạ-brī'nạ-wėrk), *n.* A variety of application embroidery, the larger parts of the design being cut out of some textile material and sewed to a background, needlework supplying the bordering and the smaller details.

A Member of the Scots Greys, a British cavalry regiment, wearing Sabretash. (After drawing by Elizabeth Butler.)

sabuline (sab'ụ-lin), *a.* [< L. *sabulum*, sand, + *-ine*[1].] Same as *sabulous*.

sabulose (sab'ụ-lōs), *a.* [< L. *sabulosus*, sandy: see *sabulous*.] **1.** Same as *sabulous*.—**2.** In *bot.*, growing in sandy places.

sabulosity (sab-ụ-los'ị-ti), *n.* [= Pg. *sabulosidade*; as *sabulose* + *-ity*.] The quality of being sabulous; sandiness; grittiness.

sabulous (sab'ụ-lus), *a.* [= Sp. Pg. *sabuloso* = It. *sabbioso*, < L. *sabulosus*, sandy, < *sabulum*, sand.] Sandy; gritty; acervulous: specifically applied—(*a*) in anatomy to the acervulus cerebri, or gritty substance of the pineal body of the brain; (*b*) in medicine to gritty sediment or deposit in urine. Also *sabulose*, *sabuline*.

Saburean (sạ-bū'rẹ-ạn), *n.* One of a class of Jewish scholars which arose soon after the publication of the Talmud and endeavored to lessen its authority by doubts and criticisms, but became extinct in less than a century.

saburra (sạ-bur'ạ), *n.* [NL., < L. *saburra*, sand, akin to *sabulum*, coarse sand, gravel.] A foulness of the stomach. [Rare.]

saburral (sạ-bur'ạl), *a.* [< *saburra* + *-al*.] Pertaining to saburra.

saburration (sab-u-rā'shọn), *n.* [< L. *saburra*, sand (see *saburra*), + *-ation*.] **1.** The application of hot sand to any part of the body; sand-bathing; arenation.—**2.** In *zoöl.*, the act of taking a sand-bath or rolling in the sand, as is done by gallinaceous birds; pulverizing. See *pulverizer*, 2.

sac[1] (sak), *n.* [< AF. *sac* (AL. *saca*, *sacca*, *sacha*, *saka*), < AS. *sacu*, strife, contention, suit, litigation, jurisdiction in litigious suits: see *sake*[1]. Cf. *soc*.] In *law*, the privilege enjoyed by the lord of a manor of holding courts, trying causes, and imposing fines. Also *saccage*.

> Every grant of *sac* and soc to an ecclesiastical corporation or to a private man established a separate jurisdiction, cut off from the regular authorities of the mark, the hundred, the shire, and the kingdom.
> *E. A. Freeman*, Norman Conquest, V. 309.

sac[2] (sak), *n.* [< F. *sac*, < L. *saccus*, a bag: see *sack*[1].] In *bot.*, *anat.*, and *zoöl.*, a sack, cyst, bag, bursa, pouch, purse, or receptacle of some kind specified by a qualifying word; a saccule; a saccus.—**Adipose, ambulacral, amniotic, ampullaceous, branchial, cardiac sac.** See the adjectives.—**Calcareous sac.** Same as *calciferous gland* (which see, under *gland*).—**Cirrus-sac.** See *cirrus*.—**Copulating sac**, the seminal reservoir of the male dragon-fly. See *genital lobe*, under *genital*.—**Dental sac.** See *dental*.—**Embryo sac.** See *embryo-sac*.—**Galactophorous sac**, the ampulla of the galactophorous duct.—**Gastric sac.** See *gastric*.—**Hernial sac**, the sac or pouch of peritoneum which is pushed outward, and surrounds the protruding portion of intestine.—**Lacrymal sac.** See *lacrymal*.—**Masticatory sac.** See *masticatory*.—**Needham's sac.** Same as *Needham's pouch* (which see, under *pouch*).—**Otolithic, peritoneal, pharyngeal, pulmonary, pyloric, respiratory sac.** See the adjectives.—**Yolk sac.** See *yolk-sac*. = **Syn.** *Sac*, *Saccule*, *Saccus*, *Sacculus*. The first two are English, the last two Latin and only technically used, chiefly in special phrases. There is no such difference in meaning as the form of the words would imply, some of the largest sacs being called *saccules* or *sacculi*, some of the smallest *sacs* or *sacci*.

Sac[3] (sak, more properly sâk), *n.* A member of a tribe of Algonkin Indians, allied to the Foxes, who lived near the upper Mississippi previous to the Black Hawk war of 1832. The greater part are now on reservations.

sacalai, *n.* Same as *crappie*.

sacar†, *n.* An obsolete form of *saker*[1].

sacatra (sak'ą-trą), *n.* The offspring of a griffe and a negro; a person seven eighths black. *Bartlett.*

sacbut†, *n.* See *sackbut.*

Sacca coffee. See *coffee.*

saccade (sa-kād'), *n.* [< OF. *sacade*, F. *saccade*, < OF. *saquer*, *sacher*, pull, draw; origin uncertain.] 1. In the *manége*, a violent check of a horse by drawing or twitching the reins suddenly and with one pull.—2. In *violin-playing*, a firm pressure of the bow on the strings, which crowds them down so that two or three can be sounded at once.

saccage[1] (sak'āj), *n.* [< *sac*[1] + *-age.*] Same as *sac*[1].

He had rights of freewarren, saccage, and sockage. *Barham*, Ingoldsby Legends, I. 76.

saccage[2]†, *n.* and *r.* See *sackage.*

Saccata (sa-kā'tą), *n. pl.* [NL., neut. pl. of *saccatus*, saccate: see *saccate.*] 1. The *Mollusca* as a branch of the animal kingdom: correlated with *Vertebrata*, *Articulata*, and *Radiata*. *A. Hyatt.* [Not used.]—2. A grade or division of *Urochorda*, containing the true tunicaries or ascidians, with the salps and doliolids, as collectively distinguished from the *Larvalia* (or *Appendiculariidæ*).

Saccatæ (sa-kā'tē), *n. pl.* [NL., fem. pl. of *saccatus*, saccate: see *saccate.*] An order of *Ctenophora* containing ovate or spheroidal comb-jellies with two tentacles and no oral lobes; saccate or sacciform ctenophorans. There are several families. For a characteristic example, see *Cydippe.*

saccate (sak'āt), *a.* [< NL. *saccatus*, < L. *saccus*, a bag: see *sack*[1].] 1. In *bot.*, furnished with or having the form of a bag or pouch: as, a *saccate* petal.—2. In *anat.* and *zoöl.*: (*a*) Forming or formed by a sac; cystic; pouch-like; sacciform; sacculate. (*b*) Having a sac, or saccate part; pouched; sacculated; sacciferous. (*c*) Specifically, of or pertaining to the *Saccata* or the *Saccatæ.*

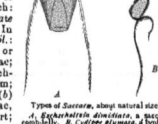

Types of *Saccatæ*, about natural size.
A, *Eschscholtzia dimidiata*, a saccate comb-jelly. *B*, *Cydippe plumosa*, a typical saccate ctenophoran.

saccated (sak'ā-ted), *a.* [< *saccate* + *-ed*[2].] Same as *saccate.*

saccharate (sak'ą-rāt), *n.* [< ML. *saccharum*, sugar (see *saccharum*), + *-ate*[1].] In *chem.*, a salt of either of the saccharic acids. (See *saccharic.*) The term is also applied to the sucrates, or compounds which cane-sugar forms with various bases and hydroxids.—**Saccharate of iron**, a preparation made from sesquioxid of iron, sugar, and soda, containing 3 per cent. of metallic iron: a valuable antidote in arsenical poisoning.—**Saccharate of lead**, an insoluble white powder made by adding, to saturation, lead carbonate to a solution of saccharic acid.—**Saccharate of lime**, a preparation consisting of sugar (16 parts), distilled water (40 parts), caustic lime (5 parts): a useful antidote in carbolic-acid poisoning.

saccharated (sak'ą-rā-ted), *a.* Mixed with some variety of sugar, either saccharose, dextrose, or milk-sugar.—**Saccharated carbonate of iron**, a greenish-gray powder composed of sulphate of iron mixed with sugar.—**Saccharated iodide of iron**, iodide of iron mixed with sugar of milk.—**Saccharated pancreatin**, pancreatin mixed with sugar of milk.—**Saccharated pepsin**, a powder consisting of sugar of milk mixed with pepsin from the stomach of the hog.—**Saccharated tar**, a mixture of tar (4 parts) with sugar (96 parts), forming an easily soluble substance for medicinal administration.

saccharic (sa-kar'ik), *a.* [< ML. *saccharum*, sugar, + *-ic.*] Pertaining to or obtained from sugar or allied substances.—**Saccharic acid.** (*a*) A monobasic acid, $C_6H_{12}O_6$, not known in the free state, but forming crystalline salts prepared by the action of bases on glucoses. (*b*) A dibasic acid, $C_6H_{10}O_8$, prepared by the action of nitric acid on sugar and various other carbohydrates. It is an amorphous solid which forms salts, many of which do not readily crystallize.

saccharide (sak'ą-rid or -rīd), *n.* [< ML. *saccharum*, sugar, + *-ide.*] A compound of sugar with a base; a sucrate.

sacchariferous (sak-ą-rif'e-rus), *a.* [< ML. *saccharum*, sugar, + *ferre* = E. *bear*[1].] Producing sugar; saccharine: as, *sacchariferous* canes. *Pop. Sci. Mo.*, XXII. 287.

saccharification (sak-ą-rif-i-kā'shon), *n.* [< *saccharify* + *-ation* (see *-fication*).] The process of converting (starch, dextrine, etc.) into sugar, as by malting.

saccharifier (sak'ą-ri-fī-ėr), *n.* [< *saccharify* + *-er*[1].] An apparatus for treating grain and potatoes by steam under high pressure, to convert the starch into sugar, previous to the alcoholic fermentation. *E. H. Knight.*

saccharify (sak'ą-ri-fī), *v. t.*; pret. and pp. *saccharified*, ppr. *saccharifying.* [< ML. *saccharum*, sugar, + L. *-ficare*, < *facere*, make: see *-fy.*] To convert into sugar, as starch; saccharize.

saccharilla (sak-ą-ril'ą), *n.* [Appar. a fanciful word, dim. of ML. *saccharum*, sugar (?).] A kind of muslin. *Simmonds.*

saccharimeter (sak-ą-rim'e-tėr), *n.* [< Gr. σάκχαρον, sugar, + μέτρον, measure.] An optical instrument used to determine the quantity of sugar in a solution. It is based upon the fact that sugar-solutions have the power of rotating the plane of polarization of a ray of light transmitted through them. Certain kinds of sugar rotate the plane to the right (dextrorotatory), as grape-sugar (dextrose) and cane-sugar; with others, the rotation is to the left (levorotatory), as levulose; further, the amount of angular rotation varies with the strength of the solution. There are many forms of saccharimeter, some of which measure directly the amount of rotation caused by a layer of the solution of given thickness; others balance the rotation of the solution against a varying thickness of some rotatory substance, as a compensating quartz plate.—**Fermentation saccharimeter**, an apparatus, chiefly used in the examination of urine, which is designed to show approximately the quantity of fermentable sugar present in solution by the volume of carbonic acid evolved on fermentation.

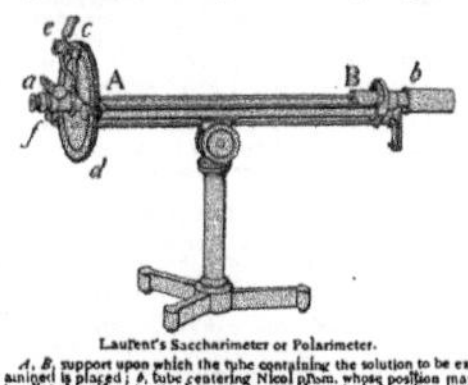

Laurent's Saccharimeter or Polarimeter.
A, *B*, support upon which the tube containing the solution to be examined is placed; *b*, tube centering Nicol prism, whose position may be slightly shifted by the lever *f*; *c*, *d*, graduated circle with mirror at *e*, and vernier at *c*; *a*, tangent screw to adjust the position of the analyzing prism, and thus remove error in the zero-point.

Fermentation Saccharimeter.

saccharimetrical (sak"ą-ri-met'ri-kal), *a.* [< *saccharimetr-y* + *-ic-al.*] Of or pertaining to or effected by saccharimetry.

saccharimetry (sak-ą-rim'e-tri), *n.* [< Gr. σάκχαρον, sugar, + -μετρία, < μέτρον, measure.] The operation or art of ascertaining the amount or proportion of sugar in solution in any liquid.

saccharin (sak'ą-rin), *n.* [< ML. *saccharum*, sugar, + *-in*[2].] 1. The anhydrid of saccharic acid, $C_6H_{10}O_5$. It is a crystalline solid having a bitter taste, dextrorotatory, and non-fermentable.—2. A complex benzin derivative, benzoyl-sulphimide, $C_6H_4SO_2.CONH$. It is a white crystalline solid, slightly soluble in cold water, odorless, but intensely sweet. It is not a sugar, nor is it assimilated, but appears to be harmless in the system, and may be useful in some cases as a substitute for sugar.

saccharinated (sak'ą-ri-nā-ted), *a.* Same as *saccharated.*

saccharine (sak'ą-rin), *a.* [< F. *saccharin* = Sp. *sacarino* = Pg. *saccharino* = It. *zuccherino*, < NL. *saccharinus*, < ML. *saccharum*, L. *saccharon*, sugar: see *saccharum.*] Of, pertaining to, or of the nature of sugar; having the qualities of sugar: as, a *saccharine* taste; the *saccharine* matter of the cane-juice; also, in *bot.*, covered with shining grains like those of sugar. Also *saccharous.*—**Saccharine diabetes.** Same as *diabetes mellitus.*—**Saccharine fermentation**, the fermentation by which starch is converted into sugar, as in the process of malting.

saccharinic (sak-ą-rin'ik), *a.* Same as *saccharic.*

saccharinity (sak-ą-rin'i-ti), *n.* [< *saccharine* + *-ity.*] The quality of being saccharine.

This is just the condition which we see, in virtue of the difference of optic refractivity produced by difference of salinity or of *saccharinity*, when we stir a tumbler of water with a quantity of undissolved sugar or salt on its bottom. *Nature*, XXXVIII. 578.

saccharite (sak'ą-rīt), *n.* [< ML. *saccharum*, sugar, + *-ite*[2].] A fine granular variety of feldspar, of a vitreous luster and white or greenish-white color.

saccharization (sak"ą-ri-zā'shon), *n.* Same as *saccharification.*

saccharize (sak'ą-rīz), *v. t.*; pret. and pp. *saccharized*, ppr. *saccharizing.* [< ML. *saccharum*, sugar, + *-ize.*] To form or convert into sugar.

saccharocolloid (sak"ą-rō-kol'oid), *n.* [< ML. *saccharum*, sugar, + *colloid.*] One of a large and important group of the carbohydrates. They are amorphous or crystallize with difficulty, diffuse through membranes very slowly if at all, are chemically indifferent, and have the general formula $_nC_6H_{10}O_5$, or differ from it slightly by the elements of water, H_2O. Here belong starch, gum, pectin, etc. *Nature*, XXXIX. 433.

saccharoid (sak'ą-roid), *a.* [< Gr. σάκχαρον, sugar, + εἶδος, form.] Same as *saccharoidal.*

saccharoidal (sak-ą-roi'dal), *a.* [< *saccharoid* + *-al.*] In *mineral.* and *geol.*, having a distinctly crystalline granular structure, somewhat resembling that of lump-sugar.

saccharometer (sak-ą-rom'e-tėr), *n.* A form of hydrometer designed to indicate the amount of sugar in a solution.—**Fermentation saccharometer**, a bent graduated tube, closed at one end, designed to indicate the amount of sugar in urine by means of the gas collected at the closed end when yeast is added to the urine.

saccharometry (sak-ą-rom'e-tri), *n.* Scientific use of a saccharometer.

Saccharomyces (sak"ą-rō-mī'sēz), *n.* [NL. (Meyen, 1838), < ML. *saccharum*, sugar, + Gr. μύκης, a mushroom.] A genus of minute saprophytic fungi; the yeast-fungi. They are unicellular fungi, destitute of true hyphæ, and increasing principally by budding or sprouting, although asci containing one to four hyaline spores are produced in a few species under certain conditions. Sexual generation is not known. The species of *Saccharomyces* occur in fermenting substances, and are well known from their power of converting sugar into alcohol and carbonic acid. Ordinary yeast, *S. cerevisiæ*, is the most familiar example; it is added to the wort of beer, the juice of fruits, etc., for the purpose of inducing fermentation. *S. ellipsoideus* and *S. Pastorianus* are also alcoholic ferments. *S. albicans*, the thrush-fungus, which lives parasitically on the mucous membrane of the human digestive organs, is also capable of exciting a weak alcoholic fermentation in a sugar solution. *S. Mycoderma* is the well-known flowers of wine. There are 31 species of *Saccharomyces* known, of which number 12 are known to produce asci. Many of these so-called species may prove to be only form-species. See *barm*[1], *flowers of wine* (under *flower*), *bloody bread* (under *bloody*), *fermentation*, and *yeast.*

saccharomycete (sak"ą-rō-mī'sēt), *n.* [< *Saccharomyces*, q. v.] A plant of the genus *Saccharomyces.*

Saccharomycetes (sak-ą-rō-mi-sē'tēz), *n. pl.* [NL., < *Saccharomyces*, q. v.] Same as *Saccharomycetaceæ.*

Saccharomycetaceæ (sak"ą-rō-mi-sē-tā'sē-ē), *n. pl.* [NL. (Reess, 1870), < *Saccharomyces* (*-cet-*) + *-aceæ.*] A monotypic group of microscopic fungi. See *Saccharomyces.*

saccharose (sak'ą-rōs), *n.* [< ML. *saccharum* + *-ose.*] 1. The general name of any crystalline sugar having the formula $C_{12}H_{22}O_{11}$ which suffers hydrolysis on heating with water or dilute mineral acid, each molecule yielding two molecules of a glucose. The saccharoses are glucose anhydrids. The best-known are saccharose or cane-sugar, milk-sugar, and maltose.
2. Specifically, the ordinary pure sugar of commerce, obtained from the sugar-cane or sorghum, from the beet-root, and from the sap of a species of maple. Chemically, pure saccharose is a solid crystalline body, odorless, having a very sweet taste, very soluble in water, less soluble in alcohol, and insoluble in absolute alcohol. Its aqueous solution is strongly dextrorotatory. It melts at 160° C., and decomposes at a higher temperature. Heated sufficiently with water or dilute mineral acid, it breaks up into equal parts of dextrose and levulose. Saccharose does not directly undergo either alcoholic or lactic fermentation; but in the presence of certain ferments it is resolved into dextrose and levulose, which are readily fermentable. It unites directly with many metallic oxids and hydrates to form compounds called *sucrates* or *saccharates.* Saccharose is extensively used both as a food and as an antiseptic. It is also used to some extent in medicine. Also called *cane-sugar.*

saccharous (sak'ą-rus), *a.* [< ML. *saccharum*, sugar, + *-ous.*] Same as *saccharine.*

saccharum (sak'ą-rum), *n.* [ML. NL., < L. *saccharon*, sugar, < Gr. σάκχαρον, also σάκχαρις, σάκχαρι, σάκχαρ, sugar: see *sugar.*] 1. Sugar.—2. [*cap.*] [NL., Linnæus, 1737.] A genus of grasses of the tribe *Andropogoneæ*, type of the group *Sacchareæ.* It is characterized by minute spikelets in pairs, one of each pair stalked and the other sessile, each spikelet composed of four awnless hyaline glumes, of which three are empty and the terminal one shorter, blunt, and including three stamens and a free oblong grain. It differs from the nearly related ornamental grass *Erianthus* in its awnless glumes, and from *Sorghum* in having a fertile and perfect flower in each spikelet of a pair. It resembles *Zea*, the Indian corn, with monœcious flowers, and *Arundo*, the cane, with several-flowered spikelets, in habit only. It includes about 12 species, natives of warm regions, probably all originally of the Old World. They are tall grasses, with leaves which are flat, or convolute when dry, and flowers in a large terminal panicle, densely sheathed everywhere with long silky hairs. By far the most important species is *S. officinarum*, the common sugar-cane. See *sugar-cane*; also *kans* and *moonja*.—**Saccharum candidum.** Same as *rock-candy*.—**Saccharum hordeatum**, barley-sugar.—**Saccharum lactis**, sugar of milk.—**Saccharum mannæ.** Same as *mannite*.—**Saccharum saturni**, sugar of lead.

sacci, *n.* Plural of *saccus*.

sacciferous (sak-sif'e-rus), *a.* [< L. *saccus*, sack, + *ferre* = E. *bear*[1].] In *anat.*, *zoöl.*, and *bot.*, having a sac, in any sense; saccate.

sacciform (sak'si-fôrm), *a.* [< L. *saccus*, sack, + *forma*, form.] Having the form of a sac; saccate or saccular; bursiform; baggy.—**Sacciform aneurism**, an aneurism with a distinct sac, and involving only part of the circumference of the artery. Also called *saccular* or *sacculated aneurism*.

Saccobranchia (sak-ō-brang'ki-ä), *n. pl.* [NL., < Gr. σάκκος, sack, + βράγχια, gills.] A division of tunicates, including the typical ascidians, as distinguished from the *Dactyliobranchia* and *Tæniobranchia*, having vascular saccate gills. Also *Saccobranchiata*. *Owen*.

saccobranchiate (sak-ō-brang'ki-āt), *a.* and *n.* [< Gr. σάκκος, sack, + βράγχια, gills, + *-ate*[1].] **I.** *a.* Having saccate gills; belonging to the *Saccobranchia*.

II. *n.* A member of the *Saccobranchia*.

Saccobranchinæ (sak"ō-brang-kī'nē), *n. pl.* [NL., < *Saccobranchus* + *-inæ*.] A subfamily of *Siluridæ*, typified by the genus *Saccobranchus*.

Saccobranchus (sak-ō-brang'kus), *n.* [NL., < Gr. σάκκος, sack, + βράγχια, gills.] A genus of East Indian catfishes of the family *Siluridæ*, having a lung-like saccular extension of the branchial cavity backward between the muscles along each side of the vertebral column: typical of the subfamily *Saccobranchinæ*.

Saccocirridæ (sak-ō-sir'i-dē), *n. pl.* [NL., < *Saccocirrus* + *-idæ*.] A family of chætopod annelids, typified by the genus *Saccocirrus*.

Saccocirridea (sak"ō-si-rid'ē-ä), *n. pl.* [NL., < *Saccocirrus* + *-idea*.] The *Saccocirridæ* elevated to the rank of a class of *Chætopoda*.

Saccocirrus (sak-ō-sir'us), *n.* [NL., < L. *saccus*, sack, + *cirrus*, a tuft of hair: see *cirrus*.] The typical genus of *Saccocirridæ*.

Saccolabium (sak-ō-lā'bi-um), *n.* [NL. (Blume, 1825), < L. *saccus*, sack, + *labium*, lip.] A genus of orchids of the tribe *Vandeæ* and subtribe *Sarcantheæ*. It is characterized by the unappendaged column, by a lip with saccate base or with a straight descending spur, and by flat and spreading sepals and petals, with the inflorescence in racemes which are often much-branched and profusely flower-bearing. It differs from the related genus *Vanda* in its smaller flowers and its commonly slender pollen-stalk. It includes about 20 species, natives of the East Indies and the Malay archipelago. They are epiphytes without pseudobulbs, but having their stems clad with two-ranked flat and spreading leaves, which are usually coriaceous or fleshy, and which cover the stem permanently by their persistent sheaths. The flowers in many cultivated species are of considerable size and great beauty, forming a dense recurving raceme. In other species they are small and scattered, or in some minute and panicled.

saccoleva, sackalever (sak-ō-lev'ä, sak-a-lev'ėr), *n.* [= F. *sacolève*.] A Levantine vessel with one lateen sail; also, a Greek vessel of about 100 tons, with a foremast raking very much forward, having a square topsail and topgallantsail, a sprit foresail, and two small masts abaft, with lateen yards and sails. *Hamersly*, Naval Encyc.

saccomyian (sak-ō-mī'i-an), *n.* [< *Saccomys* + *-ian*.] A pocket-mouse of the genus *Saccomys*; a saccomyid.

saccomyid (sak-ō-mī'id), *n.* A member of the *Saccomyidæ*; a pocket-rat or pocket-mouse. Also, improperly, *saccomyd*.

Saccomyidæ (sak-ō-mī'i-dē), *n. pl.* [NL., < *Saccomys* + *-idæ*.] 1. Same as *Saccomyina* and *Saccomyoidea*. *Lilljeborg*, 1866.—2. A family of myomorphic rodents named from the genus *Saccomys*, confined to North America and the West Indies, having external cheek-pouches and a murine aspect; the pocket-rats or pocket-mice. The genera besides *Saccomys* are *Heteromys*, *Dipodomys*, *Perognathus*, and *Cricetodipus*. The species of *Dipodomys* are known as *kangaroo-rats*. The family in this restricted sense is divided by Coues into three subfamilies, *Dipodomyinæ*, *Perognathinæ*, and *Heteromyinæ*. See cuts under *Dipodomys* and *Perognathus*.

Saccomyina (sak"ō-mi-ī'nä), *n. pl.* [NL., < *Saccomys* + *-ina*[2].] A group of myomorphic rodents, named by G. R. Waterhouse in 1848, containing all the rodents with external cheek-pouches: same as *Saccomyoidea*.

Saccomyinæ (sak"ō-mi-ī'nē), *n. pl.* [NL., < *Saccomys* + *-inæ*.] Same as *Saccomyidæ*, 2. *S. F. Baird*, 1857; *J. E. Gray*, 1868.

saccomyoid (sak-ō-mī'oid), *a.* and *n.* [< *Saccomys* + *-oid*.] **I.** *a.* Having external cheek-pouches, as a rodent; pertaining to the *Saccomyoidea*.

II. *n.* A member of the *Saccomyoidea*; a pocket-rat, pocket-mouse, or pocket-gopher.

Saccomyoidea (sak"ō-mī-oi'dē-ä), *n. pl.* [NL., < *Saccomys* + *-oidea*.] A superfamily of myomorphic rodents, named by Gill in 1872, containing all those with external cheek-pouches, or the two families *Saccomyidæ* and *Geomyidæ*. The mastoid bone is moderately developed, and the occipital correspondingly reduced. There are no postorbital processes, and the zygomatic process of the maxillary is an expanded perforated plate. The grinders are four on each side above and below. The root of the lower incisor is protuberant posteriorly. The descending process of the mandible is obliquely twisted outward and upward. There is a special muscle of the large external cheek-pouch; all the feet are five-toed; the upper lip is densely hairy, not visibly cleft, and the pelage lacks under-fur. See cuts under *Geomyidæ*, *Dipodomys*, and *Perognathus*.

Saccomys (sak'ō-mis), *n.* [NL. (F. Cuvier, 1823), < Gr. σάκκος, sack, + μῦς, a mouse.] An obscure genus of *Saccomyidæ*, giving name to the family, probably synonymous with *Heteromys* of Desmarest. A species is named *S. anthophilus*, but has never been satisfactorily identified.

saccoon†, *n.* In *fencing*, same as *seconde*.

> There were the lively Gauls, animated and chattering, ready to wound every Pillar with their Canes, as they pass'd by, either in Ters, Cart, or *Saccoon*.
> *Ashton*, Social Life in Reign of Queen Anne, I. 135.

Saccopharyngidæ (sak"ō-fä-rin'ji-dē), *n. pl.* [< *Saccopharynx* (*-pharyng-*) + *-idæ*.] A family of lyomerous fishes, represented by the genus *Saccopharynx*. They have five branchial arches, the abdominal division much longer than the rostrobranchial; the tail excessively elongated and attenuated; the eyes anterolateral; the jaws moderately extended backward (in comparison with the *Eurypharyngidæ*), and apparently not closable against each other; enlarged teeth in one or both jaws; the dorsal and anal fins feebly developed, and the pectorals short but broad. The family is represented by apparently 2 species, by some supposed to be conspecific. They reach a length of 5 or 6 feet, of which the tail forms by far the greater part. They inhabit the deep sea, and feed upon fishes, which may sometimes be as large as or larger than themselves. Individuals have been found on the surface of the sea helpless from distention by fishes swallowed superior in size to themselves. One of the species is the bottle-fish, *Saccopharynx ampullaceus*.

Bottle-fish (*Saccopharynx ampullaceus*), distended by another fish in its stomach.

Saccopharyngina (sak-ō-far-in-jī'nä), *n. pl.* [NL., < *Saccopharynx* (*-pharyng-*) + *-ina*[2].] The *Saccopharyngidæ* as a group of *Murænidæ*. *Günther*.

saccopharyngoid (sak"ō-fä-ring'goid), *n.* and *a.* **I.** *n.* A fish of the family *Saccopharyngidæ*.

II. *a.* Of or having characteristics of the *Saccopharyngidæ*.

Saccopharynx (sa-kof'a-ringks), *n.* [NL. (S. L. Mitchill, 1824), < Gr. σάκκος, sack, + φάρυγξ, throat: see *pharynx*.] A remarkable genus of deep-sea fishes, typical of the family *Saccopharyngidæ*. *S. ampullaceus* inhabits the North Atlantic, and is capable of swallowing fishes larger than itself. See cut under *Saccopharyngidæ*.

Saccophora (sa-kof'ō-rä), *n. pl.* [NL., neut. pl. of *Saccophorus*: see *saccophore*.] In J. E. Gray's classification of "mollusks" (1821), the fifth class, containing the tunicates or ascidians, and divided into 3 orders—*Holobranchia*, *Tomobranchia*, and *Diphyllobranchia*.

saccophore (sak'ō-fōr), *n.* [< NL. *Saccophorus*, q. v.] 1. A rodent mammal with external cheek-pouches.—2. A tunicate or ascidian, as a member of the *Saccophora*.

Saccophori (sa-kof'ō-rī), *n. pl.* [LL., < Gr. σακκοφόρος, wearing sackcloth, < σάκκος, sack, + φέρειν = E. *bear*[1].] A party of Christian penitents in the fourth century: probably a division of the Encratites.

Saccophorus (sa-kof'ō-rus), *n.* [NL. (cf. Gr. σακκοφόρος, wearing sackcloth), < Gr. σάκκος, sack, sackcloth, + -φορος, < φέρειν = E. *bear*[1].] 1. In *mammal.*, same as *Geomys*. *Kuhl*, 1820.—2. In *entom.*, a genus of coleopterous insects of the family *Tenebrionidæ*. *Haag-Rutenberg*, 1872.

Saccopteryx (sa-kop'te-riks), *n.* [NL., < Gr. σάκκος, sack, + πτέρυξ = E. *feather*.] A genus of South and Central American emballonurine bats, the males of which have a peculiar glandular sac of the antebrachial wing-membrane, secreting an odoriferous sebaceous substance attractive to the females; sack-winged bats. The upper incisors are one pair, the lower three pairs. There are several species, as *S. leptura* and *S. bilineata*.

saccos (sak'os), *n.* [< MGr. σάκκος (see def.), < Gr. σάκκος, sack.] A short vestment worn in the Greek Church by metropolitans and in the Russian Church by all bishops. It corresponds to the Western dalmatic.

Saccosoma (sak-ō-sō'mä), *n.* [NL., < Gr. σάκκος, sack, + σῶμα, body.] 1. A genus of encrinites, containing forms which were apparently free-swimming like the living members of the genus *Comatula*. They are found in the Oölite.—2. A genus of coleopterous insects. *Motschulsky*, 1845.

Saccostomus (sa-kos'tō-mus), *n.* [NL., < Gr. σάκκος, sack, + στόμα, mouth.] A genus of hamsters of the subfamily *Cricetinæ* and family *Muridæ*, having the molar teeth triserially tuberculate. See *hamster*.

saccular (sak'ū-lär), *a.* [< *saccule* + *-ar*[3].] Like a sac; saccate in form; sacciform: as, a *saccular* dilatation of the stomach or intestine.—**Saccular aneurism.** Same as *sacciform aneurism* (which see, under *sacciform*).—**Saccular glands**, compound glands in which the divisions of the secreting cavity assume a saccular form.

sacculate (sak'ū-lāt), *a.* [< NL. *sacculatus*, < L. *sacculus*, a little sack: see *saccule*.] Formed of or furnished with a set or series of sac-like dilatations; sacculiferous; sacculated: as, a *sacculate* stomach; a *sacculate* intestine. See cuts under *leech* and *intestine*.

sacculated (sak'ū-lā-ted), *a.* [< *sacculate* + *-ed*[2].] Same as *sacculate*.—**Sacculated aneurism.** Same as *sacciform aneurism* (which see, under *sacciform*).—**Sacculated bladder**, a bladder having a sacculus as an abnormal formation.

sacculation (sak-ū-lā'shon), *n.* [< *sacculate* + *-ion*.] The formation of a sac or saccule; a set of sacs taken together: as, the *sacculation* of the human colon, or of the stomach of a semnopithecoid ape. See cuts under *alimentary* and *intestine*.

saccule (sak'ūl), *n.* [< L. *sacculus*, dim. of *saccus*, a bag, sack: see *sack*[1].] 1. A sac or cyst; especially, a little sac; a cell; a sacculus. Specifically—2. In *anat.*, the smaller of two sacs in the vestibule of the membranous labyrinth of the ear, situated in the fovea hemispherica, in front of the utricle, connected with the membranous canal of the cochlea by the canalis reuniens, and prolonged in the aquæductus vestibuli to a pyriform dilatation, the saccus endolymphaticus.—**Saccule of the larynx.** Same as *laryngeal pouch* (which see, under *pouch*).—**Vestibular saccule.** See def. 2.=**Syn.** See *sac*[2].

sacculi, *n.* Plural of *sacculus*.

Sacculina (sak-ū-lī'nä), *n.* [NL. (J. Vaughan Thompson, about 1830), < L. *sacculus*, a little sack, + *-ina*[1].] 1. A genus of cirripeds of the division *Rhizocephala*, type of a family *Sacculinidæ*. The species are parasitic upon crabs. See cut under *Rhizocephala*.—2. [*l. c.*] A species of this genus.

sacculine (sak'ū-lin), *a.* [< NL. *Sacculina*, q. v.] Of or pertaining to the genus *Sacculina* or family *Sacculinidæ*.

> Instead of rising to its opportunities, the *sacculine* Nauplius, having reached a certain point, turned back.
> H. *Drummond*, Natural Law in the Spiritual World, p. 344.

Sacculinidæ (sak-ū-lin'i-dē), *n. pl.* [NL., < *Sacculina* + *-idæ*.] A family of rhizocephalous cirripeds, represented by the genus *Sacculina*.

sacculus (sak'ū-lus), *n.*; pl. *sacculi* (-lī). [NL., < L. *sacculus*, a little sack: see *saccule*.] A saccule.—**Sacculi of the colon**, the irregular dilatations caused by the shortness of the longitudinal muscular bands.—**Sacculus cæcalis.** Same as *laryngeal pouch* (which see, under *pouch*).—**Sacculus chylifer.** Same as *receptaculum chyli*.—**Sacculus communis, sacculus hemiellipticus.** Same as *utricle of the vestibule* (which see, under *utricle*).—**Sacculus of the larynx.** Same as *laryngeal pouch* (which see, under *pouch*).—**Sacculus proprius, sacculus rotundus.** Same as *vestibular saccule* (which see, under *saccule*).—**Sacculus semiovalis.** Same as *utricle of the vestibule* (which see, under *utricle*).—**Vesical sacculus**, a protrusion of the mucous lining of the bladder between the bundles of fibers of the muscular coat, so as to form a sort of hernia. Also called *appendix herniæ*.—**Vestibular sacculus.** Same as *saccule*, 2. =**Syn.** See *sac*[2].

saccus (sak'us), *n.*; pl. *sacci* (sak'sī). [NL., < L. *saccus*, < Gr. σάκκος, a bag, sack: see *sack*[1].] 1. In *anat.* and *zoöl.*, a sac.—2. [*cap.*] In *conch.*, a genus of gastropods: same as *Ampullaria*. *Fabricius*, 1823.—**Saccus endolymphaticus**, the dilated blind extremity of the ductus endolymphaticus, the canal leading from the utricle through the aquæductus vestibuli.—**Saccus vasculosus**, a vascular organ in the brain of some elasmobranchiate fishes, as the skate. See cut under *Elasmobranchii*.—**Saccus vitellinus**, the vitelline sac, that part of the yolk-sac which hangs out of the body of an embryo and forms the navel-sac, or umbilical vesicle. = **Syn.** See *sac*².

sacellum (sa-sel'um), *n.*; pl. *sacella* (-ä). [< L. *sacellum*, dim. of *sacrum*, a holy thing or place, neut. of *sacer*, consecrated, dedicated: see *sacre*¹, *sacred*.] In *Rom. antiq.*, a small inclosed space without a roof, consecrated to some deity, containing an altar, and sometimes also a statue of the god.

sacerdocy† (sas'ėr-dō-si), *n.* [< F. *sacerdoce*, < L. *sacerdotium*, the priesthood, < *sacerdos* (*sacerdot-*), a priest: see *sacerdotal*.] Sacerdotal system; priestly character or order.

The temporal Sceptre (as we have shown) departing from Judah, he being both Priest and Sacrificer too, their *sacerdocy* and sacrifice were brought to an end.
Evelyn, True Religion, II. 56.

sacerdotal (sas-ėr-dō'tal), *a.* [< OF. (and F.) *sacerdotal* = Pr. Sp. Pg. *sacerdotal* = It. *sacerdotale*, < L. *sacerdotalis*, of or pertaining to a priest, < *sacerdos* (*sacerdot-*) (> AS. *sacerd*), a priest, lit. 'presenter of offerings or sacred gifts,' < *sacer*, sacred, + *dare*, give (> *dos* (*dot-*), a dowry: see *dol*², *dower*²): see *sacre*¹ and *date*¹.] Of or pertaining to priests or the priesthood; priestly: as, *sacerdotal* dignity; *sacerdotal* functions or garments; *sacerdotal* character.

Duke Valentine . . . was designed by his father to a *sacerdotal* profession.
Bacon, Advancement of Learning, ii. 333.

The countries where *sacerdotal* instruction alone is permitted remain in ignorance.
Goldsmith, Citizen of the World, lxxv.

Cut off by *sacerdotal* ire
From every sympathy that Man bestowed!
Wordsworth, Eccles. Sonnets, i. 4.

sacerdotalism (sas-ėr-dō'tal-izm), *n.* [< *sacerdotal* + *-ism*.] The sacerdotal system or spirit; the methods or spirit of the priesthood; devotion to the interests or system of the priesthood: in a bad sense, priestcraft.

It is to be hoped that those Nonconformists who are so fond of pleading for grace to the Establishment on grounds of expediency, because of the good work it is doing, or because of the comprehensiveness of its policy, or, strangest of all, because of the bulwark against *sacerdotalism* which it maintains, will lay these pregnant words to heart.
British Quarterly Rev., LXXXIII. 109.

sacerdotalist (sas-ėr-dō'tal-ist), *n.* [< *sacerdotal* + *-ist*.] A supporter of sacerdotalism; one who believes in the priestly character of the clergy.

sacerdotalize (sas-ėr-dō'tal-īz), *v. t.*; pret. and pp. *sacerdotalized*, ppr. *sacerdotalizing*. [< *sacerdotal* + *-ize*.] To render sacerdotal.

Some system of actual observance, some system of custom or usage, must lie behind them [the sacred laws of the Hindus]; and it is a very plausible conjecture that it was not unlike the existing very imperfectly *sacerdotalized* customary law of the Hindus in the Punjab.
Maine, Early Law and Custom, p. 26.

sacerdotally (sas-ėr-dō'tal-i), *adv.* In a sacerdotal manner.

sacerdotism (sas'ėr-dō-tizm), *n.* [< L. *sacerdos* (*sacerdot-*), a priest, + *-ism*.] Same as *sacerdotalism*.

sachel†, *n.* An obsolete form of *satchel*.

sachem (sā'chem), *n.* [Massachusetts Ind. Cf. *sagamore*.] 1. A chief among some tribes of American Indians; a sagamore.

The Massachusets call . . . their Kings *Sachemes*.
Capt. John Smith, Works (ed. Arber), p. 939.

They [the Indians] . . . made way for ye coming of their great *Sachem*, called Massasoyt.
Coll. *Mass. Hist. Soc.*, 4th ser., III. 94.

But their *sachem*, the brave Wattawamat,
Fled not; he was dead. *Longfellow*, Miles Standish, vii.

2. One of a body of high officials in the Tammany Society of New York city. The sachems proper number twelve, and the head of the society is styled *grand sachem*.

sachemdom (sā'chem-dum), *n.* [< *sachem* + *-dom*.] The government or jurisdiction of a sachem.

sachemic (sā'chem-ik), *a.* [< *sachem* + *-ic*.] Of or pertaining to a sachem. *Stand. Nat. Hist.*, VI. 163. [Rare.]

sachemship (sā'chem-ship), *n.* [< *sachem* + *-ship*.] The office or position of a sachem.

sachet (sa-shā'), *n.* [< F. *sachet* (= Pr. *saquet* = Sp. Pg. *saquete* = It. *sacchetto*), dim. of *sac*, a bag: see *sack*¹. Cf. *sachel*, *satchel*.] A small bag, usually embroidered or otherwise ornamented, containing a perfume in the form of powder, or some perfumed substance; also, a small cushion or some similar object, the stuffing of which is strongly perfumed, placed among articles of dress, etc.

This letter, written on paper of vellum-like appearance, was put in an envelope and sealed with the armorial bearings of the sultan, and the whole enclosed in a crimson cloth *sachet* or bag, somewhat resembling a lady's small reticule, richly embroidered in gold.
Quoted in *First Year of a Silken Reign*, p. 242.

sachet-powder (sa-shā'pou'dėr), *n.* Powdered perfume for use in sachets.

sacheverel (sa-chev'e-rel), *n.* [After Dr. *Sacheverel*.] An iron door or blower for the mouth of a stove. *Halliwell*.

sack¹ (sak), *n.* [< ME. *sak*, *sac*, *sek*, *seck*, *sech*, *sack*, < AS. *sæc*, *sæcc*, *sacc* = D. *zak* = MLG. *sak*, LG. *sak*, *sack* = OHG. MHG. *sac*, G. *sack* = Icel. *sekkr* = Sw. *säkk* = Dan. *sæk* = F. *sac* (> E. *sac*) = Pr. *sac* = Sp. Pg. *saco* = It. *sacco* = OIr. Gael. *sac* = W. *sach*, sack, = Bulg. Serv. Bohem. Pol. *sak* = Russ. *sakŭ*, a bag-net, = Hung. *szák* = Albanian *sak* (OBulg. dim. *sakulŭ* = Lith. *sakrele* = NGr. σακκούλι), < L. *saccus* = Goth. *sakkus*, < Gr. σάκκος, a bag, sack, also sackcloth, a garment of sackcloth; < Heb. *saq*, Chald. *sak*, a sack for corn, stuff made of haircloth, sackcloth; prob. of Egyptian origin; cf. Coptic *sok* = Ethiopian *sak*, sackcloth. The wide diffusion of the word is prob. due to the incident in the story of Joseph in which the cup was hidden in the sack of corn (see Gen. xliv.).] 1. A bag; especially, a large bag, usually made of coarse hempen or linen cloth. (See *sackcloth*.) Sacks are used to contain grain, flour, salt, etc., potatoes and other vegetables, and coal.

One of the peasants untied closely [secretly] a *sack* of walnuttes. *Coryat*, Crudities, I. 21.

Tho' you wud gie me as much red gold
As I could haud in a *sack*.
Lambert Linkin (Child's Ballads, III. 104).

2. A unit of dry measure. English statutes previous to American independence fixed the sack of flour and meal at 5 bushels or 280 pounds, that of salt at 5 bushels, that of coal at 3 bushels (the sacks to measure 50 by 26 inches), and that of wool at 3½ hundredweight or 364 pounds. Since 1870 the British sack has been 4 imperial bushels. Locally, sacks of 2, 3, 3½, and 4 bushels were used as measures in England. The sack has been a widely diffused unit, varying in different countries, from 2 to 4 Winchester bushels. Thus, it was equal to 2 such bushels at Florence, Leghorn, Leyden, Middelburg, Tournon, etc.; to 2⅛ at Zealand and Beaumont; to 2¼ at Haarlem, Goes, Geneva, Bayonne; to 2⅜ at Amsterdam; to 2½ at Agen, Utrecht, etc.; to 2⅝ at Dort and Montauban; to 2¾ at Granada and Emden; to 2⅞ at Ghent; to 3 at Strasburg, Rotterdam, The Hague, and in Flanders (the common sack); to 3½ at Brussels; and to 3¾ at Basel. The sack of Hamburg was nearly 6 bushels, that of Toulon still greater, while the sack of Paris, used for plaster, was under a bushel.

Last Week 6 *Sacks* of Cocoa Nuts were seiz'd by a Custom House Officer, being brought up to Town for so many *sacks* of Beans. *London Post*, April 14, 1704.

3†. Sackcloth; sacking.

For forty days in *sack* and ashes fast.
Greene and Lodge, Looking Glass for Lond. and Eng.

Wearing nothing about him but a shirt of *sacke*, a paire of shooes, and a haire cappe onely.
Hakluyt's Voyages, I. 20.

The son of Nvn then . . .
Before the Ark in prostrate wise appeares.
Sack on his back, dust on his head, his eyes
Even great with teares.
Sylvester, tr. of Du Bartas's Weeks, ii., The Captaines.

4. [Also spelled *sacque*.] (*a*) A gown of a peculiar form which was first introduced from France into England toward the close of the

Woman wearing a Sack (middle of the 18th century).

seventeenth century, and continued to be fashionable throughout the greater part of the eighteenth century. It had a loose back, not held by a girdle or shaped into the waist, but hanging in straight plaits from the neck-band. See *Watteau*.

My wife this day put on first her French gown called a *sac*, which becomes her very well.
Pepys, Diary, March 2, 1668.

Madame l'Ambassadrice de Venise in a green *sack* with a straw hat. *Walpole*, Letters, II. 115.

An old-fashioned gown, which I think ladies call a *sacque*: that is, a sort of robe, completely loose in the body, but gathered into broad plaits upon the neck and shoulders, which fall down to the ground, and terminate in a species of train. *Scott*, Tapestried Chamber.

(*b*†) The loose straight back itself. The term seems to have been used in this sense in the eighteenth century.—5. [Also spelled *sacque*.] A kind of jacket or short coat, cut round at the bottom, fitting the body more or less closely, worn at the present day by both men and women: as, a sealskin *sack*; a *sack*-coat.

As for his dress, it was of the simplest kind: a summer *sack* of cheap and ordinary material, thin checkered pantaloons, and a straw hat, by no means of the finest braid.
Hawthorne, Seven Gables, iii.

A large-boned woman, dressed in a homespun stuff petticoat, with a short, loose *sack* of the same material, appeared at the door. *H. B. Stowe*, Oldtown, p. 208.

6. In *anat.* and *zoöl.*, a sac or saccule.—**To get the sack**, to be dismissed from employment, or rejected as a suitor. [Slang.]

I say, I wonder what old Fogg 'ud say, if he knew it. I should *get the sack*, I s'pose—eh? *Dickens*, Pickwick, xx.

He is no longer an officer of this gaol; he has *got the sack*, and orders to quit into the bargain.
C. *Reade*, Never too Late, xxvi.

To give one the sack, to dismiss one from employment, especially to dismiss one summarily; discharge or reject as a suitor. [Slang.]

Whenever you please, you can *give him the sack!*
Barham, Ingoldsby Legends, II. 249.

The short way would have been . . . to have requested him immediately to quit the house: or, as Mr. Gann said, "to *give him the sack* at once."
Thackeray, Shabby Genteel Story, v.

sack¹ (sak), *v. t.* [< ME. *sacken* (= MD. *sacken*, D. *zakken* = G. *sacken* = Icel. *sekka*); < *sack*¹, *n.*] 1. To put into sacks or bags, for preservation or transportation: as, to *sack* grain or salt.

The mele is *sakked* and ybounde.
Chaucer, Reeve's Tale, l. 150.

2. To inclose as in a bag; cover or incase as with a sack.

And also *sack* it in your glove.
The Elfin Knight (Child's Ballads, I. 130).

At the corners they placed pillows and bolsters *sacked* in cloth blue and crimson. *L. Wallace*, Ben-Hur, p. 253.

3. To heap or pile as by sackfuls. [Rare.]

I fly from tyrant he, whose heart more hard than flint
Hath *sack'd* on me such hugy heaps of ceaseless sorrows here,
That sure it is intolerable the torments that I bear.
Peele, Sir Clyomon and Sir Clamydes.

4. To give the sack or bag to; discharge or dismiss from office, employment, etc.; also, to reject the suit of: as, to *sack* a lover. [Slang.]

Ah! she 's a good kind creetur'; there 's no pride in her whatsumever—and she never *sacks* her servants.
Mayhew, London Labour and London Poor, II. 533.

sack² (sak), *n.* [< F. *sac* = Sp. *saco* = Pg. *saco*, *sacco*, *saque* = It. *sacco*, sack, plunder, pillage; ult. < L. *saccus*, a bag, sack (see *sack*¹), but the precise connection is uncertain. In one view, it is through a particular use of the verb represented by E. *sack*¹, 'put into a bag,' and hence, it may be supposed, 'conceal and take away' (cf. *bag*¹, and *pocket*, in similar uses); but no such use of the OF. and ML. verb appears, the Rom. verbs meaning 'sack' being secondary forms, depending on the noun (see *sack*¹, *v.*, *saccage*, *v.*); besides, the town or people 'sacked' is not 'put into a bag.' The origin is partly in the OF. "*a sac, a sac*, the word whereby a commander authorizeth his souldiers to sack a place or people" (Cotgrave), = It. *a sacco*, "*asacco, asaccomano*, to the spoile, to the sacke, ransakt" (Florio)—the exhortation *a sac*, It. *a sacco*, 'to plunder,' prob. meaning orig. 'to bag!' i. e. fill your pouches (OF. *sac* = It. *sacco*, a bag, pouch, wallet, sack: see *sack*¹, *n.*); and partly in the Sp. *sacomano*, a plunderer, also sack, plunder, pillage, = It. *saccomano*, a plunderer, freebooter, scout, soldier's servant, also plunder; < ML. *saccomannus*, a plunderer, *saccomannum*, plunder, < MHG. *sackman*, a soldier's servant, camp-servant (*sackman machen*, plunder), lit. 'sack-man,' one who carries a sack, < *sack*, = E. *sack*, + *man* = E. *man*.] 1. The plundering of a city or town after storming and capture; plunder; pillage: as, the *sack* of Magdeburg.

The people of God were moved, . . . having beheld the *sack* and combustion of his sanctuary in most lamentable manner flaming before their eyes.
Hooker, Eccles. Polity, vii. 7.

In deede he wanne it [the towne] and put it to the *sacke*.
Puttenham, Arte of Eng. Poesie, p. 217.

From her derived to Helen, and at the *sack* of Troy unfortunately lost. B. *Jonson*, Volpone, ii. 1.

The city was sure to be delivered over to fire, *sack*, and outrage. *Motley*, Dutch Republic, II. 70.

2. The plunder or booty so obtained; spoil; loot.

Everywhere
He found the *sack* and plunder of our house
All scatter'd thro' the houses of the town.
Tennyson, Geraint.

sack[2] (sak), *v. t.* [= MD. *sacken* = Sp. Pg. *saquear*, sack; from the noun: see *sack*[2], *n.* Cf. *sackage, n.*] To plunder or pillage after storming and taking: as, to *sack* a house or a town.

Burghers were fleeced, towns were now and then *sacked*, and Jews were tortured for their money.
H. *Spencer*, Social Statics, p. 462.

On Oct. 12, 1702, Sir George Rooke burnt the French and Spanish shipping in Vigo, and *sacked* the town.
J. Ashton, Social Life in Reign of Queen Anne, II. 206.

Chittore was thrice besieged and thrice *sacked* by the Mahomedans. *J. Fergusson*, Hist. Indian Arch., p. 410.

sack[3]† (sak), *n.* [Also rarely *seck* (cf. MD. *sackwijn*); < F. *sec*, dry (*vin sec*, dry wine), = Sp. *seco* = Pg. *secco* = It. *secco* (*vino secco*, dry wine), < L. *siccus*, dry; root uncertain.] Originally, one of the strong light-colored wines brought to England from the south, as from Spain and the Canary Islands, especially those which were dry and rough. These were often sweetened, and mixed with eggs and other ingredients, to make a sort of punch. The name *sweet sack* was then given to wines of similar strength and color, but requiring less artificial sweetening. In the seventeenth century the name seems to have been given alike to all strong white wines from the south, as distinguished from Rhenish on the one hand and red wines on the other.

Will 't please your lordship drink a cup of *sack?*
Shak., T. of the S., Ind., ii. 3.

For claret and *sack* they did not lack,
So drank themselves good friends.
Quoted in *Child's Ballads*, V. 211.

He and I immediately to set out, having drunk a draught of mulled *sacke*. *Pepys*, Diary, II. 313.

Burnt sack, mulled sack.

Pedro. Let's slip into a tavern for an hour;
'Tis very cold.
Uber. Content; there is one hard by.
A quart of *burnt sack* will recover us.
Beau. and Fl., Coxcomb, i. 3.

Sherris-sack, the white wine of the south of Spain, practically the same as sherris or sherry.

A good *sherris-sack* hath a two-fold operation in it.
Shak., 2 Hen. IV., iv. 3. 104.

Sweet sack. See above.

sackage (sak'āj), *n.* [Also *saccage*; < F. *saccage* (ML. *saccagium*), pillaging, < *sac*, pillage: see *sack*[2].] The act of taking by storm and with pillage; sack; plundering.

And after two yeeres *sackage* in Hungarie, they passed by the fennes of Mæotis into Tartaria, and haply had returned to make fresh spoiles in Europe, if the Embassage of Pope Innocent had not diuerted their purpose.
Purchas, Pilgrimage, p. 405.

sackage†, *v. t.* [MD. *sackageren*, < F. *saccager* (= It. *saccheggiare*, ML. *saccagere*), pillage, < *saccage*, pillaging: see *sackage*, *n.*] To sack; pillage.

Those songs of the dolorous discomfits in battaile, and other desolations in warre, or of townes *saccaged* and subuerted, were song by the remnant of the army ouerthrowen, with great skrikings and outcries.
Puttenham, Arte of Eng. Poesie (ed. Arber), p. 63.

sackalever†, *n.* See *saccoleva*.

sack-barrow (sak'bar"ō), *n.* A kind of barrow much used for moving sacks in granaries or on barn-floors from one point to another, and for loading goods in ships. See cut under *truck*.

sack-bearer (sak'bãr"ėr), *n.* Any bombycid moth of the family *Psychidæ*, whose larva carries for protection a silken case to which bits of grass, leaves, or twigs are attached; a basket-worm. See cut under *bag-worm*.

sackbut (sak'but), *n.* [Also *sacbut, sagbut*; < F. *saquebute*, OF. *saqueboute, sacheboute*, a sackbut (OF. *sacheboute*, ML. *sacabuta*, a kind of pike), = Sp. *sacabuche* (naut.), also sackbut, trombone, a tube or pipe serving for a pump, = Pg. *sacabuxa, saquebuxo*, a sackbut; origin doubtful; perhaps orig. a derisive name, 'that which exhausts the chest or belly,' < Sp. *sacar*, draw out, extract, empty (= OF. *sacquer*, draw out hastily), + *buche*, the maw, crop, stomach; perhaps < OHG. *bûh*, MHG. *bûch*, G. *bauch*, belly, = OLG. *bûc* = AS. *bûc*, belly: see *bouk*[1], *bulk*[1].] A mediæval musical instrument of the trumpet family, having a long bent tube with a movable slide so that the vibrating column of air could be varied in length and the pitch of the tone changed, as in the modern trombone. The word has been unfortunately used in Dan. iii. to translate *sabbeka*, which seems to have been a stringed instrument. Compare *sambuke*.

The trumpets, *sackbuts*, psalteries, and fifes . . .
Make the sun dance. *Shak.*, Cor., v. 4. 52.

The Hoboy, *Sagbut* deepe, Recorder, and the Flute.
Drayton, Polyolbion, iv. 365.

Alv. You must not look to have your dinner served in with trumpets.
Car. No, no, *sack-buts* shall serve us.
Middleton, Spanish Gypsy, ii. 1.

sackcloth (sak'klôth), *n.* [< *sack*[1] + *cloth*.] 1. Cloth of which sacks are made, usually a cloth of hemp or flax.—2. A coarse kind of cloth worn as a sign of grief, humiliation, or penitence; hence, the garb of mourning or penance.

Thrise every weeke in ashes shee did sitt,
And next her wrinkled skin rough *sackecloth* wore.
Spenser, F. Q., I. iii. 14.

Gird you with *sackcloth* and mourn before Abner.
2 Sam. iii. 31.

He swears
Never to wash his face, nor cut his hairs;
He puts on *sackcloth*, and to sea.
Shak., Pericles, iv. 4. 29.

sackclothed (sak'klôtht), *a.* [< *sackcloth* + *-ed*[2].] Clothed in sackcloth; penitent; humiliated.

To be jovial when God calls to mourning, . . . to glitter when he would have us *sackcloth'd* and squalid; he hates it to the death. *Bp. Hall*, Remains, p. 69. (*Latham.*)

sack-coat (sak'kōt), *n.* See *coat*[2], 2.

sack-doodle (sak'dö"dl), *v. i.* [< **sackdoodle*, *n.*, same as *doodlesack*.] To play on the bagpipe. *Scott.*

sacked (sakt), *a.* [< *sack*[1] + *-ed*[2].] Wearing a garment called a *sack*.—**Sacked friar**, a monk who wore a coarse upper garment called a *saccus*. These friars made their appearance in England about the middle of the thirteenth century.

So bene Augustyns and Cordylers,
And Carmes and eke *sacked freres*,
And alle freres shodde and bare.
Rom. of the Rose, l. 7460.

sack-emptier (sak'emp"ti-ėr), *n.* A contrivance for emptying sacks, consisting essentially of a frame or support for holding the sack, with mechanism for raising and inverting it for the discharge of its contents.

sacker[1] (sak'ėr), *n.* [< *sack*[1] + *-er*[1].] 1. One who makes or fills sacks.—2. A machine for filling sacks.—**Sacker and weigher**, in *milling*, a device for holding a sack to the spout of an elevator and weighing the grain or flour by means of a steelyard as the bag is filled. When the required weight is in the bag, the steelyard cuts off the supply automatically.

sacker[2] (sak'ėr), *n.* [< *sack*[2] + *-er*[1].] One who sacks or plunders a house or a town.

sacker[3], *n.* See *saker*[2].

sack-filter (sak'fil"tėr), *n.* A bag-filter.

sackful[1] (sak'fůl), *n.* [< *sack* + *-ful*.] As much as a sack will hold. *Swift.*

sackful[2]† (sak'fůl), *a.* [< *sack*[2] + *-ful*.] Bent on sacking or plundering; pillaging; ravaging.

Now will I sing the *sackfull* troopes Pelasgian Argos held.
Chapman, Iliad, ii. 601.

sack-hoist (sak'hoist), *n.* An adaptation of the wheel and axle to form a continuous hoist for raising sacks and bales in warehouses. The wheel is turned by an endless chain, while the hoisting-gear is passed over the axle, either raising the weight at one side and descending simultaneously for a new load at the other, or being simply wound on a drum.

sack-holder (sak'hōl"dėr), *n.* One who or that which holds a sack; specifically, a device for holding a sack open for the reception of grain, salt, or the like, consisting of a standard supporting a ring with a serrated edge.

sacking[1] (sak'ing), *n.* [< *sack*[1] + *-ing*[1].] A coarse fabric of hemp or flax, of which sacks, bags, etc., are made: also used for other purposes where strength and durability are required. Compare *sacking-bottomed*.

Getting upon the *sacking* of the bedstead, I looked over the head-board minutely at the second casement.
Poe, Murders in the Rue Morgue.

sacking[2] (sak'ing), *n.* [Verbal n. of *sack*[2], *v.*] The act of plundering or pillaging, after storming and taking, as a house or a city.

sacking-bottomed (sak'ing-bot"umd), *a.* Having a sheet of sacking stretched between the rails, as an old-fashioned bedstead, to form a support for the mattress.

New *sacking-bottom'd* Bedsteads at 11*s.* a piece.
Quoted in *Ashton's* Social Life in Reign of Queen Anne, [I. 75.

sackless (sak'les), *a.* [Also (Sc.) *saikless*; < ME. *sakles, sacless, sacles*, innocent, < AS. *sacleás* (= Icel. *saklauss* = Sw. *saklös* = Dan. *sagesløs*), without contention, quiet, peaceable, < *sacu*, strife, contention, guilt, also a cause, lawsuit, accusation, + *-leás*, E. *-less*: see *sake* and *-less*.] 1. Guiltless; innocent; free from fault or blame.

It ware worthy to be schrede and schrynede in golde,
ffor it es *sakles* of syne, sa helpe me oure Lorde!
Morte Arthure (E. E. T. S.), l. 3993.

"O, is this water deep," he said,
"As it is wondrous dun?
Or is it sic as a *saikless* maid
And a leal true knicht may swim?"
Sir Roland (Child's Ballads, I. 226).

How she was abandoned to herself, or whether she was *sackless* o' the sinfu' deed, God in Heaven knows.
Scott, Heart of Mid-Lothian, v.

2. Guileless; simple.

'Gainst slander's blast
Truth doth the silly *sackless* soul defend.
Greene, Isabel's Sonnet.

And many *sacklesse* wights and praty barnes run through the tender weambe.
Nashe, Lenten Stuffe (Harl. Misc., VI. 163).

[Obsolete or dialectal in both senses.]

Folk-free and sackless. See *folk-free*.

sack-lifter (sak'lif"tėr), *n.* Any device for lifting or raising a sack filled with grain, salt, etc. It may be a rack and pinion attached to a stationary frame or to a hand-truck to raise the sack to a height convenient for carrying, or simply a clutch or a rope to seize the gathered end of the bag.

sack-moth (sak'môth), *n.* Same as *sack-bearer*.

sack-packer (sak'pak"ėr), *n.* In *milling*, a machine for automatically weighing out a determined quantity of flour, forcing it into a flour-sack, and releasing the full sack.

sackpipe (sak'pīp), *n.* Same as *bagpipe*.

sack-posset (sak'pos"et), *n.* Posset made with sack, with or without mixture of ale: formerly brewed customarily on a wedding-night.

I must needs tell you she composes a *sack-posset* well.
B. *Jonson*, Cynthia's Revels, ii. 1.

Then my wife and I, it being a great frost, went to Mrs. Jem's, in expectation to eat a *sack-posset*, but, Mr. Edward not coming, it was put off. *Pepys*, Diary, I. 5.

sack-pot (sak'pot), *n.* A small vessel like a jug or pitcher, with a globular body, made of yellowish earthenware, and covered with a white stanniferous glaze. These pots often bear an inscribed word, as "sack," "claret," or "whit" (for white wine), and sometimes are dated, but not later than the seventeenth century. They are rarely more than 8 inches high, and were probably used for drawing wine direct from the cask.

sack-race (sak'rās), *n.* A race in which the legs of the contestants are incased in sacks gathered at the top and tied around the body.

sack-tree (sak'trē), *n.* An East Indian tree, *Antiaris toxicaria*, specifically identical with the upas-tree, though formerly separated and known as *A. innoxia, A. saccidora*, etc. Lengths of its bark after soaking and beating are turned inside out without splitting, and used as a sack, a section of wood being left as a bottom.

sack-winged (sak'wingd), *a.* Noting the bats of the genus *Saccopteryx* (which see).

sacless†, *a.* See *sackless*.

Sacodes (sā-kō'dēz), *n.* [NL. (Le Conte, 1853), < Gr. σάκος, a shield, + εἶδος, form.] A genus of beetles of the family *Cyphonidæ*, erected by Leconte for three North American forms having the last joint of the maxillary palpi acute, antennæ subserrate, body regularly elliptical, moderately convex, and the thorax semicircular, produced over the head, and strongly reflexed at the margin, as *S. thoracica*. The group is now included in the larger genus *Helodes*.

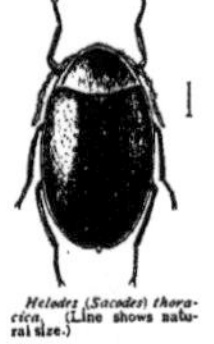
Helodes (Sacodes) thoracica. (Line shows natural size.)

Sacoglossa (sak-ō-glos'ä), *n. pl.* Same as *Sacoglossæ*.

Sacoglossæ (sak-ō-glos'ē), *n. pl.* [NL., < Gr. σάκος, a shield, + γλῶσσα, a tongue.] In Gegenbaur's system of classification, a division of opisthobranchiate gastropods, represented by such genera as *Elysia, Limapontia*, and *Placobranchus*: an inexact synonym of *Abranchiata* or *Apneusta*, and of *Pellibranchiata* (which see).

sacola, *n.* The common killifish, mummychog, or salt-water minnow, *Fundulus heteroclitus*. [Florida.]

sacque (sak), *n.* [A pseudo-F. spelling of F. *sac*, a bag: see *sack*[1].] See *sack*[1], 4 and 5.

sacra[1], *n.* Plural of *sacrum*.

sacra[2] (sā'krä), *n.*; pl. *sacræ* (-krē). [NL. (sc. *arteria*), < L. *sacra*, fem. of *sacer*, sacred: see *sacrum*.] A sacral artery.—**Sacra media**, the middle sacral artery. This is a comparatively insignificant artery in man, arising at the bifurcation of the common iliaca; it represents, however, the real continuation of the abdominal aorta, and is much larger in some animals.

sacral[1] (sā'kral), *a.* and *n.* [< NL. *sacrum* + *-al.*] I. *a.* Of or pertaining to the sacrum.—**Sacral angle**, the saliency of the sacral prominence; the acute angle, presenting anteriorly, between the base of the sacrum and the body of the last lumbar vertebra, specially marked in man.—**Sacral arteries**, arteries distributed to the anterior surface of the sacrum and the coccyx. *Lateral sacral arteries*, usually two in number on each side, arising from the posterior division of the internal iliac. *Middle sacral artery*, or *sacromedian artery*, a branch arising from the furcation of the aorta, and a vestige of the primitive condition of that vessel, descending along the middle line to terminate in Luschka's gland. Also called *sacra*.—**Sacral canal.** See *canal*[1].—**Sacral cornua.** See *cornua of the sacrum*, under *cornu*.—**Sacral curve** or **curvature**, the curved long axis of the sacrum, concentric with that of the true pelvis. It varies much in different individuals, and differs in the two sexes.—**Sacral flexure**, the curve of the rectum corresponding to the concavity of the sacrum and coccyx.—**Sacral foramina.** See *foramen*.—**Sacral ganglia.** See *ganglion*.—**Sacral glands**, four or five lymphatic glands lying in the hollow of the sacrum, in the folds of the mesorectum behind the rectum.—**Sacral index**, the ratio of the breadth to the length of the sacrum multiplied by 100.—**Sacral plexus.** See *plexus*.—**Sacral prominence** or **protuberance**, the promontory of the sacrum.—**Sacral rib.** See *rib*[1].—**Sacral veins**, the venæ comites of the sacral arteries. The *lateral sacral veins* form, by their communication with one another and with the two middle sacrals, a plexus over the anterior surface of the sacrum. The *middle sacral veins* are two veins which follow the course of the middle sacral artery, and terminate in the left common iliac vein or at the junction of the iliacs.—**Sacral vertebræ**, those vertebræ which unite to form a sacrum, usually five in number in man. They range in number from the fewest possible (two) to more than twenty. In animals with the higher numbers, especially birds, many of these ankylosed bones are really borrowed from other parts of the spinal column; they are collectively known as *false* sacral vertebræ, and distinctively as *lumbosacral* and *urosacral*. (See these words, and *sacrarium*[2].) In a few mammals (cetaceans and sirenians, without hind limbs), many reptiles (serpents, etc.), and most fishes, no sacral vertebræ are recognizable as such. See cuts under *spine*, *sacrum*, and *sacrarium*[2].

II. *n.* A sacral vertebra. Abbreviated *S.*

sacralgia (sā-kral'ji-ä), *n.* [NL., < *sacrum* + Gr. ἄλγος, pain.] Pain in the region of the sacrum.

sacrament (sak'ra-ment), *n.* [< ME. *sacrament*, *sacrement*, < OF. *sacrament*, *sagrament*, *sacrement*, an oath, consecration, F. *sacrement*, consecration, OF. vernacularly *sairement*, *serement*, *serrement*, F. *serment*, an oath, = Pr. *sagramen*, *sacrament*, *serment* = Sp. Pg. *sacramento* = It. *sacramento*, *sagramento* = D. G. Dan. Sw. *sakrament*, < L. *sacramentum*, an engagement, military oath, LL. (eccles.) a mystery, sacrament, < *sacrare*, dedicate, consecrate, render sacred or solemn: see *sacre*[1].] 1†. An oath of obedience and fidelity taken by Roman soldiers on enlistment; hence, any oath, solemn engagement, or obligation, or ceremony that binds or imposes obligation.

> Herounto the Lord addeth the Rainbow, a new *Sacrament*, to seale his mercifull Couenant with the earth, not to drowne the same any more. *Purchas*, Pilgrimage, p. 42.

> Now sure this doubtfull causes right
> Can hardly but by *Sacrament* be tride.
> *Spenser*, F. Q., V. i. 25.

> There cannot be
> A fitter drink to make this sanction in.
> Here I begin the *sacrament* to all.
> *B. Jonson*, Catiline, i. 1.

2. In *theol.*, an outward and visible sign of inward and spiritual grace; more particularly, a solemn religious ceremony enjoined by Christ, or by the church, for the spiritual benefit of the church or of individual Christians, by which their special relation to him is created or freshly recognized, or their obligations to him are renewed and ratified. In the Roman Catholic Church and the Greek Church there are seven sacraments—namely, baptism, confirmation, the eucharist, penance, holy orders, matrimony, and (in the Roman Catholic Church) extreme unction or (in the Greek Church) unction of the sick. Protestants in general acknowledge but two sacraments, baptism and the Lord's Supper. The difference of view as to the value or significance of sacraments is more important than the difference as to their true number. In general it may be said that there are three opinions respecting them: (*a*) that the sacrament is a means of grace acting directly upon the heart and life, "a sure and certain means to bring peace to our souls" (*Bishop Hay*, Sincere Christian); (*b*) that the sacrament, though not in itself the means of grace, is nevertheless a solemn ratification of a covenant between God and the individual soul; (*c*) that the sacrament is simply a visible representation of something spiritual and invisible, and that the spiritual or invisible reality may be wanting, in which case the symbol is without spiritual value or significance. The first view is held by the Roman Catholics, the Greeks, and some in the Anglican communion; the second by most Protestants; the third by the Zwinglians, the Socinians, and, in modern times, by some of the orthodox churches, especially of the Congregational denominations. The Quakers, or Friends, reject altogether the doctrine of the sacraments.

> In a word, *Sacraments* are God's secrets, discovered to none but his own people. *Hooker*, Eccles. Polity, v., App. 1.

> The Fathers, by an elegant expression, call the blessed *Sacraments* the extension of the Incarnation.
> *Jer. Taylor*, Worthy Communicant, i. 2.

> Nothing tends more to unite mens hearts than joyning together in the same Prayers and *Sacraments*.
> *Stillingfleet*, Sermons, II. vi.

3. The eucharist, or Lord's Supper: used with the definite article, and without any qualifying word.

> There offred first Melchisedeche Bred and Wyn to oure Lord, in tokene of the *Sacrement* that was to comene.
> *Mandeville*, Travels, p. 87.

> The Bishop carried *the Sacrament*, even his consecrated wafer cake, betwixt the Images of two golden Angels.
> *Coryat*, Crudities, I. 38, sig. D.

Adoration of the blessed sacrament. See *adoration*.—**Benediction of the blessed sacrament.** See *benediction*.—**Ecclesiastical sacraments**, confirmation, penance, orders, matrimony, and unction (of the sick). Also called *lesser sacraments*.—**Exposition of the sacrament.** See *exposition*.—**Sacrament of the altar**, the eucharist.

sacrament (sak'ra-ment), *v. t.* [< *sacrament*, *n.*] To bind by an oath. [Obsolete or archaic.]

> When desperate men have *sacramented* themselves to destroy, God can prevent and deliver.
> *Abp. Laud*, Works, p. 86.

> A few people at convenient distance, no matter how bad company—these, and these only, shall be your life's companions: and all those who are native, congenial, and by many an oath of the heart *sacramented* to you, are gradually and totally lost. *Emerson*, Prose Works, II. 461.

sacramental (sak-ra-men'tal), *a.* and *n.* [< ME. *sacramental*, < OF. (and F.) *sacramental*, *sacramentel* = Sp. Pg. *sacramental* = It. *sacramentale*, < LL. *sacramentalis*, sacramental, < L. *sacramentum*, an engagement, oath, sacrament: see *sacrament*.] I. *a.* 1. Of, pertaining to, or constituting a sacrament; of the nature of a sacrament; used in the sacrament: as, *sacramental* rites or elements; *sacramental* union.

> My soul is like a bird, . . . daily fed
> With sacred wine and *sacramental* bread.
> *Quarles*, Emblems, v. 10.

> But as there is a *sacramental* feeding and a spiritual feeding, and as the spiritual is the nobler of the two, and of chief concern, . . . I conceive it will be proper to treat of this first. *Waterland*, Works, VII. 101.

2. Bound or consecrated by a sacrament or oath.

> And trains, by ev'ry rule
> Of holy discipline, to glorious war
> The *sacramental* host of God's elect!
> *Cowper*, Task, ii. 349.

3. In *anc. Rom. law*, of or pertaining to the pledges deposited by the parties to a cause before entering upon litigation.

> He [the alien] could not sue by the *Sacramental* Action, a mode of litigation of which the origin mounts up to the very infancy of civilisation. *Maine*, Ancient Law, p. 48.

Sacramental communion, communion by actual bodily manducation of the eucharistic elements or species: distinguished from *spiritual communion*, or communion in will and intention at times when the communicant is unable or ritually unfitted to communicate sacramentally.—**Sacramental confession.** See *confession*.

II. *n.* 1. A rite analogous to but not included among the recognized sacraments.

> At Ester tyme, all the prestes of the same Gilde, with dyuers other, be not sufficient to mynyster the sacramentes and *sacramentalles* vnto the seyde peaple.
> *English Gilds* (E. E. T. S.), p. 247.

> It [the baptism of John] was a *sacramental* disposing to the baptism and faith of Christ.
> *Jer. Taylor*, Works (ed. 1835), I. 95.

> Sums of money were allowed by the ordinaries to be exacted by the parsons, vicars, curates, and parish priests even for the sacraments and *sacramentals* of Holy Church, which were sometimes denied until the payment was made. *R. W. Dixon*, Hist. Church of Eng., ii.

2. *pl.* Certain instruments or materials used in a sacrament, or ceremonies connected with a sacrament.

> These words, cup and testament, . . . be *sacramentals*.
> *Bp. Morton*, Discharge of Imputation, p. 80. (*Latham.*)

sacramentalism (sak-ra-men'tal-izm), *n.* [< *sacramental* + *-ism.*] The doctrine that there is in the sacraments themselves by Christ's institution a direct spiritual efficacy to confer grace upon the recipient.

sacramentalist (sak-ra-men'tal-ist), *n.* [< *sacramental* + *-ist.*] One who holds the doctrine of sacramentalism.

sacramentally (sak-ra-men'tal-i), *adv.* After the manner of a sacrament.

sacramentarian (sak'ra-men-tā'ri-an), *a.* and *n.* [< *sacramentary* + *-an.*] I. *a.* 1. Sacramentary; pertaining to a sacrament or sacraments.—2. Pertaining to sacramentarians.

> In practice she [the Church of England] gives larger scope than the Presbyterian Churches to the *sacramentarian* principle. *Schaff*, Christ and Christianity, p. 165.

II. *n.* 1†. One who holds that the sacraments are mere outward signs not connected with any spiritual grace. In the sixteenth century this name was given by the Lutherans and afterward by English reformers to the Zwinglians and Calvinists.

2. A sacramentalist.

sacramentarianism (sak'ra-men-tā'ri-an-izm), *n.* [< *sacramentarian* + *-ism.*] Sacramentarian doctrine and practices: often used opprobriously to indicate extreme views with reference to the nature, value, and efficacy of the sacraments.

> His account of the advance of sacerdotalism and *sacramentarianism*. *Athenæum*, No. 2863, p. 335.

sacramentary (sak-ra-men'ta-ri), *a.* and *n.* [= F. *sacramentaire* = Sp. Pg. It. *sacramentario*, n.; < ML. **sacramentarius*, adj., as a noun *sacramentarius*, a sacramentarian, *sacramentorium*, a service-book, < LL. *sacramentum*, sacrament: see *sacrament*.] I. *a.* 1. Of or pertaining to a sacrament or sacraments.—2. Of or pertaining to sacramentarians.

II. *n.*; pl. *sacramentaries* (-riz). 1. An office-book formerly in use, containing the rites and prayers connected with the several sacraments (the eucharist, baptism, penance, orders, etc.) and other rites. The Greek euchology is a similar book. See *missal*.

> The Western, as compared with the Oriental *Sacramentaries*, have been remarkable in all ages for the boldness with which the disposition of the several parts has been varied. *R. W. Dixon*, Hist. Church of Eng., xv.

2†. Same as *sacramentarian*, 1.

> It seemeth therefore much amiss that against them whom they term *Sacramentaries* so many invective discourses are made. *Hooker*, Eccles. Polity, v. 67.

Gelasian, Gregorian, Leonine Sacramentary. See the adjectives.

sacramentize† (sak'ra-men-tīz), *v. i.* [< *sacrament* + *-ize.*] To administer the sacraments.

> Ministers made by Presbyterian government in France and the Low Countries were owned and acknowledged by our Bishops for lawfully ordained for all intents and purposes, both to preach and *sacramentize*.
> *Fuller*, Ch. Hist., XI. v. 65.

sacrarium[1] (sā-krā'ri-um), *n.*; pl. *sacraria* (-ä). [L., a place for the keeping of sacred things, a sacristy, shrine, etc., < *sacer*, consecrated, sacred: see *sacre*[1].] 1. In *Rom. antiq.*: (*a*) Any sacred or consecrated retired place; any place where sacred objects were deposited, as that connected with the Capitoline temple where were kept the processional chariots; sometimes, a locality where a statue of an emperor was placed. (*b*) A sort of family chapel in private houses, in which the images of the Penates were kept.—2. That part of a church where the altar is situated; the sanctuary; the chancel.

Sacrarium and Entire Pelvis of a Bird (the common fowl). Upper figure, side view; lower figure, top view. *Sm*, sacrarium (in lower figure the letters at the two ends of it; in upper figure *Sm* points to bodies of dorsolumbar vertebræ ankylosed in the sacrum); *Il*, ilium; *Is*, ischium; *Pb*, pubis; *Am*, acetabulum (the line extends to the antitrochanter); the vacuity behind the acetabulum is the ilioscriatic foramen, corresponding to the sacrosciatic notch of a mammal; the vacuity below the acetabulum corresponds to the obturator foramen of a mammal.

sacrarium[2] (sā-krā'ri-um), *n.*; pl. *sacraria* (-ä). [NL., < *sacrum* + *-arium.*] In *ornith.*, the complex sacrum of any bird, consisting of dorsolumbar or lumbosacral and of urosacral vertebræ, as well as of sacrals proper. The sacrarium is ankylosed with the ilia and these with the ischia, in such manner that usually the sacrosciatic interval which exists in a mammal is converted into an iliosciatic foramen. *Coues*. See also cuts under *epipleura* and *sacrum*.

sacrary† (sak'rā-ri), *n.* [< ME. *sacrarye*, < OF. *sacrairie*, *sacraire* = Sp. Pg. *sagrario* = It. *sacrario*, < L. *sacrarium*, a place for the keeping of sacred things: see *sacrarium*[1].] A holy place.

> The purified heart is God's *sacrary*, his sanctuary, his house, his heaven. *Rev. T. Adams*, Works, I. 250.

sacrate† (sā'krāt), *v. t.* [< L. *sacratus*, pp. of *sacrare*, dedicate, consecrate: see *sacre*[1]. Cf. *consecrate*, *desecrate*, *execrate*.] To consecrate.

> The marble of some monument *sacrated* to learning.
> *Waterhouse*, Apology (1653), p. 51.

sacration† (sā-krā'shon), *n.* [< LL. *sacratio(n-)*, consecration, dedication, < L. *sacrare*, consecrate: see *sacrate*.] Consecration.

> Why then should it not as well from this be avoided as from the other find a *sacration*? *Feltham*, Resolves.

sacre¹† (sā'kėr), *v. t.* [‹ ME. *sacren, sakeren*, ‹ OF. (and F.) *sacrer* = Pr. OSp. Pg. *sagrar* = It. *sagrare, sacrare*, ‹ L. *sacrare*, render sacred, consecrate, ‹ *sacer*, sacred. Cf. *sacrate*, and see *sacred*, orig. the pp. of *sacre*¹. From the same source are ult. E. *sacrament, sacrifice, sacrilege, sacristan, sexton, sacerdotal, consecrate, desecrate, obsecrate*, etc.] To hallow; dedicate; devote; set apart; consecrate.

Than Vter went to logres, and alle the prelates of the cherche, and ther was he *sacred* and crowned. *Merlin* (E. E. T. S.), i. 57.

Amongst other reliques the Monkes shew'd us is the Holy Ampoule, the same wᵗʰ that which *sacres* their Kings at Rhemes, this being the one that anoynted Hen. IV. *Evelyn*, Diary, June 6, 1644.

sacre¹† (sā'kėr), *n.* [ME., ‹ OF. *sacre*, a consecration, sacred service, ‹ *sacrer*, consecrate: see *sacre*¹, *v.*] A sacred solemnity or service.

For the feast and for the *sacre*. *The Isle of Ladies*, l. 2135.

sacre², *n.* See *saker*¹.

sacred (sā'kred), *a.* [‹ ME. *sacred, i-sacred*, pp. of *sacren*, render holy: see *sacre*¹.] 1. Hallowed, consecrated, or made holy by association with divinity or divine things, or by solemn religious ceremony or sanction; set apart, dedicated, or appropriated to holy or religious purposes or service; regarded as holy or under divine protection: as, a *sacred* place; a *sacred* day; sacred service; the sacred lotus.

Whan the barouns saugh Arthur comynge, thei dressed alle hem a-geyn hym for that he was a kynge a-noynted and *sacred*. *Merlin* (E. E. T. S.), i. 110.

Sacred king,
Be deaf to his known malice.
Ford, Perkin Warbeck, iii. 4.

When the *Sacred* Ship returns from Delos, and is telegraphed as entering into port, may we be at peace and ready! *Thackeray*, Philip, xvii.

2. Devoted, dedicated, or consecrated with pious or filial intent: with *to*: as, a monument *sacred to* the memory of some one.

A temple *sacred* to the queen of love. *Dryden*, Pal. and Arc., ii. 459.

3†. Devoted to destruction or infamy; execrable; accursed; infamous. [A Latinism.]

O *sacred* hunger of ambitious mindes,
And impotent desire of men to raine!
Spenser, F. Q., V. xii. 1.

Sacred wit,
To villany and vengeance consecrate.
Shak., Tit. And., ii. 1. 120.

Sacred thirst of gold. *Dryden*, Æneid, iii.

4. Of or pertaining to religion or divine things; relating to the service or will of the deity: opposed to *secular* and *profane*: as, sacred music; *sacred* history.

In their *sacred* bockes or Kalendars they ordained That their names should be written after their death. *Purchas*, Pilgrimage, p. 53.

Smit with the love of *sacred* song. *Milton*, P. L., iii. 29.

5. Entitled to consideration, respect, or reverence; not to be thoughtlessly treated or intruded upon; venerable.

There is something *sacred* in misery to great and good minds. *Steele*, Spectator, No. 456.

With a soul that ever felt the sting
Of sorrow, sorrow is a *sacred* thing.
Cowper, Retirement, l. 316.

To a feather-brained school-girl nothing is *sacred*. *Charlotte Brontë*, Villette, xx.

Hence—6. To be kept inviolate; not to be violated, profaned, or made common; inviolate.

Let thy oaths be *sacred*. *Sir T. Browne*, Christ. Mor., iii. 19.

The *sacred* rights of property are to be guarded at every point. I call them *sacred* because, if they are unprotected, all other rights become worthless or visionary. *Story*, Misc. Writings, p. 519.

7. Not amenable to punishment; enjoying immunity: as, the king's person is *sacred*.—**Sacred ape** or **monkey**, a semnopithecoid; any member of the genus *Semnopithecus*. The animal to which the name specially applies is the hanuman or entellus monkey of India, *S. entellus*. The name also extends to some other monkeys which receive similar attentions, as the bunder or rhesus macaque, *Macacus rhesus*, and the talapoin. See cuts under *entellus, rhesus*, and *talapoin*.—**Sacred ax, bamboo, bean.** See the nouns.—**Sacred baboon**, the hamadryad, *Cynocephalus hamadryas*, venerated in Egypt, and often sculptured on tombs and monuments. This animal played an important part in Egyptian theology and priestcraft.—**Sacred bark**, cascara sagrada bark. See *bark*².—**Sacred beetle**, an Egyptian scarab, *Scarabæus sacer*, held sacred in antiquity. See scarab, and cuts under *Scarabæus* and *Copris*.—**Sacred cat**, the house-cat of Egypt, formerly venerated in that country as the representative of the goddess Pasht, and mummied in vast numbers at Bubastis. The "cat-cemeteries" recently opened at this place have furnished so many of these objects that they have become of commercial value as a fertilizer. This kind of cat is also interesting as indicating the origin of the present domestic cats from the *Felis maniculatus* of Rüppell, a native of Abyssinia. This is a true feline, apparently first domesticated in Egypt. The animal whose classic name (αἰλουρος) has commonly been translated *cat* was quite different, being either a musteline or a viverrine. See *Ælurus, cat*¹.—**Sacred college, fig, fir.** See the nouns.—**Sacred fish**, the mizdeh, oxyrhynch, or mormyre of the Nile, *Mormyrus oxyrhynchus*, venerated and mummied by the ancient Egyptians for the reason stated under *Mormyrus*. Some other fishes of the same river were also held in religious esteem, as the electrical catfish, *Malapterurus electricus*, and the bichir, *Polypterus bichir*. Some such fish surmounts the head of Isis in some of her representations. See cut under *Malapterurus*.—**Sacred geography.** See *geography*.—**Sacred glosses, Heart, history.** See *gloss*², *heart, history*.—**Sacred ibis**, *Ibis religiosa*, venerated and mummied by the Egyptians. See cut under *ibis*.—**Sacred lotus**, *Nelumbium speciosum*. See *lotus*, 1.—**Sacred majesty**†, a title once applied to the kings of England.—**Sacred music**, music of a religious character or connected with religious worship: opposed to *secular music*.—**Sacred place**, in *civil law*, the place where a person is buried.—**Sacred vulture.** See *vulture*. = **Syn.** *Sacred, Holy. Holy* is stronger and more absolute than any word of cognate meaning. That which is *sacred* may derive its sanction from man; that which is *holy* has its sanctity directly from God or as connected with him. Hence we speak of the Holy Bible, and the *sacred* writings of the Hindus. He who is *holy* is absolutely or essentially free from sin; *sacred* is not a word of personal character. The opposite of *holy* is *sinful* or *wicked*; that of *sacred* is *secular, profane*, or *common*.

sacredly (sā'kred-li), *adv.* In a sacred manner. (*a*) With due reverence; religiously: as, to observe the Sabbath *sacredly*; the day is *sacredly* kept. (*b*) Inviolably; strictly: as, to observe one's word *sacredly*; a secret to be *sacredly* kept.

sacredness (sā'kred-nes), *n.* [‹ *sacred* + *-ness*.] The state or character of being sacred, in any sense.

sacret† (sā'kret), *n.* [‹ OF. *sacret*, dim. of *sacre*, saker: see *saker*¹.] In *falconry*, same as *sakeret*.

sacrific¹ (sạ̄-krif'ik), *a.* [= Pg. It. *sacrifico*, ‹ L. *sacrificus*, pertaining to sacrifice, ‹ *sacrificare*, sacrifice: see *sacrify*.] Employed in sacrifice. *Johnson*.

sacrific² (sạ̄-krif'ik), *a.* [‹ NL. *sacrum*, sacrum, + L. *-ficus*, ‹ *facere*, make.] In *anat.*, entering into the composition of the sacrum: as, a *sacrific* vertebra. [Rare.]

sacrificable† (sạ̄-krif'i-ka-bl), *a.* [= Sp. *sacrificable* = Pg. *sacrificavel*; as *sacrific*¹ + *-able*.] Capable of being offered in sacrifice.

Although his [Jepthah's] vow run generally for the words "Whatsoever shall come forth," &c., yet might it be restrained in the sense, for whatsoever was *sacrificeable*, and justly subject to lawfull immolation. *Sir T. Browne*, Vulg. Err., v. 14.

sacrifical (sạ̄-krif'i-kạl), *a.* [‹ L. *sacrificalis*, pertaining to sacrifice, ‹ *sacrificare*, sacrifice: see *sacrify*.] Same as *sacrific*¹.

sacrificant (sạ̄-krif'i-kạnt), *n.* [‹ L. *sacrifican(t-)s*, ppr. of *sacrificare*, sacrifice: see *sacrifice*.] One who offers a sacrifice.

Homer did believe there were certain evil demons, who took pleasure in fumes and nidours of sacrifices; and that they were ready, as a reward, to gratify the *sacrificants* with the destruction of any person, if they so desired it. *Hallywell*, Melampronœa, p. 102.

Sacrificati (sak″ri-fi-kā'tī), *n. pl.* [L., prop. pp. pl. of *sacrificare*, sacrifice: see *sacrifice*.] In the *early church*, Christians who sacrificed to idols in times of persecution, but returned to the church when the persecution was ended, and were received as penitents.

sacrification† (sak″ri-fi-kā'shọn), *n.* [‹ L. *sacrificatio(n-)*, a sacrifice, ‹ *sacrificare*, sacrifice: see *sacrify*.] The act of sacrificing.

O son! since through the will of God I am thy father, and since to him I must again resign thee, generously suffer this *sacrification*. *Dr. A. Geddes*, Pref. to Trans. of the Bible, p. ix.

sacrificator† (sak'ri-fi-kā-tọr), *n.* [LL. *sacrificator*, ‹ L. *sacrificare*, sacrifice: see *sacrify*.] One who offers a sacrifice.

It being therefore a sacrifice so abominable unto God, although he had pursued it, it is not probable the priests and wisdom of Israel would have permitted it: and that not only in regard of the subject or sacrifice itself, but also the *sacrificator*, which the picture makes to be Jepthah. *Sir T. Browne*, Vulg. Err., v. 14.

sacrificatory (sā-krif'i-kạ̄-tọ̄-ri), *a.* [= F. *sacrificatoire*, ‹ ML. **sacrificatorius*, ‹ L. *sacrificare*, pp. *sacrificatus*, sacrifice: see *sacrify*.] Offering sacrifice. *Sherwood*.

sacrifice (sak'ri-fīs or -fīz), *n.* [‹ ME. *sacrifice, sacrifise*, ‹ OF. (and F.) *sacrifice* = Pr. *sacrifici* = Sp. Pg. *sacrificio* = It. *sagrifizio*, ‹ L. *sacrificium*, a sacrifice, lit. 'a rendering sacred,' ‹ *sacer*, sacred, + *facere*, make: see *sacre*¹ and *fact*. Cf. *sacrify*.] 1. The offering of anything to a deity; a consecratory rite.

Great pomp, and *sacrifice*, and praises loud
To Dagon. *Milton*, S. A., l. 436.

2. That which is sacrificed; specifically, that which is consecrated and offered to a deity as an expression of thanksgiving, consecration, penitence, or reconciliation. See *offering*.

I beseech you therefore, brethren, by the mercies of God, that ye present your bodies a living *sacrifice*, holy, acceptable unto God, which is your reasonable service. Rom. xii. 1.

This way the devil used to evacuate the death of Christ, that we might have affiance in other things, as in the daily *sacrifice* of the priest. *Latimer*, Sermon of the Plough.

Moloch, horrid king, besmear'd with blood
Of human *sacrifice*. *Milton*, P. L., i. 393.

3. The destruction, surrender, or giving up of some prized or desirable thing in behalf of a higher object, or to a claim considered more pressing; the loss incurred by devotion to some other person or interest; also, the thing so devoted or given up.

He made a *sacrifice* of his friendship to his interest. *Johnson*, Dict.

4. Surrender or loss of profit. [Shopkeepers' cant.]

Its patterns were last year's, and going at a *sacrifice*. *Dickens*, Chimes, ii.

Eucharistic sacrifice, sacrifice of the mass, the sacrifice of the body and blood of Christ, which, according to the doctrine of the Roman Catholic and other churches, the priest, in the celebration of the mass or eucharist, offers as a propitiation for sin and as a means of obtaining all graces and blessings from God. See *Roman Catholic Church*, under *Roman*.—**Sacrifice hit**, in *base-ball*, a hit made by the batter not for the purpose of gaining a base himself, but to enable another player already on one of the bases to score or to gain a base.

sacrifice (sak'ri-fiz or -fis), *v.*; pret. and pp. *sacrificed*, ppr. *sacrificing*. [‹ *sacrifice*, *n.*] I. *trans.* 1. To make an offering or sacrifice of; present as an expression of thanksgiving, consecration, penitence, or reconciliation.

From the herd or flock
Oft *sacrificing* bullock, lamb, or kid.
Milton, P. L., xii. 20.

2. To surrender, give up, or suffer to be lost or destroyed for the sake of something else.

My Lady will be enrag'd beyond Bounds, and *sacrifice* Neice, and Fortune, and all at that Conjuncture. *Congreve*, Way of the World, iii. 18.

Party *sacrifices* man to the measure. *Emerson*, Fortune of the Republic.

3. To dispose of regardless of gain or advantage. [Shopkeepers' cant.] = **Syn.** 1. *Sacrifice, Immolate.* By the original meaning, *sacrifice* might apply to offerings of any sort, but *immolate* only to sacrifices of life: this distinction still continues, except that, as most sacrifices have been the offering of life, *sacrifice* has come to mean that presumably. It has taken on several figurative meanings, while *immolate* has come to seem a strong word, especially appropriate to the offering of a large number of lives or of a valuable life. *Immolation* is naturally for propitiation, while *sacrifice* may be for that or only for worship.

II. *intrans.* To offer up a sacrifice; make offerings to a deity, especially by the slaughter and burning of victims, or of some part of them, on an altar.

They which *sacrificed* to the god Lunas were accounted their wiues Masters. *Purchas*, Pilgrimage, p. 75.

Whilst he [Alexander] was *sacrificing* they fell upon him, and had almost smothered him with Boughs of Palm trees and Citron trees. *Milton*, Ans. to Salmasius.

sacrificer (sak'ri-fī-zėr), *n.* [‹ *sacrifice* + *-er*¹.] 1. One who sacrifices.

The eleuenth and last persecution generally of the Church was enduring the gouernement of the Emperour Julianus, which was an idolater, and *sacrificer* to the diuel. *Guevara*, Letters (tr. by Hellowes, 1577), p. 401.

Let us be *sacrificers*, but not butchers. *Shak.*, J. C., ii. 1. 166.

2. Specifically, a priest.

So fraud was used, the *sacrificer's* trade,
Fools are more hard to conquer than persuade.
Dryden, Abs. and Achit., l. 125.

sacrificial (sak-ri-fish'ạl), *a.* [‹ L. *sacrificium*, sacrifice, + *-al*.] Of, pertaining to, or used in sacrifice; concerned with sacrificing; consisting in or including sacrifice: as, *sacrificial* robes; a *sacrificial* meal.

Now, the observation which Tertullian makes upon these *sacrificial* rites is pertinent to this rule. *Jer. Taylor*, Worthy Communicant.

sacrificially (sak-ri-fish'ạl-i), *adv.* As regards sacrifices; after the manner of a sacrifice.

sacrify† (sak'ri-fī), *v. i.* and *t.* [ME. *sacrifien*, ‹ OF. (and F.) *sacrifier* = Pr. *sacrificar, sacrifiar* = Sp. Pg. *sacrificar* = It. *sagrificare, sacrificare*, ‹ L. *sacrificare*, offer sacrifice (cf. *sacrificus*, pertaining to sacrifice), ‹ *sacer*, sacred, + *facere*, make. Cf. *sacrifice, sacrification*.] To sacrifice.

She . . . seyde that she wolde *sacrifye*,
And whanne she myghte hire tyme wel espye,
Upon the fire of sacrifice she sterte.
Chaucer, Good Women, l. 1348.

In the whiche he *sacrefied* first his blissid body and his flessh by his Bisshoppe Iosephe that he sacred with his owene hande. *Merlin* (E. E. T. S.), iii. 502.

sacrilege (sak'ri-lej), *n.* [Formerly also *sacriledge*; < ME. *sacrilege*, *sacrilegge*, *sacrilegie*, < OF. *sacrilege*, F. *sacrilège* = Sp. Pg. It. *sacrilegio*, < L. *sacrilegium*, the robbing of a temple, stealing of sacred things, < *sacrilegus*, a sacrilegious person, temple-robber, < *sacer*, sacred, + *legere*, gather, pick, purloin: see *sacred* and *legend*.] 1. The violation, desecration, or profanation of sacred things. Roman Catholics distinguish between *sacrilegium immediatum*, committed against that which in and of itself is holy, and *sacrilegium mediatum*, committed against that which is sacred because of its associations or functions.

Thou, that wlatist ydols, or mawmetis, doist *sacrilegie*? *Wyclif*, Rom. ii. 22.

The death of Ananias and Sapphira was a punishment to vow-breach and *sacrilege*. *Jer. Taylor*, Works (ed. 1835), II. 381.

I durst not tear it [a letter] after it was yours; there is some *sacrilege* in defacing anything consecrated to you. *Donne*, Letters, lxxxv.

Another great crime of near akin to the former, which was sometimes condemned and punished under the name of *sacrilege*, was robbing of graves, or defacing and spoiling the monuments of the dead. *Bingham*, Antiq. of the Christ. Church, p. 963.

2. In a more specific sense: (*a*†) The alienation to laymen or to common purposes of that which has been appropriated or consecrated to religious persons or uses. (*b*) The felonious taking of any goods out of any church or chapel. In old English law these significations of *sacrilege* were legal terms, and the crimes represented by them were for some time punished by death; in the latter sense the word is still used. =Syn. *Desecration*, etc. See *profanation*.

sacrileger† (sak'ri-lej-ėr), *n.* [< ME. *sacreleger*; < *sacrilege* + *-er*[2].] A sacrilegious person; one who is guilty of sacrilege.

The king of England [Henry VIII.], whome he [the Pope] had decreed an heretike, scismatike, a wedlocke breaker, a public murtherer, and a *sacrileger*. *Holinshed*, Chron., Hist. Scotland, an. 1535.

sacrilegie†, *n.* A Middle English form of *sacrilege*.

sacrilegious (sak-ri-lē'jus), *a.* [< *sacrilege* (L. *sacrilegium*) + *-ous*.] Guilty of or involving sacrilege; profane; impious: as, *sacrilegious* acts; *sacrilegious* hands.

Thou hast abus'd the strictness of this place,
And offer'd *sacrilegious* foul disgrace
To the sweet rest of these interred bones.
Fletcher, Faithful Shepherdess, ii. 2.

Still green with bays each ancient altar stands,
Above the reach of *sacrilegious* hands.
Pope, Essay on Criticism, l. 182.

=Syn. See *profanation*.

sacrilegiously (sak-ri-lē'jus-li), *adv.* In a sacrilegious manner; with sacrilege.

sacrilegiousness (sak-ri-lē'jus-nes), *n.* The character of being sacrilegious.

sacrilegist (sak'ri-lē-jist), *n.* [< *sacrilege* + *-ist*.] One who is guilty of sacrilege. [Rare.]

The hand of God is still upon the posterity of Antiochus Epiphanes the *sacrilegist*. *Spelman*, Hist. Sacrilege, § 6.

sacrilumbal (sā-kri-lum'bal), *a.* [< L. *sacrum*, sacrum, + *lumbus*, loin: see *lumbar*[1].] Of or pertaining to the sacrilumbalis.

sacrilumbalis (sā"kri-lum-bā'lis), *n.*; pl. *sacrilumbales* (-lēz). [NL.: see *sacrilumbal*.] The great lumbosacral muscle of the back; the erector spinæ. See *erector*. *Coues and Shute*, 1887.

sacrilumbar (sā-kri-lum'bär), *a.* Same as *sacrolumbar*. *Coues and Shute*, 1887.

sacring (sā'kring), *n.* [Formerly also *sackering*; < ME. *sakeryng*, *sacringe*, *sacrynge*; verbal n. of *sacre*[1], *v.*] 1. Consecration.

The archebisshop hadde ordeyned redy the crowne and septre, and all that longed to the *sacringe*. *Merlin* (E. E. T. S.), i. 106.

At the *sacring* of the mass, I saw
The holy elements alone. *Tennyson*, Holy Grail.

2†. The Host.

On Friday last, the Parson of Oxened "being at messe in one Parossh Chirche, evyn at levacion of the *sakeryng*, Jamys Gloys had been in the town, and come homeward by Wymondam's gate." *Paston Letters*, I. 72.

3. The sacrament; holy communion.

And on Friday after *sakeryng*, one come fro cherch warde, and schoffe doune all that was thereon. *Paston Letters*, I. 217.

Sacring bell. See *bell*[1].

sacriplex (sā'kri-pleks), *n.* [NL., < L. *sacrum*, sacrum, + *plexus*, plexus: see *plexus*, 2.] The sacral plexus of nerves. *Coues and Shute*, 1887.

sacriplexal (sā-kri-plek'sal), *a.* [< *sacriplex* + *-al*.] Entering into the composition of the sacral plexus, as a nerve; of or pertaining to the sacriplex.

sacrist (sā'krist), *n.* [= It. *sacrista*, < L. *sacrista*, a sacristan, < L. *sacer*, sacred: see *sacre*[1]. Cf. *sacristan*.] 1. A sacristan: sometimes specifically restricted to an assistant sacristan.

A *sacrist* or treasurer are not dignitaries in the church of common right, but only by custom. *Ayliffe*, Parergon.

The cellarer, the *sacrist*, and others of the brethren, disappointed in the expectation they had formed of being entertained with mirthful performances, . . . turned them out of the monastery. *Strutt*, Sports and Pastimes, p. 273.

2. A person retained in a cathedral to copy out music for the choir and take care of the books.

He would find Gervase, the *sacrist*, busy over the chronicles of the kings and the history of his own time. *Stubbs*, Medieval and Modern Hist., p. 145.

sacristan (sak'ris-tan), *n.* [< ME. *sacristane*, < OF. *sacristain*, also *segretain*, *secretain*, *soucretain*, F. *sacristain* = Pr. *sacristan*, *sagrestan* = Sp. *sacristan* = Pg. *sacristão* = It. *sagrestano*, < ML. *sacristanus*; usually *sacrista*, a sacristan, sexton: see *sacrist*. Cf. *sexton*, a contracted form of *sacristan*.] An officer of a church or monastery who has the charge of the sacristy and all its contents, and acts as custodian of the other vessels, vestments, and valuables of the church. The term *sacristan* has become corrupted into *sexton*, and these two names are sometimes used interchangeably. The *sacristan*, as distinguished from the *sexton*, however, has a more responsible and elevated office. In the Roman Catholic Church the sacristan during mass attends in a surplice at the credence-table and assists by arranging the chalice, paten, etc.; in some continental cathedrals he is a dignitary, and in the English cathedrals usually a minor canon.

The *Sacristan* shew'd us a world of rich plate, jewells, and embroder'd copes, which are kept in presses. *Evelyn*, Diary, March 23, 1646.

The *Sacristan* and old Father Nicholas had followed the Sub-Prior into the Abbot's apartment. *Scott*, Monastery, xxxiv.

sacristanry† (sak'ris-tan-ri), *n.* [ME., < *sacristan* + *-ry*.] Same as *sacristy*. *Cath. Ang.*, p. 315.

sacristy (sak'ris-ti), *n.*; pl. *sacristies* (-tiz). [< ME. **sacristie*, < OF. (and F.) *sacristie* = Pr. *sacristia*, *sagrestia* = Cat. *sagristia* = Sp. *sacristia* = Pg. *sacristia* = It. *sacristia*, *sacrestia*, *sagristia*, *sagrestia*, < ML. *sacristia*, a vestry in a church, < *sacrista*, a sacristan: see *sacrist*. Cf. *sextry*, a contracted form of the same word.] An apartment in or a building connected with a church or monastery, in which the sacred utensils are kept and the vestments used by the officiating clergymen or priests are deposited; the vestry.

sacrocaudal (sā-krō-kâ'dal), *a.* [< L. *sacrum*, the sacrum, + *cauda*, tail: see *caudal*.] Sacrococcygeal; urosacral.

sacrococcygeal (sā"krō-kok-sij'ē-al), *a.* [< *sacrococcygeus* + *-al*.] 1. Of or pertaining to the sacrum and the coccyx; sacrocaudal.—2. In *ornith.*, pertaining to that part of the sacrarium which is coccygeal; urosacral.—**Sacrococcygeal fibrocartilage, plexus**, etc. See the nouns.—**Sacrococcygeal ligaments**, the ligaments uniting the sacrum and the coccyx: an anterior, a posterior, and a lateral are distinguished.

sacrococcygean (sā"krō-kok-sij'ē-an), *a.* Same as *sacrococcygeal*.

sacrococcygeus (sā"krō-kok-sij'ē-us), *n.*; pl. *sacrococcygei* (-ī). [NL., < L. *sacrum*, the sacrum, + NL. *coccyx*: see *coccygeus*.] A sacrococcygeal muscle; a muscle connected with the sacrum and the coccyx.

sacrocostal (sā-krō-kos'tal), *a.* and *n.* [< L. *sacrum*, the sacrum, + *costa*, a rib: see *costal*.] I. *a.* Connected with the sacrum and having the character of a rib.

II. *n.* 1. A sacrocostal element of a vertebra, or so-called sacral rib.—2. In *ornith.*, specifically, a sacrocostal rib; any rib which articulates with a bird's sacrarium, or complex sacrum. *Coues*, 1890.

sacrocotyloid (sā-krō-kot'i-loid), *a.* [< L. *sacrum*, the sacrum, + Gr. κοτύλη, a vessel: see *cotyloid*.] Relating to the sacrum and to the cotyloid cavity of the hip-bone; acetabular.

sacrocotyloidean (sā-krō-kot-i-loi'dē-an), *a.* [< *sacrocotyloid* + *-e-an*.] Same as *sacrocotyloid*. —**Sacrocotyloidean diameter.** See *pelvic diameters*, under *pelvic*.

sacro-iliac (sā-krō-il'i-ak), *a.* [< L. *sacrum*, the sacrum, + *ilium*, the ilium.] Pertaining to the sacrum and the ilium: as, the *sacro-iliac* articulation.—**Sacro-iliac ligaments**, the ligaments uniting the sacrum and the ilium, which in man are anterior and posterior. The former is a short flat band of fibers which pass from the upper and anterior surface of the sacrum to the adjacent surface of the ilium. The part of the latter forming a distinct fasciculus, and running from the third transverse tubercle on the posterior surface of the sacrum to the posterior superior spine of the ilium, is sometimes called the *oblique sacro-iliac ligament*.—**Sacro-iliac synchondrosis**, the sacro-iliac articulation of man and some other animals, forming a synarthrosis between the sacrum and the ilium. It is frequently replaced by bony union, and less often forms a movable joint: but the name does not apply to either of these substitutions.

sacro-ischiac, sacro-ischiadic, sacro-ischiatic (sā-krō-is'ki-ak, -is-ki-ad'ik, -is-ki-at'ik), *a.* Pertaining to the sacrum and to the ischium; sacrosciatic.

sacrolumbal (sā-krō-lum'bal), *a.* [< L. *sacrum*, the sacrum, + *lumbus*, loin. Cf. *sacrolumbar*.] Pertaining to the sacrolumbalis; sacrilumbar: as, the *sacrolumbal* muscle.

sacrolumbalis (sā"krō-lum-bā'lis), *n.*; pl. *sacrolumbales* (-lēz). [NL.: see *sacrolumbal*.] The smaller and outer section of the erector spinæ, in man inserted by six tendons into the angles of the six lower ribs. Also called *iliocostalis*, *sacrolumbaris*, and *lumbocostalis*. In the dorsal or thoracic region of man this muscle acquires certain accessory fasciculi known in the text-books of human anatomy as *musculus accessorius ad sacrolumbalem*.

sacrolumbar (sā-krō-lum'bär), *a.* [< L. *sacrum*, the sacrum, + *lumbus*, loin: see *lumbar*[1].] 1. Pertaining to sacral and lumbar vertebræ; lumbosacral: as, the *sacrolumbar* muscle; *sacrolumbar* ligaments.—2. Combining or representing the characters of sacral and lumbar parts: as, *sacrolumbar* vertebræ; *sacrolumbar* ribs.

Also *sacrilumbar*.

sacrolumbaris (sā"krō-lum-bā'ris), *n.*; pl. *sacrolumbares* (-rēz). [NL.: see *sacrolumbar*.] Same as *sacrolumbalis*.

sacromedian (sā-krō-mē'di-an), *a.* [< L. *sacrum*, the sacrum, + *medianus*, median.] Running along the median line of the sacrum: said of an artery. See *sacra*[2].—**Sacromedian artery.** Same as *middle sacral artery*. See *sacral*.

sacropubic (sā-krō-pū'bik), *a.* [< L. *sacrum*, the sacrum, + *pubes*, the pubes: see *pubic*.] Pertaining to the sacrum and to the pubes; pubosacral: as, the *sacropubic* diameter of the pelvis.

sacrorectal (sā-krō-rek'tal), *a.* [< L. *sacrum*, the sacrum, + *rectum*, the rectum.] Pertaining to the sacrum and the rectum.—**Sacrorectal hernia**, a hernia passing down the ischiorectal fossa and appearing in the perineum, protruding between the prostate and rectum in the male, and between the vagina and rectum in the female.

sacrosanct (sak'rō-sangkt), *a.* [= F. *sacrosaint* = Sp. Pg. *sacrosanto* = It. *sacrosanto*, *sagrosanto*, < L. *sacrosanctus*, inviolable, sacred, < *sacer*, sacred, + *sanctus*, pp. of *sancire*, fix unalterably, make sacred: see *saint*[1].] Preëminently or superlatively sacred or inviolable.

The Roman church . . . makes itself so *sacrosanct* and infallible. *Dr. H. More*, Antidote against Idolatry, iii. (*Latham*.)

From *sacrosanct* and most trustworthy mouths. *Kingsley*, Hypatia, xxxi.

sacrosciatic (sā"krō-sī-at'ik), *a.* [< L. *sacrum*, the sacrum, + ML. *sciaticus*, sciatic: see *sciatic*.] Of or pertaining to the sacrum and the ischium: as, the *sacrosciatic* notch or ligaments.—**Sacrosciatic foramina**, the foramina, great and lesser, into which the great and lesser sacrosciatic notches respectively are formed by the greater and lesser sciatic ligaments. The greater transmits the pyriformis muscle, the gluteal vessels, superior gluteal nerve, sciatic vessels, greater and lesser sciatic nerves, the internal pudic vessels and nerve, and muscular branches from the sacral plexus. The lesser sacrosciatic foramen transmits the tendon of the obturator internus, the nerve which supplies that muscle, and the internal pudic vessels and nerve.—**Sacrosciatic ligaments**, two stout ligaments connecting the sacrum with the ischium. The greater or posterior passes from the posterior inferior iliac spine and the sides of the sacrum and coccyx to the ischial tuberosity; the lesser or anterior passes from the side of the sacrum and coccyx to the ischial spine.

sacrospinal (sā-krō-spī'nal), *a.* [< L. *sacrum*, the sacrum, + *spina*, the spine: see *spinal*.] Sacrovertebral; specifically, pertaining to the sacrospinalis.

sacrospinalis (sā"krō-spī-nā'lis), *n.*; pl. *sacrospinales* (-lēz). [NL.: see *sacrospinal*.] The erector spinæ muscle; the sacrolumbalis and longissimus dorsi taken together.

sacrovertebral (sā-krō-vėr'tē-bral), *a.* [< L. *sacrum*, the sacrum, + *vertebra*, a vertebra.] Of or formed by the sacrum and other vertebræ: as, the *sacrovertebral* angle or promontory (the anterior sacral angle or prominence, at the articulation of the sacrum with the last lumbar vertebra). See phrases under *sacral* and *sacrum*.—**Sacrovertebral ligament**, a ligament passing from the transverse process of the last lumbar vertebra to the lateral part of the base of the sacrum.

sacrum (sā'krum), *n.*; pl. *sacra* or *sacrums* (-krä, -krumz). [NL. (sc. *os*), the sacred bone; neut. of *sacer*, sacred: see *sacre*[1].] A compound bone resulting from the ankylosis of two or more vertebræ between the lumbar and the coccygeal region of the spine, mostly those which unite with the ilia; the os sacrum. In man the sacrum normally consists of five sacral vertebræ thus united, and is the largest, stoutest, and most solid part of the vertebral column, forming a curved pyramidal mass with the base uppermost, the keystone of the pelvic arch, wedged in posteriorly between the ilia, with which it articulates or unites by the sacro-iliac synchondrosis, all the body above being supported, so far as its bony basis is concerned, by the sacrum alone. A similar

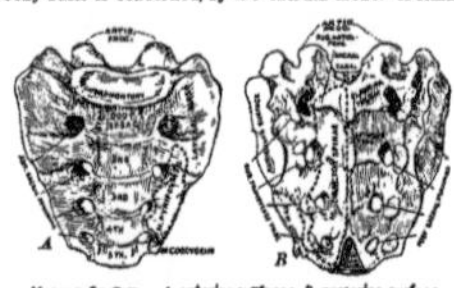

Human Sacrum. *A*, anterior surface; *B*, posterior surface.

but narrower, straighter, less pyramidal and more horizontal sacrum composed of a few bones (usually two to five, sometimes ten) characterizes *Mammalia* at large. (See *sacral*.) In birds a great number of vertebræ are ankylosed to form the sacrarium or so-called sacrum, and a large number unite with the ilia, but the greater num-

Sacrum of a Bird (young chick) before ankylosis has occurred, showing *dl*, dorsolumbar, *s*, sacral proper, and *c*, urosacral vertebræ all of which fuse together in adult life to form the sacrarium.

ber of these are borrowed from both the lumbar and the coccygeal series, and in this class it has been proposed to limit the term *sacrum* to the few (three to five) vertebræ which are in special relation with the sacral plexus. (See *urosacral*.) In some reptiles or batrachians a single rib-bearing vertebra may be united with the ilia, and so represent alone a sacrum. Also called *rump-bone*. See also cuts under *epipleura*, *Ornithoscelida*, *pelvis*, *Ichthyosauria*, *Dinornis*, *pterodactyl*, *sacrarium*[2], and *marsupial*.—**Cornua of the sacrum.** See *cornu*.—**Curve of the sacrum,** the longitudinal concavity of the sacrum, remarkably deep in man. It approximates to Carus's curve, which is the curved axis of the true pelvis of the human female.—**Promontory of the sacrum,** the sacrovertebral or sacrolumbar angle, made between the sacrum and the antecedent vertebra, remarkably salient in man.

sacry-bell† (sā'kri-bel), *n.* Same as *sacring bell* (which see, under *bell*[1]).

sad (sad), *a.* [< ME. *sad*, *sed*, < AS. *sæd*, full, sated, having had one's fill, as of food, drink, fighting, etc., = OS. *sad* = MD. *sad*, *sat*, D. *zat* = OHG. MHG. *sat*, G. *satt* = Icel. *sathr*, later *saddr* = Goth. *saths*, full, sated (cf. *sōths*, satiety); orig. pp. with suffix *-d* (as in *cold*, *old*, etc.: see *-d*[2], *-ed*[2]), < √ *sa*, fill, which appears also in L. *sat*, *satis*, sufficiently, *satur*, sated, Gr. ἄμεναι, satiate, ἄατος, insatiable, ἄδην, sufficiently, OIr. *sathach*, sated, *sasaim*, I satisfy, *saith*, satiety: see *sate*[2], *satiate*, and *satisfy*. The development of the concrete physical sense 'heavy' from that of the mental sense 'heavy' (if it does not come from the orig. sense 'filled') is parallel with the development of 'keen,' sharp-edged, from 'keen,' eager, bold.] **1†.** Full; having had one's fill; sated; surfeited; hence, satiated; wearied; tired; sick.

> *Sad* of mine londe. — *Layamon.*

> Yet of that art they can not wexen *sadde*,
> For unto hem it is a bitter swete.
> *Chaucer*, Prol. to Canon's Yeoman's Tale, l. 324.

2†. Heavy; weighty; ponderous.

> With that his hand, more *sad* then lomp of lead,
> Uplifting high, he weened with Morddure,
> His owne good sword Morddure, to cleave his head.
> *Spenser*, F. Q., II. viii. 30.

3†. Firm; solid; fixed.

> He is lyk to a man bildinge an hous, that diggide deepe, and puttide the foundement on a stoon. Sothli greet flowing maad flood was hurtlid to that hous, and it myзte not moue it, for it was foundid on a *sad* stoon.
> *Wyclif*, Luke vi. 48.

4†. Close; compact; hard; stiff; not light or soft.

> Ar then the lande be waxen *sadde* or tough.
> *Palladius*, Husbondrie (E. E. T. S.), p. 50.

> Chalky lands are naturally cold and *sad*.
> *Mortimer*, Husbandry.

5. Heavy; soggy; doughy; that has not risen well: as, *sad* bread. [Old and prov. Eng.]—**6†.** Weighty; important; momentous.

> The crowe anon hym tolde
> By *sadde* tokenes and by wordes bolde,
> How that his wyf had doon hir lecherye.
> *Chaucer*, Manciple's Tale, l. 154.

> I am on many *sad* adventures bound,
> That call me forth into the wilderness.
> *Beau. and Fl.*, Knight of Burning Pestle, iv. 2.

7†. Strong; stout: said of a person or an animal.

> It makethe a man more strong and more *sad* azenst his Enemyes. — *Mandeville*, Travels, p. 159.

> Hym selfe on a *sad* horse surely enarmyt,
> That Galathe with gomys gyuen was to nome.
> *Destruction of Troy* (E. E. T. S.), l. 6244.

> But we *saddere* men owen to susteyne the feblenesses of sijkemen, and not plese to vs silf. — *Wyclif*, Rom. xv. 1.

8†. Settled; fixed; resolute.

> Yet in the brest of hir virginitee
> Ther was enclosed rype and *sad* corage.
> *Chaucer*, Clerk's Tale, l. 164.

> If a man in synne be *sadde*,
> Ech day newe, and lith ther-inne,
> Of such a man God is moore gladde
> Than of a childe that neuere dide synne.
> *Hymns to Virgin*, etc. (E. E. T. S.), p. 75.

> Loke your hertes be seker and *sad*.
> *Lytell Geste of Robyn Hode* (Child's Ballads, V. 82).

9†. Steadfast; constant; trusty; faithful.

> O deere wyf! O gemme of lustiheed!
> That were to me so *sad*, and eek so trewe.
> *Chaucer*, Manciple's Tale, l. 171.

> Then Ecuba esely ordant a message,
> Sent to that souerain by a *sad* frynde.
> *Destruction of Troy* (E. E. T. S.), l. 10527.

10†. Sober; serious; grave; sedate; discreet; responsible; wise; sage.

> In ensaumple that men schulde se that by *sadde* resoun
> Men miзt nouзt be saued, but thoruз mercy and grace.
> *Piers Plowman* (B), xv. 541.

> In Surrye whilom dwelte a compaignye
> Of chapmen riche, and therto *sadde* and trewe.
> *Chaucer*, Man of Law's Tale, l. 37.

> And vppon these iij lordes wise and *sadde*
> A poyntid were to goo on this massage
> Onto the Sowdon and his Baronage.
> *Generydes* (E. E. T. S.), l. 3134.

> To *sadde* wise men he yaf soche thinge as hym dought sholde hem plese; and with hem he heilde companye, and enquered in the contre what myght hem beste plese.
> *Merlin* (E. E. T. S.), i. 106.

> A jest with a *sad* brow. — *Shak.*, 2 Hen. IV., v. 1. 92.

> Receive from me
> A few *sad* words, which, set against your joys,
> May make 'em shine the more.
> *Beau. and Fl.*, King and No King, ii. 1.

11. Sorrowful; melancholy; mournful; dejected.

> Methinks no body should be *sad* but I:
> Yet I remember, when I was in France,
> Young gentlemen would be as *sad* as night,
> Only for wantonness. — *Shak.*, K. John, iv. 1. 15.

> What, are you *sad* too, uncle?
> Faith, then there's a whole household down together.
> *Middleton*, Women Beware Women, i. 2.

> *Sad* for their loss, but joyful of our life.
> *Pope*, Odyssey, ix. 72.

12. Expressing or marked by sorrow or melancholy.

> Of all *sad* words of tongue or pen,
> The *saddest* are these: "It might have been!"
> *Whittier*, Maud Muller.

13. Having the external appearance of sorrow; gloomy; downcast: as, a *sad* countenance.

> Methinks your looks are *sad*, your cheer appall'd.
> *Shak.*, 1 Hen. VI., i. 2. 48.

> But while I mused came Memory with *sad* eyes,
> Holding the folded annals of my youth.
> *Tennyson*, Gardener's Daughter.

14. Distressing; grievous; disastrous: as, a *sad* accident; a *sad* disappointment.

> A *sadder* chance hath given allay
> Both to the mirth and music of this day.
> *B. Jonson*, Sad Shepherd, i. 2.

> Insulting Age will trace his cruel Way,
> And leave *sad* marks of his destructive Sway.
> *Prior*, Celia to Damon.

15. Troublesome; trying; bad; wicked: sometimes used jocularly: as, a *sad* grumbler; a *sad* rogue.

> Then does he begin to call himself the *saddest* fellow, in disappointing so many places as he was invited to elsewhere. — *Steele*, Spectator, No. 448.

> I have been told as how London is a *sad* place.
> *H. Mackenzie*, Man of Feeling, xiv.

16. Dark; somber; sober; quiet: applied to color: as, a *sad* brown.

> With him the Palmer eke in habit *sad*
> Him selfe addrest to that adventure hard.
> *Spenser*, F. Q., II. xi. 8.

> My wife is upon hanging the long chamber, where the girl lies, with the *sad* stuff that was in the best chamber.
> *Pepys*, Diary, Aug. 24, 1668.

> [Bring] the coarsest woollen cloth (so it be not flocks), and of *sad* colours, and some red.
> *Winthrop*, Hist. New England, I. 458.

=**Syn. 11** and **13.** Depressed, cheerless, desponding, disconsolate.—**14.** Dire, deplorable.

sad (sad), *v. t.*; pret. and pp. *sadded*, ppr. *sadding*. [< ME. *sadden*, < AS. *sadian*, be sated or tired, *gesadian*, fill, satisfy, satiate (= OHG. *satōn*, MHG. *saten* = Icel. *sethja*, satisfy), < *sæd*, full, sated: see *sad*, *a.* Cf. Goth. *ga-sōthjan*, fill, satisfy, < *sæd*, *sōths*, satiety.] **1†.** To make firm.

> Ancon the groundis and plauntis or solis of him ben *sadded* togidere, and he lippinge stood and wandride.
> *Wyclif*, Acts iii. 7.

2†. To strengthen; establish; confirm.

> Austyn the olde here-of he made bokes,
> And hym-self ordeyned to *sadde* vs in bileue.
> *Piers Plowman* (B), x. 242.

3. To sadden; make sorrowful; grieve.

> Nothing *sads* me so much as that; in love
> To thee and to thy blood, I had pick'd out
> A worthy match for her.
> *Middleton*, Women Beware Women, iv. 1.

> But alas! this is it that *saddeth* our hearts, and makes us look for more and more sad tidings concerning the affairs of the church, from all parts of the world.
> *Baxter*, Self-Denial, Conclusion.

sad (sad), *adv.* [< ME. *sadde*, *sade*; < *sad*, *a.*] **1†.** Strongly; stiffly.

> *Sadde* cleyed well thai save beth leide to slepe.
> *Palladius*, Husbondrie (E. E. T. S.), p. 160.

2†. Soberly; prudently; discreetly.

> Thus thi frendes wylle be glade
> That thou dispos the wyslye and *sade*.
> *Booke of Precedence* (E. E. T. S., extra ser.), i. 50.

3. Closely; firmly: as, to lie *sad*. [Scotch.]

sad-colored (sad'kul"ọrd), *a.* Of somber or sober hue.

> A *sad-coloured* stand of claiths.
> *Scott*, Monastery, Int. Epistle, p. 11.

sadden (sad'n), *v.* [< *sad* + *-en*[1].] **I.** *intrans.* **1.** To become heavy, compact, or firm; harden, as land or roads after a thaw or rain. [Prov. Eng.]—**2.** To become sad or sorrowful.

> And Mecca *saddens* at the long delay.
> *Thomson*, Summer, l. 979.

> He would pause in his swift course to admire the bright face of some cottage child; then *sadden* to think of what might be its future lot. — *E. Dowden*, Shelley, I. 80.

II. *trans.* **1†.** To make compact; make heavy or firm; harden.

> Marl is binding, and *saddening* of land is the great prejudice it doth to clay lands. — *Mortimer*, Husbandry.

2. To make sad; depress; make gloomy or melancholy.

> Her gloomy presence *saddens* all the scene.
> *Pope*, Eloisa to Abelard, l. 167.

> Accursed be he who willingly *saddens* an immortal spirit.
> *Marg. Fuller*, Woman in 19th Cent., p. 27.

3. To make dark-colored; specifically, in *dyeing* and *calico-printing*, to tone down or shade (the colors employed) by the application of certain agents, as salts of iron, copper, or bichromate of potash.

> For *saddening* olives, drabs, clarets, &c., and for cotton blacks, it [copperas] has been generally discarded in favour of nitrate of iron.
> *W. Crookes*, Dyeing and Calico-printing, p. 535.

saddle (sad'l), *n.* [< ME. *sadel*, < AS. *sadol*, *sadul*, *sadel* = OD. *sadel*, D. *zadel* = MLG. LG. *sadel* = OHG. *satal*, *satul*, MHG. *satel*, G. *sattel* = Icel. *söthull* = Sw. Dan. *sadel*, a saddle; perhaps of Slavic origin: cf. OBulg. Serv. Bohem. *sedlo* = Pol. *siodlo* = Russ. *siedlo*, a saddle (Finn. *satula*, a saddle, perhaps < Teut.); ult. < √ *sad*, sit: see *sit*. Cf. L. *sella* (for **sedla*), a seat, chair, saddle (see *sell*[2]), *sedile*, a chair, from the same root.] **1.** A contrivance secured on the back of a horse or other animal, to serve as a seat for a rider or for supporting goods packed for transportation. (*a*) The seat of wood or leather provided for a rider, especially on horseback: as, war-*saddle*,

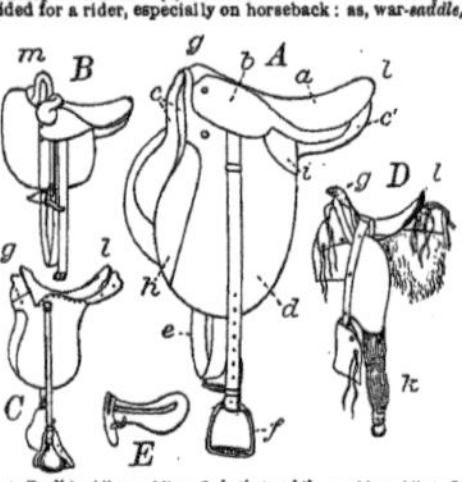

A, English riding-saddle; *B*, ladies' saddle, or side-saddle; *C*, McClellan saddle; *D*, cowboy saddle; *E*, saddletree. *a*, seat; *b*, jockey; *c*, *c'*, pad; *d*, skirt; *e*, girth; *f*, stirrup; *g*, pommel; *h*, knee-puff; *i*, thigh-puff; *k*, cinch; *l*, cantle; *m*, horn.

hunting-*saddle*, racing-*saddle*, side-*saddle*, McClellan *saddle*, Mexican *saddle*. The riders' saddle has differed greatly in construction and in use among different nations and at different times, especially as to the length of the stirrups and the posture of the rider.

> "My lorde," he seid, "that ye will in this nede
> Chaunge my *Sadyll* and sett it on this stede."
> *Generydes* (E. E. T. S.), l. 2254.

In the same Cite I sold my horse, and my *sadyll* and brydell. *Torkington*, Diarie of Eng. Travell, p. 5.

(*b*) A part of the harness used for drawing a vehicle. It is a narrow padded cushion laid across the back, and girded under the belly, and is usually held in place by a strap which passes under and around the tail: the shafts or thills are supported by it, the reins pass through rings attached to it, and the check-rein or bearing-rein is hooked to it. (*c*) A pack-saddle. See cuts under *harness* and *pad-tree*.

2. A seat prepared for a rider otherwise than on the back of an animal, but resembling an ordinary riding-saddle in design and use, as the seat on a bicycle.—3. Something resembling a saddle, or part of a saddle, in shape or use. (*a*) In *geol.*, a folded mass of rock in which the strata dip on each side away from a central axis-plane; an anticlinal.

It is a pretty high island, and very remarkable, by reason of two *saddles* or risings and fallings on the top. *Dampier*, Voyages, an. 1684.

(*b*) *Naut.*, a contrivance of wood notched or hollowed out and used to support a spar, as a wooden saddle-crutch is sometimes used to support the weight of the spanker-boom. (*c*) In *mach.*, a block with a hollowed top to sustain a round object, as a rod, upon a bench or bed. (*d*) A block, usually of cast-iron, at the top of a pier of a suspension-bridge, over which pass the suspension-cables or -chains which support the bridge platform. The saddle rests upon

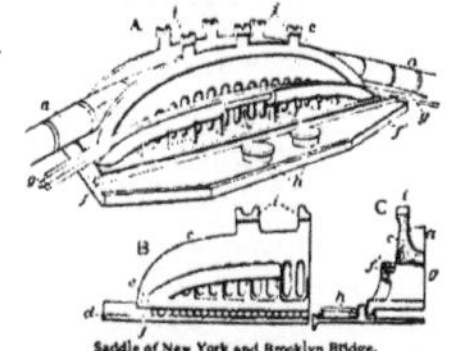

Saddle of New York and Brooklyn Bridge.

A, saddle; *B*, elevation of one half of length; *C*, section of one half of width. *a*, cable; *c*, saddle; *d*, bed-plate; *e*, steel rollers upon which the saddle rests; *f*, *f*, cradles supporting the overfloor stays, *g*; *h*, studs cast on the bed-plate, around which are looped other overfloor stays; *i*, *i*, temporary bearings for supports of strands in constructing the cable. At the completion of each strand it is lowered into the saddle. The saddles each weigh thirteen tons.

rollers, beneath which is a bed bearing upon the top of the pier. The rollers permit a slight movement that compensates for the contractions and expansions of the cables under varying temperatures, which, if the saddle were rigidly secured to the pier, would tend to lessen its stability. (*e*) In *rail.*, the bearing in the axle-box of a carriage; also, a chair or seat for the rails. See cut under *axle-box*. (*f*) In *building*, a thin board placed on the floor in the opening of a doorway, the width of the jambs. (*g*) In *zoöl.* and *anat.*, some part or configuration of parts like or likened to a saddle. Specifically—(1) The cingulum or clitellum of a worm. (2) A peculiar mark on or modification of the carapace of some crustaceans. See *ephippium*. (3) The color-mark on the back of the male harp-seal, *Phoca* (*Pagophilus*) *grœnlandica*. (4) Of mutton, veal, or venison, a butchers' cut including a part of the backbone with the ribs on one side. (5) In cephalopods, one of the elevations or saliencies of the sutures of a tetrabranchiate, separated from another by an intervening depression or reentrance called a *lobe*. (6) In poultry, the rump, or lower part of the back, which in the cock is covered with long linear hackles technically called *saddle-feathers*, which droop on each side of the root of the tail; also, these feathers collectively. See *saddle-feathers*. (*h*) In *bot.*, in the leaves of *Isoëtes*, a ridge separating the fovea and foveola. (*i*) A notched support into the recesses or notches of which a gun is laid to hold it steadily in drilling the vent or bouching. (*j*) In *gun-making*, the base of the foresight of a gun, which is soldered or brazed to the barrel.—**Boots and saddles.** See *boot*[2].—**Racing-saddle**, a small saddle of very light weight, used in horse-racing.—**The great saddle**†, the training required for accomplished or knightly horsemanship. See *to ride the great horse*, under *ride*.

The deisgne is admirable, some keeping neere an hundred brave horses, all managed to *y*ᵉ *greate saddle*. *Evelyn*, Diary, April 1, 1644.

To put the saddle on the right horse, to impute blame where it is justly deserved. [Colloq.]—**Turkish saddle**, the sella Turcica or pituitary fossa of the sphenoid bone. —**War-saddle**, a saddle used by mounted warriors, serving by its form to give such a seat as may best facilitate

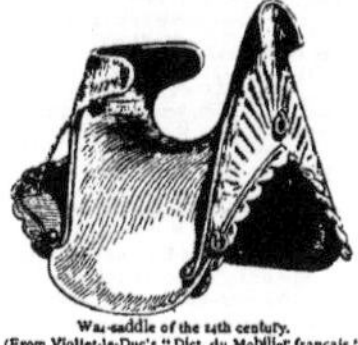

War-saddle of the 14th century.
(From Viollet-le-Duc's "Dict. du Mobilier français.")

the use of weapons, and also in some cases affording protection to the knees, thighs, etc., by appendages. (See *burl*, 3 (*c*), *leg-shield*, *saddle-bow*.) The war-saddle of the middle ages was especially adapted for charging with the lance; toward the thirteenth century it assumed a form which enabled the rider to prop himself upon the high cantle while standing almost erect in the stirrups, the body being thrown forward to aid in holding the lance straight and true.

saddle (sad'l), *v. t.*; pret. and pp. *saddled*, ppr. *saddling*. [< ME. *sadelien*, *sadlen*, < AS. *sadolian*, *sadelian*, saddle, = D. *zadelen* = MLG. *sadelen* = OHG. *satalōn*, MHG. *satelen*, G. *satteln* = Icel. *söthla* = Sw. *sadla* = Dan. *sadle*, saddle; from the noun.] 1. To put a saddle upon: as, to *saddle* a horse.

Thei ronne to here armes, that yet were in her beddys, and hadde no leyser hem to clothe, and that was yet a faire happe for hem that her horses were redy *sadellyd*. *Merlin* (E. E. T. S.), ii. 153.

And Abraham rose up early in the morning and *saddled* his ass. Gen. xxii. 3.

2. To load; encumber as with a burden; also, to impose as a burden.

Yes, Jack, the independence I was talking of is by a marriage — the fortune is *saddled* with a wife — but I suppose that makes no difference. *Sheridan*, The Rivals, ii. 1.

If you like not my company, you can *saddle* yourself on some one else. *R. L. Stevenson*, Master of Ballantrae, ii.

saddleback (sad'l-bak), *n.* 1. A hill or its summit when shaped somewhat like a saddle. —2. A bastard kind of oyster, unfit for food; a racoon-oyster.—3. The great black-backed gull: same as *blackback*, 1.—4. The harp-seal: so called from the mark on the back.

Rink says a full-grown *saddle-back* weighs about 250 lbs. *Cassell's Nat. Hist.*, II. 236. (*Encyc. Dict.*)

5. A variety of domestic geese, white, with dark feathers on the back like a saddle.—6. The larva of the bombycid moth *Empretia stimulea*:

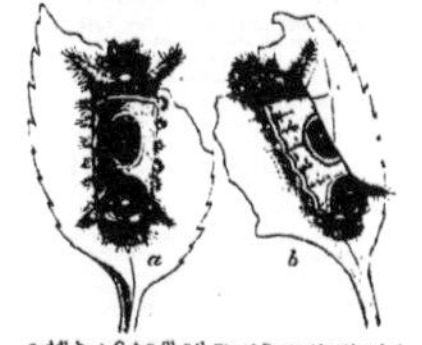

Saddleback Caterpillar (larva of *Empretia stimulea*).
a, dorsal surface; *b*, lateral surface. (Natural size, full-grown.)

so called on account of the saddle-like markings on the back. It feeds on cotton, corn, and many perennial trees and shrubs, and possesses a fringe of bristles which have urticating properties. [U. S.]—**Saddleback roof.** Same as *saddle-roof*.

saddle-backed (sad'l-bakt), *a.* 1. Hollow-backed; sway-backed: said of a horse.—2. Having the back marked or colored with the appearance of a saddle: said of various animals: as, the *saddle-backed* gull, seal, etc.—**Saddle-backed coping**, in *arch.*, a coping thicker in the middle than at the edges, so that it delivers each way the water that falls upon it.

saddle-bag (sad'l-bag), *n.* A large bag, usually one of a pair, hung from or laid over the saddle, and used to carry various articles. Those used in the East are made of cloth, especially carpeting, one long and broad strip having a kind of pocket made at each end by the application of a piece as wide as the strip. Also called *camel-bag*, from its frequent employment on camels.

The Coptic and Syriac manuscripts were stowed away in one side of a great pair of *saddle-bags*. *R. Curzon*, Monast. in the Levant, p. 90.

saddle-bar (sad'l-bär), *n.* 1. The side-bar, side-plate, or spring-bar of a saddletree.—2. In *medieval arch.*, one of several narrow iron bars extending from mullion to mullion, or through the mullions across an entire window, to hold firmly the stonework and the lead setting of the glass. When the bays are wide, upright iron bars, called *stanchions*, are sometimes used in addition to the saddle-bars, in which eyes are forged to receive the latter. Compare *stay-bar*, and see cut under *geometric*.
3. One of the bent, oblique, or straight cross-bars or pieces of lead on which the pieces of glass used in a design in a stained-glass window are placed or seated.

saddle-billed (sad'l-bild), *a.* Having a saddle on the bill: specifically applied to a large African stork, *Ephippiorhynchus senegalensis*, translating the generic name. See *Ephippiorhynchus*.

saddle-blanket (sad'l-blang"ket), *n.* A blanket, of a rather small size and coarse make, used folded under a saddle. Such blankets are almost exclusively used in western parts of the United States instead of any special saddle-cloth. The ordinary gray army blanket is generally selected.

saddle-bow (sad'l-bō), *n.* [< ME. *sadel-bowe*, *sadylle bowe*, < AS. *sadolboga*, *sadelboga*, *sadulboga* (= D. *zadelboog* = MLG. *sadelboge* = OHG. *satelbogo*, *satelpogo*, MHG. *satelboge*, G. *sattelbogen* = Icel. *söthul-bogi* = Sw. *sadelbåge* = Dan. *sadelbue*), a saddle-bow, < *sadol*, saddle, + *boga*, bow: see *saddle* and *bow*[2].] The raised front part of a saddle; hence, the front of a saddle in general; the part from which was often suspended a weapon, or the helmet, or other article requiring to be within easy reach.

She lean'd her o'er the *saddle-bow*, . . .
To give him a kiss ere she did go.
The Cruel Brother (Child's Ballads, II. 254).

One hung a pole-axe at his *saddle-bow*.
Dryden, Pal. and Arc., iii. 32.

saddle-bracket (sad'l-brak"et), *n.* In *teleg.*, a bracket shaped somewhat like a saddle, used for supporting a telegraph-wire which runs along the tops of the poles.

saddle-clip (sad'l-klip), *n.* A clip by which a spring of a vehicle is secured to the axle. The legs of the clip straddle the parts to be joined, and are fastened by bolt-nuts.

saddle-cloth (sad'l-klôth), *n.* A piece of textile material used, in connection with the saddle of a horse, for riding. Especially—(*a*) Such a piece of stuff put upon the horse under the saddle and extending some distance behind it, intended to preserve the rider's dress from contact with the horse, or to protect the horse from the saber or the like. In countries where costume is rich and varied, such saddle-cloths are sometimes of great richness. (*b*) A piece of textile material passing under the saddle of a carriage-horse. (See *saddle*, 1 (*b*).) This is sometimes decorated with the owner's crest or initials, or in other ways.

saddle-fast (sad'l-fàst), *a.* [= G. *sattelfest* = Sw. Dan. *sadelfast*; as *saddle* + *fast*[1].] Seated firmly in the saddle. *Scott*, L. of L. M., iii. 6.

saddle-feathers (sad'l-feᴛʜ"ėrz), *n. pl.* In *poultry*, saddle-hackles collectively; the long slender feathers which droop on each side of the saddle of the domestic cock.

saddle-gall (sad'l-gâl), *n.* A sore upon a horse's back made by the saddle.

saddle-girth (sad'l-gėrth), *n.* A band which is passed under a horse's belly, and secured to the saddle at each end. It is usually so made as to be drawn more or less tight by a buckle. See *cinch* and *surcingle*.

saddle-graft (sad'l-gràft), *v. t.* To ingraft by forming the stock like a wedge and fitting the end of the scion over it like a saddle: the reverse of *cleft-graft*. See cut under *grafting*.

saddle-hackle (sad'l-hak"l), *n.* A hackle from the saddle or rump of the cock, sometimes used by anglers for making artificial flies; a saddle-feather: distinguished from *neck-hackle* or *hackle*.

saddle-hill (sad'l-hil), *n.* Same as *saddleback*, 1.

A remarkable *saddle-hill*. *Cook*, First Voyage, ii. 7.

saddle-hook (sad'l-hůk), *n.* Same as *check-hook*.

saddle-horse (sad'l-hôrs), *n.* A horse used with a saddle for riding.

saddle-joint (sad'l-joint), *n.* 1. A joint made by turning up the edges of adjacent plates of tin or sheet-iron at right angles with the bodies of the sheet (one margin so turned up being nearly twice as wide as the other), and then turning down the broader margin snugly over the other so that the margins interlock.—2. In *anat.*, a joint where the articular surfaces are inversely convex in one direction and concave in the other, admitting movement in every direction except axial rotation. This joint occurs between all saddle-shaped vertebræ, as notably in the necks of all recent birds and of many reptiles. It is exemplified in man in the carpometacarpal joint of the thumb. Also called *reciprocal reception joint*.

saddle-lap† (sad'l-lap), *n.* The skirt of a saddle.

He louted ower his *saddle lap*,
To kiss her ere they part.
Lord William (Child's Ballads, III. 19).

saddle-leaf (sad'l-lēf), *n.* Same as *saddletree*, 2.

saddle-leather (sad'l-leᴛʜ"ėr), *n.* Leather prepared specially for saddlers' use. Pig-skin is much used, and, as the removal of the bristles gives this leather a peculiar indented appearance, the preparation of imitations from skins of other animals simulates it. Unlike harness-leather, it is not blackened on the grain side.

saddle-nail (sad'l-nāl), *n.* A short nail with a large smooth head, used in saddlery. *E. H. Knight.*

saddle-nosed (sad'l-nōzd), *a.* 1. Having a broad, flat nose.

His wife sate by him, who (as I verily thinke) had cut and pared her nose betweene the eyes, that she might seeme to be more flat aud *saddle-nosed*.
Hakluyt's Voyages, I. 101.

2. Having a soft nasal membrane saddled on the bill; sagmatorhine, as a bird.

saddle-plate (sad'l-plāt), *n.* In steam-boilers of the locomotive type, the bent plate which forms the arch of the furnace. Compare *crown-sheet*.

saddle-quern (sad'l-kwėrn), *n.* A form of quern the bedstone of which is hollowed on its upper surface to receive a kind of stone roller, which was used with a rocking and rubbing motion to grind the grain. See the upper example in the cut under *quern*.

Saddle-querns of the same character occur also in France. *Evans*, Ancient Stone Implements, p. 226.

saddler (sad'lėr), *n.* [< ME. *sadiler*, *sadlare*, *sadyller* (= MLG. *sadeler* = MHG. *sateler*, G. *sattler*), a saddler; as *saddle* + *-er*[1].] 1. One whose occupation is the making of saddles.

To pay the *saddler* for my mistress' crupper.
Shak., C. of E., i. 2. 56.

2. The harp-seal, *Phoca* (*Pagophilus*) *grœnlandica*, when adolescent.—**Saddlers' knife.** See *knife*.—**Saddlers' pincers.** See *pincers*.

saddle-rail (sad'l-rāl), *n.* A railway-rail of inverted-U section straddling a continuous longitudinal sleeper.

saddler-corporal (sad'lėr-kôr″pǫ-ral), *n.* A non-commissioned officer in the English service who has charge of the saddlers in the household cavalry.

saddle-reed (sad'l-rēd), *n.* In *saddlery*, a small reed used as a substitute for cord in making the edges of the sides of gig-saddles. *E. H. Knight.*

saddlerock (sad'l-rok), *n.* A variety of the oyster, *Ostrea virginica*, of large size and thick, rounded form.

saddle-roof (sad'l-röf), *n.* A roof having two gables. Sometimes termed *packsaddle-roof* and *saddle-back roof*.

saddler-sergeant (sad'lėr-sär″jent), *n.* A sergeant in the cavalry who has charge of the saddlers: in the United States a non-commissioned staff-officer of a cavalry regiment.

saddle-rug (sad'l-rug), *n.* A saddle-cloth made of carpeting.

saddlery (sad'lėr-i), *n.* [< *saddler* + *-y* (see *-ery*).] 1. The trade or employment of a saddlor.—2. A saddler's shop or establishment.—3. Saddles and their appurtenances in general; hence, by extension, all articles concerned with the equipment of horses, especially those made of leather with their necessary metal fittings.

He invested also in something of a library, and in large quantities of *saddlery*.
T. Hughes, Tom Brown at Oxford, II. xxv.

Above all, it is necessary to still further increase the reserve of mules and the reserve of horses, with all the necessary *saddlery*, harness, and carts, and to provide the whole army with the latest weapons.
Sir C. W. Dilke, Probs. of Greater Britain, iv. 1.

saddlesealing (sad'l-sē″ling), *n.* The pursuit or capture of the saddle-backed seal. See *saddle*, 3 (*g*) (3).

The majority of the vessels, after prosecuting the *saddle-sealing* at Newfoundland or Greenland, proceed direct to Disco, where they usually arrive early in May.
Encyc. Brit., XXIV. 527.

saddle-shaped (sad'l-shāpt), *a.* Having the shape of a saddle; in *bot.*, having a hollowed back and lateral lobes hanging down like the laps of a saddle, a form occurring in petals.—**Saddle-shaped articulation**, a saddle-joint.—**Saddle-shaped vertebra**, a heterocœlous vertebra. See *saddle-joint*.

saddle-shell (sad'l-shel), *n.* A shell resembling or suggesting a saddle in shape. (*a*) A species of *Placuna*, as *P. sella*. See cut under *Placuna*. (*b*) Any species of *Anomiidæ*, as *Anomia ephippium*. See cut under *Anomiidæ*.

saddle-sick (sad'l-sik), *a.* Sick or galled with much or heavy riding.

Roland of Roncesvalles too, we see well in thinking of it, found rainy weather as well as sunny, . . . was *saddle-sick*, calumniated, constipated.
Carlyle, Diamond Necklace, i. (*Davies.*)

saddle-stone (sad'l-stōn), *n.* An old name for a variety of stone containing saddle-shaped depressions. Also called *ephippite*.

saddletree (sad'l-trē), *n.* [< *saddle* + *tree*.] 1. The frame of a modern European saddle, made of wood. See cut under *saddle*.

For *saddletree* scarce reach'd had he,
His journey to begin,
When, turning round his head, he saw
Three customers come in.
Cowper, John Gilpin.

2. The American tulip-tree, *Liriodendron tulipifera*: name suggested by the form of the leaf. Also *saddle-leaf*.

Sadducæan, *a.* See *Sadducean*.

Sadducaic (sad-ū-kā'ik), *a.* [< Gr. Σαδδουκαῖοι (LL. *Sadducæi*), the Sadducees, + *-ic*.] Pertaining to or characteristic of the Sadducees: as, *Sadducaic* reasonings. [Rare.] *Imp. Dict.*

Sadducean, Sadducæan (sad-ū-sē'an), *a.* [= F. *Sadducéen*; as *Sadducee* + *-an*.] Of or pertaining to the Sadducees.

The *Sadducæan* aristocracy in particular, which formerly in the synedrium had shared the supreme power with the high priest, endeavoured to restore reality once more to the nominal ascendency which still continued to be attributed to the ethnarch and the synedrium.
Encyc. Brit., XIII. 425.

Sadducee (sad'ū-sē), *n.* [Formerly also in pl. *Saduces*, *Seduces*; < ME. *Sadducee* (in pl. *Sadduceis*) (cf. AS. pl. *Sadduceas*) = Sp. Pg. *Saduceo* = It. *Sadduceo* = D. *Sadduceer* = G. *Sadducäer* = Sw. *Saducé* = Dan. *Sadducæer*, < LL. *Sadducæus*, usually in pl. *Sadducæi*, < Gr. Σαδδουκαῖος, usually in pl. Σαδδουκαῖοι, < Heb. *Tsedūqīm*, pl., the Sadducees; so named either from their supposed founder *Zadok*, Heb. *Tsādōq*, or from their assumed or ascribed character, the word *tsedūqīm* being pl. of *tsādōq*, lit. 'the just one,' < *tsādaq*, be just.] An adherent of a skeptical school of Judaism in the time of Christ, which denied the immortality of the soul, the existence of angels, and the authority of the historical and poetical books of the Old Testament and of the oral tradition on which Pharisaic doctrine was largely founded. It is not easy to define exactly the doctrine of the Sadducees, because it was a negative rather than a positive philosophy, and a speculative rather than a practical system; and for our knowledge of it we are almost wholly dependent on the representations of its opponents. It was the doctrine of the rich, the worldly, and the compliant.

The doctrine of the *Sadducees* is this, that souls die with the bodies; nor do they regard the observation of any thing besides what the law enjoins them.
Josephus, Antiquities (trans.), XVIII. i. § 4.

In foremost rank, heer goe the *Sadduces*,
That do deny Angels and Resurrection.
Sylvester, tr. of Du Bartas's Triumph of Faith, ii. 34.

Sadduceeism (sad'ū-sē-izm), *n.* [= F. *Sadducéisme*; as *Sadducee* + *-ism*.] 1. The doctrinal system of the Sadducees.

Sadduceeism was rather a speculative than a practical system, starting from simple and well-defined principles, but wide-reaching in its possible consequences. Perhaps it may best be described as a general reaction against the extremes of Pharisaism, springing from moderate and rationalistic tendencies.
Edersheim, Life and Times of Jesus, I. 313.

2. Skepticism.

Sadduceeism has so completely become the quasi-scientific term of theology for the indifferentism or unbelief of the day, and especially for the sceptical tone of modern literature, that one might have expected the undoubted orthodoxy of the Pharisees would have saved them from reproach. H. *N. Oxenham*, Short Studies, p. 3.

Sadducism (sad'ū-sizm), *n.* [< *Sadduc*(*ee*) + *-ism*.] Same as *Sadduceeism*. [Rare.]

Atheisme and *Sadducism* disputed;
Their Tenents argued, and refuted.
Heywood, Hierarchy of Angels, p. 3.

Sadducize (sad'ū-sīz), *v. i.*; pret. and pp. *Sadducized*, ppr. *Sadducizing*. [< *Sadduc*(*ee*) + *-ize*.] To conform to the doctrines of the Sadducees; adopt the principles of the Sadducees.

Sadducizing Christians, I suppose, they were, who said there was no resurrection, neither angel or spirit.
Bp. Atterbury, Sermons, II., Pref.

sadel†, *n.* and *v.* A Middle English form of *saddle*.

sad-eyed (sad'īd), *a.* Having a sad countenance.

The *sad-eyed* justice, with his surly hum,
Delivering o'er to executors pale
The lazy yawning drone. *Shak.*, Hen. V., i. 2. 202.

sad-faced (sad'fāst), *a.* Having a sad or sorrowful face.

You *sad-faced* men, people and sons of Rome.
Shak., Tit. And., v. 3. 67.

sad-hearted (sad'här″ted), *a.* Sorrowful; melancholy.

Sad-hearted men, much overgone with care,
Here sits a king more woful than you are.
Shak., 3 Hen. VI., ii. 5. 123.

sadina (sa-dē'nạ̈), *n.* [Sp. *sardina*, a sardine: see *sardine*[1].] A clupeoid fish, *Clupea sagax*, the Californian sardine. It resembles the European sardine, C. *pilchardus*, but has no teeth, and the belly is less strongly serrate. See *sardine*[1], 1. [California.]

sad-iron (sad'ī″ėrn), *n.* A smoothing-iron for garments and textile fabrics generally, especially one differing from the ordinary flatiron in being hollow and heated by red-hot pieces of iron put into it. Compare *box-iron*.

sadly (sad'li), *adv.* [< ME. *sadly*, *sadli*; < *sad* + *-ly*[2].] 1†. Firmly; tightly.

Thus sall I fune it with a gynn,
And *sadly* sette it with symonde fyne,
Thus sall y wyrke it both more and myn[n]e.
York Plays, p. 43.

In gon the speres ful *sadly* in arest.
Chaucer, Knight's Tale, l. 1744.

2†. Steadily; constantly; persistently; industriously; eagerly.

Wigtly as a wod man the windowe he opened,
& sougt *sadli* al a-boute his semliche dougter,
but al wrougt in wast for went was that mayde.
William of Palerne (E. E. T. S.), l. 2058.

I praie thee, lord, that lore leere me,
Aftir thi loue to haue longynge,
And *sadli* to sette myn herte on thee.
Hymns to Virgin, etc. (E. E. T. S.), p. 8.

This messager drank *sadly* ale and wyn.
Chaucer, Man of Law's Tale, l. 645.

3†. Quietly.

Stand *sadly* in telling thy tale whensoeuer thou talkest.
Babees Book (E. E. T. S.), p. 75.

The fische in a dische clenly that ye lay
With vineger & powdur ther vppon, thus is vsed ay,
Than youre souerayne, whan hym semethe, *sadly* he may assay. *Babees Book* (E. E. T. S.), p. 159.

4†. In earnest; seriously; soberly; gravely; solemnly.

He that *sadly* for-soke soche a sure proffer,
And so gracius a gyste, that me is graunt here,
He might faithly for-fonnet be a fole holdyn.
Destruction of Troy (E. E. T. S.), l. 630.

The thridde day this marchant up ariseth,
And on his nedes *sadly* hym avyseth.
Chaucer, Shipman's Tale, l. 76.

This can be no trick: the conference was *sadly* borne.
Shak., Much Ado, ii. 3. 228.

Look, look, with what a discontented grace
Bruto the traveller doth *sadly* pace
'Long Westminster! *Marston*, Satires, ii. 128.

Here I *sadly* vow
Repentance and a leaving of that life
I long have died in. *Ford*, 'Tis Pity, v. 1.

5. (*a*) Sorrowfully; mournfully; miserably; grievously.

I cannot therefore but *sadly* bemoan that the Lives of these Saints are so darkened with Popish Illustrations, and farced with Fauxeties to their dishonour.
Fuller, Worthies, iii. (*Davies.*)

(*b*) In a manner to cause sadness; badly; afflictively; calamitously; deplorably.

The true principles of colonial policy were *sadly* misunderstood in the sixteenth century.
Prescott, Ferd. and Isa., ii. 26.

If his audience is really a popular audience, they bring *sadly* little information with them to the lecture.
Stubbs, Medieval and Modern Hist., p. 104.

(c) In ill health; poorly. [Colloq.]

Here's Mr. Holt, miss, wants to know if you'll give him leave to come in. I told him you was *sadly*.
George Eliot, Felix Holt, xxvii.

6. In dark or somber colors; soberly.

A gloomy, obscure place, and in it only one light, which the Genius of the house held, *sadly* attired.
B. *Jonson*, Entertainment at Theobalds.

sadness (sad'nes), *n.* [Early mod. E. also *sadnes*, *sadnesse*; < ME. *sadnes*, *sadnesse*, < AS. *sædness*, satiety, repletion, < *sæd*, full, sated: see *sad*.] 1†. Heaviness; weight; firmness; strength.

Whenne it is wel confourmed to *sadnesse*
On fleykes legge hem ichoone so from other.
Palladius, Husbondrie (E. E. T. S.), p. 154.

Whereby as I grant that it seemeth outwardlie to be verie thicke & well doone, so, if you respect the *sadnes* thereof, it dooth prooue in the end to be veric hollow & not able to hold out water.
Harrison, Descrip. of England, ii. 22 (Holinshed's Chron.).

2†. Steadiness; steadfastness; constancy.

This markis in his herte longeth so
To tempte his wyf, hir *sadnesse* for to knowe.
Chaucer, Clerk's Tale, l. 396.

3†. Seriousness; gravity; discretion; sedateness; sobriety; sober earnest.

For if that oon have beaute in hir face,
Another stant so in the peples grace
For hire *sadnesse* and hire benyngnytee,
That of the peple grettest voys hath she.
Chaucer, Merchant's Tale, l. 347.

And as for hitting the prick, because it is unpossible, it were a vain thing to go about it in good *sadness*.
Ascham, Toxophilus (ed. 1864), p. 94.

In good *sadness*, I do not know.
Shak., All's Well, iv. 3. 230.

In *sadness*, 'tis good and mature counsel.
B. *Jonson*, Epicœne, iv. 2.

4. The state of being sad or sorrowful; sorrowfulness; mournfulness; dejection of mind: as, *sadness* in the remembrance of loss.

Be sure the messenger advise his majesty
To comfort up the prince; he's full of *sadness*.
Fletcher, Humorous Lieutenant, ii. 2.

A feeling of *sadness* and longing,
That is not akin to pain,
And resembles sorrow only
As the mist resembles the rain.
Longfellow, The Day is Done.

5. A melancholy look; gloom of countenance.

Dim *sadness* did not spare
That time celestial visages. *Milton*, P. L., x. 23.

=**Syn.** 4. *Grief, Sorrow*, etc. (see *affliction*); despondency, melancholy, depression.

sadr (sad'r), *n.* [Ar.] The lote-bush, *Zizyphus Lotus*. See *lotus-tree*, 1.

sad-tree (sad'trē), *n.* The night-jasmine, *Nyctanthes Arbor-tristis*. Also called *Indian mourner*.

sae (sā), *adv.* A dialectal (Scotch) form of *so*.

sæculart, *a.* See *secular*.

Sænuridæ (sē-nū'ri-dē), *n. pl.* [NL., < *Sænuris* + *-idæ*.] A family of oligochætous annelids, named from the genus *Sænuris*.

Sænuridomorpha (sē-nū″ri-dō-môr'fä), *n. pl.* [NL., < *Sænuris* (*-id-*) + Gr. μορφή, form.] The *Sænuridæ* and their allies regarded as an order of oligochætous annelids.

Sænuris (sē-nū'ris), *n.* [NL., < Gr. σαινουρίς (-ιδ-), a fem. of σαίνουρος, wagging the tail, < σαίνειν, wag the tail, fawn, + οὐρά, the tail.] The typical genus of *Sænuridæ*. Also called *Tubifex*.

saetersbergite, sätersbergite (sā'tėrz-bėrg-īt), *n.* [< *Sætersberg* (see def.) + *-ite*[2].] A variety of loellingite, or iron arsenide, from Sætersberg near Fossum in Norway.

safe (sāf), *a.* and *n.* [< ME. *safe, saf, saaf, sauf, saulfe, sure, sauve*, < OF. *sauf, saulf, salf*, m., *sauve, saulve*, f., F. *sauf*, m., *sauve*, f., = Pr. *salv, salf, sal* = OCat. *sal* = Sp. Pg. It. *salvo*, < L. *salvus*, whole, safe, orig. **sarvus*, prob. ult. = *sollus*, whole, *sōlus*, single, sole (see *sole, solid*), orig. = Pers. *har*, every, all, every one, = Skt. *sarva*, entire. From the same L. source are ult. E. *save*[1], *save*[2], *save*[3] = *sage*[2], *salute*, etc. Cf. *vouchsafe*.] **I.** *a.* **1.** Unharmed; unscathed; without having received injury or hurt: as, to arrive *safe* and sound; to bring goods *safe* to land.

Whanne he in hond hit hade hastely hit semede
that he was al *sauf* & sound of alle his sor greues.
William of Palerne (E. E. T. S.), l. 868.

So it came to pass that they escaped all *safe* to land.
Acts xxvii. 44.

2. Free from risk or danger; secure from harm or liability to harm or injury: as, a *safe* place; a *safe* harbor; *safe* from disease, enemies, etc.

That ye sholde yeve hym trewys *saf* to come and *saf* to go by feith and suerte be-twene this and yole.
Merlin (E. E. T. S.), iii. 559.

Answer me
In what *safe* place you have bestow'd my money.
Shak., C. of E., i. 2. 78.

If to be ignorant were as *safe* as to be wise, no one would become wise. *H. Spencer*, Social Statics, p. 413.

3. Secure; not dangerous or liable to cause injury or harm; not likely to expose to danger: as, a *safe* bridge; the building was pronounced *safe*; the *safe* side of a file (the uncut side, also called the *safe-edge*).

With perfidious hatred they pursued
The sojourners of Goshen, who beheld
From the *safe* shore their floating carcases.
Milton, P. L., i. 310.

Perhaps she was sometimes too severe, which is a *safe* and pardonable error. *Swift*, Death of Stella.

4. No longer dangerous; placed beyond the power of doing harm.

Macb. Banquo's *safe*?
Mur. Aye, my good lord, *safe* in a ditch he bides.
Shak., Macbeth, iii. 4. 26.

5. Sound; whole; good.

A trade . . . that . . . I may use with a *safe* conscience.
Shak., J. C., i. 1. 14.

6. Trusty; trustworthy: as, a *safe* adviser.

My blood begins my *safer* guides to rule.
Shak., Othello, ii. 3. 205.

7. Sure; certain.

To sell away all the powder in a kingdom,
To prevent blowing up: that's *safe*, I'll able it.
Middleton, Game at Chess, ii. 1.

One or two more of the same sort are *safe* to make him an associate. *E. Yates*, Land at Last, I. 173.

=**Syn. 1** and **2**. *Safe, Secure*. These words once conformed in meaning to their derivations, *safe* implying free from danger present or prospective, and *secure* free from fear or anxiety about danger: they are so used in the quotation. Now the two words are essentially synonymous, except that *secure* is perhaps stronger, especially in emphasizing freedom from occasion to fear.

We cannot endure to be disturbed or awakened from our pleasing lethargy. For we care not to be *safe*, but to be *secure*; not to escape hell, but to live pleasantly.
Jer. Taylor, Slander and Flattery, Sermon xxiv.

II. *n.* **1†.** Safety.

If I with *safe* may graunt this deed,
I wil it not refuse.
Preston, K. Cambises (Hawkins, Eng. Dr., i. 503). (*Davies.*)

2. A place or structure for the storage of money, papers, or valuables in safety from risk of theft or fire. Safes as now made may be divided into two classes: stationary safes of stone, brick, or metal, built as part of the structure of a warehouse, store, or other building, and commonly called *vaults*; and portable safes of steel and iron. The term *safe* is usually restricted to portable safes, whatever their size or material. These safes are usually of two or more metals, as cast-iron, chilled iron, and steel, combined in various ways to resist drilling, and are made with hollow walls filled with some non-conductor of heat. A great variety of devices have been added to safes to insure greater efficiency, such as rabbeted air-tight doors, time-locks, and burglar-alarms. See *lock*[1], *alarm*, 5, *safe-deposit*, and phrases below.
3. A receptacle for the storage of meat and provisions. It is usually a skeleton frame of wood covered with fine wire netting to keep out insects.—4. Any receptacle for storing things in safety: as, a match-*safe*, milk-*safe*, coin-*safe*, etc.—5. A floating box or car for confining living fish.—6. A sheet of lead with the sides turned up, placed under a plumbing fixture to catch moisture or fluids due to leaks or carelessness, and thus protect floors and ceilings. —7. In *saddlery*, a piece of leather placed beneath a buckle to prevent chafing. *E. H. Knight.*—8. In *distilling*, a closed vessel attached by a pipe to the worm of a still, for the retention of a sample of the product, to be subsequently inspected by excise officers.—**Burglar-proof safe**, a safe constructed for protecting property against burglars. The inner compartment of the

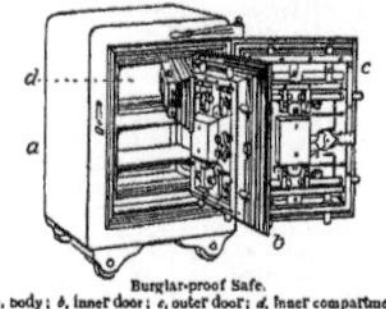

Burglar-proof Safe.
a, body; *b*, inner door; *c*, outer door; *d*, inner compartment.

burglar-proof safe (shown in the cuts) has small burglar-proof doors, each of which has its special combination-lock mechanism or may have a time-lock. All bolts and screws of this safe are made of welded steel and iron, and

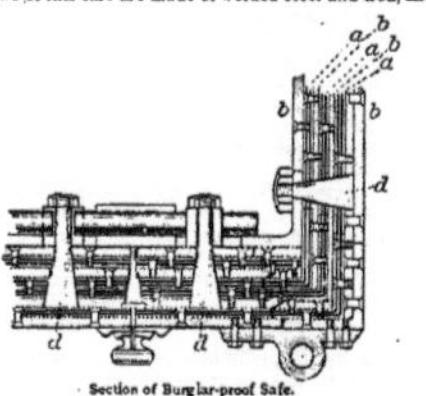

Section of Burglar-proof Safe.

twisted to produce alternate strata of steel and iron, and thus prevent their being drilled. The body (see the section) is made up of alternate plates of steel (*a*) and iron (*b*), the steel plates being interposed to obstruct drilling. The large bolts d are conical in form, and the smaller countersunk screws, as well as the lock-spindle, are all made of twisted iron and steel laminated like the bolts. In the most recent construction the lock-spindle, instead of being a single piece, is made sectional, the sections being socketed each into another to present still further obstruction to drilling. Compound hinges are also provided, whereby the door can be at first moved parallel to itself before swinging back, and an air-tight packing is interposed between the jambs and their abutments.—**Fire-proof safe**, a safe for the protection of property against fire. When the safe here figured is exposed to heat the alum gives off its water of crystallization, which becomes steam at ordinary atmospheric pressure, thus inclosing the contents in an envelop of steam at 212° F., which is maintained until the water is all expelled.

Cross-section of Fire-proof Safe.
a, outer casing of iron; *b*, door; *c*, filling of mixed alum and plaster of Paris.

safe† (sāf), *v. t.* [< *safe*, *n.* Cf. *save*[1].] **1.** To render safe.

And that which most with you should *safe* my going
Is Fulvia's death. *Shak.*, A. and C., i. 3. 55.

2. To escort to safety; safeguard.

Best you *safed* the bringer
Out of the host. *Shak.*, A. and C., iv. 6. 26.

safe-alarm (sāf'a-lärm″), *n.* An alarm-lock or other contrivance for giving notice when a safe is tampered with. Such alarms are usually electro-magnetic; but sometimes the alarm-mechanism is actuated by a body of water, or by compressed air.

safe-conduct (sāf-kon'dukt), *n.* [Early mod. E. also *salfecondite*; < ME. *safe condyth, saff condyte, saaf condyte, save conduit, save condite, saufconduit*, < OF. *sauf-conduit, salfconduit*, F. *sauf-conduit* = Sp. Pg. *salvoconducto* = It. *salvocondotto*, < ML. *salvus conductus*, a safe-conduct: L. *salvus*, safe; *conductus*, conduct: see *safe*, *a.*, and *conduct*, *n.*] A passport granted by one in authority, especially in time of war, to secure one's safety where it would otherwise be unsafe for him to go.

He had *safe conduct* for his band
Beneath the royal seal and hand.
Scott, Marmion, vi. 13.

safe-conduct (sāf-kon'dukt), *v. t.* [< *safe-conduct*, *n.*] To conduct safely; give a safe passage to, especially through a hostile country.

This sayd king . . . sayd, that he would not onely giue me passage, but also men to *safe-conduct* me.
Hakluyt's Voyages, I. 346.

Are they not now upon the western shore,
Safe-conducting the rebels from their ships?
Shak., Rich. III., iv. 4. 483.

safe-deposit (sāf'dē-poz″it), *a.* Providing safe storage for valuables of any kind, such as bullion, bonds, documents, etc.: as, a *safe-deposit* company; *safe-deposit* vaults.

safed-siris (saf'ed-sī'ris), *n.* [E. Ind.] A large deciduous tree, *Albizzia procera*, of the sub-Himalayan region. Its wood is colored dark-brown with lighter bands, is hard, straight, and durable, and is used in making agricultural implements, building bridges, etc.

safe-edged (sāf'ejd), *a.* Having an edge not liable to cause injury.—**Safe-edged file.** See *file*[1].

safeguard (sāf'gärd), *n.* [Early mod. E. also *safegard, safegarde, savegard*; ME. *saufegard, saulfegarde, salfgard*, < OF. (and F.) *sauvegarde* (= Pr. *salvagarda, salvagardia* = Sp. *salvaguardia* = Pg. *salvaguarda* = It. *salvaguardia* (ML. *salvagardia*)), safe-keeping, < *sauve*, fem. of *sauf*, safe, + *garde*, keeping, guard: see *safe* and *guard*.] **1.** Safe-keeping; defense; protection.

As our Lord knoweth, who have you in His blissid *saufegard*. *Paston Letters*, III. 366.

He tooke his penne and wrote his warrant of *sauegard*.
Ascham, The Scholemaster, p. 154.

They were . . . aduised for to accept and take treaty, if it were offered, for the *sauegard* of the common people.
Hakluyt's Voyages, II. 90.

The smallest worm will turn, being trodden on,
And doves will peck in *safeguard* of their brood.
Shak., 3 Hen. VI., ii. 2. 18.

2†. Safety.

The Admirall toke also with him al sortes of Iron tooles to th[e] intent to hyid townes and fortresses where his men might lye in *safegarde*.
R. Eden, tr. of Sebastian Munster (First Books on America, ed. Arber, p. 30).

3. One who or that which protects.

Thy sword, the *safeguard* of thy brother's throne,
Is now as much the bulwark of thy own.
Granville, To the King in the First Year of his Reign.

Specifically—(*a*) A convoy or guard to protect a traveler or merchandise. (*b*) A passport; a warrant of security given by authority of a government or a commanding officer to protect the person and property of a stranger or an enemy, or by a commanding officer to protect against the operations of his forces persons or property within the limits of his command; formerly, a protection granted to a stranger in prosecuting his rights in due course of law.

A trumpet was sent to the Earl of Essex for a *safeguard* or pass to two lords, to deliver a message from the king to the two houses. *Clarendon.*

Passports and *safeguards*, or safe conducts, are letters of protection, with or without an escort, by which the person of an enemy is rendered inviolable.
Woolsey, Introd. to Inter. Law, § 147.

4†. An outer petticoat for women's wear, intended to save their clothes from dust, etc., when on horseback or in other ways exposed to the weather. Also, contracted, *saggard*.

Make you ready straight,
And in that gown which you came first to town in,
Your *safe-guard*, cloak, and your hood suitable,
Thus on a double gelding shall you amble,
And my man Jaques shall be set before you.
Fletcher (*and another*), Noble Gentleman, ii. 1.

Enter Moll in a frieze jerkin and a black *saveguard*.
Middleton and Dekker, Roaring Girl, ii. 1.

Her mother's hood and *safe-guard* too
He brought with him.
The Suffolk Miracle (Child's Ballads, I. 220).

5. A rail-guard at railway switches and crossings.—6. A contrivance attached to a locomotive, designed to throw stones and other light obstructions from the rails.—7. In *ceram.*, a saggar.—8. In *zoöl.*, a monitor-lizard. See *monitor*, 6.

safeguard (sāf'gärd), *v. t.* [Formerly also *safegard*; ‹ *safeguard*, *n.*] To guard; protect.

Fighting men, as on a tower mounted,
Safegard themselves & doe their foes annoy.
Times' Whistle (E. E. T. S.), p. 129.

To *safeguard* thine own life
The best way is to venge my Gloucester's death.
Shak., Rich. II., i. 2. 35.

safe-keeping (sāf'kē'ping), *n.* The act of keeping or preserving in safety from injury or from escape; secure guardianship. *Imp. Dict.*

safely (sāf'li), *adv.* [‹ ME. *savely*, *saufly*, *saufliche*; ‹ *safe* + *-ly*2.] In a safe manner. (*a*) Without incurring danger or hazard of evil consequences.

For unto vertue longeth dignytee,
And nought the reverse, *savely* dar I deeme.
Chaucer, Gentilesse, l. 6.

I may *safely* say I have read over this apological oration of my Uncle Toby's a hundred times.
Sterne, Tristram Shandy, vi. 31.

(*b*) Without hurt or injury; in safety.

That my ships
Are *safely* come to road.
Shak., M. of V., v. 1. 288.

(*c*) In close custody; securely; carefully.

Till then I'll keep him dark and *safely* lock'd.
Shak., All's Well, iv. 1. 104.

safeness (sāf'nes), *n.* [‹ ME. *saafnesse*; ‹ *safe* + *-ness*.] The state or character of being safe or of conferring safety.

Saafnesse, or salvacyon. Salvacio.
Prompt. Parv., p. 440.

safe-pledge (sāf'plej), *n.* In *law*, a surety appointed for one's appearance at a day assigned.

saferay†, *n.* A Middle English form of *savory*2.

safety (sāf'ti), *n.* [‹ ME. *safte*, *savete*, ‹ OF. *sauvete*, *salveteit*, F. *sauveté* = Pr. *salvetat*, *saubetat* = Sp. *salvedad* (cf. It. *salvezza*), ‹ ML. *salvita(t-)s*, ‹ L. *salvus*, safe: see *safe*.] 1. Immunity from harm or danger; preservation or freedom from injury, loss, or hurt.

Thenking, musing hys soules *sauete*,
As will man as woman, to say in breue.
Rom. of Partenay (E. E. T. S.), l. 6170.

Would I were in an alehouse in London! I would give all my fame for a pot of ale and *safety*.
Shak., Hen. V., iii. 2. 14.

2. An unharmed or uninjured state or condition: as, to escape in *safety*.

He hadde fer contrey to ride that marched to his enmyes er he com in to his londe in *safte*.
Merlin (E. E. T. S.), iii. 471.

Edward . . .
Hath pass'd in *safety* through the narrow seas.
Shak., 3 Hen. VI., iv. 8. 3.

3. Freedom from risk or possible damage or hurt; safeness.

"Knowest thou not that Holy Writ saith, In the multitude of counsel there is *safety*?" "Ay, madam," said Walter, "but I have heard learned men say that the *safety* spoken of is for the physicians, not the patient."
Scott, Kenilworth, xv.

4†. A safeguard.

Let not my jealousies be your dishonours,
But mine own *safeties*. *Shak.*, Macbeth, iv. 3. 30.

5. Safe-keeping; close custody. [Rare.]

Imprison him; . . .
Deliver him to *safety* and return.
Shak., K. John, iv. 2. 158.

6. A safety-bicycle. See cut under *bicycle*.—7. In *foot-ball*, a safety touch-down.—**Council of safety.** See *council*.—**Safety touch-down.** See *touch-down*.

safety-arch (sāf'ti-ärch), *n.* Same as *arch of discharge* (which see, under *arch*1).

safety-beam (sāf'ti-bēm), *n.* A timber fastened at each side of the truck-frame of a railway-car, having iron straps which pass beneath the axles to support them in case of breakage.

safety-belt (sāf'ti-belt), *n.* A belt made of some buoyant material or inflated to sustain a person in water; a life-belt; a safety-buoy. See *life-preserver*.

safety-bicycle (sāf'ti-bī"si-kl), *n.* A low-wheeled bicycle, with multiplying gear, having the wheels equal, or nearly equal, in diameter.

safety-bolt (sāf'ti-bōlt), *n.* A bolt which can be locked in place by a padlock or otherwise.

safety-bridle (sāf'ti-brī"dl), *n.* In *harness*, a bridle fitted with checking apparatus for restraining a horse if he attempts to run. See *safety-rein*.

safety-buoy (sāf'ti-boi), *n.* A safety-belt.

safety-cage (sāf'ti-kāj), *n.* In *mining*, a cage fitted up with apparatus by means of which a fall will be prevented in case of breakage of the rope. Also called *parachute*.

safety-car (sāf'ti-kär), *n.* 1. A car to run on a hawser passed between a stranded vessel and the land; a life-car.—2. A barney; a small car used on inclined planes and slopes to push up a mine-car. *Penn. Geol. Surv.*, Glossary.

safety-catch (sāf'ti-kach), *n.* In *mining*, one of the catches provided to hold the cage in case of a breakage of the rope by which it is suspended. See *safety-stop*.

safety-chain (sāf'ti-chān), *n.* On a railway, an extra chain or coupling attached to a platform or other part of a car to prevent it from being detached in case of accident to the main coupling; a check-chain of a car-truck; a safety-link.—**Brake safety-chain**, a chain secured to a brake-beam and to the truck or body of a car, to hold the brake-beam if the brake-hanger should give way.

safety-disk (sāf'ti-disk), *n.* A disk of sheet-copper inserted in the skin of a boiler, so as to intervene between the steam and an escape-pipe. The copper is so light that an over-pressure of steam breaks the disk and the steam escapes through the pipe. *E. H. Knight.*

safety-door (sāf'ti-dōr), *n.* In *coal-mining*, a door hinged to the roof, and hung near a main door, so as to be ready for immediate use in case of an accident happening to the main door by an explosion or otherwise.

safety-funnel (sāf'ti-fun"el), *n.* A long-necked glass funnel for introducing acids, etc., into liquids contained in bottles or retorts and under a pressure of gas. *E. H. Knight.*

safety-fuse (sāf'ti-fūz), *n.* See *fuse*2.

safety-grate (sāf'ti-grāt), *n.* On a railway, a perforated plate placed over the fire-box of a car-heater to prevent the coals from falling out in case the heater is accidentally overturned.

safety-hanger (sāf'ti-hang"ėr), *n.* On a railway, an iron strap or loop designed to prevent a brake, rod, or other part from falling on the line in case of breakage. *E. H. Knight.*

safety-hatch (sāf'ti-hach), *n.* 1. A hatch for closing an elevator-shaft when the cage is not passing, or a hatchway when not in use.—2. A hatchway or elevator-shaft arranged with doors or traps at each floor, which are opened and closed automatically by the elevator-car in passing; or a series of traps in a shaft arranged to close in case of fire by the burning of a cord or by the release of a rope, which permits all the traps to close together.

safety-hoist (sāf'ti-hoist), *n.* 1. A hoisting-gear on the principle of the differential pulley, which will not allow its load to descend by the run.—2. A catch to prevent an elevator-cage from falling in case the rope breaks. *E. H. Knight.*

safety-hook (sāf'ti-hůk), *n.* 1. A form of safety-catch in a mine-hoist. It is a hook so arranged as to engage a support automatically in case of breakage of the hoisting-gear.

2. A hook fastened when shut by a spring or screw, intended to prevent a watch from being detached from its chain by accident or a jerk. *E. H. Knight.*

safety-ink (sāf'ti-ingk), *n.* See *ink*1.

safety-lamp (sāf'ti-lamp), *n.* In *mining*, a form of lamp intended for use in coal-mining, the object of the arrangement being to prevent the inflammable gas by which the miner is often surrounded from being set on fire, as would be the case were the flame not protected from contact with the gas. The basis of the safety-lamp, an invention of Sir Humphry Davy in 1816, is the fact, discovered by him, that flame cannot be communicated through a fine wire gauze. About 784 apertures to the square inch is the number generally adopted, the lamp being surrounded by a cylinder, about an inch and a half in diameter, made of a metallic gauze of this description. Various improvements have been made by Clanny, George Stephenson, Mueseler, and others, in the safety-lamp as originally devised by Davy. Stephenson's lamp is called by the miners a *geordie*. The Mueseler lamp is the one chiefly used in Belgium, and has been introduced in England. The essential feature of the Davy lamp remains in all these improvements, the object of which is to get more light, to secure a more complete combustion of the oil, and to prevent the miners from using the lamp without the gauze.

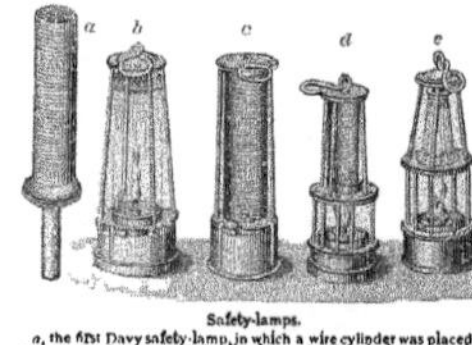

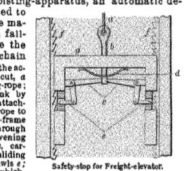

Safety-lamps.

a, the first Davy safety-lamp, in which a wire cylinder was placed as casing over the flame; *b*, English lamp, the light inclosed in a glass cylinder protected at the top by wire gauze; *c*, English lamp, the gauze cylinder protected by upright wires; *d*, French lamp (Mueseler's), with glass and gauze cylinder; *e*, petroleum lamp, glass and gauze.

safety-link (sāf'ti-lingk), *n.* A connection between a car-body and its trucks, designed to limit the swing of the latter.

safety-lintel (sāf'ti-lin"tel), *n.* A wooden lintel placed behind a stone lintel in the aperture of a door or window.

safety-lock (sāf'ti-lok), *n.* 1. A lock so contrived that it cannot be picked by ordinary means.—2. In *firearms*, a lock provided with a stop, catch, or other device to prevent accidental discharge. *E. H. Knight.*

safety-loop (sāf'ti-löp), *n.* In a vehicle, one of the loops by which the body-strap is attached to the body and perch, to prevent dangerous rolling of the body. *E. H. Knight.*

safety-match (sāf'ti-mach), *n.* See *match*2.

safety-paper (sāf'ti-pā"pėr), *n.* A paper so prepared by mechanical or chemical processes as to resist alteration by chemical or mechanical means. The paper may be colored with a pigment which must be defaced if the surface is tampered with, treated with a chemical which causes writing upon it to become fixed in the fiber, made up of several layers having special characteristics, peculiarly water-marked, incorporated in the pulp with a fiber of silk, etc. The last method is used for the paper on which United States notes are printed.

safety-pin (sāf'ti-pin), *n.* A pin bent back on itself, the bend forming a spring, and having the point fitting into a kind of sheath, so that it may not be readily withdrawn or prick the wearer or others while in use.

safety-plug (sāf'ti-plug), *n.* 1. In steam-boilers, a bolt having its center filled with a fusible metal, screwed into the top of the fire-box, so that when the water becomes too low the increased temperature melts out the metal, and thus admits steam into the fire-box or furnace to put the fire out. Also called *fusible plug*.—2. A screw-plug of fusible metal used for the same purpose in steam-heating boilers carrying pressures of from 5 to 10 pounds.—3. A form of spring-valve screwed into a barrel containing fermenting liquids to allow the gas to escape if the pressure becomes too great.

safety-rail (sāf'ti-rāl), *n.* On a railway, a guard-rail at a switch, so disposed as to bear on the inside edge of a wheel-flange and thus prevent the tread from leaving the track-rail. *E. H. Knight.*

safety-razor (sāf'ti-rā"zor), *n.* A razor with guards on each side of the edge to prevent the user from accidentally cutting himself in shaving. *E. H. Knight.*

safety-rein (sāf'ti-rān), *n.* A rein intended to prevent a horse from running away. It actuates various devices to pull the bit violently into the angles of the horse's mouth, to cover his eyes, to tighten a choking-strap about his throat, etc. *E. H. Knight.*

safety-stop (sāf'ti-stop), *n.* 1. On an elevator or other hoisting-apparatus, an automatic device designed to prevent the machine from falling in case the rope or chain breaks. In the accompanying cut, *a* is the hoisting-rope; *b*, bar or link by which the attachment of the rope to the elevator-frame *g* is made through the intervening bell-cranks *c*, carrying the sliding catches or pawls *e*; *d*, spring which, when the rope breaks, forces the inner ends of the bell-cranks downward, and the catches *e* outward into engagement with the ratches *f*, thus immediately stopping the descent of the elevator.

Safety-stop for Freight-elevator.

2. In *firearms*, a device to lock the hammer in order to prevent an accidental discharge.—3. On a pulley or sheave, a stop to prevent running backward.—4. In a spinning-machine, loom, etc., a device for arresting the motion in

case of the breakage of a yarn, thread, or sliver. *E. H. Knight.*

safety-strap (sāf'ti-strap), *n.* In *saddlery*, an extra back-band used with a light trotting-harness. It is passed over the seat of a gig-saddle, the terrets of which are inserted through holes in the strap. The ends of the strap are buckled to the shaft-tugs.—**Brake safety-strap**, an iron or steel strap so bent as to embrace the brake-beam of a car-truck, to the end-pieces or transoms of which the ends of the safety-strap are secured. Its function is to prevent the beam from falling on the track if any of the hangers give way. It is sometimes made to serve as a brake-spring to throw off the brake.

safety-switch (sāf'ti-swich), *n.* A switch which automatically returns to its normal position after being moved to shift a train to a siding.

safety-tackle (sāf'ti-tak'l), *n.* An additional tackle used to give greater support in cases where it is feared that the strain might prove too great for the tackles already in use.

safety-tube (sāf'ti-tūb), *n.* In *chem.*, a tube, usually provided with bulbs and bent to form a trap, through which such reagents as produce noxious fumes may be added to the contents of a flask or retort, or by which dangerous pressure within a vessel may be avoided.

safety-valve (sāf'ti-valv), *n.* A contrivance

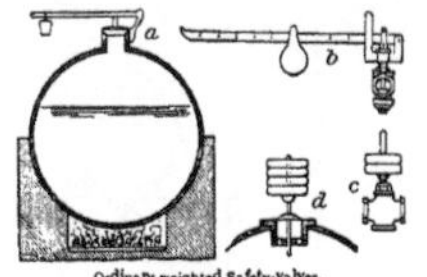

Ordinary weighted Safety-Valves.

a and *b* show the weight applied with levers as in power-boilers, while in *c* and *d* the weights are directly applied to the valve-stem —a common method with low-pressure steam-boilers used for steam-heating.

for obviating or diminishing the risk of explosion in steam-boilers. The form and construction of safety-valves are exceedingly various, but the principle of all is the same—that of opposing the pressure within the boiler by such a force as will yield before it reaches the point of danger, and permit the steam to escape. The most simple and obvious kind of safety-valve is that in which a weight is placed directly over a steam-tight plate fitted to an aperture in the boiler. When, however, the pressure is high, this form becomes inconvenient, and the lever safety-valve is adopted.—**Internal safety-valve**, in a steam-boiler, a valve which opens inward to admit air into the boiler when a partial vacuum has been formed by the condensation of the steam.—**Lock-up safety-valve**, a safety-valve having the weighted lever or spring shut in a locked chamber so that it cannot be interfered with except by the person holding the key.—**Spring safety-valve**, a form of safety-valve the pressure of which is controlled by a gaged or adjustable spring or set of springs.

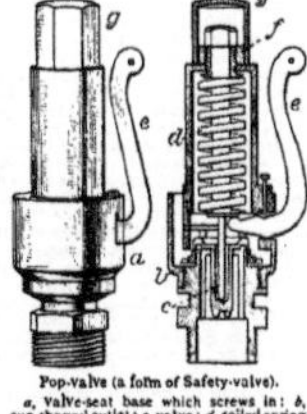

Pop-valve (a form of Safety-valve).

a, valve-seat base which screws in; *b*, cup-shaped outlet; *c*, valve; *d*, coiled spring which presses valve to its seat; *e*, lever by which the valve can be opened at will; *f*, set-nut by which the pressure of the spring is adjusted; *g*, removable cap.

saffert, *n.* An obsolete form of *sapphire*.

saffi, *n.* Plural of *saffo*.

saffian (saf'i-an), *n.* [= D. *saffiaan* = G. Sw. *saffian* = Dan. *saffian*, < Russ. *safiyanŭ*, morocco, saffian.] Goatskins or sheepskins tanned with sumac and dyed in a variety of bright colors, without a previous stuffing with oils or fats.

safflorite (saf'lor-it), *n.* [< G. *safflor*, safflower, + *-ite*[2].] An arsenide of cobalt and iron, long confounded with the isometric species smaltite.

safflowt, *n.* Same as *safflower*.

An herb they call *safflow*, or bastard saffron, dyers use for scarlet. *Mortimer*, Husbandry.

safflower (saf'lou-ėr), *n.* [Formerly also *saf-flow* (if this is not an error in the one passage cited); = D. *saffloers* = G. Sw. Dan. *safflor* = Russ. *safloru*, safflower, < OF. *saflor*, *safleur*, < OIt. *saffiore*, *asfiore*, *asfrole*, *zaffrole*, etc. (forms given by Yule and Burnell, in part simulating It. *fiore*, OF. *flor*, *fleur*, flower, and so likewise in the E., etc., forms), < Ar. *usfur*, safflower, < *sufrā*, yellow: see *saffron*.] A composite plant, *Carthamus tinctorius*; also, a drug and dyestuff consisting of its dried florets. The safflower is a thistle-like herb a foot or two high, somewhat branching above, the heads of an orange-red color. It is native perhaps from Egypt to India, and is extensively cultivated in southern

Upper Part of Stem of Safflower (*Carthamus tinctorius*), with the heads.

a, a flower; *b*, *c*, the two different kinds of involucral leaves.

Europe, Egypt, India, and China. It is sometimes planted in herb- and flower-gardens in the United States. Safflower as a medicine has little power, but is still in domestic use as a substitute for saffron. As a dyestuff (its chief application), it imparts bright but fugitive tints of red in various shades. It is extensively used at Lyons and in India and China in dyeing silks, but has been largely replaced by the aniline dyes. It is much employed in the preparation of rouge, and serves also to adulterate saffron. (See *carthamin*.) In India a lighting and culinary oil is largely expressed from its seeds. Also called *African*, *false* or *bastard*, and *dyers' saffron*.

The finest and best *safflower*, commanding the highest price, comes from China.
A. G. F. Eliot James, Indian Industries, p. 131.

safflower-oil (saf'lou-ėr-oil), *n.* Oil expressed from safflower-seed. See *safflower*. Also called *curdee-oil*.

saffot, *n.*; pl. *saffi*. [It., a bailiff, catchpoll.] A bailiff; a catchpoll.

I hear some fooling; officers, the *saffi*,
Come to apprehend us!
B. *Jonson*, Volpone, iii. 6.

saffornet, *n.* An obsolete form of *saffron*.

saffrant, *n.* and *v.* An obsolete form of *saffron*.

saffre, *n.* See *zaffre*.

saffron (saf'ron), *n.* and *a.* [Formerly also *saffran*; < ME. *saffron*, *saffroun*, *safcron*, *safforne*, *saffran*, *safrun* = D. *saffraan* = MLG. *saffarān* = MHG. *safrān*, G. *safran* = Sw. *saffran* = Dan. *safran*, < OF. *safran*, *saffran* (also *safleur*, *saflor*, > E. *safflower*), F. *safran* = Pr. *safran*, *safra* = Cat. *safra* = It. *zafferano* = (with the orig. Ar. article) Sp. *azafran* = Pg. *açafrão* = Wall. *sofran*, < Ar. (> Pers.) *za'farān*, with the article *az-za'faran*, saffron, < Ar. (> Turk. Pers.) *safrā*, yellow (as a noun, bile).] **I.** *n.* **1.** A product consisting of the dried stigmas of the flowers of the autumnal crocus, *Crocus sativus*. The true saffron of commerce is now mostly *hay saffron*—that is, it consists of the loose stigmas uncaked. The product of over four thousand flowers is required to make an ounce. It has a sweetish aromatic odor, a warm pungent bitter taste, and a deep orange color. In medicine it was formerly deemed highly stimulant, antispasmodic, and even narcotic; it was esteemed by the ancients and by the Arabians; and on the continent of Europe it is still much used as an emmenagogue. Experiments, however, have shown that it possesses little activity. It is also used to color confectionery, and in Europe and India is largely employed as a condiment. Saffron yields to water and alcohol about three fourths of its weight in an orange-red extract, which has been largely used in painting and dyeing, but in the latter use is mostly replaced by much cheaper substitutes.

Capons that ben coloured with *saffron*.
Babees Book (E. E. T. S.), p. 275.

I must have *saffron*, to colour the warden pies.
Shak., W. T., iv. 3. 48.

2. The plant which produces saffron, a low bulbous herb, *Crocus sativus*, the autumnal crocus. The saffron resembles the ordinary spring crocus. It has handsome purple flowers, the perianth funnel-shaped with a long slender tube, the style with its three stigmas, which are over an inch long, hanging out on one side. It is thought to be a native of Greece and the Levant, its wild original being perhaps a form of C. *Cartwrightianus*. It is grown for its commercial produce in parts of southern Europe, especially in Spain, and in Asia Minor, Persia, Cashmere, and China.—**African saffron.** See *safflower* and *Lyperia*.—**Aperitive saffron of Mars.** Same as *precipitated carbonate of iron* (which see, under *precipitate*).—**Bastard** or **false saffron.** Same as *safflower*.—**Dyers' saffron.** Same as *safflower*.—**Meadow saffron.** See *meadow-saffron*.—**Saffron-oil**, or **oil of saffron**, a narcotic oil extracted from the stigmata of the *Crocus sativus*.

II. *a.* Having the color given by an infusion of saffron-flowers, somewhat orange-yellow, less brilliant than chrome.

Did this companion with the *saffron* face
Revel and feast it at my house to-day?
Shak., C. of E., iv. 4. 64.

Saffron plum. See *plum*[1].

saffront (saf'ron), *v. t.* [Formerly also *saffran*; < ME. *saffronen*, < OF. *saffraner*, F. *safraner* = Sp. *azafranar* = Pg. *açafroar* = It. *zafferanare*, saffron, dye saffron; from the noun.] To tinge with saffron; make yellow; gild; give color or flavor to.

In Latyn I speke a wordes fewe
To *saffron* [var. *savore*] with my predicacioun,
And for to stire men to devocioun.
Chaucer, Prol. to Pardoner's Tale, l. 59.

Give us bacon, rinds of wallnuts,
Shells of cockels, and of small nuts;
Ribands, bells, and *saffrand* linnen.
Wits Recreations (1654). (*Nares.*)

saffron-crocus (saf'ron-krō'kus), *n.* The common saffron.

saffron-thistle (saf'ron-this'l), *n.* The safflower.

saffronwood (saf'ron-wůd), *n.* A South African tree, *Elæodendron croceum*. It has a fine-grained hard and tough wood, which is useful for beams, agricultural implements, etc., and its bark is used for tanning and dyeing.

saffrony (saf'ron-i), *a.* [< *saffron* + *-y*[1].] Having the color of saffron.

The woman was of complexion yellowish or *saffrony*, as on whose face the sun had too freely cast his beams.
Lord, Hist. of the Banians (1630), p. 9. (*Latham.*)

safranine (saf'ra-nin), *n.* [< F. *safran*, saffron, + *-ine*[2].] A coal-tar color used in dyeing, obtained by oxidizing a mixture of amido-azotoluene and toluidine. It gives yellowish-red shades on wool, silk, and cotton, and is fairly fast to light.

safranophile (saf'ran-ō-fil), *a.* [< F. *safran*, saffron, + Gr. φιλεῖν, love.] In *histol.*, staining easily and distinctively with safranine: said of cells.

safrol (saf'rol), *n.* [< F. *safr(an)*, saffron, + *-ol*.] The chief constituent of oil of sassafras ($C_{10}H_{10}O_2$).

saft (saft), *a.* and *adv.* A Scotch form of *soft*.

safyret, *n.* A Middle English form of *sapphire*.

sag (sag), *v.*; pret. and pp. *sagged*, ppr. *sagging*. [< ME. *saggen*, < Sw. *sacka*, settle, sink down (as dregs), = Dan. *sakke*, sink astern (naut.), = MLG. *sacken*, LG. *sakken* = D. *zakken*, sink (as dregs), = G. *sacken*, sink; perhaps from the non-nasal form of the root of *sink*, appearing also in AS. *sīgan*, sink (*sǣgan*, cause to sink): see *sink*, *sie*.] **I.** *intrans.* **1.** To droop, especially in the middle; settle or sink through weakness or lack of support.

The Horizons il-leuell'd circle wide
Would *sag* too much on th' one or th' other side.
Sylvester, tr. of Du Bartas's Weeks, i. 3.

Great beams *sag* from the ceiling low.
Whittier, Prophecy of Samuel Sewall.

Hence—**2.** To yield under the pressure of care, difficulties, trouble, doubt, or the like; be depressed.

The mind I sway by and the heart I bear
Shall never *sag* with doubt, nor shake with fear.
Shak., Macbeth, v. 3. 10.

3†. To go about in a careless, slovenly manner or state; slouch.

Carterly vpstarts, that out-face towne and countrey in their veluets, when Sir Rowland Russet-coat, their dad, goes *sagging* euerie day in his round gascoynes of white cotton, and hath much adoo (poore pennie-father) to keepe his vnthrift elbowes in reparations.
Nashe, Pierce Penilesse, p. 8.

4. *Naut.*, to incline to the leeward; make leeway.

II. *trans.* To cause to droop or bend in the middle, as by an excessive load or burden: opposed to *hog*.

sag (sag), *n.* [< *sag*, *v.*] A bending or drooping, as of a rope that is fastened at its extremities, or of a surface; droop. Specifically—(*a*) The dip of a telegraph-wire, or the distance from the straight line joining the points to which the wire is attached to the lowest point of the arc it forms between them. (*b*) The tendency of a vessel to drift to leeward. (*c*) Drift; tendency.

Note at the end of euery foure glasses what way the shippe hath made, . . . and howe her way hath bene through the water, considering withall for the *sagge* of the sea, to leewards, accordingly as you shall finde it growen.
Hakluyt's Voyages, I. 436.

sagt (sag), *a.* [< *sag*, *v.*] Heavy; loaded; weighed down. [Rare.]

He ventures boldly on the pith
Of sugred rush, and eats the sagge
And well bestrutted bees sweet bagge.
Herrick, Hesperides, p. 127. (*Davies.*)

saga (sä'gä), *n.* [< Icel. *saga* (gen. *sögu*, pl. *sögur*) = Sw. Dan. *saga*, saga, a tale, story, legend, tradition, history (cf. Sw. *sägen*, *sägn*, Dan. *sagn*, a tale, story, legend), = OHG. *saga*, MHG. G. *sage* = AS. *sagu*, a saying, statement, report, tale, prophecy, saw: see *saw*².] An ancient Scandinavian legend or tradition of considerable length, relating either mythical or historical events; a tale; a history: as, the Völsunga *saga;* the Knytlinga *saga*.

Sagaces (sa̤-gā'sēz), *n. pl.* [NL., < L. *sagax* (*sagac-*), sagacious: see *sagacious.*] An old division of domestic dogs, including those of great sagacity, as the spaniel: distinguished from *Celeres* and *Pugnaces.*

sagaciate (sa̤-gā'shi-āt), *v. i.*; pret. and pp. *sagaciated*, ppr. *sagaciating*. [A made word, appar. based on *sagacious* + *-ate*².] To do or be in any way; think, talk, or act, as indicating a state of mind or body: as, how do you *sagaciate* this morning? [Slang, U. S.]

"How duz yo' sym'tums seem ter *segashuate?*" sez Brer Rabbit, sezee. *J. C. Harris*, Uncle Remus, ii.

sagacious (sa̤-gā'shus), *a.* [= F. *sagace* = Sp. Pg. *sagaz* = It. *sagace*, < L. *sagax* (*sagac-*), of quick perception, acute, sagacious, < *sagire*, perceive by the senses. Not connected with *sage*¹.] 1. Keenly perceptive; discerning, as by some exceptionally developed or extraordinary natural power; especially, keen of scent: with *of*.

So scented the grim feature, and upturn'd
His nostril wide into the murky air,
Sagacious of his quarry from so far.
Milton, P. L., x. 281.

'Tis the shepherd's task the winter long
To wait upon the storms; *of* their approach
Sagacious, into sheltering coves he drives
His flock. *Wordsworth*, Prelude, viii.

2. Exhibiting or marked by keen intellectual discernment, especially of human motives and actions; having or proceeding from penetration into practical affairs in general; having keen practical sense; acute in discernment or penetration; discerning and judicious; shrewd: as, a *sagacious* mind.

Only *sagacious* heads light on these observations. *Locke.*

True charity is *sagacious*, and will find out hints for beneficence. *Sir T. Browne*, Christ. Mor., i. 6.

In Homer himself we find not a few of those *sagacious*, curt sentences, into which men unacquainted with books are fond of compressing their experience of human life. *J. S. Blackie*, Lang. and Lit. of Scottish Highlands, ii.

3. Intelligent; endowed with sagacity.

Of all the solitary insects I have ever remarked, the spider is the most *sagacious*. *Goldsmith*, The Bee, No. 4.

=**Syn.** 2 and 3. *Sage, Knowing*, etc. (see *astute*); perspicacious, clear-sighted, long-headed, sharp-witted, intelligent, well-judged, sensible.

sagaciously (sa̤-gā'shus-li), *adv.* In a sagacious manner; wisely; sagely.

Lord Coke *sagaciously* observes upon it. *Burke*, Economical Reformation.

sagaciousness (sa̤-gā'shus-nes), *n.* The quality of being sagacious; sagacity.

sagacity (sa̤-gas'i̤-ti), *n.* [< F. *sagacité* = Pr. *sagacitat* = Sp. *sagacidad* = Pg. *sagacidade* = It. *sagacità*, < L. *sagacita(t-)s*, sagaciousness, < *sagax* (*sagac-*), sagacious: see *sagacious.*] The state or character of being sagacious, in any sense; sagaciousness.

Knowledge of the world . . . consists in knowing from what principles men generally act; and it is commonly the fruit of natural *sagacity* joined with experience. *Reid*, Active Powers, III. i. 1.

=**Syn.** *Perspicacity*, etc. (see *judgment*), insight, mother-wit. See *astute* and *discernment*.

sagaie, *n.* Same as *assagai.*

sagaman (sä'gä̤-ma̤n), *n.* [< Icel. *sögumadhr* (= Dan. *sagamand*), < *saga* (gen. *sögu*), saga, + *madhr*, man.] A narrator or chanter of sagas; a Scandinavian minstrel.

You are the hero! you are the *Sagaman.* We are not worthy; we have been cowards and sluggards. *Kingsley*, Hypatia, xxix.

sagamité, *n.* [Amer. Ind. (Algonkin).] An Indian dish of coarse hominy boiled to gruel.

Corn was liberally used, and was dressed in various ways, of which the most relished was one which is still in fashion among the old French population of Louisiana, and which is called "*sagamité*." *Gayarré*, Hist. Louisiana, I. 317.

sagamore (sag'a̤-mōr), *n.* [Amer. Ind. *sagamore*, chief, king: supposed to be connected with *sachem: see sachem.*] A king or chief among some tribes of American Indians. Some writers regard *sagamore* as synonymous with *sachem*, but others distinguish between them, regarding *sachem* as a chief of the first rank, and *sagamore* as one of the second.

The next day . . . came a tall Saluage boldly amongst vs. . . . He was a *Sagamo.* *Capt. John Smith*, Works (ed. Arber), p. 754.

Wahginnacut, a *sagamore* upon the River Quonehtacut, which lies west of Naraganset, came to the governour at Boston. *Winthrop*, Hist. New England, I. 62.

The barbarous people were lords of their own; and have their *sagamores*, and orders, and forms of government under which they peaceably live. *Bp. Hall*, Cases of Conscience, iii. 8.

Foot by foot, they were driven back from the shores, until I, that am a chief and a *sagamore*, have never seen the sun shine but through the trees, and have never visited the graves of my fathers. *J. F. Cooper*, Last of Mohicans, iii.

sagapen (sag'a̤-pen), *n.* Same as *sagapenum.*

sagapenum (sag-a̤-pē'num), *n.* [NL., < L. *sagapenon, sacopenium*, < Gr. *σαγάπηνον*, a gum of some umbelliferous plant (supposed to be *Ferula Persica*) used as a medicine; cf. Σαγαπηνοί, the name of a people of Assyria.] A fetid gum-resin, the concrete juice of a Persian species of *Ferula*, formerly used in amenorrhea, hysteria, etc., or externally.

sagar†, *n.* An obsolete form of *cigar*.

Many a *sagar* have little Goldy and I smoaked together. *Colman*, Man of Business, iv. (*Davies.*)

Sagartia (sa̤-gär'ti-ä̤), *n.* [NL.] A genus of sea-anemones, typical of the family *Sagartiidæ*. *S. leucolæma* is the white-armed sea-anemone. See cut under *cancrisocial*.

Sagartiidæ (sag-är-tī'i-dē), *n. pl.* [NL., < *Sagartia* + *-idæ.*] A family of *Hexactiniæ*, typified by the genus *Sagartia*, having acontia, numerous highly contractile tentacles, a strong mesodermal circular muscle, and only the sterile septa of the first order perfect. Also *Sagartiadæ, Sagartidæ*.

sagathy† (sag'a̤-thi), *n.* [Also *sagathee;* < F. *sagatis* = Sp. *sagati*, < L. *saga, sagum*, a blanket, mantle: see *say*⁴.] A woolen stuff.

Making a panegyrick on pieces of *sagathy* or Scotch plaid. *The Tatler*, No. 270. (*Latham.*)

There were clothes of Drap du Barri, and D'Oyley suits, so called after the famous haberdasher whose name still survives in the dessert napkin. They were made of drugget and *sagathay*, camlet, but the majority of men wore cloth. *J. Ashton*, Social Life in Reign of Queen Anne, I. 151.

sagbut (sag'but), *n.* Same as *sackbut*.

sage¹ (sāj), *a.* and *n.* [< ME. *sage, sauge*, < OF. *sage*, also *saives*, F. *sage*, dial. *saige, seige* = Pr. *sage, savi, sabi* = Sp. Pg. *sabio* = It. *savio, saggio*, < LL. **sabius* (a later form of **sapius*, found only in comp. *ne-sapius*, unwise), < *sapere*, be wise: see *sapid, sapient.* Not connected with *sagacious.*] I. *a.* 1. Wise; judicious; prudent. Specifically—(*a*) Applied to persons: Discreet, far-seeing, and cool-headed; able to give good counsel.

There was A grete lorde that had A *Sage* fole, the whyche he lovyd Marvaylous well, Be Cawse of hys pastyme. *Booke of Precedence* (E. E. T. S., extra ser.), i. 77.

Very *sage*, discreet, and ancient persons. *Sir T. More*, Utopia (tr. by Robinson), ii. 1.

Cousin of Buckingham, and you *sage*, grave men. *Shak.*, Rich. III., iii. 7. 227.

(*b*) Applied to advice: Sound; well-judged; adapted to the situation.

The *sage* counsayle of Nestor. *Sir T. Elyot*, The Governour, iii. 25.

Little thought he [Elutherius] of this *sage* caution. *Milton*, Reformation in Eng., ii.

There are certain emergencies when . . . an ounce of hare-brained decision is worth a pound of *sage* doubt and cautious discussion. *Irving*, Knickerbocker, p. 203.

2. Learned; profound; having great science.

Of this wisdom, it seemeth, some of the ancient Romans, in the *sagest* and wisest times, were professors. *Bacon*, Advancement of Learning, ii. 310.

And if aught else great bards beside
In *sage* and solemn tunes have sung.
Milton, Il Penseroso, l. 117.

Fool saget. See *fool*¹. =**Syn.** 1. *Sagacious, Knowing*, etc. (see *astute*), judicious. See list under *sagacious*.—2. Oracular, venerable.

II. *n.* A wise man; a man of gravity and wisdom; particularly, a man venerable for years, and known as a man of sound judgment and prudence; a grave philosopher.

This old fader he knowit very sure,
Of vij *Saugys* called the wysest
That was in Rome.
Generydes (E. E. T. S.), l. 88.

A star,
Unseen before in heaven, proclaims him come,
And guides the eastern *sages*. *Milton*, P. L., xii. 362.

Father of all, in every age,
In every clime adored,
By saint, by savage, and by *sage*,
Jehovah, Jove, or Lord!
Pope, Universal Prayer.

The seven sages, seven men of ancient Greece, famous for their practical wisdom. A list commonly given comprises Thales, Solon, Bias, Chilo, Cleobulus, Periander, and Pittacus.

sage² (sāj), *n.* [< ME. *sauge, sawge*, also *save*, < OF. *sauge, saulge* (also **sauve*), F. *sauge* = Pr. Sp. It. *salvia* = Pg. *salva* = AS. *saluige, salfige* = MD. *salgie, saelgie, salie, savie, selfe*, D. *sali* = MLG. *salvie, salvye, salveige* = OHG. *salbeiā, salveiā*, MHG. *salveie, salbeie*, G. *salbei* = Sw. *salvia* = Dan. *salvie*, < L. *salvia*, the sage-plant: so called from the saving virtue attributed to the plant, < *salvus*, safe: see *safe*¹.] 1. A plant of the genus *Salvia*, especially *S. officinalis*, the common garden sage.

Sage (*Salvia officinalis*).
1, inflorescence; 2, lower part of stem with leaves.

This is a shrubby perennial, sometimes treated as an annual, with rough hoary-green leaves, and blue flowers variegated with white and purple and arranged in spiked whorls. Medicinally, sage is slightly tonic, astringent, and aromatic. It was esteemed by the ancients, but at present, though officinal, is little used as a remedy except in domestic practice. The great use of sage is as a condiment in flavoring dressings, sausages, cheese, etc. In Europe *S. pratensis*, the meadow-sage, a blue-flowered species growing in meadows, and *S. Sclarea*, the clary, are also officinal, and the latter is used in soups, but the taste is less agreeable. The ornamental species (which include the two last named) are numerous, and in several cases brilliant. Such are the half-hardy *S. splendens*, the scarlet sage of Brazil; *S. fulgens*, the cardinal or Mexican red sage; and the Mexican *S. patens*, with deep-blue, widely ringent corolla over two inches long. The European *S. argentea*, the silver-leafed sage, or clary, is cultivated for its foliage. Blue-flowered species fit for the garden, native in the United States, are *S. azurea* of the southern States, *S. Pitcheri*, with the leaves minutely soft-downy, found from Kansas to Texas, and the Texan *S. farinosa*, with a white hoary surface. See *chia, clary*², and phrases below.

2. A name of certain plants of other genera. See the phrases below.—**Apple-bearing sage**, a species, *Salvia triloba*, bearing the galls known as *sage-apples*. (See *sage-apple.*) The leaves and twigs of this plant form what is called *Phaskomylia tea*.—**Black sage.** (*a*) A boraginaceous shrub with sage-like leaves, *Cordia cylindristachya*, of tropical America. (*b*) In California, *Trichostema lanatum*, a labiate plant.—**Garlic-sage**, an old name of the wood-sage.—**Indian sage**, a name sometimes given to the thoroughwort or boneset, *Eupatorium perfoliatum*.—**Jerusalem sage**, a name of species of *Phlomis*, chiefly *P. fruticosa*, a half-shrubby plant 3 or 4 feet high, covered with rusty down, and producing many dense whorls of rich yellow flowers.—**Meadow-sage.** See def. 1.—**Mountain-sage.** Same as *wood-sage*.—**Sage cheese.** See *cheese*¹.—**Sage tea.** See *tea*.—**Scarlet sage.** See def. 1.—**White sage.** (*a*) A woolly chenopodiaceous plant, *Eurotia lanata*. It is a low, somewhat woody herb, abounding in some valleys of the Rocky Mountain region, and valued as a winter forage; also esteemed as a remedy for intermittent fevers. Also called *winter fat*. (*b*) See *Kochia*. (*c*) In southern California, another whitish plant of the same order, *Audibertia polystachya*, a shrub from 3 to 10 feet high, useful in bee-pastures. It is one of the plants called *greasewood*.—**Wild sage.** (*a*) In England, *Salvia Verbenaca*. Also called *wild clary*. (*b*) In Jamaica, species of *Lantana*. (*c*) At the Cape of Good Hope, a large composite shrub, *Tarchonanthus camphoratus*, having a strong balsamic odor. Also called *African fleabane*.—**Wood-sage**, the wild germander, *Teucrium Scorodonia*, of the northern Old World.

sage-apple (sāj'ap''l), *n.* A gall formed on a species of sage, *Salvia triloba*, from the puncture of the insect *Cynips salviæ*. It is eaten as a fruit at Athens.

sage-bread† (sāj'bred), *n.* Bread baked from dough mixed with a strong infusion of sage in milk.

I have known *sage-bread* do much good in drying up watery humours. *R. Sharrock*, To Boyle, April 7, 1668.

sage-brush (sāj'brush), *n.* A collective name of various species of *Artemisia* which cover immense areas on the dry, often alkaline, plains and mountains of the western United States. They are dry, shrubby, and bushy plants with a hoary sage-like aspect, but without botanical affinity with the sage. The most characteristic species is *A. tridentata*, which

Sage-brush (*Artemisia tridentata*). 1. upper part of the stem with the heads; 2, lower part of the stem with the leaves. *a*, a flower; *b*, a head; *c*, a leaf.

grows from 1 to 6 and even 12 feet high, and is prodigiously abundant. A smaller species is *A. trifida*, and a dwarf, *A. arbuscula*. Also *sage-bush* (perhaps applied more individually), *wild sage*, and *sagewood*.

sage-bush (sāj'bush), *n.* Same as *sage-brush*.

sage-cock (sāj'kok), *n.* The cock-of the plains; the male sage-grouse. See cut under *Centrocercus*.

saged†, *a.* [< *sage*[1] + *-ed*[2].] Wise.

> Begyn to synge, Amintas thou;
> For why? thy wyt is best;
> And many a *saged* sawe lies hyd
> Within thine aged brest.
>
> *Googe*, Eglogs, i. (*Davies.*)

sage-green (sāj'grēn), *n.* A gray mixed with just enough pure green to be recognized as green.

sage-grouse (sāj'grous), *n.* A large North American grouse, *Centrocercus urophasianus*, characteristic of the sage-brush regions of western North America. It is the largest grouse of that country, and nearly the largest bird of the family *Tetraonidæ*, though exceeded in size by the capercaillie. It feeds chiefly on the buds and leaves of *Artemisia*, from which its flesh acquires a bitter taste, and also on insects, especially grasshoppers, in consequence of which diet the stomach is much less muscular than is usual in this order of birds. See cut under *Centrocercus*.

sage-hare (sāj'här), *n.* Same as *sage-rabbit*.

sage-hen (sāj'hen), *n.* The female of the sage-grouse; also, this grouse without regard to sex.

> *Sage-hens* might have been easily shot, but their flesh is said to be tough and ill-flavoured.
>
> *W. Shepherd*, Prairie Experiences, p. 54.

sagely (sāj'li), *adv.* In a sage manner; wisely; with just discernment and prudence.

> Sober he seemde, and very *sagely* sad.
>
> *Spenser*, F. Q., I. i. 29.

> To whom our Saviour *sagely* thus replied.
>
> *Milton*, P. R., iv. 285.

Sagenaria (saj-e-nā'ri-ä), *n.* [NL. (Brongniart, 1822), < L. *sagena*, < Gr. σαγήνη, a large fishing-net: see *sagene*[1].] A former genus of fossil plants, occurring in the coal-measures, now united with *Lepidodendron*.

> The last [Goldenberg] fixes the characters of Lepidodendron, *Sagenaria*, Aspidiaria, and Bergeria from the relative position of the bolsters and the mode of attachment of the leaves, either on the top or on the middle of the cicatrices. These characters being unreliable, the classification has not been admitted by any recent Phyto-palæontologist.
>
> *Lesquereux*, Coal Flora, p. 366.

sagene[1] (sạ-jēn'), *n.* [< L. *sagena*, < Gr. σαγήνη, a large fishing-net: see *seine*.] A fishing-net; a net.

> Iron roads are tearing up the surface of Europe, . . . their great *sagene* is drawing and twitching the ancient frame and strength of England together.
>
> *Ruskin*, Modern Painters (ed. 1846), II. 5.

sagene[2] (sa-jen'), *n.* [= F. *sagène*, < Russ. *sazheni*.] The fundamental unit of Russian long measure, fixed by a ukase of Peter the Great at 7 feet English measure. Also *sajene*.

sageness (sāj'nes), *n.* The quality of being sage; wisdom; sagacity; prudence; gravity.

> We are not to this ende borne that we should seeme to be created for play and pastime; but we are rather borne to *sagenesse*, and to certaine graver and greater studies.
>
> *Northbrooke*, Dicing (1577). (*Nares.*)

sagenite (saj'en-īt), *n.* [F. *sagénite*, < L. *sagena*, < Gr. σαγήνη, a large drag-net, + *-ite*[2].] Acicular crystals of rutile crossing each other at angles of about 60°, and giving a reticulated appearance, whence the name (see *rutile*); also, rock-crystal inclosing a fine web of rutile needles; sometimes, also, similar acicular forms of some other mineral, as asbestos, tourmalin, etc.

sagenitic (saj-e-nit'ik), *a.* [< *sagenite* + *-ic*.] Noting quartz containing acicular crystals of other materials, most commonly rutile, also tourmalin, actinolite, and the like.

Sagenopteris (saj-e-nop'tẹ-ris), *n.* [NL., < Gr. σαγήνη, a fishing-net, + πτερίς, a fern.] The generic name given by Presl, in 1838, to an aquatic fossil plant probably belonging to the rhizocarps, and closely allied to the somewhat widely distributed and in Australia specifically important genus *Marsilea*. It is found in the Upper Trias, Rhætic, and Lias of various parts of Europe and in America.

sage-rabbit (sāj'rab"it), *n.* A small hare abounding in western North America, *Lepus artemisia*: so called from its habitat, which corresponds to the regions where sage-brush is the characteristic vegetation. It is the western representative of the common molly-cottontail, *L. sylvaticus*, from which it differs little.

Sageretia (saj-e-rē'ti-ä), *n.* [NL. (Brongniart, 1827), named after Augustin *Sageret* (1763–1852).] A genus of polypetalous plants of the order *Rhamnaceæ* and tribe *Rhamneæ*. It is characterized by opposite leaves, the flowers on opposite divaricate branches forming a terminal panicle, the calyx-tubes hemispherical or urn-shaped and lined inside by a five-lobed disk which bears the five stamens on its edge and surrounds a free three-celled ovoid ovary. There are about 12 species, natives of warmer parts of the United States, of Java, and of central and southern Asia. They are shrubs with slender or rigid opposite branches, either with or without thorns, and commonly projecting at right angles to the stem. They bear short-stalked oblong or ovate leaves with netted veins, not triple-nerved as often in the related *Ceanothus*, and furnished with minute stipules. The flowers are very small, each with five hooded and stalked petals, and followed by small globose drupes containing three hard nutlets. *S. theezans*, of China and the East Indies, is a thorny shrub with bright-green ovate leaves, the *tia* of the Chinese, among whom its leaves are said to be used by the poorer classes as a substitute for tea.

sage-rose (sāj'rōz), *n.* 1†. A plant of the genus *Cistus*.—2. An evergreen shrub, *Turnera ulmifolia*, of tropical America. It has handsome yellow flowers, and is sometimes cultivated in greenhouses. Also *holly-rose*. [West Indies.]

sage-sparrow (sāj'spar"ō), *n.* A fringilline bird of the genus *Amphispiza*, characteristic of the sage-brush of western North America. There are two distinct species, the black-throated, *A. bilineata*, and Bell's, *A. belli*. A variety of the latter is sometimes distinguished as *A. b. nevadensis*. These birds were placed in the genus *Poöspiza*, with which they have little in common, until the genus *Amphispiza* (Coues, 1874) was formed for their reception.

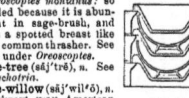

Sage-sparrow (*Amphispiza bilineata*); male adult.

sagesse†, *n.* [ME., < OF. *sagesse*, wisdom, < *sage*, wise: see *sage*[1].] Wisdom; sageness.

> I hold it no gret wisdome ne *sagesse*
> To ouermoche suffre sorew and paine.
>
> *Rom. of Partenay* (E. E. T. S.), l. 6224.

sage-thrasher (sāj'thrash"ėr), *n.* The mountain mocking-bird of western North America, *Oreoscoptes montanus*: so called because it is abundant in sage-brush, and has a spotted breast like the common thrasher. See cut under *Oreoscoptes*.

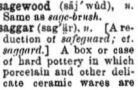

sage-tree (sāj'trē), *n.* See *Psychotria*.

sage-willow (sāj'wil"ō), *n.* A dwarf gray American willow, *Salix tristis*, growing in tufts from a strong root.

sagewood (sāj'wůd), *n.* Same as *sage-brush*.

saggar (sag'ạr), *n.* [A reduction of *safeguard*; cf. *saggard*.] A box or case of hard pottery in which porcelain and other delicate ceramic wares are inclosed for baking. The object of the saggar is to protect the vessel within from smoke, irregularities of heat, and the like. Saggars are usually so made that the bottom of one forms the cover of the next, and they are then piled in vertical columns. They vary in form and size according to the objects to be contained. Also *sagger*, *seggar*, and *case*.

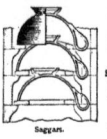

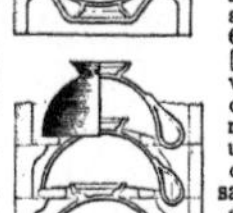

Saggars.

> Vessels resembling the crucibles or *seggars* of porcelain works.
>
> *Workshop Receipts*, 2d ser., p. 407.

saggar (sag'ạr), *v. t.* [< *saggar*, *n.*] In *ceram.*, to place in or upon a saggar.

saggard (sag'ạrd), *n.* [A reduction of *safeguard* (formerly also *safegard*) which is used in various particular senses: see *safeguard*. Cf. *saggar*.] 1. Same as *safeguard*, 4. *Halliwell and Wright* (under *seggard*).—2. A rough vessel in which all crockery, fine or coarse, is placed when taken to the oven for firing. *Halliwell.* [Prov. Eng. (Staffordshire).]

saggar-house (sag'ạr-hous), *n.* In *ceram.*, a house in which unbaked vessels of biscuit are put into saggars, in which they are to be fired.

sagging (sag'ing), *n.* That form of breakage in which the middle part sinks more than the extremities: opposed to *hogging*.

saghe†, *n.* A Middle English form of *saw*[2].

saghtel†, **saghetyl†**, *v.* See *settle*[2].

Sagina (sạ-jī'nạ), *n.* [NL. (Linnæus, 1737), so called in allusion to its abundant early growth on the thin rocky soil of the Roman Campagna, where it long furnished the spring food of the large flocks of sheep kept there; < L. *sagina*, fattening: see *saginate*.] A genus of polypetalous plants of the order *Caryophylleæ*, the pink family, and of the tribe *Alsineæ*. It is characterized by having four or five sepals, a one-celled ovary bearing four or five styles and splitting in fruit into as many valves, both styles and valves alternate with the sepals, and by the absence of stipules and sometimes of petals, which when present are entire and four or five in number. There are about 9 species, natives of temperate and colder parts of the northern hemisphere, with one species, *S. procumbens*, also widely diffused through the southern hemisphere. They are annual or perennial close-tufted little herbs with awl-shaped leaves; the herbage is at first tender, but later forms dry wiry mats, with minute white flowers generally raised on long pedicels. A general name for the species is *pearlwort*. *S. glabra* is a minute but beautiful alpine species of Europe, which in the garden can be formed into a velvety carpet, in spring and early summer dotted with white blossoms.

saginate† (saj'i-nāt), *v. t.* [< L. *saginatus*, pp. of *saginare* (> It. *saginare*, *sagginare* = Pg. *saginar*), stuff, cram, fatten, < *sagina*, stuffing, cramming; akin to Gr. σάττειν, stuff, cram.] To pamper; glut; fatten. *Blount*, Glossographia.

sagination† (saj-i-nā'shọn), *n.* [< L. *saginatio(n-)*, a fattening, < *saginare*, pp. *saginatus*, stuff: see *saginate*.] Fattening.

> They use to put them by for *sagination*, or [as it is sayd] in English for feeding, which in all countries hath a severall manner or custom.
>
> *Topsell*, Four-Footed Beasts, p. 81. (*Halliwell.*)

sagitta (sạ-jit'ạ), *n.* [NL., < L. *sagitta*, an arrow, a bolt, prob. akin to Gr. σάγαρις, a battle-ax. Hence ult. *satty*, *settee*[2].] 1. [*cap.*] An insignificant but very ancient northern constellation, the Arrow, placed between Aquila and the bill of the Swan. It is, roughly speaking, in a line with the most prominent stars of Sagittarius and Centaurus, with which it may originally have been conceived to be connected. Also called *Alahance*. 2. In *anat.*, the sagittal suture.—3. In *ichth.*, one of the otoliths of a fish's ear.—4. [*cap.*] The typical genus of *Sagittidæ*, formerly containing all the species, now restricted to those with two pairs of lateral fins besides the caudal fin. Also *Saggitta*, *Saggita*, *Sagita*. See accompanying cut.—5. An arrow-worm or sea-arrow; a member of the *Sagittidæ*.—6. The keystone of an arch. [Rare.]—7. In *geom.*: (*a*) The versed sine of an arc: so called by Kepler because it makes a figure like an arrow upon a bow. (*b*) The abscissa of a curve. *Hutton.*

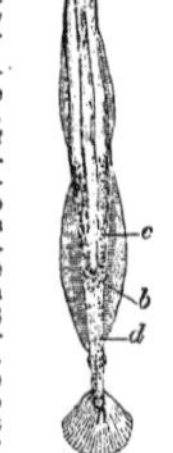

Sagitta bipunctata, enlarged. *a*, head with eyes and appendages; *b*, anus; *c*, ovary; *d*, testicular chambers. [illegible]

sagittal (saj'i-tal), *a.* [= OF. *sagitel*, F. *sagittal* = Sp. Pg. *sagital* = It. *sagittale*, < NL. **sagittalis*, < L. *sagitta*, an arrow: see *sagitta*.] 1. Shaped like or resembling an arrow or an arrow-head. Specifically—2. In *anat.*: (*a*) Pertaining to the sagittal suture. (*b*) Lying in or parallel to the plane of that suture: in this sense opposed to *coronal*.—**Sagittal axis of the cerebrum**, a sagittal line passing through the center of the cerebrum.—**Sagittal crest.** See *crest*.—**Sagittal fissure**, the great longitudinal interhemicerebral fissure of the brain, which separates the right and left cerebral hemispheres.—**Sagittal groove or furrow**, the groove for the superior longitudinal sinus.—**Sagittal line**, the intersection of any sagittal with any horizontal plane.—**Sagittal plane**, the median plane of the body, which is the plane of the sagittal suture, or any plane parallel to that plane.—**Sagittal section**, a section made in a sagittal plane.—**Sagittal semicircular canal**, the posterior semicircular canal. See cut under *ear*[1].—**Sagittal sinus.** Same as *superior longitudinal sinus* (which see, under *sinus*).—**Sagittal suture**, the suture between the two parietal bones; the rhabdoidal or interparietal suture. See cut under *cranium*.—**Sagittal triradiate.** See *triradiate*.

sagittally (saj'i-tal-i), *adv.* [< *sagittal* + *-ly*[2].] In *anat.*, so as to be sagittal in shape, situation, or direction. *B. G. Wilder.*

Sagittaria (saj-i-tā'ri-ä), *n.* [NL. (Linnæus, 1737), fem. of L. *sagittarius*, pertaining to an arrow: see *sagittary*.] A genus of monocotyledonous plants of the order *Alismaceæ* and tribe *Alismeæ*. It is characterized by unisexual flowers, commonly three in a whorl, and by very numerous broad and compressed carpels densely crowded on large globular or oblong receptacles. There are about 15 species, natives of temperate and tropical regions, growing in marshes, in ditches, and on the margins of streams. They are generally erect stemless perennials, with arrow-shaped, lanceolate, or elliptical leaves rising well above the water on long thick stalks. The flowers are spiked or panicled, each with three conspicuous white petals and three smaller green sepals, and usually numerous stamens. The general name for the species is *arrow-head*, but the fine South American species, *S. Montevidensis*, is called *arrowleaf*. The most common American species is *S. variabilis*, whose leaves are extremely various in form. The tubers of this are used for food by the Indians of the Northwest, as are those of *S. Chinensis* in China, where it is cultivated for the purpose. *S. sagittifolia* is the European species, which with *S. variabilis* is worthy of culture in artificial water.

Flowering Plant of Arrow-head (*Sagittaria variabilis*). *a*, a male flower; *b*, the fruit; *c*, a nut.

Sagittariidæ (saj"i-tā-ri'i-dē), *n. pl.* [NL., < *Sagittaria* + *-idæ*.] The most unusual name of the secretary-birds or serpent-eaters, a family of African *Raptores*, commonly called *Gypogeranidæ* or *Serpentariidæ*.

Sagittarius (saj-i-tā'ri-us), *n.* [< L. *sagittarius*, an archer: see *sagittary*.] **1.** A southern zodiacal constellation and sign, the Archer, rep-

The Constellation Sagittarius.

resenting a centaur (originally doubtless some Babylonian divinity) drawing a bow. The constellation is situated east of Scorpio, and is, especially in the latitudes of the southern United States, a prominent object on summer evenings. The symbol of the constellation ♐ shows the Archer's arrow and part of the bow. **2.** In *her.*, the representation of a centaur carrying a bow and arrow.—**3.** [NL. (Vosmaer, 1769).] The typical genus of *Sagittariidæ*: so called, it is said, from the arrowy crest; the secretary-birds. This is the earliest name of the genus, which is also known as *Serpentarius* (*Cuvier*, 1798), *Secretarius* (*Daudin*, 1800), usually *Gypogeranus* (*Illiger*, 1811), and *Ophiotheres* (*Vieillot*, 1816); but Vosmaer does not appear to have used it as a technical New Latin designation, though it has often been taken as such by subsequent writers, following H. E. Strickland. See cuts under *dermognathous* and *secretary-bird*.

sagittary (saj'i-tā-ri), *a.* and *n.* [= OF. *sagitaire*, *sagetaire*, F. *sagittaire* = Sp. Pg. *sagitario* = It. *sagittario*, one of the zodiacal signs, < L. *sagittarius*, pertaining to arrows, as a noun an archer, an arrowsmith, the constellation of the Archer, < *sagitta*, an arrow: see *sagitta*.] **I.** *a.* Pertaining to an arrow or to archery.

> With such differences of reeds, vallatory, *sagittary*, scriptory, and others, they might be furnished in Judæa.
> *Sir T. Browne*, Misc. Tracts, i.

II. *n.*; pl. *sagittaries* (-riz). **1.** [*cap.*] The constellation Sagittarius.—**2.** A centaur; specifically [*cap.*], a centaur fabled to have been in the Trojan army.

> Also in our lande been ye *Sagittary*, the whyche ben fro the myddel vpward lyke men, and fro ye myddel donwarde ben they lyke the halfe neder parte of an horse, and they bere bowes and arowes.
> *R. Eden* (First Books on America, ed. Arber, p. xxxiii.).

> The dreadful *Sagittary*
> Appals our numbers. *Shak.*, T. and C., v. 5. 14.

3. In *zoöl.*, an arrow-worm or sagitta.

sagittate (saj'i-tāt), *a.* [< NL. *sagittatus*, formed like an arrow (cf. L. *sagittare*, pp. *sagittatus*, shoot with an arrow), < L. *sagitta*, an arrow: see *sagitta*.] **1.** Shaped like the head of an arrow; sagittal; specifically, in *bot.*, triangular, with a deep sinus at the base, the lobes not pointing outward. Compare *hastate*. See also cut under *Sagittaria*.—**2.** In *entom.*, having the form of a barbed arrow-head.—**Sagittate spots**, on the wings of a noctuid moth, arrow-shaped marks with their points turned inward, between the posterior transverse line and the undulate subterminal line.

Sagittate Leaf of Calla Lily (*Richardia Africana*).

sagittated (saj'i-tā-ted), *a.* [< *sagittate* + *-ed*[2].] In *zoöl.*, sagittate; shaped like an arrow or an arrow-head: specifically noting certain decacerous cephalopods: as, the *sagittated* calamaries or squids.

Sagittidæ (sā-jit'i-dē), *n. pl.* [NL., < *Sagitta* + *-idæ*.] A family of worms, typified by the genus *Sagitta*, and the only one of the order *Chætognatha* and class *Aphanozoa*. They are small marine creatures, from half an inch to an inch long, transparent, unsegmented, without parapodia, with chitinous processes which serve as jaws, and with lateral cuticular processes. The structure is anomalous, and the *Sagittidæ* were variously considered as mollusks, annelids, and nematoids before an order was instituted for their reception. See cut under *Sagitta*.

sagittilingual (saj"i-ti-ling'gwal), *a.* [< L. *sagitta*, an arrow, + *lingua*, the tongue: see *lingual*.] Having a long slender cylindrical

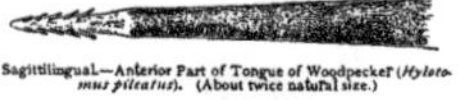

Sagittilingual.—Anterior Part of Tongue of Woodpecker (*Hylotomus pileatus*). (About twice natural size.)

tongue barbed at the end and capable of being thrust out like an arrow, as a woodpecker; belonging to the *Sagittilingues*.

Sagittilingues† (saj"i-ti-ling'gwēz), *n. pl.* [NL.: see *sagittilingual*.] In Illiger's system of classification (1811), the woodpeckers. See *Picidæ*.

sagittocyst (saj'i-tō-sist), *n.* [< L. *sagitta*, an arrow, + Gr. κύστις, bladder: see *cyst*.] One of the cutaneous cells of turbellarian worms, containing rhabdites.

Sagmarius (sag-mā'ri-us), *n.* [NL., < L. *sagmarius*, of or pertaining to a pack-saddle, < *sagma*, < Gr. σάγμα, a pack-saddle (> NL. *Sagma*, a star so called): see *seam*[2].] The constellation Pegasus, in which the star Sagma is seen.

sagmatorhine (sag-mat'ō-rin), *a.* [< NL. *Sagmatorrhina* (Bonaparte, 1851) (< Gr. σάγμα (σαγματ-), a saddle, + ῥίς (ῥιν-), the nose), a supposed genus of *Alcidæ*, based on the tufted puffin, *Lunda cirrata*, when the horny covering of the bill had been molted, leaving a saddle-shaped soft skin over the nostrils.] Saddle-nosed, as an auk.

sago (sā'gō), *n.* [= F. *sagou* = Sp. *sagú*, *sagui* = Pg. *sagu* = It. *sagù* = D. G. Dan. Sw. *sago* (NL. *sagus*), Hind. *sāgū* (*sāgū-dānā sābūdānā*), sago, < Malay *sāgu*, *sāgū*, sago, the farinaceous and glutinous pith of a tree of the palm kind named *rumbiya*.] An amylaceous food derived from the soft spongy interior, the so-called "pith," of the trunks of various palms. (See *sago-palm*.) The tree, which in the case of the proper sago-palms naturally flowers but once, is felled when just ready to flower, the trunk cut in pieces, the pith-like matter separated, and the starch washed from it. After due settling, the water is drained off, and the deposited starch may be caked, as it is for native use, or dried into a meal which is converted into pearl-sago. This is the ordinary granulated sago of the market, consisting of fine pearly grains, brownish or sometimes bleached white, prepared by making the meal into a paste and pressing this through a sieve.—**Japan sago**, a farinaceous material derived from different species of *Cycas*.—**Pearl sago.** See *pearl-sago*.—**Portland sago**, a delicate and nutritious farina extracted from the corm or tuber of the European wake-robin, *Arum maculatum*. It was formerly prepared in considerable quantity in the Isle of Portland, England. Also called *Portland arrowroot*.—**Sago-meal**, sago in a fine powder.—**Wild sago**, *Zamia integrifolia* (*Z. pumila*) of Jamaica and Florida, whose stem furnishes a sago-starch or arrowroot. See *coontie*.

sagoin, sagouin, *n.* Same as *saguin*.

sago-palm (sā'gō-päm), *n.* Either of the two palms *Metroxylon lævis* and *M. Rumphii*. See *Metroxylon* and *sago*. Other palms yielding sago are the *Phœnix farinifera* in Singapore, the ge-

Sago-palm (*Metroxylon lævis*). *a*, the fruit.

bang-palm, *Corypha Gebanga*, in Java, the jaggery palm or bastard sago, *Caryota urens*, in Mysore, and the palmyra and the areng or gomuti elsewhere in India. Species of *Cycas* are also called *sago-palm*. See *Cycas*.

sago-plant (sā'gō-plant), *n.* *Arum maculatum*. See *Portland sago*, under *sago*.

sago-spleen (sā'gō-splēn), *n.* A spleen in which the Malpighian corpuscles are enlarged and lardaceous, presenting the appearance of boiled sago.

Sagra (sā'grä), *n.* [NL. (Fabricius, 1792).] A genus of phytophagous beetles of the family *Chrysomelidæ*, giving name to the *Sagridæ*. The species inhabit tropical parts of the Old World; they are of brilliant colors, and have highly developed hind legs, whence they have received the name of *kangaroo-beetles*.

Sagridæ (sag'ri-dē), *n. pl.* [NL., < *Sagra* + *-idæ*.] A family of *Coleoptera*, typified by the genus *Sagra*. It is now merged in the *Chrysomelidæ*.

saguaro (sa-gwar'ō), *n.* [Also, corruptly, *suwarrow*; Mex. or Amer. Ind.] The giant cactus, *Cereus giganteus*, a columnar species from 25 to over 50 feet high, growing on stony mesas and low hills in Arizona and adjacent parts of Mexico. The wood of the large strong ribs is light and soft, solid, and susceptible of a beautiful polish, and is indestructible in contact with the soil. It is used by the Indians for lances and bows, and by the settlers for rafters of adobe houses, fencing, etc. The edible fruit is largely collected and dried by the Indians.—**Saguaro woodpecker**, *Centurus uropygialis*, the Gila woodpecker: so called from its nesting in the giant cactuses. It is abundant in the valley of the Gila and the lower Colorado river, and is a near relative of the red-bellied woodpecker, *C. carolinus*. See cut under *pitahaya*.

saguin (sag'win), *n.* [Also *sagoin*, *sagouin*, *sanglain*, *saglin*; = F. *sagouin*, said to be < Braz. *sahui*, native name near Bahia.] A South American monkey of the genus *Callithrix*.

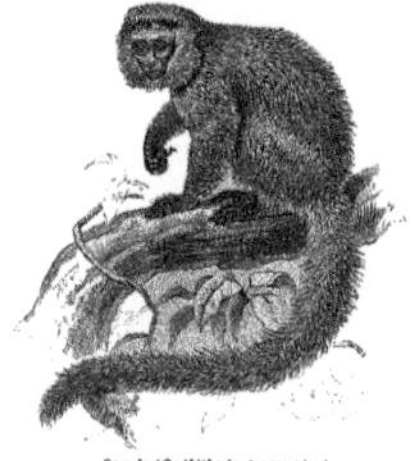

Saguin (*Callithrix personatus*).

=**Syn.** *Saguin*, *sajou*, *sai*, *saimiri*, *sapajou*. These are all native names of South American monkeys, now become inextricably confounded by the different usages of authors, if indeed they had originally specific meanings. *Sai* is the most general term, meaning monkey. *Sajou* and *sapajou* are the same, meaning a prehensile-tailed monkey of one of the genera *Cebus* and *Ateles*; but *sapajou* has become associated specially with *Ateles*, then meaning spider-monkey. *Saguin* was one of the smaller species of *Cebus*, but became confused with *saimiri*. *Saguin* and *saimiri* are now specially attached to the small non-prehensile-tailed squirrel-monkeys, respectively of the genera *Callithrix* and *Chrysothrix*, but are also loosely used for any of the marmosets.

Saguinus (sag-ū-ī'nus), *n.* [NL. (Lacépède): see *saguin*.] A genus of South American marmosets: same as *Hapale*.

sagum (sā'gum), *n.* [L., also *sagus*; = Gr. σάγος, a coarse woolen blanket or mantle: said to be of Celtic origin: see *say*[4].] A military cloak worn by ancient Roman soldiers and inferior officers, in contradistinction to the paludamentum of the superior officers. It was the garb of war, as the toga was the garb of peace.

Sagus (sā'gus), *n.* [NL. (Blume, 1830), ‹ Malay *sāgu*, sago: see *sago*.] A former genus of palms, now known as *Metroxylon*. See also *Raphia*, species of which are often cultivated under the name *Sagus*. See cut under *sago*.

sagy (sā'ji), *a.* [‹ *sage*[2] + *-y*[1].] Full of sage; seasoned with sage.

Saharan (sā-hā'ran), *a.* Same as *Saharic*.

Saharic (sā-har'ik), *a.* [‹ *Sahara* (see def.) (‹ Ar. *sahrā*, a desert plain) + *-ic*.] Of or pertaining to the desert of Sahara, a vast region in northern Africa.

sahib (sä'ib), *n.* [‹ Hind. *sāhib*, ‹ Ar. *sāhib* (with initial letter *sād*), master, lord, sovereign, ruler, a gentleman, European gentleman, sir, possessor, owner, prop. companion, associate; fem. *sāhiba*, mistress, lady.] A term of respect used by the natives of India and Persia in addressing or speaking of Europeans: equivalent to *Master* or *Sir*, and even to *Mistress*: as, Colonel *sahib*; the *sahib* did so and so; it is the mem-*sahib's* command. (See *mem-sahib*.) It is also occasionally used as a specific title among both Hindus and Mohammedans, as Tippoo *Sahib*.

sahlite (sä'līt), *n.* See *salite*[2].

sahtit, sahtet, *a.* and *n.* See *saught*.

sahtlet, *v.* See *settle*[2].

Sahuca bean. See *bean*[1] and *soy*.

sai (sä'i), *n.* [= F. *saïou*, ‹ Braz. *sai*, *çai*.] **1.** A South American monkey of the genus *Cebus* in a broad sense. See synonyms under *saguin*.—**2.** A guitguit of the genus *Cœreba*, *C. cyanea*, about 4½ inches long, bright-blue, varied with black, green, and yellow, and with red bill and feet, inhabiting tropical America. See cut under *Cœrebinæ*.

saibling (sāb'ling), *n.* The char of Europe, *Salvelinus alpinus*.

saic (sä'ik), *n.* [‹ F. *saïque* = Sp. It. *saica* = Pg. *saique* = Russ. *saikā*, ‹ Turk. *shāïqa*.] A Turkish or Grecian vessel, very common in the Levant, a kind of ketch which has no topgallantsail nor mizzen-topsail.

saice (sīs), *n.* See *sice*[2].

said (sed), *p. a.* [Pp. of *say*[1], *v.*] **1.** Declared; uttered; reported.—**2.** Mentioned; before-mentioned; aforesaid: used chiefly in legal style: as, the *said* witness.

> And ther our Savyr for gaff the synnys of the *sayd* mary Mawdleyn. *Torkington*, Diarie of Eng. Travell, p. 54.

> And so there at the *sayde* Mounte Syon we toke our asses and rode forth at the *sayd* time, and neuer we alyghted to beyte vnto tyme we come to Rama. *Sir R. Guylforde*, Pylgrymage, p. 56.

> The *said* Charles by his writing obligatory did acknowledge himself to be bound to the *said* William in the *said* sum of two hundred pounds. *Proceedings on an Action of Debt*, Blackstone's Com., [III., App. iii.

saiet, *n.* See *say*[4].

saiga (sī'gä), *n.* [= F. *saïga*, ‹ Russ. *saïga*, an antelope, saiga.] **1.** A ruminant of the genus *Saiga*, remarkable for the singular conformation of the head, which gives it a peculiar physiognomy.—**2.** [*cap.*] (sä'i-gä) [NL.] The typical and only genus of *Saigidæ*. There is only one species, the saiga or saiga-antelope, *Antilope saiga*, *Colus saiga*, or *Saiga tartarica*, inhabiting western Asia and eastern Europe. Also called *Colus*. See cut in next column.

saiga-antelope (sī'gä-an"tē-lōp), *n.* The saiga.

Saigidæ (sā-ij'i-dē), *n. pl.* [NL., ‹ *Saiga* + *-idæ*.] In J. E. Gray's classification, a family of hollow-horned ruminants, represented by the genus *Saiga*; the saiga-antelopes, having the nose peculiarly inflated and expanded, the conformation affecting not only the outward parts, but the bones of the nasal region. The nasal bones are short, arched upward, and entirely separated from the maxillaries and lacrymals; the frontal bone projects between the lacrymals and nasals, and the maxillaries and premaxillaries are both much reduced. The group would be better named *Saiginæ*, as a subfamily of *Bovidæ*.

Saiga-antelope (*Saiga tartarica*).

saikless (sāk'les), *a.* A dialectal (Scotch) form of *sackless*.

sail[1] (sāl), *n.* [‹ ME. *saile*, *sayle*, *seil*, *seyl*, ‹ AS. *segel*, *segl* = OS. *segel* = MD. *seyl*, D. *zeil* = MLG. LG. *segel*, *seil* = OHG. *segal*, MHG. G. *segel* = Icel. *segl* = Sw. *segel* = Dan. *sejl* (Goth. not recorded), a sail. Root unknown; certainly not ‹ L. *sagulum*, a mantle.] **1.** A piece of cloth, or a texture or tissue of some kind, spread to the wind to cause, or assist in causing, a vessel to move through the water. Sails are usually made of several breadths of canvas, sewed together with a double seam at the borders, and edged all round with a cord or cords called the *bolt-rope* or *bolt-ropes*. A sail extended by a yard hung (slung) by the middle is called a *square sail*; a sail set upon a gaff, boom, or stay is called a *fore-and-aft sail*. (See *fore-and-aft*.) The upper part of every sail is the *head*, the lower part the *foot*, the sides in general are called *leeches*; but the weather side or edge (that is, the side next the mast or stay to which it is attached) of any but a square sail is called the *luff*, and the other edge the *after leech*. The two lower corners of a square sail are in general *clues*; the weather clue of a fore-and-aft sail, or of a course while set, is the *tack*. Sails generally take their names, partly at least, from the mast, yard, or stay upon which they are stretched; thus, the main-course, maintopsail, and maintopgallantsail are respectively the sails on the mainmast, maintopmast, and maintopgallantmast. The principal sails in a full-rigged vessel are the courses or lower sails, the topsails, and the topgallantsails. See *topsail*, *topsail-yard*, and cut under *ship*.

> Fearing lest they should fall into the quicksands, strake *sail*, and so were driven. Acts xxvii. 17.

> Their *saile* spread forth, and with a fore-right gale
> Leaving our coast. *Massinger*, Renegado, v. 8.

2. That part of the arm of a windmill which catches the wind.

> And the whirring *sail* goes round. *Tennyson*, The Owl.

3. One of the canvas flaps of a cart or wagon. [South Africa.]

> He drew the *sails* down before and behind, and the wagon rolled away slowly. *Olive Schreiner*, Story of an African Farm, II. xii.

4. Figuratively, a wing.

> He, cutting way
> With his broad *sayles*, about him soared round;
> At last, low stouping with unweldy sway,
> Snatcht up both horse and man.
> *Spenser*, F. Q., I. xi. 18.

5. A single ship or vessel, especially a ship considered as one of a number: the same form in the singular and the plural: as, at noon we sighted a *sail* and gave chase; a fleet of twenty *sail*.

> Returning back to Legorne, suddainly in the way we met with Fiftie *saile* of the Turkes Gallies. *E. Webb*, Travels (ed. Arber), p. 19.

> How many *sail* of well-mann'd ships before us,
> As the bonito does the flying-fish,
> Have we pursu'd and scour'd.
> *Fletcher*, Double Marriage, ii. 1.

> Our great fleet goes still forward amain, of above one hundred *sail* of ships. *Court and Times of Charles I.*, I. 5.

6. A fleet. [Rare.]

> We have descried, upon our neighbouring shore,
> A portly *sail* of ships make hitherward.
> *Shak.*, Pericles, i. 4. 61.

7†. Sailing qualities; speed.

> We departed from Constantinople in the Trinity of London: a ship of better defence then *saile*. *Sandys*, Travailes, p. 68.

8. A journey or excursion upon water; a passage in a vessel or boat.

> Here is my journey's end, here is my butt,
> And very sea-mark of my utmost *sail*.
> *Shak.*, Othello, v. 2. 268.

> The other monastery, best known as the Badia, once a house of Benedictines, afterwards of Franciscans, stands on a separate island, approached by a pleasant *sail*. *E. A. Freeman*, Venice, p. 216.

9. A ride in a cart or other conveyance. [Ireland.]—**10.** In *zoöl.*, a structure or formation of parts suggesting a sail in shape or use. (*a*) A very large dorsal fin. See *sailfish*. (*b*) The arm by means of which a nautilus is wafted over the water.—**After-sail**, a term generally applied to the sails carried on the mainmast and mizzenmast of three-masted vessels, and on the mainmast of vessels having but two masts.

> When the *after sails* fill and she gathers headway, put the helm again to port, and when the wind is astern brace up the alter yards by the port braces. *Luce*, Seamanship, p. 433.

Depth of a sail. See *depth*.—**Full sail**, with all sails set.—**Lateen sail.** See *lateen*.—**Light sails.** See *light*[2].

> If it is perfectly calm and there is a swell on, furl the *light sails* to save them from chafe. *Luce*, Seamanship, p. 437.

Press of sail. See *press*[1].—**Shoulder-of-mutton sail**, a triangular sail used in boats, also called a *leg-of-mutton sail*. See cut under *sharpie*.—**Sliding-gunter sail**, a triangular boat-sail used with a sliding-gunter mast.—**To back a sail, bend a sail, crowd sail, cut the sailt, flat in the sail, flatten a sail, loose sail.** See the verbs.—To **make sail.** (*a*) To set sail; depart.

> Sonnday a for Midsom day, abowyt vij of the cloke in the mornyng we *made Sayle*, And passyd by the Costes of Slavone and Histria. *Torkington*, Diarie of Eng. Travell, p. 16.

(*b*) To spread more sail; hasten on by spreading more sail.—To **point a sail.** See *point*[1].—To **press sail.** Same as *to crowd sail*.—To **ride down a sail.** See *ride*.—To **set sail**, to expand or spread the sails; hence, to begin a voyage.—To **shorten sail**, to reduce the extent of sail, or take in a part.—To **strike sail.** (*a*) To lower the sails suddenly, as in saluting or in sudden gusts of wind. Acts xxvii. 17. (*b*) To abate show or pomp. [Rare.]

> Margaret
> Must *strike* her *sail*, and learn awhile to serve
> Where kings command. *Shak.*, 3 Hen. VI., iii. 3. 5.

To **take the wind out of one's sails**, to take away one's means of progress; deprive one of an advantage; discomfit one, especially by sudden or unexpected action.

> I've undermined Garstin's people. They'll use their authority, and give a little shabby treating, but I've *taken* all *the wind out of their sails*. *George Eliot*, Felix Holt, xvii.

Under sail, having sail spread.

sail[1] (sāl), *v.* [‹ ME. *sailen*, *saylen*, *seilen*, *seilien*, ‹ AS. *seglian* = MD. *seylen*, D. *zeilen* = MLG. LG. *segelen* = MHG. *sigelen*, *segelen*, G. *segeln* = Icel. *sigla* = Sw. *segla* = Dan. *sejle* (cf. OF. *sigler*, *singler*, F. *cingler* = Sp. *singlar* = Pg. *singrar*, ‹ MHG.), sail; from the noun.] **I.** *intrans.* **1.** To move along through or over the water by the action of the wind upon sails; by extension, to move along through or over the water by means of sails, oars, steam, or other mechanical agency.

> This seyle sette on thi mast,
> And *seyle* in-to the blisse of heuene.
> *Holy Rood* (E. E. T. S.), p. 214.

> Tewysday, the v day of Januarii, we *seyleyd* vp and down in the gulff of Venys, ffor the wynde was so straygth a yens vs that we myght not kepte the ryght wey in no wyse. *Torkington*, Diarie of Eng. Travell, p. 59.

> Say, shall my little bark attendant *sail*,
> Pursue the triumph, and partake the gale?
> *Pope*, Essay on Man, iv. 385.

2. To set sail; hoist sail and depart; begin a journey on shipboard: as, to *sail* at noon.

> The maistres, whan the mone a-ros manli in come,
> & faire at the tulle flod thei ferden to *sayle*,
> & hadde wind at wille to wende whan hem liked.
> *William of Palerne* (E. E. T. S.), l. 2745.

> On leaving Ascension we *sailed* for Bahia, on the coast of Brazil, in order to complete the chronometrical measurement of the world. *Darwin*, Voyage of Beagle, II. 297.

3. To journey by water; travel by ship.

> And when we had *sailed* over the sea of Cilicia and Pamphylia, we came to Myra, a city of Lycia. Acts xxvii. 5.

> Here's such a merry grig, I could find in my heart to *sail* to the world's end with such company. *Middleton and Dekker*, Roaring Girl, i. 1.

4. To swim, as a fish or a swan.

> Like little dolphins, when they *sail*
> In the vast shadow of the British whale.
> *Dryden*, tr. of Juvenal's Satires, x. 21.

5. To fly without visible movement of the wings, as a bird; float through the air; pass smoothly along; glide: as, the clouds *sail* across the sky.

> He bestrides the lazy-pacing clouds
> And *sails* upon the bosom of the air.
> *Shak.*, R. and J., ii. 2. 32.

> *Sails* between worlds and worlds with steady wing.
> *Milton*, P. L., v. 268.

> Across the sunny vale,
> From hill to hill the wandering rook did *sail*,
> Lazily croaking.
> *William Morris*, Earthly Paradise, I. 339.

Hence, figuratively—**6.** To move forward impressively, as if in the manner of a ship with all sail set. [Colloq.]

> Lady B. *sailed* in, arrayed in ribbons of scarlet, with many brooches, bangles, and other gimcracks ornamenting her plenteous person. *Thackeray*, Lovel the Widower.

7. To plunge forward, like a ship; rush forward: sometimes with *in*. [Colloq.]

> The fact is, a man must dismiss all thoughts of prudence and common-sense when it comes to masquerade

dresses, and just *sail in* and make an unmitigated fool of himself. *Harper's Mag.*, LXXVIII. 561.

Sailing ice. See *ice*.—**To sail close to the wind.** (a) To run great risk or hazard; leave little leeway or margin for escape from danger or difficulty. (b) To move or act with great caution; be in circumstances requiring careful action. (c) To live closely up to one's income; be straitened for money.—**To sail free.** See *free*.—**To sail on a bowline**, to sail close-hauled, or with the bowlines hauled taut.—**To sail over**, in *arch.*, to project beyond a surface. *Gwilt.*

II. *trans.* 1. To move or pass over or upon by the action of the wind upon sails, or, by extension, by the propelling power of oars, steam, etc.

> Thus time we waste, and longest leagues make short;
> *Sail* seas in cockles. *Shak.*, Pericles, iv. 4. 2.

> It was the schooner Hesperus,
> That *sailed* the wintry sea.
> *Longfellow*, Wreck of the Hesperus.

2. To direct or manage the motion, movements, and course of; navigate: as, to *sail* a ship.—**To sail a race**, to compete in a sailing-contest.

sail[2]†, *v. i.* [< ME. *saylen, salyen*, dance, < OF. *sailir, saillir, salir*, F. *saillir*, leap, issue forth, sally, dance, < L. *salire*, leap: see *salient*, and cf. *sally*[2], which is related to *sail*[2] as *rally*[2] is to *rail*[5].] To dance.

> Nother *sailen* ne sautrien ne singe with the giterne.
> *Piers Plowman* (C), xvi. 208.

sail[3]†, *v. t.* [< ME. *sailen, saylen*, by apheresis from *asailen*, assail: see *assail*.] To assail.

> "Everyman
> Now to assaut, that *sailen* can,"
> Quod Love. *Rom. of the Rose*, l. 7336.

sailable (sā'la-bl), *a.* [< *sail*[1], *v.*, + *-able*.] Capable of being sailed on or through; navigable; admitting of being passed by ships. [Rare.] *Imp. Dict.*

sail-boat (sāl'bōt), *n.* A boat propelled by or fitted for a sail or sails.

sail-borne (sāl'bōrn), *a.* Borne or conveyed by sails. *Falconer.*

sail-broad (sāl'brâd), *a.* Spreading like a sail.

> At last his *sail-broad* vans
> He spreads for flight. *Milton*, P. L., ii. 927.

sail-burton (sāl'bėr'tọn), *n.* A long tackle used for hoisting topsails aloft ready for bending.

sail-cloth (sāl'klôth), *n.* [Early mod. E. in pl. *sayleclothes, saleclothes*; < ME. *seil-cloth, seilclæth*; < *sail* + *cloth*.] Hemp or cotton canvas or duck, used in making sails for ships, etc.

> No Shippe can sayle without Hempe, ye *sayle clothes*, the shroudes, staies, tacles, yarde lines, warps & Cables can not be made. *Babees Book* (E. E. T. S.), p. 243.

> Whatsoeuer *sale-clothes* are already transported, or at any time here-after to bee transported out of England into Prussia by the English marchants, and shall there be offered to bee solde, whether they be whole cloathes or halfe cloathes, they must containe both their endes.
> *Hakluyt's Voyages*, I. 163.

sail-cover (sāl'kuv"ėr), *n.* A canvas cover placed as a protection over a furled sail.

sailed (sāld), *a.* [< *sail*[1] + *-ed*[2].] Furnished with sails; having sails set: as, full-*sailed*.

> Prostrated, in most extreme ill fare,
> He lies before his high-*sail'd* fleet.
> *Chapman*, Iliad, xix. 335. (*Davies.*)

> Over all the clouds floated like *sailed* ships anchored.
> *L. Wallace*, Ben-Hur, p. 457.

sailer (sā'lėr), *n.* [Early mod. E. also *sayler*; < ME. **sayler* = D. *zeiler* = G. *segler* = Dan. *sejler* = Sw. *seglare*, a sailer (a ship); as *sail* + *-er*[1]. Cf. *sailor*.] 1. One who sails; a seaman; a sailor. See *sailor*, an erroneous spelling now established in this sense.

> There I found my sword among some of the shrowds, wishing, I must confess, if I died, to be found with that in my hand, and withal waving it about my head, that *sailers* by might have the better glimpse of me.
> *Sir P. Sidney*, Arcadia, i.

> The inhabitants are cunning Artificers, Merchants, and *Saylers*. *Purchas*, Pilgrimage, p. 548.

> For the *Saylers* (I confesse), they daily make good cheare, but our dyet is a little meale and water.
> *Capt. John Smith*, Works, I. 202.

2. A ship or other vessel with reference to her sailing powers or manner of sailing, or as being propelled by sails, not steam.

> "You must be mad. She is the fastest *sailer* between here and the Thames." . . . "I care not!" the porter replied, snatching up a stout oaken staff that lay in a corner, "I'm an old sailor."
> *G. A. Sala*, The Ship-Chandler. (*Latham.*)

> From east and west across the horizon's edge,
> Two mighty masterful vessels, *sailers*, steal upon us.
> *Walt Whitman*, The Century, XXXIX. 553.

sailfish (sāl'fish), *n.* One of several different fishes, so called from the large or long dorsal fin. (a) A fish of the genus *Carpiodes*; the carp-sucker, *C. cyprinus*. [Local, U. S.] (b) A fish of the genus *Xiphias*; a sword-fish. See cut under *sword-fish*. (c) The basking-shark, *Cetorhinus maximus* or *Selache maxima*. See cut under *basking-shark*. (d) A fish of the genus *Histiophorus*, whose dorsal fin is very ample. The best-known and most widely distributed species is *H. gladius*, of European and some other waters, from which the American sailfish, *H. americanus*, differs so little that it has been considered specifically identical by most ichthyologists. See also *sailing-fish*. Also called *spike-fish*.

Sailfish (*Histiophorus americanus*).

sail-fluke (sāl'flök), *n.* The whiff, a pleuronectoid fish. [Orkneys.]

sail-gang (sāl'gang), *n.* The seine-gang of a sailing vessel in the menhaden-fishery, including their gear and boats. Also *sailing-gang*.

sail-hook (sāl'hůk), *n.* A small hook used to hold sail-cloth while it is being sewed.

sail-hoop (sāl'höp), *n.* One of the rings by which fore-and-aft sails are secured to masts and stays; a mast-hoop.

sailing (sā'ling), *n.* [< ME. *seylynge*, < AS. *segling*, verbal n. of *seglian*, sail: see *sail*[1], *v.*] 1. The act of one who or of that which sails.—2. The art or rules of navigation; the art or the act of directing a ship on a given line laid down in a chart; also, the rules by which a ship's track is determined and represented on a chart, and by which the problems relating to it are solved.—**Circular sailing.** See *circular*.—**Composite sailing.** See *composite*.—**Current-sailing**, the method of determining the true course and distance of a ship when her own motion is combined with that of a current.—**Globular sailing.** See *globular*.—**Great-circle sailing**, a method of navigation by which the courses of the ship are so laid as to carry her over a great circle, which is the shortest path between two points on the globe.—**Mercator's sailing**, a method in which problems are solved according to the principles applied in Mercator's projection. See *Mercator's chart*, under *chart*.—**Middle-latitude sailing.** See *latitude*.—**Oblique sailing.** See *oblique*.—**Order of sailing.** See *order*.—**Parallel sailing**, the method of sailing when the ship's track lies along a parallel of latitude. Its characteristic formula is: Distance = difference of longitude × cosine latitude. This method may be used when the ship's course is nearly east or west. Formerly, when longitude could not be determined as accurately as at present, it was a common practice to make the latitude of the port of destination, and then sail east or west as required. Hence the importance then attached to parallel sailing.—**Plain sailing**, an easy, unobstructed course in sailing, or, figuratively, in any enterprise.—**Plane sailing.** See *plane-sailing*.—**Sailing instructions**, written or printed directions delivered by the commanding officer of a convoy to the several masters of the ships under his care. By these instructions they are enabled to understand and answer the signals of the commander, and to know the place of rendezvous appointed for the fleet in case of dispersion by storm, by an enemy, or by any other accident. *Bouvier.*—**Traverse sailing**, the case in plane-sailing where a ship makes several courses in succession, the track being zigzag, and the directions of its several parts traversing or lying more or less athwart each other. For all these actual courses and distances run on each a single equivalent imaginary course and distance may be found which the ship would have described had she sailed direct for the place of destination; finding this single course is called *working* or *resolving a traverse*, which is effected by trigonometrical computation or by the aid of a traverse-table.

sailing-directions (sā'ling-di-rek'shọnz), *n. pl.* Published details respecting particular seas and coasts, useful for the purpose of navigation. Compare *pilot*, 4.

sailing-fish (sā'ling-fish), *n.* *Histiophorus indicus*, resembling the American sailfish. See *sailfish* (*d*).

sailing-gang (sā'ling-gang), *n.* Same as *sail-gang*.

sailing-ice (sā'ling-īs), *n.* An ice-pack sufficiently open to allow a vessel propelled by sails alone to force her way through.

sailing-master (sā'ling-mås"tėr), *n.* The navigating officer of a ship; specifically, a warrant-officer in the United States navy whose duties are to navigate the vessel and to attend to other matters connected with stowage, the rigging, etc., under the direction of the executive officer.

sailing-orders (sā'ling-ôr"dėrz), *n. pl.* Orders directing a ship or fleet to proceed to sea, and indicating its destination.

saillant (sal'yänt), *a.* [F., ppr. of *saillir*, leap: see *salient*.] Springing up or forth; arising; salient, as the teeth of *Astropectinidæ*.

sailless (sāl'les), *a.* [< *sail*[1] + *-less*.] Having no sails.

sail-lizard (sāl'liz"ärd), *n.* A large lizard of Amboyna, having a crested tail. See cut under *Histiurus*.

sail-loft (sāl'lôft), *n.* A loft or an apartment where sails are cut out and made.

sailmaker (sāl'mā"kėr), *n.* One whose occupation is the making, altering, or repairing of sails; in the United States navy, a warrant-officer whose duty it is to take charge of and keep in repair all sails, awnings, etc.—**Sailmaker's mate**, a petty officer in the United States navy, whose duty it is to assist the sailmaker.

sail-needle (sāl'nē"dl), *n.* A large needle with a triangular tapering end, used in sewing canvas for sails. See cut under *needle*.

sailor (sā'lọr), *n.* [Early mod. E. also *saylor*; an erroneous spelling (perhaps prob. due to conformity with *tailor*, or with the obs. *sailour*, a dancer) of *sailer*: see *sailer*.] One who sails; a seaman; a mariner; one of the crew of a ship or vessel.

> O quhar will I get guid *sailor*
> To sail this schip of mine?
> *Sir Patrick Spens* (Child's Ballads, III. 149).

> I see the cabin-window bright;
> I see the *sailor* at the wheel.
> *Tennyson*, In Memoriam, x.

Free trade and sailors' rights. See *free*.—**Paper sailor.** See *paper-sailor*.—**Pearly sailor**, the pearly nautilus.—**Sailors' Bible**, Bowditch's Navigator. [Old slang.]—**Sailors' home**, an institution where seamen may lodge and be cared for while on shore, or in which retired, aged, or infirm seafaring men are maintained. =**Syn.** *Sailor, Seaman, Mariner*. To most landsmen any one who leads a seafaring life is a *sailor*. Nelson was a great *sailor*. Technically, *sailor* applies only to the men before the mast. To a landsman *seaman* seems a business term for a *sailor*; technically, *seaman* includes sailors and petty officers. *Mariner* is an elevated, poetic, or quaint term for a *seaman*; *shipman* is a still older term. The technical use of *mariner* is now restricted to legal documents. There is no present distinction in name between the men in the navy and those in the merchant marine.

sailor-fish (sā'lọr-fish), *n.* A sword-fish of the family *Histiophoridæ*; a sail-fish. See *Histiophorus*, *sailing-fish*, and cut under *sail-fish*.

sailorman (sā'lọr-mạn), *n.*; pl. *sailormen* (-men). A sailor; a seaman.

> It is not always blowing at sea, a mercy *sailor-men* are grateful for. *W. C. Russell*, Jack's Courtship, xxix.

sailor-plant (sā'lọr-plant), *n.* The beefsteak-plant or strawberry-geranium, *Saxifraga sarmentosa*.

sailor's-choice (sā'lọrz-chois), *n.* 1. A sparine fish, the pinfish, *Lagodon rhomboides*. It has a general resemblance to a scup or porgy, but the front teeth are broad and emarginate. It is common along the eastern American coast. See cut under *Lagodon*.
2. A fish, *Orthopristis chrysopterus*; the pig-fish. The dorsal and anal fins are nearly naked, and the posterior dorsal spines are abbreviated. The fish is of a light brown above, silvery below, with numerous orange and yellow spots, which are aggregated in oblique lines above the lateral line, and in horizontal ones below it. It is an important food-fish along the eastern American coast, especially in the south.

sailor's-purse (sā'lọrz-pėrs), *n.* An egg-pouch of oviparous rays and sharks, which is mostly found empty on the sea-shore. See cut under *mermaid's-purse*. [Humorous.]

sailour†, *n.* [ME. *sailour, saillour, salyare*, < OF. **saillour, saillur, sailleur*, a dancer, < *sailir, saillir*, dance: see *sail*[2].] A dancer.

> Ther was many a tymbester
> And *saillouris*, that I dar wel swere
> Couthe her craft ful perfitly.
> *Rom. of the Rose*, l. 770.

sail-room (sāl'röm), *n.* An apartment in a vessel where sails are stowed.

sail-trimmer (sāl'trim"ėr), *n.* A man detailed to assist in working the sails of a man-of-war in action.

sail-wheel (sāl'hwēl), *n.* A name for Woltmann's tachometer. *E. H. Knight.*

saily (sā'li), *a.* [< *sail*[1], *n.*, + *-y*[1].] Like a sail. [Rare.]

> From Penmen's craggy height to try her *saily* wings . . .
> She meets with Conway first. *Drayton*, Polyolbion, x. 3.

sail-yard (sāl'yärd), *n.* [< ME. *saylezerd, seilzerd*, < AS. *segelgyrd, seglgyrd*, < *segel*, sail, + *geard, gyrd*, yard.] The yard or spar on which sails are extended. [Rare.]

saim (sām), *n.* and *v.* A form of *seam*[3].

saimiri (sī'mi-ri), *n.* [S. Amer.; cf. *sai*.] A squirrel-monkey; a small South American monkey of the genus *Saimiris* (Geoffroy) or *Chrysothrix* (Wagler), having a bushy non-prehensile tail: extended to some other small squirrel-like monkeys of the same country, and confused with *saguin* (which see). Also written *samiri, saimari*, and rarely Englished *saimir*. See cut under *squirrel-monkey*.

sain[1] (sān), *v. t.* [Also *sane*; < ME. *sainen, saynen, seinen, seinien, signen*, < AS. *segnian* = OS. *sëgnōn* = MD. *seghenen*, D. *zegenen* = MLG. *segenen, segen* = OHG. *seganōn*, MHG. *segenen*, *sēnen, seinen*, G. *segnen*, bless, = Icel. Sw. *signa* = Dan. *signe*, make the sign of the cross upon, bless, = OF. *seigner, signer* = Pr. *signar, segnar, senar* = Sp. *signar* = It. *segnare*, make the sign of the cross upon, mark, note, stamp, < L. *signare*, mark, distinguish, sign, ML. make the sign of the cross upon, bless, < *signum*, a sign (> AS. *segen*, a sign, standard, etc.): see *sign*, *n.*, and cf. *sign*, *v.*, a doublet of *sain*1.] To bless with the sign of the cross; bless so as to protect from evil influence. [Obsolete or Scotch.]

> Nade he *sayned* hym-self, segge, bot thrye,
> Er he watz war in the wod of a won in a mote.
> *Sir Gawayne and the Green Knight* (E. E. T. S.), l. 763.

> The truth ye'll tell to me, Tamlane;
> A word ye mauna lie;
> Gin e'er ye was in haly chapel,
> Or *sained* in Christentie?
> *The Young Tamlane* (Child's Ballads, I. 119).

> My stepmither put on my claithes,
> An' ill, ill, *sained* she me.
> *Tam-a-Line* (Child's Ballads, I. 261).

sain2**t, sainet.** Forms of the past participle of *say*1, conformed to original strong participles like *lain*.

sainfoin (sān'foin), *n.* [Also *saintfoin*; < F. *sain-foin*, older *sainctfoin, saintfoin*, appar. < *saint* (< L. *sanctus*), holy, + *foin* (< L. *fœnum*), hay: see *saint*1, *fennel*, and *fenugreek*; otherwise (the form *sainfoin* being then orig.) < *sain*, sound, wholesome (< L. *sanus*, sound: see *sane*1), + *foin*, hay. In this view Pg. *sanfeno* is adapted from the F.; the word does not appear in Sp. or It.] A perennial herb, *Onobrychis sativa*, native in temperate Europe and part of Asia, and widely cultivated in Europe as a forage-plant. It is suitable for pasturage, especially for sheep, and makes a good hay. It prefers light, dry, calcareous soils, and will thrive in places where clover fails. It has been introduced into the United States under the corrupt name *asperset* [F. *esparcet*, G. *esparsette*]. Also *cockshead, French grass*, and *hen's-bill*.

1. The inflorescence of sainfoin (*Onobrychis sativa*). 2. The lower part of the stem with the leaves. *a*, the pod with the persistent calyx.

saint1 (sānt), *a.* and *n.* [< ME. *saint, saynt, seint, seynt, sant, sont*, < OF. *saint, seint, sainct*, m., *saincte, sainte*, f., F. *saint*, m., *sainte*, f., = Pr. *sanct, sant, san*, m., *santa*, f., = Sp. *santo, san*, m., *santa*, f., = Pg. *santo, são*, m., *santa*, f., = It. *santo, san*, m., *santa*, f., holy, sacred, as a noun a saint (= AS. *sanct* = D. *sant* = G. *sankt, sanct* = Dan. Sw. *sankt*, saint), < L. *sanctus*, holy, consecrated, LL. as a noun a saint, prop. pp. of *sancire*, render sacred, make holy, akin to *sacer*, holy, sacred: see *sacre*1. Cf. Skt. √ *sanj*, adhere, *sakta*, attached, devoted. From the same L. verb are ult. E. *sanction, sanctify, sanctimony*, etc. Cf. *corposant, corsaint*.] **I.** *a.* Holy; sacred: only in attributive use, and now only before proper names, as *Saint* John, *Saint* Paul, *Saint* Augustine, or quasi-proper names, as *Saint* Saviour, *Saint* Sophia (Holy Wisdom), *Saint* Cross, *Saint* Sepulcher (in names of churches), where it is usually regarded as a noun appositive, a quasi-title. See II., 3.

> And sle me first, for *seynte* charitee.
> *Chaucer*, Knight's Tale, l. 863.

> It shall here-after be declared how that she was disceased of the *seint* Graal and wher-fore, and how the aventures of the *seynt* Graal were brought to fin.
> *Merlin* (E. E. T. S.), ii. 229.

II. *n.* **1.** One who has been consecrated or set apart to the service of God: applied in the Old Testament to the Israelites as a people (Ps. cxxxii. 9; compare Num. xvi. 3), and in the New Testament to all members of the Christian churches (2 Cor. i. 1).

> Paul, an apostle of Jesus Christ by the will of God, and Timothy our brother, unto the church of God which is at Corinth, with all the *saints* which are in all Achaia.
> 2 Cor. i. 1.

2. One who is pure and upright in heart and life; hence, in Scriptural and Christian usage, one who has been regenerated and sanctified by the Spirit of God; one of the redeemed: applied to them both in their earthly and in their heavenly state; also used of persons of other religions: as, a Buddhist *saint*.

> Than thei seyn that tho ben *Seyntes*, be cause that thei slowen hemself of here owne gode wille for love of here Ydole.
> *Mandeville*, Travels, p. 176.

> All faithful Christ's people, that believe in him faithfully, are *saints* and holy.
> *Latimer*, Sermons (Parker Soc.), p. 507.

> In her was found the blood of prophets, and of *saints*, and of all that were slain upon the earth.
> Rev. xviii. 24.

3. One who is eminent for consecration, holiness, and piety in life and character; specifically, one who is generally or officially recognized as an example of holiness of life, and to whose name it is customary to prefix *Saint* (abbreviated *St.* or *S.*) as a title. The persons so honored were, in the earlier centuries, the Virgin, the apostles and martyrs, and others commemorated in the diptychs or recognized by public opinion. In later times the process of canonization or beatification became a matter of strict regulation by papal or patriarchal authority in the Roman Catholic and Greek churches. Saints are classed in calendars by their rank, as apostles, bishops, archbishops, priests, deacons, kings, etc., and also as martyrs, confessors, and virgins. The title of *saint* is also given to angels, as *St.* Michael, *St.* Gabriel, *St.* Raphael. In the phrases given below many diseases will be found named from those saints whose intercession was especially sought for their cure. When *saint* is used before a person's name as a quasi-title (originally an adjective), it is commonly abbreviated *St.*; but such names, and surnames and local names derived from them, are properly alphabeted under the full form *saint*.

> We have decided and defined the Blessed Francis de Sales, Bishop of Geneva, to be a *Saint*, and have inscribed him on the catalogue of the *Saints*.
> *Bull of Alexander VII. concerning St. Francis de Sales* [(1665), quoted in Cath. Dict., p. 114.

> Any one writing on ecclesiastical history ought to know that the British and Saxon *saints* were not canonized, but acquired the name of *saint* not directly from Rome, but from the voice of the people of their own neighbourhood.
> *N. and Q.*, 7th ser., IX. 319.

4. An angel.

> The Lord came from Sinai, and rose up from Seir unto them; he shined forth from mount Paran, and he came with ten thousands of *saints*.
> Deut. xxxiii. 2.

5. One of the blessed dead: distinguished from the angels, who are superhuman beings.

> We therefore pray thee, help thy servants. . . . Make them to be numbered with thy *Saints* in glory everlasting.
> *Book of Common Prayer*, Te Deum.

> Holy! holy! holy! all the *saints* adore thee,
> Casting down their golden crowns around the glassy sea.
> *Heber*, Holy! holy! holy! Lord God Almighty.

6. An image of a saint.

> No silver *saints* by dying misers given
> Here bribed the rage of ill-requited Heaven.
> *Pope*, Eloisa to Abelard, l. 137.

All Saints' day, a feast of all martyrs and saints, observed as early as the fourth century. In the Greek Church it occurs on the first Sunday after Pentecost; in the Latin Church at first observed on the 13th of May, since Pope Gregory III. on the 1st of November. Also called *All-saints*.—**Christians of St. John.** See *Mandæan*, 1.—**Common of the Saints.** See *common*.—**Communion of saints**, the spiritual fellowship of all true believers, both living and dead, mystically united with each other in Christ their head.—**Cross of St. George, of St. James, of St. Julian, of St. Patrick.** See *cross*1.—**Herb of St. Martin.** See *herb*.—**Intercession of saints.** See *intercession*.—**Invocation of saints.** See *invocation*.—**Knights of the Order of St. Crispin.** See *knight*.—**Latter-day Saints**, the name assumed by the people popularly called Mormons. See *Mormon*2.

> For thus shall my Church be called in the last days; even the Church of Jesus Christ of Latter *Day Saints*.
> *Mormon Catechism*, p. 14.

Lion of St. Mark. See *lion*.—**Nativity of a saint, nativity of St. John Baptist.** See *nativity*.—**Oratory of St. Philip Neri.** See *oratory*.—**Order of St. Andrew, St. George, St. Michael**, etc. See *order*.—**Patron saint**, a saint who is regarded as a protector, a guardian, or a favorer: as, St. Genevieve, the *patron saint* of Paris; St. Cecilia, the *patron saint* of music; St. George is the *patron saint* of England, St. Andrew of Scotland, St. Patrick of Ireland, St. Denys of France.—**Perseverance of the saints.** See *perseverance*1.—**Proper of Saints.** See *proper*.—**St. Agatha's disease**, disease of the mammæ.—**St. Agnes's flower**, the snowflake (*Leucoium*).—**St. Aignon's disease**, tinea.—**St. Andrew's cross.** (*a*) See *cross*1, 1, and *saltier*. (*b*) A North American shrub, *Ascyrum Crux Andreæ*.—**St. Andrew's day.** See *day*1.—**St. Ann's bark.** Same as *Santa Ana bark* (which see, under *bark*2).—**St. Anthony's cross.** See *cross*1, 1.—**St. Anthony's fire.** (*a*) Epidermic gangrene, as in ergotism. (*b*) Erysipelas.—**St. Anthony's nut**, the pignut or hawknut: so called because St. Anthony was the patron of pigs.—**St. Anthony's rape** or **turnip.** See *turnip*.—**St. Apollonia's disease**, pains in the jaw, accompanied by toothache.—**St. Audrey's necklace**, a string of holy stones or "fairy beads."—**St. Augustine grass**, *Stenotaphrum Americanum*, a common coarse grass of Florida, making a firm sod, green through the year. [Local name.]—**St. Avertin's disease**, epilepsy.—**St. Barbara's cress** or **herb**, the yellow rocket, *Barbarea vulgaris*.—**St. Barnaby's thistle.** See *thistle*.—**St. Bennet's herb**, the herb-bennet.—**St. Blase's disease**, sore throat; quinsy.—**St. Bruno's lily.** See *Paradisia*.—**St. Cassian beds**, a division of the Triassic series, particularly well developed near St. Cassian in southern Tyrol, and consisting of calcareous marls, extremely rich in fossils: among these are ammonites, orthoceratites, gastropods, lamellibranchs, brachiopods, echinoderms, crinoids, corals, and sponges. The fauna of the Alpine Trias, to which the St. Cassian beds belong, is remarkable as presenting a mixture of Paleozoic and Mesozoic forms.—**St. Catherine's flower**, the *Nigella Damascena*.—**St. Christopher's herb.** Same as *herb-christopher*.—**St. Clair's disease**, ophthalmia.—**St. Crispin's day.** See *Crispin*.—**St. Cuthbert's beads, duck.** See *bead, duck*2.—**St. Dabeoc's heath.** See *heath*, 2.—**St. David's day.** See *day*1.—**Saint Distaff's day.** See *distaff*.—**St. Domingo duck**, *Erismatura* (or *Nomonyx*) *dominica*, a West Indian duck, rarely found in the United States, a near relative of the common ruddy duck.—**St. Domingo falcon.** See *falcon*.—**St. Domingo grebe**, *Podiceps* or *Sylbeocyclus* or *Tachybaptes dominicus*, the least grebe of America, about 9½ inches long, found in the West Indies and other warm parts of America, including the Rio Grande Valley of Texas.—**St. Dymphna's disease**, insanity.—**St. Elmo's fire** or **light** (*St. Elmo*, patron of navigation), a name given by seamen to brushes and jets of electric light seen on the tips of masts and yard-arms of vessels, especially during thunder-storms. This form of electric discharge occurs also on land, and most frequently on mountain summits, where it glows and hisses in brilliant tongues of white and blue light several inches in length. On Ben Nevis it is most generally seen in winter during storms of dry, hard snow-hail, with rising barometer, falling temperature, and northwesterly wind. Also called *corposant*.—**St. Emilion**, a red wine produced in the department of Gironde, on the right bank of the Dordogne, and generally classed among clarets, though different in quality and flavor from the wines grown nearer Bordeaux.—**St. Erasmus's disease**, colic.—**St. Estèphe**, a red wine produced north of the Garonne, in the department of Gironde, and belonging to the same class of wines as St. Emilion. It is generally exported from Bordeaux, and is considered a claret.—**St. Francis's fire**†. See *fire*.—**St. George**, a cross of St. George—that is, an upright red cross on a white field: as, "a *St. George* cantoned with the *Jack*." *C. Boutell*.—**St. Georges.** (*a*) A red wine of Burgundy, produced in the immediate neighborhood of wines of the highest quality, but not ranking above the second grade. (*b*) A Bordeaux wine, especially red, of medium quality. (*c*) A red wine grown near Poitiers.—**St. George's day, fish, mushroom.** See *day*1, *fish*1, etc.—**St. George's ensign**, the distinguishing flag of ships of the British navy, consisting of a red cross on a white field, with the union-flag in the upper quarter next the mast.—**St. Germain tea.** See *tea*.—**St. Giles's disease**, cancer.—**St. Gilles**, a white wine produced at St. Gilles, in the department of Gard. It is one of the best of the wines of southern France.—**St. Gothard's disease**, a disease due to the intestinal worm *Ankylostomum duodenale*.—**St. Helena blackwood** or **ebony**, a tree, *Melhania melanoxylon*, of the *Sterculiaceæ*, formerly of St. Helena, now extinct. Its dark, heavy wood was still at a recent date collected and turned into ornaments.—**St. Helen's beds.** See *Osborne series*, under *series*.—**St. Hubert's disease**, hydrophobia.—**St. Ignatius' beans.** See *bean*1.—**St. James lily.** Same as *jacobæa-lily*.—**St. James's flower.** See *Lotus*, 2.—**St. James's shell.** See *pilgrim's shell* (*a*), under *pilgrim*.—**St.-James's-wort.** Same as *rag-wort*.—**St. Job's disease**, syphilis.—**St. John's bread.** (*a*) The carob-bean: used medicinally as an expectorant and demulcent. See *Ceratonia*. (*b*) The ergot of rye (*Claviceps purpurea*). See *ergot*1 for figure and description.—**St. John's evil**, epilepsy.—**St. John's falcon.** See *falcon*.—**St. John's hawk** or **buzzard**, a blackish variety of the rough-legged buzzard, *Archibuteo lagopus*, var. *sanctijohannis*, originally described as *Falco sanctijohannis*, from St. John's in Newfoundland.—**St. Johnstone's tippet.** See *tippet*.—**St.-John's-wort.** See *Hypericum*.—**St. Julien.** (*a*) A red Bordeaux wine produced in the Médoc region, and properly in the small district of St. Julien de Reignac. The name has become known in the United States, and is commonly understood to denote claret of a medium grade without especial reference to the place of production. (*b*) A red wine produced in the neighborhood of the Rhone, not often exported.—**St. Julien plum.** See *plum*1.—**St. Lawrence's tears**†. See *tear*2.—**St. Lazarus disease.** (*a*) Leprosy. (*b*) Tinea. (*c*) Measles of the hog. See *Trichina, trichinosis*.—**St. Louis limestone**, a division of the mountain limestone, well developed in Indiana, Illinois, Iowa, and Missouri, and having a maximum thickness of 250 feet.—**St. Lucas cactus-wren**, *Campylorhynchus affinis*, closely related to *C. brunneicapillus*. See *Campylorhynchus*.—**St. Lucas gecko, robin, thrasher.** See *gecko, robin*1, etc.—**St. Lucia bark.** See *bark*2.—**St. Luke's summer**, in weather lore, a period of fine pleasant weather about October 18th.—**St. Martin's evil**, drunkenness.—**St. Martin's flower**, an ornamental plant of the *Amaryllidaceæ*, *Alstrœmeria pulchra* (*A. Flos-Martini*).—**St. Martin's herb.** See *herb of St. Martin*, under *herb*.—**St. Martin's Lent.** See *Lent*1.—**St. Martin's little summer**, a period beginning about the 11th of November, popularly considered in the Mediterranean to mark a period of warm, quiet weather.—**St. Martin's rings.** See *ring*1.—**St. Mary's trout.** See *trout*.—**St. Mathurin's disease.** (*a*) Epilepsy. (*b*) Insanity.—**St. Michael's bannock**, an oatmeal cake made especially for Michaelmas time. [Prov. Eng.]—**St. Michael's orange.** See *orange*1.—**St. Nicholas's clerk**†. See *clerk*.—**St. Nicholas's day.** See *day*1.—**St. Patrick's cabbage, day, Purgatory.** See *cabbage*1, *day*1, etc.—**St. Peter's chair.** See *chair*.—**St. Peter's corn**, a species of wheat, *Triticum monococcum*. See *wheat*.—**St. Peter's finger.** (*a*) A belemnite, or some similar fossil cephalopod. These are among many petrifactions which, like some prehistoric artificial implements, have been generally regarded superstitiously by the ignorant, and sometimes worshiped. See *ammonite, ram's-horn, thunder-stone*, and cut under *belemnite*. Compare *salagrama*. (*b*) The garfish, *Belone belone* or *B. vulgaris*. [Local, Eng.]—**St. Peter's fish**, the dory. See *dory*1, 1.—**St. Peter's sandstone.** See *sandstone*.—**St.-Peter's-wort.** (*a*) In old herbals, same as *herb-peter*. (*b*) In later books, the European *Hypericum quadrangulum*. (*c*) Perhaps transferred from the last, the American genus *Ascyrum*, especially *A. stans*. (*d*) The snowberry, *Symphoricarpos*.—**St. Peter's wreath.** Same as *Italian may* (which see, under *may*4).—**St. Pierre.** (*a*) A claret of the second grade. (*b*) A white wine produced in the department of Gironde, in the neighborhood of St. Emilion.—**St. Pierre group**, a thick mass of shales, marls, and clays covering a very extensive area in the upper Missouri region. It belongs to the Cretaceous system, is rich in fossils, especially cephalopods, and lies between the

Fox Hills and Niobrara groups. Properly called *Fort Pierre* and sometimes *Pierre group*.—**St. Roch's disease**, the bubo plague.—**Saint's day**, a day set apart by ecclesiastical authority for the commemoration of a particular saint.—**St. Swithin's day.** See *day*[1].—**St. Thomas's balsam**, balsam of Tolu. See *balsam*.—**St. Thomas tree**, a name of *Bauhinia tomentosa* and *B. variegata* of the East Indies, etc. Their yellow petals are variegated with red fancifully attributed to the blood of St. Thomas.—**St. Valentine's day.** See *valentine*.—**St. Victor's balsam**, a name given to compound tincture of benzoin.—**St. Vitus's dance**, chorea.—**St. Zachary's disease**, dumbness.—**Sunday of St. Thomas**, or **the Touching of St. Thomas.** Same as *Low Sunday* (which see, under *low*[2]).—**The O's of St. Bridget.** See *O*[2].—**To braid St. Catherine's tresses.** See *braid*[1].—**To tie with St. Mary's knott.** See *knot*[1].

saint[1] (sānt), *v.* [< ME. *sainten (see *sainted*), < OF. *saintir*; from the noun.] **I.** *trans.* **1.** To number or enroll among saints officially; canonize.

> Thou shalt be *sainted*, woman, and thy tomb
> Cut out in crystal, pure and good as thou art.
> *Beau. and Fl.*, Thierry and Theodoret, iv. 1.

> The Picture sett in Front would Martyr him and *Saint* him to befoole the people. *Milton*, Eikonoklastes, Pref.

2. To salute as a saint. [Rare.]

> However Pharisee-like they otherwise *saint* him, and call him an Holy Father, sure it is, they reject his counsel.
> *Penn*, No Cross, No Crown, ii.

> They shout, "Behold a saint!"
> And lower voices *saint* me from above.
> *Tennyson*, St. Simeon Stylites.

II. *intrans.* To act piously or with a show of piety; play the saint: sometimes with an indefinite *it*.

> Think women still to strive with men,
> To sin and never for to *saint*.
> *Shak.*, Passionate Pilgrim, l. 342.

saint[2]† (sānt), *n.* An old game: same as *cent*, 4.

> My Saints turn'd deuill. No, wee'l none of *Saint*;
> You are best at New-cut wife; you'l play at that.
> *Heywood*, Woman Killed with Kindness (Works, II. 122).

saintdom (sānt'dum), *n.* [< *saint*[1] + *-dom*.] The state or condition of being a saint; the state of being sainted or canonized; canonization.

> I will not cease to grasp the hope I hold
> Of *saintdom*. *Tennyson*, St. Simeon Stylites.

sainted (sān'ted), *p. a.* [< ME. **sainted, i-sonted*; pp. of *saint*[1], *v.*] **1.** Canonized; enrolled among the saints.—**2.** Holy; pious.

> Thy royal father
> Was a most *sainted* king.
> *Shak.*, Macbeth, iv. 3. 109.

3. Sacred.

> Amongst the enthroned gods on *sainted* seats.
> *Milton*, Comus, l. 11.

4. Entered into bliss; gone to heaven: often used as a euphemism for *dead*.

> He is the very picture of his *sainted* mother.
> *Thackeray*, Vanity Fair, viii.

saintess (sān'tes), *n.* [< *saint*[1] + *-ess*.] A female saint.

> Some of your *saintesses* have gowns and kirtles made of such dames' refuses.
> *Sheldon*, Miracles of Antichrist, p. 98. (*Latham*.)

saintfoin (sānt'foin), *n.* See *sainfoin*.

sainthood (sānt'hůd), *n.* [< *saint*[1] + *-hood*.] The character, condition, rank, or dignity of a saint.

> Theodore had none of that contemptible apathy which almost lifted our *James* the Second to the superior honour of monkish *sainthood*. *Walpole*. (*Latham*.)

saintish (sān'tish), *a.* [< *saint*[1] + *-ish*[1].] Somewhat saintly; affected with piety: used ironically.

> They be no diuels (I trow) which seme so *saintish*.
> *Gascoigne*, Steele Glas (ed. Arber), p. 82.

> I give you check and mate to your white king,
> Simplicity itself, your *saintish* king there.
> *Middleton*, Women Beware Women, ii. 2.

saintism (sān'tizm), *n.* [< *saint*[1] + *-ism*.] Sanctimonious character or profession; assumption of holiness. [Contemptuous and rare.]

> John Pointer . . . became . . . acquainted with Oliver Cromwel; who, when Protector, gave him a Canonry Ch. Ch. in Oxon, as a reward for the pains he took in converting him to godliness, i. e. to canting Puritanism and *Saintism*.
> *A. Wood*, Fasti Oxon., I. 200.

saintlike (sānt'līk), *a.* [< *saint*[1] + *like*.] **1.** Resembling a saint; saintly: as, a *saintlike* prince.—**2.** Suiting a saint; befitting a saint.

> Glossed over only with a *saint-like* show, . . .
> Still thou art bound to vice.
> *Dryden*, tr. of Persius's Satires, v. 167.

saintlily (sānt'li-li), *adv.* In a saintly manner. *Poe*, Rationale of Verse.

saintliness (sānt'li-nes), *n.* The state or character of being saintly. = **Syn.** *Piety, Sanctity*, etc. See *religion*.

saintly (sānt'li), *a.* [< *saint*[1] + *-ly*[1].] Like or characteristic of a saint; befitting a holy person; saintlike.

> I mention still
> Him whom thy wrongs, with *saintly* patience borne,
> Made famous in a land and times obscure.
> *Milton*, P. R., iii. 93.

> With eyes astray, she told mechanic beads
> Before some shrine of *saintly* womanhood.
> *Lowell*, Cathedral.

saintologist (sān-tol'ō-jist), *n.* [< *saint*[1] + *-olog-y* + *-ist*.] One who writes the lives of saints; one versed in the history of saints; a hagiologist. [Rare.] *Imp. Dict.*

Saints' bell. See *bell*[1].

> Whene'er the old exchange of profit rings
> Her silver *saint's-bell* of uncertain gains.
> *Quarles*, Emblems, iv. 3.

saint-seeming (sānt'sē"ming), *a.* Having the appearance of a saint.

> A *saint-seeming* and Bible-bearing hypocritical puritan.
> *Bp. Mountagu*, Appeal to Cæsar, p. 43. (*Latham*.)

> Those are the *Saint-seeming* Worthies of Virginia, that haue notwithstanding all this meate, drinke, and wages.
> Quoted in *Capt. John Smith's* Works, I. 199.

saintship (sānt'ship), *n.* [< *saint*[1] + *-ship*.] The character or qualities of a saint; the position of a saint; as a sort of title, saint.

> Saint Frip, Saint Trip, Saint Fill, Saint Fillie;
> Neither those other *saint-ships* will I
> Here goe about for to recite. *Herrick*, The Temple.

> Might shake the *saintship* of an anchorite.
> *Byron*, Childe Harold, i. 11.

Saint-Simonian (sānt-sī-mō'ni-an), *a.* and *n.* [< *Saint-Simon* (see *Saint-Simonism*) + *-i-an*.] **I.** *a.* Pertaining to or believing in the principles of Saint-Simon or Saint-Simonism.

> The leaders of the *Saint-Simonian* religion.
> *R. T. Ely*, French and German Socialism, p. 71.

II. *n.* A follower of Saint-Simon; a believer in the principles of Saint-Simonism.

> While the economists were discussing theories, the *Saint-Simonians* were trying courageously the hazards of practice, and were making, at their risk and peril, experiments preparatory to the future.
> *Blanqui*, Hist. Pol. Econ. (trans.), xliii.

Saint-Simonianism (sānt-si-mō'ni-an-izm), *n.* [< *Saint-Simonian* + *-ism*.] Same as *Saint-Simonism*.

Saint-Simonism (sānt-sī'mon-izm), *n.* [< *Saint-Simon* (see def.) + *-ism*.] The socialistic system founded by Claude Henri, Comte de Saint-Simon (1760–1825), and developed by his disciples. According to this system the state should become possessed of all property; the distribution of the products of the common labor of the community should not, however, be an equal one, but each person should be rewarded according to the services he has rendered the state, the active and able receiving a larger share than the slow and dull; and inheritance should be abolished, as otherwise men would be rewarded according to the merits of their parents and not according to their own. The system proposes that all should not be occupied alike, but differently, according to their vocation and capacity, the labor of each being assigned, like grades in a regiment, by the will of the directing authority. *J. S. Mill*, Pol. Econ., II. i. § 4.

Saint-Simonist (sānt-sī'mon-ist), *n.* [< *Saint-Simon* (see *Saint-Simonism*) + *-ist*.] A follower of Saint-Simon; a Saint-Simonian.

> He was reproached on all sides as a demagogue, a *Saint-Simonist*. *Nineteenth Century*, XXIV. 434.

sair[1] (sãr), *a.* and *adv.* A Scotch form of *sore*[1].

sair[2] (sãr), *v. t.* [Also North. dial. *sarra*, serve, fit, a reduced form (with the common loss of final *v* after a vowel or, as here, a semi-vowel) of *serve*[1]. Cf. E. dial. *sarrant*, a servant.] To serve; fit; be large enough for; satisfy, as with food. [Scotch.]

sairing (sãr'ing), *n.* [Verbal n. of *sair*[2], *v.*] As much as satisfies or serves the turn; enough for any one: as, he has got his *sairing*. [Scotch.]

> You couldna look your *sairin* at her face,
> So meek it was, so sweet, so fu' o' grace.
> *Ross*, Helenore, p. 16.

sairly (sãr'li), *adv.* A Scotch form of *sorely*.

saise†, *v.* A Middle English form of *seize*.

Saisne†, *n.* [ME., < OF. *Saisne*, a Saxon: see *Saxon*.] A Saxon.

> That tyme the *Saisnes* made euell waich, for thei were nothynge war till these were euein a-monge hem.
> *Merlin* (E. E. T. S.), ii. 231.

saith[1] (seth). Third person singular present indicative of *say*[1].

saith[2] (sāth), *n.* [Also *saithe*, *seth*; < Gael. *saidhean*, the coalfish, especially in its 2d, 3d, and 4th years.] The coalfish. [Scotch.]

> He proposed he should go ashore and buy a few lines with which they might fish for young *saithe* or lythe over the side of the yacht. *W. Black*, Princess of Thule, xxvii.

Saitic (sā-it'ik), *a.* [< L. *Saïticus*, < Gr. Σαϊτικός, Saitic, < Σαΐτης, L. *Saïtes*, of Sais, < Σάϊς, L. *Saïs*, Sais.] Of or pertaining to Sais, a sacred city of ancient Egypt: as, the *Saitic* Isis.

Saiva (sī'vạ̈), *n.* [Hind., < *Siva*, q. v.] A votary of Siva.

Saivism (sī'vizm), *n.* Same as *Sivism*.

saiyid, *n.* See *sayid*.

saj (saj), *n.* [E. Ind.] An East Indian tree, *Terminalia tomentosa*, affording a hard, finely variegated wood, used for many purposes, but of doubtful durability. Its bark is used for tanning and for dyeing black.

sajene, *n.* See *sagene*[1].

sajou (sa-jö'), *n.* [S. Amer.] A South American monkey, or sai, one of several kinds also called *sapajou*. See *sapajou*, and synonyms under *saguin*.

sak†, *n.* A Middle English form of *sack*[1].

saka (sä'kạ̈), *n.* [S. Amer.] The native name of the bastard purple-heart tree, a species of *Copaifera*.

Saka era. See *Çāka era*, under *era*.

sake[1] (sāk), *n.* [< ME. *sake*, *sak*, *sac*, dispute, contention, lawsuit, cause, purpose, guilt, sake, < AS. *sacu*, strife, distress, persecution, fault, a lawsuit, jurisdiction in litigious suits (see *sac*[1]), guilt, crime, = OS. *saka*, strife, crime, lawsuit, cause, thing, = MD. *saecke*, D. *zaak*, matter, case, cause, business, affair, = MLG. LG. *sake* = OHG. *sacha*, *sahha*, MHG. *sache*, strife, contention, lawsuit, case, cause, thing, G. *sache*, case, affair, thing, = Icel. *sök* (gen. *sakar*), a lawsuit, plaint, charge, offense charged, guilt, cause, sake, = Sw. *sak* = Dan. *sag*, case, cause, matter, thing; cf. Goth. *sakjō*, strife; orig. strife, contention, esp. at law; from the verb represented by AS. *sacan* (pret. *sōc*), strive, contend at law, bring a charge against, accuse (also in comp. *ætsacan*, deny, disown, *forsacan*, deny, forsake, *onsacan*, strive against, resist, deny, etc.), = Goth. *sakan* (pret. *sók*), contend, blame, rebuke; perhaps akin to L. *sancire*, render sacred, forbid, etc. (see *sanction*), Skt. *sanj*, *sajj*, adhere. From the same Teut. root are ult. *seek* and *sac*[1], *soc*, *socage*, *saught*, *settle*[2]; cf. also *forsake* and *ransack*.] **1**†. Strife; contention; dispute.

> That he with Romleode summe *sake* arerde.
> *Layamon*, l. 26290.

> Cheste and *sake*. *Owl and Nightingale*, l. 1160.

2†. Fault; guilt.

> & o thatt an [on that one] he leȝȝde thær
> All theȝȝre *sake* & sinne. *Ormulum*, l. 1335.

> This bischop bad him haf god hop,
> And asked him yef he walde tac
> Riht penanz for his sinful *sac*.
> *Eng. Metr. Homilies* (ed. Small), p. 139.

> If my gaynlych God such gref to me wolde,
> For [for?] desert of sum *sake* that I slayne were,
> At alle peryles, quoth the prophete, I aproche hit no nerre.
> *Alliterative Poems* (ed. Morris), iii. 84.

> With-outen any *sake* of felonye,
> As a schep to the slaȝtther lad watȝ he.
> *Alliterative Poems* (ed. Morris), l. 799.

3. Purpose; purpose of obtaining or achieving: as, to labor for the *sake* of subsistence.

> Ther-fore for sothe gret sorwe sche made,
> & swore for that *sake* to suffur alle peynes,
> To be honget on beiȝ or with horse to-drawe,
> Sche wold neuer be wedded to no wiȝh of grece.
> *William of Palerne* (E. E. T. S.), l. 2019.

> Thou neither dost persuade me to seek wealth
> For empire's *sake*, nor empire to affect
> For glory's *sake*. *Milton*, P. R., iii. 45.

4. Cause; account; reason; interest; regard to any person or thing: as, without *sake*: now always preceded by *for*, with a possessive: as, *for my sake*; *for heaven's sake*. When the possessive is plural, the noun is often made plural also: as, "for your fair *sakes*" (*Shak.*, L. L. L., v. 2. 765); "for both our *sakes*" (*Shak.*, T. of the S., v. 2. 16). The final *s* of the possessive is often merged with the initial *s* of *sake*, and thus disappears: as, "for heaven *sake*" (*Shak.*, K. John, iv. 1. 78); "for fashion *sake*" (*Shak.*, As you Like it, iii. 2. 271); etc. Compare "for conscience *sake*," etc.

> And faytour *for thy sake*,
> Thei sall be putte to pyne.
> *York Plays*, p. 80.

> I will not again curse the ground any more *for man's sake*. Gen. viii. 21.

> Our hope is that the God of Peace shall . . . enable us quietly and even gladly to suffer all things, *for that work sake* which we covet to perform.
> *Hooker*, Eccles. Polity, Pref., i.

For old sake's sake, for the sake of old times; for auld langsyne. [Colloq. or prov. Eng.]

> Yet *for old sake's sake* she is still, dears,
> The prettiest doll in the world.
> *Kingsley*, Water-Babies.

sake[2] (sak'e), *n.* [Jap.] **1.** A Japanese fermented liquor made from rice. It contains from 11 to 17 per cent. of alcohol, and is heated before being drunk.

Of *saké* there are many varieties, from the best quality down to shiro-zaké, or "white *saké*," and the turbid sort, drunk only in the poorer districts, known as nigori-zaké; there is also a sweet sort, called mirin.
Encyc. Brit., XIII. 574.

2. The generic name in Japan for all kinds of spirituous liquors, whether made from grain or grapes, fermented or distilled.

sake[3] (sä'ke), *n.* Same as *saki*.

sakeen, *n.* [Native name (?).] A kind of ibex found in the Himalayas.

saker[1] (sā'kėr), *n.* [Also written *sacre*, formerly also *sakre*; < OF. (and F.) *sacre* = Sp. Pg. *sacre* = It. *sagro*, formerly also *sacro*, *saccaro* (G. *saker-falk*), < ML. *sacer* (also *falco sacer*, OF. *faucon sacre*), a kind of falcon; either < Ar. *saqr*, a falcon, or < L. *sacer*, sacred (cf. Gr. ἱέραξ, a hawk, < ἱερός, sacred: see *Hierax* and *gerfalcon*). Hence *sakeret*.] A kind of hawk used in falconry, especially the female, which is larger than the male, the latter being called a *sakeret* or *sacret*. It is a true falcon of Asia and Europe, *Falco sacer*. A related falcon of western North America, *Falco polyagrus* or *F. mexicanus*, is known as the *American saker*.

Let these proud *sakers* and gerfalcons fly;
Do not thou move a wing.
Middleton, Spanish Gypsy, ii. 1.

saker[2] (sā'kėr), *n.* [Also *sacker*, *sayker*; a particular use of *saker*[1]. Cf. *falcon*, 4, *falconet*, 3, *musket*[2], etc., guns similarly named from birds.] A small piece of artillery, smaller than the demi-culverin, formerly much employed in sieges.

They set vp a mantellet, vnder the which they put three or foure pieces, as *sacres*, where with they shot against the posterns. *Hakluyt's Voyages*, II. 79.

I reckoned about eight and twenty great pieces [of ordnance], besides those of the lesser sort, as *Sakers*.
Coryat, Crudities, I. 125.

saker[3]†, *v.* See *sacre*[1].

sakeret (sā'kėr-et), *n.* [Also *sacret*; < OF. *sacret*, dim. of *sacre*, a saker: see *saker*[1].] The male of the saker.

sakeryng†, *n.* An obsolete form of *sacring*.

saki (sak'i), *n.* [= F. *saki*; < S. Amer. name (?).] A South American monkey of the family *Cebidæ* and subfamily *Pitheciinæ*, especially of the genus *Pithecia*, of which there are several species; one of the fox-tailed monkeys, with a bushy non-prehensile tail. *P. monachus* is the monk-saki; *P. satanas* is the black saki, or couxio; *P. leucocephalus* is the white-headed saki; *P. chiropotes* is sometimes called the "hand-drinking" saki, from some story which attached to this species, though all these monkeys drink in the same way. See cut under *Pithecia*. Also *sake*.

sakieh (sak'i-e), *n.* [Also *sakiah*, *sakia*; < Ar. *saqieh*, a water-wheel; cf. *segiya*, an irrigating brook, *siqâya*, an aqueduct, < *isqi*, water, irrigate.] A modification of the Persian wheel used in Egypt for raising water for purposes of irrigation. It consists essentially of a vertical wheel to which earthen pots are attached on projecting spokes, a second vertical wheel on the same axis with cogs, and a large horizontal cogged wheel, which gears with the other cogged wheel. The large wheel, being turned by oxen or other draft-animals, puts in motion the other two wheels, the one carrying the pitchers dipping into a well or a deep pit adjoining and supplied with water from a river. The pitchers are thus emptied into a tank at a higher level, whence the water is led off in a network of channels over the neighboring fields. Instead of the pitchers being attached directly to the wheel when the level of the water is very low, they are attached to an endless rope. The construction of these machines is usually very rude.

saklest, *a.* A Middle English form of *sackless*.

saksaul (sak'sâl), *n.* [Also *saksau*, *saksaw*, *saxaul*; of E. Ind. origin.] An arborescent shrub, *Anabasis ammodendron* of the *Chenopodiaceæ*. It is a typical growth of the sand-deserts of Asia, furnishes a valuable fuel, and is planted to stay shifting sands.

Sakta (sak'tä), *n.* [Hind. *sākta*, < Skt. *çākta*, concerned with (Siva's) *çakti*, or 'power' or 'energy' in female personification.] A member of one of the great divisions of Hindu sectaries, comprising the worshipers of the female principle according to the ritual of the Tantras. The Saktas are divided into two branches, the followers respectively of the right-hand and left-hand rituals. The latter practise the grossest impurities.

sakur (sā'kėr), *n.* [E. Ind.] A small rounded astringent gall formed on some species of *Tamarix*, used in medicine and dyeing.

sal[1] (sal), *n.* [< L. *sal*, salt: see *salt*[1].] Salt: a word much used by the older chemists and in pharmacy.

Grynde summe of these thingis forseid, which that ȝe wil, as strongly as ȝe can in a morter, with the 10 part of him of *sal* comen preparate to the medicyne of men.
Book of Quinte Essence (ed. Furnivall), p. 12.

Sal absinthii. Same as *salt of wormwood* (which see, under *salt*[1]).—**Sal aeratus.** See *saleratus*.—**Sal alembroth**, a solution of equal parts of corrosive sublimate and ammonium chlorid. Also called *salt of wisdom*.—**Sal ammoniac.** See *ammoniac*.—**Sal de duobus**, or **sal duplicatus**, an old chemical name applied to potassium sulphate.—**Sal diureticus**, an old name for potassium acetate.—**Sal enixum**, an old name for potassium bisulphate.—**Sal gemmæ**, a native sodium chlorid, or rock-salt.—**Sal mirabile**, sodium sulphate; Glauber's salt.—**Sal peter**†, a Middle English form of *saltpeter*.—**Sal prunella.** See *prunella*[3].—**Sal Seignette**, Rochelle salt.—**Sal tartre**, salt of tartar.—**Sal volatile**, ammonium carbonate. The name is also applied to a spirituous solution of ammonium carbonate flavored with aromatics.

sal[2] (säl), *n.* [Also *saul*; < Hind. *sāl*, Skt. *çāla*.] A large gregarious tree, *Shorea robusta*, natural order *Dipterocarpeæ*, of northern India. It affords the most extensively used timber of that region, ranking in quality next to teak. The wood is of a dark-brown color, hard, rather coarse-grained, and very durable. It is employed for building houses, bridges, and boats, for making carts and gun-carriages, for railroad-ties, etc. It yields, by tapping, a kind of resin (see *saldammar*), and its leaves are the food of the Tussa silk-worm.

salaam, salam (sa-läm'), *n.* [< Hind. Pers. *salām*, < Ar. *salām*, saluting, wishing health or peace, a salutation, peace (< *salm*, saluting), = Heb. *shelām*, peace, < *shālam*, be safe.] A ceremonious salutation of the Orientals. In India the personal salaam or salutation is an obeisance executed by bowing the head with the body downward, in extreme cases nearly to the ground, and placing the palm of the right hand on the forehead.

He [the King] . . . presenteth himselfe to the people to receiue their *Salames* or good morrow.
Purchas, Pilgrimage, p. 546.

A trace of pity in the silent *salaam* with which the grim durwan salutes you.
J. W. Palmer, The Old and the New, p. 328.

Salaam convulsion, a bilateral clonic spasm of muscles supplied by the spinal accessory nerve, confined almost wholly to children between the periods of dentition and puberty. The disease is paroxysmal, of varying duration and number of attacks; with each attack the head is bowed forward and then relaxed. Also called *nodding spasm*, *spasmus nutans*, and *eclampsia nutans*.—**To send salaam**, to send one's compliments. [Colloq.]

salaam, salam (sa-läm'), *v. i.* and *t.* [< *salaam*, *n.*] To perform the salaam; salute with a salaam; greet.

This was the place where the multitude assembled every morning to *salam* the Padishah.
J. T. Wheeler, Short Hist. India, p. 165.

salability, saleability (sā-la-bil'i-ti), *n.* [< *salable* + *-ity* (see *-bility*).] Salableness.

What can he do but spread himself into breadth and length, into superficiality and *saleability*?
Carlyle, Misc., IV. 139. (*Davies.*)

salable, saleable (sā'la-bl), *a.* [< *sale*[1] + *-able*.] Capable of being sold; purchasable; hence, finding a ready market; in demand.

Woeful is that judgment which comes from him who hath venalem animam, a *saleable* soul.
Rev. T. Adams, Works, II. 549.

Any *saleable* commodity . . . removed out of the course of trade. *Locke.*

salableness, saleableness (sā'la-bl-nes), *n.* The character of being salable; salability.

salably, saleably (sā'la-bli), *adv.* In a salable manner; so as to be salable.

salacious (sa-lā'shus), *a.* [< L. *salax* (*-ac-*), disposed to leap, lustful, < *salire*, leap: see *sail*[2], *salient*.] Lustful; lecherous.

One more *salacious*, rich, and old
Outbids, and buys her pleasure with her gold.
Dryden, tr. of Juvenal's Satires, x.

salaciously (sa-lā'shus-li), *adv.* In a salacious manner; lustfully; with eager animal appetite.

salaciousness (sa-lā'shus-nes), *n.* The quality of being salacious; lust; lecherousness; strong propensity to venery.

salacity (sa-las'i-ti), *n.* [= F. *salacité* = It. *salacità*, < L. *salacita(t-)s*, lust, < *salax* (*-ac-*), disposed to leap, lustful: see *salacious*.] Salaciousness.

salad[1] (sal'ad), *n.* [Formerly also *sallad*, *sallet*; < ME. *salade* (= D. *salade* = MHG. *salât*, G. *salat* = Dan. *salat* = Sw. *salat*, *salad*), < OF. (and F.) *salade*, < OIt. *salata* = Pg. *salada*, a salad (cf. Sp. *ensalada* = It. *insalata*, a salad); lit. 'salted,' < ML. *salata*, fem. of *salatus* (> Sp. Pg. *salado* = It. *salato*), salted, pickled (cf. It. *salato*, salt meat), pp. of *salare*, salt, < L. *sal*, salt: see *salt*[1].] 1. Raw herbs, such as lettuce, endive, radishes, green mustard, land- and water-cresses, celery, or young onions, cut up and variously dressed, as with eggs, salt, mustard, oil, vinegar, etc.

Beware of *saladis*, grene metis, & of frutes rawe,
For they make many a man haue a feble mawe.
Babees Book (E. E. T. S.), p. 124.

They haue also a *Sallet* of hearbes and a Saweer of Vinegar set on the Table. *Purchas*, Pilgrimage, p. 206.

I often gathered wholesome herbs, which I boiled, or eat as *salads* with my bread. *Swift*, Gulliver's Travels, iv. 2.

2. Herbs for use as salad: colloquially restricted in the United States to lettuce.

After that they yede aboute gaderinge
Pleasaunt *salades*, which they made hem eate.
Flower and Leaf, l. 412.

3. A dish composed of some kind of meat, chopped and mixed with uncooked herbs, and seasoned with various condiments: as, chicken *salad*; lobster *salad*.—**Salad days**, days of youthful inexperience.

My *salad days*,
When I was green in judgement.
Shak., A. and C., i. 5. 73.

salad[2]†, *n.* See *sallet*[2].

salad-burnet (sal'ad-bėr'net), *n.* The common European burnet, *Poterium Sanguisorba*. It is used as a salad, and serves also as a sheep-fodder. See *burnet*[2], 2.

salade[1]†, *n.* An obsolete form of *salad*[1].

salade[2]†, *n.* See *sallet*[2].

salad-fork (sal'ad-fôrk), *n.* A fork used in mixing salads. See *salad-spoon*.

salading† (sal'ad-ing), *n.* [Formerly also *sallading*; < *salad*[1] + *-ing*[1].] Herbs for salads; also, the making of salads.

The Dutch have instructed the Natives [Tonquinese] in the art of Gardening: by which means they have abundance of Herbage for *Sallading*; which among other things is a great refreshment to the Dutch Sea-men when they arrive here. *Dampier*, Voyages, II. i. 12.

Their *sallading* was never far to seek,
The poignant water-grass, or savoury leek.
W. King, Art of Cookery, l. 493.

salad-oil (sal'ad-oil), *n.* Olive-oil, used in dressing salads and for other culinary purposes.

salad-plate (sal'ad-plāt), *n.* A small plate intended for salad; especially, such a plate of an unusual shape, intended for use with the large dinner-plate for meat or game, and designed not to take up much room on the table.

salad-rocket (sal'ad-rok'et), *n.* The garden-rocket, *Eruca sativa*.

salad-spoon (sal'ad-spön), *n.* A large spoon with a long handle, made of some material, as wood, not affected by vinegar, oil, etc., used for stirring and mixing salads. It is common to fix a spoon and fork together by means of a rivet, somewhat like a pair of scissors.

salagane (sal'a-gān), *n.* Same as *salangane*.

salagrama (sä-la-grä'mä), *n.* [Anglo-Ind. *salgram*; Hind. *sālagrāma*, *sāligrām*, < Skt. *çālagrāma*, name of a village where the stones are found.] A sort of stone sacred to Vishnu, and employed by the Brahmans in propitiatory rites. It is a fossil cephalopod, as an ammonite, a belemnite, etc. Such a stone, when found, is preserved as a precious talisman. It appears, however, that a great variety of petrifactions receive the general name *salagrama*.

Belemnites and Orthoceratites mineralized by the same material as the ammonites (iron clay and pyrites). Their abundance in the beds of mountain torrents, especially the Gundak, had been long known, as they form an indispensable article in the sacra of the Hindu Thakoordwaree, under the name of *Salagrama*.
Dr. Gerard, Asiat. Soc. of Calcutta, Oct., 1830.

salal-berry (sal'al-ber'i), *n.* A berry-like fruit about the size of a common grape, of a dark color and sweet flavor. It is the fruit of *Gaultheria Shallon*, the salal, a small shrubby plant about 1½ feet high, growing in Oregon and California.

salam, *n.* and *v.* See *salaam*.

salamander (sal'a-man-dėr), *n.* [< ME. *salamandre*, < OF. *salamandre*, *salemandre*, *salmendre*, F. *salamandre* = Pr. Sp. Pg. It. *salamandra* = D. G. Dan. Sw. *salamander*, < L. *salamandra*, < Gr. σαλαμάνδρα, a kind of lizard supposed to be an extinguisher of fire; of Eastern origin; cf. Pers. *samandar*, a salamander.] 1. A kind of lizard or other reptile formerly supposed to live in or be able to endure fire.

The more hit [gold] is ine nere [fire], the more hit is clene and clyer and tretable, ase the *salamandre* thet loueth ine the uere. *Ayenbite of Inwyt* (E. E. T. S.), p. 167.

The cameleon liveth by the ayre, and the *salamander* by the fire. *Nashe*, Lenten Stuffe (Harl. Misc., VI. 179).

Gratiana false?
The snow shall turn a *salamander* first,
And dwell in fire. *Shirley*, The Wedding, i. 4.

2. An imaginary or immaterial being of human form living in fire; an elemental of the fire; that one of the four classes of nature-spirits which corresponds to the element fire, the others being called *sylphs*, *undines*, and *gnomes*.

The sprites of fiery termagants in flame
Mount up, and take a *Salamander's* name.
Pope, R. of the L., i. 60.

3. In *zoöl.*, a urodele batrachian, or tailed amphibian; a newt or an eft; a triton; especially, a terrestrial batrachian of this kind, not having the tail compressed like a fin, as distinguished from one of the aquatic kinds especially called *newts* or *tritons*; specifically, a

member of the restricted family *Salamandridæ*. (See *Salamandra*.) It is a name of loose and comprehensive use. The two kinds of salamanders above noted are sometimes distinguished as *land-* and *water-salamanders*. All are harmless, timid creatures, with four legs and a tail, resembling lizards, but naked instead of scaly,

Red-backed Salamander (*Plethodon erythronotus*).

and otherwise quite different from any lacertilians. The species are very numerous, representing many genera and several families of *Urodela*, and are found in most parts of the northern hemisphere, in brooks and ponds, and moist places on land. They are mostly small, a few inches long, but some, as the menopome, menobranch, hellbender, mudpuppy, etc., of America, attain a length of a foot or more, and the giant salamander of Japan, *Megalobatrachus giganteus*, is some 3 feet long. See also cuts under *axolotl*, *hellbender*, *Menobranchus*, *newt*, and *Salamandra*. **4.** In *her.*, the representation of a four-legged creature with a long tail, surrounded by flames of fire. It is a modern bearing, and the flames are usually drawn in a realistic way.—**5.** The pocket-gopher of the South Atlantic and Mexican Gulf States, *Geomys tuza* or *G. pinetis*, a rodent mammal. [Local, U. S.]—**6.** Same as *bear*[2], 7. [Rarely used.]—**7.** Anything used in connection with the fire, or useful only when very hot, as a culinary vessel, a poker, an iron used red-hot to ignite gunpowder, and the like. [Colloq. or prov.]—**8.** A fire-proof safe. [Colloq.]

Salamandra (sal-ạ-man'drạ̈), *n.* [NL. (Laurenti), < L. *salamandra* = Gr. σαλαμάνδρα, a salamander: see *salamander*.] An old genus of urodele batrachians, formerly used with great

Spotted Salamander (*Salamandra maculosa*).

latitude, now made type of a special family, *Salamandridæ*, and restricted to such species as *S. maculosa*, the common spotted salamander of central and southern Europe.

Salamandridæ (sal-ạ-man'dri-dē), *n. pl.* [NL., < *Salamandra* + *-idæ*.] A family of urodele batrachians, typified by the genus *Salamandra*; the salamanders proper. They have palatine teeth in two longitudinal series diverging behind, inserted on the inner margin of two palatine processes which are much prolonged posteriorly, the parasphenoid toothless, the vertebræ opisthocœlian, and no postfronto-squamosal arch or ligament. None are American.

Salamandridea (sal″a-man-drid'ẹ̄-ạ̈), *n. pl.* [NL., < *Salamandra* + *-idea*.] A division of saurobatrachian or urodele *Amphibia*, having no branchiæ or branchial clefts in the adult, the vertebræ usually opisthocœlous, the carpus and tarsus more or less ossified, and eyelids present: a group contrasted with *Proteidea*.

salamandriform (sal-ạ-man'dri-fôrm), *a.* [< L. *salamandra*, a salamander, + *forma*, form.] Having the form of a salamander; having the characters of such urodele batrachians as salamanders.

The Labyrinthodonta were colossal animals of a *Salamandriform* type. *Pascoe*, Zoöl. Class., p. 194.

Salamandrina (sal″ạ-man-drī'nạ̈), *n.* [NL. (Fitzinger, 1826), < *Salamandra* + *-ina*[1].] A genus of salamanders, containing such species as *S. perspicillata* of southern Europe.

Salamandrinæ (sal″ạ-man-drī'nē), *n. pl.* [NL., < *Salamandra* + *-inæ*.] A suborder or superfamily of urodele batrachians, represented by such families as *Salamandridæ*, *Plethodontidæ*, and *Amblystomidæ*.

salamandrine (sal-ạ-man'drin), *a.* and *n.* [< L. *salamandra*, a salamander, + *-ine*[1].] **I.** *a.* **1.** Resembling the imaginary salamander in being able to resist fire, or capable of living in fire.

We laid it [a coquette's heart] into a pan of burning coals, when we observed in it a certain *salamandrine* quality, that made it capable of living in the midst of fire and flame, without being consumed, or so much as singed. *Addison*, Spectator, No. 281.

2. In *zoöl.*, of or pertaining to the *Salamandridæ* or *Salamandrinæ*; resembling or related to *Salamandra*; salamandriform or salamandroid.

II. *n.* In *zoöl.*, a salamander.

salamandroid (sal-ạ-man'droid), *a.* and *n.* [< Gr. σαλαμάνδρα, a salamander, + εἶδος, form.] **I.** *a.* In *zoöl.*, resembling a salamander, in a broad sense; salamandriform.

II. *n.* A member of the *Salamandrinæ*, or some similar urodele.

Salamandroides (sal″ạ-man-droi'dēz), *n.* [NL. (Jäger, 1828), < *Salamandra* + *-oides*.] A genus of fossil labyrinthodont amphibians, based on a species originally called *Labyrinthodon salamandroides*.

salamba (sa-lam'bạ̈), *n.* [E. Ind.] A kind of fishing-apparatus used on the banks near Manila, and common in the East, fitted upon a raft composed of several tiers of bamboos. It consists of a rectangular net, two corners of which are attached to the upper extremities of two long bamboos tied crosswise, their lower extremities being fastened to a bar on the raft, which acts as a hinge; a movable pole, arranged with a counterpoise as a sort of crane, supports the bamboos at the point of junction, and thus enables the fishermen to raise or depress the net at pleasure. The lower extremities of the net are guided by a cord, which is drawn toward the raft at the same time that the long bamboos are elevated by the crane and counterpoise; only a small part of the net thus remains in the water, and is easily cleared of its contents by means of a landing-net.

Salamis (sal'ạ-mis), *n.* [NL., < L. *Salamis*, < Gr. Σαλαμίς, the island of Salamis.] **1.** A genus of lepidopterous insects. *Boisduval*, 1833.—**2.** A genus of acalephs. *Lesson*, 1837.—**3.** A genus of coleopterous insects.

salamstone (sa-lam'stōn), *n.* [Tr. G. *salamstein*, a name given by Werner; as *salaam*, *salam*, + *stone*.] A variety of sapphire from Ceylon, generally of pale-reddish and bluish colors.

salangane (sal'ang-gān), *n.* [< F. *salangane*, < *salamga*, a native name, > NL. *Salangana* (Streubel, 1848).] A swift of the genus *Collocalia*, one of the birds which construct edible nests, as *C. esculenta*. Also *salagane*. See cut under *Collocalia*.

Salangidæ (sạ-lan'ji-dē), *n. pl.* [NL., < *Salanx* (*-ang-*) + *-idæ*.] A family of malacopterygian fishes, exemplified by the genus *Salanx*. The body is elongated and compressed, naked or with deciduous scales; the head is elongate, much depressed, and produced into a flat snout; the mouth is deeply cleft, with conical teeth on the jaws and palate; the dorsal fin is far behind the ventrals, but in advance of the anal; a small adipose fin is developed; the alimentary canal is straight and without pyloric appendages. Only one species, *Salanx sinensis*, is known; it occurs along the coast of China, and is regarded as a delicacy. To the foreign residents it is known as *whitebait*.

Salangina (sal-an-jī'nạ̈), *n. pl.* The *Salangidæ* as a group of *Salmonidæ*. *Günther*.

Salanx (sā'langks), *n.* [NL. (Cuvier, 1817).] A genus of salmonoid fishes, typical of the family *Salangidæ* (which see).

salaried (sal'ạ-rid), *a.* [< *salary*[1] + *-ed*[2].] In receipt of a fixed salary or stipulated pay, as distinguished from *honorary*, or without pay, or remunerated by fees only; having a fixed or stipulated salary: as, a *salaried* inspector; a *salaried* office; a *salaried* post.

He knew he was no poet, yet he would string wretched rhymes, even when not *salaried* for them. *I. D'Israeli*, Quar. of Authors, p. 107.

I have had two professors of Arabic and Mohammedan religion and law as my regular *salaried* tutors. *E. W. Lane*, Modern Egyptians, Pref., p. viii.

salary[1] (sal'ạ-ri), *n.*; pl. *salaries* (-riz). [Formerly also *sallery*; < ME. *salary*, *salarye*, < OF. *salarie*, *salaire*, *salayre*, *sollaire*, F. *salaire* = Pr. *salari*, *selari* = Sp. Pg. It. *salario*, < L. *salarium*, a stipend, salary, pension, orig. (sc. *argentum*, money) 'salt-money,' money given to soldiers for salt, neut. of *salarius*, belonging to salt, < *sal*, salt: see *sal*[1] and *salt*[1]. Cf. *seller*[2], *cellar* in *salt-cellar*.] The recompense or consideration stipulated to be paid to a person periodically for services, usually a fixed sum to be paid by the year, half-year, or quarter. See *wages*.

And my seruauntz some tyme her *salarye* is bihynde,
Reuthe is to here the rekenynge whan we shal rede acomptes;
So with wikked wille and wraththe my werkmen I paye.
Piers Plowman (B), v. 433.

O, this is hire and *salary*, not revenge.
Shak., Hamlet, iii. 3. 79.

Never a more popular pastor than Mr. Wall the uncle, yet never a more painful duty than that of collecting, in that region, the pastor's *salary*. *W. M. Baker*, New Timothy, p. 24.

Salary grab. See *grab*[1].=**Syn.** *Salary*, *Stipend*, *Wages*, *Pay*, *Hire*, *Allowance*. An *allowance* is gratuitous or discretionary, and may be of any sort: as, an *allowance* of a pitcher of wine daily to Chaucer; the rest are given from time to time in return for regular work of some kind, and are presumably in the form of money. Of these latter *pay* is the most generic; it is especially used of the soldier. *Wages* and *hire* are for the more menial, manual, or mechanical forms of work, and commonly imply employment for short periods, as a day or a week; *salary* and *stipend* are for the more mental forms, and imply greater permanence of employment and payment at longer intervals: the *wages* of a servant or a laborer; the *salary* of a postmaster or a teacher. *Hire* is Biblical and old-fashioned. *Stipend* is used chiefly as a technical term of the English and Scotch churches. See *wages*.

salary[1] (sal'ạ-ri), *v. t.*; pret. and pp. *salaried*, ppr. *salarying*. [< *salary*[1], *n.*] To pay a salary to, or connect a salary with: chiefly used in the past participle. See *salaried*.

salary[2]† (sal'ạ-ri), *a.* [< L. *salarius*, of or belonging to salt, < *sal*, salt: see *sal*[1] and *salt*[1], and cf. *salary*[1], *n.*] Saline.

From such *salary* irradiations may those wondrous variations arise which are observable in animals. *Sir T. Browne*, Vulg. Err., p. 338.

Salda (sal'dạ̈), *n.* [NL. (Fabricius, 1803); from a proper name.] A genus of heteropterous insects, or true bugs, typical of the family *Saldidæ*. They are of small size and varied coloration, and are found mainly upon the sea-beach, where they feed upon the remains of drowned flies and other insects. The species are numerous and mostly American. About 30 are known in North America. Sometimes called *Acanthia*.

sal-dammar (sal'dam″ạ̈r), *n.* [< *sal*[2] + *dammar*.] A whitish aromatic resin obtained in India from the sal-tree by tapping. It occasionally appears in European markets.

Saldidæ (sal'di-dē), *n. pl.* [NL., < *Salda* + *-idæ*.] A family of true bugs, belonging to Westwood's section *Aurocorisa* of the *Heteroptera*, and comprising forms of small size which inhabit damp soils and are often found in countless numbers on the salt and brackish marshes of the sea-coast. They are oval in shape, with a free head and prominent eyes, and are of a black, brown, or drab color marked with yellow or white. They are mainly American.

sale[1] (sāl), *n.* [< ME. *sale*, < AS. *sala*, a sale (= OHG. *sala*, MHG. *sale*, *sal*, a delivery, = Icel. *sala*, f., *sal*, n., a sale, bargain, = Sw. *salu* = Dan. *salg*, a sale), < *sellan* (√ *sal*), give, give over, sell: see *sell*[1].] **1.** The act of selling; also, a specific act or a continuous process of selling; the exchange or disposal of a commodity, right, property, or whatever may be the subject of bargain, for a price agreed on and generally payable in money, as distinguished from barter; the transfer of all right and property in a thing for a price to be paid in money.

They shall have like portions to eat, beside that which cometh of the *sale* of his patrimony. Deut. xviii. 8.

The most considerable offices in church and state were put up to *sale*. *Prescott*, Ferd. and Isa., ii. 25.

2. In *law*, a contract for the transfer of property from one person to another, for a valuable consideration. Three things are requisite to its validity, namely the thing sold, which is the object of the contract, the price, and the consent of the contracting parties. (*Kent.*) The word *sale* is often used more specifically as indicating the consideration to be pecuniary, as distinguished from *barter* or *exchange*. It is also often used as indicating a present transfer, as distinguished from a contract to transfer at a future time, which is sometimes termed an *executory sale*. In respect to real property, *sale* usually means the executory contract or bargain, as distinguished from the deed of conveyance in fulfilment of the bargain. **3.** Opportunity to sell; demand; market.

The countrymen will be more industrious in tillage, and rearing of all husbandry commodities, knowing that they shall have a ready *sale* for them at those towns. *Spenser*.

4. Disposal by auction or public outcry.

Those that won the plate, and those thus sold, ought to be marked, so that they may never return to the race or to the *sale*. *Sir W. Temple*.

Purchase corrupted pardon of a man,
Who in that *sale* sells pardon from himself.
Shak., K. John, iii. 1. 167.

Account sales. See *account*.—**Aleatory sale.** See *aleatory*.—**Bargain and sale.** See *bargain*.—**Bill of sale.** See *bill*[3].—**Cognition and sale.** See *cognition*.—**Conditional sale.** See *conditional*.—**Conditions of sale.** See *condition*.—**Distress sale.** See *distress*.—**Executory sale,** a sale in which the thing disposed of is to be delivered at a future time.—**Forced sale**, a sale compelled by a creditor or other claimant, without regard to the interest of the owner to be favored with delay in order to secure a full price.—**Foreclosure and sale.** See *foreclosure*.—**House of sale†**, a brothel. [Slang.]

> I saw him enter such a *house of sale*,
> Videlicet, a brothel, or so forth.
> *Shak.*, Hamlet, ii. 1. 60.

Judicial sale. See *judicial*.—**Memorandum sale.** See *memorandum*.—**Of sale.** Same as *on sale*.—**On sale**, for sale, to be sold; offered to purchasers.—**Power of sale.** See *power*[1].—**Ranking and sale.** See *ranking*.—**Regular sales.** See *regular*.—**Rummage sale.** See *rummage*.—**Sale by candle.** Same as *auction by inch of candle* (which see, under *auction*).—**Sale of indulgences.** See *indulgence*.—**Sale of Land by Auction Act**, an English statute of 1867 (30 and 31 Vict., c. 48), making auction sales of land which are invalid in law (by reason of the employment of a puffer) invalid also in equity; discontinuing the practice of opening biddings by order in chancery, except for fraud; and prescribing rules to govern sales of land by auction.—**Sale to arrive**, a sale of merchandise which is in transit, the sale being dependent on its arrival.—**Terms of sale.** (a) The conditions to be imposed upon and assented to by a purchaser, as distinguished from *price*. (b) The price.—**To cover short sales.** See *cover*[1].—**To set to sale†**, to offer for sale; make merchandise of.

> His tongue is *set to sale*, he is a mere voice.
> *Burton*, Anat. of Mel., To the Reader, p. 71.

> His modesty, *set* there *to sale* in the frontispice, is not much addicted to blush.
> *Milton*, Apology for Smectymnuus.

Wash sales, in the stock-market, feigned sales, made for the sake of advantage gained by the report of a fictitious price.

sale[2]**†**, *n.* [< ME. *sale*, a hall, < AS. *sæl*, *sel*, a house, hall, = MD. *sael*, D. *zaal*, a parlor, room, = MLG. *sal*, *sâl* = OHG. MHG. *sal*, G. *saal*, a dwelling, house, hall, room, chamber, = Icel. *salr* = Sw. Dan. *sal*, a hall (cf. OF. *sale*, F. *salle* = Pr. Sp. Pg. It. *sala*, a hall, < Teut.); cf. AS. *salor*, also *sele* = OS. *seli*, a hall (OS. *selihûs* = OHG. *seli-hûs*, hall-house); OHG. *selida*, MHG. *selde* = Goth. *salithwa*, a mansion, guest-chamber, lodging; Goth. *saljan*, dwell; prob. akin to OBulg. *selo*, ground, Bulg. *selo*, a village, = Serv. *selo* = Pol. *siolo*, *sielo* = Russ. *selo*, a village, OBulg. *selitva*, a dwelling; L. *sŏlum*, soil, ground: see *sole*[2], *soil*[1]. Hence (through F.) E. *saloon*, *salon*.] A hall.

> He helpe us in alle at heuene 3ate,
> With seintis to sitte there in *sale!*
> *Hymns to Virgin*, etc. (E. E. T. S.), p. 57.

sale[3]**†** (sāl), *n.* [Ult. < AS. *seal*, *sealh*, willow: see *sallow*[1], *sally*[1].] Willow; osier; also, a basket-like net.

> To make . . . baskets of bulrushes was my wont;
> Who to entrappe the fish in winding *sale*
> Was better seene? *Spenser*, Shep. Cal., December.

saleability, saleable, etc. See *salability*, etc.

salebrosity (sal-ē-bros'i-ti), *n.* [< L. *salebrosita(t-)s, < *salebrosus*, rough, rugged: see *salebrous*.] The state or character of being salebrous, or rough or rugged. [Rare.]

> There is a blaze of honour guilding the bryers, and inticing the mind; yet is not this without its thorns and *salebrosity*. *Feltham*, On Eccles. ii. 2.

salebrous (sal'ē-brus), *a.* [< F. *salébreux*, < L. *salebrosus*, rugged, uneven, < *salebra*, i. e. *via*, a rugged, uneven road, < *salire*, leap, jump: see *sail*[2], *salient*.] Rough; rugged; uneven. [Rare.]

> We now again proceed
> Thorough a vale that's *salebrous* indeed.
> *Cotton*, Wonders of the Peake, p. 54.

saleetah (sa-lē'tä), *n.* [E. Ind. (?).] A bag of gunny-cloth, containing a soldier's bedding, tents, etc., while on the march.

Salenia (sa-lē'ni-ä), *n.* [NL. (J. E. Gray).] The typical genus of *Saleniidæ*. *S. rarispina* is an extant species. *S. petalifera* is found fossil in the greensand of Wiltshire, England.

Saleniidæ (sal-ē-nī'i-dē), *n. pl.* [NL., < *Salenia* + *-idæ*.] A family of chiefly fossil sea-urchins, typified by the genus *Salenia*, belonging to the *Endocyclica*, or regular echinoids, but having the anus displaced by one or more supernumerary apical plates.

salep, salop (sal'ep, -op), *n.* [Also *saleb*; = F. Sp. *salep* = Pg. *salepo*, *salepo* = D. G. Sw. Dan. *salep*, < Turk. *saleb*, *salleb*, < Ar. *sahleb*, salep.] A drug consisting of the decorticated and dried tubers of numerous orchidaceous plants, chiefly of the genus *Orchis*. It is composed of small hard, horny bodies, oval or ovoid in form or sometimes palmate, in different degrees translucent, and nearly scentless and tasteless. *Orchis Morio* and *O. mascula* are perhaps the leading species yielding the rounded kinds, and *O. latifolia* the chief source of the palmate. Species of *Eulophia* are assigned as sources of salep in India. The salep of the European market is prepared chiefly in Asia Minor, and in small quantities in Germany; that of the Indian market is from Persia and Tibet, or local. Salep contains 48 per cent. of mucilage and 30 per cent. of starch; it is largely insoluble in water, but swells up when steeped. In the East it is highly esteemed as a nervine restorative and fattener; but it appears to have no other properties than those of a nutrient and demulcent. In Europe it is chiefly used in making a variously seasoned demulcent drink. It is a suitable food for convalescents, etc., like tapioca and sago. It is prepared for use by pulverizing and boiling. In America it is but little known.—**Otaheite** or **Tahiti salep**, a starch derived from the tuberous roots of *Tacca pinnatifida* in the Society, Fiji, and other Pacific islands; Tahiti or South Sea arrowroot; tacca-starch.

sale-pond (sāl'pond), *n.* See *pond*[1].

saleratus (sal-e-rā'tus), *n.* [Also *salæratus* (for **salaëratus*); orig. (NL.) *sal aeratus*, aërated salt: see *aërate* and *salt*[1].] Originally potassium bicarbonate, but at present sodium bicarbonate is commonly sold under the same name. It is used in cookery for neutralizing acidity and for raising dough by the evolution of carbonic acid which takes place when it is brought in contact with an acid. It is also largely used in so-called baking-powders.

saler†, salere†, *n.* See *seller*[3].

sale-room (sāl'röm), *n.* A room in which goods are sold; specifically, an auction-room. Often also *salesroom*.

Salesian (sā-lē'shian), *n.* [< St. Francis of *Sales*: see *visitant*.] A member of a Roman Catholic order of nuns: same as *visitant*.

saleslady (sālz'lā'di), *n.*; pl. *salesladies* (-diz). A saleswoman; a woman who waits upon customers in a shop or store. [Vulgar, U. S.]

> He shows the crowded state of the poor in cities, how sewing-women, and even "*sales-ladies*," work from fourteen to sixteen hours a day for pittances scarcely sufficient to support life. *Harper's Mag.*, LXXVIII.

salesman (sālz'man), *n.*; pl. *salesmen* (-men). One whose occupation is the selling of goods or merchandise. Specifically—(a) One who sells some commodity at wholesale. (b) A commercial traveler. [U. S.] (c) A man who waits on customers in a shop or store.—**Dead salesman**, a wholesale dealer in butcher-meat; one who disposes of consignments of dead meat by auction or other mode of sale. [Eng.]

salesroom (sālz'röm), *n.* Same as *sale-room*.

saleswoman (sālz'wum"an), *n.*; pl. *saleswomen* (-wim"en). A woman who waits upon customers in a shop or store, and exhibits wares to them for sale.

salet†, *n.* An obsolete form of *sallet*[2].

sale-tongued† (sāl'tungd), *a.* Mercenary.

> So *sale-tongu'd* lawyers, wresting eloquence,
> Excuse rich wrong, and cast poore innocence.
> *Sylvester*, tr. of Du Bartas. (*Nares.*)

sale-wares† (sāl'wārz), *n. pl.* Merchandise.

> All our *sale-wares* which we had left we cast away.
> *R. Knox* (Arber's Eng. Garner, I. 415).

salewe†, *v.* and *n.* See *salue*.

salework (sāl'wėrk), *n.* [< *sale*[1] + *work*.] Work or things made for sale; hence, work carelessly done.

> I see no more in you than in the ordinary
> Of nature's *sale-work*.
> *Shak.*, As you Like it, iii. 5. 43.

Salian[1] (sā'li-an), *a.* and *n.* [< LL. *Salii*, a tribe of Franks, + *-an*.] **I.** *a.* Of or belonging to a tribe of Franks settled along the lower Rhine near the North Sea. See *Franconian* and *Frank*[1].

II. *n.* A member of this tribe of Franks.

Salian[2] (sā'li-an), *a.* [< L. *Salii*, a college of priests of Mars, lit. 'leapers,' < *salire*, leap: see *sail*[2], *salient*.] Of or pertaining to the Salii or priests of Mars in ancient Rome.—**Salian hymns**, songs sung at an annual festival by the priests of Mars, in praise of that deity, of other gods, and of distinguished men. The songs were accompanied by warlike dances, the clashing of ancilia (shields of a peculiar form), etc.

saliant (sā'li-ant), *a.* In *her.*, same as *salient*.

saliaunce†, saliance†, *n.* [Cf. *sálience*.] Assault or sally.

> Now mote I weet,
> Sir Guyon, why with so fierce *saliaunce*
> And fell intent ye did at earst me meet.
> *Spenser*, F. Q., II. i. 29.

Salic (sal'ik), *a.* [Also *Salique*; < OF. (and F.) *salique* = Sp. *sálico* = Pg. It. *salico*, < ML. *Salicus*, pertaining to the Salians (*lex Salica*, the Salic law), < LL. *Salii*, a tribe of Franks: see *Salian*[1].] Based on or contained in the code of the Salian Franks: specifically applied to one of the laws in that code which excluded women from inheriting certain lands, probably because certain military duties were connected with such inheritance. In the fourteenth century females were excluded from the throne of France by the application of this law to the succession to the crown, and it is in this sense that the phrase *Salic law* is commonly used.

> A French antiquarian (Claude Seissel) had derived the name of the *Salic Law* from the Latin word *sal*, comme une loy pleine de sel, c'est à dire pleine de sapience, and this the Doctor thought a far more rational etymology than what some one proposed, either seriously or in sport, that the law was called *Salique* because the words Si aliquis and Si aliqua were of such frequent occurrence in it. *Southey*, The Doctor, ccviii. (*Davies.*)

> The famous clause in the *Salic Law* by which, it is commonly said, women are precluded from succession to the throne, and which alone has become known in course of time as the *Salic Law*, is the fifth paragraph of chapter 59 (with the rubric "De Alodis"), in which the succession to private property is regulated. *Encyc. Brit.*, XXI. 214.

Salicaceæ (sal-i-kā'sē-ē), *n. pl.* [NL. (Lindley, 1836), < *Salix* (*Salic-*) + *-aceæ*.] Same as *Salicineæ*.

salicaceous (sal-i-kā'shius), *a.* [< L. *salix* (*salic-*), a willow, + *-aceous*.] Of or pertaining to the willow or the order *Salicineæ*.

salicarian (sal-i-kā'ri-an), *a.* [< *Salicaria*, a genus of birds, now obsolete, + *-an*.] Pertaining to the former genus *Salicaria*, now *Calamoherpe*, *Acrocephalus*, etc., as a reed-warbler; acrocephaline.

salicet (sal'i-set), *n.* [< L. *salix* (*salic-*), a willow, + *-et*.] Same as *salicional*.

salicetum (sal-i-sē'tum), *n.*; pl. *salicetums* or *saliceta* (-tumz, -tä). [L., also *salictum*, a thicket of willows, < *salix* (*salic-*), a willow: see *sallow*[1].] A willow-plantation; a scientific collection of growing willows.

salicin (sal'i-sin), *n.* [< L. *salix* (*salic-*), a willow, + *-in*[2].] A neutral crystalline glucoside ($C_{13}H_{18}O_7$), of a bitter taste. It occurs in the form of colorless or white silky crystals, and is obtained from the bark of various species of willow and poplar. It possesses tonic properties, and is sometimes used as a substitute for salicylic acid in the treatment of rheumatism.

Salicineæ (sal-i-sin'ē-ē), *n. pl.* [NL. (L. C. Richard, 1828), < *Salix* (*Salic-*) + *-in-eæ*.] A well-defined order of apetalous plants, little related to any other. It is characterized by diœcious inflorescence with both sorts of flowers in catkins, a perianth or disk either cup-shaped or reduced to gland-like scales, two or more stamens to each flower, and a one-celled ovary becoming in fruit a two- to four-valved capsule with numerous minute seeds which bear a long dense tuft of white hairs at one end. There are 178 (or, as some estimate them, 300) species, natives of temperate and cold regions, widely scattered throughout the world, rarer in the tropics, and very few in the southern hemisphere. They are trees or shrubs, bearing alternate entire or toothed leaves, tree stipules, and catkins produced before or with the leaves, often clothed with long silky hairs. The order is composed of but two genera, *Salix* (the type) and *Populus*. Also *Salicaceæ*.

salicional (sā-lish'on-al), *n.* [< L. *salix* (*salic-*), a willow, + *-ion* (as in *accordion*, etc.) + *-al*.] In *organ-building*, a stop closely resembling the dulciana, and deriving its name from its delicate reedy tone, which resembles that produced by a willow pipe. Also *salicet*.

Salicornia (sal-i-kôr'ni-ä), *n.* [NL. (Tournefort, 1700), < F. *salicorne*, *salicor*, glasswort, saltwort, < L. *sal*, salt, + *cornu*, horn.] A genus of apetalous plants of the order *Chenopodiaceæ*, type of the tribe *Salicornieæ*, having the flowers immersed in hollows of the upper joints of the stem, from which the two light-yellow anthers protrude. The small fleshy three- or four-toothed perianth becomes spongy and thickened in fruit, inclosing the ovoid utricle, which contains a single erect seed destitute of albumen, having a conduplicate embryo with two thickish seed-leaves. The 8 species are native of saline soils throughout the world, and are remarkable for their smooth, fleshy, leafless, and jointed stems, erect or decumbent, and bearing many short branches, their numerous joints dilated above into sheaths which form a socket partly inclosing the next higher joint. Their inconspicuous flowers form terminal fleshy and cylindrical spikes closely resembling the branches. See *glasswort* and *marsh-samphire*, also *crab-grass*, 2, and *jume*.

Salicornieæ (sal"i-kôr-ni'ē-ē), *n. pl.* [NL. (Dumortier, 1827), < *Salicornia* + *-eæ*.] A tribe of apetalous plants of the order *Chenopodiaceæ*. It is characterized by bisexual flowers immersed in the axils of scales of a cone or in hollows of the stem, and by the fruit which is a utricle included in an unappendaged and generally somewhat enlarged perianth. It includes 11 genera and about 81 species, many of them natives of salt-marshes. They are herbs or fleshy shrubs, with continuous or jointed branches, often leafless.

salicyl (sal'i-sil), *n.* [< L. *salix* (*salic-*), willow, + *-yl*.] The hypothetical radical of salicylic acid, $C_6H_4.OH.CO$.

> In relieving pain and lessening fever in acute rheumatism the *salicyl* treatment is undoubtedly the most effective we know of. *Lancet*, No. 3431, p. 1086.

salicylate (sal'i-sil-āt), *n.* [< *salicyl*(*ic*) + *-ate*[1].] A salt of salicylic acid.

salicylated (sal'i-si-lā-ted), *a.* [< *salicyl*(*ic*) + *-ate*[1] + *-ed*[2].] Mixed or impregnated with, or combined with, salicylic acid: as, *salicylated* cotton.—**Salicylated camphor**, an antiseptic preparation made by heating camphor (84 parts) with salicylic acid (65 parts), which gives an oily liquid, solid when cold.—**Salicylated cotton.** Same as *salicylic cotton*. See *salicylic*.

salicylic (sal-i-sil'ik), *a.* [< L. *salix* (*salic-*), willow, + *-yl* + *-ic*.] Derived from the willow: applied to a number of benzene derivatives which may be derived from the glucoside salicin found in the bark and leaves of willows.—**Salicylic acid**, an acid ($C_6H_4.OH.CO_2H$) obtained from oil of wintergreen, from salicin, and from other sources. It crystallizes in tufts of slender prisms, which are odorless, with an astringent taste and a slightly irritating effect on the fauces. It is prepared commercially by the action of carbonic acid on sodium phenol (sodium carbolate). Salicylic acid has come into very general use as an antiseptic, and, being devoid of active poisonous properties, is employed for preserving foods, etc., from decay. It is also used in acute articular rheumatism and in myalgia.—**Salicylic aldehyde**, the aldehyde of salicylic acid, $C_6H_4.OH.COH$, which occurs in the volatile oil of *Spiræa*. It is an oily liquid with aromatic odor, soluble in water, and readily oxidized to salicylic acid.—**Salicylic or salicylated cotton**, absorbent cotton impregnated with salicylic acid and used as an antiseptic dressing.—**Salicylic ether**, an ether formed by the combination of salicylic acid with an alcohol radical. Oil of wintergreen is salicylic methyl ether.

salicylism (sal'i-sil-izm), *n.* Toxic effects produced by salicylic acid.

salience (sā'li-ens), *n.* [< *salien(t)* + *-ce*. Cf. the older form *saliance*.] 1. The fact or condition of being salient; the state of projecting or being projected; projection; protrusion.

The thickness and *salience* of the external frontal table remains apparent. *Sir W. Hamilton.*

2. A projection; any part or feature of an object or whole which protrudes or juts out beyond its general surface, as a molding considered with reference to a wall which it decorates.

Saliences are indicated conventionally [in medieval illumination] by paling the colour, while depressions are expressed by deepening it. *C. H. Moore*, Gothic Architecture, p. 299.

saliency (sā'li-en-si), *n.* Same as *salience*.

salient (sā'li-ent), *a.* and *n.* [An altered form, to suit the L. spelling, of earlier *saliant* (in her.), **saillant*, < F. *saillant*, < L. *salien(t-)s*, ppr. of *salire*, leap, spring forth (> It. *salire* = Sp. *salir* = Pg. *sahir* = Pr. *salir*, *salhir*, *sallir* = F. *saillir*, > E. obs. *sail*[2]), = Gr. ἅλλεσθαι, leap (> E. *halter*[2], etc.). From the same L. verb are ult. E. *sail*[2], *assail* (*sail*[3]), *sally*[2], *assault*, *sault*[1], *saltation*, *saltier*, *exult*, *insult*, result, *desultory*, *resilient*, *salmon*, etc.] I. *a.* 1. Leaping; bounding; jumping; moving by leaps; specifically, in *herpet.*, saltatorial; habitually leaping or jumping, as a frog or toad; of or pertaining to the *Salientia*.

The legs of both sides moving together, as in frogs and *saliant* animals, is properly called leaping. *Sir T. Browne*, Vulg. Err., iv. 6.

2. In *her.*, leaping or springing: said of a beast of prey which is represented bendwise on the escutcheon, the hind feet together at the sinister base, and the fore paws raised and usually on a level, though sometimes separate, nearly as when rampant. Also *saliant*, *assailant*, *effaré*.—3. Shooting up or out; springing up.

A Lion Salient.

He had in himself a *salient* living spring of generous and manly action. *Burke*, To a Noble Lord.

Who best can send on high
The *salient* spout, far streaming to the sky?
Pope, Dunciad, ii. 162.

4. Projecting outward; convex: as, a *salient* angle.—5. Standing out; conspicuous; prominent; striking.

There are people who seem to have no notion of sketching a character, or observing and describing *salient* points, either in persons or things. *Charlotte Brontë*, Jane Eyre, xi.

The antiphonary furnished the anthems or verses for the beginning of the communion, the offertory, and other *salient* passages of the office. *A. W. Ward*, Eng. Dram. Lit., I. 20.

Mr. John Westbrook, . . . known, from his swarthy looks and *salient* features, as "Jew Westbrook." *E. Dowden*, Shelley, I. 142.

Salient angle. (*a*) In *fort.* See *bastion*. (*b*) In *geom.*, an angle bending toward the interior of a closed figure, as an ordinary angle of a polygon: opposed to *reëntrant angle*.—**Salient batrachians.** Same as *Salientia*, 1.

II. *n.* A salient angle or part; a projection.

I fired my revolver through the angle of the case, so as to make a hole in the tin. Having first made this lodgement in the *salient*, the rest of the work was easy. *W. H. Russell*, Diary in India, I. 162.

Some of them, in the impetus of the assault, went even inside one of the *salients* of the work. *N. A. Rev.*, CXLIII. 46.

Salientia (sā-li-en'shi-ä), *n. pl.* [NL., < L. *salien(t-)s*, ppr. of *salire*, leap, spring: see *salient*.] 1. In *herpet.*, an old name, originating with Laurenti, 1768, of salient or saltatorial amphibians, as frogs and toads: synonymous with *Anura*, and with *Batrachia* in a restricted sense.—2†. In Illiger's classification (1811), the third order of mammals, containing the kangaroos and potoroos—that is, those marsupials which he did not class with the *Quadrumana* in his second order *Pollicata*.

saliently (sā'li-ent-li), *adv.* In a salient manner, in any sense of *salient*.

salière (sa-liãr'), *n.* [F.: see *seller*[3].] A salt-cellar.

saliferous (sā-lif'e-rus), *a.* [< L. *sal*, salt, + *ferre* = E. *bear*[1].] In *geol.*, noting a formation containing a considerable amount of rock-salt, or yielding brine in economically valuable quantity. Saliferous beds are found in almost all the divisions of the geological series, from the lowest to the highest.—**Saliferous system**, in *geol.*, a name sometimes given to the Triassic series, because some of the most important salt-deposits of Europe occupy this geological position.

salifiable (sal'i-fi-a-bl), *a.* [= F. *salifiable* = Sp. *salificable* = It. *salificabile*; as *salify* + *-able*.] Capable of being salified, or of combining with an acid to form a salt.

salification (sal'i-fi-kā'shon), *n.* [= F. *salification*; as *salify* + *-ation* (see *-fication*).] The act of salifying, or the state of being salified.

salify (sal'i-fi), *v. t.*; pret. and pp. *salified*, ppr. *salifying*. [= F. *salifier* = It. *salificare*, < L. *sal*, salt, + *-ficare*, < *facere*, make (see *-fy*).] To form into a salt, as by combination with an acid.

saligot (sal'i-got), *n.* [Also *salligot*; < OF. *saligots*, "saligots, water caltrops, water nuts" (Cotgrave).] 1. The water-chestnut, *Trapa natans*.—2. A ragout of tripe. *Davies.*

He himself made the wedding with fine sheeps-heads, brave haslets with mustard, gallant *salligots* with garlic (tribars aux ails). *Urquhart*, tr. of Rabelais, ii. 31.

Salii (sā'li-ī), *n. pl.* [L. *Salii*: see *Salian*[2].] The priests of Mars, in ancient Rome: according to tradition their college was established by Numa Pompilius. See *Salian*[2].

salimeter (sā-lim'e-tėr), *n.* [< L. *sal*, salt, + Gr. μέτρον, measure.] Same as *salinometer*, 1.

salimetry (sā-lim'e-tri), *n.* [< L. *sal*, salt, + Gr. -μετρία, < μέτρον, measure.] Same as *salinometry*.

salina (sā-lī'nā), *n.* [Sp. *salina*: see *saline*, *n.*] A saline; salt-works; any place where salt is deposited, gathered, or manufactured.

In a large *salina*, northward of the Rio Negro, the salt at the bottom, during the whole year, is between two and three feet in thickness. *Darwin*, Geol. Observations, ii. 309.

Salina group. Same as *Onondaga salt-group*. See *salt-group*.

salination (sal-i-nā'shon), *n.* [< *saline* + *-ation*.] The act of washing with or soaking in salt liquor.

The Egyptians might have been accustomed to wash the body with the same pickle they used in *salination*. *Greenhill*, Art of Embalming, p. 59.

saline (sā-līn' or sā'līn), *a.* [< OF. (and F.) *salin* = Sp. Pg. It. *salino*, < L. **salinus* (found only in neut. *salinum*, salt-cellar, and pl. fem. *salinæ*, salt-pits: see *saline*, *n.*), < *sal*, salt: see *salt*[1] and *sal*[1].] 1. Consisting of salt or constituting salt: as, *saline* particles; *saline* substances.—2. Of, pertaining to, or characteristic of salt; salty: as, a *saline* taste.

With bacon, mass *saline*, where never lean
Beneath the brown and bristly rind was seen.
Crabbe, Works, IV. 154.

A delicious *saline* scent of sea-weed. *Harper's Mag.*, LXXVII. 630.

Saline bath, a bath used as a substitute for sea-water, containing 36 ounces of salt to 60 gallons of water.—**Saline infiltration**, the deposit of various salts in a tissue, as in calcareous degeneration.—**Saline mixture**, lemon-juice and potassium bicarbonate.—**Saline purgative**, a salt with purgative properties, such as magnesium or sodium sulphate, sodiopotassium tartrate, magnesium carbonate, etc.—**Saline waters**, waters impregnated with salts, especially spring waters which contain considerable quantities of salts of the alkalis and alkaline earths, used as medicines.

saline (sā-līn' or sā'līn), *n.* [< F. *saline* = Sp. Pg. It. *salina*, < L. *salinæ*, salt-works, salt-pits, pl. of *salina*, fem. of adj. (cf. ML. *salina*, L. and ML. *salinum*, a salt-cellar) **salinus*, of salt: see *saline*, *a.*] A salt-spring, or a place where salt water is collected in the earth; a salt-marsh or -pit.

The most part of all the salt they haue in Venice commeth from these *Salines*. *Hakluyt's Voyages*, II. 108.

The waters of the bay were already marbling over the *salines* and half across the island. *Harper's Mag.*, LXXVI. 739.

salineness (sā-līn'nes), *n.* [< *saline* + *-ness*.] Saline character or condition. *Imp. Dict.*

saliniferous (sal-i-nif'e-rus), *a.* [Irreg. < L. **salinus*, of salt (see *saline*), + *ferre* = E. *bear*[1].] Producing salt.

saliniform (sā-lin'i-fôrm), *a.* [Irreg. < L. **salinus*, of salt (see *saline*), + *forma*, form.] Having the form of salt.

salinity (sā-lin'i-ti), *n.* [= F. *salinité*; as *saline* + *-ity*.] Saline or salty character or quality; degree of saltiness; salineness.

It is shown by a glance at the charts that there are areas in the ocean of great *salinity* and areas of great dilution. *Nature*, XXX. 314.

salinometer (sal-i-nom'e-tėr), *n.* [< L. **salinus*, of salt (see *saline*), + Gr. μέτρον, measure.] 1. A form of hydrometer for measuring the amount of salt present in any given solution. The numbers on the stem (see figure) show the percentages of strength for the depths to which the instrument sinks in a solution. Also *salimeter*, *salometer*. 2. A similar apparatus used for indicating the density of brine in the boilers of marine steam-engines, and thus showing when they should be cleansed by blowing off the deposit left by the salt water, which tends to injure the boilers as well as to diminish their evaporating power. Also called *salt-gage*.

Salinometer.

salinometer-pot (sal-i-nom'e-tėr-pot), *n.* A vessel in which water from a boiler may be drawn to test it for brine by the salinometer.

salinometry (sal-i-nom'e-tri), *n.* [< L. **salinus*, of salt, + Gr. -μετρία, < μέτρον, measure.] The use of the salinometer. Also *salimetry*, *salometry*.

salinoterrene (sā-lī'nō-te-rēn'), *a.* [< L. **salinus*, of salt (see *saline*), + *terrenus*, of earth: see *terrene*.] Pertaining to or composed of salt and earth.

salinous† (sā-lī'nus), *a.* [< L. **salinus*, of salt: see *saline*.] Same as *saline*.

When wood and many other bodies do petrifie . . . we do not usually ascribe their induration to cold, but rather unto *salinous* spirits, concretive juices, and causes circumjacent, which do assimilate all bodies not indisposed for their impressions. *Sir T. Browne*, Vulg. Err., ii. 1.

Salique† (sal'ik or sa-lēk'), *a.* Same as *Salic*.

Salisburia (sal-is-bū'ri-ä), *n.* [NL. (Sir James Smith, 1798), named after R. A. *Salisbury*, an English botanist (born 1762).] A former genus of coniferous trees, now known by the earlier name *Ginkgo* (Kaempfer, 1712). The change of name was proposed on the ground that *Ginkgo* (also spelled *Gingko*) was a barbarism, a reason which is not accepted by the modern rules of nomenclature. See *maiden-hair-tree*, and cut under *gingko*.

Salisbury boot. See *boot*[2].

salite[1]† (sā'līt), *v. t.* [< L. *salitus*, pp. of *salire*, salt, < *sal*, salt: see *sal*[1], *salt*[1].] To salt; impregnate or season with salt. *Imp. Dict.*

salite[2] (sā'līt), *n.* [< *Sala* (see def.) + *-ite*[1].] A lamellar variety of pyroxene or augite, of a grayish-green color, from Sala, Sweden, and elsewhere. See *pyroxene*. Also spelled *sahlite*.

salitral (sal'i-tral), *n.* [Sp., < *salitre* = It. *salnitro*, saltpeter, < L. *sal*, salt, + *nitrum*, niter: see *niter*.] A place where saltpeter occurs or is collected.

We passed also a muddy swamp of considerable extent, which in summer dries, and becomes incrusted with various salts, and hence is called a *salitral*. *Darwin*, Voyage of Beagle, I. 90.

saliva (sā-lī'vä), *n.* [In ME. *salve*, < OF. (and F.) *salive* = Pr. Sp. Pg. It. *saliva*; < L. *saliva*, spittle, saliva, slime. Cf. Gr. σίαλον, spittle, Russ. *slina*, Gael. *seile*, spittle; perhaps akin to *slime*.] Spittle; the mixed secretion of the salivary glands and of the mucous membrane of the mouth, a colorless ropy liquid which normally has an alkaline reaction. Its physiological use is to keep moist the tongue, mouth, and fauces, thus aiding the sense of taste, and to assist mastication and deglutition. Specifically, saliva is the secretion of the salivary glands, which in man and many other animals contains a digestive ferment, ptyalin. See *ptyalin*, and cuts under *parotid* and *salivary*.

saliva-ejector (sā-lī'vä-ē-jek'tor), *n.* A saliva-pump.

salival (sā-lī'val), *a.* [= Sp. Pg. *salival* = It. *salivale*; as *saliva* + *-al*.] Same as *salivary*. *W. C. Russell*, Jack's Courtship, xxxix. [Rare.]

salivan (sā-lī'van), *a.* [< L. *saliva*, spittle, + *-an*.] Same as *salivary*. [Rare.]

salivant (sal'i-vant), *a.* and *n.* [< L. *salivan(t-)s*, ppr. of *salivare*, spit out, salivate, < *saliva*, spittle: see *saliva*.] I. *a.* Promoting the flow of saliva; exciting or producing salivation.

II. *n.* A substance which has the property of salivating.

saliva-pump (sa̤-lī'vä-pump), *n.* In *dentistry*, a device for carrying off the accumulating saliva from the mouth of a patient. A bent tube is inserted in the mouth, and is connected at the other end with a valved chamber through which is passed a small stream of water. The vacuum thus produced draws out from the mouth any excess of saliva. Also called *saliva-ejector.*

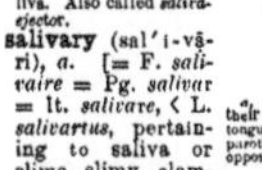

Salivary Glands. *a*, sublingual; *b*, submaxillary; their ducts opening at *d*, beside the tongue on the floor of the mouth; *c*, parotid, its duct (Stenson's), *e*, opening opposite the second upper molar tooth.

salivary (sal'i-vā-ri), *a.* [= F. *salivaire* = Pg. *salivar* = It. *salivare*, < L. *salivarius*, pertaining to saliva or slime, slimy, clammy, < *saliva*, spittle: see *saliva.*] Of or pertaining to saliva; secreting or conveying saliva: as, *salivary* glands; *salivary* ducts or canals. In man the salivary glands are three pairs — the parotid (see cut under *parotid*), submaxillary, and sublingual. Such glands are of enormous size in various animals, as the beaver and sewellel. In the latter they form a great glandular collar

Salivary Gland of Woodpecker.

Head of Woodpecker (*Colaptes auratus*), with the integument removed, showing the large salivary gland *sg*. (About two thirds natural size.)

like a goiter. They are also very large in some birds, as swifts and woodpeckers.—**Buccal salivary papilla**, the prominent opening in the cheek of the duct of the parotid gland.—**Salivary calculus**, a concretion found in the duct of Wharton, and consisting chiefly of carbonates of lime and magnesia, and phosphate of lime. These calculi are also sometimes found in the ducts of the parotid and submaxillary glands.—**Salivary corpuscles**, pale spherical nucleated bodies found in the saliva, containing numerous fine granules in incessant agitation.—**Salivary diastase.** Same as *ptyalin.*—**Salivary fistula**, an abnormal opening on the side of a salivary duct.—**Salivary tubes of Pflueger**, the intralobular ducts of the salivary glands.

salivate (sal'i-vāt), *v. t.*; pret. and pp. *salivated*, ppr. *salivating.* [< L. *salivatus*, pp. of *salivare* (> It. *salivare* = Sp. Pg. Pr. *salivar* = F. *saliver*), spit out, also salivate, < L. *saliva*, spittle: see *saliva.*] To purge by the salivary glands; produce an unusual secretion and discharge of saliva in, usually by the action of mercury; produce ptyalism in.

salivation (sal-i-vā'shon), *n.* [= F. *salivation* = Sp. *salivacion* = Pg. *salivação* = It. *salivazione*, < LL. *salivatio(n-)*, < L. *salivare*, pp. *salivatus*, spit: see *salivate.*] An abnormally abundant flow of saliva; the act or process of salivating, or producing an excessive secretion of saliva, generally by means of mercury; ptyalism.

salivin (sal'i-vin), *n.* [< L. *saliva*, saliva, + *-in*2.] Same as *ptyalin.*

salivous† (sa̤-lī'vus), *a.* [= Sp. Pg. *salivoso*, < L. *salivosus*, full of spittle, < *saliva*, spittle: see *saliva.*] Of or pertaining to saliva; partaking of the nature of saliva.

There also happeneth an elongation of the uvula, through the abundance of *salivous* humour flowing upon it.
Wiseman, Surgery, iv. 7.

Salix (sā'liks), *n.* [NL. (Tournefort, 1700), < L. *salix*, a willow: see *sallow*1.] A genus of apetalous trees and shrubs, the willows, type of the order *Salicineæ*, and characterized by a disk or perianth reduced to one or two distinct glands, and a one-celled ovary with a short two-cleft style, and two placentæ each bearing commonly from four to eight ovules, arranged in two ranks. Unlike those of *Populus*, the other genus of the order, the leaves are commonly long and narrow, the catkins are dense, erect, and at first covered by a single bud-scale, the flowers sessile, stigma short, stamens usually but two, the bracts entire, and the seeds few in each two-valved capsule. There are over 160 species enumerated, often of very difficult limitation from the number of connecting forms and of hybrids. They are natives of all northern and cold regions, rare in the tropics, and very few in the southern hemisphere. One species only is known in South Africa, and one in South America, native in Chili; none occurs in Australasia or Oceanica. About 20 are native to the northeastern United States; and they are still more numerous northward, 10 species being reported from Point Barrow in Alaska alone. They are trees or shrubs, generally with long lithe branches and elongated entire or minutely toothed leaves, often with conspicuous stipules. A few alpine species are prostrate, and form matted turfs or send up small herb-like branches from underground stems. *S. arctica*, a wide-spread species of the far north, extends to latitude 81° 44′ N., in the form, at sea-level, of dwarf shrubs a foot high, but with a trunk an inch thick. The catkins are conspicuous: in temperate climates they are usually put forth before the leaves, but in colder regions they commonly appear nearly at the same time. Most species grow along streams, and many are widely planted to consolidate banks, and thus have become extensively naturalized. Many are found in a fossil state. See *willow*, *osier*, and *sallow*1; also cuts under *ament*, *inflorescence*, *lanceolate*, and *retuse*.

sall1†, *n.* A Middle English form of *soul.*

sall2, *v.* An obsolete or dialectal form of *shall.*

sallad†, **sallade**†, *n.* Obsolete forms of *salad*1, *sallet*2.

sallee-man (sal'ē-man), *n.* 1. A Moorish pirate: so called from the port of Sallee, on the coast of Morocco.

Fleets of her Portuguese men-of-war rode down over the long swell to give battle to saucy *sallee-men.*
J. W. Palmer, Up and Down the Irrawaddi, p. 29.

2. In *zoöl.*, a physophorous oceanic hydrozoan of the family *Velellidæ*, as *Velella vulgaris.* It is about 2 inches long, of a transparent blue color, and rides on the surface of the sea with its vertical crest acting as a sail. Also *sallyman.*

sallenders (sal'en-dėrz), *n.* Same as *sellanders.*

saller†, *n.* Same as *seller*3.

sallet1† (sal'et), *n.* An obsolete form of *salad*1. [In the first quotation there is a play upon this word and *sallet*2, a helmet.]

Wherefore . . . have I climbed into this garden to see if I can eat grass or pick a *sallet*, . . . which is not amiss to cool a man's stomach this hot weather. And I think this word *sallet* was born to do me good; for many a time, but for a sallet, my brain-pan had been cleft with a brown-bill; and many a time, when I have been dry, and bravely marching, it hath served me instead of a quart-pot to drink in; and now the word *sallet* must serve me to feed on.
Shak., 2 Hen. VI., iv. 10. 9.

On Christ-masse Euen they eate a *Sallet* made of diuers Hearbs, and seeth all kindes of Pulse which they feed vpon.
Purchas, Pilgrimage, p. 618.

Wilt eate any of a young spring *sallet?*
Marston, The Fawne, ii. 1.

sallet2 (sal'et), *n.* [Early mod. E. also *sallett*, *salet*, also *salad*, *sallad*, *sallade*, *salade*, < ME. *salette* (confused in spelling with *salad*1, also spelled *sallet*), prop. *salade*, < OF. *salade*, *sallade*, a helmet, head-piece, = Sp. Pg. *celada*, a helmet (cf. Sp. *celar*, engrave, *celadura*, enamel, inlaying), < It. *celata*, a helmet, < L. *cælata*, sc. *cassis*, an engraved or ornamented helmet, fem. pp. of *cælare*, engrave: see *ceil* and *celure.*] 1. A kind of helmet, first introduced at the beginning of the fifteenth century, lighter than the helm, and having an intermediary form between this and the chapel-de-fer. Its distinguishing mark is the fixed projection behind, which replaces the articulated couvre-nuque of other forms of head-piece. The sallet is always extremely simple in form, having rounded surfaces everywhere, and especially well adapted to cause blows or thrusts to glance from the surface. Most sallets are without movable vizors; but where there are vizors the same peculiarity of small rounded surfaces is preserved.

Sallet, with vizor; Spanish, 15th century.

Sallet, without vizor, of form worn by horsemen in the first half of the 15th century.

Salad, speare, gard-brace, ne page.
The Isle of Ladies, l. 1556.

The seid Lord sent to the seid mansion a riotous peple, to the nombre of a thowsand persones, with blanket bendes of a sute as risers ageyn your pees, arrayd in maner of werre, with curesse, brigaunders, jakks, *salettes*, gleyfes, howes, arows, pavyse, gonnes, pannys with fier and teynes brennyng therein.
Paston Letters, I. 106.

2. As much as a sallet will hold. [Rare.]

No more calling of lanthorn and candle-light;
That maidenheads be valued at just nothing;
And sacke be sold by the *sallet.*
Heywood, 1 Edw. IV. (Works, ed. Pearson, 1874, I. 19).

salleting† (sal'et-ing), *n.* [< *sallet*1 + *-ing*1.] Same as *salad*1.

salliance†, *n.* An obsolete form of *salience.*

salligot† (sal'i-got), *n.* See *saligot.*

sallow1 (sal'ō), *n.* [Also *sally*, dial. (Sc.) *sauch*, *saugh*; early mod. E. also *salowe*, rarely *sale*; < ME. *salewe*, *salwe*, *saluhe*, *salwhe*, also *saly* (pl. *salewis*, *salwes*, *salyhes*), < AS. *sealh* (in inflection also *seal-*) = OHG. *salahā*, MHG. *salhe*, G. *sahl* (in *sahlweide*, the round-leafed willow) = Icel. *selja* = Sw. *sälg* = Dan. *selje* = L. *salix*, a willow (> It. *salcio*, *salce*, *salice* = Sp. *salce* = Pg. *sauze* (the F. *saule* is < OHG.) = Gael. *seileach* = Ir. *sail*, *saileach* = W. *helyg*, pl.), = Gr. ἑλίκη, a willow: prob. named from its growing near water; cf. Skt. *salila*, *saras*, *sari*, water, *sarasya*, a lotus, *sarit*, a river, < √ *sar*, flow.] 1. A willow, especially *Salix caprea*, the great sallow or goat- or hedge-willow. It is a tall shrub or bushy tree, found through the northern Old World. It puts forth its showy yellow catkins very early in spring, and in England its branches serve in church use for palms. (See *palm*2, 3.) It furnishes an osier for basket- and hoop-making: its wood is made into implements, and largely into gunpowder-charcoal; its bark is used for tanning, especially for tanning glove-leather. The gray sallow is only a variety. In Australia the name is applied to some acacias.

ȝe schulen take to ȝou in the firste day . . . braunchis of a tree of thicke bowis, and *salewis* of the rennynge streem.
Wyclif, Lev. xxiii. 40 (ed. Purvey).

In this Region of Canchieta, the gossampine trees growe of them selues commonly in many places, as doo with vs elmes, wyllowes, and *salowes.*
Peter Martyr (tr. in Eden's First Books on America, [ed. Arber, p. 95).

The fore-pillar [of the Dalway harp] appears to be *sallow*, the harmonic curve of yew.
O'Curry, Anc. Irish, II. xxxiii.

2. An osier; a willow wand.

And softe a *saly* twygge aboute him plie.
Palladius, Husbondrie (E. E. T. S.), p. 104.

Who so that buyldeth his hous al of *salwes* . . .
Is worthy to been hanged on the galwes.
Chaucer, Prol. to Wife of Bath's Tale, l. 655.

sallow2 (sal'ō), *a.* [< ME. *salow*, *salwhe*, < AS. *salo*, *salu*, *sealo*, sallow (*salo-neb*, yellow-beaked, *salu-pād*, with pale garment, *sealo-brūn*, sallow-brown), = MD. *salwe*, D. *zaluw*, *saluwe*, tawny, sallow, = OHG. *salo*, dusky (> F. *sale* = It. *salavo*, dirty), MHG. *sale*, *sal*, G. dial. *sal*, *sahl* = Icel. *sölr*, yellowish; root uncertain.] Having a yellowish color; of a brownish-yellow and unhealthy-looking color: said of the skin or complexion.

What a deal of brine
Hath wash'd thy *sallow* cheeks for Rosaline!
Shak., R. and J., ii. 3. 70.

Then the judge's face had lost the ruddy English hue, that showed its warmth through all the duskiness of the colonel's weather-beaten cheek, and had taken a *sallow* shade, the established complexion of his countrymen.
Hawthorne, Seven Gables, viii.

sallow2 (sal'ō), *v. t.* [< *sallow*2, *a.*] To tinge with a sallow or yellowish color.

July breathes hot, *sallows* the crispy fields.
Lowell, Under the Willows.

sallow3 (sal'ō), *n.* [Abbr. of *sallow-moth.*] An English collectors' name for certain noctuid moths; a sallow-moth. Thus, *Cirrœdia xerampelina* is the center-barred *sallow.*—**Bordered sallow.** See *Heliothis.*—**Orange sallow.** See *orange*1.

sallow-kitten (sal'ō-kit"n), *n.* A kind of puss-moth, *Dicranura furcula*: so called by British collectors.

sallow-moth (sal'ō-môth), *n.* A British moth of the genus *Xanthia*, as *X. cerago*, *X. sulphurago*, etc., of a pale-yellowish color; a sallow.

sallowness (sal'ō-nes), *n.* [< *sallow*2 + *-ness.*] The quality of being sallow; paleness, tinged with brownish yellow: as, *sallowness* of complexion.

With the *sallowness* from the face flies the bitterness from the heart.
W. M. Baker, New Timothy, p. 319.

sallow-thorn (sal'ō-thôrn), *n.* See *Hippophaë.*

sallowy (sal'ō-i), *a.* [< *sallow* + *-y*1.] Abounding in sallows or willows.

The brook,
Vocal, with here and there a silence, ran
By *sallowy* rims.
Tennyson, Aylmer's Field.

sally1 (sal'i), *n.*; pl. *sallies* (-iz). Same as *sallow*1.

sally2 (sal'i), *n.*; pl. *sallies* (-iz). [Early mod. E. also *sallie*; < OF. (and F.) *saillie* (= Pr. *salhia* = Sp. *salida* = Pg. *sahida*), a sally, eruption, leap, < *saillir*, rush forth, leap: see *sally*2, *v.*] 1†. A leap or spring; a darting; a dance.—2. A sudden rush, dash, or springing forth; specifically, a sudden and determined rush or eruption of troops from a besieged place to attack the besiegers; a sortie: as, the garrison made a *sally.*

I come from haunts of coot and hern,
I make a sudden *sally*,
And sparkle out among the fern,
To bicker down a valley.
Tennyson, The Brook.

3. A run or excursion; a trip or jaunt; a going out in general.

Bellmour, good Morrow—Why, truth on 't is, these early *Sallies* are not usual to me; but Business, as you see, Sir — Congreve, Old Batchelor, i. 1.

Every one shall know a country better that makes often *sallies* into it, and traverses it up and down, than he that like a mill-horse goes still round in the same track. Locke.

Every step in the history of political liberty is a *sally* of the human mind into the untried Future. Emerson, Amer. Civilization.

4. In *arch.*, a projection; the end of a piece of timber cut with an interior angle formed by two planes across the fibers, as the feet of common rafters.—5. An outburst, as of imagination, fancy, merriment, etc.; a flight; hence, a freak, frolic, or escapade.

The Dorien [measure] because his falls, *sallyes*, and compasse be diuers from those of the Phrigien. Puttenham, Arte of Eng. Poesie, p. 70.

These passages were intended for *sallies* of wit. Stillingfleet.

'Tis but a *sally* of youth. Sir J. Denham, The Sophy. (Latham.)

She was apt to fall into little *sallies* of passion. Steele, Tatler, No. 172.

sally[2] (sal'i), *v.*; pret. and pp. *sallied*, ppr. *sallying*. [Early mod. E. also *sallie*, *salie*; < ME. *saillen*, *saillyn*, < OF. *saillir*, leap, jump, bound, issue forth, < L. *salire*, leap: see *sail*[2], of which *sally*[2] is a doublet. The verb *sally*[2], however, depends in part on the noun.] I. *intrans.* 1†. To leap; spring; dance.

Herod also made a promise to the daughter of Herodias when she danced and *salied* so pleasantly before him and his lords. Becon, Works, I. 378. (Davies.)

2. To leap, dash, or spring forth; burst out; specifically, to make a sally, as a body of troops from a besieged place to attack the besiegers; hence, to set out briskly or energetically.

At his first coming, the Turkes *sallied* upon the Germane quarter. Capt. John Smith, True Travels, I. 10.

Then they opened their gate,
Sallying forth with vigor and might.
Undaunted Londonderry (Child's Ballads, VII. 250).

How merrily we would *sally* forth into the fields! Lamb, Christ's Hospital.

So enfeebled and disheartened were they that they offered no resistance if attacked; . . . even the women of Malaga *sallied* forth and made prisoners. Irving, Granada, p. 98.

II.† *trans.* To mount; copulate with: said of horses. Urquhart, tr. of Rabelais, iii. 36.

sally[3] (sal'i), *n.* [A particular use of *sally*, var. of *sallow*[2]. Cf. *sallow*[3].] 1. The wren, *Troglodytes parvulus*. [Ireland.]—2. A kind of stone-fly; one of the *Perlidæ*: as, the yellow *sally*, *Chloroperla viridis*, much used by anglers in England.

sally-lunn (sal'i-lun'), *n.* [Named after *Sally Lunn*, a young woman who sold this species of bun through the streets of Bath, about the end of the 18th century.] A kind of sweet spongy teacake, larger than a muffin: in the United States usually baked in loaves or forms, not in muffin-rings.

It's a sort of night that's meant for muffins. Likewise crumpets. Also *sally-luns*. Dickens, Chimes, iv.

Phillis trifling with a plover's
Egg, while Corydon uncovers with a grace the *Sally Lunn*.
C. S. Calverley, In the Gloaming.

sallyman (sal'i-man), *n.* Same as *sallee-man*, 2.

sally-picker (sal'i-pik'ėr), *n.* [< *sally*[1] + *picker*.] One of several different warblers: so called in Ireland. (*a*) The least willow-wren, or chiff-chaff, *Phylloscopus rufus*; also, P. *trochilus*. (*b*) The sedge-warbler, *Acrocephalus phragmitis*.

sally-port (sal'i-pōrt), *n.* 1. In *fort.*, a gate or a passage to afford free egress to troops in making a sally. The name is applied to the postern leading from under the rampart into the ditch; or in more modern use to a cutting through the glacis, by which a sally may be made through the covered way. See diagram under *barbican*.

At a small distance from it [a rocky hill] on one side there is a *sally port*, cut down through the rock to the sea. Pococke, Description of the East, II. ii. 26.

The direction taken by Hawk-eye soon brought the travellers to the level of the plain, nearly opposite to a *sally-port* in the western curtain of the fort. J. F. Cooper, Last of Mohicans, xiv.

2. A large port on each quarter of a fire-ship, for the escape of the crew into boats when the train is fired.

sally-wood (sal'i-wůd), *n.* Willow-wood.

salm†, *n.* An obsolete form of *psalm*.

salmagundi (sal-ma-gun'di), *n.* [Also *salmagundy*, dial. *salmon-gundy*; < OF. *salmigondin*, *salmigondins*, F. *salmigondis*, orig. 'seasoned salt meats'; prob. < It. *salame* (pl. *salami*), salt meat (< L. *sal*, salt), + *conditi*, pl. of *condito*, < L. *conditus*, seasoned, savory, pp. of *condire*, pickle, preserve: see *condiment*, *condite*[2].] 1. Originally, an Italian dish consisting of chopped meat, eggs, anchovies, onions, oil, etc.

The descendant of Caractacus returned, and, ordering the boy to bring a piece of salt beef from the brine, cut off a slice and mixed it with an equal quantity of onions, which, seasoning with a moderate proportion of pepper and salt, he brought into a consistence with oil and vinegar; then, tasting the dish, assured us it was the best *salmagundy* that he had ever made. Smollett, Roderick Random, xxvi.

Hence—2. A mixture of various ingredients; an olio or medley; a hotchpotch; a miscellany. *W. Irving.*

salmi, salmis (sal'mi), *n.* [< F. *salmis*, orig. 'salted meats,' a double pl., < It. *salame* (pl. *salami*), salt meat: see *salmagundi*.] A ragout of roasted woodcocks, larks, thrushes, or other species of game, minced and stewed with wine, little pieces of bread, and other ingredients to stimulate the appetite.

As it is, though in one way still a striking picture, it is too much of a "*salmi* of frogs' legs," as they said of Correggio's famous dome at Parma. Nineteenth Century, XXIV. 42.

salmiac (sal'mi-ak), *n.* [= F. *salmiac* = G. Sw. Dan. *salmiak*, corruptions of *sal ammoniac*: see *sal ammoniac*, under *ammoniac*.] A contraction of *sal ammoniac* (which see, under *ammoniac*).

salmis, *n.* See *salmi*.

salmite (sal'mit), *n.* [< (Viel)-*Salm* (see def.) + *-ite*[2].] In *mineral.*, a manganesian variety of chloritoid, from Viel-Salm in Belgium.

Salmo (sal'mō), *n.* [NL. (Artedi; Linnæus), < L. *salmo*, a salmon: see *salmon*.] The leading genus of *Salmonidæ*. It was formerly more than coextensive with the family as now understood, but is usually restricted to forms having the anal fin short, of only nine to eleven developed rays; the vomer flat, its surface plane and toothed; and the body spotted with black (not with red or silvery gray). In this sense the genus *Salmo* is exclusive of the chars (*Salvelinus*) and of the Pacific salmon (*Oncorhynchus*). But even thus restricted it contains two sets of species: (*a*) True salmon, marine and anadromous, as *S. salar*, with the vomerine teeth little developed, no hyoid teeth, scales large, caudal fin well forked (truncate in old individuals), and sexual distinctions strong, the breeding males having the lower jaw hooked upward. Such salmon are sometimes landlocked, as the variety found in Sebago Lake, in Maine. See cut under *parr*. (*b*) River-salmon, not anadromous, with vomerine teeth highly developed, and sexual differences not strong. Such salmon are among the many fishes called *trout* or *salmon-trout* in the United States, as *S. irideus*, the rainbow-trout of California, which is a variety or subspecies of *S. gairdneri*, the steel-head or hard-head salmon-trout of the Sacramento river and northward, attaining a weight of twenty pounds (see cut under *rainbow-trout*); *S. purpuratus*, var. *spilurus*, the trout of the Rio Grande, Utah Basin, etc.; and *S. purpuratus*, the salmon-trout of the Columbia river, Rocky Mountain brook-trout, Yellowstone trout, etc. (See *lake-trout*, 1; *lake-trout*, 2, is a char.) Genera of *Salmoninæ* which have been detached from *Salmo* proper are *Salvelinus*, the chars (including *Cristivomer*) and *Oncorhynchus*. The river and lake species of *Salmo* which are not anadromous form a section or subgenus called *Fario*.

Salmon-trout (*Salmo purpuratus*).

salmoid (sal'moid), *n.* [< *salm*(*on*) + *-oid*.] Same as *salmonoid*.

salmon (sam'un), *n.* [Early mod. E. also *salmond*, *samon*; < ME. *salmon*, *salmond*, usually *saumon*, *samon*, *saumoun*, *samowne*, < OF. *saumon*, *saumun*, *saulmone*, *saulmon*, *salmun*, F. *saumon*, a salmon (fish), = Pr. *salmo* = Sp. *salmon* = Pg. *salmão* = It. *salamone* = OS. OHG. *salmo*, MHG. *salme*, G. *salm*, < L. *salmo*(*-n*), a salmon, lit. 'leaper,' < *salire*, leap: see *sail*[2], *salient*.] 1. A fish of the genus *Salmo* (*S. salar*), found in all the northern parts of Europe, America, and Asia. The salmon is both a marine and a fresh-water fish. Its normal locality may be said to be off the mouth or estuary of the larger rivers, whence, in the season of sexual excitement, it ascends to the spawning-beds, which are frequently far inland, near the head-waters of the rivers. On reaching the spawning-station, the female by means of her tail makes a furrow in the gravelly bed of the river, in which she deposits her spawn or eggs, numbering many thousands, which, when impregnated by the male accompanying her, she carefully covers up by rapid sweeps of her tail. At this season the snout of the male undergoes a strange transformation, the under jaw becoming hooked upward with a cartilaginous excrescence, which is used as a weapon in the combats which are frequent when two or more males attach themselves to one female. In this condition he is known as a *kipper*. The time occupied in spawning is from three to twelve days, and the season extends from the end of autumn till spring. After spawning, the salmon, both male and female, die or go to sea under the name of *spent fish*, *foul fish*, or *kelts*, the females being further distinguished as *shedders* or *baggits*. In from 80 to 140 days the young fish hatches from the egg. Then it is about five eighths of an inch long. In this embryonic state it is nourished from a vitellicle, or umbilical vesicle, suspended under the belly, containing the red yolk of the egg and oil-globules, to be absorbed later. When about fifty days old it is about an inch in length, and becomes a *samlet* or *parr* (see cut under *parr*). It continues in the shallows of its native stream till the following spring, when it is from 3 to 4 inches long and is known as the *May parr*. It now descends into deeper parts of the river, where the weaker fish remain till the end of the second spring, the stronger ones till the end of the first spring only. When the season of its migration arrives, generally the month of May or June, the fins have become darker, and the fish has assumed a silvery hue. It is now known as a *smolt* or *salmon-fry*. The smolts now congregate into shoals and proceed leisurely seaward. On reaching the estuary they remain in its brackish water for a short time, and then proceed to the open sea. Of their life there nothing is known, except that they grow with such rapidity that a fish which reaches the estuary weighing, it may be, not more than 2 ounces, may return to it from the sea, after a few months, as a *grilse*, weighing 8 or 10 pounds. A grilse under 2 pounds is called a *salmon-peal*. In between two and three years the grilse becomes a *salmon*. The salmon returns in preference to the river in which it passed its earlier existence. It has been known to grow to the weight of 83 pounds; more generally it weighs from 15 to 25 pounds. It furnishes a delicious dish for the table, and is an important article of commerce. Its flesh is of a pinkish-orange color. The synonyms of *salmon* are very numerous. Nearly or quite exact local ones are *mort*, *simen*, *sprod*. Salmon under two years old, which have not entered the sea, are generally called *parr*, *pink*, and *smolt*, or, more locally, *black-fin*, *brandling*, *brood*, *cocksper*, *fingerling*, *ginkin*, *graveling*, *gravel-laspring*, *heppet*, *jerkin*, *laspring*, *salmon-fry*, *salmon-spring*, *samlet*, *skegger*, *skerling*, *smelt*, *sparling*, *sprag*. One which has returned from the sea a second time is a *gerling*; one which has remained in fresh water during summer is a *laurel*; a milter, or spawning male, may be called a *gib-fish* or *summer-cock*. In the Ribble, in Willughby's time, a two-year old salmon was called *sprod*; a supposed three-year fish *mort*, or perhaps *pug*; a four-year fish, a *forktail*; a five-year fish, a *half-fish*, and a six-year one, a *salmon* specifically.

Atlantic Salmon (*Salmo salar*).

2. One of various fishes of the same family as the above, but of different genera. Some of these species are recognizable by an increased number of the anal rays (14 to 20), and by the fact that the jaws in the males at the breeding-season become peculiarly developed and hooked. They form the genus *Oncorhynchus*, and are collectively called *Pacific salmon*. Five such species occur in the North Pacific. (*a*) One of these, the humpbacked salmon, *O. gorbuscha*, has from 25 to 30 short gill-rakers and very small scales (over 200 in a longitudinal row). It reaches a weight of from 3 to 6 pounds, and is found as far south as Oregon or even in the Sacramento river. (*b*) Another, the dog-salmon, *O. keta* or *O. lagocephalus*, has less than 25 short gill-rakers, moderately small scales (about 150 in a longitudinal row), 13 or 14 anal rays, and 13 or 14 branchiostegal rays: the spots are faint or obsolete. It attains a weight of about 12 pounds, and extends southward (sparingly) to the Sacramento river, but is of little value. (*c*) The quinnat or king-salmon, *O. chavicha* or *O. quinnat*, has about 23 short gill-rakers, about 150 scales in a longitudinal row, 16 anal rays, 15 to 19 branchiostegal rays (those of the opposite sides often unlike), and the back and upper fins dotted with black. It reaches a weight of over 100 pounds, but the average in the Columbia river is about 22. It enters abundantly into the Sacramento river and still more numerously into the northern streams from both sides of the Pacific, and is by far the most important species of its genus. About 30,000,000 pounds are estimated to have been the average take for several years in the Columbia river alone, along whose banks extensive canneries are established to preserve the fish. (*d*) The silver or kisutch salmon, *O. kisutch*, has about 23 rather slender gill-rakers, rather large scales (about 130 in a row), and is bluish-green on the back, silvery on the sides, and punctulated with blackish, but without decided spots except on the top of the head, back, dorsal and adipose fins, and the upper rudimentary rays of the caudal fin. It grows to a weight of from 3 to 8 pounds, and is abundant southward to the Sacramento river, but is of little economic value. (*e*) The blue-back salmon, *O. nerka* or *O. lycaodon*, has about 30 or 40 comparatively long gill-rakers, rather large scales (about 130 in a row), and is normally colored bright-blue above and silvery on the sides, but the males in the fall become deep-red, and are then known in the interior as *redfish*. It attains a weight of from 4 to 8 pounds, and ascends the Columbia river and tributaries in abundance. It ranks next in value to the quinnat. In canning salmon in America the fish are cooked in the cans in which they are put up, unlike any fish canned in Europe, which are all cooked first and then canned and cooked again. (See *sardine*[1], 1.) The salmon are first

Quinnat, or California Salmon (*Oncorhynchus chavicha*).

cleaned and scaled, and have their heads, tails, and fins cut off. Then they are placed in tanks filled with salted water, where they remain some time to "slime" or be cleansed before being brought into the factory. They are then cut into pieces of the proper size to fill the can. These pieces are placed in cans, which are subsequently filled with brine. The raw fish, thus pickled, are soldered in the cans, which are next placed on forms holding many hundreds and lowered by machinery into steam-boilers, where they are cooked for an hour. The next step is a nice process called *venting*. A little hole is pricked in the can to allow the gas within to escape, when the vent-hole is instantly soldered. A second cooking now takes place, after which the cans are taken from the boilers and showered with cold water. If the vacuum is perfect, showing a sound can, the top hollows in with the cooling process. If a can is in the least swollen, it is rejected.

3. One of various fishes, not of the family *Salmonidæ*, suggestive of or mistaken for a salmon. (*a*) A sciænoid fish, *Cynoscion maculatus*. See *squeteague*. [Southern coast of the U. S.] (*b*) A percoideous fish of the genus *Stizostedium*; a pike-perch: more fully called *jack-salmon*. (*c*) In New Zealand, a serranoid fish, *Arripis salar*. (See also the phrases below.)

4. The upper bricks in a kiln, which in firing receive the least heat: so called from their color.

The arches, from necessity, are overburdened in consequence of prolonging the firing sufficiently to burn the top and sides of the kiln into respectable *salmon*.
Ure, Dict., IV. 157.

Black salmon, a local name of the great lake-trout, *Salvelinus (Cristivomer) namaycush*.—**Burnett salmon**, a ceratodontoid fish, *Ceratodus (Neoceratodus) forsteri*, with reddish flesh like that of the salmon. See *Ceratodus*.—**Calvered salmon**, pickled salmon. See *calver*, *v. t.*

Did I ever think . . .
That my too curious appetite, that turn'd
At the sight of godwits, pheasant, partridge, quails,
Larks, woodcocks, calver'd *salmon*, as coarse diet,
Would leap at a mouldy crust?
Massinger, Maid of Honour, iii. 1.

Cornish salmon, the pollack. [Local, Eng.]—**Kelp salmon**, of California (Monterey), a serranoid fish, *Paralabrax clathratus*.—**King of the salmon**. See *king*[1].—**Land-locked salmon**, *Salmo salar sebago*, confined to lakes, etc., and manifest as a variety.—**Quoddy salmon**, a gadoid fish, *Pollachius carbonarius* or *virens*; the pollack.—**Salmon brick**. See def. 4, and *brick*[2].—**Sea-salmon**, a gadoid fish, the pollack, *Pollachius carbonarius*. [Gulf of St. Lawrence.]—**White salmon**, of California, a carangoid fish, *Seriola dorsalis*.—**Wide-mouthed salmon**, any member of the *Scopelidæ*.

salmon (sam'un), *v. t.* [< *salmon*, *n.*] To sicken or poison with salmon, as dogs. [Pacific coast, U. S.]

salmon-belly (sam'un-bel″i), *n.* The belly of a salmon prepared for eating by salting and curing. [Oregon.]

salmon-berry (sam'un-ber″i), *n.* See *flowering raspberry*, under *raspberry*.

salmon-color (sam'un-kul″or), *n.* A reddish-orange color of high luminosity but low chroma; an orange pink. The name is associated with the pink color of salmon-flesh, but, as in the cases of other color-names, departs somewhat widely from the color of the thing suggested.

salmon-colored (sam'un-kul″ord), *a.* Of a salmon-color.

salmond†, *n.* An obsolete form of *salmon*.

salmon-disease (sam'un-di-zēz″), *n.* A destructive disease of fish, especially of salmon, caused by a fungus, *Saprolegnia ferax*. See *Saprolegnia*.

Salmones (sal-mō'nēz), *n. pl.* Same as *Salmonidæ* (*a*).

salmonet (sam'un-et), *n.* [= Sp. Pg. *salmonete*, samlet, red mullet; as *salmon* + *-et*. Doublet of *samlet*.] A young or small salmon; a samlet.

salmon-fishery (sam'un-fish″ėr-i), *n.* 1. A place where salmon-fishing is regularly or systematically carried on.—2. Salmon-fishing.

salmon-fishing (sam'un-fish″ing), *n.* The act or practice of fishing for salmon; salmon-fishery.

salmon-fly (sam'un-flī), *n.* Any kind of artificial fly used for taking salmon with rod and line.

salmon-fry (sam'un-frī), *n.* Salmon under two years old.

salmonic (sal-mon'ik), *a.* [< *salmon* + *-ic*.] Pertaining to or derived from salmon: as, *salmonic* acid (a peculiar kind of coloring matter found in the muscles of the trout).

salmonid (sal'mọ-nid), *n.* and *a.* I. *n.* A fish of the family *Salmonidæ*.

II. *a.* Salmonoid.

Salmonidæ (sal-mon'i-dē), *n. pl.* [NL., < *Salmo(n-)* + *-idæ*.] A family of malacopterygian fishes, exemplified by the genus *Salmo*, to which various limits have been ascribed by different ichthyologists. (*a*) In Bonaparte's earlier classification, a family coextensive with Cuvier's *Salmonoides*, the fourth family of *Malacopterygii abdominales*, with scaly body, soft dorsal followed by a second small and adipose fin, numerous cæca, and a natatory bladder. (*b*) In Günther's system, a family of physostomous fishes, with the margin of the upper jaw formed by the intermaxillaries mesially, and by the maxillaries laterally, the head naked, body covered with scales, belly rounded, a small adipose fin behind the dorsal, pyloric appendages generally numerous (rarely absent), pseudobranchiæ present, and the ova discharged into the cavity of the abdomen before exclusion. (*c*) By Cope restricted to such fishes as have the parietals separated by the supra-occipital, and with two tail-vertebræ—the *Coregonidæ* being separated in another family, distinguished (erroneously) by the contiguous parietals and the presence of only one tail-vertebra. (*d*) By Gill restricted to species having the parietals separated by the supra-occipital, accessory costal bones, the stomach siphonal, and the pyloric cæca many. It was divided into two subfamilies, *Coregoninæ* and *Salmoninæ*, containing the whitefish, chars, and trout, as well as the salmon, but not the *Thymallidæ*, the *Argentinidæ*, nor the *Plecoglossidæ*. See cuts under *char*, *hypural*, *inconnu*, *lake-trout*, *parr*, *rainbow-trout*, *Salmo*, *salmon*, and *trout*.

salmoniform (sal-mon'i-fôrm), *a.* [< L. *salmo(n-)*, a salmon, + *forma*, form.] Same as *salmonoid*. *Huxley*.

Salmonina (sal-mō-nī'nạ̈), *n. pl.* [NL., < *Salmo(n-)* + *-ina*.] In Günther's classification, the first group of his *Salmonidæ* (see *Salmonidæ* (*b*)), with the dorsal fin opposite or nearly opposite the ventrals. It included all the genera of his *Salmonidæ* except *Salanx*.

Salmoninæ (sal-mọ-nī'nē), *n. pl.* [NL., < *Salmo(n-)* + *-inæ*.] A subfamily of *Salmonidæ*, typified by the genus *Salmo*, to which different limits have been assigned. (*a*) Same as *Salmonina* of Günther. (*b*) By Jordan and Gilbert restricted to species with many pyloric cæca, distinct conic teeth to the jaws, and mostly small scales. It includes the genera *Salmo*, *Thymallus*, etc. (*c*) By Gill further restricted to *Salmonidæ* with the parietal bones separated by the supra-occipital, well-developed teeth in the jaws, and mostly small and adherent scales. It thus includes only the genera *Salmo*, *Oncorhynchus*, *Salvelinus*, and their subdivisions. In senses (*b*) and (*c*) the group is contrasted with *Coregoninæ*.

salmoning (sam'un-ing), *n.* [< *salmon* + *-ing*[1].] 1. The pursuit or capture of salmon; also, the salmon industry, as canning. [Oregon.]—2. The habit of feeding on salmon; also, a disease of dogs due to this diet. [Oregon.]

salmon-killer (sam'un-kil″ėr), *n.* A sort of stickleback, *Gasterosteus aculeatus*, var. *cataphractus*, found from San Francisco to Alaska and Kamchatka, and destructive to salmon-fry and -spawn. [Columbia river, U. S.]

salmon-ladder (sam'un-lad″ėr), *n.* 1. A fishway.—2. A contrivance resembling a fishway in construction, used in the chemical treatment of sewage for thoroughly mixing the chemicals with the sewage.

salmon-leap (sam'un-lēp), *n.* [< ME. *samounlepe*; < *salmon* + *leap*[1].] A series of steps or ladders, etc., so constructed on a dam as to permit salmon to pass up-stream.

salmon-louse (sam'un-lous), *n.* A parasitic crustacean, *Caligus piscinus*, which adheres to the gills of the salmon.

salmonoid (sal'mọ-noid), *a.* and *n.* [< L. *salmo(n-)*, a salmon, + *-oid*.] I. *a.* Resembling a salmon; of or pertaining to the *Salmonidæ* in a broad sense; related to the salmon family. Also *salmoniform*.

II. *n.* A salmonoid fish. Also *salmoid*, *salmonid*.

Salmonoidea (sal-mọ-noi'dẹ-ạ̈), *n. pl.* [NL., < *Salmo(n-)* + *-oidea*.] A superfamily of malacopterygian fishes, comprising the *Salmonidæ*, *Thymallidæ*, *Argentinidæ*, etc.

salmon-peal, salmon-peel (sam'un-pēl), *n.* A young salmon under two pounds weight.

salmon-pink (sam'un-pingk), *n.* A salmon-color verging upon a scarlet pink.

salmon-pool (sam'un-pöl), *n.* See *pool*[1].

salmon-spear (sam'un-spēr), *n.* 1. An instrument used in spearing salmon.—2. In *her.*, a bearing representing a three-pronged or four-pronged fish-spear, the prongs being usually barbed.

salmon-spring (sam'un-spring), *n.* A smolt, or young salmon of the first year. [Prov. Eng.]

salmon-stair (sam'un-stãr), *n.* Same as *salmon-ladder*.

salmon-tackle (sam'un-tak″l), *n.* The rod, line, and hook or fly with which salmon are taken.

salmon-trout (sam'un-trout), *n.* A kind of salmon. Specifically—(*a*) The *Salmo trutta*, a species which in value ranks next to the salmon itself. It resembles the salmon in form and color, and is, like it, migratory, ascending rivers to deposit its spawn. See cut under *trout*. (*b*) In the United States, one of several different fishes which resemble both salmon and trout—the former in size, the latter in having red or silvery spots. Some are true trout, as *Salmo gairdneri*; others are chars, as all species of *Salvelinus*; none is the same as *Salmo trutta* of Europe. See cuts under *rainbow-trout* and *Salmo*.

salmon-twine (sam'un-twīn), *n.* Linen or cotton twine used in the manufacture of salmon-nets. It is a strong twine of various sizes, corresponding to the varying sizes of nets.

salmon-weir (sam'un-wēr), *n.* A weir especially designed or used to take salmon.

salnatron (sal-nā'trọn), *n.* [< L. *sal*, salt, + E. *natron*.] Crude sodium carbonate: a word used by dyers, soap-makers, and others.

salol (sal'ol), *n.* [< *sal(icyl)* + *-ol*.] Phenyl salicylate, $C_6H_4.OHCO_2.C_6H_5$, a salicylic ether forming odorless crystals. It is used as an antiseptic, and internally as a substitute for salicylic acid, being less irritating to the stomach.

salometer (sạ̈-lom'e-tėr), *n.* [< L. *sal*, salt, + Gr. *μέτρον*, measure.] Same as *salinometer*, 1.

salometry (sạ̈-lom'e-tri), *n.* Same as *salinometry*.

salomon† (sal'ō-mọn), *n.* The mass. [Thieves' slang or cant.]

He will not beg out of his limit though hee starve; nor breake his oath if hee sweare by his *Salomon* [the rogues' inviolable oath], though you hang him.
Sir T. Overbury, Characters, A Canting Rogue.

I have, by the *Salomon*, a doxy that carries a kinchinmort in her slate at her back.
Middleton, Roaring Girl, v. 1.

Salomonian (sal-ọ-mō'ni-ạn), *a.* [< LL. *Solomon*, Solomon, + *-ian*.] Same as *Salomonic*.

Salomonic (sal-ọ-mon'ik), *a.* [< LL. *Solomon*, < LGr. *Σαλωμών*, *Σολομών*, Solomon, King of Israel, + *-ic*.] Pertaining or relating to Solomon, or composed by him.

The collection of *Salomonic* proverbs formed by the scholars in the service of King Hezekiah.
W. R. Smith, The Old Testament in the Jewish Church, [p. 122.

salon (sa-lôṅ'), *n.* [F.: see *saloon*.] An apartment for the reception of company; a saloon; hence, a fashionable gathering or assemblage.

saloon[1] (sạ-lön'), *n.* [< F. *salon* (= Sp. *salon* = Pg. *salão* = It. *salone*), a large room, a hall, < OF. *sole*, F. *salle* = Pr. Sp. Pg. It. *sala*, a room, chamber, < ML. *sala*, a hall, room, chamber, < OHG. MHG. *sal*, a dwelling, house, hall, room, chamber: see *sale*[2].] 1. Any spacious or elegant apartment for the reception of company, or for the exhibition of works of art; a hall of reception.

What Mr. Lovelace saw of the house—which were the *saloon* and the parlours—was perfectly elegant.
Richardson, Clarissa Harlowe, III. 352 (Hall's Mod. Eng., [p. 251).

2. A hall for public entertainments or amusement; also, an apartment for specific public use: as, the *saloon* of a steamer (that is, the main cabin); a refreshment *saloon*.

The gilded *saloons* in which the first magnates of the realm . . . gave banquets and balls. *Macaulay*.

3. A place where intoxicating liquors are sold and drunk; a grog-shop. [U. S.]

The restriction of one *saloon* to every 500 people would diminish the number in New York from 10,000 to 2,500.
Harper's Weekly, XXXIII. 42.

Saloon rifle. See *rifle*[2].

saloon[2]†, *n.* An erroneous form of *shalloon*.

saloon-car (sạ-lön'kär), *n.* A drawing-room car on a railroad. [U. S.]

saloonist (sạ-lö'nist), *n.* [< *saloon*[1] + *-ist*.] A saloon-keeper; one who supports the saloons. [U. S.]

Any persistent effort to enforce the Sunday laws against the saloon is met by the *saloonist* with the counter-effort to enforce the laws against legitimate business.
Pop. Sci. Mo., XXX. 16.

saloon-keeper (sạ-lön'kē″pėr), *n.* One who keeps a saloon for the retailing of liquors. [U. S.]

saloop (sa-löp'), *n.* A drink prepared from sassafras-bark; sassafras-tea.

There is a composition, the ground-work of which I have understood to be the sweet wood yclept sassafras. This wood boiled down to a kind of tea, and tempered with an infusion of milk and sugar, hath to some tastes a delicacy beyond the China luxury. . . . This is *saloop*.
Lamb, Chimney-sweepers.

Sassafras tea, flavoured with milk and sugar, is sold at daybreak in the streets of London under the name of *saloop*.
Pereira's Materia Medica, quoted in N. and Q., 7th ser., [VII. 35.

Considered as a sovereign cure for drunkenness, and pleasant withal, *saloop*, first sold at street corners, where it was consumed principally about the hour of midnight, eventually found its way into the coffee houses. The ingredients used in the preparation of this beverage were of several kinds—sassafras and plants of the genus known by the simplers as cuckoo-flowers being the principal among them. Tuer, London Cries, p. 13.

saloop-bush (sa-löp'bush), *n.* See *Rhagodia*.

salop, *n.* See *salep*.

Salopian[1] (sa-lō'pi-ạn), *a.* and *n.* [< *Salop* (see def.) + *-ian*.] I. *a.* Of or pertaining to Salop, or Shropshire, a western county of England.—**Salopian ware**, a name given to the Roman pottery found in Shropshire, or thought to have been made there.

II. *n.* An inhabitant of Shropshire.

salopian[2] (sa-lō′pi-an), *a.* [< *saloop* + *-ian.*] Pertaining or relating to saloop; consisting of or prepared from saloop; producing or making t preparation of saloop.

A shop . . . for the vending of this "wholesome and pleasant beverage," on the south side of Fleet-street, as thou approachest Bridge-street—the only *Salopian* house.
Lamb, Chimney-sweepers.

salp (salp), *n.* [= F. *saupe* = Sp. *salpa*, < L. *salpa*, a kind of stock-fish: see *Salpa.*] A species of *Salpa*; one of the *Salpidæ*; a salpian.

Salpa (sal′pä), *n.* [NL. (Forskål, 1775), < L. *salpa*, < Gr. σάλπη, a kind of stock-fish.] 1. The typical genus of *Salpidæ*. There are two groups of species, in one of which the intestine is extended along the ventral aspect of the body, as in *S. pinnata*; in the other it is compacted in globular form posteriorly, as in

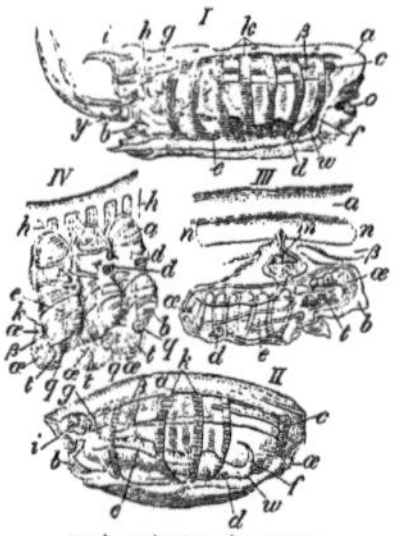

Development and Structure of *Salpa*.
I. Salpa democratica, the sexless ascidiozoöid. *II. Salpa mucronata*, the free sexual ascidiozoöid. *III.* Fetal *Salpa democratica*, attached by placenta to wall of atrial cavity of *S. mucronata*. *IV.* Part of the stolon of *S. democratica*, with buds of *S. mucronata* attached. In all the figures—*o*, oral orifice; *b*, atrial orifice; *c*, endostyle; *d*, ganglion; *e*, hypopharyngeal band; *f*, languet; *g*, heart; *h*, gemmiparous stolon; *i*, visceral mass, or nucleus; *k*, muscular bands; *m*, placenta; *n*, blood-sinus; *q*, ovisac and ovum; *t*, stomach; *w*, ciliated sac; *α*, elæoblast; *a*, ectoderm and test; *β*, endoderm.

S. fusiformis, and forms the so-called nucleus. About 15 species are known, of nearly all seas. All are brilliantly luminous or phosphorescent (like the pyrosomes, with which they were formerly associated), and all occur under two forms—an asexual form, in which the individual salps are solitary, and the mature sexual form, in which a number of salps are linked together to form a chain. Also called *Thalia*.
2. [*l. c.*; pl. *salpæ* (-pē).] A species of this genus; a salp.—3†. A kind of stockfish.

Salpa is a fowle fisshe and lytell set by, for it will neuer be ynough for no maner of dressinge tyll it haue ben beten with grete hamers & staues.
Babees Book (E. E. T. S.), p. 237.

Salpacea (sal-pā′sẹ-ạ̈), *n. pl.* [NL., < *Salpa* + *-acea.*] In De Blainville's classification, one of two families of his *Heterobranchiata*, contrasted with *Ascidiacea*.

salpaceous (sal-pā′shius), *a.* Same as *salpian*.

salpeter†, salpetre†, *n.* Obsolete forms of *saltpeter*.

salpetry†, *a.* [< *salpetre* (now *saltpeter*) + *-y*[1].] Abounding in or impregnated with saltpeter; nitrous.

Rich Iericho's (sometimes) *sal-peetry* soil,
Through brinie springs that did about it boil,
Brought forth no fruit.
Sylvester, tr. of Du Bartas's Weeks, ii., The Schisme.

salpian (sal′pi-ạn), *a.* and *n.* [< NL. *Salpa* + *-i-an.*] I. *a.* Resembling a salp; of or pertaining to the *Salpidæ*; salpiform. Also *salpaceous*.
II. *n.* A salp.

The *salpians* and pyrosomes.
Adams, Man. Nat. Hist., p. 164.

salpicon† (sal′pi-kon), *n.* [< F. *salpicon*, < Sp. *salpicon*, a mixture, salmagundi, bespattering, < *salpicar*, bespatter, besprinkle (= Pg. *salpicar*, corn, powder), < *sal*, salt, + *picar*, pick: see *pike*[1], *pick*[1].] Stuffing; farce; chopped meat or bread, etc., used to stuff legs of veal. *Bacon.* (*Imp. Dict.*)

Salpidæ (sal′pi-dē), *n. pl.* [NL., < *Salpa* + *-idæ.*] A family of hemimyarian ascidians, typified by the genus *Salpa*; the salps. They are placed with the *Doliolidæ* in the order *Thaliacea* (which see). They are free-swimming oceanic organisms, which are colonial when sexually mature, and exhibit alternation of generation; the larvæ are not tailed; the alimentary canal is ventral; the sac is well developed; and the musculation does not form complete rings (is hemimyarian, as distinguished from the cyclomyarian muscles of the *Doliolidæ*). The branchial and peribranchial spaces are continuous, opening by the branchial and atrial pores. The *Salpidæ* include but one genus; as a related form, *Octacnemus*, lately discovered and not yet well known, serves as type of another family (*Octacnemidæ*).

salpiform (sal′pi-fôrm), *a.* [< L. *salpa*, salp, + *forma*, form.] Having the form or structure of a salp; of or pertaining to the *Salpiformes*.

Salpiformes (sal-pi-fôr′mēz), *n. pl.* [NL.: see *salpiform.*] A suborder of ascidians, constituted by the firebodies or *Pyrosomatidæ* alone, forming free-swimming colonies in the shape of a hollow cylinder closed at one end: more fully called *Ascidiæ salpiformes*, and contrasted with *Ascidiæ compositæ* and *Ascidiæ simplices*, as one of three suborders of *Ascidiacea* proper. This group does not include the salps (which belong to a different order), to which, however, the pyrosomes were formerly approximated in some classifications, in view of their resemblance in some respects.

Salpiglossidæ (sal-pi-glos′i-dē), *n. pl.* [NL. (Bentham and Hooker, 1876), < *Salpiglossis* + *-idæ.*] A tribe of gamopetalous plants of the order *Solanaceæ*, characterized by flower-buds with the lobes folded in and also somewhat imbricated, and with the two upper lobes outside of the others and often a little larger. The stamens are sometimes two, usually four, perfect and didynamous, accompanied commonly by a smaller or rudimentary or rarely perfect fifth stamen. The tribe forms the link between the *Solanaceæ*—to which it conforms in centrifugal inflorescence and plicate petals—and the large order *Scrophularineæ*, which it resembles in its didynamous stamens. It includes 18 genera, mostly of tropical America, of which *Salpiglossis* (the type), *Petunia*, *Schizanthus*, *Browallia*, and *Nierembergia* are cultivated for their handsome flowers.

Salpiglossis (sal-pi-glos′is), *n.* [NL. (Ruiz and Pavon, 1798), irreg. < Gr. σάλπιγξ, a trumpet, + γλῶσσα, tongue.] A genus of gamopetalous plants of the order *Solanaceæ*, type of the tribe *Salpiglossidæ*, and characterized by four perfect didynamous stamens, two-cleft capsule-valves, and an obliquely funnel-shaped corolla slightly two-lipped and with ample throat, the lobes both plicate and imbricated. It includes 2 or 3 closely allied and variable species, natives of Chili. They are viscid and hairy herbs, annual or perennial, bearing leaves which are entire, or toothed or pinnately cleft, and a few long-pedicelled showy flowers, with the aspect of petunias. *S. sinuata* is a beautiful half-hardy garden annual with many hybrids, the corolla feathered and veined with dark lines on a ground-color varying from pure white to deep crimson, yellow, orange, or purple.

Salpinctes (sal-pingk′tēz), *n.* [NL. (Cabanis, 1847), < Gr. σαλπιγκτής, a trumpeter, < σάλπιγξ, a war-trumpet.] An American genus of *Troglodytidæ*; the rock-wrens. The leading species is *S. obsoletus*. See cut under *rock-wren*.

salpingectomy (sal-pin-jek′tọ-mi), *n.* [< NL. *salpinx* (*salping-*), q. v., + Gr. ἐκτομή, a cutting out.] The excision of a Fallopian tube.

salpingemphraxis (sal″pin-jem-frak′sis), *n.* [NL., < *salpinx* (*salping-*), q. v., + Gr. ἔμφραξις, a stopping, stoppage.] Obstruction of a Fallopian or of a Eustachian tube.

salpinges, *n.* Plural of *salpinx*.

salpingian (sal-pin′ji-an), *a.* [< NL. *salpinx* (*salping-*), q. v., + *-ian.*] Pertaining to a Fallopian or to a Eustachian tube.—**Salpingian dropsy**, hydrosalpinx.

salpingitic (sal-pin-jit′ik), *a.* [< *salpingit*(*is*) + *-ic.*] Of or pertaining to salpingitis.

salpingitis (sal-pin-jī′tis), *n.* [NL., < *salpinx* (*salping-*) + *-itis.*] 1. Inflammation of a Fallopian tube.—2†. Inflammation of a Eustachian tube; syringitis.

salpingocyesis (sal-ping″gọ-sī-ē′sis), *n.* [NL., < *salpinx* (*salping-*), q. v., + Gr. κύησις, pregnancy, < κυεῖν, be pregnant.] Tubal pregnancy.

Salpingœca (sal-pin-jē′kạ̈), *n.* [NL., < Gr. σάλπιγξ, a trumpet, + οἶκος, a dwelling.] The typical genus of *Salpingœcidæ*, founded by H. J. Clark in 1866. *S. amphoridium* is an example.

Salpingœcidæ (sal-pin-jē′si-dē), *n. pl.* [NL., < *Salpingœca* + *-idæ.*] A family of infusorians, represented by the genera *Salpingœca*, *Lagenœca*, and *Polyœca*, inhabiting both fresh and salt water. They secrete and inhabit protective sheaths or loricæ, which are either free, or attached and sessile or pedunculate. The flagellum is single and collared; there are usually two or more contractile vacuoles, situated posteriorly; and there is an endoplast.

salpingomalleus (sal-ping-gọ-mal′ẹ-us), *n.*; pl. *salpingomallei* (-ī). [NL., < *salpinx* (*salping-*), q. v., + *malleus.*] The tensor tympani muscle. See *tensor*.

salpingonasal (sal-ping-gō-nā′zạl), *a.* [< NL. *salpinx* (*salping-*), q. v., + L. *nasalis*, of the nose: see *nasal.*] Of or pertaining to the Eustachian tube and the nose; syringonasal.—**Salpingonasal fold**, a fold of mucous membrane extending from the opening of the Eustachian tube to the posterior nares.

salpingo-oöphorectomy (sal-ping-gō-ō″ọ-fọ-rek′tọ-mi), *n.* [< *salpinx* (*salping-*) + *oöphorectomy.*] The excision of the ovaries and Fallopian tubes.

salpingopharyngeal (sal-ping″gō-fạ-rin′jẹ-ạl), *a.* [< *salpingopharynge-us* + *-al.*] Of or pertaining to the Eustachian tube and the pharynx: specifically noting the salpingopharyngeus.

salpingopharyngeus (sal-ping-gō-far-in-jē′us), *n.*; pl. *salpingopharyngei* (-ī). [NL., < *salpinx* (*salping-*) + *pharynx* (*pharyng-*): see *pharyngeus.*] The salpingopharyngeal muscle, or that part of the palatopharyngeus which arises from the mouth of the Eustachian tube.

salpingostaphylinus (sal-ping-gō-staf-i-lī′nus), *n.*; pl. *salpingostaphylini* (-nī). [NL., < *salpinx* (*salping-*), q. v., + Gr. σταφυλή, uvula.] Either one of two muscles of the soft palate, external and internal.—**Salpingostaphylinus externus.** Same as *circumflexus palati* (which see, under *palatum*).—**Salpingostaphylinus internus.** Same as *levator palati* (which see, under *levator*).

salpingotomy (sal-ping-got′ọ-mi), *n.* [< NL. *salpinx* (*salping-*), q. v., + Gr. τομία, < τέμνειν, ταμεῖν, cut.] The surgical division or exsection of a Fallopian tube.

salpingysterocyesis (sal-pin-jis″tẹr-ọ-sī-ē′sis), *n.* [NL., < *salpinx* (*salping-*), q. v., + Gr. ὑστέρα, the womb, + κύησις, pregnancy.] Pregnancy occurring at the junction of a Fallopian tube with the uterus.

salpinx (sal′pingks), *n.*; pl. *salpinges* (sal-pin′jēz), rarely *salpinxes* (sal′pingk-sez). [NL., < Gr. σάλπιγξ, a trumpet.] 1. A Fallopian tube.—2. A Eustachian tube, or syrinx.—3. [*cap.*] In *entom.*, a genus of lepidopterous insects. *Hübner*, 1816.

Salpornis (sal-pôr′nis), *n.* [NL. (G. R. Gray, 1847), shortened form of *Salpingornis, < Gr. σάλπιγξ, a trumpet, + ὄρνις, a bird.] A notable genus of creepers, of the family *Certhiidæ*, inhabiting parts of Asia and Africa. The leading species is *S. spilonotus*, under 5 inches long, the slender curved bill 1 inch. The upper parts are dark-brown, profusely spotted with white; the wings and tail are barred with white; the under parts are whitish or pale-buff with numerous dark-brown bars. This creeper inhabits central India. A second species, *S. salvadorii*, is African, forming the type of the subgenus *Hylypsornis*.

Indian Creeper (*Salpornis spilonotus*).

salsafy, *n.* See *salsify*.

salsamentarious† (sal″sạ-men-tā′ri-us), *a.* [< L. *salsamentarius*, pertaining to pickle or salted fish, < *salsamentum*, pickle, salted fish, < *salsus*, pp. of *salire*, salt, < *sal*, salt: see *salt*[1], *sauce.*] Pertaining to or containing salt; salted. *Bailey*, 1731.

salse[1]**†**, *n.* A Middle English form of *sauce*.

salse[2] (sals), *n.* [< F. *salse*, < L. *salsus*, pp. of *salire*, salt, < *sal*, salt: see *salt*[1], *sauce.*] A mud volcano; a conical hill of soft, muddy material, formed from the decomposition of volcanic rock, and forced upward by the currents of gas escaping from the solfataric region beneath.

The *salses*, or hillocks of mud, which are common in some parts of Italy and in other countries.
Darwin, Geol. Obs., i. 127.

Upper Part of the Stem of Salsify (*Tragopogon porrifolius*), with heads. *a*, a flower; *b*, the fruit.

Lightning Source UK Ltd.
Milton Keynes UK
UKHW020341090219
336963UK00010B/658/P

9 780265 69969